Macworld® Office 98 Bible

Macworld® Office 98 Bible

Bob LeVitus, Deborah Shadovitz, Edward Jones, and Derek Sutton

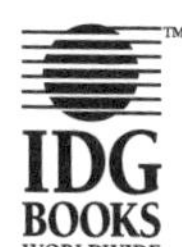

IDG Books Worldwide, Inc.
An International Data Group Company

Foster City, CA ✦ Chicago, IL ✦ Indianapolis, IN ✦ New York, NY

Macworld® Office 98 Bible

Published by
IDG Books Worldwide, Inc.
An International Data Group Company
919 E. Hillsdale Blvd., Suite 400
Foster City, CA 94404
http: www.idgbooks.com (IDG Books Worldwide Web site)

Library of Congress Catalog Card No.: 98-70591

ISBN: 0-7645-4041-6

Printed in the United States of America

10 9 8 7 6 5 4 3 2 1

1E/SY/QV/ZY/FC

Distributed in the United States by IDG Books Worldwide, Inc.

Distributed by Macmillan Canada for Canada; by Transworld Publishers Limited in the United Kingdom; by IDG Norge Books for Norway; by IDG Sweden Books for Sweden; by Woodslane Pty. Ltd. for Australia; by Woodslane (NZ) Ltd. for New Zealand; by Addison Wesley Longman Singapore Pte Ltd. for Singapore, Malaysia, Thailand, Indonesia, and Korea; by Norma Comunicaciones S.A. for Colombia; by Intersoft for South Africa; by International Thomson Publishing for Germany, Austria, and Switzerland; by Toppan Company Ltd. for Japan; by Distribuidora Cuspide for Argentina; by Livraria Cultura for Brazil; by Ediciencia S.A. for Ecuador; by Ediciones ZETA S.C.R. Ltda. for Peru; by WS Computer Publishing Corporation, Inc., for the Philippines; by Unalis Corporation for Taiwan; by Contemporanea de Ediciones for Venezuela; by Computer Book & Magazine Store for Puerto Rico; by Express Computer Distributors for the Caribbean and West Indies. Authorized Sales Agent: Anthony Rudkin Associates for the Middle East and North Africa.

For general information on IDG Books Worldwide's books in the U.S., please call our Consumer Customer Service department at 800-762-2974. For reseller information, including discounts and premium sales, please call our Reseller Customer Service department at 800-434-3422.

For information on where to purchase IDG Books Worldwide's books outside the U.S., please contact our International Sales department at 650-655-3200 or fax 650-655-3297.

For information on foreign language translations, please contact our Foreign & Subsidiary Rights department at 650-655-3021 or fax 650-655-3281.

For sales inquiries and special prices for bulk quantities, please contact our Sales department at 650-655-3200 or write to the address above.

For information on using IDG Books Worldwide's books in the classroom or for ordering examination copies, please contact our Educational Sales department at 800-434-2086.

For press review copies, author interviews, or other publicity information, please contact our Public Relations department at 650-655-3000 or fax 650-655-3299.

For authorization to photocopy items for corporate, personal, or educational use, please contact Copyright Clearance Center, 222 Rosewood Drive, Danvers, MA 01923, or fax 978-750-4470.

ABOUT IDG BOOKS WORLDWIDE

Welcome to the world of IDG Books Worldwide.

IDG Books Worldwide, Inc., is a subsidiary of International Data Group, the world's largest publisher of computer-related information and the leading global provider of information services on information technology. IDG was founded more than 25 years ago and now employs more than 8,500 people worldwide. IDG publishes more than 275 computer publications in over 75 countries (see listing below). More than 90 million people read one or more IDG publications each month.

Launched in 1990, IDG Books Worldwide is today the #1 publisher of best-selling computer books in the United States. We are proud to have received eight awards from the Computer Press Association in recognition of editorial excellence and three from *Computer Currents*' First Annual Readers' Choice Awards. Our best-selling *...For Dummies®* series has more than 50 million copies in print with translations in 38 languages. IDG Books Worldwide, through a joint venture with IDG's Hi-Tech Beijing, became the first U.S. publisher to publish a computer book in the People's Republic of China. In record time, IDG Books Worldwide has become the first choice for millions of readers around the world who want to learn how to better manage their businesses.

Our mission is simple: Every one of our books is designed to bring extra value and skill-building instructions to the reader. Our books are written by experts who understand and care about our readers. The knowledge base of our editorial staff comes from years of experience in publishing, education, and journalism — experience we use to produce books for the '90s. In short, we care about books, so we attract the best people. We devote special attention to details such as audience, interior design, use of icons, and illustrations. And because we use an efficient process of authoring, editing, and desktop publishing our books electronically, we can spend more time ensuring superior content and spend less time on the technicalities of making books.

You can count on our commitment to deliver high-quality books at competitive prices on topics you want to read about. At IDG Books Worldwide, we continue in the IDG tradition of delivering quality for more than 25 years. You'll find no better book on a subject than one from IDG Books Worldwide.

John Kilcullen
CEO
IDG Books Worldwide, Inc.

Steven Berkowitz
President and Publisher
IDG Books Worldwide, Inc.

Eighth Annual Computer Press Awards 1992

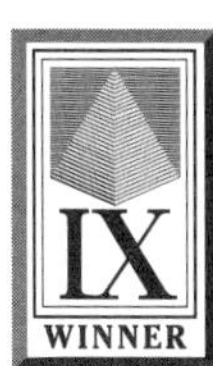

Ninth Annual Computer Press Awards 1993

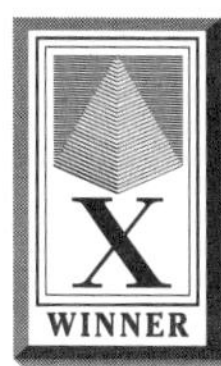

Tenth Annual Computer Press Awards 1994

Eleventh Annual Computer Press Awards 1995

IDG Books Worldwide, Inc., is a subsidiary of International Data Group, the world's largest publisher of computer-related information and the leading global provider of information services on information technology. International Data Group publishes over 275 computer publications in over 75 countries. More than 90 million people read one or more International Data Group publications each month. International Data Group's publications include: **ARGENTINA:** Buyer's Guide, Computerworld Argentina, PC World Argentina; **AUSTRALIA:** Australian Macworld, Australian PC World, Australian Reseller News, Computerworld, IT Casebook, Network World, Publish, Webmaster; **AUSTRIA:** Computerwelt Osterreich, Networks Austria, PC Tip Austria; **BANGLADESH:** PC World Bangladesh; **BELARUS:** PC World Belarus; **BELGIUM:** Data News; **BRAZIL:** Annuário de Informática, Computerworld, Connections, Macworld, PC Player, PC World, Publish, Reseller News, Supergamepower; **BULGARIA:** Computerworld Bulgaria, Network World Bulgaria, PC & MacWorld Bulgaria; **CANADA:** CIO Canada, Client/Server World, ComputerWorld Canada, InfoWorld Canada, NetworkWorld Canada, WebWorld; **CHILE:** Computerworld Chile, PC World Chile; **COLOMBIA:** Computerworld Colombia, PC World Colombia; **COSTA RICA:** PC World Centro America; **THE CZECH AND SLOVAK REPUBLICS:** Computerworld Czechoslovakia, Macworld Czech Republic, PC World Czechoslovakia; **DENMARK:** Communications World Danmark, Computerworld Danmark, Macworld Danmark, PC World Danmark, Techworld Denmark; **DOMINICAN REPUBLIC:** PC World Republica Dominicana; **ECUADOR:** PC World Ecuador; **EGYPT:** Computerworld Middle East, PC World Middle East; **EL SALVADOR:** PC World Centro America; **FINLAND:** MikroPC, Tietoverkko, Tietoviikko; **FRANCE:** Distributique, Hebdo, Info PC, Le Monde Informatique, Macworld, Reseaux & Telecoms, WebMaster France; **GERMANY:** Computer Partner, Computerwoche, Computerwoche Extra, Computerwoche FOCUS, Global Online, Macwelt, PC Welt; **GREECE:** Amiga Computing, GamePro Greece, Multimedia World; **GUATEMALA:** PC World Centro America; **HONDURAS:** PC World Centro America; **HONG KONG:** Computerworld Hong Kong, PC World Hong Kong, Publish in Asia; **HUNGARY:** ABCD CD-ROM, Computerworld Szamitastechnika, Internetto online Magazine, PC World Hungary, PC-X Magazin Hungary; **ICELAND:** Tolvuheimur PC World Island; **INDIA:** Information Communications World, Information Systems Computerworld, PC World India, Publish in Asia; **INDONESIA:** InfoKomputer PC World, Komputek Computerworld, Publish in Asia; **IRELAND:** ComputerScope, PC Live!; **ISRAEL:** Macworld Israel, People & Computers/Computerworld; **ITALY:** Computerworld Italia, Macworld Italia, Networking Italia, PC World Italia; **JAPAN:** DTP World, Macworld Japan, Nikkei Personal Computing, OS/2 World Japan, SunWorld Japan, Windows NT World, Windows World Japan; **KENYA:** PC World East African; **KOREA:** Hi-Tech Information, Macworld Korea, PC World Korea; **MACEDONIA:** PC World Macedonia; **MALAYSIA:** Computerworld Malaysia, PC World Malaysia, Publish in Asia; **MALTA:** PC World Malta; **MEXICO:** Computerworld Mexico, PC World Mexico; **MYANMAR:** PC World Myanmar; **NETHERLANDS:** Computer! Totaal, LAN Internetworking Magazine, LAN World Buyers Guide, Macworld Netherlands, Net, WebWereld; **NEW ZEALAND:** Absolute Beginners Guide and Plain & Simple Series, Computer Buyer, Computer Industry Directory, Computerworld New Zealand, MTB, Network World, PC World New Zealand; **NICARAGUA:** PC World Centro America; **NORWAY:** Computerworld Norge, CW Rapport, Datamagasinet, Financial Rapport, Kursguide Norge, Macworld Norge, Multimediaworld Norge, PC World Ekspress Norge, PC World Nettverk, PC World Norge, PC World ProduktGuide Norge; **PAKISTAN:** Computerworld Pakistan; **PANAMA:** PC World Panama; **PEOPLE'S REPUBLIC OF CHINA:** China Computer Users, China Computerworld, China InfoWorld, China Telecom World Weekly, Computer & Communication, Electronic Design China, Electronics Today, Electronics Weekly, Game Software, PC World China, Popular Computer Week, Software Weekly, Software World, Telecom World; **PERU:** Computerworld Peru, PC World Profesional Peru, PC World SoHo Peru; **PHILIPPINES:** Click!, Computerworld Philippines, PC World Philippines, Publish in Asia; **POLAND:** Computerworld Poland, Computerworld Special Report Poland, Cyber, Macworld Poland, Networld Poland, PC World Komputer; **PORTUGAL:** Cerebro/PC World, Computerworld/Correio Informático, Dealer World Portugal, Mac*In/PC*In Portugal, Multimedia World; **PUERTO RICO:** PC World Puerto Rico; **ROMANIA:** Computerworld Romania, PC World Romania, Telecom Romania; **RUSSIA:** Computerworld Russia, Mir PK, Publish, Seti; **SINGAPORE:** Computerworld Singapore, PC World Singapore, Publish in Asia; **SLOVENIA:** Monitor; **SOUTH AFRICA:** Computing SA, Network World SA, Software World SA; **SPAIN:** Communicaciones World España, Computerworld España, Dealer World España, Macworld España, PC World España; **SRI LANKA:** Infolink PC World; **SWEDEN:** CAP&Design, Computer Sweden, Corporate Computing Sweden, Internetworld Sweden, it.branschen, Macworld Sweden, MaxiData Sweden, MikroDatorn, Nätverk & Kommunikation, PC World Sweden, PCaktiv, Windows World Sweden; **SWITZERLAND:** Computerworld Schweiz, Macworld Schweiz, PCtip; **TAIWAN:** Computerworld Taiwan, Macworld Taiwan, NEW ViSiON/Publish, PC World Taiwan, Windows World Taiwan; **THAILAND:** Publish in Asia, Thai Computerworld; **TURKEY:** Computerworld Turkiye, Macworld Turkiye, Network World Turkiye, PC World Turkiye; **UKRAINE:** Computerworld Kiev, Multimedia World Ukraine, PC World Ukraine; **UNITED KINGDOM:** Acorn User UK, Amiga Action UK, Amiga Computing UK, Apple Talk UK, Computing, Macworld, Parents and Computers UK, PC Advisor, PC Home, PSX Pro, The WEB; **UNITED STATES:** Cable in the Classroom, CIO Magazine, Computerworld, DOS World, Federal Computer Week, GamePro Magazine, InfoWorld, I-Way, Macworld, Network World, PC Games, PC World, Publish, Video Event, THE WEB Magazine, and WebMaster; online webzines: JavaWorld, NetscapeWorld, and SunWorld Online; **URUGUAY:** InfoWorld Uruguay; **VENEZUELA:** Computerworld Venezuela, PC World Venezuela; and **VIETNAM:** PC World Vietnam.

5/7/98

Credits

Acquisitions Editor
Michael Roney

Development Editors
Alex Miloradovich
Claire Keaveney
Kenyon Brown

Technical Editor
Terence Worley

Copy Editors
Suki Gear
Nate Holdread
Richard H. Adin
Anne Friedman

Project Coordinator
Tom Debolski

Quality Control Specialists
Mick Arellano
Mark Schumann

Graphics and Production Specialist
Jude Levinson

Illustrators
Linda Marousek
Hector Mendoza

Cover Design
Murder By Design

Proofreader
Nancy Reinhardt

Indexer
Lynnzee Elze Spence

About the Authors

Bob LeVitus (pronounced Love-eye-tis) was the editor-in-chief of the wildly popular *MACazine* until its untimely demise in 1988. Since 1989, he has been a contributing editor/columnist for *MacUser* magazine, writing the "Help Folder," "Beating the System," "Personal Best," and "Game Room" columns at various times in his illustrious career. In his spare time, LeVitus has written 26 popular computer books, including *WebMaster Macintosh, Second Edition*—the "everything you need to build your own Web site on a Mac" book and CD-ROM — and *ClarisWorks Office For Dummies* (with Deborah Shadovitz).

Always a popular speaker at Macintosh user groups and trade shows, LeVitus has spoken at more than 100 international seminars, presented keynote addresses in several countries, and serves on the Macworld Expo Advisory Board. He was also the host of *Mac Today,* a half-hour television show syndicated in over 100 markets, which aired in late 1992.

LeVitus has forgotten more about the Macintosh than most people ever knew. He won the Macworld Expo MacJeopardy World Championship an unbelievable four times before retiring his crown. But most of all, LeVitus is known for his clear, understandable writing, his humorous style, and his ability to translate techie jargon into usable and fun advice for the rest of us. He lives in Austin, Texas with his wife, two children, and a small pack of dogs.

Deborah Shadovitz started playing with computers in high school, where a terminal called into a mainframe at a local university. Throughout her years in video and audio/visual production, computers kept coming back into her life. Then came the Mac. . . . Deborah got into the Mac for its creative capabilities, did some art and desktop publishing, and then found herself being called a Mac "expert" and asked to teach. Today you can find her teaching Mac usage all over Los Angeles, leading special interest groups at the Los Angeles Macintosh Group, or speaking at MacFair LA and Macworld Expo when she's not writing articles or books about the Mac. Deborah began using Word with version 4.0 and has been training people in its efficient use since then.

Deborah has been active on the LAMG Board of Directors since 1993. She's also on the board of the Association of Database Developers, on the steering committee of Webgrrls-LA, and is a member of the Association of Macintosh Trainers. Before writing this book, she cowrote *ClarisWorks Office For Dummies* with Bob LeVitus. She is also the Mac columnist for *ComputerUser* magazine.

To Lisa, Allison, and Jacob: I do it all for you.

—Bob LeVitus

To my family (especially my parents, Rosalie and Herbert) for the value placed on learning and communication, with special remembrance to my Uncle Sidney.

To my good friends (you know who you are) for your encouragement and understanding when I dropped out of touch to write. Also to my neighbor and confidant, Harry Robbins, rest in peace. I miss you.

—Deborah S. Shadovitz

Foreword

In the Macintosh's early days, one of the only places you could get authoritative and friendly information about your Mac was from your local user group. I remember meeting Bob LeVitus more than ten years ago at a Los Angeles Macintosh Group (LAMG) meeting; he was one of the first gurus spawned by what would become the Macintosh industry and was the expert on anything Mac-related. Bob has gone on to write dozens of popular books and continues as one of the best-known and best-loved authors in the Mac community. Bob's coauthor Deborah Shadovitz has been one of the most popular instructors at the LAMG for many years and has taught thousands of people in Southern California, both through the LAMG Education Program and at our annual spring trade show, MacFair LA.

In the past eight years, as the executive director of one of the three largest Macintosh user groups in the world, it has given me great pleasure to be a part of the community "for the rest of us." I've seen thousands of computer users stretch themselves personally and professionally by using Macintosh computers. The LAMG exists to help people get more out of their computers, and it's writers like Bob and Deborah that make this effort feasible. In this book, they've managed to take Microsoft Office, certainly one of the most robust programs ever developed, and explain its inner workings in a friendly and informative manner.

Recognizing the cross-platform use of a program such at Office, this book uses IDG Books Worldwide's *Office 97 Bible* (for Windows users) as its basis. But thanks to the aforementioned talents of Bob and Deborah, the book has been revamped, updated, seriously supercharged, and polished into a 100% Mac book for Mac people.

With this book, you can hit the ground running. Whether you're a beginner or an expert, you should benefit from the information found between its covers.

Suzy Prieto

Executive Director, Los Angeles Macintosh Group (LAMG)

Preface

Welcome to the *Macworld Office 98 Bible*. This is your personal guide to the Microsoft Office 98 applications: Word, Excel, PowerPoint, Outlook Express, and Internet Explorer. This book tells you all the stuff you need to learn about any or all of the Microsoft Office applications, regardless of how much you already know about Office. While first and foremost a comprehensive reference, the *Macworld Office 98 Bible* also helps you learn by example. The book gives you special tips and techniques to get the most out of the Office applications, as they stand alone and as they work in conjunction with their fellow applications. All in all, this book helps you integrate the use of the Office applications into your life for maximum efficiency and shows you how to share information among the applications to produce impressive documents and presentations.

Although each chapter is an integral part of the book as a whole, each chapter can also stand on its own. You can read the book in any order you want, skipping from chapter to chapter and from topic to topic. (This book's index is particularly thorough: Rely on the index to find the topics that interest you.)

For each of the major applications (Word, Excel, and PowerPoint) we've included chapters that answer the ten most common user questions, based on user feedback to Microsoft. We've also included At Work chapters that show you how to accomplish common, everyday office tasks with Office. In case you've never touched Word, Excel, or PowerPoint, we've included appendixes that provide the basics for each application.

Is This Book for You?

If you use (or will soon use) Microsoft Office, this book is for you. As we describe fully in the next section, this book is divided into parts. If you're an Office beginner, start with the first chapter in each part and work to the end. (If you've never used any kind of word processor, spreadsheet, database manager, or presentation graphics program before, start with the appendixes!) If you have some Office experience, at least breeze through the chapters that cover topics you already know. They introduce you to the new features and provide tips and techniques that help you work better with Office.

How This Book Is Organized

We've divided this book into five parts: one part that gives an overview of Office; one part each for Word, Excel, and PowerPoint; and one part that describes the Office Internet tools — Outlook Express (for e-mail) and Internet Explorer (for viewing Web pages).

Part I: Introducing Microsoft Office 98

This tiny, one-chapter part introduces the tools Office gives you to work more efficiently.

Part II: Word

Ah, Word: the 800-pound gorilla of word processors. This part tells you what Word can do for you.

Part III: Excel

This part describes Office's spreadsheet application, Excel.

Part IV: PowerPoint

This part tells you how to use PowerPoint to create great presentations.

Part V: The Internet Office

This part tells you about Outlook Express, Office's Internet messaging application, and Internet Explorer, a Web browser that enables you to view Web pages efficiently.

Appendixes

If you haven't installed Office on your Mac yet, check out Appendix A. If you are new to any of the Office applications, visit the appendix dedicated to that program; it will get you going.

Appendix A tells you how to install Office 98 and goes over each of the Value Pack additions you can install.

Appendix B shows the new Word user how to launch Word, how to create a document, how to open an existing document, how to navigate a document, how to enter and edit text, how to print a document, and how to save a document.

Appendix C shows the new Excel user how to launch Excel, what a workbook is, how to navigate a workbook, how to enter and edit data and formulas, how to do basic formatting, and how to save and print a workbook.

Appendix D shows the new PowerPoint user how to launch PowerPoint; how to create, move around in, and save presentations; and how to enter text and graphics.

Appendix E gives you the full lowdown on how to change your Office menus and toolbars to best fit your own use. This appendix is for *after* you've worked with any of the applications.

Conventions This Book Uses

We've written a thick book: There's a lot to say about Office! Therefore, we've used several devices that help you find your way.

You'll see eye-catching icons in the margin from time to time. They alert you to critical information, warn you about problems, tell you where to go for more information, and highlight useful tips.

This icon highlights a special point of interest about the current topic.

This icon helps you work faster by pointing out shortcuts and killer techniques. If you've worked with the Office applications before and want to expand your knowledge quickly, skim the book for these icons.

Sometimes it's important to be aware of potential problems that can develop if you're not aware of them. This icon points out those situations so you can avoid them.

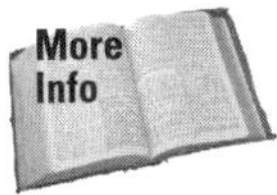

This icon sends you to other places in the book for more information about something we mention.

While each Office application stands on its own and does an excellent job, many times having the applications work together increases your productivity. This icon highlights examples where we've used more than one Office application to accomplish a task.

Sidebars

We use sidebars to highlight related information, give an example, or discuss an item in greater detail. For example, one sidebar tells you where to get graphics you can add to documents, spreadsheets, and presentations — cool information, but not critical. If you don't want to delve too deeply into a subject, stick to the body of the text and skip the sidebars.

When we write command names, we use a convention that shows you the menus you need to use to execute the command. So, when we want you to execute the Print command from the File menu, we've written File ⇨ Print. When we want you to execute the Define command from the Name submenu of the Insert menu, we've written Insert ⇨ Name ⇨ Define.

Where Should I Start?

If you want to learn about Word, start with Chapter 2. If you've never used a word processor before, read Appendix B first.

If you want to work with Excel, go to Chapter 15. Appendix C teaches the basics of Excel, for those who've never used a spreadsheet program.

If you want to create presentations in PowerPoint, start with Chapter 27 (or Appendix D, if you don't know the first thing about presentation-creation software).

If you want to use Outlook Express, go to Chapter 35.

If you want to use Internet Explorer, go to Chapter 36.

Acknowledgments

First, thanks to the IDG folks: Michael Roney for asking us to do this book and for all his work to make it a great experience, Claire Keaveney for her excellent editing expertise, and the entire staff who make working with IDG Books Worldwide such a pleasure for us writers.

Thanks to some really cool programmers at Microsoft: program managers Todd Roshak (Word), Richard Brown (Excel), and handsome Hillel Cooperman (Internet Explorer) for sharing their knowledge and insights; programmer Fred Kesler for his insights into his programming of Office's drawing capabilities; and programmer Terence Worley for his insights into his programs — MOM, Outlook, and more. Thanks, too, to Deanna Meyer for fielding our first questions and putting us in touch with these great guys.

Thanks to Irving Kwong and his minions at Waggener-Edstrom Public Relations for keeping us current with news of Office 98's development.

Thanks also to superagent Carole "stop calling me Swifty in the acknowledgments" McClendon of Waterside Productions for her deal-making and coordination beyond the call of duty. Carole, you're the greatest!

Finally, thanks to all the software and hardware makers who provided the tools we used to create this book, including Microsoft, Apple, Adobe, Newer, APS, Iomega, Dantz, Aladdin, PowerOn, and others too numerous to mention.

Contents at a Glance

Preface xiii
Acknowledgments xvii

Part I: Introducing Microsoft Office 98 1

Chapter 1: Getting to Know Microsoft Office....3

Part II: Word....19

Chapter 2: Creating and Working with Documents....21
Chapter 3: Formatting Documents 71
Chapter 4: Previewing and Printing Your Documents 103
Chapter 5: Working with Tables and Outlines....117
Chapter 6: Working with Fields 149
Chapter 7: Building Tables of Contents and Indexes 173
Chapter 8: Working with Styles and Templates....189
Chapter 9: Working with Word Macros....213
Chapter 10: Desktop Publishing with Word....225
Chapter 11: Word on the Web 251
Chapter 12: Word and Visual Basic for Applications 263
Chapter 13: Word 98 at Work....273
Chapter 14: The Word Top Ten 283

Part III: Excel....293

Chapter 15: Making the Most of Workbooks 295
Chapter 16: Getting Information into Excel 319
Chapter 17: Excel Formatting....361
Chapter 18: Adding Graphics to Worksheets....387
Chapter 19: Working with Excel Charts 407
Chapter 20: Printing and Page Setup 431
Chapter 21: Working with Excel Databases 447
Chapter 22: Working with Excel Macros....467
Chapter 23: Excel and the Web 481
Chapter 24: Excel and Visual Basic for Applications 491
Chapter 25: Excel at Work 503
Chapter 26: The Excel Top Ten 523

Part IV: PowerPoint 529

Chapter 27: Working with PowerPoint 531
Chapter 28: Enhancing a Presentation 557
Chapter 29: Working with Charts in PowerPoint 577
Chapter 30: Producing Your Work 597
Chapter 31: Working with PowerPoint Macros 611
Chapter 32: PowerPoint and the Web 619
Chapter 33: PowerPoint at Work 631
Chapter 34: The PowerPoint Top Ten 641

Part V: The Internet Office 645

Chapter 35: Using Outlook Express 647
Chapter 36: Overview of Internet Explorer 693

Appendixes 731

Appendix A: Installing Microsoft Office 98 733
Appendix B: Word Quick Start 745
Appendix C: Excel Quick Start 761
Appendix D: PowerPoint Quick Start 779
Appendix E: Customizing Toolbars and Menus 793

Index 803

Contents

Preface ... xiii
Acknowledgments ... xvii

Part I: Introducing Microsoft Office 98 — 1

Chapter 1: Getting to Know Microsoft Office ... 3

- Getting to Know Microsoft Office ... 3
- Installing Office 98 ... 4
- Launching Office Applications ... 5
- Creating New Documents ... 6
- Opening Existing Documents ... 7
- Using the Microsoft Office Manager ... 9
  - Installing MOM ... 9
  - Customizing the MOM menu ... 9
  - Using QuickSwitch ... 10
- Learning About Toolbars ... 11
  - Turning toolbars on or off ... 11
  - Docking, undocking, and moving toolbars ... 12
  - Enabling ScreenTips ... 12
- Working with the Office Assistant ... 13
  - Getting help through your assistant ... 13
  - Tips ... 14
  - Setting your Assistant's behavior ... 14
  - More help ... 15
- Using Command Underlines ... 15
  - Summary ... 16
  - Where to go next ... 17

Part II: Word — 19

Chapter 2: Creating and Working with Documents ... 21

- Launching the Program ... 21
- Creating and Opening Documents ... 21
- Understanding Templates ... 22
  - Exploring template categories ... 23
  - Looking at template wizards ... 25
  - Editing templates ... 30
- Working with Text ... 31
  - Using AutoComplete ... 31
  - Copying and Pasting ... 31

Selecting text 32
Deleting text 33
Inserting Graphics 33
Navigating Within a Document 34
Customizing keyboard commands 35
Using the Document Map view 35
Saving Your Documents 36
Looking at Word's Views 37
Setting Margins, Tabs, and Line Spacing 38
Changing margins 39
Applying tabs 39
Adjusting Line spacing 42
Adjusting Paragraph spacing 44
Moving and Copying Text 44
Searching and Replacing Text 45
Searching for regular text 45
Replacing text 47
Checking Spelling and Grammar 48
Interactive spell-checking 49
Spell-checking manually 49
Interactive grammar-checking 50
Grammar-checking manually 51
Spelling and grammar preferences 52
Changing dictionaries 53
Using AutoCorrect 55
AutoCorrect's features and capabilities 55
Working with AutoText entries 56
Accessing Word's Thesaurus 59
Hyphenating Your Document 59
Adding Bullets or Paragraph Numbers 60
Collaborating on a Document 62
Tracking changes to your document 62
Comparing documents 63
Creating comments 63
Finding comments 65
Locking the document 65
Working with Document Summaries 65
Viewing or editing a summary 66
Using the AutoSummarize feature 67
Summary 68
Where to go next 69

Chapter 3: Formatting Documents 71

Discovering Formatting 71
Formatting Documents 72
Orientation 73
Page Size 74
Margins 74

Formatting Paragraphs 75
Applying paragraph formatting....77
Indenting paragraphs 80
Aligning paragraphs....82
Applying line spacing 83
Applying paragraph spacing....83
Applying borders to paragraphs....84
Formatting Characters 86
Using character formatting options 86
Using character formatting shortcuts....89
Changing character fonts and point sizes 90
Applying superscript and subscript....91
Adjusting kerning....92
Copying character formatting 92
Formatting Sections....92
Headers and footers 94
Deleting a header or footer....95
Adjusting margin settings 95
Positioning headers and footers....95
Page numbers 96
Footnotes....97
Editing existing footnotes 100
Moving and deleting footnotes....100
Exploring footnote options....101
Changing footnotes to endnotes....101
Summary....102
Where to go next....102

Chapter 4: Previewing and Printing Your Documents....103

Previewing Documents....103
The Print Preview toolbar....103
Adjusting margins 104
Adjusting object locations and text wrap....105
Printing Documents....106
General (standard) printing options 107
Word's special printing options 108
Printing Document Information 111
Changing Your Printer....112
Printing Envelopes....113
Summary....115
Where to go next....116

Chapter 5: Working with Tables and Outlines 117

Understanding Tables in Word 98....117
Creating Tables....118
Navigating within a table 120
Creating your own table....122

Editing Tables 123
Inserting and deleting columns or rows 124
Inserting and deleting cells..124
Merging cells 127
Splitting a table...127
Formatting Tables 128
Setting column widths...128
Adjusting the space between columns 130
Making row adjustments 130
Applying borders...131
Converting text to tables 132
Exploring Other Uses for Tables..133
Creating side-by-side paragraphs 134
Sorting information...134
Understanding Outlines in Word 135
Selecting text 136
Changing the structure of an outline..136
Changing Outline Headings 138
Converting body text..138
Expanding or collapsing outline headings..139
Moving headings 139
Applying numbering to outlines 140
Creating Your Own Outline...141
Collapsing and expanding the sample outline 144
Changing headings in the sample outline...145
Creating Tables of Contents from Outlines 146
Adding a table of contents...147
Updating a table of contents 147
Printing Outlines 148
Summary 148
Where to go next...148

Chapter 6: Working with Fields 149

Defining Fields 149
Using Fields..150
Inserting fields 150
Viewing field codes 153
Updating fields..153
Moving between fields...154
Formatting fields 154
Locking a field's contents..155
Using fields in an example 155
Creating a Mail Merge...157
How to finish your mail merge 157
Specifying a main document..158
Creating a data source...158

Adding merge fields to the main document 159
Merging data 160
Printing Envelopes and Mailing Labels 161
Printing envelopes 161
Printing mailing labels 163
Creating Data Documents with Other Software 165
Copying Excel data 166
Embedding Excel data 167
Embedding data from other sources 171
Summary 171
Where to go next 172

Chapter 7: Building Tables of Contents and Indexes 173

Building Tables of Contents 173
Using style and outline headings 174
Using nonstandard styles 176
Using TC entries 176
Creating Your Own Table of Contents 178
Building tables of figures 180
Building indexes 181
Marking the index entries 181
Inserting the index 183
Creating multilevel index entries 184
Using page number ranges in indexes 185
Using additional index options 185
Building Large Indexes 186
Summary 186
Where to go next 187

Chapter 8: Working with Styles and Templates 189

Discovering Styles and Templates 189
Applying Styles 191
Using the Formatting toolbar 191
Using the keyboard 193
Defining Styles 193
Using the Style command 194
Defining styles by example 196
Assigning a shortcut key to a style 196
Basing a style on another style 197
Copying, deleting, and renaming styles 199
Redefining Styles 200
Finding Styles When You Need Them 201
Displaying style names as you work 201
Using the Style Gallery 202

Defining and Applying Styles: An Exercise 203
Understanding Templates 205
Working with Templates 207
Applying templates 207
Creating a template 208
Basing a new template on an existing template 208
Changing the default template 208
Creating and Applying a Template: An Exercise 210
Summary 211
Where to go next 212

Chapter 9: Working with Word Macros 213

Defining Macros 213
Storing Macros 215
Creating Macros 215
Preparing to create your macro 216
Recording the macro 217
Running Macros 220
Deleting Unwanted Macros 221
Understanding the Macros Dialog Box 221
Using Macros in an Example 222
Creating Macros That Run Automatically 223
Summary 224
Where to go next 224

Chapter 10: Desktop Publishing with Word 225

Working with Columns 225
Using the AutoFormat Command 227
Understanding Graphic Images 229
Bitmapped images 230
Object images 232
Using Graphic Images 233
Inserting images into Word 233
Changing the look of the image 235
Editing images 238
Inserting Graphs into Word 238
Working with Text Boxes 240
Creating a text box around existing text 241
Inserting an empty text box into a document 241
Linking text boxes 241
Formatting text boxes 242
Moving text boxes 243
Sizing text boxes 244
Wrapping text around text boxes 245
Applying the Organizational Tools 246
Columns and margins 246
Headlines and subheads 246

Graphic images 247
Graphs and tables 248
Using the Newsletter Wizard 248
Summary 249
Where to go next 249

Chapter 11: Word on the Web 251

Making the Network Connection 251
Discovering the Web and the Internet 252
About the World Wide Web 252
About Internet addresses 253
About intranets 253
About HTML 253
About the Web toolbar 253
Using Word to Open Web Documents 255
Creating Hyperlinks in Documents 256
Linking to office documents with Copy and Paste 256
Linking to Web sites or files with Insert Hyperlink 257
Publishing Documents on the Web 258
Saving existing Word documents as HTML 258
Using the Web Page Wizard to create Web pages 260
Summary 261
Where to go next 262

Chapter 12: Word and Visual Basic for Applications 263

Using Macros to Learn VBA 263
Understanding VBA Code 265
About comments 267
About headers and footers 268
About VBA code 268
About displaying dialog boxes 268
Editing VBA Code 269
Printing Visual Basic Code 270
About the Visual Basic Toolbar 270
Just a Beginning 271
Summary 271
Where to go next 271

Chapter 13: Word 98 at Work 273

Designing a Fax Cover Sheet 273
Writing an Interoffice Memo 276
Summary 281
Where to go next 281

Chapter 14: The Word Top Ten 283

Summary 291
Where to go next 291

Part III: Excel 293

Chapter 15: Making the Most of Workbooks 295

Understanding Excel Workbooks 295
- Opening a new workbook 297
- Opening an existing workbook 297

Working with Worksheets 298
- Navigating within your worksheet 299
- Moving among worksheets 301
- Renaming the worksheet tabs 302
- Selecting multiple worksheets 302
- Selecting a range of cells 303
- Adding and deleting worksheets 304
- Moving and copying information in worksheets 305
- Splitting the worksheet window 307

Working with Excel's Toolbars 307
- The formula bar 308
- The status bar 308

Saving and Closing a Workbook 309
- Adding summary information to your workbook 310
- Using the AutoSave feature 311
- Creating a backup file 312
- Saving in other file formats 312
- Saving Excel data as HTML 313
- Saving a workspace file 313
- Closing a workbook and exiting Excel 314

Finding Workbooks 314

Organizing Your Files 316

Summary 316
- Where to go next 317

Chapter 16: Getting Information into Excel 319

Entering Data 319
- Entering numbers 321
- Entering text 322
- Using the AutoComplete feature 322
- Entering dates and times 324
- Displayed values versus underlying values 325

Adding Comments to Cells 326

Editing Data 328
- Editing using the formula bar 328
- Using in-cell editing 328

Clearing Data from Cells 328

Copying and Moving Cells 329
- Copying and moving data with Cut, Copy, and Paste 330
- Copying and moving data with drag-and-drop 331
- Copying data with Fill and AutoFill 331

Building series 334
Using Paste Special 336
Working with Cells, Rows, and Columns 338
Inserting cells, rows, and columns 338
Deleting cells, rows, and columns 339
Working with Named Ranges....340
Creating and Using Formulas 341
In the formula bar or with Edit directly in cell 342
Creating formulas by pointing....342
Allowed elements 343
Displaying and editing formulas 345
Changing the recalculation options....346
Using Functions....347
Average, Maximum, Minimum, and Sum....348
Using AutoSum 349
Using the Function Wizard....349
Validating Your Data 351
Using Find and Replace....354
Finding data 354
Finding and replacing data 355
Correcting Your Spelling 356
AutoCorrect....356
Checking spelling 357
Adding a custom dictionary 358
Summary 358
Where to go next 359

Chapter 17: Excel Formatting 361

Using the AutoFormat Feature....361
Changing Widths and Heights....365
Column widths....365
Row heights 366
Hiding and Unhiding Elements....366
Hiding columns....367
Hiding rows 367
Hiding gridlines 367
Changing Alignments....367
Formatting Text....369
Centering text 370
Wrapping text 370
Justifying text....370
Rotating text 371
Applying fonts and style formats....372
Applying Borders, Patterns, and Colors 373
Working with Number Formats....376
Date and time formats....377
Custom number formats 378
Using the Format Painter....381
Creating Your Own Styles 382

Protecting Your Formatting Changes 384
Summary 385
Where to go next 386

Chapter 18: Adding Graphics to Worksheets 387

Discovering a Need for Graphics 387
Inserting Graphics into Worksheets 388
Working with Graphic Objects 389
Inserting AutoShapes 391
Drawing lines, arcs, ellipses, and rectangles 393
Selecting and grouping objects 394
Using Bring To Front and Send To Back 395
Moving and copying objects 396
Resizing objects 396
Formatting objects 397
Adding Text Boxes 399
Editing text 400
Formatting text 400
Rotating text 401
Using WordArt 402
Changing colors and sizes 405
Changing shapes 406
Rotating objects 406
Summary 406
Where to go next 406

Chapter 19: Working with Excel Charts 407

Learning About Charts 407
Embedding Charts and Chart Sheets 408
Creating an embedded chart or chart sheet 410
Using the Chart Wizard 410
Creating a Sample Chart 413
Saving and Printing Charts 415
Understanding the Parts of a Chart 415
Working with Charts 417
Selecting parts of a chart 418
Working with the Chart toolbar 418
Adding titles 419
Adding unattached text 420
Formatting text 420
Formatting chart axes 421
Adding legends 421
Adding gridlines 422
Customizing a chart's area 422
Working with Chart Types 423
Understanding How Excel Plots a Chart 426
Summary 429
Where to go next 430

Chapter 20: Printing and Page Setup 431

Learning Printing Basics 431
Printing worksheets 431
About the Print dialog box 433
Setting Up Your Pages 434
Paper size 436
Orientation 436
Scaling 437
First page number 437
Print quality 437
Margins 438
Headers and footers 438
Print titles 440
Row and column headings 441
Printing gridlines 441
Printing comments 441
Setting Print Ranges 441
Setting a Page Order 442
Previewing Print Jobs 443
Controlling Page Breaks 444
E-mailing a File 445
Summary 446
Where to go next 446

Chapter 21: Working with Excel Databases 447

Learning About Databases 447
Creating a Database 449
Working with Database Records 450
Adding new records 451
Editing records 451
Deleting records 451
Finding data by using criteria 451
Using the AutoFormat Command 454
Sorting a Database 454
How it works 454
Custom sort orders 458
Using the AutoFilter Command 459
Printing a report based on specific data 461
Using complex criteria with AutoFilter 461
The Top 10 option 462
Turning off the effects of AutoFilter 463
Performing a Mail Merge 463
Designing Databases 464
About data and attributes 464
Steps in database design 465
Summary 466
Where to go next 466

Chapter 22: Working with Excel Macros 467

Understanding Macro Types 467
Creating a Macro 468
Assigning Macros 471
  Assigning macros to a worksheet button 471
  Assigning macros to graphic objects 473
  Assigning macros to toolbar buttons 474
  Assigning macros to menus 475
Running a Macro 476
Changing Macro Options 476
Making Macros Available 477
Summary 478
  Where to go next 479

Chapter 23: Excel and the Web 481

Working with Excel 98 on the Web 481
Learning the Ropes 482
  The World Wide Web 483
  The Internet 483
  About intranets 483
  About HTML 483
  About the Web toolbar 484
Creating Hyperlinks 484
  Linking to Office documents with Copy and Paste 485
  Linking to Web sites or files with Insert Hyperlink 486
Publishing Worksheets and Charts 487
Summary 489
  Where to go next 489

Chapter 24: Excel and Visual Basic for Applications 491

Learning VBA with Macros 491
Understanding VBA Code 494
  About comments 495
  About headers and footers 496
  About selecting and entering data 496
  About control statements 497
  About displaying dialog boxes 497
  About user input 498
Editing VBA Code 499
Printing Visual Basic Code 499
Using the Visual Basic Toolbar 499
Getting Started 500
Summary 501
  Where to go next 501

Chapter 25: Excel at Work 503

Managing Cash Flow 503
Performing Break-Even Analysis 505

Using the IRA calculator 510
Working with Mortgages and Amortization 518
Summary 521
Where to go next 521

Chapter 26: The Excel Top Ten 523

Summary 528
Where to go next 528

Part IV: PowerPoint 529

Chapter 27: Working with PowerPoint 531

Discovering the Presentation Window 531
Working with Shortcuts and Toolbars 534
Using shortcut menus 535
Using the toolbars 536
Using PowerPoint's Default Presentations 537
Working with Presentations 540
Creating a new presentation 540
Saving a presentation 541
Entering summary information 542
Entering and editing text 543
Working with slides 544
Working with objects 548
Working with shapes 552
Summary 555
Where to go next 556

Chapter 28: Enhancing a Presentation 557

Using the AutoContent Wizard 557
Using the AutoLayout Feature 560
Using the Slide Master 561
Working with Lists and Columns 564
Creating bulleted lists 564
Creating columns 566
Adding Formatting and Special Effects 567
Fonts, styles, and colors 567
Special effects with WordArt 568
Excel Worksheets and Word Tables 571
Sound, slide animation, and action buttons 574
Summary 576
Where to go next 576

Chapter 29: Working with Charts in PowerPoint 577

Looking at a Typical Chart 577
Working with Chart Types 579
Inserting Charts 580

Entering Data and Editing Charts 582
Legends and headings 582
Adjusting the column width 583
Number formats 583
Editing charts 583
Changing the data series 584
Changing the chart type 587
Enhancing a Chart's Appearance 588
Changing fonts 588
Changing chart colors 590
Adding titles 590
Changing axes 591
Changing borders 591
Enhancing 3-D charts 592
Creating Organizational Charts 593
Summary 594
Where to go next 596

Chapter 30: Producing Your Work 597

Printing Presentations 597
Setting up your slides for printing 597
Printing parts of your presentation 598
Producing Onscreen Slide Shows 600
Creating progressive slides 602
Hiding and unhiding slides 604
Adding Speaker Notes and Handouts 604
Creating Custom Shows 607
Using the PowerPoint Viewer 609
Summary 610
Where to go next 610

Chapter 31: Working with PowerPoint Macros 611

Approaching Visual Basic 611
Creating a Macro 612
Using the Macro dialog box 612
Getting help with Visual Basic 614
Running Macros During Slide Shows 614
Assigning macros to toolbar buttons 615
Running the macro 615
Deleting a macro 616
About the macro code 616
Summary 617
Where to go next 617

Chapter 32: PowerPoint and the Web 619

Getting Started 619
Exploring what's possible 619
Connecting to a network 620

Defining Some Terms and Concepts....620
The Internet....621
The World Wide Web....621
About Intranets....621
About HTML....621
Using the Web Toolbar....622
Creating Hyperlinks in Documents....623
Linking to Office documents with Copy and Paste....623
Linking to Web sites or files with Insert Hyperlink....623
Publishing PowerPoint Slides on the Web....624
Summary....630
Where to go next....630

Chapter 33: PowerPoint at Work....631

Creating an Organization Chart....631
Creating a Travel Presentation....635
Applying a template....635
Applying a background....637
Adding notes and handouts....637
Adding headers and footers....638
Printing your notes pages....639
Adding transitions....639
Summary....640
Where to go next....640

Chapter 34: The PowerPoint Top Ten....641

Summary....643
Where to go next....643

Part V: The Internet Office 645

Chapter 35: Using Outlook Express....647

Introducing Outlook Express....647
How it works....647
Looking at the window....648
Working with E-Mail Accounts....653
Setting up your e-mail account....654
Dealing with contacts....657
Working with Messages....661
Creating a message....661
Sending a message....666
Receiving and reading messages....667
Making attachments....670
Printing a message....672
Saving a message....672
Replying to a message....672

Forwarding a message 674
Deleting messages 675
Filing your messages 676
Automating your incoming mail 677
Sorting messages 679
Searching for messages 679
Working with Multiple Users 680
Setting up multiple users 681
Switching between users 682
Deleting a user 683
Transferring users from Mac to Mac 683
Working with Newsgroups 683
Setting up a news account 685
Viewing messages 688
Keeping messages 689
Automating actions 690
Posting to a newsgroup 691
Replying to a message 691
Summary 692
Where to go next 692

Chapter 36: Overview of Internet Explorer 693

Looking at the Window 693
Using the button bar 696
Using the Explorer bar 697
Working with Web Pages and Sites 701
Visiting a Web site 702
Getting to a site 702
Subscribing to a site 706
Subscribing to a channel 709
Marking favorite sites for easy return 710
Controlling how you see Web sites 712
Searching Web sites 715
Browsing offline 717
Downloading and Saving Files 718
Copying 719
Saving a file 719
Downloading 720
Stopping a download 721
Reviewing your downloads 721
Setting the Download Manager's preferences 722
Printing Web Pages 723
Dealing with Security Concerns 723
SSL and Windows NT 723
Site certificates 723
Security zones 723
Security alerts 725
Working with Internet Ratings Support 726

Reading Mail and News 727
Getting More Help 728
Summary 729
Where to go next 729

Appendixes 731

Appendix A: Installing Microsoft Office 98 733

Appendix B: Word Quick Start 745

Appendix C: Excel Quick Start 761

Appendix D: PowerPoint Quick Start 779

Appendix E: Customizing Toolbars and Menus 795

Index 803

Introducing Microsoft Office 98

PART

I

✦ ✦ ✦ ✦

In This Part

Chapter 1
Getting to Know Microsoft Office

✦ ✦ ✦ ✦

Getting to Know Microsoft Office

✦ ✦ ✦ ✦

In This Chapter

Getting to know Microsoft Office

Installing Office 98

Launching Office applications

Creating new documents

Opening existing documents

Using the Microsoft Office Manager

Learning about toolbars

Working with the Office Assistant

Using Command Underlines

✦ ✦ ✦ ✦

This chapter introduces Microsoft Office, showing you what comes with Office 98 and how to install its core components. We introduce the various ways you can launch your Office applications and the basics for opening documents. You'll also be introduced to toolbars and the Office Assistant, your Office Help venue.

Getting to Know Microsoft Office

Microsoft Office consists of a group of applications that complement each other to accomplish things in a similar way and provide easy access to data shared between the individual applications. Office is designed to make you more productive with less hassle. With Microsoft Office, you can create business documents to meet virtually any need, handle complex financial analysis, and produce professional presentations. Microsoft Office includes the following applications:

- ✦ Word—Word provides all the power you need in a word processor along with a range of tools that make complex formatting tasks easier.
- ✦ Excel—In Microsoft Excel, you have a spreadsheet that is powerful yet simple to use. Besides offering powerful spreadsheet capabilities and the capability to work with multiple pages in the same spreadsheet file (the workbook concept), Excel provides powerful charting and graphing features and can readily use spreadsheets you have saved in other popular spreadsheet formats.
- ✦ PowerPoint—PowerPoint is a presentation graphics program that can provide you with overheads for team meetings, slides for sales meetings, animated special effects for video presentations, and more. PowerPoint's tools combined with its simple approach make it easy for you to create presentations that clearly emphasize what you are trying to say.

✦ Outlook Express—Outlook Express is a contact and e-mail management program. The Contacts feature provides a basic address book in which you can list a name, address, four numbers, and e-mail and Web information as well as take notes. Outlook enables you to send and receive e-mail, including Newsgroup e-mail, and to manage your messages. Filters and actions can be applied to incoming mail. (Outlook Express must be custom installed. It is not a core application.)

✦ Internet Explorer—Internet Explorer is a Web browser, an application that brings the pages of the World Wide Web to your screen. Features such as the Favorites list help you bookmark sites of interest for easy access. (Internet Explorer is not a core application. It must be installed separately.)

Office 98 also includes some "shared" applications, which are accessed from any of the individual programs. These include such programs as Word Art, Equation Editor, and Microsoft Graph:

✦ Word Art—Word art is actually art with words. You type in any text, pick a shape and colors for your text, and in a moment you have decorative text. You can then make several adjustments to the text. It can be edited or changed at any time, too. Although Word Art works in any of the core Office applications, we cover Word Art in the PowerPoint section.

✦ Equation Editor—The Equation Editor enables you to create true mathematical equations. Equations can be inserted into Word, Excel, or PowerPoint using the Insert Object command. Equation Editor is part of the Value Pack install.

✦ Microsoft Graph—Microsoft Graph enables you to create charts and graphs easily. We show you how to use it in the Word section in Chapter 10.

Installing Office 98

Microsoft Office 98 introduces a refreshing new twist on the original Mac software installation technique. Installation couldn't be simpler. Just insert the CD-ROM and drag the folder called Microsoft Office 98 onto your hard drive. That's it! The icons for each of the core Office 98 applications—Word, Excel, and PowerPoint—are in this main folder. You don't need to search through buried folders to find and launch any of the applications. Simply double-click the one you want to run, and launch it. Each of the Office applications self-install and reinstall themselves as needed. Each time you launch any Office application, it looks to see that all necessary pieces are in your System folder. If you turn off or remove any necessary pieces, the pieces are reinstalled.

The drag install provides all the basics of Microsoft Office 98; it's commonly called a *standard install,* and this is what most people want. If you find the drag install is more than you want, you can do a custom install instead by running the Microsoft Office Installer (located inside the Office Custom Install folder on your install CD-ROM). For details, see Appendix A.

How Does Office Do It?

The Office folder, within the Microsoft Office 98 folder, contains all the necessary extensions. If Microsoft Office First Run, an application within the Office folder, sees any extensions missing from your active extensions folder, it invisibly copies what it needs into your extensions folder.

If you happen to disable any necessary extensions, Office places a new copy in your active extensions folder. Therefore, it is possible that you'll end up with duplicate copies of an extension. An extensions manager, such as Conflict Catcher, will notice this duplication and ask you if you want to delete one version. You can delete the disabled version.

The installation performed by dragging the Microsoft Office 98 folder is the basic installation. Additional Office components, such as the Microsoft Office Manager, small business templates, and Word Speak, are available in the Value Pack on the CD-ROM. For details on these options and their installation, see Appendix A.

Office 98 also comes with more than what the drag install provides. You can find these additions in the Value Pack folder on your Office CD-ROM. These elements are installed via the Value Pack Installer inside the Value Pack folder. For the lowdown on what's in the Value Pack and installation instructions, see Appendix A.

Should you wish to remove Office 98 from your hard drive, you can use the Remove Office 98 application located in the Administration Tools folder within the Value Pack folder. Again, see Appendix A.

Outlook Express and Internet Explorer are separate installs. You can find their installers in the Microsoft Internet folder on your install CD-ROM. Just double-click the program icon to install, and then follow the directions as with any installer. (See Appendix A.)

Launching Office Applications

As with all Macintosh software, launching an Office application is as easy as double-clicking the application's icon. The standard shortcuts, such as placing an alias on your desktop or in you Apple menu, are also available. Microsoft provides one more launching option—the Microsoft Office Manager, an optional install via the Value Pack folder. Microsoft Office Manager (MOM) is a simple control panel that places a new menu in the menu bar to the left of the Application menu in the upper-right corner of your monitor. With MOM installed, you can select Word, Excel, or PowerPoint from the menu bar, as shown in Figure 1-1. (For more about MOM, see "Using thc Microsoft Office Manager" later in this chapter.)

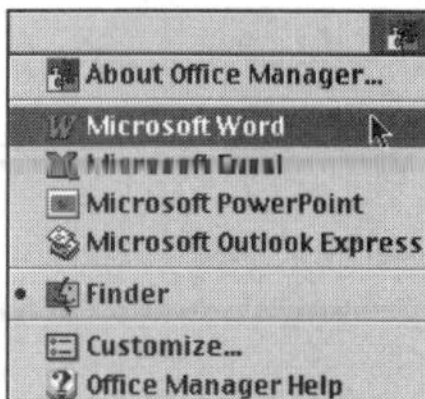

Figure 1-1: The Microsoft Office Manager menu

Aliases and the Apple Menu

You can save yourself considerable time by adding an alias of each Office icon to your Apple menu. This provides the same effect as using MOM, but also provides access to folders. (Except it doesn't provide MOM's cool application switching.)

An alias is a small file that points to, and opens, the actual program, file, or folder that it represents. You can place an alias anywhere on your Mac, but placing it in the Apple menu provides universal access. To create an alias, click the icon to select it, and then choose File ⇨ Make Alias (⌘-M). Alternatively, if you're using OS 8, press ⌘-Option as you click the desired icon and drag the icon to your destination. (These are the standard Mac procedures for creating aliases. See you Mac documentation for more information.) For example, to create an alias of Word, open the Microsoft Office 98 folder, click the Word icon, and then choose File ⇨ Make Alias. Or, in OS 8, press ⌘-Option as you click the Microsoft Word icon and drag the icon to your destination.

The point is, if you place an alias of Word, Excel, or PowerPoint (or any other application) in the Apple Menu Items folder, you can start that program without bothering to open the hard drive and the applications folder. Instead, you simply select the application's name in the Apple menu. If you place an alias of a file directly in the Apple menu, you can select it from this menu at any time to launch that file easily. If you place an alias of a folder in the Apple menu, you can go down to the folder to open it or slide over to any file within that folder to launch that file.

Don't skip the creation of an alias by dragging the Word, Excel, or PowerPoint icons from the Microsoft Office 98 folder to your desired location. If you do this, you are literally moving the program file from the application's folder (from which it is designed to work).

You can also place aliases of your Office applications on your desktop. This comes in handy when you want to open a file that was created in another application.

Creating New Documents

When you have any Office application (Word, Excel, or PowerPoint) open, you can use the New Document button to create new documents within that application. Of course, you can also use the standard Mac commands, File ⇨ New or ⌘-N.

The button directly opens a generic new document (from the standard template). So does the New document shortcut, ⌘-N. File ⇨ New provides more flexibility by taking you to the New Document window, enabling you to use a specialized template or wizard.

In the New Document window, you can peruse the various document choices, categorized by tabs. For example, while in Word, if you wanted to create a fax sheet, you click the Letters and Faxes tab and then choose Contemporary Fax. Or, if you want to create a sales presentation using PowerPoint, you might click the Presentations tab and select one of the sales presentations in the list box. Clicking a template (which selects it) presents a preview to help you decide what template is right for you. Figure 1-2 shows you the New Document window provided by the default install of Excel. After you select the template you want to use, clicking the OK button opens a new document based upon that template. (Or, if you've selected a wizard, it launches the wizard.) You can also open a template by double-clicking it, rather than clicking it once to select it and then clicking OK. (This works because the OK button is the default selection, as designated by the black ring around it.)

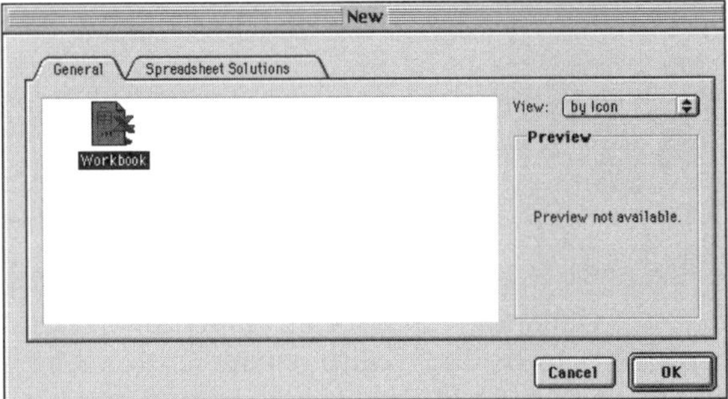

Figure 1-2: Excel's New Document dialog box

Opening Existing Documents

Opening an existing Office document is exactly the same as opening any document on the Mac. From within Word, Excel, or PowerPoint, you can use File⇨Open. Or, in the Finder you can directly select your document and open it, which launches the application in which the document was created (if it isn't already running) or brings the application forward (if it is already running).

Using File⇨Open from within a Word, Excel, or PowerPoint document enables you to open another Word, Excel, or PowerPoint document. (That is, from Word you can open a Word document, from Excel you can open an Excel document, and so on.) The Open Document dialog box is shown in Figure 1-3. You can filter the documents that appear in the open document list by selecting a filter from the List Files of Type pop-up box at the bottom of the window.

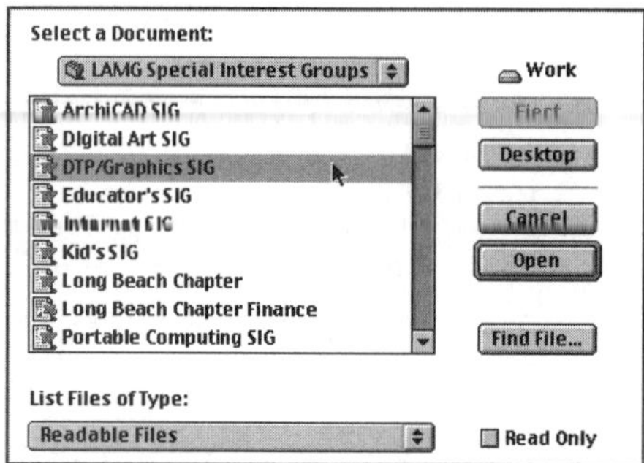

Figure 1-3: The Open Document dialog box revealing all document types

To open a document from the Finder, go directly to the folder that houses the document, and then double-click the document. If you have placed an alias of the document (or the document's folder) in the Apple menu, you can select the document directly from the Apple menu.

You can often open a document created in another, similar application. For example, you can be in Word and use the File ➪ Open command to select a word processing document that was created in ClarisWorks or WordPerfect. Word will translate it for you. Another way to do this is to drag the ClarisWorks or WordPerfect document onto the Word icon or an alias of the Word icon.

Office 97, the Windows equivalent of Office 98, has a feature called the Binder, which allows several Office documents to be bound into one file. If someone gives you an Office 97 document but you can't open it, the file may be one of these Binder files. It's easy to separate a Binder file into individual Office documents that you can work with. To do so, you use the Unbinder, a small application installed via the Value Pack Installer.

If you receive a document that has been bound, follow these steps:

1. Launch the Unbinder. Once installed, it should be located in the Microsoft Office 98 folder.
2. Select File ➪ Open Binder. Locate the file to unbind and click Open. A dialog box will appear, telling you the name of each file as it unbinds, and also reporting how many files there are in all.
3. The files will appear in the Office 98 folder. You can double-click any of the files and use them as normal.

Using the Microsoft Office Manager

As we said earlier, MOM, the Microsoft Office Manager, is a control panel that adds an extra menu to your Mac's menu bar. Unlike the other Office menus, MOM stays in view at all times, similar to the Apple menu and other such menus you may have installed. MOM also provides you with QuickSwitch—the capability to move between your open applications by pressing ⌘-Tab. You can use the Customize window to change the combination to Control or Option along with the Tab key, if you prefer.

Installing MOM

MOM doesn't install by default. (If you use your Apple menu effectively, you may not find MOM necessary.) To install MOM, insert your Microsoft Office 98 CD-ROM, open the Value Pack folder, and then double-click the Value Pack Installer. Locate Microsoft Office Manager in the list of items to install and click the box next to it. Check that each of the other option's check boxes are blank. (Any checked options will also be installed. A dash in the check box means at least one component of that option will be installed. Click the arrow at its left to view the components.) After checking the option you want to install (MOM), click the Install button. Upon restarting your Mac you'll find the new control panel activated.

Customizing the MOM menu

MOM's fairly smart; knowing which Office applications to list in its menu. For example, if you've done the standard (drag the folder) install, you have Word, Excel, and PowerPoint, so MOM lists those applications. If you add Outlook Express and restart, MOM adds Outlook Express to the menu. MOM also automatically recognizes Internet Explorer if you happen to have it installed. MOM enables you to add other programs—and files—to it, turning MOM into your Mac's launcher if you want. A business may appreciate MOM as the universal application launcher for company computers. For example, you can add a file, such as a FileMaker Pro database, your Quicken file, or any application you use in addition to Office. After adding items to the MOM menu, you can change their order.

To customize MOM, select Customize from the MOM menu. This brings up the Microsoft Office Manager control panel, as shown in Figure 1-4. Simply click New, locate and select the application or file you wish to add to the menu, and then click Add. To change an item's location in the menu, select Customize from the MOM menu, click once on the item you wish to move, and click the up or down Move arrows until the item is where you want it.

Figure 1-4: The. Microsoft Office Manager control panel

MOM gives you a head start in customization by listing all Microsoft software for you. If you own any of these programs and want them to appear, all you need to do is check the box next to the application. Likewise, you can remove any application from the menu by unchecking the box by that item. Some separators are also ready and waiting for you to select, deselect, or move around.

You can also rename any item in the MOM menu by opening the MOM control panel, selecting the item to be renamed, and then clicking Edit. In the text field that appears, rename your item and click OK.

By default, MOM shows you the icon for each application in the menu. You can uncheck this option—Include menu icons—if you wish. You can also stop the MOM menu from appearing in your menu bar by unchecking Enable Microsoft Office Manager. To turn it back on, select the MOM control panel as you access any control panel (Apple menu ➪ Control panels).

In case you'd like more help with MOM, you can click the Help icon (the question mark, located at the bottom of MOM's control panel window). This brings up a Help window specifically dedicated to MOM.

Using QuickSwitch

QuickSwitch gives you the capability to move between your open applications via the keyboard, rather than by moving your mouse to the Mac's Application menu. By default, QuickSwitch is turned on and ⌘-Tab does the switching.

With QuickSwitch on, simply press ⌘-Tab at any time, from any program you happen to be in. You will see a list of your open applications flash in the middle of your screen. Your Mac will switch you from the application that was active to the one that comes next in the list of active applications under your Application menu.

For more control, keep the ⌘ key pressed, thereby keeping the open applications list onscreen. Then press Tab once for each time you want to move down once in the list of open applications. When your target application becomes active, release the ⌘ key.

You can use MOM's control panel window to turn QuickSwitch off or to change the combination to Control-Tab or Option-Tab. To turn QuickSwitch off, simply click the check box to remove the check mark. To change the key combination, click the pop-up menu in the QuickSwitch area and select the preferred key. The Include extra information option enables you to see the status of your computer's memory use as you switch programs. (This is the same memory information you get by selecting About this Computer from the Apple menu when you're in the Finder.)

You can use QuickSwitch even if you opt not to keep the MOM menu turned on in your menu bar.

Learning About Toolbars

When you activate Word, Excel, or PowerPoint, you will see a gray area containing toolbars—rows full of symbols—across the top of your screen (unless your toolbars were turned off). Toolbars are strips of buttons you can use to perform common tasks. Word, Excel, and PowerPoint each have a standard toolbar as well as several function-specific toolbars. As you rest your mouse over any button, a little yellow information window pops up, telling you what that button does. Using the toolbars is a great way to accomplish an action with as few motions as possible. In this section, we introduce toolbars so you can use them comfortably as you work.

Toolbars are highly customizable. You can add or remove buttons as you wish, swap button positions, and customize button icons. In Appendix E you can learn how to customize your toolbars.

Outlook and Internet Explorer also have toolbars, so you can enjoy the same convenience you are used to in Office. However, these toolbars are not customizable.

Turning toolbars on or off

Toolbars provide great shortcuts; but of course, if you had every toolbar in view, there would be no room onscreen to see your document. Therefore, you can turn each of these toolbars on and off as desired. Turning a toolbar on or off is easy. The toolbar control is under the View menu. Simply click the View menu, and then move (in OS 8) or drag (in OS 7.5.5) down to the Toolbars option and over to the toolbar you want to turn on or off. A check mark in the menu indicates the menu is on. (Of course, you can also see the menu onscreen.) Office applications often turn on toolbars, as appropriate, when you call upon a function.

Docking, undocking, and moving toolbars

You can change a toolbar's position or undock the toolbars. Rather than keeping your toolbars attached to the top of the screen, you may prefer to move a toolbar to the left or right edge of your monitor. Simply click any edge of a toolbar and drag left or right.

Toolbars can also float freely as palettes, rather than remaining attached to the top of your screen. Notice that the left side of the toolbar has a few rows of dots. To undock a toolbar, click these dots and drag the toolbar down and away from the docked area. (Actually, you can click any edge of any toolbar to undock it.) The toolbar then gains the standard Mac window features: a close box, a title bar, and a resize corner (bottom right). Like any window, you can drag this palette anywhere onscreen and resize it. Resizing the palette doesn't add a scrollbar; it rearranges the buttons. To redock the toolbar, drag it back up into the toolbar area until your mouse overlaps the toolbar below which you want it to fall.

Enabling ScreenTips

We mentioned that a little yellow information window pops up when you rest your mouse over a button. These windows are called ScreenTips. You can turn them on and off at any time. Select Tools ➪ Customize, click the Options tab of the Customize dialog box that opens (see Figure 1-5). Click the check box to turn on or turn off Show ScreenTips on toolbars. ScreenTips are turned on by default. In Word and PowerPoint, you have another ScreenTip option—Show shortcut keys in ScreenTips—which shows you a keyboard equivalent to pressing the button (when there is one). Enabling this feature is a great way to become more familiar with your keyboard shortcuts. Show shortcut keys in ScreenTips is turned off by default.

By the way, Large icons sets your buttons to a (very) large size.

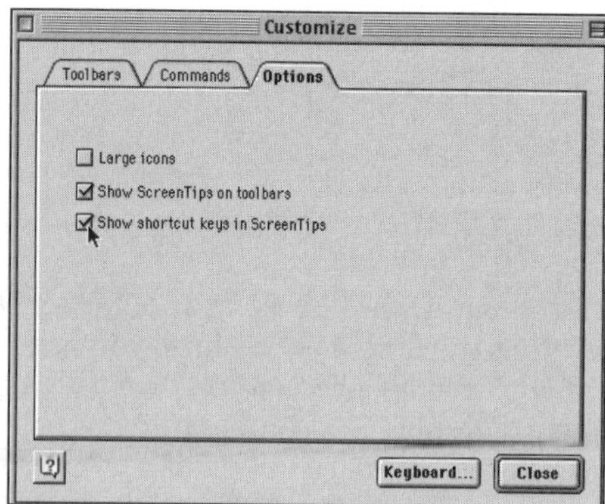

Figure 1-5: The Options tab of the Customize dialog box

When you select Tools ➪ Customize, you will most likely be greeted by the Office Assistant. He pops up once in a while to guide you when he feels you may need help (as described in the following section). Because selecting options is so easy, you probably won't need to consult the Office Assistant in this case.

Working with the Office Assistant

The Office Assistant is another element common to the core Office applications (Word, Excel, and PowerPoint). The Office Assistant provides you with help, tips, advice, and warnings. You can call it up at any time by pressing the Help key or selecting ". . . Help" from the Help menu. From time to time, the Assistant pops up on its own, offering to tell you about something you're about to do. It may even pop up to suggest a way to do something easier, for example, by suggesting you use a Wizard.

The default Assistant is Max, an original Mac. Several more are included in the Value Pack. Each has a unique personality and can prove entertaining as it hangs out watching you work, waiting to be useful. By default, the assistants are quiet, but you can program them to speak.

Getting help from your Assistant

To get help, click your Assistant, press the Help key or select ". . . Help" from the Help menu. If the Assistant isn't already onscreen, he'll pop up at your beck and call. In a yellow balloon, he'll ask, "What would you like to do?" There's a text area below, requesting you to type your question and click Search. You don't have to place your cursor anywhere. Just type. The Assistant understands plain English, so you can ask it any question. If it doesn't respond with what you need, try removing unnecessary instructions. For example, you don't need to say "Show me . . ." or "Tell me about . . . ." You can experiment with cutting down your questions to phrases. After you type your question, press Return or Enter, or click Search. The Assistant will then present a list of all topics that may meet your needs. Click the blue bullet next to the offering you want. A new window opens, providing details. When appropriate, there will be other symbols to click for more information on a related topic.

If you switch help pages and want to return to one you visited, click the History button. This brings up a list of help pages you've been to in that session. Double-click any topic to return to it.

You can bookmark a help page so you can find it again later. While on the page, select Bookmark ➪ Define. Rename the bookmark if you want. Bookmarks show at the bottom of the Bookmark menu. To return to a bookmarked page, simply choose it from the Bookmark menu. You can also copy help text. While on the page, choose Edit ➪ Copy (⌘-C). The entire page's text will appear, all selected. Click Copy to copy the entire text. To copy only part, select that part using the standard drag-over-the-text selection method, and then click the Copy button.

Tips

A yellow light bulb by the Assistant's head lets you know a tip is waiting for you. Click the light bulb to view the tip. You can determine whether you see tips and what tip topics are offered. (See "Setting your Assistant's behavior," which follows.)

Setting your Assistant's behavior

You can change your Assistant or its behavior at any time. This Assistant and behavior is common throughout each of the core Office applications. When you call up the Assistant, an Options button appears in its dialog box. Click the Options button. Click the Gallery tab (see Figure 1-6) to select a new Assistant (after you've installed alternatives via the Value Pack Installer). The Back and Next buttons move through each installed Assistant. Each Assistant is shown and described. Click the Options tab (see Figure 1-7) to determine what your Assistant will help you with and how.

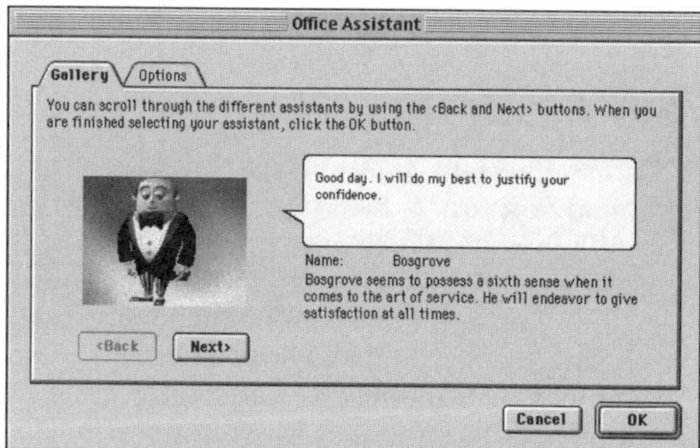

Figure 1-6: The Gallery tab of the Office Assistant dialog box

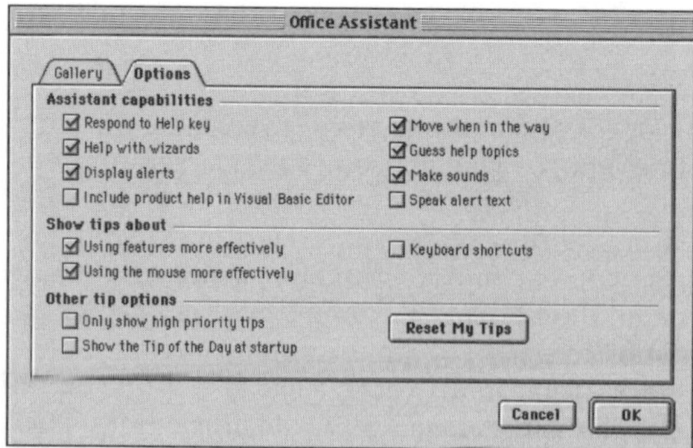

Figure 1-7: The Options tab of the Office Assistant dialog box

The options available to you are fairly self-explanatory, but a few are worth pointing out. Guess help topics is the option that enables the Assistant to anticipate your needs, suggesting help relevant to what you are doing. The Help with wizards option triggers help to come up whenever you start a wizard. The Display alerts option enables the Assistant to deliver alerts. Alerts can also be spoken when the Speak alert text option is checked. When the Display alerts option is not checked, alert messages are shown in an alternative dialog box.

After you have set your Assistant and/or chosen your options, click OK.

More help

When the Assistant fails to find what you are looking for, you can go to the Help menu and select Contents and Index. You now have two options: You can delve into a subject or go directly to a subtopic.

If you see a subject that looks like what you want, double-click to "open the book" on a subject, and then double-click any of the question mark documents.

If you don't see your subject, click the Index button at the top. Type a topic into the box at the top. (You're there automatically.) Matches appear in the top half of the dialog box. When you see one of interest, click it to select it, and then click Show Topics. In the lower dialog box, view the topics, and when one interests you, select it and click Go To.

Using Command Underlines

Chances are, if you've seen a Windows program, you've noticed menus and commands each have one letter underlined. Those underlined characters, when pressed with the Alt key, pull down the menu or issue the command—an alternative to using the mouse for those who prefer to keep their hands on the keyboard. Each of the core Office 98 programs (Word, Excel, and PowerPoint) now provide those same hot keys. So, if you are one of the people who like your hands on the keys, you can press F10 when you need to issue a menu command.

Pressing F10 makes command underlines appear temporarily. Note the letter that's underlined in your desired menu and type that letter. When the elected menu pulls down, the commands under it will also be underlined. Again, press the letter that corresponds to your command. If that's the end of your action, the underlines disappear and turn off. If the command you select opens a dialog box, each option in the dialog box also has an underline. While in the dialog box, press ⌘ as you press the underlined character. This moves you to the option or selects a radio button or check box for you. When you close the dialog box, completing the command, the underlines turn off.

If you open a dialog box without pressing F10 to use hot keys, you can still turn the underlines on by pressing the ⌘ key two or three times. Or, if you happen to recall what hot key you need to select your option or activate your desired button, you can press ⌘ and the key to select the option and activate underline mode at the same time.

As long as keys appear underlined, they are active as hot keys. When the underlines go away, press F10 the next time you want to take advantage of them.

In Excel, there is a Preference option to keep Command underline (as it is called there) on or off all the time and one to have it be automatic. This F10 method is the Automatic option in Excel (which happens to be the default). In Word, you have the option of changing keyboard commands or adding your own instead of using F10. Word calls this command MenuMode.

Summary

This chapter showed how to access the Microsoft Office applications—via standard Mac methods or the optional Microsoft Office Manager (MOM). MOM also helps you switch between all running applications using its QuickSwitch feature. You also learned about getting help. This chapter covered these points:

- ✦ Microsoft Office includes Word (for word processing), Excel (for spreadsheets), PowerPoint (for presentations), Outlook Express (for managing contacts and e-mail), and Internet Explorer (for using the Web).
- ✦ Some Windows users bind their documents. Use the Unbinder to access those documents.
- ✦ You can customize the Microsoft Office Manager (MOM) by adding applications and files to it.
- ✦ You can easily switch between all running applications using MOM's QuickSwitch feature.
- ✦ In addition to the standard Mac install, you can install complementary productivity (Value Pack) features. Appendix A covers the Value Pack.
- ✦ You can customize Word, Excel, or PowerPoint's toolbars. Appendix E shows you how.
- ✦ The Office Assistant is always standing by to help you. You can ask questions in real English. If the Assistant can't help, you can find topics in the Help Index.
- ✦ The Office Assistant can even anticipate your needs. You can set the Assistant's behavior—which remains consistent between each core application.
- ✦ Command underlines provide a new alternative to the other methods of selecting commands. They turn on when you press F10.

Where to go next

- ✦ The remainder of this book details how you can get the most out of Microsoft Office.
- ✦ If you want to work in Word, go to Chapter 2. If you're a Word neophyte, Appendix B gets you started.
- ✦ If you want to use Excel, go to Chapter 15. Appendix C provides Excel basics for those who have never used a spreadsheet before.
- ✦ If you want to create presentations in PowerPoint, see Chapter 27. If you are a beginner, see Appendix D.
- ✦ If you'd like to customize your toolbars, visit Appendix E.
- ✦ If you'd like to custom install Office, or add Value Pack features, go directly to Appendix A.

✦ ✦ ✦

P A R T

Word

✦ ✦ ✦ ✦

In This Part

Chapter 2
Creating and Working with Documents

Chapter 3
Formatting Documents

Chapter 4
Previewing and Printing Your Documents

Chapter 5
Working with Tables and Outlines

Chapter 6
Working with Fields

Chapter 7
Building Tables of Contents and Indexes

Chapter 8
Working with Styles and Templates

Chapter 9
Working with Word Macros

Chapter 10
Desktop Publishing with Word

Chapter 11
Word on the Web

Chapter 12
Word and Visual Basic for Applications

Chapter 13
Word at Work

Chapter 14
The Word Top Ten

✦ ✦ ✦ ✦

Creating and Working with Documents

✦ ✦ ✦ ✦

In This Chapter

Launching the program

Creating and opening documents

Understanding templates

Working with text

Inserting graphics

Navigating within a document

Saving your documents

Setting margins, tabs, and line spacing

Moving and copying text

Searching and replacing text

Checking spelling and grammar

Hyphenating your document

Adding bullets or paragraph numbers

Collaborating on a document

✦ ✦ ✦ ✦

Because the first thing you will do in Word is create documents, it makes sense for us to cover the basics of creating documents in the first Word chapter. You also need to know about the many techniques you can use to edit the documents you create. These techniques will help you find mistakes in your documents so you can create the best documents possible.

Launching the Program

Of course, before you can work with documents in Word, you have to launch the Word application. You can start Word by opening the Microsoft Office 98 folder and double-clicking the Microsoft Word icon, located directly inside. If you have placed an alias of Word in your Apple menu, you can select the alias from there to launch Word. If an alias of Word is on your desktop, you can double-click it. If you have another application that enables you to create a shortcut to launch applications, you can assign a shortcut to Word and use the shortcut. If you have installed the Microsoft Office Manager (MOM), you can select Word from MOM's menu. (See Chapter 1 for more information on MOM.) If Word is already running on your Mac, but it's not the active program, you can bring Word to the front (make it active) by selecting it in the Application menu at the far right of your menu bar. If Word is already running, all the other methods also still work.

Creating and Opening Documents

Each time you launch Word, a blank document automatically appears, ready for you to begin typing. It is a common mistake to think that because there is no document showing on your screen, Word (or any other application for that matter) is not running. Some people quit Word and relaunch it to have a new document open for them. Of course, this isn't necessary. To create more documents, simply select New from the File menu (⌘-N) or click the New Document button on Word's Standard (top) toolbar. File➪New opens the New Document dialog box so you can select a template or wizard. ⌘-N or the New Document button provides a generic document based on your default margins, font, and such. (See the next section, "Understanding Templates.") You can create new documents any time Word is the active application.

If you already have a document created and saved, simply double-click the document. This launches Word automatically as it opens your document.

Understanding Templates

You may not have thought about it before, but when you create a new document in any program, you are, in effect, opening up a template. A template is a collection of settings that determine how the document created from it will look. In Word, any time you use the New Document button or use the ⌘-N shortcut, you are launching a copy of Word's default template, which is named Normal. When you use the File ➪New command, the New dialog box opens and in it you can actually see the New template. It is always the selected template, so when you immediately click OK, Word opens this template.

Word gives you two ways to create documents: You can use the Normal template or a template of your choosing—be it one of Word's specialty templates or one you create yourself. You will probably use both methods in your work. Templates help you streamline the creation of documents that you produce on a regular basis.

When Word is first opened, it contains a document with default settings ready for you to use. This is the Normal template (stored in the Templates folder), which contains a set of standard margins and no formatting. Remember that clicking the New button in the Standard toolbar or using the ⌘-N keys always creates a new document based on this Normal template. After you begin to enter text, you can change all these settings.

If you do not want to use the default Normal template, you can use one of the other Word templates that may be better suited to your needs. To open one of these templates, choose New from the File menu (not ⌘-N). The New dialog box appears, in which you can make the selection that is best for your needs (see Figure 2-1). The dialog box is divided by a series of tabs, and each tab contains one or more templates appropriate to a specific task. For example, if most of the documents you create are memos, you can click the Memos tab to display a group of templates appropriate for creating memos. (The tab also lists one wizard; see the section "Looking at template wizards" a little later in this chapter for information about using wizards.) After you create a document based on a template, the template controls the appearance of the document.

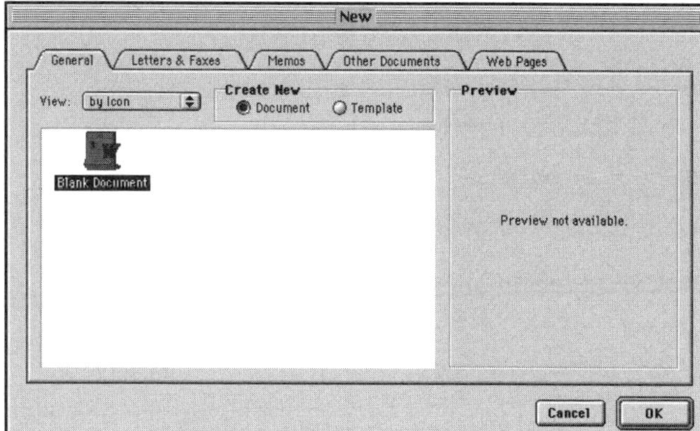

Figure 2-1: The New dialog box

Many documents are made up of standard parts. For example, an interoffice memo often contains a company name and address heading; To, From, Date, and Subject headings; and closing information, such as a routing list of persons receiving the memo. Assuming a template is designed for your interoffice memos, the template can contain your boilerplate (standard) text. You can even design your templates to prompt you for the specific information (such as the recipient's name) needed each time the template is used. (See "About user input" in Chapter 24 for more about this.)

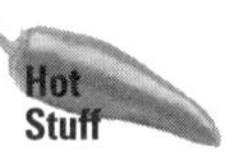

Another benefit of using templates is that in Word, all toolbar, menu, and keyboard customization is stored within the document—in the Normal template, by default. If you want to distribute customized toolbars, menus, or shortcuts, store them in a template and send it along to those who should use those customizations. (See Appendix E for the story on customizing toolbars, menus, and keyboard shortcuts.)

Exploring template categories

Table 2-1 lists the template categories and the templates in each category. The name of each template explains its function.

You can view the available templates by icon (the default view), by small icon, or by name (called Details). Select your desired view in the pop-up View menu.

Table 2-1
Templates Available in Microsoft Word

Template Category	*Name of Template*
General	Blank Document (uses Normal template)
Letters & Faxes	Contemporary Fax
	Contemporary Letter
	Elegant Fax
	Elegant Letter
	Professional Fax
	Professional Letter
	Envelope Wizard
	Fax Wizard
	Letter Wizard
	Mailing Label Wizard
Memos	Contemporary Memo
	Elegant Memo
	Professional Memo
	Memo Wizard
Other Documents	Brochure*
	Contemporary Report
	Contemporary Resume
	Elegant Resume
	Invoice (US, Australian, and UK versions)*
	Legal Pleading Wizard*
	Manual*
	Press Release*
	Professional Resume
	Purchase Order (US, Australian, and UK versions)*
	Thesis*
	Agenda Wizard*
	Calendar Wizard*
	Newsletter Wizard*
	Resume Wizard

Template Category	*Name of Template*
Web Pages	Blank Web Page
	Web Page Wizard

*These templates or wizards may only be available through the Value Pack installation. (The Newsletter Wizard may also be available through the custom installation.)

In addition to all these templates, you find a tab full of Windows templates, all named with the Windows-standard .dot extension. These templates are provided to make it easier for users in a cross-platform environment. The Mac templates are specifically created with a Mac look, using Mac fonts, and so on.

Looking at template wizards

Word 98 also includes template wizards, which help you create a document when you may not be sure of its layout or even its content. To activate any of these wizards, choose New from the File menu. Scroll through the Template list and double-click the wizard that best fits the document you want to create.

Use the Resume Wizard, found under the Other Documents tab, to create professionally formatted résumés tailored to your experience (see Figure 2-2). The Resume Wizard can create a résumé in various forms—contemporary, classic, or professional. The Resume Wizard also provides some tips on the best way to lay out a résumé. You can choose to create a professional, chronological, entry-level, or functional résumé. Finally, you can omit any elements you don't want to include.

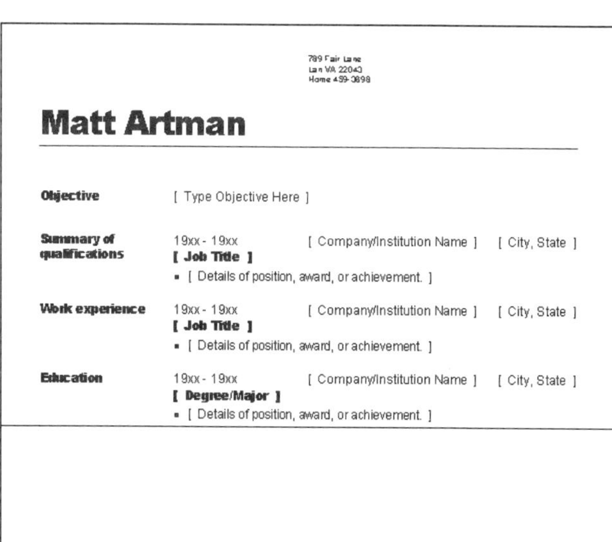

789 Fair Lane
Lan VA 22043
Home 459-0898

Matt Artman

Objective [Type Objective Here]

Summary of qualifications 19xx - 19xx [Company/Institution Name] [City, State]
[Job Title]
▪ [Details of position, award, or achievement.]

Work experience 19xx - 19xx [Company/Institution Name] [City, State]
[Job Title]
▪ [Details of position, award, or achievement.]

Education 19xx - 19xx [Company/Institution Name] [City, State]
[Degree/Major]
▪ [Details of position, award, or achievement.]

Figure 2-2: A résumé created with the Resume Wizard

As you step through the dialog boxes in the Resume Wizard, you are prompted to select a style (professional, contemporary, or elegant) and add elements that are appropriate for the type of résumé you have chosen. For example, you are prompted to add your phone number, e-mail address, fax number, and physical address. Next, you are prompted for the categories you wish to include, such as your work experience, volunteer history, and educational background. The wizard next gives you the chance to add any additional headings and change the order in which they appear. Figure 2-2 shows a résumé created by the Resume Wizard; yours may differ, based on the choices you make in the wizard.

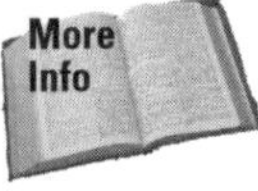

The Envelope Wizard is on the Letters & Faxes tab. When you choose this wizard, the animated help is activated and you are asked to choose between creating a single envelope or using the Mail Merge feature (Chapter 6 covers Mail Merge in detail). If you choose to make a single envelope, the Envelopes and Labels box is opened with the Envelope tab selected, so you can enter To and Return addresses for the envelope. If you choose the Mailing list option from the animated help, you will see the Mail Merge Helper appear, which will aid you in creating envelopes from a mailing list. This is covered in detail in Chapter 6.

The Fax Wizard, found under the Letters & Faxes tab, creates a fax sheet that you can customize. The fax sheet can be a contemporary, modern, or jazzy fax sheet. In the Fax Wizard, you also have the luxury of not having to look for your names and addresses. If they are stored in Microsoft Office Address Book, you can click the Address Book button, and then double-click the name of the person to which you want to send the fax. Figure 2-3 shows a fax sheet created by the Fax Wizard.

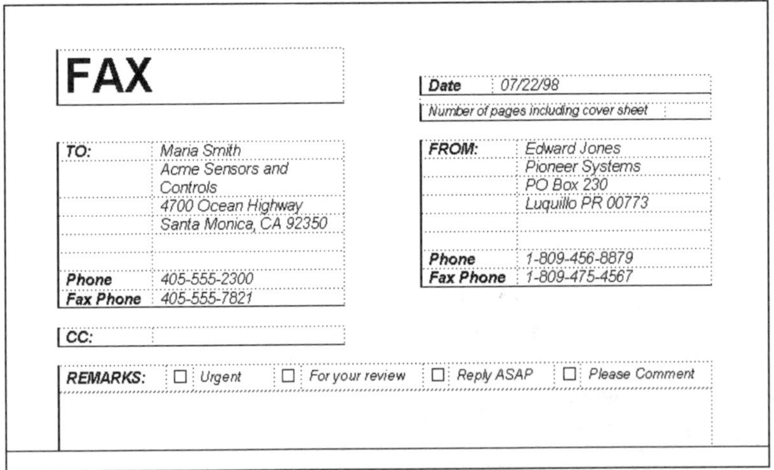

FAX

Date	07/22/98
Number of pages including cover sheet	

TO:	Maria Smith Acme Sensors and Controls 4700 Ocean Highway Santa Monica, CA 92350
Phone	405-555-2300
Fax Phone	405-555-7821

FROM:	Edward Jones Pioneer Systems PO Box 230 Luquillo PR 00773
Phone	1-809-456-8879
Fax Phone	1-809-475-4567

CC:	

REMARKS: ☐ Urgent ☐ For your review ☐ Reply ASAP ☐ Please Comment

Figure 2-3: A fax sheet created with the Fax Wizard

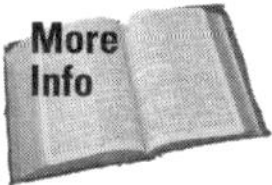

Use the Mailing Label Wizard, located on the Letters & Faxes tab, to create mailing labels for letters you create. After you activate this wizard, you have the option of creating a single label or a sheet of mailing labels, or accessing the Mail Merge Helper. For additional details about mail merges, see Chapter 6.

The Award Wizard, also found under the Other Documents tab, creates a customized award for any occasion by providing the art for the award certificate (which save you the annoyance of finding clip art and appropriately inserting it). The wizard enables you to choose award certificates of a more modern, formal, or decorative manner. Each one of the styles has corresponding art for the certificate. Figure 2-4 shows a document created with the Award Wizard.

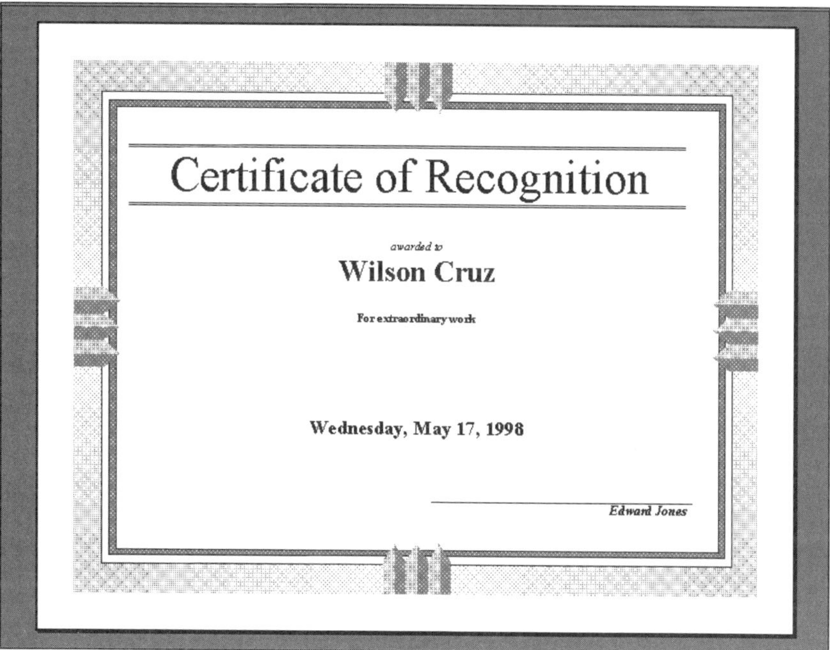

Figure 2-4: A document created with the Award Wizard

The Calendar Wizard, found under the Other Documents tab, creates a monthly calendar in various styles, such as the one shown in Figure 2-5. You can design the calendar in either a portrait or a landscape orientation. You can show the month name in different formats, such as a banner or box and border. You can add pictures to the calendar if you want. Finally, one of the Calendar Wizard's most impressive features is that it can create a calendar that starts and ends with the months you specify.

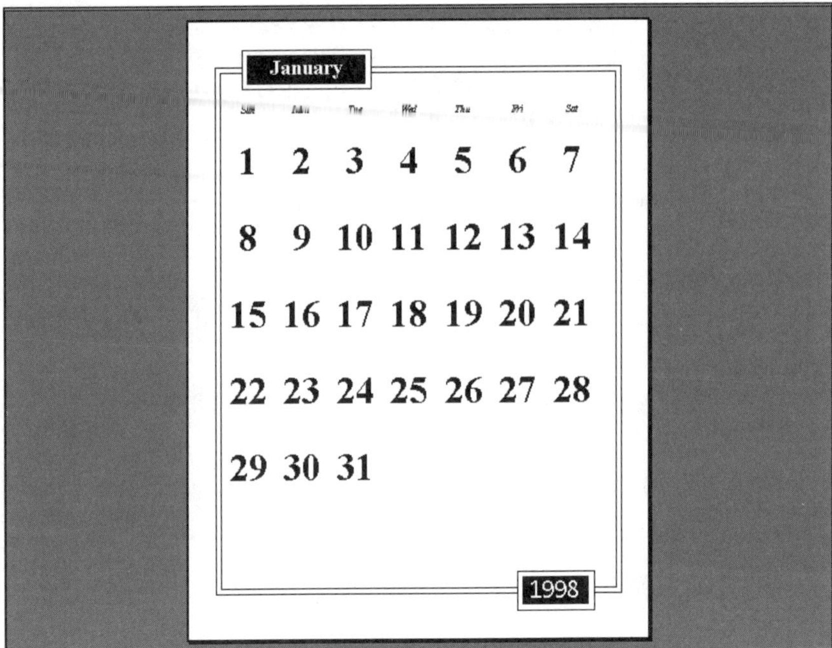

Figure 2-5: A calendar created with the Calendar Wizard

The Letter Wizard, located under the Letters & Faxes tab, can create prewritten letters or help in the design of your own letters. Again, you have the choice of creating a letter via a mailing list or just one letter. You then have the option of choosing a page design for your letter—contemporary, elegant, or professional. You can also choose different styles for your letters, block or semi-block. You can tell the wizard you are using preprinted letterhead, and then tell it where the letterhead is located and how much space it needs. The Letter Wizard then asks you to enter recipient information or take this information from the Address Book. A few more handy options are available; then the wizard ends with sender information. Yes, that would be you. Figure 2-6 shows a letter created using the Letter Wizard.

The Memo Wizard, found under the Memos tab, is very similar to the Letter wizard, helping you create customized memos (see Figure 2-7). You can create office memos (the default) or any other kind of memo. Addresses here can also be drawn from the Address Book.

March 3, 1998

Alberta Sutton
PO Box 3450
Fredericksburg VA 22043

Dear Mom,

How are you doing? Everything is fine with me!

I'm sorry that I haven't written for a while, but I've been really busy! As you know, I really like computers, and I'm spending long hours in front of a screen both at work and at home.

In fact, I just bought a great program. It's really neat — a collection of business letters that I can customize any way I want. For example, there's a letter to people who are late paying their bills and another one that complains about a defective product.

I'm sure it'll save me a lot of time and energy— you know how hard it is for me to write letters! Now I'll be able to think about business instead of worrying about what to say in letters.

Too bad they don't have one for writing to you! Ha ha ha. They should also have one for thanking Aunt Patty for the cookies! Nah — form letters could never replace the personal touch!

Gotta run now, Mom! All my love!

Figure 2-6: A letter created with the Letter Wizard

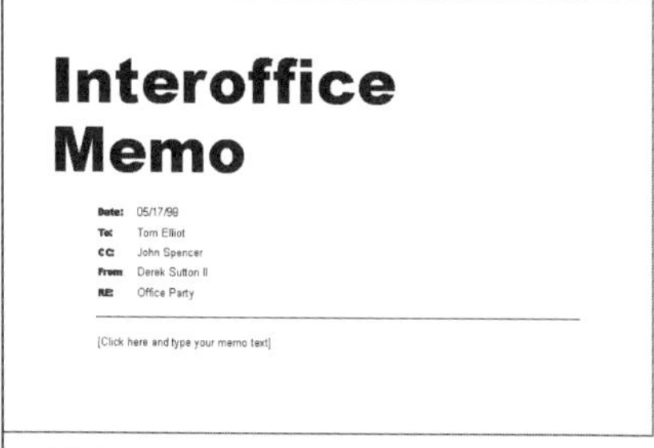
Interoffice Memo

Date: 05/17/98
To: Tom Elliot
CC: John Spencer
From: Derek Sutton II
RE: Office Party

[Click here and type your memo text]

Figure 2-7: An office memo created with the Memo Wizard

The Newsletter Wizard, found under the Other Documents tab, helps you create an attractive newsletter. You can create the newsletter in professional, contemporary, or elegant style. You can also include the date and volume number. Options, such as the number of columns and table of contents, are determined by the style you choose. Figure 2-8 shows a newsletter created with the Newsletter Wizard. As you can see, the wizard handles what would manually be a challenging task by creating a professional-looking newsletter in a short amount of time. The Newsletter Wizard, part of the Value Pack (see Appendix A), is covered in Chapter 10.

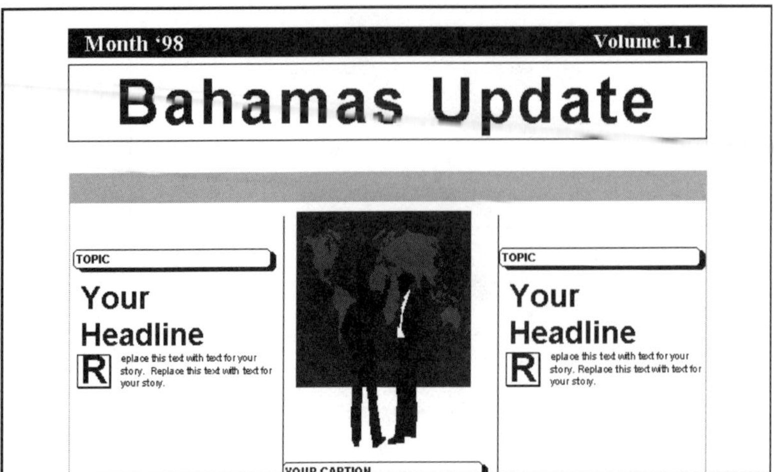

Figure 2-8: A newsletter created with the Newsletter Wizard

The Pleading Wizard, found under the Other Documents tab, provides a quick and easy way to create a legal pleading (see Figure 2-9). The legal pleading that results includes the name of the court, inserted in the correct location in the document for the style you choose. The alignment and style can be modified by using the various options presented as you move through the Pleading Wizard. Footnotes can also be added to the pleading. The Pleading Wizard is part of the Value Pack (see Appendix A).

Dario Sutton
Petro Venezuela
456 Calle Quezal
Maracaibo, Estado Zulia
Venezuela
Telephone: 011-454-454-4571-1471

Attorney for: Dirk Johnson

UNITED STATES DISTRICT COURT

CENTRAL DISTRICT OF CALIFORNIA

PLAINTIFF'S NAME, Plaintiff, vs. DEFENDANT'S NAME, Defendant	)	No. 12-3-456789-1 PLEADING TITLE

Figure 2-9: A legal pleading created with the Pleading Wizard

Avoiding Bad Typing Habits

If you are upgrading to the world of Word from a very old environment (such as a typewriter or a very early-generation word processor), there are some habits you need to drop. First, and probably the most obvious, is you don't have to press Return at the end of every line because word processors automatically wrap text.

Second, don't use spaces (inserted with the spacebar) to center or indent text. To center text, use the Center button on the Formatting toolbar (discussed in Chapter 3). To indent, use tabs or indented paragraphs (also discussed in Chapter 3). If you need to create columns, don't use spaces or tabs—use Word's Columns feature (see Chapter 3), or use tables (see Chapter 5).

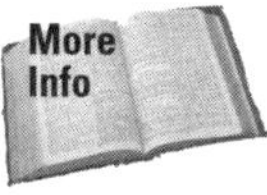

The Web Page Wizard, located on the Web Pages tab, enables you to create a Web page painlessly. You can create various types of Web pages, such as a personal page, calendar, survey form, or registration form. Chapter 11 discusses the Web Page Wizard in detail.

Editing templates

You can change the templates so they better fit your needs. We give you the full lowdown on how to create your own templates based on any of Word's templates—after we fill you in on some of the cool things you can do to format your documents.

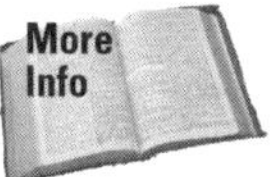

Look for the details on editing templates in Chapter 8. In fact, you'll find all the information you need about templates in Chapter 8.

Working with Text

You can get text into your document by typing it or pasting text copied from another source. Text is entered at the right of the insertion point (which we sometimes call the cursor). Don't press Return or Enter at the end of each line—Word automatically wraps your text from line to line. Press the Return key only when you want to create a new paragraph. As you work, previously entered text is moved up to keep the insertion point visible.

Using AutoComplete

From time to time, as you type you may see a yellow box pop up and suggest a word to you. This is Word's AutoComplete feature. If Word recognizes that you may be typing a specific word, it will suggest the word inside the pop-up box. If that's your intended word, press Return. Word will complete that word for you so you can go on typing as normal. In this case, pressing Return does not create a new paragraph. (If the suggestion isn't your desired word, just ignore it.)

Word also recognizes AutoText entries (covered in detail later in this chapter).

Copying and Pasting

You can paste text from another document into your current document by using the Clipboard. The Clipboard, part of the Mac OS, is an area of memory that stores temporary information. Edit ➪ Paste(⌘-V) pastes whatever is in the Clipboard into the current document at the insertion point. (Of course, the Clipboard must contain something before you can paste it into your document.)

To place text into the Clipboard, select it, and then choose Edit ➪ Copy (⌘-C) or click the Copy button on the Standard toolbar. Then move the insertion point to the desired position for the text and choose Edit ➪ Paste (⌘-V), or click the Paste button on the Standard toolbar. The text or graphic stored in the Clipboard appears at the insertion point. The Clipboard's contents remain there for repeated pasting until another piece of data is copied. This means you can copy part of your own document and paste it into another part of the same document.

You can also use the Clipboard to move text from one place in a document to another. Highlight the text you want to move and then use Edit ➪ Cut (⌘-X) or click the Cut button on the Standard toolbar. This places the selection into the Clipboard. Move the insertion point to the desired location and use Edit ➪ Paste (⌘-V), or click the Paste button on the Standard toolbar. The text comes in at the insertion point location.

Selecting text

Before you can make any changes to text, you need to select it. Clicking and dragging is the most common way to select text. If you're not proficient with a mouse, spend time practicing. In the long run, the time you spend practicing with the mouse will save you hours. The following list contains practical techniques for selecting text:

- To select a word, double-click anywhere in the word. You can then select adjacent words by keeping the mouse button pressed after the second click and dragging through the additional words.
- To select entire paragraphs, triple-click anywhere within the paragraph.
- To select entire lines, move the mouse pointer to the left of the line (where it becomes an arrow) and click once. This lets you select lines but not parts of a line.
- To select entire sentences, hold down the ⌘ key while you click anywhere in the sentence.
- To select the entire document, choose Edit ➪ Select All or press ⌘-A.
- To select a large portion of a document, click the start of the portion you want to select. Then move to the end of the desired portion, hold down the Shift key, and click again. Your initial selection determines the level to which

you can select. For example, if your initial selection is one character, you can select by character; if you first select a word, you can select to the end of any word. The same goes for lines or sentences. Use this method in conjunction with the scroll bars or navigation keys to avoid having to drag through your entire document.

If you select too much text, you can even deselect some. Just press Shift again as you click at the place you want your selection to end.

Deleting text

You can delete text (or graphics) in several ways. One method is by using the Delete key. When you use the Delete key, the text to the left of the insertion point is removed. Another method is using the Forward Delete key, which is marked by an arrow with an *x* inside and is located under the Help key. The Forward Delete key deletes text that appears to the right of the insertion point.

You can also delete blocks of text by selecting (highlighting) the block of text and then pressing Delete.

Inserting Graphics

Word 98 is rich in graphic abilities. You can create graphic objects within Word, insert existing graphics, and do quite a bit of manipulation to make them look just right. We discuss graphics in Chapter 10 and in Part IV, "PowerPoint." But while we're on the topic of pasting, you can also paste graphics into your document. To paste graphics, first get into the drawing or graphics program that contains the image you want to use in your Word document. Use the selection tool within the drawing or graphics program to select the desired image; choose Edit ➪ Copy (or press ⌘-C) to copy the selection into the Clipboard. Leave or quit the drawing or graphics program and click a visible portion of your document to come back to it, or select Word from the Application menu (top right) to make Word the active program. With the insertion point at the desired location, choose Edit ➪ Paste (or press ⌘-V). The graphic appears at the insertion point.

You can also add graphics to your documents by means of clip art. Word includes plenty to get you started. Position the insertion point where you want the clip art to go. Then, simply choose Insert ➪ Picture ➪ Clip Art. This opens Microsoft Clip Gallery, as shown in Figure 2-10. In the Clip Art tab, select the category of graphic you seek. A preview appears in the area to the right. Select the art you want, and click Insert. The clip art appears at the insertion point in your document.

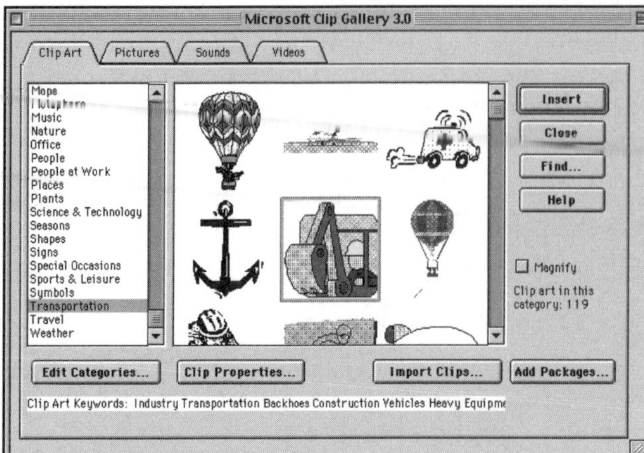

Figure 2-10: Preview the clip art file before you insert it into your document.

Navigating Within a Document

For basic navigation within a Word document, you can use the arrow keys and the navigation keys on the keyboard. Table 2-2 lists the keyboard combinations that help you move around in your document.

Table 2-2
Navigation Shortcuts

Keyboard Combination	*What it Does*
⌘-up arrow	Moves the cursor up one paragraph
⌘-down arrow	Moves the cursor down one paragraph
⌘-left arrow	Moves the cursor one word to the left
⌘-right arrow	Moves the cursor one word to the right
Page Up key	Moves the cursor up one screen page
Page Down key	Moves the cursor down one screen page
Home key	Moves the cursor to the beginning of the current line of text
⌘-Home key	Moves the cursor to the beginning of the document
End key	Moves the cursor to the end of the current line of text
⌘-End key	Moves the cursor to the end of the document

You can also scroll through a document. Scroll controls, standard on the Mac, are located at the right side and bottom of every document window. Click the up or down arrow to move in the direction you want to go. Use the left or right arrow to view longer lines of text. As long as you press the mouse button, the document will scroll. To move more quickly, click the scroll box (the square inside the scroll bars) and drag it up or down or left or right to move in the direction you want to go. You can also click within the shaded areas of the scroll bars to scroll more roughly.

If you click the scroll box, drag it, and hold the mouse button down for approximately half a second, a small window appears showing the page number of the document represented by the position of the scroll box. In a large document, this can provide an easy way to reach a desired page quickly.

If you want to jump to a specific page number in a document, press F5 and enter a page number in the dialog box that appears.

Customizing keyboard commands

All Mac applications provide you with keyboard equivalents you can press to invoke a command without going to the menus and/or dialog boxes. In Word, you can change the keys used. For example, if you are used to a certain key combination from using another program, you can assign that combination the parallel command in Word.

To alter (or just to discover) a keyboard combination, Control-click in any blank spot on a toolbar and select Customize (or select Tools ⇨ Customize). When the Customize dialog box appears, click the Keyboard button to open the Customize Keyboard dialog box. Select the category the command falls under (or select All Commands), and then click the command in the Commands list. If a shortcut already exists, it will appear in the Current keys list.

To add a key combination, after selecting the command from the Commands list, click in the box that aptly says Press new shortcut key, and then type your new combination. A message appears in the dialog box to tell you if this combination is available or already taken and, if so, what command uses it. If these keys are already assigned to something you want to keep, use the Delete key to delete your combination, and then try a new one. When you are happy with a new key combination, click Assign.

A word about locating commands in the Commands list: Built-in menu commands are composed of the name of their menu attached to the name of the command, rather than just the name of the command. For example, the Save command isn't under S for save, but under F for FileSave.

If a key combination makes you crazy and you want to change it, you can, but you have to figure out what that command is called first—and that can be a challenge with Word's mysterious key command names. The trick is to open the Customize Keyboard dialog box, and then click in the Press new shortcut key box and type the keys in question. The dialog box will report that the keys you entered are already in use and tell you the name of the command using them. That's all you need to know. Now you can follow the customization steps listed previously, knowing what command to change.

Using the Document Map view

The Document Map view provides another useful way of navigating in a document. This view is especially useful when you are working with long documents. Document Map analyzes a document, finds the patterns for the headings you have included, and places them in a frame to the left of your document. This will give you a quick view of your entire document without the use of the scroll bar. As you look at the headings, you can click one and move to that heading in your document. To view the Document Map, click the button with a magnifying glass icon or choose View➪Document Map.

Control-clicking the heading on the right enables a specific level of headings to be shown. This feature is much like the Outline view, which is discussed in detail in Chapter 5.

Saving Your Documents

Saving is a fundamental part of working with documents. (Your documents won't be permanent if you don't save them for later use.) As soon as you begin your document, save it using Save in the File menu. After the initial save, each save makes changes to the existing document. To create a duplicate document under a new name or to save a document under a file format different from Word's native file format, choose File➪Save As. In addition to the normal Save and Save As commands that enable you to save a document or change the name, Word 98 offers additional options for saving documents.

You can choose File➪Save as HTML to save a Word document as an HTML file. (HTML, Hypertext Markup Language, is the language used to store information on the World Wide Web.) The HTML files you create using Word can be uploaded to a Web server for availability on the Web or to a corporate intranet. When you save a word document as an HTML file, the document is closed by Word and then reopened in HTML format with Word acting as a Web browser. Note that formatting not supported by HTML is removed from the document. Here are examples of formatting that would be dropped from a document when you save it as HTML:

- Comments
- Paragraph formatting
- Tabs
- Fields
- Tables of contents and authorities
- Indexes
- Drawing objects
- User-defined styles

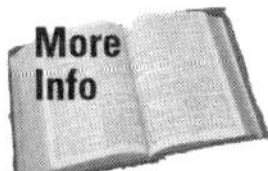

For more specifics on working with Word and the Web, see Chapter 11.

You can also save multiple versions of the same document to a single file. By choosing File➪Versions, you display a dialog box that enables you to save a new version of the same document. The versions are identified within the dialog box by the date of creation and the author of the version.

When you choose File➪Versions, you see a listing of the existing versions of the document, the date they were last saved, and the modifier of that version. After clicking the Save now button in the dialog box, you can add comments about the particular version of the document that can further aid as an identifier of the document.

Looking at Word's Views

Word enables you to work with your document in one of five possible views: Normal, Page Layout, Outline, Online Layout, and Master Document. Normal is the default view. You can access these views by selecting the appropriate command on the View menu. A check mark to the left of the command in the View menu indicates your current view. You can also switch among Normal, Online Layout, Outline, and Page Layout views by clicking the View buttons at the bottom-left of your document's window. (The left-most button is Normal, the next button is Online Layout, then Page Layout, and Outline.) Master Document view is only accessed from the View menu.

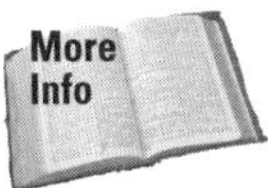

If you are using line numbering and wish to see the line numbers, you need to switch to Page Layout view, see Chapter 3.

Use Normal view for basic typing and editing. Normal view shows a simple version of the document and is the best all-purpose view. Should you change views, you can return to Normal view at any time by clicking the Normal View button in the lower-left corner of the document or selecting it from the View menu.

Use Outline view for outlining and organizing a document. Outline view enables you to see only the main headings of a document or the entire document. In this view, you can easily move text over long distances or change the order of your topics, as detailed in Chapter 5. To change to Outline view, choose View➪Outline.

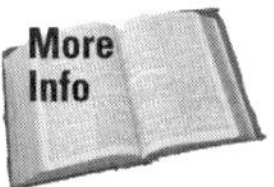

You control how much you see of the document in Outline view by clicking the plus signs located next to the headings for each section. When you double-click a plus sign, the text under the heading is hidden to show only the heading. Double-click again to reveal the hidden information. Chapter 5 discusses outlines in detail.

Use Page Layout view to see the printed page. This view lets you see how the elements of the document will appear when printed. To switch to Page Layout view, click the Page Layout View button on the lower-left corner of the document window, or choose View➪Page Layout.

Use the Online Layout view to create your online documents as HTML documents. HTML documents behave differently from standard word processing documents. By default, the Document Map appears to give you an overview of your page and aid you in navigation. Fonts appear larger and text wraps to the document window, Web browser style. Graphics default to inline. Outline elements do not show. Remember, though, this is only a bit of an approximation. If you're creating a document to use online, use Online Layout view. When you browse Web pages directly in Word, this is the view Word uses.

Use Master Document view to work with long documents. This view helps you divide long documents into several shorter documents to make them easier to work with, because you can see all the components of a document when you are in Master Document view. To switch to Master Document view, click the Master Document View button at the lower-left corner of the document window, or choose View➪Master Document.

Word 98 also lets you change options in each of the views. To change the default settings, choose Preferences from the Tools menu. The Preferences dialog box appears, from which you can change options for the current view. The Preferences dialog box contains ten tabs, each with its own set of options, as shown in Figure 2-11. Click a tab to bring it to the front of the dialog box so you can view and make changes to its options. When you click OK, the new settings take effect in all the tabs that you have changed.

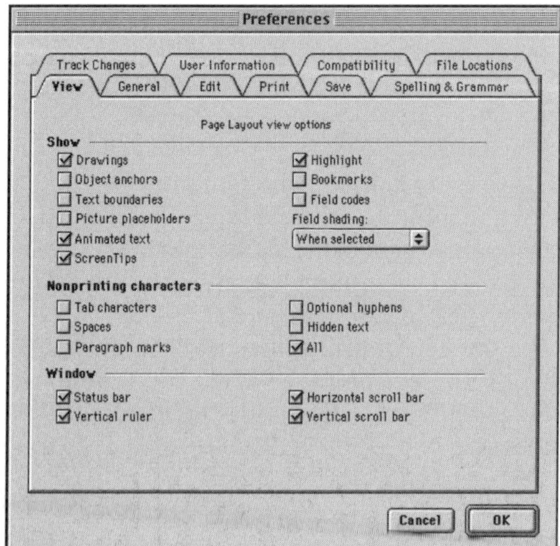

Figure 2-11: The Preferences dialog box

Setting Margins, Tabs, and Line Spacing

The three most elementary aspects of formatting—margins, tabs, and line spacing—can be found even on the most basic typewriters. These elements are very important to setting up your pages appropriately. This section shows you how to apply these formatting elements to all or part of a document. To control page margins, select Format ⇨ Document; to set default tab stops, select Format ⇨ Tabs; and to change line spacing, select Format ⇨ Paragraph. However, these commands are not the only ways to change parameters that affect margins, tabs, and line spacing in Word, as you discover shortly.

Changing margins

When you start a new Word document, default margins are already set at 1 inch for the top and bottom margins and 1.25 inches for the left and right margins. To change the default settings, choose Format ⇨ Document. The Document dialog box contains two tabs. The Margins tab lets you set the top, bottom, right, and left margins to your desired measurements. You also can click the Mirror Margins check box to force the left-facing and right-facing pages to have the same margins between the edge of the text and the center of the binding.

Margins can be changed visually as well. Switch your view to Page Layout. Page Layout view shows your margins as gray bars in the rulers. Position your mouse where the margin (gray) and text area (white) meet. As you do, your cursor becomes a two-headed arrow. With this cursor in effect, you can drag left or right (or up or down) to resize your margin.

Applying tabs

Tabs are the only way (aside from tables) to ensure you text will line up. Word has tab stops set to every 0.5 inch by default. These tab stops are depicted by the gray tick marks at the bottom of the ruler. The ruler should appear at the top of your document window. (If the ruler is not on, select View ⇨ Ruler. A check mark appears beside it.) To change the default tab stops, select the Format ⇨ Tabs command. In the Tabs dialog box, change the measurement in the Default tab stops box to any desired value. The value is measured in inches, centimeters, picas, or points, depending upon your ruler's units. (This measurement can be changed in the General tab of the Preferences dialog box.)

Default tab stops are only a starting point. When you need to move text 2 inches for example, it's a very bad idea to press tab four times. Instead, you should set a custom tab stop 2 inches in. This setting would be only for the paragraph that needs it. (You can have different ruler settings for each paragraph.) Custom tab stops take precedence over the default tab stops; therefore, whenever you set a custom tab stop, Word clears all default tab stops that occur to the left of the custom tab stop. When you set one or more custom tab stops, these remain in effect until you change the tab setting. When you start a new line, the ruler formatting, including tabs, of the previous paragraph is carried down. Once you begin a new paragraph, you can assign that paragraph it's own tab settings.

Understanding the types of tabs

Word has five types of tabs; left, center, right, decimal, and bar. The type of tab you choose controls where the text aligns with the tab. When you use a left tab, the left edge of the text aligns with the tab stop. With right tabs, the right edge of the text aligns with the tab stop. When you use centered tabs, the text centers at the tab stop. Decimal tabs are used when the decimal point in numbers must align with the tab stop. Finally, bar tabs are thin vertical lines that can be used to separate columns created by tabs within a document.

Setting custom tabs

You can set custom tabs visually, using your mouse and one of the Tab buttons on the ruler (the easier method) or with the Tabs command on the Format menu. To set tabs with the mouse, first click the Tab button on the ruler (the button to the far left of the ruler) until you get the tab alignment you want, and then click the gray strip just under the ruler at the desired location. For example, to set a center tab at the 2-inch location on the ruler, you would first click the Tab button until the marker for the center tab appears and then click just under or on the 2-inch marker on the ruler. To verify the position of the tab stop numerically, choose Format ➪ Tabs to open the Tabs dialog box (see Figure 2-12).

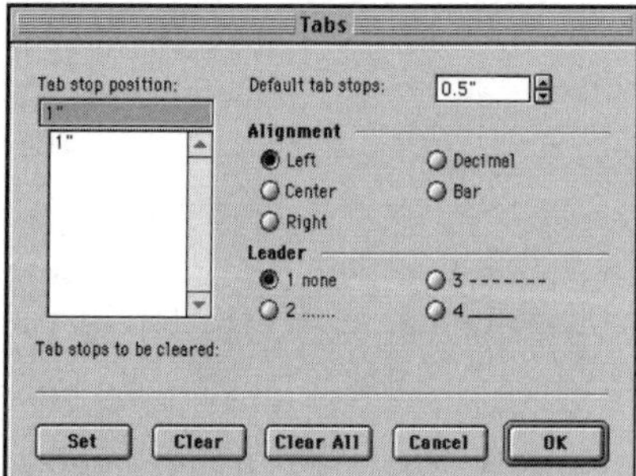

Figure 2-12: The Tabs dialog box

If the 2-inch tab stop isn't in the exact position you want, you can click it and drag it to whatever position you want on the ruler. After you drag it to its new location, verify the new position of the tab stop by opening the Tabs dialog box again. Alternately, you can manually enter a measurement in the Tab stop position text box. The Tabs dialog box gives you unlimited control of how to position the tabs in your documents.

Figure 2-13 shows some of the different tab alignments in Word. In the figure, a left tab stop has been set at the 1-inch position, a center tab at the 2-inch position, a right tab at the 4-inch position, and a decimal tab stop at the 5-inch position. Actually, you can have all these tabs on one line. You can place as many custom tab stops on one line as you need. The first time you press Tab, your text jumps to the first tab stop. The next tab character causes the text that comes after it to jump to the second tab stop, and so on. Remember that one tab on your line of text should equal one tab stop on the ruler. The number of tabs in your line of text should be the number of tabs on the ruler for that line.

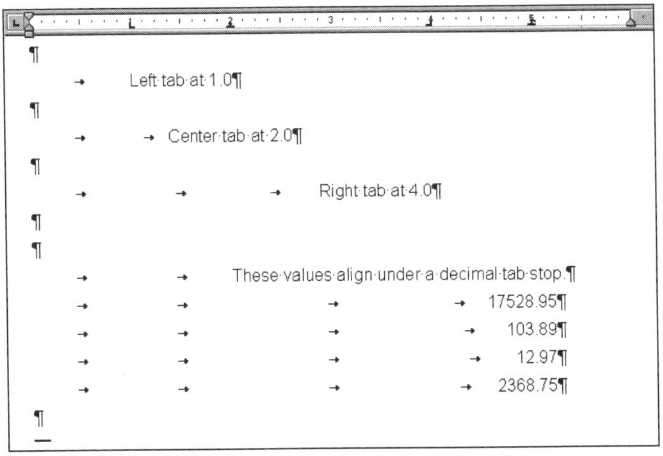

Figure 2-13: The different Tab alignments shown in Word

To set tabs with the Tabs command, choose Format ⇨ Tabs. The Tabs dialog box (refer to Figure 2-12) appears. In this dialog box, you can enter or clear tab stops. Enter the desired location for the tab stop in the Tab stop position text box and then choose the type of tab you want (Left, Center, Right, Decimal, or Bar) from the Alignment options. If you have additional tabs to set, click the Set button to set the current tab, and then go back to the Tab stop position box to enter the location for the next tab and to choose its alignment. After you finish setting the tabs, click OK.

Try experimenting with the tab stop techniques to find the one that suits you best (see Figure 2-14). You can use the following steps to see the effects of the different tab stops you can set in Word:

1. Create a new document with a left tab at 1.0 inch, a center tab at 2.5 inches, a right tab at 3.5 inches, and a decimal tab at 5.0 inches.
2. Press the Tab key once (to reach the left-aligned tab at the 1 inch mark), and type the words **left-aligned**. Then, press Return.
3. Press the Tab key twice (to reach the center tab at the 2.5-inch mark), and type the word **centered**. Notice that as you type, the word remains centered at the tab stop. When done, press Return.
4. Press the Tab key three times (to reach the right-aligned tab at the 3.5-inch mark), and type the words **right-aligned**. Notice that as you type, the words remain right aligned with the tab stop. When done, press Return.

5. Press the Tab key four times (to reach the decimal tab), type the value **103.99**, and press Return.

6. Press the Tab key four times (to reach the decimal tab), type the value **1342.23**, and press Return. Notice that the second number correctly aligns with the first, based on the location of the decimal point.

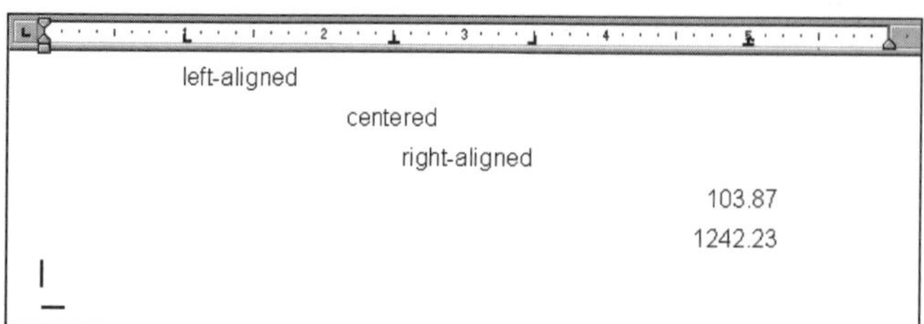

Figure 2-14: A document with different tab stops

Moving and clearing tabs

As with setting tabs, you can move tabs and clear tabs using your mouse and the ruler or with the Tabs command on the Format menu. Again, the mouse excels in ease of use. To move a tab, simply click the tab and drag it to the desired location. To clear a tab, simply drag the tab up or down off the ruler.

You can also use the Tabs command from the Format menu to move or clear tabs. The Tab stop position area of the Tabs dialog box displays all tab settings for custom tabs in the document. From the list of tab positions, select the tab you want to delete, and then click Clear. To clear all custom tabs, click Clear All and then click OK. To move a tab stop, select it in the dialog box, click Clear, and then enter a new location for the tab.

Creating leader tabs

Some documents, such as tables of contents, make use of leader tabs—characters that fill the space prior to the tab. To set a leader tab, set the tab as you normally would, then open the Tabs dialog box with the Tabs command. Word offers three kinds of leader tabs: periods, hyphens, and underlines. After you select the desired type of leader, click OK.

Adjusting Line spacing

Line spacing affects the amount of space between lines of a paragraph. You can also change the spacing between paragraphs. To change the line spacing, place the insertion point anywhere within the desired paragraph and choose Format ➪ Paragraph. The Paragraph dialog box appears, with the Indents and Spacing tab visible, as shown in Figure 2-15. Use the options in this tab to enter the desired line and paragraph spacing. In the Line spacing list box, select the kind of spacing you desire: Single, Double, 1.5, At Least, Exactly, or Multiple. You can adjust the preset spacing of these options by clicking the arrows next to the At box. The Exactly option makes the spacing only the specified amount. The At Least choice can be used to set the spacing to a specified amount or greater.

In the Indentation area, you can specify the amount of indentation you want to apply to the left and right margins of the document. The Special box also allows for the addition of a hanging indent or other custom indent. However, indents are more commonly done on the ruler, which we cover later.

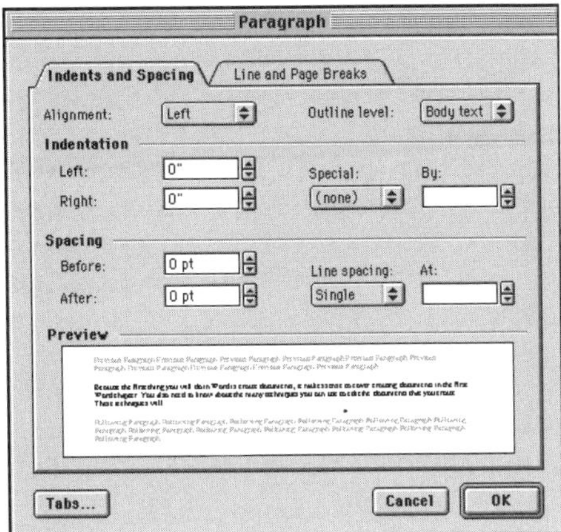

Figure 2-15: The Indents and Spacing tab of the Paragraph dialog box

If you don't want to use the default unit of measurements, enter one of the abbreviations for alternate measurements. In the At box to the right of the Line spacing list box, enter one of the following abbreviations: inches (in.), centimeters (cm.), picas (pi.), points (pt.), or lines (li.). Picas and points are units of measurement used by typesetters: 6 picas equal 1 inch, and 72 points equal 1 inch. If you enter a numeric value alone, Word assumes that value is in points.

To set the three commonly used variations of line spacing, you can use key combinations without entering the dialog box. With the insertion point anywhere in the desired paragraph, press ⌘-1 for single line spacing, ⌘-2 for double line spacing, or ⌘-5 for one-and-a-half line spacing.

Paragraph formatting only applies to the paragraph your cursor is in, or the paragraphs that are selected when you apply the formatting. If you want to apply spacing to a specific paragraph only, click in that paragraph (or select it), and then choose Format ⇨ Paragraph. In the Paragraph dialog box, select the desired spacing and click OK. (You can also use the ⌘ key combinations to change the spacing in the paragraph.)

Adjusting Paragraph spacing

Word also enables you to control the amount of space that appears before or after paragraphs. In the Paragraph dialog box, you may have noticed the Before and After text boxes in the Spacing area. You can enter numeric values in the Before or After boxes to place additional spacing before or after a paragraph. For example, placing 12 points after a paragraph automatically adds 12 points of space when you press Return. This would be the same as pressing Return an extra time, when your text is 12-point size.

Paragraph spacing is an important part of formatting styles, which we cover in Chapter 8. For now, here's an idea as to why: If you have a document in which you've used a style that includes the space-after or space-before settings to control the space between your paragraphs, but then find yourself short on space, you're in luck. All you need to do is place your cursor in one paragraph that contains that style, and then return to the Paragraph dialog box and change the space before or after to 10 or 11 points. Then, with a couple of clicks, you can redefine that style—all the paragraphs that have that style tighten up by a point or two and ideally give you the room you need to fit everything in your document. And if you still need more room, you can go back and try 9 points.

As with line spacing, you can enter any value for paragraph spacing that Word understands: inches (in.), centimeters (cm.), picas (pi.), points (pt.), or lines (li.). Word assumes points as a default value of measurement (one point being 1⁄72 of an inch).

Moving and Copying Text

The original way to move text or graphics is to use the standard cut (or copy) and paste method. With this method, you use the menu commands or their keyboard shortcuts to transfer the information to the invisible Clipboard as a staging area. This method works best when moving information long distances within a document or between documents, or even applications. To use this method, select your text and either cut it by using Edit⇨Cut or ⌘-X or copy it by using Edit⇨Copy or ⌘-C. Then move your cursor to the location where you want the data to land and use Edit⇨Paste or ⌘-V. Word also provides buttons for cutting, copying, and pasting. Cutting removes your text or graphic from its place. Copying keeps it there and makes a copy to be used elsewhere.

If you are moving information from one Word document to another, you can use the Arrange All command under the Window menu to have Word tile your documents for you. Alternately, you can move between open Word documents by selecting any document name from the bottom of the Window menu. Any Word documents you have open will appear there. If a desired document is not open yet, use the Open command under the File menu or return to the Finder to locate the document in its folder and double-click it from there.

Rather than using cut and paste to move text, you can use drag-and-drop. There are two benefits to drag-and-drop: it's faster when moving text short distances and it doesn't use the Clipboard, so your Clipboard's contents remain intact. Notice that when you select text, your cursor becomes an arrow. Immediately click the text and drag it to the desired position in your document. As you drag the selection, the mouse pointer consists of the usual pointer arrow and a small rectangle; the rectangle indicates that you are dragging text. You will also notice a dotted cursor-type line as you drag. This line indicates where the text will land when you release the mouse. When that line is in the desired position, release the mouse button.

The same method can be used to copy information. Simply select the text you want to copy, and then press Option as you click the selected text and drag it to the new location.

Searching and Replacing Text

Like all full-featured word processors, Word 98 offers a search-and-replace capability. You'll find these commands in the Edit menu: Find (⌘-F) and Replace (⌘-H). These commands may offer more search capabilities than you are accustomed to, because you can look for more than just text. You can search for specific formatting as well as for special characters, such as paragraph marks, new-line characters, and tabs.

Searching for regular text

To search for text, choose Edit➪Find. In the Find dialog box (see Figure 2-16), enter the desired word or phrase in the Find what text box. Click the Find Next button, which is the default option, or press Return or Enter. Word finds the first occurrence of the text, starting its search at the position of your cursor. You may continue the search for subsequent occurrences by pressing Return or Enter or clicking Find Next.

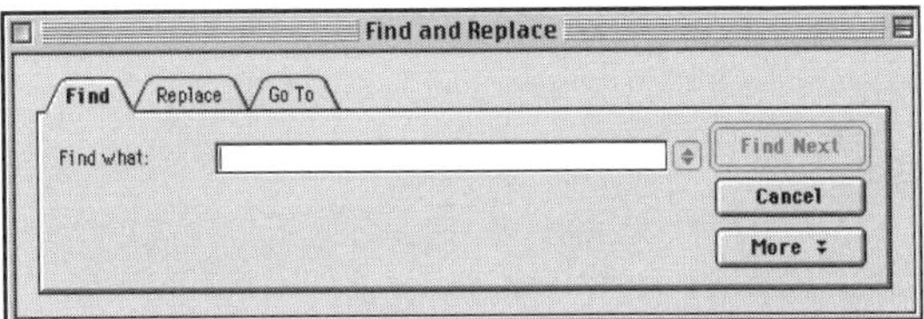

Figure 2-16: The Find tab of the Find and Replace dialog box

Clicking the More button gives you additional search options. The choices in the dialog box are fairly self-explanatory. The Match case option tells Word you want the search to be case-sensitive. When checked, Word searches for a match that uses the same case as the letters you entered. When the option is not checked, case does not matter during the search. The Use wildcards option tells Word to let you use wildcards, such as a question mark, for any single character and an asterisk for any combination of characters within the search text.

The Find whole words only option specifies that only whole words matching the search text will be found. For example, if you search for the word *move* in the sample document and the Find whole words only option is not checked, Word finds occurrences of move, moves, and moved in the document. If Find whole words only is checked, only occurrences of the word *move* are found. The Sounds like option finds words that sound like the word entered but are spelled differently. The Find all word forms option, when checked, tells Word to locate all matching noun forms or verb tenses. (Word can do this based on logic built into its grammar checking.) The Search list box lets you set the direction of the search. The default choice is All, which tells Word to search through the entire document. If you select Up or Down from this list box, Word begins its search at the current insertion point and searches up or down in the document for the desired search term. If the end of the document is reached and the search term has not been found, Word displays an alert box telling you that a match has not been found.

Searching for special characters

If you want to find special characters, such as paragraph marks or tab characters, you can also use the Find dialog box. Click the Special button to open a pop-up menu (see Figure 2-17) for special characters for which you want to search, and select the desired character from the menu.

If you want to search for a format, click the Format button and select the format you want to find. This option lets you search for fonts, paragraph formats, languages, styles, tabs, frames, and highlighting.

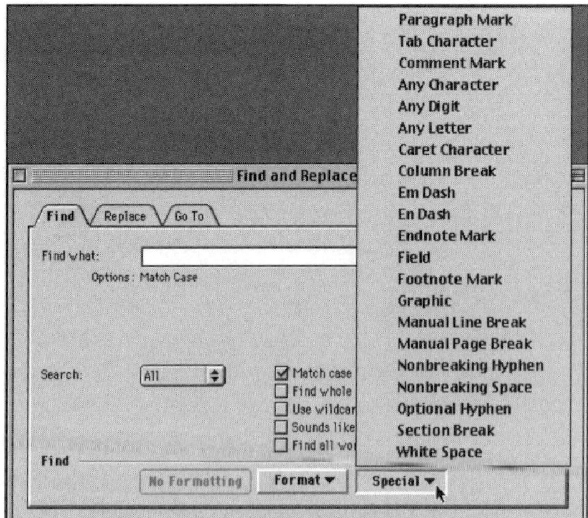

Figure 2-17: The pop-up menu for special characters

Replacing text

You can use the same search techniques to replace the search text with other text as well. For example, you may want to replace every occurrence of the word *version* with the word *level* throughout a document. Or perhaps a certain word has been underlined at every occurrence in a document and you want to replace it with the same word without the underline. To replace text, you use Edit ⇨ Replace (⌘-H), which displays the Replace dialog box, as shown in Figure 2-18. (It's actually the same dialog box as Find, but with the Replace tab in front.)

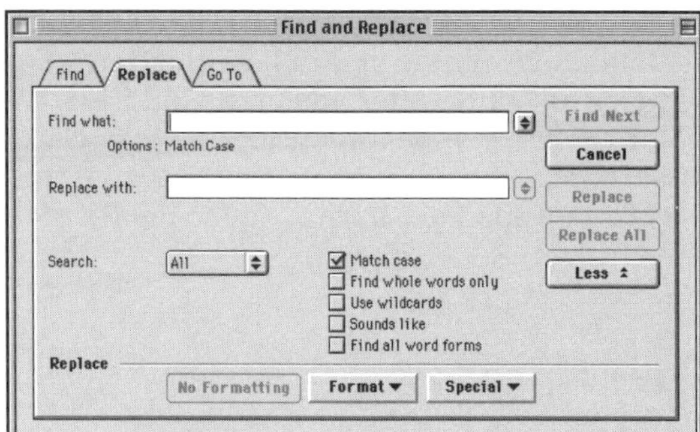

Figure 2-18: The Replace tab of the Find and Replace dialog box

As with searches, you enter the search text in the Find what text box. By default, Word intelligently replaces what it calls "all grammatically inflected forms of a word." For example, Word will replace the word *versions* with the word *levels.* You can also use the Format and Special buttons to find special characters or formats that you want to replace. The Find whole words only and Match case options can also be used. Turn on the Find whole words only option if you want the search to find only complete words, and turn on the Match case option if the case of the letters found must match that of the search text. The Use Pattern Matching and the Sounds like options work just as they do in the Find dialog box. In the Replace with text box, enter the text that should replace the search text when it is found.

After you click the Find Next button, Word stops and asks for confirmation when the first occurrence of the search term is located. Click the Replace button to make the change at this occurrence of the found text. Click Replace All to make all the subsequent changes for you automatically without asking for confirmation. After the changes are made, Word tells you the number of replacements it made.

Be careful when using the Replace All button because it may make some replacements you do not intend. For example, if you want to replace the word *Figure*, as in *Figure 2-18* with the word *Item*, and you choose Replace All, the phrase *Figure out the answer* also gets changed to *Item out the answer.* Or, while changing *go* to *travel*, *I have gone to the store* will become *I have travelne to the store.* Oops! Not exactly what you intended. Therefore, if you are not sure that the word is used only in the one context that you want to replace, click the Replace button to make the first replacement, and then use the Find Next button to find the next occurrence of the text so you can view it and decide if you want to replace it.

If you choose the Replace button, the replacement of the word is made. If you do not care to replace that word, skip it by using the Find Next button. Word then finds the next occurrence of the word and, again, you have the option of replacing it.

You can search for and replace formatting in the Replace dialog box. For example, you can replace all instances of a word in bold formatting with the same word in italic formatting. With the cursor in the Find what text box, click the Bold button (for bold formatting). Beneath the Find what text box, you will see Format: Bold appear to reflect the bold formatting you've applied to the search text. Then tab to the Replace with text box and click the Italic button (for italic formatting). Figure 2-19 shows an example of this search procedure. After you click Find Next, Word finds the first occurrence of the word *Figure* in bold formatting. You can click Replace or Replace All to make the change to italic formatting. (Note that the keyboard commands such as ⌘-B and ⌘-I don't work here, due to another feature that uses the I key.)

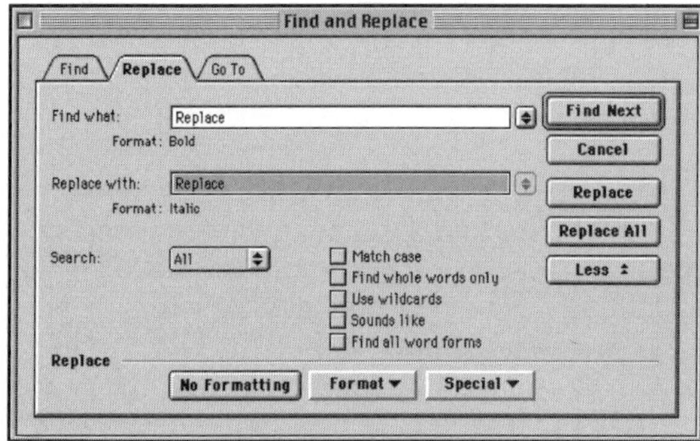

Figure 2-19: Replacing formatting in the Replace dialog box

If you are searching for an occurrence of a word or format by using the Find dialog box, and you decide to change the word or format, simply click the Replace tab, which brings up the Replace dialog box. In the Replace dialog box, you can replace what you are looking for in your search by entering text in the Replace with text box.

Checking Spelling and Grammar

Word's spell-checker and grammar-checker features check your documents for spelling errors and for proper—but real-world—grammatical construction. Multiple dictionaries enable you to create your own custom dictionaries, and permit you to use different dictionaries for special uses. You can check spelling and grammar as you work, or check a word, section, or entire document at any time. As part of the grammar-checking process, Word also checks for grammatical errors—including many commonly confused words. If Word finds an error, it often suggests ways to correct the sentence containing the error. You can make changes based on Word's suggestions, make changes based on your own preferences, or bypass the error altogether (the "error" may be okay as is).

Word's spell- and grammar-checkers use a main dictionary and a custom dictionary to check for potential misspellings. The main dictionary is supplied with the program and cannot be changed. The default supplemental dictionary is called Custom Dictionary. When you add new words to the dictionary (which you can do when the spell-checker finds a word it does not know, but you know is spelled correctly), you are adding them to the Custom Dictionary file unless you specify a different dictionary. Those of you used to previous versions of Word will be impressed by Word's new vocabulary. Your name and organization, as entered upon registration or edited in Preferences, are now recognized. Many Fortune 1,000 names are now known, as are many new technological terms. Country names and most U.S. cities (with a population of 30,000 or more, to quote the Office Assistant) are recognized. Internet addresses are not only flagged, they can be automatically converted into clickable links to your e-mail program.

Interactive spell-checking

Word 98 provides excellent interactive spell-checking. With this option on, misspelled words are underlined with a wavy red line to alert you. The preference to turn this on or off is under Tools ➪ Preferences in the Spelling & Grammar tab. It is the top option: Check spelling as you type. If you turn on interactive spell-checking while you're already in a document, Word takes a moment to go through and mark up your document.

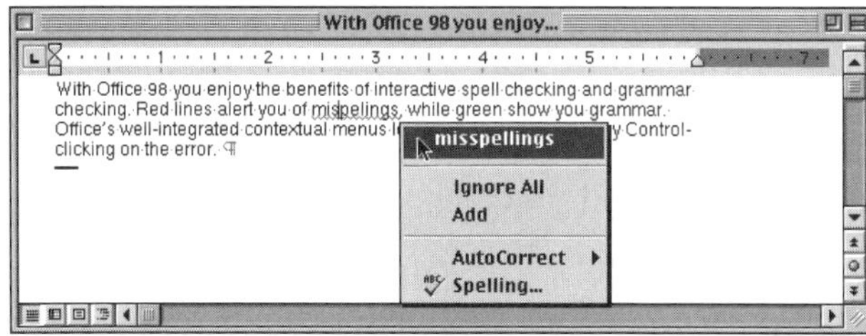

Figure 2-20: Word 98 alerts you to misspelled words as you type.

While interactive spell-checking is on, you can Control-click any misspelled word to reveal a list of possible correct spellings for that word. Simply drag to the spelling you'd like and click to replace the misspelled word with your choice. You can also choose to add the word to the selected user dictionary, ignore the spelling, or open the spell-checker.

Spell-checking manually

When spell-checking manually, you check a selected portion of a document or the entire document. To check the spelling or grammar in only part of a document, first select the part you want checked, and then choose Tools ➪ Spelling and Grammar. If no selection has been made, Word assumes you want to check the entire document.

After you choose the Spelling and Grammar command from the Tools menu, or you click the Spelling button on the Standard toolbar, Word checks all words and grammar constructions against those in the dictionaries. If a suspected misspelled word or improper use of grammar is found, Word stops, and the Spelling dialog box shown in Figure 2-21 appears. After Word finds a misspelling or misuse of grammar, it tries to provide a number of options for a correct spelling of the word, or offers an alternate grammar construction that can be used.

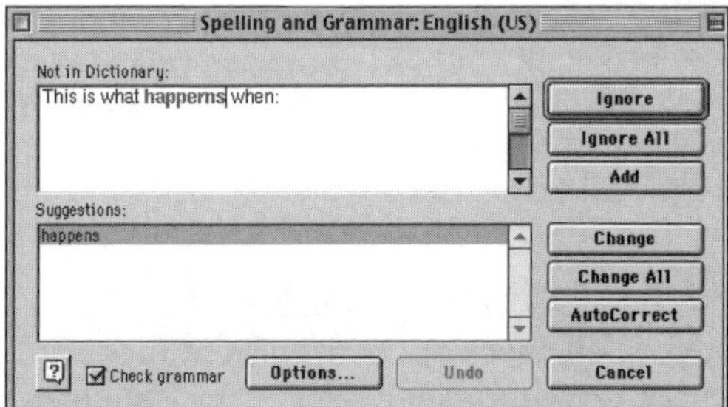

Figure 2-21: The Spelling and Grammar dialog box

Any suggestions for the misspelled word are presented in the Suggestions list below a display of the incorrect word. If one of the suggestions is the desired spelling, select it in the list box, and then click the Change button. The Ignore button lets you leave a word as is; the Cancel button cancels the entire spell-checking operation. The Add button lets you add a word to the selected user dictionary.

As a shortcut to selecting the Spelling and Grammar command from the Tools menu or clicking the Spelling button on the Standard toolbar, you can press F7 (as in Windows) to start checking the spelling of a selection or a document. The same applies for the grammar-checker. If you wish to keep the grammar construction you presently have, choose Ignore from the dialog box, and Word leaves the sentence as it is.

Interactive grammar-checking

As with spell-checking, you can have Word do interactive grammar-checking and underline any questionable grammar. Grammar receives a wavy green line to alert you.

With interactive grammar-checking on, Control-clicking any questionable phrase tells you the error and reveals suggestions. Simply drag to the correction you would like to make and click to replace the error word with your choice. Or, you can open the grammar-checker from this contextual menu.

The preference to turn this on or off is under Tools ➪ Preferences in the Spelling & Grammar tab. It is the top option under Grammar: Check grammar as you type. If you turn on interactive grammar-checking while you're already in a document, Word goes through and marks up your document.

Hot Stuff

While interactive spelling and grammar are turned on, you can tell the document is being checked by looking at your status bar. As Word is checking, you see a pen writing in the book. When an error is found, an *x* appears over the book and awaits your attention. Double-click this status bar icon and Word points out the potential error, presenting the shortcut menu you'd see if you Control-clicked the error. You can correct the error from the shortcut menu. If there are no errors found in your document (or if you've approved all the potential errors), the icon will show a check mark.

Grammar-checking manually

To check grammar in a document, first select the passage of text you wish to check or make no selection to check the entire document. Then choose Spelling and Grammar from the Tools menu. If an error is found, Word displays the Grammar dialog box and the animated help (if you haven't turned it off). A suggestion may appear that explains the error or offers a way to fix it. If you agree with the suggestion to fix the error, click the Change button. You can ignore the error by clicking Ignore. Sometimes you may want to edit the sentence yourself. Click in the Sentence text box and edit the sentence as you normally would, and then click the Change button. You can also start the grammar-checker by clicking the Spelling button on the Standard toolbar.

The Suggestions box contains alternatives to the construction you used in your sentence. Animated help provides you with some explanations as to why the grammar construction is incorrect. The explanation appears in an automated help window, as shown in Figure 2-22. You can ignore this rule in the rest of the grammar-check by clicking the Ignore button in the Grammar dialog box.

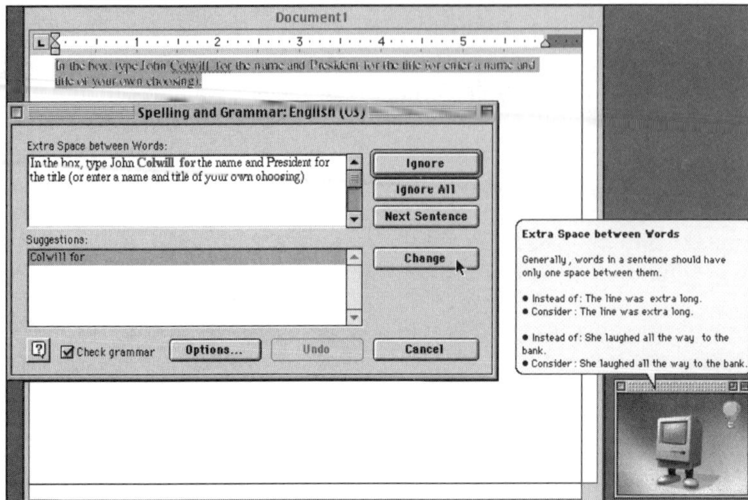

Figure 2-22: The Spelling and Grammar dialog box with an automated help window

Spelling and grammar preferences

To see the options available to you, choose Tools ➪ Preferences, and then select the Spelling & Grammar tab. Alternatively, if you are in the Spelling and Grammar dialog box, click the Options button. Either way, the same Spelling and Grammar preferences appear. The options are fairly self explanatory. Figure 2-23 shows the contents of the Spelling & Grammar Preferences dialog box as selected from Tools ➪ Preferences. Notice that you can tell Word which grammar rules to follow. The default setting is Standard, but the Writing style pop-up list enables you to choose the rules group you prefer: casual, technical, formal, or a custom style that you create by removing or changing the settings. To customize the type of grammar checking you want for your documents, click the Settings button.

As mentioned earlier, when you check spelling, Word also checks your grammar. If you prefer not to have Word check grammar, turn it off by removing the check mark from the Check grammar with spelling box on the Spelling & Grammar tab of the Preferences dialog box.

You can also obtain readability statistics on your document. After Word has completed the grammar check, it analyzes the document and provides a summary of readability statistics. These statistics let you evaluate whether an adult reader can easily understand your document. You can turn this analysis on and off through the Grammar tab of the Preferences menu.

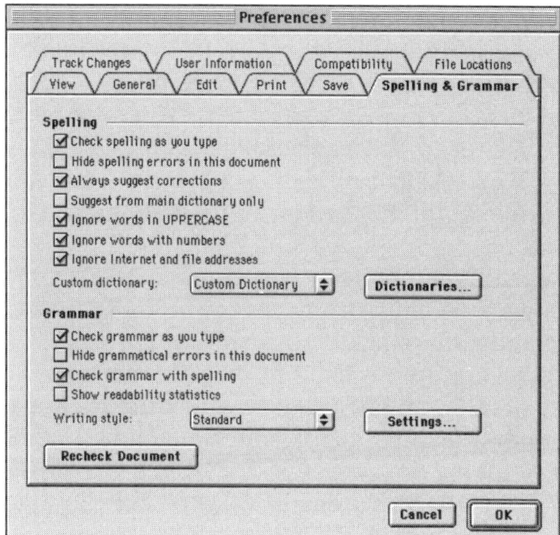

Figure 2-23: The Spelling & Grammar tab of the Preferences dialog box

Changing dictionaries

As mentioned, Word always uses the main dictionary and at least one supplemental dictionary. You normally add words to the Custom Dictionary when you click the Add button in the Spelling dialog box, but you can also add words to any supplemental dictionary that you have created (or intend to create).

At times you may want to create a new custom dictionary. For example, if you work with many medical terms, you can create a medical dictionary and call it something like Medical Dictionary. Then, you can add the medical words to this new dictionary as they are found in the spell-checker. To create a new dictionary, first click the Options button in the Spelling and Grammar dialog box. When Spelling & Grammar Preferences appears, click the Dictionaries button to bring up the Custom Dictionaries dialog box, shown in Figure 2-24.

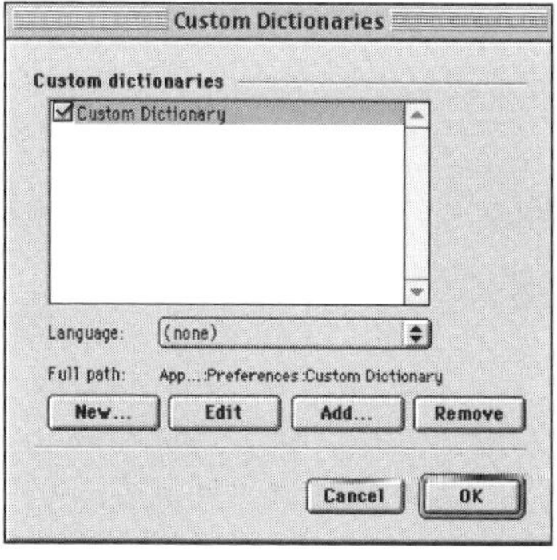

Figure 2-24: The Custom Dictionaries dialog box

Click the New button in the Custom Dictionaries dialog box. You are presented with a save dialog box that says Save Current Dictionary as. (Don't let this throw you. Word isn't saving an existing dictionary; it's creating a new, blank one.) Name your new dictionary and choose a location in which to save it. You may want to save it in the folder along with the provided dictionaries. Just don't forget to copy the dictionary if you ever uninstall Word. Your new dictionary is automatically added to the list of custom dictionaries and checked for immediate use.

In case you are provided with an existing supplemental dictionary (for example, from someone in your office), you need to tell Word to recognize it. To do so, click the Options button in the Spelling and Grammar dialog box. The Spelling & Grammar Preferences dialog box appears. In the Custom Dictionaries area, you should see Custom Dictionary, the default, already chosen. Click the Dictionaries button to bring up the Custom Dictionaries dialog box, and then click the Add button. The Add Custom Dictionary dialog box opens (see Figure 2-25). Navigate to the dictionary you want to install, select it, and then click Open. The dictionary appears in the custom dictionaries list as active.

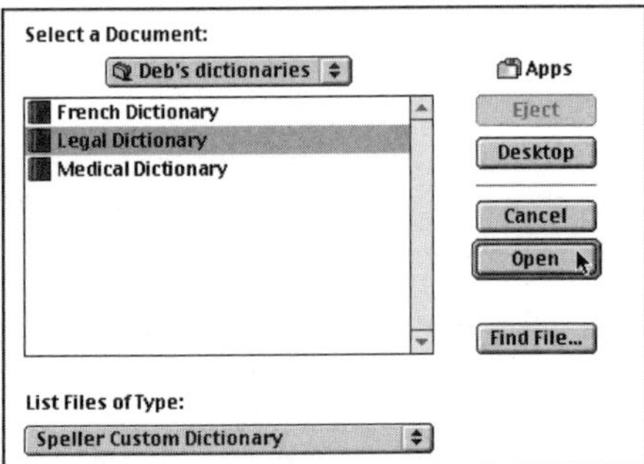

Figure 2-25: The Add Custom Dictionary dialog box

You can also turn a supplemental dictionary on or off at any time by opening the same Custom Dictionaries dialog box and checking or unchecking any dictionary in the list.

Hot Stuff

You can check and edit any custom dictionary from the Custom Dictionaries dialog box by clicking the Edit button. This button opens the dictionary as a Word document in which you can make your changes.

Why Should You Use More Than One Custom Dictionary?

Many Word users leave Word set to the default Custom Dictionary. But, depending on your needs, you may have good reason to create and use more than one custom dictionary. If you tend to bounce back and forth between projects that involve a good deal of technical lingo or other nonstandard terms, you can make the overall process of spell-checking a bit faster by using different custom dictionaries, with each one specific to the task you are working on.

Word spends less time searching a smaller, specific custom dictionary than a large custom dictionary that contains terms for many subjects. Just remember to turn on the custom dictionary of your choice when it's needed by using the Spelling tab, available through the Tools⇨Preferences command.

Using AutoCorrect

As with the spell- and grammar-checkers, AutoCorrect works with you to ease you work load. When your fingers get tangled, this feature tries to figure out what you meant to type and automatically repairs the word for you. For example, if you type *wnat*, it automatically changes to *want* and *witht he* becomes *with the*. AutoCorrect can also become your shorthand manager. You can tell it which letter combinations to turn into words or phrases.

AutoCorrect is also available in Excel and PowerPoint. Each Office application shares your AutoCorrect list.

AutoCorrect's features and capabilities

To gain insight into AutoCorrect's features and capabilities, and to customize the correction and shorthand list, select Tools⇨AutoCorrect. The scrolling list contains all words to be corrected. To avoid redundancy and confusion, take a look before you add your own words. When you are ready to add a new AutoCorrect entry, type your key combination in the Replace box, and then type the word, phrase, or symbol you want entered in place of the combination in the With box. Finally, click Add. To change an existing AutoCorrect entry, select the correction from the list and enter your change in the Replace or With box. Click Replace. To remove an AutoCorrect entry, select it from the list and click Delete.

By the way, AutoCorrect is intelligent. If you happen to request that *jd* be replaced by *John Doe* (your name, of course), when you type *jd's,* Word will substitute *John Doe's*.

Working with AutoText entries

AutoText entries are stored entries of text that you frequently use and want to have handy for easy entry. Phrases such as closings to business or personal letters are candidates for AutoText entries. To store an AutoText entry, type the text you want or import the graphic, and then select it. Next, choose Insert ⇨ AutoText ⇨ New. The Create AutoText box appears, with the entry as the default name. If you want to keep the suggested name, simply click OK. This is the name as it will appear under the AutoText submenu to help you select it later. If you prefer to make changes to the menu listing, do so in the text box before clicking OK. Word then places the entry on the submenu that appears under Insert ⇨ AutoText ⇨ Normal.

Word provides some default entries, such as common openings and closings to letters, signatures, and filenames. You can view them by choosing Insert ⇨ Auto Text ⇨ Auto Text. This brings up the AutoText tab of the AutoCorrect dialog box shown in Figure 2-26. The menu title appears in the top area. Click any menu title to view the entire entry in the preview area, below.

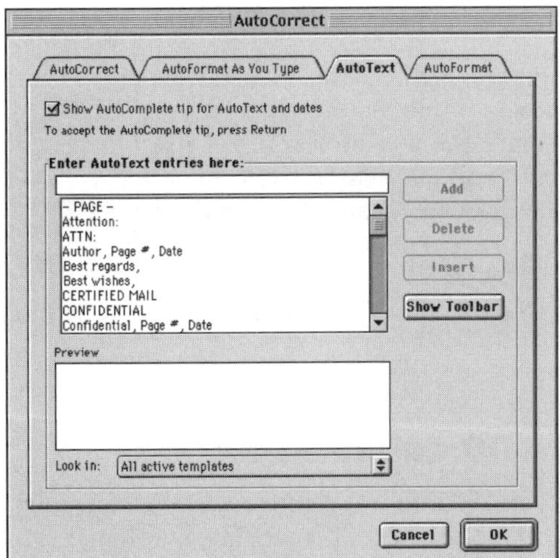

Figure 2-26: The AutoText tab of the AutoCorrect dialog box

To insert an AutoText entry, place your cursor where you want the entry to go and then choose Insert ⇨ AutoText ⇨ AutoText. In the dialog box that appears, click the AutoText tab and double-click the desired AutoText entry from the list box.

Word also gives you the option of assigning an AutoText entry to a toolbar so you can insert the AutoText entry by clicking that toolbar button. If you want to assign an AutoText entry to a toolbar, perform the following steps:

1. From the View menu, choose Toolbars and choose Customize from the submenu.
2. In the Customize dialog box, click the Commands tab (see Figure 2-27).

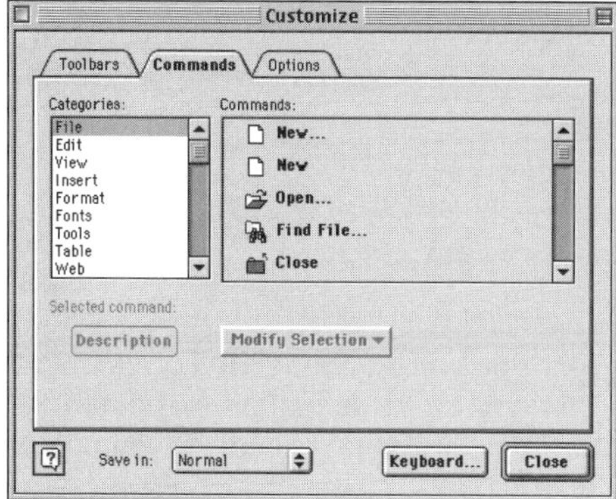

Figure 2-27: The Commands tab of the Customize dialog box

3. In the Categories list box, scroll down to AutoText and click this category. The adjacent box becomes the AutoText box, which displays the names of all your AutoText entries (and the default entries) in alphabetical order.
4. Click the name of the entry to which you want to assign a button. You will see the outline of a toolbar button appear.
5. Click the entry. Your cursor will have a special *x* at its bottom right. Drag the button to the toolbar and position where you want the AutoText button. (The toolbar must be displayed to do this.)
6. The name of the AutoText entry appears as the default name for the button, but you can change the name. With the Customize window open, press ⌘ and Option as you click the button you created. To change the text that appears on the button, drag to the Name field, stop, and change or delete the text that appears. To add a default button image, continue dragging to the Change Button Image of your choice, if you like one of them. Otherwise, see Step 7.
7. If you choose to create your own button, drag to Edit Button Image to open the Button Editor dialog box (see Figure 2-28). The editor is a miniature paint program for you to redraw your button. You can also paste an image from the Clipboard.

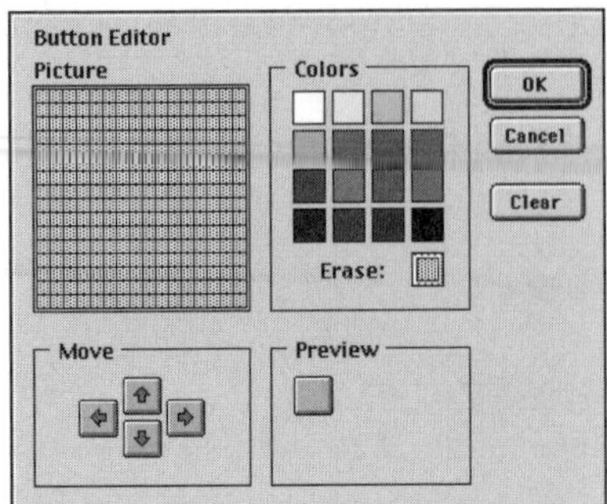

Figure 2-28: The Button Editor dialog box

Changes can be made to an AutoText entry at any time. You might want to begin by placing the AutoText into a document. Edit this text as you desire, and then select the edited text. Create a new entry, but give it the same name as the original. When asked if you want to redefine your existing entry, click Yes.

If you no longer need an AutoText entry, you can delete it. Return to the AutoText tab of the AutoCorrect dialog box (Insert ➪ AutoText ➪ AutoText). Select the name of the AutoText entry you want to delete and click the Delete button. The entry is removed.

You can also print your AutoText entries. Select Print from the File menu. The Print dialog box appears. Select Word from the pop-up menu that typically says General. This presents you with printing options specific to Word. Next, select AutoText Entries from the first Print pop-up list, as shown in Figure 2-29. After you click OK, the AutoText entries print.

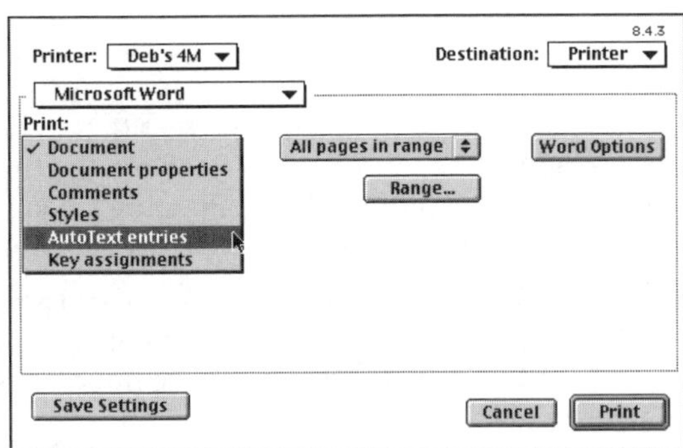

Figure 2-29: Word-specific print options as seen in a laser printer's Print dialog box

Accessing Word's Thesaurus

Word's Thesaurus enables you to find synonyms for specific words in your documents. The fastest way to do so is to move your cursor over the desired word, and then Control-click to bring up the shortcut menu. At the bottom of the menu is a submenu that lists all the synonyms Word can find for your word. Simply drag to the word you desire (if any) and click that word. (In case you are a cross-platform user, we should point out that this method is not available in Office 97 for Windows.)

If you prefer not to Control-click or you want to further explore your synonym options, you can always go the long route. First select the desired word (remember, you can double-click anywhere in a word to select it) and then choose the Tools ⇨ Language ⇨ Thesaurus (⌘-Option-R or Shift-F7). The Thesaurus dialog box appears, as shown in Figure 2-30.

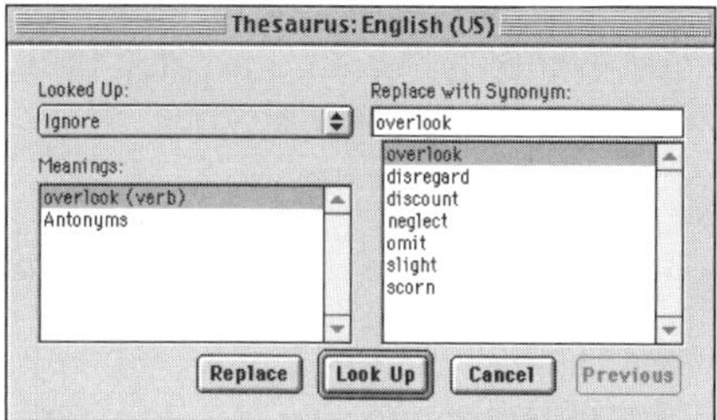

Figure 2-30: The Thesaurus dialog box

The dialog box shows any synonyms found for the selected word in the Replace with Synonym list box. To replace the selected word with a synonym, select the desired synonym from the list box and then click the Replace button.

In the Meanings list box, you'll see one or more definitions for the selected word. The list of available synonyms changes when you select a different meaning. You can use the mouse to move between the Replace with Synonym and the Meanings list boxes. If you want to look up one of the words in the Meanings list box, simply select the word and click the Look Up button.

Hyphenating Your Document

Word provides different ways to handle hyphenation, the process of adding hyphens to reduce the ragged appearance of a document's right margin. If the text is justified, hyphens reduce the space between words to fill out a line. In Word, you can add hyphens manually or automatically.

To enter hyphens manually, choose Tools ➪ Language ➪ Hyphenation. This displays the Hyphenation dialog box (see Figure 2-31). After you click the Manual button, Word switches to Page Layout view and stops to let you confirm the desired location for each hyphen. If you don't want to add a hyphen to a word, click No, and the word is skipped untouched.

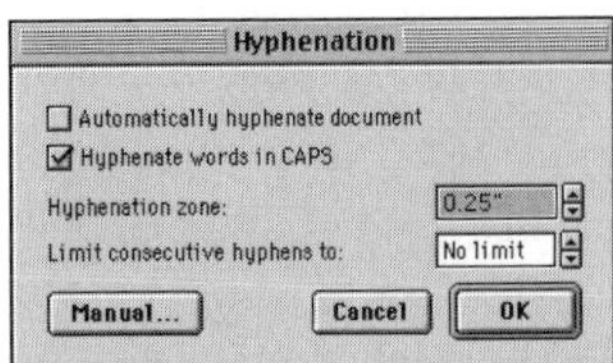

Figure 2-31: The Hyphenation dialog box

With automatic hyphenation, Word adds hyphens automatically, making its best guess as to where hyphenation should occur. In the Hyphenation dialog box, click the Automatically hyphenate document check box to activate automatic hyphenation.

If you choose to hyphenate as you type, you can use one of two types of hyphens: optional or nonbreaking. Optional hyphens appear only if the word is at the end of the line. Optional hyphens are the kind Word inserts when you use semiautomatic or automatic hyphenation. To insert an optional hyphen, press ⌘-- (hyphen). Use nonbreaking hyphens (also called hard hyphens) when you do not want a hyphenated word to be broken at the end of a line. To insert a nonbreaking hyphen, press ⌘-Shift-- (hyphen).

Adding Bullets or Paragraph Numbers

With Word, you can automatically add paragraph numbers to your documents or bullets to each paragraph. This feature can be very useful when you are working with legal documents. Also, documents that are numbered are easy to edit and revise. As you add or delete paragraphs, Word maintains the correct numbering for the paragraphs.

In addition to typing an asterisk and space to create a bulleted list, you can also type one hyphen, two hyphens, a greater-than sign (>), or a hyphen or equal sign followed by a greater than sign. The number followed by a period,), -, or > creates the numbered list with that specific character.

The next-fastest way to add simple bullets or numbers to paragraphs as you type is to use the buttons on the Formatting toolbar. Select the paragraphs or section to which you want to add numbers or bullets, and then click the Bullets button to add bullets or the Numbering button to add numbers.

Using the AutoFormat Feature

The newest and coolest way to add paragraph numbers or bullets is to use Word's new AutoFormat feature. To create a bullet list, simply type an asterisk and a space or a tab, and then type your list text and press Return to begin your next list element. By default, Word automatically converts the asterisk and space (or tab) into a bullet and tab. Word also places the next bullet and tab for you, so all you need to do is type your list text.

To create a numbered list, type your first number and a period or closing parenthesis, then a space or tab, and then type your text and press Return to begin your next list item. Word converts this into a proper numbered list (a number, period, and tab) and places the next number on the page for you. The ever-courteous Office Assistant lets you know when one of these conversions has been made and gives you the option of undoing it. When you are done with your list, press Return twice to end. Should you prefer to deactivate this AutoFormat feature, you can deselect it under Tools ➪ AutoCorrect in the AutoFormat as you type tab.

When you add numbers, using either of the fast methods, Word automatically checks the preceding paragraph for its numbering style. If it is numbered, Word uses the same style of numbering for the selected paragraph. If the paragraph is not numbered, Word applies the style of numbering that you selected last. (You select numbering style in the dialog box mentioned next.)

You can also add paragraph numbering or bullets the old-fashioned way. Select the paragraphs or section to which you want to apply the numbering or bullets. Next, choose Format ➪ Bullets and Numbering. The Bullets and Numbering dialog box appears, from which you can choose from seven different bullet layouts on the Bulleted tab or seven different numbering layouts from the Numbered tab. The Outline Numbered tab lets you create outline-style numbering with numbers and letters. Each bullet or numbering effect is depicted visually. Click the one you want, and then click OK or simply double-click the one you want.

Hot Stuff

With the advent of the Web, bulleted lists using images rather than bullets or symbols have gained popularity. Word 98 even has a quick way for you to create this specialized list using AutoFormat. For a bulleted list using a symbol, select Insert ➪ Symbol to insert a symbol, close the Symbol dialog box, and then type two or more spaces, add your list text, and press Return. For an image as a bullet, insert your image as an inline graphic, type two or more spaces, add your list text, and then press Return. In each case, as with bullets and numbers, Word automatically creates your next line until you press Return twice to end the list. One important rule applies to using an image: The graphic must not be more than 1.5 times the height of the text in that list. (Note: The easiest way to get the graphic inline is to go to its source and copy it. Then use Edit ➪ Paste Special, select Picture from the list, and uncheck Float over Text.)

Collaborating on a Document

Often several people must work together to create a final document. Word offers a full complement of collaboration tools. There is even a Reviewing Toolbar to help. To activate this toolbar, select View➪Toolbars➪Reviewing. This toolbar may also open automatically when you select certain reviewing options. Using the Track Changes feature, you can see what each person suggests, and then accept or reject each change. When you use the Comments feature, each person can add his or her own two cents without messing up the document.

Tracking changes to your document

When two or more people are working together on a document, being able to track the changes (called Revisions in Word 6) is a very handy feature. To begin tracking changes, select Tools➪Track Changes➪Highlight Changes (see Figure 2-32). Then click to place a check by the Track changes while editing option. In addition, you can choose to see those changes onscreen while you work by checking Highlight changes on screen. (This means you will see the revision marks.) You can also see those changes printed by checking Highlight changes in printed document.

Figure 2-32: The Highlight Changes dialog box

If you choose to highlight the changes onscreen, whenever a change is made to your document, deleted text shows in strikethrough font and new text is underlined. (These are the defaults. You can change the markings.) Each person who edits shows up in a different color. (Word doesn't know you as a person, but it knows it's on a different machine.) To get a feel for how this feature works, from the Highlight Changes dialog box, click Options, or select Tools➪Preferences and select the Track Changes tab. Either way, you end up in the same place. In this Preferences tab, you can determine what changes will track. By default, only inserting and deleting text is tracked, but you can also follow formatting changes and line changes.

As your document is passed around, each person can make the changes visible and see what happened to the document so far. (You may not want to keep the revisions visible most of the time while you are trying to read the document.) After the document has made the rounds, you can decide whether to keep each change. Select Tools ➪ Track Changes ➪ Accept or Reject Changes to bring up the dialog box of the same name. You can move through the entire document, change by change, by clicking the Find button. There's a button for moving forward and one to go backward through the document. As you get to each change, you can see it in the document (you may have to move the dialog box window at times). Click Accept or Reject. Or, you can simply view the document with or without changes, decide you love or hate all the changes, and then Accept All or Reject All of the changes.

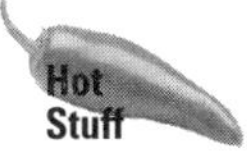

Another, fast way to turn Track Changes on and off is to double-click the letters TRK in the status bar. When changes are being tracked, these letters are black. When changes are off, the letters are grayed out (dimmed).

Comparing documents

Perhaps you've kept a copy of a document you created and want to see how it stacks up to the final version. With one version open, select Tools ➪ Track Changes ➪ Compare documents. This opens the Mac's Open dialog box. Locate and open the other copy. Word will now go through and place revision marks so you can see the changes between the two documents.

Creating comments

You can easily create and edit comments—notes regarding your document—as a part of your Word document. Think of comments as annotations added to a document: They are not normally visible in the document, but can easily be seen by using the Comments command from the View menu. Comments are very useful when multiple Word users want to make comments on a proposed document. Because each comment includes the initials of the person making the comment, you can view the comments and contact the persons who have made the comments for help in incorporating the changes. Even when you are working on documents alone, you may find comments useful for reminding yourself about revisions that you plan to make to the document.

To create a comment, place the insertion point at the desired location for the comment and choose Comment from the Insert menu. Word splits the current window and inserts your initials within a bracket at the comment point (see Figure 2-33). In addition to your initials, Word provides an annotation number so you can add more comments later. Each comment is assigned a number in sequential order.

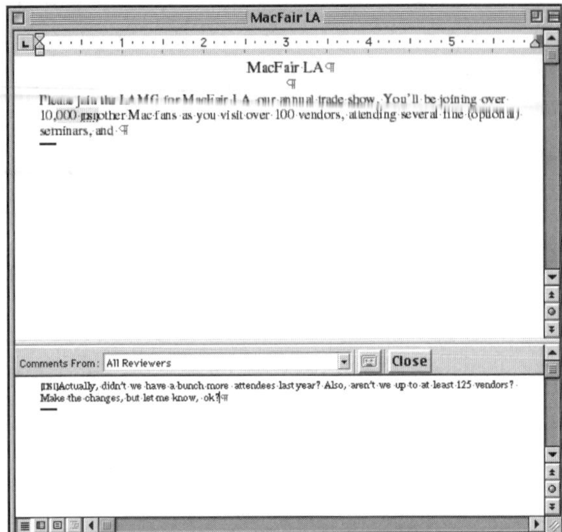

Figure 2-33: A document with comments

The active insertion point is automatically placed in the comments pane—the lower half of the split window. Type any desired comments here, as there is no limit to the length of an annotation. Refer to Figure 2-33 to see a document with a comment added. You can even add sound, which can be especially useful by giving specific instruction that should be delivered with the touch of a human voice. You can do this by clicking the Insert Sound Object button in the comments window. (The Insert Sound Object button will only be enabled if you have the Voice Annotation OLE server installed. If Voice Annotation is not in your Custom Installer or Value Pack Installer, look for it at Microsoft's Web site.)

When you finish writing the comments, close the comments pane of the window by clicking the Close button on the pane, using the View⇨Comments command again or by double-clicking the split line. You can also drag the split bar to the bottom of the window.

To view a comment, move your mouse over the highlight that indicates the comment and rest it a moment until the comment pops up. To view all comments that you have added to a document, select View⇨Comments. The command is a toggle, so choosing it repeatedly will turn comments viewing on or off. To edit the text of an existing comment if the comments pane is not already open, choose View⇨Comments or Control-click the highlight that indicates a comment in the document and select Edit Comment. This opens the comment pane. Edit the comment text as you would edit any other text.

To delete a comment, go to that comment's marker in the document (the yellow highlight), Control-click the highlighted word and choose Delete Comment from the shortcut menu. You can also print all the comments in a document by choosing the

Print command from the File menu, selecting Word from the top pop-up menu, and then selecting Comments from the Word-specific pop-up menu.

You can use the Cut and Paste commands to move text from the comments pane into the document. This technique is particularly helpful when some of the comments that have been added to your documents by other people should be incorporated into the actual document.

Finding comments

In a large document, you can quickly get to a desired annotation with the Go To command from the Edit menu (F5 or ⌘-G). In the Go To dialog box, choose Comments in the Go to What list on the left. A reviewer's name field appears. Select the name of a specific reviewer by clicking the arrow to the right of the box, or keep the default, Any Reviewer if you prefer. Click the Next button to go to the first qualifying comment. Each time you click Next, you are moved to the next qualifying annotation.

Locking the document

When multiple persons are commenting on a document, you may find it helpful to lock the document so no one but the author can change the actual document—others can only add or edit comments. If you lock a document and allow comments only, you can safely pass the file around for comments, while ensuring that others cannot make any changes to the document.

To lock a file for comments only, choose File⇨Save As and click the Options button in the Save As dialog box. In the Save tab, enter a password under Password to modify. Those opening the document without this password cannot make changes. You can also restrict the editing of your document by clicking the Read-Only Recommended box. After you've entered your password(s), perform the save. Use the same document name if you want to replace the current document.

Working with Document Summaries

Document summaries are not exactly an aid to the editing process, but they can be helpful in the long run. If you take the time to fill in a summary, you can later use the information stored in it as a way to search for desired documents.

When you want to open a document but can't recall a filename, you can find the file by searching document summaries. Choose File⇨Open, and then click Find File. This brings up a basic search dialog box. From here you can search for a document by title, although you can also do that within the Mac OS. More importantly, you can select which hard drive (volume) to search—handy for partitioned hard drives or networked computers. Click Advanced Search to present more search criteria (see Figure 2-34). Enter the desired search criteria. Special characters may also be used to create approximate criteria (see “Searching for special characters” earlier in this chapter). Click OK to close the Advanced dialog box and click OK again to begin the search.

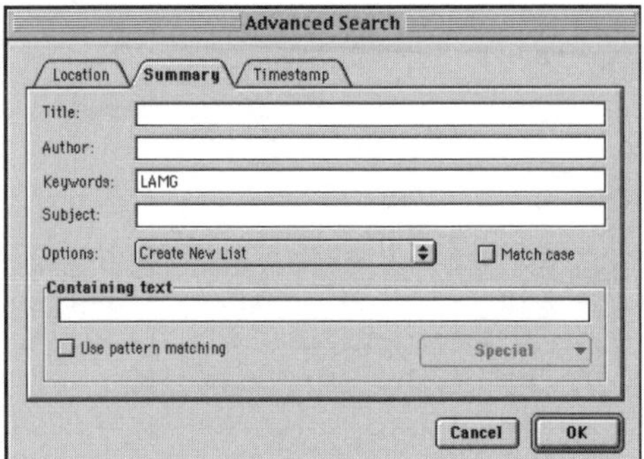

Figure 2-34: The Advanced Search dialog box

Viewing or editing a summary

To view or edit a document summary, make sure the document is open, choose File➪Properties. This brings up the Summary tab in the Properties dialog box that opens. The Summary tab is shown in Figure 2-35.

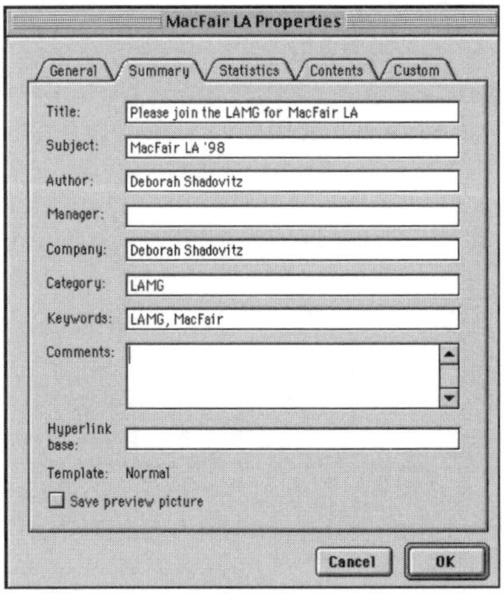

Figure 2-35: The Summary tab of the Properties dialog box

The fields are self-explanatory—you can enter the desired document title, subject, and keywords that may help you identify the document later. Word inserts the author's name, based on the name that is stored in the dialog box on the User Info tab of the Preferences dialog box (accessed from the Tools menu). When you change the author's name in the Summary dialog box, the change takes effect only for the current document.

The Statistics tab in the Properties dialog box can be useful for getting information about the productivity of the document. This tab displays all sorts of useful information regarding your document (see Figure 2-36).

The Statistics tab shows the document's creation date; when it was last saved; how many times it has been revised; the total time you have spent editing it; and how many characters, words, and pages are in the document.

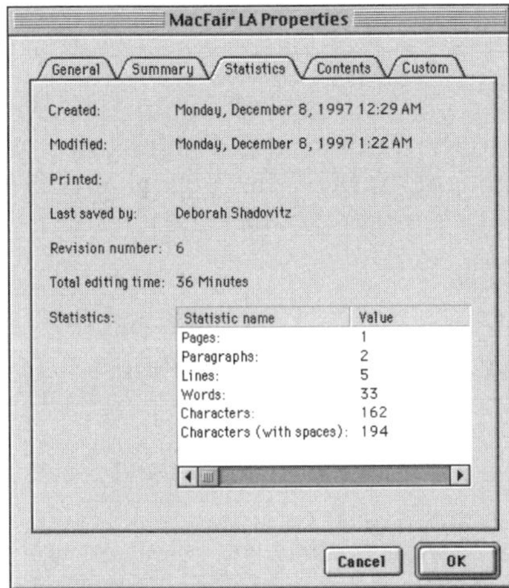

Figure 2-36: The Statistics tab of the Properties dialog box

Using the AutoSummarize feature

AutoSummarize is another feature of Office 98. This feature enables you to summarize the key points in a document. It analyzes documents and assigns scores to each of the sentences in a document by analyzing the frequency of words in sentences. You can also choose a percentage of the high-scoring sentences that you wish to display in your summary. Figure 2-37 shows the AutoSummarize window that appears when you choose Tools ➪ AutoSummarize.

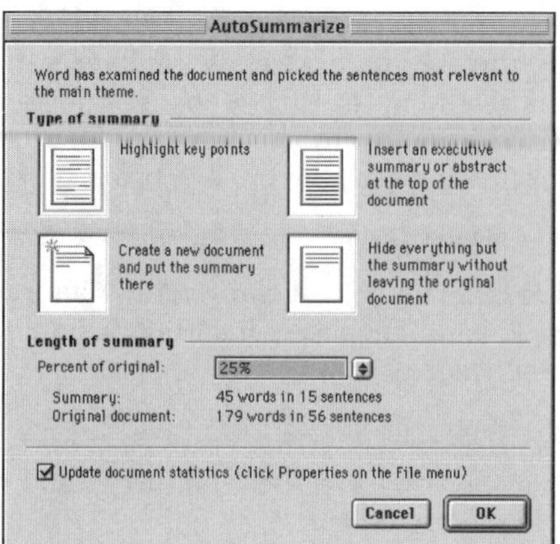

Figure 2-37: The AutoSummarize dialog box

You will find that this feature works best with well-structured documents. Also, the use of the Find All Word Forms Tool will help produce quality summaries. With your well-structured document, you can add the summary as a highlighted section at the top of your document, in a new document, or hide the original and just show the summary. You do this by making the corresponding choices from the AutoSummarize dialog box.

Next, you will want to choose the percentage of the document you want to summarize, using the options in the Length of Summary section of the AutoSummarize box. There, you have choices between sentences, percentages, or number of words in your document on which you wish to base the summary. This gives you the power to control the length of the summary Word creates for you.

After the summary is created, the results appear, based on the selection you made in the Type of Summary section of the AutoSummarize dialog box. By default, the AutoSummarize box also updates the document statistics automatically.

Summary

This chapter provided you with useful techniques for working with documents in Word. The following points were covered:

✦ Word's File➪New command displays a dialog box containing tabs you can use to create new documents. New documents are based on a blank document or on one of Word's predefined templates. You can base your documents on different templates containing certain formatting and, in many cases, boilerplate text.

- Word includes a number of wizards that ask you a series of questions and then create a basic document based on your responses.
- You can see your document in one of five possible views: Normal, Outline, Online Layout, Page Layout, or Master Document.
- You can change your margin settings with the Format⇨Document command, your tabs with the Format⇨Tabs command, and your line spacing with the Format⇨Paragraph command.
- You can search for text with the Edit⇨Find command, or search for and replace text with the Edit⇨Replace command. Word provides a full-featured search-and-replace capability that lets you search for text, formatting, and special characters such as paragraph marks and tabs.
- You can use the spell- and grammar-checkers to find and fix misspellings and/or grammatical errors. Word can do this checking as you type. Word will even fix common spelling or spacing errors automatically, and let you create your own shorthand to have an entire phrase replace your shorthand combination.
- You can mark and track revisions made to your documents.
- You can use the Insert⇨Comments command to add comments to a document.

Where to go next

- Chapter 3 takes you to the next step: formatting documents.
- Ready to print your work? Chapter 4 tells you how.
- Do you need to create tables, outlines, tables of contents, or indexes? See Chapters 5 and 7 for help.

✦ ✦ ✦

Formatting Documents

✦ ✦ ✦ ✦

In This Chapter

Discovering formatting

Formatting documents

Formatting paragraphs

Formatting characters

Formatting sections

✦ ✦ ✦ ✦

As you create and refine your text, you will need to control the appearance of the document. This is where Word's formatting features come in. In the previous chapter, you were introduced to some of the basic ways to format your text. This chapter details formatting as it applies to the pages, sections, paragraphs, and individual characters of your document. We begin with the entire-document level, and then go into paragraphs and characters. Finally, we talk about sections, another alternative for formatting.

Discovering Formatting

Later in this chapter, you'll use many of the options in Word's Format menu, which offers many of the features that control Word's formatting. In the meantime, the following are some basic points you should know about formatting in Word:

- ✦ The largest unit in terms of formatting your document is *page* formatting. With page formatting, you control the appearance of every page for the entire document. Page formatting affects such settings as page size, default tab stops, and margins for the document.
- ✦ Optionally, you can apply *section* formatting to entire sections of a document. A document can consist of a single section, as most do, or you can divide a document into multiple sections. When you format a section of a document, you change certain formatting aspects for pages within that section. For example, you may want to change the number of columns in a portion of the document, or you may want to change the look of the headers and footers in another section. After you divide a document into sections, you can use many formatting commands to format each section individually. If you're a beginner and won't be creating

documents such as newsletters from scratch, you can skip the information about sections.

✦ The next level in the formatting arena is *paragraph* formatting. With paragraph formatting, the formatting you apply controls the appearance of the text from one paragraph mark to the next. Paragraph marks appear whenever you press the Return key. If you press Return once, type seven lines of text and press Return again, those seven lines of text are one paragraph. After you select paragraphs, you can change the formatting for those particular paragraphs. For example, you can change a paragraph's alignment or its line spacing. To change only one paragraph, you only need to place your cursor within that paragraph.

✦ Because paragraphs consist of characters, it is easy to confuse character and paragraph formatting. It may help to remember that paragraph formatting generally controls the appearance of lines, because a group of lines typically makes up a paragraph. Paragraph formatting controls the alignment of lines, the spacing between lines, the indents in lines, and borders around the paragraph.

✦ The smallest unit of formatting is the character. With *character* formatting, any formatting you apply affects all the characters within a selected area of text or all the characters you type after you select the formatting. When you select a sentence and click the Bold button in the Formatting toolbar, you're applying character formatting. Character formatting is often used to make a word or phrase stand out.

Formatting Documents

The broadest degree of formatting you can do applies to your entire document. Document formatting affects such settings as page size, orientation, and page margins for the overall appearance of each page in your document. In the Macintosh version of Word, two menus work together to provide full document formatting control. File⇨Page Setup, a regular feature of every Mac program, offers controls for Paper Size, Orientation, and Scale. Other document formatting options, such as Margins, are accessed from the Format⇨Document menu. Because the Page Setup dialog box can also be accessed from the Document dialog box, you can just remember that to affect the format of the entire document, seek the Format menu and select Document. You can also start with the Page Setup command and access the other document formatting from there.

Changes made within the Document dialog box can apply to the entire document or just from the position of your insertion point onward, as you specify in the Apply To pop-up list. Accordingly, your choices are: Whole Document or This Point Forward. (By default, This Point Forward creates a section break and moves your cursor into the new section where your changes begin to apply. However, if you want the change to take place within one page, go to the Layout tab of the Document dialog box and change the Section start option from New Page to

Continuous. (See "Formatting Sections," later in this chapter, for details.) The Preview window provides a visual representation of how the formatting changes appear when applied to the printed page.

Changes made within the Document dialog box apply only to the document in which you are currently working. However, with the Default button, you can make them the default and have these settings apply to all future Word documents. (We're assuming you are using the default Normal template. If you are using any other template, the changes are applied to the template you are using. Templates are explained in detail in Chapter 8.)

Orientation

The first thing to consider about your document's look is the orientation. The default orientation of a Word document is Portrait, the tall, letter-writing format of most written documents. If this suits your needs, as it probably does, there is nothing you need to do. You can change the orientation to Landscape, the wide or horizontal format, by choosing File ➪ Page Setup to open the Page Setup dialog box and clicking the image that represents the orientation you want. The Page Setup dialog box is shown in Figure 3-1.

Orientation can be changed at any point of your work. The default margins for the new orientation take over automatically so your text doesn't get clipped.

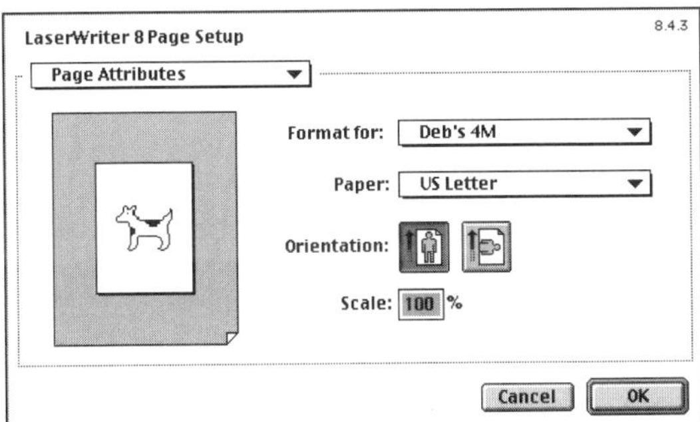

Figure 3-1: The Page Setup dialog box

Backgrounds

You may notice a command called Background under the Format menu. Adding a background is indeed formatting that can enhance the appearance of your documents.

Word enables you to choose a color that you want to appear as the background for the entire document. However, it is viewable only in Online Layout view, as it's a Web-page-creation feature. We cover Word and the Web in Chapter 11.

Page size

The default page size for the U.S. version of Word 98 is the standard 8 ½" × 11". If this is appropriate for you, there is no need to adjust anything. If not, select File ➪ Page Setup (or click the Page Setup button from within the Document dialog box) to make your adjustments. In the Paper pop-up menu (refer to Figure 3-1), you can select a desired paper size. The available choices are Letter, Legal, A4 (European), Executive, Env Comm 10 (legal-sized envelope), Env Monarch (the smaller envelope size), Env DL, Env C5, and Env ISO B5, or Custom Size. You can also create a custom size. To do so, click the pop-up menu at the top of the dialog box and select Microsoft Word. This brings you to another view of the Page Setup dialog box. Here you have a Custom button. Click Custom, and then simply enter any desired width and height for the paper size. (Of course you need a printer that can handle the size you set up.)

Margins

Now that you have your page's most basic setup down, margins are your next possible concern. Margins are the distance between the top of the page and the first printed line, between the bottom of the page and the last printed line, and between the printed lines and paper's right and left edges. You can see your document's margins by looking at the ruler while in Page Layout view. The gray on the left reflects the left margin and gray on the right is the right margin. By default, Word uses a 1.25" margin on the sides. Corporate letterhead is often printed with only 1" from the letterhead to the sides of the page. If you want your text to align with your letterhead, you may need to change these side margins. Word's default top and bottom margins are 1".

You can change your document's margins visually via the ruler or in the Margins tab of the Document dialog box (Format ➪ Document). To use the ruler, switch to Page Layout view, and then move your cursor to the place on the ruler where the margin (gray) section meets the white (text) section. At this meeting point of the margin and document area, your cursor becomes a double-headed arrow. Simply drag the margin to reduce or enlarge the margin area. This works for all margins: sides, top, and bottom.

Figure 3-2 shows you this tab. Simply enter the appropriate number in each margin box. You can type the number or use the arrows.

The From edge settings control the distance from the top and bottom edge of the page to the header and footer. Word measures the distance from the top edge of the header and the bottom edge of the footer to the page edges.

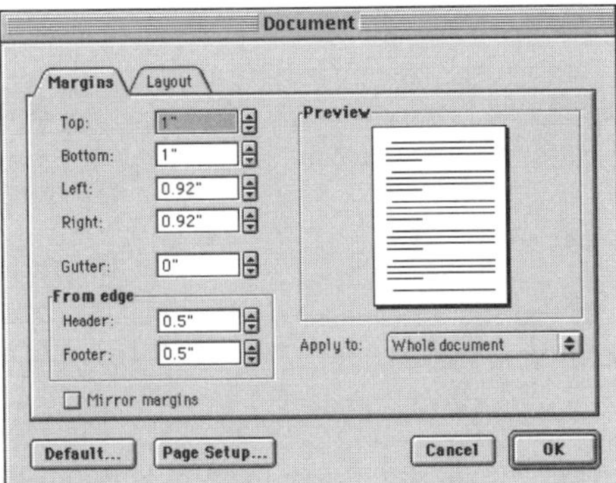

Figure 3-2: The Margins tab of the Document dialog box

There is also a Mirror Margins option. Turn on Mirror Margins to have margins on facing pages mirror each other. You should use this option when you want to print on both sides of a page. With this option turned on, inside margins will have the same width as outside margins. In fact, the Left and Right margin options change to say Inside and Outside. You can also enter a numeric value to determine the width of an optional gutter, an additional white space that is allowed when a document will be bound.

Finally, you need to tell Word where to apply your new margin settings. In the Apply to pop-up menu, you can choose to apply the changes to the entire document—Whole document—or apply the changes to all text following the current location of the insertion point—This Point Forward. Whole Document is fine for most common letters.

Formatting Paragraphs

For the most part, documents consist of paragraphs. Therefore, Word lets you apply formatting to words on the paragraph level. It's important to remember that Word considers a paragraph to be any text between one paragraph mark and the next. While you are working on formatting your document, it helps to see the paragraph marks. Clicking the Show/Hide button on the Standard toolbar (the button with the paragraph symbol resembling a backwards P), or using its keyboard shortcut (⌘-8), toggles these marks along with other invisible formatting characters. (A similar command, Reveal Formatting, works a little differently, but is located under the View menu. You might want to try it as well.)

Figure 3-3 shows you what paragraph marks look like.

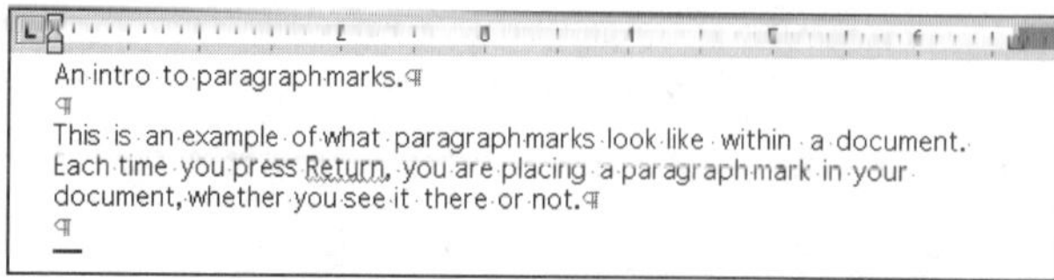

An intro to paragraph marks.¶
¶
This is an example of what paragraph marks look like within a document. Each time you press Return, you are placing a paragraph mark in your document, whether you see it there or not.¶
¶

Figure 3-3: Paragraph marks in a document

The most common paragraph formatting is the alignment of lines at the left and right edges, and the indentation of each paragraph's first line. Paragraph formatting also lets you control the length of lines, the space between lines, and the space between paragraphs. You can also control the placement of tab stops and how text is aligned at the tab stops. When deciding where paragraph formatting is necessary, remember that paragraphs are basically collections of lines. Paragraph formatting affects the appearance of a collection of one or more lines that end with a paragraph marker, which appears when you press Return.

At times your paragraph formatting may include automatic space after or before each Return. You may find yourself with a single word oddly hanging out at the end of a line, or prefer to place some words at the start of a new line, and you'll find yourself with unwanted space if you use the Return key to move those words down to a new line. To avoid this space, use a soft Return by pressing Shift as you press Return. Word does not consider the soft return character (a left-pointing arrow when you reveal formatting) to be the start of a paragraph.

Carrying Down Formatting

It's very helpful to understand how formatting gets carried down from one paragraph to your next new paragraph. Begin a new document, turn Show Formatting on or press ⌘-8, and then type a few lines of text. Don't press Return. Notice that you can't place your insertion point after the paragraph marker, only before it. (Go ahead and try.) Center that paragraph. Each paragraph marker invisibly holds its paragraph's formatting so your marker now holds the code for centering. Now press Return. When you do, the paragraph marker at the end of your first paragraph is carried down or cloned so the new marker carries the identical formatting. This helps you to create consistent documents. (Your second paragraph is now centered.)

Often, beginners press Return without realizing the repercussions. Each time you press Return you place a marker that contains formatting codes. Each might contain different codes, depending on when you created the Return marker (by pressing Return). Therefore, if you use your mouse (or arrow keys) to move your insertion point in from of another marker, you may end up with a paragraph that looks nothing like the paragraph above. People commonly do so, and wonder why each paragraph looks different. Now you know why.

Applying paragraph formatting

You can apply paragraph formatting in different ways. The easiest way is to use the toolbar buttons and the indent controls on the ruler. For more in-depth control, you can use Format ⇨ Paragraph to bring up the Paragraph dialog box shown in Figure 3-4. Whichever method you use, remember that the formatting you select will apply to either the paragraph your cursor is in or the paragraphs selected at the time you make the changes. And remember that each paragraph can have its own formatting.

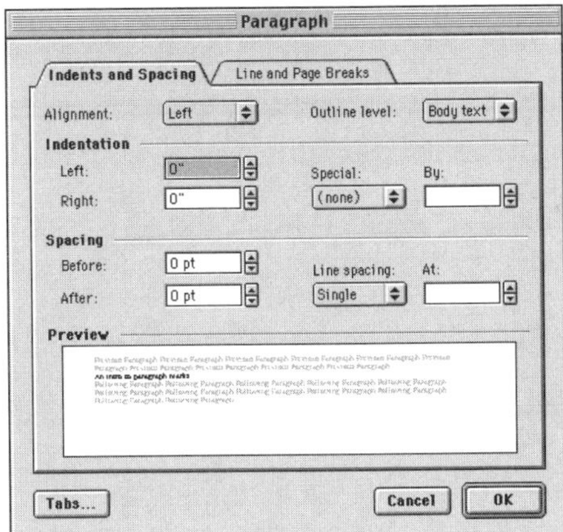

Figure 3-4: The Indents and Spacing tab of the Paragraph dialog box

Any time you wonder what type of formatting a paragraph contains, you can simply place your insertion point within any paragraph and look at the ruler and Formatting toolbar. For example, place your insertion point within any paragraph and look at the alignment buttons (Align Left, Center, Align Right, and Justify). The one that looks pressed reflects the alignment of the paragraph your cursor is in. The positions of the indents and tabs in effect for that paragraph are also evident on the ruler.

The Paragraph dialog box contains two tabs. On the Indents and Spacing tab, you can control the amount of left and right indentation and create a first-line indent or hanging indent (and how much of an indent). This can also be done by dragging the indent controls on the ruler at the top of each document. Using the ruler enables you to see the results more quickly and work visually. In the Spacing area, you can choose the amount of spacing above each new paragraph (before), after each new paragraph (after), and between each line within the paragraph. This is best done from the dialog box or with the keyboard shortcuts you learn in Table 3-1. Spacing can't be done with the ruler.

Table 3-1
Shortcut Keys for Paragraph Formatting

Format	*Shortcut Key*
Left-align text	⌘-L
Center text	⌘-E
Right-align text	⌘-R
Justify text	⌘-J
Indent from left margin	⌘-M
Decrease indent	⌘-Shift-M
Create a hanging indent	⌘-T
Decrease a hanging indent	⌘-Shift-T
Single-space lines	⌘-1
Create 1.5-line spacing	⌘-5
Double-space lines	⌘-2
Add/remove 12 points of space before a paragraph	⌘-0 (zero)
Restore default formatting (reapply the Normal style)	⌘-Shift-N
Show/hide formatting (nonprinting) characters	⌘-8

What Are First-Line Indents and Hanging Indents?

In some paragraphs, you might want to align the first line of the paragraph differently than the remaining lines.

A *first-line indent* begins a paragraph's first line to the right of the paragraph's margin. You probably remember the two-finger first-line indent you learned in elementary school—this is the high-tech version.

A *hanging indent,* sometimes called an outdent, begins a paragraph's first line to the left of the paragraph's margin. You can use a hanging indent to create a bulleted list, for example. Use Format ➪ Paragraph to bring up the Paragraph dialog box. In the Special pop-up menu of the Indents and Spacing tab, choose Hanging. In the By entry, type **.25"**. Click OK. In your document, type a bullet symbol, a tab, and then type the text of the bullet item. The text wraps cleanly along that quarter-inch margin.

The Line and Page Breaks tab of the Paragraph dialog box (see Figure 3-5) contains options that control how text flows within a paragraph. These controls don't have ruler or button equivalents, although you can add them to your menus or create buttons for them in case you find yourself adjusting the controls often. You can turn on the following options:

- ✦ The Widow/Orphan control option prevents a widow (a single line at the bottom of the page) from appearing by itself at the bottom of the page, and it prevents an orphan (a single line at the top of a page) from appearing by itself at the top of the page.
- ✦ The Keep lines together option prevents a page break within the paragraph.
- ✦ The Keep with next option prevents a page break between the paragraph and the one that follows.
- ✦ The Page break before option inserts a page break before the paragraph.
- ✦ The Suppress line numbers option suppresses line numbers for the selected paragraph when line numbering is turned on in a document.
- ✦ The Don't hyphenate option excludes the paragraph from automatic hyphenation.

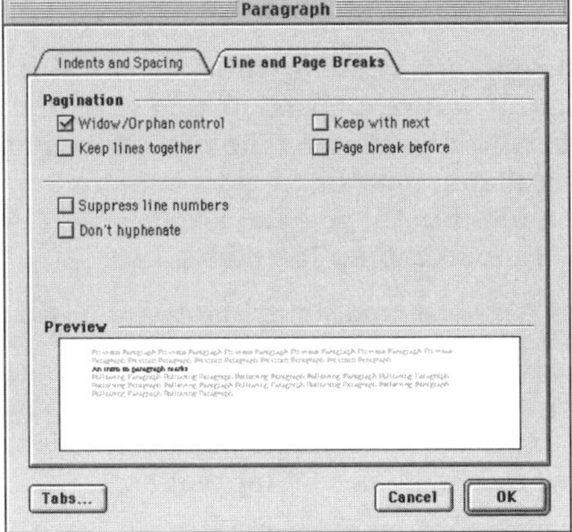

Figure 3-5: The Line and Page Breaks tab of the Paragraph dialog box

Word also provides what it calls a shortcut menu to do character and paragraph formatting. (As a Mac user, you are more likely to call it a Contextual menu.) To call up this menu, Control-click (press Control as you click) over any location in your paragraph. Figure 3-6 shows the formatting shortcut menu that appears. Here you can choose Cut or Copy (if text is selected), Paste (if something is on the Clipboard), or the Font, Paragraph, or Bullets and Numbering dialog boxes. If a single word is selected or your cursor is next to or within a word, you will also have a Synonym's menu. This menu displays that word's synonyms in a submenu from which you can select a replacement. In addition to those options, you can choose Draw Table, which is discussed in Chapter 5.

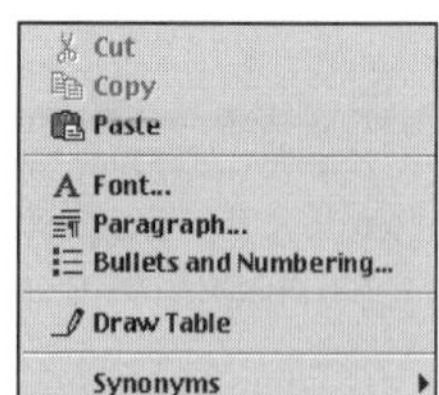

Figure 3-6: The formatting shortcut menu

Indenting paragraphs

Indenting the first line of each paragraph is perhaps the most common formatting effect. However, entire paragraphs can also be indented—on either the left, the right, or both (which creates a block quote). For practice, type the following text (or your own words) and follow the steps to experiment with paragraph formatting:

1. *Type the following text* (not in bold):

   Choices, choices, choices

   It seems you always have three ways to do anything on the Mac. Margins and indents are no exception. If you're a visual person, you'll love using the ruler so you can see where you're moving the text. More numerically based? You'll prefer opening dialog boxes and entering numbers to set indents and such. If you're a bit of both, you can use the ruler, but double-click any ruler element any time to call up the dialog box.

   Experiment to discover how it's most comfortable for you to work.

2. *Center your title.* Place the insertion point anywhere on the first line, and click the Center button (on the Formatting toolbar). Notice the first paragraph ("Choices, choices, choices") takes on a centered alignment. It is actually centered between the left and right margins set for that line.

3. *Indent the paragraph from the left.* Place the insertion point anywhere within the first full paragraph. (Text does not need to be selected.)

   Visually: Click the rectangle (called the left indent), located below the two left triangles on the ruler, and drag it about ½" to the right. This moves both the top and bottom arrows, which affects the indent of both the first line of the paragraph and all following lines. You see the effect when you release the mouse.

   — or —

   Numerically: Choose Format➪Paragraph to open the Paragraph dialog box. In the Indentation area on the Indents and Spacing tab, enter **0.5** as a value in the Left box. You see the effect after you click OK and close the dialog box.

4. *Indent the paragraph from the right.* (Keep the insertion point within the first paragraph.)

   Visually: Click the triangle at the right on the ruler and drag it about ½" to the left. This brings the end of the line (for this paragraph) inward. Your text will wrap when it reaches that triangle. In effect, you have changed the margin for that paragraph. You see the effect when you release the mouse.

   — or —

   Numerically: If you've closed the Paragraph dialog box, open it again (as in Step 3). In the Indentation area, enter **0.5** as a value in the Right box. Click OK. The paragraph appears indented by one-half inch on both sides.

5. *Indent the first line of the paragraph.* Keep your cursor in the same paragraph.

   Visually: Click the top arrow on the left side of the ruler and drag it to the 1" mark. When you release the mouse, the first line of the paragraph is indented to that 1" mark.

   — or —

   Numerically: Return to the Paragraph dialog box and the Indents and Spacing tab. By Indentation, select First Line from the pop-up menu under Special. Enter **1** under By. When you click OK, the first line of the paragraph is now indented by 1 inch.

Figure 3-7 shows the results of all this paragraph formatting.

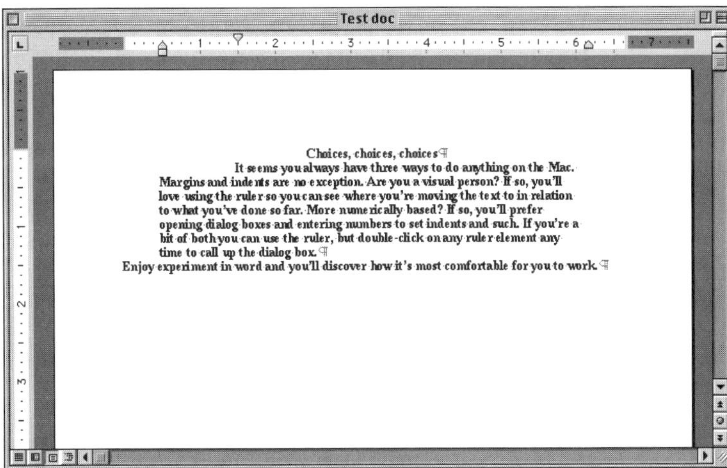

Figure 3-7: Paragraphs after formatting has been applied

If you use the visual method and open the dialog box later, you'll notice that the numbers in the dialog box reflect your ruler movement. Regardless of the method you use, you can change the settings for any paragraph any time. Of course, you can drag the left-indent symbol (the rectangle) back to the zero mark on the ruler to realign the paragraph with the zero marker on the ruler (which is your document's left margin). The first line is indented by one inch unless you drag the first-line indent symbol (top-left triangle) back to the zero mark on the ruler.

When you set indentations on the ruler, remember that the measurement set by the first-line symbol is always relative to that set by the left-indent symbol. Therefore, to indent an entire paragraph by ½ inch and the first line by another ½ inch, you should drag the left-indent symbol to the right by ½ inch and then drag the first-line symbol to the right another ½ inch past the left-indent symbol. The best way to do this is to move the entire paragraph first, using the left-indent (rectangle) symbol and then moving the first-line indent marker. To move the first-line symbol independently of the other controls, drag the top triangle.

While we've been using ½" as indents in our examples, ½" isn't necessarily the correct indent to use. The typographic standard is to indent one em space, which is the width of a capitol letter M for the font you are using. Usually that's two ticks on the ruler. Look closely at books and experiment with your own document to decide what works best for you. The ½" standard is a hold-over from the days of typewriters, but typewriters never had the proper typesetting power that word processing has.

Aligning paragraphs

Paragraphs can be aligned in four ways: left, right, centered, and justified (aligned on both sides). The text in the previous exercise is all left-aligned, meaning that the left edge of the paragraph is even and the right edge is ragged. By comparison, there may be times you need justified text (where both edges of the paragraph are aligned) or centered paragraphs (as in titles or headings). In rare instances, you may need to right-align a paragraph; in such cases, the right side aligns flush, and the left edge of the paragraph is ragged. You can change these settings by clicking the alignment buttons on the Formatting toolbar or from within the Alignment box of the Indents and Spacing tab in the Paragraph dialog box.

To see an example of the available paragraph alignments, return to the text from the last exercise or open any existing Word document, place the insertion point anywhere within a paragraph, and click each alignment button. Watch how the text moves from left to center to right to justified.

Justified text is most often seen in books and magazines to give them a neater appearance. Justification is accomplished by adjusting the space between words to make the right edge of the line even with the edge of the paragraph.

Depending on the type of document, the appearance of justified text may be improved by hyphenation. To enable Word to hyphenate automatically, choose Tools ➪ Language ➪ Hyphenation and turn on the Automatically hyphenate document option in the Hyphenation dialog box, and then click OK.

To Justify, or Not to Justify?

Many people consider the look of fully justified text (that is, justified both left and right) to have a professional, typeset quality. Justification also provides an appearance of formality. In multicolumn documents, the justified right edge creates a line that serves as a clear delimiter between columns. On the other hand, if you want your document to appear more friendly, avoid full justification.

Also, note that full justification can cause uneven spacing and vertical rivers of white space in paragraphs. If you don't allow hyphenation, full justification creates some lines that are excessively loose (lots of space between words), and some lines that are excessively tight (too little space between words). If you allow hyphenation when you use full justification, Word hyphenates many words to create evenly spaced lines—far more than if you left the right margin ragged.

Applying line spacing

Line spacing affects the amount of space between lines in a paragraph. To change the line spacing, place the insertion point anywhere within the desired paragraph or, to set several existing paragraphs identically, select all of the paragraphs to change. Choose the desired line spacing by using shortcut keys (see Table 3-1) or by setting the Line spacing option in the Indents and Spacing tab of the Paragraph dialog box.

The common choices for line spacing are Single, 1.5 Lines (for 1.5-times single spacing), and Double. You can also select At Least, Exactly, or Multiple. (When you choose any of the last three options, you must enter or select a corresponding amount in the At box.) The At Least choice sets a minimum line spacing that Word adjusts, when needed, to allow for larger font sizes or graphics. The Exactly choice sets a fixed line spacing that Word cannot adjust. The Multiple choice lets you enter incremental values (such as 1.2) to increase or decrease spacing by a fractional amount. For example, choosing Multiple and entering 1.2 in the At box results in line spacing that is 120 percent of single spacing.

Applying paragraph spacing

Word also lets you control the amount of space that appears before or after paragraphs. This is set within the Spacing area on the Indents and Spacing tab of the Paragraph dialog box. You can enter numeric values in the Before or After boxes to indicate the additional space that you want. As with line spacing, you can enter the value in points (pt.), each point being 1⁄72 of an inch.

Applying borders to paragraphs

You may find borders useful for emphasizing a particular portion of text, such as in newsletter layouts, fliers, and data sheets. Borders will appear around any text selected when you choose your border options. You can easily apply a border to paragraphs by clicking the arrow next to the border button on the Formatting toolbar. However, for the most control, select Format ⇨ Borders and Shading to use the Borders and Shading dialog box. If you apply borders often, click the Show Toolbar button in the Borders and Shading dialog box. The Borders toolbar that appears makes adding borders to your documents much easier, although it offers fewer options than the dialog box.

Word offers several border choices:

- Top Border—a line above the paragraph
- Bottom Border—a line below the paragraph
- Left Border—a line to the left of the paragraph
- Right Border—a line to the right of the paragraph
- Inside Border—a line within the paragraph
- Outside Border—lines that surround the paragraph
- Box Border—a line around all sides of the paragraph
- Shadow Border—a shadowed line around the paragraph
- 3-D—a 3-D line around the paragraph
- Custom—a custom line of your choice around the paragraph
- No Border

When using the dialog box, after you select the type of border you want for you paragraph, you still need to tell Word where you want the border to appear. On the right side of the Borders tab in the Preview box, you can click on the side of the paragraph on which you want the border to appear. This will give you a general idea of what the border will look like once it is applied to your paragraph.

You can even change the line width for the different borders in your document. Both the dialog box and the optional menu make it easy to select a line width from the pop-up menu each provides. The default width is ½". In Figure 3-8, you can see the Width pop-up menu, located in the Style section of the Borders tab (in the Paragraph Borders and Shading dialog box).

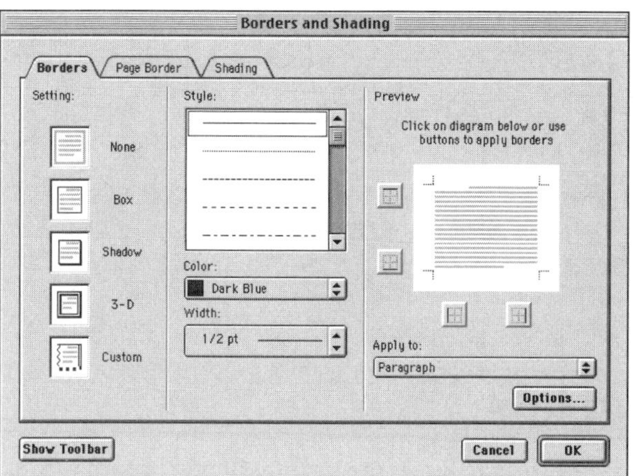

Figure 3-8: The Borders tab of the Borders and Shading dialog box

Besides adding borders, you can also apply various kinds of shading to your text. To do so, click Custom in the Borders tab of the Borders and Shading dialog box. Then move to the Shading tab (see Figure 3-9). In the Fill palette, click a shade of gray or another color to select it. You also have the option to apply a pattern to the fill. Just select a percentage from the Style pop-up menu. To have the pattern be a different color, select any color from the Color pop-up menu of the Patterns area. The Preview area to the right will give you a general idea of how that will appear in your document. Click OK to apply the effects.

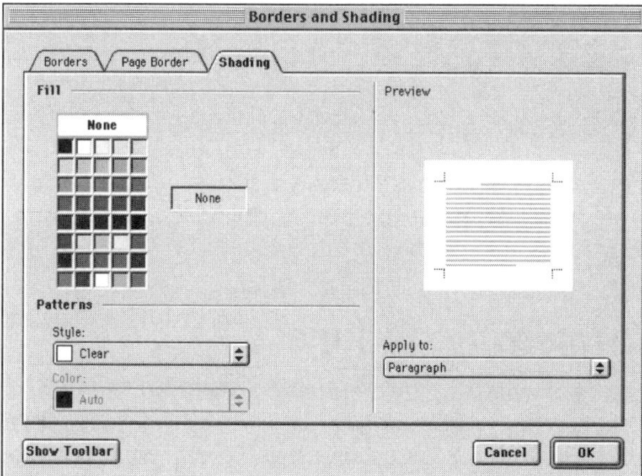

Figure 3-9: The Shading tab of the Borders and Shading dialog box

A Word About Styles

Character, paragraph, and page formatting are known as direct formatting options. Another way to control formatting is with styles. When you use styles, you apply a group of formatting settings to an entire document.

As an example, if a certain style defines indented paragraphs, and you apply that style to a document, that document's paragraphs will be indented. Chapter 8 explores the use of styles.

Formatting Characters

As mentioned earlier, character formatting is the smallest level of formatting. Character formatting—the most common type of formatting—governs how your characters look. When you apply character formatting, you are changing the format for each character. When you look at a newspaper or a book, character formatting is evident. Headlines appear in boldface characters and in large fonts. Secondary headlines, however, are in smaller fonts and may not be bold. The role of character formatting is to emphasize text:

Characters and lines

can be produced

in a number of ways,

even in combination,

TO HELP MAKE

different points.

You can also add color formatting to any characters. Of course, you need a color monitor to see the colors onscreen. To print the colors properly, you need a color printer, too. Colors will show in shades of gray on good laser or ink jet printers.

Using character formatting options

We can further divide character formatting into specific areas that are controlled by the options in the Font dialog box, which appears after you select the Font command from the Format menu. Table 3-2 explains these formatting options.

The most frequently used character formats are on the Formatting toolbar. From there, you can choose the font and point size, and then apply bold, italics, and underlining. It is also easy to use the keyboard equivalents for bold (⌘-B), italics (⌘-I), and underline (⌘-U). Any other character formatting you use often can also be added to the toolbar or menus.

To add formatting that isn't on the toolbar, you need to select Format ➪ Font to bring up the Font tab of the Font dialog box. It may also be easier to open this dialog box when you need to change several formats at one time, The Font dialog box reveals many options, as shown in Figure 3-10. Here you can choose a font, select a style, change text color, specify the type of underlining you desire, and add effects such as strikethrough, all caps, or small caps.

Table 3-2
Formatting Options

Option	*Description*
Font	A character set with a consistent and identifiable typeface, such as Times, Courier, or Helvetica.
Font Style	Defines a style for the chosen font, such as regular text, italic, bold, or bold italic.
Size	Specifies what point size to use—essentially, how big the text should be. Strictly speaking, point size measures character height, but characters proportionally increase in width as they increase in height. A point is 1/72 of an inch, so a 72-point font can take up an inch from top to bottom (not counting descenders, which dangle from the bottom of y, g, q, and so on). This does not mean, however, that a 72-point p is always an inch tall. Each font has other characteristics that determine its actual size. (This is why a p in one font may look bigger than a p in another font, even when they're the same point size.)
Color	16 possible colors can be selected from the list box.
Underline	Specifies a type of underlining (none, single, double, dotted).
Effects	Specifies appearance attributes, such as strikethrough, hidden (which means the text does not appear, but is actually still there), superscript, subscript, small caps (in which all letters are in caps, but those created by pressing Shift are slightly larger), and all caps.
Spacing	Controls the amount of space that appears between characters (under the Character Spacing tab). Word places a default amount of space between characters, but you can expand or condense this allowance.
Position	The position of the characters on a line. Options are normal, raised (the characters appearing above the baseline by half a line), or lowered (the characters appearing below the baseline by half a line). Position is located on the Character Spacing tab.
Drop Caps	Inserts an oversized drop capital, a large first letter as in the following example: Once upon a time there were two boys who lived in LA. They were very good boys, but they were very curious.
Animation	Controls different animating effects to your document such as a Las Vegas lights effect with blinking, moving borders. Animation is set under the Animation tab.

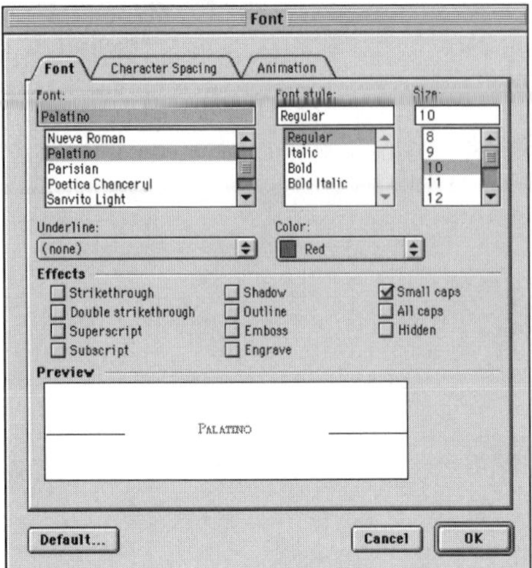

Figure 3-10: The Font tab of the Font dialog box

You can use the options in the Font and Font Style list boxes to choose a desired font and font style, and you can choose a desired size in the Size list box. You can select a type of underlining (Single, Words Only, Double, or Dotted) from the Underline pop-up menu, and you can select a color for the text in the Color pop-up list. In the Effects portion of the tab, you can turn on as many effects at one time as you want.

The Character Spacing tab of the Font dialog box (see Figure 3-11) provides options for changing the amount of spacing between characters (Normal, Expanded, or Condensed), the position (whether text appears raised or lowered relative to the baseline of normal text), and kerning (the precise amount of space between characters, as detailed shortly).

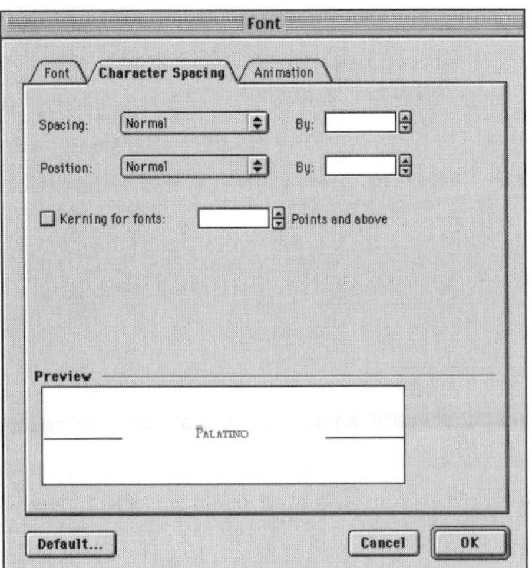

Figure 3-11: The Character Spacing tab of the Font dialog box

The Animation tab of the Font dialog box applies animation to characters in your document. You may find this useful to draw attention to certain words. Select the text you wish to animate, choose Format ➪ Font to open the Font dialog box, and then click the Animation tab. (The Animation tab is shown in Figure 3-12.) Select the type of animation you wish to apply. The preview box at the bottom of the Animation tab demonstrates the effect. Click OK to apply the selected animation to your text.

To remove or apply character formats, simply select the text you want to affect, or position the cursor where you want to begin typing the formatted characters. Then, click on the formatting option in the Formatting toolbar, or choose Format ➪ Font to choose your options.

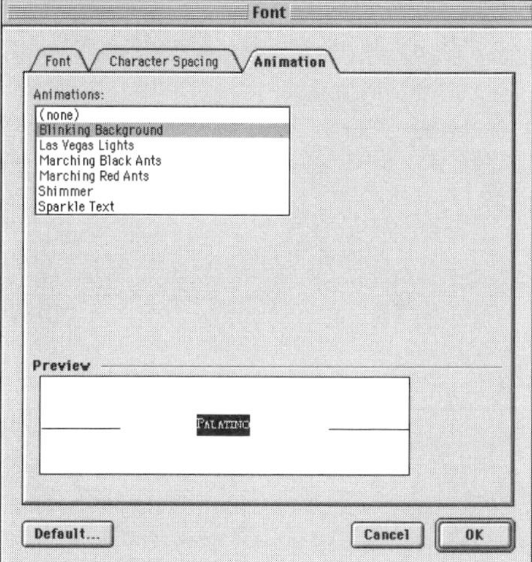

Figure 3-12: The Animation tab of the Font dialog box

Using character formatting shortcuts

You can also apply most of these character formats with shortcut keys, which are sometimes easier to use than the mouse. The shortcut keys act as switches to turn the various Format commands on and off. Table 3-3 contains several shortcut keys that you can use to apply character formatting.

The Hows and Whens of Formatting

You can apply formatting before you enter your text (but you must turn it off when you're done with the effect), or you can enter all the new text in a single format and change the formatting later. The latter enables you to get all of your thoughts out first, without distracting yourself with formatting.

You can also finish a sentence or chunk of text, and then go back and format that section before writing some more. There is no right or wrong way; you can use either method at any time.

Table 3-3
Shortcut Keys for Character Formatting

Format	*Shortcut Key*
Bold	⌘-B
Italic	⌘-I***Format Shortcut Key***
Underline	⌘-U
Word underline	⌘-Shift-W
Double underline	⌘-Shift-D
Subscript (H_2O)	⌘-= (Equal Sign)
Superscript (X^2)	⌘-Shift-= (Equal Sign)
Small caps	⌘-Shift-K
All caps	⌘-Shift-A
Change case of letters, cycling through	Shift-F3
Hidden text	⌘-Shift-H
Remove formats	⌘-Spacebar
Font	⌘-Shift-F
Symbol font	⌘-Shift-Q
Point size	⌘- Shift-P
Next larger size	⌘- Shift ->
Next smaller size	⌘- Shift -<
Up one point	⌘-]
Down one point	⌘- [

You can turn off all character formatting for a selection—returning to plain text—by pressing Control-Spacebar. This is especially useful when you've applied various formatting features to a selection, and you want to return to normal, plain text.

Changing character fonts and point sizes

You can use various fonts within any document and see how they look as you work. The font used initially as the default is Times, but you can change this to whatever you wish. Any fonts installed on you Mac (or turned on by a font management program, such as Font Reserve) are available to you. You can use the following steps to change the default font used for your documents:

1. From the menus, choose Format ⇨ Font.
2. Click the Font tab in the Font dialog box (if it isn't already visible).
3. Choose the desired font, font style, and size you want to use as the default.
4. Click the Default button in the dialog box.
5. When asked if you really want to change the default font, click Yes.

In addition to choosing appropriate fonts, you can also select various point sizes with the Formatting toolbar or the Font dialog box. Each point is 1⁄72 of an inch, so in a 10-point font size, the characters would be roughly 10⁄72 of an inch high. The following lines demonstrate the effects of various point sizes:

This is 12-point Times New Roman.

This is 14-point Times New Roman.

This is 16-point Times New Roman.

This is 18-point Times New Roman.

With varied fonts and font sizes, you can easily get carried away. A document with too many different fonts and font sizes can take on a busy look and be visually distracting to the reader.

Applying superscript and subscript

You can create superscript (raised) text or subscript (lowered) text by selecting the Superscript or Subscript options on the Font tab of the Font dialog box. Examples of both types of text are as follows:

This is ^{superscript} text

This is $_{\text{subscript}}$ text.

You can apply super- or subscripting to text by using either the Font dialog box or the shortcut keys (see Table 3-3). If you use the Font dialog box, you can also change the font size you use for the superscript or subscript while you're in the Font tab.

Adjusting kerning

You can also control kerning—the adjusting of the space between characters, relative to the specific type of font used. Kerning can give a document a better appearance, although you need a high-resolution printer (600 dpi or better) for the effects of minor changes in kerning to be noticeable. Kerning can be used only with proportionally spaced PostScript or TrueType fonts. This feature is available in the Character Spacing tab of the Font dialog box.

Copying character formatting

If you use a particular type of formatting often in a document (but not in all places), you can save time by copying the format from one place in the document to another. Word makes this simple with the Format Painter button. To copy a character format, first select some text that has the format you want to copy. Next, click the Format Painter button on the Standard toolbar (it's the button with the small brush). A small plus sign appears on your cursor as you click the button. Then select the characters or section to which you want to apply the format. If you are applying it to just one word, simply click the word—no need to select the word first. The formatting is automatically applied to the new characters. This only works to apply the formatting once. If you wish to apply the same formatting to several areas, double-click the Format Painter button initially. The plus sign and format painting will remain in effect until you place the cursor and type.

Formatting Sections

Sections are portions of documents that carry formatting characteristics independent of other sections in the same document. Section formatting isn't required; by default, Word treats an entire document as a single section. By giving you the power to add multiple sections to a document, Word gives you a way to apply different formatting settings to each section. At first, the concept of sections may be difficult to understand. However, knowledge of how sections operate in Word is worth the effort because sections add flexibility to how a document can be formatted. If you have used older versions of Word or desktop publishing software, such as Adobe PageMaker, the concept of formatting in sections will be more familiar to you. (If you are coming from an old version of Word for DOS, you may be familiar with divisions, which are equivalent to sections.)

Typically, you use section formatting to change the number of columns or the style of page numbering for a section of the document. Changes that affect all pages of a document, such as page margins, are part of page formatting.

Even in a very short document, you are still using sections, although you may not give them any thought. In a short document (such as a one-page memo), the entire document consists of a single section, so you can use Word's section formatting commands to control certain elements of its layout.

If you want to apply a specific set of formatting to a section, select the text and choose Format ⇨ Document. In the Document dialog box, click the Layout tab (see Figure 3-13). In the Apply to pop-up menu, you will see Selected text, the default option. (At times this will say Whole document or Selected sections as the default; it changes to suit what you're doing.) In this tab, you can control the section breaks for a document, headers and footers, and vertical alignment.

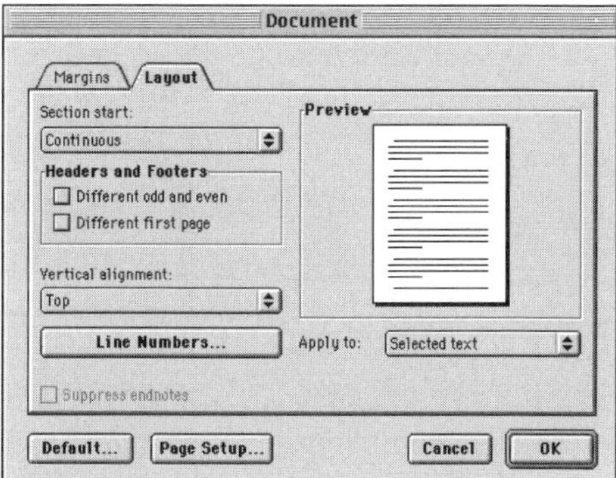

Figure 3-13: The Layout tab of the Document dialog box

To control the section breaks in a document, select an option in the Section start pop-up menu. Here, you can control where you want the section to begin and where the preceding section should end.

- ✦ Continuous — This option causes the selected section to follow the preceding section immediately, without a page break.
- ✦ New Column — This option starts printing the selected section's text at the top of the next column.
- ✦ New Page — This option breaks the page at the section break.
- ✦ Even Page — This option starts the selected section at the next even-numbered page.
- ✦ Odd Page — This option starts the selected section at the next odd-numbered page.

The Layout tab also lets you control vertical alignment. Vertical alignment is the spacing of a document from the top to the bottom of the page. The document can be vertically centered to the top, centered, or justified.

You can also add line numbers by clicking the Line Numbers button and turning on the Add line numbering option in the dialog box that appears (see Figure 3-14). You can apply line numbers to the whole document or only to a selected section.

You can apply line numbers in various ways: They can start at the beginning of the document and go to the end; they can start at a specified line or section; they can begin from line 1 at the start of each new page; or they can begin at a specified number on the selected page. Line numbers are useful in legal documents where you may need to examine a specific line of a contract or other legal document.

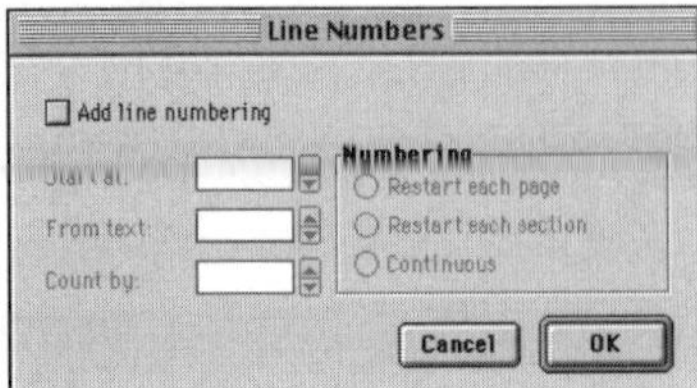

Figure 3-14: The Line Numbers dialog box

Headers and footers

Word makes it easy to add headers and footers to a document. A header is text or a graphic that is printed at the top of every page in a document; a footer is text or a graphic that is printed at the bottom of every page. Headers and footers can be different for odd and even pages.

You can create headers and footers by choosing the View➪Header and Footer command. Word switches to Page Layout view, the body of your document grays out, and the cursor activates in the Header area. The Header and Footer toolbar also appears, as shown in Figure 3-15 You can switch between headers and footers by clicking the Switch Between Header and Footer button (which shows both a header and a footer) on the toolbar, or you can scroll up or down the document with the vertical scroll bar.

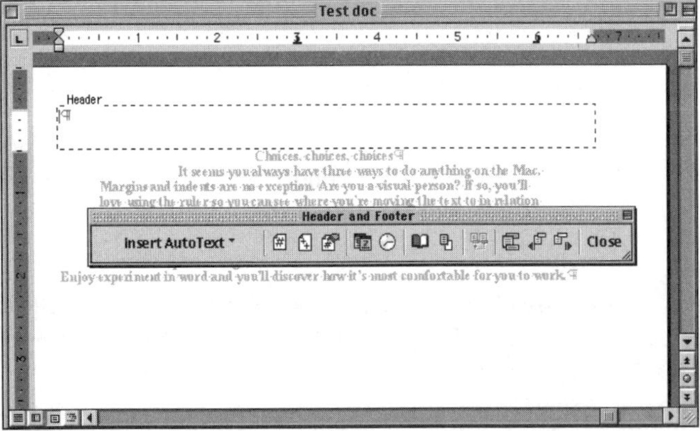

Figure 3-15: The Header and Footer toolbar in Page Layout view

You type and format text in headers and footers the same way you type text in a normal document. You can also enter page numbers, the date, and the time as a header or footer in a document. Click the Page Numbers, Date, and Time buttons on the Header and Footer toolbar. If you want the time, page number, or date centered, you can do so the way you center text in a document.

After entering your header or footer information, click the Close button on the Header and Footer toolbar, and Word returns to Normal layout. From now on, when you switch to Page Layout view, Word displays the header and footer as dimmed (grayed out) so you can read it but not edit it. (To edit, select View⇨Header and Footer again.)

You may want to use a different header or footer for the first page, as in a case where page numbering isn't appropriate. Or, you may want a different header on odd and even pages, as in books. Both options are check boxes in the Layout tab of the Document dialog box. Just click to select either one.

Deleting a header or footer

Deleting a header or footer is also simple. Choose View ⇨Header and Footer, and then Select All (⌘-A) within the header or footer. Press Delete or use the Cut command (⌘-X), emptying the header or footer. The header or footer area still appears when you choose View⇨Header and Footer, but when this area is empty, it won't appear in print or in Page Preview. To delete other headers or footers, click the Show Next button on the Header and Footer toolbar to display the next header or footer, and then delete that text.

Adjusting margin settings

Headers and footers are printed inside the top and bottom margins. If the header or footer is too large to fit in the margin, Word adjusts the top or bottom margin so the header or footer fits. If you don't want Word to adjust the margins, choose Format⇨Document and go to the Margins tab. Enter a hyphen before the Top or Bottom margin setting. However, if the header or footer is too large, it may overwrite the main document.

Positioning headers and footers

You may want to adjust the position of your headers and footers in your document. You can adjust the horizontal position by centering it, running it into the left or right margin, or aligning it with the left or right margin. There are two preset tabs in the header and footer areas. One is centered between the left and right margins, and one is right aligned at the default right margin. You can use these tabs to place a page number flush right and to center text in the headers and footers. (If you change the margins, you may also want to adjust the tab stops.)

For a left-aligned header or footer, type the text where the cursor first appears in the text box. For a centered header or footer, tab once to the center and begin typing. You may also use the alignment buttons on the Formatting toolbar to center, left align, right align, or justify your headers or footers. If you want to add a negative indent to your header or footer, drag the indent markers on the ruler or use the Paragraph command from the Format menu to place a negative indent in your header or footer. (Remember, you need to select the header or footer before using the Paragraph command.)

You can adjust the distance of the footer from the top or bottom of the page. To do so numerically, click the Document Layout button on the Headers and Footers toolbar or select Format⇨Document. Select the Margins tab. In the From edge section, type or select the distance you want from the edge of the paper. To move the header up or down visually, with the header active, move your pointer to the vertical ruler at the left of your screen and point to the top margin boundary. The header area is the white area on the otherwise gray ruler, so it's easy to see. The pointer becomes a double-headed arrow. Click and drag upward to move the header toward the top of the paper's edge or drag downward to increase the distance. Do the same to move the footer in the footer area but, of course, with the direction reversed.

You can also adjust the space between the header or footer and the main document. This is done visually almost exactly as described previously. To add more space after the header, go to the header you want to adjust. Move your pointer to the vertical ruler at the left of your screen and point to the bottom margin boundary. The header area is the white area on the otherwise gray ruler, so it's easy to see. The pointer becomes a double-headed arrow. Click and drag downward to enlarge the space allotted to the header. You can see the effect whenever you release the mouse. Do the same to add space before the footer in the footer area but, of course, with the direction reversed.

Page numbers

Inserting page numbers is one of the easiest of all formatting jobs.

To add page numbers visually, place your cursor in the header or footer. Type any opening text, such as **Page #** and a space. Then click the Page Number button on the Header and Footer toolbar. Type another space and the word **of** if you want, and then click the Insert Number of Pages button. The result of this would read "Page # 1 of 2" in a two-page document and always reflect the correct page numbering and total page count. A third button enables you to change the number format by opening the Page Number Format dialog box (for example, letters instead of numbers or roman numerals). You can also add chapter numbers to your document, but you have to tell Word where a new chapter begins. To indicate where a new chapter begins, use the Chapter starts with style list box, which causes Word to look for the style that is designated as the chapter heading for each chapter. You also have the option of numbering from a previous section if you don't want to number the entire document. And finally, you can ask Word to start numbering from a specific page.

To add page numbers numerically, choose Insert⇨Page Numbers to bring up the Page Numbers dialog box shown in Figure 3-16. In this dialog box, you can use the pop-up menus to position your page numbers in the header or footer and align them. Click the Format button to open the Page Number Format dialog box, which lets you change the number format as mentioned previously.

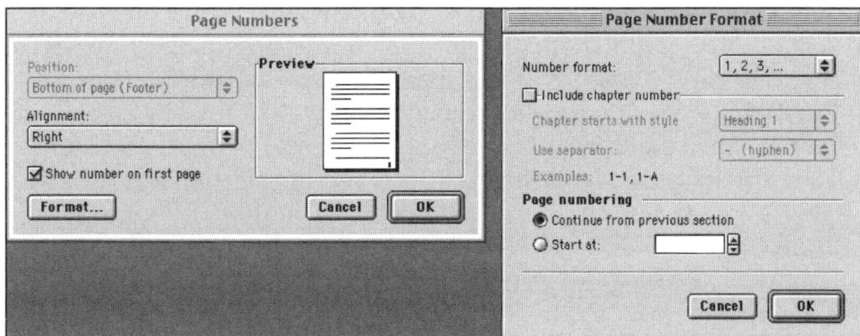

Figure 3-16: The Page Numbers and Page Number Format dialog boxes

Footnotes

Word's capability to display multiple portions of a document simultaneously makes adding footnotes to a Word document a simple matter. You can look at and work with the text of a footnote in a separate pane, while the related portion of your document remains visible. Word, like most word processors, lets you position footnotes either at the bottom of each page or collectively at the end of the document. (When footnotes are placed at the end of a document, they are called endnotes.) However, in Word you can also put a footnote directly beneath the text to which it applies or at the end of a section.

To add a footnote, first place the insertion point where the footnote reference mark (such as a superscript number) is to appear in the text. Then choose the Insert ⇨ Footnote command to bring up the Footnote and Endnote dialog box shown in Figure 3-17.

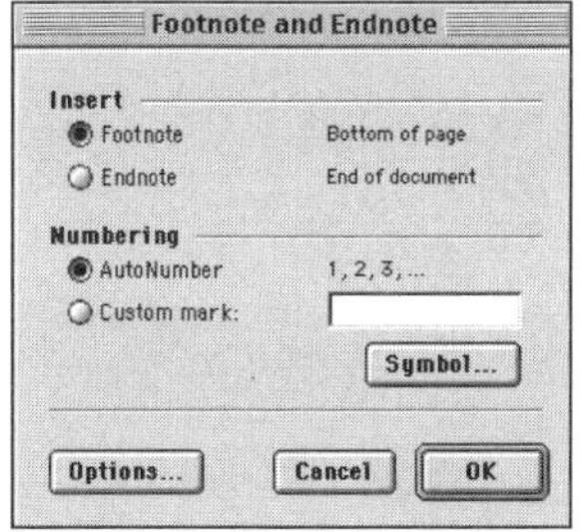

Figure 3-17: The Footnote and Endnote dialog box

In this dialog box, you can specify whether you want the footnote to be automatically numbered by Word (the default), or you can enter a reference mark of your own choosing, such as an asterisk or a number in parentheses. The Options button displays another dialog box that lets you control the placement of footnotes and the number format.

You also have the option to choose the symbol you wish to appear as your default foot or endnote indicator. In the Footnote and Endnote dialog box, click the Symbol button. This opens the Symbol dialog box shown in Figure 3-18. Here you can select a font from the pop-up list and see all the characters for that font. If there is a subset for the font, the Subset list box appears and provides you more choices for the font. Click the symbol you wish to use to indicate a foot or endnote. An enlarged view of the character appears so you can check it out. If you like the symbol, click OK. Click OK to close the Footnote and Endnote dialog box.

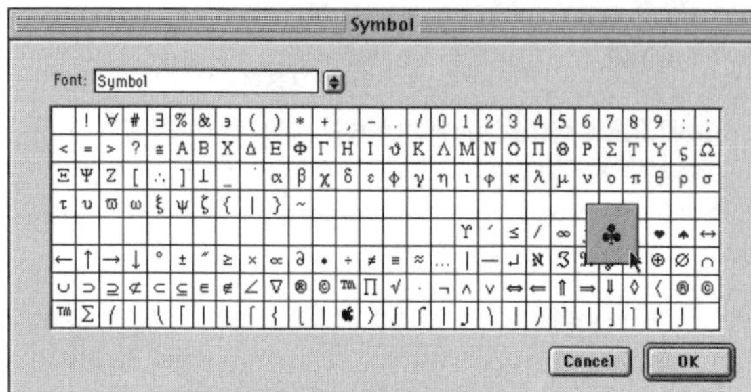

Figure 3-18: The Symbol dialog box

After you close the dialog box(es), a footnote pane opens in the bottom portion of the screen (see Figure 3-19). This is where you type the desired footnote. When the footnote pane is open, a split bar appears in the vertical scroll bar. Using the mouse, you can drag the split bar up or down to change the size of the pane. At any time when you are working with footnotes, you can return to the main part of the document while leaving the footnote pane open; simply click back in the document's body. You can also press F6, which issues the Other Pane command. When you are finished typing the footnote, you can drag the split bar down to close the footnote pane or click the Close button. You can see footnotes in your document only if you are in Page Layout view.

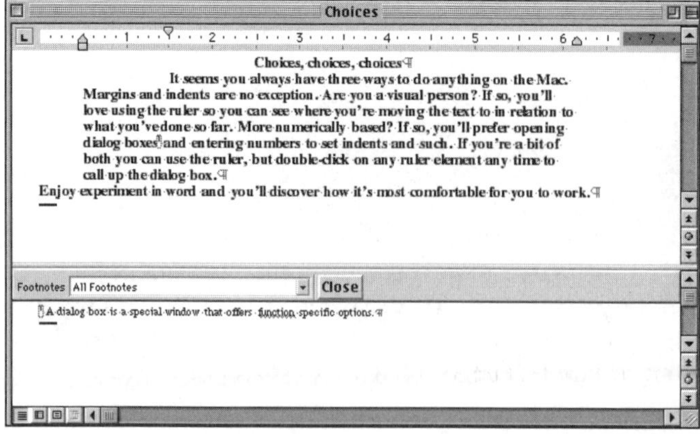

Figure 3-19: The footnote pane

Try adding a footnote to the sample document you created earlier in this chapter or to any paragraph. After you create the footnote, read on to see how to edit and delete it, position reference marks and footnotes, and define the separator line at the bottom of the page. Follow these steps to add a footnote:

1. Switch to Normal view and put the insertion point anywhere within any Word 98 document. You can use the document you created earlier, or any other document.
2. Choose Insert⇨Footnote.
3. To accept automatic numbering for footnotes, leave the radio button at the default—AutoNumber—and click OK. Word places a superscript reference number at the cursor position in the document and opens the footnote pane for the footnote text.
4. Enter some text in the footnote pane. You might type the following as we did:

   A dialog box is a special window that offers function-specific options.
5. Click the Close button to close the footnote pane. Or, keep it open and simply click back in your main document to continue working there.

If you have used the sample document for your exercise, your footnote should look like the one in Figure 3-20.

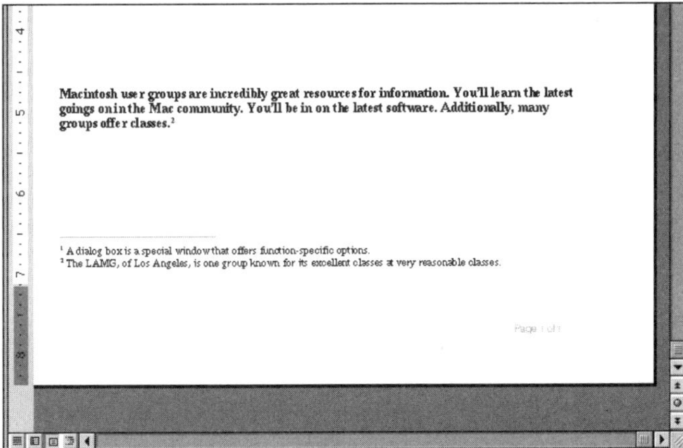

Figure 3-20: Page Layout view showing a footnote added to the end of a document

Editing existing footnotes

To edit an existing footnote, open the footnote pane with the View⇨Footnotes command. Scroll within the footnote pane to find the desired footnote and edit it as you would regular text.

You can move from footnote to footnote with your mouse. However, the footnotes may not all be on the same page. In that case, you can quickly jump between footnotes using the Go To key (F5). Press F5 and click Footnote in the Go to What list box. Then use the Next and Previous buttons to jump through the footnotes until you find the one that you want, or enter the footnote number in the Footnote Number box and click OK to go to that footnote.

Moving and deleting footnotes

Footnotes are indicated by the reference marks in the document, so moving or deleting a footnote is as easy as moving or deleting the reference mark.

- ✦ To move a footnote, select the reference mark within the document and move it to the desired new location.
- ✦ To delete a footnote, select the reference mark and press Delete or use Edit ⇨ Cut. If you used Word's automatic footnote numbering, the footnotes are renumbered accordingly. If you numbered footnotes manually, you need to renumber them yourself as necessary.

Exploring footnote options

In the Footnote and Endnote dialog box is an Options button. After you click this button, the Note Options dialog box appears, as shown in Figure 3-21. Click the All Footnotes tab to choose options that apply to footnotes, or click the All Endnotes tab to choose options that apply to endnotes.

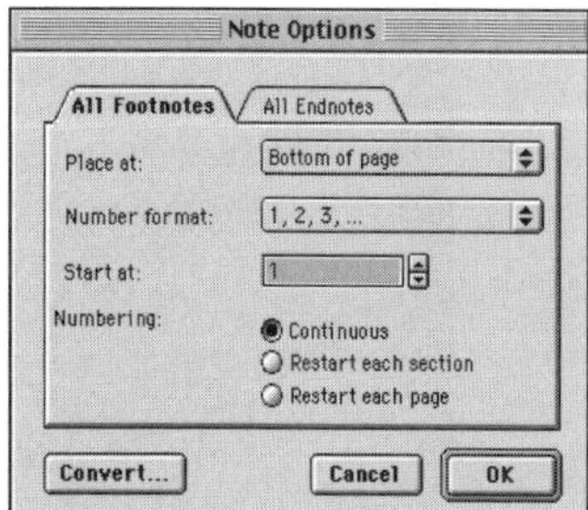

Figure 3-21: The Note Options dialog box

The Place at pop-up menu in the All Footnotes tab enables you to determine the placement of the footnotes. You can choose between Bottom of page or Beneath text. Select Bottom of page to place the footnotes for a given page at the bottom of that page. The Beneath text choice places the footnote directly after the text containing the footnote reference mark.

The Number format pop-up menu enables you to choose the type of numbers you want to use for the footnotes. The Start at box lets you change the starting number for automatically numbered footnotes. If you want Word to restart the automatic numbering each time a new section begins, turn on the Restart each section option in the Numbering area.

Changing footnotes to endnotes

Changing all your footnotes (or just one footnote) to endnotes is easy. Begin in Normal view. Activate the Footnote area by choosing View⇨Footnotes. In the separator bar above the footnotes, select All Footnotes from the pop-up menu (or All Endnotes if working in reverse). Now that all possible footnotes (or endnotes) are visible, select the footnotes (or endnotes) you want to convert. Control-click the selected footnotes (endnotes) to open the shortcut menu. Select Convert to Endnote to convert the footnote to an endnote. Now, to see the kind of note you want, choose it from the Notes box in the footnote window.

You can also copy and move a footnote by using the regular Cut, Copy, and Paste commands or by clicking and dragging it to its new location.

Summary

In this chapter, you have read about all sorts of formatting techniques that you will use often if you work in Word on a regular basis. The chapter covered these points:

- ✦ In Word, you can apply formatting to characters, paragraphs, pages, or sections of a document.
- ✦ You can change page formatting in the Format⇨Document and File⇨Page Setup dialog boxes.
- ✦ To apply formatting to paragraphs, you can use the various buttons of the Formatting toolbar that apply to paragraph formatting, or you can use the Format⇨Paragraph command.
- ✦ You can apply borders and shadings to paragraphs by using the Format⇨Borders and Shading command.
- ✦ To apply formatting to characters, you can use the various buttons of the Formatting toolbar that apply to character formatting, or you can use the Format⇨Font command.
- ✦ Section formatting can also be applied through the use of the Format⇨Document command, by using the options that appear on the Layout tab of the resulting dialog box.
- ✦ You can add headers and footers to a document with the View⇨Header and Footer command.

✦ You can add footnotes and endnotes to a document with the Insert⇨Footnote command.

Where to go next

✦ Now that you've explored so many aspects of document formatting, you're probably anxious to try printing some examples of your work. Chapter 4 will set you right up.

✦ You can make many common formatting tasks easier by applying styles to portions of your document. You find details in Chapter 8.

✦ ✦ ✦

CHAPTER 4

Previewing and Printing Your Documents

✦ ✦ ✦ ✦

In This Chapter

Previewing documents

Printing documents

Printing document information

Changing your printer

Printing envelopes

✦ ✦ ✦ ✦

This chapter details how to print your documents and how you can preview them prior to printing. Of course, your printer must be connected to your computer and turned on before you can print.

Previewing Documents

Using Print Preview saves trees: you don't waste paper printing draft copies to see if everything looks right. With File ➪ Print Preview (or the button on the Standard toolbar that looks like a document with a magnifying glass) you see onscreen what a document will look like when you print it. This includes footnotes, headers, footers, page numbers, multiple columns, and graphics. You can view more than one page at a time by clicking the Multiple Pages button in the Print Preview toolbar and selecting the number of pages you want to see simultaneously. While in Print Preview mode, you can easily move between pages, change some ruler settings, and even move graphics, but you cannot edit text.

The Print Preview toolbar

In Print Preview mode, the Print Preview toolbar (see Figure 4-1) appears, providing preview-specific options. Click the appropriate button to perform a task, as outlined in Table 4-1.

Figure 4-1: The Print Preview toolbar

Table 4-1
Print Preview Toolbar Buttons

Button	*Function*
Print	Brings up the Mac's Print dialog box.
Magnifier	Clicking the preview with the magnifier enlarges the preview so you can read the text better or inspect the document more closely.
One Page	Lets you see the current page in Print Preview mode.
Multiple Pages	Lets you see up to six pages at once onscreen. These pages appear so you can see the layout of each page.
Zoom Control	Lets you control the distance at which you see the pages (magnification) in the Print Preview window.
View Ruler	Toggles the ruler on and off so you can get a fuller idea of sizes and move the margins.
Shrink to Fit	Attempts to shrink your document so it will all fit on one page by reducing the font size. For example, two pages of 10-point text becomes one page of 6-point text.
Full Screen	Takes away all standard window scrolling and controls. Provides a button to click to return you to the traditional window type. (This feature is more commonly used in Windows.)
Close	Closes the preview window and returns you to Normal view.

To leave Print Preview mode and return to your document, you can click the Close button, click the standard close box in the preview window or press the Esc key.

Many commands from the normal Word menus are not available in Print Preview mode. These commands appear dimmed on the menus. Remember that you cannot open files or change windows while in Print Preview mode.

Adjusting margins

Although you cannot edit text in Print Preview mode, you can move text around. You can also make changes to some aspects of the document, such as the location of page margins, headers, and footers.

In order to make changes to page margins or indentations, the ruler must be showing. If it's not already on, turn on the ruler using the ruler button in the Preview toolbar or choose View⇨Ruler. When you enter Preview mode, your cursor becomes a magnifier. Click the Magnifier button to switch to a standard cursor.

To change the indentations for a section of text, using any normal selection technique, select the text you wish to change. Next, move the triangles (or rectangle) on the ruler until the text starts and ends where you want.

To change the margins for the entire document, move your cursor to the place on the ruler where the gray section of the ruler meets the white section. The gray represents your page margin. There is gray on the left for the left margin and gray on the right for the right margin. When your cursor is the meeting point of the margin and document area, it becomes a double-headed arrow. Simply drag the margin left or right to reduce or enlarge the margin area. (You don't need to select any text.)

To move text around within your document, select the text as you normally would, and then drag it to the new location. Don't forget that you can also Control-click any highlighted text to see a shortcut menu to cut, paste, make font changes, add paragraph modifications, add bullets and numbering, and draw tables.

Adjusting object locations and text wrap

You can also move your graphics while in Print Preview. Again, if your mouse pointer is Preview's default magnifier, you must first switch to a standard cursor by clicking the Magnifier button on the toolbar. Then simply click the graphic and drag it.

You may also want to set your picture apart visually by placing a frame around it. To frame the object while you are in Print Preview, first click the Magnifier button to turn off the magnifier (if it's on) and then Control-click the picture you want to frame. Choose Format Picture from the shortcut menu. From the Format Picture dialog box, shown in Figure 4-2, choose the Colors and Lines tab. In the Line area, choose the type of frame lines desired. When you do so, the frame appears around the picture.

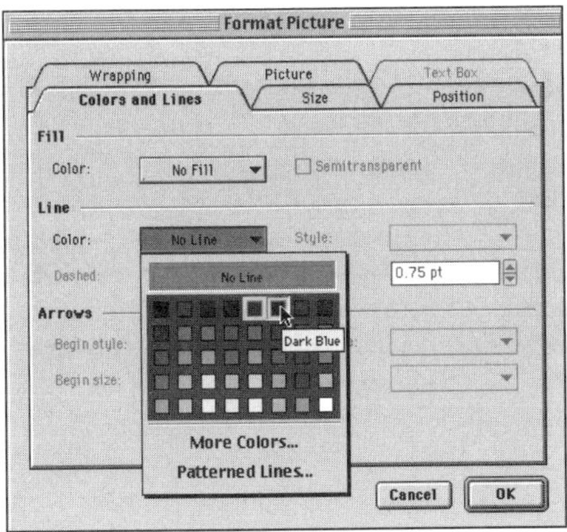

Figure 4-2: Selecting a dark blue border for a graphic object

An object, such as a picture, will sit on top of your text by default. If you want text to wrap around the object, you need to turn on wrapping. Control-click the picture and choose Format Picture from the shortcut menu. Next, choose the Wrapping tab, as shown in Figure 4-3. Choose the desired type of wrapping from the diagrams and the text will wrap accordingly.

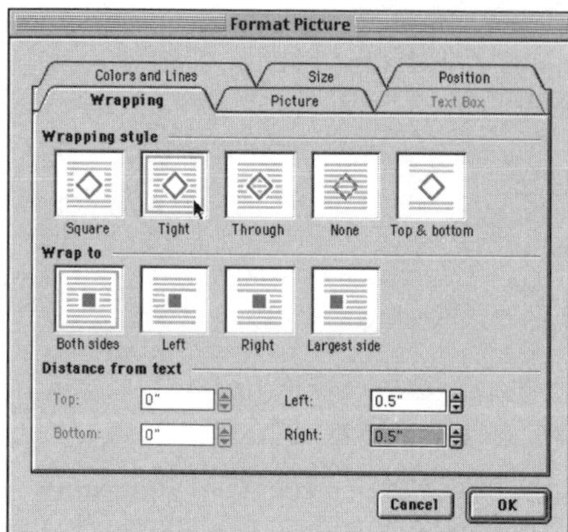

Figure 4-3: Selecting a tight text wrap with a half-inch distance from image to text

Sometimes it can be difficult to select an object in order to move or set text wrap. You know you've selected the image when the open square handles appear at its corners and Control-clicking yields Format Picture as a choice. Selecting an object may become easier if you place a frame around the object. If you select a white frame, it won't appear when you print on white paper.

Using the Distance from text section of the Wrapping tab, you can control the distance of the text from the picture. Simply adjust the numbers in the Top, Bottom, Left, and Right sections of the Distance from text section.

Printing Documents

Word 98 isn't limited to simply printing your documents or a range of pages; it enables you to print specifically selected text blocks as well as other related information, such as summary information, annotations, AutoText entries, and style sheets. In the "Formatting Documents" section of Chapter 3, we covered page orientation and page size, as they relate to setting up your document. In this chapter, we cover the standard printing options and then introduce Word's unique printing capabilities.

General (standard) printing options

To print your document, choose File⇨Print (⌘-P) or click the printer icon in the Standard toolbar. The standard Print dialog box appears. There is a pop-up menu that typically opens with General and enables you to select the usual Mac printing options. The look of your Print dialog box may be different, depending on the printer you have or the version of the LaserWriter software you have installed on your Mac. However, the options available are basically the same. A typical Print dialog box is shown in Figure 4-4.

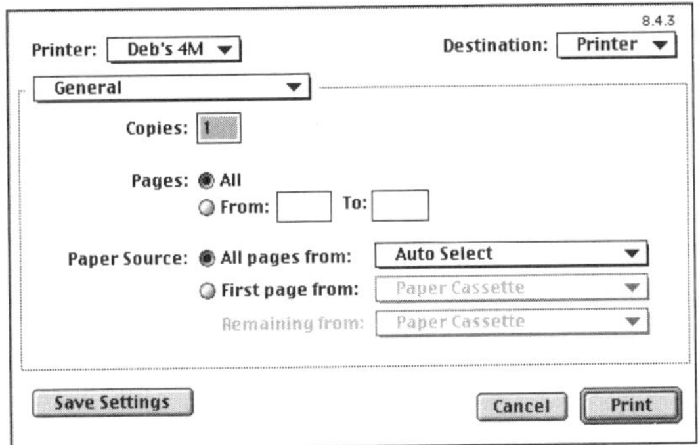

Figure 4-4: A typical Mac Print dialog box (yours may vary)

Here's a rundown of the standard Mac (General) printing options:

- ✦ Printer—This pop-up menu tells you which printer you will print to.
- ✦ Destination—This pop-up menu enables you to tell Word (or any application from which you are printing, such as Excel) to print to a printer or to print to a file. The latter is not commonly used, but is helpful when you don't have a printer handy and want to prepare (spool) the document for printing at a later time.
- ✦ Copies—This tells the printer how many copies to print. The default is 1. Notice the 1 in the Copies field is selected (highlighted). This makes it easy for you to enter the number of copies you wish to print by just typing the number.
- ✦ Pages—With the Pages fields, you can choose which pages of the document you will print. All is the default so your entire document prints. To print only a range of pages, enter the first page to print in the From field and the last page in the To field. For example, to print only Pages 3, 4, and 5, enter **3** in the From field and **5** in the To field. What if you want to begin at Page 3 and print the rest of the document, but don't know exactly how many pages there are? Simply enter **3** in the From box and leave the To field empty. Likewise, you can leave the From field blank and enter a **5** in the To field to print all

pages up to Page 5. Of course, you know the document begins on Page 1, but this saves you a key stroke, so what the heck?

✦ Paper Source—This feature enables you to control which paper trays you print from. For example, the main tray, a secondary tray (if you have one), or the manual feed. Each tray may hold a different type of paper. Most commonly, you won't change this from the default, which is to print all pages from the main tray. To print onto an envelope or a paper not in the main tray, you would click in the pop-up menu and select Manual Feed. Or, if you have a specialty tray, or second main tray, you may keep stock in there and select that tray.

In the corporate world, it is common to print a first page on letterhead and the rest of the document to plain paper. To do so, click the First page from button, and, in that pop-up menu, select the tray containing your letterhead (choose Manual Feed if you need to hand-feed the paper). In the pop-up menu below, Remaining from, select the tray that holds plain paper.

In most cases, these options are all you need to print. After you've set your options (if any are desired), click Print.

On occasion, you may want your document laid out with a vertical orientation, or in what is known as landscape orientation. This is particularly useful with very wide documents, such as those that contain a table of numbers or documents containing pictures. This is covered in the "Formatting Documents" in Chapter 3. Page sizing is also covered there.

Word's special printing options

In addition to the usual Mac printing options, Word provides a few more. To access these unique options, you click the pop-up menu that opens with General and drag down to the selection that says Microsoft Word. (This pop-up menu is clear in Figure 4-5 as the pointer is still at the pop-up menu location.)

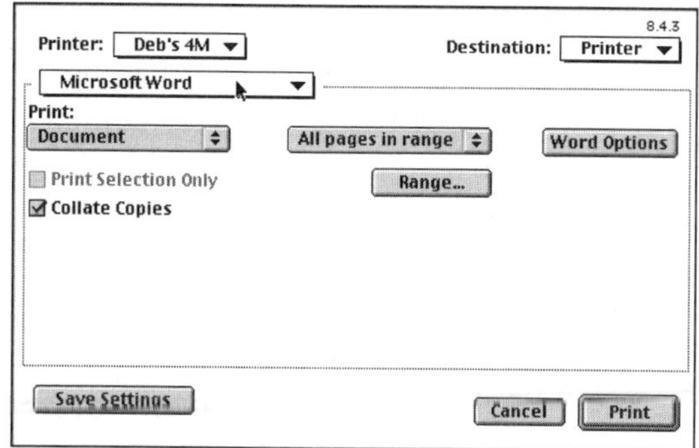

Figure 4-5: The Word section of the Print dialog box

Figure 4-5 shows you one version of the Microsoft Word section of the Print dialog box. The available options in the Print dialog box include:

Printing portions of a document

Previously, we discussed how to print a range of pages from your document, as opposed to printing the entire document. This is always possible on the Mac and can be set in the print dialog box. However, there may be times when you want to print only a section of a page, or one and a half pages. This is easy to do.

Simply select a portion of text you want to print, whether it's part of one page or a selection that spans many pages. You can use any of the usual selection techniques. Then issue the print command as usual (⌘-P or File⇨Print). Click the pop-up menu that opens with General and drag down to the selection that says Microsoft Word. Click in the check box next to Print selection only. (If no text or graphics are selected in the document, this option is grayed out.) When this option is checked, the message "Selected text will be printed" appears below the option. Click Print when all your options are checked and you are ready to print.

Printing several ranges of full pages

At times, you may want to print more than one range of pages. For example, you may want to print Pages 3–5, but you also want to print 7, 9, and 10–12. You could issue the Print command four times, naming one range each time, but Word 98 provides a more convenient way. In the Word section of the Print dialog box, click the Range button to bring up a range-specific dialog box. As shown in Figure 4-6, this box provides very clear instructions. You can fully control your print range(s) from here. To print several ranges, list the pages in the Pages box. If you want to print consecutive page numbers, separate them with a hyphen. Use a comma to separate nonconsecutive page numbers. For the previous example, you would enter **3-5, 7, 9, 10-12**. Click OK, and then click Print when all your options are checked and you are ready to print.

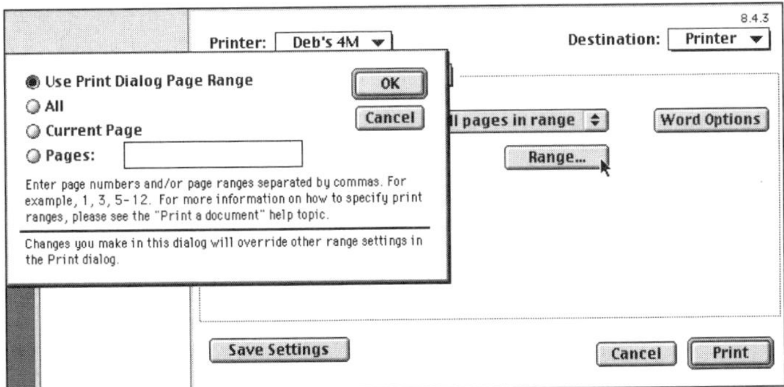

Figure 4-6: The Range dialog box in the Word section of the Print dialog box

Collating a document

Normally, when you print more than one copy of a document, Word prints all copies of Page 1, followed by all copies of Page 2, followed by all copies of Page 3, and so on. The Collate option tells Word to print all the pages of your document once, before it goes on to the next set. This is a true time-saver. To have Word print in a collating manner, simply check the Collate box in the Microsoft Word section of the Print dialog box.

Printing odd or even pages

By default, Word prints all the pages in the page range you specify, whether it's the full document, one range, or a series of ranges. You can easily tell Word to print only the odd pages within that range, or only the even pages. To do so, go to the Word section of the Print dialog box by clicking the General pop-up menu and selecting Microsoft Word. Then click the pop-up menu that reads All pages in range, and select Odd pages or Even pages. That's it! When you've selected all desired options, click Print.

Printing in reverse order

Should you find you want to have Word print your last page first and work forward, rather than beginning with Page 1, you can—easily. In the Word section of the Print dialog box, click Word Options. This brings up the Print tab of the Preferences dialog (shown in Figure 4-7). By the way, you can also arrive at this tab from Tools ➪ Preferences. Just click the check box next to Reverse print order. While you're there, select any other printing options, click OK, and then proceed to click Print whenever you're ready.

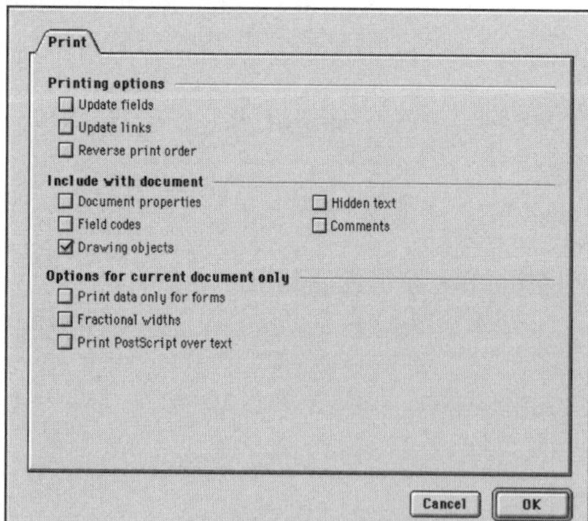

Figure 4-7: The Print tab of the Options dialog box

This option is helpful with laser printers that are based on the first-generation Canon engine (such as the original Hewlett-Packard LaserJet). The design of such printers causes printed pages to come out face up, so a multiple-page document would be stacked with the last page on top (which is usually not where you want it). The Reverse Print Order option requests that the printed document end up in the proper order.

Note that Printing options checked in the Preferences dialog box stay with the document and are in effect next time you print (unless you deselect them). In fact, this option becomes effective for all new documents you create as long as it's checked.

Printing documents containing links

By default, Word updates any links within your document every time the document is opened. However, there is a Preference option that provides an extra safety to ensure that your links update before printing. The Update links check box is located under the Print tab of the Preferences dialog box, shown in Figure 4-7. (Select Tools ➪ Preferences and click the Print tab, or choose Word Options from the Word section of the Print dialog box.) To turn it on, simply check Update links. Once checked, this option is effective for your current document and all new documents unless you deselect it.

Printing documents containing fields

Fields are placeholders that contain information that is melded into your document in text form. By default, Word updates all fields within your document every time the document is opened. Just to be on the safe side, you can set a preference to ensure fields update before printing. From your document, go to Tools ➪ Preferences, select the Print tab, and then check the option called Update fields. If you are in the Print dialog box, select the Word pop-up menu, and then click the Word Options button to access the same Print Preferences tab. As this is a preference, it is effective for your current document and all new documents unless you deselect it.

Printing Document Information

When you go to the Print dialog box, by default you print your current document. However, you can select Microsoft Word from the main pop-up menu, and then use the Print pop-up list to specify what you'd like to print (see Figure 4-8). (This is the pop-up menu that lists the document as its default.) You can print information pertaining to your document, or the comments, styles, or AutoText entries related to your document. Specifically, you can print the following:

✦ Document properties — Reports all the information found under File ➪ Properties, including your document's name and location, the template from which it was created, the author's name, keywords and comments you've entered in the document summary, the creation date, last save information, and last date printed. It also includes the total editing time and gives you a page, word, and character count. (You can also set a preference in Word to always print the document properties whenever you print the document.)

- ✦ Comments—Prints the comments stored within the document. Comments are sorted by page number and report the initials of each author. (You can also set Word's preferences to always print the comments whenever you print the document.)
- ✦ Styles—Prints the style sheet for the document.
- ✦ AutoText entries—Prints the AutoText entries belonging to the template you are using.
- ✦ Key assignments—Prints the names and descriptions of macros along with the keys to which they are assigned.

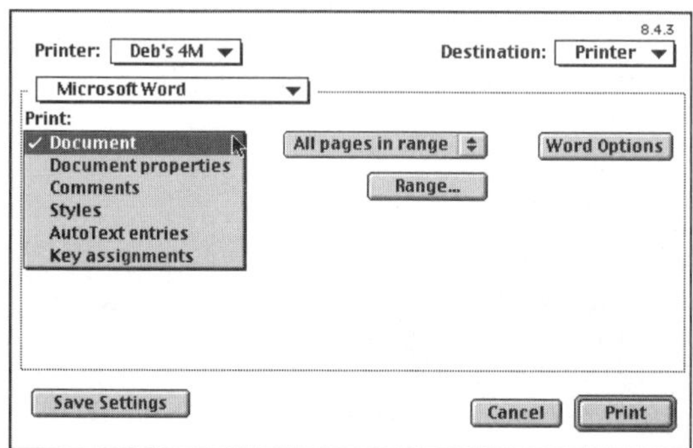

Figure 4-8: The Print choices provided by the Print dialog box

Changing Your Printer

Changing your printer is part of your Mac's operating system, rather than a part of Word. If you are using the Desktop Printer feature, you should have an icon of your printer somewhere on your desktop. If you have several printers available, the printer currently selected should have a black border. To select another printer, simply click the icon of the desired printer and, in the Printing menu that appears, select Set Default Printer. (This printer now has the black border.) Alternatively, you can go to the Chooser (in your Apple menu) and click the desired printer.

After you change printers, it's a good idea to go to the File➪Page Setup command. Open the dialog box, double-check your settings, and then click OK. This tells word the parameters of your chosen printer.

Printing Ancillary Information with Your Document

You can also set Word's preferences to always print certain document information whenever you print the document. These options are found in the Print tab of the Preferences dialog box. You can get to this tab by selecting Tools ➪ Preferences and clicking the Print tab; Or, from the Print dialog box, by clicking Word Options. Remember that these are preferences. Once checked, these preferences are effective for your current document and all new documents you create unless you deselect them.

Use the Include with Document options to specify which information should be included with the printed document. If you turn on Document properties, the document properties (as in File➪Properties) sheet is printed along with the document. Turn on Field Codes to print field codes instead of the results of the fields. If you turn on Annotations, Word prints the document and any annotation comments added to the document. Turn on Hidden Text to print the document and any text that you hid with the Hidden option from the Character dialog box. Click the Drawing Objects check box to print the drawing objects you may have included in your document.

Printing Envelopes

Word has an envelope-printing feature that makes printing envelopes simple, if your printer can handle envelopes. If you have already created your document, select the addressee's name and address. Then choose Tools➪Envelopes and Labels to open the Envelopes and Labels dialog box (see Figure 4-9).

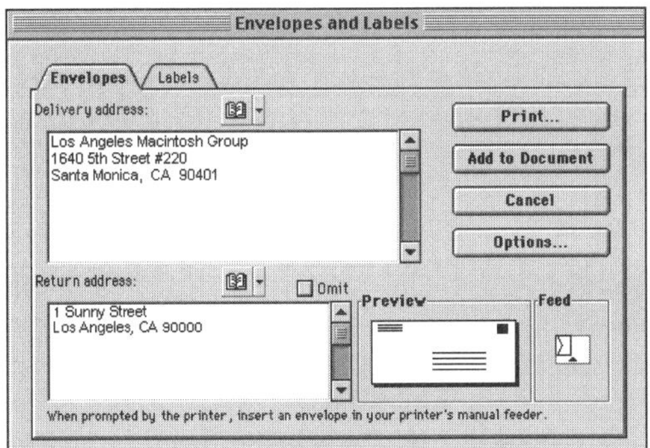

Figure 4-9: The Envelopes and Labels dialog box

In the Envelopes tab of this dialog box, there are two text boxes for the delivery and return addresses. If you've selected the addressee's name and address, Word automatically places them in the Delivery address text box. In the Return address area, Word enters the name and address stored under the User Info tab of the Preferences dialog box. (The name is automatically taken from your Mac if you entered it during Mac setup. The address must be hand-entered via the Preferences dialog box.) Both addresses can be hand-edited within these text boxes.

If you use the Address Book within Word, you can also select a delivery address or return address from the Address Book pop-up menu above each text box.

If you use Word's Address Book feature, rather than typing an address each time you create a letter, you can select Tools ➪ Envelopes and Labels, select a delivery address from the Address Book pop-up menu above the Delivery address text box, and then click the Add to Document button. This places the selected address into your document for you.

Once your address information is complete, you may want to check or change the kind of envelope on which you are printing. Click the envelope in the Preview window, or click the Options button to open the Envelope Options dialog box shown in Figure 4-10.

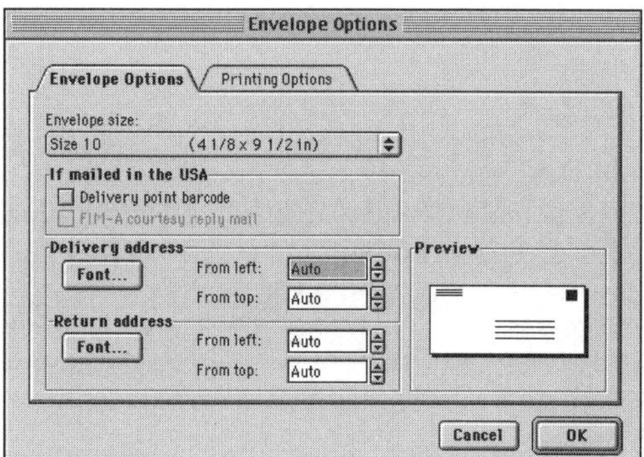

Figure 4-10: The Envelope Options dialog box

If You Have Problems Printing

If your Mac has problems printing, a dialog box should come up and tell you what is wrong. Follow the instructions to solve the problem. There are some basic things to check, such as whether your printer is turned on (don't laugh), and if you have more than one printer, make sure the wrong printer is not selected. If you are using the Desktop Printer feature, you can easily see which printer is selected as your print destination. (The icon of the printer currently selected to print has a black border.) If the desired printer is already selected, the icon may provide clues about the problem.

For example, if a stop-sign-styled hand appears, you have told the printer to stop printing. Simply select Start Print Queue from the Printing menu. If an alert (exclamation point) symbol appears, double-click the printer's icon to open the Print Monitor dialog box and read the messages in this dialog box for clues. If the message says a printer can't be found, check that the cables connecting your Mac to the printer are all firmly connected.

The Envelope Options dialog box contains two tabs. The Envelope Options tab lets you change the kind of envelope on which you are printing, add delivery point barcodes and courtesy facing ID marks, format the delivery and return addresses, and control the positioning of the text on the envelope. The Printing Options tab of the Envelope Options dialog box lets you control the way envelopes are printed (see Figure 4-11). First select Face up or Face down. Next, select the icon that represents the way your envelopes feed into your printer. Check or uncheck the Clockwise rotation option to help. If you are using an envelope feeder, check the Use envelope feeder option.

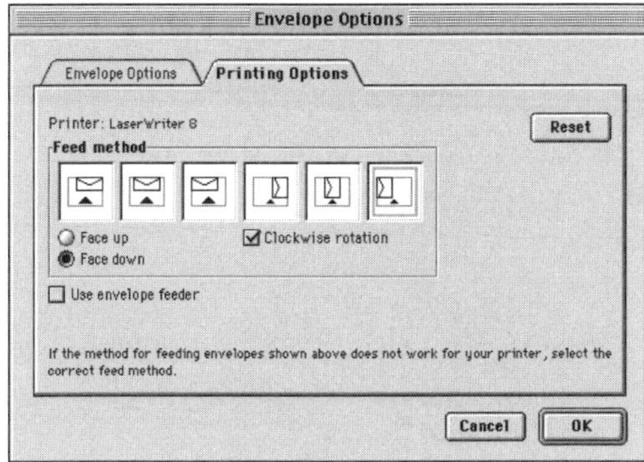

Figure 4-11: The Printing Options tab of the Envelope Options dialog box

After you have made all the necessary formatting changes, close the Envelope Options dialog box and click the Print button in the Envelopes and Labels dialog box. This calls up your Mac's Print dialog box. Select the appropriate paper tray, and then click Print to print your envelope.

Summary

In this chapter, you learned how to examine the appearance of documents before you print them and how to print the documents in Word. The following points were covered:

✦ Choosing File➪Print Preview provides a useful way to see what a document looks like before it is printed.

✦ You can use Print Preview to make changes to margins and indents as well as to move images around in your document.

✦ Using the Microsoft Word view in the Print dialog box, you can print portions of the document, and you can print other items (such as document properties, style sheets, comments, styles, and macro assignments).

Where to go next

✦ In the next chapter, you learn how to work with tables and outlines in Word.

✦ Macros enable you to automate the printing of documents that you print regularly. Chapter 9 gives you the lowdown on macros.

✦ The appearance of your printed document depends on how your document is formatted. Chapter 3 teaches you how to format your documents.

✦ ✦ ✦

CHAPTER 5

Working with Tables and Outlines

✦ ✦ ✦ ✦

In This Chapter

Understanding tables in Word 98

Creating tables

Editing tables

Formatting tables

Exploring other uses for tables

Understanding outlines in Word

Changing outline headings

Creating your own outline

Creating tables of contents from outlines

Printing outlines

✦ ✦ ✦ ✦

Tables are an excellent way to organize document content, and with Word they are easy to create and highly flexible. Outlines are also an important organizational aid. For many people who work with words, creating an outline is the first step to putting their thoughts on paper. If you've been working with a program less powerful than Word in the past, you may be accustomed to creating outlines by means of tabs and manually typed headings. Word's automatic outlining enables you to number headings and create tables of contents automatically based on the outline headings.

Understanding Tables in Word 98

A table is any grouping of information arranged in rows and columns, as illustrated in Figure 5-1. Tables have two or more columns and one or more rows. Each intersection of a row and a column is called a *cell* of the table. If you are familiar with computer spreadsheets, such as Excel, you should easily understand the concept of a cell.

Detective	Book Title	Author
Elvis Cole	Sunset Express	Robert Crais
Phillip Marlowe	The Big Sleep	Raymond Chandler
Sam Spade	The Maltese Falcon	Dashiell Hammett

Figure 5-1: A sample table

Before Word's Table feature came along, users typically set up tables using tabs or indented paragraphs. Although this method works, it is cumbersome and awkward. A table set up with tabs gets tricky and becomes inefficient when any cell in the table contains more than one line of text. At that point, any changes you make to the table's text also throw off the alignment of the tabs, so you constantly have to add and delete tabs to line up the information in columns. Manually creating a table is more trouble than it is worth.

In comparison, Word's Table feature creates a group of cells that expands as needed to fit all your required text or graphics. The only limit to the size of your table is that a single cell cannot be larger than a page. You can resize columns and cells, and you can add rows, columns, and cells. Word also provides useful commands that make life easier when you need to edit the tables. All in all, Word's Table feature is the best way for you to create a table.

By default, a table appears with gridlines surrounding the cells. If you do not see the gridlines surrounding the tables you create, choose Table ⇨ Gridlines to turn on the gridlines. Gridlines do not print in your document; they are simply an aid for entering and editing text in tables. You can also add borders (which do appear when printed) to cells or to an entire table (see "Formatting Tables" later in the chapter).

Creating Tables

You have several ways to add a table in Word 98. You can click and drag, use a dialog box, custom draw a table, or type in a table. Before you begin any table, it helps to place your cursor where you want the table to come into your document.

To add a table via click-and-drag, place your cursor in the document where you want the table. Then click the Insert Table button on the Standard toolbar and drag down in the pictorial submenu that appears. Drag across until you reach the number of columns you want. The submenu shows five columns, but if you drag past that, the submenu grows to accommodate you. Then drag down to define the number of rows. Just enter a minimum number of rows, such as two; your table grows automatically when you get to the last cell in the last row and press Tab. It's even easy to add more rows (or columns) between existing rows (or columns) later.

You can also add a table numerically. To do so, place the cursor where you want the table to enter. Then choose Table ⇨ Insert Table, which brings up the Insert Table dialog box shown in Figure 5-2. In the Number of columns text box, enter the desired number of columns for the table. Word proposes 2, but you can enter any value up to 31. If you are not sure how many columns you need, don't worry. You can add columns at any time.

In the Number of rows text box, enter the desired number of rows for the table. If you are not sure how many rows you need, enter a minimum number of rows, such as two. It's easy to add more later. Actually, your table grows automatically when you get to the last cell in the last row and press the Tab key. You can also add rows between existing rows.

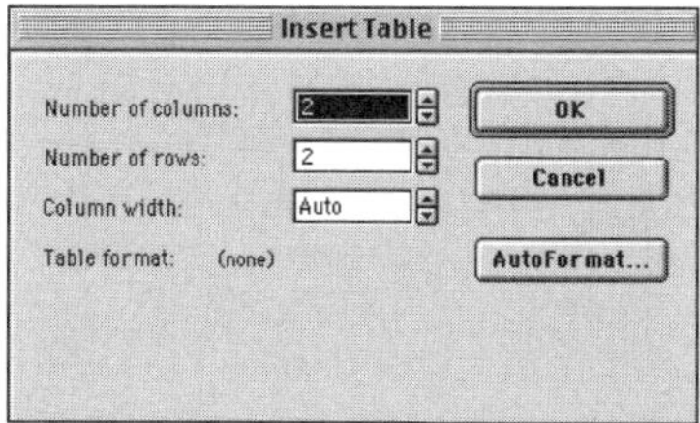

Figure 5-2: The Insert Table dialog box

In the Column width text box, you can leave the setting at Auto, which is the default, or enter a decimal measurement for the width of the columns. If you use Auto, Word makes all columns an equal width. We discuss how to set different column widths later. To add a table via the Insert Table dialog box, follow these steps:

1. Place the insertion point in the document where you want the table placed.
2. Choose Table ⇨ Insert Table.
3. Enter the number of columns desired in the Number of columns text box, and enter the number of rows desired in the Number of rows text box.
4. Enter the desired column width in the Column width text box (or accept the Auto default).
5. If you want to add borders or other formatting, click the AutoFormat button. In the Table AutoFormat dialog box, you can choose from a wide range of effects. (This is covered under "Formatting Tables" later in this chapter.) You can apply predefined lines, borders, and shading to different sections of the table.
6. When you are finished making your selections, click OK to add the table at the insertion point location. The insertion point automatically waits in the first cell so you can begin typing the desired data.

The Insert Table button and dialog box both create uniform tables—each row has the same number of columns, each column has the same number of rows, and all rows and columns are equal in their height and width. After you create the table, you can select any two or more cells in a row or column and use the Table ⇨ Merge Cells command to create one cell that transcends the selected columns or rows. (For more information, see the "Merging cells" section.)

The most flexible way to create a table is by custom-drawing it yourself, using Word's intuitive Draw Table feature. Using this method, you can immediately create nonuniform tables without first creating the table and then merging cells.

To create a table using Draw Table, click the Tables and Borders button on the Standard toolbar, or choose Table ⇨ Draw Table. The mouse pointer then becomes a pencil. Click and drag to draw the outer sides of the table. Next, create the cells within the table by drawing horizontal and vertical lines where desired. Lines do not have to be the full width or length of the table. You can draw a line between individual rows or columns. Again, if you are not sure how many cells you will need, you can always add cells and columns to the table as needed by drawing additional lines or by tabbing at the end to create new rows. If you find after you have drawn the table that you need to remove some of the cells or lines, press and hold the Shift key to turn the pencil into an eraser, and then drag the eraser over the lines you want to delete. If you use the Draw Table feature, you will not see the Insert Table dialog box shown earlier in Figure 5-2.

Finally, you can take advantage of Word's AutoFormat feature to create a table. When you type plus sign (+) followed by a hyphen (-), or hyphens and another plus sign, Word creates a table. AutoFormat converts each plus sign to a column border and determines the width of the columns between plus signs by the number of hyphens you type. For example, three plus signs with at least one hyphen between each plus sign translates to two columns. This method provides a one-row table. As with any table in Word, a new row is automatically created when you reach the last cell and press Tab.

Navigating within a table

To move forward from cell to cell in the table, press the Tab key; to move in reverse, press Shift-Tab. If you reach the end of a table and press Tab, you add a new row to the table and move into it. The arrow keys also move the insertion point around in the table. In addition, the arrow keys move into and out of a table. You can also use the mouse to click in any cell and place the insertion point in that cell. For a complete summary of the keys used for navigation in tables, see Table 5-1.

Navigating inside a table with the mouse works in the same way as navigating in regular text: you point and click in the location where you want to place the insertion point. However, you need to know some additional mouse techniques beyond the obvious ones. Tables provide special selection areas for mouse use. At the left edge of each cell is a selection bar, an area where the mouse pointer changes to an arrow pointing upward and to the right. If you click the left edge of a cell while the pointer is shaped like this arrow, you will select the entire cell. You can also double-click in any cell's selection bar to select the entire row of the table, or you can click and drag across cell boundaries to select a group of cells.

At the top of a table is a column-selection area. If you place the mouse pointer above the border at the top of the table, the pointer changes to the shape of a downward-pointing arrow, which indicates the column-selection mode. If you click while the pointer is shaped like the downward-pointing arrow, you select the entire column below the pointer.

How Can I Type a Tab?

Because you use the Tab key to move around within a table, you can't use the Tab key to enter a Tab character. In some ways this is good, because tabs inside tables are dangerous. In the first place, you don't have much horizontal space in the cells to play with.

In the second place, the tabs may mess up your overall formatting for the table. Nevertheless, if you must have a tab character inside a table, you can add one by pressing Option-Tab.

Within a single cell, you can use the same keys you use to navigate in any Word document. Table 5-1 summarizes the keys that you use to navigate within a table.

Table 5-1
Navigation Keys To Use within Tables

Key	*Purpose*
Tab	Moves the cursor to the next cell in the table. If the cursor is in the last cell in the table, the Tab key adds a new row and moves the cursor to the first cell of the new row.
Shift-Tab	Moves the cursor to the preceding cell.
Option-Home	Moves the cursor to the first cell in a row.
Option-End	Moves the cursor to the last cell in a row.
Option-PgUp	Moves the cursor to the top cell in a column.
Option-PgDn	Moves the cursor to the bottom cell in a column.
Option-Clear	Selects the entire table.
Shift	Activates the eraser if you used the Draw Table feature, so you can use the eraser to erase unwanted lines.
Arrow keys	Moves the cursor within the text in a cell and between cells. If the insertion point is at the edge of a table, you can use the arrow keys to move in or out of the table.

If you press Tab while the insertion point is in the last cell of a table, a new row is automatically added, and Word places the insertion point in the first cell of the new row. You can add new rows by choosing Table ⇨ Insert Rows or by clicking the Insert Rows button on the Standard tool bar, but it is generally easier to add new rows as needed by using the Tab key.

Cells Can Contain Mucho Texto . . .

As you type within a cell, your text wraps automatically, expanding the height of the cell. This alone is useful, but there's more. You can also have more than a single paragraph of text within a cell. At any time, you can press Return to create a new paragraph and keep right on typing.

Longtime users of Word have often taken advantage of this design trait to create side-by-side columns of unequal size, although newer versions of Word (like yours) offer specific commands for handling multiple-column documents. You can also format every paragraph in a table just like paragraphs that are not in cells of a table; you can assign your paragraphs indentation settings, alignments, line spacing, and the like.

Creating your own table

To practice setting up a table, entering information, and revising a table, follow along with this next exercise. You can also create your own table with your own data if you want. Follow these steps to create a sample table:

1. Begin a new document by clicking the New button on the Standard toolbar (or typing **⌘-N** for File➪New). Type the following phrase:

   Food arrangements for Herb's visit with us

2. Press Return to begin a new paragraph.
3. Click the Insert Table button and drag across four columns and down six rows. (You can also use the Draw table method to frame your table, and then add the rows and columns. Otherwise, choose Table➪Insert Table and enter **4** in the Number of columns text box and **6** for the number of rows, and then click OK.) The insertion point is in the first cell.
4. Enter the information shown in Figure 5-3. Use the Tab key to advance to each new cell. (Do not press Return or Enter to advance to a new cell—doing so simply creates new paragraphs within the same cell.)

   Notice that as you enter the information shown in the table, the text in the right-most column will often be too long to fit on a single line. When this happens, the cell expands in height automatically. This example illustrates one advantage of Word's Table feature: You do not need to calculate the space you need between rows of a table because Word does this automatically. You can enter as little or as much text as you want in a cell (up to the limit of one page in size).

Day	Who	What	Where
Monday	David & Orly	Salads	Orly's Home Cooking Kitchen
Tuesday	Shira & Elysa	Veggies	Mimi's
Wednesday	Donna	Indian	The Curry House by the Sea
Thursday	Rosalie & Herb	Sushi	To be determined.
Friday	Yekutiel & Tani	Pizza	Nagila

Figure 5-3: A sample table containing lunch arrangements

5. After you have finished entering the information in Step 4, move your cursor into the cell containing the text "To be determined." Press End to get to the end of the existing text, and then press Return to begin a new paragraph. Type the following text:

   (They are looking into a central location.)

   Notice how Word expands the table downward to accommodate all the necessary information (see Figure 5-4).

Day	Who	What	Where
Monday	David & Orly	Salads	Orly's Home Cooking Kitchen
Tuesday	Shira & Elysa	Veggies	Mimi's
Wednesday	Donna	Indian	The Curry House by the Sea
Thursday	Rosalie & Herb	Sushi	To be determined. (They are looking into a central location.)
Friday	Yekutiel & Tani	Pizza	Nagila

Figure 5-4: Word expands the table to accommodate more information.

Remember that you can insert graphics into the cells of a table. To do so, use the cut-and-paste technique for graphic images detailed in Chapter 10.

Editing Tables

After you have created a table, you can add or delete columns and rows, merge the information from more than one cell, and split your table into more than one part. This section looks at how to do all these things in a table.

Before you can edit a table, however, you must learn how to select the cells in a table. To select cells in a table, use the same selection methods you use in regular text. Briefly, you can click and drag across text in one or more cells with the mouse, or you can hold down the Shift key while you use the arrow keys. You can also use any of the Option key combinations shown in Table 5-1. While selecting, as you move the insertion point past the end of text in a particular cell, text in the adjacent cell is selected. If no text is in a cell, the entire cell is selected as you move through it while dragging.

To select an entire column most efficiently, move your cursor just above the table, close to the top of the column to be selected. The cursor becomes a downward-pointing arrow. While the cursor is an arrow, click to select the entire column. This action tells Word you're specifying columns, not just cells that are next to each other. Therefore, Word provides you with column commands rather than generic cell commands.

To select an entire row most efficiently, move your cursor just to the left of the table, close to the side of the column to be selected, until the cursor becomes a right-pointing arrow. While the cursor is an arrow, click to select the entire row. If you want to select several rows, keep the mouse pressed as you drag up or down to select those rows, too. This tells Word you're specifying rows, not just cells that are above each other. Therefore, Word provides you with row commands rather than generic cell commands.

Inserting and deleting columns or rows

You can add columns at any time. Select the column(s) as an entire column(s) in the manner described in the previous section—move your mouse to the top of the column until the cursor becomes a downward-pointing arrow. To select one entire column, click above the row. To select more than one column, drag over those columns. Then choose Insert Columns from the Table menu or click the Insert Columns button on the Standard toolbar. (The Insert Table button and menu item changes to Insert Columns.) This action inserts the new column to the left of the selected column.

To delete an entire column, select it using the arrow pointer, and then select Table ⇨ Delete Columns. The column(s) simply disappears, taking with it any text inside.

New rows are added automatically when you get to the last cell in the last row and press the Tab key. You can also insert new rows between existing rows. The new rows are inserted above any row selected when you issue the command. Choose the now-showing Insert Rows option from the Table menu. (The Insert Table button and menu item changes to Insert Rows.) If one row was selected, one new row is added. If two rows were selected, two are added, and so on.

To delete an entire row, first select it as a row when the cursor becomes the arrow pointer. Then choose Table ⇨ Delete Rows. The rows are removed, along with the data in them.

Inserting and deleting cells

You don't have to add entire rows or columns at a time. You can click in a single cell or select just a few cells in a row or column, and then insert or delete new cells or columns, shifting the existing ones right or down.

To add cells, first select the cell(s) you want to add new cells next to, and then choose Table ⇨ Insert Cells or click the Insert Cells button on the Standard toolbar. The Insert Cells dialog box, shown in Figure 5-5, asks whether you want to insert an entire row of cells or whether you want only the selected cells to shift after you add them to the table. The dialog box preselects the option Word anticipates you'll want. For example, if you select two cells next to each other, Shift cells down is the default option. If you click OK, two new cells land above the selected ones, pushing the selected cells down. The rest of the cells in the row remain in place.

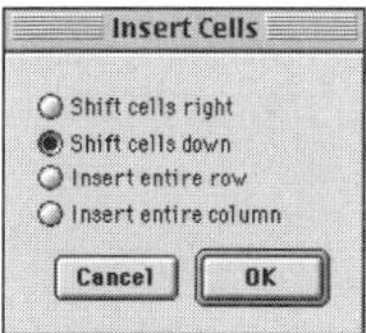

Figure 5-5: The Insert Cells dialog box

When you need to remove rows, columns, or cells from a table, first select the cells you want to delete. Then choose Table ➪ Delete Cells or click the Delete Cells button on the Standard toolbar. The Delete Cells dialog box (see Figure 5-6) lets you shift the cells left after deletion, shift the cells up after deletion, or delete entire rows or columns.

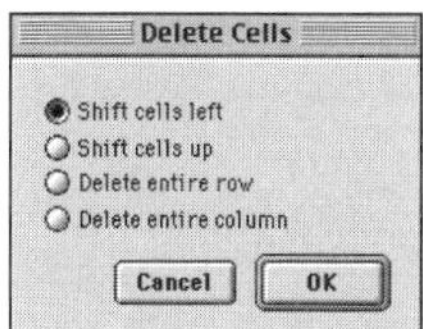

Figure 5-6: The Delete Cells dialog box

How the insertion or deletion of cells affects the table depends on what you delete or add, and whether you choose to shift the cells horizontally or vertically. As an example, Figure 5-7 shows a table measuring five rows by two columns: ten cells.

FIRST	SECOND
THIRD	FOURTH
FIFTH	SIXTH
SEVENTH	EIGHTH
NINTH	TENTH

Figure 5-7: A 5 × 2 table

If you select a cell or a group of cells (third and fourth) *and not the entire row*, choose Table ➪ Insert Cells. Then choose Shift cells right in the dialog box, The new cell or group of cells is inserted at the selection location, and the existing cells move to the right, as shown in Figure 5-8.

FIRST	SECOND		
		THIRD	FOURTH
FIFTH	SIXTH		
SEVENTH	EIGHTH		
NINTH	TENTH		

Figure 5-8: The table from Figure 5-7 after choosing Shift cells right from the Insert Cells dialog box

If you select a cell or a group of cells (third and fourth) but not the entire row, choose Table⇨Insert Cells. Then choose Shift cells down in the dialog box. The new cell, or group of cells, is inserted at the selection location, and the existing cells move down, as illustrated in Figure 5-9.

FIRST	SECOND
THIRD	FOURTH
FIFTH	SIXTH
SEVENTH	EIGHTH
NINTH	TENTH

Figure 5-9: The table from Figure 5-7 after choosing Shift cells down from the Insert Cells dialog box

If you select a cell or a group of cells (not the entire row) and choose Table⇨Delete Cells, you again have the choice of choosing to shift the cells up or to the left. Figure 5-10 shows the example table if the fifth and seventh cells were selected and the Shift cells left option was chosen.

FIRST	SECOND
THIRD	FOURTH
SIXTH	
EIGHTH	
NINTH	TENTH

Figure 5-10: The table from Figure 5-7 after choosing Shift cells left from the Insert Cells dialog box

The quickest way to add one full row is to place your cursor in any cell in the row below where you want the new row to land. Then Control-click and select Insert Row. You can also quickly delete an entire row by selecting the entire row, Control-clicking, and then selecting Delete row. If you select less than an entire row, your only delete option is to delete cells, which brings up the Delete Cells dialog box.

Merging cells

Any number of adjacent cells in any one direction can be merged to become one larger cell. This is commonly done to create a header in which text is centered across an entire table. Once in a while, you may also want to merge information from one group of cells into one cell. There are a few ways to merge cells in Word 98. As an example, consider the simple table shown in Figure 5-11.

Detective	Book Title	Author	Carries Gun?
Elvis Cole	Sunset Express	Robert Crais	Yes
Phillip Marlowe	The Big Sleep	Raymond Chandler	Yes
Sam Spade	The Maltese Falcon	Dashiell Hammett	Yes

Figure 5-11: A table before cells are merged

The traditional way to merge a group of horizontally adjacent cells into a single cell is to first select the cells you want to merge, and then choose Table⇨Merge Cells. After choosing the command, the information merges into one cell.

If you were to select the two cells at the right end of the top row of the table and choose Table⇨Merge Cells, the result would resemble that shown in Figure 5-12, where the adjoining cells are merged into one cell. Note that any text in the cells is also merged into a single entry, as demonstrated in the example.

Detective	Book Title	Author Carries Gun?	
Elvis Cole	Sunset Express	Robert Crais	Yes
Phillip Marlowe	The Big Sleep	Raymond Chandler	Yes
Sam Spade	The Maltese Falcon	Dashiell Hammett	Yes

Figure 5-12: The same table after cells are merged

The next, and perhaps easiest, way to merge cells is to select the cells you want to merge, and then Control-click and select Merge Cells from the shortcut menu.

The last way to merge cells is to use the eraser from the Draw Table toolbar. If it's not already showing, Control-click in any table cell and select Draw Table. Then click the Eraser tool so your cursor becomes an eraser. Move the eraser over the line you want to remove and drag over that line. Close the Draw Table toolbar window to return to your regular cursor.

If you merge cells and don't like the result, remember that you can undo the operation by immediately choosing Edit⇨Undo (which will read Undo Merge Cells).

Splitting a table

In case a table becomes to intricate or unwieldy, you can also split your table horizontally. When you choose Table⇨Split Table, the table splits in two just above the insertion point, and Word inserts a paragraph marker between the two tables. Splitting the table makes the groups more visible. Splitting a table is also useful if you want to insert text between the rows of an existing table, and you do not want the text to be a part of the table.

Formatting Tables

In Word you can format the contents of your tables (usually text), and you can format the full table. You can apply formatting to the contents of tables the same way you apply formatting to characters or paragraphs. This means you can change the text alignment within a cell, rotate the text, highlight the text or change its color, and even add numbering or bullets to the text. Control-clicking a cell of text gives you an idea of the options available. (See Chapter 3 for more on character and paragraph formatting.) For example, if you want to apply bold character formatting to a portion of text in a table, you can select the text and click the Bold button in the Standard toolbar, or press ⌘-B to apply the formatting.

If you want to format aspects of the actual table (as opposed to its contents), select Table➪Table AutoFormat to open the Table AutoFormat dialog box (see Figure 5-13). In this dialog box, you see a selection of various formats you can apply to your table. Choose the format you want to use, and select the areas to which you want to apply the format by clicking as many check boxes as you want. The Preview box lets you see what the table will look like after the formatting is complete. When you finish making your selections, click OK to apply the formatting to the table.

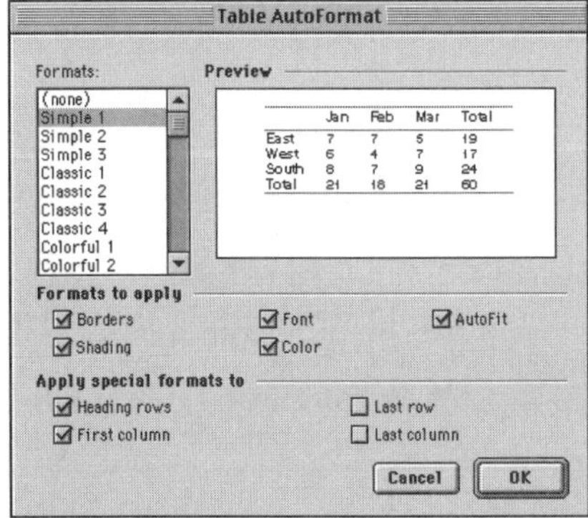

Figure 5-13: The Table AutoFormat dialog box

Setting column widths

Choose Table➪Cell Height and Width to open the Cell Height and Width dialog box (see Figure 5-14). In this dialog box, you can specify the width of one or more cells of the table. In the Row tab of the dialog box, you can change the row height, the indentation from the left, and the alignment. You can also tell Word whether to allow rows to break across the ends of pages. In the Column tab, you can set the width of the columns and the amount of space between columns.

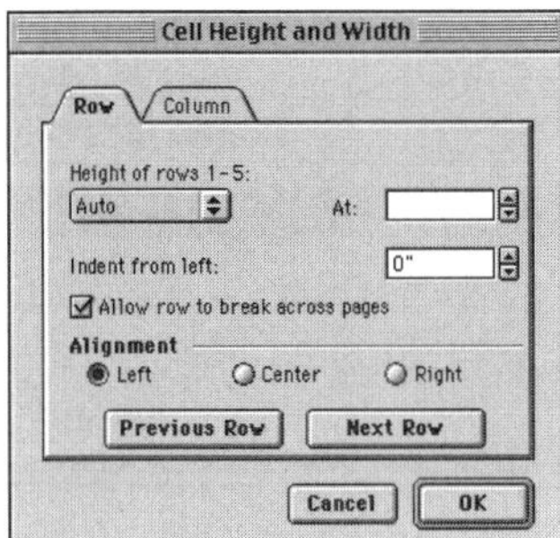

Figure 5-14: The Cell Height and Width dialog box

Another way to resize cells is to work visually. You can physically drag the gridline between cells or move the gray box on the ruler that corresponds to the gridlines. Move your pointer over the gridline of the desired row or column (or over the gray box on the ruler) until the pointer changes into a two-sided arrow. Then click and drag to the desired height or width.

After you have adjusted the column width, all the columns to the right of the adjusted column are resized in proportion to their previous widths, but the overall width of the table is not changed when you drag the gridline or the column marker. The following list contains your options for adjusting your current column:

- ✦ To adjust the current column and one column to the right, press the Shift key while you drag. The overall table width remains unchanged.
- ✦ To adjust the current column and make all columns to the right equal in width, press ⌘-Shift as you drag. The overall table width remains unchanged.
- ✦ To adjust the current column without changing the width of the other columns, hold down the Option and Shift keys while you drag. This changes the overall table width.

To see the actual width measurement in the ruler, add the Option key to any combination as you drag column widths.

From time to time, the use of the Draw Table feature to create your tables will result in cells or columns that are not the same height. Or, you may find the default cell sizes too big for your needs. In these cases, you can take advantage of the Table menu's Distribute Rows Evenly or Distribute Columns Evenly commands. These options even out the columns and the rows, averaging their sizes.

Adjusting the space between columns

You can adjust the spacing between columns by choosing Table➪Cell Height and Width and clicking the Column tab in the Cell Height and Width dialog box . In this tab, you can use the Space between columns box to adjust the horizontal space that Word places between the text of adjacent cells. (The default value is 0.15 inches.) If you click the AutoFit button, Word automatically sizes the columns to best fit the text contained in them.

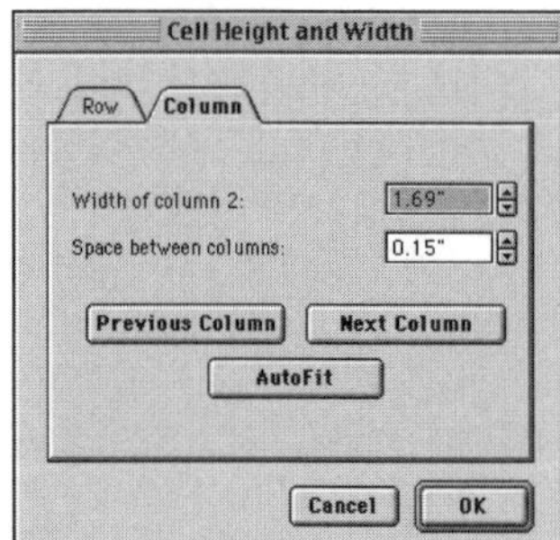

Figure 5-15: The Column tab of the Cell Height and Width dialog box

Making row adjustments

To set the height of a row, select Table➪Cell Height and Width, and then select the Row tab in the dialog box. Use the Height of Rows list box to set the minimum height of one or more rows. By default, this value is set to Auto, which means the row will be high enough to contain any text in the row. If you choose the At Least option from the Height of Rows list box, Word makes the row at least as tall as the value you enter. If any text within a cell is larger than the minimum height, Word increases the height to accommodate the text. You can also choose the Exactly option from the list box, which causes Word to make the cell exactly the height that you enter in the box. Using the Exactly option, however, may cause text to be cut off.

To add indents to your cells, click the Indent from left box on the Row tab. The row is indented from the left page margin by the decimal amount you enter. For example, if you enter 0.5 in., the row will be indented half an inch from the left page margin. You can enter a negative value to shift the row to the left, past the left margin. If you want to apply the indent to one row, select the entire row or just one cell in the row before you open the dialog box. After you make your entries on the Row tab of the Cell Height and Width dialog box, those entries are applied to the entire row. If you don't make a selection first, the changes are applied to the entire table.

To determine the alignment of rows with respect to the page margins, choose from among the Left, Center, or Right options in the Alignment area of the Row tab. These options are comparable to the ones found in the Paragraph dialog box (select Format ⇨ Paragraph). As with paragraphs, you can left-align, center, or right-align rows horizontally on a page. In fact, you can select the entire table and then use the Alignment buttons on the default toolbar, as you do with text. By default, the selected row is left-aligned, which causes the left edge of the row to align with the left margin (assuming you have not specified an indentation). Choose Center to center the row or choose Right to align the right edge of the row with the right page margin.

For the Row Alignment options to have any visible effect, your table must be smaller than the width of the page margins. If you used the default options in the Insert Table dialog box when you created the table, the table is already as wide as the page margins, and choosing an alignment option will have no visible effect. The alignment options are useful when you specify your own widths for the table columns rather than letting Word automatically size the table. They may also be handy after you change your document's margin.

Remember that adjusting the Alignment options in the dialog box moves the horizontal position of the entire row, not the text within the row. For example, if you choose the Center option from the Alignment area, Word centers the row within the page margins, but individual text within the cells is not centered. If you want to left-align, center, or right-align text within a cell, select the desired text and then use the alignment options of the Format ⇨ Paragraph command (or the alignment buttons on the Formatting toolbar).

If you don't select any text to which to apply the text alignment, the alignment you choose applies to the specific cell that contains the insertion point. To apply the alignment to the current row, select the row and then choose one of the alignment buttons on the Formatting toolbar.

Applying borders

You can use the various options within the Cell Borders and Shading dialog box (see Figure 5-16) to place borders around a cell or a group of cells in the table. Select one or more cells and open this dialog box by choosing Format ⇨ Borders and Shading while the insertion point is in a table. The borders you create in this dialog box will be printed, unlike the table gridlines that are visible by default. The borders you specify are added directly on top of the table gridlines.

How Word applies the borders depends on the selections you make in the Cell Borders and Shading dialog box. As with other options in this dialog box, Word applies borders and shading according to the cell or cells you select in the table.

From the Borders and Shading toolbar, you can also select the Line Style list box. Doing so gives you a list of choices for line styles that you can use for the table you have created. After selecting the line style, the cursor becomes a pencil.

Simply draw on the line you want to change the style of, and Word applies the style to the line. If you decide you don't like a style after it has been applied, simply Undo (⌘-Z) and the style will be removed.

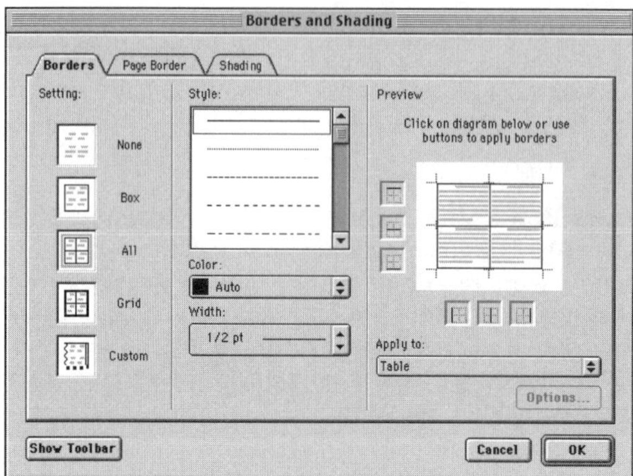

Figure 5-16: The Borders tab of the Borders and Shading dialog box

You can also use Table⇨Table AutoFormat to add borders and shading to a table. When you choose this command, Word provides a list of different formats for shading and borders you can use (see "Formatting Tables" earlier in this chapter). Simply select the format you want in the Table AutoFormat dialog box and click OK.

Besides specifying the presence of a border, Word lets you select from among different types of borders. After you choose the desired option (Outline, Inside, Top, Bottom, Left, or Right) in the Cell Borders and Shading dialog box, you can select the style of borders you want and the colors to be used for the border.

Converting text to tables

Word's tables certainly provide a lot of flexibility and make it easy to organize your information to look great. But what if you already started using tabs or spaces between columns to create the equivalent of a table? Rest easy. Word converts tab or space-created tables with the Text to Table command (Table⇨Convert Text to Table). We definitely recommend this conversion.

You can also use the Text to Table feature to convert data that's been exported from databases in a comma-delimited or tab-delimited format. (See your database documentation for directions on creating comma-delimited or tab-delimited files.) Any text that is separated by either tabs, commas, or paragraph marks can be converted into a table.

To convert text into a table, first select the text and then choose Table ➪ Convert Text to Table. When the Convert Text to Table dialog box appears, choose the Paragraph, Tabs, or Comma option (based on the text to be converted) from the Separate Text At area of the dialog box. Then click OK. Word will recommend a number of columns and a number of rows. It will see each tab or comma as forming a new column, and each paragraph marker as creating a new line. (You can change the recommendations by entering any desired values in the Number of columns and Number of rows text boxes.) To complete the conversion of the text to a table, click OK.

For example, consider the text shown in Figure 5-17. (You can easily duplicate this example by opening a new document, typing the text shown, pressing Tab once between columns, and pressing Return at the end of each line.)

```
¶
¶
Detective → Book Title → Author → Carries Gun?¶
Elvis Cole → Sunset Express → Robert Crais → Yes¶
Phillip Marlowe → The Big Sleep → Raymond Chandler → Yes¶
Sam Spade → The Maltese Falcon → Dashiell Hammett → Yes¶
¶
¶
```

Figure 5-17: Text separated by tab marks can form the basis of a table.

To convert this text into a table, select all three rows of text and choose Table ➪ Convert Text to Table. In the Convert Text to Table dialog box, accept Word's suggestions for a table measuring four columns by three rows by clicking OK. The table shown in Figure 5-18 is the result of Word's efforts. (In the figure, we've added borders to the table to make the effects of the table more visible.)

Detective	Book Title	Author	Carries Gun?
Elvis Cole	Sunset Express	Robert Crais	Yes
Phillip Marlowe	The Big Sleep	Raymond Chandler	Yes
Sam Spade	The Maltese Falcon	Dashiell Hammett	Yes

Figure 5-18: A newly created table based on the text in Figure 5-17

If the makeshift table you are converting contains more than one tab between any single column in any row, remove the extra tabs. Removing extra tabs keeps everything in the proper columns.

Exploring Other Uses for Tables

You can do more with tables than just create them and enter text. You can use tables to lay out large amounts of textual data in the form of side-by-side paragraphs. You can also convert existing text to table form, and you can sort information stored in your tables.

Creating side-by-side paragraphs

Word's capability to store up to one page-length of text in any column of a table makes it easy to set up side-by-side paragraphs with the Table feature. (Side-by-side paragraphs are one way to create newspaper-style columns. You can create side-by-side paragraphs in other ways as well, and Chapter 10 provides additional details regarding this and other desktop publishing topics.) To create side-by-side paragraphs, simply insert a table with two or more columns into your document and use the Cell Height and Width dialog box to size the columns as desired. Remember that you visually set the column widths by clicking the gridlines and dragging them to the appropriate width. Then type as much text as you want in the columns, but keep in mind the rule that a table cannot extend beyond the length of a single page. The table will automatically display the paragraphs of text side-by-side onscreen. You can also add borders to differentiate the text.

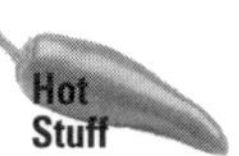

If you are creating a legal pleading page, you'll find a two-column, one-row table useful on Page 1 to format the information about the parties.

Sorting information

Sometimes you may want to arrange a list of data (often within a table) in alphabetical or numerical order. You can use Word's Sort command for this task.

Remember that the Sort command is by no means limited to tables. You can use the Sort command to sort any list of data, whether the information is in a table or in a simple list with paragraph marks separating the lines.

When Word sorts a list, it rearranges the list entries in alphabetical or numerical order. You can choose whether to sort in ascending or descending order or whether to sort by date, text, or number. Follow these steps to sort the data in a table:

1. Select the column, row, or items in the table that you want to sort.
2. Choose Table⇨Sort. (If the selected information is not a table, the command is Sort Text.) The Sort dialog box appears, as shown in Figure 5-19.

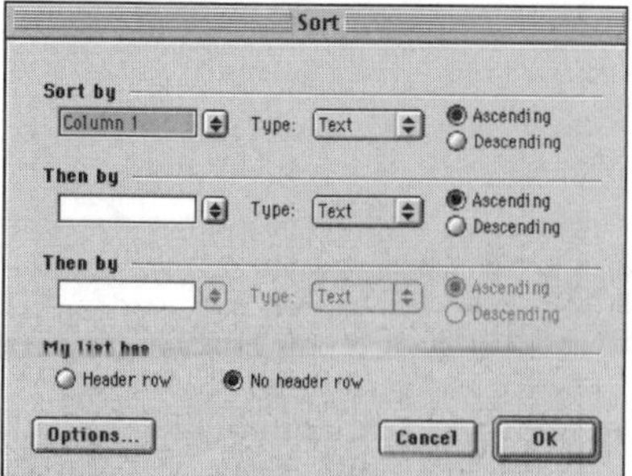

Figure 5-19: The Sort dialog box

3. If you have headings you don't want sorted, click the Header row radio button in the My list has area of the dialog box.
4. In the Sort by area, make your selection for the column by which you want to sort.
5. In the Type pop-up menu of the Sort by area, choose the Text, Number, or Date option, and then click the Ascending or Descending radio button. To choose additional columns to sort by, repeat Steps 4 and 5.
6. Click OK to sort the data.

Understanding Outlines in Word

For many people who work with words, an outline is the first step to putting cohesive thoughts down on paper. Even with the earliest word processors, simple outlining was possible using tabs and manually typed headings. Word, however, offers automatic outlining and its significant advantages. In addition to aiding the organizing process, Word's outlining lets you number headings automatically and create tables of contents based on an outline. When you create an outline in Word, you can easily rearrange parts of the outlining without giving thought to precise formatting.

In Word, outlining is built into a document. With Word, the only difference between a normal document and an outline is the view you use to examine the document. When you are in Normal view, Draft view, or Page Layout view, you are looking at the document in its normal (nonoutline) form. When you turn on Outline view, however, you look at the document in the form of an outline. Figure 5-20 shows an example of a document in outline form (you will duplicate this document in a later exercise).

Outlines consist of headings and body text. A *heading* is any paragraph that has been assigned a special paragraph style. Word provides these styles specifically for the creation of outlines. There are eight predefined styles, from Heading 1 through Heading 8. The numbers define the importance of headings in an outline: A top-level heading is assigned the Heading 1 style, the next level heading is assigned the Heading 2 style, and so on. Word automatically places all top-level headings at the left margin by default, and each lower-level heading style is successively indented (placed farther to the right than the preceding heading level).

Body text is any text within an outline that hasn't been given a heading style. Word also uses the term *subtext* to refer to all headings and body text that appear below a particular heading.

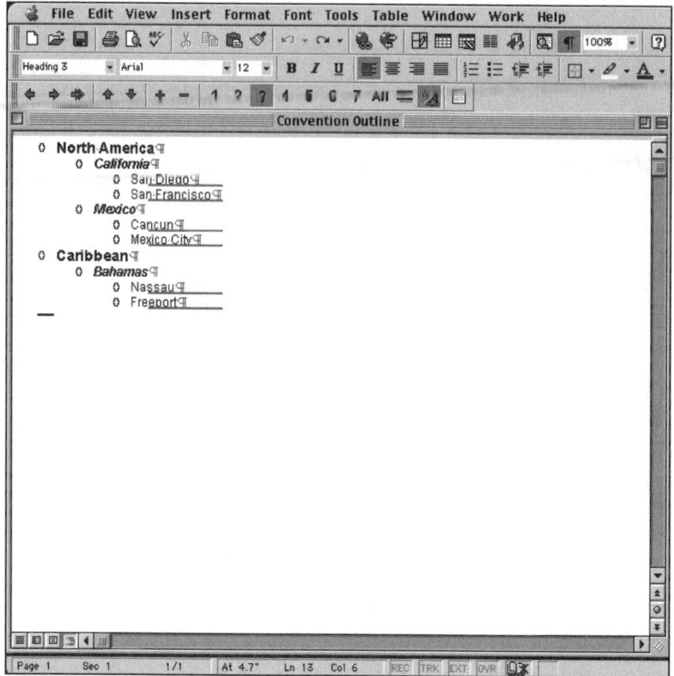

Figure 5-20: A sample document viewed in outline form

Selecting text

When you are in Outline view, selecting text is basically the same as selecting text in other areas of Word—with two differences. The most significant difference is that text is selectable, not by part of a paragraph, but by the entire paragraph only. Normally, you can select a full paragraph along with only part of another paragraph. In Outline view, any paragraph partially selected becomes fully selected. (You can get around this by turning off Outline view while editing.)

You can select any heading or body text by clicking once in the margin to the left of it. Double-clicking selects not only the heading or subtext, but also all the subtext below it. Alternately, you can press Shift along with the arrow keys. There are no other keyboard equivalents.

Changing the structure of an outline

To work with a document in Outline view, choose View⇨Outline. In Outline view, small icons appear to the left of each paragraph, and character formatting such as bolding appears to differentiate headings levels and subtext. Additionally, the Outlining toolbar appears at the top of your window to help structure the outline. When you rest your mouse over any button, its function appears in a yellow pop-up box, so you don't have to memorize all the functions right away. Figure 5-21 shows the Outlining toolbar and its functions.

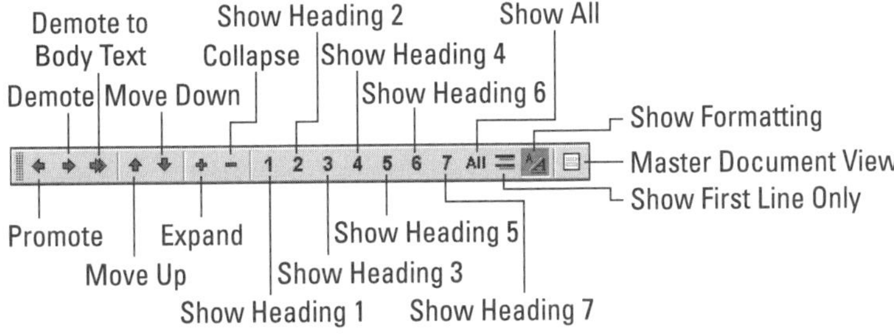

Figure 5-21: The Outlining toolbar

You can use Word's outlining features and benefits at any time. You can create a document and later come back and structure it in outline form, or you can create the document in outline form and then switch to Normal view. You can add additional portions of a document, whether headings or body text, at any time.

At any time, you can promote a paragraph to a higher level or demote it to a lower level of importance. You can also move any element up or down in the order of the document, even placing it under another heading. Making such changes is simple. All you need to do is drag text from one place to another. (See the next section, "Changing Outline Headings.") In case you're not comfortable dragging, you can select the desired paragraph and click the appropriate button on the Outlining toolbar, or you can use keyboard equivalents. To get an idea of what you can do with outlines, see Table 5-2, which explains the function of the Outlining toolbar's buttons.

Table 5-2
The Outlining Toolbar Buttons and Their Functions

Button	*Function*
Promote	Promotes a paragraph to a higher level
Demote	Demotes a paragraph to a lower level
Demote to Body Text	Demotes a heading to body text
Move Up and Move Down	Moves a heading up or down to a new location in the outline
Expand	Expands all text within a heading
Collapse	Collapses a paragraph so only the heading shows
Show Heading	Controls how many levels of the outline are displayed
All	Expands or collapses the entire outline
Show First Line Only	When All is selected, shows just the first line of body text
Show Formatting	Shows or hides character formatting
Master Document View	Switches to Master Document view

There are keyboard equivalents for every Outlining toolbar button. When you rest your mouse over any button, you not only learn what each button does but also see its keyboard equivalent. Table 5-3 summarizes these equivalents for you.

Table 5-3
Keyboard Equivalents for the Outlining Toolbar

Keyboard combination	*Function*
Option-Shift-left arrow or Tab	Promotes a paragraph
Option-Shift-right arrow or Shift-Tab	Demotes a paragraph
Option-Shift-up arrow	Moves a paragraph up
Option-Shift-down arrow	Moves a paragraph down
Control-Shift-+ (plus sign)	Expands body text
Control-Shift– (minus sign)	Collapses body text
Control-Shift-1 through Control-Shift-9	Expands or collapses headings to specified levels (1 through 8), or to show body text (9)
Control-Shift-L	When All is selected, shows just the first line of fbody text

Changing Outline Headings

You can drag, use the Promote and Demote buttons, or use keyboard equivalents to change heading levels, convert body text to headings, or convert headings to body text. To promote a heading level with the mouse, select the heading and drag the heading's icon to the left. Otherwise, select the heading and click the Promote button on the Outlining toolbar. To demote a heading level, select the heading and drag the heading's icon to the right or click the Demote button.

When you promote a heading, it is assigned the next highest heading level, and it moves farther to the left. The opposite happens when you demote a heading: it is assigned the next lower level, and it is indented farther to the right.

Converting body text

To demote a heading to body text, click the double-right arrow in the Outlining toolbar. The appearance of the selected text changes from a heading to regular body text.

You can convert body text to a heading simply by promoting the body text. Select the body text and click the Promote button. When promoted, the body text is converted to a heading that has the same level as the heading above it.

Expanding or collapsing outline headings

As an aid in organizing your thoughts, you can expand or collapse outline headings. When you expand a heading, all the subtext (lower-level headings and body text) below the heading is made visible. On the other hand, when you collapse a heading, all subtext below the heading is hidden from view. Figure 5-22 shows an outline with its body text collapsed; it then shows the same outline with its body text expanded.

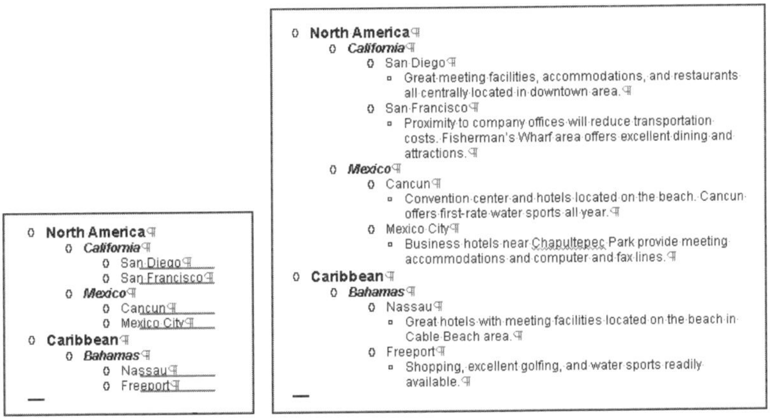

- **North America**
  - ***California***
    - San Diego
    - San Francisco
  - ***Mexico***
    - Cancun
    - Mexico City
- **Caribbean**
  - ***Bahamas***
    - Nassau
    - Freeport

- **North America**
  - ***California***
    - San Diego
      - Great meeting facilities, accommodations, and restaurants all centrally located in downtown area.
    - San Francisco
      - Proximity to company offices will reduce transportation costs. Fisherman's Wharf area offers excellent dining and attractions.
  - ***Mexico***
    - Cancun
      - Convention center and hotels located on the beach. Cancun offers first-rate water sports all year.
    - Mexico City
      - Business hotels near Chapultepec Park provide meeting accommodations and computer and fax lines.
- **Caribbean**
  - ***Bahamas***
    - Nassau
      - Great hotels with meeting facilities located on the beach in Cable Beach area.
    - Freeport
      - Shopping, excellent golfing, and water sports readily available.

Figure 5-22: Left—an outline with collapsed body text. Right—the same outline with body text expanded.

To expand or collapse a single heading, simply double-click the heading's symbol. If you prefer, you can also use the buttons. To expand a heading, select the desired heading and then click the Expand button on the Outlining toolbar. To collapse a heading, select the heading and then click the Collapse button.

To collapse or expand an entire outline, use the Show buttons on the Outlining toolbar. The numbered buttons correspond to the possible heading levels within an outline: clicking the 1 button causes level-one headings to be visible; clicking the 2 button causes all level-one and level-two headings to be visible; clicking the 3 button causes all heading levels of 1, 2, and 3 to be visible; and so on. Clicking the All button causes all headings and all body text in an outline to be visible.

Moving headings

Word provides considerable flexibility regarding the movement of headings and associated subtext. You can move headings around in an outline, you can move associated subtext with or without the headings, and you can move multiple headings and associated subtext by selecting more than one heading prior to the move operation.

To move a heading, first select it by moving your cursor to the left of the heading symbol (the hollow plus sign) so your cursor becomes an arrow. When the arrow points to the heading's symbol, click to select that heading. After you have selected the heading you want to move, click the up or down arrow on the Outlining toolbar to move the heading up or down in the outline.

Note that if you select only a heading in an expanded outline (the subtext is visible), Word moves only the heading and leaves the subtext in its current position. If the heading is collapsed, however, any movement of the heading causes the associated subtext to be moved, even if only the heading is selected.

You can also drag headings to new locations. After selecting the heading, move your cursor over the selected text until it becomes an arrow. Then drag as you normally would to move text. It appears as if your selected heading will merely become part of the line to which you are dragging. The trick is to release the mouse when the dragged heading looks as if it will land between the first word and the symbol of the heading you are placing the dragged heading in front of.

Applying numbering to outlines

You may want to apply numbering to the headings of an outline. You can manually number an outline by typing the numbers as you type the headings, but the drawback to this is evident as soon as you rearrange the outline and have to renumber the headings manually. The efficient way to do it is to take advantage of Word's Bullets and Numbering command to apply numbering to your outline headings. Click either the Numbering button or the Bullets button, call up the Bullets and Numbering dialog box by selecting Format⇨Bullets and Numbering, or Command-click in the outline.

To number or bullet an outline using the buttons, perform the following steps:

1. Select the paragraphs you want to number. (To number the entire document, select the entire document—⌘-A.)
2. Click the Numbering button to apply numbers or the Bullets button to apply bullets. The buttons don't open the dialog box. Instead, they automatically apply whichever format was last selected in the dialog box. (To remove the numbers or bullets, click the button again. If you've deselected the text, select it again and then click.)

To number or bullet an outline with the dialog box, perform the following steps:

1. Select the paragraphs you want to number. If you want to number the entire document, select the entire document by pressing ⌘-A.
2. Choose Format⇨Bullets and Numbering or Control-click in the outline and select Bullets and Numbering to open the Bullets and Numbering dialog box.
3. Select the desired tab and effect. There are six possible number formats and six bullet formats.

If you want to customize the effect, click Customize. In the Number format box type a number as an example for Word to follow. If you don't want the numbers to start with 1, enter a new starting number in the Start at box. You can also align the numbers and set an indent for them.

4. Click OK. Paragraph numbers or bullets appear beside each selected topic in your outline.

You can remove paragraph numbering from the outline at any time by opening the Bullets and Numbering dialog box again and clicking None as the format.

Creating Your Own Outline

To demonstrate the concepts you can use in building outlines, it's best to create an outline of your own on which to experiment. Follow along with this exercise to create an outline:

1. Use any method to create a new document (File⇨New, ⌘-N, or the New document button).
2. Choose View⇨Outline to switch to Outline view. (Do this now, before you enter the text. If you do it later, your outline will behave a bit differently. More on this soon.)
3. Choose File⇨Save (⌘-S) to save the document with the name Sample Outline #1. (The sooner you save your document, the less you have to redo if you lose it. Continue saving as you work.)
4. To begin your outline, type the following text and press Return after each line:

   North America

   California

   San Diego

   San Francisco

   Mexico

   Cancun

   Mexico City

   Caribbean

   Bahamas

   Nassau

   Freeport

Each of these words is automatically assigned a level-one heading. (If they are not, you didn't begin entering your text while in Outline view. In that case, see the Note that follows Step 6 in this list.)

5. Because California is to be a subheading under North America, you want to create a second level in your outline. Click in the California heading and then click the Demote button. (If any words under California move right along with it, you probably didn't begin entering your text while in Outline view. In that case, see the Note below.) Repeat this step for the Mexico and Bahamas headings.

6. Because San Diego and San Francisco are categories under California, they should be a third level in your outline. Select San Diego and San Francisco and click the Demote button twice to indent them one step further than California. Repeat this step for the San Francisco, Cancun, Mexico City, Nassau, and Freeport headings.

At this point, the structure of the sample outline is apparent. If you have been following the directions, your outline should resemble the example shown in Figure 5-23.

If you enter the text while in Normal view, or decide to make an outline after beginning the document in Normal view, headings act differently when demoted or later promoted. All text may begin as Normal, so you need to begin by promoting the level-one headings once to the left. Next you need to demote the level-two headings (California, Mexico, and Bahamas) once. (Look in the Style pop-up box on the Formatting toolbar to see the level of your heading.) As you demote the level-two headings, notice that anything under it, up to the next level-one heading, moves along with it. As you move a line, rather than that line moving alone, all lines under a line move with it. Lines following the current line are assumed to be part of the current heading, so they are indented below the current heading. Continue to demote or promote your headings until they look like the ones in Figures 5-23, 5-24, and 5-25.

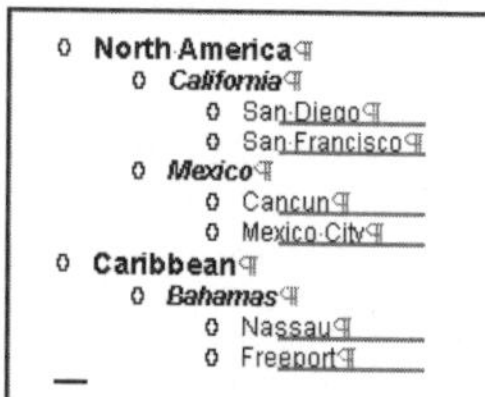

Figure 5-23: The structure of the sample outline

Now you can begin adding body text to the various parts of the outline. Keep in mind that Word's flexibility means you do not necessarily have to create your outlines in this same manner. This example follows the common technique of creating outline headings first and then filling in the details; however, you can create headings and body text as you go along. To add some body text to the sample outline, perform the following steps:

1. Move the cursor to the end of the San Diego line. Press Return to begin a new line. Note that the icon aligns with the existing level directly above it; hence, the new line is initially a heading. Before you begin typing, convert this new line to body text.
2. Click the Demote to Body Text button on the Outlining toolbar, and type the following text:

   Great meeting facilities, accommodations, and restaurants all centrally located in downtown area.
3. Move the cursor to the end of the San Francisco line. Press Return to begin a new line, and click the Demote to Body Text button on the Outlining toolbar. Then type the following text:

   Proximity to company offices will reduce transportation costs. Fisherman's Wharf area offers excellent dining and attractions.
4. Move the cursor to the end of the Cancun line. Press Return to begin a new line, and click the Demote to Body Text button on the Outlining toolbar. Then type the following text:

   Convention center and hotels located on the beach. Cancun offers first-rate water sports all year.
5. Move the cursor to the end of the Mexico City line. Press Return to begin a new line, and click the Demote to Body Text button on the Outlining toolbar. Then type the following text:

   Business hotels near Chapultepec Park provide meeting accommodations and computer fax lines.
6. Move the cursor to the end of the Nassau line. Press Return to begin a new line, and click the Demote to Body Text button on the Outlining toolbar. Then type the following text:

   Great hotels with meeting facilities located on the beach in Cable Beach area.
7. Move the cursor to the end of the Freeport line. Press Return to begin a new line, and click the Demote to Body Text button on the Outlining toolbar. Then type the following text:

   Shopping, excellent golfing, and water sports readily available.

At this point, your outline should resemble the one shown in Figure 5-24.

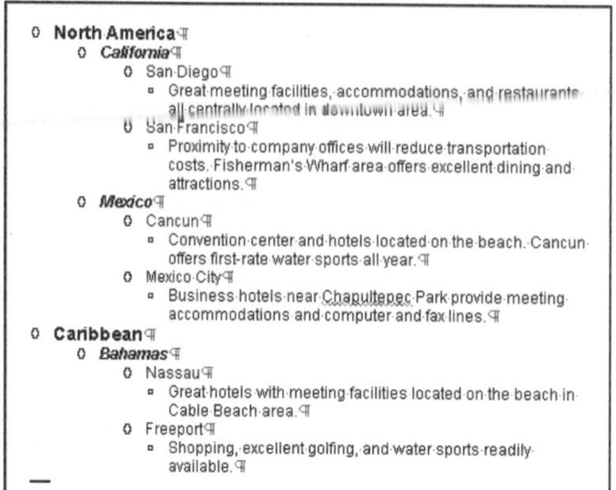

Figure 5-24: Adding body text to the sample outline

Collapsing and expanding the sample outline

As we mentioned earlier, it's often helpful to collapse an outline so you can see the major points without being distracted by the less important points or by the body text. The easiest way to collapse an entire outline is by using the numbered Show buttons on the Outlining toolbar or their keyboard equivalents.

To experiment with collapsing your own outline, open it. (Sample Outline #1, if you followed along.) Click the 1 button on the Outlining toolbar to show only level-one headings in your outline. Only the North America and Caribbean lines should be visible. To expose the next level of headings, click the 2 button. Now you should also be able to see the California, Mexico, and Bahamas lines. When you click the 3 button, the level-three headings (the names of the cities) become visible beneath the level-two headings. Finally, click the All button. The body text becomes visible along with all headings of the outline.

Of course, you can also individually expand or collapse headings using the Expand and Collapse buttons on the Outlining toolbar or by double-clicking any heading's symbol. To see how these buttons work, place the cursor anywhere in the Mexico heading and click the Collapse button. Notice that the Cancun and Mexico City headings collapse underneath and hide the body text. If you click the Expand button, the subheadings expand to reveal the body text underneath. To see how double-clicking works, move your cursor directly over the heading's symbol, causing your cursor to become two crossed, double-headed arrows, and then just double-click. If your heading is expanded, it will collapse.

Changing headings in the sample outline

You can use the Promote and Demote buttons on the Outlining toolbar to promote and demote headings, or you can simply drag any outline part into a new position. Remember that body text for a heading is promoted or demoted along with the heading, but subheadings are not. To see how this concept works using the toolbar's buttons, click in the line of the San Francisco heading and click Promote. Notice that the San Francisco heading is promoted to the same level as the California and Mexico headings. Notice, too, that the text immediately below the San Francisco heading moved along with the heading. With the cursor still in the same line, click the Demote button to demote the heading and subtext back to its original level. Then go one level further to see the effect.

To try dragging, move your cursor directly over the heading's symbol, causing your cursor to become two crossed, double-headed arrows. Click and begin to drag your cursor left or right. A gray horizontal line appears to help you see how far in or out you are moving the heading. The cursor also changes to indicate the direction in which you are dragging. Stop anywhere you want. How far you go determines the level your dragged header will take on. Dragging has the same effect as using the buttons.

Use the Move Up and Move Down buttons (or their keyboard equivalents) to move headings up or down within an outline. Remember: If any subtext is collapsed, subtext moves with the heading. If subtext is not collapsed, it moves with the heading only if you have selected it with the heading. To demonstrate this concept, click All to give yourself a fresh start and be sure all text is revealed. Then place the cursor in the Mexico City heading and click the Move Up button (Option-Shift-up arrow). The Mexico City heading moves up in the outline. The body text associated with the heading remains in its original location, however. While Mexico City is still the selected paragraph, click the Move Down button (Option-Shift-down arrow) to restore the heading to its proper location.

Next, select the Mexico City heading and the subtext underneath the heading. Click the Move Up button twice. This step moves the heading and its subtext above the Cancun heading and its subtext, as shown in Figure 5-25.

In most cases you'll want the body text to move with the headings. To make this move easier, first collapse the outline to the level of the heading to be moved (use the numbered Show buttons or their keyboard equivalents). After you have collapsed the outline, you can move headings without worrying about selecting the subtext, because the subtext automatically follows the headings. (If you are using the dragging method to move your text, you don't have to collapse the headings because contents below the heading also move with it.)

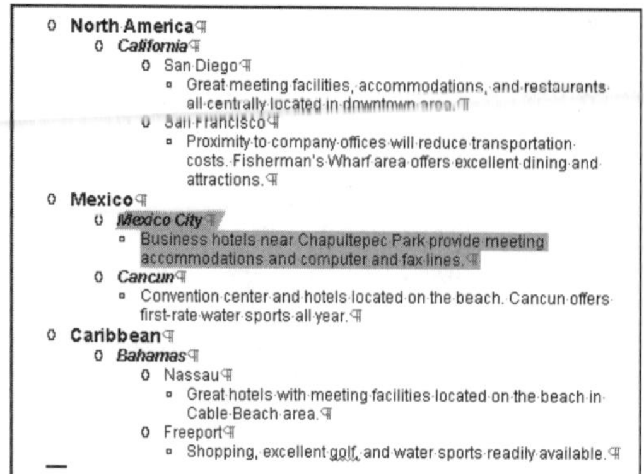

Figure 5-25: Moving the Mexico City heading and subtext

It is also possible to promote body text to headline stature at any time.

Creating Tables of Contents from Outlines

One powerful feature that Word provides is the capability to generate a table of contents quickly based on the headings within an outline. Use the Insert ➪ Index and Tables command to insert a table of contents at the location of the insertion point.

After your document exists in outline form, perform the following steps to create a table of contents:

1. Place the insertion point where you want to insert the table of contents.
2. Choose Insert ➪ Index and Tables to open the Index and Tables dialog box.
3. Click the Table of Contents tab, and then choose the type of format you want for the table of contents from the Formats list box. The Preview box gives you an idea of how the format will look before you apply the style. Of course, Word provides a lot of customization options. For more on Table of Contents options, see "Building Tables of Contents" in Chapter 7.
4. Click OK. Word inserts a table of contents at the insertion point.

It doesn't matter whether you are in Outline view when inserting a table of contents in this manner. All that matters is that your document contains headings. Because it is common to place a table of contents on a separate page from the main content, however, you probably want to switch to Normal view first. This way you can add a page break above your document's main content, and then position the cursor in the new blank page. (You probably want to put a page break above the table of contents, too.)

Adding a table of contents

You can see how easy it is to create a table of contents by trying it with the sample outline you created earlier. Perform the following steps to add a table of contents to the sample outline or to any existing outline:

1. Choose View➪Normal to turn off the Outline view. (In Normal or Page Layout you can add a page break to put the table of contents on the first page. You cannot add page breaks while in Outline view.)
2. Scroll to the top of your document (or press ⌘-Home). Press Return once to add a new line, and then press Shift-Enter (not Return) to insert a page break. (In case you don't recall this shortcut, you can use Insert➪Break.) Place your cursor back to the start of the document again. (It appears on the page break's line.) Add the table of contents on what is now Page 1 of the document, with the remainder of the document appearing on Page 2.
3. Choose Insert➪Index and Tables, and click the Table of Contents tab.
4. Leave the default options set as they are for now, or select a style from the Formats list.
5. Click OK to have Word create your table of contents.

Because the entire outline is on Page 2, all topics of the outline are shown in the table of contents as being on Page 2. If your sample document was longer, Word would assign the proper page numbers automatically.

Updating a table of contents

Tables of contents are not updated automatically. If changing your document's content changes page numbers, you must tell it to update. To do so, select the table of contents, issue the Update Fields command, and tell Word to update the TOC. The table of contents is based on fields, so this is an Update Fields command. For more information on fields, see Chapter 6. Word can do a lot more when it comes to tables of contents and indexes. See Chapter 7 for additional details on these subjects.

To update a table of contents follow these steps:

1. Move your cursor the left of the document so the cursor turns into an up and right-pointing arrow, like the one that normally selects a line. Point the arrow cursor toward the first line of the table of contents, and then click to select the entire TOC.
2. Press F9 or ⌘-Option-Shift. This brings up the Update Table of Contents dialog box.
3. Select from your two options: Update page numbers only or Update entire table. Then click OK.

Printing Outlines

Although you print outlines the same way you print any other document, keep in mind that what you get varies, depending on what view you are using when you print. Just as the document looks different onscreen in the various views, the document also prints differently in the different views. If you are in Outline view, the document prints much like it appears onscreen in Outline view. The only items that don't appear on the printed copy are the outline icons. Word uses whatever tabs are in effect for the document to indent the headings and body text.

If you are not in Outline view, Word prints the document somewhat differently. Heading styles are still printed, but all text is printed at the left margin, without any indentation. In short, it prints as it looks onscreen.

Summary

This chapter covered topics related to tables and outlines. Specifically, you learned the following:

- Creating tables using Word's Table feature
- Editing the contents of a table and how to delete, insert, and merge cells
- Using the tools needed to add borders, control table alignment, and sort table contents
- Converting text to a table
- Using the Outlining toolbar
- Promoting, demoting, and moving headings in an outline
- Creating a table of contents from your outline

Where to go next

- In the next chapter, you learn how to work with fields and form letters in Word.
- Tables are a routine part of documents that demand a desktop-published appearance. For more tips and techniques on performing desktop publishing tasks, see Chapter 10.
- If you regularly use outlining in complex documents, keep in mind that you can quickly create tables of contents based on your outline. For details on using an outline to create a table of contents, see Chapter 7.

✦ ✦ ✦

Working with Fields

✦ ✦ ✦ ✦

In This Chapter

Defining fields

Using fields

Creating a mail merge

Printing envelopes and mailing labels

Creating data documents with other software

✦ ✦ ✦ ✦

This chapter covers topics related to working with fields—or special codes—that can be inserted in documents to perform various tasks. In this chapter you learn some of the common uses for fields when working in Word and how to create form letters.

Defining Fields

In Word, a *field* is a special set of instructions that tells Word to insert certain information at a given location in a document. The basic difference between fields and normal text is that with fields, the computer provides the information for you. Using fields does more than just save you the effort of typing the information, however. Fields are dynamic; they can change as circumstances change. You already may have used fields at various times in your work with Word. For example, when you insert the current date or page numbers in a document, you are inserting a certain kind of field.

Think of fields as special codes that you include in documents. The codes tell Word to insert information at the location where the code appears. The codes can automatically update the text of your document, or you can tell Word to update the information produced by the fields only when you specify. Typically, you use fields to add text or graphics to a document, to update information that changes on a regular basis, and to perform calculations.

Word has dozens of types of fields. Some, like page numbers and the current date, are simple to understand and use. Others are more complex and are beyond the scope of this book. But all fields can be inserted into a document and updated using the same procedures, and this chapter details those procedures.

You can effectively work with fields after you learn four skills: how to insert fields in a document, how to update fields so they show the most current results, how to view fields, and how to move between fields.

Using Fields

A field consists of three parts: field characters, a field type, and instructions. It is not necessary to know about these components because they are compiled for you when you use the Insert➪Field command or place a field using Insert Date. However, in case you are curious, here's an explanation. Consider the following example date field:

```
{Date\@M/d/yy}
```

The field characters are the curly braces that enclose the field. The curly braces indicate the presence of a field in Word to the user. Inside the curly braces you find the special code or instruction that tells Word what is to appear in this area. Although curly braces are used to indicate the presence of a field, you cannot insert a field in a document by typing curly braces. If you are manually entering your field, you must use the key combination (⌘-F9) specifically designed to insert fields. (If you use Insert➪Field to choose a field function, the brackets are automatically placed, along with all the field coding.)

The field type is the first word that appears after the left field character. In the preceding example, the word *date* is the field type; this particular field type tells Word to insert the current date—based on your computer's clock—into the document.

The instructions follow the field type. Instructions are optional, depending on the field type, but most field types have instructions. The instructions tell Word exactly how the information specified by the field type will be displayed. In this example, `\@M/d/yy` is an instruction that tells Word to display the current date in the American numeric format with the month, day, and year separated by slashes. The instruction `\* MERGEFORMAT` tells the field to retain its formatting during updates. The contents of the instructions may appear somewhat cryptic, but you need not be concerned with what they mean because Word inserts the proper instructions for you automatically.

Inserting fields

Many commands in Word insert fields indirectly. When you insert page numbers or a table of contents, for example, you are inserting fields to produce the page numbers or the table of contents. But when you specifically want to insert fields into a document, you use Insert➪Field. Follow these steps to use the Field command to insert a field into your document:

1. After placing the insertion point where you want to insert the field, choose Insert⇨Field. The Field dialog box appears, as shown in Figure 6-1.

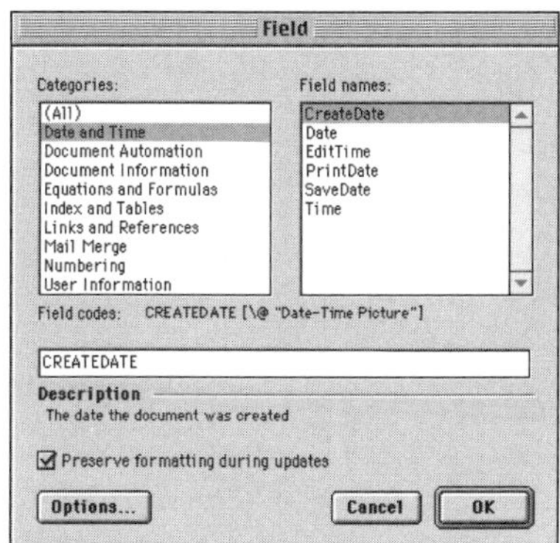

Figure 6-1: The Field dialog box

2. From the Categories list box, select the field category you want to insert. The All category enables you to see all the fields in alphabetical order in the Field names list box.

3. From the Field names list box, select the field you want to insert. The Field codes text box at the bottom of the dialog box displays the field you have selected. (You can also use this text box to enter the name of the desired field; however, it's generally easier to pick the field by name from the Field names list box.)

4. Click the Options button if you want to add switches to the field. (*Switches* are options that change the characteristics of a field's results, such as the way a date appears, displaying characters as uppercase, or converting numbers to Roman numerals.) The Field Options dialog box is shown in Figure 6-2. To add switches or formatting, select the desired formatting from the list, and then click the Add to Field button. If you change your mind and decide to remove the formatting or switches, click the Undo Add button.

   In the Field dialog box, check the Preserve formatting during updates option so any formatting you apply to the resulting text won't be lost during updates.

5. Click OK to insert the field into the document.

Hot Stuff

Word also provides an Insert Field shortcut key combination (⌘-F9). This shortcut inserts the field characters (curly braces) into the document, which enables you to type the field name and instructions manually. This method for entering fields is typically used by programmers who are familiar with the Visual Basic programming language built into Word. Unless you are familiar with field types and their instructions, you will probably find it much easier to add fields using Insert⇨Field and letting Word build your fields for you.

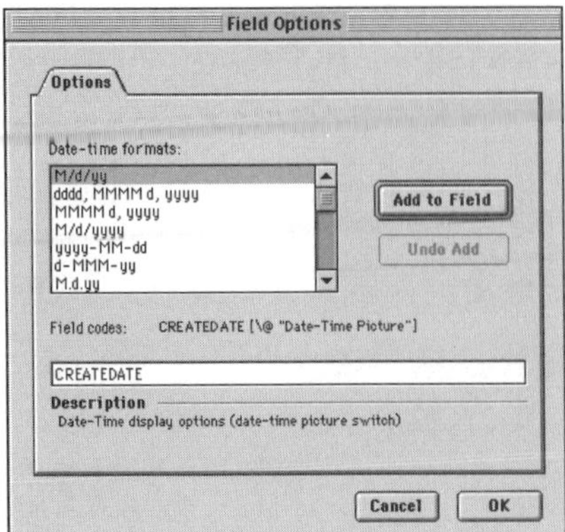

Figure 6-2: The Field Options dialog box

More About Switches

Switches are not an easy topic to tackle, and there is probably no reason for you to do so. However, in case you are interested:

✦ Switches determine the data to be inserted into your field, the order, and even what the data look like. There are two kinds of field switches. Field-specific switches set certain options for a given field, such as \l for the hyperlink field, and other switches affect formatting. The switches you are most likely to deal with are the ones that affect formatting. These formatting switches serve to enforce the formatting during field updates.

✦ You can tell Word what to put in a switch. Use the Options button from within the Field dialog box when you first insert your field. While you are in the Insert⇨Field dialog box, choose your category as normal, and then choose the specific field from the Field names list. Then click the Options button. The General Switches tab appears, in which is a list of options specific to the category you've chosen. These options are mostly formatting options. Select the format you want and click the Add to Field button. The other tab, Field Specific Switches, offers more options. In each tab, a description appears, telling you about the switch you are considering. When you click OK, the field comes into your document in the form you've selected.

✦ After your field appears in your document, you can manually type another switch to tell Word how to format the results of the field. This procedure is covered in the "Formatting fields" section.

Viewing field codes

By default, when you insert a field, you see the results of that field. For example, when you insert a date field, you see the current date. When you are editing documents, however, you may find it useful to see the actual contents of the fields rather than the results. Here's how to see one field's contents, instead of its results:

1. Place the cursor in the field and Control-click to display a shortcut menu.
2. Choose Toggle Field Codes to turn on the codes for the field. Perform the same steps if you want to turn off the codes again.

If you prefer the keyboard, you can place the insertion pointer anywhere in the desired field and press Shift-F9 to toggle between showing the codes and showing the results.

If you want to see the codes for all fields, choose Tools ➪ Preferences, click the View tab, check Field Codes, and click OK. With this option turned on, the default for all fields inserted with the Insert ➪ Field command is to see the code immediately, rather than the results.

If you are working with a large document that contains a number of fields, you may find it helpful to split the document into two panes. You can then scroll so the same text shows in both panes, and you can turn on Field Codes in one pane while viewing the resulting text in the other. Place your cursor in one pane, and then click Option-F9. If you prefer, you can go to the View tab of Tools ➪ Preferences and check the Field Codes check box, but this may affect both panes identically unless you select all the text (⌘-A) in one pane first. (Note that although Control-clicking while in a field also reveals a Toggle Field command, this command has a different effect than the one suggested in this paragraph. This command affects both panels, toggling each panel from whatever state each was in.)

Updating fields

You can update fields by selecting the text containing the field, Control-clicking the text, and choosing Update Field from the shortcut menu that appears. Some fields, such as those used in page numbering, are automatically updated whenever you print or repaginate a document. Other fields, such as in tables of contents, are not updated until you tell Word to update the fields.

To update fields in the entire document, select the entire document (⌘-A) and Control-click anywhere in the document. Choose Update Field from the shortcut menu that appears.

It is important to realize that when you update a field, it can lose any formatting you apply. To help prevent this, check the Preserve formatting during updates option when you insert your fields via the Field dialog box.

Moving between fields

To move to the next field, just click the field you want to move to. If you prefer keyboard commands, use F11 to move to the next field and Shift-F11 to move to a previous field.

Formatting fields

You have two ways to format fields. You can either insert the field and then apply font and paragraph formatting, or set the code of the field to format the field results automatically. The latter method is called adding switches to the field codes.

To format the field if the code is showing, first Control-click the field and choose Toggle Field Codes to display the results. That way you can see your formatting more clearly. Then Control-click the field and choose the desired formatting option from the shortcut menu. (Choose Font to format the fonts used, or choose Paragraph to apply paragraph formatting.)

If you're brave, to format the field by manually typing switches, display the code for the field and then manually type the command into the code. Your switch options change certain characteristics of the field results, such as displaying characters as uppercase or converting numbers to Roman numerals. For example, a simple DATE field looks like this:

```
{DATE}
```

However, a field with the DATE code and a switch that tells Word how to display the date looks like this:

```
{DATE\@d-M-yy }
```

Table 6-1 lists some of the general switches and their functions.

Table 6-1
Commonly Used Switches and Their Functions

Switch	*Function*
* caps	Capitalizes the initial letter of each word in the result.
* firstcap	Capitalizes the initial letter of the first word in the result.
* lower	Makes all letters in the result appear as lowercase.
* upper	Makes all letters in the result appear as uppercase.
* arabic	Converts a number to Arabic (standard) format, overriding any default set elsewhere in Windows.

Switch	Function
* dollartext	Spells out a number with two decimal places as words with initial capital letters, the word *and*, and the numbers that follow the decimal places (suitable for producing checks with currency amounts spelled out).
* roman	Converts a number to lowercase Roman numerals.
* Roman	Converts a number to uppercase Roman numerals.
\@ dddd,MMMM,d,yyyy	Displays a date as spelled out, such as Wednesday, May 24, 1995.
* mergeformat	Preserves manual formatting in the fields, such as character and paragraph formatting in text, and scaling and cropping dimensions in graphics.
* charformat	Applies the formatting on the first character of the field name to the entire field result.

Locking a field's contents

At times, you may want to prevent the results of a field from being updated. You can lock a field to prevent it from being updated until you unlock it. To lock a field, place the cursor anywhere in the desired field and press ⌘-3 or ⌘-F11. To unlock the field, place the cursor anywhere in the field and press ⌘-4 or Shift-⌘-F11.

Using fields in an example

To see how fields can be used within a document, open a new document in the usual manner and perform the following steps:

1. Choose Insert ➪ Field to display the Field dialog box. In the Categories list, select Date and Time. Then click Date in the Field Names list and click OK. The current date, as measured by your Mac's clock, appears at the insertion point. (If you see the actual field type and instructions for the field instead of the current date, choose Tools ➪ Preferences, click the View tab, turn off the Field Codes option, and then click OK.)
2. Press Return twice and type the following words:

   This document was written by

   Add a space after *by*, and then select Insert ➪ Field. In the Categories list of the Field dialog box, choose Document Information. In the Field names list box, choose Author and then click OK to insert the author's name into the document.

   Word automatically fills in the name that was entered when Word was first installed and launched. This name can be changed in the User Info tab of Word's Preferences (found under the Tools menu).

3. Add a period after the author's name, and then start a new sentence by typing the following:

   The document contains

   Add a space after *contains*, and then choose Insert ⇨ Field. In the Categories list box, choose Document Information. In the Field names list box, scroll and choose NumWords (an abbreviation for *number of words*), and then click OK.

4. Add a space after the number that was just inserted, and finish the sentence by typing the following text:

   words, and the time of day is now

5. Add a space after *now* and choose Insert ⇨ Field. In the Insert Categories list, choose Date and Time. In the Field names list box, choose Time and click OK to place the field.

6. Add a period after the time that was just inserted.

At this point, your document should resemble the one shown in Figure 6-3. Of course, the date and time will be different, the word count may differ, and you may have a different font in use. If you have interactive grammar-checking, you will probably have a green squiggly line beneath the first sentence. This line indicates that Word has a suggestion for better wording of the sentence. If so, you can resolve that issue when you do your spelling and grammar check.

Notice that the word count is accurate only to the point that *11* was inserted. It has not updated to include words after *11*. To update the word count without closing the document, click anywhere on the word count field (the number 11, in this example) to select it, and then Control-click and select the Update Field command. Doing so changes the number in this example to 22.

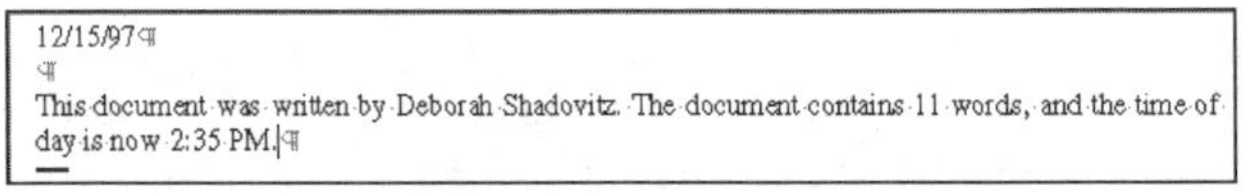

12/15/97¶
¶
This document was written by Deborah Shadovitz. The document contains 11 words, and the time of day is now 2:35 PM.¶

Figure 6-3: The sample document containing fields

Printing Field Codes

When you print a document containing fields, Word prints the results of the fields by default and does not print the actual field codes themselves. At times, you may want to print the field codes themselves so you can get a concrete idea of what codes are actually in your documents.

The printing of field codes is a preference set in the Print tab of the Tools ⇨ Preferences menu. If you are already in the Print dialog box, you can set Word to print the field codes by selecting Microsoft Word from the pop-up menu in the Print dialog box, and then clicking the Word Options button and checking Field Codes.

Creating a Mail Merge

One way to take advantage of fields in your documents is to use them in mail merges to create personalized form letters. You can also create mailing labels and put together legal documents, data sheets, catalogs, and other documents of this kind. Mail merges let you print multiple copies of a document, where certain information (such as a name or address) changes for each document. The form letters you receive from businesses are examples of mail merges at work.

Mail merges combine two kinds of documents: a *main document*, which contains identical text for each printed copy, and a *data source*, which contains the text specific to each copy printed. The main document also contains fields that tell Word where to find the information stored in the data source. These fields are referred to as *merge fields*. As you type the main document, you can insert the fields at any desired location.

In the data source, you type the information Word needs to fill in the fields inserted in the main document. For example, if your main document contains a name field and an address field, your data document should have names and addresses of all the people who should receive the letter. Just like a table in which the first row typically contains labels describing what information follows, the first line of a data document normally contains a *header record*, a single line that identifies the order in which you place the data in the data document. When you use a table as your data source, the first row becomes your header. When you use a database as your data source, field names become your header.

If you aren't dealing with a ton of names, you can create a data source by typing the desired information into a Word document. This is best done by setting up a table. (You can actually use any word processing document and separate each piece of merge data by a tab or a comma, with a return at the end of each contact; however, that's more confusing to read and takes more time to set up from scratch.) If you are managing a lot of names or contacts, you will find it easier in the long run to use a database (such as FileMaker Pro, ACI US 4th Dimension, or Provue Panorama) or Word's Address Book or Outlook Express's contact list. You can also store and manage your information in database form within spreadsheet programs. In the section "Creating a data source," you'll learn how to create a data source by using data stored in a spreadsheet or in a database.

How to finish your mail merge

After the data source and main document both exist, you can print multiple copies of the main document, based on the data contained in the data source. When you print the file, Word reads the first record in the data source, inserts the fields of that record into the main document, and sends the information to your printer to print a copy. It repeats this process for as many records as are contained in the data source. If a data source has five entries that contain the name and address for five individuals, a mail merge operation would print five copies of the document, each addressed to a different individual.

Specifying a main document

The first step in the process of creating a form letter is to choose your main document. This may be a new blank document, or it may be an existing one, such as letterhead, complete with text and graphics. To choose the main document, perform the following steps:

1. For this exercise, open a new document. Then choose Tools ➪ Mail Merge to activate the Mail Merge Helper dialog box shown in Figure 6-4. (The option will be grayed out if you don't have a document open.)
2. Select Form Letters from the pop-up Create menu. Word then asks whether you want to use the active document or create a new document as your main document. Click the Active Window button to use the active document.

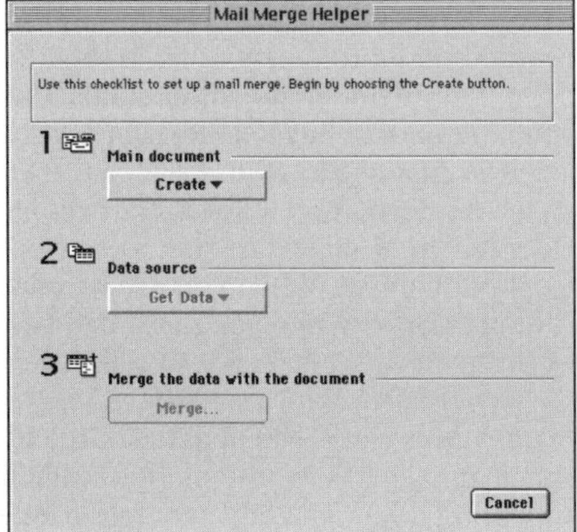

Figure 6-4: The Mail Merge Helper dialog box

Creating a data source

Now that you have created your main document (the document that will be your actual form letter), you need to designate the source from which you will get the data to use in the form letter's fields. In this case, you will create one from scratch.

Follow these steps to create a data source:

1. After designating the main document, choose Tools ➪ Mail Merge to activate the Mail Merge Helper dialog box.
2. Now select Create Data Source from the Get Data pop-up menu. This activates the Create Data Source dialog box shown in Figure 6-5. This dialog box aids you in the creation of the fields you are going to use in your form letter. The Field names in header row box lists commonly used fields for form letters.

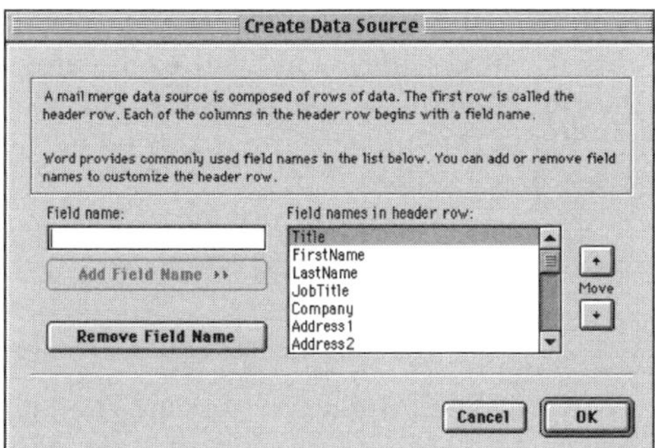

Figure 6-5: The Create Data Source dialog box

3. In the Field names in header row box is a list of all the fields Word includes by default. One by one, highlight the names of the fields you do *not* need, and then click the Remove Field Name button. If you have a field you want to use that is not included in the list, type the name in the Field name entry and click the Add Field Name button, which activates after you enter a name. When the Field names in header row list contains all the fields from which you want to merge data, click OK. The Save As dialog box opens. Enter a name for your data source (note the location where you're saving it) and save it.
4. Word then displays a message telling you that your data source has no data. Click the Edit Data Source button to open a data source into which you can enter information for your mail merge. If you have no information for one of the fields, press Return (or Enter) to skip it. Don't enter any spaces in the boxes. (They will print and drive you crazy.) To record the completed information and add a new record, click the Add New button. Repeat this procedure until you have entered all the information needed in your data source.
5. Now that you have created your data source, return to your main document by clicking OK.
6. If you later decide that you want to add information to your data source, click the Edit data source button on the Mail Merge toolbar that has appeared. You go directly to the Data Form you used to enter information in your data source. You can click the Add New button to add a new record. Alternatively, you can click the Mail Merge Helper button on the Mail Merge toolbar, or select Tools ⇨ Mail Merge again to bring up the Mail Merge Helper. Then click the Edit button under Data source and choose the data source you created.

Adding merge fields to the main document

After you finish creating a data document or opening the one you want to use, you can finish the main document.

First, you can add any text or graphics you want to complete your document. Then you add the fields by inserting a merge field where you want each category of information to appear in printed form. You can format the information any way you want using the Formatting toolbar. When the information is placed in the main document, it takes on the formatting you applied.

To add merge fields to your main document, follow these steps:

1. Enter the graphics and text that you want in each version of the form letter.
2. Place your cursor where you want the first field to appear. Then click the Insert Merge Field button on the Mail Merge toolbar and choose the appropriate merge field. Be sure to add any spaces and punctuation that you want to include between merge fields. You can move your cursor freely and perform any other document creation as you add the merge fields.(You must use the Insert Merge Field command because a merge field cannot be typed directly into a document.)
3. Save the main document to complete your work.

Merging data

Now it's time to merge the data with the main document. Before continuing, be sure you have done the following:

✦ Entered all the information into the data document

✦ Inserted all the merge fields into the main document

You can use the Mail Merge toolbar to see the form letter onscreen, enabling you to make sure the records contain everything you want to have in the form letter. Click the View Merged Data button (which has an ABC with a bracket above it) on the Mail Merge toolbar to see the result of merging the first record. You can scan more records using the forward and reverse arrows—First record, Previous record, Next record, and Last record. The record number you are viewing appears in the box between them. You can also enter any record number in the box and press Return or Enter to go directly to that record. You can also print a test document.

As you perform your inspection, you can make any changes to your document. When you have completed your inspection, you can print each letter using the Print command from the File menu.

Follow these steps to merge the data document with the main document:

1. Make sure the main document is active, and then click the View Merged Data button on the Mail Merge toolbar. The information from the first data record appears in the main document. Click the Next Record button on the Mail Merge toolbar to see the information inserted from the next records. To see the printed result of one sample page, tell Word to print (File⇨Print or ⌘-P) as normal. Only the record you are viewing prints.

2. Merge the data document into the main document by doing one of the following:
   - To print the form letters, click the Merge to Printer button. Then select any print options and print as normal.
   - You also have the option of creating a new single document that contains one copy of each document, complete with the merged data. This may be desirable as a historic record of your mailing. You can also use this document to reprint the same document at a later date. To create this historic merged document, click the Merge to New Document button on the Mail Merge toolbar.

Printing Envelopes and Mailing Labels

You can also print mailing labels and envelopes using the Mail Merge command. You can either create a new data document or use an existing one. This feature can prove invaluable: it prevents you from having to address many envelopes by hand.

Printing envelopes

The steps for printing envelopes and mailing labels are similar to the steps used to create a form letter. Follow these steps for printing envelopes:

1. First you need to set up the main document; in this case, the one representing the face of the envelope. Note that Word uses the information from the currently selected printer. If you want to print on a different printer, go to the Chooser or select a new default Desktop Printer before continuing.
2. Choose Tools ⇨ Mail Merge and select Envelopes from the Main Document pop-up menu.
3. Click the Active Window button in the next dialog box. It doesn't matter how the new document you started with was formatted—Word will adjust it.
4. For the Data Source, you'll likely want to get existing data if you already printed letters. To do so, Choose Open Data Source from the Get Data pop-up menu, find your way to your data source, and then click OK. (If your document doesn't show in the Open window, select All from the pop-up menu under List Files of Type.) Then click the Set Up Main Document button.

   Your other option is to choose Create Data Source from the Get Data menu. Cull the Field names in header row list box down to only the fields you want merged, and then click OK. Next, name and save the file, and then enter the data and click OK. Then click the Set Up Main Document button
5. The Envelope Options dialog box appears (see Figure 6-6). In the Envelope Options tab, select an envelope size (10 is standard business size). Click the Font button under Delivery address or under Return address to format the appearance of each address. You can also adjust the position of the addresses

by clicking the arrows to change their margins. Watch the Preview window for feedback.

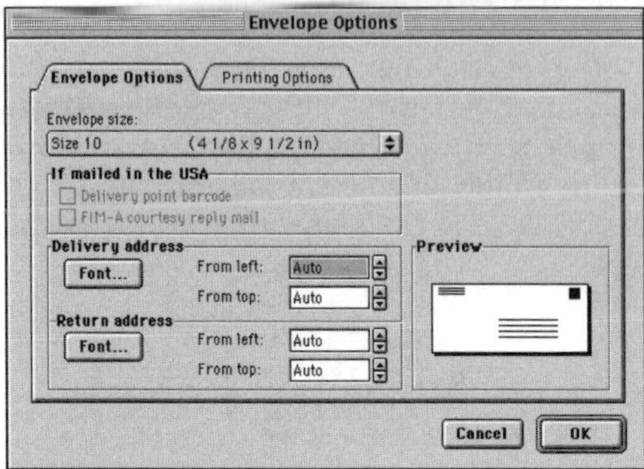

Figure 6-6: The Envelope Options tab of the Envelope Options dialog box

Now select the Printing Options tab (see Figure 6-7) to tell Word how your printer needs the envelope fed. Begin by selecting either Face up or Face down. If the diagrams (which are buttons) don't match, check or uncheck Clockwise rotation. Click the button/diagram that fits your envelope feed. Click OK when you're finished.

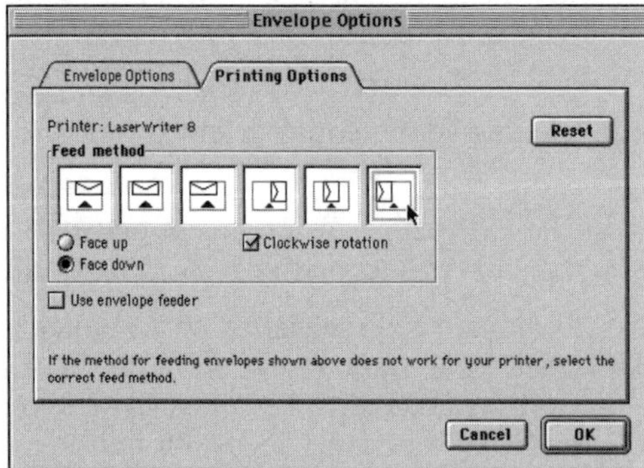

Figure 6-7: The Printing Options tab of the Envelope Options dialog box

6. Click OK to close the dialog box. The Envelope Address dialog box appears (see Figure 6-8).

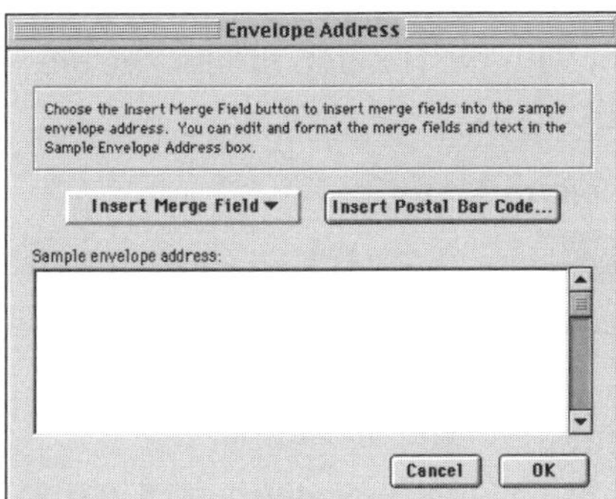

Figure 6-8: The Envelope Address dialog box

7. Position the insertion point in the Sample envelope address box, and insert the appropriate merge fields by selecting each, in turn, from the Insert Merge Field pop-up menu. Enter the appropriate punctuation between fields, and press Return to create each new line. You can even add a postal bar code to identify the delivery address. Click the Insert Postal Bar Code button, and then select the fields that contain the zip code and delivery address.
8. Click OK to close the Envelope Address dialog box and return to the Mail Merge Helper dialog box.
9. Under Main Document area, select the envelope document from the list of envelope documents in the Edit pop-up menu.
10. The envelope is now displayed in Page Layout view. Click the View Merged Data button on the Mail Merge toolbar to verify that data is in the correct place. Make any changes as needed. Finally, click the Merge to Printer button and print as normal.

Note

You can skip the preview in Step 10: While in the Mail Merge Helper dialog box at the end of Step 8, click the Merge button. In the Merge dialog box, select Printer from the Merge to pop-up menu. Leave the All radio button set under Records to be merged, or designate a range to print. Click Merge when ready to print. Again, you'll see the Mac's Print dialog box, in which you can make any final changes. From there, print as normal.

After your perform all the steps, your printer should turn out one envelope after another.

Printing mailing labels

You can also use Word to print mailing labels. If you have used the Merge command in earlier versions of Word, you can reuse your main document. If this is the first time you are printing labels, or you want to change the size of the labels, select Tools ➪ Mail Merge and set up a new main document. A document is automatically set up for most Avery brand labels. If you need to use another brand, specify an

Avery label of the same size or specify a custom label. Remember to choose your destination printer (in the Chooser or with the Desktop Printer) before you begin so Word can set up the margins correctly.

To print mailing labels, perform the following steps:

1. Start a new document, and then choose Tools ➪ Mail Merge. In the Mail Merge Helper dialog box that opens, select Create and choose Mailing Labels from the pop-up menu.
2. In the next dialog box, click the Active Window button.
3. Back in the Mail Merge Helper dialog box, move down to the Data Source area and click the Get Data pop-up menu. In this step you have four options:
   - **Create Data Source** enables you to create your own data document, as explained previously in the "Creating a Mail Merge" section. In the Create Data Source dialog box, name and save the new data document. When the next message is displayed, click the Edit Data Source button to bring up the Data Form dialog box. Enter the address information. Click OK and then click the Mail Merge Helper button on the Mail Merge toolbar. Then click the Setup button under Main Document.
   - **Open Data Source** enables you to locate, select, and open an existing data file via the Open dialog box. After doing so, click the Set Up Main Document button in the next message box displayed.
   - **Use Address Book** enables you to use an existing address book you created in Word. Choose which address book you want to use. Word tells you it needs to set up the main document, and then it takes you there.
   - **Header Options** is for those who use several data sources. Word's built-in help explains the header options under the heading "About using a header source for a mail merge." In the Header Options dialog box, click the Create button to create a header. You can also use a current data source as a header by clicking the Open button and choosing the file you want to use. If you're managing a lot of data, chances are you're using a database. Because your database export can include a header, it's just as well to use that method instead.
4. Each of the four options brings you to the Main Document in Layout view to continue the document's setup, and calls up the Label Options dialog box. Change your printer type from Laser and ink jet to Dot matrix if necessary. In the Label products pop-up menu, select a label type. In the Product number list box, select the product number for the labels you are printing to. (Most label packages have such a designated number code.) The Details button shows you the exact specifications of the label you've selected. You can make alterations to your label layout, seeing the effect as you make the change, and then give it a custom name. The New Label button lets you set up your own custom label size.

5. The Sample Label text box, shown in Figure 6-9, comes up next. Enter the merge fields here by placing the cursor within the text box and selecting your desired field from the Insert Merge Field pop-up menu. Be sure to enter any spaces or punctuation that you want between the fields. Press Return at the end of each line.

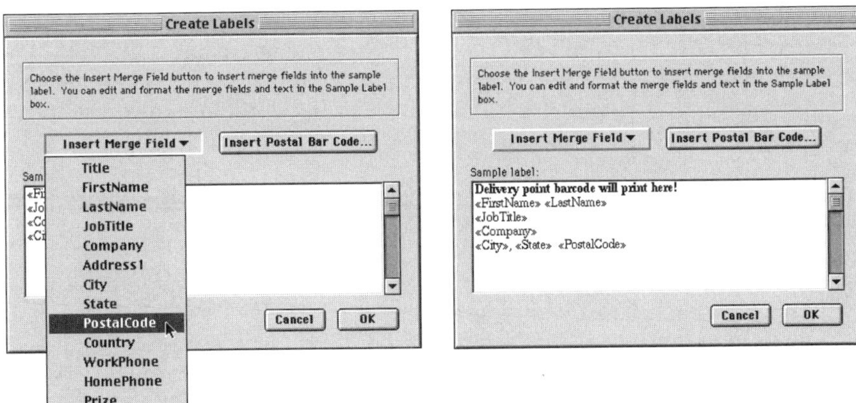

Figure 6-9: At left, the Create Labels dialog box as fields are being added to the merge. At right, a completed Create Labels dialog box.

6. You can easily insert a postal barcode. Just click the Insert Postal Bar Code button, select the fields that contain the zip code and delivery address, and then click OK.
7. Click OK to close the Create Labels dialog box after you have inserted the merge fields. This returns you to the Mail Merge Helper dialog box.
8. Be sure the printer is ready to print, and then click the Merge button. In the resulting Merge dialog box, select Printer from the Merge to pop-up menu. To print one label for each address in the data file, leave the All radio button set under Records to be merged. Otherwise, designate a range to print. Click Merge when ready to print.

Creating Data Documents with Other Software

So far in this chapter, you've used data documents that were created by typing the data directly into a Word table. However, there's a good chance your company's or personal contacts are already stored in another software package, such as in a spreadsheet or database. (PIMs—Personal Information Managers—such as Apple's Organizer, Now Contact, or Symantec's ACT, are actually databases. They count here, too.) If this is the case, it's very easy to export your information from there.

Every good database or spreadsheet has an export function. The most basic export formats are tab-delimited and comma-delimited. (See your spreadsheet or database manager documentation for details on how to create a tab- or comma-delimited file. There should be an Export command under the File menu. From there you should be able to select a format and determine which fields to export.)

Tab- or comma-delimited exports result in a simple text file where each chunk of information (field) is separated by a tab or a comma (see Figure 6-10). A paragraph mark is placed between each contact to tell the importing software where to begin a new record/page/envelope/label. Sometimes quotation marks are placed around each field. Quotation marks are not needed by Word, but Word has no problem with them.

To bring a tab-delimited or comma-delimited file into Word, just drag the file onto Word's icon, and it coverts automatically. Then you can select the text as it appears in Word and use the Convert Text to Table command under the Table menu to turn the newly imported text into a table. That's all you need to do if your end result is a table. If your end result is to be a merged document, after you've created the table, you can merge it as demonstrated earlier in this chapter. However, if your goal is a mail merge, you don't even have to turn the text into a Word table. Simply begin your merge process and select the raw export file as your data source from the Mail Merge Helper.

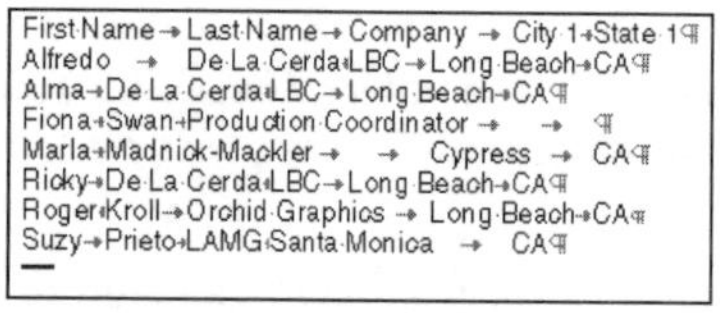

```
First·Name→Last·Name→Company → City·1→State·1¶
Alfredo → De·La·Cerda→LBC→Long·Beach→CA¶
Alma→De·La·Cerda→LBC→Long·Beach→CA¶
Fiona→Swan→Production·Coordinator → → ¶
Marla→Madnick-Mackler→ → Cypress → CA¶
Ricky→De·La·Cerda→LBC→Long·Beach→CA¶
Roger→Kroll→Orchid·Graphics → Long·Beach→CA¶
Suzy→Prieto→LAMG→Santa·Monica → CA¶
```

Figure 6-10: A tab-delimited exported file, complete with headers

Copying Excel data

You can easily use any data you have stored in Excel to create a table or to create your mail merge documents. When a portion of any Excel worksheet is selected and copied and then pasted into a Word document, the Excel data automatically appears as a table. If the selection includes your column headers, your new Word table is complete with headers. If not, you can add a header and save the table as a Word document. Then you use the Mail Merge commands to do the merge.

To transfer data from an Excel worksheet into a Word document, perform the following steps:

1. Start Excel and open the desired worksheet.
2. Using the selection techniques common to Excel, select the worksheet range that contains the desired data. If the data is not contiguous to the column names in the first row, press the ⌘ key as you select that row. Use the same

selection method to select any other noncontiguous rows or columns. (In case you miss selecting information, you can always add it as described in the following steps.)

3. Choose Edit➪Copy (⌘-C) to copy the selection to the Clipboard.
4. Launch (or return to) Word and open a new document.
5. Choose Edit➪Paste (⌘-V). The data selected in the Excel document appears as a table in Word.

If for some reason your copy and paste didn't include information such as the column names to create a header row, choose Table➪Insert Rows to add a new row where needed. Then enter or paste the missing information into this row.

After the data exists in table form in Word, you can use the techniques outlined earlier in this chapter to complete the mail merge process.

This method is a straight copy and paste. For more flexibility, see the method described in the next section, "Embedding Excel data."

Embedding Excel data

If the data you are using for your merge already exists in Excel, there is a more flexible way to use the data than by copying or exporting/importing it. By establishing a link to existing data in Excel, you gain the advantage of having your mail merge information automatically sorted, filtered, and even updated when the data changes.

If you think you will regularly update the information in your data document, you will want to use the field code method. If you won't be updating the information, insert it directly into the data document. In both cases, follow these steps:

1. Click the Insert Database button on the Database toolbar to open the Database dialog box shown in Figure 6-11.

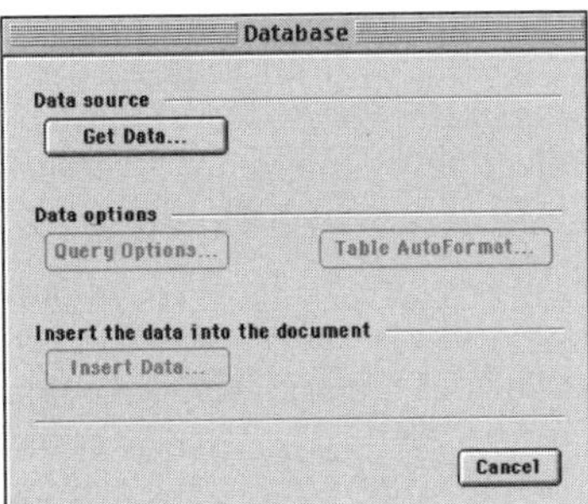

Figure 6-11: The Database dialog box

2. Click the Get Data button to open the Open Data Source dialog box shown in Figure 6-12. This box looks like the standard Open dialog box from the File menu. Choose the data document you want to use. Because you're in Word, the Files of type pop up filter is probably set to show only Word documents. Select the appropriate filter so you can see your document. If your source is in an Excel version file listed, choose that filter. Otherwise, the link is created using Excel via DDE, which is much slower. Double-click your Excel worksheet to choose it. (It doesn't matter whether Excel is running or whether the spreadsheet is open.)

   The status bar in Word keeps you apprised of what is happening. If necessary, Excel launches and the worksheet opens.

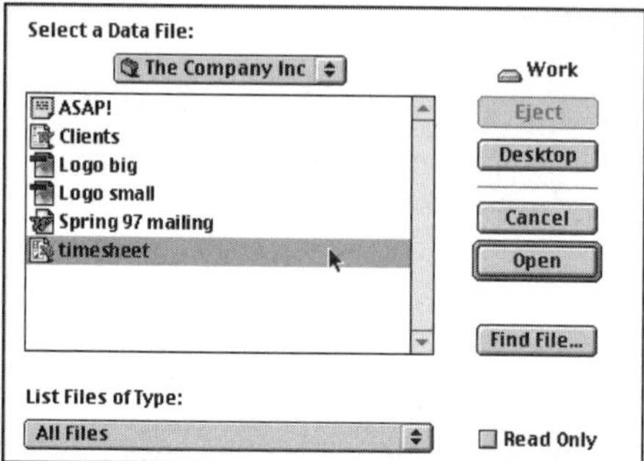

Figure 6-12: The Open Data Source dialog box

3. In a moment a dialog box asks what you want to import. Depending on your source, you are asked to choose a specific worksheet from a pop-up menu or if you want to import the entire spreadsheet or a range, in which case you double-click your choice of selection. (Note: *Entire spreadsheet* doesn't mean the tons of empty cells. An entire spreadsheet simply includes all cells that contain data or a formula. You learn how to further filter your import in a moment.)

4. The Database dialog box reappears, so you have the option of performing a query on the information you are importing. Click the Query Options button in the Database dialog box to open the Query Options dialog box. In here you can filter records by entering conditions in the Filter Records tab, select the fields you want to include using the Select fields tab, or sort records by choosing the desired sort fields in the Sort Records tab.

   If your goal is to limit the number of imported records or show only certain records, click the Filter Records tab and choose a field from the pop-up list. Next, move to the Comparison box and select a comparison, such as equal to, not equal to, greater than, less than, and so forth. The final part of the query is to enter a value to which the field can be compared in the Compare to box. You can also enter additional conditions for the filter. On each successive line of the dialog box, select an And or an Or relationship, and then enter the rest of your conditions (see Figure 6-13).

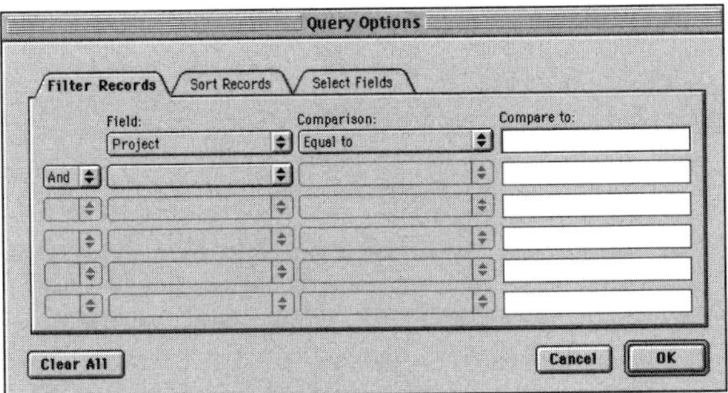

Figure 6-13: The Filter Records tab of the Query Options Dialog box

The records can also be sorted to help organize the presentation of your data. Click the Sort Records tab of the Query Options dialog box (see Figure 6-14). Select the primary field by which to sort, and then choose an ascending or descending sort. To have a secondary sort, select a field from the next pop-up menu (Then by) and again choose between ascending or descending. The same goes for a third sort criteria.

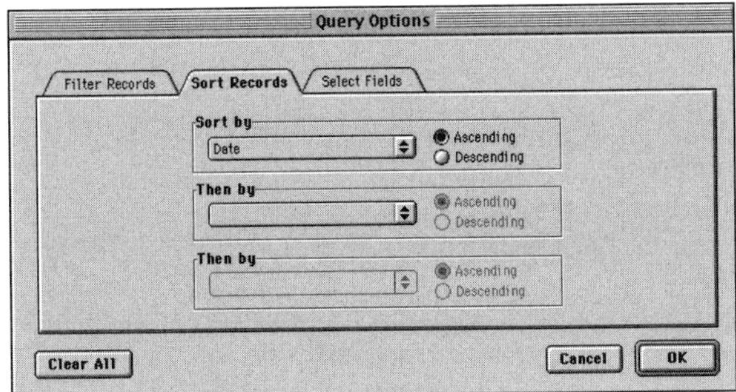

Figure 6-14: The Sort Records tab of the Query Options dialog box

Because you may not want to present all the fields from your spreadsheet, you can use the Select Fields tab (see Figure 6-15) to determine which fields to exclude. By default, all fields are included. Click a field in the Selected fields list on the right, and then click Remove to exclude it. Or, you may prefer to begin by clicking Remove All and then selectively including your fields. To include a field, click it once in the list on the left to select it, and then click Select. (Double-clicking the field name closes the dialog box.)

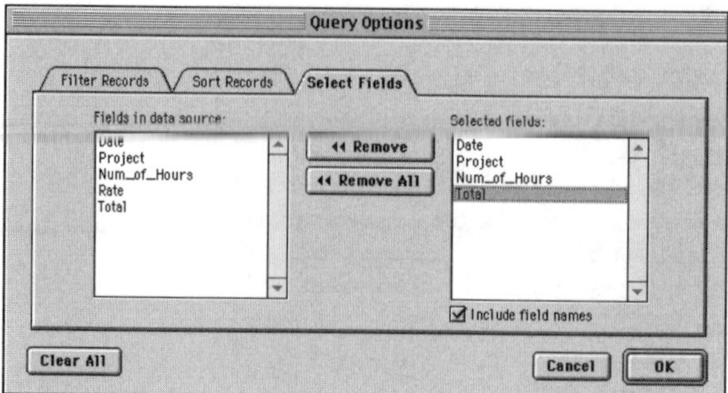

Figure 6-15: The Select Fields tab of the Query Options dialog box

After you have finished in all three tabs, click OK. You are again returned to the Database dialog box.

5. Click Table AutoFormat if you want to format the table. The Preview window lets you see what the data will look like after the formatting is applied. After choosing the format you want for the table, click OK.

6. Click the Insert Data button in the Database dialog box. The Insert Data dialog box appears, as shown in Figure 6-16. This dialog box gives you one more opportunity to choose a range for the information being imported; otherwise, retain the default choice—All. Click OK to import the information.

If you want the information to be linked, check the Insert data as a field option in the Insert Data dialog box. When information is linked, the data can be updated to reflect changes made to the Excel data. If Insert data as a field is not checked, automatic updating is not an option, and you'll have to enter any changes manually.

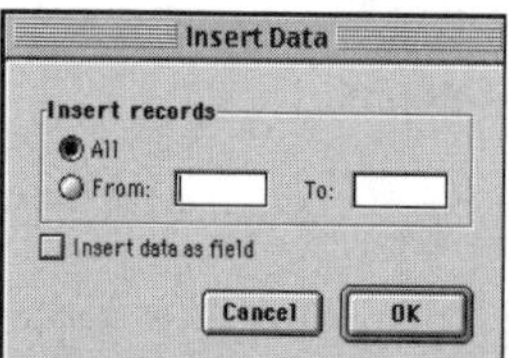

Figure 6-16: The Insert Data dialog box

After you click OK, Word and Excel communicate, as reflected by the messages in the status bar, and then your new table appears in Word.

If you have selected the Insert data as a field option, when the data is updated in Excel, you can tell Word to talk to Excel and update your table in Word. Click the Update Fields button on the Database toolbar, or Control-click in any cell of your table (in Word), and choose Update Fields from the shortcut menu that appears. Word initiates communication to Excel, as reported in the status bar, and then the data within your table changes to match the data in Excel. If you do not choose the Insert data as a field option, the Update Fields button will have no effect, and you will not see Update Fields in the shortcut menu when you Control-click in a cell in your table.

Embedding data from other sources

You can also use the Get Data button to insert data from other Microsoft sources, such as Outlook Express's contact list, Word's Address Book, or FoxPro databases. Doing so is similar to the method for embedding Excel data, except that, depending on the source, different dialog boxes will present appropriate choices. To make this procedure a bit easier, begin by selecting that source's filter in the Files of Type pop-up filter when you are getting the data source.

You may also be able to embed data from other sources. Again, begin with the Get Data button.

Summary

This chapter has detailed the following topics related to working with fields:

- ✦ Fields are instructions that Word uses to insert certain information, such as the current date, into a document.
- ✦ You can insert fields by choosing Insert⇨Field or using the Insert Field shortcut key combination (⌘-F9).
- ✦ You can update a field's results by Control-clicking the field and choosing Update Fields from the shortcut menu.
- ✦ Fields can be formatted like other text.
- ✦ Fields aid in the creation of form letters, which can be handled with the Mail Merge Helper.
- ✦ Fields can also be used in the creation of envelopes.
- ✦ We also covered the creation of data sources in other software applications—useful for large mailing lists or other cases where you need to work with large amounts of data that would be better handled in a database.

Where to go next

✦ After you have created your form letters, you want them to look their best. This requires some formatting work. For more information on formatting, see Chapter 3.

✦ ✦ ✦

CHAPTER 7

Building Tables of Contents and Indexes

✦ ✦ ✦ ✦

In This Chapter

Building tables of contents

Creating your own table of contents

Building large indexes

✦ ✦ ✦ ✦

This chapter covers two elements of a document that are similar in many ways: tables of contents and indexes. Both are essentially lists that are arranged in slightly different ways. A *table of contents* is a list of the major portions of a document (such as sections of a report), including the page numbers for each section. By comparison, an *index* is a list of important words or subjects in a document with page numbers where the subjects can be found.

Word lets you avoid much of the work in preparing both tables of contents and indexes. With the Index and Tables command from the Insert menu, you can automatically create tables of contents and similar lists or indexes based on special fields that you insert while writing your document. Besides saving you from all that typing and formatting, Index and Tables enables you to update the table of contents and index easily to reflect changes you make to the document.

Building Tables of Contents

You can use several methods for building a table of contents. You can base the table of contents on built-in heading styles or outline headings; you can change the default styles so Word creates the tables of contents based on your chosen styles; or you can build the table of contents by using TC fields, a special type of field that you insert into a document by using the steps outlined in this chapter. The easiest method for creating a table of contents—to base it on the styles within your document—requires only that you structure your document with styles such as headings or that you use an outline form. Figure 7-1 shows an example of a typical table of contents in Word. In this case, the table of contents was generated on the default heading styles used throughout the document.

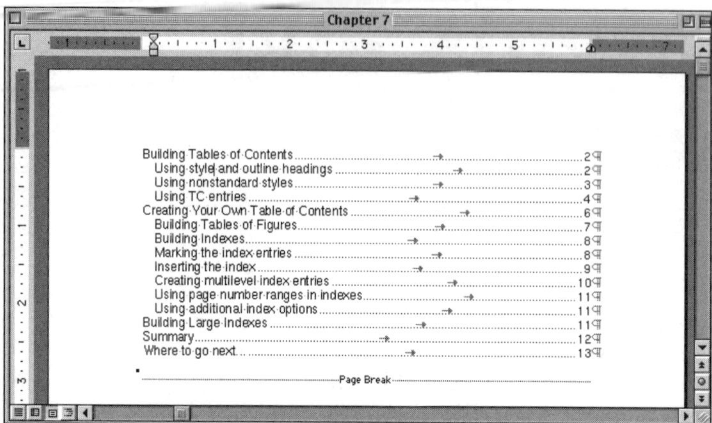

Figure 7-1: A typical table of contents generated in Word

If you need both a table of contents and an index in the same document, create the index first (use the techniques discussed in the second part of this chapter). This way you can include an entry for the index in your table of contents.

Using style and outline headings

In any document, Word includes the default styles of Normal, Heading 1, Heading 2, Heading 3, and Heading 4. You can apply these styles (or outline headings, if you've added these to your documents) to lines of text in your document to make the creation of tables of contents a simple matter. Follow these steps:

1. Check the headings of your document to be sure they are formatted in one of the heading styles. To do so, simply place your cursor (insertion point) anywhere in the heading text and then note the style reported in the Style box on the Formatting toolbar. To apply a heading style, with the insertion point anywhere within the heading, click the pop-up arrow to the right of the Style box on the Formatting toolbar and drag down or up to select any available style. (For more about the use of styles, see Chapter 8.)
2. Move the insertion point to the place where you want the table of contents.
3. Choose Insert ⇨ Index and Tables and then click the Table of Contents tab in the Index and Tables dialog box (see Figure 7-2).

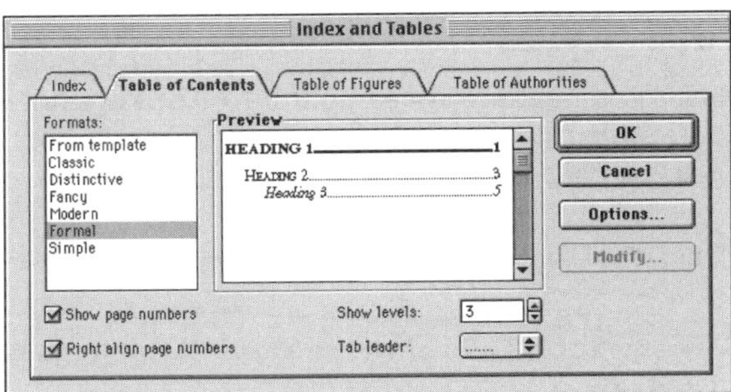

Figure 7-2: The Table of Contents tab of the Index and Tables dialog box

4. In the Formats list box, select the format you want for your table of contents. As you click each format, a representative sample of how the table of contents will look appears in the Preview area of the dialog box.

   You can include page numbers, along with the format, by leaving the Show page numbers check box turned on. You can also specify the number of heading levels by entering the desired value in the Show levels box. (When you select 1, only Heading 1 styles are included in the table of contents; when you select 2, Heading 1 and Heading 2 styles are included in the table of contents; and so on.) Clicking the Options button displays the Table of Contents Options dialog box that lets you designate styles (other than Word's default heading styles) that Word should use to build the table of contents.

5. After you select the options you want, click OK. Word constructs the table of contents at the insertion point location.

The Funny Codes Dilemma

If you see a series of codes, such as {TOC}, rather than actual text after you generate your table of contents, your table of contents is displaying field codes. If you want to see the actual text of the table of contents, select Tools⇨Preferences, select the View tab in the Preferences dialog box, and uncheck the Field Codes check box in the Show area. This displays all the field results instead of the codes.

If you like seeing the codes but want to see page number results in individual instances, place the cursor in the field code and press Shift-F9, or Control-click and select Toggle Codes.

Using nonstandard styles

Sometimes you may find that the heading styles built into Word are not the styles you prefer for building your table of contents. If you want to base the table of contents on different styles, you can do so by performing these steps:

1. Position the cursor in the area where you want to insert the table of contents.
2. Choose Insert ⇨ Index and Tables and click the Table of Contents tab in the Index and Tables dialog box.
3. In the Formats list box, select the format you want to use. Then click the Options button to open the Table of Contents Options dialog box (see Figure 7-3).

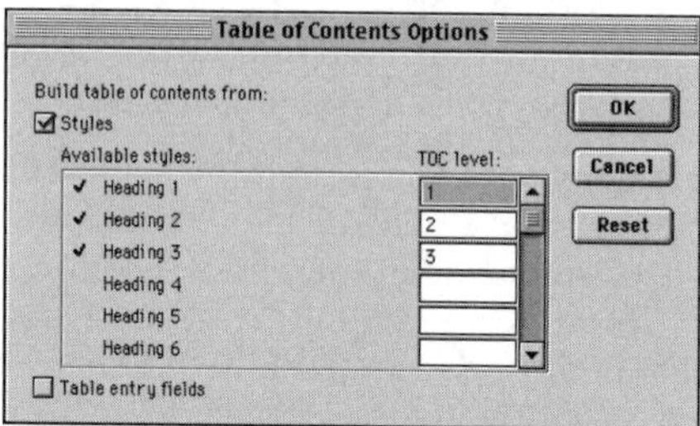

Figure 7-3: The Table of Contents Options dialog box

4. Scroll down in the Available styles list box to find the first style you want to use for the table of contents. In the TOC level list to the right of the style name, type **1**. Notice that a check mark automatically appeared in the column to the left of the style. This style is now designated as the first level of importance in your table of contents. Continue, entering a 2, 3, 4, and so on depending on how many styles you'd like to include in your table of contents. You can renumber any style at any time. Styles with no TOC level indicated are not part of the table of contents.
5. Click OK to close the Table of Contents Options dialog box and preview the table of contents in the Index and Tables dialog box.
6. Click OK in the Index and Tables dialog box. Word compiles the table of contents at the insertion point location.

Using TC entries

Another method for building a table of contents involves adding fields called TC entries (an abbreviation for table of contents entries) to your document. This involves manually building the field by using ⌘-F9 to insert field brackets. The overall technique involves two main steps: identifying and marking items to include in the table of contents, and generating the table of contents itself.

You can insert TC entries in a document and generate the table of contents by performing the following steps:

1. Be sure that hidden text is showing on the screen. (If you can see paragraph markers at the end of your paragraphs, hidden text is showing.) If hidden text is not showing, click the Show/Hide button on the Standard toolbar.
2. Place the insertion point at the location in the document where you want to insert a TC entry. (A good place for TC entries is right after the section titles or headings in your document.)
3. Press ⌘-F9 to insert an empty field. You see the field braces with the insertion point placed between them. The field code resembles the following: {_}
4. Type the letters **TC** and a space. Then type a quotation mark, the entry that you want to have appear in the table of contents, and then another quotation mark. (The letters *TC* can be either uppercase or lowercase.) For example, if you want to add a table of contents entry that reads "Unpacking your new lawn mower," your entry would resemble the following:

   {tc "Unpacking your new lawn mower"}

5. Repeat Steps 2 through 4 for each table of contents entry you want to add.
6. When all the TC entry fields have been placed in the document, move the insertion point to the place in your document where you would like the table of contents to appear.
7. Choose Insert ➪ Index and Tables and click the Table of Contents tab. Next click the Options button and, in the dialog box that appears, turn on the Table Entry Fields check box. This action tells Word to base the table of contents on the TC entries that you have added to the document. Click OK.
8. Click OK in the Index and Tables dialog box. Word builds the table of contents at the insertion point location.

   If the Field Codes option is turned on, you will see field codes in the table of contents rather than text. You can turn off the field codes by choosing Tools ➪ Preferences, clicking the View tab in the Preferences dialog box, and turning off the Field Codes option. (Another easy way to turn off the field codes is to Control-click in the field code and choose Toggle Field Codes from the shortcut menu that appears.)

Formatting on the Fly

Probably the easiest way to make a quick format change to your table of contents or index is to Control-click anywhere within the table of contents or index. Then choose the Font, Paragraph, or Bullets and Numbering command from the shortcut menu that appears.

Depending on which menu option you select, you can then make appropriate changes in the dialog box that appears.

Remember that the table of contents is based on a Word field. If you make changes to the document that changes the page count, you need to update the table of contents to reflect those changes. To update a table of contents, place the insertion point anywhere within the table of contents and Control-click. Choose Update Field from the shortcut menu that appears.

Remember that TC entries are fields. If you want to delete or move a TC entry to another location, select the entire field and move it or delete it as you would move or delete any text.

Creating Your Own Table of Contents

To see how to build a table of contents by inserting TC fields, you can follow the steps in the next exercise. Or, if you have a sizable document of your own, you may want to apply these steps to create a table of contents based on your own document:

1. Choose File⇨New (⌘-N) and then click OK to create a new document and save it right away. (Always save and keep saving.)
2. Type the following lines (press Return after each one) and press Shift-Enter after each line to insert a page break between each line and the next:

   Principles of Flight

   Aircraft and Engines

   Flight Instruments

   Navigation

3. If the hidden text option is not turned on, click the Show/Hide button on the Standard toolbar to show the hidden characters.
4. Place the insertion point at the end of the first line of text. Press ⌘-F9 and then type the following inside the brackets:

   tc "Principles of Flight"

5. Move the insertion point to the end of the next line of text. Press ⌘-F9 and then type the following inside the brackets:

   tc "Aircraft and Engines"

6. Move the insertion point to the end of the next line of text. Press ⌘-F9 and then type the following inside the brackets:

   tc "Flight Instruments"

7. Move the insertion point to the end of the next line of text. Press ⌘-F9 and then type the following inside the brackets:

   tc "Navigation"

8. Insert you cursor at the beginning of the document (or press ⌘-Home as the shortcut). Press Return once to add a new line, and then press Shift-Enter to insert a page break. Then with your cursor, the arrows, or ⌘-Home, move back to the start of the document. You will add the table of contents on what is now Page 1 of the document, with the remainder of the document appearing on the following four pages.

9. Choose Insert ⇨ Index and Tables. Then click the Table of Contents tab in the Index and Tables dialog box.

10. Click the Options button to open the Table of Contents Options dialog box and turn on the Table Entry Fields check box. Click OK.

11. Click OK in the Index and Tables dialog box to have Word insert your table of contents. It should look like the one in Figure 7-4.

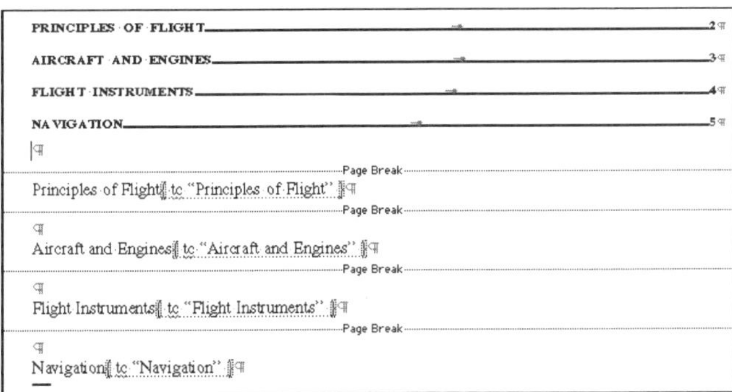

Figure 7-4: The sample table of contents

Banishing Strange Codes

By default, TC entries are stored as hidden text. If you cannot see them, however, they are rather difficult to enter because you will not see what you're typing.

However, if they are visible, the entries may become annoying when you are trying to proof your text. You can easily toggle this hidden text between visible and invisible by clicking the Show/Hide button, a backwards fancy *P* on the Standard toolbar.

Building tables of figures

A table of figures is another type of list you can easily create in Word. Like a table of contents and an index, a table of figures is a list of items. In this case, the items are figure captions, shown in the order in which the figures appear in the document. A table of figures can include such items as illustrations, figures, charts, or graphs. Examples of figure captions appear throughout this book; every figure in this book includes a caption that describes the figure. You can do the same kind of thing in your own Word documents.

All the captions you create in your documents can be easily included in a table of figures that you can place at any location within your document. There are two ways to create a table of figures. You can use the Insert ⇨ Caption command, or you can assign a style to each caption.

To create your table of figures with the Insert ⇨ Caption command, you work on your document as normal, using this command as you come to each caption location. (Or you can create your document, and then go back and insert the captions by choosing Insert ⇨ Caption.) This command brings up the Caption dialog box, which presents you with a field into which you type the name of the caption. You repeat this process for every caption you want to insert.

After inserting all your captions, you can perform the following steps to insert the table of figures:

1. Position the cursor where you want to place the table of figures.
2. Choose Insert ⇨ Index and Table and click the Table of Figures tab in the Index and Tables dialog box (see Figure 7-5).

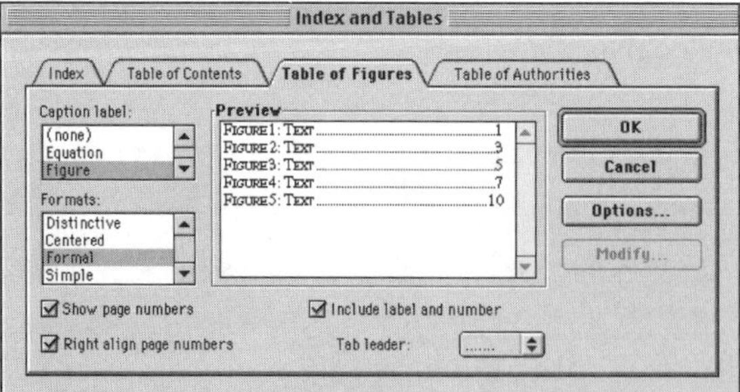

Figure 7-5: The Table of Figures tab in the Index and Tables dialog box

3. Choose the kind of caption label you want for your table of figures.

4. Select the format you want for your table. As with tables of contents, you can choose to build your table of figures from a template or use a Classic, Distinctive, Centered, Formal, or Simple style. (These formats are displayed in the Preview portion of the dialog box.) The Show Page Numbers option, when checked, causes page numbers to be included with the table of figures. The Right Align Page Numbers option, when checked, causes the page numbers to be aligned with the right margin.
5. After making your choices, click OK to insert the table of figures at the insertion point.

To create your table of figures based on styles, you enter your caption by typing within your document as normal, and then assign a style to each caption. For example, to write this book, we typed the words, "Figure 7-5: The Table of Figures tab in the Index and Tables dialog box." We then assigned this line a style, which we happen to call Caption. (For more information on styles, see Chapter 8.) After all your text is entered, you select Insert⇨Index and Table, as with the previously described method. This time, however, click the Options button and click the check box next to Style, telling Word to build the table of figures from a style. In the pop-up menu next to the selection, choose the style you used for your captions. We would select Caption as our style because that's the style we assigned to our caption text. Click OK. Then choose your Table of Figures options and click OK to have word build your table.

Building indexes

Word enables you to build indexes in a manner similar to the one for building tables of contents. You insert special fields, called index entries, into the document at locations where you mention the indexed topics. In the case of index entries, Word provides a command just for this purpose, or you can use the Insert Field command (⌘-F9). After you mark all the index entries, you use Insert⇨Index and Tables to place the index at the insertion point. As with a table of contents, the index that Word generates is based on a field, which you can easily change by updating the field as the document changes.

Word offers considerable control over the index. You can generate an index for the entire document or for a range of letters in the alphabet. Index entries can all appear flush left in the index, or they can be indented to multiple levels. And you can easily add bold or italics to the page numbers of the index entries.

Marking the index entries

Every item that is to appear in the index must have an index entry. You can mark index entries by performing the following steps:

1. Select the text in the document that you want to use for an index entry or place the insertion point immediately after the text.

2. Choose Insert⇨Index and Tables, and then click the Index tab. Click the Mark Entry button to reveal the Mark Index Entry dialog box (see Figure 7-6). By default, any selected text appears in the Main entry text box. If you want the text to appear in the index as a subentry (a secondary-level index heading), delete any entry in the Main entry text box and enter the entry in the Subentry text box.

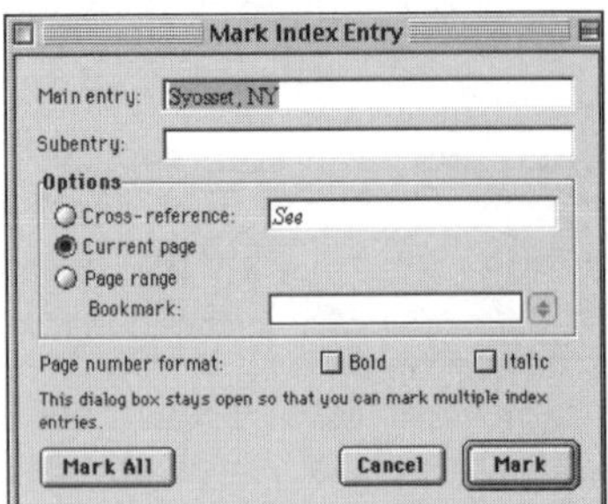

Figure 7-6: The Mark Index Entry dialog box

3. After entering the desired entry, click the Mark button. Word inserts the index entry at the insertion point location. (Like the fields you use to insert tables of contents, index entries are stored as hidden text. You will not see them in the document unless you click the Show/Hide button on the Standard toolbar.)

The Mark Index Entry dialog box contains various options you can use to determine how Word should handle the index entries. In the Cross-reference text box, you can type the text you want to use as a cross-reference for the index entry. You can also specify a range of pages in an index entry by turning on the Page Range option and typing or selecting a bookmark name that you used to mark a range of pages. Finally, the Page number format options apply bold or italic formatting to page numbers in the index.

If you don't like using menus and dialog boxes, an alternative way of inserting index entries exists. Because an index entry is a field, you can use the Insert Field key (⌘-F9) to insert an index entry. To do so, press Insert Field (⌘-F9), type the letters **xe** followed by a space, and then type the index entry surrounded by quotation marks. If you want the page number of the index entry to be in bold or italic, you must also add a \b or \i switch; type **\b** for bold or **\i** for italic (you can add both options in the same field). With hidden text showing, a sample index entry may resemble the following:

{xe "Adding Oil to the Lawn Mower" \b}

One important note: an index entry should follow the topic to which it refers in the text; that is, the index entry should be placed immediately after the sentence that concludes the subject that is indexed. (If you select the text before you use the Index and Tables command—rather than typing the index entry yourself—Word automatically places the index entry immediately after the selection.) This rule of thumb is important because if you place the index entry before the subject being indexed, and the subject is near the bottom of the page, Word may add a page break between the index entry and the text. The result would be an index with an incorrect page number.

Inserting the index

After you mark all the index entries, you can use Insert➪Index and Tables to place the index in the document. To insert the index, perform the following steps:

1. Place the insertion point at the desired location for the index. (With most documents, indexes are customarily placed at the end of the document.)
2. Choose Insert➪Index and Tables and click the Index tab, as shown in Figure 7-7.

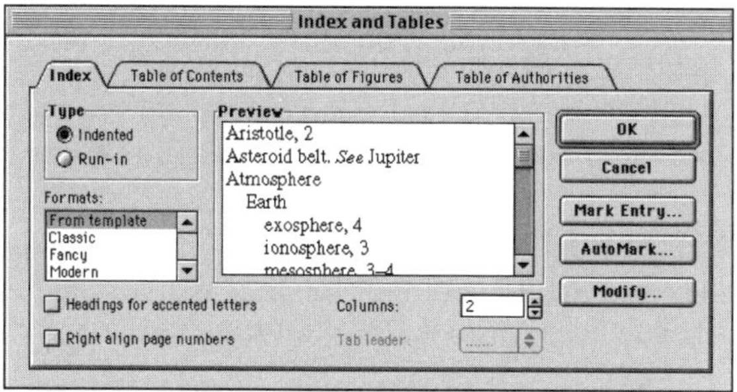

Figure 7-7: The Index tab of the Index and Tables dialog box

3. Choose the type of index (Indented or Run-in) that you want and choose the desired format for the index. As you select among the available formats, a preview of each format appears in the Preview area of the dialog box.
4. After you click OK, Word generates the index. Note that if Field Codes is turned on, you will see the fields that built the index and not the index itself. You can turn off the field codes by choosing the Preferences command from the Tools menu and clicking the View tab of the Preferences dialog box. Just turn off the Field Codes option in the Show area of the tab.

Creating multilevel index entries

You can insert index entries that indicate multiple levels. As an example, the following part of an index is designed with two levels:

Data

Copying, 104
Definition, 251
Deleting, 92
Editing, 91
Linking, 216
Reporting, 251

Data Menu, 64, 216

Database

Attributes of, 251
Creating, 216
Criteria, 230

To create an index based on multiple levels, enter the text of the secondary entry in the Subentry text box rather than in the Main entry text box of the Mark Entry dialog box. If you are typing the entries manually, simply add a colon (:) when you type the index entry into the dialog box to separate the levels. You can create a multilevel index by performing the following steps to mark your index entries:

1. Place the insertion point at the desired location for the index.
2. Choose Insert ⇨ Index and Tables and click the Index tab of the Index and Tables dialog box. Then click the Mark Entry button.
3. In the Main entry text box, type the first-level entry. In the Subentry text box, type the second-level entry.
4. Click the Mark button to place the index entry.

When you specify multiple levels, remember that you now have a choice of how Word structures a multilevel index when you use the Index and Tables command. You can choose either the Indented or the Run-in type of index. The default is Indented, which results in an index where sublevel entries are indented, as shown in the following example:

Database

Attributes of, 251
Creating, 216
Criteria, 230

On the other hand, if you choose the Run-in option in the dialog box, Word inserts all sublevel entries in the same paragraph as the main entry in the index. The main entry is separated from the subentries with a colon, and all remaining subentries are separated by semicolons. The preceding indented example now appears as a run-in example in the following:

Database; Attributes of, 251; Creating, 216; Criteria, 230

Using page number ranges in indexes

In those cases where a subject covered by an index entry spans several pages in a document, you may want the reference in the index to include the range of pages in the document. In the following example, the entries for the Go To command and Hardware both contain a range of pages:

Get Info command, 41

Go To command, 62-65

Gridlines command, 145

Hardware, 19-20

Help menu, 12

With the methods described so far for inserting index entries, you get only the first page of the subject referred to by the index, even if you make a selection that spans multiple pages. If you want page numbers that span a range of pages, you must do things a little differently. First you must select the range of text and insert a bookmark that refers to the selection by following these steps:

1. Use your preferred selection method to select the range of text you want to index.
2. Choose Insert⇨Bookmark. In the Bookmark dialog box, type a name for the bookmark, and then click Add.
3. Choose Insert⇨Index and Tables, click the Index tab, and click Mark Entry. In the Mark Index Entry dialog box, click the Page Range Bookmark radio button and enter the bookmark name in the list box. When you create the index using the steps described earlier in this chapter, your entry includes your specified range of pages.

Using additional index options

Additional switches (programming codes) are available for you to use in index fields in Word to add sophistication to your indexes. These features include changing the separator character used between ranges of page numbers (normally a hyphen) and restricting an index to include only index items that begin with a certain letter. These special index switches are beyond the scope of this book, but Word's Help talks more about them.

Building Large Indexes

If you are generating a large index (one with 4,000 entries or more), Word may run out of memory when you attempt to use the Index and Tables command. Microsoft recommends that you generate indexes for large documents in multiple steps. First, for example, you build an index that contains entries only for the letters *A* through *L*, and then you build an index for the letters *M* through *Z*. You choose the Field command from the Insert menu rather than the Index and Tables to insert a separate field for each portion of the index after you have marked all the entries that you want in the document.

To create a separate field for each portion of the index, do the following:

1. Place the insertion point at the location in the document where the index is to appear.
2. Choose Insert ➪ Field.
3. Type the word **index** followed by a space, a backslash, the letter p, a space, and a range of letters (such as *A-L*); for example, **index \p A-L**.
4. Click OK to insert the first index field into the document. If the hidden text option is turned on, the field may resemble the following:

   {index \p A - L}

5. Move the insertion point to the right of the existing index field and press Return to start a new line.
6. Repeat Steps 2 through 5 for each additional range of letters that you need.

Summary

In this chapter you learned how to use Word's capabilities to generate tables of contents and indexes. The chapter covered the following topics:

- ✦ Tables of contents can be based on heading styles, outline headings, or TC fields (a special kind of field inserted into a document).
- ✦ If you use Word's default heading styles or outlining in your document, you can quickly generate a table of contents by choosing Insert ➪ Index and Tables, clicking the Table of Contents tab, and selecting the desired format in the dialog box.
- ✦ You can create tables of contents based on any text in your document by adding fields called TC fields to your document. After adding these fields, you can generate a table of contents with the Table of Contents tab, which appears in the dialog box when you choose Insert ➪ Index and Tables from the menus.

- You can create indexes by adding fields called index entries to your document. After adding index entries, you can generate an index with the Index tab, which appears in the dialog box when you choose Insert⇨Index and Tables from the menus.

Where to go next

- In the next chapter, you learn how to work effectively with styles and templates to govern the overall appearance of your document in Word.
- If you make full use of Word's predefined styles or of outlines in your documents, the creation of tables of contents becomes an easy task. You can find more information on working with Word's predefined styles in Chapter 8. For the lowdown on using outlines in Word, see Chapter 5.
- Also, an important part of any complex document is page number formatting, and possibly the inclusion of headers and footers. These topics are detailed in Chapter 3.

✦ ✦ ✦

Working with Styles and Templates

✦ ✦ ✦ ✦

In This Chapter

Discovering styles and templates

Applying styles

Defining styles

Redefining styles

Finding styles when you need them

Defining and applying styles

Understanding templates

Working with templates

Creating and applying a template

✦ ✦ ✦ ✦

Word provides styles and templates, which are tools that make it easy to mold the appearance of routinely produced or long documents. The first part of the chapter deals with styles; the second part of the chapter deals with templates. The two concepts are closely related.

Discovering Styles and Templates

Too many users of Word find styles to be an esoteric subject and avoid it. It is quite possible to use Word day after day and never learn about the strength and flexibility of styles. The same can be said for templates, which offer another way to reduce repetitive work while aiding in design consistency. You're doing yourself a disservice if you avoid styles or templates — they can be time-savers.

So what is a style? A style is a collection of character formatting and/or paragraph formatting settings. Styles save time you might otherwise spend formatting your documents — and give your documents a consistent look. For example, you may routinely apply a 0.5-inch left indent, a first-line indent, and Times font to paragraphs in a document. You can define this set of formatting aspects to a style. After the style has been defined, you can apply all these formatting aspects to any paragraph in a document in a single operation.

Word has a number of built-in styles. They may be all you need, but you can also create your own. Figure 8-1 shows a letter that contains a number of different styles. Notice the names of the styles to the left of the document. (You can display style names at the far left like this by choosing Tools ➪ Preferences, clicking the View tab, and changing the Style Area Width. This is discussed further in the section

"Displaying style names as you work.") All available styles appear in the pop-up Style list on the left side of the Formatting toolbar as you create a document.

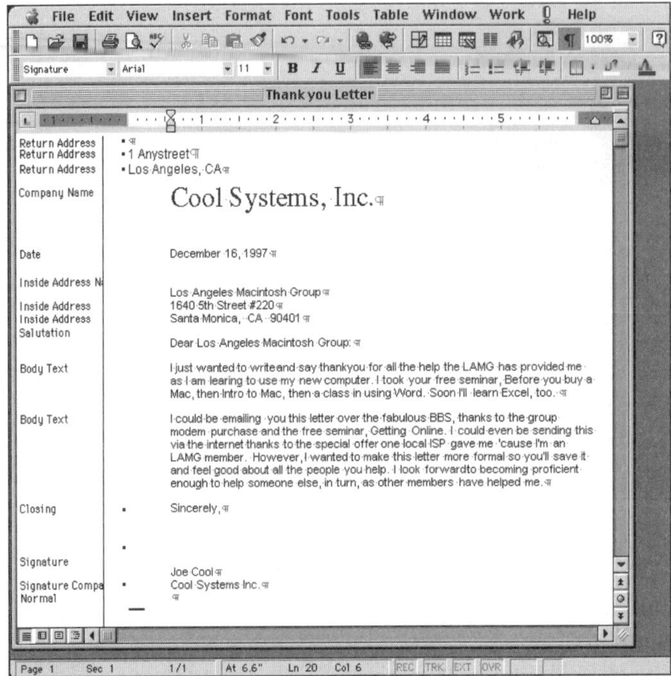

Figure 8-1: An example of a letter containing various styles

Besides making formatting easier to apply, styles also offer an advantage when you revise document formats. When you change the formatting in the style, all paragraphs that are formatted with this style automatically change. For example, you may decide to apply a border and shading to all paragraphs with a particular style. By changing the definition of the style to include the border and shading, you automatically add the border and shading to all paragraphs in all documents that use that particular style.

Word offers two overall kinds of styles: character and paragraph. Character styles apply a variety of formatting to the individual letters and punctuation in a document. Character styles are those that appear in the Font command of the Format menu. This is the formatting that includes font size and style; bold, italics, or underlining; small caps; and other text-related settings. These attributes can be applied with buttons, keyboard commands, or from within the Font dialog box. Paragraph styles govern the overall appearance of the paragraph. You apply paragraph styles with the Format ➪ Paragraph command or from the ruler. Paragraph formatting includes indentation, line spacing, and paragraph alignment. It also includes character formatting. Word normally saves styles along with the active document, but you can easily copy the styles you create to a specific template, which brings us to the strength of templates.

A document template, also called a *stationery document* on the Mac, is like a blank page of stationery that has your name, address and logo already printed and waiting to go. For example, in the case of an interoffice memo, you can create a template that already contains the text for a company name, date, to, from, and subject headings. In addition to this boilerplate text, templates can also contain margin settings, headers and footers, styles, macros, and custom keyboard, menu, or toolbar assignments. By storing styles in a template, you make the stored styles available for use whenever you use that template. When you click the drop-down arrow in the Style list on the Formatting toolbar, the styles you see are all stored in the template that you are using.

By starting with a template you arrive directly at a particular format, rather than having to begin from scratch defining everything from the page margins to the most intricate of styles. The second part of this chapter explains templates in more detail. Because templates include collections of styles, it's important to understand styles before you begin working with templates.

Applying Styles

You can apply styles throughout your Word documents in two ways. You can use the pop-up Style list that's in the Formatting toolbar or you can use keyboard shortcuts.

Using the Formatting toolbar

Because Word comes with a number of default styles, putting styles to work is as easy as choosing the desired style from the Style list on the Formatting toolbar. To apply any of the available styles to paragraphs in your document, follow these steps:

1. If the Formatting toolbar isn't already showing, choose View ⇨ Toolbars ⇨ Formatting. (Because this is the most useful Word toolbar, we recommend that you keep it open at all times.)
2. To apply a paragraph style to one paragraph, place the insertion pointer anywhere in that paragraph. To apply the style to more than one paragraph, select at least part of each paragraph.

   To apply a character style, select the desired portion of text.
3. Click the arrow to the right of the Style list in the Formatting toolbar to reveal the list of available styles (see Figure 8-2) and drag to the style you wish to apply.

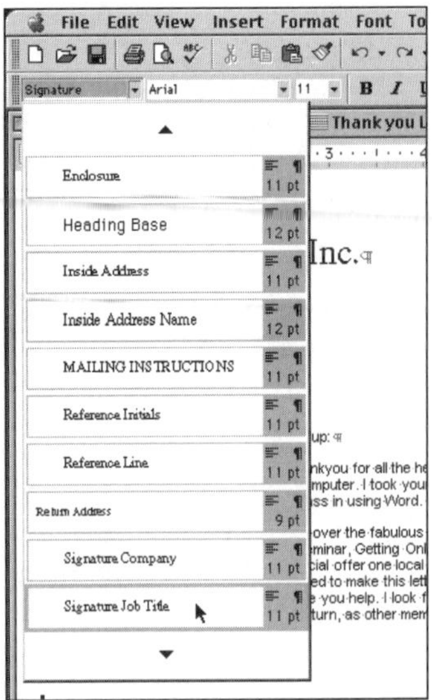

Figure 8-2: The pop-up Style list on the Formatting toolbar

The style list also provides a Style preview to help you select the appropriate style. The style name doubles as a view of any indentation and shows the font size if it's between 8 and 16 points. If the style's font is below 8 points, it is still seen at 8 points. If the style's font is above 16 points, it is still seen at 16 points. The information on the right states the font size of that style, shows you the alignment, then tells you that style is a character style (with an underlined *a*) or a paragraph style (paragraph mark).

If you don't like the effects of a style you apply, you can undo its effects by immediately choosing Edit ➪ Undo (Style).

Why Is My Style List Different?

If you look at the available styles shown in Figure 8-2 and compare them to the styles shown in your own Style list, you may find the lists don't match. "Where are all these styles?" you may ask. Remember that each template contains a collection of styles. When you look in the Style list, the styles you see are part of the template you are using. If we are using a different template, the styles are different.

For now, remember that you can choose from among different templates in the New dialog box that appears when you select File ➪ New. Each template in the New dialog box has its own list of styles that are useful for that particular type of document.

Using the keyboard

If you are using a document that is based on Word's default (Normal) template, you can use keyboard shortcuts to apply the available styles. Table 8-1 shows the available styles in the Normal template and the keyboard shortcuts that apply the styles.

Table 8-1
Styles That Have Keyboard Shortcuts

Style Name	*Formatting Applied*	*Keyboard Shortcut*
Heading 1	Normal; Helvetica 14 point; Bold; Space Before 12 pts; After 3 pts	⌘-Option-1
Heading 2	Normal; Helvetica 12 point; Bold; Italic; Space Before 12 pts; After 3 pts	⌘-Option-2
Heading 3	Normal; Helvetica 12 point; Space Before 12 pts; After 3 pts	⌘-Option-3

You can quickly apply the same style to a number of items in your document. After applying the style to the first selection, select the additional text that you want formatted with the same style and press the ⌘ key.

Why Do Italicized Words Become Normal?

If you apply a style that includes bold or italics to selected text that already contains bold or italic formatting, the existing bold or italicized text in the selection changes to normal text.

This change happens because in Word, bold and italic character formatting is a "switch" that is either on or off for a given selection. Thus, any style-applied bold or italic formatting toggles that switch, removing any bold or italic formatting that had been previously applied to the selection.

Defining Styles

Word provides two overall methods for creating (defining) styles. For the first method, you choose Format⇨Style and click the New button in the Style dialog box. In the New Style dialog box that appears, enter a name for the new style, and then click the Format pop-up menu to define the style, choosing the characteristics you desire. (Yes, this is a lot to describe in one paragraph, but the next section gives you the complete scoop.)

Styles can also be defined by example. This means that you can format your paragraph until you like the way it looks, then define a style based on that paragraph. This method is friendlier and easier.

Using the Style command

The more powerful (and, yes, more complex) method of defining a style is using Format ➪ Style. This command opens the Style dialog box shown in Figure 8-3. Click the New button in the dialog box to reveal the New Style dialog box shown in Figure 8-4.

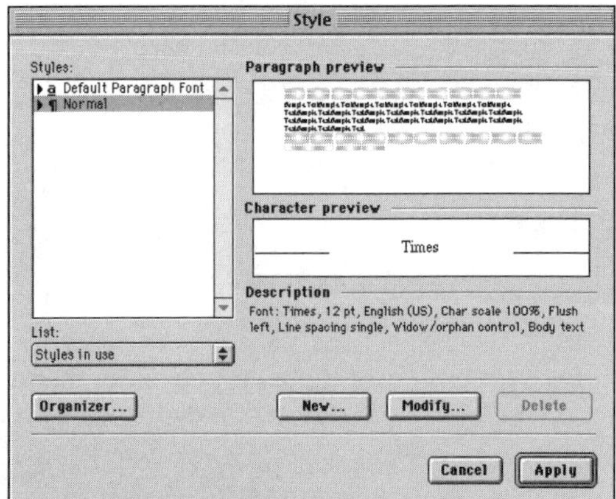

Figure 8-3: The Style dialog box

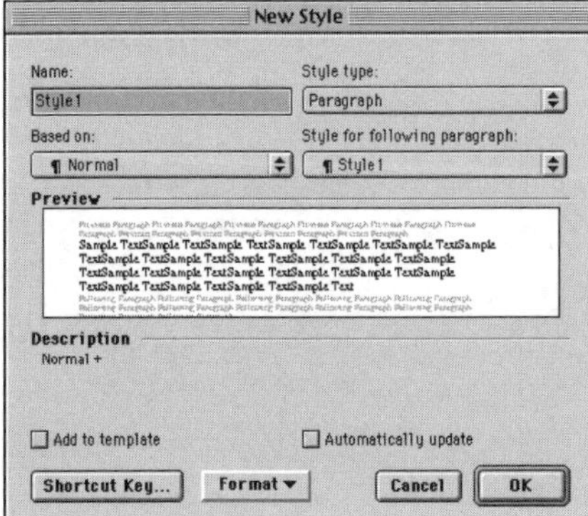

Figure 8-4: The New Style dialog box

You can change the formatting for the style by clicking on the Format pop-up and selecting the appropriate category to format. Each of the menu choices displayed in the Format list (Font, Paragraph, Tabs, Border, Language, Frame, and

Numbering) takes you directly to the dialog box that particular formatting command uses. For example, choosing Font displays the same Font dialog box displayed with Format ➪ Font; choosing Paragraph displays the same Paragraph dialog box as Format ➪ Paragraph. The Style type pop-up menu offers a choice of Character or Paragraph, which is where you indicate whether your new style is a character style or a paragraph style.

Make the desired changes in the respective dialog boxes and then click OK to return to the New Style dialog box. (The only formatting option not covered elsewhere in this text is the one provided by the Language option. This menu option brings up a dialog box that lets you change the language used by the spell-checker, thesaurus, and grammar-checker.)

You can use the Based on pop-up in the New Style dialog box to base the style you are creating on an existing style. (If the style you are defining is not based on any other style, this box will be blank.) To base a new style on an existing one, select it from this pop-up menu. (This technique is covered in more detail in "Basing a style on another style" later in this chapter.)

You can turn on the Add to template check box at the bottom of the New Styles dialog box if you want to add the style that you've defined to the current template. (If you are using the default Normal template, the style will be added to that template and will be available in all documents that you create in Word.)

After you have made all the desired formatting changes, enter a name for the style in the Name box. Remember that each style name must be unique. It doesn't make sense to have two styles with the same name so Word doesn't let you make this mistake. Because style names are case-sensitive, you can use "Figures" and "figures" as two different style names (although that would confuse most people). Style names can be up to 253 characters in length, and they can use any combination of characters except for the backslash (\), the curly braces ({}), or the semicolon (;).

After giving your style a name, click OK to return to the Style dialog box. From here you can apply the style to the current paragraph or selection by clicking the Apply button. When you do, the dialog box closes and you are back in your document. After the style has been defined, you can apply that style to the desired paragraphs of the document by using the techniques covered under "Using the Formatting toolbar" earlier in this chapter.

In addition to the Apply button, the Style dialog box contains other interesting buttons. Use the Modify button to change the formatting of an existing style that you have selected in the Styles list box. Use the Delete button to remove an unwanted style from the Styles list box. Click the Organizer button to display the Organizer dialog box, which lets you rename and copy a style (see "Copying, deleting, and renaming styles" later in this chapter).

Defining styles by example

The easy way to define a new style is to base it on an existing paragraph and then use the buttons on the Formatting toolbar. (This includes starting with Normal as the style as when you've simply typed new text.) To create a new style based on an existing paragraph, follow these steps:

1. Be sure the Formatting toolbar is displayed. Place the insertion pointer anywhere in the paragraph on which you want to base the style. Of course, it is more efficient to make the changes to the paragraph you really want to change. Make any desired changes to the formatting for that paragraph using the ruler and formatting Toolbar, the menus, and the dialog boxes. (Any changes made are reflected in the new style.)
2. Click once in the Style list box on the Formatting toolbar. Yes, you're clicking where the name of the current style is displayed. This selects or highlights the name of the style (see Figure 8-5). Remember that you can always type over selected text. Here you can type a new name.
3. Type a name for the style and press Return or Enter. Word adds the new style name to the list of styles for the document.

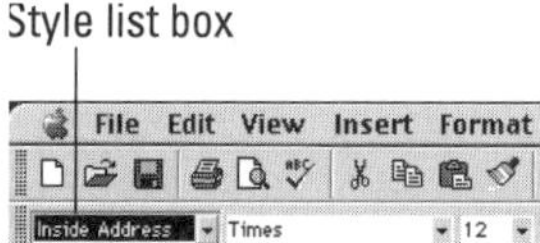

Figure 8-5: A highlighted entry in the Style list box

Assigning a shortcut key to a style

As a time-saving feature, Word lets you assign shortcut keys to styles. Then, to apply a style you use regularly to selected paragraphs, you just press a key combination. To assign a shortcut key to a style, follow these steps:

1. Choose Format ➪ Style.
2. In the Style dialog box (refer to Figure 8-3), select the desired style and click the Modify button to open the Modify Style dialog box.
3. Click the Shortcut Key button to open the Customize Keyboard dialog box (see Figure 8-6). A shortcut key is assigned to your style in this dialog box.
4. Press the desired shortcut key combination. Your key combination appears in the Press new shortcut key box (where the cursor was waiting for you when you got there.)
5. Below the new shortcut key box, a message appears. This Currently assigned to message tells you whether the key combination you have chosen is

currently selected for another use in Word. If you see an existing description for that particular key combination, you can overwrite the existing key assignment or choose another.

6. Click the Assign button to assign the shortcut key to the style.

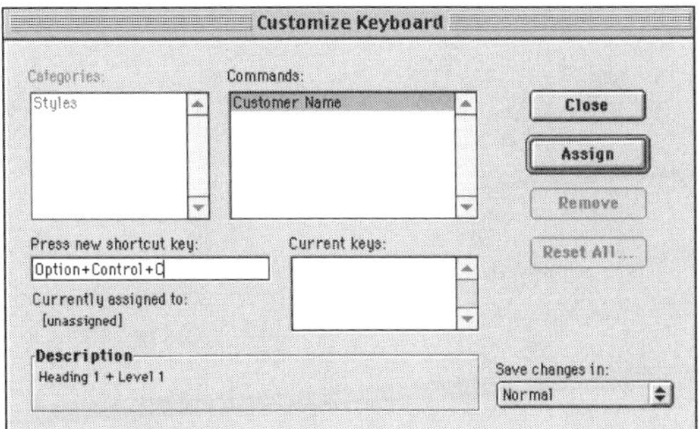

Figure 8-6: The Customize Keyboard dialog box

Before you create a large number of styles on your own, take the time to become familiar with the styles that are already in Word's templates. Word may already have a style that will accomplish what you want.

Basing a style on another style

You can base a new style on an existing style. Suppose you have an existing paragraph of text that uses the Normal style. If you indent that paragraph by 0.5 inch, you can define that as a new style based on the way the paragraph now appears. That new style you created is based on the Normal style. If you then change the font used for the Normal style, the font used for your new style would also change. In such a case, the Normal style would be the base style for the new style that you created.

You can see which (if any) style is used as a base style by opening the Style dialog box (Format ⇨ Style). As you select any style in the Styles list box at the left, the Description area at the bottom of the dialog box shows whether that style is based on another style. For example, Figure 8-7 shows the Style dialog box with the Body Text style selected. The Description area tells you that the Body Text style is based on the Normal style with 6-point line spacing after paragraphs are added.

Be aware that this capability to base a style on another style can create quite a chain of interdependencies. For example, if the Signature Name style is based on the Signature style, the Signature style is based on the Body Text style, and the Body Text style is based on the Normal style, any change to the Normal style affects all the other named styles.

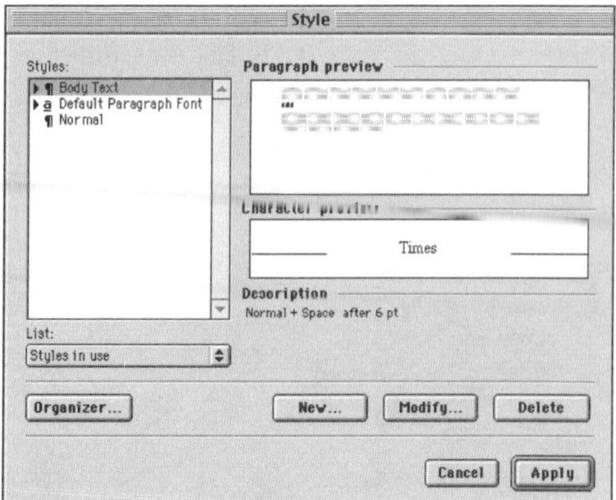

Figure 8-7: The Body Text style is based on the Normal style, according to the Description area in this dialog box.

You can change the base style for any style by using the options found in the Modify Style dialog box. To change a style's base style, follow these steps:

1. Choose Format ⇨ Style to display the Style dialog box.
2. In the Styles list box, select the style for which you want to change the base style.
3. Click the Modify button to reveal the Modify Style dialog box, as shown in Figure 8-8. In the Name box, you should see the name of the style that you want to change. In the Based on list box, you should see the base style that is currently used.

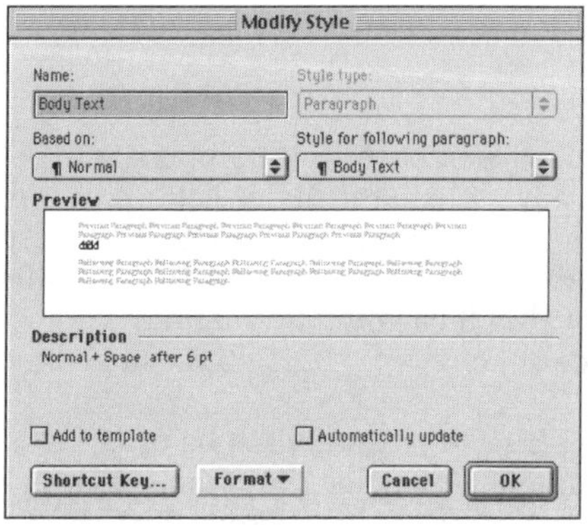

Figure 8-8: The Modify Style dialog box

The Dangers of Redefining Normal

Word takes advantage of the fact that styles can be based on other styles by basing many of its built-in styles on the Normal style. Therefore, redefining the Normal style can cause major repercussions elsewhere including some that may prove undesirable.

For example, if you redefine the Normal style to use 12-point Palatino font, every style based on the Normal style will use 12-point Palatino, whether you like it or not.

4. Click the arrow at the right side of the Based on pop-up menu to display all available styles in the document and to find a desired style to serve as the base style. Then click OK.

If you turn on the Add to template check box before clicking OK, the changes to the base style are recorded in the template that you used to create the document.

Copying, deleting, and renaming styles

Word enables you to copy styles from one document to another. In many cases, this capability helps you to avoid the work necessary to create the same style twice. To copy styles from one document to another and to delete and rename styles, follow these steps:

1. Choose Format ➪ Style.
2. In the Style dialog box, click the Organizer button. Word displays the Organizer dialog box shown in Figure 8-9.

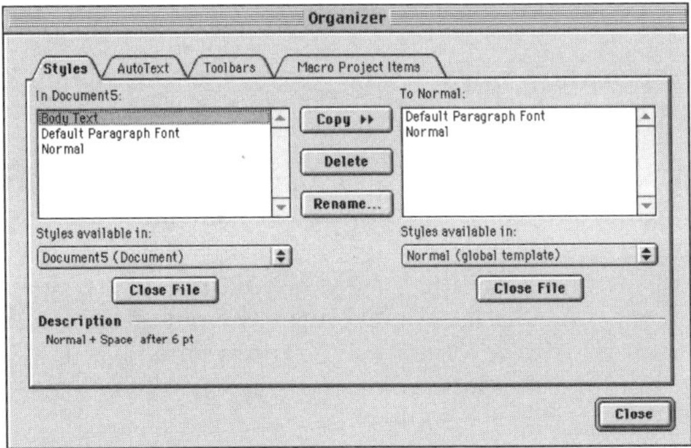

Figure 8-9: The Styles tab of the Organizer dialog box

3. To copy a style to or from a different document or template, click the Close File button (which toggles to Open File) and then click the Open File button to open the desired document or template that contains the style. Select the desired style in the list box to the left and click the Copy button to copy the style to the other document or template.
4. To delete a style, click the desired style in the list box to the left and click the Delete button. (Note that Word will not let you delete its built-in styles; you can delete only custom styles.)
5. To rename a style, click the desired style in the list box to the left, then click Rename and enter a new name in the dialog box that appears. Then click Close.

Redefining Styles

As you create your document, you won't always be certain exactly how you'll want every bit of it to look. That's an opportunity to call on the power of styles. For example, assume you're doing a ten-page document, such as a contract. Perhaps you create a style that is 12-point type with 12 points of space after each paragraph. (Does this sound the same as pressing Return an extra time between paragraphs?) What if after entering all the text, you find the document looks silly with only six lines on the last page? Or what if your boss decides it should be done in a different font and in 10-point type? And, to make it worse, what if your boss doesn't like your half-inch indents at the start of each paragraph? None of this is a problem as long as you've used styles. All you need to do is change one paragraph to the way you want them all to be. Then you just redefine the existing style that's applied to all the paragraphs in question.

To redefine a style, follow these steps:

1. Place the cursor in the paragraph you want to change. Then make your changes.
2. Click in the style menu box, which selects the entire contents of the box. Press Return to bring up the Modify Style dialog box.

   The default choice in this dialog box is to "Update the style to reflect the recent changes." This is the option you want, so you can click OK.

   The other choice is to "Reapply the formatting of the style to the selection." This option removes your changes and returns the paragraph to the way it was before you messed with it. There will be times when being able to do this will be handy.

After updating the style, all paragraphs containing the style automatically change to the new look. Just imagine—ten pages can all be changed with so few clicks of the mouse!

Finding Styles When You Need Them

Word provides two ways to find and use styles. Using Word's Help feature, you can display information about your styles as you work, or you can use Format ➪ Style Gallery.

Displaying style names as you work

You can see which styles are in effect in your documents in two ways. One is to have the style names appear in Formatting balloons; the other way is to see the style names onscreen in the left margin area.

To have the Formatting balloons appear, select View ➪ Reveal Formatting. When this feature is on (checked in the menu), your cursor looks like a text balloon. When you click this cursor on any text, a balloon full of style information about that text pops up. Balloons will continue to reveal style information until you return to View ➪ Reveal Formatting to uncheck the feature or until you begin to type again. (Typing automatically turns off Reveal Formatting.)

You can see the styles you have used in your document by displaying them onscreen in the left margin area. In Figure 8-10, you can see the styles displayed in such a manner. To do so, first make sure you are in either Normal or Outline view (you can't show styles in the margin in any of the other views of Word), and then follow these steps:

1. Choose Tools ➪ Preferences.
2. Click the View tab in the Preferences dialog box.
3. In the Style Area Width box, enter or use the arrows to select a desired width. (One inch works well for showing the names of most styles, unless you've added very long style names to your document.)
4. Click OK. The style names in your document appear to the left of the document.

You can easily resize the style width area visually. Move your mouse over the line that divides the style area from the rest of the document until the cursor becomes a line with arrows pointing left and right. When it does, you can click and drag in either direction to enlarge or reduce the style column.

There are two ways to remove the style names from view. One is to return to the Preferences dialog box and change the Style Area Width setting back to zero. The faster way is to use the visual resizing technique and drag the dividing line all the way to the left of your document window.

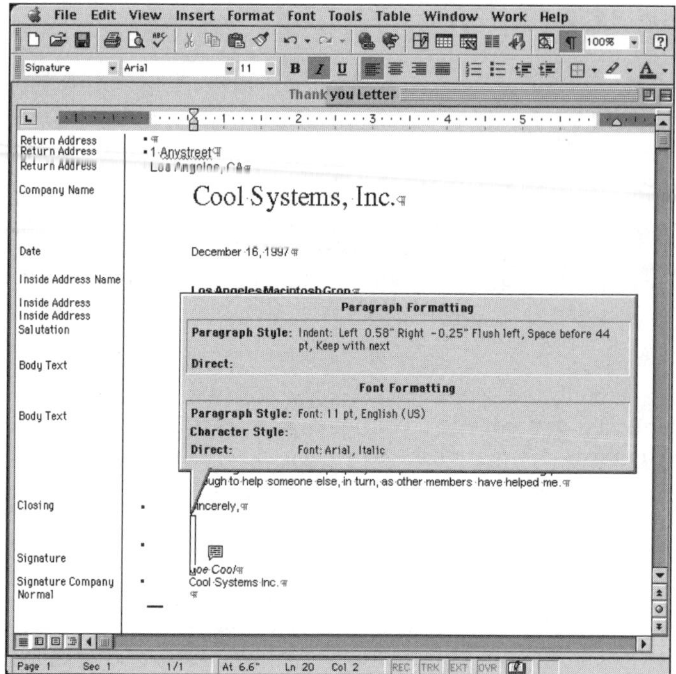

Figure 8-10: A document displaying style information both ways

Using the Style Gallery

With Word's plethora of built-in styles scattered across numerous templates, it can be challenging to find where a useful style is located. To help you find the styles you seek, use Word's Style Gallery dialog box (see Figure 8-11). To open this dialog box, choose the command from the Format Style Gallery menu.

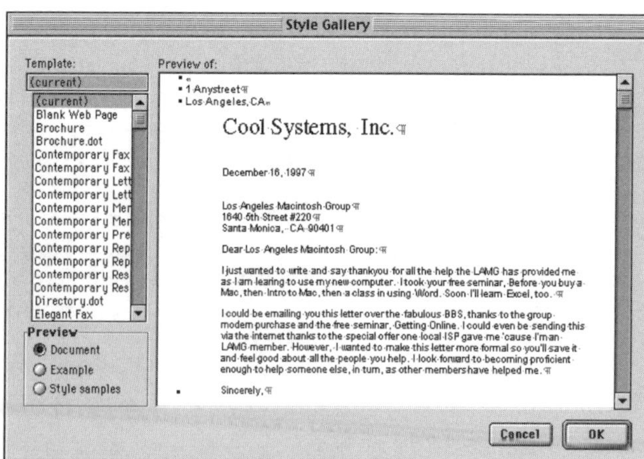

Figure 8-11: The Style Gallery dialog box

The Template list box contains all the available templates. You can click any template name in the list box to see a preview of your own document as it uses the styles contained in that particular template. At the lower-left corner of the dialog box, you can click the Style samples radio button to view samples of the different styles instead of viewing a preview of the document. You can also click the Example radio button to see an example document formatted with the various available styles. The Style Gallery is helpful when you're trying to locate a style that will work in a given situation.

Defining and Applying Styles: An Exercise

To try your hand at using the dialog boxes to create and apply a new style to a document, follow these steps:

1. Open any existing document that contains two or more paragraphs and place the insertion point anywhere in the first paragraph.
2. From the Format menu, choose the Style command. When the Style dialog box appears, click the New button.
3. In the Name text box, type My Style as a name for the new style.
4. Select Font from the Format pop-up list to display the Font dialog box (see Figure 8-12). In the Font list box, choose any font other than the one you are currently using and then click OK.

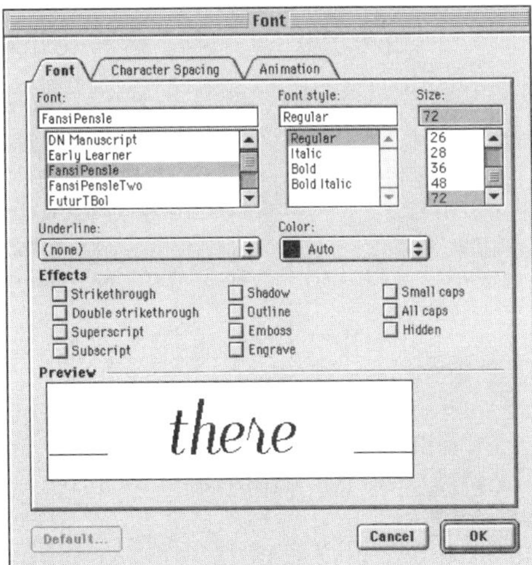

Figure 8-12: The Font dialog box

5. Select Paragraph from the Format pop-up list to display the Paragraph dialog box (see Figure 8-13). In the Indentation area, set the Left value to 0.5 inches, and then click the Special list box, choose First line, and set the First-line indentation to 0.5 inches. Set the Line spacing to 1.5 lines and click OK.

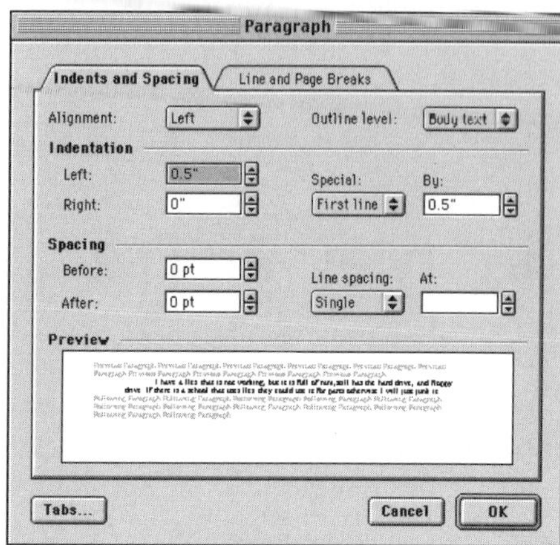

Figure 8-13: The Indents and Spacing tab of the Paragraph dialog box

The Preview box shows your formatting changes, including your selected font, the new paragraph indentations, and the new line spacing.

6. Click OK to add the new style to the list.
7. Click the Apply button to apply the style and close the Style dialog box.

Remember that this is one of the two ways to define a style. The other method was described earlier in the section "Defining styles by example."

To apply the new style to another paragraph in the document, follow these steps:

1. Place the insertion pointer anywhere in a different paragraph of the document.
2. If the Formatting toolbar is not visible, choose it from the View➪Toolbars submenu.
3. Click the arrow to the right of the Styles list box and choose My Style from the list. When you choose the style, the paragraph assumes the style's formatting as shown in Figure 8-14.

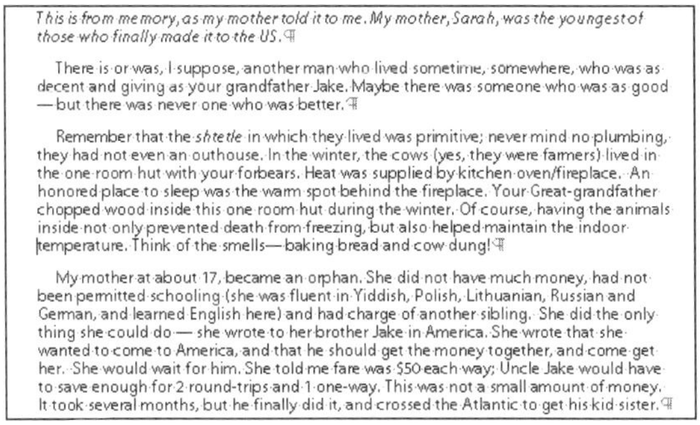

This is from memory, as my mother told it to me. My mother, Sarah, was the youngest of those who finally made it to the US.¶

There is or was, I suppose, another man who lived sometime, somewhere, who was as decent and giving as your grandfather Jake. Maybe there was someone who was as good — but there was never one who was better.¶

Remember that the *shtetle* in which they lived was primitive; never mind no plumbing, they had not even an outhouse. In the winter, the cows (yes, they were farmers) lived in the one room hut with your forbears. Heat was supplied by kitchen oven/fireplace. An honored place to sleep was the warm spot behind the fireplace. Your Great-grandfather chopped wood inside this one room hut during the winter. Of course, having the animals inside not only prevented death from freezing, but also helped maintain the indoor temperature. Think of the smells— baking bread and cow dung!¶

My mother at about 17, became an orphan. She did not have much money, had not been permitted schooling (she was fluent in Yiddish, Polish, Lithuanian, Russian and German, and learned English here) and had charge of another sibling. She did the only thing she could do — she wrote to her brother Jake in America. She wrote that she wanted to come to America, and that he should get the money together, and come get her. She would wait for him. She told me fare was $50 each way; Uncle Jake would have to save enough for 2 round-trips and 1 one-way. This was not a small amount of money. It took several months, but he finally did it, and crossed the Atlantic to get his kid sister.¶

Figure 8-14: The results of applying the styles to paragraphs

Understanding Templates

To carry document design consistency even further than character and paragraph formatting, use templates. As mentioned earlier, templates are models that serve as molds for your documents. Templates include such items as margins, text, and page setup in addition to collections of styles.

When you create a new document with the New command from the File menu, Word always asks which template you want to use by displaying the available templates on several tabs in the New dialog box (see Figure 8-15). The tabs group Word's predefined templates according to their functions. Any new templates that you create appear under the General tab. If you click OK in the New document dialog box without making a selection, Word uses the default Normal template to create the new document.

The Easiest Way to Apply a Heading

Word's AutoFormat feature makes it incredibly simple to apply Word's built-in Heading 1 style to text. Simply type your line of text and press Return twice without adding any punctuation to the end of the line.

If you change the style called Heading 1 in any way, those changes will also apply to text that was styled Heading 1 using this method.

Hint: If it doesn't work for you, make sure the headings are turned on in the AutoFormat tab (click the Options button in the Format ➪ AutoFormat dialog box).

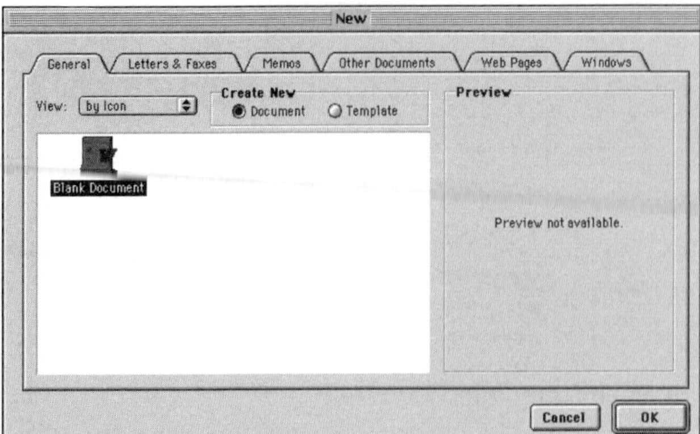

Figure 8-15: The General tab of the New dialog box

When you select a template from this dialog box, your new document takes on all the features of that template—including any text stored in the template; any character, paragraph, and page layout formatting; any preset styles; and any new styles that you added to the document. Any macros, AutoText entries, or keyboard, menu, or toolbar definitions stored in the template are also available to the document.

You can use any of Word's predefined templates or you can create and save your own. If you take the time to examine the templates provided with Word, you may find many that can be useful in your work. When you click any template (except Normal), Word provides a preview to help you determine whether this template is right for you. Predefined Word templates include:

- Contemporary fax
- Contemporary letter
- Elegant fax
- Elegant letter
- Professional fax
- Professional letter
- Contemporary memo
- Elegant memo
- Professional memo
- Contemporary resume
- Elegant resume
- Professional resume
- Blank web page

Because a template is a document, you use the same procedure to create and save a template as you use for a document. Word lets you specify whether you want to create a document or a template when you use the New command from the File menu. At the lower-right corner of the New dialog box, simply click the Template radio button to make the new document a template and then click OK. When the new document appears onscreen, you can add whatever boilerplate text, formatting, and styles that you want, and then save the file with the Save command from the File menu.

You can also specify that a file be saved as a template after you have created it. For example, if you have created a boilerplate document, and you want to store that document as a template, you can do so with the Save As command from the File menu. In the Save As dialog box, choose Document Template from the Save as Type pop-up menu. Be sure to name your new template appropriately. By default it will use the name you've previously used. Remember that two documents with the same name will lead to confusion. To have this template accessible from the New dialog box with the File⇨New command, be sure to save it in the Templates folder in the Microsoft Office 98 folder.

Working with Templates

When you need to set standards for more than just the character and paragraph formatting of your documents, you can use templates. Templates can contain styles, boilerplate text or graphics, macros, and even custom menu, keyboard, and toolbar assignments.

Applying templates

To begin a new document using one of Word's templates, simply use the File⇨New command, then click your desired template and click OK. You can also access your own templates this from dialog box if you've saved them within the Templates folder of the Microsoft Office 98 folder. Otherwise, you can go directly to your template from the Finder and double-click it to open it, just as you would any other document.

What's "Normal"?

Some new users of Word get confused about what "Normal" refers to. Word has both a Normal style and a Normal template, and the two don't mean the same thing. The Normal style refers to one particular style (available in all Word's default templates) that defines the character and paragraph formatting for ordinary text.

The Normal template, on the other hand, is a template file (saved as Normal) that contains Word's default styles along with the default keyboard, menu, and toolbar macro assignments. All styles and default keyboard, menu, and toolbar macro assignments that are saved to the Normal template are available for use from anywhere within Word.

Creating a template

To create a new template for use with Word, follow these steps:

1. From the File menu choose the New command.
2. In the New dialog box, click the Template radio button and click OK. (This will start you with the Normal document.)
3. Design your template as desired. Set margins. Add graphics. Add any desired character, paragraph, section, or page layout formatting, and create any desired styles. Define any desired AutoText entries or desired macros.
4. From the File menu, choose the Save command.
5. In the File Name text box, enter a name for the template.
6. Select a folder in which to save your template.
7. Click the Save button to save the template.

Hot Stuff

If you save your template in the Templates folder of the Microsoft Office 98 folder, it will always be available in the General tab of the New document dialog box. (However, you may lose your templates if you ever reinstall your software.) You can create your own tab by simply creating a new folder in the Templates folder. If you save your own templates in your own folder, you will always know which templates are your own, and you will always be able to identify them for saving during a software reinstall. You can even make several personalized folders/tabs.

Basing a new template on an existing template

You can use a simple variation of the steps in the preceding section to create a new template based on an existing template. In the New dialog box, click the Template radio button. Then, click the desired tab under which the existing template is stored, or choose the name of the template on which you want to base the new template, and click OK. When you save the template, be sure to save it under a different name than the original template.

To modify an existing template, simply open the template as normal, make the desired changes, and save it using an appropriate name.

Changing the default template

Word uses its default template, Normal, to store all its global settings—those settings that are available no matter what document you are using. Because Normal is the default template, it is worth spending time to customize it so that it meets the needs of your work. And because the Normal template is a template like all other templates, you can modify it (and save the changes) as you would any other template. Remember that the Default button present in some dialog boxes also lets you change the default settings in the Normal template. You can change the defaults for the character font, the page setup, and the language used by the proofing tools.

The Normal template is in the Templates folder of the Microsoft Office 98 folder. Either go there and double-click the document called Normal, or use the File⇨Open command to get to it and open it.

To change the default font, choose Format⇨Font, select the desired font and point size in the Font dialog box, then click the Default button. Click Yes in the next dialog box to verify that the changes should be stored in the Normal template.

To change the margins, choose File⇨Document and select the desired options from the Margins tab. Make any other appropriate changes you want in this dialog box. Click the Default button, and then click Yes in the next dialog box to verify that the changes should be stored in Normal. Click OK to close the Document dialog box. (You can also get to the Margins tab from the Word-specific screen of the Page Setup dialog box—File⇨Page Setup.)

To change the default page setup, choose File⇨Page Setup and select the desired options in the Page Setup dialog box. To change the orientation and paper size, do so in the first screen that appears by default, and then click the pop-up menu and select Microsoft Word from the pop-up menu. This brings you to the Word-specific screen. On this screen, click the Default button, and then click Yes in the next dialog box to verify that the changes should be stored in Normal. There are other page-customizing choices on the Word-specific screen. When you've made all your selections, click the Default button, and then click Yes in the next dialog box to verify that the changes should be stored in Normal.

To change the default language used by the proofing tools, choose Tools⇨Language⇨Set Language to open the Language dialog box shown in Figure 8-16. Select the desired language from the list, click the Default button, and click Yes in the next dialog box to verify that the changes should be stored in Normal. Click OK to close the Language dialog box. (You may need to purchase optional dictionaries to use a language other than the one supplied with the version of Word for your country.)

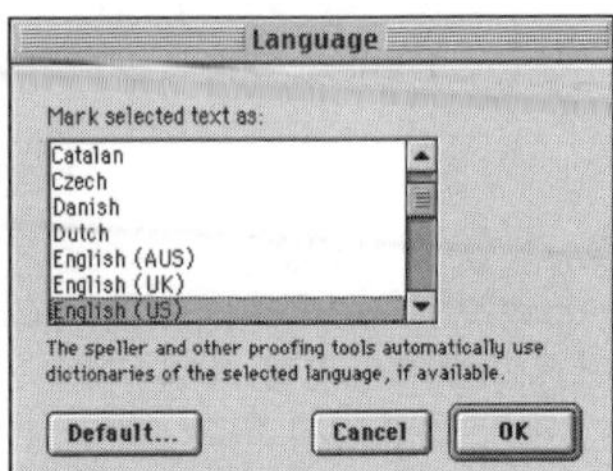

Figure 8-16: The Language dialog box

When you are finished making changes to the Normal template, use the Save command from the File menu to save the changes.

If you find you don't like the changes you've made to your Normal template, you can trash it. If Word can't find the Normal template it creates a new one. To trash it, simply go to the folder it's in, drag it to the Trash, then empty the Trash. Unless you've assigned a custom location for your Normal template (using the File Locations tab of the Preference dialog box), Word looks for the Normal template directly inside the Templates folder of the Microsoft Office 98 folder.

Creating and Applying a Template: An Exercise

Create your own business letterhead as a template for practice in creating templates. You can later create documents based on that template and the documents will automatically include your letterhead. To create your own business letterhead as a template, follow these steps:

1. Choose File⇨New.
2. In the New dialog box, click the Template radio button and then click OK. A blank document appears with the title Template1. (Or, if you've already tried this, Template2, Template3, and so on.)
3. On the first three lines of the document type your name and address. Add a blank line after the last line of your address.

4. This is a good time to save your document. From the File menu, choose the Save command. Enter Letterhead in the File Name text box. Select the Templates folder within the Microsoft Office 98 folder, and then select the folder whose tab you want your letterhead to show under. Click Save to save the template.
5. Select all three lines and click the Center button on the Formatting toolbar (or press ⌘-E) to center the text.
6. Format your characters. With the three lines still selected, click the arrow next to the Font box on the Formatting toolbar and drag down to select a font that you like. In the same manner, select the desired point size from the Font Size pop-up list next to the Font list. If you'd like to bold your name and address, click the Bold button next to the Font Size list (or use ⌘-B).
7. Place your cursor at the end of your text (or press ⌘-End) and press Return or Enter twice.
8. Close the document by clicking the close box in the top left of the document window (or use ⌘-W).

You can now create documents based on the template that you saved. Choose File ⇨ New, and then click your Letterhead template to select it. (If you saved it directly in the Templates folder, it appears in the General tab of the New dialog box. If you saved it in another folder within the Templates folder, your Letterhead template appears under the tab with the name of that folder.) Click OK to open the template. A new document that already contains your letterhead, such as the example shown in Figure 8-17, appears. Notice that this document is not called Letterhead and is unnamed. This is because you've opened a template rather than a regular document. Doing a save will not affect the original document.

Figure 8-17: A sample letterhead produced with the new template

This chapter gives you an idea of what you can do with styles and templates—a detailed discussion of the possibilities could fill a book of its own. You can obtain more ideas about creating styles and templates of your own by examining the sample templates provided with Word.

Summary

In this chapter, you learned how you can use styles and templates to mold the appearance of your documents to suit your needs and to make document creation easier. These points were discussed:

- ✦ Styles are collections of character and paragraph formatting decisions; templates are collections of styles, macros, and keyboard and toolbar assignments.
- ✦ You can choose a variety of styles from the Style list on the Formatting toolbar.
- ✦ You can easily create new styles and can base new styles on existing styles.
- ✦ You can copy styles between documents and between templates.
- ✦ Word provides a number of predefined templates that contain different collections of styles.
- ✦ All of Word's global settings regarding formatting are stored in the Normal template.

Where to go next

- ✦ In the next chapter, you learn how to use macros to automate many of the tasks that you normally perform in Word.
- ✦ Because styles are, in effect, collections of character and paragraph formatting, it makes sense to be familiar with the mechanics of formatting when you want to put styles to work in your Word documents. You can find more details about those formatting specifics in Chapter 3.
- ✦ Styles and templates are useful when you want to do desktop publishing in Word. Chapter 10 has the lowdown on desktop publishing.

✦ ✦ ✦

Working with Word Macros

✦ ✦ ✦ ✦

In This Chapter

Defining macros

Storing macros

Creating macros

Running macros

Deleting unwanted macros

Understanding the Macros dialog box

Using macros in an example

Creating macros that run automatically

✦ ✦ ✦ ✦

Macros bring to mind scary connotations for some people, while others, such as QuicKeys users, would hate to use a Mac without them. If you're one of the former, you can relax. Word 98's macros require no programming genius. If you're one of the former, check out Word 98's macro feature. You might just be surprised.

Macros are easy to create, and they can accomplish a great deal by saving time in your everyday work. In this chapter, you learn what macros are and how you can create them. You can then take a look at step-by-step examples that illustrate how you can use macros to automate common Word tasks.

Defining Macros

Macros are recorded combinations of keystrokes and certain mouse actions. Macros can automate many of the tasks that are normally performed manually, keystroke by keystroke, within Word. In a macro, you can record a sequence of keyboard and mouse entries and link them to a single key combination, or to a menu option, or to a toolbar button. Later, you can "play back" the recorded sequence by pressing a key combination, or clicking a toolbar button, or choosing the menu option that you've assigned to it. When the macro plays back, Word performs as if you had manually executed the operations contained within the macro. When your work involves highly repetitive tasks such as the production of daily reports, or the repeating of certain formatting tasks, you can often save many keystrokes by creating a few macros.

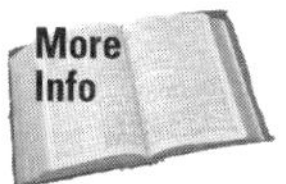

At first glance, macros may seem similar to AutoText entries (see Chapter 2), but there are significant differences. AutoText entries can reproduce text, but macros can do much more than simulate typing. Macros can perform menu and dialog box selections—something that you cannot do with AutoText entries. For example, if you routinely print two copies of a certain weekly report, you can create a macro that opens the document, chooses File⇨Print from the menus, and marks the dialog box options needed to send two copies of the report to the printer.

Word records your macros as instructions in the programming language used by the Microsoft Office applications: Visual Basic for Applications (or VBA for short). Don't panic at the sound of the name (or the implication that you need to learn programming). You can create macros in Word without knowing one iota about Visual Basic for Applications. You can create macros in either of the following two ways:

- ✦ You can record a series of keyboard and mouse actions (the most commonly used method). This method requires no knowledge of Word's programming language.
- ✦ You can type a macro directly into a VBA Editor window. This method lets you do some advanced tricks by means of VBA commands that you can't do by recording actions, but it requires that you get your hands dirty with VBA.

Not only can you use a macro to combine a sequence of commands that you use regularly, but you can also use a macro to perform routine editing and formatting tasks faster. You can also create a macro to reach buried dialog boxes more quickly.

Macros are especially useful when you format documents. You may have to change a document's font and spacing, enter heading styles, change margins, and check spelling and grammar. If you make these changes regularly, create a macro so you don't have to invoke the same commands over and over again. The following sections show you how to make your life easier with macros.

Alternatives to Macros

After spending this much time touting the benefits of macros, you should know that sometimes a macro might not be the most effective solution to a specific need. Before you jump into the task of designing macros for a task, consider whether another feature of Word can handle the task with less effort on your part.

If you want to use a macro to apply several character or paragraph formatting options to selected text, consider using a style instead. If you want to use a macro to type long, repetitive phrases, consider using AutoCorrect instead to designate an abbreviation of your choice to serve as the phrase. And if you are trying to use a macro to automate the process of filling out a form, consider using fields to make this task easier.

Storing Macros

Where you store macros depends on two things: the settings in the Template and Add-ins dialog box (which appears when you choose Tools⇨Templates and Add-Ins) and whether you are using the default template (Normal). If you are using the default template, macros are stored in Normal.

When you quit Word, you are asked whether you want to store the macros you've created during your session in the Normal template; you can answer Yes to store the macros or No to discard the macros.

When you choose Tools⇨Templates and Add-ins, the Templates and Add-ins dialog box appears, as shown in Figure 9-1.

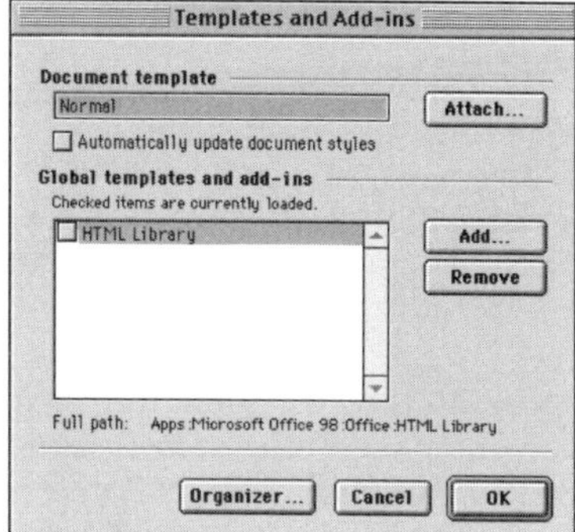

Figure 9-1: The Templates and Add-ins dialog box

If you are using a template different from Normal, the storage location for new macros depends on the settings in the Templates and Add-ins dialog box. If you turn on the check box for the template you are using, Word saves macros in that template. You can click the Add button to display all your templates and double-click any template to add it to the list in the Templates and Add-ins dialog box. In addition to saving macros to templates you've checked in the Templates and Add-ins dialog box, on exit Word will ask if you want to save the new macros to the Normal template file. All macros saved to Normal are global in nature, which means that they are available from any document in Word.

Creating Macros

The easiest way to record a macro is to use Word's macro recorder and follow the steps in the dialog boxes that appear. You then perform the desired actions with your keyboard and mouse and tell Word to stop recording. To turn the macro recorder on you can choose Tools➪Macro➪Record New Macro or you can double-click the letters REC in the status bar at the bottom of the screen. Both provide the same result.

You can also create macros manually by using Visual Basic for Applications, the programming language used with Word. Using Visual Basic for Applications to write and edit macros is beyond the scope of this chapter, but in short, you open a window into the VBA Editor and type macro instructions using VBA code. (Word and VBA programming is discussed in greater detail in Chapter 12 .)

The macro recorder is limited in an important way: you cannot record mouse actions within a document, such as selecting text with the mouse. If you try to use the mouse within a document, Word just beeps. However, you can use the mouse to select menu options and choose dialog box settings. If you want to select text as part of a macro, use the keyboard. (Hold down the Shift key and use the arrow keys to select large amounts of text; use ⌘-A to select all text in a document.)

Preparing to create your macro

Before you record your macro, you need to make some decisions about how it will be invoked, in what kinds of documents it will be used, and so on. Keep these points in mind when making these decisions:

- ✦ Give some thought to the overall workspace and how it should appear when the macro runs. You want to organize the workspace in the same manner as it should appear when the macro runs. For example, if you will use the macro in a blank document, you should have a blank document onscreen before you begin recording the macro.
- ✦ Think about all the steps that you need to take to accomplish the task for which you are creating the macro. Write the steps down if this will help you remember them. You don't want to forget an important step as you are recording the macro.
- ✦ If you want the macro to apply to a selected piece of text, select the text before you begin to record the macro.
- ✦ Think of a name for the macro that reminds you of the macro's function. For example, if you have a bad habit of typing two periods at the end of a sentence and you want a macro that deletes the extra period, you can call the macro Delete_period.
- ✦ Decide how you want to invoke your macro. You can assign a key combination to your macro, place it in a menu in the menu bar, or create a button for it in a toolbar.
- ✦ When you choose to assign a key combination to a macro, you can use Shift, Control, Option, or ⌘ key, or a combination of these modifier keys along with all letters, numbers, and the function keys F2 through F12. Word also lets you use some keys such as the Forward Delete key alone or with a modifier key or keys. If you assign a key combination, you simply press it to execute the

macro. If you assign ⌘-Option-P to a macro that prints two copies of the document that's currently open, and then you open a document and press ⌘-Option-P, the newly opened document will print twice.

While Word may let you assign macros to such keys as the Forward Delete key, it's not a good idea to do so because this disables the normal editing function of that key. (Even if you're aware of the change, your guest-users may not be and this might wreak havoc on your documents.) Also, be aware that Word has several shortcut keys that have already been assigned to execute other functions. You can assign a macro to these preassigned key combinations, but if you do, their preassigned function will be lost. For example, ⌘-B makes typed or selected text appear in bold font. If you assign ⌘-B to a macro, you would not be able to use that key combination to apply bold to any text. Don't worry about accidentally overwriting a key combination, however, because Word tells you whether it's already assigned to another function.

Recording the macro

To record a macro, follow these steps:

1. Choose Tools➪Macro➪Record New Macro (or double-click the letters REC in the status bar) to bring up the Macro dialog box shown in Figure 9-2.

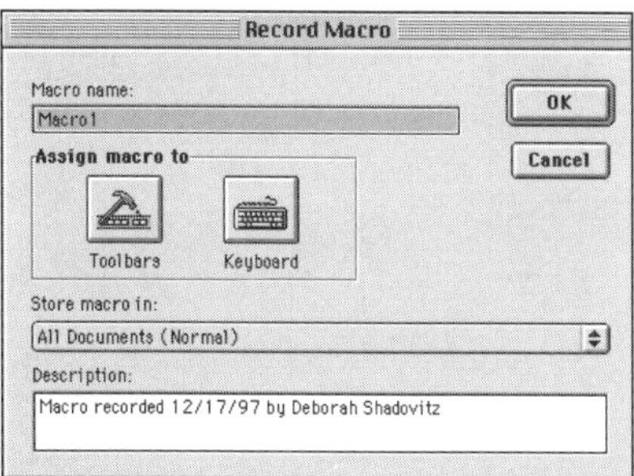

Figure 9-2: The Record Macro dialog box

2. Type a name for your macro in the Macro name text box. (Macro names cannot contain spaces, commas, or periods.) Word creates a new macro, saves it in the Normal template, and makes the macro available to all active templates unless you choose a different template in the Store macro in pop-up menu.
3. If desired, add an optional description in the Description text box. (It may help you later when you can't recall what you did or what you were thinking. See the section "Understanding the Macros Dialog Box.")
4. Click the Toolbars button or the Keyboard button, respectively, to assign the macro to a toolbar button or to a key combination. (The choice is up to you;

one isn't necessarily better than the other. People who aren't wild about the use of the mouse generally prefer keyboard shortcuts. People who don't want to memorize tons of commands generally prefer menus or buttons.)

5. After you choose how you want to activate the macro, the Customize dialog box appears.

   If you choose to add the macro to a toolbar, click the Toolbars tab of the Customize dialog box (see Figure 9-3). If the desired toolbar it isn't already visible onscreen, click the Toolbars tab and click to place a check by it to turn it on. In the Commands tab, drag the name of the macro from the Commands list out of the dialog box to the area on the toolbar where you want to place the button. Your cursor will give you a dotted line as feedback to tell you where the new button will land. Release the mouse when the cursor is where you want your button. (You can then click the button and use the Modify Selection pop-up menu of the Command tab of the Customize dialog box to edit the button.)

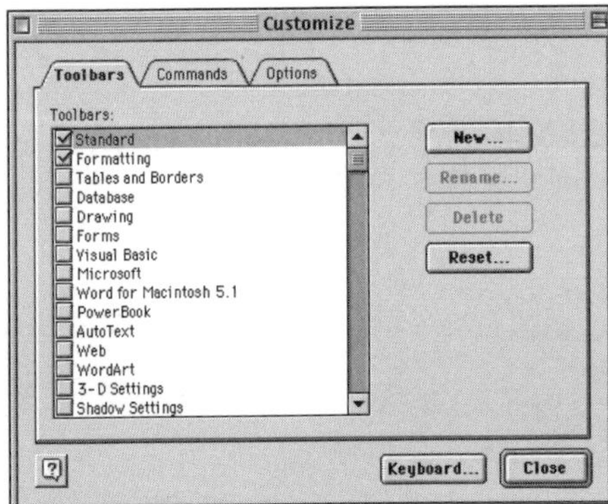

Figure 9-3: The Toolbars tab of the Customize dialog box

If you choose to assign your macro to a key combination, the Customize Keyboard dialog box appears (see Figure 9-4). The cursor is waiting in the Press new shortcut key text box so just press the key combination you want to assign to the macro. If these keys are already assigned to something you want to keep, use the Delete key to delete your combination and try a new one. When you are happy with the keys you've chosen, click the Assign button. The keys you've chosen are reported in the Current keys list. You can assign more than one key combination if you'd like.

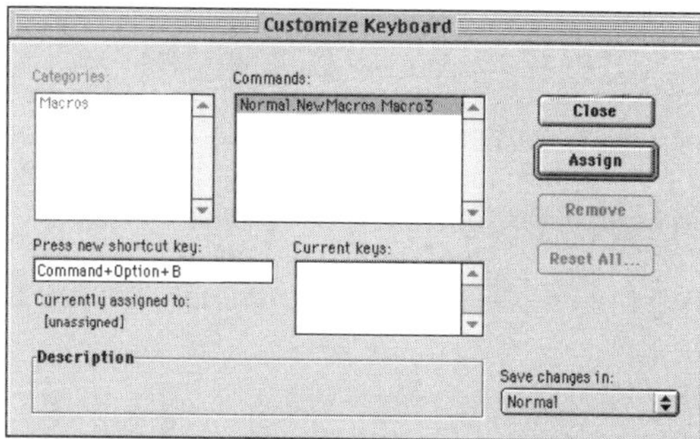

Figure 9-4: The Customize Keyboard dialog box

6. After assigning the activation command(s) click the Close button to start recording the macro. The Macro Recorder toolbar appears (see Figure 9-5). This toolbar contains just two buttons: a Stop button (on the left) and a Pause button (on the right).
7. Perform the steps that you want to record in the macro.

   If you want to pause the recording of the macro while you carry out actions that you don't want recorded, click the Pause button. When you want to start recording again, click the Pause button again.

Figure 9-5: The Macro Recorder toolbar, with the Stop button on the left and the Pause button on the right

8. After you finish recording, click the Stop button on the Macro Recorder toolbar. (Alternately, you can choose Tools➪Macro➪Stop Recording or double-click the letters REC in the status bar.)

Now you can activate the macro in the way you chose in Step 4: either from the toolbar or by pressing the key combination. You can also choose Tools➪Macro➪Macros, as detailed in the following section.

There are two ways you can tell you are in record mode. You will see the Macro Recorder toolbar and the letters REC in the status bar will be active rather than grayed out.

What's Recorded? What Isn't?

Word's macro recorder doesn't actually record your actions; instead, it records the commands and the keystrokes you enter. Remember that the macro recorder doesn't record mouse movements. If you want to create a macro that depends on selecting text, select the text by using the keyboard and not the mouse. Clicking the OK button in a dialog box while you are recording a macro records the state of every option in the tab that is visible in the dialog box.

If you want to select options in another tab of the same dialog box, you must click OK to accept the options in the first tab and then reopen the dialog box. Click the new tab, select the options in it, and click OK to accept the options in the second tab. You do all these steps while you are recording the macro.

Running Macros

If you assigned your macro to a key combination, menu, or toolbar, you execute the macro by using the chosen method. To run macros with Tools⇨Macro⇨Macros, follow these steps:

1. Choose Tools⇨Macro⇨Macros. The Macros dialog box appears, as shown in Figure 9-6.

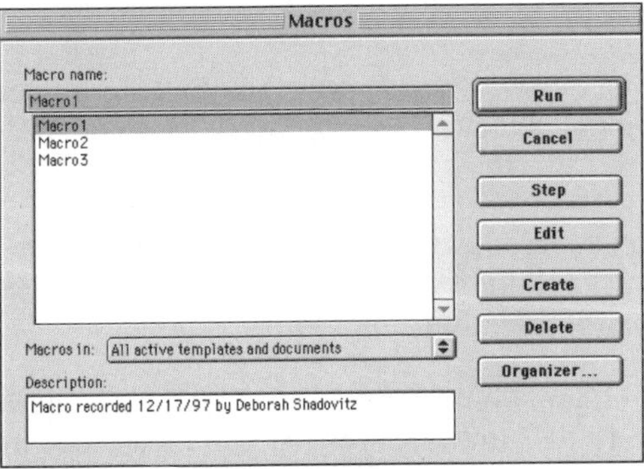

Figure 9-6: The Macros dialog box

2. Choose a macro from the list or type the name of the macro in the Macro name text box.

   If the macro you want to execute isn't listed, Word may not be configured to run macros from all active templates. If the Macros in pop-up menu does not say either All active templates and documents or the name of the template in which you created the macro, select either of those values. This pop-up menu controls available macros based on the templates in which they were created.

3. Click Run. Word executes the chosen macro. (Or, to run the macro, double-click the name of the macro.)

If you try to run a macro and you can't find it, chances are that your document is using a different template from the one to which your macro was originally saved.

Deleting Unwanted Macros

If you create a macro and later decide that you no longer need it, you can delete it. To delete a macro, choose Tools⇨Macro⇨Macros. In the Macros dialog box that appears, click the unwanted macro to select it and click Delete. Click Yes in the confirmation dialog box that appears and the macro is deleted.

Understanding the Macros Dialog Box

As noted earlier, you enter the name of the desired macro in the Macro name text box. After a name is entered (or chosen from the list box), all the buttons at the right side of the dialog box are made available. Also, if you entered a description when you created the macro, the description appears in the Description text box at the bottom of the dialog box. The buttons in the dialog box perform the functions shown in Table 9-1.

Table 9-1
Macro Dialog Box Buttons

Button	***Purpose***
Run	Runs the selected macro.
Cancel	Closes the dialog box without running the macro.
Step	Opens the selected macro in the VBA Editor and runs the macro one step at a time.
Edit	Opens the selected macro in the VBA Editor where you can edit the code.
Create	Creates a macro by using the Visual Basic for Applications program code.
Delete	Deletes the selected macro.
Organizer	Displays the Organizer dialog box, which can be used to copy macros between templates.

Macros can be copied from one template to another, which is very useful when you have created a macro in one template that you want to use in another. This is done by clicking the Organizer button in the Macro dialog box and selecting the Macro

Project Items tab of the Organizer dialog box to copy macros from one template to another. To copy a macro from one template to another, follow these steps:

1. Choose Tools ➪ Macro ➪ Macros to bring up the Macros dialog box.
2. Click the Organizer button to bring up the Organizer dialog box shown in Figure 9-7. The Macro Project Items tab should be in the front of the dialog box.

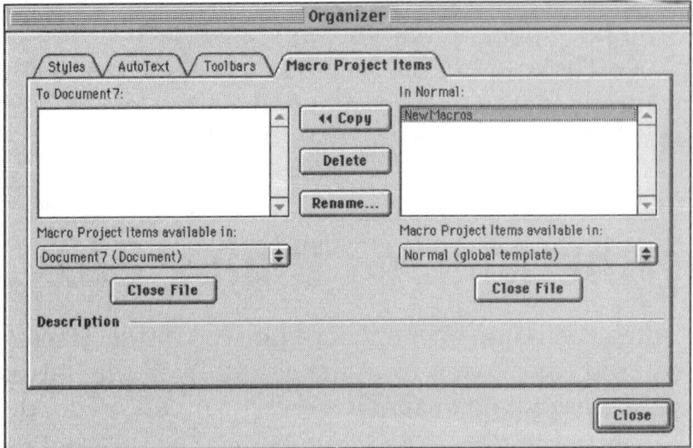

Figure 9-7: The Macro Project Items tab of the Organizer dialog box

3. You may need to close the open file. If so, click the Close File button on the left side of the dialog box. It then toggles to say Open File. Click this Open File button and choose the template in which you created the macro that you want to copy. On the right side of the dialog box do these steps again: Click the Close File button; click the Open File button; choose the template to which you want to copy the macro.
4. The Copy button now appears active so you can copy the macro to the other template. You can also rename the macro by clicking the Rename button and entering a new name in the Rename dialog box.

Word stores your macros in the Normal default template so you can use them with every document. You can use the Organizer dialog box to sort your macros by putting them into the templates in which you will use the macros most often.

Using Macros in an Example

To show you that macros aren't intimidating, try your hand at creating the following macro. After following these steps to create the macro, try one of your own.

In this example, assume that you regularly switch to Page Layout view from Normal view so you can see as much of your document as possible. You routinely choose View⇨Page Layout menu and turn off the ruler. These steps are time-consuming if you do them often in a day, so you can save time by creating a macro to carry out the commands for you. To set the stage, first turn on your ruler (if it is not already on) by choosing View⇨Ruler and check that you are in Normal view. To record the macro, follow these steps:

1. Choose Tools⇨Macro⇨Record New Macro to bring up the Record Macro dialog box.
2. In the Macro name text box, enter MoreSpace as the name for this macro.
3. Click the Keyboard button to assign the macro to a key combination. The Customize Keyboard dialog box appears.
4. Because Word doesn't use Control-. (period) for anything, it makes a good key combination. Press Control-. (period) and then click the Assign button to assign this key combination to the MoreSpace macro.
5. Click the Close button to begin recording the macro.
6. Choose the Ruler command from the View menu to turn off the ruler.
7. Choose View⇨Page Layout to activate this view.
8. Click the Stop button (the one on the left) on the Macro Recorder toolbar to end the recording.

To try out the macro, go back to the Normal view and redisplay the ruler. Then run the macro by pressing Control-.(period). Word turns off the ruler and switches to Page Layout view. Now you can create a macro that switches it back!

For another example of a useful Macro, see Chapter 12.

Creating Macros That Run Automatically

You can assign a specific name to a macro that will cause the macro to run automatically when a certain action is performed. For example, if you want a macro to run whenever you start Word, you would name that macro AutoExec. If you want a macro to run each time that you open a new document, you would name that macro AutoNew. Table 9-2 lists the names that you can assign macros to make them run when you perform the related action.

You can have only one AutoExec macro for your copy of Word. However, you can have a different AutoOpen macro for each template. A good use for an AutoOpen macro is to activate a special toolbar that you need in that template or to add a special message to the screen. Note that an AutoClose macro, which runs whenever you close a document, will also run whenever you quit Word before closing a Word document (because Word automatically closes documents when you attempt to quit Word).

Table 9-2
Automatic Macros and the Actions That Trigger Them

Macro Name	*Action That Triggers the Macro*
AutoExec	Runs when you launch Word.
AutoExit	Runs when you quit Word.
AutoOpen	Runs when you choose File⇨Open.
AutoNew	Runs when you choose File⇨New.
AutoClose	Runs when you close the current document.

An excellent use for an AutoOpen macro is one that automatically changes to your favorite folder for your Word files. When you create this macro, name it AutoOpen, and during recording use the Open dialog box from the File menu to switch to your favorite folder. After switching folders, click Stop to stop recording the macro.

Summary

In this chapter on using macros in Word, you learned the following:

✦ Macros are actually Visual Basic for Applications programs, but you don't need to know programming to create a macro. You can record a series of keystrokes and mouse actions as a macro.

✦ Macros can be assigned to toolbar buttons and key combinations.

✦ Some macros can be associated with launching or quitting Word, with creating a file, and with opening or closing a file. Such macros execute automatically when the event occurs.

Where to go next

✦ Macros can perform a number of tasks. Printing is one of them. Chapter 4 has the details.

✦ You may also create macros to format your documents. For some ideas on the different formatting options you have and how you can implement them, see Chapter 3.

✦ ✦ ✦

Desktop Publishing with Word

✦ ✦ ✦ ✦

In This Chapter

Working with columns

Using the AutoFormat command

Understanding graphic images

Using graphic images

Inserting graphs into Word

Working with text boxes

Applying the organizational tools

Using the Newsletter Wizard

✦ ✦ ✦ ✦

This chapter explains several techniques for using Word's desktop publishing capabilities. You learn to create documents that contain graphic images, text boxes, frames, and columns. You also learn how to create newsletters and other documents that contain headlines.

Word provides significant drawing and charting tools to create business graphs (also called charts). It is easy to insert into Word documents graphs created with the built-in Microsoft Graph, the popular FastTrack Schedule, or with many other programs.

Many programs let you save files in a common format. These saved files can easily be imported into Office documents. For example, Photoshop files can be saved as JPEG, GIF, TIFF, or PICT (among others) and are an ideal addition to a Word, PowerPoint, or Excel document.

Working with Columns

There are times when you will want columns in your documents. This section explains how to add columns. You can set your entire document in newspaper-style columns or add columns to just a section of it. Word lets you have up to eight columns. To insert columns into a document, follow these steps:

1. Select the text that you want to place in columns.
2. Click the Columns button on the Standard toolbar and drag to the number of columns that you want for your text, or choose Format ➪ Columns. The Columns dialog box appears (see Figure 10-1).

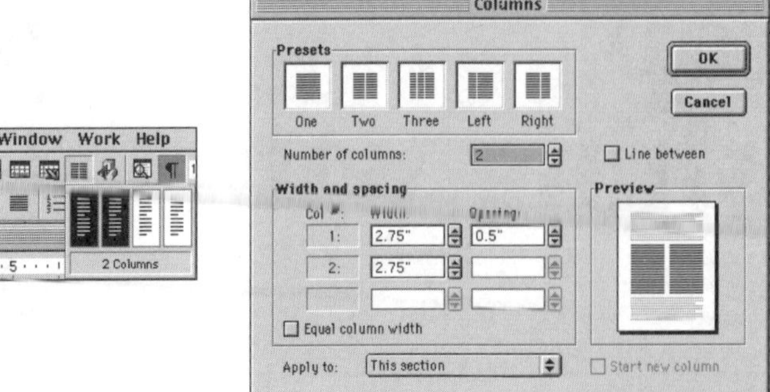

Figure 10-1: At left, the Columns button. At right, the Columns dialog box.

When you click the Columns button on the Standard toolbar, a pop-up box lets you choose the number of columns that you want in your document. Only four columns show when you click the button, but if you drag right, the selection will grow, allowing you to select up to eight columns. These columns are preset in width. They are adjustable as explained in the next section.

In the dialog box, you use the arrows next to number of columns box to set up to eight columns for your document. You can also choose the width of each column. For example, you can have two columns, one column smaller than the other column. The smaller column can be placed on the left or the right side of the page. Adjusting the settings in the Width and Spacing area of the dialog box easily sets column width and spacing. To place a thin ruled line between each column, check the Line between option. The Preview area lets you see the document layout with the chosen settings.

After choosing the number of columns for the document, you may need to change the preset column widths. There are two ways to change the width of the columns. To use the Columns dialog box, first select the text that you formatted for columns, and then choose Format ➪ Columns to open the Columns dialog box. In the Width and spacing area, choose the desired width for the columns and click OK to make the changes to your document.

Column width can also be adjusted visually in the document itself. This method is useful if you are not sure what width you want the column to be. To change the column width in the document, move the mouse pointer to the column marker on the ruler until the pointer turns into a double-sided arrow. Then click and drag to make the columns the desired width.

So Where Are My Columns?

When you add columns to a document, Word automatically switches to Page Layout view so you can see the columns. If you switch to Normal view, you'll probably wonder what happened to your columns. Don't think you've done something horribly wrong. Columns aren't visible side-by-side in Normal view.

To see your columns side by side (the way they will actually appear when printed), switch to Page Layout view (View⇨Page Layout). Many of Word's desktop publishing features are not evident unless you are in Page Layout view. If you are desktop publishing in Word, you may want to switch to Page Layout view after you have entered your basic text.

Using the AutoFormat Command

Automatic formatting is a relatively new feature, first introduced in Word version 6.0. Word's AutoFormat command provides a quick and easy way to format a document that you have created. AutoFormat makes Word analyze each of the paragraphs in your document to determine how the paragraph is used. Even though you may have formatted the text, the AutoFormat command may change the formatting to improve the overall appearance of the document. However, styles you have applied are not changed unless you permit Word to do so. To accept the changes that Word makes, choose Accept from the AutoFormat dialog box.

Remember the differences between the AutoFormat button and Format⇨AutoFormat. To format your document quickly, click the AutoFormat button. If you use this method, however, you are on your own to review the changes and to change things back. If you're at all worried about Word wantonly reformatting your text, and you wish to review each of the changes AutoFormat makes, use Format⇨AutoFormat and select the AutoFormat and review each change radio button. When Word is finished formatting the document, it presents another dialog box that gives you the opportunity to accept all changes, reject all changes, or review the changes one by one. Simply select the option you want.

AutoFormat removes extra returns or paragraph marks at the end of each line of body text. It also replaces straight quotation marks and apostrophes with "smart" (curly) quotation marks and apostrophes. AutoFormat can also replace hyphens, asterisks, and other characters used in a bulleted list with another kind of bullet character. It indents your paragraphs to replace horizontal spacing that you inserted with the Tab key or the spacebar. It makes e-mail addresses into live mailto links and Uniform Resource Locators (URLs) into Web links. You can program AutoFormat to add copyright (©), trademark (™), and registered trademark (®) symbols to a document. It can even add borders and shading for a professional look.

To use AutoFormat, open the desired document and click the AutoFormat button on the Standard toolbar or choose Format➪AutoFormat for the dialog box. If you use the AutoFormat button, you will not have the opportunity to review your changes. The AutoFormat dialog box provides the opportunity to review each change and then accept or reject each change separately.

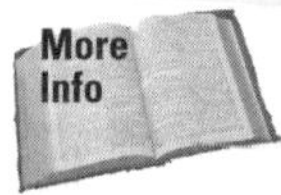

The AutoFormat command is very valuable. It can take the monotony out of formatting documents for users who don't do it along the way. See Chapter 8 for more information about the styles Word uses as it formats your document.

Of course, you may not be comfortable permitting Word to make such global changes to your document. For this reason, you can allow or disallow changes to be made by choosing Format➪AutoFormat, and clicking the Options button. This brings you to the AutoFormat tab of the Options dialog box (see Figure 10-2). The AutoFormat tab lets you control the changes Word makes to your document when you select the AutoFormat command. You can control whether Word preserves the styles that you apply or whether Word applies styles to lists, headings, and other paragraphs. You can also control whether Word makes adjustments to paragraph marks, spaces, tabs, and empty paragraphs. In the Replace area of the AutoFormat tab, you can control the replacements Word makes as it formats. It is a good idea to review these options before you begin the AutoFormat process to prevent unwanted changes.

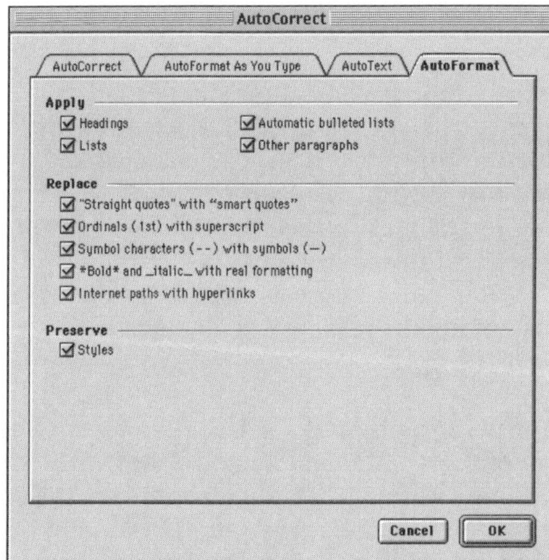

Figure 10-2: The AutoFormat tab

When Not to Use AutoFormat

Word's AutoFormat command shares an interesting trait with that of Excel's: they both work well with documents (in Excel's case, worksheets) that follow a conventional format. If your document is very unusual in terms of how it is structured, you may not like the kind of changes that AutoFormat applies.

If you happen to click the Accept button in the AutoFormat dialog box, and you don't like what Word does to your document, you can reverse the changes by choosing Edit➪Undo.

If you had selected the option to review the formatting results, when the formatting is complete, a second AutoFormat dialog box appears. It contains the Review Changes button. Click this button to display the Review AutoFormat Changes dialog box (see Figure 10-3), which enables you to review the changes that were made. Using this box, you can review the changes one by one by clicking the Find right arrow button to move forward, or clicking the Find left arrow button to move backward in the document. Each change is explained in the dialog box, as well as highlighted in the document.

Hot Stuff

If you forgot to ask Word to let you review changes, or if you gambled and let Word do its thing, but don't like the effect, you can always use the Edit➪Undo command to revert your document to its former glory. As another safety measure save your document before beginning the AutoFormat. That way, in addition to the Undo command, you can simply close your document without saving it, and then reopen it in its pre-AutoFormat form.

Figure 10-3: The Review AutoFormat Changes dialog box

Understanding Graphic Images

Word's capability to import graphic images from other software adds much to its desktop publishing capabilities. The basic installation of Word enables you to import any of the image types listed in Table 10-1.

Table 10-1
Image Types That Are Importable into Word

File Type	*Popular Abbreviation*
Encapsulated PostScript	EPS
Enhanced Windows Metafile	EMF
[CompuServe] Graphics Interchange Format	GIF
Joint Photographic Experts Group File Interchange Format	JPEG
Macintosh Picture	PICT
Macintosh Paint	PNTG
Portable Network Graphics	PNG
Tagged Image File Format	TIFF
Windows Bitmap	BMP
Windows Metafile	WMF

Word uses graphic filters to convert these image file formats to an image that appears in your document. If you try to import a picture (Insert⇨Picture) that your copy of Word lacks a filter for, you will have to install the necessary filter. This is easily done by running the Microsoft Office Installer located in the Office Custom Install folder of your installation CD or by running the Value Pack Installer. See Appendix A or your Word documentation for details.

As programs grow in popularity, new graphic filters are added to Word, so your version of Word may be able to import more file types than are listed in Table 10-1. Refer to your Word documentation to determine which file types your version of Word can import.

There are two kinds of graphic images: *bitmapped images*, which are created in painting programs, and *object images*, which are created in drawing programs. Because both types of images have definite advantages and disadvantages, you should be familiar with both.

Bitmapped images

Bitmapped images are images composed of dots or pixels. These images are called bitmaps because the image is literally defined within the computer by assigning each onscreen pixel to a storage bit (location) within the computer's memory. You can create your own bitmapped images using any painting program, such as Painter or Dabbler 2 (by MetaCreations) or use clip-art (predrawn images). Figure 10-4 shows an example of a ready-to-use bitmapped image from a clip-art collection.

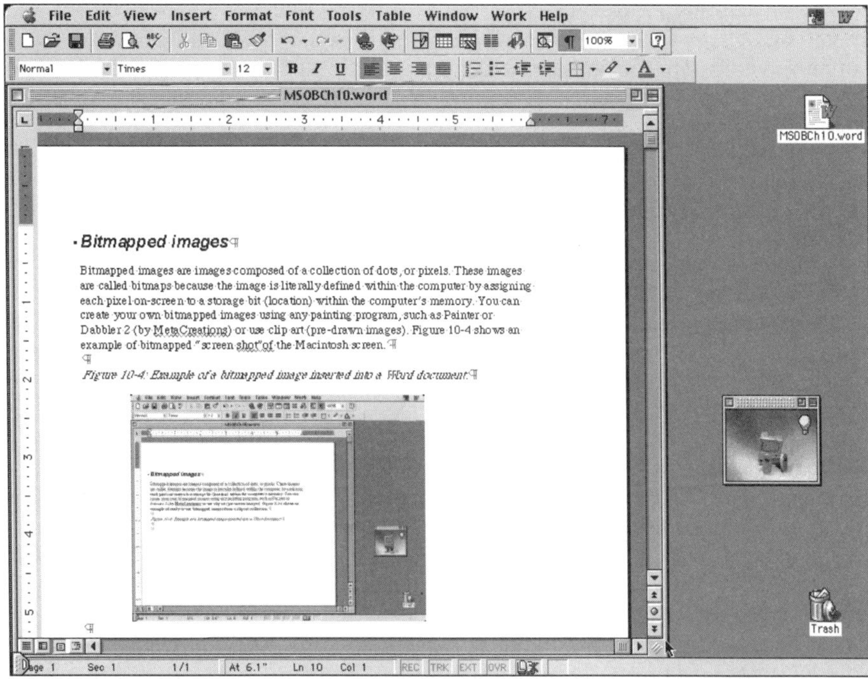

Figure 10-4: Example of a bitmapped image inserted in a Word document

Photographs are also stored as bitmapped images. If you have access to a scanner, you can scan photographs and store them on disk as bitmapped images by using the directions supplied with your scanner. You can then import the bitmapped image of the photo into your Word document. Note that black-and-white photographs typically scan with greater clarity than color photographs. Figure 10-5 shows an example of a photograph scanned into a bitmapped image.

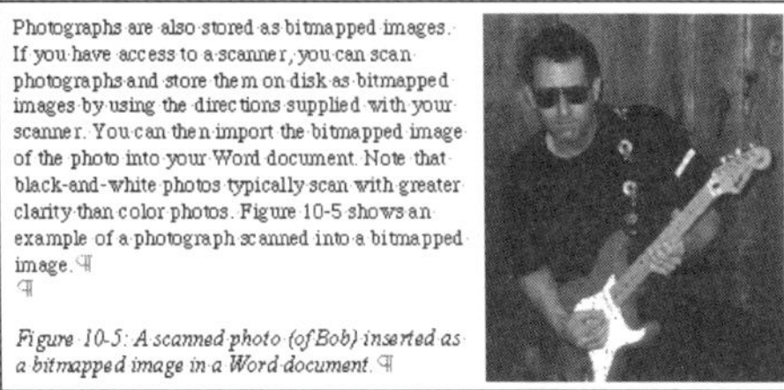

Figure 10-5: A scanned photo (of Bob) inserted as a bitmapped image in a Word document

Bitmapped images have one major advantage and one major disadvantage. The strength of bitmapped images is that you can easily modify them. Most painting programs enable you to modify existing parts of a bitmapped image by selectively adding or deleting bits. You can "zoom in" on the image as if it was under a magnifying glass, and you can turn individual pixels black, white, or any one of a range of colors. The disadvantage of bitmapped images is that you typically cannot modify their size by scaling (stretching or shrinking the image in one or more directions).

Object images

Drawing programs, such as Adobe Illustrator or ClarisWorks, create object images. Drawing programs work better than painting programs for creating line drawings such as company logos, maps, and images of constructed objects (houses, cars, planes, bridges, and so on). Painting programs work better than drawing programs for projects that you would sketch on paper without using a ruler such as drawing a person's portrait.

The disadvantage of painting programs becomes the advantage of drawing programs, and vice versa. For example, object images can easily be scaled, which means that you can change the size of the object by stretching it or shrinking it in one or more directions. Because the object is based on a collection of mathematically defined lines, the software simply expands or contracts the lines to expand or contract the entire image. The disadvantage of object images, however, is that you don't easily get a handpainted look. Paint programs allow you to work pixel by pixel, adding the tiniest of touches.

You can paste or import a bitmapped image into a PostScript-based drawing program. However, this does not convert the bitmapped image, which consists of pixels, into an image of PostScript-based lines. Curved lines in a bitmapped image are made up of "stepped" pixels (squares) of light and dark pixels. Bringing a bitmapped image into a PostScript-based program doesn't make the lines perfectly straight. If you bring a bitmapped image into a drawing program and then try to scale the image, the jagged patterns change disproportionately. The result is often a distorted image. Similarly, you can place a PostScript-based image in a painting program. It will probably look fine at its original size, but is unlikely to enlarge well as the lines become "stepped."

Getting Some Snazzy Graphics

If you'd like to jazz up your documents with some snazzy graphics but don't happen to be an artist, don't worry. There's no shortage of artwork available. In fact, the default installation of Office 98 even gives you some to start with. (It's stored in the Clipart folder in the Microsoft Office 98 folder.) In addition, you can find clipart and stock photos in many inexpensive commercial disk packages.

There are plenty of advertisements for specialized packages in the back pages of your favorite Mac magazines. Macintosh user groups may also be another good source of clipart. Lastly, commercial online services may have shareware clipart online.

Using Graphic Images

The addition of graphic images to your desktop publishing documents is very useful. After inserting the images, you will need to perform various tasks to make the object look presentable in your document. This includes tasks such as cropping, or adding borders or callouts to your graphic image. In Chapter 2, we discussed pasting graphics and inserting clipart. In this chapter, we show you how to insert images from other files.

Inserting images into Word

Insert ➪ Picture is used to insert images from a wide range of software. To insert a picture into your document, follow these steps:

1. Place the insertion pointer where the image is to appear.
2. Choose Insert ➪ Picture ➪ From file to open the Insert Picture dialog box, as shown in Figure 10-6.

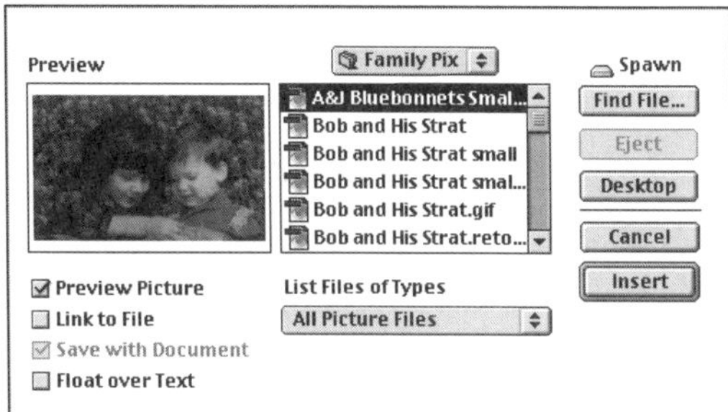

Figure 10-6: The Insert Picture dialog box

3. Using the normal Mac technique to open a file, select the folder your image is in. By default all picture files will appear in the list of files within that folder. To make it easier to find the correct image, you can control what type of files you see in the window (although this is not necessary). To see files of a particular type, click the List Files of Types pop-up menu and choose your desired file format from the list.

   As you select a file, a preview appears. Preview is a great timesaver when searching for an image. If you'd rather not see a preview, uncheck the Preview Picture option.

   If you want to link the image in Word to the original graphic file, turn on the Link to File check box. Word inserts the image as a field, and you can use the Update Field key (F9) to update the picture if you later make changes to the image.

4. Click the Insert button to close the dialog box and to insert the image into your Word document. (You can also double-click the image name, or press Return or Enter to issue the Insert command.) The image appears at the insertion pointer location. Figure 10-7 shows an example of a clipart image pasted into a Word document using this technique.

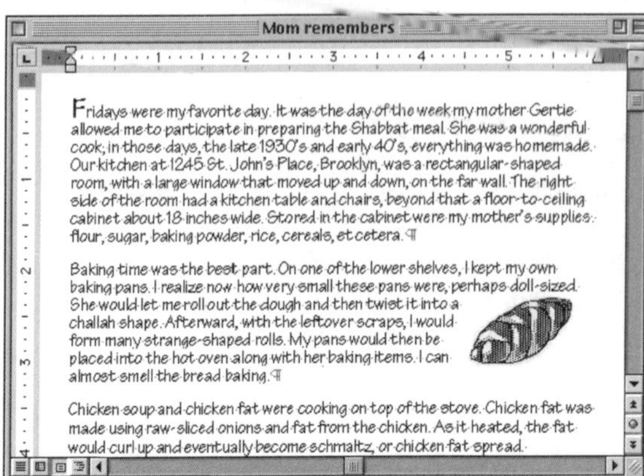

Figure 10-7: Clipart inserted into a Word document

Normally, you can think of an image that you insert into a document as a single large character, such as a giant letter A. As such, you cannot place text around the image because the image takes up one giant line of text. However, you can surround the image with a frame. You can position the frame containing the image anywhere in your document. Using a frame around the image makes available the option of text wrapping; that is, text will automatically reposition itself around the frame. (Wrapped text is visible only in Page Layout view.) See "Working with Text Boxes" later in this chapter for details about using frames in Word.

In addition to importing graphics, you can also create graphics directly from Word. To do so, make the Drawing toolbar visible (View➪Toolbars➪Drawing) if it isn't already. This toolbar contains several tools for creating shapes and images. Some buttons provide pop-up selections of tools to create shapes, while other buttons turn your cursor into a drawing tool so you can draw your own shape directly within your document.

Don't Forget Copy and Paste

In addition to using the Insert command to place images in your document, you can paste them in. Just open the image you want, select it, and copy it (Edit➪Copy or ⌘-C). Return to Word, place the insertion pointer at the desired location, and paste (Edit➪Paste or ⌘-V).

The image from the other program is inserted into your Word document at the insertion point.

Changing the look of the image

An inserted image can be scaled (resized) or cropped (trimmed). It is easier to use the mouse than the keyboard to change the size of the image. Select the image with the mouse and drag the sizing handles that appear; with the keyboard, select Format ⇨ Picture, and then enter dimensions in the dialog box that appears.

You can also apply borders to an image by using Format ⇨ Borders and Shading or by clicking the Borders button on the Formatting toolbar. You cannot apply shading to an image as you can to a paragraph. Notice that when you select a picture and choose Format ⇨ Borders and Shading, the Shading tab is dimmed in the dialog box.

Scaling an image

To scale an image, you must first select it. Instead of dragging over the image, as you do for text, click it. Word selects the image and displays sizing handles. Your cursor also changes to a pointer. (If you're really not into using your mouse, you can select an image by placing the insertion pointer anywhere inside the image, hold down the Shift key and press the right-arrow key once.)

Drawn objects can be scaled by dragging sizing handles, but not by using the Format Picture dialog box.

To scale (resize) a graphic visually with the mouse, drag one of the handles until the image reaches the desired size. Dragging the center-left or the center-right handle resizes the width of the image. Dragging the center-top or the center-bottom handle resizes the height of the image. Dragging any of the corner handles resizes both the width and height of the image. To maintain the image's proportions, press the Shift key while you click and drag one of the corner handles. To scale an image numerically, select the image and choose Format ⇨ Picture to open the Format Picture dialog box. Then select the Size tab, as shown in Figure 10-8.

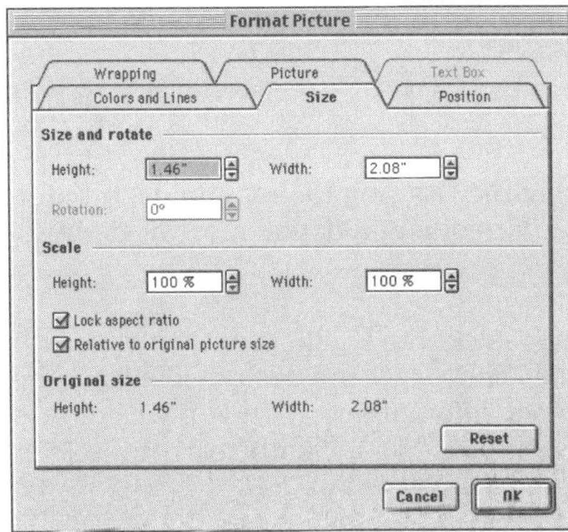

Figure 10-8: The Size tab of the Format Picture dialog box

The scaling can be changed by either entering a percentage in the Width and Height text boxes in the Scale area (in which case the Size and rotate measurements change accordingly), or by entering a measurement in the Width and Height boxes in the Size and rotate area (in which case the Scale percentages change accordingly). To maintain the image's proportions, use the Scale feature and be sure to enter the same number in the Height and Width boxes. After you have made your desired changes, click OK or press Return.

Word remembers the original size of an image, regardless of how you scale or crop it, so you can later undo your modifications—even after you've saved and closed your document. Use the Reset button in the Size tab of the Format Picture dialog box to restore an image to its original size.

Cropping an image

To crop a graphic, select the Crop tool (which looks like two corners overlapping) from the Picture toolbar. (This toolbar should activate automatically when you place a picture in your document. If it doesn't turn it on by selecting it using the View ⇨ Toolbars ⇨ Picture toolbar command.) Your cursor takes on the appearance of the Crop tool. Using this cursor, drag any handle to crop your image.

Dragging a handle on either center side crops the image on that side; dragging a handle on the center top or the center bottom crops the image from the top or the bottom; and dragging any of the corner handles crops from both the side nearest that corner and the top or bottom nearest that corner.

You can also crop a graphic by using a dialog box. Select the image and then choose Format ⇨ Picture and make sure you're in the Picture tab. In the Picture dialog box, use the measurement boxes in the Crop From area to enter the amounts by which you want to crop the image. A measurement in the Left and Right text boxes specifies how much the image will be cropped on the left and right sides, and a measurement in the Top and Bottom text boxes specifies how much the image will be cropped on the top and bottom. Use the Reset button to restore the original measurements if you need to start fresh. After you have made your desired changes, click OK (or press Return or Enter). As with scaling, you can always go back and use the Reset button to restore an image that you have cropped to its original size.

Adding borders

You can apply a border to an image using the Drawing toolbar, the Picture toolbar, or the Format Picture dialog box. Regardless of method, you must begin by selecting the image.

If you have the Drawing toolbar showing, select the image, and then click either one of the two buttons that look like lines and select the desired line from the menu that pops up. (Each button provides different lines.) To apply a color to your border, click the Line Color button (which looks like a Paintbrush) and select your color from the list that pops up. Selecting More lines opens the Colors and Lines tab of the Format Picture dialog box.

If you want to create a simple border the full width of your paragraph, you can take advantage of one of Word's many AutoFormat features. Simply type three or more consecutive hyphens (-) or equal signs (=) in a row and press Return. The hyphens create a single border while the equal signs create a double border.

If you have the Picture toolbar showing, select the image, then click the button with the lines and select the desired line from the pop-up menu. Selecting More lines opens the Colors and Lines tab of the Format Picture dialog box.

Alternately, you can choose Format⇨Borders and Shading. This brings you to the Colors and Lines tab of the Format Picture dialog box. In the Line area, select the type of border you want.

Borders can be applied to text, not just to tables and images. In fact, in Word 98 you can apply a border to any word or phrase, not just to an entire paragraph. However, borders are applied to text differently than they are to graphics or tables. Select the text to which you want to add the border, and then select Format⇨Borders and Shading to make your selection. This dialog box is highly visual so you will clearly see the effect before applying it. A quicker way to add a border around selected text is to click the pop-up arrow next to the Border button on the Formatting toolbar. This allows you to apply a border to the top, bottom, right, or left (or any combination) of the text. However, the color, width, and pattern will be whatever was last set in the Borders and Shading dialog box.

Adding Callouts to Your Art

You may want to add callouts to the images you insert in your documents. There are several ways to insert callouts. The most flexible way is to click the Text Box button on the Drawing toolbar, which selects the Text Box tool. Then bring your cursor to the approximate place in your document where you want to place the callout. Your cursor becomes a cross hair (+). Click and drag to define a text box and then release the mouse button. You now have a free-floating text box with a text insertion cursor ready and waiting for you to enter your text. At any time you can click this text box and drag it into the desired position.

The other way is to use Word's Table feature. Add a table with the Table⇨Insert Table command (or toolbar button) and insert the image into one cell of the table. Then type the text of your callout in an adjacent cell of the table and format the table so the text appears where you want.

Editing images

After you have placed an image into Word, you can edit it. To edit an image, double-click the image or Control-click and choose Picture Object➪Open from the shortcut menu. Then you can edit the picture by using the Drawing toolbar.

After you are finished editing the image, click the Close Picture button located on the tiny free-floating Edit Picture toolbar that has automatically appeared.

Word's drawing capabilities are object-based, so you may get unsatisfactory results if you import a bitmapped image into a Word document and then modify it with the Drawing toolbar.

Inserting Graphs into Word

You can insert graphs (charts) into Word by using Microsoft Graph, a program designed for creating business graphs. Graphs can also be inserted from spreadsheet programs. To insert a graph from Microsoft Graph, follow these steps:

1. Choose Insert➪Object to open the Object dialog box. In the Object Type list box, select Microsoft Graph 98 Chart and click OK. This adds a default graph and a Datasheet window. A new set of menus also appears to enable you to work with the chart. In the cells of the datasheet that appears over the graph, you can type the values that you want to use for the graph. Figure 10-9 shows the graph and the Datasheet window in a document.

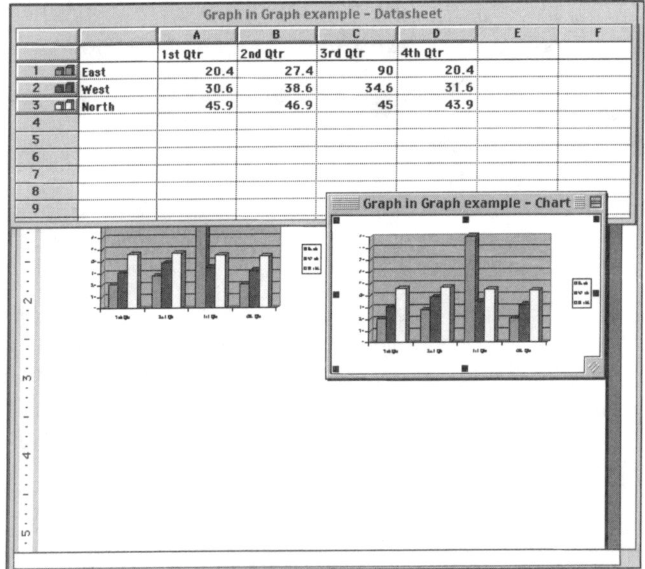

Figure 10-9: A graph and Datasheet window in a Word document

Notice the Float over text check box option. Checking this inserts the graph as a free-floating object that can be freely moved and have text wrap around it. Without this option checked, your graph is inserted into your line of text.

2. The default chart appears in your document, but is grayed out. Two chart windows appear—one that's a spreadsheet and the other that's the chart you'll edit.

   Enter the desired numeric data into the cells of the Datasheet window. The names of the headings in the cells are used as the categories of the chart. You can change them, too.

3. Choose Chart ➪ Chart Type to select the type of chart you want. In the Chart Type dialog box that appears, choose a chart type from the list and click the image of the desired chart subtype. Then click OK.

4. Control-click any desired part of the chart to display a shortcut menu that enables you to add any desired titles, legends, gridlines, or other items to the chart.

5. When you are finished making the desired refinements to the chart, select File ➪ Quit and Return to Document (⌘-Q). Figure 10-10 shows a document with a chart that's been customized and inserted.

You can make changes to your chart at any time. You can either double-click the chart, or Control-click the chart, and then select Chart Object ➪ Edit. Both actions relaunch Microsoft Graph and call the Datasheet windows back up.

You can also use Copy and Paste to copy graphs from another program to your Word documents. Simply display the graph in a window, select the graph, and choose Edit ➪ Copy. Then leave or quit that program and switch to Word in the usual manner. Place the insertion pointer at the desired location and choose Edit ➪ Paste to insert the graph into your document.

You can use the Clipboard techniques to copy information from any other Mac software into a Word document.

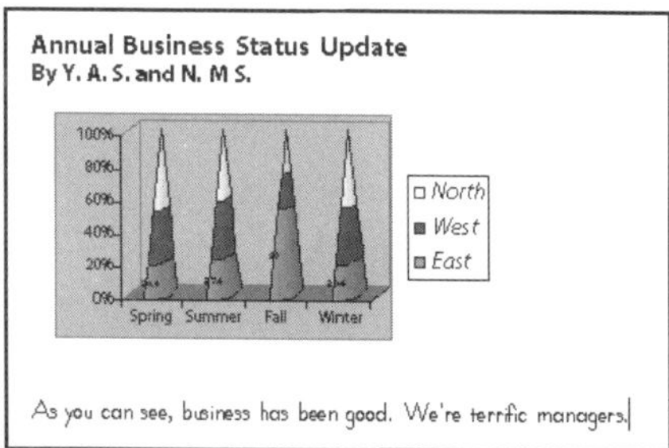

Figure 10-10: The sample document with a bar graph inserted from Microsoft Graph

Because Microsoft Graph shows a simple bar graph by default whenever it is launched, you can easily use the program to insert a graph into a document. For practice, follow these steps to place a graph in a document using Microsoft Graph:

1. Open a new document and enter this text:

   Word makes inserting graphs very easy. There are many options provided for the formatting of a chart that will be discussed as we move along in the chapter.

2. Place the insertion pointer at the end of the paragraph and press Return to begin a new line.
3. Choose Insert ➪ Object and choose Microsoft Graph 98 Chart from the dialog box that appears. Click OK to open the Microsoft Graph window. (Actually, you can save time by double-clicking your selection — Microsoft Graph 98 Chart.) A default bar graph appears in the document and two new windows open.
4. In the Data window that contains the spreadsheet, click the cell that contains East, type the name **Karen**, and press Return or Enter. For the cell that contains West, type **Cori**; and for the cell containing North, type **Alex**. Change a few of the numbers using the same methods.
5. Select File ➪ Quit and Return to Document (⌘-Q).
6. Back in your document, press Return twice to move your cursor down two lines, and then type:

   Here it is — my first chart.

You now have a chart that looks something like the chart in Figure 10-10, depending upon how you customized yours. (The text is also different.)

If you later want to make more changes to the graph's design, you can double-click the graph to switch back to the windows, menus, and toolbar of Microsoft Graph. For now, leave the document open onscreen because you will use it in an upcoming exercise involving frames.

Working with Text Boxes

As you work with text in Word, you will find times when you want to place text into a freestanding container. One common use for a text box is to draw attention to the text within it. Another great reason to use a text box is that you can move it and have other text wrap around it, creating a nice, refined look. However, perhaps the strongest benefit of a text box, is that you can link text boxes and have text flow from one to another. This is particularly useful when you have a multipage document such as a newsletter. Text will flow and reflow as you edit the text, resize the text boxes, or make changes to the graphics that your text flows around. Links don't even have to flow forward over pages; text just flows from the first box you create, to the next, and so on. In any case, within the text box, your text can be formatted as normal.

Creating a text box around existing text

You can place a text box around an existing section of text by following these steps:

1. Select the text you wish to create a box for by using your favorite selection method.
2. Choose Format⇨Insert Text Box or Insert⇨Text Box. Word then inserts a text box around the text you selected and a small floating Text Box toolbar appears. The document switches to Page Layout view if it's not in Page Layout view already.

If all you want is to draw attention to the text in the box or have other text wrap around the box, skip to "Formatting text boxes" and continue from there. If you want to create linked text boxes, continue here, following the steps to insert an empty text box into a document.

Inserting an empty text box into a document

At times you may want to insert an empty text box into a document to serve as a placeholder for text you will be entering later. Such is the case when you plan to link text boxes, or when you are planning your document's layout but don't yet have the text. Wrapping will apply in the text box, so you will not need to press Return or Enter at the end of your lines. To insert an empty text box, follow these steps:

1. Be sure that no text or object is selected. (For example, if you just created a text box, it is selected so click outside of that text box to deselect it.)
2. Choose Insert⇨Text Box. The cursor then turns into a crosshair.
3. Click and drag to draw the text box to the size you wish. (You can always resize the text box later.)

You can create as many empty text boxes as you'd like on any pages within your document. If you plan to link the text boxes, don't worry about their order of creation, as it doesn't matter.

Linking text boxes

To link text boxes, first follow the steps in the earlier section "Creating a text box around existing text." Then follow the steps in the section "Inserting an empty text box into a document" (immediately prior to this section). Finally, the floating Text

Box toolbar comes into play. It enables you to link your text boxes. Follow these steps:

1. Click the first text box to select it.
2. Click the Create Text Box Link button on the Text Box toolbar (it's the button that looks like a closed chain). If you happen to close the Text Box toolbar, you can open it again from the View⇨Toolbars menu. In case you hadn't noticed this toolbar option before and you're wondering why, it's because the Text Box toolbar can only be activated when you have a text box in your document.
3. Now click inside the text box that you want your text to flow to (if it doesn't fit inside the first text box). This must be an empty, unlinked text box.
4. To link to another box, click the second text box again (because it was the one last linked) and repeat Steps 2 and 3. Clicking the box that was last linked and repeating Steps 2 and 3 can link additional boxes.

Instead of using the Text Box toolbar, you can use the shortcut menu. In Step 1, after you select the first text box, move your cursor to the text box's border so the cursor becomes a four-sided arrow. Control-click and select Create Text Box Link and then proceed with Step 3.

Text flows in the order of your links regardless of the order in which you created the text boxes or the order in which you dragged them. To unlink text boxes, select the last box you wish to have in the link, then click the Break Forward Link button (which just happens to look like a broken link).

Linked text boxes may be formatted as any other text boxes so continue on with the rest of the sections on text boxes. The fun of linked text boxes is in resizing them. As you do, your text reflows.

Formatting text boxes

After you have placed the text box(es) in your document, you may want to change the lines and text wrapping that Word uses as defaults. You have the option to change many of the aspects of the text box, such as its location. You can also change whether adjacent text should be permitted to wrap around the text box. All text box movement and most text box formatting can be done using the mouse, by dragging, or by using the ruler and toolbars. At times you may prefer to work numerically, or find a setting that can't be done with the mouse (such as setting the top or bottom margin for the text within the box). In this case, you can double-click your text frame to open and use the Format Text Box dialog box shown in Figure 10-11. (You can also choose Format⇨Text Box to work within the Format Text Box dialog box.)

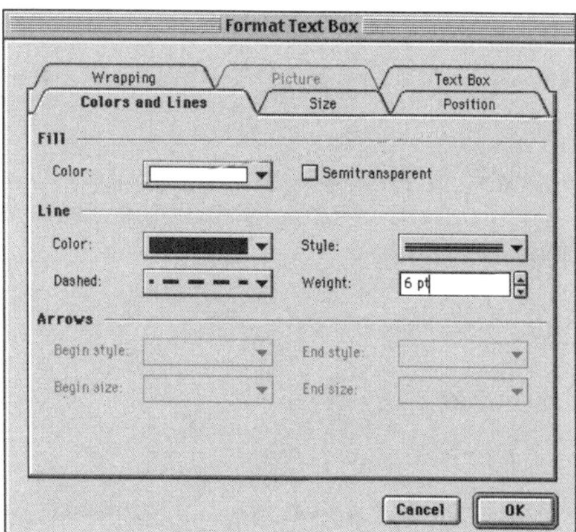

Figure 10-11: Format Text Box dialog box

The Format Text Box dialog box has six tabs. Each of these tabs aids in formatting a text box after you have inserted the text box in your document. The Colors and Lines tab enables you to change the color and line size of the text box. Clicking each option reveals a pop-up list full of choices. Just click and drag to make your selections.

The Size tab is where you manipulate the size of the text box by changing its height and width. This tab even allows you to rotate the box. Scaling the text box is also an option.

The Position tab controls the position of the text box on your document page. Clicking the arrows next to the Horizontal and Vertical settings changes the position of the text box on the page.

When a text box containing a picture is active, the Picture tab can control the cropping, brightness, and contrast of the image.

The Wrapping tab controls the wrapping of the text around your text box.

The Text Box tab determines the internal margins of the text box, enabling you to create space between the frame's border and the text inside the frame. The Convert to Frame button enables you to convert your text box to a frame. Frames are similar to text boxes and do less in the way of text flow, but they are the necessary choice when you want your box to include comment marks, notes, or fields.

Moving text boxes

After you have inserted a text box, you can easily move it to any location in a document. To move a text box visually with the mouse, follow these steps:

1. Choose View➪Page Layout to turn on Page Layout view.
2. Place the insertion pointer on the border of the frame. The mouse pointer changes to a four-headed arrow.
3. Click and drag the text box to the new location. As you drag the text box, a dotted line indicates its position. The content of the text box moves to the new location after you release the mouse button.

To move a text box using the dialog box, follow these steps:

1. Choose View➪Page Layout to turn on Page Layout view.
2. Position the insertion pointer inside the frame to move.
3. Choose Format➪Text Box from the menus and select the Position tab.
4. In the Format Text Box dialog box, enter the horizontal location you want for the frame in the Horizontal Position box. Use the From pop-up menu to choose whether the measurement that you enter is relative to the margin, the page, or a column.
5. Enter the vertical location you want for the frame in the Vertical Position box on the Position Tab. Use the From pop-up menu to choose whether the measurement you enter is relative to the margin, the page, or a paragraph.
6. Click OK (or press Return or Enter).

Sizing text boxes

To resize a text box, you can select the text box and drag one of the sizing handles, or you can select the text box and use the Size tab of the Format Text Box dialog box, entering the desired height and width.

To resize a text box using the mouse, follow these steps:

1. Choose View➪Page Layout to turn on Page Layout view.
2. Click anywhere in the text box that you want to resize. Eight black sizing handles appear on the edges of the text box.
3. Point to one of the sizing handles so that the mouse pointer becomes a two-headed arrow.
4. Drag the handle to resize the text box.

To resize a text box using the dialog box and keyboard, follow these steps:

1. Choose View➪Page Layout to turn on Page Layout view.
2. Use the arrow keys to position the insertion pointer inside the text box that you want to resize.
3. Choose Format➪Text Box.

4. Click the Size tab of the Format Text Box dialog box and enter the height and width to apply to the text box.
5. Click OK (or press Return or Enter).

Wrapping text around text boxes

By default Word wraps adjacent text around text boxes. You can turn this trait on or off for a particular text box with the Text tab of the Format Text Box dialog box. To turn on (or off) text wrapping around text boxes, follow these steps:

1. Choose View➪Page Layout to turn on Page Layout view.
2. Use the mouse or the arrow keys to place the insertion pointer inside the text box.
3. Choose Format➪Text Box to open the Format Text Box dialog box.
4. On the Wrapping tab of the dialog box, choose one of the options listed. Diagrams will give you an idea of what the text will look like when it is wrapped around the text box.
5. You can also make adjustments to the distance the text appears from the text box. After you have made your choices, click OK (or press Return or Enter).

Figure 10-12 shows the difference between text wrapping that is on and text wrapping that is off. On the left, the text box containing the graph has been placed in the center of the paragraph, and the surrounding type of wrapping was chosen. Notice how the text wraps around the text box in this figure. On the right, the text box is at the same location, but the text wrapping option has been set to None and Float over picture is turned off. As a result, the text does not wrap around the text box that contains the graph. Note that the option applies to the selected text box.

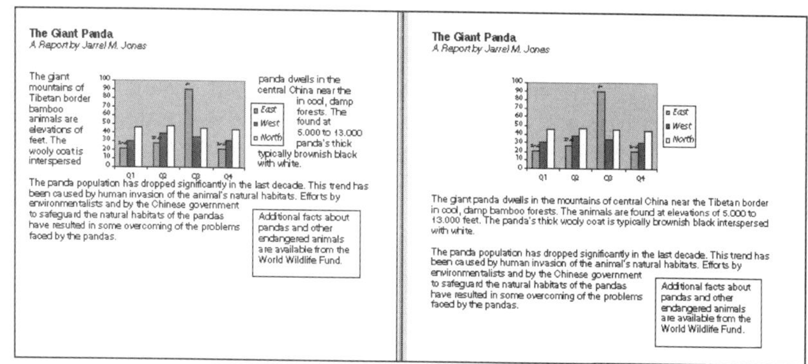

The Giant Panda
A Report by Jarrel M. Jones

The giant mountains of Tibetan border bamboo animals are elevations of feet. The wooly coat is interspersed panda dwells in the central China near the in cool, damp forests. The found at 5.000 to 13.000 panda's thick typically brownish black with white.

The panda population has dropped significantly in the last decade. This trend has been caused by human invasion of the animal's natural habitats. Efforts by environmentalists and by the Chinese government to safeguard the natural habitats of the pandas have resulted in some overcoming of the problems faced by the pandas.

Additional facts about pandas and other endangered animals are available from the World Wildlife Fund.

The Giant Panda
A Report by Jarrel M. Jones

The giant panda dwells in the mountains of central China near the Tibetan border in cool, damp bamboo forests. The animals are found at elevations of 5.000 to 13.000 feet. The panda's thick wooly coat is typically brownish black interspersed with white.

The panda population has dropped significantly in the last decade. This trend has been caused by human invasion of the animal's natural habitats. Efforts by environmentalists and by the Chinese government to safeguard the natural habitats of the pandas have resulted in some overcoming of the problems faced by the pandas.

Additional facts about pandas and other endangered animals are available from the World Wildlife Fund.

Figure 10-12: At left, text wraps around the graph. At right, text wrapping has been turned off.

Applying the Organizational Tools

To create a document with a professionally published appearance, use the organizational tools and techniques that Word provides. The combination of these techniques and the use of graphics will turn an ordinary-looking document into a professional-looking document. These organizational tools include such things as columns, gutter margins, headlines and subheads, headers and footers, and the integration of graphics. Later you learn how to use the Newsletter Wizard to create newsletters, another form of desktop publishing.

Before you attempt to apply desktop publishing techniques to any document, you should first sketch out, on paper, exactly how you want the document to look. It is much easier to create a document when you have a good idea of where you're going with it. This step also helps you avoid mistakes that may detract from the appearance of the finished document.

Columns and margins

The layout of your columns comprises a significant part of your design. One- and two-column layouts are the most popular, although you can have more. With text there is a "visual" limit. As the number of columns increases, you will eventually reach the point where readability suffers. Readers don't read individual words; they read phrases or groups of words. Therefore, column width has a direct impact on readability. Overly wide columns make it difficult for the reader to follow phrases from line to line. Overly narrow columns can also be hard to read because the eyes must often jump lines before absorbing a complete phrase. Page margins, number of columns, and the width between columns all have an impact here. Point size also impacts readability and the number of columns. Small point sizes tend to work better in narrow columns; wide columns generally need larger point sizes. Also, remember that hyphenation helps reduce that jagged-text look that is often prevalent with narrow columns, but too much hyphenation is also distracting.

When working with columns in Word, remember that columns do not need to be the same width. Also remember the effect that page margins have on the space available for your columns and on the overall design of your document. Larger margins result in a "lighter" document; smaller margins result in a "denser" appearance. Take a close look at the publications you like or dislike visually and note their designs.

Headlines and subheads

Headlines are vital in calling attention to your message. You can differentiate your headlines from your body text by setting the headlines in larger point sizes and using a sans serif font. You can also block headlines with borders or shading, or separate them from the body text by means of white space or with rules (vertical or horizontal lines drawn with Format ⇨ Borders and Shading or the Borders toolbar). Avoid setting your headlines in all uppercase letters, as this reduces readability. Also, keep your headlines short—certainly no more than three lines.

Subheads are a good way to clarify a headline. You may also want to use subheads within your text to break large expanses of text into smaller groups. Smaller text blocks tend to be visually easier to follow. Figure 10-13 shows an example of a headline and subhead.

Digital way to speed up: Learn to use all 10 of them!
The cheapest, easiest way to make your Mac faster — learn to type better...

Figure 10-13: A headline with a subheadline

Avoid a common blunder when using subheads to divide your text blocks: keep your subheads visually tied to the text they introduce by using appropriate spacing. Ideally, you want a bit more space above the subhead than below it. Otherwise, the subhead may be too close to the prior text and not close enough to the text that follows it. In such cases, the subhead appears disconnected from the text it's about. To position the subhead accurately, place the insertion pointer within the subhead, then select Format ⇨ Paragraph, and then the Indents and Spacing tab in the Paragraph dialog box. In the Spacing area, set the value of the Before measurement to one that is greater than the value in the After measurement. (Remember that this is measured in points. If your font is 12 points, 12 points of spacing equal one full line.)

Graphic images

By placing graphics in frames, you have a great deal of flexibility when you integrate graphics into the text. Alternatively, you can place a graphic image in a table cell and use table formatting to control the location of the graphic. There is no correct method to placing graphics—use whichever method feels the most comfortable and achieves the desired results.

You can use the sizing (scaling) and cropping techniques discussed earlier to add visual interest to many graphics. In some cases, you may be able to add interest to an illustration by purposely stretching it out of proportion. For example, you can use a stretched image of a dollar bill to convey an increase in buying power.

With graphics the possibilities are endless. Professionally published documents are often a source of inspiration for effective graphics. You can obtain ideas about graphic design by examining publications such as *USA Today, Time,* and *Newsweek,* which are abundant in graphics.

Graphs and tables

With Microsoft Graph, you can design business graphs and insert them into your Word documents. With Word's Table feature, you can design tables of data. Use graphs when you want the reader to see a visual representation of the underlying data. Use tables when you want the reader to see the underlying data itself. With tables that display business figures, visually set off any headings or column titles within the table from the remaining contents of the table. You can set the headings apart by formatting the headings or titles or by adding borders or shading.

Informational graphics (such as pie and bar charts) can go a long way in getting business information across to readers. You may want to consider combining clipart or drawings with your charts or graphs.

Using the Newsletter Wizard

Creating newsletters is a common task in many organizations, and one that presents design challenges. Word's Newsletter Wizard greatly reduces the tedium and challenges involved in creating newsletters. It also provides examples of how to use headings, columns, and graphics in a document.

To create a newsletter, choose File⇨New and select the Publications tab in the New dialog box. Select the Newsletter Wizard and click OK (or simply double-click the Newsletter Wizard) to launch it.

The first Newsletter Wizard page is an introduction. Click the Next button to continue. The dialog box that appears lets you choose between style options: Professional, Contemporary, or Elegant. It also asks you to determine whether you'll be printing in black and white or in color. After making these choices, click Next.

The next dialog box asks you to enter a name for your newsletter. If you can't think of one, just keep the default text, which is probably "Newsletter." You can change this later, after you complete the setup of the newsletter. If you want to include a date, keep this option selected and enter the appropriate date. Volume and issue numbers are also an option and await customization.

The final dialog box gives you the opportunity to leave room for a mailing label on the back of your newsletter. Select Yes or No, then click Next. The Wizard tells you it's done. Click Finish to have Word create your newsletter.

Remember that the format the wizard sets can be modified at any time after the newsletter is generated. If you later want to add another column to it, or want to change the look in any way, you can use the normal Word commands and dialogs to do so.

After you've set up your newsletter, whether manually or by using the Wizard, it's a good idea to enter your redundant (boilerplate) text, and then save it as a template. This ensures that your future editions will be consistent in their look.

Summary

This chapter provided an overall look at how you can combine the various tools of Word to perform desktop publishing tasks. The chapter discussed these points:

✦ You can set up multiple columns side by side using the Column button or Format ⇨ Columns. You can customize the widths of each using Format ⇨ Columns.

✦ You can quickly add attractive formatting to a document by using Word's AutoFormat command (in the Format menu).

✦ You can import graphic images of various types into a document.

✦ You can add business graphs to your Word document by pasting them in from other programs or by using Insert ⇨ Object. You can create a graph or chart in Microsoft Graph and then insert it into your document.

✦ You can add text boxes or frames to your documents. These frames can contain text or graphics. You can size text boxes or frames and drag them to any location in your document.

Where to go next

✦ For information on using Word on the World Wide Web, check out the next chapter.

✦ Chapter 13 shows you how to create typical business documents in Word 98.

✦ Much of what you do in desktop publishing involves the use of Word's different formatting tools. You can find out more about these tools in Chapter 3.

✦ If you desktop publish documents on a regular basis, you'll want to make use of Word's styles and templates. Chapter 8 has the details.

✦ ✦ ✦

CHAPTER 11

Word on the Web

✦ ✦ ✦ ✦

In This Chapter

Making the network connection

Discovering the Web and the Internet

Using Word to open Web documents

Creating hyperlinks in documents

Publishing documents on the Web

✦ ✦ ✦ ✦

Word 98 differs significantly from its predecessors in that it comes with many features for working with the Internet and with intranets. Using Word 98, you can perform a number of Net-related tasks as you work with documents. You can insert hyperlinks in a document that link to other Office 98 documents or to Web sites. When users of the documents click these hyperlinks, they jump directly to that location in the other file or to the Web site. You can also save documents as HTML (Hypertext Markup Language), the publishing lingua franca of the World Wide Web, and you can take advantage of a Web Publishing Wizard, to produce professional-looking Web pages. These topics are discussed in further detail throughout this chapter.

This chapter assumes a familiarity with the basics of Word. If you are familiar with the Web or with intranets but you haven't yet learned to work with Word, you should read Chapters 2 through 4 before proceeding with this chapter.

Making the Network Connection

To accomplish most of the tasks described in this chapter, you need to be connected to a network. This can be a dial-up connection to the Internet by means of a commercial Internet service provider (ISP) or by a direct connection through your organization's local area network. You may be connected directly to a corporate intranet, in which case you'll be able to retrieve or publish data to your company's private network. This chapter won't discuss the specifics of making a network connection because that topic is a book in itself. IDG publishes several good books on the Internet to help you get connected.

Discovering the Web and the Internet

Because intranets and the Internet may be a newer concept to you than spreadsheets, term explanations are in order. (If you're intimately familiar with the Internet, intranets, and the World Wide Web, you may want to skip this section and the next, and dive right into working with Word and the Web.) First, the Internet is a global collection of computers, linked together by means of telephone and microwave lines, and accessible to the public by means of various connections in offices and in homes. The Internet grew out of a research project that originally linked university and government computers in the United States. Since its inception, the Internet has grown to encompass thousands of computers spread throughout dozens of nations. Any PC user with an Internet connection (either by means of a phone line or a direct hookup) can connect to the Internet and gain access to the volumes of information located there.

About the World Wide Web

One major component of the Internet is the World Wide Web. There are other parts to the Internet, but the World Wide Web is the best known part. The World Wide Web is that part of the Internet that makes use of graphical software known as Web browsers and of files stored as HTML. The computers on the Internet that store the HTML files are known as Web servers. When computers connect to the Internet to retrieve this data, they use Web browser software, which converts the incoming information (encoded in HTML) to graphical pages displayed as a combination of text, graphics, and sometimes audio and video. Commonly used Web browsers include Microsoft Internet Explorer, Netscape Navigator, and the custom Web browsers provided by America Online and CompuServe.

About Internet addresses

Each site on the Internet has a unique address, or Internet address, commonly known by the official name of URL (Uniform Resource Locator). When you establish an Internet connection, open a Web browser, and enter an Internet address such as `http://www.whitehouse.gov`, you are entering the address for the Web server that provides the home page at the entered address (in the example, the President of the United States' office). Web addresses like these can be stored in Word documents and displayed as hyperlinks.

About intranets

Many Net-related uses of Office 98 involve making data available on intranets. An intranet is a private network of computers that is available only to the members of a specific organization. Intranets make use of World Wide Web technology—Web servers, network connections, and Web browser software—to enable members of an organization to share information. Intranets are very popular with corporations, as intranets let employees share work-related information in a confidential manner.

About HTML

HTML is the language used for publishing information to the World Wide Web and to intranets that use World Wide Web technology. HTML is a text-based language that makes use of special codes called *tags*. These tags are included in the text of the HTML documents. The tags provide instructions to the Web browser software, which determine how the data appears when it is viewed by the end user. Although you don't need to know the nuts and bolts of HTML coding to work with Word and the Web, it's a good idea to be familiar with the concept of saving your data in HTML file format. To publish Word data on the Internet or an intranet, you need to save that data in HTML format and upload it to your Web server. If you are dealing with an intranet, your company's Webmaster can tell you how to upload the HTML files that Word produces to the company's Web server. If you are managing a Web site on the Internet or an intranet, you already know how to do this; much of the rest of this chapter deals with getting that Word data ready for uploading to your server.

About the Web toolbar

Word provides a Web toolbar, which is a toolbar to help you browse through the resources on an intranet or the Web. Using the Web toolbar, you can quickly open, search, and browse through any document or through a Web page. You can jump between documents, and you can add favorite sites you find on the Web to the Favorites folder, enabling you to quickly go back to those sites at a later time.

In Word, you display the Web toolbar by clicking the Web toolbar button in the Standard toolbar or by choosing View⇨Toolbars and selecting Web from the submenu that appears. Figure 11-1 shows the Web toolbar.

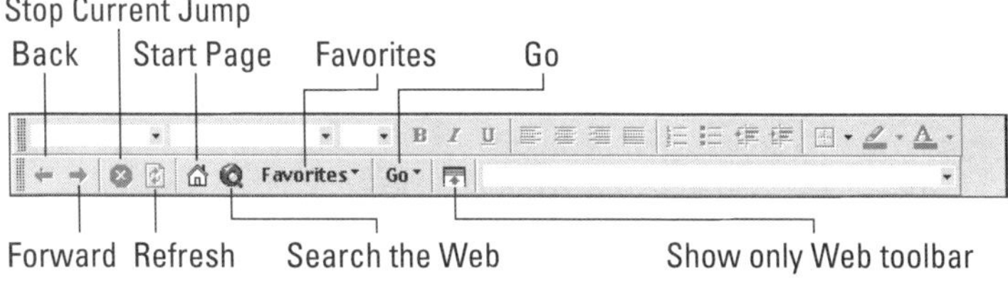

Figure 11-1: The Web toolbar

The Web toolbar is handy when you happen to be in Word and you have a need to go to the Web (or to your company's intranet) for information. For example, you can click the Search the Web button to launch your default Web browser and search the Web, or you can click the Favorites button to open a list of your favorite Web sites. Table 11-1 shows the purpose of the buttons on the Web toolbar.

Table 11-1
The Web Toolbar

Button	*Purpose*
Back	Moves backward among previously viewed Web pages
Forward	Moves forward among previously viewed Web pages
Stop Current Jump	Halts the current loading of a Web page
Refresh	Refreshes (reloads) the current Web page
Start Page	Jumps to the designated start page
Search the Web	Jumps to Microsoft's Search page on the World Wide Web
Favorites	Displays a list of favorite sites
Go	Opens the Go menu, which can be used in place of the navigation buttons
Show Only Web Toolbar	Turns off all toolbars except the Web toolbar

Using Word to Open Web Documents

You can open Web pages in Word, effectively using Word as a Web browser.

A word of caution here: Word, as a browser, can be excruciatingly slow. And we found that many pages are too complex to load properly (see Figure 11-2). If you want to do serious Web surfing, dedicated Web browsers such as Microsoft Internet Explorer and Netscape Navigator are better choices; however, if you just want to view a Web page without leaving Word, you can do so.

To open a Web page in Word, choose File⇨Open Web Page, enter the URL (Web address) in the dialog box that appears, and click OK. If you've already visited the desired page using Word 98, instead of typing the URL, you can click the arrows to the right of the address field and select it from the pop-up list. If you've set your Point-to-Point Protocol (PPP) control panel to allow applications to connect as needed, Word will connect to the Internet or intranet via your default connection and load the Web page. (If not, you'll need to connect to the Net before Word can call up the page.) Figure 11-2 shows an example of a Web page loaded using Word; in this case, the Web page is from Yahoo!, the popular Internet search directory.

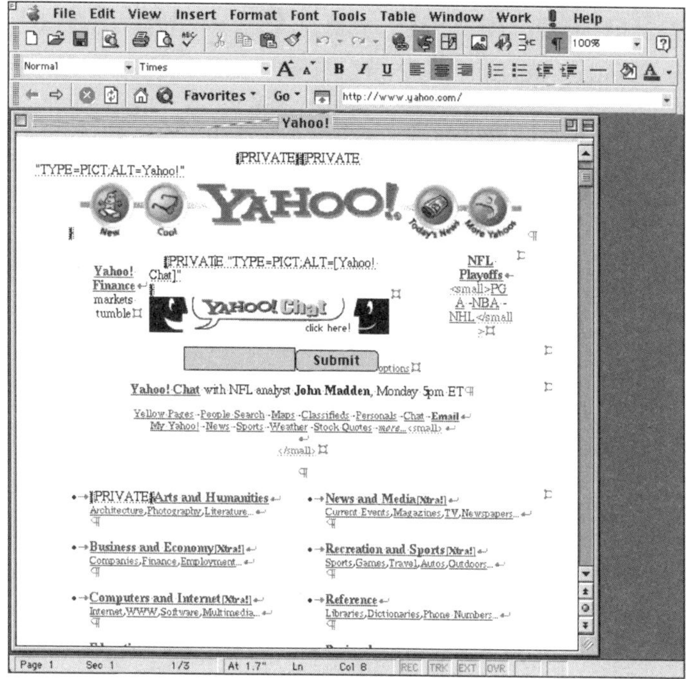

Figure 11-2: Yahoo! Web page loaded in Word

Once you open and navigate among Web pages in Word, the Forward, Back, Stop, and Refresh buttons of the Web toolbar become active. You can use the buttons to navigate forward and backward among Web pages you previously viewed. Also, the Address list box in the Web toolbar keeps a list of the sites you've visited during any Word Web session. To revisit a site, you can open the list and choose the address you want.

As you visit a site, you can add it to the Favorites list of the Web toolbar, so you can quickly go back to it later. While at a Web site, click Favorites on the Web toolbar and choose Add to Favorites.

Creating Hyperlinks in Documents

A significant feature of Word 98 is its capability to use hyperlinks in documents. You can create hyperlinks to jump to other Office documents stored on your Mac, on your company's network, on a company intranet, or on the Internet.

Linking to office documents with Copy and Paste

If you want to create a hyperlink to a location in Word, in an Excel worksheet, or in a PowerPoint presentation, the easiest way is to use the Copy and Paste as Hyperlink commands of the Edit menu. To create a hyperlink from another Office document using the Copy and Paste as Hyperlink commands, follow these steps:

1. Open the document containing the location to which you want to link. (If it is in Word, it can be in the same document or in a different document that's open. If the location is in an Excel or a PowerPoint file, it can be in any area of the worksheet or presentation.)
2. Select the portion of the document to which you want to link.
3. Choose Edit ➪ Copy (⌘-C).
4. In Word, place the insertion pointer at the location where you want to insert the hyperlink.
5. Choose Edit ➪ Paste as Hyperlink.

Note that the Paste as Hyperlink will be grayed out if the document to be linked to has not been saved.

When you perform these steps, Word inserts a hyperlink back to the original document at the selected location. You can then click the hyperlink at any time to jump to the linked document.

Another way to create a hyperlink to a portion of a Word document is to select the data to be linked and press ⌘-Option as you drag the information to the location that is to serve as the hyperlink. When you release the mouse button, choose Create Hyperlink Here from the Shortcut menu that appears.

Linking to Web sites or files with Insert Hyperlink

To establish a hyperlink to a Web site on an intranet or the Internet, follow these steps (you can use these same steps to link to another Office document, but it's easier to use the copy and paste methods described earlier):

1. Select the text in the document that will serve as the hyperlink.
2. Click the Insert Hyperlink button in the Standard toolbar, or choose Insert ➪ Hyperlink. The Insert Hyperlink dialog box appears, as shown in Figure 11-3.
3. In the Link to file or URL text box, enter the Web address (or the path for the file) of the destination for the link.
4. If you are establishing a link to a file and you want to jump to a specific location, enter that location in the Named location in file text box. (This can

be a cell reference or named range in an Excel worksheet, a Word bookmark, or the name of a PowerPoint slide.) If you link to a file and leave this entry blank, the hyperlink jumps to the beginning of the file.

…rlink dialog
…e page

… shared network directory to find the linked file … ive to the location where your current document … lative path for hyperlink check box. If you want a … rk directory to use the same address regardless … ent is stored, turn off the Use relative path for …

…erlink.

…rlinks

… converts any recognizable Internet address to a … and press the spacebar, Return, Enter, or Tab. For … ighit.com, `lamg@lamg.com`, or `ftp://ftp.` … it will become an active link, ready to start a Web browser and carry anyone who clicks it to the specified site.

Actually, what Word acts on is the identifying part of the address, such as `ftp://ftp`, `http://www`, or any text with the @ symbol between it.

This AutoFormat feature is on by default, but can be turned off by selecting Tools➪ AutoCorrect, going to the AutoFormat tab, and unchecking the option under Replace that says Internet paths with hyperlinks.

Publishing Documents on the Web

Word 98 enables you to create documents and save them as HTML files for Web publication. This is a very simple matter in Word. Before we go on, a word of caution about saving Word documents as HTML files. Many of the formatting features of Word are not supported on conversion to HTML format. Table 11-2 indicates which formats are retained after conversion to HTML.

Saving existing Word documents as HTML

You can use the Save as HTML option of the File menu to convert existing documents into HTML files. Once converted, you can upload the documents to your Internet or intranet Web server using the procedures applicable to your server.

To save an existing document in HTML format, choose File ➪ Save as HTML. When you do this, the normal Save As dialog box opens and HTML is automatically selected as the file type. Enter the desired filename and click Save. Word will save the existing document in HTML format. (Don't use the same name as your existing document or you'll replace the existing document with the HTML version. Give the new document a unique name or add the Web standard .html to the document's name.) When saving existing documents as HTML, remember the limitations of HTML documents, as emphasized in Table 11-2.

Table 11-2
Limitations of Word Conversions to HTML

Word Formatting	*Supported by HTML?*	*Comments*
Font sizes	See comments	Fonts are converted to the closest HTML font size.
Comments	See comments	Comments don't appear in the document after Web publication.
Emboss, shadow, engrave, caps, small caps, strikethrough, and outline text features	No	These formatting options are lost after conversion to HTML format.
Fields	See comments	The information in a field is retained but the field will not continue to update; the field is converted to text.
Tabs	Yes	Tabs are converted to an HTML tab character. These appear as spaces in some browsers. As an alternate use indents or a table.

Word Formatting	*Supported by HTML?*	*Comments*
Tables of contents or authorities and indexes	See comments	The information in the tables is converted, but these will not be converted because they are based on field codes. The page numbers are displayed as asterisks that are hyperlinks that readers can click to navigate the Web page. You can replace the asterisks with the text that you want to have displayed.
Drop caps	No	These are removed but you can increase the size of the letter by increasing the font size and then clicking it in the Web page environment.
Table widths	See comments	The tables are converted to a fixed width.
Tables	Yes	Tables are converted but the color and width borders settings are not retained.
Highlights	No	Highlights are lost.
Page numbering	No	An HTML document is considered a single Web page, therefore page numbers are lost.
Margins	No	Controlling layout of a page is done via tables.
Page borders	No	There is no HTML equivalent.
Headers and footers	No	There are no HTML equivalents.
Footnotes	No	There is no HTML equivalent.
Newspaper columns	No	For multicolumn effect, use tables.
Styles	No	User-defined styles are converted to direct formatting if the formatting is supported by HTML.

Using the Web Page Wizard to create Web pages

You can also create Web pages using Word's Web Page Wizard, which also produces HTML files. To produce Web-ready files based on your Word documents with the Web Page Wizard, follow these steps:

1. Choose File➪New and click the Web Pages tab.

2. Select the Web Page Wizard. The Web Page Wizard is activated. Figure 11-4 shows the First Window of the Web Page Wizard.

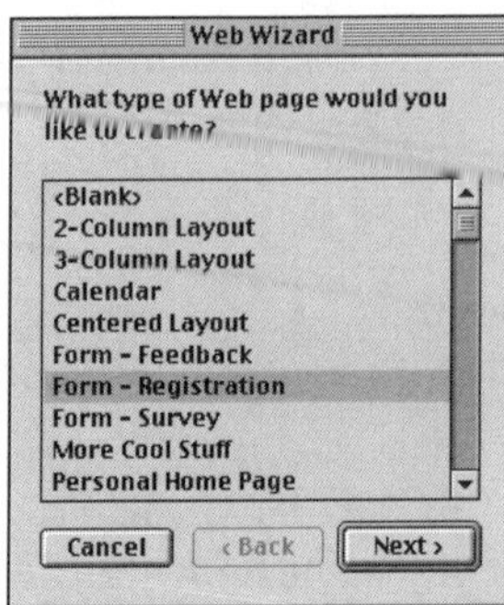

Figure 11-4: The first dialog box of the Web Page Wizard

3. In the first dialog box of the Web Page Wizard, choose the type of Web page. As you click any Web page type, it draws in the document window to give you an idea what kind of page you will be creating. After you select a page type, click next.
4. The second dialog box enables you to choose a visual style for your Web page. Again, you can see the visual style in the document window. After selecting a visual style, click Next. Figure 11-5 shows the Visual Style dialog of the Web Page Wizard.

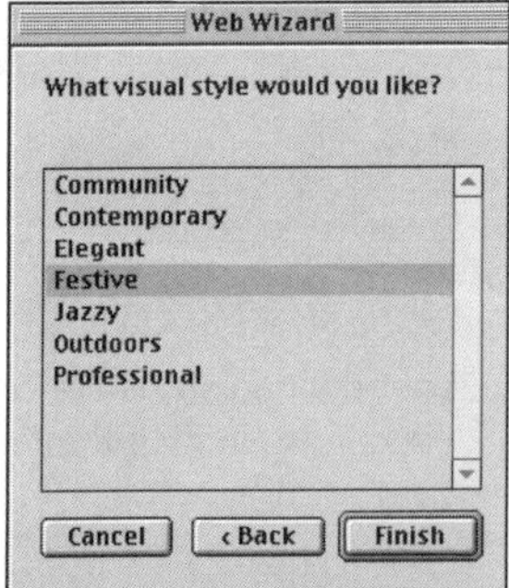

Figure 11-5: The Visual Style dialog box of the Web Page Wizard

5. After selecting the visual style for your Web page, click Finish to create the actual Web page.

The Web page that you created then shows up preformatted. Using it as a starting point, add the text you wish to appear on your Web page.

When creating HTML files based on Word documents, remember that Word has a much wider range of formatting than is possible with HTML. Hypertext Markup Language is a fairly simple formatting language, and if you use some of Word's more unusual features, they may be lost in the translation, or translated in ways you didn't expect. For example, if you place text in text boxes within a Word document and then save the document as HTML, the text stored in the text boxes does not appear in the HTML file. If you place a graphic in a document and save it as HTML, Word does write the graphic to a .GIF file and includes a reference in the HTML code for the graphic. However, the graphic often does not appear (in relation to the paragraph placement) at the same place it was originally stored in the Word document.

Summary

This chapter discussed the details behind sharing your Word data with Internet/intranet users. In this chapter, you learned the following:

- ✦ Word 98 can open files that are stored on the Internet.
- ✦ Hyperlinks can be added to the text of a document and you can store Web addresses or jump locations to other Office documents in Word documents.
- ✦ You can use the Save as HTML option of the File menu to save existing Word documents as HTML files for publishing on the Internet or an intranet.
- ✦ You can use the Web Page Wizard to quickly create Web pages that use various styles and formats.

Where to go next

- ✦ In the next chapter, you learn how to further extend the power of Word by using Visual Basic for Applications.
- ✦ Word is just one component of the Web publishing capabilities provided by Office 98. Excel and PowerPoint also offer Web publishing and Web interaction features. See Chapter 23 for specifics on Excel and the Web; and Chapter 32 for specifics on PowerPoint and the Web.

✦ ✦ ✦

CHAPTER 12

Word and Visual Basic for Applications

✦ ✦ ✦ ✦

In This Chapter

Using macros to learn VBA

Understanding VBA code

Editing VBA code

Printing Visual Basic code

About the Visual Basic toolbar

✦ ✦ ✦ ✦

This chapter details the use of Visual Basic for Applications (VBA), the programming language on which Word macros are based. VBA is heavily based on Microsoft's Visual Basic programming language. Because Word macros are based on VBA, you can use VBA to automate common tasks in Word.

VBA can take you much farther than simply duplicating keystrokes. VBA gives you full access to all of Word's commands. You can modify Word's own menus by adding your own commands and options, you can create custom dialog boxes to present messages and query users for information, and you can even construct complete applications that users with a limited knowledge of Word can use. To accomplish these kinds of tasks, you need more than a familiarity with the recording and playing of macros—you need a basic understanding of VBA.

Using Macros to Learn VBA

Chapter 9 detailed the basics of using macros, which are sequences of instructions that cause Word to perform a particular task. As Chapter 9 demonstrates, macros can be very handy to use in your work because they greatly reduce the time you spend performing routine, repetitive tasks. Macros are also an excellent starting point for understanding how VBA works and what you can do with the language. As Word's macro recorder stores all the actions that you perform or the commands that you choose, it interprets these actions or commands into statements, or lines of code, using VBA. These statements are automatically placed in a procedure, which is a block of VBA code. Procedures are stored in modules, which you can think of as containers for all VBA code.

To get an idea of how all Word macros use VBA, you should practice with a worksheet and a sample macro. This chapter familiarizes you with Visual Basic code by examining the procedure that results when you record the sample macro. The following exercise produces two printed copies of a document, along with a document summary sheet to accompany each printout. Because you can't print multiple copies of a document with nonstandard options (such as the document summaries) using just the Print icon in the toolbar, this exercise represents a typical task that can be automated by creating a macro.

Follow these steps to create the worksheet and the sample macro:

1. Open an existing document.
2. Choose Tools ➪ Macro ➪ Record New Macro.
3. In the Record New Macro dialog box, enter the name **PrintTwo** and then click OK. The Stop Recording toolbar, which you can use to stop recording the macro, appears in the document.
4. Choose File ➪ Print. The Print dialog box appears, as shown in Figure 12-1.

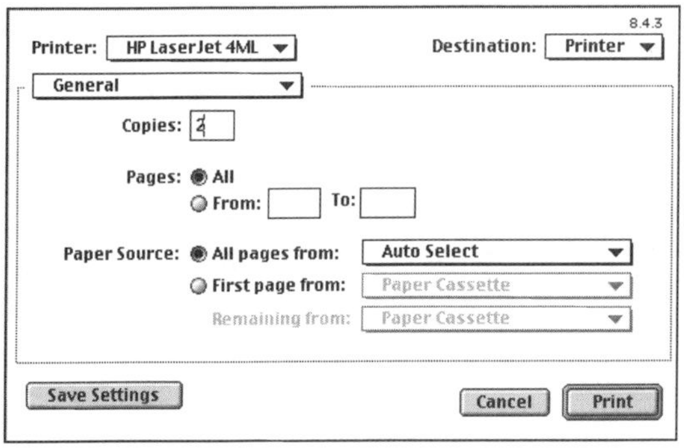

Figure 12-1: The Print dialog box

5. In the Copies portion of the dialog box, change the number of copies to 2.
6. Select Microsoft Word from the top pop-up menu. Then click the Word Options button to open the Print tab of the Preferences dialog box.
7. In the dialog box that appears, turn on the Document Properties check box, and then click OK. (If Document Properties is already on, you don't have to do anything.)
8. Click OK to close the Print dialog box and begin printing.

9. (Optional) As soon as your Mac finishes the basic printing preparation, select Tools ➪ Preferences. In the Print tab, turn off Document Properties again. (Otherwise, Document Properties is left on whenever you use this macro.)

10. Click the Stop Recording button to stop the recording of the macro.

You can verify the effects of the macro by opening any document, choosing Tools ➪ Macro ➪ Macros, clicking PrintTwo to select the macro, and then clicking the Run button. (You can also just double-click PrintTwo.) Word prints two copies of the current document, along with document summary sheets for each copy.

Understanding VBA Code

Of course, the purpose of the exercise you just completed is not to demonstrate how to create a macro but to show how VBA code works as the basis of any macro. Choose Tools ➪ Macro ➪ Macros to open the Macros dialog box, select the PrintTwo macro, and click Edit. The Visual Basic Editor opens, shown in Figure 12-2. As shown in the figure, the VBA code behind the macro appears in the module window.

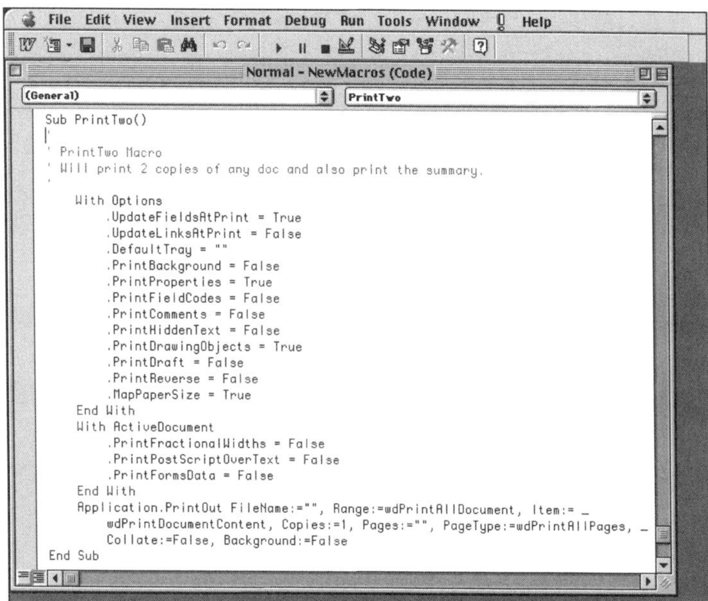

Figure 12-2: An example of macro code within the Visual Basic Editor

Here's the VBA code:

```
Sub PrintTwo()
'
' PrintTwo Macro
' Macro recorded 12/29/97 by Deborah Shadovitz
'
  With Options
    .UpdateFieldsAtPrint = True
    .UpdateLinksAtPrint = False
    .DefaultTray = ""
    .PrintBackground = False
    .PrintProperties = True
    .PrintFieldCodes = False
    .PrintComments = False
    .PrintHiddenText = False
    .PrintDrawingObjects = True
    .PrintDraft = False
    .PrintReverse = False
    .MapPaperSize = True
  End With
  With ActiveDocument
    .PrintFractionalWidths = False
    .PrintPostScriptOverText = False
    .PrintFormsData = False
  End With
  Application.PrintOut FileName:="", Range:=wdPrintAllDocument,
Item:= _
    wdPrintDocumentContent, Copies:=1, Pages:="",
PageType:=wdPrintAllPages, _
    Collate:=False, Background:=False
  With Options
    .UpdateFieldsAtPrint = True
    .UpdateLinksAtPrint = False
    .DefaultTray = ""
    .PrintBackground = False
    .PrintProperties = False
    .PrintFieldCodes = False
    .PrintComments = False
    .PrintHiddenText = False
    .PrintDrawingObjects = True
    .PrintDraft = False
    .PrintReverse = False
    .MapPaperSize = True
  End With
  With ActiveDocument
    .PrintFractionalWidths = False
    .PrintPostScriptOverText = False
    .PrintFormsData = False
  End With
End Sub
```

Note that the Paste as Hyperlink will be grayed out in the Edit menu if the document to which you want to link has not been saved yet.

How VBA Relates to Visual Basic

If you've already worked with Microsoft's Visual Basic as a development language, you'll find Visual Basic for Applications to be a familiar friend; in fact, sibling is more accurate. VBA is solidly based on Microsoft's Visual Basic programming language. The whole idea in developing VBA was to replace the old macro-based languages, such as Word Basic and Excel's macro language, with a common development language so that developers familiar with applications development in Word could easily develop applications in Excel (or in Access, if using Windows) and vice versa.

Microsoft uses Visual Basic as the base language, and it has added extensions to the language as implemented in the other Office applications. All the commands, functions, methods, procedures, and program structures used in Visual Basic can be used in VBA for Word, Excel, and PowerPoint (and Access, if using Windows). If you are a Visual Basic programmer, you're on very familiar ground.

Each of the steps you took during the recording of this procedure resulted in the addition of one or more lines of Visual Basic code in the module. The code appears in color—comments are displayed in green, key words of the Visual Basic language appear in blue, and all other code appears in black. When you run this (or any) macro, you are in effect running the Visual Basic for Applications code contained in the module recorded by the macro recorder. As the module runs, each line of Visual Basic code executes in turn, and Word performs an appropriate action as a result.

About comments

You can include comments (lines not acted upon by Word when the code runs) by preceding the text with a single quotation mark. In the sample procedure, you can see that the second and third lines are comments:

```
' PrintTwo Macro
'Will print 2 copies of any doc and also print the summary
'
```

In this case, Word added the comments based on the entries in the Macro Name and Description text boxes of the Record Macro dialog box, but you can place comments wherever you desire in your Visual Basic code by typing a single quote mark followed by the text of the comment. Comments can be quite helpful in your more complex procedures because they can help you remember what's going on at a specific point in the procedure. Comments can occupy an entire line, or you can put them at the end of a valid line of code by starting the comment with a single quotation mark. When the procedure runs, everything that follows the single quotation mark is ignored until Word finds a new line of code.

About headers and footers

If you look just above the comments, you see that the first line of the procedure reads:

```
Sub PrintTwo()
```

The matching last line reads:

```
End sub
```

Think of these lines as the header and footer for the procedure. Every VBA procedure starts with a header that begins with Sub or Function and ends with a footer that says End Sub or End Function. VBA allows two types of procedures: function procedures and sub procedures. Function procedures accept a value(s), act on the data, and return a value(s). Sub procedures do not return a value (although you can pass values from within a sub procedure using statements inside the procedure). Any arguments used by a function procedure are placed inside the parentheses of the header. The footer tells Word that it has reached the end of the procedure. When Word reaches the footer in the module, it passes program control back to any other VBA procedure that called this procedure. If the procedure was not called by another procedure, Word returns control from the procedure to Word itself.

About VBA code

The code between the Sub and the End Sub lines makes up the actual procedure that does all the work. In this example, many of the lines are assignment statements; these lines assign a value to a property in Word. For example, the following line of code tells Word to include the document properties with the printout:

```
.PrintProperties = True
```

Also included in the VBA code are statements that perform direct actions within Word. For example, the following statement tells Word to print the document:

```
Application.Printout Filename:=
```

Because this macro first tells Word to set the printing options to include document properties and then later tells Word to turn off this option, you will see the full list of preferences (`with options and with active document`) appear once to set the preferences, then another time to reset them.

About displaying dialog boxes

One reason you may want to do some Visual Basic programming yourself (rather than using only the macro recorder) is that you can do some custom programming—such as displaying dialog boxes—that you cannot do with recorded macros. To display a dialog box onscreen that contains a message with custom text, you use VBA's MsgBox function. The syntax of the statement is simple: you add a line of code that reads MsgBox("your custom text"). Put your desired text between the double quotation marks.

If you duplicated the example earlier in the chapter, go to the end of the line prior to where the macro resets the printing preferences, and place your insertion point there. The text to follow is `Background:=False`, which is right above the second occurrence of the text `Background:=False`.

Press Return to add a new, blank line. With the insertion point at the start of the blank line, enter the following:

```
MsgBox("Now printing two copies with summaries.")
```

After typing this code, choose File ➪ Close and Return to Word (⌘-Q) to exit the Visual Basic Editor. When you are back in the document, choose Tools ➪ Macro ➪ Macros. In the Macros dialog box, select the PrintTwo macro and click Run. When the macro completes this time, you see the dialog box shown in Figure 12-3. Dialog boxes such as this one can inform users, providing needed guidance about tasks the user needs to perform. After Word displays this dialog box, it continues on to reset your preferences to turn off the document properties printout.

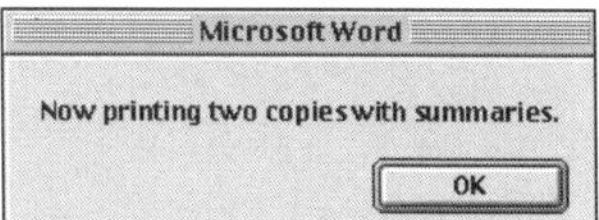

Figure 12-3: The dialog box presented by the MsgBox function

When entering code, it's important to have smart quotes turned off (or to copy and paste a straight quote from somewhere else in the code window). Use of a smart quotation mark results in a compilation error, and your script won't run. To turn off smart quotes, select Tools ➪ AutoCorrect, and then choose the AutoFormat As You Type tab. Under Replace as you type, deselect (clear) the Straight quotes with smart quotes check box.

Editing VBA Code

When you open a module, you can enter program code just like you type text in any word processor. You don't have to know the mechanics of entering text and correcting mistakes. You can use the same text-entry and editing techniques (including cutting and pasting) that you use in any Mac word processor.

While you are in the Visual Basic Editor, you can also insert text from another file into your existing program code. If you want to insert text into the program code, place the insertion point at the location in the module where you want to insert the code and choose Insert ➪ File. In the File dialog box, select the file that contains the text you want to insert. Click OK to transfer the text into the file.

Printing Visual Basic Code

You can print the code contained in your Visual Basic modules. Open the module that contains the desired code by choosing Tools ➪ Macro ➪ Macros, selecting the desired macro, and clicking the Edit button. Then choose the Print command from the File menu.

About the Visual Basic Toolbar

If you do a lot of work in VBA programming, you'll find the Visual Basic toolbar (see Figure 12-4) to be useful. You can activate the Visual Basic toolbar by Control-clicking the toolbar area and choosing Visual Basic from the shortcut menu. (Or select View ➪ Toolbars ➪ Visual Basic.) Table 12-1 describes the different buttons on the Visual Basic toolbar.

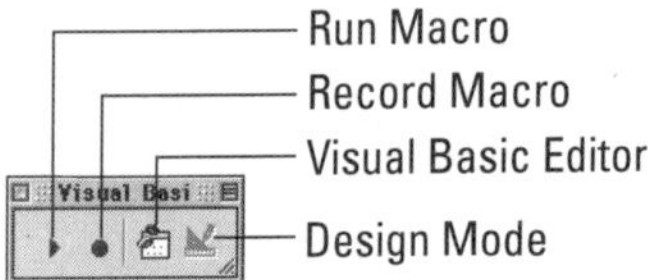

Figure 12-4: The Visual Basic toolbar

Table 12-1
Buttons on the Visual Basic Toolbar

Name	*Function*
Run Macro	Opens the Run Macro dialog box, in which you can run, delete, or modify a selected macro.
Record Macro	Opens the Record Macro dialog box, in which you can fill in the desired options used to begin recording a macro.
Visual Basic Editor	Opens the Visual Basic Editor, in which you can create, edit, and step through macros using Visual Basic.
Design Mode	Switches in and out of Design mode.

Just a Beginning . . .

Make no mistake about it, using VBA falls well into the realm of programming. (If you're completely new to programming, you should be congratulated for pressing this deeply into, for many readers, a subject of mystifying complexity.) Not only have you learned how VBA lies at the heart of everything you do with macros, you've also learned how you can extend the power of your macros by adding your own Visual Basic code to provide items such as dialog boxes and customized prompts. Still, you've only scratched the surface of what you can do with this language. VBA is a full-featured programming language you can use to automate or customize virtually any conceivable task that can be done with Word. If the challenges of programming catch your fancy, you should look into additional resources for learning about Visual Basic programming. It's a subject about which entire books have been written.

Summary

This chapter provided an introduction to programming using Visual Basic for Applications, the underlying language behind Word macros. The chapter covered the following points:

- Every Word macro exists as a series of Visual Basic program statements.
- The Visual Basic statements are stored in procedures, and one or more procedures are placed in modules.
- Visual Basic procedures can be function procedures or sub procedures. Function procedures accept a value(s), act on the data, and return a value(s). Sub procedures do not return a value (although you can pass values from within a sub procedure using statements inside the procedure).
- You can modify the Visual Basic code that Word's macro recorder creates to add special features, such as dialog boxes and custom prompts.

Where to go next

- The next chapter shows how you can put Word to work. It demonstrates how you can create and use various documents for common business tasks.
- Because Visual Basic for Applications lies at the heart of macros you create in Word, you should also be intimately familiar with the use of macros before getting deeply involved with Visual Basic for Applications. See Chapter 9.

✦ ✦ ✦

CHAPTER 13

Word 98 at Work

◆ ◆ ◆ ◆

In This Chapter

Designing a fax cover sheet

Writing an interoffice memo

◆ ◆ ◆ ◆

In this chapter, you find two step-by-step exercises you can follow to put Word 98 to work quickly. These exercises use Word's wizards, which enable you to produce professional-looking documents with ease.

Designing a Fax Cover Sheet

Figure 13-1 shows an example of a fax cover sheet you can quickly create using Word's Fax Wizard.

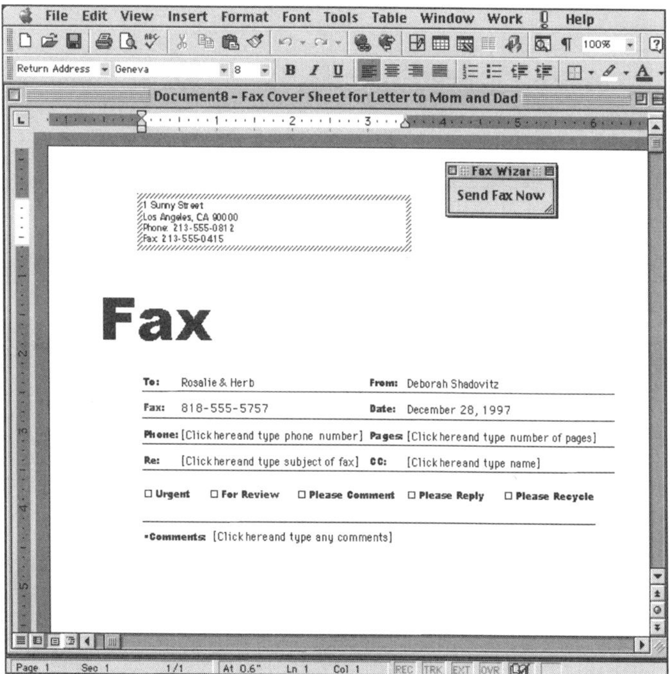

Figure 13-1: An example of a fax cover sheet

To create a fax cover sheet, perform the following steps:

1. Choose File➪New. The New dialog box appears.
2. Click the Letters and Faxes tab, and then double-click Fax Wizard. In a moment, the first Fax Wizard dialog box appears (see Figure 13-2).
3. As the dialog box notes, this Fax Wizard helps you create a cover sheet. Click Next to proceed. In a moment, the second Fax Wizard dialog box appears (see Figure 13-3).

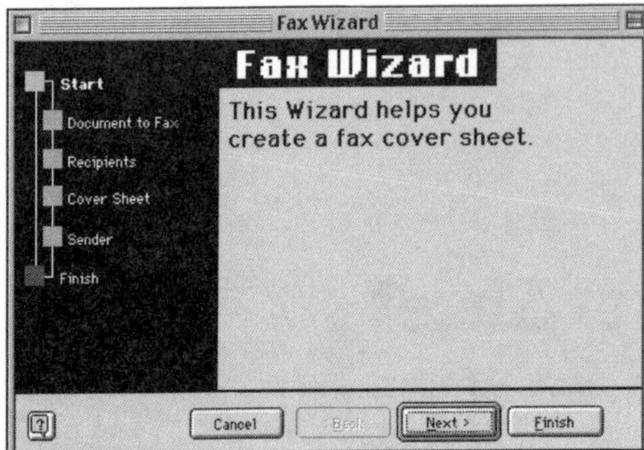

Figure 13-2: The Fax Wizard's introductory dialog box

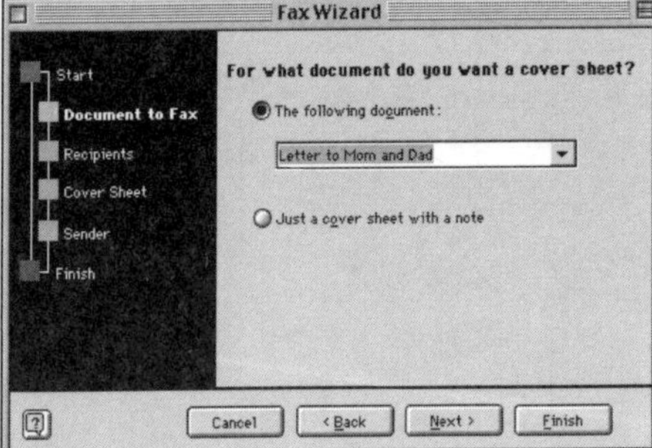

Figure 13-3: The second Fax Wizard dialog box

4. The Fax Wizard gives you the option to create the cover sheet for a letter you are currently working on or send the cover sheet without a letter.

   To have the cover sheet accompany a letter you are working on, keep the default radio button—The following document—selected. Your front-most document is entered in the box as the document to send. All other open Word 98 documents appear in the pop-up list. You can select any open document from this pop-up menu.

The other alternative is to click the Just a cover sheet with a note option.

After selecting your accompanying document, click Next to proceed to the third Fax Wizard dialog box.

5. The third dialog box asks for the recipient's name and the fax number (see Figure 13-4). Enter the desired name and number and click Next. If you have been using Word's Address Book feature, you can select your recipients' names from it by clicking the Address Book button.

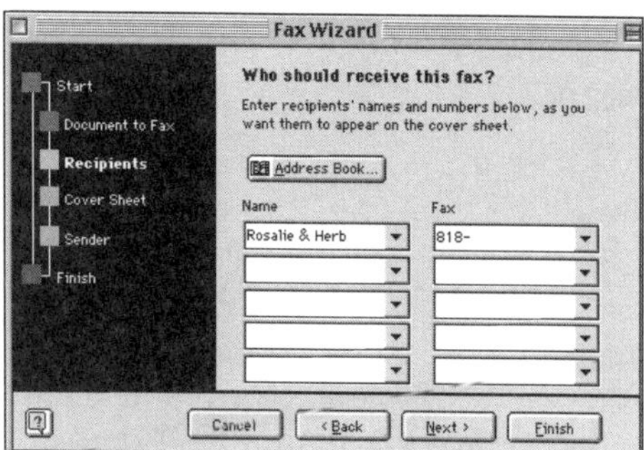

Figure 13-4: The third Fax Wizard dialog box—addressing your fax

6. The next dialog box gives you a choice of three styles: Professional, Contemporary, and Elegant (see Figure 13-5). Choose a desired style and click Next.

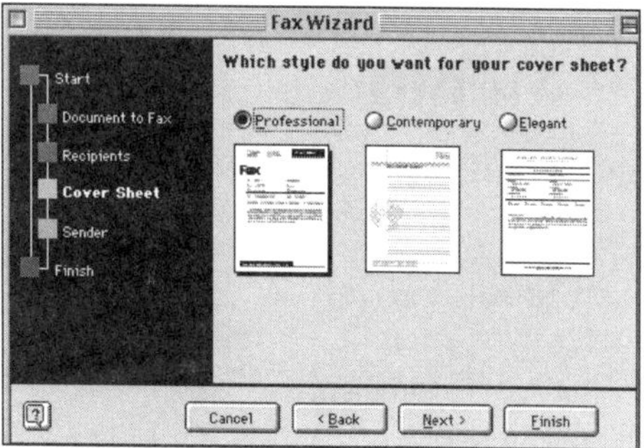

Figure 13-5: The fourth Fax Wizard dialog box—selecting a style

7. The next dialog box that appears asks for the name of the sender (see Figure 13-6). Word 98 picks up your name from the Preferences you've entered. Make any changes or additions to this information and click Next.

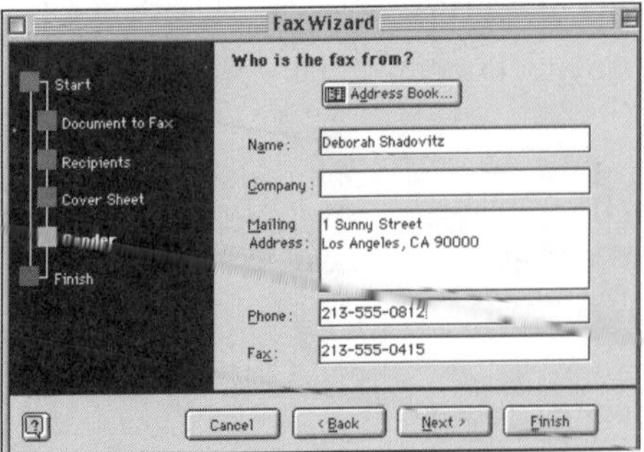

Figure 13-6: The fifth Fax Wizard dialog box—who's the sender?

8. The last dialog box indicates that the process of building the fax cover sheet is complete, and it displays the Finish button. Click Finish to produce the cover sheet.
9. In the fax cover sheet, select the "click here and type . . ." text and replace it with the appropriate information, or just delete the existing text.
10. When the fax cover sheet appears onscreen, a button bar with one button—Send Fax Now—opens. Clicking this button sends the fax cover sheet to whatever device is selected in your Chooser, which is most likely your printer.

After creating your cover sheet, print it, along with your document. Then fax it or use your fax software to fax directly from your Mac.

Writing an Interoffice Memo

Figure 13-7 shows an example of an interoffice memo. You can easily produce a memo like this with Word's Memo Wizard.

To create an interoffice memo, follow these steps:

1. Choose File ⇨ New. The New dialog box appears.
2. In the New dialog box, click the Memos tab and then double-click Memo Wizard.
3. In the first Memo Wizard dialog box that appears, click Next (see Figure 13-8).

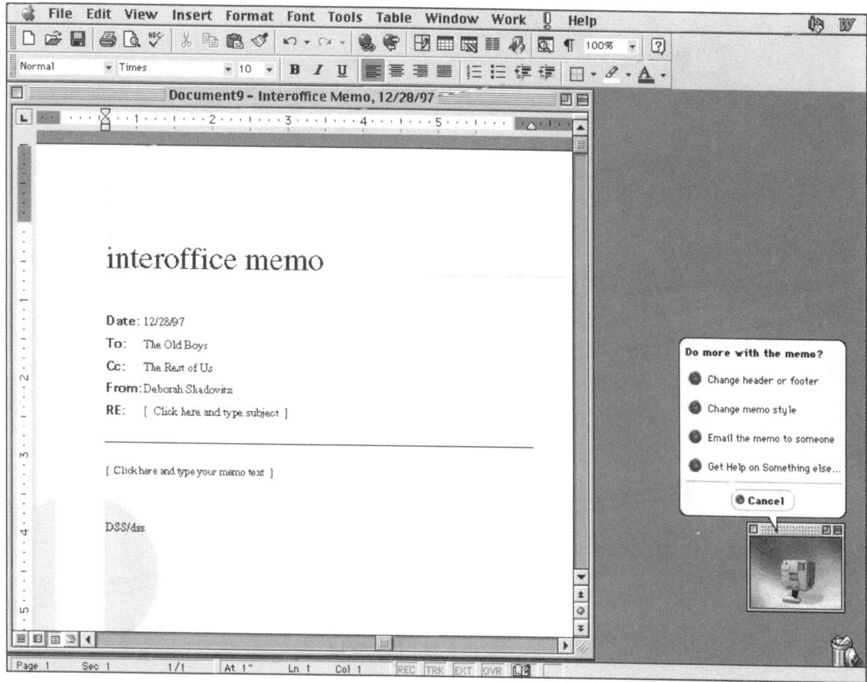

Figure 13-7: An example of an interoffice memo

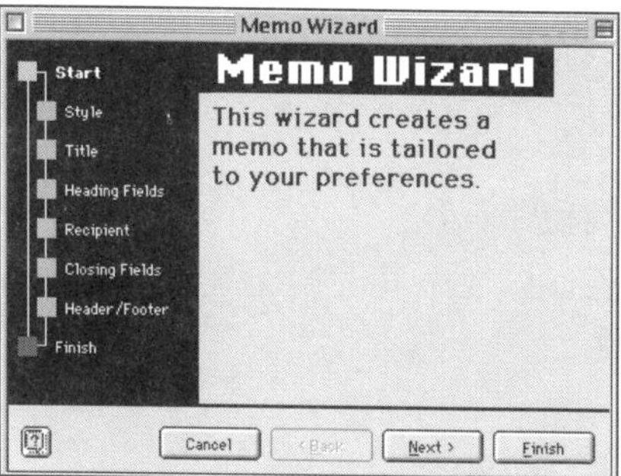

Figure 13-8: The introductory Memo Wizard dialog box

4. The second dialog box of the Memo Wizard, shown in Figure 13-9, provides a choice of three possible memo styles: Professional, Contemporary, and Elegant. Choose Professional and click Next.

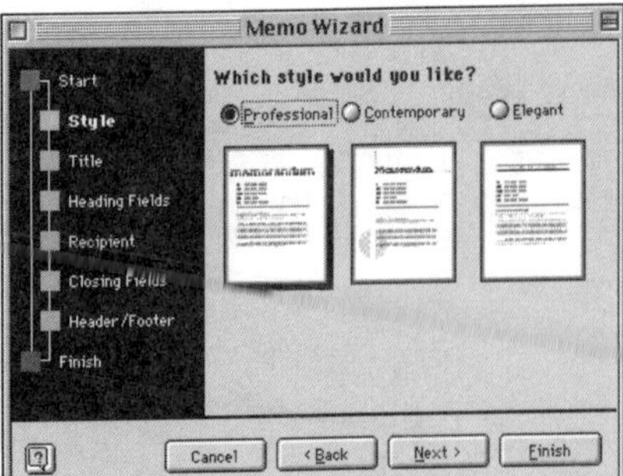

Figure 13-9: The second Memo Wizard dialog box—applying a style

5. The next dialog box of the Memo Wizard, shown in Figure 13-10, asks for a title. For this exercise, you can accept the default title of Interoffice Memo, and then click Next. However, you can easily edit the default title by typing in the text box.

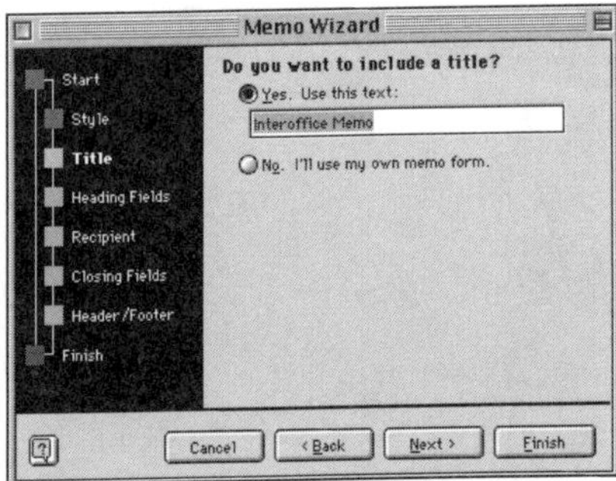

Figure 13-10: The third Memo Wizard dialog box—a title for your memo

6. The next dialog box of the Memo Wizard, shown in Figure 13-11, asks which header items should be included in your memo. The current date is inserted by default, as is your name (which is taken from the Preferences dialog box). You can change the text in either text box. You can also uncheck the information to be included or add Priority to the header information. For now, leave the defaults selected, enter a subject if desired, and then click Next.

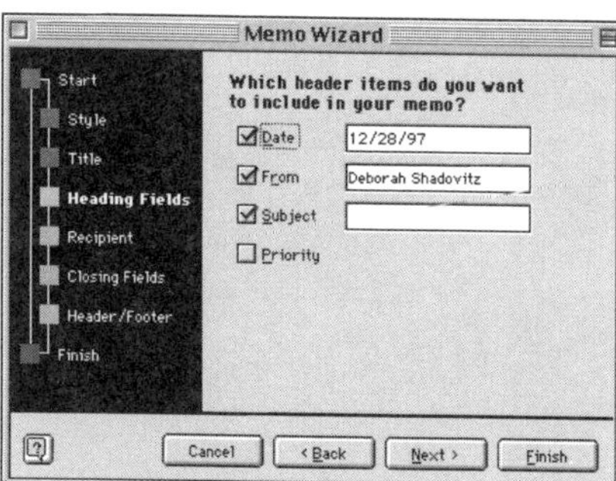

Figure 13-11: The fourth Memo Wizard dialog box—headers

7. The next dialog box of the Memo Wizard, shown in Figure 13-12, asks for recipients of the memo. Enter a desired addressee name in the To box and any names to be copied, and then click Next.

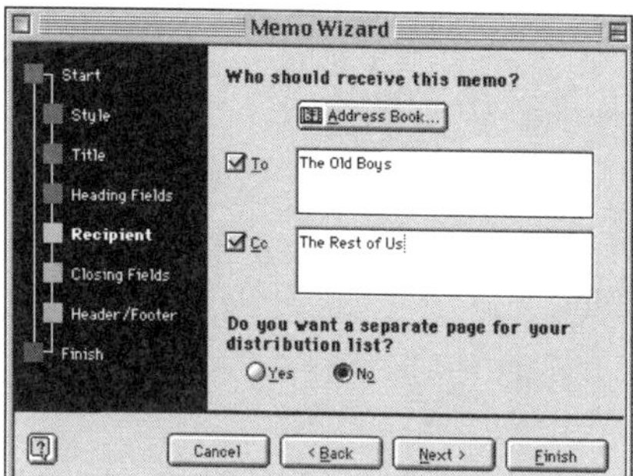

Figure 13-12: The fifth Memo Wizard dialog box—recipients

8. The next dialog box of the Memo Wizard, shown in Figure 13-13, asks which closing items you want in the memo. All these fields are optional, and you can click in any check box to turn on any desired options that are not checked, and vice versa. Check Writer's initials and enter your own initials. Then check Typist's initials and enter the appropriate initials there, too. Click Next to proceed.

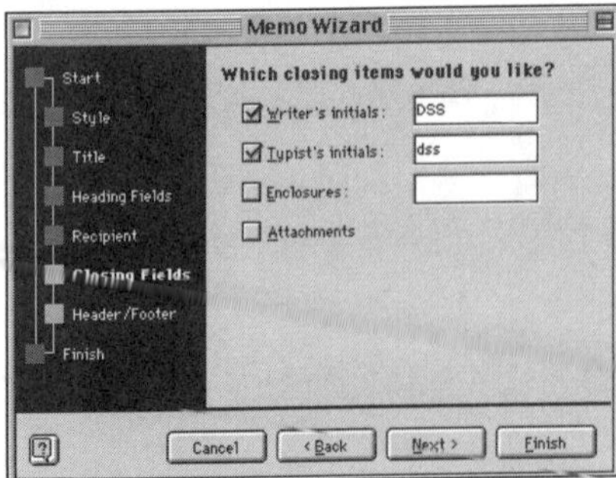

Figure 13-13: The sixth Memo Wizard dialog box—closings

9. The next dialog box of the Memo Wizard, shown in Figure 13-14, asks which items you desire in the header and the footer. In the header, you can choose the Date, Topic (which you fill in), and Page Number options. For the footer, you can choose the Date, Confidential, and Page Number options. For this example, leave the default options selected and click Next.

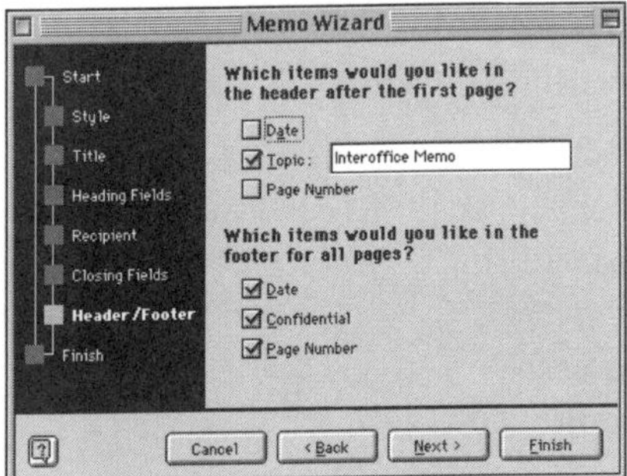

Figure 13-14: The seventh Memo Wizard dialog box—headers and footers

10. The last dialog box tells you the process is complete. Click Finish to produce the interoffice memo.

11. After the interoffice memo appears, you can edit the content as you edit any text. Word's Assistant pops up, suggesting it help you with further refinements or processes. Figure 13-15 shows the Assistant's suggestions.

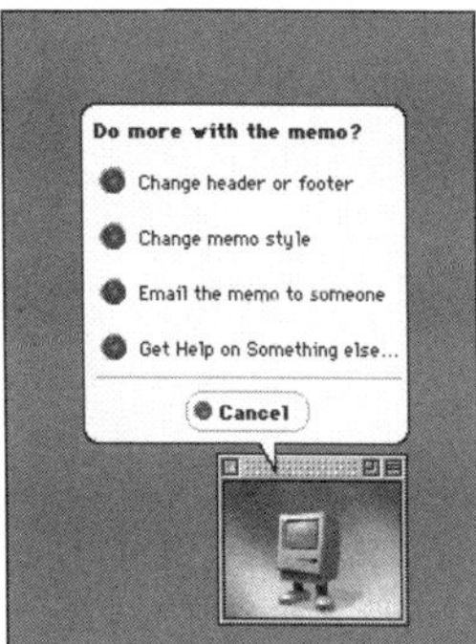

Figure 13-15: The Office Assistant offers suggestions.

One of the Office Assistant's suggestions is to e-mail the memo to someone. If you click this help item, the Assistant opens your default e-mail program, creates a new e-mail document for you, and automatically attaches the memo. You will probably need to close the memo before your e-mail program can actually send the document.

Summary

This chapter has provided a step-by-step look at what's involved in using Word 98's wizards to create typical business documents. You can use the different templates and wizards to ease the drudgery of creating many common types of documents:

✦ Use the Fax Wizard to create a fax cover sheet.

✦ Use the Memo Wizard to create an attractive memo form, complete with sender, date, recipient(s), and subject, into which you can type your message.

Where to go next

✦ The next chapter answers common questions that arise when you use Word 98.

✦ Many of the examples demonstrated in this chapter use the templates that come with Word. Chapter 8 tells the whole story about working with templates.

✦ ✦ ✦

The Word Top Ten

This chapter answers ten common Word 98 questions. These questions are based on inquiries to Microsoft Technical Support.

1. I have a document that was created with another word processing program. Can I work on this file in Word?

For the most part, Word converts files that have been created in other programs when you open them using the File⇨Open command or when you drag and drop the document onto Word's icon. If you use the File⇨Open method and don't see the desired document in the Open and Save dialog box, select All Files from the List Files of Type pop-up menu so you can be sure it isn't being filtered out.

Note, too, that Word uses file converters when it opens files created by other programs. If you did the default (drag the folder) installation of Word, the most common Microsoft converters were installed. However, you may need to add the converters by running the Value Pack Installer. Quit any running Office applications, and then perform these steps to add converters:

1. Insert the Office CD-ROM, open the Value Pack folder, and then double-click the Value Pack Installer.
2. In the Installer window, scroll to Text Converters. To install them all, click the check box next to Text Converters. To install just a few of the converters, click the arrow by the option; this reveals the selection of available converters. Check off the ones you wish to install.
3. Click Install. When installation is done, click Quit. The newly installed converters will be in the Text Converters folders, inside the Shared Files folder (which is in the Microsoft Office 98 folder, of course).

Word comes with these converters when drag-installed:

- ✦ HTML
- ✦ Microsoft Excel 2.*x*–8.0
- ✦ Recover Text Converter
- ✦ RTF—Rich Text Format
- ✦ Word 4.*x* and 5.*x* for the Macintosh
- ✦ Word 6.0/95 Export
- ✦ Word 6.0/95 Import
- ✦ Word 97–98 Import

The Value Pack Installer offers these converters:

- ✦ FoxPro–dBASE
- ✦ Text with Layout
- ✦ Word 1.*x* and 2.*x* for Windows
- ✦ Word 3.*x* for the Macintosh
- ✦ Word 3.*x*-6.0 for MS-DOS
- ✦ WordPerfect 5.*x*
- ✦ WordPerfect Graphics
- ✦ Works 2.*x*, 3.*x*, and 4.0 for the Macintosh

2. Why do addresses print on envelopes in the wrong position?

Envelope printing can be tricky to set up, but once you've figured out the setting for your printer, it's a cinch. The problem is that each printer feeds envelopes differently. Some place the envelope in the center of the feed tray; others place the envelope to the left or the right. Some printers need the envelope to be fed face down, while others want face up. If you're using a laser printer, chances are good that the paper tray and manual feeds require different positions. Ink jet printers usually have an icon somewhere inside the lid to show you how your envelope should feed. On laser printers, there should be an icon on the manual feed tray. You're on your own with the paper tray, so you may have to resort to your printer manual. Another thing to consider is that business envelopes and personal letter envelopes are different sizes.

To print an envelope, follow these steps:

1. (Optional) In your document, select the addressee information. (If you don't, Word will guess at the address for you by copying the top several lines of your document.)

2. Choose Tools ⇨ Envelopes and Labels, and select the Envelopes tab of the Envelopes and Labels dialog box (shown in Figure 14-1). If you selected the addressee information before opening this dialog box, you see the address in the Delivery address text box. If not, you see Word's guess. You can edit this guess, or any text in the Delivery address text box. Alternatively, you can select an addressee from the Address Book pop-up button or type in the delivery address. The Return address text box contains the name you entered during your initial user setup.

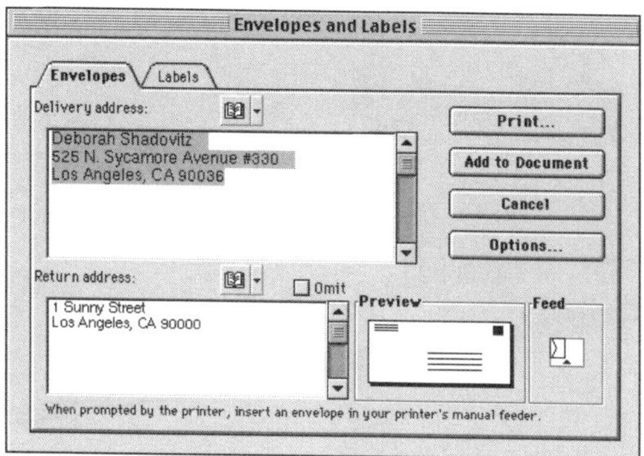

Figure 14-1: The Envelopes and Labels dialog box

3. To change the envelope size, click in the Preview area. This opens the Envelope Options tab of the Envelopes Options dialog box. Here you can change the size of the envelope and the position of the delivery and return addresses.

4. To change the feed orientation—which is the tricky part you'll need to experiment with—click the Feed button in the Envelopes and Labels dialog box or, if you're already in the Envelopes Options dialog box, go to the Printing Options tab.

   The Feed method icons represent all the various possibilities, as long as you recognize and take advantage of the Face up/Face down option and properly check or uncheck the Clockwise rotation option. The icons change as you select these options. Click the icon that finally represents the way your envelope looks in its printer tray.

5. On the Envelopes tab of the Envelopes and Labels dialog box, you see an Add to Document button. This button adds the envelope to the beginning of your document, creating a next-page section break after the envelope. Then, when you print, you can print the envelope followed by the letter (a convenient feature for writing letters).

6. To print the envelope, click Print.

3. How can I prevent page breaks from appearing in my document where I don't want them?

Unwanted page breaks can occur for any number of reasons. You may have applied paragraph formats that affect line and page breaks, or you may have inserted a "hard" page break or a section break that begins a new page. The following paragraphs should help you solve the problem. Your problem may not be an unwanted page break but one of Word's automatic paginations that simply falls in an inconvenient place. This problem is addressed, too. Figure 14-2 demonstrates the look of some breaks.

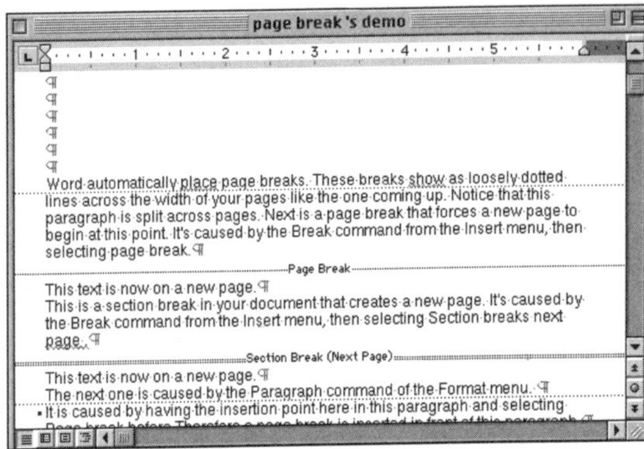

Figure 14-2: A document containing some types of breaks

You may have a page break in your document. As you work, Word automatically paginates your document for you, placing page breaks determined by your margin settings. In Normal view, these breaks show as loosely dotted lines across the width of your pages. However, people sometimes want to ensure that a new page will fall at a certain area, and therefore place a hard page break at that point. These breaks often end up falling in undesirable places as you add or delete text or change font size or line spacing. To remove a hard page break, place your insertion point immediately after the break—basically at the start of the text following the break. Then use the Delete key to remove it as you remove any unwanted character. (You'll know the hard page break from Word's automatic soft break because the hard break is labeled "page break" at the break point.)

Similarly, you may have a section break in your document. A section break can be one within a page or one that creates a new page. (It will say "section break, next page" at the break point.) You can remove this break the same way you remove a page break—by placing the cursor in the section immediately after the section break and pressing Delete.

To discover paragraph formatting that produces unwanted page breaks, select the paragraph immediately following the page break, choose Format ➪ Paragraph, and go to the Line and Page Breaks tab. In the Pagination section, you see which options you have checked and can uncheck the culprit. (The options are Keep lines together, Keep with next, or Page break before.) These breaks look like Word's automatic breaks.

You may also have a table in Word that is divided in the middle of a cell. If the entire table does not have to be on the same page, your solution is simple. Place your insertion pointer anywhere on the row that is being split. Choose Table ⇨ Cell Height and Width. In the dialog box, click the Row tab and clear the Allow Row to Break Across Pages check box. (If the table has to fit on one page, you have no choice but to rearrange adjoining text to allow the table to fit.)

If your problem is that Word's automatic pagination leaves you with a few lines of a paragraph moved over to the following page in a document, you will see the loosely dotted page-break line dividing the paragraph. To keep all of the paragraph on one page, your best options are to make your margins smaller or reduce the space between paragraphs. Both options allow more text per page so the extra lines can move up to the first page. To adjust the margins, switch to Print Preview and, in the ruler, move each margin area closer to the paper's edge. Alternatively, you can use the Format ⇨ Document command. There are two ways to reduce the space between paragraphs: If you have used styles, place the cursor within one paragraph, choose Format ⇨ Paragraph, select the Indents and Spacing tab, lessen the Space before or Space after, and then redefine the style. (For more on styles, see Chapter 8.) If you pressed Return to create space between paragraphs, reducing space between lines is more tedious. Showing the paragraph markers, select one marker character and make it a smaller font size. Then copy that marker and paste it, one by one, over all other markers that provide your space between paragraphs. Another option is to make your entire font size smaller. Finally, you can let Word reduce the document size for you. In Print Preview, click the Shrink to Fit button on the Print Preview toolbar.

4. Why doesn't Word print the gridlines in my table?

A table's gridlines appear only onscreen. If you want to add lines to your table printouts, you need to apply borders to the table. You can use the Table ⇨ Table AutoFormat command to select from predefined borders and shading. Figure 14-3 shows the Table AutoFormat dialog box.

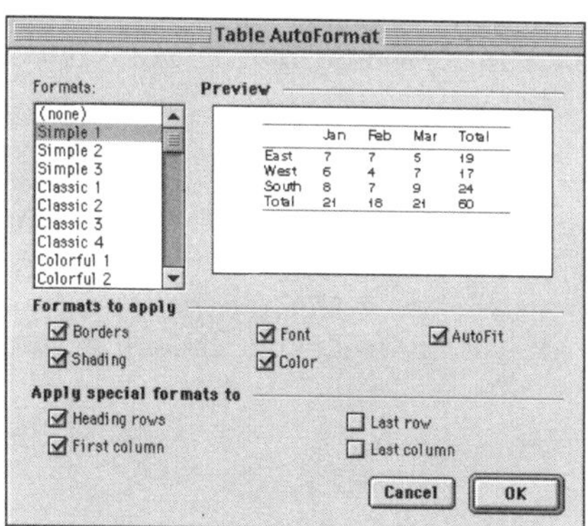

Figure 14-3: The Table AutoFormat dialog box

If you want to make a custom border, however, choose Format⇨Borders and Shading to bring up the Borders and Shading dialog box, as shown in Figure 14-4. In this dialog box, you can apply formatting to the table gridlines or to the text paragraph within a cell. If you want to apply formatting to the gridlines, be sure that you select the end-of-cell mark in the table.

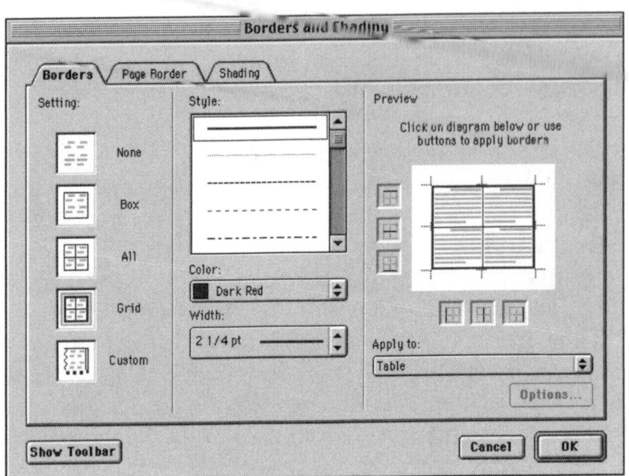

Figure 14-4: The Borders and Shading dialog box

Another option is to turn on the Tables and Borders toolbar and work from there.

5. Can I run Word 98 and an earlier version of Word on the same computer, or do I need to remove my earlier version(s) in order to run Word 98?

You can run two or three versions of Word on your computer simultaneously. Just keep each program in the folder in which it was installed.

When you install Word 5.1a, it creates its own folder. Keep this version in that folder. When you install Word 6, it installs two folders: one called Microsoft and one called Microsoft Word 6. Keep this version in those folders. Word 98 is installed in the folder called Microsoft Office 98. Keep all Office 98 components where they were installed, too.

To ensure that a document will open in the desired version, keep an alias of each version (clearly named by version) on your desktop and drag your document onto the desired version's icon.

You can launch the desired version of Word by double-clicking its icon or alias.

6. Can I delete Word documents while Word is running?

As is standard on the Mac, you can delete any document that is not open at the time. To delete a document, first close it by clicking the close box on the top left of the document's window. Then click the desktop to return to the Finder (or select Finder in the Applications menu). In the Finder, double-click your hard drive icon, locate the file, and drag it to the trash.

7. Why can't my associate using Word 4, 5, or 6 read my Word 98 documents?

When Word 4, 5, and 6 were created, Word 98 didn't exist. There is no way for any programmer to write software to accommodate things that don't exist. However, because Word programmers know about older software while writing new programs, they can make the newer software "downwardly compatible" with the older. Therefore, your solution is to work in your newer software (Word 98), but after saving a version as the normal Word 98 format, do a Save As and select the older format from the Save File as Type pop-up menu. Follow these steps:

1. In Word 98, open the document that you want to save in the earlier Word format.
2. Choose File⇨Save As to open the Save As dialog box.
3. In the Save File as Type pop-up menu, select Word 4, Word 5, Word 5.1, or Word 6 as appropriate. Make any desired change to the file's name, specify the folder in which you want to store the file, and then click OK.

8. Why aren't all my changes saved in a document, even with AutoRecover turned on?

AutoRecover is not the same as the AutoSave feature—it does not automatically save your files. There is no substitute for using the Save command each time you do something you want to be sure to keep. AutoRecover is designed to recover work after a power outage or system crash. AutoRecover periodically makes a copy of your document. If Word or your Mac freezes while you have documents open, Word automatically opens the saved recovery document when you restart and relaunch Word. The recovery files are temporary. They are erased when your document is saved and are deleted when you close the file.

If you want to turn on the AutoRecover feature or adjust the time intervals on the saves, choose Tools⇨Preferences and select the Save tab (see Figure 14-5.) Enter the desired time interval in the Save AutoRecover info every *x* minutes text box.

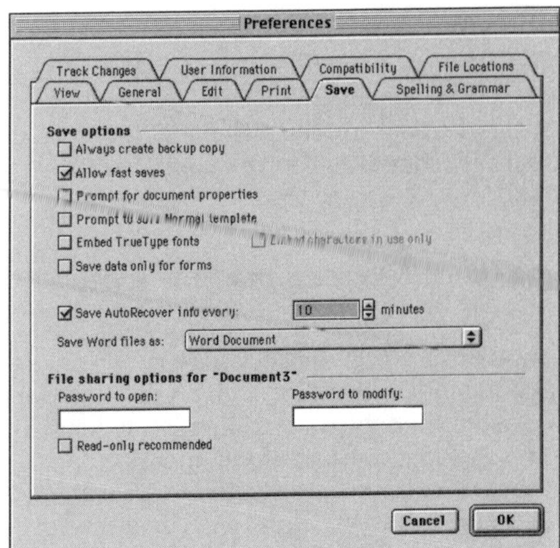

Figure 14-5: The Save Tab of the Preferences dialog box

Don't put more faith in AutoRecover than it deserves; it is not a substitute for proper saving or backup habits. The best defense is always to back up important work to another media source (such as a floppy, Zip, or Jazz disk) regularly.

9. How can I set a different font (or font size or style) as the default?

You may want to use a font different from the default font Word uses in the Normal template. Fortunately, changing that font is a piece of cake. Open the Font dialog box by choosing Format ➪ Font. In the dialog box, select the desired font, font style, and font size. Then click the Default button. Word displays a dialog box asking you to confirm the change to the default font; click OK in this dialog box to put the change into effect.

10. How can I create a bulleted or numbered list?

Word offers an easy way to create a bulleted or numbered list, add the bullets or numbers quickly, and apply a hanging indent to each of the paragraphs. To add bullets or numbers to a list, select all the paragraphs in the list and click either the Numbering button in the Formatting toolbar (to add numbers), or the Bullets button (to add bullets). If the Formatting toolbar isn't visible, choose View ➪ Toolbars ➪ Formatting.

Word's AutoFormat technology helps you automatically create bulleted and numbered lists. If you begin typing using a number, asterisk, or another form of bullet, Word will keep that format after the second bullet or number is entered. From then on, Word will automatically add the number or bullet followed by the space with which you began the first two lines of text. When you are done typing bulleted or numbered paragraphs, start a new paragraph and use the Delete key to delete the bullet. Word stops adding the bullets or numbers to successive paragraphs.

Summary

This chapter provided answers to some of the most common Word questions.

This chapter concludes the Word part of the book. The following part deals with Microsoft Excel, the spreadsheet package provided with Office 98.

Where to go next

- ✦ Printing is a task you will find yourself doing on a regular basis. For more information on the particulars of printing in Word, see Chapter 4.
- ✦ Formatting question are also common in Word. For answers to your formatting questions, see Chapter 3.

✦ ✦ ✦

Excel

P A R T

✦ ✦ ✦ ✦

In This Part

Chapter 15
Making the Most of Workbooks

Chapter 16
Getting Information into Excel

Chapter 17
Excel Formatting

Chapter 18
Adding Graphics to Worksheets

Chapter 19
Working with Excel Charts

Chapter 20
Printing and Page Setup

Chapter 21
Working with Excel Databases

Chapter 22
Working with Excel Macros

Chapter 23
Excel and the Web

Chapter 24
Excel and Visual Basic for Applications

Chapter 25
Excel at Work

Chapter 26
The Excel Top Ten

✦ ✦ ✦ ✦

CHAPTER 15

Making the Most of Workbooks

◆ ◆ ◆ ◆

In This Chapter

Understanding Excel workbooks

Working with worksheets

Working with Excel's toolbars

Saving and closing a workbook

Finding workbooks

Organizing your files

◆ ◆ ◆ ◆

This chapter covers topics related to working with Excel workbooks, which are collections of worksheet pages saved to the same disk file. Before you can effectively work with Excel, you need to become familiar with workbooks.

Understanding Excel Workbooks

Excel uses a workbook concept, which places multiple pages, each containing a worksheet, inside of a "notebook" (*workbook* in Excel lingo). Excel's designers assumed that most people who use spreadsheets have different but related groups of number-based data that would best occupy different pages. If you lived generations before the advent of the computer and you worked with numbers to earn a living, you would have different pieces of paper on your desk, each with related number-based information about a particular project. At the day's end, all the pages would go back into a file folder that was stored in your desk. In Excel, each of these pages becomes a separate worksheet, and the worksheets are identified by tabs at the bottom. All the worksheet pages make up a workbook (the file folder in the analogy).

Before spreadsheet designers implemented the workbook concept, spreadsheets first accommodated a user's desire for more power by providing increasingly larger spreadsheets in the form of a single page. But finding information became quite a challenge as spreadsheet pages approached the physical size of small houses. The next step in spreadsheet design was to give users the capability to base formulas in one spreadsheet on cells of another. This capability partially solved the organizational problem, but you had to remember to open all the spreadsheet files you needed. The workbook concept overcomes the limitations of earlier spreadsheet designs by placing all your information in an easily accessible notebook.

With the workbook concept, you can easily find information by navigating among the multiple pages of the workbook. And you can name the tabs that indicate each page (worksheet) of the workbook so the tabs represent what is stored in each worksheet. Figure 15-1 shows a typical workbook in Excel, with the House Sales worksheet page of the workbook currently active.

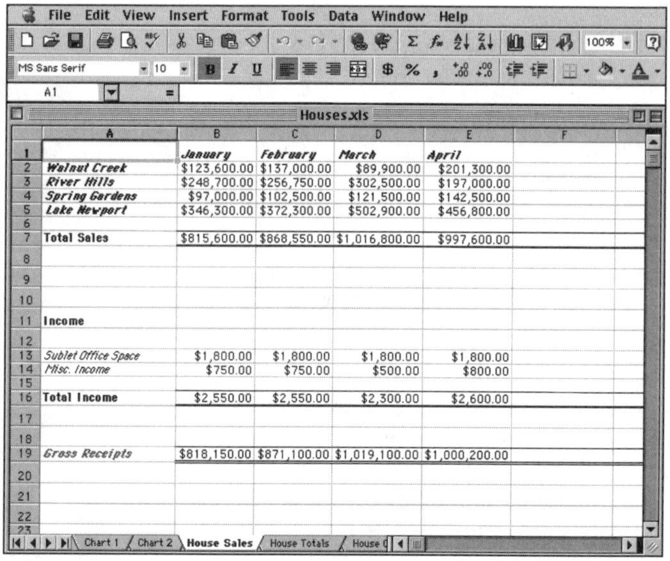

Figure 15-1: A typical Excel workbook

Each workbook can contain up to 255 separate worksheet pages. Each worksheet can have up to 65,536 rows (up from 16,384 in the previous version) and 256 columns—more than you should ever need on a single page. Each intersection of a row and column comprises a cell. Cells are identified by their row and column coordinates (for example, A1 is the cell in the upper-left corner of the worksheet). To make row and column coordinates easy to see, the row header and column header become highlighted when you select a cell. In addition to containing worksheet pages, an Excel workbook can also contain chart sheets (used to store charts), macros, and modules (collections of program code written in Visual Basic for Applications, the programming language used by Excel).

When You Need More Worksheets

By default, each workbook has three worksheet tabs. You can copy, add, or delete worksheets, at any time. However, you might find it more convenient to change this default in case it is more convenient to begin your workbooks with more (or fewer) worksheets.

To change the default number of worksheets, select Tools⇨Preferences, then select the General tab. In this tab, click the up or down arrows next to the Sheets in the new workbook field (or select the existing number and enter a new number).

Opening a new workbook

When you launch Excel, it opens a new workbook, and you can begin entering your information. If you want to create a new workbook at any time, click the New Workbook button on the Standard toolbar, or choose File⇨New.

Opening an existing workbook

You open an existing workbook the same way you open any document on the Mac. (See Chapter 1 for details.) Basically, your options are to double-click the file you want to open, select the file from the Apple menu if you stored it there, or choose File⇨Open to select the file from the Open dialog box, as shown in Figure 15-2. If you've placed the document in the MOM (Microsoft Office Manager) list, you can launch the file from there, too.

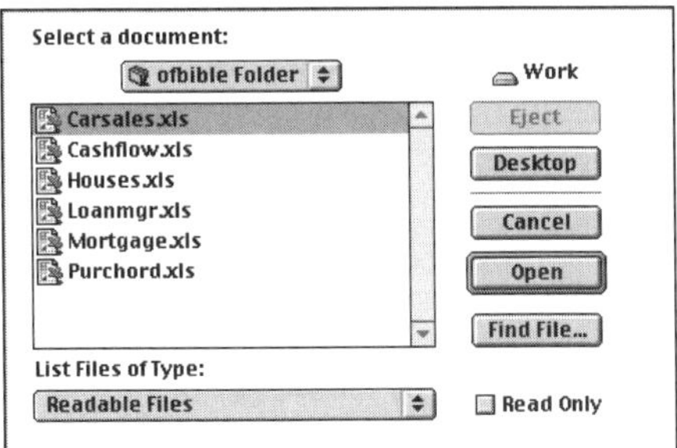

Figure 15-2: The Open dialog box

You may also be able to open a workbook you have recently worked with by selecting it from the File menu. By default, Excel remembers the last four files you worked with and lists them at the bottom of the File menu. If the list of recently used workbooks is not displayed in your File menu, the option for displaying them has been turned off. To turn it back on, choose Tools⇨Preferences, and then click the General tab in the Preferences dialog box. Click the Recently Used File List check box to activate the option, and then enter a number of files to be remembered. (You can show up to nine files.) Click OK.

The More Workbooks, the Merrier

You can have more than one workbook file open at a time. The number of workbooks you keep open at once is only limited by the memory you allot to Excel. Each workbook you open is in its own document window. You can move and size the windows containing your workbooks by using standard Mac moving and sizing techniques. To work with a specific workbook, bring it to the front.

As with any Mac document, if you see even the tiniest edge of a worksheet on your desktop, you can simply click it to bring it forward. Therefore, if you size the windows so they don't take up the entire screen, you can navigate among multiple windows by using the mouse to make any desired window the active window. You can bring the worksheet to the front by selecting it by name from the Window menu. Pressing Control-F6 also rotates through all open worksheets.

Working with Worksheets

As you work with Excel worksheets, you use various techniques to move around in the sheet and to select areas of the sheet in which to perform common operations. First, though, it makes sense to become familiar with the parts of a worksheet. The parts of a worksheet window are illustrated in Figure 15-3, and Table 15-1 describes the parts.

Table 15-1
Parts of a Worksheet

Worksheet Part	*Purpose*
Scroll bars	Use these to view sections of the worksheet that are not currently visible by clicking the arrows, or by dragging the scroll box.
Split bars	Use these to split the worksheet window into two panes horizontally and/or two panes vertically to view different portions of the worksheet. To split the window, move the pointer to the thick line by the up or right arrows and drag when the cursor becomes a two-headed arrow.
Row headers	Identifies each row and can be used to select rows (by clicking the headers).
Column headers	Identifies each column and can be used to select columns (by clicking the headers).
Cursor	Indicates the currently selected (or active) cell.
Tabs	Select each worksheet in the workbook.

Worksheet Part	*Purpose*
Standard toolbar	Provides buttons to access common operations, such as opening and saving files, and cutting, copying, and pasting data.
Formatting toolbar	Provides buttons to access common formatting tasks, such as changing the fonts and alignments used to display data.
Formula bar	Displays the contents of the active cell.
Status bar	Displays various messages as you use Excel.
Scroll buttons	Scrolls among the worksheet tabs in a workbook.

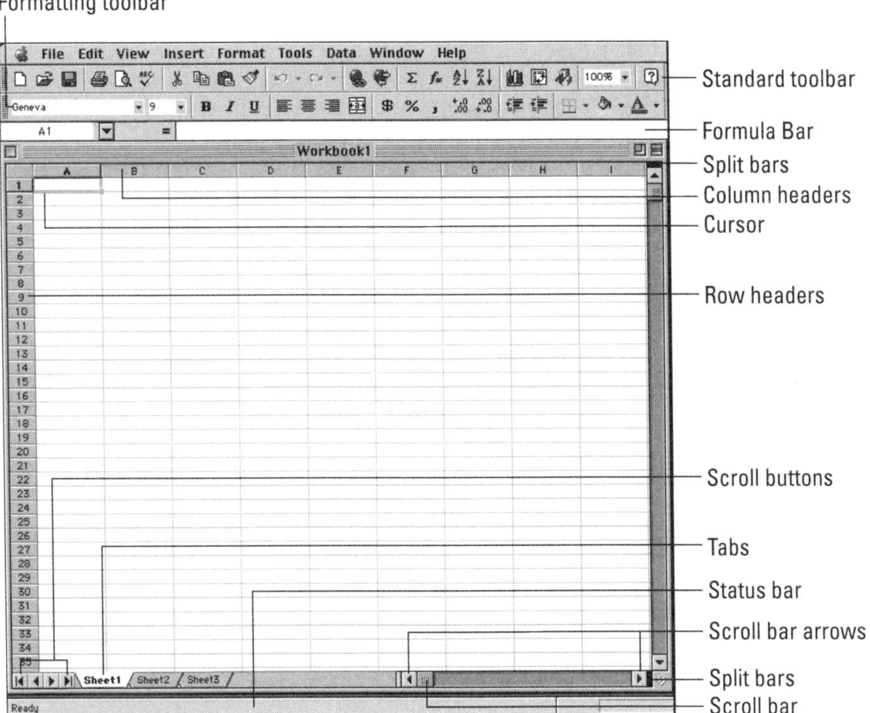

Figure 15-3: The parts of a worksheet

Navigating within your worksheet

Using the mouse is the primary method of navigating within a worksheet. As you move the mouse pointer around the worksheet, the pointer changes shape depending on its location. In most areas of the worksheet, the pointer resembles a plus sign. In most areas outside of the worksheet or over the scroll bars, the pointer changes shape to resemble an arrow. You can scroll the worksheet one row or one column at a time by pointing to the arrows at the ends of the scroll bars and clicking them with the mouse button. As always with the Mac, the longer your press the mouse, the further you travel within your document. You can also drag the scroll box, the square block in each scroll bar area. As you drag, a yellow pop-up box tells you the row or column you will be at when you release the mouse. By pressing Shift as you drag the scroll box, you scroll huge distances at a time.

The Tab and Return keys, used alone or in combination with the Shift key, also move the cursor. Pressing Tab moves the cursor to the right; pressing Shift-Tab moves the cursor to the left. Pressing Return moves the cursor down; pressing Shift-Return moves the cursor up.

If you've lost the cursor and you want to locate it quickly, press Control-Delete. This causes the window to scroll as needed to reveal the active cell.

You can also use Edit ➪ Go To (F5) to move quickly within a worksheet if you know your destination cell. Press F5 to open the Go To dialog box, as shown in Figure 15-4. In the Reference text box, enter the name of the cell you want to go to and click OK, or press Return or Enter. Excel jumps you to that cell. For example, if you enter AZ400 into the Reference text box and press Return or Enter, the cursor moves to cell AZ400.

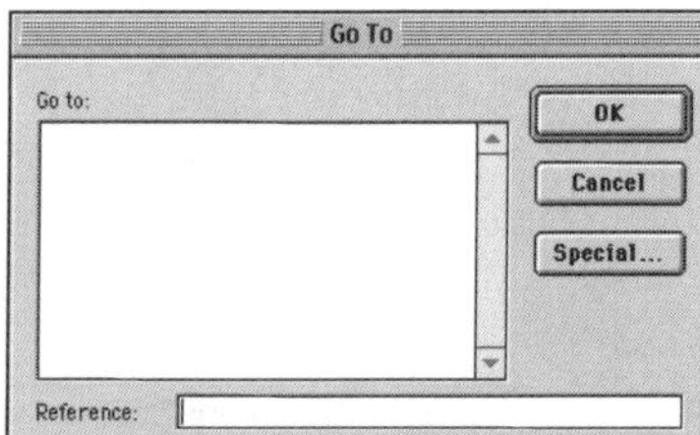

Figure 15-4: The Go To dialog box

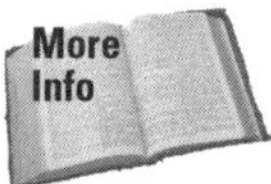

If you're curious, you can use the Go To list box to select a named range to go to in a worksheet. Chapter 16 provides details about working with named ranges.

You can also navigate within your worksheet by using arrow keys. As you reach the right side or the bottom row of the worksheet, pressing the same cursor key once more causes the worksheet to scroll, which brings an additional row or column into view.

Remember that the part of the worksheet you can see is just a small part of the entire sheet. Table 15-2 shows various other key combinations you may find useful for moving around in an Excel worksheet.

Table 15-2
Useful Keys for Worksheet Navigation

Key	*Function*
Arrow keys	Move the cursor in direction of the arrow.
Control-↑ or Control-↓	Moves the cursor to the top or bottom of a region of data.
Control-← or Control-→	Moves the cursor to the left-most or right-most region of data.
Page Up or Page Down	Moves the cursor up or down one screen.
Control-Page Up or Control-Page Down	Moves the cursor to the preceding or the following worksheet.
Home	Moves the cursor to the first cell in a row.
Control-Home	Moves the cursor to the upper-left corner of the worksheet.
Option-End	Moves the cursor to the last cell in a row.
Control-End	Moves the cursor to the last cell in the used area of a worksheet.
End-Enter	Moves the cursor to the last column in a row.

Moving among worksheets

To move among the individual worksheets of the workbook, click the worksheets' tabs at the bottom of the workbook. At the lower-left corner of the worksheet (refer to Figure 15-1) are scroll buttons that enable you to scroll among all the worksheet tabs. If a tab is not visible, click the buttons to scroll the tab into view. Clicking the left- or right-arrow button scrolls you by one tab to the left or right. Clicking the left-end or right-end button (the one with the line to the left or right of the arrow) scrolls you to the first or last tab in the worksheet. By default, new workbooks in Excel have 16 worksheets, but you can add more (up to the limit of 255 worksheets per workbook) by inserting new worksheets, a topic covered later in this chapter.

Remember that you can use the Control-Page Up command to move to the prior worksheet or Control-Page Down to move to the next worksheet.

Scrolling among the tabs works well if your workbook contains relatively few worksheets, but if your workbook is fairly large (for example, four years' worth of projected budgets stored on 48 worksheets), there's an easier way to get around the worksheets: You can use Edit⇨Go To (F5). When the Go To dialog box appears, enter the name of the tab followed by an exclamation point and the cell you want to go to. Follow these steps to use the Go To key:

1. Press F5 to open the Go To dialog box.

2. In the Reference text box, enter the tab name, an exclamation point, and the cell reference. Then click OK.

   For example, to jump to the first cell in the sixth worksheet, you would press F5 and enter Sheet6!A1 in the Reference text box.

Unfortunately, this technique doesn't work when your tab names include spaces, such as "House Sales." In this case, Excel interprets the first word you type in the Reference text box as a named range, and when Excel can't find a range by that name, it displays an error message. The only way around this problem (if you want to be able to jump across pages with the Go To key) is to rename the tab, removing spaces, or to create named ranges in the other worksheets so Excel can find the named range.

Renaming the worksheet tabs

As you work with different worksheets within a workbook, you may find it helpful to rename the tabs something meaningful. Face it, Sheet4 means a lot less to most people than May 98 Slush Fund. You can easily rename the tabs to whatever you want by Control-clicking the desired tab and choosing Rename from the shortcut menu. This highlights the existing name within the tab, ready for you to type a replacement name. Excel doesn't limit what you call your tabs, but keeping tab names short enables you to view the most tabs at the bottom of the workbook.

Selecting multiple worksheets

For many common operations (such as inserting or deleting sheets or applying formatting), you need a way to select more than one worksheet at a time. You can Shift-click to select multiple adjacent sheets (directly beside one another) by performing these steps:

1. Use the scroll buttons to bring the first tab you want to select into view, and click the tab to select that worksheet.
2. Use the scroll buttons (if needed) to bring the last tab of the group you want to select into view. Press the Shift key and click the last tab.

To select multiple nonadjacent sheets, perform the following steps:

1. Use the scroll buttons to bring the first tab you want to select into view and click the tab to select that worksheet.
2. Use the scroll buttons (if needed) to bring the next tab you want to select into view. Press the ⌘ key and click the desired tab.
3. Repeat Steps 1 and 2 for each additional tab you want to select.

Selecting a range of cells

For many operations, you will need to select large areas of cells, or ranges of cells. To select all cells from A1 to F6, for example, you would click in cell A1, hold down the mouse button, and drag down to cell F6 (see Figure 15-5). As you select the A1:F6 cell range, the first cell does not appear in your highlight color, as the others do; nevertheless, it is one of the selected cells. By placing the cursor at any cell and clicking and dragging the mouse, you can select any range of cells.

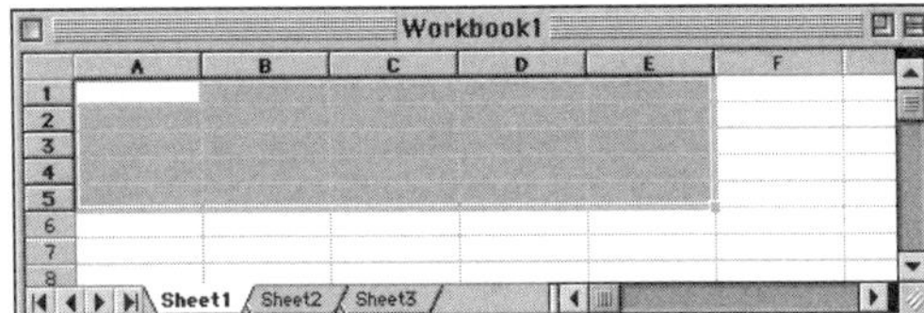

Figure 15-5: Selecting a range of cells in an Excel worksheet

Rather than drag over a large selection, you can Shift-click. Simply click in the first cell of the range, and then press Shift while you click in the last cell of the range. This selects the entire range, leaving the first cell that you selected as the active cell. For example, if you click in cell B2, press Shift, and click in cell E15, the entire range from B2 to E15 is selected, and the active cell becomes cell B2.

To select a very large range of cells, you can combine Shift-clicking and the Go To command to make your selection process faster. Follow these steps:

1. Select the first cell in the range that you want to select.
2. Press F5 to open the Go To dialog box.
3. In the Reference text box, enter the cell reference for the last cell in the range.
4. Press Shift while you click OK.

You can also use other methods to select a range of cells. Clicking a row header at the left edge of the worksheet selects an entire row, while clicking the column header at the top of the column selects an entire column. To select more than one complete row or column of a worksheet, click and drag across a series of column headers or down a series of row headers. For example, if you want to select all cells in rows 4, 5, and 6, you click the row 4 header and drag across rows 5 and 6.

You can also select noncontiguous ranges, or nonadjacent areas. For example, you can select A1:C4 and then select F3:G8. To make this selection, select the first range in any usual manner. Then press the ⌘ key and select the second range by clicking and dragging. Excel selects the second area without deselecting the first. Figure 15-6 shows the result of selecting these two ranges.

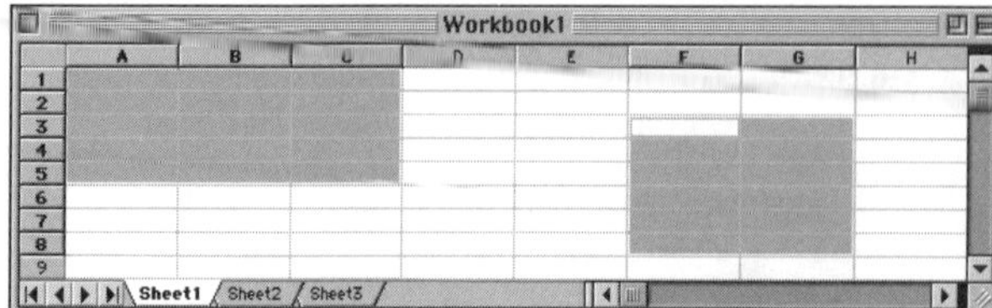

Figure 15-6: A selection of noncontiguous cells

You may also find it helpful to select multiple ranges, such as both rows and columns, as one unit so you can apply the same formatting to them. (Chapter 17 goes into more detail about formatting your worksheets.) To select rows and columns at the same time, select the first row(s) or column(s) you want and hold down the ⌘ key as you select the other rows or columns. Figure 15-7 shows the results of selecting rows 1 and 2 and columns A and B with this technique.

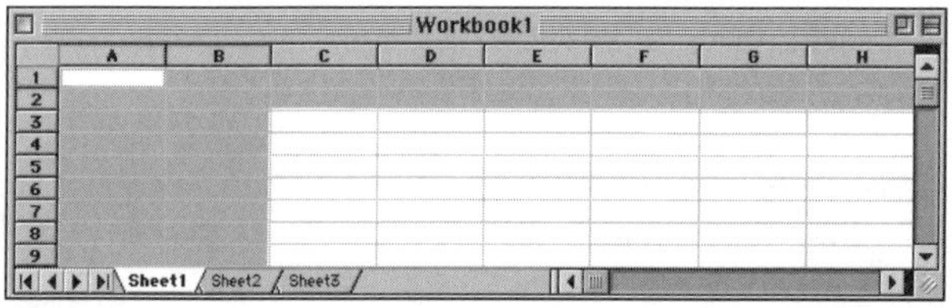

Figure 15-7: The result of selecting rows and columns as one unit

Adding and deleting worksheets

As you work in an Excel workbook, you may have to rearrange the worksheets within it. Control-clicking one of the worksheet tabs causes a shortcut menu to open. You can use this shortcut menu to add, delete, and move your worksheets.

Follow these steps to add a worksheet to a workbook:

1. Control-click the tab of the worksheet that will appear after the worksheet you want to add.
2. Choose Insert from the shortcut menu to open the Insert dialog box with the General tab displayed, as shown in Figure 15-8.

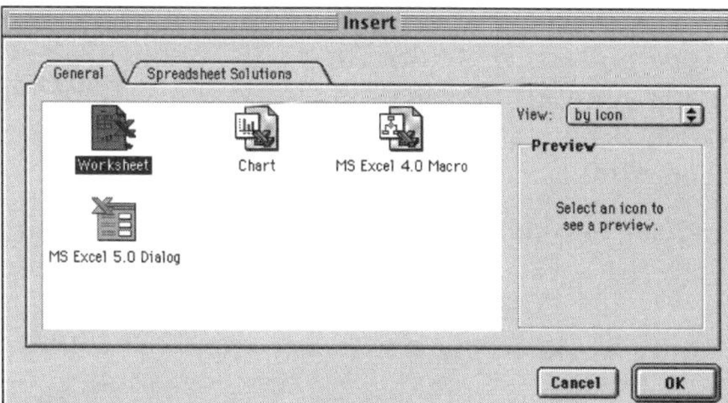

Figure 15-8: The Insert dialog box

3. Click the Worksheet icon to insert a new worksheet and click OK (or double-click the Worksheet icon).

You can also delete a worksheet by using the shortcut menu. Simply select the tab of the sheet you want to delete, Control-click it, choose Delete, and click OK to confirm the deletion.

Moving and copying information in worksheets

You can move or copy information within worksheets and between workbooks in a variety of ways. To copy information from any worksheet to another, perform the following steps:

1. Select the information you want to copy.
2. Choose Edit ➪ Copy (⌘-C) or click the Copy button in the Standard toolbar.
3. Move to the cell (in any worksheet) where you want to begin the insertion of the information. If you are pasting to a new worksheet, go to Step 4. If you are pasting into a worksheet that already contains information, select the area into which you will paste. This area must have the same number of cells as were copied in order to prevent overwriting existing information.
4. Press Enter (not Return) to place the information in the worksheet. Of course you can also choose Edit ➪ Paste (⌘-V) or click the Paste button in the Standard toolbar.

You can move information in the same worksheet or to another worksheet or workbook by following these steps:

1. Select the information you want to move.
2. Choose Edit ➪ Cut (⌘-X) or click the Cut button in the Standard toolbar.

3. Move to the cell in the worksheet where you want the paste to begin. If you are pasting to a new worksheet, go to Step 4. If you are pasting into a worksheet that already contains information, select the area into which you will paste. This area must have the same number of cells as were copied in order to prevent overwriting existing information.
4. Choose Edit ⇨ Paste (⌘-V) or click the Paste button in the Standard toolbar to insert the information.

Moving and copying an entire worksheet is also easy to do. Follow these steps:

1. Select the tab you want to move or copy.
2. Control-click the tab of the sheet and choose Move or Copy from the shortcut menu. This opens the Move or Copy dialog box. Identify the workbook to which you want to move or copy your worksheet. All available workbooks appear in the To Book pop-up list. You can also move or copy to a new workbook by selecting the (new book) option.
3. In the Before sheet portion of the Move or Copy dialog box select the tab you want your worksheet to land in front of, or select (move to end).
4. If you just want to move the worksheet, leave the Create a copy check box empty. To keep the worksheet in place but also copy it to the new location, check the copy option.
5. Click OK.

Remember, this moves or copies the entire worksheet, not just a part of it, even if only a part of it is selected when you begin.

Viewing As Much As Possible

Toolbars, the formula bar, and the status bar are very handy. However, they take up room on your screen and at times you may need to dedicate every inch to viewing your spreadsheet. You have two options to help you with this. One is to turn off each of the toolbars, the formula bar and the status bar. However, that requires several steps to turn off each element (regardless of whether you do this from the View menu or by Control-clicking any visible toolbar). Later, turning each element back on requires the same actions again.

Your other option is to use Excel's Full Screen command, available on the View menu. Simply select View ⇨ Full Screen and the worksheet expands to fit the entire screen, removing all status and toolbars. While in Full Screen mode, a small floating button bar appears, providing a button to Close Full Screen and return to normal mode. You probably don't need this button taking up screen space; you can return to the View menu any time to turn off Full Screen mode.

Splitting the worksheet window

With large worksheets, you may find it helpful to view entirely different parts of the worksheet at the same time by splitting the worksheet window into different panes (see Figure 15-9). To split a worksheet window, drag one of the split bars. You can also select a row where you want the window to split and choose Window ➪ Split. (If you select a cell and choose Window ➪ Split, the panes will split both horizontally and vertically.)

You can drag the split bar at the top right side of the window to create a horizontal split, or drag the split bar at the bottom right of the window to create a vertical split, or both. You can then switch between panes by clicking in the pane where you want to work. You can reposition your splits any time. When you are finished using multiple panes, double-click the split to close it. (Or drag the split bar back to the right or bottom of the window, or choose Window ➪ Remove Split.)

While a window is split, you can keep the top or left pane from scrolling by choosing Window ➪ Freeze Panes. This menu option freezes the window panes above and to the left of the split.

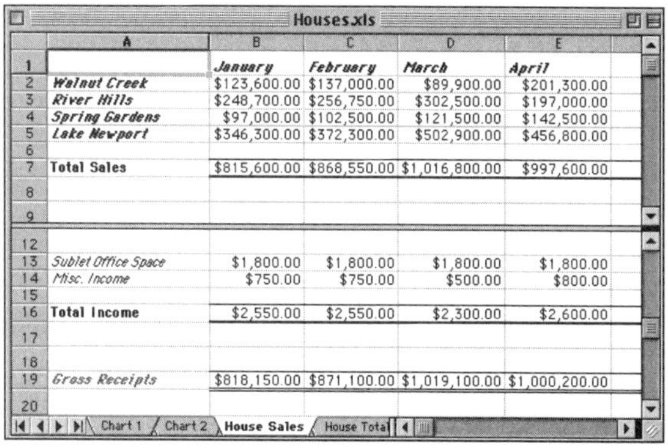

Houses.xls

	A	B	C	D	E
1		*January*	*February*	*March*	*April*
2	*Walnut Creek*	$123,600.00	$137,000.00	$89,900.00	$201,300.00
3	*River Hills*	$248,700.00	$256,750.00	$302,500.00	$197,000.00
4	*Spring Gardens*	$97,000.00	$102,500.00	$121,500.00	$142,500.00
5	*Lake Newport*	$346,300.00	$372,300.00	$502,900.00	$456,800.00
6					
7	**Total Sales**	$815,600.00	$868,550.00	$1,016,800.00	$997,600.00
8					
9					
12					
13	*Sublet Office Space*	$1,800.00	$1,800.00	$1,800.00	$1,800.00
14	*Misc. Income*	$750.00	$750.00	$500.00	$800.00
15					
16	**Total Income**	$2,550.00	$2,550.00	$2,300.00	$2,600.00
17					
18					
19	*Gross Receipts*	$818,150.00	$871,100.00	$1,019,100.00	$1,000,200.00
20					

Chart 1 / Chart 2 / House Sales / House Total

Figure 15-9: A worksheet window split into multiple panes

Working with Excel's Toolbars

Like the other Office applications, Excel provides several toolbars you can use to accomplish common tasks. By default, Excel displays the Standard and the Formatting toolbars, shown earlier in Figure 15-3. In addition, Excel has several other toolbars you may find useful. Figure 15-10 shows the rest of the Excel toolbars.

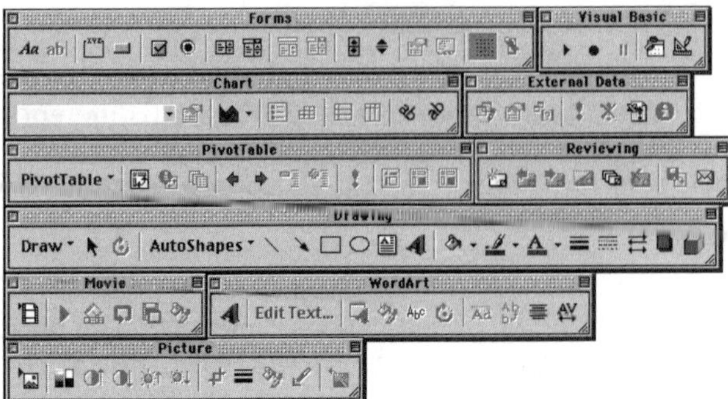

Figure 15-10: The additional Excel toolbars

To turn a toolbar on or off, choose View➪Toolbars, and then select the toolbar name. To learn what a button does, rest your mouse pointer over the button. In a moment, a yellow rectangle pops up, telling you what that button does. If this rectangle doesn't appear, ScreenTips have been turned off. (Toolbars and ScreenTips were introduced in Chapter 1.)

You can change a toolbar's position, change the buttons that appear, and change the buttons' order. And you can create your own toolbar. Toolbar customization is covered in detail in Appendix E.

The formula bar

Below the toolbars is the formula bar, unless it has been turned off. To turn the status bar on or off, select View➪Formula Bar. The formula bar is where you enter data and formulas. It also shows you any formula contained in a cell. The formula bar is key to Excel and will be discussed in many places in this section.

The status bar

At the bottom of your screen, you find a status bar, unless it has been turned off. To turn the status bar on or off, select View➪Status Bar. Occasionally, the status bar displays pertinent messages about what Excel is doing or gives you tips about how to do something.

Another cool thing the status bar shows is the result of Excel's AutoCalulate feature. When you select any range of cell within your spreadsheet, the sum of those cells appears to the right of the status bar, showing "Sum=" followed by the sum. AutoCalulate is new to Excel 98.

Saving and Closing a Workbook

Until you save a workbook, it exists only in the temporary memory of your Mac. It's a good idea to save your workbook (and any document) as soon as you create something you wouldn't want to re-create.

To save a workbook, use the standard Mac save command, File➪Save (⌘-S). You can also click the Save button on the Standard toolbar. In the Save dialog box that opens, name your workbook. Notice where your workbook is being saved and use the pop-up list at the top of the dialog box to switch folders as desired. To password-protect the workbook, click the Options button, as shown in Figure 15-11. The Save Options dialog box (see Figure 15-12) appears. Here, you can add a password for opening the workbook, or a modify password for making changes. You can also check the Read-only recommended check box to make the workbook read-only, so no edits can be added. Checking Always create backup saves the preceding version of the worksheet to a backup file each time you save the latest version. (See "Creating a backup file" later in this chapter.) Click OK to close the Save Options dialog box. Finally, click OK in the Save dialog box to perform the save.

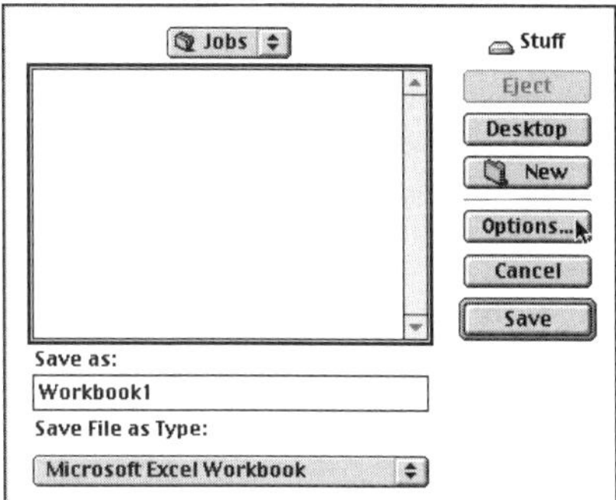

Figure 15-11: The Save dialog box

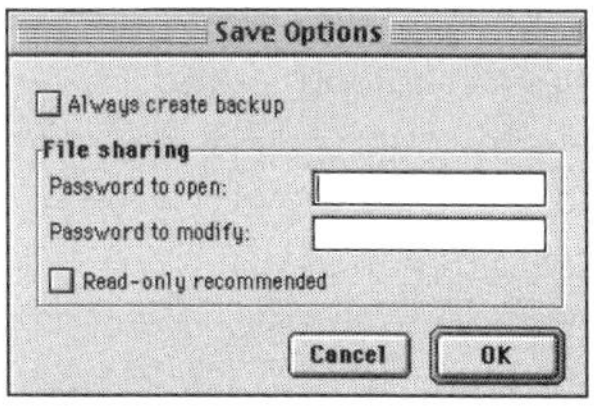

Figure 15-12: The Save Options dialog box

Once a file has been saved, you won't see the dialog box again (because you already assigned a name). If you forget to name your document when saving, the document receives the default name, such as Workbook1. You can close the workbook, locate it in the Finder, and then rename it. Never rename a file while it is open.

You can add a password at any time, even after you've saved your workbook. Select File➪Save As. This takes you to the same Save dialog box as when you first saved, providing you with the same Options button mentioned previously. Click the Options button, enter your password in the Save Options dialog box, and then click OK. Back in the Save dialog box, either give your document a new name or keep the same name. By keeping the same name and saving the document to the same place, you replace the new password-protected version with the former version.

You can set a specific folder as the default folder that opens in the Open and Save/Save As dialog boxes. To set a default folder, follow these steps:

1. Select Tools➪Preferences, and then click the General tab.
2. Click the Select button next to the Default file location field, and select your folder. The path name appears in the field.

   If you are so inclined, you can type the path for the folder you want to display as the default working folder, or click the Select button and choose the folder you want. For example, type **Macintosh HD:accounts**. If, for some reason, your default folder is directly on your desktop, add **Desktop Folder** to the path. In this example, if the Accounts folder is on the desktop, type **Macintosh HD:Desktop Folder:accounts**. (We don't endorse folders on your desktop; we advise keeping folders within the Hard Drive icon and placing aliases of the folders on your desktop—or better, in your Apple menu.)

Adding summary information to your workbook

As part of the information saved with your workbook, you can include details such as a title, author name, key words, and comments about the workbook. You can view and edit this information by choosing File➪Properties, which brings up the Properties dialog box. If it's not already in front, click the Summary tab (see Figure 15-13) and add any information you want. The information you enter can later help you locate files for which you may need to search.

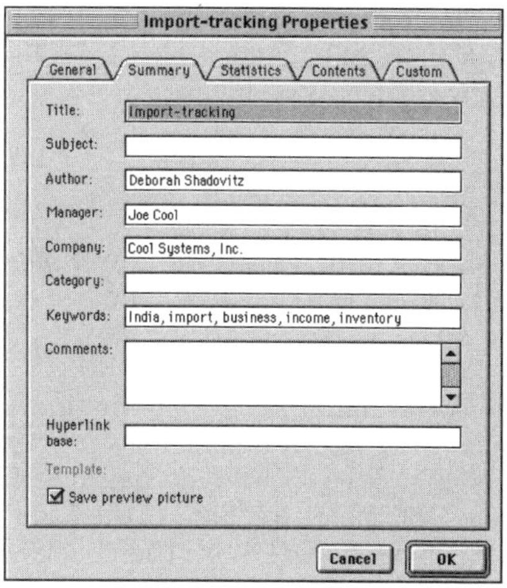

Figure 15-13: The Summary tab of the Properties dialog box

Using the AutoSave feature

Excel's AutoSave option can protect you from losing significant amounts of work in the event of a power failure or system crash. (It is not infallible, however.)

To enable AutoSave, choose Tools ➪ AutoSave. (If you don't see this menu option, skip to the next paragraph.) In the AutoSave dialog box, check the Automatic Save Every check box, and enter the time interval you want Excel to use for the AutoSave. Then choose whether you want AutoSave to save only the active workbook or all open workbooks and whether you want to be prompted before each AutoSave.

If you don't see the AutoSave option on the Tools menu, choose Tools ➪ Add-Ins to bring up the Add-Ins dialog box, as shown in Figure 15-14. This dialog box contains additional Excel options you can activate. Check the box by the AutoSave option to make the option available on the Tools menu. Then follow the steps in the preceding paragraph to turn on the AutoSave option.

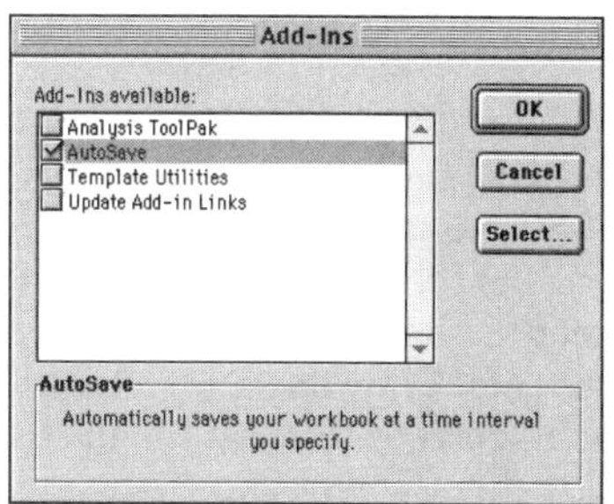

Figure 15-14: The Add-Ins dialog box

The AutoSave add-in is part of the normal Office drag-install so it should be listed in the Add-Ins dialog box. If the feature is not there, you can install it by using the Office Custom Installer. Details on this installer are in Appendix A.

Creating a backup file

Another way to protect your work from being lost after a crash or power failure is to create a backup file for each "parent file" you are working with. The backup file again minimizes the chances of losing your work.

You can take advantage of this option during your initial save or at any time after. During your first save, click Options to open the Save Options dialog box. If you have already saved your document, choose File⇨Save As to open the Save dialog box, and then click Options to open the Save Options dialog box. In the Save Options dialog box, check the Always Create Backup check box. Then click OK to close the Save Options dialog box. During your first save, continue with the normal save process. If you are doing a Save As, make sure to keep the same document name and save it to the file's original location. That way the new file you created by doing a Save As replaces the original, avoiding the confusion of duplicate documents.

After you activate the backup option, Excel creates a file named "Backup of..." whenever you save.

Saving in other file formats

You often need to save files in formats other than that used by your current version of Excel. Other users may be using earlier versions of Excel, or they may be using other spreadsheets, and you need to provide them with spreadsheet data they can work with. Saving files in other formats is relatively simple if you follow these steps:

1. Choose File⇨Save As to open the Save As dialog box.
2. In the Save File as Type pop-up list, select the format in which you want to save the file.
3. After selecting the file type, enter a name for the file or accept the default. (You may want to add the new file type as part of the name.)
4. Click Save to save the file.

If you save files in a format that is not the native Excel format, some features of the worksheet may be lost if they are not supported by the other program's file format. For example, if you save a file in an Excel 4.0 (or older) format, only the current page of the workbook will be saved to a worksheet file because that version of Excel did not support workbooks with multiple sheets. The Office Assistant will remind you of this when you save a workbook as Excel 4.0 or older. It will advise you to save each sheet separately by making each sheet active and then saving it.

Saving Excel data as HTML

New to Excel 98 is the capability to create HTML files. (HTML—Hypertext Markup Language—is the language used to store information on the World Wide Web.) The HTML files you create using Excel can be uploaded to a Web server for availability on the Web, or to a corporate intranet.

When you choose File➪Save As HTML, Excel launches the Internet Assistant Wizard. You can use this wizard to create Web pages based on worksheet data, or on charts. See Chapter 23 for additional details on saving worksheet and chart data as HTML, and on publishing Excel data on the Web.

Saving a workspace file

If you work with more than one workbook simultaneously on a regular basis, you may grow tired of opening the same workbooks day in and day out. With Excel's workspace file feature, you can avoid this monotony. You can use this workspace file to save the workbooks you are working on, the order they are in, and the sheets that are open at the time. The next time you need to work with these same workbooks, you can open the workspace file and all the workbooks open in the same position they were in when you created the workspace file. Follow these steps to create a workspace file:

1. Open the workbooks you want to include in the workspace file and arrange them the way that you want them to be when you open the workspace file.
2. Choose File➪Save Workspace to open the Save Workspace dialog box, as shown in Figure 15-15.

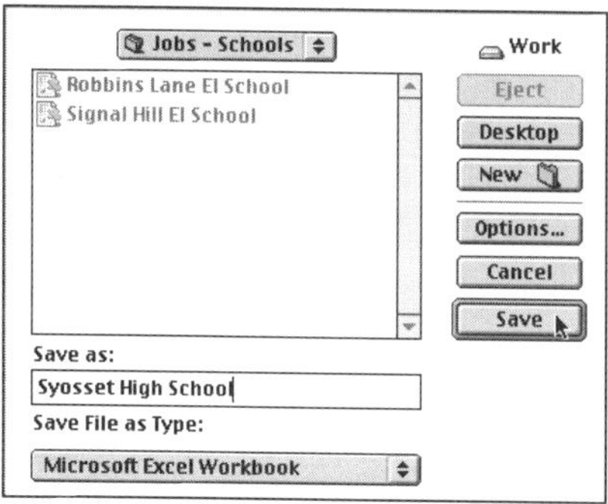

Figure 15-15: The Save Workspace dialog box

3. Enter a name for the workspace file and click OK.

The workspace file keeps track of the arrangement of your work area and opens your files when you double-click it, but you still need to save your changes to the workbook files.

Closing a workbook and exiting Excel

You close a workbook the same way you close any Mac document or window—by clicking the close box in the top left corner of the document window or choosing File ⇨ Close (⌘-W). If you made any changes to the workbook that were not saved, Excel asks whether you want to save the changes. (This safeguard is provided to avoid your exiting Excel without saving your work.)

You also quit Excel as you quit any Mac program—File ⇨ Quit. If you have any unsaved work, Excel asks whether you want to save the changes and waits for your response before continuing. To make quitting easier, Excel 98 introduces a Save All option. If you have more than one worksheet open that has not been saved since your last change, when you quit, the dialog box offers a button to save all changed worksheets with one click.

Finding Workbooks

In case the Mac Find feature isn't enough for you to locate a misplaced file, you can use Excel's Find feature—if you have diligently filled in the Summary tab of the Properties dialog box for your worksheets. This same search system is in Word and PowerPoint so you can search for files created in either application from here, and vice versa. (It also means you can refer back here if you need help searching from Word or PowerPoint.)

To do a search, select File ⇨ Open (⌘-O), and then click the Find File button. This brings up the Search dialog box shown in Figure 15-16. In this dialog box, you can enter a filename for which to search. However, this dialog box offers far less searching capacity than the Mac's Find feature.

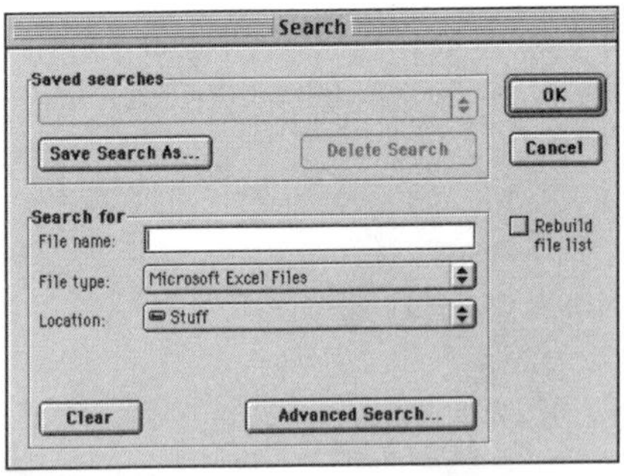

Figure 15-16: The Search dialog box

To perform an advanced search, click the Advanced Search button. This opens the Advanced Search dialog box shown in Figure 15-17. This dialog box enables you to search based upon any Summary information you have entered for any Excel, Word, or PowerPoint document.

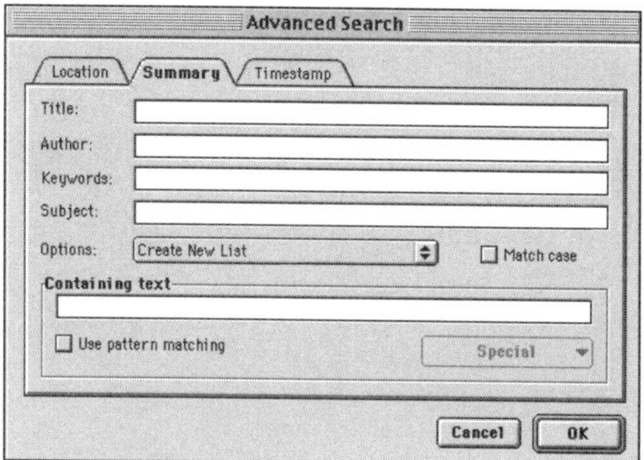

Figure 15-17: The Summary tab of the Advanced Search dialog box

To do an advanced search, follow these steps:

1. Select File➪Open (⌘-O), and then click the Find File button to open the Search dialog box.
2. Clear any existing searches by clicking the Clear button.
3. Click Advanced Search to open the Advanced Search dialog box, and then select the Summary tab.

   This is where you can perform searches based on the different sections of the Summary tab of the Properties dialog box. This is the information—filename, author name, or other elements of the document—that you enter when you save a file for the first time.
4. Enter any word on which you want to search. For example, if seeking a keyword, enter that word in the Keywords field.
5. Check the Match case option if you want to search only on words that are capitalized or not capitalized, exactly as you've entered words in the search fields.
6. Click the Location tab to specify where you want to search. To add more locations to search, click Add. In the dialog box that opens, navigate to the location you want and click the Select button at the bottom of the dialog box.
7. Make an entry in the Value text box to work with your property and condition choices. For example, if you choose Ends with in the Conditions list box, enter the ending value in this field.

8. To specify a date range to search, such as the date created or date last modified, click the Timestamp tab, and then enter the dates. You can also enter the name of the person who modified the document.

After you have set the criteria for your search and specified the location in which you want to look, you can click OK to search for your file.

You can name and save your search in case you want to use it again later. Click the Save Search As button, and then give it a name. Later, select the name of the search you want to activate from the Saved searches pop-up list. As time goes on, your saved searches may become old and you may want to get rid of them. To remove an old search, select the name of the search and click the Delete button.

Organizing Your Files

The best way to find your work when you need it is to save it to a logical place. There is no substitute for good organization. As you begin a project, create a folder for it on your hard drive. Then save that project's worksheets to that folder. If you have begun the Save procedure and realize you don't have a folder for your current project yet, just make a new folder from the Save dialog box. The Mac makes it easy.

If you create a folder for each project, you can save all project-related files to it— not just Excel files. The same folder can contain a FileMaker Pro database, letters in Word, a PageMaker file, art done in Illustrator, and so on.

There is no right or wrong way to organize your files as long as your organization makes sense to you. The one thing you should not do is save your Excel files to the Microsoft Office 98 folder. That folder should only contain the files needed to run the applications.

Summary

This chapter covered topics related to making good use of workbooks. You learned many different techniques that you can use for working with workbooks. This chapter covered the following topics:

- ✦ Excel uses the workbook concept, where each file contains a workbook of multiple worksheets occupying different tabbed pages. You can store related information in the different worksheets of the workbook, and the worksheets are saved to a single filename.
- ✦ You can open one or more workbooks, and in each workbook, you can move among the worksheets by using the worksheet tabs.

✦ Excel provides a variety of methods for navigating throughout a worksheet and for moving among worksheets.

✦ You can add and delete sheets in a workbook, and you can move sheets from one location to another in a workbook.

✦ You can save files to Excel format or to a variety of other file formats.

✦ Excel has a Find feature that enables you to search for a specific workbook based on certain search parameters that you can enter in a dialog box.

Where to go next

✦ Now that you have become familiar with workbooks, the next step is to learn the best ways to handle data entry and editing in Excel. See Chapter 16 for more information on entering data.

✦ ✦ ✦

CHAPTER 16

Getting Information into Excel

✦ ✦ ✦ ✦

In This Chapter

Entering data

Adding comments to cells

Editing data

Clearing data from cells

Copying and moving cells

Working with cells, rows, and columns

Working with named ranges

Creating and using formulas

Using functions

Validating your data

Using Find and Replace

Correcting your spelling

✦ ✦ ✦ ✦

In this chapter, you learn how to put data into your worksheets, how to insert cells, and how to add and delete selected ranges, columns, and rows. This chapter also describes great features like AutoSum, which sums a row or column of numbers at the click of a button; AutoFill, which can fill a range with successive numbers or dates; and the Function Wizard, which quickly helps you find a needed function. The chapter wraps up by explaining how to use formulas and named ranges in your worksheets.

Entering Data

A spreadsheet is nothing without data, so learning how to enter data is the best place to begin. You can enter either a value or a formula in any cell of an Excel worksheet.

Values are exactly that—constant amounts or sets of characters, dates, or times; for example, 234.78, 5/23/95, 9:35 PM, or John Doe. Formulas are combinations of values, cell references, and operators that Excel uses to calculate a result. For more information about formulas, see "Creating and Working with Formulas" later in this chapter.

When you place the cursor in a given cell and begin typing, your entry appears in the formula bar at the top of the window, as shown in Figure 16-1. In the formula bar, the insertion pointer (the flashing vertical bar) indicates where the characters you type will appear. As you type an entry, a Check (Accept) button and an X (Cancel) button appear enabled in the formula bar. You can click the Check button when you finish typing the entry to accept the entry, or just press Enter or Return. If you decide you don't want to use an entry, you can either click the X button in the formula bar or press the Esc key.

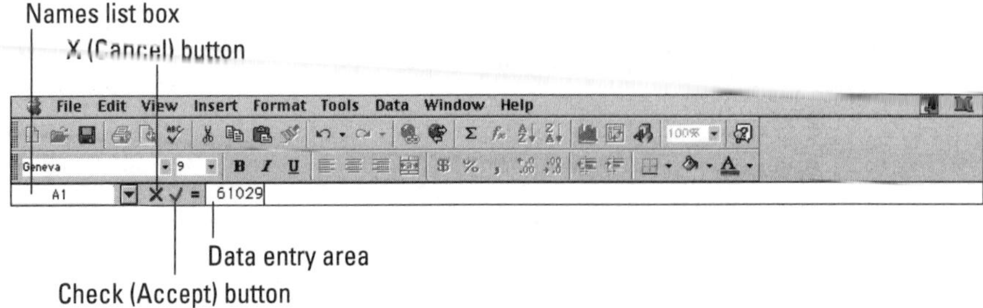

Figure 16-1: Data entered into Excel's formula bar

You may notice a Names list box (to the left of the X button). The Names list box displays the name or cell reference of the currently active cell. Use the pop-up arrow next to the Names list box to view a list of named ranges for the current workbook (after you've named some ranges, of course) . See "Working with Named Ranges" and "Using the Function Wizard" later in this chapter for more information.

You can also enter data directly into the cells of a worksheet by turning on Excel's Edit Directly in Cell option. Follow these steps:

1. Choose Tools ⇨ Preferences. In the Preferences dialog box that appears, select the Edit tab (shown in Figure 16-2).
2. Turn on the Edit directly in cell check box. (This may already be on by default.)
3. Click OK.

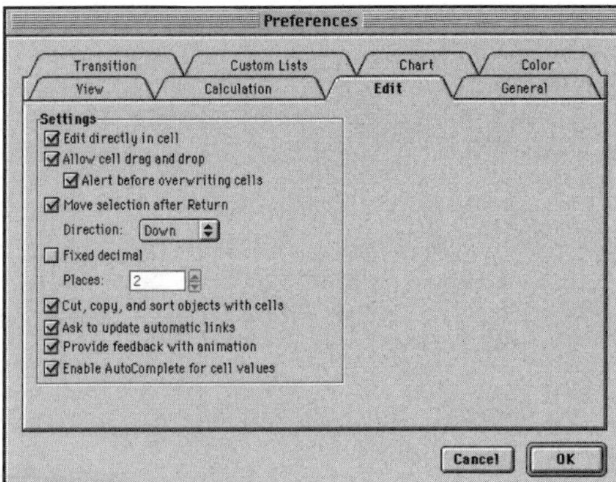

Figure 16-2: The Edit tab of the Preferences dialog box

When the Edit directly in cell option has been turned on, you can double-click the cell in which you want to enter the data—which places the insertion point directly in the cell—and then begin typing. To abort an entry, press the Esc key.

A cell can hold up to 32,000 characters (increased from 255 in previous versions); however, all characters will not be displayed unless you widen the column. (See Chapter 17 for information on formatting.)

Entering numbers

You can enter numbers into your spreadsheet in several ways. When a number is entered, Excel tries to figure out how the number will be used. This prevents you from having to format each cell for each number. The worksheet in Figure 16-3 shows some of the ways you can enter numbers in Excel.

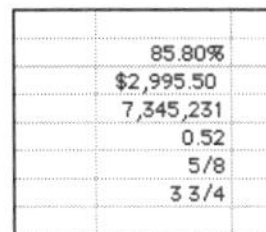

Figure 16-3: Cells with numbers entered in various formats

To enter a number, click or double-click in the target cell to select the cell, type the number, and then press Enter or click the Check button. (You can also press Return, but when using a spreadsheet, it's better to get used to using the Enter key, which is on the number keypad.) You can enter numbers as integers (226), as integer fractions (1/8 or 13/5), as decimal fractions (987.326 or 43.65), or in scientific notation (2.5849E+8). Table 16-1 shows some number entries and how Excel formats them.

What the Heck Is ######?

If you're new to Excel, you're likely to be unpleasantly surprised at some point by the dramatic appearance of the dreaded ###### in one or more of your cells. Don't panic; Excel has not suddenly absorbed all of your data into some mystical black hole. The #s tell you that the cell is too narrow to display your data or your formula's results. After you resize the cell to fit the entire value, your number will appear.

To change the width of the column to see the value, move your cursor to the column's header (A,B,C . . .) and over the line that divides the cell in question from the next cell. When your pointer becomes double-headed, click and drag. If you don't like the idea of changing the column's width, you can try reducing the size of the font used to display the data. Select the cells containing the data, and then select Format ⇨ Cells or Control-click the selection and choose Format Cells from the shortcut menu that appears. When the Format Cells dialog box appears, click the Font tab and choose a smaller font size.

Table 16-1 **How Excel Formats Number Entries**	
Number Entered	***Format Chosen by Excel***
97.9%	Number, percentage format
9705 Becker Ct.	Text, left-aligned
$200.00	Number, currency format
7862	Number, general
144,000	Number, thousands format
-27	Negative number
(27)	Negative number
0 4/5	Fraction
2 4/5	Fraction

As you can see, even in cases where the numbers are mixed with text, Excel detects what needs to be stored as text. This feature makes a big difference when you're entering database information such as street addresses.

One thing to remember is that you need to enter an integer in order to enter a fraction. If, as in the next-to-last example in Table 16-1, you need only the fractional part of a number, you must enter a zero and a space before that fraction; otherwise, Excel interprets the number as a date, and you can't use it in calculations.

Entering text

Your text entries can be any combination of letters, numbers, or other special characters. To enter text, select the desired cell and start typing, just like entering numbers. When you finish with the entry, press Enter or click the Check button in the formula bar. (Remember, a single cell can hold a maximum of 32,000 characters.) By default, Excel aligns text at the left side of the cell. The fastest way to change the alignment used for text, or any cell, is by selecting the cell and clicking the Center or Align Right buttons in the Formatting toolbar. You can also use the other formatting techniques covered in Chapter 17.

Using the AutoComplete feature

Recognizing that you often end up entering some words over and over, Excel 98 introduces AutoComplete. For example, you are keeping a worksheet of family records and repeatedly need to enter the same names: Steven, Stacey, and Amy. The first time you type Steven, Excel silently notes it. The second time it pays more attention. When you begin to type the name the fourth or fifth time, Excel gives you a hand by completing the word for you. If Steven is the only word you've entered several times that begins with the letter *S*, all you need to type is an **S**, and Excel finishes Steven for you. If you've been typing Stacey, too, Excel waits until you get past the common letters—St—before completing the word. Therefore, when you type **Sta**, the entire name Stacey will pop in automatically, and **Ste** will give you Steven.

There's a bit more to this. If you type **St** under the word Stacey, Excel guesses Stacey. If you type **St** under Steven, Excel gives you Steven. This is because Excel looks at what was last typed in that row or column and guesses that pattern. If you've just typed **Amy** a few times, just typing **A** completes Amy, even though the letter *a* is common and even a word by itself. AutoComplete works for all words and not only with names.

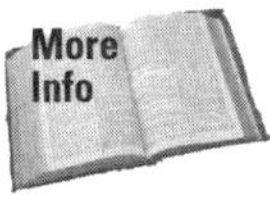

By the way, if the names used with the AutoComplete feature in the previous example were to be used repeatedly in precise order, you could use the Custom Fill option to enter them. For more information on this feature, see "Copying data with Fill and AutoFill" later in this chapter.

Sometimes, you may need to enter a number and have Excel accept it as text rather than as a numeric value. You can do so by preceding the value with a foot mark (single quote) character. For example, if you enter **"2758"** in a cell of a worksheet, Excel stores the entry as a text string made up of the characters 2758 and not as a numeric value.

To Format, or Not to Format?

Excel automatically formats a cell upon data entry—when you provide clues by means of how you enter the data. For example, when you enter a percent sign, Excel formats the cell as a percentage so you don't have to call up Format⇨Cells. But do you always want to use such clues in the data-entry process? Maybe, but maybe not, depending on how much data you have to enter.

For example, typing a dollar sign in front of an amount tells Excel to format the entry as currency. If you're faced with typing 200 entries, however, putting a dollar sign in front of each currency amount is a lot of added work. It's easier to enter all the numbers, letting Excel accept them as a general format, and then go back, select all the entries, and apply a formatting change to the entire range of cells to format it as currency. (Chapter 17 gives details on formatting a range of cells in your worksheet.)

Entering dates and times

You can also store dates and times within an Excel worksheet (see Figure 16-4). This can be useful for recording chronological data, such as employee dates of hire or the time spent on billable tasks.

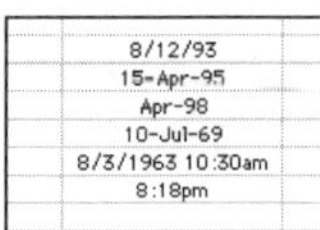

Figure 16-4: Cells with dates and times entered in various formats

Dates and times entered in acceptable date and time formats are recognized by Excel as valid date or time values. Excel converts the times and dates you enter into serial numbers, with dates being the number of days from the beginning of the century until the date value you entered. Excel sees a time entry as a decimal fraction of a 24-hour day. If Excel recognizes the entry as a valid date or time, it properly displays the date or time on the screen. If you look in the formula bar for any cell that contains a date you entered, you'll see that all dates appear in the m/dd/yyyy form, regardless of how you entered them. Time entries all appear in the formula bar in AM/PM format with seconds displayed, regardless of how you enter them.

The following examples show ways that Excel can accept valid date entries. You can use a slash, a hyphen, or a space to separate the different parts of the entry:

7/3/97

3/Jul/97

3/Jul (the current system year is used)

Jul/97

07/03/1997

Time values can be entered in these forms:

7:50

7:50 AM

15:23

15:23:22

3:23 PM

3:23:22 PM

11/13/97 15:23

Oops? Whadaya Mean, Oops?

As you enter data into Excel, keep in mind how useful Undo is. Undo can get you out of just about anything you can do to a worksheet. (However, some actions, like saving files, can't be undone.) There's the Edit⇨Undo menu command, ⌘-Z, and an Undo button on the Standard toolbar. Excel 98 provides multiple undo capability, and you can undo up to the last 16 actions. To undo multiple steps, click the arrow next to the left-pointing arrow on the Standard toolbar, drag down to the action you want to undo, and then click. A status message below the action list reports the number of actions you are undoing.

If you undo something in haste, you can use Edit⇨Redo to correct that, too. You can redo up to 16 actions. The right arrow lists your redo options and functions, the same as the Undo arrow button.

You can enter both the current date and time using shortcut keys. To enter the current date, press Control-; (semicolon). To insert the current time, press Control-Shift-; (semicolon) or ⌘-; (semicolon).

You can display time using a 12- or 24-hour clock, depending on how you enter your times. If you decide to use a 24-hour format, you don't need to use AM or PM. If you decide to use a 12-hour time entry, be sure to place a space before AM or PM (or A or P). If you choose to store dates and times within the same cell, the dates and times should be separated by a space.

Excel's capability to handle dates and times as real values is a significant benefit in some applications, because you can use Excel's computational capabilities to perform math on dates and times. For example, Excel can subtract one date from another to provide the number of days between the two dates.

Displayed values versus underlying values

Excel displays values according to precise rules; *which* rules depends on what formats you've applied to the cells in a worksheet.

Here's an example. In a blank worksheet with no formatting applied, try entering the following data exactly as shown in the cells listed.

In this cell	*Enter*
A1	**1234567890.1234**
A2	**$100.5575**
A3	**2.14159E10**

The results appear as displayed values, as shown in the worksheet in Figure 16-5.

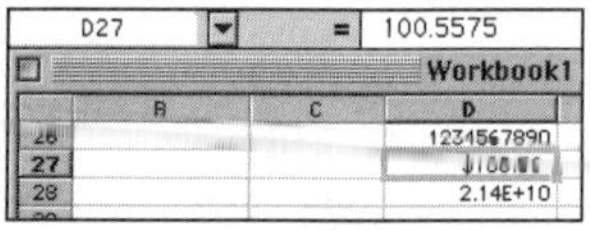

Figure 16-5: A worksheet with displayed values

As you move the cursor between the cells containing the data and note the contents of each cell in the formula bar, you will notice that Excel may display data differently than it is actually stored. For example, notice cell D27 in Figure 16-5.

Excel stores the data as you enter it, but it displays the data according to the formatting rules you establish (or according to the rules of the General format if you applied no formatting). Because the entries in cells D27 and D28 of the example include symbols, Excel formats those cells and displays their contents according to the formats dictated by those symbols. (You can also assign formats using menu commands; Chapter 17 covers this topic in more detail.) In the case of cell D26, because the value is so large, Excel displayed the whole numbers only.

In each case, what appears in the cell is the displayed value. What appears in the formula bar is the underlying value. Excel always uses the underlying value when calculating your formulas, unless you tell it otherwise. Be aware of the possible differences between underlying values and displayed values.

Adding Comments to Cells

To make collaboration on a project easier, Excel enables you to add comments to any cell of a worksheet. Comments, new to Excel 98, are like little yellow sticky notes—except neater. Comments replace Notes that were available in earlier versions of Excel. (Sound Notes, which provided the capability to add sounds to notes in Excel 4.0 for Mac and Excel 7.0 for Windows, are no longer available.)

To attach a comment, Control-click the desire cell and select Insert Comment from the shortcut list that pops up. Alternatively, you can place the cursor in the desired cell and choose Insert ➪ Comment. Either way, a comment for the cell opens. The user's name is automatically placed in the comment with a colon, and the insertion point awaits after the colon, as shown in Figure 16-6. You can enter the desired text directly into the comment.

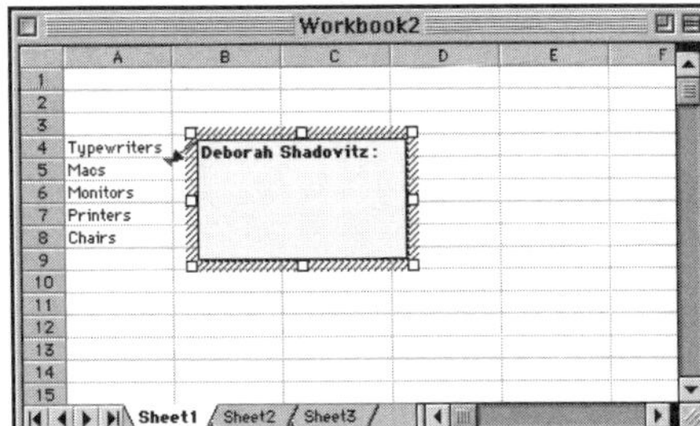

Figure 16-6: A comment added to a cell

A cell with a comment attached includes a tiny red triangle in the upper-right corner—a nondistracting visible indication of the comment. You can read the comment's contents by moving your mouse pointer over the cell containing the comment. When you do this, a window like the one in Figure 16-7 appears with the text of the comment.

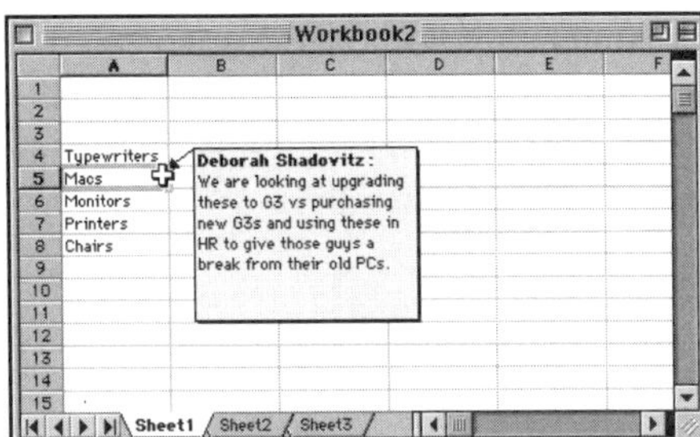

Figure 16-7: The contents of a comment displayed within a worksheet

After a comment exists for a cell, the Insert ➪ Comment command in the menubar becomes Insert ➪ Edit Comment. To edit an existing comment, select the cell containing the comment, and then select the Insert ➪ Edit Comment command. You can also Control-click the cell containing the note and then select Edit Comment.

You can review all the comments in a workbook by choosing View ➪ Comment. All comments are made visible, and the Reviewing toolbar becomes visible. In the Reviewing toolbar are Previous Comment and Next Comment buttons that enable you to move between comments. Moving between comments enables you to perform a sequential review of the comments, ensuring that you don't miss any during collaboration. (Sequential review is new to Excel 98.) Choosing View ➪ Comment again hides the comments.

To remove a comment, Control-click the cell containing the note, and then select Delete Comment.

Editing Data

Excel gives you two ways to make changes to cells. One way is to edit the entry within the formula bar; the other is to perform editing within the cell itself.

If you're a spreadsheet user from way back, you may prefer to type your entry into the formula bar as you have in the past. But if you have a worksheet set up like a database of sorts, with a large amount of data to edit, you may prefer to use the edit-in-cell method. (If you find you cannot edit in the cell, you need to turn on Edit directly in cell. It's an option in the Edit tab under Tools ➪ Preferences.) Instructions for both methods follow. By the way, a formula can contain up to 1,024 characters.

Editing using the formula bar

When you want to use the formula bar to edit a cell that already contains data:

1. Click in the cell containing the data you want to edit.
2. Move the mouse pointer to the area over the formula bar. (As you do so, the pointer takes on the shape of an I-beam as in Word's word processing.)
3. Place the I-beam at the location where you want to start editing, and then click. As with word processing, the flashing insertion pointer in the formula bar indicates where your editing will occur. Simply edit your text as you would any other text.

If the cell you are entering text into does not contain text, you don't need to click in the formula bar at all. Simply select the cell and then begin typing. The text should automatically land in the formula bar.

Using in-cell editing

To edit using in-cell editing, follow these steps:

1. Double-click the desired cell, or move the cursor to the cell and press F2. Either action causes the insertion point to appear directly within the cell.
2. Edit your text as you normally do when word processing. Use the arrow keys to move the insertion point around within the cell.
3. Make your edits and then press Enter.

Clearing Data from Cells

Excel provides several ways to clear—erase—the contents of existing cells. The most obvious way is to select the cell or range of cells and press the Delete key. This does indeed clear the cell of its contents—any values or formulas entered into the cell—but you can clear a cell of formatting and comments as well.

To clear the contents of a cell and remove more than just the data entered, first select the cell or range of cells you want to clear. Then choose Clear from the Edit menu and select the appropriate choice from the submenu. Table 16-2 lists the Clear menu's suboptions.

Table 16-2
Edit⇨Clear Submenu Options

Option	*What It Does*
All	Clears everything from the selected cells, including formatting, the contents of the cell, and any notes attached to the cell. Formatting for the cell returns to the General format.
Formats	Clears formatting only. Formatting for the cell returns to the General format.
Contents	Clears the formulas or values entered in the cell but leaves formatting and notes untouched. (This is the functional equivalent of making a selection and pressing the Delete key.)
Comments	Clears any comments that were attached to the cell but does not change the cell's contents or its formatting.
Hyperlinks	Clears any hyperlinks to other files or Web sites stored in the cell.

Excel's Edit menu contains two commands that remove the contents of cells: the Clear command and the Delete command. If you want to clear the contents in cells, stick with Edit⇨Clear; the Edit⇨Delete command does more than just clear cells. (For specifics, see the sidebar "Edit⇨Clear and Edit⇨Delete: Understanding the Difference" later in this chapter.)

You can also clear the contents of a cell by Control-clicking the cell and selecting Clear Contents from the shortcut menu that appears.

Copying and Moving Cells

As your work with Excel becomes more complex, you'll find yourself regularly needing to move and copy entire portions of worksheets from one area to another. (How often does the boss make a request like, "Oh, could we also see last quarter's sales, too?" after you've spent hours getting your worksheet just right?)

Sometimes you can make the changes you need by inserting or deleting entire blank rows and columns. In many cases, however, you'll want to leave the overall structure of a worksheet alone and copy or move selected areas of the worksheet around.

Excel lets you copy or move data from place to place using either of two methods. You can use the Cut, Copy, and Paste commands (the menus, keyboard commands, or buttons on the Standard toolbar), or you can use drag-and-drop to move and copy data. The two methods work equally well. Generally, keyboard fans prefer using the Cut, Copy, and Paste commands, whereas mouse fans usually lean toward the drag-and drop techniques. If you are moving data a long way, using Cut, Copy, and Paste works better. Over a short distance, dragging is faster and easier on your hands.

You can use any of the techniques detailed in the following paragraphs to copy data across worksheets, as well as within the same worksheet. When you want to copy across worksheets, first select the desired data, as detailed in the following steps in the next section. Then go to the worksheet where you want to place the copy, and continue with the steps outlined in the next section.

Copying and moving data with Cut, Copy, and Paste

To copy cells using the Copy and Paste method, perform these steps:

1. Select the cell or cells that you want to copy, and choose Edit ⇨ Copy (⌘-C), or click the Copy button on the Standard toolbar, or Control-click the selection and choose Copy. The cells to be copied will be marked with a dotted-line border, as shown in Figure 16-8.

10			
11		Widgets	387
12		Gadgets	402
13		Whoosits	565
14		Whatsist	118
15			

Figure 16-8: Cells in a worksheet marked for copying

2. Click the cell or select the cells in which you want to begin your copying. (You can move to cells in a different worksheet, if you want.)

3. Choose Edit ⇨ Paste (⌘-V), click the Paste button (on the Standard toolbar), or Control-click in the destination cell or selection and choose Paste from the shortcut menu. All three methods place the copied information into the chosen cell or cells.

While the highlight is still visible around the source cells, you can copy the cells again if you wish by repeating Steps 2 and 3, or you can press the Esc key to remove the highlight.

Copying information keeps it in the original location while making a copy you can paste any number of times into any number of places. If you want to actually remove the data from its original location, use the Cut command rather than the Copy command. The steps are the same; just substitute Cut (⌘-X) for Copy.

Copying and moving data with drag-and-drop

At times, using the drag-and-drop technique is easier for moving or copying data between cells or ranges. Follow these steps:

1. Select the cell or group of cells you want to move.
2. Move your mouse pointer so it points to the border of the selected cell(s). The pointer turns from the plus sign into an arrow. When it changes, click once and hold down the mouse button.
3. Drag your cells to the new location. As you drag, an outline of the selected area appears, and a yellow box tells you the address of the cell range (top-left and bottom-right cells) your cell(s) will land in. Figure 16-9 demonstrates. (Don't forget that if you move cells over others that contain information, these other cells will be overwritten.)

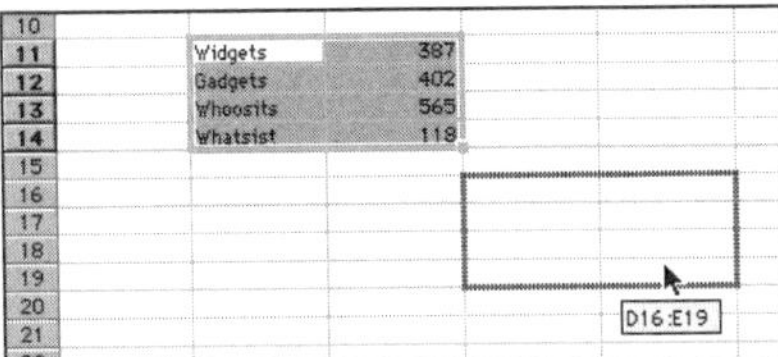

Figure 16-9: The outline of selected cells and their destination when you drag data

4. Release the mouse button.

The same steps can be used to copy a cell or a range of cells. The one difference is that when you want to copy the selection instead of just moving it, you need to press Option as you drag and drop.

Copying data with Fill and AutoFill

Excel offers two features that help you quickly fill cells with data: Fill and AutoFill. The Fill feature fills the range of cells you select with the data in the original cell. The AutoFill feature recognizes patterns or items that traditionally are entered in a pattern (such as months and days), and it fills in a range of cells intelligently, incrementing each successive cell. For example, if you enter January in a cell and then use AutoFill to fill the next 11 cells to the right, Excel fills in the names of the successive months. Actually, it would fill in any number of cells following the month pattern. You can Fill or AutoFill toward the left, right, up, or down. You can Fill or AutoFill using just the mouse, or you can use menu commands.

Excel even tells you what text will land in any cell as you drag over it during a Fill or AutoFill.

You can copy any existing data from a cell into adjacent cells using the Fill feature. Perform the following steps:

1. Move the cursor into the cell you want to copy to the adjacent cells.
2. Point the mouse pointer to the Fill handle—the tiny rectangle at the lower-right corner of the selected cell. As you do, your cursor becomes a thin black plus sign. With this cursor active, drag in any direction over all cells that are to receive this data. As you drag, a yellow information box shows you the value being copied. Release the mouse button to copy the data into the cells.

If you prefer using menu commands, perform the following steps to complete Fill:

1. Move the cursor into the cell you want to copy to the adjacent cells.
2. Place the mouse pointer over the selected cell. Click in the center of that cell and drag over all the cells that should get a copy of the original cell.
3. Choose Edit ➪ Fill, and then select Up, Down, Left, or Right from the submenu. (Choose the direction in which you've selected your cells. When you make the submenu selection, the data is copied into the adjacent cells, as shown in Figure 16-10.)

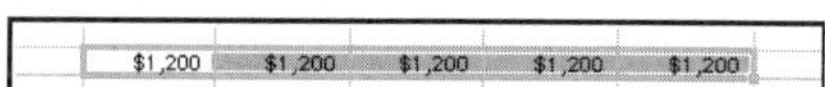

Figure 16-10: The results of using the Edit ➪ Fill command

It's possible to copy data across worksheets with the Fill command, as well. First select both the worksheet you want to copy from and the worksheet you want to copy to by holding down the Shift key while clicking both worksheet tabs. Next select the cells to be copied, choose Edit ➪ Fill, and choose Across Worksheets from the submenu. In the dialog box that appears, choose what you want to copy (All, Contents, or Formats) and click OK.

The AutoFill feature saves you time and keystrokes by providing intelligent copying. By default, AutoFill fills in days of the week and months of the year. You can also add your own custom lists to AutoFill so it can handle other requirements that you have on a regular basis.

To use AutoFill to fill in dates, type the desired day of the week or month of the year into a cell. Next drag the Fill handle (the tiny rectangle at the lower-right corner of the selected cell) to highlight the cells in which you want AutoFill to add the data. When you release the mouse button, the successive days of the week or months of the year appear. Figure 16-11 shows the results of AutoFill when January is entered into a cell and the Fill Handle is dragged across the next five cells.

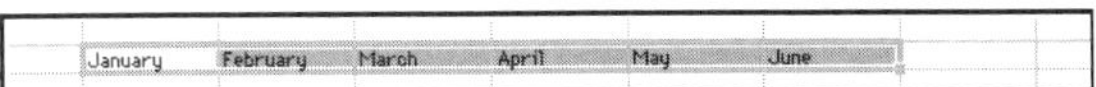

Figure 16-11: The results of using AutoFill

If you AutoFill into more cells than the length of the list used by AutoFill, Excel repeats the AutoFill pattern until all selected cells are filled. To prevent the list from repeating, you can watch the yellow information box that reports the fill data as you drag to AutoFill. (Or you can count the number of entries and the number of cells you are dragging over.)

If you regularly fill in a list of your own, you can add it to the lists that AutoFill generates. Choose Tools⇨Preferences. In the dialog box that appears, click the Custom Lists tab (shown in Figure 16-12). Click the words NEW LIST at the left side of the dialog box (even though they're already selected). An insertion point appears in the List entries box at the right. Type your own list in the List entries box, separating each entry with a comma and a space. (In Figure 16-12, a custom list of classrooms in a high school has been entered in the List entries box.) When you finish, click Add to add the list, and click OK. From then on, you can type any entry in your list into a cell and use AutoFill to fill in the successive entries based on your own list. This list can also be edited later. (We'll get to that shortly.)

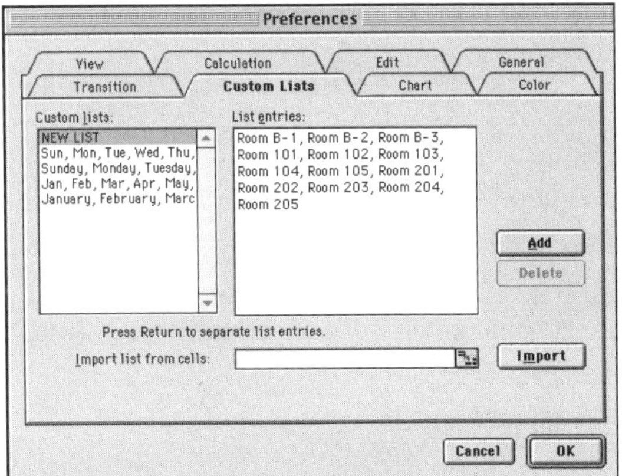

Figure 16-12: Adding a custom list via the Custom Lists tab of the Preferences dialog box

Perhaps you've already gone through the trouble of entering your text into your spreadsheet. You can turn this cell data into a custom AutoFill list without having to retype the data. To turn your cell data into a custom AutoFill list, follow these steps:

1. Select the cells that contain the data you want to turn into an AutoFill list.
2. Choose Tools⇨Preferences, and then select the Custom Lists tab.

   The range of cells you have selected should be reported in the field at the bottom of the tab (Import list from cells). (A cell range is reported as the first cell address, followed by a colon, and then the last cell address.)
3. Click Import.

   The first words in your list appear as the name of the list in the Custom Lists area. On the right you see the elements of your list.
4. Click OK.

Making changes to the custom lists used by AutoFill is a simple matter. If you want to edit one of your custom lists, follow these steps:

1. Choose Tools⇨Preferences, and then select the Custom Lists tab.
2. Click the name of your list in the Custom Lists area of the Custom Lists tab. The elements of your list appear in the List entries side of the tab.
3. Click any list entries and make the necessary changes to the list.
4. Click OK.

If you want to delete a custom list that you've created, follow these steps:

1. Choose the name of the custom list from the Custom Lists box of the Custom Lists tab.
2. Click the Delete button to delete the list.

When making your list, remember:

✦ Error values and formulas are ignored.

✦ Each list entry can contain up to 80 characters.

✦ Lists cannot start with a number. (If you want an increasing or decreasing series of numbers, use the Series command, described in the following section.)

✦ A custom list can contain a maximum of 2,000 characters.

Building series

Although AutoFill does wonders with simple and straightforward lists, sometimes you may need more flexibility in generating a list of values that change across some kind of series. For those occasions, you can use the Edit menu's Fill Series command.

Excel can work with four types of series:

✦ **Linear** simply increases a number by its step value, such as 1, 2, 3, 4, 5, 6, and so on, where the start value is 1 and the step value is 1; or 5, 10, 15, 20, 25, and so on, where the start value is 5 and the step value is 5.

✦ **Growth** multiplies the previous number by a specific value, such as 5, 10, 20, 40, 80, and so on, where the start value is 5 and the step value is 2.

✦ **Date-based**, such as 1995, 1996, 1997, 1998, and so on.

✦ **AutoFill** is based on the lists entered in the Custom List tab of the Preferences dialog box.

Create a series of values in a range of cells by following these steps:

1. Enter a value in a cell. (The value you enter serves as the starting or ending value in the series.)
2. Starting with the cell containing your value, select the cells into which you want to extend the series.
3. Choose Edit ⇨ Fill ⇨ Series, or Control-click and select Series from the bottom of the shortcut menu that pops up. The Series dialog box appears, as shown in Figure 16-13.

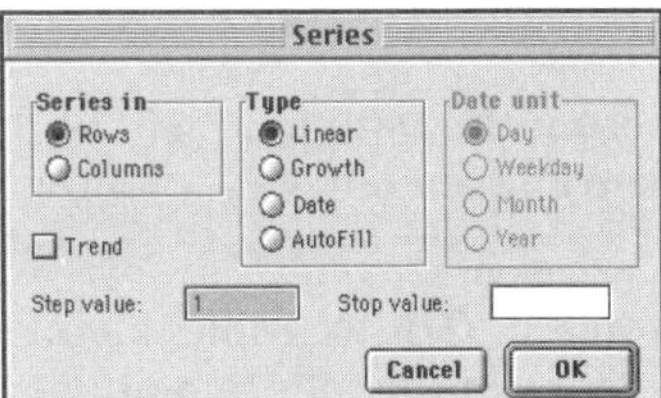

Figure 16-13: The Series dialog box

4. In the Series in field of the dialog box, make sure the Rows or Columns selection matches the type of range you want to fill.
5. If you want the selected values to be replaced by values for a linear or exponential best fit, turn on the Trend check box. (If you do this, your options in Step 6 are limited to Linear and Growth.)
6. In the Type field of the dialog box, choose the appropriate Type option:

   ✦ **Linear** adds the step value to the number that preceded the current cell in the series. When you select Trend, the trend values become a linear trend.

   ✦ **Growth** multiplies the step value by the number that preceded the current cell in the series.

✦ **Date** is used with date values; it lets you set the Date Unit options to Day, Week, Month, or Year choices.

✦ **AutoFill** creates a series automatically, based on entries in the Custom List tab of the Options dialog box (choose Tools ➪ Preferences to get there).

If you choose AutoFill, Excel fills the selected range based on the entries in the Custom List tab of the Options dialog box.

If you choose Linear or Growth, continue with the following steps up to Step 9 to finish generating your series. (If you choose Date, go to Step 10.)

7. Enter a step value. The step value is the number by which the entries change from cell to cell. For example, a step value of 2 causes numbers to increment by two, such as 2, 4, 6, 8, and so on.
8. If you don't want the entries to exceed a certain number, you can enter a stop value. (If you leave this blank, Excel continues until it fills the selected range.)
9. Click OK.

   Excel stops either at the stop value or when it reaches the end of the selected cells. If the step value is negative and you enter a stop value, the stop value needs to be less than your starting value. Dates and times can be entered in any date or time format Excel understands.

   If you chose to enter a series of dates by choosing Date in Step 6, continue with these steps.
10. Choose Day, Weekday, Month, or Year from the Date unit field of the Series dialog box to apply the step value to the chosen entry type in the Date unit area.
11. Enter the step value to specify an increment. (For example, if you chose Month as the date unit, the entries increase in the month amount by the step value.) Again, a stop value may be entered if you think you have chosen too many cells.
12. Choose OK.

Using Paste Special

Sometimes, after copying cells, you may want to invoke special options when you paste the cells. You can do this using the Paste Special command.

To see these special options, choose any cell in a worksheet, copy it (⌘-C), move the cursor to another cell, and choose Edit ➪ Paste Special. You see the Paste Special dialog box shown in Figure 16-14.

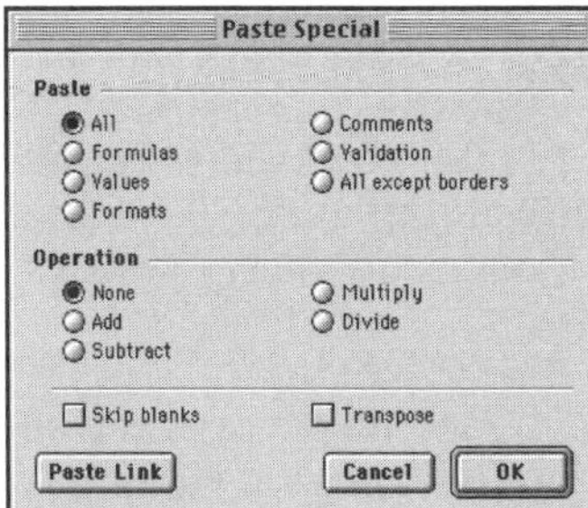

Figure 16-14: The Paste Special dialog box

You can choose any one of the options in the Paste portion of the Paste Special dialog box to select the information to be pasted. For example, if you want to copy only a cell's format, you would choose the Formats option, which copies only the cell's format so you don't have to format the new cell.

You can also combine the contents of the copy and paste areas. First select Formulas or Values in the Paste portion of the Paste Special dialog box. Next, under the Operation portion of the dialog box, select the operation you want. This combines the copy and paste areas by performing the chosen operation. For example, if cell A:6 contains the formula =SUM(A1:A5), and you want to add this formula to the contents of cell D:6, first select cell A:6 and then choose the Copy command. Next choose Edit ⇨ Paste Special, choose Formulas in the Paste portion of the Paste Special dialog box, and choose Add under the Operation portion of the same dialog box. The result is that the formula is copied in the new cell with the new cell references. (Formulas are discussed in "Creating and Using Formulas" later in this chapter.)

The Paste Special dialog box also enables you to transpose copied rows and columns by selecting the Transpose option. This option is used to transfer information entered in rows to columns, and vice versa.

The Skip blanks option prevents the copying of blank cells from the copy area to the paste area; a blank cell cannot delete existing cell data in the paste area.

The Paste Link button is also a useful option for pasting and establishing a link with the source of the data pasted into the selected cells. (The source has to be a single cell or a range.) In cases where the source is more than one cell, an *array*—a collection of cells that takes on a single value in relation to a formula—is posted. When the paste area is a single cell, the cell becomes the upper-left corner of the paste area, with the rest of the range filled in accordingly.

Working with Cells, Rows, and Columns

Another important aspect of manipulating existing data in worksheets is inserting and deleting cells and adding or deleting entire rows and columns. The first three options that Excel provides on the Insert menu let you insert cells, rows, or columns into an existing worksheet.

Before you perform major insertions, be warned that inserting cells in the midst of existing data causes cells in the area of the insertion to be pushed either down or to the right. If your worksheet contains formulas that rely on the location of cells, and you move those cells by inserting new cells, you will create errors in your worksheet's calculations.

Inserting cells, rows, and columns

To insert cells, rows, or columns, follow these steps:

1. Select the cell or range of cells in which the new cells must be inserted, or select any cells in the rows or columns in which the new rows or columns are to be inserted.

   With rows and columns, note that a new row or column is inserted for each row or column cell you select. If you drag across three columns and then choose to insert columns, you insert three new columns.

2. Choose Insert ⇨ Cells, or Control-click the selection and choose Insert from the shortcut menu, to reveal the Insert dialog box (see Figure 16-15).

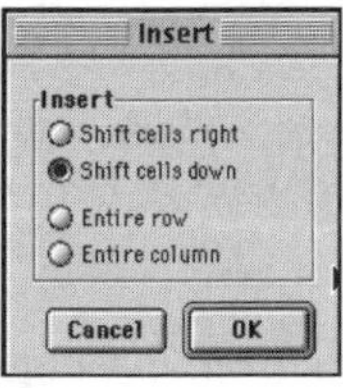

Figure 16-15: The Insert dialog box

3. If you're inserting cells, choose either Shift cells right or Shift cells down to move existing cells in the direction you want. If you want to insert entire rows or columns, choose Entire row or Entire column.

4. Click OK.

To insert only rows or columns, just select the number of rows or columns to insert at the point of insertion. For example, say you want to insert two columns ahead of column D. Click and drag across the headers for columns D and E, open the Insert menu, and then choose either Rows or Columns.

Deleting cells, rows, and columns

To delete cells, rows, or columns, follow these steps:

1. Select the cell or range of cells in which the cells must be deleted, or select any cells in the rows or columns in which the rows or columns are to be deleted.

   Note that a row or column will be deleted for each row or column cell you select. If you drag across three columns and then choose to delete columns, you will delete three columns.

2. Choose Edit ➪ Delete, or Control-click the selection and choose Delete from the shortcut menu to reveal the Delete dialog box, shown in Figure 16-16. (If you select an entire row or column, you won't see this dialog box; Excel assumes you want to delete the entire row or the entire column, and it does so. If the deletion of a row or column was not what you had in mind, choose Edit ➪ Undo.)

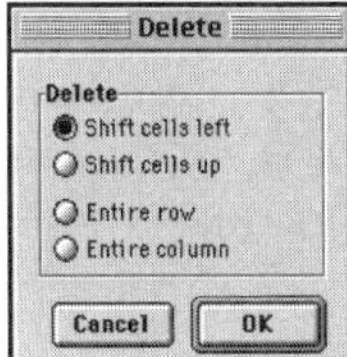

Figure 16-16: The Delete dialog box

3. If you're deleting cells, choose either Shift cells left or Shift cells up to move existing cells to fill in the space left by the deletion. If you want to delete entire rows or columns, choose Entire row or Entire column.

4. Click OK.

If you want to delete one entire row or column, the fastest way is to Control-click the row header or column header and select Delete from the shortcut menu. To delete more than one entire row or column quickly, select the rows or columns by dragging across the row or column headers (rather than selecting cells in the rows or columns). Then choose Edit ➪ Delete (⌘-K). Excel annihilates your selections, no questions asked.

Edit➪Clear and Edit➪Delete: Understanding the Difference

In Excel there's a fundamental difference between the way Edit➪Clear and Edit➪Delete work. The two commands may appear to do the same thing when applied to a range of blank cells with no adjacent data nearby, but in reality they behave very differently.

Edit➪Clear clears the selected cells of the information in them but does not move cells out of the worksheet. Edit➪Delete, on the other hand, removes the cells completely; other cells must take the place of the removed cells, even if the new cells are blank.

Compare the results of Edit➪Delete to pulling out toy blocks from a wall made of those blocks; other blocks must be moved into the empty spaces, or the wall becomes unstable. Likewise, understanding how Edit➪Delete works ensures the stability of the remaining areas of your worksheet.

Working with Named Ranges

Names are always friendlier to use and easier to remember than numbers. Therefore, Excel lets you refer to a cell or group of cells by a name rather than a cell reference, and use these names within your formulas. For example, you could name row 1 of a worksheet Income, and call row 3 Expenses. A formula in row 5 that computes net profits could then read =Income-Expenses rather than =B1-B3. (Formulas are discussed in "Creating and Using Formulas" later in this chapter.)

To assign a name to a cell or group of cells, follow these steps:

1. Select the range of cells you want to name. (You can select an entire row or an entire column by clicking the row or column header.)
2. Choose Insert➪Name➪Define, or press ⌘-L. The Define Name dialog box appears, as shown in Figure 16-17.

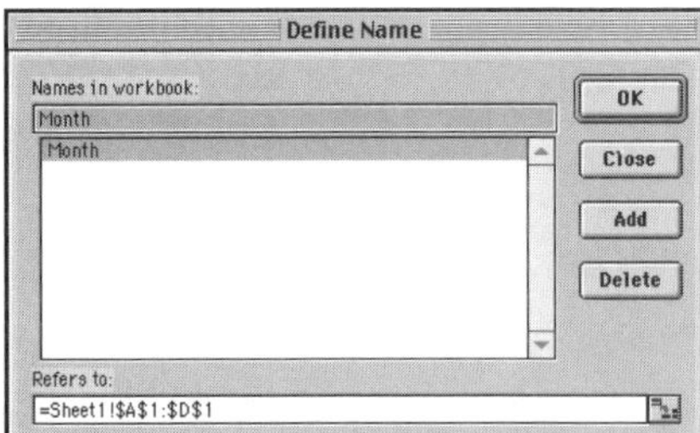

Figure 16-17: The Define Name dialog box

3. In the text box at the top of the dialog box, either type a name for the range or accept any default. (Don't use spaces in a range name; see the Note at the end of this section.)

   When Excel sees a heading at the top of a row or at the left of a column of cells you've selected, it uses the text of that heading as a default range name.

4. Click Add to add the new name to the list, and then click Close. (Or just click Close or press Return or Enter.)

Figure 16-18 shows an example of named ranges in a worksheet. In this worksheet, columns B, C, D, and E have been assigned the names of the months, at the top of the respective columns, as named ranges. As shown in the formula bar, column F uses formulas like =January+February+March+April to calculate the totals.

	A	B	C	D	E	F
1		*January*	*February*	*March*	*April*	*Total*
2	*Walnut Creek*	$123,600.00	$137,000.00	$89,900.00	$201,300.00	$551,800.00
3	*River Hills*	$248,700.00	$256,750.00	$302,500.00	$197,000.00	$1,004,950.00
4	*Spring Gardens*	$97,000.00	$102,500.00	$121,500.00	$142,500.00	$463,500.00
5	*Lake Newport*	$346,300.00	$372,300.00	$502,900.00	$456,800.00	$1,678,300.00
6						$0.00
7	Total Sales	$815,600.00	$868,550.00	$1,016,800.00	$997,600.00	$3,698,550.00
8						

Figure 16-18: An example of named ranges in a worksheet

After you've performed the preceding steps, you can refer to the range in your formulas by typing its name rather than using its cells' addresses.

The names you use for ranges can be up to 255 characters in length, and they can include letters, numbers, periods, or underscores but not spaces.

Creating and Using Formulas

In addition to entering values, you will use formulas throughout your worksheets. Excel uses the formulas you enter to perform calculations based on the values in other cells of your worksheets. Formulas let you perform common math operations (addition, subtraction, multiplication, and division) using the values in the worksheet cells.

For example, say you want to add the values in cells B1 and B2 and display the sum in cell B5. You can do so by placing the cursor in cell B5 and entering the simple formula =B1+B2.

With Excel, you build a formula by indicating which values should be used and which calculations should apply to these values. Remember that formulas always begin with an equal symbol. Figure 16-19 shows examples of various formulas within a typical worksheet.

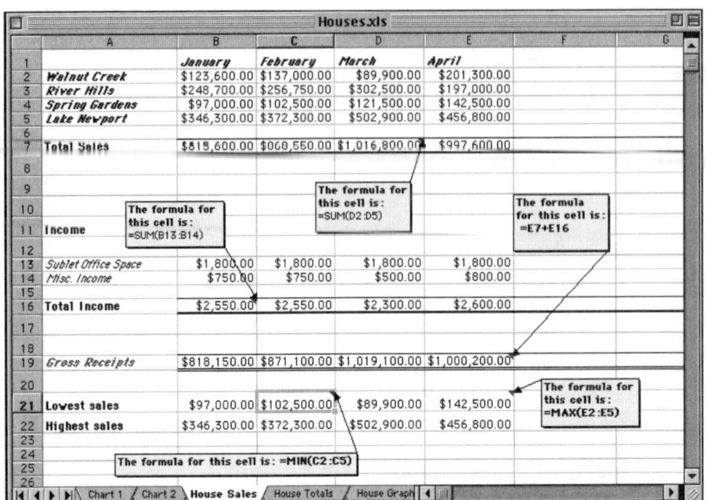

Figure 16-19: Examples of formulas within a worksheet

In the formula bar or with Edit directly in cell

If you place the cursor in any cell and type an equal symbol, the symbol and a flashing cursor appear in the formula bar. As you enter the formula, it appears within the formula bar. When you press Enter, Excel performs the calculation based on the formula and then displays, in the cell, the results of the calculation. If you've turned on Edit directly in cell as described earlier in the chapter, you can double-click the cell and type the formula directly into the cell.

Creating formulas by pointing

One handy way to enter the cell references that make up a major part of formulas is to click the cells that make up the formula. Typing the entire formula manually invites mistakes you can avoid by entering the cell references this way:

1. Place the cursor in the cell in which you want to enter the formula.
2. Click the equal sign (=) that appears in the formula bar. This starts the formula. Alternatively, you can type an equal sign (=).
3. Point to the cell you want as the first cell reference and click. (Alternatively, you can move the cursor there with the arrow keys.)
4. Type an operator (such as a plus or minus symbol) or other character to continue the desired formula.

5. Point to the next cell you want to use as a cell reference and click (or move the cursor there with the arrow keys).
6. Repeat Steps 4 and 5 as needed to complete the formula.

While using the pointing technique to create formulas, you can enter cell ranges as references. Just click and drag from the starting cell in the range to the ending cell (or hold down the Shift key as you move the cursor from the starting cell to the ending cell).

Allowed elements

Formulas are used to calculate a value based on a combination of other values. These other values can be numbers, cell references, operators (+, -, *, /), or other formulas. Formulas can also include names of other areas in the worksheet, as well as cell references in other worksheets. Individual cells are referred to by their coordinates (such as B5), and ranges of cells are referred to by the starting cell reference, followed by a colon, followed by the ending cell reference (such as D10:D18). Cells in other worksheets are referred to by the name of the worksheet, followed by an exclamation point, followed by the cell reference (such as Sheet2!E5).

You use math operators within your formulas to produce numeric results. Table 16-3 lists the operators.

References: Relative Versus Absolute

In Excel, you can have absolute or relative cell references. An *absolute* cell reference does not change when the cell containing the formula is copied to another location. A *relative* cell reference changes when the cell containing the formula is copied to another location.

You determine whether a cell reference will be relative or absolute by placing a dollar sign in front of the row or column reference. The presence of a dollar sign tells Excel not to muck around with your cell reference, no matter what. For example, perhaps cell B5 of a worksheet contains the formula =B3+B4. If you copy that cell's contents to cell D5, Excel adjusts the references, and the formula in cell D5 reads =D3+D4.

In most cases you want Excel to adjust references when you copy formulas elsewhere, but in some cases you don't. You can make cell references absolute by adding the dollar sign in front of the letter and number that make up the cell address. With the preceding example of a formula in cell B5, if the formula were entered as =$B$3+$B$4, the formula could be copied anywhere in the worksheet—and it would still refer back to cells B3 and B4.

Table 16-3
Arithmetic Operators

Operator	*Function*
+	Addition
-	Subtraction
*	Multiplication
/	Division
^	Exponentiation (for example, 3^2 is 3-squared, or 9)
%	Percentage

In addition to the math operators, Excel accepts an ampersand (&) as a text operator for strings of text. The ampersand is used to combine text strings—a process known as *concatenation*. For example, if cell B12 contains *John* followed by a space, and cell B13 contains *Smith,* the formula B12 & B13 would yield *John Smith.*

Comparison operators are used to compare values and provide a logical value (true or false) based on the comparison. Table 16-4 describes the comparison operators.

Table 16-4
Comparison Operators

Operator	*Function*
<	less than
>	greater than
=	equal to
<>	not equal to
<=	less than or equal to
>=	greater than or equal to

In a cell, the simple comparison = 6 < 7 would result in a value of true because 6 is less than 7. The result of = 6 < Number depends on the value of Number.

Typically, you use comparison operators with cell references to determine whether a desired result is true or false. For example, consider the worksheet shown in

Figure 16-20. In this example the formulas in cells C2 through C5 are based on a comparison. Cell C2 contains the formula =B2>48000. Cells C3, C4, and C5 contain similar formulas. The comparison translates to this: If the value in B2 is greater than 48,000, then display a value of true in C2; otherwise, display a value of false in C2.

54,050	TRUE
47,999.95	FALSE
48,000.01	TRUE
37	FALSE

Figure 16-20: Use of comparison operators in formulas of a worksheet

Excel has the following precise order of precedence in building formulas:

1. - (unary minus or negation)
2. % (percent)
3. ^ (exponentiation)
4. * or / (multiplication or division)
5. + or - (addition or subtraction)
6. & (text operator)
7. < > = (comparison operators)

Depending on how you structure your formulas, you may want to alter the preceding order of precedence. For example, if you want to add the contents of cells B2 and B3 and divide the resulting total by five, you cannot use the simple formula =B2 + B3 / 5 because Excel performs division before addition in its order of precedence. If you used this formula, the value in B3 would be divided by five, and that value would be added to the value of B2, producing an erroneous result. To change the order of precedence, insert parentheses around calculations that are to be performed first. Calculations surrounded by parentheses are always performed first, no matter where they fall in the order of precedence. In this example, the formula =(B2 + B3) / 5 yields the desired result. Excel would calculate the expression within the parentheses first and then divide that figure by the constant (in this example, 5).

Displaying and editing formulas

By default, Excel shows the results of the formulas you enter in cells and not the actual formulas. (Of course, you can examine any formula by clicking the cell that contains it and looking in the formula bar.) You can also see all the formulas in your worksheet. Choose Tools ⇨ Preferences, and then click the View tab in the Preferences dialog box. Under Window Options, turn on the Formulas check box and click OK. Your worksheet then shows all your formulas in the cells, rather than showing the results of the formula. By the way, Excel automatically widens the columns to provide room to view the formulas.

You can edit formulas just as you'd edit any other contents of a cell. Select the desired cell, click in the formula bar, and do your editing there; or double-click the cell and edit the formula within the cell itself.

Changing the recalculation options

By default, Excel recalculates all dependent formulas in your worksheet each time you make a change to a cell. In a large worksheet, recalculation can adversely affect performance, because Excel has to do a lot of calculating every time you change an entry in a cell. You may prefer to turn off Excel's automatic recalculation and let the worksheet recalculate only when you tell it to.

You can change the recalculation options used by Excel through the Calculation tab of the (yes, you guessed it) Tools ➪ Preferences command. Choose Tools ➪ Preferences, and then click the Calculation tab in the Preferences dialog box that appears. Under Calculation, choose Manual. Excel now recalculates only when you tell it to by pressing the Calc Now key (F9).

Don't forget you have turned off automatic recalculation, or things may get confusing. Things that appear to be errors may really be changes made when automatic recalculation was turned off and left off. Some operations (including opening and printing a worksheet) will force a recalculation, even if automatic recalculation has been turned off.

What, Me Make a Mistake?

One of the most frustrating aspects of building complex worksheets is the possibility of errors in your formulas. Watching out for common causes of formula errors can help.

Watch out for these causes in particular:

- Attempts to divide by zero
- References to blank cells
- Leaving out commas between arguments
- Deleting cells being used by formulas elsewhere in the worksheet

The codes Excel displays in the cell when an error occurs give you a clue to what's wrong. The code #DIV/0! says your formula is trying to divide by zero. The code #N/A! means that data needed to perform the calculation is not available, and #NAME? means that Excel thinks you're referring to a name that doesn't exist. The code #NUM says Excel has a problem with a numeric argument you've supplied, #REF says that a cell reference is incorrect, and #VALUE! indicates that a value supplied isn't the type of value the formula's argument expected.

Using Functions

Typing each cell reference is fine when you're adding a short column of numbers, but doing this with larger columns can be time-consuming. Fortunately, Excel offers functions to be used in your formulas.

You can think of functions as ready-to-run tools that take a group of values and perform some specialized sort of calculation on those values. For example, the commonly used SUM function adds a range of values. Instead of having to enter a formula like =B2+B3+B4+B5+B6+B7+B8, you could enter the much simpler formula of =SUM(B2:B8).

Hot Stuff

Another benefit of using a function such as SUM and naming a range becomes evident when you add a new column between those involved in the formula. If you hand-typed each cell (=B2+B3+B4+B5+B6+B7+B8), the new cell won't be included. However, if you used the cell range (B2.B8), the new column becomes included in the range.

Besides making for less typing, functions can perform specialized calculations that would take some digging on your part if you needed to duplicate the calculations manually. For example, you can use the PMT function to calculate the monthly principal and interest on a mortgage. (Few of us carry the logic for that sort of calculation around in our heads.) Excel's functions can make use of range references (such as A2:A10), named ranges (such as January Sales), or actual numeric values. Figure 16-21 shows examples of the use of functions in a worksheet.

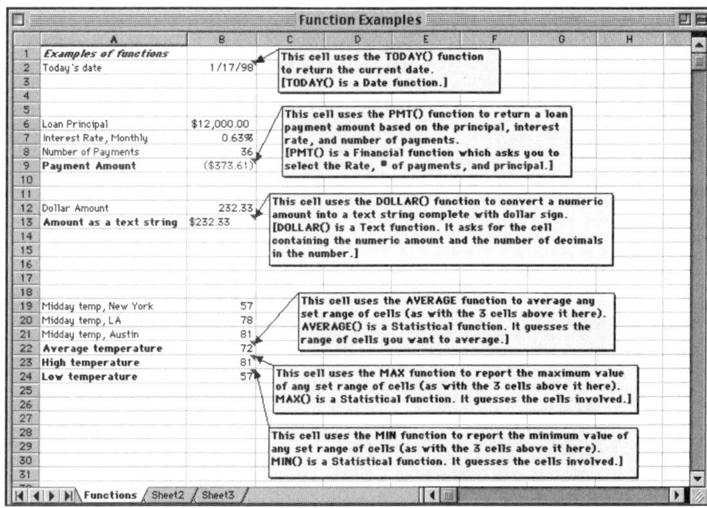

Figure 16-21: Examples of functions used in a worksheet

Every function consists of two parts:

✦ **The function name**—such as SUM, PMT, or AVERAGE—indicates what the function does.

✦ **The argument**—such as B2:B12—tells Excel what cell addresses to apply to the function. (Note that in this example the argument is a range of cells, but arguments may be references to single cells, to a group of single cells, or to actual values.)

You can enter functions just as you enter values—by typing them directly into the formula bar or into the cell. You can also use the AutoSum tool and Paste Function (both discussed shortly) to find help with the entry of your functions.

Excel has many different functions for tasks that range from calculating the square root of a number to finding the future value of an investment. You should know about some statistical functions commonly used in spreadsheet work: the AVERAGE, MAXIMUM, MINIMUM, and SUM functions.

AVERAGE, MAXIMUM, MINIMUM, and SUM

The AVERAGE function calculates the average of a series of values. This function may be expressed as:

```
=AVERAGE(1st value, 2nd value, 3rd value...last value)
```

As an example, the expression =AVERAGE(6,12,15,18) yields 12.75. Similarly, the expression =AVERAGE(B10:B15) averages the values from cells B10 through B15.

The MAXIMUM and MINIMUM functions provide the maximum and minimum values, respectively, of all values in the specified range or list of numbers. These functions may be expressed as

```
=MAX(1st value, 2nd value, 3rd value...last value)
=MIN(1st value, 2nd value, 3rd value...last value)
```

For example, consider the worksheet shown earlier in Figure 16-19. The formula in cell B21 is =MIN(B3:B5). The value that results from this formula is the smallest value in the range of cells from B2 through B5. The formula in cell B21, which is =MAX(B2:B5), produces precisely the opposite effect—the largest value of those found in the specified range of cells is displayed.

The SUM function is used to provide a sum of a list of values, commonly indicated by referencing a range of cells. For example, the SUM function =SUM(5,10,12) would provide a value of 27. The formula =SUM(B5:B60) would provide the sum of all numeric values contained in the range of cells from B5 to B60. The SUM function is an easy way to add a column of numbers; you can most easily use it when using AutoSum, too.

Using AutoSum

Because the SUM function is the most commonly used function in Excel, a toolbar button is dedicated to the SUM function's use—the AutoSum tool. Using AutoSum is simple:

1. Place the cursor in the cell below or to the right of the column or row you want to sum.
2. Click the AutoSum button on the Standard toolbar (it contains the Greek letter S).

When you do this, Excel makes its best guess about what you would like summed, based on the current cell's location relative to the row or column. (In case Excel guesses wrong, you can always edit the formula to your liking.) When you click the AutoSum button, Excel outlines the area it thinks you want summed, and it places the appropriate formula using the SUM function in the current cell, as shown in Figure 16-22. If you don't like the range that Excel selected, you can click and drag to a different range, and Excel changes the formula accordingly. When you're happy with the formula, press Enter to accept it.

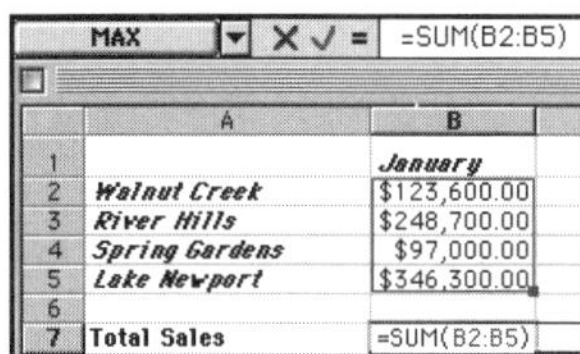

Figure 16-22: Using the AutoSum button

Using the Function Wizard

One of Excel's most useful features is Paste Function. With the help of Paste Function, you can do serious work in Excel without keeping a reference dictionary of functions handy or constantly looking in the help screens to see how particular functions should be used.

Paste Function steps you through the process of inserting a function into the formula you're building. To use Paste Function, follow these steps:

1. Click in the cell in which you want to insert the function. (If you want to insert the function into an existing formula, you can click in the formula bar at the point where the function should go to place the pointer there.)
2. Click the Paste Function button (which contains the letters *fx*) on the Standard toolbar, or choose Insert ➪ Function. The Paste Function dialog box appears, as shown in Figure 16-23.

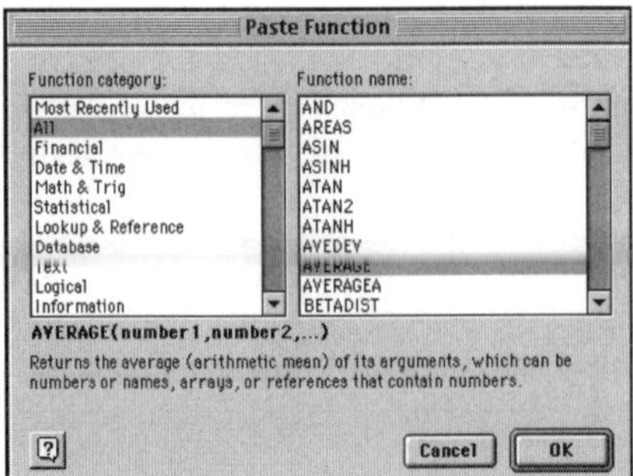

Figure 16-23: Paste Function dialog box

3. In the Function category list box at the left, click a category of functions to choose it. All the functions in the selected category appear in the Function name list box at the right. (You can leave the category set to All, but viewing all the functions can make it difficult to find your function from among Excel's hundreds of functions.)

4. From the Function name list, click the function you want to insert into your formula. A description of the function appears below the list to aid you in your decision. Click OK to place the selected function. If you are certain of the function you want and don't need to see the description, you can just double-click the desired function.

5. The next dialog box appears below the function bar, asking for values appropriate to that function. Enter the necessary values or cell ranges for the arguments needed by the function in the dialog box. You can enter the values by

   - ✦ Typing your values
   - ✦ Clicking the cells you need to refer to
   - ✦ Dragging across the cells in the range you need to refer to
   - ✦ Clicking the row or column header to select an entire row or column
   - ✦ Dragging across several row or column headers
   - ✦ Typing the names of the ranges, if you have named ranges

6. Finally, click OK in the dialog box to add the function to your formula. Click Cancel or the X in the function bar if you don't want to add that function to your formula.

Instead of Step 2, you can also take a longer route. Click the equal sign to begin your formula, and then click the down arrow on the formula bar. (Because you've begun a formula, the arrow's list contains formulas rather than the named ranges it normally lists.) The last functions you've used appear in this function list. If the function you desire is in view on the list that pops up, drag to it to select it. If not, select More functions from the bottom of the list to bring up the Paste Function dialog box (refer to Figure 16-23).

The Office Assistant can be of great help if you aren't familiar with the formulas, or if you don't happen to know which formula you need. For function help, while you are in the Paste Function dialog box, click the Help icon (question mark) or press the Help key.

The Office Assistant appears and asks, "What kind of help would you like?" and offers two choices: "Help with this feature" or "Help with something else." Accept help with this function. The Assistant next either offers help with the currently selected function or invites you to type a brief description of what you want to do. After you enter a description, the suggested function becomes selected in the Paste Function dialog box, and again you have the opportunity to get help with the currently selected function. Choosing Help with the currently selected function brings up the details of the function, complete with examples and tips.

Validating Your Data

Sometimes it is imperative that data fall within certain confines. For example, if you are tracking sales records for the year 1998, the date in the Date Sold field has to be within the year 1998. In Excel 98 you can set up data validation to totally prevent data entry unless it falls within your specifications, or just to provide a warning but enable the user to enter the incorrect data if so desired. Follow these steps:

1. Select the cells that are to have your data verification.
2. Choose Data ⇨ Validation and click the Settings tab (see Figure 16-24).

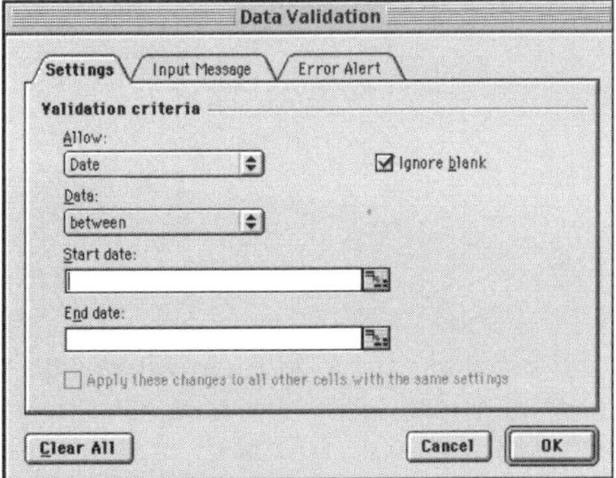

Figure 16-24: The Settings tab of the Data Validation dialog box

3. From the Allow pop-up menu, choose your validation criteria. Depending on your choice of criteria, more text boxes will appear so you can specify the acceptable data.

4. Click the Input Message tab (see Figure 16-25) to control whether the user will see a guiding message.

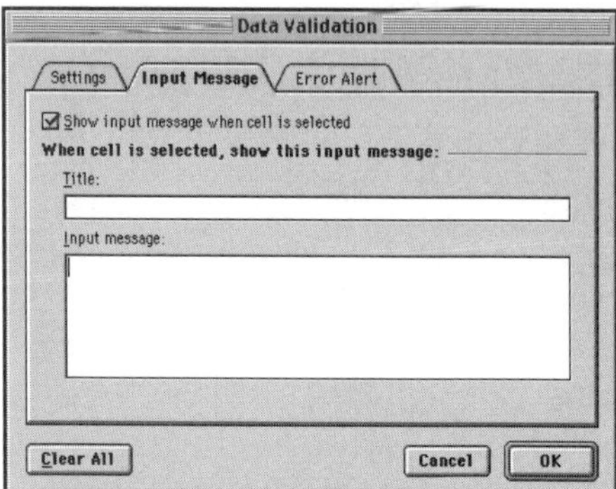

Figure 16-25: The Input Message tab of the Data Validation dialog box

5. The default option, Show input message when cell is selected, is checked. If you don't want a guiding message, uncheck this option. (Error validation will still be in effect.) With this option on, when the cell is clicked, any text you type in the Title and Input message fields appears in a yellow pop-up box when the Office Assistant isn't onscreen or in the Office Assistant's balloon (if the Assistant is turned on). Figure 16-26 shows an example of a custom message entered in this tab.

Figure 16-26: The result of an input message—guiding the user

6. Enter the text for your title and input message in the appropriate fields. In the example shown in Figure 16-26, there is no title text, and the input message text entered is "This must be a date in 1998."

7. Click the Error Alert tab, shown in Figure 16-27, to control what happens when the data entered doesn't meet the criteria you set up in the Settings tab.

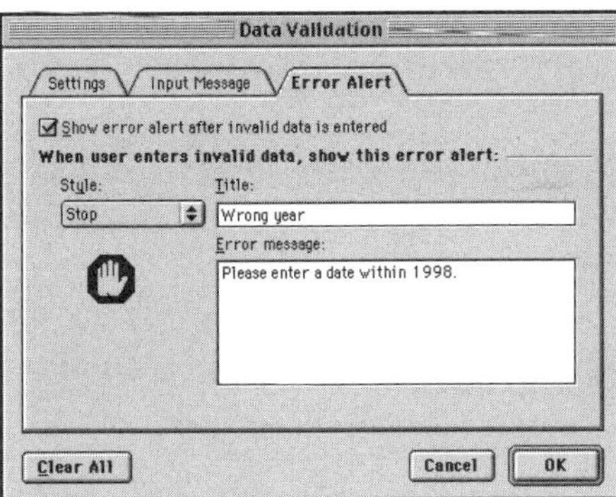

Figure 16-27: The Error Alert tab of the Data Validation dialog box

8. From the Style pop-up menu, select the results you want:

   ✦ **Stop** prevents the user from overriding your criteria. The user's only choice is to click Retry or Cancel. Clicking in another cell only causes a beep.

   ✦ **Warning** asks if the user wants to continue and allows the user to click Yes, No, or Cancel.

   ✦ **Information** asks if the user wants to continue and allows the user to click Yes or Cancel. In both of the latter choices, Yes allows the data to remain in the cell even if it doesn't meet the criteria.

9. Enter your custom Alert message of up to 225 characters in the Error message field. To start a new line within the message, press Return. If you leave this message box empty, the default message—The value you entered is not valid. A user has restricted values that can be entered into this cell.—is displayed. The title and error message appear in the Office Assistant's balloon. If the Assistant isn't onscreen, the error message appears (without the title) in a plain dialog box.

   In the example shown in Figure 16-28, the text typed into the Title field is "Wrong year." The text in the Error message field is "Please enter a date with 1998."

Figure 16-28: The result of an error message–preventing invalid data entry

Making Your Own Pop-Up List

You can even create a pop-up list of your own so that users see pop-up arrows and click them to select an acceptable value. First type your list values into a column or row in your worksheet. Then, in Step 3 (in the section on validating your data), select List as your criteria. (Make sure In-cell dropdown is checked.)

To define the list, click in the Source field (shown in Figure 16-24), and then click back in the worksheet and drag to select the values you pre-entered. Press Enter to return to the dialog box and continue.

Data validation only works for hand-typed data. If data is entered via macro or as the result of a formula, invalid data will be accepted. For more info on this topic, click the Office Assistant and enter **data validation**.

Using Find and Replace

Just like in the word-processing world, you can search and replace with Edit➪Find and Edit➪Replace. Like their counterparts in Word, these commands search for data and, optionally, replace that data with other data. The data you search for can be stored as values, as part or all of a formula, or as a cell note.

Finding data

To search for data in a worksheet using Edit➪Find, follow these steps:

1. Select the cells you want to search. If you want to search the entire worksheet, select any single cell.
2. Choose Edit➪Find (⌘-F). You'll see the Find dialog box, as shown in Figure 16-29.

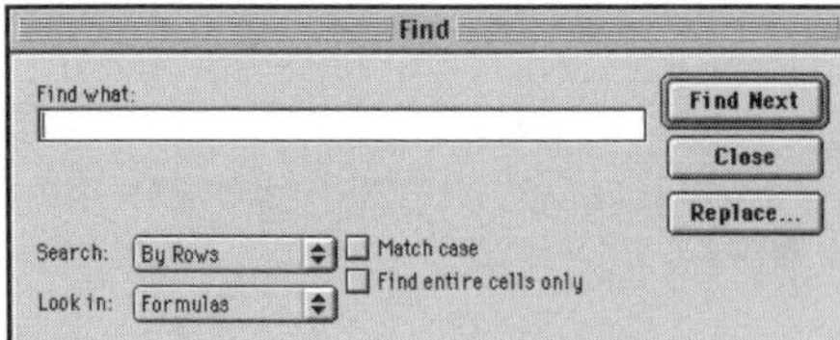

Figure 16-29: The Find dialog box

3. In the Find what text box, enter your search term. If you are not certain what you are searching for, use an asterisk (*) as a wildcard to indicate any combination of characters, or a question mark to indicate any single character.
4. From the Search pop-up, choose By Rows if you want to search across rows starting with the current cell, or By Columns to search across columns starting at the current cell.
5. From the Look in pop-up menu, choose Formulas to search through formulas, Values to search through values stored in cells, or Comments to search all comments attached to cells.
6. If you want your search to be case-sensitive, check the Match case check box. (This means when you search for *weekdays,* you will not find *Weekdays.*)
7. Check the Find entire cells only check box if you want the entire cell's contents to match your search term. If you leave this option turned off, Excel will find matches where either part or all of the cells' contents match the search term.
8. Click the Find Next button to find the next occurrence of the search term. (You can also press Return or Enter because Find Next is the default button.) When you finish searching, click Close.

When you have entered the parameters for a search in the Find dialog box, you can close the dialog box and press ShiftF4 rather than clicking Find Next to continue searching for the same data.

Finding and replacing data

Use the Replace command of the Edit menu to search for data in a worksheet and replace it with other data. The process is similar to using Edit➪Find (in fact, the dialog box you see is nearly identical). Here are the steps:

1. Select the cells you want to search. To search the entire worksheet, select any single cell.
2. Choose Edit➪Replace (⌘-H). The Replace dialog box appears, as shown in Figure 16-30.

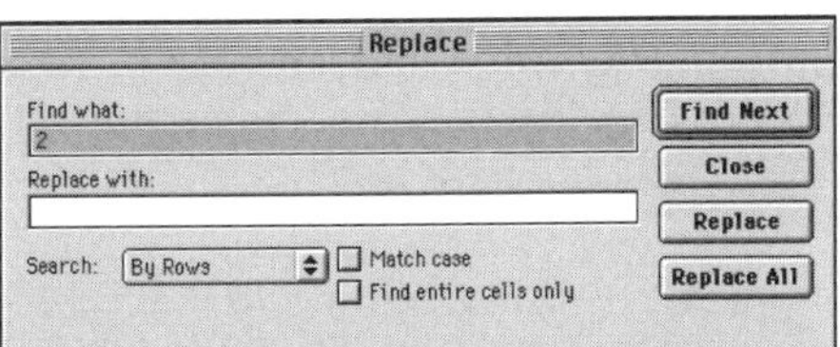

Figure 16-30: The Replace dialog box

3. In the Find what text box, enter your search term. Use an asterisk (*) to indicate any combination of characters. Use the question mark (?) to indicate any single character when you are unsure of the spelling of a word you seek or of the elements for which you are searching.
4. In the Replace with text box, type the replacement text.
5. From the Search pop-up list, choose By Rows if you want to search across rows starting with the current cell. Choose By Columns to search across columns starting at the current cell.
6. For a case-sensitive search, check the Match case check box.
7. Check the Find entire cells only box if you want the entire cell's contents to match your search term. If you leave this option off, Excel replaces data where either part or all of the cell's contents matches the search term.
8. Click the Replace All button if you want to find and replace all occurrences of the search term with your new term. A more cautious approach is to click Find Next to find the next match in the worksheet, and, after examining it, click the Replace button to replace only that match. When you're finished making your replacements, click Close.

Edit ➪ Undo (⌘-Z) rolls back the effects of a replace operation.

Correcting Your Spelling

Despite the best-looking document and most meticulously laid-out numbers, you're in for embarrassment if you're caught with spelling errors in your worksheet. Excel 98 does a lot to save you from such errors.

In Office 98, Word, Excel, and PowerPoint share the same AutoCorrect lists and dictionaries, so you don't have to enter custom words multiple times. The spelling interface for each is also shared, except that Word includes grammar checking.

AutoCorrect

How many times have your fingers typed a word incorrectly as you race to get your data into your spreadsheet? You know how to spell the word but your fingers are just not always cooperative. In Word 6, autocorrection was introduced. The good news is that AutoCorrect is now in Excel 98—and it's simple. To see for yourself, type **teh** and watch it turn into **the** in a flash as you continue to work without missing a step.

The AutoCorrect list Excel refers to as it watches your typing is the same list as the one Word uses. In fact, PowerPoint also has the AutoCorrect feature and shares the same list. There are bound to be words you mistype regularly that Microsoft hasn't thought of, so you can add any forms of a word that you want. You can also remove words from the default list.

AutoCorrect can do more than just fix your typos. It can act as a shorthand translator for you by automatically typing full words, symbols, or phrases when you type the key combination of your choice. For example, you can set up AutoCorrect so that typing **mye** types your e-mail address, saving you from finger-twisting combinations.

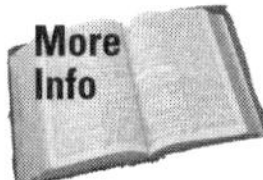

To learn how to customize your AutoCorrect list, see "Using AutoCorrect" in Chapter 2.

Checking spelling

You can save yourself from possibly embarrassing blunders by checking your worksheet's spelling before you pass out those copies at the annual board meeting. You can check any part of a selection (even a single word) or the entire worksheet, including any embedded charts. You can also add words to your own custom dictionaries in order to handle specialized words you use often (such as medical and legal terms).

To spell-check a worksheet, follow these steps:

1. Select the cells you want to spell-check. If you want to check the spelling of the entire worksheet, select any single cell.
2. Choose Tools➪Spelling, or click the Spelling button (ABC-check mark) on the Standard toolbar. Excel checks the spelling in the worksheet. If it finds what it thinks is a misspelled word, you'll see the Spelling dialog box, as shown in Figure 16-31.

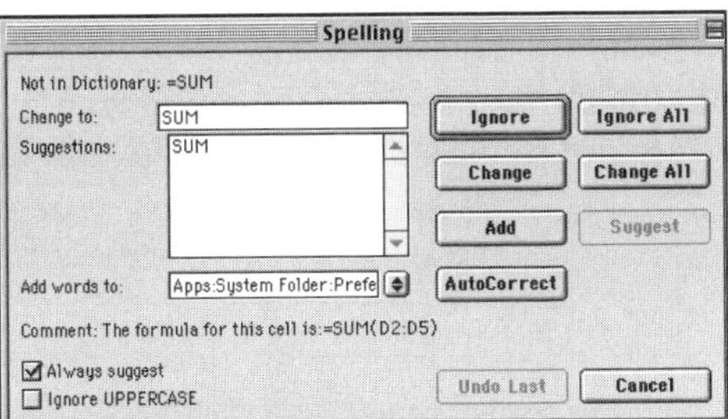

Figure 16-31: The Spelling dialog box

When Excel finds a misspelling, it tries to provide several options for a correct spelling of the word. If the Always suggest check box is turned on, Word suggests proper spellings whenever it can. In the Change to text box, enter the correct spelling, or click one of the suggested spellings in the Suggestions list box, which adds that spelling to the Change to box.

If the Always suggest check box is turned off, click the Suggest button (which appears) to see a list of possible spellings in the Suggestions list box. If one of the suggestions is the spelling you want, select it in the list box and click Change. The Ignore button lets you leave a word as is. Cancel cancels the entire spell-checking operation. Clicking Ignore All tells Excel to ignore all suspected misspellings of the term in question. Change All tells Excel to change all misspellings of the work in question to the entry in the Change to box. The Add button lets you add a word to the selected custom dictionary. When the Ignore UPPERCASE check box is turned on, Excel skips words composed of all uppercase letters.

During the spell-checking process, Excel takes a little extra time to suggest corrections to misspelled words. You can speed the process slightly by turning off the Always suggest check box and using the Suggest button to ask for help when you need it.

Adding a custom dictionary

If you make regular use of specialized terms (such as medical or legal terms) in your worksheets, the spell-checking capability will be useless unless it can work with those terms as part of Excel's dictionaries. You can add words to Excel's default custom dictionary, but another option is to create additional custom dictionaries. Follow these steps:

1. Place the cursor in any worksheet containing some of your custom terms. (This way, the spell-check operation will find them.)
2. Choose Tools ➪ Spelling. When Excel stops at the first word it doesn't recognize, the Spelling dialog box appears, as shown earlier in Figure 16-31.
3. To begin a new custom dictionary, click in the Add words to box and type a name for the new dictionary you want to create.
4. Click the Add button to add the current word to the dictionary. If Excel displays a dialog box asking if you want to create a new dictionary, click Yes.

   From this point on, you can use the dictionary by choosing from the Add words to pop-up list.

Summary

This chapter examined the many different ways you can enter data into an Excel worksheet and manipulate that data. The chapter covered the following points:

✦ You can enter values or formulas into cells of a worksheet. Values can be numbers, text, dates, or times.

✦ You can attach notes to cells by using the Comment command of the Insert menu. When a note is attached, the Comment command changes to Edit Comment so you can make changes to the note.

- You can move and copy data from place to place on a worksheet or between worksheets.
- Excel's Fill, AutoFill, and Series features can fill ranges of cells with data.
- You can insert and delete ranges of cells, as well as entire rows and columns.
- Formulas manage the calculations within your worksheets.
- Excel provides hundreds of functions, which you can think of as tools for performing specific types of calculations.
- Excel's Function Wizard can help you quickly find and properly enter the correct function for a specific task.
- You can use the Edit⇨Find and Edit⇨Replace commands to search for data and to replace data with other data.
- You can use the Tools⇨Spelling command to correct the spelling of text in a worksheet.

Where to go next

- The next chapter tells you how to format your worksheets so they look good.
- You'll soon want to print what you've created. You find the complete scoop on printing in Chapter 20.

✦ ✦ ✦

CHAPTER 17

Excel Formatting

Most spreadsheet users know that a spreadsheet is more than just a collection of raw numbers. Since the days of the first spreadsheets, users have resorted to formatting tricks to enhance the appearance of the numbers presented. (How many seasoned spreadsheet pros remember filling rows of cells with characters like asterisks or hyphens to enclose information within crude borders?) Excel offers many ways to format worksheets to give them the most effective visual impact possible. You can change the fonts, sizes, styles, and colors of the characters within your worksheets. You can also control the alignment of text within cells, both vertically and horizontally. You can change row heights and column widths, add borders to selected cells, and use Excel's powerful AutoFormat feature to enhance the appearance of part or all of a worksheet quickly—without the need to use any formatting commands!

✦ ✦ ✦ ✦

In This Chapter

Using the AutoFormat feature

Changing widths and heights

Hiding and unhiding elements

Changing alignments

Formatting text

Applying borders, patterns, and colors

Working with number formats

Using the format painter

Creating your own styles

Protecting your formatting changes

✦ ✦ ✦ ✦

Using the AutoFormat Feature

The easiest way to whip your Excel spreadsheet into shape is by using AutoFormat. This relatively new feature applies automatic formatting from a number of well-thought-out styles. You activate the AutoFormat feature by choosing Format⇨AutoFormat to call up the AutoFormat dialog box. From the dialog box, you view and select a sample format. With AutoFormat, nice-looking documents are only a few clicks away—even if you know little or nothing about formatting. Figures 17-1, 17-2, and 17-3 show some of the AutoFormat looks available.

In Figure 17-1, the Classic 1 style of AutoFormat uses traditional accounting-style fonts and simple borderlines to separate the data visually.

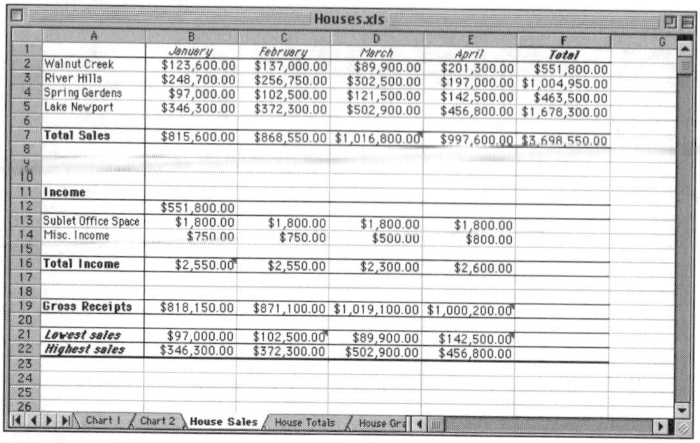

Houses.xls

	A	B	C	D	E	F
1		January	February	March	April	Total
2	Walnut Creek	$123,600.00	$137,000.00	$89,900.00	$201,300.00	$551,800.00
3	River Hills	$248,700.00	$256,750.00	$302,500.00	$197,000.00	$1,004,950.00
4	Spring Gardens	$97,000.00	$102,500.00	$121,500.00	$142,500.00	$463,500.00
5	Lake Newport	$346,300.00	$372,300.00	$502,900.00	$456,800.00	$1,678,300.00
7	Total Sales	$815,600.00	$868,550.00	$1,016,800.00	$997,600.00	$3,698,550.00
11	Income					
12		$551,800.00				
13	Sublet Office Space	$1,800.00	$1,800.00	$1,800.00	$1,800.00	
14	Misc. Income	$750.00	$750.00	$500.00	$800.00	
16	Total Income	$2,550.00	$2,550.00	$2,300.00	$2,600.00	
19	Gross Receipts	$818,150.00	$871,100.00	$1,019,100.00	$1,000,200.00	
21	Lowest sales	$97,000.00	$102,500.00	$89,900.00	$142,500.00	
22	Highest sales	$346,300.00	$372,300.00	$502,900.00	$456,800.00	

Chart 1 / Chart 2 / House Sales / House Totals / House Gr

Figure 17-1: The Classic 1 style AutoFormat

In Figure 17-2, the Colorful 1 style of AutoFormat makes extensive use of various background choices to highlight the worksheet data.

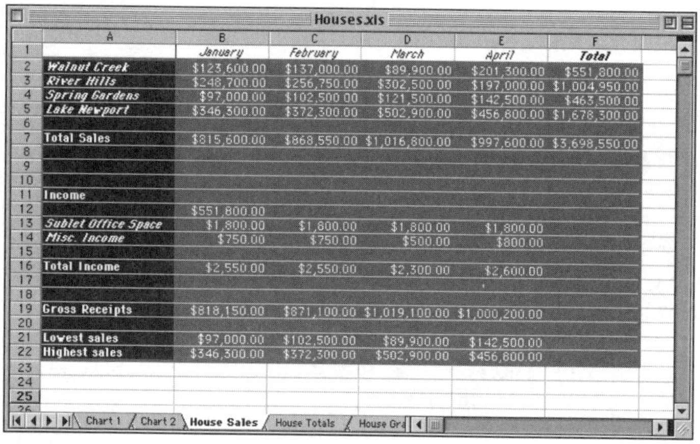

Houses.xls

	A	B	C	D	E	F
1		January	February	March	April	Total
2	Walnut Creek	$123,600.00	$137,000.00	$89,900.00	$201,300.00	$551,800.00
3	River Hills	$248,700.00	$256,750.00	$302,500.00	$197,000.00	$1,004,950.00
4	Spring Gardens	$97,000.00	$102,500.00	$121,500.00	$142,500.00	$463,500.00
5	Lake Newport	$346,300.00	$372,300.00	$502,900.00	$456,800.00	$1,678,300.00
7	Total Sales	$815,600.00	$868,550.00	$1,016,800.00	$997,600.00	$3,698,550.00
11	Income					
12		$551,800.00				
13	Sublet Office Space	$1,800.00	$1,800.00	$1,800.00	$1,800.00	
14	Misc. Income	$750.00	$750.00	$500.00	$800.00	
16	Total Income	$2,550.00	$2,550.00	$2,300.00	$2,600.00	
19	Gross Receipts	$818,150.00	$871,100.00	$1,019,100.00	$1,000,200.00	
21	Lowest sales	$97,000.00	$102,500.00	$89,900.00	$142,500.00	
22	Highest sales	$346,300.00	$372,300.00	$502,900.00	$456,800.00	

Chart 1 / Chart 2 / House Sales / House Totals / House Gr

Figure 17-2: The Colorful 1 style AutoFormat

In Figure 17-3, the List 1 style of AutoFormat uses shading in alternate rows of the worksheet.

Houses.xls

	January	February	March	April	Total
Walnut Creek	$123,600.00	$137,000.00	$89,900.00	$201,300.00	$551,800.00
River Hills	$248,700.00	$256,750.00	$302,500.00	$197,000.00	$1,004,950.00
Spring Gardens	$97,000.00	$102,500.00	$121,500.00	$142,500.00	$463,500.00
Lake Newport	$346,300.00	$372,300.00	$502,900.00	$456,800.00	$1,678,300.00
Total Sales	$815,600.00	$868,550.00	$1,016,800.00	$997,600.00	$3,698,550.00
Income					
	$551,800.00				
Sublet Office Space	$1,800.00	$1,800.00	$1,800.00	$1,800.00	
Misc. Income	$750.00	$750.00	$500.00	$800.00	
Total Income	$2,550.00	$2,550.00	$2,300.00	$2,600.00	
Gross Receipts	$818,150.00	$871,100.00	$1,019,100.00	$1,000,200.00	
Lowest sales	$97,000.00	$102,500.00	$89,900.00	$142,500.00	
Highest sales	$346,300.00	$372,300.00	$502,900.00	$456,800.00	

Chart 1 / Chart 2 / House Sales / House Totals / House Gra

Figure 17-3: The List 1 style AutoFormat

Excel examines the current range to determine levels of summary and detail. It also looks for text, values, and formulas, then applies formats accordingly. AutoFormats are combinations of several different elements: number, alignment, font, border, pattern, column, and row formats. To apply AutoFormat to your worksheet, follow these steps:

1. Select the range of cells to which you want to apply the format. If you want to select the entire worksheet, click the row and column header intersection at the upper-left corner of the worksheet.
2. Choose Format ➪ AutoFormat to open the AutoFormat dialog box shown in Figure 17-4.

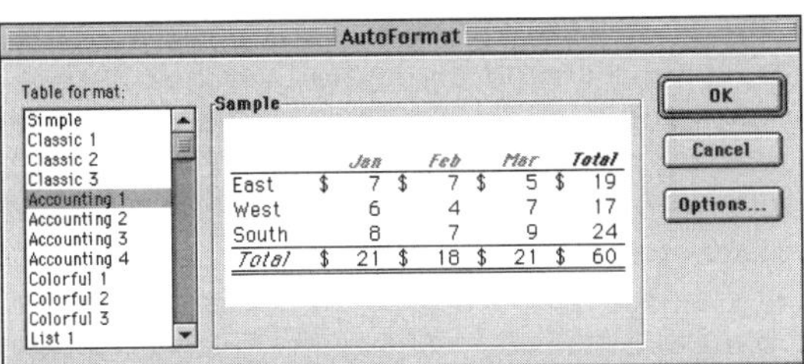

Figure 17-4: The AutoFormat dialog box

3. From the Table format list, click a format name to see a preview of it in the Sample window or to choose the desired format.

4. If you want more control over what formatting will be applied, click the Options button. This expands the dialog box to reveal check boxes for Number, Border, Font, Patterns, Alignment, and Width/Height (see Figure 17-5). By default, all the boxes are turned on. You can turn off any formatting.
5. Click OK to apply the formatting to the selection.

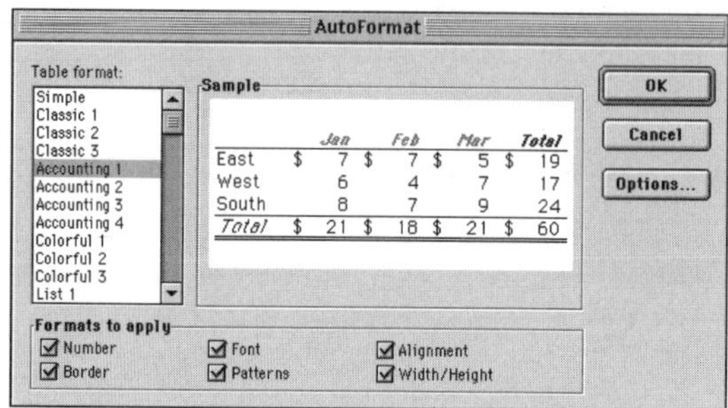

Figure 17-5: AutoFormat options—the expanded AutoFormat dialog box

If you don't like the effects of the AutoFormat command, choose Edit ⇨ Undo (⌘-Z). Or, if you have performed other tasks since applying the AutoFormat to the selection, don't worry. You can simply select the range, choose Format ⇨ Auto-Format, and select None from the bottom of the list of styles.

You don't have to settle for Excel's default formatting selections in its AutoFormats. You can mix and match styles or mix an AutoFormat style with your own by using the Options button in the AutoFormat dialog box to accept or reject certain AutoFormatting. For example, if you spent a great deal of time formatting different ranges of numeric values with different fonts, you might not want AutoFormat to mess with the fonts. Turn off the Font check box in the Formats to apply area of the AutoFormat dialog box. Then, when you apply AutoFormat to the selection, Excel won't override the already applied fonts.

You can turn off one formatting option or several formatting options depending on the selection and formatting you want applied. After turning off the desired options, you can choose the format that you want from the Table format list and click OK to apply it to your selection. Options you turn off in this manner aren't carried over to the next time you use AutoFormat. You'll need to turn off any options you don't want each time you use AutoFormat.

When to Stay Away from AutoFormat

As helpful a feature as AutoFormat is, it has its limits. Excel has to make judgment calls when it applies AutoFormat to your worksheet. For example, Excel tries to determine which parts of the selection contain column headings so it can apply a pleasing format to those headings. AutoFormat is designed to work well with worksheets that follow a traditional row-and-column format.

If your worksheet doesn't follow tradition—perhaps it contains a large number of scientific formulas laid out more like a flowchart—AutoFormat may not give you the results you'd like. In these cases, apply your desired formats manually using the formatting techniques covered later in this chapter.

Changing Widths and Heights

Excel does a good job of automatically adjusting row height to accommodate wrapped text and large fonts so you may never need to make such an adjustment. However, you will probably need to adjust your columns from time to time. For maximum flexibility, Excel enables you to adjust column width and row height at any time.

Column widths

You can adjust the standard width setting of the columns, or you can change only a few columns. There are two methods for adjusting column width. The first method, clicking and dragging the column to size it, is easier and enables you to size your columns visually. The second method is numerically accurate but requires the use of commands and dialog boxes.

To use the mouse to adjust the size of the columns, follow these steps:

1. Move the mouse pointer to the heading of the column you want to adjust and move it over the right edge of the column so the pointer becomes a double-headed arrow.
2. Drag the column-heading border to size it manually to the desired width.

Hot Stuff

You can also double-click the column header instead, which automatically sizes the column to the width of the widest entry in all the selected rows.

If you know the exact column width you want, or want to make several columns exactly the same size, you can use a dialog box. Control-click a column header and choose Column Width or choose Format ⇨ Column ⇨ Width, and enter a numeric value in the Width dialog box that appears. Control-clicking also offers other choices because Format ⇨ Column offers other submenus. For example, you can choose the Standard Width command, then accept the standard width that appears in the Standard Width dialog box. The AutoFit Selection command in the submenu automatically sizes a column to accommodate the largest entry in the column.

The AutoFit Selection command applies its magic only to selected cells, so you must first make a selection for the command to have the desired effect. If you leave the mouse cursor in a blank cell, using AutoFit Selection accomplishes nothing. Usually, it's a good idea to select the entire column before using AutoFit Selection. (To select a column, click the column header.)

Row heights

A row can range in height from 0 points to 409 points. When it comes to adjusting row height there are again two methods: clicking and dragging or the Format menu options. To use the click-and-drag method, follow these steps:

1. Move the pointer over the bottom border of the row heading so the pointer becomes a double-headed arrow.
2. Drag the bottom border of the row heading until the row reaches the desired size.

You can also AutoSize a row's height by double-clicking the bottom border of a row header. This adjusts the row to fit the tallest entry. If you want to AutoSize a number of rows, first select the desired row and then double-click the bottom border of any of the selected rows.

As with columns, you can numerically adjust row height by Control-clicking in a row heading and selecting a command, or by choosing Format ➪ Row and selecting a command from the submenu. To set the row height, for example, choose Height and enter a value for the height in the Row Height dialog box (see Figure 17-6), or choose AutoFit to adjust the row height to the largest entry in the row.

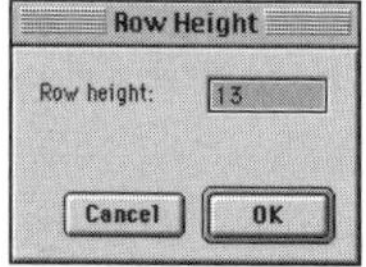

Figure 17-6: The Row Height dialog box

Hiding and Unhiding Elements

You can hide selected columns or rows from view, and later reveal rows or columns that have been previously hidden. You may want to hide rows or columns so that they don't appear in printed copies of the worksheets, or you may want to hide rows or columns so a viewer's attention is focused on important parts of the worksheet. For example, you may need to compare the data in columns B and D.

With column C between B and D the data is difficult to analyze. If you hide column C, however, the data now appear side by side and is easy to compare.

Hiding columns

To hide a column, Control-click the column header and select Hide from the shortcut menu, or click in the column header to select the column and choose Format ⇨ Column ⇨ Hide. To bring the column back, select the two columns (which are now next to each other) that surround the hidden column, Control-click the column headers, and select Unhide from the shortcut menu. Alternatively, choose Edit ⇨ Go To (F5), enter the address of any cell in that column, and click OK. Then, choose Format ⇨ Column ⇨ Unhide.

Hiding rows

Hiding rows is similar to hiding columns. Select the desired row and choose Format ⇨ Row ⇨ Hide. To bring the row back, select the two rows (which are now next to each other) that surround the hidden row, Control-click the row headers and select Unhide from the shortcut menu. Alternatively, choose Edit ⇨ Go To (F5), enter the address of any cell in that row, and click OK. Then choose Format ⇨ Row ⇨ Unhide.

Hiding gridlines

With some worksheets you may not want the gridlines that are normally displayed to appear. To hide the gridlines, first activate the worksheet page, then choose Tools ⇨ Preferences. In the Preferences dialog box, click the View tab, turn off the Gridlines option, and click OK. The gridlines disappear from the current worksheet.

The Gridlines option affects only the current worksheet in a workbook. To turn off gridlines for another worksheet, repeat the above steps. You can also turn off the gridlines for multiple worksheets at one time by selecting each of the worksheets before choosing Tools ⇨ Preferences and before turning off the Gridlines. To select several worksheets, press Shift as you click each worksheet tab that you want included in the selection.

Changing Alignments

In your quest to give your worksheet a more professional and refined look, you may want to change the alignment of data in your cells. By default, the following alignment applies to cells: right-aligned for numbers, left-aligned for text, and centered for logical and error values. Changing the alignment of text in a cell is especially important because what works with text in one area of your worksheet may not work in another area. You may want to enhance the appearance of certain parts of your worksheet by right-aligning or centering text, for example.

To change the alignment of the cells, first select the range of cells to which you want to apply the new alignment. Then you can choose between two methods to change the alignment. The fastest way—clicking the buttons on the Formatting toolbar—provides basic alignment. The other way, which presents more advanced options, is to select Format ⇨ Cells to open the Format Cells dialog box, and then click the Alignment tab to bring up your alignment options. (You can also open the Format Cells dialog box by Control-clicking the selection and choosing Format Cells from the shortcut menu.) Figure 17-7 shows the Alignment tab of the Format Cells dialog box.

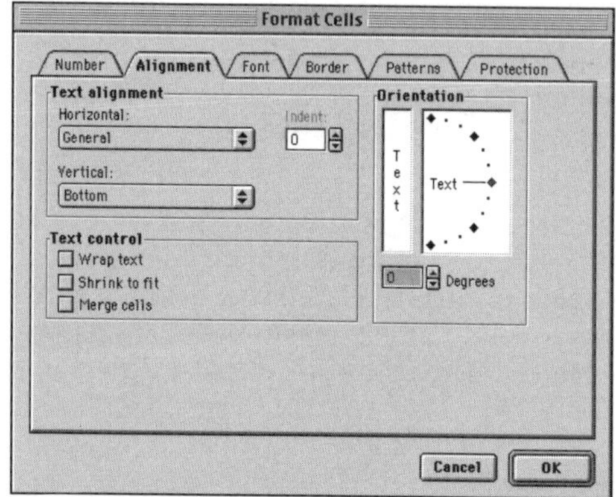

Figure 17-7: The Alignment tab of the Format Cells dialog box

In the Horizontal pop-up menu, you can choose the Left, Center, or Right alignment options. (You can also use the Wrap text and Justify options with text that occupies multiple lines of a cell.) If you've changed the row height of a cell so that the cell is much taller than the text entry, the options in the Vertical list box of the dialog box become equally useful. You can align the text to the top, bottom, or center of the cell, and you can vertically justify it. You can also use the Orientation portion of the dialog box to change the alignment of the entry within the cell.

In the Text control portion of the dialog box, turning on Wrap text allows a long entry to wrap within a cell. The Shrink to fit option, when turned on, reduces the font of an entry as needed to fit within a cell. You can use the Merge cells option to merge any selection of cells within a row or column into a single cell.

To use the Formatting toolbar buttons to change the basic alignment of data in cells, follow these steps:

1. Select the cells in which you want to change the alignment.
2. Click the Align Left button to left-align the selection, the Center button to center entries in the selection, and the Align Right button to right-align the selection.

The disadvantage of using the Formatting toolbar is that it does not offer the range of options that the Format Cells dialog box offers. You can't vertically align text from the toolbar, and you can't use the wrap and justify options, but you can center text across columns, as detailed in the next section.

Formatting Text

As you build worksheets with lots of text headings, you'll discover that you need to center headings across a series of multiple cells. Spreadsheet pros from way back centered titles across multiple columns through trial and error. Excel sends this technique back to the Stone Age where it belongs with the Merge and Center button on the Formatting toolbar and the corresponding Center across selection option on the Alignment tab of the Format Cells dialog box. Figure 17-8 shows the Projected Sales title before and after it was centered across the selected range of cells.

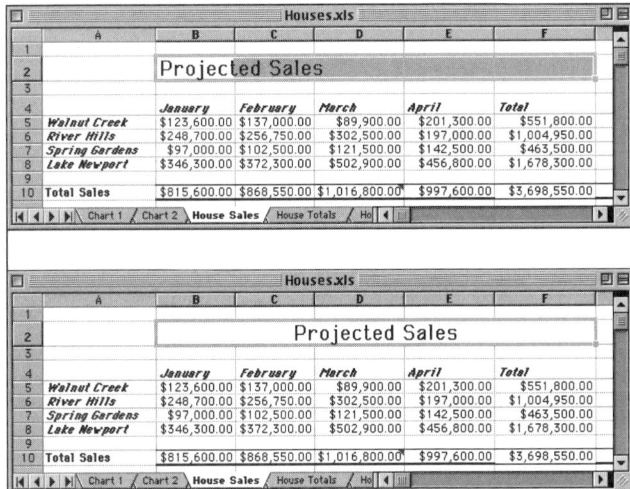

Figure 17-8: Top—a title before centering across a range of cells. Bottom—the title after centering across a range of cells.

Centering text

To center the contents of a cell across a selection of blank cells, follow these steps:

1. Select the cells the text is to be centered across. (For proper results, the left-most cell in the selection should contain the text to be centered across the range of cells.)
2. Click the Merge and Center button in the Formatting toolbar.

Alternatively, you can make the selection, Control-click it, and choose Format Cells from the shortcut menu that appears. In the Alignment tab of the Format Cells dialog box, choose Center across selection from the Horizontal pop-up menu. But unless you've turned off the display of the Formatting toolbar, it's generally easier to use the toolbar button.

Wrapping text

When you make lengthy text entries within cells, you can tell Excel to wrap the text so it fits into an attractive paragraph inside the cell. When text is wrapped, Excel automatically adjusts the row height so all of the text fits within the width of the cell. Figure 17-9 shows the before-and-after effects of using the Wrap text option. In the figure, both cells containing text contain the same information. In the upper cell that contains text, the Wrap text option has not been turned on; in the lower cell that contains text, Wrap text has been turned on.

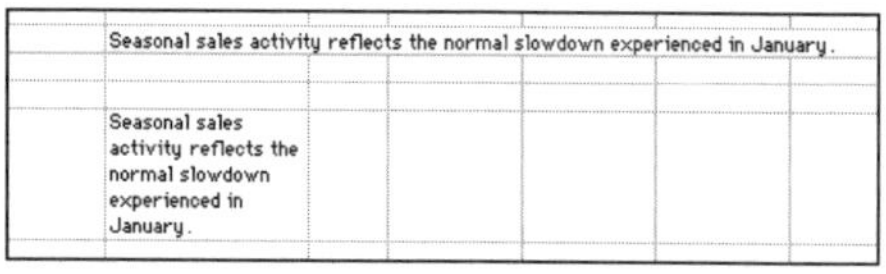

Figure 17-9: Examples of using Wrap text in a worksheet

To wrap text in a cell, follow these steps:

1. Make any desired change to the column width.
2. Select the cell(s) containing the text that you want to wrap.
3. Choose Format ➪ Cells.
4. Check Wrap text in the Text control portion of the dialog box.

Justifying text

From time to time you may want to justify your text so that every line of a paragraph (except the last if it is too short to fill a line) is aligned on both sides. For example, you may want a smooth look after you turn on text Wrap. (A cell has to contain at least two lines of text for justification to have any effect.) Figure 17-10 shows the before and after effects of using text alignment in a worksheet. In the figure, the text in the top cell is not justified (it is left-aligned); the lower cell shows the text after applying the Justify option.

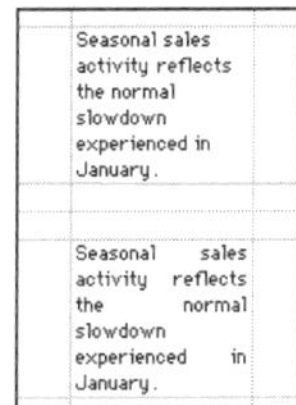

Figure 17-10: Top – left-aligned (right-ragged text). Bottom – left- and right-aligned (justified) text.

To justify entries in selected cells, follow these steps:

1. Select the cell(s) whose text you want to justify.
2. Choose Format ➪ Cells. (You can use the menu bar or the shortcut menu.)
3. Select Justify from the Horizontal pop-up menu. The text is automatically justified. (The effect is only noticed if it contains two or more lines.)

Rotating text

There is bound to be a time when you need to cram tons of data on a single page and need to save every bit of space possible. The capability to rotate text certainly is handy in a case such as this. For example, in Figure 17-11, long cell headings would waste space if they were not rotated.

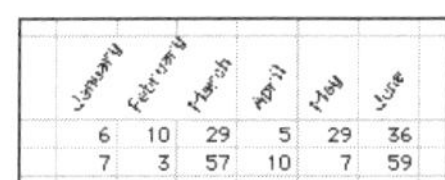

Figure 17-11: Rotated text saves valuable column space.

To rotate text, follow these steps:

1. Select the cell(s) whose text you want to rotate.
2. Choose Format ➪ Cells, then click the Alignment tab shown in Figure 17-12. (You can Control-click and select Format Cells from the shortcut menu.)
3. At the right side of the dialog box, notice the diagram that shows you the angle of the text. (It says Text and has a line following it.) Click the word *Text* and drag it to the angle you want for your text. If you prefer, you can click the up or down arrows where the degrees of the angle are reported (below the diagram), or type a number into the degrees field. Click OK or press Return or Enter when you've set the angle.

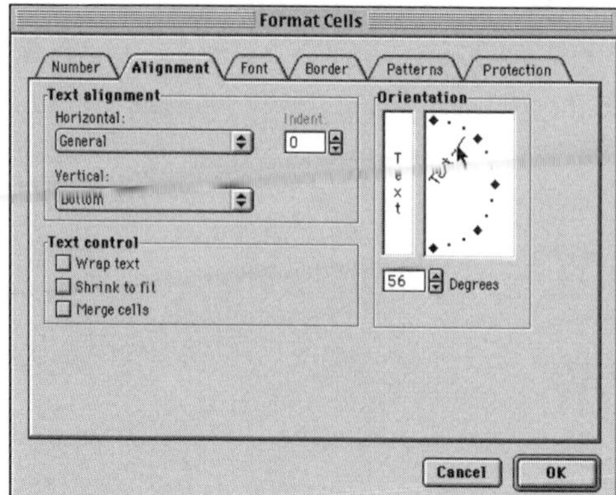

Figure 17-12: Rotating text in the Format Cells dialog box

After rotating your text, you will probably want to adjust the height and width of the cells.

Applying fonts and style formats

Just as in Word, you can apply different fonts to your entries. Applying fonts in Excel is as simple as it is in Word. Just select the cells you want to change and choose the font you want to apply from the pop-up Font menu on the Formatting toolbar. (There isn't a Font menu in Excel.) You can also choose a font size from the toolbar, and you can use the Bold, Italic, and Underline buttons to apply these types of formatting to the characters in the selected cells. Alternatively, you can use the Format Cells dialog box. Select the cells, Control-click the selection and choose Format Cells from the shortcut menu, or select the cells and choose Format ➪ Cells. In the Format Cells dialog box, click the Font tab to display your font choices, as shown in Figure 17-13.

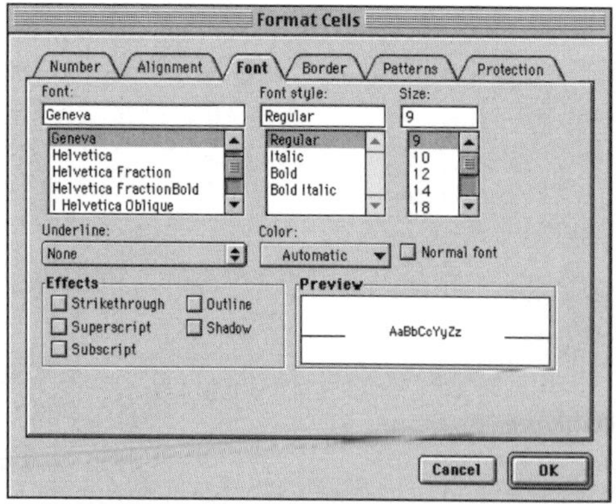

Figure 17-13: The Font tab of the Format Cells dialog box

On the Font tab, you can use the options in the Font and Font style lists to choose a desired font and font style, and you can choose a point size from the Size list. You can select a type of underlining (Single, Double, Single Accounting, or Double Accounting) from the Underline pop-up list, and a text color from the pop-up Color menu. In the Effects area, you can turn on special effects (Strikethrough, Superscript, Subscript, Outline, and Shadow).

You don't have to apply styles or fonts to the entire contents of a cell. You can choose to apply formatting to just some of the characters. To accomplish this, place the cursor in the cell that contains the text you want to change so the text appears in the formula bar. In the formula bar, click and drag to select the characters you want to change. Next, use the Formatting toolbar to apply your formatting. Otherwise, choose Format➪Cells to bring up the Format Cells dialog box (which now displays only the Font tab). Here you can choose the Font you want for those characters, along with the character size and style. Make the desired selections and click OK to apply them. (In case you're wondering, you can also double-click the cell whose text you want to edit and do the character selection directly in the cell.)

Applying Borders, Patterns, and Colors

Excel provides plenty of border types for your visual pleasure. Each border type has different widths, patterns, and colors. You can use these choices to make your worksheets more attractive and easier to read. To apply a border to a selection, follow these steps:

1. Select the cells to which you want to add the border.
2. Click the down arrow to the right of the Borders button on the Formatting toolbar and drag to the border of your choice from the menu that pops up (see Figure 17-14). The border you choose is applied to the selected cells.

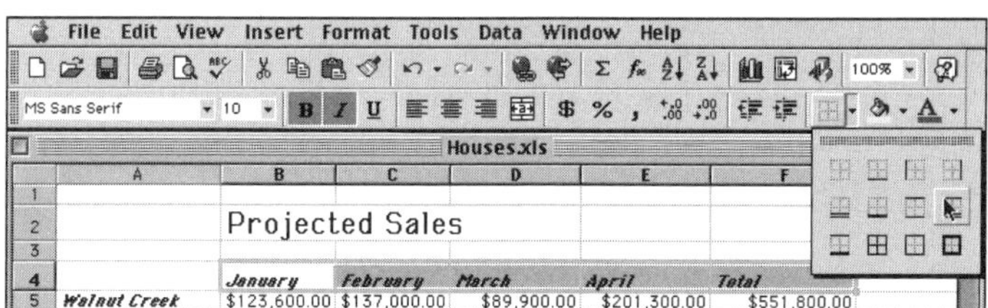

Figure 17-14: The border pop-up menu

You can also quickly apply shading to a selection by clicking the down arrow to the right of the Fill Color buttons on the Formatting toolbar and choosing a desired color from the box of colors that appears.

For fuller control over your borders, such as color and line styles, use the Format Cells dialog box. As with the button, select the cells to which you want to add the border. Choose Format ➪ Cells, or Control-click the selected cells to open the Format Cells dialog box, and click the Border tab, which is shown in Figure 17-15. You can use the options within this tab to apply your border to the selected cells. The left side of this tab basically provides the same options as the button. The right side enables you to select a line style and color.

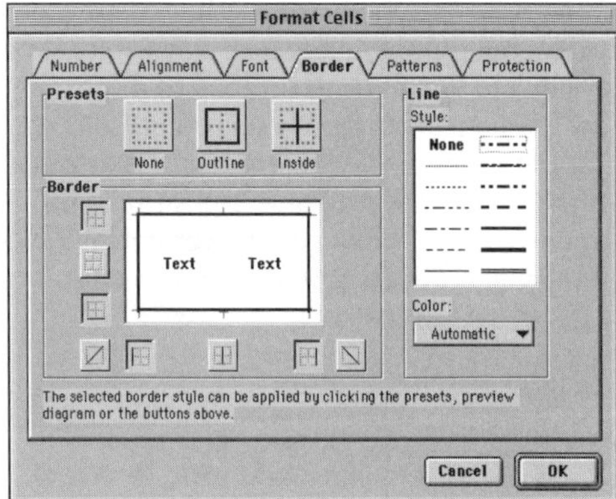

Figure 17-15: The Border tab of the Format Cells dialog box

You can also add colors and patterns to the cells you have selected. To apply a color or a pattern, select the desired cells, Control-click the selection, and choose Format Cells from the shortcut menu, or chose Format ➪ Cells. When the Format Cells dialog box appears, click the Patterns tab to bring it to the front, as shown in Figure 17-16.

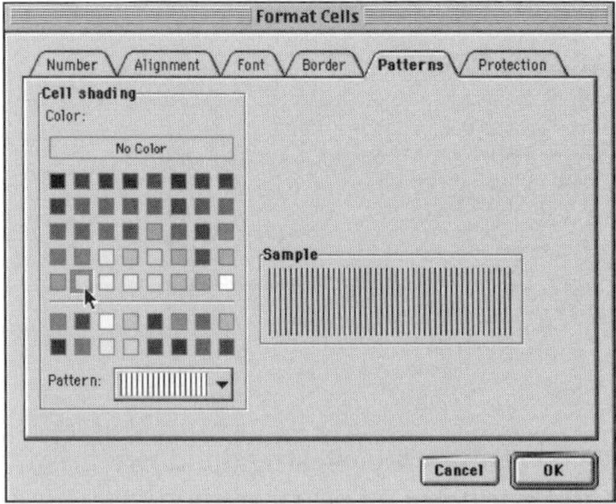

Figure 17-16: The Patterns tab of the Format Cells dialog box

In the Cell shading area of the dialog box, click the desired color or shade of gray to apply it. Then click the Pattern pop-up list and choose a pattern from the choices that appear. After you make your desired color and pattern selections, click OK to close the Format Cells dialog box and to apply your choices.

When applied, some patterns can make cell entries very difficult to read. Remember you can use Edit ⇨ Undo (⌘-Z) if you don't like the looks of your selection.

Sometimes, you may want to apply a color to the characters that you enter rather than to the background of the cell. Applying color to the characters can make a specific number or title stand out. To make the total earnings for the year stand out, for example, you can apply red formatting to the characters in that cell if the earnings were less than the previous year.

To apply a color to the characters in your worksheet quickly, select the characters to which you want to apply the color and then click the down arrow to the right of the Font Color button on the Formatting toolbar to reveal the color selection box. Choose a color to apply to the characters. (You can also open the Format Cells dialog box and go to the Font tab.)

Hot Stuff

With both the Font Color and the regular (cell) Color buttons, you can apply the color that was last chosen to another selection by simply clicking the button. This is a great shortcut feature.

Working with Number Formats

By default, Excel applies the General format to numbers in a cell. This format displays up to 11 digits if the entry exceeds the cell's width. All the numbers entered in the General format are displayed as integers (such as 21,947 or 12,382), decimal numbers (such as 21.57 or 3.14159), or in scientific notation (such as 9.43E+7 or 21.212E-5).

When you enter a numeric value in a cell, Excel tries to find the number format that is most appropriate for your entry number and assigns that format to the number. If you enter nothing but numbers and they aren't excessively large or small, Excel is pretty much clueless as to how you want them formatted. In these cases, Excel settles for the General format for the cell.

You can, however, give Excel clues as to how you want it to format an entry by including symbols with your numeric entries. For example, if you enter a dollar amount and precede it with a dollar sign, Excel automatically formats the entry as a currency value. If you want the entry formatted as a percent, you can follow the entry with a percent sign. You can enter scientific notation directly into the cell. For example, if you enter 17.409E+10 in a cell, Excel stores the value of 174,090,000,000,000 in the cell and displays 1.74E+14 in the cell.

If you've already entered your values, using the Formatting toolbar is the simplest way to apply the most commonly used number formats. After selecting the entry you want to change, click one of the number formatting buttons to apply the format. Table 17-1 lists the number formatting buttons and their functions.

Table 17-1
Number Formatting Buttons on the Formatting Toolbar

Button	*Function*
Currency Style	Changes the cell to a currency format
Percent Style	Changes the cell to a percent format
Comma Style	Changes the cell to a comma format
Increase Decimal	Increases the decimal place of the number
Decrease Decimal	Decreases the decimal place of the number

You can also apply number formats via the Number tab of the Format Cells dialog box. To activate the Format Cells dialog box, choose Format ➪ Cells (or Control-click the selection and choose Format Cells from the shortcut menu). Click the Number tab to display the Format Cells dialog box shown in Figure 17-17.

To apply number formats by using the Number tab of the Format Cells dialog box, follow these steps:

1. Select the cells to format.
2. Choose Format ➪ Cells or Control-click the selection and choose Format Cells from the shortcut menu.
3. Click the Number tab.
4. In the Category list on the left of the tab, click the category your number falls into.
5. If a list of Types appears to the right, choose the specific way you want your number to appear. As you click a format, a sample appears above the list. (Some categories, such as Text and Accounting, don't offer a list box of types.)
6. Click OK to apply the formatting.

Remember that occasions may arise when you want to format numbers as text. You can do so as you enter the value in a cell of the worksheet by entering an apostrophe before the number. You can also select the cell, choose Format ➪ Cells, click the Number tab of the Format Cells dialog box, and choose Text from the Category list.

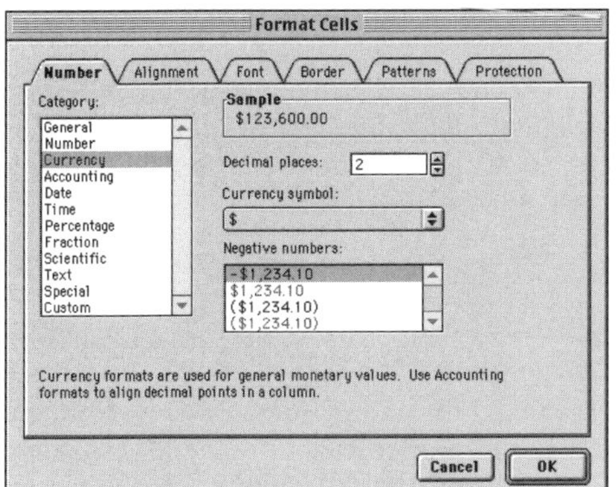

Figure 17-17: The Number tab of the Format Cells dialog box

Date and time formats

If you enter data in an acceptable date or time format, Excel stores the value as a date or time value. For example, if you type 7/3/57 into a cell, Excel stores the entry as a date value of July 3, 1957. Excel also recognizes a value such as 3-Feb-98 as a valid date. Similarly, with an entry of 9:45 PM, Excel stores a time value representing that time. (Chapter 16 provides additional specifics on the entry of dates and times in a worksheet.)

To change the format that Excel uses to display dates and times, follow these steps:

1. Select the cell or range of cells containing the date or time values.
2. Choose Format ➪ Cells, or Control-click the selection and choose Format Cells from the shortcut menu.
3. Click the Number tab.
4. In the Category list, choose Date or Time as desired. Figure 17-18 shows the Date category selected.

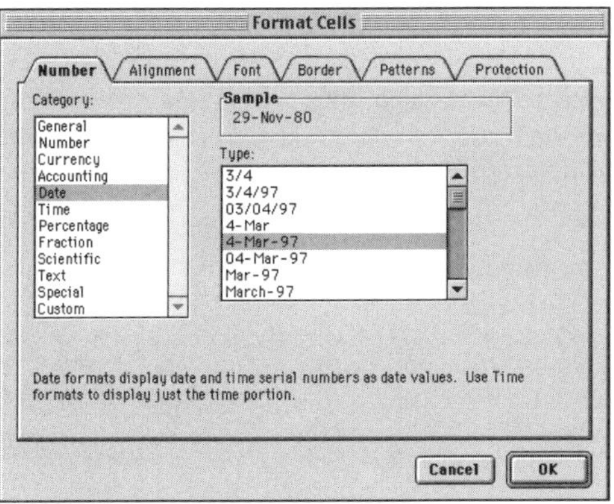

Figure 17-18: Choosing the Date category in the Number tab

5. In the Type list, choose the desired date or time format and click OK.

When you enter a date or time in a format that Excel recognizes, Excel displays the value on the right side of the cell by default. If a value appears on the left side of the cell, Excel has not recognized it as an acceptable date or time value and has instead formatted the entry as text. You should re-enter the value in an acceptable format to get the correct date or time into the cell.

Custom number formats

Besides using the variety of built-in standard formats, you can design your own custom formats. Custom formats are useful for specialized financial or scientific displays of values, or for handling such information as phone numbers, part numbers, or other data that has to appear in a specific format. Figure 17-19 shows some examples of custom formats in columns A, B, and, C.

Data Entered	Custom Format Used	How Data Appears
1505.99596	#.####	1505.9960
23562.7678	$#,##0.0000	$23,562.7678
0.15852	0.00%	15.8520%
3/15/95 14:40	d-mmm-yy h:mm:ss AM/PM	15-Mar-95 2:40:00 PM
2125551212	(###) ###-####	(212) 555-1212
1274542	"Part number" ###-####	Part number 127-4542

Figure 17-19: Examples of custom formats

When working with custom formats, it helps to understand the number format codes Excel uses. These formats are automatically stored in the correct number format category. Whenever you want to access them, open the Format Cells dialog box and choose Custom from the Category list in the Number tab. Table 17-2 explains the function of the most common symbols you use to make custom formats.

Table 17-2
Symbols Used in Custom Formats

Symbol	*Function*
?	Acts as a placeholder for digits in much the same way as zeros. Zeros that are not important are removed and spaces are inserted to keep alignment together.
/	Denotes that the slash symbol is to be used after the integer portion with fractional custom formats. This causes the number to appear as a fractional value, such as 5 ⅔.
0	Acts as a placeholder. You can use this number to display a zero when no number is entered. Also note that decimal fractions are rounded up to the number of zeros that appear to the right of the decimal.

Symbol	*Function*
#	Acts as a placeholder for digits, just as the 0zero does. The difference between # and 0zero as placeholders is that if a number is not entered, no number is displayed. Decimal fractions are rounded up to the number of #s that appear to the right of the value.
General	Denotes the default format for cells that are not formatted.
, (comma)	Marks the thousands position. (Only one comma is needed to specify the use of commas.)
. (decimal)	Marks the decimal point position. For a leading zero, enter a zero to the left of the decimal.
_(underscore)	Followed by the character of your choice, inserts a space the size of the character that follows the underscore before the character itself appears. As an example, if you enter _) to end a positive format, a blank space the size of the parenthesis is inserted. This lets you align a positive number with a negative one that's surrounded by parentheses.
:$_+()	These characters are displayed in the same positions in which they are entered in the number code.
E_E+e_e+	Displays a number in scientific notation. The zeroes or values to the right of the e denotes the power of the exponent.
%	The entry is multiplied by 100 and displayed as a percentage.
@	Takes the role of a format code to indicate where text typed by the user appears in a custom format.
*character	Fills the remainder of the column width with the character that follows the asterisk.
"text"	Displays the text between the quotation marks.
[color]	Indicates that the cell is formatted with the specified color.
\ (backslash)	When this precedes an entry, it indicates a single character or symbol.

Format codes include three sections for numbers and one for text. Semicolons separate the sections. The first section is the format for positive numbers; the second section is the format for negative numbers; the third section is the format for zeros; the fourth section is the format for text.

The section you include in your custom format determines the format for positive numbers, negative numbers, zeros, and text, in that order. If you include only two sections, the first section is used for positive numbers and zeros, and the second section is used for negative numbers. If you include only one number section, all the numbers use that format.

The text format section, if it is there, is always last. If you have text that you always want to include, enter it in double quotation marks. If your format has no text section, the text you enter in the cell is not affected by the formatting.

To create your own custom format, follow these steps:

1. Make a selection and choose Format ➪ Cells, or Control-click the selection and choose Format Cells from the shortcut menu.
2. In the Format Cells dialog box, select the Number tab.
3. Choose Custom from the Category box. From the Type list (see Figure 17-20), choose a custom format that is closest to the one you want. (You can modify it to meet your needs. See Step 4.)

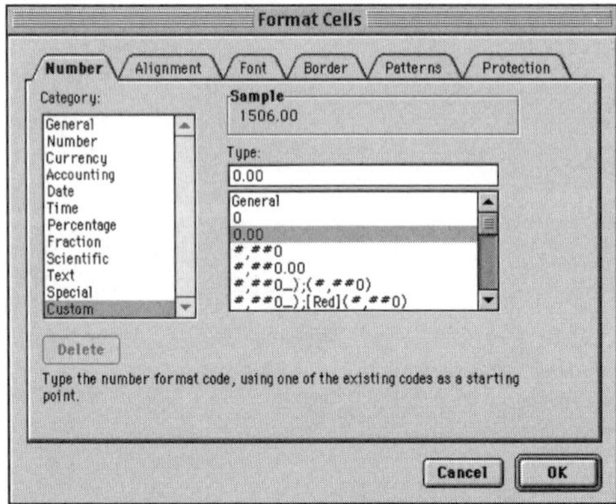

Figure 17-20: The Type list box with the Custom entries

4. Make the desired changes to the format by editing the entry in the Type text box. As you do, if you have anything entered in the selected cell, the sample will reflect that data, giving you feedback as to how your formatting is taking shape in "real life."
5. Click the OK button to save the custom number format.

Remember these points when you create custom formats:

- ✦ Excel uses zeros and number signs as digit placeholders. If you use a zero, the digit is always displayed, and the number sign suppresses the nonsignificant zeros.
- ✦ If you follow an underscore by a character, Excel creates a space the width of the character. For example, if you follow an underscore with a right parenthesis, positive numbers will line up correctly with negative numbers that are enclosed in parentheses.

✦ If you want to set a color for a section of the format, type the name of the color in square brackets in the section. An example is available in the custom format starters.

✦ Add commas to your format so the displayed numbers appear in multiples of 1,000. (The commas that are not surrounded by digit placeholders can be used to scale the numbers by thousands.)

Using the Format Painter

If you've already spent time and effort creating formats in certain areas of a worksheet and want to use them elsewhere, you can easily do so with the format painter. As its name implies, the format painter lets you take an existing format and literally "paint" that format across any other cells in a worksheet. (The same feature is also available in Word.) When you use the format painter, you copy all formatting—including text, number, and alignment formats, and cell shading, color, and borders—from the currently active cell to the range of cells that you paint. The format painter is accessible from the Standard toolbar; look for the button with the paintbrush. Use the format painter to copy the formatting information from one cell to another cell or to a range of cells, or from a range of cells to another range of cells.

To copy formatting from one cell to another cell or to a range of cells, follow these steps:

1. Select the cell that contains the formatting to copy.
2. Click the Format Painter button on the Standard toolbar. Your cursor gains a paintbrush beside it.
3. Click and drag across the range of cells that are to receive the format. (If copying to only one cell, just click that cell.) When you release the mouse button, the format of the original cell is applied to the selected range and your cursor is back to normal.

To copy formatting from a range of cells to another range of cells, follow these steps:

1. Select the entire range of cells that contains the formatting to copy. (Yes, each cell may have different formatting.)
2. Click the Format Painter button on the Formatting toolbar. A paintbrush now appears beside the usual mouse pointer.
3. Click the upper-left cell in the range of cells that should receive the format. When you release the mouse button, the format of the original range of cells is applied to a range of cells of the same size as the original range.

You can copy the format to a larger number of cells. The formatting pattern will simply repeat after the original number of cells. Rather than clicking the upper-left cell, click and drag over all the cells you want to receive the formatting.

Creating Your Own Styles

As this chapter emphasizes, Excel's formatting options give you the power to apply formatting to your worksheets in just about every conceivable manner. If you find yourself applying the same formatting choices repeatedly to different parts of a worksheet, it makes sense to save your formatting choices as a style so that you can easily apply the formatting to a selection of cells. In Excel, a *style* is a collection of formatting options that you apply to a cell or a range of cells.

The nice thing about styles is that if you apply them to your worksheets and subsequently decide to change some aspect of the style, all the parts of your worksheet that use that style will automatically change. For example, if you create a style, use it in half a dozen worksheets, and later change the font used by that style, the font will automatically change in those worksheets.

(If you are accustomed to working with styles in Word, you will find the concept of Excel styles to be similar. However, in Excel you can't format the cells first, then define the style based on those cells.)

You can easily define your own styles by choosing Format ➪ Style. To define the style, follow these steps:

1. Choose Format ➪ Style. (There is no choice in the shortcut menu for this command.) The Style dialog box appears, as shown in Figure 17-21.

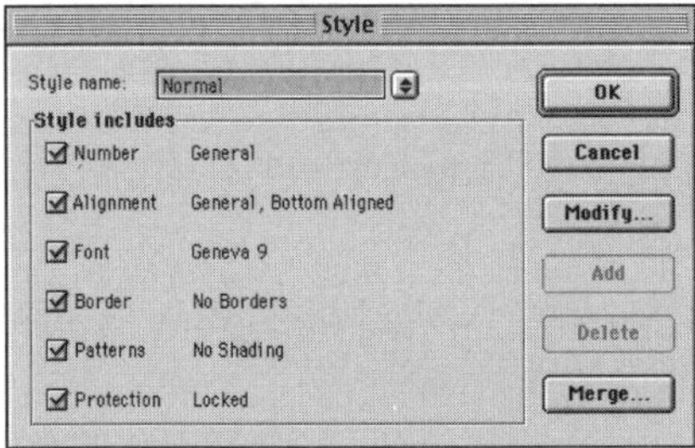

Figure 17-21: The Style dialog box

2. In the Style name box, enter a name for your new style and click the Add button that appears to add the new style to the list.
3. Turn off the check boxes for any of the attributes that you don't want included in the style.

4. If you want to change any of the attributes for the format settings shown in the list, click Modify to bring up the Format Cells dialog box.

   Click any of the tabs in the Format Cells dialog box and change the settings for the formats.

5. When you are finished setting the formats in the Format Cells dialog box, click OK to return to the Style dialog box.

6. Click OK to save the new style.

After your custom style exists, using it is simple. Just select the range of cells to which you want to apply the style and choose Format ➪ Style. In the Style dialog box, click the arrow to the right of the Style name box and drag to the name of your custom style. Click OK to apply the style to the selected range of cells.

Protecting Your Formatting Changes

You can protect cells so their formats and other data cannot be changed. (By default, the cells of a worksheet have protection turned on, but the protection does not take effect until you choose Tools ➪ Protection and choose Protect Workbook from the resulting dialog box.) To make sure that the cells of a worksheet are protected when you turn on overall protection for the workbook, follow these steps:

1. Choose any range of cells that should not be protected. Because the default setting for the cells is to be protected, you want to turn off protection for any cells that you want to retain the ability to change.

2. Choose Format ➪ Cells.

3. Click the Protection tab of the Format Cells dialog box (see Figure 17-22).

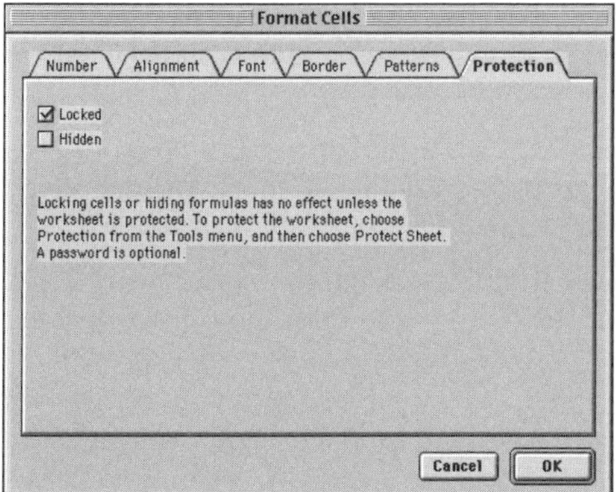

Figure 17-22: The Protection tab of the Format Cells dialog box

4. Uncheck the Locked check box if you want the selected cells to remain unprotected. You can also turn on the Hidden check box to specify that the selected cells' contents do not appear in the formula bar.
5. Click OK and repeat Steps 1 through 4 for every range of cells that should remain unprotected.
6. Choose Tools➪Protection➪Protect Workbook.
7. In the Protect Workbook dialog box, enter a password, if one is desired. If you omit the password, you can still protect the workbook, but others can remove the protection without the use of a password. (Please read the sidebar "Fair Warning.") Also, check the Windows check box if you want to protect the windows in the workbook from being moved or resized.
8. Click OK to implement the protection.

Passwords that you enter to protect a workbook are case-sensitive.

After you have protected the contents of a workbook, you can remove the protection by choosing Tools➪Protection➪Unprotect Workbook. If you entered a password during the protection process, you are asked for the password before Excel will unprotect the document.

Summary

This chapter covered formatting your worksheets. You learned how to use formatting to give a worksheet a more appealing look and to enhance its appearance. We discussed the following topics:

- ✦ You can quickly give a worksheet a professional look by selecting a worksheet range, choosing Format➪AutoFormat, and selecting the desired options.
- ✦ You can easily change row heights and column widths to accommodate your entries by clicking and dragging the column or row header edges, or by choosing the Column or Row commands (as appropriate) from the Format menu.
- ✦ You can apply specific fonts, font sizes, and styles, borders, patterns, and colors to a group of cells or to characters within a cell by choosing Format➪Cells and using the options in various tabs of the Format Cells dialog box.
- ✦ In addition to the variety of standard formats provided with Excel, you can create custom formats for the values you enter in your worksheets.

Fair Warning

If you protect a workbook with a password, *do not, do not, do not* (did we repeat that enough?) forget the password! If you forget the password, you may as well start recreating the workbook from scratch.

Even the technical support people at Microsoft cannot help you get into a workbook that is password-protected when you don't have the password.

Where to go next

- In the next chapter, you learn how you can add graphic objects to your worksheets and your charts.
- You can make charts out of the data in your worksheet. Chapter 19 has the details.

✦ ✦ ✦

CHAPTER 18

Adding Graphics to Worksheets

✦ ✦ ✦ ✦

In This Chapter

Discovering a need for graphics

Inserting graphics into worksheets

Working with graphic objects

Adding text boxes

Using WordArt

✦ ✦ ✦ ✦

Worksheets can be far more than just tables of numbers with a chart added here and there. You can emphasize the points expressed by those numbers, add visual information, and (by means of macro buttons) literally make your worksheets easier for others to use. You can draw lines, circles, rectangles, and squares, and you can add text boxes for anything from short titles to multiple paragraphs of text. You can also make use of clip-art, which is professionally drawn artwork from other programs. If you have an artistic personality (or if your worksheets are facing a demanding audience and you need all the help you can get), you can really get carried away with Excel's graphics.

Discovering a Need for Graphics

Perhaps you hadn't thought of Excel and graphics together. Because Excel is a spreadsheet package, many Excel users crunch numbers with it and leave graphics entirely to drawing programs and artists. If you don't use Excel's graphic capabilities, however, you miss out on some of Excel's best power. From its humble origin years ago as a Macintosh product, Excel provided spreadsheet capability with built-in flexible graphics. Excel 98 really packs a graphics punch with the power to add visual oomph to your work. Figure 18-1 is an example.

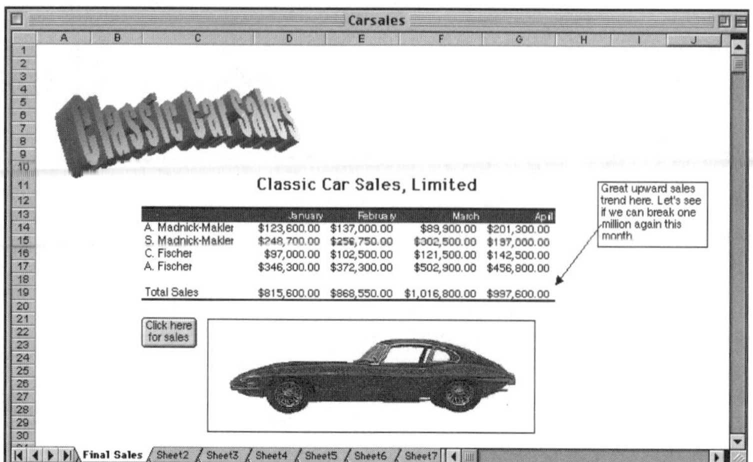

Figure 18-1: A worksheet jazzed up with graphics

In the Figure 18-1 worksheet, the gridlines were turned off and a text box with an arrow was added to describe the point that the numbers in the worksheet are attempting to get across. WordArt was used to create the title. Clip-art was added and a button that runs a macro (to display another worksheet) was drawn. You can add all these effects and more with Excel's graphics features.

Inserting Graphics into Worksheets

You can insert graphics into an Excel worksheet using drag-and-drop, copy and paste, or the Insert ➪ Picture command.

Drag-and-drop is probably the easiest way to insert graphics into a worksheet. Open the folder the graphic is in, drag it into place in the Excel worksheet, and release the mouse button. You can also store your graphics in the Mac's Scrapbook and drag them from there into your worksheet.

Another way to insert graphic files into an Excel worksheet is to use the Insert ➪ Picture command. This lets you pull graphic pictures from files created in other programs without opening the file's folder. To insert graphics with the Picture command, follow these steps:

1. Place the insertion pointer in the cell where you want the upper-left corner of the picture to appear.
2. Choose Insert ➪ Picture ➪ From File. The Insert Picture dialog box appears (see Figure 18-2).
3. In the dialog box, navigate to the folder that contains the clipart or graphics file you want to insert, as shown in Figure 18-2.

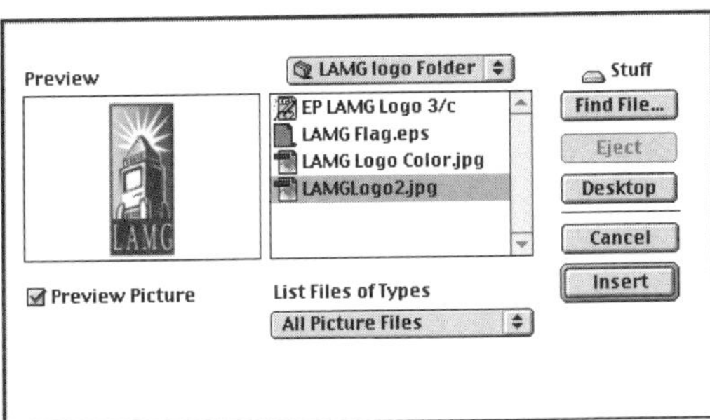

Figure 18-2: The Insert Picture dialog box

4. Click Insert to place the graphic into the worksheet. You can then use the normal sizing and moving methods to change the size or location of the graphic.

To use the copy and paste method, you need to have the program the graphic was originally created in and to follow these steps:

1. Double-click the graphic's file to open the graphic in the program it was created in and select the graphic.
2. Choose Edit⇨Copy (⌘-C).
3. Bring your Excel worksheet forward (launching it if it is not already running). Select the cell or the object where you want the upper-left corner of the graphic to appear.
4. Choose Edit⇨Paste (⌘-V). The graphic appears in the worksheet. You can then use the normal sizing and moving methods to change the size or location of the graphic.

Working with Graphic Objects

With the tools on the Drawing toolbar (see Figure 18-3) you can create your own graphic objects in Excel. If the Drawing toolbar is not displayed, choose View⇨Toolbars⇨Drawing. Another way to open the Drawing toolbar is to Control-click any open toolbar and choose Drawing from the shortcut menu that appears. After the Drawing toolbar is displayed, you can move it by clicking any blank area of the toolbar and dragging the toolbar to a desired location, just as you would move any toolbar.

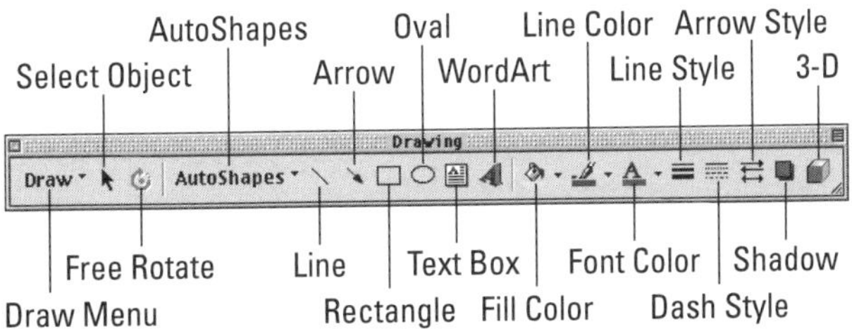

Figure 18-3: The Drawing toolbar

The Excel Drawing toolbar has a variety of drawing tools that help you enhance your worksheets. You can create items from lines, polygons, arrows, WordArt, and even 3-D shapes. Table 18-1 gives the name of each tool and its function.

Table 18-1
The Drawing Toolbar's Tools

Tool Name	*Function*
Draw Menu	Opens a menu of additional commands for drawing-related tasks
Select Arrow	Selection pointer used to select objects
Free Rotate	Rotates a selected object to any degree
AutoShapes	Opens a menu used to add AutoShape graphic objects
Line	Draws straight lines
Arrow	Creates a line with an arrowhead
Rectangle	Draws rectangles or squares
Oval	Draws ovals or circles
Text Box	Creates a text box for word-wrapped text
WordArt	Creates a WordArt object
Fill Color	Changes the fill color for an object
Line Color	Changes the line color for an object
Font Color	Changes the font color for an object
Line Style	Used to change the style of the selected solid line
Dash Style	Used to change the style of the selected dashed line
Arrow Style	Used to change the style of the selected arrow
Shadow	Adds a variety of shadow effects to the selected object
3-D	Adds a variety of three-dimensional effects to the selected object

For a real time-saver, use the shortcut menus while you are working with objects. The shortcut menu that is displayed when you Control-click an object is shown in Figure 18-4. These shortcut menus provide the Cut, Copy, and Paste commands, as well as other commands related to formatting the object.

Figure 18-4: An object shortcut menu

Inserting AutoShapes

One of Excel 98's additions is the capability to add AutoShapes as graphics to your spreadsheets. AutoShapes are groups of ready-made shapes including lines, rectangles, ovals, circles, arrows, flowchart symbols, and callouts. (If you're curious as to where the freeform and freehand tools of earlier Excel versions vanished, they are now part of the AutoShapes collection of graphics.) The worksheet shown in Figure 18-5 contains several graphics created with the AutoShapes menu in the Graphics toolbar.

What Graphic Files Can I Import?

Excel's graphic filters let you import graphic files that have been saved in any of these file formats:

File type	*Filename extension*
Macintosh Picture	PICT
Macintosh MacPaint	PNTG
Tagged Image File Format	TIFF
Encapsulated PostScript	EPS
CompuServe GIF	GIF
JPEG Filter	JPG
Portable Network Graphics	PNG
Windows Metafile	WMF
Enhanced Windows Metafile	EMF
Windows Bitmap	BMP

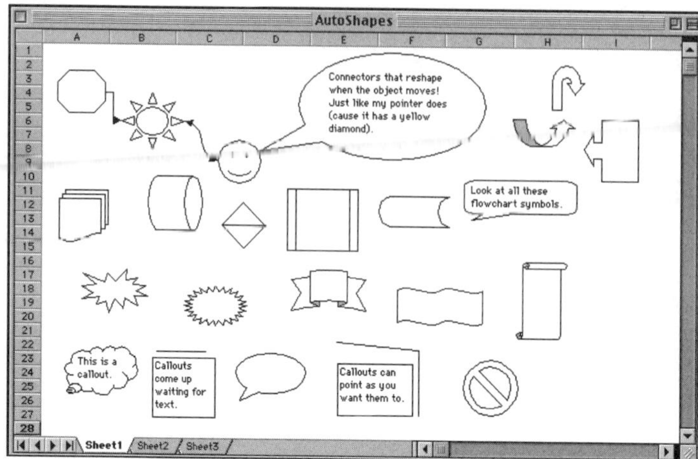

Figure 18-5: Examples of AutoShapes in an Excel worksheet

To add an AutoShapes graphic to a chart, follow these steps:

1. If the Drawing toolbar isn't visible, Control-click any visible toolbar and select Drawing from the shortcut menu (or choose View➪Toolbars➪Drawing) to display the toolbar.

   By the way, we didn't forget the hotkey for "Drawing." For whatever reason, Microsoft didn't add hotkeys for any of the toolbar menu options.

2. On the Drawing toolbar, click AutoShapes and move your mouse to the name of the desired category of shapes to see the shape. Click the desired shape. Your cursor becomes a cross hair.

3. To add a shape in a preset size, click the worksheet or chart where you want to add the shape. To make the shape your own size, click and drag the shape to the desired size.

You can align a shape with the gridlines of cells by holding the ⌘ (Command) key while dragging the shape. You can set the shape in perfect proportion by pressing the Shift key while dragging the shape.

When the AutoShapes menu opens, you are presented with seven options: lines, connectors, basic shapes, block arrows, flowcharts, stars and banners, and callouts. Figure 18-6 shows the shapes that are available under each of these menu choices.

Given that well over 100 shapes are provided, to describe how to place each shape in detail would take more text than you'd likely care to read. But you can easily view a help screen specific to the use of any AutoShape tool. Press Shift-F1 to bring up the help balloon mode, then point to a shape in the AutoShapes menu. A help balloon that explains how to draw or manipulate the chosen shape appears.

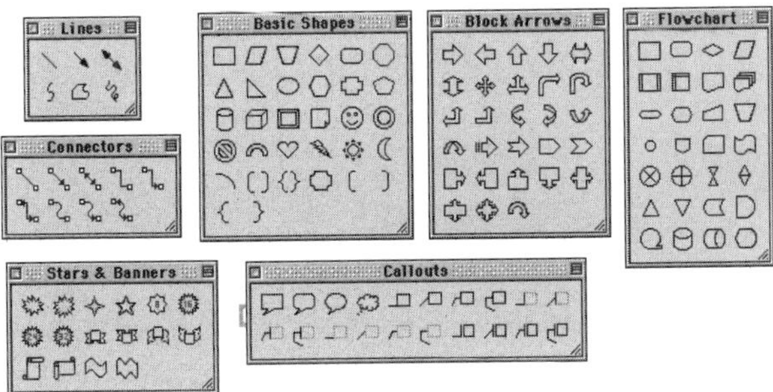

Figure 18-6: Available AutoShapes

Drawing lines, arcs, ellipses, and rectangles

The Drawing toolbar lets you create lines, arcs, ellipses, and rectangles easily. You can combine these basic drawing elements to create more complex shapes. You draw an object by clicking the desired tool to select it, then clicking and dragging in the worksheet to place the item.

While drawing lines, ellipses, and arcs, press Shift as you drag to keep the lines vertical, at a 45° angle, or horizontal. You can also hold down the ⌘ (Command) key to align the corners of the object with a cell's gridlines.

When you click a tool to select it, that tool is effective only while you draw one shape with it. If you plan to create multiple shapes with a tool, double-click it to select it. A double-click-selected tool remains effective until you select another tool.

Lines

To draw a line, click the Line tool to select it, click the beginning location for the line, and then drag to the ending location. To draw a line with an arrowhead, click the Arrow tool, click the point where the line should begin, and drag to the point where the arrowhead should appear. After you've drawn your arrow, with it still selected, you can click the Arrow Style list and select an arrow style. Your arrow will take on that style. You can turn any line or arrow into any arrow style by selecting it and choosing a style.

Squares and rectangles

To draw a square or a rectangle, click the Rectangle tool to select it, click a corner of the rectangle, and drag to size the rectangle as desired. To draw a square, press Shift while you drag to size the square.

Ovals (ellipses) and circles

To draw an Oval (ellipse), click the Oval tool to select it, click an edge of the ellipse, and drag to size the ellipse as desired. To draw a circle, press the Shift key while you drag to size the circle.

Filled objects

To fill an object, click the desired object to select it, click the down arrow to the right of the Fill Color button (in the Drawing toolbar), and choose a desired fill color. You can also apply a fancy line to an object. Again, select the object and choose a style from the pop-up Line Style or Dash Style buttons.

Arcs

To draw an arc, open the AutoShapes menu on the Drawing toolbar, choose Basic Shapes, and select the arc tool. Next, click and drag to create the arc where you want it on the worksheet. Drag the yellow handles on the arc to create more or less of the arc shape.

Many shapes are customizable. Look for yellow diamond-shaped handles, then drag the handles to experiment and discover what you can do.

Selecting and grouping objects

Most of the items that you add while drawing are considered objects. This includes text boxes, graphics brought in from other sources, and shapes you draw. Selecting an object is the key to working with it. Once you select it, you can easily manipulate it. You can have as many objects as you want in a worksheet, and you can manipulate as many as are selected.

To select the object you want to work with, click it when the cursor turns into crossed double-headed arrows along with the arrow pointer. You can then change the object's orientation, shape, color, or pattern by using the Drawing toolbar's Color, Style, Shadow, and 3-D tools. You can also select a single object by Control-clicking the object, which calls up the shortcut menu so you can choose Format AutoShape. In the Format AutoShape dialog box, select a tab and assign attributes.

To select multiple objects, press Shift while you select each object. To unselect an object, press Shift and click the object again. Even after you've let go of the Shift key, you can press it again to select or unselect another object.

Don't Let Others Mess with Your Graphics

If you want to keep others from changing your graphics, you can protect them by protecting cell contents and scenarios.

By default, all graphics are protected when you turn on cell protection. However, you can exclude individual graphics from protection. To do so, before turning on protection, Control-click a graphic, choose Format AutoShape (or Format WordArt) from the shortcut menu, and click the Protection tab. (To affect several graphics at once, first press Shift as you click each graphic, then Control-click any one of the selected graphics.) In the Protection tab, uncheck Locked and click OK.

Once you have excluded any graphics you don't want to protect, select Tools⇨Protection ⇨Protect Sheet (or Protect Workbook). Make sure Graphics is checked. While in the Protection dialog box, you can also choose to protect the data within all the cells and to protect your scenarios. You can also enter a password, if desired. If you leave the password text box blank, the worksheet will be protected from changes, but you won't need a password to turn off the protection. If you do enter a password, don't forget it! (Or be prepared to re-create the work when you want to make changes.) Click OK to enable the chosen protection. Of course, you can always go back and select Tools⇨Protection⇨Unprotect Sheet (or Unprotect Workbook).

By the way, you can also exclude cells from protection the same way you exclude graphics: Select the cells, Control-click, and select Format Cells to uncheck Locked in the Protection tab. Then protect the entire sheet or workbook.

You can also group objects together, which is useful when you want to change the colors for a group of objects or move or align them as a group. All the objects that you include in the group act as one object; if you perform an action on one of the items, the action affects all the items in the group. To group objects, follow these steps:

1. Select the objects you want to group. Remember to press Shift while you select each object.
2. Control-click any one of the selected objects and choose Grouping⇨Group from the shortcut menu that appears.

Using Bring To Front and Send To Back

Each object you draw is drawn on a layer on top of the last object. As you draw and position multiple objects, you may need to place one object on top of another (for example, a company logo may consist of a circle on top of a rectangle). If the wrong object appears on top, you can adjust its placement by using the Bring To Front or Send To Back options, which are available from the object's shortcut menu. Control-click the desired object and choose Order⇨Bring to Front to make the object appear on top of another object. You can also Control-click the object and choose Order➪Send to Back to make the selected object appear underneath the other object. You can use the Bring Forward and Send Backward options on the same menu to move a selected object one step closer to the top or to the bottom of a stack of selected objects. Figure 18-7 shows the effects of using the Bring To Front and Send To Back tools.

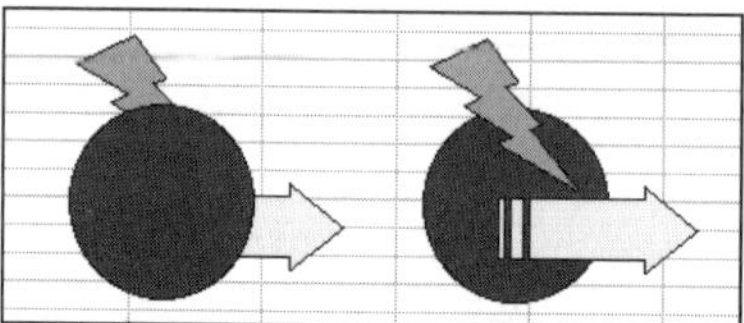

Figure 18-7: Left—the original layers. Right—Send To Back sends the circle to the back and Bring To Front brings the arrow to the front.

Moving and copying objects

As you work, you may need to move or copy objects. You have two options to move or copy objects: you can either cut or copy and then paste, or you can click and drag. To move or copy objects with the Cut or Copy commands, follow these steps:

1. Select the object(s) that you want to move or copy.
2. Choose Edit➪Cut (⌘-C) or click the Cut button on the Standard toolbar to remove the object and place it on the Clipboard. Choose Edit➪Copy if you prefer to leave the existing object intact while copying it to a new location.
3. Move the cursor to the location where you want to place the object.
4. Choose Edit➪Paste (⌘-V) or click the Paste button on the Standard toolbar to place the Clipboard information in the worksheet. The cell that contains the insertion pointer becomes the upper-left corner of the entry.

The click-and-drag method for moving objects is equally simple. Simply click the object and (while holding down the mouse button) drag it to the area where you want it placed. Release the mouse button to place the object. This is the equivalent of cutting and pasting the object. You can copy an object by pressing Option as you click and drag it.

To remove an object, select it and press the Delete key or choose Edit➪Clear.

Resizing objects

You resize objects in Excel in the same way that you resize objects in other programs. First, select the object you want to resize. You will see small squares, called handles, appear around the object. To resize the object's width, drag one of the side handles to the desired width. (The arrows on the cursor are a clue as to what you can do.) To change the height of the object, drag a top or bottom handle.

If you want to resize the length and width of the object simultaneously, drag a corner handle. However, be aware that these resizing techniques distort your object. To resize without distortion, press Shift as you resize. This constrains the object to its original proportions.

Formatting objects

You can apply a variety of formatting options to an object by selecting it and then applying the Color, Style, Shadow, or 3-D options from the Drawing toolbar. You can accomplish the same thing by Control-clicking the object, choosing Format ⇨ AutoShape, and using the various options on the Colors and Lines tabs of the dialog box.

Formatting Colors

To change the color of an object, click the object to select it and click the arrow to the right of the Fill Color button in the Drawing toolbar. A Colors dialog box appears (see Figure 18-8) and you can choose the desired color.

Figure 18-8: The Colors dialog box

If you want to change the patterns or the effects for the color, click Fill Effects at the bottom of the dialog box to open the Fill Effects dialog box shown in Figure 18-9.

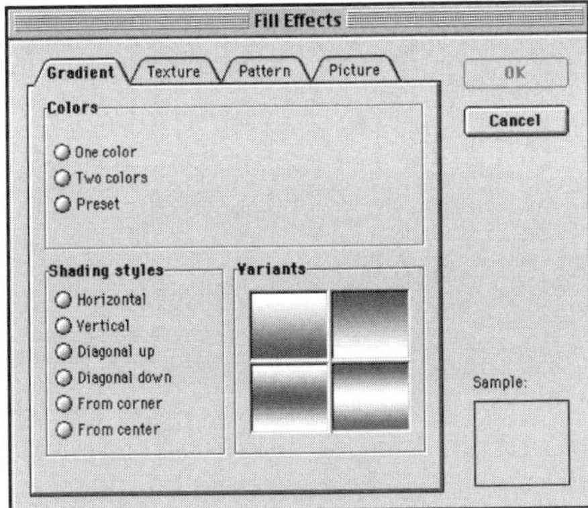

Figure 18-9: The Fill Effects dialog box

Using the tabs of this dialog box, you can change the colors and shading used for the gradient, the texture of the colors, the pattern, and whether a picture should be used as a fill. Under the Gradient tab, you can select the number of colors (one or two), the shading style, and a shading variant. Using the Texture tab, you can select one of 24 possible preset textures, or you can click the Other Texture button and choose an image file, which appears for use as a texture, in the dialog box. Using the Pattern tab, you can choose from one of 48 possible patterns. And the Picture tab lets you choose an image file to serve as a picture contained within the object. Once you make the desired selections in the Fill Effects dialog box and click OK, the changes are applied to the object.

Formatting Lines

You can change the style, thickness, and colors of lines using either of two methods. You can select the object and use the Line Color, Line Style, Dash Style, and Arrow Style buttons of the Drawing toolbar. Each button reveals a menu of possible colors or styles from which you can select the desired option.

You can also Control-click the desired object and choose Format ➪ AutoShape from the menu. In the Format AutoShape dialog box that appears, click Colors and Lines. Figure 18-10 shows what the Colors and Lines tab looks like when an arrow is selected.

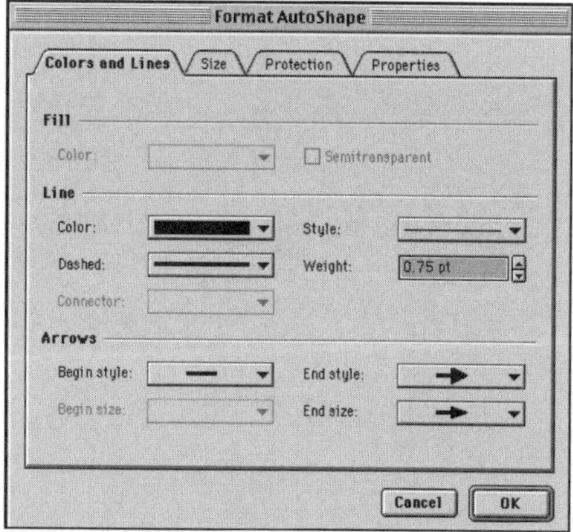

Figure 18-10: The Colors and Lines tab of the Format AutoShape dialog box when you select an arrow

In the Fill Area of the dialog box, you can choose a fill color for enclosed objects such as rectangles and ovals. However, the Fill Color toolbar button (discussed earlier) offers more options including the capability to change patterns and gradients.

Hiding Objects for Better Spreadsheet Performance

If you have a lot of graphic objects in your worksheet, Excel is forced to redraw the graphics as you scroll within the worksheet. This extra effort can slow your system's speed, especially on hardware that meets only the minimum configuration for Excel.

You can speed worksheet display by hiding the graphic objects from view or by displaying them as graphic placeholders. Choose Tools⇨Preferences and click the View tab. In the Objects area of the dialog box, turn on the Show Placeholders option to show the graphic objects as placeholders (empty white rectangles) or turn on the Hide All option to hide the graphic objects. When you need to see the objects again, you can return to this dialog box and turn on the Show All option.

In the Line area of the dialog box, you can change line colors, styles, weight (the thickness of the line), and whether the line should be dashed or solid. In the Arrows portion of the dialog box, you can choose styles and sizes for the arrowheads. Once you make the desired selections within the dialog box, click OK to apply them to the arrow.

Adding Shadows and 3-D Effects

You can use the Shadow and 3-D Effects buttons of the Drawing toolbar to add shadows or three-dimensional effects to graphic objects. To do so, click the desired object to select it, click the Shadow or 3-D button on the Drawing toolbar, and then select the desired effect from the submenu that pops up.

Adding Text Boxes

Excel lets you place text boxes in your worksheets. Text boxes make excellent titles for worksheets because they float in a layer over the worksheet. Therefore, you can position a title of any size without affecting worksheet row or column positions. You can edit and format text in these boxes using typical word processing techniques. To add a text box to your worksheet, follow these steps:

1. In the Drawing toolbar, click the Text Box button. Notice that the mouse pointer changes to a thin arrow.
2. Click and drag to form the box in which you will enter the text. To create a square text box, press Shift as you drag. If you want a box aligned with the grid, hold down the ⌘ (Command) key as you drag. When the text box reaches the desired size release the mouse button.

3. The insertion pointer now appears inside the text box (see Figure 18-11), which permits you to begin entering text. You can continue typing until the end of the text box. As you type, the text scrolls up so part of it is hidden. To make all the text visible, select the text box and drag a handle to make the box larger to accommodate the extra text.

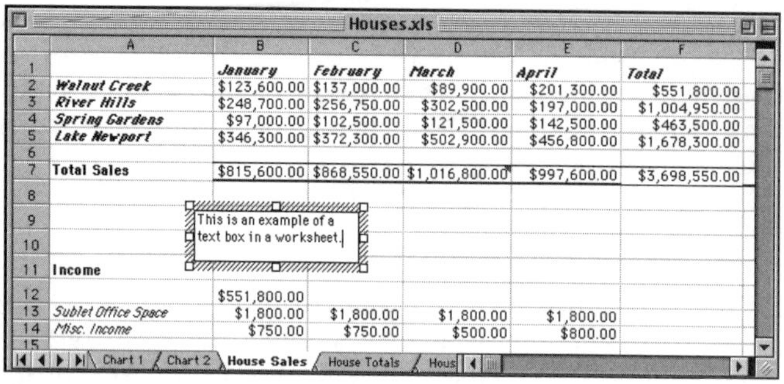

Figure 18-11: A text box added to a worksheet

Editing text

To edit text within a text box, use the normal navigation methods. To move the cursor, use the arrow keys or the mouse. Select any text to format it or type over it. Use the Delete key to delete any unwanted entry.

Formatting text

You can also format the text within a text box just as you format any other text in Excel or in Word. You can select the entire text or select individual characters. After selecting the text or characters, use the buttons and lists available on the Formatting toolbar, or use Control-click and call up the Format Text Box from the shortcut menu. If you Control-click the box without any text selected, you affect the entire contents of the box. If you first select characters within the text box and then Control-click, your changes only affect the selected text. When you use Control-click, the dialog box contains only the Font tab, as shown in Figure 18-12. Using the options on this tab, you can change your font, font style, and font point size, as well as turn on special effects such as underlining, bold, italics, strikethrough, superscript, subscript, outline, and shadow. With the Color menu you can also change the font's color. Remember, however, that this dialog box changes the font, not the text box's background. The Fill Color button on the Drawing toolbar affects the background.

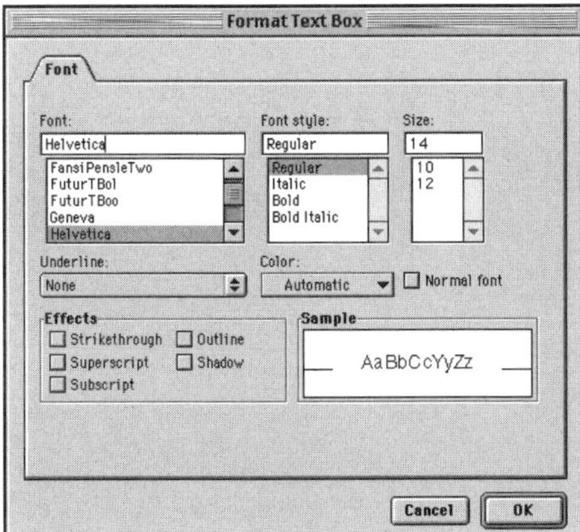

Figure 18-12: The Font tab of the Format Text Box dialog box

Rotating text

Excel also lets you rotate text within a text box, but to a lesser extent than you can rotate text within a cell. Figure 18-13 shows how text in a text box can rotate in Excel.

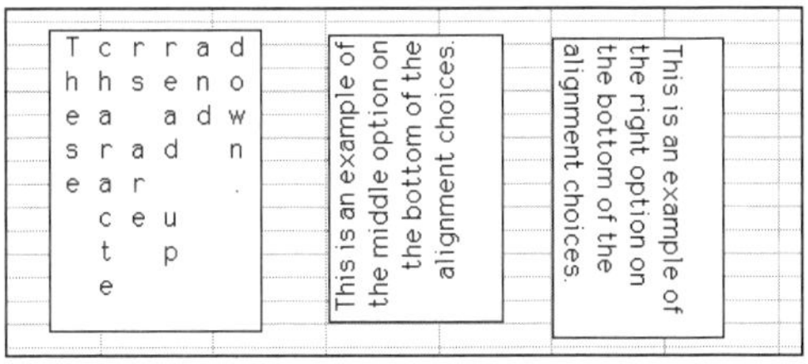

Figure 18-13: Examples of rotated text in boxes

To rotate text in a text box, follow these steps:

1. After creating the text box and entering the text, select the text box and Control-click the edge of the box (not the text within the box) and choose Format Text Box to open the Format Text Box dialog box.
2. Choose the Alignment tab (see Figure 18-14). The Text Alignment area lets you control both the horizontal and vertical alignment of the text within the text box.
3. In the Orientation area, click the desired orientation for the box.

You can use the Automatic Size option in the Alignment tab to size your entries automatically.

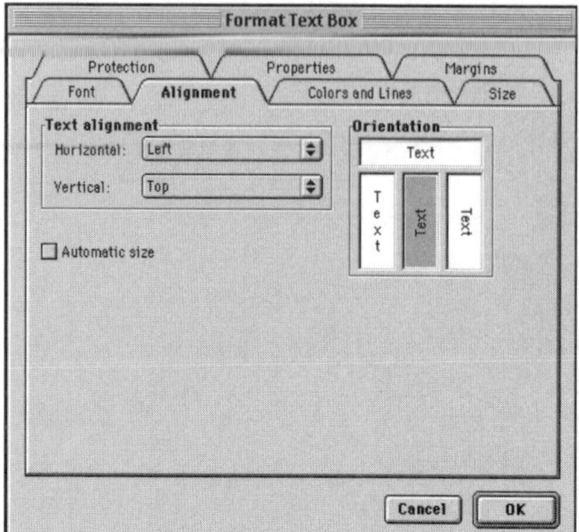

Figure 18-14: Changing text alignment in the Alignment tab when you select a text box

Using WordArt

Microsoft WordArt is an applet (actually, it is an object linking and embedding (OLE) application) that lets you create special effects using text. You can enter any text, then bend and stretch the text, or fit the text into a variety of different shapes. You can also add three-dimensional effects. This text, or WordArt, is inserted in your document as a graphic. Figure 18-15 shows an example of what you can do with WordArt.

Figure 18-15: Examples of WordArt

To add WordArt to a worksheet, first make the Drawing toolbar visible (if it isn't already) by Control-clicking any visible toolbar and selecting Drawing or by choosing View➪Toolbars➪Drawing. In the Drawing toolbar, click the WordArt button to call up the WordArt Gallery dialog box, which is shown in Figure 18-16.

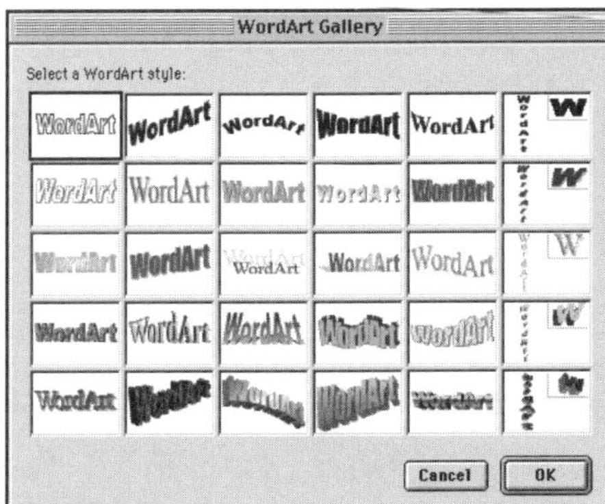

Figure 18-16: WordArt Gallery dialog box shows the available styles of WordArt.

Click a desired style to select it and then click OK. The Edit WordArt Text dialog box shown in Figure 18-17 appears.

Replace the default text with your own text by typing over this preselected message. Select a font and font size from the pop-up menus at the top of the dialog box. If you want bold or italic applied to the text, click their respective buttons.

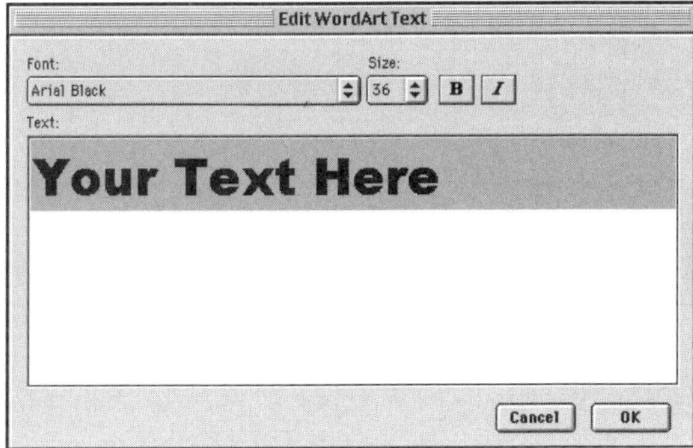

Figure 18-17: The Edit WordArt Text dialog box displays the WordArt text.

Changes you make to the selected font will override the chosen selection in the WordArt Gallery dialog box. You can always reopen the dialog box by clicking the Gallery button on the WordArt toolbar.

Click OK in the Edit WordArt Text dialog box to place the completed WordArt into your worksheet. The WordArt toolbar appears, as shown in Figure 18-18.

Figure 18-18: WordArt added to a worksheet

As with other graphic objects, you can move and size WordArt using standard techniques.

Additionally, the WordArt toolbar lets you change the appearance of a WordArt object in several ways. Figure 18-19 shows the parts of the WordArt toolbar and Table 18-2 gives the name of each tool and its function.

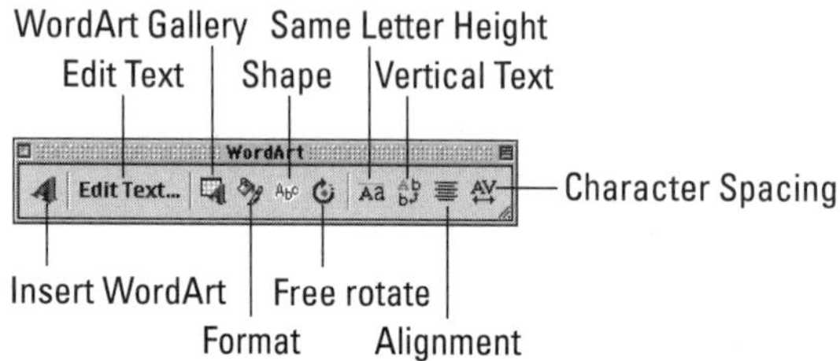

Figure 18-19: The parts of the WordArt toolbar

Table 18-2
The WordArt Toolbar's Tools

Tool Name	***Function***
Edit Text	Displays the Edit WordArt Text dialog box so you can change the text.
WordArt Gallery	Displays the WordArt Gallery dialog box so you can change the overall shape and effect.
Format WordArt	Displays the Format WordArt dialog box.
Shape	Opens a dialog box of available WordArt shapes.
Free Rotate	Rotates the selected WordArt object to any degree.

Tool Name	*Function*
Same Letter Heights	Sets all letters in WordArt to the same height; click again to toggle the text height back.
Vertical Text	Stacks text in the WordArt object vertically.
Alignment	Aligns the text left, center, or right within the dimensions of the WordArt object.
Character Spacing	Applies a variety of character spacing to the text of the WordArt object.

The WordArt toolbar performs many WordArt tasks. You can change the shape and rotation, modify the character spacing, and display the text vertically.

Changing colors and sizes

The Format WordArt button opens the Format WordArt dialog box shown in Figure 18-20. Here you can change the text colors and modify the size and rotation of the object.

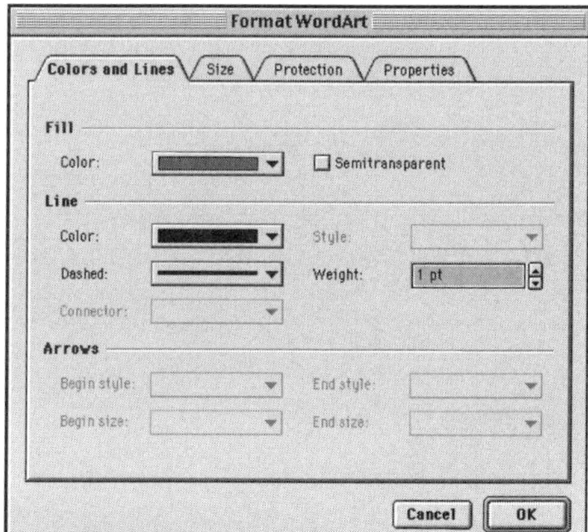

Figure 18-20: The Format WordArt dialog box with the Colors and Lines tab visible

The Fill color affects the color of the letters, whereas the Line color affects the color of the letter shading. In the Size tab, you can change the size and rotation of the object. Note, however, that it is easier to change the size by selecting and dragging the object and the rotation by using the WordArt toolbar's Free Rotate button.

Changing shapes

You can change the overall shape of a WordArt object. To do so, click the WordArt Shape button in the WordArt toolbar. When you do this, a window of shapes appears, as shown in Figure 18-21.

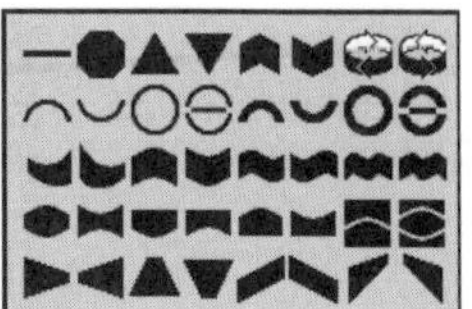

Figure 18-21: Dialog box containing the available WordArt shapes

The different shapes that you see here represent the way the WordArt text will appear in the worksheet. As you make a selection, the effect is immediately applied to the text.

Rotating objects

Finally, you can use the Free Rotate tool to rotate a selected object to any degree. Select the desired WordArt object, click the Free Rotate button in the WordArt toolbar, and then click and drag a corner of the WordArt object in the direction you want it to rotate.

Summary

In this chapter, you learned about using Excel's graphics capabilities to add pictures and other graphic objects to a worksheet. The following points were discussed:

- ✦ You can insert graphics in a worksheet with the Insert menu's Picture command.
- ✦ You can use a variety of tools from Excel's Drawing toolbar to draw different shapes in a worksheet.
- ✦ You can select multiple objects to manipulate them as a group and to apply formatting, color, or other design choices.
- ✦ You can add text boxes to worksheets by using the Text Box tool on the Drawing toolbar.

Where to go next

- ✦ For adding visual oomph to your worksheet based presentations, graphics and charts often go hand in hand. You find full details in Chapter 19.

✦ ✦ ✦

CHAPTER 19

Working with Excel Charts

This chapter details Excel's powerful capabilities for displaying and printing charts. You can create charts that emphasize numeric trends, support data analysis, and help supply presentation-quality reports. Excel provides you with a rich assortment of formatting features and options for changing and enhancing the appearance of your charts.

In This Chapter

Learning about charts

Embedding charts and chart sheets

Creating a sample chart

Saving and printing charts

Understanding the chart parts

Working with charts

Working with chart types

Understanding how Excel plots a chart

Learning About Charts

Charts graphically represent worksheet data. A collection of values from worksheet cells you select can be illustrated in charts as columns, lines, bars, pie slices, or other types of markers. Figure 19-1 shows some examples of typical charts. The appearance of the markers that are used to represent the data varies, depending on the type of marker you choose. In a bar or column chart, the markers appear as columns; in a line chart, the markers appear as lines composed of small symbols. The markers in a pie chart appear as wedges of the pie.

Most charts (with the exception of pie charts) have two axes: a horizontal axis called the *category axis* and a vertical axis called the *value axis*. Three-dimensional charts add a third axis (called the *series axis*). Figure 19-2 shows an example of a three-dimensional chart.

Charts also contain *gridlines*, which provide a frame of reference for the values displayed on the value axis. You can add descriptive text to a chart, such as a title, and you can place the text in different locations. Your charts can also contain legends, which indicate which data are represented by the markers of the chart.

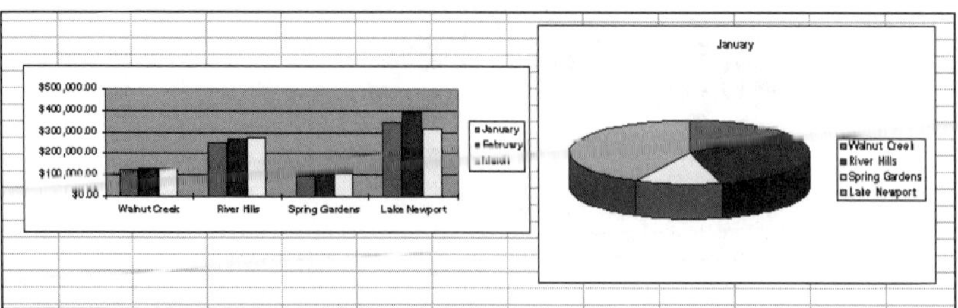

Figure 19-1: Examples of typical charts

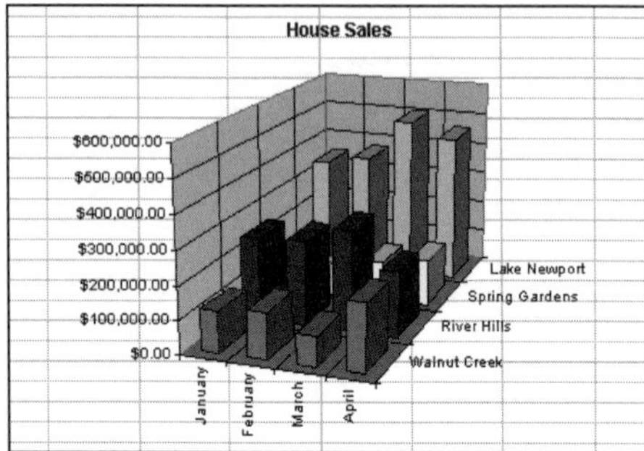

Figure 19-2: An example of a 3-D chart

Excel makes adding charts simple. The Office Assistant offers to provide a Chart Wizard whenever you add a new chart to a worksheet. If you accept the help, the Chart Wizard, like all Office wizards, produces the desired results by asking a series of questions. During each step of the wizard process, the dialog box displays a sample of the chart so you can see how your choices in the dialog box affect the final result.

Embedding Charts and Chart Sheets

You can add charts to Excel worksheets in one of two ways: as embedded charts or as chart sheets. Embedded charts are inserted into an existing worksheet page; hence, the page can show worksheet data with the chart. Figure 19-3 shows an embedded chart.

Houses

	A	B	C	D	E	F
1		*January*	*February*	*March*	*April*	*Total*
2	*Walnut Creek*	$123,600.00	$137,000.00	$89,900.00	$201,300.00	$551,800.00
3	*River Hills*	$248,700.00	$256,750.00	$302,500.00	$197,000.00	$1,004,950.00
4	*Spring Gardens*	$97,000.00	$102,500.00	$121,500.00	$142,500.00	$463,500.00
5	*Lake Newport*	$346,300.00	$372,300.00	$502,900.00	$456,800.00	$1,678,300.00
6						
7	Total Sales	$815,600.00	$868,550.00	$1,016,800.00	$997,600.00	$3,698,550.00
8						
9						
10						
11	Income					
12		$551,800.00				
13	*Sublet Office Space*	$1,800.00	$1,800.00	$1,800.00	$1,800.00	
14	*Misc. Income*	$750.00	$750.00	$500.00	$800.00	
15						
16	Total Income	$2,550.00	$2,550.00	$2,300.00	$2,600.00	
17						
18						
19	*Gross Receipts*	$818,150.00	$871,100.00	$1,019,100.00	$1,000,200.00	

House Sales w.chart / House Graph (2) / Chart 1 / Chart 2 / House Sales / House Totals / House Graph

Figure 19-3: An embedded chart

Chart sheets, on the other hand, are charts that are placed on separate sheets of a workbook, apart from any worksheet data. Figure 19-4 shows a chart added as a chart sheet.

Embedded charts work best when you need to display or print the chart along with worksheet data; chart sheets work best when all you want to show is the chart. Whether you use embedded charts or chart sheets, the data used to produce the chart is always linked to the worksheet. Therefore, as you change the data in the underlying worksheet, the chart changes to reflect the new data.

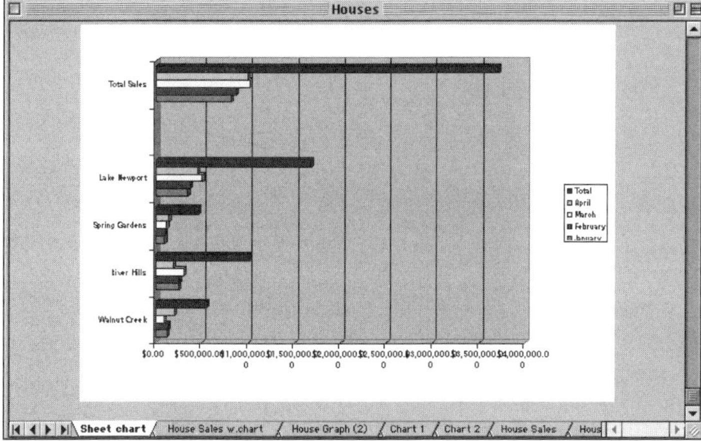

Figure 19-4: An example of a chart sheet

Creating an embedded chart or chart sheet

You can add an embedded chart to an existing worksheet page or create a chart that resides separately on a chart sheet by performing the following steps:

1. In the worksheet, select the data you want to chart. Include any labels that should be used as legends in the chart.
2. Select Insert ➪ Chart or click the Chart Wizard button on the Standard toolbar. When you do this, your Office Assistant appears and asks you whether you'd like help with this feature. Along with the Assistant, the first Chart Wizard dialog box appears, showing the available chart types. If you say yes to the help, the Assistant tells you about the Chart Wizard. If you decline, the Assistant leaves you with the Chart Wizard.
3. Choose a desired chart type, click the Next button, and follow the directions in the successive Chart Wizard dialog boxes to specify the data range, the chart's format, and the desired options for category labels and for the legend text. (The Chart Wizard dialog boxes are described in detail in a later section of this chapter.)
4. The last Chart Wizard dialog box (labeled Step 4 of 4), is where you choose to embed your chart or have it appear on a new sheet. The default is As object in, which embeds the chart. By default, Excel expects to place the chart on the sheet that contains the charting data. However, you can choose another sheet from the pop-up list.

   To place the chart on a separate worksheet, select As New Sheet and name the new sheet in the text box provided.
5. Click Finish.

Using the Chart Wizard

With either method of adding a chart, the Chart Wizard displays a series of dialog boxes that help you define precisely how the chart will appear. The first Chart Wizard dialog box appears, as shown in Figure 19-5.

In this dialog box, you can select the chart type that you want from one of the 14 available chart types. For each chart type selected in the Chart type list box (at the left side of the dialog box), you can choose any of the available sub-types from the right side of the dialog box.

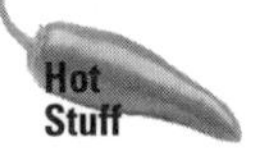

To help you decide upon a chart type, you can easily preview the potential chart. Just select the type and sub-type, and then click the Press and Hold to View Sample button (at the lower-right corner of the dialog box).

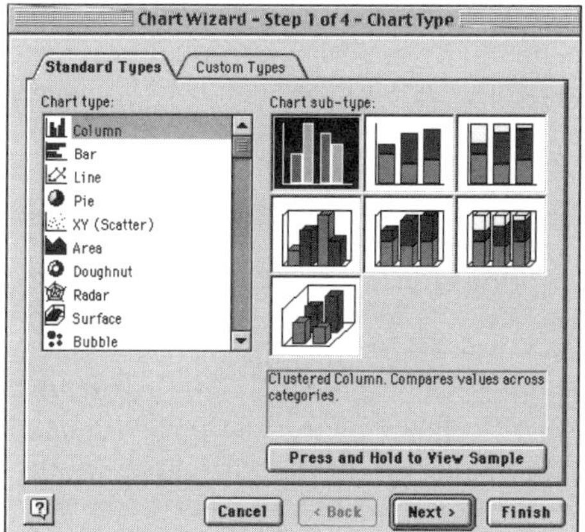

Figure 19-5: The first Chart Wizard dialog box

If none of the dozens of standard type and sub-type combinations suit your taste, you can click the Custom Types tab and choose from one of 20 available custom chart types. (For more specifics on the available chart types, see "Working with Chart Types" later in the chapter.)

Once you've selected the desired chart type and sub-type, click Next to proceed.

After you click the Next button, the second dialog box, shown in Figure 19-6, appears. You can use this dialog box to define the range of cells within the worksheet that is used as the underlying data for the chart. When you select a range in the worksheet and then use the Chart Wizard, the range automatically appears in the dialog box, as shown in Figure 19-6. If for any reason you want to change the range, you can do so by typing a different range.

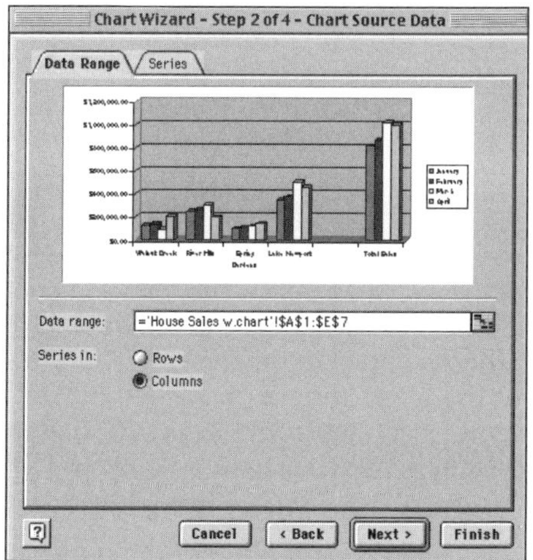

Figure 19-6: The second Chart Wizard dialog box asks for the range of cells to be plotted.

You can use the Series in option to determine whether the data series appears as rows or columns in the chart, and you can click the Series tab to add or remove a data series from the chart. (For more specifics on how you can use data series in charts, see "Understanding How Excel Plots a Chart" later in the chapter.) When done choosing the desired data range and series options, click Next to proceed.

The third Chart Wizard dialog box appears, as shown in Figure 19-7. In this dialog box, you can turn on or off a variety of options for the chart you've selected. The dialog box is divided into six tabs: Titles, Axes, Gridlines, Legend, Data Labels, and Data Table. (In case the terminology used throughout this dialog box is unfamiliar, you learn more about these terms throughout the remainder of this chapter.) You can use the Titles tab to specify titles for the chart, for the category axis, and for the value axis of the chart. On the Axis tab, you can turn on or off the display of the category axis and the value axis. On the Gridlines tab, you can specify whether gridlines are added to each axis of the chart. The Legend tab lets you show and position the chart's legend. The Data Labels tab lets you add labels to the data points plotted by the chart, and the Data Table tab lets you add an optional data table below the chart. As you change these various settings, you can look at the preview of the chart that is visible in the dialog box, to make sure you obtain the desired look for the chart. When done selecting the desired chart options, click Next to proceed.

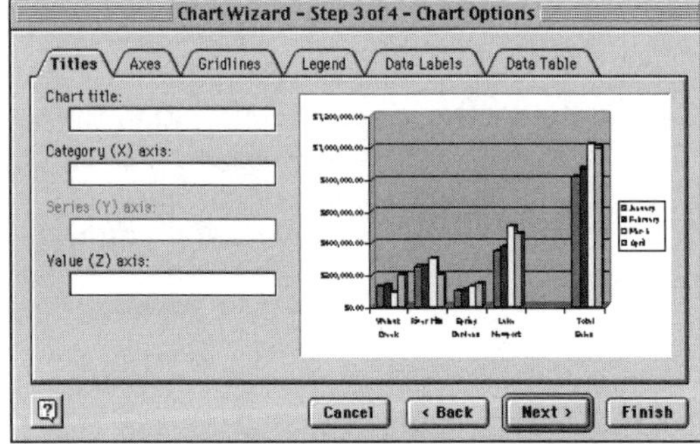

Figure 19-7: The third Chart Wizard dialog box provides various formatting options for the chart.

The fourth Chart Wizard dialog box appears, as shown in Figure 19-8. Here you specify whether the chart should be inserted as an embedded chart in the existing worksheet or placed into a separate chart sheet. If you click the As new sheet button, you can enter a name for the new sheet or accept the default name (Chart1, Chart2, and so on). If you click the As object in button, you can then choose the desired sheet by name where the chart should be placed; the default is the same worksheet where you selected the chart data. Click Finish, and your desired chart appears in the chosen location. Remember that, if you embed the chart in an existing worksheet, you can select the entire chart and drag it to any location in that worksheet.

Figure 19-8: The fourth Chart Wizard dialog box asks where the chart should be placed.

After a chart exists, you can run the Chart Wizard on this chart at any time by clicking the chart to select it, and then clicking the Chart Wizard button on the Standard toolbar.

Creating a Sample Chart

The examples shown throughout this chapter make use of the Houses workbook, which you can find at the IDG Books Web site (`www.idgbooks.com`). You can use the House Totals page to generate the charts shown throughout this chapter, and you can duplicate the examples by opening the House Sales workbook in Excel. Figure 19-9 shows the House Totals page of the Houses workbook.

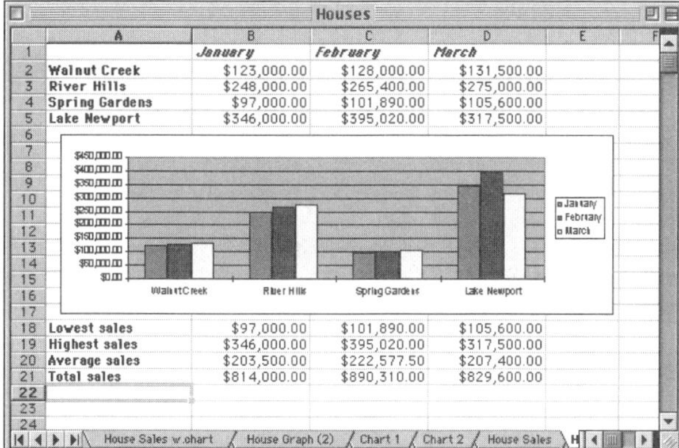

Figure 19-9: The House Totals page of House Sales workbook in Excel

After you open the workbook and move to the House Totals worksheet, follow these steps to get an idea of how you can easily create charts within Excel:

1. Click in cell A1 and drag to cell D5 to select the range that contains the house sales for all four developments for January, February, and March.
2. Choose Insert ⇨ Chart. The first Chart Wizard dialog box appears (shown earlier, in Figure 19-5).
3. This dialog box asks for a desired format for the chart. Leave the desired chart type selected as Column, choose the first sub-type shown in the dialog box and then click Next. In a moment, the second Chart Wizard dialog box appears (shown earlier, in Figure 19-6).
4. Because the range matches the cells that you selected in the worksheet, there's nothing to do here. Click Next in the dialog box to display the third Chart Wizard dialog box (shown earlier in Figure 19-7). Click Next to accept all the default options for the chart.
5. (In this case, you insert a chart as a separate sheet; you can just as easily insert the chart onto the existing worksheet page.) In the last dialog box (shown earlier in Figure 19-8), click As new sheet, enter **House Chart** in the text box, and then click Finish to create the chart and add it to the workbook. Your sample chart should resemble the one shown in Figure 19-10.

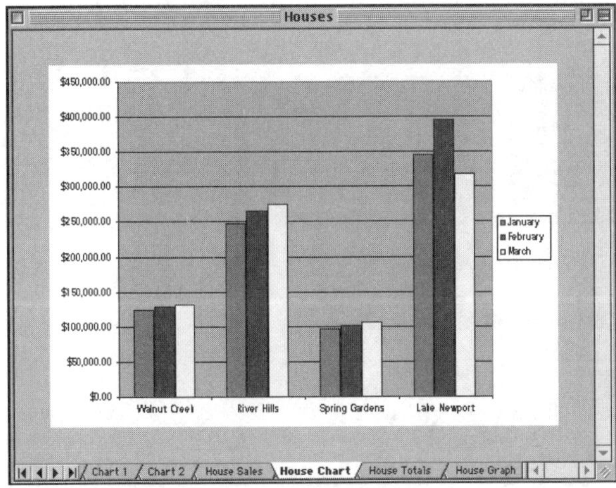

Figure 19-10: The House Chart worksheet

Saving and Printing Charts

Because charts are stored with worksheet pages, saving and printing charts is no different from saving and printing worksheets. When you save the worksheet by choosing File➪Save (⌘-S), the chart is saved along with the worksheet. You can print the chart by activating the page that contains the chart and choosing File➪Print (⌘-P). The Print dialog box that appears contains the same options you have for printing worksheets.

To print pie charts in the proper proportion to fit a single sheet of paper, first choose File➪Page Setup, and then click the Chart tab of the dialog box that appears. Turn on the Scale to Fit Page option.

Understanding the Parts of a Chart

Before you explore the options that Excel offers for creating charts, you should know the parts of a chart and the terminology used to describe these parts. Figure 19-11 shows the parts of a two-dimensional chart.

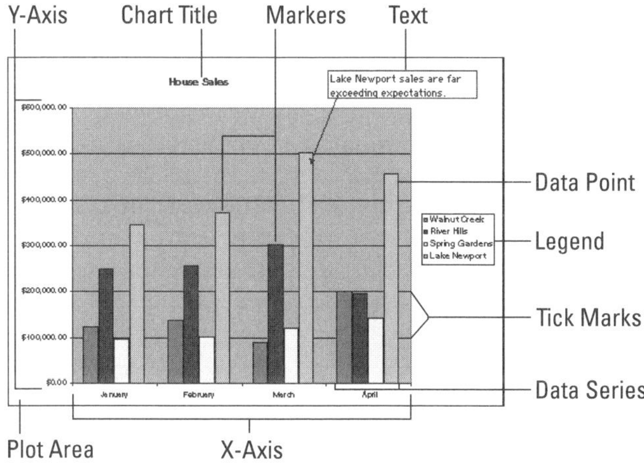

Figure 19-11: The parts of a two-dimensional chart

Three-dimensional charts have an additional axis that two-dimensional charts do not have. Three-dimensional charts also have a wall, a floor, and corners. The additional parts of a three-dimensional chart are shown in Figure 19-12.

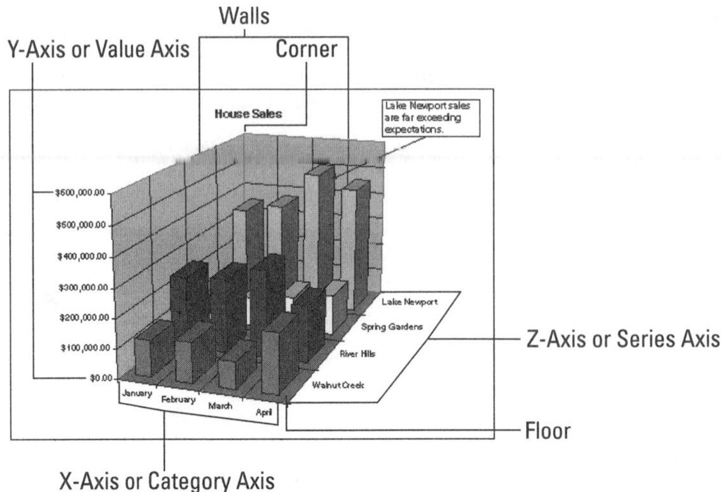

Figure 19-12: The parts of a three-dimensional chart

The following parts can be found on two- and three-dimensional charts:

✦ **Chart**—The chart is the entire area contained within the chart sheet (on charts placed in separate sheets) or in the chart frame in an embedded chart.

✦ **Plot area**—The plot area contains the chart's essential data: the value axis, the category axis, and all the markers that indicate the relative values of your data.

✦ **Markers**—Markers are the bars, lines, points, or pie wedges that represent the actual data in the chart. The form of the markers depends on the type of chart you choose. In a pie chart, the markers are wedges, or slices, of the pie. In a line chart, the markers are solid lines; although at some sharp angles, the lines may appear jagged or broken due to the limitations of screen resolution. In a column chart, such as the one shown in Figure 19-10, the markers appear as columns.

Each set of markers in the chart represents a set of values within the worksheet. The set of values represented by the markers is referred to as a *data series*. If a chart displays data from more than one data series, each data series is represented by a different pattern or symbol. In Figure 19-10, for example, the January data is one data series, and the February data is another. Data series are further differentiated by the patterns of shadings of the columns.

If you selected a range in the worksheet that contains just one row or column of data, the resulting chart contains just one data series. In a chart with a single data series, Excel takes any label in the extreme left column or top row of the selected range and automatically suggests that name as a title for the chart by default.

- **Chart title**—The title is a text label that Excel places as a title within the chart.
- **Axis**—An axis is the horizontal or vertical frame of reference that appears in all types of charts except pie charts. In two-dimensional charts, the horizontal X-axis is called the category axis because categories of data are normally plotted along this line. The vertical Y-axis is called the value axis because values are normally shown along this line. With three-dimensional charts, a series axis is added to show multiple data series within the chart.
- **Tick marks**—Tick marks are reference marks that separate the scales of the value axis and the categories of the category axis.
- **Text**—Excel lets you create text labels as titles and as data labels (associated with data points). You can have unattached, or free-floating, text that you can place anywhere in the chart.
- **Data series**—A data series is a collection of data points, such as one month's sales for a housing development.
- **Data point**—A data point is a single piece of information inside any data series. In the example shown earlier in Figure 19-10, one month's sales for a specific housing development is a single data point.
- **Series name**—You can assign a series name to each series of data contained within a chart. Excel automatically assigns default series names based on headings entered within your worksheets.
- **Gridlines**—Gridlines are reference lines that extend the tick marks across the entire area of the graph.
- **Legends**—A legend defines the patterns or shadings that are used by the chart markers. A legend consists of a sample of the pattern followed by the series name (or the category name, if the chart displays only one data series). If you include labels as series names in the top row or the left column of the selected worksheet range, Excel can use these names in the legend.
- **Arrows**—These are lines with arrowheads that can be moved and sized as desired.

Working with Charts

Excel charts are object-oriented. This means that when you need to change the appearance of an object within a chart, the easiest way to do so is to Control-click the object and choose the desired options from the dialog box or menu that appears. You can also double-click any part of a chart and be taken directly to the chart's formatting options. Users of older versions of Excel may notice a significant change in the ways in which you make modifications to charts. In older versions, you would double-click the chart, and Excel's menus would change to reflect specialized chart options.

Selecting parts of a chart

It's simple to change the parts of a chart. Just double-click the part to bring up the relevant dialog box, and then make the changes. Or, you can Control-click any part, and then make your choices from the object-specific shortcut list that appears. In most cases, the choices from the shortcut menu open up the same dialog box that double-clicking the object brings up, so double-clicking the chart part is the most efficient way to go.

If, for some reason you don't want to use the mouse to select parts of your chart, you can use the arrow keys. The left-arrow and right-arrow keys first move you among items in the same class of objects (such as markers) and then from class to class (such as from the markers to the legend to the axis and so on). When you select an object, it is marked with square handles. While the object is selected, the name of the object also appears on the left side of the formula bar. Figure 19-13 shows a set of markers selected in a chart—the marker name would also be seen in the formula bar.

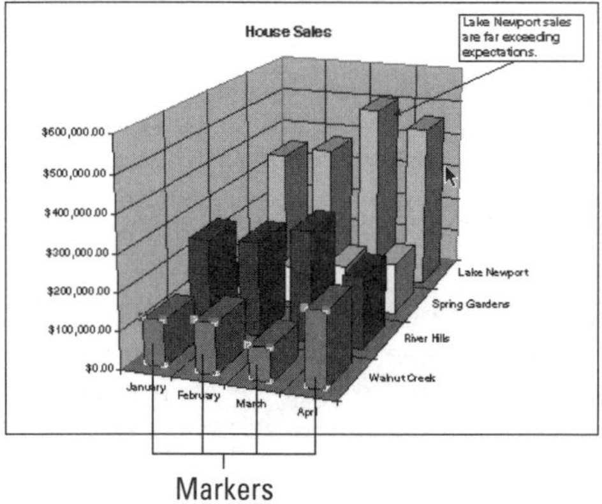

Figure 19-13: A set of markers selected in a chart

Working with the Chart toolbar

You can make use of the Chart toolbar to add new charts or to change existing charts. Figure 19-14 shows the Chart toolbar. If the Chart toolbar is not visible, you can bring it into view by Control-clicking any visible menu and selecting Chart or by choosing View ➪ Toolbars ➪ Chart. Table 19-1 describes this toolbar's buttons.

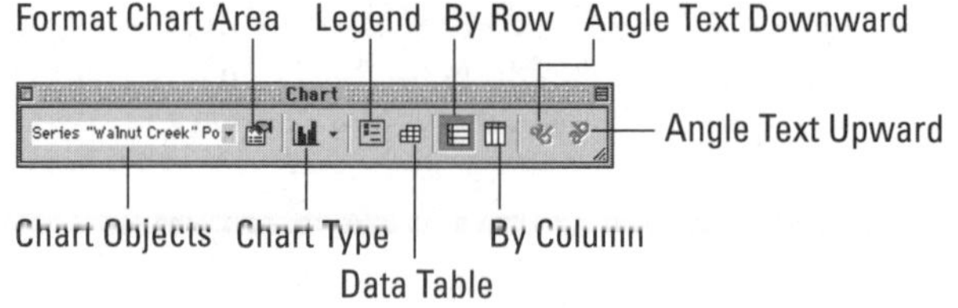

Figure 19-14: The Chart toolbar

Table 19-1
Chart Toolbar Buttons

Button	*Function*
Chart Objects	Lets you select any part of the chart by choosing it from the list box.
Format Chart Area	Displays the Format Chart Area dialog box, which lets you apply formatting to the selected chart area.
Chart Type	Selects a chart type for the chart.
Legend	Adds or removes the legend from the chart.
Data Table	Adds a data table to the chart.
By Row	Arranges the series data by row.
By Column	Arranges the series data by column.
Angle Text Downward	Arranges selected text object downward.
Angle Text Upward	Arranges selected text object upward.

Adding titles

Text boxes containing titles are typically used with charts to help describe the purpose of the chart or to clarify the purpose of the various chart axes. You can add titles to a chart by performing the following steps:

1. Control-click the chart and select Chart Options from the shortcut menu that appears, and then click the Titles tab (see Figure 19-15).

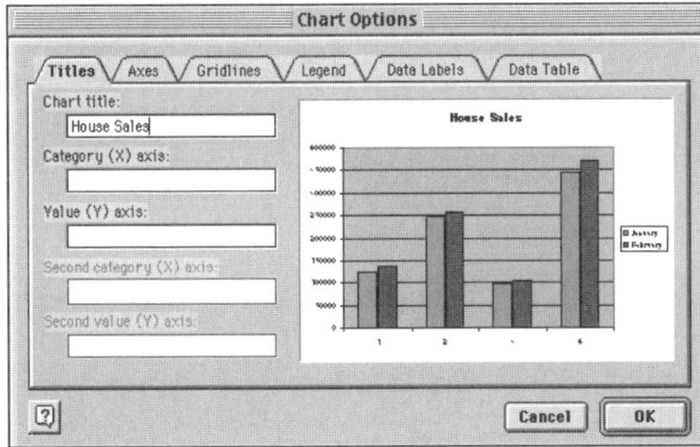

Figure 19-15: The Titles tab of the Chart Options dialog box

2. In the dialog box, shown in Figure 19-15, enter the desired titles in the text boxes and then click OK. Excel inserts text boxes for each title you add, and you can format the text by using the steps under the "Formatting text" section.

Adding unattached text

At times, you may want to add text that is not attached to a title or to a specific axis. Such text is referred to as unattached text. You can add unattached text to a chart by displaying the Drawing toolbar, clicking the Text Box button, and then clicking and dragging in the chart to create a text box of the desired size. The area you drag over defines the text area. When you release the mouse, an insertion point appears in the text box, and you can type the desired text. You can always resize the text box later by dragging its handles.

Formatting text

With all the text you can have in text boxes, you may want to change the formatting properties—the fonts and styles used—to something other than the default text formats. You can format the text in your charts by performing the following steps:

1. Control-click the text you want to format and choose Format Chart Title (for titles), Format Legend (for legends), or Format Text Box (for unattached text) from the shortcut menu.
2. In the dialog box that appears, click the Font tab to reveal the options shown in Figure 19-16.

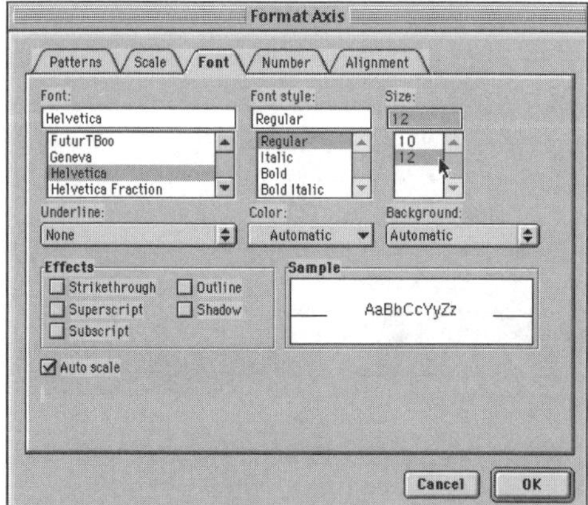

Figure 19-16: The Font tab of the Format Axis dialog box

3. Choose the desired font, font style, and font size by clicking each. You can also choose underlining, color, and background. For special text effects you can select strikethrough, superscript, subscript, outline, and/or shadow. When you are finished selecting the desired options, click OK to place them into effect.

Formatting chart axes

Excel lets you enhance the appearance of the various axes that you use in your charts. You can change the font and modify the scale. You change the format of any chart axis by Control-clicking the axis you want to format and choosing Format Axis from the shortcut menu. The Format Axis dialog box appears, as shown in Figure 19-17.

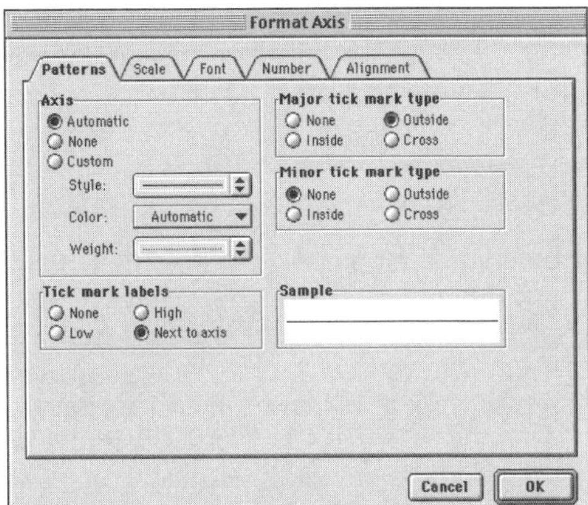

Figure 19-17: The Patterns tab of the Format Axis dialog box

The resulting dialog box contains five tabs, which you can use to change various formatting aspects of the axis. Use the options in the Patterns tab to change the patterns you use for the axis, the tick mark labels, and the types of tick marks. The Scale tab options enable you to change the values that you use to create the axis scale. The Font tab contains options to modify the font of the axis. The Number tab contains number formatting by category so you can choose the desired formatting for numbers along an axis, and the Alignment tab lets you choose an orientation for the text.

Adding legends

If a chart does not have a legend by default, you can add one at any time by Control-clicking the chart, choosing Chart Options, clicking the Legend tab, and checking Show Legend. After you add a legend to the chart, you can change its appearance by double-clicking the legend or by Control-clicking it and choosing Format Legend from the shortcut menu. Either method brings up the Format Legend dialog box, which contains tabs for Patterns, Font, and Placement of the legend. Use the options on the Patterns tab to change the patterns the legend uses to identify the markers in the chart. The Font tab contains options to modify the legend's fonts. The Placement tab lets you specify where in the chart the legend appears (top, bottom, left, right, center, or corner). Actually, because the legend is just another object in the chart, you can also move the legend by dragging it to any desired location within the chart.

Adding gridlines

To add gridlines to an existing chart, Control-click the chart, and then select the Gridlines tab in the Chart Options dialog box that appears. In the Gridlines dialog box that appears, you can choose between major or minor gridlines along either the category axis or the value axis. Major gridlines are heavier lines, widely spaced. Minor gridlines are fine lines, closely spaced. After you make the desired options and click OK, the gridlines appear within the selected chart.

Customizing a chart's area

You can add visual pizzazz to a chart by customizing the default settings for the chart's area. You can change the background colors, the borders, and the fonts used throughout the chart. Control-click in any blank area of the chart and choose Format Chart Area from the shortcut menu. Alternatively, click in any blank area of the chart to select the entire chart (handles appear around the entire chart), and then choose Format ⇨ Selected Chart Area. The Format Chart Area dialog box appears, as shown in Figure 19-18. The dialog box has multiple tabs from which you can choose all sorts of options. (If the chart is embedded, you see three tabs labeled Patterns, Font, and Properties. If the chart is on a separate sheet, you see two tabs labeled Patterns and Font.)

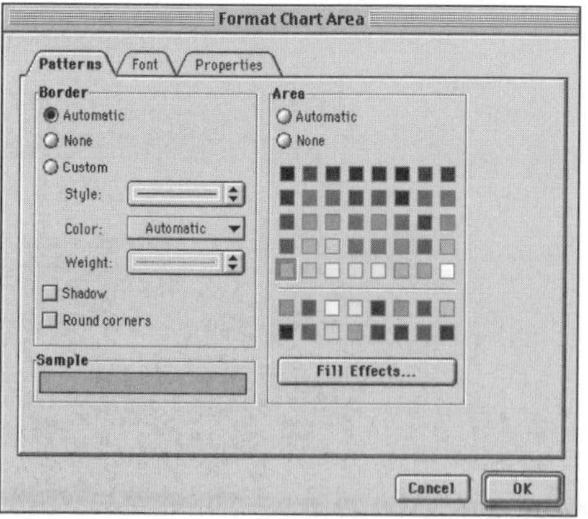

Figure 19-18: The Patterns tab of the Format Chart Area dialog box

In the Patterns tab of the Format Chart Area dialog box, you can click the Custom radio button to choose your own style, color, and weight for the border. Checking the Shadow option adds a shadow to the border and Round corners gives you Mac-like rounded corners so your border looks less boxy. In the Area section of the Patterns tab, you can choose a background color. Selecting Automatic sets the color to the default, which is usually white. Selecting None establishes no background color. To add color, click one of the Color boxes. To add a fancier background, such as a pattern or gradient, click Fill Effects, and then choose a desired pattern or effect.

This Font tab sets your font for the entire chart (which is over-ridden when you custom-choose a font for a specific chart area). Choose a font, font style, and font size. Select underlining, color, and background if you want. Then select any special font effects, such as strikethrough, superscript, subscript, outline, and/or shadow.

On the Properties tab (which appears if the chart is embedded), you can select options that determine whether the chart will move and resize with the underlying cells, whether the chart should print when the worksheet prints, and whether the chart should be locked (protected against changes) if the worksheet is locked.

After you finish selecting the desired options, click OK and the chart takes on the chosen effects.

Working with Chart Types

Excel offers several different chart types. Each of these chart types has sub-types that you can also select. The following list describes the types of charts, and how they can best be used.

Area charts—Show the significance of change during a given time period. The top line of the chart totals the individual series, so area charts make it visually apparent how each individual series contributes to the overall picture. Area charts emphasize the magnitude of change as opposed to the rate of change. (If you want to emphasize the rate of change, use line charts instead.)

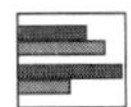

Bar charts—Use horizontal bars to show distinct figures at a specified time. Each horizontal bar in the chart shows a specific amount of change from the base value used in the chart. Bar charts visually emphasize different values, arranged vertically.

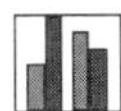

Column charts—Very much like bar charts, using columns to show distinct figures over a time period. The difference is that the markers in column charts are oriented along a horizontal plane, with the columns running vertically up or down from a base value used in the chart.

Line charts—Perfect for showing trends in data over a period of time. Like area charts, line charts show the significance of change, but line charts emphasize the rate instead of the magnitude of change.

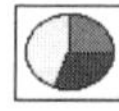

Pie charts—Show relationships between the pieces of a picture. They also can show a relationship between a piece of the picture and the entire picture. A pie chart can display only one series of data at a time because each piece of a pie chart represents part of a total series. If you have a large number of series to plot, however, you are probably better off with a column chart because a pie crowded with slices is difficult to interpret.

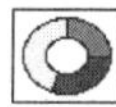

Doughnut charts—Show relationships between pieces of a picture, as do pie charts. The difference is that the doughnut chart has a hollow center.

Radar charts—Show the changes or frequencies of a data series in relation to a central point and to each other. (Every category has an axis value that radiates from a center point. Lines connect all data in the same series.) Radar charts can be difficult to interpret, unless you're accustomed to working with them.

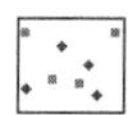

Scatter charts—Show relationships between different points of data, to compare trends across uneven time periods, or to show patterns as a set of X and Y coordinates. These charts are commonly used to plot scientific data.

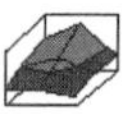

Surface charts—Show trends in values across two dimensions in a continuous curve.

Bubble charts—Compare sets of three values. In appearance, these are similar to scatter charts, with the third value interpreted by the size of the bubbles.

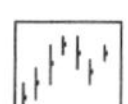

Stock charts—Also known as open-hi-lo-close charts. They are used to display the day-to-day values of stocks, commodities, or other financial market data. Stock charts require series containing four values to plot the four points (open, high, low, and close).

Cylinder charts—Column charts with the columns appearing as cylindrical shapes.

Cone charts—Column charts with the columns appearing as cone shapes.

Pyramid charts—Column charts with the columns appearing as pyramid shapes.

An important decision for you to make is which type of chart will work best to get the desired point across. Excel offers 20 different chart types. All the available chart types can be two-dimensional, and nine of the available chart types can be three-dimensional. When you create a chart by using the Chart Wizard, Excel asks you which chart type you want to use.

You also may want to change the chart type of an existing chart. Follow these steps when you want to change the type of an existing chart:

1. Control-click in an empty space on the chart and choose Chart Type from the shortcut menu. Or, if you prefer not to Control-click, select the chart and choose Chart ⇨ Chart Type. Either way, the Chart Type dialog box appears, as shown in Figure 19-19.

2. In the Chart type list at the left, choose the desired chart type.
3. In the Chart Sub-type area at the right, choose a desired sub-type. To preview the sub-type, click the button that aptly says Press and Hold to View Sample.
4. Once you have made your final type and sub-type selection, click OK.

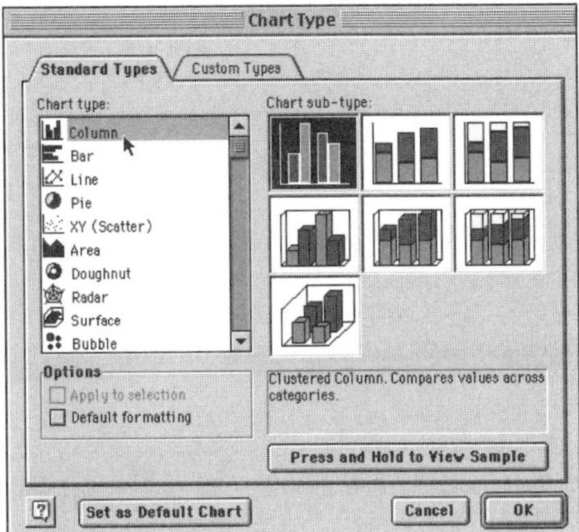

Figure 19-19: The Standard Types tab of the Chart Type dialog box

The exact appearance of the Sub-type tab will vary, depending on which type you select. Figure 19-20 shows the available sub-types that appear when you choose a pie chart.

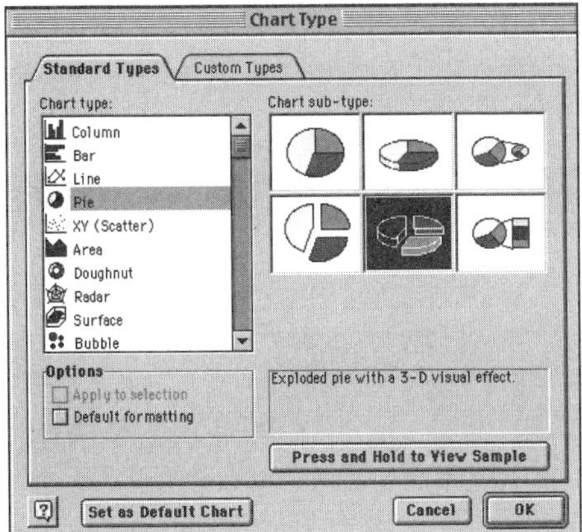

Figure 19-20: The available sub-types for a pie chart

In the Chart Type dialog box shown in Figure 19-20, note the presence of the Apply to selection option in the lower-left corner. By default, the chart type you've selected applies to the entire chart. If you select a single data series before selecting the Chart Type command, you will have the option of applying the chart type to the selected data series as opposed to the entire chart.

You can create combination charts of your own by applying different chart types to different data series. You can also use the Chart Wizard to select a Combination chart type, but you gain more flexibility by selecting each series and applying the types individually.

If you need to change the type of chart but not the chart sub-type, you can also use the Chart toolbar. To display the Chart toolbar, Control-click a visible toolbar and select Chart, or choose View⇨Toolbars⇨Chart. Click the Chart Type arrow button to drop down a list of chart types, and then click a chart type in the list. If you select an individual data series before using the Chart Type list box in the Chart toolbar, your selection gets applied to the individual data series.

Understanding How Excel Plots a Chart

When you select a group of cells and create a new chart, Excel follows specific steps to plot the chart. It first organizes the values contained within the selected range into a data series, based on the responses that you gave in the Chart Wizard dialog boxes. Then it plots the data series in the chart.

As an example, consider the chart shown in Figure 19-21. In this chart, the blue markers are based on one series of data, the sales for January. The red (dark) markers are based on another series of data, the sales for February. The yellow (lightest) markers represent March sales. In the same chart, dollar amounts are plotted along the value (Y) axis, and subdivision names are plotted along the category (X) axis. The chart values appear as dollars because the worksheet values are formatted in dollars. Excel obtains the category axis labels from cells A2 through A5 of the worksheet shown earlier in Figure 19-9, which contains the names of the subdivisions.

The chart shown in Figure 19-21 is actually the same one you created earlier (which is the one in Figure 19-10). If it isn't still open, either open it or replot the chart again by selecting cells A1 through D5 in the House Totals worksheet. Then choose Insert⇨Chart. Click Finish in the first Chart Wizard dialog box to accept the default options.

The exact points that Excel uses to graph the data are contained in a series formula that Excel builds for you. A series formula is similar to other formulas in that you can edit it from within the formula bar. To see the formula, select the chart marker by clicking the desired group of markers (or by pressing the left- or right-arrow key until the group is selected). Selecting one marker selects all the markers in that group. When you select a group of markers, Excel places small rectangles inside them.

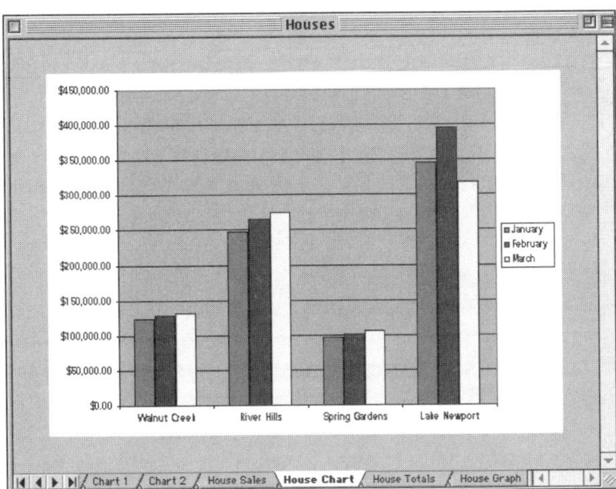

Figure 19-21: A chart based on three data series

As an exercise, select the markers representing January by clicking any of the markers for January. When the markers are selected, the series formula appears in the formula bar, as shown in Figure 19-22.

Excel uses a special function called the series function to build the data series for each set of markers in the chart. If you click the second set of markers in the chart, the series formula in the formula bar changes to reflect the points that Excel uses for the second data series.

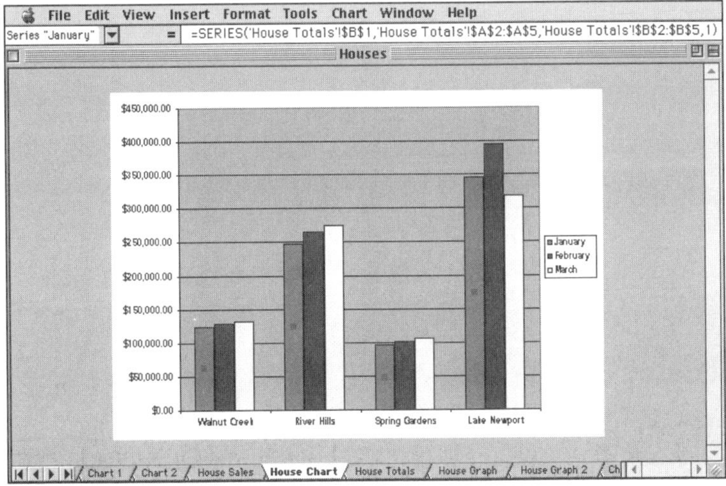

Figure 19-22: The series formula for January sales

Excel can use named ranges from a worksheet rather than absolute cell references. If you create a chart that uses absolute references and later insert rows or columns in the worksheet so the data referred to by the chart is no longer in the same location, the chart will be unable to plot the data. The result will be a chart with zero values, or even worse, incorrect data. If you use named ranges in the series formula for the chart, Excel can find the data, even if you insert rows or columns in the worksheet.

It is important to understand how Excel builds a chart automatically because, in some cases, Excel's assumptions may not be what you want, and you can make changes to adjust for those assumptions. For example, when you tell Excel to create a chart and you accept the default entries regarding the data series in the Chart Wizard dialog boxes, Excel plots the data based on certain default assumptions. One significant decision Excel makes is whether a data series should be based on the contents of rows or columns. Excel assumes that a chart should contain fewer data series than data points within each series. When you tell Excel to create the chart, Excel examines your selected range of cells. If the selected range is wider than it is tall, Excel organizes the data series based on the contents of rows. On the other hand, if the selected range is taller than it is wide, Excel organizes the data series based on the contents of the columns.

To illustrate this operation, consider the worksheet shown in Figure 19-23. In this example, the selected range of cells to be plotted is wider than it is tall. With this type of selection, Excel uses any text found in the left-most columns as series names. Text labels in the top row are used as categories, and each row becomes a data series in the chart.

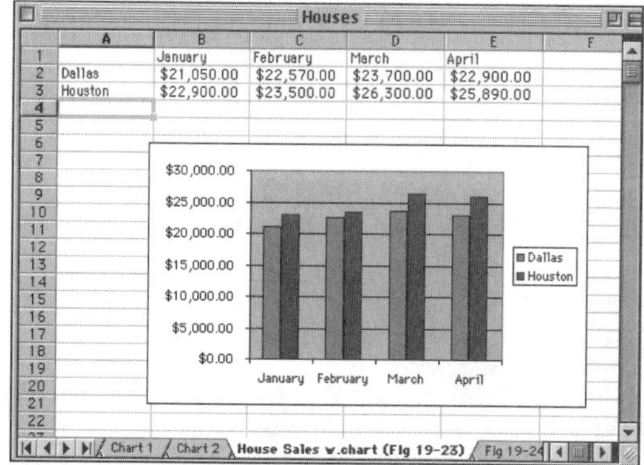

Figure 19-23: A chart oriented by rows

If the data to be plotted is square (the number of rows is equal to the number of columns) and you accept the default options in the Chart Source Data dialog box (the second dialog box) of the Chart Wizard, Excel handles the orientation of the chart in the same manner. On the other hand, if the selected range is taller than it is wide and you accept the default Chart Wizard options, Excel orients the chart differently. In such cases, the text in the top row is used as the series names, text entries appearing in the left columns are used as categories, and each column becomes a data series. This type of worksheet, and the chart resulting from it, are shown in Figure 19-24.

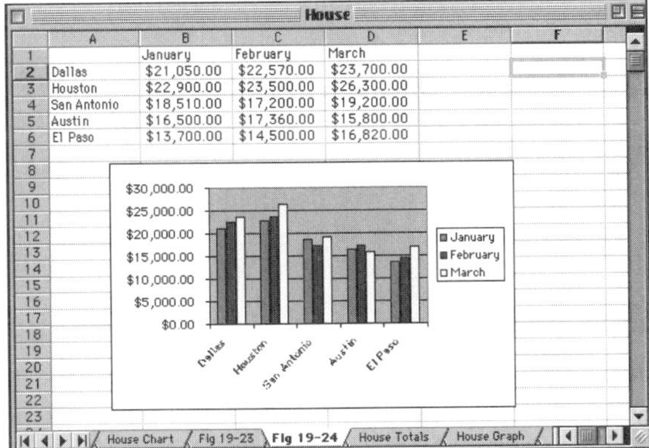

Figure 19-24: A chart oriented by columns

You can change the method Excel uses to plot the data series by changing the selection in the Data Range tab of the second Chart Wizard dialog box. With an existing chart, make the chart active. (If it's embedded, click the chart; if it's a sheet, make it the active worksheet.) Then click the Chart Wizard button on the Chart toolbar to bring up the Chart Wizard dialog box. After you click Next to bypass the first dialog box, you can change the data series in the Data Range tab by choosing Series in Rows or Series in Columns.

Summary

In this chapter, you learned how to create charts, how to change the appearance and the basis for the charts, and how to add such items as titles, legends, and text to your charts. The following points were covered:

- ✦ You can add a chart as an embedded chart (included in an existing worksheet page) or as a chart sheet (included on its own worksheet page).
- ✦ You can easily add charts to a worksheet by selecting the range of data and selecting Insert ⇨ Chart, or by clicking the Chart Wizard button on the Standard toolbar. In each case, you can accept or decline help from the Office Assistant, and then follow the instructions in the wizard dialog boxes.
- ✦ You can modify most aspects of a chart by double-clicking a specific area or object in the chart to bring up the appropriate dialog box. You can also

Control-click, and then choose the appropriate format command from the shortcut menu that appears.

Where to go next

- In the next chapter, you learn about the various printing options in Excel, which provide you with different ways to produce your work.
- You may want to embellish your charts by adding graphics, such as clip art or callouts. For tips on working with graphics, see Chapter 18.

✦ ✦ ✦

CHAPTER 20

Printing and Page Setup

✦ ✦ ✦ ✦

In This Chapter

Learning printing basics

Setting up your pages

Setting print ranges

Setting a page order

Previewing print jobs

Controlling page breaks

E-mailing a file

✦ ✦ ✦ ✦

As with word processing, you have full control over various aspects of printing that affect the appearance of a worksheet, such as margins, page orientation, horizontal and vertical alignment, and the use of headers and footers. You can print entire workbooks, individual sheets from a workbook, or a section in a worksheet. As with any Mac application, the print command is File⇨Print (⌘-P). As with the other Office applications, Excel also provides a Print button on the Standard toolbar.

Learning Printing Basics

Printing the active page of a worksheet is the most common event, so Excel makes it the default. Printing is as simple as choosing File⇨Print, or clicking the Print button, then clicking Print (or pressing Return or Enter).

Printing worksheets

To print, follow these steps:

1. To print all the data in one full worksheet make that worksheet active.

   To print only a portion of a worksheet, select the area you want to print.

   To print multiple worksheets within a workbook, select the worksheets by pressing ⌘ (Command) as you click each desired tab. (If you select a worksheet in error, press ⌘ and click again on its tab to deselect that tab.)

2. Choose File⇨Print (⌘-P) to open the Print dialog box, as shown in Figure 20-1. (Depending on your printer and printer software version, your dialog may look slightly different. This dialog box is determined by your system, not by Excel.)

3. The default prints all of the data in the current worksheet. If this is your intention, skip to Step 4.

   To print a specific selection of the worksheet, or to print more worksheets within the workbook, select the Microsoft Excel options from the pop-up menu at the top of the dialog box. Then select the appropriate radio button (Selection, Active Sheets, or Entire Workbook) in the Excel options dialog. (Note that if you have a chart selected, the only option is to print Selected Chart.)

   To see a preview of what will be printed, click the Preview button. Use the forward and backward arrows to see the entire preview.

4. Click Print to begin printing.

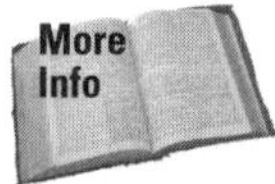

You can also print multiple selections from your spreadsheet or even print selections from several pages, all with one issue of the print command. To do so, utilize the Sheet tab of the Page Setup dialog box. To learn how, see “Setting Print Ranges” later in this chapter.

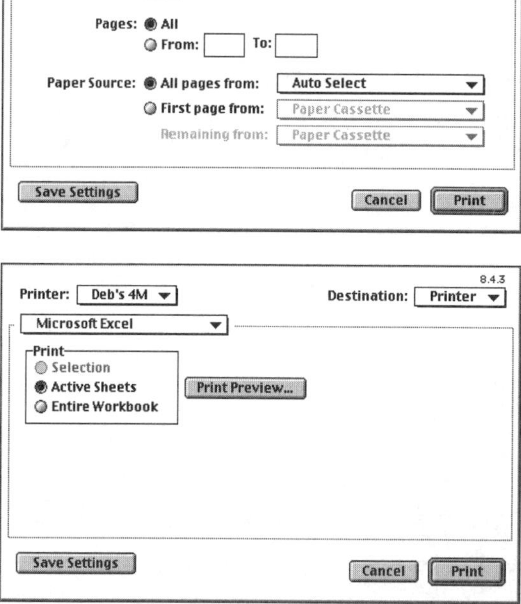

Figure 20-1: Top – the Print dialog box's main screen. Bottom – the Excel options screen.

About the Print dialog box

When you select File⇨Print, you call up the standard Mac Print dialog box. The first piece of information in the Print dialog box is the name of the printer you currently have selected in the Chooser or with your Desktop Printer. If you don't see the correct printer named there, click Cancel, select the correct printer, and issue the print command (⌘-P) again. The Destination reported should also say Printer. The next pop-up menu most likely says General. This is the default, common print dialog page.

Your first decision is to set the number of copies (of each page) that you want to print. By default there is a 1 in that box so one copy will print. To print one copy, leave it set at the default. Notice the Copies box is preselected. To print more than one copy, just type the new number. This is the same as any printing done on the Mac.

The Pages area looks the same as any Print dialog box on the Mac, with one difference. Rather than determining which pages of your entire document will print, this area only affects the current worksheet. The All option (default) prints all of the pages of the current worksheet. The From and To boxes tell Excel which pages of the current worksheet to print. For example, if a worksheet produces a 12-page printout and you need only Pages 4 through 8, you can enter 4 in the From box and 8 in the To box. As a shortcut, if you want to begin printing from Page 1, you can leave the From box blank and only enter the page you want to print in the To box. The same works in reverse, so you can leave the To box blank if you want to print from a specific page to the last page.

In the Paper Source area, you tell the printer which paper trays you print from: the main tray, a secondary tray (if you have one), or the manual feed. Often you don't have to do anything here because the default, Auto Select prints from the main tray. To use a different paper, or an envelope, you can place it in the manual feed tray and select Manual Feed from the pop-up. If your printer has an extra print tray, you would keep another commonly used paper there and select that tray from the pop-up menu as needed. You can also print the first page from one tray and the remainder from another tray. To do so, click the First page from button, then, in that pop-up, select the tray containing the paper on which you want the first page printed (if it is to be hand-fed, choose Manual Feed). In the pop-up menu below, Remaining from, select the tray that holds the second sheets.

If you want to print only a portion of your current worksheet, or print multiple pages of your worksheet, your next visit is to the Excel-specific options page of the Print dialog box. If you have preselected a portion of your current worksheet and only want to print that area, click the radio button next to Selection. If you have preselected more than one worksheet and want to print all of the sheets you've selected, click the radio button by Active Sheets. To print the entire workbook, select Entire Workbook.

At times you may want to save paper by printing smaller versions of your worksheet pages; that is, by printing two or more worksheet pages per paper page. To do so, select the Layout page from the pop-up menu at the top of your dialog box. Here you can select the number of pages per page to print and also place a border around each page if you'd like.

There are also more standard Mac printing options in the Print dialog box. You can explore them by selecting the various options pages from the pop-up menu from which you selected Microsoft Excel or Layout.

Setting Up Your Pages

There are several ways you can customize the look of your printed page. You can set margins, add headers and footers, print gridlines, turn column and row headings on or off, scale your pages, change the print orientation and more. All of these page-printing decisions are Page Setup commands.

Select File➪Page Setup to access the Page Setup dialog box. This dialog box, shown in Figure 20-2, contains four tabs: Page, Margins, Header/Footer, and Sheet. In addition to the tabs, the dialog box contains Print and Print Preview buttons. After making the desired changes to the settings, you can click the Print button to begin printing or the Print Preview button to see the worksheet in Print Preview mode.

✦ **Page tab**—The first tab in the Page Setup dialog box is the Page tab (Figure 20-2). In this tab, you control print-related settings that affect all the pages of your print job such as page orientation, scaling, paper size, and print quality. This section looks at the printing controls found on the Page tab or the Page Setup dialog box.

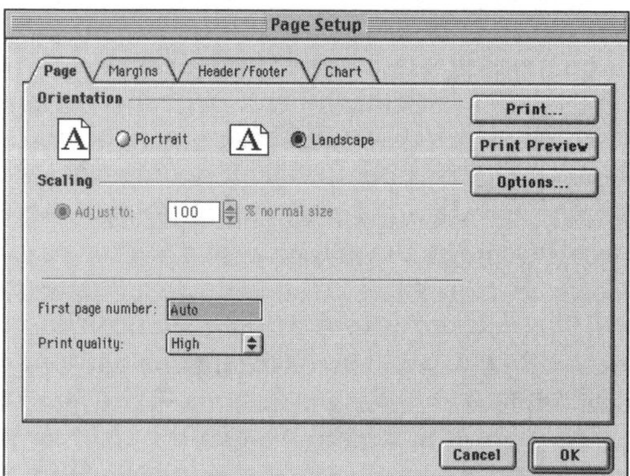

Figure 20-2: The Page tab of the Page Setup dialog box

✦ **Margins tab**—Margins, as you probably know, are the white or unprinted area of each page. In Excel, you set the margins similarly to the way you set them in a word processing program. However, the setting dialog box looks different than it does in a program such as Word (see Figure 20-3).

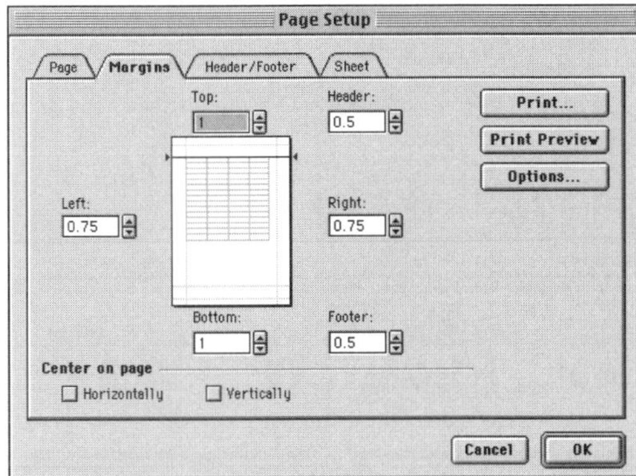

Figure 20-3: The Margins tab of the Page Setup dialog box

✦ **Header/Footer tab**—The Header/Footer tab's options control the appearance and placement of headers and footers printed on your worksheet pages. If you click the Header/Footer tab of the Page Setup dialog box, you see the options shown in Figure 20-4.

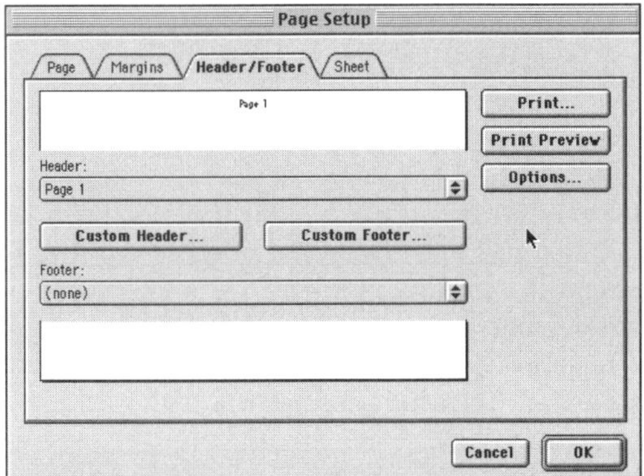

Figure 20-4: The Header/Footer tab of the Page Setup dialog box

✦ **Sheet tab**—The Sheet tab's options control various print-related settings that affect individual worksheets. If you click the Sheet tab of the Page Setup dialog box, you see the options shown in Figure 20-5.

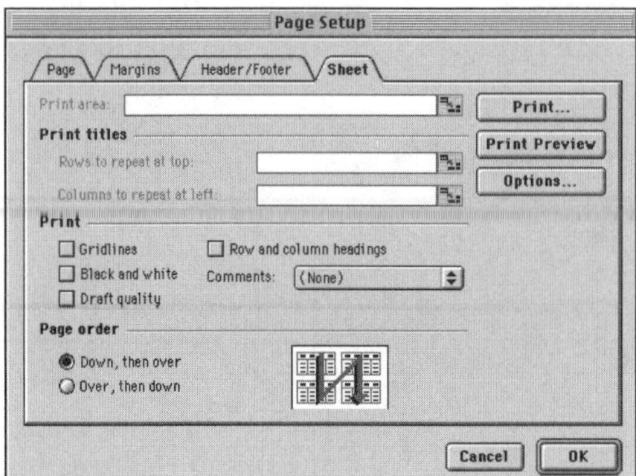

Figure 20-5: The Sheet tab of the Page Setup dialog box

Each of the options available in these tabs is explained in detail in the sections that follow.

Paper size

One of the most basic print choices is the paper size to which you print. The default paper size is Letter size (8.5 × 11 inches). To change the paper size, select File⇨Page Setup, and then click the Options button. This takes you to a printer setup dialog box. In the pop-up menu next to the word Paper, select the desired paper size.

Orientation

Orientation is the direction in which text is printed across the paper. Most text documents such as letters are printed so they are taller up and down, which is called a Portrait orientation. Think of a photograph: a portrait is taller than it is wide, whereas a picture of a beautiful mountain scene is wider than it is tall. So it goes with printing: portrait orientation prints lengthwise (like the pages of this book), whereas landscape orientation prints widthwise. If your spreadsheet has a lot of columns, you are likely to want to print across the width of the paper in order to fit all of the columns on one page.

Changing the orientation in which your document will print is very easy. On the Page tab or the Page Setup dialog box (File⇨Page Setup), simply click the radio button for Portrait or Landscape orientation.

What Happened to the Sheet Tab?

Have you selected File⇨Page Setup and seen the Page, Margins, and Header/Footer tabs but found a Chart tab where you expected the Sheet tab to be? Confusing, isn't it? This happens when you have a chart selected in your worksheet when you select File⇨Page Setup.

To get the Sheet tab back, close the Page Setup dialog box. In your worksheet, deselect the chart by clicking an empty cell, then select File⇨Page Setup again.

Scaling

Scaling enables you to reduce or enlarge your worksheets. This is useful for making a worksheet that is slightly too big for a page fit on a single page. You can choose a specific percentage to scale to, or you can try to force the spreadsheet data to fit a specific number of pages. Scaling is set on the Page tab or the Page Setup dialog box (File⇨Page Setup).

To choose a specific percentage enter a number smaller or larger than 100 in the Adjust to box or use the arrows next to the box to select a larger or smaller number. To take the other approach, use the Fit to option to fit the printed worksheet to a specific number of pages wide by a specific number of pages tall. Enter the dimensions, by pages, in the boxes to the right of the option, or use the up and down arrows to arrive at your desired number.

First page number

As is common on documents, Excel assumes that the page number of the first page to be printed is 1. This is the number assumed by the Auto default, located on the Page tab or the Page Setup dialog box (File⇨Page Setup). You can start page numbering at any page number by selecting the word Auto and entering any page number in its place.

Print quality

By default the Print Quality for your document is set to high. There may be no reason for you to change this but you can set the level if you want. The higher the setting, the nicer the appearance. If your printer prints at 600 dots per inch (dpi), keep the default high as the print setting. If your printer is only capable of printing at 300 dpi, you can choose 300 dpi without seeing any difference. A lower dpi may speed up printing but may affect the quality of the printed output. To set Print Quality select File⇨Page Setup, then the Page tab of the Page Setup dialog box.

There is also another print quality option, which is to print in draft quality. This mode ignores most formatting and graphics. To do so, select File⇨Page Setup, then the Sheet tab. Then simply check the box by the Draft quality option.

Another somewhat related print setting is the choice to print only in black and white. Without this option selected on a black and white printer colors are printed in shades of gray. When this option is selected, there are no shades of gray; color fonts and borders print in black instead.

Margins

Margins are the distance from each edge of the paper to where printing begins. The amount of space you leave between your text and the paper's edge has a great visual impact. You'll need to balance the need for white space and the need to fit all your data on the page(s). There are three margin controls described here. (You can refer back to Figure 20-3 to see these controls.)

- ✦ **Top, Bottom, Left, and Right**—You can set each margin independent of the others. Use the Top, Bottom, Left, and Right options to specify a distance from the edge of the paper for its respective margin. Note that many printers will not print closer than 0.5 inches from the edge of the paper; however, with some laser printers, you can go down to 0.3 inches.
- ✦ **Header and Footer**—The Header and Footer settings determine how far headers or footers print from the top or bottom edges. By default, the header begins 0.5 inches from the top of the page and extends down as low as it must to accommodate your header text. Similarly, the footer begins 0.5 inches from the bottom of the page and extends up as high as it must to accommodate your footer text.
- ✦ **Center on Page**—The Center on Page option determines whether printing should be centered horizontally (between the left and right margins) and vertically (between the top and bottom margins) on the page.

You can also modify the margins of your document visually while in Print Preview mode. See the Print Preview section for details.

Headers and footers

Excel lets you place headers and footers in a worksheet or workbook when you print. A header, for example, might be a title that appears at the top of every page. A footer appears at the bottom of every page and might include a page number or the current date. Adding headers and footers is relatively simple and painless. They can be very effective in giving a document a more refined and professional look.

To add a header or footer to a worksheet, follow these steps:

1. Choose File➪Page Setup.
2. Choose the Header/Footer tab from the Page Setup dialog box (refer back to Figure 20-4).
3. In this tab, you can select a header or footer, or create a custom header or footer. One pop-up list contains several headers from which you can choose, while the other contains footers. Several generic choices are available by default such as combinations that include your name and page information. If you have titled the tab of your worksheet, it will appear in the list as a choice for a header or footer. If you want more control over your header or footer, you can create your own.

   To add a custom header or footer to your worksheet, click the corresponding Custom button: Custom Header or Custom Footer.
4. In the next dialog box, enter the header or footer text. The Header dialog box is pictured in Figure 20-6.

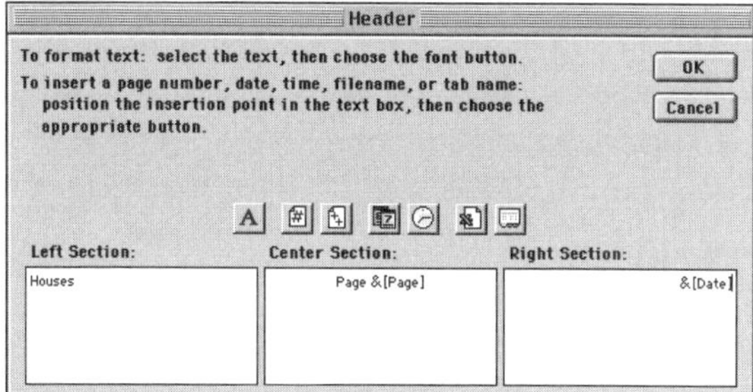

Figure 20-6: The Header dialog box

5. In the Left Section, Center Section, or Right Section portion of the dialog box, enter the desired header or footer text. Use the buttons in the dialog box to add items, insert page numbers, insert the date or time, or change the font.

   Table 20-1 explains the custom header and footer buttons that appear in the dialog box after you click either the Custom Header or Custom Footer button on the Header/Footer tab.
6. Click OK.

Table 20-1
Header/Footer Buttons and Their Functions

Button	*Function*
Font	Opens the Font dialog box from which you can change the header or footer's font.
Page Number	Inserts the page number.
Total Pages	Inserts the total number of pages in the active worksheet.
Date	Inserts the system date.
Time	Inserts the system time.
Filename	Inserts the active workbook's filename.
Sheet Name	Inserts the active worksheet's name.

Print titles

Titles are the words you place in a row or column to identify the content of the rows or columns to follow. Printing the titles on every page of your printout makes it easier to read, particularly in a long worksheet. If you don't select any titles to print, and a column or row carries on to a second or third page, your readers won't have any heading to know what the numbers refer to. Print titles lets your headings repeat on all secondary pages.

The Print Titles options are available on the Sheet tab of the Page Setup dialog box. In the Print titles area, you can specify the row(s) or column(s) you would like to see repeated on every page. To print a title on each page of a sheet, follow these steps:

1. Choose File⇨Page Setup.
2. Choose the Sheet tab from the Page Setup dialog box. (Refer to Figure 20-5 for an image of this tab.)
3. Place the insertion point in the Rows to repeat at top text box or the Columns to repeat at left text box.
4. Click the worksheet and drag to select the rows or columns that you want to repeat. You may have to move the dialog box if it covers the cells you need to select. (Remember that multiple rows and columns must be adjacent.)
5. Click OK.

If you change your mind and want to delete the entries that you have made as titles, simply return to the Sheet tab of the Page Setup dialog box and delete the cell references from the Rows to repeat at top and Columns to repeat at left text boxes.

Row and column headings

In addition to printing titles, you may want to print the row and column headings, which are the letters that identify the columns and the numbers that identify the rows. By default these headings don't print. If you prefer that they do print, you can turn them on. Select File⇨Page Setup, and select the Sheet tab. Then simply check the box by the Row and column headings option.

Printing gridlines

By default the gridlines you see onscreen don't print on paper. However, if you prefer, you can turn them on so they do print. Select File⇨Page Setup, and select the Sheet tab. Then simply check the box by the Gridlines option.

Printing comments

At times it may be helpful to have your comments appear in print. You have two such options: that comments print at the end of your document or that they print where they actually appear on your worksheet. Either way, to have comments print, select File⇨Page Setup, and select the Sheet tab. Then choose your option from the pop-up list next to the Comments label.

Setting Print Ranges

When you tell Excel to print a worksheet, it prints the entire worksheet unless you tell it otherwise. When you want to print a specific portion of a worksheet, you first need to tell Excel what area of the worksheet you want printed. If you only want to print one area of cells from one worksheet you have two choices. The first way is described at the beginning of this chapter in the section on the basics of printing. The second option is to specify the portion of the worksheet by choosing File⇨Page Setup and using the Print Area option of the Sheet tab. This method also enables you to select multiple ranges to print at the same time.

To define one print range using the second method, follow these steps:

1. Choose File⇨Page Setup. In the Page Setup dialog box that appears, click the Sheet tab.
2. Click in the Print Area text box to place the insertion pointer there.
3. Click your worksheet and select the range of cells that to print. When you click in the worksheet, the dialog box is reduced to this single field so you can see the selection you need to make. As you select the range, a dotted line appears around it and the coordinates for the range appear in the Print Area text box. When you release the mouse after making your selection, the entire Page Setup dialog box reappears.

In case you're wondering, the Print Area text box is blank by default. When it's blank, you print all cells that contain data in the sheet you are in.

4. While in the Page Setup dialog box, you can continue to set the other page setup options. If you are ready to print, you can click the Print button from the Page Setup dialog box.

You can also print multiple selections from your spreadsheet with one print command. Each range is printed on its own sheet and each can be printed with titles. Printing multiple worksheet page ranges is similar to setting a print range as in the section above. To set multiple print ranges, follow these steps (which are similar to Steps 1 to 3 of printing a print range):

1. Choose File ➪ Page Setup to open the Page Setup dialog box and select the Sheet tab as shown in Figure 20-5.
2. Click in the Print Area box to place the insertion pointer there.
3. In the document, click and drag to select the first range you want to print. When you click in the worksheet, the dialog box is reduced to this single field so you can see the selection you need to make. As you select the range, a dotted line appears around it, and the coordinates for the range appear in the Print Area text box. When you release the mouse after making your selection, the entire Page Setup dialog box reappears and your insertion pointer is once again in the Print Area text box.
4. Enter a colon in the Print Area text box.
5. Click in the document and select the next area you want to print. Again, the dialog box is reduced while you make your selection, and you are returned to the Print Area text box when you release the mouse.
6. Repeat Steps 4 and 5 until you select all the areas that you want to print. The areas are printed in the order that you selected them, and they are printed on separate pages.

Whether printing one range or several, to cancel the effects of the selection and return to printing the complete worksheet, return to File ➪ Page Setup, click the Sheet tab, delete the coordinates of the selected range, and click OK.

Setting a Page Order

You can specify whether printing of multiple-page worksheets should occur from top to bottom and then from left to right, or from left to right and then from top to bottom. To do so select File ➪ Page Setup, select the Sheet tab, and click the desired radio button at the bottom of the dialog box. A diagram shows you the result of your choice.

This page order affects page numbering. If you print downward first, Page 2 is the page that falls below Page 1 (the top-left page). If you print across first, Page 2 is the page to the right of Page 1.

Previewing Print Jobs

By previewing your work before you print, you can see how your layout looks and make any changes before wasting paper. In addition, by using the preview's Zoom feature, you can take a closer look at the document and its contents.

To preview a worksheet, choose File➪Print Preview, or click the Print Preview button on the Standard toolbar. Figure 20-7 shows an example of a document in Print Preview mode. From Print Preview mode, you can also access the Page Setup dialog box to make modifications as needed.

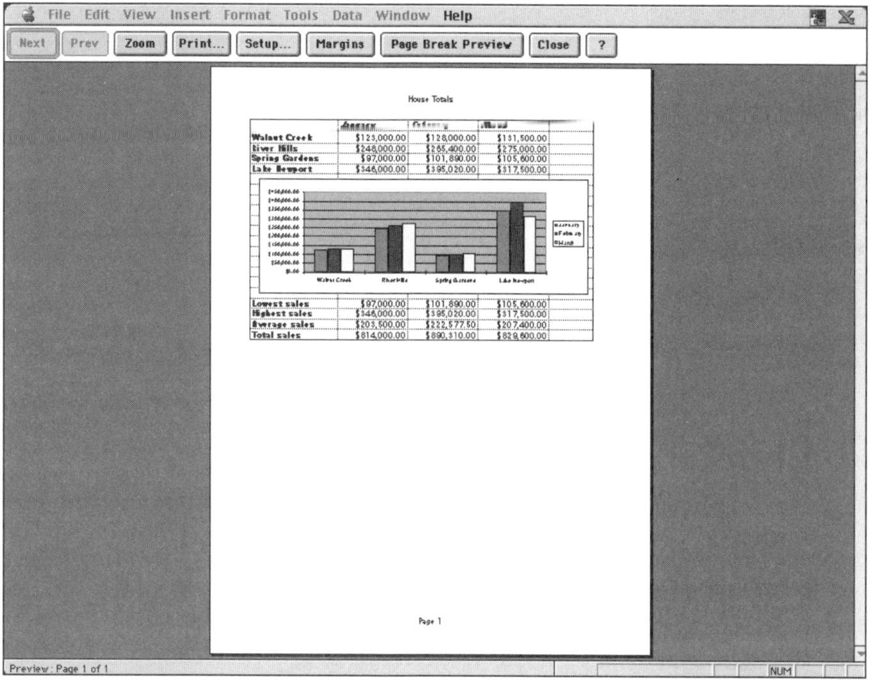

Figure 20-7: Excel's Print Preview mode

You can also modify the margins of your document in Print Preview by clicking the Margins button at the top of the screen. Clicking the Margins button activates the "margin grid" (see Figure 20-8). The margin lines can be moved using the mouse. The margin grid feature is helpful because it lets you see the document as it is being adjusted, and you can get an idea as to whether the document will fit on a single page. Setting margins in Print Preview is easier if you use the Zoom feature so you can see the page in better detail. Click the Zoom button at the top of the Print Preview window to move in closer for detail.

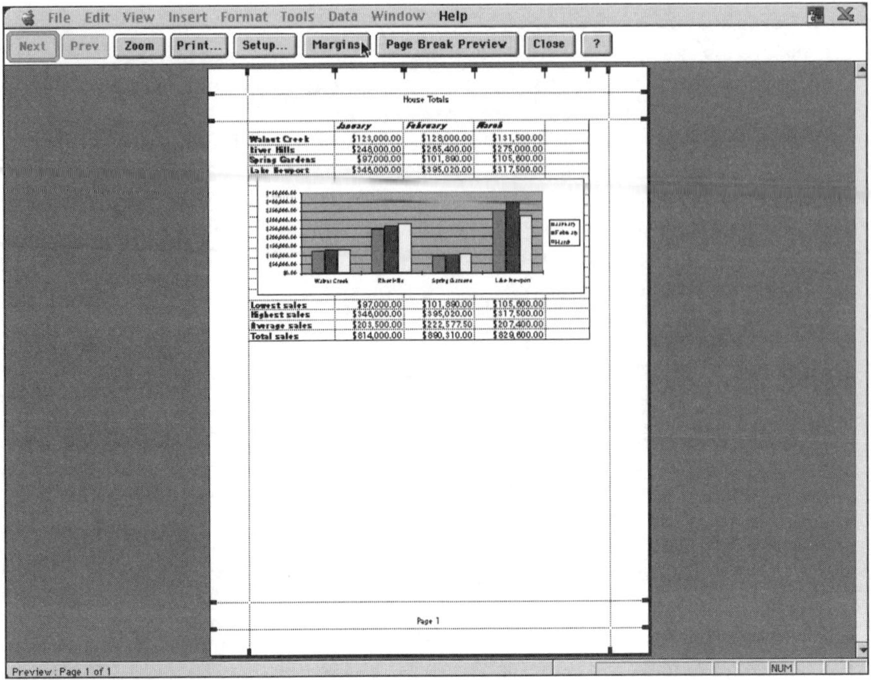

Figure 20-8: The margin grid in Print Preview mode

Controlling Page Breaks

Sometimes automatic page breaks, which are based on paper size, margins, and other settings in the Page Setup dialog box, come at inconvenient places, especially in larger worksheets. When a page breaks at a bad location, you can fix the break by inserting a manual page break. Manual page breaks are especially useful when you want to print one section per page. To insert manual page breaks, follow these steps:

1. In your worksheet, place the insertion point below and to the right of the place where you want to insert the page break.
2. Choose Insert ➪ Page Break. The page break appears onscreen and is indicated by lines with dashes.

The page breaks you insert remain in the same location until you remove them. The automatic page breaks are also repositioned after the insertion of a manual page break. If you want to remove a page break you have inserted, return to the cell in which you entered the page break and choose Insert ➪ Remove Page Break. You can also select the entire document and choose Insert ➪ Remove Page Break to remove all manual page breaks in the worksheet.

You can also set page breaks horizontally and vertically. To do so, select the column or row where you want the page break to appear and click in its header. Next choose Insert ➪ Page Break. The page break is set horizontally or vertically as you specified.

At times you will want to view your manual page breaks. These page breaks can be difficult to see, though, because of the gridlines in your worksheet. To turn off the gridlines so you can see the manual page breaks, choose Tools ➪ Preferences. Click the View tab and uncheck the Gridlines check box. Then click OK to remove the gridlines.

E-mailing a File

Excel makes it simple to e-mail your workbook. To send a workbook over the network by e-mail, follow these steps:

1. Open the workbook you want to send.
2. Select File ➪ Send To ➪ Mail Recipient. This opens your designated default e-mail program, such as Outlook Express (which comes with Office 98), Claris E-mailer, or Eudora. A new e-mail document is started and your workbook is automatically attached to the new e-mail. Figure 20-9 depicts a spreadsheet called Houses that is attached to e-mail and ready to be sent.
3. Proceed to complete your message as normal by entering a recipient and writing a note. When done, send your message as normal.

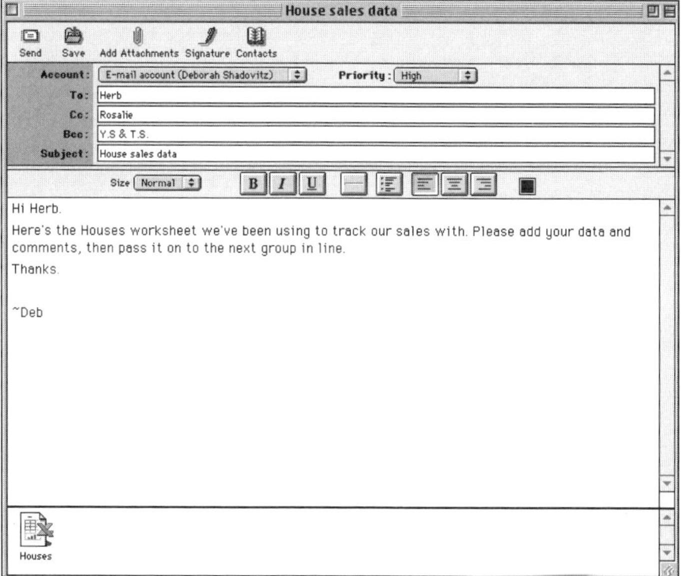

Figure 20-9: A spreadsheet attached to an Outlook Express e-mail document

Summary

This chapter detailed the features that Excel offers to help you get your facts and figures on paper. The chapter discussed these points:

- ✦ You can print a selected area of the current worksheet, selected sheets, or the entire workbook by choosing File➪Print (⌘-P).
- ✦ By choosing File➪Page Setup, you reveal the Page Setup dialog box, which lets you change various settings for printing, such as orientation, paper size, margins, headers, and footers.
- ✦ Excel's Print Preview feature can be very useful in helping find errors in a document's layout before printing occurs.
- ✦ You can use the File➪Send command to e-mail your workbook within your current e-mail program's capabilities.

Where to go next

- ✦ The next chapter explains how to create and work with databases in Excel.
- ✦ If you find yourself doing a lot of repetitive printing on a regular basis, you'll want to automate your printing by putting the power of macros to work. Chapter 22 tells you how.
- ✦ Your document's printed appearance is greatly affected by how you format it. Formatting specifics are covered in Chapter 17.
- ✦ To find out more about using Outlook Express to send e-mail, see Chapter 35.

✦ ✦ ✦

CHAPTER 21

Working with Excel Databases

✦ ✦ ✦ ✦

In This Chapter

Learning about databases

Creating a database

Working with database records

Using the AutoFormat command

Sorting a database

Using the AutoFilter command

Performing a mail merge

Designing databases

✦ ✦ ✦ ✦

This chapter details the use of databases (also called lists) that are stored in Excel worksheets. Whether or not you were aware of it at the time, you have probably used databases on numerous occasions. Any time you reference a list of business contacts, or a Rolodex file, or something as familiar as the Yellow Pages, you are working with a database. You can use Excel to manage data in a database, and this chapter shows you how.

Learning About Databases

A database is any system in which information is cataloged, stored, and used; that is, a collection of related information that is grouped as a single item. Figure 21-1 shows an example of a simple database. Metal filing cabinets containing customer records, a card file of names and telephone numbers, and even a notebook filled with a handwritten list of store inventory are all databases. The physical container—the filing cabinet or the notebook, for example—is not the database. The database is the contents of the container and the way the information is organized. Objects such as cabinets and notebooks are only tools for organizing information. Excel is one such tool for storing information.

Information in a database is usually organized and stored in a table by rows and columns. Figure 21-1, for example, is an employee list in database form. Each row contains a name, a job title, and an extension. Because the list is a collection of information arranged in a specific order it is a database.

Employee Info database

	A	B	C	D
1	Employee Information Database			
2				
3	**First Name**	**Last Name**	**Job Title**	**Extension**
4	Allison	LeVitus	Soccer Coach	0350
5	Jacob	LeVitus	Soccer Coach	0351
6	Dexter	Horthy	Mac Support	0352
7	Alma	de la Cerda	Mac Support	0353
8	Ricky	de la Cerda	Art Director	0354
9	Alfredo	de la Cerda	Mac Support	0355
10	[illegible]	Madnick-Makler	Social Director	0356
11	Shira	Madnick-Makler	Basketball Coach	0357
12	Corinne	Fischer	Teacher	0358
13	Alex	Fischer	Fireman	0359
14	Caleb	Landis	PC Support	0360
15	Naomi	Nesenoff	Orchestra Leader	0361
16	Rachael	Nesenoff	Orchestra Leader	0362

Job Titles / Sheet2 / Sheet3

Figure 21-1: A typical database in Excel

Rows in a database file are called records, and columns are called fields. Figure 21-2 illustrates this idea by showing an address filing system kept on file cards. Each card in the box is a single record, and each category of information on that card is a field. Fields can contain any type of information that can be categorized. In the card box, each record contains five fields: name, address, city, state, and zip code. Because every card in the box contains the same type of information, the information in the card box is a database.

In Excel, you design a database by following this row-and-column analogy: each column of the spreadsheet contains a different field and each row contains an additional record. Data is organized by devoting a specific column to each specific category (field) of data. You must enter each specific chunk of data in a separate cell of the worksheet. For example, in the worksheet shown in Figure 21-1, a person's first name goes into a cell of the First Name column, the person's last name goes into a cell of the Last Name column, and so on. You begin the design of any database by placing the cursor at the top of the worksheet and entering labels for the names of your fields in successive columns.

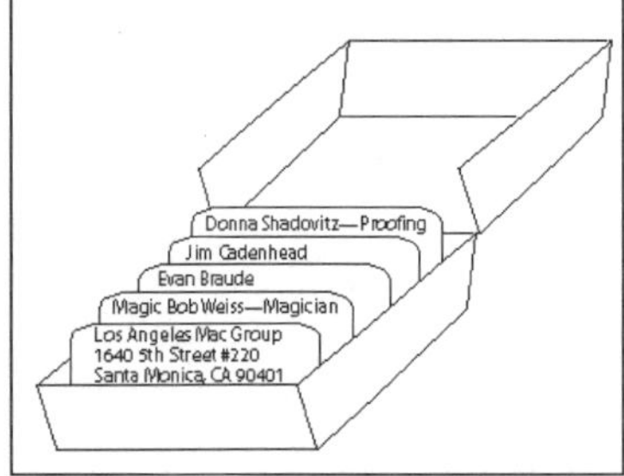

Figure 21-2: A card file shows the logical design of a database

Creating a Database

To create a database in an Excel worksheet, follow these steps:

1. In a blank row of the worksheet, enter the desired names of the fields.
2. In each cell of a row, directly underneath the field names, type the desired entries for that field into the cell. Don't leave an empty row between the field names and the data because Excel will have problems recognizing where your database begins.
3. To add entries consisting of numbers that really should be stored as text (such as zip codes), begin the entry with an apostrophe or format the cells as text (more on this very shortly).

When you finish adding records to your database, you'll have an organized collection of row-and-column data in a format somewhat like our example shown in Figure 21-1.

If you need to enter a large number of entries that comprise numbers that should be stored as text (such as zip codes or telephone numbers), format the column containing that field as text. Control-click the header for that column (which automatically selects the entire column), and choose Format Cells from the shortcut menu that appears. Click the Number tab of the Format Cells dialog box. Next, click the Text option in the Category list and then click OK. If you don't use this trick, or if you don't begin each entry with an apostrophe, zip codes that begin with zeroes (such as 00742) will appear without the zeroes.

Your database work will be easier for you to handle if you have only one database per worksheet. To store more than one database in a single worksheet, you need to define database ranges for each database, which adds an unnecessary layer of complexity. Instead, place each database on a different worksheet tab. (Each worksheet can contain up to 255 tabs.) You'll also avoid long-term organizational problems if you don't put other data below your database in the same worksheet. As the database grows, new rows are added to the bottom of the list. If other spreadsheet data exists below the list, you run the risk of overwriting the existing data.

As you work with databases in Excel, remember that the database must have its row of field names at the top of the list and you can't have any blank lines between the row containing the field names and the data. Also, each field name should be unique (having two fields named Date, for example, would be confusing). You can have other rows above the list if you want, but Excel only recognizes the row immediately above the data as the row containing field names. Field names can include 255 characters, although for readability reasons you'll probably want to keep your field names relatively short.

A New Approach to Excel Databases

If you've worked with databases in previous versions of Excel, you'll recall the procedures as being considerably more complex. In the past, for example, you had to define a specific range for your data to occupy (called a database range). When you wanted to retrieve specific data, you had to tell Excel what data you wanted by setting up a criteria range and an extract range.

You can still use these methods in Excel 98 or in Excel 97 (the Windows version), but the new approach is much easier. Excel now makes intelligent guesses regarding your database range (the size of the database), provides a data form for data entry and basic searches, and provides an AutoFilter for intricate data retrieval.

Avoid putting other important data (such as formulas) to the left or to the right of your database because if you later use Excel's AutoFilter capability to filter the data in the database, the other data may be hidden.

Working with Database Records

You can add and edit records by typing the desired data directly into the cells. You can delete rows by selecting the unwanted row and choosing Edit ⇨ Delete. Most users, however, find basic data entry and editing easier when they use a data form, a convenient form that Excel provides for you to enter and display data. To display a data form onscreen, place the cursor in any cell of your database and choose Data ⇨ Form. A data form, such as the one in Figure 21-3, containing the fields of your database appears.

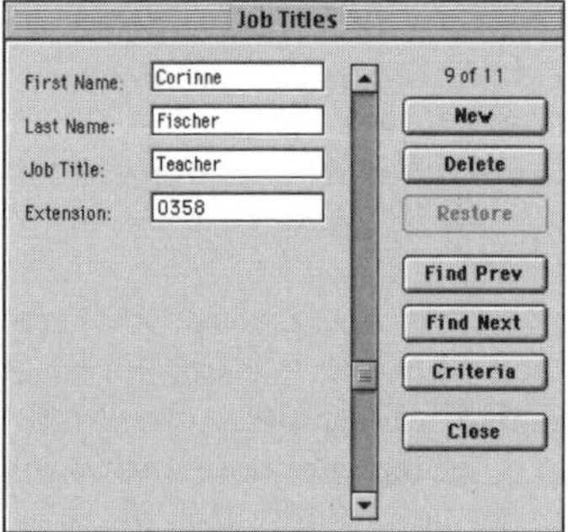

Figure 21-3: A sample data form for a database

Adding new records

To add a record, click the New button in the data form. A new record data form with blank fields for the new information appears. Repeat this process for each record that you want to add to the database.

If you're adding new records to an existing database, don't be concerned about the order of the records in the database. You can always sort the database to put the records in any order that you want (see "Sorting a Database" later in the chapter).

Editing records

You can also edit a record by using the data form. To get to the record you need to edit, use the Find Next or Find Prev(ious) buttons, use the data form's scroll bars, or press the up- and down-arrow keys to scroll through the records. In a large database, you can use the Criteria button to perform a search. When the desired record appears, click in the appropriate fields and make the desired edits.

Deleting records

To delete a record by using the data form, first locate the desired record. Again, you can use the Find Next or Find Prev(ious) buttons, the scroll bar, or the up- and down-arrow keys. When the record appears, click the Delete button in the data form.

If you have a large number of records to delete, it may be faster not to use a data form. Instead, use Excel's AutoFilter capability (discussed later in this chapter) to display all the records you want to delete. Then, you drag across the row headers to select the records. With all the desired rows selected, choose the Edit⇨Delete.

Finding data by using criteria

Another way to locate data in a database is to specify a search criterion in a data form. The criterion identifies the specific data you want to find. For example, in a large database of names and addresses, you may want to locate all records in a particular city. Excel also lets you make use of a computed criterion to find records that pass certain tests based on the contents of a formula. By using a computed criterion with a database of expenses, for example, you can find all expenses that exceed $500 by entering >500. When you specify a computed criterion in a data form, you make use of Excel's comparison operators (the same ones you can use as part of formulas in the cells of a worksheet). Table 21-1 lists the comparison operators you can use.

Table 21-1
Comparison Operators

Operator	*Function*
<	Less than
>	Greater than
=	Equal to
<>	Not equal to
<=	Less than or equal to
>=	Greater than or equal to

To use criteria to find individual records in a database, follow these steps:

1. Place the cursor anywhere in the database.
2. Choose Data ➪ Form to bring up a data form dialog box.
3. Click the Criteria button in the data form. When you do this, the data form changes in appearance to resemble the one shown in Figure 21-4. The data form now says Criteria in the upper-right corner, the Criteria button on the data form changes into the Form button, and the fields are all blank.
4. Enter the desired criteria in the appropriate fields. You need to fill in only the fields on which you want to base the search. For example, if you want to search for all San Francisco records, you would enter San Francisco in the City field of the form. In Figure 21-4, a search by first name is being entered.

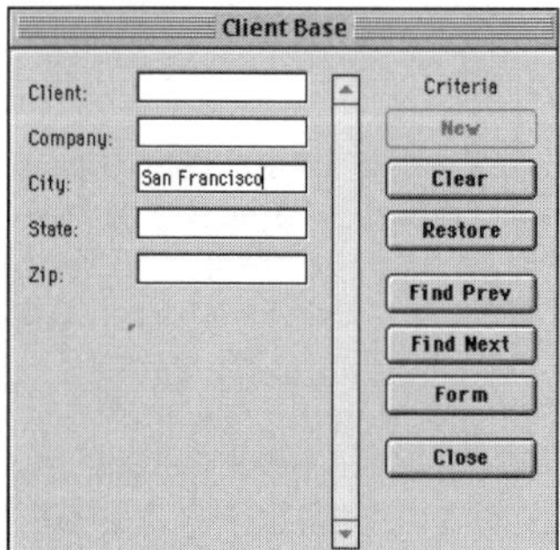

Figure 21-4: The Criteria mode of the data form

5. Press Return or Enter, or click the Form button to find the first record that meets the search criterion.

6. Use the Find Next and Find Prev(ious) buttons in the data form to locate the records that match the desired criterion. (Using the scroll bars or arrow keys takes you through all the records, not just the matches.)
7. When you are finished examining the records, click the Close button.

You can also use wildcards to represent characters in your criterion. Use the question mark to represent a single character or the asterisk (*) to represent multiple characters. As an example, the criteria `H?ll` in a Name field would locate names such as Hall, Hill, and Hull. The criterion entry `*der` would locate all strings of text ending with the letters der, such as chowder and loader.

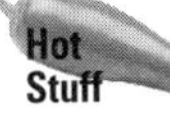

If you're familiar with databases in general, you may be wondering how you can perform searches based on multiple criteria, where you find records based on more than a single argument. In some cases, you'll want to find records by using and-based criteria, where one condition and another condition meet certain requirements. You can easily search using multiple criteria by entering multiple conditions in the different fields of the data form while in Criteria mode. For example, in a table of names and addresses, you may want to find any employee whose first name begins with an A and whose job is Mac Support. Figure 21-5 shows a data form that is set up to search on these criteria.

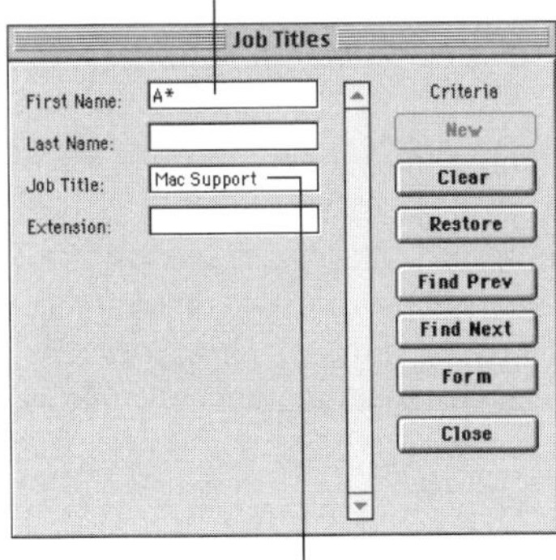

Figure 21-5: The data form set up in Criteria mode to search for multiple criteria

A search for or-based criteria is a little more complex. Or-based criteria describe those cases where the contents of a field meet one criterion or another criterion. For example, you may want to find records where the City field contains either San Francisco or San Diego. Unfortunately, you can't do searches with or-based criteria by using a data form, but you can use the AutoFilter command.

How to Get a Report

How can you get a printed copy of all records that meet a certain criterion? You can't use the data form to isolate and print a group of records, but you can filter the data in a database by using the AutoFilter command.

After you filter the records to show the ones you want, you can print the worksheet to produce a report. For details, see "Using the AutoFilter Command" later in this chapter.

Using the AutoFormat Command

You can quickly improve the appearance of your database by using Excel's AutoFormat command. To apply automatic formatting to a database, place the cursor anywhere within the database and then choose Format ➪ AutoFormat. In the AutoFormat dialog box, choose one of the available formats, check out the sample, and click OK to apply the formatting. If you don't like the effects of the formatting, you can always remove it with the Undo command (⌘-Z), which will say Edit ➪ Undo AutoFormat.

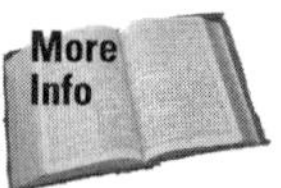

As detailed in Chapter 17, AutoFormat applies automatic formatting to parts or all of your worksheet to give the worksheet a presentation-quality appearance quickly.

Sorting a Database

At times you may want your data arranged in a more effective manner. You can do this by sorting the data by field information, which changes the order of the records. When Excel sorts a database, it rearranges all records in the database according to a specified order. If you sort a database of names alphabetically, the sorted database contains all the same records, but the names are arranged in alphabetical order.

When you sort fields that contain dates or times, Excel sorts correctly if the data is in an acceptable date or time format. If you use some format of your own devising that Excel doesn't recognize to store dates or times, the data will sort as text, and you probably won't get the results that you want.

How it works

When Excel sorts a database in ascending order, it sorts by numbers first, followed by text, and then the logical values True or False. Excel is not case sensitive; it ignores both case and accent marks while sorting. Blank cells appear at the end of the sort, whether you are sorting in ascending or descending order. To sort, you choose a field, called the *key field*, which is the field that the data is sorted by. In some cases, you may need to sort a database on more than one field. For example, if you sort a database alphabetically by using Last Name as the key field, you get groups of records with the last names arranged alphabetically but with the first names in random order. In such a case, you can sort the database by using Last Name as the first key field and First Name as the second key field. To sort a database, use Data➪Sort.

Sorting involves a major rearrangement of data so that there's always a possibility you'll make a selection that causes your data to sort in a way you didn't expect. If you have any doubts about how a sort will turn out, save the workbook under a different name before sorting. (Choose File➪Save As and enter a different name for the workbook file in the Save As dialog box.) Then if you perform a sort that produces undesirable results and you're unable to undo the sort (⌘-Z), you can always reload the original file to get your original data back.

To sort your database, follow these steps:

1. To sort a specific number of rows in your database, select those rows by dragging across the row headers. To sort the entire database, place the cursor anywhere within the database.
2. Choose Data➪Sort to open the Sort dialog box (see Figure 21-6).

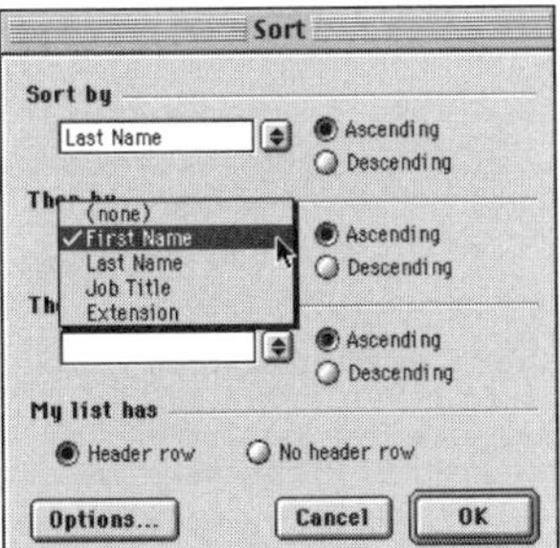

Figure 21-6: The Sort dialog box as a second sort field is being selected

3. Click the arrows next to the Sort by (top) field of the dialog box, to choose the field you want to sort by. Then select Ascending or Descending to specify the direction of the sort.
4. If you want to use additional fields as the basis for the sort, select a secondary field from the available fields in the Then by list as in Step 3. When you sort on multiple fields, the Sort by field takes first priority, followed by the first Then by field, then the second Then by field.

5. If you did not select a range of rows to sort, make sure the Header row radio button at the bottom of the dialog box remains selected. This tells Excel there's a header row that contains the field names that are not to be included in the sort.

6. Click OK to perform the sort.

Figure 21-7 shows the effects of sorting. At the top, you see a database that contains records entered in random order. Below it, you see the same database that has been sorted by Last Name and, where Last Name values are equal, by First Name fields.

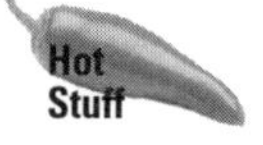

You can quickly sort a database on any single field in ascending or descending order by placing the cursor in any desired field and clicking the Sort Ascending or Sort Descending button on the Standard toolbar.

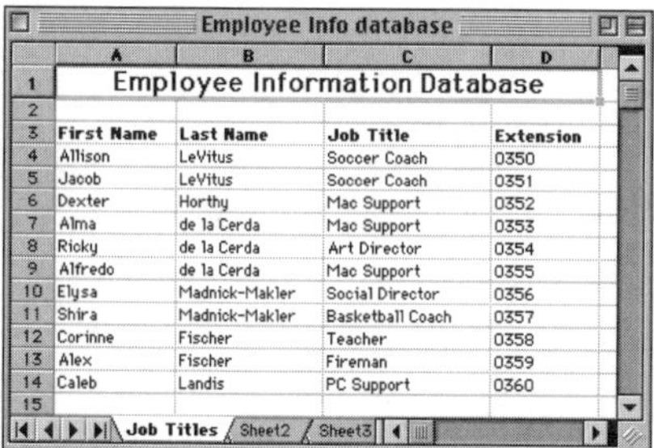

Employee Info database

Employee Information Database

First Name	Last Name	Job Title	Extension
Allison	LeVitus	Soccer Coach	0350
Jacob	LeVitus	Soccer Coach	0351
Dexter	Horthy	Mac Support	0352
Alma	de la Cerda	Mac Support	0353
Ricky	de la Cerda	Art Director	0354
Alfredo	de la Cerda	Mac Support	0355
Elysa	Madnick-Makler	Social Director	0356
Shira	Madnick-Makler	Basketball Coach	0357
Corinne	Fischer	Teacher	0358
Alex	Fischer	Fireman	0359
Caleb	Landis	PC Support	0360

Job Titles / Sheet2 / Sheet3

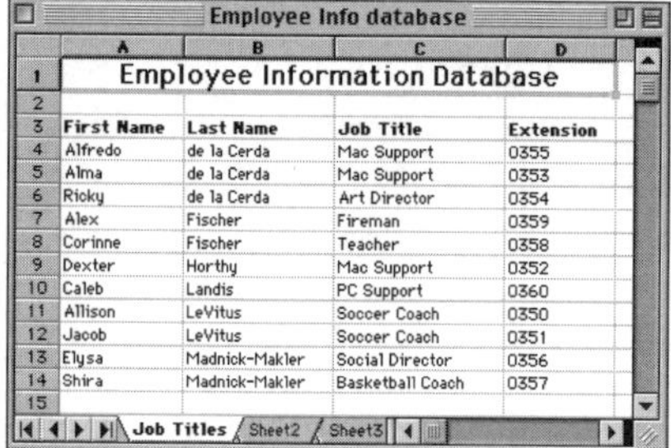

Employee Info database

Employee Information Database

First Name	Last Name	Job Title	Extension
Alfredo	de la Cerda	Mac Support	0355
Alma	de la Cerda	Mac Support	0353
Ricky	de la Cerda	Art Director	0354
Alex	Fischer	Fireman	0359
Corinne	Fischer	Teacher	0358
Dexter	Horthy	Mac Support	0352
Caleb	Landis	PC Support	0360
Allison	LeVitus	Soccer Coach	0350
Jacob	LeVitus	Soccer Coach	0351
Elysa	Madnick-Makler	Social Director	0356
Shira	Madnick-Makler	Basketball Coach	0357

Job Titles / Sheet2 / Sheet3

Figure 21-7: Top—a database containing records in random order. Bottom—the same database containing records sorted by Last Name and First Name fields.

Occasionally you may need to sort a database on more than three fields. Suppose that you have a large mailing list in Excel, and you want to sort the database by State, then by City within each state, then by Last Name within each city, and then by First Name within each group of last names. Because Excel provides only three fields from which to select in the Sort dialog box, this type of sort appears to be impossible. In fact, Excel can handle such a task if you break down the job into multiple sorts. Begin with the least important group of sorts and progress toward the most important group of sorts. Put the most important field first within each group of sorts. In the example, you would first sort by using the Last Name field as the first field and the First Name field as the second field. Then you would perform another sort by using the State field as the first field, the City field as the second field, and the Last Name field as the third field.

If you make a selection before sorting (as opposed to sorting the entire list by just placing the cursor anywhere within the list), make sure you select all the data that you want sorted. If you select most columns and leave some adjacent columns containing data unselected, the sort will affect only the data in the selected columns. The result will be a seriously garbled database. When selecting data for sorting purposes, the safest method is to drag across row headings, which selects all of the fields for that row (record). In this way, you're assured of selecting all data in the rows.

Sorting Bizarre Numbers

What happens when you need to sort by something such as product part numbers that are made up of alphanumeric combinations of varying widths? For example, a list of such part numbers with entries like:

1R9

4R32

12P182

67S2024

109P182

If you did a sort based on those values, your results would not be what you really want. 12P182 would fall above 1R9, even though in the company's grand scheme, 1R9 is a lower part number than 12P182. This is because the part numbers actually consist of three components: a number of one or more digits, followed by a letter, followed by another multi-digit number. In such a list, all parts beginning with the number 1 appear first in the sorted list, followed by all parts beginning with the number 2, then all parts beginning with the number 3, and so on.

You can correctly sort this type of a list by breaking the codes into their component parts and using a separate cell for each part. Storing each of these components in a separate cell and sorting based on all three cells solves the problem.

Can You Undo the Effects of a Sort? Maybe

If you sort a database and then go on to do other things with the data, you cannot later undo the effects of the sort. (The Undo command works only if you perform it as the first action after the sort.) If you want to retain your database in the manner in which the records were originally entered, you have two options. You can save a copy of the database worksheet under another worksheet tab or save the entire workbook under another file name by using Save As. The Save As copy of the worksheet can then be recalled if you want to see how the database was originally organized. However, it is difficult to keep two databases containing the same data updated.

A better approach is to add a column of record numbers to the database. The first record entered becomes record 1; the second record entered becomes record 2; and so on. That way, to reorganize the database in the order that the records were originally entered, you simply sort on the field that contains the record numbers. It's easy to fill a column with sequential numbers. See Chapter 16 for details.

Custom sort orders

In addition to sorting in ascending or descending order, you can have your primary sort field sort by the date or month custom orders Excel provides, or create your own custom order to sort by. For example, you may need to sort a list by manager or teacher's names but not alphabetically. Or you may need to sort by priority or by location.

To create your own sort order, follow these steps:

1. Select Tools ➪ Preferences, and then select the Custom Lists tab.
2. If you have not entered the text to sort by in your spreadsheet, click in the List entries box and type the word (letters, numbers, or combination) that you want to have first in the sort order. Press Return or Enter and type the second sort word. Repeat until you have entered all your sort elements. Then click Add.

   If you have already entered the text to sort by in your spreadsheet, select the list before selecting Tools ➪ Preferences and the Custom Lists tab. Then click Import.

   If you have already entered the text but haven't preselected the text, you can click the button attached to the Import list from cells text box. This collapses the dialog box to reveal your worksheet. In the worksheet, drag to select the cells that contain your sort data, then press Return or Enter. Back in the dialog box, click Import.
3. Click OK.

Custom sort lists can also be deleted. Just click the list name in the Custom lists and click Delete.

If you read "Copying data with Fill and AutoFill" in Chapter 16, these instructions may sound familiar. In fact, the custom lists you create in your Preferences dialog box are the same lists you use to automatically complete a data series entry when using AutoFill.

To put your custom sort order into effect, follow these steps:

1. Select Data⇨Sort and choose a field to sort on (from the pop-up list).
2. Click Options to bring up the Sort Options dialog box. Here you'll find a pop-up menu that lets you choose a custom order to sort your first sort field by. Simply select an order from the pop-up menu.

   By default the two date options and the two month options Excel provides are in this list. Any custom orders you create in the Preferences dialog box also appear in this pop-up list.
3. (Optional) Sensitive enables you to include the case of your text in the sort criteria. Check it if it makes a difference whether or not a word is capitalized. For example, do you want all Low to fall together sorting by priority, or would you want all low to fall in a different place in order from Low (as in low, medium, high, Low, Medium, High versus low, Low, medium, Medium, high, High).
4. Click a radio button to determine whether the sort will be from top to bottom or bottom to top.
5. Click OK.

Remember that a custom list can mix text and numbers and sort it however you want. Just make sure you format the cells as text before you enter the sort data.

Using the AutoFilter Command

Excel's AutoFilter enables you to define criteria to filter your database so that only records meeting the specified criteria appear. AutoFilter capability comes into play to set more complex retrieval criteria than is possible with the data form (and to print reports based on the selected data).

The AutoFilter command is a toggle, which means that after you turn it on, it's on until you turn it off. There are two clues that AutoFilter is on. You see a pop-up list next to each field name in the worksheet and the AutoFilter submenu under Data⇨Filter is checked. Turn AutoFilter off to clear the previous filters, then turn it on again to use AutoFilter on your database.

To put an AutoFilter in effect on a database, follow these steps:

1. Place the cursor anywhere in the database.
2. Choose Data⇨Filter⇨AutoFilter.

3. A pop-up list appears next to each field name in the database (see Figure 21-8). You can use these lists to filter out rows that don't match specified criteria.

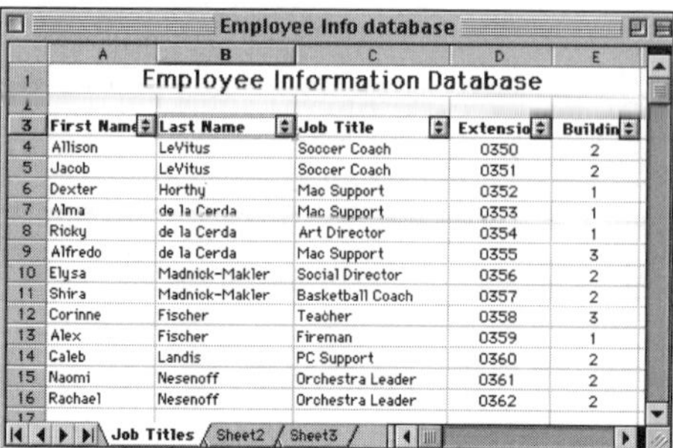

First Nam	Last Name	Job Title	Extensio	Buildin
Allison	LeVitus	Soccer Coach	0350	2
Jacob	LeVitus	Soccer Coach	0351	2
Dexter	Horthy	Mac Support	0352	1
Alma	de la Cerda	Mac Support	0353	1
Ricky	de la Cerda	Art Director	0354	1
Alfredo	de la Cerda	Mac Support	0355	3
Elysa	Madnick-Makler	Social Director	0356	2
Shira	Madnick-Makler	Basketball Coach	0357	2
Corinne	Fischer	Teacher	0358	3
Alex	Fischer	Fireman	0359	1
Caleb	Landis	PC Support	0360	2
Naomi	Nesenoff	Orchestra Leader	0361	2
Rachael	Nesenoff	Orchestra Leader	0362	2

Figure 21-8: Pop-up lists for using AutoFilter

4. Click the pop-up list for the field you want to filter and choose the entry you want as the filter. You can also select the Custom option from the pop-up list to create more complex criteria, as described later in this section.

As you make your selections from the pop-up list, Excel filters the records per your selections. You can create and-based criteria by choosing filters from more than one field. For example, in Figure 21-9, a Mac Support filter is selected in the Job Title field, and the number 1 is filtering the Building field. In this case, choosing Mac Support in the Job Title field is not enough because records would appear for all Mac Support staff, not just those working in building 1. If you choose multiple conditions, records must meet all of the conditions before they will be visible in the database when the AutoFilter is in effect.

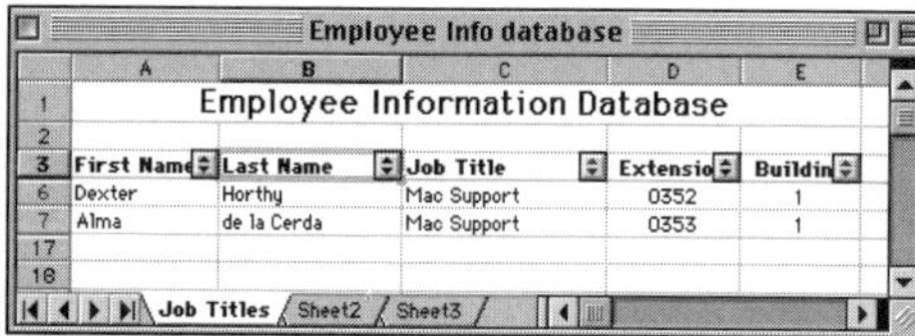

First Nam	Last Name	Job Title	Extensio	Buildin
Dexter	Horthy	Mac Support	0352	1
Alma	de la Cerda	Mac Support	0353	1

Figure 21-9: An example of AutoFilter used on two fields of a database

Keeping a Filtered Copy Handy

You may find it useful to keep a copy of the filtered data. For example, perhaps you know that during the week you'll need to refer to a listing of records that meet a certain condition several times. First use AutoFilter to filter the desired records, and then select all the records and choose Edit⇨Copy (⌘-C). Move to another worksheet and paste a copy of the filtered data there using Edit⇨Paste (⌘-V).

Just remember that if you make changes to one set of data, the other set isn't automatically updated and won't fully match the changed set.

Printing a report based on specific data

The AutoFilter capability makes it easy to get a report of records that meet a specified condition. After you have filtered your database using AutoFilter you can print the visible records by choosing File⇨Print (⌘-P) or by clicking the Print button on the Standard toolbar. Before the addition of AutoFilter, you would have had to use some of Excel's advanced database features to declare a criterion range and an extract range to manage the same sort of task. That process is no longer necessary, except in very specialized cases, so we won't bore you with the sordid details here. If you're curious, check out the specifics in Excel's Help files.

Using complex criteria with AutoFilter

You can also set more complex criteria (such as records falling within a certain range, records that use computed criteria, or records meeting or-based conditions) with AutoFilter. To do so, select Custom from the pop-up lists. This calls up the Custom AutoFilter dialog box, shown in Figure 21-10.

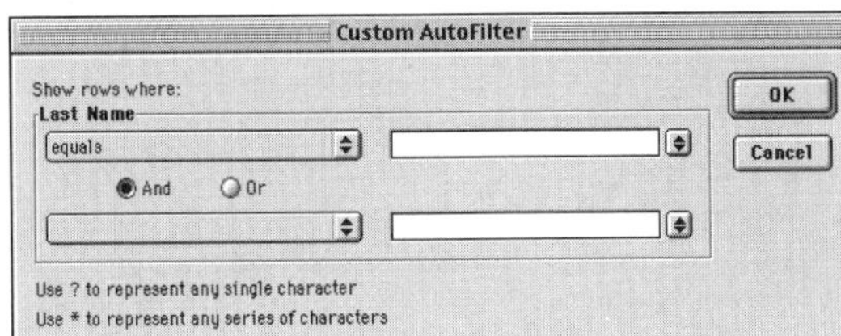

Figure 21-10: The Custom AutoFilter dialog box

Use the options in this dialog box to specify ranges of acceptable data and to specify or-based criteria (such as all records with a State value of CA or TX). Choose a desired comparison operator from the first pop-up list and enter a desired value in the text box to its right. To add a second comparison, select the And or the Or radio button as desired, and use the second pop-up list and text box for the other desired value.

You can see examples of the use of complex criteria by examining the dialog boxes shown in Figure 21-11. At the top, the expressions greater than or equal to M and less than or equal to Zz are used to retrieve all last names that start with M through Z. Note the addition of the second z. If this z was omitted, the criterion would actually find all names beginning with M through the letter Z alone, but would find no names of more than one character beginning with Z. In the middle dialog box, the expression greater than 2 retrieves all records with a value over 2 (but not equal to 2) in the Building field of the Employee Info database. At the bottom, the expression equals Mac Support or equals PC Support retrieve all entries with either of these job descriptions.

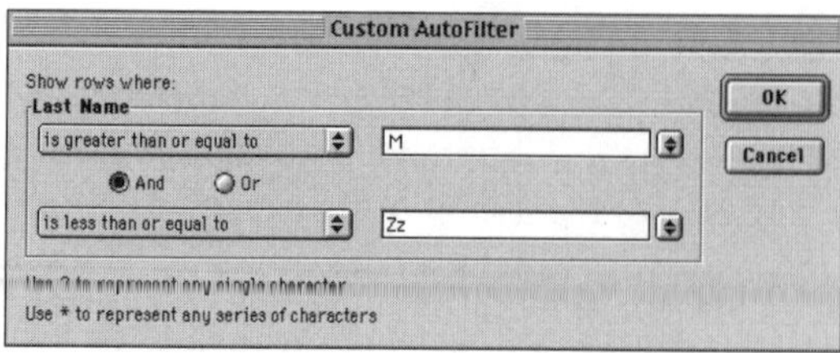

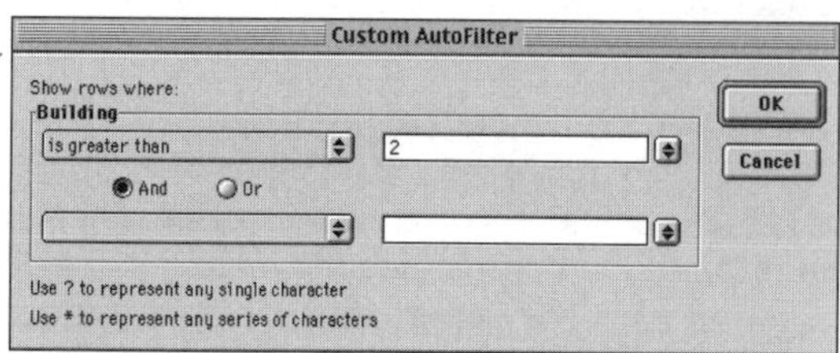

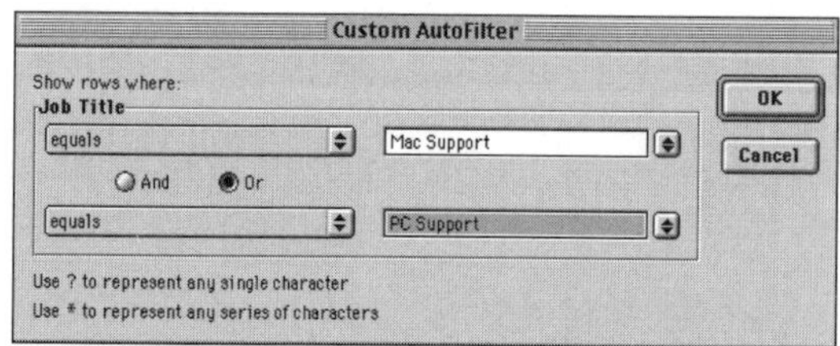

Figure 21-11: Top—complex criteria for finding all records with last names starting with M through Z. Middle—complex criteria for finding all records with a value greater than 2 in the Building field. Bottom—complex criteria for finding all records that say Mac Support or PC Support in the Job Title field.

Remember that you can use the Custom option in more than one field. By specifying Custom options in multiple fields, you can filter data based on complex criteria. To clear the effects of a Custom option, choose All from the pop-up list.

The Top 10 option

Another option you have when using the AutoFilter is to filter your lists to show only the top or bottom ten values in your list. It's called Top 10, but you can show any number of values. It's easy. To show the Top 10 values, follow these steps:

1. Select Top 10 from the AutoFilter pop-up menu to bring up the Top 10 dialog box.
2. Select Top or Bottom. Enter a number of top or bottom values to show. Finally, select Items or Percent. Then click OK to perform the filtering.

Turning off the effects of AutoFilter

When you're finished working with a filtered subset of records, remember to turn off the AutoFilter command by choosing Data ⇨ Filter ⇨ AutoFilter. Alternatively, you can click the pop-up list for any filters you have set and choose All from each of the lists for which you've set a filter.

Performing a Mail Merge

If you have names and addresses stored in an Excel database, you can combine the power of Excel and Word to create mail merge documents and generate form letters and envelopes. To generate form letters by using a mailing list stored in Excel, follow these steps:

1. Use AutoFilter, if necessary, to show only those records for which you want to print a merged document.
2. Select the entire range of data that contains the records.

Outgrowing Excel

At what point do your database needs outgrow Excel? If you cross that point and stick with Excel as your database, you're making unnecessary work for yourself. As an obvious example, consider this simple list of sales data for a small mail-order operation:

Date	*Name*	*Phone*	*Item*	*Cost*
6/15/95	Smith, R.	723-1020	calendar	18.00
6/15/95	Williams, E.	853-6723	calendar	18.00
6/15/95	Smith, R.	723-1020	portfolio	21.00
6/15/95	Smith, R.	723-1020	calendar	18.00

What may look like a simple, effective list in reality is (to a professional database developer's eye) the beginnings of a logistical nightmare. When you find yourself regularly entering any kind of data—the same employee names, customer names, item numbers, or descriptions—over and over, you're using the wrong product for your database. This kind of data cries out for "normalization," the separation of data into individual tables, with relationships established between the tables to avoid redundancy. This is something that isn't possible with Excel but falls right in line with the power of a relational database, such as FileMaker Pro or ACI US's 4th Dimension. (Go for FileMaker Pro if you're setting up the database yourself. If you're hiring a developer, both FileMaker and 4th Dimension are terrific, so go with the professional's recommendation.)

Another time to move up from Excel is when your database grows to thousands of records, putting unusual demands on the database power of a spreadsheet.

3. Choose Edit ➪ Copy (⌘-C).
4. Switch to Word and open a new document.
5. Choose Edit ➪ Paste (⌘-V) to paste the Excel data into Word as a table.
6. Save the Word document under any desired filename.
7. Open the Word document to which you are merging your data (or create a new document with the desired text).
8. Still in Word, choose Tools ➪ Mail Merge to display the Mail Merge Helper dialog box.
9. Follow the instructions that appear in the dialog box. When you are asked for a data source, choose the Word document that contains the Excel data.

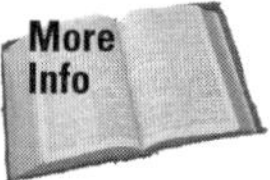

Mail merge is more specific to Word, so we give it much more detail in the Word section of this book (see Chapter 6).

If you outgrow Excel as a database and move into a relational database, don't worry about still being able to use Mail Merge. It's very easy to use this feature with any application that can export data in simple tab-delimited form—as all databases can.

Designing Databases

Planning is vital to effective database management. All too often users create a database and begin storing data only to discover that the database doesn't provide all the necessary information. Correcting mistakes that you make during the design of a database, or later trying to compensate for design shortcomings, can be tedious. To avoid such time-consuming mistakes, give some thought to designing your database.

Think about how the data should be stored and about how you and others will ask for the data. Outline the business' needs, which Excel's database capabilities can help solve. Just as you would not haphazardly toss a bunch of files into a filing cabinet without designing some type of filing system, you should not place information in a database without first designing the database. As you design the database, you must define the kinds of information to be stored in it.

About data and attributes

Data and attributes are two important terms in database design. *Data* is the information that goes into your database. *Attributes* are the types of data that make up the database. For example, an individual's last name is data. An attribute, on the other hand, is another name for a field, so an entire group of last names is considered to be an attribute. Names, telephone numbers, customer numbers, descriptions, locations, and stock numbers are all common examples of attributes that your database may contain.

In addition to thinking about what kinds of information should go into the database, give careful consideration to the ways in which Excel will retrieve the information. Information comes from a database in the form of reports. A report is a summary of information. Whether Excel displays a single row of data through a data form or dozens of rows by means of an AutoFilter, Excel is providing a report based on the data contained within the database file.

Steps in database design

Designing a database in Excel, regardless of its purpose, involves two major parts:

✦ Data definition (analyzing existing data)

✦ Data refinement (refining necessary data)

During the first phase—data definition—list (on paper) all the important attributes that are involved in your application. To do this, examine your needs carefully to determine exactly what kind of information must be stored in the database. List all possible attributes of your database even though they may not actually be needed by your particular application. You can eliminate unnecessary attributes during the data refinement stage.

During data refinement, refine your initial list of attributes so that the list forms an accurate description of the types of data you will need. At this stage, it is vital to include suggestions from as many other users of the database as possible. The people who use the database are likely to know what kinds of information they will need from it. What kinds of reports do they need? What kinds of queries will employees ask of the database? By continually asking these types of questions, you begin to think in terms of your database. This thought process helps you determine what is important and what is not important.

An example is the best way to demonstrate what we mean by considering usage and queries. Consider addresses. If you are going to store addresses, rather than creating one field called Address, break the address into its components so you have separate fields for Street, City, State, Zip and even the plus-4 zip extension. This way you can sort or filter by city or state, or find common zips for bulk rate mailing. Now consider names. Break names into first name and last name—even middle name. Create separate fields for name titles such as Dr., Mr., Ms., and so on. That way you can send a letter to Ms. Smith or to Jane. If the entire name was in one field, you'd be stuck saying "Dear Jane Smith." Using the text command concatenate, you can easily join text fields together. This is far easier than breaking up a name.

Of course, even after you begin using your database, you can change it. If you follow the systematic approach of database design for your specific application, however, the chances are better that you won't create a database that fails to provide the information you need, and you will avoid extensive redesign.

By inserting rows and columns as needed, you can change the design of a database at any time, but such changes are often inconvenient to make after the database is designed. For example, if you created a database to handle a customer mailing list, you might include fields for names, addresses, cities, states, and zip codes. At first glance, these fields seem sufficient. Gradually you build a sizable mailing list. But if your company later decides to begin telemarketing by using the same mailing list, the database you designed is inadequate because it does not include a field for telephone numbers. Although a field for telephone numbers can easily be added by inserting a new column, there is still the task of going back and adding a telephone number for every name currently in the mailing list. If this information had been entered as you developed the mailing list, there wouldn't be the inconvenience of having to enter the telephone numbers as a separate operation. Careful planning during the database design process can help avoid such pitfalls.

Summary

In this chapter, you learned how to work with databases stored within Excel worksheets. The chapter discussed these topics:

✦ In Excel, a database is a list of data that is organized into columns of data directly underneath a row of field names.

✦ You can add data to a database by typing it directly into the cells below the field names or by using a data form.

✦ In addition to adding data, you can use data forms to find specific records and to edit or delete records.

✦ Data⇨Sort enables you to sort the data in a database. You can even create your own sorting orders.

✦ You can use Excel's AutoFilter to filter a database so only records meeting certain criteria appear. You can then copy these records to a different area of the worksheet or to a different worksheet, or you can print the records.

Where to go next

✦ In the next chapter, you learn how you can put macros to work to automate many routine tasks within Excel.

✦ A major part of setting up and maintaining a database is the tedious but necessary task of data entry. Chapter 16 has some tips and techniques that you can use to make data entry easier.

✦ When you've entered data into your database, you'll want to make the most of Excel's printing capabilities to generate reports. Chapter 20 has the story.

✦ ✦ ✦

CHAPTER 22

Working with Excel Macros

✦ ✦ ✦ ✦

In This Chapter

Understanding macro types

Creating a macro

Assigning macros

Running a macro

Changing macro options

Making macros available

✦ ✦ ✦ ✦

Macros are combinations of keystrokes that automate many of the tasks you normally perform manually. Macros enable you to record a sequence of actions that you can assign to a keystroke combination, a graphic object, a toolbar button, or a button on the screen. Later, you can play back the sequence by pressing the keys, clicking the button, or selecting the menu command assigned to the macro. When you run the macro, Excel performs the steps as if you had just typed the characters, made the menu choices, or performed whatever actions you recorded for that macro. If you produce daily reports or perform repetitive tasks, macros can save you many keystrokes and a lot of time.

You don't have to be a programmer to create macros. All you have to do is turn on the macro recorder and perform the Excel steps in your worksheet as you normally do, and then turn off the macro recorder.

Understanding Macro Types

Excel provides two types of macros:

- **Command macros** carry out a series of commands. For example, you can create a command macro that marks a specific range of worksheet cells and chooses File⇨Print to begin printing. You can also create a macro that applies a preferred format to an entire worksheet. Command macros can range from simple to extremely complex.
- **Function macros** are similar to Excel's functions because they act on values by performing calculations and returning a value. For example, you can create a macro that takes the dimensions of an area in feet and returns the area in square yards.

Command macros are similar to commands because they perform tasks. Function macros are similar to functions because they are stored in formulas and accept and return a value. You can create command macros using the macro recorder. To create function macros, you must write Visual Basic for Applications code (see Chapter 24).

Creating a Macro

To create a macro, first perform every action you don't want to include in the macro, such as opening a worksheet or moving to a specific location in the worksheet. As a result, you won't include unnecessary steps in the macro. As soon as you begin recording the macro, everything you do will be included in it.

Some steps shouldn't be included in a macro. For example, although you may always want to gather redundant data, you may not always want the data to land in the same worksheet. In this case, it is better to have the user manually go to the worksheet location prior to running the macro.

To begin creating a macro, choose Tools ➪ Macro ➪ Record New Macro. The Record Macro dialog box prompts you for the name and description of your new macro (see Figure 22-1).

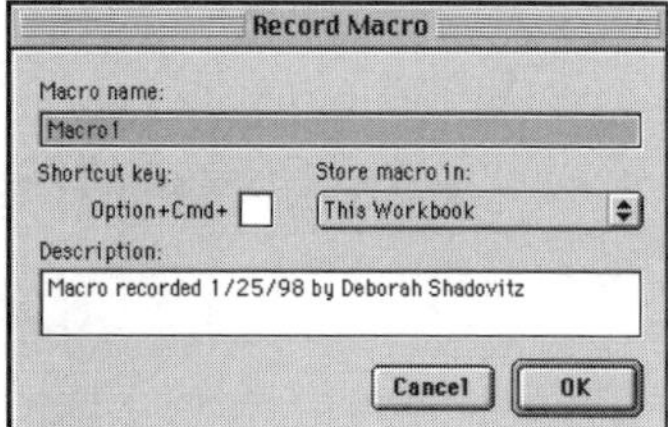

Figure 22-1: The Record Macro dialog box

Name your macro descriptively so you know what it is and what it does when you need to assign it to a button or menu, or when you need to call on its actions. You can give the macro any name, as long as the first character of the macro name is a letter and you don't include spaces. Letters, numbers, and underscore characters are fair game. An underscore or hyphen works well in lieu of a space to separate words.

In the Description area, you can enter a description of the macro. A description can be helpful, reminding you what the macro does somewhere down the line when you are bound not to remember. You can assign a keystroke combination to your macro by entering a key to add to the ⌘-Option combination assigned by default. Just click in the Shortcut key text field and press the desired key.

When Do I Really Need Macros?

The kinds of macros you can record with Excel's macro recorder are best at eliminating any kind of redundant work you perform regularly. Here are the kinds of tasks for which you can create macros to save yourself time and effort:

- ✦ Selecting several ranges on one or more sheets of a workbook and printing those selected ranges
- ✦ Opening a new workbook, entering titles, formatting different ranges in the worksheet, and adjusting row heights and column widths
- ✦ Opening a database, sorting it in a desired order, applying a filter to the data, and printing the result

By default, the macro expects to be stored in your current workbook—This Workbook. This option places the macro in a module sheet that appears at the end of the workbook. Click the pop-up list to specify where you want to store the new macro. The Personal Macro Workbook option makes the macro available to all open worksheets by attaching the macro to a hidden notebook that opens each time you launch Excel. If you need to see the macro sheet, choose Window⇨ Unhide. (This option is only available after you've saved a macro to the Personal Macro Workbook.) The New Workbook option opens a new workbook and attaches the new module sheet to it.

After you complete the information in this dialog box and click OK, a small floating button bar appears to provide a Stop button. You are now in record mode, and any actions you perform are recorded.

Stopping the macro recorder isn't too difficult—click the Stop Recording button. This button appears onscreen when you begin to record a macro. Alternatively, you can choose Tools⇨Macro⇨Stop Recording.

You can also use the Visual Basic toolbar to record macros. To activate the Visual Basic toolbar, Control-click in any visible toolbar area and choose Visual Basic from the shortcut menu. You can then click the Record button on the Visual Basic toolbar to begin recording a macro. For everyday use of macros outside the world of programming, only two buttons on the Visual Basic toolbar will be of any interest to you—Record Macro and Run Macro. For an explanation of the remaining buttons, see Chapter 24, which provides details on programming in Visual Basic for Applications.

Now that you have had a general look at creating macros, you need to see how the specifics work. The following steps show you how to create a macro that selects a range in one of your worksheets and prints that range:

1. Open the worksheet to which you want to apply the macro.

2. Choose Tools ➪ Macro ➪ Record New Macro.
3. In the Record New Macro dialog box, enter **ReportIt** in the Macro name text box.
4. Click in the Shortcut key field and enter any letter key you want to use (when combined with the ⌘-Option keys) to activate the macro.
5. After you click OK, you are ready to perform the macro steps. In this case, that means making the choices you need to print the range.
6. Select a range of data from your worksheet. Then choose File ➪ Print (⌘-P) to open the Print dialog box, as shown in Figure 22-2.

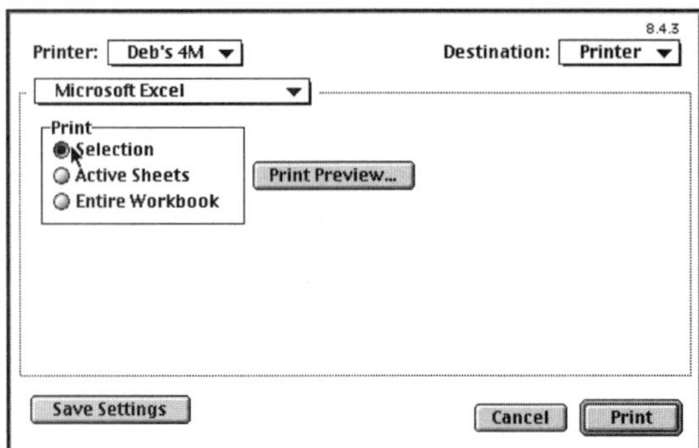

Figure 22-2: The Excel screen of the Print dialog box

7. In the pop-up menu (located below the printer name in this LaserWriter software dialog box), select Microsoft Excel. On the Excel screen, click the radio button for Selection. Then click Print to print the selected part of your worksheet.
8. Click the Stop Recording button or choose Tools ➪ Macro ➪ Stop Recording to stop recording the macro.

From this point on, you can repeatedly select and print the same range of worksheets just by running the macro. To see how this works, press the keystroke combination that you assigned to the macro. If you didn't assign a key or don't recall the key, you can select Tools ➪ Macro ➪ Macros and then double-click the Reportit macro name in the Macro dialog box (or click once on the name and click Run). With either method, the macro runs and the worksheet range is again printed. That's the beauty of macros: you can automate any task you perform regularly.

The macros you create will differ because you will have different tasks to automate. By the way, in this exercise, you may need to change the orientation to Landscape so the selection fits on one page. To do so, after selecting your range of data in the worksheet, select File➪Page Setup, click Landscape (perhaps selecting High for the Print quality) and OK, and then go on to the Print command.

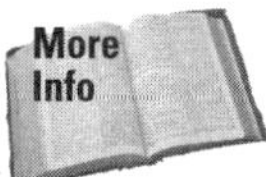

For another exercise in creating a useful macro see the first exercise—a time sheet—under "Learning VBA with Macros" in Chapter 24.

Assigning Macros

By assigning a macro to a button placed on a worksheet, a graphic object, a toolbar button, or a menu, you can probably provide the ultimate in user ease. The following sections cover each of these possibilities in detail.

Using the same techniques described in this chapter, you can even assign the macro to a topic in a Help file.

Assigning macros to a worksheet button

Assigning a macro to a button—within reach, within sight, reminding you that the macro is available—can be very handy when you are working in a worksheet. One such macro button might be set up to open another worksheet page from the current worksheet page. While you look at one set of data, the macro button provides an easy way to access the other relative data.

Placing the button

To place a button in your spreadsheet and attach a macro to it, you can use the Button tool on the Forms toolbar. You activate the macro by clicking the button.

To add a macro button to a worksheet, follow these steps:

1. Turn on the Forms toolbar by choosing View➪Toolbars➪Forms.
2. Click the Button tool in the Forms toolbar.
3. In the worksheet, click and drag to place your button and define its size.
4. When you release the mouse button, the macro button and the Assign Macro dialog box appear, as shown in Figure 22-3.

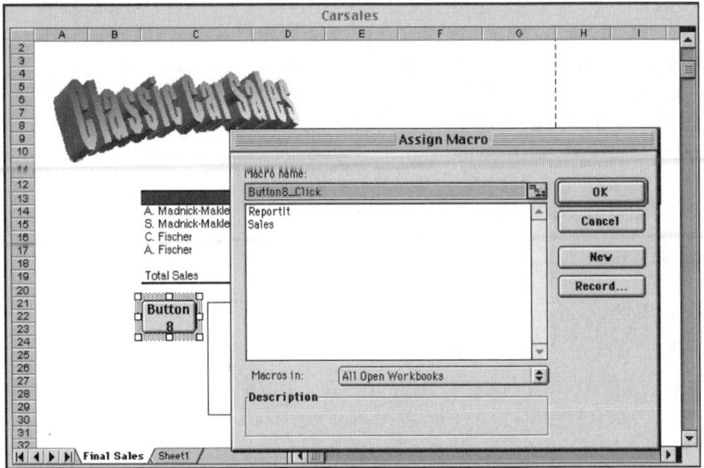

Figure 22-3: The new button and the Assign Macro dialog box

5. In the Macro name list, double-click the macro you want to assign to the button, or click once on the macro name to select it and then click OK.

If you haven't already created your macro, you can create the button and then record the macro at the same time. Create the button, and then click the Record button in the Assign Macro dialog box. In the Record New Macro dialog box, enter a name (optional), description, and key combination (optional) for the macro you will record. Then click OK and perform your macro steps.

Changing the button assignment

Excel also lets you assign a macro to a completed button or change the macro you have assigned to the button. You can perform these tasks by following these steps:

1. Control-click or ⌘-click the button and choose Assign Macro from the shortcut menu to bring up the Assign Macro dialog box. (If Control-clicking the button causes the currently assigned macro to run, ⌘-click instead.)
2. If you want to assign an existing macro, double-click the name in the Macro name list (or click once on the name and then click OK).
3. If you want to record a macro, type the name for the new macro in the Macro name text box and click the Record button (which becomes active after you type the new macro name). Then use the standard macro recording procedures detailed earlier in the chapter.

Naming Buttons

When you create a button, it is assigned a default name, such as Button 1 or Button 2. Of course, you can change this name. Before the name has been assigned to a macro, it's a plain object, so you can simply select the text and edit and format it as you do with any text. After the text has been assigned to a button, you need to Control-click the button and select Edit Text from the shortcut menu. This provides the text cursor so you can edit the text and format it using the buttons on the Formatting toolbar. To change the formatting, you can also Control-click the button and select Format Control from the shortcut menu.

Assigning macros to graphic objects

You can get visually creative and make your spreadsheets more appealing by assigning a macro to a graphic object. The visual clues of the graphic can also make your macro easier to remember. The procedure for adding a macro to a graphic object is much the same as the procedure for adding a macro to a toolbar button. An example of a macro assigned to a graphic is Figure 22-4. In the figure, a macro that prints a report is attached to a picture of a car. To print the report, the user clicks the car.

The Old Versus the New Way

If you've upgraded to Excel 98 from version 4.0 or 5.0, and you've used macros and the Excel macro language, you'll discover that many things have changed. In earlier versions of Excel you recorded macros in Excel's macro language, a language with some similarities to (and a lot of differences from) Visual Basic for Applications.

Programs were known as macros and were recorded on macro sheets. In Excel 98 each individual program (written in Visual Basic for Applications) is a procedure, and procedures are stored in modules. Each workbook can have an unlimited number of modules and procedures.

There are also differences in the languages. For example, Visual Basic for Applications brings object-oriented techniques into the picture, something that just didn't exist in the old Excel macro language.

You don't have to throw away all those macros you wrote in Excel 4.0. You can run an old macro from Excel 98 the same way you run a new macro, or you can use the following Visual Basic for Applications statement in the Module tab of the macro:

RUN("*macrosheetname!macroname*")

In this statement, *macrosheetname* is the name of the old macro sheet, and *macroname* is the name of the macro you want to run. For more specifics on using Visual Basic for Applications code in your macros, refer to Chapter 24.

Follow these steps to assign a macro to a graphic object:

1. Add the graphic object to your worksheet using the steps outlined in Chapter 18.
2. Control-click the graphic. This automatically selects the graphic object (selection handles appear on its borders) as it reveals the shortcut menu.

   If the object currently has another macro assigned to it, Control-clicking may cause the macro to run Instead, try holding down the ⌘ key as you select the object.
3. Select Assign Macro from the shortcut menu. In a moment, the Assign Macro dialog box appears.
4. If you want to assign an existing macro to the object, double-click the name of the macro in the Macro name list, or click once on the name to select it and then click OK.
5. If you want to create a new macro to the graphic object, name the macro, click Record, and then perform the steps to create a macro.

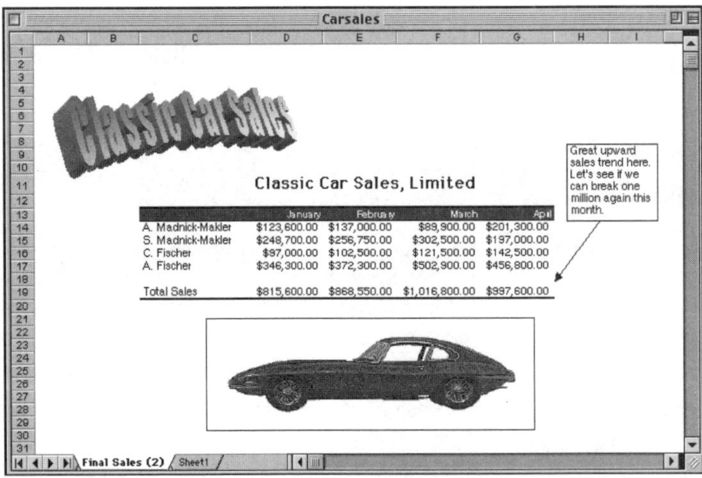

Figure 22-4: A macro attached to a graphic object (the car) in a worksheet

Assigning macros to toolbar buttons

Macros can also be assigned to buttons on the toolbar. This can prove useful if you perform certain tasks on a regular basis or create task-specific or job-specific toolbars for office staff. Typically, people create a custom button to assign a macro to, but you can also assign a macro to an existing toolbar button, which cancels the previous function. To assign a macro to a toolbar button, perform these steps:

1. Choose Tools ➪ Customize.
2. If the toolbar that contains the desired button isn't visible, click the Toolbars tab of the dialog box and check the check box beside the toolbar name.
3. To assign a macro to an existing toolbar button, skip to Step 4. If you want to run the macro from a button not on a toolbar, click the Commands tab and then click Macros in the Categories list. In the Commands list that appears, drag the Custom button onto a toolbar.
4. Control-click the toolbar button that is to receive the macro command, and choose Assign Macro from the shortcut menu.
5. In the Macro name text box, double-click the name of an existing macro in the Macro name list (or record a new macro by entering a name for the new macro, clicking Record, and then performing the macro steps.)
6. By default, the name of any new button is Custom Button, which is not highly descriptive. It is easiest to change the name right way, while the Customize dialog box is still open and the button is still selected. Just click the Modify Selection button in the Customize dialog box. When a menu pops up, move your mouse up to the Name field. Click in this field, select the existing text, type in your new button name, and press Enter. This name appears as the ScreenTip to guide you (and your users) as to its function when the mouse pauses over the button.
7. Close the Customize dialog box.

You can change the name of your buttons any time. First select Tools ➪ Customize because the toolbar cannot be modified without this Customize dialog box open. Then Control-click the button you want to change, move to the Name field, select the existing text, and enter your new button name.

Assigning macros to menus

Macros can also be assigned to menus. You can place the macro command on an existing menu or create a specialized menu. If you are creating the worksheet for office use, creating task-specific or job-specific menus can be helpful. Adding commands to the menu is covered in detail in Appendix E. However, we'll go over it here as well. To assign a macro to a menu, follow these steps:

1. Choose Tools ➪ Customize.
2. In the toolbars tab, check Worksheet Menu Bar. A customizable copy of the menu bar opens, located at the top of your screen below the normal menu bar.

   (Optional) If you want to create a new custom menu, click the Commands tab and then click New Menu in the Categories list. In the Commands list that appears, click New Menu and drag the words into place as desired on the customizable menu bar. In the Customize dialog box, click Modify Selection, move your mouse up the pop-up list to where the menu item appears in a white field, edit the command name to your liking, and then click Enter.

3. Click the Commands tab, and then click Macros in the Categories list. In the Commands list that appears, click Custom Menu Item and drag it onto the customizable menu bar. The menu drop downs and reveals the menu's commands, and your cursor gains a field and a plus sign. Move your cursor (pointer) to the exact location on the menu where you want the new command to fall. A horizontal black line will show you where the command is due to fall as you release the mouse button. Release the mouse button when the command will fall where you want it.
4. In the customizable menu bar, click the menu in which you've placed the command, and select the newly placed Custom Menu Item command. Then click the Modify Selection button in the Customize dialog box. Move your mouse up to where the menu item appears in a white field, edit the command name to your liking, and click Enter. Then click Close to close the Customize dialog box.
5. You still have to assign the macro to the menu item. Click the menu item. The Assign Macro dialog box appears, listing all available macros and asking you to assign a macro. Click the macro you want to assign and click OK.

For more on naming, renaming, and customizing menus, see Appendix E.

Running a Macro

You can run a macro several ways. After reading this section, you can decide for yourself which method is best for you.

The method always available to you for running a macro is to choose Tools ➪ Macro ➪ Macros and then double-click the name of the macro in the Macro dialog box. Or, if you want to read the macro's description, click once on the macro's name to see a description (if you or the creator entered one), and then click the Run button.

Another method for running macros is to use the keyboard combination you assign to a macro in the Record New Macro dialog box. Keyboard combinations easily coexist with buttons, so you can use the combination or click any button you may have assigned to your macro.

You can also run the macro from the menu if you've placed it there. Last, if you've created any type of button for a macro, you can click the button.

Changing Macro Options

After recording a macro, you may have to change its description or the keyboard combination that runs it. You can also change the name of the macro as it appears in a menu or on a button. (See "Assigning macros to toolbar buttons" or "Assigning macros to menus" in this chapter, or see Appendix E for more information on this subject.)

Perform these steps to change the options for an existing macro:

1. Choose Tools ➪ Macro ➪ Macros to open the Macro dialog box.
2. In the Macro name list box, select the name of the macro with the options you want to change.
3. Click the Options button to open the Macro Options dialog box, as shown in Figure 22-5.
4. Make the changes you want for the different options, and click OK.

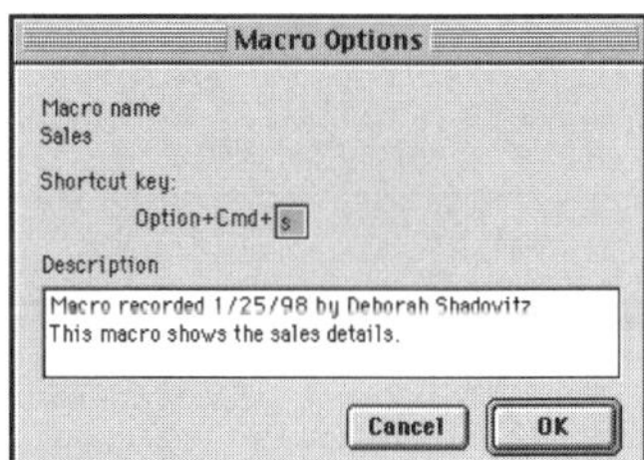

Figure 22-5: The Macro Options dialog box

Making Macros Available

You can store macros in many different places, which directly affects the availability of the macro. You can store a macro in the Personal Macro Workbook, in the active workbook, or in a new workbook.

If you want to make a macro available at all times, store it in the Personal Macro Workbook, which is an invisible workbook that is always open, unless you specify otherwise. The Personal Macro Workbook is like the depository for workbooks you use in a variety of areas throughout Excel. Because this workbook is always open, the macros are all always available, which lets you use them with all worksheets you have open.

The first time you quit Excel after the first time you save a macro to your Personal Macro Workbook, you are asked if you want to save the Personal Macro Workbook. Choose Yes. The Personal Macro Workbook is stored in the Excel folder (Microsoft Office 98/Office/Startup/Excel).

To control where you store your macro, choose Tools ➪ Macro ➪ Record New Macro. In the Store macro in list box, choose the Personal Macro Workbook option to store this and all successive macros in that workbook. This option remains in effect for all macros until you change it. In addition to placing the macros in the Personal Macro Workbook, you can also put them in the current workbook or in a new workbook.

The Personal Macro Workbook is similar to other workbooks, with the exception that it begins with one worksheet where all the macros you specify are stored. If you are into Visual Basic, you may want to add other Visual Basic module items to the Personal Macro Workbook.

To display the Personal Macro Workbook (after you have created it by saving a macro to it), choose Window⇨Unhide and choose Personal Macro Workbook from the dialog box that appears. Figure 22-6 shows what the code stored in the Personal Macro Workbook looks like when the Visual Basic for Applications Editor is opened, using the Visual Basic toolbar. (For more specifics on VBA, see Chapter 24.) Remember, the Unhide menu option is visible only if a worksheet has been hidden (as the Personal Macro Workbook normally is).

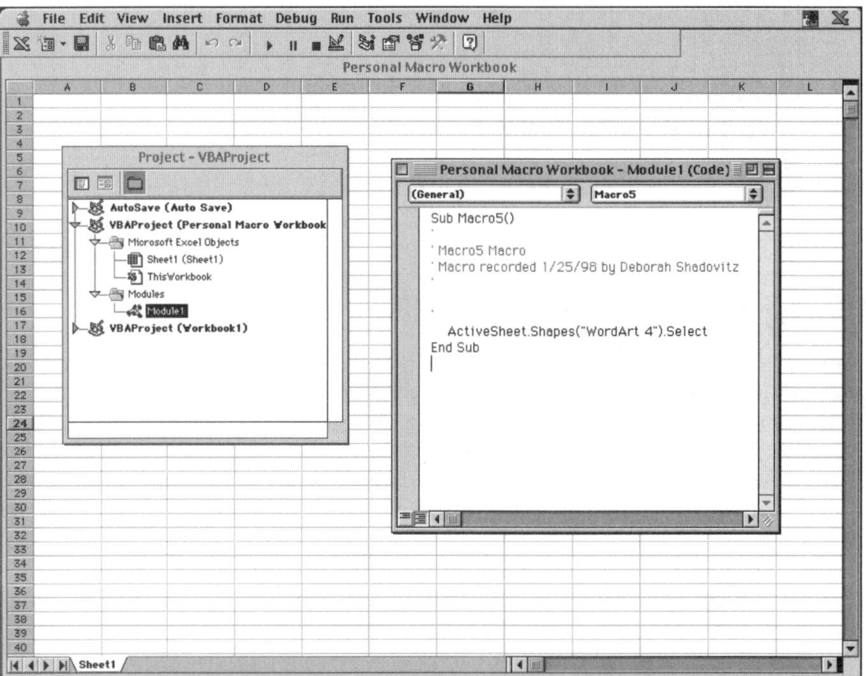

Figure 22-6: The Personal Macro Workbook

Summary

This chapter covered different topics related to macros. Now you have the tools you need to record macros efficiently and put them to use for yourself. We covered the following areas related to macros:

- ✦ Excel provides two different types of macros.
- ✦ You can easily create macros with Excel's macro recorder.

- You can run macros by choosing Tools ⇨ Macro ⇨ Macros and selecting the desired macro in the dialog box that appears.
- You can attach macros to keyboard combinations, menu options, toolbar buttons, custom buttons, and graphic images.
- Macros are recorded in Visual Basic for Applications (VBA) code, the underlying programming language of Excel.

Where to go next

- Macros can take much of the repetitive drudgery out of formatting and printing tasks. For an explanation of the kinds of formatting tasks you can automate, see Chapter 17. For specifics on printing in Excel, refer to Chapter 20.
- Excel macros are the key to learning Visual Basic for Applications. Chapter 24 delves more deeply into Visual Basic for Applications programming.

✦ ✦ ✦

Excel and the Web

✦ ✦ ✦ ✦

In This Chapter

Working with Excel 98 on the Web

Learning the ropes

Creating hyperlinks

Publishing worksheets and charts

✦ ✦ ✦ ✦

Excel 98 introduces numerous options for working with the Internet and with intranets. Excel 98 enables you to attach hyperlinks to other Office 98 documents or to Web sites. The table-like structure of a spreadsheet makes it easy for you to publish Web pages in table form. You can easily export worksheets or charts in HTML format, ready for inclusion on your Web pages.

Working with Excel 98 on the Web

Figure 23-1 shows data in an Excel worksheet, published as a Web page on a corporate intranet and viewed using Netscape Navigator, a popular Web browser. You can also place hyperlink fields in the cells of a worksheets, and you can use these cells to display links in other Web pages on an intranet or the Internet. If you need to retrieve or publish worksheet data across the Internet, Excel 98 can be a powerful tool for accomplishing such a task.

To accomplish most of the tasks described in this chapter, you'll need to be connected to the Internet or an intranet. You can obtain a dial-up connection to the Internet, by means of a commercial Internet service provider. Your connection can also be a direct connection through your organization's local area network, and you may be connected directly to a corporate intranet, in which case you'll be able to retrieve or publish data to your company's private network. This chapter won't go into specifics on getting connected, as that topic is a book in itself. IDG Books Worldwide, Inc. publishes many great books covering all aspects of the Web.

This chapter also assumes a familiarity with the basics of Excel. If you are familiar with the World Wide Web or with intranets but you haven't yet learned to work with Excel, you should peruse Chapters 15 through 20 before proceeding with this chapter.

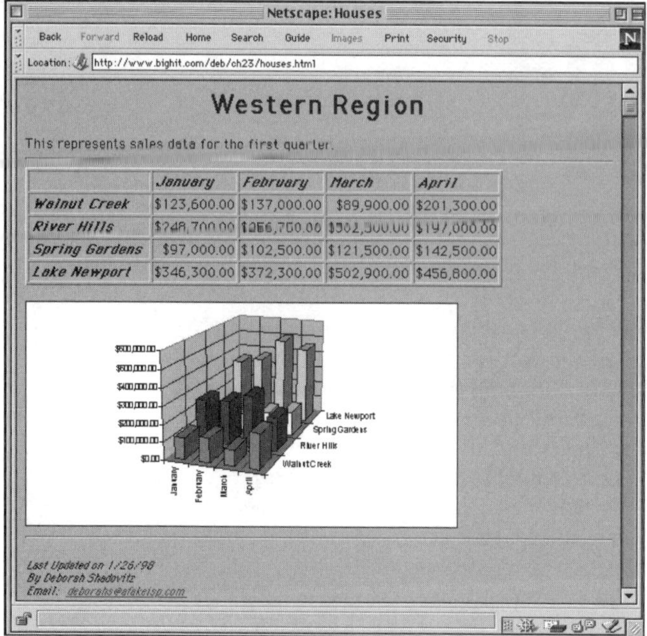

Figure 23-1: An Excel worksheet published as a Web page

Using Excel 98, you can perform a number of Internet-related tasks as you work with worksheets and charts. You can format text or objects in Excel worksheet cells as hyperlinks that link to other Office 98 documents or to Web sites. (Your Web site can be on the Internet or on your company intranet.) When users of the worksheets click in these cells, they can jump directly to that location in the other file or to a specified Web site. You can open workbooks that are stored on the Internet, and you can save worksheet data as HTML (Hypertext Markup Language), the publishing language of the Web. These topics will be covered in more detail throughout this chapter.

Learning the Ropes

Because intranets and the Internet are new concepts to many readers, an explanation of terms may be in order. (If you're intimately familiar with the Internet, intranets, and the Web, you may want to skip this section and the next and dive right into working with Excel and the Web.) First, the *Internet* is a global collection of computers linked together by means of telephone and microwave lines and accessible to the public by means of various connections in offices and in homes. The Internet grew out of a research project in the 1970s, which originally linked university and government computers in the United States. Since its inception, the Internet has grown to encompass millions of computers spread throughout dozens of nations. Any computer user with an Internet connection (either by means of a phone line or a direct hookup) can connect to the Internet and gain access to the volumes of information located there.

The World Wide Web

One major component of the Internet is the *World Wide Web.* There are other parts of the Internet, but the World Wide Web made the Internet fun and caught the public's eye. The World Wide Web is that part of the Internet that makes use of graphical software, known as *Web browsers,* and of files stored as HTML (which the browsers can read). The computers on the Internet that store the HTML files are called *Web servers.* When computers connect to the Internet to retrieve this data, they use Web browser software, which converts the incoming information (encoded in HTML) to graphical pages displayed as a combination of text, graphics, and in some cases audio and video. On the Mac, Mosaic was the first Web browser. Then came Netscape Navigator, followed by Microsoft Explorer. (These are the two most popular browsers on both the Mac and Windows platforms.) America Online and Prodigy also provide versions of Web browsers built into their software.

The Internet

Each site on the Internet has a unique address, known as a *URL (Uniform Resource Locator).* When you establish an Internet connection, open a Web browser, and enter an Internet address, you are entering the address that tells the Web server to send you Web pages stored on the server at that address. For example, `http://www.whitehouse.gov` connects you to the Web server that provides the pages for the U.S. White House. If the address you enter specifies a page after the domain name (`whitehouse.gov` or `bighit.com`, for example), that page is served to you. Otherwise the server brings you to the page designated at the default for the domain name you entered (the president's page, in this example). Web addresses like these can be stored in Excel worksheets and displayed as hyperlinks.

About intranets

Office 98 helps you make data available on intranets. An *intranet* is a private network of computers that is available only to the members of a specific organization. Intranets make use of World Wide Web technology—Web servers, network connections, and Web browser software—to enable members of an organization to share information. Intranets are very popular with corporations, as intranets let employees share work-related information in a confidential manner.

About HTML

As mentioned earlier, HTML is the language used for publishing information to the World Wide Web and to intranets that use World Wide Web technology. HTML is a text-based language that makes use of special codes called *tags.* These tags are included in the text of the HTML documents and provide instructions to the Web browser software, determining how the data appears when viewed by the end-user. You don't need to know the nuts and bolts of HTML coding to work with Excel and the Web; Excel does the coding for you. You just need to be familiar with the concept of saving your data in HTML file format. To publish Excel data on the Internet or on an intranet, you save that data in HTML format, and then upload it to your Web server. If you are dealing with a corporate intranet, your company's Webmaster can tell you how to upload the HTML files (that Excel produces) to your company's Web server. If you are renting space on a commercial server, your site host can give you directions. If you are managing a Web site on the Internet or on an intranet, you already know how to do this; the rest of this chapter will deal mostly with getting that Excel data ready for uploading to your server.

About the Web toolbar

Like all the core Office 98 applications, Excel provides the Web toolbar to help you browse through the resources on an intranet or on the Web. Using the Web toolbar, you can quickly open, search, and browse through any document or through a Web page. You can jump between documents, and you can add favorite sites you find on the Web to the Favorites folder, enabling you to go back to those sites at a later time.

In Excel, you can display the Web toolbar by choosing View ⇨ Toolbars ⇨ Web or by clicking the Web toolbar button in the Standard toolbar. Figure 23-2 shows the Web toolbar.

Figure 23-2: The Web toolbar

You may find the Web toolbar handy when you are in Excel and need to get to the Web (or to your company's intranet) for information. For example, you can click the Search the Web button to launch your default Web browser and search the Web, or click the Favorites button to select a destination from a list of your favorite Web sites. For more specifics on the Web toolbar, see Chapter 11. That chapter provides a description of how you can use the Web toolbar and how Word 98 can serve as a Web browser if you aren't using Microsoft Internet Explorer or Netscape Navigator.

Creating Hyperlinks

A significant feature of Excel 98 is its capability to use hyperlinks in worksheets. You can create hyperlinks to jump to other Office documents stored on your Mac, on your company's network, on a company intranet, or on the Internet. You can also turn the text in a cell or a graphic into a hyperlink.

Linking to Office documents with Copy and Paste

Creating a hyperlink from cells in Excel to other cells in Excel, to a Word document, or to a PowerPoint presentation, is as easy as copy and paste (actually Paste Hyperlink, in this case). To create a link to another Office document, follow these steps:

1. Open the document containing the location to which you want to link. (If the location is in Excel, it can be in the same workbook, or in a different, open workbook. If the location is in a Word or PowerPoint file, it can be in any area of the document or presentation.)
2. Select the portion of the document to which you want to link.
3. Choose Edit ➪ Copy.
4. In Excel, place the cell pointer at the cell where you want to insert the hyperlink. If you want any explanatory text in the cell, enter that text in the cell now.
5. Choose Edit ➪ Paste as Hyperlink. The cell you are in (from Step 4) becomes underlined indicating a link.

From this point on, any time you click the hyperlink, you jump to the linked document.

To create a link from one Excel worksheet to the next, follow these steps:

1. Go to the worksheet containing the cell(s) where you want the link to appear and enter the link text in the cell (by that we mean the text that will be underlined as the actual link).

   Note that links connect to an entire cell or cells, not just to a few characters within any cell.
2. Go to the worksheet containing the cell(s) you want the link to jump to and select the cell(s).
3. Copy those cells using Edit ➪ Copy, or ⌘-C.
4. Return to the worksheet containing the cell(s) where you want the link to appear and select the cell(s).
5. Choose Edit ➪ Paste as Hyperlink. The cell(s) become underlined, indicating a link.

Your link will now jump you to the linked document.

Hot Stuff

There's a faster way to create a hyperlink if you are linking from one portion of a worksheet to another portion of the same worksheet. Simply select the cell(s) to be linked to and Control-click the border of the selection. Then drag to the cell (or top-left cell) where you want the link to appear and release the Control key and mouse button, which causes the shortcut menu to appear. From this menu, choose Create Hyperlink Here to complete the link back to the original selection.

Linking to Web sites or files with Insert Hyperlink

If you need to establish a hyperlink to a Web site on an intranet or on the Internet, you can use the following steps to do so: (Technically, you can use these same steps to link to another Office document, but it's easier to copy and paste in that situation, as described earlier.)

1. Select the cell(s) that will serve as the hyperlink.
2. Click the Insert Hyperlink button in the Standard toolbar, or choose Insert ➪ Hyperlink. When you do this, the Insert Hyperlink dialog box appears, as shown in Figure 23-3.

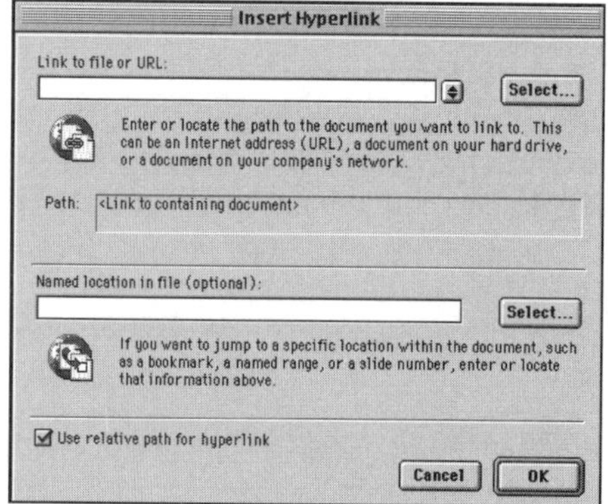

Figure 23-3: The Insert Hyperlink dialog box

3. To tell Excel to link to a file you have access to on your hard drive or network, click the top Select button (by the Link to file or URL text box). This opens an Open/Save-type dialog box. In this dialog box, navigate to the desired file, and then double-click it (or click once on the file and click OK). You can also manually enter the path.

   To tell Excel to link to a Web destination, manually enter the Web address of the destination for the link in the Link to file or URL text box. To save a bit of typing and make sure you get the address format right, you can click the pop-up arrow next to the text field and select http://, ftp://, or mailto: from the list.
4. If you are establishing a link to a file and want to jump to a specific location within that file, enter that location in the Named location in file text box. (This can be a cell reference or named range, a Word bookmark, or the name of a PowerPoint slide.) If you link to a file and leave this entry blank, the hyperlink jumps to the beginning of the file.
5. If you want a link to an item on a shared network, you have to consider that the destination file may be moved around within the hard drive on which it

resides. Relative Paths can accommodate this. By checking the Use relative path for hyperlink option, the document can be found even if it moved. If you don't check this option, the link will go only to the exact path specified. If the document is moved, the link will fail.

6. Click OK to establish the hyperlink.

When you rest your cursor over a hyperlink, a ScreenTip appears and tells you the link's destination.

Publishing Worksheets and Charts

Excel 98 includes an Internet Assistant Wizard—a wizard that enables you to convert worksheet ranges or Excel charts to HTML format, so you can publish the data on the Internet or on an intranet. The Internet Assistant lets you produce static Web pages; these appear on Web sites as fixed, unchanging data. If you change the data in your worksheet, the data will not automatically change on the Web page.

When you select File➪Save as HTML, the Internet Assistant Wizard appears, asking if you'd like help. Whether you accept the help or refuse it, the procedure discussed here is the same. The help is in the form of extra wizard dialog boxes that explain what's going on. Use the following steps to produce Web-ready files based on your worksheets or charts in Excel:

1. Choose File➪Save as HTML. In a moment, the first Internet Assistant Wizard dialog box appears, as shown in Figure 23-4.

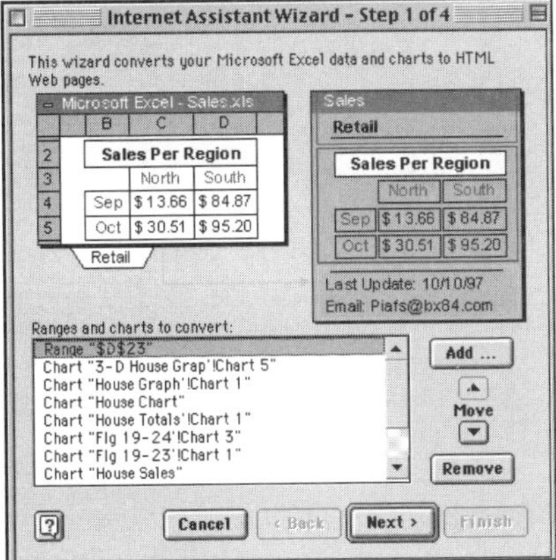

Figure 23-4: The first Internet Assistant Wizard dialog box

2. In the dialog box, add any desired ranges that don't appear in the list box by clicking the Add button and entering the cell range in the next dialog box that appears. Remove any cell ranges or charts you don't want converted by selecting them in the list and clicking Remove. The cell ranges and charts will appear in the HTML document in the same order they appear in the list. If you want to change this order, click a desired range or chart and use the up and down arrows to move it up or down as desired in the list. When done choosing the ranges and charts you want to convert to HTML, click Next. In a moment, the second Internet Assistant Wizard dialog box appears, as shown in Figure 23-5.

3. Here, you can choose whether to create a new page containing this data or whether to insert the converted data into an existing Web page. Make your desired selection and click Next.

4. The next dialog box to appear (see Figure 23-6) lets you enter additional information and add horizontal lines, if desired, before and after the converted data. The title appears as the window name. The header appears at the top of your page. In the description, you can explain to the viewer what is being displayed or say anything you'd like. This dialog box also enables you to list the date the page was last updated, the name of the updater, and an e-mail address that becomes a mailto link. Select the desired options and click Next.

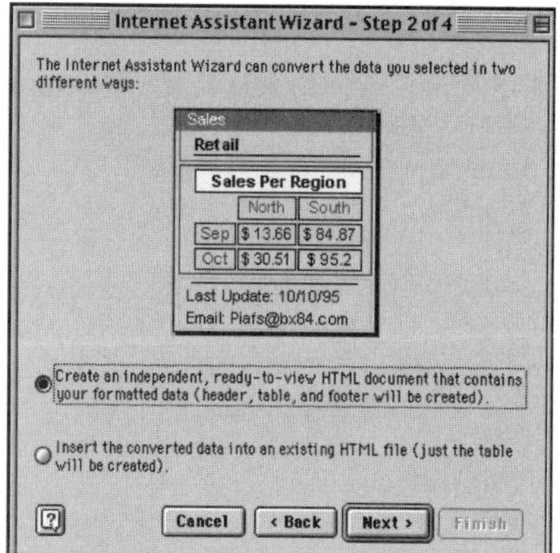

Figure 23-5: The second Internet Assistant Wizard dialog box

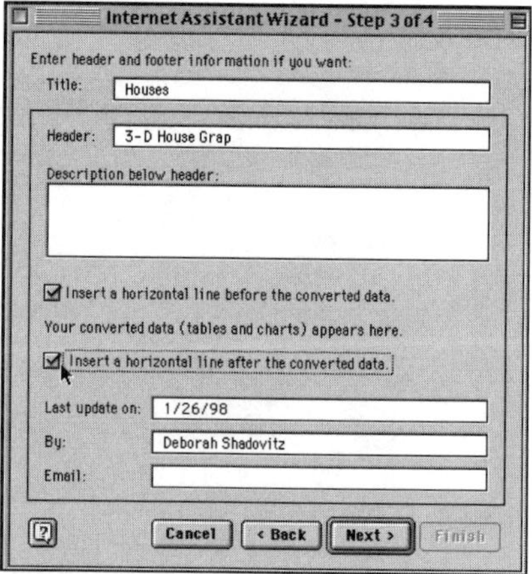

Figure 23-6: The third Internet Assistant Wizard dialog box

5. In the final dialog box to appear (see Figure 23-7), you determine where your new HTML file will be saved. You can accept the default or click the Select button, navigate to the folder you want to save to, and then click Save.

Alternatively, you can also type the desired path for the file. Notice that by default the document will be named MyHTML.html (as shown after the last colon in the file path). To change the name of your file, select MyHTML and replace it with the name you want to give your file. (It's best not to use spaces, so use an underscore—Shift-hyphen—instead.) Then click Finish to produce the HTML files.

Figure 23-7: The final Internet Assistant Wizard dialog box

Summary

This chapter covered the details involved in sharing your Excel data with Internet/intranet users. The following points were covered in this chapter:

- ✦ Hyperlinks can be added to the cells of a worksheet, and you can store Web addresses or jump locations to other Office documents in those fields.
- ✦ Use File➪Save as HTML to convert ranges of worksheets or charts to HTML files for publishing on the Internet or on an intranet. The Internet Assistant Wizard automatically launches to step you through the process.

Where to go next

- ✦ Excel is just one component of the Web publishing capabilities provided by Office 98. Word and PowerPoint also offer Web publishing and Web interaction features. For specifics on Word and the Web, see Chapter 11. For PowerPoint and the Web, see Chapter 32.
- ✦ In the next chapter, you learn how to further extend the power of Excel by using Visual Basic for Applications.

✦ ✦ ✦

CHAPTER 24

Excel and Visual Basic for Applications

✦ ✦ ✦ ✦

In This Chapter

Learning VBA with macros

Understanding VBA code

Editing VBA code

Printing Visual Basic code

Using the Visual Basic toolbar

Getting started

✦ ✦ ✦ ✦

This chapter details the use of Visual Basic for Applications (VBA), the programming language that is the basis for Excel macros. VBA is heavily based on Microsoft's Visual Basic programming language. Because Excel macros are based on VBA, you can use VBA to automate common tasks in Excel.

VBA can take you much further than simply duplicating keystrokes. VBA gives you full access to all of Excel's commands. You can modify Excel's own menus by adding your own commands and options, you can create custom dialog boxes to present messages and query users for information, and you can even construct complete applications for users with a limited knowledge of Excel. To accomplish these kinds of tasks, you need more than a familiarity with the recording and playing of macros; you need a basic understanding of VBA.

Learning VBA with Macros

Macros are an excellent starting point for understanding how VBA works and what you can do with the language. As Excel's Macro recorder stores all the actions you perform or the commands you choose, it interprets these actions or commands into statements, or lines of code, by using VBA. These statements are automatically placed in a procedure, which is a block of VBA code. Procedures are stored in modules, which you can think of as containers for all VBA code.

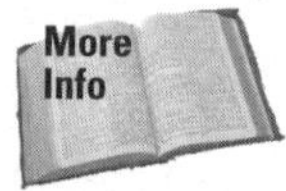

Chapter 22 detailed the basics of using macros, which are sequences of instructions that cause Excel to perform a particular task. As that chapter demonstrated, macros greatly reduce the time you spend performing routine, repetitive tasks.

To give you an idea of how all Excel macros use VBA, you should practice on an example. This chapter familiarizes you with Visual Basic code by examining the procedure that results when you record this sample macro. The following steps create the simple time sheet shown in Figure 24-1. Because time sheets are typically created weekly, this procedure represents a typical task that can be automated by creating a macro.

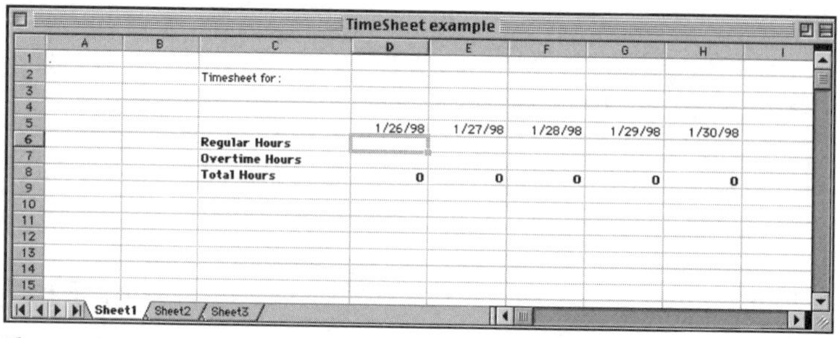

Figure 24-1: A time sheet that results from creating the sample macro

Follow these steps to create the worksheet and the sample macro:

1. Open a new workbook, save it, and name the workbook ("Timesheet Example," for instance).
2. Choose Tools ➪ Macro ➪ Record New Macro.
3. In the Record New Macro dialog box, enter the name **TimeEntry** and click OK. The Stop Macro button, which you can use to stop recording the macro, appears in the Macro toolbar. This button may be floating above the worksheet in its own toolbar or may appear in the Macro toolbar, wherever it was last used.
4. Click in cell C2 and enter **Timesheet for:**.
5. Click in cell D5, enter =**Today()**, and press Enter to end the entry within that cell.
6. Click in the center of D5 and drag from cell D5 to H5 to select D5 and the next four cells to the right.
7. Choose Edit ➪ Fill ➪ Series.
8. In the Series dialog box, click OK to accept the default options.
9. Click in cell C6 and enter **Regular Hours**.

10. Click in cell C7 and enter **Overtime Hours**.
11. Click in cell C8, enter **Total Hours**, and press Enter.
12. Select the range of cells from C6 to C8, and click the Bold button on the Formatting toolbar to add bold formatting.
13. In the column header, click the border between cells C and D and drag to widen column C until it is wide enough to display the longest text in the column.
14. Click in cell D8. Click the equal sign, and then click in cell D6 and click in D7 to create the formula =D6+D7 (or manually enter the formula =D6+D7 in the cell). Then click OK to enter the formula.
15. Click in the center of D8 and drag from cells D8 to H8 to select cell D8 and the four cells to the right of it.
16. Choose Edit ➪ Fill ➪ Right (⌘-R)
17. Click the Bold button on the Formatting toolbar to apply bold formatting to the selected cells.
18. Click in cell D6 (this repositions the cursor to prepare the worksheet for data entry).
19. Click the Stop Macro button (on the floating Macro toolbar) or select Tools ➪ Macro ➪ Stop Recording to stop recording the macro.
20. Save your worksheet again—as you should do frequently.

You can verify the effects of the macro by moving to a blank worksheet, choosing Tools ➪ Macro ➪ Macros, double-clicking TimeEntry to run it (or click once on TimeEntry to select it and click the Run button). The time sheet duplicates in the blank worksheet.

The Similarities of VBA and Visual Basic

If you've already worked with Microsoft's Visual Basic as a development language, you'll find Visual Basic for Applications similar. Visual Basic for Applications is solidly based on Microsoft's Visual Basic programming language. Visual Basic for Applications replaces the old macro-based languages, such as Excel's old macro language, with a common development language. Developers now need only learn one language to develop in all Office applications easily, on both the Mac and in Windows.

Microsoft uses Visual Basic as the base language and has added extensions to the language as implemented in the other Office applications. The commands, functions, methods, procedures, and program structures used in Visual Basic can all be used in Visual Basic for Applications for Word, Excel, and PowerPoint. So if you're a Visual Basic programmer, you're on very familiar ground.

Understanding VBA Code

Of course, the purpose of the exercise you just completed is not to demonstrate how to create a macro but to show how Visual Basic for Applications code works as the basis of any macro.

To open the Macro so you can edit it, follow these steps:

1. If the macro is stored in the Personal Macro Workbook, this workbook must be unhidden before you can edit it. Select Window ⇨ Unhide. In the Unhide dialog box that appears, double-click Personal Macro Workbook. (If you are not sure whether you need to perform this step, you can try skipping it. The Office Assistant lets you know if you need to go back.)
2. Choose Tools ⇨ Macro ⇨ Macros to open the Macro dialog box. (If you stored your macro in the Personal Macro Workbook and unhid it, you can do this while the worksheet you created the macro in is the active document or while the Personal Macro Workbook is the active window.)
3. Select the TimeEntry macro, and click Edit. This opens the Visual Basic Editor, shown in Figure 24-2. As shown in the figure, the VBA code behind the macro appears in the Module window at the right.

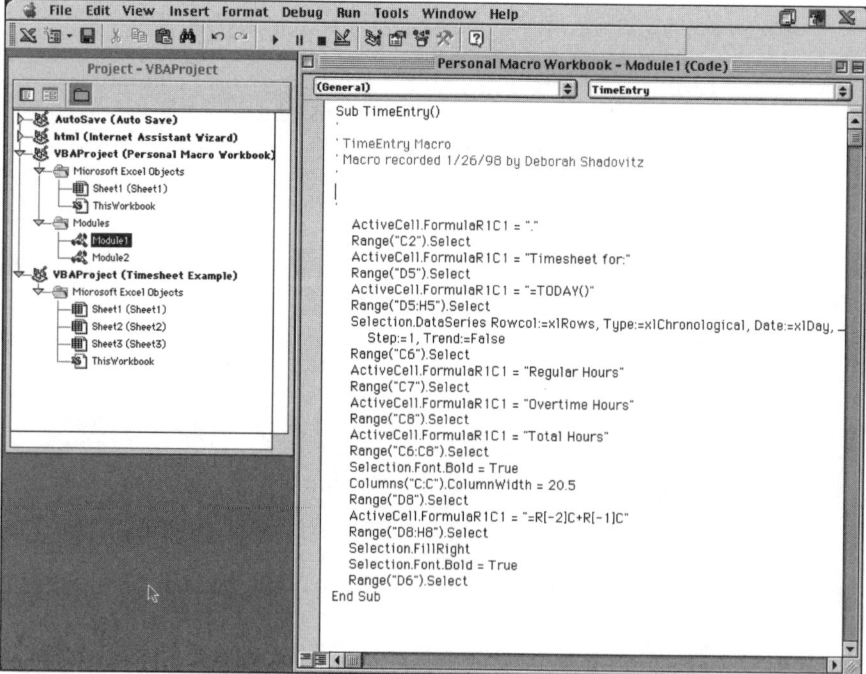

Figure 24-2: An example of macro code within the Visual Basic Editor

The code looks like this:

```
Sub TimeEntry()
'
' TimeEntry Macro
' Macro recorded 1/26/98 by Deborah Shadovitz
'
'
    ActiveCell.FormulaR1C1 = "."
    Range("C2").Select
    ActiveCell.FormulaR1C1 = "Timesheet for:"
    Range("D5").Select
    ActiveCell.FormulaR1C1 = "=TODAY()"
    Range("D5:H5").Select
    Selection.DataSeries Rowcol:=xlRows, Type:=xlChronological,
Date:=xlDay, _
        Step:=1, Trend:=False
    Range("C6").Select
    ActiveCell.FormulaR1C1 = "Regular Hours"
    Range("C7").Select
    ActiveCell.FormulaR1C1 = "Overtime Hours"
    Range("C8").Select
    ActiveCell.FormulaR1C1 = "Total Hours"
    Range("C6:C8").Select
    Selection.Font.Bold = True
    Columns("C:C").ColumnWidth = 20.5
    Range("D8").Select
    ActiveCell.FormulaR1C1 = "=R[-2]C+R[-1]C"
    Range("D8:H8").Select
    Selection.FillRight
    Selection.Font.Bold = True
    Range("D6").Select
End Sub
```

Each step you took during the recording of this procedure resulted in the addition of one or more lines of Visual Basic code in the module. The code appears in color: comments are displayed in green; key words of the Visual Basic language appear in blue; and all other code appears in black. When you run this (or any) macro, you are in effect running the Visual Basic for Applications code that is contained in the module that was recorded by the macro recorder. As the module runs, each line of Visual Basic code is executed in turn, and Excel performs an appropriate action as a result.

About comments

You can include comments (lines that aren't acted upon by Excel when the code runs) by preceding the text with a single quotation mark. In the sample procedure, you can see that the first two lines are comments:

```
' TimeEntry Macro
' Macro recorded 1/26/98 by Deborah Shadovitz
```

In this case, Excel added the comments based on the entries in the Macro name and Description text boxes of the Record Macro dialog box. If you assigned a keyboard command, the command would appear as a comment there, too. You can place comments wherever you desire in your Visual Basic code by typing a single quote mark followed by the text of the comment. Comments can be quite helpful in your more complex procedures to help you remember what's going on at any specific point in the procedure. Comments can occupy an entire line, or you can put them at the end of a valid line of code by starting the comment with a single quotation mark. When the procedure runs, everything that follows the single quotation mark is ignored until Excel finds a new line of code.

About headers and footers

The macro begins with an introductory header to the procedure.

```
Sub TimeEntry()
```

The matching footer (last line) reads:

```
End sub
```

Every VBA procedure starts with a header that begins with Sub or Function and ends with a footer that says End Sub or End Function. VBA allows two types of procedures: function procedures and sub procedures. *Function* procedures are like Excel's built-in functions. They accept a value(s), act on the data, and return a value(s). *Sub* procedures do not return a value (although you can pass values from within a sub procedure through the use of statements inside the procedure). Any arguments used by a function procedure are placed inside the parentheses of the header. The footer tells Excel that it has reached the end of the procedure. When Excel reaches the footer in the module, it passes program control back to any other VBA procedure that called this one. If the procedure was not called by another procedure, Excel returns control from the procedure to Excel itself.

About selecting and entering data

Following the header statement are two lines of code that select cell C2 and insert a text entry into that cell. The Visual Basic code for these two lines is:

```
Range("C2").Select
ActiveCell.FormulaR1C1 = "Timesheet for:"
```

The Range statement tells Excel to select a range. Because only one cell's address is given (cell C2), Excel selects only that cell. The next statement tells Excel to enter a text value (in this case, the words *Timesheet for:*) in the active cell of the worksheet, which is now cell C2.

About control statements

Besides containing lines of code that cause cursor movement and data entry in the worksheet, various lines of code within the program control certain characteristics of the worksheet in Excel. For example, when you apply bold formatting to a selection, the following code results:

```
Selection.Font.Bold = True
```

This line of code, when executed, takes the current selection and turns on bold character formatting. The following lines of code result from opening the Series dialog box (after choosing Edit ➪ Fill ➪ Series) and accepting the default options in the dialog box:

```
Selection.DataSeries Rowcol:=xlRows, Type:=xlChronological, Date:=xlDay, _
        Step:=1, Trend:=False
```

While examining this line, you should also notice the presence of the continuation character used in VBA. The underscore at the end of the first line is the continuation character, and it denotes that a line of program code is to be continued onto the line that follows. (Without this character, VBA considers any single line to be a complete program statement.)

As you grow accustomed to working in VBA, you'll find that you can accomplish a great deal of useful work by means of the various cell selection and control statements that can be used in the language.

About displaying dialog boxes

One of the reasons you may actually want to do some Visual Basic programming yourself (rather than using only the macro recorder) is that you can do some custom programming—such as displaying dialog boxes—that you cannot do with recorded macros. To display a dialog box onscreen that contains a message with custom text, you can use VBA's MsgBox function. The syntax of the statement is simple—you add a line of code that reads MsgBox("your custom text"), where you put your desired text between the double quotation marks.

If you duplicated the example earlier in the chapter, go to the end of the line prior to the End Sub and press Return to add a new, blank line to the very end of the procedure. With the insertion point at the start of the blank line, enter the following:

```
MsgBox("Enter your week's time and save under a new name.")
```

Choose File ➪ Close and Return to Microsoft Excel (⌘-Q) to quit the Visual Basic Editor. Go to a blank worksheet page and choose Tools ➪ Macro ➪ Macros. In the Macro dialog box, select the TimeEntry macro and click Run. This time, when the macro completes, you see the dialog box shown in Figure 24-3. Dialog boxes such as this one can serve to inform users, providing needed guidance about tasks the user needs to perform.

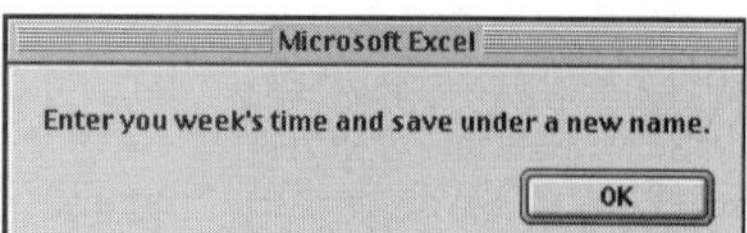

Figure 24-3: The dialog box presented by the MsgBox function

About user input

Another useful task that you can handle by adding your own Visual Basic code is prompting users for information and acting on a user's response. The InputBox function acts in a manner similar to the MsgBox function, but with InputBox, a text box appears within the dialog box. The value that the user enters in the text box is returned by the function.

You can try using the InputBox function by getting back into the module that you created as part of this exercise. Choose Tools ➪ Macro ➪ Macros to open the Macro dialog box. Click the TimeEntry macro, and click Edit to open the Visual Basic Editor. Find the following line:

```
ActiveCell.FormulaR1C1 = "Timesheet for:"
```

Place the cursor at the end of the line, and press Return to add a new line underneath this one. Enter the following two lines as new code in the procedure:

```
Range("D2").Select
ActiveCell.FormulaR1C1 = InputBox("Employee Name:")
```

(It's okay to copy and paste text in the Editor to save time and ensure the proper code. In this case, you can actually copy the line that says *Range("D5")*. Select the line, paste it into the new space, and then change the 5 to a 2.)

Choose File ➪ Close and Return to Microsoft Excel (⌘-Q) to quit the Visual Basic Editor. Move to a blank worksheet and run the macro again. (Choose Tools ➪ Macro ➪ Macros. In the Macro dialog box, double-click the TimeEntry macro.) When the macro runs, a dialog box like the one shown in Figure 24-4 appears, asking for an employee name. After you enter a name, the macro stores that name in cell D2 of the worksheet.

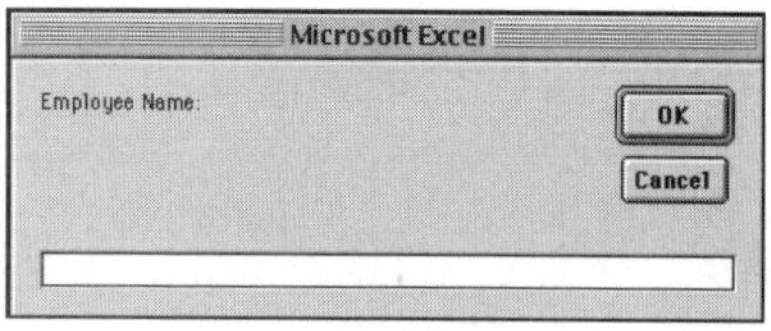

Figure 24-4: The dialog box presented by the InputBox function

Learn by Example

If you really want to do VBA programming, one of the best ways to learn the language is to examine working applications and macros ranging from simple to complex. Microsoft provides examples. To install them, use the Value Pack Installer, open the Programmability option, and then select Excel Sample VBA Code.

After they are installed, you'll find the samples in the Examples folder directly within the Microsoft Office 98 folder. Double-click this worksheet to open it, or use the File⇨Open command.

Editing VBA Code

When you click a module tab, select a macro in the Macro dialog box and click Edit to open the Visual Basic Editor, you can enter program code just like you type text in any word processor. You don't have to know the mechanics of entering text and correcting mistakes; you can use the same text entry and editing techniques—including cutting and pasting—that you can use in any Mac word processor.

In text or spreadsheet documents, it is nice to use smart quotes, which curl inward toward quoted text rather than the straight tick marks typewriters used. In Visual Basic code, you must use the old-fashioned tick marks, so if you've pasted in text that contains the curly-style quotes, delete them and retype the quote marks.

Printing Visual Basic Code

You can print the code that is contained in your Visual Basic modules. To print the code, open the module that contains the desired code by choosing Tools⇨Macro⇨Macros, selecting the desired macro, and clicking Edit to reveal the code. Then, choose the File⇨Print (⌘-P) to bring up a simple Print VBAProject dialog box. There may be several macro modules on the page. By default the current one (the one you selected to edit) is printed. You can choose to print all modules in the project if you want.

Using the Visual Basic Toolbar

If you do much work in Visual Basic for Applications programming, you'll find the Visual Basic toolbar (see Figure 24-5) useful. You can activate the Visual Basic toolbar by Control-clicking the toolbar area and choosing Visual Basic from the shortcut menu, or by selecting View⇨Toolbars⇨Visual Basic. Table 24-1 provides an explanation for the different buttons on the Visual Basic toolbar.

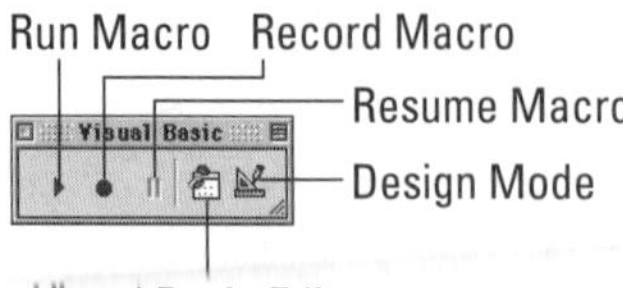

Figure 24-5: The Visual Basic toolbar

Table 24-1
Buttons on the Visual Basic Toolbar

Name	*Function*
Run Macro	Opens the Run Macro dialog box, where you can run, delete, or edit any macro you select.
Record Macro	Opens the Record Macro dialog box, where you can fill in the desired options used to begin recording a macro.
Resume Macro	Resumes playing a macro that you have paused.
Visual Basic Editor	Opens the Visual Basic Editor, where you can create, edit, and step through macros using Visual Basic.
Design Mode	Switch in and out of Design mode.

Because you may likely create macros in each of the Office applications, you should know that the Visual Basic toolbar in Word does not include the Pause button, while PowerPoint simply has the Run Macro and Visual Basic Editor buttons.

Going Forward

Make no mistake about it, using Visual Basic for Applications falls well into the realm of programming. (If you're completely new to programming, you should be congratulated for pressing this deeply into what, for many readers, is a subject of mystifying complexity.) You've not only learned how VBA lies at the heart of everything you do with macros, you've also learned how you can extend the power of your macros by adding your own Visual Basic code to provide items like dialog boxes and customized prompts.

Still, you've only scratched the surface of what you can do with this language. VBA is a full-featured programming language that you can use to automate or customize virtually any conceivable task that can be done with Excel. If you're encouraged (dare we even say excited?) by the challenges of programming, you should look into additional resources for learning about Visual Basic programming. It's a subject about which entire books have been written.

Summary

This chapter has provided an introduction to programming using Visual Basic for Applications, the underlying language behind Excel macros. The chapter covered the following points:

- Every Excel macro exists as a series of Visual Basic program statements.
- The Visual Basic statements are stored in procedures, and one or more procedures are placed in modules. Modules are part of the workbook, edited through the Visual Basic Editor. (They don't show up as sheets in the workbook.)
- Visual Basic procedures can be sub procedures or function procedures. Function procedures are like Excel's built-in functions because they accept a value(s), act on the data, and return a value(s). Sub procedures do not return a value (although you can pass values from within a sub procedure through the use of statements inside the procedure).
- You can modify the Visual Basic code that Excel's macro recorder creates to add special features like dialog boxes and custom prompts.

Where to go next

- The next chapter shows how you can use Excel to create and use worksheets for common business tasks.
- Because Visual Basic for Applications lies at the heart of macros that you create in Excel, you should be familiar with the use of macros before getting involved with Visual Basic for Applications. See Chapter 22.

✦ ✦ ✦

25

CHAPTER

Excel at Work

✦ ✦ ✦ ✦

In This Chapter

Managing cash flow

Performing break-even analysis

Using the IRA calculator

Working with mortgages and amortization

✦ ✦ ✦ ✦

This chapter gets you started on your own applications by providing some examples and step-by-step instructions you can use to build models of worksheets for various tasks.

Managing Cash Flow

Managing cash flow, or your accounts receivable and accounts payable, is a basic job that virtually every modern business must face. The following cash-flow worksheet is relatively simple to set up and keeps a clear "picture" of available funds. The worksheet is patterned after the common single-entry debits and credits bookkeeping system. You enter a starting balance into cell H4. Use column A to record the dates of each transaction, whether a credit or a debit. Use columns B, C, and D to record credits by listing the creditor, the description, and the amount. Use columns E, F, and G to record debits by listing to whom the amount is paid, the description, and the amount. Column H contains the formulas you use to keep a running total of the cash on hand. You compute the total by taking the preceding entry's running balance, adding the credits, and subtracting the debits. You can maintain this type of system by creating a separate worksheet for each month. At the end of the year, you can consolidate the totals into another worksheet to show yearly figures for cash flow. The worksheet is shown in Figure 25-1.

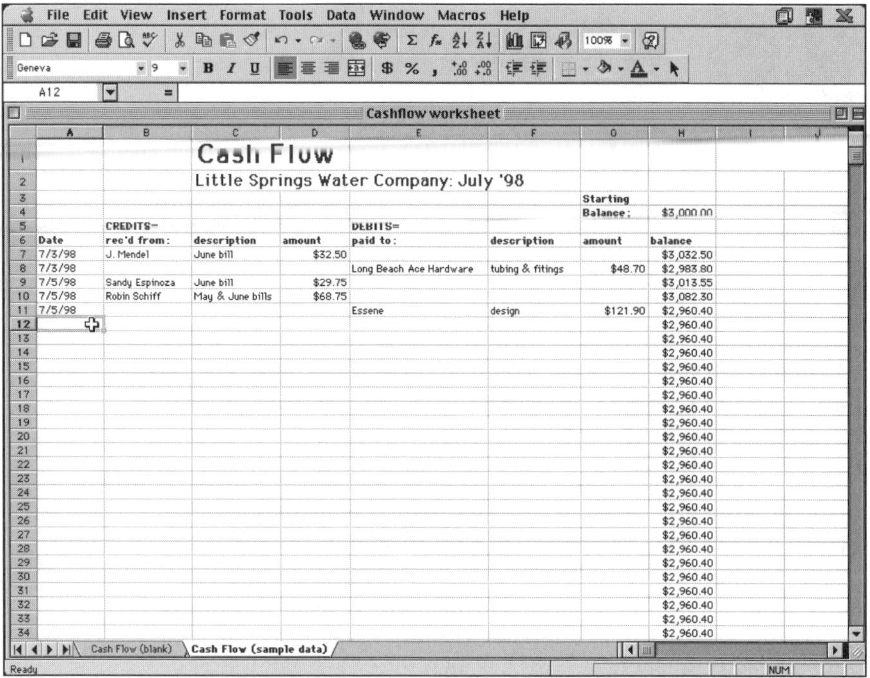

Figure 25-1: A cash flow worksheet

To build the worksheet, enter the following labels and formulas into the cells as shown:

Cell	*Entry*
A6	Date
B5	CREDITS=
B6	rec'd from:
C1	Cash Flow
C6	description
D6	amount
E5	DEBITS=
E6	paid to:
F6	description
G3	Starting
G4	Balance:

Cell	*Entry*
G6	amount
H6	balance
H7	=H4+D7-G7
H8	=H7+D8-G8

In the area below cell C1, you may want to add the name of your company or organization. In the example, we used "Little Springs Water Company."

To copy the formula into successive cells in column H, select the range of cells from H8 to H40. Choose Edit ⇨ Fill ⇨ Down. To format the cells in column H, select the range of cells from H4 to H40. Then choose Format ⇨ Cells to open the Format Cells dialog box and click the Number tab. Click the Currency option in the list, and then click OK. Using the same steps, choose the same currency format for the cells from D7 to D40 and from G7 to G40. To format a range of cells to display dates, select the range of cells from A7 to A40, choose Format ⇨ Cells to open the Format Cells dialog box, click the Number tab, click the Date option in the list, and select the second (d-m-yy) format.

At this point, the worksheet is ready to use. Size the columns and format the text as you'd like. Although you may want to use your own figures, Figure 25-1 shows part of the cash-flow worksheet that has been filled in with figures from a hypothetical small business.

Performing Break-Even Analysis

A common what-if scenario for almost any firm is the break-even analysis, which determines how many units of a given product must be sold before the producer shows a profit. A break-even analysis requires the juggling of two groups of figures: fixed costs and variable costs. *Fixed costs* do not directly increase with each unit sold. Such costs include the rental of the manufacturing plant, utilities to power the production line, and advertising expenses. Variable costs directly increase with each unit sold. Such costs include the cost of the materials to assemble each unit, labor costs per unit, packaging costs, and shipping costs.

A typical break-even analysis performs a one-time deduction of the fixed costs and then calculates the per-unit costs for each unit produced. These negative amounts are balanced against the net profits (the net sales cost times the number of units sold). As the number of units sold increases, a break-even point is reached where the total profit equals the negative fixed and variable costs. Figure 25-2 shows an example of a break-even analysis worksheet illustrating the break-even point for a child's bicycle.

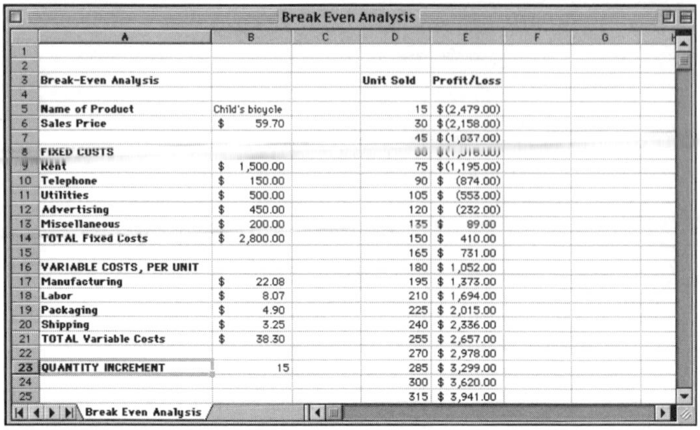

Figure 25-2: A break-even analysis worksheet

To build the model, open a new worksheet. Widen column A to roughly three times its default width and widen column B to roughly twice its default width. The other columns can remain at the default widths. Enter the following formulas into the cells shown:

Cell	*Entry*
A3	Break-Even Analysis
A5	Name of Product:
A6	Sales Price:
A8	FIXED COSTS
A9	Rent
A10	Telephone
A11	Utilities
A12	Advertising
A13	Miscellaneous
A14	TOTAL Fixed Costs
A16	VARIABLE COSTS, PER UNIT
A17	Manufacturing
A18	Labor
A19	Packaging
A20	Shipping
A21	TOTAL Variable Costs
A23	QUANTITY INCREMENT

Cell	Entry
B5	Child's bicycle
B6	59.7
B9	1500
B10	150
B11	500
B12	450
B13	200
B14	=SUM(B9:B13)
B17	22.08
B18	8.07
B19	4.9
B20	3.25
B21	=SUM(B17:B20)
B23	15
D3	Units Sold
D5	=B23
D6	=D5+$B$23

You can create the remaining formulas in column D quickly by selecting the range from D6 to D41. Then choose Edit ➪ Fill ➪ Down.

Cell	Entry
D7	=D6+$B$23
D8	=D7+$B$23
D9	=D8+$B$23
D10	=D9+$B$23
D11	=D10+$B$23
D12	=D11+$B$23
D13	=D12+$B$23
D14	=D13+$B$23
D15	=D14+$B$23
D16	=D15+$B$23

(continued)

(continued)

Cell	*Entry*
D17	=D16+$B$23
D18	=D17+$B$23
D19	=D18+$B$23
D20	=D19+$B$23
D21	=D20+$B$23
D22	=D21+$B$23
D23	=D22+$B$23
D24	=D23+$B$23
D25	=D24+$B$23
D26	=D25+$B$23
D27	=D26+$B$23
D28	=D27+$B$23
D29	=D28+$B$23
D30	=D29+$B$23
D31	=D30+$B$23
D32	=D31+$B$23
D33	=D32+$B$23
D34	=D33+$B$23
D35	=D34+$B$23
D36	=D35+$B$23
D37	=D36+$B$23
D38	=D37+$B$23
D39	=D38+$B$23
D40	=D39+$B$23
D41	=D40+$B$23

In column E, enter the following values and formulas:

Cell	*Entry*
E3	Profit/Loss
E5	=D5*$B$6-($B$14+($B$21*D5))

You can create the remaining formulas in column E quickly by selecting the range from E5 to E41. Then choose Edit ➪ Fill ➪ Down.

Cell	Entry
E6	=D6*$B$6-($B$14+($B$21*D6))
E7	=D7*$B$6-($B$14+($B$21*D7))
E8	=D8*$B$6-($B$14+($B$21*D8))
E9	=D9*$B$6-($B$14+($B$21*D9))
E10	=D10*$B$6-($B$14+($B$21*D10))
E11	=D11*$B$6-($B$14+($B$21*D11))
E12	=D12*$B$6-($B$14+($B$21*D12))
E13	=D13*$B$6-($B$14+($B$21*D13))
E14	=D14*$B$6-($B$14+($B$21*D14))
E15	=D15*$B$6-($B$14+($B$21*D15))
E16	=D16*$B$6-($B$14+($B$21*D16))
E17	=D17*$B$6-($B$14+($B$21*D17))
E18	=D18*$B$6-($B$14+($B$21*D18))
E19	=D19*$B$6-($B$14+($B$21*D19))
E20	=D20*$B$6-($B$14+($B$21*D20))
E21	=D21*$B$6-($B$14+($B$21*D21))
E22	=D22*$B$6-($B$14+($B$21*D22))
E23	=D23*$B$6-($B$14+($B$21*D23))
E24	=D24*$B$6-($B$14+($B$21*D24))
E25	=D25*$B$6-($B$14+($B$21*D25))
E26	=D26*$B$6-($B$14+($B$21*D26))
E27	=D27*$B$6-($B$14+($B$21*D27))
E28	=D28*$B$6-($B$14+($B$21*D28))
E29	=D29*$B$6-($B$14+($B$21*D29))
E30	=D30*$B$6-($B$14+($B$21*D30))
E31	=D31*$B$6-($B$14+($B$21*D31))
E32	=D32*$B$6-($B$14+($B$21*D32))
E33	=D33*$B$6-($B$14+($B$21*D33))
E34	=D34*$B$6-($B$14+($B$21*D34))

(continued)

(continued)

Cell	Entry
E35	=D35*$B$6-($B$14+($B$21*D35))
E36	=D36*$B$6-($B$14+($B$21*D36))
E37	=D37*$B$6-($B$14+($B$21*D37))
E38	=D38*$B$6-($B$14+($B$21*D38))
E39	=D39*$B$6-($B$14+($B$21*D39))
E40	=D40*$B$6-($B$14+($B$21*D40))
E41	=D41*$B$6-($B$14+($B$21*D41))

Use Format⇨Cells to format the ranges from B6 to B21 and from E5 to E41 with the currency format (click the Number tab, choose Currency in the list, and then click OK). (Or, select the cells and click the Currency Format button on the Formatting toolbar.) To use the worksheet, enter your respective fixed and variable costs in the cells provided. In the QUANTITY INCREMENT cell, enter the quantity you want to use as a scale for the break-even analysis. For example, to see how many hundreds of units it will take to break even, enter **100** for a quantity increment. For a more detailed analysis, enter a smaller increment. You can extend the analysis to cover even more units by simply copying the respective formulas down the column past row 41. However, if you're not breaking even by row 41 of the worksheet, the analysis is trying to tell you that your pricing or manufacturing strategy has a serious flaw!

Using the IRA calculator

An IRA calculator is a straightforward financial tool designed to plot the increasing value of an IRA (individual retirement account). Four columns within the worksheet contain a beginning balance in the account, a yearly contribution, an interest rate, and an ending balance. A less complex worksheet would assume a standard interest rate and yearly contribution, but in real life, your yearly contribution may vary, and it is virtually impossible to plan for a standard interest rate. Keeping separate columns for these values for each year gives you the ability to insert each year's interest rate and the amount of the IRA contribution.

Figure 25-3 shows an example of an IRA calculator worksheet. In column C, you enter the beginning balance (starting with zero in the first row). Column D contains the yearly contribution, which in this example is $1,700 the first year, $1,850 the second, $1,900 the third, and assumed to be $2,000 per year afterwards. Column E contains the interest rate, assumed to be 8.5 percent the first year, 7.25 percent the second year, 6.75 percent the third year, and 6.5 percent per year afterwards. Column F contains the formula that calculates the effect of the accumulating interest and the added yearly investment. The formula calculates on the basis of simple interest by adding the current balance to the yearly contribution and adding the result multiplied by the yearly interest rate to provide the new balance. Each year's new balance is then carried to the successive balance column.

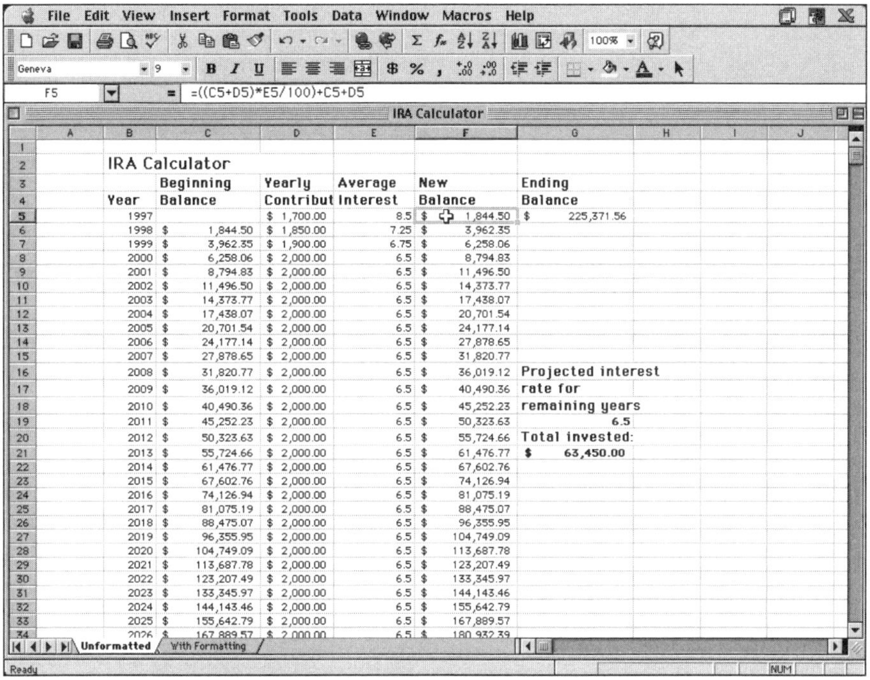

Figure 25-3: An IRA calculator worksheet

To build the worksheet, enter the following formulas into the cells shown:

Cell	*Entry*
B2	IRA Calculator
B4	Year
B5	1997
B6	=B5+1

To create the following formulas, select the range from B6 to B37. Then choose Edit ➪ Fill ➪ Down.

Cell	*Entry*
B7	=B6+1
B8	=B7+1
B9	=B8+1
B10	=B9+1
B11	=B10+1
B12	=B11+1
B13	=B12+1
B14	=B13+1
B15	=B14+1
B16	=B15+1
B17	=B16+1
B18	=B17+1
B19	=B18+1
B20	=B19+1
B21	=B20+1
B22	=B21+1
B23	=B22+1
B24	=B23+1
B25	=B24+1
B26	=B25+1
B27	=B26+1
B28	=B27+1
B29	=B28+1
B30	=B29+1
B31	=B30+1
B32	=B31+1
B33	=B32+1
B34	=B33+1
B35	=B34+1
B36	=B35+1
B37	=B36+1

In column C of the worksheet, enter the following values and formulas:

Cell	Entry
C3	Beginning
C4	Balance
C6	=F5

To create the following formulas, select the range from C6 to C37. Then choose Edit⇨Fill⇨Down.

Cell	Entry
C7	=F6
C8	=F7
C9	=F8
C10	=F9
C11	=F10
C12	=F11
C13	=F12
C14	=F13
C15	=F14
C16	=F15
C17	=F16
C18	=F17
C19	=F18
C20	=F19
C21	=F20
C22	=F21
C23	=F22
C24	=F23
C25	=F24
C26	=F25
C27	=F26
C28	=F27

(continued)

(continued)

Cell	**Entry**
C29	=F28
C30	=F29
C31	=F30
C32	=F31
C33	=F32
C34	=F33
C35	=F34
C36	=F35
C37	=F36

In column D of the worksheet, enter the following values:

Cell	**Entry**
D3	Yearly
D4	Contribution
D5	1700
D6	1850
D7	1900
D8	2000

To create the following entries, select the range from D8 to D37. Then choose Edit ➪ Fill ➪ Down.

Cell	**Entry**
D9	2000
D10	2000
D11	2000
D12	2000
D13	2000
D14	2000
D15	2000

Cell	Entry
D16	2000
D17	2000
D18	2000
D19	2000
D20	2000
D21	2000
D22	2000
D23	2000
D24	2000
D25	2000
D26	2000
D27	2000
D28	2000
D29	2000
D30	2000
D31	2000
D32	2000
D33	2000
D34	2000
D35	2000
D36	2000
D37	2000

In column E of the worksheet, enter the following values and formulas:

Cell	Entry
E3	Average
E4	Interest
E5	8.5
E6	7.25
E7	6.75
E8	=$G$19

To create the following formulas, select the range from E8 to E37. Then choose Edit ⇨ Fill ⇨ Down.

Cell	*Entry*
E9	=$G$19
E10	=$G$19
E11	=$G$19
E12	=$G$19
E13	=$G$19
E14	=$G$19
E15	=$G$19
E16	=$G$19
E17	=$G$19
E18	=$G$19
E19	=$G$19
E20	=$G$19
E21	=$G$19
E22	=$G$19
E23	=$G$19
E24	=$G$19
E25	=$G$19
E26	=$G$19
E27	=$G$19
E28	=$G$19
E29	=$G$19
E30	=$G$19
E31	=$G$19
E32	=$G$19
E33	=$G$19
E34	=$G$19
E35	=$G$19
E36	=$G$19
E37	=$G$19

In column F of the worksheet, enter the following:

Cell	*Entry*
F3	New
F4	Balance
F5	=((C5+D5)*E5/100)+C5+D5

Select the range of cells from F5 to F37. Then choose Edit➪Fill➪Down to copy the formula into the successive cells.

In column G of the worksheet, enter the following values and formulas:

Cell	*Entry*
G3	Ending
G4	Balance
G5	=F37
G16	Projected interest
G17	rate for
G18	remaining years
G19	6.5
G20	Total invested:
G21	=SUM(D4:D36)

Using Format➪Cells, select the ranges from C6 to C37, D5 to D37, and F5 to F37 one range at a time. Click the Currency Format button (the dollar sign) on the Formatting toolbar to format these cell in the currency format. Also format cells G5 and G21 for the same type of display.

After you have entered the formulas, the worksheet displays the interest accumulation and yearly balances, as shown in Figure 25-3. You can change the interest rates and investment amounts to correspond to your desired investment rates.

Working with Mortgages and Amortization

The mortgage analysis worksheet has a straightforward design. It uses the PMT (payment) function to calculate the payments on a loan and displays an amortization schedule for the term of the loan. Figure 25-4 shows the worksheet.

Cells D5, D6, and D7 of the worksheet contain the principal loan amount, interest rate, and term of the loan in years. In cell D9, the following formula supplies the rate, number of periods, and present value:

```
=PMT((D6/12),(D7*12),-D5)
```

The rate and the number of periods are converted to months, and the present value is shown as a negative value representing cash paid out.

Mortgage & Amortization

	A	B	C	D	E	F
1						
2						
3		Mortgage Analysis				
4						
5		Principal amount of loan:		70,000.00		
6		Interest rate, in percent:		8.75%		
7		Term of loan, in years:		30		
8						
9		Monthly mortgage payment		$550.69		
10						
11						
12						
13						
14						
15	YEAR	Starting balance	Ending balance	TOTAL PAID	PRINCIPAL	INTEREST
16						
17	1	70,000.00	69,496.86	6,608.28	503.14	$6,105.14
18	2	69,496.86	68,947.88	6,608.28	548.98	$6,059.31
19	3	68,947.88	68,348.89	6,608.28	598.99	$6,009.30
20	4	68,348.89	67,695.34	6,608.28	653.55	$5,954.73
21	5	67,695.34	66,982.25	6,608.28	713.09	$5,895.19
22	6	66,982.25	66,204.20	6,608.28	778.05	$5,830.23
23	7	66,204.20	65,355.27	6,608.28	848.93	$5,759.36
24	8	65,355.27	64,429.01	6,608.28	926.26	$5,682.02
25	9	64,429.01	63,418.38	6,608.28	1,010.64	$5,597.65
26	10	63,418.38	62,315.67	6,608.28	1,102.70	$5,505.58
27	11	62,315.67	61,112.52	6,608.28	1,203.15	$5,405.13
28	12	61,112.52	59,799.76	6,608.28	1,312.76	$5,295.53
29	13	59,799.76	58,367.42	6,608.28	1,432.34	$5,175.94
30	14	58,367.42	56,804.60	6,608.28	1,562.82	$5,045.46
31	15	56,804.60	55,099.41	6,608.28	1,705.19	$4,903.09
32	16	55,099.41	53,238.88	6,608.28	1,860.53	$4,747.76

Mortgage Analysi

Figure 25-4: A mortgage analysis worksheet

Year one of the amortization schedule begins in row 17. The starting balance is derived from the amount entered in cell D5. To arrive at the ending balance in column C for the first year, use a formula containing the following variation of Excel's PV (Present Value) function:

```
=PV(($D$6/12),(12*($D$7-A17)),-$D$9)
```

Now calculate the remaining forms in the row. The total paid (column D of the amortization schedule) is the monthly payment (cell D9) multiplied by 12 to compute a yearly amount. The principal in column E is calculated by subtracting column C of the schedule (the ending balance) from column B (the starting balance).

You calculate the interest (column F) by subtracting the difference between the starting and ending balance from the total paid. As the formulas are duplicated down the worksheet, relative references are adjusted upwards for each successive row location.

Choose Format ➪ Column ➪ Width to change the width of column A to 5 spaces and the width of columns B, C, D, E, and F to 15 spaces. (You can format column A by dragging the right column border in the column header. As you drag, the ScreenTip reports the column width.)

To build the worksheet, enter the following formulas in the cells shown:

Cell	*Entry*
A15	YEAR
A17	1

To enter the rest of the year numbers, select the range from A17 to A46. Then choose Edit ➪ Fill ➪ Series. (Make sure you choose Edit ➪ Fill ➪ Series and not Edit ➪ Fill ➪ Down.) Click OK in the dialog box to fill the range. When you do so, cells A17 through A46 contain values from 1 through 30 representing 30 years of mortgage payments.

In column B of the worksheet, enter the following information:

Cell	*Entry*
B3	Mortgage Analysis
B5	Principal amount of loan:
B6	Interest rate, in percent:
B7	Term of loan, in years:
B9	Monthly mortgage payment
B15	Starting balance
B17	=D5
B18	=C17

In column C of the worksheet, enter the following information and formulas:

Cell	*Entry*
C15	Ending balance
C17	=PV(($D$6/12),(12*($D$7-A17)),-$D$9)
C18	=PV(($D$6/12),(12*($D$7-A18)),-$D$9)

In column D of the worksheet, enter the following values and formulas:

Cell	*Entry*
D5	70000
D6	8.75%
D7	30
D9	=PMT((D6/12),(D7*12),-D5)
D15	TOTAL PAID
D17	=$D$9*12
D18	=$D$9*12

In column E of the worksheet, enter the following information and formulas:

Cell	*Entry*
E15	PRINCIPAL
E17	=B17-C17
E18	=B18-C18

In column F of the worksheet, enter the following information and formulas:

Cell	*Entry*
F15	INTEREST
F17	=D17-(B17-C17)
F18	=D18-(B18-C18)

When you have entered these formulas, select the range of cells from B18 to F46. Choose Edit ⇨ Fill ⇨ Down to fill the successive formulas into the selected rows. To apply formatting to a range, select the range from B17 to F46. Choose Format ⇨ Cells and click the Number tab in the Format Cells dialog box. Click Currency in the list and click OK. Apply the same formatting for D5. At this point, your worksheet should resemble the example in Figure 25-4.

The range in this example assumes a 30-year loan. However, if you enter a period of 15 years but leave the formulas intact for 30 years, you will get the interesting benefit of a nest egg that has been calculated as an increasing negative balance when the mortgage ends and the amortization schedule shows mortgage payments still being added. To avoid this situation, just adjust the range when you fill down to match the number of years for the mortgage. If you want to get fancy, you can record a macro that clears the range, takes the number of years from cell D7, selects a new range equivalent to that number of years, and performs a Fill Down command.

Summary

This chapter provided step-by-step instructions for creating various models that you may find useful in Excel. You learned how to create worksheets to handle the following:

- mortgage loan calculation and amortization
- break-even analysis
- cash-flow management
- IRA calculations

Where to go next

As these examples demonstrate, much of the basic work behind creating and using spreadsheets involves routine data and formula entry and simple to moderately complex formatting. For many spreadsheet users, these tasks are 90 percent of what they do in Excel.

- The next chapter answers common questions that arise when you use Excel.
- You can find tips and techniques that help ease the tedium of basic data and formula entry in Chapter 16.
- For the complete scoop on how you can format your Excel worksheets, see Chapter 17.

✦ ✦ ✦

The Excel Top Ten

Excel users routinely find the same questions arising as they gain proficiency with the program. To save you time and effort, we've compiled the top ten Excel questions and their answers, based on inquiries to Microsoft Technical Support.

1. Can I set up a workbook to open when I launch Excel?

You can open a workbook each time you start Excel by placing the workbook in the Excel Startup folder. The full path to this folder is Microsoft Office 98/Office/Startup/Excel. All the workbooks placed in this folder will open automatically whenever you launch Excel. These workbooks can include worksheets, chart sheets, Visual Basic modules, Excel dialog sheets, and older Excel macro sheets.

Normally, we do not recommend storing a worksheet anywhere within an application folder. This can be disastrous if someone unknowingly trashes the Microsoft Office 98 folder to perform a clean reinstall. We hope by the time you read this, Microsoft will have released an update enabling you to place an alias of the workbook in the Startup/Excel folder instead. (Try this trick with an alias instead of the original workbook. If you get an error message, you need to delete the alias and use the original. If the workbook launches, you're in luck.)

Another option is to place the workbook in the Microsoft Office Manager (MOM) menu so you can easily open it when you need it. (See Chapter 1 to learn how.)

2. Can I change the folder Excel jumps to during an open or save? While I'm at it, can I change the default font?

Changing the default folder and the standard font are simple tasks in Excel 98. To set these preferences for all workbooks, use the General tab of the Preferences dialog box, which appears after you choose Tools ➪ Preferences. Follow these steps to change the default working directory:

1. Choose Tools ➪ Preferences and click the General tab in the Preferences dialog box.
2. Click the Select button next to the Default file location text box. Use the resulting dialog box to select the folder you want Excel to jump to in all Open and Save dialog boxes.
3. Click OK when you've made all your preferences changes.

To change the default font for all new workbooks, follow these steps:

1. Choose Tools ➪ Preferences and click the General tab in the Preferences dialog box.
2. Click the arrows next to the Standard font list and select from the list of available fonts. Do the same with the Size arrows.
3. Click OK when you've made all your preferences changes.

While you're in the Preferences dialog box, you can also change the default number of tabs per workbook if you want, or change any of the other default options.

3. How can I display more than one workbook at a time?

Each workbook you open is its own window. You can move each window around as you please. However, when you create a new workbook and then another, they open on top of one another. Follow these steps to view multiple workbooks simultaneously:

1. Open as many workbooks as you want to view. (Double-click to open a worksheet, use File ➪ Open, use the MOM menu, or open them any way you prefer.)
2. Choose Window ➪ Arrange.
3. In the Arrange Windows dialog box that appears, choose tiled, horizontal, vertical, or cascade as desired, and then click OK to arrange the workbooks so you can see them all.

4. How can I prevent slashes or hyphens from being formatted as dates?

Excel automatically applies built-in number formats to values entered in an unformatted cell. Normally the appearance of the value is not altered because the format is a general number format. However, Excel tries to help you with formatting, so if the entry contains a slash or a hyphen that separates values, Excel interprets the value as a date. If the entry contains a colon, Excel expects that the value represents a time value (hours, minutes, seconds, and so on). If you want to display the value exactly as it was entered—with slashes, hyphens, or colons—and don't want Excel to confuse the value with a date or time, you must format the value as a text value. To create a text value, simply precede the entry with a single quotation mark (') or follow these steps:

1. Select the cells in which you want to enter data.
2. Choose Format ⇨ Cells and select the Number tab from the dialog box that appears.
3. In the Category list, select Text.
4. Click OK.

When you enter values in the selected cells, the values are displayed as you typed them. Remember that the cells must be formatted as text prior to entering your data.

5. What are some shortcuts for selecting cells and ranges?

Rather than clicking and dragging to select a range, you can use the Name list on the left side of the formula bar to select cells and ranges. This not only selects ranges on the active sheet—it selects ranges on other sheets within the workbook, too!

The Name list displays the cell reference or the cell name of the currently selected cell and provides a list of all the defined names in your workbook when you click the arrow to the right of the list box. When you click the arrow and select a name or enter a cell reference in this list box, Excel selects the specified cell or range, moving to the other worksheet if needed.

Hot Stuff

You can also use the Name list to define a name and insert the name into a formula. If you want to define a name for a cell or cell range so you can select it later or use it in a formula, select the cell or range, click in the Name list box, type a new name, and press Enter.

Table 26-1 contains a list of shortcuts for selecting cells and ranges.

Table 26-1 **Shortcuts for Selecting Cells and Ranges**	
To select	***Do the following***
A named cell or range on the active or another worksheet	In the Name list box, type or select the name.
An unnamed cell	In the Name list box, enter the cell reference and press Enter.
An unnamed range	With your mouse, select the first cell in the range. If the last cell in your range is an unnamed cell, enter a cell reference and press Shift-Enter. If the last cell in your range is a named cell, press Shift as you select the name from the Name list.
Nonadjacent named and unnamed cells	With your mouse, select the first cell or range. To make subsequent selections, press the ⌘ key as you click in other cells, drag over a range of cells, select a name from the Name list box, or enter a cell reference in the Name list box.

6. How do I format characters in superscript, subscript, or a different font?

In Excel, you can add such character formatting as superscript, subscript, different fonts, styles, size, underlining, color, and so on to individual characters in a single cell. Table 26-2 contains a few examples of different kinds of formatting you can add to the characters in a cell.

Table 26-2 **Formatting You Can Add to Characters in a Cell**	
Formatting	***Example***
Italics	*4th Quarter*
Superscript	2^3
Subscript	10_2
Different font	Φ(R-S)=Φ-1(S)

The phi character (Φ) is a capital F in the Symbol font. (Use the Font list in the toolbars to change to the Symbol font, and type **F**.)

You can format text just as you do in any word processor, except you select the text within the formula bar or in the cell (if you have in-cell editing turned on). To select individual text in a cell, select the cell, and then click in the formula bar and drag over the text. If you are using in-cell editing, you can double-click in the cell and drag to select the text you want to format. To select text in a text box, double-click in the text box and drag to make the selection you want. After the text is selected, you can choose Format ⇨ Cells or Control-click the selected text and choose Format Cells. Either way, you bring up the Format Cells dialog box. Select the Font tab and choose the options you want. The multiple-character formatting applies only to text.

To enter superscript and subscript, you must enter the values as text by preceding the value with a single quotation mark ('). For example, 2^3 and 10_2 would be displayed as 23 and 102 if they are not entered as text. A second option is to format the cell with the text number format before the value is entered.

7. How can I combine the contents of two cells into one?

If you have information in two separate cells that you want to combine into one cell, or if you want to combine text with a formula in a cell, use the CONCATENATE( ) function, which takes up to 30 arguments (the contents of up to 30 cells) and can consist of cell references, text, and formulas. Note that the text arguments must be enclosed in quotation marks.

Suppose someone's first name is stored in cell C1 and the last name is stored in cell D1. If you want to combine the text in those cells, enter the following formula in cell E1:

```
=CONCATENATE(C1, " ",D1)
```

The second argument in the formula is a space enclosed in quotation marks, so there will be a space between the first and last names. If you want to combine the text *Amount Payable: $* with the sum of cells A1:B1, you could enter the following formula in cell E1:

```
=CONCATENATE("Amount Payable: $",SUM(A1:B1))
```

8. How can I define a worksheet area for printing?

To define a print area, choose File ⇨ Page Setup and click the Sheet tab of the Page Setup dialog box. Place the insertion pointer in the Print Area text box and, on your worksheet, select the range or ranges you want to print. You can also enter references or names for the print area yourself. You may even want to add the Set Print Area button to a toolbar.

Another way to define a print area is to simply select your range, choose File ⇨ Print, choose Microsoft Excel in the pop-up menu in the Print dialog box, and then click the Selection radio button and click Print.

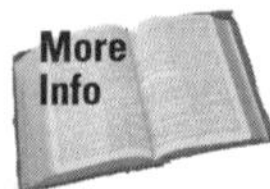

These options are explained in Chapter 20.

9. How can I make titles print on each page?

If you want to print titles on each page, choose File➪Page Setup and click the Sheet tab. Place your insertion pointer in the Rows to repeat at top box or the Columns to repeat at left box, and then select the rows or columns on your worksheet that you want to have print on each page. You may also enter references or names for the rows or columns in these boxes yourself.

10. Can I open a spreadsheet created in ClarisWorks Office?

The answer is yes . . . and no. A spreadsheet saved as a ClarisWorks document doesn't open as a spreadsheet in Excel 98. However, ClarisWorks 5.0 comes with many filters. A ClarisWorks user can easily do a Save As and select a format Excel can read. For example, the file can be saved as an Excel (for Mac) 5.0 file or as an Excel (for Windows) 5.0/7.0 file. When you receive the file, it will have the familiar Excel icon. Just double-click to open the file. By the way, ClarisWorks 5.0 uses DataViz translators.

Summary

This chapter covered the top ten Excel questions and their answers. This chapter concludes the Excel section of this book. The section that follows describes Microsoft PowerPoint, the presentation graphics package provided with Office 98.

Where to go next

- ✦ If you have questions regarding formatting that aren't covered here, look in Chapter 17.
- ✦ Chapter 20 answers your printing questions.

✦ ✦ ✦

PowerPoint

PART

IV

✦ ✦ ✦ ✦

In This Part

Chapter 27
Working in PowerPoint

Chapter 28
Enhancing a Presentation

Chapter 29
Working with Charts in PowerPoint

Chapter 30
Producing Your Work

Chapter 31
Working with PowerPoint Macros

Chapter 32
PowerPoint and the Web

Chapter 33
PowerPoint at Work

Chapter 34
The PowerPoint Top Ten

✦ ✦ ✦ ✦

CHAPTER 27

Working with PowerPoint

✦ ✦ ✦ ✦

In This Chapter

Discovering the Presentation window

Working with shortcuts and toolbars

Using PowerPoint's default presentations

Working with presentations

✦ ✦ ✦ ✦

This chapter teaches methods for moving your toolbars, saving presentations, aligning objects, rearranging a slide show, and changing the slide layout itself. Objects become more important in PowerPoint as you experiment with different layouts. You will also learn how to perform different tasks with the objects that you add to your presentation.

Discovering the Presentation Window

PowerPoint's presentation window is where you create slides and arrange them in your presentation—this is the bulk of the work you do in PowerPoint. Familiarizing yourself with the PowerPoint window (see Figure 27-1) is very important for easy functioning in PowerPoint.

At the lower-left corner of the presentation window are the view buttons (see Figure 27-2), which enable you to switch among different views in the PowerPoint presentation window. The view buttons include, from left to right: Slide view, Outline view, Slide Sorter view, Notes Pages view, and Slide Show. You can also change views by choosing the appropriate commands from the View menu.

Click the Slide view button when you want only one slide to appear onscreen. Slide view is a WYSIWYG (What You See Is What You Get) representation of your slide. (Figure 27-1 shows Slide view.)

Click the Outline view button to show the slide in outline form so that you can move headings and other information by clicking and dragging (see Figure 27-3). Outline view enables you to see the title and body text of all your slides simultaneously.

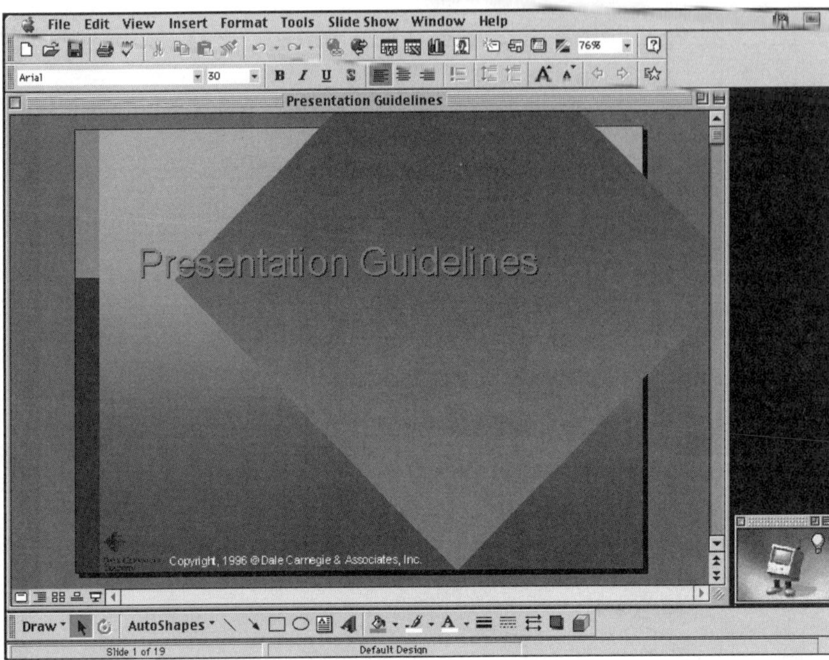

Figure 27-1: The PowerPoint window

Figure 27-2: The view buttons (close up)

Click the Slide Sorter view button for a view of all the slides in a presentation so that you can quickly see their layout and sequence (see Figure 27-4).

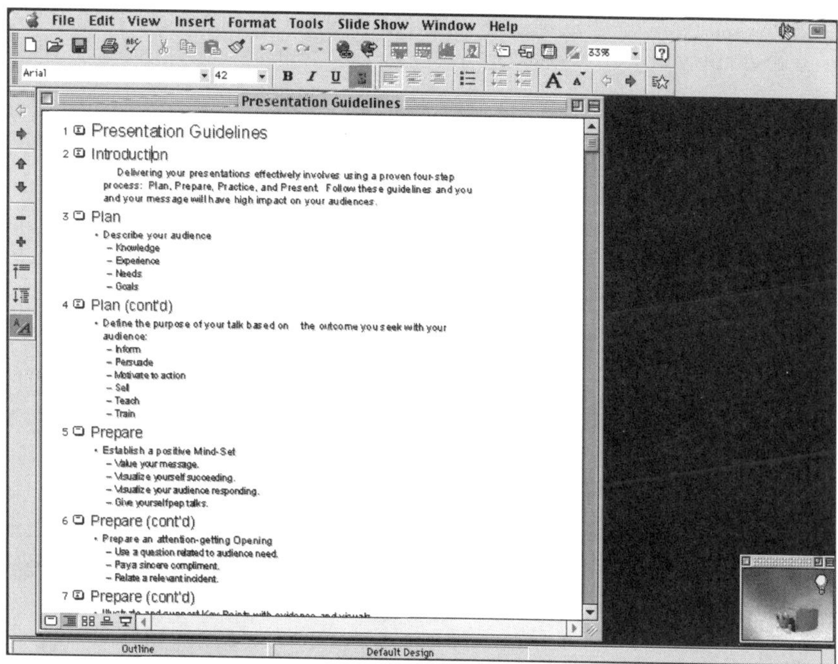

Figure 27-3: Outline view

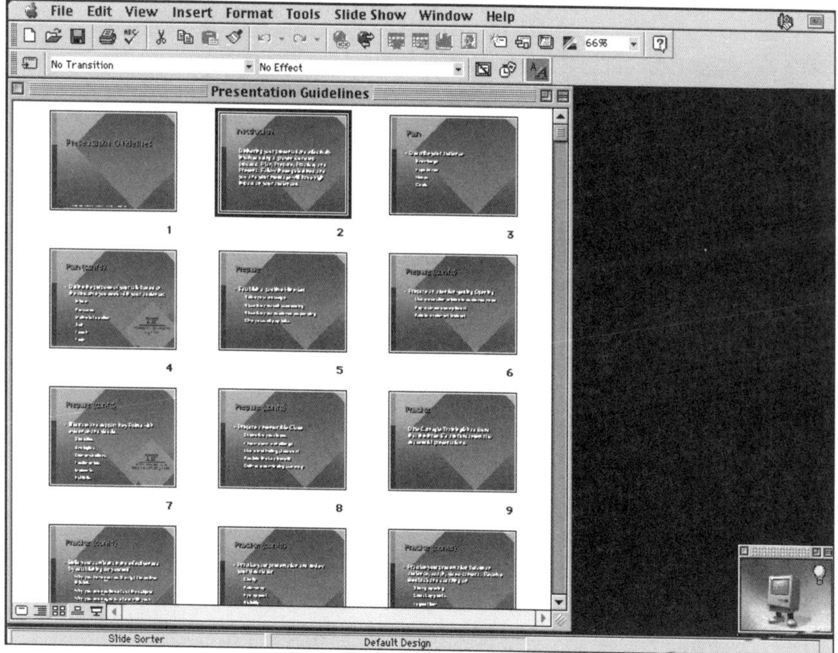

Figure 27-4: Slide Sorter view

Click the Notes Page view button to enter any notes you may want to attach to the slide or to display any notes that you may have already written (see Figure 27-5).

Click the Slide Show button to run the slide show after you have completed the slides. Notice how the slide now fills the screen (see Figure 27-6). You can also view your slides as a timed presentation.

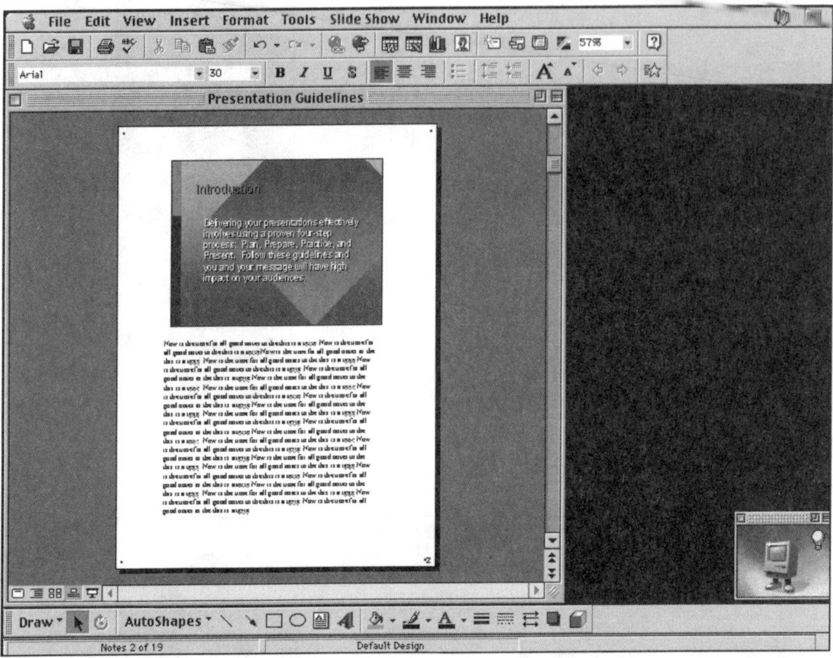

Figure 27-5: Notes Page view

Working with Shortcuts and Toolbars

Just as with other Microsoft programs, PowerPoint offers shortcut menus, shortcut buttons, and toolbars to make it as easy as possible to create a presentation.

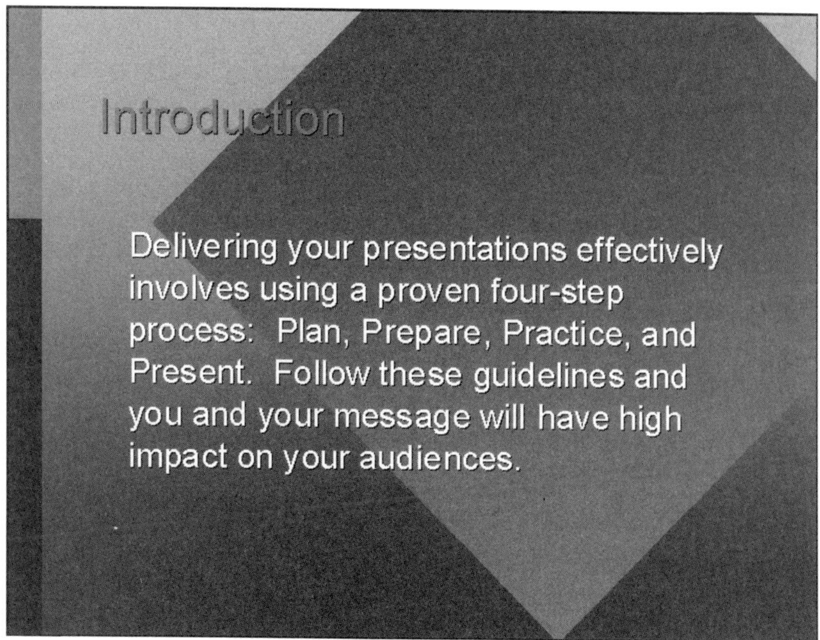

Figure 27-6: Slide Show view

Using shortcut menus

PowerPoint provides shortcut menus so you can perform different commands without having to use the pull-down menus. Shortcut menus can save lots of time. To activate any of the shortcut menus, move the pointer to the object that you want the command to act on, press and hold down the Control key, and click with the mouse. Figure 27-7 shows a shortcut menu in PowerPoint.

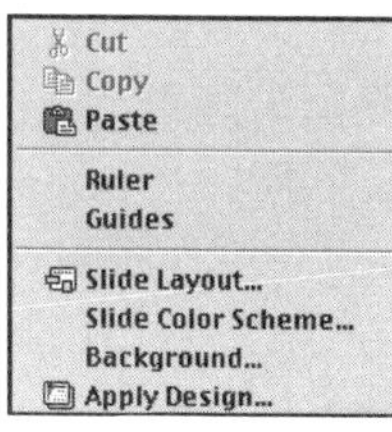

Figure 27-7: A shortcut menu in a PowerPoint slide window

Using the toolbars

When you open the PowerPoint window and enter Slide view, you see three toolbars. The Standard toolbar appears at the very top of the screen (see Figure 27-8) to open presentations, to save, to print, or to insert objects and charts. Below it is the Formatting toolbar (see Figure 27-9); use it to perform tasks related to formatting such as applying different fonts and styles and changing the indentation of the presentation. At the bottom of the screen is the Drawing toolbar (see Figure 27-10), which is used to perform tasks related to controlling the appearance of shapes. You can draw shapes, rotate them, and control different aspects of their appearance onscreen.

Figure 27-8: The Standard toolbar

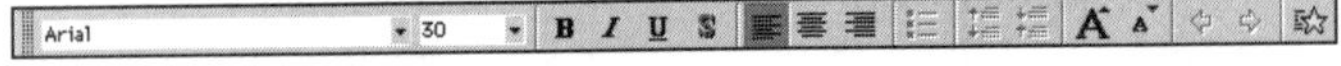

Figure 27-9: The Formatting toolbar

Figure 27-10: The Drawing toolbar

Hot Stuff

Hold the cursor over any item on a toolbar without clicking and a "tip" will pop up and tell you what it is.

You can activate the other PowerPoint toolbars by choosing the Toolbars command from the View menu and selecting other toolbars from the list in the Toolbars drop-down menu (see Figure 27-11), or you can Control-click the toolbar area of the screen and select the toolbars you want from the shortcut menu that appears.

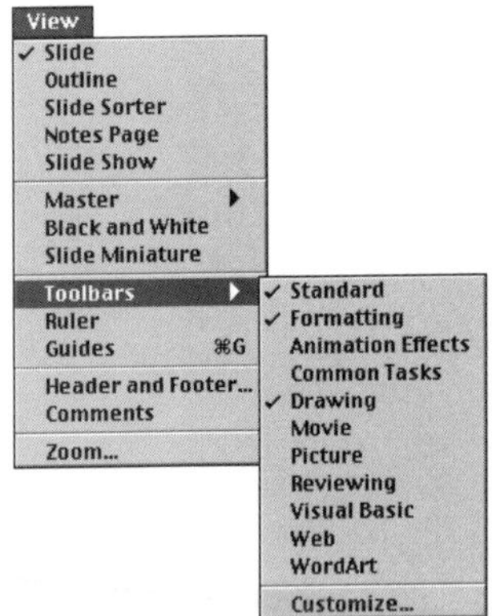

Figure 27-11: The Toolbars drop-down menu

As with all Office toolbars, you can grab and drag any or all PowerPoint toolbars anywhere onscreen. Just click the dots on the left end and drag.

Using PowerPoint's Default Presentations

By far, the easiest way to create a presentation in PowerPoint is to use one of the many default presentation formats that are provided with the software. The advantage of using a default format is that it already contains slides with content guidelines that you can follow to quickly build a presentation for a typical business need. PowerPoint provides one blank presentation, many presentation designs, and complete presentations.

The following is a list of just some of the types of default presentations available in the New Presentation dialog box shown in Figure 27-12. Some of the templates shown are only available after installing the additional templates in the Value Pack folder. Note that the presentations that are listed as Online are used to create presentations that can be saved as Hypertext Markup Language (HTML) files for viewing on the Internet:

- ✦ **Company Meeting** creates a presentation for a company meeting.
- ✦ **Corporate Financial Overview** creates a presentation that enables you to give a financial overview of your company.
- ✦ **Marketing Plan** creates a presentation that enables you to show a marketing plan for a company.
- ✦ **Project Status (Online)** shows the progress of a company project. This is one of the online presentations, which means it will be saved as an HTML file.
- ✦ **Recommending a Strategy** offers a slide layout that is useful for determining a strategy.
- ✦ **General** creates a blank presentation—you have to provide all the formatting, layout, and content.

The last default presentation format is the Blank option, which enables you to create your own layout. You need to be an experienced PowerPoint user to feel comfortable using this option.

To create a presentation by using a default presentation format, follow these steps:

1. Start a new presentation by choosing New from the File menu. The New Presentation dialog box appears, as shown in Figure 27-12.

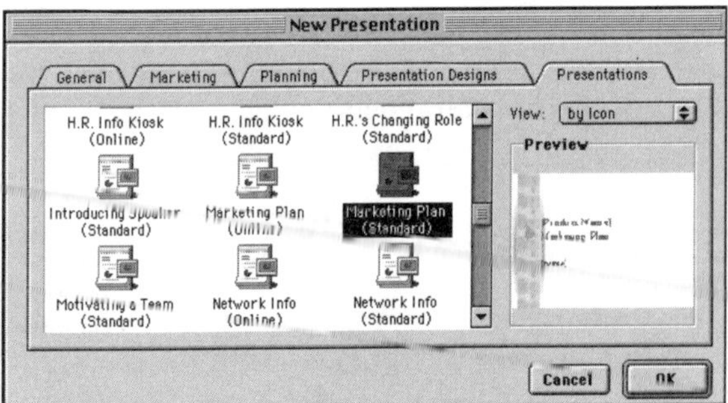

Figure 27-12: The New Presentation dialog box

2. Click the Presentations tab, if it is not already open, to show the default presentation formats.

3. Click the desired presentation format and then click OK (or double-click the desired presentation format). PowerPoint loads the presentation format and the first slide of the presentation appears. Figure 27-13 shows the first slide of the Project Status presentation format.

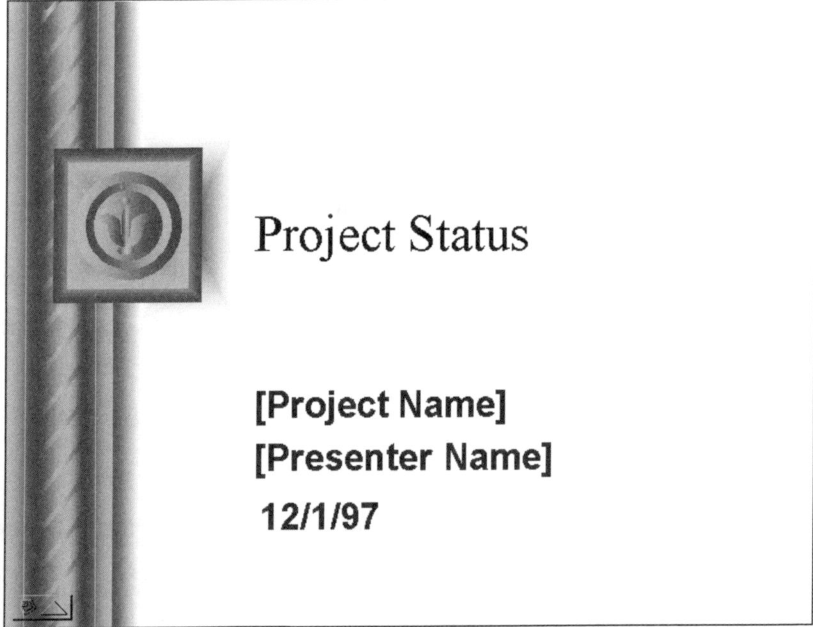

Figure 27-13: The first slide of the Project Status presentation

After you use these steps to create a presentation, you can modify the text in the slides by clicking the text to select each item you see (titles, subtitles, or text within the presentation) and typing your desired text. You can use the Page Up and Page Down keys or click the Previous Slide and Next Slide buttons at the lower-right side of the window to move among the various slides of your presentation.

Each slide contains text in the form of suggestions that you can modify. Figure 27-14, for example, shows the second of ten available slides in the Project Status presentation. You can click the existing text and edit it as desired while in Slide view.

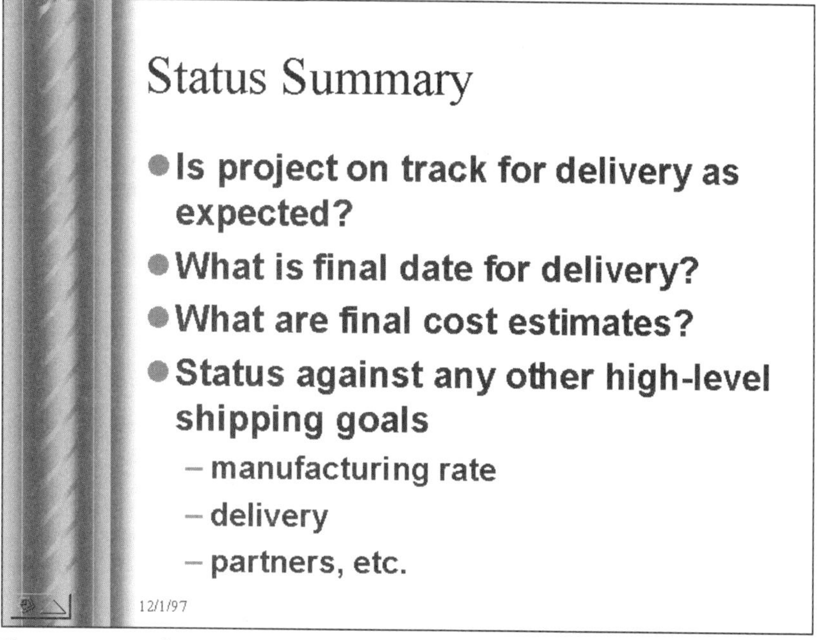

Figure 27-14: The second slide of the Project Status presentation

If you don't want one of the default slides in your presentation, just move to the unwanted slide and choose Edit ⇨ Delete Slide. If you want to add a new slide to the presentation, move to the slide that you want the new slide to follow and choose Insert ⇨ New Slide. The New Slide dialog box appears. Now choose your slide layout. Then click the boxes and type the desired text for the slide. (You learn more about adding slides and about adding items to slides later in this chapter.)

After you've finished adding the needed text to the pages of your presentation, save it by choosing File ⇨ Save. When you save a presentation for the first time, the Save dialog box shown in Figure 27-15 appears. Enter a name for the file in the Save text box and, if you want, choose a different folder in which to save the file. Then click the Save button to save the presentation.

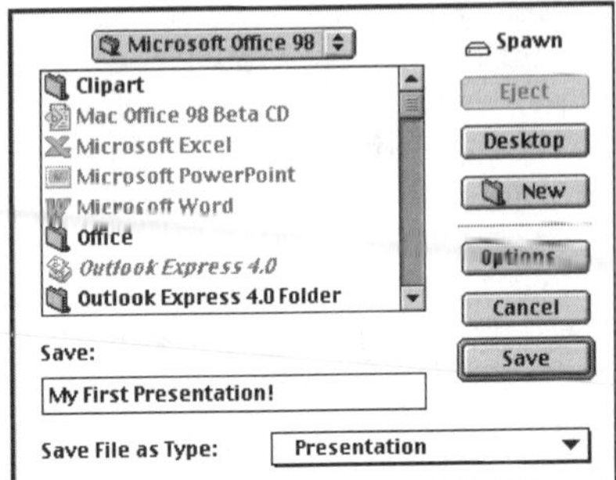

Figure 27-15: The Save dialog box

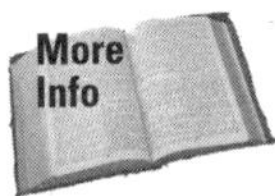

You can print your finished presentation by choosing File➪Print to open the Print dialog box. Choose All if you want to print all the slides in the presentation or type numbers in the From and To fields to print only part of the presentation. After you make your selection, click OK to begin printing. You can print information in PowerPoint in several ways. You find a full description of printing and of the other options in the Print dialog box in Chapter 30.

When you're finished with the presentation, choose File➪Close if you want to do other work in PowerPoint or File➪Quit to exit PowerPoint.

Working with Presentations

With the information that has been provided so far, you can easily start creating effective business presentations. However, you can do a lot more with PowerPoint, and the rest of this chapter gives you the basics.

Creating a new presentation

When you want to create a new presentation, choose File➪New to open the New Presentation dialog box (refer to Figure 27-12). The dialog box contains three tabs: General, Presentation Designs, and Presentations (unless you've installed additional templates from the Value Pack). By default, the General tab is selected; to choose a presentation format, select another tab (see "Using PowerPoint's Default Presentations" earlier in the chapter).

The General tab offers icons for a Blank Presentation or the AutoContent Wizard (see Figure 27-16). (See Chapter 28 for more on the AutoContent Wizard.)

The other tabs contain a host of designs you can use for your slide backgrounds (see Figure 27-17). Use the Preview window to view a design after you single-click the icon of your choice.

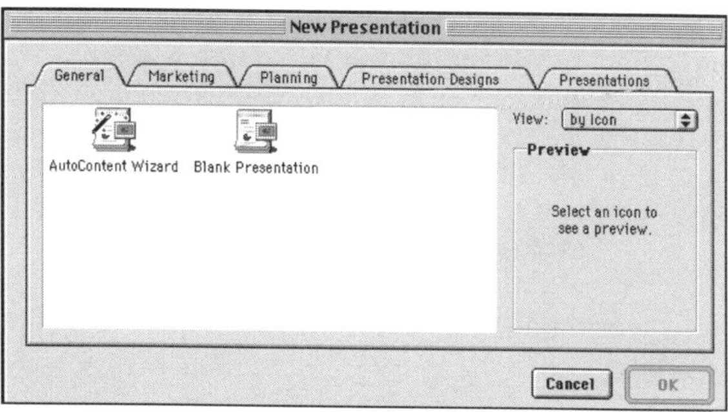

Figure 27-16: The General tab in the New Presentation dialog box

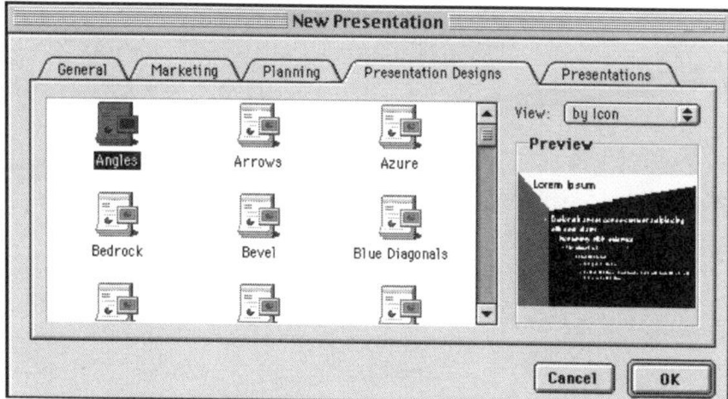

Figure 27-17: The Presentation Designs tab in the New Presentation dialog box

After you have chosen the template you want for your presentation, click OK to begin filling out the template.

You can also create a template using the design of another presentation. Choose Format➪Apply Template and choose from the Open dialog box the presentation from which you want to borrow the design.

Saving a presentation

You save a presentation in PowerPoint the same way that you save a file in most Mac programs: by choosing File➪Save or by using the keyboard shortcut ⌘-S. If you have not previously saved the presentation, the Save As dialog box opens, and you are prompted to enter a name for the presentation. If you have already given the presentation a name, it is saved under that name.

You can also perform other tasks in the Save As dialog box. You can change the name of a presentation by entering a new name in the File name text box. You can save files in a variety of formats including older versions of PowerPoint, PICT, JPEG, GIF, and Macintosh Scrapbook by choosing a new file type from the Save as type pop-up menu and then clicking OK to save the file. Remember that you need to save a presentation as a PowerPoint 4.0 file if you want to use it with PowerPoint 4.0.

When you have completed your work in PowerPoint and you want to exit the program, choose File➪Quit.

Entering summary information

You can include summary information with the presentations that you save. You enter summary information—which includes a title, subject, and other key information to help you keep track of the presentations—in the Summary Information dialog box. To enter summary information for your presentation, follow these steps:

1. Choose File➪Properties. The Properties dialog box appears with the Summary tab open, as shown in Figure 27-18.

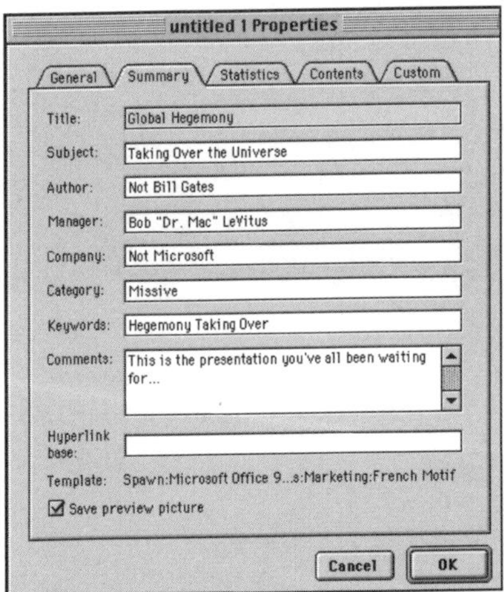

Figure 27-18: The Summary tab of the Properties dialog box

2. Enter the information you want in each of the following text boxes:
   - Title—Enter a name for the presentation.
   - Subject—Enter a brief description of the contents of the presentation.

- Author—Enter the name of the author. The default name is the name that you entered when you installed Microsoft Office.
- Manager—Enter a manager name, if you wish.
- Company—Enter a company name, if you wish.
- Category—Enter a category for the presentation if you wish to categorize it.
- Keywords—Enter keywords that you associate with the presentation. These words can help you in a Find File search, if you need to use this command from the File menu. You can use the Copy and Paste commands from the Edit menu to insert the titles of your slides in the Keywords list box.
- Comments—Enter any needed comments.

3. When are finished entering the information, click OK to store the information.
4. The summary information can be viewed by choosing File⇨Properties, which displays the properties for the presentation, and then choosing the Summary tab to display the summary info.

Entering and editing text

After you have opened a new presentation, it will not contain the text you want to use, so you will have to add and edit your own text. This section teaches the basics of editing text in Outline view and Slide view. Later in the chapter, you learn how to add objects to your presentation.

Editing in Outline view

Outline view is excellent for editing text because it enables you to see the overall content of your presentation while you are editing the text. You can switch to Outline view by choosing View⇨Outline or by clicking the Outline view button in the status bar. After you are in Outline view, you can edit text by simply clicking it and moving the cursor to the area you want to change. Use the Delete key to remove characters that are to the right of the cursor and use the Backspace key to delete characters that are to the left of the cursor. Figure 27-19 shows a slide in Outline view ready for editing.

Hot Stuff

When you select text in PowerPoint, the program selects whole words. If you want to select individual characters, choose Tools⇨Preferences. In the Preferences dialog box, choose the Edit tab. Next, uncheck the Automatic Word Selection option and click OK to turn it off.

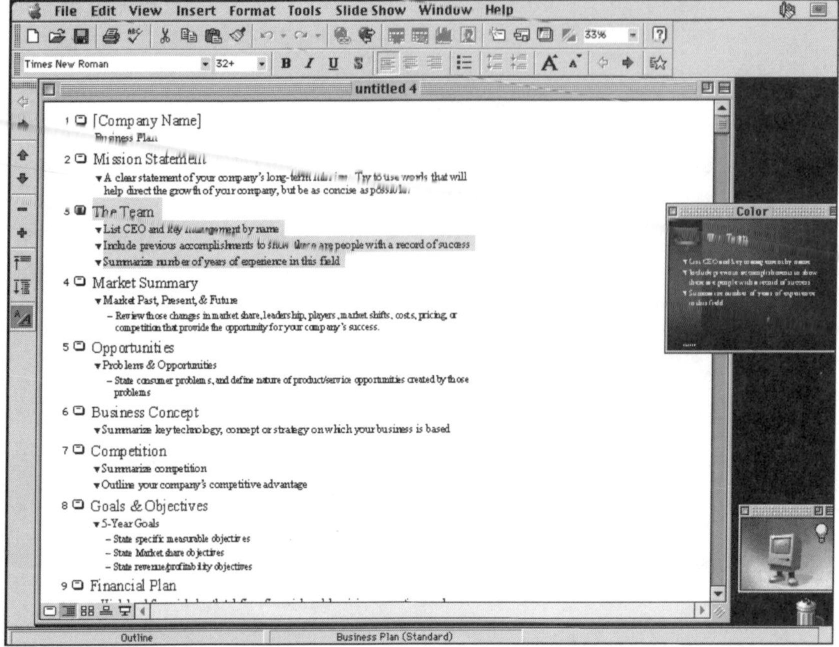

Figure 27-19: A slide in Outline view

Editing in Slide view

Slide view also provides an easy way to edit text, and it provides a good opportunity to see an individual slide's appearance. You can switch to Slide view by choosing View ⇨ Slide or by clicking the Slide view button in the status bar. As Figure 27-20 illustrates, you can edit either text or an object by clicking the text or the object to select it, clicking the space where you want the cursor to appear, and then making the changes.

Working with slides

You use Slide view to do most of your work with slides. Slide view lets you see each slide pretty much as it will appear in your presentation. It also lets you move between the slides in your presentations, and it lets you use click-and-drag to move the slide within your presentation.

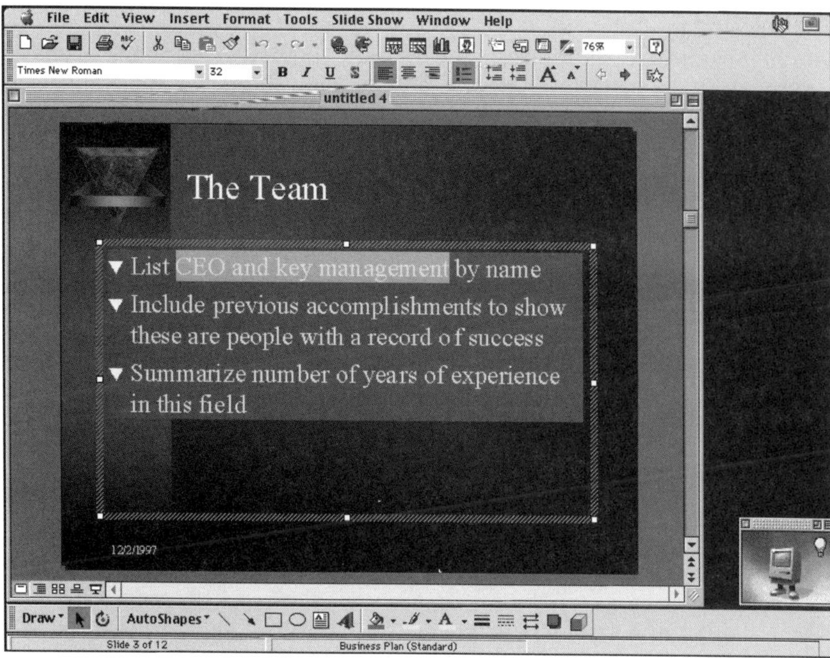

Figure 27-20: A slide in Slide view

Moving between slides

When you have more than one slide in a presentation, you must be able to move easily among the slides so that you can quickly work on all of them. (Remember that in all views except Slide Show you can perform edits by double-clicking the slide.) How you move among the slides depends on the view that you are in at the time. Table 27-1 shows how you can move among slides in each of the views.

Table 27-1
Moving Among Slides in Different Views

View	*How to Move Among Slides*
Outline	Use the scroll bar to move to the slide, click the slide icon to the left of the slide's title, or click the text to perform the changes.
Slide Sorter	Click the slide that you want to see. A border appears around the slide. If you then double-click the slide, you are switched to Slide view where you can make changes to your slide.
Slide	Drag the scroll bar until the slide that you want appears, or press the Page Up or Page Down key.
Notes Pages	Drag the scroll bar until the slide that you want appears, or press the Page Up or Page Down key.

Inserting slides

As you build your presentations in PowerPoint, you may need to make changes to the presentation by inserting, deleting, and copying slides. To add a slide to a presentation, follow these steps:

1. In any view, choose the slide after which you want the new slide to appear.
2. Choose Insert ➪ New Slide or use the keyboard shortcut ⌘-M.
3. The New Slide dialog box appears. Choose the slide layout you want and click OK to choose that slide layout.

To change the new slide's layout (or create a slide layout), follow these steps:

1. In Slide view, Control-click the slide and choose Slide Layout from the shortcut menu. The Slide Layout dialog box appears.
2. Choose the layout you want and click the Reapply button. (If you are creating a slide layout, the button is Apply.)

The layout is then applied to the slide.

Hot Stuff

Another way to add a new slide is by clicking the New Slide button on the Standard toolbar.

You can also add slides from a previous presentation to your current presentation. This shortcut is useful because it prevents you from taking the time to create an entirely new presentation when you already have slides that you can use from an old presentation. First, you must open the presentation to which you want to add the slides and choose the place where you want to insert the slides. The new slides will appear after the chosen slide. Then choose Insert ➪ Slides from Files and find the previous presentation in the Open dialog box and click the Insert button. All the slides contained in that presentation are inserted into the new presentation. Note that the inserted slides take on the look of the presentation in which they are inserted. This prevents you from having to make any changes to the look of the imported slides.

Deleting slides

Deleting a slide is relatively simple and can be performed in any view except Slide Show. Navigate to the slide and choose Edit ➪ Delete Slide to remove the slide. If you delete a slide by accident, choose Edit ➪ Undo or click the Undo button on the Standard toolbar to bring back the slide.

Copying and moving slides

You copy slides in PowerPoint just like you copy items in other Mac programs by using the Copy and Paste commands from the Edit menu. To copy a slide, follow these steps:

1. Switch to Slide Sorter view.
2. Choose the slide(s) you want to copy. To select more than one slide, press the Shift key while you select the slides.
3. Choose Edit ⇨ Copy.
4. Move to the slide after which you want to place the copied slide.
5. Choose Edit ⇨ Paste.

You use the same method to move a slide, except that you use the Cut command rather than the Copy command.

Rearranging slides

Occasionally you will need to change the order in which the slides appear in your presentation. PowerPoint provides for this need in Slide Sorter view and Outline view. In these views, you can use the drag-and-drop technique to move slides around.

To rearrange the order of your slides in Outline view, follow these steps:

1. Click the icon for the slide that you want to move.
2. Drag the icon up or down in the outline.

You can also select just one piece of information on a slide and move it to another slide by clicking and dragging it to the desired place.

To rearrange slides in Slide Sorter view, follow these steps:

1. Select the slide you want to move to a new location.
2. Drag the slide to its new location. As you drag the slide, a vertical line marks the place where it will appear.
3. Release the mouse button to insert the slide in its new location.

Changing the slide layout

You can also change the slide layout after you have created a slide. To change a slide layout, follow these steps:

1. In Slide Sorter view, move to the side you want to change.
2. Choose Format ⇨ Slide Layout.
3. In the Slide Layout dialog box, choose the layout you want to apply to the slide and click Apply (see Figure 27-21).

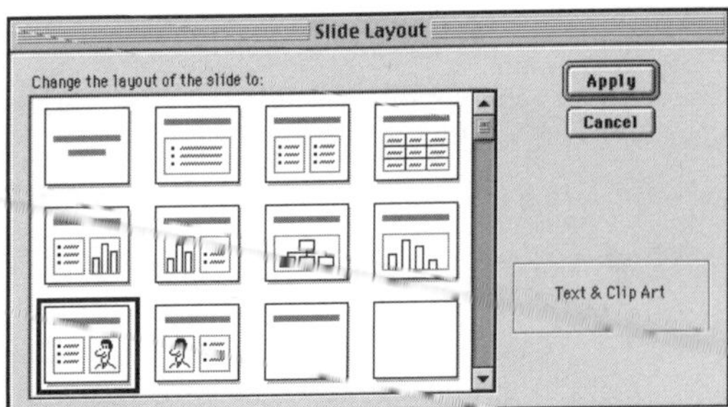

Figure 27-21: The Slide Layout dialog box

Working with objects

In PowerPoint, the basic component that you use to create a slide is an *object*. An object can be the box where you enter text, a picture brought in from another source, or the shape that you draw. You can have as many objects as you want on a slide.

Selecting and grouping objects

To select the object you want to work with, click it. After selecting the object, you can add text to it and change its orientation, shape, color, or pattern. You can also select multiple objects by holding down the Shift key as you select the objects. To deselect an object, simply hold down the Shift key and click the object again.

You can also group objects together, which is useful when you want to change the colors for a group of objects or align them horizontally. All the objects that you include in the group will act as one object. To group objects, select them then choose Draw⇨Group from the Drawing toolbar. Thereafter, if you perform an action on one of the objects, the action will affect all the objects in the group. When you group objects, you can flip, resize, or rotate them. If you want to change the grouping, choose Draw⇨Regroup from the Drawing toolbar after the objects have been grouped and ungrouped. Remember that the Regroup command will affect only the objects that were included in the original group.

You can also select and deselect noncontiguous objects in PowerPoint by clicking the objects while pressing the Shift key.

Moving and copying objects

As you work out a presentation, you may need to move your objects around. PowerPoint provides for this need nicely with two options: the cut-and-copy method or the click-and-drag method.

To use the cut-and-copy method to move objects to a different slide, follow these steps:

1. Switch to Slide view and select the object(s) that you want to move or copy.
2. Choose Edit ➪ Cut to move the object to a new location via the Clipboard, or choose Edit ➪ Copy to copy it.
3. Move to the slide on which you want to place the information.
4. Choose Edit ➪ Paste to place the Clipboard information onto the slide.

Using the click-and-drag method to move objects around on the same slide is equally simple. To use this method, click the object and hold down the mouse button. Then move to the area where you want to place the object. Release the mouse button to place the object.

Sometimes you may find that you need to remove an object from a slide. To remove an object, select it and press the Delete key or choose Edit ➪ Clear.

Cropping objects

In your quest to give your presentation a refined look, it may be necessary to crop the objects—both pictures and graphics—that you added to your presentation. Cropping is the trimming of an object to remove elements that you don't want from the picture. To crop an object, follow these steps:

1. After you add an object to a slide and the Picture toolbar appears, click the Crop button.
2. Place the mouse pointer over a selection handle. If you want to crop two sides at once, use a corner handle. If you want to crop only one side, use a top or bottom handle. Figure 27-22 shows a cropped image and the Picture toolbar with the Crop tool selected. Click and drag the handle to do the cropping.

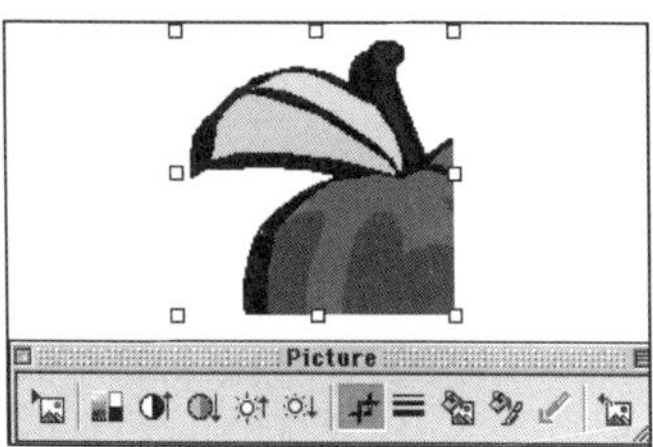

Figure 27-22: An image cropped in PowerPoint (top) and the Picture toolbar with the Crop tool selected (bottom)

Aligning objects

When you create presentations, it is important that the objects have the same sort of alignment. Figure 27-23 shows a before and after shot of some objects on a slide in PowerPoint. As you can see, the slide with aligned objects has a better appearance than the one in which the objects are not aligned. Aligned objects appear more organized than unaligned objects.

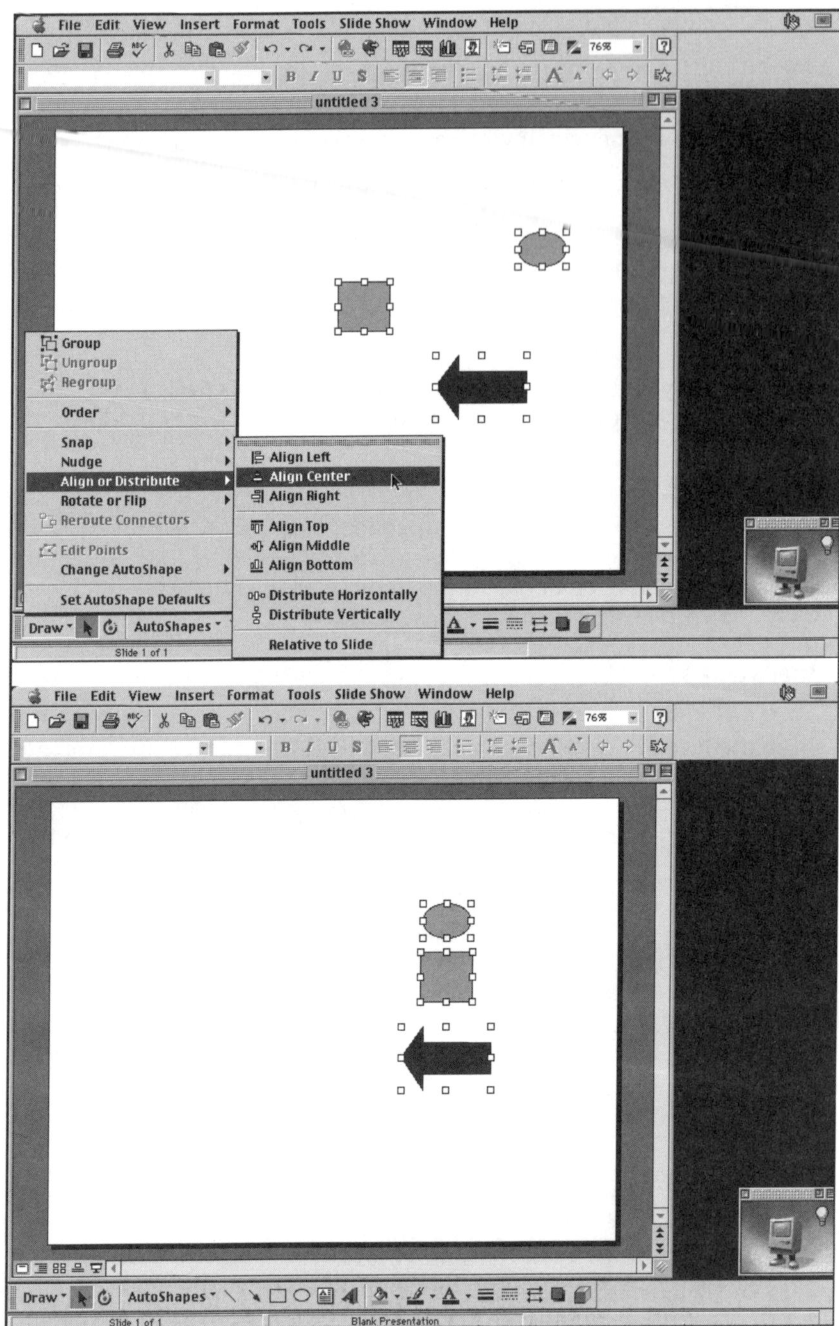

Figure 27-23: Objects before (top) and after (bottom) alignment

The Align command gives you a choice of alignment methods. You can select objects and then align them, or you can use the rulers available in the PowerPoint window. PowerPoint is equipped with a reference system for aligning objects on slides. The system uses a grid and guides. The invisible grid covers the slide with twelve gridlines per inch and five lines per centimeter. When the objects are drawn, their corners align on the nearest intersection of the grid, which is how PowerPoint helps you to align objects.

The guides that PowerPoint provides are two rulers: one horizontal and one vertical. When the corners or center of an object (whichever is closer) is close to the guide, it snaps to the guide, which is how you align the object. You can even align a group of objects.

To align an object, follow these steps:

1. Select the object(s) to align.
2. Choose Draw ⇨ Align, or Distribute from the Drawing toolbar, and then choose the alignment that you want from the submenu. You can choose from left, center, right, top, middle, or bottom.

If you want to align your objects automatically, choose Draw ⇨ Snap ⇨ To Grid from the Drawing toolbar. If the grid is on, you will see a check mark beside the choice on the menu. The Draw ⇨ Nudge choice enables you to align objects by moving the image in the direction you choose, a little at a time.

Hot Stuff

For aligning objects, there are a number of helpful toolbar buttons in the Customize dialog box. Choosing Tools ⇨ Customize opens the Customize dialog box with the Toolbars tab chosen. Choose the Commands tab and other useful toolbar buttons appear. To add any of these buttons to your toolbar, click the name of the button you wish to add from the Commands box. Next, drag the name up to a toolbar (hint: if you like, first create a new toolbar). The outline of a button appears and each of the dragged buttons is added to that toolbar. If you are not sure of what each of the buttons does, the box at the bottom of the tab gives a description of the selected button.

Stacking objects

Sometimes you have to overlap objects to give them the correct effect. You may even want to change the order of overlapped objects. You can also stack groups of objects by moving a group of objects forward or backward. You can use the Tab key to navigate through the stacked objects.

Objects in a stack can be moved up or down one level at a time, or you can send an object to the back or to the front at once. This feature prevents you from having to keep track of the objects as you draw them: in other words, you don't have to draw the bottom object first or the top object last and so on.

To bring an object to the front or to the back of a stack, click the object that you want to move and choose Draw➪Order either Bring Forward, Send Backward, Send to Back, or Bring to Front from the Drawing toolbar. Figure 27-24 shows the original positions of objects on a slide and how Bring Forward can change their positions.

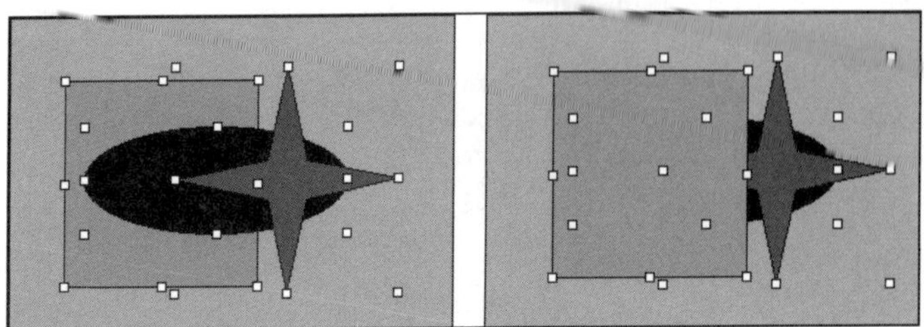

Figure 27-24: Left—the original positions of objects on a slide. Right—changing the position of the objects with the Bring Forward command.

Working with shapes

Sometimes when you work with PowerPoint, you will want to add your own shapes or art to the presentation. (Remember that these shapes are still considered objects by PowerPoint.) You can draw lines, arcs, rectangles, and ovals with the Drawing toolbar. Figure 27-25 shows some examples of shapes that you can create in PowerPoint.

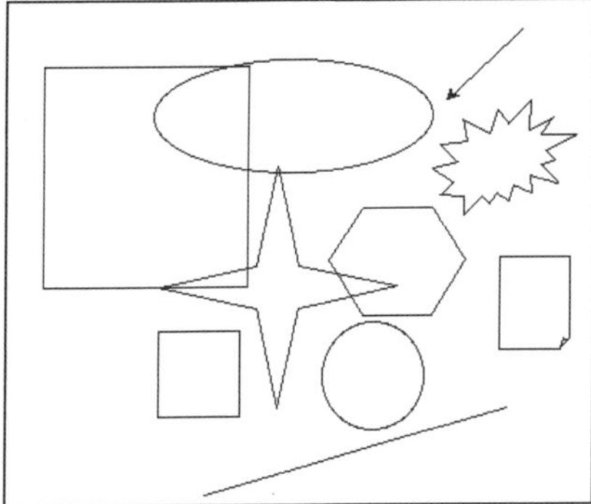

Figure 27-25: Examples of shapes that you can create in PowerPoint

You can also add different attributes to the lines and shapes that you create. For example, you can insert dotted lines, color the lines, fill in the shapes, and add arrowheads to lines. Remember that you can't add text to your shapes except by grouping.

Drawing shapes

There are many tools you can use to perform your drawing tasks. On the Drawing toolbar, use the Rectangle tool to draw rectangles and the Line tool to draw lines. You can also use the Oval and AutoShapes tools to create shapes.

To draw shapes in your slides, follow these steps:

1. Switch to Slide view if you are not already there.
2. On the Drawing toolbar, click the button for the object you want to draw. Click the Line tool button if you want to draw a line; click the Oval tool button if you want to draw an oval or a circle; click the Rectangle tool button if you want to draw a rectangle; and so on. You can also click the AutoShapes Button on the Drawing toolbar and select any of a variety of shapes.
3. Click the place where you want the shape to begin and drag to the place where you want the shape to end.
4. Release the mouse button.

Constraint keys are used to create shapes that are difficult to create freehand. These constraint keys are available:

✦ Hold down the Shift key to draw perfectly round circles and perfectly square squares.

✦ Hold down the Option key to double the size of the object you're drawing.

Drawing freeform shapes

You may want to add a freeform shape, such as a flower or an ice cream cone, to a slide. You can create any kind of drawing that you want by clicking the AutoShapes button on the Drawing toolbar, choosing Lines from the menu, and selecting the freeform button in the submenu that appears (see Figure 27-26). You draw the shape that you want by clicking and holding down the mouse button as you draw. Double-click to stop drawing.

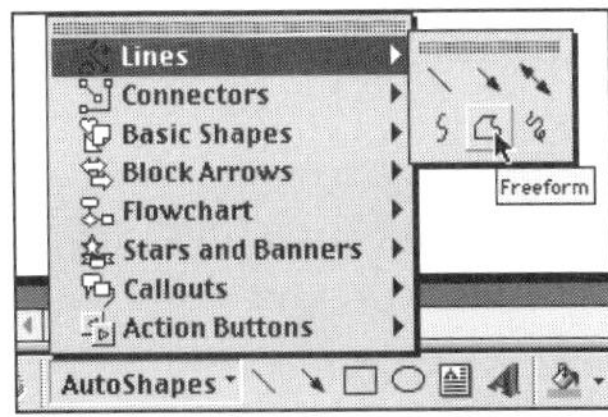

Figure 27-26: Choosing the Freeform tool from the AutoShapes menu

You can also use the Freeform tool to draw a polygon, which is a series of points joined by lines. After you click the Freeform tool button, click the point where you want the first vertex of the polygon to appear and release the mouse button. Then you click the point where you want the second point to appear and release the mouse button. Continue to click the desired points and release the mouse button until you create the polygon shape you want.

Changing the color and style of shapes

You can change the color or style of the lines in a shape. You can also apply a fill color to a shape. To change the color or style of a line in a shape, follow these steps:

1. Select the shape to change.
2. Choose Format⇨Colors and Lines to go to the Colors and Lines tab of the Format AutoShape dialog box shown in Figure 27-27. In the Line area, you can choose to change the color or style of the line in any shape. You also can add dashed lines and an arrowhead.

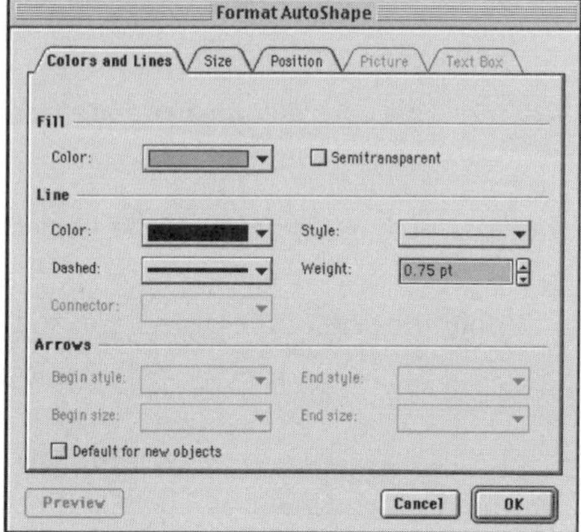

Figure 27-27: The Colors and Lines tab of the Format AutoShape dialog box

3. Clicking the Preview button applies the selected options to the slide so you can see what they look like before making the changes. You may need to drag the dialog box out of the way to see the results because the box appears on top of the slide.

You may also want to add a fill color to a shape. Simply select the shape that you want to fill with color and choose Format⇨Colors and Lines. In the Colors and Lines tab, select a color in the Fill list box and then click OK.

Rotating and sizing shapes

Rotating and changing the size of a shape is also a simple matter with PowerPoint. To rotate a shape on its center point, first select the shape. Then click the Free Rotate tool button on the Drawing toolbar. Now drag a handle of the shape to rotate it. Figure 27-28 shows the difference.

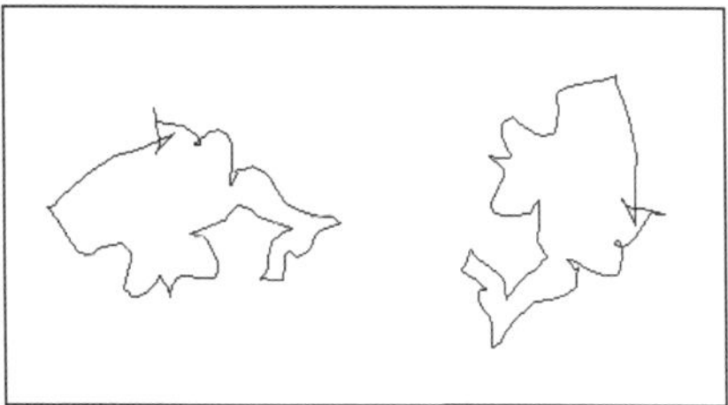

Figure 27-28: Left—a freeform object. Right—the same object rotated.

To change the size of a shape, select the shape. Small black squares, called handles, appear around the shape. To resize the width of the shape, drag one of the side handles to the desired width. To change the height of the shape, drag a top or bottom handle. If you want to resize the shape proportionally, drag a corner handle while holding down the Shift key. A shape can also be resized from its center by holding down the Option key and dragging the handles.

Using AutoShapes and clip-art

PowerPoint has many standard shapes and pieces of clip-art. To activate the Drawing toolbar, switch to Slide view, choose View ➪ Toolbars, and click Drawing. Click the AutoShapes button in the toolbar and choose the type of shape you want to add to your presentation. A submenu for each of them appears. Make your choice from the submenu. Next, move to the area of the presentation where you want to add the shape. Click to add the shape and then size it by using the resizing techniques. Remember that you can also add color to the shapes by choosing Format ➪ Colors and Lines, which brings up the Colors and Lines tab.

PowerPoint comes with a whole bunch of clip-art, which is invaluable in creating presentations. The clip-art comes in many different categories. To access the ClipArt Gallery, follow these steps:

1. Click the Insert Clip Art button on the Standard toolbar.
2. The Microsoft ClipArt Gallery dialog box appears.
3. Choose the category of clip-art you want.
4. Select the clip-art you want and click Insert. PowerPoint inserts it at the insertion point.

Summary

This chapter described many techniques for the everyday use of PowerPoint. With these skills, you can build presentations, enter the text you want, and choose the correct slide layout. This chapter discussed how to do the following:

- Use the convenient shortcut menus that make life easy and provide quick access to the commands you may need in Power Point.
- Experiment with the different methods for laying out new slides and editing text, including slides with placeholders for clip-art and other slide layouts.
- Insert objects into presentations and edit the objects. Using objects will make for nicer presentations.
- Use the built-in templates and prefabricated presentations to make creating a presentation less time-consuming.
- Save your presentations and enter summary information that will help you find the presentations if you tend to forget where they are. This is quite useful if you create many presentations.

Where to go next

- Now that you have the tools to begin your work in PowerPoint, you can begin refining the presentations you create. Chapter 28 gets you started.
- The obvious goal when you use PowerPoint is to produce a finished presentation from the slides you created with the software. Chapter 30 tells you how.

✦ ✦ ✦

CHAPTER 28

Enhancing a Presentation

◆ ◆ ◆ ◆

In This Chapter

Using the AutoContent Wizard

Using the AutoLayout feature

Using the Slide Master

Working with lists and columns

Adding formatting and special effects

◆ ◆ ◆ ◆

PowerPoint gives you lots of tools to give your presentation a more professional look. To help you along, PowerPoint provides several wizards, most notably the AutoContent Wizard, that provide simple ways to help you make your presentations look better. Creating columns and bulleted lists also helps you set up the information in a way that grabs the attention of your audience. Using different fonts and colors is another technique that can help your presentation take on a different look. This chapter discusses these methods and a few others that will enhance the appearance of your presentation.

Using the AutoContent Wizard

PowerPoint includes the AutoContent Wizard to help you define your presentation's look and contents. To use the AutoContent wizard, follow these steps:

1. Choose AutoContent from the dialog box that appears after you activate PowerPoint. If you have already activated PowerPoint, choose File➪New. From the New Presentation dialog box that appears, choose the Presentations tab. From the Presentations tab choose AutoContent Wizard. This activates the AutoContent Wizard (see Figure 28-1); click Next to proceed.

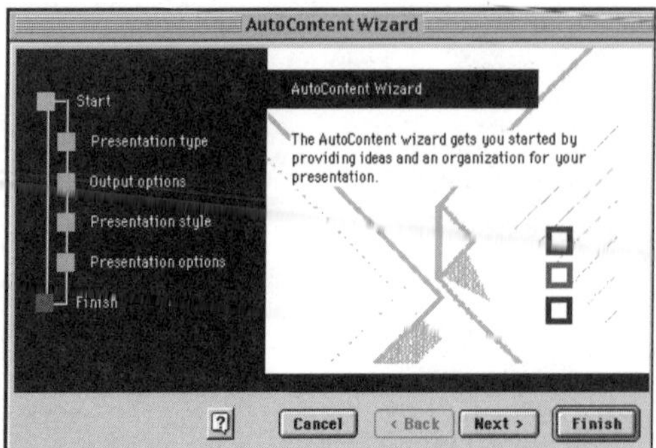

Figure 28-1: The first AutoContent Wizard dialog box

2. The second dialog box asks you to choose the type of presentation you want to give. The choices are divided into several categories. Clicking the button that corresponds to the category makes all the choices for that category appear. The default is All, which shows all the listings from all the categories. Figure 28-2 shows the second dialog box of the AutoContent Wizard.

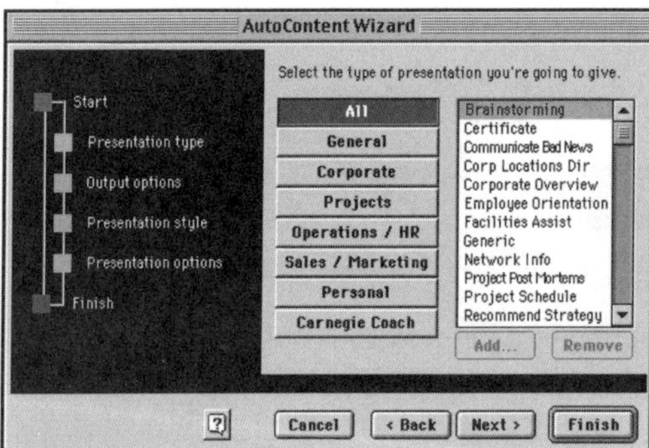

Figure 28-2: The second AutoContent Wizard dialog box

3. After you choose the type of presentation you want to create, click the Next button. You will see the third AutoContent Wizard dialog box, which is shown in Figure 28-3. In this dialog box, you can select the manner in which your presentation will be used. Your two choices are Presentations, informal meetings, handouts or Internet, kiosk. After you choose an option, click the Next button to move to the fourth dialog box.

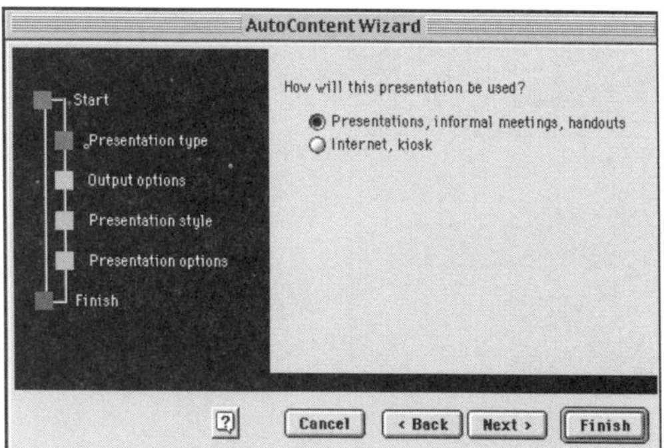

Figure 28-3: The third Auto Content Wizard dialog box

4. The fourth dialog box (see Figure 28-4) is used to choose the presentation output option. Under the type of output section, select the way you will present your slides. You can choose from On-screen presentations, Black and white overheads, Color overheads, or 35mm slides. Also, you can tell the wizard whether you will be printing out the slides. After you have made your selections, click Next to go to the fifth window of the AutoContent Wizard. When you are finished click Next to move to the fifth dialog box. If you choose Internet, kiosk, you will not see the Presentation Style dialog box. For more information on PowerPoint presentations and the Web, see Chapter 32.

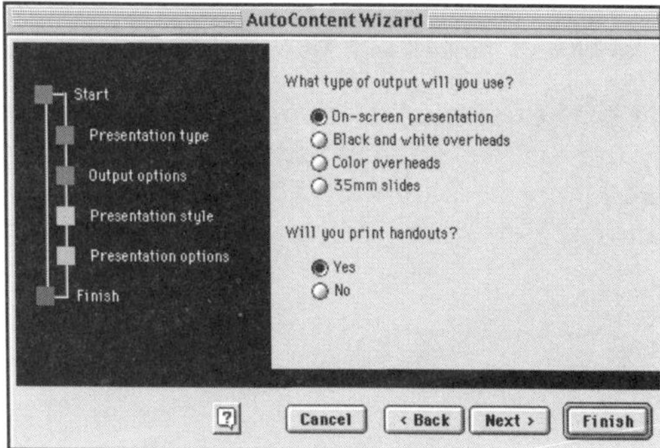

Figure 28-4: The fourth AutoContent Wizard dialog box

5. The fifth dialog box of the AutoContent Wizard (see Figure 28-5) is used to set up your title slide. Here your system profile information is entered in the boxes. If you wish to change the information, click and change the information. The wizard also allows space for any additional information that you wish to add to the title slide of the presentation. After you have finished making your entries, click Next to go to the final window of the AutoContent Wizard.

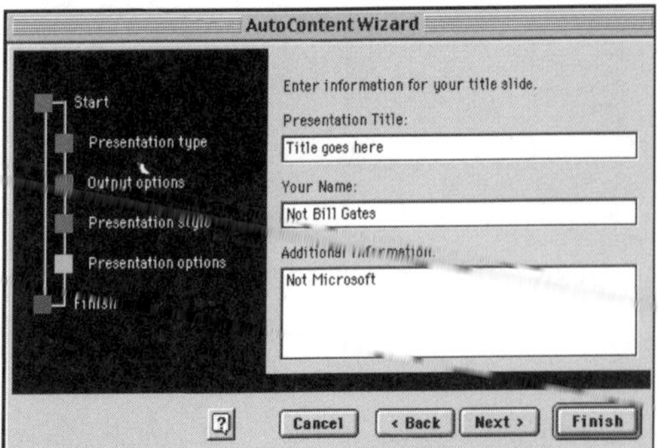

Figure 28-5: The fifth AutoContent Wizard dialog box

6. In the final AutoContent Wizard dialog box, you can change any of the choices you made if you wish. To do so, click the Back button to return to the box you used to make the choice and make the necessary changes.

7. After you have made your final choices on all your settings, click the Finish button. PowerPoint then creates the presentation using the settings you chose. Remember that if you wish to change the layout of the slides at a later time, you can do so by simply choosing the Apply Design command from the Format menu.

Using the AutoLayout Feature

The AutoLayout feature provides a series of slide layouts that you can use to speed up the process of laying out a slide. The layouts vary greatly. Layouts can include graphs, clip-art, or text. Figure 28-6 shows the Slide Layout dialog box. This is very useful when creating a presentation or adding slides to an existing one.

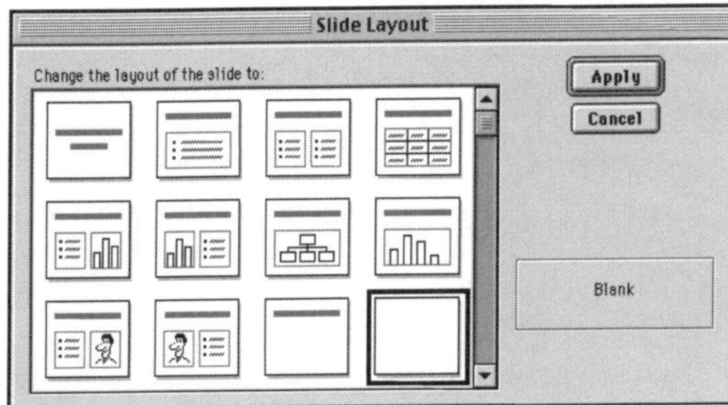

Figure 28-6: The Slide Layout dialog box

To use the AutoLayout feature, follow these steps:

1. After opening a presentation, switch to Slide view by clicking the Slide view button at the lower-right corner of the PowerPoint window. Then move to the slide that you wish to change.
2. Next choose Format ⇨ Slide Layout or click the Slide Layout button on the Standard toolbar.
3. In the Slide Layout dialog box, select the layout that you want to apply to the slide.
4. After selecting the layout, click the Apply button to apply the layout to the slide.

Using the Slide Master

You can use the Slide Master to control the overall appearance and layout of each slide in a presentation. Editing with the Slide Master is very useful because you can change all the slides in your presentation, not just one slide at a time. You can add graphics or other layouts to the Slide Master, and they will automatically appear in all the slides in that presentation. Make all the changes that you want on the Slide Master, and these new formats are applied to all the slides in your presentation.

The Slide Master contains two important elements: a title area and an object area. The formatting in the title area is specific to the title of each slide in your presentation. The title area tells PowerPoint the font size, style, and color to use for the text. The object area contains the formatting for the remaining text on the slide. The object area also sets the specifications for bulleted lists, which include the indents for each of the lists, the font styles, and size of the fonts. Figure 28-7 shows the Slide Master.

Along with the usual text formats and object setups, you can use the Slide Master to include borders, page numbers, logos, clip-art, and many other elements in the slides. To view the Slide Master, follow these steps:

1. Open a presentation and choose View ⇨ Master ⇨ Slide Master. The Slide Master appears, as shown in Figure 28-7.

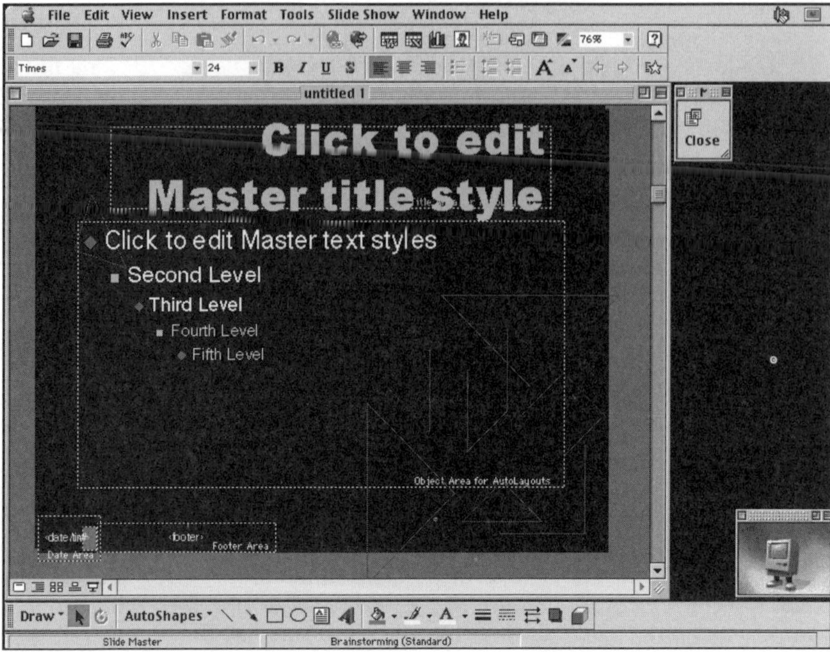

Figure 28-7: The Slide Master

2. Make any adjustment that you want to the Slide Master. To bring up a shortcut menu of available formatting options, Control-click the area outside the slide. You can change the Master Layout dialog box (see Figure 28-8), the Background dialog box (see Figure 28-9), or the Color Scheme dialog box (see Figure 28-10) options.

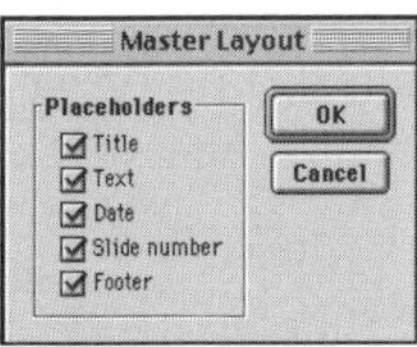

Figure 28-8: The Master Layout dialog box

Figure 28-9: The Background dialog box

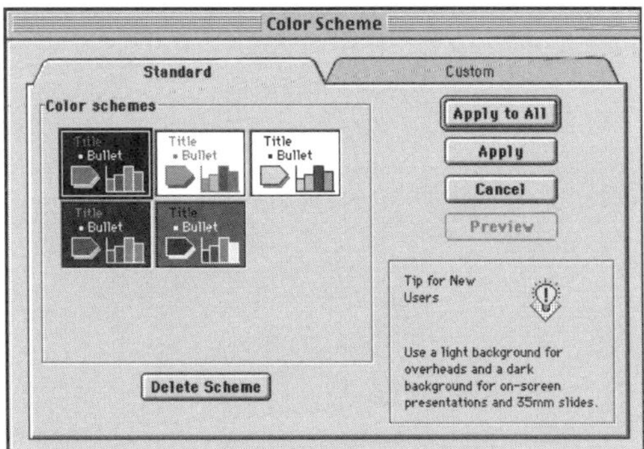

Figure 28-10: The Color Scheme dialog box

3. When you finish making the adjustments to Slide Master, you return to your regular slide by choosing the Slides command from the View menu or by clicking the Slide view button at the lower-left corner of the PowerPoint window. The changes apply to all slides.

You can create a custom color scheme for your slides by clicking the Custom tab in the Color Scheme dialog box (see Figure 28-11). In the Scheme colors area, click the box whose color you want to change and then click the Change Color button. A color dialog box appears appropriate for the box you selected. For example, if you selected a Fill box, the dialog box is titled Fill Color, whereas if you selected an Accent box, the dialog box is titled Accent Color, as shown in Figure 28-12. After creating the color scheme you want, you can add it to the standard color schemes available by clicking the Add As Standard Scheme button.

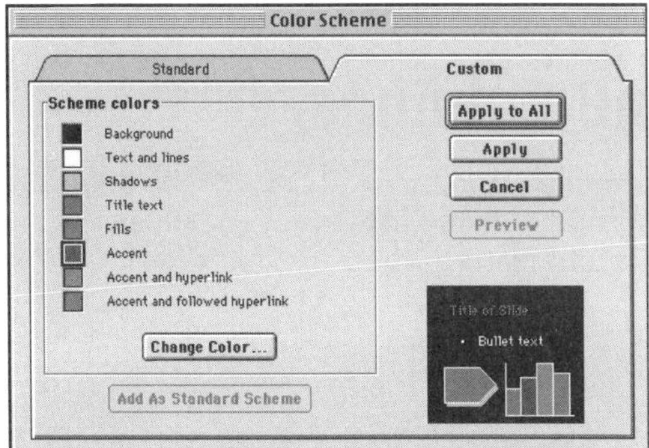

Figure 28-11: The Custom tab of the Color Scheme dialog box

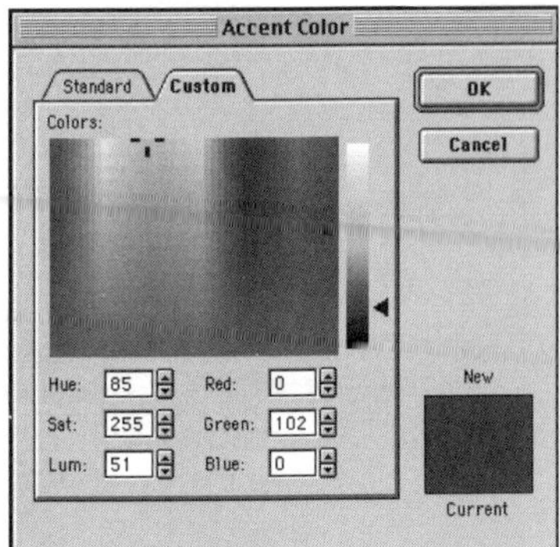

Figure 28-12: The Custom tab of the Accent Color dialog box

After you apply the editing in the Slide Master to all your slides, you can still edit and change individual slides in whatever way you want. You can even change the headings or the formatting that you added with the Slide Master. If you don't like the editing that you have done to a slide, however, and want to return it to its Slide Master state, just reapply the Slide Master formatting. To reapply the Slide Master formatting, follow these steps:

1. Move to the slide to which you want to reapply the Slide Master formatting.
2. Choose Format ➪ Slide Layout. The Slide Layout dialog box appears with the current layout selected.
3. Click the Reapply button to reapply the format. The slide now contains the formatting of the Slide Master.

Working with Lists and Columns

When creating your presentations, columns and bulleted lists can be important parts of your slides. Putting columns and bulleted lists into your slides is easy with PowerPoint. This is another useful layout feature when creating slides.

Creating bulleted lists

In PowerPoint, indents are used to create bulleted lists. You can use this technique for objects (shapes you can add), too. Figure 28-13 shows a bulleted list in PowerPoint.

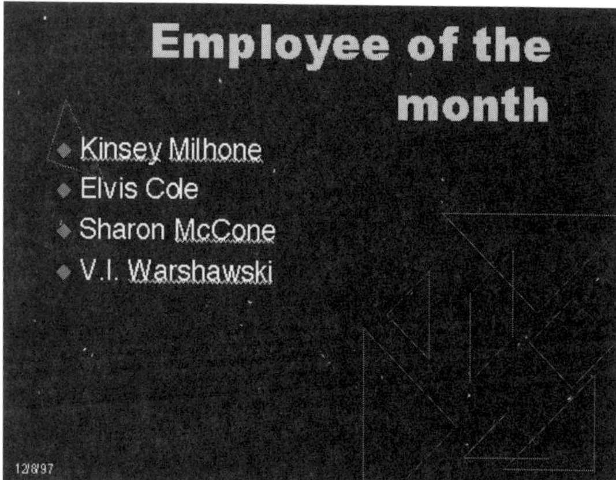

Figure 28-13: A bulleted list in PowerPoint

To create a bulleted list, follow these steps:

1. After opening a presentation, switch to Slide view and select the New Slide button in the toolbar. Then choose the Bulleted List layout from the AutoLayout dialog box.
2. Choose View ➪ Ruler so that the PowerPoint ruler is displayed onscreen.
3. Now enter the following names so you can get an idea of how the indent markers affect the text that you have entered on the bulleted list:

   Kinsey Milhone

   Elvis Cole

   Sharon McCone

   V.I. Warshawski

4. Now drag the bottom indent marker in the ruler to the right. Notice that the bottom marker moves the text away from the bullets, and the top marker moves the bullets away from the text. You can use this to set indentations.

A text box can have up to five indent levels. To add an indent level, select the item to indent and click the Demote (Indent more) button on the Formatting toolbar. You may find it easier to handle your indents in Outline view where you can create the headings by using the Demote and Promote buttons.

You can also change bullet characters. To do so, choose the paragraph with the bullet that you want to change. Then choose Format ➪ Bullet to open the Bullet dialog box. Figure 28-14 shows the many different characters in PowerPoint that can be used as a bullet. From the list, select the character that you want to use as your bullet. If you want to change the color or size of the bullet, make the changes in the corresponding list boxes.

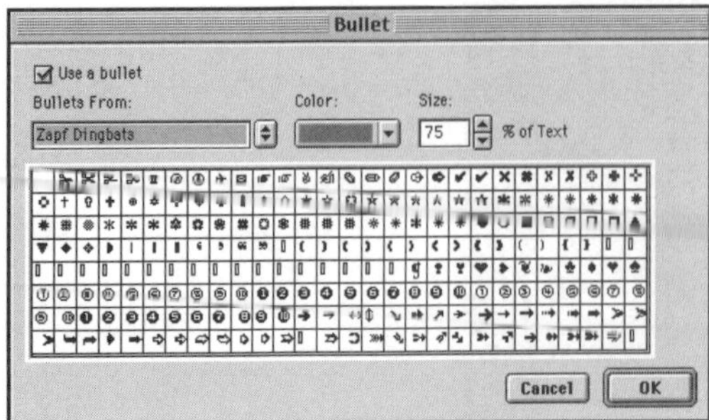

Figure 28-14: The Bullet dialog box

In the Bullets From pop-up menu, choose the font from which you want to select the bullet; remember that each font has a set of bullet characters that go with it. Along with a bullet type you can select a color and size for the bullet.

Creating columns

Columns are also useful things that can be created in PowerPoint (see Figure 28-15). Most people have an easier time reading shorter lines of text, and columns are a good way to make them narrower. This is why newspapers contain multiple columns. If you have a large amount of textual information to get across in your presentation, you can take advantage of columns to make the information easier to comprehend.

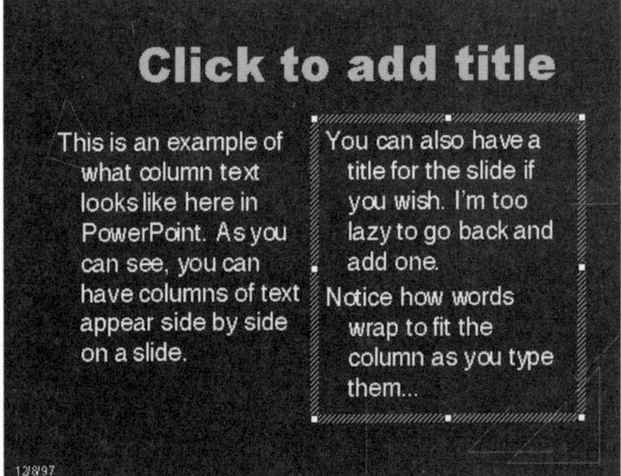

Figure 28-15: Columns displayed on a PowerPoint slide

To add columns to a slide, follow these steps:

1. Before entering the text, choose the Slide Layout button from the Standard toolbar and select 2 Column Text as the layout for the slide.
2. Click in either column and click the Left Alignment button in the Formatting toolbar.

Remember that these changes can be performed on the Slide Master if you want them to apply to all your slides.

Adding Formatting and Special Effects

When it comes to enhancing a presentation, fonts, styles, colors, and WordArt (an Office program for creating text in a variety of shapes) can be effective tools. PowerPoint also lets you embed Excel worksheets and Word tables in slides. Finally, the capability to add sound, slide animation, and action buttons can really bring your presentations to life. The following sections detail all these formatting enhancements.

Fonts, styles, and colors

Fonts, styles, and colors contribute to the look of a presentation. Just as with most Macintosh applications and the other Office 98 applications, the Formatting toolbar in PowerPoint makes it easy to change the font or apply styles to the text in your presentation. Select the text that you want to change and click a button on the Formatting toolbar to change the font or the point size or to apply bold, italic, underlining, shadow, or color. The two font-sizing buttons enable you to change the font of the selected text painlessly by just clicking them. If you click a formatting button before you begin to type, the formatting is applied to all the text that you type until you click the button again.

Applying shadowing and embossing

Shadowing and embossing are techniques that you can use to add emphasis to text in a presentation. These techniques are extremely effective in making certain words or phrases stand out. They also add a more refined look to a presentation when you use them correctly.

Shadowing adds a drop shadow behind your text to emphasize it. This effect is useful in headings. To add shadowing to your presentation, select the text and click the Shadow button on the Formatting toolbar.

Embossing is similar to shadowing, but it adds a highlight rather than a shadow to words. This effect gives the text the appearance of being slightly raised. To add embossing to your presentation, select the text and choose Format➪Font. In the Font dialog box, click the Emboss check box in the Effects area (see Figure 28-16) and click OK.

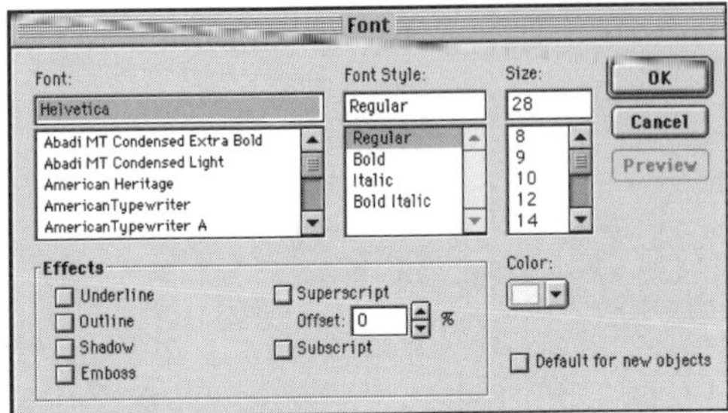

Figure 28-16: The Font dialog box

Applying superscript and subscript

You can also apply superscript and subscript to text in your slides. Choose Format➪Font. In the Effects area of the font dialog box, you will see the two check boxes for these options. After you click one of the options, enter a percentage by which to offset the text in the Offset box and click OK. Superscript looks like ^{this}; subscript looks like $_{\text{this}}$.

Special effects with WordArt

You can also enhance a presentation by using WordArt, a program in Office98 that lets you make text take on a variety of shapes. To use WordArt to change the shape of your text, follow these steps:

1. Highlight the text where you wish to apply WordArt. Choose Insert➪Picture➪WordArt.
2. Microsoft WordArt Gallery, shown in Figure 28-17, appears.
3. Choose the form you wish your text to take on. Click OK.
4. A window appears for you to enter your text. Do so. Click OK.
5. The text is then inserted into the slide. You can make any other changes to WordArt-created text with the WordArt toolbar that appears at the bottom of the slide window.

If you use WordArt frequently, you may want to set it as one of your active toolbars. You can do this by choosing Tools ⇨ Customize. On the Toolbars tab, click the check box for WordArt. This will activate the WordArt toolbar as a toolbar that is active each time you start PowerPoint. Now simply dock the toolbar where desired on the screen, and it will be there for your use during each of your PowerPoint sessions.

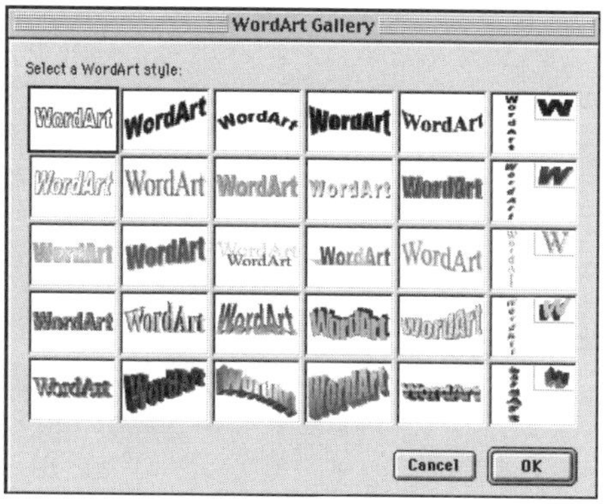

Figure 28-17: The WordArt Gallery dialog box

After your toolbar is active, click the left-most button of the WordArt toolbar to open the WordArt Gallery and see the effects that WordArt offers. Next, choose a shape for your WordArt. To do so, press and hold down the WordArt Shape button on the WordArt toolbar. This displays the Shape options pop-up menu for your WordArt (see Figure 28-18). Slide the cursor over the one you like and release the mouse button to make your desired selection.

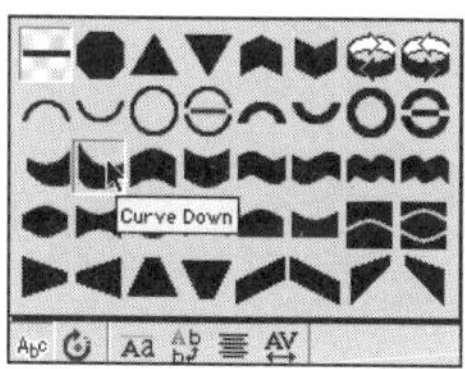

Figure 28-18: The WordArt Shape options pop-up menu

Table 28-1 explains the menu options available on the WordArt toolbar.

Table 28-1
WordArt Toolbar Options

Button	*Function*
WordArt Character Spacing	Opens the Spacing Between Characters pop-up menu shown in Figure 28-19, which lets you adjust the spacing between the characters.
WordArt Alignment	Enables you to choose an alignment for the WordArt you have inserted in your slide.
WordArt Vertical Text	Changes the WordArt text to a vertical appearance.
WordArt Same Letter Heights	Changes all the WordArt letters to the same height.
Free Rotate	Rotates the WordArt object to any degree.
WordArt Shape	Gives text the shape you select from the Layout options box.
Format WordArt	Enables you to change the color and fill for the WordArt (see Figure 28-20).
WordArt Gallery	Enables you to choose a style for the WordArt you are inserting. If you want to change the WordArt text after you have inserted it in the slide, double-click the text to activate the text box and make changes to it. Figure 28-21 shows an example of text that was formatted with WordArt.

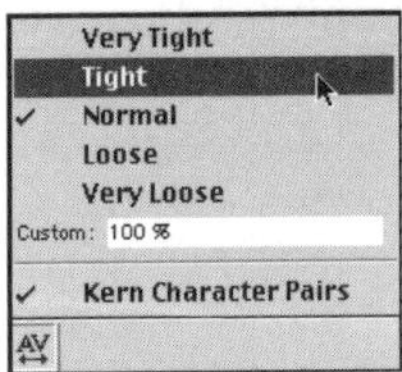

Figure 28-19: The Spacing Between Characters pop-up menu

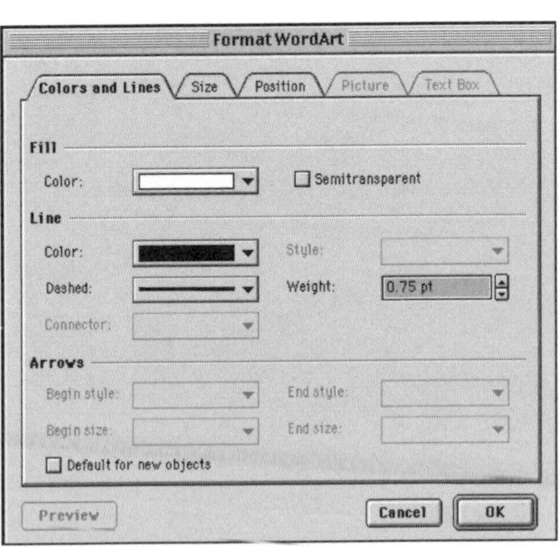

Figure 28-20: The Format WordArt dialog box

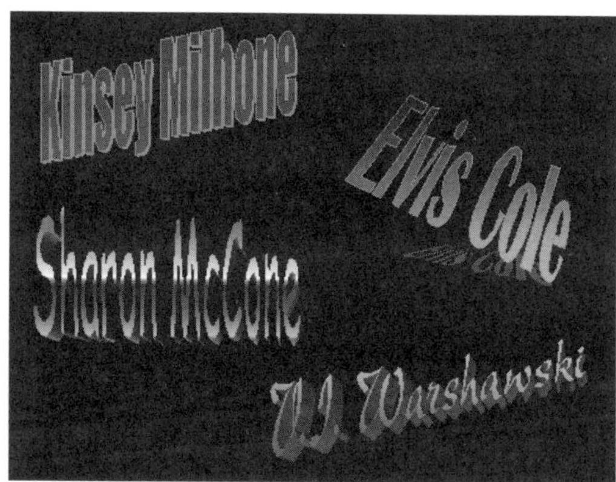

Figure 28-21: Examples of what you can do with WordArt

Excel Worksheets and Word Tables

Another strong feature of PowerPoint is it enables you to embed Excel worksheets and Word tables in the slides. The following sections show you, step-by-step, how to do this.

The capability to insert Excel worksheets and Word tables in your PowerPoint presentations saves a lot of time because you don't have to retype the information. You can use information that already exists.

It is important to explain the difference between the two methods that can be used to insert information into PowerPoint. One method uses Edit ➪ Copy and Edit ➪ Paste. The other method uses Insert ➪ Object. Although the two methods accomplish the same goal, they do work differently. If you want to insert a workbook, you need to use Insert ➪ Object. If you want to insert more than one worksheet, you need to use copy and paste. (To select the worksheets, Shift-click the worksheets you wish to insert; use File ➪ Copy to copy the worksheets; move to where you want to paste the worksheets; choose File ➪ Paste to place them there.)

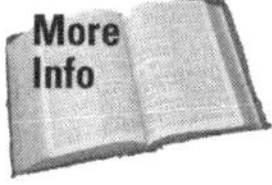

You may not want to insert an entire worksheet because it may be too hard to see on a slide. It is often better to just paste in the table that you created in Excel.

Double-clicking the sheet after it is inserted activates Excel. Now you can also perform maintenance on the workbook or worksheet. Remember that the embedding principles that are explained here apply to all applications that support object linking and embedding (OLE).

Inserting Excel worksheets

To insert an Excel worksheet into a PowerPoint slide using Edit⇨Copy and Edit⇨Paste, follow these steps:

1. From Excel, choose the worksheet you want to insert into your presentation.
2. Select the information by using the standard selection methods. Remember that you need to select just the area of the worksheet you wish to paste on the slide. This will let you size your insertion to fit the slide. If you don't do this, the worksheet will appear to flow off the slide.
3. Click the Copy button on the Standard toolbar or choose Edit⇨Copy.
4. Switch to PowerPoint and the slide in which you want to place the information.
5. Click the Paste button on the Standard toolbar or choose Edit⇨Paste.
6. Size the worksheet as you please.

Figure 28-22 shows an Excel worksheet on a PowerPoint slide.

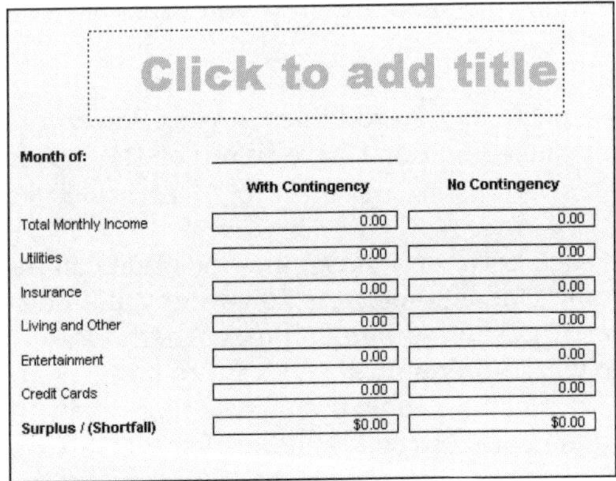

Figure 28-22: A PowerPoint slide with an Excel worksheet

You can also select cells in Excel and drag and drop them on a PowerPoint slide.

To add an Excel worksheet to a PowerPoint presentation with Insert⇨Object, follow these steps:

1. From PowerPoint, choose Insert⇨Object to bring up the Insert Object dialog box shown in Figure 28-23.

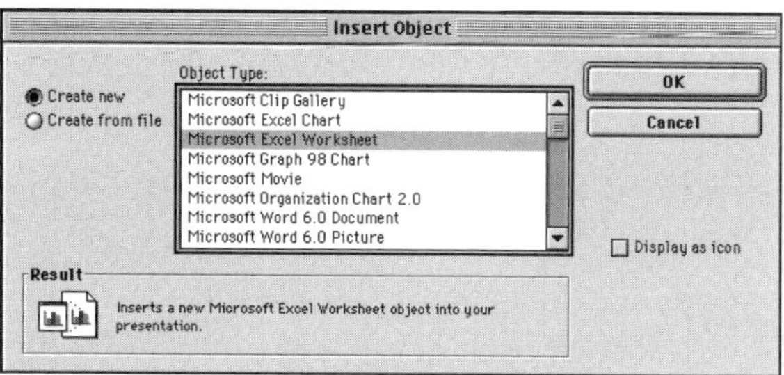

Figure 28-23: The Insert Object dialog box

2. Click the Create from file button and choose Microsoft Excel Worksheet. An Excel worksheet is then inserted onto the slide.
3. After placing the worksheet on the slide, you may want to insert an object or create a new object from another application to insert into the Excel worksheet. To do this, choose Insert ➪ Object again, click the Create new button to create a new object, and select the application you wish to use. If you want to create another object from an existing file, click the Create from file button.

Inserting Word tables

Word tables can also be inserted into PowerPoint slides. Because Word tables are the easiest way to insert tabular information, many prefer to use Word tables when they need to insert table information on a slide in PowerPoint. To insert a Word table into a PowerPoint slide, follow these steps:

1. Choose Insert ➪ Picture ➪ Microsoft Word Table to bring up the Insert Word Table dialog box (see Figure 28-24).

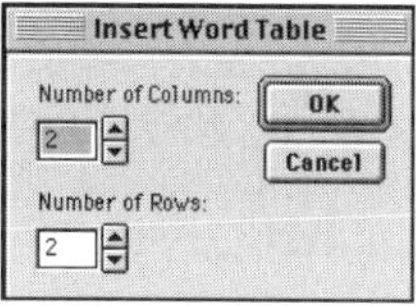

Figure 28-24: The Insert Word Table dialog box

2. Enter the number of columns and rows you want for the table. A Word table is then placed on the slide (see Figure 28-25).
3. Enter the desired text in the table. When done, click anywhere outside of the table.

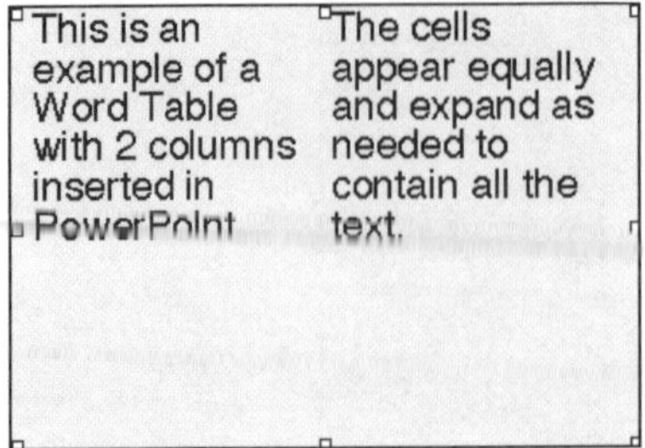

This is an example of a Word Table with 2 columns inserted in PowerPoint
The cells appear equally and expand as needed to contain all the text.

Figure 28-25: A Word table inserted in PowerPoint

Sound, slide animation, and action buttons

When it comes to enhancing a presentation, sound can also be an effective tool. If you have sound files (Mac OS sounds, .wav, or .snd files) stored on your computer, you can place sound in your presentation. To add sound to your presentation, follow these steps:

1. Move to the slide to which you want to add sound.
2. Choose Insert ➪ Movies and Sounds ➪ Sound from File.
3. After finding the desired sound file, click OK. A small icon appears in the center of the slide.

You can use the usual selection techniques to drag the icon to a desired location on the slide. When you run the presentation, clicking the icon plays the sound.

Alternatively, you can choose Insert ➪ Movies and Sounds ➪ Sound From Gallery and choose a sound from those supplied with PowerPoint.

Adding narration to a presentation

PowerPoint also offers you the capability to add narration for the slides in your presentation. This is very useful as a backup for presentation in case of absence, loss of voice, or other events that may occur unexpectedly. To record narration for a slide, first move the slide in Slide view and then follow these steps:

1. Choose Record Narration from the Slide Show menu and click OK. PowerPoint changes to Slide Show view and you can begin recording.
2. After recording, Control-click the screen and choose End show. You are asked if you want to save times for the slides or review time settings in Slide Sorter view.
3. Answer the question as desired and continue for subsequent slides in the presentation.

Slide animation

As you progress in setting up your slide show, you'll work with techniques where you can make truly professional slide shows. Along with the transition effects and timing settings that you can set using the Slide Transition dialog box, you can add animation to your presentation and function buttons to your presentation.

Animation effects can especially help hold the attention of your audience. PowerPoint offers some interesting animation effects. First, you need to activate the Animation toolbar. To do so, choose Toolbars from the View menu and turn on the Animation toolbar.

To animate the text of a slide, follow these steps:

1. Move to the slide in which you want to animate the title in Slide view.
2. Click the Animate Title button on the Animation toolbar.
3. Choose from one of the following for the effect that you want applied to the title animation:

   ✦ **Drive-in effect**—causes the title to come in from the right side.

   ✦ **Flying effect**—causes the title to come in from the left side.

   ✦ **Camera effect**—causes the title to appear with the click of a camera.

   ✦ **Flash Once effect**—causes the title to flash on the slide once.

   ✦ **Laser Text effect**—causes the letters of the title to appear one by one with the sound of a laser.

   ✦ **Typewriter effect**—causes the text to appear as if being typed with the sound of a typewriter.

   ✦ **Drop-in effect**—causes the title to fall from the top of the slide.

Adding action buttons to a slide

Action buttons are another way to enhance a presentation. PowerPoint has the capability to set a button to perform an action that you specify. This action can include sounds, links to Web pages, links to other slides in the presentation, or links to other files of any kind. One good use for an action button is if you need to show a worksheet in Excel that you cannot readily show on a slide. Another use for an action button is to link your presentation to a Web site page, which you can view with your default Web browser.

To add an action button to your presentation, follow these steps:

1. Move to the slide in which you want to place the button.
2. Choose Action Buttons from the AutoShapes menu of the Drawing toolbar.
3. Select the kind of button you wish to have represent your action.

4. You are next prompted to save your work if you have not done so already.
5. The Action settings dialog box is then activated.
6. Choose either the Mouse Click tab or the Mouse Over tab, depending on the mouse action you want to activate the hyperlink.
7. Click the Hyperlink To: radio button.
8. Specify the type of hyperlink you want to create (to another slide, a Web page, or another choice from the pop-up list).
9. If you wish it to run a program, choose the Run Program radio button.
10. After you have set up your button action, click OK.

Now, you are all set. Test the object you have linked to make sure that it works properly. To make any adjustments, simply repeat the steps and make the changes.

Summary

This chapter discussed techniques to enhance the appearance of a presentation including:

- ✦ The different methods of formatting text
- ✦ How WordArt can be used to enhance text entries
- ✦ How the Slide Master can be used to apply universal options to your presentation
- ✦ How you can use the AutoContent Wizard to create a presentation

Where to go next

- ✦ Now that you have learned the steps to enhance a presentation, you will want to produce your work. Chapter 30 tells you how.

✦ ✦ ✦

CHAPTER 29

Working with Charts in PowerPoint

✦ ✦ ✦ ✦

In This Chapter

Looking at a typical chart

Working with chart types

Inserting charts

Entering data and editing charts

Enhancing a chart's appearance

Creating organizational charts

✦ ✦ ✦ ✦

Among PowerPoint's strong features is its capability to create charts you can include in your business presentations. Charts in PowerPoint are based on numeric data you enter into a spreadsheet-like window called a *datasheet*. The charts are generated by Microsoft Graph, a mini-application included with Office 98.

Looking at a Typical Chart

Figure 29-1 shows an example of a typical chart in a PowerPoint presentation. (Note that charts are sometimes referred to as graphs; in fact, Microsoft uses the terms interchangeably.) Each chart consists of a series of markers, which represent the data you enter in the datasheet. The appearance of the markers varies according to the type of chart you decide to insert in your presentation. In a bar chart, the markers appear as a series of horizontal bars. In a column chart, the markers look like a series of vertical columns. Line charts use markers that look like a series of thin lines. In pie charts the markers are the wedges of the pie, and doughnut charts use markers that appear as slices of the doughnut.

With the exceptions of pie charts and doughnut charts, all charts use at least two axes: a horizontal axis (also known as the category axis) and a vertical axis (also known as the value axis). With three-dimensional charts, you also have a third axis, called the series axis.

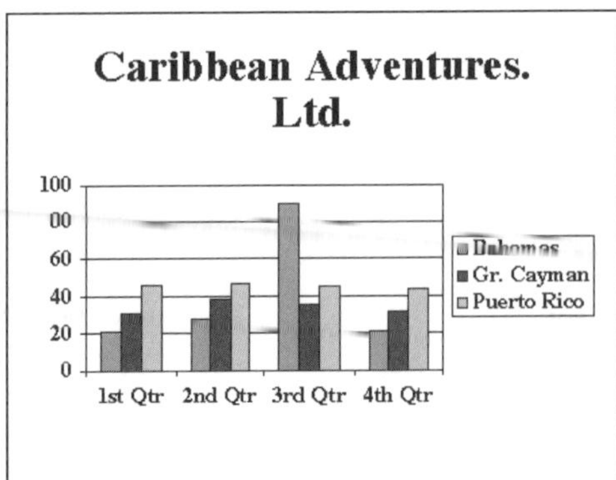

Figure 29-1: A typical chart

In addition to the markers aligned along the axes, charts can also contain titles and legends (which serve to identify the categories indicated by the various markers). Microsoft Graph, running from within PowerPoint, lets you customize any of these items in your charts.

Charts in Excel or in PowerPoint?

You can create charts in PowerPoint using Microsoft Graph and the techniques detailed in this chapter, or you can create charts in Excel using the techniques detailed in Chapter 19. Because Excel charts can be selected, copied, and pasted into a PowerPoint presentation, you have two ways of creating charts in PowerPoint. So, where should you create your charts?

If you don't mind the added complexities of a spreadsheet (maybe you're already an accomplished Excel user), you're probably better off creating your charts in Excel and then pasting them into PowerPoint. Why? Because Excel's charting capabilities exceed those of Microsoft Graph, and Excel has Chart Wizards that help you quickly design the precise kind of chart you need. Also, you can take advantage of Excel's capability to perform calculations on the data used as the basis of the chart. In contrast, the Microsoft Graph Datasheet window won't let you add two and two, much less perform any complex calculations.

On the other hand, if you're not an Excel user and have no desire to become one, stick with Microsoft Graph within PowerPoint to produce your charts.

Working with Chart Types

Microsoft Graph, the program used to insert charts in PowerPoint, provides area, bar, column, line, pie, doughnut, radar, XY scatter, surface, bubble, stock, cylinder, cone, and pyramid charts. Each chart type has optional subtypes that can also be chosen. You choose the chart type after choosing Chart⇨Chart Types in Microsoft Graph. The following descriptions identify the various standard chart types you'll find in the Chart Types dialog box (see "Changing the chart type" later in this chapter for details):

- **Area charts** show the significance of change during a given time period. The top line of the chart totals the individual series, so area charts make it visually apparent how each individual series contributes to the overall picture. Area charts emphasize the magnitude of change as opposed to the rate of change. (If you want to emphasize the rate of change, use line charts instead.)
- **Bar charts** use horizontal bars to show distinct figures at a specified time. Each horizontal bar in the chart shows a specific amount of change from the base value used in the chart. Bar charts visually emphasize different values, arranged vertically.
- **Column charts** use columns, much like bar charts, to show distinct figures over a time period. The difference is that the markers in column charts are oriented along a horizontal plane, with the columns running vertically up or down from a base value used in the chart.
- **Line charts** are perfect for showing trends in data over a period of time. Like area charts, line charts show the significance of change, but line charts emphasize the rate instead of the magnitude of change.
- **Pie charts** show relationships between the pieces of a picture. They also can show a relationship between a piece of the picture and the entire picture. You can use a pie chart to display only one series of data at a time, because each piece of a pie chart represents part of a total series. If you have a large number of series to plot, however, you are probably better off with a column chart because a pie crowded with slices is hard to interpret.
- **Doughnut charts** show relationships between pieces of a picture, as do pie charts. The difference is that the doughnut chart has a hollow center.
- **Radar charts** show the changes or frequencies of a data series in relation to a central point and to each other. (Every category has an axis value that radiates from a center point. Lines connect all data in the same series.) Radar charts can be difficult to interpret, unless you're accustomed to working with them.
- **XY Scatter charts** show relationships between different points of data either to compare trends across uneven time periods or to show patterns as a set of X and Y coordinates. These charts are commonly used to plot scientific data.
- **Surface charts** show trends in values across two dimensions in a continuous curve.
- **Bubble charts** compare sets of three values. In appearance, these charts are similar to scatter charts, with the third value interpreted by the size of the bubbles.

✦ **Stock charts** are also known as *open-hi-lo-close* charts. These charts are used to display the day-to-day values of stocks, commodities, or other financial market data. Stock charts require series containing four values to plot the four points (open, high, low, and close).

✦ **Cylinder charts** are column charts with the columns appearing as cylindrical shapes.

✦ **Cone charts** are column charts with the columns appearing as cone shapes.

✦ **Pyramid charts** are column charts with the columns appearing as pyramid shapes.

Inserting Charts

PowerPoint includes a mini-application, Microsoft Graph, that helps you create charts. Microsoft Graph displays a Datasheet window, in which you can enter the numeric data that will serve as the chart's basis. After you enter your data, Microsoft Graph translates it into professional-looking charts.

To insert a chart on a PowerPoint slide, follow these steps:

1. Choose Insert ➪ Chart or click the Insert Chart button on the Standard toolbar. A column chart appears in your presentation (this is the default type, but you can easily change it), and you're switched into Microsoft Graph, which launches automatically. A Datasheet window appears atop the chart, as shown in Figure 29-2 (with PowerPoint running in the background).

   Note that the menus and toolbar change to reflect the fact that Microsoft Graph is now the active application.

2. Enter your data directly into the Datasheet window. (See "Entering Data and Editing Charts" later in this chapter for more details.)

3. Choose Chart ➪ Chart Type to select the type of chart you want. After selecting the chart type you want, click OK. (You can also Control-click the chart and choose Chart Type from the shortcut menu that appears.)

4. Open the Chart menu and choose Chart Options to use the various options to add titles, axes, gridlines, legends, data labels, and data tables. The Chart Options dialog box contains the following options (see Figure 29-3):

   ✦ **Titles** displays chart title fields, which you can use to add titles to the chart or its axes.

   ✦ **Axes** enables you to show or hide axes in the chart.

   ✦ **Gridlines** gives you the option to show or hide major and minor gridlines along any of the chart axes.

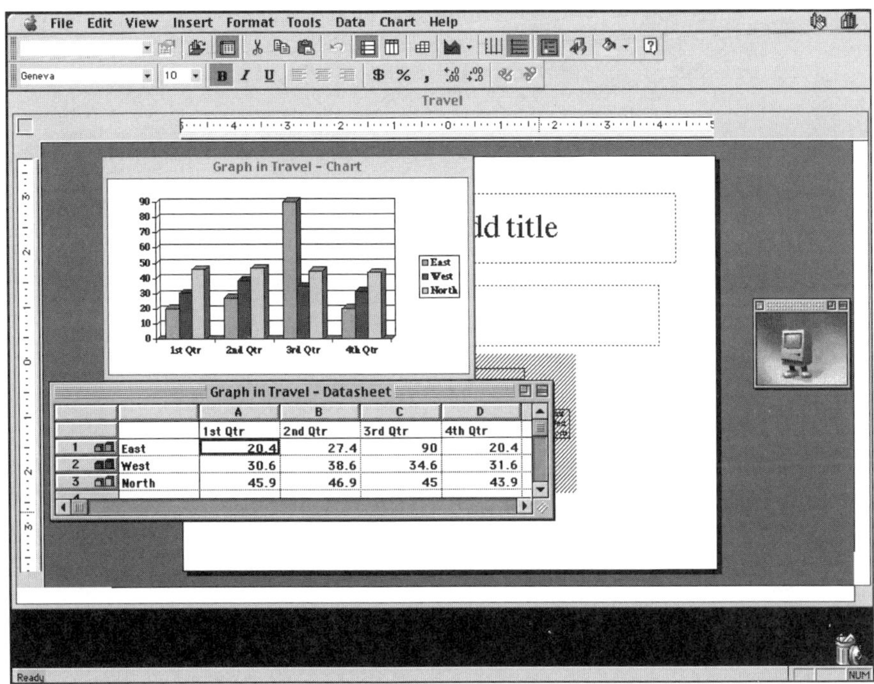

Figure 29-2: Microsoft Graph's default column chart and Datasheet windows (with PowerPoint running in the background)

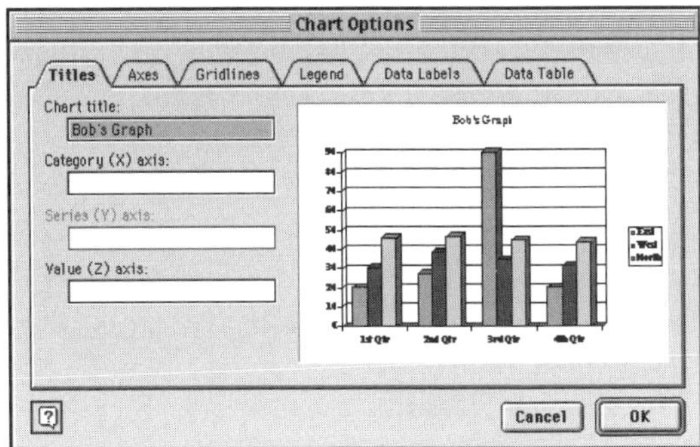

Figure 29-3: The Chart Options dialog box

✦ **Legend** enables you to add legends to your chart.

✦ **Data Labels** enables you to add data labels to a data series or to all data points in the chart.

✦ **Data Table** enables you to show or hide a data table for your chart.

5. When you're finished refining the chart, quit Microsoft Graph. You automatically return to PowerPoint, where the chart appears inside your presentation, and the menus and toolbars revert back to those of PowerPoint.

If you later want to make more changes to the chart's design, you can double-click the chart to switch back to the Microsoft Graph application.

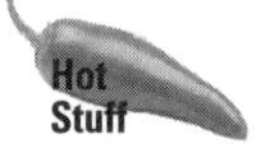

You can move and size your completed chart as you would any other object in a presentation—either by dragging it to the desired location or by dragging its size handles.

Entering Data and Editing Charts

To enter data in the Datasheet window, just move to the desired cell and type the data. You'll also want to enter the names for each data series into the left-most column, and enter the labels for each category into the top row. (The default data that appears in the Datasheet window gives you a model to follow when you enter your own data.) When you enter text in the top row and the left-most column, Microsoft Graph assigns that text as category names and legend names in the resulting chart.

Legends and headings

The default data provided in the Datasheet window shown in Figure 29-4, and the text labels in the left-most column of the datasheet—Bahamas, Grand Caymans, and Puerto Rico—are automatically used for the legend that accompanies the chart. The headings entered in the top row of the datasheet—1st, 2nd, 3rd, and 4th Qtr—appear as labels for the markers in the chart.

Graph in Bob's Slides - Datasheet

		A	B	C	D
		1st Qtr	2nd Qtr	3rd Qtr	4th Qtr
1	Bahamas	20.4	27.4	90	20.4
2	Grand Cayman	30.6	38.6	34.6	31.6
3	Puerto Rico	45.9	46.9	45	43.9

Figure 29-4: The Datasheet window

Adjusting the column width

Navigate within the Datasheet window with either the mouse or the arrow keys. You can widen the columns if they're too narrow to display the numbers you enter. To widen the columns, either drag the column's right edge with the mouse or click in any cell in the column you want to widen, choose Format ➪ Column Width, and then enter a width for the column.

Excel Users May Prefer Excel Charts

If you're familiar with Excel, you may prefer using Excel's worksheet and charting techniques for producing charts to use in your PowerPoint presentations.

To add an existing Excel chart to a PowerPoint presentation, go into Excel, select the chart, and choose Edit⇨Copy. Switch to PowerPoint, move to the slide on which you want to insert the chart, and choose Edit⇨Paste. The Excel chart appears in the slide, and you can move and size it to your liking using the usual Mac moving and sizing techniques.

To add a new Excel chart to a PowerPoint presentation, go into PowerPoint and move to the slide on which you want to place the chart. Next, select Insert⇨Object and then choose Microsoft Excel Chart from the list of objects to insert. PowerPoint then inserts a default Excel chart on the PowerPoint slide and launches Excel (memory permitting). You can then use Excel techniques (detailed in the Excel section of this book) to manipulate the data that produces the chart and to change the chart's appearance.

Number formats

When typing numeric data into cells, you can include dollar signs in front of the numbers to cause them to appear as currency values. When you do this, Microsoft Graph automatically includes the dollar sign with the values in the value axis in the chart. To apply a specific format by selecting a cell or group of cells in the datasheet, open the Format menu and choose Number. In the Number Format dialog box that appears, choose a desired number format and then click OK.

After the chart exists on a slide, you can bring up the Datasheet window at any time by double-clicking the chart to make it active and choosing View⇨Datasheet.

Editing charts

Changing circumstances may require the figures used to create a chart to change. When these figures change, you need to make adjustments to the chart's datasheet. At times you many also want to edit a chart for the sake of altering a presentation. To update figures used when you created a chart, choose View⇨Datasheet and then make the necessary changes in the datasheet (using the customary methods of editing).

Changing the data series

In some cases you may want to swap the data series for a chart. For example, you'd want to swap if you had set up a chart to show total sales over four years for divisions of a company, and you wanted the columns—which represent years—to symbolize each division. Swapping the data series would fix that.

You can swap data series for a chart by choosing either Data➪Series in Rows or Data➪Series in Columns. Alternatively, you can click the By Row or By Column buttons in the Standard toolbar while the datasheet is active. To see an example of the effects of the selection of data series, take a look at Figure 29-5, which shows a data series arranged by rows.

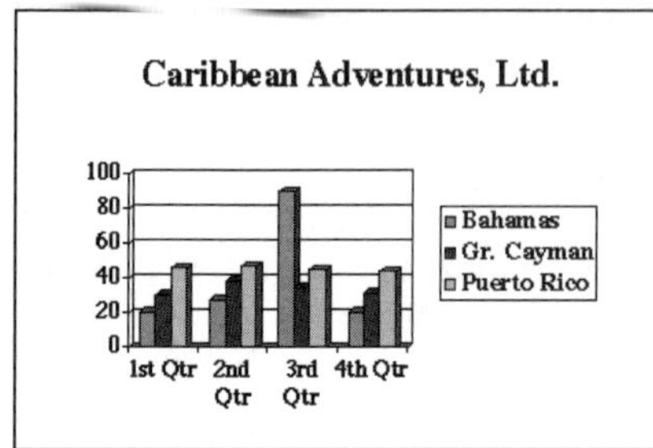

Figure 29-5: A data series arranged by rows

In contrast, note the same data shown in Figure 29-6. Here the data in the datasheet is arranged by columns in the resulting graph.

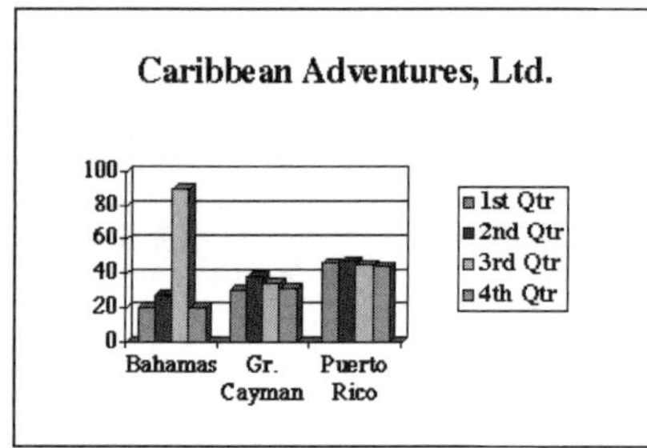

Figure 29-6: A data series arranged by columns

You can also change the actual display of the information. Do this using the shortcut menu that appears when you Control-click the bars, columns, lines, or pie slices of the chart. The shortcut menu that appears contains commands related to changes in the display of the chart information. The shortcut menu is shown in Figure 29-7 and includes the following commands:

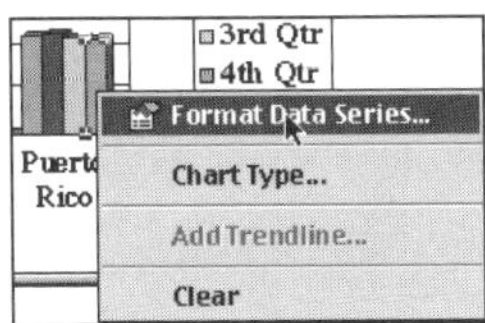

Figure 29-7: The shortcut menu for a data series

✦ **Format Data Series** lets you add labels or change the color of the data series. When you choose this option, the Format Data Series dialog box appears, shown in Figure 29-8, with the Patterns tab visible. Using the Patterns tab, you can add a border to the data series by setting the options in the Borders portion of the dialog box. You can vary the border's style, color, and thickness by selecting what you want in the Style, Color, and Weights list boxes.

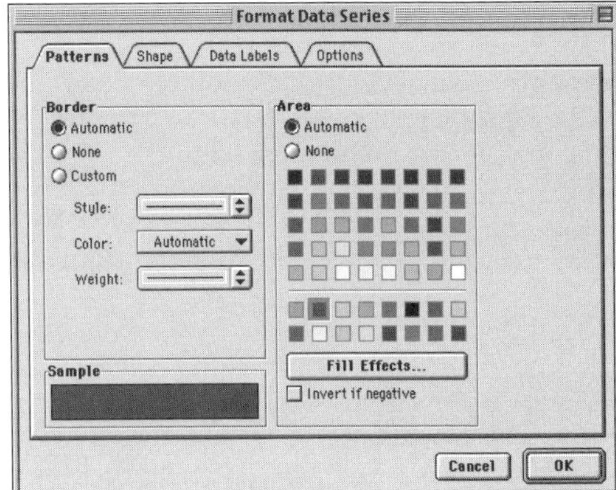

Figure 29-8: The Patterns tab of the Format Data Series dialog box

✦ In the **Area** portion of the dialog box, you can change the color of the data series to your liking. You can select a color or turn on the Automatic option, which applies the document default. Choosing None makes the marker invisible. Turning on the Invert If Negative option in the dialog box reverses the foreground and background colors for a marker if the value is negative.

✦ The **Shape** tab of the dialog box lets you choose the 3D shape you want for the selected data series.

✦ The **Data Labels** tab (see Figure 29-9) of this dialog box lets you determine whether labels appear beside the markers to the data series. You can also have a legend appear next to the label—turn on the corresponding check box.

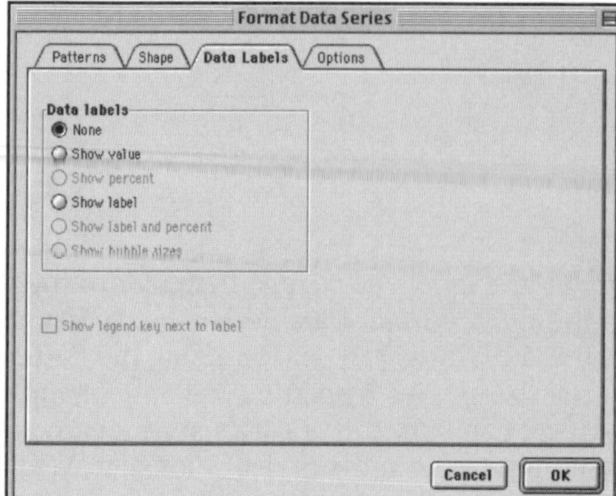

Figure 29-9: The Data Labels tab of the Format Data Series dialog box

- ✦ **Chart Type** lets you change the chart type. When you choose this option from the shortcut menu, the Chart Type dialog box appears (see Figure 29-10). The options for this dialog box are discussed in the next section.
- ✦ **Add Trendline** adds trendlines to area, bar, column, lines, and scatter charts.
- ✦ **Clear** removes a data series, the actual markers related to that series of numbers.

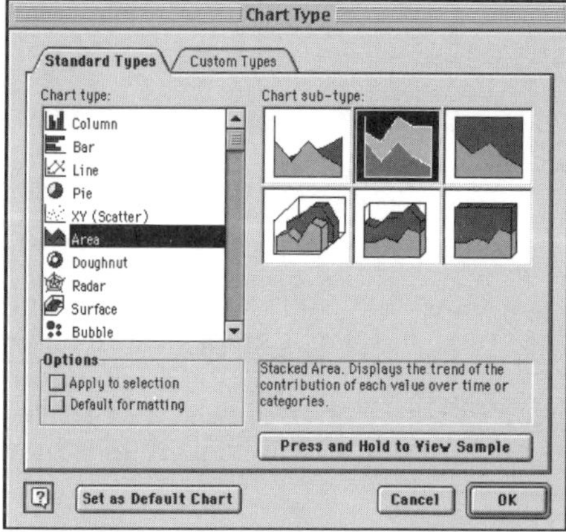

Figure 29-10: The Chart Type dialog box

Changing the chart type

After creating a chart, you can experiment to be sure you've selected the type that best represents your data. Microsoft Graph provides a range of chart types that can be viewed with a few mouse clicks. Table 29-1 lists these chart types.

Table 29-1
PowerPoint's Chart Types

Two-dimensional Charts	*Three-dimensional Charts*
Column	3-D Column
Bar	3-D Bar
Line	3-D Line
Pie	3-D Pie
Area	3-D Area
Doughnut	3-D Surface
Radar	3-D Bubble
Scatter	3-D Cylinder
Area	3-D Cone
Bubble	3-D Pyramid
Stock	
Cylinder	
Cone	
Pyramid	
Surface	

You can select chart types using different methods. The fastest method is to click the down arrow at the right of the Chart Type button on the Standard toolbar. This gives you a pop-up list of chart types, as shown in Figure 29-11. Select the chart you like and the values will be applied to it. As with many pop-up menus in Office 98, this one can be dragged off as a floating window or dragged onto a toolbar for easier access.

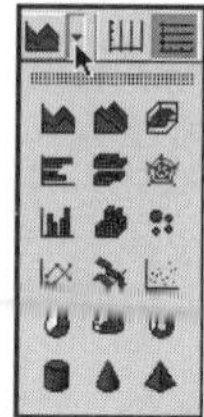

Figure 29-11: The Chart types available from the Chart Type button on the Standard toolbar

The other methods of changing the chart type include choosing Chart Type from the Chart menu, and Control-clicking the chart and choosing Chart Type from the shortcut menu. The Chart Type dialog box appears.

When you select a chart type, you can also click the Custom Types tab to use built-in custom chart types or user-defined chart types. The Custom Types tab contains many combinations of formatting, such as exploded pie charts, floating bars, and other chart types that can be useful for specialized chart needs.

Enhancing a Chart's Appearance

You can do several things to enhance the appearance of a chart. A few are simple, such as changes to fonts and colors. Others, however, are a little more involved, such as adding text boxes. All can make a difference in the appearance of the presentation.

Changing fonts

You can easily change the fonts used for text anywhere in your chart. These fonts include those used for titles, legends, or axes.

To change the fonts, Control-click the text you want to change. For example, if you want to change the fonts used for a legend, Control-click the legend. From the shortcut menu that appears, choose either the Format Axis or Format Legend option. Depending on which option you select, you will see either the Format Axis dialog box or the Format Legend dialog box. Both dialog boxes contain the same three tabs (we discuss the additional ones shortly): *Pattern*, for making pattern changes to the chart; *Font*, for making font changes to the chart; and *Placement*, for controlling the placement of the object. Figure 29-12 shows the Font tab of the Format Axis dialog box.

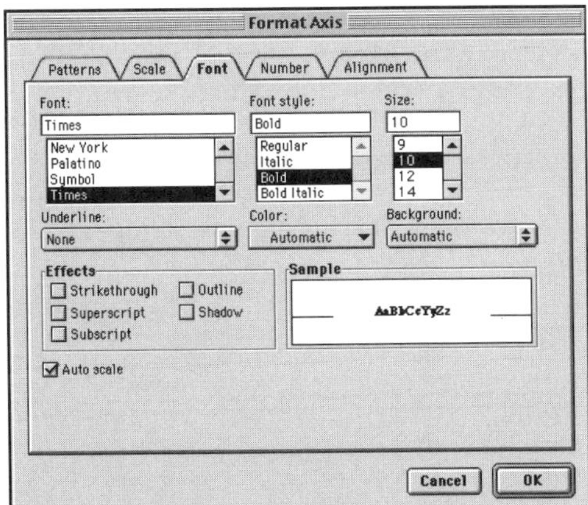

Figure 29-12: The Font tab of the Format Axis dialog box

Under the Font tab you'll see your options for setting the fonts used by the selected item. Choose a font, font style, and font size using the options displayed. You can also select underlining, color, and background, and you can turn on special effects such as strikethrough, superscript, and subscript. Under the Patterns tab you can change various options that control the style and color of the background pattern for the object.

Looks Aren't Everything, But . . .

As you work with fonts, colors, and other appearance-related aspects of a chart, remember the principles of good design by using fonts and colors wisely. It's easy to get carried away with fonts and colors and produce a chart so visually busy it distracts the reader.

You should rarely need more than two and never more than three fonts in the same chart. You'll probably need more colors, because each set of markers typically uses its own color—again, be judicious. Stick with complementary colors. PowerPoint does this automatically, but if you customize the colors, avoid clashing combinations such as bright pink against lime green. (Some designers argue strongly against using these two colors anywhere, anytime!) Keep colors elsewhere in the chart to a minimum. Before committing the chart to your presentation, step back and give it a critical, overall review for visual clarity and organization. Better charts in your presentations make for better overall presentations.

Changing chart colors

Creating and changing color schemes is another effective way to improve your chart's appearance. *Color schemes* are sets of colors designed to be used as main colors for presentations and to ensure that the presentations have a professional look.

Each presentation you open in PowerPoint has a default color scheme, but as you work with the program more and more, you'll want to create your own schemes. Chapter 27 discusses in detail what's involved in creating color schemes for an entire presentation. This section focuses on changing chart colors.

Changing the colors of your chart is relatively simple, thanks to shortcut menus. Follow these steps:

1. After choosing a chart and setting it up on your slide, double-click the chart to launch Microsoft Graph. Then Control-click the bar or section of the chart you want to change to open the shortcut menu shown earlier in Figure 29-7.
2. From the shortcut menu, choose Format Data Series. The Format Data Series dialog box opens with the Patterns tab visible, as shown earlier in Figure 29-8. This dialog box enables you to change the border settings, selecting from a range of line styles.
3. To change the color of the particular section of the chart you want to change, move to the Area portion of the Patterns tab and then click the color you want. You can also add patterns if you want by clicking the Patterns list box and then choosing a pattern from the list. When you're finished, click OK to accept the changes.

Adding titles

You may find it useful to add titles to your charts. Titles help an audience understand what a chart means, and they help you quickly find values you want to point out when giving your presentation.

To add titles to a chart area, Control-click the area to open the shortcut menu. Next, choose the Titles tab of the Chart Options dialog box, shown in Figure 29-13.

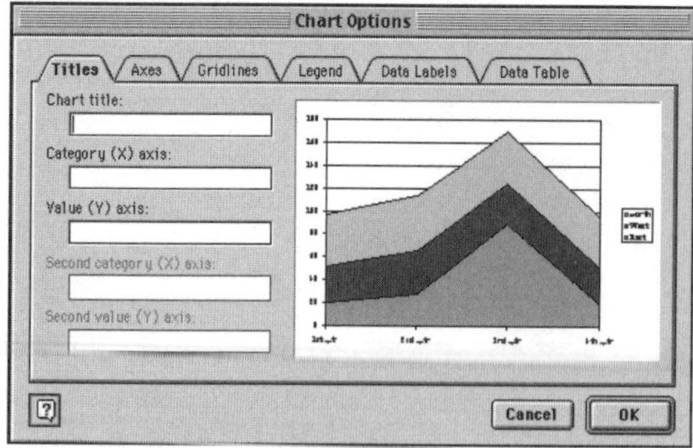

Figure 29-13: Titles tab of the Chart Options dialog box

The Titles tab enables you to add a title either to your entire chart or to just one of the available axes. Turn on the option you want and then click OK; the cursor appears in a text box in which you insert the title. If you choose more than one area to receive a title, use the mouse and click the text boxes for each of the titles. To enter the titles, click in the text boxes and type the titles you want.

You can also format the text on a chart after the text has been entered. Double-click the text and choose the formats you want from the Format dialog box.

Changing axes

You can modify the axes used by your charts to emphasize the points you're trying to get across. You can change the line style, the font of the axes' text, the scale used by the numbers, and the alignment.

To change any of these formats, select one of the axes by clicking it. Next, either choose Format ⇨ Selected Axis, Control-click the axis and choose Format Axis, or double-click the selected axis. The Format Axis dialog box opens, as shown in Figure 29-12. You can now select the options you want from the various tabs. Table 29-2 tells what you can accomplish with each of these tabs.

Table 29-2
Tabs of the Format Axis Dialog Box

Tab	*Purpose*
Patterns	Change axis formatting or choose tick mark types, both major and minor.
Scale	Control the scale settings for axis values. Logarithmic scales can also be set, along with reversing the order of the values and setting the Floor XY Plane (the floor of the chart) at a value other than zero.
Font	Change font settings for the axis.
Number	Control the number formats for the numbers used for the axis.
Alignment	Control the alignment of text used in the axis.

Changing borders

You can also change a chart by changing its borders. Control-click outside the chart's area and choose Format Chart Area from the shortcut menu. The Format Chart Area dialog box appears, as shown in Figure 29-14. This dialog box has two tabs, Patterns and Font. Make the changes you want and then click OK.

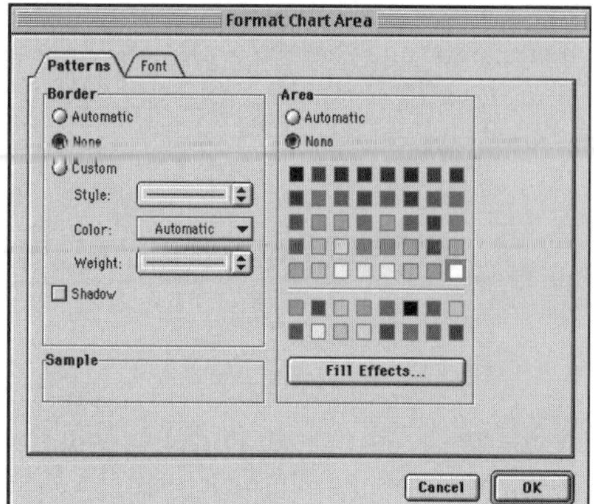

Figure 29-14: The Format Chart Area dialog box

Enhancing 3-D charts

Three-dimensional (3-D) charts are a popular variation of basic charts. Creating 3-D charts is simple in PowerPoint. When you choose Chart ⇨ Chart Type, the Chart Type dialog box that appears (shown earlier in Figure 29-10) gives you the option of selecting a 2-D or a 3-D chart.

If you use 3-D charts often, it's good to know about the flexibility that Microsoft Graph offers for changing various aspects of the appearance of 3-D charts. You can change the elevation, the rotation, and the perspective used for the chart with the following steps:

1. Double-click the 3-D chart to activate it, and choose Chart ⇨ 3-D View. (Alternatively, you can Control-click the area of the chart and select 3-D View from the shortcut menu that appears.) The 3-D View dialog box appears (see Figure 29-15). As you change the settings in this dialog box, the picture of a chart near the center of the dialog box reflects your changes.

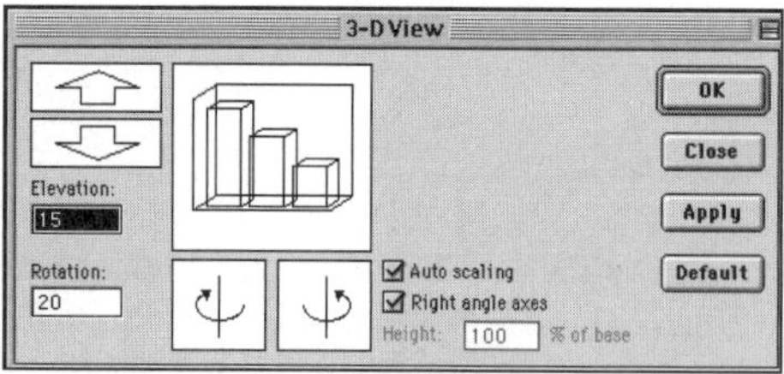

Figure 29-15: The 3-D View dialog box

2. To change the chart's elevation, click the up or down arrow buttons above Elevation or enter a value in the Elevation text box.

3. To change the chart's rotation, either click the left or right rotation buttons or enter a value in the Rotation text box.

4. To change the chart's perspective (if Right angle axes is not turned on), click the up or down arrow buttons above Perspective or enter a value in the Perspective text box. The Format 3-D View dialog box also contains options for Auto scaling, Right angle axes, and Height % of base, which work as follows:

   ✦ **Right angle axes**—This option, when turned on, sets the chart's axes at right angles independent of what you set the rotation or elevation to. (If you want to see the axes in perspective, you must turn off this option.)

   ✦ **Auto scaling**—If Right angle axes is turned on, this option is enabled. The Auto scaling option scales 3-D charts so they are closer in size to 2-D charts.

   ✦ **Height % of base**—This option controls the height of the value axis and walls of the chart, relative to the length of the category axis (the base of the chart). For example, if you enter **300%** in this box, the chart's height becomes three times the length of the base.

To see how your changes will affect your chart in PowerPoint, while leaving the dialog box open, click the Apply button. When you're finished making changes, click OK. You can use the Default button to undo your changes and return the settings to their defaults.

Creating Organizational Charts

Organizational charts are useful in a presentation for showing the hierarchy of an organization. You can create this type of chart from scratch, but PowerPoint provides an application called Microsoft Organizational Chart that greatly simplifies the process.

The following steps tell you how to create a simple organizational chart. (See Chapter 33 for an example of creating a more complex organizational chart.)

1. Choose Insert ➪ Object and then select MS Organization Chart from the Insert Object dialog box (or click the Insert Chart button on the Standard toolbar).

   Note that you should select a slide layout with the organizational chart placeholder on it. Also remember that the chart you create will be significantly smaller when placed in the placeholder area; if you have a large chart, you may want to use a blank slide.

2. Microsoft Organizational Chart launches, and a window opens with a simple chart layout. You can proceed with this default layout if you want, adding boxes to the chart as needed. On the toolbar you'll see buttons for adding boxes for the different levels of an organization. Each of the buttons lets you add boxes for the respective level of the chart. Choose the button that corresponds to the level of organization you want, and then click next to the box you want to add the selection under or next to; the box is then added to the chart.

3. After creating your chart, you may want to edit it. First click the box containing the name or entry you want to change, and then make the changes. Afterward, be sure to update the presentation within PowerPoint by choosing File➪Update or Quit and Return to (your document). Then if you want to save the changes to the presentation, choose File➪Save from within PowerPoint.

4. If you prefer, you can create an organizational chart from scratch. Choosing Style from the menu bar gives you a selection of organizational chart types. As Figure 29-16 shows, you can lay out these charts several ways from the Styles menu.

   After choosing a chart style, you can add boxes to it using the toolbar. Choose the level of the chart to which you want to add boxes, and then click the box you want connected.

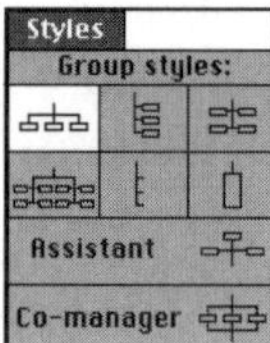

Figure 29-16: The organizational chart Styles menu

When the chart is placed in PowerPoint, you can size it to your liking by selecting the object and clicking the handles.

Summary

This chapter showed you the different options for using charts in your PowerPoint presentations. The following topics were covered:

✦ You can add a chart to any slide of a presentation either by choosing Insert➪Chart or by clicking the Insert Chart button on the Standard toolbar.

✦ When you add a chart, a Datasheet window appears in which you can enter the numeric information that serves as the chart's basis.

3-D Charts Can Lie (Or at Least, Greatly Mislead)

With 3-D charts, it's easy to get carried away with changing the various viewing angles by modifying the chart's elevation and perspective. Get too carried away, and you can wind up with a chart that's so hard to interpret, it becomes meaningless. Get even slightly carried away, and you can produce charts that distort the meaning of the underlying numbers.

For example, changing the elevation so that a chart is viewed from a high angle tends to overemphasize growth; presenting the chart as viewed from a low angle tends to minimize growth. (Could that be why many advertisements in business and financial magazines use 3-D charts viewed at high angles?) The example shown here is a 3-D chart with an elevation of 30, which severely distorts the visual growth represented by the chart.

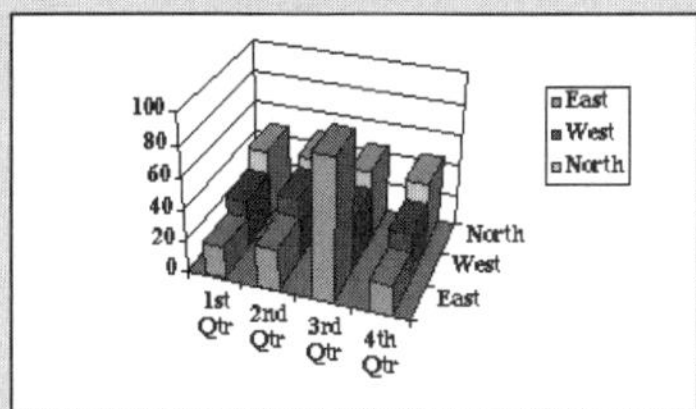

By comparison, the next example shows the same 3-D chart with a moderate elevation of 10, which avoids the visual distortion produced by the earlier chart.

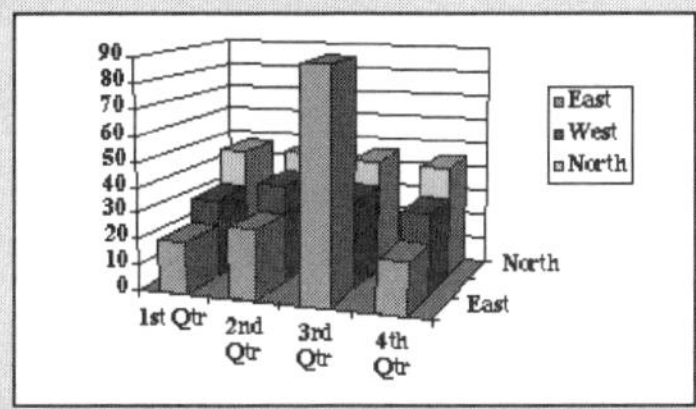

Be aware of the effects that such changes can have on your charts, and use them only when you intend to obtain such distorted results.

- ✦ After adding a chart to a presentation, you can double-click the chart and then choose Chart ⇨ Chart Type to change the chart's type.
- ✦ You can Control-click any object in a chart and then choose Format from the shortcut menu that appears to display a dialog box that lets you change the appearance of the selected object.
- ✦ In addition to conventional charts, you can create organizational charts in PowerPoint.

Where to go next

✦ Now that you have completed charts in PowerPoint, you will want to produce your work. Chapter 30 has the story.

✦ If you want to produce more elaborate charts, use Excel's chart-making feature. Head straight for Chapter 19.

✦ ✦ ✦

Producing Your Work

✦ ✦ ✦ ✦

In This Chapter

Printing presentations

Producing onscreen slide shows

Adding speaker notes and handouts

Creating custom shows

Using the PowerPoint Viewer

After you have created all the slides, you will want to prepare your work for presentation. This chapter covers the methods you can use to produce your work, including printing presentations, creating slide shows, and creating speaker's notes and audience handouts.

Printing Presentations

PowerPoint enables you to print slides, outlines, speaker's notes, and audience handouts. These items all can be printed on overhead transparencies or on paper. Slides can also be saved to a file or shipped to an outside graphics shop to create them. The printing process is basically the same, regardless of whether you are printing outlines, notes, or handouts: you open the presentation, identify what you want printed, specify the range of slides to be printed, and choose the number of copies.

Setting up your slides for printing

Before you print your presentation, you need to open the presentation and set it up for printing. Follow these steps:

1. Choose File➪Page Setup. The Page Setup dialog box appears, as shown in Figure 30-1.

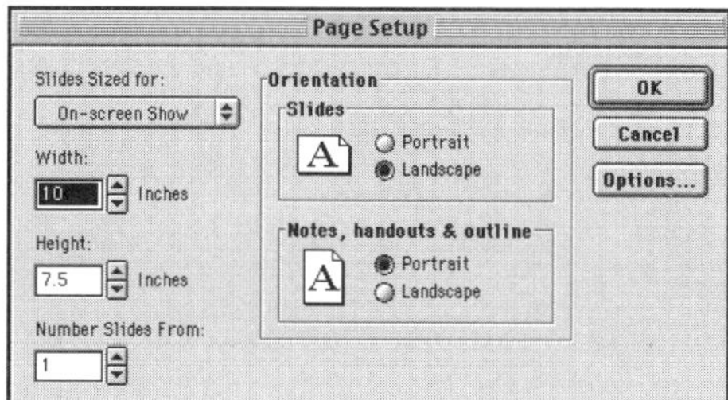

Figure 30-1: The Page Setup dialog box

2. In this dialog box, select the desired size for the slides. Note that, by default, PowerPoint is set up to create and print slides in Landscape orientation. Also remember that, by default, the slides are set up to print 10 inches wide by 7.5 inches tall. The Slides Sized for pop-up menu is set at Custom, which lets you change the following settings:

   - **On-screen Show**—This option sets the width at 10 inches and the height at 7.5 inches with Landscape orientation.
   - **Letter Paper (8.5 × 11 inches)**—This option sets the width at 10 inches and the height at 7.5 inches with Landscape orientation. These measurements cause the slides to fill the page. Choose this option when you want to print on paper and fill the entire page.
   - **A4 Paper (210 × 297 mm)**—This option sets the width at 10.83 inches and the height at 7.5 inches with Landscape orientation. The slides then fill A4 (European size) paper.
   - **35mm Slides**—This option sets the width at 11.25 inches and the height at 7.5 inches. These measurements allow the contents to fill the slide area in Landscape orientation, ideal for reduction to a 35mm slide.
   - **Overhead**—Use this option when you want to create transparencies. It makes slides fill the transparencies, making them easier to see when they are placed on an overhead projector.
   - **Banner**—Use this option to change the layout of your slides to a banner layout. This is both for printing and an onscreen presentation.
   - **Custom**—This option lets you set dimensions of your own choosing, either by entering values in the Width and Height boxes or by clicking the up and down arrows to enter the desired value.

3. In the Orientation portion of the dialog box, choose the desired orientation (Portrait or Landscape). Note that you can separately set the orientation for your speaker's notes, handouts, and outlines.
4. If you want to use a starting number other than 1 for your slides, enter a desired number in the Number Slides from pop-up menu.
5. Click OK.

The Options button brings up the standard Mac OS Page Setup dialog box.

Printing parts of your presentation

After your printing dimensions have been set by means of the Page Setup dialog box options, you can choose File➪Print to reveal the Print dialog box (see Figure 30-2).

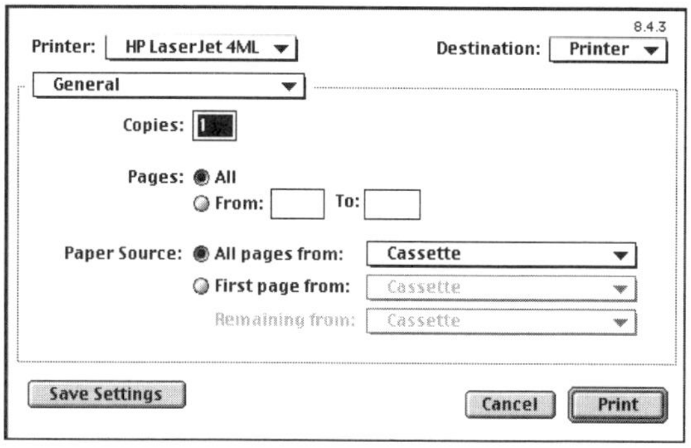

Figure 30-2: The Print dialog box

In this dialog box, you can choose what parts of the presentation you want to print. In the Pages area, choose All to print all slides, or choose From and To and type the starting and ending pages you desire. In the Copies box, you can enter the number of copies you want, and you can choose a paper source for all pages or the first page, if your printer supports multiple paper sources.

If you click the pop-up menu at top left (it says General in Figure 30-2) and choose Microsoft PowerPoint, you'll see several additional choices (see Figure 30-3).

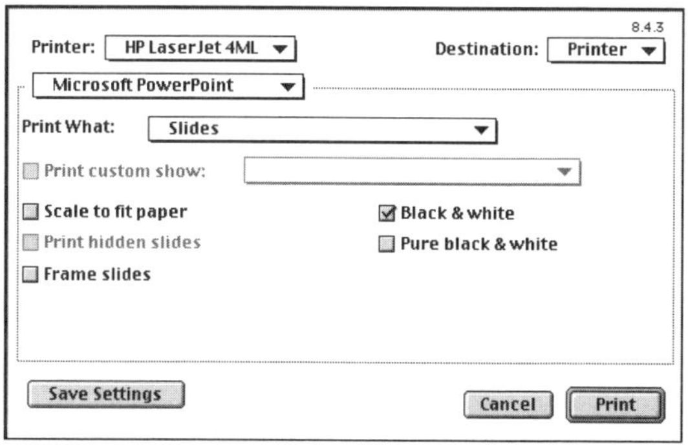

Figure 30-3: The Print dialog box after choosing Microsoft PowerPoint from the pop-up menu at top left

Use the Print What pop-up menu to tell PowerPoint exactly which parts of your presentation you want to print. The choices you have from the Print What menu include the following:

- **Slides**—This option prints your slides on paper or on overhead transparencies.

✦ **Notes Pages**—This option prints the speaker's notes pages that correspond to the slides that you decide to print.

✦ **Handouts**—You can print audience handouts that contain two, three, or six slides per page. Two slides per page is a good choice for a large image with great detail. Use three slides per page if you want to leave space for the audience to write notes. If you want to provide a presentation outline with the most information on each page of the audience handout, use six slides per page.

✦ **Outline View**—This option prints the outline that appears onscreen in Outline view.

If any slides in the presentation have been hidden (by choosing Slide Show ➪ Hide Slide), the Print Hidden Slides check box becomes available in the Print dialog box (choose File ➪ Print), and you can click it to tell PowerPoint to include hidden slides in the printout. The Black & White option tells PowerPoint to optimize the printing of color slides when printed on a black-and-white printer. The Pure Black and White option is used to print the slides in black and white while printing on a color printer; this will change all the shades of gray to either black or white. (This option is useful only if you have a color printer and, for some reason, you don't want the presentation in color.)

The Frame Slides option frames the printouts so they best fit transparencies when they are reduced, and the Scale to Fit Paper option scales the printout to the paper you have loaded in the printer. Choose your desired printing options in the dialog box and then click OK.

Producing Onscreen Slide Shows

Slide shows are another strength of PowerPoint because you can create professional-looking slide shows without much hassle. You can create a slide show by accepting PowerPoint's defaults and then choosing the Slide Show command from the View menu. The Slide Show will then begin. If you wish to change the default settings, the time settings between each of the slides, and any transition effects you wish to add to the presentation slide, you first need to go to Slide Sorter view. In Slide Sorter view, follow these steps to change the timing settings to the slide presentation:

1. Select the slide for which you want to set timings or effects. Click the Slide Transitions button on the Slide Sorter toolbar or choose Slide Show and then Slide Transitions. This will open the Slide Transition dialog box shown in Figure 30-4.
2. Choose the effects you want for the slide from the pop-up menu in the Effect area.
3. Move on to the Advance section to set your timings or choose the mouse as the signal to move to the next slide.

4. In the Sound area of the dialog box, you can add one of the default sounds or open another sound file that will play as you move to the next slide. Remember that all the effects you set are for the slide you currently have selected in Slide Sorter view unless you click Apply to all.

5. Move through your presentation, setting the effects you want for each of the slides (if you want them to vary).

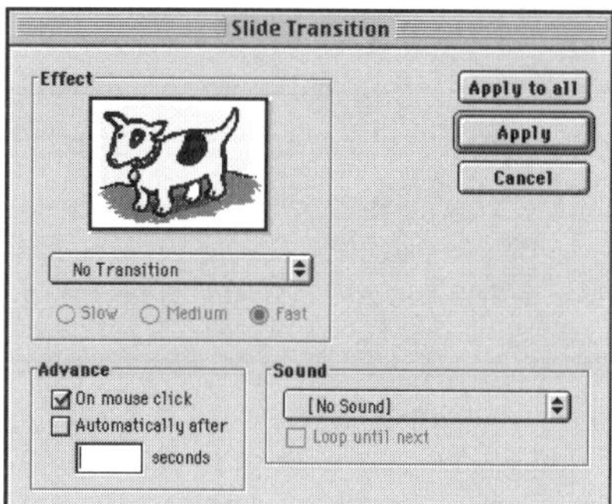

Figure 30-4: The Slide Transition dialog box

Each of the effects you set in the Slide Transition box can be set using the Slide Sorter toolbar. The toolbar begins with a transition button that opens the Slide Transition dialog box discussed earlier. Next is a Slide Transition Effects pop-up menu that allows for the setting of slide transitions. This is followed by a Text Body Animation list box that enables you to set the effects for the slide. Next you see the Hide Slide button used to hide slides in a show. This is followed by the Rehearse Timings button. This button is used to set and rehearse the slide show timings and how long each of the slides is visible. The Show Formatting button switches between showing the text and graphics for each of the slides and showing just the title. You will find this toolbar very useful for quickly assigning settings to each of your slides for a slide show.

In the Advance area of the dialog box, choose Manual Advance if you want to move from slide to slide manually during the show, or choose Use Slide Timings if you want the slides to advance automatically at timed intervals. (You learn how to change the intervals later.)

Getting the Results You Want

Don't rush to print by clicking the Print button on the Standard toolbar or by immediately clicking the OK button in the Print dialog box to accept the defaults.

Because PowerPoint has so many options for what you can print and how you can print, you may not get what you want by fast clicking. Think of the Print dialog box and the Slide Setup dialog box as working in combination to give you exactly what you want. Be sure that you set the options correctly before you start printing.

Giving Slide Shows with Polish

Giving a good presentation isn't entirely a matter of mastering PowerPoint techniques. Most of what creates a presentation that captivates (rather than enslaves) your audience falls under the more general heading of "tips for better presentations."

Always, always, always, always (did we say that enough?) test your presentation on the hardware that you plan to use before the audience starts taking their seats. No matter how well things worked back in the home office and at the last 27 on-site presentations you've given, there's no guarantee that the hardware you're using at the 28th site is correctly set up or will behave as well as the rest.

Try not to spend too much time on a single slide. If a slide stays onscreen for five minutes or more, rethink your content. Believe it or not, five minutes is a long time when a speaker drones—this has put many an audience to sleep. The audience stays with you if you break up big chunks of information into two or three separate slides.

Add a blank slide (or a slide with nothing more than an attractive background) as the last slide in your presentation. Then when you finish, the audience has an attractive slide to look at, as opposed to being dumped back in Slide view of PowerPoint.

As you verbally emphasize points, you can use the mouse pointer as an onscreen pointer. (A commercial laser pointer is nicer but costs a lot more.)

Creating progressive slides

Have you ever seen a presentation that included a slide that was nearly blank at first, but as the speaker talked, points seemed to appear on it magically? That savvy speaker used a progressive disclosure slide to create that effect. Progressive slides let your audience see your presentation develop and help them remember the last point you made. You may remember a progressive slide as a build slide from earlier versions of PowerPoint because you progressively build the points of your presentation. You can create a progressive slide by following these steps:

1. Switch to Slide view and locate the text or text object you want to show up first in your progressive slide.
2. Control-click the text or object and choose Custom Animation from the shortcut menu. The Custom Animation dialog box appears, as shown in Figure 30-5.
3. Click the Effects tab and choose the type of effects you want for the text or object.
4. Click OK.

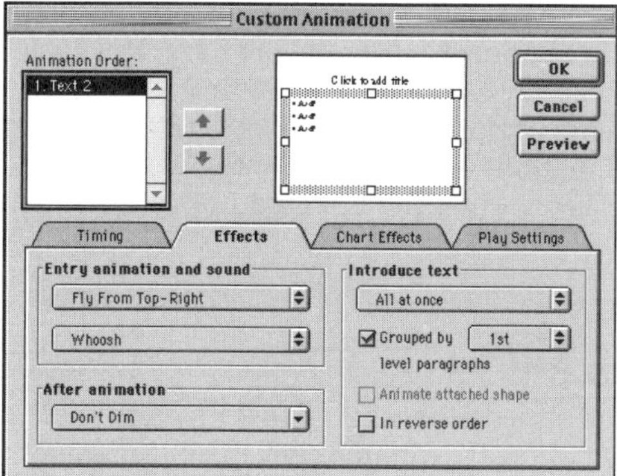

Figure 30-5: The Custom Animation dialog box

You just created the first animation in your progressive slide. To continue with your second object, repeat Steps 1 through 4 and follow these steps:

1. Click the Timing tab of the Custom Animation box.
2. In the Timing tab, you see a list of the objects without animation in your slide. From this point on, you can continue building your slide and selecting objects without returning to the slide.
3. In the Slide objects without animation box, select the next object you want in your slide by double-clicking it.
4. Choose the effects you want to attach to the object from the Effects tab.
5. If you have a chart on your slide, you can use the Chart Effects tab to add animation to the chart. First select the chart and choose from options on the Chart Effects tab. Your choices as similar to the options in the other tabs: you can introduce the chart by series category, elements of the series, and elements of the category. As with all of your animation, sound is also available for introduction of your chart. Use the Entry Animation and Sound section to make sound choices.

   The animation appears as the next item on the Animation Order list in the top-left corner of the dialog box.

If you wish to change the order of the text presentation, simply use the arrows beside the Animation Order box to change the position of the animation. Note that the default is for these actions to begin after a click of the mouse. If you want the actions to start automatically, click the Automatically button, which enables you to set a time interval for the beginning of the next part of the slide. These options are also available if you insert a sound or a chart into a PowerPoint presentation.

You can make other changes to the animation order using the Play Settings tab. In this tab, you can play the movie or sound automatically or on the click of the mouse, depending on the option you selected in the Timing tab. This action would occur before the other animations of the slide run. If you prefer to have the options run after the slide's animations have run, clear the check from the check box. Note that this tab is only active when the selected object is a movie, sound, or an OLE object.

Hiding and unhiding slides

The capability to hide or unhide slides is another useful PowerPoint feature. You may want to give similar presentations to different groups but modify the content to fit each group. For example, you might want to present revenue data to each department in a company. For example, it might make sense to show detailed financial data to Sales but more general numbers to production workers. PowerPoint lets you use one presentation for both groups—but you can hide slides so they do not appear for one group and then unhide the slides so they appear for the other group. To hide a slide, follow these steps:

1. Display the slide you want to hide. In Slide Sorter view, you can select more than one slide by holding down the Shift key while you click each slide you want to hide. When you do this, the slide's number is marked with a line through it.
2. Choose Slide Show ⇨ Hide Slide. (If you are in Slide Sorter view, you can also click the Hide Slide button in the Slide Sorter toolbar.) During the slide show, the slide will not appear, but you will know that you have a hidden slide because a hidden slide icon appears in the lower-right corner of the preceding slide.

   The menu option is a toggle, so you can unhide a hidden slide by selecting it in Slide Sorter view and choosing Slide Show ⇨ Hide Slide or you can simply click the Hide Slide button again.

During a slide show, you can display a hidden slide. Simply click the hidden slide icon that appears on the preceding slide in the lower-right corner of the screen.

You can also unhide slides before you give a presentation. To do this, Control-click the slide in Slide Sorter view and choose Hide Slide from the shortcut menu.

Adding Speaker Notes and Handouts

In PowerPoint, you can add two items to your presentation that help improve the presentation: speaker's notes and audience handouts. Each of the slides has a companion notes page that includes a small version of the slide and room for typed notes. You can print the notes and use them to recall the points you want to make for each slide. You can also print audience handouts. Audience handouts make it easy for the audience to follow your presentation and give the audience members something to take with them after the presentation is over. The handouts can contain two, three, or six slides per page.

To create speaker's notes for a presentation, follow these steps:

1. Select the slide to which you want to add a notes page. Choose View ➪ Notes Pages. The notes page appears, as shown in Figure 30-6.

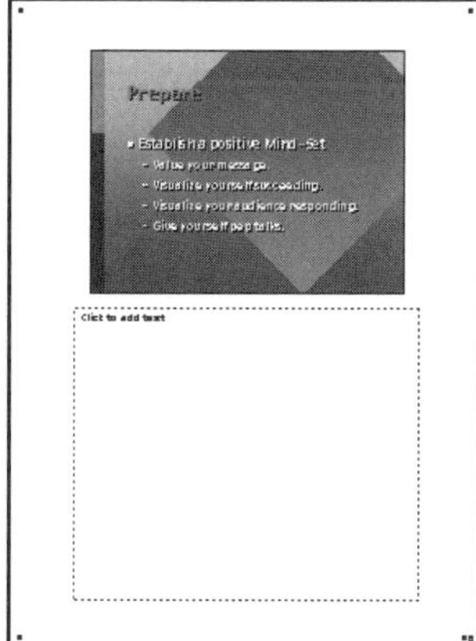

Figure 30-6: A typical notes page

2. At this size, you will have difficulty reading the notes you add to the notes page. Use the Zoom control on the Standard toolbar to increase the size of the notes page to 75 percent (see Figure 30-7).
3. To enter the notes, click the box provided for notes and type your entry. After you have added speaker's notes to a presentation, you can print the notes by using the steps outlined in "Printing parts of your presentation" earlier in this chapter.

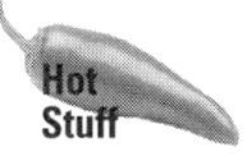

It's generally easier to see the text you type in the notes box if you change the default magnification. From the Zoom control pop-up menu on the Standard toolbar, zoom to 75 percent or larger.

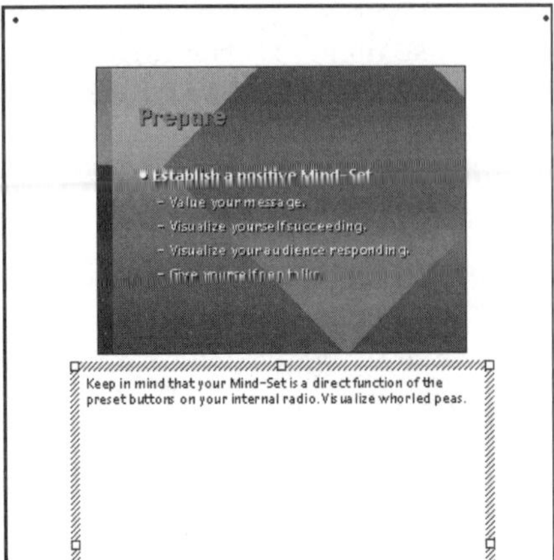

Figure 30-7: The notes page magnified by 75 percent

You can create audience handouts by performing the following steps:

1. Choose View ➪ Master ➪ Handout Master. Your screen takes on the appearance shown in Figure 30-8. In the figure, the areas outlined by dotted lines represent where your slides will appear, depending on whether you've selected two, three, or six slides per page. Figure 30-8 shows six slides per page. To select the number of slides you want to appear per page, use the Handout Master toolbar.

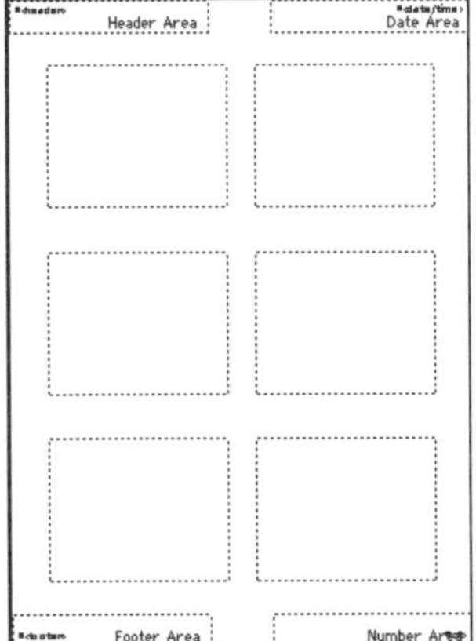

Figure 30-8: The Handout Master screen

2. Choose Insert ➪ Text Box and click and drag the desired text box to the desired size. You can then type the desired text (see Figure 30-9).

Figure 30-9: Adding a text box and text to the Handout Master

You can add the date and time or page numbers to text boxes in your handouts. To do so, place the insertion point where you want the text inside the text box, open the Insert menu, and choose the Date and Time or Page Number command. Then select the format you want in the dialog box that appears. To customize your header or footer, choose View ➪ Header and Footer.

Creating Custom Shows

PowerPoint 98 offers you the flexibility of custom slide shows. These are basically variations of the same presentation. You can give the same presentation to different sections of a company, for example. Follow these steps to create custom shows:

1. From the Slide Show menu, choose Custom Shows. You then see the Custom Shows dialog box, as shown in Figure 30-10.

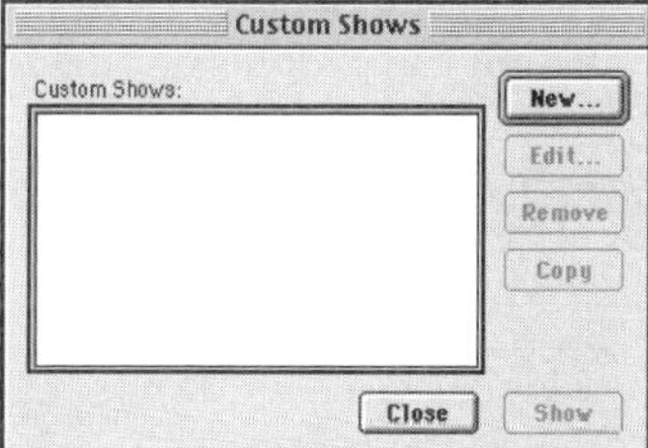

Figure 30-10: The Custom Shows dialog box

2. Choose the New button. This activates the Define Custom Show dialog box shown in Figure 30-11.
3. In the Slides in Presentation area of the dialog box, choose the desired slides and click Add. (If you want to select multiple slides, hold the ⌘ key while clicking.)
4. Using the arrows beside the Slides in Custom Show box, move the slides to appear in the order you want.
5. Give the slide show a name and save it.

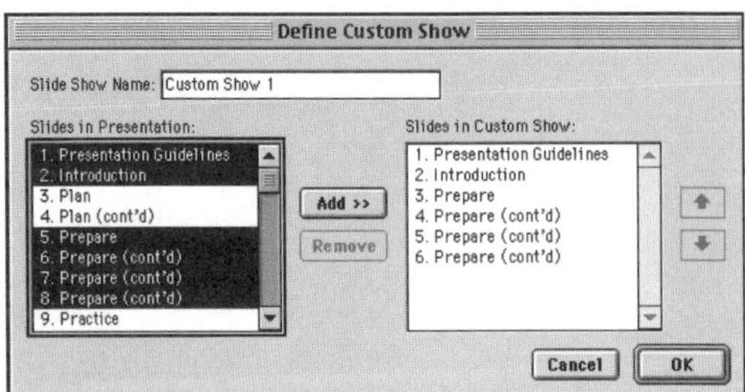

Figure 30-11: The Define Custom Show dialog box

The Custom Shows feature comes in handy when making on-the-fly adjustments to a presentation, which is fairly common. This feature also provides you with a way to make a presentation more adaptable to the circumstances. While at one time you may have had to create three presentations on the same topic, directed at different audiences with some slides in common, you can now create one presentation with several ways of running the presentation.

To see a preview of a custom show, select the name of the show in the Custom Shows dialog box and then Show.

Just before you run your slide show, you will want to select Slide Show and then Set Up Show, enabling you to make some final adjustments to the slide show. Figure 30-12 shows the Set Up Show dialog box. This dialog box offers you the option to select a type of show you want to give (for example, for browsing, where the presentation shows up in a window, or the typical slide show in full screen). You are also able to show the presentation in a looping manner or without the animation. You can make these choices by clicking the corresponding check boxes.

You can also specify which slides you wish to show in that particular session or whether you want to use one of your previously created custom shows. Pen Color and Advance slides options are also included here.

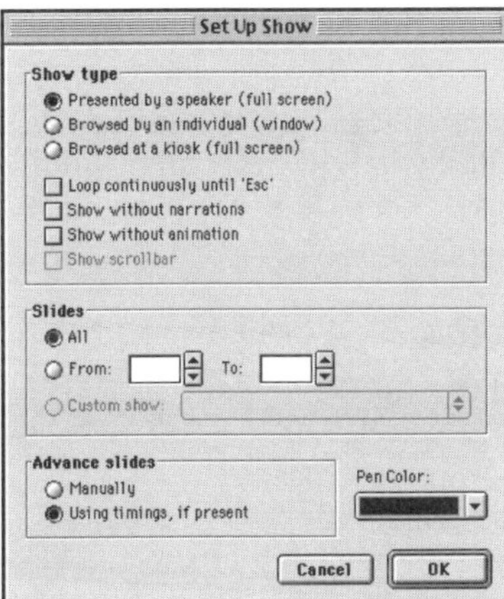

Figure 30-12: The Set Up Show dialog box

Using the PowerPoint Viewer

Your Microsoft Office package may include the PowerPoint Viewer, a separate program that is useful when you want to view a presentation with another computer that does not have PowerPoint installed. The PowerPoint Viewer provides the software needed to load and view any presentation created in PowerPoint. Then all you need to give your presentation at a site lacking PowerPoint is the PowerPoint Viewer on a disk as well as the disks containing your presentation.

Microsoft freely gives permission for this program to be copied and installed on other systems.

If you are traveling and you don't have the PowerPoint Viewer disk handy, or your copy of Microsoft Office didn't include the PowerPoint Viewer (copies shipped in early 1998 did not include it), you can download the PowerPoint Viewer from Microsoft's Web site at `www.microsoft.com`.

The E-mail Connection

One other common option that you have for "producing" your presentation is the Send To command from the File menu. With this command, you can send the presentation to another person via electronic mail. This command requires that you have an e-mail client program—for example, Outlook Express, Eudora, or Claris Emailer—installed and have used the Configuration Manager control panel to set up your mail preferences.

Using the Send To Mail Recipient command creates a new e-mail message with your presentation attached in most e-mail clients, enabling you to send the presentation to the desired recipient easily.

Summary

As demonstrated in this chapter, producing your work in PowerPoint is not an incredibly involved process. This chapter showed you how you can print presentations and how you can use different methods to improve your slide presentations. The chapter covered the following points:

✦ You can print presentation slides by choosing File ⇨ Print, but you should first set up your presentation for the type of printing you want. First choose File ⇨ Page Setup and then select the desired options in the Slide Setup dialog box.

✦ You can produce onscreen slide shows by using Slide Show menu and selecting the desired options from the Slide Show dialog box.

✦ You can add transitions or builds to each slide to enhance the effects of an onscreen presentation.

✦ You can add speaker's notes or audience handouts to presentations. You can print these items separately for distribution to the speaker or the audience.

Where to go next

✦ The next chapter demonstrates how you can use macros within PowerPoint to automate various tasks.

✦ PowerPoint offers many ways to enhance your presentation. It's never too late to make a better presentation! See Chapter 28 for details.

✦ ✦ ✦

Working with PowerPoint Macros

✦ ✦ ✦ ✦

In This Chapter

Approaching Visual Basic

Creating a macro

Running macros during slide shows

✦ ✦ ✦ ✦

Macros are combinations of keystrokes that automate many of the tasks you normally perform with a program. Macros enable you to record a sequence of characters that you can then assign to text or a graphic on a slide or to a button on a toolbar. Later, you can play back the character sequence by choosing a menu option used for running macros or by clicking the slide object or toolbar button assigned to the macro. When you run the macro, PowerPoint performs the steps as if you had just typed the characters, made the menu choices, or done whatever actions you recorded for that macro. If you must perform any repetitive tasks in PowerPoint, you can save many keystrokes and mouse option choices with macros.

Approaching Visual Basic

Unfortunately, Windows users have it better than us Mac folk when it comes to macros in Office 98. *They* get a PowerPoint macro recorder that isn't available in the Mac version. Which is a pity because, as you'll soon see, creating a macro using Visual Basic is a lot like programming.

If the idea of macros appeals to you, you'll get a lot more done in a lot less time with one of the commercial Mac macro programs—QuicKeys from CE Software and OneClick from Westcode Software are the two most popular—than you will using Visual Basic. Still, because this is a "Bible," we'll show you how to create a simple macro as well as where (within Office, of course) to find help creating more sophisticated ones.

Each of the macros you create is stored in a new Visual Basic module and attached to the open presentation. Note that you should store your macros with your presentation and not with a PowerPoint template because macros that are stored in templates are not attached to the presentation.

Creating a Macro

In this section, you create a simple macro that changes the text contained in the title text box of slide 1 to 36-point Palatino italic.

Using the Macro dialog box

To begin creating your macro, open the desired presentation and choose Tools ➪ Macro ➪ Macros. The Macro dialog box appears (see Figure 31-1).

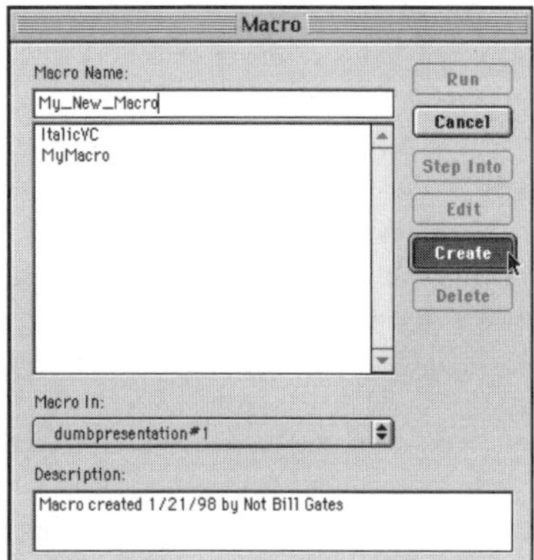

Figure 31-1: The Macro dialog box

Follow these steps:

1. Type **My_new_macro** in the Macro Name field. Note that you cannot use spaces in macro names.
2. Click the Create button. The Microsoft Visual Basic Editor window appears (see Figure 31-2).
3. Click the blank line just above the words *End sub* and type the following:

```
With
ActivePresentation.Slides(1).Shapes.Title.TextFrame.TextRange
    With .Font
        .italic = True
        .Name = "Palatino"
        .Size = 36
    End With
End With
```

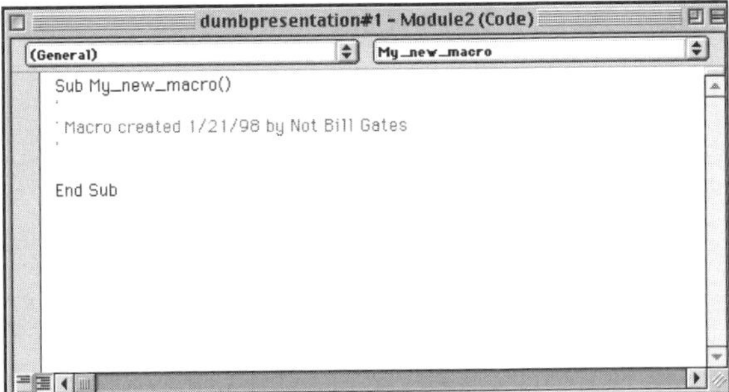

Figure 31-2: The Visual Basic Editor window

Be sure to type everything exactly as you see it or the macro won't work. Spaces, periods, and indenting all count. Also note that lines that begin with an apostrophe are considered comments and are ignored by Visual Basic when you run the macro. Finally, don't forget to type some text into the title block of slide 1 or you won't be able to see the effect of the macro when you run it.

When you're through typing the text, it should look exactly like Figure 31-3.

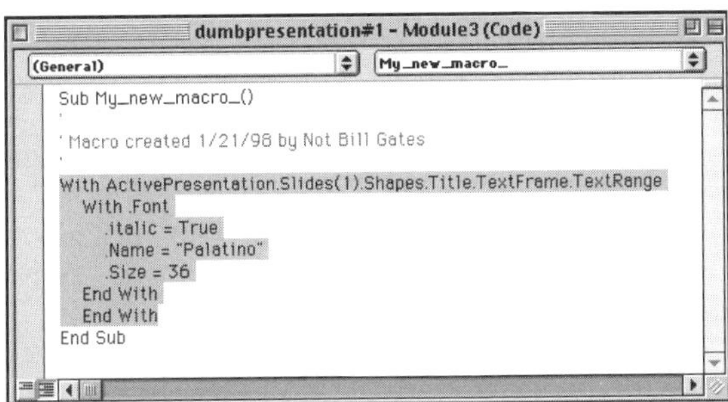

Figure 31-3: The Visual Basic Editor window with the text you typed

4. Choose File ➪ Close and Return to Microsoft PowerPoint or use the keyboard shortcut, ⌘-Q.

   The Visual Basic Editor closes and you are returned to PowerPoint.

5. Choose Tools ➪ Macro ➪ Macros.
6. Click My_new_macro, and then click the Run button.

That's it. Assuming you did everything correctly and there is text in the title text box of slide 1 for the macro to work on, the macro changes that text to 36-point Palatino italic.

Getting help with Visual Basic

If you want to learn more about creating macros with Visual Basic, you must make sure you selected the Help for Microsoft PowerPoint check box during installation. If you didn't do so when you first installed Office, install the help files now.

Once the help files have been installed, follow these steps to learn more about Visual Basic:

1. Choose Tools ➪ Macro ➪ Visual Basic Editor.
2. Click the Office Assistant.
3. In the Assistant, type the method, property, function, statement, or object you want Help on, or type a query.
4. Click Search, and then click the topic you want.

To browse through a list of all Visual Basic methods, properties, functions, and objects for PowerPoint in Visual Basic Editor, choose View ➪ Object Browser. In the list of libraries, click the library for PowerPoint. For help on an item, click the item, and then click the question mark button in the Object Browser dialog box.

To show help for Visual Basic Editor, click Contents and Index on the Help menu.

Running Macros During Slide Shows

You can assign a macro to an object (such as text or a graphic) that's placed on a slide. This technique enables you to access the macro by clicking the object.

Follow these steps to attach a macro button to an object on a slide:

1. In Slide View, select the text or graphic you want to use to run the macro.
2. Choose Slide Show ➪ Action Settings. The Action Settings dialog box appears, as shown in Figure 31-4.
3. If you want to run the macro by clicking the selected object during the slide show, click the Mouse Click tab. If you want to run the macro by moving the mouse pointer over the object, click the Mouse Over tab.
4. Click Run macro and then choose the desired macro in the pop-up menu.
5. Choose any other desired options in the dialog box.
6. Click OK, and the object in the slide takes on a highlighted appearance. When you click the object during a slide show, the macro will run.

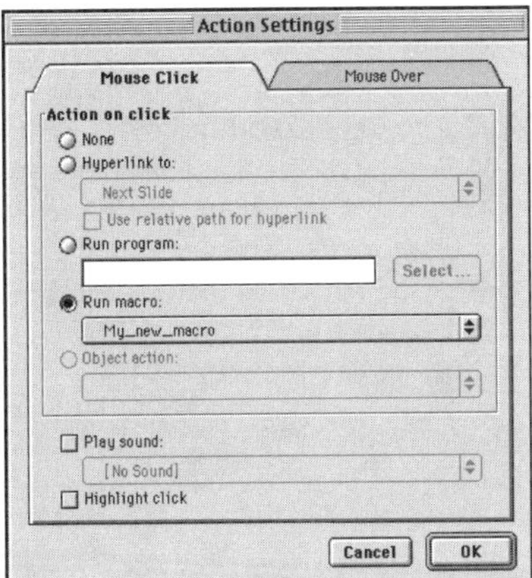

Figure 31-4: The Action Settings dialog box

Assigning macros to toolbar buttons

You can assign macros to buttons on a toolbar, which is useful if you perform some tasks on a regular basis. The macro button to which the macro is assigned is usually a custom button, but you also have the option of assigning the macro to an existing button on the toolbar, which cancels the previous function. To assign a macro to a toolbar button, follow these steps:

1. Choose Tools ➪ Customize.
2. If the toolbar to which you want to add a button isn't visible, click the Toolbars tab of the dialog box and turn on the check box beside the toolbar name.
3. Click the Commands tab of the Customize dialog box.
4. Scroll down in the Categories list and click Macros to select it.
5. In the right half of the dialog box, click and drag the desired macro onto the desired toolbar. When you release the mouse button, a button appears on the toolbar for the macro.

Running the macro

After you create a macro, you can run it in different ways. After reading this section, decide for yourself which method is best for your needs.

One obvious way to run a macro is to choose Tools ➪ Macro ➪ Macros. In the Macro dialog box, click the name of the desired macro and click the Run button.

Another method for running macros is to click an object in a slide that you assigned to the macro.

You can stop a running macro at any time by pressing ⌘-. (period).

A Note About Macro Viruses

Macro viruses are computer viruses that are stored in macros within PowerPoint presentations. PowerPoint does not have the capability to scan a floppy disk, hard disk, or network drive for a macro virus and remove it. (You can obtain this kind of protection from antivirus software, commonly available from your software retailer.) PowerPoint warns you about the possibility of viruses every time you open a presentation with macros, because the presentation may contain harmful macros. When you receive the warning, you are given the option of opening the presentation with or without the macros.

A good rule of thumb is if the presentation contains useful macros, you may want to open it with the macros, but if you don't know the source of the presentation (if it is attached to an e-mail, for example), you may want to open it without the macros; this will prevent you from running the risk of contamination.

If you want to avoid the warning, you can turn off the Always ask before opening presentations with macros check box. If you decide to turn off the option later, choose Tools ➪ Preferences, click the General tab, and uncheck the Macro virus protection check box. If you want more information on macro viruses, you can download virus protection information from Microsoft's Web site (`www.microsoft.com`).

Deleting a macro

After you have created a presentation, you may want to eliminate the macros; this is another task you can accomplish with relative ease. Follow these steps to delete a macro:

1. Choose Tools ➪ Macro ➪ Macros.
2. In the Macro dialog box, choose the name of the macro.
3. Click the Delete button.

When you perform these steps, the macro is removed from the presentation. (This if also useful when you mess up a macro and want to start over.)

About the macro code

Without a knowledge of Visual Basic for Applications (VBA), you can't easily create new or edit existing macros. And unfortunately, an in-depth discussion of VBA is far beyond the scope of this book. If you'd like to learn more about programming in Visual Basic, take a look at *Excel for Windows 95 Power Programming with VBA,* 2nd Edition, by John Walkenbach (IDG Books Worldwide, Inc.).

However, if you are familiar with the workings of VBA, you can make changes to an existing macro by editing the VBA code that lies at the heart of the macro. Choose Tools ⇨ Macro ⇨ Macros, select the desired macro in the Macro dialog box that appears, and click Edit. When you do this, the VBA code of the macro appears in a VBA Editor window. (Figure 31-3 shows the code for the macro you created earlier.)

Summary

This chapter covered the basics of using macros in PowerPoint. Now you have the tools you need to record macros efficiently and put them to work. We covered the following points:

- Macros are created in Visual Basic for Applications (VBA) code, the underlying programming language of Word, Excel, PowerPoint, and Access.
- You can run macros by choosing the Macro command from the Tools menu and selecting the desired macro in the dialog box that appears.
- You can attach macros to objects on slides and to toolbar buttons.

Where to go next

- The next chapter discusses how to use PowerPoint on the Internet and on intranets.
- Macros can take much of the repetitive drudgery out of formatting and printing tasks. For an explanation of the kinds of formatting tasks you can automate, see Chapter 28.

✦ ✦ ✦

CHAPTER 32

PowerPoint and the Web

◆ ◆ ◆ ◆

In This Chapter

Getting started

Defining some terms and concepts

Using the Web toolbar

Creating hyperlinks in documents

Publishing PowerPoint slides on the Web

◆ ◆ ◆ ◆

PowerPoint 98 differs significantly from its predecessors. This version comes enabled with specific features for producing presentation-quality Web pages for use with the Internet and with intranets. Using PowerPoint 98, you can attach hyperlinks to other Office 98 documents or to Web sites. These hyperlinks let you easily jump to locations in other Office 98 documents. You can easily save PowerPoint slides in HTML format, ready for inclusion on your Web pages, and you can take advantage of a Web Publishing Wizard to produce professional Web pages.

Getting Started

This chapter assumes a familiarity with the basics of PowerPoint. If you are familiar with the Web or with intranets but haven't yet learned to work with PowerPoint, you should consider reading Chapters 27 through 30 before proceeding with this chapter.

Exploring what's possible

Using PowerPoint 98, you can perform a number of Net-related tasks as you work with presentations. You can insert hyperlinks at any desired location in a presentation to link to other Office 98 documents or to Web sites. When you click these hyperlinks while viewing a presentation, you can jump directly to that location in the other file or to a specified Web site. You can also save PowerPoint slides as HTML (Hypertext Markup Language), the publishing language of the World Wide Web. These topics are covered in further detail throughout this chapter.

Figure 32-1 shows a PowerPoint slide. This slide was published as a Web page on a corporate intranet and viewed using Microsoft Internet Explorer (see Chapter 36), the popular Web browser included with Office 98.

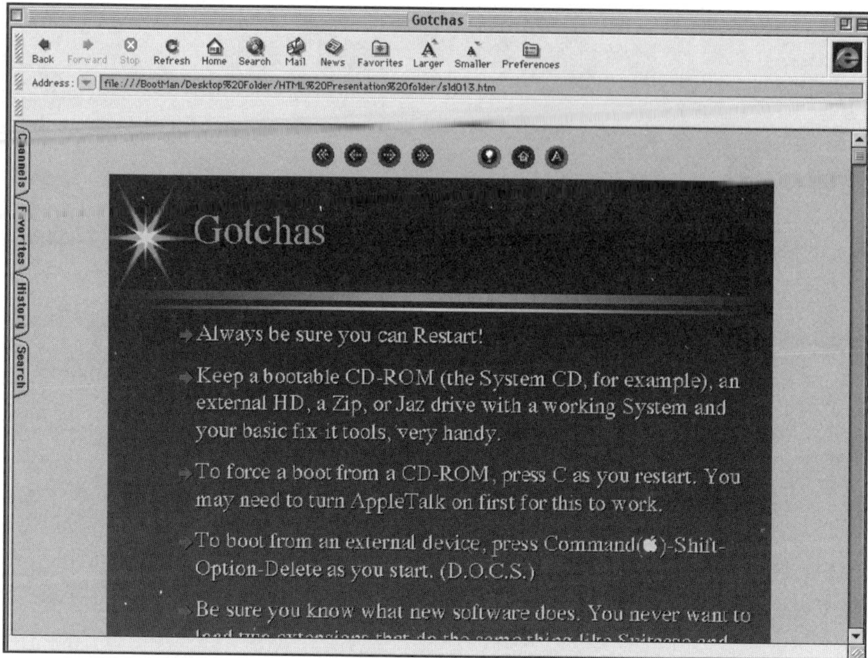

Figure 32-1: A PowerPoint slide published as a Web page

Connecting to a network

To accomplish most of the tasks described in this chapter, obviously you need to be connected to a network. This connection can be a dial-up connection to the Internet by means of a commercial Internet service provider such as AT&T WorldNet, MCINet, or NetCom. Your connection can also be a direct connection through your organization's local area network, and you may be connected directly to a corporate intranet, in which case you're able to retrieve or publish data to your company's private network.

This chapter doesn't go into specifics on making a network connection, because that topic is an entire book in itself. If you need help in this area, you can take a look at *Creating Cool Interactive Web Sites* or *Creating Cool FrontPage Web Sites* by Paul and Mary Summitt (IDG Books Worldwide, Inc.).

Defining Some Terms and Concepts

Because intranets and the Internet are newer concepts to many readers than presentations, a few explanations of terms may be in order. (If you're intimately familiar with the Internet, intranets, and the World Wide Web, you may want to skip this section and the next and dive right into working with PowerPoint and the Web.)

The Internet

First, the Internet is a global collection of computers, linked together by means of telephone and microwave lines and accessible to the public by means of various connections in offices and in homes. The Internet grew out of a research project in the 1970s that originally linked university and government computers in the United States. Since its inception, the Internet has grown to encompass millions of computers spread throughout dozens of nations. Any Mac (or PC) user with an Internet connection can connect to the Internet (either by means of a phone line or a direct hookup) and gain access to the volumes of information located there.

The World Wide Web

One major component of the Internet is the World Wide Web. There are other parts of the Internet, but the World Wide Web is the most well known. The World Wide Web uses graphical software known as *Web browsers* and files stored as HTML. The computers on the Internet that store the HTML files are known as *Web servers*. When PCs connect to the Internet to retrieve this data, they use Web browser software, which converts the incoming information (encoded in HTML) to graphical pages displayed as a combination of text, graphics, and in some cases, audio and video. Commonly used Web browsers include Microsoft Internet Explorer, Netscape Navigator, and the custom Web browsers built into the software provided by America Online and CompuServe.

Each site on the Internet has a unique address, commonly known as the Internet address (and less commonly known by the official name of URL, or *Uniform Resource Locator*). When you establish an Internet connection, open a Web browser, and enter an Internet address such as `http://www.whitehouse.gov`, you are entering the address for the Web server that provides the home page for the President's office in the United States. Web addresses like these can be stored in PowerPoint slides and displayed as hyperlinks.

About Intranets

Many Net-related uses of Office 98 involve making data available on intranets. An *intranet* is a private network of computers available only to the members of a specific organization. Intranets make use of World Wide Web technology—Web servers, network connections, and Web browser software—to enable members of an organization to share information. Intranets are popular with corporations because they enable employees to share work-related information in a confidential manner.

About HTML

As mentioned earlier, HTML is the language used for publishing information to the World Wide Web and to intranets that use World Wide Web technology. HTML is a text-based language that makes use of special codes called *tags*. These tags are included in the text of the HTML documents, and they provide instructions to the Web browser software that determine how the data appears when it is viewed by the end-user. Although you don't need to know the nuts and bolts of HTML coding to work with PowerPoint and the Web, it's a good idea to at least be familiar with the concept of saving your data in HTML file format. To publish PowerPoint data on the Internet or on an intranet, you need to save that data in HTML format and upload it to your Web server. If you are dealing with a corporate intranet, your company's Webmaster can tell you how to upload the HTML files that PowerPoint produces to your company's Web server. If you are managing a Web site on the Internet or on an intranet, you already know how to do this; much of the rest of this chapter deals with getting that PowerPoint data ready for uploading to your server.

Using the Web Toolbar

Like all the major Office 98 applications, PowerPoint provides the Web toolbar, a toolbar that helps you browse through the resources on an intranet or on the Web. Using the Web toolbar, you can quickly open, search, and browse through any document or through a Web page. You can jump between documents, and you can add favorite sites you find on the Web to the Favorites folder, enabling you to go back to those sites quickly at a later time.

In PowerPoint you can display the Web toolbar by choosing View➪Toolbars and then selecting Web from the submenu that appears, or you can click the Web toolbar button in the Standard toolbar. Figure 32-2 shows the Web toolbar.

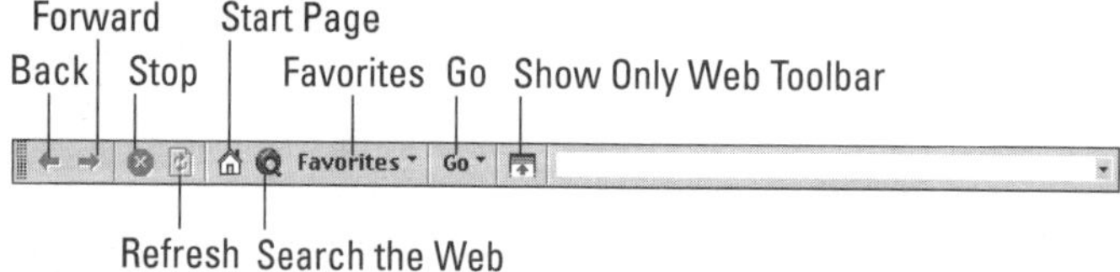

Figure 32-2: The Web toolbar

You'll find the Web toolbar to be handy when you happen to be in PowerPoint and need to go to the Web (or to your company's intranet) for information. For example, you can click the Search the Web button to launch your default Web browser and search the Web, or you can click the Favorites button to open a list of your favorite Web sites. Refer to Chapter 11 for more specifics on the use of the Web toolbar.

Creating Hyperlinks in Documents

A significant feature of PowerPoint 98 is its capability to use hyperlinks in documents. You can create hyperlinks to jump to other Office documents stored on your Mac, on your company's network, on a company intranet, or on the Internet.

Linking to Office documents with Copy and Paste

If you want to create a hyperlink to a Word document, in an Excel worksheet, or to another location in the PowerPoint presentation, the easiest way is to use the Copy and Paste Hyperlink commands of the Edit menu. In a nutshell, first select a location in the PowerPoint slide, Excel worksheet, or Word document to which you want the hyperlink to lead. Then choose Copy from the Edit menu. Finally, go back to PowerPoint. At the point you want the hyperlink to appear, choose Paste as Hyperlink from the Edit menu. In more detail, here are the steps you can use to create a hyperlink from another Office document:

1. Open the document containing the location to which you want to link. (If the location is in PowerPoint, it can be in the same presentation or in a different presentation that's open. If the location is in an Excel or a Word file, it can be in any area of the worksheet or document.)
2. Select the portion of the document to which you want to link.
3. Choose Edit ⇨ Copy.
4. In PowerPoint, go into Slide view or Outline view and place the insertion pointer at the location you want to insert the hyperlink.
5. Choose Edit ⇨ Paste as Hyperlink.

When you perform these steps, PowerPoint inserts a hyperlink back to the original document at the selected location. When you view the presentation in Slide view mode, you can click the hyperlink to jump to the linked document.

Linking to Web sites or files with Insert Hyperlink

If you need to establish a hyperlink from a PowerPoint slide to a Web site on an intranet or on the Internet, you can use the following steps. (Technically, you can use these same steps to link to another Office document, but it's easier to use the copy and paste methods described earlier.)

1. In Slide view or in Outline view, select the text in the slide that will serve as the hyperlink.

2. Click the Insert Hyperlink button in the Standard toolbar, or choose Insert ➪ Hyperlink. The Insert Hyperlink dialog box appears, as shown in Figure 32-3.

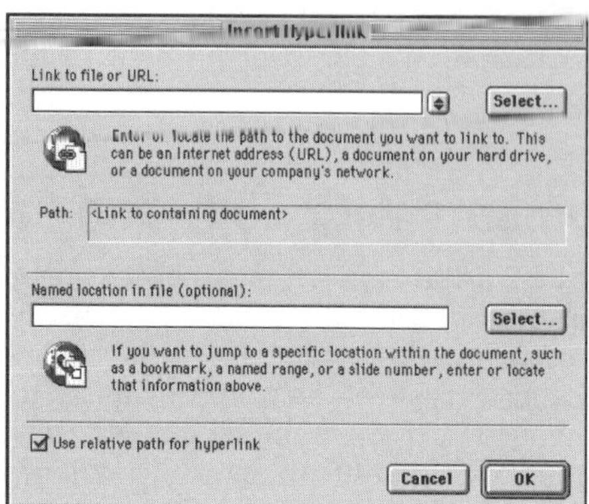

Figure 32-3: The Insert Hyperlink dialog box

3. In the Link to file or URL text box, enter the Web address (or the path for the file) of the destination for the link.

4. If you are establishing a link to a file and want to jump to a specific location, enter that location in the Named location in file text box. (The location can be a cell reference or named range in an Excel worksheet, a Word bookmark, or the name of another PowerPoint slide.) If you link to a file and leave this entry blank, the hyperlink jumps to the beginning of the file.

5. If you want a hyperlink to a shared network directory to find the linked file based on a path relative to the location where your current document is stored, turn on the Use relative path for hyperlink check box. If you want a hyperlink to a shared network directory to use the same address regardless of where the current document is stored, turn off the Use relative path for hyperlink check box.

6. Click OK to establish the hyperlink.

Publishing PowerPoint Slides on the Web

The Save as HTML option of the File menu enables you to save existing presentations as HTML files for Web publication. You can use the Save as HTML option of the File menu to convert existing PowerPoint slides into HTML files. Once converted, you can then upload the HTML files to your Internet or intranet Web server, using the procedures applicable to your server. Choosing File ➪ Save as HTML starts the Save as HTML Wizard, which displays a series of dialog boxes that let you control the content and format of the resulting Web pages.

To save an existing presentation in HTML format, choose File➪Save as HTML. The Save as HTML Wizard launches. Figure 32-4 shows the first dialog box of the Save as HTML Wizard.

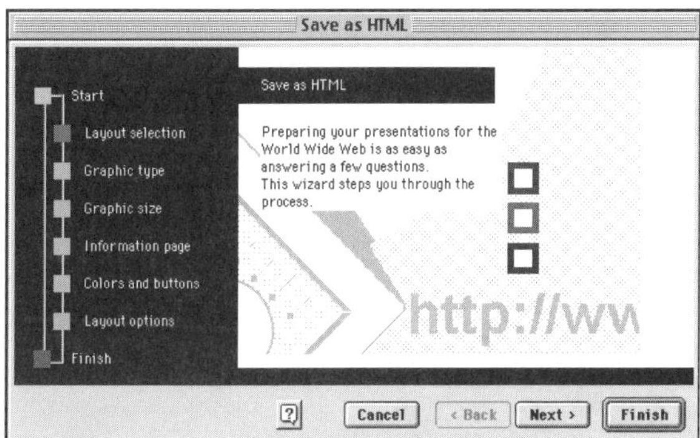

Figure 32-4: The first dialog box of the Save as HTML Wizard

Click Next to begin preparing to save your presentation as an HTML file. If you haven't chosen an existing layout, you next see the dialog box shown in Figure 32-5. This dialog box enables you to choose a standard page style for the design of the Web pages or a page style that makes use of browser frames, a popular feature of Web pages.

Before choosing browser frames, note that most but not all Web browsers support the use of frames. If the general public will be viewing your presentation on the Internet, you may want to use the Standard page style option instead.

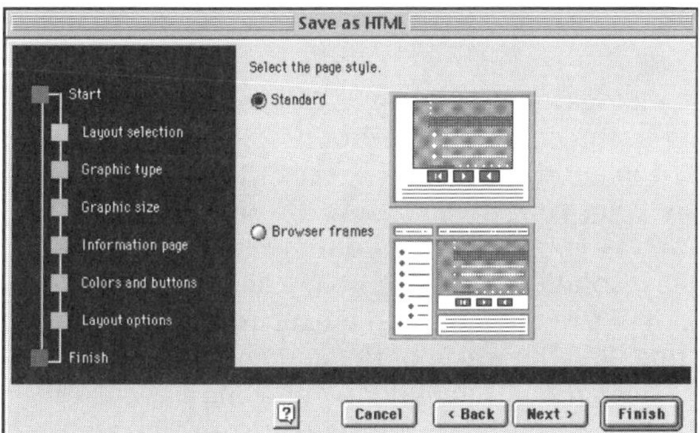

Figure 32-5: The layout selection dialog box of the Save as HTML File Wizard

After clicking Next, you see the graphic Type dialog box shown in Figure 32-6. Here, you need to select the type of graphics you want to use to produce images and backgrounds on your Web pages. You can select GIF or JPEG files as your format.

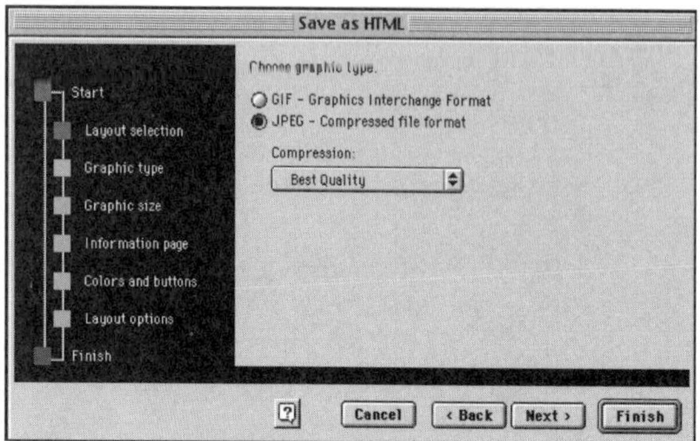

Figure 32-6: The graphics type dialog box

When deciding which graphics file formats to use, remember that either of these commonly used formats, GIF and JPEG, have advantages and disadvantages. GIF files offer good all-around image quality but tend to be larger in size than JPEG files. JPEG files are usually smaller than GIF files, but at a cost of image quality. If you use JPEG, you also need to set a Compression Value from the pop-up menu. (Best Quality is the default; other choices are Good Quality, Compromise, and Best Compression.) The higher the value, the better the image quality. The lower the value, the smaller the image files that are produced.

In our opinion, the best use of JPEG is for photographic images. JPEG was designed with this in mind, allowing high compression with almost no visual loss. GIF is best for computer-generated artwork. Using JPEG on computer art creates blurry, messy lines.

Clicking Next takes you to the dialog box that lets you choose how the graphics should be sized in comparison to the common monitor resolutions used by Macs (see Figure 32-7). Using the options in the dialog box, select the monitor resolution you think will work best for showing your presentation. (You should avoid resolutions above 800 × 600, unless you know that your viewing audiences all have monitors that make use of that resolution or better.) You can also set a width for the presentation with the Width of Graphics pop-up menu. Your choices here are the full width of the screen, three-fourths-width of the screen, half-width of the screen, and a quarter-width of the screen. When done choosing the desired options, click Next.

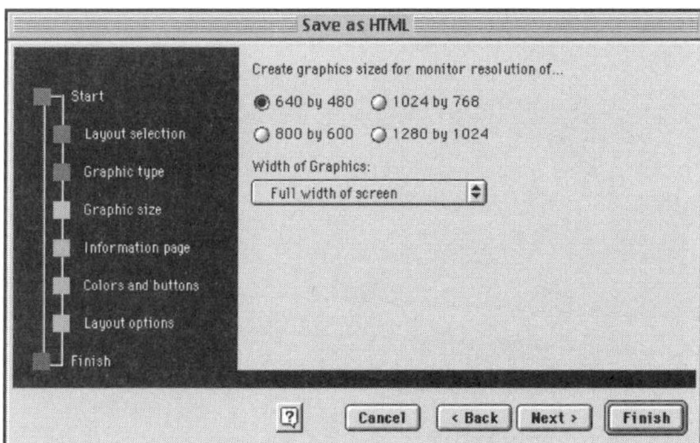

Figure 32-7: The graphic size dialog box

Next you see the information page dialog box shown in Figure 32-8. Here you can enter your e-mail address, home page, and other information you may want to add to an information page included in the Web pages produced by the wizard. You can also include buttons that enable users to download the original presentation or the latest version of Microsoft Internet Explorer by checking the corresponding check boxes.

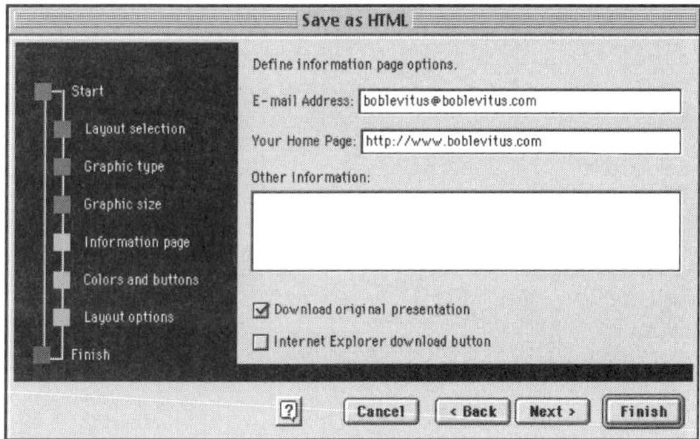

Figure 32-8: The information page dialog box

The page colors dialog box that appears next (see Figure 32-9) enables you to choose a page color and the text, background, link, or visited link colors for the presentation. You can leave the Use browser colors option selected to use the default browser colors, or you can select the Custom colors option to use custom colors of your own choosing. If you choose Custom colors, click the arrow to the right of each option to display its color palette.

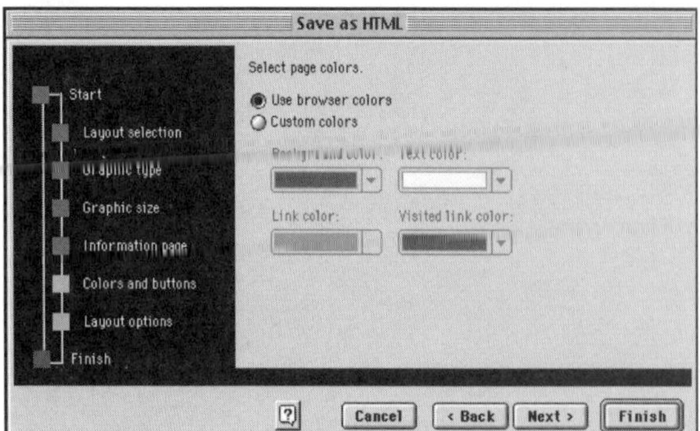

Figure 32-9: The colors and buttons dialog box

Clicking Next takes you to the button style dialog box shown in Figure 32-10. Here you can select a button style to be used for the navigation buttons in your presentation. Select a desired button style and click Next.

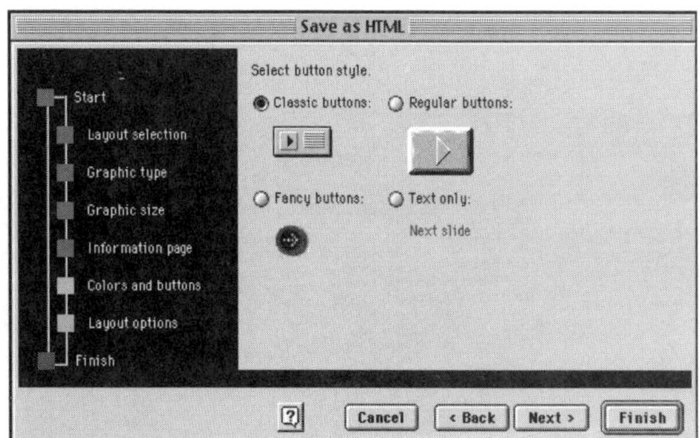

Figure 32-10: The button style dialog box

Clicking Next takes you to the layout options dialog box shown in Figure 32-11. In this dialog box you choose the layout for the navigation buttons used to move between the Web pages of the presentation. You can also choose to include the slide notes page by clicking the corresponding check box.

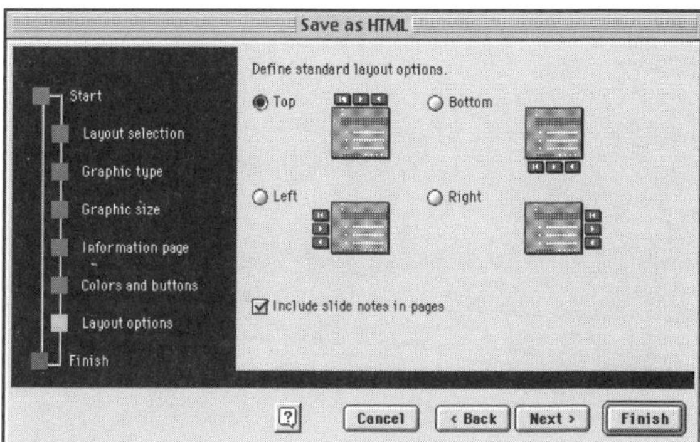

Figure 32-11: The layout options dialog box

Clicking Next takes you to the folder dialog box of the wizard, shown in Figure 32-12. This dialog box asks you to select a folder in which to save the HTML file. After choosing the desired folder, click Next, and then click Finish.

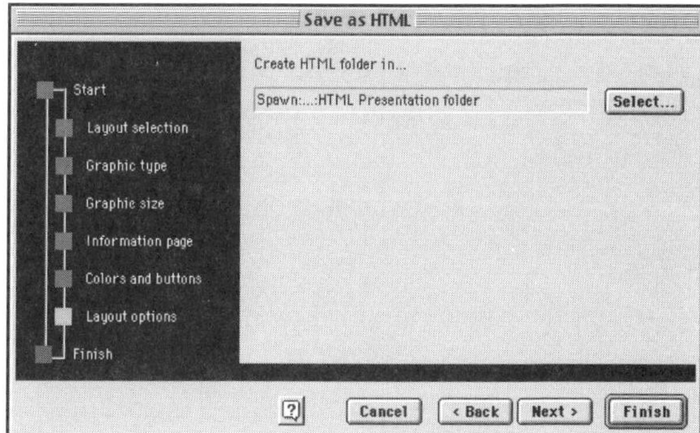

Figure 32-12: The folder dialog box of the Save as HTML Wizard

After you click Finish, PowerPoint proceeds to produce the HTML files needed for the presentation, and it stores them in the folder you specified earlier. You can then use the procedures appropriate to your Web server or your Internet service provider to upload the HTML files to your Web site.

Using the Online Presentation Templates

Note that you can also create Web pages using PowerPoint's online presentation templates. Many of the presentations included with PowerPoint are online presentations, which means they are easily prepared for Web publication.

If you wish to use one of these presentations, simply choose File⇨New and then select the Presentations tab of the New dialog box. This enables you to see some of the presentations available for easy Web publication. Remember, if you don't find one that meets your needs, you can always alter the presentation using the techniques described in Chapters 27 and 28.

Summary

This chapter detailed how to share your PowerPoint data with Internet/intranet users. Points covered in this chapter included the following:

- ✦ Hyperlinks can be added to PowerPoint slides, and you can store Web addresses or jump locations to other Office documents in PowerPoint slides.
- ✦ You can use the Save as HTML option of the File menu to save existing PowerPoint slides as HTML files so you can publish on the Internet or on an intranet.

Where to go next

- ✦ The next chapter demonstrates how you can put PowerPoint to work in real-world applications.
- ✦ PowerPoint is just one component of the Web-publishing capabilities provided by Office 98. Excel and Word also offer Web publishing and Web-interaction features. For specifics on Excel and the Web, see Chapter 23; for Word and the Web, see Chapter 11.

✦ ✦ ✦

PowerPoint at Work

✦ ✦ ✦ ✦

In This Chapter

Creating an organization chart

Creating a travel presentation

✦ ✦ ✦ ✦

This chapter shows you a nifty trick—how to create organization charts in PowerPoint. Executive secretaries throughout the corporate world rejoice in this feature, because so many companies regularly play Musical Vice Presidents in these days of downsizing.

This chapter also walks you step by step through creating a presentation for choosing a site for a convention. In this case the presentation's contents are less important than the general ideas you learn—you can use these ideas to create any kind of presentation.

Creating an Organization Chart

PowerPoint's organization chart feature lets you create company hierarchy diagrams in a hurry. By way of example, follow these steps to create a chart for the fictitious Trejo Music Corporation (see Figure 33-1):

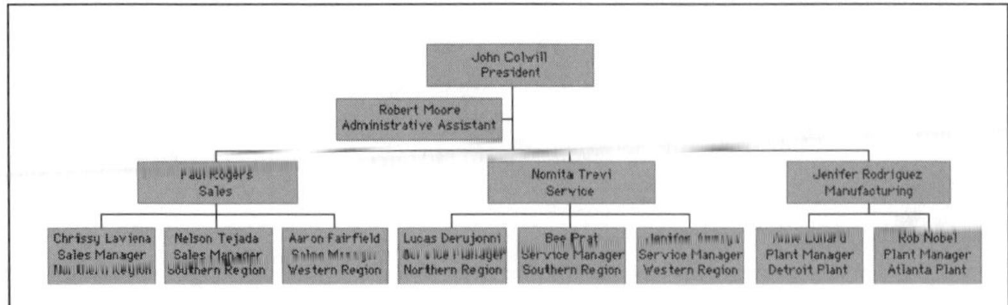

Figure 33-1: The completed organization chart in PowerPoint for the Trejo Music Company

1. Create a new presentation in PowerPoint by choosing the Template option from the opening PowerPoint window. You then see the New Presentation dialog box shown in Figure 33-2.

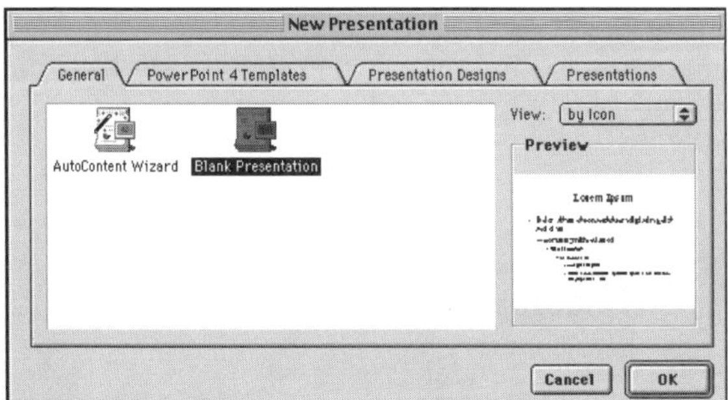

Figure 33-2: The New Presentation dialog box

The New Presentation dialog box contains three tabs:

- ✦ **General**—Contains the AutoContent Wizard and a template for a blank presentation.
- ✦ **Presentation Designs**—Has templates that can be used to create new presentations.
- ✦ **Presentations**—Used to design Web pages (see Chapter 32) and contains templates for presenting presentations for different occasions.

A fourth tab may appear if you've installed the additional templates in the Value Pack:

- ✦ **PowerPoint 4 Templates**—Used to design Web pages (see Chapter 32) and contains templates for giving presentations for different occasions.

These templates are useful when time is an important factor because they simplify the creation of your presentation. The templates also have placeholders that make suggestions on what you can include in the presentation.

2. From the General tab of the New Presentation dialog box, choose Blank Presentation and click OK.

3. The New Slide dialog box appears. Choose the Organization Chart layout (see Figure 33-3).

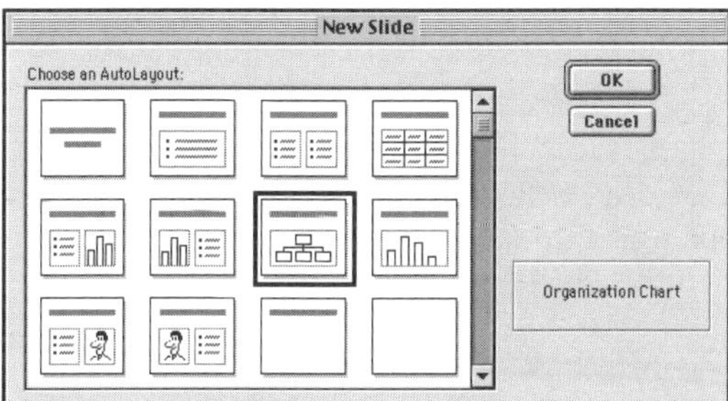

Figure 33-3: Choosing the Organization Chart layout in the New Slide dialog box

4. Double-click the Organization Chart placeholder to activate the Microsoft Organization Chart application and to display a default chart. Organization Chart opens with the default chart shown in Figure 33-4.

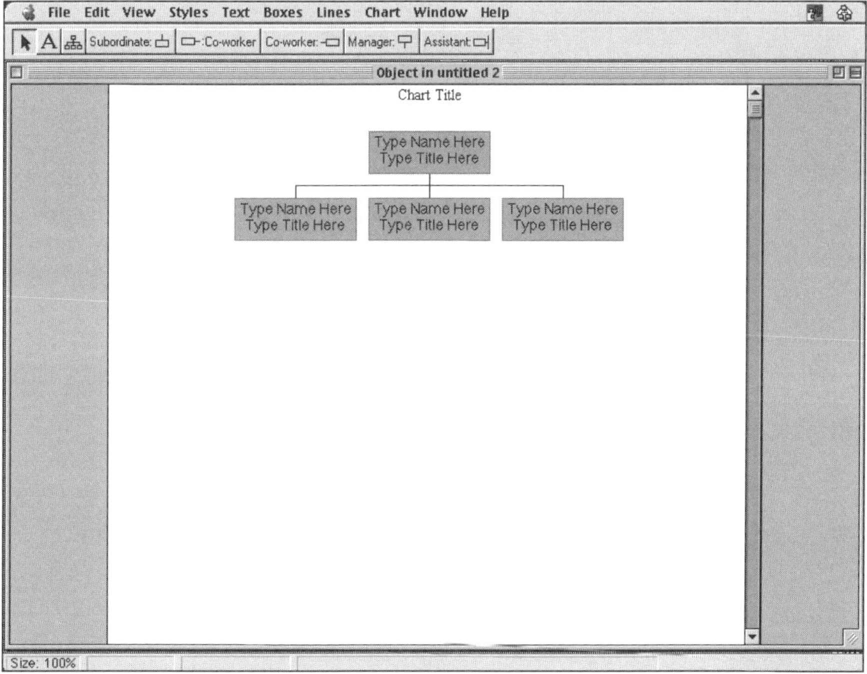

Figure 33-4: The default organization chart

5. Click in the first box of the chart. In the box type **John Colwill** for the name and **President** for the title (or enter a name and title of your own choosing). Use the Tab or down arrow key to move from the name to the title. If you want to add a comment in the chart box, simply move to the comment area and begin entering your information.

6. Next you add the administrative assistant. Click the Assistant button on the toolbar, and move the pointer and click in the President's box. Enter **Robert Moore** for the name and **Administrative Assistant** for the title (or enter a name and title of your own choosing).

7. Enter the following names and titles for the division managers (or names and titles of your own choosing) from left to right in the next level of boxes that appear below Administrative Assistant:

   Paul Rogers, Sales

   Nomita Trevi, Service

   Jenifer Rodriguez, Manufacturing

8. Click the Styles menu to drop down its Group styles options. Click the upper-left icon shown in Figure 33-5 to create subordinate levels in the chart levels.

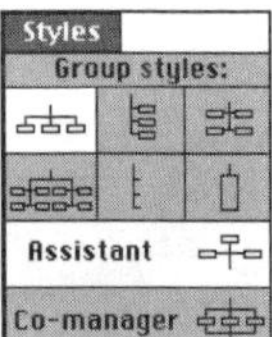

Figure 33-5: The Group styles menu

9. Click the Subordinate button on the Organization Chart toolbar and then click Paul Rogers's box. Enter the following names and titles (or use names and titles of your own choosing). Remember that you need to click the Subordinate button for each of the subordinate entries you make:

   Chrissy Laviena, Sales Manager, Northern Region

   Nelson Tejada, Sales Manager, Southern Region

   Aaron Fairfield, Sales Manager, Western Region

10. Using the procedure in Step 9, enter the following names and titles (or use names and titles of your own choosing) underneath Nomita Trevi's box:

    Lucas Derujonni, Service Manager, Northern Region

    Bee Prat, Service Manager, Southern Region

    Jenifer Arroyo, Service Manager, Western Region

11. Using the procedure in Step 9, enter the following names and titles (or use names and titles of your own choosing) underneath the box of Jenifer Rodriguez:

    Anne Edhard, Plant Manager, Detroit Plant

    Rob Nobel, Plant Manager, Atlanta Plant

12. Now choose File⇨Update Presentation to update your presentation and place the chart on the blank slide.
13. Choose File⇨Quit and Return to return to PowerPoint to see the chart.
14. Choose File⇨Save to save the presentation. Save your presentation as Chart. Your finished chart should look like the one shown in Figure 33-1.

Creating a Travel Presentation

Suppose you head the committee to choose the site for your company's annual convention this year. Your first meeting with the committee is right around the corner. It's PowerPoint to the rescue.

Applying a template

The following example applies a template to the presentation. The template gives the presentation's slides a consistent look. PowerPoint comes with many different templates you can apply to your presentation—choose the one that works best for you. Follow these steps:

1. Choose File⇨New. Click the Blank Presentation option in the New Presentation dialog box and then click OK.
2. Choose the Blank Slide option from the New Slide dialog box and then click OK. A slide appears without any formatting.
3. Control-click the slide and choose Slide Layout from the shortcut menu. You then see the Slide Layout dialog box. In the Slide Layout dialog box, choose Title Slide as the slide layout and then click Apply.
4. Enter the title **Convention Site Option for 1997.**
5. Control-click the PowerPoint window. In the shortcut menu that appears, choose Apply Design to open the Apply Design dialog box shown in Figure 33-6. Choose a template design you like and click Apply.

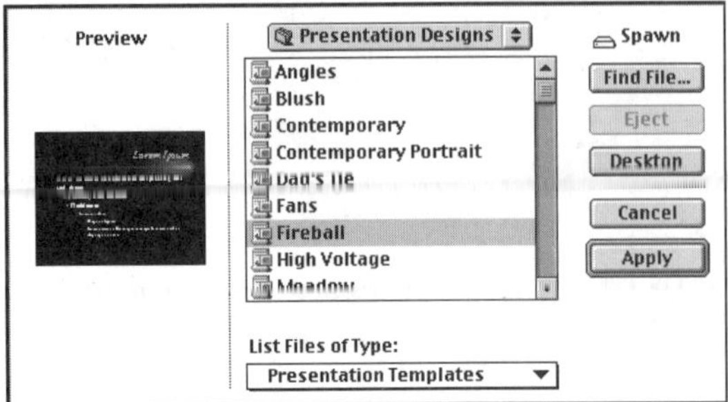

Figure 33-6: The Apply Design dialog box

6. Click the Insert New Slide button on the Standard toolbar and select Bulleted List as the slide layout. Enter **San Diego** as the title, and in the bulleted list, enter the following:

   Wide range of pricing regarding accommodations

   Excellent restaurants and entertainment

   Close to Mexico

   Beautiful scenery

7. Click the Insert New Slide button on the Standard toolbar and select Bulleted List as the slide layout. Enter **San Francisco** as the title, and in the bulleted list, enter the following:

   Excellent dining and attractions in Fisherman's Wharf area

   Proximity to sites of interest reduces transportation costs

8. Click the Insert New Slide button on the Standard toolbar and select Bulleted List as the slide layout. Enter **Cancun, Mexico** as the title, and in the bulleted list, enter the following:

   Favorable currency exchange rate maximizes dollar usage

   Outstanding water sports in close proximity to hotels

9. Click the Insert New Slide button on the Standard toolbar and select Bulleted List as the slide layout. Enter **San Juan, PR** as the title, and in the bulleted list, enter the following:

   Excellent hotel and conference facilities with casino-based entertainment

   Spanish flavor to cultural attractions

   No need for passport/visa or currency exchange

Applying a background

Now that you have applied the template to the presentation and entered the text, apply a background to all the slides in the presentation by performing the following steps:

1. Switch to Slide Master view by choosing View ⇨ Master ⇨ Slide Master.
2. Choose Format ⇨ Background to open the Background dialog box (see Figure 33-7).

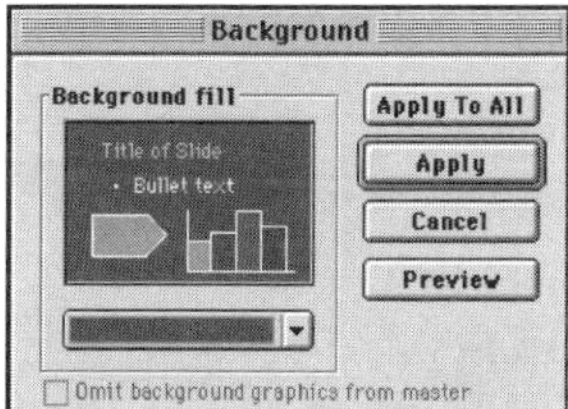

Figure 33-7: The Background dialog box

3. Choose gray as the background color by clicking the arrow in the Background fill area to open the list box. Select gray from the submenu of colors that appears and click the Apply To All button.

Adding notes and handouts

After you have created the presentation and applied a template to it, you can create a set of speaker's notes. Perform the following steps to create these items:

1. The notes page that appears onscreen corresponds to the slide you are currently working on. Therefore, switch to Slide view and move to the San Diego slide.
2. Choose View ⇨ Notes Page.
3. Click inside the notes box to make it active. You may need to use the Zoom control to see the text better. Click the Zoom control button on the Standard toolbar and choose a larger percentage to increase the size of the box.
4. Enter the following notes:

   To Garfinkles/$75 and up a meal/two persons

   Broadway shows at San Diego Theater

   Venture to Tijuana to purchase authentic Mexican arts and crafts

   Genuine Mexican food available (not those so-called imitations)

5. Move to the San Francisco slide and create a notes page by entering the following notes:

   From Hilton/double occupancy/$200 per night

   To La Quinta/double occupancy/$75 per night

   From Fisherman's Wharf/$20-$75 a meal/two persons

   Down by the Sea Restaurant rated best in San Francisco, widest selection of seafood

   12 other wharf restaurants to choose from

   5 different options of transportation with low costs as opposed to cabs

6. Move to the Cancun, Mexico slide and create a notes page by entering the following notes:

   5 pesos to a dollar

   Outstanding snorkeling and scuba diving

   Most hotels offer snorkeling gear onsite and are located on the beach

7. Move to the San Juan, Puerto Rico slide and create a notes page by entering the following notes:

   ESJ Hotel facilities perfect for working vacation

   Many Puerto Rican art museums

   Puerto Rico is a commonwealth of the United States, so you need no special paperwork to visit there.

Adding headers and footers

After creating the notes pages, you can add page numbers by choosing View➪Header and Footer. The Header and Footer dialog box appears, as shown in Figure 33-8.

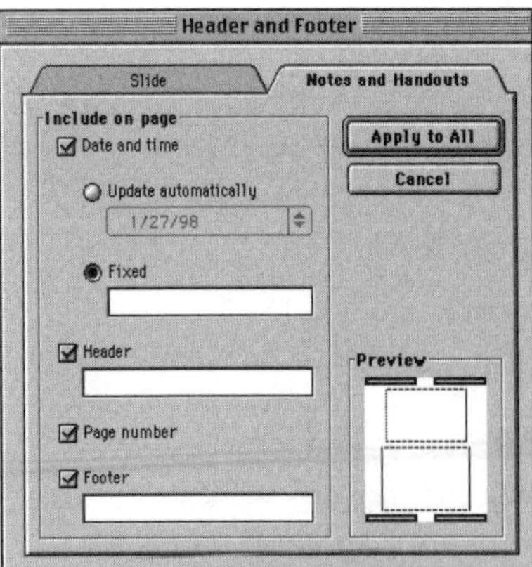

Figure 33-8: The Notes and Handouts tab of the Header and Footer dialog box

You can use this dialog box to include headers and footers on the slides and slide notes. (You can do this only from the Slide Master.) If you click the Slide tab, you can add the date, time, and slide numbers to your slides. While you're at it, you can exclude the title slide from getting these additions. Apply these items by clicking the corresponding check boxes on the Slide tab.

You use the Notes and Handouts tab to apply these same elements to the notes pages and handouts that may be included with a presentation. The one additional option you have here is the addition of headers. You may need to add headers to identify your handouts or notes. You can click the Page number box to add page numbers to your speaker's notes. The Preview box shows you where the page numbers will appear.

Printing your notes pages

To print your notes pages, follow these steps:

1. Be sure your printer is ready (check to see if it is online).
2. Choose File⇨Print.
3. In the Print What pop-up menu of the Print dialog box, choose Notes Pages.
4. Click OK.

Adding transitions

Transitions are another feature you can add to the presentation. Transitions are visual changes between the slides. For example, one kind of transition makes one slide appear to dissolve into another. Transitions can make a presentation more appealing to an audience and can be a good special effect to add to a presentation. Perform the following steps to create a transition between two slides. You must perform these steps for each slide transition.

1. Switch to Slide Sorter view by clicking its button on the left side of the status bar.
2. Choose the slide transition you want by clicking the Slide Transition box on the Slide Sorter toolbar that appears (see Figure 33-9).

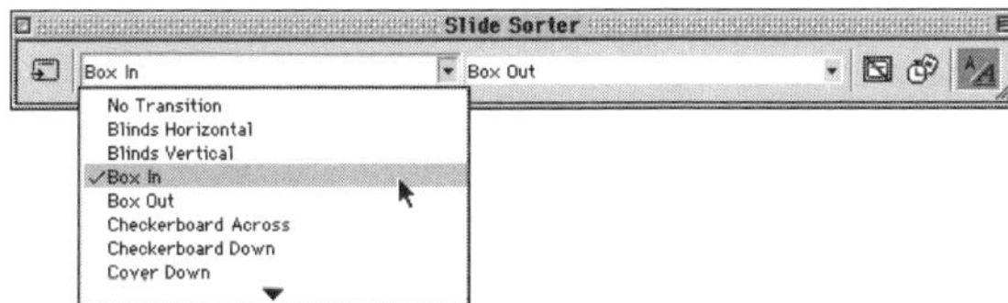

Figure 33-9: The Slide Transition list

3. In the Effect list box, choose Box Out for the transition. You can see the effect of this transition in the Preview box.

You can also insert transitions using the Transition Effects list box on the Slide Sorter toolbar at the top of your screen. Use the arrow keys to move to the slide for which you want to set a transition. Then click the arrow of the list box and choose the effect you want to apply to the slide.

The benefit of using the dialog box is that you have a chance to preview the transition before it is applied and adjust the speed of the transition. However, you can click the Transition button on the Slide Sorter toolbar to open the Transitions dialog box. Here you can preview the transition by selecting it from the list of transitions.

Finally, save the completed presentation by choosing the Save command from the File menu. When asked for a name, you can call the presentation Travel 1. Run the presentation by clicking the Slide Show button on the left side of the status bar.

Summary

This chapter provided a step-by-step look at creating an organization chart and walked you through creating a presentation. The following were key points discussed in the chapter:

- ✦ You can use the Organization Chart layout in the New Slide dialog box to create organization charts.
- ✦ To apply a design to a presentation, Control-click any blank part of the PowerPoint window and choose Apply Design Template from the shortcut menu.
- ✦ While in Slide View, you can create notes pages that provide speaker's notes you can work from while giving your presentation.
- ✦ While in Slide Sorter view, you can use Tools ➪ Slide Transition to add transitions to your slides.

Where to go next

- ✦ The next chapter answers common questions PowerPoint users have.
- ✦ Now that you have created a presentation in PowerPoint, you may want to take some time to make it more visually appealing. Chapter 28 tells you how.
- ✦ You may also want to produce the presentation you created in this chapter. See Chapter 30.

✦ ✦ ✦

CHAPTER 34

The PowerPoint Top Ten

✦ ✦ ✦ ✦

In this chapter, you find questions and answers detailing the most common problems encountered by PowerPoint users. As usual, the answers are based on information we picked up from Microsoft Technical Support and the Microsoft forums on CompuServe.

1. How can I format titles and text for entire presentations?

Sometimes you will need to make formatting changes to an entire presentation, whether those changes are for the text or for the layout of your slides. Choose View⇨Master⇨Slide Master. When you make the changes in the Slide Master, they are applied to the entire presentation.

2. How can I group and edit objects as one?

To group objects, select them and choose Draw⇨Group on the Drawing toolbar. This action groups the selected objects as one. If you want to edit the objects, use the editing techniques you learned in the PowerPoint section of this book.

3. How can I copy the formatting of one object to another?

First, highlight the object that contains the formatting you want to copy. Next, double-click the Format Painter button on the Standard toolbar. Finally, select the object(s) to which you want to apply the formatting, and the formatting is automatically applied.

4. How can I apply a PowerPoint presentation as a template?

Applying a PowerPoint presentation as a template is, in essence, creating a new template. First, create the presentation exactly the way you want it with all the formatting and objects. Next, choose File➪Save As. In the Save As dialog box, choose Presentation Template from the Save File as Type pop-up menu. The file is then saved as a template file that you can later use to create new presentations.

5. How can I change a slide's layout without losing existing work?

If you decide to change the layout of your slide while you are working on it, first click the Layout button on the right side of the status bar to open the Slide Layout dialog box. From this dialog box, choose the desired slide layout. After you click OK, the layout is applied to the slide.

6. How can I preview all my slide transitions?

To preview all your slide transitions, switch to the Slide Sorter view by clicking its button on the left of the status bar. After switching to Slide Sorter view, click the transition icon underneath each slide to see the transition.

7. How can I view my presentations without installing PowerPoint?

Download the PowerPoint Viewer from the Microsoft Web Site (`www.microsoft.com`). The PowerPoint Viewer enables you to view PowerPoint presentations on a computer that does not have PowerPoint installed on it. Install the PowerPoint Viewer on the other computer, open a copy of the presentation in PowerPoint Viewer, and run it. Remember you must save the presentation on a separate disk. You can also give the presentation and the PowerPoint Viewer to others so they can view the presentation you have created—without pressure from you. Microsoft lets you freely copy and distribute the PowerPoint Viewer disk.

8. How can I print slides in reverse order?

You can't. Actually, you can, but it's a lot of work. In the Slide Sorter view, rearrange your slides so the first is last and the last is first, and then print. (The Windows version *does* let you print in reverse order using the Print dialog box; Mac users got gypped.)

9. How can I add and erase onscreen annotations?

Annotations are useful in a slide show to make different points in your presentation. To add annotations, switch to the Slide Show view and control-click any portion of the screen. In the shortcut menu that appears, choose Pen. The pointer then becomes a pen, enabling you to make the necessary annotations to your slide show. You can also change the color of the marks by using the same shortcut menu. Choose Pointer Options and then Pen Color. From the next menu that appears, choose the color of your choice.

If you want to draw a straight line with the pen cursor in Slide Show view, hold down the Shift key while you draw the line.

After you have made the marks you need, you can press the E key to remove them. Remember that all annotation marks are temporary. When you advance to the next slide, the marks are automatically erased.

10. How can I create new slides without the New Slide dialog box?

If you want to create new slides without using the New Slide dialog box, you need to make an adjustment in the Options dialog box. To do so, choose Tools⇨ Preferences to open the Preferences dialog box. Click the View tab, and then turn off the Show New Slide Dialog check box. With this option turned off, you can add new slides without using the New Slide dialog box each time. PowerPoint adds a slide with a title box and text area each time you ask for a new slide.

Summary

This chapter has covered the top ten PowerPoint questions and their answers. The chapter also concludes the PowerPoint section of this book.

Where to go next

- ✦ Many of the common PowerPoint questions relate to working with presentation formats and layouts. Chapter 28 gives you specifics that will help you change your presentation's appearance.
- ✦ Producing finished presentations generates many questions, too. Chapter 30 takes you by the hand and leads you through it.

✦ ✦ ✦

The Internet Office

PART

V

✦ ✦ ✦ ✦

In This Part

Chapter 35
Using Outlook Express

Chapter 36
Using Internet Explorer

✦ ✦ ✦ ✦

Using Outlook Express

✦ ✦ ✦ ✦

In This Chapter

Introducing Outlook Express

Working with e-mail accounts

Working with messages

Working with multiple users

Newsgroups

✦ ✦ ✦ ✦

E-mail is where it's at these days. Type a message and send it, and in moments your message completes its trip across town or across the world to be read and addressed at the convenience of the recipient. With e-mail you can correspond several times a day, or have a message wait weeks to be read. This chapter familiarizes you with the newest member of the Microsoft Mac family—the Outlook Express Internet mail and news client e-mail program—and the benefits of using it in conjunction with Office 98.

Introducing Outlook Express

In response to e-mail's popularity, Microsoft has introduced Outlook Express, which replaces Microsoft Internet Mail and News. If you are already using e-mail, you may be using Netscape not only as your browser but also for e-mail, or you may be using one of the e-mail-specific applications: Eudora Lite, Eudora, or E-mailer. In either case, you will find many of the Outlook Express features new and exciting.

If you ever tried Cyberdog, you may find a lot of features familiar, but Cyberdog is no longer developed or supported by Apple.

How it works

Outlook Express enables you to send, receive, and store your e-mail. It also enables you to manage e-mail as it comes in to make reading it easier. Outlook Express can also handle your newsgroup mail. (A newsgroup is a list to which subscribers can send and receive each other's messages. Each newsgroup covers a specific topic, and you subscribe to a group because of its topic.)

Probably most exciting is the ability to view your e-mail not only as plain text but also in HTML format, allowing your messages to be fully creative—with active links and formatted text. Corporations will appreciate the fact that Outlook Express allows Macs to fully interact with Exchange (5.5 or newer).

Looking at the window

The Outlook Express window consists of three sections with a toolbar at the top. Figure 35-1 shows you this window as it first appears when you launch Outlook Express and read your first e-mail—the welcome letter.

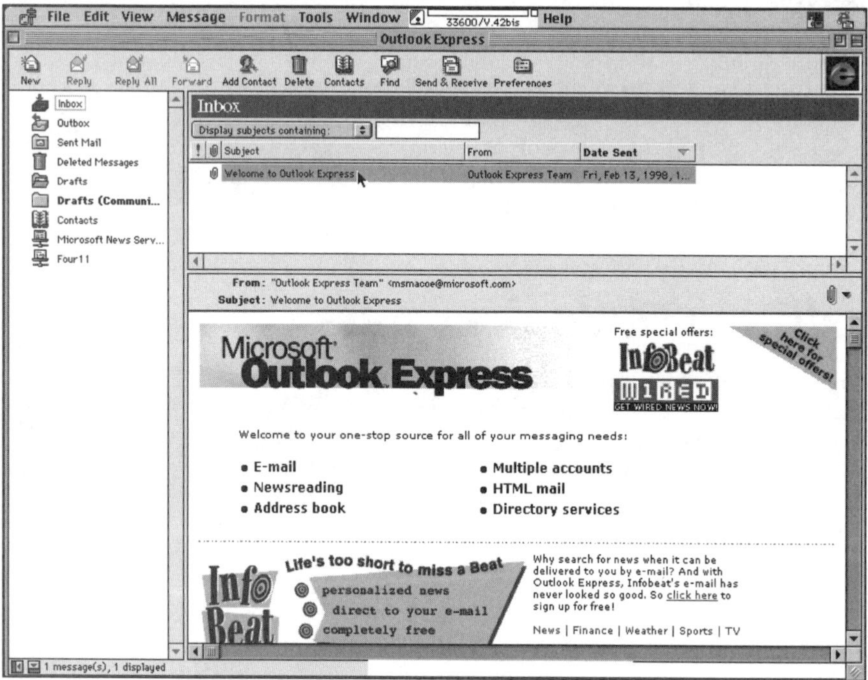

Figure 35-1: The Outlook Express window

The toolbar

As with each of the Office applications and most software these days, Outlook Express has a toolbar to make common tasks easier, without demanding you memorize keyboard shortcuts. Three clues help you identify the function of each button: a representative icon; a label below each button, which becomes underlined when selected; and a ScreenTip, which appears when you rest your mouse over the button to offer a description of each button. You have control over the option to show the underlined label and ScreenTips. To turn these options on or off, choose Edit ➪ Preferences and then click the Display icon.

Creating More Folders

The Folder list is, in effect, your filing cabinet. If all your mail remained in your inbox, you'd never find anything. Therefore, you can create as many other folders as you want. If your mail is being downloaded to your hard drive for storage and handling, each folder you create appears below the Drafts folder. If you are using an IMAP account, your online folders will appear as subfolders of your server icon, but you can also create folders on your hard drive.

It is common to create a new folder for each project you are working on, each list you subscribe to, or for any other category by which you want to file your messages. To create a new folder, select File⇨New⇨Folder. You can also add subfolders within any folder. Click the folder you want the subfolder to land in, and then select File⇨New⇨Subfolder. For more about folders, see "Filing your messages" later in this chapter.

The Folder list

For lack of a better name, the area to the left of the Outlook Express window is called the Folder list. Actually, this area also lists your contact list and the servers you are set up to connect with—perhaps you can stretch your imagination just a bit and consider your contacts file and servers as a folders. (Good thing Mac users are used to custom icons on folders.) Clicking any icon in this section reveals the corresponding information and, in the case of the Accounts (the server-type icons), ultimately initiates the corresponding connection. This section provides the lowdown on the Folder list contents.

The first items in the Folder list are folders. Each of these folders holds messages that are actually on your hard drive. Each of the following default folders serves a different purpose. Soon you'll learn how to make all the folders you want so you can file your mail as desired. You can drag messages from any Message list that appears on the right side of the Outlook Express window to any message folder in this area.

✦ **Inbox**—Your incoming messages land in this folder unless you set up an *Inbox Rule* that tells Outlook Express to take other action for a message. The Inbox name appears in bold when unread messages are waiting. Additionally, the number of unread messages appears in parentheses beside the Inbox name. Clicking the Inbox icon displays a list of its contents in the area to the right. (If you are a corporate user accessing e-mail from an IMAP server, note that only mail you transfer to your hard drive lands here.) In Figure 35-1 the Inbox is the selected folder.

✦ **Outbox**—All messages within this folder are sent when you issue the command to send your e-mail. When you compose a message, it is stored in the Drafts folder automatically, unless you click the Send button in the message composition window to move the message to the Outbox. To view and/or edit this mail, click this folder. Its contents will appear in the messages list.

✦ **Sent Mail**—Messages are filed in this folder after you send them, unless you set your preferences to do something else to the messages. You can choose not to have messages move here by choosing Edit ➪ Preferences, selecting General, and then unchecking the action. To review your sent mail, click this folder. You'll see its contents in the messages list.

✦ **Deleted Messages**—This folder, which looks like a trash can, is where you drag any message you wish to delete. (You drag them from the Folder list.) Alternatively, you can select a message in the Message list and click the Delete button. Sometimes the Deleted Messages trash can's label appears in bold, with a number beside it in parentheses. This number indicates how many unread messages you have in the folder. (If you are using an IMAP server, your messages aren't on your local hard drive, so this folder is not used. It is only for downloaded messages.)

✦ **Drafts**—This folder is where all newly composed messages are stored. A new outgoing message remains in this folder until you decide it is ready to send and move it to the Outbox. To view and/or edit your drafts, click this folder. Its contents appear in the messages list.

✦ **Contacts**—The Contacts list is a miniature address book that, most importantly, includes your addressees and their e-mail address or addresses. When you click the address book-like icon labeled Contacts, your entire list of contacts is revealed to the right of the Folder list. After you create mailing lists, an arrow appears beside the Contacts folder icon. Just like the Mac's Finder, clicking the arrow reveals the lists. (See the section on contacts for more information.)

Below your Contacts folder you'll find your Accounts—identified by their server-type icons—shown in the following list. You set up these servers by selecting Edit ➪ Preferences and then selecting each server type under the Accounts header on the left. The name you enter in the Account name field appears in the Folder list area in the main Outlook Express window. Back in the main Outlook Express window, when you click a server icon, the server information appears to the right.

✦ **E-mail server**—If you have an IMAP server (or, for some reason, you've set up your POP account to allow online access), clicking this icon connects you to your mail server and provides a live view into the messages waiting there. Your messages appear in the right side of the Outlook Express window.

Before you click this icon to connect, hide your Preview pane (View ➪ Preview Pane). If the Preview pane is showing, Outlook Express assumes you want to download your messages, and it sends all of them to your hard drive.

When you delete a message from this list, Outlook Express deletes the message from the server, not from your hard drive. When you double-click a message here or drag a message from this list to a folder, you tell Outlook Express to download it to your hard drive. See "Working with E-Mail Accounts" for more information.

- **Microsoft News Server**—This is a preset link to the news lists hosted by the Microsoft News Server. (Newsgroups are covered in detail at the end of this chapter.) You can change this server or add another one.
- **Four11**—By default, this button is a link to the popular Web-based e-mail directory, Four11. When you're looking for a person's e-mail address, simply click this Account icon, enter the search criteria, and then click Find. (The Find button only becomes available when criteria is entered. Although it doesn't show the standard Mac signs of being the default button, pressing Return or Enter does issue the Find command.)

At `http://www.four11.com`, you can find a lot more than just e-mail addresses. If you're searching for telephone book content or even directions, check out this full-featured Web site. While you're there, you may want to list yourself. There's no charge and it's a great way to let old friends or schoolmates find you—if you want to be found.

If you prefer another online directory, choose Edit ⇨ Preferences, click Directory Services on the left, and then select another directory from the Directory Services pop-up list. If you have a username and password, they can also be stored here. You can have more than one Directory button appear in the main Outlook Express window. Just click New Directory before choosing another directory from the Directory Services pop-up list, and check the option to display it in the Folder list.

If you use a dial-up account (your phone line) to access the Internet, an application has to be allowed to initiate your PPP connection. To give Outlook Express this permission (and all other Web-based applications), open your PPP control panel, click Options, select the Connections tab, and then check Connect automatically when starting TCP/IP applications. Also go to your TCP/IP control panel, click Options, and check Load only when needed, or your Mac will mysteriously try to connect every time you start it.

Outlook Express and Exchange

If you're part of a large company that uses Exchange to handle its corporate e-mail, having Macs in the system may have presented a question or issue in the past. Good news: Mac users can now fully interact with Exchange (if your company is running Exchange 5.5).

In case you're wondering why, read on.

First, as of Exchange 5.5, IMAP is fully supported and Outlook Express also provides IMAP support. Next, Outlook Express takes care of the user authentication issue by providing the secure logon protocol used by Exchange. Therefore, Mac users can connect to the Exchange server, send their passwords, and be online along with any PC user.

The Message list

When you click an item in the Folder list, its contents appear to the right in the Message list. Depending on what you are viewing, clicking or double-clicking an item in this list reveals the item's contents. If you are viewing a mail folder, clicking a message once reveals the message in the Preview area below, while double-clicking the message reveals the message in a new, separate window. If you are viewing contacts, you see a bit of information in the columns shown, but you must double-click the contact to see all the contact information or edit the contact. If an account is selected in the Folder list, the Folder list area provides the pertinent account information in list form; again, double-clicking reveals more information. This list cannot be turned on and off in the View menu. In Figure 35-1 there is one message in the Inbox, therefore one message appears in the Message list. That message was clicked once and is selected.

The Preview pane

This area is only available when viewing your e-mail. In the Preview pane you can easily view the contents of your message by clicking the message once, as shown in Figure 35-1. In case you prefer more room to see the contents of your folders, you can resize the space given to the Folder list and Preview pane or turn off the Preview pane.

To change the size of the Preview pane, move your pointer over the double line between the two areas so your pointer becomes a double-headed arrow, and then click and drag to size. To turn off the Preview pane, click the second small icon in the lower-left corner or go to the View➪Preview pane to turn it off, removing the check mark by it.

What Internet Services Can I Access?

Outlook Express supports many common Internet standard protocols, such as SMTP, POP3 (for e-mail), NNTP (for newsgroups), IMAP4 (for message server access), and LDAP (for accessing directories such as Four11). If an Internet service complies with any one of these protocols, you can access it using Outlook Express. The best way to know if a service supports one of these standards is to check the service's Web site or ask the service provider—or just try.

At the time of this writing America Online (AOL) doesn't support an Internet standard, so you can't access AOL accounts from Outlook Express. If AOL changes its protocol or works with Outlook Express to create an interface, this may change. If it does change, chances are the Microsoft Office Web site (`www.microsoft.com/macoffice`) will announce it, so check there from time to time.

Working with E-Mail Accounts

You have two ways to access your e-mail: downloading it to your hard drive for handling, or keeping your mail on the server and connecting to the server to access and handle your messages.

If you are a normal home user or small business user, chances are you use Post Office Protocol (POP). By default this method downloads your mail to your hard drive for storage and handling. That way your Internet service provider (ISP) doesn't have to provide tons of hard drive space storing your messages, and you can handle your mail on your own time without having to remain connected for long periods of time, driving up the cost of Internet access.

If you are accessing a corporate server, you may be using Internet Message Access Protocol (IMAP). IMAP servers keep your e-mail on the server, so you must connect to the server to read and handle your messages. IMAP is handy in business because you can access all your e-mail from anywhere. IMAP server-based folders can be shared by a group of people for collaboration or set up as private. If you are using IMAP, chances are your network administrator will set up your account and explain how to use it. Just in case, however, we discuss the basics of IMAP usage here, too.

Outlook Express can handle multiple accounts, so it is possible to have one POP Outlook Express account and one IMAP account.

Hot Stuff

If you are on the road, you'll love this feature: Outlook Express can extend the capabilities of POP to let you use your POP account by connecting to the server and working directly on the server instead of having your mail transferred to your hard drive. (When you do this, the Preview pane must be hidden, or clicking a message in the Message list downloads the message.) If you see your account in the Folder list (with a server-type icon), you have such access and can access your account from any computer. This gives you the best of both worlds. Instead of always connecting and downloading unwanted messages, you can connect this way, read the subjects and sender information, and then download only the messages you want and delete the rest from the server. You can also select View ➪ Columns ➪ Size to see the message size in the Message list. That way you can elect not to download a message if it will take too long or is too large. More details about this are scattered throughout this chapter.

Regardless of the way you access your e-mail, composing it and sending it is the same. In fact, most of what you do in Outlook Express is the same. Some things, however—such as where your mail filing folders are located and appear in Outlook Express, and how mail is deleted—can be different. We point out those differences as we go along.

Setting up your e-mail account

To set up an e-mail account, you enter the information needed to connect to your mail server. You do this by telling Outlook Express the name of your account and the server your mail comes into and goes out of. When you first launch Outlook Express, a message comes up, inviting you to set up your account. If you click Yes, the necessary dialog boxes open, so you are, in effect, taken directly to Step 3 in the following steps. Follow these steps to set up your e-mail account:

1. Select Edit ⇨ Preferences.
2. Click E-mail to select it from the list of preference settings at the left of the Preferences dialog box.
3. Click the New Account button at the top to open the New Account dialog box shown in Figure 35-2.
4. Enter a descriptive name for your account. This name is not an official name; it is only for your own use so you can identify the account in the Folder list and in menus.
5. Click the POP or IMAP radio button, depending on your type of mail server.

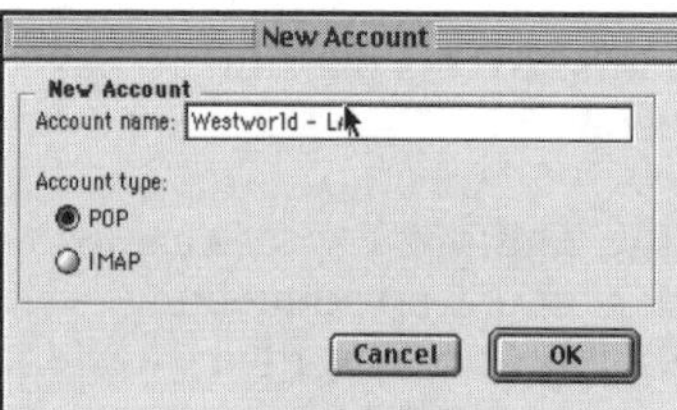

Figure 35-2: Naming your new account in the New Account dialog box

6. Click OK to close this dialog box and return to the E-mail section of the main Preferences dialog box, shown in Figure 35-3. At this point the account appears in the Account name pop-up menu.
7. Enter your first and last name in the Full name field. (If you have already set up a default account, your name automatically appears there.) This is your name as you want people to see it.
8. Enter your e-mail address in the E-mail address field. This is the address you want the world to see. It's the one used when someone clicks Reply to respond to your message. Therefore, this address should be your exact e-mail address. For example, in Figure 35-3 the address people would see and respond to is Michael@wgn.net.
9. Enter your company or group name, if you have one, in the Organization field. Again, Outlook Express takes this from your default account if you already have one set up.

10. Now you set up how your mail will be sent, which is via SMTP (Simple Mail Transport Protocol). Enter the name of your outgoing mail server in the SMTP server field. (When you sign up with an ISP, your outgoing mail server is one of the pieces of information your ISP gives you.)

11. Enter the name of your mail account in the Account ID field. You select this part of your e-mail address when you sign up with your ISP; it is how your ISP identifies you during sign-in. Unless your ISP tells you differently, this name is the same as the part of your e-mail address that goes in front of the @ sign.

12. Enter the name of your incoming mail server in the POP server box. (Again, your ISP provides this name. It is usually the same as the SMTP address.)

13. To avoid having to enter your password every time you connect, click the Save password check box. Then enter your e-mail password. This is a password you set up with your ISP when you signed up. If other users have access to your Mac, you may prefer to keep this check box blank and enter the password when you connect.

14. By default, one account (address) will be used when you send your mail or post to a newsgroup. If this is the account you wish to have as the default, click Make Default. The default account is always the one used to post to newsgroups, but you can send a message from any of your other accounts by selecting another address from the Mail From menu.

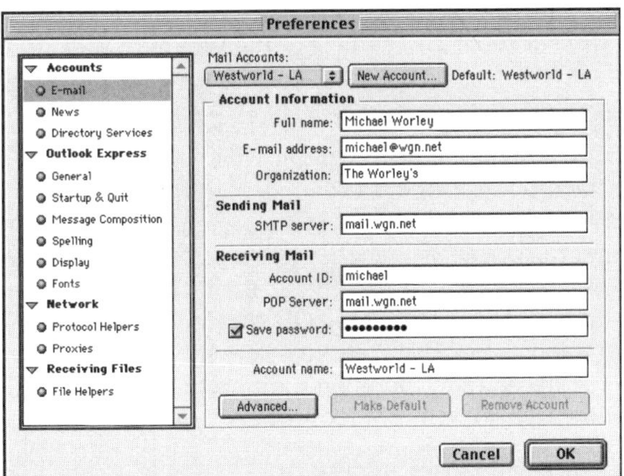

Figure 35-3: Completed New Account preferences

15. (Optional) You can click the Advanced button to set up more specific preferences, shown in Figure 35-4. Some of these preferences are determined by your ISP or mail server administrator; others are up to you.

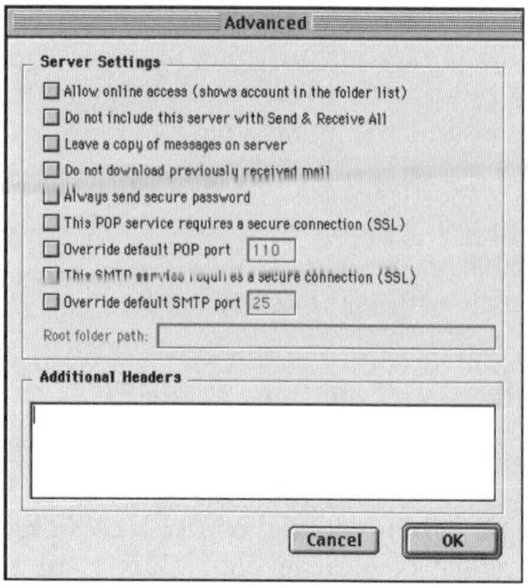

Figure 35-4: Advanced New Account preferences

For example, from the main Outlook Express window, you can send and receive mail from all your accounts. If you don't want this account included in that mass mail exchange, you can exclude it from here. Another option you might change from here is to have your ISP leave all your collected messages on the server after you collect them. This is not commonly done because it takes up room on the server, but while traveling you may want to do this. If you do, you'll also want to select the next option so you don't keep receiving the same e-mail over and over.

Some servers provide a secure connection in which your messages are encrypted to prevent interception and reading. Another advanced option allows retrieval from a secure server. If your account doesn't support a secure server connections and you enable this option, you will probably receive an error when you try to receive your mail. However, if you do require a secure connection, check This POP service requires a secure connection, and/or check This SMTP service requires a secure connection. If you are told your secure connection is on a different port, check Override default port and enter the port number. (Your ISP should help you with these options.)

If you've set up a POP account and want to give yourself online access to it, check Allow online access. Your mail server appears in the Folder list, which is where you initiate the online connection.

16. Click OK in the Advanced dialog box, if it's open, and then click OK in the Preferences dialog box.

The account is now ready to send and receive from. It appears under the Tools ➪ Send & Receive submenu from the Outlook Express main window.

Dealing with contacts

To send an e-mail message, you need to address the message to the recipient. This is where the Contacts list comes into play. You can address a note to someone without placing the name in your Contacts list, but unless you'll never write to that person again, it's more efficient to enter the names.

Creating contacts

To create a new contact while you are in the Contacts folder (it's selected in the Folder list), click the New (Contact) button or press ⌘-N. To create a new contact while in another folder, select File⇨New⇨Contact. Alternatively, you can open the Contact window by clicking the Contacts button, or you can Control-click anywhere in the Outlook Express window, select Contacts from the shortcut menu, and then click the New (Contact) button. All these methods open a new, empty Contact window so you can enter your contact information (see Figure 35-5).

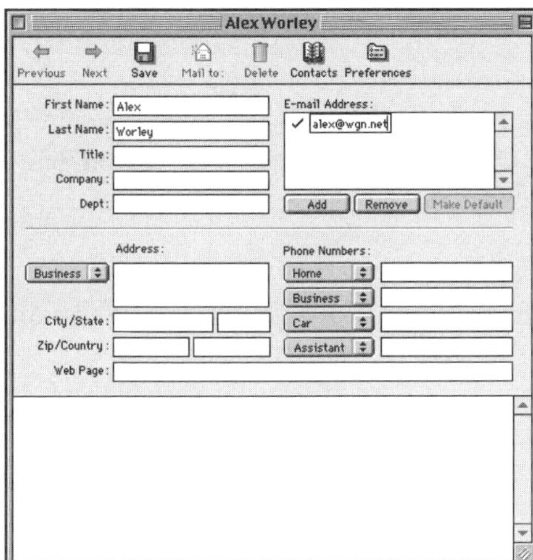

Figure 35-5: The Contact window as a contact is being entered

Enter information in the Contact window as you do in any other window. Type, paste, or drag the data into the appropriate field. Press Tab to move to the next field or Shift-Tab to move backwards. Of course, you can also click in any field to enter information into it. You can also select text to copy or delete it.

The Contact window is fairly straightforward. Pop-up menus provide options at times. Click in any pop-up menu to select your best choice. The large area at the bottom of the menu is for notes. The E-mail Address area bears some explaining, however. This area is capable of storing several e-mail addresses for one person. The first time you tab or click here, a check mark appears along with a text box with an insertion point. Just type your address as normal. To add another address, either click the Add button or click below the existing address. When you have more than one address, you must choose one to be the default. Click the desired address and click Make Default, or, as a shortcut, just click in the check mark area of the desired address.

When you're finished entering new contact information (or editing an existing contact), you can click the Save button or use ⌘-S to save the contact before closing the window. However, in case you don't remember, a dialog box will ask if you want to save your information or changes.

If you are entering your contacts manually, as opposed to importing them, just enter the ones to which you are sending a message right away. That way you can wait until you receive e-mail from your other contacts and add them the easy way. As you receive each e-mail, if you want to add the sender to your contact list, click the message in the Message list and then click the Add Contact button. The sender is invisibly added to your Contact list. Alternatively, you can Control-click any message and select Add Sender To Contacts from the shortcut menu.

Importing contacts

If you are already using an e-mail application, you probably have an ton of e-mail addresses already listed. Rather than entering all that information again, you can import those addresses into Outlook Express. Follow these steps:

1. Open your current e-mail application.
2. Export your contacts per that application's export method. (For example, from Claris E-mailer select File ⇨ Export.)

   If you are exporting from a regular address book, export the file as text. If you have the ability to control the order in which the fields are exported, match the order to that of Outlook Express.
3. Select File ⇨ Import ⇨ Contacts, and then select the list you just exported. As you import, if Outlook Express comes across a name that already exists, you are asked if you'd like to add this redundant name or replace the one already in Outlook Express.

You can also import your contact information from another contact manager into the Outlook Express address book. However, if your current contact manager accommodates more information, that may not be appropriate. For example, Apple's Claris Organizer, Now Contact, and ACT manage dual addresses and business contact information as well as store e-mail addresses. The cool thing is that each program can be set to launch Outlook Express, so you can keep one of these as your contact manager and also take advantage of Outlook Express. When you click an e-mail address in Organizer, Now Contact, or ACT, you're automatically taken to a new e-mail page that already contains the recipient's name and address.

Viewing contacts

You have two ways to see your contact list (see Figure 35-6):

✦ Click Contacts in the folder pane on the left of your window. Your list of contacts opens in the Outlook Express window.

✦ Click the Contacts button in the toolbar. This opens the same list, but as a separate window.

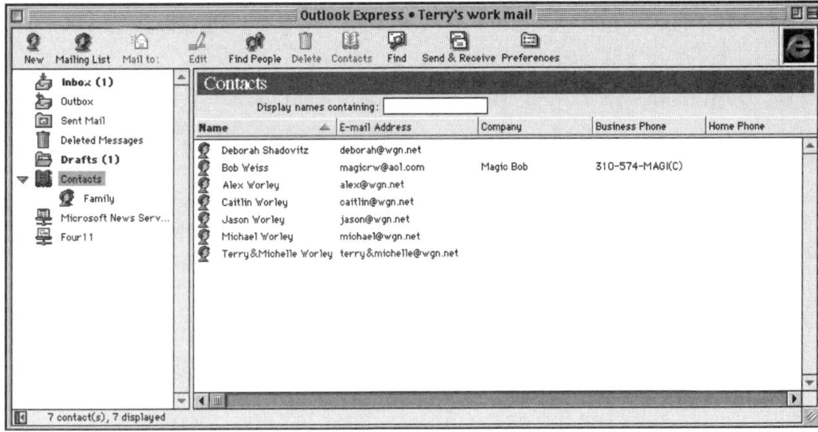

Figure 35-6: Viewing contacts within the Outlook Express window

Deleting contacts

Click the contact and click the Delete button. A dialog box message asks whether you really want to delete the message. Click Yes. To avoid the confirmation message, press Option as you click the Delete button.

Creating mailing lists

One of the most powerful (and simple) things you can do in Outlook Express is create a mailing list. A mailing list is simply a selection of your contacts that are grouped together for whatever reason you may have. Rather than individually adding the names of tons of people as message recipients, you just enter the list name.

Another advantage of using a mailing list is the ability to suppress the recipient's names when you send your message. That way you don't publicize recipients' addresses. There's another benefit, too. Have you ever been one of several recipients and had to endure a bombardment of unwanted messages and complaints when one recipient failed to respond to the sender only and responded to every original recipient? By suppressing your recipient's names, any replies come back only to you.

The same contact can be part of many lists. Names can be added or deleted at any time, and the cool thing is that it's almost all done by dragging.

To create a mailing list, follow these steps:

1. Select File➪New➪Mailing List. The Contacts window opens if it's not already open, and your new list appears as a subfolder of your Contacts folder.
2. The default list name (untitled) is preselected, so you don't have to click anywhere. Just type a short descriptive name for your list.
3. Click your main contacts list to draw your list names from it.
4. Select the name(s) you want for your list using any comfortable method, and then drag the names to the new list's icon, as shown in Figure 35-7.

   To select a contiguous range, click the first message or contact, and then press Shift as you click the last message or contact to be selected. To select non-contiguous messages or contacts, click the first message or contact, and then press ⌘ as you click the next message or contact to be selected. You can also use the list filter at the top of the list window to display only certain names or messages.
5. (Optional) To hide your recipient's names from other recipients, double-click the list name in the Folder list. A dedicated list window opens that contains the Hide recipient names option. Check this check box if desired. (You can always click the list name in the Folder list and check or uncheck this option.)

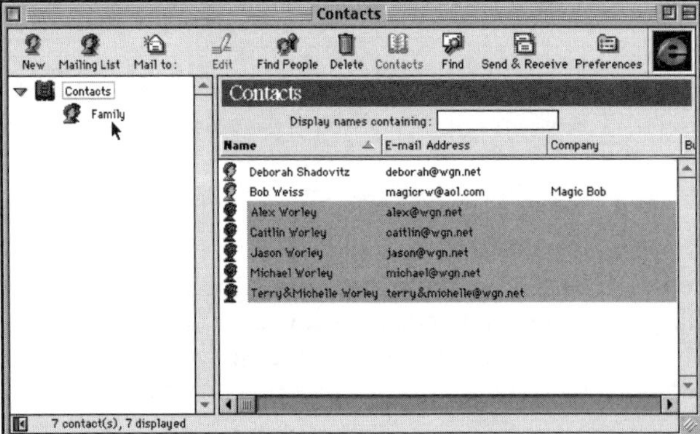

Figure 35-7: Dragging contacts to a mailing list called Family

The names in the mailing list are actually aliases. Therefore, you can delete a name from a list without really removing the contact. The easiest way to delete a name is to select it—from the mailing list, not from the "real" Contact list—and then press Delete or click the Delete button. Notice that when you are asked for confirmation, the message asks whether you want to delete from the mailing list, not from the Contact list.

Working with Messages

Your messages can take either of two forms: plain text or HTML. Plain text is just that; there is no fancy formatting—only spaces and characters. Plain text messages can be read by anyone on any computer, old or new, with any e-mail software. HTML format provides the capability to use text formatting, color, and such, as with the Web pages that have made the World Wide Web so popular. Outlook Express does its best to give you the best of both worlds. You can create your messages using the Rich Text (HTML) formatting, as is done in Figure 35-8. When the message is received, most e-mail software reads and presents the Rich Text formatting or presents a plain-text version (perhaps attaching the HTML version). In case you don't want to risk the recipient's ability to recognize Rich Text (HTML) formatting or switch to plain text, you can switch off HTML prior to sending the message by choosing Format➪Rich Text (HTML).

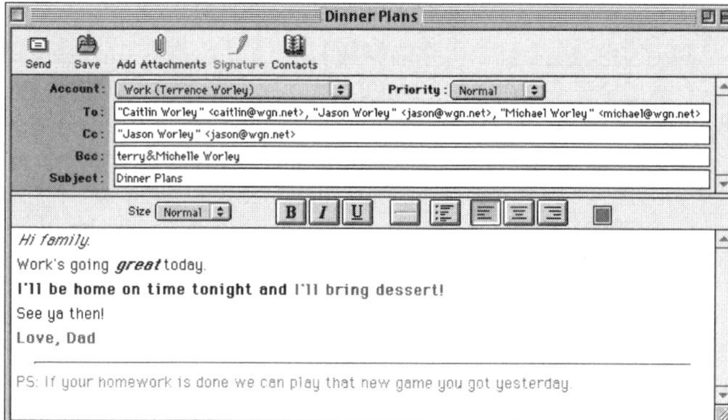

Figure 35-8: A Rich Text (HTML) message in the message creation window

Creating a message

Creating a new e-mail message is almost just like creating any new document. Simply select File➪New and then, because you also have the option of creating new contacts or folders, slide over to New Message. Alternatively, you can press ⌘-Option-N. If you're viewing the contents of a folder, you can also use the ⌘-N keyboard shortcut.

Don't forget to save your work as you create it. You can press the Save button in the message composition window's toolbar, or you can select File➪Save (⌘-S). All begun but unsent messages are stored in the Drafts folder when you save them. You can come back to work on any message in this folder until you send it.

Addressing a message

Reflecting the common style of sending business letters, Outlook Express lets you send your message to (To) a person or persons, send a (carbon) copy (Cc) to a person or persons, and send a blind (carbon) copy (Bcc) to others still. As demonstrated in Figure 35-8, each new message window has an area to enter all these recipients. When a message is a blind carbon copy, the other recipients don't see the Bcc recipient's name or address in the recipient list.

There are several ways to enter the e-mail addresses of your recipients:

✦ You can type the address if you have it handy and feel like typing. This way is best if your contact with the recipient(s) is a one-time effort.

✦ If you have entered your recipient in your Contacts list, you can begin typing the recipient's name. As Outlook Express matches the letters you type, it AutoFills the name for you. If the match is correct, stop typing. If not, keep typing. Outlook Express will guess again as it can.

Speed tip: To add another name, type a comma while the AutoFilled name is still highlighted. This automatically takes you to the end of the name and places a comma to prepare for the next name.

✦ If you have created a mailing list, begin typing the list's name. AutoFill will probably finish typing it before you do. (Remember the benefit of suppressing the recipient list: easy addressing, respect of recipient's privacy, and prevention of readers from replying to the entire group along with a response to you.)

✦ If you have entered your recipient in your Contacts list, you can also view the Contacts list and drag the contact from the Folder list pane into the To, Cc, or Bcc area of your message.

✦ You can use drag-and-drop to drag a name and/or address from the body of another e-mail or other document into place on your new message. (When you select the name or address to be dragged, your cursor turns into a hand. When you click the mouse to drag, the hand "grabs" the text to drag it.)

✦ You can copy the address from any other source and paste it into the appropriate addressee field.

If you are using an organizer, such as Apple's Claris Organizer or Now Contact, click the appropriate icon in the organizer and let it address your e-mail for you. In fact, you won't need to start your e-mail message in Outlook Express because the organizer application will start the message for you as well as address it automatically.

✦ To begin your new message and address it to the primary recipient(s) at the same time, select your contact(s) or mailing list and then click the Mail To button.

In each of the previous cases, if you have more than one recipient to send To, Cc, or Bcc, type a comma or semicolon between each recipient, as shown in Figure 35-8.

Hot Stuff

After you define a mailing list, you can create a message and address it to everyone on the list with just two clicks. Simply control-click the list name in the Folder list and select Mail To, or click the list name once in the Folder list and click the Mail To button.

Formatting your message

By sending your messages in HTML, you can create appealing, emphatic, or even decorative messages. Formatting your message is easy. If you've already used Word or just about any other word processor on the Mac, you already know how. All you need to do is select the text to be formatted, and then click the formatting buttons at the top of the message window or choose the formatting commands from the Format menu.

If you don't see buttons you are in plain-text mode. To switch, select Format ⇨ Rich Text (HTML).

Outlook Express's Rich Text (HTML) allows for all the standard text document formatting: font size, bold, italic, underline, align text left, center text, and align text right. You can also create a bulleted list and change text color. Additionally, as this is actually an HTML document after all, you can add what is known in Web page design as a *horizontal rule* (a line drawn horizontally across the page), and you can apply text emphasis by using HTML headers.

If your recipient's e-mail program doesn't read HTML-formatted e-mail, the document should appear in plain text, perhaps with the HMTL code as an attached file. However, sometimes an Internet gateway or the e-mail reader can't handle the HTML version and doesn't discriminate to display the plain text version. In that case, the recipient may end up viewing the raw HTML code. If you're not sure whether your recipient's e-mail program can appreciate an HTML-formatted e-mail, perhaps it's not a good idea to send it in this format. You might want to try a test among friends and associates.

Figure 35-8 showed you a message in Rich Text (HTML). Figure 35-9 shows a message with Rich Text (HTML) deselected.

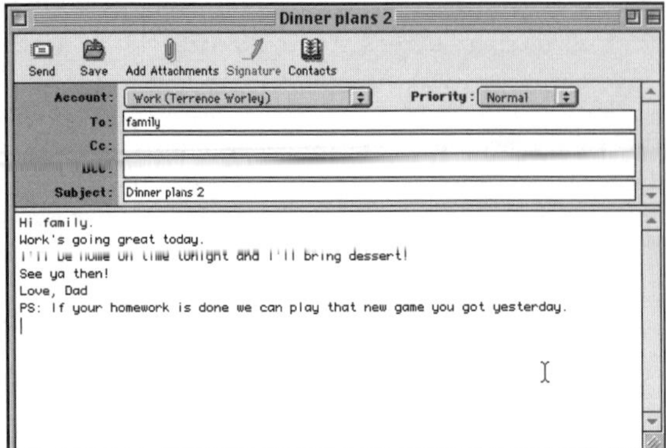

Figure 35-9: A plain text message in the message creation window

Attaching files to a message

An attached file is a document that gets sent along with your message. For example, while writing this book, we wrote each chapter as a Word document and sent chapters one or two at a time as attachments via e-mail. There are two ways to attach a file:

✦ Open the folder that contains your attachment and drag it onto the message window. You can select multiple items and drag them all at once, too.

✦ Click the Add Attachment button in the message window, and then navigate to the document, select it, and click Add. If you want to attach the entire contents of a folder, open that folder and then click Add All. Added attachments are reported in the bottom of the Open dialog box.

Attachments show up in the lower part of your message window or are noted below the subject line.

If you decide you don't want to send the attachment, click it once in the message window to select it, and then choose Edit⇨Clear. To select all the attachments, click one, choose Select All (⌘-A), and then choose Edit⇨Clear.

When you send your message, all attachments are encoded and prepared for transit. Several types of such encoding can be used. By default, the encoding used is BinHex, the method preferred when the recipient is on a Mac. However, when the recipient is on a Windows machine, Base64, the basic MIME encoding format, is a better encoding process. The method you use is set in Preferences. You can check this or change it by choosing Edit⇨Preferences, selecting Message Composition, and then noting the pop-up next to Attachment encoding.

You can send a Word, Excel, or PowerPoint document from within that document. With the document open, select File ➪ Send to ➪ Mail Recipient. Outlook Express launches, starts a new outgoing message, and attaches your document automatically. (You'll see its icon in the attachments section of the message window.) All you need to do is address the message and compose the message body text as normal, and then send it.

Adding a signature

To create your signature, select Edit ➪ Preferences, select Message Composition, and then type or paste your signature text into the large text area at the bottom of this preference window. If you want your signature added to each new message by default, check Automatically add this signature to all messages—the option above the signature text area. If you prefer not to always add the signature, you can add your signature to any message by clicking the Signature button or selecting Format ➪ Insert Signature. Figure 35-10 shows you a message that has a signature. When this message is viewed by the recipient, the e-mail address and Web site will be live links. These live links would also show in the Preview pane if the sender previewed this outgoing message.

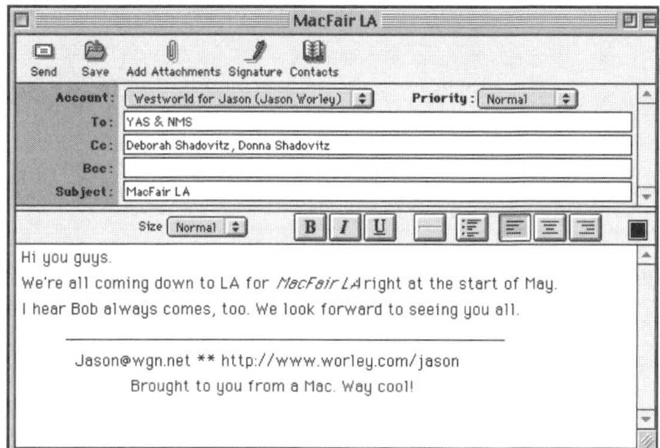

Figure 35-10: An outgoing message with a signature

Outlook Express installs and supports Internet Config, a popular extension that provides across-the-board settings. With Internet Config, you can have multiple signatures and generate them at random. However, Internet Config is beyond the scope of this book.

As of this writing, the text area provided for entering your signature is narrower than the width of a common e-mail message and not a comfortable place in which to compose your signature. This may change by the time you read this, so you may be provided with a nice full window and (Rich Text) HTML-mode formatting controls. If it hasn't changed, you'll find it easiest to compose your signature in a regular message window, and then copy it and paste it into the signature text box.

Quoting another message or other text

In the world of e-mail it has become common practice to quote the text of a message you are responding to, and then respond to each line, sentence, topic, or such below the quoted text. That way, your recipient is reminded of the conversation you two are having and can consider your responses in context. The common quote character of the day is >, so a quoted sentence and its response might look like this:

```
>Hi Auntie Donna. Can we come play on your Mac and swim on
Sunday?
That's the best idea ever! Bring Auntie Deborah too!
```

If you do not have a quote indicator, select Edit ➪ Preferences, click Message Composition, and look for quote options there. (In the first release, version 4.0, you must enter the character in the text field next to Quote plain text message using. In subsequent releases, the greater-than sign [>] is standard and options are different.)

You have two ways to apply your quote character to text. One is to select that text in an e-mail message before you click Reply. The other is to copy text from any source, and then place your insertion point in your outgoing message and select Edit ➪ Paste As Quotation. See "Replying to a message" for more details.

Sending a message

After you compose your message, you can click the Send button at the top of the button bar while you're in the message composition window. If you are composing and responding to several messages, you may opt to save the message first and then connect and send all your messages at the same time when you're finished composing. Either way, all saved and unsent messages are stored in the Drafts folder by default. They remain there until you click the Send button in the message composition window.

Rather than sending each message as you complete it, you can send all your outgoing messages at the same time. Select Tools ➪ Send & Receive ➪ Send All. Another option is to receive your new incoming e-mail at the same time you send your outgoing messages. Either click the Send & Receive button on the toolbar or select Tools ➪ Send & Receive ➪ Send & Receive All. We discuss this option further in the next section.

As you send or receive messages, a Progress dialog box lets you know what's happening, as shown in Figure 35-11. It informs you when it logs on, checks for messages, gets messages, sends messages, and so on.

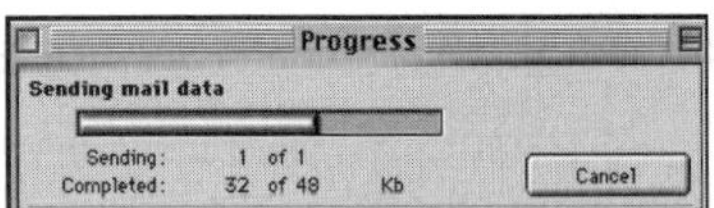

Figure 35-11: The Progress dialog box as a message is sent

Receiving and reading messages

Depending on whether you have a regular POP account (which is typical for the home user and non-business user) or an IMAP account (which is common in large businesses), you will either download your messages or read them on the server. We cover both procedures in the following sections, so you can read only the section that pertains to you.

With a POP account

If you have a POP account, you will be connecting to your ISP only long enough to download your messages (and send any outgoing messages, too). You can disconnect after you've downloaded your e-mail. That way, you can read your mail, respond at your leisure, and then connect again when you're ready to send your reply (and download any new messages that have come in for you).

To send your outgoing messages and receive your new incoming e-mail at the same time, just click the Send & Receive button on the toolbar. Or, if you prefer, select Tools ⇨ Send & Receive and then choose an option from the Send & Receive submenu. If you have only one account, as most people, both options are the same. If you have multiple accounts, you may prefer to exchange your messages from only one account at any time. The Tools menu provides this flexibility. Select Tools ⇨ Send & Receive, and then select one specific account from the bottom part of the Send & Receive submenu. (All your accounts appear under this submenu.)

Perhaps you have more than one account but like to check only one of the accounts. To make life easier, you can exclude any account(s) from the Send & Receive All command. Select Edit ⇨ Preferences and click E-mail, and then select your account and click Advanced. Place a check mark next to Do not include this server with Send & Receive All. By selecting this preference, you can use the Send & Receive button to collect mail on a regular basis, and the Tools menu command to check mail at the excluded account on demand.

Another option is to receive your messages without sending any. Select Tools ⇨ Send & Receive ⇨ Receive All. This collects all your messages from all your accounts.

If you take advantage of this option, be sure not to abuse it. Leaving all your mail on the server causes the ISP to need more servers and drives up the cost of service for everyone. Your ISP may limit the amount of space you can use for storing your messages on the server, or it may ask you to purge them from time to time.

After you've downloaded your messages, you can read them. Unless you've set up a mail filter (Inbox Rule), your messages land in the Inbox. You can tell you have unread mail when the folder name appears in boldface and the number of unread messages appears in parentheses next to the name. Click the Inbox folder to reveal the headers of each message in the Message list to the right of the window. You have two options for viewing any message. If you click the message in the Message list to select it, the message appears in the Preview pane (if the pane is showing).

See Figure 35-12, which shows a Rich Text (HTML) message, marked as high priority. If you prefer to view a message in a larger area, double-click the message in the Message list. The message opens in its own window. If you've opened the message as a separate window, click the close box the same as you close any Mac window when you're finished looking at it.

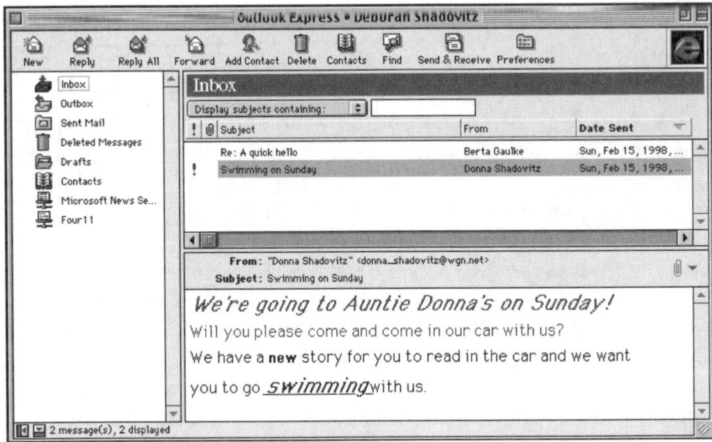

Figure 35-12: A received message being read in the Preview pane

With an IMAP account

If your e-mail is on an IMAP server, you don't download your messages to read them. Instead, you deal with messages completely while connected to the server and read the messages directly from the server. Outlook Express merely caches the message to your hard disk. (A *cache* is a temporary file. You have no control over when it will be replaced, and when the message the cache pertains to is deleted from the server, it is gone.)

Keeping the Original Message

By default, when you download a message, it is deleted from your ISP's mail server so it doesn't use up space unnecessarily. In some cases, however, such as when you are checking your e-mail from someone else's computer, you may want to keep the original message on the server so you can download it again later and have it on your own Mac.

Click the Preferences button or select Edit ➪ Preferences. Then click E-mail, select your account, and click Advanced. Place a check mark next to Leave a copy of messages on server. While you're at it, click Do not download previously received mail. Otherwise, each time you collect your mail, you will be sent every message on the server again, ending up with multiple copies of each message. Remember, you don't want to set these preferences on your own Mac. Set them on the computer you are borrowing to check your e-mail.

Before you can view your e-mail, you have to subscribe to the folders you have the option of seeing. There's a good chance your MIS person will do this for you or show you how, providing company-specific instructions. Basically, you click the server icon after setting it up. This connects you to the mail server and automatically provides a complete list of available folders. Click any unsubscribed folder to which you want access, and then click the Subscribe button in the toolbar. The full list of folders appears in the list on the right, while currently subscribed folders appear in the Folder list on the left.

You can update your list of available folders at any time. Click the server icon to connect to the mail server, and then choose View ⇨ Get Complete Folder List to get the list of available folders.

To view your e-mail, click the account's icon in the Folder list. (If you have access to more than one folder on the server, click the arrow next to the account's icon to reveal those folders. Then click the folder you want to view.) Your connection to the server opens (if it's not already open), and you see the subject of each message on the right side of your window. To read a message in the Preview pane, click the subject once. To see it in a larger, separate window, double-click the message subject.

While you are connected, more new messages may arrive. To check, click the folder to select it and then choose View ⇨ Refresh Folder Messages.

It is important to realize that messages you read from the server are *not* on your hard drive. If a message is important to you, you must save it to your own server-based folder or your hard drive, or the message can disappear without warning. To save a message to your own server-based folder, drag it from the Message list to your own folder, which appears in your Folder list. To save a message to your own hard drive, drag it from the Message list into a folder you've created on your hard drive. Folders on your hard drive appear between the Drafts folder and the Contacts folder. Folders on your server appear under your server icon when you click the triangle next to the server's icon.

From a POP account online

Outlook Express provides the capability to set up online access for POP accounts so you can access them from any computer without having to download the messages. More accurately, you can view the subject, from, sent, size, date, to, and account information—or message headers. To actually read the message you must download it. This type of access, however, saves you from unnecessarily downloading messages that aren't of interest at that particular time. It also enables you to delete any unwanted messages from the server without ever downloading them.

To connect online, click the account icon in the Folder list. But, if you connect while the Preview pane is open in your Outlook Express window, Outlook Express assumes you want to download the selected message and sends it to you. This defeats the idea behind online access. If the Preview pane is open, click the second icon in the lower-left corner of the window. (The icon depicts the Preview pane area.) Alternatively, you can select View➪Preview pane to close it. This menu command is a toggle. A check mark by the command indicates the pane is active.

To refresh your Message list in case any new messages have arrived while you were online, select View➪Refresh Message List.

To read any message of interest, double-click the message in the Message list. A full message window opens and downloads the message.

If you're curious as to what route a message took to get to you or when it was sent, you can reveal its Internet header. If you always want to see these headers, set your preferences. Choose Edit➪Preferences and then select Display and check Show Internet Headers. If you are just curious about one message here and there, while the message is being viewed, select View➪Internet Headers.

Making attachments

When a document contains an attachment, the paper clip icon located above the message has an arrow beside it. Click that arrow and choose the attachment you want to view. The attachment automatically opens if your preferences already name the necessary file helper. (Several helpers are set by default.) If Outlook Express doesn't know which file helper to use, it offers you the opportunity to select an application (via a dialog box). Otherwise you can save and file the attachment for later, or you can save the message so you can open or save the attachment later.

When GIF or JPEG images are sent to you as attachments, they should automatically appear in your message by default. If they don't, choose Edit➪Preferences, click Display, and then check the option Show attached pictures in messages. This feature uses Apple's QuickTime, so you need to have the QuickTime extension turned on for it to work. Figure 35-13 displays a plain text message sent with a JPEG attachment as the message is viewed in the Preview pane.

About file helpers

File helpers are actually regular software programs. They are simply applications elected to be automatically called into play when the associated file type is called on—for instance, when you click the arrow next to the paper clip (see Figure 35-14) and select an attachment to view. To assign a file type to a file helper, choose Edit➪Preferences and then click File Helpers. If you have an application that works as a helper, it appears in full color in the list. If you don't have the default application, that default is grayed out. You can assign your own helpers by clicking Add, and you can change a helper by clicking Change. Click Delete to delete a helper.

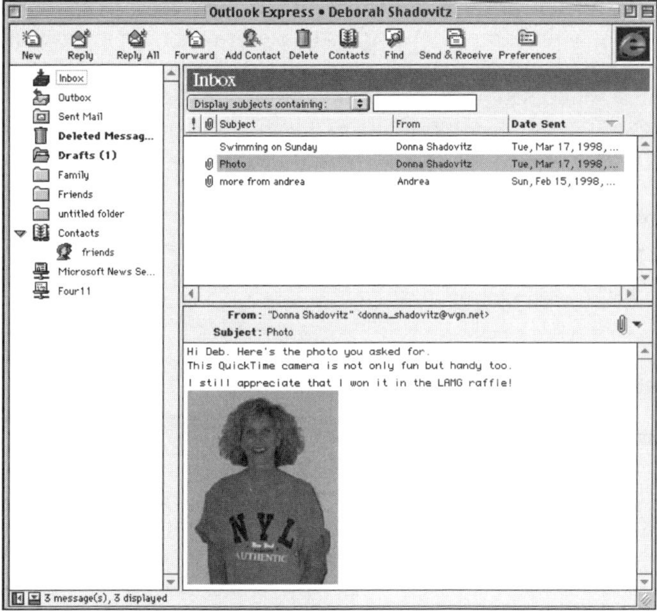

Figure 35-13: A received plain text message with a JPEG image attached

When you click the arrow next to the paper clip, if you see a Save dialog box instead of having your files open for viewing, either you don't have a File Helper assigned to that file type or you have the necessary preference turned off. To turn it back on, choose Edit ➪ Preferences, click Send & Receive, and check Use File Helpers To View File Attachments. You can also still view an attachment when this option is off by pressing Option as you select the attachment. This has the effect of temporarily turning on the option so the Helper can function for you.

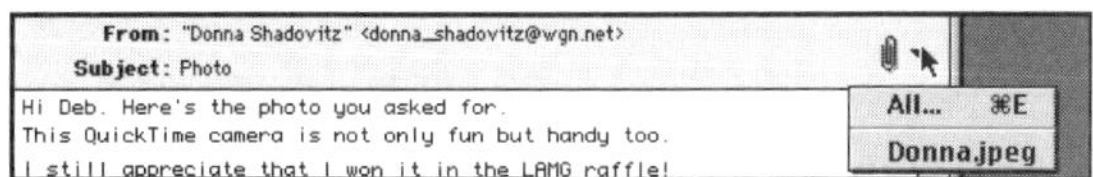

Figure 35-14: Selecting an attachment for viewing or saving

Saving file attachments

As you are viewing a message, either in the Preview pane or in its own window, you can save any attachments that came along with the message. Simply select Message ➪ Save Attachment and choose the attachment, or select Message ➪ Save All Attachments. As with any saving you do on the Mac, you should navigate to the target folder before clicking Save.

Attachments are typically compressed and encoded in order to travel the Internet. Outlook Express decodes your attachments. (That takes care of the mysterious .hqx extension on the filename.) Outlook Express continues to decode your document unless it is stuffed with Aladdin's StuffIt—a popular compression program. In that case, Aladdin's freeware decompression utility—StuffIt Expander—does the job (taking care of the .sit or .sea part of the filename). Depending on the options you set in StuffIt Expander, the document unstuffs and lands in the same folder as the download, or it requests your attention and asks where you want the file to decompress. StuffIt Expander is also available from `www.Aladdinsys.com`. Just place it on your hard drive, and Outlook Express will recognize it as a helper. StuffIt Expander is a must-have for all Mac owners and Mac BBS or Internet users.

Printing a message

You can print a message while it is open in its own window or while it is simply selected (clicked on) in the Message list. The latter offers the advantage of allowing you to print more than one message at a time because you can select more than one message at a time in the Message list. Press Shift to select a range of messages, or press ⌘ to select messages that are not next to each other in the list. After making your selection (or with a single message window open), select File⇨Print or press ⌘-P as usual. From there it's printing as normal.

Saving a message

When you file a message in any folder in your Folder list, you save it. You can only read messages in these folders, however, when you have Outlook Express open. Sometimes you'll want to save a message as a SimpleText document so you can pass it along to others. Open the message in its own window by double-clicking it in the Message list. Then select File⇨Save As. Navigate to the destination folder (or click Desktop), name your document, and then click Save.

Replying to a message

To reply to a message you basically just click Reply and type your response, and then you handle it the same as any other outgoing e-mail. The common practice with e-mail, however, is to "quote" the message you receive and add your response beneath the quoted text. That's the e-mail equivalent to having a conversation and addressing each subject as it is talked about. The common quote character of the day is the greater-than symbol (>), which is located on the same key as the period.

If you are using the first version of Outlook Express (version 4.0), you need to set up a quote character in the Message Composition area of Preferences. Just type a > in the empty text field next to Quote plain text message using.

Future revisions of Outlook Express standardize on the commonly used greater-than symbol and will add the capability to visualize quotes and quotes of quotes in color. Check the Composition area of Preferences to discover your options.

The message shown in Figure 35-15 has gone back and forth several times, so a trace of two previous exchanges is displayed. Berta is being quoted where there is one quote character because this text is being sent back to Berta and she had the most recent new text. Where there is a double quote character at the start of a paragraph, the sender is quoting Berta, who is quoting the sender from the previous message. The newest words are on the lines that have no quotation marks. Remember, you may have the option of seeing not only double greater-than symbols but also color-coding.

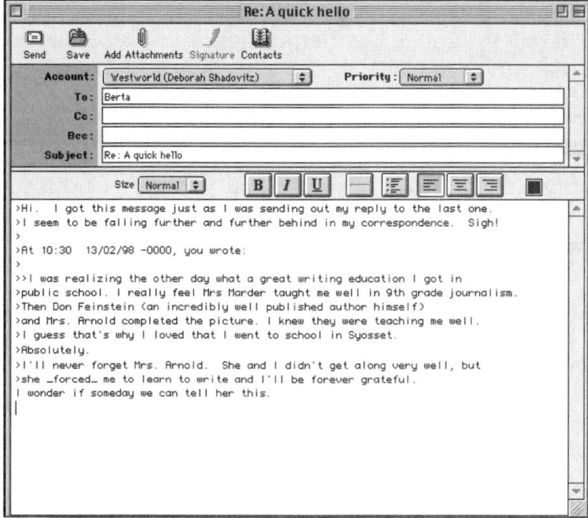

Figure 35-15: A reply being composed

You should also consider whether your correspondent's e-mail program recognizes Rich Text (HTML) formatting or at least knows to discard the HTML message and deliver the plain text version. This is discussed in the "Working with Messages" section. One step you can take to ensure smooth e-mailing is to select Edit ⇨ Preferences, choose Message Composition, and then check Reply to messages using the format in which they were sent. Outlook Express will then look at the incoming message and respond in kind.

When you respond, you may want to quote the entire letter you're responding to, or just a part of it. If you've set up a quote character, when you click the Reply or Reply All button, the entire message is quoted in your new reply. If you select specific text, only that text will be quoted. There's a trick you can use if you want to quote noncontiguous sections of text. Select the first section and click a reply button. After the new outgoing document opens, return to the incoming message and select and copy the next section to be quoted. Then click back in the outgoing message, place the insertion point, and choose Edit ⇨ Paste as Quotation. You can do this as many times as you like. You can also use the Paste as Quotation command to paste in text you copy from anywhere on your Mac.

You may notice there are two reply buttons: Reply and Reply All. If your incoming message was sent only to you, it doesn't matter which button you click. If the message was sent to several people, however, you definitely want to be sure you reply only to the sender—unless you really want all other recipients of the incoming message to see your response. If the message sent to you says Recipient list suppressed, you can simply reply to the sender and the other recipients should not receive your response. It is usually better to be safe than sorry, however, and you should get into the habit of replying wisely. We recommend you click Reply when you want to reply only to the sender. Should the message come from a list (which is a group correspondence), watch the results of clicking Reply. This may address your message to the sender, but it may also address it to the entire list. Instead of clicking buttons, you can use the Message➪Reply to Sender or Message➪Reply to All commands or their keyboard equivalents, as noted in the command menu.

When you use either Reply button to create your response, the subject of the incoming note is copied to your response and *Re:* is appended to it. This creates a thread and helps you identify your messages. Some e-mail software enables users to follow the thread via buttons, as Outlook Express does with Newsgroups. It is considered impolite to rename a message to which you are replying. If you change the topic within the body of your reply, however, you might change the subject line so people can see that the original discussion has changed direction. It is common to place the original subject in brackets ([ ]) after the new subject . For example, "Re: Office 98 meeting [was LAMG]." Get used to e-mail and notice proper practices before you begin renaming responses.

When you reply to a message, any attachments that came with the original message are removed, so they are not unnecessarily bandied back and forth.

Forwarding a message

After you read a message, you may want to send it to another person. This is called *forwarding* the message. To forward a message, click the Forward button in the toolbar or select Message➪Forward. A new message window opens, complete with the entire message; the From, Date, To, and Subject information; and any attachments included originally. The insertion point waits for you in the new To field so you can address the message. The Subject line is automatically filled in with the original message name preceded by *FW:*, indicating the message is being forwarded. You can change the subject if you like. In the message body a dotted line is added one line down. This line enables you to place the cursor in the blank top line and compose a note to the recipient. When you're ready, send the new message the same way you send any other message.

By default the body of a forwarded message appears in its original form. Some people prefer to have quotation marks appear to designate that the message wasn't composed by them. If you want quotation marks, select Edit➪Preferences, click Message Composition, and then check Use quoting characters when forwarding.

Deleting messages

It's not always necessary to keep a message. After a while even the largest hard drives get crowded, so we thought we'd better tell you how to get rid of some of your messages.

From your hard drive

If your messages are on your hard drive, you have several ways to delete them. You can click any message in the Folder list and then either choose Edit ⇨ Delete Message, press ⌘-D, click the Delete button, or press the Delete key. Each method moves the message to the Deleted Messages folder without confirmation. You can also drag any message or messages from the Folder list pane to the Trash can, which is labeled Deleted Messages and is located in the Folder list. To provide feedback about what you are deleting, if the Trash can holds any unread messages, its label appears in boldface and the number of unread messages to be deleted appears next to it in parentheses.

Messages remain in the Deleted Messages folder until you Control-click the trash icon in the Folder list and select Empty Deleted Messages, or you select Edit ⇨ Empty Deleted Messages to empty this folder. For an extra measure of safety, you must confirm this action. If you prefer to turn off the confirmation dialog box, select Edit ⇨ Preferences and choose General (the first option). You can also set the trash to empty whenever you quit Outlook Express by selecting Edit ⇨ Preferences, selecting Startup & Quit, and then checking Empty Deleted Messages Folder.

If you decide you don't want to delete a message after all, and the message is still in the Deleted Messages folder, you can open that folder (click it) and drag the message to any other folder. After you empty the Deleted Messages folder, the message is not retrievable.

From an IMAP server

If you are accessing your message from an IMAP server, you don't actually delete the message immediately but rather mark the message for deletion. To mark a message, select the message in the Message list and click the Delete button (trash can) or use any of the other deletion methods previously mentioned. The marked message appears with a line struck though it. (If you are using version 4.0 as opposed to 4.0.1 or above, the message appears in italics.) If you select Hide deleted IMAP messages in the General area of Preferences, messages marked for deletion do not appear at all. The number at the bottom of the window indicates how many deleted messages exist.

If you are accessing your messages live on the server and you've marked one for deletion, you can change your mind by selecting the message and choosing Edit ➪ Undelete. If you've already deleted the message, however, it's gone and you're out of luck.

When you are certain you absolutely don't want to keep messages any longer, you can purge them from the server. You purge folder by folder or the entire account rather than message by message. Click the account icon or the folder you want to purge. Then choose Edit ➪ Purge Deleted Items.

While online with a POP server

If you have a POP server and are viewing your messages online, click any message in the list to select it and then either choose Edit ➪ Delete Message, press ⌘-D, click the Delete button, or press the Delete key. Unless you've disabled deletion warnings, a dialog box asks whether you want to delete the message and reminds you that this deletion can't be undone. When you click Yes, Outlook Express sends the message directly to the server and the message is removed immediately.

Filing your messages

The first step to organizing your messages is to create folders. As with the file cabinets in your office or home, or with the folders on your Mac, use whatever filing system works best for you. Typically users organize files by project, category, or topic. You may even file news list messages into a folder along with "regular" e-mail if the topic matches.

You can create a new folder at any time—it's never too late—by selecting File ➪ New ➪ Folder (⌘-Shift-N). It's a good idea to begin by giving yourself a few basic folders, so you may want to try that now to get the hang of it.

To create a new folder on your hard drive, follow these steps:

1. Select File ➪ New ➪ Folder (⌘-Shift-N) or Control-click any existing folder (Drafts or Inbox are your choices to start with) and select New Folder from the shortcut menu. This method is shown in Figure 35-16. The new folder appears in the Folder list. Just like in the Mac Finder, the new folder is named *untitled folder* and the name is preselected so you can easily name it.

   The Outlook Express window does not have to be open to choose File ➪ New ➪ Folder (⌘-Shift-N), but it is less confusing to have it open when you do.

2. Without clicking anywhere, type the name for your new folder. As in the Mac Finder, the name you type replaces the words *untitled folder*. When you finish typing, press Return or Enter to set the name, or click anywhere but on the folder's name.

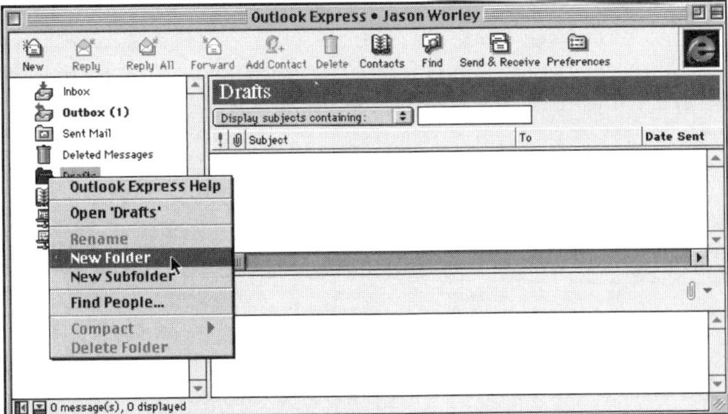

Figure 35-16: Control-clicking to create a new folder on the hard drive

To create a new subfolder within a folder, Control-click the folder you want the subfolder to land in and select New Subfolder from the shortcut menu. Alternatively, click the folder you want the subfolder to land in and then select File ⇨ New ⇨ Subfolder. The subfolder appears with the generic name preselected just like a main-level folder. Type the new name and press Return or Enter to set the name, or click anywhere but on the folder's name.

As with the Mac's Finder, you can easily rename a folder at any time. You do this the same way you do in the Finder—click the folder's name to select it and then type the new name.

After you have begun to create folders, you can begin to file your mail. Filing is easy. All you do is click a message and drag it to the folder of choice. Files can be moved from any folder to any other folder at any time. How's that for flexibility? Simply view a folder's contents so you see the message's name, and then drag the message to the new folder. Your messages can also be set up for automatic filing based on a set of criteria. Outlook Express calls this criteria *Inbox Rules*.

If you are creating folders on your IMAP server, you will see an extra dialog box in which you name your folder (as opposed to naming the folder as you name any other Mac folder). If you are unsure whether your folder has landed on the server or your hard drive, note its location. If the folder is on the server, it appears below the server icon. If the folder is on the hard drive, it appears between the Drafts folder and the Contacts list.

Automating your incoming mail

Some people find life easier when certain mail gets filed automatically. For example, if you subscribe to a list about magic but it's just a hobby, it's easier to have all those list messages go directly into a folder called Magic. Then, when you have time, you can click the Magic folder and read through the messages.

Meanwhile, the messages are out of the way rather than clogging up your Inbox, preventing you from easily noticing more important messages or, at least, more timely messages. Then perhaps you want to keep other important messages in the Inbox to make sure you act on them. As your Inbox gets full, however, you may find it difficult to notice this important mail among your numerous, plain-black messages. Maybe you even have some not-so-timely mail you'd like to identify. To accommodate easy mail identification, you can assign a color code to your messages. For example, messages about your current work project can be assigned a bright red, while notes from your family and friends can be made light blue.

Before you can set up an automatic message filter, you need to identify some characteristics with which to filter your mail. For example, if all messages from Dexter Horthy are about your current project, you can use the name Dexter Horthy as a criterion (see Figure 35-17). If all messages from your client's domain name are about the project, use the domain name as the filter (shown in Figure 35-17). If you're really lucky, all of you involved with the project have agreed to place a word or project code in the subject line, so that's all you need for the criteria.

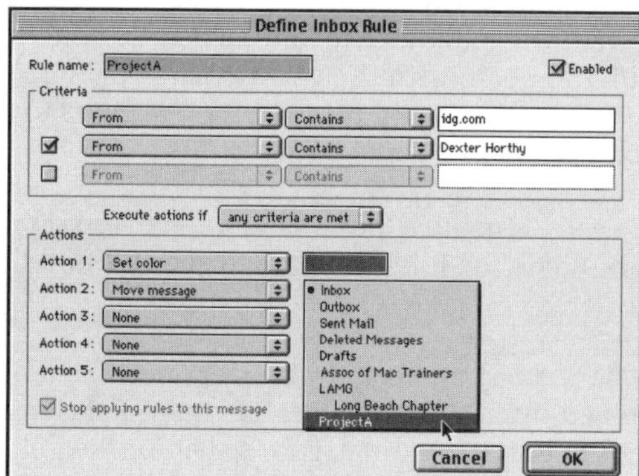

Figure 35-17: The Define Inbox Rule dialog box

When you have some criteria in mind, you can set up the filter by following these steps:

1. Choose Tools ⇨ Inbox Rules to open the Inbox Rules window.
2. Click the New Rule button at the top of the window. The Define Inbox Rule dialog box opens with the new rule enabled by default.
3. The Rule name field is preselected, so begin by typing a descriptive name for your rule.
4. The top part of the dialog box contains criteria settings. You can apply up to three filtering criteria. Use the first pop-up list to select the part of the message you are scanning for your criteria. Use the second pop-up to narrow your filter. In the text box enter (or paste) the text by which you are filtering.

For example, for this book we might have set up a filter that said *From contains @idg.com.*

To apply a second filter action, click the check box in the next line and then set that line's criterion. Do the same for one more criterion if desired.

5. In the Execute actions pop-up, tell Outlook Express whether to apply your actions only if *all* the criteria are met or if *any* of the criteria are met.
6. You can apply up to five actions. Determine what the first action should be, and then select that action from the first Actions pop-up menu. When you select an action, menus or dialog boxes appear so you can enter the rest of the action's details.

   Continue to set your criteria in the order you want the actions processed and carried out.
7. To activate the filter, click OK. This rule now appears in the Inbox Rules dialog box.

Place the rules in the order in which you want them performed. Click a rule to select it, and then click the Move Up or Move Down buttons to arrange your priorities.

At times you may not want to apply a rule. You can temporarily disable any rule by returning to the rule's dialog box and unchecking the Enabled check box.

When a rule is no longer needed, choose Tools ⇨ Inbox Rules to open the Inbox Rules window. Click the rule to select it and then click the Delete Rule button.

If you already have an Inbox full of messages you want to run through the mail filter, select the messages in the Message list, and then select Tools ⇨ Apply Rules and choose the rule from the submenu.

Sorting messages

Messages can easily be sorted to make it easier to identify the newest or oldest message, a message from a specific person, or a message about a specific topic. As with the Mac's Finder and most Mac software, click any column heading to sort by that column's criteria. Click the triangle in that column to switch the sort from ascending to descending, or vice versa.

If you are looking for a specific message, sometimes filtering the Message list helps. See "Searching for messages" for more information.

Searching for messages

If you're trying to locate a message(s) containing specific words or characters, you can perform a Find. Sometimes that's more than you need, however. For example, at times you may need to view all messages within a specific folder whose subjects, senders, or recipients contain a word or name. This is more of a filter than a search.

When you're not sure where to look or you want to be sure to find all pertinent messages, use the Find command. Choose Edit ⇨ Find (⌘-F) and then enter the text you seek into the Find field. You can narrow your search by searching for this text in a specific area(s) of your messages. Check From, To, Subject, and/or Body. Next tell Outlook Express to search the current message only, all of your Outlook Express mail folders, or a specific folder. Finally, click Find or press Return or Enter (because Find is the default button).

When you just need a clearer view of a folder's contents or you pretty much know where you want to look, use the Message list's filtering capability. Click the folder in the Folder list so you are viewing all messages within that folder. Then select a field to search by choosing it from the pop-up menu at the top of the list's column headers. Finally, enter the text you are searching for. Only messages that meet your filtering criteria will appear in the Message list. This viewing filter remains in effect until you delete the text from the criteria field.

Working with Multiple Users

If several people share your Mac, you can set up Outlook Express so all users can share the same copy of the program. Each user has his or her own folders and contacts so mail is not confused among users. You can also maintain privacy by creating a password for each user.

Accessing Another User's E-Mail

A power user trick is having users access each other's e-mail. (This doesn't work over a network or with file sharing turned on for security reasons.) For example, suppose Michael will access Caitlin's mail. Open the Outlook Express 4.0 Folder, then the Outlook Express User(s) folder, and then Caitlin's folder. To let Michael access all of Caitlin's mail, make an alias of Caitlin's Internet Mail folder. To allow Michael access to only some of Caitlin's mail, open her Internet Mail folder and alias only those folders Michael should access. Place the alias(es) into the Internet Mail folder that resides within Michael's folder. Now when Michael is using Outlook Express, he sees Caitlin's folders—either all of her folders or just the ones that were aliased.

This trick also works if the user's mail is on a removable disk—as long as the removable disk is available. Simply open Caitlin's user folder (on her removable disk) and then alias her Internet Mail folder or any folder within it.

Setting up multiple users

To set up multiple users, follow these steps:

1. Choose File➪Change Current User. A dialog box asks you to confirm that you want to change users, warning that you will be closing the current user's folders and connection. Click Yes and you're presented with a dialog box that handles your user accounts, as shown in Figure 35-18.

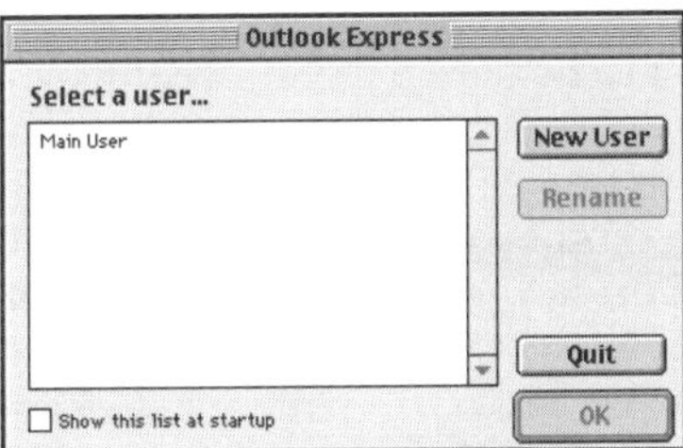

Figure 35-18: The dialog box for creating new users and renaming or selecting existing users

2. Click New User. The Edit User dialog box opens, as shown in Figure 35-19.

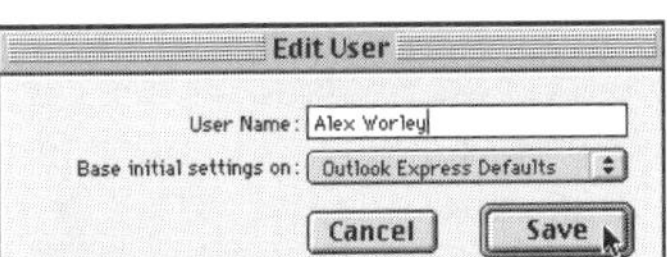

Figure 35-19: Naming a new user

3. By default the User Name is something like User1. This field is preselected, so you can type your new user's name immediately.

When you have more than one account, it will be helpful to rename your first account if it is still called Main User. This is a good time to do so because you're in the right place. Click the Main User name and then click Rename. Type the new name and click Save.

4. If you have already set up a user, you can have that user's organization name, server information, and account name entered as the basis for this new user. You'll save a bit of typing while setting up this new account. Each user's settings are available for selection from the Base initial settings on pop-up list.
5. Click Save to move to this user's set-up area in the Preferences dialog box.

6. Setting up any new user is the same, whether it's the first user or the third. See "Setting up your e-mail account" at the beginning of this chapter if you need guidance in setting up the new user's preferences. Customize the new user's preferences to reflect the user's e-mail address, username, and password. Click OK when you're finished.

When you set up a new user account, it remains as the open account until you switch users. You can tell which account you are in because the username appears as part of the window name.

When you create a new user, a folder with the user's name is created within the OE User(s) folder in the Outlook Express 4.0 Folder, which is in the Microsoft Internet Applications folder. Each user's folder contains a folder for Contacts, Internet Mail, Outlook Express Prefs, and Internet News. You can take advantage of this knowledge—and the fact that Outlook Express recognizes aliases within the OE User(s) folder—to transfer a user from one Mac to another, to have multiple users share a Mac, or to carry your e-mail with you to access your account and manage your messages from any Mac. This is power user stuff—and it's all covered soon.

Switching between users

If you have more than one user, the last user to have used Outlook Express at quitting time is the active user upon relaunch. To switch users, select File⇨Change Current User.

Hot Stuff

You may prefer to have Outlook Express let you select a user whenever it starts up. Choose File⇨Change Current User, and then click Yes and check Show This List On Startup. (This is Step 1 under "Setting up multiple users.") The dialog box in which you select a user upon startup (or when switching users anytime) is shown in Figure 35-20.

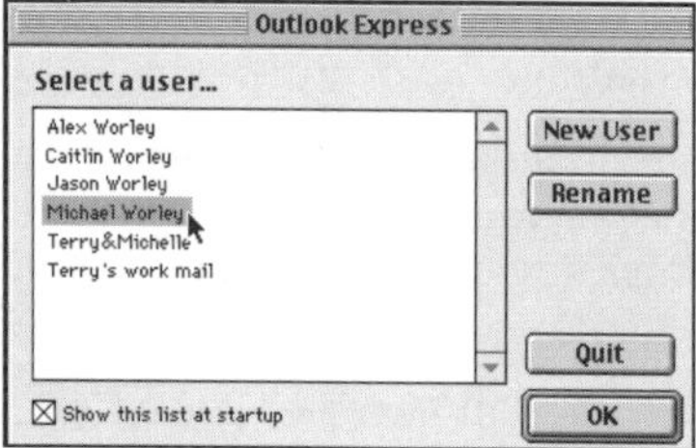

Figure 35-20: The user selection dialog box

Deleting a user

Deleting a user is a bit crude because there isn't an interface to do so. To remove a user, go to that user's folder and drag it to the Trash, just as you trash any unwanted folders or files. To get to any user's folder, open the Microsoft Internet Applications folder (if you still have Outlook Express stored there). Then open the folder labeled Outlook Express 4.0 Folder. Now open the folder called OE User(s). You'll see one folder for each of your users. You don't have to open a user's folder to trash it; just drag the entire folder to the Trash. (And empty the Trash, of course.)

Transferring users from Mac to Mac

When you don't intend to have a user access mail from your Mac any longer, you can give that user his or her user's folder for transfer to another Mac. Open the OE User(s) folder (which is in the Outlook Express 4.0 Folder in the Microsoft Internet Applications folder). Drag the user's entire folder to a removable disk. Then delete the user's folder from your hard drive. Later the user can copy his or her folder to the OE User(s) folder on another Mac. If your Mac is directly connected to the other Mac's hard drive, instead of copying to a removable disk, you can drag the user's folder directly to that other drive.

Taking It with You

What if you are in business and need your e-mail with you, but you move from office to office? What if multiple students/employees share your Mac, but you don't want all their mail on the hard drive. Perhaps you have a Mac and want to access, read, and respond to your e-mail but don't have steady net access from where you're living. All of these situations are possible. This definitely is power user stuff, however, and is not commonly necessary. If you don't fit one of the user profiles just mentioned, don't bother with this stuff.

The bottom line is that Outlook Express recognizes alias-to-mail folders, so you can store your mail on any removable medium, such as a Zip or a Jaz disk, and then access your account from any copy of Outlook Express, downloading your mail to—and uploading mail from—the disk rather than the hard drive on which Outlook Express is installed. The key to carrying mail with you is having a disk to carry it on, so you or each user must have a removable disk, such as a Zip or a Jaz, to begin with.

To carry your own mail (or have your users carry their own mail), follow these steps:

1. On the removable disk, create a new folder the same way you create any normal folder—using the File⇨New Folder (⌘-N) command. Give that folder the name you want your account to have.
2. Insert the disk into the Mac where mail will be accessed.
3. Open the folder called OE User(s), which is in the Outlook Express 4.0 Folder.

continued

4. If you're using OS 8, press ⌘-Option as you click the user folder (on the removable disk) and drag that folder into the OE User(s) folder on the hard drive. If you are using System 7, make an alias of the user folder (on the removable disk) and drag that alias into the OE User(s) folder on the hard drive to copy the alias.

   The alias on the removable disk can be copied to another OE User(s) folder on any hard drive over and over, or it can be trashed.) A user can place an alias of his folder in multiple Macs—and should place an alias on any machine from which he wants to access his mail.

5. Restart Outlook Express before continuing use of the program if it was running.

The next time you select a new user (see "Switching between users"), the aliased user appears as a choice, looking just like any other user. When you select that user, however, a dialog box asks you to insert the disk that contains the user's folder. (By the way, the dialog box asks for the disk by name, so changing the disk's name is not a good idea.) If you are not that user and don't have that disk, or if the user doesn't have the disk handy, click Cancel. Otherwise, insert the disk. The dialog box disappears and the account opens. From there use the account as normal.

With this setup the user doesn't have Outlook Express on his disk. He must use his disk with a Mac that has Outlook Express installed. (If ownership of Outlook Express remains free, there is no legal problem with letting each user have a fully installed copy of Outlook Express on the removable disk. See the next section for those details.)

As a portable user, to be able to read or compose mail while away from the Mac that provides your link to the net, Outlook Express must be installed on the removable disk. If that disk happens to contain the Mac's System folder, you can perform a normal install of Outlook Express onto that disk while it is the startup disk for the Mac to which it's attached. Otherwise, you need to follow these steps:

1. Place the disk in the drive, insert the Office 98 CD-ROM, and run the Outlook Express Installer, selecting the removable disk as the destination. When installation is complete, the Outlook Express window opens.

2. Open the Extensions folder (within the System folder) on the host hard drive. Then double-click the MS Library Folder to open it. Choose File⇨Select All and then drag the MS Library Folder contents into the new Outlook Express folder on your removable disk. This copies those necessary extensions.

3. Run your new copy of Outlook Express and set yourself up as the user. Your Users folder will appear in the OE User(s) folder. This folder is the one you alias to the OE User(s) folder on any hard drive you plan to run off of. (See the previous section and steps for details.)

Working with Newsgroups

A newsgroup is like a community bulletin board where the board addresses one specific issue. A newsgroup is a folder set up on a computer somewhere, to which anyone can post and read messages others have posted. A list may have hundreds of messages posted at one time. To read the messages within a newsgroup, you must subscribe to the list. Of course, it wouldn't be logical to have all these messages download to your hard drive, so newsgroups function with their own protocol, NNTP, rather than POP or IMAP. This protocol enables all subscribers to access the messages live over the Net. Thousands and thousands of newsgroups are scattered all over the Internet. Chances are your ISP hosts thousands of them. If so, you received the news server's address when you signed up.

After you subscribe to a news group, you read and respond to its messages the same as with an e-mail message. In this section we get you started.

Setting up a news account

There are two parts to setting up a news server account. First you tell Outlook Express what server to call into. Then you view the available newsgroups and subscribe to the ones in which you are interested.

Defining a news account

Setting up a news account is much like setting up an e-mail account. Follow these steps:

1. Click the Preferences button or choose Edit ➪ Preferences. Then select News from under the accounts heading and click New Server.
2. In the dialog box that opens, name your server as you want it to appear in the Folder list. The server in Figures 35-21 and 35-22 was named Westworld (WGN) because that's the name of the user's ISP. Then click OK to return to the Preferences dialog box.
3. Enter the address for your news server (which was probably provided by your ISP) in the Server address field, as shown in Figure 35-21.
4. Check the box marked Display this new server in the folder list to provide the one-click access to the newsgroups on this server.

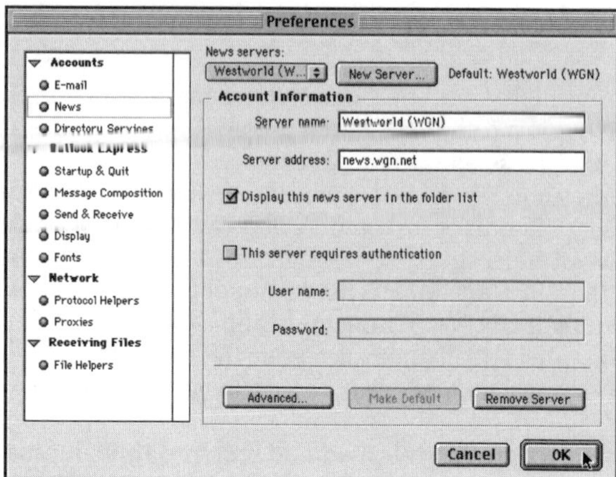

Figure 35-21: Setting up a news server in the Preferences dialog box

5. If your ISP requires a password to allow access to this server, you have already been told so and have already chosen a username and a password. In that case, check the box to tell Outlook Express the server will ask for authentication, and then enter the username and password you and your ISP agreed on.
6. Your ISP may require you to specify a port or provide header information. (You would already have been told and provided with the NNTP port number and/or header text.) If so, click the Advanced button and enter the specific information as instructed. Click OK to close the Advance features window when you're finished.
7. Click OK to close the Preferences dialog box.

Subscribing to a newsgroup

After you designate your news server, it appears in the Folder list, as shown in Figure 35-22 (where Westworld provides the news server). Now it's time to connect to the server, get the listing of available newsgroups, and subscribe. Follow these steps:

1. Click the server's icon in the Folder list. The server's name appears in the right side of the Outlook Express window, and a connection indicator appears at the lower right of the window.
2. Select View ➪ Get Complete Newsgroup List (⌘-L). This initiates the connection to your news server. The connection indicator becomes active and the list of newsgroups appears. The total number of lists is reported at the bottom left of the window.

Remember, if you are using a modem to access the Net, you need to set your PPP access to permit applications to make connections. Otherwise you need to open the PPP control panel and connect manually to access the news server, or you'll receive an error message.

3. To subscribe to a list, click the list's name and then click the Subscribe button in the toolbar, as shown in Figure 35-22. The list's name appears below the server name in the Folder list. (An arrow appears beside the server name so you can hide or reveal the lists, just like in the Mac's Finder, later on.

   Your list of available lists may contain thousands of list names, making it hard (not to mention tedious) to find the lists that interest you. Use the window's filter to make this search easier. Enter a key word to act as a filter. See Figure 35-22, where only lists with the word *travel* are displayed.

   You can subscribe to as many newsgroups as you like. Simply select each list and click Subscribe. Changing the words you filter by doesn't affect your connection.

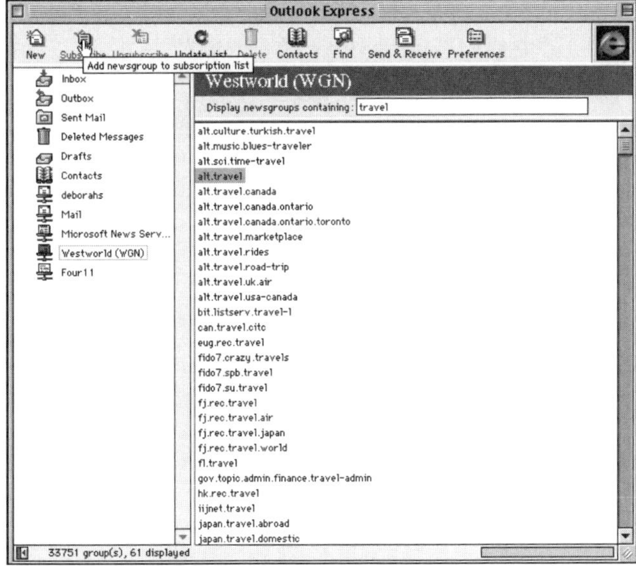

Figure 35-22: Subscribing to the `alt.travel` newsgroup list on the Westworld server

At any time you can connect to the news server and check to see if any new newsgroups are available. Rather than repeat the entire listing, click your news server and select View ➪ Check for New Newsgroups. That way only new groups will appear in the list on the right side of the window.

Unsubscribing from a newsgroup

To unsubscribe to a newsgroup, click the server icon in your Folder list. Choose View⇨Subscribed Only. Then, in the group list on the right, click the newsgroup to select it and choose Tools⇨Unsubscribe.

Viewing messages

To view the messages in a newsgroup, all you have to do is click the name of the newsgroup. (If you don't see the names of your subscribed lists in your Folder list, click the arrow beside the server name so it points downward and reveals the folder's contents.) Outlook Express automatically connects to the server and displays the list's messages. Click once to view a message in the Preview pane. (If it's not open choose View⇨Preview pane.) Double-click a message to have it open in its own window.

When viewing messages in a separate window, the window gains four new buttons to help you move through the messages. To help you understand these buttons, we should explain that a *thread* is a subject. When someone posts a message and someone else replies, the reply receives the same subject name. This reply becomes the second message in that thread. When viewing the messages in a separate window, you can't see the subject headers in the list, so instead you use the Previous Thread and Next Thread buttons to move from subject to subject. While viewing a message, to see its replies you click the Next button to move to the next message for that subject. Likewise, click Previous to move to the previous message (if there is any) that has to do with the subject (thread).

If you are viewing messages in the Preview pane in the main Outlook Express window, rather than clicking buttons to move from subject to subject, use the scroll bars and then click any message to read it. An arrow beside a message indicates that there are responses. Click the arrow to point it downward and reveal the responses. Then click any response to read it (see Figure 35-23).

After you've read some of the messages in the newsgroup list, you have the option of filtering out the ones you've read. To filter messages, select View⇨Unread Only.

Sometimes there are so many messages that the server only shows you a few hundred at a time. You'll know by viewing the status report at that bottom left of the window. To see the next bunch of messages, select View⇨Get Next 500 News Messages.

You can also select View⇨Refresh Article List to reconnect to your news server and view any new articles for that newsgroup.

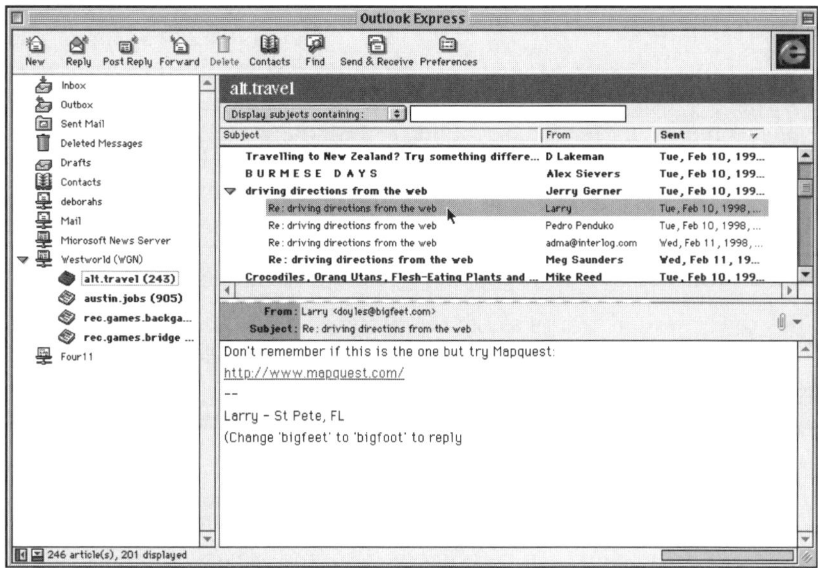

Figure 35-23: Reading a newsgroup message

Keeping messages

Remember, the messages you are reading in a newsgroup are on the news server or another computer feeding the server, not on your hard drive or in your e-mail folders, wherever they may be. If you want to keep a message, you need to transfer it to your own drive. There are two ways to transfer a message: by keeping a message in its e-mail form or by saving it as a standalone document. To keep the message as e-mail, drag the message from the Message list into the folder in which you want it stored. To save the message as a document, click the message in the Message list and then select File⇨Save (⌘-S). If you're viewing the message in its own window, you can also select File⇨Save (⌘-S).

Working Offline

Suppose you have a PowerBook and are spending time in transit. With the Work Offline feature, you can keep up with your newsgroup, IMAP-served or POP-served messages. While connected to the server, when you click a newsgroup message, IMAP-served or POP-served, the message is cached to your hard drive.

Later, select File⇨Work Offline. When you click the News Server icon to look at the messages, Outlook Express won't attempt to connect to the server.

Automating actions

Rather than wading through tons of newsgroup messages to find a message that interests you, you can set up Newsgroup Rules to search the messages. When messages meeting your criteria are found, you can have Outlook Express set them to a certain color and/or download and file them for you. Outlook Express can also mark the message as read if you want. If you've read the section "Automating your incoming mail," you will find this procedure familiar. Follow these steps:

1. Choose Tools ⇨ Newsgroup Rules to open the Newsgroup Rules window.
2. Click the New Rule button at the top of the window. The Define Newsgroup Rule dialog box opens with the new rule enabled by default.
3. The Rule name field is preselected, so begin by typing a descriptive name for your rule.
4. The top part of the dialog box contains criteria settings. In the first line tell Outlook Express what the newsgroup name should contain or not contain, be or not be, and start with or end with by selecting one of these options from the pop-up menu and then entering the text you are interested in. The example shown in Figure 35-24 searches newsgroups whose subject contains the word *travel*.

   Use the first pop-up list to select the part of the message you are scanning for your criteria. Use the second pop-up to narrow your filter. In the text box, enter (or paste) the text you are filtering by. In Figure 35-24, we search the subject for the words *Indonesia* or *London*.

   To apply a second filter action, click the check box in the next line and set that line's criteria. Do the same for one more criteria if desired.

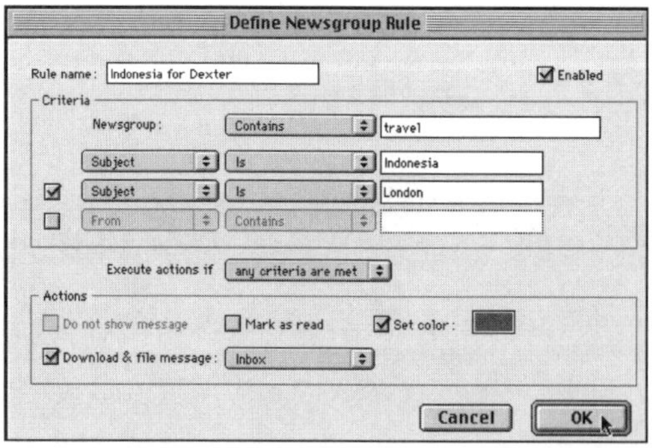

Figure 35-24: Setting up a Newsgroup Rule

5. In the Execute actions if pop-up menu, tell Outlook Express whether to apply your actions only if *all* the criteria are met or if *any* of the criteria are met.

6. In the Actions area, tell Outlook Express what to do when the criteria is met. Check Do not show message if you want Outlook Express to filter out the messages that meet your criteria. Check Set color and then select a color if you want to color code these messages. If you want these messages to be marked as already read, check that option. To have Outlook Express download these messages and file them in any one of your Outlook Express folders, check Download & File Message and then select the folder in which you want the messages filed. In Figure 35-24, we have all travel messages about Indonesia or London downloaded to the Inbox and color coded in green.
7. Click OK to activate the filter. This rule now appears in the Newsgroup Rules dialog box.

Posting to a newsgroup

Composing a new message for a newsgroup is just like composing a regular e-mail message—perhaps just a tad easier. While you are viewing the newsgroup list or a newsgroup message, click the New (Message) button. The new message window that opens is preaddressed to the newsgroup you are currently in. You can cc the message to another recipient if you want. Give your message a subject and then type your message. To send the message, click the Post button. You can also add attachments and sign it, just like any other e-mail message. If you are not ready to post the message, click Save to place it in the Drafts folder until you are ready to complete and post it.

Replying to a message

When responding to a newsgroup message, you can send your response to the newsgroup for the entire group to see, or you can send it to the author only. The most important thing is to pay attention to whom you are sending your message. Otherwise, the results can be embarrassing, or you may be posting personal information to (potentially) the entire world.

To reply only to the sender, with the message being responded to as the active message, click the Reply button or select Message ➪ Reply To Author. The message window you are presented with is a regular e-mail message window because you are sending a regular e-mail message.

To send your reply to the newsgroup for public viewing, with the message being responded to as the active message, click the Post Reply button or select Message ➪ Reply To Newsgroup. The outgoing message window is similar to a regular e-mail message window except that there is a Post button in lieu of a Send button, and the addressing is to a news server and a newsgroup instead of to a person. By default, newsgroup messages are in plain text. You can change this under the Composition area of Preferences.

Summary

This chapter familiarized you with Outlook Express—Microsoft's Internet mail and news client e-mail program. We covered the following main points:

- Whether you have a POP dial-up account or an IMAP corporate server, Outlook Express can handle your e-mail with ease.
- Multiple users can share the same copy of Outlook Express, each maintaining separate access, files, passwords, and so on.
- The Folder list is your e-mail and newsgroup filing cabinet. You can create as many other folders as you want and store messages by topic or by any organizational method. Folders residing on your hard drive appear below the Drafts folder. IMAP account folders appear as subfolders of your server icon.
- You can take advantage of Inbox Rules to filter and file your incoming messages for you. Unwanted mail can be deleted, while other mail can be filed by topic or content. It's all up to you.
- To send a message to many people at once, you can create a mailing list simply by clicking the Mailing List button and then dragging the desired names onto the list icon. Then, rather than individually adding each message recipients, you just enter the list name. With the list, you can suppress recipient's names, keeping their addresses private and preventing them from accidentally replying to all recipients rather than replying only to you. The same contact can be part of many lists. Names can be added or deleted at any time.
- Outgoing messages can be sent with color and styles or in plain text format.
- Newsgroup messages can also be handled in Outlook Express, almost exactly like regular e-mail.

Where to go next

- Need to compose the documents you'll be enclosing with your e-mail? Check out Part I: Word, Part II: Excel, and Part III: PowerPoint.
- Ready to cruise the Web? Check out Chapter 36 for information on using Internet Explorer.

✦ ✦ ✦

CHAPTER 36

Overview of Internet Explorer

✦ ✦ ✦ ✦

In This Chapter

Working with Web pages and sites

Downloading and saving files

Printing Web pages

Dealing with security concerns

Working with Internet ratings support

Reading mail and news

Getting more help

✦ ✦ ✦ ✦

Internet Explorer's main function is to enable you to visit the World Wide Web and view today's Web pages in their fullest glory. Today's Web makes it easy to seek out a page on any topic, and some Web sites even bring their content to you by enabling you to subscribe to the page or set up a channel. Internet Explorer 4.0 supports these new technologies and makes it easy for you to take advantage of the technologies. Because the Internet also includes newsgroups and e-mail, some browsers have concentrated too hard on these features. Happily, Internet Explorer has opted not to go in this direction. Instead, Internet Explorer does the Web and nothing but the Web, while allowing you easy access to your newsgroups and e-mail with the click of a button.

Internet Explorer's sister application, Outlook Express, is designed specifically to handle news and mail. By default, when you click Internet Explorer's Mail button, you are taken to Outlook Express. However, it is very easy to change this preference to open E-mailer or Eudora if you prefer to use one of them to handle your e-mail or news (see "Reading Mail and News" later in the chapter).

Looking at the Window

The first time you launch Internet Explorer, you may be taken to a preset page. After that, you can set Internet Explorer to take you to the page of your choice, called your *home page,* or to leave the browser window blank. Figure 36-1 illustrates a blank window.

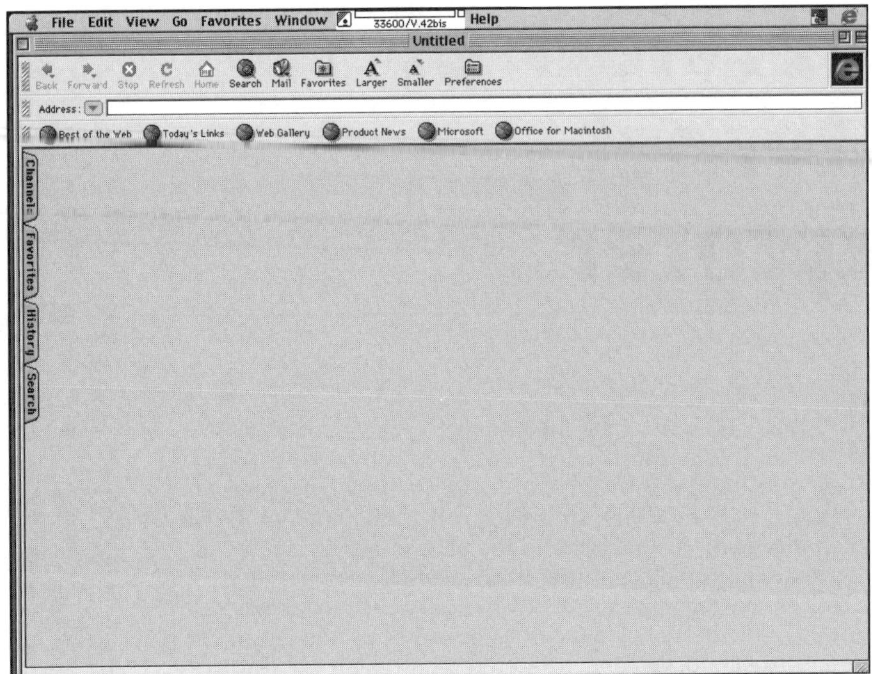

Figure 36-1: A blank Internet Explorer window—no page loaded

The Internet Explorer window begins with the *title bar,* as does any Mac program. The name in the title bar usually reflects the Web page you are on. That title is determined by the page's creator. In Figure 36-1 there is no page so the title is *untitled*. The title bar also contains the standard Mac close box, size box, and windowshade button (if you have OS 8).

Below the title bar are Internet Explorer's buttons. While the core Office 98 applications refer to the strip of buttons as a *toolbar,* Internet Explorer refers to this area as the *button bar.*

Next you find the *address bar.* This is where you type the URL, or address, of the page you want to visit. Alternatives to hand-entering an address are clicking a bookmark, clicking a link—that appears in another page or in any document that contains live links—or using Apple's Data Detectors to Control-click a destination and go there. As you enter a site's address, or just part of it, a feature called AutoComplete searches all addresses you've visited before that contain that address or word you entered. Click the arrow in the address bar to display the list of matching addresses, and then select any address from this list to go to that page. (See "Using the address bar" later in this chapter.)

The next strip of buttons is the *favorites bar.* Don't confuse this with the list of preferred Web sites that you build for yourself. Each of these buttons is a link to a page Microsoft has set up to provide information about and provide links to areas that may be of interest to you.

Along the left side of the window is the Explorer bar—another tool designed to make your Internet travels easier and more efficient. There are four tabs: Channels, Favorites, History, and Search. These tabs hang out quietly on the side trying not to encroach on the Web page until you click one of them to call it into action. When you're done with the information in the tab, click the tab again and it slides back to the side. This is a new alternative to selecting an item from a pop-up list or opening a separate window.

At the bottom of the window is the *status bar.* This is where you are kept informed of what Internet Explorer is doing, where a link will take you, whether the page you are accessing is from the Web or from your hard drive, and so on. For example, while a page is loading, the status bar tells you as it retrieves each component and what percent of the download is complete.

Next to the status bar is the scroll bar and arrows when applicable. The right side of the window also has a scroll bar and arrows as needed. And, of course, you can always click in the bottom-right corner and drag to custom-size your window.

Completing the picture in the Internet Explorer window, smack dab in the center, is the reason you're in Internet Explorer in the first place—the Web page you are visiting.

In more detail, here's how each part of the Internet Explorer window can serve you.

Changing the Window's Look

Each of the bars—the button, address, favorites, Explorer, and status bar—can be turned on and off by default or per session. To effect the default, click the Preferences button (or choose Edit⇨Preferences), and then click Browser Display and check or uncheck each bar. To turn one on or off temporarily, select the bar in the View menu. (The View menu is a toggle.)

When you rest your mouse over any button, a balloon appears to tell you about that button's function. This is called a ToolTip. You can turn ToolTips on or off by checking or unchecking Show ToolTips in the Browser Display page of the Preferences dialog box.

You can move the button, address, and favorites bars so they reside next to each other or fall in a different order. (You cannot move these bars to the bottom of the window and you can't drag the striped area to the right to resize.) These bars move using the same method as the toolbars in the core Office applications. Click the gray-striped bar at the left of each bar, and then drag the bar into place when your cursor becomes a hand. A blue highlight lets you know where the bar is due to land when you release the mouse. These button bar location changes remain in effect for new browser windows.

Using the button bar

The button bar performs an action with a single click. Table 36-1 lists the function of each button.

Table 36-1
The Functions of the Button Bar

Button	*How It Works*
Back	With each click, the Back button takes you back one page through the pages you've visited in this browser window. To move back several pages at a time, click the Back button and hold the mouse button until a list of all sites visited in this browser window appears, and then select a site's address from the list. If you have two browser windows open, use the History tab to return to a site you visited in another browser window.
Forward	Each click moves you forward through the pages you've visited during this session in this browser window. Hold the mouse down to jump several sites forward at once by selecting an address from the pop-up list. (See Back for more details.)
Stop	Stops the current page that's being downloaded from continuing. Refresh reinitiates the loading of the page you stopped.
Refresh	Reloads the Web page currently designated in the address bar. If you've deleted the last URL, it will reappear and reload. Refresh is handy when a page fails to load properly, hangs up, or may have newer information since the last time you loaded it. If you stop a page, Refresh continues the load.
Home	Takes you to the page you designate as your home page. When you set a home page, Internet Explorer also accesses it upon each launch.
Search	Opens the search page you set as a preference. To access other search pages, use the Search tab instead.
Mail	Opens your mail reader for you to read your mail, create a new message, or send the current URL within a new message. It also lets you read your news. For each of these actions, your designated mail or news reader opens.
Favorites	Opens your Favorites list as a separate window. An alternative is the Favorites tab.
Larger	Displays all the text in the page one size larger, up to the maximum possible. There are five sizes in all: smallest, small, medium, large, and largest. This size change remains in effect when you switch pages, but only for the current browser window. It does not change your preferences.
Smaller	Displays all the text in the page one size smaller, to the minimum size. (See Larger for details.)
Preferences	Opens the Preferences dialog box so you can customize your settings. The Help icon in each page of the dialog box takes you directly to Help on that page's content.

Using the Explorer bar

The Explorer bar is like a windowshade that conveniently rolls out the left side of your window and then folds back when you're done. To access the Explorer bar, move your mouse over the desired tab and hover a moment. The tab scrolls out on top of the current Web page. Move your mouse back to the page area, off of the Explorer bar and the bar rolls back to the side, uncovering your page again. Alternatively, you can click the tab you want and the bar will pull out; this has the effect of pushing the Web page to the right. Clicking the tab again scrolls it back in and pushes the Web page back to the left.

Channels tab

Channels are the most dynamic Web sites. Channels offer regularly updated, ever-changing, custom information. Because they change more often than their more static counterparts, channels are proactive in finding their way to you rather than waiting for you to find them. This is done via subscription. When you find a channel that interests you (as they all hope to do), you can choose to subscribe to it. Internet Explorer does a good job of making that easy by providing the Channels tab (see Figure 36-2). You can read Internet Explorer's introduction to channels by (what else?) clicking Introduction to channels. You can subscribe to any channel at any time. In the Channels tab, you'll find Internet Explorer's Active Channel Guide, which is an excellent starting point for finding channels. Each of the channels in this guide is supposed to be designed to work well on the Mac.

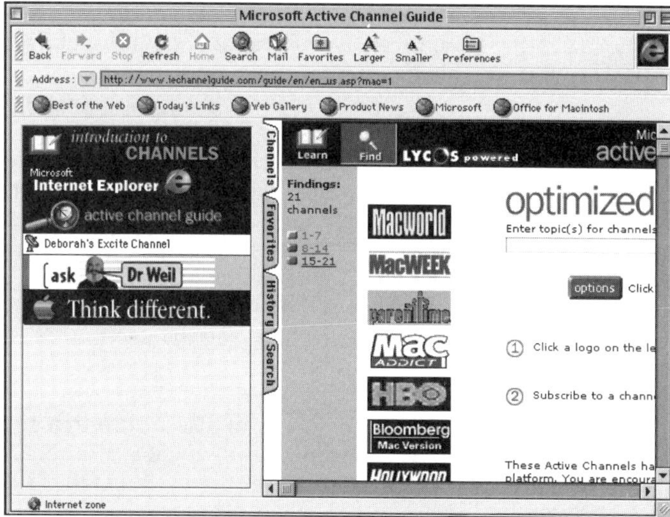

Figure 36-2: The Channels tab with three channels added

To check out a channel, click the icon for the channel you are interested in. Take a look and, if you want to subscribe, click the Add Active Channel button. Click Add or Customize, depending on what you want to do with the channel. (This is covered later in "Subscribing to a channel" and "Browsing offline.")

As you add channels, the tab fills up with colorful bars representing each channel. When you click any channel's bar, it expands to reveal the various offerings within that channel. As you click another channel's bar, the previously opened bar closes to make room in the tab. Clicking any offering within a channel connects you to the channel.

While viewing a page, you can give it more screen space by rolling back the entire Explorer bar. To do so, click the Channels tab. If you click a different tab from the tab you are in, you switch tabs but do not roll back the Explorer bar.

Channels are actually Favorites that are handled a bit differently. To move channels around in the tab, open the Favorites list by clicking the Favorites button, and then open the Channels folder and drag the channels into place. (See the following section, "Favorites tab.") Rather than delete a channel, you should unsubscribe. (See "Subscribing to a channel" for more information.)

Favorites tab

Cyberspace is vast and so easy to move around in that you are bound to forget where you've been. Placing a site's address in your Favorites list makes the site easier to return to. Organizing your Favorites list into logical folders makes it even easier. (Your list will grow and grow—believe us!) This organization is done in a separate Favorites window, rather than in the Favorites tab. See the section on marking your favorite sites, later in this chapter.

One globe icon appears for each site you bookmark as a favorite. If you've organized your sites into folders, click the triangle beside the folder to reveal its contents. As you click a folder, any previously open folder automatically closes. Each site usually has a name attached to it. That name is assigned by the page's designer. At times the name can be helpful; other times it may just say *index* or something equally vague. You can see where a site actually leads by resting your mouse over the icon until the ToolTip pops up and displays the site's URL. You can also rename the item in the Favorites list. To learn how, see the section "Marking favorite sites for easy return," later in this chapter.

To visit a site, click the icon or name of the site. (You can also return to a site by selecting it from the Favorites menu.) The tab won't automatically disappear, as you may want it again. To give your page more room onscreen, remember to click the Favorites tab.

To rearrange items in your Favorites list, click the item (icon or name), hold the mouse a moment, and then drag. After you move the item a bit, it's outline appears, along with a black bar. The black bar shows you where the icon will land when you release the mouse. You can move an item anywhere in the Favorite tab—between other icons, into a folder, or from folder to folder—just like in the Finder. (Favorites can also be rearranged from within the Favorites window, as discussed in "Marking favorite sites for easy return.")

To remove an item from your Favorites list while in this tab, drag the item to the Mac's Trash folder.

History tab

This tab tracks all the pages you visit in your travels on the Web. Whether you work within one browser window or open several browser windows in a session, they are all tracked in this tab and show in the History tab or any browser window. Histories don't begin and end with one Web session; they are carried over from one session to the next. This means if you visit a site on Monday, and then close your connection and/or quit Internet Explorer, the sites you visited are still in the History list when you connect on Wednesday and open a new browser window. To make your exploration history even more clear to you, Internet Explorer creates a folder for each day's travels.

One globe icon appears for each site you visit, each time you visit that site. The name you see on each icon is the page name assigned by the page's designer. To see a site address, rest your mouse over the icon until the ToolTip pops up.

To revisit a site, click the icon or name of the site. If you plan to visit a site again, rather than keeping it in the History tab, designate the site as a favorite. To do so, click the icon of the site (your cursor becomes a hand) and drag it, resting your mouse over the Favorites tab. In a moment, the Favorites tab becomes the active tab. Continue dragging until the site's icon lands where you want it; it can land in a folder or between any other existing favorites icons. A black line indicates where the icon will land when you release the mouse.

You can remove a site from your History list. (A great feature if your boss may see it.) Just drag the site's icon to your Mac's Trash. (You can't click the icon and select Clear because clicking the icon in the tab initiates a connection.)

To switch to another tab, click the desired tab. If you are finished using the Explorer bar and want it to roll back to the left side of the window, click the History tab.

Hot Stuff

In addition to learning the address of a site in your History list, you can also learn the date you first visited and last visited the site. To see this information, open the History list as a separate window by selecting Go⇨Open History. In the History window, click the site to select it and choose File⇨Get Info (⌘-I), as in the Finder.

Taking Control of Your History

Internet Explorer's history of your Web page visits is not infinite. There is a point at which the memory of a visited site drops off the list. By default, Internet Explorer recalls approximately 300 pages; however, you can change the number of recorded visits.

To do so, click the Preferences button, and then select the Advanced preference pane. The first option in this pane determines the number of pages that are remembered by your History list. After that, the older pages are dropped from the record (which is a good reason to add pages to your Favorites list). To change the number of pages tracked, enter a new number and click OK to close the Preferences window and effect the change.

Search tab

This tab (see Figure 36-3) is a miniature one-stop shop for quick and easy searches. At the top of the tab's area, a pop-up list automatically cycles through several providers (or search engines) and offers you the provider of the day. You can use that provider or select your preference from the menu.

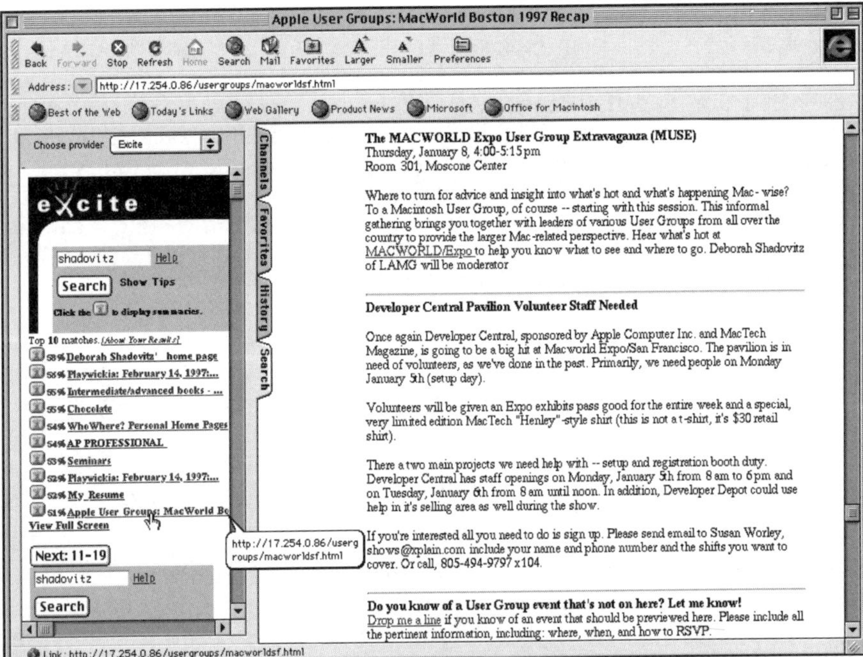

Figure 36-3: The Search tab displays results while one link is accessed

Before You Visit the Web

To access a Web site, you need to be able to connect to the Web. If you are using your Mac at home, you are probably using a modem and your phone line to create a PPP connection via a local Internet service provider (ISP). If you don't yet have an ISP, we recommend checking with your local Macintosh User's Group for recommendations. You want to find an ISP with a good modem-to-user ratio, reliable lines, knowledge of the Mac (for good technical support), and a good reputation. Other faster connections, such as an Integrated Services Digital Network (ISDN) or cable connections are also possible to have at home, although they are more expensive and therefore less common. Beginning with System 7.6, the Mac OS comes complete with all the software you need to initiate your Internet connection. If you are running any operating system prior to 7.6, let your ISP know; it should be able to provide you with the control panels you need.

If you are accessing the Internet from a corporate office, your company most likely provides your connection via its company network. In that case, you may be connected all the time. Office setups may include a *firewall,* which acts as a protective buffer, and your setup may include a *proxy server*. Your network administrator or MIS personnel most likely handle these setups in your company and will make sure you are properly configured.

A small text field is the next item of interest. Here you enter the text you are seeking information on from the Web. Enter your text, and then click the Search button—whatever it might be labeled. In a few moments, you have a list of sites that met your criteria (contained your text) listed below in the Search tab. Each found site contains a link to the found site. Clicking any returned link takes you to that site. To view a site in a larger window, click the Search tab; this rolls back to the left side of the window. Your current Web page slides over, too. To check out another found link, click the Search tab again. The information from your search remains intact until you search again. Therefore, you can look through each found site while looking at the other options simultaneously.

See the section "Searching Web sites" for more on searches.

When you are completely done with the Explorer bar, click the last tab you used to roll it back. If you click a different tab from the tab you are in, you switch tabs but do not roll back the Explorer bar.

Working with Web Pages and Sites

A Web page is a document written with HTML tags, which make the document deliverable to the Web. In the earlier days of the Web, most people posted one page of any length and used hyperlinks to take you from one part of that page to another. These days, people tend to create Web sites, rather than post single pages. A Web site is a collection of HTML pages that link together. Like the hyperlinks that take a user from one part of a page to another, hyperlinks (called *links* in everyday language) take visitors from one page to another. The same hyperlinks take a user from one Web site to another.

Rather than create redundant page parts, such as strips of buttons along the side or top of page after page, some people have moved toward using *frames*. Frames are sections of a browser window. A small frame across the top of a page may contain a banner ad, while another frame along the side contains navigational buttons. The rest of the window is reserved for the page that displays the actual information. Because that's the section visitors are most likely to be interested in, that's the frame they would click in to print the desired information or save the address of the page as a favorite.

Web pages are not actually solid pages; they are really text documents that contain references to graphics, movies, sounds, other pages, or e-mail addresses. As any page loads into your browser, watch the status bar at the bottom of the screen and you'll see messages wizzing by, telling you as Internet Explorer calls for a page, then a graphic, then another graphic. For each call there is a request, a download, and more. The status bar is quite entertaining to watch at times. The status bar also informs you of any problems the host site may be having if, for example, Internet Explorer makes a request and no response comes for a long period of time.

Visiting a Web site

Web pages appear within the Internet Explorer window, which is called a browser window. When Internet Explorer is launched, one browser window opens automatically. At times, links from pages you visit may open additional browser windows. This enables you to view the information contained in each window the same time, rather than switching pages by reloading them. You can also create additional windows at any time by selecting File⇨New Window or by clicking and holding the mouse button down in the browser window and selecting Clone Window from the contextual menu that appears. Both methods enable you to use one of the windows to move on to another site while also viewing the current site. A clone takes the new window to the same site as the current window. New Window either takes you to your home page or to a blank page, depending on your preference settings under Home/Search. If you plan to follow a link from your current page, Clone Window is your best option. Otherwise, New Window is faster (if you've deselected the option to have every new window take you to your home page).

Getting to a site

There are basically two ways to arrive at a Web page the first time: by entering its address (URL) into the address bar and pressing Enter or Return, or by clicking a link that takes you there. After you've been to a site once, you can return to it in several ways—and you can also come across links in several places. The option to subscribe to a site or have a channel deliver its content add to the number of ways you can get to a site—or how a site can get to you. This section covers getting to a Web page.

Remember that while you're at the site, you can mark that site as a favorite site, and then return to it by clicking that favorites icon later. After you leave a site, you can seek it in the History list and return to it by clicking that site's icon.

Using the address bar

As we just mentioned, you can visit a site by clicking in the address bar's text field, typing in the address, and then pressing Enter or Return. This submits the request to the Web and soon your page is sent to you.

To enter an address, you can have Internet Explorer automatically type the http://www part of the address by pressing Control and the right arrow. Alternatively, you can type the address manually—make sure you enter the address correctly. Another way to enter an address is to type only the domain part of the address. For example, type **Apple** and Internet Explorer will change it to **http://www.apple.com/**. Technically, with this method, Explorer first attempts to find a local intranet site with this name before looking for it out on the Internet, but this doesn't take much time.

Note

Some addresses don't include *www* but use other text instead. If the URL you enter doesn't locate the desired site, look closely at the address, edit it if needed, and then press Enter or Return to resubmit the request.

If you have already visited a site, as you begin to enter a site's address, AutoComplete jumps into action, searching your Favorites and History lists for all addresses that contain the address. If AutoComplete finds what it thinks may be the URL you are typing, it suggests that URL by automatically entering it. If this URL is indeed your desired destination, simply press Return or Enter to go there. If AutoComplete guessed wrong, keep typing. AutoComplete will try again, and again, until you accept its guess or type your own.

AutoComplete is actually a full automatic search. As you enter a site's address, or just part of it, Internet Explorer searches your Favorites and History lists for all addresses that contain the address or word you entered. The results of this search appear in a pop-up list when you click the arrow in the address bar. If you drag down to select any address from this list, you are taken to that page. The cool thing here is that you can enter only part of an address and Internet Explorer lists all matches for that word. For example, if you know you once visited a site about balloons, just begin typing **balloons**. By the time you type **bal**, AutoComplete may already fill in the first balloons site you've visited. If there was more than one, the arrow also becomes active so you can click the arrow to see the complete list of balloon sites you've been to. By selecting any one of those balloon sites from the list, you are returned to that site.

AutoComplete can be turned off or on by clicking the Preferences button, selecting the section called Browser Display, and clicking the check box to place a check or remove a check by this option.

When You Can't Get Through to a Site

When the server you are accessing has a problem, it sends Internet Explorer a message. Internet Explorer should display that error message. If the message isn't being displayed, perhaps you have turned off this capability. To check or change this, choose Edit ⇨ Preferences, and then click Advanced. You want to have Show Server Messages checked.

One message you may receive is, "The specified server could not be found." In this case, you've most likely mistyped the URL, the URL was given to you incorrectly, or it is no longer a valid address. Try entering it again or use a search site to verify the address. If you are accessing the Web from a corporate work site, you may be behind a firewall and have the proxy server setting wrong. In that case, check with your computer personnel.

Another message you receive may be, "The attempt to load 'http://www.something.com' failed." In case you typed the URL incorrectly, try retyping it. While you're at it, check that you entered the right addressing protocol (for example, http://, http://www, or ftp://). Also try deleting any extra path information—the text after the domain name that is divided by slashes—and see if you can get to the main page. If you are using a modem to connect to the Web, and Internet Explorer initiated the connection (started PPP and dialed the modem), when you entered the address the connection may not have gone through. Open your PPP control panel, disconnect and reconnect, and then try the URL again. There's also a chance the site's server is down or busy. In that case, the answer is to try again later.

Using the Open command

Another way to visit a page is to choose File ⇨ Open Location and type, or begin to type, the address. The Open Internet Address dialog box appears (see Figure 36-4), offering you the option to check Open in new window and have the forthcoming page open in a new window. AutoComplete is alive and well within this dialog box. However, you don't enjoy the benefit of the pop-up menu to see the entire found set of addresses.

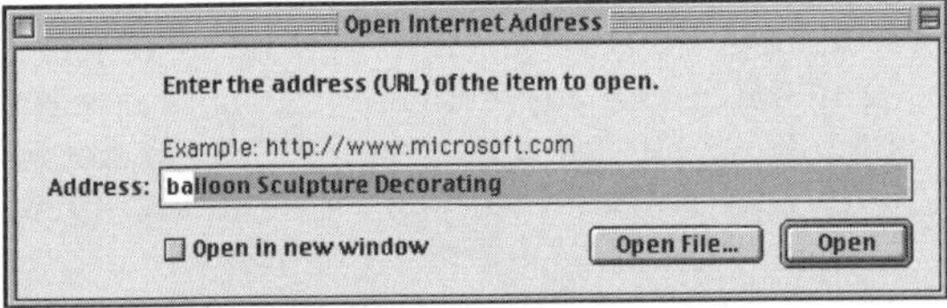

Figure 36-4: An address automatically completed in the Open Internet Address dialog box

Using Apple's Data Detectors

Apple's Data Detectors intelligently extract Internet-related data from bodies of text, and offer you various appropriate actions. For example, if you have a sentence that contains a URL, you can double-click the URL, and then Control-click it to reveal contextual menu (or shortcut menu) of actions from which to choose. With the Internet Explorer Data Detectors installed, you can launch Internet Explorer and be taken to the address noted in your text.

Using the History tab

The History tab retains a complete list of the sites you've visited. As days pass, sites are automatically filed into folders according to the day they were visited. You can click any address in the History tab to return to that site. See the section on the History tab for details.

Using the Favorites tab

When you think you may want to return to a site, it's a good idea to designate that site as a favorite. You fully control what sites are listed here, what order they appear in, what folder (if any) a site appears in, where dividing lines are placed, and so on. See the section on the Favorites tab for details.

Clicking links

More than anything else, you're most likely to use links to get around the Web. Regardless of how you get to the first page you visit, links are what take you to the subsequent pages within a site. By the way, buttons or graphics you click within a page are also links. As often as not, links lead you out of your original site and into another, and another. . . . In the earlier days of the Web, you probably arrived at your first destination by entering an address. These days, links can be found in any Office 98 (Mac) or Office 97 (Windows) document, in any ClarisWorks Office (Mac or Windows) document, in e-mail from Outlook Express, and in several other types of documents. Clicking any of these links connect you to the Web and take you to their destinations (as long as your Mac has an Internet connection or allows connections). The process is very straightforward: click and go.

You can tell you're at a link when your cursor changes from an arrow to a pointing hand icon. Unless you're in a frame, you can also tell where the link leads to by looking in the status bar (at the bottom-left of the browser window).

Normally when you click a link, the new page replaces the one you're in within your current browser window. If you prefer to open a link within a new window, instead of clicking quickly on the link, keep the mouse pressed a bit longer until a pop-up menu appears, and then select Open Link in New Window.

Stopping a page

If a page is taking too long to appear, or you decide it's not of interest to you, click the Stop button, choose View ⇨ Stop Loading, or press ⌘-. (period) (the Mac's universal stop command).

Speeding Up Your Viewing Time

We have written about you visiting a Web page, but actually the page visits you. When you view a page, that page is downloaded to your Mac. Although it appears to you as one page, it is not one element. Often a page is composed of several elements—and that requires several separate downloads from the page's host to your own computer. That's why you see the text appear first (as the text is downloaded), and then a graphic appear (as it is downloaded), and then another graphic appear (as it is downloaded), and so on. By enabling Internet Explorer to make several concurrent connections, several elements can download simultaneously.

By default, Internet Explorer is set to allow four simultaneous connections, as the Internet Explorer programmers found this most efficient when downloading one page from one server. You can check or change this option by choosing Edit⇨Preferences, and then clicking Advanced. The Support Multiple Connections box should be checked. The Max Connections number should be 4. You can set this number as high as 8, but any number over 4 will only be a benefit if you are downloading many files from several servers simultaneously. If you have a fast Mac with a fast connection, you might as well set the number higher.

Subscribing to a site

Subscriptions can either be like the ones that bring newspapers to your home (by bringing a Web site to you) or simply bring you the notification that a Web site has changed, so you can return to the site and check out the new information. You can subscribe to any site and handle each one differently. There is no cost or registration process. It's totally up to you to tell Internet Explorer how often to check the site for changes and what to do when the site does change.

If you have not yet marked a site as a favorite, you can subscribe to it and add it to your Favorites list at the same time. To do so, while at the site, select Favorites⇨Subscribe. This opens the Subscribe dialog box shown in Figure 36-5. To use the default notification and scheduling, simply click Subscribe. Click Customize to open the Get Info dialog box and set unique scheduling and notification for this site. If you click Customize, you are presented with the set of tabs shown in Figure 36-6.

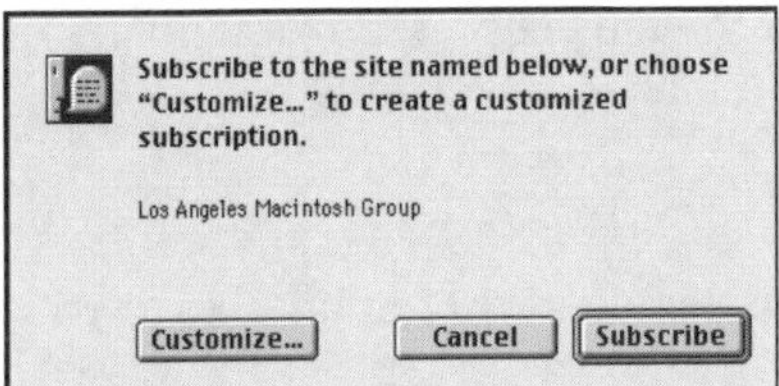

Figure 36-5: The Subscription dialog box

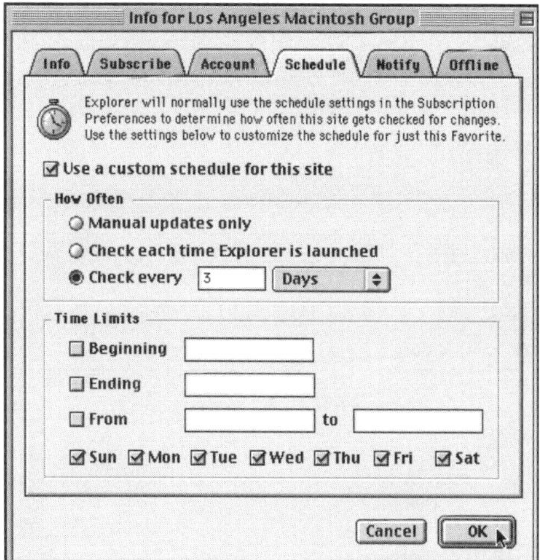

Figure 36-6: Customizing a subscription

If the site you want to subscribe to is already one of your favorites, the fastest way to subscribe is to click in the column to the left of the site's icon (either in the Favorites tab or in the Favorites window). When you do, a subscription (newspaper) icon appears to mark it as subscribed and the default subscription preferences go into effect. Double-click the subscription icon to customize these settings in the Get Info dialog box.

A longer route to subscribing to one of your favorites is to click the Favorites button (or choose Favorites ➪ Open Favorites), click the site to select it, and then choose File ➪ Get Info. In the Get Info dialog box, click the Subscribe tab, and then check the Check This Site For Changes box.

Across-the-board subscription preferences can be changed any time. To change them, click the Preferences button (or select Edit ➪ Preferences), and then click Subscriptions. First click a radio button to tell Internet Explorer how often you want it to check for updates (manual updates only, check each time Explorer is launched, or check every *x* minutes, hours, or days—you determine *x*). Then tell Explorer how to inform you of the change. This can be by sound, an alert, flashing the Explorer icon, and/or by sending an e-mail.

If you tell Explorer to check a subscription's content at a specific time interval, Explorer checks that site at that interval when it is running. This means if you use a modem to dial into the Internet and have set PPP to start when an application needs it, PPP will automatically dial up your account and connect. This can be bothersome if you are working on something at the time.

Icons help keep you informed about the status of your subscriptions, as demonstrated in Figure 36-7. The yellow diamond icon tells you the page has changed since your last visited. The alert icon—an exclamation point—informs you the page could not be checked for updates. Double-click this icon to learn more about the alert.

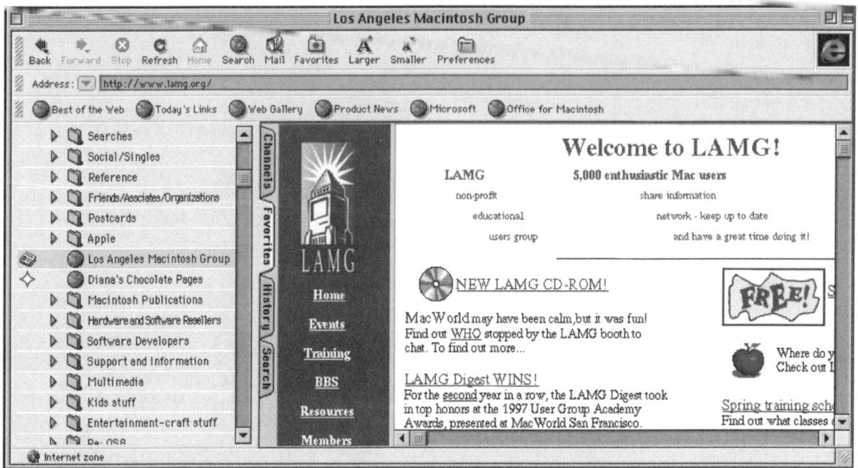

Figure 36-7: Two subscribed sites—one changed, one up to date

You can check for updates manually by choosing Favorites ➪ Update Subscriptions, which is handy if you need to check for updates in between Internet Explorer's designated checks. You'll also need this if, for some reason, you elected not to have an icon or other notification tell you about a site change.

When you no longer want to subscribe to a page, simply click the subscription icon to turn it off. Alternatively, you can double-click the subscription icon and uncheck the option to check the site for changes.

Hot Stuff

If you prefer to have the site's contents delivered to you as an archive you can read while offline, you can do so in the Get Info box for that site. This feature works the same for a subscription as it does for a channel; it's basically an automatic archive feature. (See "Browsing offline" for more information on archives.) By selecting the offline option in the Offline tab, you tell Explorer to archive the site to your hard drive. While you're there, designate a folder to have your site downloaded into. By clicking Options, you can set the components to download. Use this tab in conjunction with the default timing options or the Schedule tab to control the frequency and time of your downloads. Don't forget that if you set the download for the middle of the night, your Mac must be on. You can use the Energy Saver control panel along with this option to turn your Mac on for downloading or off after downloading.

Subscribing to a channel

While any page can be subscribed to, not any page can be a channel. Sites with channels are much more intricate, set up by programmers to deliver specific information that is usually updated on a timely basis. One example of an intricate channel is Excite's channel. You can customize this channel to bring you news, weather, television schedules, and much more—all specifically to deliver (or not deliver) information of your own choosing. Another example is the Discovery Channel Online. As shown in Figure 36-8, it provides new stories every day and delivers it to you each morning.

Internet Explorer makes channels easy to subscribe to by providing links to many Mac-considerate channels right inside the Channels tab. Click Active Channel Guide to check out the offered selection of channels. Internet Explorer also makes channels easy to access or check the status of by putting all the channel information in the Channels tab and displaying the same visual clues showing the status of the pages. (See "Subscribing to a site.")

When you come across a page that offers a channel, you see an opportunity to subscribe. (It is to the site's benefit to make that option clear to you.) When you click the Add Active Channel button or click the offered link, a dialog box opens. Click Add in this dialog box to subscribe and accept the provider's recommended subscription schedule. If you prefer to set up your own subscription options, click Customize instead. Regardless of your initial subscription, you can change your subscription settings any time.

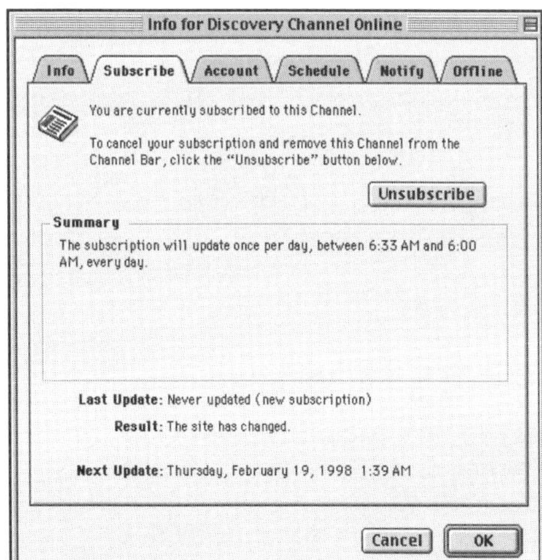

Figure 36-8: The Subscribe tab for this channel tells you about your subscription.

Doing Some Offline Browsing

As with a subscription, you can set up a channel for offline browsing. This is explained in the section "Offline browsing" and a bit in "Subscribing to a site," but briefly, here's how it's done. Click the Favorites button (or choose Favorites⇨Open Favorites), and then click the arrow beside the Channels folder to open it and click once on the channel. Double-click the subscription (newspaper) icon (or choose File⇨Get Info), and then click the Offline tab. Check Select the Download Channel For Offline Browsing.

The name of the file as it will be called when downloaded, appears in the Archive File edit field. You can change this name if you'd like. Note the folder in which the file is set to land. Click Change location and select another folder if preferred.

When you want to change the settings for a channel you subscribe to, click the Favorites tab or button, and then click the arrow next to the Channels folder to reveal its contents. Double-click the subscription (newspaper) icon next to the channel. This selects that channel and opens the Get Info dialog box from which you control the settings for the selected channel.

Select the Schedule tab to set up a custom subscription schedule. Begin by checking Use a custom schedule for this channel, and then enter your preferred schedule.

Note

Unfortunately, platform differences sometimes make something designed for the Mac unsuitable for Windows users, and vice versa. Explorer's Help points out that sites that use VBScript or an ActiveX control developed for Windows may not deliver content well to a Mac. In those cases, Internet Explorer does its best to alert you. However, there's no harm in trying a channel. After all, it's easy to unsubscribe.

When you no longer want to receive information on a channel, double-click the subscription (newspaper) icon next to the channel, and then click the Unsubscribe button located under the Subscribe tab.

Marking favorite sites for easy return

Cyberspace is vast—and incredibly easy to take exciting detours in as you follow links from one page to another. As you come across a page you are interested in, you may want to note its location so you can return to it later. In Internet Explorer, this bookmarking is called adding an address to your list of favorites.

Some people go wild marking every site they come across as a favorite site. Others explore several pages within a site or as the result of a search, and then return to the one of most interest and only add that one. The History tab tracks your travels as you explore. That enables you to relax and enjoy the trip, and then look over your History list later on and move sites of interest into the Favorites tab. This has a downside, though, as the titles of each page may not be enough to remind you which pages were worthy of your return.

If you don't mark a site in your Favorites list, you might still find it another way. You may opt to save e-mail messages with links (of course, you'd have to return to that e-mail to find the link). And you can always perform a search by keyword(s) to return to sites of interest.

One thing is certain, however: you will find yourself with an ever-growing list of favorites as you spend more time in cyberspace.

Adding a favorite

There are several ways to add a page to your list of favorites, depending on what you're doing, where you are, or what you've done.

The most obvious time to add a page to your Favorites list is while you are visiting the page. The easiest way to do so is to click within the page and hold the mouse until the pop-up menu appears. Then drag down to the Add Page to Favorites command and release the mouse button. Another option is to select Favorites ⇨ Add Page to Favorites. (You could use the keyboard equivalent, ⌘-D, but because that's often the Delete command in most Mac software, we don't recommend you get in the habit of using it.)

Hot Stuff

At times you may be on a page and see a link you are interested in, but not have time to visit that page first. You can add that link to your favorites list by clicking that link and holding down the mouse button until the shortcut menu pops up, and then selecting Add Link To Favorites.

If you've already visited the page, but didn't add it to your Favorites list, you can open the History tab and drag it from the History tab into the Favorites tab. Because the Favorites tab is not open, move the icon over the Favorites tab and rest it there until the Favorites tab becomes active. Then release the mouse when the icon will land where you want it. A black line indicates where the icon will land when you release the mouse.

There's another way to move an item from the History to the Favorites list. Click the Favorites tab so it is showing. Then choose Go ⇨ Open History and drag an icon from the History window into the Favorites list. A black line indicates where the icon will land when you release the mouse.

Adding a folder

To make a folder, choose Favorites ➪ New Folder. Your Favorites list opens in a separate window and the new folder appears there. Naming a folders works the same as naming a folder in the Finder; it is preselected so you can type a name for it immediately. To rename a folder, click the folder's title to select it and enter a new name. As in the Finder, you can click any favorite in the Favorites window and drag it into any folder. You can also move a folder into a folder. Better than in the Finder, you can move folders into any position in the list.

Renaming a folder or favorite

As we've mentioned, the page designer determines the name a site is given when you mark it as a favorite—and not all designers are savvy. By renaming a page and giving it a name you can recognize, you'll make it much easier to find later when you want to return to the site. To rename a site in your Favorites list, click the Favorites button (or choose Favorites ➪ Open Favorites) to open the Favorites window. While you're in the Favorites window, you can rename items the same way you do in the Finder. Click the name, keep the mouse button pressed for about two seconds, and then release to select the entire name. Type a new name or click to place the insertion point, and then edit the item's name.

Adding a divider

Dividing lines can do a lot to make your list easier to use. To add a dividing line, select Favorites ➪ New Divider. The Favorites window automatically opens and a new dividing line appears. Click the line and drag it into place between any favorites or folders. As you drag the divider, a black line appears to show you where the line is due to land when you release the mouse. After you've added a few lines, you can move favorites and/or folders into any order between the dividers.

Deleting a favorite

Deleting is easy—another reason that marking a site as a favorite is better than not marking it and trying to find it again later. When you no longer want to save a favorite, click the Favorites button (or choose Favorites ➪ Open Favorites) to open the Favorites window. Then drag the item to the Trash as you do with any file in a Finder window. You can also click the item to select it, and then choose Edit ➪ Clear. This removes the item without placing it in the Trash.

Controlling how you see Web sites

Much of how you—a visitor to a site—see the pages delivered to your Mac is controlled by you. You can select colors, turn images, videos, and sounds on or off, and more. Distributed among the various panes of the Preferences dialog box are the many changes you can make (see Figure 36-9). In many cases, you may be happy with the default. However, it's worth a visit to this dialog box to see what your options are. For page-viewing options, check out the Web Content, Browser Display, and Language/Fonts panes.

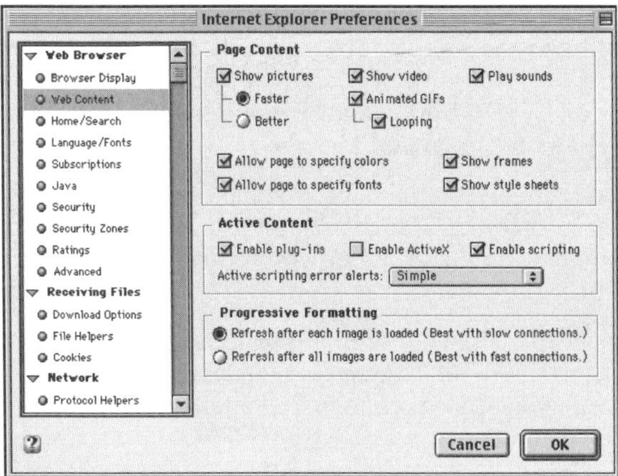

Figure 36-9: The Web Content pane and its options

Fonts

Fonts play a large role in how we perceive a message. However, a Web page is not like a printed page, as a Web page designer has no control over what fonts viewers have on their hard drives. It is quite possible for a viewer to select any font and make it any size. One option is to make messages into images, therefore protecting the look of the text. However, a viewer can turn off image loading to speed up delivery of information over his or her modem. That means the viewer doesn't get the message the image contained. If the designer is savvy, alternate image tags may present at least part of the image's text message, but it's not the same as seeing the works nicely laid out. To address this issue, HTML now includes something known as style sheets (the first bullet point). Among the choices you can make within the Web Content pane are the following:

✦ **Style Sheets**—Style sheets are similar to the styles you can set up in Word to predefine the look of a body of text. With style sheets, a Web page designer can control margins, line spacing, text placement, text colors, font faces, font sizes, and graphics placement. Designers have to worry about style sheets; all you have to do is take advantage of them. You, as the viewer have the ability to recognize the use of style sheets or not, although there is really no reason not to. To make sure style sheets are recognized, click the Preferences button, and then select the Web Content pane and check the Show style sheets box.

✦ **Colors**—Designers work hard to make their pages look good, but if the colors don't work for you or if you're color-blind, you can take control of the colors you see by turning this option off in the Web Content pane.

✦ **Fonts**—As with colors, you can use what is sent to you or choose to override them by unchecking Allow page to specify fonts in the Web Content pane. This forces the page to use the fonts you select. (See the next point. Yes, we know it's also about fonts, but it's a different preference.)

- **Font**—If you find pages hard to read, choose Edit⇨Preferences, and then click Language/Fonts and choose a font(s) that is easier on your eyes. You can designate one for display of all proportional text and one for fixed-width text. Most fonts on your Mac are proportional. The two common fixed-width fonts are Courier (the typewriter font) and Monaco.
- **Font Size**—If the text on Web pages appears too small or too large, select Edit⇨Preferences and then Browser/Display. At the top of the dialog box, select a font size from the pop-up menu. When you return to your current page, it will reload to reflect the change.
- **Language**—You can select the language selected by default in cases where a site offers its pages in more than one language. English is the default if you have an English version of Office 98. To change the language, choose Edit⇨Preferences and then Language/Fonts.

Other page content

As we mentioned, you have the option to turn off each of the special effects available. You'll find many in the Web Content pane of the Preferences dialog box, but there are other effects you can change. If speed is an issue, you can try turning off sound, video, and/or pictures. While viewing a site, if you feel you need to see any or all of the pictures, you can do so. Either click the image-missing icon for any single image, and then click and hold while you select Load Missing Image. Or, choose View⇨Load Images to view them all.

The Mac can do some incredible things thanks to QuickTime, QuickTime VR, and QuickDraw 3D/VRML. These are all extensions that come with your system installer. We recommend you install them and keep them on if you really want to take advantage of the Mac. (Actually, this technology has become the standard, so everyone will have it soon.)

Plug-ins

A plug-in is a small program that adds extra functionality to a browser. If a page designer has created a page that calls for a certain plug-in, you must download and install that plug-in before you can see that page properly. Sometimes you can still enjoy a page without the plug-in; other times the entire page depends upon the plug-in. You will most likely be alerted when a plug-in is required. You will also be given the opportunity to download the plug-in. To install a plug-in, you need to place it in the Plug-ins folder inside your Internet Explorer 4.0 folder—after decompressing it. You also need to relaunch Internet Explorer. Plug-ins share RAM with Internet Explorer, so as you add plug-ins, you may need to allot more memory to Explorer. The Help files recommend raising the Preferred Size to 8,000K.

Working with Cookies

There has been a lot of controversy over *cookies* since their inception. A spy doesn't sneak a cookie into your computer to steal data. A cookie is just a bit of information a Web page's server sends to a file on your computer. Later, when you revisit that page or site, the information in that cookie is returned to the Web site so it can recognize you. Don't worry—a cookie doesn't have your social security number or any such thing; a cookie is usually a randomly generated number. Databases often rely on cookies to make sure the information you request gets back to you.

You have full control of cookies on your own Mac. To see for yourself and review your options, click the Preferences button, and then select the Cookies pane. The following controls are offered:

✦ Use the When Receiving Cookies pop-up menu to select the option you are most comfortable with. Perhaps you want to decide on a site-to-site basis, or maybe you don't mind accepting any cookie. If you choose Ask for each site, you can predetermine whether you accept a site or not. To do so, click the cookie in question, and then click the button that pertains to your options. For example, if you previously had your preference set to Always accept cookies, and then switch to Ask for each site, the option you have for each cookie is to Decline.

✦ You can view the information within a cookie by clicking the cookie and clicking the View button.

✦ You can delete a cookie by clicking the cookie and clicking the Delete button. If you delete a cookie, the next time you visit that cookie's site, a new cookie downloads.

Searching Web sites

The Web is full of information just waiting to be discovered. Knowing how to search for it is the key to finding it. Internet Explorer provides several search options.

Using search engines

While Internet Explorer provides several ways to search, it's the *search engines* on the Web that do the actual searching. Internet Explorer simply makes the pages of the search engines easily accessible. To search, you visit—download—the search engine's search page. In the fields provided, you enter your search criteria. Then you click Search (or something to that affect) and your request is processed, returning a results page to you. A results page always contains some sort of brief description of the sites found and a link to each site found.

To access the search engines, use one of the following methods:

✦ **The Go menu**—Selecting Go⇨Search The Internet takes you directly to one specific preset search engine. By default, Internet Explorer takes you to a special search page set up by Microsoft. On it you can select any of the available search engines. The engine options are the same as those provided in the Search tab.

If you have a preferred search page, you can set it as the one this command goes to. The easiest way to do so is to go to that page, click anywhere on that page, and keep the mouse button down until a menu pops up. (You'll get the same menu if you Control-click.) From the menu that pops up, select Set Search Page. Alternatively, you can click the Preferences button or select Edit⇨Preferences, click Home/Search (in the Preferences dialog box), and then enter the address of your preferred search page in the Address field. To reset the Go menu command to call up the default page, use the Preferences dialog box and click the Default button. If for some reason you prefer not to have a search page under the Go menu, click Use None in the Preferences dialog box.

✦ **The Search tab in the Explorer bar**—The Search tab of the Explorer bar provides quick access to several search engines. Click the Search tab, and then either use the provider of the day, which is automatically chosen, or select the provider of your choice from the pop-up list. (If the Explorer bar is not showing, select it from the View menu.) One excellent benefit to this tab is you can see the results of your search in the tab while you click the resulting links to see where they lead.

✦ **The address bar**—Internet Explorer's AutoSearch and its partnership with Yahoo! (a popular search engine) enables you to search Yahoo! directly from the address bar without going to the Yahoo! search page first. Click in the address bar and type **go** or **?** (a question mark), then a space, followed by the word you want to search for. Then press Enter or Return, as you do whenever you enter an address in this field. Internet Explorer does the rest, taking you to a special search page co-provided by Microsoft and Yahoo!, where your results are displayed.

Searching for text

As in a regular document, you can search for specific text within a Web page. The command is the same as it usually is on the Mac—Find and Find Again. To find text, select Edit⇨Find (⌘-F).

In the Find dialog box, enter the text you are seeking. Check Match Case if you want only the same pattern of capital and lowercase letters to be found. Leave it unchecked if you don't care about capitalization. In the example in Figure 36-10, we are searching for Chocolate, but only for occurrences of the word with a capital C. To begin your search from wherever your cursor is, leave the Start From Top option unchecked. To start your search at the top of the page, check Start From Top, as we did in our quest for Chocolate.

After entering your criteria, click Find to locate the first occurrence of the text you seek. To find subsequent occurrences of that text, select Edit⇨Find Again (⌘-G). ⌘-G is easier to use. Keep pressing ⌘-G and each occurrence of your desired text appears highlighted on the Web page.

To search beyond the current page and check an entire Web site, you need to use a search engine.

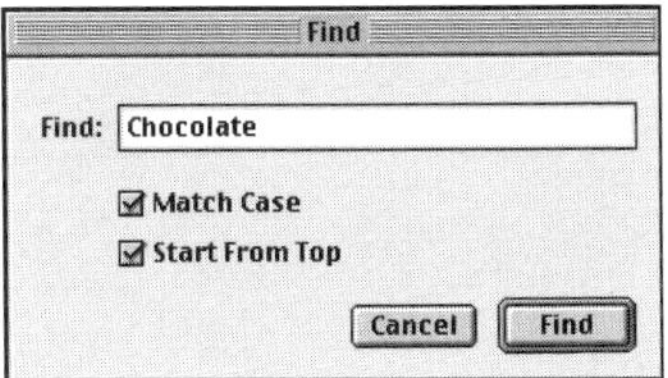

Figure 36-10: The Find dialog box—searching for Chocolate

Browsing offline

Internet Explorer provides a few features that make it possible to review Web content without being connected to the Internet. This is a terrific feature if you want to work while commuting, access the Web at school but not at home, or if you pay for your connection time. To check a site on a regular basis, subscribe to the site or channel and set it to download for offline browsing.

While you are still online, visit the site(s) you are interested in, but instead of reading it, archive it. An archive is a single file that can contain every graphic, sound, movie, and link, in addition to all the site's text. By double-clicking the file, the archive opens and you have, in effect, the entire Web site, complete with working links. That way you can read the site at your leisure—even when you're not connected to the Internet.

When you create your archive, you set the option to save any number of links that connect from the site. While viewing offline, eventually, you may get to a link that is beyond what you elected to save. (After all, the Web keeps going and going.) If you click a link that was not included in your archive, you see a message, as shown in Figure 36.11. While offline, click Cancel.

For more on saving a site as an archive, see the following section, "Downloading and Saving Files."

When you subscribe to a site (see "Subscribing to a site"), rather than accepting the default options, click Customize to bring up the Get Info window. In this window, be sure to select the Offline tab, as shown in Figure 36-12 and check the offline option as shown. As with archiving, click Options to determine which accompanying files will be downloaded.

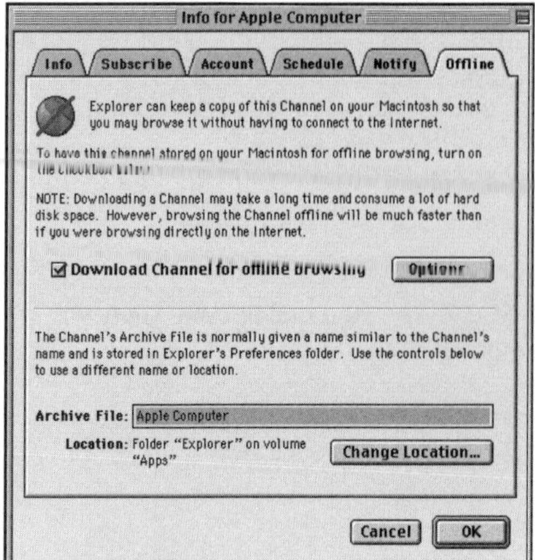

Figure 36-11: The offline alert asking to connect

Figure 36-12: Automatic delivery of a site archive is set in this tab.

Even while you do have access to the Internet, at times you may not wish to connect. In that case, be sure to select File ⇨ Offline Browsing. That way when you click links that would otherwise attempt a Web connection, they will not do so.

Downloading and Saving Files

There are several ways you can save the information found on the Web and keep it for your own reference. This section covers your options. Please remember that material on the Web was created by people who may have worked very hard on it and the creators of material retain the rights to the material. (Just because it's easy to copy material doesn't make it legal.)

Copying

The easiest way to transfer text from a Web page is to copy it, and then paste in into your Notepad, organizer, document, and so on. Simply drag over the text to select it and choose Edit⇨Copy (⌘-C) the same way you select text and copy it in any Mac document. Then paste the text into your destination document.

Links can be tricky to copy by selecting. Try starting at the end of the link text, rather than the left side. The easiest way to copy a link is to click the link, and then hold the mouse button down until the shortcut menu pops up. From the menu, select Copy Link to Clipboard. Then paste as normal.

To copy an image for pasting, click the image, holding the mouse button down until the shortcut menu pops up, and then select Copy Image. Paste this copied image as normal.

Saving a file

While you are viewing a Web page, you can save it as plain text, as HTML code, or as an Internet Explorer archive. All of these are done via the File⇨Save As command.

- ✦ Saving as plain text is easiest if you want to show someone the content of the page. You'll be able to open the document in SimpleText, or in a word processor. However, images and formatting are lost this way.
- ✦ Saving as HTML enables you to see the page as it was created. It's a great way to learn how to create your own Web pages. This method doesn't download the images, however.
- ✦ Saving as an archive saves the entire site, not just the page you are on. Saving as an archive can also download the page's images, sounds, movies, and/or links at the same time. (Click the Options button to determine what will be downloaded.) You can also choose how many links deep you want to go. Archiving a site, page, or channel enables you to read it offline. To view an archived site, double-click it in the Finder.

Choose File⇨Save As, and then click the Format pop-up menu to select Plain Text, HTML format, or Web Archive. As your download takes place, the Download Manager window reports its progress. To learn more about the downloaded item, double-click the item in the window. See "Reviewing your downloads."

Note

To preserve the look of text, it has become common for designers to use graphics that contain text, rather than using plain text. Therefore, if you save a site without saving the graphics, you may be missing important information. When saving as HTML, you need to be sure to save each important graphic as a separate save. The easiest solution is to save the site as an archive, remembering to click the Options button and make sure you are saving the images and any other components that are important to your appreciation of the site.

Decoding Files

To travel through cyberspace, files must be encoded and often compressed to make transfers faster. Aladdin's StuffIt Expander is the de facto standard for compression on the Mac (and also available for Windows). You'll know these files by the extension .hqx (which stands for a process called BinHex). At present, StuffIt Expander is not installed by Internet Explorer or any of the other Office 98 programs. We highly recommend that you download this application if you don't already have StuffIt Deluxe. StuffIt Expander is freeware and is available at `Aladdinsys.com`. Once StuffIt Expander is installed, you can drag any .hqx, or .sit file onto the program's icon to decode and expand the file.

Another popular decoding freeware application, by Peter N. Lewis, is called MacBinary. Both MacBinary and BinHex decoding are turned on by default in Internet Explorer's Preferences under Download Options.

Downloading

Downloading a file, text, link, or image creates a new file on your hard drive (as does the Save As command but not the Copy command). This file can be opened later and handled however you want.

Note

For easy access to your downloads, make the folder you elect to collect your downloaded files easily accessible. Make an alias of this folder, and then place that alias in the Apple menu, or in a folder within that menu.

- ✦ To download an image, click the image, hold the mouse button down until the shortcut menu pops up, and then select Download Image To Disk from the shortcut menu.
- ✦ Sounds, and sometimes videos, are not actually in the Web page but are links the page retrieves at the user's request. Therefore, to download sounds, select Download Link To Disk from the pop-up menu. (Clicking quickly on a sound link plays the sound instead of presenting the menu, so be sure to hold the mouse button down when you click the sound's link or icon.)
- ✦ If a movie has been embedded in the page, the pop-up menu offers Save Movie As, rather than the Download Link To Disk command. To download an embedded movie, select Save Movie As. In this case, the Download Manager won't track the download.

In each case, as when you save any file, you must choose a folder in which to save the file, and then name or rename the file and click Save.

The truth is that images are also not actually in a Web page; they are referred to by the page and downloaded separately. It just so happens that the command to save them to disk is a different one from the command to download a sound or movie link.

To download an entire page, copy the URL of that page if you are already there. Then select File➪Download File to open the dialog box shown in Figure 36-13. If you've copied the URL of the file to be downloaded, paste it in the URL field. Otherwise type in the URL. (This field doesn't accept drag-and-drop as of this writing.) Note the folder the download is set to land in. To change folders, click the Change button and select a new folder. When ready, click Download. This opens the Download Manager window so you can watch the progress, as shown in Figure 36-14. It's okay to continue working in Internet Explorer as a file downloads. Internet Explorer works in the background.

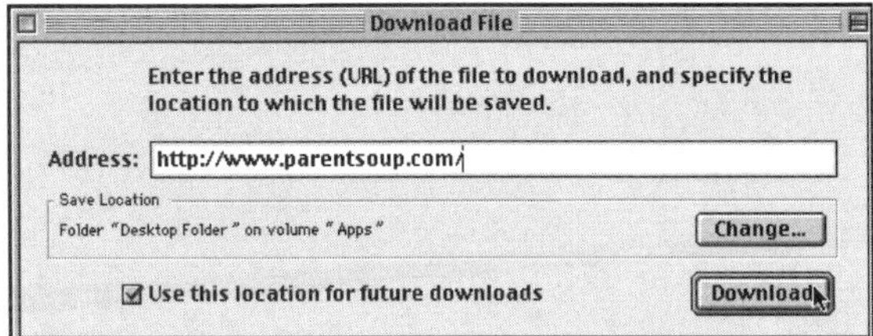

Figure 36-13: Entering a URL for a page download

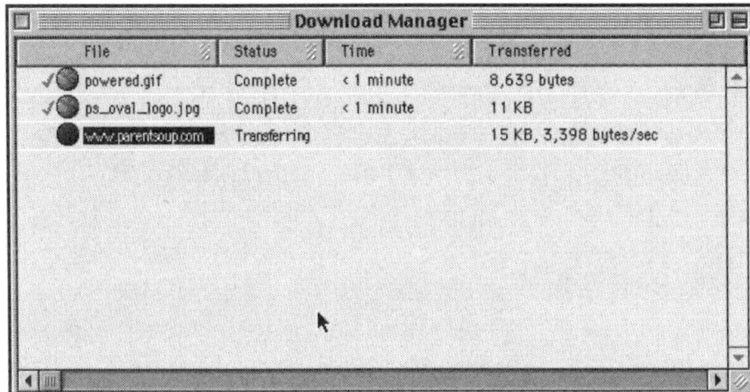

Figure 36-14: The Download Manager tracking a download's progress

Stopping a download

To stop a file from downloading once you've started the download, select View➪Stop Loading. This file will be listed as Canceled in the Download Manager.

Reviewing your downloads

If you can't recall where you saved a file or aren't sure the file downloaded successfully, check with the Download Manager, shown in Figure 36-14. To open the Download Manager, select File➪Download Manager. When a file is downloaded successfully, a green check mark appears beside it. You can sort the list by any column header by clicking that header. Therefore, you can sort by filename, status, the time it took to download, or the size of the file transferred. To resize a column for easier reading, move your mouse pointer over the cross-hatched area in the header until your pointer becomes a hand. Then click and drag the column to size. Double-click a filename to reveal information about the file, such as the folder that file landed in. The file in Figure 36-15 was successful and landed on the desktop.

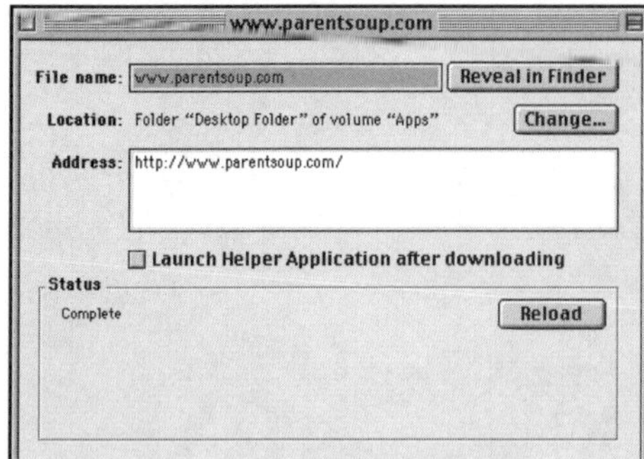

Figure 36-15: Details of a download

Setting the Download Manager's preferences

You can determine where downloads will be saved by default. This, and all the other Download Manager's settings are saved in the Preferences dialog box, so click the Preferences button or choose Edit ⇨ Preferences, and then click Download Options.

The currently selected location is noted in the top portion of the dialog box. To change folders, click the Change Location button, and then navigate to the folder you want your downloaded files to land in. If you always want your files to land in that folder, click the radio button for this option. The alternative is to let files go to folders that the appropriate helpers send files to. For example, if you use StuffIt Expander to translate and decompress files, and you've set StuffIt Expander to decompress to a folder called InBox, then a downloaded unstuffed file would land in the InBox rather than the folder designated by the Download Manager.

You can control how many files you can download at one time by choosing a number from the pop-up box labeled Maximum Number of Concurrent Downloads.

If the Download Manager does not list the files you download, select the radio button marked Immediately Remove Items After They Have Been Downloaded. Otherwise, keep the default, which is to track all downloads and enter the maximum number of downloads you want tracked in the list. By the way, you can always delete a listing from the Download Manager's window by dragging it from the window to the Mac's Trash folder.

Automatic decoding of files is very handy and makes the Internet less confusing. Keep the two decoding options checked.

Printing Web Pages

Web pages are printed just like any other document. Go to the page, and then select File⇨Print or ⌘-P. Frames are the only tricky thing to print. To print the page contained within a frame, click inside the frame before you give the print command. If you want images to print, be sure to turn them on in Preferences first. If you see images on your screen, they are on. If they are off, you see a red circle and white X.

Dealing with Security Concerns

To make your exchanges on the Web as secure as possible, Internet Explorer supports these security standards:

SSL and Windows NT

This is Web-server-level security. When a Web server supports one of these standards, unauthorized people won't see any data sent to or from those sites, so you can be comfortable knowing your information is safe. Internet Explorer supports these servers, doing whatever it needs to do on the user's (your) end of the Web equation. When you are on a Web page sent from a secure server, you see a lock in the status bar.

Site certificates

When a Web site wants its users to be confident of the site's security, it can apply for a certificate. These certificates are not given out lightly. They are costly and the site is rigorously tested to make sure it meets the demands of the issuer. Internet Explorer is set up to recognize trusted certificates. You can choose which ones you want to accept or ignore by checking or unchecking each one in the Security pane of the Preferences dialog box.

Security zones

Security zones are a set of four zones, set by you, each bearing a security level. You then assign any site to a zone. As you call on a site, Internet Explorer notes the zone and checks the security setting for that site's zone. You can always tell which zone you are accessing by looking in the status bar.

The four zones are:

✦ **Local Intranet**—assigned a Medium security level by default. These are the addresses on your company or group's intranet, placed there by your system administrator. This administrator can also add new addresses to this zone

✦ **Trusted Sites**—assigned a Low security by default, which is probably all that is needed here. These are the sites you trust. They feel safe to download or run files from.

✦ **Restricted Sites**—assigned a High security by default, which is probably needed here. These are the sites you aren't sure of. They may be fine, but you have no way of knowing whether accessing files from these sites is safe.

✦ **Internet zone**—Medium security is assigned here. This is the rest of the Internet. You've weeded out and marked the sites you don't trust, and marked the sites you do trust. You know your intranet and your own hard drive are safe. This is everything else. You don't assign every single site in existence to a level; this is the catch-all for that.

Each zone is preset with a set of permitted actions and alerts. You can use these or customize your own permissions for each zone. For example, you can allow full access—running and downloading—of files in your intranet zone; therefore setting security to Low. For sites in the restricted zone, you can prevent any active exchange—no running of scripts, no downloading, no active content.

The first step is to determine what security level you want for each zone. To do so, click the Preferences button, and then click Security Zones, as shown in Figure 36-16. Select the zone you want to effect from the Zone pop-up menu, and then click one of the four radio buttons to set a security level.

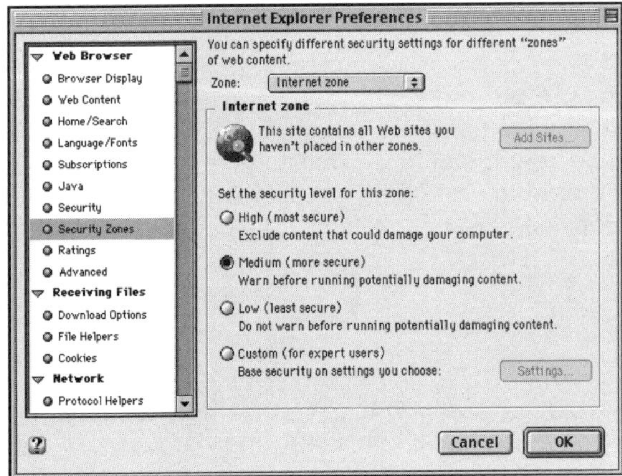

Figure 36-16: The Security Zones pane in the Preferences dialog box

The next step is to assign each Web site to a security zone. To do so, click the Preferences button, and then click Security Zones. Only the system administrator sets up the Local Intranet zone, and the Internet zone is all the sites that are otherwise not assigned. That leaves the Trusted Sites zone and the Restricted Sites zone for site assignment, so choose one of these from the Zone menu. When you do, the Add Sites button becomes active. Click Add Sites to open a sites list dialog box. Click the next Add button, and then enter a URL for the Web site you are assigning to that zone and click OK. For example, in Figure 36-17 we show the addition of bighit.com into our zone. Figure 36-18 shows the sites in our Trusted Sites list.

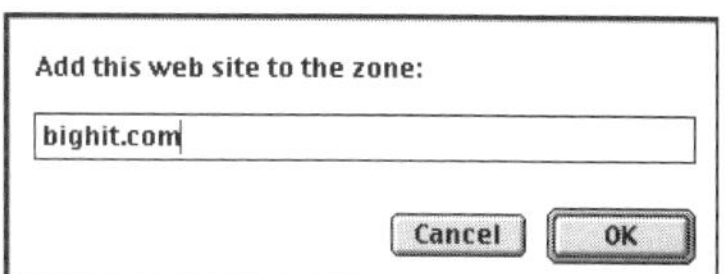

Figure 36-17: Adding a site to a zone

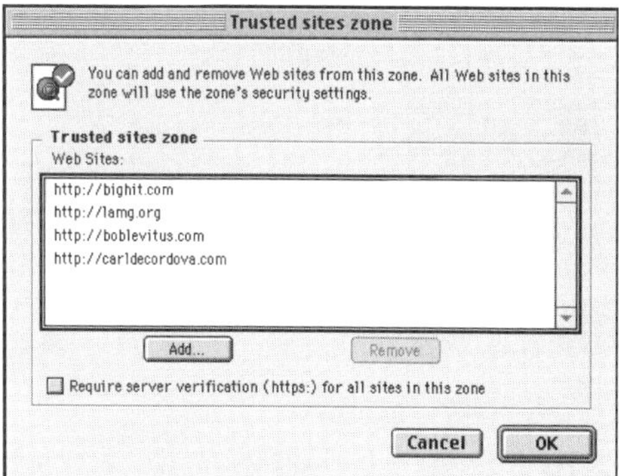

Figure 36-18: The Trusted Sites zone list

Security alerts

Security alerts are warnings that appear when you attempt to access, submit, or download items that are potential security risks. An alert may be helpful to remind you—or the users of the Mac in use—that a site is not secure. It may help users think twice before sending such things as account or client information.

To display security alerts, click the Preferences button, and then click Security. This brings up the Security pane, as shown in Figure 36-19. Add or remove checks to activate or deactivate the alerts you want in effect.

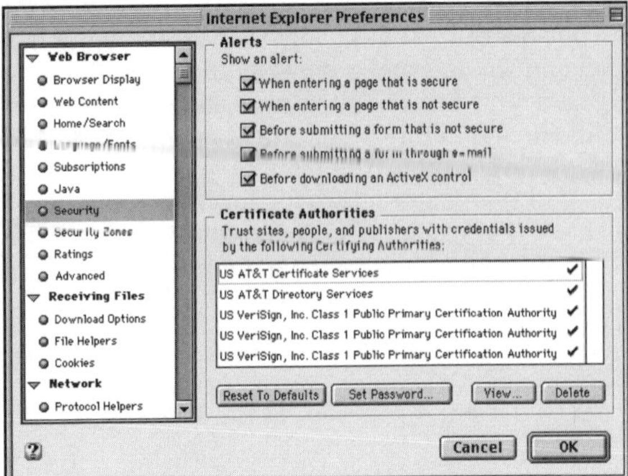

Figure 36-19: Security alerts and certificates settings

Besides relying on alerts, it is helpful to train yourself and users to notice the lock icon (or lack thereof) in the status bar.

Working with Internet Ratings Support

In case you have family or business members accessing the Internet from your Mac, Internet Explorer provides the capability to control the types of content that your computer can access on the Internet. By turning on Internet Ratings and password-protecting your settings, you can ensure that only the content that meets your criteria is accessed and viewed.

To set up your content-screening, click the Preferences button, and then click Ratings to select the Ratings Preferences pane, as shown in Figure 36-20. Then, follow these steps:

1. By default ratings are turned off, so click Enabled to turn them on.
2. Ratings screening doesn't mean much if anyone can change the settings. By default there is no password, so click Change Password and enter a password in the New Password field—not the top field. To make sure you've entered the desired word correctly, you must type it again.

   Notice you can change your password at any time. But no matter what—remember your password! You will need it to change the ratings.
3. Use the pop-up menu by each of the four categories: Violence, Sex, Nudity, and Language to tell Internet Explorer the level you are comfortable with. Figure 36-20 demonstrates the types of choices you can make.

4. (Optional) You can allow users to have access to sites that are unrated. To do so, click the Options button, and then check User can view sites that have no rating.

5. (Optional) You can opt to set up Internet Explorer so you can enter your password at any time and allow your users access to all restricted sites. To do so, check the option that says Supervisor can type a password to allow users to view restricted content.

6. (Optional) If you want to use a Ratings Bureau, enter the name of the bureau in the Ratings Bureau text field.

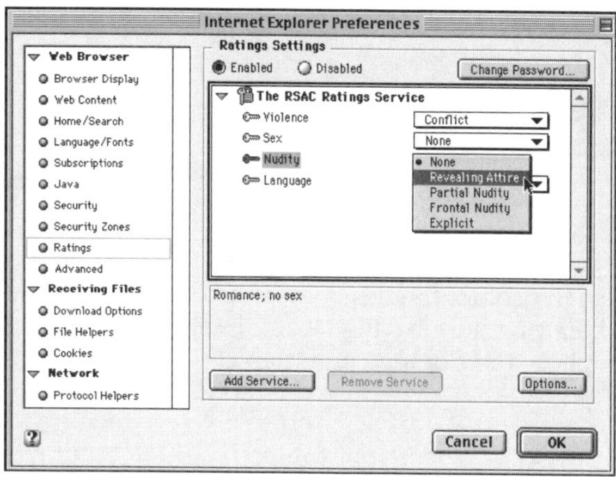

Figure 36-20: Setting up ratings screening

The default rating system is that of the Recreational Software Advisory Council (RSAC) at `http://www.rsac.org/`. If you prefer, you can elect to choose from other rating services instead. To do so, download these services. Then click Add Service in the Ratings Preferences pane and select the new service.

Reading Mail and News

From Internet Explorer, you can read your e-mail or read your news. You can also send a new e-mail message or even send a new message that automatically includes the URL of the page you are currently on. To do either of these things, click the Mail button, which is actually a pop-up menu, and then make your selection. By default, any of these selections opens Outlook Express, Internet Explorer's sister application. You can change this so the button opens another program. In fact, you can have one program selected to handle e-mail and another to handle news.

To change your Mail and News program, select Edit⇨Preferences, and then click Protocol Helpers. Click Mail to in the Helpers list, and then click the Change button. In the Protocol Helper Editor that opens, click Choose Helper. Navigate to your e-mail program of choice and click Open. You see the chosen helper noted in the Protocol Helper Editor dialog box. Click OK. Next click News in the Protocol list and repeat the steps to elect your preferred helper. By default, the protocols and the helpers available are sorted by protocol (as shown by the underline). To sort by application, click the word *Application*.

To create a new message and have the body of the message list the URL you are at, go to the Web site you want to note, and then select Send Link from the Mail button's pop-up menu.

Getting More Help

To access Internet Explorer's Help, go to Help⇨Internet Explorer Help. This Help is a system of linked Web pages presented via Internet Explorer. You can print the pages and change their look the same way you change any other Web pages.

Note

As with most Web pages, the colors the designer set up work well. If you have altered your colors and are therefore having trouble seeing the information, click the Preferences button, click Web Content, and then check Allow Page To Specify Colors.

Click Index to view the Index and select your topic from there. After each topic is a list of related topics. Each related topic is a link, so you can click it to follow it immediately. As with all links, the color changes after you follow it so you can tell where you've already been.

Tips & Tricks is a good place to pick up not only tips and tricks, but also menu command definitions.

The Glossary will help you understand terms you may be unfamiliar with.

There is also an entire newsgroup dedicated to using Internet Explorer for the Macintosh. Because it's a newsgroup, its subscription and message exchanges are handled by Outlook Express or another newsgroup e-mail client if you have another you prefer. Please refer to Chapter 35 to learn about Outlook Express and newsgroups. You can subscribe to the Internet Explorer for Macintosh list at `microsoft.public.inetexplorer.mac`.

Finally, at `www.microsoft.com/ie/mac`, you find updated announcements about Internet Explorer and possibly more help, tips, and so on.

Summary

This chapter provided an overview of Internet Explorer, Microsoft's Web browser. Points covered in this chapter included the following:

- ✦ Marking a site as a favorite enables you to revisit it easily.
- ✦ You can have Internet Explorer notify you when a site's content changes by subscribing to that site.
- ✦ As you visit sites, Internet Explorer keeps a history of those sites. (You can limit the number of sites tracked by setting this in the Advanced section of your Preferences under Web Browser.)
- ✦ The Search tab of the Explorer bar makes it easier than ever to seek out Web sites by content. You can do your search within the Explorer bar and continue to view the search results while visiting the found sites.
- ✦ Internet Explorer supports several security standards. It recognizes site certificates, enables you to set up security zones, and uses security alerts to warn users they are entering an unsecured Web site. It also enables you to use the standardized ratings to help you restrict access to sites by content.

Where to go next

- ✦ Are you considering placing your own documents on the Web? Chapter 11 covers Word and the Web; Chapter 23 covers Excel and the Web; and Chapter 32 covers PowerPoint and the Web.
- ✦ Wondering how to send and receive e-mail or access newsgroups? Chapter 35 is standing by to help you do so with Outlook Express.

✦ ✦ ✦

Appendixes

In This Part

Appendix A
Installing Microsoft Office

Appendix B
Word Quick Start

Appendix C
Excel Quick Start

Appendix D
PowerPoint Quick Start

Appendix E
Customizing Toolbars and Menus

Installing Microsoft Office 98

✦ ✦ ✦ ✦

In This Appendix

Getting started

Making a custom installation

Working with the Value Pack

Removing Office 98

Removing previous versions of Office

Installing Internet Explorer

Installing Outlook Express

✦ ✦ ✦ ✦

The Microsoft Office 98 CD-ROM includes two installation options—basic and custom—for installing the core Office 98 applications: Word, Excel, and PowerPoint. In addition, Microsoft provides several extras for Office 98 and two Internet programs.

Getting Started

The basic installation is incredibly easy. You simply drag the Microsoft Office 98 folder to your hard drive. (This is covered in Chapter 1.) This basic installation may well include all you need—or even more than you need (in which case, you may prefer a custom install).

The Office custom install is an alternative to the standard drag-install, enabling you to install only portions of the standard Office software. It may also contain functions that are not part of the drag-install, but those options are likely to also be available in the Value Pack Installer, which you are more likely to use. The custom install also helps you remove Office. The Value Pack folder provides more Office software that complements the standard install. In the Value Pack section of this appendix, we explore each of the options and what it provides for you. The Microsoft Internet folder provides Microsoft Internet Explorer, a browser, and Outlook Express, an e-mail handler.

Making a Custom Installation

When should you use the custom installer?

- ✦ If all the programs and options the basic Office installation offers are more than you need, you can choose to do a custom install instead, opting to install only part of the full offering.
- ✦ If you've installed Office 98 and find you need to reinstall part of the program, a custom install may be your solution.
- ✦ If you have installed only parts of the Office installation and later decide to install other components, use the custom install.

To perform a custom install, follow these steps:

1. Insert the Office CD-ROM and double-click the Microsoft Office Install folder to open it. (If you press the Option key as you double-click this—or any—folder, its enclosing folder closes automatically and reduces screen clutter.)
2. Double-click the Microsoft Office Installer to launch this installer application. (Press Option as you do, if you want to close the Microsoft Office Install folder automatically.)

   Upon launch, the installer searches your drive(s) for any previously installed Office software, such as an older version of Office. If any are found, Office notifies you and asks if you'd like to delete them.
3. The Microsoft Office Installer dialog box should be familiar to you if you have ever performed a software installation on the Mac. At the top of the dialog box is a pop-up menu. Click it and drag to the option of your choice: Easy Install, Custom Install, or Remove. Figure A-1 shows the first installer dialog box as Custom Install is being selected.

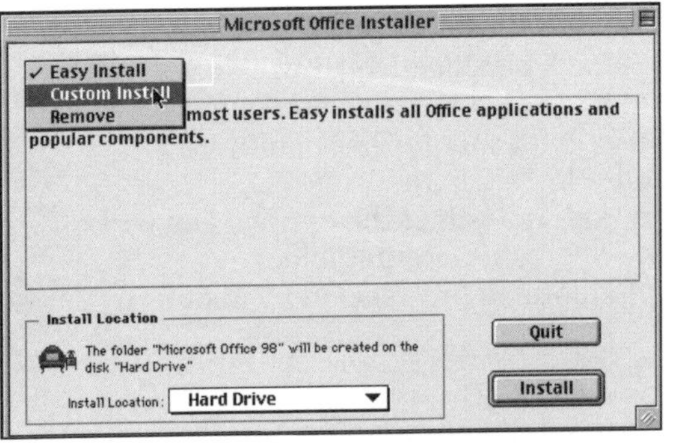

Figure A-1: The Microsoft Office Installer dialog box

- ✦ **Easy Install** is the equivalent of the drag-install: it places the same applications and components. If you want this option, select it in the menu and skip to Step 5.

- ✦ **Remove** deletes all traces of Office 98. (It doesn't affect Internet Explorer or Outlook Express.) If opting for Remove, select it in the menu and skip to Step 5.
- ✦ **Custom Install** is the option you most likely want. If so, check out the next steps.

4. If you choose the Custom Install option, you are presented with another dialog box in which you select the software you want to install. As you click the arrows beside folders in the Finder, you can click the arrows here to reveal smaller components to install. An X beside a software category indicates that all components within the category will be installed. A horizontal line means not all but some parts will be installed. Check or uncheck each part you want to install or not install. In Figure A-2, all wizards and templates will be installed, but only part of the Help files.

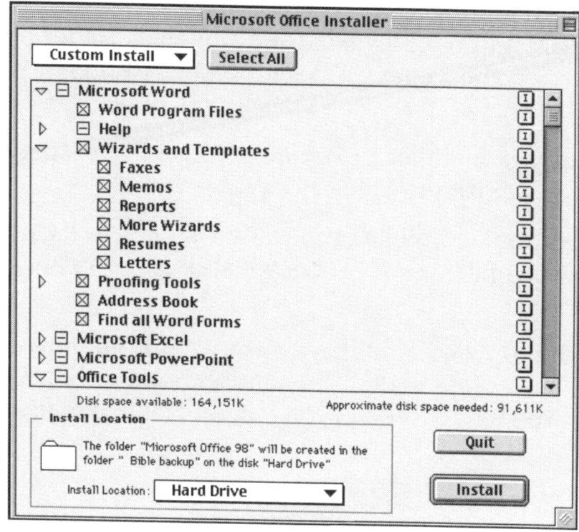

Figure A-2: Selecting software to install

5. Select an install location from the pop-up menu at the bottom of the dialog box. In Figure A-2, Hard Drive is the location where Office will be stored.

   Alternatively, if you are removing Office, choose the drive from which Office will be deleted.

   You can also choose to select a folder into which Office, or the installed components will be installed. In Figure A-3, this option is being selected. When you choose Select Folder, you see an open dialog box in which you can navigate to the folder you want, and then click.

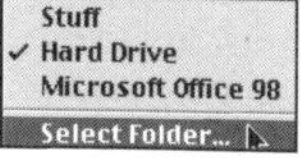

Figure A-3: Selecting a new destination for the custom installation

Regardless of where you install to, a folder called Microsoft Office 98 is created—unless you elect to install into an existing Microsoft Office 98 folder.

6. Click Install (or Remove).

Working with the Value Pack

The Value Pack is one of two places to go for items that will enhance your Office productivity. (The other place to go is `http://www.Microsoft.com/macoffice`—a site that promises to have new and useful files and tips.)

Installing Value Pack

To install any part of the Value Pack, follow these steps:

1. Insert the Office CD-ROM and double-click the Value Pack folder to open it. (Press Option as you open the folder to close the Microsoft Office 98 CD window automatically.)
2. Double-click the Value Pack Installer to launch it. (Again, pressing Option as you do will automatically close the Value Pack folder.)
3. The Value Pack Installer dialog box has the same install interface common to most Mac programs—except there is no Easy Install and you are taken directly to the Custom Install.

   The pop-up menu at the top also contains a Remove option; however, you cannot remove individual components. This option removes all Value Pack files. Figure A-4 shows the first screen of the Value Pack Installer dialog box.

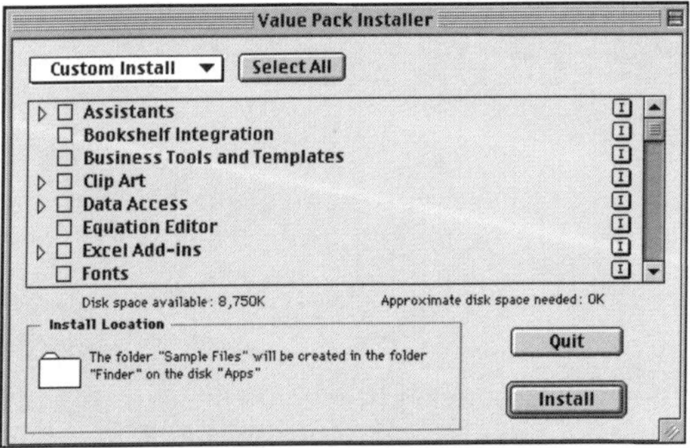

Figure A-4: Value Pack Installer dialog box

4. Check each part you want to install and uncheck what you don't want to install. If an option has more than one component, it has an arrow beside it (similar to the Finder). Click the arrow to reveal the components. When all components within the category are to be installed, there is an X beside the

option. A horizontal line means some but not all parts will be installed. In Figure A-4, nothing is set to be installed. To learn a bit more about an option, click the I (Information) button to its right.

As you select items to install, the installer reports the space it will require and lets you know how much space you have available. If you want to install the entire Value Pack, click Select All at the top of the dialog box. Select All is also handy if you want to install many components; it checks everything so all you have to do is uncheck what you don't want. To see your options better, you can make the box longer by dragging the sizing corner at the bottom right.

5. Click Install (the button says Remove if you selected Remove in the pop-up menu in Step 1).

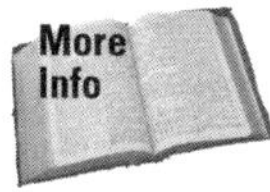

To learn more about the Value Pack and its components, double-click About the Value Pack—a Help file inside the Value Pack folder on the Office CD-ROM.

Value Pack Contents

To help you decide which Value Pack items are right for you, here's an overview of what each item does.

Assistants

If you have already launched Word, Excel, or PowerPoint, you have probably met the default Office Assistant, Max. He's cute and entertaining, but he's not your only Assistant. By clicking the arrow next to Assistants in the Value Pack Installer, you reveal several more Assistants. Each has its own personality, as described when you click the Information (I) button to its right.

After you do the Value Pack installation, you can give Max a rest and change Assistants at any time. To do so, call up your Assistant, and then click Options in the Assistant's dialog box. Next, click the Gallery tab. Then click the Next and/or Back buttons to check out all your installed Assistants. When you arrive at the one you want, click OK.

Bookshelf integration

Microsoft Bookshelf is a collection of several online multimedia references. You can search its article titles or article contents in one reference or in every reference at once. Searches can also be done by zip code.

If you own Microsoft Bookshelf 98 (and have it installed), you'll find Bookshelf Integration helpful. Integration adds specific Bookshelf commands to your Word and PowerPoint menus. For example, you can select Tools⇨Look Up Reference to look up information in Bookshelf or Control-click a word and choose Define from the shortcut menu to find a definition—all without leaving your document. Of course, you can also copy articles, selected text, or images from Bookshelf—and when you do, Bookshelf includes copyright information so you won't get in trouble over plagiarism.

Bookshelf 98 includes: *The American Heritage Dictionary (3rd Edition), Roget's Thesaurus, The Columbia Dictionary of Quotations, The People's Chronology, The World Almanac and Book of Facts (1997), The Encarta 98 Desk Encyclopedia, The Encarta 98 Desk World Atlas, The Microsoft Bookshelf Internet Directory 98, The Microsoft Bookshelf Computer and Internet Dictionary,* and the U.S. Postal Service Zip Code database.

Business tools and templates

If you're using Office 98 for business—especially if it's your own small business—you may find these templates and documents helpful. There are more than 43 of them, so install them and see what helps you best. Once you install them, you can access these templates just like any other template.

Clip-art

Clip-art, which is discussed in Chapters 10, is predrawn artwork that (when you own the license for it) you may use to spice up your documents or presentations. Office 98 provides plenty of clip-art, divided into categories. Click the arrow by the check box to reveal the various libraries of art you can install and use.

Data access

If you're working with databases, you should probably install these files and explore what they can do for you. There are two options after you click the arrow next to data access:

- **ODBC** installs ODBC 3.0 and an ODBC driver. If you are working with ODBC-compliant databases, you know what this is. If you aren't, don't worry.
- **Microsoft Query** lets you construct queries and retrieve data from external data sources. This data is then available for use in Excel or Word.

Equation editor

Into mathematical equations? If so, this is for you. This application is specifically designed to enable you to create any kind of equation. If you're using such formulas (and don't already own a full-blown version of an Equation editor), this is a must-have.

Excel add-ins

The following is a list of the various Excel add-ins that come with the Office 98 Value Pack:

- **File Conversion Wizard** converts a group of files to Excel format. After installation, you can access the wizard by selecting Tools ➪ Wizard ➪ File Conversion. This wizard provides three easy steps for you to follow.

✦ **Report Manager** is, as it sounds, an aid in creating reports. After installation, you can access it from View ➪ Report Manager. Report Manager is a simple interface that enables you to add reports with a click of a button.

✦ **Solver** calculates solutions to your what-if scenarios. You'll find Solver in the Tools menu if it has been installed.

✦ **Template Wizard** creates special templates that record the data entered into worksheets so the data is available for analysis. The Template Wizard is directly in the Data menu after installation.

Fonts

Want more fonts to jazz up your documents? Check out these fonts. There are 58 True-Type fonts for you to explore.

If you're going to load up on fonts, you might want to try Font Reserve (`www.fontreserve.com`) by DiamondSoft; that way you don't have to install all the fonts into your system, but you have easy access to them.

Genigraphics

After you've created your terrific presentation materials, you may want to have them professionally prepared as slides, overheads, or such. Genigraphics has long been an expert in such materials creation. This file is actually a wizard that assists you in preparing and sending your documents to Genigraphics.

Microsoft Movie

When you're ready to add QuickTime videos to your documents, adding another dimension to them, you're ready to install Microsoft Movie. This is the application you'll need to add the QuickTime elements. As it is used for all Office applications, Microsoft Movie is stored in the Shared Applications folder. After you install it, you can go to Insert ➪ Object, and then select Microsoft Movie in the Object type list.

Microsoft Office Manager

MOM, which enables easy application launching and cool program switching, is covered in Chapter 1. Take a look there at what it can do for you.

More help

This selection is the full complement of help for using Visual Basic for Applications, Office's macro or automation programming language. VBA, as it's known, is covered in each section of the book (Word, Excel, and PowerPoint) as an introduction to its power. These Help files can take you a long way if you want to learn VBA.

Proofing tools

Proofing tools consist of the Hyphenation files, and the Spelling and Thesaurus dictionaries. They come in nine languages in addition to English. These tools are stored in the Proofing Tools folder, which is in the Shared Applications folder inside the main Microsoft Office 98 folder. Of course, if you are using an English version of Office, English tools are installed by default.

Programmability

If you're into automation, you'll want these files; there are some macros for Word and some macros and VBA code for Excel.

In case you are using VBA macros written in a language other than English, you can install other language type libraries. Language support is there for Danish, Dutch, French, German, Italian, Japanese, Norwegian, Portuguese, Spanish, and Swedish. Excel type library files are stored in the Type Libraries folder inside the Extensions folder in your System folder.

Templates

Here you can choose to install extra templates for Word, Excel, or PowerPoint, and even install templates for Word for Windows (in case you are in a cross-platform environment that needs to cater to Windows). In Chapter 2, we list the Word templates and wizards that come with Office 98 and let you know which ones are part of this install. There are nine Excel spreadsheet solutions, a ton of presentations, and a whole lot of presentation design elements.

Text converters

Converters help you open files that were created in other programs and help you save your own Office documents in other file formats. When you click the arrow by the Text Converters option, you see a full list of available converters. Check the ones you may find useful and install them to have them on hand when needed.

Unbinder

Windows has a feature called the Binder. With it, users can create a Binder into which they can place one or more Word, Excel, or PowerPoint documents. If you receive a file that's a Binder, you'll need to be able to open it. That's when the Unbinder comes in handy.

Word Speak

For many years, you've been able to create a text document on the Mac and have it read back (aloud) to yourself. To do so with Word 98, you need to install Word Speak. After installing Word Speak, you see two new commands in Word's Tools menu: Pick Voice and Speak Selection. Pick Voice opens a dialog box so you can listen to, select, and modify MacinTalk voices. Tools ➪ Speak Selection is the command that loads the voice and reads your words to you—after you select the text to be read.

Removing Office 98

Office 98 doesn't provide a custom deinstaller. The only removal option offered is the full removal of all Office applications (with the Microsoft Office Installer) or full removal of all Value Pack items (with the Value Pack Installer). Internet Explorer and Outlook Express have their own removal so they are unaffected by these deinstallers.

To remove Office 98, insert your Office 98 CD-ROM. Open the Office Custom Install folder. Launch the Microsoft Office Installer. In the pop-up list at the top of the dialog box, select Remove. Then click the Remove button. That's it. The Value Pack is the same, except you open the Value Pack folder and launch the Value Pack Installer.

Removing Previous Versions of Office

After you're up and running with Office 98—or perhaps even before then—you will most likely (believe us) want to remove your older Office, Word, Excel, or PowerPoint applications. An application to do just that is available in the Value Pack. Specifically, the application will remove Word 6.0, Word 5.1, Excel 5.0, Excel 4.0, PowerPoint 4.0, and PowerPoint 3.0.

As mentioned earlier, when you do a custom install of Office 98, you are asked if you'd like to remove old versions of Office. This is the same tool. But you may wish to wait until you're safely up and running with Office 98 and therefore skip the Remove option at that time. Instead, you can run Remove Old Office Versions whenever you're ready. To use it, follow these steps:

1. Open the Value Pack folder, and then open the Administration Tools folder.
2. Double-click the Remove Old Office Versions application.
3. The pop-up list at the top of the dialog box gives you two choices: Remove All, which removes all files from previous versions of Office, and Custom Remove, which lets you remove only selected programs by checking the check boxes for the parts you want removed.

The Remove Old Office Versions program doesn't remove your own documents, templates, or data files. Pretty cool.

Installing Internet Explorer

These Internet applications are each a separate installation process from the core applications (Word, Excel, and PowerPoint) that you are used to getting with Office.

To install Internet Explorer, follow these steps:

1. Install the Office CD-ROM and double-click the Microsoft Internet folder to open it. (Press Option as you open it to close the Microsoft Office 98 CD window automatically.)
2. Double-click the Internet Explorer Installer to launch it. (Pressing Option as you do will automatically close the Microsoft Internet folder.)
3. Select Easy Install, Custom Install, or Remove from the pop-up list at the top of the dialog box.
   - **Easy Install** places everything you'll need.
   - **Custom Install** lets you install Internet Explorer without Internet Config, or vice versa. (Internet Config is like SimpleText—small, harmless, and being installed by tons of applications these days. You only need it once on your hard drive. However, as you install Internet Config, preferences that work for Outlook Express and Internet Explorer are set. So if you are using Outlook Express and Internet Explorer, you might as well let the installer give you a hand, and get the latest version of Internet Config while you're at it.) If you select Custom install, check the box for the application you want to install.
   - **Remove** deletes all Internet Explorer files, but not those that are needed by other applications.
4. Click Install (The button says Remove if you selected Remove in the pop-up menu in Step 3.).

Installing Outlook Express

As we mentioned, the Internet applications are each a separate installation process from the core applications (Word, Excel, and PowerPoint) that you are used to getting with Office.

To install Outlook Express, follow these steps:

1. Install the Office CD-ROM and double-click the Microsoft Internet folder to open it. (Press Option as you open it to close the Microsoft Office 98 CD window automatically.)
2. Double-click the Outlook Express 4.0 Installer to launch it. (Pressing Option as you do will automatically close the Microsoft Internet folder.)
3. Select Easy Install, Custom Install, or Remove from the pop-up list at the top of the dialog box.
   - **Easy Install** places everything you'll need.

- **Custom Install** lets you install Outlook Express without Internet Config, or vice versa. (Internet Config is like SimpleText—small, harmless, and installed by tons of applications these days. You only need it once on your hard drive. However, when you install Internet Config, preferences that work for Outlook Express and Internet Explorer are also set. So, if you are using Outlook Express and Internet Explorer, you might as well let the installer give you a hand—and get the latest version of Internet Config while you're at it.) If you select Custom install, check the box for the application you want to install.
- **Remove** deletes all Outlook Express files, but not those that are needed by other applications.

4. Click Install (the button says Remove if you selected Remove in the pop-up menu in Step 3).

✦ ✦ ✦

APPENDIX B

Word Quick Start

◆ ◆ ◆ ◆

In This Appendix

Launching Word

Learning about the screen

Opening new or existing documents

Entering and editing text

Saving documents

Printing your documents

◆ ◆ ◆ ◆

This appendix provides a fast-paced overview of Word 98 basics, particularly the details of the Word menus and document window. It also introduces text editing for beginners. If you've never used Word, start here.

Launching Word

You can launch Word several ways. If you've done the simplest install—by dragging the Microsoft Office 98 folder to your hard drive and letting Word do the installation for you—you can launch Word as you launch any program on your Mac. Word is located directly in the Microsoft Office 98 folder, which is either immediately on your hard drive, or within a folder such as Applications, depending upon where you've placed it. The icon for the actual Word program is a blue W; this is the icon you double-click to launch Word. Rather than having to open the hard drive, then open the Microsoft Office 98 folder every time you launch Word, we recommend that you place an alias of the Word icon under your Apple menu.

If you've installed the Microsoft Office Manager control panel from the Value Pack, you have a custom menu on the top, right side of your menus. With Microsoft Office Manager (MOM), all you have to do is click the menu and select Word.

In Chapter 1, we discuss launching all Office applications.

Learning About the Screen

Each time you launch Word, a new blank document is automatically started for you to begin entering text. Figure B-1 shows the different parts of the screen. Menus, located in the white strip at the top of your screen, are one of the founding principles of all Macintosh applications.

The rest of your screen area, your desktop, is where Word's toolbars and document windows reside when active. At the top of your desktop, immediately below the menus, you find Word-specific tools. Word's default setup is to show you its Standard toolbar (top) and the Formatting toolbar (below). The numerous buttons on the toolbars may seem daunting at first, but move your mouse pointer (cursor) over any button and let it rest a moment (without clicking). Notice a yellow box appears, telling you what that button does. These are called ScreenTips. ScreenTips can also list the key combinations you can press if you prefer not to use the mouse. The presence of ScreenTips is a preference you can set (covered in Chapter 1). Now that you know Word will tell you what each button does, you needn't worry about memorizing the buttons. Some of the buttons, especially the ones on the Formatting toolbar, are also clearly depicted for you. For example, the button with the lines all to the left represents left-alignment.

When you're working with a document, the document appears onscreen in its own free-floating window (as do all Mac documents). When you're not working with a document, you just see your desktop (unless you've set your Mac to hide the desktop). The document window appears below the toolbars. Word's document window is the same as any other Mac application's—but with a few more controls. You can resize it or move it at any time. The top of the window has strips going across it and a name in the center. This is the title bar for your document window. The name reflected there is the name of your document ("Document" followed by a number, if unsaved). To move your document around onscreen, click in the title bar area and drag. This is a basic Mac function. (If you're coming to the Mac from a Windows background, the title bar is in a new location for you, as are the close window and windowshade boxes.) Everything on the title bar is standard on the Mac. However, Word introduces a few of its own window controls: view controls at that bottom left (discussed in Chapter 2) and Next, Previous, and Select Browse Object on the right side.

By default, Next and Previous jump the onscreen view of your document to the top of the next or previous page. In addition, they jump your text insertion point to the top of the page you are viewing. Select Browse Object is a pop-up menu that enables you to jump through your document, landing at the object you select. These objects include fields, comments, and other such Word features. Whatever object is selected in this pop-up menu is the object that the Next and Previous buttons jump to.

Below the title bar, if it is showing, is the ruler. The ruler lets you use the mouse to change paragraph indents, adjust page margins, change the width of columns, and set tab stops. See Chapters 2, 3, and 5 for more information. If you don't see a ruler, you can turn it on by selecting Ruler from the View menu. A check mark tells you it's on. Of course, so does seeing it.

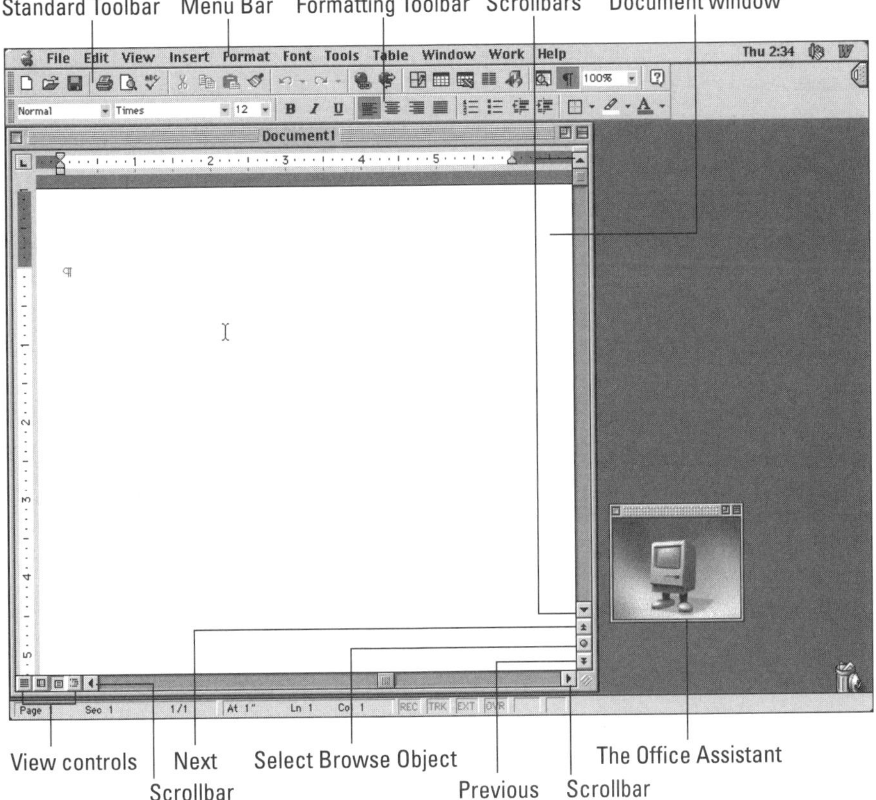

Figure B-1: The Word window

Figure B-2 shows the toolbars that, by default, appear when you launch Word: the Standard and Formatting toolbars. Table B-1 describes the Standard toolbar's buttons; Table B-2 briefly describes the Formatting toolbar's buttons. For detailed information, see Chapter 3.

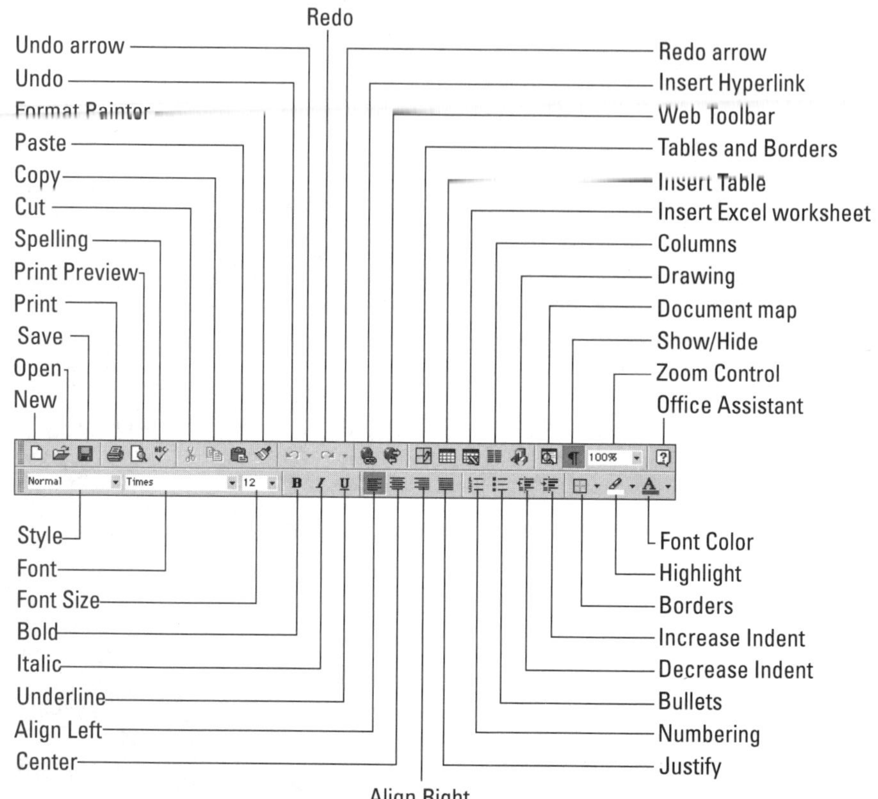

Figure B-2: The Standard and Formatting toolbars

Table B-1 **Standard Toolbar Buttons**		
Button	***Name***	***Description***
	New	Opens a new document using the default page settings
	Open	Opens the Open/Save dialog box so you can open an existing document
	Save	Saves the current document under its present name; if no name exists, the Save As dialog box appears so you can provide one
	Print	Opens the Print dialog box to print the current document
	Print Preview	Lets you see what your current document will look like when printed and lets you make layout changes

Button	Name	Description
	Spelling	Checks the spelling of the current section (see Chapter 3 for an explanation), of the entire document if no section exists, or of the current selection if any text is selected.
	Cut	Removes a section of selected (highlighted) text and places it on the Clipboard
	Copy	Makes a copy of the current section of text and places it on the Clipboard
	Paste	Pastes the contents of the Clipboard into the document at the insertion point
	Format Painter	Copies formatting characteristics from one selection of text to another
	Undo	Reverses the last action; the arrow lets you choose the action that you wish to undo
	Redo	Redoes the last action that was undone; the arrow lets you choose the undone action that you wish to redo
	Insert Hyperlink	Inserts a link to a URL or another file in Word
	Web Toolbar	Activates the Web toolbar (see Chapter 11)
	Tables and Borders	Activates the Tables and Borders toolbar, and enables creation of tables (for more information, see Chapter 5)
	Insert Table	Inserts a table in your document (Chapter 5 tells you all about tables)
	Insert Microsoft Excel Worksheet	Inserts a Microsoft Excel worksheet into your Word document
	Columns	Formats the current selection or section into columns
	Drawing	Shows or hides the Drawing toolbar
	Document Map	Activates the Document Map pane (for more information, see Chapter 5)
¶	Show/Hide	Shows or hides all nonprinting characters
100%	Zoom Control	Lets you zoom in closer to your document so text and symbols appear closer. Also enables you to zoom out so more of your document fits onscreen. This doesn't affect the actual characteristic of the text—only its appearance onscreen. (8-point Helvetica, zoomed so it's larger, is still 8-point Helvetica.)
	Office Assistant	Activates the Office Assistant, which provides general help

Table B-2
Formatting Toolbar Buttons

Button	*Name*	*Description*
Normal	Style	Lets you choose a style for your text
Times	Font	Lets you choose a font for your text
12	Font Size	Lets you choose a size for your text's font
	Bold	Applies or removes boldface from text
	Italic	Applies or removes italics from text
	Underline	Applies or removes underlining from text
	Align Left	Aligns text to the left margin
	Center	Centers text between margins
	Align Right	Aligns text to the right margin
	Justify	Aligns text to both the left and the right margins
	Numbering	Creates a numbered list from a selected set of items
	Bullets	Creates a bulleted list from a selected set of items
	Decrease Indent	Indents a paragraph to the previous tab stop
	Increase Indent	Indents a paragraph to the next tab stop
	Borders	Lets you apply borders and shading to your text
	Highlight	Applies or removes highlighting from text (this is highlighting as one uses a highlight marker, not as in selecting text to format it)
	Font Color	Applies a color to the selected text

Starting from the left side of the Formatting toolbar, you first see the Style menu. This menu lets you apply any of Word's styles to a selection (or the paragraph where the insertion point is placed). Next comes the Font menu, which lets you change the appearance of selected characters by choosing different typefaces. Next to the Font menu is the Font Size menu, which lets you change the size of the selected characters. Next are the three character-formatting buttons: **Bold**, *Italic*, and Underline.

The four alignment buttons come next—Align Left, Center, Align Right, and Justify. Following those are the Numbering, Bullets, Decrease Indent, and Increase Indent buttons used for outlining.

The Borders button comes next, enabling you to place various types of borders and shading on sections of a document. Next, you see the Highlight button, which lets you highlight text in a color as you would do with a highlight marker on paper. Finally, you have the Font Color button, with which you can change the color of any selected text. (When using color, remember that highlight color uses a lot of ink on an ink-jet printer and comes out in shades of gray on a black-and-white laser printer.)

Each component of the Formatting toolbar is discussed in detail in the corresponding section.

Opening New or Existing Documents

Each time you launch Microsoft Word, a blank document automatically appears, ready for you to begin typing. This automatic document is the "default." In Chapter 2, you learn how to adjust its margins, font, and so on by changing your preferences. If you are starting a new document from scratch, this document is usually the best starting place; it's the document you work with in Chapter 2 as you become familiar with the basics of word processing with Word.

Creating new documents

As you use Word, the chances are you'll create more than one document in one session. It's common to create one document, close it when done, and then start another. To create more documents, simply select New from the File menu (⌘-N) or click the New Document button on Word's Standard (top) toolbar. You can create new documents any time Word is the active application. If you press ⌘-N or click the New Document button, you get the same default document. If you choose New from the File menu, you see what's called the New Document dialog box. To open a new default page, you locate the document called Normal (which is in the General tab), click it to select it, and then click OK. If you want to begin with a specific style document, click once on your desired template, and then click OK.

Rather than selecting the document and then clicking OK, you can simply double-click the document. This is possible because OK is the default option (that Word assumes you'll want), and there is a black line around the OK button.

Opening Existing Documents

To open an existing document, either click the Open icon on the toolbar, choose File⇨Open, or press ⌘-O. The Open dialog box appears. When you see the name of the desired document in the immediate list, simply double-click it.

To open an existing document, you can also go to the desktop and open the folder that contains the document and double-click the document. This action launches Word if it's not already running.

If you do not immediately see the desired document, you need to navigate to the folder that contains it. The pop-up menu at the top of the Open dialog box states the folder, disk, or hard drive that you are currently viewing. The list box shows you the contents of that folder, disk, or hard drive. By clicking the pop-up menu, you can travel from the current folder to any location between that folder and your desktop. To get to another disk, return to the desktop so you can view the contents of the desktop. Double-click any folder, disk, or hard drive in the list box to open it. Click the pop-up menu at the top to travel back out of the current folder. You can select the folder, disk, or hard drive you want to see. You can peruse your entire hard drive and all connected volumes from here. For more understanding of the Open or Open and Save dialog box, see your Macintosh manual.

Entering and Editing Text

If you already have text in your computer, you can copy and paste it into your new document. Otherwise, the common way to get text into your document is to type it. Assuming you are starting with the blank new document Word provides when you launch Word, you see a flashing line at the top of your new document page. That line, called the insertion point, shows you where your typed or pasted text will be entered. If you're completely new to Word, practice by typing the following text. Humor us on this; we use this example again later, and it will help if you've already typed it:

Choices, choices, choices

It seems you always have three ways to do anything on the Mac. Margins and indents are no exception. If you're a visual person, you'll love using the ruler so you can see where you're moving the text to. More numerically based? You'll prefer opening dialog boxes and entering numbers to set indents and such. If you're a bit of both, you can use the ruler, but double-click any ruler element any time to call up the dialog box.

Basic Navigation

Now that you have some text in your new document, you can practice some basic navigation skills. To place text, you need to have the insertion point (that flashing line) at the place you want your text to appear. You can use the arrow keys to move the insertion point in the direction of the arrow you press. However, this can be tedious. The standard way to move your insertion point on the Mac is to use your mouse. When your mouse pointer is in the text area of a page, the pointer turns into an I-beam. Click this I-beam in your document to place the insertion point there. To move from page to page within your document, use the scroll bars on the side of your document window.

If you prefer not to take your fingers off the keyboard, you can use the built-in key combinations to move through chunks of text, and so on. Table B-3 lists keystrokes that move you around your documents. You can learn the keystrokes if you like; however, you don't have to learn any of them.

Table B-3
Navigation Keystrokes

Keystroke	*Function*
Arrow keys	Move the insertion point around in your document
⌘-↑	Moves the cursor up one paragraph
⌘-↓	Moves the cursor down one paragraph
⌘-←	Moves the cursor one word to the left
⌘-→	Moves the cursor one word to the right
Page Up key	Moves the cursor up one screen page
Page Down key	Moves the cursor down one screen page
Home key	Moves the cursor to the beginning of the current line of text
⌘-Home key	Moves the cursor to the beginning of the document
End key	Moves the cursor to the end of the current line of text
⌘-End key	Moves the cursor to the end of the document

The scroll bars move you through a document, too. There are four ways to scroll with the scroll bar: click the arrows incrementally, hold down the mouse button on the scroll arrow, drag the scroll bar box, or click in the gray area above or below the scroll bar.

Basic Text Editing

There are two basic rules of text editing. First, as mentioned above, you can type or paste text at the insertion point. The second is that any text that is selected can be changed.

To try adding text, return to the second line of the "Choices" document you typed earlier (or any practice document). Move your I-beam until it's in front of the first line of the text you just typed, and then click to place the insertion point there. Now type **Wow**. *Wow* lands in front of the word *it.* In some word processors, this is known as Insert mode. (The term *Insert mode* is used in Word for Windows but isn't common on the Mac.)

To try deleting text, with the insertion point flashing after Wow, press the Delete key. Press once and the w is removed. Press again and the o is removed. As the insertion point travels backward over text, via the Delete key, it removes the text is moves back over. Now try deleting an entire word: double-click the middle word *choices* in the title. With the word *choices* selected, press Delete. The selected text (*choices*) is gone and the insertion point is left flashing in the space. You can type a new word there if you'd like. For now, type **many**. Pressing Delete isn't even necessary, however. Whenever text is selected, it is automatically replaced by whatever is typed at the time it is selected. In other words, if you select text, and then type, the selected text is deleted and the new text is entered in place of it. This is standard for the Mac.

Word provides another editing feature those of you used to non-Mac word processors may already be familiar with. In Overtype mode, text you type replaces existing text, letter for letter. Overtype mode is not the default. You enter Overtype mode by double-clicking the letters *OVR* in the status bar at the bottom of your screen. If OVR appears in black letters, you're in Overtype mode; if it's dimmed, you're in the normal Insert mode. When you are in Overtype mode, the cursor moves forward as normal and enters your new text. However, it erases your existing type as you type the new text. To see the effect, double-click OVR in the status bar (if it's not on yet), and then go back to the first line you typed and place your insertion point in front of the m in many. Now type the letters **oh**. Notice your word is no longer *many,* but is now *ohny.* You typed two letters so two letters were deleted. Overtype mode replaces all text until you stop typing, so be careful not to overwrite what you want to keep. Rather than overtyping, it is more common on the Mac to select the text you don't want and then type new text in its place.

The status bar is on by default, but it may be turned off. To do so, choose Tools ⇨ Preferences, click the View tab, and then click in the box next to Status bar. A check means the status bar is showing; no check means it's off.

Saving Documents

When you create a document, it exists only in the temporary memory of your computer. When you turn the power off, or a power outage turns it off for you, your document is lost—unless you've saved it. Saving is the act of writing the document to the hard drive or disk. Once the document is saved, you can open it again later. Word provides a variety of save options. You can save a file under a new name or an existing one. You can save files in Word's own file format, or you can save them in the formats of other popular word processors.

Using the Save command

To save a file, go to the File menu and select Save, or press ⌘-S—the keyboard equivalent. Word also provides a Save button you can click in the Standard toolbar. The first time you save a document, Word displays the Save dialog box (see Figure B-3). Enter a filename, select the folder you want to save it to, and then click Save. You can save to your hard drive or to any removable disk. When you do subsequent saves, Word saves the file without prompting you for any information. It's a good idea to save often.

If you created the example document "Choices," save it now by following these steps:

1. Choose File➪Save. Because you have never saved this file, the Save dialog box appears.
2. Word gives you a head start on naming the document by taking the first few words of your first page and automatically placing them in the Save Current Document as field. In this case, the name field probably already says "Choices." You can select the entire name or any part of it, or enter any name you'd like.
3. Click the pop-up box at the top of the dialog box and navigate to the disk or folder to which you want your document saved. If you are not yet comfortable with navigating folders this way, just click Desktop. That way the document will be saved to the desktop and you can drag it to a folder later.
4. Click OK. You now have a document named Choices.

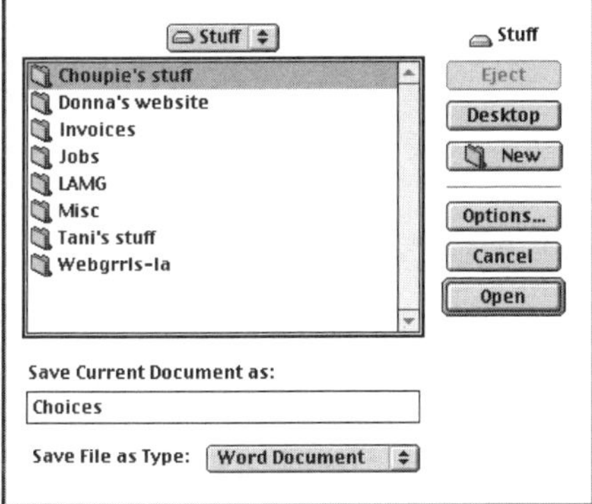

Figure B-3: The Save dialog box

When you quit Word, you are asked if you want to save any documents you have not yet saved or have made changes to since your last save. It is not a good idea to get dependent on that dialog box, however. It is much better to save your document each time you make a change you want to keep. Developing the ⌘-S reflex will save you a lot of grief.

Using the Save As command

At times you will find that you like a document you created but want to try another version of it. This is where Save As comes in. The Save As command silently and invisibly makes a copy of your document, safely putting your original away. Word then presents you with a new Save dialog box (the same as the one shown earlier in Figure B-3) so you can give the copy a new name and even choose a new location to save it to. Save As is also handy when you've finished your document and need to create a copy of it in another file format (for example, when you need to give a document to a friend who uses an older version of Word or Word for Windows, or another word processing program).

When you do a Save As, the original name of the file appears in the Save Current Document as field (if the document has ever been saved). On the Mac, two files within the same folder cannot have the same name. If you don't give your new document a different name, you are asked if you want to replace the original. You can save the file with the same name if you save it to another location, but it is very confusing to have two files with the same name. To avoid confusion, give this document a new name. For example, if you are saving a version for WordPerfect, you might want to name it with WP at the end.

If you are using File⇨Save As to save a document in the format of another word processor, in addition to naming your new copy, you need to choose the new format. Click the arrow of the Save File as Type pop-up menu to reveal the installed formats in which you can save your document (see Figure B-4). Drag up or down to the format you desire, and then release the mouse button.

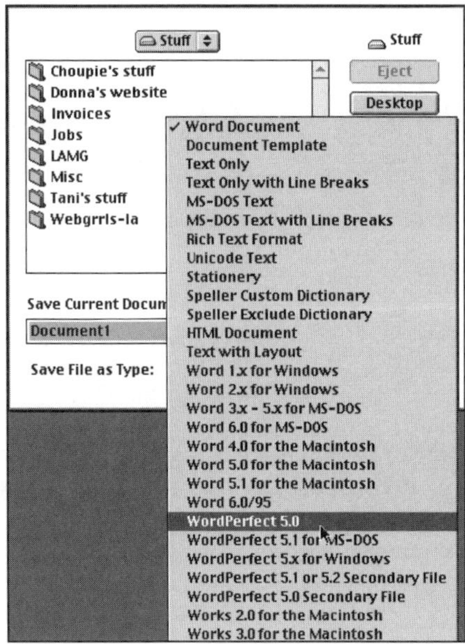

Figure B-4: The Save File as Type list box

Note that the available formats depends on what converters you've installed. If you need a popular file format and you don't see it in the pop-up menu, the Value Pack Installer may provide it. Microsoft may also provide other format converters from time to time. If so, the converters will be on the Microsoft Web site for you to download and install (`www.microsoft.com`).

Word enables you to set certain preferences for your saving pleasure. You can see and change these preferences by selecting Tools ➪ Preferences or by clicking the Options button in the Save dialog box. Your options include: Always Create Backup Copy, Allow Fast Saves, Prompt for Document Properties, Prompt to Save Normal Template, Embed True Type Fonts, Save Data Only for Forms, and Save AutoRecover Info every *x* Minutes. The following sections cover the most basic options for saving files.

The Always Create Backup Copy option

In case your original document somehow becomes corrupted, you'll be happy to have a backup copy of your document. When the Always Create Backup Copy option is on, Word creates a backup file every time you save. The backup file will have the name "Backup (or Bkup) of *document name*." The backup is saved to the folder where the original document is stored. You can open the backup file the same way you open any document.

The Allow Fast Saves option

Some of Word's behavior when saving files depends on how much editing you've done to the file since it was saved last.

Word saves files using either of two methods: a fast save or a full save. When you save, Word saves your file using the method indicated by the circumstances. Normally, Word performs a fast save, where your changes are appended onto the end of an existing file. With a full save, Word saves the entire document, including unchanged parts, as if you were saving the file for the first time.The first time a document is saved, Word performs a full save. After that, Word usually performs a fast save whenever you save updates to your document. (If you make extensive changes, Word may perform a full save automatically.)

Operationally, you'll see no difference between the two methods other than speed. Full saves take somewhat longer than fast saves; exactly how much longer varies greatly depending on the speed of your hardware. Fast-saved files become larger as all changes are included. To turn fast saves on or off, go to the Save tab of the Preferences dialog box or click the Options button from the Save dialog box, and check or uncheck the Allow Fast Saves check box.

The Prompt for Document Properties option

The Prompt for Document Properties option shows the Summary tab of the Properties dialog box the first time you save a document. This tab lets you store general information about the document, such as title, subject, or author.

The Save AutoRecover Every *x* Minutes option

AutoRecover may help you recover your document in the case of a power outage or system crash. You determine how often AutoRecover makes a copy of your document by entering a time interval in the Preferences Save tab. The recovery files are temporary. They are erased when your document is saved and are deleted when you close the file. Recovery files come into play after a freeze and are automatically opened when you restart and relaunch Word.

Printing Your Documents

This section quickly shows how to print to the printer you've chosen in the Chooser. (Printing is covered in detail in Chapter 4.)

To print a document, choose File⇨Print (or press ⌘-P). The Print dialog box appears, as shown in Figure B-5.

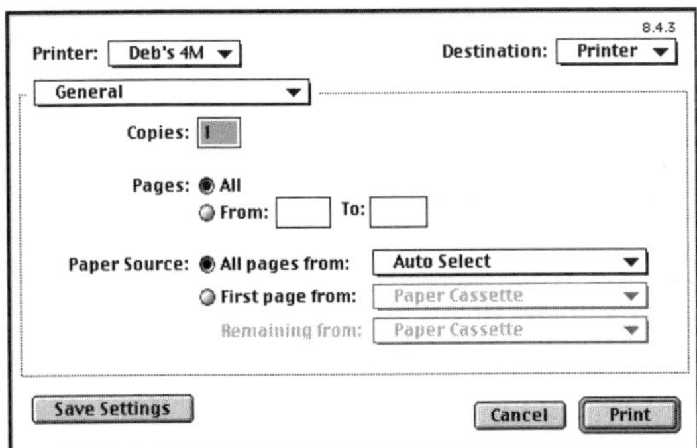

Figure B-5: The Print dialog box

Choosing the printer and number of copies

Check that the printer name that appears at the top of the dialog box is the printer to which you want to print. If it's not, use the Chooser to select the correct printer and try again. The default options in the dialog box assume you want one copy of the document and that you want all pages in the document printed. The Copies field is preselected so you can easily type a different number of copies.

After reviewing or selecting the options you want, click Print.

Printing part of a document

You can also enter a specific page at which to begin printing (in the From box), a specific page to end printing (in the To box), or a page to begin with and end with (by entering a number in each box). You can print several ranges of pages by entering the range in the Microsoft Word section of the Print dialog box. You can even print a selected portion of a document by highlighting the selection and choosing File ⇨ Print, going to the Microsoft Word section of the Print dialog box, and checking Print Selection. Again, this is all covered in detail in Chapter 4.

You can even print a document without opening it. Just locate the document in its folder and drag it to your desktop printer icon. Your Mac launches Word, opens the document, prompts you for a number of copies (and other options), and then quits Word when done.

✦ ✦ ✦

Excel Quick Start

In This Appendix

Getting started

Opening and using workbooks

Entering and editing data

Building formulas

Printing your worksheets

Saving your worksheets

This appendix provides a fast-paced overview of Excel 98 basics, particularly the details of the Excel menus and workbook window. If you're new to Excel, start here.

Getting Started

You can launch Excel the same way you launch any Mac program—by double-clicking the application's icon or alias, or selecting it from the Apple menu (if you've placed it there). If you've installed MOM, the Microsoft Office Manager, you can select Excel from there to launch it. For details on MOM, see the section devoted to it in Chapter 1.

Understanding spreadsheets

A spreadsheet is an electronic version of bookkeeping tools: the ledger pad, pencil, and calculator. Excel spreadsheets, called *worksheets* in Microsoft terminology, can be likened to huge sheets of ledger paper. Each worksheet measures 65,536 rows by 256 columns—realistically, more size than you should ever need on a single page. Each cell is made up of the intersection of a row and column. Therefore cells are identified by their row and column coordinates. A1 is the cell in the upper-left corner of the worksheet. When you click any cell to select it, the row and column that cell is in become highlighted in the row and column headings to help you identify where you are. In addition, as you drag across a cell, a yellow ScreenTip is likely to report that cell's address to you so you know where you're going.

Dealing with data

Data you enter in a worksheet can take the form of constant values or of variables that are based on formulas. Constant values, such as a number (13) or a name (Lani Speer), do not change. They are the data you enter to track your information. Values are the information Excel calculates for you. They are the result of formulas you place in cells. Behind the scenes is the formula (which shows in the formula bar). In the spreadsheet, the result of the formula shows so you can do your work. Formulas most often refer to other cells in the worksheet to get their data and do their calculations. For example, a cell might contain the formula C5+C6+C7 or C5:C7, which adds the contents of those three cells.

Excel's worksheets can display data in a wide variety of formats. You can display numeric values with or without decimals, currency amounts, or exponential values. You can also enter text, such as the name of a month or a product model name. And you can store and display date and time-of-day data in worksheet cells.

Introducing calculations and formulas

Calculations are what nearly all spreadsheet models are about. Formulas can be as simple as the addition of cells or be highly intricate. Excel helps you with formulas by providing a rich assortment of functions, which are special built-in formulas that provide a variety of calculations (the average of a series of values, for example, or the square root of a number). Excel provides functions for mathematical, statistical, financial, logical, date and time, text, and special-purpose operations.

At first glance, Excel can be scary and seem to appeal only to numbers-oriented people who must manage numbers on a day-to-day basis. However, if you give it a chance, you may find Excel easy to use and quite handy. In addition to tracking numeric-based things, Excel can build you some excellent charts and graphs. Excel 98 also introduces rich graphics capabilities to jazz up documents for presentations.

Understanding the Excel screen

By default, Excel provides two toolbars when it launches—the Standard toolbar and the Formatting toolbar—directly below the menus. Some toolbar buttons may be familiar to you if you're used another version of Excel or used Word or PowerPoint. Below the toolbars, you'll see the formula bar. Next you'll see the workbook, which you can move and resize as you can with any Mac document. At the bottom of your screen is the status bar. If you've used other Microsoft products, you are probably familiar with status bars.

Figure C-1 shows what Excel looks like when first opened; you'll see a new workbook with the title "Workbook1."

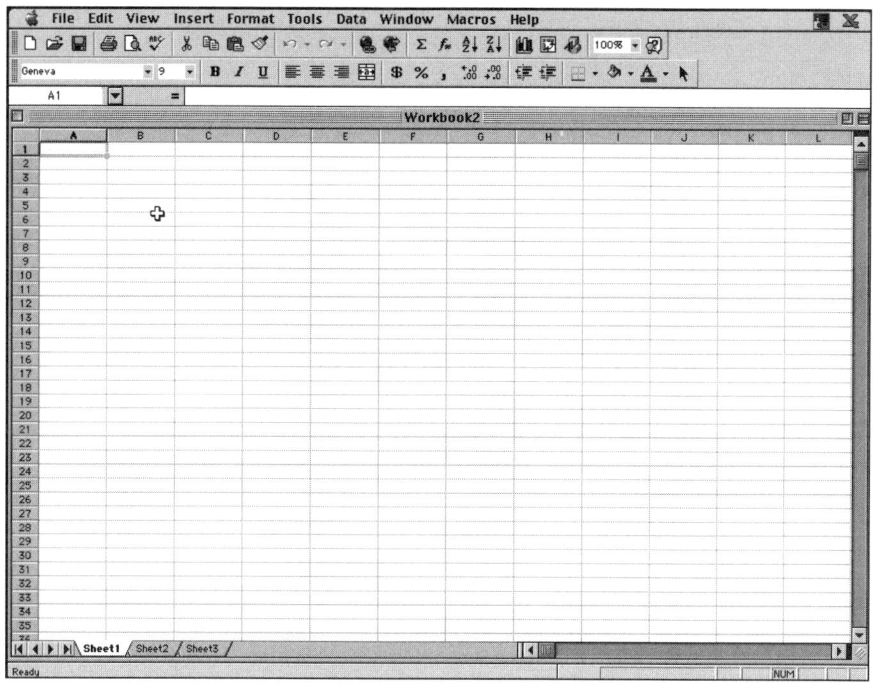

Figure C-1: A new Excel workbook

The components of Excel's workbook window are explained in Chapter 15.

Excel's toolbars

Toolbars are customizable sections of buttons. Each button, when clicked once, performs a function. Some buttons provide pop-up selections you drag to and click instead. This section describes Excel's toolbars. Although each button has an icon that attempts to convey its function, some can be rather mystical. You can always tell what a button does by bringing your mouse over the button and pausing there. After a moment a ScreenTip appears presenting the name of the button. (Figure C-3 demonstrates ScreenTips.)

Note

Excel—and the other core Office applications—makes good use of ScreenTips. You'll see them appear occasionally to provide various bits of information.

Figure C-2 shows Excel's Standard toolbar. Table C-1 shows its buttons.

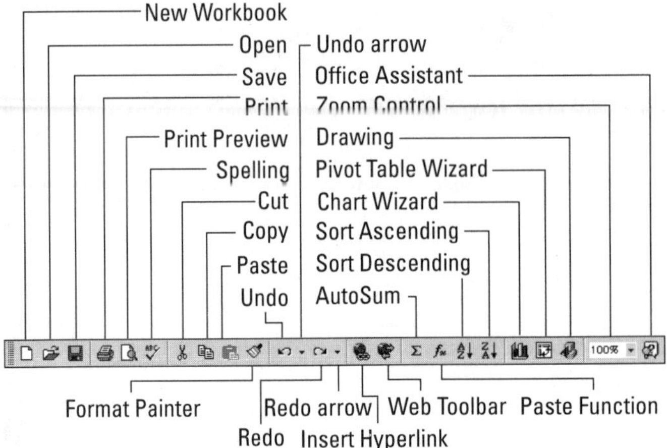

Figure C-2: The Standard toolbar

Table C-1
Standard Toolbar Buttons

Button	*Name*	*Function*
	New Workbook	Opens a new workbook
	Open	Opens a workbook file
	Save	Saves a current workbook; if it has not been saved before, you are prompted to enter a name for the workbook
	Print	Opens the Print dialog box for printing
	Print Preview	Shows you what the workbook will look like when printed
	Spelling	Checks the spelling for the current sheet or the selected section
	Cut	Cuts the selected information and places it on the Clipboard
	Copy	Copies selected text and places it on a Clipboard
	Paste	Pastes selected text in the document at the insertion point

Button	*Name*	*Function*
	Format Painter	Copies text formatting from one area to another
	Undo	Reverses last action; the arrow lets you choose the action that you wish to undo
	Redo	Redoes the last action that was undone; the arrow lets you choose the undone action that you wish to redo
	Insert Hyperlink	Inserts a link to another file or to a Web site on the Internet or on an intranet
	Web Toolbar	Displays the Web toolbar, which can be used for various Web-related tasks
Σ	AutoSum	Invokes the SUM function, which adds a column of numbers
fx	Paste Function	Activates the Function Wizard, which quickly locates a desired function for use in a formula
A Z ↓	Sort Ascending	Sorts list information in ascending order
Z A ↓	Sort Descending	Sorts list information in descending order
	ChartWizard	Activates the Chart Wizard, which creates a chart based on worksheet data
	PivotTable Wizard	Activates the PivotTable Wizard, to help you create a PivotTable. (PivotTables are beyond the scope of this book.) (If you switch to Excel 97—for Windows—you see a Map Wizard button in this position.)
	Drawing	Displays the Drawing toolbar, which contains various tools that can be used to draw graphic shapes in a worksheet
100%	Zoom Control	Controls the size of a document's appearance onscreen
	Office Assistant	Activates the Office Assistant Help system

Figure C-3 shows Excel's Formatting toolbar with the mouse resting over a button, revealing a ScreenTip. Table C-2 explains the Formatting toolbar buttons.

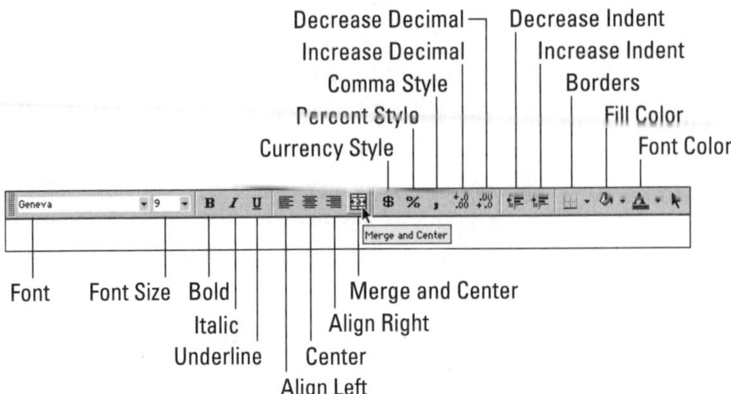

Figure C-3: The Formatting toolbar with a ScreenTip revealed

Table C-2 **Formatting Toolbar Buttons**

Button	*Name*	*Function*
Geneva	Font	Displays list of fonts
9	Font Size	Displays available font sizes
B	Bold	Changes the selected text to boldface
I	Italic	Changes the selected text to italics
U	Underline	Underlines the selected text
	Align Left	Left-aligns cell entries
	Center	Centers cell entries
	Align Right	Right-aligns cell entries
	Merge and Center	Centers cell entries across the columns
$	Currency Style	Applies currency formatting to the current selection
%	Percent Style	Applies percent formatting to the current selection
,	Comma Style	Applies comma formatting to the current selection
+.0 .00	Increase Decimal	Increases the number of digits shown after the decimal point in the selection
.00 +.0	Decrease Decimal	Decreases the number of digits shown after the decimal point in the selection
	Decrease Indent	Reduces the amount of indentation of the selection
	Increase Indent	Increases the amount of indentation of the selection

Button	Name	Function
	Borders	Displays a Borders palette, which can be used to apply a border to the current selection
	Fill Color	Displays a Color palette, which can be used to apply a color choice to the current selection
	Font Color	Displays a Font Color palette, which can be used to apply a font color choice to the current selection

Understanding the workbook concept

Workbooks were introduced to Excel with version 5.0, so if you discuss Excel with someone using version 4.0, the concept of workbooks may be new. In a nutshell, a workbook is a collection of worksheets. Each of the worksheets consists of columns and rows that form cells. There is a tab at the bottom of each of sheet so you can click a tab to go to that sheet. The tabs can be easily renamed so you can know what information is on each sheet.

The advantage of using workbooks is you can keep more than one spreadsheet in a file. This is especially useful when you have a series of worksheets that track time-related data, such as sales or expenses for a series of months. Instead of storing several files, you can place all the worksheets in the same workbook—a single file.

Opening and Using Workbooks

The following sections cover the basics of opening and navigating within Excel files—workbooks and worksheets.

Opening an existing file

You can open an existing (previously saved) workbook the same way you open any file on the Mac—by double-clicking the document's icon or alias, or using the Open dialog box via File ⇨ Open. Another option is the MOM menu, if the file has been added to this menu. Opening files is discussed fully in Chapter 1, and opening workbooks is discussed briefly in Chapter 15.

Workbook and worksheet navigation

This section teaches the basics of navigation within a worksheet and workbook. As always, you can use either the mouse or the keyboard, depending on your preference.

Navigating in the workbook window

When you launch Excel, a new workbook opens and takes you to the first worksheet. If you launch a workbook, it opens to the worksheet that was in front when the worksheet was last saved. To switch to another worksheet, just click the tab of the desired worksheet. You can see the tabs in Figure C-1, but Figure C-4 shows a close-up of a workbook's worksheet tabs. (If you can't see the needed tab, use the four arrows—which are scroll buttons—at the lower left or the use the workbook window scroll bar.)

You can also move from worksheet to worksheet by pressing ⌘-PgDn to move to the next sheet or ⌘-PgUp to move to the preceding sheet.

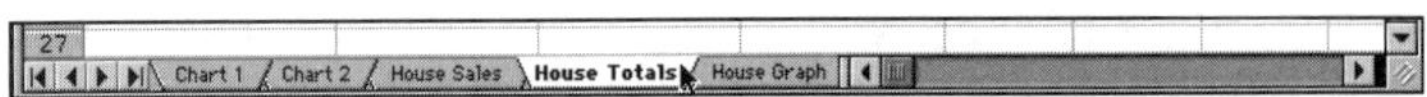

Figure C-4: The tabs of an Excel workbook

Navigating in a worksheet

After selecting your worksheet, you'll want to move around within it. (Remember that the part of the spreadsheet you see onscreen is only a small section of the entire worksheet.) This section introduces four navigation methods.

To make a cell active, just point your cursor at the center of the cell and click. If the desired cell isn't in view, use the scroll arrows to move sideways or up and down until you can see it. You can use the arrows or the scroll box to move through your worksheet. Click any arrow quickly to move a bit or keep the mouse pressed longer to move it farther. Or drag the scroll bar box any distance—note the ScreenTip that tells you what row or column you're on. A less accurate but sometimes faster way to move long distances is to click in the gray area above or below the scroll box. The farther away from the box you click, the farther you'll move within the spreadsheet.

If you prefer to keep your hands on the keys, you can use the key combinations noted in Table C-3 to move around in any Excel worksheet. (This table also appears in Chapter 15.)

Table C-3
Keys and Key Combinations for Navigating in a Worksheet

Keys	*Function*
Arrow keys	Move the cursor in direction of the arrow
Control-↑ or Control-↓	Moves the cursor to the top or bottom of a region of data
Control-← or Control-→	Moves the cursor to the left-most or right-most region of data

Keys	*Function*
Page Up or Page Down	Moves the cursor up or down one screen
Control-Page Up or Control-Page Down	Moves the cursor to the preceding or the following worksheet
Home	Moves the cursor to the first cell in a row
Control-Home	Moves the cursor to the upper-left corner of the worksheet
Option-End	Moves the cursor to the last cell in a row
Control-End	Moves the cursor to the last cell in the used area of a worksheet
End-Enter	Moves the cursor to the last column in a row

Using the Go To command

Yet another option for moving is with the Go To command. You can move to a specific cell on a worksheet by selecting Edit ⇨ Go To or pressing F5. Both moves open the Go To dialog box, as shown in Figure C-5. The text insertion point should be waiting for you in the Reference box or the box will be preselected. Just enter the cell address you want to move to, and then click OK to go directly to that cell. If the insertion point is not awaiting you in the Reference box and it's not preselected (highlighted), click in that cell to place the cursor there, and then type.

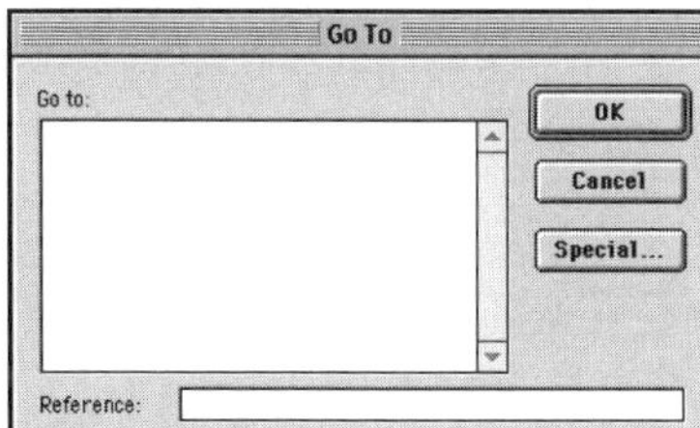

Figure C-5: The Excel Go To dialog box

Using the Name box

The last method for moving to a cell or area of your worksheet becomes available after you begin to assign names to your cells or to ranges of cells. (Naming cell ranges is covered in Chapter 16.) If there are any ranges defined in your worksheet, they appear in the pop-up list when you click the arrow next to the Name box in the formula bar. (The Name box is farthest left in formula bar.) By dragging down to a name in this list and clicking, you move to this range. At the same time, the entire range will also become selected. The unique thing about this method is if the named range is on a different worksheet in your workbook, Excel jumps you to that other worksheet.

Entering and Editing Data

Cells can contain text, numbers, or combinations of both. This data lands in whatever cell is currently selected. If a range of cells is selected, the data lands in the top-left cell of that range. Just move to any cell and start typing. When done with your entry, you must tell Excel you are done entering data and want that data to be entered into that cell. Until you do, you remain in an entry mode and are adding data to your cell or to your formula. We go into detail about how to enter and edit data in a moment.

Two kinds of data can be entered into a worksheet: values and formulas.

- ✦ Values are data, such as dates, time, percents, scientific notation, or text; values don't change unless the cell is edited.
- ✦ Formulas are sequences of cell references, names, functions, or operators that produce a new value based on existing values in other cells of the worksheet.

Formulas can be tricky so Excel provides some coaching to make them easier. (This is covered in detail in Chapter 16.)

Figure C-6 shows a typical worksheet containing both values and formulas.

F2 =SUM(B2:E2)

Sales

	A	B	C	D	E	F
1		January	February	March	April	Total
2	Fiona Swan	$13,600.00	$13,700.00	$89,900.00	$89,900.00	$207,100.00
3	Andrea Czurd	$48,700.00	$25,675.00	$32,500.00	$17,000.00	$123,875.00
4	Karen Fischer	$53,000.00	$10,250.00	$11,500.00	$48,700.00	$123,450.00
5	Nancy Greenberger	$34,630.00	$37,230.00	$50,200.00	$46,800.00	$168,860.00
6	Dexter Horthy	$10,250.00	$456,800.00	$21,300.00	$48,700.00	$537,050.00
7	Donna Shadovitz	$25,675.00	$48,700.00	$25,675.00	$50,200.00	$150,250.00
8	Amelia Wallerstien	$502,900.00	$25,675.00	$48,700.00	$13,700.00	$590,975.00
9						
10	Total Sales	$185,855.00	$592,355.00	$231,075.00	$301,300.00	$1,310,585.00

Figure C-6: A typical worksheet with values and formulas stored in cells

Entering data

If you are new to using a spreadsheet, you may find data entry a bit disconcerting. You select a cell and type, but rather than having the characters you type appear directly in the cell you've selected, the data you are entering appears above the spreadsheet in the formula bar. The data doesn't appear in the cell until after you tell Excel to accept the data.

Excel 98 introduces an alternative to the traditional spreadsheet data entry method. You can enter data directly into the cell, which may be more comfortable for you. You simply double-click in the cell into which you want to enter data. The insertion point flashes directly in the cell and as you enter your data, the data appears right there in the cell. Actually, it also appear in the formula bar. (In-cell editing works for editing as well as initial data entry.)

In-cell editing is turned on by default. If double-clicking in a cell doesn't place the insertion point in the cell, in-cell editing may not be turned on. To check, or to turn it on, select Tools ⇨ Preferences, and then click the Edit tab and check Edit directly in cell.

Whether you enter your data into the formula bar or directly into the cell, after you've entered it, you must tell Excel to accept your data. There are a few ways to do so.

- ✦ You can click the green check mark in the formula bar or press Enter. Both methods store the data in the cell but don't move you out of that cell.
- ✦ Another option is to accept the data and move to another cell at the same time. To do so, you can press Return or use the arrow keys. The arrow keys move you the next cell to the left, right, up, or down, depending on the direction of the arrow you pressed. The effect of pressing Return is controlled by you in your Excel Preferences. (Select Tools ⇨ Preferences, and then click the Edit tab.) By default, Excel moves you down the column to the next cell, but it can move you left, right, or up instead. If you prefer, you can uncheck the option and have Return act the same as Enter.

If you decide you don't really want to enter the data you typed, click the Cancel button in the formula bar (the red X, as shown in Figure C-7) or press Esc. If you've already entered the text and told Excel to accept it, you can undo your entry or changes with the Undo command by selecting Edit ⇨ Undo, pressing ⌘-Z, or by clicking the Undo button on the Standard toolbar.

Figure C-7: The Cancel button of the formula bar

Editing data

As you enter text, you'll sometimes want to edit it. After you select your cell or place your insertion point, editing data is the same as entering it.

Follow these steps to edit existing data in cells using the traditional formula bar entry technique:

1. Move the cursor to the cell containing the data you want to edit. As you select any cell, the data or formula it contains appears in the formula bar.
2. Move the mouse pointer over the formula bar. (As you do so, the pointer becomes an I-beam—as used in text entry.)
3. Click the I-beam at the location where you want to start editing, just as you do to edit text in word processing. (The flashing insertion point in the formula bar indicates where your editing will occur.) Edit as in word processing, and then tell Excel to accept the changes using one of the same methods you use when you originally enter data (most commonly by pressing Return or Enter).

To edit existing data using in-cell editing, follow these steps:

1. Move the mouse pointer over the cell you want to edit and double-click. The insertion point appears in the cell and the your pointer becomes an I-beam while over that cell.

   With practice, you can even control where the insertion point lands within the cell. (It lands at the left edge of the vertical part of the fat cross.)
2. Click the I-beam at the location where you want to start editing, or use the arrow keys to move the insertion point, just as you do to edit text in word processing. (The flashing insertion point indicates where your editing will occur.) Edit as in word processing, and then tell Excel to accept the changes using one of the same methods you use when you originally enter data (most commonly by pressing Return or Enter).

If you have data in a cell, be careful. It is quite possible to click a cell, enter new data, and accept it. This replaces the existing data or formula with the new entry. If you mean to edit the contents of a cell, be sure to place your cursor within the contents of that cell before typing and accepting the change.

If you decide you don't like your changes, click the Cancel button (the red X, as shown earlier in Figure C-7) in the formula bar or press Esc. If you've already told Excel to accept changes, you can undo your changes with the Undo command by selecting Edit⇨Undo (⌘-Z) or by clicking the Undo button on the Standard toolbar.

Numbers

By default, cells are formatted with the General Number format. This causes Excel to display numbers as accurately as possible using the integer, decimal fraction, and—if the number is longer than the cell—scientific notation. You can easily format any cell or group of cells to take on any number format (or make the cell text format). However, you don't always have to format cells, as Excel tries to do it for you. As you enter your data, you can give Excel clues to assign the correct format. If you enter a dollar sign before the number, the number is assigned a currency format. If you enter a percent sign, the number is assigned the percent format.

Sometimes your number will be larger than the default column width. When the number is too large to fit in the column, Excel displays a series of # symbols. To see the entire number, simply widen the column. The fastest way to make the column wide enough to fit the entire number is by double-clicking the column's right border in the column header.

At times you may want to enter numbers as text, as may be the case with zip codes. To do this, you can format the column as text—or, as you enter each zip code, you can tell Excel to format the numbers as text and left-align them by entering a single quotation mark (') before the number.

You can enter numbers in your worksheet using any of the following special characters:

+ - () , / $ % . E e

Dates and times

Dates and times are common in spreadsheets. Excel provides several standard date and time formats, as shown in Table C-4 and C-5. In addition, you can create your own custom formats. (Chapter 16 tells you how.) If you use any of Table C-4 and C-5's formats to enter dates and times, the dates and times revert to that format automatically. Otherwise, you can enter the dates or times in any format, select the cells, and choose a format any time. You can also always change a format.

Table C-4
Date Formats

Format	*Example*
D/M	3/5
D/M/YY	1/1/99
DD/MM/YY	01/01/99
D-MON	1-Apr
D-MON-YY	3-Aug-63
DD-MON-YY	03-Aug-63
MON-YY	Apr 98

(continued)

Table C-4 (continued)

Format	*Example*
MONTH-YY	April 98
MONTH-D-YYYY	February-3-1989
D/M/YY H:MM 24-hour	3/4/95 14:30 PM
D/M/YY H:MM AM/PM	5/12/93 2:30 PM (This defaults to 24 hour until you reformat it.)

Table C-5
Time Formats

Format	*Example*
HH:MM	10:30
HH:MM AM/PM	02:30 PM
HH:MM:SS	10:30:55
HH:MM:SS (24-hour)	14:30:55
HH:MM:SS AM/PM	01:30:55 PM
HH:MM.n (with tenths)	02:30.7
D/M/YY H:MM (12 or 24-hour)	3/4/95 2:30

Text entry

To enter text in Excel, select the cell and type. You can type up to 32,000 characters in a cell. Entries can include text and numbers and, as mentioned earlier, numbers can also be entered as text.

You may want to format large amounts of text in a way that presents an attractive display. Rather than using the method of typing a single quote in front of the text, it is easier to format the cell properly. To do this, choose Format⇨Cells to bring up the Format Cells dialog box shown in Figure C-8. In the Number tab, select Text.

To accommodate a long display of text, you can set text wrap. This allows text to wrap within the width of the cell (regardless of the cell width), therefore preventing long strips of text from overflowing into other cells. Instead, you will have multiple lines of text in your cells and the cell will grow to any height necessary to accommodate the number of lines.

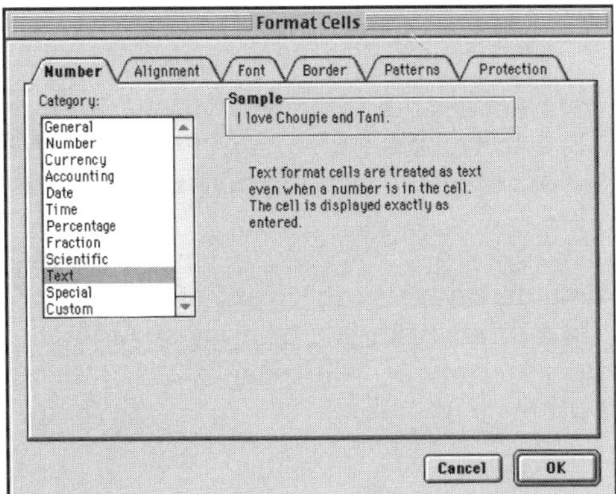

Figure C-8: The Format Cells dialog box

To activate text wrap, click the Alignment tab in the Format Cells dialog box and click in the box next to Wrap Text. You can change the column width any time and the text will wrap accordingly.

Building Formulas

The whole point of spreadsheets is to manipulate the numbers: Add them. Multiply them. Calculate their cosines, if you're trigonometrically inclined. You use formulas to do this. You build a formula by indicating which values should be used and which calculations should apply to these values.

For example, if you wanted to add the values in cells B1 and B2 and then display the results of that calculation in cell B5, you could place the cursor in cell B5 and enter the simple formula =B1+B2. The equal sign tells Excel this cell will be calculating a result based on a formula. Formulas always start with an equal sign.

A formula calculates a value based on a combination of other values. These other values can be numbers, cell references, operators (+, -, *, and /), or other formulas. Formulas can also include the names of other areas in the worksheet, as well as cell references in other worksheets.

Math operators produce numeric results. Besides addition (+), subtraction (-), multiplication (*), and division (/) symbols, Excel accepts as math operators the exponentiation (^) and percentage (%) symbols. A number of other types of characters can be used in formulas for manipulating text and numbers. Chapter 16 covers formula entry in detail.

Printing Your Worksheets

For the most part, you print an Excel worksheet the same way you print any other document on the Mac—by choosing File➪Print (⌘-P). This brings up the Print dialog box. Here you enter the number of copies, select a paper tray if applicable, and then click Print.

This prints the active worksheet by default. However, there are other options, such as printing a part of a page, printing an entire workbook, printing several worksheets within a workbook at once, and even printing several disconnected cell ranges. (Chapter 20 covers printing options in detail.)

Saving Your Worksheets

Although we didn't mention it in this appendix, we highly recommend saving your worksheet periodically. Even before it's complete? Yes! Definitely. Doing so reduces the possibility of losing large amounts of information due to a freeze or power failure. The commands used for saving worksheets—Save, Save As, and Save Workspace—are found in the File menu.

The Save and Save As commands save worksheets to disk. Save saves the worksheet under the existing name (after it has been saved once). Save As enables you to save a second copy of your workbook by prompting you for a new filename.

Save As is handy when you need to make a second copy so you can alter one without ruining the original. It also lets you save files in formats other than Excel's normal format. You can save the data in many other database and spreadsheet file formats. You can also save your worksheet as HTML for publishing on the Internet or on an intranet.

To save your worksheet, choose File➪Save (⌘-S). When you do this the first time, the dialog box shown in Figure C-9 appears. This enables you to name your workbook and select the folder to which the file is saved.

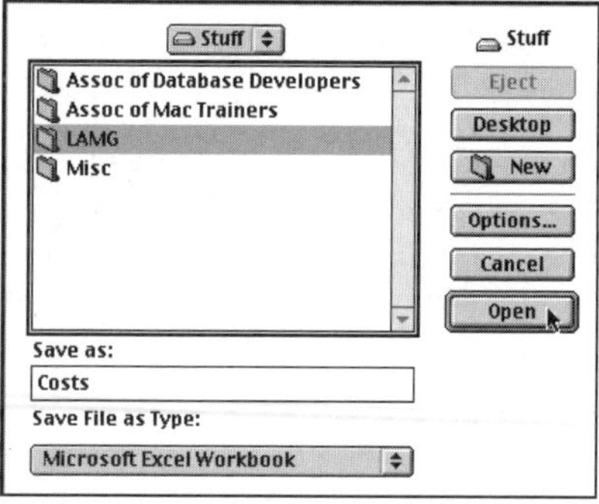

Figure C-9: The Save As dialog box

In Figure C-9, the file is being saved with the name Costs. It will land in a folder called LAMG when the user clicks Open and then Save. (The Open button turns into a Save button once you are in a folder.) The drive being saved to is called Stuff. (You can always move the file later, after closing it, but that's an extra step that can be avoided by paying attention to where you save to initially.) Saving is covered in detail in Chapter 15.

✦ ✦ ✦

PowerPoint Quick Start

✦ ✦ ✦ ✦

In This Appendix

Understanding PowerPoint

Creating presentations

Opening, saving, and closing presentations

Using PowerPoint's views

Working with slides

Adding clip-art

Printing your presentation

✦ ✦ ✦ ✦

This introduction to PowerPoint covers basic PowerPoint skills and is designed to familiarize readers who have never worked with PowerPoint. In this introduction, you learn how to create presentations with and without the aid of the wizards, how to enter and edit text, how to add clip-art to slides, and how to print your slides. You also learn some basic terminology that applies to using PowerPoint. When you feel familiar with the basics, you'll find the more advanced details of PowerPoint in Chapters 27 through 34.

Understanding PowerPoint

As you work with PowerPoint, you'll encounter some common terms. Being familiar with these terms will maximize your effectiveness in using PowerPoint. Look over the following list and familiarize yourself with these common PowerPoint terms:

- ✦ **Presentation:** In PowerPoint, a presentation is the container holding all the individual slides, text, graphics, drawings, and other objects that make up your presentation. PowerPoint stores each presentation in a separate file on your hard disk.
- ✦ **Template:** A template is a kind of formatting model in PowerPoint. You use templates to apply a chosen group of styles, colors, and fonts to the slides you are working with. PowerPoint comes with over 150 different templates; you can see examples of the style and layout of each of these in Appendix F of the *PowerPoint User's Guide*.
- ✦ **Slides:** Slides are the individual screens or pages that you see within your presentation.
- ✦ **Slide masters:** Slide masters are master documents that control the appearance and layout of the slides you create. If you make a design change to a slide master,

the same change is reflected in all the new slides that you create based on that master.

- **Layout:** This term refers to the overall appearance of a single slide. You can change the layout for any slide on an individual basis without affecting other slides in the presentation.

Creating Presentations

To create a new presentation, choose File⇨New to open the New Presentation dialog box shown in Figure D-1. When the New Presentation dialog box opens, the General tab is displayed along with the Blank Presentation icon. Choose from among these options:

- **General**: This tab contains the Blank Presentation icon as well as the AutoContent Wizard. Use the Blank Presentation icon to create a presentation that contains no preformatted slides, or use the AutoContent Wizard to help you create a presentation if those listed in the other tabs do not meet your needs. The AutoContent Wizard produces six styles of presentations, including strategy, sales, training, progress report, and bad news.
- **Presentation Designs:** This tab contains templates you can use for the presentations you create. PowerPoint contains 17 template designs you can use to design your presentations.
- **Presentations:** This tab contains 40 different presentations you can use for different subjects.

After you choose the way in which you want to create the new presentation, click OK. If you chose a wizard, you may be asked additional questions to help determine the layout and content of your presentation. When you are finished answering the questions, the basis of your presentation appears onscreen, and you can edit it as you see fit.

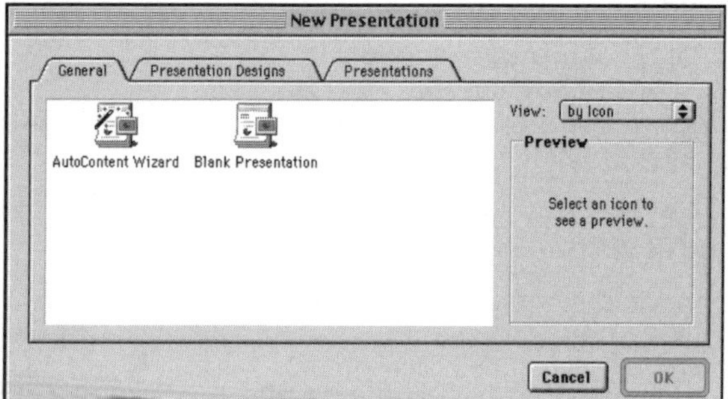

Figure D-1: The General tab of the New Presentation dialog box

Using the AutoContent Wizard

When you start a new presentation with the AutoContent Wizard, the first AutoContent Wizard dialog box appears, explaining the purpose of the wizard. After you click the Next button, the second AutoContent Wizard dialog box appears, as shown in Figure D-2.

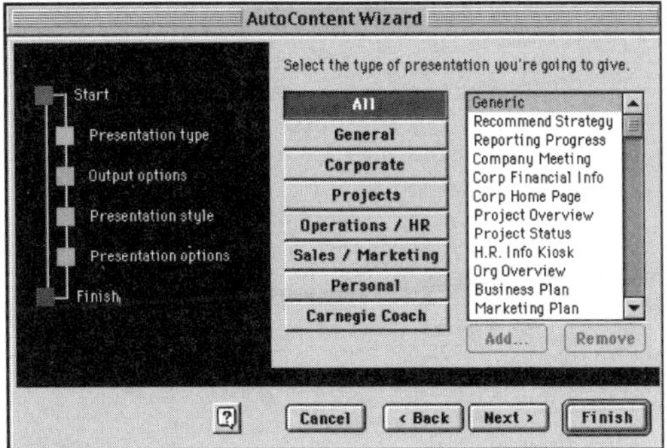

Figure D-2: The second AutoContent Wizard dialog box

The second dialog box asks you to choose the type of presentation you want to create. You have choices divided into several categories. Clicking the button corresponding to the desired category makes all the choices for that category appear. The default is All, which shows all the listings from all the categories. After you choose the type of presentation you want to create, click the Next button; you see the third AutoContent Wizard dialog box, as shown in Figure D-3.

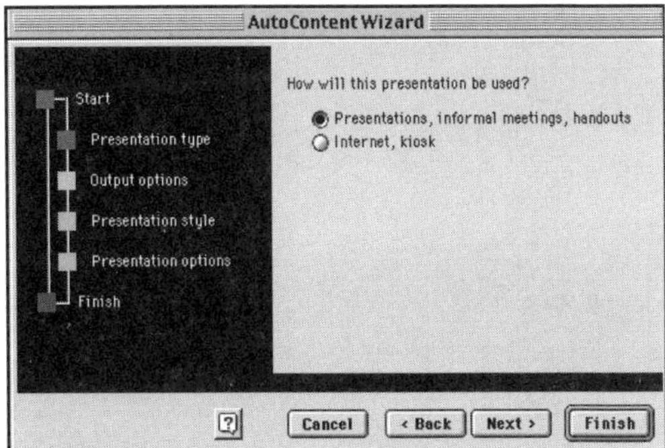

Figure D-3: The third AutoContent Wizard dialog box

In this dialog box, you can select the manner in which your presentation will be used. Your choices are Presentations, informal meetings, handouts or Internet, kiosk. After you choose an option, click the Next button to show the fourth dialog box (see Figure D-4).

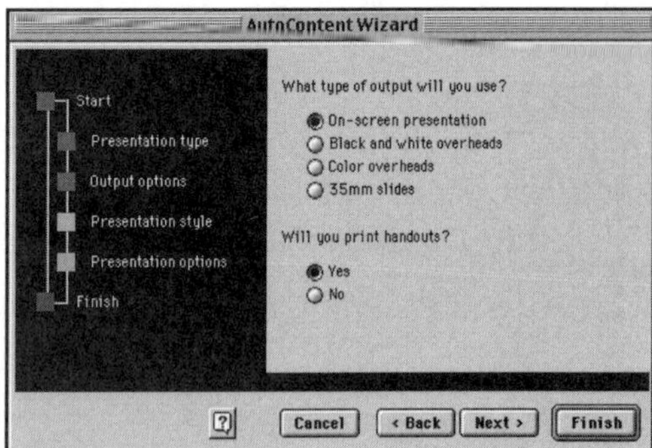

Figure D-4: The fourth AutoContent Wizard dialog box

The fourth dialog box is used to choose the desired style of your presentation. Under the type of output section, select the way you will be presenting your slides. You can choose from On-screen presentation, Black and White overheads, Color overheads, or 35mm slides. Also, you can tell the wizard whether you will be printing out the slides. After you have made your selections, click Next to go to the fifth window of the AutoContent Wizard (see Figure D-5).

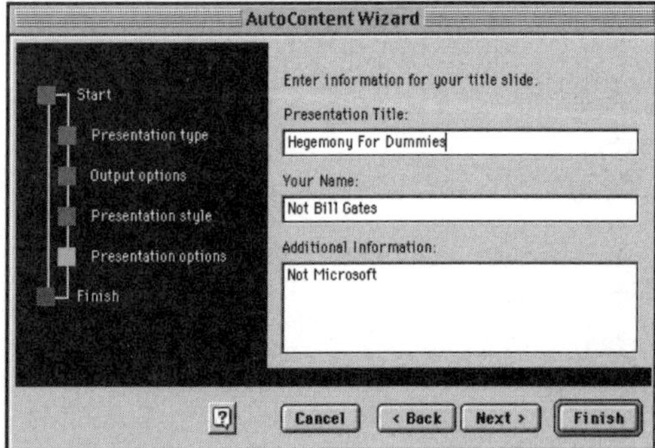

Figure D-5: The fifth AutoContent Wizard dialog box

This fifth dialog box to the AutoContent Wizard is used to set up your title slide. Here, you enter a title for your first slide. After entering a title, you may want to include your name. If so, enter it in the Your Name field. The wizard also allows space for any additional information that you wish to add to the title slide of the presentation. After you have completed making your choices, click Next to go to the final dialog box of the AutoContent Wizard. This dialog box asks for confirmation before creating the presentation, and you click Finish to complete the presentation.

Using a template

To use a template, choose File⇨New, and then select the Presentations tab. Now choose the template on which you want to base your presentation. Choose the desired template and click OK. Next, you see the New Slide dialog box, as shown in Figure D-6.

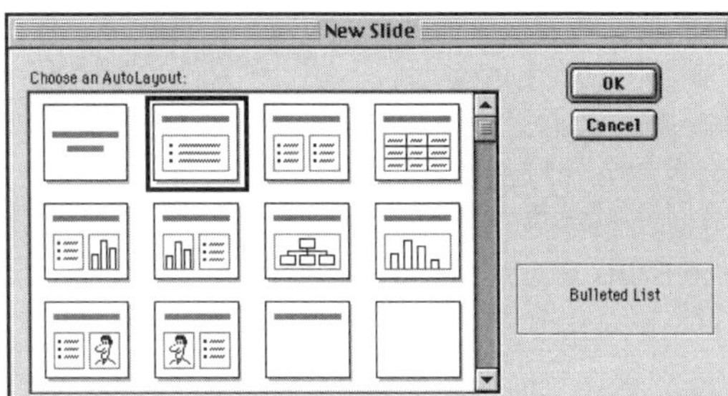

Figure D-6: The New Slide dialog box

After you choose one of the layouts shown in the dialog box, click OK. PowerPoint creates a presentation containing a single slide that uses the style and layout you have specified. You can then add text and graphics to the slide and insert additional slides into the presentation.

Starting a blank presentation

The Blank Presentation option is suited to PowerPoint users who are familiar with the package. This option assumes you want to handle all the design and content decisions on your own. After you choose the Blank Presentation option from the General tab of the New Presentation dialog box, the New Slide dialog box appears. After you select the layout you want, click OK. The result is a blank presentation containing a single slide, similar to the one shown in Figure D-7. You can add text and slides as desired.

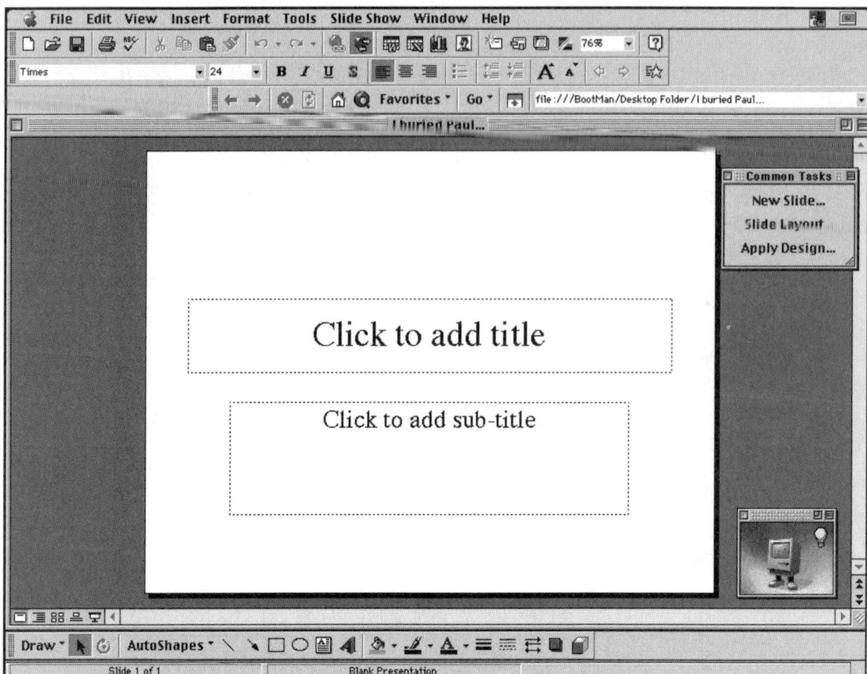

Figure D-7: The result of selecting the Blank Presentation option

Opening, Saving, and Closing Presentations

You can open an existing presentation by choosing File⇨Open or by clicking the Open button on the Standard toolbar. Either method results in the appearance of the Open dialog box. Choose the presentation you want and click OK. You can open and work with multiple presentations simultaneously. As you open each presentation, its name is added to the bottom of the Window menu.

PowerPoint uses the standard Mac methods to save files. When you choose File⇨Save or click the Save button on the Standard toolbar, PowerPoint saves the presentation to a file. If you are saving the presentation for the first time, a Save As dialog box appears, where you provide a filename for the presentation. You can save an existing presentation under a different filename by choosing File⇨Save As and entering the new name for the presentation.

To close a presentation, choose File⇨Close, or click the close box in the top-left corner of the presentation's window.

Using PowerPoint's Views

As you work with your presentations, you can switch between any one of five different views: Slide, Outline, Slide Sorter, Notes Pages, and Slide Show. Each of these views provides you with a different way of looking at the same presentation. To switch between the available views, click the appropriate view button at the lower-left corner of your screen. You can also choose the corresponding view from the View menu. For example, choosing View ⇨ Outline switches you to Outline view. Here is a description of the available views:

✦ **Slide view**—fills the window with a view of the current slide. In this view, you can add and edit text and graphics or change the layout of the slide. Figure D-8 shows an example of a presentation in Slide view.

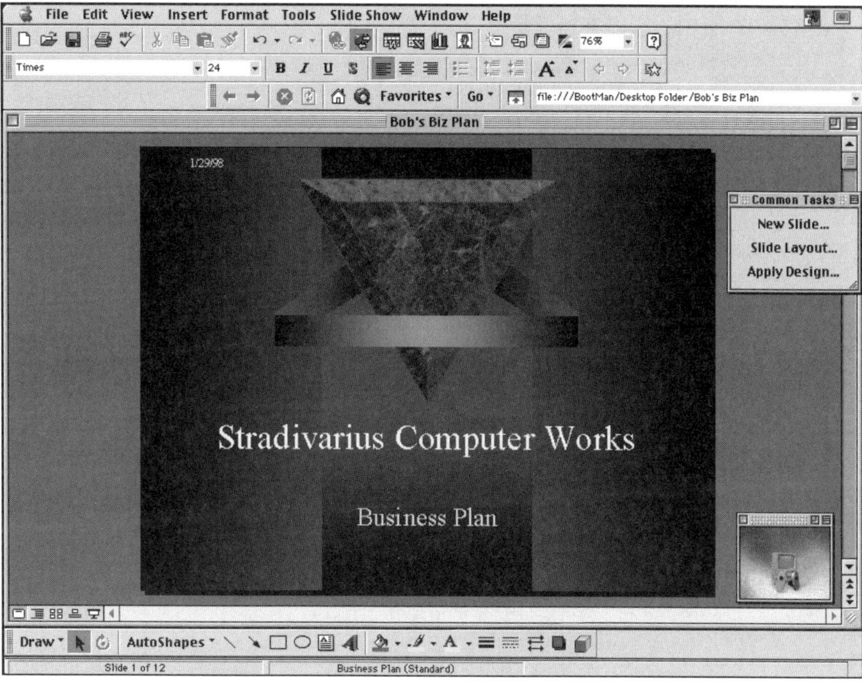

Figure D-8: An example of a presentation in Slide view

✦ **Outline view**—provides a view of the overall organization of the text in your presentation. In this view, it's easier to see a large portion of your presentation's contents. Although you can't change the slide layouts or modify graphics in this view, you can add and edit the slide titles and the main text. Figure D-9 shows an example of a presentation in Outline view.

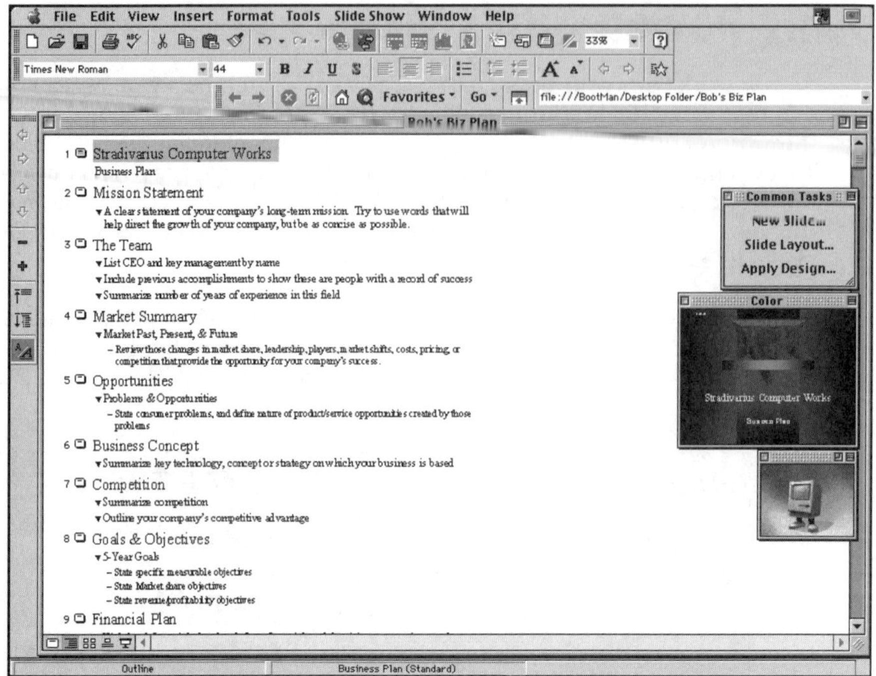

Figure D-9: An example of a presentation in Outline view

- **Slide Sorter view**—provides a window containing multiple slides, each in reduced form. This view is best when you want an overall view of your presentation or when you want to see the overall appearance of the text and the graphics. You can't edit text or graphics in this view, but you can reorder the slides. When you are working with electronic slide shows, you can also add transitions between slides and set the timing in this view (see Chapter 30). Figure D-10 shows an example of Slide Sorter view.
- **Notes Pages view**—provides a view where a single slide is placed in the top half of a page, and the bottom half of the page is reserved for typing notes. This view is useful when you want to add speaker's notes that you can refer to during your presentation. PowerPoint lets you print the notes pages separately from the slides or overheads that you produce for your presentation. Figure D-11 shows an example of Notes Pages view.
- **Slide Show view**—fills the screen with a view of one slide at a time. In this view, you also see the effects of any transitions and timing that you have added to the presentation.

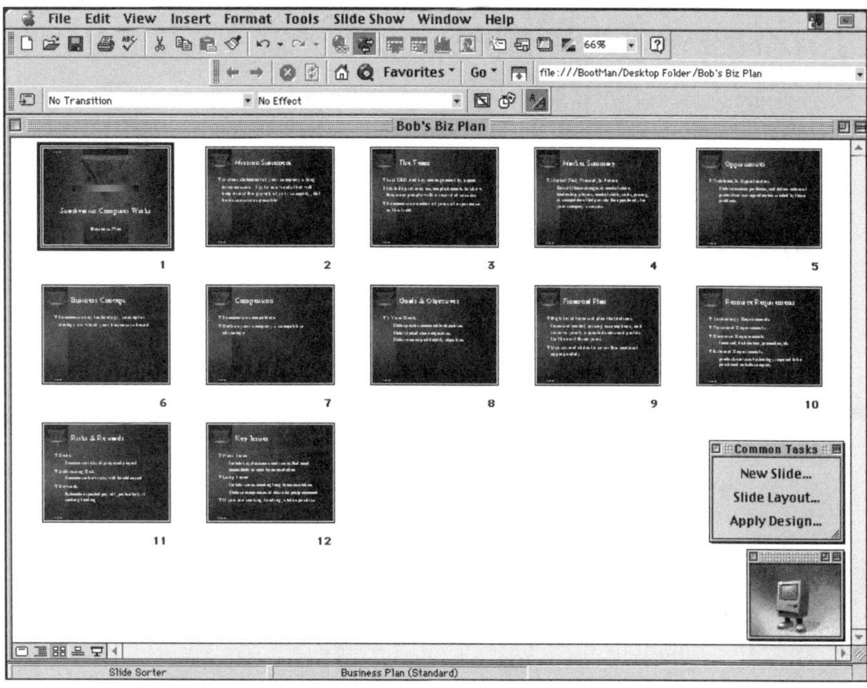

Figure D-10: An example of a presentation in Slide Sorter view

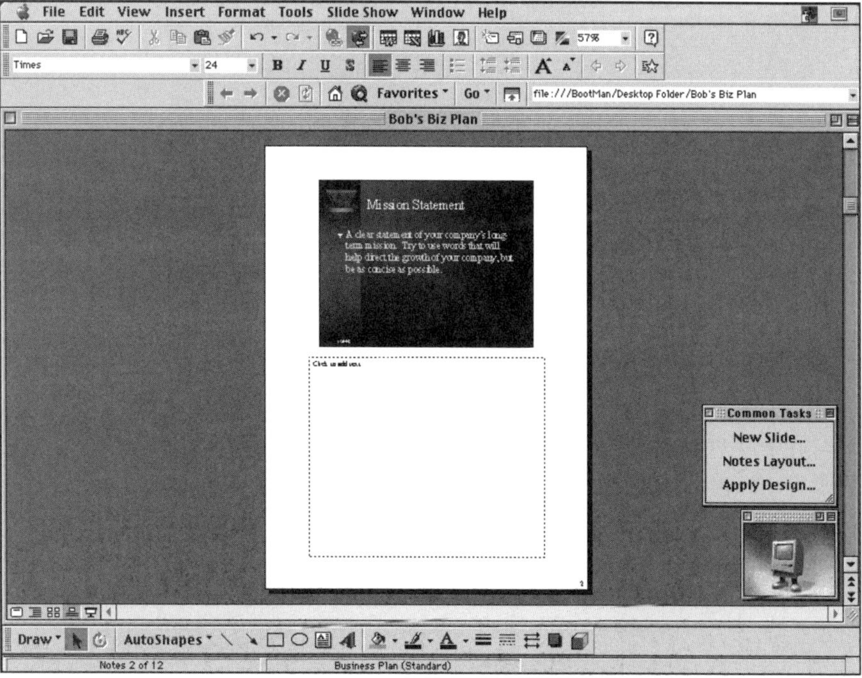

Figure D-11: An example of a presentation in Notes Pages view

Working with Slides

If you use PowerPoint much, you'll often find yourself adding slides, moving among slides, and editing the contents of your slides. The following sections cover these eventualities in brief.

Adding slides

To add a slide to your presentation, follow these steps:

1. In any view, choose Insert➪New Slide. (You can also use ⌘-M as a shortcut.) The New Slide dialog box appears.
2. Choose the layout you want for the new slide and click OK.

The slide is then added to the end of your presentation; it has the same design as the other slides in your presentation.

Moving among slides

Most presentations have more than one slide, so you must be able to move among slides to work on your whole presentation. How you move among slides depends on which view you're in. Table D-1 shows the different methods for moving around within the different slide views.

Table D-1
Methods of Moving Among Slides

View	*How to Move Among Slides*
Outline view	Drag the scroll box to display the desired slide. Click the slide icon to the left of the slide's title to select the slide. Click anywhere within the slide's text to edit it.
Slide view	Drag the scroll box until you reach the desired slide number or click the Previous Slide or Next Slide button at the bottom of the vertical scroll bar.
Slide Sorter view	Click the desired slide.
Notes Pages view	Drag the scroll box until you reach the desired slide number or click the Previous Slide or Next Slide button at the bottom of the vertical scroll bar.

Editing a slide's contents

If you've created a presentation based on a blank slide, you must enter all the required text. If you used an AutoContent Wizard, you've got a fair amount of text in your presentation already, but it's probably not precisely what you want. In either case, you need to add or edit the text you want in your presentation. This section details how you can add or edit text in Slide view or in Outline view.

Editing text in Slide view

In Slide view, you see your text along with any graphics you have added to the slide, and you can edit any object in the slide by clicking the object. To add text, click in the placeholder labeled Click to add title and type the text, as shown in Figure D-12. To edit existing text, click the text to select it and then edit as you normally would. If you're working with a bulleted list of topics, you can add a new topic by placing the insertion point at the end of an existing topic and pressing Enter.

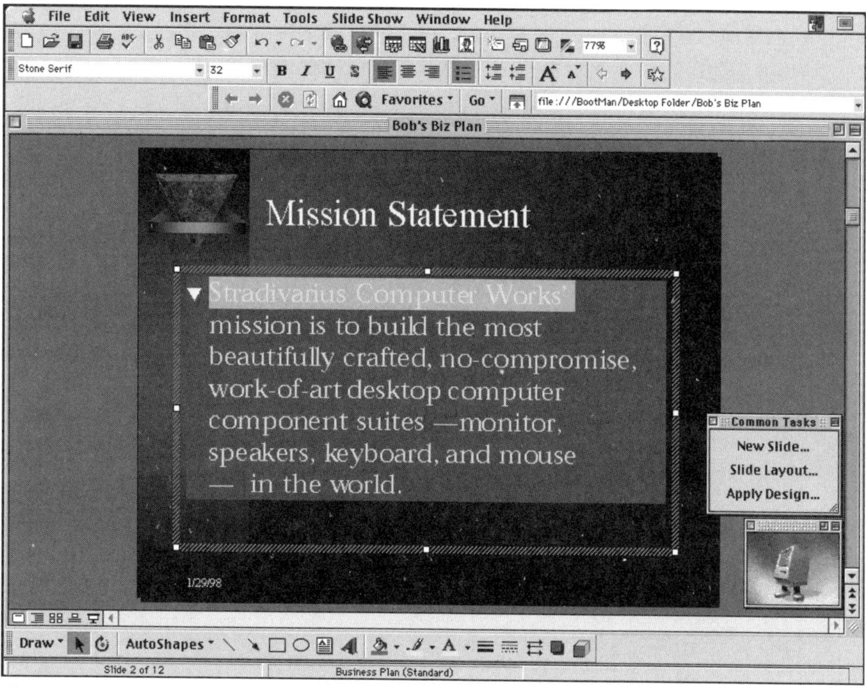

Figure D-12: Editing text in Slide view

Editing text in Outline view

Outline view provides an easy way to edit text because you can view much of your presentation at one time. To edit text, just click to place the insertion point where you want it and type the desired text, as shown in Figure D-13. You can use the Delete or Backspace keys to remove unwanted text.

As you work with text in Outline view, remember that you can use the Promote, Demote, Move Up, and Move Down buttons on the Outlining toolbar to the left of the screen to change the levels or the locations of the items with which you are working. Simply place the insertion point anywhere inside the desired entry and then click the appropriate button. The outlining buttons perform the following tasks:

- **Promote (Indent less)**—Click this button to remove an indent and move the entry one level higher (in importance) within the list. The item moves to the left, and in most cases, the font size increases.
- **Demote (Indent more)**—Click this button to add an indent and move the entry one level lower (in importance) within the list. The item moves to the right, and in most cases, the font size decreases.
- **Move Up**—Click this button to move the entry up in the list by one line.
- **Move Down**—Click this button to move the entry down in the list by one line.

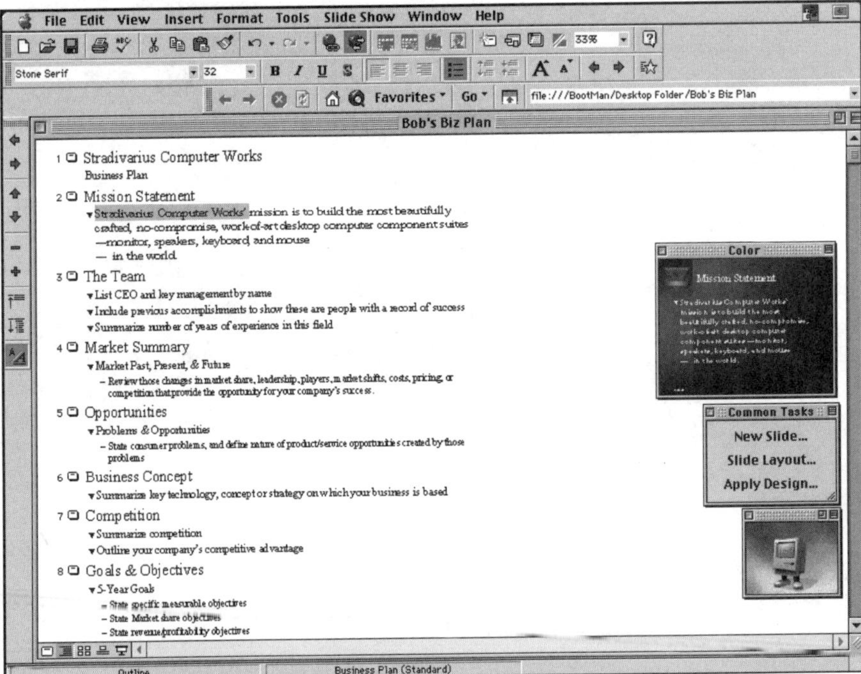

Figure D-13: Editing text in Outline view

Adding Clip-art

PowerPoint comes with hundreds of clip-art images that you can easily add to your presentations to add pizzazz to your slides. Note that before you can insert clip-art, you must have installed the ClipArt Gallery along with PowerPoint. You can add clip-art by following these steps:

1. Switch to Slide view and display the slide where you want to add the clip-art.
2. Choose Insert ⇨ Picture, and then choose Clip Art or click the Insert Clip Art button on the Standard toolbar to open the Microsoft Clip Gallery dialog box, as shown in Figure D-14.

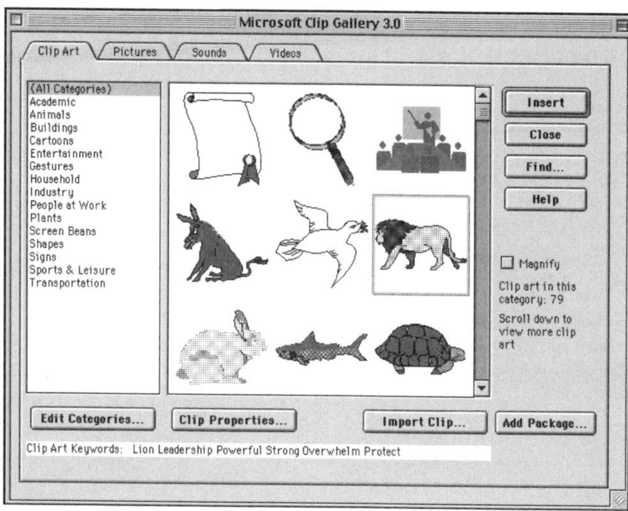

Figure D-14: The Clip Art tab of the Microsoft Clip Gallery dialog box

If you're inserting clip-art for the first time, you'll see a dialog box warning you that the process may take some time because PowerPoint has to organize the files first.

3. In the categories list box at the top of the dialog box, click the desired category.
4. In the right half of the dialog box, click the desired image. You can use the scroll bar at the right side of the dialog box to see additional images.
5. Click the Insert button to place the clip-art in the slide.

After the clip-art appears in the slide, you can click it to select it. Then hold down the mouse button while you drag the clip-art to the location you want. You can resize the clip-art by clicking one of the sizing handles (the small rectangles that surround the clip-art when you select it) and dragging it until the clip-art reaches the desired size.

You may often want to add clip-art to an area that has existing text, but by default, any clip-art you add covers the existing text. To solve this problem, go into Slide view and select the clip-art by clicking it. Then choose the Send to Back command from the Draw menu to place the clip-art underneath the text, which makes the text visible.

Printing Your Presentation

You can print various parts of your presentation or all of your presentation. To print your presentation, choose File➪Print or click the Print button on the Standard toolbar. The Print dialog box appears, as shown in Figure D-15.

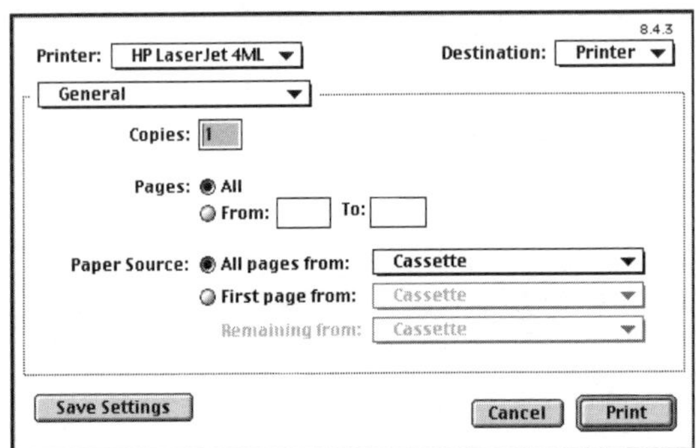

Figure D-15: The Print dialog box

You learn more about the Print dialog box in Chapter 30, but for now, the most important point is to select exactly what you want to print. First, choose Microsoft PowerPoint from the pop-up menu (it says General when you first open the dialog box and has a downward-pointing arrow on it). Then, in the Print What list box, you can choose Slides, Note Pages, Handouts, or Outline View. Finally, choose General from the pop-up menu and choose the pages you want to print (the default option is All). Select any other desired options in the dialog box and click OK to begin printing.

✦ ✦ ✦

Customizing Toolbars and Menus

✦ ✦ ✦ ✦

In This Appendix

About toolbars

Turning toolbars on or off

Repositioning toolbars

Customizing toolbars

Creating a new toolbar

Customizing menus

Changing Word's keyboard shortcuts

✦ ✦ ✦ ✦

This appendix is your one-stop shop for the lowdown on customizing Microsoft Office toolbars and menus.

About Toolbars

Toolbars are strips of buttons you click to perform certain common tasks. Toolbars are a great way to accomplish an action with as few motions as possible. While buttons are helpful, you don't need every button all the time, so each Office application has a Standard toolbar you can keep on all the time as well as several function-specific toolbars you can turn on as needed. Office even turns on some of these function-specific toolbars for you when appropriate. (Of course, you can turn them off if you want.) In Office 98, toolbars can also contain menus. This new feature means you can place a menu in a toolbar.

There's only one main rule to remember: You have to be in an application to work with its toolbars, so remember to launch your Office application before you try to do any of these customizations.

Turning Toolbars on or off

Turning a toolbar on or off is very easy. There are several ways to do so:

✦ In the View menu, select Toolbars, and then select the toolbar you wish to turn on or off. A check mark in the menu indicates the toolbar is on. (Of course, you can also see the toolbar onscreen.)

✦ Control-click any blank part of any visible toolbar. This brings up the list of toolbars. Checks indicate which toolbars are active. Click any toolbar to open or close it.

✦ Go to Tools ➪ Customize, and then click the Toolbars tab. Check or uncheck any toolbar.

Repositioning Toolbars

Rather than keeping toolbars at the top of the screen, you may prefer to move a toolbar to the left or right edge of your monitor or have it float freely as a palette. Simply click the rows of dots at the left side of the toolbar, or any edge of a toolbar, and drag. If you drag to an edge of the monitor, the toolbar docks there; if you drag to the middle of your screen, the toolbar floats freely. To move a toolbar back to the top or to redock the toolbar, drag it back up into the toolbar area until your mouse overlaps the toolbar you want it to fall below.

When floating, a toolbar has the standard Mac window features: a close box, a title bar, and a resize corner (bottom right). Like any window, you can drag this palette anywhere onscreen and resize it. Resizing the palette doesn't add a scroll bar; instead it rearranges the buttons. Double-clicking the top of the palette window windowshades it (collapses the palette to just the title bar) as with any Mac window. (In Word 97 for Windows this would redock the toolbar.)

Customizing Toolbars

To customize a toolbar, launch the application for the toolbar you want to customize. Then Control-click in any blank spot on the toolbar and select Customize (or select Tools ➪ Customize). The Customize dialog box appears. Notice it has three tabs and a Keyboard button; these are your keys to making all sorts of changes to the toolbars. It's a good idea to explore the Commands tab of the Customize dialog box, just to discover some the possibilities available to you. Figure E-1 shows you the Customize dialog box with the Commands tab chosen.

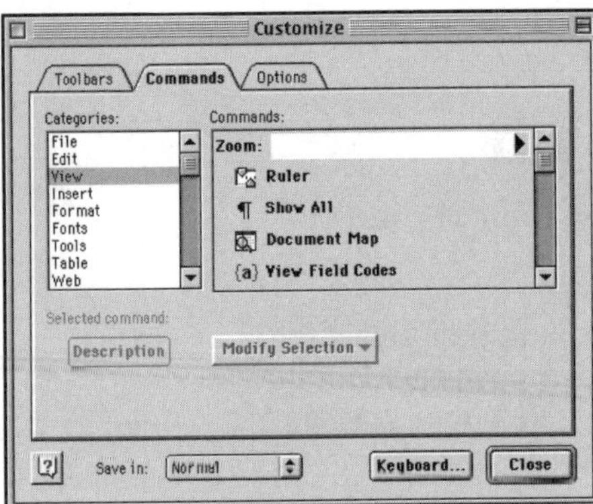

Figure E-1: The Commands tab of the Customize dialog box

Adding or deleting a button (or menu)

To add or remove a button from a toolbar, the Customize dialog box must be open. Select Tools ➪ Customize from the menus or Control-click any toolbar and select Customize from the shortcut menu.

Adding a button is easy—you just drag it to the toolbar. Follow these steps:

1. Select the Commands tab of the Customize dialog box so you can locate the command (button) you want to add.
2. In the Categories list, click a category. On the right, you see a list of all commands within that category. (To make it easier for you to find a command, all commands are categorized.) You will also see All Commands, which, of course, lists every command available.

   To add a menu, choose Built-in Menus.
3. Scroll through the Commands list until you locate the desired command. To learn exactly what a command does, click it, and then click the Description button.
4. To add the button to the toolbar, click the command and drag it into place on the toolbar. As you drag it to the toolbar, a black bar shows you where the button will land. When it is where you want, release the mouse button. Toolbars grow to accommodate a new button. If the button doesn't land where you want, you can drag it to the desired location. (If the toolbar you want to add the button or menu to is not showing, first click the Toolbars tab, and then check the appropriate box to turn on any toolbar. Then proceed with this step.)

You may notice that some commands have an image on their left while others don't. If a command has an image, this image will be shown on its button. If not, the command name (text) appears on the button. You can change this later (read on to learn how).

To remove a button from a toolbar, select Tools ➪ Customize, and then simply click the button and drag it off the toolbar. While the Customize dialog box is open, clicking a button doesn't issue a command. You'll notice that when you click the button and begin to drag it, your cursor gains an X.

To restore a toolbar, select Tools ➪ Customize, and then select the Toolbars tab. In the Toolbars list, click the toolbar to select it, and then click the Reset button.

Customizing a button icon

After you add a new button, you may want to change its icon. You can assign the button a predrawn image, paste in your own image, or draw your own image with the Button Editor.

Adding an existing image

To give your button an existing image, follow these steps:

1. Select Tools ➪ Customize to open the Customize dialog box.
2. Control-click the button to be changed to bring up the shortcut menu. (After you Control-click, you can release the Control key.)
3. Select Change Button Image, and then drag over to the image of your choice and click to set the image. Figure E-2 shows the images menu.

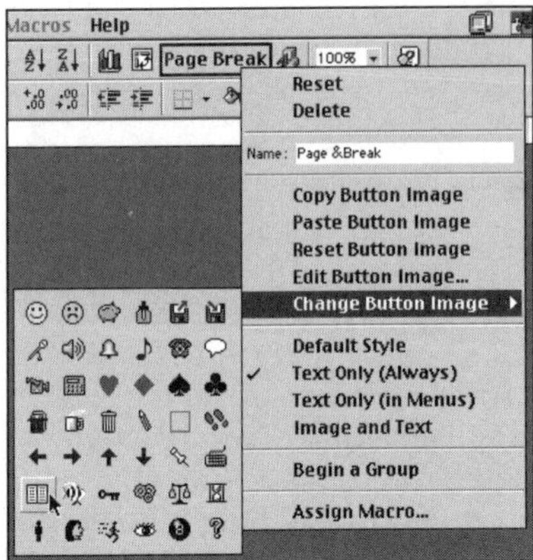

Figure E-2: Selecting a predrawn image for your button

4. If your button contains text, the icon appears along with the text. To remove the text from the button, Control-click the button again, select Text Only (in Menus) on the shortcut menu, and click.
5. Close the Customize dialog box by clicking Close.

Pasting an image from another source

A cool way to give your new button an image is to copy an image from another source and paste in into your button. To paste an image from another source onto your button, follow these steps:

1. Open the program that contains the image you want to use, select the image, and copy it. To achieve the best look for your button, the copied image should be 16 × 16 pixels.
2. Select Tools ➪ Customize to open the Customize dialog box. You can actually reverse Steps 1 and 2. While the Customize dialog box is open, it is quite possible to switch to another program and copy an image.
3. Control-click the button to be changed and select Paste Button Image from the shortcut menu.

4. Close the Customize dialog box by clicking Close.

Drawing your own image

You can draw your own button icon by using the Button Editor—a miniature paint program for drawing buttons. As a shortcut, you can assign a button a precreated image, as shown previously, and then use the Button Editor to make changes to that image. To give your button your own image, follow these steps:

1. Select Tools⇨Customize to open the Customize dialog box.
2. Control-click the button to be changed and select Edit Button Image from the shortcut menu. This brings up the Button Editor dialog box as shown in Figure E-3. The existing button image appears in the Picture section of the Editor. A preview of your button appears in the Preview box.

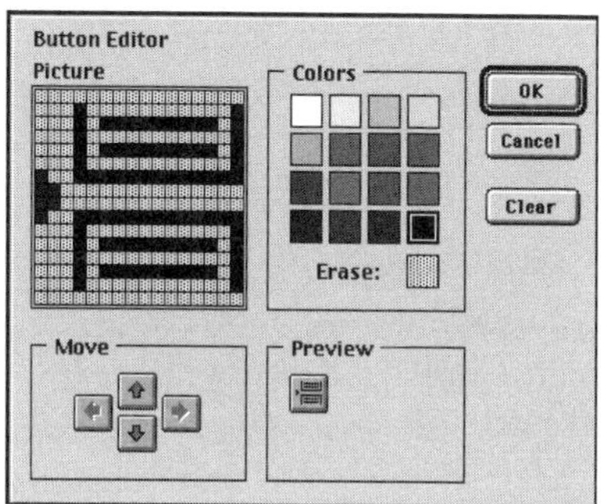

Figure E-3: The Button Editor dialog box

3. To edit the existing image, keep the image in the Picture section. To start fresh, click Clear. Click any color from the Colors section to choose it. Then bring your cursor over to the picture and click in any square to place the color in that square. You can keep your mouse button pressed and drag your mouse to draw. Click the Erase "color" to remove any color from a square.
4. To see your new button appear on the toolbar, click OK to close the Button Editor dialog box. After that, either finish or Control-click the button and select Edit Button Image to edit it again.
5. When you're all done, click Close in the Customize dialog box.

It's common to misjudge size or dimensions as you draw. To make this less of a problem, you can move your image within the button by clicking the arrows in the dialog box.

Customizing the text on a button

The text that appears on your button is actually the name of your button. To change the text that appears, follow the directions in the next section.

Naming buttons

1. Select Tools ➪ Customize to open the Customize dialog box.
2. Control-click the button to be changed. Drag to the Name field in the shortcut menu that appears. (You can see this field in Figure E-2.) Click in that field to place an insertion point in the field, and then edit the name text as you would any text. (Use an ampersand [&] to create a space in this field.)
3. Press Enter to enforce the change.
4. Click Close in the Customize dialog box.

Creating a New Toolbar

You can create a new toolbar easily by following these steps:

1. Control-click in any blank spot on a toolbar and select Customize (or select Tools ➪ Customize). When the Customize dialog box appears, click the Toolbars tab.
2. Click the New button. In the New Toolbar dialog box, name your new toolbar.

   In Word, you can also set where you want that toolbar to be available. When you save the toolbar, you are given the option of saving it to any open template. By default, the toolbar is saved to the Normal template. (See Chapter 2 to learn about templates.)

   That's it. Behind or near the dialog box, a new, empty floating toolbar appears, ready for you to add buttons to it.

Customizing Menus

Office's menus are also very flexible. You can add or remove commands (including styles, AutoText entries, and macros) to make the menus most efficient for your use. To customize a menu, launch the application containing the menu you want to customize.

Customize commands in an existing menu

To customize the commands in an existing menu, follow these steps:

1. Control-click any blank spot on a toolbar and select Customize (or select Tools ➪ Customize). When the Customize dialog box appears, click the Toolbars tab.
2. In the Toolbars list, check Menu Bar (Word and PowerPoint), or Worksheet Menu bar or Chart Menu bar (Excel). This brings up a customizable copy of the menu bar you are altering. You'll find this customizable menu bar at the top of your screen, below the normal menu bar.

3. Click the Commands tab (of the Customize dialog box).
4. In the Categories list, select the category of the command you wish to add.
5. Scroll to the command you want. If you don't see the command you want, try another category or click All Commands.
6. Click the desired command in the Commands box and drag it over the customizable menu bar. The menu drop downs and reveals a list of its commands, and your cursor gains a field and a plus sign. Move your cursor (pointer) to the exact location on the menu where you want the new command to fall. A horizontal black line shows you where it is due to fall as you release the mouse button. Release the mouse button when the command is in place.

To remove a command from a menu, repeat Steps 1 and 2. Then, in the customizable version of the menu bar, click the menu that contains your command. This reveals all of that menu's commands. Click the command you want to remove and drag it off the menu. (You can stop dragging as soon as it's off the menu area.)

You can also change the order of commands on your menus or move them to another menu. In the customizable version of the menu bar, click the menu that contains your command. When the menu's commands appear, click the command you want to reorder and drag it to a new position on that menu. To move the command to another menu, drag the command on top of that menu's name, and move it into place when the menu's contents appear.

Adding your own menus

You can even add your own menu. This is a great option if you're hesitant to alter the standard menu. If you are using Office in an office environment, you should consider creating task or job-specific menus. To do so, follow these steps:

1. Control-click in any blank spot on a toolbar and select Customize (or select Tools ➪ Customize). When the Customize dialog box appears, click the Toolbars tab.
2. In the Toolbars list, check Menu Bar (Word and PowerPoint), or Worksheet Menu bar or Chart Menu bar (Excel). This brings up a customizable copy of the menu bar you are altering. You'll find this customizable menu bar at the top of your screen, below the normal menu bar.
3. Click the Commands tab (of the Customize dialog box).
4. In the Categories list, select New Menu.
5. Click New Menu in the Commands list and drag it over the customizable menu bar. The menu drop downs and reveals a list of its commands and your cursor gains a field and a plus sign. Move your cursor (pointer) to the exact location between existing menus where you want the new menu to fall. A horizontal black line shows you where the menu is due to fall as you release the mouse button. Release the mouse button when it's in place.

More Help with Customization

For more information about customizing Office 98's menus and toolbars, check out the Help within each application. Go to Help⇨Contents and Indexes. In Word, open Customizing Microsoft Word, and then choose Customizing Toolbars and Menus; in Excel, see Customizing Microsoft Excel for the Way You Work, and then choose Customizing Toolbars and Menus; in PowerPoint, see Customizing Toolbars and Menus.

Renaming menus or menu items

To rename any menu command or menu name, follow Steps 1 and 2 under "Customizing Menus."

If you want to change a menu name, in the customizable menu, click that menu name. If you want to rename a command, click the menu name, and then click the command you want to rename. Now that the item to be renamed is selected, click Modify Selection in the Customize dialog box. In the list of options that pops up, drag to the option that says Name. The Name box appears highlighted. Type the name you want for that menu, and then press Return or Enter. (Alternatively, once you have selected the item to be renamed, you can also Control-click the item to be renamed, move down to the Name box, select the existing name, and alter it.)

Restoring menus

After you've customized the built-in menus for an Office application, you can restore the original settings—their look, commands, and submenus—at any time.

If you are in an office and inheriting your Mac from another employee, restoring menus is a good way to make sure you are working with the default settings. However, you should check with your Mac manager first to make sure the menus weren't specifically customized for your office or position.

To restore your menus, follow these steps:

1. As with any menu or toolbar customization, the Customize dialog box must be open. Select Tools⇨Customize (or Control-click a toolbar and select Customize). In the Customize dialog box that appears, click the Toolbars tab.
2. In the Toolbars list, check the Menu Bar check box. This displays the customizable copy of the menu bar below the regular menu bar.
3. Control-click the menu you want to restore, and select Reset from the shortcut menu.
4. Close the Customize dialog box.

If you completely removed a built-in menu, go to the Commands tab of the Customize dialog box and select Built-in Menus from the Categories list. From the Commands list, drag the desired menu name into place on the customizable menu bar (which is below the normal menu bar).

Changing Word's Keyboard Shortcuts

By default, Office's applications provide you with keyboard command (shortcuts) that you can press to invoke a command without going to the menus and/or dialog boxes. In Word, you can change these shortcuts. For example, if you are used to a certain key combination from another program, you can assign that combination the parallel command in Word.

To alter (or just to discover) a keyboard combination, launch the application containing the commands you want to customize. Then Control-click in any blank spot on a toolbar and select Customize (or select Tools ➪ Customize). When the Customize dialog box appears, click the Keyboard button to open the Customize Keyboard dialog box. Select the category the command falls under (or select All Commands), and then click the command in the Commands list. If a shortcut already exists, it appears in the Current keys list. In Figure E-4, the command selected has two shortcut combinations already.

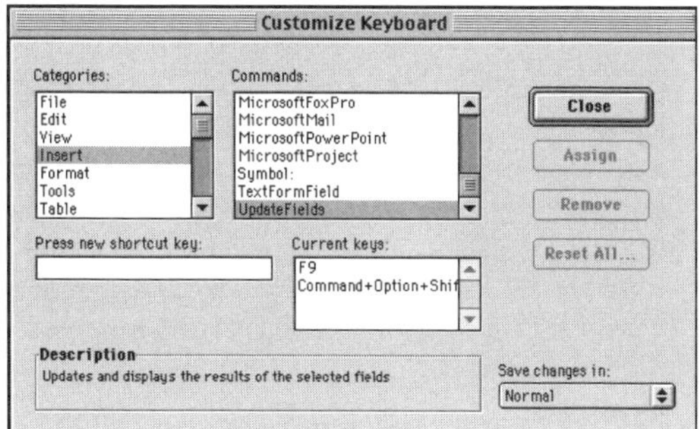

Figure E-4: The Customize Keyboard dialog box

To add a key combination, after selecting the command from the Commands list, click in the box that aptly says Press new shortcut key, and then press your new combination. A message appears in the dialog box, telling you if this combination is available or already taken and, if so, what command uses it. If these keys are already assigned to something you want to keep, use the Delete key to delete your combination, and then try a new one. When you are happy with a new key combination, click Assign.

A word about locating commands in the Commands list: Built-in menu commands are represented by the name of their menu, attached to the name of the command, rather than the name of the command. For example, the Save command isn't under S for Save, but under F for FileSave.

✦ ✦ ✦

Index

NUMBERS

3-D effects in Excel graphics, 399
3-D PowerPoint charts, 592–593, 595
3-D View dialog box, 592–593

A

absolute cell references in Excel, 343
Accent Color dialog box, 563–564
accessing
  e-mail from other computers, 653, 669
    e-mail of other users, 680
  Internet, 701
  Internet on POP servers, 653, 669
  search engines, 715–716
  Web sites, 702–706
action buttons in slides, 575–576
Action Settings dialog box, 614–615
Add Custom Dictionary dialog box, 54
adding. *See also* inserting
  buttons to toolbars, 795
  callouts, 237, 391–393
  dividing lines to Favorites list, 712
  Excel worksheets to workbooks, 304
  favorites in Internet Explorer, 711
  file converters to Word 98, 283–284
  folders to Favorites list, 712
  footnotes, 97–99
  images to toolbar buttons, 796–797
  menus, 795, 799
  merge fields to main documents, 159–160
  Office application aliases to Apple menus, 6
  patterns to paragraphs, 85
  patterns to worksheets, 374–375
  records to Excel databases, 450–451
  shadows to Excel graphics, 399
  signatures to e-mail messages, 665
  summary data to Excel workbooks, 310–311
Add-Ins dialog box, 311–312
address bar in Internet Explorer, 694, 703, 716
addresses, Internet, 252, 483, 621
addressing e-mail messages, 662–663
Advanced pane of Internet Explorer Preferences
    dialog box, 700
Advanced Search dialog box, 65–66, 315–316
Aladdin StuffIt and StuffIt Expander programs,
    672, 720
aliases, 6
aligning
  document sections, 93
  graphic objects, 549–551
  table rows, 131
  text in Excel worksheets, 367–372, 401–402
Alignment tab
  of Format Cells dialog box, 368, 371–372
  of Format Text Box dialog box, 401–402
all caps text option, 87–88, 89–90
All Footnotes tab of Note Options dialog box,
    100–101
Allow Fast Saves option, 757
alphanumeric values in sorting Excel data, 457
Always Create Backup Copy option, 757
animating
  slides, 602–604
  text in PowerPoint presentations, 575
  text in Word documents, 87, 89
Animation tab of Font dialog box, 89
annotations in onscreen slides, 642–643
AOL (America Online), 652
Apple Data Detectors, 704–705
Apple menus, adding aliases to, 6
applications in Office 98, 3–6
Apply Design dialog box, 635–636
applying
  backgrounds to PowerPoint slides, 637
  custom sort orders to Excel databases, 459
  headings with AutoFormat feature, 205
  new styles, 203–205
  Normal (default) styles, 191–193
  templates, 207, 210–211
archiving Web sites, 708, 717
arcs, creating, 394
area charts, 423, 579
arguments in Excel functions, 348
arithmetic operators in Excel, 344
arrays of cells, 337
arrows in Excel charts, 417
art. *See* graphic objects
Assign Macro dialog box, 471–472

assigning
  AutoText entries to toolbars, 56–58
  Excel macros
    changing assignments, 472
    to graphic objects, 473–474
    to keyboard shortcuts, 468, 476
    to menus, 475–476
    overview of, 471
    to toolbar buttons, 474–475
    to worksheet buttons, 471–473
  PowerPoint macros to objects in slides, 614–615
  PowerPoint macros to toolbar buttons, 615
  styles to keyboard shortcuts, 196–197
  Word macros to keyboard shortcuts, 216–217, 218–219
Assistants, Value Pack, 737. *See also* Office Assistant
attachments, e-mail. *See also* Outlook Express
  encoding, 664
  file helpers for viewing, 670–671
  GIF or JPEG images as, 670, 671
  overview of, 664–665, 670, 671
  saving, 671–672
attributes in Excel databases, 464
audience handouts, creating, 606–607
AutoCalculate feature, 308
AutoComplete feature, 31, 322–323, 703
AutoContent Wizard, 557–560, 780, 781–783
AutoCorrect dialog box, 56
AutoCorrect feature, 55–58, 356–357
AutoFill feature, 331–334
AutoFill series option in Excel, 338–339
AutoFilter command, 459–463. *See also* Excel databases; filtering
  copying and pasting filtered data, 460
  custom options for, 461–462
  overview of, 454, 459–460
  printing filtered data, 454, 461
  Top 10 option, 462
  turning on or off, 459, 463
AutoFormat dialog box, 227–229, 363–364
AutoFormat features
  applying headings, 205
  converting Internet addresses to hyperlinks, 257
  creating borders, 237, 287
  creating tables, 120, 128, 132, 287
  formatting Excel databases, 454
  formatting Excel worksheets, 361–365
  formatting Word documents, 227–229
  overview of, 61
AutoLayout feature, 560–561
automatic macros, 223–224
automating incoming e-mail messages, 677–679
automating newsgroup messages, 690–691
AutoRecover feature, 289–290, 758
AutoSave feature, 311–312
AutoSearch feature, 716
AutoShapes feature, 391–393, 553–555
AutoSum tool, 349
AutoSummarize feature, 67–68
AutoText entries. *See also* Word documents
  assigning to toolbars, 56–58
  deleting, 58
  editing, 58
  inserting, 56
  versus macros, 213–214
  printing, 58, 112
  storing, 56
  viewing default entries, 56
AutoText tab of AutoCorrect dialog box, 56
AVERAGE function in Excel, 348
Award Wizard, 27
axes in charts, 415–416, 417, 421, 591

B

backgrounds, formatting, 73, 562, 637
backup files
  saving Excel workbooks in, 312
  saving Word documents in, 290, 757
bar charts, 423, 579
bar tabs, 40
bars, Internet Explorer, 694–703. *See also* toolbars
  address bar, 694, 703, 716
  button bar, 694, 696
  Explorer bar
    Channels tab, 697–698
    Favorites tab, 698–699, 705
    History tab, 699–700, 705
    overview of, 695, 697
    Search tab, 700–701, 716
  favorites bar, 694–695
  moving, 695
  scroll bars, 695
  status bar, 695, 702
  title bar, 694

ToolTips and, 695
turning on or off, 695
Binder feature, 8, 740
bitmapped images, importing, 230–232
Blank Presentation option, PowerPoint, 537, 540–541, 780, 783–784
bolding text, 87–88, 89–90, 193
bookmarking help pages, 13
Border tab of Format Cells dialog box, 374
borders. *See also* text boxes
borders, adding
to Excel worksheets, 373–374
to images, 105–106, 236–237
to paragraphs, 84–85
to tables, 131–132, 287–288
while previewing printing, 105–106
borders, formatting
border line widths, 84
in Excel charts, 422–423
in PowerPoint charts, 591–592
in tables, 131–132
Borders and Shading dialog box, 84–85, 288
break-even analysis example, 505–510
breaks
inserting in Excel worksheets, 444–445
line and page breaks in paragraphs, 79
preventing and removing, 286–287
section breaks, 93
Bring to Front option for graphics, 395–396
browser frames, 625, 702
browser windows, 702
browsers, Web, 252, 483, 621. *See also* Internet Explorer
browsing offline
in Internet Explorer, 708, 710, 717–718
in Outlook Express, 689
bubble charts, 424, 579
bulleted lists
in PowerPoint presentations, 564–566
in Word documents, 60–61, 78, 290–291
bullets
formatting, 565–566
images as, 61
in outline headings, 140–141
overview of, 60–61
button bar in Internet Explorer, 694, 696
Button Editor dialog box, 57–58, 797
buttons. *See also* bars; toolbars
adding action buttons to slides, 575–576
assigning Excel macros to, 471–475
Excel number formatting buttons, 376
PowerPoint view buttons, 531–532
toolbar buttons
adding, 795
adding existing images to, 796
assigning AutoText entries to, 56–58
assigning macros to, 474–475, 615
copying and pasting images onto, 796
deleting, 795
drawing images onto, 797
naming, 798
overview of, 794
underlined labels on, 648

C

calculation options in Excel, changing, 346
Calculation tab of Preferences dialog box, 346
Calendar Wizard, 27–28
callouts, adding, 237, 391–393
Cancel button in formula bar, 771
captions, figure, creating tables of, 180–181
case, changing, 90
category axis in charts, 416, 417, 577
Cell Borders and Shading dialog box, 131–132
Cell Height and Width dialog box, 128–129, 130–131
cells. *See* Excel worksheets; tables
center tabs, 40–41
centering text in Excel worksheets, 369–370
certificates, site, 723
changing. *See also* customizing; editing
base styles, 197–199
case, 90
column widths
in Excel worksheets, 321, 365–366
in PowerPoint charts, 582
in Word documents, 226
in Word tables, 128–129
default fonts, 524
default number of Excel worksheets, 297
Excel chart data plotting, 429
Excel default options, 524
Excel recalculation options, 346
Excel worksheet row heights, 366
footnotes to endnotes, 101
Normal (default) styles, 197–199
outline headings, 145–146

(continued)

changing (*continued*)
outline structure, 136–138
point sizes, 87–88, 90–91
printers, 112
slide layout, 547–548, 642, 780
slide show timing, 600–601
style of PowerPoint graphics, 554
Word document styles, 200
WordArt shapes, 406
channels in Internet Explorer, 697–698, 709–710
Character Spacing tab of Font dialog box, 88, 91
characters. *See also* formatting, Word documents; text
character styles, 190
field characters, 150
spacing between, 87–88, 91, 570
special, entering in Excel worksheets, 773
special, searching and replacing, 46–48
tab characters in Word tables, 121
Chart Options dialog box, 419–420, 580–581, 590–591
Chart toolbar, 418–419, 426
Chart Type dialog box, 424–426, 586–588
Chart Wizard, 408–413
charts from Microsoft Graph, 238–240, 248. *See also* Excel charts; PowerPoint charts
checking spelling and grammar, 48–55. *See also* Word documents
creating custom dictionaries, 53–55, 358
grammar-checking, 51–52
overview of, 48–49
setting options for, 52–53
spell-checking Excel worksheets, 356–358
spell-checking Word documents, 49–50
circles, creating, 394
ClarisWorks Office documents, opening in Excel, 528
Classic 1 AutoFormat style, 361–362
clearing. *See also* deleting; removing
Excel worksheet cells, 328–329, 340
tab stops, 42
clip-art. *See also* graphic objects
adding to PowerPoint presentations, 555, 791–792
adding to Word documents, 33–34
importing into Word documents, 232, 234
overview of, 738
ClipArt Gallery, 33–34, 555, 791–792
cloning browser windows, 702
closing
Excel workbooks, 314
PowerPoint presentations, 784
codes. *See also* fields; VBA
error codes in Excel worksheets, 321, 340
printing field codes, 156
viewing field codes, 152–153, 175
collaborating on Word documents, 62–65
collating Word documents while printing, 110
Color Scheme dialog box, 562, 563–564
color schemes, 590
Colorful 1 AutoFormat style, 362
coloring
Excel charts, 422–423
Excel graphics, 397–398
Excel worksheets, 373–375
PowerPoint charts, 589–590
PowerPoint graphics, 554
Web sites, 713, 728
Word paragraphs, 85
Word text, 87–88
WordArt, 405
Colors dialog box, 397
Colors and Lines tab
of Format AutoShape dialog box, 398–399, 554
of Format Picture dialog box, 105, 237
of Format Text Box dialog box, 243
of Format WordArt dialog box, 405, 570
column charts, 423, 579
Column tab of Cell Height and Width dialog box, 130
columns
in Excel databases, 447–448
in Excel worksheets
deleting, 339–340
formatting widths of, 321, 365–366
hiding and unhiding, 367
inserting, 338
printing headings, 441
in PowerPoint charts, 582
of text
in PowerPoint presentations, 566–567
in Word documents, 225–227, 246
in Word tables, 134
in Word tables
adjusting space between, 130
deleting, 124, 126
formatting widths of, 128–129

inserting, 124, 126
selecting, 123–124
of text, 134
Columns button, 226
Columns dialog box, 226
comma-delimited export files, 166
command macros, Excel, 467–468
command underlines, 15–16
commands, menu, 798–800
Commands tab of Customize dialog box, 57, 794–795, 801
comments
adding to Excel worksheets, 326–327
creating, 63–65
cutting and pasting, 64–65
defined, 63
deleting, 64
finding, 65
printing, 64–65, 112
printing in Excel worksheets, 441
VBA code for inserting, 267, 495–496
viewing, 64
comparison operators in Excel, 344–345, 451–452
compressed files, decoding, 720
concatenating data in Excel, 527
cone charts, 424, 580
contact lists, 657–658
Contacts folder in Outlook Express, 650
Contents and Index option in Help menu, 15
control statements in VBA code, 497
converters, file, 283–284, 740
converting
text to outline headings, 138
text to tables, 132–133, 166
cookies, 715
copying
Excel data, 329–337
with Fill and AutoFill features, 331–334
with Fill Series command, 334–336
overview of, 305–306, 329–330
files with Save As command, 755–757
formatting, 92, 381–382, 641
graphic objects in PowerPoint, 548–549
help text, 13
macros to templates, 221–222
styles, 199–200
copying and pasting. *See also* cutting and pasting
Excel data
in AutoFilter command, 460
graphics, 396
into PowerPoint slides, 571, 572
in mail merges, 166–167
overview of, 305, 330, 336–337
graphics, 33
hyperlinks, 256, 485, 623
images into Word documents, 234
images onto toolbar buttons, 796
slides, 546–547
text, 32, 44
Web page data, 719
Create Data Source dialog box, 158–159
Create Labels dialog box, 165
creating
aliases, 6
audience handouts, 606–607
backup files, 312
comments, 63–65
contact lists, 657–658
custom database sort orders, 458
custom dictionaries, 53–55, 358
custom number formats, 378–381
custom slide shows, 607–609
e-mail messages, 661–666
Excel charts, 413–414
Excel databases, 449–450
Excel formulas, 341–343
Excel macros, 468–471
folders for e-mail, 649, 676–677
form letters, 157–161, 463–464
headers and footers, 94–95
Internet Explorer browser windows, 702
mail merge documents, 157–161, 463–464
mailing lists, 659–660, 692
newsgroup messages, 691
numbered lists, 60–61, 290–291
organization charts, 593–594, 631–635
outlines, 141–144
PowerPoint macros, 611–613
PowerPoint slides, 643
progressive slides, 602–604
side-by-side paragraphs, 134
tables of figures, 181
templates, 207, 208–209, 210–211
text boxes, 241
Web pages, 259–261
cropping graphic objects, 236, 549

cursors, pen, 642–643
Custom Animation dialog box, 602–604
Custom AutoFilter dialog box, 461–462
Custom Dictionary, 49
Custom Dictionary dialog box, 54–55
Custom Lists tab of Preferences dialog box, 333–334
Custom Shows dialog box, 607
Custom tabs
of Accent Color dialog box, 563–564
of Color Scheme dialog box, 563–564
Custom Types tab of Chart Type dialog box, 588
Customize dialog box
Commands tab, 57, 794–795, 801
Keyboard button, 35
Options tab, 12
Toolbars tab, 218, 795–800
Customize Keyboard dialog box, 196–197, 218–219, 801
customizing. *See also* changing; editing
dictionaries, 53–55, 358
Excel database sort orders, 458–459
Excel number formats, 378–381
keyboard shortcuts, 35, 801
menus and menu commands, 798–801
MOM (Microsoft Office Manager) menu, 9–10
Normal (default) templates, 209–210
slide shows, 607–609
tab stops, 40–42
toolbars, 793–798
cutting and pasting. *See also* copying and pasting
comments, 64–65
Excel data, 305–306, 330
Excel graphics, 396
text, 44
Cyberdog, 647
cylinder charts, 424, 580

D

danger zones
assigning macros to shortcut keys, 217
bad typing habits, 31
browser frames, 625
changing Normal (default) styles, 197, 199
creating new styles, 197
data validation, 354
entering numbers in Excel, 322
inserting cells in Excel worksheets, 338
passwords, 384, 385
Replace All button, 47–48
saving Word documents as HTML files, 36, 258–259, 261
sorting Excel databases, 454, 455, 457
storing Excel workbooks in application folders, 523
VBA code and smart quotes, 269
Word as Web browser, 254
data. *See also* Excel databases
data access software in Value Pack, 738
data forms for Excel databases, 450–453
data points in Excel charts, 415, 417
data series in Excel charts, 415, 416, 417
data series in PowerPoint charts, 583–586
in Excel databases, 464
plotting in Excel charts, 426–429
VBA code for entering, 496
Data Detectors, Apple, 704–705
Data Labels tab of Format Data Series dialog box, 585–586
data sources. *See also* mail merges
creating from other software, 165–171
creating manually, 158–159
defined, 157
embedding, 171
for envelopes, 161
exporting, 165–166
for mailing labels, 164
merging with main documents, 160–161
Data Validation dialog box, 351–353
Database dialog box, 167, 168, 170
Datasheet windows for PowerPoint charts, 580–581, 582
Date series option in Excel, 338–339
dates
entering in Excel worksheets, 324–325, 773–774
formatting in Excel worksheets, 377–378
preventing slashes and hyphens from being formatted as, 525
decimal tabs, 40–42
decoding compressed files, 720
default AutoText entries, 56
default Excel workbook folders, 310, 524
default fonts, 290
default (Normal) styles, 191–193, 197–199
default (Normal) templates, 22, 208, 209–210
default number of Excel worksheets, 297

default PowerPoint templates, 537–541
default tab stops, 39
Define Custom Show dialog box, 608
Define Inbox Rule dialog box, 678–679
Define Name dialog box, 340–341
Define Newsgroup Rule dialog box, 690–691
Delete Cells dialog box, 125–126
Delete dialog box, 339
Deleted Messages folder in Outlook Express, 650
deleting. *See also* clearing; removing
  AutoText entries, 58
  comments, 64
  e-mail contacts, 659
  e-mail messages, 675–676
  Excel database records, 451
  Excel graphics, 396
  Excel worksheet data, 339–340
  Excel worksheets, 304
  favorites, 699, 712
  footnotes, 100
  headers or footers, 95
  macros, 221, 616
  menus, 795
  onscreen slide annotations, 643
  Outlook Express users, 683
  slides, 539, 546
  styles, 200
  table cells, columns, and rows, 124–126
  toolbar buttons, 795
  Word documents, 289
  Word text, 33, 753
desktop publishing, 225–249. *See also* formatting, Word documents; publishing on the Web; Word documents
  with AutoFormat command, 227–229
  images
    adding borders to, 236–237
    adding callouts to, 237
    creating, 234
    cropping (trimming), 236
    editing, 235, 238
    overview of, 247
    scaling (sizing), 235–236
  importing images
    bitmapped images, 230–232
    by copying and pasting, 234
    by scanning photographs, 231
    clip-art, 232, 234
    with Insert Picture command, 233–234
    object images, 230, 232
    overview of, 229–230
  inserting
    columns of text, 225–227, 246
    graphs (charts), 238–240, 248
    headlines, 246–247
    subheads, 246–247
    tables, 248
  margins and, 246
  with Newsletter Wizard, 248–249
  Normal and Page Layout views, 227
  organizational tools in, 246–248
  overview of, 225, 249
  text boxes
    creating, 241
    formatting, 242–243
    for images, 234
    linking, 241–242
    moving, 243–244
    overview of, 240–241
    sizing, 244–245
    wrapping text around, 245
  Undo command and, 229
dialog boxes, VBA code, 268–269, 497–498
dial-up e-mail accounts, 651
DiamondSoft Font Reserve, 739
dictionaries, 49, 53–55, 358
Discovery Channel Online, 709
disks, removable, 683–684
docking toolbars, 12
Document dialog box, 74–75, 92–94
Document Map view, 36
documents. *See* Word documents
doughnut charts, 424, 579
downloading files, 718–723. *See also* Internet Explorer
  by copying and pasting, 719
  decoding and, 720
  Download Manager and, 721, 722–723
  images, 720
  movies, 720
  overview of, 718, 720–721
  reviewing downloads, 721–722
  and saving, 719
  setting options for, 706, 721, 722–723
  sounds, 720
  stopping downloads, 721
Drafts folder in Outlook Express, 650

dragging-and-dropping
  Excel data, 330, 331
  Excel graphics, 396
  hyperlinks, 256, 485
  text, 45
Draw Table feature, 119–120, 129
drawing images with Button Editor, 797
Drawing toolbar
  in Excel, 389–390, 393–394
  in PowerPoint, 536–537, 552–554
  in Word, 234
drop caps text option, 87

E

Edit tab of Preferences dialog box, 320–321
Edit User dialog box, 681
Edit WordArt Text dialog box, 403
editing. *See also* changing; customizing
  AutoText entries, 58
  document summaries, 66–67
  Excel charts, 417–419
  Excel data, 328, 771–772
  Excel database records, 450, 451
  Excel formulas, 345–346
  Excel text, 400
  footnotes, 99–100
  images in Word documents, 235, 238
  PowerPoint charts, 583
  PowerPoint graphics, 641
  slide text in Outline view, 543–544, 790
  slide text in Slide view, 539, 544, 545, 789
  VBA code, 269–270, 494, 499, 617
  Word document text, 753–754
  Word tables, 123–128
  Word templates, 31
ellipses, creating, 394
e-mail and news in Internet Explorer, 727
E-mail server icon in Outlook Express, 650
e-mailing. *See also* Outlook Express
  Excel workbooks, 445
  PowerPoint presentations, 609
embedding
  data from other sources in mail merges, 171
  Excel charts in worksheets, 408–413
  Excel data in mail merges, 167–171
  Excel worksheets in slides, 571–573
  Word tables in slides, 571, 573–574
embossing text, 568
endnotes, 97, 101. *See also* footnotes
Envelope Address dialog box, 162–163
Envelope Options dialog box, 114, 115, 161–162
Envelope Wizard, 26
envelopes, printing, 113–115, 161–163, 284–285
Envelopes and Labels dialog box, 113–114, 115, 285
Equation Editor, 4, 738
Error Alert tab of Data Validation dialog box, 352–353
error codes in Excel worksheets, 321, 346
error messages in Internet Explorer, 704
Excel 98
  add–in software in Value Pack, 738–739
  AutoCalculate feature, 308
  AutoCorrect feature, 356–357
  AutoFill series option in, 338–339
  AutoFilter command, 453–454, 459–463
  AutoSave feature, 311–312
  changing default options in, 524
  character formatting in, 526–527
  Date series option in, 338–339
  exiting, 314
  File Conversion Wizard, 738
  formula bar
    editing cells with, 328
    entering values in, 319–320
    overview of, 299, 308
  Growth series option in, 338
  launching, 761
  Linear series option in, 338
  main screen, 762–763
  New Document dialog box in, 7
  opening ClarisWorks Office documents in, 528
  overview of, 3
  Report Manager, 739
  Solver, 739
  status bar, 299, 308
  Template Wizard, 739
  toolbars
    Formatting toolbar, 299, 766–767
    overview of, 307–308, 762–763
    Standard toolbar, 299, 764–765
  on the Web, 481–489
    creating hyperlinks in worksheets, 484–487
    Internet Assistant Wizard, 487–489
    overview of, 481–484, 489

publishing worksheets and charts, 487–489
saving Excel data as HTML files, 313, 487–489
Web toolbar, 484
Excel charts, 407–430. *See also* PowerPoint charts
adding to PowerPoint presentations, 583
adding to worksheets, 408–413
axes in, 415–416, 417
changing data plotting in, 429
changing types of, 424–426
chart sheets, 408–410
creating, 413–414
data plotting in, 426–429
data series in, 415, 416, 417
embedding in worksheets, 408–413
formatting, 417–423
adding gridlines, 417, 422
adding legends, 415, 417, 421–422
adding titles, 417, 419–420
adding unattached text, 420
axes, 421
borders, 422–423
with Chart toolbar, 418–419, 426
colors, 422–423
overview of, 417
selecting parts of, 418
text, 420–421, 422–423
markers in, 415, 416
overview of, 407–408, 417, 429–430
parts of, 415–417
versus PowerPoint charts, 578
printing, 415
publishing on the Web, 487–489
saving, 415
series formulas in, 426–427
toolbar, 418–419, 426
types of, 423–426
Excel databases, 447–466
adding records to, 450–451
attributes in, 464
AutoFormatting, 454
columns in, 447–448
comparison operators and, 451–452
copying and pasting data in mail merges, 166–167
creating, 449–450
creating mail merge documents from, 463–464
data forms for, 450–453
data in, 464
deleting records from, 451
designing, 464–466
editing records in, 450, 451
embedding data in mail merges, 167–171
fields in, 448
filtering with AutoFilter
copying and pasting filtered data, 460
custom options for, 461–462
overview of, 454, 459–460
printing filtered data, 454, 461
Top 10 option for, 462
turning on or off, 459, 463
finding records, 451–453
formatting characters in, 526–527
formatting numbers as text in, 323, 376, 449, 525, 773
outgrowing, 463, 464
overview of, 447–448
ranges in, 450
records in
adding, 450–451
defined, 448
deleting, 451
editing, 450, 451
finding, 451–453
rows in, 447–448
sorting
alphanumeric values, 457
custom sort orders, 458–459
danger zones in, 454, 455, 457
key fields in, 455
overview of, 454–457
undoing effects of, 458
Excel macros. *See* macros in Excel
Excel for Windows 95 Power Programming with VBA (Walkenbach), 616
Excel workbooks, 295–317
adding summary data to, 310–311
closing, 314
defined, 295
e-mailing, 445
finding, 314–316
navigating in, 767–768
opening, 297–298, 523, 767

(continued)

Excel workbooks (*continued*)
organizing, 316
overview of, 295–296, 316–317, 767
password-protecting, 309–310
saving, 309–314
adding passwords after, 310
with AutoSave feature, 311–312
in backup files, 312
in folders, 316
as HTML files, 313, 487–489
in other formats, 312
overview of, 309–310
setting default folders for, 310, 524
setting options for, 309
summary information, 310–311
in workspace files, 313–314
storing in application folders, 523
tabs, 768
viewing multiple workbooks, 524
Excel worksheets, 319–359, 503–528, 761–777
adding to PowerPoint presentations, 571–573
adding to workbooks, 304
assigning macros to buttons on, 471–473
AutoCorrect feature and, 55–58, 356–357
cells in
adding comments to, 326–327
clearing, 328–329, 340
concatenating data in, 527
deleting, 339–340
editing data in, 328, 771–772
error codes in, 321, 346
formatting characters in, 526–527
formatting ranges of, 323
inserting, 338
naming, 340–341
overview of, 329–330
printing ranges of, 441–442, 527–528
relative versus absolute cell references, 343
selecting ranges of, 303–304
changing default number of, 297
checking spelling in, 356–358
copying data in
with AutoFill feature, 331–334
with Fill feature, 331–334
with Fill Series command, 334–336
overview of, 329–330
and pasting, 305, 330, 336–337
creating custom dictionaries from, 358
creating hyperlinks in, 484–487
defined, 295, 761
deleting, 304
deleting columns and rows in, 339–340
editing data in, 328
embedding in PowerPoint slides, 571–573
entering values in
with AutoComplete feature, 322–323
with AutoFill feature, 331–334
dates, 324–325, 773–774
displayed values versus underlying values, 325–326
with Fill feature, 331–334
with Fill Series command, 334–336
formatting numbers as text, 323, 376, 449, 525, 773
numbers, 321–322, 772–773
overview of, 319–321, 761–762, 770–771
special characters, 773
text, 322, 774–775
times, 324–325, 773–774
Undo and, 325
examples
break-even analyses, 505–510
IRA calculators, 510–517
managing cash flow, 503–505
mortgage/amortization analyses, 518–521
expanding view of, 306
finding data in, 354–355
finding and replacing data in, 355–356
formatting characters in, 526–527
formatting ranges of cells in, 323
formulas in
allowed elements in, 343–345
arithmetic operators in, 344
changing recalculation options for, 346
comparison operators in, 344–345
creating, 341–345
editing, 345–346
entering, 341–343, 770–771
error codes for, 346
order of precedence in, 345
overview of, 341–342, 762, 775
relative versus absolute cell references and, 343
viewing, 345
functions in
AutoSum tool, 349
AVERAGE function, 348

defined, 762
MAXIMUM and MINIMUM functions, 348
overview of, 347–348
Paste Function Wizard, 349–351
SUM function, 348
inserting columns and rows in, 338
moving among, 301–302, 768
moving data in
by cutting and pasting, 305–306, 330
by dragging-and-dropping, 330, 331
overview of, 329–330
Paste Special options for, 336–337
navigating
with Go To command, 300, 769
keyboard shortcuts for, 300–301, 768–769
with Name box in formula bar, 769
overview of, 299–301, 767–769
in workbook windows, 768
overview of, 295–296, 358
parts of, 298–299
publishing on the Web, 487–489
renaming tabs in, 302
rows in
changing heights of, 366
deleting, 339–340
hiding and unhiding, 367
inserting, 338
printing row headings, 441
saving, 776–777
selecting multiple worksheets, 302
selecting ranges of cells in, 303–304
spell-checking, 356–358
splitting worksheet windows, 307
tabs on
moving among worksheets with, 301–302, 768
overview of, 295–296
renaming, 302
viewing, 301, 768
validating data in, 351–354
viewing multiple worksheets, 524
Exchange, Microsoft, 648, 651
expanding. *See also* sizing
Internet Explorer screen space, 698
outline headings, 139
outlines, 144
view of Excel worksheets, 306
Explorer bar. *See also* Internet Explorer
Channels tab, 697–698
Favorites tab, 698–699, 705
History tab, 699–700, 705
overview of, 697
Search tab, 700–701, 716
extensions folder in Office 98, 5

F

fast saves option, 757
favorites bar, 694–695
Favorites list. *See also* Internet Explorer
adding dividing lines to, 712
adding favorites, 711
adding folders to, 712
deleting favorites, 699, 712
marking favorites, 710–711
overview of, 698–699
rearranging favorites in, 698–699
renaming folders or favorites, 712
Favorites tab, 698–699, 705
Fax Wizard, 26, 273–276
Field dialog box, 151, 152
Field Options dialog box, 151–152
fields, 149–171
components of, 150
example, 155–156
in Excel databases, 448, 455
field switches, 152, 154–155
formatting, 154–155
inserting
index entry fields, 181–183
overview of, 150–152
TC entry fields, 176–177
key fields in Excel databases, 455
locking, 155
in mail merges, 157–171
adding merge fields to main documents, 159–160
choosing main documents, 158
copying and pasting Excel data, 166–167
creating data sources from other software, 165–171
creating data sources manually, 158–159
creating form letters, 157–161
embedding data from other sources, 171
embedding Excel data, 167–171
exporting data sources, 165–166
merging data with main documents, 160–161

(continued)

fields, in mail merges (*continued*)
    overview of, 157
    printing envelopes, 161–163
    printing mailing labels, 163–165
  merge fields, 157–160
  moving between, 154
  overview of, 149–150, 171
  printing field codes, 156
  updating
    before printing, 111
    linked to other data sources, 170–171
    overview of, 153
    in tables of contents, 147, 178
  viewing field codes, 152–153, 175
figure captions, tables of, 180–181
File Conversion Wizard, 738
file converters, 283–284, 740
file extensions folder in Office 98, 5
files, tab or comma-delimited, 166
filing e-mail messages, 676–677
Fill Effects dialog box, 397–398
Fill feature, copying Excel data with, 331–334
Fill Series command, 334–336
fills for Excel graphics, 394, 397–398
Filter Records tab of Query Options dialog box, 168–169
filtering
  e-mail messages, 678–680
  Excel databases with AutoFilter, 459–463
    copying and pasting filtered data, 460
    custom options for, 461–462
    overview of, 454, 459–460
    printing filtered data, 454, 461
    Top 10 option for, 462
    turning on or off, 459, 463
  newsgroup messages, 690–691
Find dialog box, 354–355, 716–717
Find and Replace dialog box, 45–46, 47–48
finding. *See also* searching
  comments, 65
  e-mail messages, 679–680
  Excel database records, 451–453
  Excel workbooks, 314–316
  Excel worksheet data, 354–355
  styles in Style Gallery, 202–203
  synonyms, 59
finding and replacing
  Excel worksheet data, 355–356
  Word document text, 45–48
firewalls, 701
first-line indents, 77–78
Folder list in Outlook Express, 649–651, 692
folders
  adding to Favorites list, 712
  creating for e-mail messages, 649, 676–677
  extensions folder in Office 98, 5
  saving Excel workbooks in, 310, 316, 524
Font dialog box
  Animation tab, 89
  Character Spacing tab, 88, 91
  effects options, 568
  Font tab, 87–88, 91, 203
  overview of, 86
Font Reserve, DiamondSoft, 739
Font tab
  of Format Axis dialog box, 420–421, 588–589
  of Format Cells dialog box, 372–373
  of Format Chart Area dialog box, 423
  of Format Text Box dialog box, 400–401
fonts, formatting
  in Excel charts, 420–421, 423
  in Excel text boxes, 400–401
  in Excel worksheets, 321, 372–373, 524, 526–527
  in PowerPoint charts, 588–589
  in Web sites, 713–714
  in Word documents, 87–88, 90–91, 290
fonts in Value Pack, 739
footers. *See also* headers
  adding to PowerPoint presentations, 638–639
  adjusting margins for, 95–96
  creating, 94–95
  deleting, 95
  positioning, 95–96
  printing in Excel worksheets, 438–440
  in VBA code, 268, 496
Footnote and Endnote dialog box, 97–98, 100–101
footnotes
  adding, 97–99
  changing to endnotes, 101
  deleting, 100
  editing, 99–100
  moving, 100
  options for, 100–101
form letters, creating, 157–161, 463–464. *See also* mail merges
Format AutoShape dialog box, 398–399, 554

Format Axis dialog box
Font tab, 420–421, 588–589
overview of, 588, 591
Patterns tab, 421
Format Cells dialog box
Alignment tab, 368, 371–372
Border tab, 374
Font tab, 372–373
Number tab, 376–378, 380, 774–775
Patterns tab, 374–375
Protection tab, 383–384
Format Chart Area dialog box
Font tab, 423
overview of, 591
Patterns tab, 422–423, 592
Properties tab, 423
Format Data Series dialog box, 585–586, 590
Format Legend dialog box, 588
Format Painter button, 92, 381–382, 641
Format Picture dialog box
Colors and Lines tab, 105, 237
Picture tab, 236
Size tab, 235–236
Wrapping tab, 106
Format Text Box dialog box
Alignment tab, 401–402
Colors and Lines tab, 243
Font tab, 400–401
overview of, 242–243
Format WordArt dialog box, 405, 570
formats, searching and replacing, 46–48
formatting
bullets, 565–566
e-mail messages, 663–664
formatting, Excel charts, 417–423
adding gridlines, 417, 422
adding legends, 415, 417, 421–422
adding titles, 417, 419–420
adding unattached text, 420
axes, 421
borders, 422–423
with Chart toolbar, 418–419, 426
colors, 422–423
overview of, 417
selecting parts of, 418
text, 420–421, 422–423
formatting, Excel worksheets, 361–385
adding borders, 373–374
adding colors, 373–375
adding patterns, 374–375
with AutoFormat feature, 361–365
changing alignments, 367–369
changing column widths, 321, 365–366
changing row heights, 366
copying formatting, 92, 381–382
creating custom number formats, 378–381
creating styles from, 382–383
dates, 377–378
graphics
colors, 397–398
fills, 397–398
lines, 398–399
overview of, 397
shadows, 399
3-D effects, 399
hiding columns, rows, and gridlines, 367
numbers, 375–377
numbers as text, 323, 376, 449, 525, 773
overview of, 361, 384
protecting, 383–384
saving as styles, 382–383
text
aligning, 367–369
centering, 369–370
fonts and font styles, 372–373
justifying, 370–371
overview of, 369
rotating, 371–372
in text boxes, 400–401
wrapping, 370, 774–775
times, 377–378
unhiding columns, rows, and gridlines, 367
formatting, PowerPoint charts, 588–593
axes, 591
borders, 591–592
colors, 589–590
data series, 583–586
fonts, 588–589
numbers, 583
3-D charts, 592–593, 595
formatting, PowerPoint presentations
with AutoLayout, 560–561
copying formatting, 641
entire presentations, 561, 641
with Formatting toolbar, 536–537
with Slide Master, 561–564, 641
text fonts, colors, and styles, 567–568
text with WordArt, 568–571

formatting, Word documents, 71–102. *See also* desktop publishing; styles; Word documents
with AutoFormat feature, 227–229
backgrounds, 73
characters, 86–92
all caps option, 87–88, 89–90
animating, 87, 89
applying formats, 89
bolding, 87–88, 89–90, 193
changing case, 90
changing fonts and point sizes, 87–88, 90–91, 290
coloring, 87–88
copying formatting, 92
drop caps option, 87
hiding text, 87–88, 89–90
italicizing, 87–88, 89–90, 193
kerning, 91
keyboard shortcuts for, 89–90
options for, 86–89
overview of, 72, 86
positioning text, 87, 88
removing formats, 89, 90
sizing, 87–88, 89–90
small caps option, 87–88, 89–90
spacing between, 87–88, 91
styling fonts, 87–88, 90–91
superscript and subscript options, 87–88, 90, 91
underlining, 87–88, 89–90
copying formatting, 92, 381–382
fields, 154–155
indexes, 177
margins, 74–75
orientation, 73
overview of, 71–73, 101–102
page size, 74
pages, 71
paragraphs, 75–86
adding borders, 84–85
adding patterns, 85
avoiding unwanted space in, 76
carrying down formatting, 76
coloring, 85
hiding paragraph marks, 75–76
indenting, 77–78, 80–82
keyboard shortcuts for, 78
line and page breaks, 79, 286–287
overview of, 72, 75–77
shading, 85
shortcut menus for, 79–80
showing paragraph marks, 75–76
spacing text in, 42–44, 77–78, 83
styles and, 86
viewing formatting in, 77
sections, 92–101
adding footnotes, 97–99
adding line numbers, 93–94
adding page numbers, 96–97
adjusting margins, 95–96
aligning, 93
changing footnotes to endnotes, 101
creating headers and footers, 94–95
deleting footnotes, 100
deleting headers and footers, 95
editing footnotes, 99–100
footnote options, 100–101
moving footnotes, 100
overview of, 71–72, 92–94
positioning headers and footers, 95–96
section break options, 93, 286–287
tables, 128–133
borders, 131–132, 287–288
column widths, 128–129
converting text to tables, 132–133, 166
indenting rows, 130
overview of, 128
row alignment, 131
row height, 130
space between columns, 130
text, 122, 128, 131
tables of contents, 177
text boxes, 242–243
text in tables, 122, 128, 131
unsupported by HTML, 36, 258–259, 261
Formatting toolbars
in Excel, 376
in PowerPoint, 536–537
in Word, 191–192, 748, 750–751
formula bar, Excel
editing cells with, 328
entering values in, 319–320
overview of, 299, 308
formulas, Excel, 341–346. *See also* Excel worksheets
allowed elements in, 343–345
arithmetic operators in, 344

- changing recalculation options for, 346
- comparison operators in, 344–345
- creating, 341–345
- editing, 345–346
- entering, 341–343, 770–771
- error codes for, 346
- order of precedence in, 345
- overview of, 341–342, 762, 775
- relative versus absolute cell references and, 343
- series formulas in charts, 426–427
- viewing, 345

forwarding e-mail messages, 674–675
Four11 e-mail directory, 651
frames, browser, 625, 702
framing graphics, 105–106. *See also* borders; text boxes
freeform shapes, drawing, 553–554
Full Screen command, 306
function macros, Excel, 467–468
functions, Excel, 347–351. *See also* Excel worksheets
- AutoSum tool, 349
- AVERAGE function, 348
- defined, 762
- overview of, 347–348
- Paste Function Wizard, 349–351
- SUM function, 348

G

Gallery tab of Office Assistant, 14
General tab
- of New dialog box, 22–23, 205–207
- of New Presentation dialog box, 540–541, 632, 780

Genigraphics, 739
Get Info dialog box
- Offline tab, 717–718
- Schedule tab, 707
- Subscribe tab, 709

GIF graphics file format, 626, 670, 671
Go To dialog box in Excel, 300, 769
grammar-checking. *See* checking spelling and grammar
Graph, Microsoft, 4, 238–240, 248. *See also* charts
graphic objects. *See also* text boxes
- adding to toolbar buttons, 796–797
- clip-art
  - adding to PowerPoint presentations, 555, 791–792
  - adding to Word documents, 33–34
  - importing into Word documents, 232, 234
  - overview of, 738
- downloading, 720
- file formats for, 626
- GIF images, 670, 671
- JPEG images, 626, 670, 671

graphic objects in Excel, 387–406
- assigning macros to, 473–474
- AutoShapes, 391–393
- Bring to Front option, 395–396
- creating
  - arcs, 394
  - circles, 394
  - filled objects, 394
  - lines, 393, 394
  - ovals (ellipses), 394
  - overview of, 389–390, 393
  - rectangles, 393
  - squares, 393
- cutting or copying, and pasting, 396
- deleting, 396
- dragging-and-dropping, 396
- formatting
  - colors, 397–398
  - fills, 397–398
  - lines, 398–399
  - overview of, 397
  - shadows, 399
  - 3-D effects, 399
- grouping, 395
- hiding, 399
- importing, 391
- inserting, 388–389
- layering, 395–396
- moving, 396
- overview of, 387–388, 406
- protecting, 395
- resizing, 396–397
- selecting, 394
- Send to Back option, 395–396
- shortcut menus and, 390–391
- showing as placeholders, 399
- text boxes
  - adding, 399–400
  - editing text in, 400

(continued)

graphic objects in Excel (*continued*)
formatting text in, 400–401
rotating text in, 401–402
WordArt
adding to worksheets, 402–403
changing shapes of, 406
coloring, 405
examples, 571
overview of, 4, 402
rotating, 406
shape options, 569
sizing, 405
toolbar, 569–570
graphic objects in PowerPoint, 548–555
aligning, 549–551
assigning macros to, 614–615
AutoShapes, 553–555
changing style of, 554
clip-art, 555, 791–792
coloring, 554
copying, 548–549
copying formatting of, 641
cropping, 549
defined, 548, 552
Drawing toolbar and, 536–537, 552–554
editing, 641
grouping, 548, 641
moving, 548–549
overview of, 552
removing, 549
rotating, 554–555
selecting, 548
sizing, 555
stacking, 551–552
WordArt, 568–571
graphic objects in Word, 229–238. *See also* desktop publishing
adding borders to, 236–237
adding callouts to, 237
adding to documents, 33–34
as bullets, 61
copying and pasting, 33
creating, 234
cropping, 236
Drawing toolbar and, 234
editing, 235, 238
framing while previewing printing, 105–106
importing
bitmapped images, 230–232
by copying and pasting, 234
by scanning photographs, 231
clip-art, 232, 234
with Insert Picture command, 233–234
into Excel worksheets, 391
object images, 230, 232
overview of, 229–230
overview of, 247
scaling (sizing), 235–236
text boxes for, 234
trimming, 236
graphs, from Microsoft Graph, 238–240, 248. *See also* Excel charts; PowerPoint charts
gridlines
adding to Excel charts, 422
hiding and unhiding in Excel worksheets, 367
in PowerPoint charts, 580
printing in Excel worksheets, 441
printing in tables, 287–288
Group styles menu in Microsoft Organization Chart, 634
grouping graphic objects, 395, 548, 641
Growth series option in Excel, 338

H

handouts, audience, 606–607
hanging indents, 77–78
Header dialog box, 439
Header and Footer dialog box, 638–639
Header and Footer toolbar, 94–95, 96
header records, 157
Header/Footer tab of Page Setup dialog box, 435, 438–440
headers. *See also* footers
adding to PowerPoint presentations, 638–639
adjusting margins for, 95–96
creating, 94–95
deleting, 95
in Excel worksheets, printing, 438–440
positioning, 95–96
in VBA code, 268, 496
headings
in charts, 582
defined, 135
in Excel worksheets, printing, 441
headings, in outlines
bulleting, 140–141
changing, 145–146
collapsing, 139

converting body text to, 138
creating tables of contents from, 146–147, 174–175
demoting, 138, 145
expanding, 139
moving, 139–140, 145–146
numbering, 140–141
overview of, 138
promoting, 138, 145–146
headlines, inserting, 246–247
heights of rows in Excel worksheets, 366
heights of tables, 130
Help. *See also* Office Assistant
bookmarking help pages, 13
Contents and Index menu option, 15
copying help text, 13
customizing toolbars and menus, 800
file helpers for viewing attachments, 670–671
in Internet Explorer, 728
in MOM (Microsoft Office Manager), 10
overview of, 15
returning to previous help pages, 13
ScreenTips, 12, 766
ToolTips, 695
Value Pack Assistants, 737
with VBA, 614, 616, 739
hidden text option, 87–88, 89–90
hiding and unhiding. *See also* showing and hiding; turning on or off
Excel worksheet elements, 367
Personal Macro Workbook, 478
slides in slide shows, 604
Highlight Changes dialog box, 62
History tab in Internet Explorer, 699–700, 705
horizontal rules, 663
hot keys. *See* keyboard shortcuts
HTML (Hypertext Markup Language)
defined, 36
formatting unsupported by, 36, 258–259, 261
overview of, 253, 484, 621–622
Rich Text (HTML) format, 661, 663, 668
saving Excel data as, 313, 487–489
saving PowerPoint slides as, 624–629
saving Word documents as, 36, 258–259, 261
hyperlinks
accessing Web sites via, 705
converting Internet addresses to, 257
copying and pasting, 256, 485
dragging-and-dropping, 256, 485
to embedded Excel data in mail merges, 167–171
in Excel worksheets, 484–487
from slides to Office documents, 623
from slides to Web sites, 623–624
updating before printing, 111
in Word documents, 255–257
hyphenating text, 59–60, 82–83
Hyphenation dialog box, 60
hyphens, preventing date formatting of, 525

I

images. *See* graphic objects
IMAP (Internet Message Access Protocol) servers. *See also* Outlook Express
deleting messages from, 675–676
overview of, 651, 653
reading mail with, 668–669
importing e-mail contacts, 658
importing images. *See also* desktop publishing
bitmapped images, 230–232
by copying and pasting, 234
by scanning photographs, 231
clip-art, 232, 234
with Insert Picture command, 233–234
into Excel worksheets, 391
object images, 230, 232
overview of, 229–230
Inbox folder in Outlook Express, 649
indented indexes, 184
indenting paragraphs, 77–78, 80–82
indenting table cells and rows, 130
Indents and Spacing tab of Paragraph dialog box, 42–44, 77–78, 80–81, 83, 204
Index and Tables dialog box
Index tab, 183–184
Table of Contents tab, 174–177, 179
Table of Figures tab, 180–181
indexes, 181–187
creating
indented indexes, 184
for large documents, 186
with multiple levels, 184–185
overview of, 181
run-in indexes, 185
defined, 173
formatting, 177
index switches, 185

(continued)

- indexes (*continued*)
  - inserting in documents, 183
  - Internet Explorer Index, 728
  - marking index entries, 181–183
  - overview of, 173, 187
  - page number ranges in, 185
- input boxes, VBA code for, 498
- Input Message tab of Data Validation dialog box, 352
- Insert Cells dialog box, 124–126
- Insert Data dialog box, 170–171
- Insert dialog box, 338
- Insert Hyperlink dialog box, 256–257, 486–487, 624
- Insert Object dialog box, 572–573
- Insert Picture dialog box, 233–234
- Insert Table dialog box, 118–119
- Insert Word Table dialog box, 573
- inserting. *See also* adding
  - comments, VBA code for, 267, 495–496
  - drop caps in text, 87
  - Excel worksheet elements, 338
  - Excel worksheets in PowerPoint slides, 571–573
  - graphics in Excel worksheets, 388–389
  - hyperlinks
    - in Excel worksheets, 486–487
    - in PowerPoint slides, 624
    - in Word documents, 256–257
  - manual page breaks in Excel worksheets, 444–445
  - PowerPoint charts in slides, 580–582
  - slides in PowerPoint presentations, 539, 546, 788
  - in Word documents
    - AutoText entries, 56
    - columns of text, 225–227, 246
    - fields, 150–152
    - graphics, 33–34
    - graphs (charts), 238–240, 248
    - headlines, 246–247
    - hyperlinks, 256–257
    - index entries, 181–183
    - indexes, 183
    - subheads, 246–247
    - tables, 248
    - TC entries, 176–177
  - Word table elements, 124–126
  - Word tables in PowerPoint slides, 571, 573–574
- insertion points, 752
- installing, 733–743
  - Internet Explorer, 741–742
  - MOM (Microsoft Office Manager), 9
  - Office 98
    - custom install, 733–736
    - overview of, 4–5, 733
    - standard drag-install, 4, 733
    - uninstalling, 735–736, 741
    - Value Pack, 736–737
  - Outlook Express, 684, 742–743
  - plug-ins, 714
- Internet. *See also* World Wide Web
  - accessing on POP servers, 653, 669
  - connection options, 701
  - overview of, 252, 483, 621
- Internet Assistant Wizard, 487–489
- Internet Config, 665, 743
- Internet Explorer, 693–729
  - accessing the Internet, 701
  - accessing search engines, 715–716
  - accessing Web sites, 702–706
    - with address bars, 703
    - with Apple Data Detectors, 704–705
    - AutoComplete in, 703
    - by clicking links, 705
    - error messages in, 704
    - with Favorites tab, 705
    - with History tab, 705
    - multiple connections option for, 706
    - with Open command, 704
    - overview of, 702–703
    - stopping, 705
  - archives, 708, 717
  - AutoSearch, 716
  - browsing offline, 708, 710, 717–718
  - channels, 697–698, 709–710
  - creating browser windows, 702
  - Discovery Channel Online and, 709
  - downloading files
    - by copying and pasting, 719
    - decoding and, 720
    - images, 720
    - movies, 720
    - overview of, 718, 720–721
    - reviewing downloads, 721–722
    - and saving, 719

setting options for, 706, 721, 722–723
sounds, 720
stopping downloads, 721
error messages, 704
expanding screen space, 698
Explorer bar
Channels tab, 697–698
Favorites tab, 698–699, 705
History tab, 699–700, 705
overview of, 695, 697
Search tab, 700–701, 716
favorites bar, 694–695
Favorites list
adding dividing lines to, 712
adding favorites, 711
adding folders to, 712
deleting favorites, 699, 712
marking favorites, 710–711
overview of, 698–699
rearranging favorites, 698–699
renaming folders or favorites, 712
Favorites tab, 698–699, 705
Help, 728
History tab, 699–700, 705
Index, 728
installing, 741–742
Internet connection options, 701
main window, 693–703
address bar, 694, 703, 716
button bar, 694, 696
cloning, 702
Explorer bar, 695, 697–701
favorites bar, 694–695
frames in, 702
moving bars, 695
overview of, 693–695, 702
scroll bars, 695
status bar, 695, 702
title bar, 694
ToolTips, 695
turning bars on or off, 695
overview of, 4, 693, 729
printing Web pages, 723
reading mail and news, 727
searching
with AutoComplete, 703
with search engines, 715–716
with Search tab, 700–701, 716
for text, 716–717
security standards
security alerts, 725–726
security zones, 723–725
site certificates, 723
SSL servers, 723
Windows NT servers, 723
setting options
buttons and bars, 695
downloading files, 706, 721, 722–723
History lists, 700
screening ratings, 726–727
security, 724–726
subscriptions, 707–710
Web page viewing, 712–714
Tips & Tricks, 728
Web pages
copying and pasting data from, 719
frames in, 702
overview of, 701–702
plug-ins and, 714
printing, 723
saving, 719
Web sites, 701–718
accessing, 702–706
archiving, 708, 717
browsing offline, 708, 710, 717–718
color options, 713, 728
cookies and, 715
defined, 701–702
font options, 713–714
getting to, 702–706
language options, 714
screening content of, 726–727
searching, 700–701, 703, 715–717
setting viewing options, 712–714
special effects options, 714
style sheets option, 713
subscribing to, 706–708
subscribing to channels in, 709–710
tracking visits to, 699–700, 705
visiting, 702
Internet Message Access Protocol. *See* IMAP
Internet protocols supported by Outlook Express, 652
Internet security zone in Internet Explorer, 724
Internet service providers (ISPs), 701
intranets, 252, 483, 621
italicizing text, 87–88, 89–90, 193

J

JPEG graphics file format, 626, 670, 671
justifying text, 82–83, 370–371

K

kerning characters, 91
key fields in Excel databases, 455
Keyboard button in Customize dialog box, 35
keyboard shortcuts
  applying Normal (default) styles with, 193
  assigning Excel macros to, 468, 476
  assigning styles to, 196–197
  assigning Word macros to, 216–217, 218–219
  command underlines, 15–16
  customizing, 35, 801
  for entering Excel dates and times with, 325
  for formatting characters, 89–90
  for formatting paragraphs, 78
  for inserting fields, 151
  for line spacing, 43, 78
  for navigating
    Excel worksheets, 300–301, 768–769
    Word documents, 34–35, 752–753
    Word tables, 120–121
  for outlines, 138
  QuickSwitch, 10–11
  in ScreenTips, 12
  for spell-checking, 50
  Tab keys, Word tables and, 121

L

labels, mailing, 163–165
Landscape orientation, 73
Language dialog box, 209–210
language options for Web sites, 714
Layout tab of Document dialog box, 92–94
layouts for slide shows, 547–548, 642, 780
leader tab stops, 42
left tabs, 40–41
legends in Excel charts, 415, 417, 421–422
legends in PowerPoint charts, 582
Letter Wizard, 28, 29
letters, form, 157–161
Lewis, Peter N., 720
line breaks. *See* breaks
line charts, 423, 579
line numbers in Word documents, 93–94
Line and Page Breaks tab of Paragraph dialog box, 79
line spacing in Word documents, 42–43, 77–78, 83
Linear series option in Excel, 338
lines
  adding dividing lines to Favorites list, 712
  creating in Excel, 393, 394, 398–399
  horizontal lines (rules), 663
linking text boxes, 241–242
links. *See* hyperlinks
List 1 AutoFormat style, 362–363
lists, bulleted or numbered, 60–61, 78, 290–291, 564–566
Local Intranet security zone in Internet Explorer, 724
locking. *See* security

M

MacBinary decoding software, 720
Macro dialog box, PowerPoint, 612
Macro Options dialog box, 477
Macro Project Items tab of Organizer dialog box, 222
Macro Recorder toolbar, 219
macros, 611
Macros dialog box, Word, 221–222
macros in Excel, 467–479. *See also* VBA
  assigning
    changing assignments, 472
    to graphic objects, 473–474
    to keyboard shortcuts, 468, 476
    to menus, 475–476
    overview of, 471
    to toolbar buttons, 474–475
    to worksheet buttons, 471–473
  changing options for, 476–477
  command macros, 467–468
  creating, 468–471, 492–493
  function macros, 467–468
  naming, 468
  naming macro buttons, 473
  overview of, 467, 478–479, 740
  from previous versions of Excel, 473
  for printing, 469–471
  running, 473, 476
storing, 469, 477–478
types of, 467–468
macros in PowerPoint, 611–617. *See also* VBA
  assigning to objects on slides, 614–615
  assigning to toolbar buttons, 615

creating with VBA, 611–613
deleting, 616
editing VBA code for, 617
getting help with VBA, 614, 616, 739
overview of, 611–612
running, 614–615
storing, 612
viruses in, 616
macros in Word, 213–224. *See also* VBA
alternatives to, 214
assigning to keyboard shortcuts, 216–217, 218–219
versus AutoText entries, 213–214
copying to templates, 221–222
creating
examples of, 222–223, 264–265
manually, 216
overview of, 214, 215–217
to run automatically, 223–224
with Word macro recorder, 217–220
defined, 213
deleting, 221
overview of, 213–214, 224, 740
printing, 112
running, 220–221
storing, 215
Mail Merge Helper dialog box, 158, 163, 164–165
mail merges, 157–171. *See also* fields
adding merge fields to main documents, 159–160
choosing main documents, 158
creating form letters with, 157–161
creating from Excel databases, 463–464
data sources
copying and pasting Excel data, 166–167
creating from other software, 165–171
creating manually, 158–159
embedding data from other sources, 171
embedding Excel data, 167–171
exporting, 165–166
merging with main documents, 160–161
overview of, 157
printing envelopes, 161–163
printing mailing labels, 163–165
mail messages. *See* Outlook Express
Mailing Label Wizard, 27
mailing labels, printing, 163–165
mailing lists, creating, 659–660, 692
margins
adjusting for headers and footers, 95–96
adjusting while previewing printing, 104–105, 443–444
applying, 75
changing, 39, 74
defined, 74
desktop publishing and, 246
Mirror Margins option, 39, 74–75
setting up in Excel printing, 434–435, 438, 443–444
Margins tab
of Document dialog box, 74–75, 95, 96
of Page Setup dialog box, 434–435, 438
Mark Index Entry dialog box, 182
markers in charts, 415, 416, 577
marking favorites, 710–711
marking index entries, 181–183
Master Document view in Word, 37–38
Master Layout dialog box, 562
MAXIMUM and MINIMUM functions in Excel, 348
Memo Wizard, 28–29, 276–281
menus. *See also* shortcut menus
adding, 795, 799
assigning Excel macros to, 475–476
customizing menu commands, 798–799
customizing MOM menus, 9–10
deleting, 795
in Microsoft Office Manager, 5–6, 9–10
renaming menu commands and, 800
restoring, 800–801
merge fields, 157–160. *See also* mail merges
merging table cells, 127
Message list in Outlook Express, 652
messages. *See* Outlook Express
Microsoft Bookshelf 98, 737–738
Microsoft ClipArt Gallery, 33–34, 555, 791–792
Microsoft Excel. *See* Excel
Microsoft Exchange, 648, 651
Microsoft Graph, 4, 238–240, 248. *See also* charts
Microsoft Internet Explorer. *See* Internet Explorer
Microsoft Internet Mail and News. *See* Outlook Express
Microsoft Movie, 739
Microsoft News Server, 651
Microsoft Office 98. *See* Office 98
Microsoft Office Installer dialog box, 734–735

Microsoft Office Manager. *See* MOM
Microsoft Organization Chart, 593–594, 633–635
Microsoft Outlook Express. *See* Outlook Express
Microsoft PowerPoint. *See* PowerPoint
Microsoft Query, 738
Microsoft Visual Basic, 267, 493
Microsoft Web site, 609, 616, 756
Microsoft Windows NT servers, 723
Microsoft Word 98. *See* Word 98
Microsoft WordArt. *See* WordArt
Mirror Margins option, 39, 74–75
Modify Style dialog box, 198–199
MOM (Microsoft Office Manager). *See also* Office 98
- customizing MOM menu, 9–10
- Help, 10
- installing, 9
- overview of, 5–6, 9, 739
- QuickSwitch option, 10–11

movies, downloading, 720
moving
- among Excel worksheets, 301–302, 768
- among slides, 539, 545, 788
- Excel data
  - by cutting and pasting, 305–306, 330
  - with drag-and-drop, 330, 331
  - overview of, 329–330
  - Paste Special options for, 336–337
- between fields, 154
- footnotes, 100
- graphic objects
  - in Excel, 396
  - in PowerPoint, 548–549
  - while previewing printing, 105–106
- Internet Explorer bars, 695
- outline headings, 139–140, 145–146
- slides, 547
- tab stops, 42
- text, 44–45, 104–105
- text boxes, 243–244
- toolbars, 12

N

naming
- Excel macro buttons, 473
- Excel macros, 468
- Excel worksheet cells, 340–341
- Excel worksheet tabs, 302
- favorites and favorites folders, 712
- menu commands and menus, 800
- styles, 200
- toolbar buttons, 798

narration in PowerPoint presentations, 574
navigating
- Excel workbook windows, 767–768
- Excel worksheets, 299–301, 767–769
- Word documents, 34–36, 752–753
- Word tables, 120–121

New Account dialog box, 654
New dialog box
- General tab, 22–23, 206
- overview of, 192, 205–207

New Document dialog box, 7
New Presentation dialog box
- General tab, 540–541, 632, 780
- PowerPoint 4 Templates tab, 632
- Presentation Designs tab, 541, 632, 780
- Presentations tab, 537–538, 630, 632, 780

New Slide dialog box, 633, 783
New Style dialog box, 194–195
news in Internet Explorer, 727
News Server, Microsoft, 651
newsgroups, 685–691. *See also* Outlook Express
Newsletter Wizard, 29–30, 248–249
Normal (default) styles, 191–193, 197–199
Normal (default) templates, 22, 208, 209–210
Normal view in Word, 37, 227
Note Options dialog box, 100–101
Notes, Excel, 326
Notes Page view in PowerPoint, 534, 786, 787
notes for speakers in PowerPoint presentations, 604–606, 637–639
Number tab of Format Cells dialog box, 376–378, 380, 774–775
numbering
- index page ranges, 185
- lines of text, 93–94
- lists, 60–61, 290–291
- outline headings, 140–141
- pages in Excel printing, 437
- pages in Word documents, 96–97
- paragraphs, 60–61

numbers
- alphanumeric values in sorting Excel databases, 457
- custom number formats in Excel, 378–381
- entering in Excel worksheets, 321–322
- formatting

in Excel worksheets, 375–377
in PowerPoint charts, 583
as text in Excel worksheets, 323, 376, 449, 525, 773

O

object images, 230, 232
objects. *See* graphic objects
OE User(s) folder in Outlook Express, 682, 683
Office 98, 3–16, 733–743
adding application aliases to Apple menus, 6
applications, 3–4
command underlines, 15–16
creating documents, 6–7
creating hyperlinks from slides to Office documents, 623
extensions folder, 5
Help, 15
installing
custom install, 733–736
Internet Explorer, 741–742
MOM (Microsoft Office Manager), 9
Outlook Express, 684, 742–743
overview of, 4–5, 733
standard drag-install, 4, 733
uninstalling, 735–736, 741
Value Pack, 736–737
launching Office applications, 5–6
MOM (Microsoft Office Manager), 5–6, 9–10, 739
Office Assistant, 13–15
opening documents, 7–8
overview of, 16
Proofing tools, 740
removing, 735, 741
removing old Office versions, 741
toolbars, 11–13
Unbinder, 8, 740
Value Pack
contents, 737–740
Help, 737
installing, 736–737
removing, 741
Web site, 652, 736
Office Assistant
for function help, 351
Gallery tab, 14
getting help from, 13
Options tab, 14–15
overview of, 13
setting options for, 14–15
Value Pack Assistants and, 737
viewing tips from, 14
offline browsing in Internet Explorer, 708, 710, 717–718
offline browsing in Outlook Express, 689
Offline tab of Get Info dialog box, 717–718
online access for POP servers, 653, 669
online directories, 651
Online Layout view in Word, 37–38
online presentation templates, 537–538, 630
onscreen annotations in slides, 642–643
Open command in accessing Web sites, 704
Open Data Source dialog box, 168
Open dialog box, 297
Open Document dialog box, 7–8
Open Internet Address dialog box, 704
opening
ClarisWorks Office documents in Excel, 528
Excel workbooks, 297–298, 523, 767
PowerPoint presentations, 784
Web documents in Word, 254–255
Word documents, 7–8, 21–22, 751–752
operators in Excel formulas, 344–345
options. *See* setting options
Options tab
of Customize dialog box, 12
of Office Assistant, 14–15
organization charts, PowerPoint, 593–594, 631–635
Organizer dialog box, 199–200, 222
orientation
in Excel printing, 436
in formatting documents, 73
orphan text lines, 79
Outbox folder in Outlook Express, 649
Outline view in PowerPoint
editing text in, 543–544, 790
overview of, 532, 533, 785–786
Outline view in Word, 37, 135, 136
outlines, in Word documents, 135–148. *See also* Word documents
changing structure of, 136–138
collapsing, 144
creating, 141–144
creating tables of contents from, 146–147, 174–175

(continued)

outlines, in Word documents (*continued*)
defined, 135
expanding, 144
headings in
bulleting, 140–141
changing, 145–146
collapsing, 139
converting body text to, 138
demoting, 138, 145
expanding, 139
moving, 139–140, 145–146
numbering, 140–141
overview of, 138
promoting, 138, 145–146
keyboard shortcuts for, 138
Outlining toolbar, 136–138, 790
overview of, 135–136, 148
printing, 148
selecting text in Outline view, 136
Outlook Express, 647–692
attachments
encoding, 664
file helpers for viewing, 670–671
GIF or JPEG images as, 670, 671
overview of, 664–665, 670, 671
saving, 671–672
Contacts folder, 650
Deleted Messages folder, 650
deleting messages
from hard drives, 675
from IMAP servers, 675–676
while online with POP servers, 676
Drafts folder, 650
e-mail accounts, 653–660
accessing from other computers, 653, 669
Accounts icons, 650–651
AOL (America Online) and, 652
creating contact lists, 657–658
creating mailing lists, 659–660, 692
deleting contacts, 659
dial-up accounts, 651
with IMAP servers, 651, 653, 668–669
importing contacts, 658
overview of, 653
with POP servers, 653, 667–668, 669–670
setting up, 654–656
viewing contacts, 659
e-mail messages, 661–680
accessing from other computers, 653, 669
accessing mail of other users, 680
adding signatures to, 665
addressing, 662–663
attaching files to, 664–665
automating incoming mail, 677–679
carrying on disk, 683–684
creating, 661–666
creating folders for, 649, 676–677
defining rules for, 678–679
deleting, 675–676
filing, 676–677
filtering, 678–680
finding, 679–680
formatting, 663–664
forwarding, 674–675
overview of, 661
plain text format for, 661, 663–664
printing, 672
quoting other messages or text, 666, 672–673
receiving and reading, 667–670
replying to, 672–674
Rich Text (HTML) format for, 661, 663, 668
saving, 661, 669, 672
saving attachments, 671–672
searching for, 679–680
sending, 666
sending to multiple recipients, 659–660, 692
setting options for, 668
sorting, 679
storing on removable disks, 683–684
storing on servers, 668
viewing attachments, 670–671
Exchange and, 648, 651
IMAP servers
deleting messages from, 675–676
overview of, 651, 653
reading mail with, 668–669
Inbox folder, 649
installing, 742–743
installing on removable disks, 684
Internet Config and, 665, 743
Internet protocols supported by, 652
main window
Contacts folder, 650
Deleted Messages folder, 650
Drafts folder, 650

E-mail server icon, 650
Folder list, 649–651, 692
Four11 icon, 651
Inbox folder, 649
Message list, 652
Microsoft News Server icon, 651
Outbox folder, 649
overview of, 648
Preview pane, 652, 668
Sent Mail folder, 650
toolbar, 648
viewing contact lists in, 659
multiple users
accessing mail of other users, 680
carrying mail on removable disks, 683–684
deleting users, 683
overview of, 680
setting up, 681–682
switching between users, 682
transferring users from Mac to Mac, 683
newsgroup messages
automating, 690–691
creating, 691
defining rules for, 690–691
filtering, 690–691
reading, 688–689
replying to, 691
saving, 689
sending, 691
threads in, 688
viewing, 688–689
newsgroups
defined, 647, 685
sending messages to, 691
setting up accounts with, 685–686
subscribing to, 686–687
unsubscribing to, 688
OE User(s) folder, 682, 683
Outbox folder, 649
overview of, 4, 647–648, 692
POP servers
deleting mail while online with, 676
overview of, 653
reading mail with, 667–668, 669–670
setting up online access for, 653, 669
reading mail
from any computers, 653, 669
with IMAP accounts, 668–669
overview of, 667
with POP accounts, 667–668, 669–670
Sent Mail folder, 650
Work Offline feature, 689
ovals, creating, 394
overtyping Word document text, 754

P

page breaks. *See* breaks
page formatting, 71
Page Layout view in Word, 37–38, 39, 227
Page Number Format dialog box, 96–97
page numbers. *See* numbering; numbers
Page Numbers dialog box, 96–97
page order in printing, 442
page ranges in printing, 109
Page Setup dialog box
formatting Word documents in, 72–74
Header/Footer tab, 435, 438–440
Margins tab, 434–435, 438
Page tab, 434, 436, 437
in PowerPoint, 597–598
Sheet tab, 435–436, 437, 438, 440–442
page size in formatting Word documents, 74
paper size in Excel printing, 436
Paragraph dialog box, 42–44, 77–81, 83, 204
paragraph styles, 190
paragraphs. *See* formatting, Word documents
password-protecting. *See also* security
Excel formatting, 384, 385
Excel graphics, 395
Excel workbooks, 309–310
Paste Function Wizard, 349–351
Paste Special dialog box, 336–337
pasting. *See* copying and pasting; cutting and pasting
patterns
adding to Excel worksheets, 374–375
adding to paragraphs, 85
Patterns tab
of Format Axis dialog box, 421
of Format Cells dialog box, 374–375
of Format Chart Area dialog box, 422–423, 592
of Format Data Series dialog box, 585
pen cursors in onscreen slides, 642–643
Personal Macro Workbook, Excel, 469, 477–478
photographs, 231
Picture tab of Format Picture dialog box, 236

Picture toolbar, 549
pie charts, 424, 579
plain text format, 661, 663–664, 719
Pleading Wizard, 30
plot areas in Excel charts, 415, 416
plotting data in Excel charts, 426–429
plug-in software, 714
point sizes, changing, 87–88, 90–91
points in line spacing, 44
POP (Post Office Protocol) servers. *See also* Outlook Express
  deleting messages while online with, 676
  overview of, 653
  reading mail with, 667–668, 669–670
  setting up online access for, 653, 669
Portrait orientation, 73
PowerPoint 4 Templates tab of New Presentation dialog box, 632
PowerPoint charts, 577–595. *See also* Excel charts
  adding titles to, 590–591
  changing column widths, 582
  changing types, 586–588
  creating organization charts, 593–594, 631–635
  Datasheet windows for, 580–581, 582
  designing, 589
  editing, 583
  entering data in, 582–583
  versus Excel charts, 578
  formatting
    3-D charts, 592–593, 595
    axes, 591
    borders, 591–592
    colors, 589–590
    data series, 583–586
    fonts, 588–589
    numbers, 583
  headings in, 582
  inserting in slides, 580–582
  legends in, 582
  overview of, 577–578, 594–595
  setting options for, 580–581
  swapping data series in, 583–584
  types of, 578–580, 586–588
PowerPoint macros. *See* macros in PowerPoint
PowerPoint presentations, 531–643, 779–792
  adding to
    action buttons, 575–576
    clip-art, 555, 791–792
    Excel charts, 583
    Excel worksheets, 571–573
    headers and footers, 638–639
    narration, 574
    onscreen annotations, 642–643
    sound, 574
    speaker notes, 604–606, 637–638
    transitions, 639–640
    Word tables, 571, 573–574
    WordArt, 568–571
  animating slides in, 602–604
  animating text in, 575
  applying backgrounds to, 637
  AutoLayout feature and, 560–561
  closing, 784
  creating
    audience handouts for, 606–607
    with AutoContent Wizard, 557–560, 780, 781–783
    Blank Presentation option for, 537, 540–541, 780, 783–784
    bulleted lists in, 564–566
    columns of text in, 566–567
    custom slide shows, 607–609
    overview of, 540–541
    with templates, 537–540
    templates, 541
    with templates, 635–637, 780, 783
    travel presentation example, 635–640
  default formats for, 537–541
  defined, 779
  Drawing toolbar and, 536–537, 552–554
  e-mailing, 609
  enhancing, 557, 576
  entering summary information for, 542–543
  entering text in, 543
  formatting
    copying object formatting, 641
    entire presentations, 561, 641
    with Formatting toolbar, 536–537
    slides with AutoLayout, 560–561
    slides with Slide Master, 561–564, 641
    text fonts, colors, and styles, 567–568
    text with WordArt, 568–571
  graphic objects in, 548–555
    aligning, 549–551
    assigning macros to, 614–615
    AutoShapes, 553–555

changing style of, 554
clip-art, 555, 791–792
coloring, 554
copying, 548–549
copying formatting of, 641
cropping, 549
defined, 548, 552
drawing shapes, 536–537, 552–554
editing, 641
grouping, 548, 641
moving, 548–549
overview of, 552
removing, 549
rotating, 554–555
selecting, 548
sizing, 555
stacking, 551–552
WordArt, 568–571
macros in, 611–617
assigning to slides, 614–615
assigning to toolbar buttons, 615
creating with VBA, 611–613
deleting, 616
editing VBA code for, 617
getting VBA help, 614, 616, 739
overview of, 611–612
running during slide shows, 614–615
storing, 612
viruses in, 616
Notes Page view, 534, 786, 787
opening, 784
Outline view
editing text in, 543–544, 790
overview of, 532, 533, 785–786
overview of, 3, 531, 555–556, 610, 640
Picture toolbar and, 549
PowerPoint Viewer, 609, 642
presentation window, 531–534
printing
overview of, 540, 597, 792
portions of, 598–600
setting options for, 597–598, 601
slides in reverse order, 642
speaker notes, 639
publishing on the Web, 624–629
saving
as HTML files, 624–629
overview of, 539, 541–542, 784
as templates, 642
shortcut menus for, 535
Slide Show view, 534, 535, 786
slide shows
changing timing settings, 600–601
creating custom slide shows, 607–609
creating progressive slides, 602–604
hiding and unhiding slides, 604
running macros during, 614–615
setting options for, 601
tips for, 602
Slide Sorter view, 532, 533, 786, 787
Slide view
editing text in, 539, 544, 545, 789
overview of, 531–532, 785
slides in, 543–548
adding action buttons to, 575–576
animating, 602–604
assigning macros to, 614–615
changing layout of, 547–548, 642, 780
copying and pasting, 546–547
creating, 643
defined, 779
deleting, 539, 546
editing text in Outline view, 543–544, 790
editing text in Slide view, 539, 544, 545, 789
formatting with AutoLayout, 560–561
formatting with Slide Master, 561–564, 641
hiding, 604
inserting, 539, 546, 788
inserting charts in, 580–582
moving, 547
moving among, 539, 545, 788
overview of, 544
previewing transitions between, 642
printing in reverse order, 642
publishing on the Web, 624–629
rearranging, 547
saving as HTML files, 624–629
slide masters, 779–780
unhiding, 604
Standard toolbar and, 536–537
templates
creating, 541
creating presentations with, 537–540, 635–637, 780, 783
default templates, 537–541
defined, 779

(continued)

PowerPoint presentations (*continued*)
for online presentations, 537–538, 630
overview of, 540–541, 632, 780
saving presentations as, 642
text in
animating, 575
coloring, 567–568
editing in Outline view, 543–544, 790
editing in Slide view, 539, 544, 545, 789
embossing, 568
entering, 543
formatting fonts and styles, 567–568
headers and footers, 638–639
laying out in columns, 566–567
onscreen annotations, 642–643
shadowing, 567
speaker notes, 604–606, 637–638
superscript and subscript text, 568
WordArt, 568–571
toolbars for, 536–537
view buttons for, 531–532
viewing on non-PowerPoint computers, 609, 642
views, 531–535, 785–787
on the Web, 619–630
connecting to networks, 620
creating hyperlinks to Office documents, 623
creating hyperlinks to Web sites, 623–624
online presentation templates, 537–538, 630
overview of, 619–622, 630
publishing slides, 624–629
saving slides as HTML files, 624–629
Web toolbar, 622
PowerPoint Viewer, 609, 642
preferences. *See also* setting options
Preferences dialog box
Calculation tab, 346
Custom Lists tab, 333–334
Edit tab, 320–321
overview of, 38
Print tab, 110–111, 113, 156
Save tab, 289–290
Spelling & Grammar tab, 49, 51, 52–53
Track Changes tab, 62
View tab, 38, 175
Preferences dialog box, Internet Explorer
Advanced pane, 700
overview of, 712
Ratings pane, 726–727
Security pane, 725–726
Security Zones pane, 724–725
Web Content pane, 712–714
Presentation Designs tab of New Presentation dialog box, 541, 632, 780
presentations. *See* PowerPoint presentations
Presentations tab of New Presentation dialog box, 537–538, 630, 632, 780
President of the United States Web site, 621
preventing
date formatting of slashes and hyphens, 525
page and line breaks, 286–287
Preview pane in Outlook Express, 652, 668
previewing. *See also* viewing
Excel printing, 443–444
slide transitions, 642
Word printing, 103–106
Print dialog box
default (General) screen, 107–108, 264, 431, 432–434, 599
in Excel, 432, 433–434, 470
in PowerPoint, 599–600, 792
in Word, 58, 108–112
Print Preview toolbar, 103–104
print quality in Excel printing, 437–438
print ranges in Excel printing, 441–442, 527–528
Print tab of Preferences dialog box, 110–111, 113
printing
e-mail messages, 672
VBA code, 270, 499
Web pages, 723
printing, Excel worksheets, 431–446
column headings, 441
comments, 441
creating macros for, 469–471
filtered database records, 454, 461
gridlines, 441
headers and footers, 438–440
inserting manual page breaks, 444–445
macros for, 469–471
overview of, 431–432, 446, 776
previewing, 443–444
Print dialog box and, 431–434, 470
row headings, 441
setting up, 434–442
margins, 434–435, 438, 443–444

orientation, 436
overview of, 434–436
page numbering, 437
page order, 442
paper size, 436
print quality, 437–438
print ranges, 441–442, 527–528
scaling, 437
Sheet tab and, 435–436, 437
titles on successive pages, 440, 528
printing, PowerPoint presentations
overview of, 540, 597, 792
portions of, 598–600
setting options for, 597–598, 601
slides in reverse order, 642
speaker notes, 639
printing, Word, 103–115
AutoText entries, 58, 112
changing printers, 112
comments, 64–65, 112
document information, 111–112, 113
documents
collating while, 110
with document information, 113
General options for, 107–108
odd or even pages, 110
overview of, 106
portions of, 109
in reverse order, 110–111
several page ranges, 109
special options for, 108–112, 113, 156
updating fields and links before, 111
envelopes, 113–115, 161–163, 284–285
Excel charts, 415
field codes, 156
key assignments (macros), 112
mailing labels, 163–165
outlines, 148
overview of, 115
portions of documents, 109, 759
previewing
adjusting margins, 104–105
framing graphics, 105–106
moving graphics, 105–106
moving text, 104–105
overview of, 103
toolbar options for, 103–104
wrapping text, 106
problems with, 114
style sheets, 112
without opening documents, 759
Printing Options tab of Envelope Options dialog box, 115, 162
problems. *See also* danger zones
accessing Web sites, 704
error codes in Excel cells, 321, 346
error messages in Internet Explorer, 704
with Excel data entry, 321
with Excel formulas, 346
with printing, 114
Progress dialog box, 666
progressive slides, creating, 602–604
Prompt for Document Properties option, 757
Proofing tools in Value Pack, 740
Properties dialog box, 66–67, 310–311
Properties tab of Format Chart Area dialog box, 423
protecting. *See* security
Protection tab of Format Cells dialog box, 383–384
protocols supported by Outlook Express, 652
publishing on the Web. *See also* desktop publishing
Excel worksheets and charts, 487–489
PowerPoint presentations, 624–629
Word documents, 258–259
pyramid charts, 424, 580

Q

Query Options dialog box, 168–170
QuickSwitch option, 10–11
quotes, smart, 269
quoting text in e-mail messages, 666, 672–673

R

radar charts, 424, 579
ranges
in Excel databases, 450
formatting ranges of Excel cells, 323
page number ranges in indexes, 185
print ranges in Excel, 441–442, 527–528
print ranges in Word, 109
selecting ranges of Excel cells, 303–304, 525–526
ratings of Web site content, 726–727
reading e-mail. *See also* Outlook Express
from any computers, 653, 669
with IMAP servers, 668–669

(continued)

reading e-mail (*continued*)
from newsgroups, 688–689
overview of, 667
with POP servers, 667–668, 669–670
reading mail and news in Internet Explorer, 727
recalculation options in Excel, 346
Record Macro dialog box, 217, 468–469
recorded narration in PowerPoint presentations, 574
recording macros, 217–220
records. *See* Excel databases
Recreational Software Advisory Council (RSAC), 727
rectangles, creating, 393
relative cell references in Excel, 343
removing. *See also* clearing; deleting
character formatting, 89, 90
graphic objects in PowerPoint, 549
page and line breaks, 286–287
renaming. *See* naming
Replace All button, dangers of, 47–48
Replace dialog box, 355–356
Replace tab of Find and Replace dialog box, 47–48
replacing. *See* finding and replacing; searching
replying to messages, 672–674, 691
Report Manager software, 739
resizing. *See* sizing
restoring menus, 800–801
Restricted Sites security zone in Internet Explorer, 724, 725
Resume Wizard, 25–26
reversing print orders, 110–111, 642
Review AutoFormat Changes dialog box, 229
Rich Text (HTML) format for e-mail messages, 661, 663, 668
right tabs, 40–41
rotating graphic objects, 406, 554–555
rotating text in Excel, 371–372, 401–402
Row Height dialog box, 366
Row tab of Cell Height and Width dialog box, 128–129, 130–131
rows, Excel worksheet. *See also* Excel worksheets
changing heights of, 366
deleting, 339–340
hiding and unhiding, 367
inserting, 338
printing row headings, 441
rows, table. *See also* tables
adjusting height of, 130
aligning, 131
deleting, 124, 126
indenting, 130
inserting, 124, 126
selecting, 123–124
rows in Excel databases, 447–448
RSAC (Recreational Software Advisory Council), 727
rulers
indenting paragraphs with, 80–82
and setting tabs, 39, 40
rules
for filtering e-mail messages, 678–679
for filtering newsgroup messages, 690–691
rules, horizontal, 663
run-in indexes, 185
running
earlier Word versions with Word 98, 288
Excel macros, 473, 476
PowerPoint macros, 614–615
Word macros, 220–221

S

Save As command, 755–757
Save As dialog box, 776–777
Save As HTML Wizard, 624–629
Save AutoRecover Every *x* Minutes option, 758
Save command, 754–755
Save dialog box, 309–310, 539–540, 755
Save File as Type list box, 756
Save Options dialog box, 309–310
Save tab of Preferences dialog box, 289–290
Save Workspace dialog box, 313
saving. *See also* storing
document summaries option for, 757
e-mail attachments, 671–672
e-mail messages, 661, 669, 672
Excel charts, 415
Excel formatting as styles, 382–383
Excel workbooks
adding passwords after, 310
with AutoSave feature, 311–312
in backup files, 312
in folders, 316
in other formats, 312
overview of, 309–310
setting default folders for, 310, 524

setting options for, 309
in workspace files, 313–314
Excel worksheets, 776–777
as HTML files
Excel workbooks, 313, 487–489
PowerPoint slides, 624–629
Web pages, 719
Word documents, 36, 258–259, 261
newsgroup messages, 689
PowerPoint presentations
as HTML files, 624–629
overview of, 539, 541–542, 784
as templates, 642
Web pages, 719
Word documents
AutoRecover option, 289–290, 758
in backup files, 290, 757
document summaries option, 757
as earlier Word formats, 289
overview of, 36–37
with Save As command, 755–757
with Save command, 754–755
setting options for, 289–290, 757–758
as templates, 207
scaling. *See also* sizing
Excel worksheets for printing, 437
images, 235–236
scanning photographs, 231
scatter charts, 424
Schedule tab of Get Info dialog box, 707
screening Web site content, 726–727
ScreenTips
overview of, 12, 766
ToolTips and, 695
turning on or off, 648
scroll bars, navigating with, 34–35, 752, 753
Search dialog box, 314
searching. *See also* finding
for e-mail messages, 679–680
Internet
with AutoComplete, 703
with search engines, 715–716
with Search tab, 700–701, 716
for text, 716–717
and replacing Excel data, 355–356
and replacing Word text, 45–48
sections. *See* formatting, Word documents
security
in Internet Explorer, 723–726
locking fields, 155
locking Word documents, 65
password-protecting Excel formatting, 383–384
password-protecting Excel graphics, 395
password-protecting Excel workbooks, 309–310
Security pane of Internet Explorer Preferences dialog box, 725–726
Security Zones pane of Internet Explorer Preferences dialog box, 724–725
Select Fields tab of Query Options dialog box, 169–170
selecting
cells, VBA code for, 496
cells and ranges, shortcuts for, 525–526
graphics in Excel, 394
graphics in PowerPoint, 548
multiple Excel worksheets, 302
online directories, 651
parts of Excel charts, 418
ranges of Excel cells, 303–304, 525–526
table cells, columns, and rows, 123–124
text, 32–33
text in Outline view, 136
Send to Back option in Excel graphics, 395–396
sending messages, 659–660, 666, 691–692
Sent Mail folder in Outlook Express, 650
series, data
in Excel charts, 415, 416, 417
in PowerPoint charts, 583–586
series axis in charts, 416, 417, 577
Series dialog box, 335–336
series formulas in Excel charts, 426–427
series names in Excel charts, 417
servers
IMAP servers
deleting messages from, 675–676
overview of, 651, 653
reading mail with, 668–669
POP servers
deleting messages while online with, 676
reading mail with, 667–668, 669–670
setting up online access for, 653, 669
SSL servers, 723
Web servers, 252, 483, 621
Windows NT servers, 723
Set Up Show dialog box, 608–609

setting default folders for Excel workbooks, 310, 524
setting margins, 39, 74–75
setting options
  for checking spelling and grammar, 52–53
  for downloading files, 706, 721, 722–723
  for e-mail messages, 668
  in Internet Explorer
    buttons and bars, 695
    downloading files, 706, 721, 722–723
    History lists, 700
    screening ratings, 726–727
    security, 724–726
    subscriptions, 707–710
    Web page viewing, 712–714
  for Office Assistant, 14–15
  for PowerPoint charts, 580–581
  for printing PowerPoint presentations, 597–598, 601
  for saving Excel workbooks, 309
  for saving Word documents, 289–290, 757–758
setting up
  e-mail accounts, 654–656
  multiple users in Outlook Express, 681–682
  newsgroup accounts, 685–686
  online access for POP servers, 653, 669
Settings tab of Data Validation dialog box, 351–352
shading paragraphs, 85
shadowing Excel graphics, 399
Shape tab of Format Data Series dialog box, 585
shapes. *See* graphic objects
Sheet tab of Page Setup dialog box, 435–436, 437, 438, 440–442
shortcut keys. *See* keyboard shortcuts
shortcut menus. *See also* menus
  for chart data series, 584–585
  for Excel graphics, 390–391
  for PowerPoint presentations, 535
shortcuts for selecting cells and ranges, 525–526
showing and hiding. *See also* hiding and unhiding; turning on or off
  Excel graphics, 399
  index entries, 182
  paragraph marks, 75–76
  PowerPoint chart elements, 580–581
  TC entries, 179
signatures in e-mail messages, 665
site certificates in Internet Explorer, 723
Size tab of Format Picture dialog box, 235–236
sizing. *See also* expanding; scaling
  document pages, 74
  Excel graphics, 396–397
  fonts in Web pages, 714
  graphic objects in PowerPoint, 555
  images, 235–236
  paper size in Excel printing, 436
  resizing Excel graphics, 396–397
  text, 87–88, 89–90
  text boxes, 244–245
  WordArt, 405
slashes, preventing date formatting of, 525
Slide Layout dialog box, 547–548, 560–561
Slide Master feature, 561–564, 641
slide presentations. *See* PowerPoint presentations
Slide Show view in PowerPoint, 534, 535, 786
Slide Sorter toolbar, 639–640
Slide Sorter view in PowerPoint, 532, 533, 786, 787
Slide Transition dialog box, 600–601
Slide Transition list, 639–640
Slide view in PowerPoint
  editing text in, 539, 544, 545, 789
  overview of, 531–532, 785
small caps text option, 87–88, 89–90
smart quotes, 269
Solver software, 739
Sort dialog box, 134–135, 455–456
Sort Records tab of Query Options dialog box, 169
sorting
  e-mail messages, 679
  Excel databases
    alphanumeric values, 457
    custom sort orders, 458–459
    danger zones in, 454, 455, 457
    key fields in, 455
    overview of, 454–457
    undoing effects of, 458
  Word table data, 134–135
Sound Notes, Excel, 326
sound in PowerPoint presentations, 574
sounds, downloading, 720
space
  avoiding unwanted space in paragraphs, 76

expanding Internet Explorer screen space, 698
spacing
between table columns, 130
between text characters, 87–88, 91, 570
text in Word documents, 42–44, 77–78, 83
speaker notes in PowerPoint presentations, 604–606, 637–639
special characters. *See* characters
special effects options for Web sites, 714
spell–checking. *See* checking spelling and grammar
Spelling & Grammar tab of Preferences dialog box, 49, 51, 52–53
Spelling dialog box, 357–358
Spelling and Grammar dialog box, 50–52
splitting
Excel worksheet windows, 307
Word tables, 127–128
spreadsheets. *See* Excel workbooks; Excel worksheets
squares, creating, 393
SSL servers, 723
stacking graphic objects, 551–552
Standard tab of Color Scheme dialog box, 562, 563
Standard toolbars
in Excel, 299, 764–765
in PowerPoint, 536–537
in Word, 748–749
Standard Types tab of Chart Type dialog box, 424–426
stationery documents. *See* templates
Statistics tab of Properties dialog box, 67
status bars
in Excel, 299, 308
in Internet Explorer, 695, 702
turning on or off, 754
stock charts, 424, 580
stopping downloads, 705, 721
storing. *See also* saving
AutoText entries, 56
e-mail on removable disks, 683–684
e-mail on servers, 668
Excel macros, 469, 477–478
Excel workbooks, 523
PowerPoint macros, 612
Word macros, 215
StuffIt and StuffIt Expander programs, 672, 720
Style dialog box, 194–195, 197–198, 382–383
Style Gallery dialog box, 202–203
style sheets, 112, 713
styles, 189–205. *See also* formatting, Word documents; templates
applying new styles, 203–205
applying Normal (default) styles, 191–193
assigning to shortcut keys, 196–197
changing, 200
changing base styles, 197–199
changing graphic object styles, 554
character styles, 190
copying, 199–200
creating
based on examples, 196
based on existing styles, 195, 197–199
example, 203–205
from Excel formatting, 382–383
overview of, 193–194
with Style command, 194–195
creating tables of contents using, 174–176
creating tables of figures using, 181
defined, 189
deleting, 200
finding in Style Gallery, 202–203
formatting font styles in Excel, 372–373, 526–527
and formatting paragraphs, 86
Normal (default) styles, 191–193, 197, 199
overview of, 189–191, 212
paragraph styles, 190
redefining, 200
renaming, 200
saving Excel formatting as, 382–383
Style list box, 191–192, 195–196, 197–198
viewing while working, 201–202
Styles menu in Microsoft Organization Chart, 594, 634
Styles tab of Organizer dialog box, 199–200
styling fonts, 87–88, 90–91
subheads, inserting, 246–247
Subscribe tab of Get Info dialog box, 709
subscribing
to channels, 709–710
to newsgroups, 686–687
and unsubscribing, 688
to Web sites, 706–708
subscript text option, 87–88, 90, 91, 526–527, 568

Subscription dialog box, 706
subtext, 135
SUM function in Excel, 348
summaries, document. *See* Word documents
Summary tab
of Advanced Search dialog box, 65–66, 315–316
of Properties dialog box, 66–67, 310–311
superscript text option, 87–88, 90, 91, 526–527, 568
surface charts, 424, 579
switches
defined, 151
field switches, 152, 154–155
index switches, 185
Symbol dialog box, 98
symbols in custom number formats, 378–379
synonyms, finding, 59

T

3-D effects in Excel graphics, 399
Tab keys and tab characters in Word tables, 121
tab stops. *See also* Word documents
clearing, 42
custom tabs, 40–42
default tabs, 39
leader tabs, 42
moving, 42
overview of, 39–40
types of, 40
tab-delimited export files, 166
Table AutoFormat dialog box, 128, 132, 287
Table of Contents Options dialog box, 176
Table of Contents tab of Index and Tables dialog box, 174–177, 179
Table of Figures tab of Index and Tables dialog box, 180–181
tables, Word, 117–135
adding callouts to images in, 237
adding to PowerPoint presentations, 571, 573–574
cells in
defined, 117
deleting, 125–126
indenting, 130
inserting, 124–126
merging, 127
selecting, 123–124
columns in
adjusting space between, 130
deleting, 124, 126
formatting widths of, 128–129
inserting, 124, 126
selecting, 123–124
of text, 134
creating
with AutoFormat feature, 120, 128, 132, 287
with click-and-drag, 118
from dialog boxes, 118–119
with Draw Table feature, 119–120, 129
example, 122–123
overview of, 118
editing
deleting table elements, 124–126
inserting table elements, 124–126
merging cells, 127
overview of, 123
selecting table elements, 123–124
splitting tables, 127–128
formatting
borders, 131–132, 287–288
column widths, 128–129
converting text to tables, 132–133, 166
indenting rows, 130
overview of, 128
row alignment, 131
row height, 130
space between columns, 130
text, 122, 128, 131
gridlines in, 287–288
inserting in PowerPoint presentations, 571, 573–574
inserting in Word documents, 248
navigating within, 120–121
overview of, 117–118, 148
rows in
adjusting height of, 130
aligning, 131
deleting, 124, 126
indenting, 130
inserting, 124, 126
selecting, 123–124
sorting information in, 134–135
Tab keys, tab characters, and, 121
uses for, 133–135
wrapping text in, 122
tables of contents, 173–179

creating
from outline headings, 146–147, 174–175
overview of, 173–174
from TC entries, 176–179
using heading styles, 174–176
defined, 173
formatting, 177
overview of, 173, 186
updating fields in, 147, 178
tables of figures, 180–181
tabs, Excel worksheet
overview of, 295–296
renaming, 302
scrolling through, 301–302, 768
viewing, 301, 768
Tabs dialog box, 40–41
tags, HTML, 253, 483–484, 621–622
TC (table of contents) entries, 176–179
Template Wizard in Excel, 739
templates, PowerPoint. *See also* PowerPoint presentations
creating, 541
creating presentations with, 537–540, 635–637, 780, 783
default templates, 537–541
defined, 779
for online presentations, 537–538, 630
overview of, 540–541, 632, 780
saving presentations as, 642
templates, Word, 22–31, 205–212. *See also* styles; Word documents
applying, 207, 210–211
categories of, 23–25
copying macros to, 221–222
creating, 207, 208–209, 210–211
defined, 191, 205
editing, 31
finding in Style Gallery, 202–203
Normal (default) templates, 208–210
overview of, 22–23, 189, 205–207, 212
predefined templates, 206
saving Word documents as, 207
template wizards, 25–31
Templates and Add-ins dialog box, 215
templates in Value Pack, 738, 740
text. *See also* desktop publishing; formatting; WordArt
columns of text
in PowerPoint presentations, 566–567
in Word documents, 225–227, 246
in Word tables, 134
in Excel charts
adding unattached text to, 420
formatting, 420–421, 422–423
overview of, 415, 417
in Excel worksheets
aligning, 367–369
centering, 369–370
entering, 322, 774–775
formatting fonts and styles, 372–373
formatting numbers as text, 323, 376, 449, 525, 773
justifying, 370–371
overview of, 369
rotating, 371–372
plain text format, 661, 663–664, 719
in PowerPoint presentations
animating, 575
coloring, 567–568
editing in Outline view, 543–544, 790
editing in Slide view, 539, 544, 545, 789
embossing, 568
entering, 543
formatting fonts and styles, 567–568
headers and footers, 638–639
onscreen annotations, 642–643
shadowing, 567
speaker notes, 604–606, 637–638
superscript and subscript text, 568
WordArt, 568–571
Rich Text (HTML) format, 661, 663, 668
searching Internet for, 716–717
in Word documents
animating, 87, 89
AutoComplete feature and, 31
body text, 135
bolding, 87–88, 89–90, 193
coloring, 87–88
converting outline headings to body text, 138
converting to tables, 132–133, 166
copying and pasting, 32, 44
cutting and pasting, 44
deleting, 33, 753
dragging and dropping, 45
editing, 753–754
entering, 31, 752, 753

(continued)

text (*continued*)
finding synonyms for, 59
formatting in tables, 122, 128, 131
hiding, 87–88, 89–90
hyphenating, 59–60, 82–83
inserting drop caps in, 87
italicizing, 87–88, 89–90, 193
justifying, 82–83
moving, 44–45
moving while previewing printing, 104–105
overtyping, 754
positioning, 87, 88
searching and replacing, 45–48
selecting, 32–33
selecting in Outline view, 136
sizing, 87–88, 89–90
spacing between characters, 87–88, 91, 570
spacing in paragraphs, 42–44, 77–78, 83
subtext, 135
underlining, 87–88, 89–90
wrapping around text boxes, 245
wrapping in tables, 122
wrapping while previewing printing, 106
Text Box toolbar, 242
text boxes, 240–245. *See also* desktop publishing; graphic objects
creating, 241
in Excel worksheets
adding, 399–400
editing text in, 400
formatting text in, 400–401
rotating text in, 401–402
formatting, 242–243
for images, 234
linking, 241–242
moving, 243–244
overview of, 240–241
sizing, 244–245
wrapping text around, 245
text converters, 283–284, 740
Thesaurus, Word 98, 59
3-D PowerPoint charts, 592–593, 595
3-D View dialog box, 592–593
threads in newsgroup messages, 688
tick marks in Excel charts, 415, 417
times
entering in Excel, 324–325, 773–774
formatting in Excel, 377–378
timing settings for slide shows, 600–601
Tips & Tricks in Internet Explorer, 728
titles
adding to Excel charts, 417, 419–420
adding to PowerPoint charts, 580, 590–591
printing on successive Excel pages, 440, 528
Titles tab of Chart Options dialog box, 419–420, 581, 590–591
toolbars, 793–798. *See also* bars
adding menus to, 795
buttons
adding, 795
adding existing images to, 796
assigning AutoText entries to, 56–58
assigning macros to, 474–475, 615
copying and pasting images onto, 796
deleting, 795
drawing images onto, 797
naming, 798
overview of, 794
Chart toolbar, 418–419, 426
creating, 798
customizing, 793–798
docking, 12
Drawing toolbars
in Excel, 389–390, 393–394
in PowerPoint, 536–537, 552–554
in Word, 234
in Excel, 299, 307–308
Formatting toolbars
in Excel, 376
in PowerPoint, 536–537
in Word, 191–192
Header and Footer toolbar, 94–95, 96
Macro Recorder toolbar, 219
moving, 12, 794
Office Assistant and, 13
Outlining toolbar, 136–138, 790
in Outlook Express, 648
overview of, 11, 793
Picture toolbar, 549
in PowerPoint, 536–537
Print Preview toolbar, 103–104
restoring, 795
ScreenTips, 12
Standard toolbars
in Excel, 299, 764–765
in PowerPoint, 536–537

in Word, 748–749
Text Box toolbar, 242
turning on or off, 11, 793–794
undocking, 12
Visual Basic toolbar, 270, 469, 499–500
Web toolbars
in Excel, 484
in PowerPoint, 622
in Word, 253–254
WordArt toolbar, 404–405, 569–570
Toolbars tab of Customize dialog box, 218, 795–800
ToolTips, 695. *See also* ScreenTips
Top 10 option in AutoFilter command, 462
Track Changes tab of Preferences dialog box, 62
tracking
document changes, 62–63
visits to Web sites, 699–700, 705
transitions in PowerPoint presentations, 639–640, 642
travel presentation example, 635–640
trimming images, 236
troubleshooting
accessing Web sites, 704
Excel data entry errors, 321
Excel formula errors, 346
printing, 114
Trusted Sites security zone in Internet Explorer, 724, 725
turning on or off. *See also* hiding and unhiding; showing and hiding
AutoComplete, 703
AutoFilter, 459, 463
field codes, 175, 177
gridlines, 445
Internet Explorer bars, 695
ScreenTips, 648
smart quotes, 269
status bars, 754
text wrapping around text boxes, 245
toolbars, 11, 793–794
ToolTips, 695
underlined labels on buttons, 648

U

Unbinder application, 8, 740
underlined button labels, 648
underlined commands, 15–16
underlining text, 87–88, 89–90
Undo command
desktop publishing and, 229
Excel worksheets and, 325, 771
sorting Excel databases and, 458
undocking toolbars, 12
unhiding. *See* hiding and unhiding; showing and hiding
updating fields. *See also* fields
linked to other data sources, 170–171
and links before printing, 111
overview of, 153
in tables of contents, 147, 178
URLs (Uniform Resource Locators), 252, 483, 621
user input boxes, VBA code for, 498

V

validating Excel data, 351–354
value axis in charts, 416, 417, 577
values, 319. *See also* Excel worksheets
VBA (Visual Basic for Applications), 263–271, 491–501. *See also* macros
creating PowerPoint macros with, 611–613
examples, 499
getting help with, 614, 616, 739
in macros, 263–268, 491–497, 740
Microsoft Visual Basic and, 267, 493
overview of, 263, 271, 491, 500–501
VBA code
control statements in, 497
for dialog boxes, 268–269, 497–498
editing, 269–270, 494, 499, 617
for entering data, 496
headers and footers in, 268, 496
for inserting comments, 267, 495–496
in macro examples, 265–268, 494–497, 612–613
printing, 270, 499
for selecting cells, 496
smart quotes and, 269
for user input boxes, 498
viewing, 265, 494
Visual Basic toolbar, 270, 499–500
View tab of Preferences dialog box, 38, 175
viewing. *See also* previewing; showing and hiding
comments, 64
default AutoText entries, 56

(continued)

viewing (*continued*)
document summaries, 66–67
e-mail attachments, 670–671
e-mail contacts, 659
Excel formulas, 345
field codes, 152–153, 175
multiple Excel worksheets, 524
newsgroup messages, 688–689
Office Assistant tips, 14
paragraph formatting, 77
presentations on non-PowerPoint computers, 609, 642
styles while working, 201–202
VBA code, 265, 494
Web page options for, 712–714
views
expanding in Excel worksheets, 306
in PowerPoint, 531–535, 785–787
in Word, 37–38
viruses in PowerPoint macros, 616
Visual Basic, Microsoft, 267, 493
Visual Basic for Applications. *See* VBA
Visual Basic Editor, 265
Visual Basic toolbar, 270, 469, 499–500

W

Walkenbach, John, 616
warnings. *See* danger zones
Web. *See also* World Wide Web
Web browsers, 252, 483, 621. *See also* Internet Explorer
Web Content pane of Internet Explorer Preferences dialog box, 712–714
Web Page Wizard, 31, 259–261
Web pages. *See also* Internet Explorer; Web sites
copying and pasting data in, 719
frames in, 702
overview of, 701–702
plug-ins and, 714
printing, 723
saving, 719
Web servers, 252, 483, 621
Web site addresses
Aladdin, 672, 720
DiamondSoft Font Reserve, 739
file format converters, 756
Four11 e-mail directory, 651
Microsoft Internet Explorer, 728
Microsoft Office 98, 652
Microsoft PowerPoint Viewer, 609, 642
President of the United States, 621
RSAC (Recreational Software Advisory Council), 727
StuffIt Expander, 672, 720
virus protection information, 616
Web sites, 701–718. *See also* Internet Explorer; Web pages
accessing
with address bars, 703
with Apple Data Detectors, 704–705
AutoComplete and, 703
by clicking links, 705
error messages in, 704
with Favorites tab, 705
with History tab, 705
multiple connections option for, 706
with Open command, 704
overview of, 702–703
stopping, 705
archiving, 708, 717
browsing offline, 708, 710, 717–718
color options, 713, 728
cookies and, 715
creating hyperlinks from slides to, 623–624
defined, 701–702
font options, 713–714
getting to, 702–706
language option, 714
screening content of, 726–727
searching, 700–701, 703, 715–717
setting viewing options, 712–714
special effects options, 714
style sheets option, 713
subscribing to, 706–708
subscribing to channels in, 709–710
tracking visits to, 699–700, 705
visiting, 702
Web toolbars
in Excel, 484
in PowerPoint, 622
in Word, 253–254
Whitehouse Web site, 621
widow text lines, 79
widths
of border lines, 84
of Excel worksheet columns, 321, 365–366
of PowerPoint chart columns, 582

of table columns, 128–129
of Word document columns, 226
windows, splitting, 307
Windows NT servers, 723
wizards
AutoContent Wizard, 557–560, 780, 781–783
Award Wizard, 27
Calendar Wizard, 27–28
Chart Wizard, 408–413
Envelope Wizard, 26
Fax Wizard, 26
File Conversion Wizard, 738
Internet Assistant Wizard, 487–489
Letter Wizard, 28, 29
Mailing Label Wizard, 27
Memo Wizard, 28–29
Newsletter Wizard, 29–30, 248–249
Paste Function Wizard, 349–351
Pleading Wizard, 30
Resume Wizard, 25–26
Save As HTML Wizard, 624–629
Template Wizard in Excel, 739
Web Page Wizard, 259–261
Word document template wizards, 25–31
Word 98, 251–261, 745–759
adding file converters to, 283–284
AutoComplete feature, 31
AutoCorrect feature, 55–58, 356–357
AutoFormat features
applying headings, 205
converting Internet addresses to hyperlinks, 257
creating borders, 237, 288
creating tables, 120, 128, 132, 287
formatting documents, 227–229
overview of, 61
AutoRecover feature, 289–290
Draw Table feature, 119–120, 129
launching, 21, 745
main screen
Formatting toolbar, 748, 750–751
overview of, 745–747
Standard toolbar, 748–749
opening Web documents in, 254–255
overview of, 3, 21, 68–69
running earlier versions of Word with, 288
saving documents as earlier Word formats, 289
special printing options, 108–111
Thesaurus, 59
on the Web, 251–261
creating hyperlinks in Word documents, 255–257
creating Web pages, 259–261
opening Web documents, 254–255
overview of, 251–252, 261
publishing Word documents, 258–259
saving Word documents as HTML files, 36, 258–259, 261
Web toolbar, 253–254
Word formatting unsupported by HTML, 36, 258–259, 261
Word documents, 21–69. *See also* formatting, Word documents; styles
adding
bulleted lists, 60–61, 78, 290–291
bullets to outline headings, 140–141
graphics, 33–34
paragraph numbers, 60–61
AutoComplete feature and, 31
AutoCorrect feature and, 55–58, 356–357
AutoFormat feature and, 61
AutoSummarize feature and, 67–68
AutoText entries and
assigning to toolbars, 56–58
deleting, 58
editing, 58
inserting, 56
versus macros, 213–214
printing, 58, 112
storing, 56
viewing default entries, 56
avoiding bad typing habits, 31
checking spelling and grammar
with custom dictionaries, 53–55, 358
grammar-checking, 51–52
overview of, 48–49
setting options for, 52–53
spell-checking, 49–50
collaborating on
and comparing, 63
creating comments, 63–65
cutting and pasting comments, 64–65
deleting comments, 64
finding comments, 65
inserting comments, 267, 495–496
and locking, 65

(continued)

Word documents (*continued*)
printing comments, 64–65
and tracking changes, 62–63
viewing comments, 64
comparing, 63
copying and pasting graphics, 33
copying and pasting text, 32, 44
creating, 6–7, 21–22, 751
creating hyperlinks in, 255–257
cutting and pasting text, 44
deleting, 289
deleting text in, 33, 753
document summaries
AutoSummarize feature, 67–68
editing, 66–67
for Excel workbooks, 310–311
option for saving, 757
overview of, 65–66
for PowerPoint presentations, 542–543
viewing, 66–67
dragging and dropping text, 45
editing text, 753–754
entering text, 31, 752, 753
hyphenating text, 59–60, 82–83
inserting graphics, 33–34
line spacing in, 42–43, 77–78, 83
locking, 65
margin settings, 39
Master Document view, 37–38
moving text, 44–45
navigating
with Document Map view, 36
with keyboard shortcuts, 34–35, 752–753
with mouse, 752
with scroll bars, 34–35, 752, 753
Normal view, 37
Online Layout view, 37–38
opening, 7–8, 21–22, 751–752
Outline view, 37, 135
overview of, 68–69
Page Layout view, 37–38, 39
paragraph spacing in, 44, 77–78, 83
preventing unwanted page breaks in, 286–287
printing
collating while, 110
document information, 111–112, 113
General options for, 107–108
odd or even pages, 110
overview of, 106, 758
portions of, 109, 759
in reverse order, 110–111
several page ranges, 109
special options for, 108–112, 113
updating fields and links before, 111
without opening, 759
publishing on the Web, 258–259
removing unwanted page breaks in, 286–287
saving
AutoRecover option for, 289–290, 758
in backup files, 290, 757
document summaries option, 757
as earlier Word formats, 289
fast saves option, 757
as HTML files, 36, 258–259, 261
overview of, 36–37, 754
with Save As command, 755–757
with Save command, 754–755
setting options for, 289–290, 757–758
as templates, 207
searching and replacing text, 45–48
selecting text, 32–33
spacing between characters in, 87–88, 91, 570
spacing text in, 42–44, 77–78, 83
tab stops
clearing, 42
custom tabs, 40–42
default tabs, 39
leader tabs, 42
moving, 42
overview of, 39–40
types of, 40
templates, 22–31, 205–212
applying, 207, 210–211
categories of, 23–25
copying macros to, 221–222
creating, 207, 208–209, 210–211
defined, 191, 205
editing, 31
finding in Style Gallery, 202–203
Normal (default) templates, 208–210
overview of, 22–23, 189, 205–207, 212
predefined templates, 206
saving Word documents as, 207
template wizards, 25–31
text
AutoComplete feature and, 31

copying and pasting, 32, 44
cutting and pasting, 44
deleting, 33, 753
dragging and dropping, 45
editing, 753–754
entering, 31, 752, 753
finding synonyms for, 59
hyphenating, 59–60, 82–83
moving, 44–45
overtyping, 754
searching and replacing, 45–48
selecting, 32–33
spacing, 42–44, 77–78, 83
tracking changes to, 62–63
view options for, 37–38
Word 98 Thesaurus and, 59
Word macros. *See* macros in Word
Word Speak, 740
Word tables. *See* tables
WordArt, 402–406. *See also* graphic objects; text
adding to Excel worksheets, 402–403
adding to PowerPoint presentations, 568–571
changing shapes of, 406
coloring, 405
examples, 571
overview of, 4, 402
rotating, 406
shape options, 569
sizing, 405
toolbar, 404–405, 569–570
WordArt Gallery dialog box, 402–403, 568–569
Work Offline feature in Outlook Express, 689
World Wide Web. *See also* Internet; Web pages; Web sites
addresses, 252, 483, 621
defined, 252, 483, 621
Excel 98 and, 481–489
creating hyperlinks in worksheets, 484–487
Internet Assistant Wizard, 487–489
overview of, 481–484, 489
publishing worksheets and charts on the Web, 487–489
saving Excel data as HTML files, 313, 487–489
Web toolbar, 484
HTML and, 253, 483–484, 621–622
Internet and, 252, 482, 621
intranets and, 252, 483, 621
PowerPoint 98 and, 619–630
connecting to networks, 620
creating hyperlinks to Office documents, 623
creating hyperlinks to Web sites, 623–624
online presentation templates, 537–538, 630
overview of, 619–622, 630
publishing presentations on the Web, 624–629
saving slides as HTML files, 624–629
Web toolbar, 622
Web browsers, 252, 483, 621
Web servers, 252, 483, 621
Word 98 and, 251–261
creating hyperlinks in documents, 255–257
creating Web pages, 259–261
opening Web documents, 254–255
overview of, 251–252, 261
publishing documents on the Web, 258–259
saving Word documents as HTML files, 36, 258–259, 261
Web toolbar, 253–254
Wrapping tab of Format Picture dialog box, 106
wrapping text
around text boxes, 245
in Excel worksheets, 370, 774–775
while previewing printing, 106
in Word tables, 122

X

XY scatter charts, 579

Y

Yahoo! search en 254–255

CW00E90363

Collins

OFFICIAL SCRABBLE™ BRAND Crossword Game WORDS

S

1

Published by Collins
An imprint of HarperCollins Publishers
Westerhill Road
Bishopbriggs
Glasgow G64 2QT

Fifth Edition 2019

10 9 8 7 6 5 4 3 2 1

ISBN 978-0-00-832012-6

www.harpercollins.co.uk/scrabble

Typeset by Davidson Publishing Solutions, Glasgow

Printed in Great Britain by Clays Ltd, Elcograf S.p.A

A catalogue record for this book is available from the British Library.

If you would like to comment on any aspect of this book, please contact us at the given address or online.
E-mail: puzzles@harpercollins.co.uk
facebook.com/collinsdictionary
@collinsdict

MIX
Paper from responsible sources
FSC™ C007454

This book is produced from independently certified FSC™ paper to ensure responsible forest management.

For more information visit: www.harpercollins.co.uk/green

Contents

Foreword by Philip Nelkon	v
Introduction	vii
Other Scrabble resources	viii
Alphabetical list of two-letter words	x
Alphabetical list of three-letter words	xi
Two to nine letter words	1
Ten to fifteen letter words	691

Scrabble Consultants
Darryl Francis
David Sutton

Editor
Mary O'Neill

Computing Support
Claire Dimeo

For the Publisher
Gerry Breslin
Kerry Ferguson

Foreword by Philip Nelkon

Is it already four years since we got to play *lolz* and *xed* on a Scrabble board? Congratulations to the Collins team led by Darryl Francis and David Sutton for the hard work they have done in identifying nearly 3,000 new words for us to use and abuse in this new edition of *Collins Official Scrabble Words* (OSW). Now, for the first time, there is a word to describe OSW aficionados – *wordies*! There's also *boardies*, which would be a great collective noun for Scrabble fanatics, though it's actually an Australian term for men's shorts.

There's more good news. We all know that 2-letter words are the lifeblood of high-score Scrabble, enabling us to make those high-scoring parallel plays involving many words. Now, for the first time since 2007, there are three new 2-letter words to enhance our Scrabble firepower. If you've been following the media, you'll have seen that one of these – *ok* – has been the source of much controversy. Well, the word list compilers have gone *judgy* and made their decision – it's in.

A fair smattering of words that I have seen played incorrectly over the board in the past make it, at last, into this edition, words like *zen*, *earnt* and *laxed*. On publication of the last list, I was personally accosted by two irate elderly gentlemen who were fans of 'figgy pie' and couldn't believe that *figgy* wasn't allowed, but the word has now been included. That's the sort of passion Scrabble can engender. You might also be getting emotional over the political situation at the moment but there is one incontestable benefit of Brexit (not shown due to being a proper noun) – *remainer* has finally made it into the Dictionary.

With all these new terms, it's tempting to fantasize over their source. A couple of editions ago, a large number of cricketing terms appeared, this time it's the turn of obscure currencies. The undoubted star is *qapik*, from Azerbaijan, that's going to be helpful if you don't have a U with your Q. There's also *thetri*, *togrog*, *metica*, *maraca* and even *kopiyky*, though I think that one is unlikely to come in useful on a regular basis. Another regular contributor is food, which gives us a couple of potentially fruitful 3's – *bao* and *ume*. There are other foodie terms like *nduja*, *jollof*, *labneh* and *arancini*, which I predict will start to appear regularly on Scrabble boards in the future.

What else will enhance our play? Well, there are some useful 7- and 8-letter words; these are the most effective for playing all your tiles in one go and getting a 50-point bonus. *Rendang* could have been included in the food section and also has a high probability of turning up on your rack, as do *galants*, *othered*, *roguier* and *telogen*. Amongst 8-letter words there are *transmen*, *nonstate* and *sonliest*.

No matter how you enjoy your Scrabble – in tournaments, online or at home – this is the go-to book for adjudication and for adding ammunition to your Scrabble armoury.

Philip Nelkon
Four-time National Scrabble Champion

Introduction

This new edition of *Collins Official Scrabble Words* marks the completion of an epic amount of work carried out by the World English-Language Scrabble Players Association (WESPA) Dictionary Committee, comprising Darryl Francis, Chairman, with David Sutton and others, working in tandem with Collins lexicographers. The team at Collins had just completed work on the largest single-volume English dictionary in print, *Collins English Dictionary*, and presented the WESPA Dictionary Committee with a huge selection task to identify the candidates for inclusion according to the rules that apply to the Scrabble word list, which now boasts 279,496 word forms and will be officially adopted for use in WESPA tournaments by 1st July 2019.

Rules for the Scrabble word list

- Only includes words of between 2 and 15 letters in length
- Does not include proper nouns, place names, and words with an initial capital letter, unless such words can also be spelt with a lowercase initial letter
- Does not include abbreviations, prefixes, suffixes, words requiring apostrophes or hyphens
- Includes foreign words that are considered to have been absorbed into the English language
- Includes inflected forms, such as plurals and verb forms, eg plumb, plumbs, plumbed, plumbing
- Includes words that are old, obsolete, dialectal, historical and/or literary
- Includes World English, including spelling and variants from the US, South Africa, Australia, New Zealand, etc
- Includes words that are denoted contractions, short forms and slang
- Includes words which may be deemed rude or offensive

Disclaimer

The words in this list are published in accordance with the rules of the WESPA Dictionary Committee and based on the strict criteria above. They are valid for use in Scrabble games under the aegis of WESPA, and no word is excluded on the grounds of religion, gender, race, or for any reason other than that it is an invalid word form for the game of Scrabble. The presence or exclusion of any word does not in any way represent the views of WESPA or the Publisher, HarperCollins.

The Collins Editorial Team and WESPA

Other Scrabble resources

Associations

World English-Language Scrabble Players Association (WESPA) – www.wespa.org

The WESPA website also provides access to resources for national associations, tournament organizers, players and youth players.

Association of British Scrabble Players (ABSP) – www.absp.org.uk

The ABSP website includes details of UK Scrabble clubs and UK tournaments.

North American Scrabble Players Association (NASPA) – www.scrabbleplayers.org

The NASPA website contains numerous word lists and lists of further Scrabble resources.

Mindsports Academy – www.mindsportsacademy.com

Facebook

Several Scrabble groups, including:

World English-Language Scrabble Players Association

Scrabble International

Scrabble Snippetz

Collins Scrabble Players

Mindsports Academy

Interactive Scrabble games

Internet Scrabble Club (ISC) – www.isc.ro

Mobile phone – Real Networks

Sky Interactive – Sky TV platform

iTouch / iPhone / Android / iPad – Electronic Arts (EA)

Collins Scrabble App

Download the Collins Official SCRABBLE™ app from the App Store.

Perfect for adjudication, solving and training.

Collins Scrabble Tools online

www.collinsdictionary.com/scrabble/scrabble-tools

Tools and tips, plus *Collins Scrabble Word Finder*, giving instant access to all official playable Scrabble words and scores.

Alphabetical list of two-letter words

AA
AB
AD
AE
AG
AH
AI
AL
AM
AN
AR
AS
AT
AW
AX
AY
BA
BE
BI
BO
BY
CH
DA
DE
DI
DO
EA
ED
EE
EF
EH
EL
EM
EN
ER
ES
ET
EW
EX
FA
FE
FY
GI
GO
GU
HA
HE
HI
HM
HO
ID
IF
IN
IO
IS
IT
JA
JO
KA
KI
KO
KY
LA
LI
LO
MA
ME
MI
MM
MO
MU
MY
NA
NE
NO
NU
NY
OB
OD
OE
OF
OH
OI
OK
OM
ON
OO
OP
OR
OS
OU
OW
OX
OY
PA
PE
PI
PO
QI
RE
SH
SI
SO
ST
TA
TE
TI
TO
UG
UH
UM
UN
UP
UR
US
UT
WE
WO
XI
XU
YA
YE
YO
YU
ZA
ZE
ZO

Alphabetical list of three-letter words

AAH
AAL
AAS
ABA
ABB
ABO
ABS
ABY
ACE
ACH
ACT
ADD
ADO
ADS
ADZ
AFF
AFT
AGA
AGE
AGO
AGS
AHA
AHI
AHS
AIA
AID
AIL
AIM
AIN
AIR
AIS
AIT
AJI
AKA
AKE
ALA
ALB
ALE
ALF
ALL
ALP
ALS
ALT
ALU
AMA
AME
AMI
AMP
AMU
ANA
AND
ANE
ANI
ANN
ANS
ANT
ANY
APE
APO
APP
APT
ARB
ARC
ARD
ARE
ARF
ARK
ARM
ARS
ART
ARY
ASH
ASK
ASP
ASS
ATE
ATS
ATT
AUA
AUE
AUF
AUK
AVA
AVE
AVO
AWA
AWE
AWK
AWL
AWN
AXE
AYE
AYS
AYU
AZO
BAA
BAC
BAD
BAE
BAG
BAH
BAL
BAM
BAN
BAO
BAP
BAR
BAS
BAT
BAY
BED
BEE
BEG
BEL
BEN
BES
BET
BEY
BEZ
BIB
BID
BIG
BIN
BIO
BIS
BIT
BIZ
BOA
BOB
BOD
BOG
BOH
BOI
BOK
BON
BOO
BOP
BOR
BOS
BOT
BOW
BOX
BOY
BRA
BRO
BRR
BRU
BUB
BUD
BUG
BUM
BUN
BUR
BUS
BUT
BUY
BYE
BYS
CAA
CAB

CAD
CAF
CAG
CAL
CAM
CAN
CAP
CAR
CAT
CAW
CAY
CAZ
CEE
CEL
CEP
CHA
CHE
CHI
CID
CIG
CIS
CIT
CLY
COB
COD
COG
COL
CON
COO
COP
COR
COS
COT
COW

COX
COY
COZ
CRU
CRY
CUB
CUD
CUE
CUM
CUP
CUR
CUT
CUZ
CWM
DAB
DAD
DAE
DAG
DAH
DAK
DAL
DAM
DAN
DAP
DAS
DAW
DAY
DEB
DEE
DEF
DEG
DEI
DEL
DEN

DEP
DEV
DEW
DEX
DEY
DIB
DID
DIE
DIF
DIG
DIM
DIN
DIP
DIS
DIT
DIV
DOB
DOC
DOD
DOE
DOF
DOG
DOH
DOL
DOM
DON
DOO
DOP
DOR
DOS
DOT
DOW
DOX
DOY

DRY
DSO
DUB
DUD
DUE
DUG
DUH
DUI
DUM
DUN
DUO
DUP
DUX
DYE
DZO
EAN
EAR
EAS
EAT
EAU
EBB
ECH
ECO
ECU
EDH
EDS
EEK
EEL
EEN
EEW
EFF
EFS
EFT
EGG

EGO
EHS
EIK
EKE
ELD
ELF
ELK
ELL
ELM
ELS
ELT
EME
EMO
EMS
EMU
END
ENE
ENG
ENS
EON
ERA
ERE
ERF
ERG
ERK
ERM
ERN
ERR
ERS
ESS
EST
ETA
ETH
EUK

EVE
EVO
EWE
EWK
EWT
EXO
EYE
FAA
FAB
FAD
FAE
FAG
FAH
FAN
FAP
FAR
FAS
FAT
FAW
FAX
FAY
FED
FEE
FEG
FEH
FEM
FEN
FER
FES
FET
FEU
FEW
FEY
FEZ
FIB
FID
FIE
FIG
FIL
FIN
FIR
FIT
FIX
FIZ
FLU
FLY
FOB
FOE
FOG
FOH
FON
FOO
FOP
FOR
FOU
FOX
FOY
FRA
FRO
FRY
FUB
FUD
FUG
FUM
FUN
FUR
GAB
GAD
GAE
GAG
GAK
GAL
GAM
GAN
GAP
GAR
GAS
GAT
GAU
GAW
GAY
GED
GEE
GEL
GEM
GEN
GEO
GER
GET
GEY
GHI
GIB
GID
GIE
GIF
GIG
GIN
GIO
GIP
GIS
GIT
GJU
GNU
GOA
GOB
GOD
GOE
GON
GOO
GOR
GOS
GOT
GOV
GOX
GOY
GRR
GUB
GUE
GUL
GUM
GUN
GUP
GUR
GUS
GUT
GUV
GUY
GYM
GYP
HAD
HAE
HAG
HAH
HAJ
HAM
HAN
HAO
HAP
HAS
HAT
HAW
HAY
HEH
HEM
HEN
HEP
HER
HES
HET
HEW
HEX
HEY
HIC
HID
HIE
HIM
HIN
HIP
HIS
HIT
HMM
HOA
HOB
HOC
HOD
HOE
HOG
HOH
HOI
HOM

HON	INS	JOT	KIS	LES
HOO	ION	JOW	KIT	LET
HOP	IOS	JOY	KOA	LEU
HOS	IRE	JUD	KOB	LEV
HOT	IRK	JUG	KOI	LEW
HOW	ISH	JUN	KON	LEX
HOX	ISM	JUS	KOP	LEY
HOY	ISO	JUT	KOR	LEZ
HUB	ITA	KAB	KOS	LIB
HUE	ITS	KAE	KOW	LID
HUG	IVY	KAF	KUE	LIE
HUH	IWI	KAI	KYE	LIG
HUI	JAB	KAK	KYU	LIN
HUM	JAG	KAM	LAB	LIP
HUN	JAI	KAS	LAC	LIS
HUP	JAK	KAT	LAD	LIT
HUT	JAM	KAW	LAG	LOB
HYE	JAP	KAY	LAH	LOD
HYP	JAR	KEA	LAM	LOG
ICE	JAW	KEB	LAP	LOO
ICH	JAY	KED	LAR	LOP
ICK	JEE	KEF	LAS	LOR
ICY	JET	KEG	LAT	LOS
IDE	JEU	KEN	LAV	LOT
IDS	JEW	KEP	LAW	LOU
IFF	JIB	KET	LAX	LOW
IFS	JIG	KEX	LAY	LOX
IGG	JIN	KEY	LEA	LOY
ILK	JIZ	KHI	LED	LUD
ILL	JOB	KID	LEE	LUG
IMP	JOE	KIF	LEG	LUM
ING	JOG	KIN	LEI	LUN
INK	JOL	KIP	LEK	LUR
INN	JOR	KIR	LEP	LUV

LUX
LUZ
LYE
LYM
MAA
MAC
MAD
MAE
MAG
MAK
MAL
MAM
MAN
MAP
MAR
MAS
MAT
MAW
MAX
MAY
MED
MEE
MEG
MEH
MEL
MEM
MEN
MES
MET
MEU
MEW
MHO
MIB
MIC

MID
MIG
MIL
MIM
MIR
MIS
MIX
MIZ
MMM
MNA
MOA
MOB
MOC
MOD
MOE
MOG
MOI
MOL
MOM
MON
MOO
MOP
MOR
MOS
MOT
MOU
MOW
MOY
MOZ
MUD
MUG
MUM
MUN
MUS

MUT
MUX
MYC
NAB
NAE
NAG
NAH
NAM
NAN
NAP
NAS
NAT
NAV
NAW
NAY
NEB
NED
NEE
NEF
NEG
NEK
NEP
NET
NEW
NIB
NID
NIE
NIL
NIM
NIP
NIS
NIT
NIX
NOB

NOD
NOG
NOH
NOM
NON
NOO
NOR
NOS
NOT
NOW
NOX
NOY
NTH
NUB
NUG
NUN
NUR
NUS
NUT
NYE
NYM
NYS
OAF
OAK
OAR
OAT
OBA
OBE
OBI
OBO
OBS
OCA
OCH
ODA

ODD
ODE
ODS
OES
OFF
OFT
OHM
OHO
OHS
OIK
OIL
OIS
OKA
OKE
OLD
OLE
OLM
OMA
OMS
ONE
ONO
ONS
ONY
OOF
OOH
OOM
OON
OOP
OOR
OOS
OOT
OPA
OPE
OPS

OPT
ORA
ORB
ORC
ORD
ORE
ORF
ORG
ORS
ORT
OSE
OUD
OUK
OUP
OUR
OUS
OUT
OVA
OWE
OWL
OWN
OWT
OXO
OXY
OYE
OYS
PAC
PAD
PAH
PAK
PAL
PAM
PAN
PAP

PAR
PAS
PAT
PAV
PAW
PAX
PAY
PEA
PEC
PED
PEE
PEG
PEH
PEL
PEN
PEP
PER
PES
PET
PEW
PHI
PHO
PHT
PIA
PIC
PIE
PIG
PIN
PIP
PIR
PIS
PIT
PIU
PIX

PLU
PLY
POA
POD
POH
POI
POL
POM
POO
POP
POS
POT
POW
POX
POZ
PRE
PRO
PRY
PSI
PST
PUB
PUD
PUG
PUH
PUL
PUN
PUP
PUR
PUS
PUT
PUY
PWN
PYA
PYE

PYX
QAT
QIN
QIS
QUA
RAD
RAG
RAH
RAI
RAJ
RAM
RAN
RAP
RAS
RAT
RAV
RAW
RAX
RAY
REB
REC
RED
REE
REF
REG
REH
REI
REM
REN
REO
REP
RES
RET
REV

REW
REX
REZ
RHO
RHY
RIA
RIB
RID
RIF
RIG
RIM
RIN
RIP
RIT
RIZ
ROB
ROC
ROD
ROE
ROK
ROM
ROO
ROT
ROW
RUB
RUC
RUD
RUE
RUG
RUM
RUN
RUT
RYA
RYE

RYU
SAB
SAC
SAD
SAE
SAG
SAI
SAL
SAM
SAN
SAP
SAR
SAT
SAU
SAV
SAW
SAX
SAY
SAZ
SEA
SEC
SED
SEE
SEG
SEI
SEL
SEN
SER
SET
SEV
SEW
SEX
SEY
SEZ
SHA
SHE
SHH
SHO
SHY
SIB
SIC
SIF
SIG
SIK
SIM
SIN
SIP
SIR
SIS
SIT
SIX
SKA
SKI
SKY
SLY
SMA
SNY
SOB
SOC
SOD
SOG
SOH
SOL
SOM
SON
SOP
SOS
SOT
SOU
SOV
SOW
SOX
SOY
SOZ
SPA
SPY
SRI
STY
SUB
SUD
SUE
SUG
SUI
SUK
SUM
SUN
SUP
SUQ
SUR
SUS
SWY
SYE
SYN
TAB
TAD
TAE
TAG
TAI
TAJ
TAK
TAM
TAN
TAO
TAP
TAR
TAS
TAT
TAU
TAV
TAW
TAX
TAY
TEA
TEC
TED
TEE
TEF
TEG
TEL
TEN
TES
TET
TEW
TEX
THE
THO
THY
TIC
TID
TIE
TIG
TIK
TIL
TIN
TIP
TIS
TIT
TIX
TIZ
TOC
TOD
TOE
TOG
TOM
TON
TOO
TOP
TOR
TOT
TOW
TOY
TRY
TSK
TUB
TUG
TUI
TUM
TUN
TUP
TUT
TUX
TWA
TWO
TWP
TYE
TYG
UDO
UDS
UEY
UFO

UGH
UGS
UKE
ULE
ULU
UME
UMM
UMP
UMS
UMU
UNI
UNS
UPO
UPS
URB
URD
URE
URN
URP
USE
UTA
UTE
UTS
UTU
UVA
VAC
VAE
VAG
VAN
VAR
VAS
VAT
VAU
VAV
VAW
VAX
VEE
VEG
VET
VEX
VIA
VID
VIE
VIG
VIM
VIN
VIS
VLY
VOE
VOG
VOL
VOM
VOR
VOW
VOX
VUG
VUM
WAB
WAD
WAE
WAG
WAI
WAN
WAP
WAR
WAS
WAT
WAW
WAX
WAY
WAZ
WEB
WED
WEE
WEM
WEN
WET
WEX
WEY
WHA
WHO
WHY
WIG
WIN
WIS
WIT
WIZ
WOE
WOF
WOG
WOK
WON
WOO
WOP
WOS
WOT
WOW
WOX
WRY
WUD
WUS
WUZ
WYE
WYN
XED
XIS
YAD
YAE
YAG
YAH
YAK
YAM
YAP
YAR
YAS
YAW
YAY
YEA
YEH
YEN
YEP
YER
YES
YET
YEW
YEX
YEZ
YGO
YID
YIN
YIP
YOB
YOD
YOK
YOM
YON
YOU
YOW
YUG
YUK
YUM
YUP
YUS
ZAG
ZAP
ZAS
ZAX
ZEA
ZED
ZEE
ZEK
ZEL
ZEN
ZEP
ZEX
ZHO
ZIG
ZIN
ZIP
ZIT
ZIZ
ZOA
ZOL
ZOO
ZOS
ZUZ
ZZZ

two to nine letter words

A

AA
AAH
AAHED
AAHING
AAHS
AAL
AALII
AALIIS
AALS
AARDVARK
AARDVARKS
AARDWOLF
AARGH
AARRGH
AARRGHH
AARTI
AARTIS
AAS
AASVOGEL
AASVOGELS
AB
ABA
ABAC
ABACA
ABACAS
ABACI
ABACK
ABACS
ABACTINAL
ABACTOR
ABACTORS
ABACUS
ABACUSES
ABAFT
ABAKA
ABAKAS
ABALONE
ABALONES
ABAMP
ABAMPERE
ABAMPERES
ABAMPS
ABAND
ABANDED
ABANDING
ABANDON
ABANDONED
ABANDONEE
ABANDONER
ABANDONS
ABANDS
ABAPICAL
ABAS
ABASE
ABASED
ABASEDLY
ABASEMENT
ABASER
ABASERS
ABASES
ABASH
ABASHED
ABASHEDLY
ABASHES
ABASHING
ABASHLESS
ABASHMENT
ABASIA
ABASIAS
ABASING
ABASK
ABATABLE
ABATE
ABATED
ABATEMENT
ABATER
ABATERS
ABATES
ABATING
ABATIS
ABATISES
ABATOR
ABATORS
ABATTIS
ABATTISES
ABATTOIR
ABATTOIRS
ABATTU
ABATURE
ABATURES
ABAXIAL
ABAXILE
ABAYA
ABAYAS
ABB
ABBA
ABBACIES
ABBACY
ABBAS
ABBATIAL
ABBE
ABBED
ABBES
ABBESS
ABBESSES
ABBEY
ABBEYS
ABBOT
ABBOTCIES
ABBOTCY
ABBOTS
ABBOTSHIP
ABBS
ABCEE
ABCEES
ABCOULOMB
ABDABS
ABDICABLE
ABDICANT
ABDICANTS
ABDICATE
ABDICATED
ABDICATES
ABDICATOR
ABDOMEN
ABDOMENS
ABDOMINA
ABDOMINAL
ABDUCE
ABDUCED
ABDUCENS
ABDUCENT
ABDUCES
ABDUCING
ABDUCT
ABDUCTED
ABDUCTEE
ABDUCTEES
ABDUCTING
ABDUCTION
ABDUCTOR
ABDUCTORS
ABDUCTS
ABEAM
ABEAR
ABEARING
ABEARS
ABED
ABEGGING
ABEIGH
ABELE
ABELES
ABELIA
ABELIAN
ABELIAS
ABELMOSK
ABELMOSKS
ABER
ABERNETHY
ABERRANCE
ABERRANCY
ABERRANT
ABERRANTS
ABERRATE
ABERRATED
ABERRATES
ABERS
ABESSIVE
ABESSIVES
ABET
ABETMENT
ABETMENTS
ABETS
ABETTAL
ABETTALS
ABETTED
ABETTER
ABETTERS
ABETTING
ABETTOR
ABETTORS
ABEYANCE
ABEYANCES
ABEYANCY
ABEYANT
ABFARAD
ABFARADS
ABHENRIES
ABHENRY
ABHENRYS
ABHOR
ABHORRED
ABHORRENT
ABHORRER
ABHORRERS
ABHORRING
ABHORS
ABID
ABIDANCE
ABIDANCES
ABIDDEN
ABIDE
ABIDED
ABIDER
ABIDERS
ABIDES
ABIDING
ABIDINGLY
ABIDINGS
ABIES

ABIETES
ABIETIC
ABIGAIL
ABIGAILS
ABILITIES
ABILITY
ABIOGENIC
ABIOSES
ABIOSIS
ABIOTIC
ABITUR
ABITURS
ABJECT
ABJECTED
ABJECTING
ABJECTION
ABJECTLY
ABJECTS
ABJOINT
ABJOINTED
ABJOINTS
ABJURE
ABJURED
ABJURER
ABJURERS
ABJURES
ABJURING
ABLATE
ABLATED
ABLATES
ABLATING
ABLATION
ABLATIONS
ABLATIVAL
ABLATIVE
ABLATIVES
ABLATOR
ABLATORS
ABLAUT
ABLAUTS
ABLAZE
ABLE
ABLED
ABLEGATE
ABLEGATES
ABLEISM
ABLEISMS
ABLEIST
ABLEISTS
ABLER
ABLES
ABLEST
ABLET
ABLETS
ABLING
ABLINGS
ABLINS
ABLOOM
ABLOW
ABLUENT
ABLUENTS
ABLUSH
ABLUTED
ABLUTION
ABLUTIONS
ABLY
ABMHO
ABMHOS
ABNEGATE
ABNEGATED
ABNEGATES
ABNEGATOR
ABNORMAL
ABNORMALS
ABNORMITY
ABNORMOUS
ABO
ABOARD
ABODE
ABODED
ABODEMENT
ABODES
ABODING
ABOHM
ABOHMS
ABOIDEAU
ABOIDEAUS
ABOIDEAUX
ABOIL
ABOITEAU
ABOITEAUS
ABOITEAUX
ABOLISH
ABOLISHED
ABOLISHER
ABOLISHES
ABOLITION
ABOLLA
ABOLLAE
ABOLLAS
ABOMA
ABOMAS
ABOMASA
ABOMASAI
ABOMASI
ABOMASUM
ABOMASUS
ABOMINATE
ABONDANCE
ABOON
ABORAL
ABORALLY
ABORD
ABORDED
ABORDING
ABORDS
ABORE
ABORIGEN
ABORIGENS
ABORIGIN
ABORIGINE
ABORIGINS
ABORNE
ABORNING
ABORT
ABORTED
ABORTEE
ABORTEES
ABORTER
ABORTERS
ABORTING
ABORTION
ABORTIONS
ABORTIVE
ABORTS
ABORTUARY
ABORTUS
ABORTUSES
ABOS
ABOUGHT
ABOULIA
ABOULIAS
ABOULIC
ABOUND
ABOUNDED
ABOUNDING
ABOUNDS
ABOUT
ABOUTS
ABOVE
ABOVES
ABRACHIA
ABRACHIAS
ABRADABLE
ABRADANT
ABRADANTS
ABRADE
ABRADED
ABRADER
ABRADERS
ABRADES
ABRADING
ABRAID
ABRAIDED
ABRAIDING
ABRAIDS
ABRAM
ABRASAX
ABRASAXES
ABRASION
ABRASIONS
ABRASIVE
ABRASIVES
ABRAXAS
ABRAXASES
ABRAY
ABRAYED
ABRAYING
ABRAYS
ABRAZO
ABRAZOS
ABREACT
ABREACTED
ABREACTS
ABREAST
ABREGE
ABREGES
ABRI
ABRICOCK
ABRICOCKS
ABRIDGE
ABRIDGED
ABRIDGER
ABRIDGERS
ABRIDGES
ABRIDGING
ABRIM
ABRIN
ABRINS
ABRIS
ABROACH
ABROAD
ABROADS
ABROGABLE
ABROGATE
ABROGATED
ABROGATES
ABROGATOR
ABROOKE
ABROOKED
ABROOKES
ABROOKING
ABROSIA
ABROSIAS
ABRUPT
ABRUPTER
ABRUPTEST
ABRUPTION
ABRUPTLY
ABRUPTS
ABS
ABSCESS
ABSCESSED
ABSCESSES
ABSCIND
ABSCINDED
ABSCINDS
ABSCISE
ABSCISED
ABSCISES
ABSCISIC
ABSCISIN
ABSCISING
ABSCISINS
ABSCISS
ABSCISSA
ABSCISSAE
ABSCISSAS
ABSCISSE
ABSCISSES

ABSCISSIN
ABSCOND
ABSCONDED
ABSCONDER
ABSCONDS
ABSEIL
ABSEILED
ABSEILER
ABSEILERS
ABSEILING
ABSEILS
ABSENCE
ABSENCES
ABSENT
ABSENTED
ABSENTEE
ABSENTEES
ABSENTER
ABSENTERS
ABSENTING
ABSENTLY
ABSENTS
ABSEY
ABSEYS
ABSINTH
ABSINTHE
ABSINTHES
ABSINTHS
ABSIT
ABSITS
ABSOLUTE
ABSOLUTER
ABSOLUTES
ABSOLVE
ABSOLVED
ABSOLVENT
ABSOLVER
ABSOLVERS
ABSOLVES
ABSOLVING
ABSONANT
ABSORB
ABSORBANT
ABSORBATE
ABSORBED
ABSORBENT
ABSORBER
ABSORBERS
ABSORBING
ABSORBS
ABSTAIN
ABSTAINED
ABSTAINER
ABSTAINS
ABSTERGE
ABSTERGED
ABSTERGES
ABSTINENT
ABSTRACT
ABSTRACTS
ABSTRICT
ABSTRICTS
ABSTRUSE
ABSTRUSER
ABSURD
ABSURDER
ABSURDEST
ABSURDISM
ABSURDIST
ABSURDITY
ABSURDLY
ABSURDS
ABTHANE
ABTHANES
ABUBBLE
ABUILDING
ABULIA
ABULIAS
ABULIC
ABUNA
ABUNAS
ABUNDANCE
ABUNDANCY
ABUNDANT
ABUNE
ABURST
ABUSABLE
ABUSAGE
ABUSAGES
ABUSE
ABUSED
ABUSER
ABUSERS
ABUSES
ABUSING
ABUSION
ABUSIONS
ABUSIVE
ABUSIVELY
ABUT
ABUTILON
ABUTILONS
ABUTMENT
ABUTMENTS
ABUTS
ABUTTAL
ABUTTALS
ABUTTED
ABUTTER
ABUTTERS
ABUTTING
ABUZZ
ABVOLT
ABVOLTS
ABWATT
ABWATTS
ABY
ABYE
ABYEING
ABYES
ABYING
ABYS
ABYSM
ABYSMAL
ABYSMALLY
ABYSMS
ABYSS
ABYSSAL
ABYSSES
ACACIA
ACACIAS
ACADEME
ACADEMES
ACADEMIA
ACADEMIAS
ACADEMIC
ACADEMICS
ACADEMIES
ACADEMISM
ACADEMIST
ACADEMY
ACAI
ACAIS
ACAJOU
ACAJOUS
ACALCULIA
ACALEPH
ACALEPHAE
ACALEPHAN
ACALEPHE
ACALEPHES
ACALEPHS
ACANTH
ACANTHA
ACANTHAE
ACANTHAS
ACANTHI
ACANTHIN
ACANTHINE
ACANTHINS
ACANTHOID
ACANTHOUS
ACANTHS
ACANTHUS
ACAPNIA
ACAPNIAS
ACARBOSE
ACARBOSES
ACARI
ACARIAN
ACARIASES
ACARIASIS
ACARICIDE
ACARID
ACARIDAN
ACARIDANS
ACARIDEAN
ACARIDIAN
ACARIDS
ACARINE
ACARINES
ACAROID
ACAROLOGY
ACARPOUS
ACARUS
ACATER
ACATERS
ACATES
ACATHISIA
ACATOUR
ACATOURS
ACAUDAL
ACAUDATE
ACAULINE
ACAULOSE
ACAULOUS
ACCA
ACCABLE
ACCAS
ACCEDE
ACCEDED
ACCEDENCE
ACCEDER
ACCEDERS
ACCEDES
ACCEDING
ACCEND
ACCENDED
ACCENDING
ACCENDS
ACCENSION
ACCENT
ACCENTED
ACCENTING
ACCENTOR
ACCENTORS
ACCENTS
ACCENTUAL
ACCEPT
ACCEPTANT
ACCEPTED
ACCEPTEE
ACCEPTEES
ACCEPTER
ACCEPTERS
ACCEPTING
ACCEPTIVE
ACCEPTOR
ACCEPTORS
ACCEPTS
ACCESS
ACCESSARY
ACCESSED
ACCESSES
ACCESSING
ACCESSION
ACCESSORY
ACCIDENCE
ACCIDENT
ACCIDENTS

ACCIDIA
ACCIDIAS
ACCIDIE
ACCIDIES
ACCINGE
ACCINGED
ACCINGES
ACCINGING
ACCIPITER
ACCITE
ACCITED
ACCITES
ACCITING
ACCLAIM
ACCLAIMED
ACCLAIMER
ACCLAIMS
ACCLIMATE
ACCLIVITY
ACCLIVOUS
ACCLOY
ACCLOYED
ACCLOYING
ACCLOYS
ACCOAST
ACCOASTED
ACCOASTS
ACCOIED
ACCOIL
ACCOILS
ACCOLADE
ACCOLADED
ACCOLADES
ACCOMPANY
ACCOMPT
ACCOMPTED
ACCOMPTS
ACCORAGE
ACCORAGED
ACCORAGES
ACCORD
ACCORDANT
ACCORDED
ACCORDER
ACCORDERS
ACCORDING
ACCORDION
ACCORDS
ACCOST
ACCOSTED
ACCOSTING
ACCOSTS
ACCOUNT
ACCOUNTED
ACCOUNTS
ACCOURAGE
ACCOURT
ACCOURTED
ACCOURTS
ACCOUTER
ACCOUTERS
ACCOUTRE
ACCOUTRED
ACCOUTRES
ACCOY
ACCOYED
ACCOYING
ACCOYLD
ACCOYS
ACCREDIT
ACCREDITS
ACCRETE
ACCRETED
ACCRETES
ACCRETING
ACCRETION
ACCRETIVE
ACCREW
ACCREWED
ACCREWING
ACCREWS
ACCROIDES
ACCRUABLE
ACCRUAL
ACCRUALS
ACCRUE
ACCRUED
ACCRUES
ACCRUING
ACCUMBENT
ACCURACY
ACCURATE
ACCURSE
ACCURSED
ACCURSES
ACCURSING
ACCURST
ACCUSABLE
ACCUSABLY
ACCUSAL
ACCUSALS
ACCUSANT
ACCUSANTS
ACCUSE
ACCUSED
ACCUSER
ACCUSERS
ACCUSES
ACCUSING
ACCUSTOM
ACCUSTOMS
ACE
ACED
ACEDIA
ACEDIAS
ACELDAMA
ACELDAMAS
ACELLULAR
ACENTRIC
ACENTRICS
ACEPHALIC
ACEQUIA
ACEQUIAS
ACER
ACERATE
ACERATED
ACERB
ACERBATE
ACERBATED
ACERBATES
ACERBER
ACERBEST
ACERBIC
ACERBITY
ACEROLA
ACEROLAS
ACEROSE
ACEROUS
ACERS
ACERVATE
ACERVULI
ACERVULUS
ACES
ACESCENCE
ACESCENCY
ACESCENT
ACESCENTS
ACETA
ACETABULA
ACETAL
ACETALS
ACETAMID
ACETAMIDE
ACETAMIDS
ACETATE
ACETATED
ACETATES
ACETIC
ACETIFIED
ACETIFIER
ACETIFIES
ACETIFY
ACETIN
ACETINS
ACETONE
ACETONES
ACETONIC
ACETOSE
ACETOUS
ACETOXYL
ACETOXYLS
ACETUM
ACETYL
ACETYLATE
ACETYLENE
ACETYLIC
ACETYLIDE
ACETYLS
ACH
ACHAENIA
ACHAENIUM
ACHAGE
ACHAGES
ACHALASIA
ACHAR
ACHARNE
ACHARS
ACHARYA
ACHARYAS
ACHATES
ACHE
ACHED
ACHENE
ACHENES
ACHENIA
ACHENIAL
ACHENIUM
ACHENIUMS
ACHES
ACHIER
ACHIEST
ACHIEVE
ACHIEVED
ACHIEVER
ACHIEVERS
ACHIEVES
ACHIEVING
ACHILLEA
ACHILLEAS
ACHIMENES
ACHINESS
ACHING
ACHINGLY
ACHINGS
ACHIOTE
ACHIOTES
ACHIRAL
ACHKAN
ACHKANS
ACHOLIA
ACHOLIAS
ACHOO
ACHOOS
ACHROMAT
ACHROMATS
ACHROMIC
ACHROMOUS
ACHY
ACICLOVIR
ACICULA
ACICULAE
ACICULAR
ACICULAS
ACICULATE
ACICULUM
ACICULUMS
ACID
ACIDEMIA
ACIDEMIAS
ACIDER

ACIDEST
ACIDHEAD
ACIDHEADS
ACIDIC
ACIDIER
ACIDIEST
ACIDIFIED
ACIDIFIER
ACIDIFIES
ACIDIFY
ACIDITIES
ACIDITY
ACIDLY
ACIDNESS
ACIDOPHIL
ACIDOSES
ACIDOSIS
ACIDOTIC
ACIDS
ACIDULATE
ACIDULENT
ACIDULOUS
ACIDURIA
ACIDURIAS
ACIDY
ACIERAGE
ACIERAGES
ACIERATE
ACIERATED
ACIERATES
ACIFORM
ACINAR
ACING
ACINI
ACINIC
ACINIFORM
ACINOSE
ACINOUS
ACINUS
ACKEE
ACKEES
ACKER
ACKERS
ACKNEW
ACKNOW
ACKNOWING
ACKNOWN
ACKNOWNE
ACKNOWS
ACLINIC
ACMATIC
ACME
ACMES
ACMIC
ACMITE
ACMITES
ACNE
ACNED
ACNES
ACNODAL
ACNODE
ACNODES
ACOCK
ACOELOUS
ACOEMETI
ACOLD
ACOLUTHIC
ACOLYTE
ACOLYTES
ACOLYTH
ACOLYTHS
ACONITE
ACONITES
ACONITIC
ACONITINE
ACONITUM
ACONITUMS
ACORN
ACORNED
ACORNS
ACOSMISM
ACOSMISMS
ACOSMIST
ACOSMISTS
ACOUCHI
ACOUCHIES
ACOUCHIS
ACOUCHY
ACOUSTIC
ACOUSTICS
ACQUAINT
ACQUAINTS
ACQUEST
ACQUESTS
ACQUIESCE
ACQUIGHT
ACQUIGHTS
ACQUIRAL
ACQUIRALS
ACQUIRE
ACQUIRED
ACQUIREE
ACQUIREES
ACQUIRER
ACQUIRERS
ACQUIRES
ACQUIRING
ACQUIS
ACQUIST
ACQUISTS
ACQUIT
ACQUITE
ACQUITES
ACQUITING
ACQUITS
ACQUITTAL
ACQUITTED
ACQUITTER
ACRASIA
ACRASIAS
ACRASIN
ACRASINS
ACRATIC
ACRAWL
ACRE
ACREAGE
ACREAGES
ACRED
ACRES
ACRID
ACRIDER
ACRIDEST
ACRIDIN
ACRIDINE
ACRIDINES
ACRIDINS
ACRIDITY
ACRIDLY
ACRIDNESS
ACRIMONY
ACRITARCH
ACRITICAL
ACRO
ACROBAT
ACROBATIC
ACROBATS
ACRODONT
ACRODONTS
ACRODROME
ACROGEN
ACROGENIC
ACROGENS
ACROLECT
ACROLECTS
ACROLEIN
ACROLEINS
ACROLITH
ACROLITHS
ACROMIA
ACROMIAL
ACROMION
ACRONIC
ACRONICAL
ACRONYCAL
ACRONYM
ACRONYMIC
ACRONYMS
ACROPETAL
ACROPHOBE
ACROPHONY
ACROPOLIS
ACROS
ACROSOMAL
ACROSOME
ACROSOMES
ACROSPIRE
ACROSS
ACROSTIC
ACROSTICS
ACROTER
ACROTERIA
ACROTERS
ACROTIC
ACROTISM
ACROTISMS
ACRYLATE
ACRYLATES
ACRYLIC
ACRYLICS
ACRYLYL
ACRYLYLS
ACT
ACTA
ACTABLE
ACTANT
ACTANTS
ACTED
ACTIN
ACTINAL
ACTINALLY
ACTING
ACTINGS
ACTINIA
ACTINIAE
ACTINIAN
ACTINIANS
ACTINIAS
ACTINIC
ACTINIDE
ACTINIDES
ACTINISM
ACTINISMS
ACTINIUM
ACTINIUMS
ACTINOID
ACTINOIDS
ACTINON
ACTINONS
ACTINOPOD
ACTINS
ACTION
ACTIONED
ACTIONER
ACTIONERS
ACTIONING
ACTIONIST
ACTIONS
ACTIVATE
ACTIVATED
ACTIVATES
ACTIVATOR
ACTIVE
ACTIVELY
ACTIVES
ACTIVISE
ACTIVISED
ACTIVISES
ACTIVISM
ACTIVISMS
ACTIVIST

A

ACTIVISTS
ACTIVITY
ACTIVIZE
ACTIVIZED
ACTIVIZES
ACTON
ACTONS
ACTOR
ACTORISH
ACTORLIER
ACTORLY
ACTORS
ACTRESS
ACTRESSES
ACTRESSY
ACTS
ACTUAL
ACTUALISE
ACTUALIST
ACTUALITE
ACTUALITY
ACTUALIZE
ACTUALLY
ACTUALS
ACTUARIAL
ACTUARIES
ACTUARY
ACTUATE
ACTUATED
ACTUATES
ACTUATING
ACTUATION
ACTUATOR
ACTUATORS
ACTURE
ACTURES
ACUATE
ACUATED
ACUATES
ACUATING
ACUITIES
ACUITY
ACULEATE
ACULEATED
ACULEATES
ACULEI
ACULEUS
ACUMEN
ACUMENS
ACUMINATE
ACUMINOUS
ACUPOINT
ACUPOINTS
ACUSHLA
ACUSHLAS
ACUTANCE
ACUTANCES
ACUTE
ACUTELY
ACUTENESS
ACUTER
ACUTES
ACUTEST
ACYCLIC
ACYCLOVIR
ACYL
ACYLATE
ACYLATED
ACYLATES
ACYLATING
ACYLATION
ACYLOIN
ACYLOINS
ACYLS
AD
ADAGE
ADAGES
ADAGIAL
ADAGIO
ADAGIOS
ADAMANCE
ADAMANCES
ADAMANCY
ADAMANT
ADAMANTLY
ADAMANTS
ADAMSITE
ADAMSITES
ADAPT
ADAPTABLE
ADAPTED
ADAPTER
ADAPTERS
ADAPTING
ADAPTION
ADAPTIONS
ADAPTIVE
ADAPTOGEN
ADAPTOR
ADAPTORS
ADAPTS
ADAW
ADAWED
ADAWING
ADAWS
ADAXIAL
ADAYS
ADBOT
ADBOTS
ADD
ADDABLE
ADDAX
ADDAXES
ADDEBTED
ADDED
ADDEDLY
ADDEEM
ADDEEMED
ADDEEMING
ADDEEMS
ADDEND
ADDENDA
ADDENDS
ADDENDUM
ADDENDUMS
ADDER
ADDERBEAD
ADDERS
ADDERWORT
ADDIBLE
ADDICT
ADDICTED
ADDICTING
ADDICTION
ADDICTIVE
ADDICTS
ADDIES
ADDING
ADDINGS
ADDIO
ADDIOS
ADDITION
ADDITIONS
ADDITIVE
ADDITIVES
ADDITORY
ADDLE
ADDLED
ADDLEMENT
ADDLES
ADDLING
ADDOOM
ADDOOMED
ADDOOMING
ADDOOMS
ADDORSED
ADDRESS
ADDRESSED
ADDRESSEE
ADDRESSER
ADDRESSES
ADDRESSOR
ADDREST
ADDS
ADDUCE
ADDUCED
ADDUCENT
ADDUCER
ADDUCERS
ADDUCES
ADDUCIBLE
ADDUCING
ADDUCT
ADDUCTED
ADDUCTING
ADDUCTION
ADDUCTIVE
ADDUCTOR
ADDUCTORS
ADDUCTS
ADDY
ADEEM
ADEEMED
ADEEMING
ADEEMS
ADELGID
ADELGIDS
ADEMPTION
ADENINE
ADENINES
ADENITIS
ADENOID
ADENOIDAL
ADENOIDS
ADENOMA
ADENOMAS
ADENOMATA
ADENOSES
ADENOSINE
ADENOSIS
ADENYL
ADENYLATE
ADENYLIC
ADENYLS
ADEPT
ADEPTER
ADEPTEST
ADEPTLY
ADEPTNESS
ADEPTS
ADEQUACY
ADEQUATE
ADERMIN
ADERMINS
ADESPOTA
ADESSIVE
ADESSIVES
ADHAN
ADHANS
ADHARMA
ADHARMAS
ADHERABLE
ADHERE
ADHERED
ADHERENCE
ADHEREND
ADHERENDS
ADHERENT
ADHERENTS
ADHERER
ADHERERS
ADHERES
ADHERING
ADHESION
ADHESIONS
ADHESIVE
ADHESIVES
ADHIBIT
ADHIBITED
ADHIBITS

ADHOCRACY
ADIABATIC
ADIAPHORA
ADIEU
ADIEUS
ADIEUX
ADIOS
ADIOSES
ADIPIC
ADIPOCERE
ADIPOCYTE
ADIPOSE
ADIPOSES
ADIPOSIS
ADIPOSITY
ADIPOUS
ADIPSIA
ADIPSIAS
ADIT
ADITS
ADJACENCE
ADJACENCY
ADJACENT
ADJACENTS
ADJECTIVE
ADJIGO
ADJIGOS
ADJOIN
ADJOINED
ADJOINING
ADJOINS
ADJOINT
ADJOINTS
ADJOURN
ADJOURNED
ADJOURNS
ADJUDGE
ADJUDGED
ADJUDGES
ADJUDGING
ADJUNCT
ADJUNCTLY
ADJUNCTS
ADJURE
ADJURED
ADJURER
ADJURERS
ADJURES
ADJURING
ADJUROR
ADJURORS
ADJUST
ADJUSTED
ADJUSTER
ADJUSTERS
ADJUSTING
ADJUSTIVE
ADJUSTOR
ADJUSTORS
ADJUSTS
ADJUTAGE
ADJUTAGES
ADJUTANCY
ADJUTANT
ADJUTANTS
ADJUVANCY
ADJUVANT
ADJUVANTS
ADLAND
ADLANDS
ADMAN
ADMASS
ADMASSES
ADMEASURE
ADMEN
ADMIN
ADMINICLE
ADMINS
ADMIRABLE
ADMIRABLY
ADMIRAL
ADMIRALS
ADMIRALTY
ADMIRANCE
ADMIRE
ADMIRED
ADMIRER
ADMIRERS
ADMIRES
ADMIRING
ADMISSION
ADMISSIVE
ADMIT
ADMITS
ADMITTED
ADMITTEE
ADMITTEES
ADMITTER
ADMITTERS
ADMITTING
ADMIX
ADMIXED
ADMIXES
ADMIXING
ADMIXT
ADMIXTURE
ADMONISH
ADMONITOR
ADNASCENT
ADNATE
ADNATION
ADNATIONS
ADNEXA
ADNEXAL
ADNOMINAL
ADNOUN
ADNOUNS
ADO
ADOBE
ADOBELIKE
ADOBES
ADOBO
ADOBOS
ADONIS
ADONISE
ADONISED
ADONISES
ADONISING
ADONIZE
ADONIZED
ADONIZES
ADONIZING
ADOORS
ADOPT
ADOPTABLE
ADOPTED
ADOPTEE
ADOPTEES
ADOPTER
ADOPTERS
ADOPTING
ADOPTION
ADOPTIONS
ADOPTIOUS
ADOPTIVE
ADOPTS
ADORABLE
ADORABLY
ADORATION
ADORE
ADORED
ADORER
ADORERS
ADORES
ADORING
ADORINGLY
ADORKABLE
ADORN
ADORNED
ADORNER
ADORNERS
ADORNING
ADORNMENT
ADORNS
ADOS
ADOWN
ADOZE
ADPRESS
ADPRESSED
ADPRESSES
ADRAD
ADRATE
ADRATES
ADREAD
ADREADED
ADREADING
ADREADS
ADRED
ADRENAL
ADRENALIN
ADRENALLY
ADRENALS
ADRIFT
ADROIT
ADROITER
ADROITEST
ADROITLY
ADRY
ADS
ADSCRIPT
ADSCRIPTS
ADSORB
ADSORBATE
ADSORBED
ADSORBENT
ADSORBER
ADSORBERS
ADSORBING
ADSORBS
ADSPEAK
ADSPEAKS
ADSUKI
ADSUKIS
ADSUM
ADUKI
ADUKIS
ADULARIA
ADULARIAS
ADULATE
ADULATED
ADULATES
ADULATING
ADULATION
ADULATOR
ADULATORS
ADULATORY
ADULT
ADULTERER
ADULTERY
ADULTHOOD
ADULTLIKE
ADULTLY
ADULTNESS
ADULTRESS
ADULTS
ADUMBRAL
ADUMBRATE
ADUNC
ADUNCATE
ADUNCATED
ADUNCITY
ADUNCOUS
ADUST
ADUSTED
ADUSTING
ADUSTS
ADVANCE
ADVANCED
ADVANCER
ADVANCERS

A

ADVANCES
ADVANCING
ADVANTAGE
ADVECT
ADVECTED
ADVECTING
ADVECTION
ADVECTIVE
ADVECTS
ADVENE
ADVENED
ADVENES
ADVENING
ADVENT
ADVENTIVE
ADVENTS
ADVENTURE
ADVERB
ADVERBIAL
ADVERBS
ADVERSARY
ADVERSE
ADVERSELY
ADVERSER
ADVERSEST
ADVERSITY
ADVERT
ADVERTED
ADVERTENT
ADVERTING
ADVERTISE
ADVERTIZE
ADVERTS
ADVEW
ADVEWED
ADVEWING
ADVEWS
ADVICE
ADVICEFUL
ADVICES
ADVISABLE
ADVISABLY
ADVISE
ADVISED
ADVISEDLY
ADVISEE
ADVISEES
ADVISER
ADVISERS
ADVISES
ADVISING
ADVISINGS
ADVISOR
ADVISORS
ADVISORY
ADVOCAAT
ADVOCAATS
ADVOCACY
ADVOCATE
ADVOCATED
ADVOCATES
ADVOCATOR
ADVOUTRER
ADVOUTRY
ADVOWSON
ADVOWSONS
ADWARD
ADWARDED
ADWARDING
ADWARDS
ADWARE
ADWARES
ADWOMAN
ADWOMEN
ADYNAMIA
ADYNAMIAS
ADYNAMIC
ADYTA
ADYTUM
ADZ
ADZE
ADZED
ADZELIKE
ADZES
ADZING
ADZUKI
ADZUKIS
AE
AECIA
AECIAL
AECIDIA
AECIDIAL
AECIDIUM
AECIUM
AEDES
AEDICULE
AEDICULES
AEDILE
AEDILES
AEDINE
AEFALD
AEFAULD
AEGIRINE
AEGIRINES
AEGIRITE
AEGIRITES
AEGIS
AEGISES
AEGLOGUE
AEGLOGUES
AEGROTAT
AEGROTATS
AEMULE
AEMULED
AEMULES
AEMULING
AENEOUS
AENEUS
AENEUSES
AEOLIAN
AEOLIPILE
AEOLIPYLE
AEON
AEONIAN
AEONIC
AEONS
AEPYORNIS
AEQUORIN
AEQUORINS
AERADIO
AERADIOS
AERATE
AERATED
AERATES
AERATING
AERATION
AERATIONS
AERATOR
AERATORS
AERIAL
AERIALIST
AERIALITY
AERIALLY
AERIALS
AERIE
AERIED
AERIER
AERIES
AERIEST
AERIFIED
AERIFIES
AERIFORM
AERIFY
AERIFYING
AERILY
AERO
AEROBAT
AEROBATIC
AEROBATS
AEROBE
AEROBES
AEROBIA
AEROBIC
AEROBICS
AEROBIONT
AEROBIUM
AEROBOMB
AEROBOMBS
AEROBOT
AEROBOTS
AEROBRAKE
AEROBUS
AEROBUSES
AERODART
AERODARTS
AERODROME
AERODUCT
AERODUCTS
AERODYNE
AERODYNES
AEROFOIL
AEROFOILS
AEROGEL
AEROGELS
AEROGRAM
AEROGRAMS
AEROGRAPH
AEROLITE
AEROLITES
AEROLITH
AEROLITHS
AEROLITIC
AEROLOGIC
AEROLOGY
AEROMANCY
AEROMETER
AEROMETRY
AEROMOTOR
AERONAUT
AERONAUTS
AERONOMER
AERONOMIC
AERONOMY
AEROPAUSE
AEROPHAGY
AEROPHOBE
AEROPHONE
AEROPHORE
AEROPHYTE
AEROPLANE
AEROPULSE
AEROS
AEROSAT
AEROSATS
AEROSCOPE
AEROSHELL
AEROSOL
AEROSOLS
AEROSPACE
AEROSPIKE
AEROSTAT
AEROSTATS
AEROTAXES
AEROTAXIS
AEROTONE
AEROTONES
AEROTRAIN
AERUGO
AERUGOS
AERY
AESC
AESCES
AESCULIN
AESCULINS
AESIR
AESTHESES
AESTHESIA
AESTHESIS
AESTHETE
AESTHETES

AESTHETIC
AESTIVAL
AESTIVATE
AETATIS
AETHER
AETHEREAL
AETHERIC
AETHERS
AETIOLOGY
AFALD
AFAR
AFARA
AFARAS
AFARS
AFAWLD
AFEAR
AFEARD
AFEARED
AFEARING
AFEARS
AFEBRILE
AFF
AFFABLE
AFFABLY
AFFAIR
AFFAIRE
AFFAIRES
AFFAIRS
AFFEAR
AFFEARD
AFFEARE
AFFEARED
AFFEARES
AFFEARING
AFFEARS
AFFECT
AFFECTED
AFFECTER
AFFECTERS
AFFECTING
AFFECTION
AFFECTIVE
AFFECTS
AFFEER
AFFEERED
AFFEERING
AFFEERS
AFFERENT
AFFERENTS
AFFIANCE
AFFIANCED
AFFIANCES
AFFIANT
AFFIANTS
AFFICHE
AFFICHES
AFFIDAVIT
AFFIED
AFFIES
AFFILIATE
AFFINAL
AFFINE
AFFINED
AFFINELY
AFFINES
AFFINITY
AFFIRM
AFFIRMANT
AFFIRMED
AFFIRMER
AFFIRMERS
AFFIRMING
AFFIRMS
AFFIX
AFFIXABLE
AFFIXAL
AFFIXED
AFFIXER
AFFIXERS
AFFIXES
AFFIXIAL
AFFIXING
AFFIXMENT
AFFIXTURE
AFFLATED
AFFLATION
AFFLATUS
AFFLICT
AFFLICTED
AFFLICTER
AFFLICTS
AFFLUENCE
AFFLUENCY
AFFLUENT
AFFLUENTS
AFFLUENZA
AFFLUX
AFFLUXES
AFFLUXION
AFFOGATO
AFFOGATOS
AFFOORD
AFFOORDED
AFFOORDS
AFFORCE
AFFORCED
AFFORCES
AFFORCING
AFFORD
AFFORDED
AFFORDING
AFFORDS
AFFOREST
AFFORESTS
AFFRAP
AFFRAPPED
AFFRAPS
AFFRAY
AFFRAYED
AFFRAYER
AFFRAYERS
AFFRAYING
AFFRAYS
AFFRENDED
AFFRET
AFFRETS
AFFRICATE
AFFRIGHT
AFFRIGHTS
AFFRONT
AFFRONTE
AFFRONTED
AFFRONTEE
AFFRONTS
AFFUSION
AFFUSIONS
AFFY
AFFYDE
AFFYING
AFGHAN
AFGHANI
AFGHANIS
AFGHANS
AFIELD
AFIRE
AFLAJ
AFLAME
AFLATOXIN
AFLOAT
AFLUTTER
AFOCAL
AFOOT
AFORE
AFOREHAND
AFORESAID
AFORETIME
AFOUL
AFRAID
AFREET
AFREETS
AFRESH
AFRIT
AFRITS
AFRO
AFRONT
AFROS
AFT
AFTER
AFTERBODY
AFTERBURN
AFTERCARE
AFTERCLAP
AFTERDAMP
AFTERDECK
AFTEREYE
AFTEREYED
AFTEREYES
AFTERGAME
AFTERGLOW
AFTERHEAT
AFTERINGS
AFTERLIFE
AFTERMAST
AFTERMATH
AFTERMOST
AFTERNOON
AFTERPAIN
AFTERPEAK
AFTERS
AFTERSHOW
AFTERSUN
AFTERSUNS
AFTERTAX
AFTERTIME
AFTERWARD
AFTERWORD
AFTMOST
AFTOSA
AFTOSAS
AG
AGA
AGACANT
AGACANTE
AGACERIE
AGACERIES
AGAIN
AGAINST
AGALACTIA
AGALLOCH
AGALLOCHS
AGALWOOD
AGALWOODS
AGAMA
AGAMAS
AGAMETE
AGAMETES
AGAMI
AGAMIC
AGAMID
AGAMIDS
AGAMIS
AGAMOGONY
AGAMOID
AGAMOIDS
AGAMONT
AGAMONTS
AGAMOUS
AGAPAE
AGAPAI
AGAPE
AGAPEIC
AGAPES
AGAR
AGARIC
AGARICS
AGAROSE
AGAROSES
AGARS
AGARWOOD
AGARWOODS

AGAS
AGAST
AGASTED
AGASTING
AGASTS
AGATE
AGATES
AGATEWARE
AGATISE
AGATISED
AGATISES
AGATISING
AGATIZE
AGATIZED
AGATIZES
AGATIZING
AGATOID
AGAVE
AGAVES
AGAZE
AGAZED
AGE
AGED
AGEDLY
AGEDNESS
AGEE
AGEING
AGEINGS
AGEISM
AGEISMS
AGEIST
AGEISTS
AGELAST
AGELASTIC
AGELASTS
AGELESS
AGELESSLY
AGELONG
AGEMATE
AGEMATES
AGEN
AGENCIES
AGENCY
AGENDA
AGENDAS
AGENDER
AGENDUM
AGENDUMS
AGENE
AGENES
AGENESES
AGENESIA
AGENESIAS
AGENESIS
AGENETIC
AGENISE
AGENISED
AGENISES
AGENISING
AGENIZE
AGENIZED
AGENIZES
AGENIZING
AGENT
AGENTED
AGENTIAL
AGENTING
AGENTINGS
AGENTIVAL
AGENTIVE
AGENTIVES
AGENTRIES
AGENTRY
AGENTS
AGER
AGERATUM
AGERATUMS
AGERS
AGES
AGEUSIA
AGEUSIAS
AGFLATION
AGGADA
AGGADAH
AGGADAHS
AGGADAS
AGGADIC
AGGADOT
AGGADOTH
AGGER
AGGERS
AGGIE
AGGIES
AGGRACE
AGGRACED
AGGRACES
AGGRACING
AGGRADE
AGGRADED
AGGRADES
AGGRADING
AGGRATE
AGGRATED
AGGRATES
AGGRATING
AGGRAVATE
AGGREGATE
AGGRESS
AGGRESSED
AGGRESSES
AGGRESSOR
AGGRI
AGGRIEVE
AGGRIEVED
AGGRIEVES
AGGRO
AGGROS
AGGRY
AGHA
AGHAS
AGHAST
AGILA
AGILAS
AGILE
AGILELY
AGILENESS
AGILER
AGILEST
AGILITIES
AGILITY
AGIN
AGING
AGINGS
AGINNER
AGINNERS
AGIO
AGIOS
AGIOTAGE
AGIOTAGES
AGISM
AGISMS
AGIST
AGISTED
AGISTER
AGISTERS
AGISTING
AGISTMENT
AGISTOR
AGISTORS
AGISTS
AGITA
AGITABLE
AGITANS
AGITAS
AGITATE
AGITATED
AGITATES
AGITATING
AGITATION
AGITATIVE
AGITATO
AGITATOR
AGITATORS
AGITPOP
AGITPOPS
AGITPROP
AGITPROPS
AGLARE
AGLEAM
AGLEE
AGLET
AGLETS
AGLEY
AGLIMMER
AGLITTER
AGLOO
AGLOOS
AGLOSSAL
AGLOSSATE
AGLOSSIA
AGLOSSIAS
AGLOW
AGLU
AGLUS
AGLY
AGLYCON
AGLYCONE
AGLYCONES
AGLYCONS
AGMA
AGMAS
AGMINATE
AGNAIL
AGNAILS
AGNAME
AGNAMED
AGNAMES
AGNATE
AGNATES
AGNATHAN
AGNATHANS
AGNATHOUS
AGNATIC
AGNATICAL
AGNATION
AGNATIONS
AGNISE
AGNISED
AGNISES
AGNISING
AGNIZE
AGNIZED
AGNIZES
AGNIZING
AGNOLOTTI
AGNOMEN
AGNOMENS
AGNOMINA
AGNOMINAL
AGNOSIA
AGNOSIAS
AGNOSIC
AGNOSTIC
AGNOSTICS
AGO
AGOG
AGOGE
AGOGES
AGOGIC
AGOGICS
AGOING
AGON
AGONAL
AGONE
AGONES
AGONIC
AGONIES
AGONISE
AGONISED
AGONISES

AGONISING
AGONISM
AGONISMS
AGONIST
AGONISTES
AGONISTIC
AGONISTS
AGONIZE
AGONIZED
AGONIZES
AGONIZING
AGONS
AGONY
AGOOD
AGORA
AGORAE
AGORAS
AGOROT
AGOROTH
AGOUTA
AGOUTAS
AGOUTI
AGOUTIES
AGOUTIS
AGOUTY
AGRAFE
AGRAFES
AGRAFFE
AGRAFFES
AGRAPHA
AGRAPHIA
AGRAPHIAS
AGRAPHIC
AGRAPHON
AGRARIAN
AGRARIANS
AGRASTE
AGRAVIC
AGREE
AGREEABLE
AGREEABLY
AGREED
AGREEING
AGREEMENT
AGREES
AGREGE
AGREGES
AGREMENS
AGREMENT
AGREMENTS
AGRESTAL
AGRESTIAL
AGRESTIC
AGRIA
AGRIAS
AGRIMONY
AGRIN
AGRINS
AGRIOLOGY
AGRISE
AGRISED
AGRISES
AGRISING
AGRIZE
AGRIZED
AGRIZES
AGRIZING
AGRO
AGRODOLCE
AGROLOGIC
AGROLOGY
AGRONOMIC
AGRONOMY
AGROS
AGROUND
AGRYPNIA
AGRYPNIAS
AGRYZE
AGRYZED
AGRYZES
AGRYZING
AGS
AGTERSKOT
AGUACATE
AGUACATES
AGUE
AGUED
AGUELIKE
AGUES
AGUEWEED
AGUEWEEDS
AGUISE
AGUISED
AGUISES
AGUISH
AGUISHLY
AGUISING
AGUIZE
AGUIZED
AGUIZES
AGUIZING
AGUNA
AGUNAH
AGUNOT
AGUNOTH
AGUTI
AGUTIS
AGYRIA
AGYRIAS
AH
AHA
AHCHOO
AHEAD
AHEAP
AHED
AHEIGHT
AHEM
AHEMERAL
AHENT
AHI
AHIGH
AHIMSA
AHIMSAS
AHIND
AHING
AHINT
AHIS
AHISTORIC
AHOLD
AHOLDS
AHORSE
AHOY
AHS
AHULL
AHUNGERED
AHUNGRY
AHURU
AHURUHURU
AHURUS
AI
AIA
AIAS
AIBLINS
AID
AIDA
AIDANCE
AIDANCES
AIDANT
AIDANTS
AIDAS
AIDE
AIDED
AIDER
AIDERS
AIDES
AIDFUL
AIDING
AIDLESS
AIDMAN
AIDMEN
AIDOI
AIDOS
AIDS
AIERIES
AIERY
AIGA
AIGAS
AIGHT
AIGLET
AIGLETS
AIGRET
AIGRETS
AIGRETTE
AIGRETTES
AIGUILLE
AIGUILLES
AIKIDO
AIKIDOS
AIKONA
AIL
AILANTHIC
AILANTHUS
AILANTO
AILANTOS
AILED
AILERON
AILERONS
AILETTE
AILETTES
AILING
AILMENT
AILMENTS
AILS
AIM
AIMED
AIMER
AIMERS
AIMFUL
AIMFULLY
AIMING
AIMLESS
AIMLESSLY
AIMS
AIN
AINE
AINEE
AINGA
AINGAS
AINS
AINSELL
AINSELLS
AIOLI
AIOLIS
AIR
AIRBAG
AIRBAGS
AIRBALL
AIRBALLED
AIRBALLS
AIRBASE
AIRBASES
AIRBOARD
AIRBOARDS
AIRBOAT
AIRBOATS
AIRBORNE
AIRBOUND
AIRBRICK
AIRBRICKS
AIRBRUSH
AIRBURST
AIRBURSTS
AIRBUS
AIRBUSES
AIRBUSSES
AIRCHECK
AIRCHECKS
AIRCOACH
AIRCON
AIRCONS

A

AIRCRAFT
AIRCREW
AIRCREWS
AIRDATE
AIRDATES
AIRDRAWN
AIRDROME
AIRDROMES
AIRDROP
AIRDROPS
AIRED
AIRER
AIRERS
AIREST
AIRFARE
AIRFARES
AIRFIELD
AIRFIELDS
AIRFLOW
AIRFLOWS
AIRFOIL
AIRFOILS
AIRFRAME
AIRFRAMES
AIRGAP
AIRGAPS
AIRGLOW
AIRGLOWS
AIRGRAPH
AIRGRAPHS
AIRGUN
AIRGUNS
AIRHEAD
AIRHEADED
AIRHEADS
AIRHOLE
AIRHOLES
AIRIER
AIRIEST
AIRILY
AIRINESS
AIRING
AIRINGS
AIRLESS
AIRLIFT
AIRLIFTED
AIRLIFTS
AIRLIKE
AIRLINE
AIRLINER
AIRLINERS
AIRLINES
AIRLOCK
AIRLOCKS
AIRMAIL
AIRMAILED
AIRMAILS
AIRMAN
AIRMEN
AIRMOBILE
AIRN
AIRNED
AIRNING
AIRNS
AIRPARK
AIRPARKS
AIRPLANE
AIRPLANES
AIRPLAY
AIRPLAYS
AIRPORT
AIRPORTS
AIRPOST
AIRPOSTS
AIRPOWER
AIRPOWERS
AIRPROOF
AIRPROOFS
AIRPROX
AIRPROXES
AIRS
AIRSCAPE
AIRSCAPES
AIRSCREW
AIRSCREWS
AIRSHAFT
AIRSHAFTS
AIRSHED
AIRSHEDS
AIRSHIP
AIRSHIPS
AIRSHOT
AIRSHOTS
AIRSHOW
AIRSHOWS
AIRSICK
AIRSIDE
AIRSIDES
AIRSOME
AIRSPACE
AIRSPACES
AIRSPEED
AIRSPEEDS
AIRSTOP
AIRSTOPS
AIRSTREAM
AIRSTRIKE
AIRSTRIP
AIRSTRIPS
AIRT
AIRTED
AIRTH
AIRTHED
AIRTHING
AIRTHS
AIRTIGHT
AIRTIME
AIRTIMES
AIRTING
AIRTRAM
AIRTRAMS
AIRTS
AIRVAC
AIRVACS
AIRWARD
AIRWARDS
AIRWAVE
AIRWAVES
AIRWAY
AIRWAYS
AIRWISE
AIRWOMAN
AIRWOMEN
AIRWORTHY
AIRY
AIS
AISLE
AISLED
AISLELESS
AISLES
AISLEWAY
AISLEWAYS
AISLING
AISLINGS
AIT
AITCH
AITCHBONE
AITCHES
AITS
AITU
AITUS
AIVER
AIVERS
AIYEE
AIZLE
AIZLES
AJAR
AJEE
AJI
AJIES
AJIS
AJIVA
AJIVAS
AJOWAN
AJOWANS
AJUGA
AJUGAS
AJUTAGE
AJUTAGES
AJWAN
AJWANS
AKA
AKARYOTE
AKARYOTES
AKARYOTIC
AKAS
AKATEA
AKATEAS
AKATHISIA
AKE
AKEAKE
AKEAKES
AKEBIA
AKEBIAS
AKED
AKEDAH
AKEDAHS
AKEE
AKEES
AKELA
AKELAS
AKENE
AKENES
AKENIAL
AKES
AKHARA
AKHARAS
AKIMBO
AKIN
AKINESES
AKINESIA
AKINESIAS
AKINESIS
AKINETIC
AKING
AKIRAHO
AKIRAHOS
AKITA
AKITAS
AKKAS
AKOLUTHOS
AKRASIA
AKRASIAS
AKRATIC
AKVAVIT
AKVAVITS
AL
ALA
ALAAP
ALAAPS
ALABAMINE
ALABASTER
ALACHLOR
ALACHLORS
ALACK
ALACKADAY
ALACRITY
ALAE
ALAIMENT
ALAIMENTS
ALALAGMOI
ALALAGMOS
ALALIA
ALALIAS
ALAMEDA
ALAMEDAS
ALAMO
ALAMODE
ALAMODES
ALAMORT

A

ALAMOS
ALAN
ALAND
ALANDS
ALANE
ALANG
ALANGS
ALANIN
ALANINE
ALANINES
ALANINS
ALANNAH
ALANNAHS
ALANS
ALANT
ALANTS
ALANYL
ALANYLS
ALAP
ALAPA
ALAPAS
ALAPS
ALAR
ALARM
ALARMABLE
ALARMED
ALARMEDLY
ALARMING
ALARMISM
ALARMISMS
ALARMIST
ALARMISTS
ALARMS
ALARUM
ALARUMED
ALARUMING
ALARUMS
ALARY
ALAS
ALASKA
ALASKAS
ALASTOR
ALASTORS
ALASTRIM
ALASTRIMS
ALATE
ALATED
ALATES
ALATION
ALATIONS
ALAY
ALAYED
ALAYING
ALAYS
ALB
ALBA
ALBACORE
ALBACORES
ALBARELLI
ALBARELLO
ALBAS
ALBATA
ALBATAS
ALBATROSS
ALBE
ALBEDO
ALBEDOES
ALBEDOS
ALBEE
ALBEIT
ALBERGHI
ALBERGO
ALBERT
ALBERTITE
ALBERTS
ALBESCENT
ALBESPINE
ALBESPYNE
ALBICORE
ALBICORES
ALBINAL
ALBINESS
ALBINIC
ALBINISM
ALBINISMS
ALBINO
ALBINOISM
ALBINOS
ALBINOTIC
ALBITE
ALBITES
ALBITIC
ALBITICAL
ALBITISE
ALBITISED
ALBITISES
ALBITIZE
ALBITIZED
ALBITIZES
ALBIZIA
ALBIZIAS
ALBIZZIA
ALBIZZIAS
ALBRICIAS
ALBS
ALBUGO
ALBUGOS
ALBUM
ALBUMEN
ALBUMENS
ALBUMIN
ALBUMINS
ALBUMOSE
ALBUMOSES
ALBUMS
ALBURNOUS
ALBURNUM
ALBURNUMS
ALBUTEROL
ALCADE
ALCADES
ALCAHEST
ALCAHESTS
ALCAIC
ALCAICS
ALCAIDE
ALCAIDES
ALCALDE
ALCALDES
ALCARRAZA
ALCATRAS
ALCAYDE
ALCAYDES
ALCAZAR
ALCAZARS
ALCHEMIC
ALCHEMIES
ALCHEMISE
ALCHEMIST
ALCHEMIZE
ALCHEMY
ALCHERA
ALCHERAS
ALCHYMIES
ALCHYMY
ALCID
ALCIDINE
ALCIDS
ALCO
ALCOHOL
ALCOHOLIC
ALCOHOLS
ALCOLOCK
ALCOLOCKS
ALCOOL
ALCOOLS
ALCOPOP
ALCOPOPS
ALCORZA
ALCORZAS
ALCOS
ALCOVE
ALCOVED
ALCOVES
ALDEA
ALDEAS
ALDEHYDE
ALDEHYDES
ALDEHYDIC
ALDER
ALDERFLY
ALDERMAN
ALDERMEN
ALDERN
ALDERS
ALDICARB
ALDICARBS
ALDOL
ALDOLASE
ALDOLASES
ALDOLS
ALDOSE
ALDOSES
ALDOXIME
ALDOXIMES
ALDRIN
ALDRINS
ALE
ALEATORIC
ALEATORY
ALEBENCH
ALEC
ALECITHAL
ALECK
ALECKS
ALECOST
ALECOSTS
ALECS
ALECTRYON
ALEE
ALEF
ALEFS
ALEFT
ALEGAR
ALEGARS
ALEGGE
ALEGGED
ALEGGES
ALEGGING
ALEHOUSE
ALEHOUSES
ALEMBIC
ALEMBICS
ALEMBROTH
ALENCON
ALENCONS
ALENGTH
ALEPH
ALEPHS
ALEPINE
ALEPINES
ALERCE
ALERCES
ALERION
ALERIONS
ALERT
ALERTED
ALERTER
ALERTEST
ALERTING
ALERTLY
ALERTNESS
ALERTS
ALES
ALETHIC
ALEURON
ALEURONE
ALEURONES
ALEURONIC
ALEURONS

ALEVIN
ALEVINS
ALEW
ALEWASHED
ALEWIFE
ALEWIVES
ALEWS
ALEXANDER
ALEXIA
ALEXIAS
ALEXIC
ALEXIN
ALEXINE
ALEXINES
ALEXINIC
ALEXINS
ALEYE
ALEYED
ALEYES
ALEYING
ALF
ALFA
ALFAKI
ALFAKIS
ALFALFA
ALFALFAS
ALFAQUI
ALFAQUIN
ALFAQUINS
ALFAQUIS
ALFAS
ALFERECES
ALFEREZ
ALFILARIA
ALFILERIA
ALFORJA
ALFORJAS
ALFREDO
ALFRESCO
ALFS
ALGA
ALGAE
ALGAECIDE
ALGAL
ALGAROBA
ALGAROBAS
ALGARROBA
ALGARROBO
ALGAS
ALGATE
ALGATES
ALGEBRA
ALGEBRAIC
ALGEBRAS
ALGERINE
ALGERINES
ALGESES
ALGESIA
ALGESIAS
ALGESIC
ALGESIS
ALGETIC
ALGICIDAL
ALGICIDE
ALGICIDES
ALGID
ALGIDITY
ALGIDNESS
ALGIN
ALGINATE
ALGINATES
ALGINIC
ALGINS
ALGOID
ALGOLOGY
ALGOMETER
ALGOMETRY
ALGOR
ALGORISM
ALGORISMS
ALGORITHM
ALGORS
ALGUACIL
ALGUACILS
ALGUAZIL
ALGUAZILS
ALGUM
ALGUMS
ALIAS
ALIASED
ALIASES
ALIASING
ALIASINGS
ALIBI
ALIBIED
ALIBIES
ALIBIING
ALIBIS
ALIBLE
ALICANT
ALICANTS
ALICYCLIC
ALIDAD
ALIDADE
ALIDADES
ALIDADS
ALIEN
ALIENABLE
ALIENAGE
ALIENAGES
ALIENATE
ALIENATED
ALIENATES
ALIENATOR
ALIENED
ALIENEE
ALIENEES
ALIENER
ALIENERS
ALIENING
ALIENISM
ALIENISMS
ALIENIST
ALIENISTS
ALIENLY
ALIENNESS
ALIENOR
ALIENORS
ALIENS
ALIF
ALIFORM
ALIFS
ALIGARTA
ALIGARTAS
ALIGHT
ALIGHTED
ALIGHTING
ALIGHTS
ALIGN
ALIGNED
ALIGNER
ALIGNERS
ALIGNING
ALIGNMENT
ALIGNS
ALIKE
ALIKENESS
ALIMENT
ALIMENTAL
ALIMENTED
ALIMENTS
ALIMONIED
ALIMONIES
ALIMONY
ALINE
ALINED
ALINEMENT
ALINER
ALINERS
ALINES
ALINING
ALIPED
ALIPEDS
ALIPHATIC
ALIQUANT
ALIQUOT
ALIQUOTS
ALISMA
ALISMAS
ALISON
ALISONS
ALIST
ALIT
ALITERACY
ALITERATE
ALIUNDE
ALIVE
ALIVENESS
ALIYA
ALIYAH
ALIYAHS
ALIYAS
ALIYOS
ALIYOT
ALIYOTH
ALIZARI
ALIZARIN
ALIZARINE
ALIZARINS
ALIZARIS
ALKAHEST
ALKAHESTS
ALKALI
ALKALIC
ALKALIES
ALKALIFY
ALKALIN
ALKALINE
ALKALIS
ALKALISE
ALKALISED
ALKALISER
ALKALISES
ALKALIZE
ALKALIZED
ALKALIZER
ALKALIZES
ALKALOID
ALKALOIDS
ALKALOSES
ALKALOSIS
ALKALOTIC
ALKANE
ALKANES
ALKANET
ALKANETS
ALKANNIN
ALKANNINS
ALKENE
ALKENES
ALKIE
ALKIES
ALKINE
ALKINES
ALKO
ALKOS
ALKOXIDE
ALKOXIDES
ALKOXY
ALKY
ALKYD
ALKYDS
ALKYL
ALKYLATE
ALKYLATED
ALKYLATES
ALKYLIC
ALKYLS
ALKYNE
ALKYNES

ALL
ALLANITE
ALLANITES
ALLANTOIC
ALLANTOID
ALLANTOIN
ALLANTOIS
ALLATIVE
ALLATIVES
ALLAY
ALLAYED
ALLAYER
ALLAYERS
ALLAYING
ALLAYINGS
ALLAYMENT
ALLAYS
ALLCOMERS
ALLEDGE
ALLEDGED
ALLEDGES
ALLEDGING
ALLEE
ALLEES
ALLEGE
ALLEGED
ALLEGEDLY
ALLEGER
ALLEGERS
ALLEGES
ALLEGGE
ALLEGGED
ALLEGGES
ALLEGGING
ALLEGIANT
ALLEGING
ALLEGORIC
ALLEGORY
ALLEGRO
ALLEGROS
ALLEL
ALLELE
ALLELES
ALLELIC
ALLELISM
ALLELISMS
ALLELS
ALLELUIA
ALLELUIAH
ALLELUIAS
ALLEMANDE
ALLENARLY
ALLERGEN
ALLERGENS
ALLERGIC
ALLERGICS
ALLERGIES
ALLERGIN
ALLERGINS
ALLERGIST
ALLERGY
ALLERION
ALLERIONS
ALLETHRIN
ALLEVIANT
ALLEVIATE
ALLEY
ALLEYCAT
ALLEYCATS
ALLEYED
ALLEYS
ALLEYWAY
ALLEYWAYS
ALLHEAL
ALLHEALS
ALLIABLE
ALLIAK
ALLIAKS
ALLIANCE
ALLIANCES
ALLICE
ALLICES
ALLICHOLY
ALLICIN
ALLICINS
ALLIED
ALLIES
ALLIGARTA
ALLIGATE
ALLIGATED
ALLIGATES
ALLIGATOR
ALLIS
ALLISES
ALLIUM
ALLIUMS
ALLNESS
ALLNESSES
ALLNIGHT
ALLOBAR
ALLOBARS
ALLOCABLE
ALLOCARPY
ALLOCATE
ALLOCATED
ALLOCATES
ALLOCATOR
ALLOD
ALLODIA
ALLODIAL
ALLODIUM
ALLODIUMS
ALLODS
ALLODYNIA
ALLOGAMY
ALLOGENIC
ALLOGRAFT
ALLOGRAPH
ALLOMERIC
ALLOMETRY
ALLOMONE
ALLOMONES
ALLOMORPH
ALLONGE
ALLONGED
ALLONGES
ALLONGING
ALLONS
ALLONYM
ALLONYMS
ALLOPATH
ALLOPATHS
ALLOPATHY
ALLOPATRY
ALLOPHANE
ALLOPHONE
ALLOPLASM
ALLOSAUR
ALLOSAURS
ALLOSTERY
ALLOT
ALLOTMENT
ALLOTROPE
ALLOTROPY
ALLOTS
ALLOTTED
ALLOTTEE
ALLOTTEES
ALLOTTER
ALLOTTERS
ALLOTTERY
ALLOTTING
ALLOTYPE
ALLOTYPES
ALLOTYPIC
ALLOTYPY
ALLOVER
ALLOVERS
ALLOW
ALLOWABLE
ALLOWABLY
ALLOWANCE
ALLOWED
ALLOWEDLY
ALLOWING
ALLOWS
ALLOXAN
ALLOXANS
ALLOY
ALLOYED
ALLOYING
ALLOYS
ALLOZYME
ALLOZYMES
ALLS
ALLSEED
ALLSEEDS
ALLSORTS
ALLSPICE
ALLSPICES
ALLUDE
ALLUDED
ALLUDES
ALLUDING
ALLURE
ALLURED
ALLURER
ALLURERS
ALLURES
ALLURING
ALLUSION
ALLUSIONS
ALLUSIVE
ALLUVIA
ALLUVIAL
ALLUVIALS
ALLUVION
ALLUVIONS
ALLUVIUM
ALLUVIUMS
ALLY
ALLYING
ALLYL
ALLYLIC
ALLYLS
ALLYOU
ALMA
ALMAGEST
ALMAGESTS
ALMAH
ALMAHS
ALMAIN
ALMAINS
ALMANAC
ALMANACK
ALMANACKS
ALMANACS
ALMANDINE
ALMANDITE
ALMAS
ALME
ALMEH
ALMEHS
ALMEMAR
ALMEMARS
ALMERIES
ALMERY
ALMES
ALMIGHTY
ALMIRAH
ALMIRAHS
ALMNER
ALMNERS
ALMOND
ALMONDIER
ALMONDITE
ALMONDS
ALMONDY
ALMONER
ALMONERS

A

ALMONRIES
ALMONRY
ALMOST
ALMOUS
ALMS
ALMSGIVER
ALMSHOUSE
ALMSMAN
ALMSMEN
ALMSWOMAN
ALMSWOMEN
ALMUCE
ALMUCES
ALMUD
ALMUDE
ALMUDES
ALMUDS
ALMUG
ALMUGS
ALNAGE
ALNAGER
ALNAGERS
ALNAGES
ALNICO
ALNICOS
ALOCASIA
ALOCASIAS
ALOD
ALODIA
ALODIAL
ALODIUM
ALODIUMS
ALODS
ALOE
ALOED
ALOES
ALOESWOOD
ALOETIC
ALOETICS
ALOFT
ALOGIA
ALOGIAS
ALOGICAL
ALOHA
ALOHAS
ALOIN
ALOINS
ALONE
ALONELY
ALONENESS
ALONG
ALONGSIDE
ALONGST
ALOO
ALOOF
ALOOFLY
ALOOFNESS
ALOOS
ALOPECIA
ALOPECIAS
ALOPECIC
ALOPECOID
ALOUD
ALOW
ALOWE
ALP
ALPACA
ALPACAS
ALPACCA
ALPACCAS
ALPARGATA
ALPEEN
ALPEENS
ALPENGLOW
ALPENHORN
ALPHA
ALPHABET
ALPHABETS
ALPHAS
ALPHASORT
ALPHATEST
ALPHORN
ALPHORNS
ALPHOSIS
ALPHYL
ALPHYLS
ALPINE
ALPINELY
ALPINES
ALPINISM
ALPINISMS
ALPINIST
ALPINISTS
ALPS
ALREADY
ALRIGHT
ALS
ALSIKE
ALSIKES
ALSO
ALSOON
ALSOONE
ALT
ALTAR
ALTARAGE
ALTARAGES
ALTARS
ALTARWISE
ALTER
ALTERABLE
ALTERABLY
ALTERANT
ALTERANTS
ALTERCATE
ALTERED
ALTERER
ALTERERS
ALTERING
ALTERITY
ALTERN
ALTERNANT
ALTERNAT
ALTERNATE
ALTERNATS
ALTERNE
ALTERNES
ALTERS
ALTESSE
ALTESSES
ALTEZA
ALTEZAS
ALTEZZA
ALTEZZAS
ALTHAEA
ALTHAEAS
ALTHEA
ALTHEAS
ALTHO
ALTHORN
ALTHORNS
ALTHOUGH
ALTIGRAPH
ALTIMETER
ALTIMETRY
ALTIPLANO
ALTISSIMO
ALTITUDE
ALTITUDES
ALTO
ALTOIST
ALTOISTS
ALTOS
ALTRICES
ALTRICIAL
ALTRUISM
ALTRUISMS
ALTRUIST
ALTRUISTS
ALTS
ALU
ALUDEL
ALUDELS
ALULA
ALULAE
ALULAR
ALULAS
ALUM
ALUMIN
ALUMINA
ALUMINAS
ALUMINATE
ALUMINE
ALUMINES
ALUMINIC
ALUMINIDE
ALUMINISE
ALUMINIUM
ALUMINIZE
ALUMINOUS
ALUMINS
ALUMINUM
ALUMINUMS
ALUMISH
ALUMIUM
ALUMIUMS
ALUMNA
ALUMNAE
ALUMNI
ALUMNUS
ALUMROOT
ALUMROOTS
ALUMS
ALUMSTONE
ALUNITE
ALUNITES
ALURE
ALURES
ALUS
ALVAR
ALVARS
ALVEARIES
ALVEARY
ALVEATED
ALVEOLAR
ALVEOLARS
ALVEOLATE
ALVEOLE
ALVEOLES
ALVEOLI
ALVEOLUS
ALVINE
ALWAY
ALWAYS
ALYSSUM
ALYSSUMS
AM
AMA
AMABILE
AMADAVAT
AMADAVATS
AMADODA
AMADOU
AMADOUS
AMAH
AMAHS
AMAIN
AMAKHOSI
AMAKOSI
AMALGAM
AMALGAMS
AMANDINE
AMANDINES
AMANDLA
AMANDLAS
AMANITA
AMANITAS
AMANITIN
AMANITINS
AMARACUS
AMARANT

AMARANTH
AMARANTHS
AMARANTIN
AMARANTS
AMARELLE
AMARELLES
AMARETTI
AMARETTO
AMARETTOS
AMARNA
AMARONE
AMARONES
AMARYLLID
AMARYLLIS
AMAS
AMASS
AMASSABLE
AMASSED
AMASSER
AMASSERS
AMASSES
AMASSING
AMASSMENT
AMATE
AMATED
AMATES
AMATEUR
AMATEURS
AMATING
AMATION
AMATIONS
AMATIVE
AMATIVELY
AMATOL
AMATOLS
AMATORIAL
AMATORIAN
AMATORY
AMAUROSES
AMAUROSIS
AMAUROTIC
AMAUT
AMAUTI
AMAUTIK
AMAUTIKS
AMAUTIS
AMAUTS
AMAZE
AMAZED
AMAZEDLY
AMAZEMENT
AMAZES
AMAZING
AMAZINGLY
AMAZON
AMAZONIAN
AMAZONITE
AMAZONS
AMBACH
AMBACHES
AMBAGE
AMBAGES
AMBAGIOUS
AMBAN
AMBANS
AMBARI
AMBARIES
AMBARIS
AMBARY
AMBASSAGE
AMBASSIES
AMBASSY
AMBATCH
AMBATCHES
AMBEER
AMBEERS
AMBER
AMBERED
AMBERGRIS
AMBERIER
AMBERIES
AMBERIEST
AMBERINA
AMBERINAS
AMBERITE
AMBERITES
AMBERJACK
AMBEROID
AMBEROIDS
AMBEROUS
AMBERS
AMBERY
AMBIANCE
AMBIANCES
AMBIENCE
AMBIENCES
AMBIENT
AMBIENTS
AMBIGUITY
AMBIGUOUS
AMBIPOLAR
AMBIT
AMBITION
AMBITIONS
AMBITIOUS
AMBITS
AMBITTY
AMBIVERT
AMBIVERTS
AMBLE
AMBLED
AMBLER
AMBLERS
AMBLES
AMBLING
AMBLINGS
AMBLYOPIA
AMBLYOPIC
AMBO
AMBOINA
AMBOINAS
AMBONES
AMBOS
AMBOYNA
AMBOYNAS
AMBRIES
AMBROID
AMBROIDS
AMBROSIA
AMBROSIAL
AMBROSIAN
AMBROSIAS
AMBROTYPE
AMBRY
AMBSACE
AMBSACES
AMBULACRA
AMBULANCE
AMBULANT
AMBULANTS
AMBULATE
AMBULATED
AMBULATES
AMBULATOR
AMBULETTE
AMBUSCADE
AMBUSCADO
AMBUSH
AMBUSHED
AMBUSHER
AMBUSHERS
AMBUSHES
AMBUSHING
AME
AMEARST
AMEBA
AMEBAE
AMEBAN
AMEBAS
AMEBEAN
AMEBIASES
AMEBIASIS
AMEBIC
AMEBOCYTE
AMEBOID
AMEER
AMEERATE
AMEERATES
AMEERS
AMEIOSES
AMEIOSIS
AMELCORN
AMELCORNS
AMELIA
AMELIAS
AMEN
AMENABLE
AMENABLY
AMENAGE
AMENAGED
AMENAGES
AMENAGING
AMENAUNCE
AMEND
AMENDABLE
AMENDE
AMENDED
AMENDER
AMENDERS
AMENDES
AMENDING
AMENDMENT
AMENDS
AMENE
AMENED
AMENING
AMENITIES
AMENITY
AMENS
AMENT
AMENTA
AMENTAL
AMENTIA
AMENTIAS
AMENTS
AMENTUM
AMERCE
AMERCED
AMERCER
AMERCERS
AMERCES
AMERCING
AMERICIUM
AMES
AMESACE
AMESACES
AMETHYST
AMETHYSTS
AMETROPIA
AMETROPIC
AMI
AMIA
AMIABLE
AMIABLY
AMIANTHUS
AMIANTUS
AMIAS
AMICABLE
AMICABLY
AMICE
AMICES
AMICI
AMICUS
AMID
AMIDASE
AMIDASES
AMIDE
AMIDES
AMIDIC
AMIDIN

A

A

AMIDINE
AMIDINES
AMIDINS
AMIDMOST
AMIDO
AMIDOGEN
AMIDOGENS
AMIDOL
AMIDOLS
AMIDONE
AMIDONES
AMIDS
AMIDSHIP
AMIDSHIPS
AMIDST
AMIE
AMIES
AMIGA
AMIGAS
AMIGO
AMIGOS
AMILDAR
AMILDARS
AMIN
AMINE
AMINES
AMINIC
AMINITIES
AMINITY
AMINO
AMINOS
AMINS
AMIR
AMIRATE
AMIRATES
AMIRS
AMIS
AMISES
AMISS
AMISSES
AMISSIBLE
AMISSING
AMITIES
AMITOSES
AMITOSIS
AMITOTIC
AMITROLE
AMITROLES
AMITY
AMLA
AMLAS
AMMAN
AMMANS
AMMETER
AMMETERS
AMMINE
AMMINES
AMMINO
AMMIRAL
AMMIRALS
AMMO
AMMOCETE
AMMOCETES
AMMOCOETE
AMMOLITE
AMMOLITES
AMMON
AMMONAL
AMMONALS
AMMONATE
AMMONATES
AMMONIA
AMMONIAC
AMMONIACS
AMMONIAS
AMMONIATE
AMMONIC
AMMONICAL
AMMONIFY
AMMONITE
AMMONITES
AMMONITIC
AMMONIUM
AMMONIUMS
AMMONO
AMMONOID
AMMONOIDS
AMMONS
AMMOS
AMNESIA
AMNESIAC
AMNESIACS
AMNESIAS
AMNESIC
AMNESICS
AMNESTIC
AMNESTIED
AMNESTIES
AMNESTY
AMNIA
AMNIC
AMNIO
AMNION
AMNIONIC
AMNIONS
AMNIOS
AMNIOTE
AMNIOTES
AMNIOTIC
AMNIOTOMY
AMOEBA
AMOEBAE
AMOEBAEAN
AMOEBAN
AMOEBAS
AMOEBEAN
AMOEBIC
AMOEBOID
AMOK
AMOKS
AMOKURA
AMOKURAS
AMOLE
AMOLES
AMOMUM
AMOMUMS
AMONG
AMONGST
AMOOVE
AMOOVED
AMOOVES
AMOOVING
AMORAL
AMORALISM
AMORALIST
AMORALITY
AMORALLY
AMORANCE
AMORANCES
AMORANT
AMORCE
AMORCES
AMORET
AMORETS
AMORETTI
AMORETTO
AMORETTOS
AMORINI
AMORINO
AMORISM
AMORISMS
AMORIST
AMORISTIC
AMORISTS
AMORNINGS
AMOROSA
AMOROSAS
AMOROSITY
AMOROSO
AMOROSOS
AMOROUS
AMOROUSLY
AMORPHISM
AMORPHOUS
AMORT
AMORTISE
AMORTISED
AMORTISES
AMORTIZE
AMORTIZED
AMORTIZES
AMOSITE
AMOSITES
AMOTION
AMOTIONS
AMOUNT
AMOUNTED
AMOUNTING
AMOUNTS
AMOUR
AMOURETTE
AMOURS
AMOVE
AMOVED
AMOVES
AMOVING
AMOWT
AMOWTS
AMP
AMPACITY
AMPASSIES
AMPASSY
AMPED
AMPERAGE
AMPERAGES
AMPERE
AMPERES
AMPERSAND
AMPERZAND
AMPHIBIA
AMPHIBIAN
AMPHIBOLE
AMPHIBOLY
AMPHIGORY
AMPHIOXI
AMPHIOXUS
AMPHIPATH
AMPHIPOD
AMPHIPODS
AMPHOLYTE
AMPHORA
AMPHORAE
AMPHORAL
AMPHORAS
AMPHORIC
AMPING
AMPLE
AMPLENESS
AMPLER
AMPLEST
AMPLEXUS
AMPLIDYNE
AMPLIFIED
AMPLIFIER
AMPLIFIES
AMPLIFY
AMPLITUDE
AMPLOSOME
AMPLY
AMPOULE
AMPOULES
AMPS
AMPUL
AMPULE
AMPULES
AMPULLA
AMPULLAE
AMPULLAR
AMPULLARY
AMPULS

AMPUTATE
AMPUTATED
AMPUTATES
AMPUTATOR
AMPUTEE
AMPUTEES
AMREETA
AMREETAS
AMRIT
AMRITA
AMRITAS
AMRITS
AMSINCKIA
AMTMAN
AMTMANS
AMTRAC
AMTRACK
AMTRACKS
AMTRACS
AMTRAK
AMTRAKS
AMU
AMUCK
AMUCKS
AMULET
AMULETIC
AMULETS
AMUS
AMUSABLE
AMUSE
AMUSEABLE
AMUSED
AMUSEDLY
AMUSEMENT
AMUSER
AMUSERS
AMUSES
AMUSETTE
AMUSETTES
AMUSIA
AMUSIAS
AMUSIC
AMUSING
AMUSINGLY
AMUSIVE
AMYGDAL
AMYGDALA
AMYGDALAE

AMYGDALE
AMYGDALES
AMYGDALIN
AMYGDALS
AMYGDULE
AMYGDULES
AMYL
AMYLASE
AMYLASES
AMYLENE
AMYLENES
AMYLIC
AMYLOGEN
AMYLOGENS
AMYLOID
AMYLOIDAL
AMYLOIDS
AMYLOPSIN
AMYLOSE
AMYLOSES
AMYLS
AMYLUM
AMYLUMS
AMYOTONIA
AMYTAL
AMYTALS
AN
ANA
ANABAENA
ANABAENAS
ANABANTID
ANABAS
ANABASES
ANABASIS
ANABATIC
ANABIOSES
ANABIOSIS
ANABIOTIC
ANABLEPS
ANABOLIC
ANABOLISM
ANABOLITE
ANABRANCH
ANACHARIS
ANACLINAL
ANACLISES
ANACLISIS
ANACLITIC

ANACONDA
ANACONDAS
ANACRUSES
ANACRUSIS
ANADEM
ANADEMS
ANAEMIA
ANAEMIAS
ANAEMIC
ANAEROBE
ANAEROBES
ANAEROBIA
ANAEROBIC
ANAGEN
ANAGENS
ANAGLYPH
ANAGLYPHS
ANAGLYPHY
ANAGOGE
ANAGOGES
ANAGOGIC
ANAGOGIES
ANAGOGY
ANAGRAM
ANAGRAMS
ANAL
ANALCIME
ANALCIMES
ANALCIMIC
ANALCITE
ANALCITES
ANALECTA
ANALECTIC
ANALECTS
ANALEMMA
ANALEMMAS
ANALEPTIC
ANALGESIA
ANALGESIC
ANALGETIC
ANALGIA
ANALGIAS
ANALITIES
ANALITY
ANALLY
ANALOG
ANALOGA
ANALOGIC

ANALOGIES
ANALOGISE
ANALOGISM
ANALOGIST
ANALOGIZE
ANALOGON
ANALOGONS
ANALOGOUS
ANALOGS
ANALOGUE
ANALOGUES
ANALOGY
ANALYSAND
ANALYSE
ANALYSED
ANALYSER
ANALYSERS
ANALYSES
ANALYSING
ANALYSIS
ANALYST
ANALYSTS
ANALYTE
ANALYTES
ANALYTIC
ANALYTICS
ANALYZE
ANALYZED
ANALYZER
ANALYZERS
ANALYZES
ANALYZING
ANAMNESES
ANAMNESIS
ANAMNIOTE
ANAN
ANANA
ANANAS
ANANASES
ANANDA
ANANDAS
ANANDROUS
ANANKE
ANANKES
ANANTHOUS
ANAPAEST
ANAPAESTS
ANAPEST

ANAPESTIC
ANAPESTS
ANAPHASE
ANAPHASES
ANAPHASIC
ANAPHOR
ANAPHORA
ANAPHORAL
ANAPHORAS
ANAPHORIC
ANAPHORS
ANAPLASIA
ANAPLASTY
ANAPTYXES
ANAPTYXIS
ANARCH
ANARCHAL
ANARCHIAL
ANARCHIC
ANARCHIES
ANARCHISE
ANARCHISM
ANARCHIST
ANARCHIZE
ANARCHS
ANARCHY
ANARTHRIA
ANARTHRIC
ANAS
ANASARCA
ANASARCAS
ANASTASES
ANASTASIS
ANASTATIC
ANATA
ANATAS
ANATASE
ANATASES
ANATEXES
ANATEXIS
ANATHEMA
ANATHEMAS
ANATMAN
ANATMANS
ANATOMIC
ANATOMIES
ANATOMISE
ANATOMIST

A

ANATOMIZE
ANATOMY
ANATOXIN
ANATOXINS
ANATROPY
ANATTA
ANATTAS
ANATTO
ANATTOS
ANAXIAL
ANBURIES
ANBURY
ANCE
ANCESTOR
ANCESTORS
ANCESTRAL
ANCESTRY
ANCHO
ANCHOR
ANCHORAGE
ANCHORED
ANCHORESS
ANCHORET
ANCHORETS
ANCHORING
ANCHORITE
ANCHORMAN
ANCHORMEN
ANCHORS
ANCHOS
ANCHOVETA
ANCHOVIES
ANCHOVY
ANCHUSA
ANCHUSAS
ANCHUSIN
ANCHUSINS
ANCHYLOSE
ANCIENT
ANCIENTER
ANCIENTLY
ANCIENTRY
ANCIENTS
ANCILE
ANCILIA
ANCILLA
ANCILLAE
ANCILLARY
ANCILLAS
ANCIPITAL
ANCLE
ANCLES
ANCOME
ANCOMES
ANCON
ANCONAL
ANCONE
ANCONEAL
ANCONES
ANCONOID
ANCORA
ANCRESS
ANCRESSES
AND
ANDANTE
ANDANTES
ANDANTINI
ANDANTINO
ANDESINE
ANDESINES
ANDESITE
ANDESITES
ANDESITIC
ANDESYTE
ANDESYTES
ANDIRON
ANDIRONS
ANDOUILLE
ANDRADITE
ANDRO
ANDROECIA
ANDROGEN
ANDROGENS
ANDROGYNE
ANDROGYNY
ANDROID
ANDROIDS
ANDROLOGY
ANDROMEDA
ANDROS
ANDS
ANDVILE
ANDVILES
ANE
ANEAR
ANEARED
ANEARING
ANEARS
ANEATH
ANECDOTA
ANECDOTAL
ANECDOTE
ANECDOTES
ANECDOTIC
ANECDYSES
ANECDYSIS
ANECHOIC
ANELACE
ANELACES
ANELASTIC
ANELE
ANELED
ANELES
ANELING
ANELLI
ANEMIA
ANEMIAS
ANEMIC
ANEMOGRAM
ANEMOLOGY
ANEMONE
ANEMONES
ANEMOSES
ANEMOSIS
ANENST
ANENT
ANERGIA
ANERGIAS
ANERGIC
ANERGIES
ANERGY
ANERLY
ANEROID
ANEROIDS
ANES
ANESTRA
ANESTRI
ANESTROUS
ANESTRUM
ANESTRUS
ANETHOL
ANETHOLE
ANETHOLES
ANETHOLS
ANETIC
ANEUPLOID
ANEURIN
ANEURINS
ANEURISM
ANEURISMS
ANEURYSM
ANEURYSMS
ANEW
ANGA
ANGAKOK
ANGAKOKS
ANGARIA
ANGARIAS
ANGARIES
ANGARY
ANGAS
ANGASHORE
ANGEKKOK
ANGEKKOKS
ANGEKOK
ANGEKOKS
ANGEL
ANGELED
ANGELFISH
ANGELHOOD
ANGELIC
ANGELICA
ANGELICAL
ANGELICAS
ANGELING
ANGELS
ANGELUS
ANGELUSES
ANGER
ANGERED
ANGERING
ANGERLESS
ANGERLY
ANGERS
ANGICO
ANGICOS
ANGINA
ANGINAL
ANGINAS
ANGINOSE
ANGINOUS
ANGIOGRAM
ANGIOLOGY
ANGIOMA
ANGIOMAS
ANGIOMATA
ANGISHORE
ANGKLUNG
ANGKLUNGS
ANGLE
ANGLED
ANGLEDUG
ANGLEDUGS
ANGLEPOD
ANGLEPODS
ANGLER
ANGLERS
ANGLES
ANGLESITE
ANGLEWISE
ANGLEWORM
ANGLICE
ANGLICISE
ANGLICISM
ANGLICIST
ANGLICIZE
ANGLIFIED
ANGLIFIES
ANGLIFY
ANGLING
ANGLINGS
ANGLIST
ANGLISTS
ANGLO
ANGLOPHIL
ANGLOS
ANGOLA
ANGOPHORA
ANGORA
ANGORAS
ANGOSTURA
ANGRIER
ANGRIES
ANGRIEST
ANGRILY
ANGRINESS
ANGRY
ANGST
ANGSTIER
ANGSTIEST

ANGSTROM
ANGSTROMS
ANGSTS
ANGSTY
ANGUIFORM
ANGUINE
ANGUIPED
ANGUIPEDE
ANGUIPEDS
ANGUISH
ANGUISHED
ANGUISHES
ANGULAR
ANGULARLY
ANGULATE
ANGULATED
ANGULATES
ANGULOSE
ANGULOUS
ANHEDONIA
ANHEDONIC
ANHEDRAL
ANHEDRALS
ANHINGA
ANHINGAS
ANHUNGRED
ANHYDRASE
ANHYDRIDE
ANHYDRITE
ANHYDROUS
ANI
ANICCA
ANICCAS
ANICONIC
ANICONISM
ANICONIST
ANICUT
ANICUTS
ANIDROSES
ANIDROSIS
ANIGH
ANIGHT
ANIL
ANILE
ANILIN
ANILINE
ANILINES
ANILINGUS
ANILINS
ANILITIES
ANILITY
ANILS
ANIMA
ANIMACIES
ANIMACY
ANIMAL
ANIMALIAN
ANIMALIC
ANIMALIER
ANIMALISE
ANIMALISM
ANIMALIST
ANIMALITY
ANIMALIZE
ANIMALLY
ANIMALS
ANIMAS
ANIMATE
ANIMATED
ANIMATELY
ANIMATER
ANIMATERS
ANIMATES
ANIMATEUR
ANIMATI
ANIMATIC
ANIMATICS
ANIMATING
ANIMATION
ANIMATISM
ANIMATIST
ANIMATO
ANIMATOR
ANIMATORS
ANIMATOS
ANIME
ANIMES
ANIMI
ANIMIS
ANIMISM
ANIMISMS
ANIMIST
ANIMISTIC
ANIMISTS
ANIMOSITY
ANIMUS
ANIMUSES
ANION
ANIONIC
ANIONS
ANIRIDIA
ANIRIDIAS
ANIRIDIC
ANIS
ANISE
ANISEED
ANISEEDS
ANISES
ANISETTE
ANISETTES
ANISIC
ANISOGAMY
ANISOLE
ANISOLES
ANKER
ANKERITE
ANKERITES
ANKERS
ANKH
ANKHS
ANKLE
ANKLEBONE
ANKLED
ANKLES
ANKLET
ANKLETS
ANKLING
ANKLONG
ANKLONGS
ANKLUNG
ANKLUNGS
ANKUS
ANKUSES
ANKUSH
ANKUSHES
ANKYLOSE
ANKYLOSED
ANKYLOSES
ANKYLOSIS
ANKYLOTIC
ANLACE
ANLACES
ANLAGE
ANLAGEN
ANLAGES
ANLAS
ANLASES
ANN
ANNA
ANNAL
ANNALISE
ANNALISED
ANNALISES
ANNALIST
ANNALISTS
ANNALIZE
ANNALIZED
ANNALIZES
ANNALS
ANNAS
ANNAT
ANNATES
ANNATS
ANNATTA
ANNATTAS
ANNATTO
ANNATTOS
ANNEAL
ANNEALED
ANNEALER
ANNEALERS
ANNEALING
ANNEALS
ANNECTENT
ANNELID
ANNELIDAN
ANNELIDS
ANNEX
ANNEXABLE
ANNEXE
ANNEXED
ANNEXES
ANNEXING
ANNEXION
ANNEXIONS
ANNEXMENT
ANNEXURE
ANNEXURES
ANNICUT
ANNICUTS
ANNO
ANNONA
ANNONAS
ANNOTATE
ANNOTATED
ANNOTATES
ANNOTATOR
ANNOUNCE
ANNOUNCED
ANNOUNCER
ANNOUNCES
ANNOY
ANNOYANCE
ANNOYED
ANNOYER
ANNOYERS
ANNOYING
ANNOYS
ANNS
ANNUAL
ANNUALISE
ANNUALIZE
ANNUALLY
ANNUALS
ANNUITANT
ANNUITIES
ANNUITISE
ANNUITIZE
ANNUITY
ANNUL
ANNULAR
ANNULARLY
ANNULARS
ANNULATE
ANNULATED
ANNULATES
ANNULET
ANNULETS
ANNULI
ANNULLED
ANNULLING
ANNULMENT
ANNULOSE
ANNULS
ANNULUS
ANNULUSES
ANOA
ANOAS
ANOBIID
ANOBIIDS

ANODAL
ANODALLY
ANODE
ANODES
ANODIC
ANODISE
ANODISED
ANODISER
ANODISERS
ANODISES
ANODISING
ANODIZE
ANODIZED
ANODIZER
ANODIZERS
ANODIZES
ANODIZING
ANODONTIA
ANODYNE
ANODYNES
ANODYNIC
ANOESES
ANOESIS
ANOESTRA
ANOESTRI
ANOESTRUM
ANOESTRUS
ANOETIC
ANOINT
ANOINTED
ANOINTER
ANOINTERS
ANOINTING
ANOINTS
ANOLE
ANOLES
ANOLYTE
ANOLYTES
ANOMALIES
ANOMALOUS
ANOMALY
ANOMIC
ANOMIE
ANOMIES
ANOMY
ANON
ANONYM
ANONYMA
ANONYMAS
ANONYMISE
ANONYMITY
ANONYMIZE
ANONYMOUS
ANONYMS
ANOOPSIA
ANOOPSIAS
ANOPHELES
ANOPIA
ANOPIAS
ANOPSIA
ANOPSIAS
ANORAK
ANORAKS
ANORECTAL
ANORECTIC
ANORETIC
ANORETICS
ANOREXIA
ANOREXIAS
ANOREXIC
ANOREXICS
ANOREXIES
ANOREXY
ANORTHIC
ANORTHITE
ANOSMATIC
ANOSMIA
ANOSMIAS
ANOSMIC
ANOTHER
ANOUGH
ANOUROUS
ANOVULANT
ANOVULAR
ANOW
ANOXAEMIA
ANOXAEMIC
ANOXEMIA
ANOXEMIAS
ANOXEMIC
ANOXIA
ANOXIAS
ANOXIC
ANS
ANSA
ANSAE
ANSAPHONE
ANSATE
ANSATED
ANSATZ
ANSATZES
ANSERINE
ANSERINES
ANSEROUS
ANSWER
ANSWERED
ANSWERER
ANSWERERS
ANSWERING
ANSWERS
ANT
ANTA
ANTACID
ANTACIDS
ANTAE
ANTALGIC
ANTALGICS
ANTALKALI
ANTAR
ANTARA
ANTARAS
ANTARCTIC
ANTARS
ANTAS
ANTBEAR
ANTBEARS
ANTBIRD
ANTBIRDS
ANTE
ANTEATER
ANTEATERS
ANTECEDE
ANTECEDED
ANTECEDES
ANTECHOIR
ANTED
ANTEDATE
ANTEDATED
ANTEDATES
ANTEED
ANTEFIX
ANTEFIXA
ANTEFIXAE
ANTEFIXAL
ANTEFIXES
ANTEING
ANTELOPE
ANTELOPES
ANTELUCAN
ANTENATAL
ANTENATI
ANTENNA
ANTENNAE
ANTENNAL
ANTENNARY
ANTENNAS
ANTENNULE
ANTEPAST
ANTEPASTS
ANTERIOR
ANTEROOM
ANTEROOMS
ANTES
ANTETYPE
ANTETYPES
ANTEVERT
ANTEVERTS
ANTHELIA
ANTHELION
ANTHELIX
ANTHEM
ANTHEMED
ANTHEMIA
ANTHEMIC
ANTHEMING
ANTHEMION
ANTHEMIS
ANTHEMS
ANTHER
ANTHERAL
ANTHERID
ANTHERIDS
ANTHERS
ANTHESES
ANTHESIS
ANTHILL
ANTHILLS
ANTHOCARP
ANTHOCYAN
ANTHODIA
ANTHODIUM
ANTHOID
ANTHOLOGY
ANTHOTAXY
ANTHOZOAN
ANTHOZOIC
ANTHRACES
ANTHRACIC
ANTHRAX
ANTHRAXES
ANTHRO
ANTHROPIC
ANTHROS
ANTHURIUM
ANTI
ANTIABUSE
ANTIACNE
ANTIAGING
ANTIAIR
ANTIALIEN
ANTIAR
ANTIARIN
ANTIARINS
ANTIARMOR
ANTIARS
ANTIATOM
ANTIATOMS
ANTIAUXIN
ANTIBIAS
ANTIBLACK
ANTIBODY
ANTIBOSS
ANTIBUG
ANTIBUSER
ANTIC
ANTICAL
ANTICALLY
ANTICAR
ANTICHLOR
ANTICISE
ANTICISED
ANTICISES
ANTICITY
ANTICIVIC
ANTICIZE
ANTICIZED
ANTICIZES
ANTICK
ANTICKE
ANTICKED

ANTICKES
ANTICKING
ANTICKS
ANTICLINE
ANTICLING
ANTICLY
ANTICODON
ANTICOLD
ANTICOUS
ANTICRACK
ANTICRIME
ANTICS
ANTICULT
ANTICULTS
ANTIDORA
ANTIDORON
ANTIDOTAL
ANTIDOTE
ANTIDOTED
ANTIDOTES
ANTIDRAFT
ANTIDRUG
ANTIDUNE
ANTIDUNES
ANTIELITE
ANTIENT
ANTIENTS
ANTIFA
ANTIFAS
ANTIFAT
ANTIFLU
ANTIFOAM
ANTIFOG
ANTIFRAUD
ANTIFUR
ANTIGANG
ANTIGAY
ANTIGEN
ANTIGENE
ANTIGENES
ANTIGENIC
ANTIGENS
ANTIGLARE
ANTIGRAFT
ANTIGUN
ANTIHELIX
ANTIHERO
ANTIHUMAN
ANTIJAM
ANTIKING
ANTIKINGS
ANTIKNOCK
ANTILABOR
ANTILEAK
ANTILEFT
ANTILIFE
ANTILIFER
ANTILOCK
ANTILOG
ANTILOGS
ANTILOGY
ANTIMACHO
ANTIMALE
ANTIMAN
ANTIMASK
ANTIMASKS
ANTIMEN
ANTIMERE
ANTIMERES
ANTIMERIC
ANTIMINE
ANTIMONIC
ANTIMONY
ANTIMONYL
ANTIMUON
ANTIMUONS
ANTIMUSIC
ANTIMYCIN
ANTING
ANTINGS
ANTINODAL
ANTINODE
ANTINODES
ANTINOISE
ANTINOME
ANTINOMES
ANTINOMIC
ANTINOMY
ANTINOVEL
ANTINUKE
ANTINUKER
ANTINUKES
ANTIPAPAL
ANTIPARTY
ANTIPASTI
ANTIPASTO
ANTIPATHY
ANTIPHON
ANTIPHONS
ANTIPHONY
ANTIPILL
ANTIPODAL
ANTIPODE
ANTIPODES
ANTIPOLAR
ANTIPOLE
ANTIPOLES
ANTIPOPE
ANTIPOPES
ANTIPORN
ANTIPOT
ANTIPRESS
ANTIPYIC
ANTIPYICS
ANTIQUARK
ANTIQUARY
ANTIQUATE
ANTIQUE
ANTIQUED
ANTIQUELY
ANTIQUER
ANTIQUERS
ANTIQUES
ANTIQUEY
ANTIQUIER
ANTIQUING
ANTIQUITY
ANTIRADAR
ANTIRAPE
ANTIRED
ANTIRIOT
ANTIROCK
ANTIROLL
ANTIROYAL
ANTIRUST
ANTIRUSTS
ANTIS
ANTISAG
ANTISCIAN
ANTISENSE
ANTISERA
ANTISERUM
ANTISEX
ANTISHAKE
ANTISHARK
ANTISHIP
ANTISHOCK
ANTISKID
ANTISLEEP
ANTISLIP
ANTISMOG
ANTISMOKE
ANTISMUT
ANTISNOB
ANTISNOBS
ANTISOLAR
ANTISPAM
ANTISPAST
ANTISTAT
ANTISTATE
ANTISTATS
ANTISTICK
ANTISTORY
ANTISTYLE
ANTITANK
ANTITAX
ANTITHEFT
ANTITHET
ANTITHETS
ANTITOXIC
ANTITOXIN
ANTITRADE
ANTITRAGI
ANTITRUST
ANTITUMOR
ANTITYPAL
ANTITYPE
ANTITYPES
ANTITYPIC
ANTIULCER
ANTIUNION
ANTIURBAN
ANTIVAX
ANTIVAXER
ANTIVENIN
ANTIVENOM
ANTIVIRAL
ANTIVIRUS
ANTIWAR
ANTIWEAR
ANTIWEED
ANTIWHITE
ANTIWOMAN
ANTIWORLD
ANTLER
ANTLERED
ANTLERS
ANTLIA
ANTLIAE
ANTLIATE
ANTLIKE
ANTLION
ANTLIONS
ANTONYM
ANTONYMIC
ANTONYMS
ANTONYMY
ANTPITTA
ANTPITTAS
ANTRA
ANTRAL
ANTRE
ANTRES
ANTRORSE
ANTRUM
ANTRUMS
ANTS
ANTSIER
ANTSIEST
ANTSINESS
ANTSY
ANTWACKIE
ANUCLEATE
ANURA
ANURAL
ANURAN
ANURANS
ANURESES
ANURESIS
ANURETIC
ANURIA
ANURIAS
ANURIC
ANUROUS
ANUS
ANUSES
ANVIL
ANVILED
ANVILING
ANVILLED

ANVILLING
ANVILS
ANVILTOP
ANVILTOPS
ANXIETIES
ANXIETY
ANXIOUS
ANXIOUSLY
ANY
ANYBODIES
ANYBODY
ANYHOW
ANYMORE
ANYON
ANYONE
ANYONES
ANYONS
ANYPLACE
ANYROAD
ANYTHING
ANYTHINGS
ANYTIME
ANYWAY
ANYWAYS
ANYWHEN
ANYWHERE
ANYWHERES
ANYWISE
ANZIANI
AORIST
AORISTIC
AORISTS
AORTA
AORTAE
AORTAL
AORTAS
AORTIC
AORTITIS
AOUDAD
AOUDADS
APACE
APACHE
APACHES
APADANA
APADANAS
APAGE
APAGOGE
APAGOGES
APAGOGIC
APAID
APANAGE
APANAGED
APANAGES
APAREJO
APAREJOS
APART
APARTHEID
APARTMENT
APARTNESS
APATETIC
APATHATON
APATHETIC
APATHIES
APATHY
APATITE
APATITES
APATOSAUR
APAY
APAYD
APAYING
APAYS
APE
APEAK
APED
APEDOM
APEDOMS
APEEK
APEHOOD
APEHOODS
APELIKE
APEMAN
APEMEN
APEPSIA
APEPSIAS
APEPSIES
APEPSY
APER
APERCU
APERCUS
APERIENT
APERIENTS
APERIES
APERIODIC
APERITIF
APERITIFS
APERITIVE
APERS
APERT
APERTNESS
APERTURAL
APERTURE
APERTURED
APERTURES
APERY
APES
APESHIT
APETALIES
APETALOUS
APETALY
APEX
APEXES
APGAR
APHAGIA
APHAGIAS
APHAKIA
APHAKIAS
APHANITE
APHANITES
APHANITIC
APHASIA
APHASIAC
APHASIACS
APHASIAS
APHASIC
APHASICS
APHELIA
APHELIAN
APHELION
APHELIONS
APHERESES
APHERESIS
APHERETIC
APHESES
APHESIS
APHETIC
APHETISE
APHETISED
APHETISES
APHETIZE
APHETIZED
APHETIZES
APHICIDE
APHICIDES
APHID
APHIDES
APHIDIAN
APHIDIANS
APHIDIOUS
APHIDS
APHIS
APHOLATE
APHOLATES
APHONIA
APHONIAS
APHONIC
APHONICS
APHONIES
APHONOUS
APHONY
APHORISE
APHORISED
APHORISER
APHORISES
APHORISM
APHORISMS
APHORIST
APHORISTS
APHORIZE
APHORIZED
APHORIZER
APHORIZES
APHOTIC
APHRODITE
APHTHA
APHTHAE
APHTHOUS
APHYLLIES
APHYLLOUS
APHYLLY
APIACEOUS
APIAN
APIARIAN
APIARIANS
APIARIES
APIARIST
APIARISTS
APIARY
APICAL
APICALLY
APICALS
APICES
APICIAN
APICULATE
APICULI
APICULUS
APIECE
APIEZON
APIMANIA
APIMANIAS
APING
APIOL
APIOLOGY
APIOLS
APISH
APISHLY
APISHNESS
APISM
APISMS
APIVOROUS
APLANAT
APLANATIC
APLANATS
APLANETIC
APLASIA
APLASIAS
APLASTIC
APLENTY
APLITE
APLITES
APLITIC
APLOMB
APLOMBS
APLUSTRE
APLUSTRES
APNEA
APNEAL
APNEAS
APNEIC
APNEUSES
APNEUSIS
APNEUSTIC
APNOEA
APNOEAL
APNOEAS
APNOEIC
APO
APOAPSES
APOAPSIS
APOCARP
APOCARPS

APOCARPY
APOCOPATE
APOCOPE
APOCOPES
APOCOPIC
APOCRINE
APOCRYPHA
APOD
APODAL
APODE
APODES
APODICTIC
APODOSES
APODOSIS
APODOUS
APODS
APOENZYME
APOGAEIC
APOGAMIC
APOGAMIES
APOGAMOUS
APOGAMY
APOGEAL
APOGEAN
APOGEE
APOGEES
APOGEIC
APOGRAPH
APOGRAPHS
APOLLO
APOLLOS
APOLOG
APOLOGAL
APOLOGIA
APOLOGIAE
APOLOGIAS
APOLOGIES
APOLOGISE
APOLOGIST
APOLOGIZE
APOLOGS
APOLOGUE
APOLOGUES
APOLOGY
APOLUNE
APOLUNES
APOMICT
APOMICTIC
APOMICTS
APOMIXES
APOMIXIS
APOOP
APOPHASES
APOPHASIS
APOPHATIC
APOPHENIA
APOPHONY
APOPHYGE
APOPHYGES
APOPHYSES
APOPHYSIS
APOPLAST
APOPLASTS
APOPLEX
APOPLEXED
APOPLEXES
APOPLEXY
APOPTOSES
APOPTOSIS
APOPTOTIC
APORETIC
APORIA
APORIAS
APORT
APOS
APOSITIA
APOSITIAS
APOSITIC
APOSPORIC
APOSPORY
APOSTACY
APOSTASY
APOSTATE
APOSTATES
APOSTATIC
APOSTIL
APOSTILLE
APOSTILS
APOSTLE
APOSTLES
APOSTOLIC
APOTHECE
APOTHECES
APOTHECIA
APOTHEGM
APOTHEGMS
APOTHEM
APOTHEMS
APOZEM
APOZEMS
APP
APPAID
APPAIR
APPAIRED
APPAIRING
APPAIRS
APPAL
APPALL
APPALLED
APPALLING
APPALLS
APPALOOSA
APPALS
APPALTI
APPALTO
APPANAGE
APPANAGED
APPANAGES
APPARAT
APPARATS
APPARATUS
APPAREL
APPARELED
APPARELS
APPARENCY
APPARENT
APPARENTS
APPARITOR
APPAY
APPAYD
APPAYING
APPAYS
APPEACH
APPEACHED
APPEACHES
APPEAL
APPEALED
APPEALER
APPEALERS
APPEALING
APPEALS
APPEAR
APPEARED
APPEARER
APPEARERS
APPEARING
APPEARS
APPEASE
APPEASED
APPEASER
APPEASERS
APPEASES
APPEASING
APPEL
APPELLANT
APPELLATE
APPELLEE
APPELLEES
APPELLOR
APPELLORS
APPELS
APPEND
APPENDAGE
APPENDANT
APPENDED
APPENDENT
APPENDING
APPENDIX
APPENDS
APPERIL
APPERILL
APPERILLS
APPERILS
APPERTAIN
APPESTAT
APPESTATS
APPETENCE
APPETENCY
APPETENT
APPETIBLE
APPETISE
APPETISED
APPETISER
APPETISES
APPETITE
APPETITES
APPETIZE
APPETIZED
APPETIZER
APPETIZES
APPLAUD
APPLAUDED
APPLAUDER
APPLAUDS
APPLAUSE
APPLAUSES
APPLE
APPLECART
APPLEJACK
APPLES
APPLET
APPLETINI
APPLETS
APPLEY
APPLIABLE
APPLIANCE
APPLICANT
APPLICATE
APPLIED
APPLIER
APPLIERS
APPLIES
APPLIEST
APPLIQUE
APPLIQUED
APPLIQUES
APPLY
APPLYING
APPOINT
APPOINTED
APPOINTEE
APPOINTER
APPOINTOR
APPOINTS
APPORT
APPORTION
APPORTS
APPOSABLE
APPOSE
APPOSED
APPOSER
APPOSERS
APPOSES
APPOSING
APPOSITE
APPRAISAL
APPRAISE
APPRAISED
APPRAISEE
APPRAISER

APPRAISES
APPREHEND
APPRESS
APPRESSED
APPRESSES
APPRISE
APPRISED
APPRISER
APPRISERS
APPRISES
APPRISING
APPRIZE
APPRIZED
APPRIZER
APPRIZERS
APPRIZES
APPRIZING
APPRO
APPROACH
APPROBATE
APPROOF
APPROOFS
APPROS
APPROVAL
APPROVALS
APPROVE
APPROVED
APPROVER
APPROVERS
APPROVES
APPROVING
APPS
APPUI
APPUIED
APPUIS
APPULSE
APPULSES
APPULSIVE
APPUY
APPUYED
APPUYING
APPUYS
APRACTIC
APRAXIA
APRAXIAS
APRAXIC
APRES
APRICATE
APRICATED
APRICATES
APRICOCK
APRICOCKS
APRICOT
APRICOTS
APRIORISM
APRIORIST
APRIORITY
APRON
APRONED
APRONFUL
APRONFULS
APRONING
APRONLIKE
APRONS
APROPOS
APROTIC
APSARAS
APSARASES
APSE
APSES
APSIDAL
APSIDES
APSIDIOLE
APSIS
APSO
APSOS
APT
APTAMER
APTAMERS
APTED
APTER
APTERAL
APTERIA
APTERISM
APTERISMS
APTERIUM
APTEROUS
APTERYX
APTERYXES
APTEST
APTING
APTITUDE
APTITUDES
APTLY
APTNESS
APTNESSES
APTOTE
APTOTES
APTOTIC
APTS
APYRASE
APYRASES
APYRETIC
APYREXIA
APYREXIAS
AQUA
AQUABATIC
AQUABOARD
AQUACADE
AQUACADES
AQUADROME
AQUAE
AQUAFABA
AQUAFABAS
AQUAFARM
AQUAFARMS
AQUAFER
AQUAFERS
AQUAFIT
AQUAFITS
AQUALUNG
AQUALUNGS
AQUANAUT
AQUANAUTS
AQUAPHOBE
AQUAPLANE
AQUAPORIN
AQUARELLE
AQUARIA
AQUARIAL
AQUARIAN
AQUARIANS
AQUARIIST
AQUARIST
AQUARISTS
AQUARIUM
AQUARIUMS
AQUAROBIC
AQUAS
AQUASCAPE
AQUASHOW
AQUASHOWS
AQUATIC
AQUATICS
AQUATINT
AQUATINTA
AQUATINTS
AQUATONE
AQUATONES
AQUAVIT
AQUAVITS
AQUEDUCT
AQUEDUCTS
AQUEOUS
AQUEOUSLY
AQUIFER
AQUIFERS
AQUILEGIA
AQUILINE
AQUILON
AQUILONS
AQUIVER
AR
ARAARA
ARAARAS
ARABA
ARABAS
ARABESK
ARABESKS
ARABESQUE
ARABIC
ARABICA
ARABICAS
ARABICISE
ARABICIZE
ARABILITY
ARABIN
ARABINOSE
ARABINS
ARABIS
ARABISE
ARABISED
ARABISES
ARABISING
ARABIZE
ARABIZED
ARABIZES
ARABIZING
ARABLE
ARABLES
ARACEOUS
ARACHIS
ARACHISES
ARACHNID
ARACHNIDS
ARACHNOID
ARAGONITE
ARAHUANA
ARAHUANAS
ARAISE
ARAISED
ARAISES
ARAISING
ARAK
ARAKS
ARALIA
ARALIAS
ARAME
ARAMES
ARAMID
ARAMIDS
ARANCINI
ARANEID
ARANEIDAN
ARANEIDS
ARANEOUS
ARAPAIMA
ARAPAIMAS
ARAPONGA
ARAPONGAS
ARAPUNGA
ARAPUNGAS
ARAR
ARAROBA
ARAROBAS
ARARS
ARAUCARIA
ARAWANA
ARAWANAS
ARAYSE
ARAYSED
ARAYSES
ARAYSING
ARB
ARBA
ARBALEST
ARBALESTS
ARBALIST
ARBALISTS
ARBAS

ARBELEST
ARBELESTS
ARBITER
ARBITERS
ARBITRAGE
ARBITRAL
ARBITRARY
ARBITRATE
ARBITRESS
ARBITRIUM
ARBLAST
ARBLASTER
ARBLASTS
ARBOR
ARBOREAL
ARBORED
ARBOREOUS
ARBORES
ARBORET
ARBORETA
ARBORETS
ARBORETUM
ARBORIO
ARBORIOS
ARBORISE
ARBORISED
ARBORISES
ARBORIST
ARBORISTS
ARBORIZE
ARBORIZED
ARBORIZES
ARBOROUS
ARBORS
ARBOUR
ARBOURED
ARBOURS
ARBOVIRAL
ARBOVIRUS
ARBS
ARBUSCLE
ARBUSCLES
ARBUTE
ARBUTEAN
ARBUTES
ARBUTUS
ARBUTUSES
ARC
ARCADE
ARCADED
ARCADES
ARCADIA
ARCADIAN
ARCADIANS
ARCADIAS
ARCADING
ARCADINGS
ARCANA
ARCANAS
ARCANE
ARCANELY
ARCANIST
ARCANISTS
ARCANUM
ARCANUMS
ARCATURE
ARCATURES
ARCCOSINE
ARCED
ARCH
ARCHAEA
ARCHAEAL
ARCHAEAN
ARCHAEANS
ARCHAEI
ARCHAEON
ARCHAEUS
ARCHAIC
ARCHAICAL
ARCHAISE
ARCHAISED
ARCHAISER
ARCHAISES
ARCHAISM
ARCHAISMS
ARCHAIST
ARCHAISTS
ARCHAIZE
ARCHAIZED
ARCHAIZER
ARCHAIZES
ARCHANGEL
ARCHDRUID
ARCHDUCAL
ARCHDUCHY
ARCHDUKE
ARCHDUKES
ARCHEAN
ARCHED
ARCHEI
ARCHENEMY
ARCHER
ARCHERESS
ARCHERIES
ARCHERS
ARCHERY
ARCHES
ARCHEST
ARCHETYPE
ARCHEUS
ARCHFIEND
ARCHFOE
ARCHFOES
ARCHFOOL
ARCHFOOLS
ARCHI
ARCHICARP
ARCHIL
ARCHILOWE
ARCHILS
ARCHIMAGE
ARCHINE
ARCHINES
ARCHING
ARCHINGS
ARCHITECT
ARCHITYPE
ARCHIVAL
ARCHIVE
ARCHIVED
ARCHIVES
ARCHIVING
ARCHIVIST
ARCHIVOLT
ARCHLET
ARCHLETS
ARCHLIKE
ARCHLUTE
ARCHLUTES
ARCHLY
ARCHNESS
ARCHOLOGY
ARCHON
ARCHONS
ARCHONTIC
ARCHOSAUR
ARCHRIVAL
ARCHSTONE
ARCHWAY
ARCHWAYS
ARCHWISE
ARCIFORM
ARCING
ARCINGS
ARCKED
ARCKING
ARCKINGS
ARCMIN
ARCMINS
ARCMINUTE
ARCO
ARCOGRAPH
ARCOLOGY
ARCOS
ARCS
ARCSEC
ARCSECOND
ARCSECS
ARCSINE
ARCSINES
ARCTIC
ARCTICS
ARCTIID
ARCTIIDS
ARCTOID
ARCTOPHIL
ARCUATE
ARCUATED
ARCUATELY
ARCUATION
ARCUS
ARCUSES
ARD
ARDEB
ARDEBS
ARDENCIES
ARDENCY
ARDENT
ARDENTLY
ARDOR
ARDORS
ARDOUR
ARDOURS
ARDRI
ARDRIGH
ARDRIGHS
ARDRIS
ARDS
ARDUOUS
ARDUOUSLY
ARE
AREA
AREACH
AREACHED
AREACHES
AREACHING
AREAD
AREADING
AREADS
AREAE
AREAL
AREALLY
AREAR
AREARS
AREAS
AREAWAY
AREAWAYS
ARECA
ARECAS
ARECOLINE
ARED
AREDD
AREDE
AREDES
AREDING
AREFIED
AREFIES
AREFY
AREFYING
AREG
AREIC
ARENA
ARENAS
ARENATION
ARENE
ARENES
ARENITE
ARENITES
ARENITIC
ARENOSE

ARENOUS
AREOLA
AREOLAE
AREOLAR
AREOLAS
AREOLATE
AREOLATED
AREOLE
AREOLES
AREOLOGY
AREOMETER
AREOMETRY
AREOSTYLE
AREPA
AREPAS
ARERE
ARES
ARET
ARETE
ARETES
ARETHUSA
ARETHUSAS
ARETS
ARETT
ARETTED
ARETTING
ARETTS
AREW
ARF
ARFS
ARGAL
ARGALA
ARGALAS
ARGALI
ARGALIS
ARGALS
ARGAN
ARGAND
ARGANDS
ARGANS
ARGEMONE
ARGEMONES
ARGENT
ARGENTAL
ARGENTIC
ARGENTINE
ARGENTITE
ARGENTOUS
ARGENTS
ARGENTUM
ARGENTUMS
ARGH
ARGHAN
ARGHANS
ARGIL
ARGILLITE
ARGILS
ARGINASE
ARGINASES
ARGININE
ARGININES
ARGLE
ARGLED
ARGLES
ARGLING
ARGOL
ARGOLS
ARGON
ARGONAUT
ARGONAUTS
ARGONON
ARGONONS
ARGONS
ARGOSIES
ARGOSY
ARGOT
ARGOTIC
ARGOTS
ARGUABLE
ARGUABLY
ARGUE
ARGUED
ARGUER
ARGUERS
ARGUES
ARGUFIED
ARGUFIER
ARGUFIERS
ARGUFIES
ARGUFY
ARGUFYING
ARGUING
ARGULI
ARGULUS
ARGUMENT
ARGUMENTA
ARGUMENTS
ARGUS
ARGUSES
ARGUTE
ARGUTELY
ARGYLE
ARGYLES
ARGYLL
ARGYLLS
ARGYRIA
ARGYRIAS
ARGYRITE
ARGYRITES
ARHAT
ARHATS
ARHATSHIP
ARHYTHMIA
ARHYTHMIC
ARIA
ARIARIES
ARIARY
ARIAS
ARID
ARIDER
ARIDEST
ARIDITIES
ARIDITY
ARIDLY
ARIDNESS
ARIEL
ARIELS
ARIETTA
ARIETTAS
ARIETTE
ARIETTES
ARIGHT
ARIKI
ARIKIS
ARIL
ARILED
ARILLARY
ARILLATE
ARILLATED
ARILLI
ARILLODE
ARILLODES
ARILLOID
ARILLUS
ARILS
ARIOSE
ARIOSI
ARIOSO
ARIOSOS
ARIOT
ARIPPLE
ARIS
ARISE
ARISEN
ARISES
ARISH
ARISHES
ARISING
ARISTA
ARISTAE
ARISTAS
ARISTATE
ARISTO
ARISTOS
ARISTOTLE
ARK
ARKED
ARKING
ARKITE
ARKITES
ARKOSE
ARKOSES
ARKOSIC
ARKS
ARLE
ARLED
ARLES
ARLING
ARM
ARMADA
ARMADAS
ARMADILLO
ARMAGNAC
ARMAGNACS
ARMAMENT
ARMAMENTS
ARMATURE
ARMATURED
ARMATURES
ARMBAND
ARMBANDS
ARMCHAIR
ARMCHAIRS
ARMED
ARMER
ARMERIA
ARMERIAS
ARMERS
ARMET
ARMETS
ARMFUL
ARMFULS
ARMGAUNT
ARMGUARD
ARMGUARDS
ARMHOLE
ARMHOLES
ARMIES
ARMIGER
ARMIGERAL
ARMIGERO
ARMIGEROS
ARMIGERS
ARMIL
ARMILLA
ARMILLAE
ARMILLARY
ARMILLAS
ARMILS
ARMING
ARMINGS
ARMISTICE
ARMLESS
ARMLET
ARMLETS
ARMLIKE
ARMLOAD
ARMLOADS
ARMLOCK
ARMLOCKED
ARMLOCKS
ARMOIRE
ARMOIRES
ARMONICA
ARMONICAS
ARMOR
ARMORED
ARMORER
ARMORERS
ARMORIAL

ARMORIALS
ARMORIES
ARMORING
ARMORIST
ARMORISTS
ARMORLESS
ARMORS
ARMORY
ARMOUR
ARMOURED
ARMOURER
ARMOURERS
ARMOURIES
ARMOURING
ARMOURS
ARMOURY
ARMOZEEN
ARMOZEENS
ARMOZINE
ARMOZINES
ARMPIT
ARMPITS
ARMREST
ARMRESTS
ARMS
ARMSFUL
ARMURE
ARMURES
ARMY
ARMYWORM
ARMYWORMS
ARNA
ARNAS
ARNATTO
ARNATTOS
ARNICA
ARNICAS
ARNOTTO
ARNOTTOS
ARNUT
ARNUTS
AROBA
AROBAS
AROHA
AROHAS
AROID
AROIDS
AROINT
AROINTED
AROINTING
AROINTS
AROLLA
AROLLAS
AROMA
AROMAS
AROMATASE
AROMATIC
AROMATICS
AROMATISE
AROMATIZE
AROSE
AROUND
AROUSABLE
AROUSAL
AROUSALS
AROUSE
AROUSED
AROUSER
AROUSERS
AROUSES
AROUSING
AROW
AROWANA
AROWANAS
AROYNT
AROYNTED
AROYNTING
AROYNTS
ARPA
ARPAS
ARPEGGIO
ARPEGGIOS
ARPEN
ARPENS
ARPENT
ARPENTS
ARPILLERA
ARQUEBUS
ARRACACHA
ARRACK
ARRACKS
ARRAH
ARRAIGN
ARRAIGNED
ARRAIGNER
ARRAIGNS
ARRANGE
ARRANGED
ARRANGER
ARRANGERS
ARRANGES
ARRANGING
ARRANT
ARRANTLY
ARRAS
ARRASED
ARRASENE
ARRASENES
ARRASES
ARRAUGHT
ARRAY
ARRAYAL
ARRAYALS
ARRAYED
ARRAYER
ARRAYERS
ARRAYING
ARRAYMENT
ARRAYS
ARREAR
ARREARAGE
ARREARS
ARRECT
ARREEDE
ARREEDES
ARREEDING
ARREST
ARRESTANT
ARRESTED
ARRESTEE
ARRESTEES
ARRESTER
ARRESTERS
ARRESTING
ARRESTIVE
ARRESTOR
ARRESTORS
ARRESTS
ARRET
ARRETS
ARRHIZAL
ARRIAGE
ARRIAGES
ARRIBA
ARRIDE
ARRIDED
ARRIDES
ARRIDING
ARRIERE
ARRIERO
ARRIEROS
ARRIS
ARRISES
ARRISH
ARRISHES
ARRIVAL
ARRIVALS
ARRIVANCE
ARRIVANCY
ARRIVE
ARRIVED
ARRIVER
ARRIVERS
ARRIVES
ARRIVING
ARRIVISME
ARRIVISTE
ARROBA
ARROBAS
ARROCES
ARROGANCE
ARROGANCY
ARROGANT
ARROGATE
ARROGATED
ARROGATES
ARROGATOR
ARROW
ARROWED
ARROWHEAD
ARROWIER
ARROWIEST
ARROWING
ARROWLESS
ARROWLIKE
ARROWROOT
ARROWS
ARROWWOOD
ARROWWORM
ARROWY
ARROYO
ARROYOS
ARROZ
ARROZES
ARS
ARSE
ARSED
ARSEHOLE
ARSEHOLED
ARSEHOLES
ARSENAL
ARSENALS
ARSENATE
ARSENATES
ARSENIATE
ARSENIC
ARSENICAL
ARSENICS
ARSENIDE
ARSENIDES
ARSENIOUS
ARSENITE
ARSENITES
ARSENO
ARSENOUS
ARSES
ARSEY
ARSHEEN
ARSHEENS
ARSHIN
ARSHINE
ARSHINES
ARSHINS
ARSIER
ARSIEST
ARSINE
ARSINES
ARSING
ARSINO
ARSIS
ARSON
ARSONIST
ARSONISTS
ARSONITE
ARSONITES
ARSONOUS
ARSONS
ARSY
ART
ARTAL

ARTEFACT
ARTEFACTS
ARTEL
ARTELS
ARTEMISIA
ARTERIAL
ARTERIALS
ARTERIES
ARTERIOLE
ARTERITIS
ARTERY
ARTESIAN
ARTFUL
ARTFULLY
ARTHOUSE
ARTHOUSES
ARTHRITIC
ARTHRITIS
ARTHRODIA
ARTHROPOD
ARTHROSES
ARTHROSIS
ARTI
ARTIC
ARTICHOKE
ARTICLE
ARTICLED
ARTICLES
ARTICLING
ARTICS
ARTICULAR
ARTIER
ARTIES
ARTIEST
ARTIFACT
ARTIFACTS
ARTIFICE
ARTIFICER
ARTIFICES
ARTIGI
ARTIGIS
ARTILLERY
ARTILY
ARTINESS
ARTIS
ARTISAN
ARTISANAL
ARTISANS
ARTIST
ARTISTE
ARTISTES
ARTISTIC
ARTISTRY
ARTISTS
ARTLESS
ARTLESSLY
ARTMAKER
ARTMAKERS
ARTMAKING
ARTS
ARTSIE
ARTSIER
ARTSIES
ARTSIEST
ARTSINESS
ARTSMAN
ARTSMEN
ARTSY
ARTWORK
ARTWORKS
ARTY
ARUANA
ARUANAS
ARUGOLA
ARUGOLAS
ARUGULA
ARUGULAS
ARUHE
ARUHES
ARUM
ARUMS
ARUSPEX
ARUSPICES
ARVAL
ARVEE
ARVEES
ARVICOLE
ARVICOLES
ARVO
ARVOS
ARY
ARYBALLOS
ARYL
ARYLS
ARYTENOID
ARYTHMIA
ARYTHMIAS
ARYTHMIC
AS
ASAFETIDA
ASANA
ASANAS
ASAR
ASARUM
ASARUMS
ASBESTIC
ASBESTINE
ASBESTOS
ASBESTOUS
ASBESTUS
ASCARED
ASCARID
ASCARIDES
ASCARIDS
ASCARIS
ASCARISES
ASCAUNT
ASCEND
ASCENDANT
ASCENDED
ASCENDENT
ASCENDER
ASCENDERS
ASCENDEUR
ASCENDING
ASCENDS
ASCENSION
ASCENSIVE
ASCENT
ASCENTS
ASCERTAIN
ASCESES
ASCESIS
ASCETIC
ASCETICAL
ASCETICS
ASCI
ASCIAN
ASCIANS
ASCIDIA
ASCIDIAN
ASCIDIANS
ASCIDIATE
ASCIDIUM
ASCITES
ASCITIC
ASCITICAL
ASCLEPIAD
ASCLEPIAS
ASCOCARP
ASCOCARPS
ASCOGONIA
ASCON
ASCONCE
ASCONOID
ASCONS
ASCORBATE
ASCORBIC
ASCOSPORE
ASCOT
ASCOTS
ASCRIBE
ASCRIBED
ASCRIBES
ASCRIBING
ASCUS
ASDIC
ASDICS
ASEA
ASEISMIC
ASEITIES
ASEITY
ASEMANTIC
ASEPALOUS
ASEPSES
ASEPSIS
ASEPTATE
ASEPTIC
ASEPTICS
ASEXUAL
ASEXUALLY
ASH
ASHAKE
ASHAME
ASHAMED
ASHAMEDLY
ASHAMES
ASHAMING
ASHCAKE
ASHCAKES
ASHCAN
ASHCANS
ASHED
ASHEN
ASHERIES
ASHERY
ASHES
ASHET
ASHETS
ASHFALL
ASHFALLS
ASHIER
ASHIEST
ASHINE
ASHINESS
ASHING
ASHIVER
ASHKEY
ASHKEYS
ASHLAR
ASHLARED
ASHLARING
ASHLARS
ASHLER
ASHLERED
ASHLERING
ASHLERS
ASHLESS
ASHMAN
ASHMEN
ASHORE
ASHPAN
ASHPANS
ASHPLANT
ASHPLANTS
ASHRAF
ASHRAM
ASHRAMA
ASHRAMAS
ASHRAMITE
ASHRAMS
ASHTANGA
ASHTANGAS
ASHTRAY
ASHTRAYS
ASHY
ASIAGO
ASIAGOS
ASIDE
ASIDES

ASINICO
ASINICOS
ASININE
ASININELY
ASININITY
ASK
ASKANCE
ASKANCED
ASKANCES
ASKANCING
ASKANT
ASKANTED
ASKANTING
ASKANTS
ASKARI
ASKARIS
ASKED
ASKER
ASKERS
ASKESES
ASKESIS
ASKEW
ASKEWNESS
ASKING
ASKINGS
ASKLENT
ASKOI
ASKOS
ASKS
ASLAKE
ASLAKED
ASLAKES
ASLAKING
ASLANT
ASLEEP
ASLOPE
ASLOSH
ASMEAR
ASMOULDER
ASOCIAL
ASOCIALS
ASP
ASPARAGUS
ASPARKLE
ASPARTAME
ASPARTATE
ASPARTIC
ASPECT
ASPECTED
ASPECTING
ASPECTS
ASPECTUAL
ASPEN
ASPENS
ASPER
ASPERATE
ASPERATED
ASPERATES
ASPERGE
ASPERGED
ASPERGER
ASPERGERS
ASPERGES
ASPERGILL
ASPERGING
ASPERITY
ASPERMIA
ASPERMIAS
ASPEROUS
ASPERS
ASPERSE
ASPERSED
ASPERSER
ASPERSERS
ASPERSES
ASPERSING
ASPERSION
ASPERSIVE
ASPERSOIR
ASPERSOR
ASPERSORS
ASPERSORY
ASPHALT
ASPHALTED
ASPHALTER
ASPHALTIC
ASPHALTS
ASPHALTUM
ASPHERIC
ASPHERICS
ASPHODEL
ASPHODELS
ASPHYXIA
ASPHYXIAL
ASPHYXIAS
ASPHYXIED
ASPHYXIES
ASPHYXY
ASPIC
ASPICK
ASPICKS
ASPICS
ASPIDIA
ASPIDIOID
ASPIDIUM
ASPIE
ASPIES
ASPINE
ASPINES
ASPIRANT
ASPIRANTS
ASPIRATA
ASPIRATAE
ASPIRATE
ASPIRATED
ASPIRATES
ASPIRATOR
ASPIRE
ASPIRED
ASPIRER
ASPIRERS
ASPIRES
ASPIRIN
ASPIRING
ASPIRINS
ASPIS
ASPISES
ASPISH
ASPLENIUM
ASPORT
ASPORTED
ASPORTING
ASPORTS
ASPOUT
ASPRAWL
ASPREAD
ASPRO
ASPROS
ASPROUT
ASPS
ASQUAT
ASQUINT
ASRAMA
ASRAMAS
ASS
ASSAGAI
ASSAGAIED
ASSAGAIS
ASSAI
ASSAIL
ASSAILANT
ASSAILED
ASSAILER
ASSAILERS
ASSAILING
ASSAILS
ASSAIS
ASSAM
ASSAMS
ASSART
ASSARTED
ASSARTING
ASSARTS
ASSASSIN
ASSASSINS
ASSAULT
ASSAULTED
ASSAULTER
ASSAULTS
ASSAY
ASSAYABLE
ASSAYED
ASSAYER
ASSAYERS
ASSAYING
ASSAYINGS
ASSAYS
ASSEGAAI
ASSEGAAIS
ASSEGAI
ASSEGAIED
ASSEGAIS
ASSEMBLE
ASSEMBLED
ASSEMBLER
ASSEMBLES
ASSEMBLY
ASSENT
ASSENTED
ASSENTER
ASSENTERS
ASSENTING
ASSENTIVE
ASSENTOR
ASSENTORS
ASSENTS
ASSERT
ASSERTED
ASSERTER
ASSERTERS
ASSERTING
ASSERTION
ASSERTIVE
ASSERTOR
ASSERTORS
ASSERTORY
ASSERTS
ASSES
ASSESS
ASSESSED
ASSESSES
ASSESSING
ASSESSOR
ASSESSORS
ASSET
ASSETLESS
ASSETS
ASSEVER
ASSEVERED
ASSEVERS
ASSEZ
ASSHOLE
ASSHOLES
ASSIDUITY
ASSIDUOUS
ASSIEGE
ASSIEGED
ASSIEGES
ASSIEGING
ASSIENTO
ASSIENTOS
ASSIGN
ASSIGNAT
ASSIGNATS
ASSIGNED
ASSIGNEE
ASSIGNEES
ASSIGNER
ASSIGNERS
ASSIGNING

ASSIGNOR
ASSIGNORS
ASSIGNS
ASSIST
ASSISTANT
ASSISTED
ASSISTER
ASSISTERS
ASSISTING
ASSISTIVE
ASSISTOR
ASSISTORS
ASSISTS
ASSIZE
ASSIZED
ASSIZER
ASSIZERS
ASSIZES
ASSIZING
ASSLIKE
ASSOCIATE
ASSOIL
ASSOILED
ASSOILING
ASSOILS
ASSOILZIE
ASSONANCE
ASSONANT
ASSONANTS
ASSONATE
ASSONATED
ASSONATES
ASSORT
ASSORTED
ASSORTER
ASSORTERS
ASSORTING
ASSORTIVE
ASSORTS
ASSOT
ASSOTS
ASSOTT
ASSOTTED
ASSOTTING
ASSUAGE
ASSUAGED
ASSUAGER
ASSUAGERS
ASSUAGES
ASSUAGING
ASSUASIVE
ASSUETUDE
ASSUMABLE
ASSUMABLY
ASSUME
ASSUMED
ASSUMEDLY
ASSUMER
ASSUMERS
ASSUMES
ASSUMING
ASSUMINGS
ASSUMPSIT
ASSURABLE
ASSURANCE
ASSURE
ASSURED
ASSUREDLY
ASSUREDS
ASSURER
ASSURERS
ASSURES
ASSURGENT
ASSURING
ASSUROR
ASSURORS
ASSWAGE
ASSWAGED
ASSWAGES
ASSWAGING
ASSWIPE
ASSWIPES
ASTABLE
ASTANGA
ASTANGAS
ASTARE
ASTART
ASTARTED
ASTARTING
ASTARTS
ASTASIA
ASTASIAS
ASTATIC
ASTATIDE
ASTATIDES
ASTATINE
ASTATINES
ASTATKI
ASTATKIS
ASTEISM
ASTEISMS
ASTELIC
ASTELIES
ASTELY
ASTER
ASTERIA
ASTERIAS
ASTERID
ASTERIDS
ASTERISK
ASTERISKS
ASTERISM
ASTERISMS
ASTERN
ASTERNAL
ASTEROID
ASTEROIDS
ASTERS
ASTERT
ASTERTED
ASTERTING
ASTERTS
ASTHANGA
ASTHANGAS
ASTHENIA
ASTHENIAS
ASTHENIC
ASTHENICS
ASTHENIES
ASTHENY
ASTHMA
ASTHMAS
ASTHMATIC
ASTHORE
ASTHORES
ASTICHOUS
ASTIGMIA
ASTIGMIAS
ASTILBE
ASTILBES
ASTIR
ASTOMATAL
ASTOMOUS
ASTONE
ASTONED
ASTONES
ASTONIED
ASTONIES
ASTONING
ASTONISH
ASTONY
ASTONYING
ASTOOP
ASTOUND
ASTOUNDED
ASTOUNDS
ASTRACHAN
ASTRADDLE
ASTRAGAL
ASTRAGALI
ASTRAGALS
ASTRAKHAN
ASTRAL
ASTRALLY
ASTRALS
ASTRAND
ASTRANTIA
ASTRAY
ASTRICT
ASTRICTED
ASTRICTS
ASTRIDE
ASTRINGE
ASTRINGED
ASTRINGER
ASTRINGES
ASTROCYTE
ASTRODOME
ASTROFELL
ASTROID
ASTROIDS
ASTROLABE
ASTROLOGY
ASTRONAUT
ASTRONOMY
ASTROPHEL
ASTRUT
ASTUCIOUS
ASTUCITY
ASTUN
ASTUNNED
ASTUNNING
ASTUNS
ASTUTE
ASTUTELY
ASTUTER
ASTUTEST
ASTYLAR
ASUDDEN
ASUNDER
ASURA
ASURAS
ASWARM
ASWAY
ASWIM
ASWING
ASWIRL
ASWOON
ASYLA
ASYLEE
ASYLEES
ASYLLABIC
ASYLUM
ASYLUMS
ASYMMETRY
ASYMPTOTE
ASYNAPSES
ASYNAPSIS
ASYNDETA
ASYNDETIC
ASYNDETON
ASYNERGIA
ASYNERGY
ASYSTOLE
ASYSTOLES
ASYSTOLIC
AT
ATAATA
ATAATAS
ATABAL
ATABALS
ATABEG
ATABEGS
ATABEK
ATABEKS
ATABRIN
ATABRINE
ATABRINES
ATABRINS
ATACAMITE

ATACTIC
ATAGHAN
ATAGHANS
ATALAYA
ATALAYAS
ATAMAN
ATAMANS
ATAMASCO
ATAMASCOS
ATAP
ATAPS
ATARACTIC
ATARAXIA
ATARAXIAS
ATARAXIC
ATARAXICS
ATARAXIES
ATARAXY
ATAVIC
ATAVISM
ATAVISMS
ATAVIST
ATAVISTIC
ATAVISTS
ATAXIA
ATAXIAS
ATAXIC
ATAXICS
ATAXIES
ATAXY
ATCHIEVE
ATCHIEVED
ATCHIEVES
ATE
ATEBRIN
ATEBRINS
ATECHNIC
ATECHNICS
ATELIC
ATELIER
ATELIERS
ATEMOYA
ATEMOYAS
ATEMPORAL
ATENOLOL
ATENOLOLS
ATES
ATHAME
ATHAMES
ATHANASY
ATHANOR
ATHANORS
ATHEISE
ATHEISED
ATHEISES
ATHEISING
ATHEISM
ATHEISMS
ATHEIST
ATHEISTIC
ATHEISTS
ATHEIZE
ATHEIZED
ATHEIZES
ATHEIZING
ATHELING
ATHELINGS
ATHEMATIC
ATHENAEUM
ATHENEUM
ATHENEUMS
ATHEOLOGY
ATHEOUS
ATHERINE
ATHERINES
ATHEROMA
ATHEROMAS
ATHETESES
ATHETESIS
ATHETISE
ATHETISED
ATHETISES
ATHETIZE
ATHETIZED
ATHETIZES
ATHETOID
ATHETOSES
ATHETOSIC
ATHETOSIS
ATHETOTIC
ATHIRST
ATHLETA
ATHLETAS
ATHLETE
ATHLETES
ATHLETIC
ATHLETICS
ATHODYD
ATHODYDS
ATHRILL
ATHROB
ATHROCYTE
ATHWART
ATIGI
ATIGIS
ATILT
ATIMIES
ATIMY
ATINGLE
ATISHOO
ATISHOOS
ATLANTES
ATLAS
ATLASES
ATLATL
ATLATLS
ATMA
ATMAN
ATMANS
ATMAS
ATMOLOGY
ATMOLYSE
ATMOLYSED
ATMOLYSES
ATMOLYSIS
ATMOLYZE
ATMOLYZED
ATMOLYZES
ATMOMETER
ATMOMETRY
ATMOS
ATMOSES
ATOC
ATOCIA
ATOCIAS
ATOCS
ATOK
ATOKAL
ATOKE
ATOKES
ATOKOUS
ATOKS
ATOLL
ATOLLS
ATOM
ATOMIC
ATOMICAL
ATOMICITY
ATOMICS
ATOMIES
ATOMISE
ATOMISED
ATOMISER
ATOMISERS
ATOMISES
ATOMISING
ATOMISM
ATOMISMS
ATOMIST
ATOMISTIC
ATOMISTS
ATOMIZE
ATOMIZED
ATOMIZER
ATOMIZERS
ATOMIZES
ATOMIZING
ATOMS
ATOMY
ATONABLE
ATONAL
ATONALISM
ATONALIST
ATONALITY
ATONALLY
ATONE
ATONEABLE
ATONED
ATONEMENT
ATONER
ATONERS
ATONES
ATONIA
ATONIAS
ATONIC
ATONICITY
ATONICS
ATONIES
ATONING
ATONINGLY
ATONY
ATOP
ATOPIC
ATOPIES
ATOPY
ATRAMENT
ATRAMENTS
ATRAZINE
ATRAZINES
ATREMBLE
ATRESIA
ATRESIAS
ATRESIC
ATRETIC
ATRIA
ATRIAL
ATRIP
ATRIUM
ATRIUMS
ATROCIOUS
ATROCITY
ATROPHIA
ATROPHIAS
ATROPHIC
ATROPHIED
ATROPHIES
ATROPHY
ATROPIA
ATROPIAS
ATROPIN
ATROPINE
ATROPINES
ATROPINS
ATROPISM
ATROPISMS
ATROPOUS
ATS
ATT
ATTABOY
ATTABOYS
ATTACH
ATTACHE
ATTACHED
ATTACHER
ATTACHERS
ATTACHES
ATTACHING
ATTACK
ATTACKED
ATTACKER

ATTACKERS
ATTACKING
ATTACKMAN
ATTACKMEN
ATTACKS
ATTAGIRL
ATTAIN
ATTAINDER
ATTAINED
ATTAINER
ATTAINERS
ATTAINING
ATTAINS
ATTAINT
ATTAINTED
ATTAINTS
ATTAP
ATTAPS
ATTAR
ATTARS
ATTASK
ATTASKED
ATTASKING
ATTASKS
ATTASKT
ATTEMPER
ATTEMPERS
ATTEMPT
ATTEMPTED
ATTEMPTER
ATTEMPTS
ATTEND
ATTENDANT
ATTENDED
ATTENDEE
ATTENDEES
ATTENDER
ATTENDERS
ATTENDING
ATTENDS
ATTENT
ATTENTAT
ATTENTATS
ATTENTION
ATTENTIVE
ATTENTS
ATTENUANT
ATTENUATE
ATTERCOP
ATTERCOPS
ATTEST
ATTESTANT
ATTESTED
ATTESTER
ATTESTERS
ATTESTING
ATTESTOR
ATTESTORS
ATTESTS
ATTIC
ATTICISE
ATTICISED
ATTICISES
ATTICISM
ATTICISMS
ATTICIST
ATTICISTS
ATTICIZE
ATTICIZED
ATTICIZES
ATTICS
ATTIRE
ATTIRED
ATTIRES
ATTIRING
ATTIRINGS
ATTITUDE
ATTITUDES
ATTOLASER
ATTOLLENS
ATTOLLENT
ATTOMETER
ATTOMETRE
ATTONCE
ATTONE
ATTONED
ATTONES
ATTONING
ATTORN
ATTORNED
ATTORNEY
ATTORNEYS
ATTORNING
ATTORNS
ATTOTESLA
ATTRACT
ATTRACTED
ATTRACTER
ATTRACTOR
ATTRACTS
ATTRAHENS
ATTRAHENT
ATTRAP
ATTRAPPED
ATTRAPS
ATTRIBUTE
ATTRIST
ATTRISTED
ATTRISTS
ATTRIT
ATTRITE
ATTRITED
ATTRITES
ATTRITING
ATTRITION
ATTRITIVE
ATTRITS
ATTRITTED
ATTUENT
ATTUITE
ATTUITED
ATTUITES
ATTUITING
ATTUITION
ATTUITIVE
ATTUNE
ATTUNED
ATTUNES
ATTUNING
ATUA
ATUAS
ATWAIN
ATWEEL
ATWEEN
ATWITTER
ATWIXT
ATYPIC
ATYPICAL
AUA
AUAS
AUBADE
AUBADES
AUBERGE
AUBERGES
AUBERGINE
AUBRETIA
AUBRETIAS
AUBRIETA
AUBRIETAS
AUBRIETIA
AUBURN
AUBURNS
AUCEPS
AUCEPSES
AUCTION
AUCTIONED
AUCTIONS
AUCTORIAL
AUCUBA
AUCUBAS
AUDACIOUS
AUDACITY
AUDAD
AUDADS
AUDIAL
AUDIBLE
AUDIBLED
AUDIBLES
AUDIBLING
AUDIBLY
AUDIENCE
AUDIENCES
AUDIENCIA
AUDIENT
AUDIENTS
AUDILE
AUDILES
AUDING
AUDINGS
AUDIO
AUDIOBOOK
AUDIOGRAM
AUDIOLOGY
AUDIOPHIL
AUDIOS
AUDIOTAPE
AUDIPHONE
AUDISM
AUDISMS
AUDIST
AUDISTS
AUDIT
AUDITABLE
AUDITED
AUDITEE
AUDITEES
AUDITING
AUDITINGS
AUDITION
AUDITIONS
AUDITIVE
AUDITIVES
AUDITOR
AUDITORIA
AUDITORS
AUDITORY
AUDITRESS
AUDITS
AUE
AUF
AUFGABE
AUFGABES
AUFS
AUGEND
AUGENDS
AUGER
AUGERS
AUGH
AUGHT
AUGHTS
AUGITE
AUGITES
AUGITIC
AUGMENT
AUGMENTED
AUGMENTER
AUGMENTOR
AUGMENTS
AUGUR
AUGURAL
AUGURED
AUGURER
AUGURERS
AUGURIES
AUGURING
AUGURS
AUGURSHIP
AUGURY
AUGUST
AUGUSTE

AUGUSTER
AUGUSTES
AUGUSTEST
AUGUSTLY
AUGUSTS
AUK
AUKLET
AUKLETS
AUKS
AULA
AULARIAN
AULARIANS
AULAS
AULD
AULDER
AULDEST
AULIC
AULNAGE
AULNAGER
AULNAGERS
AULNAGES
AULOI
AULOS
AUMAIL
AUMAILED
AUMAILING
AUMAILS
AUMBRIES
AUMBRY
AUMIL
AUMILS
AUNE
AUNES
AUNT
AUNTER
AUNTERS
AUNTHOOD
AUNTHOODS
AUNTIE
AUNTIES
AUNTLIER
AUNTLIEST
AUNTLIKE
AUNTLY
AUNTS
AUNTY
AURA
AURAE
AURAL
AURALITY
AURALLY
AURAR
AURAS
AURATE
AURATED
AURATES
AUREATE
AUREATELY
AUREI
AUREITIES
AUREITY
AURELIA
AURELIAN
AURELIANS
AURELIAS
AUREOLA
AUREOLAE
AUREOLAS
AUREOLE
AUREOLED
AUREOLES
AUREOLING
AURES
AUREUS
AURIC
AURICLE
AURICLED
AURICLES
AURICULA
AURICULAE
AURICULAR
AURICULAS
AURIFIED
AURIFIES
AURIFORM
AURIFY
AURIFYING
AURIS
AURISCOPE
AURIST
AURISTS
AUROCHS
AUROCHSES
AURORA
AURORAE
AURORAL
AURORALLY
AURORAS
AUROREAN
AUROUS
AURUM
AURUMS
AUSFORM
AUSFORMED
AUSFORMS
AUSLANDER
AUSPEX
AUSPICATE
AUSPICE
AUSPICES
AUSTENITE
AUSTERE
AUSTERELY
AUSTERER
AUSTEREST
AUSTERITY
AUSTRAL
AUSTRALES
AUSTRALIS
AUSTRALS
AUSUBO
AUSUBOS
AUTACOID
AUTACOIDS
AUTARCH
AUTARCHIC
AUTARCHS
AUTARCHY
AUTARKIC
AUTARKIES
AUTARKIST
AUTARKY
AUTECIOUS
AUTECISM
AUTECISMS
AUTEUR
AUTEURISM
AUTEURIST
AUTEURS
AUTHENTIC
AUTHOR
AUTHORED
AUTHORESS
AUTHORIAL
AUTHORING
AUTHORISE
AUTHORISH
AUTHORISM
AUTHORITY
AUTHORIZE
AUTHORS
AUTISM
AUTISMS
AUTIST
AUTISTIC
AUTISTICS
AUTISTS
AUTO
AUTOBAHN
AUTOBAHNS
AUTOBANK
AUTOBANKS
AUTOBODY
AUTOBUS
AUTOBUSES
AUTOCADE
AUTOCADES
AUTOCAR
AUTOCARP
AUTOCARPS
AUTOCARS
AUTOCIDAL
AUTOCLAVE
AUTOCOID
AUTOCOIDS
AUTOCRACY
AUTOCRAT
AUTOCRATS
AUTOCRIME
AUTOCRINE
AUTOCROSS
AUTOCUE
AUTOCUES
AUTOCUTIE
AUTOCYCLE
AUTODIAL
AUTODIALS
AUTODROME
AUTODYNE
AUTODYNES
AUTOECISM
AUTOED
AUTOFLARE
AUTOFOCUS
AUTOGAMIC
AUTOGAMY
AUTOGENIC
AUTOGENY
AUTOGIRO
AUTOGIROS
AUTOGRAFT
AUTOGRAPH
AUTOGUIDE
AUTOGYRO
AUTOGYROS
AUTOHARP
AUTOHARPS
AUTOICOUS
AUTOING
AUTOLATRY
AUTOLOAD
AUTOLOADS
AUTOLOGY
AUTOLYSE
AUTOLYSED
AUTOLYSES
AUTOLYSIN
AUTOLYSIS
AUTOLYTIC
AUTOLYZE
AUTOLYZED
AUTOLYZES
AUTOMAGIC
AUTOMAKER
AUTOMAN
AUTOMAT
AUTOMATA
AUTOMATE
AUTOMATED
AUTOMATES
AUTOMATIC
AUTOMATON
AUTOMATS
AUTOMEN
AUTOMETER
AUTONOMIC
AUTONOMY
AUTONYM
AUTONYMS
AUTOPEN

A

A

AUTOPENS
AUTOPHAGY
AUTOPHOBY
AUTOPHONY
AUTOPHYTE
AUTOPILOT
AUTOPISTA
AUTOPOINT
AUTOPSIA
AUTOPSIAS
AUTOPSIC
AUTOPSIED
AUTOPSIES
AUTOPSIST
AUTOPSY
AUTOPTIC
AUTOPUT
AUTOPUTS
AUTOREPLY
AUTOROUTE
AUTOS
AUTOSAVE
AUTOSAVED
AUTOSAVES
AUTOSCOPY
AUTOSOMAL
AUTOSOME
AUTOSOMES
AUTOSPORE
AUTOSPORT
AUTOTELIC
AUTOTEST
AUTOTESTS
AUTOTIMER
AUTOTOMIC
AUTOTOMY
AUTOTOXIC
AUTOTOXIN
AUTOTROPH
AUTOTUNE
AUTOTUNES
AUTOTYPE
AUTOTYPED
AUTOTYPES
AUTOTYPIC
AUTOTYPY
AUTOVAC
AUTOVACS
AUTUMN
AUTUMNAL
AUTUMNIER
AUTUMNS
AUTUMNY
AUTUNITE
AUTUNITES
AUXESES
AUXESIS
AUXETIC
AUXETICS
AUXILIAR
AUXILIARS
AUXILIARY
AUXIN
AUXINIC
AUXINS
AUXOCYTE
AUXOCYTES
AUXOMETER
AUXOSPORE
AUXOTONIC
AUXOTROPH
AVA
AVADAVAT
AVADAVATS
AVAIL
AVAILABLE
AVAILABLY
AVAILE
AVAILED
AVAILES
AVAILFUL
AVAILING
AVAILS
AVAL
AVALANCHE
AVALE
AVALED
AVALEMENT
AVALES
AVALING
AVANT
AVANTI
AVANTIST
AVANTISTS
AVARICE
AVARICES
AVAS
AVASCULAR
AVAST
AVATAR
AVATARS
AVAUNT
AVAUNTED
AVAUNTING
AVAUNTS
AVE
AVEL
AVELLAN
AVELLANE
AVELS
AVENGE
AVENGED
AVENGEFUL
AVENGER
AVENGERS
AVENGES
AVENGING
AVENIR
AVENIRS
AVENS
AVENSES
AVENTAIL
AVENTAILE
AVENTAILS
AVENTRE
AVENTRED
AVENTRES
AVENTRING
AVENTURE
AVENTURES
AVENTURIN
AVENUE
AVENUES
AVER
AVERAGE
AVERAGED
AVERAGELY
AVERAGER
AVERAGERS
AVERAGES
AVERAGING
AVERMENT
AVERMENTS
AVERRABLE
AVERRED
AVERRING
AVERS
AVERSE
AVERSELY
AVERSION
AVERSIONS
AVERSIVE
AVERSIVES
AVERT
AVERTABLE
AVERTED
AVERTEDLY
AVERTER
AVERTERS
AVERTIBLE
AVERTING
AVERTS
AVES
AVGAS
AVGASES
AVGASSES
AVIAN
AVIANISE
AVIANISED
AVIANISES
AVIANIZE
AVIANIZED
AVIANIZES
AVIANS
AVIARIES
AVIARIST
AVIARISTS
AVIARY
AVIATE
AVIATED
AVIATES
AVIATIC
AVIATING
AVIATION
AVIATIONS
AVIATOR
AVIATORS
AVIATRESS
AVIATRICE
AVIATRIX
AVICULAR
AVID
AVIDER
AVIDEST
AVIDIN
AVIDINS
AVIDITIES
AVIDITY
AVIDLY
AVIDNESS
AVIETTE
AVIETTES
AVIFAUNA
AVIFAUNAE
AVIFAUNAL
AVIFAUNAS
AVIFORM
AVIGATOR
AVIGATORS
AVINE
AVION
AVIONIC
AVIONICS
AVIONS
AVIRULENT
AVISANDUM
AVISE
AVISED
AVISEMENT
AVISES
AVISING
AVISO
AVISOS
AVITAL
AVIZANDUM
AVIZE
AVIZED
AVIZEFULL
AVIZES
AVIZING
AVO
AVOCADO
AVOCADOES
AVOCADOS
AVOCATION
AVOCET
AVOCETS
AVODIRE
AVODIRES
AVOID

AVOIDABLE
AVOIDABLY
AVOIDANCE
AVOIDANT
AVOIDED
AVOIDER
AVOIDERS
AVOIDING
AVOIDS
AVOISION
AVOISIONS
AVOPARCIN
AVOS
AVOSET
AVOSETS
AVOUCH
AVOUCHED
AVOUCHER
AVOUCHERS
AVOUCHES
AVOUCHING
AVOURE
AVOURES
AVOUTERER
AVOUTRER
AVOUTRERS
AVOUTRIES
AVOUTRY
AVOW
AVOWABLE
AVOWABLY
AVOWAL
AVOWALS
AVOWED
AVOWEDLY
AVOWER
AVOWERS
AVOWING
AVOWRIES
AVOWRY
AVOWS
AVOYER
AVOYERS
AVRUGA
AVRUGAS
AVULSE
AVULSED
AVULSES
AVULSING
AVULSION
AVULSIONS
AVUNCULAR
AVYZE
AVYZED
AVYZES
AVYZING
AW
AWA
AWAIT
AWAITED
AWAITER
AWAITERS
AWAITING
AWAITS
AWAKE
AWAKED
AWAKEN
AWAKENED
AWAKENER
AWAKENERS
AWAKENING
AWAKENS
AWAKES
AWAKING
AWAKINGS
AWANTING
AWARD
AWARDABLE
AWARDED
AWARDEE
AWARDEES
AWARDER
AWARDERS
AWARDING
AWARDS
AWARE
AWARENESS
AWARER
AWAREST
AWARN
AWARNED
AWARNING
AWARNS
AWASH
AWATCH
AWATO
AWATOS
AWAVE
AWAY
AWAYDAY
AWAYDAYS
AWAYES
AWAYNESS
AWAYS
AWDL
AWDLS
AWE
AWEARIED
AWEARY
AWEATHER
AWED
AWEE
AWEEL
AWEIGH
AWEING
AWELESS
AWES
AWESOME
AWESOMELY
AWESTRIKE
AWESTRUCK
AWETO
AWETOS
AWFUL
AWFULLER
AWFULLEST
AWFULLY
AWFULNESS
AWFY
AWHAPE
AWHAPED
AWHAPES
AWHAPING
AWHATO
AWHATOS
AWHEEL
AWHEELS
AWHETO
AWHETOS
AWHILE
AWHIRL
AWING
AWK
AWKS
AWKWARD
AWKWARDER
AWKWARDLY
AWL
AWLBIRD
AWLBIRDS
AWLESS
AWLS
AWLWORT
AWLWORTS
AWMOUS
AWMRIE
AWMRIES
AWMRY
AWN
AWNED
AWNER
AWNERS
AWNIER
AWNIEST
AWNING
AWNINGED
AWNINGS
AWNLESS
AWNS
AWNY
AWOKE
AWOKEN
AWOL
AWOLS
AWORK
AWRACK
AWRONG
AWRY
AWSOME
AX
AXAL
AXE
AXEBIRD
AXEBIRDS
AXED
AXEL
AXELIKE
AXELS
AXEMAN
AXEMEN
AXENIC
AXES
AXIAL
AXIALITY
AXIALLY
AXIL
AXILE
AXILEMMA
AXILEMMAS
AXILLA
AXILLAE
AXILLAR
AXILLARS
AXILLARY
AXILLAS
AXILS
AXING
AXINITE
AXINITES
AXIOLOGY
AXIOM
AXIOMATIC
AXIOMS
AXION
AXIONS
AXIS
AXISED
AXISES
AXITE
AXITES
AXLE
AXLED
AXLES
AXLETREE
AXLETREES
AXLIKE
AXMAN
AXMEN
AXOID
AXOIDS
AXOLEMMA
AXOLEMMAS
AXOLOTL
AXOLOTLS
AXON
AXONAL
AXONE
AXONEMAL
AXONEME
AXONEMES

AXONES
AXONIC
AXONS
AXOPLASM
AXOPLASMS
AXSEED
AXSEEDS
AY
AYAH
AYAHS
AYAHUASCA
AYAHUASCO
AYATOLLAH
AYAYA
AYAYAS
AYE
AYELP
AYENBITE
AYENBITES
AYES
AYGRE
AYIN
AYINS
AYONT
AYRE
AYRES
AYRIE
AYRIES
AYS
AYU
AYURVEDA
AYURVEDAS
AYURVEDIC
AYUS
AYWORD
AYWORDS
AZALEA
AZALEAS
AZAN
AZANS
AZEDARACH
AZEOTROPE
AZEOTROPY
AZERTY
AZIDE
AZIDES
AZIDO
AZIMUTH
AZIMUTHAL
AZIMUTHS
AZINE
AZINES
AZIONE
AZIONES
AZLON
AZLONS
AZO
AZOIC
AZOLE
AZOLES
AZOLLA
AZOLLAS
AZON
AZONAL
AZONIC
AZONS
AZOTAEMIA
AZOTAEMIC
AZOTE
AZOTED
AZOTEMIA
AZOTEMIAS
AZOTEMIC
AZOTES
AZOTH
AZOTHS
AZOTIC
AZOTISE
AZOTISED
AZOTISES
AZOTISING
AZOTIZE
AZOTIZED
AZOTIZES
AZOTIZING
AZOTOUS
AZOTURIA
AZOTURIAS
AZUKI
AZUKIS
AZULEJO
AZULEJOS
AZURE
AZUREAN
AZURES
AZURIES
AZURINE
AZURINES
AZURITE
AZURITES
AZURN
AZURY
AZYGIES
AZYGOS
AZYGOSES
AZYGOUS
AZYGOUSLY
AZYGY
AZYM
AZYME
AZYMES
AZYMITE
AZYMITES
AZYMOUS
AZYMS

B

BA
BAA
BAAED
BAAING
BAAINGS
BAAL
BAALEBOS
BAALIM
BAALISM
BAALISMS
BAALS
BAAS
BAASES
BAASKAAP
BAASKAAPS
BAASKAP
BAASKAPS
BAASSKAP
BAASSKAPS
BABA
BABACO
BABACOOTE
BABACOS
BABACU
BABACUS
BABALAS
BABAS
BABASSU
BABASSUS
BABBELAS
BABBITRY
BABBITT
BABBITTED
BABBITTRY
BABBITTS
BABBLE
BABBLED
BABBLER
BABBLERS
BABBLES
BABBLIER
BABBLIEST
BABBLING
BABBLINGS
BABBLY
BABE
BABEL
BABELDOM
BABELDOMS
BABELISH
BABELISM
BABELISMS
BABELS
BABES
BABESIA
BABESIAE
BABESIAS
BABICHE
BABICHES
BABIED
BABIER
BABIES
BABIEST
BABIRUSA
BABIRUSAS
BABIRUSSA
BABKA
BABKAS
BABLAH
BABLAHS
BABOO
BABOOL
BABOOLS
BABOON
BABOONERY
BABOONISH
BABOONS
BABOOS
BABOOSH
BABOOSHES
BABOUCHE
BABOUCHES
BABU
BABUCHE
BABUCHES
BABUDOM
BABUDOMS
BABUISM
BABUISMS
BABUL
BABULS
BABUS
BABUSHKA
BABUSHKAS
BABY
BABYCCINO
BABYCINO
BABYCINOS
BABYDADDY
BABYDOLL
BABYDOLLS
BABYFOOD
BABYFOODS
BABYHOOD
BABYHOODS
BABYING
BABYISH
BABYISHLY
BABYLIKE
BABYMOON
BABYMOONS
BABYPROOF
BABYSAT
BABYSIT
BABYSITS
BAC
BACALAO
BACALAOS
BACALHAU
BACALHAUS
BACCA
BACCAE
BACCALA
BACCALAS
BACCARA
BACCARAS
BACCARAT
BACCARATS
BACCARE
BACCAS
BACCATE
BACCATED
BACCHANAL
BACCHANT
BACCHANTE
BACCHANTS
BACCHIAC
BACCHIAN
BACCHIC
BACCHII
BACCHIUS
BACCIES
BACCIFORM
BACCO
BACCOES
BACCOS
BACCY
BACH
BACHA
BACHARACH
BACHAS
BACHATA
BACHATAS
BACHCHA
BACHCHAS
BACHED
BACHELOR
BACHELORS
BACHES
BACHING
BACHS
BACILLAR
BACILLARY
BACILLI
BACILLUS
BACK
BACKACHE
BACKACHES
BACKACTER
BACKARE
BACKBAND
BACKBANDS
BACKBAR
BACKBARS
BACKBEAT
BACKBEATS
BACKBENCH
BACKBEND
BACKBENDS
BACKBIT
BACKBITE
BACKBITER
BACKBITES
BACKBLOCK
BACKBOARD
BACKBOND
BACKBONDS
BACKBONE
BACKBONED
BACKBONES
BACKBURN
BACKBURNS
BACKCAST
BACKCASTS
BACKCHAT
BACKCHATS
BACKCHECK
BACKCLOTH
BACKCOMB
BACKCOMBS
BACKCOURT
BACKCROSS
BACKDATE
BACKDATED
BACKDATES
BACKDOOR
BACKDOWN
BACKDOWNS
BACKDRAFT
BACKDROP

B

BACKDROPS
BACKDROPT
BACKED
BACKER
BACKERS
BACKET
BACKETS
BACKFALL
BACKFALLS
BACKFAT
BACKFATS
BACKFIELD
BACKFILE
BACKFILES
BACKFILL
BACKFILLS
BACKFIRE
BACKFIRED
BACKFIRES
BACKFISCH
BACKFIT
BACKFITS
BACKFLIP
BACKFLIPS
BACKFLOW
BACKFLOWS
BACKHAND
BACKHANDS
BACKHAUL
BACKHAULS
BACKHOE
BACKHOED
BACKHOES
BACKHOUSE
BACKIE
BACKIES
BACKING
BACKINGS
BACKLAND
BACKLANDS
BACKLASH
BACKLESS
BACKLIFT
BACKLIFTS
BACKLIGHT
BACKLINE
BACKLINER
BACKLINES
BACKLIST
BACKLISTS
BACKLIT
BACKLOAD
BACKLOADS
BACKLOG
BACKLOGS
BACKLOT
BACKLOTS
BACKMOST
BACKOUT
BACKOUTS
BACKPACK
BACKPACKS
BACKPEDAL
BACKPIECE
BACKPLANE
BACKPLATE
BACKRA
BACKRAS
BACKREST
BACKRESTS
BACKRONYM
BACKROOM
BACKROOMS
BACKRUSH
BACKS
BACKSAW
BACKSAWS
BACKSEAT
BACKSEATS
BACKSET
BACKSETS
BACKSEY
BACKSEYS
BACKSHISH
BACKSHORE
BACKSIDE
BACKSIDES
BACKSIGHT
BACKSLAP
BACKSLAPS
BACKSLASH
BACKSLID
BACKSLIDE
BACKSPACE
BACKSPEER
BACKSPEIR
BACKSPIN
BACKSPINS
BACKSPLIT
BACKSTAB
BACKSTABS
BACKSTAGE
BACKSTAIR
BACKSTALL
BACKSTAMP
BACKSTAY
BACKSTAYS
BACKSTOP
BACKSTOPS
BACKSTORY
BACKSTRAP
BACKSWEPT
BACKSWING
BACKSWORD
BACKTALK
BACKTALKS
BACKTRACK
BACKUP
BACKUPS
BACKVELD
BACKVELDS
BACKWALL
BACKWALLS
BACKWARD
BACKWARDS
BACKWASH
BACKWATER
BACKWIND
BACKWINDS
BACKWOOD
BACKWOODS
BACKWORD
BACKWORDS
BACKWORK
BACKWORKS
BACKWRAP
BACKWRAPS
BACKYARD
BACKYARDS
BACLAVA
BACLAVAS
BACLOFEN
BACLOFENS
BACON
BACONER
BACONERS
BACONS
BACRONYM
BACRONYMS
BACS
BACTERIA
BACTERIAL
BACTERIAN
BACTERIAS
BACTERIC
BACTERIN
BACTERINS
BACTERISE
BACTERIUM
BACTERIZE
BACTEROID
BACULA
BACULINE
BACULITE
BACULITES
BACULUM
BACULUMS
BAD
BADASS
BADASSED
BADASSES
BADDER
BADDEST
BADDIE
BADDIES
BADDISH
BADDY
BADE
BADGE
BADGED
BADGELESS
BADGER
BADGERED
BADGERING
BADGERLY
BADGERS
BADGES
BADGING
BADINAGE
BADINAGED
BADINAGES
BADINERIE
BADIOUS
BADLAND
BADLANDS
BADLY
BADMAN
BADMASH
BADMASHES
BADMEN
BADMINTON
BADMOUTH
BADMOUTHS
BADNESS
BADNESSES
BADS
BADWARE
BADWARES
BAE
BAEL
BAELS
BAES
BAETYL
BAETYLS
BAFF
BAFFED
BAFFIES
BAFFING
BAFFLE
BAFFLED
BAFFLEGAB
BAFFLER
BAFFLERS
BAFFLES
BAFFLING
BAFFS
BAFFY
BAFT
BAFTS
BAG
BAGARRE
BAGARRES
BAGASS
BAGASSE
BAGASSES
BAGATELLE
BAGEL
BAGELED
BAGELING
BAGELLED

BAGELLING
BAGELS
BAGFUL
BAGFULS
BAGGAGE
BAGGAGES
BAGGED
BAGGER
BAGGERS
BAGGIE
BAGGIER
BAGGIES
BAGGIEST
BAGGILY
BAGGINESS
BAGGING
BAGGINGS
BAGGIT
BAGGITS
BAGGY
BAGH
BAGHOUSE
BAGHOUSES
BAGHS
BAGIE
BAGIES
BAGLESS
BAGLIKE
BAGMAN
BAGMEN
BAGNETTE
BAGNETTES
BAGNIO
BAGNIOS
BAGPIPE
BAGPIPED
BAGPIPER
BAGPIPERS
BAGPIPES
BAGPIPING
BAGS
BAGSFUL
BAGUET
BAGUETS
BAGUETTE
BAGUETTES
BAGUIO
BAGUIOS
BAGWASH
BAGWASHES
BAGWIG
BAGWIGS
BAGWORM
BAGWORMS
BAH
BAHADA
BAHADAS
BAHADUR
BAHADURS
BAHOOKIE
BAHOOKIES
BAHT
BAHTS
BAHU
BAHUS
BAHUT
BAHUTS
BAHUVRIHI
BAIDAR
BAIDARKA
BAIDARKAS
BAIDARS
BAIGNOIRE
BAIL
BAILABLE
BAILBOND
BAILBONDS
BAILED
BAILEE
BAILEES
BAILER
BAILERS
BAILEY
BAILEYS
BAILIE
BAILIES
BAILIFF
BAILIFFS
BAILING
BAILIWICK
BAILLI
BAILLIAGE
BAILLIE
BAILLIES
BAILLIS
BAILMENT
BAILMENTS
BAILOR
BAILORS
BAILOUT
BAILOUTS
BAILS
BAILSMAN
BAILSMEN
BAININ
BAININS
BAINITE
BAINITES
BAIRN
BAIRNISH
BAIRNLIER
BAIRNLIKE
BAIRNLY
BAIRNS
BAISA
BAISAS
BAISEMAIN
BAIT
BAITED
BAITER
BAITERS
BAITFISH
BAITH
BAITING
BAITINGS
BAITS
BAIZA
BAIZAS
BAIZE
BAIZED
BAIZES
BAIZING
BAJADA
BAJADAS
BAJAN
BAJANS
BAJILLION
BAJRA
BAJRAS
BAJREE
BAJREES
BAJRI
BAJRIS
BAJU
BAJUS
BAKE
BAKEAPPLE
BAKEBOARD
BAKED
BAKEHOUSE
BAKELITE
BAKELITES
BAKEMEAT
BAKEMEATS
BAKEN
BAKEOFF
BAKEOFFS
BAKER
BAKERIES
BAKERS
BAKERY
BAKES
BAKESHOP
BAKESHOPS
BAKESTONE
BAKEWARE
BAKEWARES
BAKGAT
BAKHSHISH
BAKING
BAKINGS
BAKKIE
BAKKIES
BAKLAVA
BAKLAVAS
BAKLAWA
BAKLAWAS
BAKRA
BAKRAS
BAKSHEESH
BAKSHISH
BAL
BALACLAVA
BALADIN
BALADINE
BALADINES
BALADINS
BALAFON
BALAFONS
BALALAIKA
BALANCE
BALANCED
BALANCER
BALANCERS
BALANCES
BALANCING
BALANITIS
BALAS
BALASES
BALATA
BALATAS
BALAYAGE
BALAYAGED
BALAYAGES
BALBOA
BALBOAS
BALCONET
BALCONETS
BALCONIED
BALCONIES
BALCONY
BALD
BALDACHIN
BALDAQUIN
BALDED
BALDER
BALDEST
BALDFACED
BALDHEAD
BALDHEADS
BALDICOOT
BALDIE
BALDIER
BALDIES
BALDIEST
BALDING
BALDISH
BALDLY
BALDMONEY
BALDNESS
BALDPATE
BALDPATED
BALDPATES
BALDRIC
BALDRICK
BALDRICKS
BALDRICS
BALDS
BALDY
BALE

BALECTION
BALED
BALEEN
BALEENS
BALEFIRE
BALEFIRES
BALEFUL
BALEFULLY
BALER
BALERS
BALES
BALING
BALINGS
BALISAUR
BALISAURS
BALISE
BALISES
BALISTA
BALISTAE
BALISTAS
BALK
BALKANISE
BALKANIZE
BALKED
BALKER
BALKERS
BALKIER
BALKIEST
BALKILY
BALKINESS
BALKING
BALKINGLY
BALKINGS
BALKLINE
BALKLINES
BALKS
BALKY
BALL
BALLABILE
BALLABILI
BALLAD
BALLADE
BALLADED
BALLADEER
BALLADES
BALLADIC
BALLADIN
BALLADINE
BALLADING
BALLADINS
BALLADIST
BALLADRY
BALLADS
BALLAN
BALLANS
BALLANT
BALLANTED
BALLANTS
BALLAST
BALLASTED
BALLASTER
BALLASTS
BALLAT
BALLATED
BALLATING
BALLATS
BALLBOY
BALLBOYS
BALLCLAY
BALLCLAYS
BALLCOCK
BALLCOCKS
BALLED
BALLER
BALLERINA
BALLERINE
BALLERS
BALLET
BALLETED
BALLETIC
BALLETING
BALLETS
BALLFIELD
BALLGAME
BALLGAMES
BALLGIRL
BALLGIRLS
BALLGOWN
BALLGOWNS
BALLHAWK
BALLHAWKS
BALLIER
BALLIES
BALLIEST
BALLING
BALLINGS
BALLISTA
BALLISTAE
BALLISTAS
BALLISTIC
BALLIUM
BALLIUMS
BALLOCKS
BALLON
BALLONET
BALLONETS
BALLONNE
BALLONNES
BALLONS
BALLOON
BALLOONED
BALLOONS
BALLOT
BALLOTED
BALLOTEE
BALLOTEES
BALLOTER
BALLOTERS
BALLOTING
BALLOTINI
BALLOTS
BALLOW
BALLOWS
BALLPARK
BALLPARKS
BALLPEEN
BALLPOINT
BALLROOM
BALLROOMS
BALLS
BALLSED
BALLSES
BALLSIER
BALLSIEST
BALLSING
BALLSY
BALLUP
BALLUPS
BALLUTE
BALLUTES
BALLY
BALLYARD
BALLYARDS
BALLYHOO
BALLYHOOS
BALLYRAG
BALLYRAGS
BALM
BALMACAAN
BALMED
BALMIER
BALMIEST
BALMILY
BALMINESS
BALMING
BALMLIKE
BALMORAL
BALMORALS
BALMS
BALMY
BALNEAL
BALNEARY
BALONEY
BALONEYS
BALOO
BALOOS
BALS
BALSA
BALSAM
BALSAMED
BALSAMIC
BALSAMIER
BALSAMING
BALSAMS
BALSAMY
BALSAS
BALSAWOOD
BALTHASAR
BALTHAZAR
BALTI
BALTIC
BALTIS
BALU
BALUN
BALUNS
BALUS
BALUSTER
BALUSTERS
BALZARINE
BAM
BAMBI
BAMBINI
BAMBINO
BAMBINOS
BAMBIS
BAMBOO
BAMBOOS
BAMBOOZLE
BAMMED
BAMMER
BAMMERS
BAMMING
BAMPOT
BAMPOTS
BAMS
BAN
BANAK
BANAKS
BANAL
BANALER
BANALEST
BANALISE
BANALISED
BANALISES
BANALITY
BANALIZE
BANALIZED
BANALIZES
BANALLY
BANANA
BANANAS
BANAUSIAN
BANAUSIC
BANC
BANCO
BANCOS
BANCS
BAND
BANDA
BANDAGE
BANDAGED
BANDAGER
BANDAGERS
BANDAGES
BANDAGING
BANDAID
BANDALORE
BANDANA
BANDANAS
BANDANNA

BANDANNAS
BANDAR
BANDARI
BANDARIS
BANDARS
BANDAS
BANDBOX
BANDBOXES
BANDBRAKE
BANDEAU
BANDEAUS
BANDEAUX
BANDED
BANDEIRA
BANDEIRAS
BANDELET
BANDELETS
BANDELIER
BANDER
BANDEROL
BANDEROLE
BANDEROLS
BANDERS
BANDFISH
BANDH
BANDHS
BANDICOOT
BANDIED
BANDIER
BANDIES
BANDIEST
BANDINESS
BANDING
BANDINGS
BANDIT
BANDITO
BANDITOS
BANDITRY
BANDITS
BANDITTI
BANDITTIS
BANDLIKE
BANDMATE
BANDMATES
BANDOBAST
BANDOBUST
BANDOG
BANDOGS
BANDOLEER
BANDOLEON
BANDOLERO
BANDOLIER
BANDOLINE
BANDONEON
BANDONION
BANDOOK
BANDOOKS
BANDORA
BANDORAS
BANDORE
BANDORES
BANDPASS
BANDROL
BANDROLS
BANDS
BANDSAW
BANDSAWED
BANDSAWS
BANDSHELL
BANDSMAN
BANDSMEN
BANDSTAND
BANDSTER
BANDSTERS
BANDURA
BANDURAS
BANDURIST
BANDWAGON
BANDWIDTH
BANDY
BANDYING
BANDYINGS
BANDYMAN
BANDYMEN
BANE
BANEBERRY
BANED
BANEFUL
BANEFULLY
BANES
BANG
BANGALAY
BANGALAYS
BANGALORE
BANGALOW
BANGALOWS
BANGBELLY
BANGED
BANGER
BANGERS
BANGING
BANGKOK
BANGKOKS
BANGLE
BANGLED
BANGLES
BANGS
BANGSRING
BANGSTER
BANGSTERS
BANGTAIL
BANGTAILS
BANI
BANIA
BANIAN
BANIANS
BANIAS
BANING
BANISH
BANISHED
BANISHER
BANISHERS
BANISHES
BANISHING
BANISTER
BANISTERS
BANJAX
BANJAXED
BANJAXES
BANJAXING
BANJO
BANJOES
BANJOIST
BANJOISTS
BANJOLELE
BANJOS
BANJULELE
BANK
BANKABLE
BANKBOOK
BANKBOOKS
BANKCARD
BANKCARDS
BANKED
BANKER
BANKERLY
BANKERS
BANKET
BANKETS
BANKING
BANKINGS
BANKIT
BANKITS
BANKNOTE
BANKNOTES
BANKROLL
BANKROLLS
BANKRUPT
BANKRUPTS
BANKS
BANKSIA
BANKSIAS
BANKSIDE
BANKSIDES
BANKSMAN
BANKSMEN
BANKSTER
BANKSTERS
BANLIEUE
BANLIEUES
BANNABLE
BANNED
BANNER
BANNERALL
BANNERED
BANNERET
BANNERETS
BANNERING
BANNEROL
BANNEROLS
BANNERS
BANNET
BANNETS
BANNING
BANNINGS
BANNISTER
BANNOCK
BANNOCKS
BANNS
BANOFFEE
BANOFFEES
BANOFFI
BANOFFIS
BANQUET
BANQUETED
BANQUETER
BANQUETS
BANQUETTE
BANS
BANSELA
BANSELAS
BANSHEE
BANSHEES
BANSHIE
BANSHIES
BANT
BANTAM
BANTAMS
BANTED
BANTENG
BANTENGS
BANTER
BANTERED
BANTERER
BANTERERS
BANTERING
BANTERS
BANTIES
BANTING
BANTINGS
BANTLING
BANTLINGS
BANTS
BANTU
BANTUS
BANTY
BANXRING
BANXRINGS
BANYA
BANYAN
BANYANS
BANYAS
BANZAI
BANZAIS
BAO
BAOBAB
BAOBABS
BAOS
BAP
BAPS

BAPTISE
BAPTISED
BAPTISER
BAPTISERS
BAPTISES
BAPTISIA
BAPTISIAS
BAPTISING
BAPTISM
BAPTISMAL
BAPTISMS
BAPTIST
BAPTISTRY
BAPTISTS
BAPTIZE
BAPTIZED
BAPTIZER
BAPTIZERS
BAPTIZES
BAPTIZING
BAPU
BAPUS
BAR
BARACAN
BARACANS
BARACHOIS
BARAGOUIN
BARASINGA
BARATHEA
BARATHEAS
BARATHRUM
BARAZA
BARAZAS
BARB
BARBAL
BARBARIAN
BARBARIC
BARBARISE
BARBARISM
BARBARITY
BARBARIZE
BARBAROUS
BARBASCO
BARBASCOS
BARBASTEL
BARBATE
BARBATED
BARBE
BARBECUE
BARBECUED
BARBECUER
BARBECUES
BARBED
BARBEL
BARBELL
BARBELLS
BARBELS
BARBEQUE
BARBEQUED
BARBEQUES
BARBER
BARBERED
BARBERING
BARBERRY
BARBERS
BARBES
BARBET
BARBETS
BARBETTE
BARBETTES
BARBICAN
BARBICANS
BARBICEL
BARBICELS
BARBIE
BARBIES
BARBING
BARBITAL
BARBITALS
BARBITONE
BARBLESS
BARBOLA
BARBOLAS
BARBOT
BARBOTINE
BARBOTS
BARBOTTE
BARBOTTES
BARBS
BARBULE
BARBULES
BARBUT
BARBUTS
BARBWIRE
BARBWIRES
BARBY
BARCA
BARCAROLE
BARCAS
BARCHAN
BARCHANE
BARCHANES
BARCHANS
BARCODE
BARCODED
BARCODES
BARD
BARDASH
BARDASHES
BARDE
BARDED
BARDES
BARDIC
BARDIE
BARDIER
BARDIES
BARDIEST
BARDING
BARDISM
BARDISMS
BARDLING
BARDLINGS
BARDO
BARDOS
BARDS
BARDSHIP
BARDSHIPS
BARDY
BARE
BAREBACK
BAREBACKS
BAREBOAT
BAREBOATS
BAREBONE
BAREBONED
BAREBONES
BARED
BAREFACED
BAREFIT
BAREFOOT
BAREGE
BAREGES
BAREGINE
BAREGINES
BAREHAND
BAREHANDS
BAREHEAD
BARELAND
BARELY
BARENESS
BARER
BARES
BARESARK
BARESARKS
BAREST
BARF
BARFED
BARFI
BARFING
BARFIS
BARFLIES
BARFLY
BARFS
BARFUL
BARGAIN
BARGAINED
BARGAINER
BARGAINS
BARGANDER
BARGE
BARGED
BARGEE
BARGEES
BARGEESE
BARGELIKE
BARGELLO
BARGELLOS
BARGEMAN
BARGEMEN
BARGEPOLE
BARGES
BARGEST
BARGESTS
BARGHEST
BARGHESTS
BARGING
BARGOON
BARGOONS
BARGOOSE
BARGUEST
BARGUESTS
BARHOP
BARHOPPED
BARHOPS
BARIATRIC
BARIC
BARILLA
BARILLAS
BARING
BARISH
BARISTA
BARISTAS
BARITE
BARITES
BARITONAL
BARITONE
BARITONES
BARIUM
BARIUMS
BARK
BARKAN
BARKANS
BARKED
BARKEEP
BARKEEPER
BARKEEPS
BARKEN
BARKENED
BARKENING
BARKENS
BARKER
BARKERS
BARKHAN
BARKHANS
BARKIER
BARKIEST
BARKING
BARKLESS
BARKLIKE
BARKS
BARKY
BARLEDUC
BARLEDUCS
BARLESS
BARLEY
BARLEYS
BARLOW
BARLOWS
BARM
BARMAID

BARMAIDS
BARMAN
BARMBRACK
BARMEN
BARMIE
BARMIER
BARMIEST
BARMILY
BARMINESS
BARMKIN
BARMKINS
BARMPOT
BARMPOTS
BARMS
BARMY
BARN
BARNACLE
BARNACLED
BARNACLES
BARNBOARD
BARNBRACK
BARNED
BARNET
BARNETS
BARNEY
BARNEYED
BARNEYING
BARNEYS
BARNIER
BARNIEST
BARNING
BARNLIKE
BARNS
BARNSTORM
BARNWOOD
BARNWOODS
BARNY
BARNYARD
BARNYARDS
BAROCCO
BAROCCOS
BAROCK
BAROCKS
BAROGRAM
BAROGRAMS
BAROGRAPH
BAROLO
BAROLOS
BAROMETER
BAROMETRY
BAROMETZ
BARON
BARONAGE
BARONAGES
BARONESS
BARONET
BARONETCY
BARONETS
BARONG
BARONGS
BARONIAL
BARONIES
BARONNE
BARONNES
BARONS
BARONY
BAROPHILE
BAROQUE
BAROQUELY
BAROQUES
BAROSAUR
BAROSAURS
BAROSCOPE
BAROSTAT
BAROSTATS
BAROTITIS
BAROUCHE
BAROUCHES
BARP
BARPERSON
BARPS
BARQUE
BARQUES
BARQUETTE
BARRA
BARRABLE
BARRACAN
BARRACANS
BARRACE
BARRACES
BARRACK
BARRACKED
BARRACKER
BARRACKS
BARRACOON
BARRACUDA
BARRAGE
BARRAGED
BARRAGES
BARRAGING
BARRANCA
BARRANCAS
BARRANCO
BARRANCOS
BARRAS
BARRASWAY
BARRAT
BARRATED
BARRATER
BARRATERS
BARRATING
BARRATOR
BARRATORS
BARRATRY
BARRATS
BARRE
BARRED
BARREED
BARREFULL
BARREING
BARREL
BARRELAGE
BARRELED
BARRELFUL
BARRELING
BARRELLED
BARRELS
BARREN
BARRENER
BARRENEST
BARRENLY
BARRENS
BARRES
BARRET
BARRETOR
BARRETORS
BARRETRY
BARRETS
BARRETTE
BARRETTER
BARRETTES
BARRICADE
BARRICADO
BARRICO
BARRICOES
BARRICOS
BARRIE
BARRIER
BARRIERED
BARRIERS
BARRIES
BARRIEST
BARRING
BARRINGS
BARRIO
BARRIOS
BARRIQUE
BARRIQUES
BARRISTER
BARRO
BARROOM
BARROOMS
BARROW
BARROWFUL
BARROWS
BARRULET
BARRULETS
BARRY
BARS
BARSTOOL
BARSTOOLS
BARTEND
BARTENDED
BARTENDER
BARTENDS
BARTER
BARTERED
BARTERER
BARTERERS
BARTERING
BARTERS
BARTISAN
BARTISANS
BARTIZAN
BARTIZANS
BARTON
BARTONS
BARTSIA
BARTSIAS
BARWARE
BARWARES
BARWOOD
BARWOODS
BARYE
BARYES
BARYON
BARYONIC
BARYONS
BARYTA
BARYTAS
BARYTE
BARYTES
BARYTIC
BARYTON
BARYTONE
BARYTONES
BARYTONS
BAS
BASAL
BASALLY
BASALT
BASALTES
BASALTIC
BASALTINE
BASALTS
BASAN
BASANITE
BASANITES
BASANS
BASANT
BASANTS
BASCINET
BASCINETS
BASCULE
BASCULES
BASE
BASEBALL
BASEBALLS
BASEBAND
BASEBANDS
BASEBOARD
BASEBORN
BASED
BASEEJ
BASEHEAD
BASEHEADS
BASELARD
BASELARDS
BASELESS
BASELINE

BASELINER
BASELINES
BASELOAD
BASELOADS
BASELY
BASEMAN
BASEMEN
BASEMENT
BASEMENTS
BASEN
BASENESS
BASENJI
BASENJIS
BASEPATH
BASEPATHS
BASEPLATE
BASER
BASES
BASEST
BASH
BASHAW
BASHAWISM
BASHAWS
BASHED
BASHER
BASHERS
BASHES
BASHFUL
BASHFULLY
BASHING
BASHINGS
BASHLESS
BASHLIK
BASHLIKS
BASHLYK
BASHLYKS
BASHMENT
BASHMENTS
BASHO
BASHTAG
BASHTAGS
BASIC
BASICALLY
BASICITY
BASICS
BASIDIA
BASIDIAL
BASIDIUM
BASIFIED
BASIFIER
BASIFIERS
BASIFIES
BASIFIXED
BASIFUGAL
BASIFY
BASIFYING
BASIJ
BASIL
BASILAR
BASILARY
BASILECT
BASILECTS
BASILIC
BASILICA
BASILICAE
BASILICAL
BASILICAN
BASILICAS
BASILICON
BASILISK
BASILISKS
BASILS
BASIN
BASINAL
BASINED
BASINET
BASINETS
BASINFUL
BASINFULS
BASING
BASINLIKE
BASINS
BASION
BASIONS
BASIPETAL
BASIS
BASK
BASKED
BASKET
BASKETFUL
BASKETRY
BASKETS
BASKING
BASKS
BASMATI
BASMATIS
BASNET
BASNETS
BASOCHE
BASOCHES
BASON
BASONS
BASOPHIL
BASOPHILE
BASOPHILS
BASQUE
BASQUED
BASQUES
BASQUINE
BASQUINES
BASS
BASSE
BASSED
BASSER
BASSERS
BASSES
BASSEST
BASSET
BASSETED
BASSETING
BASSETS
BASSETT
BASSETTED
BASSETTS
BASSI
BASSIER
BASSIEST
BASSINET
BASSINETS
BASSING
BASSIST
BASSISTS
BASSLINE
BASSLINES
BASSLY
BASSNESS
BASSO
BASSOON
BASSOONS
BASSOS
BASSWOOD
BASSWOODS
BASSY
BAST
BASTA
BASTARD
BASTARDLY
BASTARDRY
BASTARDS
BASTARDY
BASTE
BASTED
BASTER
BASTERS
BASTES
BASTI
BASTIDE
BASTIDES
BASTILE
BASTILES
BASTILLE
BASTILLES
BASTINADE
BASTINADO
BASTING
BASTINGS
BASTION
BASTIONED
BASTIONS
BASTIS
BASTLE
BASTLES
BASTO
BASTOS
BASTS
BASUCO
BASUCOS
BAT
BATABLE
BATARD
BATARDS
BATATA
BATATAS
BATAVIA
BATAVIAS
BATBOY
BATBOYS
BATCH
BATCHED
BATCHER
BATCHERS
BATCHES
BATCHING
BATCHINGS
BATE
BATEAU
BATEAUX
BATED
BATELESS
BATELEUR
BATELEURS
BATEMENT
BATEMENTS
BATES
BATFISH
BATFISHES
BATFOWL
BATFOWLED
BATFOWLER
BATFOWLS
BATGIRL
BATGIRLS
BATH
BATHCUBE
BATHCUBES
BATHE
BATHED
BATHER
BATHERS
BATHES
BATHETIC
BATHHOUSE
BATHING
BATHINGS
BATHLESS
BATHMAT
BATHMATS
BATHMIC
BATHMISM
BATHMISMS
BATHOLITE
BATHOLITH
BATHORSE
BATHORSES
BATHOS
BATHOSES
BATHROBE
BATHROBES
BATHROOM
BATHROOMS

BATHS
BATHTUB
BATHTUBS
BATHWATER
BATHYAL
BATHYBIUS
BATHYLITE
BATHYLITH
BATIK
BATIKED
BATIKING
BATIKS
BATING
BATISTE
BATISTES
BATLER
BATLERS
BATLET
BATLETS
BATLIKE
BATMAN
BATMEN
BATOLOGY
BATON
BATONED
BATONING
BATONNIER
BATONS
BATOON
BATOONED
BATOONING
BATOONS
BATRACHIA
BATS
BATSHIT
BATSMAN
BATSMEN
BATSWING
BATSWOMAN
BATSWOMEN
BATT
BATTA
BATTALIA
BATTALIAS
BATTALION
BATTAS
BATTEAU
BATTEAUX
BATTED
BATTEL
BATTELED
BATTELER
BATTELERS
BATTELING
BATTELLED
BATTELS
BATTEMENT
BATTEN
BATTENED
BATTENER
BATTENERS
BATTENING
BATTENS
BATTER
BATTERED
BATTERER
BATTERERS
BATTERIE
BATTERIES
BATTERING
BATTERO
BATTEROS
BATTERS
BATTERY
BATTIER
BATTIES
BATTIEST
BATTIK
BATTIKS
BATTILL
BATTILLED
BATTILLS
BATTILY
BATTINESS
BATTING
BATTINGS
BATTLE
BATTLEAX
BATTLEAXE
BATTLEBUS
BATTLED
BATTLER
BATTLERS
BATTLES
BATTLING
BATTOLOGY
BATTS
BATTU
BATTUE
BATTUES
BATTUTA
BATTUTAS
BATTUTO
BATTUTOS
BATTY
BATWING
BATWOMAN
BATWOMEN
BAUBEE
BAUBEES
BAUBLE
BAUBLES
BAUBLING
BAUCHLE
BAUCHLED
BAUCHLES
BAUCHLING
BAUD
BAUDEKIN
BAUDEKINS
BAUDRIC
BAUDRICK
BAUDRICKE
BAUDRICKS
BAUDRICS
BAUDRONS
BAUDS
BAUERA
BAUERAS
BAUHINIA
BAUHINIAS
BAUK
BAUKED
BAUKING
BAUKS
BAULK
BAULKED
BAULKER
BAULKERS
BAULKIER
BAULKIEST
BAULKILY
BAULKING
BAULKLINE
BAULKS
BAULKY
BAUR
BAURS
BAUSOND
BAUXITE
BAUXITES
BAUXITIC
BAVARDAGE
BAVAROIS
BAVIN
BAVINED
BAVINING
BAVINS
BAWBEE
BAWBEES
BAWBLE
BAWBLES
BAWCOCK
BAWCOCKS
BAWD
BAWDIER
BAWDIES
BAWDIEST
BAWDILY
BAWDINESS
BAWDKIN
BAWDKINS
BAWDRIC
BAWDRICS
BAWDRIES
BAWDRY
BAWDS
BAWDY
BAWK
BAWKS
BAWL
BAWLED
BAWLER
BAWLERS
BAWLEY
BAWLEYS
BAWLING
BAWLINGS
BAWLS
BAWN
BAWNEEN
BAWNEENS
BAWNS
BAWR
BAWRS
BAWSUNT
BAWTIE
BAWTIES
BAWTY
BAXTER
BAXTERS
BAY
BAYADEER
BAYADEERS
BAYADERE
BAYADERES
BAYAMO
BAYAMOS
BAYARD
BAYARDS
BAYBERRY
BAYE
BAYED
BAYER
BAYES
BAYEST
BAYFRONT
BAYFRONTS
BAYING
BAYLE
BAYLES
BAYMAN
BAYMEN
BAYNODDY
BAYONET
BAYONETED
BAYONETS
BAYOU
BAYOUS
BAYS
BAYSIDE
BAYSIDES
BAYT
BAYTED
BAYTING
BAYTS
BAYWOOD
BAYWOODS
BAYWOP
BAYWOPS

B

BAYYAN
BAYYANS
BAZAAR
BAZAARS
BAZAR
BAZARS
BAZAZZ
BAZAZZES
BAZILLION
BAZOO
BAZOOKA
BAZOOKAS
BAZOOM
BAZOOMS
BAZOOS
BAZOUKI
BAZOUKIS
BAZZ
BAZZAZZ
BAZZAZZES
BAZZED
BAZZES
BAZZING
BDELLIUM
BDELLIUMS
BE
BEACH
BEACHBALL
BEACHBOY
BEACHBOYS
BEACHCOMB
BEACHED
BEACHES
BEACHGOER
BEACHHEAD
BEACHIER
BEACHIEST
BEACHING
BEACHSIDE
BEACHWEAR
BEACHY
BEACON
BEACONED
BEACONING
BEACONS
BEAD
BEADBLAST
BEADED
BEADER
BEADERS
BEADHOUSE
BEADIER
BEADIEST
BEADILY
BEADINESS
BEADING
BEADINGS
BEADLE
BEADLEDOM
BEADLES
BEADLIKE
BEADMAN
BEADMEN
BEADROLL
BEADROLLS
BEADS
BEADSMAN
BEADSMEN
BEADWORK
BEADWORKS
BEADY
BEAGLE
BEAGLED
BEAGLER
BEAGLERS
BEAGLES
BEAGLING
BEAGLINGS
BEAK
BEAKED
BEAKER
BEAKERFUL
BEAKERS
BEAKIER
BEAKIEST
BEAKLESS
BEAKLIKE
BEAKS
BEAKY
BEAL
BEALING
BEALINGS
BEALS
BEAM
BEAMED
BEAMER
BEAMERS
BEAMIER
BEAMIEST
BEAMILY
BEAMINESS
BEAMING
BEAMINGLY
BEAMINGS
BEAMISH
BEAMISHLY
BEAMLESS
BEAMLET
BEAMLETS
BEAMLIKE
BEAMS
BEAMY
BEAN
BEANBAG
BEANBAGS
BEANBALL
BEANBALLS
BEANED
BEANERIES
BEANERY
BEANFEAST
BEANIE
BEANIES
BEANING
BEANLIKE
BEANO
BEANOS
BEANPOLE
BEANPOLES
BEANS
BEANSTALK
BEANY
BEAR
BEARABLE
BEARABLY
BEARBERRY
BEARBINE
BEARBINES
BEARCAT
BEARCATS
BEARD
BEARDED
BEARDIE
BEARDIER
BEARDIES
BEARDIEST
BEARDING
BEARDLESS
BEARDLIKE
BEARDS
BEARDY
BEARE
BEARED
BEARER
BEARERS
BEARES
BEARGRASS
BEARHUG
BEARHUGS
BEARING
BEARINGS
BEARISH
BEARISHLY
BEARLIKE
BEARNAISE
BEARPAW
BEARPAWS
BEARS
BEARSKIN
BEARSKINS
BEARWARD
BEARWARDS
BEARWOOD
BEARWOODS
BEAST
BEASTED
BEASTHOOD
BEASTIE
BEASTIES
BEASTILY
BEASTING
BEASTINGS
BEASTLIER
BEASTLIKE
BEASTLY
BEASTS
BEAT
BEATABLE
BEATBOX
BEATBOXED
BEATBOXER
BEATBOXES
BEATDOWN
BEATDOWNS
BEATEN
BEATER
BEATERS
BEATH
BEATHED
BEATHING
BEATHS
BEATIER
BEATIEST
BEATIFIC
BEATIFIED
BEATIFIES
BEATIFY
BEATING
BEATINGS
BEATITUDE
BEATLESS
BEATNIK
BEATNIKS
BEATS
BEATY
BEAU
BEAUCOUP
BEAUCOUPS
BEAUFET
BEAUFETS
BEAUFFET
BEAUFFETS
BEAUFIN
BEAUFINS
BEAUISH
BEAUS
BEAUT
BEAUTEOUS
BEAUTER
BEAUTEST
BEAUTIED
BEAUTIES
BEAUTIFUL
BEAUTIFY
BEAUTS
BEAUTY
BEAUTYING
BEAUX
BEAUXITE
BEAUXITES

BEAVER
BEAVERED
BEAVERIES
BEAVERING
BEAVERS
BEAVERY
BEBEERINE
BEBEERU
BEBEERUS
BEBLOOD
BEBLOODED
BEBLOODS
BEBOP
BEBOPPED
BEBOPPER
BEBOPPERS
BEBOPPING
BEBOPS
BEBUNG
BEBUNGS
BECALL
BECALLED
BECALLING
BECALLS
BECALM
BECALMED
BECALMING
BECALMS
BECAME
BECAP
BECAPPED
BECAPPING
BECAPS
BECARPET
BECARPETS
BECASSE
BECASSES
BECAUSE
BECCACCIA
BECCAFICO
BECHALK
BECHALKED
BECHALKS
BECHAMEL
BECHAMELS
BECHANCE
BECHANCED
BECHANCES
BECHARM
BECHARMED
BECHARMS
BECK
BECKE
BECKED
BECKES
BECKET
BECKETS
BECKING
BECKON
BECKONED
BECKONER
BECKONERS
BECKONING
BECKONS
BECKS
BECLAMOR
BECLAMORS
BECLAMOUR
BECLASP
BECLASPED
BECLASPS
BECLOAK
BECLOAKED
BECLOAKS
BECLOG
BECLOGGED
BECLOGS
BECLOTHE
BECLOTHED
BECLOTHES
BECLOUD
BECLOUDED
BECLOUDS
BECLOWN
BECLOWNED
BECLOWNS
BECOME
BECOMES
BECOMING
BECOMINGS
BECOWARD
BECOWARDS
BECQUEREL
BECRAWL
BECRAWLED
BECRAWLS
BECRIME
BECRIMED
BECRIMES
BECRIMING
BECROWD
BECROWDED
BECROWDS
BECRUST
BECRUSTED
BECRUSTS
BECUDGEL
BECUDGELS
BECURL
BECURLED
BECURLING
BECURLS
BECURSE
BECURSED
BECURSES
BECURSING
BECURST
BED
BEDABBLE
BEDABBLED
BEDABBLES
BEDAD
BEDAGGLE
BEDAGGLED
BEDAGGLES
BEDAMN
BEDAMNED
BEDAMNING
BEDAMNS
BEDARKEN
BEDARKENS
BEDASH
BEDASHED
BEDASHES
BEDASHING
BEDAUB
BEDAUBED
BEDAUBING
BEDAUBS
BEDAWIN
BEDAWINS
BEDAZE
BEDAZED
BEDAZES
BEDAZING
BEDAZZLE
BEDAZZLED
BEDAZZLES
BEDBATH
BEDBATHS
BEDBOARD
BEDBOARDS
BEDBUG
BEDBUGS
BEDCHAIR
BEDCHAIRS
BEDCOVER
BEDCOVERS
BEDDABLE
BEDDED
BEDDER
BEDDERS
BEDDING
BEDDINGS
BEDE
BEDEAFEN
BEDEAFENS
BEDECK
BEDECKED
BEDECKING
BEDECKS
BEDEGUAR
BEDEGUARS
BEDEHOUSE
BEDEL
BEDELL
BEDELLS
BEDELS
BEDELSHIP
BEDEMAN
BEDEMEN
BEDERAL
BEDERALS
BEDES
BEDESMAN
BEDESMEN
BEDEVIL
BEDEVILED
BEDEVILS
BEDEW
BEDEWED
BEDEWING
BEDEWS
BEDFAST
BEDFELLOW
BEDFRAME
BEDFRAMES
BEDGOWN
BEDGOWNS
BEDHEAD
BEDHEADS
BEDIAPER
BEDIAPERS
BEDIDE
BEDIGHT
BEDIGHTED
BEDIGHTS
BEDIM
BEDIMMED
BEDIMMING
BEDIMPLE
BEDIMPLED
BEDIMPLES
BEDIMS
BEDIRTIED
BEDIRTIES
BEDIRTY
BEDIZEN
BEDIZENED
BEDIZENS
BEDLAM
BEDLAMER
BEDLAMERS
BEDLAMISM
BEDLAMITE
BEDLAMP
BEDLAMPS
BEDLAMS
BEDLESS
BEDLIKE
BEDLINER
BEDLINERS
BEDMAKER
BEDMAKERS
BEDMATE
BEDMATES
BEDOTTED
BEDOUIN
BEDOUINS
BEDPAN

BEDPANS
BEDPLATE
BEDPLATES
BEDPOST
BEDPOSTS
BEDQUILT
BEDQUILTS
BEDRAGGLE
BEDRAIL
BEDRAILS
BEDRAL
BEDRALS
BEDRAPE
BEDRAPED
BEDRAPES
BEDRAPING
BEDRENCH
BEDREST
BEDRESTS
BEDRID
BEDRIDDEN
BEDRIGHT
BEDRIGHTS
BEDRITE
BEDRITES
BEDRIVEL
BEDRIVELS
BEDROCK
BEDROCKS
BEDROLL
BEDROLLS
BEDROOM
BEDROOMED
BEDROOMS
BEDROP
BEDROPPED
BEDROPS
BEDROPT
BEDRUG
BEDRUGGED
BEDRUGS
BEDS
BEDSHEET
BEDSHEETS
BEDSIDE
BEDSIDES
BEDSIT
BEDSITS
BEDSITTER
BEDSKIRT
BEDSKIRTS
BEDSOCK
BEDSOCKS
BEDSONIA
BEDSONIAS
BEDSORE
BEDSORES
BEDSPREAD
BEDSPRING
BEDSTAND
BEDSTANDS
BEDSTEAD
BEDSTEADS
BEDSTRAW
BEDSTRAWS
BEDTICK
BEDTICKS
BEDTIME
BEDTIMES
BEDU
BEDUCK
BEDUCKED
BEDUCKING
BEDUCKS
BEDUIN
BEDUINS
BEDUMB
BEDUMBED
BEDUMBING
BEDUMBS
BEDUNCE
BEDUNCED
BEDUNCES
BEDUNCING
BEDUNG
BEDUNGED
BEDUNGING
BEDUNGS
BEDUST
BEDUSTED
BEDUSTING
BEDUSTS
BEDWARD
BEDWARDS
BEDWARF
BEDWARFED
BEDWARFS
BEDWARMER
BEDWETTER
BEDYDE
BEDYE
BEDYED
BEDYEING
BEDYES
BEE
BEEBEE
BEEBEES
BEEBREAD
BEEBREADS
BEECH
BEECHEN
BEECHES
BEECHIER
BEECHIEST
BEECHMAST
BEECHNUT
BEECHNUTS
BEECHWOOD
BEECHY
BEEDI
BEEDIE
BEEDIES
BEEF
BEEFALO
BEEFALOES
BEEFALOS
BEEFCAKE
BEEFCAKES
BEEFEATER
BEEFED
BEEFIER
BEEFIEST
BEEFILY
BEEFINESS
BEEFING
BEEFLESS
BEEFS
BEEFSTEAK
BEEFWOOD
BEEFWOODS
BEEFY
BEEGAH
BEEGAHS
BEEHIVE
BEEHIVED
BEEHIVES
BEEKEEPER
BEELIKE
BEELINE
BEELINED
BEELINES
BEELINING
BEEN
BEENAH
BEENAHS
BEENTO
BEENTOS
BEEP
BEEPED
BEEPER
BEEPERS
BEEPING
BEEPS
BEER
BEERAGE
BEERAGES
BEERFEST
BEERFESTS
BEERHALL
BEERHALLS
BEERIER
BEERIEST
BEERILY
BEERINESS
BEERMAT
BEERMATS
BEERNUT
BEERNUTS
BEERS
BEERSIES
BEERY
BEES
BEESOME
BEESTING
BEESTINGS
BEESTUNG
BEESWAX
BEESWAXED
BEESWAXES
BEESWING
BEESWINGS
BEET
BEETED
BEETFLIES
BEETFLY
BEETING
BEETLE
BEETLED
BEETLER
BEETLERS
BEETLES
BEETLING
BEETROOT
BEETROOTS
BEETS
BEEVES
BEEYARD
BEEYARDS
BEEZER
BEEZERS
BEFALL
BEFALLEN
BEFALLING
BEFALLS
BEFANA
BEFANAS
BEFELD
BEFELL
BEFFANA
BEFFANAS
BEFINGER
BEFINGERS
BEFINNED
BEFIT
BEFITS
BEFITTED
BEFITTING
BEFLAG
BEFLAGGED
BEFLAGS
BEFLEA
BEFLEAED
BEFLEAING
BEFLEAS
BEFLECK
BEFLECKED
BEFLECKS
BEFLOWER
BEFLOWERS
BEFLUM

BEFLUMMED
BEFLUMS
BEFOAM
BEFOAMED
BEFOAMING
BEFOAMS
BEFOG
BEFOGGED
BEFOGGING
BEFOGS
BEFOOL
BEFOOLED
BEFOOLING
BEFOOLS
BEFORE
BEFORTUNE
BEFOUL
BEFOULED
BEFOULER
BEFOULERS
BEFOULING
BEFOULS
BEFRET
BEFRETS
BEFRETTED
BEFRIEND
BEFRIENDS
BEFRINGE
BEFRINGED
BEFRINGES
BEFUDDLE
BEFUDDLED
BEFUDDLES
BEG
BEGAD
BEGALL
BEGALLED
BEGALLING
BEGALLS
BEGAN
BEGAR
BEGARS
BEGAT
BEGAZE
BEGAZED
BEGAZES
BEGAZING
BEGEM
BEGEMMED
BEGEMMING
BEGEMS
BEGET
BEGETS
BEGETTER
BEGETTERS
BEGETTING
BEGGAR
BEGGARDOM
BEGGARED
BEGGARIES
BEGGARING
BEGGARLY
BEGGARS
BEGGARY
BEGGED
BEGGING
BEGGINGLY
BEGGINGS
BEGHARD
BEGHARDS
BEGIFT
BEGIFTED
BEGIFTING
BEGIFTS
BEGILD
BEGILDED
BEGILDING
BEGILDS
BEGILT
BEGIN
BEGINNE
BEGINNER
BEGINNERS
BEGINNES
BEGINNING
BEGINS
BEGIRD
BEGIRDED
BEGIRDING
BEGIRDLE
BEGIRDLED
BEGIRDLES
BEGIRDS
BEGIRT
BEGLAD
BEGLADDED
BEGLADS
BEGLAMOR
BEGLAMORS
BEGLAMOUR
BEGLERBEG
BEGLOOM
BEGLOOMED
BEGLOOMS
BEGNAW
BEGNAWED
BEGNAWING
BEGNAWS
BEGO
BEGOES
BEGOGGLED
BEGOING
BEGONE
BEGONIA
BEGONIAS
BEGORAH
BEGORED
BEGORRA
BEGORRAH
BEGOT
BEGOTTEN
BEGRIM
BEGRIME
BEGRIMED
BEGRIMES
BEGRIMING
BEGRIMMED
BEGRIMS
BEGROAN
BEGROANED
BEGROANS
BEGRUDGE
BEGRUDGED
BEGRUDGER
BEGRUDGES
BEGS
BEGUILE
BEGUILED
BEGUILER
BEGUILERS
BEGUILES
BEGUILING
BEGUIN
BEGUINAGE
BEGUINE
BEGUINES
BEGUINS
BEGULF
BEGULFED
BEGULFING
BEGULFS
BEGUM
BEGUMS
BEGUN
BEGUNK
BEGUNKED
BEGUNKING
BEGUNKS
BEHALF
BEHALVES
BEHAPPEN
BEHAPPENS
BEHATTED
BEHAVE
BEHAVED
BEHAVER
BEHAVERS
BEHAVES
BEHAVING
BEHAVIOR
BEHAVIORS
BEHAVIOUR
BEHEAD
BEHEADAL
BEHEADALS
BEHEADED
BEHEADER
BEHEADERS
BEHEADING
BEHEADS
BEHELD
BEHEMOTH
BEHEMOTHS
BEHEST
BEHESTS
BEHIGHT
BEHIGHTED
BEHIGHTS
BEHIND
BEHINDS
BEHOLD
BEHOLDEN
BEHOLDER
BEHOLDERS
BEHOLDING
BEHOLDS
BEHOOF
BEHOOFS
BEHOOVE
BEHOOVED
BEHOOVES
BEHOOVING
BEHOTE
BEHOTES
BEHOTING
BEHOVE
BEHOVED
BEHOVEFUL
BEHOVELY
BEHOVES
BEHOVING
BEHOWL
BEHOWLED
BEHOWLING
BEHOWLS
BEIGE
BEIGEL
BEIGELS
BEIGER
BEIGES
BEIGEST
BEIGIER
BEIGIEST
BEIGNE
BEIGNES
BEIGNET
BEIGNETS
BEIGY
BEIN
BEINED
BEING
BEINGLESS
BEINGNESS
BEINGS
BEINING
BEINKED
BEINNESS
BEINS
BEJABBERS
BEJABERS

BEJADE
BEJADED
BEJADES
BEJADING
BEJANT
BEJANTS
BEJASUS
BEJASUSES
BEJEEBERS
BEJEEZUS
BEJESUIT
BEJESUITS
BEJESUS
BEJESUSES
BEJEWEL
BEJEWELED
BEJEWELS
BEJUMBLE
BEJUMBLED
BEJUMBLES
BEKAH
BEKAHS
BEKISS
BEKISSED
BEKISSES
BEKISSING
BEKNAVE
BEKNAVED
BEKNAVES
BEKNAVING
BEKNIGHT
BEKNIGHTS
BEKNOT
BEKNOTS
BEKNOTTED
BEKNOWN
BEL
BELABOR
BELABORED
BELABORS
BELABOUR
BELABOURS
BELACE
BELACED
BELACES
BELACING
BELADIED
BELADIES
BELADY
BELADYING
BELAH
BELAHS
BELAMIES
BELAMOUR
BELAMOURE
BELAMOURS
BELAMY
BELAR
BELARS
BELATE
BELATED
BELATEDLY
BELATES
BELATING
BELAUD
BELAUDED
BELAUDING
BELAUDS
BELAY
BELAYED
BELAYER
BELAYERS
BELAYING
BELAYS
BELCH
BELCHED
BELCHER
BELCHERS
BELCHES
BELCHING
BELDAM
BELDAME
BELDAMES
BELDAMS
BELEAGUER
BELEAP
BELEAPED
BELEAPING
BELEAPS
BELEAPT
BELEE
BELEED
BELEEING
BELEES
BELEMNITE
BELEMNOID
BELFRIED
BELFRIES
BELFRY
BELGA
BELGARD
BELGARDS
BELGAS
BELGICISM
BELIE
BELIED
BELIEF
BELIEFS
BELIER
BELIERS
BELIES
BELIEVE
BELIEVED
BELIEVER
BELIEVERS
BELIEVES
BELIEVING
BELIKE
BELIQUOR
BELIQUORS
BELITTLE
BELITTLED
BELITTLER
BELITTLES
BELIVE
BELL
BELLBIND
BELLBINDS
BELLBIRD
BELLBIRDS
BELLBOY
BELLBOYS
BELLBUOY
BELLBUOYS
BELLCAST
BELLCOTE
BELLCOTES
BELLE
BELLED
BELLEEK
BELLEEKS
BELLES
BELLETER
BELLETERS
BELLHOP
BELLHOPS
BELLIBONE
BELLICOSE
BELLIED
BELLIES
BELLING
BELLINGS
BELLINI
BELLINIS
BELLMAN
BELLMEN
BELLOCK
BELLOCKED
BELLOCKS
BELLOW
BELLOWED
BELLOWER
BELLOWERS
BELLOWING
BELLOWS
BELLPULL
BELLPULLS
BELLS
BELLWORT
BELLWORTS
BELLY
BELLYACHE
BELLYBAND
BELLYBOAT
BELLYFLOP
BELLYFUL
BELLYFULS
BELLYING
BELLYINGS
BELLYLIKE
BELOMANCY
BELON
BELONG
BELONGED
BELONGER
BELONGERS
BELONGING
BELONGS
BELONS
BELOVE
BELOVED
BELOVEDS
BELOVES
BELOVING
BELOW
BELOWS
BELS
BELT
BELTED
BELTER
BELTERS
BELTING
BELTINGS
BELTLESS
BELTLIKE
BELTLINE
BELTLINES
BELTMAN
BELTMEN
BELTS
BELTWAY
BELTWAYS
BELUGA
BELUGAS
BELVEDERE
BELYING
BEMA
BEMAD
BEMADAM
BEMADAMED
BEMADAMS
BEMADDED
BEMADDEN
BEMADDENS
BEMADDING
BEMADS
BEMAS
BEMATA
BEMAUL
BEMAULED
BEMAULING
BEMAULS
BEMAZED
BEMBEX
BEMBEXES
BEMBIX
BEMBIXES
BEMEAN
BEMEANED
BEMEANING

BEMEANS
BEMEANT
BEMEDAL
BEMEDALED
BEMEDALS
BEMETE
BEMETED
BEMETES
BEMETING
BEMINGLE
BEMINGLED
BEMINGLES
BEMIRE
BEMIRED
BEMIRES
BEMIRING
BEMIST
BEMISTED
BEMISTING
BEMISTS
BEMIX
BEMIXED
BEMIXES
BEMIXING
BEMIXT
BEMOAN
BEMOANED
BEMOANER
BEMOANERS
BEMOANING
BEMOANS
BEMOCK
BEMOCKED
BEMOCKING
BEMOCKS
BEMOIL
BEMOILED
BEMOILING
BEMOILS
BEMONSTER
BEMOUTH
BEMOUTHED
BEMOUTHS
BEMUD
BEMUDDED
BEMUDDING
BEMUDDLE
BEMUDDLED
BEMUDDLES
BEMUDS
BEMUFFLE
BEMUFFLED
BEMUFFLES
BEMURMUR
BEMURMURS
BEMUSE
BEMUSED
BEMUSEDLY
BEMUSES
BEMUSING
BEMUZZLE
BEMUZZLED
BEMUZZLES
BEN
BENADRYL
BENADRYLS
BENAME
BENAMED
BENAMES
BENAMING
BENCH
BENCHED
BENCHER
BENCHERS
BENCHES
BENCHIER
BENCHIEST
BENCHING
BENCHLAND
BENCHLESS
BENCHMARK
BENCHTOP
BENCHTOPS
BENCHY
BEND
BENDABLE
BENDAY
BENDAYED
BENDAYING
BENDAYS
BENDED
BENDEE
BENDEES
BENDER
BENDERS
BENDIER
BENDIEST
BENDINESS
BENDING
BENDINGLY
BENDINGS
BENDLET
BENDLETS
BENDS
BENDWAYS
BENDWISE
BENDY
BENDYS
BENE
BENEATH
BENEDICK
BENEDICKS
BENEDICT
BENEDICTS
BENEDIGHT
BENEFACT
BENEFACTS
BENEFIC
BENEFICE
BENEFICED
BENEFICES
BENEFIT
BENEFITED
BENEFITER
BENEFITS
BENEMPT
BENEMPTED
BENES
BENET
BENETS
BENETTED
BENETTING
BENGA
BENGALINE
BENGAS
BENI
BENIGHT
BENIGHTED
BENIGHTEN
BENIGHTER
BENIGHTS
BENIGN
BENIGNANT
BENIGNER
BENIGNEST
BENIGNITY
BENIGNLY
BENIS
BENISEED
BENISEEDS
BENISON
BENISONS
BENITIER
BENITIERS
BENJ
BENJAMIN
BENJAMINS
BENJES
BENNE
BENNES
BENNET
BENNETS
BENNI
BENNIES
BENNIS
BENNY
BENOMYL
BENOMYLS
BENS
BENT
BENTGRASS
BENTHAL
BENTHIC
BENTHOAL
BENTHON
BENTHONIC
BENTHONS
BENTHOS
BENTHOSES
BENTIER
BENTIEST
BENTO
BENTONITE
BENTOS
BENTS
BENTWOOD
BENTWOODS
BENTY
BENUMB
BENUMBED
BENUMBING
BENUMBS
BENZAL
BENZALS
BENZENE
BENZENES
BENZENOID
BENZIDIN
BENZIDINE
BENZIDINS
BENZIL
BENZILS
BENZIN
BENZINE
BENZINES
BENZINS
BENZOATE
BENZOATES
BENZOIC
BENZOIN
BENZOINS
BENZOL
BENZOLE
BENZOLES
BENZOLINE
BENZOLS
BENZOYL
BENZOYLS
BENZYL
BENZYLIC
BENZYLS
BEPAINT
BEPAINTED
BEPAINTS
BEPAT
BEPATCHED
BEPATS
BEPATTED
BEPATTING
BEPEARL
BEPEARLED
BEPEARLS
BEPELT
BEPELTED
BEPELTING
BEPELTS
BEPEPPER
BEPEPPERS
BEPESTER
BEPESTERS

B

BEPIMPLE
BEPIMPLED
BEPIMPLES
BEPITIED
BEPITIES
BEPITY
BEPITYING
BEPLASTER
BEPLUMED
BEPOMMEL
BEPOMMELS
BEPOWDER
BEPOWDERS
BEPRAISE
BEPRAISED
BEPRAISES
BEPROSE
BEPROSED
BEPROSES
BEPROSING
BEPUFF
BEPUFFED
BEPUFFING
BEPUFFS
BEQUEATH
BEQUEATHS
BEQUEST
BEQUESTS
BERAKE
BERAKED
BERAKES
BERAKING
BERASCAL
BERASCALS
BERATE
BERATED
BERATES
BERATING
BERAY
BERAYED
BERAYING
BERAYS
BERBER
BERBERE
BERBERES
BERBERIN
BERBERINE
BERBERINS
BERBERIS
BERBERS
BERBICE
BERCEAU
BERCEAUX
BERCEUSE
BERCEUSES
BERDACHE
BERDACHES
BERDASH
BERDASHES
BERE
BEREAVE
BEREAVED
BEREAVEN
BEREAVER
BEREAVERS
BEREAVES
BEREAVING
BEREFT
BERES
BERET
BERETS
BERETTA
BERETTAS
BERG
BERGALL
BERGALLS
BERGAMA
BERGAMAS
BERGAMASK
BERGAMOT
BERGAMOTS
BERGANDER
BERGEN
BERGENIA
BERGENIAS
BERGENS
BERGERE
BERGERES
BERGFALL
BERGFALLS
BERGHAAN
BERGHAANS
BERGMEHL
BERGMEHLS
BERGOMASK
BERGS
BERGYLT
BERGYLTS
BERHYME
BERHYMED
BERHYMES
BERHYMING
BERIBERI
BERIBERIS
BERIMBAU
BERIMBAUS
BERIME
BERIMED
BERIMES
BERIMING
BERINGED
BERK
BERKELIUM
BERKO
BERKS
BERLEY
BERLEYED
BERLEYING
BERLEYS
BERLIN
BERLINE
BERLINES
BERLINS
BERM
BERME
BERMED
BERMES
BERMING
BERMS
BERMUDAS
BERNICLE
BERNICLES
BEROB
BEROBBED
BEROBBING
BEROBED
BEROBS
BEROUGED
BERRET
BERRETS
BERRETTA
BERRETTAS
BERRIED
BERRIES
BERRIGAN
BERRIGANS
BERRY
BERRYING
BERRYINGS
BERRYLESS
BERRYLIKE
BERSEEM
BERSEEMS
BERSERK
BERSERKER
BERSERKLY
BERSERKS
BERTH
BERTHA
BERTHAGE
BERTHAGES
BERTHAS
BERTHE
BERTHED
BERTHES
BERTHING
BERTHINGS
BERTHS
BERYL
BERYLINE
BERYLLIA
BERYLLIAS
BERYLLIUM
BERYLS
BES
BESAINT
BESAINTED
BESAINTS
BESANG
BESAT
BESAW
BESCATTER
BESCORCH
BESCOUR
BESCOURED
BESCOURS
BESCRAWL
BESCRAWLS
BESCREEN
BESCREENS
BESEE
BESEECH
BESEECHED
BESEECHER
BESEECHES
BESEEING
BESEEKE
BESEEKES
BESEEKING
BESEEM
BESEEMED
BESEEMING
BESEEMLY
BESEEMS
BESEEN
BESEES
BESES
BESET
BESETMENT
BESETS
BESETTER
BESETTERS
BESETTING
BESHADOW
BESHADOWS
BESHAME
BESHAMED
BESHAMES
BESHAMING
BESHINE
BESHINES
BESHINING
BESHIVER
BESHIVERS
BESHONE
BESHOUT
BESHOUTED
BESHOUTS
BESHREW
BESHREWED
BESHREWS
BESHROUD
BESHROUDS
BESIDE
BESIDES
BESIEGE
BESIEGED
BESIEGER
BESIEGERS
BESIEGES

BESIEGING
BESIGH
BESIGHED
BESIGHING
BESIGHS
BESING
BESINGING
BESINGS
BESIT
BESITS
BESITTING
BESLAVE
BESLAVED
BESLAVER
BESLAVERS
BESLAVES
BESLAVING
BESLIME
BESLIMED
BESLIMES
BESLIMING
BESLOBBER
BESLUBBER
BESMEAR
BESMEARED
BESMEARER
BESMEARS
BESMILE
BESMILED
BESMILES
BESMILING
BESMIRCH
BESMOKE
BESMOKED
BESMOKES
BESMOKING
BESMOOTH
BESMOOTHS
BESMUDGE
BESMUDGED
BESMUDGES
BESMUT
BESMUTCH
BESMUTS
BESMUTTED
BESNOW
BESNOWED
BESNOWING
BESNOWS
BESOGNIO
BESOGNIOS
BESOIN
BESOINS
BESOM
BESOMED
BESOMING
BESOMS
BESONIAN
BESONIANS
BESOOTHE
BESOOTHED
BESOOTHES
BESORT
BESORTED
BESORTING
BESORTS
BESOT
BESOTS
BESOTTED
BESOTTING
BESOUGHT
BESOULED
BESPAKE
BESPANGLE
BESPAT
BESPATE
BESPATTER
BESPEAK
BESPEAKS
BESPECKLE
BESPED
BESPEED
BESPEEDS
BESPICE
BESPICED
BESPICES
BESPICING
BESPIT
BESPITS
BESPOKE
BESPOKEN
BESPORT
BESPORTED
BESPORTS
BESPOT
BESPOTS
BESPOTTED
BESPOUSE
BESPOUSED
BESPOUSES
BESPOUT
BESPOUTED
BESPOUTS
BESPREAD
BESPREADS
BESPRENT
BEST
BESTAD
BESTADDE
BESTAIN
BESTAINED
BESTAINS
BESTAR
BESTARRED
BESTARS
BESTEAD
BESTEADED
BESTEADS
BESTED
BESTEST
BESTI
BESTIAL
BESTIALLY
BESTIALS
BESTIARY
BESTICK
BESTICKS
BESTIE
BESTIES
BESTILL
BESTILLED
BESTILLS
BESTING
BESTIR
BESTIRRED
BESTIRS
BESTIS
BESTORM
BESTORMED
BESTORMS
BESTOW
BESTOWAL
BESTOWALS
BESTOWED
BESTOWER
BESTOWERS
BESTOWING
BESTOWS
BESTREAK
BESTREAKS
BESTREW
BESTREWED
BESTREWN
BESTREWS
BESTRID
BESTRIDE
BESTRIDES
BESTRODE
BESTROW
BESTROWED
BESTROWN
BESTROWS
BESTS
BESTUCK
BESTUD
BESTUDDED
BESTUDS
BESUITED
BESUNG
BESWARM
BESWARMED
BESWARMS
BET
BETA
BETACISM
BETACISMS
BETAINE
BETAINES
BETAKE
BETAKEN
BETAKES
BETAKING
BETAS
BETATOPIC
BETATRON
BETATRONS
BETATTER
BETATTERS
BETAXED
BETCHA
BETE
BETED
BETEEM
BETEEME
BETEEMED
BETEEMES
BETEEMING
BETEEMS
BETEL
BETELNUT
BETELNUTS
BETELS
BETES
BETH
BETHANK
BETHANKED
BETHANKIT
BETHANKS
BETHEL
BETHELS
BETHESDA
BETHESDAS
BETHINK
BETHINKS
BETHORN
BETHORNED
BETHORNS
BETHOUGHT
BETHRALL
BETHRALLS
BETHS
BETHUMB
BETHUMBED
BETHUMBS
BETHUMP
BETHUMPED
BETHUMPS
BETHWACK
BETHWACKS
BETID
BETIDE
BETIDED
BETIDES
BETIDING
BETIGHT
BETIME
BETIMED
BETIMES
BETIMING
BETING

B

BETISE
BETISES
BETITLE
BETITLED
BETITLES
BETITLING
BETOIL
BETOILED
BETOILING
BETOILS
BETOKEN
BETOKENED
BETOKENS
BETON
BETONIES
BETONS
BETONY
BETOOK
BETOSS
BETOSSED
BETOSSES
BETOSSING
BETRAY
BETRAYAL
BETRAYALS
BETRAYED
BETRAYER
BETRAYERS
BETRAYING
BETRAYS
BETREAD
BETREADS
BETRIM
BETRIMMED
BETRIMS
BETROD
BETRODDEN
BETROTH
BETROTHAL
BETROTHED
BETROTHS
BETS
BETTA
BETTAS
BETTED
BETTER
BETTERED
BETTERING
BETTERS
BETTIES
BETTING
BETTINGS
BETTONG
BETTONGS
BETTOR
BETTORS
BETTY
BETUMBLED
BETWEEN
BETWEENS
BETWIXT
BEUNCLED
BEURRE
BEURRES
BEVATRON
BEVATRONS
BEVEL
BEVELED
BEVELER
BEVELERS
BEVELING
BEVELLED
BEVELLER
BEVELLERS
BEVELLING
BEVELMENT
BEVELS
BEVER
BEVERAGE
BEVERAGES
BEVERED
BEVERING
BEVERS
BEVIES
BEVOMIT
BEVOMITED
BEVOMITS
BEVOR
BEVORS
BEVUE
BEVUES
BEVVIED
BEVVIES
BEVVY
BEVVYING
BEVY
BEWAIL
BEWAILED
BEWAILER
BEWAILERS
BEWAILING
BEWAILS
BEWARE
BEWARED
BEWARES
BEWARING
BEWEARIED
BEWEARIES
BEWEARY
BEWEEP
BEWEEPING
BEWEEPS
BEWENT
BEWEPT
BEWET
BEWETS
BEWETTED
BEWETTING
BEWHORE
BEWHORED
BEWHORES
BEWHORING
BEWIG
BEWIGGED
BEWIGGING
BEWIGS
BEWILDER
BEWILDERS
BEWINGED
BEWITCH
BEWITCHED
BEWITCHER
BEWITCHES
BEWORM
BEWORMED
BEWORMING
BEWORMS
BEWORRIED
BEWORRIES
BEWORRY
BEWRAP
BEWRAPPED
BEWRAPS
BEWRAPT
BEWRAY
BEWRAYED
BEWRAYER
BEWRAYERS
BEWRAYING
BEWRAYS
BEY
BEYLIC
BEYLICS
BEYLIK
BEYLIKS
BEYOND
BEYONDS
BEYS
BEZ
BEZANT
BEZANTS
BEZAZZ
BEZAZZES
BEZEL
BEZELLESS
BEZELS
BEZES
BEZIL
BEZILS
BEZIQUE
BEZIQUES
BEZOAR
BEZOARDIC
BEZOARS
BEZONIAN
BEZONIANS
BEZZANT
BEZZANTS
BEZZAZZ
BEZZAZZES
BEZZIE
BEZZIES
BEZZLE
BEZZLED
BEZZLES
BEZZLING
BEZZY
BHAGEE
BHAGEES
BHAI
BHAIS
BHAJAN
BHAJANS
BHAJEE
BHAJEES
BHAJI
BHAJIA
BHAJIS
BHAKTA
BHAKTAS
BHAKTI
BHAKTIS
BHANG
BHANGRA
BHANGRAS
BHANGS
BHARAL
BHARALS
BHAT
BHATS
BHAVAN
BHAVANS
BHAWAN
BHAWANS
BHEESTIE
BHEESTIES
BHEESTY
BHEL
BHELPURI
BHELPURIS
BHELS
BHIKHU
BHIKHUS
BHIKKHUNI
BHINDI
BHINDIS
BHISHTI
BHISHTIS
BHISTEE
BHISTEES
BHISTI
BHISTIE
BHISTIES
BHISTIS
BHOONA
BHOONAS
BHOOT
BHOOTS
BHUNA
BHUNAS

BHUT
BHUTS
BI
BIACETYL
BIACETYLS
BIACH
BIACHES
BIALI
BIALIES
BIALIS
BIALY
BIALYS
BIANNUAL
BIANNUALS
BIAS
BIASED
BIASEDLY
BIASES
BIASING
BIASINGS
BIASNESS
BIASSED
BIASSEDLY
BIASSES
BIASSING
BIATCH
BIATCHES
BIATHLETE
BIATHLON
BIATHLONS
BIAXAL
BIAXIAL
BIAXIALLY
BIB
BIBACIOUS
BIBASIC
BIBATION
BIBATIONS
BIBB
BIBBED
BIBBER
BIBBERIES
BIBBERS
BIBBERY
BIBBING
BIBBINGS
BIBBLE
BIBBLES
BIBBS
BIBCOCK
BIBCOCKS
BIBE
BIBELOT
BIBELOTS
BIBES
BIBFUL
BIBFULS
BIBIMBAP
BIBIMBAPS
BIBLE
BIBLES
BIBLESS
BIBLICAL
BIBLICISM
BIBLICIST
BIBLIKE
BIBLIOTIC
BIBLIST
BIBLISTS
BIBS
BIBULOUS
BICAMERAL
BICARB
BICARBS
BICAUDAL
BICCIES
BICCY
BICE
BICENTRIC
BICEP
BICEPS
BICEPSES
BICES
BICHIR
BICHIRS
BICHORD
BICHROME
BICIPITAL
BICKER
BICKERED
BICKERER
BICKERERS
BICKERING
BICKERS
BICKIE
BICKIES
BICOASTAL
BICOLOR
BICOLORED
BICOLORS
BICOLOUR
BICOLOURS
BICONCAVE
BICONVEX
BICORN
BICORNATE
BICORNE
BICORNES
BICORNS
BICRON
BICRONS
BICURIOUS
BICUSPID
BICUSPIDS
BICYCLE
BICYCLED
BICYCLER
BICYCLERS
BICYCLES
BICYCLIC
BICYCLING
BICYCLIST
BID
BIDARKA
BIDARKAS
BIDARKEE
BIDARKEES
BIDDABLE
BIDDABLY
BIDDEN
BIDDER
BIDDERS
BIDDIES
BIDDING
BIDDINGS
BIDDY
BIDE
BIDED
BIDENT
BIDENTAL
BIDENTALS
BIDENTATE
BIDENTS
BIDER
BIDERS
BIDES
BIDET
BIDETS
BIDI
BIDING
BIDINGS
BIDIS
BIDON
BIDONS
BIDS
BIELD
BIELDED
BIELDIER
BIELDIEST
BIELDING
BIELDS
BIELDY
BIEN
BIENNALE
BIENNALES
BIENNIA
BIENNIAL
BIENNIALS
BIENNIUM
BIENNIUMS
BIER
BIERS
BIERWURST
BIESTINGS
BIFACE
BIFACES
BIFACIAL
BIFARIOUS
BIFF
BIFFED
BIFFER
BIFFERS
BIFFIES
BIFFIN
BIFFING
BIFFINS
BIFFO
BIFFOS
BIFFS
BIFFY
BIFID
BIFIDA
BIFIDITY
BIFIDLY
BIFIDUM
BIFIDUMS
BIFIDUS
BIFIDUSES
BIFILAR
BIFILARLY
BIFLEX
BIFOCAL
BIFOCALED
BIFOCALS
BIFOLD
BIFOLDS
BIFOLIATE
BIFORATE
BIFORKED
BIFORM
BIFORMED
BIFTAH
BIFTAHS
BIFTER
BIFTERS
BIFURCATE
BIG
BIGA
BIGAE
BIGAMIES
BIGAMIST
BIGAMISTS
BIGAMOUS
BIGAMY
BIGARADE
BIGARADES
BIGAROON
BIGAROONS
BIGARREAU
BIGEMINAL
BIGEMINY
BIGENER
BIGENERIC
BIGENERS
BIGEYE
BIGEYES
BIGFEET
BIGFOOT
BIGFOOTED
BIGFOOTS

BIGG
BIGGED
BIGGER
BIGGEST
BIGGETIER
BIGGETY
BIGGIE
BIGGIES
BIGGIN
BIGGING
BIGGINGS
BIGGINS
BIGGISH
BIGGITIER
BIGGITY
BIGGON
BIGGONS
BIGGS
BIGGY
BIGHA
BIGHAS
BIGHEAD
BIGHEADED
BIGHEADS
BIGHORN
BIGHORNS
BIGHT
BIGHTED
BIGHTING
BIGHTS
BIGLY
BIGMOUTH
BIGMOUTHS
BIGNESS
BIGNESSES
BIGNONIA
BIGNONIAS
BIGOS
BIGOSES
BIGOT
BIGOTED
BIGOTEDLY
BIGOTRIES
BIGOTRY
BIGOTS
BIGS
BIGSTICK
BIGTIME

BIGUANIDE
BIGUINE
BIGUINES
BIGWIG
BIGWIGS
BIHOURLY
BIJECTION
BIJECTIVE
BIJOU
BIJOUS
BIJOUX
BIJUGATE
BIJUGOUS
BIJURAL
BIJWONER
BIJWONERS
BIKE
BIKED
BIKER
BIKERS
BIKES
BIKEWAY
BIKEWAYS
BIKIE
BIKIES
BIKING
BIKINGS
BIKINI
BIKINIED
BIKINIS
BIKKIE
BIKKIES
BILABIAL
BILABIALS
BILABIATE
BILANDER
BILANDERS
BILATERAL
BILAYER
BILAYERS
BILBERRY
BILBIES
BILBO
BILBOA
BILBOAS
BILBOES
BILBOS
BILBY

BILE
BILECTION
BILED
BILES
BILESTONE
BILEVEL
BILEVELS
BILGE
BILGED
BILGES
BILGIER
BILGIEST
BILGING
BILGY
BILHARZIA
BILIAN
BILIANS
BILIARIES
BILIARY
BILIMBI
BILIMBING
BILIMBIS
BILINEAR
BILING
BILINGUAL
BILIOUS
BILIOUSLY
BILIRUBIN
BILITERAL
BILK
BILKED
BILKER
BILKERS
BILKING
BILKS
BILL
BILLABLE
BILLABONG
BILLBOARD
BILLBOOK
BILLBOOKS
BILLBUG
BILLBUGS
BILLED
BILLER
BILLERS
BILLET
BILLETED

BILLETEE
BILLETEES
BILLETER
BILLETERS
BILLETING
BILLETS
BILLFISH
BILLFOLD
BILLFOLDS
BILLHEAD
BILLHEADS
BILLHOOK
BILLHOOKS
BILLIARD
BILLIARDS
BILLIE
BILLIES
BILLING
BILLINGS
BILLION
BILLIONS
BILLIONTH
BILLMAN
BILLMEN
BILLON
BILLONS
BILLOW
BILLOWED
BILLOWIER
BILLOWING
BILLOWS
BILLOWY
BILLS
BILLY
BILLYBOY
BILLYBOYS
BILLYCAN
BILLYCANS
BILLYCOCK
BILLYO
BILLYOH
BILLYOHS
BILLYOS
BILOBAR
BILOBATE
BILOBATED
BILOBED
BILOBULAR

BILOCULAR
BILSTED
BILSTEDS
BILTONG
BILTONGS
BIMA
BIMAH
BIMAHS
BIMANAL
BIMANOUS
BIMANUAL
BIMAS
BIMBASHI
BIMBASHIS
BIMBETTE
BIMBETTES
BIMBLE
BIMBO
BIMBOES
BIMBOS
BIMENSAL
BIMESTER
BIMESTERS
BIMETAL
BIMETALS
BIMETHYL
BIMETHYLS
BIMINI
BIMINIS
BIMODAL
BIMONTHLY
BIMORPH
BIMORPHS
BIN
BINAL
BINARIES
BINARISM
BINARISMS
BINARY
BINATE
BINATELY
BINAURAL
BIND
BINDABLE
BINDER
BINDERIES
BINDERS
BINDERY

BINDHI
BINDHIS
BINDI
BINDING
BINDINGLY
BINDINGS
BINDIS
BINDLE
BINDLES
BINDS
BINDWEED
BINDWEEDS
BINE
BINER
BINERS
BINERVATE
BINES
BING
BINGE
BINGEABLE
BINGED
BINGEING
BINGEINGS
BINGER
BINGERS
BINGES
BINGHI
BINGHIS
BINGIES
BINGING
BINGINGS
BINGLE
BINGLED
BINGLES
BINGLING
BINGO
BINGOED
BINGOES
BINGOING
BINGOS
BINGS
BINGY
BINIOU
BINIOUS
BINIT
BINITS
BINK
BINKS
BINMAN
BINMEN
BINNACLE
BINNACLES
BINNED
BINNING
BINOCLE
BINOCLES
BINOCS
BINOCULAR
BINOMIAL
BINOMIALS
BINOMINAL
BINOVULAR
BINS
BINT
BINTS
BINTURONG
BINUCLEAR
BIO
BIOACTIVE
BIOASSAY
BIOASSAYS
BIOBANK
BIOBANKS
BIOBLAST
BIOBLASTS
BIOCENOSE
BIOCHEMIC
BIOCHIP
BIOCHIPS
BIOCIDAL
BIOCIDE
BIOCIDES
BIOCLEAN
BIOCYCLE
BIOCYCLES
BIODATA
BIODIESEL
BIODOT
BIODOTS
BIOENERGY
BIOETHIC
BIOETHICS
BIOFACT
BIOFACTS
BIOFIBERS
BIOFIBRES
BIOFILM
BIOFILMS
BIOFOULER
BIOFUEL
BIOFUELED
BIOFUELS
BIOG
BIOGAS
BIOGASES
BIOGASSES
BIOGEN
BIOGENIC
BIOGENIES
BIOGENOUS
BIOGENS
BIOGENY
BIOGRAPH
BIOGRAPHS
BIOGRAPHY
BIOGS
BIOHACKER
BIOHAZARD
BIOHERM
BIOHERMS
BIOLOGIC
BIOLOGICS
BIOLOGIES
BIOLOGISM
BIOLOGIST
BIOLOGY
BIOLYSES
BIOLYSIS
BIOLYTIC
BIOMARKER
BIOMASS
BIOMASSES
BIOME
BIOMES
BIOMETER
BIOMETERS
BIOMETRIC
BIOMETRY
BIOMINING
BIOMORPH
BIOMORPHS
BIONIC
BIONICS
BIONOMIC
BIONOMICS
BIONOMIES
BIONOMIST
BIONOMY
BIONT
BIONTIC
BIONTS
BIOPARENT
BIOPHILIA
BIOPHOR
BIOPHORE
BIOPHORES
BIOPHORS
BIOPIC
BIOPICS
BIOPIRACY
BIOPIRATE
BIOPLASM
BIOPLASMS
BIOPLAST
BIOPLASTS
BIOPLAY
BIOPLAYS
BIOPSIC
BIOPSIED
BIOPSIES
BIOPSY
BIOPSYING
BIOPTIC
BIOREGION
BIORHYTHM
BIOS
BIOSAFETY
BIOSCOPE
BIOSCOPES
BIOSCOPY
BIOSENSOR
BIOSOCIAL
BIOSOLID
BIOSOLIDS
BIOSPHERE
BIOSTABLE
BIOSTATIC
BIOSTROME
BIOTA
BIOTAS
BIOTECH
BIOTECHS
BIOTERROR
BIOTIC
BIOTICAL
BIOTICS
BIOTIN
BIOTINS
BIOTITE
BIOTITES
BIOTITIC
BIOTOPE
BIOTOPES
BIOTOXIN
BIOTOXINS
BIOTRON
BIOTRONS
BIOTROPH
BIOTROPHS
BIOTURBED
BIOTYPE
BIOTYPES
BIOTYPIC
BIOVULAR
BIOWASTE
BIOWASTES
BIOWEAPON
BIPACK
BIPACKS
BIPAROUS
BIPARTED
BIPARTITE
BIPARTY
BIPED
BIPEDAL
BIPEDALLY
BIPEDS
BIPHASIC
BIPHENYL
BIPHENYLS
BIPINNATE
BIPLANE
BIPLANES
BIPOD
BIPODS
BIPOLAR
BIPRISM
BIPRISMS
BIPYRAMID
BIRACIAL

BIRADIAL
BIRADICAL
BIRAMOSE
BIRAMOUS
BIRCH
BIRCHBARK
BIRCHED
BIRCHEN
BIRCHES
BIRCHING
BIRCHINGS
BIRCHIR
BIRCHIRS
BIRCHWOOD
BIRD
BIRDBATH
BIRDBATHS
BIRDBRAIN
BIRDCAGE
BIRDCAGES
BIRDCALL
BIRDCALLS
BIRDDOG
BIRDDOGS
BIRDED
BIRDER
BIRDERS
BIRDFARM
BIRDFARMS
BIRDFEED
BIRDFEEDS
BIRDHOUSE
BIRDIE
BIRDIED
BIRDIEING
BIRDIES
BIRDING
BIRDINGS
BIRDLIFE
BIRDLIFES
BIRDLIKE
BIRDLIME
BIRDLIMED
BIRDLIMES
BIRDMAN
BIRDMEN
BIRDS
BIRDSEED
BIRDSEEDS
BIRDSEYE
BIRDSEYES
BIRDSFOOT
BIRDSHOT
BIRDSHOTS
BIRDSONG
BIRDSONGS
BIRDWATCH
BIRDWING
BIRDWINGS
BIREME
BIREMES
BIRETTA
BIRETTAS
BIRIANI
BIRIANIS
BIRIYANI
BIRIYANIS
BIRK
BIRKEN
BIRKIE
BIRKIER
BIRKIES
BIRKIEST
BIRKS
BIRL
BIRLE
BIRLED
BIRLER
BIRLERS
BIRLES
BIRLIEMAN
BIRLIEMEN
BIRLING
BIRLINGS
BIRLINN
BIRLINNS
BIRLS
BIRO
BIROS
BIRR
BIRRED
BIRRETTA
BIRRETTAS
BIRRING
BIRROTCH
BIRRS
BIRSE
BIRSED
BIRSES
BIRSIER
BIRSIEST
BIRSING
BIRSLE
BIRSLED
BIRSLES
BIRSLING
BIRSY
BIRTH
BIRTHDATE
BIRTHDAY
BIRTHDAYS
BIRTHDOM
BIRTHDOMS
BIRTHED
BIRTHER
BIRTHERS
BIRTHING
BIRTHINGS
BIRTHMARK
BIRTHNAME
BIRTHRATE
BIRTHROOT
BIRTHS
BIRTHWORT
BIRYANI
BIRYANIS
BIS
BISCACHA
BISCACHAS
BISCOTTI
BISCOTTO
BISCUIT
BISCUITS
BISCUITY
BISE
BISECT
BISECTED
BISECTING
BISECTION
BISECTOR
BISECTORS
BISECTRIX
BISECTS
BISERIAL
BISERIATE
BISERRATE
BISES
BISEXUAL
BISEXUALS
BISH
BISHES
BISHOP
BISHOPDOM
BISHOPED
BISHOPESS
BISHOPING
BISHOPRIC
BISHOPS
BISK
BISKS
BISMAR
BISMARCK
BISMARCKS
BISMARS
BISMILLAH
BISMUTH
BISMUTHAL
BISMUTHIC
BISMUTHS
BISNAGA
BISNAGAS
BISOM
BISOMS
BISON
BISONS
BISONTINE
BISPHENOL
BISQUE
BISQUES
BISSON
BISSONED
BISSONING
BISSONS
BIST
BISTABLE
BISTABLES
BISTATE
BISTER
BISTERED
BISTERS
BISTORT
BISTORTS
BISTOURY
BISTRE
BISTRED
BISTRES
BISTRO
BISTROIC
BISTROS
BISULCATE
BISULFATE
BISULFIDE
BISULFITE
BIT
BITABLE
BITCH
BITCHED
BITCHEN
BITCHERY
BITCHES
BITCHFEST
BITCHIER
BITCHIEST
BITCHILY
BITCHING
BITCHY
BITCOIN
BITCOINS
BITE
BITEABLE
BITEPLATE
BITER
BITERS
BITES
BITESIZE
BITEWING
BITEWINGS
BITING
BITINGLY
BITINGS
BITLESS
BITMAP
BITMAPPED
BITMAPS
BITO
BITONAL
BITOS
BITOU
BITRATE
BITRATES

BITS
BITSER
BITSERS
BITSIER
BITSIEST
BITSTOCK
BITSTOCKS
BITSTREAM
BITSY
BITT
BITTACLE
BITTACLES
BITTE
BITTED
BITTEN
BITTER
BITTERED
BITTERER
BITTEREST
BITTERING
BITTERISH
BITTERLY
BITTERN
BITTERNS
BITTERNUT
BITTERS
BITTIE
BITTIER
BITTIES
BITTIEST
BITTILY
BITTINESS
BITTING
BITTINGS
BITTOCK
BITTOCKS
BITTOR
BITTORS
BITTOUR
BITTOURS
BITTS
BITTUR
BITTURS
BITTY
BITUMED
BITUMEN
BITUMENS
BITURBO
BITURBOS
BITWISE
BIUNIQUE
BIVALENCE
BIVALENCY
BIVALENT
BIVALENTS
BIVALVATE
BIVALVE
BIVALVED
BIVALVES
BIVARIANT
BIVARIATE
BIVIA
BIVINYL
BIVINYLS
BIVIOUS
BIVIUM
BIVOUAC
BIVOUACKS
BIVOUACS
BIVVIED
BIVVIES
BIVVY
BIVVYING
BIWEEKLY
BIYEARLY
BIZ
BIZARRE
BIZARRELY
BIZARRES
BIZARRO
BIZARROS
BIZAZZ
BIZAZZES
BIZCACHA
BIZCACHAS
BIZE
BIZES
BIZJET
BIZJETS
BIZNAGA
BIZNAGAS
BIZONAL
BIZONE
BIZONES
BIZZAZZ
BIZZAZZES
BIZZES
BIZZIES
BIZZO
BIZZOS
BIZZY
BLAB
BLABBED
BLABBER
BLABBERED
BLABBERS
BLABBIER
BLABBIEST
BLABBING
BLABBINGS
BLABBY
BLABS
BLACK
BLACKBALL
BLACKBAND
BLACKBIRD
BLACKBODY
BLACKBOY
BLACKBOYS
BLACKBUCK
BLACKBUTT
BLACKCAP
BLACKCAPS
BLACKCOCK
BLACKDAMP
BLACKED
BLACKEN
BLACKENED
BLACKENER
BLACKENS
BLACKER
BLACKEST
BLACKFACE
BLACKFIN
BLACKFINS
BLACKFISH
BLACKFLY
BLACKGAME
BLACKGUM
BLACKGUMS
BLACKHEAD
BLACKING
BLACKINGS
BLACKISH
BLACKJACK
BLACKLAND
BLACKLEAD
BLACKLEG
BLACKLEGS
BLACKLIST
BLACKLY
BLACKMAIL
BLACKNESS
BLACKOUT
BLACKOUTS
BLACKPOLL
BLACKS
BLACKSPOT
BLACKTAIL
BLACKTIP
BLACKTIPS
BLACKTOP
BLACKTOPS
BLACKWASH
BLACKWOOD
BLAD
BLADDED
BLADDER
BLADDERED
BLADDERS
BLADDERY
BLADDING
BLADE
BLADED
BLADELESS
BLADELIKE
BLADER
BLADERS
BLADES
BLADEWORK
BLADIER
BLADIEST
BLADING
BLADINGS
BLADS
BLADY
BLAE
BLAEBERRY
BLAER
BLAES
BLAEST
BLAFF
BLAFFED
BLAFFING
BLAFFS
BLAG
BLAGGED
BLAGGER
BLAGGERS
BLAGGING
BLAGGINGS
BLAGS
BLAGUE
BLAGUER
BLAGUERS
BLAGUES
BLAGUEUR
BLAGUEURS
BLAH
BLAHED
BLAHER
BLAHEST
BLAHING
BLAHS
BLAIN
BLAINS
BLAISE
BLAIZE
BLAM
BLAMABLE
BLAMABLY
BLAME
BLAMEABLE
BLAMEABLY
BLAMED
BLAMEFUL
BLAMELESS
BLAMER
BLAMERS
BLAMES
BLAMING
BLAMMED
BLAMMING
BLAMS
BLANCH
BLANCHED
BLANCHER
BLANCHERS
BLANCHES
BLANCHING

BLANCO
BLANCOED
BLANCOING
BLANCOS
BLAND
BLANDED
BLANDER
BLANDEST
BLANDING
BLANDISH
BLANDLY
BLANDNESS
BLANDS
BLANK
BLANKED
BLANKER
BLANKEST
BLANKET
BLANKETED
BLANKETS
BLANKETY
BLANKIE
BLANKIES
BLANKING
BLANKINGS
BLANKLY
BLANKNESS
BLANKS
BLANKY
BLANQUET
BLANQUETS
BLARE
BLARED
BLARES
BLARING
BLARNEY
BLARNEYED
BLARNEYS
BLART
BLARTED
BLARTING
BLARTS
BLASE
BLASH
BLASHED
BLASHES
BLASHIER
BLASHIEST
BLASHING
BLASHY
BLASPHEME
BLASPHEMY
BLAST
BLASTED
BLASTEMA
BLASTEMAL
BLASTEMAS
BLASTEMIC
BLASTER
BLASTERS
BLASTHOLE
BLASTIE
BLASTIER
BLASTIES
BLASTIEST
BLASTING
BLASTINGS
BLASTMENT
BLASTOFF
BLASTOFFS
BLASTOID
BLASTOIDS
BLASTOMA
BLASTOMAS
BLASTOPOR
BLASTS
BLASTULA
BLASTULAE
BLASTULAR
BLASTULAS
BLASTY
BLAT
BLATANCY
BLATANT
BLATANTLY
BLATE
BLATED
BLATER
BLATES
BLATEST
BLATHER
BLATHERED
BLATHERER
BLATHERS
BLATING
BLATS
BLATT
BLATTANT
BLATTED
BLATTER
BLATTERED
BLATTERS
BLATTING
BLATTS
BLAUBOK
BLAUBOKS
BLAUD
BLAUDED
BLAUDING
BLAUDS
BLAW
BLAWED
BLAWING
BLAWN
BLAWORT
BLAWORTS
BLAWS
BLAY
BLAYS
BLAZAR
BLAZARS
BLAZE
BLAZED
BLAZER
BLAZERED
BLAZERS
BLAZES
BLAZING
BLAZINGLY
BLAZON
BLAZONED
BLAZONER
BLAZONERS
BLAZONING
BLAZONRY
BLAZONS
BLEACH
BLEACHED
BLEACHER
BLEACHERS
BLEACHERY
BLEACHES
BLEACHING
BLEAK
BLEAKER
BLEAKEST
BLEAKISH
BLEAKLY
BLEAKNESS
BLEAKS
BLEAKY
BLEAR
BLEARED
BLEARER
BLEAREST
BLEAREYED
BLEARIER
BLEARIEST
BLEARILY
BLEARING
BLEARS
BLEARY
BLEAT
BLEATED
BLEATER
BLEATERS
BLEATING
BLEATINGS
BLEATS
BLEB
BLEBBIER
BLEBBIEST
BLEBBING
BLEBBINGS
BLEBBY
BLEBS
BLECH
BLED
BLEE
BLEED
BLEEDER
BLEEDERS
BLEEDING
BLEEDINGS
BLEEDS
BLEEP
BLEEPED
BLEEPER
BLEEPERS
BLEEPING
BLEEPS
BLEES
BLELLUM
BLELLUMS
BLEMISH
BLEMISHED
BLEMISHER
BLEMISHES
BLENCH
BLENCHED
BLENCHER
BLENCHERS
BLENCHES
BLENCHING
BLEND
BLENDABLE
BLENDE
BLENDED
BLENDER
BLENDERS
BLENDES
BLENDING
BLENDINGS
BLENDS
BLENNIES
BLENNIOID
BLENNY
BLENT
BLEOMYCIN
BLERT
BLERTS
BLESBOK
BLESBOKS
BLESBUCK
BLESBUCKS
BLESS
BLESSED
BLESSEDER
BLESSEDLY
BLESSER
BLESSERS
BLESSES
BLESSING
BLESSINGS
BLEST
BLET
BLETHER
BLETHERED
BLETHERER
BLETHERS

BLETS
BLETTED
BLETTING
BLEUATRE
BLEW
BLEWART
BLEWARTS
BLEWIT
BLEWITS
BLEWITSES
BLEY
BLEYS
BLIGHT
BLIGHTED
BLIGHTER
BLIGHTERS
BLIGHTIES
BLIGHTING
BLIGHTS
BLIGHTY
BLIKSEM
BLIMBING
BLIMBINGS
BLIMEY
BLIMP
BLIMPED
BLIMPERY
BLIMPING
BLIMPISH
BLIMPS
BLIMY
BLIN
BLIND
BLINDAGE
BLINDAGES
BLINDED
BLINDER
BLINDERS
BLINDEST
BLINDFISH
BLINDFOLD
BLINDGUT
BLINDGUTS
BLINDING
BLINDINGS
BLINDLESS
BLINDLY
BLINDNESS
BLINDS
BLINDSIDE
BLINDWORM
BLING
BLINGED
BLINGER
BLINGEST
BLINGIER
BLINGIEST
BLINGING
BLINGLISH
BLINGS
BLINGY
BLINI
BLINIS
BLINK
BLINKARD
BLINKARDS
BLINKED
BLINKER
BLINKERED
BLINKERS
BLINKING
BLINKS
BLINNED
BLINNING
BLINS
BLINTZ
BLINTZE
BLINTZES
BLINY
BLIP
BLIPPED
BLIPPING
BLIPS
BLIPVERT
BLIPVERTS
BLISS
BLISSED
BLISSES
BLISSFUL
BLISSING
BLISSLESS
BLIST
BLISTER
BLISTERED
BLISTERS
BLISTERY
BLIT
BLITE
BLITES
BLITHE
BLITHEFUL
BLITHELY
BLITHER
BLITHERED
BLITHERS
BLITHEST
BLITS
BLITTED
BLITTER
BLITTERS
BLITTING
BLITZ
BLITZED
BLITZER
BLITZERS
BLITZES
BLITZING
BLIVE
BLIZZARD
BLIZZARDS
BLIZZARDY
BLOAT
BLOATED
BLOATER
BLOATERS
BLOATING
BLOATINGS
BLOATS
BLOATWARE
BLOB
BLOBBED
BLOBBIER
BLOBBIEST
BLOBBING
BLOBBY
BLOBS
BLOC
BLOCK
BLOCKABLE
BLOCKADE
BLOCKADED
BLOCKADER
BLOCKADES
BLOCKAGE
BLOCKAGES
BLOCKBUST
BLOCKED
BLOCKER
BLOCKERS
BLOCKHEAD
BLOCKHOLE
BLOCKIE
BLOCKIER
BLOCKIES
BLOCKIEST
BLOCKING
BLOCKINGS
BLOCKISH
BLOCKS
BLOCKSHIP
BLOCKWORK
BLOCKY
BLOCS
BLOG
BLOGGABLE
BLOGGED
BLOGGER
BLOGGERS
BLOGGIER
BLOGGIEST
BLOGGING
BLOGGINGS
BLOGGY
BLOGPOST
BLOGPOSTS
BLOGRING
BLOGRINGS
BLOGROLL
BLOGROLLS
BLOGS
BLOKART
BLOKARTS
BLOKE
BLOKEDOM
BLOKEDOMS
BLOKEISH
BLOKES
BLOKEY
BLOKIER
BLOKIEST
BLOKISH
BLONCKET
BLOND
BLONDE
BLONDER
BLONDES
BLONDEST
BLONDINE
BLONDINED
BLONDINES
BLONDING
BLONDINGS
BLONDISH
BLONDNESS
BLONDS
BLOOD
BLOODBATH
BLOODED
BLOODFIN
BLOODFINS
BLOODIED
BLOODIER
BLOODIES
BLOODIEST
BLOODILY
BLOODING
BLOODINGS
BLOODLESS
BLOODLIKE
BLOODLINE
BLOODLUST
BLOODRED
BLOODROOT
BLOODS
BLOODSHED
BLOODSHOT
BLOODWOOD
BLOODWORM
BLOODWORT
BLOODY
BLOODYING
BLOOEY
BLOOIE
BLOOK
BLOOKS
BLOOM
BLOOMED
BLOOMER
BLOOMERS
BLOOMERY

B

BLOOMIER BLOOMIEST BLOOMING BLOOMINGS BLOOMLESS BLOOMS BLOOMY BLOOP BLOOPED BLOOPER BLOOPERS BLOOPIER BLOOPIEST BLOOPING BLOOPS BLOOPY BLOOSME BLOOSMED BLOOSMES BLOOSMING BLOOTERED BLOQUISTE BLORE BLORES BLOSSOM BLOSSOMED BLOSSOMS BLOSSOMY BLOT BLOTCH BLOTCHED BLOTCHES BLOTCHIER BLOTCHILY BLOTCHING BLOTCHY BLOTLESS BLOTS BLOTTED BLOTTER BLOTTERS BLOTTIER BLOTTIEST BLOTTING BLOTTINGS BLOTTO BLOTTY BLOUBOK

BLOUBOKS BLOUSE BLOUSED BLOUSES BLOUSIER BLOUSIEST BLOUSILY BLOUSING BLOUSON BLOUSONS BLOUSY BLOVIATE BLOVIATED BLOVIATES BLOW BLOWBACK BLOWBACKS BLOWBALL BLOWBALLS BLOWBY BLOWBYS BLOWDART BLOWDARTS BLOWDOWN BLOWDOWNS BLOWED BLOWER BLOWERS BLOWFISH BLOWFLIES BLOWFLY BLOWGUN BLOWGUNS BLOWHARD BLOWHARDS BLOWHOLE BLOWHOLES BLOWIE BLOWIER BLOWIES BLOWIEST BLOWINESS BLOWING BLOWINGS BLOWJOB BLOWJOBS BLOWKART BLOWKARTS

BLOWLAMP BLOWLAMPS BLOWN BLOWOFF BLOWOFFS BLOWOUT BLOWOUTS BLOWPIPE BLOWPIPES BLOWS BLOWSE BLOWSED BLOWSES BLOWSIER BLOWSIEST BLOWSILY BLOWSY BLOWTORCH BLOWTUBE BLOWTUBES BLOWUP BLOWUPS BLOWY BLOWZE BLOWZED BLOWZES BLOWZIER BLOWZIEST BLOWZILY BLOWZY BLUB BLUBBED BLUBBER BLUBBERED BLUBBERER BLUBBERS BLUBBERY BLUBBING BLUBS BLUCHER BLUCHERS BLUD BLUDE BLUDES BLUDGE BLUDGED BLUDGEON BLUDGEONS

BLUDGER BLUDGERS BLUDGES BLUDGING BLUDIE BLUDIER BLUDIEST BLUDS BLUDY BLUE BLUEBACK BLUEBACKS BLUEBALL BLUEBALLS BLUEBEARD BLUEBEAT BLUEBEATS BLUEBELL BLUEBELLS BLUEBERRY BLUEBILL BLUEBILLS BLUEBIRD BLUEBIRDS BLUEBLOOD BLUEBOOK BLUEBOOKS BLUEBUCK BLUEBUCKS BLUEBUSH BLUECAP BLUECAPS BLUECOAT BLUECOATS BLUECURLS BLUED BLUEFIN BLUEFINS BLUEFISH BLUEGILL BLUEGILLS BLUEGOWN BLUEGOWNS BLUEGRASS BLUEGUM BLUEGUMS BLUEHEAD BLUEHEADS

BLUEING BLUEINGS BLUEISH BLUEJACK BLUEJACKS BLUEJAY BLUEJAYS BLUEJEANS BLUELINE BLUELINER BLUELINES BLUELY BLUEMOUTH BLUENESS BLUENOSE BLUENOSED BLUENOSES BLUEPOINT BLUEPRINT BLUER BLUES BLUESHIFT BLUESIER BLUESIEST BLUESMAN BLUESMEN BLUEST BLUESTEM BLUESTEMS BLUESTONE BLUESY BLUET BLUETICK BLUETICKS BLUETIT BLUETITS BLUETS BLUETTE BLUETTES BLUEWEED BLUEWEEDS BLUEWING BLUEWINGS BLUEWOOD BLUEWOODS BLUEY BLUEYS BLUFF

BLUFFABLE
BLUFFED
BLUFFER
BLUFFERS
BLUFFEST
BLUFFING
BLUFFLY
BLUFFNESS
BLUFFS
BLUGGIER
BLUGGIEST
BLUGGY
BLUID
BLUIDIER
BLUIDIEST
BLUIDS
BLUIDY
BLUIER
BLUIEST
BLUING
BLUINGS
BLUISH
BLUME
BLUMED
BLUMES
BLUMING
BLUNDER
BLUNDERED
BLUNDERER
BLUNDERS
BLUNGE
BLUNGED
BLUNGER
BLUNGERS
BLUNGES
BLUNGING
BLUNK
BLUNKED
BLUNKER
BLUNKERS
BLUNKING
BLUNKS
BLUNT
BLUNTED
BLUNTER
BLUNTEST
BLUNTHEAD
BLUNTING
BLUNTISH
BLUNTLY
BLUNTNESS
BLUNTS
BLUR
BLURB
BLURBED
BLURBING
BLURBIST
BLURBISTS
BLURBS
BLURRED
BLURREDLY
BLURRIER
BLURRIEST
BLURRILY
BLURRING
BLURRY
BLURS
BLURT
BLURTED
BLURTER
BLURTERS
BLURTING
BLURTINGS
BLURTS
BLUSH
BLUSHED
BLUSHER
BLUSHERS
BLUSHES
BLUSHET
BLUSHETS
BLUSHFUL
BLUSHING
BLUSHINGS
BLUSHLESS
BLUSTER
BLUSTERED
BLUSTERER
BLUSTERS
BLUSTERY
BLUSTROUS
BLUTWURST
BLYPE
BLYPES
BO
BOA
BOAB
BOABS
BOAK
BOAKED
BOAKING
BOAKS
BOAR
BOARD
BOARDABLE
BOARDED
BOARDER
BOARDERS
BOARDIES
BOARDING
BOARDINGS
BOARDLIKE
BOARDMAN
BOARDMEN
BOARDROOM
BOARDS
BOARDWALK
BOARFISH
BOARHOUND
BOARISH
BOARISHLY
BOARS
BOART
BOARTS
BOAS
BOAST
BOASTED
BOASTER
BOASTERS
BOASTFUL
BOASTING
BOASTINGS
BOASTLESS
BOASTS
BOAT
BOATABLE
BOATBILL
BOATBILLS
BOATED
BOATEL
BOATELS
BOATER
BOATERS
BOATFUL
BOATFULS
BOATHOOK
BOATHOOKS
BOATHOUSE
BOATIE
BOATIES
BOATING
BOATINGS
BOATLIFT
BOATLIFTS
BOATLIKE
BOATLOAD
BOATLOADS
BOATMAN
BOATMEN
BOATNECK
BOATNECKS
BOATPORT
BOATPORTS
BOATS
BOATSMAN
BOATSMEN
BOATSWAIN
BOATTAIL
BOATTAILS
BOATYARD
BOATYARDS
BOB
BOBA
BOBAC
BOBACS
BOBAK
BOBAKS
BOBAS
BOBBED
BOBBEJAAN
BOBBER
BOBBERIES
BOBBERS
BOBBERY
BOBBIES
BOBBIN
BOBBINET
BOBBINETS
BOBBING
BOBBINS
BOBBISH
BOBBITT
BOBBITTED
BOBBITTS
BOBBLE
BOBBLED
BOBBLES
BOBBLIER
BOBBLIEST
BOBBLING
BOBBLY
BOBBY
BOBBYSOCK
BOBBYSOX
BOBCAT
BOBCATS
BOBECHE
BOBECHES
BOBFLOAT
BOBFLOATS
BOBLET
BOBLETS
BOBO
BOBOL
BOBOLINK
BOBOLINKS
BOBOLLED
BOBOLLING
BOBOLS
BOBOS
BOBOTIE
BOBOTIES
BOBOWLER
BOBOWLERS
BOBS
BOBSKATE
BOBSKATES
BOBSLED
BOBSLEDS
BOBSLEIGH
BOBSTAY
BOBSTAYS
BOBTAIL
BOBTAILED
BOBTAILS
BOBWEIGHT
BOBWHEEL
BOBWHEELS
BOBWHITE
BOBWHITES

B

BOBWIG
BOBWIGS
BOCACCIO
BOCACCIOS
BOCAGE
BOCAGES
BOCCA
BOCCAS
BOCCE
BOCCES
BOCCI
BOCCIA
BOCCIAS
BOCCIE
BOCCIES
BOCCIS
BOCHE
BOCHES
BOCK
BOCKED
BOCKEDY
BOCKING
BOCKS
BOCONCINI
BOD
BODACH
BODACHS
BODACIOUS
BODDLE
BODDLES
BODE
BODED
BODEFUL
BODEGA
BODEGAS
BODEGUERO
BODEMENT
BODEMENTS
BODES
BODGE
BODGED
BODGER
BODGERS
BODGES
BODGIE
BODGIER
BODGIES
BODGIEST
BODGING
BODHI
BODHIS
BODHRAN
BODHRANS
BODICE
BODICES
BODIED
BODIES
BODIKIN
BODIKINS
BODILESS
BODILY
BODING
BODINGLY
BODINGS
BODKIN
BODKINS
BODLE
BODLES
BODRAG
BODRAGS
BODS
BODY
BODYBOARD
BODYBUILD
BODYBUILT
BODYCHECK
BODYGUARD
BODYING
BODYLINE
BODYLINES
BODYMAN
BODYMEN
BODYSHELL
BODYSIDE
BODYSIDES
BODYSUIT
BODYSUITS
BODYSURF
BODYSURFS
BODYWASH
BODYWORK
BODYWORKS
BOEHMITE
BOEHMITES
BOEP
BOEPS
BOERBUL
BOERBULL
BOERBULLS
BOERBULS
BOEREWORS
BOERTJIE
BOERTJIES
BOET
BOETS
BOEUF
BOEUFS
BOFF
BOFFED
BOFFIN
BOFFING
BOFFINIER
BOFFINS
BOFFINY
BOFFO
BOFFOLA
BOFFOLAS
BOFFOS
BOFFS
BOG
BOGAN
BOGANS
BOGART
BOGARTED
BOGARTING
BOGARTS
BOGBEAN
BOGBEANS
BOGEY
BOGEYED
BOGEYING
BOGEYISM
BOGEYISMS
BOGEYMAN
BOGEYMEN
BOGEYS
BOGGARD
BOGGARDS
BOGGART
BOGGARTS
BOGGED
BOGGER
BOGGERS
BOGGIER
BOGGIEST
BOGGINESS
BOGGING
BOGGISH
BOGGLE
BOGGLED
BOGGLER
BOGGLERS
BOGGLES
BOGGLING
BOGGY
BOGHEAD
BOGHOLE
BOGHOLES
BOGIE
BOGIED
BOGIEING
BOGIES
BOGLAND
BOGLANDS
BOGLE
BOGLED
BOGLES
BOGLING
BOGMAN
BOGMEN
BOGOAK
BOGOAKS
BOGONG
BOGONGS
BOGS
BOGUE
BOGUES
BOGUS
BOGUSLY
BOGUSNESS
BOGWOOD
BOGWOODS
BOGY
BOGYISM
BOGYISMS
BOGYMAN
BOGYMEN
BOH
BOHEA
BOHEAS
BOHEMIA
BOHEMIAN
BOHEMIANS
BOHEMIAS
BOHO
BOHOS
BOHRIUM
BOHRIUMS
BOHS
BOHUNK
BOHUNKS
BOI
BOIL
BOILABLE
BOILED
BOILER
BOILERIES
BOILERMAN
BOILERMEN
BOILERS
BOILERY
BOILING
BOILINGLY
BOILINGS
BOILOFF
BOILOFFS
BOILOVER
BOILOVERS
BOILS
BOING
BOINGED
BOINGING
BOINGS
BOINK
BOINKED
BOINKING
BOINKS
BOIS
BOISERIE
BOISERIES
BOITE
BOITES
BOK
BOKE
BOKED
BOKEH
BOKEHS
BOKES
BOKING
BOKKEN

BOKKENS
BOKO
BOKOS
BOKS
BOLA
BOLAR
BOLAS
BOLASES
BOLD
BOLDED
BOLDEN
BOLDENED
BOLDENING
BOLDENS
BOLDER
BOLDEST
BOLDFACE
BOLDFACED
BOLDFACES
BOLDING
BOLDLY
BOLDNESS
BOLDS
BOLE
BOLECTION
BOLERO
BOLEROS
BOLES
BOLETE
BOLETES
BOLETI
BOLETUS
BOLETUSES
BOLIDE
BOLIDES
BOLINE
BOLINES
BOLIVAR
BOLIVARES
BOLIVARS
BOLIVIA
BOLIVIANO
BOLIVIAS
BOLIX
BOLIXED
BOLIXES
BOLIXING
BOLL
BOLLARD
BOLLARDS
BOLLED
BOLLEN
BOLLETRIE
BOLLING
BOLLIX
BOLLIXED
BOLLIXES
BOLLIXING
BOLLOCK
BOLLOCKED
BOLLOCKS
BOLLOX
BOLLOXED
BOLLOXES
BOLLOXING
BOLLS
BOLLWORM
BOLLWORMS
BOLO
BOLOGNA
BOLOGNAS
BOLOGNESE
BOLOGRAPH
BOLOMETER
BOLOMETRY
BOLONEY
BOLONEYS
BOLOS
BOLSHEVIK
BOLSHIE
BOLSHIER
BOLSHIES
BOLSHIEST
BOLSHY
BOLSON
BOLSONS
BOLSTER
BOLSTERED
BOLSTERER
BOLSTERS
BOLT
BOLTED
BOLTER
BOLTERS
BOLTHEAD
BOLTHEADS
BOLTHOLE
BOLTHOLES
BOLTING
BOLTINGS
BOLTLESS
BOLTLIKE
BOLTONIA
BOLTONIAS
BOLTROPE
BOLTROPES
BOLTS
BOLUS
BOLUSES
BOMA
BOMAS
BOMB
BOMBABLE
BOMBARD
BOMBARDE
BOMBARDED
BOMBARDER
BOMBARDES
BOMBARDON
BOMBARDS
BOMBASINE
BOMBAST
BOMBASTED
BOMBASTER
BOMBASTIC
BOMBASTS
BOMBAX
BOMBAXES
BOMBAZINE
BOMBE
BOMBED
BOMBER
BOMBERS
BOMBES
BOMBESIN
BOMBESINS
BOMBILATE
BOMBINATE
BOMBING
BOMBINGS
BOMBLET
BOMBLETS
BOMBLOAD
BOMBLOADS
BOMBO
BOMBORA
BOMBORAS
BOMBOS
BOMBPROOF
BOMBS
BOMBSHELL
BOMBSIGHT
BOMBSITE
BOMBSITES
BOMBYCID
BOMBYCIDS
BOMBYCOID
BOMBYX
BOMBYXES
BOMMIE
BOMMIES
BON
BONA
BONACI
BONACIS
BONAMANI
BONAMANO
BONAMIA
BONAMIAS
BONANZA
BONANZAS
BONASSUS
BONASUS
BONASUSES
BONBON
BONBONS
BONCE
BONCES
BOND
BONDABLE
BONDAGE
BONDAGER
BONDAGERS
BONDAGES
BONDED
BONDER
BONDERS
BONDING
BONDINGS
BONDLESS
BONDMAID
BONDMAIDS
BONDMAN
BONDMEN
BONDS
BONDSMAN
BONDSMEN
BONDSTONE
BONDUC
BONDUCS
BONDWOMAN
BONDWOMEN
BONE
BONEBED
BONEBEDS
BONEBLACK
BONED
BONEFISH
BONEHEAD
BONEHEADS
BONELESS
BONELIKE
BONEMEAL
BONEMEALS
BONER
BONERS
BONES
BONESET
BONESETS
BONETIRED
BONEY
BONEYARD
BONEYARDS
BONEYER
BONEYEST
BONFIRE
BONFIRES
BONG
BONGED
BONGING
BONGO
BONGOES
BONGOIST
BONGOISTS
BONGOS
BONGRACE
BONGRACES
BONGS
BONHAM
BONHAMS

BONHOMIE
BONHOMIES
BONHOMMIE
BONHOMOUS
BONIATO
BONIATOS
BONIBELL
BONIBELLS
BONIE
BONIER
BONIEST
BONIFACE
BONIFACES
BONILASSE
BONINESS
BONING
BONINGS
BONISM
BONISMS
BONIST
BONISTS
BONITA
BONITAS
BONITO
BONITOES
BONITOS
BONJOUR
BONK
BONKED
BONKERS
BONKING
BONKINGS
BONKS
BONNE
BONNES
BONNET
BONNETED
BONNETING
BONNETS
BONNIBELL
BONNIE
BONNIER
BONNIES
BONNIEST
BONNILY
BONNINESS
BONNOCK
BONNOCKS
BONNY
BONOBO
BONOBOS
BONSAI
BONSELA
BONSELAS
BONSELLA
BONSELLAS
BONSOIR
BONSPELL
BONSPELLS
BONSPIEL
BONSPIELS
BONTBOK
BONTBOKS
BONTEBOK
BONTEBOKS
BONUS
BONUSED
BONUSES
BONUSING
BONUSINGS
BONUSSED
BONUSSES
BONUSSING
BONXIE
BONXIES
BONY
BONZA
BONZE
BONZER
BONZES
BOO
BOOAI
BOOAIS
BOOAY
BOOAYS
BOOB
BOOBED
BOOBHEAD
BOOBHEADS
BOOBIALLA
BOOBIE
BOOBIES
BOOBING
BOOBIRD
BOOBIRDS
BOOBISH
BOOBOISIE
BOOBOO
BOOBOOK
BOOBOOKS
BOOBOOS
BOOBS
BOOBY
BOOBYISH
BOOBYISM
BOOBYISMS
BOOCOO
BOOCOOS
BOODIE
BOODIED
BOODIES
BOODLE
BOODLED
BOODLER
BOODLERS
BOODLES
BOODLING
BOODY
BOODYING
BOOED
BOOFHEAD
BOOFHEADS
BOOFIER
BOOFIEST
BOOFY
BOOGALOO
BOOGALOOS
BOOGER
BOOGERMAN
BOOGERMEN
BOOGERS
BOOGEY
BOOGEYED
BOOGEYING
BOOGEYMAN
BOOGEYMEN
BOOGEYS
BOOGIE
BOOGIED
BOOGIEING
BOOGIEMAN
BOOGIEMEN
BOOGIES
BOOGY
BOOGYING
BOOGYMAN
BOOGYMEN
BOOH
BOOHAI
BOOHAIS
BOOHED
BOOHING
BOOHOO
BOOHOOED
BOOHOOING
BOOHOOS
BOOHS
BOOING
BOOINGS
BOOJUM
BOOJUMS
BOOK
BOOKABLE
BOOKBAG
BOOKBAGS
BOOKCASE
BOOKCASES
BOOKED
BOOKEND
BOOKENDED
BOOKENDS
BOOKER
BOOKERS
BOOKFUL
BOOKFULS
BOOKIE
BOOKIER
BOOKIES
BOOKIEST
BOOKING
BOOKINGS
BOOKISH
BOOKISHLY
BOOKLAND
BOOKLANDS
BOOKLESS
BOOKLET
BOOKLETS
BOOKLICE
BOOKLIGHT
BOOKLIKE
BOOKLORE
BOOKLORES
BOOKLOUSE
BOOKMAKER
BOOKMAN
BOOKMARK
BOOKMARKS
BOOKMEN
BOOKOO
BOOKOOS
BOOKPLATE
BOOKRACK
BOOKRACKS
BOOKREST
BOOKRESTS
BOOKS
BOOKSHELF
BOOKSHOP
BOOKSHOPS
BOOKSIE
BOOKSIER
BOOKSIEST
BOOKSTALL
BOOKSTAND
BOOKSTORE
BOOKSY
BOOKWORK
BOOKWORKS
BOOKWORM
BOOKWORMS
BOOKY
BOOL
BOOLED
BOOLING
BOOLS
BOOM
BOOMBOX
BOOMBOXES
BOOMBURB
BOOMBURBS
BOOMED
BOOMER
BOOMERANG
BOOMERS
BOOMIER
BOOMIEST
BOOMING
BOOMINGLY
BOOMINGS

BOOMKIN
BOOMKINS
BOOMLET
BOOMLETS
BOOMS
BOOMSLANG
BOOMSTICK
BOOMTOWN
BOOMTOWNS
BOOMY
BOON
BOONDOCK
BOONDOCKS
BOONER
BOONERS
BOONEST
BOONG
BOONGA
BOONGARY
BOONGAS
BOONGS
BOONIES
BOONLESS
BOONS
BOOR
BOORD
BOORDE
BOORDES
BOORDS
BOORISH
BOORISHLY
BOORKA
BOORKAS
BOORS
BOORTREE
BOORTREES
BOOS
BOOSE
BOOSED
BOOSES
BOOSHIT
BOOSING
BOOST
BOOSTED
BOOSTER
BOOSTERS
BOOSTING
BOOSTS
BOOT
BOOTABLE
BOOTBLACK
BOOTCUT
BOOTED
BOOTEE
BOOTEES
BOOTERIES
BOOTERY
BOOTH
BOOTHOSE
BOOTHS
BOOTIE
BOOTIES
BOOTIKIN
BOOTIKINS
BOOTING
BOOTJACK
BOOTJACKS
BOOTLACE
BOOTLACES
BOOTLAST
BOOTLASTS
BOOTLEG
BOOTLEGS
BOOTLESS
BOOTLICK
BOOTLICKS
BOOTMAKER
BOOTS
BOOTSTRAP
BOOTY
BOOZE
BOOZED
BOOZER
BOOZERS
BOOZES
BOOZEY
BOOZIER
BOOZIEST
BOOZILY
BOOZINESS
BOOZING
BOOZINGS
BOOZY
BOP
BOPEEP
BOPEEPS
BOPPED
BOPPER
BOPPERS
BOPPIER
BOPPIEST
BOPPING
BOPPISH
BOPPY
BOPS
BOR
BORA
BORACES
BORACHIO
BORACHIOS
BORACIC
BORACITE
BORACITES
BORAGE
BORAGES
BORAK
BORAKS
BORAL
BORALS
BORANE
BORANES
BORAS
BORATE
BORATED
BORATES
BORATING
BORAX
BORAXES
BORAZON
BORAZONS
BORD
BORDAR
BORDARS
BORDE
BORDEAUX
BORDEL
BORDELLO
BORDELLOS
BORDELS
BORDER
BORDEREAU
BORDERED
BORDERER
BORDERERS
BORDERING
BORDERS
BORDES
BORDS
BORDURE
BORDURES
BORE
BOREAL
BOREALIS
BOREAS
BOREASES
BORECOLE
BORECOLES
BORED
BOREDOM
BOREDOMS
BOREE
BOREEN
BOREENS
BOREES
BOREHOLE
BOREHOLES
BOREL
BORELS
BORER
BORERS
BORES
BORESCOPE
BORESOME
BORGHETTO
BORGO
BORGOS
BORIC
BORIDE
BORIDES
BORING
BORINGLY
BORINGS
BORK
BORKED
BORKING
BORKINGS
BORKS
BORLOTTI
BORM
BORMED
BORMING
BORMS
BORN
BORNA
BORNE
BORNEOL
BORNEOLS
BORNITE
BORNITES
BORNITIC
BORNYL
BORNYLS
BORON
BORONIA
BORONIAS
BORONIC
BORONS
BOROUGH
BOROUGHS
BORREL
BORRELIA
BORRELIAS
BORRELL
BORROW
BORROWED
BORROWER
BORROWERS
BORROWING
BORROWS
BORS
BORSCH
BORSCHES
BORSCHT
BORSCHTS
BORSHCH
BORSHCHES
BORSHT
BORSHTS
BORSIC
BORSICS
BORSTAL
BORSTALL
BORSTALLS
BORSTALS
BORT
BORTIER
BORTIEST
BORTS
BORTSCH
BORTSCHES

BORTY
BORTZ
BORTZES
BORZOI
BORZOIS
BOS
BOSBERAAD
BOSBOK
BOSBOKS
BOSCAGE
BOSCAGES
BOSCHBOK
BOSCHBOKS
BOSCHE
BOSCHES
BOSCHVARK
BOSCHVELD
BOSH
BOSHBOK
BOSHBOKS
BOSHES
BOSHTA
BOSHTER
BOSHVARK
BOSHVARKS
BOSIE
BOSIES
BOSK
BOSKAGE
BOSKAGES
BOSKER
BOSKET
BOSKETS
BOSKIER
BOSKIEST
BOSKINESS
BOSKS
BOSKY
BOSOM
BOSOMED
BOSOMIER
BOSOMIEST
BOSOMING
BOSOMS
BOSOMY
BOSON
BOSONIC
BOSONS
BOSQUE
BOSQUES
BOSQUET
BOSQUETS
BOSS
BOSSBOY
BOSSBOYS
BOSSDOM
BOSSDOMS
BOSSED
BOSSER
BOSSES
BOSSEST
BOSSET
BOSSETS
BOSSIER
BOSSIES
BOSSIEST
BOSSILY
BOSSINESS
BOSSING
BOSSINGS
BOSSISM
BOSSISMS
BOSSY
BOSTANGI
BOSTANGIS
BOSTHOON
BOSTHOONS
BOSTON
BOSTONS
BOSTRYX
BOSTRYXES
BOSUN
BOSUNS
BOT
BOTA
BOTANIC
BOTANICA
BOTANICAL
BOTANICAS
BOTANICS
BOTANIES
BOTANISE
BOTANISED
BOTANISER
BOTANISES
BOTANIST
BOTANISTS
BOTANIZE
BOTANIZED
BOTANIZER
BOTANIZES
BOTANY
BOTARGO
BOTARGOES
BOTARGOS
BOTAS
BOTCH
BOTCHED
BOTCHEDLY
BOTCHER
BOTCHERS
BOTCHERY
BOTCHES
BOTCHIER
BOTCHIEST
BOTCHILY
BOTCHING
BOTCHINGS
BOTCHY
BOTE
BOTEL
BOTELS
BOTES
BOTFLIES
BOTFLY
BOTH
BOTHAN
BOTHANS
BOTHER
BOTHERED
BOTHERING
BOTHERS
BOTHIE
BOTHIES
BOTHOLE
BOTHOLES
BOTHRIA
BOTHRIUM
BOTHRIUMS
BOTHY
BOTHYMAN
BOTHYMEN
BOTNET
BOTNETS
BOTONE
BOTONEE
BOTONNEE
BOTOXED
BOTRYOID
BOTRYOSE
BOTRYTIS
BOTS
BOTT
BOTTARGA
BOTTARGAS
BOTTE
BOTTED
BOTTEGA
BOTTEGAS
BOTTES
BOTTIES
BOTTINE
BOTTINES
BOTTING
BOTTLE
BOTTLED
BOTTLEFUL
BOTTLER
BOTTLERS
BOTTLES
BOTTLING
BOTTLINGS
BOTTOM
BOTTOMED
BOTTOMER
BOTTOMERS
BOTTOMING
BOTTOMRY
BOTTOMS
BOTTOMSET
BOTTONY
BOTTS
BOTTY
BOTULIN
BOTULINAL
BOTULINS
BOTULINUM
BOTULINUS
BOTULISM
BOTULISMS
BOUBOU
BOUBOUS
BOUCHE
BOUCHEE
BOUCHEES
BOUCHES
BOUCLE
BOUCLEE
BOUCLEES
BOUCLES
BOUDERIE
BOUDERIES
BOUDIN
BOUDINS
BOUDOIR
BOUDOIRS
BOUFFANT
BOUFFANTS
BOUFFE
BOUFFES
BOUGE
BOUGED
BOUGES
BOUGET
BOUGETS
BOUGH
BOUGHED
BOUGHLESS
BOUGHPOT
BOUGHPOTS
BOUGHS
BOUGHT
BOUGHTEN
BOUGHTS
BOUGIE
BOUGIES
BOUGING
BOUILLI
BOUILLIS
BOUILLON
BOUILLONS
BOUK
BOUKS
BOULDER
BOULDERED
BOULDERER
BOULDERS
BOULDERY
BOULE
BOULES

BOULEVARD
BOULLE
BOULLES
BOULT
BOULTED
BOULTER
BOULTERS
BOULTING
BOULTINGS
BOULTS
BOUN
BOUNCE
BOUNCED
BOUNCER
BOUNCERS
BOUNCES
BOUNCIER
BOUNCIEST
BOUNCILY
BOUNCING
BOUNCY
BOUND
BOUNDABLE
BOUNDARY
BOUNDED
BOUNDEN
BOUNDER
BOUNDERS
BOUNDING
BOUNDLESS
BOUNDNESS
BOUNDS
BOUNED
BOUNING
BOUNS
BOUNTEOUS
BOUNTIED
BOUNTIES
BOUNTIFUL
BOUNTREE
BOUNTREES
BOUNTY
BOUNTYHED
BOUQUET
BOUQUETS
BOURASQUE
BOURBON
BOURBONS
BOURD
BOURDED
BOURDER
BOURDERS
BOURDING
BOURDON
BOURDONS
BOURDS
BOURG
BOURGEOIS
BOURGEON
BOURGEONS
BOURGS
BOURKHA
BOURKHAS
BOURLAW
BOURLAWS
BOURN
BOURNE
BOURNES
BOURNS
BOURREE
BOURREES
BOURRIDE
BOURRIDES
BOURSE
BOURSES
BOURSIER
BOURSIERS
BOURSIN
BOURSINS
BOURTREE
BOURTREES
BOUSE
BOUSED
BOUSES
BOUSIER
BOUSIEST
BOUSING
BOUSOUKI
BOUSOUKIA
BOUSOUKIS
BOUSY
BOUT
BOUTADE
BOUTADES
BOUTIQUE
BOUTIQUES
BOUTIQUEY
BOUTON
BOUTONNE
BOUTONNEE
BOUTONS
BOUTS
BOUVARDIA
BOUVIER
BOUVIERS
BOUZOUKI
BOUZOUKIA
BOUZOUKIS
BOVATE
BOVATES
BOVID
BOVIDS
BOVINE
BOVINELY
BOVINES
BOVINITY
BOVVER
BOVVERS
BOW
BOWAT
BOWATS
BOWBENT
BOWED
BOWEL
BOWELED
BOWELING
BOWELLED
BOWELLESS
BOWELLING
BOWELS
BOWER
BOWERBIRD
BOWERED
BOWERIES
BOWERING
BOWERS
BOWERY
BOWES
BOWET
BOWETS
BOWFIN
BOWFINS
BOWFRONT
BOWGET
BOWGETS
BOWHEAD
BOWHEADS
BOWHUNT
BOWHUNTED
BOWHUNTER
BOWHUNTS
BOWIE
BOWING
BOWINGLY
BOWINGS
BOWKNOT
BOWKNOTS
BOWL
BOWLDER
BOWLDERS
BOWLED
BOWLEG
BOWLEGGED
BOWLEGS
BOWLER
BOWLERS
BOWLESS
BOWLFUL
BOWLFULS
BOWLIKE
BOWLINE
BOWLINES
BOWLING
BOWLINGS
BOWLLIKE
BOWLS
BOWMAN
BOWMEN
BOWNE
BOWNED
BOWNES
BOWNING
BOWPOT
BOWPOTS
BOWR
BOWRS
BOWS
BOWSAW
BOWSAWS
BOWSE
BOWSED
BOWSER
BOWSERS
BOWSES
BOWSEY
BOWSEYS
BOWSHOT
BOWSHOTS
BOWSIE
BOWSIES
BOWSING
BOWSMAN
BOWSMEN
BOWSPRIT
BOWSPRITS
BOWSTRING
BOWSTRUNG
BOWWOOD
BOWWOODS
BOWWOW
BOWWOWED
BOWWOWING
BOWWOWS
BOWYANG
BOWYANGS
BOWYER
BOWYERS
BOX
BOXBALL
BOXBALLS
BOXBERRY
BOXBOARD
BOXBOARDS
BOXCAR
BOXCARS
BOXED
BOXEN
BOXER
BOXERCISE
BOXERS
BOXES
BOXFISH
BOXFISHES
BOXFUL
BOXFULS
BOXHAUL
BOXHAULED
BOXHAULS
BOXIER
BOXIEST

B

BOXILY
BOXINESS
BOXING
BOXINGS
BOXKEEPER
BOXLA
BOXLAS
BOXLIKE
BOXPLOT
BOXPLOTS
BOXROOM
BOXROOMS
BOXTHORN
BOXTHORNS
BOXTIES
BOXTY
BOXWALLAH
BOXWOOD
BOXWOODS
BOXY
BOY
BOYAR
BOYARD
BOYARDS
BOYARISM
BOYARISMS
BOYARS
BOYAU
BOYAUX
BOYCHICK
BOYCHICKS
BOYCHIK
BOYCHIKS
BOYCOTT
BOYCOTTED
BOYCOTTER
BOYCOTTS
BOYED
BOYF
BOYFRIEND
BOYFS
BOYG
BOYGS
BOYHOOD
BOYHOODS
BOYING
BOYISH
BOYISHLY
BOYKIE
BOYKIES
BOYLA
BOYLAS
BOYO
BOYOS
BOYS
BOYSHORTS
BOYSIER
BOYSIEST
BOYSY
BOZO
BOZOS
BOZZETTI
BOZZETTO
BRA
BRAAI
BRAAIED
BRAAIING
BRAAIS
BRAATA
BRAATAS
BRAATASES
BRABBLE
BRABBLED
BRABBLER
BRABBLERS
BRABBLES
BRABBLING
BRACCATE
BRACCIA
BRACCIO
BRACE
BRACED
BRACELET
BRACELETS
BRACER
BRACERO
BRACEROS
BRACERS
BRACES
BRACH
BRACHAH
BRACHAHS
BRACHES
BRACHET
BRACHETS
BRACHIA
BRACHIAL
BRACHIALS
BRACHIATE
BRACHIUM
BRACHIUMS
BRACHOT
BRACHS
BRACING
BRACINGLY
BRACINGS
BRACIOLA
BRACIOLAS
BRACIOLE
BRACIOLES
BRACK
BRACKEN
BRACKENS
BRACKET
BRACKETED
BRACKETS
BRACKISH
BRACKS
BRACONID
BRACONIDS
BRACT
BRACTEAL
BRACTEATE
BRACTED
BRACTEOLE
BRACTLESS
BRACTLET
BRACTLETS
BRACTS
BRAD
BRADAWL
BRADAWLS
BRADDED
BRADDING
BRADOON
BRADOONS
BRADS
BRAE
BRAEHEID
BRAEHEIDS
BRAES
BRAG
BRAGGART
BRAGGARTS
BRAGGED
BRAGGER
BRAGGERS
BRAGGEST
BRAGGIER
BRAGGIEST
BRAGGING
BRAGGINGS
BRAGGY
BRAGLY
BRAGS
BRAHMA
BRAHMAN
BRAHMANI
BRAHMANIS
BRAHMANS
BRAHMAS
BRAHMIN
BRAHMINS
BRAID
BRAIDE
BRAIDED
BRAIDER
BRAIDERS
BRAIDEST
BRAIDING
BRAIDINGS
BRAIDS
BRAIL
BRAILED
BRAILING
BRAILLE
BRAILLED
BRAILLER
BRAILLERS
BRAILLES
BRAILLING
BRAILLIST
BRAILS
BRAIN
BRAINBOX
BRAINCASE
BRAINDEAD
BRAINED
BRAINFART
BRAINFOOD
BRAINIAC
BRAINIACS
BRAINIER
BRAINIEST
BRAINILY
BRAINING
BRAINISH
BRAINLESS
BRAINPAN
BRAINPANS
BRAINS
BRAINSICK
BRAINSTEM
BRAINWASH
BRAINWAVE
BRAINWORK
BRAINY
BRAIRD
BRAIRDED
BRAIRDING
BRAIRDS
BRAISE
BRAISED
BRAISES
BRAISING
BRAIZE
BRAIZES
BRAK
BRAKE
BRAKEAGE
BRAKEAGES
BRAKED
BRAKELESS
BRAKEMAN
BRAKEMEN
BRAKES
BRAKESMAN
BRAKESMEN
BRAKIER
BRAKIEST
BRAKING
BRAKINGS
BRAKS
BRAKY
BRALESS
BRAMBLE
BRAMBLED
BRAMBLES
BRAMBLIER
BRAMBLING

BRAMBLY
BRAME
BRAMES
BRAN
BRANCARD
BRANCARDS
BRANCH
BRANCHED
BRANCHER
BRANCHERS
BRANCHERY
BRANCHES
BRANCHIA
BRANCHIAE
BRANCHIAL
BRANCHIER
BRANCHING
BRANCHLET
BRANCHY
BRAND
BRANDADE
BRANDADES
BRANDED
BRANDER
BRANDERED
BRANDERS
BRANDIED
BRANDIES
BRANDING
BRANDINGS
BRANDISE
BRANDISES
BRANDISH
BRANDLESS
BRANDLING
BRANDRETH
BRANDS
BRANDY
BRANDYING
BRANE
BRANES
BRANGLE
BRANGLED
BRANGLES
BRANGLING
BRANK
BRANKED
BRANKIER
BRANKIEST
BRANKING
BRANKS
BRANKY
BRANLE
BRANLES
BRANNED
BRANNER
BRANNERS
BRANNIER
BRANNIEST
BRANNIGAN
BRANNING
BRANNY
BRANS
BRANSLE
BRANSLES
BRANT
BRANTAIL
BRANTAILS
BRANTLE
BRANTLES
BRANTS
BRAP
BRAS
BRASCO
BRASCOS
BRASERO
BRASEROS
BRASES
BRASH
BRASHED
BRASHER
BRASHES
BRASHEST
BRASHIER
BRASHIEST
BRASHING
BRASHLY
BRASHNESS
BRASHY
BRASIER
BRASIERS
BRASIL
BRASILEIN
BRASILIN
BRASILINS
BRASILS
BRASS
BRASSAGE
BRASSAGES
BRASSARD
BRASSARDS
BRASSART
BRASSARTS
BRASSED
BRASSERIE
BRASSES
BRASSET
BRASSETS
BRASSICA
BRASSICAS
BRASSIE
BRASSIER
BRASSIERE
BRASSIES
BRASSIEST
BRASSILY
BRASSING
BRASSISH
BRASSWARE
BRASSY
BRAST
BRASTING
BRASTS
BRAT
BRATCHET
BRATCHETS
BRATLING
BRATLINGS
BRATPACK
BRATPACKS
BRATS
BRATTICE
BRATTICED
BRATTICES
BRATTIER
BRATTIEST
BRATTISH
BRATTLE
BRATTLED
BRATTLES
BRATTLING
BRATTY
BRATWURST
BRAUNCH
BRAUNCHED
BRAUNCHES
BRAUNITE
BRAUNITES
BRAVA
BRAVADO
BRAVADOED
BRAVADOES
BRAVADOS
BRAVAS
BRAVE
BRAVED
BRAVELY
BRAVENESS
BRAVER
BRAVERIES
BRAVERS
BRAVERY
BRAVES
BRAVEST
BRAVI
BRAVING
BRAVO
BRAVOED
BRAVOES
BRAVOING
BRAVOS
BRAVURA
BRAVURAS
BRAVURE
BRAW
BRAWER
BRAWEST
BRAWL
BRAWLED
BRAWLER
BRAWLERS
BRAWLIE
BRAWLIER
BRAWLIEST
BRAWLING
BRAWLINGS
BRAWLS
BRAWLY
BRAWN
BRAWNED
BRAWNIER
BRAWNIEST
BRAWNILY
BRAWNS
BRAWNY
BRAWS
BRAXIES
BRAXY
BRAY
BRAYED
BRAYER
BRAYERS
BRAYING
BRAYS
BRAZA
BRAZAS
BRAZE
BRAZED
BRAZELESS
BRAZEN
BRAZENED
BRAZENING
BRAZENLY
BRAZENRY
BRAZENS
BRAZER
BRAZERS
BRAZES
BRAZIER
BRAZIERS
BRAZIERY
BRAZIL
BRAZILEIN
BRAZILIN
BRAZILINS
BRAZILS
BRAZING
BREACH
BREACHED
BREACHER
BREACHERS
BREACHES
BREACHING
BREAD
BREADBIN
BREADBINS
BREADBOX
BREADED
BREADHEAD
BREADIER

B

BREADIEST
BREADING
BREADLESS
BREADLIKE
BREADLINE
BREADNUT
BREADNUTS
BREADROOM
BREADROOT
BREADS
BREADTH
BREADTHS
BREADY
BREAK
BREAKABLE
BREAKAGE
BREAKAGES
BREAKAWAY
BREAKBACK
BREAKBEAT
BREAKBONE
BREAKDOWN
BREAKER
BREAKERS
BREAKEVEN
BREAKFAST
BREAKING
BREAKINGS
BREAKNECK
BREAKOFF
BREAKOFFS
BREAKOUT
BREAKOUTS
BREAKS
BREAKTIME
BREAKUP
BREAKUPS
BREAKWALL
BREAM
BREAMED
BREAMING
BREAMS
BREARE
BREARES
BREASKIT
BREASKITS
BREAST
BREASTED
BREASTFED
BREASTING
BREASTPIN
BREASTS
BREATH
BREATHE
BREATHED
BREATHER
BREATHERS
BREATHES
BREATHFUL
BREATHIER
BREATHILY
BREATHING
BREATHS
BREATHY
BRECCIA
BRECCIAL
BRECCIAS
BRECCIATE
BRECHAM
BRECHAMS
BRECHAN
BRECHANS
BRED
BREDE
BREDED
BREDES
BREDIE
BREDIES
BREDING
BREDREN
BREDRENS
BREDRIN
BREDRINS
BREDS
BREE
BREECH
BREECHED
BREECHES
BREECHING
BREED
BREEDER
BREEDERS
BREEDING
BREEDINGS
BREEDS
BREEKS
BREEM
BREENGE
BREENGED
BREENGES
BREENGING
BREER
BREERED
BREERING
BREERS
BREES
BREESE
BREESES
BREEST
BREESTS
BREEZE
BREEZED
BREEZES
BREEZEWAY
BREEZIER
BREEZIEST
BREEZILY
BREEZING
BREEZY
BREGMA
BREGMAS
BREGMATA
BREGMATE
BREGMATIC
BREHON
BREHONS
BREI
BREID
BREIDS
BREIING
BREINGE
BREINGED
BREINGES
BREINGING
BREIS
BREIST
BREISTS
BREKKIE
BREKKIES
BREKKY
BRELOQUE
BRELOQUES
BREME
BREN
BRENNE
BRENNES
BRENNING
BRENS
BRENT
BRENTER
BRENTEST
BRENTS
BRER
BRERE
BRERES
BRERS
BRESAOLA
BRESAOLAS
BRETASCHE
BRETESSE
BRETESSES
BRETHREN
BRETON
BRETONS
BRETTICE
BRETTICED
BRETTICES
BREVE
BREVES
BREVET
BREVETCY
BREVETE
BREVETED
BREVETING
BREVETS
BREVETTED
BREVIARY
BREVIATE
BREVIATES
BREVIER
BREVIERS
BREVIS
BREVISES
BREVITIES
BREVITY
BREW
BREWAGE
BREWAGES
BREWED
BREWER
BREWERIES
BREWERS
BREWERY
BREWHOUSE
BREWING
BREWINGS
BREWIS
BREWISES
BREWPUB
BREWPUBS
BREWS
BREWSKI
BREWSKIES
BREWSKIS
BREWSTER
BREWSTERS
BREY
BREYED
BREYING
BREYS
BRIAR
BRIARD
BRIARDS
BRIARED
BRIARIER
BRIARIEST
BRIARROOT
BRIARS
BRIARWOOD
BRIARY
BRIBABLE
BRIBE
BRIBEABLE
BRIBED
BRIBEE
BRIBEES
BRIBER
BRIBERIES
BRIBERS
BRIBERY
BRIBES
BRIBING
BRICABRAC
BRICHT
BRICHTER
BRICHTEST
BRICK
BRICKBAT
BRICKBATS
BRICKCLAY

BRICKED
BRICKEN
BRICKIE
BRICKIER
BRICKIES
BRICKIEST
BRICKING
BRICKINGS
BRICKKILN
BRICKLE
BRICKLES
BRICKLIKE
BRICKS
BRICKWALL
BRICKWORK
BRICKY
BRICKYARD
BRICOLAGE
BRICOLE
BRICOLES
BRICOLEUR
BRIDAL
BRIDALLY
BRIDALS
BRIDE
BRIDECAKE
BRIDED
BRIDEMAID
BRIDEMAN
BRIDEMEN
BRIDES
BRIDESMAN
BRIDESMEN
BRIDEWELL
BRIDGABLE
BRIDGE
BRIDGED
BRIDGES
BRIDGING
BRIDGINGS
BRIDIE
BRIDIES
BRIDING
BRIDLE
BRIDLED
BRIDLER
BRIDLERS
BRIDLES
BRIDLEWAY
BRIDLING
BRIDOON
BRIDOONS
BRIE
BRIEF
BRIEFCASE
BRIEFED
BRIEFER
BRIEFERS
BRIEFEST
BRIEFING
BRIEFINGS
BRIEFLESS
BRIEFLY
BRIEFNESS
BRIEFS
BRIER
BRIERED
BRIERIER
BRIERIEST
BRIERROOT
BRIERS
BRIERWOOD
BRIERY
BRIES
BRIG
BRIGADE
BRIGADED
BRIGADES
BRIGADIER
BRIGADING
BRIGALOW
BRIGALOWS
BRIGAND
BRIGANDRY
BRIGANDS
BRIGHT
BRIGHTEN
BRIGHTENS
BRIGHTER
BRIGHTEST
BRIGHTISH
BRIGHTLY
BRIGHTS
BRIGS
BRIGUE
BRIGUED
BRIGUES
BRIGUING
BRIGUINGS
BRIK
BRIKI
BRIKIS
BRIKS
BRILL
BRILLER
BRILLEST
BRILLIANT
BRILLO
BRILLOS
BRILLS
BRIM
BRIMFUL
BRIMFULL
BRIMFULLY
BRIMING
BRIMINGS
BRIMLESS
BRIMMED
BRIMMER
BRIMMERS
BRIMMING
BRIMS
BRIMSTONE
BRIMSTONY
BRIN
BRINDED
BRINDISI
BRINDISIS
BRINDLE
BRINDLED
BRINDLES
BRINE
BRINED
BRINELESS
BRINER
BRINERS
BRINES
BRING
BRINGDOWN
BRINGER
BRINGERS
BRINGING
BRINGINGS
BRINGS
BRINIER
BRINIES
BRINIEST
BRININESS
BRINING
BRINISH
BRINJAL
BRINJALS
BRINJARRY
BRINK
BRINKMAN
BRINKMEN
BRINKS
BRINNIES
BRINNY
BRINS
BRINY
BRIO
BRIOCHE
BRIOCHES
BRIOLETTE
BRIONIES
BRIONY
BRIOS
BRIQUET
BRIQUETS
BRIQUETTE
BRIS
BRISANCE
BRISANCES
BRISANT
BRISE
BRISES
BRISK
BRISKED
BRISKEN
BRISKENED
BRISKENS
BRISKER
BRISKEST
BRISKET
BRISKETS
BRISKIER
BRISKIEST
BRISKING
BRISKISH
BRISKLY
BRISKNESS
BRISKS
BRISKY
BRISLING
BRISLINGS
BRISS
BRISSES
BRISTLE
BRISTLED
BRISTLES
BRISTLIER
BRISTLING
BRISTLY
BRISTOL
BRISTOLS
BRISURE
BRISURES
BRIT
BRITANNIA
BRITCHES
BRITH
BRITHS
BRITS
BRITSCHKA
BRITSKA
BRITSKAS
BRITT
BRITTANIA
BRITTLE
BRITTLED
BRITTLELY
BRITTLER
BRITTLES
BRITTLEST
BRITTLING
BRITTLY
BRITTS
BRITZKA
BRITZKAS
BRITZSKA
BRITZSKAS
BRIZE
BRIZES
BRO
BROACH
BROACHED
BROACHER
BROACHERS
BROACHES

BROACHING
BROAD
BROADAX
BROADAXE
BROADAXES
BROADBAND
BROADBEAN
BROADBILL
BROADBRIM
BROADCAST
BROADEN
BROADENED
BROADENER
BROADENS
BROADER
BROADEST
BROADISH
BROADLEAF
BROADLINE
BROADLOOM
BROADLY
BROADNESS
BROADS
BROADSIDE
BROADTAIL
BROADWAY
BROADWAYS
BROADWISE
BROAST
BROASTED
BROASTING
BROASTS
BROCADE
BROCADED
BROCADES
BROCADING
BROCAGE
BROCAGES
BROCARD
BROCARDS
BROCATEL
BROCATELS
BROCCOLI
BROCCOLIS
BROCH
BROCHAN
BROCHANS
BROCHE
BROCHED
BROCHES
BROCHETTE
BROCHING
BROCHO
BROCHOS
BROCHS
BROCHURE
BROCHURES
BROCK
BROCKAGE
BROCKAGES
BROCKED
BROCKET
BROCKETS
BROCKIT
BROCKRAM
BROCKRAMS
BROCKS
BROCOLI
BROCOLIS
BROD
BRODDED
BRODDING
BRODDLE
BRODDLED
BRODDLES
BRODDLING
BRODEKIN
BRODEKINS
BRODKIN
BRODKINS
BRODS
BROEKIES
BROG
BROGAN
BROGANS
BROGGED
BROGGING
BROGH
BROGHS
BROGS
BROGUE
BROGUEISH
BROGUERY
BROGUES
BROGUISH
BROIDER
BROIDERED
BROIDERER
BROIDERS
BROIDERY
BROIL
BROILED
BROILER
BROILERS
BROILING
BROILS
BROKAGE
BROKAGES
BROKE
BROKED
BROKEN
BROKENLY
BROKER
BROKERAGE
BROKERED
BROKERIES
BROKERING
BROKERS
BROKERY
BROKES
BROKING
BROKINGS
BROLGA
BROLGAS
BROLLIES
BROLLY
BROMAL
BROMALS
BROMANCE
BROMANCES
BROMANTIC
BROMATE
BROMATED
BROMATES
BROMATING
BROME
BROMELAIN
BROMELIA
BROMELIAD
BROMELIAS
BROMELIN
BROMELINS
BROMEOSIN
BROMES
BROMIC
BROMID
BROMIDE
BROMIDES
BROMIDIC
BROMIDS
BROMIN
BROMINATE
BROMINE
BROMINES
BROMINISM
BROMINS
BROMISE
BROMISED
BROMISES
BROMISING
BROMISM
BROMISMS
BROMIZE
BROMIZED
BROMIZES
BROMIZING
BROMMER
BROMMERS
BROMO
BROMOFORM
BROMOS
BRONC
BRONCHI
BRONCHIA
BRONCHIAL
BRONCHIUM
BRONCHO
BRONCHOS
BRONCHUS
BRONCO
BRONCOS
BRONCS
BROND
BRONDE
BRONDER
BRONDES
BRONDEST
BRONDS
BRONDYRON
BRONZE
BRONZED
BRONZEN
BRONZER
BRONZERS
BRONZES
BRONZIER
BRONZIEST
BRONZIFY
BRONZING
BRONZINGS
BRONZITE
BRONZITES
BRONZY
BROO
BROOCH
BROOCHED
BROOCHES
BROOCHING
BROOD
BROODED
BROODER
BROODERS
BROODIER
BROODIEST
BROODILY
BROODING
BROODINGS
BROODLESS
BROODMARE
BROODS
BROODY
BROOK
BROOKABLE
BROOKED
BROOKIE
BROOKIES
BROOKING
BROOKITE
BROOKITES
BROOKLET
BROOKLETS
BROOKLIKE
BROOKLIME
BROOKS
BROOKWEED
BROOL
BROOLS
BROOM
BROOMBALL
BROOMCORN

BROOMED
BROOMIER
BROOMIEST
BROOMING
BROOMRAPE
BROOMS
BROOMY
BROOS
BROOSE
BROOSES
BROS
BROSE
BROSES
BROSIER
BROSIEST
BROSY
BROTH
BROTHA
BROTHAS
BROTHEL
BROTHELS
BROTHER
BROTHERED
BROTHERLY
BROTHERS
BROTHIER
BROTHIEST
BROTHS
BROTHY
BROUGH
BROUGHAM
BROUGHAMS
BROUGHS
BROUGHT
BROUGHTA
BROUGHTAS
BROUHAHA
BROUHAHAS
BROUZE
BROUZES
BROW
BROWALLIA
BROWBAND
BROWBANDS
BROWBEAT
BROWBEATS
BROWBONE
BROWBONES
BROWED
BROWLESS
BROWN
BROWNED
BROWNER
BROWNERS
BROWNEST
BROWNIE
BROWNIER
BROWNIES
BROWNIEST
BROWNING
BROWNINGS
BROWNISH
BROWNNESS
BROWNNOSE
BROWNOUT
BROWNOUTS
BROWNS
BROWNTAIL
BROWNY
BROWRIDGE
BROWS
BROWSABLE
BROWSE
BROWSED
BROWSER
BROWSERS
BROWSES
BROWSIER
BROWSIEST
BROWSING
BROWSINGS
BROWST
BROWSTS
BROWSY
BRR
BRRR
BRU
BRUCELLA
BRUCELLAE
BRUCELLAS
BRUCHID
BRUCHIDS
BRUCIN
BRUCINE
BRUCINES
BRUCINS
BRUCITE
BRUCITES
BRUCKLE
BRUGH
BRUGHS
BRUHAHA
BRUHAHAS
BRUILZIE
BRUILZIES
BRUIN
BRUINS
BRUISE
BRUISED
BRUISER
BRUISERS
BRUISES
BRUISING
BRUISINGS
BRUIT
BRUITED
BRUITER
BRUITERS
BRUITING
BRUITS
BRULE
BRULES
BRULOT
BRULOTS
BRULYIE
BRULYIES
BRULZIE
BRULZIES
BRUMAL
BRUMBIES
BRUMBY
BRUME
BRUMES
BRUMMAGEM
BRUMMER
BRUMMERS
BRUMOUS
BRUNCH
BRUNCHED
BRUNCHER
BRUNCHERS
BRUNCHES
BRUNCHING
BRUNET
BRUNETS
BRUNETTE
BRUNETTES
BRUNG
BRUNIZEM
BRUNIZEMS
BRUNT
BRUNTED
BRUNTING
BRUNTS
BRUS
BRUSH
BRUSHABLE
BRUSHBACK
BRUSHED
BRUSHER
BRUSHERS
BRUSHES
BRUSHFIRE
BRUSHIER
BRUSHIEST
BRUSHING
BRUSHINGS
BRUSHLAND
BRUSHLESS
BRUSHLIKE
BRUSHMARK
BRUSHOFF
BRUSHOFFS
BRUSHUP
BRUSHUPS
BRUSHWOOD
BRUSHWORK
BRUSHY
BRUSK
BRUSKER
BRUSKEST
BRUSQUE
BRUSQUELY
BRUSQUER
BRUSQUEST
BRUSSELS
BRUSSEN
BRUST
BRUSTING
BRUSTS
BRUT
BRUTAL
BRUTALISE
BRUTALISM
BRUTALIST
BRUTALITY
BRUTALIZE
BRUTALLY
BRUTE
BRUTED
BRUTELIKE
BRUTELY
BRUTENESS
BRUTER
BRUTERS
BRUTES
BRUTEST
BRUTIFIED
BRUTIFIES
BRUTIFY
BRUTING
BRUTINGS
BRUTISH
BRUTISHLY
BRUTISM
BRUTISMS
BRUTS
BRUX
BRUXED
BRUXES
BRUXING
BRUXISM
BRUXISMS
BRYOLOGY
BRYONIES
BRYONY
BRYOPHYTE
BRYOZOAN
BRYOZOANS
BUAT
BUATS
BUAZE
BUAZES
BUB
BUBA
BUBAL
BUBALE
BUBALES
BUBALINE
BUBALIS

BUBALISES
BUBALS
BUBAS
BUBBA
BUBBAS
BUBBE
BUBBES
BUBBIE
BUBBIES
BUBBLE
BUBBLED
BUBBLEGUM
BUBBLER
BUBBLERS
BUBBLES
BUBBLIER
BUBBLIES
BUBBLIEST
BUBBLING
BUBBLY
BUBBY
BUBINGA
BUBINGAS
BUBKES
BUBKIS
BUBO
BUBOED
BUBOES
BUBONIC
BUBS
BUBU
BUBUKLE
BUBUKLES
BUBUS
BUCARDO
BUCARDOS
BUCATINI
BUCCAL
BUCCALLY
BUCCANEER
BUCCANIER
BUCCINA
BUCCINAS
BUCELLAS
BUCENTAUR
BUCHU
BUCHUS
BUCK
BUCKAROO
BUCKAROOS
BUCKAYRO
BUCKAYROS
BUCKBEAN
BUCKBEANS
BUCKBOARD
BUCKBRUSH
BUCKED
BUCKEEN
BUCKEENS
BUCKER
BUCKEROO
BUCKEROOS
BUCKERS
BUCKET
BUCKETED
BUCKETFUL
BUCKETING
BUCKETS
BUCKEYE
BUCKEYES
BUCKHORN
BUCKHORNS
BUCKHOUND
BUCKIE
BUCKIES
BUCKING
BUCKINGS
BUCKISH
BUCKISHLY
BUCKLE
BUCKLED
BUCKLER
BUCKLERED
BUCKLERS
BUCKLES
BUCKLING
BUCKLINGS
BUCKO
BUCKOES
BUCKOS
BUCKRA
BUCKRAKE
BUCKRAKES
BUCKRAM
BUCKRAMED
BUCKRAMS
BUCKRAS
BUCKS
BUCKSAW
BUCKSAWS
BUCKSHEE
BUCKSHEES
BUCKSHISH
BUCKSHOT
BUCKSHOTS
BUCKSKIN
BUCKSKINS
BUCKSOM
BUCKTAIL
BUCKTAILS
BUCKTEETH
BUCKTHORN
BUCKTOOTH
BUCKU
BUCKUS
BUCKWHEAT
BUCKYBALL
BUCKYTUBE
BUCOLIC
BUCOLICAL
BUCOLICS
BUD
BUDA
BUDAS
BUDDED
BUDDER
BUDDERS
BUDDHA
BUDDHAS
BUDDIED
BUDDIER
BUDDIES
BUDDIEST
BUDDING
BUDDINGS
BUDDLE
BUDDLED
BUDDLEIA
BUDDLEIAS
BUDDLES
BUDDLING
BUDDY
BUDDYING
BUDGE
BUDGED
BUDGER
BUDGEREE
BUDGERO
BUDGEROS
BUDGEROW
BUDGEROWS
BUDGERS
BUDGES
BUDGET
BUDGETARY
BUDGETED
BUDGETEER
BUDGETER
BUDGETERS
BUDGETING
BUDGETS
BUDGIE
BUDGIES
BUDGING
BUDI
BUDIS
BUDLESS
BUDLIKE
BUDMASH
BUDMASHES
BUDO
BUDOS
BUDS
BUDTENDER
BUDWOOD
BUDWOODS
BUDWORM
BUDWORMS
BUFF
BUFFA
BUFFABLE
BUFFALO
BUFFALOED
BUFFALOES
BUFFALOS
BUFFAS
BUFFE
BUFFED
BUFFEL
BUFFER
BUFFERED
BUFFERING
BUFFERS
BUFFEST
BUFFET
BUFFETED
BUFFETER
BUFFETERS
BUFFETING
BUFFETS
BUFFI
BUFFIER
BUFFIEST
BUFFING
BUFFINGS
BUFFO
BUFFOON
BUFFOONS
BUFFOS
BUFFS
BUFFY
BUFO
BUFOS
BUFOTALIN
BUFTIE
BUFTIES
BUFTY
BUG
BUGABOO
BUGABOOS
BUGBANE
BUGBANES
BUGBEAR
BUGBEARS
BUGEYE
BUGEYES
BUGGAN
BUGGANE
BUGGANES
BUGGANS
BUGGED
BUGGER
BUGGERED
BUGGERIES
BUGGERING
BUGGERS
BUGGERY
BUGGIER
BUGGIES
BUGGIEST

BUGGIN
BUGGINESS
BUGGING
BUGGINGS
BUGGINS
BUGGY
BUGHOUSE
BUGHOUSES
BUGLE
BUGLED
BUGLER
BUGLERS
BUGLES
BUGLET
BUGLETS
BUGLEWEED
BUGLING
BUGLOSS
BUGLOSSES
BUGONG
BUGONGS
BUGOUT
BUGOUTS
BUGS
BUGSEED
BUGSEEDS
BUGSHA
BUGSHAS
BUGWORT
BUGWORTS
BUHL
BUHLS
BUHLWORK
BUHLWORKS
BUHR
BUHRS
BUHRSTONE
BUHUND
BUHUNDS
BUIBUI
BUIBUIS
BUIK
BUIKS
BUILD
BUILDABLE
BUILDDOWN
BUILDED
BUILDER
BUILDERS
BUILDING
BUILDINGS
BUILDOUT
BUILDOUTS
BUILDS
BUILDUP
BUILDUPS
BUILT
BUIRDLIER
BUIRDLY
BUIST
BUISTED
BUISTING
BUISTS
BUKE
BUKES
BUKKAKE
BUKKAKES
BUKSHEE
BUKSHEES
BUKSHI
BUKSHIS
BULB
BULBAR
BULBED
BULBEL
BULBELS
BULBIL
BULBILS
BULBING
BULBLET
BULBLETS
BULBOSITY
BULBOUS
BULBOUSLY
BULBS
BULBUL
BULBULS
BULGAR
BULGARS
BULGE
BULGED
BULGER
BULGERS
BULGES
BULGHUR
BULGHURS
BULGIER
BULGIEST
BULGINE
BULGINES
BULGINESS
BULGING
BULGINGLY
BULGUR
BULGURS
BULGY
BULIMIA
BULIMIAC
BULIMIACS
BULIMIAS
BULIMIC
BULIMICS
BULIMIES
BULIMUS
BULIMUSES
BULIMY
BULK
BULKAGE
BULKAGES
BULKED
BULKER
BULKERS
BULKHEAD
BULKHEADS
BULKIER
BULKIEST
BULKILY
BULKINESS
BULKING
BULKINGS
BULKS
BULKY
BULL
BULLA
BULLACE
BULLACES
BULLAE
BULLARIES
BULLARY
BULLATE
BULLBARS
BULLBAT
BULLBATS
BULLBRIER
BULLCOOK
BULLCOOKS
BULLDIKE
BULLDIKES
BULLDOG
BULLDOGS
BULLDOZE
BULLDOZED
BULLDOZER
BULLDOZES
BULLDUST
BULLDUSTS
BULLDYKE
BULLDYKES
BULLED
BULLER
BULLERED
BULLERING
BULLERS
BULLET
BULLETED
BULLETIN
BULLETING
BULLETINS
BULLETRIE
BULLETS
BULLEY
BULLEYS
BULLFIGHT
BULLFINCH
BULLFROG
BULLFROGS
BULLGINE
BULLGINES
BULLHEAD
BULLHEADS
BULLHORN
BULLHORNS
BULLIED
BULLIER
BULLIES
BULLIEST
BULLING
BULLINGS
BULLION
BULLIONS
BULLISH
BULLISHLY
BULLNECK
BULLNECKS
BULLNOSE
BULLNOSED
BULLNOSES
BULLOCK
BULLOCKED
BULLOCKS
BULLOCKY
BULLOSA
BULLOUS
BULLPEN
BULLPENS
BULLPOUT
BULLPOUTS
BULLRING
BULLRINGS
BULLRUSH
BULLS
BULLSEYE
BULLSEYES
BULLSHAT
BULLSHIT
BULLSHITS
BULLSHOT
BULLSHOTS
BULLSNAKE
BULLWADDY
BULLWEED
BULLWEEDS
BULLWHACK
BULLWHIP
BULLWHIPS
BULLY
BULLYBOY
BULLYBOYS
BULLYCIDE
BULLYING
BULLYINGS
BULLYISM
BULLYISMS
BULLYRAG
BULLYRAGS
BULNBULN
BULNBULNS
BULRUSH
BULRUSHES
BULRUSHY

BULSE
BULSES
BULWADDEE
BULWADDY
BULWARK
BULWARKED
BULWARKS
BUM
BUMALO
BUMALOTI
BUMALOTIS
BUMBAG
BUMBAGS
BUMBAZE
BUMBAZED
BUMBAZES
BUMBAZING
BUMBLE
BUMBLEBEE
BUMBLED
BUMBLEDOM
BUMBLER
BUMBLERS
BUMBLES
BUMBLING
BUMBLINGS
BUMBO
BUMBOAT
BUMBOATS
BUMBOS
BUMBOY
BUMBOYS
BUMELIA
BUMELIAS
BUMF
BUMFLUFF
BUMFLUFFS
BUMFS
BUMFUCK
BUMFUCKS
BUMFUZZLE
BUMKIN
BUMKINS
BUMMALO
BUMMALOS
BUMMALOTI
BUMMAREE
BUMMAREES
BUMMED
BUMMEL
BUMMELS
BUMMER
BUMMERS
BUMMEST
BUMMING
BUMMLE
BUMMLED
BUMMLES
BUMMLING
BUMMOCK
BUMMOCKS
BUMP
BUMPED
BUMPER
BUMPERED
BUMPERING
BUMPERS
BUMPH
BUMPHS
BUMPIER
BUMPIEST
BUMPILY
BUMPINESS
BUMPING
BUMPINGS
BUMPKIN
BUMPKINLY
BUMPKINS
BUMPOLOGY
BUMPS
BUMPTIOUS
BUMPY
BUMS
BUMSTER
BUMSTERS
BUMSUCKER
BUMWAD
BUMWADS
BUN
BUNA
BUNAS
BUNBURIED
BUNBURIES
BUNBURY
BUNCE
BUNCED
BUNCES
BUNCH
BUNCHED
BUNCHER
BUNCHERS
BUNCHES
BUNCHIER
BUNCHIEST
BUNCHILY
BUNCHING
BUNCHINGS
BUNCHY
BUNCING
BUNCO
BUNCOED
BUNCOES
BUNCOING
BUNCOMBE
BUNCOMBES
BUNCOS
BUND
BUNDE
BUNDED
BUNDH
BUNDHS
BUNDIED
BUNDIES
BUNDING
BUNDIST
BUNDISTS
BUNDLE
BUNDLED
BUNDLER
BUNDLERS
BUNDLES
BUNDLING
BUNDLINGS
BUNDOBUST
BUNDOOK
BUNDOOKS
BUNDS
BUNDT
BUNDTS
BUNDU
BUNDUS
BUNDWALL
BUNDWALLS
BUNDY
BUNDYING
BUNFIGHT
BUNFIGHTS
BUNG
BUNGALOID
BUNGALOW
BUNGALOWS
BUNGED
BUNGEE
BUNGEES
BUNGER
BUNGERS
BUNGEY
BUNGEYS
BUNGHOLE
BUNGHOLES
BUNGIE
BUNGIES
BUNGING
BUNGLE
BUNGLED
BUNGLER
BUNGLERS
BUNGLES
BUNGLING
BUNGLINGS
BUNGS
BUNGWALL
BUNGWALLS
BUNGY
BUNHEAD
BUNHEADS
BUNIA
BUNIAS
BUNION
BUNIONS
BUNJE
BUNJEE
BUNJEES
BUNJES
BUNJIE
BUNJIES
BUNJY
BUNK
BUNKED
BUNKER
BUNKERED
BUNKERING
BUNKERS
BUNKHOUSE
BUNKIE
BUNKIES
BUNKING
BUNKMATE
BUNKMATES
BUNKO
BUNKOED
BUNKOING
BUNKOS
BUNKS
BUNKUM
BUNKUMS
BUNN
BUNNET
BUNNETS
BUNNIA
BUNNIAS
BUNNIES
BUNNS
BUNNY
BUNODONT
BUNRAKU
BUNRAKUS
BUNS
BUNSEN
BUNSENS
BUNT
BUNTAL
BUNTALS
BUNTED
BUNTER
BUNTERS
BUNTIER
BUNTIEST
BUNTING
BUNTINGS
BUNTLINE
BUNTLINES
BUNTS
BUNTY
BUNYA
BUNYAS
BUNYIP
BUNYIPS
BUOY
BUOYAGE

BUOYAGES
BUOYANCE
BUOYANCES
BUOYANCY
BUOYANT
BUOYANTLY
BUOYED
BUOYING
BUOYS
BUPKES
BUPKIS
BUPKUS
BUPLEVER
BUPLEVERS
BUPPIE
BUPPIES
BUPPY
BUPRESTID
BUPROPION
BUQSHA
BUQSHAS
BUR
BURA
BURAN
BURANS
BURAS
BURB
BURBLE
BURBLED
BURBLER
BURBLERS
BURBLES
BURBLIER
BURBLIEST
BURBLING
BURBLINGS
BURBLY
BURBOT
BURBOTS
BURBS
BURD
BURDASH
BURDASHES
BURDEN
BURDENED
BURDENER
BURDENERS
BURDENING
BURDENOUS
BURDENS
BURDIE
BURDIES
BURDIZZO
BURDIZZOS
BURDOCK
BURDOCKS
BURDS
BUREAU
BUREAUS
BUREAUX
BURET
BURETS
BURETTE
BURETTES
BURFI
BURFIS
BURG
BURGAGE
BURGAGES
BURGANET
BURGANETS
BURGEE
BURGEES
BURGEON
BURGEONED
BURGEONS
BURGER
BURGERS
BURGESS
BURGESSES
BURGH
BURGHAL
BURGHER
BURGHERS
BURGHS
BURGHUL
BURGHULS
BURGLAR
BURGLARED
BURGLARS
BURGLARY
BURGLE
BURGLED
BURGLES
BURGLING
BURGONET
BURGONETS
BURGOO
BURGOOS
BURGOUT
BURGOUTS
BURGRAVE
BURGRAVES
BURGS
BURGUNDY
BURHEL
BURHELS
BURIAL
BURIALS
BURIED
BURIER
BURIERS
BURIES
BURIN
BURINIST
BURINISTS
BURINS
BURITI
BURITIS
BURK
BURKA
BURKAS
BURKE
BURKED
BURKER
BURKERS
BURKES
BURKHA
BURKHAS
BURKING
BURKINI
BURKINIS
BURKITE
BURKITES
BURKS
BURL
BURLADERO
BURLAP
BURLAPS
BURLED
BURLER
BURLERS
BURLESK
BURLESKS
BURLESQUE
BURLETTA
BURLETTAS
BURLEY
BURLEYCUE
BURLEYED
BURLEYING
BURLEYS
BURLIER
BURLIEST
BURLIKE
BURLILY
BURLINESS
BURLING
BURLS
BURLY
BURN
BURNABLE
BURNABLES
BURNED
BURNER
BURNERS
BURNET
BURNETS
BURNIE
BURNIES
BURNING
BURNINGLY
BURNINGS
BURNISH
BURNISHED
BURNISHER
BURNISHES
BURNOOSE
BURNOOSED
BURNOOSES
BURNOUS
BURNOUSE
BURNOUSED
BURNOUSES
BURNOUT
BURNOUTS
BURNS
BURNSIDE
BURNSIDES
BURNT
BUROO
BUROOS
BURP
BURPED
BURPEE
BURPEES
BURPING
BURPS
BURQA
BURQAS
BURQUINI
BURQUINIS
BURR
BURRAMYS
BURRATA
BURRATAS
BURRAWANG
BURRED
BURREL
BURRELL
BURRELLS
BURRELS
BURRER
BURRERS
BURRFISH
BURRHEL
BURRHELS
BURRIER
BURRIEST
BURRING
BURRITO
BURRITOS
BURRO
BURROS
BURROW
BURROWED
BURROWER
BURROWERS
BURROWING
BURROWS
BURRS
BURRSTONE
BURRY
BURS
BURSA
BURSAE
BURSAL
BURSAR
BURSARIAL
BURSARIES

BURSARS
BURSARY
BURSAS
BURSATE
BURSE
BURSEED
BURSEEDS
BURSERA
BURSES
BURSICON
BURSICONS
BURSIFORM
BURSITIS
BURST
BURSTED
BURSTEN
BURSTER
BURSTERS
BURSTIER
BURSTIEST
BURSTING
BURSTONE
BURSTONES
BURSTS
BURSTY
BURTHEN
BURTHENED
BURTHENS
BURTON
BURTONS
BURWEED
BURWEEDS
BURY
BURYING
BUS
BUSBAR
BUSBARS
BUSBIES
BUSBOY
BUSBOYS
BUSBY
BUSED
BUSERA
BUSERAS
BUSES
BUSGIRL
BUSGIRLS
BUSH

BUSHBABY
BUSHBUCK
BUSHBUCKS
BUSHCRAFT
BUSHED
BUSHEL
BUSHELED
BUSHELER
BUSHELERS
BUSHELFUL
BUSHELING
BUSHELLED
BUSHELLER
BUSHELMAN
BUSHELMEN
BUSHELS
BUSHER
BUSHERS
BUSHES
BUSHFIRE
BUSHFIRES
BUSHFLIES
BUSHFLY
BUSHGOAT
BUSHGOATS
BUSHIDO
BUSHIDOS
BUSHIE
BUSHIER
BUSHIES
BUSHIEST
BUSHILY
BUSHINESS
BUSHING
BUSHINGS
BUSHLAND
BUSHLANDS
BUSHLESS
BUSHLIKE
BUSHLOT
BUSHLOTS
BUSHMAN
BUSHMEAT
BUSHMEATS
BUSHMEN
BUSHPIG
BUSHPIGS
BUSHTIT

BUSHTITS
BUSHVELD
BUSHVELDS
BUSHWA
BUSHWAH
BUSHWAHS
BUSHWALK
BUSHWALKS
BUSHWAS
BUSHWHACK
BUSHWOMAN
BUSHWOMEN
BUSHY
BUSIED
BUSIER
BUSIES
BUSIEST
BUSILY
BUSINESS
BUSINESSY
BUSING
BUSINGS
BUSK
BUSKED
BUSKER
BUSKERS
BUSKET
BUSKETS
BUSKIN
BUSKINED
BUSKING
BUSKINGS
BUSKINS
BUSKS
BUSKY
BUSLOAD
BUSLOADS
BUSMAN
BUSMEN
BUSS
BUSSED
BUSSES
BUSSING
BUSSINGS
BUSSU
BUSSUS
BUST
BUSTARD

BUSTARDS
BUSTED
BUSTEE
BUSTEES
BUSTER
BUSTERS
BUSTI
BUSTIC
BUSTICATE
BUSTICS
BUSTIER
BUSTIERS
BUSTIEST
BUSTINESS
BUSTING
BUSTINGS
BUSTIS
BUSTLE
BUSTLED
BUSTLER
BUSTLERS
BUSTLES
BUSTLINE
BUSTLINES
BUSTLING
BUSTS
BUSTY
BUSULFAN
BUSULFANS
BUSUUTI
BUSUUTIS
BUSY
BUSYBODY
BUSYING
BUSYNESS
BUSYWORK
BUSYWORKS
BUT
BUTADIENE
BUTANE
BUTANES
BUTANOIC
BUTANOL
BUTANOLS
BUTANONE
BUTANONES
BUTCH
BUTCHER

BUTCHERED
BUTCHERER
BUTCHERLY
BUTCHERS
BUTCHERY
BUTCHES
BUTCHEST
BUTCHING
BUTCHINGS
BUTCHNESS
BUTE
BUTENE
BUTENES
BUTEO
BUTEONINE
BUTEOS
BUTES
BUTLE
BUTLED
BUTLER
BUTLERAGE
BUTLERED
BUTLERIES
BUTLERING
BUTLERS
BUTLERY
BUTLES
BUTLING
BUTMENT
BUTMENTS
BUTOH
BUTOHS
BUTS
BUTSUDAN
BUTSUDANS
BUTT
BUTTALS
BUTTE
BUTTED
BUTTER
BUTTERBUR
BUTTERCUP
BUTTERED
BUTTERFAT
BUTTERFLY
BUTTERIER
BUTTERIES
BUTTERINE

BUTTERING
BUTTERNUT
BUTTERS
BUTTERY
BUTTES
BUTTHEAD
BUTTHEADS
BUTTIES
BUTTING
BUTTINSKI
BUTTINSKY
BUTTLE
BUTTLED
BUTTLES
BUTTLING
BUTTOCK
BUTTOCKED
BUTTOCKS
BUTTON
BUTTONED
BUTTONER
BUTTONERS
BUTTONIER
BUTTONING
BUTTONS
BUTTONY
BUTTRESS
BUTTS
BUTTSTOCK
BUTTY
BUTTYMAN
BUTTYMEN
BUTUT
BUTUTS
BUTYL
BUTYLATE
BUTYLATED
BUTYLATES
BUTYLENE
BUTYLENES
BUTYLS
BUTYRAL
BUTYRALS
BUTYRATE
BUTYRATES
BUTYRIC
BUTYRIN
BUTYRINS
BUTYROUS
BUTYRYL
BUTYRYLS
BUVETTE
BUVETTES
BUXOM
BUXOMER
BUXOMEST
BUXOMLY
BUXOMNESS
BUY
BUYABLE
BUYABLES
BUYBACK
BUYBACKS
BUYER
BUYERS
BUYING
BUYINGS
BUYOFF
BUYOFFS
BUYOUT
BUYOUTS
BUYS
BUZKASHI
BUZKASHIS
BUZUKI
BUZUKIA
BUZUKIS
BUZZ
BUZZARD
BUZZARDS
BUZZBAIT
BUZZBAITS
BUZZCUT
BUZZCUTS
BUZZED
BUZZER
BUZZERS
BUZZES
BUZZIER
BUZZIEST
BUZZING
BUZZINGLY
BUZZINGS
BUZZKILL
BUZZKILLS
BUZZSAW
BUZZSAWS
BUZZWIG
BUZZWIGS
BUZZWORD
BUZZWORDS
BUZZY
BWANA
BWANAS
BWAZI
BWAZIS
BY
BYCATCH
BYCATCHES
BYCOKET
BYCOKETS
BYDE
BYDED
BYDES
BYDING
BYE
BYELAW
BYELAWS
BYES
BYGONE
BYGONES
BYKE
BYKED
BYKES
BYKING
BYLANDER
BYLANDERS
BYLANE
BYLANES
BYLAW
BYLAWS
BYLINE
BYLINED
BYLINER
BYLINERS
BYLINES
BYLINING
BYLIVE
BYNAME
BYNAMES
BYNEMPT
BYPASS
BYPASSED
BYPASSES
BYPASSING
BYPAST
BYPATH
BYPATHS
BYPLACE
BYPLACES
BYPLAY
BYPLAYS
BYPRODUCT
BYRE
BYREMAN
BYREMEN
BYRES
BYREWOMAN
BYREWOMEN
BYRL
BYRLADY
BYRLAKIN
BYRLAW
BYRLAWS
BYRLED
BYRLING
BYRLS
BYRNIE
BYRNIES
BYROAD
BYROADS
BYROOM
BYROOMS
BYS
BYSSAL
BYSSI
BYSSINE
BYSSOID
BYSSUS
BYSSUSES
BYSTANDER
BYSTREET
BYSTREETS
BYTALK
BYTALKS
BYTE
BYTES
BYTOWNITE
BYWAY
BYWAYS
BYWONER
BYWONERS
BYWORD
BYWORDS
BYWORK
BYWORKS
BYZANT
BYZANTINE
BYZANTS

C

CAA
CAAED
CAAING
CAAS
CAATINGA
CAATINGAS
CAB
CABA
CABAL
CABALA
CABALAS
CABALETTA
CABALETTE
CABALISM
CABALISMS
CABALIST
CABALISTS
CABALLED
CABALLER
CABALLERO
CABALLERS
CABALLINE
CABALLING
CABALS
CABANA
CABANAS
CABARET
CABARETS
CABAS
CABBAGE
CABBAGED
CABBAGES
CABBAGEY
CABBAGIER
CABBAGING
CABBAGY
CABBALA
CABBALAH
CABBALAHS
CABBALAS
CABBALISM
CABBALIST
CABBED
CABBIE
CABBIES
CABBING
CABBY
CABDRIVER
CABER
CABERNET
CABERNETS
CABERS
CABESTRO
CABESTROS
CABEZON
CABEZONE
CABEZONES
CABEZONS
CABILDO
CABILDOS
CABIN
CABINED
CABINET
CABINETRY
CABINETS
CABINING
CABINMATE
CABINS
CABLE
CABLECAST
CABLED
CABLEGRAM
CABLER
CABLERS
CABLES
CABLET
CABLETS
CABLEWAY
CABLEWAYS
CABLING
CABLINGS
CABMAN
CABMEN
CABOB
CABOBBED
CABOBBING
CABOBS
CABOC
CABOCEER
CABOCEERS
CABOCHED
CABOCHON
CABOCHONS
CABOCS
CABOMBA
CABOMBAS
CABOODLE
CABOODLES
CABOOSE
CABOOSES
CABOSHED
CABOTAGE
CABOTAGES
CABOVER
CABOVERS
CABRE
CABRESTA
CABRESTAS
CABRESTO
CABRESTOS
CABRETTA
CABRETTAS
CABRIE
CABRIES
CABRILLA
CABRILLAS
CABRIO
CABRIOLE
CABRIOLES
CABRIOLET
CABRIOS
CABRIT
CABRITS
CABS
CABSTAND
CABSTANDS
CACA
CACAFOGO
CACAFOGOS
CACAFUEGO
CACAO
CACAOS
CACAS
CACHACA
CACHACAS
CACHAEMIA
CACHAEMIC
CACHALOT
CACHALOTS
CACHE
CACHECTIC
CACHED
CACHEPOT
CACHEPOTS
CACHES
CACHET
CACHETED
CACHETING
CACHETS
CACHEXIA
CACHEXIAS
CACHEXIC
CACHEXIES
CACHEXY
CACHING
CACHOLONG
CACHOLOT
CACHOLOTS
CACHOU
CACHOUS
CACHUCHA
CACHUCHAS
CACIQUE
CACIQUES
CACIQUISM
CACK
CACKED
CACKIER
CACKIEST
CACKING
CACKLE
CACKLED
CACKLER
CACKLERS
CACKLES
CACKLING
CACKS
CACKY
CACODEMON
CACODOXY
CACODYL
CACODYLIC
CACODYLS
CACOEPIES
CACOEPY
CACOETHES
CACOETHIC
CACOGENIC
CACOLET
CACOLETS
CACOLOGY
CACOMIXL
CACOMIXLE
CACOMIXLS
CACONYM
CACONYMS
CACONYMY
CACOON
CACOONS
CACOPHONY
CACOTOPIA
CACTI
CACTIFORM
CACTOID
CACTUS
CACTUSES
CACUMEN
CACUMENS
CACUMINA
CACUMINAL

CAD
CADAGA
CADAGAS
CADAGI
CADAGIS
CADASTER
CADASTERS
CADASTRAL
CADASTRE
CADASTRES
CADAVER
CADAVERIC
CADAVERS
CADDICE
CADDICES
CADDIE
CADDIED
CADDIES
CADDIS
CADDISED
CADDISES
CADDISFLY
CADDISH
CADDISHLY
CADDY
CADDYING
CADDYSS
CADDYSSES
CADE
CADEAU
CADEAUX
CADEE
CADEES
CADELLE
CADELLES
CADENCE
CADENCED
CADENCES
CADENCIES
CADENCING
CADENCY
CADENT
CADENTIAL
CADENZA
CADENZAS
CADES
CADET
CADETS
CADETSHIP
CADGE
CADGED
CADGER
CADGERS
CADGES
CADGIER
CADGIEST
CADGING
CADGY
CADI
CADIE
CADIES
CADIS
CADMIC
CADMIUM
CADMIUMS
CADRANS
CADRANSES
CADRE
CADRES
CADS
CADUAC
CADUACS
CADUCEAN
CADUCEI
CADUCEUS
CADUCITY
CADUCOUS
CAECA
CAECAL
CAECALLY
CAECILIAN
CAECITIS
CAECUM
CAEOMA
CAEOMAS
CAERULE
CAERULEAN
CAESAR
CAESAREAN
CAESARIAN
CAESARISM
CAESARS
CAESE
CAESIOUS
CAESIUM
CAESIUMS
CAESTUS
CAESTUSES
CAESURA
CAESURAE
CAESURAL
CAESURAS
CAESURIC
CAF
CAFARD
CAFARDS
CAFE
CAFES
CAFETERIA
CAFETIERE
CAFETORIA
CAFF
CAFFEIN
CAFFEINE
CAFFEINES
CAFFEINIC
CAFFEINS
CAFFEISM
CAFFEISMS
CAFFILA
CAFFILAS
CAFFS
CAFILA
CAFILAS
CAFS
CAFTAN
CAFTANED
CAFTANS
CAG
CAGANER
CAGANERS
CAGE
CAGED
CAGEFUL
CAGEFULS
CAGELIKE
CAGELING
CAGELINGS
CAGER
CAGERS
CAGES
CAGEWORK
CAGEWORKS
CAGEY
CAGEYNESS
CAGIER
CAGIEST
CAGILY
CAGINESS
CAGING
CAGMAG
CAGMAGGED
CAGMAGS
CAGOT
CAGOTS
CAGOUL
CAGOULE
CAGOULES
CAGOULS
CAGS
CAGY
CAGYNESS
CAHIER
CAHIERS
CAHOOT
CAHOOTS
CAHOUN
CAHOUNS
CAHOW
CAHOWS
CAID
CAIDS
CAILLACH
CAILLACHS
CAILLE
CAILLEACH
CAILLES
CAILLIACH
CAIMAC
CAIMACAM
CAIMACAMS
CAIMACS
CAIMAN
CAIMANS
CAIN
CAINS
CAIQUE
CAIQUES
CAIRD
CAIRDS
CAIRN
CAIRNED
CAIRNGORM
CAIRNIER
CAIRNIEST
CAIRNS
CAIRNY
CAISSON
CAISSONS
CAITIFF
CAITIFFS
CAITIVE
CAITIVES
CAJAPUT
CAJAPUTS
CAJEPUT
CAJEPUTS
CAJOLE
CAJOLED
CAJOLER
CAJOLERS
CAJOLERY
CAJOLES
CAJOLING
CAJON
CAJONES
CAJUN
CAJUPUT
CAJUPUTS
CAKE
CAKEAGE
CAKEAGES
CAKEBOX
CAKEBOXES
CAKED
CAKEHOLE
CAKEHOLES
CAKES
CAKEWALK
CAKEWALKS
CAKEY
CAKIER
CAKIEST
CAKINESS
CAKING
CAKINGS
CAKY
CAL
CALABASH
CALABAZA

C

CALABAZAS
CALABOGUS
CALABOOSE
CALABRESE
CALADIUM
CALADIUMS
CALALOO
CALALOOS
CALALU
CALALUS
CALAMANCO
CALAMANSI
CALAMAR
CALAMARI
CALAMARIS
CALAMARS
CALAMARY
CALAMATA
CALAMATAS
CALAMI
CALAMINE
CALAMINED
CALAMINES
CALAMINT
CALAMINTS
CALAMITE
CALAMITES
CALAMITY
CALAMUS
CALAMUSES
CALANDO
CALANDRIA
CALANTHE
CALANTHES
CALASH
CALASHES
CALATHEA
CALATHEAS
CALATHI
CALATHOS
CALATHUS
CALAVANCE
CALCANEA
CALCANEAL
CALCANEAN
CALCANEI
CALCANEUM
CALCANEUS
CALCAR
CALCARATE
CALCARIA
CALCARINE
CALCARS
CALCEATE
CALCEATED
CALCEATES
CALCED
CALCEDONY
CALCES
CALCIC
CALCICOLE
CALCIFIC
CALCIFIED
CALCIFIES
CALCIFUGE
CALCIFY
CALCIMINE
CALCINE
CALCINED
CALCINES
CALCINING
CALCITE
CALCITES
CALCITIC
CALCIUM
CALCIUMS
CALCRETE
CALCRETES
CALCSPAR
CALCSPARS
CALCTUFA
CALCTUFAS
CALCTUFF
CALCTUFFS
CALCULAR
CALCULARY
CALCULATE
CALCULI
CALCULOSE
CALCULOUS
CALCULUS
CALDARIA
CALDARIUM
CALDERA
CALDERAS
CALDRON
CALDRONS
CALECHE
CALECHES
CALEFIED
CALEFIES
CALEFY
CALEFYING
CALEMBOUR
CALENDAL
CALENDAR
CALENDARS
CALENDER
CALENDERS
CALENDRER
CALENDRIC
CALENDRY
CALENDS
CALENDULA
CALENTURE
CALESA
CALESAS
CALESCENT
CALF
CALFDOZER
CALFHOOD
CALFHOODS
CALFLESS
CALFLICK
CALFLICKS
CALFLIKE
CALFS
CALFSKIN
CALFSKINS
CALIATOUR
CALIBER
CALIBERED
CALIBERS
CALIBRATE
CALIBRE
CALIBRED
CALIBRES
CALICES
CALICHE
CALICHES
CALICLE
CALICLES
CALICO
CALICOES
CALICOS
CALICULAR
CALID
CALIDITY
CALIF
CALIFATE
CALIFATES
CALIFONT
CALIFONTS
CALIFS
CALIGO
CALIGOES
CALIGOS
CALIMA
CALIMAS
CALIMOCHO
CALIOLOGY
CALIPASH
CALIPEE
CALIPEES
CALIPER
CALIPERED
CALIPERS
CALIPH
CALIPHAL
CALIPHATE
CALIPHS
CALISAYA
CALISAYAS
CALIVER
CALIVERS
CALIX
CALIXES
CALK
CALKED
CALKER
CALKERS
CALKIN
CALKING
CALKINGS
CALKINS
CALKS
CALL
CALLA
CALLABLE
CALLAIDES
CALLAIS
CALLALOO
CALLALOOS
CALLALOU
CALLALOUS
CALLAN
CALLANS
CALLANT
CALLANTS
CALLAS
CALLBACK
CALLBACKS
CALLBOARD
CALLBOY
CALLBOYS
CALLED
CALLEE
CALLEES
CALLER
CALLERS
CALLET
CALLETS
CALLID
CALLIDITY
CALLIGRAM
CALLING
CALLINGS
CALLIOPE
CALLIOPES
CALLIPASH
CALLIPEE
CALLIPEES
CALLIPER
CALLIPERS
CALLOP
CALLOPS
CALLOSE
CALLOSES
CALLOSITY
CALLOUS
CALLOUSED
CALLOUSES
CALLOUSLY
CALLOUT
CALLOUTS
CALLOW
CALLOWER
CALLOWEST
CALLOWLY
CALLOWS

CALLS
CALLTIME
CALLTIMES
CALLUNA
CALLUNAS
CALLUS
CALLUSED
CALLUSES
CALLUSING
CALM
CALMANT
CALMANTS
CALMATIVE
CALMED
CALMER
CALMEST
CALMIER
CALMIEST
CALMING
CALMINGLY
CALMINGS
CALMLY
CALMNESS
CALMS
CALMSTANE
CALMSTONE
CALMY
CALO
CALOMEL
CALOMELS
CALORIC
CALORICS
CALORIE
CALORIES
CALORIFIC
CALORISE
CALORISED
CALORISES
CALORIST
CALORISTS
CALORIZE
CALORIZED
CALORIZES
CALORY
CALOS
CALOTTE
CALOTTES
CALOTYPE
CALOTYPES
CALOYER
CALOYERS
CALP
CALPA
CALPAC
CALPACK
CALPACKS
CALPACS
CALPAIN
CALPAINS
CALPAS
CALPS
CALQUE
CALQUED
CALQUES
CALQUING
CALS
CALTHA
CALTHAS
CALTHROP
CALTHROPS
CALTRAP
CALTRAPS
CALTROP
CALTROPS
CALUMBA
CALUMBAS
CALUMET
CALUMETS
CALUMNIED
CALUMNIES
CALUMNY
CALUTRON
CALUTRONS
CALVADOS
CALVARIA
CALVARIAE
CALVARIAL
CALVARIAN
CALVARIAS
CALVARIES
CALVARIUM
CALVARY
CALVE
CALVED
CALVER
CALVERED
CALVERING
CALVERS
CALVES
CALVING
CALVITIES
CALX
CALXES
CALYCATE
CALYCEAL
CALYCES
CALYCINAL
CALYCINE
CALYCLE
CALYCLED
CALYCLES
CALYCOID
CALYCULAR
CALYCULE
CALYCULES
CALYCULI
CALYCULUS
CALYPSO
CALYPSOES
CALYPSOS
CALYPTER
CALYPTERA
CALYPTERS
CALYPTRA
CALYPTRAS
CALYX
CALYXES
CALZONE
CALZONES
CALZONI
CAM
CAMA
CAMAIEU
CAMAIEUX
CAMAIL
CAMAILED
CAMAILS
CAMAN
CAMANACHD
CAMANS
CAMARILLA
CAMARON
CAMARONS
CAMAS
CAMASES
CAMASH
CAMASHES
CAMASS
CAMASSES
CAMBER
CAMBERED
CAMBERING
CAMBERS
CAMBIA
CAMBIAL
CAMBIFORM
CAMBISM
CAMBISMS
CAMBIST
CAMBISTRY
CAMBISTS
CAMBIUM
CAMBIUMS
CAMBOGE
CAMBOGES
CAMBOGIA
CAMBOGIAS
CAMBOOSE
CAMBOOSES
CAMBREL
CAMBRELS
CAMBRIC
CAMBRICS
CAMCORD
CAMCORDED
CAMCORDER
CAMCORDS
CAME
CAMEL
CAMELBACK
CAMELEER
CAMELEERS
CAMELEON
CAMELEONS
CAMELHAIR
CAMELIA
CAMELIAS
CAMELID
CAMELIDS
CAMELINE
CAMELINES
CAMELISH
CAMELLIA
CAMELLIAS
CAMELLIKE
CAMELOID
CAMELOIDS
CAMELOT
CAMELOTS
CAMELRIES
CAMELRY
CAMELS
CAMEO
CAMEOED
CAMEOING
CAMEOS
CAMERA
CAMERAE
CAMERAL
CAMERAMAN
CAMERAMEN
CAMERAS
CAMERATED
CAMES
CAMESE
CAMESES
CAMI
CAMION
CAMIONS
CAMIS
CAMISA
CAMISADE
CAMISADES
CAMISADO
CAMISADOS
CAMISAS
CAMISE
CAMISES
CAMISIA
CAMISIAS
CAMISOLE
CAMISOLES
CAMLET
CAMLETS
CAMMED
CAMMIE
CAMMIES
CAMMING
CAMO
CAMOGIE

C

CAMOGIES
CAMOMILE
CAMOMILES
CAMOODI
CAMOODIS
CAMORRA
CAMORRAS
CAMORRIST
CAMOS
CAMOTE
CAMOTES
CAMOUFLET
CAMP
CAMPAGNA
CAMPAGNAS
CAMPAGNE
CAMPAIGN
CAMPAIGNS
CAMPANA
CAMPANAS
CAMPANERO
CAMPANILE
CAMPANILI
CAMPANIST
CAMPANULA
CAMPCRAFT
CAMPEACHY
CAMPEADOR
CAMPED
CAMPER
CAMPERIES
CAMPERS
CAMPERY
CAMPESINO
CAMPEST
CAMPFIRE
CAMPFIRES
CAMPHANE
CAMPHANES
CAMPHENE
CAMPHENES
CAMPHINE
CAMPHINES
CAMPHIRE
CAMPHIRES
CAMPHOL
CAMPHOLS
CAMPHONE
CAMPHONES
CAMPHOR
CAMPHORIC
CAMPHORS
CAMPI
CAMPIER
CAMPIEST
CAMPILY
CAMPINESS
CAMPING
CAMPINGS
CAMPION
CAMPIONS
CAMPLE
CAMPLED
CAMPLES
CAMPLING
CAMPLY
CAMPNESS
CAMPO
CAMPODEID
CAMPONG
CAMPONGS
CAMPOREE
CAMPOREES
CAMPOS
CAMPOUT
CAMPOUTS
CAMPS
CAMPSHIRT
CAMPSITE
CAMPSITES
CAMPSTOOL
CAMPUS
CAMPUSED
CAMPUSES
CAMPUSING
CAMPY
CAMS
CAMSHAFT
CAMSHAFTS
CAMSHO
CAMSHOCH
CAMSTAIRY
CAMSTANE
CAMSTANES
CAMSTEARY
CAMSTONE
CAMSTONES
CAMUS
CAMUSES
CAMWHORE
CAMWHORED
CAMWHORES
CAMWOOD
CAMWOODS
CAN
CANADA
CANADAS
CANAIGRE
CANAIGRES
CANAILLE
CANAILLES
CANAKIN
CANAKINS
CANAL
CANALBOAT
CANALED
CANALING
CANALISE
CANALISED
CANALISES
CANALIZE
CANALIZED
CANALIZES
CANALLED
CANALLER
CANALLERS
CANALLING
CANALS
CANAPE
CANAPES
CANARD
CANARDS
CANARIED
CANARIES
CANARY
CANARYING
CANASTA
CANASTAS
CANASTER
CANASTERS
CANBANK
CANBANKS
CANCAN
CANCANS
CANCEL
CANCELBOT
CANCELED
CANCELEER
CANCELER
CANCELERS
CANCELIER
CANCELING
CANCELLED
CANCELLER
CANCELLI
CANCELS
CANCER
CANCERATE
CANCERED
CANCEROUS
CANCERS
CANCHA
CANCHAS
CANCRINE
CANCROID
CANCROIDS
CANDELA
CANDELAS
CANDENT
CANDID
CANDIDA
CANDIDACY
CANDIDAL
CANDIDAS
CANDIDATE
CANDIDER
CANDIDEST
CANDIDLY
CANDIDS
CANDIE
CANDIED
CANDIES
CANDIRU
CANDIRUS
CANDLE
CANDLED
CANDLELIT
CANDLENUT
CANDLEPIN
CANDLER
CANDLERS
CANDLES
CANDLING
CANDOCK
CANDOCKS
CANDOR
CANDORS
CANDOUR
CANDOURS
CANDY
CANDYGRAM
CANDYING
CANDYMAN
CANDYMEN
CANDYTUFT
CANE
CANEBRAKE
CANED
CANEFRUIT
CANEGRUB
CANEGRUBS
CANEH
CANEHS
CANELLA
CANELLAS
CANELLINI
CANEPHOR
CANEPHORA
CANEPHORE
CANEPHORS
CANER
CANERS
CANES
CANESCENT
CANEWARE
CANEWARES
CANFIELD
CANFIELDS
CANFUL
CANFULS
CANG
CANGLE
CANGLED
CANGLES
CANGLING
CANGS
CANGUE
CANGUES
CANICULAR
CANID

CANIDS
CANIER
CANIEST
CANIKIN
CANIKINS
CANINE
CANINES
CANING
CANINGS
CANINITY
CANISTEL
CANISTELS
CANISTER
CANISTERS
CANITIES
CANKER
CANKERED
CANKERIER
CANKERING
CANKEROUS
CANKERS
CANKERY
CANKLE
CANKLES
CANN
CANNA
CANNABIC
CANNABIN
CANNABINS
CANNABIS
CANNACH
CANNACHS
CANNAE
CANNAS
CANNED
CANNEL
CANNELON
CANNELONI
CANNELONS
CANNELS
CANNELURE
CANNER
CANNERIES
CANNERS
CANNERY
CANNIBAL
CANNIBALS
CANNIE
CANNIER
CANNIEST
CANNIKIN
CANNIKINS
CANNILY
CANNINESS
CANNING
CANNINGS
CANNISTER
CANNOLI
CANNOLIS
CANNON
CANNONADE
CANNONED
CANNONEER
CANNONIER
CANNONING
CANNONRY
CANNONS
CANNOT
CANNS
CANNULA
CANNULAE
CANNULAR
CANNULAS
CANNULATE
CANNY
CANOE
CANOEABLE
CANOED
CANOEING
CANOEINGS
CANOEIST
CANOEISTS
CANOEMAN
CANOEMEN
CANOER
CANOERS
CANOES
CANOEWOOD
CANOLA
CANOLAS
CANON
CANONESS
CANONIC
CANONICAL
CANONISE
CANONISED
CANONISER
CANONISES
CANONIST
CANONISTS
CANONIZE
CANONIZED
CANONIZER
CANONIZES
CANONRIES
CANONRY
CANONS
CANOODLE
CANOODLED
CANOODLER
CANOODLES
CANOPIC
CANOPIED
CANOPIES
CANOPY
CANOPYING
CANOROUS
CANS
CANSFUL
CANSO
CANSOS
CANST
CANSTICK
CANSTICKS
CANT
CANTABANK
CANTABILE
CANTAL
CANTALA
CANTALAS
CANTALOUP
CANTALS
CANTAR
CANTARS
CANTATA
CANTATAS
CANTATE
CANTATES
CANTDOG
CANTDOGS
CANTED
CANTEEN
CANTEENS
CANTER
CANTERED
CANTERING
CANTERS
CANTEST
CANTHAL
CANTHARI
CANTHARID
CANTHARIS
CANTHARUS
CANTHI
CANTHIC
CANTHITIS
CANTHOOK
CANTHOOKS
CANTHUS
CANTIC
CANTICLE
CANTICLES
CANTICO
CANTICOED
CANTICOS
CANTICOY
CANTICOYS
CANTICUM
CANTICUMS
CANTIER
CANTIEST
CANTILENA
CANTILY
CANTINA
CANTINAS
CANTINESS
CANTING
CANTINGLY
CANTINGS
CANTION
CANTIONS
CANTLE
CANTLED
CANTLES
CANTLET
CANTLETS
CANTLING
CANTO
CANTON
CANTONAL
CANTONED
CANTONING
CANTONISE
CANTONIZE
CANTONS
CANTOR
CANTORIAL
CANTORIS
CANTORS
CANTOS
CANTRAIP
CANTRAIPS
CANTRAP
CANTRAPS
CANTRED
CANTREDS
CANTREF
CANTREFS
CANTRIP
CANTRIPS
CANTS
CANTUS
CANTUSES
CANTY
CANULA
CANULAE
CANULAR
CANULAS
CANULATE
CANULATED
CANULATES
CANVAS
CANVASED
CANVASER
CANVASERS
CANVASES
CANVASING
CANVASS
CANVASSED
CANVASSER
CANVASSES
CANY
CANYON
CANYONEER
CANYONING
CANYONS
CANZONA
CANZONAS
CANZONE
CANZONES

C

C

CANZONET
CANZONETS
CANZONI
CAP
CAPA
CAPABLE
CAPABLER
CAPABLEST
CAPABLY
CAPACIOUS
CAPACITOR
CAPACITY
CAPARISON
CAPAS
CAPCOM
CAPCOMS
CAPE
CAPED
CAPEESH
CAPELAN
CAPELANS
CAPELET
CAPELETS
CAPELIKE
CAPELIN
CAPELINE
CAPELINES
CAPELINS
CAPELLET
CAPELLETS
CAPELLINE
CAPELLINI
CAPER
CAPERED
CAPERER
CAPERERS
CAPERING
CAPERS
CAPES
CAPESKIN
CAPESKINS
CAPEWORK
CAPEWORKS
CAPEX
CAPEXES
CAPFUL
CAPFULS
CAPH
CAPHS
CAPI
CAPIAS
CAPIASES
CAPICHE
CAPICOLLA
CAPICOLLO
CAPILLARY
CAPING
CAPISCE
CAPISH
CAPITA
CAPITAL
CAPITALLY
CAPITALS
CAPITAN
CAPITANI
CAPITANO
CAPITANOS
CAPITANS
CAPITATE
CAPITATED
CAPITATES
CAPITAYN
CAPITAYNS
CAPITELLA
CAPITOL
CAPITOLS
CAPITULA
CAPITULAR
CAPITULUM
CAPIZ
CAPIZES
CAPLE
CAPLES
CAPLESS
CAPLET
CAPLETS
CAPLIKE
CAPLIN
CAPLINS
CAPMAKER
CAPMAKERS
CAPO
CAPOCCHIA
CAPOEIRA
CAPOEIRAS
CAPON
CAPONATA
CAPONATAS
CAPONIER
CAPONIERE
CAPONIERS
CAPONISE
CAPONISED
CAPONISES
CAPONIZE
CAPONIZED
CAPONIZES
CAPONS
CAPORAL
CAPORALS
CAPOS
CAPOT
CAPOTASTO
CAPOTE
CAPOTES
CAPOTS
CAPOTTED
CAPOTTING
CAPOUCH
CAPOUCHES
CAPPED
CAPPER
CAPPERS
CAPPING
CAPPINGS
CAPRATE
CAPRATES
CAPRESE
CAPRESES
CAPRI
CAPRIC
CAPRICCI
CAPRICCIO
CAPRICE
CAPRICES
CAPRID
CAPRIDS
CAPRIFIED
CAPRIFIES
CAPRIFIG
CAPRIFIGS
CAPRIFOIL
CAPRIFOLE
CAPRIFORM
CAPRIFY
CAPRINE
CAPRIOLE
CAPRIOLED
CAPRIOLES
CAPRIS
CAPROATE
CAPROATES
CAPROCK
CAPROCKS
CAPROIC
CAPRYLATE
CAPRYLIC
CAPS
CAPSAICIN
CAPSICIN
CAPSICINS
CAPSICUM
CAPSICUMS
CAPSID
CAPSIDAL
CAPSIDS
CAPSIZAL
CAPSIZALS
CAPSIZE
CAPSIZED
CAPSIZES
CAPSIZING
CAPSOMER
CAPSOMERE
CAPSOMERS
CAPSTAN
CAPSTANS
CAPSTONE
CAPSTONES
CAPSULAR
CAPSULARY
CAPSULATE
CAPSULE
CAPSULED
CAPSULES
CAPSULING
CAPSULISE
CAPSULIZE
CAPTAIN
CAPTAINCY
CAPTAINED
CAPTAINRY
CAPTAINS
CAPTAN
CAPTANS
CAPTCHA
CAPTCHAS
CAPTION
CAPTIONED
CAPTIONS
CAPTIOUS
CAPTIVATE
CAPTIVE
CAPTIVED
CAPTIVES
CAPTIVING
CAPTIVITY
CAPTOPRIL
CAPTOR
CAPTORS
CAPTURE
CAPTURED
CAPTURER
CAPTURERS
CAPTURES
CAPTURING
CAPUCCIO
CAPUCCIOS
CAPUCHE
CAPUCHED
CAPUCHES
CAPUCHIN
CAPUCHINS
CAPUERA
CAPUERAS
CAPUL
CAPULS
CAPUT
CAPYBARA
CAPYBARAS
CAR
CARABAO
CARABAOS
CARABID
CARABIDS
CARABIN
CARABINE
CARABINER
CARABINES
CARABINS

CARACAL
CARACALS
CARACARA
CARACARAS
CARACK
CARACKS
CARACOL
CARACOLE
CARACOLED
CARACOLER
CARACOLES
CARACOLS
CARACT
CARACTS
CARACUL
CARACULS
CARAFE
CARAFES
CARAGANA
CARAGANAS
CARAGEEN
CARAGEENS
CARAMBA
CARAMBOLA
CARAMBOLE
CARAMEL
CARAMELS
CARANGID
CARANGIDS
CARANGOID
CARANNA
CARANNAS
CARAP
CARAPACE
CARAPACED
CARAPACES
CARAPAX
CARAPAXES
CARAPS
CARASSOW
CARASSOWS
CARAT
CARATE
CARATES
CARATS
CARAUNA
CARAUNAS
CARAVAN
CARAVANCE
CARAVANED
CARAVANER
CARAVANS
CARAVEL
CARAVELLE
CARAVELS
CARAWAY
CARAWAYS
CARB
CARBACHOL
CARBAMATE
CARBAMIC
CARBAMIDE
CARBAMINO
CARBAMOYL
CARBAMYL
CARBAMYLS
CARBANION
CARBARN
CARBARNS
CARBARYL
CARBARYLS
CARBAZOLE
CARBEEN
CARBEENS
CARBENE
CARBENES
CARBIDE
CARBIDES
CARBIDOPA
CARBIES
CARBINE
CARBINEER
CARBINES
CARBINIER
CARBINOL
CARBINOLS
CARBO
CARBOLIC
CARBOLICS
CARBOLISE
CARBOLIZE
CARBON
CARBONADE
CARBONADO
CARBONARA
CARBONATE
CARBONIC
CARBONISE
CARBONIUM
CARBONIZE
CARBONOUS
CARBONS
CARBONYL
CARBONYLS
CARBORA
CARBORAS
CARBORNE
CARBOS
CARBOXYL
CARBOXYLS
CARBOY
CARBOYED
CARBOYS
CARBS
CARBUNCLE
CARBURATE
CARBURET
CARBURETS
CARBURISE
CARBURIZE
CARBY
CARCAJOU
CARCAJOUS
CARCAKE
CARCAKES
CARCANET
CARCANETS
CARCASE
CARCASED
CARCASES
CARCASING
CARCASS
CARCASSED
CARCASSES
CARCEL
CARCELS
CARCERAL
CARCINOID
CARCINOMA
CARD
CARDAMINE
CARDAMOM
CARDAMOMS
CARDAMON
CARDAMONS
CARDAMUM
CARDAMUMS
CARDAN
CARDBOARD
CARDCASE
CARDCASES
CARDECU
CARDECUE
CARDECUES
CARDECUS
CARDED
CARDER
CARDERS
CARDI
CARDIA
CARDIAC
CARDIACAL
CARDIACS
CARDIAE
CARDIALGY
CARDIAS
CARDIE
CARDIES
CARDIGAN
CARDIGANS
CARDINAL
CARDINALS
CARDING
CARDINGS
CARDIO
CARDIOID
CARDIOIDS
CARDIOS
CARDIS
CARDITIC
CARDITIS
CARDON
CARDONS
CARDOON
CARDOONS
CARDPHONE
CARDPUNCH
CARDS
CARDSHARP
CARDUUS
CARDUUSES
CARDY
CARE
CARED
CAREEN
CAREENAGE
CAREENED
CAREENER
CAREENERS
CAREENING
CAREENS
CAREER
CAREERED
CAREERER
CAREERERS
CAREERING
CAREERISM
CAREERIST
CAREERS
CAREFREE
CAREFUL
CAREFULLY
CAREGIVER
CARELESS
CARELINE
CARELINES
CAREME
CAREMES
CARER
CARERS
CARES
CARESS
CARESSED
CARESSER
CARESSERS
CARESSES
CARESSING
CARESSIVE
CARET
CARETAKE
CARETAKEN
CARETAKER
CARETAKES
CARETOOK
CARETS
CAREWARE
CAREWARES
CAREWORN
CAREX
CARFARE

C

CARFARES
CARFAX
CARFAXES
CARFOX
CARFOXES
CARFUFFLE
CARFUL
CARFULS
CARGEESE
CARGO
CARGOED
CARGOES
CARGOING
CARGOOSE
CARGOS
CARHOP
CARHOPPED
CARHOPS
CARIACOU
CARIACOUS
CARIAMA
CARIAMAS
CARIBE
CARIBES
CARIBOO
CARIBOOS
CARIBOU
CARIBOUS
CARICES
CARIED
CARIERE
CARIERES
CARIES
CARILLON
CARILLONS
CARINA
CARINAE
CARINAL
CARINAS
CARINATE
CARINATED
CARING
CARINGLY
CARINGS
CARIOCA
CARIOCAS
CARIOLE
CARIOLES
CARIOSE
CARIOSITY
CARIOUS
CARITAS
CARITASES
CARITATES
CARJACK
CARJACKED
CARJACKER
CARJACKS
CARJACOU
CARJACOUS
CARK
CARKED
CARKING
CARKS
CARL
CARLE
CARLES
CARLESS
CARLIN
CARLINE
CARLINES
CARLING
CARLINGS
CARLINS
CARLISH
CARLOAD
CARLOADS
CARLOCK
CARLOCKS
CARLOT
CARLOTS
CARLS
CARMAKER
CARMAKERS
CARMAN
CARMELITE
CARMEN
CARMINE
CARMINES
CARN
CARNAGE
CARNAGES
CARNAHUBA
CARNAL
CARNALISE
CARNALISM
CARNALIST
CARNALITY
CARNALIZE
CARNALLED
CARNALLY
CARNALS
CARNAROLI
CARNATION
CARNAUBA
CARNAUBAS
CARNELIAN
CARNEOUS
CARNET
CARNETS
CARNEY
CARNEYED
CARNEYING
CARNEYS
CARNIE
CARNIED
CARNIER
CARNIES
CARNIEST
CARNIFEX
CARNIFIED
CARNIFIES
CARNIFY
CARNITINE
CARNIVAL
CARNIVALS
CARNIVORA
CARNIVORE
CARNIVORY
CARNOSAUR
CARNOSE
CARNOSITY
CARNOTITE
CARNS
CARNY
CARNYING
CARNYX
CARNYXES
CAROACH
CAROACHES
CAROB
CAROBS
CAROCH
CAROCHE
CAROCHES
CAROL
CAROLED
CAROLER
CAROLERS
CAROLI
CAROLING
CAROLINGS
CAROLLED
CAROLLER
CAROLLERS
CAROLLING
CAROLS
CAROLUS
CAROLUSES
CAROM
CAROMED
CAROMEL
CAROMELS
CAROMING
CAROMS
CARON
CARONS
CAROTENE
CAROTENES
CAROTID
CAROTIDAL
CAROTIDS
CAROTIN
CAROTINS
CAROUSAL
CAROUSALS
CAROUSE
CAROUSED
CAROUSEL
CAROUSELS
CAROUSER
CAROUSERS
CAROUSES
CAROUSING
CARP
CARPACCIO
CARPAL
CARPALE
CARPALES
CARPALIA
CARPALS
CARPED
CARPEL
CARPELS
CARPENTER
CARPENTRY
CARPER
CARPERS
CARPET
CARPETBAG
CARPETED
CARPETING
CARPETS
CARPHONE
CARPHONES
CARPI
CARPING
CARPINGLY
CARPINGS
CARPLIKE
CARPOLOGY
CARPOOL
CARPOOLED
CARPOOLER
CARPOOLS
CARPORT
CARPORTS
CARPS
CARPUS
CARR
CARRACK
CARRACKS
CARRACT
CARRACTS
CARRAGEEN
CARRAT
CARRATS
CARRAWAY
CARRAWAYS
CARRECT
CARRECTS
CARREFOUR
CARREL
CARRELL
CARRELLS
CARRELS
CARRIAGE
CARRIAGES
CARRICK
CARRIED

CARRIER
CARRIERS
CARRIES
CARRIOLE
CARRIOLES
CARRION
CARRIONS
CARRITCH
CARROCH
CARROCHES
CARROM
CARROMED
CARROMING
CARROMS
CARRON
CARRONADE
CARROT
CARROTIER
CARROTIN
CARROTINS
CARROTS
CARROTTOP
CARROTY
CARROUSEL
CARRS
CARRY
CARRYALL
CARRYALLS
CARRYBACK
CARRYCOT
CARRYCOTS
CARRYING
CARRYON
CARRYONS
CARRYOUT
CARRYOUTS
CARRYOVER
CARRYTALE
CARS
CARSE
CARSES
CARSEY
CARSEYS
CARSHARE
CARSHARED
CARSHARES
CARSICK
CARSPIEL
CARSPIELS
CART
CARTA
CARTABLE
CARTAGE
CARTAGES
CARTAS
CARTE
CARTED
CARTEL
CARTELISE
CARTELISM
CARTELIST
CARTELIZE
CARTELS
CARTER
CARTERS
CARTES
CARTFUL
CARTFULS
CARTHORSE
CARTILAGE
CARTING
CARTLOAD
CARTLOADS
CARTOGRAM
CARTOLOGY
CARTON
CARTONAGE
CARTONED
CARTONING
CARTONS
CARTOON
CARTOONED
CARTOONS
CARTOONY
CARTOP
CARTOPPER
CARTOUCH
CARTOUCHE
CARTRIDGE
CARTROAD
CARTROADS
CARTS
CARTULARY
CARTWAY
CARTWAYS
CARTWHEEL
CARUCAGE
CARUCAGES
CARUCATE
CARUCATES
CARUNCLE
CARUNCLES
CARVACROL
CARVE
CARVED
CARVEL
CARVELS
CARVEN
CARVER
CARVERIES
CARVERS
CARVERY
CARVES
CARVIES
CARVING
CARVINGS
CARVY
CARWASH
CARWASHES
CARYATIC
CARYATID
CARYATIDS
CARYOPSES
CARYOPSIS
CARYOTIN
CARYOTINS
CASA
CASABA
CASABAS
CASAS
CASAVA
CASAVAS
CASBAH
CASBAHS
CASCABEL
CASCABELS
CASCABLE
CASCABLES
CASCADE
CASCADED
CASCADES
CASCADING
CASCADURA
CASCARA
CASCARAS
CASCHROM
CASCHROMS
CASCO
CASCOS
CASE
CASEASE
CASEASES
CASEATE
CASEATED
CASEATES
CASEATING
CASEATION
CASEBOOK
CASEBOOKS
CASEBOUND
CASED
CASEFIED
CASEFIES
CASEFY
CASEFYING
CASEIC
CASEIN
CASEINATE
CASEINS
CASELAW
CASELAWS
CASELOAD
CASELOADS
CASEMAKER
CASEMAN
CASEMATE
CASEMATED
CASEMATES
CASEMEN
CASEMENT
CASEMENTS
CASEMIX
CASEMIXES
CASEOSE
CASEOSES
CASEOUS
CASERN
CASERNE
CASERNES
CASERNS
CASES
CASETTE
CASETTES
CASEVAC
CASEVACED
CASEVACS
CASEWORK
CASEWORKS
CASEWORM
CASEWORMS
CASH
CASHABLE
CASHAW
CASHAWS
CASHBACK
CASHBACKS
CASHBOOK
CASHBOOKS
CASHBOX
CASHBOXES
CASHED
CASHES
CASHEW
CASHEWS
CASHIER
CASHIERED
CASHIERER
CASHIERS
CASHING
CASHLESS
CASHMERE
CASHMERES
CASHOO
CASHOOS
CASHPOINT
CASHSPIEL
CASIMERE
CASIMERES
CASIMIRE
CASIMIRES
CASING
CASINGS
CASINI
CASINO
CASINOS
CASITA
CASITAS
CASK
CASKED
CASKET

C

CASKETED
CASKETING
CASKETS
CASKIER
CASKIEST
CASKING
CASKS
CASKSTAND
CASKY
CASPASE
CASPASES
CASQUE
CASQUED
CASQUES
CASSABA
CASSABAS
CASSAREEP
CASSATA
CASSATAS
CASSATION
CASSAVA
CASSAVAS
CASSENA
CASSENAS
CASSENE
CASSENES
CASSEROLE
CASSETTE
CASSETTES
CASSIA
CASSIAS
CASSIE
CASSIES
CASSIMERE
CASSINA
CASSINAS
CASSINE
CASSINES
CASSINGLE
CASSINO
CASSINOS
CASSIOPE
CASSIOPES
CASSIS
CASSISES
CASSOCK
CASSOCKED
CASSOCKS
CASSONADE
CASSONE
CASSONES
CASSOULET
CASSOWARY
CASSPIR
CASSPIRS
CAST
CASTABLE
CASTANET
CASTANETS
CASTAWAY
CASTAWAYS
CASTE
CASTED
CASTEISM
CASTEISMS
CASTELESS
CASTELLA
CASTELLAN
CASTELLUM
CASTER
CASTERED
CASTERS
CASTES
CASTIGATE
CASTING
CASTINGS
CASTLE
CASTLED
CASTLES
CASTLING
CASTLINGS
CASTOCK
CASTOCKS
CASTOFF
CASTOFFS
CASTOR
CASTOREUM
CASTORIES
CASTORS
CASTORY
CASTRAL
CASTRATE
CASTRATED
CASTRATER
CASTRATES
CASTRATI
CASTRATO
CASTRATOR
CASTRATOS
CASTS
CASUAL
CASUALISE
CASUALISM
CASUALIZE
CASUALLY
CASUALS
CASUALTY
CASUARINA
CASUIST
CASUISTIC
CASUISTRY
CASUISTS
CASUS
CAT
CATABASES
CATABASIS
CATABATIC
CATABOLIC
CATACLASM
CATACLYSM
CATACOMB
CATACOMBS
CATAFALCO
CATAGEN
CATAGENS
CATALASE
CATALASES
CATALATIC
CATALEPSY
CATALEXES
CATALEXIS
CATALO
CATALOES
CATALOG
CATALOGED
CATALOGER
CATALOGIC
CATALOGNE
CATALOGS
CATALOGUE
CATALOS
CATALPA
CATALPAS
CATALYSE
CATALYSED
CATALYSER
CATALYSES
CATALYSIS
CATALYST
CATALYSTS
CATALYTIC
CATALYZE
CATALYZED
CATALYZER
CATALYZES
CATAMARAN
CATAMENIA
CATAMITE
CATAMITES
CATAMOUNT
CATAPAN
CATAPANS
CATAPHOR
CATAPHORA
CATAPHORS
CATAPHYLL
CATAPLASM
CATAPLEXY
CATAPULT
CATAPULTS
CATARACT
CATARACTS
CATARHINE
CATARRH
CATARRHAL
CATARRHS
CATASTA
CATASTAS
CATATONIA
CATATONIC
CATATONY
CATAWBA
CATAWBAS
CATBIRD
CATBIRDS
CATBOAT
CATBOATS
CATBRIAR
CATBRIARS
CATBRIER
CATBRIERS
CATCALL
CATCALLED
CATCALLER
CATCALLS
CATCH
CATCHABLE
CATCHALL
CATCHALLS
CATCHCRY
CATCHED
CATCHEN
CATCHER
CATCHERS
CATCHES
CATCHFLY
CATCHIER
CATCHIEST
CATCHILY
CATCHING
CATCHINGS
CATCHLINE
CATCHMENT
CATCHPOLE
CATCHPOLL
CATCHT
CATCHUP
CATCHUPS
CATCHWEED
CATCHWORD
CATCHY
CATCLAW
CATCLAWS
CATCON
CATCONS
CATE
CATECHIN
CATECHINS
CATECHISE
CATECHISM
CATECHIST
CATECHIZE
CATECHOL
CATECHOLS
CATECHU
CATECHUS
CATEGORIC
CATEGORY
CATELOG
CATELOGS

CATENA
CATENAE
CATENANE
CATENANES
CATENARY
CATENAS
CATENATE
CATENATED
CATENATES
CATENOID
CATENOIDS
CATER
CATERAN
CATERANS
CATERED
CATERER
CATERERS
CATERESS
CATERING
CATERINGS
CATERS
CATERWAUL
CATES
CATFACE
CATFACES
CATFACING
CATFALL
CATFALLS
CATFIGHT
CATFIGHTS
CATFISH
CATFISHED
CATFISHES
CATFLAP
CATFLAPS
CATFOOD
CATFOODS
CATGUT
CATGUTS
CATHARISE
CATHARIZE
CATHARSES
CATHARSIS
CATHARTIC
CATHEAD
CATHEADS
CATHECT
CATHECTED
CATHECTIC
CATHECTS
CATHEDRA
CATHEDRAE
CATHEDRAL
CATHEDRAS
CATHEPSIN
CATHEPTIC
CATHETER
CATHETERS
CATHETUS
CATHEXES
CATHEXIS
CATHINONE
CATHISMA
CATHISMAS
CATHODAL
CATHODE
CATHODES
CATHODIC
CATHOLE
CATHOLES
CATHOLIC
CATHOLICS
CATHOLYTE
CATHOOD
CATHOODS
CATHOUSE
CATHOUSES
CATION
CATIONIC
CATIONS
CATJANG
CATJANGS
CATKIN
CATKINATE
CATKINS
CATLIKE
CATLIN
CATLING
CATLINGS
CATLINITE
CATLINS
CATMINT
CATMINTS
CATNAP
CATNAPER
CATNAPERS
CATNAPPED
CATNAPPER
CATNAPS
CATNEP
CATNEPS
CATNIP
CATNIPS
CATOLYTE
CATOLYTES
CATOPTRIC
CATRIGGED
CATS
CATSKIN
CATSKINS
CATSPAW
CATSPAWS
CATSUIT
CATSUITS
CATSUP
CATSUPS
CATTABU
CATTABUS
CATTAIL
CATTAILS
CATTALO
CATTALOES
CATTALOS
CATTED
CATTERIES
CATTERY
CATTIE
CATTIER
CATTIES
CATTIEST
CATTILY
CATTINESS
CATTING
CATTISH
CATTISHLY
CATTLE
CATTLEMAN
CATTLEMEN
CATTLEYA
CATTLEYAS
CATTY
CATWALK
CATWALKS
CATWORKS
CATWORM
CATWORMS
CAUCHEMAR
CAUCUS
CAUCUSED
CAUCUSES
CAUCUSING
CAUCUSSED
CAUCUSSES
CAUDA
CAUDAD
CAUDAE
CAUDAL
CAUDALLY
CAUDATE
CAUDATED
CAUDATES
CAUDATION
CAUDEX
CAUDEXES
CAUDICES
CAUDICLE
CAUDICLES
CAUDILLO
CAUDILLOS
CAUDLE
CAUDLED
CAUDLES
CAUDLING
CAUDRON
CAUDRONS
CAUF
CAUGHT
CAUK
CAUKER
CAUKERS
CAUKS
CAUL
CAULD
CAULDER
CAULDEST
CAULDRIFE
CAULDRON
CAULDRONS
CAULDS
CAULES
CAULICLE
CAULICLES
CAULICULI
CAULIFORM
CAULINARY
CAULINE
CAULIS
CAULK
CAULKED
CAULKER
CAULKERS
CAULKING
CAULKINGS
CAULKS
CAULOME
CAULOMES
CAULS
CAUM
CAUMED
CAUMING
CAUMS
CAUMSTANE
CAUMSTONE
CAUP
CAUPS
CAURI
CAURIS
CAUSA
CAUSABLE
CAUSAE
CAUSAL
CAUSALGIA
CAUSALGIC
CAUSALITY
CAUSALLY
CAUSALS
CAUSATION
CAUSATIVE
CAUSE
CAUSED
CAUSELESS
CAUSEN
CAUSER
CAUSERIE
CAUSERIES
CAUSERS
CAUSES
CAUSEWAY
CAUSEWAYS
CAUSEY

C

CAUSEYED
CAUSEYS
CAUSING
CAUSTIC
CAUSTICAL
CAUSTICS
CAUTEL
CAUTELOUS
CAUTELS
CAUTER
CAUTERANT
CAUTERIES
CAUTERISE
CAUTERISM
CAUTERIZE
CAUTERS
CAUTERY
CAUTION
CAUTIONED
CAUTIONER
CAUTIONRY
CAUTIONS
CAUTIOUS
CAUVES
CAVA
CAVALCADE
CAVALERO
CAVALEROS
CAVALETTI
CAVALIER
CAVALIERS
CAVALLA
CAVALLAS
CAVALLIES
CAVALLY
CAVALRIES
CAVALRY
CAVAS
CAVASS
CAVASSES
CAVATINA
CAVATINAS
CAVATINE
CAVE
CAVEAT
CAVEATED
CAVEATING
CAVEATOR
CAVEATORS
CAVEATS
CAVED
CAVEFISH
CAVEL
CAVELIKE
CAVELS
CAVEMAN
CAVEMEN
CAVENDISH
CAVEOLA
CAVEOLAE
CAVEOLAR
CAVER
CAVERN
CAVERNED
CAVERNING
CAVERNOUS
CAVERNS
CAVERS
CAVES
CAVESSON
CAVESSONS
CAVETTI
CAVETTO
CAVETTOS
CAVIAR
CAVIARE
CAVIARES
CAVIARIE
CAVIARIES
CAVIARS
CAVICORN
CAVICORNS
CAVIE
CAVIER
CAVIERS
CAVIES
CAVIL
CAVILED
CAVILER
CAVILERS
CAVILING
CAVILLED
CAVILLER
CAVILLERS
CAVILLING
CAVILS
CAVING
CAVINGS
CAVITARY
CAVITATE
CAVITATED
CAVITATES
CAVITIED
CAVITIES
CAVITY
CAVORT
CAVORTED
CAVORTER
CAVORTERS
CAVORTING
CAVORTS
CAVY
CAW
CAWED
CAWING
CAWINGS
CAWK
CAWKER
CAWKERS
CAWKS
CAWS
CAXON
CAXONS
CAY
CAYENNE
CAYENNED
CAYENNES
CAYMAN
CAYMANS
CAYS
CAYUSE
CAYUSES
CAZ
CAZH
CAZIQUE
CAZIQUES
CEANOTHUS
CEAS
CEASE
CEASED
CEASEFIRE
CEASELESS
CEASES
CEASING
CEASINGS
CEAZE
CEAZED
CEAZES
CEAZING
CEBADILLA
CEBID
CEBIDS
CEBOID
CEBOIDS
CECA
CECAL
CECALLY
CECILS
CECITIES
CECITIS
CECITISES
CECITY
CECROPIA
CECROPIAS
CECROPIN
CECROPINS
CECUM
CEDAR
CEDARBIRD
CEDARED
CEDARIER
CEDARIEST
CEDARN
CEDARS
CEDARWOOD
CEDARY
CEDE
CEDED
CEDER
CEDERS
CEDES
CEDI
CEDILLA
CEDILLAS
CEDING
CEDIS
CEDRATE
CEDRATES
CEDRINE
CEDULA
CEDULAS
CEE
CEES
CEIBA
CEIBAS
CEIL
CEILED
CEILER
CEILERS
CEILI
CEILIDH
CEILIDHS
CEILING
CEILINGED
CEILINGS
CEILIS
CEILS
CEINTURE
CEINTURES
CEL
CELADON
CELADONS
CELANDINE
CELEB
CELEBRANT
CELEBRATE
CELEBRITY
CELEBS
CELECOXIB
CELERIAC
CELERIACS
CELERIES
CELERITY
CELERY
CELESTA
CELESTAS
CELESTE
CELESTES
CELESTIAL
CELESTINE
CELESTITE
CELIAC
CELIACS
CELIBACY
CELIBATE
CELIBATES
CELIBATIC
CELL
CELLA
CELLAE

CELLAR
CELLARAGE
CELLARED
CELLARER
CELLARERS
CELLARET
CELLARETS
CELLARING
CELLARIST
CELLARMAN
CELLARMEN
CELLAROUS
CELLARS
CELLARWAY
CELLBLOCK
CELLED
CELLI
CELLING
CELLINGS
CELLIST
CELLISTS
CELLMATE
CELLMATES
CELLO
CELLOIDIN
CELLOS
CELLOSE
CELLOSES
CELLPHONE
CELLS
CELLULAR
CELLULARS
CELLULASE
CELLULE
CELLULES
CELLULITE
CELLULOID
CELLULOSE
CELLULOUS
CELOM
CELOMATA
CELOMIC
CELOMS
CELOSIA
CELOSIAS
CELOTEX
CELOTEXES
CELS
CELSITUDE
CELT
CELTS
CEMBALI
CEMBALIST
CEMBALO
CEMBALOS
CEMBRA
CEMBRAS
CEMENT
CEMENTA
CEMENTED
CEMENTER
CEMENTERS
CEMENTING
CEMENTITE
CEMENTS
CEMENTUM
CEMENTUMS
CEMETERY
CEMITARE
CEMITARES
CENACLE
CENACLES
CENDRE
CENOBITE
CENOBITES
CENOBITIC
CENOTAPH
CENOTAPHS
CENOTE
CENOTES
CENOZOIC
CENS
CENSE
CENSED
CENSER
CENSERS
CENSES
CENSING
CENSOR
CENSORED
CENSORIAL
CENSORIAN
CENSORING
CENSORS
CENSUAL
CENSURE
CENSURED
CENSURER
CENSURERS
CENSURES
CENSURING
CENSUS
CENSUSED
CENSUSES
CENSUSING
CENT
CENTAGE
CENTAGES
CENTAI
CENTAL
CENTALS
CENTARE
CENTARES
CENTAS
CENTAUR
CENTAUREA
CENTAURIC
CENTAURS
CENTAURY
CENTAVO
CENTAVOS
CENTENARY
CENTENIER
CENTER
CENTERED
CENTERING
CENTERS
CENTESES
CENTESIMI
CENTESIMO
CENTESIS
CENTIARE
CENTIARES
CENTIGRAM
CENTILE
CENTILES
CENTIME
CENTIMES
CENTIMO
CENTIMOS
CENTINEL
CENTINELL
CENTINELS
CENTIPEDE
CENTNER
CENTNERS
CENTO
CENTOIST
CENTOISTS
CENTONATE
CENTONEL
CENTONELL
CENTONELS
CENTONES
CENTONIST
CENTOS
CENTRA
CENTRAL
CENTRALER
CENTRALLY
CENTRALS
CENTRE
CENTRED
CENTREING
CENTREMAN
CENTREMEN
CENTRES
CENTRIC
CENTRICAL
CENTRIES
CENTRING
CENTRINGS
CENTRIOLE
CENTRISM
CENTRISMS
CENTRIST
CENTRISTS
CENTRODE
CENTRODES
CENTROID
CENTROIDS
CENTRUM
CENTRUMS
CENTRY
CENTS
CENTU
CENTUM
CENTUMS
CENTUMVIR
CENTUPLE
CENTUPLED
CENTUPLES
CENTURIAL
CENTURIES
CENTURION
CENTURY
CEORL
CEORLISH
CEORLS
CEP
CEPACEOUS
CEPAGE
CEPAGES
CEPE
CEPES
CEPHALAD
CEPHALATE
CEPHALIC
CEPHALICS
CEPHALIN
CEPHALINS
CEPHALOUS
CEPHEID
CEPHEIDS
CEPS
CERACEOUS
CERAMAL
CERAMALS
CERAMIC
CERAMICS
CERAMIDE
CERAMIDES
CERAMIST
CERAMISTS
CERASIN
CERASINS
CERASTES
CERASTIUM
CERATE
CERATED
CERATES
CERATIN
CERATINS
CERATITIS
CERATODUS
CERATOID
CERBEREAN
CERBERIAN
CERCAL
CERCARIA

CERCARIAE
CERCARIAL
CERCARIAN
CERCARIAS
CERCI
CERCIS
CERCISES
CERCLAGE
CERCLAGES
CERCOPID
CERCOPIDS
CERCUS
CERE
CEREAL
CEREALIST
CEREALS
CEREBELLA
CEREBRA
CEREBRAL
CEREBRALS
CEREBRATE
CEREBRIC
CEREBROID
CEREBRUM
CEREBRUMS
CERECLOTH
CERED
CEREMENT
CEREMENTS
CEREMONY
CEREOUS
CERES
CERESIN
CERESINE
CERESINES
CERESINS
CEREUS
CEREUSES
CERGE
CERGES
CERIA
CERIAS
CERIC
CERING
CERIPH
CERIPHS
CERISE
CERISES
CERITE
CERITES
CERIUM
CERIUMS
CERMET
CERMETS
CERNE
CERNED
CERNES
CERNING
CERNUOUS
CERO
CEROC
CEROCS
CEROGRAPH
CEROMANCY
CEROON
CEROONS
CEROS
CEROTIC
CEROTYPE
CEROTYPES
CEROUS
CERRADO
CERRADOS
CERRIAL
CERRIS
CERRISES
CERT
CERTAIN
CERTAINER
CERTAINLY
CERTAINTY
CERTES
CERTIE
CERTIFIED
CERTIFIER
CERTIFIES
CERTIFY
CERTITUDE
CERTS
CERTY
CERULE
CERULEAN
CERULEANS
CERULEIN
CERULEINS
CERULEOUS
CERUMEN
CERUMENS
CERUSE
CERUSES
CERUSITE
CERUSITES
CERUSSITE
CERVELAS
CERVELAT
CERVELATS
CERVEZA
CERVEZAS
CERVICAL
CERVICES
CERVICUM
CERVICUMS
CERVID
CERVIDS
CERVINE
CERVIX
CERVIXES
CESAREAN
CESAREANS
CESAREVNA
CESARIAN
CESARIANS
CESIOUS
CESIUM
CESIUMS
CESPITOSE
CESS
CESSATION
CESSE
CESSED
CESSER
CESSERS
CESSES
CESSING
CESSION
CESSIONS
CESSPIT
CESSPITS
CESSPOOL
CESSPOOLS
CESTA
CESTAS
CESTI
CESTODE
CESTODES
CESTOI
CESTOID
CESTOIDS
CESTOS
CESTOSES
CESTUI
CESTUIS
CESTUS
CESTUSES
CESURA
CESURAE
CESURAL
CESURAS
CESURE
CESURES
CETACEAN
CETACEANS
CETACEOUS
CETANE
CETANES
CETE
CETERACH
CETERACHS
CETES
CETOLOGY
CETRIMIDE
CETUXIMAB
CETYL
CETYLS
CETYWALL
CETYWALLS
CEVADILLA
CEVAPCICI
CEVICHE
CEVICHES
CEVITAMIC
CEYLANITE
CEYLONITE
CEZVE
CEZVES
CH
CHA
CHABAZITE
CHABLIS
CHABOUK
CHABOUKS
CHABUK
CHABUKS
CHACE
CHACED
CHACES
CHACHKA
CHACHKAS
CHACING
CHACK
CHACKED
CHACKING
CHACKS
CHACMA
CHACMAS
CHACO
CHACOES
CHACONINE
CHACONNE
CHACONNES
CHACOS
CHAD
CHADAR
CHADARIM
CHADARS
CHADDAR
CHADDARS
CHADDOR
CHADDORS
CHADLESS
CHADO
CHADOR
CHADORS
CHADOS
CHADRI
CHADS
CHAEBOL
CHAEBOLS
CHAETA
CHAETAE
CHAETAL
CHAETODON
CHAETOPOD
CHAFE
CHAFED
CHAFER
CHAFERS
CHAFES
CHAFF
CHAFFED

CHAFFER
CHAFFERED
CHAFFERER
CHAFFERS
CHAFFERY
CHAFFIER
CHAFFIEST
CHAFFINCH
CHAFFING
CHAFFINGS
CHAFFRON
CHAFFRONS
CHAFFS
CHAFFY
CHAFING
CHAFT
CHAFTS
CHAGAN
CHAGANS
CHAGRIN
CHAGRINED
CHAGRINS
CHAI
CHAIN
CHAINE
CHAINED
CHAINER
CHAINERS
CHAINES
CHAINFALL
CHAINING
CHAINLESS
CHAINLET
CHAINLETS
CHAINMAN
CHAINMEN
CHAINS
CHAINSAW
CHAINSAWS
CHAINSHOT
CHAINWORK
CHAIR
CHAIRBACK
CHAIRDAYS
CHAIRED
CHAIRING
CHAIRLIFT
CHAIRMAN
CHAIRMANS
CHAIRMEN
CHAIRS
CHAIS
CHAISE
CHAISES
CHAKALAKA
CHAKRA
CHAKRAS
CHAL
CHALAH
CHALAHS
CHALAN
CHALANED
CHALANING
CHALANNED
CHALANS
CHALAZA
CHALAZAE
CHALAZAL
CHALAZAS
CHALAZIA
CHALAZION
CHALCID
CHALCIDS
CHALCOGEN
CHALDER
CHALDERS
CHALDRON
CHALDRONS
CHALEH
CHALEHS
CHALET
CHALETS
CHALICE
CHALICED
CHALICES
CHALK
CHALKED
CHALKFACE
CHALKIER
CHALKIEST
CHALKING
CHALKLAND
CHALKLIKE
CHALKMARK
CHALKPIT
CHALKPITS
CHALKS
CHALKY
CHALLA
CHALLAH
CHALLAHS
CHALLAN
CHALLANS
CHALLAS
CHALLENGE
CHALLIE
CHALLIES
CHALLIS
CHALLISES
CHALLOT
CHALLOTH
CHALLY
CHALONE
CHALONES
CHALONIC
CHALOT
CHALOTH
CHALS
CHALUMEAU
CHALUPA
CHALUPAS
CHALUTZ
CHALUTZES
CHALUTZIM
CHALYBEAN
CHALYBITE
CHAM
CHAMADE
CHAMADES
CHAMBER
CHAMBERED
CHAMBERER
CHAMBERS
CHAMBRAY
CHAMBRAYS
CHAMBRE
CHAMELEON
CHAMELOT
CHAMELOTS
CHAMETZ
CHAMETZES
CIIAMFER
CHAMFERED
CHAMFERER
CHAMFERS
CHAMFRAIN
CHAMFRON
CHAMFRONS
CHAMISA
CHAMISAL
CHAMISALS
CHAMISAS
CHAMISE
CHAMISES
CHAMISO
CHAMISOS
CHAMLET
CHAMLETS
CHAMMIED
CHAMMIES
CHAMMY
CHAMMYING
CHAMOIS
CHAMOISED
CHAMOISES
CHAMOIX
CHAMOMILE
CHAMP
CHAMPAC
CHAMPACA
CHAMPACAS
CHAMPACS
CHAMPAGNE
CHAMPAIGN
CHAMPAK
CHAMPAKS
CHAMPART
CHAMPARTS
CHAMPAS
CHAMPED
CHAMPER
CHAMPERS
CHAMPERTY
CHAMPIER
CHAMPIEST
CHAMPING
CHAMPION
CHAMPIONS
CHAMPLEVE
CHAMPS
CHAMPY
CHAMS
CHANA
CHANAS
CHANCE
CHANCED
CHANCEFUL
CHANCEL
CHANCELS
CHANCER
CHANCERS
CHANCERY
CHANCES
CHANCEY
CHANCIER
CHANCIEST
CHANCILY
CHANCING
CHANCRE
CHANCRES
CHANCROID
CHANCROUS
CHANCY
CHANDELLE
CHANDLER
CHANDLERS
CHANDLERY
CHANFRON
CHANFRONS
CHANG
CHANGA
CHANGE
CHANGED
CHANGEFUL
CHANGER
CHANGERS
CHANGES
CHANGEUP
CHANGEUPS
CHANGING
CHANGS
CHANK
CHANKS
CHANNEL
CHANNELED
CHANNELER
CHANNELS
CHANNER
CHANNERS
CHANOYO

C

CHANOYOS
CHANOYU
CHANOYUS
CHANSON
CHANSONS
CHANT
CHANTABLE
CHANTAGE
CHANTAGES
CHANTED
CHANTER
CHANTERS
CHANTEUSE
CHANTEY
CHANTEYS
CHANTIE
CHANTIES
CHANTILLY
CHANTING
CHANTINGS
CHANTOR
CHANTORS
CHANTRESS
CHANTRIES
CHANTRY
CHANTS
CHANTY
CHANUKIAH
CHAO
CHAOLOGY
CHAORDIC
CHAOS
CHAOSES
CHAOTIC
CHAP
CHAPARRAL
CHAPATI
CHAPATIES
CHAPATIS
CHAPATTI
CHAPATTIS
CHAPBOOK
CHAPBOOKS
CHAPE
CHAPEAU
CHAPEAUS
CHAPEAUX
CHAPEL
CHAPELESS
CHAPELRY
CHAPELS
CHAPERON
CHAPERONE
CHAPERONS
CHAPES
CHAPESS
CHAPESSES
CHAPITER
CHAPITERS
CHAPKA
CHAPKAS
CHAPLAIN
CHAPLAINS
CHAPLESS
CHAPLET
CHAPLETED
CHAPLETS
CHAPMAN
CHAPMEN
CHAPPAL
CHAPPALS
CHAPPATI
CHAPPATIS
CHAPPED
CHAPPESS
CHAPPIE
CHAPPIER
CHAPPIES
CHAPPIEST
CHAPPING
CHAPPY
CHAPRASSI
CHAPS
CHAPSTICK
CHAPT
CHAPTER
CHAPTERAL
CHAPTERED
CHAPTERS
CHAPTREL
CHAPTRELS
CHAQUETA
CHAQUETAS
CHAR
CHARA
CHARABANC
CHARACID
CHARACIDS
CHARACIN
CHARACINS
CHARACT
CHARACTER
CHARACTS
CHARADE
CHARADES
CHARANGA
CHARANGAS
CHARANGO
CHARANGOS
CHARAS
CHARASES
CHARBROIL
CHARCOAL
CHARCOALS
CHARCOALY
CHARD
CHARDS
CHARE
CHARED
CHARES
CHARET
CHARETS
CHARETTE
CHARETTES
CHARGE
CHARGED
CHARGEFUL
CHARGER
CHARGERS
CHARGES
CHARGING
CHARGINGS
CHARGRILL
CHARIDEE
CHARIDEES
CHARIER
CHARIEST
CHARILY
CHARINESS
CHARING
CHARIOT
CHARIOTED
CHARIOTS
CHARISM
CHARISMA
CHARISMAS
CHARISMS
CHARITIES
CHARITY
CHARIVARI
CHARK
CHARKA
CHARKAS
CHARKED
CHARKHA
CHARKHAS
CHARKING
CHARKS
CHARLADY
CHARLATAN
CHARLEY
CHARLEYS
CHARLIE
CHARLIER
CHARLIES
CHARLOCK
CHARLOCKS
CHARLOTTE
CHARM
CHARMED
CHARMER
CHARMERS
CHARMEUSE
CHARMFUL
CHARMING
CHARMLESS
CHARMONIA
CHARMS
CHARNECO
CHARNECOS
CHARNEL
CHARNELS
CHAROSET
CHAROSETH
CHAROSETS
CHARPAI
CHARPAIS
CHARPIE
CHARPIES
CHARPOY
CHARPOYS
CHARQUI
CHARQUID
CHARQUIS
CHARR
CHARREADA
CHARRED
CHARRIER
CHARRIEST
CHARRING
CHARRO
CHARROS
CHARRS
CHARRY
CHARS
CHART
CHARTA
CHARTABLE
CHARTAS
CHARTED
CHARTER
CHARTERED
CHARTERER
CHARTERS
CHARTING
CHARTISM
CHARTISMS
CHARTIST
CHARTISTS
CHARTLESS
CHARTS
CHARVER
CHARVERS
CHARWOMAN
CHARWOMEN
CHARY
CHAS
CHASE
CHASEABLE
CHASED
CHASEPORT
CHASER
CHASERS
CHASES
CHASING
CHASINGS
CHASM
CHASMAL
CHASMED
CHASMIC

CHASMIER
CHASMIEST
CHASMS
CHASMY
CHASSE
CHASSED
CHASSEED
CHASSEING
CHASSEPOT
CHASSES
CHASSEUR
CHASSEURS
CHASSIS
CHASTE
CHASTELY
CHASTEN
CHASTENED
CHASTENER
CHASTENS
CHASTER
CHASTEST
CHASTISE
CHASTISED
CHASTISER
CHASTISES
CHASTITY
CHASUBLE
CHASUBLES
CHAT
CHATBOT
CHATBOTS
CHATCHKA
CHATCHKAS
CHATCHKE
CHATCHKES
CHATEAU
CHATEAUS
CHATEAUX
CHATELAIN
CHATLINE
CHATLINES
CHATON
CHATONS
CHATOYANT
CHATROOM
CHATROOMS
CHATS
CHATTA
CHATTAS
CHATTED
CHATTEL
CHATTELS
CHATTER
CHATTERED
CHATTERER
CHATTERS
CHATTERY
CHATTI
CHATTIER
CHATTIES
CHATTIEST
CHATTILY
CHATTING
CHATTIS
CHATTY
CHAUFE
CHAUFED
CHAUFER
CHAUFERS
CHAUFES
CHAUFF
CHAUFFED
CHAUFFER
CHAUFFERS
CHAUFFEUR
CHAUFFING
CHAUFFS
CHAUFING
CHAUMER
CHAUMERS
CHAUNCE
CHAUNCED
CHAUNCES
CHAUNCING
CHAUNGE
CHAUNGED
CHAUNGES
CHAUNGING
CHAUNT
CHAUNTED
CHAUNTER
CHAUNTERS
CHAUNTING
CHAUNTRY
CHAUNTS
CHAUSSES
CHAUSSURE
CHAUVIN
CHAUVINS
CHAV
CHAVE
CHAVENDER
CHAVETTE
CHAVETTES
CHAVISH
CHAVS
CHAVVIER
CHAVVIEST
CHAVVY
CHAW
CHAWBACON
CHAWDRON
CHAWDRONS
CHAWED
CHAWER
CHAWERS
CHAWING
CHAWK
CHAWKS
CHAWS
CHAY
CHAYA
CHAYAS
CHAYOTE
CHAYOTES
CHAYROOT
CHAYROOTS
CHAYS
CHAZAN
CHAZANIM
CHAZANS
CHAZZAN
CHAZZANIM
CHAZZANS
CHAZZEN
CHAZZENIM
CHAZZENS
CHE
CHEAP
CHEAPED
CHEAPEN
CHEAPENED
CHEAPENER
CHEAPENS
CHEAPER
CHEAPEST
CHEAPIE
CHEAPIES
CHEAPING
CHEAPISH
CHEAPJACK
CHEAPLY
CHEAPNESS
CHEAPO
CHEAPOS
CHEAPS
CHEAPSHOT
CHEAPY
CHEAT
CHEATABLE
CHEATED
CHEATER
CHEATERS
CHEATERY
CHEATING
CHEATINGS
CHEATS
CHEBEC
CHEBECS
CHECHAKO
CHECHAKOS
CHECHAQUO
CHECHIA
CHECHIAS
CHECK
CHECKABLE
CHECKBOOK
CHECKBOX
CHECKED
CHECKER
CHECKERED
CHECKERS
CHECKIER
CHECKIEST
CHECKING
CHECKINGS
CHECKLESS
CHECKLIST
CHECKMARK
CHECKMATE
CHECKOFF
CHECKOFFS
CHECKOUT
CHECKOUTS
CHECKRAIL
CHECKREIN
CHECKROOM
CHECKROW
CHECKROWS
CHECKS
CHECKSTOP
CHECKSUM
CHECKSUMS
CHECKUP
CHECKUPS
CHECKY
CHEDARIM
CHEDDAR
CHEDDARS
CHEDDARY
CHEDDITE
CHEDDITES
CHEDER
CHEDERS
CHEDITE
CHEDITES
CHEECHAKO
CHEEK
CHEEKBONE
CHEEKED
CHEEKFUL
CHEEKFULS
CHEEKIER
CHEEKIEST
CHEEKILY
CHEEKING
CHEEKLESS
CHEEKS
CHEEKY
CHEEP
CHEEPED
CHEEPER
CHEEPERS
CHEEPING
CHEEPS
CHEER
CHEERED
CHEERER
CHEERERS
CHEERFUL

CHEERIER
CHEERIEST
CHEERILY
CHEERING
CHEERINGS
CHEERIO
CHEERIOS
CHEERLEAD
CHEERLED
CHEERLESS
CHEERLY
CHEERO
CHEEROS
CHEERS
CHEERY
CHEESE
CHEESED
CHEESES
CHEESEVAT
CHEESIER
CHEESIEST
CHEESILY
CHEESING
CHEESY
CHEETAH
CHEETAHS
CHEEWINK
CHEEWINKS
CHEF
CHEFDOM
CHEFDOMS
CHEFED
CHEFFED
CHEFFIER
CHEFFIEST
CHEFFING
CHEFFY
CHEFING
CHEFS
CHEGOE
CHEGOES
CHEILITIS
CHEKA
CHEKAS
CHEKIST
CHEKISTS
CHELA
CHELAE
CHELAS
CHELASHIP
CHELATE
CHELATED
CHELATES
CHELATING
CHELATION
CHELATOR
CHELATORS
CHELICERA
CHELIFORM
CHELIPED
CHELIPEDS
CHELLUP
CHELLUPS
CHELOID
CHELOIDAL
CHELOIDS
CHELONE
CHELONES
CHELONIAN
CHELP
CHELPED
CHELPING
CHELPS
CHEM
CHEMIC
CHEMICAL
CHEMICALS
CHEMICKED
CHEMICS
CHEMISE
CHEMISES
CHEMISM
CHEMISMS
CHEMISORB
CHEMIST
CHEMISTRY
CHEMISTS
CHEMITYPE
CHEMITYPY
CHEMMIES
CHEMMY
CHEMO
CHEMOKINE
CHEMOS
CHEMOSORB
CHEMOSTAT
CHEMPADUK
CHEMS
CHEMSEX
CHEMSEXES
CHEMTRAIL
CHEMURGIC
CHEMURGY
CHENAR
CHENARS
CHENET
CHENETS
CHENILLE
CHENILLES
CHENIX
CHENIXES
CHENOPOD
CHENOPODS
CHEONGSAM
CHEQUE
CHEQUER
CHEQUERED
CHEQUERS
CHEQUES
CHEQUIER
CHEQUIEST
CHEQUING
CHEQUY
CHER
CHERALITE
CHERE
CHERIMOYA
CHERISH
CHERISHED
CHERISHER
CHERISHES
CHERMOULA
CHERNOZEM
CHEROOT
CHEROOTS
CHERRIED
CHERRIER
CHERRIES
CHERRIEST
CHERRY
CHERRYING
CHERT
CHERTIER
CHERTIEST
CHERTS
CHERTY
CHERUB
CHERUBIC
CHERUBIM
CHERUBIMS
CHERUBIN
CHERUBINS
CHERUBS
CHERUP
CHERUPED
CHERUPING
CHERUPS
CHERVIL
CHERVILS
CHESHIRE
CHESHIRES
CHESIL
CHESILS
CHESNUT
CHESNUTS
CHESS
CHESSEL
CHESSELS
CHESSES
CHESSMAN
CHESSMEN
CHEST
CHESTED
CHESTFUL
CHESTFULS
CHESTIER
CHESTIEST
CHESTILY
CHESTING
CHESTNUT
CHESTNUTS
CHESTS
CHESTY
CHETAH
CHETAHS
CHETH
CHETHS
CHETNIK
CHETNIKS
CHETRUM
CHETRUMS
CHEVAL
CHEVALET
CHEVALETS
CHEVALIER
CHEVELURE
CHEVEN
CHEVENS
CHEVEREL
CHEVERELS
CHEVERIL
CHEVERILS
CHEVERON
CHEVERONS
CHEVERYE
CHEVERYES
CHEVET
CHEVETS
CHEVIED
CHEVIES
CHEVILLE
CHEVILLES
CHEVIN
CHEVINS
CHEVIOT
CHEVIOTS
CHEVRE
CHEVRES
CHEVRET
CHEVRETS
CHEVRETTE
CHEVRON
CHEVRONED
CHEVRONS
CHEVRONY
CHEVROTIN
CHEVY
CHEVYING
CHEW
CHEWABLE
CHEWED
CHEWER
CHEWERS
CHEWET
CHEWETS
CHEWIE
CHEWIER
CHEWIES
CHEWIEST
CHEWINESS

CHEWING
CHEWINK
CHEWINKS
CHEWS
CHEWY
CHEZ
CHHERTUM
CHI
CHIA
CHIACK
CHIACKED
CHIACKING
CHIACKS
CHIANTI
CHIANTIS
CHIAO
CHIAOS
CHIAREZZA
CHIAREZZE
CHIAS
CHIASM
CHIASMA
CHIASMAL
CHIASMAS
CHIASMATA
CHIASMI
CHIASMIC
CHIASMS
CHIASMUS
CHIASTIC
CHIAUS
CHIAUSED
CHIAUSES
CHIAUSING
CHIB
CHIBBED
CHIBBING
CHIBOL
CHIBOLS
CHIBOUK
CHIBOUKS
CHIBOUQUE
CHIBS
CHIC
CHICA
CHICALOTE
CHICANA
CHICANAS
CHICANE
CHICANED
CHICANER
CHICANERS
CHICANERY
CHICANES
CHICANING
CHICANO
CHICANOS
CHICAS
CHICCORY
CHICER
CHICEST
CHICH
CHICHA
CHICHAS
CHICHES
CHICHI
CHICHIER
CHICHIEST
CHICHIS
CHICK
CHICKADEE
CHICKAREE
CHICKEE
CHICKEES
CHICKEN
CHICKENED
CHICKENS
CHICKLING
CHICKORY
CHICKPEA
CHICKPEAS
CHICKS
CHICKWEED
CHICLE
CHICLES
CHICLY
CHICNESS
CHICO
CHICON
CHICONS
CHICORIES
CHICORY
CHICOS
CHICOT
CHICOTS
CHICS
CHID
CHIDDEN
CHIDE
CHIDED
CHIDER
CHIDERS
CHIDES
CHIDING
CHIDINGLY
CHIDINGS
CHIDLINGS
CHIEF
CHIEFDOM
CHIEFDOMS
CHIEFER
CHIEFERY
CHIEFESS
CHIEFEST
CHIEFLESS
CHIEFLING
CHIEFLY
CHIEFRIES
CHIEFRY
CHIEFS
CHIEFSHIP
CHIEFTAIN
CHIEL
CHIELD
CHIELDS
CHIELS
CHIFFON
CHIFFONS
CHIFFONY
CHIGETAI
CHIGETAIS
CHIGGA
CHIGGAS
CHIGGER
CHIGGERS
CHIGNON
CHIGNONED
CHIGNONS
CHIGOE
CHIGOES
CHIGRE
CHIGRES
CHIHUAHUA
CHIK
CHIKARA
CHIKARAS
CHIKHOR
CHIKHORS
CHIKOR
CHIKORS
CHIKS
CHILBLAIN
CHILD
CHILDBED
CHILDBEDS
CHILDCARE
CHILDE
CHILDED
CHILDER
CHILDES
CHILDHOOD
CHILDING
CHILDISH
CHILDLESS
CHILDLIER
CHILDLIKE
CHILDLY
CHILDNESS
CHILDREN
CHILDS
CHILE
CHILES
CHILI
CHILIAD
CHILIADAL
CHILIADIC
CHILIADS
CHILIAGON
CHILIARCH
CHILIASM
CHILIASMS
CHILIAST
CHILIASTS
CHILIDOG
CHILIDOGS
CHILIES
CHILIS
CHILL
CHILLADA
CHILLADAS
CHILLAX
CHILLAXED
CHILLAXES
CHILLED
CHILLER
CHILLERS
CHILLEST
CHILLI
CHILLIER
CHILLIES
CHILLIEST
CHILLILY
CHILLING
CHILLINGS
CHILLIS
CHILLNESS
CHILLS
CHILLUM
CHILLUMS
CHILLY
CHILOPOD
CHILOPODS
CHILTEPIN
CHIMAERA
CHIMAERAS
CHIMAERIC
CHIMAR
CHIMARS
CHIMB
CHIMBLEY
CHIMBLEYS
CHIMBLIES
CHIMBLY
CHIMBS
CHIME
CHIMED
CHIMENEA
CHIMENEAS
CHIMER
CHIMERA
CHIMERAS
CHIMERE
CHIMERES
CHIMERIC
CHIMERID
CHIMERIDS
CHIMERISM
CHIMERS
CHIMES
CHIMINEA

C

CHIMINEAS
CHIMING
CHIMLA
CHIMLAS
CHIMLEY
CHIMLEYS
CHIMNEY
CHIMNEYED
CHIMNEYS
CHIMO
CHIMP
CHIMPS
CHIN
CHINA
CHINAMAN
CHINAMEN
CHINAMPA
CHINAMPAS
CHINAR
CHINAROOT
CHINARS
CHINAS
CHINAWARE
CHINBONE
CHINBONES
CHINCAPIN
CHINCH
CHINCHED
CHINCHES
CHINCHIER
CHINCHING
CHINCHY
CHINCOUGH
CHINDIT
CHINDITS
CHINE
CHINED
CHINES
CHINESE
CHING
CHINGS
CHINING
CHINK
CHINKAPIN
CHINKARA
CHINKARAS
CHINKED
CHINKIE
CHINKIER
CHINKIES
CHINKIEST
CHINKING
CHINKS
CHINKY
CHINLESS
CHINNED
CHINNING
CHINO
CHINOIS
CHINOISES
CHINONE
CHINONES
CHINOOK
CHINOOKS
CHINOS
CHINOVNIK
CHINS
CHINSE
CHINSED
CHINSES
CHINSING
CHINSTRAP
CHINTS
CHINTSES
CHINTZ
CHINTZES
CHINTZIER
CHINTZILY
CHINTZY
CHINWAG
CHINWAGS
CHIP
CHIPBOARD
CHIPMAKER
CHIPMUCK
CHIPMUCKS
CHIPMUNK
CHIPMUNKS
CHIPOCHIA
CHIPOLATA
CHIPOTLE
CHIPOTLES
CHIPPABLE
CHIPPED
CHIPPER
CHIPPERED
CHIPPERER
CHIPPERS
CHIPPIE
CHIPPIER
CHIPPIES
CHIPPIEST
CHIPPING
CHIPPINGS
CHIPPY
CHIPS
CHIPSET
CHIPSETS
CHIRAGRA
CHIRAGRAS
CHIRAGRIC
CHIRAL
CHIRALITY
CHIRIMOYA
CHIRK
CHIRKED
CHIRKER
CHIRKEST
CHIRKING
CHIRKS
CHIRL
CHIRLED
CHIRLING
CHIRLS
CHIRM
CHIRMED
CHIRMING
CHIRMS
CHIRO
CHIROLOGY
CHIRONOMY
CHIROPODY
CHIROPTER
CHIROS
CHIRP
CHIRPED
CHIRPER
CHIRPERS
CHIRPIER
CHIRPIEST
CHIRPILY
CHIRPING
CHIRPINGS
CHIRPS
CHIRPY
CHIRR
CHIRRE
CHIRRED
CHIRREN
CHIRRES
CHIRRING
CHIRRS
CHIRRUP
CHIRRUPED
CHIRRUPER
CHIRRUPS
CHIRRUPY
CHIRT
CHIRTED
CHIRTING
CHIRTS
CHIRU
CHIRUS
CHIS
CHISEL
CHISELED
CHISELER
CHISELERS
CHISELING
CHISELLED
CHISELLER
CHISELS
CHIT
CHITAL
CHITALS
CHITCHAT
CHITCHATS
CHITIN
CHITINOID
CHITINOUS
CHITINS
CHITLIN
CHITLING
CHITLINGS
CHITLINS
CHITON
CHITONS
CHITOSAN
CHITOSANS
CHITS
CHITTED
CHITTER
CHITTERED
CHITTERS
CHITTIER
CHITTIES
CHITTIEST
CHITTING
CHITTY
CHIV
CHIVALRIC
CHIVALRY
CHIVAREE
CHIVAREED
CHIVAREES
CHIVARI
CHIVARIED
CHIVARIES
CHIVE
CHIVED
CHIVES
CHIVIED
CHIVIES
CHIVING
CHIVS
CHIVVED
CHIVVIED
CHIVVIES
CHIVVING
CHIVVY
CHIVVYING
CHIVY
CHIVYING
CHIWEENIE
CHIYOGAMI
CHIZ
CHIZZ
CHIZZED
CHIZZES
CHIZZING
CHLAMYDES
CHLAMYDIA
CHLAMYS
CHLAMYSES
CHLOASMA
CHLOASMAS
CHLORACNE
CHLORAL
CHLORALS
CHLORATE

CHLORATES
CHLORDAN
CHLORDANE
CHLORDANS
CHLORELLA
CHLORIC
CHLORID
CHLORIDE
CHLORIDES
CHLORIDIC
CHLORIDS
CHLORIN
CHLORINE
CHLORINES
CHLORINS
CHLORITE
CHLORITES
CHLORITIC
CHLOROSES
CHLOROSIS
CHLOROTIC
CHLOROUS
CHOANA
CHOANAE
CHOBDAR
CHOBDARS
CHOC
CHOCCIER
CHOCCIES
CHOCCIEST
CHOCCY
CHOCHO
CHOCHOS
CHOCK
CHOCKED
CHOCKER
CHOCKERS
CHOCKFUL
CHOCKFULL
CHOCKIE
CHOCKIER
CHOCKIES
CHOCKIEST
CHOCKING
CHOCKO
CHOCKOS
CHOCKS
CHOCKY
CHOCO
CHOCOLATE
CHOCOLATY
CHOCOS
CHOCS
CHOCTAW
CHOCTAWS
CHODE
CHOENIX
CHOENIXES
CHOG
CHOGS
CHOICE
CHOICEFUL
CHOICELY
CHOICER
CHOICES
CHOICEST
CHOIL
CHOILS
CHOIR
CHOIRBOY
CHOIRBOYS
CHOIRED
CHOIRGIRL
CHOIRING
CHOIRLIKE
CHOIRMAN
CHOIRMEN
CHOIRS
CHOKE
CHOKEABLE
CHOKEBORE
CHOKECOIL
CHOKED
CHOKEDAMP
CHOKEHOLD
CHOKER
CHOKERMAN
CHOKERMEN
CHOKERS
CHOKES
CHOKEY
CHOKEYS
CHOKIDAR
CHOKIDARS
CHOKIER
CHOKIES
CHOKIEST
CHOKING
CHOKINGLY
CHOKO
CHOKOS
CHOKRA
CHOKRAS
CHOKRI
CHOKRIS
CHOKY
CHOLA
CHOLAEMIA
CHOLAEMIC
CHOLAS
CHOLATE
CHOLATES
CHOLECYST
CHOLELITH
CHOLEMIA
CHOLEMIAS
CHOLENT
CHOLENTS
CHOLER
CHOLERA
CHOLERAIC
CHOLERAS
CHOLERIC
CHOLEROID
CHOLERS
CHOLI
CHOLIAMB
CHOLIAMBS
CHOLIC
CHOLINE
CHOLINES
CHOLIS
CHOLLA
CHOLLAS
CHOLLERS
CHOLO
CHOLOS
CHOLTRIES
CHOLTRY
CHOMETZ
CHOMETZES
CHOMMIE
CHOMMIES
CHOMP
CHOMPED
CHOMPER
CHOMPERS
CHOMPING
CHOMPS
CHON
CHONDRAL
CHONDRE
CHONDRES
CHONDRI
CHONDRIFY
CHONDRIN
CHONDRINS
CHONDRITE
CHONDROID
CHONDROMA
CHONDRULE
CHONDRUS
CHONS
CHOOF
CHOOFED
CHOOFING
CHOOFS
CHOOK
CHOOKED
CHOOKIE
CHOOKIES
CHOOKING
CHOOKS
CHOOM
CHOOMS
CHOON
CHOONS
CHOOSE
CHOOSER
CHOOSERS
CHOOSES
CHOOSEY
CHOOSIER
CHOOSIEST
CHOOSILY
CHOOSING
CHOOSY
CHOP
CHOPHOUSE
CHOPIN
CHOPINE
CHOPINES
CHOPINS
CHOPLOGIC
CHOPPED
CHOPPER
CHOPPERED
CHOPPERS
CHOPPIER
CHOPPIEST
CHOPPILY
CHOPPING
CHOPPINGS
CHOPPY
CHOPS
CHOPSOCKY
CHOPSTICK
CHORAGI
CHORAGIC
CHORAGUS
CHORAL
CHORALE
CHORALES
CHORALIST
CHORALLY
CHORALS
CHORD
CHORDA
CHORDAE
CHORDAL
CHORDATE
CHORDATES
CHORDED
CHORDEE
CHORDEES
CHORDING
CHORDINGS
CHORDLIKE
CHORDS
CHORDWISE
CHORE
CHOREA
CHOREAL
CHOREAS
CHOREATIC
CHOREBOY
CHOREBOYS
CHORED
CHOREE
CHOREES

CHOREGI
CHOREGIC
CHOREGUS
CHOREIC
CHOREMAN
CHOREMEN
CHOREOID
CHORES
CHOREUS
CHOREUSES
CHORIA
CHORIAL
CHORIAMB
CHORIAMBI
CHORIAMBS
CHORIC
CHORINE
CHORINES
CHORING
CHORIOID
CHORIOIDS
CHORION
CHORIONIC
CHORIONS
CHORISES
CHORISIS
CHORISM
CHORISMS
CHORIST
CHORISTER
CHORISTS
CHORIZO
CHORIZONT
CHORIZOS
CHOROID
CHOROIDAL
CHOROIDS
CHOROLOGY
CHORRIE
CHORRIES
CHORTEN
CHORTENS
CHORTLE
CHORTLED
CHORTLER
CHORTLERS
CHORTLES
CHORTLING
CHORUS
CHORUSED
CHORUSES
CHORUSING
CHORUSSED
CHORUSSES
CHOSE
CHOSEN
CHOSES
CHOTA
CHOTT
CHOTTS
CHOU
CHOUGH
CHOUGHS
CHOULTRY
CHOUNTER
CHOUNTERS
CHOUSE
CHOUSED
CHOUSER
CHOUSERS
CHOUSES
CHOUSH
CHOUSHES
CHOUSING
CHOUT
CHOUTS
CHOUX
CHOW
CHOWCHOW
CHOWCHOWS
CHOWDER
CHOWDERED
CHOWDERS
CHOWDOWN
CHOWDOWNS
CHOWED
CHOWHOUND
CHOWING
CHOWK
CHOWKIDAR
CHOWKS
CHOWRI
CHOWRIES
CHOWRIS
CHOWRY
CHOWS
CHOWSE
CHOWSED
CHOWSES
CHOWSING
CHOWTIME
CHOWTIMES
CHRESARD
CHRESARDS
CHRISM
CHRISMA
CHRISMAL
CHRISMALS
CHRISMON
CHRISMONS
CHRISMS
CHRISOM
CHRISOMS
CHRISTEN
CHRISTENS
CHRISTIAN
CHRISTIE
CHRISTIES
CHRISTOM
CHRISTOMS
CHRISTY
CHROMA
CHROMAKEY
CHROMAS
CHROMATE
CHROMATES
CHROMATIC
CHROMATID
CHROMATIN
CHROME
CHROMED
CHROMEL
CHROMELS
CHROMENE
CHROMENES
CHROMES
CHROMIC
CHROMIDE
CHROMIDES
CHROMIDIA
CHROMIER
CHROMIEST
CHROMING
CHROMINGS
CHROMISE
CHROMISED
CHROMISES
CHROMITE
CHROMITES
CHROMIUM
CHROMIUMS
CHROMIZE
CHROMIZED
CHROMIZES
CHROMO
CHROMOGEN
CHROMOLY
CHROMOLYS
CHROMOS
CHROMOUS
CHROMY
CHROMYL
CHROMYLS
CHRONAXIE
CHRONAXY
CHRONIC
CHRONICAL
CHRONICLE
CHRONICS
CHRONON
CHRONONS
CHRYSALID
CHRYSALIS
CHRYSANTH
CHTHONIAN
CHTHONIC
CHUB
CHUBASCO
CHUBASCOS
CHUBBIER
CHUBBIEST
CHUBBILY
CHUBBY
CHUBS
CHUCK
CHUCKED
CHUCKER
CHUCKERS
CHUCKHOLE
CHUCKIE
CHUCKIES
CHUCKING
CHUCKLE
CHUCKLED
CHUCKLER
CHUCKLERS
CHUCKLES
CHUCKLING
CHUCKS
CHUCKY
CHUDDAH
CHUDDAHS
CHUDDAR
CHUDDARS
CHUDDER
CHUDDERS
CHUDDIES
CHUDDY
CHUFA
CHUFAS
CHUFF
CHUFFED
CHUFFER
CHUFFEST
CHUFFIER
CHUFFIEST
CHUFFING
CHUFFS
CHUFFY
CHUG
CHUGALUG
CHUGALUGS
CHUGGED
CHUGGER
CHUGGERS
CHUGGING
CHUGGINGS
CHUGS
CHUKAR
CHUKARS
CHUKKA
CHUKKAR
CHUKKARS
CHUKKAS
CHUKKER
CHUKKERS
CHUKOR
CHUKORS
CHUM
CHUMASH

CHUMASHES
CHUMASHIM
CHUMLEY
CHUMLEYS
CHUMMAGE
CHUMMAGES
CHUMMED
CHUMMIER
CHUMMIES
CHUMMIEST
CHUMMILY
CHUMMING
CHUMMY
CHUMP
CHUMPED
CHUMPING
CHUMPINGS
CHUMPS
CHUMS
CHUMSHIP
CHUMSHIPS
CHUNDER
CHUNDERED
CHUNDERS
CHUNK
CHUNKED
CHUNKIER
CHUNKIEST
CHUNKILY
CHUNKING
CHUNKINGS
CHUNKS
CHUNKY
CHUNNEL
CHUNNELS
CHUNNER
CHUNNERED
CHUNNERS
CHUNTER
CHUNTERED
CHUNTERS
CHUPATI
CHUPATIS
CHUPATTI
CHUPATTIS
CHUPATTY
CHUPPA
CHUPPAH
CHUPPAHS
CHUPPAS
CHUPPOT
CHUPPOTH
CHUPRASSY
CHUR
CHURCH
CHURCHED
CHURCHES
CHURCHIER
CHURCHING
CHURCHISM
CHURCHLY
CHURCHMAN
CHURCHMEN
CHURCHWAY
CHURCHY
CHURIDAR
CHURIDARS
CHURINGA
CHURINGAS
CHURL
CHURLISH
CHURLS
CHURN
CHURNED
CHURNER
CHURNERS
CHURNING
CHURNINGS
CHURNMILK
CHURNS
CHURR
CHURRED
CHURRING
CHURRO
CHURROS
CHURRS
CHURRUS
CHURRUSES
CHUSE
CHUSED
CHUSES
CHUSING
CHUT
CHUTE
CHUTED
CHUTES
CHUTING
CHUTIST
CHUTISTS
CHUTNEE
CHUTNEES
CHUTNEY
CHUTNEYS
CHUTS
CHUTZPA
CHUTZPAH
CHUTZPAHS
CHUTZPAS
CHYACK
CHYACKED
CHYACKING
CHYACKS
CHYLDE
CHYLE
CHYLES
CHYLIFIED
CHYLIFIES
CHYLIFY
CHYLOUS
CHYLURIA
CHYLURIAS
CHYME
CHYMES
CHYMIC
CHYMICS
CHYMIFIED
CHYMIFIES
CHYMIFY
CHYMIST
CHYMISTRY
CHYMISTS
CHYMOSIN
CHYMOSINS
CHYMOUS
CHYND
CHYPRE
CHYPRES
CHYRON
CHYRONS
CHYTRID
CHYTRIDS
CIABATTA
CIABATTAS
CIABATTE
CIAO
CIBATION
CIBATIONS
CIBOL
CIBOLS
CIBORIA
CIBORIUM
CIBORIUMS
CIBOULE
CIBOULES
CICADA
CICADAE
CICADAS
CICALA
CICALAS
CICALE
CICATRICE
CICATRISE
CICATRIX
CICATRIZE
CICELIES
CICELY
CICERO
CICERONE
CICERONED
CICERONES
CICERONI
CICEROS
CICHLID
CICHLIDAE
CICHLIDS
CICHLOID
CICINNUS
CICISBEI
CICISBEO
CICISBEOS
CICLATON
CICLATONS
CICLATOUN
CICOREE
CICOREES
CICUTA
CICUTAS
CICUTINE
CICUTINES
CID
CIDARIS
CIDARISES
CIDE
CIDED
CIDER
CIDERIER
CIDERIEST
CIDERKIN
CIDERKINS
CIDERS
CIDERY
CIDES
CIDING
CIDS
CIEL
CIELED
CIELING
CIELINGS
CIELS
CIERGE
CIERGES
CIG
CIGAR
CIGARET
CIGARETS
CIGARETTE
CIGARILLO
CIGARLIKE
CIGARS
CIGGIE
CIGGIES
CIGGY
CIGS
CIGUATERA
CILANTRO
CILANTROS
CILIA
CILIARY
CILIATE
CILIATED
CILIATELY
CILIATES
CILIATION
CILICE
CILICES
CILICIOUS
CILIOLATE
CILIUM
CILL
CILLS

C

CIMAR
CIMARS
CIMBALOM
CIMBALOMS
CIMELIA
CIMEX
CIMICES
CIMIER
CIMIERS
CIMINITE
CIMINITES
CIMMERIAN
CIMOLITE
CIMOLITES
CINCH
CINCHED
CINCHES
CINCHING
CINCHINGS
CINCHONA
CINCHONAS
CINCHONIC
CINCINNUS
CINCT
CINCTURE
CINCTURED
CINCTURES
CINDER
CINDERED
CINDERIER
CINDERING
CINDEROUS
CINDERS
CINDERY
CINE
CINEAST
CINEASTE
CINEASTES
CINEASTS
CINEMA
CINEMAS
CINEMATIC
CINEOL
CINEOLE
CINEOLES
CINEOLS
CINEPHILE
CINEPLEX
CINERAMIC
CINERARIA
CINERARY
CINERATOR
CINEREA
CINEREAL
CINEREAS
CINEREOUS
CINERIN
CINERINS
CINES
CINGULA
CINGULAR
CINGULATE
CINGULUM
CINNABAR
CINNABARS
CINNAMIC
CINNAMON
CINNAMONS
CINNAMONY
CINNAMYL
CINNAMYLS
CINQ
CINQS
CINQUAIN
CINQUAINS
CINQUE
CINQUES
CION
CIONS
CIOPPINO
CIOPPINOS
CIPAILLE
CIPAILLES
CIPHER
CIPHERED
CIPHERER
CIPHERERS
CIPHERING
CIPHERS
CIPHONIES
CIPHONY
CIPOLIN
CIPOLINS
CIPOLLINO
CIPPI
CIPPUS
CIRCA
CIRCADIAN
CIRCAR
CIRCARS
CIRCINATE
CIRCITER
CIRCLE
CIRCLED
CIRCLER
CIRCLERS
CIRCLES
CIRCLET
CIRCLETS
CIRCLING
CIRCLINGS
CIRCLIP
CIRCLIPS
CIRCS
CIRCUIT
CIRCUITAL
CIRCUITED
CIRCUITRY
CIRCUITS
CIRCUITY
CIRCULAR
CIRCULARS
CIRCULATE
CIRCUS
CIRCUSES
CIRCUSIER
CIRCUSSY
CIRCUSY
CIRE
CIRES
CIRL
CIRLS
CIRQUE
CIRQUES
CIRRATE
CIRRHOSED
CIRRHOSES
CIRRHOSIS
CIRRHOTIC
CIRRI
CIRRIFORM
CIRRIPED
CIRRIPEDE
CIRRIPEDS
CIRROSE
CIRROUS
CIRRUS
CIRRUSES
CIRSOID
CIS
CISALPINE
CISCO
CISCOES
CISCOS
CISELEUR
CISELEURS
CISELURE
CISELURES
CISGENDER
CISLUNAR
CISPADANE
CISPLATIN
CISSIER
CISSIES
CISSIEST
CISSIFIED
CISSING
CISSINGS
CISSOID
CISSOIDS
CISSUS
CISSUSES
CISSY
CIST
CISTED
CISTERN
CISTERNA
CISTERNAE
CISTERNAL
CISTERNS
CISTIC
CISTRON
CISTRONIC
CISTRONS
CISTS
CISTUS
CISTUSES
CISTVAEN
CISTVAENS
CIT
CITABLE
CITADEL
CITADELS
CITAL
CITALS
CITATION
CITATIONS
CITATOR
CITATORS
CITATORY
CITE
CITEABLE
CITED
CITER
CITERS
CITES
CITESS
CITESSES
CITHARA
CITHARAS
CITHARIST
CITHER
CITHERN
CITHERNS
CITHERS
CITHREN
CITHRENS
CITIED
CITIES
CITIFIED
CITIFIES
CITIFY
CITIFYING
CITIGRADE
CITING
CITIZEN
CITIZENLY
CITIZENRY
CITIZENS
CITO
CITOLA
CITOLAS
CITOLE
CITOLES
CITRAL
CITRALS
CITRANGE
CITRANGES
CITRATE
CITRATED

CITRATES
CITREOUS
CITRIC
CITRIN
CITRINE
CITRINES
CITRININ
CITRININS
CITRINS
CITRON
CITRONS
CITROUS
CITRUS
CITRUSES
CITRUSIER
CITRUSSY
CITRUSY
CITS
CITTERN
CITTERNS
CITY
CITYFIED
CITYFIES
CITYFY
CITYFYING
CITYSCAPE
CITYWARD
CITYWIDE
CIVE
CIVES
CIVET
CIVETLIKE
CIVETS
CIVIC
CIVICALLY
CIVICISM
CIVICISMS
CIVICS
CIVIE
CIVIES
CIVIL
CIVILIAN
CIVILIANS
CIVILISE
CIVILISED
CIVILISER
CIVILISES
CIVILIST
CIVILISTS
CIVILITY
CIVILIZE
CIVILIZED
CIVILIZER
CIVILIZES
CIVILLY
CIVILNESS
CIVILS
CIVISM
CIVISMS
CIVVIES
CIVVY
CIZERS
CLABBER
CLABBERED
CLABBERS
CLACH
CLACHAN
CLACHANS
CLACHED
CLACHES
CLACHING
CLACHS
CLACK
CLACKBOX
CLACKDISH
CLACKED
CLACKER
CLACKERS
CLACKING
CLACKS
CLAD
CLADDAGH
CLADDAGHS
CLADDED
CLADDER
CLADDERS
CLADDIE
CLADDIES
CLADDING
CLADDINGS
CLADE
CLADES
CLADISM
CLADISMS
CLADIST
CLADISTIC
CLADISTS
CLADODE
CLADODES
CLADODIAL
CLADOGRAM
CLADS
CLAES
CLAFOUTI
CLAFOUTIS
CLAG
CLAGGED
CLAGGIER
CLAGGIEST
CLAGGING
CLAGGY
CLAGS
CLAIM
CLAIMABLE
CLAIMANT
CLAIMANTS
CLAIMED
CLAIMER
CLAIMERS
CLAIMING
CLAIMS
CLAM
CLAMANCY
CLAMANT
CLAMANTLY
CLAMBAKE
CLAMBAKES
CLAMBE
CLAMBER
CLAMBERED
CLAMBERER
CLAMBERS
CLAME
CLAMES
CLAMLIKE
CLAMMED
CLAMMER
CLAMMERS
CLAMMIER
CLAMMIEST
CLAMMILY
CLAMMING
CLAMMY
CLAMOR
CLAMORED
CLAMORER
CLAMORERS
CLAMORING
CLAMOROUS
CLAMORS
CLAMOUR
CLAMOURED
CLAMOURER
CLAMOURS
CLAMP
CLAMPDOWN
CLAMPED
CLAMPER
CLAMPERED
CLAMPERS
CLAMPING
CLAMPINGS
CLAMPS
CLAMS
CLAMSHELL
CLAMWORM
CLAMWORMS
CLAN
CLANG
CLANGBOX
CLANGED
CLANGER
CLANGERS
CLANGING
CLANGINGS
CLANGOR
CLANGORED
CLANGORS
CLANGOUR
CLANGOURS
CLANGS
CLANK
CLANKED
CLANKIER
CLANKIEST
CLANKING
CLANKINGS
CLANKS
CLANKY
CLANNISH
CLANS
CLANSHIP
CLANSHIPS
CLANSMAN
CLANSMEN
CLAP
CLAPBOARD
CLAPBREAD
CLAPDISH
CLAPNET
CLAPNETS
CLAPPED
CLAPPER
CLAPPERED
CLAPPERS
CLAPPING
CLAPPINGS
CLAPS
CLAPT
CLAPTRAP
CLAPTRAPS
CLAQUE
CLAQUER
CLAQUERS
CLAQUES
CLAQUEUR
CLAQUEURS
CLARAIN
CLARAINS
CLARENCE
CLARENCES
CLARENDON
CLARET
CLARETED
CLARETING
CLARETS
CLARIES
CLARIFIED
CLARIFIER
CLARIFIES
CLARIFY
CLARINET
CLARINETS
CLARINI
CLARINO
CLARINOS
CLARION
CLARIONED
CLARIONET
CLARIONS

C

CLARITIES
CLARITY
CLARKIA
CLARKIAS
CLARO
CLAROES
CLAROS
CLARSACH
CLARSACHS
CLART
CLARTED
CLARTHEAD
CLARTIER
CLARTIEST
CLARTING
CLARTS
CLARTY
CLARY
CLASH
CLASHED
CLASHER
CLASHERS
CLASHES
CLASHING
CLASHINGS
CLASP
CLASPED
CLASPER
CLASPERS
CLASPING
CLASPINGS
CLASPS
CLASPT
CLASS
CLASSABLE
CLASSED
CLASSER
CLASSERS
CLASSES
CLASSIBLE
CLASSIC
CLASSICAL
CLASSICO
CLASSICS
CLASSIER
CLASSIEST
CLASSIFIC
CLASSIFY
CLASSILY
CLASSING
CLASSINGS
CLASSIS
CLASSISM
CLASSISMS
CLASSIST
CLASSISTS
CLASSLESS
CLASSMAN
CLASSMATE
CLASSMEN
CLASSON
CLASSONS
CLASSROOM
CLASSWORK
CLASSY
CLAST
CLASTIC
CLASTICS
CLASTS
CLAT
CLATCH
CLATCHED
CLATCHES
CLATCHING
CLATHRATE
CLATS
CLATTED
CLATTER
CLATTERED
CLATTERER
CLATTERS
CLATTERY
CLATTING
CLAUCHT
CLAUCHTED
CLAUCHTS
CLAUGHT
CLAUGHTED
CLAUGHTS
CLAUSAL
CLAUSE
CLAUSES
CLAUSTRA
CLAUSTRAL
CLAUSTRUM
CLAUSULA
CLAUSULAE
CLAUSULAR
CLAUT
CLAUTED
CLAUTING
CLAUTS
CLAVATE
CLAVATED
CLAVATELY
CLAVATION
CLAVE
CLAVECIN
CLAVECINS
CLAVER
CLAVERED
CLAVERING
CLAVERS
CLAVES
CLAVI
CLAVICLE
CLAVICLES
CLAVICORN
CLAVICULA
CLAVIE
CLAVIER
CLAVIERS
CLAVIES
CLAVIFORM
CLAVIGER
CLAVIGERS
CLAVIS
CLAVULATE
CLAVUS
CLAW
CLAWBACK
CLAWBACKS
CLAWED
CLAWER
CLAWERS
CLAWING
CLAWLESS
CLAWLIKE
CLAWS
CLAXON
CLAXONS
CLAY
CLAYBANK
CLAYBANKS
CLAYED
CLAYEY
CLAYIER
CLAYIEST
CLAYING
CLAYISH
CLAYLIKE
CLAYMORE
CLAYMORES
CLAYPAN
CLAYPANS
CLAYS
CLAYSTONE
CLAYTONIA
CLAYWARE
CLAYWARES
CLEAN
CLEANABLE
CLEANED
CLEANER
CLEANERS
CLEANEST
CLEANING
CLEANINGS
CLEANISH
CLEANLIER
CLEANLILY
CLEANLY
CLEANNESS
CLEANOUT
CLEANOUTS
CLEANS
CLEANSE
CLEANSED
CLEANSER
CLEANSERS
CLEANSES
CLEANSING
CLEANSKIN
CLEANTECH
CLEANUP
CLEANUPS
CLEAR
CLEARABLE
CLEARAGE
CLEARAGES
CLEARANCE
CLEARCOLE
CLEARCUT
CLEARCUTS
CLEARED
CLEARER
CLEARERS
CLEAREST
CLEAREYED
CLEARING
CLEARINGS
CLEARLY
CLEARNESS
CLEAROUT
CLEAROUTS
CLEARS
CLEARSKIN
CLEARWAY
CLEARWAYS
CLEARWEED
CLEARWING
CLEAT
CLEATED
CLEATING
CLEATS
CLEAVABLE
CLEAVAGE
CLEAVAGES
CLEAVE
CLEAVED
CLEAVER
CLEAVERS
CLEAVES
CLEAVING
CLEAVINGS
CLECHE
CLECK
CLECKED
CLECKIER
CLECKIEST
CLECKING
CLECKINGS
CLECKS
CLECKY
CLEEK
CLEEKED
CLEEKING
CLEEKIT
CLEEKS
CLEEP

CLEEPED
CLEEPING
CLEEPS
CLEEVE
CLEEVES
CLEF
CLEFS
CLEFT
CLEFTED
CLEFTING
CLEFTS
CLEG
CLEGS
CLEIDOIC
CLEIK
CLEIKS
CLEITHRAL
CLEM
CLEMATIS
CLEMENCY
CLEMENT
CLEMENTLY
CLEMMED
CLEMMING
CLEMS
CLENCH
CLENCHED
CLENCHER
CLENCHERS
CLENCHES
CLENCHING
CLEOME
CLEOMES
CLEOPATRA
CLEPE
CLEPED
CLEPES
CLEPING
CLEPSYDRA
CLEPT
CLERGIES
CLERGY
CLERGYMAN
CLERGYMEN
CLERIC
CLERICAL
CLERICALS
CLERICATE
CLERICITY
CLERICS
CLERID
CLERIDS
CLERIHEW
CLERIHEWS
CLERISIES
CLERISY
CLERK
CLERKDOM
CLERKDOMS
CLERKED
CLERKESS
CLERKING
CLERKISH
CLERKLIER
CLERKLIKE
CLERKLING
CLERKLY
CLERKS
CLERKSHIP
CLERUCH
CLERUCHIA
CLERUCHS
CLERUCHY
CLEUCH
CLEUCHS
CLEUGH
CLEUGHS
CLEVE
CLEVEITE
CLEVEITES
CLEVER
CLEVERER
CLEVEREST
CLEVERISH
CLEVERLY
CLEVES
CLEVIS
CLEVISES
CLEW
CLEWED
CLEWING
CLEWS
CLIANTHUS
CLICHE
CLICHED
CLICHEED
CLICHES
CLICK
CLICKABLE
CLICKBAIT
CLICKED
CLICKER
CLICKERS
CLICKET
CLICKETED
CLICKETS
CLICKING
CLICKINGS
CLICKLESS
CLICKS
CLICKWRAP
CLIED
CLIENT
CLIENTAGE
CLIENTAL
CLIENTELE
CLIENTS
CLIES
CLIFF
CLIFFED
CLIFFHANG
CLIFFHUNG
CLIFFIER
CLIFFIEST
CLIFFLIKE
CLIFFS
CLIFFSIDE
CLIFFTOP
CLIFFTOPS
CLIFFY
CLIFT
CLIFTED
CLIFTIER
CLIFTIEST
CLIFTS
CLIFTY
CLIMACTIC
CLIMATAL
CLIMATE
CLIMATED
CLIMATES
CLIMATIC
CLIMATING
CLIMATISE
CLIMATIZE
CLIMATURE
CLIMAX
CLIMAXED
CLIMAXES
CLIMAXING
CLIMB
CLIMBABLE
CLIMBDOWN
CLIMBED
CLIMBER
CLIMBERS
CLIMBING
CLIMBINGS
CLIMBS
CLIME
CLIMES
CLINAL
CLINALLY
CLINAMEN
CLINAMENS
CLINCH
CLINCHED
CLINCHER
CLINCHERS
CLINCHES
CLINCHING
CLINE
CLINES
CLING
CLINGED
CLINGER
CLINGERS
CLINGFILM
CLINGFISH
CLINGIER
CLINGIEST
CLINGING
CLINGS
CLINGWRAP
CLINGY
CLINIC
CLINICAL
CLINICIAN
CLINICS
CLINIQUE
CLINIQUES
CLINK
CLINKED
CLINKER
CLINKERED
CLINKERS
CLINKING
CLINKS
CLINOAXES
CLINOAXIS
CLINOSTAT
CLINQUANT
CLINT
CLINTONIA
CLINTS
CLIOMETRY
CLIP
CLIPART
CLIPARTS
CLIPBOARD
CLIPE
CLIPED
CLIPES
CLIPING
CLIPPABLE
CLIPPED
CLIPPER
CLIPPERS
CLIPPIE
CLIPPIES
CLIPPING
CLIPPINGS
CLIPS
CLIPSHEAR
CLIPSHEET
CLIPT
CLIQUE
CLIQUED
CLIQUES
CLIQUEY
CLIQUIER
CLIQUIEST
CLIQUING
CLIQUISH
CLIQUISM
CLIQUISMS
CLIQUY
CLIT
CLITELLA
CLITELLAR

CLITELLUM
CLITHRAL
CLITIC
CLITICISE
CLITICIZE
CLITICS
CLITURAL
CLITORIC
CLITORIS
CLITS
CLITTER
CLITTERED
CLITTERS
CLIVERS
CLIVIA
CLIVIAS
CLOACA
CLOACAE
CLOACAL
CLOACAS
CLOACINAL
CLOACITIS
CLOAK
CLOAKED
CLOAKING
CLOAKROOM
CLOAKS
CLOAM
CLOAMS
CLOBBER
CLOBBERED
CLOBBERS
CLOCHARD
CLOCHARDS
CLOCHE
CLOCHES
CLOCK
CLOCKED
CLOCKER
CLOCKERS
CLOCKFACE
CLOCKING
CLOCKINGS
CLOCKLIKE
CLOCKS
CLOCKWISE
CLOCKWORK
CLOD
CLODDED
CLODDIER
CLODDIEST
CLODDING
CLODDISH
CLODDY
CLODLY
CLODPATE
CLODPATED
CLODPATES
CLODPOLE
CLODPOLES
CLODPOLL
CLODPOLLS
CLODS
CLOFF
CLOFFS
CLOG
CLOGDANCE
CLOGGED
CLOGGER
CLOGGERS
CLOGGIER
CLOGGIEST
CLOGGILY
CLOGGING
CLOGGINGS
CLOGGY
CLOGMAKER
CLOGS
CLOISON
CLOISONNE
CLOISONS
CLOISTER
CLOISTERS
CLOISTRAL
CLOKE
CLOKED
CLOKES
CLOKING
CLOMB
CLOMP
CLOMPED
CLOMPING
CLOMPS
CLON
CLONAL
CLONALLY
CLONE
CLONED
CLONER
CLONERS
CLONES
CLONIC
CLONICITY
CLONIDINE
CLONING
CLONINGS
CLONISM
CLONISMS
CLONK
CLONKED
CLONKIER
CLONKIEST
CLONKING
CLONKS
CLONKY
CLONS
CLONUS
CLONUSES
CLOOP
CLOOPS
CLOOT
CLOOTIE
CLOOTS
CLOP
CLOPPED
CLOPPING
CLOPS
CLOQUE
CLOQUES
CLOSABLE
CLOSE
CLOSEABLE
CLOSED
CLOSEDOWN
CLOSEHEAD
CLOSELY
CLOSENESS
CLOSEOUT
CLOSEOUTS
CLOSER
CLOSERS
CLOSES
CLOSEST
CLOSET
CLOSETED
CLOSETFUL
CLOSETING
CLOSETS
CLOSEUP
CLOSEUPS
CLOSING
CLOSINGS
CLOSURE
CLOSURED
CLOSURES
CLOSURING
CLOT
CLOTBUR
CLOTBURS
CLOTE
CLOTES
CLOTH
CLOTHE
CLOTHED
CLOTHES
CLOTHIER
CLOTHIERS
CLOTHING
CLOTHINGS
CLOTHLIKE
CLOTHS
CLOTPOLL
CLOTPOLLS
CLOTS
CLOTTED
CLOTTER
CLOTTERED
CLOTTERS
CLOTTIER
CLOTTIEST
CLOTTING
CLOTTINGS
CLOTTISH
CLOTTY
CLOTURE
CLOTURED
CLOTURES
CLOTURING
CLOU
CLOUD
CLOUDAGE
CLOUDAGES
CLOUDED
CLOUDIER
CLOUDIEST
CLOUDILY
CLOUDING
CLOUDINGS
CLOUDLAND
CLOUDLESS
CLOUDLET
CLOUDLETS
CLOUDLIKE
CLOUDS
CLOUDTOWN
CLOUDY
CLOUGH
CLOUGHS
CLOUR
CLOURED
CLOURING
CLOURS
CLOUS
CLOUT
CLOUTED
CLOUTER
CLOUTERLY
CLOUTERS
CLOUTING
CLOUTS
CLOVE
CLOVEN
CLOVER
CLOVERED
CLOVERIER
CLOVERS
CLOVERY
CLOVES
CLOVIS
CLOW
CLOWDER
CLOWDERS
CLOWED
CLOWING
CLOWN
CLOWNED
CLOWNERY
CLOWNFISH
CLOWNING
CLOWNINGS

CLOWNISH
CLOWNS
CLOWS
CLOY
CLOYE
CLOYED
CLOYES
CLOYING
CLOYINGLY
CLOYLESS
CLOYMENT
CLOYMENTS
CLOYS
CLOYSOME
CLOZAPINE
CLOZE
CLOZES
CLUB
CLUBABLE
CLUBBABLE
CLUBBED
CLUBBER
CLUBBERS
CLUBBIER
CLUBBIEST
CLUBBILY
CLUBBING
CLUBBINGS
CLUBBISH
CLUBBISM
CLUBBISMS
CLUBBIST
CLUBBISTS
CLUBBY
CLUBFACE
CLUBFACES
CLUBFEET
CLUBFOOT
CLUBHAND
CLUBHANDS
CLUBHAUL
CLUBHAULS
CLUBHEAD
CLUBHEADS
CLUBHOUSE
CLUBLAND
CLUBLANDS
CLUBLIKE
CLUBMAN
CLUBMATE
CLUBMATES
CLUBMEN
CLUBMOSS
CLUBROOM
CLUBROOMS
CLUBROOT
CLUBROOTS
CLUBRUSH
CLUBS
CLUBWOMAN
CLUBWOMEN
CLUCK
CLUCKED
CLUCKER
CLUCKERS
CLUCKIER
CLUCKIEST
CLUCKING
CLUCKS
CLUCKY
CLUDGIE
CLUDGIES
CLUE
CLUED
CLUEING
CLUELESS
CLUES
CLUEY
CLUIER
CLUIEST
CLUING
CLUMBER
CLUMBERS
CLUMP
CLUMPED
CLUMPER
CLUMPERED
CLUMPERS
CLUMPET
CLUMPETS
CLUMPIER
CLUMPIEST
CLUMPING
CLUMPISH
CLUMPLIKE
CLUMPS
CLUMPY
CLUMSIER
CLUMSIEST
CLUMSILY
CLUMSY
CLUNCH
CLUNCHES
CLUNG
CLUNK
CLUNKED
CLUNKER
CLUNKERS
CLUNKIER
CLUNKIEST
CLUNKING
CLUNKS
CLUNKY
CLUPEID
CLUPEIDS
CLUPEOID
CLUPEOIDS
CLUSIA
CLUSIAS
CLUSTER
CLUSTERED
CLUSTERS
CLUSTERY
CLUTCH
CLUTCHED
CLUTCHES
CLUTCHIER
CLUTCHING
CLUTCHY
CLUTTER
CLUTTERED
CLUTTERS
CLUTTERY
CLY
CLYING
CLYPE
CLYPEAL
CLYPEATE
CLYPED
CLYPEI
CLYPES
CLYPEUS
CLYPING
CLYSTER
CLYSTERS
CNEMIAL
CNEMIDES
CNEMIS
CNIDA
CNIDAE
CNIDARIAN
COACH
COACHABLE
COACHDOG
COACHDOGS
COACHED
COACHEE
COACHEES
COACHER
COACHERS
COACHES
COACHIER
COACHIES
COACHIEST
COACHING
COACHINGS
COACHLINE
COACHLOAD
COACHMAN
COACHMEN
COACHROOF
COACHWHIP
COACHWOOD
COACHWORK
COACHY
COACT
COACTED
COACTING
COACTION
COACTIONS
COACTIVE
COACTOR
COACTORS
COACTS
COADAPTED
COADIES
COADJUTOR
COADMIRE
COADMIRED
COADMIRES
COADMIT
COADMITS
COADUNATE
COADY
COAEVAL
COAEVALS
COAGENCY
COAGENT
COAGENTS
COAGULA
COAGULANT
COAGULASE
COAGULATE
COAGULUM
COAGULUMS
COAITA
COAITAS
COAL
COALA
COALAS
COALBALL
COALBALLS
COALBIN
COALBINS
COALBOX
COALBOXES
COALDUST
COALDUSTS
COALED
COALER
COALERS
COALESCE
COALESCED
COALESCES
COALFACE
COALFACES
COALFIELD
COALFISH
COALHOLE
COALHOLES
COALHOUSE
COALIER
COALIEST
COALIFIED
COALIFIES
COALIFY
COALING
COALISE
COALISED
COALISES

C

COALISING
COALITION
COALIZE
COALIZED
COALIZES
COALIZING
COALLESS
COALMAN
COALMEN
COALMINE
COALMINER
COALMINES
COALPIT
COALPITS
COALS
COALSACK
COALSACKS
COALSHED
COALSHEDS
COALY
COALYARD
COALYARDS
COAMING
COAMINGS
COANCHOR
COANCHORS
COANNEX
COANNEXED
COANNEXES
COAPPEAR
COAPPEARS
COAPT
COAPTED
COAPTING
COAPTS
COARB
COARBS
COARCTATE
COARSE
COARSELY
COARSEN
COARSENED
COARSENS
COARSER
COARSEST
COARSISH
COASSIST
COASSISTS
COASSUME
COASSUMED
COASSUMES
COAST
COASTAL
COASTALLY
COASTED
COASTER
COASTERS
COASTING
COASTINGS
COASTLAND
COASTLINE
COASTS
COASTWARD
COASTWISE
COAT
COATDRESS
COATE
COATED
COATEE
COATEES
COATER
COATERS
COATES
COATI
COATING
COATINGS
COATIS
COATLESS
COATLIKE
COATRACK
COATRACKS
COATROOM
COATROOMS
COATS
COATSTAND
COATTAIL
COATTAILS
COATTEND
COATTENDS
COATTEST
COATTESTS
COAUTHOR
COAUTHORS
COAX
COAXAL
COAXED
COAXER
COAXERS
COAXES
COAXIAL
COAXIALLY
COAXING
COAXINGLY
COAXINGS
COB
COBAEA
COBAEAS
COBALAMIN
COBALT
COBALTIC
COBALTINE
COBALTITE
COBALTOUS
COBALTS
COBB
COBBED
COBBER
COBBERS
COBBIER
COBBIEST
COBBING
COBBLE
COBBLED
COBBLER
COBBLERS
COBBLERY
COBBLES
COBBLING
COBBLINGS
COBBS
COBBY
COBIA
COBIAS
COBLE
COBLES
COBLOAF
COBLOAVES
COBNUT
COBNUTS
COBRA
COBRAS
COBRIC
COBRIFORM
COBS
COBURG
COBURGS
COBWEB
COBWEBBED
COBWEBBY
COBWEBS
COBZA
COBZAS
COCA
COCAIN
COCAINE
COCAINES
COCAINISE
COCAINISM
COCAINIST
COCAINIZE
COCAINS
COCAPTAIN
COCAS
COCCAL
COCCI
COCCIC
COCCID
COCCIDIA
COCCIDIAN
COCCIDIUM
COCCIDS
COCCO
COCCOID
COCCOIDAL
COCCOIDS
COCCOLITE
COCCOLITH
COCCOS
COCCOUS
COCCUS
COCCYGEAL
COCCYGES
COCCYGIAN
COCCYX
COCCYXES
COCH
COCHAIR
COCHAIRED
COCHAIRS
COCHES
COCHIN
COCHINEAL
COCHINS
COCHLEA
COCHLEAE
COCHLEAR
COCHLEARE
COCHLEARS
COCHLEAS
COCHLEATE
COCINERA
COCINERAS
COCK
COCKADE
COCKADED
COCKADES
COCKAMAMY
COCKAPOO
COCKAPOOS
COCKATEEL
COCKATIEL
COCKATOO
COCKATOOS
COCKBILL
COCKBILLS
COCKBIRD
COCKBIRDS
COCKBOAT
COCKBOATS
COCKCROW
COCKCROWS
COCKED
COCKER
COCKERED
COCKEREL
COCKERELS
COCKERING
COCKERS
COCKET
COCKETS
COCKEYE
COCKEYED
COCKEYES
COCKFIGHT
COCKHORSE
COCKIER
COCKIES
COCKIEST
COCKILY
COCKINESS

COCKING
COCKISH
COCKLE
COCKLEBUR
COCKLED
COCKLEERT
COCKLEMAN
COCKLEMEN
COCKLER
COCKLERS
COCKLES
COCKLIKE
COCKLING
COCKLINGS
COCKLOFT
COCKLOFTS
COCKMATCH
COCKNEY
COCKNEYFY
COCKNEYS
COCKNIFY
COCKPIT
COCKPITS
COCKROACH
COCKS
COCKSCOMB
COCKSFOOT
COCKSHIES
COCKSHOT
COCKSHOTS
COCKSHUT
COCKSHUTS
COCKSHY
COCKSIER
COCKSIEST
COCKSMAN
COCKSMEN
COCKSPUR
COCKSPURS
COCKSURE
COCKSWAIN
COCKSY
COCKTAIL
COCKTAILS
COCKUP
COCKUPS
COCKY
COCO
COCOA
COCOANUT
COCOANUTS
COCOAS
COCOBOLA
COCOBOLAS
COCOBOLO
COCOBOLOS
COCOMAT
COCOMATS
COCONUT
COCONUTS
COCONUTTY
COCOON
COCOONED
COCOONER
COCOONERS
COCOONERY
COCOONING
COCOONS
COCOPAN
COCOPANS
COCOPLUM
COCOPLUMS
COCOS
COCOTTE
COCOTTES
COCOUNSEL
COCOYAM
COCOYAMS
COCOZELLE
COCREATE
COCREATED
COCREATES
COCREATOR
COCTILE
COCTION
COCTIONS
COCULTURE
COCURATE
COCURATED
COCURATES
COCURATOR
COCUSWOOD
COD
CODA
CODABLE
CODAS
CODDED
CODDER
CODDERS
CODDING
CODDLE
CODDLED
CODDLER
CODDLERS
CODDLES
CODDLING
CODE
CODEBOOK
CODEBOOKS
CODEBTOR
CODEBTORS
CODEC
CODECS
CODED
CODEIA
CODEIAS
CODEIN
CODEINA
CODEINAS
CODEINE
CODEINES
CODEINS
CODELESS
CODEN
CODENAME
CODENAMES
CODENS
CODER
CODERIVE
CODERIVED
CODERIVES
CODERS
CODES
CODESIGN
CODESIGNS
CODETTA
CODETTAS
CODEVELOP
CODEWORD
CODEWORDS
CODEX
CODEXES
CODFISH
CODFISHES
CODGER
CODGERS
CODICES
CODICIL
CODICILS
CODIFIED
CODIFIER
CODIFIERS
CODIFIES
CODIFY
CODIFYING
CODILLA
CODILLAS
CODILLE
CODILLES
CODING
CODINGS
CODIRECT
CODIRECTS
CODIST
CODISTS
CODLIN
CODLING
CODLINGS
CODLINS
CODOLOGY
CODOMAIN
CODOMAINS
CODON
CODONS
CODPIECE
CODPIECES
CODRIVE
CODRIVEN
CODRIVER
CODRIVERS
CODRIVES
CODRIVING
CODROVE
CODS
COECILIAN
COED
COEDIT
COEDITED
COEDITING
COEDITOR
COEDITORS
COEDITS
COEDS
COEFFECT
COEFFECTS
COEHORN
COEHORNS
COELIAC
COELIACS
COELOM
COELOMATA
COELOMATE
COELOME
COELOMES
COELOMIC
COELOMS
COELOSTAT
COEMBODY
COEMPLOY
COEMPLOYS
COEMPT
COEMPTED
COEMPTING
COEMPTION
COEMPTS
COENACLE
COENACLES
COENACT
COENACTED
COENACTS
COENAMOR
COENAMORS
COENAMOUR
COENDURE
COENDURED
COENDURES
COENOBIA
COENOBITE
COENOBIUM
COENOCYTE
COENOSARC
COENURE
COENURES
COENURI
COENURUS
COENZYME
COENZYMES
COEQUAL
COEQUALLY
COEQUALS

C

COEQUATE
COEQUATED
COEQUATES
COERCE
COERCED
COERCER
COERCERS
COERCES
COERCIBLE
COERCIBLY
COERCING
COERCION
COERCIONS
COERCIVE
COERECT
COERECTED
COERECTS
COESITE
COESITES
COETERNAL
COEVAL
COEVALITY
COEVALLY
COEVALS
COEVOLVE
COEVOLVED
COEVOLVES
COEXERT
COEXERTED
COEXERTS
COEXIST
COEXISTED
COEXISTS
COEXTEND
COEXTENDS
COFACTOR
COFACTORS
COFEATURE
COFF
COFFED
COFFEE
COFFEEPOT
COFFEES
COFFER
COFFERDAM
COFFERED
COFFERING
COFFERS
COFFIN
COFFINED
COFFING
COFFINING
COFFINITE
COFFINS
COFFLE
COFFLED
COFFLES
COFFLING
COFFRET
COFFRETS
COFFS
COFINANCE
COFIRING
COFIRINGS
COFOUND
COFOUNDED
COFOUNDER
COFOUNDS
COFT
COG
COGENCE
COGENCES
COGENCIES
COGENCY
COGENER
COGENERS
COGENT
COGENTLY
COGGED
COGGER
COGGERS
COGGIE
COGGIES
COGGING
COGGINGS
COGGLE
COGGLED
COGGLES
COGGLIER
COGGLIEST
COGGLING
COGGLY
COGIE
COGIES
COGITABLE
COGITATE
COGITATED
COGITATES
COGITATOR
COGITO
COGITOS
COGNAC
COGNACS
COGNATE
COGNATELY
COGNATES
COGNATION
COGNISANT
COGNISE
COGNISED
COGNISER
COGNISERS
COGNISES
COGNISING
COGNITION
COGNITIVE
COGNIZANT
COGNIZE
COGNIZED
COGNIZER
COGNIZERS
COGNIZES
COGNIZING
COGNOMEN
COGNOMENS
COGNOMINA
COGNOSCE
COGNOSCED
COGNOSCES
COGNOVIT
COGNOVITS
COGON
COGONS
COGS
COGUE
COGUES
COGWAY
COGWAYS
COGWHEEL
COGWHEELS
COHAB
COHABIT
COHABITED
COHABITEE
COHABITER
COHABITOR
COHABITS
COHABS
COHEAD
COHEADED
COHEADING
COHEADS
COHEIR
COHEIRESS
COHEIRS
COHEN
COHENS
COHERE
COHERED
COHERENCE
COHERENCY
COHERENT
COHERER
COHERERS
COHERES
COHERING
COHERITOR
COHESIBLE
COHESION
COHESIONS
COHESIVE
COHIBIT
COHIBITED
COHIBITS
COHO
COHOBATE
COHOBATED
COHOBATES
COHOE
COHOES
COHOG
COHOGS
COHOLDER
COHOLDERS
COHORN
COHORNS
COHORT
COHORTS
COHOS
COHOSH
COHOSHES
COHOST
COHOSTED
COHOSTESS
COHOSTING
COHOSTS
COHOUSING
COHUNE
COHUNES
COHYPONYM
COIF
COIFED
COIFFE
COIFFED
COIFFES
COIFFEUR
COIFFEURS
COIFFEUSE
COIFFING
COIFFURE
COIFFURED
COIFFURES
COIFING
COIFS
COIGN
COIGNE
COIGNED
COIGNES
COIGNING
COIGNS
COIL
COILED
COILER
COILERS
COILING
COILS
COIN
COINABLE
COINAGE
COINAGES
COINCIDE
COINCIDED
COINCIDES
COINED
COINER
COINERS
COINFECT
COINFECTS
COINFER
COINFERS

COINHERE
COINHERED
COINHERES
COINING
COININGS
COINMATE
COINMATES
COINOP
COINS
COINSURE
COINSURED
COINSURER
COINSURES
COINTER
COINTERS
COINTREAU
COINVENT
COINVENTS
COINVEST
COINVESTS
COIR
COIRS
COISTREL
COISTRELS
COISTRIL
COISTRILS
COIT
COITAL
COITALLY
COITION
COITIONAL
COITIONS
COITS
COITUS
COITUSES
COJOIN
COJOINED
COJOINING
COJOINS
COJONES
COKE
COKED
COKEHEAD
COKEHEADS
COKELIKE
COKERNUT
COKERNUTS
COKES
COKESES
COKIER
COKIEST
COKING
COKINGS
COKULORIS
COKY
COL
COLA
COLANDER
COLANDERS
COLAS
COLBIES
COLBY
COLBYS
COLCANNON
COLCHICA
COLCHICUM
COLCOTHAR
COLD
COLDBLOOD
COLDCOCK
COLDCOCKS
COLDER
COLDEST
COLDHOUSE
COLDIE
COLDIES
COLDISH
COLDLY
COLDNESS
COLDS
COLE
COLEAD
COLEADER
COLEADERS
COLEADING
COLEADS
COLECTOMY
COLED
COLEOPTER
COLES
COLESEED
COLESEEDS
COLESLAW
COLESLAWS
COLESSEE
COLESSEES
COLESSOR
COLESSORS
COLETIT
COLETITS
COLEUS
COLEUSES
COLEWORT
COLEWORTS
COLEY
COLEYS
COLIBRI
COLIBRIS
COLIC
COLICIN
COLICINE
COLICINES
COLICINS
COLICKIER
COLICKY
COLICROOT
COLICS
COLICWEED
COLIES
COLIFORM
COLIFORMS
COLIN
COLINEAR
COLINS
COLIPHAGE
COLISEUM
COLISEUMS
COLISTIN
COLISTINS
COLITIC
COLITIS
COLITISES
COLL
COLLAB
COLLABS
COLLAGE
COLLAGED
COLLAGEN
COLLAGENS
COLLAGES
COLLAGING
COLLAGIST
COLLAPSAR
COLLAPSE
COLLAPSED
COLLAPSES
COLLAR
COLLARD
COLLARDS
COLLARED
COLLARET
COLLARETS
COLLARING
COLLARS
COLLATE
COLLATED
COLLATES
COLLATING
COLLATION
COLLATIVE
COLLATOR
COLLATORS
COLLEAGUE
COLLECT
COLLECTED
COLLECTOR
COLLECTS
COLLED
COLLEEN
COLLEENS
COLLEGE
COLLEGER
COLLEGERS
COLLEGES
COLLEGIA
COLLEGIAL
COLLEGIAN
COLLEGIUM
COLLET
COLLETED
COLLETING
COLLETS
COLLICULI
COLLIDE
COLLIDED
COLLIDER
COLLIDERS
COLLIDES
COLLIDING
COLLIE
COLLIED
COLLIER
COLLIERS
COLLIERY
COLLIES
COLLIGATE
COLLIMATE
COLLINEAR
COLLING
COLLINGS
COLLINS
COLLINSES
COLLINSIA
COLLISION
COLLOCATE
COLLODION
COLLODIUM
COLLOGUE
COLLOGUED
COLLOGUES
COLLOID
COLLOIDAL
COLLOIDS
COLLOP
COLLOPS
COLLOQUE
COLLOQUED
COLLOQUES
COLLOQUIA
COLLOQUY
COLLOTYPE
COLLOTYPY
COLLS
COLLUDE
COLLUDED
COLLUDER
COLLUDERS
COLLUDES
COLLUDING
COLLUSION
COLLUSIVE
COLLUVIA
COLLUVIAL
COLLUVIES
COLLUVIUM
COLLY
COLLYING
COLLYRIA
COLLYRIUM
COLOBI

C

COLOBID
COLOBIDS
COLOBOMA
COLOBOMAS
COLOBUS
COLOBUSES
COLOCATE
COLOCATED
COLOCATES
COLOCYNTH
COLOG
COLOGNE
COLOGNED
COLOGNES
COLOGS
COLOMBARD
COLON
COLONE
COLONEL
COLONELCY
COLONELS
COLONES
COLONI
COLONIAL
COLONIALS
COLONIC
COLONICS
COLONIES
COLONISE
COLONISED
COLONISER
COLONISES
COLONIST
COLONISTS
COLONITIS
COLONIZE
COLONIZED
COLONIZER
COLONIZES
COLONNADE
COLONS
COLONUS
COLONY
COLOPHON
COLOPHONS
COLOPHONY
COLOR
COLORABLE
COLORABLY
COLORADO
COLORANT
COLORANTS
COLORBRED
COLORCAST
COLORED
COLOREDS
COLORER
COLORERS
COLORFAST
COLORFUL
COLORIER
COLORIEST
COLORIFIC
COLORING
COLORINGS
COLORISE
COLORISED
COLORISER
COLORISES
COLORISM
COLORISMS
COLORIST
COLORISTS
COLORIZE
COLORIZED
COLORIZER
COLORIZES
COLORLESS
COLORMAN
COLORMEN
COLORS
COLORWASH
COLORWAY
COLORWAYS
COLORY
COLOSSAL
COLOSSEUM
COLOSSI
COLOSSUS
COLOSTOMY
COLOSTRAL
COLOSTRIC
COLOSTRUM
COLOTOMY
COLOUR
COLOURANT
COLOURED
COLOUREDS
COLOURER
COLOURERS
COLOURFUL
COLOURIER
COLOURING
COLOURISE
COLOURISM
COLOURIST
COLOURIZE
COLOURMAN
COLOURMEN
COLOURS
COLOURWAY
COLOURY
COLPITIS
COLPOTOMY
COLS
COLT
COLTAN
COLTANS
COLTED
COLTER
COLTERS
COLTHOOD
COLTHOODS
COLTING
COLTISH
COLTISHLY
COLTS
COLTSFOOT
COLTWOOD
COLTWOODS
COLUBRIAD
COLUBRID
COLUBRIDS
COLUBRINE
COLUGO
COLUGOS
COLUMBARY
COLUMBATE
COLUMBIC
COLUMBINE
COLUMBITE
COLUMBIUM
COLUMBOUS
COLUMEL
COLUMELLA
COLUMELS
COLUMN
COLUMNAL
COLUMNALS
COLUMNAR
COLUMNEA
COLUMNEAS
COLUMNED
COLUMNIST
COLUMNS
COLURE
COLURES
COLY
COLZA
COLZAS
COMA
COMADE
COMAE
COMAKE
COMAKER
COMAKERS
COMAKES
COMAKING
COMAL
COMANAGE
COMANAGED
COMANAGER
COMANAGES
COMARB
COMARBS
COMART
COMARTS
COMAS
COMATE
COMATES
COMATIC
COMATIK
COMATIKS
COMATOSE
COMATULA
COMATULAE
COMATULID
COMB
COMBAT
COMBATANT
COMBATED
COMBATER
COMBATERS
COMBATING
COMBATIVE
COMBATS
COMBATTED
COMBE
COMBED
COMBER
COMBERS
COMBES
COMBI
COMBIER
COMBIES
COMBIEST
COMBINATE
COMBINE
COMBINED
COMBINEDS
COMBINER
COMBINERS
COMBINES
COMBING
COMBINGS
COMBINING
COMBIS
COMBLE
COMBLES
COMBLESS
COMBLIKE
COMBO
COMBOS
COMBOVER
COMBOVERS
COMBRETUM
COMBS
COMBUST
COMBUSTED
COMBUSTOR
COMBUSTS
COMBWISE
COMBY
COME
COMEBACK
COMEBACKS
COMEDDLE
COMEDDLED
COMEDDLES
COMEDIAN

COMEDIANS
COMEDIC
COMEDIES
COMEDIST
COMEDISTS
COMEDO
COMEDONES
COMEDOS
COMEDOWN
COMEDOWNS
COMEDY
COMELIER
COMELIEST
COMELILY
COMELY
COMEMBER
COMEMBERS
COMEOVER
COMEOVERS
COMER
COMERS
COMES
COMET
COMETARY
COMETH
COMETHER
COMETHERS
COMETIC
COMETS
COMFIER
COMFIEST
COMFILY
COMFINESS
COMFIT
COMFITS
COMFITURE
COMFORT
COMFORTED
COMFORTER
COMFORTS
COMFREY
COMFREYS
COMFY
COMIC
COMICAL
COMICALLY
COMICE
COMICES
COMICS
COMING
COMINGLE
COMINGLED
COMINGLES
COMINGS
COMIQUE
COMIQUES
COMITADJI
COMITAL
COMITATUS
COMITIA
COMITIAL
COMITIAS
COMITIES
COMITY
COMIX
COMM
COMMA
COMMAND
COMMANDED
COMMANDER
COMMANDO
COMMANDOS
COMMANDS
COMMAS
COMMATA
COMMENCE
COMMENCED
COMMENCER
COMMENCES
COMMEND
COMMENDAM
COMMENDED
COMMENDER
COMMENDS
COMMENSAL
COMMENT
COMMENTED
COMMENTER
COMMENTOR
COMMENTS
COMMER
COMMERCE
COMMERCED
COMMERCES
COMMERE
COMMERES
COMMERGE
COMMERGED
COMMERGES
COMMERS
COMMIE
COMMIES
COMMINATE
COMMINGLE
COMMINUTE
COMMIS
COMMISH
COMMISHES
COMMISSAR
COMMIT
COMMITS
COMMITTAL
COMMITTED
COMMITTEE
COMMITTER
COMMIX
COMMIXED
COMMIXES
COMMIXING
COMMIXT
COMMO
COMMODE
COMMODES
COMMODIFY
COMMODITY
COMMODO
COMMODORE
COMMON
COMMONAGE
COMMONED
COMMONER
COMMONERS
COMMONEST
COMMONEY
COMMONEYS
COMMONING
COMMONLY
COMMONS
COMMORANT
COMMOS
COMMOT
COMMOTE
COMMOTES
COMMOTION
COMMOTS
COMMOVE
COMMOVED
COMMOVES
COMMOVING
COMMS
COMMUNAL
COMMUNARD
COMMUNE
COMMUNED
COMMUNER
COMMUNERS
COMMUNES
COMMUNING
COMMUNION
COMMUNISE
COMMUNISM
COMMUNIST
COMMUNITY
COMMUNIZE
COMMUTATE
COMMUTE
COMMUTED
COMMUTER
COMMUTERS
COMMUTES
COMMUTING
COMMUTUAL
COMMY
COMODO
COMONOMER
COMORBID
COMOSE
COMOUS
COMP
COMPACT
COMPACTED
COMPACTER
COMPACTLY
COMPACTOR
COMPACTS
COMPADRE
COMPADRES
COMPAGE
COMPAGES
COMPAND
COMPANDED
COMPANDER
COMPANDOR
COMPANDS
COMPANIED
COMPANIES
COMPANING
COMPANION
COMPANY
COMPARE
COMPARED
COMPARER
COMPARERS
COMPARES
COMPARING
COMPART
COMPARTED
COMPARTS
COMPAS
COMPASS
COMPASSED
COMPASSES
COMPAST
COMPEAR
COMPEARED
COMPEARS
COMPED
COMPEER
COMPEERED
COMPEERS
COMPEL
COMPELLED
COMPELLER
COMPELS
COMPEND
COMPENDIA
COMPENDS
COMPER
COMPERE
COMPERED
COMPERES
COMPERING
COMPERS
COMPESCE
COMPESCED
COMPESCES
COMPETE
COMPETED
COMPETENT
COMPETES

C

COMPETING
COMPILE
COMPILED
COMPILER
COMPILERS
COMPILES
COMPILING
COMPING
COMPINGS
COMPITAL
COMPLAIN
COMPLAINS
COMPLAINT
COMPLEAT
COMPLEATS
COMPLECT
COMPLECTS
COMPLETE
COMPLETED
COMPLETER
COMPLETES
COMPLEX
COMPLEXED
COMPLEXER
COMPLEXES
COMPLEXLY
COMPLEXUS
COMPLIANT
COMPLICE
COMPLICES
COMPLICIT
COMPLIED
COMPLIER
COMPLIERS
COMPLIES
COMPLIN
COMPLINE
COMPLINES
COMPLINS
COMPLISH
COMPLOT
COMPLOTS
COMPLUVIA
COMPLY
COMPLYING
COMPO
COMPONE
COMPONENT
COMPONY
COMPORT
COMPORTED
COMPORTS
COMPOS
COMPOSE
COMPOSED
COMPOSER
COMPOSERS
COMPOSES
COMPOSING
COMPOSITE
COMPOST
COMPOSTED
COMPOSTER
COMPOSTS
COMPOSURE
COMPOT
COMPOTE
COMPOTES
COMPOTIER
COMPOTS
COMPOUND
COMPOUNDS
COMPRADOR
COMPRESS
COMPRINT
COMPRINTS
COMPRISAL
COMPRISE
COMPRISED
COMPRISES
COMPRIZE
COMPRIZED
COMPRIZES
COMPS
COMPT
COMPTABLE
COMPTED
COMPTER
COMPTERS
COMPTIBLE
COMPTING
COMPTROLL
COMPTS
COMPULSE
COMPULSED
COMPULSES
COMPUTANT
COMPUTE
COMPUTED
COMPUTER
COMPUTERS
COMPUTES
COMPUTING
COMPUTIST
COMRADE
COMRADELY
COMRADERY
COMRADES
COMS
COMSAT
COMSATS
COMSYMP
COMSYMPS
COMTE
COMTES
COMUS
COMUSES
CON
CONACRE
CONACRED
CONACRES
CONACRING
CONARIA
CONARIAL
CONARIUM
CONATION
CONATIONS
CONATIVE
CONATUS
CONCAUSE
CONCAUSES
CONCAVE
CONCAVED
CONCAVELY
CONCAVES
CONCAVING
CONCAVITY
CONCEAL
CONCEALED
CONCEALER
CONCEALS
CONCEDE
CONCEDED
CONCEDER
CONCEDERS
CONCEDES
CONCEDING
CONCEDO
CONCEIT
CONCEITED
CONCEITS
CONCEITY
CONCEIVE
CONCEIVED
CONCEIVER
CONCEIVES
CONCENT
CONCENTER
CONCENTRE
CONCENTS
CONCENTUS
CONCEPT
CONCEPTI
CONCEPTS
CONCEPTUS
CONCERN
CONCERNED
CONCERNS
CONCERT
CONCERTED
CONCERTI
CONCERTO
CONCERTOS
CONCERTS
CONCETTI
CONCETTO
CONCH
CONCHA
CONCHAE
CONCHAL
CONCHAS
CONCHATE
CONCHE
CONCHED
CONCHES
CONCHIE
CONCHIES
CONCHING
CONCHITIS
CONCHO
CONCHOID
CONCHOIDS
CONCHOS
CONCHS
CONCHY
CONCIERGE
CONCILIAR
CONCISE
CONCISED
CONCISELY
CONCISER
CONCISES
CONCISEST
CONCISING
CONCISION
CONCLAVE
CONCLAVES
CONCLUDE
CONCLUDED
CONCLUDER
CONCLUDES
CONCOCT
CONCOCTED
CONCOCTER
CONCOCTOR
CONCOCTS
CONCOLOR
CONCORD
CONCORDAL
CONCORDAT
CONCORDED
CONCORDS
CONCOURS
CONCOURSE
CONCREATE
CONCRETE
CONCRETED
CONCRETES
CONCREW
CONCREWED
CONCREWS
CONCUBINE
CONCUPIES
CONCUPY
CONCUR
CONCURRED
CONCURS
CONCUSS
CONCUSSED
CONCUSSES

CONCYCLIC
COND
CONDEMN
CONDEMNED
CONDEMNER
CONDEMNOR
CONDEMNS
CONDENSE
CONDENSED
CONDENSER
CONDENSES
CONDER
CONDERS
CONDIDDLE
CONDIE
CONDIES
CONDIGN
CONDIGNLY
CONDIMENT
CONDITION
CONDO
CONDOES
CONDOLE
CONDOLED
CONDOLENT
CONDOLER
CONDOLERS
CONDOLES
CONDOLING
CONDOM
CONDOMS
CONDONE
CONDONED
CONDONER
CONDONERS
CONDONES
CONDONING
CONDOR
CONDORES
CONDORS
CONDOS
CONDUCE
CONDUCED
CONDUCER
CONDUCERS
CONDUCES
CONDUCING
CONDUCIVE
CONDUCT
CONDUCTED
CONDUCTI
CONDUCTOR
CONDUCTS
CONDUCTUS
CONDUIT
CONDUITS
CONDYLAR
CONDYLE
CONDYLES
CONDYLOID
CONDYLOMA
CONE
CONED
CONELESS
CONELIKE
CONELRAD
CONELRADS
CONENOSE
CONENOSES
CONEPATE
CONEPATES
CONEPATL
CONEPATLS
CONES
CONEY
CONEYS
CONF
CONFAB
CONFABBED
CONFABS
CONFECT
CONFECTED
CONFECTS
CONFER
CONFEREE
CONFEREES
CONFERRAL
CONFERRED
CONFERREE
CONFERRER
CONFERS
CONFERVA
CONFERVAE
CONFFRVAL
CONFERVAS
CONFESS
CONFESSED
CONFESSES
CONFESSOR
CONFEST
CONFESTLY
CONFETTI
CONFETTO
CONFIDANT
CONFIDE
CONFIDED
CONFIDENT
CONFIDER
CONFIDERS
CONFIDES
CONFIDING
CONFIGURE
CONFINE
CONFINED
CONFINER
CONFINERS
CONFINES
CONFINING
CONFIRM
CONFIRMED
CONFIRMEE
CONFIRMER
CONFIRMOR
CONFIRMS
CONFISEUR
CONFIT
CONFITEOR
CONFITS
CONFITURE
CONFIX
CONFIXED
CONFIXES
CONFIXING
CONFLATE
CONFLATED
CONFLATES
CONFLICT
CONFLICTS
CONFLUENT
CONFLUX
CONFLUXES
CONFOCAL
CONFORM
CONFORMAL
CONFORMED
CONFORMER
CONFORMS
CONFOUND
CONFOUNDS
CONFRERE
CONFRERES
CONFRERIE
CONFRONT
CONFRONTE
CONFRONTS
CONFS
CONFUSE
CONFUSED
CONFUSES
CONFUSING
CONFUSION
CONFUTE
CONFUTED
CONFUTER
CONFUTERS
CONFUTES
CONFUTING
CONGA
CONGAED
CONGAING
CONGAS
CONGE
CONGEAL
CONGEALED
CONGEALER
CONGEALS
CONGED
CONGEE
CONGEED
CONGEEING
CONGEES
CONGEING
CONGENER
CONGENERS
CONGENIAL
CONGENIC
CONGER
CONGERIES
CONGERS
CONGES
CONGEST
CONGESTED
CONGESTS
CONGIARY
CONGII
CONGIUS
CONGLOBE
CONGLOBED
CONGLOBES
CONGO
CONGOES
CONGOS
CONGOU
CONGOUS
CONGRATS
CONGREE
CONGREED
CONGREES
CONGREET
CONGREETS
CONGRESS
CONGRUE
CONGRUED
CONGRUENT
CONGRUES
CONGRUING
CONGRUITY
CONGRUOUS
CONI
CONIA
CONIAS
CONIC
CONICAL
CONICALLY
CONICINE
CONICINES
CONICITY
CONICS
CONIDIA
CONIDIAL
CONIDIAN
CONIDIUM
CONIES
CONIFER
CONIFERS
CONIFORM
CONIINE
CONIINES
CONIMA
CONIMAS

C

CONIN
CONINE
CONINES
CONING
CONINS
CONIOLOGY
CONIOSES
CONIOSIS
CONIUM
CONIUMS
CONJECT
CONJECTED
CONJECTS
CONJEE
CONJEED
CONJEEING
CONJEES
CONJOIN
CONJOINED
CONJOINER
CONJOINS
CONJOINT
CONJUGAL
CONJUGANT
CONJUGATE
CONJUNCT
CONJUNCTS
CONJUNTO
CONJUNTOS
CONJURE
CONJURED
CONJURER
CONJURERS
CONJURES
CONJURIES
CONJURING
CONJUROR
CONJURORS
CONJURY
CONK
CONKED
CONKER
CONKERS
CONKIER
CONKIEST
CONKING
CONKOUT
CONKOUTS
CONKS
CONKY
CONLANG
CONLANGER
CONLANGS
CONMAN
CONMEN
CONN
CONNATE
CONNATELY
CONNATION
CONNATURE
CONNE
CONNECT
CONNECTED
CONNECTER
CONNECTOR
CONNECTS
CONNED
CONNER
CONNERS
CONNES
CONNEXION
CONNEXIVE
CONNIE
CONNIES
CONNING
CONNINGS
CONNIVE
CONNIVED
CONNIVENT
CONNIVER
CONNIVERS
CONNIVERY
CONNIVES
CONNIVING
CONNOR
CONNORS
CONNOTATE
CONNOTE
CONNOTED
CONNOTES
CONNOTING
CONNOTIVE
CONNS
CONNUBIAL
CONODONT
CONODONTS
CONOID
CONOIDAL
CONOIDIC
CONOIDS
CONOMINEE
CONQUER
CONQUERED
CONQUERER
CONQUEROR
CONQUERS
CONQUEST
CONQUESTS
CONQUIAN
CONQUIANS
CONS
CONSCIENT
CONSCIOUS
CONSCRIBE
CONSCRIPT
CONSEIL
CONSEILS
CONSENSUS
CONSENT
CONSENTED
CONSENTER
CONSENTS
CONSERVE
CONSERVED
CONSERVER
CONSERVES
CONSIDER
CONSIDERS
CONSIGN
CONSIGNED
CONSIGNEE
CONSIGNER
CONSIGNOR
CONSIGNS
CONSIST
CONSISTED
CONSISTS
CONSOCIES
CONSOL
CONSOLATE
CONSOLE
CONSOLED
CONSOLER
CONSOLERS
CONSOLES
CONSOLING
CONSOLS
CONSOLUTE
CONSOMME
CONSOMMES
CONSONANT
CONSONOUS
CONSORT
CONSORTED
CONSORTER
CONSORTIA
CONSORTS
CONSPIRE
CONSPIRED
CONSPIRER
CONSPIRES
CONSPUE
CONSPUED
CONSPUES
CONSPUING
CONSTABLE
CONSTANCY
CONSTANT
CONSTANTS
CONSTATE
CONSTATED
CONSTATES
CONSTER
CONSTERED
CONSTERS
CONSTRAIN
CONSTRICT
CONSTRUAL
CONSTRUCT
CONSTRUE
CONSTRUED
CONSTRUER
CONSTRUES
CONSUL
CONSULAGE
CONSULAR
CONSULARS
CONSULATE
CONSULS
CONSULT
CONSULTA
CONSULTAS
CONSULTED
CONSULTEE
CONSULTER
CONSULTOR
CONSULTS
CONSUME
CONSUMED
CONSUMER
CONSUMERS
CONSUMES
CONSUMING
CONSUMPT
CONSUMPTS
CONTACT
CONTACTED
CONTACTEE
CONTACTOR
CONTACTS
CONTADINA
CONTADINE
CONTADINI
CONTADINO
CONTAGIA
CONTAGION
CONTAGIUM
CONTAIN
CONTAINED
CONTAINER
CONTAINS
CONTANGO
CONTANGOS
CONTE
CONTECK
CONTECKS
CONTEMN
CONTEMNED
CONTEMNER
CONTEMNOR
CONTEMNS
CONTEMPER
CONTEMPO
CONTEMPT
CONTEMPTS
CONTEND
CONTENDED
CONTENDER
CONTENDS
CONTENT

CONTENTED
CONTENTLY
CONTENTS
CONTES
CONTESSA
CONTESSAS
CONTEST
CONTESTED
CONTESTER
CONTESTS
CONTEXT
CONTEXTS
CONTICENT
CONTINENT
CONTINUA
CONTINUAL
CONTINUE
CONTINUED
CONTINUER
CONTINUES
CONTINUO
CONTINUOS
CONTINUUM
CONTLINE
CONTLINES
CONTO
CONTORNI
CONTORNO
CONTORNOS
CONTORT
CONTORTED
CONTORTS
CONTOS
CONTOUR
CONTOURED
CONTOURS
CONTRA
CONTRACT
CONTRACTS
CONTRAIL
CONTRAILS
CONTRAIR
CONTRALTI
CONTRALTO
CONTRARY
CONTRAS
CONTRAST
CONTRASTS
CONTRASTY
CONTRAT
CONTRATE
CONTRATS
CONTRIST
CONTRISTS
CONTRITE
CONTRIVE
CONTRIVED
CONTRIVER
CONTRIVES
CONTROL
CONTROLE
CONTROLS
CONTROUL
CONTROULS
CONTUMACY
CONTUMELY
CONTUND
CONTUNDED
CONTUNDS
CONTUSE
CONTUSED
CONTUSES
CONTUSING
CONTUSION
CONTUSIVE
CONUNDRUM
CONURBAN
CONURBIA
CONURBIAS
CONURE
CONURES
CONUS
CONVECT
CONVECTED
CONVECTOR
CONVECTS
CONVENE
CONVENED
CONVENER
CONVENERS
CONVENES
CONVENING
CONVENOR
CONVENORS
CONVENT
CONVENTED
CONVENTS
CONVERGE
CONVERGED
CONVERGES
CONVERSE
CONVERSED
CONVERSER
CONVERSES
CONVERSO
CONVERSOS
CONVERT
CONVERTED
CONVERTER
CONVERTOR
CONVERTS
CONVEX
CONVEXED
CONVEXES
CONVEXING
CONVEXITY
CONVEXLY
CONVEY
CONVEYAL
CONVEYALS
CONVEYED
CONVEYER
CONVEYERS
CONVEYING
CONVEYOR
CONVEYORS
CONVEYS
CONVICT
CONVICTED
CONVICTS
CONVINCE
CONVINCED
CONVINCER
CONVINCES
CONVIVE
CONVIVED
CONVIVES
CONVIVIAL
CONVIVING
CONVO
CONVOCATE
CONVOKE
CONVOKED
CONVOKER
CONVOKERS
CONVOKES
CONVOKING
CONVOLUTE
CONVOLVE
CONVOLVED
CONVOLVES
CONVOS
CONVOY
CONVOYED
CONVOYING
CONVOYS
CONVULSE
CONVULSED
CONVULSES
CONWOMAN
CONWOMEN
CONY
COO
COOCH
COOCHES
COOCOO
COOED
COOEE
COOEED
COOEEING
COOEES
COOER
COOERS
COOEY
COOEYED
COOEYING
COOEYS
COOF
COOFS
COOING
COOINGLY
COOINGS
COOK
COOKABLE
COOKABLES
COOKBOOK
COOKBOOKS
COOKED
COOKER
COOKERIES
COOKERS
COOKERY
COOKEY
COOKEYS
COOKHOUSE
COOKIE
COOKIES
COOKING
COOKINGS
COOKLESS
COOKMAID
COOKMAIDS
COOKOFF
COOKOFFS
COOKOUT
COOKOUTS
COOKROOM
COOKROOMS
COOKS
COOKSHACK
COOKSHOP
COOKSHOPS
COOKSTOVE
COOKTOP
COOKTOPS
COOKWARE
COOKWARES
COOKY
COOL
COOLABAH
COOLABAHS
COOLAMON
COOLAMONS
COOLANT
COOLANTS
COOLDOWN
COOLDOWNS
COOLED
COOLER
COOLERS
COOLEST
COOLHOUSE
COOLIBAH
COOLIBAHS
COOLIBAR
COOLIBARS
COOLIE
COOLIES
COOLING
COOLINGLY

C

COOLINGS
COOLISH
COOLIST
COOLISTS
COOLLY
COOLNESS
COOLS
COOLTH
COOLTHS
COOLY
COOM
COOMB
COOMBE
COOMBES
COOMBS
COOMED
COOMIER
COOMIEST
COOMING
COOMS
COOMY
COON
COONCAN
COONCANS
COONDOG
COONDOGS
COONHOUND
COONS
COONSHIT
COONSHITS
COONSKIN
COONSKINS
COONTIE
COONTIES
COONTY
COOP
COOPED
COOPER
COOPERAGE
COOPERATE
COOPERED
COOPERIES
COOPERING
COOPERS
COOPERY
COOPING
COOPS
COOPT
COOPTED
COOPTING
COOPTION
COOPTIONS
COOPTS
COORDINAL
COORIE
COORIED
COORIEING
COORIES
COOS
COOSEN
COOSENED
COOSENING
COOSENS
COOSER
COOSERS
COOSIN
COOSINED
COOSINING
COOSINS
COOST
COOT
COOTCH
COOTCHED
COOTCHES
COOTCHING
COOTER
COOTERS
COOTIE
COOTIES
COOTIKIN
COOTIKINS
COOTS
COOZE
COOZES
COP
COPACETIC
COPAIBA
COPAIBAS
COPAIVA
COPAIVAS
COPAL
COPALM
COPALMS
COPALS
COPARCENY
COPARENT
COPARENTS
COPARTNER
COPASETIC
COPASTOR
COPASTORS
COPATAINE
COPATRIOT
COPATRON
COPATRONS
COPAY
COPAYMENT
COPAYS
COPE
COPECK
COPECKS
COPED
COPEMATE
COPEMATES
COPEN
COPENS
COPEPOD
COPEPODS
COPER
COPERED
COPERING
COPERS
COPES
COPESETIC
COPESTONE
COPIABLE
COPIED
COPIER
COPIERS
COPIES
COPIHUE
COPIHUES
COPILOT
COPILOTED
COPILOTS
COPING
COPINGS
COPIOUS
COPIOUSLY
COPITA
COPITAS
COPLANAR
COPLOT
COPLOTS
COPLOTTED
COPOLYMER
COPOUT
COPOUTS
COPPED
COPPER
COPPERAH
COPPERAHS
COPPERAS
COPPERED
COPPERIER
COPPERING
COPPERISH
COPPERS
COPPERY
COPPICE
COPPICED
COPPICES
COPPICING
COPPIES
COPPIN
COPPING
COPPINS
COPPLE
COPPLES
COPPRA
COPPRAS
COPPY
COPRA
COPRAEMIA
COPRAEMIC
COPRAH
COPRAHS
COPRAS
COPREMIA
COPREMIAS
COPREMIC
COPRESENT
COPRINCE
COPRINCES
COPRODUCE
COPRODUCT
COPROLITE
COPROLITH
COPROLOGY
COPROSMA
COPROSMAS
COPROZOIC
COPS
COPSE
COPSED
COPSES
COPSEWOOD
COPSHOP
COPSHOPS
COPSIER
COPSIEST
COPSING
COPSY
COPTER
COPTERS
COPUBLISH
COPULA
COPULAE
COPULAR
COPULAS
COPULATE
COPULATED
COPULATES
COPURIFY
COPY
COPYABLE
COPYBOOK
COPYBOOKS
COPYBOY
COPYBOYS
COPYCAT
COPYCATS
COPYDESK
COPYDESKS
COPYEDIT
COPYEDITS
COPYFIGHT
COPYGIRL
COPYGIRLS
COPYGRAPH
COPYHOLD
COPYHOLDS
COPYING
COPYINGS
COPYISM
COPYISMS
COPYIST
COPYISTS
COPYLEFT
COPYLEFTS

COPYREAD
COPYREADS
COPYRIGHT
COPYTAKER
COQUET
COQUETRY
COQUETS
COQUETTE
COQUETTED
COQUETTES
COQUI
COQUILLA
COQUILLAS
COQUILLE
COQUILLES
COQUINA
COQUINAS
COQUIS
COQUITO
COQUITOS
COR
CORACLE
CORACLES
CORACOID
CORACOIDS
CORAGGIO
CORAL
CORALLA
CORALLINE
CORALLITE
CORALLOID
CORALLUM
CORALROOT
CORALS
CORALWORT
CORAM
CORAMINE
CORAMINES
CORANACH
CORANACHS
CORANTO
CORANTOES
CORANTOS
CORBAN
CORBANS
CORBE
CORBEAU
CORBEAUS
CORBEIL
CORBEILLE
CORBEILS
CORBEL
CORBELED
CORBELING
CORBELLED
CORBELS
CORBES
CORBICULA
CORBIE
CORBIES
CORBINA
CORBINAS
CORBY
CORCASS
CORCASSES
CORD
CORDAGE
CORDAGES
CORDATE
CORDATELY
CORDED
CORDELLE
CORDELLED
CORDELLES
CORDER
CORDERS
CORDGRASS
CORDIAL
CORDIALLY
CORDIALS
CORDIFORM
CORDINER
CORDINERS
CORDING
CORDINGS
CORDITE
CORDITES
CORDLESS
CORDLIKE
CORDOBA
CORDOBAS
CORDON
CORDONED
CORDONING
CORDONNET
CORDONS
CORDOTOMY
CORDOVAN
CORDOVANS
CORDS
CORDUROY
CORDUROYS
CORDWAIN
CORDWAINS
CORDWOOD
CORDWOODS
CORDYLINE
CORE
CORED
COREDEEM
COREDEEMS
COREGENT
COREGENTS
COREIGN
COREIGNS
CORELATE
CORELATED
CORELATES
CORELESS
CORELLA
CORELLAS
COREMIA
COREMIUM
COREOPSIS
CORER
CORERS
CORES
COREY
COREYS
CORF
CORFHOUSE
CORGI
CORGIS
CORIA
CORIANDER
CORIES
CORING
CORIOUS
CORIUM
CORIUMS
CORIVAL
CORIVALRY
CORIVALS
CORIXID
CORIXIDS
CORK
CORKAGE
CORKAGES
CORKBOARD
CORKBORER
CORKED
CORKER
CORKERS
CORKIER
CORKIEST
CORKINESS
CORKING
CORKIR
CORKIRS
CORKLIKE
CORKS
CORKSCREW
CORKTREE
CORKTREES
CORKWING
CORKWINGS
CORKWOOD
CORKWOODS
CORKY
CORM
CORMEL
CORMELS
CORMIDIA
CORMIDIUM
CORMLET
CORMLETS
CORMLIKE
CORMOID
CORMORANT
CORMOUS
CORMS
CORMUS
CORMUSES
CORN
CORNACRE
CORNACRES
CORNAGE
CORNAGES
CORNBALL
CORNBALLS
CORNBORER
CORNBRAID
CORNBRASH
CORNBREAD
CORNCAKE
CORNCAKES
CORNCOB
CORNCOBS
CORNCRAKE
CORNCRIB
CORNCRIBS
CORNEA
CORNEAE
CORNEAL
CORNEAS
CORNED
CORNEITIS
CORNEL
CORNELIAN
CORNELS
CORNEMUSE
CORNEOUS
CORNER
CORNERED
CORNERING
CORNERMAN
CORNERMEN
CORNERS
CORNET
CORNETCY
CORNETIST
CORNETS
CORNETT
CORNETTI
CORNETTO
CORNETTOS
CORNETTS
CORNFED
CORNFIELD
CORNFLAG
CORNFLAGS
CORNFLAKE
CORNFLIES
CORNFLOUR
CORNFLY
CORNHUSK
CORNHUSKS
CORNI
CORNICE
CORNICED

C

CORNICES
CORNICHE
CORNICHES
CORNICHON
CORNICING
CORNICLE
CORNICLES
CORNICULA
CORNIER
CORNIEST
CORNIFIC
CORNIFIED
CORNIFIES
CORNIFORM
CORNIFY
CORNILY
CORNINESS
CORNING
CORNIST
CORNISTS
CORNLAND
CORNLANDS
CORNLOFT
CORNLOFTS
CORNMEAL
CORNMEALS
CORNMILL
CORNMILLS
CORNMOTH
CORNMOTHS
CORNO
CORNOPEAN
CORNPIPE
CORNPIPES
CORNPONE
CORNPONES
CORNRENT
CORNRENTS
CORNROW
CORNROWED
CORNROWS
CORNS
CORNSILK
CORNSILKS
CORNSTALK
CORNSTONE
CORNU
CORNUA
CORNUAL
CORNUS
CORNUSES
CORNUTE
CORNUTED
CORNUTES
CORNUTING
CORNUTO
CORNUTOS
CORNWORM
CORNWORMS
CORNY
COROCORE
COROCORES
COROCORO
COROCOROS
CORODIES
CORODY
COROLLA
COROLLARY
COROLLAS
COROLLATE
COROLLINE
CORONA
CORONACH
CORONACHS
CORONAE
CORONAL
CORONALLY
CORONALS
CORONARY
CORONAS
CORONATE
CORONATED
CORONATES
CORONEL
CORONELS
CORONER
CORONERS
CORONET
CORONETED
CORONETS
CORONIAL
CORONIS
CORONISES
CORONIUM
CORONIUMS
CORONOID
COROTATE
COROTATED
COROTATES
COROZO
COROZOS
CORPORA
CORPORAL
CORPORALE
CORPORALS
CORPORAS
CORPORATE
CORPOREAL
CORPORIFY
CORPOSANT
CORPS
CORPSE
CORPSED
CORPSES
CORPSING
CORPSMAN
CORPSMEN
CORPULENT
CORPUS
CORPUSCLE
CORPUSES
CORRADE
CORRADED
CORRADES
CORRADING
CORRAL
CORRALLED
CORRALS
CORRASION
CORRASIVE
CORREA
CORREAS
CORRECT
CORRECTED
CORRECTER
CORRECTLY
CORRECTOR
CORRECTS
CORRELATE
CORRETTO
CORRETTOS
CORRIDA
CORRIDAS
CORRIDOR
CORRIDORS
CORRIE
CORRIES
CORRIGENT
CORRIVAL
CORRIVALS
CORRODANT
CORRODE
CORRODED
CORRODENT
CORRODER
CORRODERS
CORRODES
CORRODIES
CORRODING
CORRODY
CORROSION
CORROSIVE
CORRUGATE
CORRUPT
CORRUPTED
CORRUPTER
CORRUPTLY
CORRUPTOR
CORRUPTS
CORS
CORSAC
CORSACS
CORSAGE
CORSAGES
CORSAIR
CORSAIRS
CORSE
CORSELET
CORSELETS
CORSES
CORSET
CORSETED
CORSETIER
CORSETING
CORSETRY
CORSETS
CORSEY
CORSEYS
CORSITE
CORSITES
CORSIVE
CORSIVES
CORSLET
CORSLETED
CORSLETS
CORSNED
CORSNEDS
CORSO
CORSOS
CORTEGE
CORTEGES
CORTEX
CORTEXES
CORTICAL
CORTICATE
CORTICES
CORTICOID
CORTICOSE
CORTILE
CORTILI
CORTIN
CORTINA
CORTINAS
CORTINS
CORTISOL
CORTISOLS
CORTISONE
CORULER
CORULERS
CORUNDUM
CORUNDUMS
CORUSCANT
CORUSCATE
CORVEE
CORVEES
CORVES
CORVET
CORVETED
CORVETING
CORVETS
CORVETTE
CORVETTED
CORVETTES
CORVID
CORVIDS
CORVINA
CORVINAS
CORVINE
CORVUS
CORVUSES

CORY
CORYBANT
CORYBANTS
CORYDALIS
CORYLUS
CORYLUSES
CORYMB
CORYMBED
CORYMBOSE
CORYMBOUS
CORYMBS
CORYPHAEI
CORYPHE
CORYPHEE
CORYPHEES
CORYPHENE
CORYPHES
CORYZA
CORYZAL
CORYZAS
COS
COSCRIPT
COSCRIPTS
COSE
COSEC
COSECANT
COSECANTS
COSECH
COSECHS
COSECS
COSED
COSEISMAL
COSEISMIC
COSES
COSET
COSETS
COSEY
COSEYS
COSH
COSHED
COSHER
COSHERED
COSHERER
COSHERERS
COSHERIES
COSHERING
COSHERS
COSHERY
COSHES
COSHING
COSIE
COSIED
COSIER
COSIERS
COSIES
COSIEST
COSIGN
COSIGNED
COSIGNER
COSIGNERS
COSIGNING
COSIGNS
COSILY
COSINE
COSINES
COSINESS
COSING
COSMEA
COSMEAS
COSMESES
COSMESIS
COSMETIC
COSMETICS
COSMIC
COSMICAL
COSMID
COSMIDS
COSMIN
COSMINE
COSMINES
COSMINS
COSMISM
COSMISMS
COSMIST
COSMISTS
COSMOCRAT
COSMOGENY
COSMOGONY
COSMOID
COSMOLINE
COSMOLOGY
COSMONAUT
COSMORAMA
COSMOS
COSMOSES
COSMOTRON
COSPHERED
COSPLAY
COSPLAYS
COSPONSOR
COSS
COSSACK
COSSACKS
COSSES
COSSET
COSSETED
COSSETING
COSSETS
COSSETTED
COSSIE
COSSIES
COST
COSTA
COSTAE
COSTAL
COSTALGIA
COSTALLY
COSTALS
COSTAR
COSTARD
COSTARDS
COSTARRED
COSTARS
COSTATE
COSTATED
COSTE
COSTEAN
COSTEANED
COSTEANS
COSTED
COSTER
COSTERS
COSTES
COSTING
COSTINGS
COSTIVE
COSTIVELY
COSTLESS
COSTLIER
COSTLIEST
COSTLY
COSTMARY
COSTOTOMY
COSTREL
COSTRELS
COSTS
COSTUME
COSTUMED
COSTUMER
COSTUMERS
COSTUMERY
COSTUMES
COSTUMEY
COSTUMIER
COSTUMING
COSTUS
COSTUSES
COSY
COSYING
COT
COTAN
COTANGENT
COTANS
COTE
COTEAU
COTEAUS
COTEAUX
COTED
COTELETTE
COTELINE
COTELINES
COTENANCY
COTENANT
COTENANTS
COTERIE
COTERIES
COTES
COTH
COTHS
COTHURN
COTHURNAL
COTHURNI
COTHURNS
COTHURNUS
COTICULAR
COTIDAL
COTIJA
COTIJAS
COTILLION
COTILLON
COTILLONS
COTING
COTINGA
COTINGAS
COTININE
COTININES
COTISE
COTISED
COTISES
COTISING
COTLAND
COTLANDS
COTQUEAN
COTQUEANS
COTRUSTEE
COTS
COTT
COTTA
COTTABUS
COTTAE
COTTAGE
COTTAGED
COTTAGER
COTTAGERS
COTTAGES
COTTAGEY
COTTAGIER
COTTAGING
COTTAR
COTTARS
COTTAS
COTTED
COTTER
COTTERED
COTTERING
COTTERS
COTTID
COTTIDS
COTTIER
COTTIERS
COTTING
COTTISE
COTTISED
COTTISES
COTTISING
COTTOID
COTTON
COTTONADE
COTTONED
COTTONIER

C

COTTONING
COTTONS
COTTONY
COTTOWN
COTTOWNS
COTTS
COTTUS
COTTUSES
COTURNIX
COTWAL
COTWALS
COTYLAE
COTYLE
COTYLEDON
COTYLES
COTYLOID
COTYLOIDS
COTYPE
COTYPES
COUCAL
COUCALS
COUCH
COUCHANT
COUCHE
COUCHED
COUCHEE
COUCHEES
COUCHER
COUCHERS
COUCHES
COUCHETTE
COUCHING
COUCHINGS
COUDE
COUDES
COUGAN
COUGANS
COUGAR
COUGARS
COUGH
COUGHED
COUGHER
COUGHERS
COUGHING
COUGHINGS
COUGHS
COUGUAR
COUGUARS
COULD
COULDEST
COULDST
COULEE
COULEES
COULIBIAC
COULIS
COULISSE
COULISSES
COULOIR
COULOIRS
COULOMB
COULOMBIC
COULOMBS
COULTER
COULTERS
COUMARIC
COUMARIN
COUMARINS
COUMARONE
COUMAROU
COUMAROUS
COUNCIL
COUNCILOR
COUNCILS
COUNSEL
COUNSELED
COUNSELEE
COUNSELOR
COUNSELS
COUNT
COUNTABLE
COUNTABLY
COUNTBACK
COUNTDOWN
COUNTED
COUNTER
COUNTERED
COUNTERS
COUNTESS
COUNTIAN
COUNTIANS
COUNTIES
COUNTING
COUNTINGS
COUNTLESS
COUNTLINE
COUNTRIES
COUNTROL
COUNTROLS
COUNTRY
COUNTS
COUNTSHIP
COUNTY
COUP
COUPE
COUPED
COUPEE
COUPEES
COUPER
COUPERS
COUPES
COUPING
COUPLE
COUPLED
COUPLEDOM
COUPLER
COUPLERS
COUPLES
COUPLET
COUPLETS
COUPLING
COUPLINGS
COUPON
COUPONING
COUPONS
COUPS
COUPURE
COUPURES
COUR
COURAGE
COURAGES
COURANT
COURANTE
COURANTES
COURANTO
COURANTOS
COURANTS
COURB
COURBARIL
COURBED
COURBETTE
COURBING
COURBS
COURD
COURE
COURED
COURES
COURGETTE
COURIE
COURIED
COURIEING
COURIER
COURIERED
COURIERS
COURIES
COURING
COURLAN
COURLANS
COURS
COURSE
COURSED
COURSER
COURSERS
COURSES
COURSING
COURSINGS
COURT
COURTED
COURTEOUS
COURTER
COURTERS
COURTESAN
COURTESY
COURTEZAN
COURTIER
COURTIERS
COURTING
COURTINGS
COURTLET
COURTLETS
COURTLIER
COURTLIKE
COURTLING
COURTLY
COURTROOM
COURTS
COURTSHIP
COURTSIDE
COURTYARD
COUSCOUS
COUSIN
COUSINAGE
COUSINLY
COUSINRY
COUSINS
COUTA
COUTAS
COUTEAU
COUTEAUX
COUTER
COUTERS
COUTH
COUTHER
COUTHEST
COUTHIE
COUTHIER
COUTHIEST
COUTHS
COUTHY
COUTIL
COUTILLE
COUTILLES
COUTILS
COUTURE
COUTURES
COUTURIER
COUVADE
COUVADES
COUVERT
COUVERTS
COUZIN
COUZINS
COVALENCE
COVALENCY
COVALENT
COVARIANT
COVARIATE
COVARIED
COVARIES
COVARY
COVARYING
COVE
COVED
COVELET
COVELETS
COVELLINE
COVELLITE
COVEN
COVENANT
COVENANTS
COVENS

COVENT
COVENTS
COVER
COVERABLE
COVERAGE
COVERAGES
COVERALL
COVERALLS
COVERED
COVERER
COVERERS
COVERING
COVERINGS
COVERLESS
COVERLET
COVERLETS
COVERLID
COVERLIDS
COVERS
COVERSED
COVERSINE
COVERSLIP
COVERT
COVERTER
COVERTEST
COVERTLY
COVERTS
COVERTURE
COVERUP
COVERUPS
COVES
COVET
COVETABLE
COVETED
COVETER
COVETERS
COVETING
COVETISE
COVETISES
COVETOUS
COVETS
COVEY
COVEYS
COVIN
COVINE
COVINES
COVING
COVINGS
COVINOUS
COVINS
COVYNE
COVYNES
COW
COWABUNGA
COWAGE
COWAGES
COWAL
COWALS
COWAN
COWANS
COWARD
COWARDED
COWARDICE
COWARDING
COWARDLY
COWARDRY
COWARDS
COWBANE
COWBANES
COWBELL
COWBELLS
COWBERRY
COWBIND
COWBINDS
COWBIRD
COWBIRDS
COWBOY
COWBOYED
COWBOYING
COWBOYS
COWED
COWEDLY
COWER
COWERED
COWERING
COWERS
COWFEEDER
COWFISH
COWFISHES
COWFLAP
COWFLAPS
COWFLOP
COWFLOPS
COWGIRL
COWGIRLS
COWGRASS
COWHAGE
COWHAGES
COWHAND
COWHANDS
COWHEARD
COWHEARDS
COWHEEL
COWHEELS
COWHERB
COWHERBS
COWHERD
COWHERDS
COWHIDE
COWHIDED
COWHIDES
COWHIDING
COWHOUSE
COWHOUSES
COWIER
COWIEST
COWING
COWINNER
COWINNERS
COWISH
COWISHES
COWITCH
COWITCHES
COWK
COWKED
COWKING
COWKS
COWL
COWLED
COWLICK
COWLICKS
COWLIKE
COWLING
COWLINGS
COWLS
COWLSTAFF
COWMAN
COWMEN
COWORKER
COWORKERS
COWP
COWPAT
COWPATS
COWPEA
COWPEAS
COWPED
COWPIE
COWPIES
COWPING
COWPLOP
COWPLOPS
COWPOKE
COWPOKES
COWPOX
COWPOXES
COWPS
COWPUNK
COWPUNKS
COWRIE
COWRIES
COWRITE
COWRITER
COWRITERS
COWRITES
COWRITING
COWRITTEN
COWROTE
COWRY
COWS
COWSHED
COWSHEDS
COWSKIN
COWSKINS
COWSLIP
COWSLIPS
COWTOWN
COWTOWNS
COWTREE
COWTREES
COWY
COX
COXA
COXAE
COXAL
COXALGIA
COXALGIAS
COXALGIC
COXALGIES
COXALGY
COXCOMB
COXCOMBIC
COXCOMBRY
COXCOMBS
COXED
COXES
COXIB
COXIBS
COXIER
COXIEST
COXINESS
COXING
COXITIDES
COXITIS
COXLESS
COXSACKIE
COXSWAIN
COXSWAINS
COXY
COY
COYAU
COYAUS
COYDOG
COYDOGS
COYED
COYER
COYEST
COYING
COYISH
COYISHLY
COYLY
COYNESS
COYNESSES
COYOTE
COYOTES
COYOTILLO
COYPOU
COYPOUS
COYPU
COYPUS
COYS
COYSTREL
COYSTRELS
COYSTRIL
COYSTRILS
COZ
COZE
COZED
COZEN
COZENAGE
COZENAGES

COZENED
COZENER
COZENERS
COZENING
COZENS
COZES
COZEY
COZEYS
COZIE
COZIED
COZIER
COZIERS
COZIES
COZIEST
COZILY
COZINESS
COZING
COZY
COZYING
COZZES
COZZIE
COZZIES
CRAAL
CRAALED
CRAALING
CRAALS
CRAB
CRABAPPLE
CRABBED
CRABBEDLY
CRABBER
CRABBERS
CRABBIER
CRABBIEST
CRABBILY
CRABBING
CRABBIT
CRABBY
CRABEATER
CRABGRASS
CRABLIKE
CRABMEAT
CRABMEATS
CRABS
CRABSTICK
CRABWISE
CRABWOOD
CRABWOODS
CRACHACH
CRACK
CRACKA
CRACKAS
CRACKBACK
CRACKDOWN
CRACKED
CRACKER
CRACKERS
CRACKET
CRACKETS
CRACKHEAD
CRACKIE
CRACKIER
CRACKIES
CRACKIEST
CRACKING
CRACKINGS
CRACKJAW
CRACKJAWS
CRACKLE
CRACKLED
CRACKLES
CRACKLIER
CRACKLING
CRACKLY
CRACKNEL
CRACKNELS
CRACKPOT
CRACKPOTS
CRACKS
CRACKSMAN
CRACKSMEN
CRACKUP
CRACKUPS
CRACKY
CRACOWE
CRACOWES
CRADLE
CRADLED
CRADLER
CRADLERS
CRADLES
CRADLING
CRADLINGS
CRAFT
CRAFTED
CRAFTER
CRAFTERS
CRAFTIER
CRAFTIEST
CRAFTILY
CRAFTING
CRAFTLESS
CRAFTS
CRAFTSMAN
CRAFTSMEN
CRAFTWORK
CRAFTY
CRAG
CRAGFAST
CRAGGED
CRAGGER
CRAGGERS
CRAGGIER
CRAGGIEST
CRAGGILY
CRAGGY
CRAGS
CRAGSMAN
CRAGSMEN
CRAIC
CRAICS
CRAIG
CRAIGS
CRAKE
CRAKED
CRAKES
CRAKING
CRAM
CRAMBE
CRAMBES
CRAMBO
CRAMBOES
CRAMBOS
CRAME
CRAMES
CRAMESIES
CRAMESY
CRAMFULL
CRAMMABLE
CRAMMED
CRAMMER
CRAMMERS
CRAMMING
CRAMMINGS
CRAMOISIE
CRAMOISY
CRAMP
CRAMPBARK
CRAMPED
CRAMPER
CRAMPERS
CRAMPET
CRAMPETS
CRAMPFISH
CRAMPIER
CRAMPIEST
CRAMPING
CRAMPIT
CRAMPITS
CRAMPON
CRAMPONED
CRAMPONS
CRAMPOON
CRAMPOONS
CRAMPS
CRAMPY
CRAMS
CRAN
CRANACHAN
CRANAGE
CRANAGES
CRANAPPLE
CRANBERRY
CRANCH
CRANCHED
CRANCHES
CRANCHING
CRANE
CRANED
CRANEFLY
CRANELIKE
CRANES
CRANIA
CRANIAL
CRANIALLY
CRANIATE
CRANIATES
CRANING
CRANIUM
CRANIUMS
CRANK
CRANKBAIT
CRANKCASE
CRANKED
CRANKER
CRANKEST
CRANKIER
CRANKIEST
CRANKILY
CRANKING
CRANKISH
CRANKLE
CRANKLED
CRANKLES
CRANKLING
CRANKLY
CRANKNESS
CRANKOUS
CRANKPIN
CRANKPINS
CRANKS
CRANKY
CRANNIED
CRANNIES
CRANNOG
CRANNOGE
CRANNOGES
CRANNOGS
CRANNY
CRANNYING
CRANREUCH
CRANS
CRANTS
CRANTSES
CRAP
CRAPAUD
CRAPAUDS
CRAPE
CRAPED
CRAPELIKE
CRAPES
CRAPIER
CRAPIEST
CRAPING
CRAPLE
CRAPLES
CRAPOLA
CRAPOLAS
CRAPPED
CRAPPER

CRAPPERS
CRAPPIE
CRAPPIER
CRAPPIES
CRAPPIEST
CRAPPING
CRAPPY
CRAPS
CRAPSHOOT
CRAPULENT
CRAPULOUS
CRAPY
CRARE
CRARES
CRASES
CRASH
CRASHED
CRASHER
CRASHERS
CRASHES
CRASHING
CRASHPAD
CRASHPADS
CRASIS
CRASS
CRASSER
CRASSEST
CRASSLY
CRASSNESS
CRATCH
CRATCHES
CRATE
CRATED
CRATEFUL
CRATEFULS
CRATER
CRATERED
CRATERING
CRATERLET
CRATEROUS
CRATERS
CRATES
CRATHUR
CRATHURS
CRATING
CRATON
CRATONIC
CRATONS
CRATUR
CRATURS
CRAUNCH
CRAUNCHED
CRAUNCHES
CRAUNCHY
CRAVAT
CRAVATE
CRAVATES
CRAVATS
CRAVATTED
CRAVE
CRAVED
CRAVEN
CRAVENED
CRAVENER
CRAVENEST
CRAVENING
CRAVENLY
CRAVENS
CRAVER
CRAVERS
CRAVES
CRAVING
CRAVINGS
CRAW
CRAWDAD
CRAWDADDY
CRAWDADS
CRAWFISH
CRAWL
CRAWLED
CRAWLER
CRAWLERS
CRAWLIER
CRAWLIEST
CRAWLING
CRAWLINGS
CRAWLS
CRAWLWAY
CRAWLWAYS
CRAWLY
CRAWS
CRAY
CRAYER
CRAYERS
CRAYEST
CRAYFISH
CRAYON
CRAYONED
CRAYONER
CRAYONERS
CRAYONING
CRAYONIST
CRAYONS
CRAYS
CRAYTHUR
CRAYTHURS
CRAZE
CRAZED
CRAZES
CRAZIER
CRAZIES
CRAZIEST
CRAZILY
CRAZINESS
CRAZING
CRAZINGS
CRAZY
CRAZYWEED
CREACH
CREACHS
CREAGH
CREAGHS
CREAK
CREAKED
CREAKIER
CREAKIEST
CREAKILY
CREAKING
CREAKS
CREAKY
CREAM
CREAMCUPS
CREAMED
CREAMER
CREAMERS
CREAMERY
CREAMIER
CREAMIEST
CREAMILY
CREAMING
CREAMLAID
CREAMLIKE
CREAMPUFF
CREAMS
CREAMWARE
CREAMWOVE
CREAMY
CREANCE
CREANCES
CREANT
CREASE
CREASED
CREASER
CREASERS
CREASES
CREASIER
CREASIEST
CREASING
CREASOTE
CREASOTED
CREASOTES
CREASY
CREATABLE
CREATE
CREATED
CREATES
CREATIC
CREATIN
CREATINE
CREATINES
CREATING
CREATINS
CREATION
CREATIONS
CREATIVE
CREATIVES
CREATOR
CREATORS
CREATRESS
CREATRIX
CREATURAL
CREATURE
CREATURES
CRECHE
CRECHES
CRED
CREDAL
CREDENCE
CREDENCES
CREDENDA
CREDENDUM
CREDENT
CREDENZA
CREDENZAS
CREDIBLE
CREDIBLY
CREDIT
CREDITED
CREDITING
CREDITOR
CREDITORS
CREDITS
CREDO
CREDOS
CREDS
CREDULITY
CREDULOUS
CREE
CREED
CREEDAL
CREEDS
CREEING
CREEK
CREEKIER
CREEKIEST
CREEKS
CREEKSIDE
CREEKY
CREEL
CREELED
CREELING
CREELS
CREEP
CREEPAGE
CREEPAGES
CREEPED
CREEPER
CREEPERED
CREEPERS
CREEPIE
CREEPIER
CREEPIES
CREEPIEST
CREEPILY
CREEPING
CREEPMICE
CREEPS
CREEPY
CREES
CREESE

C

CREESED
CREESES
CREESH
CREESHED
CREESHES
CREESHIER
CREESHING
CREESHY
CREESING
CREM
CREMAINS
CREMANT
CREMASTER
CREMATE
CREMATED
CREMATES
CREMATING
CREMATION
CREMATOR
CREMATORS
CREMATORY
CREME
CREMES
CREMINI
CREMINIS
CREMOCARP
CREMONA
CREMONAS
CREMOR
CREMORNE
CREMORNES
CREMORS
CREMOSIN
CREMS
CREMSIN
CRENA
CRENAS
CRENATE
CRENATED
CRENATELY
CRENATION
CRENATURE
CRENEL
CRENELATE
CRENELED
CRENELING
CRENELLE
CRENELLED
CRENELLES
CRENELS
CRENSHAW
CRENSHAWS
CRENULATE
CREODONT
CREODONTS
CREOLE
CREOLES
CREOLIAN
CREOLIANS
CREOLISE
CREOLISED
CREOLISES
CREOLIST
CREOLISTS
CREOLIZE
CREOLIZED
CREOLIZES
CREOPHAGY
CREOSOL
CREOSOLS
CREOSOTE
CREOSOTED
CREOSOTES
CREOSOTIC
CREPANCE
CREPANCES
CREPE
CREPED
CREPELIKE
CREPERIE
CREPERIES
CREPES
CREPEY
CREPIER
CREPIEST
CREPINESS
CREPING
CREPITANT
CREPITATE
CREPITUS
CREPOLINE
CREPON
CREPONS
CREPS
CREPT
CREPUSCLE
CREPY
CRESCENDI
CRESCENDO
CRESCENT
CRESCENTS
CRESCIVE
CRESOL
CRESOLS
CRESS
CRESSES
CRESSET
CRESSETS
CRESSIER
CRESSIEST
CRESSY
CREST
CRESTA
CRESTAL
CRESTALS
CRESTED
CRESTING
CRESTINGS
CRESTLESS
CRESTON
CRESTONS
CRESTS
CRESYL
CRESYLIC
CRESYLS
CRETIC
CRETICS
CRETIN
CRETINISE
CRETINISM
CRETINIZE
CRETINOID
CRETINOUS
CRETINS
CRETISM
CRETISMS
CRETONNE
CRETONNES
CRETONS
CREUTZER
CREUTZERS
CREVALLE
CREVALLES
CREVASSE
CREVASSED
CREVASSES
CREVETTE
CREVETTES
CREVICE
CREVICED
CREVICES
CREW
CREWCUT
CREWCUTS
CREWE
CREWED
CREWEL
CREWELIST
CREWELLED
CREWELS
CREWES
CREWING
CREWLESS
CREWMAN
CREWMATE
CREWMATES
CREWMEN
CREWNECK
CREWNECKS
CREWS
CRIA
CRIANT
CRIAS
CRIB
CRIBBAGE
CRIBBAGES
CRIBBED
CRIBBER
CRIBBERS
CRIBBING
CRIBBINGS
CRIBBLE
CRIBBLED
CRIBBLES
CRIBBLING
CRIBELLA
CRIBELLAR
CRIBELLUM
CRIBLE
CRIBLES
CRIBRATE
CRIBROSE
CRIBROUS
CRIBS
CRIBWORK
CRIBWORKS
CRICETID
CRICETIDS
CRICK
CRICKED
CRICKET
CRICKETED
CRICKETER
CRICKETS
CRICKEY
CRICKING
CRICKS
CRICKY
CRICOID
CRICOIDS
CRIED
CRIER
CRIERS
CRIES
CRIKEY
CRIM
CRIME
CRIMED
CRIMEFUL
CRIMELESS
CRIMEN
CRIMES
CRIMEWAVE
CRIMINA
CRIMINAL
CRIMINALS
CRIMINATE
CRIMINE
CRIMING
CRIMINI
CRIMINIS
CRIMINOUS
CRIMINY
CRIMMER
CRIMMERS
CRIMP
CRIMPED
CRIMPER
CRIMPERS
CRIMPIER

CRIMPIEST
CRIMPING
CRIMPLE
CRIMPLED
CRIMPLES
CRIMPLING
CRIMPS
CRIMPY
CRIMS
CRIMSON
CRIMSONED
CRIMSONS
CRINAL
CRINATE
CRINATED
CRINE
CRINED
CRINES
CRINGE
CRINGED
CRINGER
CRINGERS
CRINGES
CRINGEY
CRINGIER
CRINGIEST
CRINGING
CRINGINGS
CRINGLE
CRINGLES
CRINGY
CRINING
CRINITE
CRINITES
CRINKLE
CRINKLED
CRINKLES
CRINKLIER
CRINKLIES
CRINKLING
CRINKLY
CRINOID
CRINOIDAL
CRINOIDS
CRINOLINE
CRINOSE
CRINUM
CRINUMS
CRIOLLO
CRIOLLOS
CRIOS
CRIOSES
CRIP
CRIPE
CRIPES
CRIPPLE
CRIPPLED
CRIPPLER
CRIPPLERS
CRIPPLES
CRIPPLING
CRIPS
CRIS
CRISE
CRISES
CRISIC
CRISIS
CRISP
CRISPATE
CRISPATED
CRISPED
CRISPEN
CRISPENED
CRISPENS
CRISPER
CRISPERS
CRISPEST
CRISPHEAD
CRISPIER
CRISPIES
CRISPIEST
CRISPILY
CRISPIN
CRISPING
CRISPINS
CRISPLY
CRISPNESS
CRISPS
CRISPY
CRISSA
CRISSAL
CRISSUM
CRISTA
CRISTAE
CRISTATE
CRISTATED
CRIT
CRITERIA
CRITERIAL
CRITERION
CRITERIUM
CRITH
CRITHS
CRITIC
CRITICAL
CRITICISE
CRITICISM
CRITICIZE
CRITICS
CRITIQUE
CRITIQUED
CRITIQUES
CRITS
CRITTER
CRITTERS
CRITTUR
CRITTURS
CRIVENS
CRIVVENS
CROAK
CROAKED
CROAKER
CROAKERS
CROAKIER
CROAKIEST
CROAKILY
CROAKING
CROAKINGS
CROAKS
CROAKY
CROC
CROCEATE
CROCEIN
CROCEINE
CROCEINES
CROCEINS
CROCEOUS
CROCHE
CROCHES
CROCHET
CROCHETED
CROCHETER
CROCHETS
CROCI
CROCINE
CROCK
CROCKED
CROCKERY
CROCKET
CROCKETED
CROCKETS
CROCKING
CROCKPOT
CROCKPOTS
CROCKS
CROCODILE
CROCOITE
CROCOITES
CROCOSMIA
CROCS
CROCUS
CROCUSES
CROFT
CROFTED
CROFTER
CROFTERS
CROFTING
CROFTINGS
CROFTS
CROG
CROGGED
CROGGIES
CROGGING
CROGGY
CROGS
CROISSANT
CROJIK
CROJIKS
CROKINOLE
CROMACK
CROMACKS
CROMB
CROMBEC
CROMBECS
CROMBED
CROMBING
CROMBS
CROME
CROMED
CROMES
CROMING
CROMLECH
CROMLECHS
CROMORNA
CROMORNAS
CROMORNE
CROMORNES
CRON
CRONE
CRONES
CRONET
CRONETS
CRONIES
CRONISH
CRONK
CRONKER
CRONKEST
CRONS
CRONY
CRONYISM
CRONYISMS
CROODLE
CROODLED
CROODLES
CROODLING
CROOK
CROOKBACK
CROOKED
CROOKEDER
CROOKEDLY
CROOKER
CROOKERY
CROOKEST
CROOKING
CROOKNECK
CROOKS
CROOL
CROOLED
CROOLING
CROOLS
CROON
CROONED
CROONER
CROONERS
CROONIER
CROONIEST
CROONING
CROONINGS
CROONS
CROONY

CROOVE
CROOVES
CROP
CROPBOUND
CROPFUL
CROPFULL
CROPFULLS
CROPFULS
CROPLAND
CROPLANDS
CROPLESS
CROPPED
CROPPER
CROPPERS
CROPPIE
CROPPIES
CROPPING
CROPPINGS
CROPPY
CROPS
CROPSICK
CROQUANTE
CROQUET
CROQUETED
CROQUETS
CROQUETTE
CROQUIS
CRORE
CROREPATI
CRORES
CROSIER
CROSIERED
CROSIERS
CROSS
CROSSABLE
CROSSARM
CROSSARMS
CROSSBAND
CROSSBAR
CROSSBARS
CROSSBEAM
CROSSBILL
CROSSBIT
CROSSBITE
CROSSBOW
CROSSBOWS
CROSSBRED
CROSSBUCK
CROSSCUT
CROSSCUTS
CROSSE
CROSSED
CROSSER
CROSSERS
CROSSES
CROSSEST
CROSSETTE
CROSSFALL
CROSSFIRE
CROSSFISH
CROSSHAIR
CROSSHEAD
CROSSING
CROSSINGS
CROSSISH
CROSSJACK
CROSSLET
CROSSLETS
CROSSLIKE
CROSSLY
CROSSNESS
CROSSOVER
CROSSPLY
CROSSROAD
CROSSRUFF
CROSSTALK
CROSSTIE
CROSSTIED
CROSSTIES
CROSSTOWN
CROSSTREE
CROSSWALK
CROSSWAY
CROSSWAYS
CROSSWIND
CROSSWIRE
CROSSWISE
CROSSWORD
CROSSWORT
CROST
CROSTATA
CROSTATAS
CROSTINI
CROSTINIS
CROSTINO
CROTAL
CROTALA
CROTALE
CROTALES
CROTALINE
CROTALISM
CROTALS
CROTALUM
CROTCH
CROTCHED
CROTCHES
CROTCHET
CROTCHETS
CROTCHETY
CROTON
CROTONBUG
CROTONIC
CROTONS
CROTTLE
CROTTLES
CROUCH
CROUCHED
CROUCHES
CROUCHING
CROUP
CROUPADE
CROUPADES
CROUPE
CROUPED
CROUPER
CROUPERS
CROUPES
CROUPIER
CROUPIERS
CROUPIEST
CROUPILY
CROUPING
CROUPON
CROUPONS
CROUPOUS
CROUPS
CROUPY
CROUSE
CROUSELY
CROUSTADE
CROUT
CROUTE
CROUTES
CROUTON
CROUTONS
CROUTS
CROW
CROWBAIT
CROWBAITS
CROWBAR
CROWBARS
CROWBERRY
CROWBOOT
CROWBOOTS
CROWD
CROWDED
CROWDEDLY
CROWDER
CROWDERS
CROWDFUND
CROWDIE
CROWDIES
CROWDING
CROWDS
CROWDY
CROWEA
CROWEAS
CROWED
CROWER
CROWERS
CROWFEET
CROWFOOT
CROWFOOTS
CROWING
CROWINGLY
CROWINGS
CROWLIKE
CROWN
CROWNED
CROWNER
CROWNERS
CROWNET
CROWNETS
CROWNING
CROWNINGS
CROWNLAND
CROWNLESS
CROWNLET
CROWNLETS
CROWNLIKE
CROWNS
CROWNWORK
CROWS
CROWSFEET
CROWSFOOT
CROWSTEP
CROWSTEPS
CROZE
CROZER
CROZERS
CROZES
CROZIER
CROZIERS
CROZZLED
CRU
CRUBEEN
CRUBEENS
CRUCES
CRUCIAL
CRUCIALLY
CRUCIAN
CRUCIANS
CRUCIATE
CRUCIATES
CRUCIBLE
CRUCIBLES
CRUCIFER
CRUCIFERS
CRUCIFIED
CRUCIFIER
CRUCIFIES
CRUCIFIX
CRUCIFORM
CRUCIFY
CRUCK
CRUCKS
CRUD
CRUDDED
CRUDDIER
CRUDDIEST
CRUDDING
CRUDDLE
CRUDDLED
CRUDDLES
CRUDDLING
CRUDDY
CRUDE
CRUDELY
CRUDENESS
CRUDER

CRUDES
CRUDEST
CRUDIER
CRUDIEST
CRUDITES
CRUDITIES
CRUDITY
CRUDO
CRUDOS
CRUDS
CRUDY
CRUE
CRUEL
CRUELER
CRUELEST
CRUELLER
CRUELLEST
CRUELLS
CRUELLY
CRUELNESS
CRUELS
CRUELTIES
CRUELTY
CRUES
CRUET
CRUETS
CRUFT
CRUFTS
CRUISE
CRUISED
CRUISER
CRUISERS
CRUISES
CRUISEWAY
CRUISEY
CRUISIE
CRUISIER
CRUISIES
CRUISIEST
CRUISING
CRUISINGS
CRUISY
CRUIVE
CRUIVES
CRUIZIE
CRUIZIES
CRULLER
CRULLERS
CRUMB
CRUMBED
CRUMBER
CRUMBERS
CRUMBIER
CRUMBIEST
CRUMBING
CRUMBLE
CRUMBLED
CRUMBLES
CRUMBLIER
CRUMBLIES
CRUMBLING
CRUMBLY
CRUMBS
CRUMBUM
CRUMBUMS
CRUMBY
CRUMEN
CRUMENAL
CRUMENALS
CRUMENS
CRUMHORN
CRUMHORNS
CRUMMACK
CRUMMACKS
CRUMMIE
CRUMMIER
CRUMMIES
CRUMMIEST
CRUMMILY
CRUMMOCK
CRUMMOCKS
CRUMMY
CRUMP
CRUMPED
CRUMPER
CRUMPEST
CRUMPET
CRUMPETS
CRUMPIER
CRUMPIEST
CRUMPING
CRUMPLE
CRUMPLED
CRUMPLES
CRUMPLIER
CRUMPLING
CRUMPLY
CRUMPS
CRUMPY
CRUNCH
CRUNCHED
CRUNCHER
CRUNCHERS
CRUNCHES
CRUNCHIE
CRUNCHIER
CRUNCHIES
CRUNCHILY
CRUNCHING
CRUNCHY
CRUNK
CRUNKED
CRUNKLE
CRUNKLED
CRUNKLES
CRUNKLING
CRUNKS
CRUNODAL
CRUNODE
CRUNODES
CRUOR
CRUORES
CRUORS
CRUPPER
CRUPPERS
CRURA
CRURAL
CRUS
CRUSADE
CRUSADED
CRUSADER
CRUSADERS
CRUSADES
CRUSADING
CRUSADO
CRUSADOES
CRUSADOS
CRUSE
CRUSES
CRUSET
CRUSETS
CRUSH
CRUSHABLE
CRUSHED
CRUSHER
CRUSHERS
CRUSHES
CRUSHING
CRUSHINGS
CRUSIAN
CRUSIANS
CRUSIE
CRUSIES
CRUSILY
CRUST
CRUSTA
CRUSTACEA
CRUSTAE
CRUSTAL
CRUSTAS
CRUSTATE
CRUSTATED
CRUSTED
CRUSTIER
CRUSTIES
CRUSTIEST
CRUSTILY
CRUSTING
CRUSTLESS
CRUSTLIKE
CRUSTOSE
CRUSTS
CRUSTY
CRUSY
CRUTCH
CRUTCHED
CRUTCHES
CRUTCHING
CRUVE
CRUVES
CRUX
CRUXES
CRUZADO
CRUZADOES
CRUZADOS
CRUZEIRO
CRUZEIROS
CRUZIE
CRUZIES
CRWTH
CRWTHS
CRY
CRYBABIES
CRYBABY
CRYER
CRYERS
CRYING
CRYINGLY
CRYINGS
CRYOBANK
CRYOBANKS
CRYOCABLE
CRYOGEN
CRYOGENIC
CRYOGENS
CRYOGENY
CRYOLITE
CRYOLITES
CRYOMETER
CRYOMETRY
CRYONIC
CRYONICS
CRYOPHYTE
CRYOPROBE
CRYOSCOPE
CRYOSCOPY
CRYOSTAT
CRYOSTATS
CRYOTRON
CRYOTRONS
CRYPT
CRYPTADIA
CRYPTAL
CRYPTIC
CRYPTICAL
CRYPTO
CRYPTOGAM
CRYPTON
CRYPTONS
CRYPTONYM
CRYPTOS
CRYPTS
CRYSTAL
CRYSTALS
CSARDAS
CSARDASES
CTENE
CTENES
CTENIDIA
CTENIDIUM

CTENIFORM
CTENOID
CUADRILLA
CUATRO
CUATROS
CUB
CUBAGE
CUBAGES
CUBANE
CUBANELLE
CUBANES
CUBATURE
CUBATURES
CUBBED
CUBBIER
CUBBIES
CUBBIEST
CUBBING
CUBBINGS
CUBBISH
CUBBISHLY
CUBBY
CUBBYHOLE
CUBE
CUBEB
CUBEBS
CUBED
CUBELIKE
CUBER
CUBERS
CUBES
CUBHOOD
CUBHOODS
CUBIC
CUBICA
CUBICAL
CUBICALLY
CUBICAS
CUBICITY
CUBICLE
CUBICLES
CUBICLY
CUBICS
CUBICULA
CUBICULUM
CUBIFORM
CUBING
CUBISM
CUBISMS
CUBIST
CUBISTIC
CUBISTS
CUBIT
CUBITAL
CUBITI
CUBITS
CUBITUS
CUBITUSES
CUBLESS
CUBOID
CUBOIDAL
CUBOIDS
CUBS
CUCKING
CUCKOLD
CUCKOLDED
CUCKOLDLY
CUCKOLDOM
CUCKOLDRY
CUCKOLDS
CUCKOO
CUCKOOED
CUCKOOING
CUCKOOS
CUCULLATE
CUCUMBER
CUCUMBERS
CUCURBIT
CUCURBITS
CUD
CUDBEAR
CUDBEARS
CUDDEN
CUDDENS
CUDDIE
CUDDIES
CUDDIN
CUDDINS
CUDDLE
CUDDLED
CUDDLER
CUDDLERS
CUDDLES
CUDDLIER
CUDDLIEST
CUDDLING
CUDDLY
CUDDY
CUDGEL
CUDGELED
CUDGELER
CUDGELERS
CUDGELING
CUDGELLED
CUDGELLER
CUDGELS
CUDGERIE
CUDGERIES
CUDS
CUDWEED
CUDWEEDS
CUE
CUED
CUEING
CUEINGS
CUEIST
CUEISTS
CUES
CUESTA
CUESTAS
CUFF
CUFFABLE
CUFFED
CUFFIN
CUFFING
CUFFINS
CUFFLE
CUFFLED
CUFFLES
CUFFLESS
CUFFLING
CUFFLINK
CUFFLINKS
CUFFO
CUFFS
CUFFUFFLE
CUIF
CUIFS
CUING
CUIRASS
CUIRASSED
CUIRASSES
CUISH
CUISHES
CUISINART
CUISINE
CUISINES
CUISINIER
CUISSE
CUISSER
CUISSERS
CUISSES
CUIT
CUITER
CUITERED
CUITERING
CUITERS
CUITIKIN
CUITIKINS
CUITS
CUITTLE
CUITTLED
CUITTLES
CUITTLING
CUKE
CUKES
CULCH
CULCHES
CULCHIE
CULCHIER
CULCHIES
CULCHIEST
CULET
CULETS
CULEX
CULEXES
CULICES
CULICID
CULICIDS
CULICINE
CULICINES
CULINARY
CULL
CULLAY
CULLAYS
CULLED
CULLENDER
CULLER
CULLERS
CULLET
CULLETS
CULLIED
CULLIES
CULLING
CULLINGS
CULLION
CULLIONLY
CULLIONS
CULLIS
CULLISES
CULLS
CULLY
CULLYING
CULLYISM
CULLYISMS
CULM
CULMED
CULMEN
CULMINA
CULMINANT
CULMINATE
CULMING
CULMS
CULOTTE
CULOTTES
CULPA
CULPABLE
CULPABLY
CULPAE
CULPATORY
CULPRIT
CULPRITS
CULSHIE
CULSHIER
CULSHIES
CULSHIEST
CULT
CULTCH
CULTCHES
CULTER
CULTERS
CULTI
CULTIC
CULTIER
CULTIEST
CULTIGEN
CULTIGENS
CULTISH
CULTISHLY
CULTISM

CULTISMS
CULTIST
CULTISTS
CULTIVAR
CULTIVARS
CULTIVATE
CULTLIKE
CULTRATE
CULTRATED
CULTS
CULTURAL
CULTURATI
CULTURE
CULTURED
CULTURES
CULTURING
CULTURIST
CULTUS
CULTUSES
CULTY
CULVER
CULVERIN
CULVERINS
CULVERS
CULVERT
CULVERTED
CULVERTS
CUM
CUMACEAN
CUMACEANS
CUMARIC
CUMARIN
CUMARINS
CUMARONE
CUMARONES
CUMBENT
CUMBER
CUMBERED
CUMBERER
CUMBERERS
CUMBERING
CUMBERS
CUMBIA
CUMBIAS
CUMBRANCE
CUMBROUS
CUMBUNGI
CUMBUNGIS
CUMEC
CUMECS
CUMIN
CUMINS
CUMMED
CUMMER
CUMMERS
CUMMIN
CUMMING
CUMMINS
CUMQUAT
CUMQUATS
CUMS
CUMSHAW
CUMSHAWS
CUMULATE
CUMULATED
CUMULATES
CUMULET
CUMULETS
CUMULI
CUMULOSE
CUMULOUS
CUMULUS
CUMULUSES
CUNABULA
CUNCTATOR
CUNDIES
CUNDUM
CUNDUMS
CUNDY
CUNEAL
CUNEATE
CUNEATED
CUNEATELY
CUNEATIC
CUNEI
CUNEIFORM
CUNETTE
CUNETTES
CUNEUS
CUNIFORM
CUNIFORMS
CUNIT
CUNITS
CUNJEVOI
CUNJEVOIS
CUNNER
CUNNERS
CUNNING
CUNNINGER
CUNNINGLY
CUNNINGS
CUNT
CUNTS
CUP
CUPBEARER
CUPBOARD
CUPBOARDS
CUPCAKE
CUPCAKES
CUPEL
CUPELED
CUPELER
CUPELERS
CUPELING
CUPELLED
CUPELLER
CUPELLERS
CUPELLING
CUPELS
CUPFERRON
CUPFUL
CUPFULS
CUPGALL
CUPGALLS
CUPHEAD
CUPHEADS
CUPHOLDER
CUPID
CUPIDITY
CUPIDS
CUPLIKE
CUPMAN
CUPMEN
CUPOLA
CUPOLAED
CUPOLAING
CUPOLAR
CUPOLAS
CUPOLATED
CUPPA
CUPPAS
CUPPED
CUPPER
CUPPERS
CUPPIER
CUPPIEST
CUPPING
CUPPINGS
CUPPY
CUPREOUS
CUPRESSUS
CUPRIC
CUPRITE
CUPRITES
CUPROUS
CUPRUM
CUPRUMS
CUPS
CUPSFUL
CUPULA
CUPULAE
CUPULAR
CUPULATE
CUPULE
CUPULES
CUR
CURABLE
CURABLY
CURACAO
CURACAOS
CURACIES
CURACOA
CURACOAS
CURACY
CURAGH
CURAGHS
CURANDERA
CURANDERO
CURARA
CURARAS
CURARE
CURARES
CURARI
CURARINE
CURARINES
CURARIS
CURARISE
CURARISED
CURARISES
CURARIZE
CURARIZED
CURARIZES
CURASSOW
CURASSOWS
CURAT
CURATE
CURATED
CURATES
CURATING
CURATION
CURATIONS
CURATIVE
CURATIVES
CURATOR
CURATORS
CURATORY
CURATRIX
CURATS
CURB
CURBABLE
CURBED
CURBER
CURBERS
CURBING
CURBINGS
CURBLESS
CURBS
CURBSIDE
CURBSIDES
CURBSTONE
CURCH
CURCHEF
CURCHEFS
CURCHES
CURCULIO
CURCULIOS
CURCUMA
CURCUMAS
CURCUMIN
CURCUMINE
CURCUMINS
CURD
CURDED
CURDIER
CURDIEST
CURDINESS
CURDING
CURDLE
CURDLED
CURDLER

C

CURDLERS
CURDLES
CURDLING
CURDS
CURDY
CURE
CURED
CURELESS
CURER
CURERS
CURES
CURET
CURETS
CURETTAGE
CURETTE
CURETTED
CURETTES
CURETTING
CURF
CURFEW
CURFEWS
CURFS
CURFUFFLE
CURIA
CURIAE
CURIAL
CURIALISM
CURIALIST
CURIAS
CURIE
CURIES
CURIET
CURIETS
CURING
CURINGS
CURIO
CURIOS
CURIOSA
CURIOSITY
CURIOUS
CURIOUSER
CURIOUSLY
CURITE
CURITES
CURIUM
CURIUMS
CURL
CURLED
CURLER
CURLERS
CURLEW
CURLEWS
CURLI
CURLICUE
CURLICUED
CURLICUES
CURLIER
CURLIES
CURLIEST
CURLILY
CURLINESS
CURLING
CURLINGS
CURLPAPER
CURLS
CURLY
CURLYCUE
CURLYCUES
CURN
CURNEY
CURNIER
CURNIEST
CURNS
CURNY
CURPEL
CURPELS
CURR
CURRACH
CURRACHS
CURRAGH
CURRAGHS
CURRAJONG
CURRAN
CURRANS
CURRANT
CURRANTS
CURRANTY
CURRAWONG
CURRED
CURREJONG
CURRENCY
CURRENT
CURRENTLY
CURRENTS
CURRICLE
CURRICLES
CURRICULA
CURRIE
CURRIED
CURRIER
CURRIERS
CURRIERY
CURRIES
CURRIJONG
CURRING
CURRISH
CURRISHLY
CURRS
CURRY
CURRYCOMB
CURRYING
CURRYINGS
CURS
CURSAL
CURSE
CURSED
CURSEDER
CURSEDEST
CURSEDLY
CURSENARY
CURSER
CURSERS
CURSES
CURSI
CURSILLO
CURSILLOS
CURSING
CURSINGS
CURSITOR
CURSITORS
CURSITORY
CURSIVE
CURSIVELY
CURSIVES
CURSOR
CURSORARY
CURSORES
CURSORIAL
CURSORILY
CURSORS
CURSORY
CURST
CURSTNESS
CURSUS
CURT
CURTAIL
CURTAILED
CURTAILER
CURTAILS
CURTAIN
CURTAINED
CURTAINS
CURTAL
CURTALAX
CURTALAXE
CURTALS
CURTANA
CURTANAS
CURTATE
CURTATION
CURTAXE
CURTAXES
CURTER
CURTESIES
CURTEST
CURTESY
CURTILAGE
CURTLY
CURTNESS
CURTSEY
CURTSEYED
CURTSEYS
CURTSIED
CURTSIES
CURTSY
CURTSYING
CURULE
CURVATE
CURVATED
CURVATION
CURVATIVE
CURVATURE
CURVE
CURVEBALL
CURVED
CURVEDLY
CURVES
CURVESOME
CURVET
CURVETED
CURVETING
CURVETS
CURVETTED
CURVEY
CURVIER
CURVIEST
CURVIFORM
CURVINESS
CURVING
CURVITAL
CURVITIES
CURVITY
CURVY
CUSCUS
CUSCUSES
CUSEC
CUSECS
CUSH
CUSHAT
CUSHATS
CUSHAW
CUSHAWS
CUSHES
CUSHIE
CUSHIER
CUSHIES
CUSHIEST
CUSHILY
CUSHINESS
CUSHION
CUSHIONED
CUSHIONET
CUSHIONS
CUSHIONY
CUSHTY
CUSHY
CUSK
CUSKS
CUSP
CUSPAL
CUSPATE
CUSPATED
CUSPED
CUSPID
CUSPIDAL
CUSPIDATE
CUSPIDES
CUSPIDOR
CUSPIDORE
CUSPIDORS

CUSPIDS
CUSPIER
CUSPIEST
CUSPIS
CUSPLIKE
CUSPS
CUSPY
CUSS
CUSSED
CUSSEDLY
CUSSER
CUSSERS
CUSSES
CUSSING
CUSSO
CUSSOS
CUSSWORD
CUSSWORDS
CUSTARD
CUSTARDS
CUSTARDY
CUSTOCK
CUSTOCKS
CUSTODE
CUSTODES
CUSTODIAL
CUSTODIAN
CUSTODIER
CUSTODIES
CUSTODY
CUSTOM
CUSTOMARY
CUSTOMED
CUSTOMER
CUSTOMERS
CUSTOMISE
CUSTOMIZE
CUSTOMS
CUSTOS
CUSTREL
CUSTRELS
CUSTUMAL
CUSTUMALS
CUSTUMARY
CUSUM
CUSUMS
CUT
CUTANEOUS
CUTAWAY
CUTAWAYS
CUTBACK
CUTBACKS
CUTBANK
CUTBANKS
CUTBLOCK
CUTBLOCKS
CUTCH
CUTCHA
CUTCHERRY
CUTCHERY
CUTCHES
CUTDOWN
CUTDOWNS
CUTE
CUTELY
CUTENESS
CUTER
CUTES
CUTESIE
CUTESIER
CUTESIEST
CUTEST
CUTESY
CUTEY
CUTEYS
CUTGLASS
CUTGRASS
CUTICLE
CUTICLES
CUTICULA
CUTICULAE
CUTICULAR
CUTIE
CUTIES
CUTIKIN
CUTIKINS
CUTIN
CUTINISE
CUTINISED
CUTINISES
CUTINIZE
CUTINIZED
CUTINIZES
CUTINS
CUTIS
CUTISES
CUTLAS
CUTLASES
CUTLASS
CUTLASSES
CUTLER
CUTLERIES
CUTLERS
CUTLERY
CUTLET
CUTLETS
CUTLETTE
CUTLETTES
CUTLINE
CUTLINES
CUTOFF
CUTOFFS
CUTOUT
CUTOUTS
CUTOVER
CUTOVERS
CUTPURSE
CUTPURSES
CUTS
CUTSCENE
CUTSCENES
CUTTABLE
CUTTAGE
CUTTAGES
CUTTER
CUTTERS
CUTTHROAT
CUTTIER
CUTTIES
CUTTIEST
CUTTING
CUTTINGLY
CUTTINGS
CUTTLE
CUTTLED
CUTTLES
CUTTLING
CUTTO
CUTTOE
CUTTOES
CUTTY
CUTUP
CUTUPS
CUTWATER
CUTWATERS
CUTWORK
CUTWORKS
CUTWORM
CUTWORMS
CUVEE
CUVEES
CUVETTE
CUVETTES
CUZ
CUZES
CUZZES
CUZZIE
CUZZIES
CWM
CWMS
CWTCH
CWTCHED
CWTCHES
CWTCHING
CYAN
CYANAMID
CYANAMIDE
CYANAMIDS
CYANATE
CYANATES
CYANIC
CYANID
CYANIDE
CYANIDED
CYANIDES
CYANIDING
CYANIDS
CYANIN
CYANINE
CYANINES
CYANINS
CYANISE
CYANISED
CYANISES
CYANISING
CYANITE
CYANITES
CYANITIC
CYANIZE
CYANIZED
CYANIZES
CYANIZING
CYANO
CYANOGEN
CYANOGENS
CYANOSE
CYANOSED
CYANOSES
CYANOSIS
CYANOTIC
CYANOTYPE
CYANS
CYANURATE
CYANURET
CYANURETS
CYANURIC
CYATHI
CYATHIA
CYATHIUM
CYATHUS
CYBER
CYBERCAFE
CYBERCAST
CYBERNATE
CYBERNAUT
CYBERPET
CYBERPETS
CYBERPORN
CYBERPUNK
CYBERSEX
CYBERWAR
CYBERWARS
CYBORG
CYBORGS
CYBRARIAN
CYBRID
CYBRIDS
CYCAD
CYCADEOID
CYCADS
CYCAS
CYCASES
CYCASIN
CYCASINS
CYCLAMATE
CYCLAMEN
CYCLAMENS
CYCLAMIC
CYCLASE
CYCLASES

CYCLE
CYCLECAR
CYCLECARS
CYCLED
CYCLEPATH
CYCLER
CYCLERIES
CYCLERS
CYCLERY
CYCLES
CYCLEWAY
CYCLEWAYS
CYCLIC
CYCLICAL
CYCLICALS
CYCLICISM
CYCLICITY
CYCLICLY
CYCLIN
CYCLING
CYCLINGS
CYCLINS
CYCLISE
CYCLISED
CYCLISES
CYCLISING
CYCLIST
CYCLISTS
CYCLITOL
CYCLITOLS
CYCLIZE
CYCLIZED
CYCLIZES
CYCLIZINE
CYCLIZING
CYCLO
CYCLOGIRO
CYCLOID
CYCLOIDAL
CYCLOIDS
CYCLOLITH
CYCLONAL
CYCLONE
CYCLONES
CYCLONIC
CYCLONITE
CYCLOPEAN
CYCLOPES
CYCLOPIAN
CYCLOPIC
CYCLOPS
CYCLORAMA
CYCLOS
CYCLOSES
CYCLOSIS
CYCLOTRON
CYCLUS
CYCLUSES
CYDER
CYDERS
CYESES
CYESIS
CYGNET
CYGNETS
CYLICES
CYLIKES
CYLINDER
CYLINDERS
CYLINDRIC
CYLIX
CYMA
CYMAE
CYMAGRAPH
CYMAR
CYMARS
CYMAS
CYMATIA
CYMATICS
CYMATIUM
CYMBAL
CYMBALEER
CYMBALER
CYMBALERS
CYMBALIST
CYMBALO
CYMBALOES
CYMBALOM
CYMBALOMS
CYMBALOS
CYMBALS
CYMBIDIA
CYMBIDIUM
CYMBIFORM
CYMBLING
CYMBLINGS
CYME
CYMENE
CYMENES
CYMES
CYMLIN
CYMLING
CYMLINGS
CYMLINS
CYMOGENE
CYMOGENES
CYMOGRAPH
CYMOID
CYMOL
CYMOLS
CYMOPHANE
CYMOSE
CYMOSELY
CYMOUS
CYNANCHE
CYNANCHES
CYNEGETIC
CYNIC
CYNICAL
CYNICALLY
CYNICISM
CYNICISMS
CYNICS
CYNODONT
CYNODONTS
CYNOMOLGI
CYNOSURAL
CYNOSURE
CYNOSURES
CYPHER
CYPHERED
CYPHERING
CYPHERS
CYPRES
CYPRESES
CYPRESS
CYPRESSES
CYPRIAN
CYPRIANS
CYPRID
CYPRIDES
CYPRIDS
CYPRINE
CYPRINES
CYPRINID
CYPRINIDS
CYPRINOID
CYPRIS
CYPRUS
CYPRUSES
CYPSELA
CYPSELAE
CYST
CYSTEIN
CYSTEINE
CYSTEINES
CYSTEINIC
CYSTEINS
CYSTIC
CYSTID
CYSTIDEAN
CYSTIDS
CYSTIFORM
CYSTINE
CYSTINES
CYSTITIS
CYSTOCARP
CYSTOCELE
CYSTOID
CYSTOIDS
CYSTOLITH
CYSTOTOMY
CYSTS
CYTASE
CYTASES
CYTASTER
CYTASTERS
CYTE
CYTES
CYTIDINE
CYTIDINES
CYTIDYLIC
CYTISI
CYTISINE
CYTISINES
CYTISUS
CYTODE
CYTODES
CYTOGENY
CYTOID
CYTOKINE
CYTOKINES
CYTOKININ
CYTOLOGIC
CYTOLOGY
CYTOLYSES
CYTOLYSIN
CYTOLYSIS
CYTOLYTIC
CYTOMETER
CYTOMETRY
CYTON
CYTONS
CYTOPATHY
CYTOPENIA
CYTOPLASM
CYTOPLAST
CYTOSINE
CYTOSINES
CYTOSOL
CYTOSOLIC
CYTOSOLS
CYTOSOME
CYTOSOMES
CYTOTAXES
CYTOTAXIS
CYTOTOXIC
CYTOTOXIN
CZAPKA
CZAPKAS
CZAR
CZARDAS
CZARDASES
CZARDOM
CZARDOMS
CZAREVICH
CZAREVNA
CZAREVNAS
CZARINA
CZARINAS
CZARISM
CZARISMS
CZARIST
CZARISTS
CZARITSA
CZARITSAS
CZARITZA
CZARITZAS
CZARS

D

DA
DAAL
DAALS
DAB
DABBA
DABBAS
DABBED
DABBER
DABBERS
DABBING
DABBITIES
DABBITY
DABBLE
DABBLED
DABBLER
DABBLERS
DABBLES
DABBLING
DABBLINGS
DABCHICK
DABCHICKS
DABS
DABSTER
DABSTERS
DACE
DACES
DACHA
DACHAS
DACHSHUND
DACITE
DACITES
DACK
DACKED
DACKER
DACKERED
DACKERING
DACKERS
DACKING
DACKS
DACOIT
DACOITAGE
DACOITIES
DACOITS
DACOITY
DACQUOISE
DACRON
DACRONS
DACTYL
DACTYLAR
DACTYLI
DACTYLIC
DACTYLICS
DACTYLIST
DACTYLS
DACTYLUS
DAD
DADA
DADAH
DADAHS
DADAISM
DADAISMS
DADAIST
DADAISTIC
DADAISTS
DADAS
DADBOD
DADBODS
DADCHELOR
DADDED
DADDIES
DADDING
DADDLE
DADDLED
DADDLES
DADDLING
DADDOCK
DADDOCKS
DADDY
DADGUM
DADO
DADOED
DADOES
DADOING
DADOS
DADS
DAE
DAEDAL
DAEDALEAN
DAEDALIAN
DAEDALIC
DAEING
DAEMON
DAEMONES
DAEMONIC
DAEMONS
DAES
DAFF
DAFFED
DAFFIER
DAFFIES
DAFFIEST
DAFFILY
DAFFINESS
DAFFING
DAFFINGS
DAFFODIL
DAFFODILS
DAFFS
DAFFY
DAFT
DAFTAR
DAFTARS
DAFTER
DAFTEST
DAFTIE
DAFTIES
DAFTLY
DAFTNESS
DAG
DAGABA
DAGABAS
DAGGA
DAGGAS
DAGGED
DAGGER
DAGGERED
DAGGERING
DAGGERS
DAGGIER
DAGGIEST
DAGGING
DAGGINGS
DAGGLE
DAGGLED
DAGGLES
DAGGLING
DAGGY
DAGLOCK
DAGLOCKS
DAGO
DAGOBA
DAGOBAS
DAGOES
DAGOS
DAGS
DAGWOOD
DAGWOODS
DAH
DAHABEAH
DAHABEAHS
DAHABEEAH
DAHABIAH
DAHABIAHS
DAHABIEH
DAHABIEHS
DAHABIYA
DAHABIYAH
DAHABIYAS
DAHABIYEH
DAHL
DAHLIA
DAHLIAS
DAHLS
DAHOON
DAHOONS
DAHS
DAIDLE
DAIDLED
DAIDLES
DAIDLING
DAIDZEIN
DAIDZEINS
DAIKER
DAIKERED
DAIKERING
DAIKERS
DAIKO
DAIKON
DAIKONS
DAIKOS
DAILIES
DAILINESS
DAILY
DAILYNESS
DAIMEN
DAIMIO
DAIMIOS
DAIMOKU
DAIMOKUS
DAIMON
DAIMONES
DAIMONIC
DAIMONS
DAIMYO
DAIMYOS
DAINE
DAINED
DAINES
DAINING
DAINT
DAINTIER
DAINTIES
DAINTIEST
DAINTILY
DAINTS
DAINTY
DAIQUIRI
DAIQUIRIS
DAIRIES
DAIRY

DAIRYING
DAIRYINGS
DAIRYMAID
DAIRYMAN
DAIRYMEN
DAIS
DAISES
DAISHIKI
DAISHIKIS
DAISIED
DAISIES
DAISY
DAISYLIKE
DAK
DAKER
DAKERED
DAKERHEN
DAKERHENS
DAKERING
DAKERS
DAKOIT
DAKOITI
DAKOITIES
DAKOITIS
DAKOITS
DAKOITY
DAKS
DAL
DALAPON
DALAPONS
DALASI
DALASIS
DALE
DALED
DALEDH
DALEDHS
DALEDS
DALES
DALESMAN
DALESMEN
DALETH
DALETHS
DALGYTE
DALGYTES
DALI
DALIS
DALLE
DALLES
DALLIANCE
DALLIED
DALLIER
DALLIERS
DALLIES
DALLOP
DALLOPS
DALLY
DALLYING
DALMAHOY
DALMAHOYS
DALMATIAN
DALMATIC
DALMATICS
DALS
DALT
DALTON
DALTONIAN
DALTONIC
DALTONISM
DALTONS
DALTS
DAM
DAMAGE
DAMAGED
DAMAGER
DAMAGERS
DAMAGES
DAMAGING
DAMAN
DAMANS
DAMAR
DAMARS
DAMASCENE
DAMASK
DAMASKED
DAMASKEEN
DAMASKIN
DAMASKING
DAMASKINS
DAMASKS
DAMASQUIN
DAMASSIN
DAMASSINS
DAMBOARD
DAMBOARDS
DAMBROD
DAMBRODS
DAME
DAMEHOOD
DAMEHOODS
DAMES
DAMEWORT
DAMEWORTS
DAMFOOL
DAMFOOLS
DAMIANA
DAMIANAS
DAMMAR
DAMMARS
DAMME
DAMMED
DAMMER
DAMMERS
DAMMING
DAMMIT
DAMN
DAMNABLE
DAMNABLY
DAMNATION
DAMNATORY
DAMNDEST
DAMNDESTS
DAMNED
DAMNEDER
DAMNEDEST
DAMNER
DAMNERS
DAMNEST
DAMNESTS
DAMNIFIED
DAMNIFIES
DAMNIFY
DAMNING
DAMNINGLY
DAMNS
DAMOISEL
DAMOISELS
DAMOSEL
DAMOSELS
DAMOZEL
DAMOZELS
DAMP
DAMPED
DAMPEN
DAMPENED
DAMPENER
DAMPENERS
DAMPENING
DAMPENS
DAMPER
DAMPERS
DAMPEST
DAMPIER
DAMPIEST
DAMPING
DAMPINGS
DAMPISH
DAMPLY
DAMPNESS
DAMPS
DAMPY
DAMS
DAMSEL
DAMSELFLY
DAMSELS
DAMSON
DAMSONS
DAN
DANAZOL
DANAZOLS
DANCE
DANCEABLE
DANCECORE
DANCED
DANCEHALL
DANCELIKE
DANCER
DANCERS
DANCES
DANCETTE
DANCETTEE
DANCETTES
DANCETTY
DANCEWEAR
DANCEY
DANCICAL
DANCICALS
DANCIER
DANCIEST
DANCING
DANCINGS
DANCY
DANDELION
DANDER
DANDERED
DANDERING
DANDERS
DANDIACAL
DANDIER
DANDIES
DANDIEST
DANDIFIED
DANDIFIES
DANDIFY
DANDILY
DANDIPRAT
DANDLE
DANDLED
DANDLER
DANDLERS
DANDLES
DANDLING
DANDRIFF
DANDRIFFS
DANDRUFF
DANDRUFFS
DANDRUFFY
DANDY
DANDYFUNK
DANDYISH
DANDYISM
DANDYISMS
DANDYPRAT
DANEGELD
DANEGELDS
DANEGELT
DANEGELTS
DANELAGH
DANELAGHS
DANELAW
DANELAWS
DANEWEED
DANEWEEDS
DANEWORT
DANEWORTS
DANG
DANGED
DANGER
DANGERED
DANGERING
DANGEROUS

DANGERS
DANGEST
DANGING
DANGLE
DANGLED
DANGLER
DANGLERS
DANGLES
DANGLIER
DANGLIEST
DANGLING
DANGLINGS
DANGLY
DANGS
DANIO
DANIOS
DANISH
DANISHES
DANK
DANKER
DANKEST
DANKISH
DANKLY
DANKNESS
DANKS
DANNEBROG
DANNIES
DANNY
DANS
DANSAK
DANSAKS
DANSEUR
DANSEURS
DANSEUSE
DANSEUSES
DANT
DANTED
DANTHONIA
DANTING
DANTON
DANTONED
DANTONING
DANTONS
DANTS
DAP
DAPHNE
DAPHNES
DAPHNIA
DAPHNIAS
DAPHNID
DAPHNIDS
DAPPED
DAPPER
DAPPERER
DAPPEREST
DAPPERLY
DAPPERS
DAPPING
DAPPLE
DAPPLED
DAPPLES
DAPPLING
DAPS
DAPSONE
DAPSONES
DAQUIRI
DAQUIRIS
DARAF
DARAFS
DARB
DARBAR
DARBARS
DARBIES
DARBS
DARCIES
DARCY
DARCYS
DARE
DARED
DAREDEVIL
DAREFUL
DARER
DARERS
DARES
DARESAY
DARG
DARGA
DARGAH
DARGAHS
DARGAS
DARGLE
DARGLES
DARGS
DARI
DARIC
DARICS
DARING
DARINGLY
DARINGS
DARIOLE
DARIOLES
DARIS
DARK
DARKED
DARKEN
DARKENED
DARKENER
DARKENERS
DARKENING
DARKENS
DARKER
DARKEST
DARKEY
DARKEYS
DARKFIELD
DARKIE
DARKIES
DARKING
DARKISH
DARKLE
DARKLED
DARKLES
DARKLIER
DARKLIEST
DARKLING
DARKLINGS
DARKLY
DARKMANS
DARKNESS
DARKNET
DARKNETS
DARKROOM
DARKROOMS
DARKS
DARKSOME
DARKY
DARLING
DARLINGLY
DARLINGS
DARN
DARNATION
DARNDEST
DARNDESTS
DARNED
DARNEDER
DARNEDEST
DARNEL
DARNELS
DARNER
DARNERS
DARNEST
DARNESTS
DARNING
DARNINGS
DARNS
DAROGHA
DAROGHAS
DARRAIGN
DARRAIGNE
DARRAIGNS
DARRAIN
DARRAINE
DARRAINED
DARRAINES
DARRAINS
DARRAYN
DARRAYNED
DARRAYNS
DARRE
DARRED
DARRES
DARRING
DARSHAN
DARSHANS
DART
DARTBOARD
DARTED
DARTER
DARTERS
DARTING
DARTINGLY
DARTITIS
DARTLE
DARTLED
DARTLES
DARTLING
DARTRE
DARTRES
DARTROUS
DARTS
DARZI
DARZIS
DAS
DASH
DASHBOARD
DASHCAM
DASHCAMS
DASHED
DASHEEN
DASHEENS
DASHEKI
DASHEKIS
DASHER
DASHERS
DASHES
DASHI
DASHIER
DASHIEST
DASHIKI
DASHIKIS
DASHING
DASHINGLY
DASHIS
DASHLIGHT
DASHPOT
DASHPOTS
DASHY
DASSIE
DASSIES
DASTARD
DASTARDLY
DASTARDS
DASTARDY
DASYMETER
DASYPOD
DASYPODS
DASYURE
DASYURES
DATA
DATABANK
DATABANKS
DATABASE
DATABASED
DATABASES
DATABLE
DATABUS
DATABUSES
DATACARD
DATACARDS
DATACOMMS

D

DATAFLOW
DATAGLOVE
DATAGRAM
DATAGRAMS
DATAL
DATALLER
DATALLERS
DATALS
DATARIA
DATARIAS
DATARIES
DATARY
DATCHA
DATCHAS
DATE
DATEABLE
DATEBOOK
DATEBOOKS
DATED
DATEDLY
DATEDNESS
DATELESS
DATELINE
DATELINED
DATELINES
DATER
DATERS
DATES
DATING
DATINGS
DATIVAL
DATIVE
DATIVELY
DATIVES
DATO
DATOLITE
DATOLITES
DATOS
DATTO
DATTOS
DATUM
DATUMS
DATURA
DATURAS
DATURIC
DATURINE
DATURINES
DAUB
DAUBE
DAUBED
DAUBER
DAUBERIES
DAUBERS
DAUBERY
DAUBES
DAUBIER
DAUBIEST
DAUBING
DAUBINGLY
DAUBINGS
DAUBRIES
DAUBRY
DAUBS
DAUBY
DAUD
DAUDED
DAUDING
DAUDS
DAUGHTER
DAUGHTERS
DAULT
DAULTS
DAUNDER
DAUNDERED
DAUNDERS
DAUNER
DAUNERED
DAUNERING
DAUNERS
DAUNT
DAUNTED
DAUNTER
DAUNTERS
DAUNTING
DAUNTLESS
DAUNTON
DAUNTONED
DAUNTONS
DAUNTS
DAUPHIN
DAUPHINE
DAUPHINES
DAUPHINS
DAUR
DAURED
DAURING
DAURS
DAUT
DAUTED
DAUTIE
DAUTIES
DAUTING
DAUTS
DAVEN
DAVENED
DAVENING
DAVENPORT
DAVENS
DAVIDIA
DAVIDIAS
DAVIES
DAVIT
DAVITS
DAVY
DAW
DAWAH
DAWAHS
DAWBAKE
DAWBAKES
DAWBRIES
DAWBRY
DAWCOCK
DAWCOCKS
DAWD
DAWDED
DAWDING
DAWDLE
DAWDLED
DAWDLER
DAWDLERS
DAWDLES
DAWDLING
DAWDLINGS
DAWDS
DAWED
DAWEN
DAWING
DAWISH
DAWK
DAWKS
DAWN
DAWNED
DAWNER
DAWNERED
DAWNERING
DAWNERS
DAWNEY
DAWNING
DAWNINGS
DAWNLIKE
DAWNS
DAWS
DAWSONITE
DAWT
DAWTED
DAWTIE
DAWTIES
DAWTING
DAWTS
DAY
DAYAN
DAYANIM
DAYANS
DAYBED
DAYBEDS
DAYBOAT
DAYBOATS
DAYBOOK
DAYBOOKS
DAYBOY
DAYBOYS
DAYBREAK
DAYBREAKS
DAYCARE
DAYCARES
DAYCATION
DAYCENTRE
DAYCH
DAYCHED
DAYCHES
DAYCHING
DAYDREAM
DAYDREAMS
DAYDREAMT
DAYDREAMY
DAYFLIES
DAYFLOWER
DAYFLY
DAYGIRL
DAYGIRLS
DAYGLO
DAYGLOW
DAYGLOWS
DAYLIGHT
DAYLIGHTS
DAYLILIES
DAYLILY
DAYLIT
DAYLONG
DAYMARE
DAYMARES
DAYMARK
DAYMARKS
DAYNT
DAYNTS
DAYPACK
DAYPACKS
DAYROOM
DAYROOMS
DAYS
DAYSACK
DAYSACKS
DAYSAIL
DAYSAILED
DAYSAILER
DAYSAILOR
DAYSAILS
DAYSHELL
DAYSHELLS
DAYSIDE
DAYSIDES
DAYSMAN
DAYSMEN
DAYSPRING
DAYSTAR
DAYSTARS
DAYTALE
DAYTALER
DAYTALERS
DAYTALES
DAYTIME
DAYTIMES
DAYWEAR
DAYWEARS
DAYWORK
DAYWORKER
DAYWORKS
DAZE
DAZED
DAZEDLY

DAZEDNESS
DAZER
DAZERS
DAZES
DAZING
DAZZLE
DAZZLED
DAZZLER
DAZZLERS
DAZZLES
DAZZLING
DAZZLINGS
DE
DEACIDIFY
DEACON
DEACONED
DEACONESS
DEACONING
DEACONRY
DEACONS
DEAD
DEADBEAT
DEADBEATS
DEADBOLT
DEADBOLTS
DEADBOY
DEADBOYS
DEADED
DEADEN
DEADENED
DEADENER
DEADENERS
DEADENING
DEADENS
DEADER
DEADERS
DEADEST
DEADEYE
DEADEYES
DEADFALL
DEADFALLS
DEADHEAD
DEADHEADS
DEADHOUSE
DEADING
DEADLIER
DEADLIEST
DEADLIFT
DEADLIFTS
DEADLIGHT
DEADLINE
DEADLINED
DEADLINES
DEADLOCK
DEADLOCKS
DEADLY
DEADMAN
DEADMEN
DEADNESS
DEADPAN
DEADPANS
DEADS
DEADSTOCK
DEADWATER
DEADWOOD
DEADWOODS
DEAERATE
DEAERATED
DEAERATES
DEAERATOR
DEAF
DEAFBLIND
DEAFEN
DEAFENED
DEAFENING
DEAFENS
DEAFER
DEAFEST
DEAFISH
DEAFLY
DEAFNESS
DEAIR
DEAIRED
DEAIRING
DEAIRS
DEAL
DEALATE
DEALATED
DEALATES
DEALATION
DEALBATE
DEALER
DEALERS
DEALFISH
DEALIGN
DEALIGNED
DEALIGNS
DEALING
DEALINGS
DEALMAKER
DEALS
DEALT
DEAMINASE
DEAMINATE
DEAMINISE
DEAMINIZE
DEAN
DEANED
DEANER
DEANERIES
DEANERS
DEANERY
DEANING
DEANS
DEANSHIP
DEANSHIPS
DEAR
DEARE
DEARED
DEARER
DEARES
DEAREST
DEARESTS
DEARIE
DEARIES
DEARING
DEARLING
DEARLINGS
DEARLY
DEARN
DEARNED
DEARNESS
DEARNFUL
DEARNING
DEARNLY
DEARNS
DEARS
DEARTH
DEARTHS
DEARY
DEASH
DEASHED
DEASHES
DEASHING
DEASIL
DEASILS
DEASIUL
DEASIULS
DEASOIL
DEASOILS
DEATH
DEATHBED
DEATHBEDS
DEATHBLOW
DEATHCARE
DEATHCUP
DEATHCUPS
DEATHFUL
DEATHIER
DEATHIEST
DEATHLESS
DEATHLIER
DEATHLIKE
DEATHLY
DEATHS
DEATHSMAN
DEATHSMEN
DEATHTRAP
DEATHWARD
DEATHY
DEAVE
DEAVED
DEAVES
DEAVING
DEAW
DEAWED
DEAWIE
DEAWING
DEAWS
DEAWY
DEB
DEBACLE
DEBACLES
DEBAG
DEBAGGED
DEBAGGING
DEBAGS
DEBAR
DEBARK
DEBARKED
DEBARKER
DEBARKERS
DEBARKING
DEBARKS
DEBARMENT
DEBARRASS
DEBARRED
DEBARRING
DEBARS
DEBASE
DEBASED
DEBASER
DEBASERS
DEBASES
DEBASING
DEBATABLE
DEBATABLY
DEBATE
DEBATED
DEBATEFUL
DEBATER
DEBATERS
DEBATES
DEBATING
DEBATINGS
DEBAUCH
DEBAUCHED
DEBAUCHEE
DEBAUCHER
DEBAUCHES
DEBBIER
DEBBIES
DEBBIEST
DEBBY
DEBE
DEBEAK
DEBEAKED
DEBEAKING
DEBEAKS
DEBEARD
DEBEARDED
DEBEARDS
DEBEL
DEBELLED
DEBELLING
DEBELS
DEBENTURE
DEBES
DEBILE
DEBILITY

D

DEBIT
DEBITED
DEBITING
DEBITOR
DEBITORS
DEBITS
DEBONAIR
DEBONAIRE
DEBONE
DEBONED
DEBONER
DEBONERS
DEBONES
DEBONING
DEBOSH
DEBOSHED
DEBOSHES
DEBOSHING
DEBOSS
DEBOSSED
DEBOSSES
DEBOSSING
DEBOUCH
DEBOUCHE
DEBOUCHED
DEBOUCHES
DEBRIDE
DEBRIDED
DEBRIDES
DEBRIDING
DEBRIEF
DEBRIEFED
DEBRIEFER
DEBRIEFS
DEBRIS
DEBRUISE
DEBRUISED
DEBRUISES
DEBS
DEBT
DEBTED
DEBTEE
DEBTEES
DEBTLESS
DEBTOR
DEBTORS
DEBTS
DEBUD
DEBUDDED
DEBUDDING
DEBUDS
DEBUG
DEBUGGED
DEBUGGER
DEBUGGERS
DEBUGGING
DEBUGS
DEBUNK
DEBUNKED
DEBUNKER
DEBUNKERS
DEBUNKING
DEBUNKS
DEBUR
DEBURR
DEBURRED
DEBURRING
DEBURRS
DEBURS
DEBUS
DEBUSED
DEBUSES
DEBUSING
DEBUSSED
DEBUSSES
DEBUSSING
DEBUT
DEBUTANT
DEBUTANTE
DEBUTANTS
DEBUTED
DEBUTING
DEBUTS
DEBYE
DEBYES
DECACHORD
DECAD
DECADAL
DECADE
DECADENCE
DECADENCY
DECADENT
DECADENTS
DECADES
DECADS
DECAF
DECAFF
DECAFFS
DECAFS
DECAGON
DECAGONAL
DECAGONS
DECAGRAM
DECAGRAMS
DECAHEDRA
DECAL
DECALCIFY
DECALED
DECALING
DECALITER
DECALITRE
DECALLED
DECALLING
DECALOG
DECALOGS
DECALOGUE
DECALS
DECAMETER
DECAMETRE
DECAMP
DECAMPED
DECAMPING
DECAMPS
DECAN
DECANAL
DECANALLY
DECANE
DECANES
DECANI
DECANOIC
DECANS
DECANT
DECANTATE
DECANTED
DECANTER
DECANTERS
DECANTING
DECANTS
DECAPOD
DECAPODAL
DECAPODAN
DECAPODS
DECARB
DECARBED
DECARBING
DECARBS
DECARE
DECARES
DECASTERE
DECASTICH
DECASTYLE
DECATHLON
DECAUDATE
DECAY
DECAYABLE
DECAYED
DECAYER
DECAYERS
DECAYING
DECAYLESS
DECAYS
DECCIE
DECCIES
DECEASE
DECEASED
DECEASEDS
DECEASES
DECEASING
DECEDENT
DECEDENTS
DECEIT
DECEITFUL
DECEITS
DECEIVE
DECEIVED
DECEIVER
DECEIVERS
DECEIVES
DECEIVING
DECELERON
DECEMVIR
DECEMVIRI
DECEMVIRS
DECENARY
DECENCIES
DECENCY
DECENNARY
DECENNIA
DECENNIAL
DECENNIUM
DECENT
DECENTER
DECENTERS
DECENTEST
DECENTLY
DECENTRE
DECENTRED
DECENTRES
DECEPTION
DECEPTIVE
DECEPTORY
DECERN
DECERNED
DECERNING
DECERNS
DECERTIFY
DECESSION
DECHEANCE
DECIARE
DECIARES
DECIBEL
DECIBELS
DECIDABLE
DECIDE
DECIDED
DECIDEDLY
DECIDER
DECIDERS
DECIDES
DECIDING
DECIDUA
DECIDUAE
DECIDUAL
DECIDUAS
DECIDUATE
DECIDUOUS
DECIGRAM
DECIGRAMS
DECILE
DECILES
DECILITER
DECILITRE
DECILLION
DECIMAL
DECIMALLY
DECIMALS
DECIMATE
DECIMATED
DECIMATES
DECIMATOR

DECIME
DECIMES
DECIMETER
DECIMETRE
DECIPHER
DECIPHERS
DECISION
DECISIONS
DECISIVE
DECISORY
DECISTERE
DECK
DECKCHAIR
DECKED
DECKEL
DECKELS
DECKER
DECKERS
DECKHAND
DECKHANDS
DECKHOUSE
DECKING
DECKINGS
DECKLE
DECKLED
DECKLES
DECKLESS
DECKO
DECKOED
DECKOING
DECKOS
DECKS
DECLAIM
DECLAIMED
DECLAIMER
DECLAIMS
DECLARANT
DECLARE
DECLARED
DECLARER
DECLARERS
DECLARES
DECLARING
DECLASS
DECLASSE
DECLASSED
DECLASSEE
DECLASSES
DECLAW
DECLAWED
DECLAWING
DECLAWS
DECLINAL
DECLINALS
DECLINANT
DECLINATE
DECLINE
DECLINED
DECLINER
DECLINERS
DECLINES
DECLINING
DECLINIST
DECLIVITY
DECLIVOUS
DECLUTCH
DECLUTTER
DECO
DECOCT
DECOCTED
DECOCTING
DECOCTION
DECOCTIVE
DECOCTS
DECOCTURE
DECODABLE
DECODE
DECODED
DECODER
DECODERS
DECODES
DECODING
DECODINGS
DECOHERER
DECOKE
DECOKED
DECOKES
DECOKING
DECOLLATE
DECOLLETE
DECOLOR
DECOLORED
DECOLORS
DECOLOUR
DECOLOURS
DECOMMIT
DECOMMITS
DECOMPLEX
DECOMPOSE
DECONGEST
DECONTROL
DECOR
DECORATE
DECORATED
DECORATES
DECORATOR
DECOROUS
DECORS
DECORUM
DECORUMS
DECOS
DECOUPAGE
DECOUPLE
DECOUPLED
DECOUPLER
DECOUPLES
DECOY
DECOYED
DECOYER
DECOYERS
DECOYING
DECOYS
DECREASE
DECREASED
DECREASES
DECREE
DECREED
DECREEING
DECREER
DECREERS
DECREES
DECREET
DECREETS
DECREMENT
DECREPIT
DECRETAL
DECRETALS
DECRETIST
DECRETIVE
DECRETORY
DECREW
DECREWED
DECREWING
DECREWS
DECRIAL
DECRIALS
DECRIED
DECRIER
DECRIERS
DECRIES
DECROWN
DECROWNED
DECROWNS
DECRY
DECRYING
DECRYPT
DECRYPTED
DECRYPTS
DECTET
DECTETS
DECUBITAL
DECUBITI
DECUBITUS
DECUMAN
DECUMANS
DECUMBENT
DECUPLE
DECUPLED
DECUPLES
DECUPLING
DECURIA
DECURIAS
DECURIES
DECURION
DECURIONS
DECURRENT
DECURSION
DECURSIVE
DECURVE
DECURVED
DECURVES
DECURVING
DECURY
DECUSSATE
DEDAL
DEDALIAN
DEDANS
DEDENDA
DEDENDUM
DEDENDUMS
DEDICANT
DEDICANTS
DEDICATE
DEDICATED
DEDICATEE
DEDICATES
DEDICATOR
DEDIMUS
DEDIMUSES
DEDUCE
DEDUCED
DEDUCES
DEDUCIBLE
DEDUCIBLY
DEDUCING
DEDUCT
DEDUCTED
DEDUCTING
DEDUCTION
DEDUCTIVE
DEDUCTS
DEE
DEED
DEEDED
DEEDER
DEEDEST
DEEDFUL
DEEDIER
DEEDIEST
DEEDILY
DEEDING
DEEDLESS
DEEDS
DEEDY
DEEING
DEEJAY
DEEJAYED
DEEJAYING
DEEJAYS
DEEK
DEELY
DEEM
DEEMED
DEEMING
DEEMS
DEEMSTER
DEEMSTERS
DEEN
DEENS
DEEP

DEEPEN
DEEPENED
DEEPENER
DEEPENERS
DEEPENING
DEEPENS
DEEPER
DEEPEST
DEEPFELT
DEEPFROZE
DEEPIE
DEEPIES
DEEPLY
DEEPMOST
DEEPNESS
DEEPS
DEEPWATER
DEER
DEERBERRY
DEERE
DEERES
DEERFLIES
DEERFLY
DEERGRASS
DEERHORN
DEERHORNS
DEERHOUND
DEERLET
DEERLETS
DEERLIKE
DEERS
DEERSKIN
DEERSKINS
DEERWEED
DEERWEEDS
DEERYARD
DEERYARDS
DEES
DEET
DEETS
DEEV
DEEVE
DEEVED
DEEVES
DEEVING
DEEVS
DEEWAN
DEEWANS
DEF
DEFACE
DEFACED
DEFACER
DEFACERS
DEFACES
DEFACING
DEFAECATE
DEFALCATE
DEFAME
DEFAMED
DEFAMER
DEFAMERS
DEFAMES
DEFAMING
DEFAMINGS
DEFANG
DEFANGED
DEFANGING
DEFANGS
DEFAST
DEFASTE
DEFAT
DEFATS
DEFATTED
DEFATTING
DEFAULT
DEFAULTED
DEFAULTER
DEFAULTS
DEFEAT
DEFEATED
DEFEATER
DEFEATERS
DEFEATING
DEFEATISM
DEFEATIST
DEFEATS
DEFEATURE
DEFECATE
DEFECATED
DEFECATES
DEFECATOR
DEFECT
DEFECTED
DEFECTING
DEFECTION
DEFECTIVE
DEFECTOR
DEFECTORS
DEFECTS
DEFENCE
DEFENCED
DEFENCES
DEFENCING
DEFEND
DEFENDANT
DEFENDED
DEFENDER
DEFENDERS
DEFENDING
DEFENDS
DEFENSE
DEFENSED
DEFENSES
DEFENSING
DEFENSIVE
DEFER
DEFERABLE
DEFERENCE
DEFERENT
DEFERENTS
DEFERMENT
DEFERRAL
DEFERRALS
DEFERRED
DEFERRER
DEFERRERS
DEFERRING
DEFERS
DEFFER
DEFFEST
DEFFLY
DEFFO
DEFI
DEFIANCE
DEFIANCES
DEFIANT
DEFIANTLY
DEFICIENT
DEFICIT
DEFICITS
DEFIED
DEFIER
DEFIERS
DEFIES
DEFILADE
DEFILADED
DEFILADES
DEFILE
DEFILED
DEFILER
DEFILERS
DEFILES
DEFILING
DEFINABLE
DEFINABLY
DEFINE
DEFINED
DEFINER
DEFINERS
DEFINES
DEFINIENS
DEFINING
DEFINITE
DEFINITES
DEFIS
DEFLATE
DEFLATED
DEFLATER
DEFLATERS
DEFLATES
DEFLATING
DEFLATION
DEFLATOR
DEFLATORS
DEFLEA
DEFLEAED
DEFLEAING
DEFLEAS
DEFLECT
DEFLECTED
DEFLECTOR
DEFLECTS
DEFLEX
DEFLEXED
DEFLEXES
DEFLEXING
DEFLEXION
DEFLEXURE
DEFLORATE
DEFLOWER
DEFLOWERS
DEFLUENT
DEFLUXION
DEFO
DEFOAM
DEFOAMED
DEFOAMER
DEFOAMERS
DEFOAMING
DEFOAMS
DEFOCUS
DEFOCUSED
DEFOCUSES
DEFOG
DEFOGGED
DEFOGGER
DEFOGGERS
DEFOGGING
DEFOGS
DEFOLIANT
DEFOLIATE
DEFORCE
DEFORCED
DEFORCER
DEFORCERS
DEFORCES
DEFORCING
DEFOREST
DEFORESTS
DEFORM
DEFORMED
DEFORMER
DEFORMERS
DEFORMING
DEFORMITY
DEFORMS
DEFOUL
DEFOULED
DEFOULING
DEFOULS
DEFRAG
DEFRAGGED
DEFRAGGER
DEFRAGS
DEFRAUD
DEFRAUDED
DEFRAUDER
DEFRAUDS
DEFRAY
DEFRAYAL

DEFRAYALS
DEFRAYED
DEFRAYER
DEFRAYERS
DEFRAYING
DEFRAYS
DEFREEZE
DEFREEZES
DEFRIEND
DEFRIENDS
DEFROCK
DEFROCKED
DEFROCKS
DEFROST
DEFROSTED
DEFROSTER
DEFROSTS
DEFROZE
DEFROZEN
DEFT
DEFTER
DEFTEST
DEFTLY
DEFTNESS
DEFUEL
DEFUELED
DEFUELING
DEFUELLED
DEFUELS
DEFUNCT
DEFUNCTS
DEFUND
DEFUNDED
DEFUNDING
DEFUNDS
DEFUSE
DEFUSED
DEFUSER
DEFUSERS
DEFUSES
DEFUSING
DEFUZE
DEFUZED
DEFUZES
DEFUZING
DEFY
DEFYING
DEG
DEGAGE
DEGAME
DEGAMES
DEGAMI
DEGAMIS
DEGARNISH
DEGAS
DEGASES
DEGASSED
DEGASSER
DEGASSERS
DEGASSES
DEGASSING
DEGAUSS
DEGAUSSED
DEGAUSSER
DEGAUSSES
DEGEARING
DEGENDER
DEGENDERS
DEGERM
DEGERMED
DEGERMING
DEGERMS
DEGGED
DEGGING
DEGLAZE
DEGLAZED
DEGLAZES
DEGLAZING
DEGOUT
DEGOUTED
DEGOUTING
DEGOUTS
DEGRADE
DEGRADED
DEGRADER
DEGRADERS
DEGRADES
DEGRADING
DEGRAS
DEGREASE
DEGREASED
DEGREASER
DEGREASES
DEGREE
DEGREED
DEGREES
DEGS
DEGU
DEGUM
DEGUMMED
DEGUMMING
DEGUMS
DEGUS
DEGUST
DEGUSTATE
DEGUSTED
DEGUSTING
DEGUSTS
DEHAIR
DEHAIRED
DEHAIRING
DEHAIRS
DEHISCE
DEHISCED
DEHISCENT
DEHISCES
DEHISCING
DEHORN
DEHORNED
DEHORNER
DEHORNERS
DEHORNING
DEHORNS
DEHORS
DEHORT
DEHORTED
DEHORTER
DEHORTERS
DEHORTING
DEHORTS
DEHYDRATE
DEI
DEICE
DEICED
DEICER
DEICERS
DEICES
DEICIDAL
DEICIDE
DEICIDES
DEICING
DEICTIC
DEICTICS
DEID
DEIDER
DEIDEST
DEIDS
DEIF
DEIFER
DEIFEST
DEIFIC
DEIFICAL
DEIFIED
DEIFIER
DEIFIERS
DEIFIES
DEIFORM
DEIFY
DEIFYING
DEIGN
DEIGNED
DEIGNING
DEIGNS
DEIL
DEILS
DEINDEX
DEINDEXED
DEINDEXES
DEINOSAUR
DEIONISE
DEIONISED
DEIONISER
DEIONISES
DEIONIZE
DEIONIZED
DEIONIZER
DEIONIZES
DEIPAROUS
DEISEAL
DEISEALS
DEISHEAL
DEISHEALS
DEISM
DEISMS
DEIST
DEISTIC
DEISTICAL
DEISTS
DEITIES
DEITY
DEIXES
DEIXIS
DEIXISES
DEJECT
DEJECTA
DEJECTED
DEJECTING
DEJECTION
DEJECTORY
DEJECTS
DEJEUNE
DEJEUNER
DEJEUNERS
DEJEUNES
DEKAGRAM
DEKAGRAMS
DEKALITER
DEKALITRE
DEKALOGY
DEKAMETER
DEKAMETRE
DEKARE
DEKARES
DEKE
DEKED
DEKEING
DEKES
DEKING
DEKKO
DEKKOED
DEKKOING
DEKKOS
DEL
DELAINE
DELAINES
DELAPSE
DELAPSED
DELAPSES
DELAPSING
DELAPSION
DELATE
DELATED
DELATES
DELATING
DELATION
DELATIONS
DELATOR
DELATORS
DELAY
DELAYABLE

D

DELAYED
DELAYER
DELAYERS
DELAYING
DELAYS
DELE
DELEAD
DELEADED
DELEADING
DELEADS
DELEAVE
DELEAVED
DELEAVES
DELEAVING
DELEBLE
DELECTATE
DELED
DELEGABLE
DELEGACY
DELEGATE
DELEGATED
DELEGATEE
DELEGATES
DELEGATOR
DELEING
DELENDA
DELES
DELETABLE
DELETE
DELETED
DELETES
DELETING
DELETION
DELETIONS
DELETIVE
DELETORY
DELF
DELFS
DELFT
DELFTS
DELFTWARE
DELI
DELIBATE
DELIBATED
DELIBATES
DELIBLE
DELICACY
DELICATE
DELICATES
DELICE
DELICES
DELICIOUS
DELICT
DELICTS
DELIGHT
DELIGHTED
DELIGHTER
DELIGHTS
DELIME
DELIMED
DELIMES
DELIMING
DELIMIT
DELIMITED
DELIMITER
DELIMITS
DELINEATE
DELINK
DELINKED
DELINKING
DELINKS
DELIQUIUM
DELIRIA
DELIRIANT
DELIRIOUS
DELIRIUM
DELIRIUMS
DELIS
DELISH
DELIST
DELISTED
DELISTING
DELISTS
DELIVER
DELIVERED
DELIVERER
DELIVERLY
DELIVERS
DELIVERY
DELL
DELLIER
DELLIES
DELLIEST
DELLS
DELLY
DELO
DELOPE
DELOPED
DELOPES
DELOPING
DELOS
DELOUSE
DELOUSED
DELOUSER
DELOUSERS
DELOUSES
DELOUSING
DELPH
DELPHIC
DELPHIN
DELPHINIA
DELPHINS
DELPHS
DELS
DELT
DELTA
DELTAIC
DELTAS
DELTIC
DELTOID
DELTOIDEI
DELTOIDS
DELTS
DELUBRA
DELUBRUM
DELUBRUMS
DELUDABLE
DELUDE
DELUDED
DELUDER
DELUDERS
DELUDES
DELUDING
DELUGE
DELUGED
DELUGES
DELUGING
DELUNDUNG
DELUSION
DELUSIONS
DELUSIVE
DELUSORY
DELUSTER
DELUSTERS
DELUSTRE
DELUSTRED
DELUSTRES
DELUXE
DELVE
DELVED
DELVER
DELVERS
DELVES
DELVING
DEMAGOG
DEMAGOGED
DEMAGOGIC
DEMAGOGS
DEMAGOGUE
DEMAGOGY
DEMAIN
DEMAINE
DEMAINES
DEMAINS
DEMAN
DEMAND
DEMANDANT
DEMANDED
DEMANDER
DEMANDERS
DEMANDING
DEMANDS
DEMANNED
DEMANNING
DEMANS
DEMANTOID
DEMARCATE
DEMARCHE
DEMARCHES
DEMARK
DEMARKED
DEMARKET
DEMARKETS
DEMARKING
DEMARKS
DEMAST
DEMASTED
DEMASTING
DEMASTS
DEMAYNE
DEMAYNES
DEME
DEMEAN
DEMEANE
DEMEANED
DEMEANES
DEMEANING
DEMEANOR
DEMEANORS
DEMEANOUR
DEMEANS
DEMENT
DEMENTATE
DEMENTED
DEMENTI
DEMENTIA
DEMENTIAL
DEMENTIAS
DEMENTING
DEMENTIS
DEMENTS
DEMERARA
DEMERARAN
DEMERARAS
DEMERGE
DEMERGED
DEMERGER
DEMERGERS
DEMERGES
DEMERGING
DEMERIT
DEMERITED
DEMERITS
DEMERSAL
DEMERSE
DEMERSED
DEMERSES
DEMERSING
DEMERSION
DEMES
DEMESNE
DEMESNES
DEMETON
DEMETONS
DEMIC
DEMIES
DEMIGOD
DEMIGODS
DEMIJOHN
DEMIJOHNS

DEMILUNE
DEMILUNES
DEMIMONDE
DEMINER
DEMINERS
DEMINING
DEMININGS
DEMIPIQUE
DEMIREP
DEMIREPS
DEMISABLE
DEMISE
DEMISED
DEMISES
DEMISING
DEMISS
DEMISSION
DEMISSIVE
DEMISSLY
DEMIST
DEMISTED
DEMISTER
DEMISTERS
DEMISTING
DEMISTS
DEMIT
DEMITASSE
DEMITS
DEMITTED
DEMITTING
DEMIURGE
DEMIURGES
DEMIURGIC
DEMIURGUS
DEMIVEG
DEMIVEGES
DEMIVOLT
DEMIVOLTE
DEMIVOLTS
DEMIWORLD
DEMO
DEMOB
DEMOBBED
DEMOBBING
DEMOBS
DEMOCRACY
DEMOCRAT
DEMOCRATS
DEMOCRATY
DEMODE
DEMODED
DEMOED
DEMOI
DEMOING
DEMOLISH
DEMOLOGY
DEMON
DEMONESS
DEMONIAC
DEMONIACS
DEMONIAN
DEMONIC
DEMONICAL
DEMONISE
DEMONISED
DEMONISES
DEMONISM
DEMONISMS
DEMONIST
DEMONISTS
DEMONIZE
DEMONIZED
DEMONIZES
DEMONRIES
DEMONRY
DEMONS
DEMONYM
DEMONYMS
DEMOS
DEMOSCENE
DEMOSES
DEMOTE
DEMOTED
DEMOTES
DEMOTIC
DEMOTICS
DEMOTING
DEMOTION
DEMOTIONS
DEMOTIST
DEMOTISTS
DEMOUNT
DEMOUNTED
DEMOUNTS
DEMPSTER
DEMPSTERS
DEMPT
DEMULCENT
DEMULSIFY
DEMUR
DEMURE
DEMURED
DEMURELY
DEMURER
DEMURES
DEMUREST
DEMURING
DEMURRAGE
DEMURRAL
DEMURRALS
DEMURRED
DEMURRER
DEMURRERS
DEMURRING
DEMURS
DEMY
DEMYSHIP
DEMYSHIPS
DEMYSTIFY
DEMYTHIFY
DEN
DENAR
DENARI
DENARIES
DENARII
DENARIUS
DENARS
DENARY
DENATURE
DENATURED
DENATURES
DENAY
DENAYED
DENAYING
DENAYS
DENAZIFY
DENCH
DENDRIMER
DENDRITE
DENDRITES
DENDRITIC
DENDROID
DENDROIDS
DENDRON
DENDRONS
DENE
DENERVATE
DENES
DENET
DENETS
DENETTED
DENETTING
DENGUE
DENGUES
DENI
DENIABLE
DENIABLY
DENIAL
DENIALIST
DENIALS
DENIED
DENIER
DENIERS
DENIES
DENIGRATE
DENIM
DENIMED
DENIMS
DENIS
DENITRATE
DENITRIFY
DENIZEN
DENIZENED
DENIZENS
DENNED
DENNET
DENNETS
DENNING
DENOMINAL
DENOTABLE
DENOTATE
DENOTATED
DENOTATES
DENOTE
DENOTED
DENOTES
DENOTING
DENOTIVE
DENOUNCE
DENOUNCED
DENOUNCER
DENOUNCES
DENS
DENSE
DENSELY
DENSENESS
DENSER
DENSEST
DENSIFIED
DENSIFIER
DENSIFIES
DENSIFY
DENSITIES
DENSITY
DENT
DENTAL
DENTALIA
DENTALISE
DENTALITY
DENTALIUM
DENTALIZE
DENTALLY
DENTALS
DENTARIA
DENTARIAS
DENTARIES
DENTARY
DENTATE
DENTATED
DENTATELY
DENTATION
DENTED
DENTEL
DENTELLE
DENTELLES
DENTELS
DENTEX
DENTEXES
DENTICARE
DENTICLE
DENTICLES
DENTIFORM
DENTIL
DENTILED
DENTILS
DENTIN
DENTINAL
DENTINE
DENTINES
DENTING

D

DENTINS
DENTIST
DENTISTRY
DENTISTS
DENTITION
DENTOID
DENTS
DENTULOUS
DENTURAL
DENTURE
DENTURES
DENTURISM
DENTURIST
DENUDATE
DENUDATED
DENUDATES
DENUDE
DENUDED
DENUDER
DENUDERS
DENUDES
DENUDING
DENY
DENYING
DENYINGLY
DEODAND
DEODANDS
DEODAR
DEODARA
DEODARAS
DEODARS
DEODATE
DEODATES
DEODORANT
DEODORISE
DEODORIZE
DEONTIC
DEONTICS
DEORBIT
DEORBITED
DEORBITS
DEOXIDATE
DEOXIDISE
DEOXIDIZE
DEOXY
DEP
DEPAINT
DEPAINTED
DEPAINTS
DEPANNEUR
DEPART
DEPARTED
DEPARTEDS
DEPARTEE
DEPARTEES
DEPARTER
DEPARTERS
DEPARTING
DEPARTS
DEPARTURE
DEPASTURE
DEPECHE
DEPECHED
DEPECHES
DEPECHING
DEPEINCT
DEPEINCTS
DEPEND
DEPENDANT
DEPENDED
DEPENDENT
DEPENDING
DEPENDS
DEPEOPLE
DEPEOPLED
DEPEOPLES
DEPERM
DEPERMED
DEPERMING
DEPERMS
DEPICT
DEPICTED
DEPICTER
DEPICTERS
DEPICTING
DEPICTION
DEPICTIVE
DEPICTOR
DEPICTORS
DEPICTS
DEPICTURE
DEPIGMENT
DEPILATE
DEPILATED
DEPILATES
DEPILATOR
DEPLANE
DEPLANED
DEPLANES
DEPLANING
DEPLENISH
DEPLETE
DEPLETED
DEPLETER
DEPLETERS
DEPLETES
DEPLETING
DEPLETION
DEPLETIVE
DEPLETORY
DEPLORE
DEPLORED
DEPLORER
DEPLORERS
DEPLORES
DEPLORING
DEPLOY
DEPLOYED
DEPLOYER
DEPLOYERS
DEPLOYING
DEPLOYS
DEPLUME
DEPLUMED
DEPLUMES
DEPLUMING
DEPOLISH
DEPONE
DEPONED
DEPONENT
DEPONENTS
DEPONES
DEPONING
DEPORT
DEPORTED
DEPORTEE
DEPORTEES
DEPORTER
DEPORTERS
DEPORTING
DEPORTS
DEPOSABLE
DEPOSAL
DEPOSALS
DEPOSE
DEPOSED
DEPOSER
DEPOSERS
DEPOSES
DEPOSING
DEPOSIT
DEPOSITED
DEPOSITOR
DEPOSITS
DEPOT
DEPOTS
DEPRAVE
DEPRAVED
DEPRAVER
DEPRAVERS
DEPRAVES
DEPRAVING
DEPRAVITY
DEPRECATE
DEPREDATE
DEPREHEND
DEPRENYL
DEPRENYLS
DEPRESS
DEPRESSED
DEPRESSES
DEPRESSOR
DEPRIME
DEPRIMED
DEPRIMES
DEPRIMING
DEPRIVAL
DEPRIVALS
DEPRIVE
DEPRIVED
DEPRIVER
DEPRIVERS
DEPRIVES
DEPRIVING
DEPROGRAM
DEPS
DEPSIDE
DEPSIDES
DEPTH
DEPTHLESS
DEPTHS
DEPURANT
DEPURANTS
DEPURATE
DEPURATED
DEPURATES
DEPURATOR
DEPUTABLE
DEPUTE
DEPUTED
DEPUTES
DEPUTIES
DEPUTING
DEPUTISE
DEPUTISED
DEPUTISES
DEPUTIZE
DEPUTIZED
DEPUTIZES
DEPUTY
DEQUEUE
DEQUEUED
DEQUEUES
DEQUEUING
DERACINE
DERACINES
DERAIGN
DERAIGNED
DERAIGNS
DERAIL
DERAILED
DERAILER
DERAILERS
DERAILING
DERAILS
DERANGE
DERANGED
DERANGER
DERANGERS
DERANGES
DERANGING
DERAT
DERATE
DERATED
DERATES
DERATING
DERATINGS
DERATION
DERATIONS
DERATS

DERATTED
DERATTING
DERAY
DERAYED
DERAYING
DERAYS
DERBIES
DERBY
DERE
DERECHO
DERECHOS
DERED
DERELICT
DERELICTS
DEREPRESS
DERES
DERHAM
DERHAMS
DERIDE
DERIDED
DERIDER
DERIDERS
DERIDES
DERIDING
DERIG
DERIGGED
DERIGGING
DERIGS
DERING
DERINGER
DERINGERS
DERISIBLE
DERISION
DERISIONS
DERISIVE
DERISORY
DERIVABLE
DERIVABLY
DERIVATE
DERIVATED
DERIVATES
DERIVE
DERIVED
DERIVER
DERIVERS
DERIVES
DERIVING
DERM
DERMA
DERMAL
DERMAS
DERMATIC
DERMATOID
DERMATOME
DERMESTID
DERMIC
DERMIS
DERMISES
DERMOID
DERMOIDS
DERMS
DERN
DERNED
DERNFUL
DERNIER
DERNIES
DERNING
DERNLY
DERNS
DERNY
DERNYS
DERO
DEROGATE
DEROGATED
DEROGATES
DEROS
DERRICK
DERRICKED
DERRICKS
DERRIERE
DERRIERES
DERRIES
DERRINGER
DERRIS
DERRISES
DERRO
DERROS
DERRY
DERTH
DERTHS
DERV
DERVISH
DERVISHES
DERVS
DESALT
DESALTED
DESALTER
DESALTERS
DESALTING
DESALTS
DESAND
DESANDED
DESANDING
DESANDS
DESCALE
DESCALED
DESCALER
DESCALERS
DESCALES
DESCALING
DESCANT
DESCANTED
DESCANTER
DESCANTS
DESCEND
DESCENDED
DESCENDER
DESCENDS
DESCENT
DESCENTS
DESCHOOL
DESCHOOLS
DESCRIBE
DESCRIBED
DESCRIBER
DESCRIBES
DESCRIED
DESCRIER
DESCRIERS
DESCRIES
DESCRIVE
DESCRIVED
DESCRIVES
DESCRY
DESCRYING
DESECRATE
DESEED
DESEEDED
DESEEDER
DESEEDERS
DESEEDING
DESEEDS
DESELECT
DESELECTS
DESERT
DESERTED
DESERTER
DESERTERS
DESERTIC
DESERTIFY
DESERTING
DESERTION
DESERTS
DESERVE
DESERVED
DESERVER
DESERVERS
DESERVES
DESERVING
DESEX
DESEXED
DESEXES
DESEXING
DESHI
DESHIS
DESI
DESICCANT
DESICCATE
DESIGN
DESIGNATE
DESIGNED
DESIGNEE
DESIGNEES
DESIGNER
DESIGNERS
DESIGNFUL
DESIGNING
DESIGNS
DESILVER
DESILVERS
DESINE
DESINED
DESINENCE
DESINENT
DESINES
DESINING
DESIPIENT
DESIRABLE
DESIRABLY
DESIRE
DESIRED
DESIRER
DESIRERS
DESIRES
DESIRING
DESIROUS
DESIS
DESIST
DESISTED
DESISTING
DESISTS
DESK
DESKBOUND
DESKFAST
DESKFASTS
DESKILL
DESKILLED
DESKILLS
DESKING
DESKINGS
DESKMAN
DESKMEN
DESKNOTE
DESKNOTES
DESKS
DESKTOP
DESKTOPS
DESMAN
DESMANS
DESMID
DESMIDIAN
DESMIDS
DESMINE
DESMINES
DESMODIUM
DESMOID
DESMOIDS
DESMOSOME
DESNOOD
DESNOODED
DESNOODS
DESOEUVRE
DESOLATE
DESOLATED
DESOLATER
DESOLATES
DESOLATOR
DESORB
DESORBED
DESORBER

D

DESORBERS
DESORBING
DESORBS
DESOXY
DESPAIR
DESPAIRED
DESPAIRER
DESPAIRS
DESPATCH
DESPERADO
DESPERATE
DESPIGHT
DESPIGHTS
DESPISAL
DESPISALS
DESPISE
DESPISED
DESPISER
DESPISERS
DESPISES
DESPISING
DESPITE
DESPITED
DESPITES
DESPITING
DESPOIL
DESPOILED
DESPOILER
DESPOILS
DESPOND
DESPONDED
DESPONDS
DESPOT
DESPOTAT
DESPOTATE
DESPOTATS
DESPOTIC
DESPOTISM
DESPOTS
DESPUMATE
DESSE
DESSERT
DESSERTS
DESSES
DESSYATIN
DESTAIN
DESTAINED
DESTAINS
DESTEMPER
DESTINATE
DESTINE
DESTINED
DESTINES
DESTINIES
DESTINING
DESTINY
DESTITUTE
DESTOCK
DESTOCKED
DESTOCKS
DESTREAM
DESTREAMS
DESTRESS
DESTRIER
DESTRIERS
DESTROY
DESTROYED
DESTROYER
DESTROYS
DESTRUCT
DESTRUCTO
DESTRUCTS
DESUETUDE
DESUGAR
DESUGARED
DESUGARS
DESULFUR
DESULFURS
DESULPHUR
DESULTORY
DESYATIN
DESYATINS
DESYNE
DESYNED
DESYNES
DESYNING
DETACH
DETACHED
DETACHER
DETACHERS
DETACHES
DETACHING
DETAIL
DETAILED
DETAILER
DETAILERS
DETAILING
DETAILS
DETAIN
DETAINED
DETAINEE
DETAINEES
DETAINER
DETAINERS
DETAINING
DETAINS
DETANGLE
DETANGLED
DETANGLER
DETANGLES
DETASSEL
DETASSELS
DETECT
DETECTED
DETECTER
DETECTERS
DETECTING
DETECTION
DETECTIVE
DETECTOR
DETECTORS
DETECTS
DETENT
DETENTE
DETENTES
DETENTION
DETENTIST
DETENTS
DETENU
DETENUE
DETENUES
DETENUS
DETER
DETERGE
DETERGED
DETERGENT
DETERGER
DETERGERS
DETERGES
DETERGING
DETERMENT
DETERMINE
DETERRED
DETERRENT
DETERRER
DETERRERS
DETERRING
DETERS
DETERSION
DETERSIVE
DETEST
DETESTED
DETESTER
DETESTERS
DETESTING
DETESTS
DETHATCH
DETHRONE
DETHRONED
DETHRONER
DETHRONES
DETICK
DETICKED
DETICKER
DETICKERS
DETICKING
DETICKS
DETINUE
DETINUES
DETONABLE
DETONATE
DETONATED
DETONATES
DETONATOR
DETORSION
DETORT
DETORTED
DETORTING
DETORTION
DETORTS
DETOUR
DETOURED
DETOURING
DETOURS
DETOX
DETOXED
DETOXES
DETOXIFY
DETOXING
DETRACT
DETRACTED
DETRACTOR
DETRACTS
DETRAIN
DETRAINED
DETRAINS
DETRAQUE
DETRAQUEE
DETRAQUES
DETRIMENT
DETRITAL
DETRITION
DETRITUS
DETRUDE
DETRUDED
DETRUDES
DETRUDING
DETRUSION
DETRUSOR
DETRUSORS
DETUNE
DETUNED
DETUNES
DETUNING
DEUCE
DEUCED
DEUCEDLY
DEUCES
DEUCING
DEUDDARN
DEUDDARNS
DEUS
DEUTERATE
DEUTERIC
DEUTERIDE
DEUTERIUM
DEUTERON
DEUTERONS
DEUTON
DEUTONS
DEUTZIA
DEUTZIAS
DEV
DEVA
DEVALL
DEVALLED
DEVALLING
DEVALLS
DEVALUATE
DEVALUE

DEVALUED
DEVALUES
DEVALUING
DEVAS
DEVASTATE
DEVEIN
DEVEINED
DEVEINING
DEVEINS
DEVEL
DEVELED
DEVELING
DEVELLED
DEVELLING
DEVELOP
DEVELOPE
DEVELOPED
DEVELOPER
DEVELOPES
DEVELOPPE
DEVELOPS
DEVELS
DEVERBAL
DEVERBALS
DEVEST
DEVESTED
DEVESTING
DEVESTS
DEVI
DEVIANCE
DEVIANCES
DEVIANCY
DEVIANT
DEVIANTS
DEVIATE
DEVIATED
DEVIATES
DEVIATING
DEVIATION
DEVIATIVE
DEVIATOR
DEVIATORS
DEVIATORY
DEVICE
DEVICEFUL
DEVICES
DEVIL
DEVILDOM
DEVILDOMS
DEVILED
DEVILESS
DEVILET
DEVILETS
DEVILFISH
DEVILING
DEVILINGS
DEVILISH
DEVILISM
DEVILISMS
DEVILKIN
DEVILKINS
DEVILLED
DEVILLING
DEVILMENT
DEVILRIES
DEVILRY
DEVILS
DEVILSHIP
DEVILTRY
DEVILWOOD
DEVIOUS
DEVIOUSLY
DEVIS
DEVISABLE
DEVISAL
DEVISALS
DEVISE
DEVISED
DEVISEE
DEVISEES
DEVISER
DEVISERS
DEVISES
DEVISING
DEVISOR
DEVISORS
DEVITRIFY
DEVLING
DEVLINGS
DEVO
DEVOICE
DEVOICED
DEVOICES
DEVOICING
DEVOID
DEVOIR
DEVOIRS
DEVOLVE
DEVOLVED
DEVOLVES
DEVOLVING
DEVON
DEVONIAN
DEVONPORT
DEVONS
DEVORE
DEVORES
DEVOS
DEVOT
DEVOTE
DEVOTED
DEVOTEDLY
DEVOTEE
DEVOTEES
DEVOTES
DEVOTING
DEVOTION
DEVOTIONS
DEVOTS
DEVOUR
DEVOURED
DEVOURER
DEVOURERS
DEVOURING
DEVOURS
DEVOUT
DEVOUTER
DEVOUTEST
DEVOUTLY
DEVS
DEVVEL
DEVVELLED
DEVVELS
DEW
DEWAN
DEWANI
DEWANIS
DEWANNIES
DEWANNY
DEWANS
DEWAR
DEWARS
DEWATER
DEWATERED
DEWATERER
DEWATERS
DEWAX
DEWAXED
DEWAXES
DEWAXING
DEWBERRY
DEWCLAW
DEWCLAWED
DEWCLAWS
DEWDROP
DEWDROPS
DEWED
DEWFALL
DEWFALLS
DEWFULL
DEWIER
DEWIEST
DEWILY
DEWINESS
DEWING
DEWITT
DEWITTED
DEWITTING
DEWITTS
DEWLAP
DEWLAPPED
DEWLAPS
DEWLAPT
DEWLESS
DEWOOL
DEWOOLED
DEWOOLING
DEWOOLS
DEWORM
DEWORMED
DEWORMER
DEWORMERS
DEWORMING
DEWORMS
DEWPOINT
DEWPOINTS
DEWS
DEWY
DEX
DEXES
DEXIE
DEXIES
DEXTER
DEXTERITY
DEXTEROUS
DEXTERS
DEXTRAL
DEXTRALLY
DEXTRALS
DEXTRAN
DEXTRANS
DEXTRIN
DEXTRINE
DEXTRINES
DEXTRINS
DEXTRO
DEXTRORSE
DEXTROSE
DEXTROSES
DEXTROUS
DEXY
DEY
DEYS
DEZINC
DEZINCED
DEZINCING
DEZINCKED
DEZINCS
DHABA
DHABAS
DHAK
DHAKS
DHAL
DHALS
DHAMMA
DHAMMAS
DHANSAK
DHANSAKS
DHARMA
DHARMAS
DHARMIC
DHARMSALA
DHARNA
DHARNAS
DHIKR
DHIKRS
DHIMMI
DHIMMIS
DHOBI
DHOBIS

DHOL
DHOLAK
DHOLAKS
DHOLE
DHOLES
DHOLL
DHOLLS
DHOLS
DHOOLIES
DHOOLY
DHOORA
DHOORAS
DHOOTI
DHOOTIE
DHOOTIES
DHOOTIS
DHOTI
DHOTIS
DHOURRA
DHOURRAS
DHOW
DHOWS
DHURNA
DHURNAS
DHURRA
DHURRAS
DHURRIE
DHURRIES
DHUTI
DHUTIS
DHYANA
DHYANAS
DI
DIABASE
DIABASES
DIABASIC
DIABETES
DIABETIC
DIABETICS
DIABLE
DIABLERIE
DIABLERY
DIABLES
DIABOLIC
DIABOLISE
DIABOLISM
DIABOLIST
DIABOLIZE
DIABOLO
DIABOLOGY
DIABOLOS
DIACETYL
DIACETYLS
DIACHRONY
DIACHYLON
DIACHYLUM
DIACID
DIACIDIC
DIACIDS
DIACODION
DIACODIUM
DIACONAL
DIACONATE
DIACRITIC
DIACT
DIACTINAL
DIACTINE
DIACTINES
DIACTINIC
DIACTS
DIADEM
DIADEMED
DIADEMING
DIADEMS
DIADOCHI
DIADOCHY
DIADROM
DIADROMS
DIAERESES
DIAERESIS
DIAERETIC
DIAGLYPH
DIAGLYPHS
DIAGNOSE
DIAGNOSED
DIAGNOSES
DIAGNOSIS
DIAGONAL
DIAGONALS
DIAGRAM
DIAGRAMED
DIAGRAMS
DIAGRAPH
DIAGRAPHS
DIAGRID
DIAGRIDS
DIAL
DIALECT
DIALECTAL
DIALECTIC
DIALECTS
DIALED
DIALER
DIALERS
DIALING
DIALINGS
DIALIST
DIALISTS
DIALLAGE
DIALLAGES
DIALLAGIC
DIALLED
DIALLEL
DIALLELS
DIALLER
DIALLERS
DIALLING
DIALLINGS
DIALLIST
DIALLISTS
DIALOG
DIALOGED
DIALOGER
DIALOGERS
DIALOGIC
DIALOGING
DIALOGISE
DIALOGISM
DIALOGIST
DIALOGITE
DIALOGIZE
DIALOGS
DIALOGUE
DIALOGUED
DIALOGUER
DIALOGUES
DIALS
DIALYSATE
DIALYSE
DIALYSED
DIALYSER
DIALYSERS
DIALYSES
DIALYSING
DIALYSIS
DIALYTIC
DIALYZATE
DIALYZE
DIALYZED
DIALYZER
DIALYZERS
DIALYZES
DIALYZING
DIAMAGNET
DIAMANTE
DIAMANTES
DIAMETER
DIAMETERS
DIAMETRAL
DIAMETRIC
DIAMIDE
DIAMIDES
DIAMIN
DIAMINE
DIAMINES
DIAMINS
DIAMOND
DIAMONDED
DIAMONDS
DIAMYL
DIANDRIES
DIANDROUS
DIANDRY
DIANE
DIANODAL
DIANOETIC
DIANOIA
DIANOIAS
DIANTHUS
DIAPASE
DIAPASES
DIAPASON
DIAPASONS
DIAPAUSE
DIAPAUSED
DIAPAUSES
DIAPENTE
DIAPENTES
DIAPER
DIAPERED
DIAPERING
DIAPERS
DIAPHONE
DIAPHONES
DIAPHONIC
DIAPHONY
DIAPHRAGM
DIAPHYSES
DIAPHYSIS
DIAPIR
DIAPIRIC
DIAPIRISM
DIAPIRS
DIAPSID
DIAPSIDS
DIAPYESES
DIAPYESIS
DIAPYETIC
DIARCH
DIARCHAL
DIARCHIC
DIARCHIES
DIARCHY
DIARIAL
DIARIAN
DIARIES
DIARISE
DIARISED
DIARISES
DIARISING
DIARIST
DIARISTIC
DIARISTS
DIARIZE
DIARIZED
DIARIZES
DIARIZING
DIARRHEA
DIARRHEAL
DIARRHEAS
DIARRHEIC
DIARRHOEA
DIARY
DIASCIA
DIASCIAS
DIASCOPE
DIASCOPES
DIASPORA
DIASPORAS
DIASPORE

DIASPORES
DIASPORIC
DIASTASE
DIASTASES
DIASTASIC
DIASTASIS
DIASTATIC
DIASTEM
DIASTEMA
DIASTEMAS
DIASTEMS
DIASTER
DIASTERS
DIASTOLE
DIASTOLES
DIASTOLIC
DIASTRAL
DIASTYLE
DIASTYLES
DIATHERMY
DIATHESES
DIATHESIS
DIATHETIC
DIATOM
DIATOMIC
DIATOMIST
DIATOMITE
DIATOMS
DIATONIC
DIATREME
DIATREMES
DIATRETA
DIATRETUM
DIATRIBE
DIATRIBES
DIATRON
DIATRONS
DIATROPIC
DIAXON
DIAXONS
DIAZEPAM
DIAZEPAMS
DIAZEUXES
DIAZEUXIS
DIAZIN
DIAZINE
DIAZINES
DIAZINON
DIAZINONS
DIAZINS
DIAZO
DIAZOES
DIAZOLE
DIAZOLES
DIAZONIUM
DIAZOS
DIAZOTISE
DIAZOTIZE
DIB
DIBASIC
DIBBED
DIBBER
DIBBERS
DIBBING
DIBBLE
DIBBLED
DIBBLER
DIBBLERS
DIBBLES
DIBBLING
DIBBS
DIBBUK
DIBBUKIM
DIBBUKKIM
DIBBUKS
DIBROMIDE
DIBS
DIBUTYL
DICACIOUS
DICACITY
DICACODYL
DICALCIUM
DICAMBA
DICAMBAS
DICAST
DICASTERY
DICASTIC
DICASTS
DICE
DICED
DICELIKE
DICENTRA
DICENTRAS
DICENTRIC
DICER
DICERS
DICES
DICEY
DICH
DICHASIA
DICHASIAL
DICHASIUM
DICHOGAMY
DICHONDRA
DICHOPTIC
DICHORD
DICHORDS
DICHOTIC
DICHOTOMY
DICHROIC
DICHROISM
DICHROITE
DICHROMAT
DICHROMIC
DICHT
DICHTED
DICHTING
DICHTS
DICIER
DICIEST
DICING
DICINGS
DICK
DICKED
DICKENS
DICKENSES
DICKER
DICKERED
DICKERER
DICKERERS
DICKERING
DICKERS
DICKEY
DICKEYS
DICKHEAD
DICKHEADS
DICKIE
DICKIER
DICKIES
DICKIEST
DICKING
DICKINGS
DICKS
DICKTIER
DICKTIEST
DICKTY
DICKY
DICKYBIRD
DICLINIES
DICLINISM
DICLINOUS
DICLINY
DICOT
DICOTS
DICOTYL
DICOTYLS
DICROTAL
DICROTIC
DICROTISM
DICROTOUS
DICT
DICTA
DICTATE
DICTATED
DICTATES
DICTATING
DICTATION
DICTATOR
DICTATORS
DICTATORY
DICTATRIX
DICTATURE
DICTED
DICTIER
DICTIEST
DICTING
DICTION
DICTIONAL
DICTIONS
DICTS
DICTUM
DICTUMS
DICTY
DICTYOGEN
DICUMAROL
DICYCLIC
DICYCLIES
DICYCLY
DID
DIDACT
DIDACTIC
DIDACTICS
DIDACTS
DIDACTYL
DIDACTYLS
DIDAKAI
DIDAKAIS
DIDAKEI
DIDAKEIS
DIDAPPER
DIDAPPERS
DIDDER
DIDDERED
DIDDERING
DIDDERS
DIDDICOY
DIDDICOYS
DIDDIER
DIDDIES
DIDDIEST
DIDDLE
DIDDLED
DIDDLER
DIDDLERS
DIDDLES
DIDDLEY
DIDDLEYS
DIDDLIES
DIDDLING
DIDDLY
DIDDUMS
DIDDY
DIDELPHIC
DIDELPHID
DIDICOI
DIDICOIS
DIDICOY
DIDICOYS
DIDIE
DIDIES
DIDJERIDU
DIDO
DIDOES
DIDOS
DIDRACHM
DIDRACHMA
DIDRACHMS
DIDST
DIDY
DIDYMIUM

DIDYMIUMS
DIDYMO
DIDYMOS
DIDYMOUS
DIDYNAMY
DIE
DIEB
DIEBACK
DIEBACKS
DIEBS
DIECIOUS
DIED
DIEDRAL
DIEDRALS
DIEDRE
DIEDRES
DIEGESES
DIEGESIS
DIEGETIC
DIEHARD
DIEHARDS
DIEING
DIEL
DIELDRIN
DIELDRINS
DIELS
DIELYTRA
DIELYTRAS
DIEMAKER
DIEMAKERS
DIENE
DIENES
DIEOFF
DIEOFFS
DIERESES
DIERESIS
DIERETIC
DIES
DIESEL
DIESELED
DIESELING
DIESELISE
DIESELIZE
DIESELS
DIESES
DIESINKER
DIESIS
DIESTER
DIESTERS
DIESTOCK
DIESTOCKS
DIESTROUS
DIESTRUM
DIESTRUMS
DIESTRUS
DIET
DIETARIAN
DIETARIES
DIETARILY
DIETARY
DIETED
DIETER
DIETERS
DIETETIC
DIETETICS
DIETHER
DIETHERS
DIETHYL
DIETHYLS
DIETICIAN
DIETINE
DIETINES
DIETING
DIETINGS
DIETIST
DIETISTS
DIETITIAN
DIETS
DIF
DIFF
DIFFER
DIFFERED
DIFFERENT
DIFFERING
DIFFERS
DIFFICILE
DIFFICULT
DIFFIDENT
DIFFLUENT
DIFFORM
DIFFRACT
DIFFRACTS
DIFFS
DIFFUSE
DIFFUSED
DIFFUSELY
DIFFUSER
DIFFUSERS
DIFFUSES
DIFFUSING
DIFFUSION
DIFFUSIVE
DIFFUSOR
DIFFUSORS
DIFS
DIG
DIGAMIES
DIGAMIST
DIGAMISTS
DIGAMMA
DIGAMMAS
DIGAMOUS
DIGAMY
DIGASTRIC
DIGENESES
DIGENESIS
DIGENETIC
DIGERATI
DIGEST
DIGESTANT
DIGESTED
DIGESTER
DIGESTERS
DIGESTIF
DIGESTIFS
DIGESTING
DIGESTION
DIGESTIVE
DIGESTOR
DIGESTORS
DIGESTS
DIGGABLE
DIGGED
DIGGER
DIGGERS
DIGGING
DIGGINGS
DIGHT
DIGHTED
DIGHTING
DIGHTS
DIGICAM
DIGICAMS
DIGIPACK
DIGIPACKS
DIGIT
DIGITAL
DIGITALIN
DIGITALIS
DIGITALLY
DIGITALS
DIGITATE
DIGITATED
DIGITISE
DIGITISED
DIGITISER
DIGITISES
DIGITIZE
DIGITIZED
DIGITIZER
DIGITIZES
DIGITONIN
DIGITOXIN
DIGITRON
DIGITRONS
DIGITS
DIGITULE
DIGITULES
DIGLOSSIA
DIGLOSSIC
DIGLOT
DIGLOTS
DIGLOTTIC
DIGLYPH
DIGLYPHS
DIGNIFIED
DIGNIFIES
DIGNIFY
DIGNITARY
DIGNITIES
DIGNITY
DIGONAL
DIGOXIN
DIGOXINS
DIGRAPH
DIGRAPHIC
DIGRAPHS
DIGRESS
DIGRESSED
DIGRESSER
DIGRESSES
DIGS
DIGYNIAN
DIGYNOUS
DIHEDRA
DIHEDRAL
DIHEDRALS
DIHEDRON
DIHEDRONS
DIHYBRID
DIHYBRIDS
DIHYDRIC
DIKA
DIKAS
DIKAST
DIKASTS
DIKDIK
DIKDIKS
DIKE
DIKED
DIKER
DIKERS
DIKES
DIKETONE
DIKETONES
DIKEY
DIKIER
DIKIEST
DIKING
DIKKOP
DIKKOPS
DIKTAT
DIKTATS
DILATABLE
DILATABLY
DILATANCY
DILATANT
DILATANTS
DILATATE
DILATATOR
DILATE
DILATED
DILATER
DILATERS
DILATES
DILATING
DILATION
DILATIONS
DILATIVE
DILATOR

DILATORS
DILATORY
DILDO
DILDOE
DILDOES
DILDOS
DILEMMA
DILEMMAS
DILEMMIC
DILIGENCE
DILIGENT
DILL
DILLED
DILLI
DILLIER
DILLIES
DILLIEST
DILLING
DILLINGS
DILLIS
DILLS
DILLWEED
DILLWEEDS
DILLY
DILSCOOP
DILSCOOPS
DILTIAZEM
DILUENT
DILUENTS
DILUTABLE
DILUTE
DILUTED
DILUTEE
DILUTEES
DILUTER
DILUTERS
DILUTES
DILUTING
DILUTION
DILUTIONS
DILUTIVE
DILUTOR
DILUTORS
DILUVIA
DILUVIAL
DILUVIAN
DILUVION
DILUVIONS
DILUVIUM
DILUVIUMS
DIM
DIMBLE
DIMBLES
DIMBO
DIMBOES
DIMBOS
DIME
DIMENSION
DIMER
DIMERIC
DIMERISE
DIMERISED
DIMERISES
DIMERISM
DIMERISMS
DIMERIZE
DIMERIZED
DIMERIZES
DIMEROUS
DIMERS
DIMES
DIMETER
DIMETERS
DIMETHYL
DIMETHYLS
DIMETRIC
DIMIDIATE
DIMINISH
DIMISSORY
DIMITIES
DIMITY
DIMLY
DIMMABLE
DIMMED
DIMMER
DIMMERS
DIMMEST
DIMMING
DIMMINGS
DIMMISH
DIMNESS
DIMNESSES
DIMORPH
DIMORPHIC
DIMORPHS
DIMOUT
DIMOUTS
DIMP
DIMPLE
DIMPLED
DIMPLES
DIMPLIER
DIMPLIEST
DIMPLING
DIMPLY
DIMPS
DIMPSIES
DIMPSY
DIMS
DIMWIT
DIMWITS
DIMWITTED
DIMYARIAN
DIMYARY
DIN
DINAR
DINARCHY
DINARS
DINDLE
DINDLED
DINDLES
DINDLING
DINE
DINED
DINER
DINERIC
DINERO
DINEROS
DINERS
DINES
DINETTE
DINETTES
DINFUL
DING
DINGBAT
DINGBATS
DINGDONG
DINGDONGS
DINGE
DINGED
DINGER
DINGERS
DINGES
DINGESES
DINGEY
DINGEYS
DINGHIES
DINGHY
DINGIED
DINGIER
DINGIES
DINGIEST
DINGILY
DINGINESS
DINGING
DINGLE
DINGLES
DINGO
DINGOED
DINGOES
DINGOING
DINGOS
DINGS
DINGUS
DINGUSES
DINGY
DINGYING
DINIC
DINICS
DINING
DININGS
DINITRO
DINK
DINKED
DINKER
DINKEST
DINKEY
DINKEYS
DINKIE
DINKIER
DINKIES
DINKIEST
DINKING
DINKLIER
DINKLIEST
DINKLY
DINKS
DINKUM
DINKUMS
DINKY
DINMONT
DINMONTS
DINNA
DINNAE
DINNED
DINNER
DINNERED
DINNERING
DINNERS
DINNING
DINNLE
DINNLED
DINNLES
DINNLING
DINO
DINOCERAS
DINOMANIA
DINOS
DINOSAUR
DINOSAURS
DINOTHERE
DINS
DINT
DINTED
DINTING
DINTLESS
DINTS
DIOBOL
DIOBOLON
DIOBOLONS
DIOBOLS
DIOCESAN
DIOCESANS
DIOCESE
DIOCESES
DIODE
DIODES
DIOECIES
DIOECIOUS
DIOECISM
DIOECISMS
DIOECY
DIOESTRUS
DIOICOUS
DIOL
DIOLEFIN
DIOLEFINS
DIOLS
DIONYSIAC
DIONYSIAN

D

DIOPSIDE
DIOPSIDES
DIOPSIDIC
DIOPTASE
DIOPTASES
DIOPTER
DIOPTERS
DIOPTRAL
DIOPTRATE
DIOPTRE
DIOPTRES
DIOPTRIC
DIOPTRICS
DIORAMA
DIORAMAS
DIORAMIC
DIORISM
DIORISMS
DIORISTIC
DIORITE
DIORITES
DIORITIC
DIOSGENIN
DIOTA
DIOTAS
DIOXAN
DIOXANE
DIOXANES
DIOXANS
DIOXID
DIOXIDE
DIOXIDES
DIOXIDS
DIOXIN
DIOXINS
DIP
DIPCHICK
DIPCHICKS
DIPEPTIDE
DIPHASE
DIPHASIC
DIPHENYL
DIPHENYLS
DIPHONE
DIPHONES
DIPHTHONG
DIPHYSITE
DIPLEGIA
DIPLEGIAS
DIPLEGIC
DIPLEX
DIPLEXER
DIPLEXERS
DIPLOE
DIPLOES
DIPLOGEN
DIPLOGENS
DIPLOIC
DIPLOID
DIPLOIDIC
DIPLOIDS
DIPLOIDY
DIPLOMA
DIPLOMACY
DIPLOMAED
DIPLOMAS
DIPLOMAT
DIPLOMATA
DIPLOMATE
DIPLOMATS
DIPLON
DIPLONEMA
DIPLONS
DIPLONT
DIPLONTIC
DIPLONTS
DIPLOPIA
DIPLOPIAS
DIPLOPIC
DIPLOPOD
DIPLOPODS
DIPLOSES
DIPLOSIS
DIPLOTENE
DIPLOZOA
DIPLOZOIC
DIPLOZOON
DIPNET
DIPNETS
DIPNETTED
DIPNOAN
DIPNOANS
DIPNOOUS
DIPODIC
DIPODIES
DIPODY
DIPOLAR
DIPOLE
DIPOLES
DIPPABLE
DIPPED
DIPPER
DIPPERFUL
DIPPERS
DIPPIER
DIPPIEST
DIPPINESS
DIPPING
DIPPINGS
DIPPY
DIPROTIC
DIPS
DIPSADES
DIPSAS
DIPSHIT
DIPSHITS
DIPSO
DIPSOS
DIPSTICK
DIPSTICKS
DIPSWITCH
DIPT
DIPTERA
DIPTERAL
DIPTERAN
DIPTERANS
DIPTERAS
DIPTERIST
DIPTEROI
DIPTERON
DIPTERONS
DIPTEROS
DIPTEROUS
DIPTYCA
DIPTYCAS
DIPTYCH
DIPTYCHS
DIQUARK
DIQUARKS
DIQUAT
DIQUATS
DIRAM
DIRAMS
DIRDAM
DIRDAMS
DIRDUM
DIRDUMS
DIRE
DIRECT
DIRECTED
DIRECTER
DIRECTEST
DIRECTING
DIRECTION
DIRECTIVE
DIRECTLY
DIRECTOR
DIRECTORS
DIRECTORY
DIRECTRIX
DIRECTS
DIREFUL
DIREFULLY
DIRELY
DIREMPT
DIREMPTED
DIREMPTS
DIRENESS
DIRER
DIREST
DIRGE
DIRGEFUL
DIRGELIKE
DIRGES
DIRHAM
DIRHAMS
DIRHEM
DIRHEMS
DIRIGE
DIRIGENT
DIRIGES
DIRIGIBLE
DIRIGISM
DIRIGISME
DIRIGISMS
DIRIGISTE
DIRIMENT
DIRK
DIRKE
DIRKED
DIRKES
DIRKING
DIRKS
DIRL
DIRLED
DIRLING
DIRLS
DIRNDL
DIRNDLS
DIRT
DIRTBAG
DIRTBAGS
DIRTBALL
DIRTBALLS
DIRTED
DIRTIED
DIRTIER
DIRTIES
DIRTIEST
DIRTILY
DIRTINESS
DIRTING
DIRTS
DIRTY
DIRTYING
DIS
DISA
DISABLE
DISABLED
DISABLER
DISABLERS
DISABLES
DISABLING
DISABLISM
DISABLIST
DISABUSAL
DISABUSE
DISABUSED
DISABUSES
DISACCORD
DISADORN
DISADORNS
DISAFFECT
DISAFFIRM
DISAGREE
DISAGREED
DISAGREES
DISALLIED
DISALLIES
DISALLOW

DISALLOWS
DISALLY
DISANCHOR
DISANNEX
DISANNUL
DISANNULS
DISANOINT
DISAPPEAR
DISAPPLY
DISARM
DISARMED
DISARMER
DISARMERS
DISARMING
DISARMS
DISARRAY
DISARRAYS
DISAS
DISASTER
DISASTERS
DISATTIRE
DISATTUNE
DISAVOUCH
DISAVOW
DISAVOWAL
DISAVOWED
DISAVOWER
DISAVOWS
DISBAND
DISBANDED
DISBANDS
DISBAR
DISBARK
DISBARKED
DISBARKS
DISBARRED
DISBARS
DISBELIEF
DISBENCH
DISBODIED
DISBOSOM
DISBOSOMS
DISBOUND
DISBOWEL
DISBOWELS
DISBRANCH
DISBUD
DISBUDDED
DISBUDS
DISBURDEN
DISBURSAL
DISBURSE
DISBURSED
DISBURSER
DISBURSES
DISC
DISCAGE
DISCAGED
DISCAGES
DISCAGING
DISCAL
DISCALCED
DISCANDIE
DISCANDY
DISCANT
DISCANTED
DISCANTER
DISCANTS
DISCARD
DISCARDED
DISCARDER
DISCARDS
DISCASE
DISCASED
DISCASES
DISCASING
DISCED
DISCEPT
DISCEPTED
DISCEPTS
DISCERN
DISCERNED
DISCERNER
DISCERNS
DISCERP
DISCERPED
DISCERPS
DISCHARGE
DISCHURCH
DISCI
DISCIDE
DISCIDED
DISCIDES
DISCIDING
DISCIFORM
DISCINCT
DISCING
DISCIPLE
DISCIPLED
DISCIPLES
DISCLAIM
DISCLAIMS
DISCLESS
DISCLIKE
DISCLIMAX
DISCLOSE
DISCLOSED
DISCLOSER
DISCLOSES
DISCLOST
DISCO
DISCOBOLI
DISCOED
DISCOER
DISCOERS
DISCOES
DISCOID
DISCOIDAL
DISCOIDS
DISCOING
DISCOLOGY
DISCOLOR
DISCOLORS
DISCOLOUR
DISCOMFIT
DISCOMMON
DISCORD
DISCORDED
DISCORDS
DISCOS
DISCOUNT
DISCOUNTS
DISCOURE
DISCOURED
DISCOURES
DISCOURSE
DISCOVER
DISCOVERS
DISCOVERT
DISCOVERY
DISCREDIT
DISCREET
DISCRETE
DISCRETER
DISCROWN
DISCROWNS
DISCS
DISCUMBER
DISCURE
DISCURED
DISCURES
DISCURING
DISCURSUS
DISCUS
DISCUSES
DISCUSS
DISCUSSED
DISCUSSER
DISCUSSES
DISDAIN
DISDAINED
DISDAINS
DISEASE
DISEASED
DISEASES
DISEASING
DISEDGE
DISEDGED
DISEDGES
DISEDGING
DISEMBARK
DISEMBODY
DISEMPLOY
DISENABLE
DISENDOW
DISENDOWS
DISENGAGE
DISENROL
DISENROLS
DISENTAIL
DISENTOMB
DISESTEEM
DISEUR
DISEURS
DISEUSE
DISEUSES
DISFAME
DISFAMED
DISFAMES
DISFAMING
DISFAVOR
DISFAVORS
DISFAVOUR
DISFIGURE
DISFLESH
DISFLUENT
DISFOREST
DISFORM
DISFORMED
DISFORMS
DISFROCK
DISFROCKS
DISGAVEL
DISGAVELS
DISGEST
DISGESTED
DISGESTS
DISGODDED
DISGORGE
DISGORGED
DISGORGER
DISGORGES
DISGOWN
DISGOWNED
DISGOWNS
DISGRACE
DISGRACED
DISGRACER
DISGRACES
DISGRADE
DISGRADED
DISGRADES
DISGUISE
DISGUISED
DISGUISER
DISGUISES
DISGUST
DISGUSTED
DISGUSTS
DISH
DISHABIT
DISHABITS
DISHABLE
DISHABLED
DISHABLES
DISHALLOW
DISHCLOTH
DISHCLOUT
DISHDASH
DISHDASHA

DISHED
DISHELM
DISHELMED
DISHELMS
DISHERIT
DISHERITS
DISHES
DISHEVEL
DISHEVELS
DISHFUL
DISHFULS
DISHIER
DISHIEST
DISHING
DISHINGS
DISHLIKE
DISHMOP
DISHMOPS
DISHOARD
DISHOARDS
DISHOME
DISHOMED
DISHOMES
DISHOMING
DISHONEST
DISHONOR
DISHONORS
DISHONOUR
DISHORN
DISHORNED
DISHORNS
DISHORSE
DISHORSED
DISHORSES
DISHOUSE
DISHOUSED
DISHOUSES
DISHPAN
DISHPANS
DISHRAG
DISHRAGS
DISHTOWEL
DISHUMOUR
DISHWARE
DISHWARES
DISHWATER
DISHY
DISILLUDE
DISIMMURE
DISINFECT
DISINFEST
DISINFORM
DISINHUME
DISINTER
DISINTERS
DISINURE
DISINURED
DISINURES
DISINVENT
DISINVEST
DISINVITE
DISJASKIT
DISJECT
DISJECTED
DISJECTS
DISJOIN
DISJOINED
DISJOINS
DISJOINT
DISJOINTS
DISJUNCT
DISJUNCTS
DISJUNE
DISJUNED
DISJUNES
DISJUNING
DISK
DISKED
DISKER
DISKERS
DISKETTE
DISKETTES
DISKING
DISKLESS
DISKLIKE
DISKS
DISLEAF
DISLEAFED
DISLEAFS
DISLEAL
DISLEAVE
DISLEAVED
DISLEAVES
DISLIKE
DISLIKED
DISLIKEN
DISLIKENS
DISLIKER
DISLIKERS
DISLIKES
DISLIKING
DISLIMB
DISLIMBED
DISLIMBS
DISLIMN
DISLIMNED
DISLIMNS
DISLINK
DISLINKED
DISLINKS
DISLOAD
DISLOADED
DISLOADS
DISLOCATE
DISLODGE
DISLODGED
DISLODGES
DISLOIGN
DISLOIGNS
DISLOYAL
DISLUSTRE
DISMAL
DISMALER
DISMALEST
DISMALITY
DISMALLER
DISMALLY
DISMALS
DISMAN
DISMANNED
DISMANS
DISMANTLE
DISMASK
DISMASKED
DISMASKS
DISMAST
DISMASTED
DISMASTS
DISMAY
DISMAYD
DISMAYED
DISMAYFUL
DISMAYING
DISMAYL
DISMAYLED
DISMAYLS
DISMAYS
DISME
DISMEMBER
DISMES
DISMISS
DISMISSAL
DISMISSED
DISMISSES
DISMODED
DISMOUNT
DISMOUNTS
DISNATURE
DISNEST
DISNESTED
DISNESTS
DISOBEY
DISOBEYED
DISOBEYER
DISOBEYS
DISOBLIGE
DISODIUM
DISOMIC
DISOMIES
DISOMY
DISORBED
DISORDER
DISORDERS
DISORIENT
DISOWN
DISOWNED
DISOWNER
DISOWNERS
DISOWNING
DISOWNS
DISPACE
DISPACED
DISPACES
DISPACING
DISPARAGE
DISPARATE
DISPARITY
DISPARK
DISPARKED
DISPARKS
DISPART
DISPARTED
DISPARTS
DISPATCH
DISPATHY
DISPAUPER
DISPEACE
DISPEACES
DISPEL
DISPELLED
DISPELLER
DISPELS
DISPENCE
DISPENCED
DISPENCES
DISPEND
DISPENDED
DISPENDS
DISPENSE
DISPENSED
DISPENSER
DISPENSES
DISPEOPLE
DISPERSAL
DISPERSE
DISPERSED
DISPERSER
DISPERSES
DISPIRIT
DISPIRITS
DISPLACE
DISPLACED
DISPLACER
DISPLACES
DISPLANT
DISPLANTS
DISPLAY
DISPLAYED
DISPLAYER
DISPLAYS
DISPLE
DISPLEASE
DISPLED
DISPLES
DISPLING
DISPLODE
DISPLODED
DISPLODES
DISPLUME
DISPLUMED

DISPLUMES
DISPONDEE
DISPONE
DISPONED
DISPONEE
DISPONEES
DISPONER
DISPONERS
DISPONES
DISPONGE
DISPONGED
DISPONGES
DISPONING
DISPORT
DISPORTED
DISPORTS
DISPOSAL
DISPOSALS
DISPOSE
DISPOSED
DISPOSER
DISPOSERS
DISPOSES
DISPOSING
DISPOST
DISPOSTED
DISPOSTS
DISPOSURE
DISPRAD
DISPRAISE
DISPREAD
DISPREADS
DISPRED
DISPREDS
DISPRISON
DISPRIZE
DISPRIZED
DISPRIZES
DISPROFIT
DISPROOF
DISPROOFS
DISPROOVE
DISPROVAL
DISPROVE
DISPROVED
DISPROVEN
DISPROVER
DISPROVES
DISPUNGE
DISPUNGED
DISPUNGES
DISPURSE
DISPURSED
DISPURSES
DISPURVEY
DISPUTANT
DISPUTE
DISPUTED
DISPUTER
DISPUTERS
DISPUTES
DISPUTING
DISQUIET
DISQUIETS
DISRANK
DISRANKED
DISRANKS
DISRATE
DISRATED
DISRATES
DISRATING
DISREGARD
DISRELISH
DISREPAIR
DISREPUTE
DISROBE
DISROBED
DISROBER
DISROBERS
DISROBES
DISROBING
DISROOT
DISROOTED
DISROOTS
DISRUPT
DISRUPTED
DISRUPTER
DISRUPTOR
DISRUPTS
DISS
DISSAVE
DISSAVED
DISSAVER
DISSAVERS
DISSAVES
DISSAVING
DISSEAT
DISSEATED
DISSEATS
DISSECT
DISSECTED
DISSECTOR
DISSECTS
DISSED
DISSEISE
DISSEISED
DISSEISEE
DISSEISES
DISSEISIN
DISSEISOR
DISSEIZE
DISSEIZED
DISSEIZEE
DISSEIZES
DISSEIZIN
DISSEIZOR
DISSEMBLE
DISSEMBLY
DISSENSUS
DISSENT
DISSENTED
DISSENTER
DISSENTS
DISSERT
DISSERTED
DISSERTS
DISSERVE
DISSERVED
DISSERVES
DISSES
DISSEVER
DISSEVERS
DISSHIVER
DISSIDENT
DISSIGHT
DISSIGHTS
DISSIMILE
DISSING
DISSIPATE
DISSOCIAL
DISSOLUTE
DISSOLVE
DISSOLVED
DISSOLVER
DISSOLVES
DISSONANT
DISSUADE
DISSUADED
DISSUADER
DISSUADES
DISSUNDER
DISTAFF
DISTAFFS
DISTAIN
DISTAINED
DISTAINS
DISTAL
DISTALLY
DISTANCE
DISTANCED
DISTANCES
DISTANT
DISTANTLY
DISTASTE
DISTASTED
DISTASTES
DISTAVES
DISTEMPER
DISTEND
DISTENDED
DISTENDER
DISTENDS
DISTENT
DISTENTS
DISTHENE
DISTHENES
DISTHRONE
DISTICH
DISTICHAL
DISTICHS
DISTIL
DISTILL
DISTILLED
DISTILLER
DISTILLS
DISTILS
DISTINCT
DISTINGUE
DISTOME
DISTOMES
DISTORT
DISTORTED
DISTORTER
DISTORTS
DISTRACT
DISTRACTS
DISTRAIL
DISTRAILS
DISTRAIN
DISTRAINS
DISTRAINT
DISTRAIT
DISTRAITE
DISTRESS
DISTRICT
DISTRICTS
DISTRIX
DISTRIXES
DISTRUST
DISTRUSTS
DISTUNE
DISTUNED
DISTUNES
DISTUNING
DISTURB
DISTURBED
DISTURBER
DISTURBS
DISTYLE
DISTYLES
DISULFATE
DISULFID
DISULFIDE
DISULFIDS
DISUNION
DISUNIONS
DISUNITE
DISUNITED
DISUNITER
DISUNITES
DISUNITY
DISUSAGE
DISUSAGES
DISUSE
DISUSED
DISUSES
DISUSING
DISVALUE
DISVALUED
DISVALUES

D

DISVOUCH
DISYOKE
DISYOKED
DISYOKES
DISYOKING
DIT
DITA
DITAL
DITALS
DITAS
DITCH
DITCHED
DITCHER
DITCHERS
DITCHES
DITCHING
DITCHLESS
DITE
DITED
DITES
DITHECAL
DITHECOUS
DITHEISM
DITHEISMS
DITHEIST
DITHEISTS
DITHELETE
DITHELISM
DITHER
DITHERED
DITHERER
DITHERERS
DITHERIER
DITHERING
DITHERS
DITHERY
DITHIOL
DITHIOLS
DITHIONIC
DITHYRAMB
DITING
DITOKOUS
DITONE
DITONES
DITROCHEE
DITS
DITSIER
DITSIEST
DITSINESS
DITSY
DITT
DITTANDER
DITTANIES
DITTANY
DITTAY
DITTAYS
DITTED
DITTIED
DITTIES
DITTING
DITTIT
DITTO
DITTOED
DITTOING
DITTOLOGY
DITTOS
DITTS
DITTY
DITTYING
DITZ
DITZES
DITZIER
DITZIEST
DITZINESS
DITZY
DIURESES
DIURESIS
DIURETIC
DIURETICS
DIURNAL
DIURNALLY
DIURNALS
DIURON
DIURONS
DIUTURNAL
DIV
DIVA
DIVAGATE
DIVAGATED
DIVAGATES
DIVALENCE
DIVALENCY
DIVALENT
DIVALENTS
DIVAN
DIVANS
DIVAS
DIVE
DIVEBOMB
DIVEBOMBS
DIVED
DIVELLENT
DIVER
DIVERGE
DIVERGED
DIVERGENT
DIVERGES
DIVERGING
DIVERS
DIVERSE
DIVERSED
DIVERSELY
DIVERSES
DIVERSIFY
DIVERSING
DIVERSION
DIVERSITY
DIVERSLY
DIVERT
DIVERTED
DIVERTER
DIVERTERS
DIVERTING
DIVERTIVE
DIVERTS
DIVES
DIVEST
DIVESTED
DIVESTING
DIVESTS
DIVESTURE
DIVI
DIVIDABLE
DIVIDANT
DIVIDE
DIVIDED
DIVIDEDLY
DIVIDEND
DIVIDENDS
DIVIDER
DIVIDERS
DIVIDES
DIVIDING
DIVIDINGS
DIVIDIVI
DIVIDIVIS
DIVIDUAL
DIVIDUOUS
DIVIED
DIVINABLE
DIVINATOR
DIVINE
DIVINED
DIVINELY
DIVINER
DIVINERS
DIVINES
DIVINEST
DIVING
DIVINGS
DIVINIFY
DIVINING
DIVINISE
DIVINISED
DIVINISES
DIVINITY
DIVINIZE
DIVINIZED
DIVINIZES
DIVIS
DIVISIBLE
DIVISIBLY
DIVISIM
DIVISION
DIVISIONS
DIVISIVE
DIVISOR
DIVISORS
DIVNA
DIVO
DIVORCE
DIVORCED
DIVORCEE
DIVORCEES
DIVORCER
DIVORCERS
DIVORCES
DIVORCING
DIVORCIVE
DIVOS
DIVOT
DIVOTS
DIVS
DIVULGATE
DIVULGE
DIVULGED
DIVULGER
DIVULGERS
DIVULGES
DIVULGING
DIVULSE
DIVULSED
DIVULSES
DIVULSING
DIVULSION
DIVULSIVE
DIVVIED
DIVVIER
DIVVIES
DIVVIEST
DIVVY
DIVVYING
DIVYING
DIWAN
DIWANS
DIXI
DIXIE
DIXIES
DIXIT
DIXITS
DIXY
DIYA
DIYAS
DIZAIN
DIZAINS
DIZEN
DIZENED
DIZENING
DIZENMENT
DIZENS
DIZYGOTIC
DIZYGOUS
DIZZARD
DIZZARDS
DIZZIED
DIZZIER
DIZZIES
DIZZIEST
DIZZILY
DIZZINESS

DIZZY
DIZZYING
DJEBEL
DJEBELS
DJELLABA
DJELLABAH
DJELLABAS
DJEMBE
DJEMBES
DJIBBA
DJIBBAH
DJIBBAHS
DJIBBAS
DJIN
DJINN
DJINNI
DJINNS
DJINNY
DJINS
DO
DOAB
DOABLE
DOABS
DOAT
DOATED
DOATER
DOATERS
DOATING
DOATINGS
DOATS
DOB
DOBBED
DOBBER
DOBBERS
DOBBIE
DOBBIES
DOBBIN
DOBBING
DOBBINS
DOBBY
DOBCHICK
DOBCHICKS
DOBE
DOBES
DOBHASH
DOBHASHES
DOBIE
DOBIES
DOBLA
DOBLAS
DOBLON
DOBLONES
DOBLONS
DOBRA
DOBRAS
DOBRO
DOBROS
DOBS
DOBSON
DOBSONFLY
DOBSONS
DOBY
DOC
DOCENT
DOCENTS
DOCETIC
DOCHMIAC
DOCHMIACS
DOCHMII
DOCHMIUS
DOCHT
DOCIBLE
DOCILE
DOCILELY
DOCILER
DOCILEST
DOCILITY
DOCIMASY
DOCK
DOCKAGE
DOCKAGES
DOCKED
DOCKEN
DOCKENS
DOCKER
DOCKERS
DOCKET
DOCKETED
DOCKETING
DOCKETS
DOCKHAND
DOCKHANDS
DOCKING
DOCKINGS
DOCKISE
DOCKISED
DOCKISES
DOCKISING
DOCKIZE
DOCKIZED
DOCKIZES
DOCKIZING
DOCKLAND
DOCKLANDS
DOCKS
DOCKSIDE
DOCKSIDES
DOCKYARD
DOCKYARDS
DOCO
DOCOS
DOCQUET
DOCQUETED
DOCQUETS
DOCS
DOCTOR
DOCTORAL
DOCTORAND
DOCTORATE
DOCTORED
DOCTORESS
DOCTORIAL
DOCTORING
DOCTORLY
DOCTORS
DOCTRESS
DOCTRINAL
DOCTRINE
DOCTRINES
DOCU
DOCUDRAMA
DOCUMENT
DOCUMENTS
DOCUS
DOCUSOAP
DOCUSOAPS
DOD
DODDARD
DODDARDS
DODDED
DODDER
DODDERED
DODDERER
DODDERERS
DODDERIER
DODDERING
DODDERS
DODDERY
DODDIER
DODDIES
DODDIEST
DODDING
DODDIPOLL
DODDLE
DODDLES
DODDY
DODDYPOLL
DODECAGON
DODGE
DODGEBALL
DODGED
DODGEM
DODGEMS
DODGER
DODGERIES
DODGERS
DODGERY
DODGES
DODGIER
DODGIEST
DODGINESS
DODGING
DODGINGS
DODGY
DODKIN
DODKINS
DODMAN
DODMANS
DODO
DODOES
DODOISM
DODOISMS
DODOS
DODS
DOE
DOEK
DOEKS
DOEN
DOER
DOERS
DOES
DOESKIN
DOESKINS
DOEST
DOETH
DOF
DOFF
DOFFED
DOFFER
DOFFERS
DOFFING
DOFFS
DOG
DOGAN
DOGANS
DOGARESSA
DOGATE
DOGATES
DOGBANE
DOGBANES
DOGBERRY
DOGBOLT
DOGBOLTS
DOGCART
DOGCARTS
DOGDOM
DOGDOMS
DOGE
DOGEAR
DOGEARED
DOGEARING
DOGEARS
DOGEATE
DOGEATES
DOGEDOM
DOGEDOMS
DOGES
DOGESHIP
DOGESHIPS
DOGEY
DOGEYS
DOGFACE
DOGFACES
DOGFIGHT
DOGFIGHTS
DOGFISH
DOGFISHES
DOGFOOD
DOGFOODS
DOGFOUGHT

DOGFOX
DOGFOXES
DOGGED
DOGGEDER
DOGGEDEST
DOGGEDLY
DOGGER
DOGGEREL
DOGGERELS
DOGGERIES
DOGGERMAN
DOGGERMEN
DOGGERS
DOGGERY
DOGGESS
DOGGESSES
DOGGIE
DOGGIER
DOGGIES
DOGGIEST
DOGGINESS
DOGGING
DOGGINGS
DOGGISH
DOGGISHLY
DOGGO
DOGGONE
DOGGONED
DOGGONER
DOGGONES
DOGGONEST
DOGGONING
DOGGREL
DOGGRELS
DOGGY
DOGHANGED
DOGHOLE
DOGHOLES
DOGHOUSE
DOGHOUSES
DOGIE
DOGIES
DOGLEG
DOGLEGGED
DOGLEGS
DOGLIKE
DOGMA
DOGMAN
DOGMAS
DOGMATA
DOGMATIC
DOGMATICS
DOGMATISE
DOGMATISM
DOGMATIST
DOGMATIZE
DOGMATORY
DOGMEN
DOGNAP
DOGNAPED
DOGNAPER
DOGNAPERS
DOGNAPING
DOGNAPPED
DOGNAPPER
DOGNAPS
DOGPILE
DOGPILES
DOGREL
DOGRELS
DOGROBBER
DOGS
DOGSBODY
DOGSHIP
DOGSHIPS
DOGSHORES
DOGSHOW
DOGSHOWS
DOGSKIN
DOGSKINS
DOGSLED
DOGSLEDS
DOGSLEEP
DOGSLEEPS
DOGSTAIL
DOGSTAILS
DOGTAIL
DOGTAILS
DOGTEETH
DOGTOOTH
DOGTOWN
DOGTOWNS
DOGTROT
DOGTROTS
DOGVANE
DOGVANES
DOGWATCH
DOGWOOD
DOGWOODS
DOGY
DOH
DOHS
DOHYO
DOHYOS
DOILED
DOILIED
DOILIES
DOILT
DOILTER
DOILTEST
DOILY
DOING
DOINGS
DOIT
DOITED
DOITIT
DOITKIN
DOITKINS
DOITS
DOJO
DOJOS
DOL
DOLABRATE
DOLCE
DOLCES
DOLCETTO
DOLCETTOS
DOLCI
DOLDRUMS
DOLE
DOLED
DOLEFUL
DOLEFULLY
DOLENT
DOLENTE
DOLERITE
DOLERITES
DOLERITIC
DOLES
DOLESOME
DOLIA
DOLICHOS
DOLICHURI
DOLINA
DOLINAS
DOLINE
DOLINES
DOLING
DOLIUM
DOLL
DOLLAR
DOLLARED
DOLLARISE
DOLLARIZE
DOLLARS
DOLLDOM
DOLLDOMS
DOLLED
DOLLHOOD
DOLLHOODS
DOLLHOUSE
DOLLIED
DOLLIER
DOLLIERS
DOLLIES
DOLLINESS
DOLLING
DOLLISH
DOLLISHLY
DOLLOP
DOLLOPED
DOLLOPING
DOLLOPS
DOLLS
DOLLY
DOLLYBIRD
DOLLYING
DOLMA
DOLMADES
DOLMAN
DOLMANS
DOLMAS
DOLMEN
DOLMENIC
DOLMENS
DOLOMITE
DOLOMITES
DOLOMITIC
DOLOR
DOLORIFIC
DOLOROSO
DOLOROUS
DOLORS
DOLOS
DOLOSSE
DOLOSTONE
DOLOUR
DOLOURS
DOLPHIN
DOLPHINET
DOLPHINS
DOLS
DOLT
DOLTISH
DOLTISHLY
DOLTS
DOM
DOMAIN
DOMAINAL
DOMAINE
DOMAINES
DOMAINS
DOMAL
DOMANIAL
DOMATIA
DOMATIUM
DOME
DOMED
DOMELIKE
DOMES
DOMESDAY
DOMESDAYS
DOMESTIC
DOMESTICS
DOMETT
DOMETTS
DOMIC
DOMICAL
DOMICALLY
DOMICIL
DOMICILE
DOMICILED
DOMICILES
DOMICILS
DOMIER
DOMIEST
DOMINANCE
DOMINANCY
DOMINANT
DOMINANTS

DOMINATE
DOMINATED
DOMINATES
DOMINATOR
DOMINE
DOMINEE
DOMINEER
DOMINEERS
DOMINEES
DOMINES
DOMING
DOMINICAL
DOMINICK
DOMINICKS
DOMINIE
DOMINIES
DOMINION
DOMINIONS
DOMINIQUE
DOMINIUM
DOMINIUMS
DOMINO
DOMINOES
DOMINOS
DOMOIC
DOMS
DOMY
DON
DONA
DONAH
DONAHS
DONAIR
DONAIRS
DONARIES
DONARY
DONAS
DONATARY
DONATE
DONATED
DONATES
DONATING
DONATION
DONATIONS
DONATISM
DONATISMS
DONATIVE
DONATIVES
DONATOR
DONATORS
DONATORY
DONDER
DONDERED
DONDERING
DONDERS
DONE
DONEE
DONEES
DONEGAL
DONEGALS
DONENESS
DONEPEZIL
DONER
DONERS
DONG
DONGA
DONGAS
DONGED
DONGING
DONGLE
DONGLES
DONGOLA
DONGOLAS
DONGS
DONING
DONINGS
DONJON
DONJONS
DONKEY
DONKEYMAN
DONKEYMEN
DONKEYS
DONKO
DONKOS
DONNA
DONNARD
DONNART
DONNAS
DONNAT
DONNATS
DONNE
DONNED
DONNEE
DONNEES
DONNERD
DONNERED
DONNERT
DONNES
DONNICKER
DONNIES
DONNIKER
DONNIKERS
DONNING
DONNISH
DONNISHLY
DONNISM
DONNISMS
DONNOT
DONNOTS
DONNY
DONOR
DONORS
DONORSHIP
DONS
DONSHIP
DONSHIPS
DONSIE
DONSIER
DONSIEST
DONSY
DONUT
DONUTS
DONUTTED
DONUTTING
DONZEL
DONZELS
DOO
DOOB
DOOBIE
DOOBIES
DOOBREY
DOOBREYS
DOOBRIE
DOOBRIES
DOOBRY
DOOBS
DOOCE
DOOCED
DOOCES
DOOCING
DOOCOT
DOOCOTS
DOODAD
DOODADS
DOODAH
DOODAHS
DOODIES
DOODLE
DOODLEBUG
DOODLED
DOODLER
DOODLERS
DOODLES
DOODLING
DOODOO
DOODOOS
DOODY
DOOFER
DOOFERS
DOOFUS
DOOFUSES
DOOHICKEY
DOOK
DOOKED
DOOKET
DOOKETS
DOOKING
DOOKS
DOOL
DOOLALLY
DOOLAN
DOOLANS
DOOLE
DOOLEE
DOOLEES
DOOLES
DOOLIE
DOOLIES
DOOLS
DOOLY
DOOM
DOOMED
DOOMFUL
DOOMFULLY
DOOMIER
DOOMIEST
DOOMILY
DOOMING
DOOMS
DOOMSAYER
DOOMSDAY
DOOMSDAYS
DOOMSMAN
DOOMSMEN
DOOMSTER
DOOMSTERS
DOOMWATCH
DOOMY
DOON
DOONA
DOONAS
DOOR
DOORBELL
DOORBELLS
DOORCASE
DOORCASES
DOORED
DOORFRAME
DOORJAMB
DOORJAMBS
DOORKNOB
DOORKNOBS
DOORKNOCK
DOORLESS
DOORLIKE
DOORMAN
DOORMAT
DOORMATS
DOORMEN
DOORN
DOORNAIL
DOORNAILS
DOORNBOOM
DOORNS
DOORPLATE
DOORPOST
DOORPOSTS
DOORS
DOORSILL
DOORSILLS
DOORSMAN
DOORSMEN
DOORSTEP
DOORSTEPS
DOORSTONE
DOORSTOP
DOORSTOPS
DOORWAY
DOORWAYS
DOORWOMAN
DOORWOMEN

D

DOORYARD
DOORYARDS
DOOS
DOOSES
DOOSRA
DOOSRAS
DOOWOP
DOOWOPS
DOOZER
DOOZERS
DOOZIE
DOOZIES
DOOZY
DOP
DOPA
DOPAMINE
DOPAMINES
DOPANT
DOPANTS
DOPAS
DOPATTA
DOPATTAS
DOPE
DOPED
DOPEHEAD
DOPEHEADS
DOPER
DOPERS
DOPES
DOPESHEET
DOPEST
DOPESTER
DOPESTERS
DOPEY
DOPEYNESS
DOPIAZA
DOPIAZAS
DOPIER
DOPIEST
DOPILY
DOPINESS
DOPING
DOPINGS
DOPPED
DOPPER
DOPPERS
DOPPIE
DOPPIES
DOPPING
DOPPINGS
DOPPIO
DOPPIOS
DOPS
DOPY
DOR
DORAD
DORADO
DORADOS
DORADS
DORB
DORBA
DORBAS
DORBEETLE
DORBS
DORBUG
DORBUGS
DORE
DOREE
DOREES
DORES
DORHAWK
DORHAWKS
DORIC
DORIDOID
DORIDOIDS
DORIES
DORIS
DORISE
DORISED
DORISES
DORISING
DORIZE
DORIZED
DORIZES
DORIZING
DORK
DORKIER
DORKIEST
DORKINESS
DORKISH
DORKS
DORKY
DORLACH
DORLACHS
DORM
DORMANCY
DORMANT
DORMANTS
DORMER
DORMERED
DORMERS
DORMICE
DORMIE
DORMIENT
DORMIN
DORMINS
DORMITION
DORMITIVE
DORMITORY
DORMOUSE
DORMS
DORMY
DORNECK
DORNECKS
DORNICK
DORNICKS
DORNOCK
DORNOCKS
DORONICUM
DORP
DORPER
DORPERS
DORPS
DORR
DORRED
DORRING
DORRS
DORS
DORSA
DORSAD
DORSAL
DORSALLY
DORSALS
DORSE
DORSEL
DORSELS
DORSER
DORSERS
DORSES
DORSIFLEX
DORSUM
DORT
DORTED
DORTER
DORTERS
DORTIER
DORTIEST
DORTINESS
DORTING
DORTOUR
DORTOURS
DORTS
DORTY
DORY
DORYMAN
DORYMEN
DOS
DOSA
DOSAGE
DOSAGES
DOSAI
DOSAS
DOSE
DOSED
DOSEH
DOSEHS
DOSEMETER
DOSER
DOSERS
DOSES
DOSH
DOSHA
DOSHAS
DOSHES
DOSIMETER
DOSIMETRY
DOSING
DOSIOLOGY
DOSOLOGY
DOSS
DOSSAL
DOSSALS
DOSSED
DOSSEL
DOSSELS
DOSSER
DOSSERET
DOSSERETS
DOSSERS
DOSSES
DOSSHOUSE
DOSSIER
DOSSIERS
DOSSIL
DOSSILS
DOSSING
DOST
DOT
DOTAGE
DOTAGES
DOTAL
DOTANT
DOTANTS
DOTARD
DOTARDLY
DOTARDS
DOTATION
DOTATIONS
DOTCOM
DOTCOMMER
DOTCOMS
DOTE
DOTED
DOTER
DOTERS
DOTES
DOTH
DOTIER
DOTIEST
DOTING
DOTINGLY
DOTINGS
DOTISH
DOTS
DOTTED
DOTTEL
DOTTELS
DOTTER
DOTTEREL
DOTTERELS
DOTTERS
DOTTIER
DOTTIEST
DOTTILY
DOTTINESS
DOTTING
DOTTLE
DOTTLED
DOTTLER
DOTTLES

DOTTLEST
DOTTREL
DOTTRELS
DOTTY
DOTY
DOUANE
DOUANES
DOUANIER
DOUANIERS
DOUAR
DOUARS
DOUBLE
DOUBLED
DOUBLER
DOUBLERS
DOUBLES
DOUBLET
DOUBLETON
DOUBLETS
DOUBLING
DOUBLINGS
DOUBLOON
DOUBLOONS
DOUBLURE
DOUBLURES
DOUBLY
DOUBT
DOUBTABLE
DOUBTABLY
DOUBTED
DOUBTER
DOUBTERS
DOUBTFUL
DOUBTFULS
DOUBTING
DOUBTINGS
DOUBTLESS
DOUBTS
DOUC
DOUCE
DOUCELY
DOUCENESS
DOUCEPERE
DOUCER
DOUCEST
DOUCET
DOUCETS
DOUCEUR
DOUCEURS
DOUCHE
DOUCHEBAG
DOUCHED
DOUCHES
DOUCHING
DOUCHINGS
DOUCINE
DOUCINES
DOUCS
DOUGH
DOUGHBALL
DOUGHBOY
DOUGHBOYS
DOUGHFACE
DOUGHIER
DOUGHIEST
DOUGHLIKE
DOUGHNUT
DOUGHNUTS
DOUGHS
DOUGHT
DOUGHTIER
DOUGHTILY
DOUGHTY
DOUGHY
DOUK
DOUKED
DOUKING
DOUKS
DOULA
DOULAS
DOULEIA
DOULEIAS
DOUM
DOUMA
DOUMAS
DOUMS
DOUN
DOUP
DOUPIONI
DOUPIONIS
DOUPPIONI
DOUPS
DOUR
DOURA
DOURAH
DOURAHS
DOURAS
DOURER
DOUREST
DOURINE
DOURINES
DOURLY
DOURNESS
DOUSE
DOUSED
DOUSER
DOUSERS
DOUSES
DOUSING
DOUT
DOUTED
DOUTER
DOUTERS
DOUTING
DOUTS
DOUX
DOUZEPER
DOUZEPERS
DOVE
DOVECOT
DOVECOTE
DOVECOTES
DOVECOTS
DOVED
DOVEISH
DOVEISHLY
DOVEKEY
DOVEKEYS
DOVEKIE
DOVEKIES
DOVELET
DOVELETS
DOVELIKE
DOVEN
DOVENED
DOVENING
DOVENS
DOVER
DOVERED
DOVERING
DOVERS
DOVES
DOVETAIL
DOVETAILS
DOVIE
DOVIER
DOVIEST
DOVING
DOVISH
DOVISHLY
DOW
DOWABLE
DOWAGER
DOWAGERS
DOWAR
DOWARS
DOWD
DOWDIER
DOWDIES
DOWDIEST
DOWDILY
DOWDINESS
DOWDS
DOWDY
DOWDYISH
DOWDYISM
DOWDYISMS
DOWED
DOWEL
DOWELED
DOWELING
DOWELINGS
DOWELLED
DOWELLING
DOWELS
DOWER
DOWERED
DOWERIES
DOWERING
DOWERLESS
DOWERS
DOWERY
DOWF
DOWFNESS
DOWIE
DOWIER
DOWIEST
DOWING
DOWITCHER
DOWL
DOWLAS
DOWLASES
DOWLE
DOWLES
DOWLIER
DOWLIEST
DOWLNE
DOWLNES
DOWLNEY
DOWLS
DOWLY
DOWN
DOWNA
DOWNBEAT
DOWNBEATS
DOWNBOUND
DOWNBOW
DOWNBOWS
DOWNBURST
DOWNCAST
DOWNCASTS
DOWNCOME
DOWNCOMER
DOWNCOMES
DOWNCOURT
DOWNCRIED
DOWNCRIES
DOWNCRY
DOWNDRAFT
DOWNED
DOWNER
DOWNERS
DOWNFALL
DOWNFALLS
DOWNFIELD
DOWNFLOW
DOWNFLOWS
DOWNFORCE
DOWNGRADE
DOWNHAUL
DOWNHAULS
DOWNHILL
DOWNHILLS
DOWNHOLE
DOWNIER
DOWNIES
DOWNIEST
DOWNILY
DOWNINESS
DOWNING

DOWNLAND
DOWNLANDS
DOWNLESS
DOWNLIGHT
DOWNLIKE
DOWNLINK
DOWNLINKS
DOWNLOAD
DOWNLOADS
DOWNLOW
DOWNLOWS
DOWNMOST
DOWNPIPE
DOWNPIPES
DOWNPLAY
DOWNPLAYS
DOWNPOUR
DOWNPOURS
DOWNRANGE
DOWNRATE
DOWNRATED
DOWNRATES
DOWNRIGHT
DOWNRIVER
DOWNRUSH
DOWNS
DOWNSCALE
DOWNSHIFT
DOWNSIDE
DOWNSIDES
DOWNSIZE
DOWNSIZED
DOWNSIZER
DOWNSIZES
DOWNSLIDE
DOWNSLOPE
DOWNSPIN
DOWNSPINS
DOWNSPOUT
DOWNSTAGE
DOWNSTAIR
DOWNSTATE
DOWNSWEPT
DOWNSWING
DOWNTHROW
DOWNTICK
DOWNTICKS
DOWNTIME
DOWNTIMES
DOWNTOWN
DOWNTOWNS
DOWNTREND
DOWNTROD
DOWNTURN
DOWNTURNS
DOWNVOTE
DOWNVOTED
DOWNVOTES
DOWNWARD
DOWNWARDS
DOWNWARP
DOWNWARPS
DOWNWASH
DOWNWIND
DOWNY
DOWNZONE
DOWNZONED
DOWNZONES
DOWP
DOWPS
DOWRIES
DOWRY
DOWS
DOWSABEL
DOWSABELS
DOWSE
DOWSED
DOWSER
DOWSERS
DOWSES
DOWSET
DOWSETS
DOWSING
DOWSINGS
DOWT
DOWTS
DOX
DOXAPRAM
DOXAPRAMS
DOXASTIC
DOXASTICS
DOXED
DOXES
DOXIE
DOXIES
DOXING
DOXOLOGY
DOXY
DOY
DOYEN
DOYENNE
DOYENNES
DOYENS
DOYLEY
DOYLEYS
DOYLIES
DOYLY
DOYS
DOZE
DOZED
DOZEN
DOZENED
DOZENING
DOZENS
DOZENTH
DOZENTHS
DOZER
DOZERS
DOZES
DOZIER
DOZIEST
DOZILY
DOZINESS
DOZING
DOZINGS
DOZY
DRAB
DRABBED
DRABBER
DRABBERS
DRABBEST
DRABBET
DRABBETS
DRABBIER
DRABBIEST
DRABBING
DRABBISH
DRABBLE
DRABBLED
DRABBLER
DRABBLERS
DRABBLES
DRABBLING
DRABBY
DRABETTE
DRABETTES
DRABLER
DRABLERS
DRABLY
DRABNESS
DRABS
DRAC
DRACAENA
DRACAENAS
DRACENA
DRACENAS
DRACHM
DRACHMA
DRACHMAE
DRACHMAI
DRACHMAS
DRACHMS
DRACK
DRACO
DRACONE
DRACONES
DRACONIAN
DRACONIC
DRACONISM
DRACONTIC
DRAD
DRAFF
DRAFFIER
DRAFFIEST
DRAFFISH
DRAFFS
DRAFFY
DRAFT
DRAFTABLE
DRAFTED
DRAFTEE
DRAFTEES
DRAFTER
DRAFTERS
DRAFTIER
DRAFTIEST
DRAFTILY
DRAFTING
DRAFTINGS
DRAFTS
DRAFTSMAN
DRAFTSMEN
DRAFTY
DRAG
DRAGEE
DRAGEES
DRAGGED
DRAGGER
DRAGGERS
DRAGGIER
DRAGGIEST
DRAGGING
DRAGGINGS
DRAGGLE
DRAGGLED
DRAGGLES
DRAGGLING
DRAGGY
DRAGHOUND
DRAGLINE
DRAGLINES
DRAGNET
DRAGNETS
DRAGOMAN
DRAGOMANS
DRAGOMEN
DRAGON
DRAGONESS
DRAGONET
DRAGONETS
DRAGONFLY
DRAGONISE
DRAGONISH
DRAGONISM
DRAGONIZE
DRAGONNE
DRAGONS
DRAGOON
DRAGOONED
DRAGOONS
DRAGROPE
DRAGROPES
DRAGS
DRAGSMAN
DRAGSMEN
DRAGSTER
DRAGSTERS
DRAGSTRIP
DRAGWAY
DRAGWAYS

DRAIL
DRAILED
DRAILING
DRAILS
DRAIN
DRAINABLE
DRAINAGE
DRAINAGES
DRAINED
DRAINER
DRAINERS
DRAINING
DRAINPIPE
DRAINS
DRAISENE
DRAISENES
DRAISINE
DRAISINES
DRAKE
DRAKES
DRAM
DRAMA
DRAMADIES
DRAMADY
DRAMAS
DRAMATIC
DRAMATICS
DRAMATISE
DRAMATIST
DRAMATIZE
DRAMATURG
DRAMEDIES
DRAMEDY
DRAMMACH
DRAMMACHS
DRAMMED
DRAMMING
DRAMMOCK
DRAMMOCKS
DRAMS
DRAMSHOP
DRAMSHOPS
DRANGWAY
DRANGWAYS
DRANK
DRANT
DRANTED
DRANTING
DRANTS
DRAP
DRAPABLE
DRAPE
DRAPEABLE
DRAPED
DRAPER
DRAPERIED
DRAPERIES
DRAPERS
DRAPERY
DRAPES
DRAPET
DRAPETS
DRAPEY
DRAPIER
DRAPIERS
DRAPIEST
DRAPING
DRAPPED
DRAPPIE
DRAPPIES
DRAPPING
DRAPPY
DRAPS
DRASTIC
DRASTICS
DRAT
DRATCHELL
DRATS
DRATTED
DRATTING
DRAUGHT
DRAUGHTED
DRAUGHTER
DRAUGHTS
DRAUGHTY
DRAUNT
DRAUNTED
DRAUNTING
DRAUNTS
DRAVE
DRAW
DRAWABLE
DRAWBACK
DRAWBACKS
DRAWBAR
DRAWBARS
DRAWBORE
DRAWBORES
DRAWCARD
DRAWCARDS
DRAWCORD
DRAWCORDS
DRAWDOWN
DRAWDOWNS
DRAWEE
DRAWEES
DRAWER
DRAWERFUL
DRAWERS
DRAWING
DRAWINGS
DRAWKNIFE
DRAWL
DRAWLED
DRAWLER
DRAWLERS
DRAWLIER
DRAWLIEST
DRAWLING
DRAWLS
DRAWLY
DRAWN
DRAWNWORK
DRAWPLATE
DRAWS
DRAWSHAVE
DRAWTUBE
DRAWTUBES
DRAY
DRAYAGE
DRAYAGES
DRAYED
DRAYHORSE
DRAYING
DRAYMAN
DRAYMEN
DRAYS
DRAZEL
DRAZELS
DREAD
DREADED
DREADER
DREADERS
DREADEST
DREADFUL
DREADFULS
DREADING
DREADLESS
DREADLOCK
DREADLY
DREADS
DREAM
DREAMBOAT
DREAMED
DREAMER
DREAMERS
DREAMERY
DREAMFUL
DREAMHOLE
DREAMIER
DREAMIEST
DREAMILY
DREAMING
DREAMINGS
DREAMLAND
DREAMLESS
DREAMLIKE
DREAMS
DREAMT
DREAMTIME
DREAMY
DREAR
DREARE
DREARER
DREARES
DREAREST
DREARIER
DREARIES
DREARIEST
DREARILY
DREARING
DREARINGS
DREARS
DREARY
DRECK
DRECKIER
DRECKIEST
DRECKISH
DRECKS
DRECKSILL
DRECKY
DREDGE
DREDGED
DREDGER
DREDGERS
DREDGES
DREDGING
DREDGINGS
DREE
DREED
DREEING
DREER
DREES
DREEST
DREG
DREGGIER
DREGGIEST
DREGGISH
DREGGY
DREGS
DREICH
DREICHER
DREICHEST
DREIDEL
DREIDELS
DREIDL
DREIDLS
DREIGH
DREIGHER
DREIGHEST
DREK
DREKKIER
DREKKIEST
DREKKY
DREKS
DRENCH
DRENCHED
DRENCHER
DRENCHERS
DRENCHES
DRENCHING
DRENT
DREPANID
DREPANIDS
DREPANIUM
DRERE
DRERES
DRERIHEAD
DRESS
DRESSAGE

DRESSAGES
DRESSED
DRESSER
DRESSERS
DRESSES
DRESSIER
DRESSIEST
DRESSILY
DRESSING
DRESSINGS
DRESSMADE
DRESSMAKE
DRESSY
DREST
DREVILL
DREVILLS
DREW
DREY
DREYS
DRIB
DRIBBED
DRIBBER
DRIBBERS
DRIBBING
DRIBBLE
DRIBBLED
DRIBBLER
DRIBBLERS
DRIBBLES
DRIBBLET
DRIBBLETS
DRIBBLIER
DRIBBLING
DRIBBLY
DRIBLET
DRIBLETS
DRIBS
DRICE
DRICES
DRICKSIE
DRICKSIER
DRIED
DRIEGH
DRIER
DRIERS
DRIES
DRIEST
DRIFT
DRIFTAGE
DRIFTAGES
DRIFTED
DRIFTER
DRIFTERS
DRIFTIER
DRIFTIEST
DRIFTING
DRIFTINGS
DRIFTLESS
DRIFTNET
DRIFTNETS
DRIFTPIN
DRIFTPINS
DRIFTS
DRIFTWOOD
DRIFTY
DRILL
DRILLABLE
DRILLED
DRILLER
DRILLERS
DRILLHOLE
DRILLING
DRILLINGS
DRILLS
DRILLSHIP
DRILY
DRINK
DRINKABLE
DRINKABLY
DRINKER
DRINKERS
DRINKING
DRINKINGS
DRINKS
DRIP
DRIPLESS
DRIPPED
DRIPPER
DRIPPERS
DRIPPIER
DRIPPIEST
DRIPPILY
DRIPPING
DRIPPINGS
DRIPPY
DRIPS
DRIPSTONE
DRIPT
DRISHEEN
DRISHEENS
DRIVABLE
DRIVE
DRIVEABLE
DRIVEL
DRIVELED
DRIVELER
DRIVELERS
DRIVELINE
DRIVELING
DRIVELLED
DRIVELLER
DRIVELS
DRIVEN
DRIVER
DRIVERS
DRIVES
DRIVEWAY
DRIVEWAYS
DRIVING
DRIVINGLY
DRIVINGS
DRIZZLE
DRIZZLED
DRIZZLES
DRIZZLIER
DRIZZLING
DRIZZLY
DROGER
DROGERS
DROGHER
DROGHERS
DROGUE
DROGUES
DROGUET
DROGUETS
DROICH
DROICHIER
DROICHS
DROICHY
DROID
DROIDS
DROIL
DROILED
DROILING
DROILS
DROIT
DROITS
DROKE
DROKES
DROLE
DROLER
DROLES
DROLEST
DROLL
DROLLED
DROLLER
DROLLERY
DROLLEST
DROLLING
DROLLINGS
DROLLISH
DROLLNESS
DROLLS
DROLLY
DROME
DROMEDARE
DROMEDARY
DROMES
DROMIC
DROMICAL
DROMOI
DROMON
DROMOND
DROMONDS
DROMONS
DROMOS
DRONE
DRONED
DRONER
DRONERS
DRONES
DRONGO
DRONGOES
DRONGOS
DRONIER
DRONIEST
DRONING
DRONINGLY
DRONISH
DRONISHLY
DRONKLAP
DRONKLAPS
DRONY
DROOB
DROOBS
DROOG
DROOGISH
DROOGS
DROOK
DROOKED
DROOKING
DROOKINGS
DROOKIT
DROOKS
DROOL
DROOLED
DROOLIER
DROOLIEST
DROOLING
DROOLS
DROOLY
DROOME
DROOMES
DROOP
DROOPED
DROOPIER
DROOPIEST
DROOPILY
DROOPING
DROOPS
DROOPY
DROP
DROPCLOTH
DROPDOWN
DROPDOWNS
DROPFLIES
DROPFLY
DROPFORGE
DROPHEAD
DROPHEADS
DROPKICK
DROPKICKS
DROPLET
DROPLETS
DROPLIGHT
DROPLIKE
DROPLOCK
DROPLOCKS
DROPOUT
DROPOUTS

DROPPABLE
DROPPED
DROPPER
DROPPERS
DROPPING
DROPPINGS
DROPPLE
DROPPLES
DROPS
DROPSEED
DROPSEEDS
DROPSHOT
DROPSHOTS
DROPSICAL
DROPSIED
DROPSIES
DROPSONDE
DROPSTONE
DROPSY
DROPT
DROPTOP
DROPTOPS
DROPWISE
DROPWORT
DROPWORTS
DROSERA
DROSERAS
DROSHKIES
DROSHKY
DROSKIES
DROSKY
DROSS
DROSSES
DROSSIER
DROSSIEST
DROSSY
DROSTDIES
DROSTDY
DROSTDYS
DROUGHT
DROUGHTS
DROUGHTY
DROUK
DROUKED
DROUKING
DROUKINGS
DROUKIT
DROUKS
DROUTH
DROUTHIER
DROUTHS
DROUTHY
DROVE
DROVED
DROVER
DROVERS
DROVES
DROVING
DROVINGS
DROW
DROWN
DROWND
DROWNDED
DROWNDING
DROWNDS
DROWNED
DROWNER
DROWNERS
DROWNING
DROWNINGS
DROWNS
DROWS
DROWSE
DROWSED
DROWSES
DROWSIER
DROWSIEST
DROWSIHED
DROWSILY
DROWSING
DROWSY
DRUB
DRUBBED
DRUBBER
DRUBBERS
DRUBBING
DRUBBINGS
DRUBS
DRUCKEN
DRUDGE
DRUDGED
DRUDGER
DRUDGERS
DRUDGERY
DRUDGES
DRUDGING
DRUDGISM
DRUDGISMS
DRUG
DRUGGED
DRUGGER
DRUGGERS
DRUGGET
DRUGGETS
DRUGGIE
DRUGGIER
DRUGGIES
DRUGGIEST
DRUGGING
DRUGGIST
DRUGGISTS
DRUGGY
DRUGLESS
DRUGLORD
DRUGLORDS
DRUGMAKER
DRUGS
DRUGSTER
DRUGSTERS
DRUGSTORE
DRUID
DRUIDESS
DRUIDIC
DRUIDICAL
DRUIDISM
DRUIDISMS
DRUIDRIES
DRUIDRY
DRUIDS
DRUM
DRUMBEAT
DRUMBEATS
DRUMBLE
DRUMBLED
DRUMBLES
DRUMBLING
DRUMFIRE
DRUMFIRES
DRUMFISH
DRUMHEAD
DRUMHEADS
DRUMLIER
DRUMLIEST
DRUMLIKE
DRUMLIN
DRUMLINS
DRUMLY
DRUMMED
DRUMMER
DRUMMERS
DRUMMIES
DRUMMING
DRUMMINGS
DRUMMOCK
DRUMMOCKS
DRUMMY
DRUMROLL
DRUMROLLS
DRUMS
DRUMSTICK
DRUNK
DRUNKARD
DRUNKARDS
DRUNKEN
DRUNKENLY
DRUNKER
DRUNKEST
DRUNKISH
DRUNKS
DRUPE
DRUPEL
DRUPELET
DRUPELETS
DRUPELS
DRUPES
DRUSE
DRUSEN
DRUSES
DRUSIER
DRUSIEST
DRUSY
DRUTHER
DRUTHERS
DRUXIER
DRUXIEST
DRUXY
DRY
DRYABLE
DRYAD
DRYADES
DRYADIC
DRYADS
DRYAS
DRYASDUST
DRYBEAT
DRYBEATEN
DRYBEATS
DRYER
DRYERS
DRYEST
DRYING
DRYINGS
DRYISH
DRYLAND
DRYLANDS
DRYLOT
DRYLOTS
DRYLY
DRYMOUTH
DRYMOUTHS
DRYNESS
DRYNESSES
DRYPOINT
DRYPOINTS
DRYS
DRYSALTER
DRYSTONE
DRYSUIT
DRYSUITS
DRYWALL
DRYWALLED
DRYWALLER
DRYWALLS
DRYWELL
DRYWELLS
DSO
DSOBO
DSOBOS
DSOMO
DSOMOS
DSOS
DUAD
DUADS
DUAL
DUALIN
DUALINS
DUALISE
DUALISED
DUALISES
DUALISING

D

DUALISM
DUALISMS
DUALIST
DUALISTIC
DUALISTS
DUALITIES
DUALITY
DUALIZE
DUALIZED
DUALIZES
DUALIZING
DUALLED
DUALLIE
DUALLIES
DUALLING
DUALLY
DUALS
DUAN
DUANS
DUAR
DUARCHIES
DUARCHY
DUARS
DUATHLETE
DUATHLON
DUATHLONS
DUB
DUBBED
DUBBER
DUBBERS
DUBBIN
DUBBINED
DUBBING
DUBBINGS
DUBBINING
DUBBINS
DUBBO
DUBBOS
DUBIETIES
DUBIETY
DUBIOSITY
DUBIOUS
DUBIOUSLY
DUBITABLE
DUBITABLY
DUBITANCY
DUBITATE
DUBITATED
DUBITATES
DUBNIUM
DUBNIUMS
DUBONNET
DUBONNETS
DUBS
DUBSTEP
DUBSTEPS
DUCAL
DUCALLY
DUCAT
DUCATOON
DUCATOONS
DUCATS
DUCDAME
DUCE
DUCES
DUCHESS
DUCHESSE
DUCHESSED
DUCHESSES
DUCHIES
DUCHY
DUCI
DUCK
DUCKBILL
DUCKBILLS
DUCKBOARD
DUCKED
DUCKER
DUCKERS
DUCKFOOT
DUCKIE
DUCKIER
DUCKIES
DUCKIEST
DUCKING
DUCKINGS
DUCKISH
DUCKISHES
DUCKLING
DUCKLINGS
DUCKMOLE
DUCKMOLES
DUCKPIN
DUCKPINS
DUCKS
DUCKSHOVE
DUCKTAIL
DUCKTAILS
DUCKWALK
DUCKWALKS
DUCKWEED
DUCKWEEDS
DUCKY
DUCT
DUCTAL
DUCTED
DUCTILE
DUCTILELY
DUCTILITY
DUCTING
DUCTINGS
DUCTLESS
DUCTS
DUCTULE
DUCTULES
DUCTWORK
DUCTWORKS
DUD
DUDDER
DUDDERED
DUDDERIES
DUDDERING
DUDDERS
DUDDERY
DUDDIE
DUDDIER
DUDDIES
DUDDIEST
DUDDY
DUDE
DUDED
DUDEEN
DUDEENS
DUDENESS
DUDES
DUDETTE
DUDETTES
DUDGEON
DUDGEONS
DUDHEEN
DUDHEENS
DUDING
DUDISH
DUDISHLY
DUDISM
DUDISMS
DUDS
DUE
DUECENTO
DUECENTOS
DUED
DUEFUL
DUEL
DUELED
DUELER
DUELERS
DUELING
DUELINGS
DUELIST
DUELISTS
DUELLED
DUELLER
DUELLERS
DUELLI
DUELLING
DUELLINGS
DUELLIST
DUELLISTS
DUELLO
DUELLOS
DUELS
DUELSOME
DUENDE
DUENDES
DUENESS
DUENESSES
DUENNA
DUENNAS
DUES
DUET
DUETED
DUETING
DUETS
DUETT
DUETTED
DUETTI
DUETTING
DUETTINO
DUETTINOS
DUETTIST
DUETTISTS
DUETTO
DUETTOS
DUETTS
DUFF
DUFFED
DUFFEL
DUFFELS
DUFFER
DUFFERDOM
DUFFERISM
DUFFERS
DUFFEST
DUFFING
DUFFINGS
DUFFLE
DUFFLES
DUFFS
DUFUS
DUFUSES
DUG
DUGITE
DUGITES
DUGONG
DUGONGS
DUGOUT
DUGOUTS
DUGS
DUH
DUHKHA
DUHKHAS
DUI
DUIKER
DUIKERBOK
DUIKERS
DUING
DUIT
DUITS
DUKA
DUKAS
DUKE
DUKED
DUKEDOM
DUKEDOMS
DUKELING
DUKELINGS
DUKERIES
DUKERY
DUKES
DUKESHIP

DUKESHIPS
DUKING
DUKKA
DUKKAH
DUKKAHS
DUKKAS
DUKKHA
DUKKHAS
DULCAMARA
DULCE
DULCES
DULCET
DULCETLY
DULCETS
DULCIAN
DULCIANA
DULCIANAS
DULCIANS
DULCIFIED
DULCIFIES
DULCIFY
DULCIMER
DULCIMERS
DULCIMORE
DULCINEA
DULCINEAS
DULCITE
DULCITES
DULCITOL
DULCITOLS
DULCITUDE
DULCOSE
DULCOSES
DULE
DULES
DULIA
DULIAS
DULL
DULLARD
DULLARDS
DULLED
DULLER
DULLEST
DULLIER
DULLIEST
DULLING
DULLISH
DULLISHLY
DULLNESS
DULLS
DULLY
DULNESS
DULNESSES
DULOCRACY
DULOSES
DULOSIS
DULOTIC
DULSE
DULSES
DULY
DUM
DUMA
DUMAIST
DUMAISTS
DUMAS
DUMB
DUMBBELL
DUMBBELLS
DUMBCANE
DUMBCANES
DUMBED
DUMBER
DUMBEST
DUMBFOUND
DUMBHEAD
DUMBHEADS
DUMBING
DUMBLY
DUMBNESS
DUMBO
DUMBOS
DUMBS
DUMBSHIT
DUMBSHITS
DUMBSHOW
DUMBSHOWS
DUMBSIZE
DUMBSIZED
DUMBSIZES
DUMDUM
DUMDUMS
DUMELA
DUMFOUND
DUMFOUNDS
DUMKA
DUMKAS
DUMKY
DUMMERER
DUMMERERS
DUMMIED
DUMMIER
DUMMIES
DUMMIEST
DUMMINESS
DUMMKOPF
DUMMKOPFS
DUMMY
DUMMYING
DUMOSE
DUMOSITY
DUMOUS
DUMP
DUMPBIN
DUMPBINS
DUMPCART
DUMPCARTS
DUMPED
DUMPEE
DUMPEES
DUMPER
DUMPERS
DUMPIER
DUMPIES
DUMPIEST
DUMPILY
DUMPINESS
DUMPING
DUMPINGS
DUMPISH
DUMPISHLY
DUMPLE
DUMPLED
DUMPLES
DUMPLING
DUMPLINGS
DUMPS
DUMPSITE
DUMPSITES
DUMPSTER
DUMPSTERS
DUMPTRUCK
DUMPY
DUN
DUNAM
DUNAMS
DUNCE
DUNCEDOM
DUNCEDOMS
DUNCELIKE
DUNCERIES
DUNCERY
DUNCES
DUNCH
DUNCHED
DUNCHES
DUNCHING
DUNCICAL
DUNCISH
DUNCISHLY
DUNDER
DUNDERS
DUNE
DUNELAND
DUNELANDS
DUNELIKE
DUNES
DUNG
DUNGAREE
DUNGAREED
DUNGAREES
DUNGED
DUNGEON
DUNGEONED
DUNGEONER
DUNGEONS
DUNGER
DUNGERS
DUNGHEAP
DUNGHEAPS
DUNGHILL
DUNGHILLS
DUNGIER
DUNGIEST
DUNGING
DUNGMERE
DUNGMERES
DUNGS
DUNGY
DUNITE
DUNITES
DUNITIC
DUNK
DUNKED
DUNKER
DUNKERS
DUNKING
DUNKINGS
DUNKS
DUNLIN
DUNLINS
DUNNAGE
DUNNAGES
DUNNAKIN
DUNNAKINS
DUNNART
DUNNARTS
DUNNED
DUNNER
DUNNESS
DUNNESSES
DUNNEST
DUNNIER
DUNNIES
DUNNIEST
DUNNING
DUNNINGS
DUNNISH
DUNNITE
DUNNITES
DUNNO
DUNNOCK
DUNNOCKS
DUNNY
DUNS
DUNSH
DUNSHED
DUNSHES
DUNSHING
DUNT
DUNTED
DUNTING
DUNTS
DUO
DUOBINARY
DUODECIMO
DUODENA
DUODENAL
DUODENARY
DUODENUM
DUODENUMS

DUOLOG
DUOLOGS
DUOLOGUE
DUOLOGUES
DUOMI
DUOMO
DUOMOS
DUOPOLIES
DUOPOLIST
DUOPOLY
DUOPSONY
DUOS
DUOTONE
DUOTONES
DUP
DUPABLE
DUPATTA
DUPATTAS
DUPE
DUPED
DUPER
DUPERIES
DUPERS
DUPERY
DUPES
DUPING
DUPINGS
DUPION
DUPIONS
DUPLE
DUPLET
DUPLETS
DUPLEX
DUPLEXED
DUPLEXER
DUPLEXERS
DUPLEXES
DUPLEXING
DUPLEXITY
DUPLICAND
DUPLICATE
DUPLICITY
DUPLIED
DUPLIES
DUPLY
DUPLYING
DUPONDII
DUPONDIUS
DUPPED
DUPPIES
DUPPING
DUPPY
DUPS
DURA
DURABLE
DURABLES
DURABLY
DURAL
DURALS
DURALUMIN
DURAMEN
DURAMENS
DURANCE
DURANCES
DURANT
DURANTS
DURAS
DURATION
DURATIONS
DURATIVE
DURATIVES
DURBAR
DURBARS
DURDUM
DURDUMS
DURE
DURED
DUREFUL
DURES
DURESS
DURESSE
DURESSES
DURGAH
DURGAHS
DURGAN
DURGANS
DURGIER
DURGIEST
DURGY
DURIAN
DURIANS
DURICRUST
DURING
DURION
DURIONS
DURMAST
DURMASTS
DURN
DURNDEST
DURNED
DURNEDER
DURNEDEST
DURNING
DURNS
DURO
DUROC
DUROCS
DUROMETER
DUROS
DUROY
DUROYS
DURR
DURRA
DURRAS
DURRIE
DURRIES
DURRS
DURRY
DURST
DURUKULI
DURUKULIS
DURUM
DURUMS
DURZI
DURZIS
DUSH
DUSHED
DUSHES
DUSHING
DUSK
DUSKED
DUSKEN
DUSKENED
DUSKENING
DUSKENS
DUSKER
DUSKEST
DUSKIER
DUSKIEST
DUSKILY
DUSKINESS
DUSKING
DUSKISH
DUSKISHLY
DUSKLY
DUSKNESS
DUSKS
DUSKY
DUST
DUSTBALL
DUSTBALLS
DUSTBIN
DUSTBINS
DUSTCART
DUSTCARTS
DUSTCLOTH
DUSTCOAT
DUSTCOATS
DUSTCOVER
DUSTED
DUSTER
DUSTERS
DUSTHEAP
DUSTHEAPS
DUSTIER
DUSTIEST
DUSTILY
DUSTINESS
DUSTING
DUSTINGS
DUSTLESS
DUSTLIKE
DUSTMAN
DUSTMEN
DUSTOFF
DUSTOFFS
DUSTPAN
DUSTPANS
DUSTPROOF
DUSTRAG
DUSTRAGS
DUSTS
DUSTSHEET
DUSTSTORM
DUSTUP
DUSTUPS
DUSTY
DUTCH
DUTCHES
DUTCHMAN
DUTCHMEN
DUTEOUS
DUTEOUSLY
DUTIABLE
DUTIED
DUTIES
DUTIFUL
DUTIFULLY
DUTY
DUUMVIR
DUUMVIRAL
DUUMVIRI
DUUMVIRS
DUVET
DUVETINE
DUVETINES
DUVETS
DUVETYN
DUVETYNE
DUVETYNES
DUVETYNS
DUX
DUXELLES
DUXES
DUYKER
DUYKERS
DVANDVA
DVANDVAS
DVORNIK
DVORNIKS
DWAAL
DWAALS
DWALE
DWALES
DWALM
DWALMED
DWALMING
DWALMS
DWAM
DWAMMED
DWAMMING
DWAMS
DWANG
DWANGS
DWARF
DWARFED
DWARFER
DWARFEST
DWARFING
DWARFISH

DWARFISM
DWARFISMS
DWARFLIKE
DWARFNESS
DWARFS
DWARVES
DWAUM
DWAUMED
DWAUMING
DWAUMS
DWEEB
DWEEBIER
DWEEBIEST
DWEEBISH
DWEEBS
DWEEBY
DWELL
DWELLED
DWELLER
DWELLERS
DWELLING
DWELLINGS
DWELLS
DWELT
DWILE
DWILES
DWINDLE
DWINDLED
DWINDLES
DWINDLING
DWINE
DWINED
DWINES
DWINING
DYABLE
DYAD
DYADIC
DYADICS
DYADS
DYARCHAL
DYARCHIC
DYARCHIES
DYARCHY
DYBBUK
DYBBUKIM
DYBBUKKIM
DYBBUKS
DYE
DYEABLE
DYED
DYEING
DYEINGS
DYELINE
DYELINES
DYER
DYERS
DYES
DYESTER
DYESTERS
DYESTUFF
DYESTUFFS
DYEWEED
DYEWEEDS
DYEWOOD
DYEWOODS
DYEWORKS
DYING
DYINGLY
DYINGNESS
DYINGS
DYKE
DYKED
DYKES
DYKEY
DYKIER
DYKIEST
DYKING
DYKON
DYKONS
DYNAMETER
DYNAMIC
DYNAMICAL
DYNAMICS
DYNAMISE
DYNAMISED
DYNAMISES
DYNAMISM
DYNAMISMS
DYNAMIST
DYNAMISTS
DYNAMITE
DYNAMITED
DYNAMITER
DYNAMITES
DYNAMITIC
DYNAMIZE
DYNAMIZED
DYNAMIZES
DYNAMO
DYNAMOS
DYNAMOTOR
DYNAST
DYNASTIC
DYNASTIES
DYNASTS
DYNASTY
DYNATRON
DYNATRONS
DYNE
DYNEIN
DYNEINS
DYNEL
DYNELS
DYNES
DYNODE
DYNODES
DYNORPHIN
DYSBINDIN
DYSCHROA
DYSCHROAS
DYSCHROIA
DYSCRASIA
DYSCRASIC
DYSCRATIC
DYSENTERY
DYSFLUENT
DYSGENIC
DYSGENICS
DYSLALIA
DYSLALIAS
DYSLECTIC
DYSLEXIA
DYSLEXIAS
DYSLEXIC
DYSLEXICS
DYSLOGIES
DYSLOGY
DYSMELIA
DYSMELIAS
DYSMELIC
DYSODIL
DYSODILE
DYSODILES
DYSODILS
DYSODYLE
DYSODYLES
DYSPATHY
DYSPEPSIA
DYSPEPSY
DYSPEPTIC
DYSPHAGIA
DYSPHAGIC
DYSPHAGY
DYSPHASIA
DYSPHASIC
DYSPHONIA
DYSPHONIC
DYSPHORIA
DYSPHORIC
DYSPLASIA
DYSPNEA
DYSPNEAL
DYSPNEAS
DYSPNEIC
DYSPNOEA
DYSPNOEAL
DYSPNOEAS
DYSPNOEIC
DYSPNOIC
DYSPRAXIA
DYSPRAXIC
DYSTAXIA
DYSTAXIAS
DYSTAXIC
DYSTECTIC
DYSTHESIA
DYSTHETIC
DYSTHYMIA
DYSTHYMIC
DYSTOCIA
DYSTOCIAL
DYSTOCIAS
DYSTONIA
DYSTONIAS
DYSTONIC
DYSTOPIA
DYSTOPIAN
DYSTOPIAS
DYSTROPHY
DYSURIA
DYSURIAS
DYSURIC
DYSURIES
DYSURY
DYTISCID
DYTISCIDS
DYVOUR
DYVOURIES
DYVOURS
DYVOURY
DZEREN
DZERENS
DZHO
DZHOS
DZIGGETAI
DZO
DZOS

E

EA
EACH
EACHWHERE
EADISH
EADISHES
EAGER
EAGERER
EAGEREST
EAGERLY
EAGERNESS
EAGERS
EAGLE
EAGLED
EAGLEHAWK
EAGLES
EAGLET
EAGLETS
EAGLEWOOD
EAGLING
EAGRE
EAGRES
EALDORMAN
EALDORMEN
EALE
EALED
EALES
EALING
EAN
EANED
EANING
EANLING
EANLINGS
EANS
EAR
EARACHE
EARACHES
EARBALL
EARBALLS
EARBASH
EARBASHED
EARBASHER
EARBASHES
EARBOB
EARBOBS
EARBUD
EARBUDS
EARCON
EARCONS
EARD
EARDED
EARDING
EARDROP
EARDROPS
EARDRUM
EARDRUMS
EARDS
EARED
EARFLAP
EARFLAPS
EARFUL
EARFULS
EARHOLE
EARHOLES
EARING
EARINGS
EARL
EARLAP
EARLAPS
EARLDOM
EARLDOMS
EARLESS
EARLIER
EARLIES
EARLIEST
EARLIKE
EARLINESS
EARLOBE
EARLOBES
EARLOCK
EARLOCKS
EARLS
EARLSHIP
EARLSHIPS
EARLY
EARLYWOOD
EARMARK
EARMARKED
EARMARKS
EARMUFF
EARMUFFS
EARN
EARNED
EARNER
EARNERS
EARNEST
EARNESTLY
EARNESTS
EARNING
EARNINGS
EARNS
EARNT
EARPHONE
EARPHONES
EARPICK
EARPICKS
EARPIECE
EARPIECES
EARPLUG
EARPLUGS
EARRING
EARRINGED
EARRINGS
EARS
EARSHOT
EARSHOTS
EARST
EARSTONE
EARSTONES
EARTH
EARTHBORN
EARTHED
EARTHEN
EARTHFALL
EARTHFAST
EARTHFLAX
EARTHIER
EARTHIEST
EARTHILY
EARTHING
EARTHLIER
EARTHLIES
EARTHLIKE
EARTHLING
EARTHLY
EARTHMAN
EARTHMEN
EARTHNUT
EARTHNUTS
EARTHPEA
EARTHPEAS
EARTHRISE
EARTHS
EARTHSET
EARTHSETS
EARTHSTAR
EARTHWARD
EARTHWAX
EARTHWOLF
EARTHWORK
EARTHWORM
EARTHY
EARWAX
EARWAXES
EARWIG
EARWIGGED
EARWIGGY
EARWIGS
EARWORM
EARWORMS
EAS
EASE
EASED
EASEFUL
EASEFULLY
EASEL
EASELED
EASELESS
EASELS
EASEMENT
EASEMENTS
EASER
EASERS
EASES
EASIED
EASIER
EASIES
EASIEST
EASILY
EASINESS
EASING
EASINGS
EASLE
EASLES
EASSEL
EASSIL
EAST
EASTABOUT
EASTBOUND
EASTED
EASTER
EASTERLY
EASTERN
EASTERNER
EASTERS
EASTING
EASTINGS
EASTLAND
EASTLANDS
EASTLIN
EASTLING
EASTLINGS
EASTLINS
EASTMOST
EASTS
EASTWARD
EASTWARDS
EASY
EASYGOING
EASYING
EAT

EATABLE
EATABLES
EATAGE
EATAGES
EATCHE
EATCHES
EATEN
EATER
EATERIE
EATERIES
EATERS
EATERY
EATH
EATHE
EATHLY
EATING
EATINGS
EATS
EAU
EAUS
EAUX
EAVE
EAVED
EAVES
EAVESDRIP
EAVESDROP
EAVING
EBAUCHE
EBAUCHES
EBAYER
EBAYERS
EBAYING
EBAYINGS
EBB
EBBED
EBBET
EBBETS
EBBING
EBBLESS
EBBS
EBENEZER
EBENEZERS
EBENISTE
EBENISTES
EBIONISE
EBIONISED
EBIONISES
EBIONISM
EBIONISMS
EBIONITIC
EBIONIZE
EBIONIZED
EBIONIZES
EBON
EBONICS
EBONIES
EBONISE
EBONISED
EBONISES
EBONISING
EBONIST
EBONISTS
EBONITE
EBONITES
EBONIZE
EBONIZED
EBONIZES
EBONIZING
EBONS
EBONY
EBOOK
EBOOKS
EBRIATE
EBRIATED
EBRIETIES
EBRIETY
EBRILLADE
EBRIOSE
EBRIOSITY
EBULLIENT
EBURNEAN
EBURNEOUS
ECAD
ECADS
ECARINATE
ECARTE
ECARTES
ECAUDATE
ECBOLE
ECBOLES
ECBOLIC
ECBOLICS
ECCE
ECCENTRIC
ECCLESIA
ECCLESIAE
ECCLESIAL
ECCO
ECCRINE
ECCRISES
ECCRISIS
ECCRITIC
ECCRITICS
ECDEMIC
ECDYSES
ECDYSIAL
ECDYSIAST
ECDYSIS
ECDYSISES
ECDYSON
ECDYSONE
ECDYSONES
ECDYSONS
ECESIC
ECESIS
ECESISES
ECH
ECHAPPE
ECHAPPES
ECHARD
ECHARDS
ECHE
ECHED
ECHELLE
ECHELLES
ECHELON
ECHELONED
ECHELONS
ECHES
ECHEVERIA
ECHIDNA
ECHIDNAE
ECHIDNAS
ECHIDNINE
ECHINACEA
ECHINATE
ECHINATED
ECHING
ECHINI
ECHINOID
ECHINOIDS
ECHINUS
ECHINUSES
ECHIUM
ECHIUMS
ECHIURAN
ECHIURANS
ECHIUROID
ECHO
ECHOED
ECHOER
ECHOERS
ECHOES
ECHOEY
ECHOGRAM
ECHOGRAMS
ECHOGRAPH
ECHOIC
ECHOIER
ECHOIEST
ECHOING
ECHOISE
ECHOISED
ECHOISES
ECHOISING
ECHOISM
ECHOISMS
ECHOIST
ECHOISTS
ECHOIZE
ECHOIZED
ECHOIZES
ECHOIZING
ECHOLALIA
ECHOLALIC
ECHOLESS
ECHOS
ECHOVIRUS
ECHT
ECLAIR
ECLAIRS
ECLAMPSIA
ECLAMPSY
ECLAMPTIC
ECLAT
ECLATS
ECLECTIC
ECLECTICS
ECLIPSE
ECLIPSED
ECLIPSER
ECLIPSERS
ECLIPSES
ECLIPSING
ECLIPSIS
ECLIPTIC
ECLIPTICS
ECLOGITE
ECLOGITES
ECLOGUE
ECLOGUES
ECLOSE
ECLOSED
ECLOSES
ECLOSING
ECLOSION
ECLOSIONS
ECO
ECOCIDAL
ECOCIDE
ECOCIDES
ECOD
ECOFREAK
ECOFREAKS
ECOGIFT
ECOGIFTS
ECOLODGE
ECOLODGES
ECOLOGIC
ECOLOGIES
ECOLOGIST
ECOLOGY
ECOMAP
ECOMAPS
ECOMMERCE
ECOMUSEUM
ECONOBOX
ECONOMIC
ECONOMICS
ECONOMIES
ECONOMISE
ECONOMISM
ECONOMIST
ECONOMIZE
ECONOMY
ECONUT
ECONUTS
ECOPHOBIA
ECORCHE
ECORCHES

E

ECOREGION
ECOS
ECOSPHERE
ECOSSAISE
ECOSTATE
ECOSYSTEM
ECOTAGE
ECOTAGES
ECOTARIAN
ECOTONAL
ECOTONE
ECOTONES
ECOTOPIA
ECOTOPIAS
ECOTOUR
ECOTOURED
ECOTOURS
ECOTOXIC
ECOTYPE
ECOTYPES
ECOTYPIC
ECOZONE
ECOZONES
ECPHRASES
ECPHRASIS
ECRASEUR
ECRASEURS
ECRITOIRE
ECRU
ECRUS
ECSTASES
ECSTASIED
ECSTASIES
ECSTASIS
ECSTASISE
ECSTASIZE
ECSTASY
ECSTATIC
ECSTATICS
ECTASES
ECTASIA
ECTASIAS
ECTASIS
ECTATIC
ECTHYMA
ECTHYMAS
ECTHYMATA
ECTOBLAST
ECTOCRINE
ECTODERM
ECTODERMS
ECTOGENE
ECTOGENES
ECTOGENIC
ECTOGENY
ECTOMERE
ECTOMERES
ECTOMERIC
ECTOMORPH
ECTOPHYTE
ECTOPIA
ECTOPIAS
ECTOPIC
ECTOPIES
ECTOPLASM
ECTOPROCT
ECTOPY
ECTOSARC
ECTOSARCS
ECTOTHERM
ECTOZOA
ECTOZOAN
ECTOZOANS
ECTOZOIC
ECTOZOON
ECTROPIC
ECTROPION
ECTROPIUM
ECTYPAL
ECTYPE
ECTYPES
ECU
ECUELLE
ECUELLES
ECUMENE
ECUMENES
ECUMENIC
ECUMENICS
ECUMENISM
ECUMENIST
ECURIE
ECURIES
ECUS
ECZEMA
ECZEMAS
ED
EDACIOUS
EDACITIES
EDACITY
EDAMAME
EDAMAMES
EDAPHIC
EDDIED
EDDIES
EDDISH
EDDISHES
EDDO
EDDOES
EDDY
EDDYING
EDELWEISS
EDEMA
EDEMAS
EDEMATA
EDEMATOSE
EDEMATOUS
EDENIC
EDENTAL
EDENTATE
EDENTATES
EDGE
EDGEBONE
EDGEBONES
EDGED
EDGELESS
EDGER
EDGERS
EDGES
EDGEWAYS
EDGEWISE
EDGIER
EDGIEST
EDGILY
EDGINESS
EDGING
EDGINGS
EDGY
EDH
EDHS
EDIBILITY
EDIBLE
EDIBLES
EDICT
EDICTAL
EDICTALLY
EDICTS
EDIFICE
EDIFICES
EDIFICIAL
EDIFIED
EDIFIER
EDIFIERS
EDIFIES
EDIFY
EDIFYING
EDILE
EDILES
EDIT
EDITABLE
EDITED
EDITING
EDITINGS
EDITION
EDITIONED
EDITIONS
EDITOR
EDITORIAL
EDITORS
EDITRESS
EDITRICES
EDITRIX
EDITRIXES
EDITS
EDS
EDUCABLE
EDUCABLES
EDUCATE
EDUCATED
EDUCATES
EDUCATING
EDUCATION
EDUCATIVE
EDUCATOR
EDUCATORS
EDUCATORY
EDUCE
EDUCED
EDUCEMENT
EDUCES
EDUCIBLE
EDUCING
EDUCT
EDUCTION
EDUCTIONS
EDUCTIVE
EDUCTOR
EDUCTORS
EDUCTS
EE
EECH
EECHED
EECHES
EECHING
EEEW
EEJIT
EEJITS
EEK
EEL
EELFARE
EELFARES
EELGRASS
EELIER
EELIEST
EELING
EELINGS
EELLIKE
EELPOUT
EELPOUTS
EELS
EELWORM
EELWORMS
EELWRACK
EELWRACKS
EELY
EEN
EENSIER
EENSIEST
EENSY
EERIE
EERIER
EERIEST
EERILY
EERINESS
EERY
EEVEN
EEVENS
EEVN
EEVNING
EEVNINGS
EEVNS

EEW
EF
EFF
EFFABLE
EFFACE
EFFACED
EFFACER
EFFACERS
EFFACES
EFFACING
EFFECT
EFFECTED
EFFECTER
EFFECTERS
EFFECTING
EFFECTIVE
EFFECTOR
EFFECTORS
EFFECTS
EFFECTUAL
EFFED
EFFEIR
EFFEIRED
EFFEIRING
EFFEIRS
EFFENDI
EFFENDIS
EFFERE
EFFERED
EFFERENCE
EFFERENT
EFFERENTS
EFFERES
EFFERING
EFFETE
EFFETELY
EFFICACY
EFFICIENT
EFFIERCE
EFFIERCED
EFFIERCES
EFFIGIAL
EFFIGIES
EFFIGY
EFFING
EFFINGS
EFFLUENCE
EFFLUENT
EFFLUENTS
EFFLUVIA
EFFLUVIAL
EFFLUVIUM
EFFLUX
EFFLUXES
EFFLUXION
EFFORCE
EFFORCED
EFFORCES
EFFORCING
EFFORT
EFFORTFUL
EFFORTS
EFFRAIDE
EFFRAY
EFFRAYS
EFFS
EFFULGE
EFFULGED
EFFULGENT
EFFULGES
EFFULGING
EFFUSE
EFFUSED
EFFUSES
EFFUSING
EFFUSION
EFFUSIONS
EFFUSIVE
EFS
EFT
EFTEST
EFTS
EFTSOON
EFTSOONS
EGAD
EGADS
EGAL
EGALITE
EGALITES
EGALITIES
EGALITY
EGALLY
EGAREMENT
EGENCE
EGENCES
EGENCIES
EGENCY
EGER
EGERS
EGEST
EGESTA
EGESTED
EGESTING
EGESTION
EGESTIONS
EGESTIVE
EGESTS
EGG
EGGAR
EGGARS
EGGBEATER
EGGCORN
EGGCORNS
EGGCUP
EGGCUPS
EGGED
EGGER
EGGERIES
EGGERS
EGGERY
EGGFRUIT
EGGFRUITS
EGGHEAD
EGGHEADED
EGGHEADS
EGGIER
EGGIEST
EGGING
EGGLER
EGGLERS
EGGLESS
EGGLIKE
EGGMASS
EGGMASSES
EGGNOG
EGGNOGS
EGGPLANT
EGGPLANTS
EGGS
EGGSHELL
EGGSHELLS
EGGWASH
EGGWASHES
EGGWHISK
EGGWHISKS
EGGY
EGIS
EGISES
EGLANTINE
EGLATERE
EGLATERES
EGLOMISE
EGLOMISES
EGMA
EGMAS
EGO
EGOISM
EGOISMS
EGOIST
EGOISTIC
EGOISTS
EGOITIES
EGOITY
EGOLESS
EGOMANIA
EGOMANIAC
EGOMANIAS
EGOS
EGOSURF
EGOSURFED
EGOSURFS
EGOTHEISM
EGOTISE
EGOTISED
EGOTISES
EGOTISING
EGOTISM
EGOTISMS
EGOTIST
EGOTISTIC
EGOTISTS
EGOTIZE
EGOTIZED
EGOTIZES
EGOTIZING
EGREGIOUS
EGRESS
EGRESSED
EGRESSES
EGRESSING
EGRESSION
EGRESSIVE
EGRET
EGRETS
EGYPTIAN
EGYPTIANS
EH
EHED
EHING
EHS
EIDE
EIDENT
EIDER
EIDERDOWN
EIDERS
EIDETIC
EIDETICS
EIDOGRAPH
EIDOLA
EIDOLIC
EIDOLON
EIDOLONS
EIDOS
EIGENMODE
EIGENTONE
EIGHT
EIGHTBALL
EIGHTEEN
EIGHTEENS
EIGHTFOIL
EIGHTFOLD
EIGHTFOOT
EIGHTH
EIGHTHLY
EIGHTHS
EIGHTIES
EIGHTIETH
EIGHTS
EIGHTSMAN
EIGHTSMEN
EIGHTSOME
EIGHTVO
EIGHTVOS
EIGHTY
EIGNE
EIK
EIKED
EIKING
EIKON
EIKONES

EIKONS
EIKS
EILD
EILDING
EILDINGS
EILDS
EINA
EINE
EINKORN
EINKORNS
EINSTEIN
EINSTEINS
EIRACK
EIRACKS
EIRENIC
EIRENICAL
EIRENICON
EIRENICS
EISEGESES
EISEGESIS
EISEL
EISELL
EISELLS
EISELS
EISH
EISWEIN
EISWEINS
EITHER
EJACULATE
EJECT
EJECTA
EJECTABLE
EJECTED
EJECTING
EJECTION
EJECTIONS
EJECTIVE
EJECTIVES
EJECTMENT
EJECTOR
EJECTORS
EJECTS
EJIDO
EJIDOS
EKE
EKED
EKES
EKING
EKISTIC
EKISTICAL
EKISTICS
EKKA
EKKAS
EKLOGITE
EKLOGITES
EKPHRASES
EKPHRASIS
EKPWELE
EKPWELES
EKTEXINE
EKTEXINES
EKUELE
EL
ELABORATE
ELAEAGNUS
ELAEOLITE
ELAIN
ELAINS
ELAIOSOME
ELAN
ELANCE
ELANCED
ELANCES
ELANCING
ELAND
ELANDS
ELANET
ELANETS
ELANS
ELAPHINE
ELAPID
ELAPIDS
ELAPINE
ELAPSE
ELAPSED
ELAPSES
ELAPSING
ELASTANCE
ELASTANE
ELASTANES
ELASTASE
ELASTASES
ELASTIC
ELASTICS
ELASTIN
ELASTINS
ELASTOMER
ELATE
ELATED
ELATEDLY
ELATER
ELATERID
ELATERIDS
ELATERIN
ELATERINS
ELATERITE
ELATERIUM
ELATERS
ELATES
ELATING
ELATION
ELATIONS
ELATIVE
ELATIVES
ELBOW
ELBOWED
ELBOWING
ELBOWINGS
ELBOWROOM
ELBOWS
ELCHEE
ELCHEES
ELCHI
ELCHIS
ELD
ELDER
ELDERCARE
ELDERLIES
ELDERLY
ELDERS
ELDERSHIP
ELDEST
ELDESTS
ELDIN
ELDING
ELDINGS
ELDINS
ELDORADO
ELDORADOS
ELDRESS
ELDRESSES
ELDRICH
ELDRITCH
ELDS
ELECT
ELECTABLE
ELECTED
ELECTEE
ELECTEES
ELECTING
ELECTION
ELECTIONS
ELECTIVE
ELECTIVES
ELECTOR
ELECTORAL
ELECTORS
ELECTRESS
ELECTRET
ELECTRETS
ELECTRIC
ELECTRICS
ELECTRIFY
ELECTRISE
ELECTRIZE
ELECTRO
ELECTRODE
ELECTROED
ELECTRON
ELECTRONS
ELECTROS
ELECTRUM
ELECTRUMS
ELECTS
ELECTUARY
ELEDOISIN
ELEGANCE
ELEGANCES
ELEGANCY
ELEGANT
ELEGANTLY
ELEGIAC
ELEGIACAL
ELEGIACS
ELEGIAST
ELEGIASTS
ELEGIES
ELEGISE
ELEGISED
ELEGISES
ELEGISING
ELEGIST
ELEGISTS
ELEGIT
ELEGITS
ELEGIZE
ELEGIZED
ELEGIZES
ELEGIZING
ELEGY
ELEMENT
ELEMENTAL
ELEMENTS
ELEMI
ELEMIS
ELENCH
ELENCHI
ELENCHIC
ELENCHS
ELENCHTIC
ELENCHUS
ELENCTIC
ELEOPTENE
ELEPHANT
ELEPHANTS
ELEPIDOTE
ELEUTHERI
ELEVATE
ELEVATED
ELEVATEDS
ELEVATES
ELEVATING
ELEVATION
ELEVATOR
ELEVATORS
ELEVATORY
ELEVEN
ELEVENS
ELEVENSES
ELEVENTH
ELEVENTHS
ELEVON
ELEVONS
ELF
ELFED
ELFHOOD
ELFHOODS
ELFIN
ELFING
ELFINS

ELFISH
ELFISHES
ELFISHLY
ELFLAND
ELFLANDS
ELFLIKE
ELFLOCK
ELFLOCKS
ELFS
ELHI
ELIAD
ELIADS
ELICHE
ELICHES
ELICIT
ELICITED
ELICITING
ELICITOR
ELICITORS
ELICITS
ELIDE
ELIDED
ELIDES
ELIDIBLE
ELIDING
ELIGIBLE
ELIGIBLES
ELIGIBLY
ELIMINANT
ELIMINATE
ELINT
ELINTS
ELISION
ELISIONS
ELITE
ELITES
ELITISM
ELITISMS
ELITIST
ELITISTS
ELIXIR
ELIXIRS
ELK
ELKHORN
ELKHOUND
ELKHOUNDS
ELKS
ELL
ELLAGIC
ELLIPSE
ELLIPSES
ELLIPSIS
ELLIPSOID
ELLIPTIC
ELLOPS
ELLOPSES
ELLS
ELLWAND
ELLWANDS
ELM
ELMEN
ELMIER
ELMIEST
ELMS
ELMWOOD
ELMWOODS
ELMY
ELOCUTE
ELOCUTED
ELOCUTES
ELOCUTING
ELOCUTION
ELOCUTORY
ELODEA
ELODEAS
ELOGE
ELOGES
ELOGIES
ELOGIST
ELOGISTS
ELOGIUM
ELOGIUMS
ELOGY
ELOIGN
ELOIGNED
ELOIGNER
ELOIGNERS
ELOIGNING
ELOIGNS
ELOIN
ELOINED
ELOINER
ELOINERS
ELOINING
ELOINMENT
ELOINS
ELONGATE
ELONGATED
ELONGATES
ELOPE
ELOPED
ELOPEMENT
ELOPER
ELOPERS
ELOPES
ELOPING
ELOPS
ELOPSES
ELOQUENCE
ELOQUENT
ELPEE
ELPEES
ELS
ELSE
ELSEWHERE
ELSEWISE
ELSHIN
ELSHINS
ELSIN
ELSINS
ELT
ELTCHI
ELTCHIS
ELTS
ELUANT
ELUANTS
ELUATE
ELUATES
ELUCIDATE
ELUDE
ELUDED
ELUDER
ELUDERS
ELUDES
ELUDIBLE
ELUDING
ELUENT
ELUENTS
ELUSION
ELUSIONS
ELUSIVE
ELUSIVELY
ELUSORY
ELUTE
ELUTED
ELUTES
ELUTING
ELUTION
ELUTIONS
ELUTOR
ELUTORS
ELUTRIATE
ELUVIA
ELUVIAL
ELUVIATE
ELUVIATED
ELUVIATES
ELUVIUM
ELUVIUMS
ELVAN
ELVANITE
ELVANITES
ELVANS
ELVEN
ELVER
ELVERS
ELVES
ELVISH
ELVISHES
ELVISHLY
ELYSIAN
ELYTRA
ELYTRAL
ELYTROID
ELYTRON
ELYTROUS
ELYTRUM
EM
EMACIATE
EMACIATED
EMACIATES
EMACS
EMACSEN
EMAIL
EMAILABLE
EMAILED
EMAILER
EMAILERS
EMAILING
EMAILINGS
EMAILS
EMANANT
EMANATE
EMANATED
EMANATES
EMANATING
EMANATION
EMANATIST
EMANATIVE
EMANATOR
EMANATORS
EMANATORY
EMBACE
EMBACES
EMBACING
EMBAIL
EMBAILED
EMBAILING
EMBAILS
EMBALE
EMBALED
EMBALES
EMBALING
EMBALL
EMBALLED
EMBALLING
EMBALLS
EMBALM
EMBALMED
EMBALMER
EMBALMERS
EMBALMING
EMBALMS
EMBANK
EMBANKED
EMBANKER
EMBANKERS
EMBANKING
EMBANKS
EMBAR
EMBARGO
EMBARGOED
EMBARGOES
EMBARK
EMBARKED
EMBARKING
EMBARKS
EMBARRAS
EMBARRASS
EMBARRED

E

EMBARRING
EMBARS
EMBASE
EMBASED
EMBASES
EMBASING
EMBASSADE
EMBASSAGE
EMBASSIES
EMBASSY
EMBASTE
EMBATHE
EMBATHED
EMBATHES
EMBATHING
EMBATTLE
EMBATTLED
EMBATTLES
EMBAY
EMBAYED
EMBAYING
EMBAYLD
EMBAYMENT
EMBAYS
EMBED
EMBEDDED
EMBEDDING
EMBEDMENT
EMBEDS
EMBELLISH
EMBER
EMBERS
EMBEZZLE
EMBEZZLED
EMBEZZLER
EMBEZZLES
EMBIGGEN
EMBIGGENS
EMBITTER
EMBITTERS
EMBLAZE
EMBLAZED
EMBLAZER
EMBLAZERS
EMBLAZES
EMBLAZING
EMBLAZON
EMBLAZONS
EMBLEM
EMBLEMA
EMBLEMATA
EMBLEMED
EMBLEMING
EMBLEMISE
EMBLEMIZE
EMBLEMS
EMBLIC
EMBLICS
EMBLOOM
EMBLOOMED
EMBLOOMS
EMBLOSSOM
EMBODIED
EMBODIER
EMBODIERS
EMBODIES
EMBODY
EMBODYING
EMBOG
EMBOGGED
EMBOGGING
EMBOGS
EMBOGUE
EMBOGUED
EMBOGUES
EMBOGUING
EMBOIL
EMBOILED
EMBOILING
EMBOILS
EMBOLDEN
EMBOLDENS
EMBOLI
EMBOLIC
EMBOLIES
EMBOLISE
EMBOLISED
EMBOLISES
EMBOLISM
EMBOLISMS
EMBOLIZE
EMBOLIZED
EMBOLIZES
EMBOLUS
EMBOLUSES
EMBOLY
EMBORDER
EMBORDERS
EMBOSCATA
EMBOSK
EMBOSKED
EMBOSKING
EMBOSKS
EMBOSOM
EMBOSOMED
EMBOSOMS
EMBOSS
EMBOSSED
EMBOSSER
EMBOSSERS
EMBOSSES
EMBOSSING
EMBOST
EMBOUND
EMBOUNDED
EMBOUNDS
EMBOW
EMBOWED
EMBOWEL
EMBOWELED
EMBOWELS
EMBOWER
EMBOWERED
EMBOWERS
EMBOWING
EMBOWMENT
EMBOWS
EMBOX
EMBOXED
EMBOXES
EMBOXING
EMBRACE
EMBRACED
EMBRACEOR
EMBRACER
EMBRACERS
EMBRACERY
EMBRACES
EMBRACING
EMBRACIVE
EMBRAID
EMBRAIDED
EMBRAIDS
EMBRANGLE
EMBRASOR
EMBRASORS
EMBRASURE
EMBRAVE
EMBRAVED
EMBRAVES
EMBRAVING
EMBRAZURE
EMBREAD
EMBREADED
EMBREADS
EMBREATHE
EMBRITTLE
EMBROCATE
EMBROGLIO
EMBROIDER
EMBROIL
EMBROILED
EMBROILER
EMBROILS
EMBROWN
EMBROWNED
EMBROWNS
EMBRUE
EMBRUED
EMBRUES
EMBRUING
EMBRUTE
EMBRUTED
EMBRUTES
EMBRUTING
EMBRYO
EMBRYOID
EMBRYOIDS
EMBRYON
EMBRYONAL
EMBRYONIC
EMBRYONS
EMBRYOS
EMBRYOTIC
EMBUS
EMBUSED
EMBUSES
EMBUSIED
EMBUSIES
EMBUSING
EMBUSQUE
EMBUSQUES
EMBUSSED
EMBUSSES
EMBUSSING
EMBUSY
EMBUSYING
EMCEE
EMCEED
EMCEEING
EMCEES
EMDASH
EMDASHES
EME
EMEER
EMEERATE
EMEERATES
EMEERS
EMEND
EMENDABLE
EMENDALS
EMENDATE
EMENDATED
EMENDATES
EMENDATOR
EMENDED
EMENDER
EMENDERS
EMENDING
EMENDS
EMERALD
EMERALDS
EMERAUDE
EMERAUDES
EMERG
EMERGE
EMERGED
EMERGENCE
EMERGENCY
EMERGENT
EMERGENTS
EMERGES
EMERGING
EMERGS
EMERIED
EMERIES
EMERITA
EMERITAE
EMERITAS
EMERITI

EMERITUS
EMEROD
EMERODS
EMEROID
EMEROIDS
EMERSE
EMERSED
EMERSION
EMERSIONS
EMERY
EMERYING
EMES
EMESES
EMESIS
EMESISES
EMETIC
EMETICAL
EMETICS
EMETIN
EMETINE
EMETINES
EMETINS
EMEU
EMEUS
EMEUTE
EMEUTES
EMIC
EMICANT
EMICATE
EMICATED
EMICATES
EMICATING
EMICATION
EMICS
EMICTION
EMICTIONS
EMICTORY
EMIGRANT
EMIGRANTS
EMIGRATE
EMIGRATED
EMIGRATES
EMIGRE
EMIGREE
EMIGREES
EMIGRES
EMINENCE
EMINENCES
EMINENCY
EMINENT
EMINENTLY
EMIR
EMIRATE
EMIRATES
EMIRS
EMISSARY
EMISSILE
EMISSION
EMISSIONS
EMISSIVE
EMIT
EMITS
EMITTANCE
EMITTED
EMITTER
EMITTERS
EMITTING
EMLETS
EMMA
EMMARBLE
EMMARBLED
EMMARBLES
EMMAS
EMMER
EMMERS
EMMESH
EMMESHED
EMMESHES
EMMESHING
EMMET
EMMETROPE
EMMETS
EMMEW
EMMEWED
EMMEWING
EMMEWS
EMMOVE
EMMOVED
EMMOVES
EMMOVING
EMMY
EMMYS
EMO
EMOCORE
EMOCORES
EMODIN
EMODINS
EMOJI
EMOJIS
EMOLLIATE
EMOLLIENT
EMOLUMENT
EMONG
EMONGES
EMONGEST
EMONGST
EMOS
EMOTE
EMOTED
EMOTER
EMOTERS
EMOTES
EMOTICON
EMOTICONS
EMOTING
EMOTION
EMOTIONAL
EMOTIONS
EMOTIVE
EMOTIVELY
EMOTIVISM
EMOTIVITY
EMOVE
EMOVED
EMOVES
EMOVING
EMPACKET
EMPACKETS
EMPAESTIC
EMPAIRE
EMPAIRED
EMPAIRES
EMPAIRING
EMPALE
EMPALED
EMPALER
EMPALERS
EMPALES
EMPALING
EMPANADA
EMPANADAS
EMPANEL
EMPANELED
EMPANELS
EMPANOPLY
EMPARE
EMPARED
EMPARES
EMPARING
EMPARL
EMPARLED
EMPARLING
EMPARLS
EMPART
EMPARTED
EMPARTING
EMPARTS
EMPATHIC
EMPATHIES
EMPATHISE
EMPATHIST
EMPATHIZE
EMPATHY
EMPATRON
EMPATRONS
EMPAYRE
EMPAYRED
EMPAYRES
EMPAYRING
EMPEACH
EMPEACHED
EMPEACHES
EMPENNAGE
EMPEOPLE
EMPEOPLED
EMPEOPLES
EMPERCE
EMPERCED
EMPERCES
EMPERCING
EMPERIES
EMPERISE
EMPERISED
EMPERISES
EMPERISH
EMPERIZE
EMPERIZED
EMPERIZES
EMPEROR
EMPERORS
EMPERY
EMPHASES
EMPHASIS
EMPHASISE
EMPHASIZE
EMPHATIC
EMPHATICS
EMPHLYSES
EMPHLYSIS
EMPHYSEMA
EMPIERCE
EMPIERCED
EMPIERCES
EMPIGHT
EMPIGHTED
EMPIGHTS
EMPIRE
EMPIRES
EMPIRIC
EMPIRICAL
EMPIRICS
EMPLACE
EMPLACED
EMPLACES
EMPLACING
EMPLANE
EMPLANED
EMPLANES
EMPLANING
EMPLASTER
EMPLASTIC
EMPLASTRA
EMPLEACH
EMPLECTON
EMPLECTUM
EMPLONGE
EMPLONGED
EMPLONGES
EMPLOY
EMPLOYE
EMPLOYED
EMPLOYEE
EMPLOYEES
EMPLOYER
EMPLOYERS
EMPLOYES
EMPLOYING
EMPLOYS
EMPLUME
EMPLUMED

EMPLUMES
EMPLUMING
EMPOISON
EMPOISONS
EMPOLDER
EMPOLDERS
EMPORIA
EMPORIUM
EMPORIUMS
EMPOWER
EMPOWERED
EMPOWERS
EMPRESS
EMPRESSE
EMPRESSES
EMPRISE
EMPRISES
EMPRIZE
EMPRIZES
EMPT
EMPTED
EMPTIABLE
EMPTIED
EMPTIER
EMPTIERS
EMPTIES
EMPTIEST
EMPTILY
EMPTINESS
EMPTING
EMPTINGS
EMPTINS
EMPTION
EMPTIONAL
EMPTIONS
EMPTS
EMPTY
EMPTYING
EMPTYINGS
EMPTYSES
EMPTYSIS
EMPURPLE
EMPURPLED
EMPURPLES
EMPUSA
EMPUSAS
EMPUSE
EMPUSES
EMPYEMA
EMPYEMAS
EMPYEMATA
EMPYEMIC
EMPYESES
EMPYESIS
EMPYREAL
EMPYREAN
EMPYREANS
EMPYREUMA
EMS
EMU
EMULATE
EMULATED
EMULATES
EMULATING
EMULATION
EMULATIVE
EMULATOR
EMULATORS
EMULE
EMULED
EMULES
EMULGE
EMULGED
EMULGENCE
EMULGENT
EMULGES
EMULGING
EMULING
EMULOUS
EMULOUSLY
EMULSIBLE
EMULSIFY
EMULSIN
EMULSINS
EMULSION
EMULSIONS
EMULSIVE
EMULSOID
EMULSOIDS
EMULSOR
EMULSORS
EMUNCTION
EMUNCTORY
EMUNGE
EMUNGED
EMUNGES
EMUNGING
EMURE
EMURED
EMURES
EMURING
EMUS
EMYD
EMYDE
EMYDES
EMYDS
EMYS
EN
ENABLE
ENABLED
ENABLER
ENABLERS
ENABLES
ENABLING
ENACT
ENACTABLE
ENACTED
ENACTING
ENACTION
ENACTIONS
ENACTIVE
ENACTMENT
ENACTOR
ENACTORS
ENACTORY
ENACTS
ENACTURE
ENACTURES
ENALAPRIL
ENALLAGE
ENALLAGES
ENAMEL
ENAMELED
ENAMELER
ENAMELERS
ENAMELING
ENAMELIST
ENAMELLED
ENAMELLER
ENAMELS
ENAMINE
ENAMINES
ENAMOR
ENAMORADO
ENAMORED
ENAMORING
ENAMORS
ENAMOUR
ENAMOURED
ENAMOURS
ENANTHEMA
ENARCH
ENARCHED
ENARCHES
ENARCHING
ENARGITE
ENARGITES
ENARM
ENARMED
ENARMING
ENARMS
ENATE
ENATES
ENATIC
ENATION
ENATIONS
ENAUNTER
ENCAENIA
ENCAENIAS
ENCAGE
ENCAGED
ENCAGES
ENCAGING
ENCALM
ENCALMED
ENCALMING
ENCALMS
ENCAMP
ENCAMPED
ENCAMPING
ENCAMPS
ENCANTHIS
ENCAPSULE
ENCARPUS
ENCASE
ENCASED
ENCASES
ENCASH
ENCASHED
ENCASHES
ENCASHING
ENCASING
ENCASTRE
ENCAUSTIC
ENCAVE
ENCAVED
ENCAVES
ENCAVING
ENCEINTE
ENCEINTES
ENCEPHALA
ENCHAFE
ENCHAFED
ENCHAFES
ENCHAFING
ENCHAIN
ENCHAINED
ENCHAINS
ENCHANT
ENCHANTED
ENCHANTER
ENCHANTS
ENCHARGE
ENCHARGED
ENCHARGES
ENCHARM
ENCHARMED
ENCHARMS
ENCHASE
ENCHASED
ENCHASER
ENCHASERS
ENCHASES
ENCHASING
ENCHEASON
ENCHEER
ENCHEERED
ENCHEERS
ENCHILADA
ENCHORIAL
ENCHORIC
ENCIERRO
ENCIERROS
ENCINA
ENCINAL
ENCINAS
ENCIPHER
ENCIPHERS
ENCIRCLE
ENCIRCLED

ENCIRCLES
ENCLASP
ENCLASPED
ENCLASPS
ENCLAVE
ENCLAVED
ENCLAVES
ENCLAVING
ENCLISES
ENCLISIS
ENCLITIC
ENCLITICS
ENCLOSE
ENCLOSED
ENCLOSER
ENCLOSERS
ENCLOSES
ENCLOSING
ENCLOSURE
ENCLOTHE
ENCLOTHED
ENCLOTHES
ENCLOUD
ENCLOUDED
ENCLOUDS
ENCODABLE
ENCODE
ENCODED
ENCODER
ENCODERS
ENCODES
ENCODING
ENCODINGS
ENCOLOUR
ENCOLOURS
ENCOLPIA
ENCOLPION
ENCOLPIUM
ENCOLURE
ENCOLURES
ENCOMIA
ENCOMIAST
ENCOMION
ENCOMIUM
ENCOMIUMS
ENCOMPASS
ENCORE
ENCORED
ENCORES
ENCORING
ENCOUNTER
ENCOURAGE
ENCRADLE
ENCRADLED
ENCRADLES
ENCRATIES
ENCRATY
ENCREASE
ENCREASED
ENCREASES
ENCRIMSON
ENCRINAL
ENCRINIC
ENCRINITE
ENCROACH
ENCRUST
ENCRUSTED
ENCRUSTS
ENCRYPT
ENCRYPTED
ENCRYPTS
ENCUMBER
ENCUMBERS
ENCURTAIN
ENCYCLIC
ENCYCLICS
ENCYST
ENCYSTED
ENCYSTING
ENCYSTS
END
ENDAMAGE
ENDAMAGED
ENDAMAGES
ENDAMEBA
ENDAMEBAE
ENDAMEBAS
ENDAMEBIC
ENDAMOEBA
ENDANGER
ENDANGERS
ENDARCH
ENDARCHY
ENDART
ENDARTED
ENDARTING
ENDARTS
ENDASH
ENDASHES
ENDBRAIN
ENDBRAINS
ENDCAP
ENDCAPS
ENDEAR
ENDEARED
ENDEARING
ENDEARS
ENDEAVOR
ENDEAVORS
ENDEAVOUR
ENDECAGON
ENDED
ENDEICTIC
ENDEIXES
ENDEIXIS
ENDEMIAL
ENDEMIC
ENDEMICAL
ENDEMICS
ENDEMISM
ENDEMISMS
ENDENIZEN
ENDER
ENDERMIC
ENDERON
ENDERONS
ENDERS
ENDEW
ENDEWED
ENDEWING
ENDEWS
ENDEXINE
ENDEXINES
ENDGAME
ENDGAMES
ENDGATE
ENDGATES
ENDING
ENDINGS
ENDIRON
ENDIRONS
ENDITE
ENDITED
ENDITES
ENDITING
ENDIVE
ENDIVES
ENDLANG
ENDLEAF
ENDLEAFS
ENDLEAVES
ENDLESS
ENDLESSLY
ENDLONG
ENDMOST
ENDNOTE
ENDNOTES
ENDOBLAST
ENDOCARP
ENDOCARPS
ENDOCAST
ENDOCASTS
ENDOCRINE
ENDOCYTIC
ENDODERM
ENDODERMS
ENDODYNE
ENDOERGIC
ENDOGAMIC
ENDOGAMY
ENDOGEN
ENDOGENIC
ENDOGENS
ENDOGENY
ENDOLYMPH
ENDOMIXES
ENDOMIXIS
ENDOMORPH
ENDOPHAGY
ENDOPHYTE
ENDOPLASM
ENDOPOD
ENDOPODS
ENDOPROCT
ENDORPHIN
ENDORSE
ENDORSED
ENDORSEE
ENDORSEES
ENDORSER
ENDORSERS
ENDORSES
ENDORSING
ENDORSIVE
ENDORSOR
ENDORSORS
ENDOSARC
ENDOSARCS
ENDOSCOPE
ENDOSCOPY
ENDOSMOS
ENDOSMOSE
ENDOSOME
ENDOSOMES
ENDOSPERM
ENDOSPORE
ENDOSS
ENDOSSED
ENDOSSES
ENDOSSING
ENDOSTEA
ENDOSTEAL
ENDOSTEUM
ENDOSTYLE
ENDOTHERM
ENDOTOXIC
ENDOTOXIN
ENDOW
ENDOWED
ENDOWER
ENDOWERS
ENDOWING
ENDOWMENT
ENDOWS
ENDOZOA
ENDOZOIC
ENDOZOON
ENDPAPER
ENDPAPERS
ENDPLATE
ENDPLATES
ENDPLAY
ENDPLAYED
ENDPLAYS
ENDPOINT
ENDPOINTS
ENDRIN
ENDRINS
ENDS
ENDSHIP

ENDSHIPS
ENDUE
ENDUED
ENDUES
ENDUING
ENDUNGEON
ENDURABLE
ENDURABLY
ENDURANCE
ENDURE
ENDURED
ENDURER
ENDURERS
ENDURES
ENDURING
ENDURO
ENDUROS
ENDWAYS
ENDWISE
ENDYSES
ENDYSIS
ENDZONE
ENDZONES
ENE
ENEMA
ENEMAS
ENEMATA
ENEMIES
ENEMY
ENERGETIC
ENERGIC
ENERGID
ENERGIDS
ENERGIES
ENERGISE
ENERGISED
ENERGISER
ENERGISES
ENERGIZE
ENERGIZED
ENERGIZER
ENERGIZES
ENERGUMEN
ENERGY
ENERVATE
ENERVATED
ENERVATES
ENERVATOR
ENERVE
ENERVED
ENERVES
ENERVING
ENES
ENEW
ENEWED
ENEWING
ENEWS
ENFACE
ENFACED
ENFACES
ENFACING
ENFANT
ENFANTS
ENFEEBLE
ENFEEBLED
ENFEEBLER
ENFEEBLES
ENFELON
ENFELONED
ENFELONS
ENFEOFF
ENFEOFFED
ENFEOFFS
ENFESTED
ENFETTER
ENFETTERS
ENFEVER
ENFEVERED
ENFEVERS
ENFIERCE
ENFIERCED
ENFIERCES
ENFILADE
ENFILADED
ENFILADES
ENFILED
ENFIRE
ENFIRED
ENFIRES
ENFIRING
ENFIX
ENFIXED
ENFIXES
ENFIXING
ENFLAME
ENFLAMED
ENFLAMES
ENFLAMING
ENFLESH
ENFLESHED
ENFLESHES
ENFLOWER
ENFLOWERS
ENFOLD
ENFOLDED
ENFOLDER
ENFOLDERS
ENFOLDING
ENFOLDS
ENFORCE
ENFORCED
ENFORCER
ENFORCERS
ENFORCES
ENFORCING
ENFOREST
ENFORESTS
ENFORM
ENFORMED
ENFORMING
ENFORMS
ENFRAME
ENFRAMED
ENFRAMES
ENFRAMING
ENFREE
ENFREED
ENFREEDOM
ENFREEING
ENFREES
ENFREEZE
ENFREEZES
ENFROSEN
ENFROZE
ENFROZEN
ENG
ENGAGE
ENGAGED
ENGAGEDLY
ENGAGEE
ENGAGER
ENGAGERS
ENGAGES
ENGAGING
ENGAOL
ENGAOLED
ENGAOLING
ENGAOLS
ENGARLAND
ENGENDER
ENGENDERS
ENGENDURE
ENGILD
ENGILDED
ENGILDING
ENGILDS
ENGILT
ENGINE
ENGINED
ENGINEER
ENGINEERS
ENGINER
ENGINERS
ENGINERY
ENGINES
ENGINING
ENGINOUS
ENGIRD
ENGIRDED
ENGIRDING
ENGIRDLE
ENGIRDLED
ENGIRDLES
ENGIRDS
ENGIRT
ENGLACIAL
ENGLISH
ENGLISHED
ENGLISHES
ENGLOBE
ENGLOBED
ENGLOBES
ENGLOBING
ENGLOOM
ENGLOOMED
ENGLOOMS
ENGLUT
ENGLUTS
ENGLUTTED
ENGOBE
ENGOBES
ENGORE
ENGORED
ENGORES
ENGORGE
ENGORGED
ENGORGES
ENGORGING
ENGORING
ENGOULED
ENGOUMENT
ENGRACE
ENGRACED
ENGRACES
ENGRACING
ENGRAFF
ENGRAFFED
ENGRAFFS
ENGRAFT
ENGRAFTED
ENGRAFTS
ENGRAIL
ENGRAILED
ENGRAILS
ENGRAIN
ENGRAINED
ENGRAINER
ENGRAINS
ENGRAM
ENGRAMMA
ENGRAMMAS
ENGRAMME
ENGRAMMES
ENGRAMMIC
ENGRAMS
ENGRASP
ENGRASPED
ENGRASPS
ENGRAVE
ENGRAVED
ENGRAVEN
ENGRAVER
ENGRAVERS
ENGRAVERY
ENGRAVES
ENGRAVING
ENGRENAGE
ENGRIEVE
ENGRIEVED
ENGRIEVES

ENGROOVE
ENGROOVED
ENGROOVES
ENGROSS
ENGROSSED
ENGROSSER
ENGROSSES
ENGS
ENGUARD
ENGUARDED
ENGUARDS
ENGULF
ENGULFED
ENGULFING
ENGULFS
ENGULPH
ENGULPHED
ENGULPHS
ENGYSCOPE
ENHALO
ENHALOED
ENHALOES
ENHALOING
ENHALOS
ENHANCE
ENHANCED
ENHANCER
ENHANCERS
ENHANCES
ENHANCING
ENHANCIVE
ENHEARSE
ENHEARSED
ENHEARSES
ENHEARTEN
ENHUNGER
ENHUNGERS
ENHYDRITE
ENHYDROS
ENHYDROUS
ENIAC
ENIACS
ENIGMA
ENIGMAS
ENIGMATA
ENIGMATIC
ENISLE
ENISLED
ENISLES
ENISLING
ENJAMB
ENJAMBED
ENJAMBING
ENJAMBS
ENJOIN
ENJOINDER
ENJOINED
ENJOINER
ENJOINERS
ENJOINING
ENJOINS
ENJOY
ENJOYABLE
ENJOYABLY
ENJOYED
ENJOYER
ENJOYERS
ENJOYING
ENJOYMENT
ENJOYS
ENKERNEL
ENKERNELS
ENKINDLE
ENKINDLED
ENKINDLER
ENKINDLES
ENLACE
ENLACED
ENLACES
ENLACING
ENLARD
ENLARDED
ENLARDING
ENLARDS
ENLARGE
ENLARGED
ENLARGEN
ENLARGENS
ENLARGER
ENLARGERS
ENLARGES
ENLARGING
ENLEVE
ENLIGHT
ENLIGHTED
ENLIGHTEN
ENLIGHTS
ENLINK
ENLINKED
ENLINKING
ENLINKS
ENLIST
ENLISTED
ENLISTEE
ENLISTEES
ENLISTER
ENLISTERS
ENLISTING
ENLISTS
ENLIT
ENLIVEN
ENLIVENED
ENLIVENER
ENLIVENS
ENLOCK
ENLOCKED
ENLOCKING
ENLOCKS
ENLUMINE
ENLUMINED
ENLUMINES
ENMESH
ENMESHED
ENMESHES
ENMESHING
ENMEW
ENMEWED
ENMEWING
ENMEWS
ENMITIES
ENMITY
ENMOSSED
ENMOVE
ENMOVED
ENMOVES
ENMOVING
ENNAGE
ENNAGES
ENNEAD
ENNEADIC
ENNEADS
ENNEAGON
ENNEAGONS
ENNEAGRAM
ENNOBLE
ENNOBLED
ENNOBLER
ENNOBLERS
ENNOBLES
ENNOBLING
ENNOG
ENNOGS
ENNUI
ENNUIED
ENNUIS
ENNUYE
ENNUYED
ENNUYEE
ENNUYING
ENODAL
ENOKI
ENOKIDAKE
ENOKIS
ENOKITAKE
ENOL
ENOLASE
ENOLASES
ENOLIC
ENOLOGIES
ENOLOGIST
ENOLOGY
ENOLS
ENOMOTIES
ENOMOTY
ENOPHILE
ENOPHILES
ENORM
ENORMITY
ENORMOUS
ENOSES
ENOSIS
ENOSISES
ENOUGH
ENOUGHS
ENOUNCE
ENOUNCED
ENOUNCES
ENOUNCING
ENOW
ENOWS
ENPLANE
ENPLANED
ENPLANES
ENPLANING
ENPRINT
ENPRINTS
ENQUEUE
ENQUEUED
ENQUEUES
ENQUEUING
ENQUIRE
ENQUIRED
ENQUIRER
ENQUIRERS
ENQUIRES
ENQUIRIES
ENQUIRING
ENQUIRY
ENRACE
ENRACED
ENRACES
ENRACING
ENRAGE
ENRAGED
ENRAGEDLY
ENRAGES
ENRAGING
ENRANCKLE
ENRANGE
ENRANGED
ENRANGES
ENRANGING
ENRANK
ENRANKED
ENRANKING
ENRANKS
ENRAPT
ENRAPTURE
ENRAUNGE
ENRAUNGED
ENRAUNGES
ENRAVISH
ENRHEUM
ENRHEUMED
ENRHEUMS
ENRICH
ENRICHED
ENRICHER
ENRICHERS
ENRICHES

ENRICHING
ENRIDGED
ENRING
ENRINGED
ENRINGING
ENRINGS
ENRIVEN
ENROBE
ENROBED
ENROBER
ENROBERS
ENROBES
ENROBING
ENROL
ENROLL
ENROLLED
ENROLLEE
ENROLLEES
ENROLLER
ENROLLERS
ENROLLING
ENROLLS
ENROLMENT
ENROLS
ENROOT
ENROOTED
ENROOTING
ENROOTS
ENROUGH
ENROUGHED
ENROUGHS
ENROUND
ENROUNDED
ENROUNDS
ENS
ENSAMPLE
ENSAMPLED
ENSAMPLES
ENSATE
ENSCONCE
ENSCONCED
ENSCONCES
ENSCROLL
ENSCROLLS
ENSEAL
ENSEALED
ENSEALING
ENSEALS
ENSEAM
ENSEAMED
ENSEAMING
ENSEAMS
ENSEAR
ENSEARED
ENSEARING
ENSEARS
ENSEMBLE
ENSEMBLES
ENSERF
ENSERFED
ENSERFING
ENSERFS
ENSEW
ENSEWED
ENSEWING
ENSEWS
ENSHEATH
ENSHEATHE
ENSHEATHS
ENSHELL
ENSHELLED
ENSHELLS
ENSHELTER
ENSHIELD
ENSHIELDS
ENSHRINE
ENSHRINED
ENSHRINEE
ENSHRINES
ENSHROUD
ENSHROUDS
ENSIFORM
ENSIGN
ENSIGNCY
ENSIGNED
ENSIGNING
ENSIGNS
ENSILAGE
ENSILAGED
ENSILAGES
ENSILE
ENSILED
ENSILES
ENSILING
ENSKIED
ENSKIES
ENSKY
ENSKYED
ENSKYING
ENSLAVE
ENSLAVED
ENSLAVER
ENSLAVERS
ENSLAVES
ENSLAVING
ENSNARE
ENSNARED
ENSNARER
ENSNARERS
ENSNARES
ENSNARING
ENSNARL
ENSNARLED
ENSNARLS
ENSORCEL
ENSORCELL
ENSORCELS
ENSOUL
ENSOULED
ENSOULING
ENSOULS
ENSPHERE
ENSPHERED
ENSPHERES
ENSTAMP
ENSTAMPED
ENSTAMPS
ENSTATITE
ENSTEEP
ENSTEEPED
ENSTEEPS
ENSTYLE
ENSTYLED
ENSTYLES
ENSTYLING
ENSUE
ENSUED
ENSUES
ENSUING
ENSUITE
ENSUITES
ENSURE
ENSURED
ENSURER
ENSURERS
ENSURES
ENSURING
ENSWATHE
ENSWATHED
ENSWATHES
ENSWEEP
ENSWEEPS
ENSWEPT
ENTAIL
ENTAILED
ENTAILER
ENTAILERS
ENTAILING
ENTAILS
ENTAME
ENTAMEBA
ENTAMEBAE
ENTAMEBAS
ENTAMED
ENTAMES
ENTAMING
ENTAMOEBA
ENTANGLE
ENTANGLED
ENTANGLER
ENTANGLES
ENTASES
ENTASIA
ENTASIAS
ENTASIS
ENTASTIC
ENTAYLE
ENTAYLED
ENTAYLES
ENTAYLING
ENTELECHY
ENTELLUS
ENTENDER
ENTENDERS
ENTENTE
ENTENTES
ENTER
ENTERA
ENTERABLE
ENTERAL
ENTERALLY
ENTERATE
ENTERED
ENTERER
ENTERERS
ENTERIC
ENTERICS
ENTERING
ENTERINGS
ENTERITIS
ENTERON
ENTERONS
ENTERS
ENTERTAIN
ENTERTAKE
ENTERTOOK
ENTETE
ENTETEE
ENTHALPY
ENTHETIC
ENTHRAL
ENTHRALL
ENTHRALLS
ENTHRALS
ENTHRONE
ENTHRONED
ENTHRONES
ENTHUSE
ENTHUSED
ENTHUSES
ENTHUSING
ENTHYMEME
ENTIA
ENTICE
ENTICED
ENTICER
ENTICERS
ENTICES
ENTICING
ENTICINGS
ENTIRE
ENTIRELY
ENTIRES
ENTIRETY
ENTITIES
ENTITLE
ENTITLED
ENTITLES
ENTITLING
ENTITY

ENTOBLAST
ENTODERM
ENTODERMS
ENTOIL
ENTOILED
ENTOILING
ENTOILS
ENTOMB
ENTOMBED
ENTOMBING
ENTOMBS
ENTOMIC
ENTOPHYTE
ENTOPIC
ENTOPROCT
ENTOPTIC
ENTOPTICS
ENTOTIC
ENTOURAGE
ENTOZOA
ENTOZOAL
ENTOZOAN
ENTOZOANS
ENTOZOIC
ENTOZOON
ENTRAIL
ENTRAILED
ENTRAILS
ENTRAIN
ENTRAINED
ENTRAINER
ENTRAINS
ENTRALL
ENTRALLES
ENTRAMMEL
ENTRANCE
ENTRANCED
ENTRANCES
ENTRANT
ENTRANTS
ENTRAP
ENTRAPPED
ENTRAPPER
ENTRAPS
ENTREAT
ENTREATED
ENTREATS
ENTREATY
ENTRECHAT
ENTRECOTE
ENTREE
ENTREES
ENTREMES
ENTREMETS
ENTRENCH
ENTREPOT
ENTREPOTS
ENTRESOL
ENTRESOLS
ENTREZ
ENTRIES
ENTRISM
ENTRISMS
ENTRIST
ENTRISTS
ENTROLD
ENTROPIC
ENTROPIES
ENTROPION
ENTROPIUM
ENTROPY
ENTRUST
ENTRUSTED
ENTRUSTS
ENTRY
ENTRYISM
ENTRYISMS
ENTRYIST
ENTRYISTS
ENTRYWAY
ENTRYWAYS
ENTS
ENTWINE
ENTWINED
ENTWINES
ENTWINING
ENTWIST
ENTWISTED
ENTWISTS
ENUCLEATE
ENUF
ENUMERATE
ENUNCIATE
ENURE
ENURED
ENUREMENT
ENURES
ENURESES
ENURESIS
ENURETIC
ENURETICS
ENURING
ENURN
ENURNED
ENURNING
ENURNS
ENVASSAL
ENVASSALS
ENVAULT
ENVAULTED
ENVAULTS
ENVEIGLE
ENVEIGLED
ENVEIGLES
ENVELOP
ENVELOPE
ENVELOPED
ENVELOPER
ENVELOPES
ENVELOPS
ENVENOM
ENVENOMED
ENVENOMS
ENVERMEIL
ENVIABLE
ENVIABLY
ENVIED
ENVIER
ENVIERS
ENVIES
ENVIOUS
ENVIOUSLY
ENVIRO
ENVIRON
ENVIRONED
ENVIRONS
ENVIROS
ENVISAGE
ENVISAGED
ENVISAGES
ENVISION
ENVISIONS
ENVOI
ENVOIS
ENVOY
ENVOYS
ENVOYSHIP
ENVY
ENVYING
ENVYINGLY
ENVYINGS
ENWALL
ENWALLED
ENWALLING
ENWALLOW
ENWALLOWS
ENWALLS
ENWHEEL
ENWHEELED
ENWHEELS
ENWIND
ENWINDING
ENWINDS
ENWOMB
ENWOMBED
ENWOMBING
ENWOMBS
ENWOUND
ENWRAP
ENWRAPPED
ENWRAPS
ENWRAPT
ENWREATH
ENWREATHE
ENWREATHS
ENZIAN
ENZIANS
ENZONE
ENZONED
ENZONES
ENZONING
ENZOOTIC
ENZOOTICS
ENZYM
ENZYMATIC
ENZYME
ENZYMES
ENZYMIC
ENZYMS
EOAN
EOBIONT
EOBIONTS
EOCENE
EOHIPPUS
EOLIAN
EOLIENNE
EOLIENNES
EOLIPILE
EOLIPILES
EOLITH
EOLITHIC
EOLITHS
EOLOPILE
EOLOPILES
EON
EONIAN
EONISM
EONISMS
EONS
EORL
EORLS
EOSIN
EOSINE
EOSINES
EOSINIC
EOSINS
EOTHEN
EPACRID
EPACRIDS
EPACRIS
EPACRISES
EPACT
EPACTS
EPAENETIC
EPAGOGE
EPAGOGES
EPAGOGIC
EPANODOS
EPARCH
EPARCHATE
EPARCHIAL
EPARCHIES
EPARCHS
EPARCHY
EPATANT
EPATER
EPATERED
EPATERING
EPATERS
EPAULE

E

EPAULES
EPAULET
EPAULETED
EPAULETS
EPAULETTE
EPAXIAL
EPAZOTE
EPAZOTES
EPEDAPHIC
EPEE
EPEEIST
EPEEISTS
EPEES
EPEIRA
EPEIRAS
EPEIRIC
EPEIRID
EPEIRIDS
EPENDYMA
EPENDYMAL
EPENDYMAS
EPEOLATRY
EPERDU
EPERDUE
EPERGNE
EPERGNES
EPHA
EPHAH
EPHAHS
EPHAS
EPHEBE
EPHEBES
EPHEBI
EPHEBIC
EPHEBOI
EPHEBOS
EPHEBUS
EPHEDRA
EPHEDRAS
EPHEDRIN
EPHEDRINE
EPHEDRINS
EPHELIDES
EPHELIS
EPHEMERA
EPHEMERAE
EPHEMERAL
EPHEMERAS
EPHEMERID
EPHEMERIS
EPHEMERON
EPHIALTES
EPHOD
EPHODS
EPHOR
EPHORAL
EPHORALTY
EPHORATE
EPHORATES
EPHORI
EPHORS
EPIBIOSES
EPIBIOSIS
EPIBIOTIC
EPIBLAST
EPIBLASTS
EPIBLEM
EPIBLEMS
EPIBOLIC
EPIBOLIES
EPIBOLY
EPIC
EPICAL
EPICALLY
EPICALYX
EPICANTHI
EPICARDIA
EPICARP
EPICARPS
EPICEDE
EPICEDES
EPICEDIA
EPICEDIAL
EPICEDIAN
EPICEDIUM
EPICENE
EPICENES
EPICENISM
EPICENTER
EPICENTRA
EPICENTRE
EPICIER
EPICIERS
EPICISM
EPICISMS
EPICIST
EPICISTS
EPICLESES
EPICLESIS
EPICLIKE
EPICORMIC
EPICOTYL
EPICOTYLS
EPICRANIA
EPICRISES
EPICRISIS
EPICRITIC
EPICS
EPICURE
EPICUREAN
EPICURES
EPICURISE
EPICURISM
EPICURIZE
EPICYCLE
EPICYCLES
EPICYCLIC
EPIDEMIC
EPIDEMICS
EPIDERM
EPIDERMAL
EPIDERMIC
EPIDERMIS
EPIDERMS
EPIDICTIC
EPIDOSITE
EPIDOTE
EPIDOTES
EPIDOTIC
EPIDURAL
EPIDURALS
EPIFAUNA
EPIFAUNAE
EPIFAUNAL
EPIFAUNAS
EPIFOCAL
EPIGAEAL
EPIGAEAN
EPIGAEOUS
EPIGAMIC
EPIGEAL
EPIGEAN
EPIGEIC
EPIGENE
EPIGENIC
EPIGENIST
EPIGENOME
EPIGENOUS
EPIGEOUS
EPIGON
EPIGONE
EPIGONES
EPIGONI
EPIGONIC
EPIGONISM
EPIGONOUS
EPIGONS
EPIGONUS
EPIGRAM
EPIGRAMS
EPIGRAPH
EPIGRAPHS
EPIGRAPHY
EPIGYNIES
EPIGYNOUS
EPIGYNY
EPILATE
EPILATED
EPILATES
EPILATING
EPILATION
EPILATOR
EPILATORS
EPILEPSY
EPILEPTIC
EPILIMNIA
EPILITHIC
EPILOBIUM
EPILOG
EPILOGIC
EPILOGISE
EPILOGIST
EPILOGIZE
EPILOGS
EPILOGUE
EPILOGUED
EPILOGUES
EPIMER
EPIMERASE
EPIMERE
EPIMERES
EPIMERIC
EPIMERISE
EPIMERISM
EPIMERIZE
EPIMERS
EPIMYSIA
EPIMYSIUM
EPINAOI
EPINAOS
EPINASTIC
EPINASTY
EPINEURAL
EPINEURIA
EPINICIAN
EPINICION
EPINIKIAN
EPINIKION
EPINOSIC
EPIPHANIC
EPIPHANY
EPIPHRAGM
EPIPHYSES
EPIPHYSIS
EPIPHYTAL
EPIPHYTE
EPIPHYTES
EPIPHYTIC
EPIPLOA
EPIPLOIC
EPIPLOON
EPIPLOONS
EPIPOLIC
EPIPOLISM
EPIROGENY
EPIRRHEMA
EPISCIA
EPISCIAS
EPISCOPAL
EPISCOPE
EPISCOPES
EPISCOPY
EPISEMON
EPISEMONS
EPISODAL
EPISODE
EPISODES
EPISODIAL
EPISODIC
EPISOMAL

EPISOME
EPISOMES
EPISPERM
EPISPERMS
EPISPORE
EPISPORES
EPISTASES
EPISTASIS
EPISTASY
EPISTATIC
EPISTAXES
EPISTAXIS
EPISTEMIC
EPISTERNA
EPISTLE
EPISTLED
EPISTLER
EPISTLERS
EPISTLES
EPISTLING
EPISTOLER
EPISTOLET
EPISTOLIC
EPISTOME
EPISTOMES
EPISTYLE
EPISTYLES
EPITAPH
EPITAPHED
EPITAPHER
EPITAPHIC
EPITAPHS
EPITASES
EPITASIS
EPITAXES
EPITAXIAL
EPITAXIC
EPITAXIES
EPITAXIS
EPITAXY
EPITHECA
EPITHECAE
EPITHELIA
EPITHEM
EPITHEMA
EPITHEMS
EPITHESES
EPITHESIS
EPITHET
EPITHETED
EPITHETIC
EPITHETON
EPITHETS
EPITOME
EPITOMES
EPITOMIC
EPITOMISE
EPITOMIST
EPITOMIZE
EPITONIC
EPITOPE
EPITOPES
EPITRITE
EPITRITES
EPIZEUXES
EPIZEUXIS
EPIZOA
EPIZOAN
EPIZOANS
EPIZOIC
EPIZOISM
EPIZOISMS
EPIZOITE
EPIZOITES
EPIZOON
EPIZOOTIC
EPIZOOTY
EPOCH
EPOCHA
EPOCHAL
EPOCHALLY
EPOCHAS
EPOCHS
EPODE
EPODES
EPODIC
EPONYM
EPONYMIC
EPONYMIES
EPONYMOUS
EPONYMS
EPONYMY
EPOPEE
EPOPEES
EPOPOEIA
EPOPOEIAS
EPOPT
EPOPTS
EPOS
EPOSES
EPOXIDE
EPOXIDES
EPOXIDISE
EPOXIDIZE
EPOXIED
EPOXIES
EPOXY
EPOXYED
EPOXYING
EPRIS
EPRISE
EPSILON
EPSILONIC
EPSILONS
EPSOMITE
EPSOMITES
EPUISE
EPUISEE
EPULARY
EPULATION
EPULIDES
EPULIS
EPULISES
EPULOTIC
EPULOTICS
EPURATE
EPURATED
EPURATES
EPURATING
EPURATION
EPYLLIA
EPYLLION
EPYLLIONS
EQUABLE
EQUABLY
EQUAL
EQUALED
EQUALI
EQUALING
EQUALISE
EQUALISED
EQUALISER
EQUALISES
EQUALITY
EQUALIZE
EQUALIZED
EQUALIZER
EQUALIZES
EQUALLED
EQUALLING
EQUALLY
EQUALNESS
EQUALS
EQUANT
EQUANTS
EQUATABLE
EQUATE
EQUATED
EQUATES
EQUATING
EQUATION
EQUATIONS
EQUATIVE
EQUATOR
EQUATORS
EQUERRIES
EQUERRY
EQUES
EQUID
EQUIDS
EQUIFINAL
EQUIMOLAL
EQUIMOLAR
EQUINAL
EQUINE
EQUINELY
EQUINES
EQUINIA
EQUINIAS
EQUINITY
EQUINOX
EQUINOXES
EQUIP
EQUIPAGE
EQUIPAGED
EQUIPAGES
EQUIPE
EQUIPES
EQUIPMENT
EQUIPOISE
EQUIPPED
EQUIPPER
EQUIPPERS
EQUIPPING
EQUIPS
EQUISETA
EQUISETIC
EQUISETUM
EQUITABLE
EQUITABLY
EQUITANT
EQUITES
EQUITIES
EQUITY
EQUIVALVE
EQUIVOCAL
EQUIVOKE
EQUIVOKES
EQUIVOQUE
ER
ERA
ERADIATE
ERADIATED
ERADIATES
ERADICANT
ERADICATE
ERAS
ERASABLE
ERASE
ERASED
ERASEMENT
ERASER
ERASERS
ERASES
ERASING
ERASION
ERASIONS
ERASURE
ERASURES
ERATHEM
ERATHEMS
ERBIA
ERBIAS
ERBIUM
ERBIUMS
ERE
ERECT
ERECTABLE
ERECTED
ERECTER

ERECTERS
ERECTILE
ERECTING
ERECTION
ERECTIONS
ERECTIVE
ERECTLY
ERECTNESS
ERECTOR
ERECTORS
ERECTS
ERED
ERELONG
EREMIC
EREMITAL
EREMITE
EREMITES
EREMITIC
EREMITISH
EREMITISM
EREMURI
EREMURUS
ERENOW
EREPSIN
EREPSINS
ERES
ERETHIC
ERETHISM
ERETHISMS
ERETHITIC
EREV
EREVS
EREWHILE
EREWHILES
ERF
ERG
ERGASTIC
ERGATANER
ERGATE
ERGATES
ERGATIVE
ERGATIVES
ERGATOID
ERGATOIDS
ERGO
ERGODIC
ERGOGENIC
ERGOGRAM
ERGOGRAMS
ERGOGRAPH
ERGOMANIA
ERGOMETER
ERGOMETRY
ERGON
ERGONOMIC
ERGONS
ERGOS
ERGOT
ERGOTIC
ERGOTISE
ERGOTISED
ERGOTISES
ERGOTISM
ERGOTISMS
ERGOTIZE
ERGOTIZED
ERGOTIZES
ERGOTS
ERGS
ERHU
ERHUS
ERIACH
ERIACHS
ERIC
ERICA
ERICAS
ERICK
ERICKS
ERICOID
ERICS
ERIGERON
ERIGERONS
ERING
ERINGO
ERINGOES
ERINGOS
ERINITE
ERINITES
ERINUS
ERINUSES
ERIOMETER
ERIONITE
ERIONITES
ERIOPHYID
ERISTIC
ERISTICAL
ERISTICS
ERK
ERKS
ERLANG
ERLANGS
ERLKING
ERLKINGS
ERM
ERMELIN
ERMELINS
ERMINE
ERMINED
ERMINES
ERN
ERNE
ERNED
ERNES
ERNING
ERNS
ERODABLE
ERODE
ERODED
ERODENT
ERODENTS
ERODES
ERODIBLE
ERODING
ERODIUM
ERODIUMS
EROGENIC
EROGENOUS
EROS
EROSE
EROSELY
EROSES
EROSIBLE
EROSION
EROSIONAL
EROSIONS
EROSIVE
EROSIVITY
EROSTRATE
EROTEMA
EROTEMAS
EROTEME
EROTEMES
EROTESES
EROTESIS
EROTETIC
EROTIC
EROTICA
EROTICAL
EROTICAS
EROTICISE
EROTICISM
EROTICIST
EROTICIZE
EROTICS
EROTISE
EROTISED
EROTISES
EROTISING
EROTISM
EROTISMS
EROTIZE
EROTIZED
EROTIZES
EROTIZING
EROTOLOGY
ERR
ERRABLE
ERRANCIES
ERRANCY
ERRAND
ERRANDS
ERRANT
ERRANTLY
ERRANTRY
ERRANTS
ERRATA
ERRATAS
ERRATIC
ERRATICAL
ERRATICS
ERRATUM
ERRED
ERRHINE
ERRHINES
ERRING
ERRINGLY
ERRINGS
ERRONEOUS
ERROR
ERRORIST
ERRORISTS
ERRORLESS
ERRORS
ERRS
ERS
ERSATZ
ERSATZES
ERSES
ERST
ERSTWHILE
ERUCIC
ERUCIFORM
ERUCT
ERUCTATE
ERUCTATED
ERUCTATES
ERUCTED
ERUCTING
ERUCTS
ERUDITE
ERUDITELY
ERUDITES
ERUDITION
ERUGO
ERUGOS
ERUMPENT
ERUPT
ERUPTED
ERUPTIBLE
ERUPTING
ERUPTION
ERUPTIONS
ERUPTIVE
ERUPTIVES
ERUPTS
ERUV
ERUVIM
ERUVIN
ERUVS
ERVALENTA
ERVEN
ERVIL
ERVILS
ERYNGIUM
ERYNGIUMS
ERYNGO
ERYNGOES
ERYNGOS
ERYTHEMA
ERYTHEMAL

ERYTHEMAS
ERYTHEMIC
ERYTHRINA
ERYTHRISM
ERYTHRITE
ERYTHROID
ERYTHRON
ERYTHRONS
ES
ESCABECHE
ESCALADE
ESCALADED
ESCALADER
ESCALADES
ESCALADO
ESCALATE
ESCALATED
ESCALATES
ESCALATOR
ESCALIER
ESCALIERS
ESCALLOP
ESCALLOPS
ESCALOP
ESCALOPE
ESCALOPED
ESCALOPES
ESCALOPS
ESCAPABLE
ESCAPADE
ESCAPADES
ESCAPADO
ESCAPADOS
ESCAPE
ESCAPED
ESCAPEE
ESCAPEES
ESCAPER
ESCAPERS
ESCAPES
ESCAPING
ESCAPISM
ESCAPISMS
ESCAPIST
ESCAPISTS
ESCAR
ESCARGOT
ESCARGOTS
ESCAROLE
ESCAROLES
ESCARP
ESCARPED
ESCARPING
ESCARPS
ESCARS
ESCHALOT
ESCHALOTS
ESCHAR
ESCHARS
ESCHEAT
ESCHEATED
ESCHEATOR
ESCHEATS
ESCHEW
ESCHEWAL
ESCHEWALS
ESCHEWED
ESCHEWER
ESCHEWERS
ESCHEWING
ESCHEWS
ESCLANDRE
ESCOLAR
ESCOLARS
ESCOPETTE
ESCORT
ESCORTAGE
ESCORTED
ESCORTING
ESCORTS
ESCOT
ESCOTED
ESCOTING
ESCOTS
ESCOTTED
ESCOTTING
ESCRIBANO
ESCRIBE
ESCRIBED
ESCRIBES
ESCRIBING
ESCROC
ESCROCS
ESCROL
ESCROLL
ESCROLLS
ESCROLS
ESCROW
ESCROWED
ESCROWING
ESCROWS
ESCUAGE
ESCUAGES
ESCUDO
ESCUDOS
ESCULENT
ESCULENTS
ESEMPLASY
ESERINE
ESERINES
ESES
ESILE
ESILES
ESKAR
ESKARS
ESKER
ESKERS
ESKIES
ESKY
ESLOIN
ESLOINED
ESLOINING
ESLOINS
ESLOYNE
ESLOYNED
ESLOYNES
ESLOYNING
ESNE
ESNECIES
ESNECY
ESNES
ESOPHAGI
ESOPHAGUS
ESOTERIC
ESOTERICA
ESOTERIES
ESOTERISM
ESOTERY
ESOTROPIA
ESOTROPIC
ESPADA
ESPADAS
ESPAGNOLE
ESPALIER
ESPALIERS
ESPANOL
ESPANOLES
ESPARTO
ESPARTOS
ESPECIAL
ESPERANCE
ESPIAL
ESPIALS
ESPIED
ESPIEGLE
ESPIER
ESPIERS
ESPIES
ESPIONAGE
ESPLANADE
ESPOIR
ESPOIRS
ESPOUSAL
ESPOUSALS
ESPOUSE
ESPOUSED
ESPOUSER
ESPOUSERS
ESPOUSES
ESPOUSING
ESPRESSO
ESPRESSOS
ESPRIT
ESPRITS
ESPUMOSO
ESPUMOSOS
ESPY
ESPYING
ESQUIRE
ESQUIRED
ESQUIRES
ESQUIRESS
ESQUIRING
ESQUISSE
ESQUISSES
ESS
ESSAY
ESSAYED
ESSAYER
ESSAYERS
ESSAYETTE
ESSAYING
ESSAYISH
ESSAYIST
ESSAYISTS
ESSAYS
ESSE
ESSENCE
ESSENCES
ESSENTIAL
ESSES
ESSIVE
ESSIVES
ESSOIN
ESSOINED
ESSOINER
ESSOINERS
ESSOINING
ESSOINS
ESSONITE
ESSONITES
ESSOYNE
ESSOYNES
EST
ESTABLISH
ESTACADE
ESTACADES
ESTAFETTE
ESTAMINET
ESTANCIA
ESTANCIAS
ESTATE
ESTATED
ESTATES
ESTATING
ESTEEM
ESTEEMED
ESTEEMING
ESTEEMS
ESTER
ESTERASE
ESTERASES
ESTERIFY
ESTERS
ESTHESES
ESTHESIA
ESTHESIAS
ESTHESIS
ESTHETE
ESTHETES

ESTHETIC
ESTHETICS
ESTIMABLE
ESTIMABLY
ESTIMATE
ESTIMATED
ESTIMATES
ESTIMATOR
ESTIVAL
ESTIVATE
ESTIVATED
ESTIVATES
ESTIVATOR
ESTOC
ESTOCS
ESTOILE
ESTOILES
ESTOP
ESTOPPAGE
ESTOPPED
ESTOPPEL
ESTOPPELS
ESTOPPING
ESTOPS
ESTOVER
ESTOVERS
ESTRADE
ESTRADES
ESTRADIOL
ESTRAGON
ESTRAGONS
ESTRAL
ESTRANGE
ESTRANGED
ESTRANGER
ESTRANGES
ESTRAPADE
ESTRAY
ESTRAYED
ESTRAYING
ESTRAYS
ESTREAT
ESTREATED
ESTREATS
ESTREPE
ESTREPED
ESTREPES
ESTREPING
ESTRICH
ESTRICHES
ESTRIDGE
ESTRIDGES
ESTRILDID
ESTRIN
ESTRINS
ESTRIOL
ESTRIOLS
ESTRO
ESTROGEN
ESTROGENS
ESTRONE
ESTRONES
ESTROS
ESTROUS
ESTRUAL
ESTRUM
ESTRUMS
ESTRUS
ESTRUSES
ESTS
ESTUARIAL
ESTUARIAN
ESTUARIES
ESTUARINE
ESTUARY
ESURIENCE
ESURIENCY
ESURIENT
ET
ETA
ETACISM
ETACISMS
ETAERIO
ETAERIOS
ETAGE
ETAGERE
ETAGERES
ETAGES
ETALAGE
ETALAGES
ETALON
ETALONS
ETAMIN
ETAMINE
ETAMINES
ETAMINS
ETAPE
ETAPES
ETAS
ETAT
ETATISM
ETATISME
ETATISMES
ETATISMS
ETATIST
ETATISTE
ETATISTES
ETATS
ETCETERA
ETCETERAS
ETCH
ETCHANT
ETCHANTS
ETCHED
ETCHER
ETCHERS
ETCHES
ETCHING
ETCHINGS
ETEN
ETENS
ETERNAL
ETERNALLY
ETERNALS
ETERNE
ETERNISE
ETERNISED
ETERNISES
ETERNITY
ETERNIZE
ETERNIZED
ETERNIZES
ETESIAN
ETESIANS
ETH
ETHAL
ETHALS
ETHANAL
ETHANALS
ETHANE
ETHANES
ETHANOATE
ETHANOIC
ETHANOL
ETHANOLS
ETHANOYL
ETHANOYLS
ETHE
ETHENE
ETHENES
ETHEPHON
ETHEPHONS
ETHER
ETHERCAP
ETHERCAPS
ETHEREAL
ETHEREOUS
ETHERIAL
ETHERIC
ETHERICAL
ETHERIFY
ETHERION
ETHERIONS
ETHERISE
ETHERISED
ETHERISER
ETHERISES
ETHERISH
ETHERISM
ETHERISMS
ETHERIST
ETHERISTS
ETHERIZE
ETHERIZED
ETHERIZER
ETHERIZES
ETHERS
ETHIC
ETHICAL
ETHICALLY
ETHICALS
ETHICIAN
ETHICIANS
ETHICISE
ETHICISED
ETHICISES
ETHICISM
ETHICISMS
ETHICIST
ETHICISTS
ETHICIZE
ETHICIZED
ETHICIZES
ETHICS
ETHINYL
ETHINYLS
ETHION
ETHIONINE
ETHIONS
ETHIOPS
ETHIOPSES
ETHMOID
ETHMOIDAL
ETHMOIDS
ETHNARCH
ETHNARCHS
ETHNARCHY
ETHNE
ETHNIC
ETHNICAL
ETHNICISM
ETHNICITY
ETHNICS
ETHNOCIDE
ETHNOGENY
ETHNOLOGY
ETHNONYM
ETHNONYMS
ETHNOS
ETHNOSES
ETHOGRAM
ETHOGRAMS
ETHOLOGIC
ETHOLOGY
ETHONONE
ETHONONES
ETHOS
ETHOSES
ETHOXIDE
ETHOXIDES
ETHOXIES
ETHOXY
ETHOXYL
ETHOXYLS
ETHS
ETHYL
ETHYLATE
ETHYLATED
ETHYLATES
ETHYLENE

ETHYLENES
ETHYLENIC
ETHYLIC
ETHYLS
ETHYNE
ETHYNES
ETHYNYL
ETHYNYLS
ETIC
ETICS
ETIOLATE
ETIOLATED
ETIOLATES
ETIOLIN
ETIOLINS
ETIOLOGIC
ETIOLOGY
ETIQUETTE
ETNA
ETNAS
ETOILE
ETOILES
ETOUFFEE
ETOUFFEES
ETOURDI
ETOURDIE
ETRANGER
ETRANGERE
ETRANGERS
ETRENNE
ETRENNES
ETRIER
ETRIERS
ETTERCAP
ETTERCAPS
ETTIN
ETTINS
ETTLE
ETTLED
ETTLES
ETTLING
ETUDE
ETUDES
ETUI
ETUIS
ETWEE
ETWEES
ETYMA
ETYMIC
ETYMOLOGY
ETYMON
ETYMONS
ETYPIC
ETYPICAL
EUCAIN
EUCAINE
EUCAINES
EUCAINS
EUCALYPT
EUCALYPTI
EUCALYPTS
EUCARYON
EUCARYONS
EUCARYOT
EUCARYOTE
EUCARYOTS
EUCHARIS
EUCHLORIC
EUCHLORIN
EUCHOLOGY
EUCHRE
EUCHRED
EUCHRES
EUCHRING
EUCLASE
EUCLASES
EUCLIDEAN
EUCLIDIAN
EUCRITE
EUCRITES
EUCRITIC
EUCRYPHIA
EUCYCLIC
EUDAEMON
EUDAEMONS
EUDAEMONY
EUDAIMON
EUDAIMONS
EUDEMON
EUDEMONIA
EUDEMONIC
EUDEMONS
EUDIALYTE
EUGARIE
EUGARIES
EUGE
EUGENIA
EUGENIAS
EUGENIC
EUGENICAL
EUGENICS
EUGENISM
EUGENISMS
EUGENIST
EUGENISTS
EUGENOL
EUGENOLS
EUGH
EUGHEN
EUGHS
EUGLENA
EUGLENAS
EUGLENID
EUGLENIDS
EUGLENOID
EUK
EUKARYON
EUKARYONS
EUKARYOT
EUKARYOTE
EUKARYOTS
EUKED
EUKING
EUKS
EULACHAN
EULACHANS
EULACHON
EULACHONS
EULOGIA
EULOGIAE
EULOGIAS
EULOGIES
EULOGISE
EULOGISED
EULOGISER
EULOGISES
EULOGIST
EULOGISTS
EULOGIUM
EULOGIUMS
EULOGIZE
EULOGIZED
EULOGIZER
EULOGIZES
EULOGY
EUMELANIN
EUMERISM
EUMERISMS
EUMONG
EUMONGS
EUMUNG
EUMUNGS
EUNUCH
EUNUCHISE
EUNUCHISM
EUNUCHIZE
EUNUCHOID
EUNUCHS
EUOI
EUONYMIN
EUONYMINS
EUONYMUS
EUOUAE
EUOUAES
EUPAD
EUPADS
EUPATRID
EUPATRIDS
EUPEPSIA
EUPEPSIAS
EUPEPSIES
EUPEPSY
EUPEPTIC
EUPHAUSID
EUPHEMISE
EUPHEMISM
EUPHEMIST
EUPHEMIZE
EUPHENIC
EUPHENICS
EUPHOBIA
EUPHOBIAS
EUPHON
EUPHONIA
EUPHONIAS
EUPHONIC
EUPHONIES
EUPHONISE
EUPHONISM
EUPHONIUM
EUPHONIZE
EUPHONS
EUPHONY
EUPHORBIA
EUPHORIA
EUPHORIAS
EUPHORIC
EUPHORIES
EUPHORY
EUPHOTIC
EUPHRASIA
EUPHRASY
EUPHROE
EUPHROES
EUPHUISE
EUPHUISED
EUPHUISES
EUPHUISM
EUPHUISMS
EUPHUIST
EUPHUISTS
EUPHUIZE
EUPHUIZED
EUPHUIZES
EUPLASTIC
EUPLOID
EUPLOIDS
EUPLOIDY
EUPNEA
EUPNEAS
EUPNEIC
EUPNOEA
EUPNOEAS
EUPNOEIC
EUREKA
EUREKAS
EURHYTHMY
EURIPI
EURIPUS
EURIPUSES
EURO
EUROBOND
EUROBONDS
EUROCRAT
EUROCRATS
EUROCREEP
EUROKIES
EUROKOUS
EUROKY
EUROLAND

EUROLANDS
EURONOTE
EURONOTES
EUROPHILE
EUROPIUM
EUROPIUMS
EUROPOP
EUROPOPS
EUROS
EUROZONE
EUROZONES
EURYBATH
EURYBATHS
EURYOKIES
EURYOKOUS
EURYOKY
EURYTHERM
EURYTHMIC
EURYTHMY
EURYTOPIC
EUSOCIAL
EUSOL
EUSOLS
EUSTACIES
EUSTACY
EUSTASIES
EUSTASY
EUSTATIC
EUSTELE
EUSTELES
EUSTRESS
EUSTYLE
EUSTYLES
EUTAXIA
EUTAXIAS
EUTAXIES
EUTAXITE
EUTAXITES
EUTAXITIC
EUTAXY
EUTECTIC
EUTECTICS
EUTECTOID
EUTEXIA
EUTEXIAS
EUTHANASE
EUTHANASY
EUTHANAZE
EUTHANISE
EUTHANIZE
EUTHENICS
EUTHENIST
EUTHERIAN
EUTHYMIA
EUTHYMIAS
EUTHYROID
EUTRAPELY
EUTROPHIC
EUTROPHY
EUTROPIC
EUTROPIES
EUTROPOUS
EUTROPY
EUXENITE
EUXENITES
EVACUANT
EVACUANTS
EVACUATE
EVACUATED
EVACUATES
EVACUATOR
EVACUEE
EVACUEES
EVADABLE
EVADE
EVADED
EVADER
EVADERS
EVADES
EVADIBLE
EVADING
EVADINGLY
EVAGATION
EVAGINATE
EVALUABLE
EVALUATE
EVALUATED
EVALUATES
EVALUATOR
EVANESCE
EVANESCED
EVANESCES
EVANGEL
EVANGELIC
EVANGELS
EVANGELY
EVANISH
EVANISHED
EVANISHES
EVANITION
EVAPORATE
EVAPORITE
EVASIBLE
EVASION
EVASIONAL
EVASIONS
EVASIVE
EVASIVELY
EVE
EVECTION
EVECTIONS
EVEJAR
EVEJARS
EVEN
EVENED
EVENEMENT
EVENER
EVENERS
EVENEST
EVENFALL
EVENFALLS
EVENING
EVENINGS
EVENLY
EVENNESS
EVENS
EVENSONG
EVENSONGS
EVENT
EVENTED
EVENTER
EVENTERS
EVENTFUL
EVENTIDE
EVENTIDES
EVENTING
EVENTINGS
EVENTIVE
EVENTLESS
EVENTRATE
EVENTS
EVENTUAL
EVENTUATE
EVER
EVERGLADE
EVERGREEN
EVERMORE
EVERNET
EVERNETS
EVERSIBLE
EVERSION
EVERSIONS
EVERT
EVERTED
EVERTING
EVERTOR
EVERTORS
EVERTS
EVERWHERE
EVERWHICH
EVERY
EVERYBODY
EVERYDAY
EVERYDAYS
EVERYMAN
EVERYMEN
EVERYONE
EVERYWAY
EVERYWHEN
EVES
EVET
EVETS
EVHOE
EVICT
EVICTED
EVICTEE
EVICTEES
EVICTING
EVICTION
EVICTIONS
EVICTOR
EVICTORS
EVICTS
EVIDENCE
EVIDENCED
EVIDENCES
EVIDENT
EVIDENTLY
EVIDENTS
EVIL
EVILDOER
EVILDOERS
EVILDOING
EVILER
EVILEST
EVILLER
EVILLEST
EVILLY
EVILNESS
EVILS
EVINCE
EVINCED
EVINCES
EVINCIBLE
EVINCIBLY
EVINCING
EVINCIVE
EVIRATE
EVIRATED
EVIRATES
EVIRATING
EVITABLE
EVITATE
EVITATED
EVITATES
EVITATING
EVITATION
EVITE
EVITED
EVITERNAL
EVITES
EVITING
EVO
EVOCABLE
EVOCATE
EVOCATED
EVOCATES
EVOCATING
EVOCATION
EVOCATIVE
EVOCATOR
EVOCATORS
EVOCATORY
EVOE
EVOHE
EVOKE
EVOKED
EVOKER
EVOKERS
EVOKES

EVOKING
EVOLUE
EVOLUES
EVOLUTE
EVOLUTED
EVOLUTES
EVOLUTING
EVOLUTION
EVOLUTIVE
EVOLVABLE
EVOLVE
EVOLVED
EVOLVENT
EVOLVENTS
EVOLVER
EVOLVERS
EVOLVES
EVOLVING
EVONYMUS
EVOS
EVOVAE
EVOVAES
EVULGATE
EVULGATED
EVULGATES
EVULSE
EVULSED
EVULSES
EVULSING
EVULSION
EVULSIONS
EVZONE
EVZONES
EW
EWE
EWER
EWERS
EWES
EWEST
EWFTES
EWGHEN
EWHOW
EWK
EWKED
EWKING
EWKS
EWT
EWTS

EX
EXABYTE
EXABYTES
EXACT
EXACTA
EXACTABLE
EXACTAS
EXACTED
EXACTER
EXACTERS
EXACTEST
EXACTING
EXACTION
EXACTIONS
EXACTLY
EXACTMENT
EXACTNESS
EXACTOR
EXACTORS
EXACTRESS
EXACTS
EXACUM
EXACUMS
EXAHERTZ
EXALT
EXALTED
EXALTEDLY
EXALTER
EXALTERS
EXALTING
EXALTS
EXAM
EXAMEN
EXAMENS
EXAMETRE
EXAMETRES
EXAMINANT
EXAMINATE
EXAMINE
EXAMINED
EXAMINEE
EXAMINEES
EXAMINER
EXAMINERS
EXAMINES
EXAMINING
EXAMPLAR
EXAMPLARS

EXAMPLE
EXAMPLED
EXAMPLES
EXAMPLING
EXAMS
EXANIMATE
EXANTHEM
EXANTHEMA
EXANTHEMS
EXAPTED
EXAPTIVE
EXARATE
EXARATION
EXARCH
EXARCHAL
EXARCHATE
EXARCHIES
EXARCHIST
EXARCHS
EXARCHY
EXCAMB
EXCAMBED
EXCAMBING
EXCAMBION
EXCAMBIUM
EXCAMBS
EXCARNATE
EXCAUDATE
EXCAVATE
EXCAVATED
EXCAVATES
EXCAVATOR
EXCEED
EXCEEDED
EXCEEDER
EXCEEDERS
EXCEEDING
EXCEEDS
EXCEL
EXCELLED
EXCELLENT
EXCELLING
EXCELS
EXCELSIOR
EXCENTRIC
EXCEPT
EXCEPTANT
EXCEPTED

EXCEPTING
EXCEPTION
EXCEPTIVE
EXCEPTOR
EXCEPTORS
EXCEPTS
EXCERPT
EXCERPTA
EXCERPTED
EXCERPTER
EXCERPTOR
EXCERPTS
EXCERPTUM
EXCESS
EXCESSED
EXCESSES
EXCESSING
EXCESSIVE
EXCHANGE
EXCHANGED
EXCHANGER
EXCHANGES
EXCHEAT
EXCHEATS
EXCHEQUER
EXCIDE
EXCIDED
EXCIDES
EXCIDING
EXCIMER
EXCIMERS
EXCIPIENT
EXCIPLE
EXCIPLES
EXCISABLE
EXCISE
EXCISED
EXCISEMAN
EXCISEMEN
EXCISES
EXCISING
EXCISION
EXCISIONS
EXCITABLE
EXCITABLY
EXCITANCY
EXCITANT
EXCITANTS

EXCITE
EXCITED
EXCITEDLY
EXCITER
EXCITERS
EXCITES
EXCITING
EXCITON
EXCITONIC
EXCITONS
EXCITOR
EXCITORS
EXCLAIM
EXCLAIMED
EXCLAIMER
EXCLAIMS
EXCLAVE
EXCLAVES
EXCLOSURE
EXCLUDE
EXCLUDED
EXCLUDEE
EXCLUDEES
EXCLUDER
EXCLUDERS
EXCLUDES
EXCLUDING
EXCLUSION
EXCLUSIVE
EXCLUSORY
EXCORIATE
EXCREMENT
EXCRETA
EXCRETAL
EXCRETE
EXCRETED
EXCRETER
EXCRETERS
EXCRETES
EXCRETING
EXCRETION
EXCRETIVE
EXCRETORY
EXCUBANT
EXCUDIT
EXCULPATE
EXCURRENT
EXCURSE

E

EXCURSED
EXCURSES
EXCURSING
EXCURSION
EXCURSIVE
EXCURSUS
EXCUSABLE
EXCUSABLY
EXCUSAL
EXCUSALS
EXCUSE
EXCUSED
EXCUSER
EXCUSERS
EXCUSES
EXCUSING
EXCUSIVE
EXEAT
EXEATS
EXEC
EXECRABLE
EXECRABLY
EXECRATE
EXECRATED
EXECRATES
EXECRATOR
EXECS
EXECUTANT
EXECUTARY
EXECUTE
EXECUTED
EXECUTER
EXECUTERS
EXECUTES
EXECUTING
EXECUTION
EXECUTIVE
EXECUTOR
EXECUTORS
EXECUTORY
EXECUTRIX
EXECUTRY
EXED
EXEDRA
EXEDRAE
EXEDRAS
EXEEM
EXEEMED
EXEEMING
EXEEMS
EXEGESES
EXEGESIS
EXEGETE
EXEGETES
EXEGETIC
EXEGETICS
EXEGETIST
EXEME
EXEMED
EXEMES
EXEMING
EXEMPLA
EXEMPLAR
EXEMPLARS
EXEMPLARY
EXEMPLE
EXEMPLES
EXEMPLIFY
EXEMPLUM
EXEMPT
EXEMPTED
EXEMPTING
EXEMPTION
EXEMPTIVE
EXEMPTS
EXEQUATUR
EXEQUIAL
EXEQUIES
EXEQUY
EXERCISE
EXERCISED
EXERCISER
EXERCISES
EXERCYCLE
EXERGIES
EXERGONIC
EXERGUAL
EXERGUE
EXERGUES
EXERGY
EXERT
EXERTED
EXERTING
EXERTION
EXERTIONS
EXERTIVE
EXERTS
EXES
EXEUNT
EXFIL
EXFILLED
EXFILLING
EXFILS
EXFOLIANT
EXFOLIATE
EXHALABLE
EXHALANT
EXHALANTS
EXHALE
EXHALED
EXHALENT
EXHALENTS
EXHALES
EXHALING
EXHAUST
EXHAUSTED
EXHAUSTER
EXHAUSTS
EXHEDRA
EXHEDRAE
EXHIBIT
EXHIBITED
EXHIBITER
EXHIBITOR
EXHIBITS
EXHORT
EXHORTED
EXHORTER
EXHORTERS
EXHORTING
EXHORTS
EXHUMATE
EXHUMATED
EXHUMATES
EXHUME
EXHUMED
EXHUMER
EXHUMERS
EXHUMES
EXHUMING
EXIES
EXIGEANT
EXIGEANTE
EXIGENCE
EXIGENCES
EXIGENCY
EXIGENT
EXIGENTLY
EXIGENTS
EXIGIBLE
EXIGUITY
EXIGUOUS
EXILABLE
EXILE
EXILED
EXILEMENT
EXILER
EXILERS
EXILES
EXILIAN
EXILIC
EXILING
EXILITIES
EXILITY
EXIMIOUS
EXINE
EXINES
EXING
EXIST
EXISTED
EXISTENCE
EXISTENT
EXISTENTS
EXISTING
EXISTS
EXIT
EXITANCE
EXITANCES
EXITED
EXITING
EXITLESS
EXITS
EXO
EXOCARP
EXOCARPS
EXOCRINE
EXOCRINES
EXOCYCLIC
EXOCYTIC
EXOCYTOSE
EXODE
EXODERM
EXODERMAL
EXODERMIS
EXODERMS
EXODES
EXODIC
EXODIST
EXODISTS
EXODOI
EXODONTIA
EXODOS
EXODUS
EXODUSES
EXOENZYME
EXOERGIC
EXOGAMIC
EXOGAMIES
EXOGAMOUS
EXOGAMY
EXOGEN
EXOGENIC
EXOGENISM
EXOGENOUS
EXOGENS
EXOME
EXOMES
EXOMION
EXOMIONS
EXOMIS
EXOMISES
EXON
EXONERATE
EXONEREE
EXONEREES
EXONIC
EXONS
EXONUMIA
EXONUMIST
EXONYM
EXONYMS
EXOPHAGY
EXOPHORIC
EXOPLANET
EXOPLASM
EXOPLASMS
EXOPOD
EXOPODITE
EXOPODS
EXORABLE

EXORATION
EXORCISE
EXORCISED
EXORCISER
EXORCISES
EXORCISM
EXORCISMS
EXORCIST
EXORCISTS
EXORCIZE
EXORCIZED
EXORCIZER
EXORCIZES
EXORDIA
EXORDIAL
EXORDIUM
EXORDIUMS
EXOSMIC
EXOSMOSE
EXOSMOSES
EXOSMOSIS
EXOSMOTIC
EXOSPHERE
EXOSPORAL
EXOSPORE
EXOSPORES
EXOSPORIA
EXOSTOSES
EXOSTOSIS
EXOTERIC
EXOTIC
EXOTICA
EXOTICISE
EXOTICISM
EXOTICIST
EXOTICIZE
EXOTICS
EXOTISM
EXOTISMS
EXOTOXIC
EXOTOXIN
EXOTOXINS
EXOTROPIA
EXOTROPIC
EXPAND
EXPANDED
EXPANDER
EXPANDERS
EXPANDING
EXPANDOR
EXPANDORS
EXPANDS
EXPANSE
EXPANSES
EXPANSILE
EXPANSION
EXPANSIVE
EXPAT
EXPATIATE
EXPATS
EXPECT
EXPECTANT
EXPECTED
EXPECTER
EXPECTERS
EXPECTING
EXPECTS
EXPEDIENT
EXPEDITE
EXPEDITED
EXPEDITER
EXPEDITES
EXPEDITOR
EXPEL
EXPELLANT
EXPELLED
EXPELLEE
EXPELLEES
EXPELLENT
EXPELLER
EXPELLERS
EXPELLING
EXPELS
EXPEND
EXPENDED
EXPENDER
EXPENDERS
EXPENDING
EXPENDS
EXPENSE
EXPENSED
EXPENSES
EXPENSING
EXPENSIVE
EXPERT
EXPERTED
EXPERTING
EXPERTISE
EXPERTISM
EXPERTIZE
EXPERTLY
EXPERTS
EXPIABLE
EXPIATE
EXPIATED
EXPIATES
EXPIATING
EXPIATION
EXPIATOR
EXPIATORS
EXPIATORY
EXPIRABLE
EXPIRANT
EXPIRANTS
EXPIRE
EXPIRED
EXPIRER
EXPIRERS
EXPIRES
EXPIRIES
EXPIRING
EXPIRY
EXPISCATE
EXPLAIN
EXPLAINED
EXPLAINER
EXPLAINS
EXPLANT
EXPLANTED
EXPLANTS
EXPLETIVE
EXPLETORY
EXPLICATE
EXPLICIT
EXPLICITS
EXPLODE
EXPLODED
EXPLODER
EXPLODERS
EXPLODES
EXPLODING
EXPLOIT
EXPLOITED
EXPLOITER
EXPLOITS
EXPLORE
EXPLORED
EXPLORER
EXPLORERS
EXPLORES
EXPLORING
EXPLOSION
EXPLOSIVE
EXPO
EXPONENT
EXPONENTS
EXPONIBLE
EXPORT
EXPORTED
EXPORTER
EXPORTERS
EXPORTING
EXPORTS
EXPOS
EXPOSABLE
EXPOSAL
EXPOSALS
EXPOSE
EXPOSED
EXPOSER
EXPOSERS
EXPOSES
EXPOSING
EXPOSIT
EXPOSITED
EXPOSITOR
EXPOSITS
EXPOSOME
EXPOSOMES
EXPOSTURE
EXPOSURE
EXPOSURES
EXPOUND
EXPOUNDED
EXPOUNDER
EXPOUNDS
EXPRESS
EXPRESSED
EXPRESSER
EXPRESSES
EXPRESSLY
EXPRESSO
EXPRESSOS
EXPUGN
EXPUGNED
EXPUGNING
EXPUGNS
EXPULSE
EXPULSED
EXPULSES
EXPULSING
EXPULSION
EXPULSIVE
EXPUNCT
EXPUNCTED
EXPUNCTS
EXPUNGE
EXPUNGED
EXPUNGER
EXPUNGERS
EXPUNGES
EXPUNGING
EXPURGATE
EXPURGE
EXPURGED
EXPURGES
EXPURGING
EXQUISITE
EXSCIND
EXSCINDED
EXSCINDS
EXSECANT
EXSECANTS
EXSECT
EXSECTED
EXSECTING
EXSECTION
EXSECTS
EXSERT
EXSERTED
EXSERTILE
EXSERTING
EXSERTION
EXSERTS
EXSICCANT
EXSICCATE
EXSTROPHY
EXSUCCOUS
EXTANT
EXTASIES

E

EXTASY
EXTATIC
EXTEMPORE
EXTEND
EXTENDANT
EXTENDED
EXTENDER
EXTENDERS
EXTENDING
EXTENDS
EXTENSE
EXTENSES
EXTENSILE
EXTENSION
EXTENSITY
EXTENSIVE
EXTENSOR
EXTENSORS
EXTENT
EXTENTS
EXTENUATE
EXTERIOR
EXTERIORS
EXTERMINE
EXTERN
EXTERNAL
EXTERNALS
EXTERNAT
EXTERNATS
EXTERNE
EXTERNES
EXTERNS
EXTINCT
EXTINCTED
EXTINCTS
EXTINE
EXTINES
EXTIRP
EXTIRPATE
EXTIRPED
EXTIRPING
EXTIRPS
EXTOL
EXTOLD
EXTOLL
EXTOLLED
EXTOLLER
EXTOLLERS
EXTOLLING
EXTOLLS
EXTOLMENT
EXTOLS
EXTORSIVE
EXTORT
EXTORTED
EXTORTER
EXTORTERS
EXTORTING
EXTORTION
EXTORTIVE
EXTORTS
EXTRA
EXTRABOLD
EXTRACT
EXTRACTED
EXTRACTOR
EXTRACTS
EXTRADITE
EXTRADOS
EXTRAIT
EXTRAITS
EXTRALITY
EXTRANET
EXTRANETS
EXTRAPOSE
EXTRAS
EXTRAUGHT
EXTRAVERT
EXTREAT
EXTREATED
EXTREATS
EXTREMA
EXTREMAL
EXTREMALS
EXTREME
EXTREMELY
EXTREMER
EXTREMES
EXTREMEST
EXTREMISM
EXTREMIST
EXTREMITY
EXTREMUM
EXTREMUMS
EXTRICATE
EXTRINSIC
EXTROPIAN
EXTROPIES
EXTROPY
EXTRORSAL
EXTRORSE
EXTROVERT
EXTRUDE
EXTRUDED
EXTRUDER
EXTRUDERS
EXTRUDES
EXTRUDING
EXTRUSILE
EXTRUSION
EXTRUSIVE
EXTRUSORY
EXTUBATE
EXTUBATED
EXTUBATES
EXUBERANT
EXUBERATE
EXUDATE
EXUDATES
EXUDATION
EXUDATIVE
EXUDE
EXUDED
EXUDES
EXUDING
EXUL
EXULLED
EXULLING
EXULS
EXULT
EXULTANCE
EXULTANCY
EXULTANT
EXULTED
EXULTING
EXULTS
EXURB
EXURBAN
EXURBIA
EXURBIAS
EXURBS
EXUVIA
EXUVIAE
EXUVIAL
EXUVIATE
EXUVIATED
EXUVIATES
EXUVIUM
EYALET
EYALETS
EYAS
EYASES
EYASS
EYASSES
EYE
EYEABLE
EYEBALL
EYEBALLED
EYEBALLS
EYEBANK
EYEBANKS
EYEBAR
EYEBARS
EYEBATH
EYEBATHS
EYEBEAM
EYEBEAMS
EYEBLACK
EYEBLACKS
EYEBLINK
EYEBLINKS
EYEBOLT
EYEBOLTS
EYEBRIGHT
EYEBROW
EYEBROWED
EYEBROWS
EYECUP
EYECUPS
EYED
EYEDNESS
EYEDROPS
EYEFOLD
EYEFOLDS
EYEFUL
EYEFULS
EYEGLASS
EYEHOLE
EYEHOLES
EYEHOOK
EYEHOOKS
EYEING
EYELASH
EYELASHES
EYELESS
EYELET
EYELETED
EYELETEER
EYELETING
EYELETS
EYELETTED
EYELEVEL
EYELIAD
EYELIADS
EYELID
EYELIDS
EYELIFT
EYELIFTS
EYELIKE
EYELINE
EYELINER
EYELINERS
EYELINES
EYEN
EYEOPENER
EYEPATCH
EYEPIECE
EYEPIECES
EYEPOINT
EYEPOINTS
EYEPOPPER
EYER
EYERS
EYES
EYESHADE
EYESHADES
EYESHADOW
EYESHINE
EYESHINES
EYESHOT
EYESHOTS
EYESIGHT
EYESIGHTS
EYESOME
EYESORE
EYESORES
EYESPOT
EYESPOTS
EYESTALK
EYESTALKS

EYESTONE
EYESTONES
EYESTRAIN
EYETEETH
EYETOOTH
EYEWASH
EYEWASHES
EYEWATER
EYEWATERS
EYEWEAR
EYEWEARS
EYEWINK
EYEWINKS
EYING
EYLIAD
EYLIADS
EYNE
EYOT
EYOTS
EYRA
EYRAS
EYRE
EYRES
EYRIE
EYRIES
EYRIR
EYRY
EZINE
EZINES

F

FA
FAA
FAAING
FAAN
FAAS
FAB
FABACEOUS
FABBER
FABBEST
FABBIER
FABBIEST
FABBY
FABLE
FABLED
FABLER
FABLERS
FABLES
FABLET
FABLETS
FABLIAU
FABLIAUX
FABLING
FABLINGS
FABRIC
FABRICANT
FABRICATE
FABRICKED
FABRICS
FABRIQUE
FABRIQUES
FABS
FABULAR
FABULATE
FABULATED
FABULATES
FABULATOR
FABULISE
FABULISED
FABULISES
FABULISM
FABULISMS
FABULIST
FABULISTS
FABULIZE
FABULIZED
FABULIZES
FABULOUS
FABURDEN
FABURDENS
FACADE
FACADES
FACE
FACEABLE
FACEBAR
FACEBARS
FACEBOOK
FACEBOOKS
FACECLOTH
FACED
FACEDOWN
FACEDOWNS
FACELESS
FACELIFT
FACELIFTS
FACEMAIL
FACEMAILS
FACEMAN
FACEMASK
FACEMASKS
FACEMEN
FACEOFF
FACEOFFS
FACEPALM
FACEPALMS
FACEPLANT
FACEPLATE
FACEPRINT
FACER
FACERS
FACES
FACET
FACETE
FACETED
FACETELY
FACETIAE
FACETIME
FACETIMED
FACETIMES
FACETING
FACETINGS
FACETIOUS
FACETS
FACETTED
FACETTING
FACEUP
FACIA
FACIAE
FACIAL
FACIALIST
FACIALLY
FACIALS
FACIAS
FACIEND
FACIENDS
FACIES
FACILE
FACILELY
FACILITY
FACING
FACINGS
FACONNE
FACONNES
FACSIMILE
FACT
FACTA
FACTFUL
FACTICE
FACTICES
FACTICITY
FACTION
FACTIONAL
FACTIONS
FACTIOUS
FACTIS
FACTISES
FACTITIVE
FACTIVE
FACTOID
FACTOIDAL
FACTOIDS
FACTOR
FACTORAGE
FACTORED
FACTORIAL
FACTORIES
FACTORING
FACTORISE
FACTORIZE
FACTORS
FACTORY
FACTOTUM
FACTOTUMS
FACTS
FACTSHEET
FACTUAL
FACTUALLY
FACTUM
FACTUMS
FACTURE
FACTURES
FACULA
FACULAE
FACULAR
FACULTIES
FACULTY
FACUNDITY
FAD
FADABLE
FADAISE
FADAISES
FADDIER
FADDIEST
FADDINESS
FADDISH
FADDISHLY
FADDISM
FADDISMS
FADDIST
FADDISTS
FADDLE
FADDLED
FADDLES
FADDLING
FADDY
FADE
FADEAWAY
FADEAWAYS
FADED
FADEDLY
FADEDNESS
FADEIN
FADEINS
FADELESS
FADEOUT
FADEOUTS
FADER
FADERS
FADES
FADEUR
FADEURS
FADGE
FADGED
FADGES
FADGING
FADIER
FADIEST
FADING
FADINGS
FADLIKE
FADO
FADOMETER
FADOS
FADS
FADY
FAE
FAECAL
FAECES
FAENA
FAENAS
FAERIE

FAERIES
FAERY
FAFF
FAFFED
FAFFIER
FAFFIEST
FAFFING
FAFFS
FAFFY
FAG
FAGACEOUS
FAGGED
FAGGERIES
FAGGERY
FAGGIER
FAGGIEST
FAGGING
FAGGINGS
FAGGOT
FAGGOTED
FAGGOTIER
FAGGOTING
FAGGOTRY
FAGGOTS
FAGGOTY
FAGGY
FAGIN
FAGINS
FAGOT
FAGOTED
FAGOTER
FAGOTERS
FAGOTING
FAGOTINGS
FAGOTS
FAGOTTI
FAGOTTIST
FAGOTTO
FAGOTTOS
FAGS
FAH
FAHLBAND
FAHLBANDS
FAHLERZ
FAHLERZES
FAHLORE
FAHLORES
FAHS
FAIBLE
FAIBLES
FAIENCE
FAIENCES
FAIK
FAIKED
FAIKES
FAIKING
FAIKS
FAIL
FAILED
FAILING
FAILINGLY
FAILINGS
FAILLE
FAILLES
FAILOVER
FAILOVERS
FAILS
FAILURE
FAILURES
FAIN
FAINE
FAINEANCE
FAINEANCY
FAINEANT
FAINEANTS
FAINED
FAINER
FAINES
FAINEST
FAINING
FAINITES
FAINLY
FAINNE
FAINNES
FAINNESS
FAINS
FAINT
FAINTED
FAINTER
FAINTERS
FAINTEST
FAINTIER
FAINTIEST
FAINTING
FAINTINGS
FAINTISH
FAINTLY
FAINTNESS
FAINTS
FAINTY
FAIR
FAIRED
FAIRER
FAIREST
FAIRFACED
FAIRGOER
FAIRGOERS
FAIRIER
FAIRIES
FAIRIEST
FAIRILY
FAIRING
FAIRINGS
FAIRISH
FAIRISHLY
FAIRLEAD
FAIRLEADS
FAIRLY
FAIRNESS
FAIRS
FAIRWAY
FAIRWAYS
FAIRY
FAIRYDOM
FAIRYDOMS
FAIRYHOOD
FAIRYISM
FAIRYISMS
FAIRYLAND
FAIRYLIKE
FAIRYTALE
FAITH
FAITHCURE
FAITHED
FAITHER
FAITHERS
FAITHFUL
FAITHFULS
FAITHING
FAITHINGS
FAITHLESS
FAITHS
FAITOR
FAITORS
FAITOUR
FAITOURS
FAIX
FAJITA
FAJITAS
FAKE
FAKED
FAKEER
FAKEERS
FAKEMENT
FAKEMENTS
FAKER
FAKERIES
FAKERS
FAKERY
FAKES
FAKEST
FAKEY
FAKEYS
FAKIE
FAKIER
FAKIES
FAKIEST
FAKING
FAKIR
FAKIRISM
FAKIRISMS
FAKIRS
FALAFEL
FALAFELS
FALAJ
FALANGISM
FALANGIST
FALBALA
FALBALAS
FALCADE
FALCADES
FALCATE
FALCATED
FALCATION
FALCES
FALCHION
FALCHIONS
FALCIFORM
FALCON
FALCONER
FALCONERS
FALCONET
FALCONETS
FALCONINE
FALCONOID
FALCONRY
FALCONS
FALCULA
FALCULAE
FALCULAS
FALCULATE
FALDAGE
FALDAGES
FALDERAL
FALDERALS
FALDEROL
FALDEROLS
FALDETTA
FALDETTAS
FALDSTOOL
FALL
FALLACIES
FALLACY
FALLAL
FALLALERY
FALLALISH
FALLALS
FALLAWAY
FALLAWAYS
FALLBACK
FALLBACKS
FALLBOARD
FALLEN
FALLER
FALLERS
FALLFISH
FALLIBLE
FALLIBLY
FALLING
FALLINGS
FALLOFF
FALLOFFS
FALLOUT
FALLOUTS
FALLOW
FALLOWED
FALLOWER
FALLOWEST
FALLOWING
FALLOWS

F

FALLS
FALSE
FALSED
FALSEFACE
FALSEHOOD
FALSELY
FALSENESS
FALSER
FALSERS
FALSES
FALSEST
FALSETTO
FALSETTOS
FALSEWORK
FALSIE
FALSIES
FALSIFIED
FALSIFIER
FALSIFIES
FALSIFY
FALSING
FALSISH
FALSISM
FALSISMS
FALSITIES
FALSITY
FALTBOAT
FALTBOATS
FALTER
FALTERED
FALTERER
FALTERERS
FALTERING
FALTERS
FALX
FAME
FAMED
FAMELESS
FAMES
FAMILIAL
FAMILIAR
FAMILIARS
FAMILIES
FAMILISM
FAMILISMS
FAMILIST
FAMILLE
FAMILLES
FAMILY
FAMINE
FAMINES
FAMING
FAMISH
FAMISHED
FAMISHES
FAMISHING
FAMOUS
FAMOUSED
FAMOUSES
FAMOUSING
FAMOUSLY
FAMULI
FAMULUS
FAN
FANAL
FANALS
FANATIC
FANATICAL
FANATICS
FANBASE
FANBASES
FANBOY
FANBOYS
FANCIABLE
FANCIED
FANCIER
FANCIERS
FANCIES
FANCIEST
FANCIFIED
FANCIFIES
FANCIFUL
FANCIFY
FANCILESS
FANCILY
FANCINESS
FANCY
FANCYING
FANCYWORK
FAND
FANDANGLE
FANDANGO
FANDANGOS
FANDED
FANDING
FANDOM
FANDOMS
FANDS
FANE
FANEGA
FANEGADA
FANEGADAS
FANEGAS
FANES
FANFARADE
FANFARE
FANFARED
FANFARES
FANFARING
FANFARON
FANFARONA
FANFARONS
FANFIC
FANFICS
FANFOLD
FANFOLDED
FANFOLDS
FANG
FANGA
FANGAS
FANGED
FANGING
FANGIRL
FANGIRLS
FANGLE
FANGLED
FANGLES
FANGLESS
FANGLIKE
FANGLING
FANGO
FANGOS
FANGS
FANION
FANIONS
FANJET
FANJETS
FANK
FANKED
FANKING
FANKLE
FANKLED
FANKLES
FANKLING
FANKS
FANLIGHT
FANLIGHTS
FANLIKE
FANNED
FANNEL
FANNELL
FANNELLS
FANNELS
FANNER
FANNERS
FANNIED
FANNIES
FANNING
FANNINGS
FANNY
FANNYING
FANO
FANON
FANONS
FANOS
FANS
FANSITE
FANSITES
FANSUB
FANSUBS
FANTAD
FANTADS
FANTAIL
FANTAILED
FANTAILS
FANTASIA
FANTASIAS
FANTASIE
FANTASIED
FANTASIES
FANTASISE
FANTASIST
FANTASIZE
FANTASM
FANTASMAL
FANTASMIC
FANTASMS
FANTASQUE
FANTAST
FANTASTIC
FANTASTRY
FANTASTS
FANTASY
FANTEEG
FANTEEGS
FANTIGUE
FANTIGUES
FANTOD
FANTODS
FANTOM
FANTOMS
FANTOOSH
FANUM
FANUMS
FANWISE
FANWORT
FANWORTS
FANZINE
FANZINES
FAP
FAQIR
FAQIRS
FAQUIR
FAQUIRS
FAR
FARAD
FARADAIC
FARADAY
FARADAYS
FARADIC
FARADISE
FARADISED
FARADISER
FARADISES
FARADISM
FARADISMS
FARADIZE
FARADIZED
FARADIZER
FARADIZES
FARADS
FARAND
FARANDINE
FARANDOLE
FARANG
FARANGS
FARAWAY
FARAWAYS
FARCE
FARCED

FARCEMEAT
FARCER
FARCERS
FARCES
FARCEUR
FARCEURS
FARCEUSE
FARCEUSES
FARCI
FARCICAL
FARCIE
FARCIED
FARCIES
FARCIFIED
FARCIFIES
FARCIFY
FARCIN
FARCING
FARCINGS
FARCINS
FARCY
FARD
FARDAGE
FARDAGES
FARDED
FARDEL
FARDELS
FARDEN
FARDENS
FARDING
FARDINGS
FARDS
FARE
FAREBOX
FAREBOXES
FARED
FARER
FARERS
FARES
FAREWELL
FAREWELLS
FARFAL
FARFALLE
FARFALLES
FARFALS
FARFEL
FARFELS
FARFET
FARINA
FARINAS
FARING
FARINHA
FARINHAS
FARINOSE
FARL
FARLE
FARLES
FARLS
FARM
FARMABLE
FARMED
FARMER
FARMERESS
FARMERIES
FARMERS
FARMERY
FARMHAND
FARMHANDS
FARMHOUSE
FARMING
FARMINGS
FARMLAND
FARMLANDS
FARMOST
FARMS
FARMSTEAD
FARMWIFE
FARMWIVES
FARMWORK
FARMWORKS
FARMYARD
FARMYARDS
FARNARKEL
FARNESOL
FARNESOLS
FARNESS
FARNESSES
FARO
FAROLITO
FAROLITOS
FAROS
FAROUCHE
FARRAGO
FARRAGOES
FARRAGOS
FARRAND
FARRANT
FARRED
FARREN
FARRENS
FARRIER
FARRIERS
FARRIERY
FARRING
FARRO
FARROS
FARROW
FARROWED
FARROWING
FARROWS
FARRUCA
FARRUCAS
FARS
FARSE
FARSED
FARSEEING
FARSES
FARSIDE
FARSIDES
FARSING
FART
FARTED
FARTHEL
FARTHELS
FARTHER
FARTHEST
FARTHING
FARTHINGS
FARTING
FARTLEK
FARTLEKS
FARTS
FAS
FASCES
FASCI
FASCIA
FASCIAE
FASCIAL
FASCIAS
FASCIATE
FASCIATED
FASCICLE
FASCICLED
FASCICLES
FASCICULE
FASCICULI
FASCIITIS
FASCINATE
FASCINE
FASCINES
FASCIO
FASCIOLA
FASCIOLAS
FASCIOLE
FASCIOLES
FASCIS
FASCISM
FASCISMI
FASCISMO
FASCISMS
FASCIST
FASCISTA
FASCISTI
FASCISTIC
FASCISTS
FASCITIS
FASH
FASHED
FASHERIES
FASHERY
FASHES
FASHING
FASHION
FASHIONED
FASHIONER
FASHIONS
FASHIONY
FASHIOUS
FAST
FASTBACK
FASTBACKS
FASTBALL
FASTBALLS
FASTED
FASTEN
FASTENED
FASTENER
FASTENERS
FASTENING
FASTENS
FASTER
FASTERS
FASTEST
FASTI
FASTIE
FASTIES
FASTIGIUM
FASTING
FASTINGS
FASTISH
FASTLY
FASTNESS
FASTS
FASTUOUS
FAT
FATAL
FATALISM
FATALISMS
FATALIST
FATALISTS
FATALITY
FATALLY
FATALNESS
FATBACK
FATBACKS
FATBERG
FATBERGS
FATBIRD
FATBIRDS
FATE
FATED
FATEFUL
FATEFULLY
FATES
FATHEAD
FATHEADED
FATHEADS
FATHER
FATHERED
FATHERING
FATHERLY
FATHERS
FATHOM
FATHOMED
FATHOMER
FATHOMERS
FATHOMING
FATHOMS
FATIDIC
FATIDICAL

FATIGABLE
FATIGATE
FATIGATED
FATIGATES
FATIGUE
FATIGUED
FATIGUES
FATIGUING
FATING
FATISCENT
FATLESS
FATLIKE
FATLING
FATLINGS
FATLY
FATNESS
FATNESSES
FATS
FATSIA
FATSIAS
FATSO
FATSOES
FATSOS
FATSTOCK
FATSTOCKS
FATTED
FATTEN
FATTENED
FATTENER
FATTENERS
FATTENING
FATTENS
FATTER
FATTEST
FATTIER
FATTIES
FATTIEST
FATTILY
FATTINESS
FATTING
FATTISH
FATTISM
FATTISMS
FATTIST
FATTISTS
FATTRELS
FATTY
FATUITIES
FATUITOUS
FATUITY
FATUOUS
FATUOUSLY
FATWA
FATWAED
FATWAH
FATWAHED
FATWAHING
FATWAHS
FATWAING
FATWAS
FATWOOD
FATWOODS
FAUBOURG
FAUBOURGS
FAUCAL
FAUCALS
FAUCES
FAUCET
FAUCETRY
FAUCETS
FAUCHION
FAUCHIONS
FAUCHON
FAUCHONS
FAUCIAL
FAUGH
FAULCHION
FAULD
FAULDS
FAULT
FAULTED
FAULTFUL
FAULTIER
FAULTIEST
FAULTILY
FAULTING
FAULTLESS
FAULTLINE
FAULTS
FAULTY
FAUN
FAUNA
FAUNAE
FAUNAL
FAUNALLY
FAUNAS
FAUNIST
FAUNISTIC
FAUNISTS
FAUNLIKE
FAUNS
FAUNULA
FAUNULAE
FAUNULE
FAUNULES
FAUR
FAURD
FAURER
FAUREST
FAUSTIAN
FAUT
FAUTED
FAUTEUIL
FAUTEUILS
FAUTING
FAUTOR
FAUTORS
FAUTS
FAUVE
FAUVES
FAUVETTE
FAUVETTES
FAUVISM
FAUVISMS
FAUVIST
FAUVISTS
FAUX
FAUXMANCE
FAVA
FAVAS
FAVE
FAVEL
FAVELA
FAVELAS
FAVELL
FAVELLA
FAVELLAS
FAVELS
FAVEOLATE
FAVER
FAVES
FAVEST
FAVICON
FAVICONS
FAVISM
FAVISMS
FAVONIAN
FAVOR
FAVORABLE
FAVORABLY
FAVORED
FAVORER
FAVORERS
FAVORING
FAVORITE
FAVORITES
FAVORLESS
FAVORS
FAVOSE
FAVOUR
FAVOURED
FAVOURER
FAVOURERS
FAVOURING
FAVOURITE
FAVOURS
FAVOUS
FAVRILE
FAVRILES
FAVUS
FAVUSES
FAW
FAWN
FAWNED
FAWNER
FAWNERS
FAWNIER
FAWNIEST
FAWNING
FAWNINGLY
FAWNINGS
FAWNLIKE
FAWNS
FAWNY
FAWS
FAX
FAXABLE
FAXED
FAXES
FAXING
FAY
FAYALITE
FAYALITES
FAYED
FAYENCE
FAYENCES
FAYER
FAYEST
FAYING
FAYNE
FAYNED
FAYNES
FAYNING
FAYRE
FAYRES
FAYS
FAZE
FAZED
FAZENDA
FAZENDAS
FAZES
FAZING
FE
FEAGUE
FEAGUED
FEAGUES
FEAGUING
FEAL
FEALED
FEALING
FEALS
FEALTIES
FEALTY
FEAR
FEARE
FEARED
FEARER
FEARERS
FEARES
FEARFUL
FEARFULLY
FEARING
FEARLESS
FEARS
FEARSOME
FEART
FEASANCE
FEASANCES
FEASE
FEASED

FEASES
FEASIBLE
FEASIBLY
FEASING
FEAST
FEASTED
FEASTER
FEASTERS
FEASTFUL
FEASTING
FEASTINGS
FEASTLESS
FEASTS
FEAT
FEATED
FEATEOUS
FEATER
FEATEST
FEATHER
FEATHERED
FEATHERS
FEATHERY
FEATING
FEATLIER
FEATLIEST
FEATLY
FEATOUS
FEATS
FEATUOUS
FEATURE
FEATURED
FEATURELY
FEATURES
FEATURING
FEAZE
FEAZED
FEAZES
FEAZING
FEBLESSE
FEBLESSES
FEBRICITY
FEBRICULA
FEBRICULE
FEBRIFIC
FEBRIFUGE
FEBRILE
FEBRILITY
FECAL
FECES
FECHT
FECHTER
FECHTERS
FECHTING
FECHTS
FECIAL
FECIALS
FECIT
FECK
FECKED
FECKIN
FECKING
FECKLESS
FECKLY
FECKS
FECULA
FECULAE
FECULAS
FECULENCE
FECULENCY
FECULENT
FECUND
FECUNDATE
FECUNDITY
FED
FEDARIE
FEDARIES
FEDAYEE
FEDAYEEN
FEDELINI
FEDELINIS
FEDERACY
FEDERAL
FEDERALLY
FEDERALS
FEDERARIE
FEDERARY
FEDERATE
FEDERATED
FEDERATES
FEDERATOR
FEDEX
FEDEXED
FEDEXES
FEDEXING
FEDORA
FEDORAS
FEDS
FEE
FEEB
FEEBLE
FEEBLED
FEEBLER
FEEBLES
FEEBLEST
FEEBLING
FEEBLISH
FEEBLY
FEEBS
FEED
FEEDABLE
FEEDBACK
FEEDBACKS
FEEDBAG
FEEDBAGS
FEEDBOX
FEEDBOXES
FEEDER
FEEDERS
FEEDGRAIN
FEEDHOLE
FEEDHOLES
FEEDING
FEEDINGS
FEEDLOT
FEEDLOTS
FEEDPIPE
FEEDPIPES
FEEDS
FEEDSTOCK
FEEDSTUFF
FEEDWATER
FEEDYARD
FEEDYARDS
FEEING
FEEL
FEELBAD
FEELER
FEELERS
FEELESS
FEELGOOD
FEELING
FEELINGLY
FEELINGS
FEELS
FEEN
FEENS
FEER
FEERED
FEERIE
FEERIES
FEERIN
FEERING
FEERINGS
FEERINS
FEERS
FEES
FEESE
FEESED
FEESES
FEESING
FEET
FEETFIRST
FEETLESS
FEEZE
FEEZED
FEEZES
FEEZING
FEG
FEGARIES
FEGARY
FEGS
FEH
FEHM
FEHME
FEHMIC
FEHS
FEIGN
FEIGNED
FEIGNEDLY
FEIGNER
FEIGNERS
FEIGNING
FEIGNINGS
FEIGNS
FEIJOA
FEIJOADA
FEIJOADAS
FEIJOAS
FEINT
FEINTED
FEINTER
FEINTEST
FEINTING
FEINTS
FEIRIE
FEIRIER
FEIRIEST
FEIS
FEISEANNA
FEIST
FEISTIER
FEISTIEST
FEISTILY
FEISTS
FEISTY
FELAFEL
FELAFELS
FELCH
FELCHED
FELCHES
FELCHING
FELDGRAU
FELDGRAUS
FELDSCHAR
FELDSCHER
FELDSHER
FELDSHERS
FELDSPAR
FELDSPARS
FELDSPATH
FELICIA
FELICIAS
FELICIFIC
FELICITER
FELICITY
FELID
FELIDS
FELINE
FELINELY
FELINES
FELINITY
FELL
FELLA
FELLABLE
FELLAH
FELLAHEEN
FELLAHIN
FELLAHS
FELLAS
FELLATE

F

F

FELLATED
FELLATES
FELLATING
FELLATIO
FELLATION
FELLATIOS
FELLATOR
FELLATORS
FELLATRIX
FELLED
FELLER
FELLERS
FELLEST
FELLFIELD
FELLIES
FELLING
FELLINGS
FELLNESS
FELLOE
FELLOES
FELLOW
FELLOWED
FELLOWING
FELLOWLY
FELLOWMAN
FELLOWMEN
FELLOWS
FELLS
FELLY
FELON
FELONIES
FELONIOUS
FELONOUS
FELONRIES
FELONRY
FELONS
FELONY
FELQUISTE
FELSIC
FELSITE
FELSITES
FELSITIC
FELSPAR
FELSPARS
FELSTONE
FELSTONES
FELT
FELTED
FELTER
FELTERED
FELTERING
FELTERS
FELTIER
FELTIEST
FELTING
FELTINGS
FELTLIKE
FELTS
FELTY
FELUCCA
FELUCCAS
FELWORT
FELWORTS
FEM
FEMAL
FEMALE
FEMALES
FEMALITY
FEMALS
FEME
FEMERALL
FEMERALLS
FEMERELL
FEMERELLS
FEMES
FEMETARY
FEMICIDAL
FEMICIDE
FEMICIDES
FEMINACY
FEMINAL
FEMINAZI
FEMINAZIS
FEMINEITY
FEMINIE
FEMINIES
FEMININE
FEMININES
FEMINISE
FEMINISED
FEMINISES
FEMINISM
FEMINISMS
FEMINIST
FEMINISTS
FEMINITY
FEMINIZE
FEMINIZED
FEMINIZES
FEMITER
FEMITERS
FEMME
FEMMES
FEMMIER
FEMMIEST
FEMMY
FEMORA
FEMORAL
FEMS
FEMUR
FEMURS
FEN
FENAGLE
FENAGLED
FENAGLES
FENAGLING
FENCE
FENCED
FENCELESS
FENCELIKE
FENCELINE
FENCER
FENCEROW
FENCEROWS
FENCERS
FENCES
FENCEWIRE
FENCIBLE
FENCIBLES
FENCING
FENCINGS
FEND
FENDED
FENDER
FENDERED
FENDERS
FENDIER
FENDIEST
FENDING
FENDS
FENDY
FENESTRA
FENESTRAE
FENESTRAL
FENESTRAS
FENI
FENING
FENINGA
FENINGS
FENIS
FENITAR
FENITARS
FENKS
FENLAND
FENLANDS
FENMAN
FENMEN
FENNEC
FENNECS
FENNEL
FENNELS
FENNIER
FENNIES
FENNIEST
FENNING
FENNISH
FENNY
FENS
FENT
FENTANYL
FENTANYLS
FENTHION
FENTHIONS
FENTS
FENUGREEK
FENURON
FENURONS
FEOD
FEODAL
FEODARIES
FEODARY
FEODS
FEOFF
FEOFFED
FEOFFEE
FEOFFEES
FEOFFER
FEOFFERS
FEOFFING
FEOFFMENT
FEOFFOR
FEOFFORS
FEOFFS
FER
FERACIOUS
FERACITY
FERAL
FERALISED
FERALIZED
FERALS
FERBAM
FERBAMS
FERE
FERER
FERES
FEREST
FERETORY
FERIA
FERIAE
FERIAL
FERIAS
FERINE
FERITIES
FERITY
FERLIE
FERLIED
FERLIER
FERLIES
FERLIEST
FERLY
FERLYING
FERM
FERMATA
FERMATAS
FERMATE
FERMENT
FERMENTED
FERMENTER
FERMENTOR
FERMENTS
FERMI
FERMION
FERMIONIC
FERMIONS
FERMIS
FERMIUM
FERMIUMS
FERMS
FERN
FERNALLY

FERNBIRD
FERNBIRDS
FERNERIES
FERNERY
FERNIER
FERNIEST
FERNING
FERNINGS
FERNINST
FERNLESS
FERNLIKE
FERNS
FERNSHAW
FERNSHAWS
FERNTICLE
FERNY
FEROCIOUS
FEROCITY
FERRATE
FERRATES
FERREL
FERRELED
FERRELING
FERRELLED
FERRELS
FERREOUS
FERRET
FERRETED
FERRETER
FERRETERS
FERRETIER
FERRETING
FERRETS
FERRETY
FERRIAGE
FERRIAGES
FERRIC
FERRIED
FERRIES
FERRITE
FERRITES
FERRITIC
FERRITIN
FERRITINS
FERROCENE
FERROGRAM
FERROTYPE
FERROUS
FERRUGO
FERRUGOS
FERRULE
FERRULED
FERRULES
FERRULING
FERRUM
FERRUMS
FERRY
FERRYBOAT
FERRYING
FERRYMAN
FERRYMEN
FERTIGATE
FERTILE
FERTILELY
FERTILER
FERTILEST
FERTILISE
FERTILITY
FERTILIZE
FERULA
FERULAE
FERULAS
FERULE
FERULED
FERULES
FERULING
FERVENCY
FERVENT
FERVENTER
FERVENTLY
FERVID
FERVIDER
FERVIDEST
FERVIDITY
FERVIDLY
FERVOR
FERVOROUS
FERVORS
FERVOUR
FERVOURS
FES
FESCUE
FESCUES
FESS
FESSE
FESSED
FESSES
FESSING
FESSWISE
FEST
FESTA
FESTAL
FESTALLY
FESTALS
FESTAS
FESTER
FESTERED
FESTERING
FESTERS
FESTIER
FESTIEST
FESTILOGY
FESTINATE
FESTIVAL
FESTIVALS
FESTIVE
FESTIVELY
FESTIVITY
FESTIVOUS
FESTOLOGY
FESTOON
FESTOONED
FESTOONS
FESTS
FESTY
FET
FETA
FETAL
FETAS
FETATION
FETATIONS
FETCH
FETCHED
FETCHER
FETCHERS
FETCHES
FETCHING
FETE
FETED
FETERITA
FETERITAS
FETES
FETIAL
FETIALES
FETIALIS
FETIALS
FETICH
FETICHE
FETICHES
FETICHISE
FETICHISM
FETICHIST
FETICHIZE
FETICIDAL
FETICIDE
FETICIDES
FETID
FETIDER
FETIDEST
FETIDITY
FETIDLY
FETIDNESS
FETING
FETISH
FETISHES
FETISHISE
FETISHISM
FETISHIST
FETISHIZE
FETLOCK
FETLOCKED
FETLOCKS
FETOLOGY
FETOR
FETORS
FETOSCOPE
FETOSCOPY
FETS
FETT
FETTA
FETTAS
FETTED
FETTER
FETTERED
FETTERER
FETTERERS
FETTERING
FETTERS
FETTING
FETTLE
FETTLED
FETTLER
FETTLERS
FETTLES
FETTLING
FETTLINGS
FETTS
FETTUCINE
FETTUCINI
FETUS
FETUSES
FETWA
FETWAS
FEU
FEUAR
FEUARS
FEUD
FEUDAL
FEUDALISE
FEUDALISM
FEUDALIST
FEUDALITY
FEUDALIZE
FEUDALLY
FEUDARIES
FEUDARY
FEUDATORY
FEUDED
FEUDING
FEUDINGS
FEUDIST
FEUDISTS
FEUDS
FEUED
FEUILLETE
FEUING
FEUS
FEUTRE
FEUTRED
FEUTRES
FEUTRING
FEVER
FEVERED
FEVERFEW
FEVERFEWS
FEVERING
FEVERISH
FEVERLESS
FEVEROUS
FEVERROOT

F

FEVERS
FEVERWEED
FEVERWORT
FEW
FEWER
FEWEST
FEWMET
FEWMETS
FEWNESS
FEWNESSES
FEWS
FEWTER
FEWTERED
FEWTERING
FEWTERS
FEWTRILS
FEY
FEYED
FEYER
FEYEST
FEYING
FEYLY
FEYNESS
FEYNESSES
FEYS
FEZ
FEZES
FEZZED
FEZZES
FEZZY
FIACRE
FIACRES
FIANCE
FIANCEE
FIANCEES
FIANCES
FIAR
FIARS
FIASCHI
FIASCO
FIASCOES
FIASCOS
FIAT
FIATED
FIATING
FIATS
FIAUNT
FIAUNTS
FIB
FIBBED
FIBBER
FIBBERIES
FIBBERS
FIBBERY
FIBBING
FIBER
FIBERED
FIBERFILL
FIBERISE
FIBERISED
FIBERISES
FIBERIZE
FIBERIZED
FIBERIZES
FIBERLESS
FIBERLIKE
FIBERS
FIBRANNE
FIBRANNES
FIBRATE
FIBRATES
FIBRE
FIBRED
FIBREFILL
FIBRELESS
FIBRELIKE
FIBRES
FIBRIFORM
FIBRIL
FIBRILAR
FIBRILLA
FIBRILLAE
FIBRILLAR
FIBRILLIN
FIBRILS
FIBRIN
FIBRINOID
FIBRINOUS
FIBRINS
FIBRO
FIBROCYTE
FIBROID
FIBROIDS
FIBROIN
FIBROINS
FIBROLINE
FIBROLITE
FIBROMA
FIBROMAS
FIBROMATA
FIBROS
FIBROSE
FIBROSED
FIBROSES
FIBROSING
FIBROSIS
FIBROTIC
FIBROUS
FIBROUSLY
FIBS
FIBSTER
FIBSTERS
FIBULA
FIBULAE
FIBULAR
FIBULAS
FICAIN
FICAINS
FICE
FICES
FICHE
FICHES
FICHU
FICHUS
FICIN
FICINS
FICKLE
FICKLED
FICKLER
FICKLES
FICKLEST
FICKLING
FICKLY
FICO
FICOES
FICOS
FICTILE
FICTION
FICTIONAL
FICTIONS
FICTIVE
FICTIVELY
FICTOR
FICTORS
FICUS
FICUSES
FID
FIDDIOUS
FIDDLE
FIDDLED
FIDDLER
FIDDLERS
FIDDLES
FIDDLEY
FIDDLEYS
FIDDLIER
FIDDLIEST
FIDDLING
FIDDLINGS
FIDDLY
FIDEISM
FIDEISMS
FIDEIST
FIDEISTIC
FIDEISTS
FIDELISMO
FIDELISTA
FIDELITY
FIDES
FIDGE
FIDGED
FIDGES
FIDGET
FIDGETED
FIDGETER
FIDGETERS
FIDGETIER
FIDGETING
FIDGETS
FIDGETY
FIDGING
FIDIBUS
FIDIBUSES
FIDO
FIDOS
FIDS
FIDUCIAL
FIDUCIARY
FIE
FIEF
FIEFDOM
FIEFDOMS
FIEFS
FIELD
FIELDBOOT
FIELDED
FIELDER
FIELDERS
FIELDFARE
FIELDING
FIELDINGS
FIELDMICE
FIELDS
FIELDSMAN
FIELDSMEN
FIELDVOLE
FIELDWARD
FIELDWORK
FIEND
FIENDISH
FIENDLIKE
FIENDS
FIENT
FIENTS
FIER
FIERCE
FIERCELY
FIERCER
FIERCEST
FIERE
FIERES
FIERIER
FIERIEST
FIERILY
FIERINESS
FIERS
FIERY
FIEST
FIESTA
FIESTAS
FIFE
FIFED
FIFER
FIFERS
FIFES
FIFI
FIFING
FIFIS
FIFTEEN
FIFTEENER

FIFTEENS
FIFTEENTH
FIFTH
FIFTHLY
FIFTHS
FIFTIES
FIFTIETH
FIFTIETHS
FIFTY
FIFTYFOLD
FIFTYISH
FIG
FIGEATER
FIGEATERS
FIGGED
FIGGERIES
FIGGERY
FIGGIER
FIGGIEST
FIGGING
FIGGY
FIGHT
FIGHTABLE
FIGHTBACK
FIGHTER
FIGHTERS
FIGHTING
FIGHTINGS
FIGHTS
FIGJAM
FIGJAMS
FIGLIKE
FIGMENT
FIGMENTS
FIGO
FIGOS
FIGS
FIGTREE
FIGTREES
FIGULINE
FIGULINES
FIGURABLE
FIGURAL
FIGURALLY
FIGURANT
FIGURANTE
FIGURANTS
FIGURATE
FIGURE
FIGURED
FIGUREDLY
FIGURER
FIGURERS
FIGURES
FIGURINE
FIGURINES
FIGURING
FIGURIST
FIGURISTS
FIGWORT
FIGWORTS
FIKE
FIKED
FIKERIES
FIKERY
FIKES
FIKIER
FIKIEST
FIKING
FIKISH
FIKY
FIL
FILA
FILABEG
FILABEGS
FILACEOUS
FILACER
FILACERS
FILAGGRIN
FILAGREE
FILAGREED
FILAGREES
FILAMENT
FILAMENTS
FILANDER
FILANDERS
FILAR
FILAREE
FILAREES
FILARIA
FILARIAE
FILARIAL
FILARIAN
FILARIID
FILARIIDS
FILASSE
FILASSES
FILATORY
FILATURE
FILATURES
FILAZER
FILAZERS
FILBERD
FILBERDS
FILBERT
FILBERTS
FILCH
FILCHED
FILCHER
FILCHERS
FILCHES
FILCHING
FILCHINGS
FILE
FILEABLE
FILECARD
FILECARDS
FILED
FILEFISH
FILEMOT
FILEMOTS
FILENAME
FILENAMES
FILER
FILERS
FILES
FILET
FILETED
FILETING
FILETS
FILFOT
FILFOTS
FILIAL
FILIALLY
FILIATE
FILIATED
FILIATES
FILIATING
FILIATION
FILIBEG
FILIBEGS
FILICIDAL
FILICIDE
FILICIDES
FILIFORM
FILIGRAIN
FILIGRANE
FILIGREE
FILIGREED
FILIGREES
FILII
FILING
FILINGS
FILIOQUE
FILIOQUES
FILISTER
FILISTERS
FILIUS
FILK
FILKS
FILL
FILLABLE
FILLAGREE
FILLE
FILLED
FILLER
FILLERS
FILLES
FILLESTER
FILLET
FILLETED
FILLETER
FILLETERS
FILLETING
FILLETS
FILLIBEG
FILLIBEGS
FILLIES
FILLING
FILLINGS
FILLIP
FILLIPED
FILLIPEEN
FILLIPING
FILLIPS
FILLISTER
FILLO
FILLOS
FILLS
FILLY
FILM
FILMABLE
FILMCARD
FILMCARDS
FILMDOM
FILMDOMS
FILMED
FILMER
FILMERS
FILMFEST
FILMFESTS
FILMGOER
FILMGOERS
FILMGOING
FILMI
FILMIC
FILMIER
FILMIEST
FILMILY
FILMINESS
FILMING
FILMINGS
FILMIS
FILMISH
FILMLAND
FILMLANDS
FILMLESS
FILMLIKE
FILMMAKER
FILMS
FILMSET
FILMSETS
FILMSTRIP
FILMY
FILO
FILOPLUME
FILOPODIA
FILOS
FILOSE
FILOSELLE
FILOVIRUS
FILS
FILTER
FILTERED
FILTERER
FILTERERS
FILTERING
FILTERS
FILTH
FILTHIER

FILTHIEST
FILTHILY
FILTHS
FILTHY
FILTRABLE
FILTRATE
FILTRATED
FILTRATES
FILTRE
FILUM
FIMBLE
FIMBLES
FIMBRIA
FIMBRIAE
FIMBRIAL
FIMBRIATE
FIN
FINABLE
FINAGLE
FINAGLED
FINAGLER
FINAGLERS
FINAGLES
FINAGLING
FINAL
FINALE
FINALES
FINALIS
FINALISE
FINALISED
FINALISER
FINALISES
FINALISM
FINALISMS
FINALIST
FINALISTS
FINALITY
FINALIZE
FINALIZED
FINALIZER
FINALIZES
FINALLY
FINALS
FINANCE
FINANCED
FINANCES
FINANCIAL
FINANCIER
FINANCING
FINBACK
FINBACKS
FINCA
FINCAS
FINCH
FINCHED
FINCHES
FINCHLIKE
FIND
FINDABLE
FINDER
FINDERS
FINDING
FINDINGS
FINDRAM
FINDRAMS
FINDS
FINE
FINEABLE
FINED
FINEER
FINEERED
FINEERING
FINEERS
FINEISH
FINELESS
FINELY
FINENESS
FINER
FINERIES
FINERS
FINERY
FINES
FINESPUN
FINESSE
FINESSED
FINESSER
FINESSERS
FINESSES
FINESSING
FINEST
FINESTS
FINFISH
FINFISHES
FINFOOT
FINFOOTS
FINGAN
FINGANS
FINGER
FINGERED
FINGERER
FINGERERS
FINGERING
FINGERS
FINGERTIP
FINI
FINIAL
FINIALED
FINIALS
FINICAL
FINICALLY
FINICKETY
FINICKIER
FINICKIN
FINICKING
FINICKY
FINIKIN
FINIKING
FINING
FININGS
FINIS
FINISES
FINISH
FINISHED
FINISHER
FINISHERS
FINISHES
FINISHING
FINITE
FINITELY
FINITES
FINITISM
FINITISMS
FINITIST
FINITISTS
FINITO
FINITUDE
FINITUDES
FINJAN
FINJANS
FINK
FINKED
FINKING
FINKS
FINLESS
FINLIKE
FINLIT
FINLITS
FINMARK
FINMARKS
FINNAC
FINNACK
FINNACKS
FINNACS
FINNAN
FINNANS
FINNED
FINNER
FINNERS
FINNESKO
FINNICKY
FINNIER
FINNIEST
FINNING
FINNMARK
FINNMARKS
FINNOCHIO
FINNOCK
FINNOCKS
FINNSKO
FINNY
FINO
FINOCCHIO
FINOCHIO
FINOCHIOS
FINOS
FINS
FINSKO
FINTECH
FINTECHS
FIORATURA
FIORD
FIORDS
FIORIN
FIORINS
FIORITURA
FIORITURE
FIPPENCE
FIPPENCES
FIPPLE
FIPPLES
FIQH
FIQHS
FIQUE
FIQUES
FIR
FIRE
FIREABLE
FIREARM
FIREARMED
FIREARMS
FIREBACK
FIREBACKS
FIREBALL
FIREBALLS
FIREBASE
FIREBASES
FIREBIRD
FIREBIRDS
FIREBOARD
FIREBOAT
FIREBOATS
FIREBOMB
FIREBOMBS
FIREBOX
FIREBOXES
FIREBRAND
FIREBRAT
FIREBRATS
FIREBREAK
FIREBRICK
FIREBUG
FIREBUGS
FIREBUSH
FIRECLAY
FIRECLAYS
FIRECREST
FIRED
FIREDAMP
FIREDAMPS
FIREDOG
FIREDOGS
FIREDRAKE
FIREFANG
FIREFANGS
FIREFIGHT
FIREFLIES
FIREFLOAT
FIREFLOOD
FIREFLY
FIREGUARD

FIREHALL
FIREHALLS
FIREHOSE
FIREHOSES
FIREHOUSE
FIRELESS
FIRELIGHT
FIRELIT
FIRELOCK
FIRELOCKS
FIREMAN
FIREMANIC
FIREMARK
FIREMARKS
FIREMEN
FIREPAN
FIREPANS
FIREPINK
FIREPINKS
FIREPIT
FIREPITS
FIREPLACE
FIREPLUG
FIREPLUGS
FIREPOT
FIREPOTS
FIREPOWER
FIREPROOF
FIRER
FIREREEL
FIREREELS
FIREROOM
FIREROOMS
FIRERS
FIRES
FIRESCAPE
FIRESHIP
FIRESHIPS
FIRESIDE
FIRESIDES
FIRESTONE
FIRESTORM
FIRETHORN
FIRETRAP
FIRETRAPS
FIRETRUCK
FIREWALL
FIREWALLS
FIREWATER
FIREWEED
FIREWEEDS
FIREWOMAN
FIREWOMEN
FIREWOOD
FIREWOODS
FIREWORK
FIREWORKS
FIREWORM
FIREWORMS
FIRIE
FIRIES
FIRING
FIRINGS
FIRK
FIRKED
FIRKIN
FIRKING
FIRKINS
FIRKS
FIRLOT
FIRLOTS
FIRM
FIRMAMENT
FIRMAN
FIRMANS
FIRMED
FIRMER
FIRMERS
FIRMEST
FIRMING
FIRMLESS
FIRMLY
FIRMNESS
FIRMS
FIRMWARE
FIRMWARES
FIRN
FIRNS
FIRRIER
FIRRIEST
FIRRING
FIRRINGS
FIRRY
FIRS
FIRST
FIRSTBORN
FIRSTHAND
FIRSTLING
FIRSTLY
FIRSTNESS
FIRSTS
FIRTH
FIRTHS
FIRWOOD
FIRWOODS
FISC
FISCAL
FISCALIST
FISCALLY
FISCALS
FISCS
FISGIG
FISGIGS
FISH
FISHABLE
FISHBALL
FISHBALLS
FISHBOAT
FISHBOATS
FISHBOLT
FISHBOLTS
FISHBONE
FISHBONES
FISHBOWL
FISHBOWLS
FISHCAKE
FISHCAKES
FISHED
FISHER
FISHERIES
FISHERMAN
FISHERMEN
FISHERS
FISHERY
FISHES
FISHEYE
FISHEYES
FISHFUL
FISHGIG
FISHGIGS
FISHHOOK
FISHHOOKS
FISHIER
FISHIEST
FISHIFIED
FISHIFIES
FISHIFY
FISHILY
FISHINESS
FISHING
FISHINGS
FISHKILL
FISHKILLS
FISHLESS
FISHLIKE
FISHLINE
FISHLINES
FISHMEAL
FISHMEALS
FISHNET
FISHNETS
FISHPLATE
FISHPOLE
FISHPOLES
FISHPOND
FISHPONDS
FISHSKIN
FISHSKINS
FISHTAIL
FISHTAILS
FISHWAY
FISHWAYS
FISHWIFE
FISHWIVES
FISHWORM
FISHWORMS
FISHY
FISHYBACK
FISK
FISKED
FISKING
FISKS
FISNOMIE
FISNOMIES
FISSATE
FISSILE
FISSILITY
FISSION
FISSIONAL
FISSIONED
FISSIONS
FISSIPED
FISSIPEDE
FISSIPEDS
FISSIVE
FISSLE
FISSLED
FISSLES
FISSLING
FISSURAL
FISSURE
FISSURED
FISSURES
FISSURING
FIST
FISTED
FISTFIGHT
FISTFUL
FISTFULS
FISTIANA
FISTIANAS
FISTIC
FISTICAL
FISTICUFF
FISTIER
FISTIEST
FISTING
FISTINGS
FISTMELE
FISTMELES
FISTNOTE
FISTNOTES
FISTS
FISTULA
FISTULAE
FISTULAR
FISTULAS
FISTULATE
FISTULOSE
FISTULOUS
FISTY
FIT
FITCH
FITCHE
FITCHEE
FITCHES
FITCHET
FITCHETS
FITCHEW
FITCHEWS

FITCHY
FITFUL
FITFULLY
FITLIER
FITLIEST
FITLY
FITMENT
FITMENTS
FITNA
FITNAS
FITNESS
FITNESSES
FITS
FITT
FITTABLE
FITTE
FITTED
FITTER
FITTERS
FITTES
FITTEST
FITTING
FITTINGLY
FITTINGS
FITTS
FIVE
FIVEFOLD
FIVEPENCE
FIVEPENNY
FIVEPIN
FIVEPINS
FIVER
FIVERS
FIVES
FIX
FIXABLE
FIXATE
FIXATED
FIXATES
FIXATIF
FIXATIFS
FIXATING
FIXATION
FIXATIONS
FIXATIVE
FIXATIVES
FIXATURE
FIXATURES
FIXED
FIXEDLY
FIXEDNESS
FIXER
FIXERS
FIXES
FIXING
FIXINGS
FIXIT
FIXITIES
FIXITS
FIXITY
FIXIVE
FIXT
FIXTURE
FIXTURES
FIXURE
FIXURES
FIZ
FIZGIG
FIZGIGGED
FIZGIGS
FIZZ
FIZZED
FIZZEN
FIZZENS
FIZZER
FIZZERS
FIZZES
FIZZGIG
FIZZGIGS
FIZZIER
FIZZIEST
FIZZILY
FIZZINESS
FIZZING
FIZZINGS
FIZZLE
FIZZLED
FIZZLES
FIZZLING
FIZZY
FJELD
FJELDS
FJORD
FJORDIC
FJORDS
FLAB
FLABBIER
FLABBIEST
FLABBILY
FLABBY
FLABELLA
FLABELLUM
FLABS
FLACCID
FLACCIDER
FLACCIDLY
FLACK
FLACKED
FLACKER
FLACKERED
FLACKERS
FLACKERY
FLACKET
FLACKETED
FLACKETS
FLACKING
FLACKS
FLACON
FLACONS
FLAFF
FLAFFED
FLAFFER
FLAFFERED
FLAFFERS
FLAFFING
FLAFFS
FLAG
FLAGELLA
FLAGELLAR
FLAGELLIN
FLAGELLUM
FLAGEOLET
FLAGGED
FLAGGER
FLAGGERS
FLAGGIER
FLAGGIEST
FLAGGING
FLAGGINGS
FLAGGY
FLAGITATE
FLAGLESS
FLAGMAN
FLAGMEN
FLAGON
FLAGONS
FLAGPOLE
FLAGPOLES
FLAGRANCE
FLAGRANCY
FLAGRANT
FLAGS
FLAGSHIP
FLAGSHIPS
FLAGSTAFF
FLAGSTICK
FLAGSTONE
FLAIL
FLAILED
FLAILING
FLAILS
FLAIR
FLAIRS
FLAK
FLAKE
FLAKED
FLAKER
FLAKERS
FLAKES
FLAKEY
FLAKIER
FLAKIES
FLAKIEST
FLAKILY
FLAKINESS
FLAKING
FLAKS
FLAKY
FLAM
FLAMBE
FLAMBEAU
FLAMBEAUS
FLAMBEAUX
FLAMBEE
FLAMBEED
FLAMBEES
FLAMBEING
FLAMBES
FLAME
FLAMED
FLAMELESS
FLAMELET
FLAMELETS
FLAMELIKE
FLAMEN
FLAMENCO
FLAMENCOS
FLAMENS
FLAMEOUT
FLAMEOUTS
FLAMER
FLAMERS
FLAMES
FLAMFEW
FLAMFEWS
FLAMIER
FLAMIEST
FLAMINES
FLAMING
FLAMINGLY
FLAMINGO
FLAMINGOS
FLAMM
FLAMMABLE
FLAMMED
FLAMMING
FLAMMS
FLAMMULE
FLAMMULES
FLAMS
FLAMY
FLAN
FLANCARD
FLANCARDS
FLANCH
FLANCHED
FLANCHES
FLANCHING
FLANE
FLANED
FLANERIE
FLANERIES
FLANES
FLANEUR
FLANEURS
FLANGE
FLANGED
FLANGER
FLANGERS
FLANGES

FLANGING
FLANGINGS
FLANING
FLANK
FLANKED
FLANKEN
FLANKENS
FLANKER
FLANKERED
FLANKERS
FLANKING
FLANKS
FLANNEL
FLANNELED
FLANNELET
FLANNELLY
FLANNELS
FLANNEN
FLANNENS
FLANNIE
FLANNIES
FLANNY
FLANS
FLAP
FLAPERON
FLAPERONS
FLAPJACK
FLAPJACKS
FLAPLESS
FLAPLIKE
FLAPPABLE
FLAPPED
FLAPPER
FLAPPERS
FLAPPIER
FLAPPIEST
FLAPPING
FLAPPINGS
FLAPPY
FLAPS
FLAPTRACK
FLARE
FLAREBACK
FLARED
FLARES
FLAREUP
FLAREUPS
FLARIER
FLARIEST
FLARING
FLARINGLY
FLARY
FLASER
FLASERS
FLASH
FLASHBACK
FLASHBANG
FLASHBULB
FLASHCARD
FLASHCUBE
FLASHED
FLASHER
FLASHERS
FLASHES
FLASHEST
FLASHGUN
FLASHGUNS
FLASHIER
FLASHIEST
FLASHILY
FLASHING
FLASHINGS
FLASHLAMP
FLASHOVER
FLASHTUBE
FLASHY
FLASK
FLASKET
FLASKETS
FLASKS
FLAT
FLATBACK
FLATBACKS
FLATBED
FLATBEDS
FLATBOAT
FLATBOATS
FLATBREAD
FLATBROD
FLATBRODS
FLATCAP
FLATCAPS
FLATCAR
FLATCARS
FLATETTE
FLATETTES
FLATFEET
FLATFISH
FLATFOOT
FLATFOOTS
FLATFORM
FLATFORMS
FLATHEAD
FLATHEADS
FLATIRON
FLATIRONS
FLATLAND
FLATLANDS
FLATLET
FLATLETS
FLATLINE
FLATLINED
FLATLINER
FLATLINES
FLATLING
FLATLINGS
FLATLONG
FLATLY
FLATMATE
FLATMATES
FLATNESS
FLATPACK
FLATPACKS
FLATPICK
FLATPICKS
FLATS
FLATSHARE
FLATSTICK
FLATTED
FLATTEN
FLATTENED
FLATTENER
FLATTENS
FLATTER
FLATTERED
FLATTERER
FLATTERS
FLATTERY
FLATTEST
FLATTIE
FLATTIES
FLATTING
FLATTINGS
FLATTISH
FLATTOP
FLATTOPS
FLATTY
FLATULENT
FLATUOUS
FLATUS
FLATUSES
FLATWARE
FLATWARES
FLATWASH
FLATWATER
FLATWAYS
FLATWISE
FLATWORK
FLATWORKS
FLATWORM
FLATWORMS
FLAUGHT
FLAUGHTED
FLAUGHTER
FLAUGHTS
FLAUNCH
FLAUNCHED
FLAUNCHES
FLAUNE
FLAUNES
FLAUNT
FLAUNTED
FLAUNTER
FLAUNTERS
FLAUNTIER
FLAUNTILY
FLAUNTING
FLAUNTS
FLAUNTY
FLAUTA
FLAUTAS
FLAUTIST
FLAUTISTS
FLAVA
FLAVANOL
FLAVANOLS
FLAVANONE
FLAVAS
FLAVIN
FLAVINE
FLAVINES
FLAVINS
FLAVONE
FLAVONES
FLAVONOID
FLAVONOL
FLAVONOLS
FLAVOR
FLAVORED
FLAVORER
FLAVORERS
FLAVORFUL
FLAVORIER
FLAVORING
FLAVORIST
FLAVOROUS
FLAVORS
FLAVORY
FLAVOUR
FLAVOURED
FLAVOURER
FLAVOURS
FLAVOURY
FLAW
FLAWED
FLAWIER
FLAWIEST
FLAWING
FLAWLESS
FLAWN
FLAWNS
FLAWS
FLAWY
FLAX
FLAXEN
FLAXES
FLAXIER
FLAXIEST
FLAXLIKE
FLAXSEED
FLAXSEEDS
FLAXY
FLAY
FLAYED
FLAYER
FLAYERS
FLAYING
FLAYS
FLAYSOME
FLEA

FLEABAG
FLEABAGS
FLEABANE
FLEABANES
FLEABITE
FLEABITES
FLEADH
FLEADHS
FLEAM
FLEAMS
FLEAPIT
FLEAPITS
FLEAS
FLEASOME
FLEAWORT
FLEAWORTS
FLECHE
FLECHES
FLECHETTE
FLECK
FLECKED
FLECKER
FLECKERED
FLECKERS
FLECKIER
FLECKIEST
FLECKING
FLECKLESS
FLECKS
FLECKY
FLECTION
FLECTIONS
FLED
FLEDGE
FLEDGED
FLEDGES
FLEDGIER
FLEDGIEST
FLEDGING
FLEDGLING
FLEDGY
FLEE
FLEECE
FLEECED
FLEECER
FLEECERS
FLEECES
FLEECH
FLEECHED
FLEECHES
FLEECHING
FLEECIE
FLEECIER
FLEECIES
FLEECIEST
FLEECILY
FLEECING
FLEECY
FLEEING
FLEEK
FLEEKS
FLEER
FLEERED
FLEERER
FLEERERS
FLEERING
FLEERINGS
FLEERS
FLEES
FLEET
FLEETED
FLEETER
FLEETERS
FLEETEST
FLEETING
FLEETLY
FLEETNESS
FLEETS
FLEG
FLEGGED
FLEGGING
FLEGS
FLEHMEN
FLEHMENED
FLEHMENS
FLEISHIG
FLEISHIK
FLEME
FLEMED
FLEMES
FLEMING
FLEMISH
FLEMISHED
FLEMISHES
FLEMIT
FLENCH
FLENCHED
FLENCHER
FLENCHERS
FLENCHES
FLENCHING
FLENSE
FLENSED
FLENSER
FLENSERS
FLENSES
FLENSING
FLEROVIUM
FLESH
FLESHED
FLESHER
FLESHERS
FLESHES
FLESHHOOD
FLESHIER
FLESHIEST
FLESHILY
FLESHING
FLESHINGS
FLESHLESS
FLESHLIER
FLESHLING
FLESHLY
FLESHMENT
FLESHPOT
FLESHPOTS
FLESHWORM
FLESHY
FLETCH
FLETCHED
FLETCHER
FLETCHERS
FLETCHES
FLETCHING
FLETTON
FLETTONS
FLEUR
FLEURET
FLEURETS
FLEURETTE
FLEURON
FLEURONS
FLEURS
FLEURY
FLEW
FLEWED
FLEWS
FLEX
FLEXAGON
FLEXAGONS
FLEXED
FLEXES
FLEXI
FLEXIBLE
FLEXIBLY
FLEXILE
FLEXING
FLEXION
FLEXIONAL
FLEXIONS
FLEXIS
FLEXITIME
FLEXO
FLEXOR
FLEXORS
FLEXOS
FLEXTIME
FLEXTIMER
FLEXTIMES
FLEXUOSE
FLEXUOUS
FLEXURAL
FLEXURE
FLEXURES
FLEXWING
FLEXWINGS
FLEY
FLEYED
FLEYING
FLEYS
FLIBBERT
FLIBBERTS
FLIC
FLICHTER
FLICHTERS
FLICK
FLICKABLE
FLICKED
FLICKER
FLICKERED
FLICKERS
FLICKERY
FLICKING
FLICKS
FLICS
FLIED
FLIER
FLIERS
FLIES
FLIEST
FLIGHT
FLIGHTED
FLIGHTIER
FLIGHTILY
FLIGHTING
FLIGHTS
FLIGHTY
FLIM
FLIMFLAM
FLIMFLAMS
FLIMP
FLIMPED
FLIMPING
FLIMPS
FLIMS
FLIMSIER
FLIMSIES
FLIMSIEST
FLIMSILY
FLIMSY
FLINCH
FLINCHED
FLINCHER
FLINCHERS
FLINCHES
FLINCHING
FLINDER
FLINDERED
FLINDERS
FLING
FLINGER
FLINGERS
FLINGING
FLINGS
FLINKITE
FLINKITES
FLINT
FLINTED
FLINTHEAD
FLINTIER

FLINTIEST
FLINTIFY
FLINTILY
FLINTING
FLINTLIKE
FLINTLOCK
FLINTS
FLINTY
FLIP
FLIPBOARD
FLIPBOOK
FLIPBOOKS
FLIPCHART
FLIPFLOP
FLIPFLOPS
FLIPPANCY
FLIPPANT
FLIPPED
FLIPPER
FLIPPERS
FLIPPEST
FLIPPIER
FLIPPIEST
FLIPPING
FLIPPINGS
FLIPPY
FLIPS
FLIPSIDE
FLIPSIDES
FLIR
FLIRS
FLIRT
FLIRTED
FLIRTER
FLIRTERS
FLIRTIER
FLIRTIEST
FLIRTING
FLIRTINGS
FLIRTISH
FLIRTS
FLIRTY
FLISK
FLISKED
FLISKIER
FLISKIEST
FLISKING
FLISKS
FLISKY
FLIT
FLITCH
FLITCHED
FLITCHES
FLITCHING
FLITE
FLITED
FLITES
FLITING
FLITS
FLITT
FLITTED
FLITTER
FLITTERED
FLITTERN
FLITTERNS
FLITTERS
FLITTING
FLITTINGS
FLITTS
FLIVVER
FLIVVERS
FLIX
FLIXED
FLIXES
FLIXING
FLIXWEED
FLIXWEEDS
FLOAT
FLOATABLE
FLOATAGE
FLOATAGES
FLOATANT
FLOATANTS
FLOATBASE
FLOATCUT
FLOATED
FLOATEL
FLOATELS
FLOATER
FLOATERS
FLOATIER
FLOATIEST
FLOATING
FLOATINGS
FLOATS
FLOATY
FLOB
FLOBBED
FLOBBING
FLOBS
FLOC
FLOCCED
FLOCCI
FLOCCING
FLOCCOSE
FLOCCULAR
FLOCCULE
FLOCCULES
FLOCCULI
FLOCCULUS
FLOCCUS
FLOCK
FLOCKED
FLOCKIER
FLOCKIEST
FLOCKING
FLOCKINGS
FLOCKLESS
FLOCKS
FLOCKY
FLOCS
FLOE
FLOES
FLOG
FLOGGABLE
FLOGGED
FLOGGER
FLOGGERS
FLOGGING
FLOGGINGS
FLOGS
FLOKATI
FLOKATIS
FLONG
FLONGS
FLOOD
FLOODABLE
FLOODED
FLOODER
FLOODERS
FLOODGATE
FLOODING
FLOODINGS
FLOODLESS
FLOODLIT
FLOODMARK
FLOODS
FLOODTIDE
FLOODWALL
FLOODWAY
FLOODWAYS
FLOOEY
FLOOIE
FLOOR
FLOORAGE
FLOORAGES
FLOORED
FLOORER
FLOORERS
FLOORHEAD
FLOORING
FLOORINGS
FLOORLESS
FLOORPAN
FLOORPANS
FLOORS
FLOORSHOW
FLOOSIE
FLOOSIES
FLOOSY
FLOOZIE
FLOOZIES
FLOOZY
FLOP
FLOPHOUSE
FLOPOVER
FLOPOVERS
FLOPPED
FLOPPER
FLOPPERS
FLOPPIER
FLOPPIES
FLOPPIEST
FLOPPILY
FLOPPING
FLOPPY
FLOPS
FLOPTICAL
FLOR
FLORA
FLORAE
FLORAL
FLORALLY
FLORALS
FLORAS
FLOREANT
FLOREAT
FLOREATED
FLORENCE
FLORENCES
FLORET
FLORETS
FLORIATED
FLORICANE
FLORID
FLORIDEAN
FLORIDER
FLORIDEST
FLORIDITY
FLORIDLY
FLORIER
FLORIEST
FLORIFORM
FLORIGEN
FLORIGENS
FLORIN
FLORINS
FLORIST
FLORISTIC
FLORISTRY
FLORISTS
FLORS
FLORUIT
FLORUITS
FLORULA
FLORULAE
FLORULE
FLORULES
FLORY
FLOSCULAR
FLOSCULE
FLOSCULES
FLOSH
FLOSHES
FLOSS
FLOSSED
FLOSSER
FLOSSERS
FLOSSES
FLOSSIE

F

FLOSSIER
FLOSSIES
FLOSSIEST
FLOSSILY
FLOSSING
FLOSSINGS
FLOSSY
FLOTA
FLOTAGE
FLOTAGES
FLOTANT
FLOTAS
FLOTATION
FLOTE
FLOTED
FLOTEL
FLOTELS
FLOTES
FLOTILLA
FLOTILLAS
FLOTING
FLOTSAM
FLOTSAMS
FLOUNCE
FLOUNCED
FLOUNCES
FLOUNCIER
FLOUNCING
FLOUNCY
FLOUNDER
FLOUNDERS
FLOUR
FLOURED
FLOURIER
FLOURIEST
FLOURING
FLOURISH
FLOURISHY
FLOURLESS
FLOURS
FLOURY
FLOUSE
FLOUSED
FLOUSES
FLOUSH
FLOUSHED
FLOUSHES
FLOUSHING
FLOUSING
FLOUT
FLOUTED
FLOUTER
FLOUTERS
FLOUTING
FLOUTS
FLOW
FLOWABLE
FLOWAGE
FLOWAGES
FLOWCHART
FLOWED
FLOWER
FLOWERAGE
FLOWERBED
FLOWERED
FLOWERER
FLOWERERS
FLOWERET
FLOWERETS
FLOWERFUL
FLOWERIER
FLOWERILY
FLOWERING
FLOWERPOT
FLOWERS
FLOWERY
FLOWING
FLOWINGLY
FLOWMETER
FLOWN
FLOWS
FLOWSTONE
FLOX
FLU
FLUATE
FLUATES
FLUB
FLUBBED
FLUBBER
FLUBBERS
FLUBBING
FLUBDUB
FLUBDUBS
FLUBS
FLUCTUANT
FLUCTUATE
FLUE
FLUED
FLUELLEN
FLUELLENS
FLUELLIN
FLUELLINS
FLUENCE
FLUENCES
FLUENCIES
FLUENCY
FLUENT
FLUENTLY
FLUENTS
FLUERIC
FLUERICS
FLUES
FLUEWORK
FLUEWORKS
FLUEY
FLUFF
FLUFFBALL
FLUFFED
FLUFFER
FLUFFERS
FLUFFIER
FLUFFIEST
FLUFFILY
FLUFFING
FLUFFS
FLUFFY
FLUGEL
FLUGELMAN
FLUGELMEN
FLUGELS
FLUID
FLUIDAL
FLUIDALLY
FLUIDIC
FLUIDICS
FLUIDIFY
FLUIDISE
FLUIDISED
FLUIDISER
FLUIDISES
FLUIDITY
FLUIDIZE
FLUIDIZED
FLUIDIZER
FLUIDIZES
FLUIDLIKE
FLUIDLY
FLUIDNESS
FLUIDRAM
FLUIDRAMS
FLUIDS
FLUIER
FLUIEST
FLUISH
FLUKE
FLUKED
FLUKES
FLUKEY
FLUKIER
FLUKIEST
FLUKILY
FLUKINESS
FLUKING
FLUKY
FLUME
FLUMED
FLUMES
FLUMING
FLUMMERY
FLUMMOX
FLUMMOXED
FLUMMOXES
FLUMP
FLUMPED
FLUMPING
FLUMPS
FLUNG
FLUNK
FLUNKED
FLUNKER
FLUNKERS
FLUNKEY
FLUNKEYS
FLUNKIE
FLUNKIES
FLUNKING
FLUNKS
FLUNKY
FLUNKYISM
FLUOR
FLUORENE
FLUORENES
FLUORESCE
FLUORIC
FLUORID
FLUORIDE
FLUORIDES
FLUORIDS
FLUORIN
FLUORINE
FLUORINES
FLUORINS
FLUORITE
FLUORITES
FLUOROSES
FLUOROSIS
FLUOROTIC
FLUORS
FLUORSPAR
FLURR
FLURRED
FLURRIED
FLURRIES
FLURRING
FLURRS
FLURRY
FLURRYING
FLUS
FLUSH
FLUSHABLE
FLUSHED
FLUSHER
FLUSHERS
FLUSHES
FLUSHEST
FLUSHIER
FLUSHIEST
FLUSHING
FLUSHINGS
FLUSHNESS
FLUSHWORK
FLUSHY
FLUSTER
FLUSTERED
FLUSTERS
FLUSTERY
FLUSTRATE
FLUTE
FLUTED
FLUTELIKE

FLUTER
FLUTERS
FLUTES
FLUTEY
FLUTEYER
FLUTEYEST
FLUTIER
FLUTIEST
FLUTINA
FLUTINAS
FLUTING
FLUTINGS
FLUTIST
FLUTISTS
FLUTTER
FLUTTERED
FLUTTERER
FLUTTERS
FLUTTERY
FLUTY
FLUVIAL
FLUVIATIC
FLUX
FLUXED
FLUXES
FLUXGATE
FLUXGATES
FLUXING
FLUXION
FLUXIONAL
FLUXIONS
FLUXIVE
FLUXMETER
FLUYT
FLUYTS
FLY
FLYABLE
FLYAWAY
FLYAWAYS
FLYBACK
FLYBACKS
FLYBANE
FLYBANES
FLYBELT
FLYBELTS
FLYBLEW
FLYBLOW
FLYBLOWN
FLYBLOWS
FLYBOAT
FLYBOATS
FLYBOOK
FLYBOOKS
FLYBOY
FLYBOYS
FLYBRIDGE
FLYBY
FLYBYS
FLYER
FLYERS
FLYEST
FLYFISHER
FLYHAND
FLYHANDS
FLYING
FLYINGS
FLYLEAF
FLYLEAVES
FLYLESS
FLYLINE
FLYLINES
FLYMAKER
FLYMAKERS
FLYMAN
FLYMEN
FLYOFF
FLYOFFS
FLYOVER
FLYOVERS
FLYPAPER
FLYPAPERS
FLYPAST
FLYPASTS
FLYPE
FLYPED
FLYPES
FLYPING
FLYPITCH
FLYPOSTER
FLYRODDER
FLYSCH
FLYSCHES
FLYSCREEN
FLYSHEET
FLYSHEETS
FLYSPECK
FLYSPECKS
FLYSPRAY
FLYSPRAYS
FLYSTRIKE
FLYTE
FLYTED
FLYTES
FLYTIER
FLYTIERS
FLYTING
FLYTINGS
FLYTRAP
FLYTRAPS
FLYWAY
FLYWAYS
FLYWEIGHT
FLYWHEEL
FLYWHEELS
FOAL
FOALED
FOALFOOT
FOALFOOTS
FOALING
FOALINGS
FOALS
FOAM
FOAMABLE
FOAMED
FOAMER
FOAMERS
FOAMIER
FOAMIEST
FOAMILY
FOAMINESS
FOAMING
FOAMINGLY
FOAMINGS
FOAMLESS
FOAMLIKE
FOAMS
FOAMY
FOB
FOBBED
FOBBING
FOBS
FOCACCIA
FOCACCIAS
FOCAL
FOCALISE
FOCALISED
FOCALISES
FOCALIZE
FOCALIZED
FOCALIZES
FOCALLY
FOCI
FOCIMETER
FOCOMETER
FOCUS
FOCUSABLE
FOCUSED
FOCUSER
FOCUSERS
FOCUSES
FOCUSING
FOCUSINGS
FOCUSLESS
FOCUSSED
FOCUSSES
FOCUSSING
FODDER
FODDERED
FODDERER
FODDERERS
FODDERING
FODDERS
FODGEL
FOE
FOEDARIE
FOEDARIES
FOEDERATI
FOEFIE
FOEHN
FOEHNS
FOEMAN
FOEMEN
FOEN
FOES
FOETAL
FOETATION
FOETICIDE
FOETID
FOETIDER
FOETIDEST
FOETIDLY
FOETOR
FOETORS
FOETUS
FOETUSES
FOG
FOGASH
FOGASHES
FOGBOUND
FOGBOW
FOGBOWS
FOGDOG
FOGDOGS
FOGEY
FOGEYDOM
FOGEYDOMS
FOGEYISH
FOGEYISM
FOGEYISMS
FOGEYS
FOGFRUIT
FOGFRUITS
FOGGAGE
FOGGAGES
FOGGED
FOGGER
FOGGERS
FOGGIER
FOGGIEST
FOGGILY
FOGGINESS
FOGGING
FOGGINGS
FOGGY
FOGHORN
FOGHORNS
FOGIE
FOGIES
FOGLE
FOGLES
FOGLESS
FOGLIGHT
FOGLIGHTS
FOGMAN
FOGMEN
FOGOU
FOGOUS
FOGRAM
FOGRAMITE
FOGRAMITY

F

FOGRAMS
FOGS
FOGY
FOGYDOM
FOGYDOMS
FOGYISH
FOGYISM
FOGYISMS
FOH
FOHN
FOHNS
FOIBLE
FOIBLES
FOID
FOIDS
FOIL
FOILABLE
FOILBORNE
FOILED
FOILING
FOILINGS
FOILIST
FOILISTS
FOILS
FOILSMAN
FOILSMEN
FOIN
FOINED
FOINING
FOININGLY
FOINS
FOISON
FOISONS
FOIST
FOISTED
FOISTER
FOISTERS
FOISTING
FOISTS
FOLACIN
FOLACINS
FOLATE
FOLATES
FOLD
FOLDABLE
FOLDAWAY
FOLDAWAYS
FOLDBACK
FOLDBACKS
FOLDBOAT
FOLDBOATS
FOLDED
FOLDER
FOLDEROL
FOLDEROLS
FOLDERS
FOLDING
FOLDINGS
FOLDOUT
FOLDOUTS
FOLDS
FOLDUP
FOLDUPS
FOLEY
FOLEYS
FOLIA
FOLIAGE
FOLIAGED
FOLIAGES
FOLIAR
FOLIATE
FOLIATED
FOLIATES
FOLIATING
FOLIATION
FOLIATURE
FOLIC
FOLIE
FOLIES
FOLIO
FOLIOED
FOLIOING
FOLIOLATE
FOLIOLE
FOLIOLES
FOLIOLOSE
FOLIOS
FOLIOSE
FOLIOUS
FOLIUM
FOLIUMS
FOLK
FOLKIE
FOLKIER
FOLKIES
FOLKIEST
FOLKINESS
FOLKISH
FOLKLAND
FOLKLANDS
FOLKLIFE
FOLKLIFES
FOLKLIKE
FOLKLIVES
FOLKLORE
FOLKLORES
FOLKLORIC
FOLKMOOT
FOLKMOOTS
FOLKMOT
FOLKMOTE
FOLKMOTES
FOLKMOTS
FOLKS
FOLKSIER
FOLKSIEST
FOLKSILY
FOLKSONG
FOLKSONGS
FOLKSY
FOLKTALE
FOLKTALES
FOLKWAY
FOLKWAYS
FOLKY
FOLLES
FOLLICLE
FOLLICLES
FOLLIED
FOLLIES
FOLLIS
FOLLOW
FOLLOWED
FOLLOWER
FOLLOWERS
FOLLOWING
FOLLOWS
FOLLOWUP
FOLLOWUPS
FOLLY
FOLLYING
FOMENT
FOMENTED
FOMENTER
FOMENTERS
FOMENTING
FOMENTS
FOMES
FOMITE
FOMITES
FON
FOND
FONDA
FONDANT
FONDANTS
FONDAS
FONDED
FONDER
FONDEST
FONDING
FONDLE
FONDLED
FONDLER
FONDLERS
FONDLES
FONDLING
FONDLINGS
FONDLY
FONDNESS
FONDS
FONDU
FONDUE
FONDUED
FONDUEING
FONDUES
FONDUING
FONDUS
FONE
FONES
FONLY
FONNED
FONNING
FONS
FONT
FONTAL
FONTANEL
FONTANELS
FONTANGE
FONTANGES
FONTICULI
FONTINA
FONTINAS
FONTLET
FONTLETS
FONTS
FOO
FOOBAR
FOOD
FOODBANK
FOODBANKS
FOODBORNE
FOODERIES
FOODERY
FOODFUL
FOODIE
FOODIES
FOODISM
FOODISMS
FOODLAND
FOODLANDS
FOODLESS
FOODOIR
FOODOIRS
FOODS
FOODSHED
FOODSHEDS
FOODSTUFF
FOODWAYS
FOODY
FOOFARAW
FOOFARAWS
FOOL
FOOLED
FOOLERIES
FOOLERY
FOOLFISH
FOOLHARDY
FOOLING
FOOLINGS
FOOLISH
FOOLISHER
FOOLISHLY
FOOLPROOF
FOOLS
FOOLSCAP
FOOLSCAPS
FOOS
FOOSBALL
FOOSBALLS
FOOT

FOOTAGE
FOOTAGES
FOOTBAG
FOOTBAGS
FOOTBALL
FOOTBALLS
FOOTBAR
FOOTBARS
FOOTBATH
FOOTBATHS
FOOTBED
FOOTBEDS
FOOTBOARD
FOOTBOY
FOOTBOYS
FOOTBRAKE
FOOTCLOTH
FOOTED
FOOTER
FOOTERED
FOOTERING
FOOTERS
FOOTFALL
FOOTFALLS
FOOTFAULT
FOOTGEAR
FOOTGEARS
FOOTHILL
FOOTHILLS
FOOTHOLD
FOOTHOLDS
FOOTIE
FOOTIER
FOOTIES
FOOTIEST
FOOTING
FOOTINGS
FOOTLE
FOOTLED
FOOTLER
FOOTLERS
FOOTLES
FOOTLESS
FOOTLIGHT
FOOTLIKE
FOOTLING
FOOTLINGS
FOOTLONG
FOOTLONGS
FOOTLOOSE
FOOTMAN
FOOTMARK
FOOTMARKS
FOOTMEN
FOOTMUFF
FOOTMUFFS
FOOTNOTE
FOOTNOTED
FOOTNOTES
FOOTPACE
FOOTPACES
FOOTPAD
FOOTPADS
FOOTPAGE
FOOTPAGES
FOOTPATH
FOOTPATHS
FOOTPLATE
FOOTPOST
FOOTPOSTS
FOOTPRINT
FOOTPUMP
FOOTPUMPS
FOOTRA
FOOTRACE
FOOTRACES
FOOTRAS
FOOTREST
FOOTRESTS
FOOTROPE
FOOTROPES
FOOTRULE
FOOTRULES
FOOTS
FOOTSAL
FOOTSALS
FOOTSIE
FOOTSIES
FOOTSLOG
FOOTSLOGS
FOOTSORE
FOOTSTALK
FOOTSTALL
FOOTSTEP
FOOTSTEPS
FOOTSTOCK
FOOTSTONE
FOOTSTOOL
FOOTSY
FOOTWALL
FOOTWALLS
FOOTWAY
FOOTWAYS
FOOTWEAR
FOOTWEARS
FOOTWEARY
FOOTWELL
FOOTWELLS
FOOTWORK
FOOTWORKS
FOOTWORN
FOOTY
FOOZLE
FOOZLED
FOOZLER
FOOZLERS
FOOZLES
FOOZLING
FOOZLINGS
FOP
FOPLING
FOPLINGS
FOPPED
FOPPERIES
FOPPERY
FOPPING
FOPPISH
FOPPISHLY
FOPS
FOR
FORA
FORAGE
FORAGED
FORAGER
FORAGERS
FORAGES
FORAGING
FORAM
FORAMEN
FORAMENS
FORAMINA
FORAMINAL
FORAMS
FORANE
FORASMUCH
FORAY
FORAYED
FORAYER
FORAYERS
FORAYING
FORAYS
FORB
FORBAD
FORBADE
FORBARE
FORBEAR
FORBEARER
FORBEARS
FORBID
FORBIDAL
FORBIDALS
FORBIDDAL
FORBIDDEN
FORBIDDER
FORBIDS
FORBODE
FORBODED
FORBODES
FORBODING
FORBORE
FORBORNE
FORBS
FORBY
FORBYE
FORCAT
FORCATS
FORCE
FORCEABLE
FORCEABLY
FORCED
FORCEDLY
FORCEFUL
FORCELESS
FORCEMEAT
FORCEOUT
FORCEOUTS
FORCEPS
FORCEPSES
FORCER
FORCERS
FORCES
FORCIBLE
FORCIBLY
FORCING
FORCINGLY
FORCIPATE
FORCIPES
FORD
FORDABLE
FORDED
FORDID
FORDING
FORDLESS
FORDO
FORDOES
FORDOING
FORDONE
FORDONNE
FORDS
FORE
FOREANENT
FOREARM
FOREARMED
FOREARMS
FOREBAY
FOREBAYS
FOREBEAR
FOREBEARS
FOREBITT
FOREBITTS
FOREBODE
FOREBODED
FOREBODER
FOREBODES
FOREBODY
FOREBOOM
FOREBOOMS
FOREBRAIN
FOREBY
FOREBYE
FORECABIN
FORECADDY
FORECAR
FORECARS
FORECAST
FORECASTS
FORECHECK
FORECLOSE
FORECLOTH
FORECOURT

F

FOREDATE
FOREDATED
FOREDATES
FOREDECK
FOREDECKS
FOREDID
FOREDO
FOREDOES
FOREDOING
FOREDONE
FOREDOOM
FOREDOOMS
FOREFACE
FOREFACES
FOREFEEL
FOREFEELS
FOREFEET
FOREFELT
FOREFEND
FOREFENDS
FOREFOOT
FOREFRONT
FOREGLEAM
FOREGO
FOREGOER
FOREGOERS
FOREGOES
FOREGOING
FOREGONE
FOREGUT
FOREGUTS
FOREHAND
FOREHANDS
FOREHEAD
FOREHEADS
FOREHENT
FOREHENTS
FOREHOCK
FOREHOCKS
FOREHOOF
FOREHOOFS
FOREIGN
FOREIGNER
FOREIGNLY
FOREJUDGE
FOREKING
FOREKINGS
FOREKNEW
FOREKNOW
FOREKNOWN
FOREKNOWS
FOREL
FORELADY
FORELAID
FORELAIN
FORELAND
FORELANDS
FORELAY
FORELAYS
FORELEG
FORELEGS
FORELEND
FORELENDS
FORELENT
FORELIE
FORELIES
FORELIFT
FORELIFTS
FORELIMB
FORELIMBS
FORELLED
FORELLING
FORELOCK
FORELOCKS
FORELS
FORELYING
FOREMAN
FOREMAST
FOREMASTS
FOREMEAN
FOREMEANS
FOREMEANT
FOREMEN
FOREMILK
FOREMILKS
FOREMOST
FORENAME
FORENAMED
FORENAMES
FORENIGHT
FORENOON
FORENOONS
FORENSIC
FORENSICS
FOREPART
FOREPARTS
FOREPAST
FOREPAW
FOREPAWS
FOREPEAK
FOREPEAKS
FOREPLAN
FOREPLANS
FOREPLAY
FOREPLAYS
FOREPOINT
FORERAN
FORERANK
FORERANKS
FOREREACH
FOREREAD
FOREREADS
FORERUN
FORERUNS
FORES
FORESAID
FORESAIL
FORESAILS
FORESAW
FORESAY
FORESAYS
FORESEE
FORESEEN
FORESEER
FORESEERS
FORESEES
FORESHANK
FORESHEET
FORESHEW
FORESHEWN
FORESHEWS
FORESHIP
FORESHIPS
FORESHOCK
FORESHORE
FORESHOW
FORESHOWN
FORESHOWS
FORESIDE
FORESIDES
FORESIGHT
FORESKIN
FORESKINS
FORESKIRT
FORESLACK
FORESLOW
FORESLOWS
FORESPAKE
FORESPEAK
FORESPEND
FORESPENT
FORESPOKE
FOREST
FORESTAGE
FORESTAIR
FORESTAL
FORESTALL
FORESTAY
FORESTAYS
FORESTEAL
FORESTED
FORESTER
FORESTERS
FORESTIAL
FORESTINE
FORESTING
FORESTRY
FORESTS
FORESWEAR
FORESWORE
FORESWORN
FORETASTE
FORETEACH
FORETEETH
FORETELL
FORETELLS
FORETHINK
FORETIME
FORETIMES
FORETOKEN
FORETOLD
FORETOOTH
FORETOP
FORETOPS
FOREVER
FOREVERS
FOREWARD
FOREWARDS
FOREWARN
FOREWARNS
FOREWEIGH
FOREWENT
FOREWIND
FOREWINDS
FOREWING
FOREWINGS
FOREWOMAN
FOREWOMEN
FOREWORD
FOREWORDS
FOREWORN
FOREX
FOREXES
FOREYARD
FOREYARDS
FORFAIR
FORFAIRED
FORFAIRN
FORFAIRS
FORFAITER
FORFAULT
FORFAULTS
FORFEIT
FORFEITED
FORFEITER
FORFEITS
FORFEND
FORFENDED
FORFENDS
FORFEX
FORFEXES
FORFICATE
FORFOCHEN
FORGAT
FORGATHER
FORGAVE
FORGE
FORGEABLE
FORGED
FORGEMAN
FORGEMEN
FORGER
FORGERIES
FORGERS
FORGERY
FORGES
FORGET
FORGETFUL
FORGETIVE
FORGETS

FORGETTER
FORGING
FORGINGS
FORGIVE
FORGIVEN
FORGIVER
FORGIVERS
FORGIVES
FORGIVING
FORGO
FORGOER
FORGOERS
FORGOES
FORGOING
FORGONE
FORGOT
FORGOTTEN
FORHAILE
FORHAILED
FORHAILES
FORHENT
FORHENTS
FORHOO
FORHOOED
FORHOOIE
FORHOOIED
FORHOOIES
FORHOOING
FORHOOS
FORHOW
FORHOWED
FORHOWING
FORHOWS
FORINSEC
FORINT
FORINTS
FORJASKIT
FORJESKIT
FORJUDGE
FORJUDGED
FORJUDGES
FORK
FORKBALL
FORKBALLS
FORKED
FORKEDLY
FORKER
FORKERS
FORKFUL
FORKFULS
FORKHEAD
FORKHEADS
FORKIER
FORKIEST
FORKINESS
FORKING
FORKLESS
FORKLIFT
FORKLIFTS
FORKLIKE
FORKS
FORKSFUL
FORKTAIL
FORKTAILS
FORKY
FORLANA
FORLANAS
FORLEND
FORLENDS
FORLENT
FORLESE
FORLESES
FORLESING
FORLORE
FORLORN
FORLORNER
FORLORNLY
FORLORNS
FORM
FORMABLE
FORMABLY
FORMAL
FORMALIN
FORMALINE
FORMALINS
FORMALISE
FORMALISM
FORMALIST
FORMALITY
FORMALIZE
FORMALLY
FORMALS
FORMAMIDE
FORMANT
FORMANTS
FORMAT
FORMATE
FORMATED
FORMATES
FORMATING
FORMATION
FORMATIVE
FORMATS
FORMATTED
FORMATTER
FORME
FORMED
FORMEE
FORMEES
FORMER
FORMERLY
FORMERS
FORMES
FORMFUL
FORMIATE
FORMIATES
FORMIC
FORMICA
FORMICANT
FORMICARY
FORMICAS
FORMICATE
FORMING
FORMINGS
FORMLESS
FORMOL
FORMOLS
FORMS
FORMULA
FORMULAE
FORMULAIC
FORMULAR
FORMULARS
FORMULARY
FORMULAS
FORMULATE
FORMULISE
FORMULISM
FORMULIST
FORMULIZE
FORMWORK
FORMWORKS
FORMYL
FORMYLS
FORNENST
FORNENT
FORNICAL
FORNICATE
FORNICES
FORNIX
FORPET
FORPETS
FORPINE
FORPINED
FORPINES
FORPINING
FORPIT
FORPITS
FORRAD
FORRADER
FORRADS
FORRARDER
FORRAY
FORRAYED
FORRAYING
FORRAYS
FORREN
FORRIT
FORSAID
FORSAKE
FORSAKEN
FORSAKER
FORSAKERS
FORSAKES
FORSAKING
FORSAY
FORSAYING
FORSAYS
FORSLACK
FORSLACKS
FORSLOE
FORSLOED
FORSLOES
FORSLOW
FORSLOWED
FORSLOWS
FORSOOK
FORSOOTH
FORSPEAK
FORSPEAKS
FORSPEND
FORSPENDS
FORSPENT
FORSPOKE
FORSPOKEN
FORSWATT
FORSWEAR
FORSWEARS
FORSWINK
FORSWINKS
FORSWONCK
FORSWORE
FORSWORN
FORSWUNK
FORSYTHIA
FORT
FORTALICE
FORTE
FORTED
FORTES
FORTH
FORTHCAME
FORTHCOME
FORTHINK
FORTHINKS
FORTHWITH
FORTHY
FORTIES
FORTIETH
FORTIETHS
FORTIFIED
FORTIFIER
FORTIFIES
FORTIFY
FORTILAGE
FORTING
FORTIS
FORTITUDE
FORTLET
FORTLETS
FORTNIGHT
FORTRESS
FORTS
FORTUITY
FORTUNATE
FORTUNE
FORTUNED
FORTUNES
FORTUNING
FORTUNISE

FORTUNIZE
FORTY
FORTYFOLD
FORTYISH
FORUM
FORUMS
FORWANDER
FORWARD
FORWARDED
FORWARDER
FORWARDLY
FORWARDS
FORWARN
FORWARNED
FORWARNS
FORWASTE
FORWASTED
FORWASTES
FORWEARY
FORWENT
FORWHY
FORWORN
FORZA
FORZANDI
FORZANDO
FORZANDOS
FORZATI
FORZATO
FORZATOS
FORZE
FOSCARNET
FOSS
FOSSA
FOSSAE
FOSSAS
FOSSATE
FOSSE
FOSSED
FOSSES
FOSSETTE
FOSSETTES
FOSSICK
FOSSICKED
FOSSICKER
FOSSICKS
FOSSIL
FOSSILISE
FOSSILIZE
FOSSILS
FOSSOR
FOSSORIAL
FOSSORS
FOSSULA
FOSSULAE
FOSSULATE
FOSTER
FOSTERAGE
FOSTERED
FOSTERER
FOSTERERS
FOSTERING
FOSTERS
FOSTRESS
FOTHER
FOTHERED
FOTHERING
FOTHERS
FOU
FOUAT
FOUATS
FOUD
FOUDRIE
FOUDRIES
FOUDS
FOUER
FOUEST
FOUET
FOUETS
FOUETTE
FOUETTES
FOUGADE
FOUGADES
FOUGASSE
FOUGASSES
FOUGHT
FOUGHTEN
FOUGHTIER
FOUGHTY
FOUL
FOULARD
FOULARDS
FOULBROOD
FOULDER
FOULDERED
FOULDERS
FOULE
FOULED
FOULER
FOULES
FOULEST
FOULIE
FOULIES
FOULING
FOULINGS
FOULLY
FOULMART
FOULMARTS
FOULNESS
FOULS
FOUMART
FOUMARTS
FOUND
FOUNDED
FOUNDER
FOUNDERED
FOUNDERS
FOUNDING
FOUNDINGS
FOUNDLING
FOUNDRESS
FOUNDRIES
FOUNDRY
FOUNDS
FOUNT
FOUNTAIN
FOUNTAINS
FOUNTFUL
FOUNTS
FOUR
FOURBALL
FOURBALLS
FOURCHEE
FOURCHEES
FOUREYED
FOURFOLD
FOURGON
FOURGONS
FOURPENCE
FOURPENNY
FOURPLAY
FOURPLAYS
FOURPLEX
FOURS
FOURSCORE
FOURSES
FOURSOME
FOURSOMES
FOURTEEN
FOURTEENS
FOURTH
FOURTHLY
FOURTHS
FOUS
FOUSSA
FOUSSAS
FOUSTIER
FOUSTIEST
FOUSTY
FOUTER
FOUTERED
FOUTERING
FOUTERS
FOUTH
FOUTHS
FOUTRA
FOUTRAS
FOUTRE
FOUTRED
FOUTRES
FOUTRING
FOVEA
FOVEAE
FOVEAL
FOVEAS
FOVEATE
FOVEATED
FOVEIFORM
FOVEOLA
FOVEOLAE
FOVEOLAR
FOVEOLAS
FOVEOLATE
FOVEOLE
FOVEOLES
FOVEOLET
FOVEOLETS
FOWL
FOWLED
FOWLER
FOWLERS
FOWLING
FOWLINGS
FOWLPOX
FOWLPOXES
FOWLS
FOWTH
FOWTHS
FOX
FOXBERRY
FOXED
FOXES
FOXFIRE
FOXFIRES
FOXFISH
FOXFISHES
FOXGLOVE
FOXGLOVES
FOXHOLE
FOXHOLES
FOXHOUND
FOXHOUNDS
FOXHUNT
FOXHUNTED
FOXHUNTER
FOXHUNTS
FOXIE
FOXIER
FOXIES
FOXIEST
FOXILY
FOXINESS
FOXING
FOXINGS
FOXLIKE
FOXSHARK
FOXSHARKS
FOXSHIP
FOXSHIPS
FOXSKIN
FOXSKINS
FOXTAIL
FOXTAILS
FOXTROT
FOXTROTS
FOXY
FOY
FOYBOAT
FOYBOATS
FOYER
FOYERS

FOYLE
FOYLED
FOYLES
FOYLING
FOYNE
FOYNED
FOYNES
FOYNING
FOYS
FOZIER
FOZIEST
FOZINESS
FOZY
FRA
FRAB
FRABBED
FRABBING
FRABBIT
FRABJOUS
FRABS
FRACAS
FRACASES
FRACK
FRACKED
FRACKER
FRACKERS
FRACKING
FRACKINGS
FRACKS
FRACT
FRACTAL
FRACTALS
FRACTED
FRACTI
FRACTING
FRACTION
FRACTIONS
FRACTIOUS
FRACTS
FRACTUR
FRACTURAL
FRACTURE
FRACTURED
FRACTURER
FRACTURES
FRACTURS
FRACTUS
FRAE
FRAENA
FRAENUM
FRAENUMS
FRAG
FRAGGED
FRAGGING
FRAGGINGS
FRAGILE
FRAGILELY
FRAGILER
FRAGILEST
FRAGILITY
FRAGMENT
FRAGMENTS
FRAGOR
FRAGORS
FRAGRANCE
FRAGRANCY
FRAGRANT
FRAGS
FRAICHEUR
FRAIL
FRAILER
FRAILEST
FRAILISH
FRAILLY
FRAILNESS
FRAILS
FRAILTEE
FRAILTEES
FRAILTIES
FRAILTY
FRAIM
FRAIMS
FRAISE
FRAISED
FRAISES
FRAISING
FRAKTUR
FRAKTURS
FRAMABLE
FRAMBESIA
FRAMBOISE
FRAME
FRAMEABLE
FRAMED
FRAMELESS
FRAMER
FRAMERS
FRAMES
FRAMEWORK
FRAMING
FRAMINGS
FRAMPAL
FRAMPLER
FRAMPLERS
FRAMPOLD
FRANC
FRANCHISE
FRANCISE
FRANCISED
FRANCISES
FRANCIUM
FRANCIUMS
FRANCIZE
FRANCIZED
FRANCIZES
FRANCO
FRANCOLIN
FRANCS
FRANGER
FRANGERS
FRANGIBLE
FRANGLAIS
FRANION
FRANIONS
FRANK
FRANKABLE
FRANKED
FRANKER
FRANKERS
FRANKEST
FRANKFORT
FRANKFURT
FRANKING
FRANKLIN
FRANKLINS
FRANKLY
FRANKNESS
FRANKS
FRANKUM
FRANKUMS
FRANSERIA
FRANTIC
FRANTICLY
FRANZIER
FRANZIEST
FRANZY
FRAP
FRAPE
FRAPEAGE
FRAPEAGES
FRAPED
FRAPES
FRAPING
FRAPPANT
FRAPPE
FRAPPED
FRAPPEE
FRAPPES
FRAPPING
FRAPS
FRAS
FRASCATI
FRASCATIS
FRASS
FRASSES
FRAT
FRATCH
FRATCHES
FRATCHETY
FRATCHIER
FRATCHING
FRATCHY
FRATE
FRATER
FRATERIES
FRATERNAL
FRATERS
FRATERY
FRATI
FRATRIES
FRATRY
FRATS
FRAU
FRAUD
FRAUDFUL
FRAUDS
FRAUDSMAN
FRAUDSMEN
FRAUDSTER
FRAUGHAN
FRAUGHANS
FRAUGHT
FRAUGHTED
FRAUGHTER
FRAUGHTS
FRAULEIN
FRAULEINS
FRAUS
FRAUTAGE
FRAUTAGES
FRAWZEY
FRAWZEYS
FRAY
FRAYED
FRAYING
FRAYINGS
FRAYS
FRAZIL
FRAZILS
FRAZZLE
FRAZZLED
FRAZZLES
FRAZZLING
FREAK
FREAKED
FREAKERY
FREAKFUL
FREAKIER
FREAKIEST
FREAKILY
FREAKING
FREAKISH
FREAKOUT
FREAKOUTS
FREAKS
FREAKY
FRECKLE
FRECKLED
FRECKLES
FRECKLIER
FRECKLING
FRECKLY
FREDAINE
FREDAINES
FREE
FREEBASE
FREEBASED
FREEBASER
FREEBASES
FREEBEE

FREEBEES
FREEBIE
FREEBIES
FREEBOARD
FREEBOOT
FREEBOOTS
FREEBOOTY
FREEBORN
FREECYCLE
FREED
FREEDIVER
FREEDMAN
FREEDMEN
FREEDOM
FREEDOMS
FREEFALL
FREEFORM
FREEGAN
FREEGANS
FREEHAND
FREEHOLD
FREEHOLDS
FREEING
FREEKEH
FREEKEHS
FREELANCE
FREELOAD
FREELOADS
FREELY
FREEMAN
FREEMASON
FREEMEN
FREEMIUM
FREEMIUMS
FREENESS
FREEPHONE
FREEPOST
FREEPOSTS
FREER
FREERIDE
FREERIDES
FREERS
FREES
FREESHEET
FREESIA
FREESIAS
FREEST
FREESTONE
FREESTYLE
FREET
FREETIER
FREETIEST
FREETS
FREETY
FREEWARE
FREEWARES
FREEWAY
FREEWAYS
FREEWHEEL
FREEWILL
FREEWOMAN
FREEWOMEN
FREEWRITE
FREEWROTE
FREEZABLE
FREEZE
FREEZER
FREEZERS
FREEZES
FREEZING
FREEZINGS
FREIGHT
FREIGHTED
FREIGHTER
FREIGHTS
FREIT
FREITIER
FREITIEST
FREITS
FREITY
FREMD
FREMDS
FREMIT
FREMITS
FREMITUS
FRENA
FRENCH
FRENCHED
FRENCHES
FRENCHIFY
FRENCHING
FRENEMIES
FRENEMY
FRENETIC
FRENETICS
FRENNE
FRENNES
FRENULA
FRENULAR
FRENULUM
FRENULUMS
FRENUM
FRENUMS
FRENZICAL
FRENZIED
FRENZIES
FRENZILY
FRENZY
FRENZYING
FREON
FREONS
FREQUENCE
FREQUENCY
FREQUENT
FREQUENTS
FRERE
FRERES
FRESCADE
FRESCADES
FRESCO
FRESCOED
FRESCOER
FRESCOERS
FRESCOES
FRESCOING
FRESCOIST
FRESCOS
FRESH
FRESHED
FRESHEN
FRESHENED
FRESHENER
FRESHENS
FRESHER
FRESHERS
FRESHES
FRESHEST
FRESHET
FRESHETS
FRESHIE
FRESHIES
FRESHING
FRESHISH
FRESHLY
FRESHMAN
FRESHMEN
FRESHNESS
FRESNEL
FRESNELS
FRET
FRETBOARD
FRETFUL
FRETFULLY
FRETLESS
FRETS
FRETSAW
FRETSAWS
FRETSOME
FRETTED
FRETTER
FRETTERS
FRETTIER
FRETTIEST
FRETTING
FRETTINGS
FRETTY
FRETWORK
FRETWORKS
FRIABLE
FRIAND
FRIANDE
FRIANDES
FRIANDS
FRIAR
FRIARBIRD
FRIARIES
FRIARLY
FRIARS
FRIARY
FRIB
FRIBBLE
FRIBBLED
FRIBBLER
FRIBBLERS
FRIBBLES
FRIBBLING
FRIBBLISH
FRIBS
FRICADEL
FRICADELS
FRICANDO
FRICASSEE
FRICATIVE
FRICHT
FRICHTED
FRICHTING
FRICHTS
FRICKING
FRICOT
FRICOTS
FRICTION
FRICTIONS
FRIDGE
FRIDGED
FRIDGES
FRIDGING
FRIED
FRIEDCAKE
FRIEND
FRIENDED
FRIENDING
FRIENDLY
FRIENDS
FRIER
FRIERS
FRIES
FRIEZE
FRIEZED
FRIEZES
FRIEZING
FRIG
FRIGATE
FRIGATES
FRIGATOON
FRIGES
FRIGGED
FRIGGER
FRIGGERS
FRIGGING
FRIGGINGS
FRIGHT
FRIGHTED
FRIGHTEN
FRIGHTENS
FRIGHTFUL
FRIGHTING
FRIGHTS
FRIGID
FRIGIDER
FRIGIDEST

FRIGIDITY
FRIGIDLY
FRIGOT
FRIGOTS
FRIGS
FRIJOL
FRIJOLE
FRIJOLES
FRIKKADEL
FRILL
FRILLED
FRILLER
FRILLERS
FRILLERY
FRILLIER
FRILLIES
FRILLIEST
FRILLING
FRILLINGS
FRILLS
FRILLY
FRINGE
FRINGED
FRINGES
FRINGIER
FRINGIEST
FRINGING
FRINGINGS
FRINGY
FRIPON
FRIPONS
FRIPPER
FRIPPERER
FRIPPERS
FRIPPERY
FRIPPET
FRIPPETS
FRIS
FRISBEE
FRISBEES
FRISE
FRISEE
FRISEES
FRISES
FRISETTE
FRISETTES
FRISEUR
FRISEURS
FRISK
FRISKA
FRISKAS
FRISKED
FRISKER
FRISKERS
FRISKET
FRISKETS
FRISKFUL
FRISKIER
FRISKIEST
FRISKILY
FRISKING
FRISKINGS
FRISKS
FRISKY
FRISSON
FRISSONS
FRIST
FRISTED
FRISTING
FRISTS
FRISURE
FRISURES
FRIT
FRITES
FRITFLIES
FRITFLY
FRITH
FRITHBORH
FRITHS
FRITS
FRITT
FRITTATA
FRITTATAS
FRITTED
FRITTER
FRITTERED
FRITTERER
FRITTERS
FRITTING
FRITTS
FRITURE
FRITURES
FRITZ
FRITZED
FRITZES
FRITZING
FRIULANO
FRIULANOS
FRIVOL
FRIVOLED
FRIVOLER
FRIVOLERS
FRIVOLING
FRIVOLITY
FRIVOLLED
FRIVOLLER
FRIVOLOUS
FRIVOLS
FRIZ
FRIZADO
FRIZADOS
FRIZE
FRIZED
FRIZER
FRIZERS
FRIZES
FRIZETTE
FRIZETTES
FRIZING
FRIZZ
FRIZZANTE
FRIZZED
FRIZZER
FRIZZERS
FRIZZES
FRIZZIER
FRIZZIES
FRIZZIEST
FRIZZILY
FRIZZING
FRIZZLE
FRIZZLED
FRIZZLER
FRIZZLERS
FRIZZLES
FRIZZLIER
FRIZZLING
FRIZZLY
FRIZZY
FRO
FROCK
FROCKED
FROCKING
FROCKINGS
FROCKLESS
FROCKS
FROE
FROES
FROG
FROGBIT
FROGBITS
FROGEYE
FROGEYED
FROGEYES
FROGFISH
FROGGED
FROGGERY
FROGGIER
FROGGIEST
FROGGING
FROGGINGS
FROGGY
FROGLET
FROGLETS
FROGLIKE
FROGLING
FROGLINGS
FROGMAN
FROGMARCH
FROGMEN
FROGMOUTH
FROGS
FROGSPAWN
FROIDEUR
FROIDEURS
FROING
FROINGS
FROISE
FROISES
FROLIC
FROLICKED
FROLICKER
FROLICKY
FROLICS
FROM
FROMAGE
FROMAGES
FROMENTY
FROND
FRONDAGE
FRONDAGES
FRONDED
FRONDENT
FRONDEUR
FRONDEURS
FRONDLESS
FRONDOSE
FRONDOUS
FRONDS
FRONS
FRONT
FRONTAGE
FRONTAGER
FRONTAGES
FRONTAL
FRONTALLY
FRONTALS
FRONTED
FRONTENIS
FRONTER
FRONTERS
FRONTES
FRONTEST
FRONTIER
FRONTIERS
FRONTING
FRONTLESS
FRONTLET
FRONTLETS
FRONTLINE
FRONTLIST
FRONTMAN
FRONTMEN
FRONTON
FRONTONS
FRONTOON
FRONTOONS
FRONTPAGE
FRONTS
FRONTWARD
FRONTWAYS
FRONTWISE
FRORE
FROREN
FRORN
FRORNE
FRORY
FROS
FROSH
FROSHES

FROST
FROSTBIT
FROSTBITE
FROSTED
FROSTEDS
FROSTFISH
FROSTIER
FROSTIEST
FROSTILY
FROSTING
FROSTINGS
FROSTLESS
FROSTLIKE
FROSTLINE
FROSTNIP
FROSTNIPS
FROSTS
FROSTWORK
FROSTY
FROTH
FROTHED
FROTHER
FROTHERS
FROTHERY
FROTHIER
FROTHIEST
FROTHILY
FROTHING
FROTHINGS
FROTHLESS
FROTHS
FROTHY
FROTTAGE
FROTTAGES
FROTTEUR
FROTTEURS
FROUFROU
FROUFROUS
FROUGHIER
FROUGHY
FROUNCE
FROUNCED
FROUNCES
FROUNCING
FROUZIER
FROUZIEST
FROUZILY
FROUZY
FROW
FROWARD
FROWARDLY
FROWARDS
FROWIE
FROWIER
FROWIEST
FROWN
FROWNED
FROWNER
FROWNERS
FROWNIER
FROWNIEST
FROWNING
FROWNS
FROWNY
FROWS
FROWSIER
FROWSIEST
FROWSILY
FROWST
FROWSTED
FROWSTER
FROWSTERS
FROWSTIER
FROWSTING
FROWSTS
FROWSTY
FROWSY
FROWY
FROWZIER
FROWZIEST
FROWZILY
FROWZY
FROZE
FROZEN
FROZENLY
FRUCTAN
FRUCTANS
FRUCTED
FRUCTIFY
FRUCTIVE
FRUCTOSE
FRUCTOSES
FRUCTUARY
FRUCTUATE
FRUCTUOUS
FRUG
FRUGAL
FRUGALIST
FRUGALITY
FRUGALLY
FRUGGED
FRUGGING
FRUGIVORE
FRUGS
FRUICT
FRUICTS
FRUIT
FRUITAGE
FRUITAGES
FRUITCAKE
FRUITED
FRUITER
FRUITERER
FRUITERS
FRUITERY
FRUITFUL
FRUITIER
FRUITIEST
FRUITILY
FRUITING
FRUITINGS
FRUITION
FRUITIONS
FRUITIVE
FRUITLESS
FRUITLET
FRUITLETS
FRUITLIKE
FRUITS
FRUITWOOD
FRUITWORM
FRUITY
FRUMENTY
FRUMP
FRUMPED
FRUMPIER
FRUMPIEST
FRUMPILY
FRUMPING
FRUMPISH
FRUMPLE
FRUMPLED
FRUMPLES
FRUMPLING
FRUMPS
FRUMPY
FRUSEMIDE
FRUSH
FRUSHED
FRUSHES
FRUSHING
FRUST
FRUSTA
FRUSTRATE
FRUSTS
FRUSTULE
FRUSTULES
FRUSTUM
FRUSTUMS
FRUTEX
FRUTICES
FRUTICOSE
FRUTIFIED
FRUTIFIES
FRUTIFY
FRY
FRYABLE
FRYBREAD
FRYBREADS
FRYER
FRYERS
FRYING
FRYINGS
FRYPAN
FRYPANS
FUB
FUBAR
FUBBED
FUBBERIES
FUBBERY
FUBBIER
FUBBIEST
FUBBING
FUBBY
FUBS
FUBSIER
FUBSIEST
FUBSY
FUCHSIA
FUCHSIAS
FUCHSIN
FUCHSINE
FUCHSINES
FUCHSINS
FUCHSITE
FUCHSITES
FUCI
FUCK
FUCKED
FUCKER
FUCKERS
FUCKFACE
FUCKFACES
FUCKHEAD
FUCKHEADS
FUCKING
FUCKINGS
FUCKOFF
FUCKOFFS
FUCKS
FUCKUP
FUCKUPS
FUCKWIT
FUCKWITS
FUCOID
FUCOIDAL
FUCOIDS
FUCOSE
FUCOSES
FUCOUS
FUCUS
FUCUSED
FUCUSES
FUD
FUDDIER
FUDDIES
FUDDIEST
FUDDLE
FUDDLED
FUDDLER
FUDDLERS
FUDDLES
FUDDLING
FUDDLINGS
FUDDY
FUDGE
FUDGED
FUDGES
FUDGIER
FUDGIEST

FUDGING
FUDGY
FUDS
FUEHRER
FUEHRERS
FUEL
FUELED
FUELER
FUELERS
FUELING
FUELLED
FUELLER
FUELLERS
FUELLING
FUELS
FUELWOOD
FUELWOODS
FUERO
FUEROS
FUFF
FUFFED
FUFFIER
FUFFIEST
FUFFING
FUFFS
FUFFY
FUG
FUGACIOUS
FUGACITY
FUGAL
FUGALLY
FUGATO
FUGATOS
FUGGED
FUGGIER
FUGGIEST
FUGGILY
FUGGINESS
FUGGING
FUGGY
FUGHETTA
FUGHETTAS
FUGIE
FUGIES
FUGIO
FUGIOS
FUGITIVE
FUGITIVES
FUGLE
FUGLED
FUGLEMAN
FUGLEMEN
FUGLES
FUGLIER
FUGLIEST
FUGLING
FUGLY
FUGS
FUGU
FUGUE
FUGUED
FUGUELIKE
FUGUES
FUGUING
FUGUIST
FUGUISTS
FUGUS
FUHRER
FUHRERS
FUJI
FUJIS
FULCRA
FULCRATE
FULCRUM
FULCRUMS
FULFIL
FULFILL
FULFILLED
FULFILLER
FULFILLS
FULFILS
FULGENCY
FULGENT
FULGENTLY
FULGID
FULGOR
FULGOROUS
FULGORS
FULGOUR
FULGOURS
FULGURAL
FULGURANT
FULGURATE
FULGURITE
FULGUROUS
FULHAM
FULHAMS
FULL
FULLAGE
FULLAGES
FULLAM
FULLAMS
FULLAN
FULLANS
FULLBACK
FULLBACKS
FULLBLOOD
FULLED
FULLER
FULLERED
FULLERENE
FULLERIDE
FULLERIES
FULLERING
FULLERITE
FULLERS
FULLERY
FULLEST
FULLFACE
FULLFACES
FULLING
FULLISH
FULLNESS
FULLS
FULLY
FULMAR
FULMARS
FULMINANT
FULMINATE
FULMINE
FULMINED
FULMINES
FULMINIC
FULMINING
FULMINOUS
FULNESS
FULNESSES
FULSOME
FULSOMELY
FULSOMER
FULSOMEST
FULVID
FULVOUS
FUM
FUMADO
FUMADOES
FUMADOS
FUMAGE
FUMAGES
FUMARASE
FUMARASES
FUMARATE
FUMARATES
FUMARIC
FUMAROLE
FUMAROLES
FUMAROLIC
FUMATORIA
FUMATORY
FUMBLE
FUMBLED
FUMBLER
FUMBLERS
FUMBLES
FUMBLING
FUME
FUMED
FUMELESS
FUMELIKE
FUMER
FUMEROLE
FUMEROLES
FUMERS
FUMES
FUMET
FUMETS
FUMETTE
FUMETTES
FUMETTI
FUMETTO
FUMETTOS
FUMIER
FUMIEST
FUMIGANT
FUMIGANTS
FUMIGATE
FUMIGATED
FUMIGATES
FUMIGATOR
FUMING
FUMINGLY
FUMITORY
FUMOSITY
FUMOUS
FUMS
FUMULI
FUMULUS
FUMY
FUN
FUNBOARD
FUNBOARDS
FUNCKIA
FUNCKIAS
FUNCTION
FUNCTIONS
FUNCTOR
FUNCTORS
FUND
FUNDABLE
FUNDAMENT
FUNDED
FUNDER
FUNDERS
FUNDI
FUNDIC
FUNDIE
FUNDIES
FUNDING
FUNDINGS
FUNDIS
FUNDLESS
FUNDRAISE
FUNDS
FUNDUS
FUNDY
FUNEBRAL
FUNEBRE
FUNEBRIAL
FUNERAL
FUNERALS
FUNERARY
FUNEREAL
FUNEST
FUNFAIR
FUNFAIRS
FUNFEST
FUNFESTS
FUNG
FUNGAL
FUNGALS

FUNGI
FUNGIBLE
FUNGIBLES
FUNGIC
FUNGICIDE
FUNGIFORM
FUNGISTAT
FUNGO
FUNGOED
FUNGOES
FUNGOID
FUNGOIDAL
FUNGOIDS
FUNGOING
FUNGOS
FUNGOSITY
FUNGOUS
FUNGS
FUNGUS
FUNGUSES
FUNHOUSE
FUNHOUSES
FUNICLE
FUNICLES
FUNICULAR
FUNICULI
FUNICULUS
FUNK
FUNKED
FUNKER
FUNKERS
FUNKHOLE
FUNKHOLES
FUNKIA
FUNKIAS
FUNKIER
FUNKIEST
FUNKILY
FUNKINESS
FUNKING
FUNKS
FUNKSTER
FUNKSTERS
FUNKY
FUNNED
FUNNEL
FUNNELED
FUNNELING
FUNNELLED
FUNNELS
FUNNER
FUNNEST
FUNNIER
FUNNIES
FUNNIEST
FUNNILY
FUNNINESS
FUNNING
FUNNY
FUNNYMAN
FUNNYMEN
FUNPLEX
FUNPLEXES
FUNS
FUNSTER
FUNSTERS
FUR
FURACIOUS
FURACITY
FURAL
FURALS
FURAN
FURANE
FURANES
FURANOSE
FURANOSES
FURANS
FURBALL
FURBALLS
FURBEARER
FURBELOW
FURBELOWS
FURBISH
FURBISHED
FURBISHER
FURBISHES
FURCA
FURCAE
FURCAL
FURCATE
FURCATED
FURCATELY
FURCATES
FURCATING
FURCATION
FURCRAEA
FURCRAEAS
FURCULA
FURCULAE
FURCULAR
FURCULUM
FURDER
FUREUR
FUREURS
FURFAIR
FURFAIRS
FURFUR
FURFURAL
FURFURALS
FURFURAN
FURFURANS
FURFURES
FURFUROL
FURFUROLE
FURFUROLS
FURFUROUS
FURFURS
FURIBUND
FURIES
FURIOSITY
FURIOSO
FURIOSOS
FURIOUS
FURIOUSLY
FURKID
FURKIDS
FURL
FURLABLE
FURLANA
FURLANAS
FURLED
FURLER
FURLERS
FURLESS
FURLIKE
FURLING
FURLONG
FURLONGS
FURLOUGH
FURLOUGHS
FURLS
FURMENTY
FURMETIES
FURMETY
FURMITIES
FURMITY
FURNACE
FURNACED
FURNACES
FURNACING
FURNITMENT
FURNISH
FURNISHED
FURNISHER
FURNISHES
FURNITURE
FUROL
FUROLE
FUROLES
FUROLS
FUROR
FURORE
FURORES
FURORS
FURPHIES
FURPHY
FURPIECE
FURPIECES
FURR
FURRED
FURRIER
FURRIERS
FURRIERY
FURRIES
FURRIEST
FURRILY
FURRINER
FURRINERS
FURRINESS
FURRING
FURRINGS
FURROW
FURROWED
FURROWER
FURROWERS
FURROWIER
FURROWING
FURROWS
FURROWY
FURRS
FURRY
FURS
FURTH
FURTHER
FURTHERED
FURTHERER
FURTHERS
FURTHEST
FURTIVE
FURTIVELY
FURUNCLE
FURUNCLES
FURY
FURZE
FURZES
FURZIER
FURZIEST
FURZY
FUSAIN
FUSAINS
FUSARIA
FUSARIUM
FUSARIUMS
FUSAROL
FUSAROLE
FUSAROLES
FUSAROLS
FUSBALL
FUSBALLS
FUSC
FUSCOUS
FUSE
FUSED
FUSEE
FUSEES
FUSEL
FUSELAGE
FUSELAGES
FUSELESS
FUSELIKE
FUSELS
FUSES
FUSHION
FUSHIONS
FUSIBLE
FUSIBLY
FUSIDIC
FUSIFORM
FUSIL
FUSILE

FUSILEER
FUSILEERS
FUSILIER
FUSILIERS
FUSILLADE
FUSILLI
FUSILLIS
FUSILS
FUSING
FUSION
FUSIONAL
FUSIONISM
FUSIONIST
FUSIONS
FUSK
FUSKED
FUSKER
FUSKERED
FUSKERING
FUSKERS
FUSKING
FUSKS
FUSS
FUSSBALL
FUSSBALLS
FUSSED
FUSSER
FUSSERS
FUSSES
FUSSIER
FUSSIEST
FUSSILY
FUSSINESS
FUSSING
FUSSPOT
FUSSPOTS
FUSSY
FUST
FUSTED
FUSTET
FUSTETS
FUSTIAN
FUSTIANS
FUSTIC
FUSTICS
FUSTIER
FUSTIEST
FUSTIGATE
FUSTILUGS
FUSTILY
FUSTINESS
FUSTING
FUSTOC
FUSTOCS
FUSTS
FUSTY
FUSULINID
FUSUMA
FUSUMAS
FUTCHEL
FUTCHELS
FUTHARC
FUTHARCS
FUTHARK
FUTHARKS
FUTHORC
FUTHORCS
FUTHORK
FUTHORKS
FUTILE
FUTILELY
FUTILER
FUTILEST
FUTILITY
FUTON
FUTONS
FUTSAL
FUTSALS
FUTTOCK
FUTTOCKS
FUTURAL
FUTURE
FUTURES
FUTURISM
FUTURISMS
FUTURIST
FUTURISTS
FUTURITY
FUTZ
FUTZED
FUTZES
FUTZING
FUZE
FUZED
FUZEE
FUZEES
FUZELESS
FUZES
FUZIL
FUZILS
FUZING
FUZZ
FUZZBALL
FUZZBALLS
FUZZBOX
FUZZBOXES
FUZZED
FUZZES
FUZZIER
FUZZIEST
FUZZILY
FUZZINESS
FUZZING
FUZZLE
FUZZLED
FUZZLES
FUZZLING
FUZZTONE
FUZZTONES
FUZZY
FY
FYCE
FYCES
FYKE
FYKED
FYKES
FYKING
FYLE
FYLES
FYLFOT
FYLFOTS
FYNBOS
FYNBOSES
FYRD
FYRDS
FYTTE
FYTTES

G

GAB
GABARDINE
GABBA
GABBARD
GABBARDS
GABBART
GABBARTS
GABBAS
GABBED
GABBER
GABBERS
GABBIER
GABBIEST
GABBINESS
GABBING
GABBLE
GABBLED
GABBLER
GABBLERS
GABBLES
GABBLING
GABBLINGS
GABBRO
GABBROIC
GABBROID
GABBROS
GABBY
GABELLE
GABELLED
GABELLER
GABELLERS
GABELLES
GABERDINE
GABFEST
GABFESTS
GABIES
GABION
GABIONADE
GABIONAGE
GABIONED
GABIONS
GABLE
GABLED
GABLELIKE
GABLES
GABLET
GABLETS
GABLING
GABNASH
GABNASHES
GABOON
GABOONS
GABS
GABY
GACH
GACHED
GACHER
GACHERS
GACHES
GACHING
GAD
GADABOUT
GADABOUTS
GADARENE
GADDED
GADDER
GADDERS
GADDI
GADDING
GADDIS
GADE
GADES
GADFLIES
GADFLY
GADGE
GADGES
GADGET
GADGETEER
GADGETIER
GADGETRY
GADGETS
GADGETY
GADGIE
GADGIES
GADI
GADID
GADIDS
GADIS
GADJE
GADJES
GADJO
GADJOS
GADLING
GADLINGS
GADMAN
GADMEN
GADOID
GADOIDS
GADOLINIC
GADROON
GADROONED
GADROONS
GADS
GADSMAN
GADSMEN
GADSO
GADWALL
GADWALLS
GADZOOKS
GAE
GAED
GAEING
GAELICISE
GAELICISM
GAELICIZE
GAEN
GAES
GAFF
GAFFE
GAFFED
GAFFER
GAFFERS
GAFFES
GAFFING
GAFFINGS
GAFFS
GAFFSAIL
GAFFSAILS
GAG
GAGA
GAGAKU
GAGAKUS
GAGE
GAGEABLE
GAGEABLY
GAGED
GAGER
GAGERS
GAGES
GAGGED
GAGGER
GAGGERIES
GAGGERS
GAGGERY
GAGGING
GAGGLE
GAGGLED
GAGGLES
GAGGLING
GAGGLINGS
GAGING
GAGMAN
GAGMEN
GAGS
GAGSTER
GAGSTERS
GAHNITE
GAHNITES
GAID
GAIDS
GAIETIES
GAIETY
GAIJIN
GAILLARD
GAILLARDE
GAILY
GAIN
GAINABLE
GAINED
GAINER
GAINERS
GAINEST
GAINFUL
GAINFULLY
GAINING
GAININGS
GAINLESS
GAINLIER
GAINLIEST
GAINLY
GAINS
GAINSAID
GAINSAY
GAINSAYER
GAINSAYS
GAINST
GAIR
GAIRFOWL
GAIRFOWLS
GAIRS
GAIT
GAITA
GAITAS
GAITED
GAITER
GAITERED
GAITERS
GAITING
GAITS
GAITT
GAITTS
GAJO
GAJOS
GAK
GAKS
GAL
GALA
GALABEA
GALABEAH
GALABEAHS

GALABEAS
GALABIA
GALABIAH
GALABIAHS
GALABIAS
GALABIEH
GALABIEHS
GALABIYA
GALABIYAH
GALABIYAS
GALACTIC
GALACTICO
GALACTOSE
GALAGE
GALAGES
GALAGO
GALAGOS
GALAH
GALAHS
GALANGA
GALANGAL
GALANGALS
GALANGAS
GALANT
GALANTINE
GALANTS
GALANTY
GALAPAGO
GALAPAGOS
GALAS
GALATEA
GALATEAS
GALAVANT
GALAVANTS
GALAX
GALAXES
GALAXIES
GALAXY
GALBANUM
GALBANUMS
GALDRAGON
GALE
GALEA
GALEAE
GALEAS
GALEATE
GALEATED
GALED
GALEIFORM
GALENA
GALENAS
GALENGALE
GALENIC
GALENICAL
GALENITE
GALENITES
GALENOID
GALERE
GALERES
GALES
GALETTE
GALETTES
GALILEE
GALILEES
GALING
GALINGALE
GALIONGEE
GALIOT
GALIOTS
GALIPOT
GALIPOTS
GALIVANT
GALIVANTS
GALL
GALLABEA
GALLABEAH
GALLABEAS
GALLABIA
GALLABIAH
GALLABIAS
GALLABIEH
GALLABIYA
GALLAMINE
GALLANT
GALLANTED
GALLANTER
GALLANTLY
GALLANTRY
GALLANTS
GALLATE
GALLATES
GALLEASS
GALLED
GALLEIN
GALLEINS
GALLEON
GALLEONS
GALLERIA
GALLERIAS
GALLERIED
GALLERIES
GALLERIST
GALLERY
GALLET
GALLETA
GALLETAS
GALLETED
GALLETING
GALLETS
GALLEY
GALLEYS
GALLFLIES
GALLFLY
GALLIARD
GALLIARDS
GALLIASS
GALLIC
GALLICA
GALLICAN
GALLICAS
GALLICISE
GALLICISM
GALLICIZE
GALLIED
GALLIER
GALLIES
GALLIEST
GALLINAZO
GALLING
GALLINGLY
GALLINULE
GALLIOT
GALLIOTS
GALLIPOT
GALLIPOTS
GALLISE
GALLISED
GALLISES
GALLISING
GALLISISE
GALLISIZE
GALLIUM
GALLIUMS
GALLIVANT
GALLIVAT
GALLIVATS
GALLIWASP
GALLIZE
GALLIZED
GALLIZES
GALLIZING
GALLNUT
GALLNUTS
GALLOCK
GALLON
GALLONAGE
GALLONS
GALLOON
GALLOONED
GALLOONS
GALLOOT
GALLOOTS
GALLOP
GALLOPADE
GALLOPED
GALLOPER
GALLOPERS
GALLOPING
GALLOPS
GALLOUS
GALLOW
GALLOWAY
GALLOWAYS
GALLOWED
GALLOWING
GALLOWS
GALLOWSES
GALLS
GALLSTONE
GALLUMPH
GALLUMPHS
GALLUS
GALLUSED
GALLUSES
GALLY
GALLYING
GALOCHE
GALOCHED
GALOCHES
GALOCHING
GALOOT
GALOOTS
GALOP
GALOPADE
GALOPADES
GALOPED
GALOPIN
GALOPING
GALOPINS
GALOPPED
GALOPPING
GALOPS
GALORE
GALORES
GALOSH
GALOSHE
GALOSHED
GALOSHES
GALOSHING
GALOWSES
GALRAVAGE
GALS
GALTONIA
GALTONIAS
GALUMPH
GALUMPHED
GALUMPHER
GALUMPHS
GALUT
GALUTH
GALUTHS
GALUTS
GALVANIC
GALVANISE
GALVANISM
GALVANIST
GALVANIZE
GALVO
GALVOS
GALYAC
GALYACS
GALYAK
GALYAKS
GAM
GAMA
GAMAHUCHE
GAMARUCHE
GAMAS
GAMASH
GAMASHES

GAMAY
GAMAYS
GAMB
GAMBA
GAMBADE
GAMBADES
GAMBADO
GAMBADOED
GAMBADOES
GAMBADOS
GAMBAS
GAMBE
GAMBES
GAMBESON
GAMBESONS
GAMBET
GAMBETS
GAMBETTA
GAMBETTAS
GAMBIA
GAMBIAS
GAMBIER
GAMBIERS
GAMBIR
GAMBIRS
GAMBIST
GAMBISTS
GAMBIT
GAMBITED
GAMBITING
GAMBITS
GAMBLE
GAMBLED
GAMBLER
GAMBLERS
GAMBLES
GAMBLING
GAMBLINGS
GAMBO
GAMBOES
GAMBOGE
GAMBOGES
GAMBOGIAN
GAMBOGIC
GAMBOL
GAMBOLED
GAMBOLING
GAMBOLLED
GAMBOLS
GAMBOS
GAMBREL
GAMBRELS
GAMBROON
GAMBROONS
GAMBS
GAMBUSIA
GAMBUSIAS
GAME
GAMEBAG
GAMEBAGS
GAMEBOOK
GAMEBOOKS
GAMECOCK
GAMECOCKS
GAMED
GAMEFISH
GAMEFOWL
GAMEFOWLS
GAMELAN
GAMELANS
GAMELIKE
GAMELY
GAMENESS
GAMEPLAY
GAMEPLAYS
GAMER
GAMERS
GAMES
GAMESHOW
GAMESHOWS
GAMESIER
GAMESIEST
GAMESMAN
GAMESMEN
GAMESOME
GAMEST
GAMESTER
GAMESTERS
GAMESY
GAMETAL
GAMETE
GAMETES
GAMETIC
GAMEY
GAMEYNESS
GAMGEE
GAMIC
GAMIER
GAMIEST
GAMIFIED
GAMIFIES
GAMIFY
GAMIFYING
GAMILY
GAMIN
GAMINE
GAMINERIE
GAMINES
GAMINESS
GAMING
GAMINGS
GAMINS
GAMMA
GAMMADIA
GAMMADION
GAMMAS
GAMMAT
GAMMATIA
GAMMATION
GAMMATS
GAMME
GAMMED
GAMMER
GAMMERS
GAMMES
GAMMIER
GAMMIEST
GAMMING
GAMMOCK
GAMMOCKED
GAMMOCKS
GAMMON
GAMMONED
GAMMONER
GAMMONERS
GAMMONING
GAMMONS
GAMMY
GAMODEME
GAMODEMES
GAMONE
GAMONES
GAMP
GAMPISH
GAMPS
GAMS
GAMUT
GAMUTS
GAMY
GAMYNESS
GAN
GANACHE
GANACHES
GANCH
GANCHED
GANCHES
GANCHING
GANDER
GANDERED
GANDERING
GANDERISM
GANDERS
GANDY
GANE
GANEF
GANEFS
GANEV
GANEVS
GANG
GANGBANG
GANGBANGS
GANGBO
GANGBOARD
GANGBOS
GANGED
GANGER
GANGERS
GANGING
GANGINGS
GANGLAND
GANGLANDS
GANGLE
GANGLED
GANGLES
GANGLIA
GANGLIAL
GANGLIAR
GANGLIATE
GANGLIER
GANGLIEST
GANGLING
GANGLION
GANGLIONS
GANGLY
GANGPLANK
GANGPLOW
GANGPLOWS
GANGREL
GANGRELS
GANGRENE
GANGRENED
GANGRENES
GANGS
GANGSHAG
GANGSHAGS
GANGSMAN
GANGSMEN
GANGSTA
GANGSTAS
GANGSTER
GANGSTERS
GANGUE
GANGUES
GANGWAY
GANGWAYS
GANISTER
GANISTERS
GANJA
GANJAH
GANJAHS
GANJAS
GANNED
GANNET
GANNETRY
GANNETS
GANNING
GANNISTER
GANOF
GANOFS
GANOID
GANOIDS
GANOIN
GANOINE
GANOINES
GANOINS
GANS
GANSEY
GANSEYS
GANT
GANTED

GANTELOPE
GANTING
GANTLET
GANTLETED
GANTLETS
GANTLINE
GANTLINES
GANTLOPE
GANTLOPES
GANTRIES
GANTRY
GANTS
GANYMEDE
GANYMEDES
GANZFELD
GANZFELDS
GAOL
GAOLBIRD
GAOLBIRDS
GAOLBREAK
GAOLBROKE
GAOLED
GAOLER
GAOLERESS
GAOLERS
GAOLING
GAOLLESS
GAOLS
GAP
GAPE
GAPED
GAPER
GAPERS
GAPES
GAPESEED
GAPESEEDS
GAPEWORM
GAPEWORMS
GAPIER
GAPIEST
GAPING
GAPINGLY
GAPINGS
GAPLESS
GAPO
GAPOS
GAPOSIS
GAPOSISES
GAPPED
GAPPER
GAPPERS
GAPPIER
GAPPIEST
GAPPING
GAPPINGS
GAPPY
GAPS
GAPY
GAR
GARAGE
GARAGED
GARAGEMAN
GARAGEMEN
GARAGES
GARAGEY
GARAGIER
GARAGIEST
GARAGING
GARAGINGS
GARAGIST
GARAGISTE
GARAGISTS
GARB
GARBAGE
GARBAGES
GARBAGEY
GARBAGIER
GARBAGY
GARBANZO
GARBANZOS
GARBE
GARBED
GARBES
GARBING
GARBLE
GARBLED
GARBLER
GARBLERS
GARBLES
GARBLESS
GARBLING
GARBLINGS
GARBO
GARBOARD
GARBOARDS
GARBOIL
GARBOILS
GARBOLOGY
GARBOS
GARBS
GARBURE
GARBURES
GARCINIA
GARCINIAS
GARCON
GARCONS
GARDA
GARDAI
GARDANT
GARDANTS
GARDEN
GARDENED
GARDENER
GARDENERS
GARDENFUL
GARDENIA
GARDENIAS
GARDENING
GARDENS
GARDEROBE
GARDYLOO
GARDYLOOS
GARE
GAREFOWL
GAREFOWLS
GARES
GARFISH
GARFISHES
GARGANEY
GARGANEYS
GARGANTUA
GARGARISE
GARGARISM
GARGARIZE
GARGET
GARGETS
GARGETY
GARGLE
GARGLED
GARGLER
GARGLERS
GARGLES
GARGLING
GARGOYLE
GARGOYLED
GARGOYLES
GARI
GARIAL
GARIALS
GARIBALDI
GARIGUE
GARIGUES
GARIS
GARISH
GARISHED
GARISHES
GARISHING
GARISHLY
GARJAN
GARJANS
GARLAND
GARLANDED
GARLANDRY
GARLANDS
GARLIC
GARLICKED
GARLICKY
GARLICS
GARMENT
GARMENTED
GARMENTS
GARMS
GARNER
GARNERED
GARNERING
GARNERS
GARNET
GARNETS
GARNI
GARNISH
GARNISHED
GARNISHEE
GARNISHER
GARNISHES
GARNISHOR
GARNISHRY
GARNITURE
GAROTE
GAROTED
GAROTES
GAROTING
GAROTTE
GAROTTED
GAROTTER
GAROTTERS
GAROTTES
GAROTTING
GAROUPA
GAROUPAS
GARPIKE
GARPIKES
GARRAN
GARRANS
GARRE
GARRED
GARRES
GARRET
GARRETED
GARRETEER
GARRETS
GARRIGUE
GARRIGUES
GARRING
GARRISON
GARRISONS
GARRON
GARRONS
GARROT
GARROTE
GARROTED
GARROTER
GARROTERS
GARROTES
GARROTING
GARROTS
GARROTTE
GARROTTED
GARROTTER
GARROTTES
GARRULITY
GARRULOUS
GARRYA
GARRYAS
GARRYOWEN
GARS
GART
GARTER
GARTERED
GARTERING
GARTERS

G

GARTH
GARTHS
GARUDA
GARUDAS
GARUM
GARUMS
GARVEY
GARVEYS
GARVIE
GARVIES
GARVOCK
GARVOCKS
GAS
GASAHOL
GASAHOLS
GASALIER
GASALIERS
GASBAG
GASBAGGED
GASBAGS
GASCON
GASCONADE
GASCONISM
GASCONS
GASEITIES
GASEITY
GASELIER
GASELIERS
GASEOUS
GASES
GASFIELD
GASFIELDS
GASH
GASHED
GASHER
GASHES
GASHEST
GASHFUL
GASHING
GASHLIER
GASHLIEST
GASHLY
GASHOLDER
GASHOUSE
GASHOUSES
GASIFIED
GASIFIER
GASIFIERS
GASIFIES
GASIFORM
GASIFY
GASIFYING
GASKET
GASKETED
GASKETS
GASKIN
GASKING
GASKINGS
GASKINS
GASLESS
GASLIGHT
GASLIGHTS
GASLIT
GASMAN
GASMEN
GASOGENE
GASOGENES
GASOHOL
GASOHOLS
GASOLENE
GASOLENES
GASOLIER
GASOLIERS
GASOLINE
GASOLINES
GASOLINIC
GASOMETER
GASOMETRY
GASP
GASPED
GASPER
GASPEREAU
GASPERS
GASPIER
GASPIEST
GASPINESS
GASPING
GASPINGLY
GASPINGS
GASPS
GASPY
GASSED
GASSER
GASSERS
GASSES
GASSIER
GASSIEST
GASSILY
GASSINESS
GASSING
GASSINGS
GASSY
GAST
GASTED
GASTER
GASTERED
GASTERING
GASTERS
GASTFULL
GASTHAUS
GASTIGHT
GASTING
GASTNESS
GASTNESSE
GASTRAEA
GASTRAEAS
GASTRAEUM
GASTRAL
GASTREA
GASTREAS
GASTRIC
GASTRIN
GASTRINS
GASTRITIC
GASTRITIS
GASTROPOD
GASTROPUB
GASTRULA
GASTRULAE
GASTRULAR
GASTRULAS
GASTS
GASWORKS
GAT
GATCH
GATCHED
GATCHER
GATCHERS
GATCHES
GATCHING
GATE
GATEAU
GATEAUS
GATEAUX
GATECRASH
GATED
GATEFOLD
GATEFOLDS
GATEHOUSE
GATELEG
GATELEGS
GATELESS
GATELIKE
GATEMAN
GATEMEN
GATEPOST
GATEPOSTS
GATER
GATERS
GATES
GATEWAY
GATEWAYS
GATH
GATHER
GATHERED
GATHERER
GATHERERS
GATHERING
GATHERS
GATHS
GATING
GATINGS
GATLING
GATOR
GATORS
GATS
GATVOL
GAU
GAUCH
GAUCHE
GAUCHED
GAUCHELY
GAUCHER
GAUCHERIE
GAUCHERS
GAUCHES
GAUCHESCO
GAUCHEST
GAUCHING
GAUCHO
GAUCHOS
GAUCIE
GAUCIER
GAUCIEST
GAUCY
GAUD
GAUDEAMUS
GAUDED
GAUDERIES
GAUDERY
GAUDGIE
GAUDGIES
GAUDIER
GAUDIES
GAUDIEST
GAUDILY
GAUDINESS
GAUDING
GAUDS
GAUDY
GAUFER
GAUFERS
GAUFFER
GAUFFERED
GAUFFERS
GAUFRE
GAUFRES
GAUGE
GAUGEABLE
GAUGEABLY
GAUGED
GAUGER
GAUGERS
GAUGES
GAUGING
GAUGINGS
GAUJE
GAUJES
GAULEITER
GAULT
GAULTER
GAULTERS
GAULTS
GAUM
GAUMED
GAUMIER
GAUMIEST
GAUMING
GAUMLESS
GAUMS

GAUMY
GAUN
GAUNCH
GAUNCHED
GAUNCHES
GAUNCHING
GAUNT
GAUNTED
GAUNTER
GAUNTEST
GAUNTING
GAUNTLET
GAUNTLETS
GAUNTLY
GAUNTNESS
GAUNTREE
GAUNTREES
GAUNTRIES
GAUNTRY
GAUNTS
GAUP
GAUPED
GAUPER
GAUPERS
GAUPING
GAUPS
GAUPUS
GAUPUSES
GAUR
GAURS
GAUS
GAUSS
GAUSSES
GAUSSIAN
GAUZE
GAUZELIKE
GAUZES
GAUZIER
GAUZIEST
GAUZILY
GAUZINESS
GAUZY
GAVAGE
GAVAGES
GAVE
GAVEL
GAVELED
GAVELING
GAVELKIND
GAVELLED
GAVELLING
GAVELMAN
GAVELMEN
GAVELOCK
GAVELOCKS
GAVELS
GAVIAL
GAVIALOID
GAVIALS
GAVOT
GAVOTS
GAVOTTE
GAVOTTED
GAVOTTES
GAVOTTING
GAW
GAWCIER
GAWCIEST
GAWCY
GAWD
GAWDS
GAWK
GAWKED
GAWKER
GAWKERS
GAWKIER
GAWKIES
GAWKIEST
GAWKIHOOD
GAWKILY
GAWKINESS
GAWKING
GAWKISH
GAWKISHLY
GAWKS
GAWKY
GAWMOGE
GAWMOGES
GAWP
GAWPED
GAWPER
GAWPERS
GAWPING
GAWPS
GAWPUS
GAWPUSES
GAWS
GAWSIE
GAWSIER
GAWSIEST
GAWSY
GAY
GAYAL
GAYALS
GAYCATION
GAYDAR
GAYDARS
GAYER
GAYEST
GAYETIES
GAYETY
GAYLY
GAYNESS
GAYNESSES
GAYS
GAYSOME
GAYWINGS
GAZABO
GAZABOES
GAZABOS
GAZAL
GAZALS
GAZANG
GAZANGED
GAZANGING
GAZANGS
GAZANIA
GAZANIAS
GAZAR
GAZARS
GAZE
GAZEBO
GAZEBOES
GAZEBOS
GAZED
GAZEFUL
GAZEHOUND
GAZELLE
GAZELLES
GAZEMENT
GAZEMENTS
GAZER
GAZERS
GAZES
GAZETTE
GAZETTED
GAZETTEER
GAZETTES
GAZETTING
GAZIER
GAZIEST
GAZILLION
GAZING
GAZINGS
GAZOGENE
GAZOGENES
GAZON
GAZONS
GAZOO
GAZOOKA
GAZOOKAS
GAZOON
GAZOONS
GAZOOS
GAZPACHO
GAZPACHOS
GAZUMP
GAZUMPED
GAZUMPER
GAZUMPERS
GAZUMPING
GAZUMPS
GAZUNDER
GAZUNDERS
GAZY
GEAL
GEALED
GEALING
GEALOUS
GEALOUSY
GEALS
GEAN
GEANS
GEAR
GEARBOX
GEARBOXES
GEARCASE
GEARCASES
GEARE
GEARED
GEARES
GEARHEAD
GEARHEADS
GEARING
GEARINGS
GEARLESS
GEARS
GEARSHIFT
GEARSTICK
GEARWHEEL
GEASON
GEAT
GEATS
GEBUR
GEBURS
GECK
GECKED
GECKING
GECKO
GECKOES
GECKOS
GECKS
GED
GEDACT
GEDACTS
GEDDIT
GEDECKT
GEDECKTS
GEDS
GEE
GEEBAG
GEEBAGS
GEEBUNG
GEEBUNGS
GEECHEE
GEECHEES
GEED
GEEGAW
GEEGAWS
GEEING
GEEK
GEEKDOM
GEEKDOMS
GEEKED
GEEKERIES
GEEKERY
GEEKIER
GEEKIEST
GEEKINESS
GEEKISH

GEEKISM
GEEKISMS
GEEKS
GEEKSPEAK
GEEKY
GEELBEK
GEELBEKS
GEEP
GEEPOUND
GEEPOUNDS
GEEPS
GEES
GEESE
GEEST
GEESTS
GEEZ
GEEZAH
GEEZAHS
GEEZER
GEEZERS
GEFILTE
GEFUFFLE
GEFUFFLED
GEFUFFLES
GEFULLTE
GEGGIE
GEGGIES
GEHLENITE
GEISHA
GEISHAS
GEIST
GEISTS
GEIT
GEITED
GEITING
GEITS
GEL
GELABLE
GELADA
GELADAS
GELANDE
GELANT
GELANTS
GELASTIC
GELATE
GELATED
GELATES
GELATI
GELATIN
GELATINE
GELATINES
GELATING
GELATINS
GELATION
GELATIONS
GELATIS
GELATO
GELATOS
GELCAP
GELCAPS
GELCOAT
GELCOATS
GELD
GELDED
GELDER
GELDERS
GELDING
GELDINGS
GELDS
GELEE
GELEES
GELID
GELIDER
GELIDEST
GELIDITY
GELIDLY
GELIDNESS
GELIGNITE
GELLANT
GELLANTS
GELLED
GELLIES
GELLING
GELLY
GELOSIES
GELOSY
GELS
GELSEMIA
GELSEMINE
GELSEMIUM
GELT
GELTS
GEM
GEMATRIA
GEMATRIAS
GEMCLIP
GEMCLIPS
GEMEL
GEMELS
GEMFISH
GEMFISHES
GEMINAL
GEMINALLY
GEMINATE
GEMINATED
GEMINATES
GEMINI
GEMINIES
GEMINOUS
GEMINY
GEMLIKE
GEMMA
GEMMAE
GEMMAN
GEMMATE
GEMMATED
GEMMATES
GEMMATING
GEMMATION
GEMMATIVE
GEMMED
GEMMEN
GEMMEOUS
GEMMERIES
GEMMERY
GEMMIER
GEMMIEST
GEMMILY
GEMMINESS
GEMMING
GEMMOLOGY
GEMMULE
GEMMULES
GEMMY
GEMOLOGY
GEMONY
GEMOT
GEMOTE
GEMOTES
GEMOTS
GEMS
GEMSBOK
GEMSBOKS
GEMSBUCK
GEMSBUCKS
GEMSHORN
GEMSHORNS
GEMSTONE
GEMSTONES
GEMUTLICH
GEN
GENA
GENAL
GENAPPE
GENAPPES
GENAS
GENDARME
GENDARMES
GENDER
GENDERED
GENDERING
GENDERISE
GENDERIZE
GENDERS
GENE
GENEALOGY
GENERA
GENERABLE
GENERAL
GENERALCY
GENERALE
GENERALIA
GENERALLY
GENERALS
GENERANT
GENERANTS
GENERATE
GENERATED
GENERATES
GENERATOR
GENERIC
GENERICAL
GENERICS
GENEROUS
GENES
GENESES
GENESIS
GENET
GENETIC
GENETICAL
GENETICS
GENETRIX
GENETS
GENETTE
GENETTES
GENEVA
GENEVAS
GENIAL
GENIALISE
GENIALITY
GENIALIZE
GENIALLY
GENIC
GENICALLY
GENICULAR
GENIE
GENIES
GENII
GENIP
GENIPAP
GENIPAPO
GENIPAPOS
GENIPAPS
GENIPS
GENISTA
GENISTAS
GENISTEIN
GENITAL
GENITALIA
GENITALIC
GENITALLY
GENITALS
GENITIVAL
GENITIVE
GENITIVES
GENITOR
GENITORS
GENITRIX
GENITURE
GENITURES
GENIUS
GENIUSES
GENIZAH
GENIZAHS
GENIZOT
GENIZOTH
GENLOCK
GENLOCKED
GENLOCKS
GENNAKER

GENNAKERS
GENNED
GENNEL
GENNELS
GENNET
GENNETS
GENNIES
GENNING
GENNY
GENOA
GENOAS
GENOCIDAL
GENOCIDE
GENOCIDES
GENOGRAM
GENOGRAMS
GENOISE
GENOISES
GENOM
GENOME
GENOMES
GENOMIC
GENOMICS
GENOMS
GENOTOXIC
GENOTYPE
GENOTYPED
GENOTYPES
GENOTYPIC
GENRE
GENRES
GENRO
GENROS
GENS
GENSENG
GENSENGS
GENT
GENTEEL
GENTEELER
GENTEELLY
GENTES
GENTIAN
GENTIANS
GENTIER
GENTIEST
GENTIL
GENTILE
GENTILES
GENTILIC
GENTILISE
GENTILISH
GENTILISM
GENTILITY
GENTILIZE
GENTLE
GENTLED
GENTLEMAN
GENTLEMEN
GENTLER
GENTLES
GENTLEST
GENTLING
GENTLY
GENTOO
GENTOOS
GENTRICE
GENTRICES
GENTRIES
GENTRIFY
GENTRY
GENTS
GENTY
GENU
GENUA
GENUFLECT
GENUINE
GENUINELY
GENUS
GENUSES
GEO
GEOBOTANY
GEOCACHE
GEOCACHED
GEOCACHER
GEOCACHES
GEOCARPIC
GEOCARPY
GEOCODE
GEOCODED
GEOCODES
GEOCODING
GEOCORONA
GEODATA
GEODE
GEODES
GEODESIC
GEODESICS
GEODESIES
GEODESIST
GEODESY
GEODETIC
GEODETICS
GEODIC
GEODUCK
GEODUCKS
GEOFACT
GEOFACTS
GEOGENIES
GEOGENY
GEOGNOSES
GEOGNOSIS
GEOGNOST
GEOGNOSTS
GEOGNOSY
GEOGONIC
GEOGONIES
GEOGONY
GEOGRAPHY
GEOID
GEOIDAL
GEOIDS
GEOLATRY
GEOLOGER
GEOLOGERS
GEOLOGIAN
GEOLOGIC
GEOLOGIES
GEOLOGISE
GEOLOGIST
GEOLOGIZE
GEOLOGY
GEOMANCER
GEOMANCY
GEOMANT
GEOMANTIC
GEOMANTS
GEOMATICS
GEOMETER
GEOMETERS
GEOMETRIC
GEOMETRID
GEOMETRY
GEOMYOID
GEONOMICS
GEOPHAGIA
GEOPHAGY
GEOPHILIC
GEOPHONE
GEOPHONES
GEOPHYTE
GEOPHYTES
GEOPHYTIC
GEOPONIC
GEOPONICS
GEOPROBE
GEOPROBES
GEORGETTE
GEORGIC
GEORGICAL
GEORGICS
GEOS
GEOSPHERE
GEOSTATIC
GEOTACTIC
GEOTAG
GEOTAGGED
GEOTAGS
GEOTAXES
GEOTAXIS
GEOTHERM
GEOTHERMS
GEOTROPIC
GER
GERAH
GERAHS
GERANIAL
GERANIALS
GERANIOL
GERANIOLS
GERANIUM
GERANIUMS
GERARDIA
GERARDIAS
GERBE
GERBERA
GERBERAS
GERBES
GERBIL
GERBILLE
GERBILLES
GERBILS
GERE
GERENT
GERENTS
GERENUK
GERENUKS
GERES
GERFALCON
GERIATRIC
GERLE
GERLES
GERM
GERMAIN
GERMAINE
GERMAINES
GERMAINS
GERMAN
GERMANDER
GERMANE
GERMANELY
GERMANIC
GERMANISE
GERMANITE
GERMANIUM
GERMANIZE
GERMANOUS
GERMANS
GERMED
GERMEN
GERMENS
GERMFREE
GERMICIDE
GERMIER
GERMIEST
GERMIN
GERMINA
GERMINAL
GERMINANT
GERMINATE
GERMINESS
GERMING
GERMINS
GERMLIKE
GERMPLASM
GERMPROOF
GERMS
GERMY
GERNE
GERNED
GERNES

GERNING
GERONIMO
GERONTIC
GEROPIGA
GEROPIGAS
GERS
GERT
GERTCHA
GERUND
GERUNDIAL
GERUNDIVE
GERUNDS
GESNERIA
GESNERIAD
GESNERIAS
GESSAMINE
GESSE
GESSED
GESSES
GESSING
GESSO
GESSOED
GESSOES
GEST
GESTALT
GESTALTEN
GESTALTS
GESTANT
GESTAPO
GESTAPOS
GESTATE
GESTATED
GESTATES
GESTATING
GESTATION
GESTATIVE
GESTATORY
GESTE
GESTES
GESTIC
GESTICAL
GESTS
GESTURAL
GESTURE
GESTURED
GESTURER
GESTURERS
GESTURES
GESTURING
GET
GETA
GETABLE
GETAS
GETATABLE
GETAWAY
GETAWAYS
GETOUT
GETOUTS
GETS
GETTABLE
GETTER
GETTERED
GETTERING
GETTERS
GETTING
GETTINGS
GETUP
GETUPS
GEUM
GEUMS
GEWGAW
GEWGAWED
GEWGAWS
GEY
GEYAN
GEYER
GEYEST
GEYSER
GEYSERED
GEYSERING
GEYSERITE
GEYSERS
GHARIAL
GHARIALS
GHARRI
GHARRIES
GHARRIS
GHARRY
GHAST
GHASTED
GHASTFUL
GHASTING
GHASTLIER
GHASTLY
GHASTNESS
GHASTS
GHAT
GHATS
GHAUT
GHAUTS
GHAZAL
GHAZALS
GHAZEL
GHAZELS
GHAZI
GHAZIES
GHAZIS
GHEE
GHEES
GHERAO
GHERAOED
GHERAOES
GHERAOING
GHERAOS
GHERKIN
GHERKINS
GHESSE
GHESSED
GHESSES
GHESSING
GHEST
GHETTO
GHETTOED
GHETTOES
GHETTOING
GHETTOISE
GHETTOIZE
GHETTOS
GHI
GHIBLI
GHIBLIS
GHILGAI
GHILGAIS
GHILLIE
GHILLIED
GHILLIES
GHILLYING
GHIS
GHOST
GHOSTED
GHOSTIER
GHOSTIEST
GHOSTING
GHOSTINGS
GHOSTLIER
GHOSTLIKE
GHOSTLY
GHOSTS
GHOSTY
GHOUL
GHOULIE
GHOULIES
GHOULISH
GHOULS
GHRELIN
GHRELINS
GHUBAR
GHYLL
GHYLLS
GI
GIAMBEUX
GIANT
GIANTESS
GIANTHOOD
GIANTISM
GIANTISMS
GIANTLIER
GIANTLIKE
GIANTLY
GIANTRIES
GIANTRY
GIANTS
GIANTSHIP
GIAOUR
GIAOURS
GIARDIA
GIARDIAS
GIB
GIBBED
GIBBER
GIBBERED
GIBBERING
GIBBERISH
GIBBERS
GIBBET
GIBBETED
GIBBETING
GIBBETS
GIBBETTED
GIBBING
GIBBON
GIBBONS
GIBBOSE
GIBBOSITY
GIBBOUS
GIBBOUSLY
GIBBSITE
GIBBSITES
GIBE
GIBED
GIBEL
GIBELS
GIBER
GIBERS
GIBES
GIBING
GIBINGLY
GIBLET
GIBLETS
GIBLI
GIBLIS
GIBS
GIBSON
GIBSONS
GIBUS
GIBUSES
GID
GIDDAP
GIDDAY
GIDDIED
GIDDIER
GIDDIES
GIDDIEST
GIDDILY
GIDDINESS
GIDDUP
GIDDY
GIDDYAP
GIDDYING
GIDDYUP
GIDGEE
GIDGEES
GIDJEE
GIDJEES
GIDS
GIE
GIED
GIEING
GIEN
GIES

GIF
GIFS
GIFT
GIFTABLE
GIFTABLES
GIFTED
GIFTEDLY
GIFTEE
GIFTEES
GIFTING
GIFTINGS
GIFTLESS
GIFTS
GIFTSHOP
GIFTSHOPS
GIFTWARE
GIFTWARES
GIFTWRAP
GIFTWRAPS
GIG
GIGA
GIGABIT
GIGABITS
GIGABYTE
GIGABYTES
GIGACYCLE
GIGAFLOP
GIGAFLOPS
GIGAHERTZ
GIGANTEAN
GIGANTIC
GIGANTISM
GIGAS
GIGATON
GIGATONS
GIGAVOLT
GIGAVOLTS
GIGAWATT
GIGAWATTS
GIGGED
GIGGING
GIGGIT
GIGGITED
GIGGITING
GIGGITS
GIGGLE
GIGGLED
GIGGLER
GIGGLERS
GIGGLES
GIGGLIER
GIGGLIEST
GIGGLING
GIGGLINGS
GIGGLY
GIGHE
GIGLET
GIGLETS
GIGLOT
GIGLOTS
GIGMAN
GIGMANITY
GIGMEN
GIGOLO
GIGOLOS
GIGOT
GIGOTS
GIGS
GIGUE
GIGUES
GILA
GILAS
GILBERT
GILBERTS
GILCUP
GILCUPS
GILD
GILDED
GILDEN
GILDER
GILDERS
GILDHALL
GILDHALLS
GILDING
GILDINGS
GILDS
GILDSMAN
GILDSMEN
GILET
GILETS
GILGAI
GILGAIS
GILGIE
GILGIES
GILL
GILLAROO
GILLAROOS
GILLED
GILLER
GILLERS
GILLET
GILLETS
GILLFLIRT
GILLIE
GILLIED
GILLIES
GILLING
GILLION
GILLIONS
GILLNET
GILLNETS
GILLS
GILLY
GILLYING
GILLYVOR
GILLYVORS
GILPEY
GILPEYS
GILPIES
GILPY
GILRAVAGE
GILSONITE
GILT
GILTCUP
GILTCUPS
GILTHEAD
GILTHEADS
GILTS
GILTWOOD
GIMBAL
GIMBALED
GIMBALING
GIMBALLED
GIMBALS
GIMCRACK
GIMCRACKS
GIMEL
GIMELS
GIMLET
GIMLETED
GIMLETING
GIMLETS
GIMMAL
GIMMALLED
GIMMALS
GIMME
GIMMER
GIMMERS
GIMMES
GIMMICK
GIMMICKED
GIMMICKRY
GIMMICKS
GIMMICKY
GIMMIE
GIMMIES
GIMMOR
GIMMORS
GIMP
GIMPED
GIMPIER
GIMPIEST
GIMPING
GIMPS
GIMPY
GIN
GINCH
GINCHES
GING
GINGAL
GINGALL
GINGALLS
GINGALS
GINGE
GINGELEY
GINGELEYS
GINGELI
GINGELIES
GINGELIS
GINGELLI
GINGELLIS
GINGELLY
GINGELY
GINGER
GINGERADE
GINGERED
GINGERIER
GINGERING
GINGERLY
GINGEROUS
GINGERS
GINGERY
GINGES
GINGHAM
GINGHAMS
GINGILI
GINGILIS
GINGILLI
GINGILLIS
GINGIVA
GINGIVAE
GINGIVAL
GINGKO
GINGKOES
GINGKOS
GINGLE
GINGLES
GINGLYMI
GINGLYMUS
GINGS
GINHOUSE
GINHOUSES
GINK
GINKGO
GINKGOES
GINKGOS
GINKS
GINN
GINNED
GINNEL
GINNELS
GINNER
GINNERIES
GINNERS
GINNERY
GINNIER
GINNIEST
GINNING
GINNINGS
GINNY
GINORMOUS
GINS
GINSENG
GINSENGS
GINSHOP
GINSHOPS
GINZO
GINZOES
GINZOS
GIO

G

G

GIOCOSO
GIOS
GIP
GIPON
GIPONS
GIPPED
GIPPER
GIPPERS
GIPPIES
GIPPING
GIPPO
GIPPOES
GIPPOS
GIPPY
GIPS
GIPSEN
GIPSENS
GIPSIED
GIPSIES
GIPSY
GIPSYDOM
GIPSYDOMS
GIPSYHOOD
GIPSYING
GIPSYISH
GIPSYISM
GIPSYISMS
GIPSYWORT
GIRAFFE
GIRAFFES
GIRAFFID
GIRAFFIDS
GIRAFFINE
GIRAFFISH
GIRAFFOID
GIRANDOLA
GIRANDOLE
GIRASOL
GIRASOLE
GIRASOLES
GIRASOLS
GIRD
GIRDED
GIRDER
GIRDERS
GIRDING
GIRDINGLY
GIRDINGS
GIRDLE
GIRDLED
GIRDLER
GIRDLERS
GIRDLES
GIRDLING
GIRDS
GIRKIN
GIRKINS
GIRL
GIRLHOOD
GIRLHOODS
GIRLIE
GIRLIER
GIRLIES
GIRLIEST
GIRLISH
GIRLISHLY
GIRLOND
GIRLONDS
GIRLS
GIRLY
GIRN
GIRNED
GIRNEL
GIRNELS
GIRNER
GIRNERS
GIRNIE
GIRNIER
GIRNIEST
GIRNING
GIRNS
GIRO
GIROLLE
GIROLLES
GIRON
GIRONIC
GIRONNY
GIRONS
GIROS
GIROSOL
GIROSOLS
GIRR
GIRRS
GIRSH
GIRSHES
GIRT
GIRTED
GIRTH
GIRTHED
GIRTHING
GIRTHLINE
GIRTHS
GIRTING
GIRTLINE
GIRTLINES
GIRTS
GIS
GISARME
GISARMES
GISM
GISMO
GISMOLOGY
GISMOS
GISMS
GIST
GISTS
GIT
GITANA
GITANAS
GITANO
GITANOS
GITCH
GITCHES
GITE
GITES
GITS
GITTARONE
GITTED
GITTERN
GITTERNED
GITTERNS
GITTIN
GITTING
GIUST
GIUSTED
GIUSTING
GIUSTO
GIUSTS
GIVABLE
GIVE
GIVEABLE
GIVEAWAY
GIVEAWAYS
GIVEBACK
GIVEBACKS
GIVED
GIVEN
GIVENNESS
GIVENS
GIVER
GIVERS
GIVES
GIVING
GIVINGS
GIZMO
GIZMOLOGY
GIZMOS
GIZZ
GIZZARD
GIZZARDS
GIZZEN
GIZZENED
GIZZENING
GIZZENS
GIZZES
GJETOST
GJETOSTS
GJU
GJUS
GLABELLA
GLABELLAE
GLABELLAR
GLABRATE
GLABROUS
GLACE
GLACED
GLACEED
GLACEING
GLACES
GLACIAL
GLACIALLY
GLACIALS
GLACIATE
GLACIATED
GLACIATES
GLACIER
GLACIERED
GLACIERS
GLACIS
GLACISES
GLAD
GLADDED
GLADDEN
GLADDENED
GLADDENER
GLADDENS
GLADDER
GLADDEST
GLADDIE
GLADDIES
GLADDING
GLADDON
GLADDONS
GLADE
GLADELIKE
GLADES
GLADFUL
GLADIATE
GLADIATOR
GLADIER
GLADIEST
GLADIOLA
GLADIOLAR
GLADIOLAS
GLADIOLE
GLADIOLES
GLADIOLI
GLADIOLUS
GLADIUS
GLADIUSES
GLADLIER
GLADLIEST
GLADLY
GLADNESS
GLADS
GLADSOME
GLADSOMER
GLADSTONE
GLADWRAP
GLADWRAPS
GLADY
GLAIK
GLAIKET
GLAIKIT
GLAIKS
GLAIR
GLAIRE
GLAIRED
GLAIREOUS
GLAIRES

GLAIRIER
GLAIRIEST
GLAIRIN
GLAIRING
GLAIRINS
GLAIRS
GLAIRY
GLAIVE
GLAIVED
GLAIVES
GLAM
GLAMMED
GLAMMER
GLAMMEST
GLAMMIER
GLAMMIEST
GLAMMING
GLAMMY
GLAMOR
GLAMORED
GLAMORING
GLAMORISE
GLAMORIZE
GLAMOROUS
GLAMORS
GLAMOUR
GLAMOURED
GLAMOURS
GLAMPING
GLAMPINGS
GLAMS
GLANCE
GLANCED
GLANCER
GLANCERS
GLANCES
GLANCING
GLANCINGS
GLAND
GLANDERED
GLANDERS
GLANDES
GLANDLESS
GLANDLIKE
GLANDS
GLANDULAR
GLANDULE
GLANDULES
GLANS
GLARE
GLAREAL
GLARED
GLARELESS
GLAREOUS
GLARES
GLARIER
GLARIEST
GLARINESS
GLARING
GLARINGLY
GLARY
GLASNOST
GLASNOSTS
GLASS
GLASSED
GLASSEN
GLASSES
GLASSFUL
GLASSFULS
GLASSIE
GLASSIER
GLASSIES
GLASSIEST
GLASSIFY
GLASSILY
GLASSINE
GLASSINES
GLASSING
GLASSLESS
GLASSLIKE
GLASSMAN
GLASSMEN
GLASSWARE
GLASSWORK
GLASSWORM
GLASSWORT
GLASSY
GLAUCOMA
GLAUCOMAS
GLAUCOUS
GLAUM
GLAUMED
GLAUMING
GLAUMS
GLAUR
GLAURIER
GLAURIEST
GLAURS
GLAURY
GLAZE
GLAZED
GLAZEN
GLAZER
GLAZERS
GLAZES
GLAZIER
GLAZIERS
GLAZIERY
GLAZIEST
GLAZILY
GLAZINESS
GLAZING
GLAZINGS
GLAZY
GLEAM
GLEAMED
GLEAMER
GLEAMERS
GLEAMIER
GLEAMIEST
GLEAMING
GLEAMINGS
GLEAMS
GLEAMY
GLEAN
GLEANABLE
GLEANED
GLEANER
GLEANERS
GLEANING
GLEANINGS
GLEANS
GLEAVE
GLEAVES
GLEBA
GLEBAE
GLEBE
GLEBELESS
GLEBES
GLEBIER
GLEBIEST
GLEBOUS
GLEBY
GLED
GLEDE
GLEDES
GLEDGE
GLEDGED
GLEDGES
GLEDGING
GLEDS
GLEE
GLEED
GLEEDS
GLEEFUL
GLEEFULLY
GLEEING
GLEEK
GLEEKED
GLEEKING
GLEEKS
GLEEMAN
GLEEMEN
GLEENIE
GLEENIES
GLEES
GLEESOME
GLEET
GLEETED
GLEETIER
GLEETIEST
GLEETING
GLEETS
GLEETY
GLEG
GLEGGER
GLEGGEST
GLEGLY
GLEGNESS
GLEI
GLEIS
GLEN
GLENGARRY
GLENLIKE
GLENOID
GLENOIDAL
GLENOIDS
GLENS
GLENT
GLENTED
GLENTING
GLENTS
GLEY
GLEYED
GLEYING
GLEYINGS
GLEYS
GLIA
GLIADIN
GLIADINE
GLIADINES
GLIADINS
GLIAL
GLIAS
GLIB
GLIBBED
GLIBBER
GLIBBERY
GLIBBEST
GLIBBING
GLIBLY
GLIBNESS
GLIBS
GLID
GLIDDER
GLIDDERY
GLIDDEST
GLIDE
GLIDED
GLIDEPATH
GLIDER
GLIDERS
GLIDES
GLIDING
GLIDINGLY
GLIDINGS
GLIFF
GLIFFING
GLIFFINGS
GLIFFS
GLIFT
GLIFTS
GLIKE
GLIKES
GLIM
GLIME
GLIMED
GLIMES
GLIMING
GLIMMER

G

GLIMMERED
GLIMMERS
GLIMMERY
GLIMPSE
GLIMPSED
GLIMPSER
GLIMPSERS
GLIMPSES
GLIMPSING
GLIMS
GLINT
GLINTED
GLINTIER
GLINTIEST
GLINTING
GLINTS
GLINTY
GLIOMA
GLIOMAS
GLIOMATA
GLIOSES
GLIOSIS
GLISK
GLISKS
GLISSADE
GLISSADED
GLISSADER
GLISSADES
GLISSANDI
GLISSANDO
GLISSE
GLISSES
GLISTEN
GLISTENED
GLISTENS
GLISTER
GLISTERED
GLISTERS
GLIT
GLITCH
GLITCHES
GLITCHIER
GLITCHY
GLITS
GLITTER
GLITTERED
GLITTERS
GLITTERY
GLITZ
GLITZED
GLITZES
GLITZIER
GLITZIEST
GLITZILY
GLITZING
GLITZY
GLOAM
GLOAMING
GLOAMINGS
GLOAMS
GLOAT
GLOATED
GLOATER
GLOATERS
GLOATING
GLOATINGS
GLOATS
GLOB
GLOBAL
GLOBALISE
GLOBALISM
GLOBALIST
GLOBALIZE
GLOBALLY
GLOBATE
GLOBATED
GLOBBIER
GLOBBIEST
GLOBBY
GLOBE
GLOBED
GLOBEFISH
GLOBELIKE
GLOBES
GLOBESITY
GLOBETROT
GLOBI
GLOBIER
GLOBIEST
GLOBIN
GLOBING
GLOBINS
GLOBOID
GLOBOIDS
GLOBOSE
GLOBOSELY
GLOBOSITY
GLOBOUS
GLOBS
GLOBULAR
GLOBULARS
GLOBULE
GLOBULES
GLOBULET
GLOBULETS
GLOBULIN
GLOBULINS
GLOBULITE
GLOBULOUS
GLOBUS
GLOBY
GLOCHID
GLOCHIDIA
GLOCHIDS
GLODE
GLOGG
GLOGGS
GLOIRE
GLOIRES
GLOM
GLOMERA
GLOMERATE
GLOMERULE
GLOMERULI
GLOMMED
GLOMMING
GLOMS
GLOMUS
GLONOIN
GLONOINS
GLOOM
GLOOMED
GLOOMFUL
GLOOMIER
GLOOMIEST
GLOOMILY
GLOOMING
GLOOMINGS
GLOOMLESS
GLOOMS
GLOOMSTER
GLOOMY
GLOOP
GLOOPED
GLOOPIER
GLOOPIEST
GLOOPING
GLOOPS
GLOOPY
GLOP
GLOPPED
GLOPPIER
GLOPPIEST
GLOPPING
GLOPPY
GLOPS
GLORIA
GLORIAS
GLORIED
GLORIES
GLORIFIED
GLORIFIER
GLORIFIES
GLORIFY
GLORIOLE
GLORIOLES
GLORIOSA
GLORIOSAS
GLORIOUS
GLORY
GLORYING
GLOSS
GLOSSA
GLOSSAE
GLOSSAL
GLOSSARY
GLOSSAS
GLOSSATOR
GLOSSED
GLOSSEME
GLOSSEMES
GLOSSER
GLOSSERS
GLOSSES
GLOSSIER
GLOSSIES
GLOSSIEST
GLOSSILY
GLOSSINA
GLOSSINAS
GLOSSING
GLOSSIST
GLOSSISTS
GLOSSITIC
GLOSSITIS
GLOSSLESS
GLOSSY
GLOST
GLOSTS
GLOTTAL
GLOTTIC
GLOTTIDES
GLOTTIS
GLOTTISES
GLOUT
GLOUTED
GLOUTING
GLOUTS
GLOVE
GLOVEBOX
GLOVED
GLOVELESS
GLOVELIKE
GLOVER
GLOVERS
GLOVES
GLOVING
GLOVINGS
GLOW
GLOWED
GLOWER
GLOWERED
GLOWERING
GLOWERS
GLOWFLIES
GLOWFLY
GLOWING
GLOWINGLY
GLOWLAMP
GLOWLAMPS
GLOWS
GLOWSTICK
GLOWWORM
GLOWWORMS
GLOXINIA
GLOXINIAS
GLOZE
GLOZED
GLOZES
GLOZING

GLOZINGS
GLUCAGON
GLUCAGONS
GLUCAN
GLUCANS
GLUCINA
GLUCINAS
GLUCINIC
GLUCINIUM
GLUCINUM
GLUCINUMS
GLUCONATE
GLUCONIC
GLUCOSE
GLUCOSES
GLUCOSIC
GLUCOSIDE
GLUE
GLUEBALL
GLUEBALLS
GLUED
GLUEING
GLUEISH
GLUELIKE
GLUEPOT
GLUEPOTS
GLUER
GLUERS
GLUES
GLUEY
GLUEYNESS
GLUG
GLUGGABLE
GLUGGED
GLUGGING
GLUGS
GLUHWEIN
GLUHWEINS
GLUIER
GLUIEST
GLUILY
GLUINESS
GLUING
GLUISH
GLUM
GLUME
GLUMELIKE
GLUMELLA
GLUMELLAS
GLUMES
GLUMLY
GLUMMER
GLUMMEST
GLUMNESS
GLUMPIER
GLUMPIEST
GLUMPILY
GLUMPISH
GLUMPS
GLUMPY
GLUMS
GLUNCH
GLUNCHED
GLUNCHES
GLUNCHING
GLUON
GLUONS
GLURGE
GLURGES
GLUT
GLUTAEAL
GLUTAEI
GLUTAEUS
GLUTAMATE
GLUTAMIC
GLUTAMINE
GLUTCH
GLUTCHED
GLUTCHES
GLUTCHING
GLUTE
GLUTEAL
GLUTEI
GLUTELIN
GLUTELINS
GLUTEN
GLUTENIN
GLUTENINS
GLUTENOUS
GLUTENS
GLUTES
GLUTEUS
GLUTINOUS
GLUTS
GLUTTED
GLUTTING
GLUTTON
GLUTTONS
GLUTTONY
GLYCAEMIA
GLYCAEMIC
GLYCAN
GLYCANS
GLYCATION
GLYCEMIA
GLYCEMIAS
GLYCEMIC
GLYCERIA
GLYCERIAS
GLYCERIC
GLYCERIDE
GLYCERIN
GLYCERINE
GLYCERINS
GLYCEROL
GLYCEROLS
GLYCERYL
GLYCERYLS
GLYCIN
GLYCINE
GLYCINES
GLYCINS
GLYCOCOLL
GLYCOGEN
GLYCOGENS
GLYCOL
GLYCOLIC
GLYCOLLIC
GLYCOLS
GLYCONIC
GLYCONICS
GLYCOSE
GLYCOSES
GLYCOSIDE
GLYCOSYL
GLYCOSYLS
GLYCYL
GLYCYLS
GLYPH
GLYPHIC
GLYPHS
GLYPTAL
GLYPTALS
GLYPTIC
GLYPTICS
GMELINITE
GNAMMA
GNAR
GNARL
GNARLED
GNARLIER
GNARLIEST
GNARLING
GNARLS
GNARLY
GNARR
GNARRED
GNARRING
GNARRS
GNARS
GNASH
GNASHED
GNASHER
GNASHERS
GNASHES
GNASHING
GNASHINGS
GNAT
GNATHAL
GNATHIC
GNATHION
GNATHIONS
GNATHITE
GNATHITES
GNATHONIC
GNATLIKE
GNATLING
GNATLINGS
GNATS
GNATTIER
GNATTIEST
GNATTY
GNATWREN
GNATWRENS
GNAW
GNAWABLE
GNAWED
GNAWER
GNAWERS
GNAWING
GNAWINGLY
GNAWINGS
GNAWN
GNAWS
GNEISS
GNEISSES
GNEISSIC
GNEISSOID
GNEISSOSE
GNOCCHI
GNOMAE
GNOME
GNOMELIKE
GNOMES
GNOMIC
GNOMICAL
GNOMISH
GNOMIST
GNOMISTS
GNOMON
GNOMONIC
GNOMONICS
GNOMONS
GNOSES
GNOSIS
GNOSTIC
GNOSTICAL
GNOSTICS
GNOW
GNOWS
GNU
GNUS
GO
GOA
GOAD
GOADED
GOADING
GOADLIKE
GOADS
GOADSMAN
GOADSMEN
GOADSTER
GOADSTERS
GOAF
GOAFS
GOAL
GOALBALL
GOALBALLS
GOALED
GOALIE

G

GOALIES
GOALING
GOALLESS
GOALMOUTH
GOALPOST
GOALPOSTS
GOALS
GOALWARD
GOALWARDS
GOANNA
GOANNAS
GOARY
GOAS
GOAT
GOATEE
GOATEED
GOATEES
GOATFISH
GOATHERD
GOATHERDS
GOATIER
GOATIES
GOATIEST
GOATISH
GOATISHLY
GOATLIKE
GOATLING
GOATLINGS
GOATS
GOATSE
GOATSES
GOATSKIN
GOATSKINS
GOATWEED
GOATWEEDS
GOATY
GOB
GOBAN
GOBANG
GOBANGS
GOBANS
GOBAR
GOBBED
GOBBELINE
GOBBET
GOBBETS
GOBBI
GOBBIER
GOBBIEST
GOBBING
GOBBLE
GOBBLED
GOBBLER
GOBBLERS
GOBBLES
GOBBLING
GOBBO
GOBBY
GOBI
GOBIES
GOBIID
GOBIIDS
GOBIOID
GOBIOIDS
GOBIS
GOBLET
GOBLETS
GOBLIN
GOBLINS
GOBO
GOBOES
GOBONEE
GOBONY
GOBOS
GOBS
GOBSHITE
GOBSHITES
GOBURRA
GOBURRAS
GOBY
GOCHUJANG
GOD
GODAWFUL
GODCHILD
GODDAM
GODDAMMED
GODDAMMIT
GODDAMN
GODDAMNED
GODDAMNIT
GODDAMNS
GODDAMS
GODDED
GODDEN
GODDENS
GODDESS
GODDESSES
GODDING
GODET
GODETIA
GODETIAS
GODETS
GODFATHER
GODHEAD
GODHEADS
GODHOOD
GODHOODS
GODLESS
GODLESSLY
GODLIER
GODLIEST
GODLIKE
GODLILY
GODLINESS
GODLING
GODLINGS
GODLY
GODMOTHER
GODOWN
GODOWNS
GODPARENT
GODROON
GODROONED
GODROONS
GODS
GODSEND
GODSENDS
GODSHIP
GODSHIPS
GODSLOT
GODSLOTS
GODSO
GODSON
GODSONS
GODSPEED
GODSPEEDS
GODSQUAD
GODSQUADS
GODWARD
GODWARDS
GODWIT
GODWITS
GOE
GOEL
GOELS
GOER
GOERS
GOES
GOEST
GOETH
GOETHITE
GOETHITES
GOETIC
GOETIES
GOETY
GOEY
GOFER
GOFERS
GOFF
GOFFED
GOFFER
GOFFERED
GOFFERING
GOFFERS
GOFFING
GOFFS
GOGGA
GOGGAS
GOGGLE
GOGGLEBOX
GOGGLED
GOGGLER
GOGGLERS
GOGGLES
GOGGLIER
GOGGLIEST
GOGGLING
GOGGLINGS
GOGGLY
GOGLET
GOGLETS
GOGO
GOGOS
GOHONZON
GOHONZONS
GOIER
GOIEST
GOING
GOINGS
GOITER
GOITERED
GOITERS
GOITRE
GOITRED
GOITRES
GOITROGEN
GOITROUS
GOJI
GOJIS
GOLCONDA
GOLCONDAS
GOLD
GOLDARN
GOLDARNED
GOLDARNS
GOLDBRICK
GOLDBUG
GOLDBUGS
GOLDCREST
GOLDEN
GOLDENED
GOLDENER
GOLDENEST
GOLDENEYE
GOLDENING
GOLDENLY
GOLDENROD
GOLDENS
GOLDER
GOLDEST
GOLDEYE
GOLDEYES
GOLDFIELD
GOLDFINCH
GOLDFINNY
GOLDFISH
GOLDIER
GOLDIES
GOLDIEST
GOLDISH
GOLDLESS
GOLDMINER
GOLDS
GOLDSINNY
GOLDSIZE
GOLDSIZES
GOLDSMITH
GOLDSPINK
GOLDSTICK
GOLDSTONE

GOLDTAIL
GOLDTONE
GOLDTONES
GOLDURN
GOLDURNS
GOLDWORK
GOLDWORKS
GOLDY
GOLE
GOLEM
GOLEMS
GOLES
GOLF
GOLFED
GOLFER
GOLFERS
GOLFIANA
GOLFIANAS
GOLFING
GOLFINGS
GOLFS
GOLGOTHA
GOLGOTHAS
GOLIARD
GOLIARDIC
GOLIARDS
GOLIARDY
GOLIAS
GOLIASED
GOLIASES
GOLIASING
GOLIATH
GOLIATHS
GOLLAN
GOLLAND
GOLLANDS
GOLLANS
GOLLAR
GOLLARED
GOLLARING
GOLLARS
GOLLER
GOLLERED
GOLLERING
GOLLERS
GOLLIED
GOLLIES
GOLLIWOG
GOLLIWOGG
GOLLIWOGS
GOLLOP
GOLLOPED
GOLLOPER
GOLLOPERS
GOLLOPING
GOLLOPS
GOLLY
GOLLYING
GOLLYWOG
GOLLYWOGS
GOLOMYNKA
GOLOSH
GOLOSHE
GOLOSHED
GOLOSHES
GOLOSHING
GOLOSHOES
GOLP
GOLPE
GOLPES
GOLPS
GOMBEEN
GOMBEENS
GOMBO
GOMBOS
GOMBRO
GOMBROON
GOMBROONS
GOMBROS
GOMER
GOMERAL
GOMERALS
GOMEREL
GOMERELS
GOMERIL
GOMERILS
GOMERS
GOMOKU
GOMOKUS
GOMPA
GOMPAS
GOMPHOSES
GOMPHOSIS
GOMUTI
GOMUTIS
GOMUTO
GOMUTOS
GON
GONAD
GONADAL
GONADIAL
GONADIC
GONADS
GONCH
GONCHES
GONDELAY
GONDELAYS
GONDOLA
GONDOLAS
GONDOLIER
GONE
GONEF
GONEFS
GONENESS
GONER
GONERS
GONFALON
GONFALONS
GONFANON
GONFANONS
GONG
GONGED
GONGING
GONGLIKE
GONGS
GONGSTER
GONGSTERS
GONGYO
GONGYOS
GONIA
GONIATITE
GONIDIA
GONIDIAL
GONIDIC
GONIDIUM
GONIF
GONIFF
GONIFFS
GONIFS
GONION
GONIUM
GONK
GONKS
GONNA
GONOCOCCI
GONOCYTE
GONOCYTES
GONODUCT
GONODUCTS
GONOF
GONOFS
GONOPH
GONOPHORE
GONOPHS
GONOPOD
GONOPODS
GONOPORE
GONOPORES
GONORRHEA
GONOSOME
GONOSOMES
GONS
GONYS
GONYSES
GONZO
GONZOS
GOO
GOOBER
GOOBERS
GOOBIES
GOOBY
GOOD
GOODBY
GOODBYE
GOODBYES
GOODBYS
GOODFACED
GOODFELLA
GOODIE
GOODIER
GOODIES
GOODIEST
GOODINESS
GOODISH
GOODLIER
GOODLIEST
GOODLY
GOODMAN
GOODMEN
GOODNESS
GOODNIGHT
GOODS
GOODSIRE
GOODSIRES
GOODTIME
GOODWIFE
GOODWILL
GOODWILLS
GOODWIVES
GOODY
GOODYEAR
GOODYEARS
GOOEY
GOOEYNESS
GOOF
GOOFBALL
GOOFBALLS
GOOFED
GOOFIER
GOOFIEST
GOOFILY
GOOFINESS
GOOFING
GOOFS
GOOFUS
GOOFUSES
GOOFY
GOOG
GOOGLE
GOOGLED
GOOGLES
GOOGLIES
GOOGLING
GOOGLY
GOOGOL
GOOGOLS
GOOGS
GOOIER
GOOIEST
GOOILY
GOOINESS
GOOK
GOOKIER
GOOKIEST
GOOKS
GOOKY
GOOL
GOOLD
GOOLDS
GOOLEY

GOOLEYS
GOOLIE
GOOLIES
GOOLS
GOOLY
GOOMBAH
GOOMBAHS
GOOMBAY
GOOMBAYS
GOON
GOONDA
GOONDAS
GOONERIES
GOONERY
GOONEY
GOONEYS
GOONIE
GOONIER
GOONIES
GOONIEST
GOONS
GOONY
GOOP
GOOPED
GOOPIER
GOOPIEST
GOOPINESS
GOOPS
GOOPY
GOOR
GOORAL
GOORALS
GOORIE
GOORIES
GOOROO
GOOROOS
GOORS
GOORY
GOOS
GOOSANDER
GOOSE
GOOSED
GOOSEFISH
GOOSEFOOT
GOOSEGOB
GOOSEGOBS
GOOSEGOG
GOOSEGOGS
GOOSEHERD
GOOSELIKE
GOOSENECK
GOOSERIES
GOOSERY
GOOSES
GOOSEY
GOOSEYS
GOOSIER
GOOSIES
GOOSIEST
GOOSINESS
GOOSING
GOOSY
GOPAK
GOPAKS
GOPHER
GOPHERED
GOPHERING
GOPHERS
GOPIK
GOPIKS
GOPURA
GOPURAM
GOPURAMS
GOPURAS
GOR
GORA
GORAL
GORALS
GORAMIES
GORAMY
GORAS
GORBELLY
GORBLIMEY
GORBLIMY
GORCOCK
GORCOCKS
GORCROW
GORCROWS
GORDITA
GORDITAS
GORE
GORED
GOREFEST
GOREFESTS
GOREHOUND
GORES
GORGE
GORGEABLE
GORGED
GORGEDLY
GORGEOUS
GORGER
GORGERIN
GORGERINS
GORGERS
GORGES
GORGET
GORGETED
GORGETS
GORGIA
GORGIAS
GORGING
GORGIO
GORGIOS
GORGON
GORGONEIA
GORGONIAN
GORGONISE
GORGONIZE
GORGONS
GORHEN
GORHENS
GORI
GORIER
GORIEST
GORILLA
GORILLAS
GORILLIAN
GORILLINE
GORILLOID
GORILY
GORINESS
GORING
GORINGS
GORIS
GORM
GORMAND
GORMANDS
GORMED
GORMIER
GORMIEST
GORMING
GORMLESS
GORMS
GORMY
GORP
GORPED
GORPING
GORPS
GORS
GORSE
GORSEDD
GORSEDDS
GORSES
GORSIER
GORSIEST
GORSOON
GORSOONS
GORSY
GORY
GOS
GOSH
GOSHAWK
GOSHAWKS
GOSHT
GOSHTS
GOSLARITE
GOSLET
GOSLETS
GOSLING
GOSLINGS
GOSPEL
GOSPELER
GOSPELERS
GOSPELISE
GOSPELIZE
GOSPELLED
GOSPELLER
GOSPELLY
GOSPELS
GOSPODA
GOSPODAR
GOSPODARS
GOSPODIN
GOSPORT
GOSPORTS
GOSS
GOSSAMER
GOSSAMERS
GOSSAMERY
GOSSAN
GOSSANS
GOSSE
GOSSED
GOSSES
GOSSIB
GOSSIBS
GOSSING
GOSSIP
GOSSIPED
GOSSIPER
GOSSIPERS
GOSSIPIER
GOSSIPING
GOSSIPPED
GOSSIPPER
GOSSIPRY
GOSSIPS
GOSSIPY
GOSSOON
GOSSOONS
GOSSYPINE
GOSSYPOL
GOSSYPOLS
GOSTER
GOSTERED
GOSTERING
GOSTERS
GOT
GOTCH
GOTCHA
GOTCHAS
GOTCHES
GOTCHIES
GOTH
GOTHIC
GOTHICISE
GOTHICISM
GOTHICIZE
GOTHICS
GOTHIER
GOTHIEST
GOTHITE
GOTHITES
GOTHS
GOTHY
GOTTA
GOTTEN
GOUACHE
GOUACHES

GOUCH
GOUCHED
GOUCHES
GOUCHING
GOUGE
GOUGED
GOUGER
GOUGERE
GOUGERES
GOUGERS
GOUGES
GOUGING
GOUJEERS
GOUJON
GOUJONS
GOUK
GOUKS
GOULASH
GOULASHES
GOURA
GOURAMI
GOURAMIES
GOURAMIS
GOURAS
GOURD
GOURDE
GOURDES
GOURDFUL
GOURDFULS
GOURDIER
GOURDIEST
GOURDLIKE
GOURDS
GOURDY
GOURMAND
GOURMANDS
GOURMET
GOURMETS
GOUSTIER
GOUSTIEST
GOUSTROUS
GOUSTY
GOUT
GOUTFLIES
GOUTFLY
GOUTIER
GOUTIEST
GOUTILY
GOUTINESS
GOUTS
GOUTTE
GOUTTES
GOUTWEED
GOUTWEEDS
GOUTWORT
GOUTWORTS
GOUTY
GOV
GOVERN
GOVERNALL
GOVERNED
GOVERNESS
GOVERNING
GOVERNOR
GOVERNORS
GOVERNS
GOVS
GOWAN
GOWANED
GOWANS
GOWANY
GOWD
GOWDER
GOWDEST
GOWDS
GOWDSPINK
GOWF
GOWFED
GOWFER
GOWFERS
GOWFING
GOWFS
GOWK
GOWKS
GOWL
GOWLAN
GOWLAND
GOWLANDS
GOWLANS
GOWLED
GOWLING
GOWLS
GOWN
GOWNBOY
GOWNBOYS
GOWNED
GOWNING
GOWNMAN
GOWNMEN
GOWNS
GOWNSMAN
GOWNSMEN
GOWPEN
GOWPENFUL
GOWPENS
GOX
GOXES
GOY
GOYIM
GOYISCH
GOYISH
GOYISHE
GOYLE
GOYLES
GOYS
GOZZAN
GOZZANS
GRAAL
GRAALS
GRAB
GRABBABLE
GRABBED
GRABBER
GRABBERS
GRABBIER
GRABBIEST
GRABBING
GRABBLE
GRABBLED
GRABBLER
GRABBLERS
GRABBLES
GRABBLING
GRABBY
GRABEN
GRABENS
GRABS
GRACE
GRACED
GRACEFUL
GRACELESS
GRACES
GRACILE
GRACILES
GRACILIS
GRACILITY
GRACING
GRACIOSO
GRACIOSOS
GRACIOUS
GRACKLE
GRACKLES
GRAD
GRADABLE
GRADABLES
GRADATE
GRADATED
GRADATES
GRADATIM
GRADATING
GRADATION
GRADATORY
GRADDAN
GRADDANED
GRADDANS
GRADE
GRADED
GRADELESS
GRADELIER
GRADELY
GRADER
GRADERS
GRADES
GRADIENT
GRADIENTS
GRADIN
GRADINE
GRADINES
GRADING
GRADINGS
GRADINI
GRADINO
GRADINS
GRADS
GRADUAL
GRADUALLY
GRADUALS
GRADUAND
GRADUANDS
GRADUATE
GRADUATED
GRADUATES
GRADUATOR
GRADUS
GRADUSES
GRAECISE
GRAECISED
GRAECISES
GRAECIZE
GRAECIZED
GRAECIZES
GRAFF
GRAFFED
GRAFFING
GRAFFITI
GRAFFITIS
GRAFFITO
GRAFFS
GRAFT
GRAFTAGE
GRAFTAGES
GRAFTED
GRAFTER
GRAFTERS
GRAFTING
GRAFTINGS
GRAFTS
GRAHAM
GRAHAMS
GRAIL
GRAILE
GRAILES
GRAILS
GRAIN
GRAINAGE
GRAINAGES
GRAINE
GRAINED
GRAINER
GRAINERS
GRAINES
GRAINIER
GRAINIEST
GRAINING
GRAININGS
GRAINLESS
GRAINS
GRAINY
GRAIP
GRAIPS

GRAITH
GRAITHED
GRAITHING
GRAITHLY
GRAITHS
GRAKLE
GRAKLES
GRALLOCH
GRALLOCHS
GRAM
GRAMA
GRAMARIES
GRAMARY
GRAMARYE
GRAMARYES
GRAMAS
GRAMASH
GRAMASHES
GRAME
GRAMERCY
GRAMES
GRAMMA
GRAMMAGE
GRAMMAGES
GRAMMAR
GRAMMARS
GRAMMAS
GRAMMATIC
GRAMME
GRAMMES
GRAMOCHE
GRAMOCHES
GRAMP
GRAMPA
GRAMPAS
GRAMPIES
GRAMPS
GRAMPUS
GRAMPUSES
GRAMPY
GRAMS
GRAN
GRANA
GRANARIES
GRANARY
GRAND
GRANDAD
GRANDADDY
GRANDADS
GRANDAM
GRANDAME
GRANDAMES
GRANDAMS
GRANDAUNT
GRANDBABY
GRANDDAD
GRANDDADS
GRANDDAM
GRANDDAMS
GRANDE
GRANDEE
GRANDEES
GRANDER
GRANDEST
GRANDEUR
GRANDEURS
GRANDIOSE
GRANDIOSO
GRANDKID
GRANDKIDS
GRANDLY
GRANDMA
GRANDMAMA
GRANDMAS
GRANDNESS
GRANDPA
GRANDPAPA
GRANDPAS
GRANDS
GRANDSIR
GRANDSIRE
GRANDSIRS
GRANDSON
GRANDSONS
GRANFER
GRANFERS
GRANGE
GRANGER
GRANGERS
GRANGES
GRANITA
GRANITAS
GRANITE
GRANITES
GRANITIC
GRANITISE
GRANITITE
GRANITIZE
GRANITOID
GRANIVORE
GRANNAM
GRANNAMS
GRANNIE
GRANNIED
GRANNIES
GRANNOM
GRANNOMS
GRANNY
GRANNYING
GRANNYISH
GRANOLA
GRANOLAS
GRANOLITH
GRANS
GRANT
GRANTABLE
GRANTED
GRANTEE
GRANTEES
GRANTER
GRANTERS
GRANTING
GRANTOR
GRANTORS
GRANTS
GRANTSMAN
GRANTSMEN
GRANULAR
GRANULARY
GRANULATE
GRANULE
GRANULES
GRANULITE
GRANULOMA
GRANULOSE
GRANULOUS
GRANUM
GRANUMS
GRAPE
GRAPED
GRAPELESS
GRAPELICE
GRAPELIKE
GRAPERIES
GRAPERY
GRAPES
GRAPESEED
GRAPESHOT
GRAPETREE
GRAPEVINE
GRAPEY
GRAPH
GRAPHED
GRAPHEME
GRAPHEMES
GRAPHEMIC
GRAPHENE
GRAPHENES
GRAPHIC
GRAPHICAL
GRAPHICLY
GRAPHICS
GRAPHING
GRAPHITE
GRAPHITES
GRAPHITIC
GRAPHIUM
GRAPHIUMS
GRAPHS
GRAPIER
GRAPIEST
GRAPINESS
GRAPING
GRAPLE
GRAPLES
GRAPLIN
GRAPLINE
GRAPLINES
GRAPLINS
GRAPNEL
GRAPNELS
GRAPPA
GRAPPAS
GRAPPLE
GRAPPLED
GRAPPLER
GRAPPLERS
GRAPPLES
GRAPPLING
GRAPY
GRASP
GRASPABLE
GRASPED
GRASPER
GRASPERS
GRASPING
GRASPLESS
GRASPS
GRASS
GRASSBIRD
GRASSED
GRASSER
GRASSERS
GRASSES
GRASSHOOK
GRASSIER
GRASSIEST
GRASSILY
GRASSING
GRASSINGS
GRASSLAND
GRASSLESS
GRASSLIKE
GRASSPLOT
GRASSQUIT
GRASSROOT
GRASSUM
GRASSUMS
GRASSY
GRASTE
GRAT
GRATE
GRATED
GRATEFUL
GRATELESS
GRATER
GRATERS
GRATES
GRATICULE
GRATIFIED
GRATIFIER
GRATIFIES
GRATIFY
GRATIN
GRATINATE
GRATINE
GRATINEE
GRATINEED
GRATINEES
GRATING

GRATINGLY
GRATINGS
GRATINS
GRATIS
GRATITUDE
GRATTOIR
GRATTOIRS
GRATUITY
GRATULANT
GRATULATE
GRAUNCH
GRAUNCHED
GRAUNCHER
GRAUNCHES
GRAUPEL
GRAUPELS
GRAV
GRAVADLAX
GRAVAMEN
GRAVAMENS
GRAVAMINA
GRAVE
GRAVED
GRAVEL
GRAVELED
GRAVELESS
GRAVELIKE
GRAVELING
GRAVELISH
GRAVELLED
GRAVELLY
GRAVELS
GRAVELY
GRAVEN
GRAVENESS
GRAVER
GRAVERS
GRAVES
GRAVESIDE
GRAVESITE
GRAVEST
GRAVEWARD
GRAVEYARD
GRAVID
GRAVIDA
GRAVIDAE
GRAVIDAS
GRAVIDITY
GRAVIDLY
GRAVIES
GRAVING
GRAVINGS
GRAVIS
GRAVITAS
GRAVITATE
GRAVITIES
GRAVITINO
GRAVITON
GRAVITONS
GRAVITY
GRAVLAKS
GRAVLAX
GRAVLAXES
GRAVS
GRAVURE
GRAVURES
GRAVY
GRAWLIX
GRAWLIXES
GRAY
GRAYBACK
GRAYBACKS
GRAYBEARD
GRAYED
GRAYER
GRAYEST
GRAYFISH
GRAYFLIES
GRAYFLY
GRAYHEAD
GRAYHEADS
GRAYHEN
GRAYHENS
GRAYHOUND
GRAYING
GRAYISH
GRAYLAG
GRAYLAGS
GRAYLE
GRAYLES
GRAYLING
GRAYLINGS
GRAYLIST
GRAYLISTS
GRAYLY
GRAYMAIL
GRAYMAILS
GRAYNESS
GRAYOUT
GRAYOUTS
GRAYS
GRAYSCALE
GRAYSTONE
GRAYWACKE
GRAYWATER
GRAZABLE
GRAZE
GRAZEABLE
GRAZED
GRAZER
GRAZERS
GRAZES
GRAZIER
GRAZIERS
GRAZING
GRAZINGLY
GRAZINGS
GRAZIOSO
GREASE
GREASED
GREASER
GREASERS
GREASES
GREASIER
GREASIES
GREASIEST
GREASILY
GREASING
GREASY
GREAT
GREATCOAT
GREATEN
GREATENED
GREATENS
GREATER
GREATEST
GREATESTS
GREATLY
GREATNESS
GREATS
GREAVE
GREAVED
GREAVES
GREAVING
GREBE
GREBES
GREBO
GREBOES
GREBOS
GRECE
GRECES
GRECIAN
GRECIANS
GRECISE
GRECISED
GRECISES
GRECISING
GRECIZE
GRECIZED
GRECIZES
GRECIZING
GRECQUE
GRECQUES
GREE
GREEBO
GREEBOES
GREEBOS
GREECE
GREECES
GREED
GREEDHEAD
GREEDIER
GREEDIEST
GREEDILY
GREEDLESS
GREEDS
GREEDSOME
GREEDY
GREEGREE
GREEGREES
GREEING
GREEK
GREEKED
GREEKING
GREEKINGS
GREEN
GREENBACK
GREENBELT
GREENBONE
GREENBUG
GREENBUGS
GREENED
GREENER
GREENERS
GREENERY
GREENEST
GREENEYE
GREENEYES
GREENFLY
GREENGAGE
GREENHAND
GREENHEAD
GREENHORN
GREENIE
GREENIER
GREENIES
GREENIEST
GREENING
GREENINGS
GREENISH
GREENLET
GREENLETS
GREENLING
GREENLIT
GREENLY
GREENMAIL
GREENNESS
GREENROOM
GREENS
GREENSAND
GREENSICK
GREENSOME
GREENTH
GREENTHS
GREENWASH
GREENWAY
GREENWAYS
GREENWEED
GREENWING
GREENWOOD
GREENY
GREES
GREESE
GREESES
GREESING
GREESINGS
GREET
GREETE
GREETED
GREETER

G

GREETERS
GREETES
GREETING
GREETINGS
GREETS
GREFFIER
GREFFIERS
GREGALE
GREGALES
GREGARIAN
GREGARINE
GREGATIM
GREGE
GREGED
GREGES
GREGING
GREGO
GREGOS
GREIGE
GREIGES
GREIN
GREINED
GREINING
GREINS
GREISEN
GREISENS
GREISLY
GREMIAL
GREMIALS
GREMLIN
GREMLINS
GREMMIE
GREMMIES
GREMMY
GREMOLATA
GREN
GRENACHE
GRENACHES
GRENADE
GRENADES
GRENADIER
GRENADINE
GRENNED
GRENNING
GRENS
GRESE
GRESES
GRESSING
GRESSINGS
GREVE
GREVES
GREVILLEA
GREW
GREWED
GREWHOUND
GREWING
GREWS
GREWSOME
GREWSOMER
GREX
GREXES
GREY
GREYBACK
GREYBACKS
GREYBEARD
GREYED
GREYER
GREYEST
GREYHEAD
GREYHEADS
GREYHEN
GREYHENS
GREYHOUND
GREYING
GREYINGS
GREYISH
GREYLAG
GREYLAGS
GREYLIST
GREYLISTS
GREYLY
GREYNESS
GREYS
GREYSCALE
GREYSTONE
GREYWACKE
GRIBBLE
GRIBBLES
GRICE
GRICED
GRICER
GRICERS
GRICES
GRICING
GRICINGS
GRID
GRIDDED
GRIDDER
GRIDDERS
GRIDDING
GRIDDLE
GRIDDLED
GRIDDLES
GRIDDLING
GRIDE
GRIDED
GRIDELIN
GRIDELINS
GRIDES
GRIDING
GRIDIRON
GRIDIRONS
GRIDLOCK
GRIDLOCKS
GRIDS
GRIECE
GRIECED
GRIECES
GRIEF
GRIEFER
GRIEFERS
GRIEFFUL
GRIEFLESS
GRIEFS
GRIESIE
GRIESLY
GRIESY
GRIEVANCE
GRIEVANT
GRIEVANTS
GRIEVE
GRIEVED
GRIEVER
GRIEVERS
GRIEVES
GRIEVING
GRIEVINGS
GRIEVOUS
GRIFF
GRIFFE
GRIFFES
GRIFFIN
GRIFFINS
GRIFFON
GRIFFONS
GRIFFS
GRIFT
GRIFTED
GRIFTER
GRIFTERS
GRIFTING
GRIFTS
GRIG
GRIGGED
GRIGGING
GRIGRI
GRIGRIS
GRIGS
GRIKE
GRIKES
GRILL
GRILLADE
GRILLADES
GRILLAGE
GRILLAGES
GRILLE
GRILLED
GRILLER
GRILLERS
GRILLERY
GRILLES
GRILLING
GRILLINGS
GRILLION
GRILLIONS
GRILLROOM
GRILLS
GRILLWORK
GRILSE
GRILSES
GRIM
GRIMACE
GRIMACED
GRIMACER
GRIMACERS
GRIMACES
GRIMACING
GRIMALKIN
GRIME
GRIMED
GRIMES
GRIMIER
GRIMIEST
GRIMILY
GRIMINESS
GRIMING
GRIMLY
GRIMMER
GRIMMEST
GRIMNESS
GRIMOIRE
GRIMOIRES
GRIMY
GRIN
GRINCH
GRINCHES
GRIND
GRINDED
GRINDELIA
GRINDER
GRINDERS
GRINDERY
GRINDING
GRINDINGS
GRINDS
GRINGA
GRINGAS
GRINGO
GRINGOS
GRINNED
GRINNER
GRINNERS
GRINNING
GRINNINGS
GRINS
GRIOT
GRIOTS
GRIP
GRIPE
GRIPED
GRIPER
GRIPERS
GRIPES
GRIPEY
GRIPIER
GRIPIEST
GRIPING
GRIPINGLY
GRIPINGS
GRIPLE

GRIPMAN
GRIPMEN
GRIPPE
GRIPPED
GRIPPER
GRIPPERS
GRIPPES
GRIPPIER
GRIPPIEST
GRIPPING
GRIPPLE
GRIPPLES
GRIPPY
GRIPS
GRIPSACK
GRIPSACKS
GRIPT
GRIPTAPE
GRIPTAPES
GRIPY
GRIS
GRISAILLE
GRISE
GRISED
GRISELY
GRISEOUS
GRISES
GRISETTE
GRISETTES
GRISGRIS
GRISING
GRISKIN
GRISKINS
GRISLED
GRISLIER
GRISLIES
GRISLIEST
GRISLY
GRISON
GRISONS
GRISSINI
GRISSINO
GRIST
GRISTER
GRISTERS
GRISTLE
GRISTLES
GRISTLIER
GRISTLY
GRISTMILL
GRISTS
GRISY
GRIT
GRITH
GRITHS
GRITLESS
GRITS
GRITSTONE
GRITTED
GRITTER
GRITTERS
GRITTEST
GRITTIER
GRITTIEST
GRITTILY
GRITTING
GRITTINGS
GRITTY
GRIVATION
GRIVET
GRIVETS
GRIZ
GRIZE
GRIZES
GRIZZES
GRIZZLE
GRIZZLED
GRIZZLER
GRIZZLERS
GRIZZLES
GRIZZLIER
GRIZZLIES
GRIZZLING
GRIZZLY
GROAN
GROANED
GROANER
GROANERS
GROANFUL
GROANING
GROANINGS
GROANS
GROAT
GROATS
GROCER
GROCERIES
GROCERS
GROCERY
GROCKED
GROCKING
GROCKLE
GROCKLES
GRODIER
GRODIEST
GRODY
GROG
GROGGED
GROGGERY
GROGGIER
GROGGIEST
GROGGILY
GROGGING
GROGGY
GROGRAM
GROGRAMS
GROGS
GROGSHOP
GROGSHOPS
GROIN
GROINED
GROINING
GROININGS
GROINS
GROK
GROKED
GROKING
GROKKED
GROKKING
GROKS
GROMA
GROMAS
GROMET
GROMETS
GROMMET
GROMMETED
GROMMETS
GROMWELL
GROMWELLS
GRONE
GRONED
GRONEFULL
GRONES
GRONING
GROOF
GROOFS
GROOLIER
GROOLIEST
GROOLY
GROOM
GROOMED
GROOMER
GROOMERS
GROOMING
GROOMINGS
GROOMS
GROOMSMAN
GROOMSMEN
GROOVE
GROOVED
GROOVER
GROOVERS
GROOVES
GROOVIER
GROOVIEST
GROOVILY
GROOVING
GROOVY
GROPE
GROPED
GROPER
GROPERS
GROPES
GROPING
GROPINGLY
GROSBEAK
GROSBEAKS
GROSCHEN
GROSCHENS
GROSER
GROSERS
GROSERT
GROSERTS
GROSET
GROSETS
GROSGRAIN
GROSS
GROSSART
GROSSARTS
GROSSED
GROSSER
GROSSERS
GROSSES
GROSSEST
GROSSING
GROSSLY
GROSSNESS
GROSSULAR
GROSZ
GROSZE
GROSZY
GROT
GROTESQUE
GROTS
GROTTIER
GROTTIEST
GROTTO
GROTTOED
GROTTOES
GROTTOS
GROTTY
GROUCH
GROUCHED
GROUCHES
GROUCHIER
GROUCHILY
GROUCHING
GROUCHY
GROUF
GROUFS
GROUGH
GROUGHS
GROUND
GROUNDAGE
GROUNDED
GROUNDEN
GROUNDER
GROUNDERS
GROUNDHOG
GROUNDING
GROUNDMAN
GROUNDMEN
GROUNDNUT
GROUNDOUT
GROUNDS
GROUNDSEL
GROUP
GROUPABLE
GROUPAGE
GROUPAGES
GROUPED

G

GROUPER
GROUPERS
GROUPIE
GROUPIES
GROUPING
GROUPINGS
GROUPIST
GROUPISTS
GROUPLET
GROUPLETS
GROUPOID
GROUPOIDS
GROUPS
GROUPWARE
GROUPWORK
GROUPY
GROUSE
GROUSED
GROUSER
GROUSERS
GROUSES
GROUSEST
GROUSING
GROUT
GROUTED
GROUTER
GROUTERS
GROUTIER
GROUTIEST
GROUTING
GROUTINGS
GROUTS
GROUTY
GROVE
GROVED
GROVEL
GROVELED
GROVELER
GROVELERS
GROVELESS
GROVELING
GROVELLED
GROVELLER
GROVELS
GROVES
GROVET
GROVETS
GROVIER
GROVIEST
GROVY
GROW
GROWABLE
GROWER
GROWERS
GROWING
GROWINGLY
GROWINGS
GROWL
GROWLED
GROWLER
GROWLERS
GROWLERY
GROWLIER
GROWLIEST
GROWLING
GROWLINGS
GROWLS
GROWLY
GROWN
GROWNUP
GROWNUPS
GROWS
GROWTH
GROWTHIER
GROWTHIST
GROWTHS
GROWTHY
GROYNE
GROYNES
GROZING
GRR
GRRL
GRRLS
GRRRL
GRRRLS
GRUB
GRUBBED
GRUBBER
GRUBBERS
GRUBBIER
GRUBBIEST
GRUBBILY
GRUBBING
GRUBBLE
GRUBBLED
GRUBBLES
GRUBBLING
GRUBBY
GRUBS
GRUBSTAKE
GRUBWORM
GRUBWORMS
GRUDGE
GRUDGED
GRUDGEFUL
GRUDGER
GRUDGERS
GRUDGES
GRUDGING
GRUDGINGS
GRUE
GRUED
GRUEING
GRUEL
GRUELED
GRUELER
GRUELERS
GRUELING
GRUELINGS
GRUELLED
GRUELLER
GRUELLERS
GRUELLING
GRUELS
GRUES
GRUESOME
GRUESOMER
GRUFE
GRUFES
GRUFF
GRUFFED
GRUFFER
GRUFFEST
GRUFFIER
GRUFFIEST
GRUFFILY
GRUFFING
GRUFFISH
GRUFFLY
GRUFFNESS
GRUFFS
GRUFFY
GRUFTED
GRUGRU
GRUGRUS
GRUIFORM
GRUING
GRUM
GRUMBLE
GRUMBLED
GRUMBLER
GRUMBLERS
GRUMBLES
GRUMBLIER
GRUMBLING
GRUMBLY
GRUME
GRUMES
GRUMLY
GRUMMER
GRUMMEST
GRUMMET
GRUMMETED
GRUMMETS
GRUMNESS
GRUMOSE
GRUMOUS
GRUMP
GRUMPED
GRUMPH
GRUMPHED
GRUMPHIE
GRUMPHIES
GRUMPHING
GRUMPHS
GRUMPHY
GRUMPIER
GRUMPIES
GRUMPIEST
GRUMPILY
GRUMPING
GRUMPISH
GRUMPS
GRUMPY
GRUND
GRUNDIES
GRUNDLE
GRUNDLES
GRUNGE
GRUNGER
GRUNGERS
GRUNGES
GRUNGEY
GRUNGIER
GRUNGIEST
GRUNGY
GRUNION
GRUNIONS
GRUNT
GRUNTED
GRUNTER
GRUNTERS
GRUNTING
GRUNTINGS
GRUNTLE
GRUNTLED
GRUNTLES
GRUNTLING
GRUNTS
GRUPPETTI
GRUPPETTO
GRUSHIE
GRUTCH
GRUTCHED
GRUTCHES
GRUTCHING
GRUTTEN
GRUYERE
GRUYERES
GRYCE
GRYCES
GRYDE
GRYDED
GRYDES
GRYDING
GRYESY
GRYFON
GRYFONS
GRYKE
GRYKES
GRYPE
GRYPES
GRYPHON
GRYPHONS
GRYPT
GRYSBOK
GRYSBOKS
GRYSELY
GRYSIE
GU

GUACAMOLE
GUACHARO
GUACHAROS
GUACO
GUACOS
GUAIAC
GUAIACOL
GUAIACOLS
GUAIACS
GUAIACUM
GUAIACUMS
GUAIOCUM
GUAIOCUMS
GUAN
GUANA
GUANABANA
GUANACO
GUANACOS
GUANAS
GUANASE
GUANASES
GUANAY
GUANAYS
GUANAZOLO
GUANGO
GUANGOS
GUANIDIN
GUANIDINE
GUANIDINS
GUANIN
GUANINE
GUANINES
GUANINS
GUANO
GUANOS
GUANOSINE
GUANS
GUANXI
GUANXIS
GUANYLIC
GUAR
GUARACHA
GUARACHAS
GUARACHE
GUARACHES
GUARACHI
GUARACHIS
GUARANA
GUARANAS
GUARANI
GUARANIES
GUARANIS
GUARANTEE
GUARANTOR
GUARANTY
GUARD
GUARDABLE
GUARDAGE
GUARDAGES
GUARDANT
GUARDANTS
GUARDDOG
GUARDDOGS
GUARDED
GUARDEDLY
GUARDEE
GUARDEES
GUARDER
GUARDERS
GUARDIAN
GUARDIANS
GUARDING
GUARDLESS
GUARDLIKE
GUARDRAIL
GUARDROOM
GUARDS
GUARDSHIP
GUARDSMAN
GUARDSMEN
GUARISH
GUARISHED
GUARISHES
GUARS
GUAVA
GUAVAS
GUAYABERA
GUAYULE
GUAYULES
GUB
GUBBAH
GUBBAHS
GUBBED
GUBBING
GUBBINS
GUBBINSES
GUBERNIYA
GUBS
GUCK
GUCKIER
GUCKIEST
GUCKS
GUCKY
GUDDLE
GUDDLED
GUDDLES
GUDDLING
GUDE
GUDEMAN
GUDEMEN
GUDES
GUDESIRE
GUDESIRES
GUDEWIFE
GUDEWIVES
GUDGEON
GUDGEONED
GUDGEONS
GUE
GUELDER
GUENON
GUENONS
GUERDON
GUERDONED
GUERDONER
GUERDONS
GUEREZA
GUEREZAS
GUERIDON
GUERIDONS
GUERILLA
GUERILLAS
GUERITE
GUERITES
GUERNSEY
GUERNSEYS
GUERRILLA
GUES
GUESS
GUESSABLE
GUESSED
GUESSER
GUESSERS
GUESSES
GUESSING
GUESSINGS
GUESSWORK
GUEST
GUESTBOOK
GUESTED
GUESTEN
GUESTENED
GUESTENS
GUESTING
GUESTS
GUESTWISE
GUFF
GUFFAW
GUFFAWED
GUFFAWING
GUFFAWS
GUFFIE
GUFFIES
GUFFS
GUGA
GUGAS
GUGGLE
GUGGLED
GUGGLES
GUGGLING
GUGLET
GUGLETS
GUICHET
GUICHETS
GUID
GUIDABLE
GUIDAGE
GUIDAGES
GUIDANCE
GUIDANCES
GUIDE
GUIDEBOOK
GUIDED
GUIDELESS
GUIDELINE
GUIDEPOST
GUIDER
GUIDERS
GUIDES
GUIDESHIP
GUIDEWAY
GUIDEWAYS
GUIDEWORD
GUIDING
GUIDINGS
GUIDON
GUIDONS
GUIDS
GUILD
GUILDER
GUILDERS
GUILDHALL
GUILDRIES
GUILDRY
GUILDS
GUILDSHIP
GUILDSMAN
GUILDSMEN
GUILE
GUILED
GUILEFUL
GUILELESS
GUILER
GUILERS
GUILES
GUILING
GUILLEMET
GUILLEMOT
GUILLOCHE
GUILT
GUILTED
GUILTIER
GUILTIEST
GUILTILY
GUILTING
GUILTLESS
GUILTS
GUILTY
GUIMBARD
GUIMBARDS
GUIMP
GUIMPE
GUIMPED
GUIMPES
GUIMPING
GUIMPS
GUINEA
GUINEAS
GUINEP
GUINEPS

GUIPURE
GUIPURES
GUIRO
GUIROS
GUISARD
GUISARDS
GUISE
GUISED
GUISER
GUISERS
GUISES
GUISING
GUISINGS
GUITAR
GUITARIST
GUITARS
GUITGUIT
GUITGUITS
GUIZER
GUIZERS
GUL
GULA
GULAG
GULAGS
GULAR
GULARS
GULAS
GULCH
GULCHED
GULCHES
GULCHING
GULDEN
GULDENS
GULE
GULES
GULET
GULETS
GULF
GULFED
GULFIER
GULFIEST
GULFING
GULFLIKE
GULFS
GULFWEED
GULFWEEDS
GULFY
GULL
GULLABLE
GULLABLY
GULLED
GULLER
GULLERIES
GULLERS
GULLERY
GULLET
GULLETS
GULLEY
GULLEYED
GULLEYING
GULLEYS
GULLIBLE
GULLIBLY
GULLIED
GULLIES
GULLING
GULLISH
GULLS
GULLWING
GULLY
GULLYING
GULOSITY
GULP
GULPED
GULPER
GULPERS
GULPH
GULPHS
GULPIER
GULPIEST
GULPING
GULPINGLY
GULPS
GULPY
GULS
GULY
GUM
GUMBALL
GUMBALLS
GUMBO
GUMBOIL
GUMBOILS
GUMBOOT
GUMBOOTS
GUMBOS
GUMBOTIL
GUMBOTILS
GUMDROP
GUMDROPS
GUMLANDS
GUMLESS
GUMLIKE
GUMLINE
GUMLINES
GUMMA
GUMMAS
GUMMATA
GUMMATOUS
GUMMED
GUMMER
GUMMERS
GUMMI
GUMMIER
GUMMIES
GUMMIEST
GUMMILY
GUMMINESS
GUMMING
GUMMINGS
GUMMIS
GUMMITE
GUMMITES
GUMMOSE
GUMMOSES
GUMMOSIS
GUMMOSITY
GUMMOUS
GUMMY
GUMNUT
GUMNUTS
GUMP
GUMPED
GUMPHION
GUMPHIONS
GUMPING
GUMPS
GUMPTION
GUMPTIONS
GUMPTIOUS
GUMS
GUMSHIELD
GUMSHOE
GUMSHOED
GUMSHOES
GUMSUCKER
GUMTREE
GUMTREES
GUMWEED
GUMWEEDS
GUMWOOD
GUMWOODS
GUN
GUNBOAT
GUNBOATS
GUNCOTTON
GUNDIES
GUNDOG
GUNDOGS
GUNDY
GUNFIGHT
GUNFIGHTS
GUNFIRE
GUNFIRES
GUNFLINT
GUNFLINTS
GUNFOUGHT
GUNG
GUNGE
GUNGED
GUNGES
GUNGIER
GUNGIEST
GUNGING
GUNGY
GUNHOUSE
GUNHOUSES
GUNITE
GUNITES
GUNK
GUNKED
GUNKHOLE
GUNKHOLED
GUNKHOLES
GUNKIER
GUNKIEST
GUNKING
GUNKS
GUNKY
GUNLAYER
GUNLAYERS
GUNLESS
GUNLOCK
GUNLOCKS
GUNMAKER
GUNMAKERS
GUNMAN
GUNMEN
GUNMETAL
GUNMETALS
GUNNAGE
GUNNAGES
GUNNED
GUNNEL
GUNNELS
GUNNEN
GUNNER
GUNNERA
GUNNERAS
GUNNERIES
GUNNERS
GUNNERY
GUNNIES
GUNNING
GUNNINGS
GUNNY
GUNNYBAG
GUNNYBAGS
GUNNYSACK
GUNPAPER
GUNPAPERS
GUNPLAY
GUNPLAYS
GUNPOINT
GUNPOINTS
GUNPORT
GUNPORTS
GUNPOWDER
GUNROOM
GUNROOMS
GUNRUNNER
GUNS
GUNSEL
GUNSELS
GUNSHIP
GUNSHIPS
GUNSHOT
GUNSHOTS
GUNSIGHT
GUNSIGHTS
GUNSMITH

G

GUNSMITHS
GUNSTICK
GUNSTICKS
GUNSTOCK
GUNSTOCKS
GUNSTONE
GUNSTONES
GUNTER
GUNTERS
GUNWALE
GUNWALES
GUNYAH
GUNYAHS
GUP
GUPPIES
GUPPY
GUPS
GUQIN
GUQINS
GUR
GURAMI
GURAMIS
GURDIES
GURDWARA
GURDWARAS
GURDY
GURGE
GURGED
GURGES
GURGING
GURGLE
GURGLED
GURGLES
GURGLET
GURGLETS
GURGLIER
GURGLIEST
GURGLING
GURGLY
GURGOYLE
GURGOYLES
GURJUN
GURJUNS
GURL
GURLED
GURLET
GURLETS
GURLIER
GURLIEST
GURLING
GURLS
GURLY
GURN
GURNARD
GURNARDS
GURNED
GURNET
GURNETS
GURNEY
GURNEYS
GURNING
GURNS
GURRAH
GURRAHS
GURRIER
GURRIERS
GURRIES
GURRY
GURS
GURSH
GURSHES
GURU
GURUDOM
GURUDOMS
GURUISM
GURUISMS
GURUS
GURUSHIP
GURUSHIPS
GUS
GUSH
GUSHED
GUSHER
GUSHERS
GUSHES
GUSHIER
GUSHIEST
GUSHILY
GUSHINESS
GUSHING
GUSHINGLY
GUSHY
GUSLA
GUSLAR
GUSLARS
GUSLAS
GUSLE
GUSLES
GUSLI
GUSLIS
GUSSET
GUSSETED
GUSSETING
GUSSETS
GUSSIE
GUSSIED
GUSSIES
GUSSY
GUSSYING
GUST
GUSTABLE
GUSTABLES
GUSTATION
GUSTATIVE
GUSTATORY
GUSTED
GUSTFUL
GUSTIE
GUSTIER
GUSTIEST
GUSTILY
GUSTINESS
GUSTING
GUSTLESS
GUSTO
GUSTOES
GUSTOS
GUSTS
GUSTY
GUT
GUTBUCKET
GUTCHER
GUTCHERS
GUTFUL
GUTFULS
GUTLESS
GUTLESSLY
GUTLIKE
GUTROT
GUTROTS
GUTS
GUTSED
GUTSER
GUTSERS
GUTSES
GUTSFUL
GUTSFULS
GUTSIER
GUTSIEST
GUTSILY
GUTSINESS
GUTSING
GUTSY
GUTTA
GUTTAE
GUTTAS
GUTTATE
GUTTATED
GUTTATES
GUTTATING
GUTTATION
GUTTED
GUTTER
GUTTERED
GUTTERIER
GUTTERING
GUTTERS
GUTTERY
GUTTIER
GUTTIES
GUTTIEST
GUTTING
GUTTLE
GUTTLED
GUTTLER
GUTTLERS
GUTTLES
GUTTLING
GUTTURAL
GUTTURALS
GUTTY
GUTZER
GUTZERS
GUV
GUVS
GUY
GUYED
GUYING
GUYLE
GUYLED
GUYLER
GUYLERS
GUYLES
GUYLINE
GUYLINER
GUYLINERS
GUYLINES
GUYLING
GUYOT
GUYOTS
GUYS
GUYSE
GUYSES
GUZZLE
GUZZLED
GUZZLER
GUZZLERS
GUZZLES
GUZZLING
GWEDUC
GWEDUCK
GWEDUCKS
GWEDUCS
GWINE
GWINIAD
GWINIADS
GWYNIAD
GWYNIADS
GYAL
GYALS
GYAN
GYANS
GYBE
GYBED
GYBES
GYBING
GYELD
GYELDS
GYLDEN
GYM
GYMBAL
GYMBALS
GYMKHANA
GYMKHANAS
GYMMAL
GYMMALS
GYMNASIA
GYMNASIAL
GYMNASIC
GYMNASIEN

GYMNASIUM
GYMNAST
GYMNASTIC
GYMNASTS
GYMNIC
GYMNOSOPH
GYMP
GYMPED
GYMPIE
GYMPIES
GYMPING
GYMPS
GYMS
GYMSLIP
GYMSLIPS
GYMSUIT
GYMSUITS
GYNAE
GYNAECEA
GYNAECEUM
GYNAECIA
GYNAECIUM
GYNAECOID
GYNAES
GYNANDRY
GYNARCHIC
GYNARCHY
GYNECIA
GYNECIC
GYNECIUM
GYNECOID
GYNIATRY
GYNIE
GYNIES
GYNNEY
GYNNEYS
GYNNIES
GYNNY
GYNO
GYNOCRACY
GYNOECIA
GYNOECIUM
GYNOPHOBE
GYNOPHORE
GYNOS
GYNY
GYOZA
GYOZAS
GYP
GYPLURE
GYPLURES
GYPO
GYPOS
GYPPED
GYPPER
GYPPERS
GYPPIE
GYPPIES
GYPPING
GYPPO
GYPPOS
GYPPY
GYPS
GYPSEIAN
GYPSEOUS
GYPSIED
GYPSIES
GYPSTER
GYPSTERS
GYPSUM
GYPSUMS
GYPSY
GYPSYDOM
GYPSYDOMS
GYPSYHOOD
GYPSYING
GYPSYISH
GYPSYISM
GYPSYISMS
GYPSYWORT
GYRAL
GYRALLY
GYRANT
GYRASE
GYRASES
GYRATE
GYRATED
GYRATES
GYRATING
GYRATION
GYRATIONS
GYRATOR
GYRATORS
GYRATORY
GYRE
GYRED
GYRENE
GYRENES
GYRES
GYRFALCON
GYRI
GYRING
GYRO
GYROCAR
GYROCARS
GYRODYNE
GYRODYNES
GYROIDAL
GYROLITE
GYROLITES
GYROMANCY
GYRON
GYRONIC
GYRONNY
GYRONS
GYROPILOT
GYROPLANE
GYROS
GYROSCOPE
GYROSE
GYROSTAT
GYROSTATS
GYROUS
GYROVAGUE
GYRUS
GYRUSES
GYTE
GYTES
GYTRASH
GYTRASHES
GYTTJA
GYTTJAS
GYVE
GYVED
GYVES
GYVING

HA
HAAF
HAAFS
HAANEPOOT
HAAR
HAARS
HABANERA
HABANERAS
HABANERO
HABANEROS
HABDABS
HABDALAH
HABDALAHS
HABENDUM
HABENDUMS
HABERDINE
HABERGEON
HABILABLE
HABILE
HABIT
HABITABLE
HABITABLY
HABITAN
HABITANS
HABITANT
HABITANTS
HABITAT
HABITATS
HABITED
HABITING
HABITS
HABITUAL
HABITUALS
HABITUATE
HABITUDE
HABITUDES
HABITUE
HABITUES
HABITUS
HABITUSES
HABLE
HABOOB
HABOOBS
HABU
HABUS
HACEK
HACEKS
HACENDADO
HACHIS
HACHURE
HACHURED
HACHURES
HACHURING
HACIENDA
HACIENDAS
HACK
HACKABLE
HACKAMORE
HACKBERRY
HACKBOLT
HACKBOLTS
HACKBUT
HACKBUTS
HACKED
HACKEE
HACKEES
HACKER
HACKERIES
HACKERS
HACKERY
HACKETTE
HACKETTES
HACKIE
HACKIES
HACKING
HACKINGS
HACKLE
HACKLED
HACKLER
HACKLERS
HACKLES
HACKLET
HACKLETS
HACKLIER
HACKLIEST
HACKLING
HACKLY
HACKMAN
HACKMEN
HACKNEY
HACKNEYED
HACKNEYS
HACKS
HACKSAW
HACKSAWED
HACKSAWN
HACKSAWS
HACKWORK
HACKWORKS
HACQUETON
HAD
HADAL
HADARIM
HADAWAY
HADDEN
HADDEST
HADDIE
HADDIES
HADDING
HADDOCK
HADDOCKS
HADE
HADED
HADEDAH
HADEDAHS
HADES
HADING
HADITH
HADITHS
HADJ
HADJEE
HADJEES
HADJES
HADJI
HADJIS
HADROME
HADROMES
HADRON
HADRONIC
HADRONS
HADROSAUR
HADS
HADST
HAE
HAECCEITY
HAED
HAEING
HAEM
HAEMAL
HAEMATAL
HAEMATEIN
HAEMATIC
HAEMATICS
HAEMATIN
HAEMATINS
HAEMATITE
HAEMATOID
HAEMATOMA
HAEMIC
HAEMIN
HAEMINS
HAEMOCOEL
HAEMOCYTE
HAEMOID
HAEMOLYSE
HAEMOLYZE
HAEMONIES
HAEMONY
HAEMOSTAT
HAEMS
HAEN
HAEREDES
HAEREMAI
HAEREMAIS
HAERES
HAES
HAET
HAETS
HAFF
HAFFET
HAFFETS
HAFFIT
HAFFITS
HAFFLIN
HAFFLINS
HAFFS
HAFIZ
HAFIZES
HAFNIUM
HAFNIUMS
HAFT
HAFTARA
HAFTARAH
HAFTARAHS
HAFTARAS
HAFTAROS
HAFTAROT
HAFTAROTH
HAFTED
HAFTER
HAFTERS
HAFTING
HAFTORAH
HAFTORAHS
HAFTOROS
HAFTOROT
HAFTOROTH
HAFTS
HAG
HAGADIC
HAGADIST
HAGADISTS
HAGBERRY
HAGBOLT
HAGBOLTS
HAGBORN
HAGBUSH
HAGBUSHES
HAGBUT
HAGBUTEER

H

HAGBUTS
HAGBUTTER
HAGDEN
HAGDENS
HAGDON
HAGDONS
HAGDOWN
HAGDOWNS
HAGFISH
HAGFISHES
HAGG
HAGGADA
HAGGADAH
HAGGADAHS
HAGGADAS
HAGGADIC
HAGGADIST
HAGGADOT
HAGGADOTH
HAGGARD
HAGGARDLY
HAGGARDS
HAGGED
HAGGING
HAGGIS
HAGGISES
HAGGISH
HAGGISHLY
HAGGLE
HAGGLED
HAGGLER
HAGGLERS
HAGGLES
HAGGLING
HAGGLINGS
HAGGS
HAGIARCHY
HAGIOLOGY
HAGLET
HAGLETS
HAGLIKE
HAGRIDDEN
HAGRIDE
HAGRIDER
HAGRIDERS
HAGRIDES
HAGRIDING
HAGRODE
HAGS
HAH
HAHA
HAHAS
HAHNIUM
HAHNIUMS
HAHS
HAICK
HAICKS
HAIDUK
HAIDUKS
HAIK
HAIKA
HAIKAI
HAIKS
HAIKU
HAIKUS
HAIL
HAILED
HAILER
HAILERS
HAILIER
HAILIEST
HAILING
HAILS
HAILSHOT
HAILSHOTS
HAILSTONE
HAILSTORM
HAILY
HAIMISH
HAIN
HAINCH
HAINCHED
HAINCHES
HAINCHING
HAINED
HAINING
HAININGS
HAINS
HAINT
HAINTS
HAIQUE
HAIQUES
HAIR
HAIRBALL
HAIRBALLS
HAIRBAND
HAIRBANDS
HAIRBELL
HAIRBELLS
HAIRBRUSH
HAIRCAP
HAIRCAPS
HAIRCLOTH
HAIRCUT
HAIRCUTS
HAIRDO
HAIRDOS
HAIRDRIER
HAIRDRYER
HAIRED
HAIRGRIP
HAIRGRIPS
HAIRIER
HAIRIEST
HAIRIF
HAIRIFS
HAIRILY
HAIRINESS
HAIRING
HAIRLESS
HAIRLIKE
HAIRLINE
HAIRLINES
HAIRLOCK
HAIRLOCKS
HAIRNET
HAIRNETS
HAIRPIECE
HAIRPIN
HAIRPINS
HAIRS
HAIRSPRAY
HAIRST
HAIRSTED
HAIRSTING
HAIRSTS
HAIRSTYLE
HAIRTAIL
HAIRTAILS
HAIRWING
HAIRWINGS
HAIRWORK
HAIRWORKS
HAIRWORM
HAIRWORMS
HAIRY
HAIRYBACK
HAITH
HAJ
HAJES
HAJI
HAJIS
HAJJ
HAJJAH
HAJJAHS
HAJJES
HAJJI
HAJJIS
HAKA
HAKAM
HAKAMS
HAKARI
HAKARIS
HAKAS
HAKE
HAKEA
HAKEAS
HAKEEM
HAKEEMS
HAKES
HAKIM
HAKIMS
HAKU
HAKUS
HALACHA
HALACHAS
HALACHIC
HALACHIST
HALACHOT
HALACHOTH
HALAKAH
HALAKAHS
HALAKHA
HALAKHAH
HALAKHAHS
HALAKHAS
HALAKHIC
HALAKHIST
HALAKHOT
HALAKHOTH
HALAKIC
HALAKIST
HALAKISTS
HALAKOTH
HALAL
HALALA
HALALAH
HALALAHS
HALALAS
HALALLED
HALALLING
HALALS
HALATION
HALATIONS
HALAVAH
HALAVAHS
HALAZONE
HALAZONES
HALBERD
HALBERDS
HALBERT
HALBERTS
HALCYON
HALCYONIC
HALCYONS
HALE
HALED
HALENESS
HALER
HALERS
HALERU
HALES
HALEST
HALF
HALFA
HALFAS
HALFBACK
HALFBACKS
HALFBEAK
HALFBEAKS
HALFEN
HALFLIFE
HALFLIN
HALFLING
HALFLINGS
HALFLINS
HALFLIVES
HALFNESS
HALFPACE
HALFPACES

HALFPENCE
HALFPENNY
HALFPIPE
HALFPIPES
HALFS
HALFTIME
HALFTIMES
HALFTONE
HALFTONES
HALFTRACK
HALFWAY
HALFWIT
HALFWITS
HALIBUT
HALIBUTS
HALICORE
HALICORES
HALID
HALIDE
HALIDES
HALIDOM
HALIDOME
HALIDOMES
HALIDOMS
HALIDS
HALIER
HALIEROV
HALIERS
HALIEUTIC
HALIMOT
HALIMOTE
HALIMOTES
HALIMOTS
HALING
HALIOTIS
HALITE
HALITES
HALITOSES
HALITOSIS
HALITOTIC
HALITOUS
HALITUS
HALITUSES
HALL
HALLAH
HALLAHS
HALLAL
HALLALI
HALLALIS
HALLALLED
HALLALOO
HALLALOOS
HALLALS
HALLAN
HALLANS
HALLEL
HALLELS
HALLIAN
HALLIANS
HALLIARD
HALLIARDS
HALLING
HALLINGS
HALLION
HALLIONS
HALLMARK
HALLMARKS
HALLO
HALLOA
HALLOAED
HALLOAING
HALLOAS
HALLOED
HALLOES
HALLOING
HALLOO
HALLOOED
HALLOOING
HALLOOS
HALLOS
HALLOT
HALLOTH
HALLOUMI
HALLOUMIS
HALLOW
HALLOWED
HALLOWER
HALLOWERS
HALLOWING
HALLOWS
HALLS
HALLSTAND
HALLUCAL
HALLUCES
HALLUX
HALLWAY
HALLWAYS
HALLYON
HALLYONS
HALM
HALMA
HALMAS
HALMS
HALO
HALOBIONT
HALOCLINE
HALOED
HALOES
HALOGEN
HALOGENIC
HALOGENS
HALOGETON
HALOID
HALOIDS
HALOING
HALOLIKE
HALON
HALONS
HALOPHILE
HALOPHILY
HALOPHOBE
HALOPHYTE
HALOS
HALOSERE
HALOSERES
HALOTHANE
HALOUMI
HALOUMIS
HALSE
HALSED
HALSER
HALSERS
HALSES
HALSING
HALT
HALTED
HALTER
HALTERE
HALTERED
HALTERES
HALTERING
HALTERS
HALTING
HALTINGLY
HALTINGS
HALTLESS
HALTS
HALUTZ
HALUTZIM
HALVA
HALVAH
HALVAHS
HALVAS
HALVE
HALVED
HALVER
HALVERS
HALVES
HALVING
HALVINGS
HALWA
HALWAS
HALYARD
HALYARDS
HAM
HAMADA
HAMADAS
HAMADRYAD
HAMADRYAS
HAMAL
HAMALS
HAMAMELIS
HAMARTIA
HAMARTIAS
HAMATE
HAMATES
HAMATSA
HAMATSAS
HAMAUL
HAMAULS
HAMBA
HAMBLE
HAMBLED
HAMBLES
HAMBLING
HAMBONE
HAMBONED
HAMBONES
HAMBONING
HAMBURG
HAMBURGER
HAMBURGS
HAME
HAMED
HAMES
HAMEWITH
HAMFAT
HAMFATS
HAMFATTER
HAMING
HAMLET
HAMLETS
HAMMADA
HAMMADAS
HAMMAL
HAMMALS
HAMMAM
HAMMAMS
HAMMED
HAMMER
HAMMERED
HAMMERER
HAMMERERS
HAMMERING
HAMMERKOP
HAMMERMAN
HAMMERMEN
HAMMERS
HAMMERTOE
HAMMIER
HAMMIES
HAMMIEST
HAMMILY
HAMMINESS
HAMMING
HAMMOCK
HAMMOCKS
HAMMY
HAMOSE
HAMOUS
HAMPER
HAMPERED
HAMPERER
HAMPERERS
HAMPERING
HAMPERS
HAMPSTER
HAMPSTERS
HAMS
HAMSTER

HAMSTERS
HAMSTRING
HAMSTRUNG
HAMULAR
HAMULATE
HAMULI
HAMULOSE
HAMULOUS
HAMULUS
HAMZA
HAMZAH
HAMZAHS
HAMZAS
HAN
HANAP
HANAPER
HANAPERS
HANAPS
HANCE
HANCES
HANCH
HANCHED
HANCHES
HANCHING
HAND
HANDAX
HANDAXE
HANDAXES
HANDBAG
HANDBAGS
HANDBALL
HANDBALLS
HANDBELL
HANDBELLS
HANDBILL
HANDBILLS
HANDBLOWN
HANDBOOK
HANDBOOKS
HANDBRAKE
HANDCAR
HANDCARS
HANDCART
HANDCARTS
HANDCLAP
HANDCLAPS
HANDCLASP
HANDCRAFT
HANDCUFF
HANDCUFFS
HANDED
HANDER
HANDERS
HANDFAST
HANDFASTS
HANDFED
HANDFEED
HANDFEEDS
HANDFUL
HANDFULS
HANDGLASS
HANDGRIP
HANDGRIPS
HANDGUN
HANDGUNS
HANDHELD
HANDHELDS
HANDHOLD
HANDHOLDS
HANDICAP
HANDICAPS
HANDIER
HANDIEST
HANDILY
HANDINESS
HANDING
HANDISM
HANDISMS
HANDIWORK
HANDJAR
HANDJARS
HANDJOB
HANDJOBS
HANDKNIT
HANDKNITS
HANDLE
HANDLEBAR
HANDLED
HANDLER
HANDLERS
HANDLES
HANDLESS
HANDLIKE
HANDLINE
HANDLINER
HANDLINES
HANDLING
HANDLINGS
HANDLIST
HANDLISTS
HANDLOOM
HANDLOOMS
HANDMADE
HANDMAID
HANDMAIDS
HANDOFF
HANDOFFS
HANDOUT
HANDOUTS
HANDOVER
HANDOVERS
HANDPASS
HANDPHONE
HANDPICK
HANDPICKS
HANDPLAY
HANDPLAYS
HANDPRESS
HANDPRINT
HANDRAIL
HANDRAILS
HANDROLL
HANDROLLS
HANDS
HANDSAW
HANDSAWS
HANDSEL
HANDSELED
HANDSELS
HANDSET
HANDSETS
HANDSEWN
HANDSFUL
HANDSHAKE
HANDSIER
HANDSIEST
HANDSOME
HANDSOMER
HANDSOMES
HANDSPIKE
HANDSTAFF
HANDSTAMP
HANDSTAND
HANDSTURN
HANDSY
HANDTOWEL
HANDWHEEL
HANDWORK
HANDWORKS
HANDWOVEN
HANDWRIT
HANDWRITE
HANDWROTE
HANDY
HANDYMAN
HANDYMEN
HANDYWORK
HANEPOOT
HANEPOOTS
HANG
HANGABLE
HANGAR
HANGARAGE
HANGARED
HANGARING
HANGARS
HANGBIRD
HANGBIRDS
HANGDOG
HANGDOGS
HANGED
HANGER
HANGERS
HANGFIRE
HANGFIRES
HANGI
HANGING
HANGINGS
HANGIS
HANGMAN
HANGMEN
HANGNAIL
HANGNAILS
HANGNEST
HANGNESTS
HANGOUT
HANGOUTS
HANGOVER
HANGOVERS
HANGRIER
HANGRIEST
HANGRY
HANGS
HANGTAG
HANGTAGS
HANGUL
HANGULS
HANGUP
HANGUPS
HANIWA
HANIWAS
HANJAR
HANJARS
HANK
HANKED
HANKER
HANKERED
HANKERER
HANKERERS
HANKERING
HANKERS
HANKIE
HANKIES
HANKING
HANKS
HANKY
HANSA
HANSAS
HANSE
HANSEATIC
HANSEL
HANSELED
HANSELING
HANSELLED
HANSELS
HANSES
HANSOM
HANSOMS
HANT
HANTED
HANTING
HANTLE
HANTLES
HANTS
HANUKIAH
HANUKIAHS
HANUMAN
HANUMANS
HAO
HAOLE

HAOLES
HAOMA
HAOMAS
HAOS
HAP
HAPAX
HAPAXES
HAPHAZARD
HAPHTARA
HAPHTARAH
HAPHTARAS
HAPHTAROT
HAPKIDO
HAPKIDOS
HAPLESS
HAPLESSLY
HAPLITE
HAPLITES
HAPLITIC
HAPLOID
HAPLOIDIC
HAPLOIDS
HAPLOIDY
HAPLOLOGY
HAPLONT
HAPLONTIC
HAPLONTS
HAPLOPIA
HAPLOPIAS
HAPLOSES
HAPLOSIS
HAPLOTYPE
HAPLY
HAPPED
HAPPEN
HAPPENED
HAPPENING
HAPPENS
HAPPI
HAPPIED
HAPPIER
HAPPIES
HAPPIEST
HAPPILY
HAPPINESS
HAPPING
HAPPIS
HAPPOSHU
HAPPOSHUS
HAPPY
HAPPYING
HAPS
HAPTEN
HAPTENE
HAPTENES
HAPTENIC
HAPTENS
HAPTERON
HAPTERONS
HAPTIC
HAPTICAL
HAPTICS
HAPU
HAPUKA
HAPUKAS
HAPUKU
HAPUKUS
HAPUS
HAQUETON
HAQUETONS
HARAAM
HARAKEKE
HARAKEKES
HARAM
HARAMBEE
HARAMBEES
HARAMDA
HARAMDAS
HARAMDI
HARAMDIS
HARAMS
HARAMZADA
HARAMZADI
HARANGUE
HARANGUED
HARANGUER
HARANGUES
HARASS
HARASSED
HARASSER
HARASSERS
HARASSES
HARASSING
HARBINGER
HARBOR
HARBORAGE
HARBORED
HARBORER
HARBORERS
HARBORFUL
HARBORING
HARBOROUS
HARBORS
HARBOUR
HARBOURED
HARBOURER
HARBOURS
HARD
HARDASS
HARDASSES
HARDBACK
HARDBACKS
HARDBAG
HARDBAGS
HARDBAKE
HARDBAKES
HARDBALL
HARDBALLS
HARDBEAM
HARDBEAMS
HARDBOARD
HARDBODY
HARDBOOT
HARDBOOTS
HARDBOUND
HARDCASE
HARDCASES
HARDCORE
HARDCORES
HARDCOURT
HARDCOVER
HARDEDGE
HARDEDGES
HARDEN
HARDENED
HARDENER
HARDENERS
HARDENING
HARDENS
HARDER
HARDEST
HARDFACE
HARDFACES
HARDGOODS
HARDGRASS
HARDHACK
HARDHACKS
HARDHAT
HARDHATS
HARDHEAD
HARDHEADS
HARDIER
HARDIES
HARDIEST
HARDIHEAD
HARDIHOOD
HARDILY
HARDIMENT
HARDINESS
HARDISH
HARDLINE
HARDLINER
HARDLY
HARDMAN
HARDMEN
HARDNESS
HARDNOSE
HARDNOSED
HARDNOSES
HARDOKE
HARDOKES
HARDPACK
HARDPACKS
HARDPAN
HARDPANS
HARDPARTS
HARDROCK
HARDROCKS
HARDS
HARDSCAPE
HARDSET
HARDSHELL
HARDSHIP
HARDSHIPS
HARDSTAND
HARDTACK
HARDTACKS
HARDTAIL
HARDTAILS
HARDTOP
HARDTOPS
HARDWARE
HARDWARES
HARDWIRE
HARDWIRED
HARDWIRES
HARDWOOD
HARDWOODS
HARDY
HARE
HAREBELL
HAREBELLS
HARED
HAREEM
HAREEMS
HARELD
HARELDS
HARELIKE
HARELIP
HARELIPS
HAREM
HAREMS
HARES
HARESTAIL
HAREWOOD
HAREWOODS
HARIANA
HARIANAS
HARICOT
HARICOTS
HARIGALDS
HARIGALS
HARIJAN
HARIJANS
HARIM
HARIMS
HARING
HARIOLATE
HARIRA
HARIRAS
HARISH
HARISSA
HARISSAS
HARK
HARKED
HARKEN
HARKENED
HARKENER
HARKENERS
HARKENING

HARKENS
HARKING
HARKS
HARL
HARLED
HARLEQUIN
HARLING
HARLINGS
HARLOT
HARLOTRY
HARLOTS
HARLS
HARM
HARMALA
HARMALAS
HARMALIN
HARMALINE
HARMALINS
HARMAN
HARMANS
HARMATTAN
HARMDOING
HARMED
HARMEL
HARMELS
HARMER
HARMERS
HARMFUL
HARMFULLY
HARMIN
HARMINE
HARMINES
HARMING
HARMINS
HARMLESS
HARMONIC
HARMONICA
HARMONICS
HARMONIES
HARMONISE
HARMONIST
HARMONIUM
HARMONIZE
HARMONY
HARMOST
HARMOSTS
HARMOSTY
HARMOTOME
HARMS
HARN
HARNESS
HARNESSED
HARNESSER
HARNESSES
HARNS
HARO
HAROS
HAROSET
HAROSETH
HAROSETHS
HAROSETS
HARP
HARPED
HARPER
HARPERS
HARPIES
HARPIN
HARPING
HARPINGS
HARPINS
HARPIST
HARPISTS
HARPOON
HARPOONED
HARPOONER
HARPOONS
HARPS
HARPY
HARPYLIKE
HARQUEBUS
HARRIDAN
HARRIDANS
HARRIED
HARRIER
HARRIERS
HARRIES
HARROW
HARROWED
HARROWER
HARROWERS
HARROWING
HARROWS
HARRUMPH
HARRUMPHS
HARRY
HARRYING
HARSH
HARSHED
HARSHEN
HARSHENED
HARSHENS
HARSHER
HARSHES
HARSHEST
HARSHING
HARSHLY
HARSHNESS
HARSLET
HARSLETS
HART
HARTAL
HARTALS
HARTBEES
HARTBEEST
HARTELY
HARTEN
HARTENED
HARTENING
HARTENS
HARTLESSE
HARTS
HARTSHORN
HARUMPH
HARUMPHED
HARUMPHS
HARUSPEX
HARUSPICY
HARVEST
HARVESTED
HARVESTER
HARVESTS
HAS
HASBIAN
HASBIANS
HASH
HASHED
HASHEESH
HASHES
HASHHEAD
HASHHEADS
HASHIER
HASHIEST
HASHING
HASHINGS
HASHISH
HASHISHES
HASHMARK
HASHMARKS
HASHTAG
HASHTAGS
HASHY
HASK
HASKS
HASLET
HASLETS
HASP
HASPED
HASPING
HASPS
HASS
HASSAR
HASSARS
HASSEL
HASSELS
HASSES
HASSIUM
HASSIUMS
HASSLE
HASSLED
HASSLES
HASSLING
HASSOCK
HASSOCKS
HASSOCKY
HAST
HASTA
HASTATE
HASTATED
HASTATELY
HASTE
HASTED
HASTEFUL
HASTEN
HASTENED
HASTENER
HASTENERS
HASTENING
HASTENS
HASTES
HASTIER
HASTIEST
HASTILY
HASTINESS
HASTING
HASTINGS
HASTY
HAT
HATABLE
HATBAND
HATBANDS
HATBOX
HATBOXES
HATBRUSH
HATCH
HATCHABLE
HATCHBACK
HATCHECK
HATCHECKS
HATCHED
HATCHEL
HATCHELED
HATCHELS
HATCHER
HATCHERS
HATCHERY
HATCHES
HATCHET
HATCHETS
HATCHETY
HATCHING
HATCHINGS
HATCHLING
HATCHMENT
HATCHWAY
HATCHWAYS
HATE
HATEABLE
HATED
HATEFUL
HATEFULLY
HATELESS
HATER
HATERENT
HATERENTS
HATERS
HATES
HATFUL
HATFULS
HATGUARD
HATGUARDS

HATH
HATHA
HATINATOR
HATING
HATLESS
HATLIKE
HATMAKER
HATMAKERS
HATPEG
HATPEGS
HATPIN
HATPINS
HATRACK
HATRACKS
HATRED
HATREDS
HATS
HATSFUL
HATSTAND
HATSTANDS
HATTED
HATTER
HATTERED
HATTERIA
HATTERIAS
HATTERING
HATTERS
HATTING
HATTINGS
HATTOCK
HATTOCKS
HAUBERK
HAUBERKS
HAUBOIS
HAUD
HAUDING
HAUDS
HAUF
HAUFS
HAUGH
HAUGHS
HAUGHT
HAUGHTIER
HAUGHTILY
HAUGHTY
HAUL
HAULAGE
HAULAGES
HAULBACK
HAULBACKS
HAULD
HAULDS
HAULED
HAULER
HAULERS
HAULIER
HAULIERS
HAULING
HAULINGS
HAULM
HAULMIER
HAULMIEST
HAULMS
HAULMY
HAULOUT
HAULOUTS
HAULS
HAULST
HAULT
HAULYARD
HAULYARDS
HAUN
HAUNCH
HAUNCHED
HAUNCHES
HAUNCHING
HAUNS
HAUNT
HAUNTED
HAUNTER
HAUNTERS
HAUNTING
HAUNTINGS
HAUNTS
HAURIANT
HAURIENT
HAUSE
HAUSED
HAUSEN
HAUSENS
HAUSES
HAUSFRAU
HAUSFRAUS
HAUSING
HAUSTELLA
HAUSTORIA
HAUT
HAUTBOIS
HAUTBOY
HAUTBOYS
HAUTE
HAUTER
HAUTEST
HAUTEUR
HAUTEURS
HAUYNE
HAUYNES
HAVARTI
HAVARTIS
HAVDALAH
HAVDALAHS
HAVDOLOH
HAVDOLOHS
HAVE
HAVELOCK
HAVELOCKS
HAVEN
HAVENED
HAVENING
HAVENLESS
HAVENS
HAVEOUR
HAVEOURS
HAVER
HAVERED
HAVEREL
HAVERELS
HAVERING
HAVERINGS
HAVERS
HAVERSACK
HAVERSINE
HAVES
HAVILDAR
HAVILDARS
HAVING
HAVINGS
HAVIOR
HAVIORS
HAVIOUR
HAVIOURS
HAVOC
HAVOCKED
HAVOCKER
HAVOCKERS
HAVOCKING
HAVOCS
HAW
HAWALA
HAWALAS
HAWBUCK
HAWBUCKS
HAWEATER
HAWEATERS
HAWED
HAWFINCH
HAWING
HAWK
HAWKBELL
HAWKBELLS
HAWKBILL
HAWKBILLS
HAWKBIT
HAWKBITS
HAWKED
HAWKER
HAWKERS
HAWKEY
HAWKEYED
HAWKEYS
HAWKIE
HAWKIES
HAWKING
HAWKINGS
HAWKISH
HAWKISHLY
HAWKIT
HAWKLIKE
HAWKMOTH
HAWKMOTHS
HAWKNOSE
HAWKNOSES
HAWKS
HAWKSBILL
HAWKSHAW
HAWKSHAWS
HAWKWEED
HAWKWEEDS
HAWM
HAWMED
HAWMING
HAWMS
HAWS
HAWSE
HAWSED
HAWSEHOLE
HAWSEPIPE
HAWSER
HAWSERS
HAWSES
HAWSING
HAWTHORN
HAWTHORNS
HAWTHORNY
HAY
HAYBAND
HAYBANDS
HAYBOX
HAYBOXES
HAYCATION
HAYCOCK
HAYCOCKS
HAYED
HAYER
HAYERS
HAYEY
HAYFIELD
HAYFIELDS
HAYFORK
HAYFORKS
HAYIER
HAYIEST
HAYING
HAYINGS
HAYLAGE
HAYLAGES
HAYLE
HAYLES
HAYLOFT
HAYLOFTS
HAYMAKER
HAYMAKERS
HAYMAKING
HAYMOW
HAYMOWS
HAYRACK
HAYRACKS
HAYRAKE
HAYRAKES
HAYRICK

HAYRICKS
HAYRIDE
HAYRIDES
HAYS
HAYSEED
HAYSEEDS
HAYSEL
HAYSELS
HAYSTACK
HAYSTACKS
HAYWARD
HAYWARDS
HAYWIRE
HAYWIRES
HAZAN
HAZANIM
HAZANS
HAZARD
HAZARDED
HAZARDER
HAZARDERS
HAZARDING
HAZARDIZE
HAZARDOUS
HAZARDRY
HAZARDS
HAZE
HAZED
HAZEL
HAZELHEN
HAZELHENS
HAZELLY
HAZELNUT
HAZELNUTS
HAZELS
HAZELWOOD
HAZER
HAZERS
HAZES
HAZIER
HAZIEST
HAZILY
HAZINESS
HAZING
HAZINGS
HAZMAT
HAZMATS
HAZY
HAZZAN
HAZZANIM
HAZZANS
HE
HEAD
HEADACHE
HEADACHES
HEADACHEY
HEADACHY
HEADAGE
HEADAGES
HEADBAND
HEADBANDS
HEADBANG
HEADBANGS
HEADBOARD
HEADCASE
HEADCASES
HEADCHAIR
HEADCLOTH
HEADCOUNT
HEADDRESS
HEADED
HEADEND
HEADENDS
HEADER
HEADERS
HEADFAST
HEADFASTS
HEADFIRST
HEADFISH
HEADFRAME
HEADFUCK
HEADFUCKS
HEADFUL
HEADFULS
HEADGATE
HEADGATES
HEADGEAR
HEADGEARS
HEADGUARD
HEADHUNT
HEADHUNTS
HEADIER
HEADIEST
HEADILY
HEADINESS
HEADING
HEADINGS
HEADLAMP
HEADLAMPS
HEADLAND
HEADLANDS
HEADLEASE
HEADLESS
HEADLIGHT
HEADLIKE
HEADLINE
HEADLINED
HEADLINER
HEADLINES
HEADLOCK
HEADLOCKS
HEADLONG
HEADMAN
HEADMARK
HEADMARKS
HEADMEN
HEADMOST
HEADNOTE
HEADNOTES
HEADPEACE
HEADPHONE
HEADPIECE
HEADPIN
HEADPINS
HEADPOND
HEADPONDS
HEADRACE
HEADRACES
HEADRAIL
HEADRAILS
HEADREACH
HEADREST
HEADRESTS
HEADRIG
HEADRIGS
HEADRING
HEADRINGS
HEADROOM
HEADROOMS
HEADROPE
HEADROPES
HEADS
HEADSAIL
HEADSAILS
HEADSCARF
HEADSET
HEADSETS
HEADSHAKE
HEADSHIP
HEADSHIPS
HEADSHOT
HEADSHOTS
HEADSMAN
HEADSMEN
HEADSPACE
HEADSTALL
HEADSTAND
HEADSTAY
HEADSTAYS
HEADSTICK
HEADSTOCK
HEADSTONE
HEADWALL
HEADWALLS
HEADWARD
HEADWARDS
HEADWATER
HEADWAY
HEADWAYS
HEADWIND
HEADWINDS
HEADWORD
HEADWORDS
HEADWORK
HEADWORKS
HEADY
HEAL
HEALABLE
HEALD
HEALDED
HEALDING
HEALDS
HEALED
HEALEE
HEALEES
HEALER
HEALERS
HEALING
HEALINGLY
HEALINGS
HEALS
HEALSOME
HEALTH
HEALTHFUL
HEALTHIER
HEALTHILY
HEALTHISM
HEALTHS
HEALTHY
HEAME
HEAP
HEAPED
HEAPER
HEAPERS
HEAPIER
HEAPIEST
HEAPING
HEAPS
HEAPSTEAD
HEAPY
HEAR
HEARABLE
HEARD
HEARDS
HEARE
HEARER
HEARERS
HEARES
HEARIE
HEARING
HEARINGS
HEARKEN
HEARKENED
HEARKENER
HEARKENS
HEARS
HEARSAY
HEARSAYS
HEARSE
HEARSED
HEARSES
HEARSIER
HEARSIEST
HEARSING
HEARSY
HEART
HEARTACHE
HEARTBEAT
HEARTBURN
HEARTED

HEARTEN
HEARTENED
HEARTENER
HEARTENS
HEARTFELT
HEARTFREE
HEARTH
HEARTHRUG
HEARTHS
HEARTIER
HEARTIES
HEARTIEST
HEARTIKIN
HEARTILY
HEARTING
HEARTLAND
HEARTLESS
HEARTLET
HEARTLETS
HEARTLING
HEARTLY
HEARTPEA
HEARTPEAS
HEARTS
HEARTSEED
HEARTSICK
HEARTSINK
HEARTSOME
HEARTSORE
HEARTWOOD
HEARTWORM
HEARTY
HEAST
HEASTE
HEASTES
HEASTS
HEAT
HEATABLE
HEATED
HEATEDLY
HEATER
HEATERS
HEATH
HEATHBIRD
HEATHCOCK
HEATHEN
HEATHENRY
HEATHENS
HEATHER
HEATHERED
HEATHERS
HEATHERY
HEATHFOWL
HEATHIER
HEATHIEST
HEATHLAND
HEATHLESS
HEATHLIKE
HEATHS
HEATHY
HEATING
HEATINGS
HEATLESS
HEATPROOF
HEATS
HEATSPOT
HEATSPOTS
HEATWAVE
HEATWAVES
HEAUME
HEAUMES
HEAVE
HEAVED
HEAVEN
HEAVENLY
HEAVENS
HEAVER
HEAVERS
HEAVES
HEAVIER
HEAVIES
HEAVIEST
HEAVILY
HEAVINESS
HEAVING
HEAVINGS
HEAVY
HEAVYISH
HEAVYSET
HEBDOMAD
HEBDOMADS
HEBE
HEBEN
HEBENON
HEBENONS
HEBENS
HEBES
HEBETANT
HEBETATE
HEBETATED
HEBETATES
HEBETIC
HEBETUDE
HEBETUDES
HEBONA
HEBONAS
HEBRAISE
HEBRAISED
HEBRAISES
HEBRAIZE
HEBRAIZED
HEBRAIZES
HECATOMB
HECATOMBS
HECH
HECHT
HECHTING
HECHTS
HECK
HECKLE
HECKLED
HECKLER
HECKLERS
HECKLES
HECKLING
HECKLINGS
HECKS
HECKUVA
HECOGENIN
HECTARE
HECTARES
HECTIC
HECTICAL
HECTICLY
HECTICS
HECTOGRAM
HECTOR
HECTORED
HECTORER
HECTORERS
HECTORING
HECTORISM
HECTORLY
HECTORS
HEDARIM
HEDDLE
HEDDLED
HEDDLES
HEDDLING
HEDER
HEDERA
HEDERAL
HEDERAS
HEDERATED
HEDERS
HEDGE
HEDGEBILL
HEDGED
HEDGEHOG
HEDGEHOGS
HEDGEHOP
HEDGEHOPS
HEDGEPIG
HEDGEPIGS
HEDGER
HEDGEROW
HEDGEROWS
HEDGERS
HEDGES
HEDGIER
HEDGIEST
HEDGING
HEDGINGLY
HEDGINGS
HEDGY
HEDONIC
HEDONICS
HEDONISM
HEDONISMS
HEDONIST
HEDONISTS
HEDYPHANE
HEDYSARUM
HEED
HEEDED
HEEDER
HEEDERS
HEEDFUL
HEEDFULLY
HEEDIER
HEEDIEST
HEEDINESS
HEEDING
HEEDLESS
HEEDS
HEEDY
HEEHAW
HEEHAWED
HEEHAWING
HEEHAWS
HEEL
HEELBALL
HEELBALLS
HEELBAR
HEELBARS
HEELED
HEELER
HEELERS
HEELING
HEELINGS
HEELLESS
HEELPIECE
HEELPLATE
HEELPOST
HEELPOSTS
HEELS
HEELTAP
HEELTAPS
HEEZE
HEEZED
HEEZES
HEEZIE
HEEZIES
HEEZING
HEFT
HEFTE
HEFTED
HEFTER
HEFTERS
HEFTIER
HEFTIEST
HEFTILY
HEFTINESS
HEFTING
HEFTS
HEFTY
HEGARI
HEGARIS
HEGEMON
HEGEMONIC

HEGEMONS
HEGEMONY
HEGIRA
HEGIRAS
HEGUMEN
HEGUMENE
HEGUMENES
HEGUMENOI
HEGUMENOS
HEGUMENS
HEGUMENY
HEH
HEHS
HEID
HEIDS
HEIDUC
HEIDUCS
HEIFER
HEIFERS
HEIGH
HEIGHT
HEIGHTEN
HEIGHTENS
HEIGHTH
HEIGHTHS
HEIGHTISM
HEIGHTS
HEIL
HEILED
HEILING
HEILS
HEIMISH
HEINIE
HEINIES
HEINOUS
HEINOUSLY
HEIR
HEIRDOM
HEIRDOMS
HEIRED
HEIRESS
HEIRESSES
HEIRING
HEIRLESS
HEIRLOOM
HEIRLOOMS
HEIRS
HEIRSHIP
HEIRSHIPS
HEISHI
HEIST
HEISTED
HEISTER
HEISTERS
HEISTING
HEISTS
HEITIKI
HEITIKIS
HEJAB
HEJABS
HEJIRA
HEJIRAS
HEJRA
HEJRAS
HEKETARA
HEKETARAS
HEKTARE
HEKTARES
HEKTOGRAM
HELCOID
HELD
HELE
HELED
HELENIUM
HELENIUMS
HELES
HELIAC
HELIACAL
HELIAST
HELIASTS
HELIBORNE
HELIBUS
HELIBUSES
HELICAL
HELICALLY
HELICASE
HELICASES
HELICES
HELICITY
HELICLINE
HELICOID
HELICOIDS
HELICON
HELICONIA
HELICONS
HELICOPT
HELICOPTS
HELICTITE
HELIDECK
HELIDECKS
HELIDROME
HELILIFT
HELILIFTS
HELIMAN
HELIMEN
HELING
HELIO
HELIODOR
HELIODORS
HELIOGRAM
HELIOLOGY
HELIOPSES
HELIOPSIS
HELIOS
HELIOSES
HELIOSIS
HELIOSTAT
HELIOTYPE
HELIOTYPY
HELIOZOAN
HELIOZOIC
HELIPAD
HELIPADS
HELIPILOT
HELIPORT
HELIPORTS
HELISKI
HELISKIED
HELISKIS
HELISTOP
HELISTOPS
HELITACK
HELITACKS
HELIUM
HELIUMS
HELIX
HELIXES
HELL
HELLBENT
HELLBOX
HELLBOXES
HELLBROTH
HELLCAT
HELLCATS
HELLDIVER
HELLEBORE
HELLED
HELLENISE
HELLENIZE
HELLER
HELLERI
HELLERIES
HELLERIS
HELLERS
HELLERY
HELLFIRE
HELLFIRES
HELLHOLE
HELLHOLES
HELLHOUND
HELLICAT
HELLICATS
HELLIER
HELLIERS
HELLING
HELLION
HELLIONS
HELLISH
HELLISHLY
HELLKITE
HELLKITES
HELLO
HELLOED
HELLOES
HELLOING
HELLOS
HELLOVA
HELLS
HELLSCAPE
HELLUVA
HELLWARD
HELLWARDS
HELM
HELMED
HELMER
HELMERS
HELMET
HELMETED
HELMETING
HELMETS
HELMING
HELMINTH
HELMINTHS
HELMLESS
HELMS
HELMSMAN
HELMSMEN
HELO
HELOPHYTE
HELOS
HELOT
HELOTAGE
HELOTAGES
HELOTISM
HELOTISMS
HELOTRIES
HELOTRY
HELOTS
HELP
HELPABLE
HELPDESK
HELPDESKS
HELPED
HELPER
HELPERS
HELPFUL
HELPFULLY
HELPING
HELPINGS
HELPLESS
HELPLINE
HELPLINES
HELPMATE
HELPMATES
HELPMEET
HELPMEETS
HELPS
HELVE
HELVED
HELVES
HELVETIUM
HELVING
HEM
HEMAGOG
HEMAGOGS
HEMAGOGUE
HEMAL
HEMATAL
HEMATEIN
HEMATEINS

HEMATIC
HEMATICS
HEMATIN
HEMATINE
HEMATINES
HEMATINIC
HEMATINS
HEMATITE
HEMATITES
HEMATITIC
HEMATOID
HEMATOMA
HEMATOMAS
HEMATOSES
HEMATOSIS
HEMATOZOA
HEMATURIA
HEMATURIC
HEME
HEMELYTRA
HEMES
HEMIALGIA
HEMIC
HEMICYCLE
HEMIHEDRA
HEMIHEDRY
HEMIN
HEMINA
HEMINAS
HEMINS
HEMIOLA
HEMIOLAS
HEMIOLIA
HEMIOLIAS
HEMIOLIC
HEMIONE
HEMIONES
HEMIONUS
HEMIOPIA
HEMIOPIAS
HEMIOPIC
HEMIOPSIA
HEMIPOD
HEMIPODE
HEMIPODES
HEMIPODS
HEMIPTER
HEMIPTERS
HEMISPACE
HEMISTICH
HEMITROPE
HEMITROPY
HEMLINE
HEMLINES
HEMLOCK
HEMLOCKS
HEMMED
HEMMER
HEMMERS
HEMMING
HEMOCOEL
HEMOCOELS
HEMOCONIA
HEMOCYTE
HEMOCYTES
HEMOID
HEMOLYMPH
HEMOLYSE
HEMOLYSED
HEMOLYSES
HEMOLYSIN
HEMOLYSIS
HEMOLYTIC
HEMOLYZE
HEMOLYZED
HEMOLYZES
HEMOPHILE
HEMOSTAT
HEMOSTATS
HEMOTOXIC
HEMOTOXIN
HEMP
HEMPEN
HEMPIE
HEMPIER
HEMPIES
HEMPIEST
HEMPLIKE
HEMPS
HEMPSEED
HEMPSEEDS
HEMPWEED
HEMPWEEDS
HEMPY
HEMS
HEMSTITCH
HEN
HENBANE
HENBANES
HENBIT
HENBITS
HENCE
HENCH
HENCHER
HENCHEST
HENCHMAN
HENCHMEN
HENCOOP
HENCOOPS
HEND
HENDED
HENDIADYS
HENDING
HENDS
HENEQUEN
HENEQUENS
HENEQUIN
HENEQUINS
HENGE
HENGES
HENHOUSE
HENHOUSES
HENIQUEN
HENIQUENS
HENIQUIN
HENIQUINS
HENLEY
HENLEYS
HENLIKE
HENNA
HENNAED
HENNAING
HENNAS
HENNED
HENNER
HENNERIES
HENNERS
HENNERY
HENNIER
HENNIES
HENNIEST
HENNIN
HENNING
HENNINS
HENNISH
HENNISHLY
HENNY
HENOTIC
HENPECK
HENPECKED
HENPECKS
HENRIES
HENRY
HENRYS
HENS
HENT
HENTED
HENTING
HENTS
HEP
HEPAR
HEPARIN
HEPARINS
HEPARS
HEPATIC
HEPATICA
HEPATICAE
HEPATICAL
HEPATICAS
HEPATICS
HEPATISE
HEPATISED
HEPATISES
HEPATITE
HEPATITES
HEPATITIS
HEPATIZE
HEPATIZED
HEPATIZES
HEPATOMA
HEPATOMAS
HEPCAT
HEPCATS
HEPPER
HEPPEST
HEPS
HEPSTER
HEPSTERS
HEPT
HEPTAD
HEPTADS
HEPTAGLOT
HEPTAGON
HEPTAGONS
HEPTANE
HEPTANES
HEPTAPODY
HEPTARCH
HEPTARCHS
HEPTARCHY
HEPTOSE
HEPTOSES
HER
HERALD
HERALDED
HERALDIC
HERALDING
HERALDIST
HERALDRY
HERALDS
HERB
HERBAGE
HERBAGED
HERBAGES
HERBAL
HERBALISM
HERBALIST
HERBALS
HERBAR
HERBARIA
HERBARIAL
HERBARIAN
HERBARIES
HERBARIUM
HERBARS
HERBARY
HERBED
HERBELET
HERBELETS
HERBICIDE
HERBIER
HERBIEST
HERBIST
HERBISTS
HERBIVORA
HERBIVORE
HERBIVORY
HERBLESS
HERBLET
HERBLETS

HERBLIKE
HERBOLOGY
HERBORISE
HERBORIST
HERBORIZE
HERBOSE
HERBOUS
HERBS
HERBY
HERCOGAMY
HERCULEAN
HERCULES
HERCYNITE
HERD
HERDBOY
HERDBOYS
HERDED
HERDEN
HERDENS
HERDER
HERDERS
HERDESS
HERDESSES
HERDIC
HERDICS
HERDING
HERDINGS
HERDLIKE
HERDMAN
HERDMEN
HERDS
HERDSMAN
HERDSMEN
HERDWICK
HERDWICKS
HERE
HEREABOUT
HEREAFTER
HEREAT
HEREAWAY
HEREAWAYS
HEREBY
HEREDES
HEREDITY
HEREFROM
HEREIN
HEREINTO
HERENESS
HEREOF
HEREON
HERES
HERESIES
HERESY
HERETIC
HERETICAL
HERETICS
HERETO
HERETRIX
HEREUNDER
HEREUNTO
HEREUPON
HEREWITH
HERIED
HERIES
HERIOT
HERIOTS
HERISSE
HERISSON
HERISSONS
HERITABLE
HERITABLY
HERITAGE
HERITAGES
HERITOR
HERITORS
HERITRESS
HERITRIX
HERKOGAMY
HERL
HERLING
HERLINGS
HERLS
HERM
HERMA
HERMAE
HERMAEAN
HERMAI
HERMANDAD
HERMETIC
HERMETICS
HERMETISM
HERMETIST
HERMIT
HERMITAGE
HERMITESS
HERMITIC
HERMITISM
HERMITRY
HERMITS
HERMS
HERN
HERNIA
HERNIAE
HERNIAL
HERNIAS
HERNIATE
HERNIATED
HERNIATES
HERNS
HERNSHAW
HERNSHAWS
HERO
HEROES
HEROIC
HEROICAL
HEROICISE
HEROICIZE
HEROICLY
HEROICS
HEROIN
HEROINE
HEROINES
HEROINISM
HEROINS
HEROISE
HEROISED
HEROISES
HEROISING
HEROISM
HEROISMS
HEROIZE
HEROIZED
HEROIZES
HEROIZING
HERON
HERONRIES
HERONRY
HERONS
HERONSEW
HERONSEWS
HERONSHAW
HEROON
HEROONS
HEROS
HEROSHIP
HEROSHIPS
HERPES
HERPESES
HERPETIC
HERPETICS
HERPETOID
HERPTILE
HERRIED
HERRIES
HERRIMENT
HERRING
HERRINGER
HERRINGS
HERRY
HERRYING
HERRYMENT
HERS
HERSALL
HERSALLS
HERSE
HERSED
HERSELF
HERSES
HERSHIP
HERSHIPS
HERSTORY
HERTZ
HERTZES
HERY
HERYE
HERYED
HERYES
HERYING
HES
HESITANCE
HESITANCY
HESITANT
HESITATE
HESITATED
HESITATER
HESITATES
HESITATOR
HESP
HESPED
HESPERID
HESPERIDS
HESPING
HESPS
HESSIAN
HESSIANS
HESSITE
HESSITES
HESSONITE
HEST
HESTERNAL
HESTS
HET
HETAERA
HETAERAE
HETAERAS
HETAERIC
HETAERISM
HETAERIST
HETAIRA
HETAIRAI
HETAIRAS
HETAIRIA
HETAIRIAS
HETAIRIC
HETAIRISM
HETAIRIST
HETE
HETERO
HETERODOX
HETERONYM
HETEROPOD
HETEROS
HETEROSES
HETEROSIS
HETEROTIC
HETES
HETH
HETHER
HETHS
HETING
HETMAN
HETMANATE
HETMANS
HETMEN
HETS
HETTIE
HETTIES
HEUCH
HEUCHERA
HEUCHERAS

HEUCHS
HEUGH
HEUGHS
HEUREKA
HEUREKAS
HEURETIC
HEURETICS
HEURISM
HEURISMS
HEURISTIC
HEVEA
HEVEAS
HEW
HEWABLE
HEWED
HEWER
HEWERS
HEWGH
HEWING
HEWINGS
HEWN
HEWS
HEX
HEXACHORD
HEXACT
HEXACTS
HEXAD
HEXADE
HEXADECYL
HEXADES
HEXADIC
HEXADS
HEXAFOIL
HEXAFOILS
HEXAGLOT
HEXAGLOTS
HEXAGON
HEXAGONAL
HEXAGONS
HEXAGRAM
HEXAGRAMS
HEXAHEDRA
HEXAMERAL
HEXAMETER
HEXAMINE
HEXAMINES
HEXANE
HEXANES
HEXANOIC
HEXAPLA
HEXAPLAR
HEXAPLAS
HEXAPLOID
HEXAPOD
HEXAPODAL
HEXAPODIC
HEXAPODS
HEXAPODY
HEXARCH
HEXARCHY
HEXASTICH
HEXASTYLE
HEXATHLON
HEXED
HEXENE
HEXENES
HEXER
HEXEREI
HEXEREIS
HEXERS
HEXES
HEXING
HEXINGS
HEXONE
HEXONES
HEXOSAN
HEXOSANS
HEXOSE
HEXOSES
HEXYL
HEXYLENE
HEXYLENES
HEXYLIC
HEXYLS
HEY
HEYDAY
HEYDAYS
HEYDEY
HEYDEYS
HEYDUCK
HEYDUCKS
HEYED
HEYING
HEYS
HI
HIANT
HIATAL
HIATUS
HIATUSES
HIBACHI
HIBACHIS
HIBAKUSHA
HIBERNAL
HIBERNATE
HIBERNISE
HIBERNIZE
HIBISCUS
HIC
HICATEE
HICATEES
HICCATEE
HICCATEES
HICCOUGH
HICCOUGHS
HICCUP
HICCUPED
HICCUPIER
HICCUPING
HICCUPPED
HICCUPS
HICCUPY
HICK
HICKER
HICKEST
HICKEY
HICKEYS
HICKIE
HICKIES
HICKISH
HICKORIES
HICKORY
HICKS
HICKWALL
HICKWALLS
HICKYMAL
HICKYMALS
HID
HIDABLE
HIDAGE
HIDAGES
HIDALGA
HIDALGAS
HIDALGO
HIDALGOS
HIDDEN
HIDDENITE
HIDDENLY
HIDDER
HIDDERS
HIDE
HIDEAWAY
HIDEAWAYS
HIDEBOUND
HIDED
HIDELESS
HIDEOSITY
HIDEOUS
HIDEOUSLY
HIDEOUT
HIDEOUTS
HIDER
HIDERS
HIDES
HIDING
HIDINGS
HIDLING
HIDLINGS
HIDLINS
HIDROSES
HIDROSIS
HIDROTIC
HIDROTICS
HIE
HIED
HIEING
HIELAMAN
HIELAMANS
HIELAND
HIEMAL
HIEMS
HIERACIUM
HIERARCH
HIERARCHS
HIERARCHY
HIERATIC
HIERATICA
HIERATICS
HIEROCRAT
HIERODULE
HIEROGRAM
HIEROLOGY
HIERURGY
HIES
HIFALUTIN
HIGGLE
HIGGLED
HIGGLER
HIGGLERS
HIGGLES
HIGGLING
HIGGLINGS
HIGH
HIGHBALL
HIGHBALLS
HIGHBORN
HIGHBOY
HIGHBOYS
HIGHBRED
HIGHBROW
HIGHBROWS
HIGHBUSH
HIGHCHAIR
HIGHED
HIGHER
HIGHERED
HIGHERING
HIGHERS
HIGHEST
HIGHFLIER
HIGHFLYER
HIGHING
HIGHISH
HIGHJACK
HIGHJACKS
HIGHJINKS
HIGHLAND
HIGHLANDS
HIGHLIFE
HIGHLIFES
HIGHLIGHT
HIGHLY
HIGHMAN
HIGHMEN
HIGHMOST
HIGHNESS
HIGHRISE
HIGHRISES
HIGHROAD
HIGHROADS
HIGHS

H

HIGHSPOT
HIGHSPOTS
HIGHT
HIGHTAIL
HIGHTAILS
HIGHTED
HIGHTH
HIGHTHS
HIGHTING
HIGHTINGS
HIGHTOP
HIGHTOPS
HIGHTS
HIGHVELD
HIGHVELDS
HIGHWAY
HIGHWAYS
HIJAB
HIJABS
HIJACK
HIJACKED
HIJACKER
HIJACKERS
HIJACKING
HIJACKS
HIJINKS
HIJRA
HIJRAH
HIJRAHS
HIJRAS
HIKE
HIKED
HIKER
HIKERS
HIKES
HIKING
HIKINGS
HIKOI
HIKOIED
HIKOIING
HIKOIS
HILA
HILAR
HILARIOUS
HILARITY
HILCH
HILCHED
HILCHES
HILCHING
HILD
HILDING
HILDINGS
HILI
HILL
HILLBILLY
HILLCREST
HILLED
HILLER
HILLERS
HILLFOLK
HILLFORT
HILLFORTS
HILLIER
HILLIEST
HILLINESS
HILLING
HILLINGS
HILLMEN
HILLO
HILLOA
HILLOAED
HILLOAING
HILLOAS
HILLOCK
HILLOCKED
HILLOCKS
HILLOCKY
HILLOED
HILLOES
HILLOING
HILLOS
HILLS
HILLSIDE
HILLSIDES
HILLSLOPE
HILLTOP
HILLTOPS
HILLY
HILT
HILTED
HILTING
HILTLESS
HILTS
HILUM
HILUS
HIM
HIMATIA
HIMATION
HIMATIONS
HIMBO
HIMBOS
HIMS
HIMSELF
HIN
HINAHINA
HINAHINAS
HINAU
HINAUS
HIND
HINDBERRY
HINDBRAIN
HINDCAST
HINDCASTS
HINDER
HINDERED
HINDERER
HINDERERS
HINDERING
HINDERS
HINDFEET
HINDFOOT
HINDGUT
HINDGUTS
HINDHEAD
HINDHEADS
HINDLEG
HINDLEGS
HINDMILK
HINDMILKS
HINDMOST
HINDRANCE
HINDS
HINDSHANK
HINDSIGHT
HINDWARD
HINDWING
HINDWINGS
HING
HINGE
HINGED
HINGELESS
HINGELIKE
HINGER
HINGERS
HINGES
HINGING
HINGS
HINKIER
HINKIEST
HINKY
HINNIE
HINNIED
HINNIES
HINNY
HINNYING
HINS
HINT
HINTED
HINTER
HINTERS
HINTING
HINTINGLY
HINTINGS
HINTS
HIOI
HIOIS
HIP
HIPBONE
HIPBONES
HIPHUGGER
HIPLESS
HIPLIKE
HIPLINE
HIPLINES
HIPLY
HIPNESS
HIPNESSES
HIPPARCH
HIPPARCHS
HIPPED
HIPPEN
HIPPENS
HIPPER
HIPPEST
HIPPIATRY
HIPPIC
HIPPIE
HIPPIEDOM
HIPPIEISH
HIPPIER
HIPPIES
HIPPIEST
HIPPIN
HIPPINESS
HIPPING
HIPPINGS
HIPPINS
HIPPISH
HIPPO
HIPPOCRAS
HIPPODAME
HIPPOLOGY
HIPPOS
HIPPURIC
HIPPURITE
HIPPUS
HIPPUSES
HIPPY
HIPPYDOM
HIPPYDOMS
HIPPYISH
HIPS
HIPSHOT
HIPSTER
HIPSTERS
HIPT
HIRABLE
HIRAGANA
HIRAGANAS
HIRAGE
HIRAGES
HIRCINE
HIRCOSITY
HIRE
HIREABLE
HIREAGE
HIREAGES
HIRED
HIREE
HIREES
HIRELING
HIRELINGS
HIRER
HIRERS
HIRES
HIRING
HIRINGS
HIRLING
HIRLINGS
HIRPLE

HIRPLED
HIRPLES
HIRPLING
HIRRIENT
HIRRIENTS
HIRSEL
HIRSELED
HIRSELING
HIRSELLED
HIRSELS
HIRSLE
HIRSLED
HIRSLES
HIRSLING
HIRSTIE
HIRSUTE
HIRSUTISM
HIRUDIN
HIRUDINS
HIRUNDINE
HIS
HISH
HISHED
HISHES
HISHING
HISN
HISPANISM
HISPID
HISPIDITY
HISS
HISSED
HISSELF
HISSER
HISSERS
HISSES
HISSIER
HISSIES
HISSIEST
HISSING
HISSINGLY
HISSINGS
HISSY
HIST
HISTAMIN
HISTAMINE
HISTAMINS
HISTED
HISTIDIN
HISTIDINE
HISTIDINS
HISTIE
HISTING
HISTIOID
HISTOGEN
HISTOGENS
HISTOGENY
HISTOGRAM
HISTOID
HISTOLOGY
HISTONE
HISTONES
HISTORIAN
HISTORIC
HISTORIED
HISTORIES
HISTORIFY
HISTORISM
HISTORY
HISTRIO
HISTRION
HISTRIONS
HISTRIOS
HISTS
HIT
HITCH
HITCHED
HITCHER
HITCHERS
HITCHES
HITCHHIKE
HITCHIER
HITCHIEST
HITCHILY
HITCHING
HITCHY
HITHE
HITHER
HITHERED
HITHERING
HITHERS
HITHERTO
HITHES
HITLESS
HITMAKER
HITMAKERS
HITMAN
HITMEN
HITS
HITTABLE
HITTER
HITTERS
HITTING
HIVE
HIVED
HIVELESS
HIVELIKE
HIVEMIND
HIVEMINDS
HIVER
HIVERS
HIVES
HIVEWARD
HIVEWARDS
HIVING
HIYA
HIZEN
HIZENS
HIZZ
HIZZED
HIZZES
HIZZING
HIZZONER
HIZZONERS
HM
HMM
HMMM
HO
HOA
HOACTZIN
HOACTZINS
HOAED
HOAGIE
HOAGIES
HOAGY
HOAING
HOAR
HOARD
HOARDED
HOARDER
HOARDERS
HOARDING
HOARDINGS
HOARDS
HOARED
HOARFROST
HOARHEAD
HOARHEADS
HOARHOUND
HOARIER
HOARIEST
HOARILY
HOARINESS
HOARING
HOARS
HOARSE
HOARSELY
HOARSEN
HOARSENED
HOARSENS
HOARSER
HOARSEST
HOARY
HOAS
HOAST
HOASTED
HOASTING
HOASTMAN
HOASTMEN
HOASTS
HOATCHING
HOATZIN
HOATZINES
HOATZINS
HOAX
HOAXED
HOAXER
HOAXERS
HOAXES
HOAXING
HOB
HOBBED
HOBBER
HOBBERS
HOBBIES
HOBBING
HOBBISH
HOBBIT
HOBBITRY
HOBBITS
HOBBLE
HOBBLED
HOBBLER
HOBBLERS
HOBBLES
HOBBLING
HOBBLINGS
HOBBY
HOBBYISM
HOBBYISMS
HOBBYIST
HOBBYISTS
HOBBYLESS
HOBDAY
HOBDAYED
HOBDAYING
HOBDAYS
HOBGOBLIN
HOBJOB
HOBJOBBED
HOBJOBBER
HOBJOBS
HOBLIKE
HOBNAIL
HOBNAILED
HOBNAILS
HOBNOB
HOBNOBBED
HOBNOBBER
HOBNOBBY
HOBNOBS
HOBO
HOBODOM
HOBODOMS
HOBOED
HOBOES
HOBOING
HOBOISM
HOBOISMS
HOBOS
HOBS
HOC
HOCK
HOCKED
HOCKER
HOCKERS
HOCKEY
HOCKEYS
HOCKING
HOCKLE
HOCKLED

H

HOCKLES
HOCKLING
HOCKS
HOCKSHOP
HOCKSHOPS
HOCUS
HOCUSED
HOCUSES
HOCUSING
HOCUSSED
HOCUSSES
HOCUSSING
HOD
HODAD
HODADDIES
HODADDY
HODADS
HODDED
HODDEN
HODDENS
HODDIN
HODDING
HODDINS
HODDLE
HODDLED
HODDLES
HODDLING
HODIERNAL
HODJA
HODJAS
HODMAN
HODMANDOD
HODMEN
HODOGRAPH
HODOMETER
HODOMETRY
HODOSCOPE
HODS
HOE
HOECAKE
HOECAKES
HOED
HOEDOWN
HOEDOWNS
HOEING
HOELIKE
HOER
HOERS
HOES
HOG
HOGAN
HOGANS
HOGBACK
HOGBACKS
HOGEN
HOGENS
HOGFISH
HOGFISHES
HOGG
HOGGED
HOGGER
HOGGEREL
HOGGERELS
HOGGERIES
HOGGERS
HOGGERY
HOGGET
HOGGETS
HOGGIN
HOGGING
HOGGINGS
HOGGINS
HOGGISH
HOGGISHLY
HOGGS
HOGH
HOGHOOD
HOGHOODS
HOGHS
HOGLIKE
HOGMANAY
HOGMANAYS
HOGMANE
HOGMANES
HOGMENAY
HOGMENAYS
HOGNOSE
HOGNOSED
HOGNOSES
HOGNUT
HOGNUTS
HOGS
HOGSHEAD
HOGSHEADS
HOGTIE
HOGTIED
HOGTIEING
HOGTIES
HOGTYING
HOGWARD
HOGWARDS
HOGWASH
HOGWASHES
HOGWEED
HOGWEEDS
HOH
HOHA
HOHED
HOHING
HOHS
HOI
HOICK
HOICKED
HOICKING
HOICKS
HOICKSED
HOICKSES
HOICKSING
HOIDEN
HOIDENED
HOIDENING
HOIDENISH
HOIDENS
HOIED
HOIING
HOIK
HOIKED
HOIKING
HOIKS
HOING
HOIS
HOISE
HOISED
HOISES
HOISIN
HOISING
HOISINS
HOIST
HOISTED
HOISTER
HOISTERS
HOISTING
HOISTINGS
HOISTMAN
HOISTMEN
HOISTS
HOISTWAY
HOISTWAYS
HOKA
HOKAS
HOKE
HOKED
HOKES
HOKEY
HOKEYNESS
HOKI
HOKIER
HOKIEST
HOKILY
HOKINESS
HOKING
HOKIS
HOKKU
HOKONUI
HOKONUIS
HOKUM
HOKUMS
HOKYPOKY
HOLANDRIC
HOLARCHY
HOLARD
HOLARDS
HOLD
HOLDABLE
HOLDALL
HOLDALLS
HOLDBACK
HOLDBACKS
HOLDDOWN
HOLDDOWNS
HOLDEN
HOLDER
HOLDERBAT
HOLDERS
HOLDFAST
HOLDFASTS
HOLDING
HOLDINGS
HOLDOUT
HOLDOUTS
HOLDOVER
HOLDOVERS
HOLDS
HOLDUP
HOLDUPS
HOLE
HOLED
HOLELESS
HOLES
HOLESOM
HOLESOME
HOLEY
HOLEYER
HOLEYEST
HOLIBUT
HOLIBUTS
HOLIDAY
HOLIDAYED
HOLIDAYER
HOLIDAYS
HOLIER
HOLIES
HOLIEST
HOLILY
HOLINESS
HOLING
HOLINGS
HOLISM
HOLISMS
HOLIST
HOLISTIC
HOLISTS
HOLK
HOLKED
HOLKING
HOLKS
HOLLA
HOLLAED
HOLLAING
HOLLAND
HOLLANDS
HOLLAS
HOLLER
HOLLERED
HOLLERING
HOLLERS
HOLLIDAM
HOLLIDAMS
HOLLIES
HOLLO

HOLLOA
HOLLOAED
HOLLOAING
HOLLOAS
HOLLOED
HOLLOES
HOLLOING
HOLLOO
HOLLOOED
HOLLOOING
HOLLOOS
HOLLOS
HOLLOW
HOLLOWARE
HOLLOWED
HOLLOWER
HOLLOWEST
HOLLOWING
HOLLOWLY
HOLLOWS
HOLLY
HOLLYHOCK
HOLM
HOLME
HOLMES
HOLMIA
HOLMIAS
HOLMIC
HOLMIUM
HOLMIUMS
HOLMS
HOLO
HOLOCAINE
HOLOCAUST
HOLOCENE
HOLOCRINE
HOLOGAMY
HOLOGRAM
HOLOGRAMS
HOLOGRAPH
HOLOGYNIC
HOLOGYNY
HOLOHEDRA
HOLON
HOLONIC
HOLONS
HOLOPHOTE
HOLOPHYTE
HOLOPTIC
HOLOS
HOLOTYPE
HOLOTYPES
HOLOTYPIC
HOLOZOIC
HOLP
HOLPEN
HOLS
HOLSTEIN
HOLSTEINS
HOLSTER
HOLSTERED
HOLSTERS
HOLT
HOLTS
HOLUBTSI
HOLY
HOLYDAM
HOLYDAME
HOLYDAMES
HOLYDAMS
HOLYDAY
HOLYDAYS
HOLYSTONE
HOLYTIDE
HOLYTIDES
HOM
HOMA
HOMAGE
HOMAGED
HOMAGER
HOMAGERS
HOMAGES
HOMAGING
HOMALOID
HOMALOIDS
HOMAS
HOMBRE
HOMBRES
HOMBURG
HOMBURGS
HOME
HOMEBIRD
HOMEBIRDS
HOMEBIRTH
HOMEBODY
HOMEBOUND
HOMEBOY
HOMEBOYS
HOMEBRED
HOMEBREDS
HOMEBREW
HOMEBREWS
HOMEBUILT
HOMEBUYER
HOMECOMER
HOMECRAFT
HOMED
HOMEFELT
HOMEGIRL
HOMEGIRLS
HOMEGROWN
HOMELAND
HOMELANDS
HOMELESS
HOMELIER
HOMELIEST
HOMELIKE
HOMELILY
HOMELY
HOMELYN
HOMELYNS
HOMEMADE
HOMEMAKER
HOMEOBOX
HOMEOMERY
HOMEOPATH
HOMEOSES
HOMEOSIS
HOMEOTIC
HOMEOWNER
HOMEPAGE
HOMEPAGES
HOMEPLACE
HOMEPORT
HOMEPORTS
HOMER
HOMERED
HOMERIC
HOMERING
HOMEROOM
HOMEROOMS
HOMERS
HOMES
HOMESICK
HOMESITE
HOMESITES
HOMESPUN
HOMESPUNS
HOMESTALL
HOMESTAND
HOMESTAY
HOMESTAYS
HOMESTEAD
HOMESTYLE
HOMETOWN
HOMETOWNS
HOMEWARD
HOMEWARDS
HOMEWARE
HOMEWARES
HOMEWORK
HOMEWORKS
HOMEY
HOMEYNESS
HOMEYS
HOMICIDAL
HOMICIDE
HOMICIDES
HOMIE
HOMIER
HOMIES
HOMIEST
HOMILETIC
HOMILIES
HOMILIST
HOMILISTS
HOMILY
HOMINES
HOMINESS
HOMING
HOMINGS
HOMINIAN
HOMINIANS
HOMINID
HOMINIDS
HOMINIES
HOMININ
HOMININE
HOMININS
HOMINISE
HOMINISED
HOMINISES
HOMINIZE
HOMINIZED
HOMINIZES
HOMINOID
HOMINOIDS
HOMINY
HOMME
HOMMES
HOMMOCK
HOMMOCKS
HOMMOS
HOMMOSES
HOMO
HOMOCERCY
HOMODONT
HOMODYNE
HOMOEOBOX
HOMOEOSES
HOMOEOSIS
HOMOEOTIC
HOMOGAMIC
HOMOGAMY
HOMOGENY
HOMOGONY
HOMOGRAFT
HOMOGRAPH
HOMOLOG
HOMOLOGIC
HOMOLOGS
HOMOLOGUE
HOMOLOGY
HOMOLYSES
HOMOLYSIS
HOMOLYTIC
HOMOMORPH
HOMONYM
HOMONYMIC
HOMONYMS
HOMONYMY
HOMOPHILE
HOMOPHOBE
HOMOPHONE
HOMOPHONY
HOMOPHYLY
HOMOPLASY
HOMOPOLAR
HOMOS
HOMOSEX

HOMOSEXES
HOMOSPORY
HOMOSTYLY
HOMOTAXES
HOMOTAXIC
HOMOTAXIS
HOMOTONIC
HOMOTONY
HOMOTYPAL
HOMOTYPE
HOMOTYPES
HOMOTYPIC
HOMOTYPY
HOMOUSIAN
HOMS
HOMUNCLE
HOMUNCLES
HOMUNCULE
HOMUNCULI
HOMY
HON
HONAN
HONANS
HONCHO
HONCHOED
HONCHOES
HONCHOING
HONCHOS
HOND
HONDA
HONDAS
HONDLE
HONDLED
HONDLES
HONDLING
HONDS
HONE
HONED
HONER
HONERS
HONES
HONEST
HONESTER
HONESTEST
HONESTIES
HONESTLY
HONESTY
HONEWORT
HONEWORTS
HONEY
HONEYBEE
HONEYBEES
HONEYBELL
HONEYBUN
HONEYBUNS
HONEYCOMB
HONEYDEW
HONEYDEWS
HONEYED
HONEYEDLY
HONEYFUL
HONEYING
HONEYLESS
HONEYMOON
HONEYPOT
HONEYPOTS
HONEYS
HONEYTRAP
HONG
HONGI
HONGIED
HONGIES
HONGIING
HONGING
HONGIS
HONGS
HONIED
HONIEDLY
HONING
HONK
HONKED
HONKER
HONKERS
HONKEY
HONKEYS
HONKIE
HONKIES
HONKING
HONKS
HONKY
HONOR
HONORABLE
HONORABLY
HONORAND
HONORANDS
HONORARIA
HONORARY
HONORED
HONOREE
HONOREES
HONORER
HONORERS
HONORIFIC
HONORING
HONORLESS
HONORS
HONOUR
HONOURARY
HONOURED
HONOUREE
HONOUREES
HONOURER
HONOURERS
HONOURING
HONOURS
HONS
HOO
HOOCH
HOOCHES
HOOCHIE
HOOCHIES
HOOD
HOODED
HOODIA
HOODIAS
HOODIE
HOODIER
HOODIES
HOODIEST
HOODING
HOODLESS
HOODLIKE
HOODLUM
HOODLUMS
HOODMAN
HOODMEN
HOODMOLD
HOODMOLDS
HOODOO
HOODOOED
HOODOOING
HOODOOISM
HOODOOS
HOODS
HOODWINK
HOODWINKS
HOODY
HOOEY
HOOEYS
HOOF
HOOFBEAT
HOOFBEATS
HOOFBOUND
HOOFED
HOOFER
HOOFERS
HOOFING
HOOFLESS
HOOFLIKE
HOOFPRINT
HOOFROT
HOOFROTS
HOOFS
HOOK
HOOKA
HOOKAH
HOOKAHS
HOOKAS
HOOKCHECK
HOOKED
HOOKER
HOOKERS
HOOKEY
HOOKEYS
HOOKIER
HOOKIES
HOOKIEST
HOOKING
HOOKINGS
HOOKLESS
HOOKLET
HOOKLETS
HOOKLIKE
HOOKNOSE
HOOKNOSED
HOOKNOSES
HOOKS
HOOKUP
HOOKUPS
HOOKWORM
HOOKWORMS
HOOKY
HOOLACHAN
HOOLEY
HOOLEYS
HOOLICAN
HOOLICANS
HOOLIE
HOOLIER
HOOLIES
HOOLIEST
HOOLIGAN
HOOLIGANS
HOOLOCK
HOOLOCKS
HOOLY
HOON
HOONED
HOONING
HOONS
HOOP
HOOPED
HOOPER
HOOPERS
HOOPING
HOOPLA
HOOPLAS
HOOPLESS
HOOPLIKE
HOOPOE
HOOPOES
HOOPOO
HOOPOOS
HOOPS
HOOPSKIRT
HOOPSTER
HOOPSTERS
HOOR
HOORAH
HOORAHED
HOORAHING
HOORAHS
HOORAY
HOORAYED
HOORAYING
HOORAYS
HOORD
HOORDS
HOOROO
HOOROOED

HOOROOING
HOOROOS
HOORS
HOOSEGOW
HOOSEGOWS
HOOSGOW
HOOSGOWS
HOOSH
HOOSHED
HOOSHES
HOOSHING
HOOT
HOOTCH
HOOTCHES
HOOTED
HOOTER
HOOTERS
HOOTIER
HOOTIEST
HOOTING
HOOTNANNY
HOOTS
HOOTY
HOOVE
HOOVED
HOOVEN
HOOVER
HOOVERED
HOOVERING
HOOVERS
HOOVES
HOOVING
HOP
HOPAK
HOPAKS
HOPBIND
HOPBINDS
HOPBINE
HOPBINES
HOPDOG
HOPDOGS
HOPE
HOPED
HOPEFUL
HOPEFULLY
HOPEFULS
HOPELESS
HOPER
HOPERS
HOPES
HOPFIELD
HOPFIELDS
HOPHEAD
HOPHEADS
HOPING
HOPINGLY
HOPLITE
HOPLITES
HOPLITIC
HOPLOLOGY
HOPPED
HOPPER
HOPPERCAR
HOPPERS
HOPPIER
HOPPIEST
HOPPINESS
HOPPING
HOPPINGS
HOPPLE
HOPPLED
HOPPLER
HOPPLERS
HOPPLES
HOPPLING
HOPPUS
HOPPY
HOPS
HOPSACK
HOPSACKS
HOPSCOTCH
HOPTOAD
HOPTOADS
HORA
HORAH
HORAHS
HORAL
HORARY
HORAS
HORDE
HORDED
HORDEIN
HORDEINS
HORDEOLA
HORDEOLUM
HORDES
HORDING
HORDOCK
HORDOCKS
HORE
HOREHOUND
HORI
HORIATIKI
HORIS
HORIZON
HORIZONAL
HORIZONS
HORK
HORKED
HORKEY
HORKEYS
HORKING
HORKS
HORLICKS
HORME
HORMES
HORMESES
HORMESIS
HORMETIC
HORMIC
HORMONAL
HORMONE
HORMONES
HORMONIC
HORN
HORNBAG
HORNBAGS
HORNBEAK
HORNBEAKS
HORNBEAM
HORNBEAMS
HORNBILL
HORNBILLS
HORNBOOK
HORNBOOKS
HORNBUG
HORNBUGS
HORNDOG
HORNDOGS
HORNED
HORNER
HORNERS
HORNET
HORNETS
HORNFELS
HORNFISH
HORNFUL
HORNFULS
HORNGELD
HORNGELDS
HORNIER
HORNIEST
HORNILY
HORNINESS
HORNING
HORNINGS
HORNISH
HORNIST
HORNISTS
HORNITO
HORNITOS
HORNLESS
HORNLET
HORNLETS
HORNLIKE
HORNPIPE
HORNPIPES
HORNPOUT
HORNPOUTS
HORNS
HORNSTONE
HORNTAIL
HORNTAILS
HORNWORK
HORNWORKS
HORNWORM
HORNWORMS
HORNWORT
HORNWORTS
HORNWRACK
HORNY
HORNYHEAD
HORNYWINK
HOROEKA
HOROEKAS
HOROKAKA
HOROKAKAS
HOROLOGE
HOROLOGER
HOROLOGES
HOROLOGIA
HOROLOGIC
HOROLOGY
HOROMETRY
HOROPITO
HOROPITOS
HOROPTER
HOROPTERS
HOROSCOPE
HOROSCOPY
HORRENT
HORRIBLE
HORRIBLES
HORRIBLY
HORRID
HORRIDER
HORRIDEST
HORRIDLY
HORRIFIC
HORRIFIED
HORRIFIES
HORRIFY
HORROR
HORRORS
HORS
HORSE
HORSEBACK
HORSEBEAN
HORSEBOX
HORSECAR
HORSECARS
HORSED
HORSEFLY
HORSEHAIR
HORSEHEAD
HORSEHIDE
HORSELESS
HORSELIKE
HORSEMAN
HORSEMEAT
HORSEMEN
HORSEMINT
HORSEPLAY
HORSEPOND
HORSEPOX
HORSERACE
HORSES
HORSESHIT
HORSESHOD
HORSESHOE

HORSETAIL
HORSEWAY
HORSEWAYS
HORSEWEED
HORSEWHIP
HORSEY
HORSIE
HORSIER
HORSIES
HORSIEST
HORSILY
HORSINESS
HORSING
HORSINGS
HORSON
HORSONS
HORST
HORSTE
HORSTES
HORSTS
HORSY
HORTATION
HORTATIVE
HORTATORY
HORTENSIA
HOS
HOSANNA
HOSANNAED
HOSANNAH
HOSANNAHS
HOSANNAS
HOSE
HOSED
HOSEL
HOSELIKE
HOSELS
HOSEMAN
HOSEMEN
HOSEN
HOSEPIPE
HOSEPIPES
HOSER
HOSERS
HOSES
HOSEY
HOSEYED
HOSEYING
HOSEYS
HOSIER
HOSIERIES
HOSIERS
HOSIERY
HOSING
HOSPICE
HOSPICES
HOSPITAGE
HOSPITAL
HOSPITALE
HOSPITALS
HOSPITIA
HOSPITIUM
HOSPODAR
HOSPODARS
HOSS
HOSSES
HOST
HOSTA
HOSTAGE
HOSTAGES
HOSTAS
HOSTED
HOSTEL
HOSTELED
HOSTELER
HOSTELERS
HOSTELING
HOSTELLED
HOSTELLER
HOSTELRY
HOSTELS
HOSTESS
HOSTESSED
HOSTESSES
HOSTIE
HOSTIES
HOSTILE
HOSTILELY
HOSTILES
HOSTILITY
HOSTING
HOSTINGS
HOSTLER
HOSTLERS
HOSTLESS
HOSTLESSE
HOSTLY
HOSTRIES
HOSTRY
HOSTS
HOT
HOTBED
HOTBEDS
HOTBLOOD
HOTBLOODS
HOTBOX
HOTBOXED
HOTBOXES
HOTBOXING
HOTCAKE
HOTCAKES
HOTCH
HOTCHED
HOTCHES
HOTCHING
HOTCHPOT
HOTCHPOTS
HOTDOG
HOTDOGGED
HOTDOGGER
HOTDOGS
HOTE
HOTEL
HOTELDOM
HOTELDOMS
HOTELIER
HOTELIERS
HOTELING
HOTELINGS
HOTELLING
HOTELMAN
HOTELMEN
HOTELS
HOTEN
HOTFOOT
HOTFOOTED
HOTFOOTS
HOTHEAD
HOTHEADED
HOTHEADS
HOTHOUSE
HOTHOUSED
HOTHOUSES
HOTLINE
HOTLINER
HOTLINERS
HOTLINES
HOTLINK
HOTLINKS
HOTLY
HOTNESS
HOTNESSES
HOTPLATE
HOTPLATES
HOTPOT
HOTPOTS
HOTPRESS
HOTROD
HOTRODS
HOTS
HOTSHOT
HOTSHOTS
HOTSPOT
HOTSPOTS
HOTSPUR
HOTSPURS
HOTTED
HOTTENTOT
HOTTER
HOTTERED
HOTTERING
HOTTERS
HOTTEST
HOTTIE
HOTTIES
HOTTING
HOTTINGS
HOTTISH
HOTTY
HOUDAH
HOUDAHS
HOUDAN
HOUDANS
HOUF
HOUFED
HOUFF
HOUFFED
HOUFFING
HOUFFS
HOUFING
HOUFS
HOUGH
HOUGHED
HOUGHING
HOUGHS
HOUHERE
HOUHERES
HOUMMOS
HOUMMOSES
HOUMOUS
HOUMOUSES
HOUMUS
HOUMUSES
HOUND
HOUNDED
HOUNDER
HOUNDERS
HOUNDFISH
HOUNDING
HOUNDS
HOUNGAN
HOUNGANS
HOUR
HOURGLASS
HOURI
HOURIS
HOURLIES
HOURLONG
HOURLY
HOURPLATE
HOURS
HOUSE
HOUSEBOAT
HOUSEBOY
HOUSEBOYS
HOUSECARL
HOUSECOAT
HOUSED
HOUSEFLY
HOUSEFUL
HOUSEFULS
HOUSEHOLD
HOUSEKEEP
HOUSEKEPT
HOUSEL
HOUSELED
HOUSELEEK
HOUSELESS
HOUSELIKE
HOUSELINE
HOUSELING

HOUSELLED
HOUSELS
HOUSEMAID
HOUSEMAN
HOUSEMATE
HOUSEMEN
HOUSER
HOUSEROOM
HOUSERS
HOUSES
HOUSESAT
HOUSESIT
HOUSESITS
HOUSETOP
HOUSETOPS
HOUSEWIFE
HOUSEWORK
HOUSEWRAP
HOUSEY
HOUSIER
HOUSIEST
HOUSING
HOUSINGS
HOUSLING
HOUSLINGS
HOUSTONIA
HOUT
HOUTED
HOUTING
HOUTINGS
HOUTS
HOVE
HOVEA
HOVEAS
HOVED
HOVEL
HOVELED
HOVELING
HOVELLED
HOVELLER
HOVELLERS
HOVELLING
HOVELS
HOVEN
HOVER
HOVERED
HOVERER
HOVERERS
HOVERFLY
HOVERING
HOVERPORT
HOVERS
HOVES
HOVING
HOW
HOWBE
HOWBEIT
HOWDAH
HOWDAHS
HOWDIE
HOWDIED
HOWDIES
HOWDY
HOWDYING
HOWE
HOWES
HOWEVER
HOWF
HOWFED
HOWFF
HOWFFED
HOWFFING
HOWFFS
HOWFING
HOWFS
HOWITZER
HOWITZERS
HOWK
HOWKED
HOWKER
HOWKERS
HOWKING
HOWKS
HOWL
HOWLBACK
HOWLBACKS
HOWLED
HOWLER
HOWLERS
HOWLET
HOWLETS
HOWLING
HOWLINGLY
HOWLINGS
HOWLROUND
HOWLS
HOWRE
HOWRES
HOWS
HOWSO
HOWSOEVER
HOWTOWDIE
HOWZAT
HOWZIT
HOX
HOXED
HOXES
HOXING
HOY
HOYA
HOYAS
HOYDEN
HOYDENED
HOYDENING
HOYDENISH
HOYDENISM
HOYDENS
HOYED
HOYING
HOYLE
HOYLES
HOYS
HRYVNA
HRYVNAS
HRYVNIA
HRYVNIAS
HRYVNYA
HRYVNYAS
HUANACO
HUANACOS
HUAQUERO
HUAQUEROS
HUARACHE
HUARACHES
HUARACHO
HUARACHOS
HUB
HUBBIES
HUBBLIER
HUBBLIEST
HUBBLY
HUBBUB
HUBBUBOO
HUBBUBOOS
HUBBUBS
HUBBY
HUBCAP
HUBCAPS
HUBLESS
HUBRIS
HUBRISES
HUBRISTIC
HUBS
HUCK
HUCKABACK
HUCKED
HUCKERY
HUCKING
HUCKLE
HUCKLED
HUCKLES
HUCKLING
HUCKS
HUCKSTER
HUCKSTERS
HUCKSTERY
HUDDEN
HUDDLE
HUDDLED
HUDDLER
HUDDLERS
HUDDLES
HUDDLING
HUDDUP
HUDNA
HUDNAS
HUDUD
HUDUDS
HUE
HUED
HUELESS
HUER
HUERS
HUES
HUFF
HUFFED
HUFFER
HUFFERS
HUFFIER
HUFFIEST
HUFFILY
HUFFINESS
HUFFING
HUFFINGS
HUFFISH
HUFFISHLY
HUFFKIN
HUFFKINS
HUFFS
HUFFY
HUG
HUGE
HUGELY
HUGENESS
HUGEOUS
HUGEOUSLY
HUGER
HUGEST
HUGGABLE
HUGGED
HUGGER
HUGGERS
HUGGIER
HUGGIEST
HUGGING
HUGGY
HUGS
HUGY
HUH
HUHU
HUHUS
HUI
HUIA
HUIAS
HUIC
HUIPIL
HUIPILES
HUIPILS
HUIS
HUISACHE
HUISACHES
HUISSIER
HUISSIERS
HUITAIN
HUITAINS
HULA
HULAS
HULE
HULES
HULK

H

HULKED
HULKIER
HULKIEST
HULKING
HULKS
HULKY
HULL
HULLED
HULLER
HULLERS
HULLIER
HULLIEST
HULLING
HULLO
HULLOA
HULLOAED
HULLOAING
HULLOAS
HULLOED
HULLOES
HULLOING
HULLOO
HULLOOED
HULLOOING
HULLOOS
HULLOS
HULLS
HULLY
HUM
HUMA
HUMAN
HUMANE
HUMANELY
HUMANER
HUMANEST
HUMANHOOD
HUMANISE
HUMANISED
HUMANISER
HUMANISES
HUMANISM
HUMANISMS
HUMANIST
HUMANISTS
HUMANITY
HUMANIZE
HUMANIZED
HUMANIZER
HUMANIZES
HUMANKIND
HUMANLIKE
HUMANLY
HUMANNESS
HUMANOID
HUMANOIDS
HUMANS
HUMAS
HUMATE
HUMATES
HUMBLE
HUMBLEBEE
HUMBLED
HUMBLER
HUMBLERS
HUMBLES
HUMBLESSE
HUMBLEST
HUMBLING
HUMBLINGS
HUMBLY
HUMBUCKER
HUMBUG
HUMBUGGED
HUMBUGGER
HUMBUGS
HUMBUZZ
HUMBUZZES
HUMDINGER
HUMDRUM
HUMDRUMS
HUMECT
HUMECTANT
HUMECTATE
HUMECTED
HUMECTING
HUMECTIVE
HUMECTS
HUMEFIED
HUMEFIES
HUMEFY
HUMEFYING
HUMERAL
HUMERALS
HUMERI
HUMERUS
HUMF
HUMFED
HUMFING
HUMFS
HUMHUM
HUMHUMS
HUMIC
HUMICOLE
HUMICOLES
HUMID
HUMIDER
HUMIDEST
HUMIDEX
HUMIDEXES
HUMIDICES
HUMIDIFY
HUMIDITY
HUMIDLY
HUMIDNESS
HUMIDOR
HUMIDORS
HUMIFIED
HUMIFIES
HUMIFY
HUMIFYING
HUMILIANT
HUMILIATE
HUMILITY
HUMINT
HUMINTS
HUMITE
HUMITES
HUMITURE
HUMITURES
HUMLIE
HUMLIES
HUMMABLE
HUMMAUM
HUMMAUMS
HUMMED
HUMMEL
HUMMELLED
HUMMELLER
HUMMELS
HUMMER
HUMMERS
HUMMING
HUMMINGS
HUMMLE
HUMMOCK
HUMMOCKED
HUMMOCKS
HUMMOCKY
HUMMUM
HUMMUMS
HUMMUS
HUMMUSES
HUMOGEN
HUMOGENS
HUMONGOUS
HUMOR
HUMORAL
HUMORALLY
HUMORED
HUMORESK
HUMORESKS
HUMORFUL
HUMORING
HUMORIST
HUMORISTS
HUMORLESS
HUMOROUS
HUMORS
HUMORSOME
HUMOUR
HUMOURED
HUMOURFUL
HUMOURING
HUMOURS
HUMOUS
HUMOUSES
HUMP
HUMPBACK
HUMPBACKS
HUMPED
HUMPEN
HUMPENS
HUMPER
HUMPERS
HUMPH
HUMPHED
HUMPHING
HUMPHS
HUMPIER
HUMPIES
HUMPIEST
HUMPINESS
HUMPING
HUMPLESS
HUMPLIKE
HUMPS
HUMPTIES
HUMPTY
HUMPY
HUMS
HUMSTRUM
HUMSTRUMS
HUMUNGOUS
HUMUS
HUMUSES
HUMUSIER
HUMUSIEST
HUMUSY
HUMVEE
HUMVEES
HUN
HUNCH
HUNCHBACK
HUNCHED
HUNCHES
HUNCHING
HUNDRED
HUNDREDER
HUNDREDOR
HUNDREDS
HUNDREDTH
HUNG
HUNGAN
HUNGANS
HUNGER
HUNGERED
HUNGERFUL
HUNGERING
HUNGERLY
HUNGERS
HUNGOVER
HUNGRIER
HUNGRIEST
HUNGRILY
HUNGRY
HUNH
HUNK
HUNKER
HUNKERED
HUNKERING

H

HUNKERS
HUNKEY
HUNKEYS
HUNKIE
HUNKIER
HUNKIES
HUNKIEST
HUNKS
HUNKSES
HUNKY
HUNNISH
HUNS
HUNT
HUNTABLE
HUNTAWAY
HUNTAWAYS
HUNTED
HUNTEDLY
HUNTER
HUNTERS
HUNTING
HUNTINGS
HUNTRESS
HUNTS
HUNTSMAN
HUNTSMEN
HUP
HUPIRO
HUPIROS
HUPPAH
HUPPAHS
HUPPED
HUPPING
HUPPOT
HUPPOTH
HUPS
HURCHEON
HURCHEONS
HURDEN
HURDENS
HURDIES
HURDLE
HURDLED
HURDLER
HURDLERS
HURDLES
HURDLING
HURDLINGS
HURDS
HURL
HURLBAT
HURLBATS
HURLED
HURLER
HURLERS
HURLEY
HURLEYS
HURLIES
HURLING
HURLINGS
HURLS
HURLY
HURRA
HURRAED
HURRAH
HURRAHED
HURRAHING
HURRAHS
HURRAING
HURRAS
HURRAY
HURRAYED
HURRAYING
HURRAYS
HURRICANE
HURRICANO
HURRIED
HURRIEDLY
HURRIER
HURRIERS
HURRIES
HURRY
HURRYING
HURRYINGS
HURST
HURSTS
HURT
HURTER
HURTERS
HURTFUL
HURTFULLY
HURTING
HURTLE
HURTLED
HURTLES
HURTLESS
HURTLING
HURTS
HUSBAND
HUSBANDED
HUSBANDER
HUSBANDLY
HUSBANDRY
HUSBANDS
HUSH
HUSHABIED
HUSHABIES
HUSHABY
HUSHABYE
HUSHED
HUSHEDLY
HUSHER
HUSHERED
HUSHERING
HUSHERS
HUSHES
HUSHFUL
HUSHIER
HUSHIEST
HUSHING
HUSHPUPPY
HUSHY
HUSK
HUSKED
HUSKER
HUSKERS
HUSKIER
HUSKIES
HUSKIEST
HUSKILY
HUSKINESS
HUSKING
HUSKINGS
HUSKLIKE
HUSKS
HUSKY
HUSO
HUSOS
HUSS
HUSSAR
HUSSARS
HUSSES
HUSSIES
HUSSIF
HUSSIFS
HUSSY
HUSTINGS
HUSTLE
HUSTLED
HUSTLER
HUSTLERS
HUSTLES
HUSTLING
HUSTLINGS
HUSWIFE
HUSWIFES
HUSWIVES
HUT
HUTCH
HUTCHED
HUTCHES
HUTCHIE
HUTCHIES
HUTCHING
HUTIA
HUTIAS
HUTLIKE
HUTMENT
HUTMENTS
HUTS
HUTTED
HUTTING
HUTTINGS
HUTZPA
HUTZPAH
HUTZPAHS
HUTZPAS
HUZOOR
HUZOORS
HUZZA
HUZZAED
HUZZAH
HUZZAHED
HUZZAHING
HUZZAHS
HUZZAING
HUZZAS
HUZZIES
HUZZY
HWAN
HWYL
HWYLS
HYACINE
HYACINES
HYACINTH
HYACINTHS
HYAENA
HYAENAS
HYAENIC
HYALIN
HYALINE
HYALINES
HYALINISE
HYALINIZE
HYALINS
HYALITE
HYALITES
HYALOGEN
HYALOGENS
HYALOID
HYALOIDS
HYALONEMA
HYBRID
HYBRIDISE
HYBRIDISM
HYBRIDIST
HYBRIDITY
HYBRIDIZE
HYBRIDOMA
HYBRIDOUS
HYBRIDS
HYBRIS
HYBRISES
HYBRISTIC
HYDANTOIN
HYDATHODE
HYDATID
HYDATIDS
HYDATOID
HYDRA
HYDRACID
HYDRACIDS
HYDRAE
HYDRAEMIA
HYDRAGOG
HYDRAGOGS
HYDRANGEA
HYDRANT
HYDRANTH
HYDRANTHS

H

HYDRANTS
HYDRAS
HYDRASE
HYDRASES
HYDRASTIS
HYDRATE
HYDRATED
HYDRATES
HYDRATING
HYDRATION
HYDRATOR
HYDRATORS
HYDRAULIC
HYDRAZIDE
HYDRAZINE
HYDRAZOIC
HYDREMIA
HYDREMIAS
HYDRIA
HYDRIAE
HYDRIC
HYDRID
HYDRIDE
HYDRIDES
HYDRIDS
HYDRILLA
HYDRILLAS
HYDRIODIC
HYDRO
HYDROCAST
HYDROCELE
HYDROFOIL
HYDROGEL
HYDROGELS
HYDROGEN
HYDROGENS
HYDROID
HYDROIDS
HYDROLASE
HYDROLOGY
HYDROLYSE
HYDROLYTE
HYDROLYZE
HYDROMA
HYDROMAS
HYDROMATA
HYDROMEL
HYDROMELS
HYDRONAUT
HYDRONIC
HYDRONIUM
HYDROPATH
HYDROPIC
HYDROPS
HYDROPSES
HYDROPSY
HYDROPTIC
HYDROPULT
HYDROS
HYDROSERE
HYDROSKI
HYDROSKIS
HYDROSOL
HYDROSOLS
HYDROSOMA
HYDROSOME
HYDROSTAT
HYDROUS
HYDROVANE
HYDROXIDE
HYDROXIUM
HYDROXY
HYDROXYL
HYDROXYLS
HYDROZOA
HYDROZOAN
HYDROZOON
HYDYNE
HYDYNES
HYE
HYED
HYEING
HYEN
HYENA
HYENAS
HYENIC
HYENINE
HYENOID
HYENS
HYES
HYETAL
HYETOLOGY
HYGEIST
HYGEISTS
HYGGE
HYGGES
HYGIEIST
HYGIEISTS
HYGIENE
HYGIENES
HYGIENIC
HYGIENICS
HYGIENIST
HYGRISTOR
HYGRODEIK
HYGROLOGY
HYGROMA
HYGROMAS
HYGROMATA
HYGROPHIL
HYGROSTAT
HYING
HYKE
HYKES
HYLA
HYLAS
HYLDING
HYLDINGS
HYLE
HYLEG
HYLEGS
HYLES
HYLIC
HYLICISM
HYLICISMS
HYLICIST
HYLICISTS
HYLISM
HYLISMS
HYLIST
HYLISTS
HYLOBATE
HYLOBATES
HYLOIST
HYLOISTS
HYLOPHYTE
HYLOZOIC
HYLOZOISM
HYLOZOIST
HYMEN
HYMENAEAL
HYMENAEAN
HYMENAL
HYMENEAL
HYMENEALS
HYMENEAN
HYMENEANS
HYMENIA
HYMENIAL
HYMENIUM
HYMENIUMS
HYMENS
HYMN
HYMNAL
HYMNALS
HYMNARIES
HYMNARY
HYMNBOOK
HYMNBOOKS
HYMNED
HYMNIC
HYMNING
HYMNIST
HYMNISTS
HYMNLESS
HYMNLIKE
HYMNODIES
HYMNODIST
HYMNODY
HYMNOLOGY
HYMNS
HYNDE
HYNDES
HYOID
HYOIDAL
HYOIDEAN
HYOIDS
HYOSCINE
HYOSCINES
HYP
HYPALGIA
HYPALGIAS
HYPALLAGE
HYPANTHIA
HYPATE
HYPATES
HYPE
HYPED
HYPER
HYPERACID
HYPERARID
HYPERBOLA
HYPERBOLE
HYPERCUBE
HYPEREMIA
HYPEREMIC
HYPERER
HYPEREST
HYPERFINE
HYPERGAMY
HYPERGOL
HYPERGOLS
HYPERICIN
HYPERICUM
HYPERLINK
HYPERMART
HYPERNOVA
HYPERNYM
HYPERNYMS
HYPERNYMY
HYPERON
HYPERONS
HYPEROPE
HYPEROPES
HYPEROPIA
HYPEROPIC
HYPERPNEA
HYPERPURE
HYPERREAL
HYPERS
HYPERTEXT
HYPES
HYPESTER
HYPESTERS
HYPETHRAL
HYPHA
HYPHAE
HYPHAL
HYPHEMIA
HYPHEMIAS
HYPHEN
HYPHENATE
HYPHENED
HYPHENIC
HYPHENING
HYPHENISE
HYPHENISM
HYPHENIZE
HYPHENS
HYPHIES

HYPHY
HYPING
HYPINGS
HYPINOSES
HYPINOSIS
HYPNIC
HYPNICS
HYPNOGENY
HYPNOID
HYPNOIDAL
HYPNOLOGY
HYPNONE
HYPNONES
HYPNOSES
HYPNOSIS
HYPNOTEE
HYPNOTEES
HYPNOTIC
HYPNOTICS
HYPNOTISE
HYPNOTISM
HYPNOTIST
HYPNOTIZE
HYPNOTOID
HYPNUM
HYPNUMS
HYPO
HYPOACID
HYPOBARIC
HYPOBLAST
HYPOBOLE
HYPOBOLES
HYPOCAUST
HYPOCIST
HYPOCISTS
HYPOCOTYL
HYPOCRISY
HYPOCRITE
HYPODERM
HYPODERMA
HYPODERMS
HYPOED
HYPOGAEA
HYPOGAEAL
HYPOGAEAN
HYPOGAEUM
HYPOGEA
HYPOGEAL
HYPOGEAN
HYPOGENE
HYPOGENIC
HYPOGEOUS
HYPOGEUM
HYPOGYNY
HYPOID
HYPOIDS
HYPOING
HYPOMANIA
HYPOMANIC
HYPOMORPH
HYPONASTY
HYPONEA
HYPONEAS
HYPONOIA
HYPONOIAS
HYPONYM
HYPONYMS
HYPONYMY
HYPOPHYGE
HYPOPLOID
HYPOPNEA
HYPOPNEAS
HYPOPNEIC
HYPOPNOEA
HYPOPYON
HYPOPYONS
HYPOS
HYPOSTOME
HYPOSTYLE
HYPOTAXES
HYPOTAXIS
HYPOTHEC
HYPOTHECA
HYPOTHECS
HYPOTONIA
HYPOTONIC
HYPOXEMIA
HYPOXEMIC
HYPOXIA
HYPOXIAS
HYPOXIC
HYPPED
HYPPING
HYPS
HYPURAL
HYRACES
HYRACOID
HYRACOIDS
HYRAX
HYRAXES
HYSON
HYSONS
HYSSOP
HYSSOPS
HYSTERIA
HYSTERIAS
HYSTERIC
HYSTERICS
HYSTEROID
HYTE
HYTHE
HYTHES

H

I

IAMB
IAMBI
IAMBIC
IAMBICS
IAMBIST
IAMBISTS
IAMBS
IAMBUS
IAMBUSES
IANTHINE
IATRIC
IATRICAL
IATROGENY
IBADAH
IBADAT
IBERIS
IBERISES
IBEX
IBEXES
IBICES
IBIDEM
IBIS
IBISES
IBOGAINE
IBOGAINES
IBRIK
IBRIKS
IBUPROFEN
ICE
ICEBALL
ICEBALLS
ICEBERG
ICEBERGS
ICEBLINK
ICEBLINKS
ICEBOAT
ICEBOATED
ICEBOATER
ICEBOATS
ICEBOUND
ICEBOX
ICEBOXES
ICECAP
ICECAPPED
ICECAPS
ICED
ICEFALL
ICEFALLS
ICEFIELD
ICEFIELDS
ICEFISH
ICEFISHED
ICEFISHES
ICEHOUSE
ICEHOUSES
ICEKHANA
ICEKHANAS
ICELESS
ICELIKE
ICEMAKER
ICEMAKERS
ICEMAN
ICEMEN
ICEPACK
ICEPACKS
ICER
ICERS
ICES
ICESCAPE
ICESCAPES
ICESTONE
ICESTONES
ICEWINE
ICEWINES
ICEWORM
ICEWORMS
ICH
ICHABOD
ICHED
ICHES
ICHING
ICHNEUMON
ICHNITE
ICHNITES
ICHNOLITE
ICHNOLOGY
ICHOR
ICHOROUS
ICHORS
ICHS
ICHTHIC
ICHTHYIC
ICHTHYOID
ICHTHYS
ICHTHYSES
ICICLE
ICICLED
ICICLES
ICIER
ICIEST
ICILY
ICINESS
ICINESSES
ICING
ICINGS
ICK
ICKER
ICKERS
ICKIER
ICKIEST
ICKILY
ICKINESS
ICKLE
ICKLER
ICKLEST
ICKS
ICKY
ICON
ICONES
ICONIC
ICONICAL
ICONICITY
ICONIFIED
ICONIFIES
ICONIFY
ICONISE
ICONISED
ICONISES
ICONISING
ICONIZE
ICONIZED
ICONIZES
ICONIZING
ICONOLOGY
ICONOSTAS
ICONS
ICTAL
ICTERIC
ICTERICAL
ICTERICS
ICTERID
ICTERIDS
ICTERINE
ICTERUS
ICTERUSES
ICTIC
ICTUS
ICTUSES
ICY
ID
IDANT
IDANTS
IDE
IDEA
IDEAED
IDEAL
IDEALESS
IDEALISE
IDEALISED
IDEALISER
IDEALISES
IDEALISM
IDEALISMS
IDEALIST
IDEALISTS
IDEALITY
IDEALIZE
IDEALIZED
IDEALIZER
IDEALIZES
IDEALLESS
IDEALLY
IDEALNESS
IDEALOGUE
IDEALOGY
IDEALS
IDEAS
IDEATA
IDEATE
IDEATED
IDEATES
IDEATING
IDEATION
IDEATIONS
IDEATIVE
IDEATUM
IDEE
IDEES
IDEM
IDENT
IDENTIC
IDENTICAL
IDENTIFY
IDENTIKIT
IDENTITY
IDENTS
IDEOGRAM
IDEOGRAMS
IDEOGRAPH
IDEOLOGIC
IDEOLOGUE
IDEOLOGY
IDEOMOTOR
IDEOPHONE
IDEOPOLIS
IDES
IDIOBLAST
IDIOCIES
IDIOCY
IDIOGRAM

IDIOGRAMS
IDIOGRAPH
IDIOLECT
IDIOLECTS
IDIOM
IDIOMATIC
IDIOMS
IDIOPATHY
IDIOPHONE
IDIOPLASM
IDIOT
IDIOTCIES
IDIOTCY
IDIOTIC
IDIOTICAL
IDIOTICON
IDIOTISH
IDIOTISM
IDIOTISMS
IDIOTS
IDIOTYPE
IDIOTYPES
IDIOTYPIC
IDLE
IDLED
IDLEHOOD
IDLEHOODS
IDLENESS
IDLER
IDLERS
IDLES
IDLESSE
IDLESSES
IDLEST
IDLING
IDLY
IDOCRASE
IDOCRASES
IDOL
IDOLA
IDOLATER
IDOLATERS
IDOLATOR
IDOLATORS
IDOLATRY
IDOLISE
IDOLISED
IDOLISER
IDOLISERS
IDOLISES
IDOLISING
IDOLISM
IDOLISMS
IDOLIST
IDOLISTS
IDOLIZE
IDOLIZED
IDOLIZER
IDOLIZERS
IDOLIZES
IDOLIZING
IDOLON
IDOLS
IDOLUM
IDONEITY
IDONEOUS
IDS
IDYL
IDYLIST
IDYLISTS
IDYLL
IDYLLIAN
IDYLLIC
IDYLLIST
IDYLLISTS
IDYLLS
IDYLS
IF
IFF
IFFIER
IFFIEST
IFFILY
IFFINESS
IFFY
IFS
IFTAR
IFTARS
IGAD
IGAPO
IGAPOS
IGARAPE
IGARAPES
IGG
IGGED
IGGING
IGGS
IGLOO
IGLOOS
IGLU
IGLUS
IGNARO
IGNAROES
IGNAROS
IGNATIA
IGNATIAS
IGNEOUS
IGNESCENT
IGNIFIED
IGNIFIES
IGNIFY
IGNIFYING
IGNITABLE
IGNITE
IGNITED
IGNITER
IGNITERS
IGNITES
IGNITIBLE
IGNITING
IGNITION
IGNITIONS
IGNITOR
IGNITORS
IGNITRON
IGNITRONS
IGNOBLE
IGNOBLER
IGNOBLEST
IGNOBLY
IGNOMIES
IGNOMINY
IGNOMY
IGNORABLE
IGNORAMI
IGNORAMUS
IGNORANCE
IGNORANT
IGNORANTS
IGNORE
IGNORED
IGNORER
IGNORERS
IGNORES
IGNORING
IGUANA
IGUANAS
IGUANIAN
IGUANIANS
IGUANID
IGUANIDS
IGUANODON
IHRAM
IHRAMS
IJTIHAD
IJTIHADS
IKAN
IKANS
IKAT
IKATS
IKEBANA
IKEBANAS
IKON
IKONS
ILEA
ILEAC
ILEAL
ILEITIDES
ILEITIS
ILEITISES
ILEOSTOMY
ILEUM
ILEUS
ILEUSES
ILEX
ILEXES
ILIA
ILIAC
ILIACI
ILIACUS
ILIACUSES
ILIAD
ILIADS
ILIAL
ILICES
ILIUM
ILK
ILKA
ILKADAY
ILKADAYS
ILKS
ILL
ILLAPSE
ILLAPSED
ILLAPSES
ILLAPSING
ILLATION
ILLATIONS
ILLATIVE
ILLATIVES
ILLAWARRA
ILLEGAL
ILLEGALLY
ILLEGALS
ILLEGIBLE
ILLEGIBLY
ILLER
ILLEST
ILLIAD
ILLIADS
ILLIBERAL
ILLICIT
ILLICITLY
ILLIMITED
ILLINIUM
ILLINIUMS
ILLIPE
ILLIPES
ILLIQUID
ILLISION
ILLISIONS
ILLITE
ILLITES
ILLITIC
ILLNESS
ILLNESSES
ILLOGIC
ILLOGICAL
ILLOGICS
ILLS
ILLTH
ILLTHS
ILLUDE
ILLUDED
ILLUDES
ILLUDING
ILLUME
ILLUMED
ILLUMES
ILLUMINE
ILLUMINED

ILLUMINER
ILLUMINES
ILLUMING
ILLUPI
ILLUPIS
ILLUSION
ILLUSIONS
ILLUSIVE
ILLUSORY
ILLUVIA
ILLUVIAL
ILLUVIATE
ILLUVIUM
ILLUVIUMS
ILLY
ILMENITE
ILMENITES
IMAGE
IMAGEABLE
IMAGED
IMAGELESS
IMAGER
IMAGERIES
IMAGERS
IMAGERY
IMAGES
IMAGINAL
IMAGINARY
IMAGINE
IMAGINED
IMAGINEER
IMAGINER
IMAGINERS
IMAGINES
IMAGING
IMAGINGS
IMAGINING
IMAGINIST
IMAGISM
IMAGISMS
IMAGIST
IMAGISTIC
IMAGISTS
IMAGO
IMAGOES
IMAGOS
IMAM
IMAMATE
IMAMATES
IMAMS
IMARET
IMARETS
IMARI
IMARIS
IMAUM
IMAUMS
IMBALANCE
IMBALM
IMBALMED
IMBALMER
IMBALMERS
IMBALMING
IMBALMS
IMBAR
IMBARK
IMBARKED
IMBARKING
IMBARKS
IMBARRED
IMBARRING
IMBARS
IMBASE
IMBASED
IMBASES
IMBASING
IMBATHE
IMBATHED
IMBATHES
IMBATHING
IMBECILE
IMBECILES
IMBECILIC
IMBED
IMBEDDED
IMBEDDING
IMBEDS
IMBIBE
IMBIBED
IMBIBER
IMBIBERS
IMBIBES
IMBIBING
IMBITTER
IMBITTERS
IMBIZO
IMBIZOS
IMBLAZE
IMBLAZED
IMBLAZES
IMBLAZING
IMBODIED
IMBODIES
IMBODY
IMBODYING
IMBOLDEN
IMBOLDENS
IMBORDER
IMBORDERS
IMBOSK
IMBOSKED
IMBOSKING
IMBOSKS
IMBOSOM
IMBOSOMED
IMBOSOMS
IMBOSS
IMBOSSED
IMBOSSES
IMBOSSING
IMBOWER
IMBOWERED
IMBOWERS
IMBRANGLE
IMBRAST
IMBREX
IMBRICATE
IMBRICES
IMBROGLIO
IMBROWN
IMBROWNED
IMBROWNS
IMBRUE
IMBRUED
IMBRUES
IMBRUING
IMBRUTE
IMBRUTED
IMBRUTES
IMBRUTING
IMBUE
IMBUED
IMBUEMENT
IMBUES
IMBUING
IMBURSE
IMBURSED
IMBURSES
IMBURSING
IMID
IMIDAZOLE
IMIDE
IMIDES
IMIDIC
IMIDO
IMIDS
IMINAZOLE
IMINE
IMINES
IMINO
IMINOUREA
IMIPENEM
IMIPENEMS
IMITABLE
IMITANCY
IMITANT
IMITANTS
IMITATE
IMITATED
IMITATES
IMITATING
IMITATION
IMITATIVE
IMITATOR
IMITATORS
IMMANACLE
IMMANE
IMMANELY
IMMANENCE
IMMANENCY
IMMANENT
IMMANITY
IMMANTLE
IMMANTLED
IMMANTLES
IMMASK
IMMASKED
IMMASKING
IMMASKS
IMMATURE
IMMATURER
IMMATURES
IMMEDIACY
IMMEDIATE
IMMENSE
IMMENSELY
IMMENSER
IMMENSEST
IMMENSITY
IMMERGE
IMMERGED
IMMERGES
IMMERGING
IMMERSE
IMMERSED
IMMERSER
IMMERSERS
IMMERSES
IMMERSING
IMMERSION
IMMERSIVE
IMMESH
IMMESHED
IMMESHES
IMMESHING
IMMEW
IMMEWED
IMMEWING
IMMEWS
IMMIES
IMMIGRANT
IMMIGRATE
IMMINENCE
IMMINENCY
IMMINENT
IMMINGLE
IMMINGLED
IMMINGLES
IMMINUTE
IMMISSION
IMMIT
IMMITS
IMMITTED
IMMITTING
IMMIX
IMMIXED
IMMIXES
IMMIXING
IMMIXTURE
IMMOBILE
IMMODEST

IMMODESTY
IMMOLATE
IMMOLATED
IMMOLATES
IMMOLATOR
IMMOMENT
IMMORAL
IMMORALLY
IMMORTAL
IMMORTALS
IMMOTILE
IMMOVABLE
IMMOVABLY
IMMUNE
IMMUNER
IMMUNES
IMMUNEST
IMMUNISE
IMMUNISED
IMMUNISER
IMMUNISES
IMMUNITY
IMMUNIZE
IMMUNIZED
IMMUNIZER
IMMUNIZES
IMMUNOGEN
IMMURE
IMMURED
IMMURES
IMMURING
IMMUTABLE
IMMUTABLY
IMMY
IMP
IMPACABLE
IMPACT
IMPACTED
IMPACTER
IMPACTERS
IMPACTFUL
IMPACTING
IMPACTION
IMPACTITE
IMPACTIVE
IMPACTOR
IMPACTORS
IMPACTS
IMPAINT
IMPAINTED
IMPAINTS
IMPAIR
IMPAIRED
IMPAIRER
IMPAIRERS
IMPAIRING
IMPAIRS
IMPALA
IMPALAS
IMPALE
IMPALED
IMPALER
IMPALERS
IMPALES
IMPALING
IMPANATE
IMPANEL
IMPANELED
IMPANELS
IMPANNEL
IMPANNELS
IMPARITY
IMPARK
IMPARKED
IMPARKING
IMPARKS
IMPARL
IMPARLED
IMPARLING
IMPARLS
IMPART
IMPARTED
IMPARTER
IMPARTERS
IMPARTIAL
IMPARTING
IMPARTS
IMPASSE
IMPASSES
IMPASSION
IMPASSIVE
IMPASTE
IMPASTED
IMPASTES
IMPASTING
IMPASTO
IMPASTOED
IMPASTOS
IMPATIENS
IMPATIENT
IMPAVE
IMPAVED
IMPAVES
IMPAVID
IMPAVIDLY
IMPAVING
IMPAWN
IMPAWNED
IMPAWNING
IMPAWNS
IMPEACH
IMPEACHED
IMPEACHER
IMPEACHES
IMPEARL
IMPEARLED
IMPEARLS
IMPECCANT
IMPED
IMPEDANCE
IMPEDE
IMPEDED
IMPEDER
IMPEDERS
IMPEDES
IMPEDING
IMPEDOR
IMPEDORS
IMPEL
IMPELLED
IMPELLENT
IMPELLER
IMPELLERS
IMPELLING
IMPELLOR
IMPELLORS
IMPELS
IMPEND
IMPENDED
IMPENDENT
IMPENDING
IMPENDS
IMPENNATE
IMPERATOR
IMPERFECT
IMPERIA
IMPERIAL
IMPERIALS
IMPERIL
IMPERILED
IMPERILS
IMPERIOUS
IMPERIUM
IMPERIUMS
IMPETICOS
IMPETIGO
IMPETIGOS
IMPETRATE
IMPETUOUS
IMPETUS
IMPETUSES
IMPHEE
IMPHEES
IMPI
IMPIES
IMPIETIES
IMPIETY
IMPING
IMPINGE
IMPINGED
IMPINGENT
IMPINGER
IMPINGERS
IMPINGES
IMPINGING
IMPINGS
IMPIOUS
IMPIOUSLY
IMPIS
IMPISH
IMPISHLY
IMPLANT
IMPLANTED
IMPLANTER
IMPLANTS
IMPLATE
IMPLATED
IMPLATES
IMPLATING
IMPLEACH
IMPLEAD
IMPLEADED
IMPLEADER
IMPLEADS
IMPLED
IMPLEDGE
IMPLEDGED
IMPLEDGES
IMPLEMENT
IMPLETE
IMPLETED
IMPLETES
IMPLETING
IMPLETION
IMPLEX
IMPLEXES
IMPLEXION
IMPLICATE
IMPLICIT
IMPLICITY
IMPLIED
IMPLIEDLY
IMPLIES
IMPLODE
IMPLODED
IMPLODENT
IMPLODES
IMPLODING
IMPLORE
IMPLORED
IMPLORER
IMPLORERS
IMPLORES
IMPLORING
IMPLOSION
IMPLOSIVE
IMPLUNGE
IMPLUNGED
IMPLUNGES
IMPLUVIA
IMPLUVIUM
IMPLY
IMPLYING
IMPOCKET
IMPOCKETS
IMPOLDER
IMPOLDERS
IMPOLICY
IMPOLITE
IMPOLITER

IMPOLITIC
IMPONE
IMPONED
IMPONENT
IMPONENTS
IMPONES
IMPONING
IMPOROUS
IMPORT
IMPORTANT
IMPORTED
IMPORTER
IMPORTERS
IMPORTING
IMPORTS
IMPORTUNE
IMPOSABLE
IMPOSE
IMPOSED
IMPOSER
IMPOSERS
IMPOSES
IMPOSEX
IMPOSEXES
IMPOSING
IMPOST
IMPOSTED
IMPOSTER
IMPOSTERS
IMPOSTING
IMPOSTOR
IMPOSTORS
IMPOSTS
IMPOSTUME
IMPOSTURE
IMPOT
IMPOTENCE
IMPOTENCY
IMPOTENT
IMPOTENTS
IMPOTS
IMPOUND
IMPOUNDED
IMPOUNDER
IMPOUNDS
IMPOWER
IMPOWERED
IMPOWERS
IMPRECATE
IMPRECISE
IMPREGN
IMPREGNED
IMPREGNS
IMPRESA
IMPRESARI
IMPRESAS
IMPRESE
IMPRESES
IMPRESS
IMPRESSE
IMPRESSED
IMPRESSER
IMPRESSES
IMPREST
IMPRESTS
IMPRIMIS
IMPRINT
IMPRINTED
IMPRINTER
IMPRINTS
IMPRISON
IMPRISONS
IMPRO
IMPROBITY
IMPROMPTU
IMPROPER
IMPROS
IMPROV
IMPROVE
IMPROVED
IMPROVER
IMPROVERS
IMPROVES
IMPROVING
IMPROVISE
IMPROVS
IMPRUDENT
IMPS
IMPSONITE
IMPUDENCE
IMPUDENCY
IMPUDENT
IMPUGN
IMPUGNED
IMPUGNER
IMPUGNERS
IMPUGNING
IMPUGNS
IMPULSE
IMPULSED
IMPULSES
IMPULSING
IMPULSION
IMPULSIVE
IMPUNDULU
IMPUNITY
IMPURE
IMPURELY
IMPURER
IMPUREST
IMPURITY
IMPURPLE
IMPURPLED
IMPURPLES
IMPUTABLE
IMPUTABLY
IMPUTE
IMPUTED
IMPUTER
IMPUTERS
IMPUTES
IMPUTING
IMSHI
IMSHY
IN
INABILITY
INACTION
INACTIONS
INACTIVE
INAIDABLE
INAMORATA
INAMORATI
INAMORATO
INANE
INANELY
INANENESS
INANER
INANES
INANEST
INANGA
INANGAS
INANIMATE
INANITIES
INANITION
INANITY
INAPT
INAPTER
INAPTEST
INAPTLY
INAPTNESS
INARABLE
INARCH
INARCHED
INARCHES
INARCHING
INARM
INARMED
INARMING
INARMS
INASMUCH
INAUDIBLE
INAUDIBLY
INAUGURAL
INAURATE
INAURATED
INAURATES
INBEING
INBEINGS
INBENT
INBOARD
INBOARDS
INBORN
INBOUND
INBOUNDED
INBOUNDS
INBOX
INBOXES
INBREAK
INBREAKS
INBREATHE
INBRED
INBREDS
INBREED
INBREEDER
INBREEDS
INBRING
INBRINGS
INBROUGHT
INBUILT
INBURNING
INBURST
INBURSTS
INBY
INBYE
INCAGE
INCAGED
INCAGES
INCAGING
INCANT
INCANTED
INCANTING
INCANTS
INCAPABLE
INCAPABLY
INCARNATE
INCASE
INCASED
INCASES
INCASING
INCAUTION
INCAVE
INCAVED
INCAVES
INCAVI
INCAVING
INCAVO
INCEDE
INCEDED
INCEDES
INCEDING
INCEL
INCELS
INCENSE
INCENSED
INCENSER
INCENSERS
INCENSES
INCENSING
INCENSOR
INCENSORS
INCENSORY
INCENT
INCENTED
INCENTER
INCENTERS
INCENTING
INCENTIVE
INCENTRE
INCENTRES
INCENTS

I

INCEPT
INCEPTED
INCEPTING
INCEPTION
INCEPTIVE
INCEPTOR
INCEPTORS
INCEPTS
INCERTAIN
INCESSANT
INCEST
INCESTS
INCH
INCHASE
INCHASED
INCHASES
INCHASING
INCHED
INCHER
INCHERS
INCHES
INCHING
INCHMEAL
INCHOATE
INCHOATED
INCHOATES
INCHPIN
INCHPINS
INCHTAPE
INCHTAPES
INCHWORM
INCHWORMS
INCIDENCE
INCIDENT
INCIDENTS
INCIPIENT
INCIPIT
INCIPITS
INCISAL
INCISE
INCISED
INCISES
INCISING
INCISION
INCISIONS
INCISIVE
INCISOR
INCISORS
INCISORY
INCISURAL
INCISURE
INCISURES
INCITABLE
INCITANT
INCITANTS
INCITE
INCITED
INCITER
INCITERS
INCITES
INCITING
INCIVIL
INCIVISM
INCIVISMS
INCLASP
INCLASPED
INCLASPS
INCLE
INCLEMENT
INCLES
INCLINE
INCLINED
INCLINER
INCLINERS
INCLINES
INCLINING
INCLIP
INCLIPPED
INCLIPS
INCLOSE
INCLOSED
INCLOSER
INCLOSERS
INCLOSES
INCLOSING
INCLOSURE
INCLUDE
INCLUDED
INCLUDES
INCLUDING
INCLUSION
INCLUSIVE
INCOG
INCOGNITA
INCOGNITO
INCOGS
INCOME
INCOMER
INCOMERS
INCOMES
INCOMING
INCOMINGS
INCOMMODE
INCOMPACT
INCONDITE
INCONIE
INCONNU
INCONNUE
INCONNUES
INCONNUS
INCONY
INCORPSE
INCORPSED
INCORPSES
INCORRECT
INCORRUPT
INCREASE
INCREASED
INCREASER
INCREASES
INCREATE
INCREMATE
INCREMENT
INCRETION
INCRETORY
INCROSS
INCROSSED
INCROSSES
INCRUST
INCRUSTED
INCRUSTS
INCUBATE
INCUBATED
INCUBATES
INCUBATOR
INCUBI
INCUBOUS
INCUBUS
INCUBUSES
INCUDAL
INCUDATE
INCUDES
INCULCATE
INCULPATE
INCULT
INCUMBENT
INCUMBER
INCUMBERS
INCUNABLE
INCUR
INCURABLE
INCURABLY
INCURIOUS
INCURRED
INCURRENT
INCURRING
INCURS
INCURSION
INCURSIVE
INCURVATE
INCURVE
INCURVED
INCURVES
INCURVING
INCURVITY
INCUS
INCUSE
INCUSED
INCUSES
INCUSING
INCUT
INCUTS
INDABA
INDABAS
INDAGATE
INDAGATED
INDAGATES
INDAGATOR
INDAMIN
INDAMINE
INDAMINES
INDAMINS
INDART
INDARTED
INDARTING
INDARTS
INDEBTED
INDECENCY
INDECENT
INDECORUM
INDEED
INDEEDY
INDELIBLE
INDELIBLY
INDEMNIFY
INDEMNITY
INDENE
INDENES
INDENT
INDENTED
INDENTER
INDENTERS
INDENTING
INDENTION
INDENTOR
INDENTORS
INDENTS
INDENTURE
INDEVOUT
INDEW
INDEWED
INDEWING
INDEWS
INDEX
INDEXABLE
INDEXAL
INDEXED
INDEXER
INDEXERS
INDEXES
INDEXICAL
INDEXING
INDEXINGS
INDEXLESS
INDIA
INDIAS
INDICAN
INDICANS
INDICANT
INDICANTS
INDICATE
INDICATED
INDICATES
INDICATOR
INDICES
INDICIA
INDICIAL
INDICIAS
INDICIUM
INDICIUMS

INDICT
INDICTED
INDICTEE
INDICTEES
INDICTER
INDICTERS
INDICTING
INDICTION
INDICTOR
INDICTORS
INDICTS
INDIE
INDIES
INDIGEN
INDIGENCE
INDIGENCY
INDIGENE
INDIGENES
INDIGENS
INDIGENT
INDIGENTS
INDIGEST
INDIGESTS
INDIGN
INDIGNANT
INDIGNIFY
INDIGNITY
INDIGNLY
INDIGO
INDIGOES
INDIGOID
INDIGOIDS
INDIGOS
INDIGOTIC
INDIGOTIN
INDINAVIR
INDIRECT
INDIRUBIN
INDISPOSE
INDITE
INDITED
INDITER
INDITERS
INDITES
INDITING
INDIUM
INDIUMS
INDIVIDUA
INDOCIBLE
INDOCILE
INDOL
INDOLE
INDOLENCE
INDOLENCY
INDOLENT
INDOLES
INDOLS
INDOOR
INDOORS
INDORSE
INDORSED
INDORSEE
INDORSEES
INDORSER
INDORSERS
INDORSES
INDORSING
INDORSOR
INDORSORS
INDOW
INDOWED
INDOWING
INDOWS
INDOXYL
INDOXYLS
INDRAFT
INDRAFTS
INDRAUGHT
INDRAWN
INDRENCH
INDRI
INDRIS
INDRISES
INDUBIOUS
INDUCE
INDUCED
INDUCER
INDUCERS
INDUCES
INDUCIAE
INDUCIBLE
INDUCING
INDUCT
INDUCTED
INDUCTEE
INDUCTEES
INDUCTILE
INDUCTING
INDUCTION
INDUCTIVE
INDUCTOR
INDUCTORS
INDUCTS
INDUE
INDUED
INDUES
INDUING
INDULGE
INDULGED
INDULGENT
INDULGER
INDULGERS
INDULGES
INDULGING
INDULIN
INDULINE
INDULINES
INDULINS
INDULT
INDULTS
INDUMENTA
INDUNA
INDUNAS
INDURATE
INDURATED
INDURATES
INDUSIA
INDUSIAL
INDUSIATE
INDUSIUM
INDUSTRY
INDUVIAE
INDUVIAL
INDUVIATE
INDWELL
INDWELLER
INDWELLS
INDWELT
INDYREF
INDYREFS
INEARTH
INEARTHED
INEARTHS
INEBRIANT
INEBRIATE
INEBRIETY
INEBRIOUS
INEDIBLE
INEDIBLY
INEDITA
INEDITED
INEFFABLE
INEFFABLY
INELASTIC
INELEGANT
INEPT
INEPTER
INEPTEST
INEPTLY
INEPTNESS
INEQUABLE
INEQUITY
INERM
INERMOUS
INERRABLE
INERRABLY
INERRANCY
INERRANT
INERT
INERTER
INERTEST
INERTIA
INERTIAE
INERTIAL
INERTIAS
INERTLY
INERTNESS
INERTS
INERUDITE
INESSIVE
INESSIVES
INEXACT
INEXACTLY
INEXPERT
INEXPERTS
INFALL
INFALLING
INFALLS
INFAME
INFAMED
INFAMES
INFAMIES
INFAMING
INFAMISE
INFAMISED
INFAMISES
INFAMIZE
INFAMIZED
INFAMIZES
INFAMOUS
INFAMY
INFANCIES
INFANCY
INFANT
INFANTA
INFANTAS
INFANTE
INFANTEER
INFANTES
INFANTILE
INFANTINE
INFANTRY
INFANTS
INFARCT
INFARCTED
INFARCTS
INFARE
INFARES
INFATUATE
INFAUNA
INFAUNAE
INFAUNAL
INFAUNAS
INFAUST
INFECT
INFECTANT
INFECTED
INFECTER
INFECTERS
INFECTING
INFECTION
INFECTIVE
INFECTOR
INFECTORS
INFECTS
INFECUND
INFEED
INFEEDS
INFEFT
INFEFTED

INFEFTING
INFEFTS
INFELT
INFEOFF
INFEOFFED
INFEOFFS
INFER
INFERABLE
INFERABLY
INFERE
INFERENCE
INFERIAE
INFERIBLE
INFERIOR
INFERIORS
INFERNAL
INFERNO
INFERNOS
INFERRED
INFERRER
INFERRERS
INFERRING
INFERS
INFERTILE
INFEST
INFESTANT
INFESTED
INFESTER
INFESTERS
INFESTING
INFESTS
INFICETE
INFIDEL
INFIDELIC
INFIDELS
INFIELD
INFIELDER
INFIELDS
INFIGHT
INFIGHTER
INFIGHTS
INFILL
INFILLED
INFILLING
INFILLS
INFIMA
INFIMUM
INFIMUMS
INFINITE
INFINITES
INFINITY
INFIRM
INFIRMARY
INFIRMED
INFIRMER
INFIRMEST
INFIRMING
INFIRMITY
INFIRMLY
INFIRMS
INFIX
INFIXED
INFIXES
INFIXING
INFIXION
INFIXIONS
INFLAME
INFLAMED
INFLAMER
INFLAMERS
INFLAMES
INFLAMING
INFLATE
INFLATED
INFLATER
INFLATERS
INFLATES
INFLATING
INFLATION
INFLATIVE
INFLATOR
INFLATORS
INFLATUS
INFLECT
INFLECTED
INFLECTOR
INFLECTS
INFLEXED
INFLEXION
INFLEXURE
INFLICT
INFLICTED
INFLICTER
INFLICTOR
INFLICTS
INFLIGHT
INFLOW
INFLOWING
INFLOWS
INFLUENCE
INFLUENT
INFLUENTS
INFLUENZA
INFLUX
INFLUXES
INFLUXION
INFO
INFOBAHN
INFOBAHNS
INFOLD
INFOLDED
INFOLDER
INFOLDERS
INFOLDING
INFOLDS
INFOMANIA
INFORCE
INFORCED
INFORCES
INFORCING
INFORM
INFORMAL
INFORMANT
INFORMED
INFORMER
INFORMERS
INFORMING
INFORMS
INFORTUNE
INFOS
INFOTECH
INFOTECHS
INFOUGHT
INFRA
INFRACT
INFRACTED
INFRACTOR
INFRACTS
INFRARED
INFRAREDS
INFRINGE
INFRINGED
INFRINGER
INFRINGES
INFRUGAL
INFULA
INFULAE
INFURIATE
INFUSCATE
INFUSE
INFUSED
INFUSER
INFUSERS
INFUSES
INFUSIBLE
INFUSING
INFUSION
INFUSIONS
INFUSIVE
INFUSORIA
INFUSORY
ING
INGAN
INGANS
INGATE
INGATES
INGATHER
INGATHERS
INGENER
INGENERS
INGENIOUS
INGENIUM
INGENIUMS
INGENU
INGENUE
INGENUES
INGENUITY
INGENUOUS
INGENUS
INGEST
INGESTA
INGESTED
INGESTING
INGESTION
INGESTIVE
INGESTS
INGINE
INGINES
INGLE
INGLENEUK
INGLENOOK
INGLES
INGLOBE
INGLOBED
INGLOBES
INGLOBING
INGLUVIAL
INGLUVIES
INGO
INGOES
INGOING
INGOINGS
INGOT
INGOTED
INGOTING
INGOTS
INGRAFT
INGRAFTED
INGRAFTS
INGRAIN
INGRAINED
INGRAINER
INGRAINS
INGRAM
INGRAMS
INGRATE
INGRATELY
INGRATES
INGRESS
INGRESSES
INGROOVE
INGROOVED
INGROOVES
INGROSS
INGROSSED
INGROSSES
INGROUND
INGROUNDS
INGROUP
INGROUPS
INGROWING
INGROWN
INGROWTH
INGROWTHS
INGRUM
INGRUMS
INGS
INGUINAL
INGULF
INGULFED

INGULFING
INGULFS
INGULPH
INGULPHED
INGULPHS
INHABIT
INHABITED
INHABITER
INHABITOR
INHABITS
INHALABLE
INHALANT
INHALANTS
INHALATOR
INHALE
INHALED
INHALER
INHALERS
INHALES
INHALING
INHARMONY
INHAUL
INHAULER
INHAULERS
INHAULS
INHAUST
INHAUSTED
INHAUSTS
INHEARSE
INHEARSED
INHEARSES
INHERCE
INHERCED
INHERCES
INHERCING
INHERE
INHERED
INHERENCE
INHERENCY
INHERENT
INHERES
INHERING
INHERIT
INHERITED
INHERITOR
INHERITS
INHESION
INHESIONS
INHIBIN
INHIBINS
INHIBIT
INHIBITED
INHIBITER
INHIBITOR
INHIBITS
INHOLDER
INHOLDERS
INHOLDING
INHOOP
INHOOPED
INHOOPING
INHOOPS
INHUMAN
INHUMANE
INHUMANER
INHUMANLY
INHUMATE
INHUMATED
INHUMATES
INHUME
INHUMED
INHUMER
INHUMERS
INHUMES
INHUMING
INIA
INIMICAL
INION
INIONS
INIQUITY
INISLE
INISLED
INISLES
INISLING
INITIAL
INITIALED
INITIALER
INITIALLY
INITIALS
INITIATE
INITIATED
INITIATES
INITIATOR
INJECT
INJECTANT
INJECTED
INJECTING
INJECTION
INJECTIVE
INJECTOR
INJECTORS
INJECTS
INJELLIED
INJELLIES
INJELLY
INJERA
INJERAS
INJOINT
INJOINTED
INJOINTS
INJUNCT
INJUNCTED
INJUNCTS
INJURABLE
INJURE
INJURED
INJURER
INJURERS
INJURES
INJURIES
INJURING
INJURIOUS
INJURY
INJUSTICE
INK
INKBERRY
INKBLOT
INKBLOTS
INKED
INKER
INKERS
INKHOLDER
INKHORN
INKHORNS
INKHOSI
INKHOSIS
INKIER
INKIEST
INKINESS
INKING
INKJET
INKJETS
INKLE
INKLED
INKLES
INKLESS
INKLIKE
INKLING
INKLINGS
INKOSI
INKOSIS
INKPAD
INKPADS
INKPOT
INKPOTS
INKS
INKSPOT
INKSPOTS
INKSTAIN
INKSTAINS
INKSTAND
INKSTANDS
INKSTONE
INKSTONES
INKWELL
INKWELLS
INKWOOD
INKWOODS
INKY
INLACE
INLACED
INLACES
INLACING
INLAID
INLAND
INLANDER
INLANDERS
INLANDS
INLAY
INLAYER
INLAYERS
INLAYING
INLAYINGS
INLAYS
INLET
INLETS
INLETTING
INLIER
INLIERS
INLOCK
INLOCKED
INLOCKING
INLOCKS
INLY
INLYING
INMATE
INMATES
INMESH
INMESHED
INMESHES
INMESHING
INMIGRANT
INMOST
INN
INNAGE
INNAGES
INNARDS
INNATE
INNATELY
INNATIVE
INNED
INNER
INNERLY
INNERMOST
INNERNESS
INNERS
INNERSOLE
INNERVATE
INNERVE
INNERVED
INNERVES
INNERVING
INNERWEAR
INNING
INNINGS
INNINGSES
INNIT
INNKEEPER
INNLESS
INNOCENCE
INNOCENCY
INNOCENT
INNOCENTS
INNOCUITY
INNOCUOUS
INNOVATE
INNOVATED
INNOVATES
INNOVATOR
INNOXIOUS

INNS
INNUENDO
INNUENDOS
INNYARD
INNYARDS
INOCULA
INOCULANT
INOCULATE
INOCULUM
INOCULUMS
INODOROUS
INOPINATE
INORB
INORBED
INORBING
INORBS
INORGANIC
INORNATE
INOSINE
INOSINES
INOSITE
INOSITES
INOSITOL
INOSITOLS
INOTROPE
INOTROPES
INOTROPIC
INPATIENT
INPAYMENT
INPHASE
INPOUR
INPOURED
INPOURING
INPOURS
INPUT
INPUTS
INPUTTED
INPUTTER
INPUTTERS
INPUTTING
INQILAB
INQILABS
INQUERE
INQUERED
INQUERES
INQUERING
INQUEST
INQUESTS
INQUIET
INQUIETED
INQUIETLY
INQUIETS
INQUILINE
INQUINATE
INQUIRE
INQUIRED
INQUIRER
INQUIRERS
INQUIRES
INQUIRIES
INQUIRING
INQUIRY
INQUORATE
INRO
INROAD
INROADS
INRUN
INRUNS
INRUSH
INRUSHES
INRUSHING
INS
INSANE
INSANELY
INSANER
INSANEST
INSANIE
INSANIES
INSANITY
INSATIATE
INSATIETY
INSCAPE
INSCAPES
INSCIENCE
INSCIENT
INSCONCE
INSCONCED
INSCONCES
INSCRIBE
INSCRIBED
INSCRIBER
INSCRIBES
INSCROLL
INSCROLLS
INSCULP
INSCULPED
INSCULPS
INSCULPT
INSEAM
INSEAMED
INSEAMING
INSEAMS
INSECT
INSECTAN
INSECTARY
INSECTEAN
INSECTILE
INSECTION
INSECTS
INSECURE
INSECURER
INSEEM
INSEEMED
INSEEMING
INSEEMS
INSELBERG
INSENSATE
INSERT
INSERTED
INSERTER
INSERTERS
INSERTING
INSERTION
INSERTS
INSET
INSETS
INSETTED
INSETTER
INSETTERS
INSETTING
INSHALLAH
INSHEATH
INSHEATHE
INSHEATHS
INSHELL
INSHELLED
INSHELLS
INSHELTER
INSHIP
INSHIPPED
INSHIPS
INSHORE
INSHRINE
INSHRINED
INSHRINES
INSIDE
INSIDER
INSIDERS
INSIDES
INSIDIOUS
INSIGHT
INSIGHTS
INSIGNE
INSIGNIA
INSIGNIAS
INSINCERE
INSINEW
INSINEWED
INSINEWS
INSINUATE
INSIPID
INSIPIDER
INSIPIDLY
INSIPIENT
INSIST
INSISTED
INSISTENT
INSISTER
INSISTERS
INSISTING
INSISTS
INSNARE
INSNARED
INSNARER
INSNARERS
INSNARES
INSNARING
INSOFAR
INSOLATE
INSOLATED
INSOLATES
INSOLE
INSOLENCE
INSOLENT
INSOLENTS
INSOLES
INSOLUBLE
INSOLUBLY
INSOLVENT
INSOMNIA
INSOMNIAC
INSOMNIAS
INSOMUCH
INSOOTH
INSOUL
INSOULED
INSOULING
INSOULS
INSOURCE
INSOURCED
INSOURCES
INSPAN
INSPANNED
INSPANS
INSPECT
INSPECTED
INSPECTOR
INSPECTS
INSPHERE
INSPHERED
INSPHERES
INSPIRE
INSPIRED
INSPIRER
INSPIRERS
INSPIRES
INSPIRING
INSPIRIT
INSPIRITS
INSPO
INSPOS
INSTABLE
INSTAGRAM
INSTAL
INSTALL
INSTALLED
INSTALLER
INSTALLS
INSTALS
INSTANCE
INSTANCED
INSTANCES
INSTANCY
INSTANT
INSTANTER
INSTANTLY
INSTANTS
INSTAR
INSTARRED
INSTARS

INSTATE
INSTATED
INSTATES
INSTATING
INSTEAD
INSTEP
INSTEPS
INSTIGATE
INSTIL
INSTILL
INSTILLED
INSTILLER
INSTILLS
INSTILS
INSTINCT
INSTINCTS
INSTITUTE
INSTRESS
INSTROKE
INSTROKES
INSTRUCT
INSTRUCTS
INSUCKEN
INSULA
INSULAE
INSULANT
INSULANTS
INSULAR
INSULARLY
INSULARS
INSULATE
INSULATED
INSULATES
INSULATOR
INSULIN
INSULINS
INSULSE
INSULSITY
INSULT
INSULTANT
INSULTED
INSULTER
INSULTERS
INSULTING
INSULTS
INSURABLE
INSURANCE
INSURANT
INSURANTS
INSURE
INSURED
INSUREDS
INSURER
INSURERS
INSURES
INSURGENT
INSURING
INSWATHE
INSWATHED
INSWATHES
INSWEPT
INSWING
INSWINGER
INSWINGS
INTACT
INTACTLY
INTAGLI
INTAGLIO
INTAGLIOS
INTAKE
INTAKES
INTARSIA
INTARSIAS
INTEGER
INTEGERS
INTEGRAL
INTEGRALS
INTEGRAND
INTEGRANT
INTEGRATE
INTEGRIN
INTEGRINS
INTEGRITY
INTEL
INTELLECT
INTELS
INTENABLE
INTEND
INTENDANT
INTENDED
INTENDEDS
INTENDER
INTENDERS
INTENDING
INTENDS
INTENIBLE
INTENSATE
INTENSE
INTENSELY
INTENSER
INTENSEST
INTENSIFY
INTENSION
INTENSITY
INTENSIVE
INTENT
INTENTION
INTENTIVE
INTENTLY
INTENTS
INTER
INTERACT
INTERACTS
INTERAGE
INTERARCH
INTERBANK
INTERBED
INTERBEDS
INTERBRED
INTERCEDE
INTERCELL
INTERCEPT
INTERCITY
INTERCLAN
INTERCLUB
INTERCOM
INTERCOMS
INTERCOOL
INTERCROP
INTERCUT
INTERCUTS
INTERDASH
INTERDEAL
INTERDICT
INTERDINE
INTERESS
INTERESSE
INTEREST
INTERESTS
INTERFACE
INTERFERE
INTERFILE
INTERFIRM
INTERFLOW
INTERFOLD
INTERFUSE
INTERGANG
INTERGREW
INTERGROW
INTERIM
INTERIMS
INTERIOR
INTERIORS
INTERJECT
INTERJOIN
INTERKNIT
INTERKNOT
INTERLACE
INTERLAID
INTERLAP
INTERLAPS
INTERLARD
INTERLAY
INTERLAYS
INTERLEAF
INTERLEND
INTERLENT
INTERLINE
INTERLINK
INTERLOAN
INTERLOCK
INTERLOOP
INTERLOPE
INTERLUDE
INTERMALE
INTERMAT
INTERMATS
INTERMENT
INTERMESH
INTERMIT
INTERMITS
INTERMIX
INTERMONT
INTERMURE
INTERN
INTERNAL
INTERNALS
INTERNE
INTERNED
INTERNEE
INTERNEES
INTERNES
INTERNET
INTERNETS
INTERNING
INTERNIST
INTERNODE
INTERNS
INTERPAGE
INTERPLAY
INTERPLED
INTERPONE
INTERPOSE
INTERPRET
INTERRACE
INTERRAIL
INTERRED
INTERREX
INTERRING
INTERROW
INTERRUPT
INTERS
INTERSECT
INTERSERT
INTERSEX
INTERTERM
INTERTEXT
INTERTIE
INTERTIES
INTERTILL
INTERUNIT
INTERVAL
INTERVALE
INTERVALS
INTERVEIN
INTERVENE
INTERVIEW
INTERWAR
INTERWEB
INTERWEBS
INTERWIND
INTERWORD
INTERWORK
INTERWOVE
INTERZONE
INTESTACY
INTESTATE
INTESTINE
INTHRAL
INTHRALL

INTHRALLS
INTHRALS
INTHRONE
INTHRONED
INTHRONES
INTI
INTIFADA
INTIFADAH
INTIFADAS
INTIFADEH
INTIL
INTIMA
INTIMACY
INTIMAE
INTIMAL
INTIMAS
INTIMATE
INTIMATED
INTIMATER
INTIMATES
INTIME
INTIMISM
INTIMISMS
INTIMIST
INTIMISTE
INTIMISTS
INTIMITY
INTINE
INTINES
INTIRE
INTIS
INTITLE
INTITLED
INTITLES
INTITLING
INTITULE
INTITULED
INTITULES
INTO
INTOED
INTOMB
INTOMBED
INTOMBING
INTOMBS
INTONACO
INTONACOS
INTONATE
INTONATED
INTONATES
INTONATOR
INTONE
INTONED
INTONER
INTONERS
INTONES
INTONING
INTONINGS
INTORSION
INTORT
INTORTED
INTORTING
INTORTION
INTORTS
INTOWN
INTRA
INTRACITY
INTRADA
INTRADAS
INTRADAY
INTRADOS
INTRANET
INTRANETS
INTRANT
INTRANTS
INTREAT
INTREATED
INTREATS
INTRENCH
INTREPID
INTRICACY
INTRICATE
INTRIGANT
INTRIGUE
INTRIGUED
INTRIGUER
INTRIGUES
INTRINCE
INTRINSIC
INTRO
INTRODUCE
INTROFIED
INTROFIES
INTROFY
INTROIT
INTROITAL
INTROITS
INTROITUS
INTROJECT
INTROLD
INTROMIT
INTROMITS
INTRON
INTRONIC
INTRONS
INTRORSE
INTROS
INTROVERT
INTRUDE
INTRUDED
INTRUDER
INTRUDERS
INTRUDES
INTRUDING
INTRUSION
INTRUSIVE
INTRUST
INTRUSTED
INTRUSTS
INTUBATE
INTUBATED
INTUBATES
INTUIT
INTUITED
INTUITING
INTUITION
INTUITIVE
INTUITS
INTUMESCE
INTURN
INTURNED
INTURNS
INTUSE
INTUSES
INTWINE
INTWINED
INTWINES
INTWINING
INTWIST
INTWISTED
INTWISTS
INUKSHUIT
INUKSHUK
INUKSHUKS
INUKSUIT
INUKSUK
INUKSUKS
INULA
INULAS
INULASE
INULASES
INULIN
INULINS
INUMBRATE
INUNCTION
INUNDANT
INUNDATE
INUNDATED
INUNDATES
INUNDATOR
INURBANE
INURE
INURED
INUREMENT
INURES
INURING
INURN
INURNED
INURNING
INURNMENT
INURNS
INUSITATE
INUST
INUSTION
INUSTIONS
INUTILE
INUTILELY
INUTILITY
INVADABLE
INVADE
INVADED
INVADER
INVADERS
INVADES
INVADING
INVALID
INVALIDED
INVALIDER
INVALIDLY
INVALIDS
INVAR
INVARIANT
INVARS
INVASION
INVASIONS
INVASIVE
INVEAGLE
INVEAGLED
INVEAGLES
INVECKED
INVECTED
INVECTIVE
INVEIGH
INVEIGHED
INVEIGHER
INVEIGHS
INVEIGLE
INVEIGLED
INVEIGLER
INVEIGLES
INVENIT
INVENT
INVENTED
INVENTER
INVENTERS
INVENTING
INVENTION
INVENTIVE
INVENTOR
INVENTORS
INVENTORY
INVENTS
INVERITY
INVERNESS
INVERSE
INVERSED
INVERSELY
INVERSES
INVERSING
INVERSION
INVERSIVE
INVERT
INVERTASE
INVERTED
INVERTER
INVERTERS
INVERTIN
INVERTING
INVERTINS
INVERTOR
INVERTORS

INVERTS
INVEST
INVESTED
INVESTING
INVESTOR
INVESTORS
INVESTS
INVEXED
INVIABLE
INVIABLY
INVIDIOUS
INVIOLACY
INVIOLATE
INVIOUS
INVIRILE
INVISCID
INVISIBLE
INVISIBLY
INVITAL
INVITE
INVITED
INVITEE
INVITEES
INVITER
INVITERS
INVITES
INVITING
INVITINGS
INVOCABLE
INVOCATE
INVOCATED
INVOCATES
INVOCATOR
INVOICE
INVOICED
INVOICES
INVOICING
INVOKE
INVOKED
INVOKER
INVOKERS
INVOKES
INVOKING
INVOLUCEL
INVOLUCRA
INVOLUCRE
INVOLUTE
INVOLUTED
INVOLUTES
INVOLVE
INVOLVED
INVOLVER
INVOLVERS
INVOLVES
INVOLVING
INWALL
INWALLED
INWALLING
INWALLS
INWARD
INWARDLY
INWARDS
INWEAVE
INWEAVED
INWEAVES
INWEAVING
INWICK
INWICKED
INWICKING
INWICKS
INWIND
INWINDING
INWINDS
INWIT
INWITH
INWITS
INWORK
INWORKED
INWORKING
INWORKS
INWORN
INWOUND
INWOVE
INWOVEN
INWRAP
INWRAPPED
INWRAPS
INWRAPT
INWREATHE
INWROUGHT
INYALA
INYALAS
IO
IODATE
IODATED
IODATES
IODATING
IODATION
IODATIONS
IODIC
IODID
IODIDE
IODIDES
IODIDS
IODIN
IODINATE
IODINATED
IODINATES
IODINE
IODINES
IODINS
IODISE
IODISED
IODISER
IODISERS
IODISES
IODISING
IODISM
IODISMS
IODIZE
IODIZED
IODIZER
IODIZERS
IODIZES
IODIZING
IODOFORM
IODOFORMS
IODOMETRY
IODOPHILE
IODOPHOR
IODOPHORS
IODOPSIN
IODOPSINS
IODOUS
IODURET
IODURETS
IODYRITE
IODYRITES
IOLITE
IOLITES
ION
IONIC
IONICALLY
IONICITY
IONICS
IONISABLE
IONISE
IONISED
IONISER
IONISERS
IONISES
IONISING
IONIUM
IONIUMS
IONIZABLE
IONIZE
IONIZED
IONIZER
IONIZERS
IONIZES
IONIZING
IONOGEN
IONOGENIC
IONOGENS
IONOMER
IONOMERS
IONONE
IONONES
IONOPAUSE
IONOPHORE
IONOSONDE
IONOTROPY
IONS
IOPANOIC
IOS
IOTA
IOTACISM
IOTACISMS
IOTAS
IPECAC
IPECACS
IPOMOEA
IPOMOEAS
IPPON
IPPONS
IPRINDOLE
IRACUND
IRADE
IRADES
IRASCIBLE
IRASCIBLY
IRATE
IRATELY
IRATENESS
IRATER
IRATEST
IRE
IRED
IREFUL
IREFULLY
IRELESS
IRENIC
IRENICAL
IRENICISM
IRENICON
IRENICONS
IRENICS
IRENOLOGY
IRES
IRID
IRIDAL
IRIDEAL
IRIDES
IRIDIAL
IRIDIAN
IRIDIC
IRIDISE
IRIDISED
IRIDISES
IRIDISING
IRIDIUM
IRIDIUMS
IRIDIZE
IRIDIZED
IRIDIZES
IRIDIZING
IRIDOCYTE
IRIDOLOGY
IRIDOTOMY
IRIDS
IRING
IRIS
IRISATE
IRISATED
IRISATES
IRISATING
IRISATION
IRISCOPE
IRISCOPES
IRISED

IRISES
IRISING
IRITIC
IRITIS
IRITISES
IRK
IRKED
IRKING
IRKS
IRKSOME
IRKSOMELY
IROKO
IROKOS
IRON
IRONBARK
IRONBARKS
IRONBOUND
IRONCLAD
IRONCLADS
IRONE
IRONED
IRONER
IRONERS
IRONES
IRONIC
IRONICAL
IRONIER
IRONIES
IRONIEST
IRONING
IRONINGS
IRONISE
IRONISED
IRONISES
IRONISING
IRONIST
IRONISTS
IRONIZE
IRONIZED
IRONIZES
IRONIZING
IRONLESS
IRONLIKE
IRONMAN
IRONMEN
IRONNESS
IRONS
IRONSIDE
IRONSIDES
IRONSMITH
IRONSTONE
IRONWARE
IRONWARES
IRONWEED
IRONWEEDS
IRONWOMAN
IRONWOMEN
IRONWOOD
IRONWOODS
IRONWORK
IRONWORKS
IRONY
IRRADIANT
IRRADIATE
IRREAL
IRREALITY
IRREDENTA
IRREGULAR
IRRELATED
IRRIDENTA
IRRIGABLE
IRRIGABLY
IRRIGATE
IRRIGATED
IRRIGATES
IRRIGATOR
IRRIGUOUS
IRRISION
IRRISIONS
IRRISORY
IRRITABLE
IRRITABLY
IRRITANCY
IRRITANT
IRRITANTS
IRRITATE
IRRITATED
IRRITATES
IRRITATOR
IRRUPT
IRRUPTED
IRRUPTING
IRRUPTION
IRRUPTIVE
IRRUPTS
IRUKANDJI
IS
ISABEL
ISABELLA
ISABELLAS
ISABELS
ISAGOGE
ISAGOGES
ISAGOGIC
ISAGOGICS
ISALLOBAR
ISARITHM
ISARITHMS
ISATIN
ISATINE
ISATINES
ISATINIC
ISATINS
ISBA
ISBAS
ISCHAEMIA
ISCHAEMIC
ISCHEMIA
ISCHEMIAS
ISCHEMIC
ISCHIA
ISCHIADIC
ISCHIAL
ISCHIATIC
ISCHIUM
ISCHURIA
ISCHURIAS
ISEIKONIA
ISEIKONIC
ISENERGIC
ISH
ISHES
ISINGLASS
ISIT
ISLAND
ISLANDED
ISLANDER
ISLANDERS
ISLANDING
ISLANDS
ISLE
ISLED
ISLELESS
ISLEMAN
ISLEMEN
ISLES
ISLESMAN
ISLESMEN
ISLET
ISLETED
ISLETS
ISLING
ISLOMANIA
ISM
ISMATIC
ISMATICAL
ISMS
ISNA
ISNAE
ISO
ISOAMYL
ISOAMYLS
ISOBAR
ISOBARE
ISOBARES
ISOBARIC
ISOBARISM
ISOBARS
ISOBASE
ISOBASES
ISOBATH
ISOBATHIC
ISOBATHS
ISOBRONT
ISOBRONTS
ISOBUTANE
ISOBUTENE
ISOBUTYL
ISOBUTYLS
ISOCHASM
ISOCHASMS
ISOCHEIM
ISOCHEIMS
ISOCHIMAL
ISOCHIME
ISOCHIMES
ISOCHOR
ISOCHORE
ISOCHORES
ISOCHORIC
ISOCHORS
ISOCHRON
ISOCHRONE
ISOCHRONS
ISOCLINAL
ISOCLINE
ISOCLINES
ISOCLINIC
ISOCRACY
ISOCRATIC
ISOCRYMAL
ISOCRYME
ISOCRYMES
ISOCYANIC
ISOCYCLIC
ISODICA
ISODICON
ISODOMA
ISODOMON
ISODOMOUS
ISODOMUM
ISODONT
ISODONTAL
ISODONTS
ISODOSE
ISODOSES
ISOENZYME
ISOETES
ISOFORM
ISOFORMS
ISOGAMETE
ISOGAMIC
ISOGAMIES
ISOGAMOUS
ISOGAMY
ISOGENEIC
ISOGENIC
ISOGENIES
ISOGENOUS
ISOGENY
ISOGLOSS
ISOGON
ISOGONAL
ISOGONALS
ISOGONE
ISOGONES
ISOGONIC
ISOGONICS
ISOGONIES
ISOGONS

ISOGONY
ISOGRAFT
ISOGRAFTS
ISOGRAM
ISOGRAMS
ISOGRAPH
ISOGRAPHS
ISOGRIV
ISOGRIVS
ISOHEL
ISOHELS
ISOHYDRIC
ISOHYET
ISOHYETAL
ISOHYETS
ISOKONT
ISOKONTAN
ISOKONTS
ISOLABLE
ISOLATE
ISOLATED
ISOLATES
ISOLATING
ISOLATION
ISOLATIVE
ISOLATOR
ISOLATORS
ISOLEAD
ISOLEADS
ISOLEX
ISOLEXES
ISOLINE
ISOLINES
ISOLOG
ISOLOGOUS
ISOLOGS
ISOLOGUE
ISOLOGUES
ISOMER
ISOMERASE
ISOMERE
ISOMERES
ISOMERIC
ISOMERISE
ISOMERISM
ISOMERIZE
ISOMEROUS
ISOMERS
ISOMETRIC
ISOMETRY
ISOMORPH
ISOMORPHS
ISONIAZID
ISONOME
ISONOMES
ISONOMIC
ISONOMIES
ISONOMOUS
ISONOMY
ISOOCTANE
ISOPACH
ISOPACHS
ISOPHONE
ISOPHONES
ISOPHOTAL
ISOPHOTE
ISOPHOTES
ISOPLETH
ISOPLETHS
ISOPOD
ISOPODAN
ISOPODANS
ISOPODOUS
ISOPODS
ISOPOLITY
ISOPRENE
ISOPRENES
ISOPROPYL
ISOPTERAN
ISOPYCNAL
ISOPYCNIC
ISOS
ISOSCELES
ISOSMOTIC
ISOSPIN
ISOSPINS
ISOSPORY
ISOSTACY
ISOSTASY
ISOSTATIC
ISOSTERIC
ISOTACH
ISOTACHS
ISOTACTIC
ISOTHERAL
ISOTHERE
ISOTHERES
ISOTHERM
ISOTHERMS
ISOTONE
ISOTONES
ISOTONIC
ISOTOPE
ISOTOPES
ISOTOPIC
ISOTOPIES
ISOTOPY
ISOTRON
ISOTRONS
ISOTROPIC
ISOTROPY
ISOTYPE
ISOTYPES
ISOTYPIC
ISOZYME
ISOZYMES
ISOZYMIC
ISPAGHULA
ISSEI
ISSEIS
ISSUABLE
ISSUABLY
ISSUANCE
ISSUANCES
ISSUANT
ISSUE
ISSUED
ISSUELESS
ISSUER
ISSUERS
ISSUES
ISSUING
ISTANA
ISTANAS
ISTHMI
ISTHMIAN
ISTHMIANS
ISTHMIC
ISTHMOID
ISTHMUS
ISTHMUSES
ISTLE
ISTLES
IT
ITA
ITACISM
ITACISMS
ITACONIC
ITALIC
ITALICISE
ITALICIZE
ITALICS
ITAS
ITCH
ITCHED
ITCHES
ITCHIER
ITCHIEST
ITCHILY
ITCHINESS
ITCHING
ITCHINGS
ITCHWEED
ITCHWEEDS
ITCHY
ITEM
ITEMED
ITEMING
ITEMISE
ITEMISED
ITEMISER
ITEMISERS
ITEMISES
ITEMISING
ITEMIZE
ITEMIZED
ITEMIZER
ITEMIZERS
ITEMIZES
ITEMIZING
ITEMS
ITERANCE
ITERANCES
ITERANT
ITERATE
ITERATED
ITERATES
ITERATING
ITERATION
ITERATIVE
ITERUM
ITHER
ITINERACY
ITINERANT
ITINERARY
ITINERATE
ITS
ITSELF
IURE
IVIED
IVIES
IVORIED
IVORIER
IVORIES
IVORIEST
IVORIST
IVORISTS
IVORY
IVORYBILL
IVORYLIKE
IVORYWOOD
IVRESSE
IVRESSES
IVY
IVYLEAF
IVYLIKE
IWI
IWIS
IXIA
IXIAS
IXNAY
IXODIASES
IXODIASIS
IXODID
IXODIDS
IXORA
IXORAS
IXTLE
IXTLES
IZAR
IZARD
IZARDS
IZARS
IZVESTIA
IZVESTIAS
IZVESTIYA
IZZARD
IZZARDS
IZZAT
IZZATS

J

JA
JAAP
JAAPS
JAB
JABBED
JABBER
JABBERED
JABBERER
JABBERERS
JABBERING
JABBERS
JABBING
JABBINGLY
JABBLE
JABBLED
JABBLES
JABBLING
JABERS
JABIRU
JABIRUS
JABORANDI
JABOT
JABOTS
JABS
JACAL
JACALES
JACALS
JACAMAR
JACAMARS
JACANA
JACANAS
JACARANDA
JACARE
JACARES
JACCHUS
JACCHUSES
JACENT
JACINTH
JACINTHE
JACINTHES
JACINTHS
JACK
JACKAL
JACKALLED
JACKALOPE
JACKALS
JACKAROO
JACKAROOS
JACKASS
JACKASSES
JACKBOOT
JACKBOOTS
JACKDAW
JACKDAWS
JACKED
JACKEEN
JACKEENS
JACKER
JACKEROO
JACKEROOS
JACKERS
JACKET
JACKETED
JACKETING
JACKETS
JACKFISH
JACKFRUIT
JACKIES
JACKING
JACKINGS
JACKKNIFE
JACKLEG
JACKLEGS
JACKLIGHT
JACKLING
JACKLINGS
JACKMAN
JACKMEN
JACKPLANE
JACKPOT
JACKPOTS
JACKROLL
JACKROLLS
JACKS
JACKSCREW
JACKSHAFT
JACKSIE
JACKSIES
JACKSMELT
JACKSMITH
JACKSNIPE
JACKSTAFF
JACKSTAY
JACKSTAYS
JACKSTONE
JACKSTRAW
JACKSY
JACKY
JACOBIN
JACOBINS
JACOBUS
JACOBUSES
JACONET
JACONETS
JACQUARD
JACQUARDS
JACQUERIE
JACTATION
JACULATE
JACULATED
JACULATES
JACULATOR
JACUZZI
JACUZZIS
JADE
JADED
JADEDLY
JADEDNESS
JADEITE
JADEITES
JADELIKE
JADERIES
JADERY
JADES
JADING
JADISH
JADISHLY
JADITIC
JAEGER
JAEGERS
JAFA
JAFAS
JAFFA
JAFFAS
JAG
JAGA
JAGAED
JAGAING
JAGAS
JAGDWURST
JAGER
JAGERS
JAGG
JAGGARIES
JAGGARY
JAGGED
JAGGEDER
JAGGEDEST
JAGGEDLY
JAGGER
JAGGERIES
JAGGERS
JAGGERY
JAGGHERY
JAGGIER
JAGGIES
JAGGIEST
JAGGING
JAGGS
JAGGY
JAGHIR
JAGHIRDAR
JAGHIRE
JAGHIRES
JAGHIRS
JAGIR
JAGIRS
JAGLESS
JAGRA
JAGRAS
JAGS
JAGUAR
JAGUARS
JAI
JAIL
JAILABLE
JAILBAIT
JAILBAITS
JAILBIRD
JAILBIRDS
JAILBREAK
JAILBROKE
JAILED
JAILER
JAILERESS
JAILERS
JAILHOUSE
JAILING
JAILLESS
JAILOR
JAILORESS
JAILORS
JAILS
JAK
JAKE
JAKER
JAKES
JAKESES
JAKEST
JAKEY
JAKEYS
JAKFRUIT
JAKFRUITS
JAKS
JALABIB
JALAP
JALAPENO
JALAPENOS
JALAPIC
JALAPIN

JALAPINS
JALAPS
JALEBI
JALEBIS
JALFREZI
JALFREZIS
JALLEBI
JALLEBIS
JALOP
JALOPIES
JALOPPIES
JALOPPY
JALOPS
JALOPY
JALOUSE
JALOUSED
JALOUSES
JALOUSIE
JALOUSIED
JALOUSIES
JALOUSING
JAM
JAMAAT
JAMAATS
JAMADAR
JAMADARS
JAMB
JAMBALAYA
JAMBART
JAMBARTS
JAMBE
JAMBEAU
JAMBEAUS
JAMBEAUX
JAMBED
JAMBEE
JAMBEES
JAMBER
JAMBERS
JAMBES
JAMBEUX
JAMBIER
JAMBIERS
JAMBING
JAMBIYA
JAMBIYAH
JAMBIYAHS
JAMBIYAS
JAMBO
JAMBOK
JAMBOKKED
JAMBOKS
JAMBOLAN
JAMBOLANA
JAMBOLANS
JAMBONE
JAMBONES
JAMBOOL
JAMBOOLS
JAMBOREE
JAMBOREES
JAMBS
JAMBU
JAMBUL
JAMBULS
JAMBUS
JAMBUSTER
JAMDANI
JAMDANIS
JAMES
JAMESES
JAMJAR
JAMJARS
JAMLIKE
JAMMABLE
JAMMED
JAMMER
JAMMERS
JAMMIER
JAMMIES
JAMMIEST
JAMMING
JAMMINGS
JAMMY
JAMON
JAMPACKED
JAMPAN
JAMPANEE
JAMPANEES
JAMPANI
JAMPANIS
JAMPANS
JAMPOT
JAMPOTS
JAMS
JANE
JANES
JANGLE
JANGLED
JANGLER
JANGLERS
JANGLES
JANGLIER
JANGLIEST
JANGLING
JANGLINGS
JANGLY
JANIFORM
JANISARY
JANISSARY
JANITOR
JANITORS
JANITRESS
JANITRIX
JANIZAR
JANIZARS
JANIZARY
JANKER
JANKERS
JANN
JANNEY
JANNEYED
JANNEYING
JANNEYS
JANNIED
JANNIES
JANNOCK
JANNOCKS
JANNS
JANNY
JANNYING
JANNYINGS
JANSKY
JANSKYS
JANTEE
JANTIER
JANTIES
JANTIEST
JANTY
JAP
JAPAN
JAPANISE
JAPANISED
JAPANISES
JAPANIZE
JAPANIZED
JAPANIZES
JAPANNED
JAPANNER
JAPANNERS
JAPANNING
JAPANS
JAPE
JAPED
JAPER
JAPERIES
JAPERS
JAPERY
JAPES
JAPING
JAPINGLY
JAPINGS
JAPONICA
JAPONICAS
JAPPED
JAPPING
JAPS
JAR
JARARACA
JARARACAS
JARARAKA
JARARAKAS
JARFUL
JARFULS
JARGON
JARGONED
JARGONEER
JARGONEL
JARGONELS
JARGONIER
JARGONING
JARGONISE
JARGONISH
JARGONIST
JARGONIZE
JARGONS
JARGONY
JARGOON
JARGOONS
JARHEAD
JARHEADS
JARINA
JARINAS
JARK
JARKMAN
JARKMEN
JARKS
JARL
JARLDOM
JARLDOMS
JARLS
JARLSBERG
JAROOL
JAROOLS
JAROSITE
JAROSITES
JAROVISE
JAROVISED
JAROVISES
JAROVIZE
JAROVIZED
JAROVIZES
JARP
JARPED
JARPING
JARPS
JARRAH
JARRAHS
JARRED
JARRING
JARRINGLY
JARRINGS
JARS
JARSFUL
JARTA
JARTAS
JARUL
JARULS
JARVEY
JARVEYS
JARVIE
JARVIES
JASEY
JASEYS
JASIES
JASMIN
JASMINE
JASMINES
JASMINS
JASMONATE

JASP
JASPE
JASPER
JASPERIER
JASPERISE
JASPERIZE
JASPEROUS
JASPERS
JASPERY
JASPES
JASPIDEAN
JASPILITE
JASPIS
JASPISES
JASPS
JASS
JASSES
JASSID
JASSIDS
JASY
JATAKA
JATAKAS
JATO
JATOS
JATROPHA
JATROPHAS
JAUK
JAUKED
JAUKING
JAUKS
JAUNCE
JAUNCED
JAUNCES
JAUNCING
JAUNDICE
JAUNDICED
JAUNDICES
JAUNSE
JAUNSED
JAUNSES
JAUNSING
JAUNT
JAUNTED
JAUNTEE
JAUNTIE
JAUNTIER
JAUNTIES
JAUNTIEST
JAUNTILY
JAUNTING
JAUNTS
JAUNTY
JAUP
JAUPED
JAUPING
JAUPS
JAVA
JAVAS
JAVEL
JAVELIN
JAVELINA
JAVELINAS
JAVELINED
JAVELINS
JAVELLE
JAVELS
JAW
JAWAN
JAWANS
JAWARI
JAWARIS
JAWBATION
JAWBONE
JAWBONED
JAWBONER
JAWBONERS
JAWBONES
JAWBONING
JAWBOX
JAWBOXES
JAWED
JAWFALL
JAWFALLS
JAWHOLE
JAWHOLES
JAWING
JAWINGS
JAWLESS
JAWLIKE
JAWLINE
JAWLINES
JAWS
JAXIE
JAXIES
JAXY
JAY
JAYBIRD
JAYBIRDS
JAYCEE
JAYCEES
JAYGEE
JAYGEES
JAYHAWKER
JAYS
JAYVEE
JAYVEES
JAYWALK
JAYWALKED
JAYWALKER
JAYWALKS
JAZERANT
JAZERANTS
JAZIES
JAZY
JAZZ
JAZZBO
JAZZBOS
JAZZED
JAZZER
JAZZERS
JAZZES
JAZZIER
JAZZIEST
JAZZILY
JAZZINESS
JAZZING
JAZZLIKE
JAZZMAN
JAZZMEN
JAZZY
JEALOUS
JEALOUSE
JEALOUSED
JEALOUSER
JEALOUSES
JEALOUSLY
JEALOUSY
JEAN
JEANED
JEANETTE
JEANETTES
JEANS
JEANSWEAR
JEAT
JEATS
JEBEL
JEBELS
JEDI
JEDIS
JEE
JEED
JEEING
JEEL
JEELED
JEELIE
JEELIED
JEELIEING
JEELIES
JEELING
JEELS
JEELY
JEELYING
JEEP
JEEPED
JEEPERS
JEEPING
JEEPNEY
JEEPNEYS
JEEPS
JEER
JEERED
JEERER
JEERERS
JEERING
JEERINGLY
JEERINGS
JEERS
JEES
JEESLY
JEEZ
JEEZE
JEEZELY
JEEZLY
JEFE
JEFES
JEFF
JEFFED
JEFFING
JEFFS
JEGGINGS
JEHAD
JEHADEEN
JEHADI
JEHADIS
JEHADISM
JEHADISMS
JEHADIST
JEHADISTS
JEHADS
JEHU
JEHUS
JEJUNA
JEJUNAL
JEJUNE
JEJUNELY
JEJUNITY
JEJUNUM
JEJUNUMS
JELAB
JELABS
JELL
JELLABA
JELLABAH
JELLABAHS
JELLABAS
JELLED
JELLIED
JELLIES
JELLIFIED
JELLIFIES
JELLIFY
JELLING
JELLO
JELLOS
JELLS
JELLY
JELLYBEAN
JELLYFISH
JELLYING
JELLYLIKE
JELLYROLL
JELUTONG
JELUTONGS
JEMADAR
JEMADARS
JEMBE
JEMBES
JEMIDAR
JEMIDARS
JEMIMA

JEMIMAS
JEMMIED
JEMMIER
JEMMIES
JEMMIEST
JEMMINESS
JEMMY
JEMMYING
JENNET
JENNETING
JENNETS
JENNIES
JENNY
JEOFAIL
JEOFAILS
JEON
JEONS
JEOPARD
JEOPARDED
JEOPARDER
JEOPARDS
JEOPARDY
JEQUERITY
JEQUIRITY
JERBIL
JERBILS
JERBOA
JERBOAS
JEREED
JEREEDS
JEREMIAD
JEREMIADS
JEREPIGO
JEREPIGOS
JERFALCON
JERID
JERIDS
JERK
JERKED
JERKER
JERKERS
JERKIER
JERKIES
JERKIEST
JERKILY
JERKIN
JERKINESS
JERKING
JERKINGLY
JERKINGS
JERKINS
JERKS
JERKWATER
JERKY
JEROBOAM
JEROBOAMS
JERQUE
JERQUED
JERQUER
JERQUERS
JERQUES
JERQUING
JERQUINGS
JERREED
JERREEDS
JERRICAN
JERRICANS
JERRID
JERRIDS
JERRIES
JERRY
JERRYCAN
JERRYCANS
JERSEY
JERSEYED
JERSEYS
JESS
JESSAMIES
JESSAMINE
JESSAMY
JESSANT
JESSE
JESSED
JESSERANT
JESSES
JESSIE
JESSIES
JESSING
JEST
JESTBOOK
JESTBOOKS
JESTED
JESTEE
JESTEES
JESTER
JESTERS
JESTFUL
JESTING
JESTINGLY
JESTINGS
JESTS
JESUIT
JESUITIC
JESUITISM
JESUITRY
JESUITS
JESUS
JET
JETBEAD
JETBEADS
JETE
JETES
JETFOIL
JETFOILS
JETLAG
JETLAGS
JETLIKE
JETLINER
JETLINERS
JETON
JETONS
JETPACK
JETPACKS
JETPORT
JETPORTS
JETS
JETSAM
JETSAMS
JETSOM
JETSOMS
JETSON
JETSONS
JETSTREAM
JETTATURA
JETTED
JETTIED
JETTIER
JETTIES
JETTIEST
JETTINESS
JETTING
JETTISON
JETTISONS
JETTON
JETTONS
JETTY
JETTYING
JETWAY
JETWAYS
JEU
JEUNE
JEUX
JEW
JEWED
JEWEL
JEWELED
JEWELER
JEWELERS
JEWELFISH
JEWELING
JEWELLED
JEWELLER
JEWELLERS
JEWELLERY
JEWELLIKE
JEWELLING
JEWELRIES
JEWELRY
JEWELS
JEWELWEED
JEWFISH
JEWFISHES
JEWIE
JEWIES
JEWING
JEWS
JEZAIL
JEZAILS
JEZEBEL
JEZEBELS
JHALA
JHALAS
JHATKA
JHATKAS
JIAO
JIAOS
JIB
JIBB
JIBBA
JIBBAH
JIBBAHS
JIBBAS
JIBBED
JIBBER
JIBBERED
JIBBERING
JIBBERS
JIBBING
JIBBINGS
JIBBONS
JIBBOOM
JIBBOOMS
JIBBS
JIBE
JIBED
JIBER
JIBERS
JIBES
JIBING
JIBINGLY
JIBS
JICAMA
JICAMAS
JICKAJOG
JICKAJOGS
JIFF
JIFFIES
JIFFS
JIFFY
JIG
JIGABOO
JIGABOOS
JIGAJIG
JIGAJIGS
JIGAJOG
JIGAJOGS
JIGAMAREE
JIGGED
JIGGER
JIGGERED
JIGGERING
JIGGERS
JIGGIER
JIGGIEST
JIGGING
JIGGINGS
JIGGISH
JIGGLE
JIGGLED
JIGGLES

JIGGLIER
JIGGLIEST
JIGGLING
JIGGLY
JIGGUMBOB
JIGGY
JIGJIG
JIGJIGS
JIGLIKE
JIGOT
JIGOTS
JIGS
JIGSAW
JIGSAWED
JIGSAWING
JIGSAWN
JIGSAWS
JIHAD
JIHADEEN
JIHADI
JIHADIS
JIHADISM
JIHADISMS
JIHADIST
JIHADISTS
JIHADS
JILBAB
JILBABS
JILGIE
JILGIES
JILL
JILLAROO
JILLAROOS
JILLET
JILLETS
JILLFLIRT
JILLION
JILLIONS
JILLIONTH
JILLS
JILT
JILTED
JILTER
JILTERS
JILTING
JILTS
JIMCRACK
JIMCRACKS
JIMINY
JIMJAM
JIMJAMS
JIMMIE
JIMMIED
JIMMIES
JIMMINY
JIMMY
JIMMYING
JIMP
JIMPER
JIMPEST
JIMPIER
JIMPIEST
JIMPLY
JIMPNESS
JIMPSON
JIMPY
JIMSON
JIMSONS
JIN
JINGAL
JINGALL
JINGALLS
JINGALS
JINGBANG
JINGBANGS
JINGKO
JINGKOES
JINGLE
JINGLED
JINGLER
JINGLERS
JINGLES
JINGLET
JINGLETS
JINGLIER
JINGLIEST
JINGLING
JINGLY
JINGO
JINGOES
JINGOISH
JINGOISM
JINGOISMS
JINGOIST
JINGOISTS
JINJILI
JINJILIS
JINK
JINKED
JINKER
JINKERED
JINKERING
JINKERS
JINKING
JINKS
JINN
JINNE
JINNEE
JINNI
JINNIS
JINNS
JINRIKSHA
JINS
JINX
JINXED
JINXES
JINXING
JIPIJAPA
JIPIJAPAS
JIPYAPA
JIPYAPAS
JIRBLE
JIRBLED
JIRBLES
JIRBLING
JIRD
JIRDS
JIRGA
JIRGAS
JIRKINET
JIRKINETS
JIRRE
JISM
JISMS
JISSOM
JISSOMS
JITNEY
JITNEYS
JITTER
JITTERBUG
JITTERED
JITTERIER
JITTERING
JITTERS
JITTERY
JIUJITSU
JIUJITSUS
JIUJUTSU
JIUJUTSUS
JIVE
JIVEASS
JIVEASSES
JIVED
JIVER
JIVERS
JIVES
JIVEST
JIVEY
JIVIER
JIVIEST
JIVING
JIVY
JIZ
JIZZ
JIZZES
JNANA
JNANAS
JO
JOANNA
JOANNAS
JOANNES
JOANNESES
JOB
JOBATION
JOBATIONS
JOBBED
JOBBER
JOBBERIES
JOBBERS
JOBBERY
JOBBIE
JOBBIES
JOBBING
JOBBINGS
JOBCENTRE
JOBE
JOBED
JOBERNOWL
JOBES
JOBHOLDER
JOBING
JOBLESS
JOBNAME
JOBNAMES
JOBS
JOBSEEKER
JOBSHARE
JOBSHARES
JOBSWORTH
JOCK
JOCKDOM
JOCKDOMS
JOCKETTE
JOCKETTES
JOCKEY
JOCKEYED
JOCKEYING
JOCKEYISH
JOCKEYISM
JOCKEYS
JOCKIER
JOCKIEST
JOCKISH
JOCKNEY
JOCKNEYS
JOCKO
JOCKOS
JOCKS
JOCKSTRAP
JOCKTELEG
JOCKY
JOCO
JOCOS
JOCOSE
JOCOSELY
JOCOSER
JOCOSEST
JOCOSITY
JOCULAR
JOCULARLY
JOCULATOR
JOCUND
JOCUNDER
JOCUNDEST
JOCUNDITY
JOCUNDLY
JODEL
JODELLED
JODELLING
JODELS

J

JODHPUR
JODHPURS
JOE
JOES
JOEY
JOEYS
JOG
JOGGED
JOGGER
JOGGERS
JOGGING
JOGGINGS
JOGGLE
JOGGLED
JOGGLER
JOGGLERS
JOGGLES
JOGGLING
JOGPANTS
JOGS
JOGTROT
JOGTROTS
JOHANNES
JOHN
JOHNBOAT
JOHNBOATS
JOHNNIE
JOHNNIES
JOHNNY
JOHNS
JOHNSON
JOHNSONS
JOIN
JOINABLE
JOINDER
JOINDERS
JOINED
JOINER
JOINERIES
JOINERS
JOINERY
JOINING
JOININGS
JOINS
JOINT
JOINTED
JOINTEDLY
JOINTER
JOINTERS
JOINTING
JOINTINGS
JOINTLESS
JOINTLY
JOINTNESS
JOINTRESS
JOINTS
JOINTURE
JOINTURED
JOINTURES
JOINTWEED
JOINTWORM
JOIST
JOISTED
JOISTING
JOISTS
JOJOBA
JOJOBAS
JOKE
JOKED
JOKER
JOKERS
JOKES
JOKESMITH
JOKESOME
JOKESTER
JOKESTERS
JOKEY
JOKIER
JOKIEST
JOKILY
JOKINESS
JOKING
JOKINGLY
JOKINGS
JOKOL
JOKY
JOL
JOLE
JOLED
JOLES
JOLING
JOLIOTIUM
JOLL
JOLLED
JOLLER
JOLLERS
JOLLEY
JOLLEYER
JOLLEYERS
JOLLEYING
JOLLEYS
JOLLIED
JOLLIER
JOLLIERS
JOLLIES
JOLLIEST
JOLLIFIED
JOLLIFIES
JOLLIFY
JOLLILY
JOLLIMENT
JOLLINESS
JOLLING
JOLLITIES
JOLLITY
JOLLOF
JOLLOP
JOLLOPS
JOLLS
JOLLY
JOLLYBOAT
JOLLYER
JOLLYERS
JOLLYHEAD
JOLLYING
JOLLYINGS
JOLS
JOLT
JOLTED
JOLTER
JOLTERS
JOLTHEAD
JOLTHEADS
JOLTIER
JOLTIEST
JOLTILY
JOLTING
JOLTINGLY
JOLTINGS
JOLTS
JOLTY
JOMO
JOMON
JOMONS
JOMOS
JONCANOE
JONCANOES
JONES
JONESED
JONESES
JONESING
JONG
JONGLEUR
JONGLEURS
JONGS
JONNOCK
JONNYCAKE
JONQUIL
JONQUILS
JONTIES
JONTY
JOOK
JOOKED
JOOKERIES
JOOKERY
JOOKING
JOOKS
JOR
JORAM
JORAMS
JORDAN
JORDANS
JORDELOO
JORDELOOS
JORS
JORUM
JORUMS
JOSEPH
JOSEPHS
JOSH
JOSHED
JOSHER
JOSHERS
JOSHES
JOSHING
JOSHINGLY
JOSHINGS
JOSKIN
JOSKINS
JOSS
JOSSER
JOSSERS
JOSSES
JOSTLE
JOSTLED
JOSTLER
JOSTLERS
JOSTLES
JOSTLING
JOSTLINGS
JOT
JOTA
JOTAS
JOTS
JOTTED
JOTTER
JOTTERS
JOTTIER
JOTTIEST
JOTTING
JOTTINGS
JOTTY
JOTUN
JOTUNN
JOTUNNS
JOTUNS
JOUAL
JOUALS
JOUGS
JOUISANCE
JOUK
JOUKED
JOUKERIES
JOUKERY
JOUKING
JOUKS
JOULE
JOULED
JOULES
JOULING
JOUNCE
JOUNCED
JOUNCES
JOUNCIER
JOUNCIEST
JOUNCING
JOUNCY
JOUR
JOURNAL
JOURNALED

JOURNALS
JOURNEY
JOURNEYED
JOURNEYER
JOURNEYS
JOURNO
JOURNOS
JOURS
JOUST
JOUSTED
JOUSTER
JOUSTERS
JOUSTING
JOUSTINGS
JOUSTS
JOVIAL
JOVIALITY
JOVIALLY
JOVIALTY
JOW
JOWAR
JOWARI
JOWARIS
JOWARS
JOWED
JOWING
JOWL
JOWLED
JOWLER
JOWLERS
JOWLIER
JOWLIEST
JOWLINESS
JOWLING
JOWLS
JOWLY
JOWS
JOY
JOYANCE
JOYANCES
JOYED
JOYFUL
JOYFULLER
JOYFULLY
JOYING
JOYLESS
JOYLESSLY
JOYOUS
JOYOUSLY
JOYPAD
JOYPADS
JOYPOP
JOYPOPPED
JOYPOPPER
JOYPOPS
JOYRIDDEN
JOYRIDE
JOYRIDER
JOYRIDERS
JOYRIDES
JOYRIDING
JOYRODE
JOYS
JOYSTICK
JOYSTICKS
JUBA
JUBAS
JUBATE
JUBBAH
JUBBAHS
JUBE
JUBES
JUBHAH
JUBHAHS
JUBILANCE
JUBILANCY
JUBILANT
JUBILATE
JUBILATED
JUBILATES
JUBILE
JUBILEE
JUBILEES
JUBILES
JUCO
JUCOS
JUD
JUDAS
JUDASES
JUDDER
JUDDERED
JUDDERIER
JUDDERING
JUDDERS
JUDDERY
JUDGE
JUDGEABLE
JUDGED
JUDGELESS
JUDGELIKE
JUDGEMENT
JUDGER
JUDGERS
JUDGES
JUDGESHIP
JUDGEY
JUDGIER
JUDGIEST
JUDGING
JUDGINGLY
JUDGINGS
JUDGMATIC
JUDGMENT
JUDGMENTS
JUDGY
JUDICABLE
JUDICARE
JUDICARES
JUDICATOR
JUDICIAL
JUDICIARY
JUDICIOUS
JUDIES
JUDO
JUDOGI
JUDOGIS
JUDOIST
JUDOISTS
JUDOKA
JUDOKAS
JUDOS
JUDS
JUDY
JUG
JUGA
JUGAAD
JUGAADS
JUGAL
JUGALS
JUGATE
JUGFUL
JUGFULS
JUGGED
JUGGING
JUGGINGS
JUGGINS
JUGGINSES
JUGGLE
JUGGLED
JUGGLER
JUGGLERS
JUGGLERY
JUGGLES
JUGGLING
JUGGLINGS
JUGHEAD
JUGHEADS
JUGLET
JUGLETS
JUGS
JUGSFUL
JUGULA
JUGULAR
JUGULARS
JUGULATE
JUGULATED
JUGULATES
JUGULUM
JUGUM
JUGUMS
JUICE
JUICED
JUICEHEAD
JUICELESS
JUICER
JUICERS
JUICES
JUICIER
JUICIEST
JUICILY
JUICINESS
JUICING
JUICY
JUJITSU
JUJITSUS
JUJU
JUJUBE
JUJUBES
JUJUISM
JUJUISMS
JUJUIST
JUJUISTS
JUJUS
JUJUTSU
JUJUTSUS
JUKE
JUKEBOX
JUKEBOXES
JUKED
JUKES
JUKING
JUKSKEI
JUKSKEIS
JUKU
JUKUS
JULEP
JULEPS
JULIENNE
JULIENNED
JULIENNES
JULIET
JULIETS
JUMAR
JUMARED
JUMARING
JUMARRED
JUMARRING
JUMARS
JUMART
JUMARTS
JUMBAL
JUMBALS
JUMBIE
JUMBIES
JUMBLE
JUMBLED
JUMBLER
JUMBLERS
JUMBLES
JUMBLIER
JUMBLIEST
JUMBLING
JUMBLY
JUMBO
JUMBOISE
JUMBOISED
JUMBOISES
JUMBOIZE
JUMBOIZED
JUMBOIZES

J

JUMBOS
JUMBUCK
JUMBUCKS
JUMBY
JUMELLE
JUMELLES
JUMP
JUMPABLE
JUMPED
JUMPER
JUMPERS
JUMPIER
JUMPIEST
JUMPILY
JUMPINESS
JUMPING
JUMPINGLY
JUMPINGS
JUMPOFF
JUMPOFFS
JUMPROPE
JUMPROPES
JUMPS
JUMPSHOT
JUMPSHOTS
JUMPSIES
JUMPSUIT
JUMPSUITS
JUMPY
JUN
JUNCATE
JUNCATES
JUNCO
JUNCOES
JUNCOS
JUNCTION
JUNCTIONS
JUNCTURAL
JUNCTURE
JUNCTURES
JUNCUS
JUNCUSES
JUNEATING
JUNGLE
JUNGLED
JUNGLEGYM
JUNGLES
JUNGLI
JUNGLIER
JUNGLIEST
JUNGLIS
JUNGLIST
JUNGLISTS
JUNGLY
JUNIOR
JUNIORATE
JUNIORED
JUNIORING
JUNIORITY
JUNIORS
JUNIPER
JUNIPERS
JUNK
JUNKANOO
JUNKANOOS
JUNKED
JUNKER
JUNKERDOM
JUNKERS
JUNKET
JUNKETED
JUNKETEER
JUNKETER
JUNKETERS
JUNKETING
JUNKETS
JUNKETTED
JUNKETTER
JUNKIE
JUNKIER
JUNKIES
JUNKIEST
JUNKINESS
JUNKING
JUNKMAN
JUNKMEN
JUNKS
JUNKY
JUNKYARD
JUNKYARDS
JUNTA
JUNTAS
JUNTO
JUNTOS
JUPATI
JUPATIS
JUPE
JUPES
JUPON
JUPONS
JURA
JURAL
JURALLY
JURANT
JURANTS
JURASSIC
JURAT
JURATORY
JURATS
JURE
JUREL
JURELS
JURES
JURIDIC
JURIDICAL
JURIED
JURIES
JURIST
JURISTIC
JURISTS
JUROR
JURORS
JURY
JURYING
JURYLESS
JURYMAN
JURYMAST
JURYMASTS
JURYMEN
JURYWOMAN
JURYWOMEN
JUS
JUSSIVE
JUSSIVES
JUST
JUSTED
JUSTER
JUSTERS
JUSTEST
JUSTICE
JUSTICER
JUSTICERS
JUSTICES
JUSTICIAR
JUSTIFIED
JUSTIFIER
JUSTIFIES
JUSTIFY
JUSTING
JUSTLE
JUSTLED
JUSTLES
JUSTLING
JUSTLY
JUSTNESS
JUSTS
JUT
JUTE
JUTELIKE
JUTES
JUTS
JUTTED
JUTTIED
JUTTIER
JUTTIES
JUTTIEST
JUTTING
JUTTINGLY
JUTTY
JUTTYING
JUVE
JUVENAL
JUVENALS
JUVENILE
JUVENILES
JUVENILIA
JUVES
JUVIE
JUVIES
JUXTAPOSE
JYMOLD
JYNX
JYNXES

K

KA
KAAL
KAAMA
KAAMAS
KAAS
KAB
KABAB
KABABBED
KABABBING
KABABS
KABADDI
KABADDIS
KABAKA
KABAKAS
KABALA
KABALAS
KABALISM
KABALISMS
KABALIST
KABALISTS
KABAR
KABARS
KABAYA
KABAYAS
KABBALA
KABBALAH
KABBALAHS
KABBALAS
KABBALISM
KABBALIST
KABELE
KABELES
KABELJOU
KABELJOUS
KABELJOUW
KABIKI
KABIKIS
KABLOOEY
KABLOOIE
KABLOONA
KABLOONAS
KABLOONAT
KABOB
KABOBBED
KABOBBING
KABOBS
KABOCHA
KABOCHAS
KABOODLE
KABOODLES
KABOOM
KABOOMS
KABS
KABUKI
KABUKIS
KACCHA
KACCHAS
KACHA
KACHAHRI
KACHAHRIS
KACHCHA
KACHERI
KACHERIS
KACHINA
KACHINAS
KACHORI
KACHORIS
KACHUMBER
KACK
KACKS
KADAI
KADAIS
KADAITCHA
KADDISH
KADDISHES
KADDISHIM
KADE
KADES
KADI
KADIS
KAE
KAED
KAEING
KAES
KAF
KAFFIR
KAFFIRS
KAFFIYAH
KAFFIYAHS
KAFFIYEH
KAFFIYEHS
KAFILA
KAFILAS
KAFIR
KAFIRS
KAFS
KAFTAN
KAFTANS
KAFUFFLE
KAFUFFLES
KAGO
KAGOOL
KAGOOLS
KAGOS
KAGOUL
KAGOULE
KAGOULES
KAGOULS
KAGU
KAGUS
KAHAL
KAHALS
KAHAWAI
KAHAWAIS
KAHIKATEA
KAHIKATOA
KAHUNA
KAHUNAS
KAI
KAIAK
KAIAKED
KAIAKING
KAIAKS
KAID
KAIDS
KAIE
KAIES
KAIF
KAIFS
KAIK
KAIKA
KAIKAI
KAIKAIS
KAIKAS
KAIKAWAKA
KAIKOMAKO
KAIKS
KAIL
KAILS
KAILYAIRD
KAILYARD
KAILYARDS
KAIM
KAIMAKAM
KAIMAKAMS
KAIMS
KAIN
KAING
KAINGA
KAINGAS
KAINIT
KAINITE
KAINITES
KAINITS
KAINS
KAIROMONE
KAIS
KAISER
KAISERDOM
KAISERIN
KAISERINS
KAISERISM
KAISERS
KAIZEN
KAIZENS
KAJAWAH
KAJAWAHS
KAJEPUT
KAJEPUTS
KAK
KAKA
KAKAPO
KAKAPOS
KAKARIKI
KAKARIKIS
KAKAS
KAKEMONO
KAKEMONOS
KAKI
KAKIEMON
KAKIEMONS
KAKIS
KAKIVAK
KAKIVAKS
KAKODYL
KAKODYLS
KAKS
KAKURO
KAKUROS
KALAM
KALAMANSI
KALAMATA
KALAMATAS
KALAMDAN
KALAMDANS
KALAMKARI
KALAMS
KALANCHOE
KALE
KALENDAR
KALENDARS
KALENDS
KALES
KALEWIFE
KALEWIVES
KALEYARD
KALEYARDS
KALI
KALIAN
KALIANS

KALIF
KALIFATE
KALIFATES
KALIFS
KALIMBA
KALIMBAS
KALINITE
KALINITES
KALIPH
KALIPHATE
KALIPHS
KALIS
KALIUM
KALIUMS
KALLIDIN
KALLIDINS
KALLITYPE
KALMIA
KALMIAS
KALONG
KALONGS
KALOOKI
KALOOKIE
KALOOKIES
KALOOKIS
KALOTYPE
KALOTYPES
KALPA
KALPAC
KALPACS
KALPAK
KALPAKS
KALPAS
KALPIS
KALPISES
KALSOMINE
KALUKI
KALUKIS
KALUMPIT
KALUMPITS
KALYPTRA
KALYPTRAS
KAM
KAMA
KAMAAINA
KAMAAINAS
KAMACITE
KAMACITES
KAMAHI
KAMAHIS
KAMALA
KAMALAS
KAMAS
KAME
KAMEES
KAMEESES
KAMEEZ
KAMEEZES
KAMELA
KAMELAS
KAMERAD
KAMERADED
KAMERADS
KAMES
KAMI
KAMICHI
KAMICHIS
KAMIK
KAMIKAZE
KAMIKAZES
KAMIKS
KAMILA
KAMILAS
KAMIS
KAMISES
KAMME
KAMOKAMO
KAMOKAMOS
KAMOTIK
KAMOTIKS
KAMOTIQ
KAMOTIQS
KAMPONG
KAMPONGS
KAMSEEN
KAMSEENS
KAMSIN
KAMSINS
KANA
KANAE
KANAES
KANAKA
KANAKAS
KANAMYCIN
KANAS
KANBAN
KANBANS
KANDIES
KANDY
KANE
KANEH
KANEHS
KANES
KANG
KANGA
KANGAROO
KANGAROOS
KANGAS
KANGHA
KANGHAS
KANGS
KANJI
KANJIS
KANS
KANSES
KANT
KANTAR
KANTARS
KANTED
KANTELA
KANTELAS
KANTELE
KANTELES
KANTEN
KANTENS
KANTHA
KANTHAS
KANTIKOY
KANTIKOYS
KANTING
KANTS
KANUKA
KANUKAS
KANZU
KANZUS
KAOLIANG
KAOLIANGS
KAOLIN
KAOLINE
KAOLINES
KAOLINIC
KAOLINISE
KAOLINITE
KAOLINIZE
KAOLINS
KAON
KAONIC
KAONS
KAPA
KAPAS
KAPEEK
KAPEYKA
KAPH
KAPHS
KAPOK
KAPOKS
KAPOW
KAPOWS
KAPPA
KAPPAS
KAPU
KAPUKA
KAPUKAS
KAPUS
KAPUT
KAPUTT
KARA
KARABINER
KARAHI
KARAHIS
KARAISM
KARAISMS
KARAIT
KARAITS
KARAKA
KARAKAS
KARAKIA
KARAKIAS
KARAKUL
KARAKULS
KARAMU
KARAMUS
KARANGA
KARANGAED
KARANGAS
KARAOKE
KARAOKES
KARAS
KARAT
KARATE
KARATEIST
KARATEKA
KARATEKAS
KARATES
KARATS
KAREAREA
KAREAREAS
KARENGO
KARENGOS
KARITE
KARITES
KARK
KARKED
KARKING
KARKS
KARMA
KARMAS
KARMIC
KARN
KARNS
KARO
KAROO
KAROOS
KARORO
KAROROS
KAROS
KAROSHI
KAROSHIS
KAROSS
KAROSSES
KARRI
KARRIS
KARROO
KARROOS
KARSEY
KARSEYS
KARSIES
KARST
KARSTIC
KARSTIFY
KARSTS
KARSY
KART
KARTER
KARTERS
KARTING
KARTINGS
KARTS
KARYOGAMY
KARYOGRAM

KARYOLOGY
KARYON
KARYONS
KARYOSOME
KARYOTIN
KARYOTINS
KARYOTYPE
KARZIES
KARZY
KAS
KASBAH
KASBAHS
KASHA
KASHAS
KASHER
KASHERED
KASHERING
KASHERS
KASHMIR
KASHMIRS
KASHRUS
KASHRUSES
KASHRUT
KASHRUTH
KASHRUTHS
KASHRUTS
KASME
KAT
KATA
KATABASES
KATABASIS
KATABATIC
KATABOLIC
KATAKANA
KATAKANAS
KATAL
KATALS
KATANA
KATANAS
KATAS
KATCHINA
KATCHINAS
KATCINA
KATCINAS
KATHAK
KATHAKALI
KATHAKS
KATHARSES
KATHARSIS
KATHODAL
KATHODE
KATHODES
KATHODIC
KATHUMP
KATHUMPS
KATI
KATION
KATIONS
KATIPO
KATIPOS
KATIS
KATORGA
KATORGAS
KATS
KATSINA
KATSINAM
KATSINAS
KATSURA
KATSURAS
KATTI
KATTIS
KATYDID
KATYDIDS
KAUGH
KAUGHS
KAUMATUA
KAUMATUAS
KAUPAPA
KAUPAPAS
KAURI
KAURIES
KAURIS
KAURU
KAURUS
KAURY
KAVA
KAVAKAVA
KAVAKAVAS
KAVAL
KAVALS
KAVAS
KAVASS
KAVASSES
KAW
KAWA
KAWAII
KAWAIIS
KAWAKAWA
KAWAKAWAS
KAWAS
KAWAU
KAWAUS
KAWED
KAWING
KAWS
KAY
KAYAK
KAYAKED
KAYAKER
KAYAKERS
KAYAKING
KAYAKINGS
KAYAKS
KAYLE
KAYLES
KAYLIED
KAYO
KAYOED
KAYOES
KAYOING
KAYOINGS
KAYOS
KAYS
KAZACHKI
KAZACHOC
KAZACHOCS
KAZACHOK
KAZACHOKS
KAZATSKI
KAZATSKY
KAZATZKA
KAZATZKAS
KAZI
KAZILLION
KAZIS
KAZOO
KAZOOS
KBAR
KBARS
KEA
KEAS
KEASAR
KEASARS
KEAVIE
KEAVIES
KEB
KEBAB
KEBABBED
KEBABBING
KEBABS
KEBAR
KEBARS
KEBBED
KEBBIE
KEBBIES
KEBBING
KEBBOCK
KEBBOCKS
KEBBUCK
KEBBUCKS
KEBELE
KEBELES
KEBLAH
KEBLAHS
KEBOB
KEBOBBED
KEBOBBING
KEBOBS
KEBS
KECK
KECKED
KECKING
KECKLE
KECKLED
KECKLES
KECKLING
KECKLINGS
KECKS
KECKSES
KECKSIES
KECKSY
KED
KEDDAH
KEDDAHS
KEDGE
KEDGED
KEDGER
KEDGEREE
KEDGEREES
KEDGERS
KEDGES
KEDGIER
KEDGIEST
KEDGING
KEDGY
KEDS
KEECH
KEECHES
KEEF
KEEFS
KEEK
KEEKED
KEEKER
KEEKERS
KEEKING
KEEKS
KEEL
KEELAGE
KEELAGES
KEELBOAT
KEELBOATS
KEELED
KEELER
KEELERS
KEELHALE
KEELHALED
KEELHALES
KEELHAUL
KEELHAULS
KEELIE
KEELIES
KEELING
KEELINGS
KEELIVINE
KEELLESS
KEELMAN
KEELMEN
KEELS
KEELSON
KEELSONS
KEELYVINE
KEEMA
KEEMAS
KEEN
KEENED
KEENER
KEENERS
KEENEST
KEENING
KEENINGS

KEENLY
KEENNESS
KEENO
KEENOS
KEENS
KEEP
KEEPABLE
KEEPER
KEEPERS
KEEPING
KEEPINGS
KEEPNET
KEEPNETS
KEEPS
KEEPSAKE
KEEPSAKES
KEEPSAKY
KEESHOND
KEESHONDS
KEESTER
KEESTERS
KEET
KEETS
KEEVE
KEEVES
KEF
KEFFEL
KEFFELS
KEFFIYAH
KEFFIYAHS
KEFFIYEH
KEFFIYEHS
KEFIR
KEFIRS
KEFS
KEFTEDES
KEFUFFLE
KEFUFFLED
KEFUFFLES
KEG
KEGELER
KEGELERS
KEGGED
KEGGER
KEGGERS
KEGGING
KEGLER
KEGLERS
KEGLING
KEGLINGS
KEGS
KEHUA
KEHUAS
KEIGHT
KEIR
KEIREN
KEIRENS
KEIRETSU
KEIRETSUS
KEIRIN
KEIRINS
KEIRS
KEISTER
KEISTERS
KEITLOA
KEITLOAS
KEKENO
KEKENOS
KEKERENGU
KEKS
KEKSYE
KEKSYES
KELEP
KELEPS
KELIM
KELIMS
KELL
KELLAUT
KELLAUTS
KELLIES
KELLS
KELLY
KELOID
KELOIDAL
KELOIDS
KELP
KELPED
KELPER
KELPERS
KELPFISH
KELPIE
KELPIES
KELPING
KELPS
KELPY
KELSON
KELSONS
KELT
KELTER
KELTERS
KELTIE
KELTIES
KELTS
KELTY
KELVIN
KELVINS
KEMB
KEMBED
KEMBING
KEMBLA
KEMBLAS
KEMBO
KEMBOED
KEMBOING
KEMBOS
KEMBS
KEMP
KEMPED
KEMPER
KEMPERS
KEMPIER
KEMPIEST
KEMPING
KEMPINGS
KEMPLE
KEMPLES
KEMPS
KEMPT
KEMPY
KEN
KENAF
KENAFS
KENCH
KENCHES
KENDO
KENDOIST
KENDOISTS
KENDOS
KENNED
KENNEL
KENNELED
KENNELING
KENNELLED
KENNELMAN
KENNELMEN
KENNELS
KENNER
KENNERS
KENNET
KENNETS
KENNETT
KENNETTED
KENNETTS
KENNING
KENNINGS
KENO
KENOS
KENOSES
KENOSIS
KENOSISES
KENOTIC
KENOTICS
KENOTRON
KENOTRONS
KENS
KENSPECK
KENT
KENTE
KENTED
KENTES
KENTIA
KENTIAS
KENTING
KENTLEDGE
KENTS
KEP
KEPHALIC
KEPHALICS
KEPHALIN
KEPHALINS
KEPHIR
KEPHIRS
KEPI
KEPIS
KEPPED
KEPPEN
KEPPING
KEPPIT
KEPS
KEPT
KERAMIC
KERAMICS
KERATIN
KERATINS
KERATITIS
KERATOID
KERATOMA
KERATOMAS
KERATOSE
KERATOSES
KERATOSIC
KERATOSIS
KERATOTIC
KERB
KERBAYA
KERBAYAS
KERBED
KERBING
KERBINGS
KERBLOOEY
KERBS
KERBSIDE
KERBSIDES
KERBSTONE
KERCHIEF
KERCHIEFS
KERCHOO
KEREL
KERELS
KERERU
KERERUS
KERF
KERFED
KERFING
KERFLOOEY
KERFS
KERFUFFLE
KERKIER
KERKIEST
KERKY
KERMA
KERMAS
KERMES
KERMESES
KERMESITE
KERMESS
KERMESSE
KERMESSES
KERMIS
KERMISES

KERMODE
KERMODES
KERN
KERNE
KERNED
KERNEL
KERNELED
KERNELING
KERNELLED
KERNELLY
KERNELS
KERNES
KERNING
KERNINGS
KERNISH
KERNITE
KERNITES
KERNS
KERO
KEROGEN
KEROGENS
KEROS
KEROSENE
KEROSENES
KEROSINE
KEROSINES
KERPLUNK
KERPLUNKS
KERRIA
KERRIAS
KERRIES
KERRY
KERSEY
KERSEYS
KERVE
KERVED
KERVES
KERVING
KERYGMA
KERYGMAS
KERYGMATA
KESAR
KESARS
KESH
KESHES
KEST
KESTING
KESTREL
KESTRELS
KESTS
KET
KETA
KETAINE
KETAMINE
KETAMINES
KETAS
KETCH
KETCHES
KETCHING
KETCHUP
KETCHUPS
KETCHUPY
KETE
KETENE
KETENES
KETES
KETMIA
KETMIAS
KETO
KETOGENIC
KETOL
KETOLS
KETONE
KETONEMIA
KETONES
KETONIC
KETONURIA
KETOSE
KETOSES
KETOSIS
KETOTIC
KETOXIME
KETOXIMES
KETS
KETTLE
KETTLED
KETTLEFUL
KETTLES
KETTLING
KETUBAH
KETUBAHS
KETUBOT
KETUBOTH
KEVEL
KEVELS
KEVIL
KEVILS
KEWL
KEWLER
KEWLEST
KEWPIE
KEWPIES
KEX
KEXES
KEY
KEYBOARD
KEYBOARDS
KEYBUGLE
KEYBUGLES
KEYBUTTON
KEYCARD
KEYCARDS
KEYED
KEYER
KEYERS
KEYEST
KEYFRAME
KEYFRAMES
KEYHOLE
KEYHOLES
KEYING
KEYINGS
KEYLESS
KEYLINE
KEYLINES
KEYLOGGER
KEYNOTE
KEYNOTED
KEYNOTER
KEYNOTERS
KEYNOTES
KEYNOTING
KEYPAD
KEYPADS
KEYPAL
KEYPALS
KEYPRESS
KEYPUNCH
KEYRING
KEYRINGS
KEYS
KEYSET
KEYSETS
KEYSTER
KEYSTERS
KEYSTONE
KEYSTONED
KEYSTONES
KEYSTROKE
KEYWAY
KEYWAYS
KEYWORD
KEYWORDS
KEYWORKER
KGOTLA
KGOTLAS
KHADDAR
KHADDARS
KHADI
KHADIS
KHAF
KHAFS
KHAKI
KHAKILIKE
KHAKIS
KHALAT
KHALATS
KHALIF
KHALIFA
KHALIFAH
KHALIFAHS
KHALIFAS
KHALIFAT
KHALIFATE
KHALIFATS
KHALIFS
KHAMSEEN
KHAMSEENS
KHAMSIN
KHAMSINS
KHAN
KHANATE
KHANATES
KHANDA
KHANDAS
KHANGA
KHANGAS
KHANJAR
KHANJARS
KHANS
KHANSAMA
KHANSAMAH
KHANSAMAS
KHANUM
KHANUMS
KHAPH
KHAPHS
KHARIF
KHARIFS
KHAT
KHATS
KHAYA
KHAYAL
KHAYALS
KHAYAS
KHAZEN
KHAZENIM
KHAZENS
KHAZI
KHAZIS
KHEDA
KHEDAH
KHEDAHS
KHEDAS
KHEDIVA
KHEDIVAL
KHEDIVAS
KHEDIVATE
KHEDIVE
KHEDIVES
KHEDIVIAL
KHET
KHETH
KHETHS
KHETS
KHI
KHILAFAT
KHILAFATS
KHILAT
KHILATS
KHILIM
KHILIMS
KHIMAR
KHIMARS
KHIRKAH
KHIRKAHS
KHIS
KHODJA
KHODJAS
KHOJA

K

K

KHOJAS
KHOR
KHORS
KHOTBAH
KHOTBAHS
KHOTBEH
KHOTBEHS
KHOUM
KHOUMS
KHUD
KHUDS
KHURTA
KHURTAS
KHUSKHUS
KHUTBAH
KHUTBAHS
KI
KIAAT
KIAATS
KIACK
KIACKS
KIANG
KIANGS
KIAUGH
KIAUGHS
KIBBE
KIBBEH
KIBBEHS
KIBBES
KIBBI
KIBBIS
KIBBITZ
KIBBITZED
KIBBITZER
KIBBITZES
KIBBLE
KIBBLED
KIBBLES
KIBBLING
KIBBUTZ
KIBBUTZIM
KIBE
KIBEI
KIBEIS
KIBES
KIBIBYTE
KIBIBYTES
KIBITKA
KIBITKAS
KIBITZ
KIBITZED
KIBITZER
KIBITZERS
KIBITZES
KIBITZING
KIBLA
KIBLAH
KIBLAHS
KIBLAS
KIBOSH
KIBOSHED
KIBOSHES
KIBOSHING
KICK
KICKABLE
KICKABOUT
KICKBACK
KICKBACKS
KICKBALL
KICKBALLS
KICKBOARD
KICKBOX
KICKBOXED
KICKBOXER
KICKBOXES
KICKDOWN
KICKDOWNS
KICKED
KICKER
KICKERS
KICKFLIP
KICKFLIPS
KICKIER
KICKIEST
KICKING
KICKINGS
KICKOFF
KICKOFFS
KICKOUT
KICKOUTS
KICKPLATE
KICKS
KICKSHAW
KICKSHAWS
KICKSTAND
KICKSTART
KICKUP
KICKUPS
KICKY
KID
KIDDED
KIDDER
KIDDERS
KIDDIE
KIDDIED
KIDDIER
KIDDIERS
KIDDIES
KIDDING
KIDDINGLY
KIDDINGS
KIDDISH
KIDDLE
KIDDLES
KIDDO
KIDDOES
KIDDOS
KIDDUSH
KIDDUSHES
KIDDY
KIDDYING
KIDDYWINK
KIDEL
KIDELS
KIDGE
KIDGIE
KIDGIER
KIDGIEST
KIDGLOVE
KIDLET
KIDLETS
KIDLIKE
KIDLING
KIDLINGS
KIDLIT
KIDLITS
KIDNAP
KIDNAPED
KIDNAPEE
KIDNAPEES
KIDNAPER
KIDNAPERS
KIDNAPING
KIDNAPPED
KIDNAPPEE
KIDNAPPER
KIDNAPS
KIDNEY
KIDNEYS
KIDOLOGY
KIDS
KIDSKIN
KIDSKINS
KIDSTAKES
KIDULT
KIDULTS
KIDVID
KIDVIDS
KIEF
KIEFS
KIEKIE
KIEKIES
KIELBASA
KIELBASAS
KIELBASI
KIELBASY
KIER
KIERIE
KIERIES
KIERS
KIESELGUR
KIESERITE
KIESTER
KIESTERS
KIEV
KIEVE
KIEVES
KIEVS
KIF
KIFF
KIFS
KIGHT
KIGHTS
KIKE
KIKES
KIKOI
KIKOIS
KIKUMON
KIKUMONS
KIKUYU
KIKUYUS
KILD
KILDERKIN
KILERG
KILERGS
KILEY
KILEYS
KILIKITI
KILIKITIS
KILIM
KILIMS
KILL
KILLABLE
KILLADAR
KILLADARS
KILLAS
KILLASES
KILLCOW
KILLCOWS
KILLCROP
KILLCROPS
KILLDEE
KILLDEER
KILLDEERS
KILLDEES
KILLED
KILLER
KILLERS
KILLICK
KILLICKS
KILLIE
KILLIES
KILLIFISH
KILLING
KILLINGLY
KILLINGS
KILLJOY
KILLJOYS
KILLOCK
KILLOCKS
KILLOGIE
KILLOGIES
KILLS
KILLUT
KILLUTS
KILN
KILNED
KILNING
KILNS
KILO

KILOBAR
KILOBARS
KILOBASE
KILOBASES
KILOBAUD
KILOBAUDS
KILOBIT
KILOBITS
KILOBYTE
KILOBYTES
KILOCURIE
KILOCYCLE
KILOGAUSS
KILOGRAM
KILOGRAMS
KILOGRAY
KILOGRAYS
KILOHERTZ
KILOJOULE
KILOLITER
KILOLITRE
KILOMETER
KILOMETRE
KILOMOLE
KILOMOLES
KILOPOND
KILOPONDS
KILORAD
KILORADS
KILOS
KILOTON
KILOTONNE
KILOTONS
KILOVOLT
KILOVOLTS
KILOWATT
KILOWATTS
KILP
KILPS
KILT
KILTED
KILTER
KILTERS
KILTIE
KILTIES
KILTING
KILTINGS
KILTLIKE
KILTS
KILTY
KIMBO
KIMBOED
KIMBOING
KIMBOS
KIMCHEE
KIMCHEES
KIMCHI
KIMCHIS
KIMMER
KIMMERS
KIMONO
KIMONOED
KIMONOS
KIN
KINA
KINAKINA
KINAKINAS
KINARA
KINARAS
KINAS
KINASE
KINASES
KINCHIN
KINCHINS
KINCOB
KINCOBS
KIND
KINDA
KINDED
KINDER
KINDERS
KINDEST
KINDIE
KINDIES
KINDING
KINDLE
KINDLED
KINDLER
KINDLERS
KINDLES
KINDLESS
KINDLIER
KINDLIEST
KINDLILY
KINDLING
KINDLINGS
KINDLY
KINDNESS
KINDRED
KINDREDS
KINDS
KINDY
KINE
KINEMA
KINEMAS
KINEMATIC
KINES
KINESCOPE
KINESES
KINESIC
KINESICS
KINESIS
KINESISES
KINETIC
KINETICAL
KINETICS
KINETIN
KINETINS
KINFOLK
KINFOLKS
KING
KINGBIRD
KINGBIRDS
KINGBOLT
KINGBOLTS
KINGCRAFT
KINGCUP
KINGCUPS
KINGDOM
KINGDOMED
KINGDOMS
KINGED
KINGFISH
KINGHOOD
KINGHOODS
KINGING
KINGKLIP
KINGKLIPS
KINGLE
KINGLES
KINGLESS
KINGLET
KINGLETS
KINGLIER
KINGLIEST
KINGLIKE
KINGLING
KINGLINGS
KINGLY
KINGMAKER
KINGPIN
KINGPINS
KINGPOST
KINGPOSTS
KINGS
KINGSHIP
KINGSHIPS
KINGSIDE
KINGSIDES
KINGSNAKE
KINGWOOD
KINGWOODS
KININ
KININS
KINK
KINKAJOU
KINKAJOUS
KINKED
KINKIER
KINKIEST
KINKILY
KINKINESS
KINKING
KINKLE
KINKLES
KINKS
KINKY
KINLESS
KINO
KINONE
KINONES
KINOS
KINRED
KINREDS
KINS
KINSFOLK
KINSFOLKS
KINSHIP
KINSHIPS
KINSMAN
KINSMEN
KINSWOMAN
KINSWOMEN
KINTLEDGE
KIORE
KIORES
KIOSK
KIOSKS
KIP
KIPE
KIPES
KIPP
KIPPA
KIPPAGE
KIPPAGES
KIPPAH
KIPPAHS
KIPPAS
KIPPED
KIPPEN
KIPPER
KIPPERED
KIPPERER
KIPPERERS
KIPPERING
KIPPERS
KIPPING
KIPPS
KIPS
KIPSKIN
KIPSKINS
KIPUNJI
KIPUNJIS
KIR
KIRANA
KIRANAS
KIRBEH
KIRBEHS
KIRBIGRIP
KIRBY
KIRIGAMI
KIRIGAMIS
KIRIMON
KIRIMONS
KIRK
KIRKED
KIRKING
KIRKINGS
KIRKMAN
KIRKMEN

KIRKS
KIRKTON
KIRKTONS
KIRKWARD
KIRKYAIRD
KIRKYARD
KIRKYARDS
KIRMESS
KIRMESSES
KIRN
KIRNED
KIRNING
KIRNS
KIRPAN
KIRPANS
KIRRI
KIRRIS
KIRS
KIRSCH
KIRSCHES
KIRTAN
KIRTANS
KIRTLE
KIRTLED
KIRTLES
KIS
KISAN
KISANS
KISH
KISHES
KISHKA
KISHKAS
KISHKE
KISHKES
KISKADEE
KISKADEES
KISMAT
KISMATS
KISMET
KISMETIC
KISMETS
KISS
KISSABLE
KISSABLY
KISSAGRAM
KISSED
KISSEL
KISSELS
KISSER
KISSERS
KISSES
KISSIER
KISSIEST
KISSING
KISSINGS
KISSOGRAM
KISSY
KIST
KISTED
KISTFUL
KISTFULS
KISTING
KISTS
KISTVAEN
KISTVAENS
KIT
KITBAG
KITBAGS
KITCHEN
KITCHENED
KITCHENER
KITCHENET
KITCHENS
KITE
KITEBOARD
KITED
KITELIKE
KITENGE
KITENGES
KITER
KITERS
KITES
KITH
KITHARA
KITHARAS
KITHE
KITHED
KITHES
KITHING
KITHS
KITING
KITINGS
KITLING
KITLINGS
KITS
KITSCH
KITSCHES
KITSCHIER
KITSCHIFY
KITSCHILY
KITSCHY
KITSET
KITSETS
KITTED
KITTEL
KITTELS
KITTEN
KITTENED
KITTENIER
KITTENING
KITTENISH
KITTENS
KITTENY
KITTIES
KITTING
KITTIWAKE
KITTLE
KITTLED
KITTLER
KITTLES
KITTLEST
KITTLIER
KITTLIEST
KITTLING
KITTLY
KITTUL
KITTULS
KITTY
KITUL
KITULS
KIVA
KIVAS
KIWI
KIWIFRUIT
KIWIS
KLANG
KLANGS
KLAP
KLAPPED
KLAPPING
KLAPS
KLATCH
KLATCHES
KLATSCH
KLATSCHES
KLAVERN
KLAVERNS
KLAVIER
KLAVIERS
KLAXON
KLAXONED
KLAXONING
KLAXONS
KLEAGLE
KLEAGLES
KLEENEX
KLEENEXES
KLEFTIKO
KLEFTIKOS
KLENDUSIC
KLEPHT
KLEPHTIC
KLEPHTISM
KLEPHTS
KLEPTO
KLEPTOS
KLETT
KLETTS
KLEZMER
KLEZMERS
KLEZMORIM
KLICK
KLICKS
KLIEG
KLIEGS
KLIK
KLIKS
KLINKER
KLINKERS
KLINOSTAT
KLIPDAS
KLIPDASES
KLISTER
KLISTERS
KLONDIKE
KLONDIKED
KLONDIKER
KLONDIKES
KLONDYKE
KLONDYKED
KLONDYKER
KLONDYKES
KLONG
KLONGS
KLOOCH
KLOOCHES
KLOOCHMAN
KLOOCHMEN
KLOOF
KLOOFS
KLOOTCH
KLOOTCHES
KLUDGE
KLUDGED
KLUDGES
KLUDGEY
KLUDGIER
KLUDGIEST
KLUDGING
KLUDGY
KLUGE
KLUGED
KLUGES
KLUGING
KLUTZ
KLUTZES
KLUTZIER
KLUTZIEST
KLUTZY
KLYSTRON
KLYSTRONS
KNACK
KNACKED
KNACKER
KNACKERED
KNACKERS
KNACKERY
KNACKIER
KNACKIEST
KNACKING
KNACKISH
KNACKS
KNACKY
KNAG
KNAGGIER
KNAGGIEST
KNAGGY
KNAGS
KNAIDEL
KNAIDELS

KNAIDLACH
KNAP
KNAPPED
KNAPPER
KNAPPERS
KNAPPING
KNAPPLE
KNAPPLED
KNAPPLES
KNAPPLING
KNAPS
KNAPSACK
KNAPSACKS
KNAPWEED
KNAPWEEDS
KNAR
KNARL
KNARLIER
KNARLIEST
KNARLS
KNARLY
KNARRED
KNARRIER
KNARRIEST
KNARRING
KNARRY
KNARS
KNAUR
KNAURS
KNAVE
KNAVERIES
KNAVERY
KNAVES
KNAVESHIP
KNAVISH
KNAVISHLY
KNAWE
KNAWEL
KNAWELS
KNAWES
KNEAD
KNEADABLE
KNEADED
KNEADER
KNEADERS
KNEADING
KNEADS
KNEE
KNEEBOARD
KNEECAP
KNEECAPS
KNEED
KNEEHOLE
KNEEHOLES
KNEEING
KNEEJERK
KNEEL
KNEELED
KNEELER
KNEELERS
KNEELIKE
KNEELING
KNEELS
KNEEPAD
KNEEPADS
KNEEPAN
KNEEPANS
KNEEPIECE
KNEEROOM
KNEEROOMS
KNEES
KNEESIES
KNEESOCK
KNEESOCKS
KNEIDEL
KNEIDELS
KNEIDLACH
KNELL
KNELLED
KNELLING
KNELLS
KNELT
KNESSET
KNESSETS
KNEVELL
KNEVELLED
KNEVELLS
KNEW
KNICKER
KNICKERED
KNICKERS
KNICKS
KNIFE
KNIFED
KNIFELESS
KNIFELIKE
KNIFEMAN
KNIFEMEN
KNIFER
KNIFEREST
KNIFERS
KNIFES
KNIFING
KNIFINGS
KNIGHT
KNIGHTAGE
KNIGHTED
KNIGHTING
KNIGHTLY
KNIGHTS
KNIPHOFIA
KNISH
KNISHES
KNIT
KNITBONE
KNITBONES
KNITCH
KNITCHES
KNITS
KNITTABLE
KNITTED
KNITTER
KNITTERS
KNITTING
KNITTINGS
KNITTLE
KNITTLES
KNITWEAR
KNITWEARS
KNIVE
KNIVED
KNIVES
KNIVING
KNOB
KNOBBED
KNOBBER
KNOBBERS
KNOBBIER
KNOBBIEST
KNOBBING
KNOBBLE
KNOBBLED
KNOBBLES
KNOBBLIER
KNOBBLING
KNOBBLY
KNOBBY
KNOBHEAD
KNOBHEADS
KNOBLIKE
KNOBS
KNOBSTICK
KNOCK
KNOCKBACK
KNOCKDOWN
KNOCKED
KNOCKER
KNOCKERS
KNOCKING
KNOCKINGS
KNOCKLESS
KNOCKOFF
KNOCKOFFS
KNOCKOUT
KNOCKOUTS
KNOCKS
KNOLL
KNOLLED
KNOLLER
KNOLLERS
KNOLLIER
KNOLLIEST
KNOLLING
KNOLLS
KNOLLY
KNOP
KNOPPED
KNOPS
KNOSP
KNOSPS
KNOT
KNOTGRASS
KNOTHEAD
KNOTHEADS
KNOTHOLE
KNOTHOLES
KNOTLESS
KNOTLIKE
KNOTS
KNOTTED
KNOTTER
KNOTTERS
KNOTTIER
KNOTTIEST
KNOTTILY
KNOTTING
KNOTTINGS
KNOTTY
KNOTWEED
KNOTWEEDS
KNOTWORK
KNOTWORKS
KNOUT
KNOUTED
KNOUTING
KNOUTS
KNOW
KNOWABLE
KNOWE
KNOWER
KNOWERS
KNOWES
KNOWHOW
KNOWHOWS
KNOWING
KNOWINGER
KNOWINGLY
KNOWINGS
KNOWLEDGE
KNOWN
KNOWNS
KNOWS
KNUB
KNUBBIER
KNUBBIEST
KNUBBLE
KNUBBLED
KNUBBLES
KNUBBLIER
KNUBBLING
KNUBBLY
KNUBBY
KNUBS
KNUCKLE
KNUCKLED
KNUCKLER
KNUCKLERS
KNUCKLES
KNUCKLIER
KNUCKLING

KNUCKLY
KNUR
KNURL
KNURLED
KNURLIER
KNURLIEST
KNURLING
KNURLINGS
KNURLS
KNURLY
KNURR
KNURRS
KNURS
KNUT
KNUTS
KO
KOA
KOALA
KOALAS
KOAN
KOANS
KOAP
KOAPS
KOAS
KOB
KOBAN
KOBANG
KOBANGS
KOBANS
KOBO
KOBOLD
KOBOLDS
KOBOS
KOBS
KOCHIA
KOCHIAS
KOEKOEA
KOEKOEAS
KOEL
KOELS
KOFF
KOFFS
KOFTA
KOFTAS
KOFTGAR
KOFTGARI
KOFTGARIS
KOFTGARS
KOFTWORK
KOFTWORKS
KOGAL
KOGALS
KOHA
KOHANIM
KOHAS
KOHEKOHE
KOHEKOHES
KOHEN
KOHL
KOHLRABI
KOHLRABIS
KOHLS
KOI
KOINE
KOINES
KOIS
KOJI
KOJIS
KOKA
KOKAKO
KOKAKOS
KOKAM
KOKAMS
KOKANEE
KOKANEES
KOKAS
KOKER
KOKERS
KOKIRI
KOKIRIS
KOKOBEH
KOKOPU
KOKOPUS
KOKOWAI
KOKOWAIS
KOKRA
KOKRAS
KOKUM
KOKUMS
KOLA
KOLACKIES
KOLACKY
KOLAS
KOLBASI
KOLBASIS
KOLBASSA
KOLBASSAS
KOLBASSI
KOLBASSIS
KOLHOZ
KOLHOZES
KOLHOZY
KOLINSKI
KOLINSKY
KOLKHOS
KOLKHOSES
KOLKHOSY
KOLKHOZ
KOLKHOZES
KOLKHOZY
KOLKOZ
KOLKOZES
KOLKOZY
KOLO
KOLOS
KOMATIK
KOMATIKS
KOMBU
KOMBUS
KOMISSAR
KOMISSARS
KOMITAJI
KOMITAJIS
KOMONDOR
KOMONDORS
KOMPROMAT
KON
KONAKI
KONAKIS
KONBU
KONBUS
KOND
KONDO
KONDOS
KONEKE
KONEKES
KONFYT
KONFYTS
KONGONI
KONIMETER
KONINI
KONINIS
KONIOLOGY
KONISCOPE
KONK
KONKED
KONKING
KONKS
KONNING
KONS
KOODOO
KOODOOS
KOOK
KOOKED
KOOKIE
KOOKIER
KOOKIEST
KOOKILY
KOOKINESS
KOOKING
KOOKS
KOOKUM
KOOKUMS
KOOKY
KOOLAH
KOOLAHS
KOORI
KOORIES
KOORIS
KOP
KOPASETIC
KOPECK
KOPECKS
KOPEK
KOPEKS
KOPH
KOPHS
KOPIYKA
KOPIYKAS
KOPIYKY
KOPIYOK
KOPJE
KOPJES
KOPPA
KOPPAS
KOPPIE
KOPPIES
KOPS
KOR
KORA
KORAI
KORARI
KORARIS
KORAS
KORAT
KORATS
KORE
KORERO
KOREROED
KOREROING
KOREROS
KORES
KORFBALL
KORFBALLS
KORIMAKO
KORIMAKOS
KORKIR
KORKIRS
KORMA
KORMAS
KORO
KOROMIKO
KOROMIKOS
KORORA
KORORAS
KOROS
KOROWAI
KOROWAIS
KORS
KORU
KORUN
KORUNA
KORUNAS
KORUNY
KORUS
KOS
KOSES
KOSHER
KOSHERED
KOSHERING
KOSHERS
KOSMOS
KOSMOSES
KOSS
KOSSES
KOTARE
KOTARES
KOTCH
KOTCHED
KOTCHES

K

KOTCHING
KOTO
KOTOS
KOTOW
KOTOWED
KOTOWER
KOTOWERS
KOTOWING
KOTOWS
KOTTABOS
KOTUKU
KOTUKUS
KOTWAL
KOTWALS
KOULAN
KOULANS
KOUMIS
KOUMISES
KOUMISS
KOUMISSES
KOUMYS
KOUMYSES
KOUMYSS
KOUMYSSES
KOUPREY
KOUPREYS
KOURA
KOURAS
KOURBASH
KOUROI
KOUROS
KOUSKOUS
KOUSSO
KOUSSOS
KOW
KOWHAI
KOWHAIS
KOWS
KOWTOW
KOWTOWED
KOWTOWER
KOWTOWERS
KOWTOWING
KOWTOWS
KRAAL
KRAALED
KRAALING
KRAALS
KRAB
KRABS
KRAFT
KRAFTS
KRAI
KRAIS
KRAIT
KRAITS
KRAKEN
KRAKENS
KRAKOWIAK
KRAMERIA
KRAMERIAS
KRANG
KRANGS
KRANS
KRANSES
KRANTZ
KRANTZES
KRANZ
KRANZES
KRATER
KRATERS
KRAUT
KRAUTROCK
KRAUTS
KRAY
KRAYS
KREASOTE
KREASOTED
KREASOTES
KREATINE
KREATINES
KREEP
KREEPS
KREESE
KREESED
KREESES
KREESING
KREMLIN
KREMLINS
KRENG
KRENGS
KREOSOTE
KREOSOTED
KREOSOTES
KREPLACH
KREPLECH
KREUTZER
KREUTZERS
KREUZER
KREUZERS
KREWE
KREWES
KRILL
KRILLS
KRIMMER
KRIMMERS
KRIS
KRISED
KRISES
KRISING
KROMESKY
KRONA
KRONE
KRONEN
KRONER
KRONOR
KRONUR
KROON
KROONI
KROONS
KRUBI
KRUBIS
KRUBUT
KRUBUTS
KRULLER
KRULLERS
KRUMHORN
KRUMHORNS
KRUMKAKE
KRUMKAKES
KRUMMHOLZ
KRUMMHORN
KRUMPER
KRUMPERS
KRUMPING
KRUMPINGS
KRUNK
KRUNKED
KRUNKS
KRYOLITE
KRYOLITES
KRYOLITH
KRYOLITHS
KRYOMETER
KRYPSES
KRYPSIS
KRYPTON
KRYPTONS
KRYTRON
KRYTRONS
KSAR
KSARS
KUBASA
KUBASAS
KUBIE
KUBIES
KUCCHA
KUCCHAS
KUCHCHA
KUCHEN
KUCHENS
KUDLIK
KUDLIKS
KUDO
KUDOS
KUDOSES
KUDU
KUDUS
KUDZU
KUDZUS
KUE
KUEH
KUES
KUFI
KUFIS
KUFIYAH
KUFIYAHS
KUGEL
KUGELS
KUIA
KUIAS
KUKRI
KUKRIS
KUKU
KUKUS
KULA
KULAK
KULAKI
KULAKS
KULAN
KULANS
KULAS
KULBASA
KULBASAS
KULFI
KULFIS
KULTUR
KULTURS
KUMARA
KUMARAHOU
KUMARAS
KUMARI
KUMARIS
KUMBALOI
KUMERA
KUMERAS
KUMIKUMI
KUMIKUMIS
KUMIS
KUMISES
KUMISS
KUMISSES
KUMITE
KUMITES
KUMKUM
KUMKUMS
KUMMEL
KUMMELS
KUMQUAT
KUMQUATS
KUMYS
KUMYSES
KUNA
KUNDALINI
KUNE
KUNEKUNE
KUNEKUNES
KUNJOOS
KUNKAR
KUNKARS
KUNKUR
KUNKURS
KUNZITE
KUNZITES
KURBASH
KURBASHED
KURBASHES
KURFUFFLE
KURGAN
KURGANS

KURI
KURIS
KURRAJONG
KURRE
KURRES
KURSAAL
KURSAALS
KURTA
KURTAS
KURTOSES
KURTOSIS
KURU
KURUS
KURUSH
KURUSHES
KURVEY
KURVEYED
KURVEYING
KURVEYOR
KURVEYORS
KURVEYS
KUSSO
KUSSOS
KUTA
KUTAS
KUTCH
KUTCHA
KUTCHES
KUTI
KUTIS
KUTU
KUTUS
KUVASZ
KUVASZOK
KUZU
KUZUS
KVAS
KVASES
KVASS
KVASSES
KVELL
KVELLED
KVELLING
KVELLS
KVETCH
KVETCHED
KVETCHER
KVETCHERS
KVETCHES
KVETCHIER
KVETCHILY
KVETCHING
KVETCHY
KWACHA
KWACHAS
KWAITO
KWAITOS
KWANZA
KWANZAS
KWELA
KWELAS
KY
KYACK
KYACKS
KYAK
KYAKS
KYANG
KYANGS
KYANISE
KYANISED
KYANISES
KYANISING
KYANITE
KYANITES
KYANITIC
KYANIZE
KYANIZED
KYANIZES
KYANIZING
KYAR
KYARS
KYAT
KYATS
KYBO
KYBOS
KYBOSH
KYBOSHED
KYBOSHES
KYBOSHING
KYDST
KYE
KYES
KYLE
KYLES
KYLICES
KYLIE
KYLIES
KYLIKES
KYLIN
KYLINS
KYLIX
KYLIXES
KYLLOSES
KYLLOSIS
KYLOE
KYLOES
KYMOGRAM
KYMOGRAMS
KYMOGRAPH
KYND
KYNDE
KYNDED
KYNDES
KYNDING
KYNDS
KYNE
KYOGEN
KYOGENS
KYPE
KYPES
KYPHOSES
KYPHOSIS
KYPHOTIC
KYRIE
KYRIELLE
KYRIELLES
KYRIES
KYTE
KYTES
KYTHE
KYTHED
KYTHES
KYTHING
KYU
KYUS

L

LA
LAAGER
LAAGERED
LAAGERING
LAAGERS
LAARI
LAARIS
LAB
LABARA
LABARUM
LABARUMS
LABDA
LABDACISM
LABDANUM
LABDANUMS
LABDAS
LABEL
LABELABLE
LABELED
LABELER
LABELERS
LABELING
LABELLA
LABELLATE
LABELLED
LABELLER
LABELLERS
LABELLING
LABELLIST
LABELLOID
LABELLUM
LABELMATE
LABELS
LABIA
LABIAL
LABIALISE
LABIALISM
LABIALITY
LABIALIZE
LABIALLY
LABIALS
LABIATE
LABIATED
LABIATES
LABILE
LABILITY
LABIS
LABISES
LABIUM
LABLAB
LABLABS
LABNEH
LABNEHS
LABOR
LABORED
LABOREDLY
LABORER
LABORERS
LABORING
LABORIOUS
LABORISM
LABORISMS
LABORIST
LABORISTS
LABORITE
LABORITES
LABORS
LABORSOME
LABOUR
LABOURED
LABOURER
LABOURERS
LABOURING
LABOURISM
LABOURIST
LABOURITE
LABOURS
LABRA
LABRADOR
LABRADORS
LABRAL
LABRET
LABRETS
LABRID
LABRIDS
LABROID
LABROIDS
LABROSE
LABRUM
LABRUMS
LABRUSCA
LABRUSCAS
LABRYS
LABRYSES
LABS
LABURNUM
LABURNUMS
LABYRINTH
LAC
LACCOLITE
LACCOLITH
LACE
LACEBARK
LACEBARKS
LACED
LACELESS
LACELIKE
LACEMAKER
LACER
LACERABLE
LACERANT
LACERATE
LACERATED
LACERATES
LACERS
LACERTIAN
LACERTID
LACERTIDS
LACERTINE
LACES
LACET
LACETS
LACEWING
LACEWINGS
LACEWOOD
LACEWOODS
LACEWORK
LACEWORKS
LACEY
LACHES
LACHESES
LACHRYMAL
LACIER
LACIEST
LACILY
LACINESS
LACING
LACINGS
LACINIA
LACINIAE
LACINIATE
LACK
LACKADAY
LACKED
LACKER
LACKERED
LACKERING
LACKERS
LACKEY
LACKEYED
LACKEYING
LACKEYS
LACKING
LACKLAND
LACKLANDS
LACKS
LACMUS
LACMUSES
LACONIC
LACONICAL
LACONISM
LACONISMS
LACQUER
LACQUERED
LACQUERER
LACQUERS
LACQUEY
LACQUEYED
LACQUEYS
LACRIMAL
LACRIMALS
LACRIMARY
LACRIMOSO
LACROSSE
LACROSSES
LACRYMAL
LACRYMALS
LACS
LACTAM
LACTAMS
LACTARIAN
LACTARY
LACTASE
LACTASES
LACTATE
LACTATED
LACTATES
LACTATING
LACTATION
LACTEAL
LACTEALLY
LACTEALS
LACTEAN
LACTEOUS
LACTIC
LACTIFIC
LACTITOL
LACTITOLS
LACTIVISM
LACTIVIST
LACTONE
LACTONES
LACTONIC
LACTOSE
LACTOSES
LACTULOSE
LACUNA
LACUNAE
LACUNAL
LACUNAR

L

LACUNARIA
LACUNARS
LACUNARY
LACUNAS
LACUNATE
LACUNE
LACUNES
LACUNOSE
LACY
LAD
LADANUM
LADANUMS
LADDER
LADDERED
LADDERIER
LADDERING
LADDERS
LADDERY
LADDIE
LADDIER
LADDIES
LADDIEST
LADDISH
LADDISHLY
LADDISM
LADDISMS
LADDY
LADE
LADED
LADEN
LADENED
LADENING
LADENS
LADER
LADERS
LADES
LADETTE
LADETTES
LADHOOD
LADHOODS
LADIES
LADIFIED
LADIFIES
LADIFY
LADIFYING
LADING
LADINGS
LADINO
LADINOS
LADLE
LADLED
LADLEFUL
LADLEFULS
LADLER
LADLERS
LADLES
LADLING
LADRON
LADRONE
LADRONES
LADRONS
LADS
LADY
LADYBIRD
LADYBIRDS
LADYBOY
LADYBOYS
LADYBUG
LADYBUGS
LADYCOW
LADYCOWS
LADYFIED
LADYFIES
LADYFISH
LADYFLIES
LADYFLY
LADYFY
LADYFYING
LADYHOOD
LADYHOODS
LADYISH
LADYISM
LADYISMS
LADYKIN
LADYKINS
LADYLIKE
LADYLOVE
LADYLOVES
LADYNESS
LADYPALM
LADYPALMS
LADYSHIP
LADYSHIPS
LAER
LAERED
LAERING
LAERS
LAESIE
LAETARE
LAETARES
LAETRILE
LAETRILES
LAEVIGATE
LAEVO
LAEVULIN
LAEVULINS
LAEVULOSE
LAG
LAGAN
LAGANS
LAGENA
LAGENAS
LAGEND
LAGENDS
LAGER
LAGERED
LAGERING
LAGERS
LAGGARD
LAGGARDLY
LAGGARDS
LAGGED
LAGGEN
LAGGENS
LAGGER
LAGGERS
LAGGIN
LAGGING
LAGGINGLY
LAGGINGS
LAGGINS
LAGNAPPE
LAGNAPPES
LAGNIAPPE
LAGOMORPH
LAGOON
LAGOONAL
LAGOONS
LAGRIMOSO
LAGS
LAGUNA
LAGUNAS
LAGUNE
LAGUNES
LAH
LAHAL
LAHALS
LAHAR
LAHARS
LAHS
LAIC
LAICAL
LAICALLY
LAICH
LAICHS
LAICISE
LAICISED
LAICISES
LAICISING
LAICISM
LAICISMS
LAICITIES
LAICITY
LAICIZE
LAICIZED
LAICIZES
LAICIZING
LAICS
LAID
LAIDED
LAIDING
LAIDLIER
LAIDLIEST
LAIDLY
LAIDS
LAIGH
LAIGHER
LAIGHEST
LAIGHS
LAIK
LAIKA
LAIKAS
LAIKED
LAIKER
LAIKERS
LAIKING
LAIKS
LAIN
LAIPSE
LAIPSED
LAIPSES
LAIPSING
LAIR
LAIRAGE
LAIRAGES
LAIRD
LAIRDLIER
LAIRDLY
LAIRDS
LAIRDSHIP
LAIRED
LAIRIER
LAIRIEST
LAIRING
LAIRISE
LAIRISED
LAIRISES
LAIRISING
LAIRIZE
LAIRIZED
LAIRIZES
LAIRIZING
LAIRS
LAIRY
LAISSE
LAISSES
LAITANCE
LAITANCES
LAITH
LAITHLY
LAITIES
LAITY
LAKE
LAKEBED
LAKEBEDS
LAKED
LAKEFILL
LAKEFILLS
LAKEFRONT
LAKEHEAD
LAKEHEADS
LAKELAND
LAKELANDS
LAKELET
LAKELETS
LAKELIKE
LAKEPORT
LAKEPORTS
LAKER
LAKERS

LAKES
LAKESHORE
LAKESIDE
LAKESIDES
LAKEVIEW
LAKEWARD
LAKEWARDS
LAKH
LAKHS
LAKIER
LAKIEST
LAKIN
LAKING
LAKINGS
LAKINS
LAKISH
LAKSA
LAKSAS
LAKY
LALANG
LALANGS
LALDIE
LALDIES
LALDY
LALIQUE
LALIQUES
LALL
LALLAN
LALLAND
LALLANDS
LALLANS
LALLATION
LALLED
LALLING
LALLINGS
LALLS
LALLYGAG
LALLYGAGS
LAM
LAMA
LAMAISTIC
LAMANTIN
LAMANTINS
LAMAS
LAMASERAI
LAMASERY
LAMB
LAMBADA
LAMBADAS
LAMBAST
LAMBASTE
LAMBASTED
LAMBASTES
LAMBASTS
LAMBDA
LAMBDAS
LAMBDOID
LAMBED
LAMBENCY
LAMBENT
LAMBENTLY
LAMBER
LAMBERS
LAMBERT
LAMBERTS
LAMBIE
LAMBIER
LAMBIES
LAMBIEST
LAMBING
LAMBINGS
LAMBITIVE
LAMBKILL
LAMBKILLS
LAMBKIN
LAMBKINS
LAMBLIKE
LAMBLING
LAMBLINGS
LAMBOYS
LAMBRUSCO
LAMBS
LAMBSKIN
LAMBSKINS
LAMBSWOOL
LAMBY
LAME
LAMEBRAIN
LAMED
LAMEDH
LAMEDHS
LAMEDS
LAMELLA
LAMELLAE
LAMELLAR
LAMELLAS
LAMELLATE
LAMELLOID
LAMELLOSE
LAMELY
LAMENESS
LAMENT
LAMENTED
LAMENTER
LAMENTERS
LAMENTING
LAMENTS
LAMER
LAMES
LAMEST
LAMETER
LAMETERS
LAMIA
LAMIAE
LAMIAS
LAMIGER
LAMIGERS
LAMINA
LAMINABLE
LAMINAE
LAMINAL
LAMINALS
LAMINAR
LAMINARIA
LAMINARIN
LAMINARY
LAMINAS
LAMINATE
LAMINATED
LAMINATES
LAMINATOR
LAMING
LAMINGTON
LAMININ
LAMININS
LAMINITIS
LAMINOSE
LAMINOUS
LAMISH
LAMISTER
LAMISTERS
LAMITER
LAMITERS
LAMMED
LAMMER
LAMMERS
LAMMIE
LAMMIES
LAMMIGER
LAMMIGERS
LAMMING
LAMMINGS
LAMMY
LAMP
LAMPAD
LAMPADARY
LAMPADIST
LAMPADS
LAMPAS
LAMPASES
LAMPASSE
LAMPASSES
LAMPBLACK
LAMPBRUSH
LAMPED
LAMPER
LAMPERN
LAMPERNS
LAMPERS
LAMPERSES
LAMPHOLE
LAMPHOLES
LAMPING
LAMPINGS
LAMPION
LAMPIONS
LAMPLESS
LAMPLIGHT
LAMPLIT
LAMPOON
LAMPOONED
LAMPOONER
LAMPOONS
LAMPPOST
LAMPPOSTS
LAMPREY
LAMPREYS
LAMPS
LAMPSHADE
LAMPSHELL
LAMPSTAND
LAMPUKA
LAMPUKAS
LAMPUKI
LAMPUKIS
LAMPYRID
LAMPYRIDS
LAMS
LAMSTER
LAMSTERS
LANA
LANAI
LANAIS
LANAS
LANATE
LANATED
LANCE
LANCED
LANCEGAY
LANCEGAYS
LANCEJACK
LANCELET
LANCELETS
LANCELIKE
LANCEOLAR
LANCER
LANCERS
LANCES
LANCET
LANCETED
LANCETS
LANCEWOOD
LANCH
LANCHED
LANCHES
LANCHING
LANCIERS
LANCIFORM
LANCINATE
LANCING
LAND
LANDAMMAN
LANDAU
LANDAULET
LANDAUS
LANDBOARD
LANDDAMNE
LANDDROS
LANDDROST
LANDE

L

LANDED
LANDER
LANDERS
LANDES
LANDFALL
LANDFALLS
LANDFAST
LANDFILL
LANDFILLS
LANDFORCE
LANDFORM
LANDFORMS
LANDGRAB
LANDGRABS
LANDGRAVE
LANDING
LANDINGS
LANDLADY
LANDLER
LANDLERS
LANDLESS
LANDLINE
LANDLINES
LANDLOPER
LANDLORD
LANDLORDS
LANDMAN
LANDMARK
LANDMARKS
LANDMASS
LANDMEN
LANDMINE
LANDMINED
LANDMINES
LANDOWNER
LANDRACE
LANDRACES
LANDRAIL
LANDRAILS
LANDS
LANDSCAPE
LANDSHARK
LANDSIDE
LANDSIDES
LANDSKIP
LANDSKIPS
LANDSLEIT
LANDSLID
LANDSLIDE
LANDSLIP
LANDSLIPS
LANDSMAN
LANDSMEN
LANDWARD
LANDWARDS
LANDWASH
LANDWIND
LANDWINDS
LANE
LANELY
LANES
LANEWAY
LANEWAYS
LANG
LANGAHA
LANGAHAS
LANGAR
LANGARS
LANGER
LANGERED
LANGERS
LANGEST
LANGLAUF
LANGLAUFS
LANGLEY
LANGLEYS
LANGOUSTE
LANGRAGE
LANGRAGES
LANGREL
LANGRELS
LANGRIDGE
LANGSHAN
LANGSHANS
LANGSPEL
LANGSPELS
LANGSPIEL
LANGSPIL
LANGSPILS
LANGSYNE
LANGSYNES
LANGUAGE
LANGUAGED
LANGUAGES
LANGUE
LANGUED
LANGUES
LANGUET
LANGUETS
LANGUETTE
LANGUID
LANGUIDLY
LANGUISH
LANGUOR
LANGUORS
LANGUR
LANGURS
LANIARD
LANIARDS
LANIARIES
LANIARY
LANITAL
LANITALS
LANK
LANKED
LANKER
LANKEST
LANKIER
LANKIEST
LANKILY
LANKINESS
LANKING
LANKLY
LANKNESS
LANKS
LANKY
LANNER
LANNERET
LANNERETS
LANNERS
LANOLATED
LANOLIN
LANOLINE
LANOLINES
LANOLINS
LANOSE
LANOSITY
LANT
LANTANA
LANTANAS
LANTERLOO
LANTERN
LANTERNED
LANTERNS
LANTHANON
LANTHANUM
LANTHORN
LANTHORNS
LANTS
LANTSKIP
LANTSKIPS
LANUGO
LANUGOS
LANX
LANYARD
LANYARDS
LAODICEAN
LAOGAI
LAOGAIS
LAP
LAPBOARD
LAPBOARDS
LAPDOG
LAPDOGS
LAPEL
LAPELED
LAPELLED
LAPELS
LAPFUL
LAPFULS
LAPHELD
LAPIDARY
LAPIDATE
LAPIDATED
LAPIDATES
LAPIDEOUS
LAPIDES
LAPIDIFIC
LAPIDIFY
LAPIDIST
LAPIDISTS
LAPILLI
LAPILLUS
LAPIN
LAPINS
LAPIS
LAPISES
LAPJE
LAPJES
LAPPED
LAPPEL
LAPPELS
LAPPER
LAPPERED
LAPPERING
LAPPERS
LAPPET
LAPPETED
LAPPETS
LAPPIE
LAPPIES
LAPPING
LAPPINGS
LAPS
LAPSABLE
LAPSANG
LAPSANGS
LAPSE
LAPSED
LAPSER
LAPSERS
LAPSES
LAPSIBLE
LAPSING
LAPSTONE
LAPSTONES
LAPSTRAKE
LAPSTREAK
LAPSUS
LAPTOP
LAPTOPS
LAPTRAY
LAPTRAYS
LAPWING
LAPWINGS
LAPWORK
LAPWORKS
LAQUEARIA
LAR
LARBOARD
LARBOARDS
LARCENER
LARCENERS
LARCENIES
LARCENIST
LARCENOUS
LARCENY
LARCH
LARCHEN
LARCHES

LARCHWOOD
LARD
LARDALITE
LARDED
LARDER
LARDERER
LARDERERS
LARDERS
LARDIER
LARDIEST
LARDING
LARDLIKE
LARDON
LARDONS
LARDOON
LARDOONS
LARDS
LARDY
LARE
LAREE
LAREES
LARES
LARGANDO
LARGE
LARGELY
LARGEN
LARGENED
LARGENESS
LARGENING
LARGENS
LARGER
LARGES
LARGESS
LARGESSE
LARGESSES
LARGEST
LARGHETTO
LARGISH
LARGITION
LARGO
LARGOS
LARI
LARIAT
LARIATED
LARIATING
LARIATS
LARIGAN
LARIGANS
LARINE
LARIS
LARK
LARKED
LARKER
LARKERS
LARKIER
LARKIEST
LARKINESS
LARKING
LARKISH
LARKS
LARKSOME
LARKSPUR
LARKSPURS
LARKY
LARMIER
LARMIERS
LARN
LARNAKES
LARNAX
LARNED
LARNEY
LARNEYS
LARNIER
LARNIEST
LARNING
LARNS
LARNT
LAROID
LARRIGAN
LARRIGANS
LARRIKIN
LARRIKINS
LARRUP
LARRUPED
LARRUPER
LARRUPERS
LARRUPING
LARRUPS
LARS
LARUM
LARUMS
LARVA
LARVAE
LARVAL
LARVAS
LARVATE
LARVATED
LARVICIDE
LARVIFORM
LARVIKITE
LARYNGAL
LARYNGALS
LARYNGEAL
LARYNGES
LARYNX
LARYNXES
LAS
LASAGNA
LASAGNAS
LASAGNE
LASAGNES
LASCAR
LASCARS
LASE
LASED
LASER
LASERDISC
LASERDISK
LASERED
LASERING
LASERS
LASERWORT
LASES
LASH
LASHED
LASHER
LASHERS
LASHES
LASHING
LASHINGLY
LASHINGS
LASHINS
LASHKAR
LASHKARS
LASHLESS
LASING
LASINGS
LASKET
LASKETS
LASQUE
LASQUES
LASS
LASSES
LASSI
LASSIE
LASSIES
LASSIS
LASSITUDE
LASSLORN
LASSO
LASSOCK
LASSOCKS
LASSOED
LASSOER
LASSOERS
LASSOES
LASSOING
LASSOINGS
LASSOS
LASSU
LASSUS
LASSY
LAST
LASTAGE
LASTAGES
LASTBORN
LASTBORNS
LASTED
LASTER
LASTERS
LASTING
LASTINGLY
LASTINGS
LASTLY
LASTS
LAT
LATAH
LATAHS
LATAKIA
LATAKIAS
LATCH
LATCHED
LATCHES
LATCHET
LATCHETS
LATCHING
LATCHKEY
LATCHKEYS
LATE
LATECOMER
LATED
LATEEN
LATEENER
LATEENERS
LATEENS
LATELY
LATEN
LATENCE
LATENCES
LATENCIES
LATENCY
LATENED
LATENESS
LATENING
LATENS
LATENT
LATENTLY
LATENTS
LATER
LATERAD
LATERAL
LATERALED
LATERALLY
LATERALS
LATERBORN
LATERISE
LATERISED
LATERISES
LATERITE
LATERITES
LATERITIC
LATERIZE
LATERIZED
LATERIZES
LATESCENT
LATEST
LATESTS
LATEWAKE
LATEWAKES
LATEWOOD
LATEWOODS
LATEX
LATEXES
LATH
LATHE
LATHED
LATHEE
LATHEES
LATHEN
LATHER

L

LATHERED
LATHERER
LATHERERS
LATHERIER
LATHERING
LATHERS
LATHERY
LATHES
LATHI
LATHIER
LATHIEST
LATHING
LATHINGS
LATHIS
LATHLIKE
LATHS
LATHWORK
LATHWORKS
LATHY
LATHYRISM
LATHYRUS
LATI
LATICES
LATICIFER
LATICLAVE
LATIFONDI
LATIFONDO
LATIGO
LATIGOES
LATIGOS
LATILLA
LATILLAS
LATIMERIA
LATINA
LATINAS
LATINISE
LATINISED
LATINISES
LATINITY
LATINIZE
LATINIZED
LATINIZES
LATINO
LATINOS
LATISH
LATITANCY
LATITANT
LATITAT
LATITATS
LATITUDE
LATITUDES
LATKE
LATKES
LATOSOL
LATOSOLIC
LATOSOLS
LATRANT
LATRATION
LATRIA
LATRIAS
LATRINE
LATRINES
LATROCINY
LATRON
LATRONS
LATS
LATTE
LATTEN
LATTENS
LATTER
LATTERLY
LATTERS
LATTES
LATTICE
LATTICED
LATTICES
LATTICING
LATTICINI
LATTICINO
LATTIN
LATTINS
LATU
LATUS
LAUAN
LAUANS
LAUCH
LAUCHING
LAUCHS
LAUD
LAUDABLE
LAUDABLY
LAUDANUM
LAUDANUMS
LAUDATION
LAUDATIVE
LAUDATOR
LAUDATORS
LAUDATORY
LAUDED
LAUDER
LAUDERS
LAUDING
LAUDS
LAUF
LAUFS
LAUGH
LAUGHABLE
LAUGHABLY
LAUGHED
LAUGHER
LAUGHERS
LAUGHFUL
LAUGHIER
LAUGHIEST
LAUGHING
LAUGHINGS
LAUGHLINE
LAUGHS
LAUGHSOME
LAUGHTER
LAUGHTERS
LAUGHY
LAUNCE
LAUNCED
LAUNCES
LAUNCH
LAUNCHED
LAUNCHER
LAUNCHERS
LAUNCHES
LAUNCHING
LAUNCHPAD
LAUNCING
LAUND
LAUNDER
LAUNDERED
LAUNDERER
LAUNDERS
LAUNDRESS
LAUNDRIES
LAUNDRY
LAUNDS
LAURA
LAURAE
LAURAS
LAUREATE
LAUREATED
LAUREATES
LAUREL
LAURELED
LAURELING
LAURELLED
LAURELS
LAURIC
LAURYL
LAURYLS
LAUWINE
LAUWINES
LAV
LAVA
LAVABO
LAVABOES
LAVABOS
LAVAFORM
LAVAGE
LAVAGES
LAVAL
LAVALAVA
LAVALAVAS
LAVALIER
LAVALIERE
LAVALIERS
LAVALIKE
LAVANDIN
LAVANDINS
LAVAS
LAVASH
LAVASHES
LAVATERA
LAVATERAS
LAVATION
LAVATIONS
LAVATORY
LAVE
LAVED
LAVEER
LAVEERED
LAVEERING
LAVEERS
LAVEMENT
LAVEMENTS
LAVENDER
LAVENDERS
LAVER
LAVEROCK
LAVEROCKS
LAVERS
LAVES
LAVING
LAVISH
LAVISHED
LAVISHER
LAVISHERS
LAVISHES
LAVISHEST
LAVISHING
LAVISHLY
LAVOLT
LAVOLTA
LAVOLTAED
LAVOLTAS
LAVOLTED
LAVOLTING
LAVOLTS
LAVRA
LAVRAS
LAVROCK
LAVROCKS
LAVS
LAVVIES
LAVVY
LAW
LAWBOOK
LAWBOOKS
LAWCOURT
LAWCOURTS
LAWED
LAWER
LAWEST
LAWFARE
LAWFARES
LAWFUL
LAWFULLY
LAWGIVER
LAWGIVERS
LAWGIVING
LAWIN
LAWINE
LAWINES
LAWING

LAWINGS
LAWINS
LAWK
LAWKS
LAWLAND
LAWLANDS
LAWLESS
LAWLESSLY
LAWLIKE
LAWMAKER
LAWMAKERS
LAWMAKING
LAWMAN
LAWMEN
LAWMONGER
LAWN
LAWNED
LAWNIER
LAWNIEST
LAWNING
LAWNMOWER
LAWNS
LAWNY
LAWS
LAWSUIT
LAWSUITS
LAWYER
LAWYERED
LAWYERING
LAWYERLY
LAWYERS
LAX
LAXATION
LAXATIONS
LAXATIVE
LAXATIVES
LAXATOR
LAXATORS
LAXED
LAXER
LAXES
LAXEST
LAXING
LAXISM
LAXISMS
LAXIST
LAXISTS
LAXITIES
LAXITY
LAXLY
LAXNESS
LAXNESSES
LAY
LAYABOUT
LAYABOUTS
LAYAWAY
LAYAWAYS
LAYBACK
LAYBACKED
LAYBACKS
LAYDEEZ
LAYED
LAYER
LAYERAGE
LAYERAGES
LAYERED
LAYERING
LAYERINGS
LAYERS
LAYETTE
LAYETTES
LAYIN
LAYING
LAYINGS
LAYINS
LAYLOCK
LAYLOCKS
LAYMAN
LAYMANISE
LAYMANIZE
LAYMEN
LAYOFF
LAYOFFS
LAYOUT
LAYOUTS
LAYOVER
LAYOVERS
LAYPEOPLE
LAYPERSON
LAYS
LAYSHAFT
LAYSHAFTS
LAYSTALL
LAYSTALLS
LAYTIME
LAYTIMES
LAYUP
LAYUPS
LAYWOMAN
LAYWOMEN
LAZAR
LAZARET
LAZARETS
LAZARETTE
LAZARETTO
LAZARS
LAZE
LAZED
LAZES
LAZIED
LAZIER
LAZIES
LAZIEST
LAZILY
LAZINESS
LAZING
LAZO
LAZOED
LAZOES
LAZOING
LAZOS
LAZULI
LAZULIS
LAZULITE
LAZULITES
LAZURITE
LAZURITES
LAZY
LAZYBONES
LAZYING
LAZYISH
LAZZARONE
LAZZARONI
LAZZI
LAZZO
LEA
LEACH
LEACHABLE
LEACHATE
LEACHATES
LEACHED
LEACHER
LEACHERS
LEACHES
LEACHIER
LEACHIEST
LEACHING
LEACHINGS
LEACHOUR
LEACHOURS
LEACHY
LEAD
LEADABLE
LEADED
LEADEN
LEADENED
LEADENING
LEADENLY
LEADENS
LEADER
LEADERENE
LEADERS
LEADIER
LEADIEST
LEADING
LEADINGLY
LEADINGS
LEADLESS
LEADMAN
LEADMEN
LEADOFF
LEADOFFS
LEADPLANT
LEADS
LEADSCREW
LEADSMAN
LEADSMEN
LEADWORK
LEADWORKS
LEADWORT
LEADWORTS
LEADY
LEAF
LEAFAGE
LEAFAGES
LEAFBUD
LEAFBUDS
LEAFED
LEAFERIES
LEAFERY
LEAFIER
LEAFIEST
LEAFINESS
LEAFING
LEAFLESS
LEAFLET
LEAFLETED
LEAFLETER
LEAFLETS
LEAFLIKE
LEAFMOLD
LEAFMOLDS
LEAFROLL
LEAFROLLS
LEAFS
LEAFSTALK
LEAFWORM
LEAFWORMS
LEAFY
LEAGUE
LEAGUED
LEAGUER
LEAGUERED
LEAGUERS
LEAGUES
LEAGUING
LEAK
LEAKAGE
LEAKAGES
LEAKED
LEAKER
LEAKERS
LEAKIER
LEAKIEST
LEAKILY
LEAKINESS
LEAKING
LEAKLESS
LEAKPROOF
LEAKS
LEAKY
LEAL
LEALER
LEALEST
LEALLY
LEALTIES
LEALTY
LEAM
LEAMED
LEAMING

L

LEAMS
LEAN
LEANED
LEANER
LEANERS
LEANEST
LEANING
LEANINGS
LEANLY
LEANNESS
LEANS
LEANT
LEANY
LEAP
LEAPED
LEAPER
LEAPEROUS
LEAPERS
LEAPFROG
LEAPFROGS
LEAPING
LEAPOROUS
LEAPROUS
LEAPS
LEAPT
LEAR
LEARE
LEARED
LEARES
LEARIER
LEARIEST
LEARINESS
LEARING
LEARN
LEARNABLE
LEARNED
LEARNEDLY
LEARNER
LEARNERS
LEARNING
LEARNINGS
LEARNS
LEARNT
LEARS
LEARY
LEAS
LEASABLE
LEASE
LEASEBACK
LEASED
LEASEHOLD
LEASER
LEASERS
LEASES
LEASH
LEASHED
LEASHES
LEASHING
LEASING
LEASINGS
LEASOW
LEASOWE
LEASOWED
LEASOWES
LEASOWING
LEASOWS
LEAST
LEASTS
LEASTWAYS
LEASTWISE
LEASURE
LEASURES
LEAT
LEATHER
LEATHERED
LEATHERN
LEATHERS
LEATHERY
LEATS
LEAVE
LEAVED
LEAVEN
LEAVENED
LEAVENER
LEAVENERS
LEAVENING
LEAVENOUS
LEAVENS
LEAVER
LEAVERS
LEAVES
LEAVIER
LEAVIEST
LEAVING
LEAVINGS
LEAVY
LEAZE
LEAZES
LEBBEK
LEBBEKS
LEBEN
LEBENS
LEBKUCHEN
LECANORA
LECANORAS
LECCIES
LECCY
LECH
LECHAIM
LECHAIMS
LECHAYIM
LECHAYIMS
LECHED
LECHER
LECHERED
LECHERIES
LECHERING
LECHEROUS
LECHERS
LECHERY
LECHES
LECHING
LECHWE
LECHWES
LECITHIN
LECITHINS
LECTERN
LECTERNS
LECTIN
LECTINS
LECTION
LECTIONS
LECTOR
LECTORATE
LECTORS
LECTOTYPE
LECTRESS
LECTURE
LECTURED
LECTURER
LECTURERS
LECTURES
LECTURING
LECTURN
LECTURNS
LECYTHI
LECYTHIS
LECYTHUS
LED
LEDDEN
LEDDENS
LEDE
LEDES
LEDGE
LEDGED
LEDGER
LEDGERED
LEDGERING
LEDGERS
LEDGES
LEDGIER
LEDGIEST
LEDGY
LEDUM
LEDUMS
LEE
LEEAR
LEEARS
LEEBOARD
LEEBOARDS
LEECH
LEECHDOM
LEECHDOMS
LEECHED
LEECHEE
LEECHEES
LEECHES
LEECHING
LEECHLIKE
LEED
LEEING
LEEK
LEEKS
LEEP
LEEPED
LEEPING
LEEPS
LEER
LEERED
LEERIER
LEERIEST
LEERILY
LEERINESS
LEERING
LEERINGLY
LEERINGS
LEERS
LEERY
LEES
LEESE
LEESES
LEESING
LEET
LEETLE
LEETS
LEETSPEAK
LEEWARD
LEEWARDLY
LEEWARDS
LEEWAY
LEEWAYS
LEEZE
LEFT
LEFTE
LEFTER
LEFTEST
LEFTIE
LEFTIES
LEFTISH
LEFTISM
LEFTISMS
LEFTIST
LEFTISTS
LEFTMOST
LEFTMOSTS
LEFTOVER
LEFTOVERS
LEFTS
LEFTWARD
LEFTWARDS
LEFTWING
LEFTY
LEG
LEGACIES
LEGACY
LEGAL
LEGALESE
LEGALESES
LEGALISE
LEGALISED

LEGALISER
LEGALISES
LEGALISM
LEGALISMS
LEGALIST
LEGALISTS
LEGALITY
LEGALIZE
LEGALIZED
LEGALIZER
LEGALIZES
LEGALLY
LEGALS
LEGATARY
LEGATE
LEGATED
LEGATEE
LEGATEES
LEGATES
LEGATINE
LEGATING
LEGATION
LEGATIONS
LEGATO
LEGATOR
LEGATORS
LEGATOS
LEGEND
LEGENDARY
LEGENDISE
LEGENDIST
LEGENDIZE
LEGENDRY
LEGENDS
LEGER
LEGERING
LEGERINGS
LEGERITY
LEGERS
LEGES
LEGGE
LEGGED
LEGGER
LEGGERS
LEGGES
LEGGIE
LEGGIER
LEGGIERO
LEGGIES
LEGGIEST
LEGGIN
LEGGINESS
LEGGING
LEGGINGED
LEGGINGS
LEGGINS
LEGGISM
LEGGISMS
LEGGO
LEGGY
LEGHOLD
LEGHOLDS
LEGHORN
LEGHORNS
LEGIBLE
LEGIBLY
LEGION
LEGIONARY
LEGIONED
LEGIONS
LEGISLATE
LEGIST
LEGISTS
LEGIT
LEGITIM
LEGITIMS
LEGITS
LEGLAN
LEGLANS
LEGLEN
LEGLENS
LEGLESS
LEGLET
LEGLETS
LEGLIKE
LEGLIN
LEGLINS
LEGMAN
LEGMEN
LEGONG
LEGONGS
LEGROOM
LEGROOMS
LEGS
LEGSIDE
LEGSIDES
LEGUAAN
LEGUAANS
LEGUAN
LEGUANS
LEGUME
LEGUMES
LEGUMIN
LEGUMINS
LEGWARMER
LEGWEAR
LEGWEARS
LEGWORK
LEGWORKS
LEHAIM
LEHAIMS
LEHAYIM
LEHAYIMS
LEHR
LEHRJAHRE
LEHRS
LEHUA
LEHUAS
LEI
LEIDGER
LEIDGERS
LEIGER
LEIGERS
LEIOMYOMA
LEIPOA
LEIPOAS
LEIR
LEIRED
LEIRING
LEIRS
LEIS
LEISH
LEISHER
LEISHEST
LEISLER
LEISLERS
LEISTER
LEISTERED
LEISTERS
LEISURE
LEISURED
LEISURELY
LEISURES
LEISURING
LEITMOTIF
LEITMOTIV
LEK
LEKE
LEKGOTLA
LEKGOTLAS
LEKKED
LEKKER
LEKKING
LEKKINGS
LEKS
LEKU
LEKVAR
LEKVARS
LEKYTHI
LEKYTHOI
LEKYTHOS
LEKYTHUS
LEMAN
LEMANS
LEME
LEMED
LEMEL
LEMELS
LEMES
LEMING
LEMMA
LEMMAS
LEMMATA
LEMMATISE
LEMMATIZE
LEMME
LEMMING
LEMMINGS
LEMNISCAL
LEMNISCI
LEMNISCUS
LEMON
LEMONADE
LEMONADES
LEMONED
LEMONFISH
LEMONIER
LEMONIEST
LEMONING
LEMONISH
LEMONLIKE
LEMONS
LEMONWOOD
LEMONY
LEMPIRA
LEMPIRAS
LEMUR
LEMURES
LEMURIAN
LEMURIANS
LEMURINE
LEMURINES
LEMURLIKE
LEMUROID
LEMUROIDS
LEMURS
LEND
LENDABLE
LENDER
LENDERS
LENDING
LENDINGS
LENDS
LENES
LENG
LENGED
LENGER
LENGEST
LENGING
LENGS
LENGTH
LENGTHEN
LENGTHENS
LENGTHFUL
LENGTHIER
LENGTHILY
LENGTHMAN
LENGTHMEN
LENGTHS
LENGTHY
LENIENCE
LENIENCES
LENIENCY
LENIENT
LENIENTLY
LENIENTS
LENIFIED
LENIFIES
LENIFY
LENIFYING

L

LENIS
LENITE
LENITED
LENITES
LENITIES
LENITING
LENITION
LENITIONS
LENITIVE
LENITIVES
LENITY
LENO
LENOS
LENS
LENSE
LENSED
LENSES
LENSING
LENSINGS
LENSLESS
LENSLIKE
LENSMAN
LENSMEN
LENT
LENTANDO
LENTEN
LENTI
LENTIC
LENTICEL
LENTICELS
LENTICLE
LENTICLES
LENTICULE
LENTIFORM
LENTIGO
LENTIL
LENTILS
LENTISC
LENTISCS
LENTISK
LENTISKS
LENTO
LENTOID
LENTOIDS
LENTOR
LENTORS
LENTOS
LENTOUS
LENVOY
LENVOYS
LEONE
LEONES
LEONINE
LEOPARD
LEOPARDS
LEOTARD
LEOTARDED
LEOTARDS
LEP
LEPER
LEPERS
LEPID
LEPIDOTE
LEPIDOTES
LEPORID
LEPORIDAE
LEPORIDS
LEPORINE
LEPPED
LEPPING
LEPRA
LEPRAS
LEPROSE
LEPROSERY
LEPROSIES
LEPROSITY
LEPROSY
LEPROTIC
LEPROUS
LEPROUSLY
LEPS
LEPT
LEPTA
LEPTIN
LEPTINS
LEPTOME
LEPTOMES
LEPTON
LEPTONIC
LEPTONS
LEPTOPHOS
LEPTOSOME
LEPTOTENE
LEQUEAR
LEQUEARS
LERE
LERED
LERES
LERING
LERNAEAN
LERP
LERPS
LES
LESBIAN
LESBIANS
LESBIC
LESBIGAY
LESBIGAYS
LESBO
LESBOS
LESES
LESION
LESIONED
LESIONING
LESIONS
LESPEDEZA
LESS
LESSEE
LESSEES
LESSEN
LESSENED
LESSENING
LESSENS
LESSER
LESSES
LESSON
LESSONED
LESSONING
LESSONS
LESSOR
LESSORS
LEST
LESTED
LESTING
LESTS
LESULA
LESULAS
LET
LETCH
LETCHED
LETCHES
LETCHING
LETCHINGS
LETDOWN
LETDOWNS
LETHAL
LETHALITY
LETHALLY
LETHALS
LETHARGIC
LETHARGY
LETHE
LETHEAN
LETHEE
LETHEES
LETHES
LETHIED
LETOUT
LETOUTS
LETROZOLE
LETS
LETTABLE
LETTED
LETTER
LETTERBOX
LETTERED
LETTERER
LETTERERS
LETTERING
LETTERMAN
LETTERMEN
LETTERN
LETTERNS
LETTERS
LETTERSET
LETTING
LETTINGS
LETTRE
LETTRES
LETTUCE
LETTUCES
LETUP
LETUPS
LEU
LEUCAEMIA
LEUCAEMIC
LEUCEMIA
LEUCEMIAS
LEUCEMIC
LEUCH
LEUCHEN
LEUCIN
LEUCINE
LEUCINES
LEUCINS
LEUCISM
LEUCISMS
LEUCISTIC
LEUCITE
LEUCITES
LEUCITIC
LEUCO
LEUCOCYTE
LEUCOMA
LEUCOMAS
LEUCON
LEUCONS
LEUCOSES
LEUCOSIN
LEUCOSINS
LEUCOSIS
LEUCOTIC
LEUCOTOME
LEUCOTOMY
LEUD
LEUDES
LEUDS
LEUGH
LEUGHEN
LEUKAEMIA
LEUKAEMIC
LEUKEMIA
LEUKEMIAS
LEUKEMIC
LEUKEMICS
LEUKEMOID
LEUKOCYTE
LEUKOMA
LEUKOMAS
LEUKON
LEUKONS
LEUKOSES
LEUKOSIS
LEUKOTIC
LEUKOTOME
LEUKOTOMY
LEV
LEVA
LEVANT
LEVANTED

LEVANTER
LEVANTERS
LEVANTINE
LEVANTING
LEVANTS
LEVAS
LEVATOR
LEVATORES
LEVATORS
LEVE
LEVEE
LEVEED
LEVEEING
LEVEES
LEVEL
LEVELED
LEVELER
LEVELERS
LEVELING
LEVELLED
LEVELLER
LEVELLERS
LEVELLEST
LEVELLING
LEVELLY
LEVELNESS
LEVELS
LEVER
LEVERAGE
LEVERAGED
LEVERAGES
LEVERED
LEVERET
LEVERETS
LEVERING
LEVERS
LEVES
LEVIABLE
LEVIATHAN
LEVIED
LEVIER
LEVIERS
LEVIES
LEVIGABLE
LEVIGATE
LEVIGATED
LEVIGATES
LEVIGATOR
LEVIN
LEVINS
LEVIRATE
LEVIRATES
LEVIRATIC
LEVIS
LEVITATE
LEVITATED
LEVITATES
LEVITATOR
LEVITE
LEVITES
LEVITIC
LEVITICAL
LEVITIES
LEVITY
LEVO
LEVODOPA
LEVODOPAS
LEVOGYRE
LEVOGYRES
LEVS
LEVULIN
LEVULINS
LEVULOSE
LEVULOSES
LEVY
LEVYING
LEW
LEWD
LEWDER
LEWDEST
LEWDLY
LEWDNESS
LEWDSBIES
LEWDSBY
LEWDSTER
LEWDSTERS
LEWIS
LEWISES
LEWISIA
LEWISIAS
LEWISITE
LEWISITES
LEWISSON
LEWISSONS
LEX
LEXEME
LEXEMES
LEXEMIC
LEXES
LEXICA
LEXICAL
LEXICALLY
LEXICON
LEXICONS
LEXIGRAM
LEXIGRAMS
LEXIS
LEXISES
LEY
LEYLANDI
LEYLANDII
LEYLANDIS
LEYS
LEZ
LEZES
LEZZ
LEZZA
LEZZAS
LEZZES
LEZZIE
LEZZIES
LEZZY
LI
LIABILITY
LIABLE
LIAISE
LIAISED
LIAISES
LIAISING
LIAISON
LIAISONS
LIANA
LIANAS
LIANE
LIANES
LIANG
LIANGS
LIANOID
LIAR
LIARD
LIARDS
LIARS
LIART
LIAS
LIASES
LIASSIC
LIATRIS
LIATRISES
LIB
LIBANT
LIBATE
LIBATED
LIBATES
LIBATING
LIBATION
LIBATIONS
LIBATORY
LIBBARD
LIBBARDS
LIBBED
LIBBER
LIBBERS
LIBBING
LIBECCHIO
LIBECCIO
LIBECCIOS
LIBEL
LIBELANT
LIBELANTS
LIBELED
LIBELEE
LIBELEES
LIBELER
LIBELERS
LIBELING
LIBELINGS
LIBELIST
LIBELISTS
LIBELLANT
LIBELLED
LIBELLEE
LIBELLEES
LIBELLER
LIBELLERS
LIBELLING
LIBELLOUS
LIBELOUS
LIBELS
LIBER
LIBERAL
LIBERALLY
LIBERALS
LIBERATE
LIBERATED
LIBERATES
LIBERATOR
LIBERO
LIBEROS
LIBERS
LIBERTIES
LIBERTINE
LIBERTY
LIBIDINAL
LIBIDO
LIBIDOS
LIBKEN
LIBKENS
LIBLAB
LIBLABS
LIBRA
LIBRAE
LIBRAIRE
LIBRAIRES
LIBRAIRIE
LIBRARIAN
LIBRARIES
LIBRARY
LIBRAS
LIBRATE
LIBRATED
LIBRATES
LIBRATING
LIBRATION
LIBRATORY
LIBRETTI
LIBRETTO
LIBRETTOS
LIBRI
LIBRIFORM
LIBS
LICE
LICENCE
LICENCED
LICENCEE
LICENCEES
LICENCER
LICENCERS
LICENCES
LICENCING
LICENSE

LICENSED
LICENSEE
LICENSEES
LICENSER
LICENSERS
LICENSES
LICENSING
LICENSOR
LICENSORS
LICENSURE
LICENTE
LICH
LICHANOS
LICHEE
LICHEES
LICHEN
LICHENED
LICHENIN
LICHENING
LICHENINS
LICHENISM
LICHENIST
LICHENOID
LICHENOSE
LICHENOUS
LICHENS
LICHES
LICHGATE
LICHGATES
LICHI
LICHIS
LICHT
LICHTED
LICHTER
LICHTEST
LICHTING
LICHTLIED
LICHTLIES
LICHTLY
LICHTS
LICHWAKE
LICHWAKES
LICHWAY
LICHWAYS
LICIT
LICITLY
LICITNESS
LICK
LICKED
LICKER
LICKERISH
LICKERS
LICKING
LICKINGS
LICKPENNY
LICKS
LICKSPIT
LICKSPITS
LICORICE
LICORICES
LICTOR
LICTORIAN
LICTORS
LID
LIDAR
LIDARS
LIDDED
LIDDING
LIDDINGS
LIDGER
LIDGERS
LIDLESS
LIDO
LIDOCAINE
LIDOS
LIDS
LIE
LIED
LIEDER
LIEF
LIEFER
LIEFEST
LIEFLY
LIEFS
LIEGE
LIEGEDOM
LIEGEDOMS
LIEGELESS
LIEGEMAN
LIEGEMEN
LIEGER
LIEGERS
LIEGES
LIEN
LIENABLE
LIENAL
LIENEE
LIENEES
LIENOR
LIENORS
LIENS
LIENTERIC
LIENTERY
LIER
LIERNE
LIERNES
LIERS
LIES
LIEU
LIEUS
LIEVE
LIEVER
LIEVES
LIEVEST
LIFE
LIFEBELT
LIFEBELTS
LIFEBLOOD
LIFEBOAT
LIFEBOATS
LIFEBUOY
LIFEBUOYS
LIFECARE
LIFECARES
LIFEFUL
LIFEGUARD
LIFEHACK
LIFEHACKS
LIFEHOLD
LIFELESS
LIFELIKE
LIFELINE
LIFELINES
LIFELONG
LIFER
LIFERS
LIFES
LIFESAVER
LIFESOME
LIFESPAN
LIFESPANS
LIFESTYLE
LIFETIME
LIFETIMES
LIFEWAY
LIFEWAYS
LIFEWORK
LIFEWORKS
LIFEWORLD
LIFT
LIFTABLE
LIFTBACK
LIFTBACKS
LIFTBOY
LIFTBOYS
LIFTED
LIFTER
LIFTERS
LIFTGATE
LIFTGATES
LIFTING
LIFTMAN
LIFTMEN
LIFTOFF
LIFTOFFS
LIFTS
LIFULL
LIG
LIGAMENT
LIGAMENTS
LIGAN
LIGAND
LIGANDS
LIGANS
LIGASE
LIGASES
LIGATE
LIGATED
LIGATES
LIGATING
LIGATION
LIGATIONS
LIGATIVE
LIGATURE
LIGATURED
LIGATURES
LIGER
LIGERS
LIGGE
LIGGED
LIGGER
LIGGERS
LIGGES
LIGGING
LIGGINGS
LIGHT
LIGHTBULB
LIGHTED
LIGHTEN
LIGHTENED
LIGHTENER
LIGHTENS
LIGHTER
LIGHTERED
LIGHTERS
LIGHTEST
LIGHTFACE
LIGHTFAST
LIGHTFUL
LIGHTING
LIGHTINGS
LIGHTISH
LIGHTLESS
LIGHTLIED
LIGHTLIES
LIGHTLY
LIGHTNESS
LIGHTNING
LIGHTS
LIGHTSHIP
LIGHTSOME
LIGHTWAVE
LIGHTWOOD
LIGNAGE
LIGNAGES
LIGNALOES
LIGNAN
LIGNANS
LIGNE
LIGNEOUS
LIGNES
LIGNICOLE
LIGNIFIED
LIGNIFIES
LIGNIFORM
LIGNIFY
LIGNIN
LIGNINS
LIGNITE
LIGNITES

L

LIGNITIC
LIGNOSE
LIGNOSES
LIGNUM
LIGNUMS
LIGROIN
LIGROINE
LIGROINES
LIGROINS
LIGS
LIGULA
LIGULAE
LIGULAR
LIGULAS
LIGULATE
LIGULATED
LIGULE
LIGULES
LIGULOID
LIGURE
LIGURES
LIGUSTRUM
LIKABLE
LIKABLY
LIKE
LIKEABLE
LIKEABLY
LIKED
LIKELIER
LIKELIEST
LIKELY
LIKEN
LIKENED
LIKENESS
LIKENING
LIKENS
LIKER
LIKERS
LIKES
LIKEST
LIKEWAKE
LIKEWAKES
LIKEWALK
LIKEWALKS
LIKEWISE
LIKIN
LIKING
LIKINGS
LIKINS
LIKUTA
LILAC
LILACS
LILANGENI
LILIED
LILIES
LILL
LILLED
LILLING
LILLIPUT
LILLIPUTS
LILLS
LILO
LILOS
LILT
LILTED
LILTING
LILTINGLY
LILTS
LILY
LILYLIKE
LIMA
LIMACEL
LIMACELS
LIMACEOUS
LIMACES
LIMACINE
LIMACON
LIMACONS
LIMAIL
LIMAILS
LIMAN
LIMANS
LIMAS
LIMATION
LIMATIONS
LIMAX
LIMB
LIMBA
LIMBAS
LIMBATE
LIMBEC
LIMBECK
LIMBECKS
LIMBECS
LIMBED
LIMBER
LIMBERED
LIMBERER
LIMBEREST
LIMBERING
LIMBERLY
LIMBERS
LIMBI
LIMBIC
LIMBIER
LIMBIEST
LIMBING
LIMBLESS
LIMBMEAL
LIMBO
LIMBOED
LIMBOES
LIMBOING
LIMBOS
LIMBOUS
LIMBS
LIMBUS
LIMBUSES
LIMBY
LIME
LIMEADE
LIMEADES
LIMED
LIMEKILN
LIMEKILNS
LIMELESS
LIMELIGHT
LIMELIT
LIMEN
LIMENS
LIMEPIT
LIMEPITS
LIMERENCE
LIMERICK
LIMERICKS
LIMES
LIMESCALE
LIMESTONE
LIMEWASH
LIMEWATER
LIMEY
LIMEYS
LIMIER
LIMIEST
LIMINA
LIMINAL
LIMINESS
LIMING
LIMINGS
LIMIT
LIMITABLE
LIMITARY
LIMITED
LIMITEDLY
LIMITEDS
LIMITER
LIMITERS
LIMITES
LIMITING
LIMITINGS
LIMITLESS
LIMITS
LIMMA
LIMMAS
LIMMER
LIMMERS
LIMN
LIMNAEID
LIMNAEIDS
LIMNED
LIMNER
LIMNERS
LIMNETIC
LIMNIC
LIMNING
LIMNOLOGY
LIMNS
LIMO
LIMONENE
LIMONENES
LIMONITE
LIMONITES
LIMONITIC
LIMONIUM
LIMONIUMS
LIMOS
LIMOSES
LIMOSIS
LIMOUS
LIMOUSINE
LIMP
LIMPA
LIMPAS
LIMPED
LIMPER
LIMPERS
LIMPEST
LIMPET
LIMPETS
LIMPID
LIMPIDITY
LIMPIDLY
LIMPING
LIMPINGLY
LIMPINGS
LIMPKIN
LIMPKINS
LIMPLY
LIMPNESS
LIMPS
LIMPSEY
LIMPSIER
LIMPSIEST
LIMPSY
LIMULI
LIMULOID
LIMULOIDS
LIMULUS
LIMULUSES
LIMY
LIN
LINABLE
LINAC
LINACS
LINAGE
LINAGES
LINALOL
LINALOLS
LINALOOL
LINALOOLS
LINCH
LINCHES
LINCHET
LINCHETS
LINCHPIN
LINCHPINS
LINCRUSTA
LINCTURE
LINCTURES
LINCTUS

LINCTUSES
LIND
LINDANE
LINDANES
LINDEN
LINDENS
LINDIED
LINDIES
LINDS
LINDWORM
LINDWORMS
LINDY
LINDYING
LINE
LINEABLE
LINEAGE
LINEAGES
LINEAL
LINEALITY
LINEALLY
LINEAMENT
LINEAR
LINEARISE
LINEARITY
LINEARIZE
LINEARLY
LINEATE
LINEATED
LINEATION
LINEBRED
LINECUT
LINECUTS
LINED
LINELESS
LINELIKE
LINEMAN
LINEMATE
LINEMATES
LINEMEN
LINEN
LINENFOLD
LINENIER
LINENIEST
LINENS
LINENY
LINEOLATE
LINER
LINERLESS
LINERS
LINES
LINESCORE
LINESMAN
LINESMEN
LINEUP
LINEUPS
LINEY
LING
LINGA
LINGAM
LINGAMS
LINGAS
LINGBERRY
LINGCOD
LINGCODS
LINGEL
LINGELS
LINGER
LINGERED
LINGERER
LINGERERS
LINGERIE
LINGERIES
LINGERING
LINGERS
LINGIER
LINGIEST
LINGLE
LINGLES
LINGO
LINGOES
LINGOS
LINGOT
LINGOTS
LINGS
LINGSTER
LINGSTERS
LINGUA
LINGUAE
LINGUAL
LINGUALLY
LINGUALS
LINGUAS
LINGUICA
LINGUICAS
LINGUINE
LINGUINES
LINGUINI
LINGUINIS
LINGUISA
LINGUISAS
LINGUIST
LINGUISTS
LINGULA
LINGULAE
LINGULAR
LINGULAS
LINGULATE
LINGY
LINHAY
LINHAYS
LINIER
LINIEST
LINIMENT
LINIMENTS
LININ
LINING
LININGS
LININS
LINISH
LINISHED
LINISHER
LINISHERS
LINISHES
LINISHING
LINK
LINKABLE
LINKAGE
LINKAGES
LINKBOY
LINKBOYS
LINKED
LINKER
LINKERS
LINKIER
LINKIEST
LINKING
LINKMAN
LINKMEN
LINKROT
LINKROTS
LINKS
LINKSLAND
LINKSMAN
LINKSMEN
LINKSPAN
LINKSPANS
LINKSTER
LINKSTERS
LINKUP
LINKUPS
LINKWORK
LINKWORKS
LINKY
LINN
LINNED
LINNET
LINNETS
LINNEY
LINNEYS
LINNIES
LINNING
LINNS
LINNY
LINO
LINOCUT
LINOCUTS
LINOLEATE
LINOLEIC
LINOLENIC
LINOLEUM
LINOLEUMS
LINOS
LINOTYPE
LINOTYPED
LINOTYPER
LINOTYPES
LINS
LINSANG
LINSANGS
LINSEED
LINSEEDS
LINSEY
LINSEYS
LINSTOCK
LINSTOCKS
LINT
LINTED
LINTEL
LINTELED
LINTELLED
LINTELS
LINTER
LINTERS
LINTIE
LINTIER
LINTIES
LINTIEST
LINTING
LINTINGS
LINTLESS
LINTOL
LINTOLS
LINTS
LINTSEED
LINTSEEDS
LINTSTOCK
LINTWHITE
LINTY
LINUM
LINUMS
LINURON
LINURONS
LINUX
LINUXES
LINY
LION
LIONCEL
LIONCELLE
LIONCELS
LIONEL
LIONELS
LIONESS
LIONESSES
LIONET
LIONETS
LIONFISH
LIONHEAD
LIONHEADS
LIONISE
LIONISED
LIONISER
LIONISERS
LIONISES
LIONISING
LIONISM
LIONISMS
LIONIZE
LIONIZED
LIONIZER
LIONIZERS

LIONIZES
LIONIZING
LIONLIER
LIONLIEST
LIONLIKE
LIONLY
LIONS
LIP
LIPA
LIPAEMIA
LIPAEMIAS
LIPARITE
LIPARITES
LIPAS
LIPASE
LIPASES
LIPE
LIPECTOMY
LIPEMIA
LIPEMIAS
LIPES
LIPGLOSS
LIPID
LIPIDE
LIPIDES
LIPIDIC
LIPIDOSES
LIPIDOSIS
LIPIDS
LIPIN
LIPINS
LIPLESS
LIPLIKE
LIPLINER
LIPLINERS
LIPO
LIPOCYTE
LIPOCYTES
LIPOGRAM
LIPOGRAMS
LIPOIC
LIPOID
LIPOIDAL
LIPOIDS
LIPOLITIC
LIPOLYSES
LIPOLYSIS
LIPOLYTIC
LIPOMA
LIPOMAS
LIPOMATA
LIPOPLAST
LIPOS
LIPOSOMAL
LIPOSOME
LIPOSOMES
LIPOSUCK
LIPOSUCKS
LIPOTROPY
LIPPED
LIPPEN
LIPPENED
LIPPENING
LIPPENS
LIPPER
LIPPERED
LIPPERING
LIPPERS
LIPPIE
LIPPIER
LIPPIES
LIPPIEST
LIPPINESS
LIPPING
LIPPINGS
LIPPITUDE
LIPPY
LIPREAD
LIPREADER
LIPREADS
LIPS
LIPSALVE
LIPSALVES
LIPSTICK
LIPSTICKS
LIPURIA
LIPURIAS
LIQUABLE
LIQUATE
LIQUATED
LIQUATES
LIQUATING
LIQUATION
LIQUEFIED
LIQUEFIER
LIQUEFIES
LIQUEFY
LIQUESCE
LIQUESCED
LIQUESCES
LIQUEUR
LIQUEURED
LIQUEURS
LIQUID
LIQUIDATE
LIQUIDIER
LIQUIDISE
LIQUIDITY
LIQUIDIZE
LIQUIDLY
LIQUIDS
LIQUIDUS
LIQUIDY
LIQUIFIED
LIQUIFIER
LIQUIFIES
LIQUIFY
LIQUITAB
LIQUITABS
LIQUOR
LIQUORED
LIQUORICE
LIQUORING
LIQUORISH
LIQUORS
LIRA
LIRAS
LIRE
LIRI
LIRIOPE
LIRIOPES
LIRIPIPE
LIRIPIPES
LIRIPOOP
LIRIPOOPS
LIRK
LIRKED
LIRKING
LIRKS
LIROT
LIROTH
LIS
LISENTE
LISK
LISKS
LISLE
LISLES
LISP
LISPED
LISPER
LISPERS
LISPING
LISPINGLY
LISPINGS
LISPOUND
LISPOUNDS
LISPS
LISPUND
LISPUNDS
LISSES
LISSOM
LISSOME
LISSOMELY
LISSOMLY
LIST
LISTABLE
LISTBOX
LISTBOXES
LISTED
LISTEE
LISTEES
LISTEL
LISTELS
LISTEN
LISTENED
LISTENER
LISTENERS
LISTENING
LISTENS
LISTER
LISTERIA
LISTERIAL
LISTERIAS
LISTERS
LISTETH
LISTFUL
LISTICLE
LISTICLES
LISTING
LISTINGS
LISTLESS
LISTS
LISTSERV
LISTSERVS
LIT
LITAI
LITANIES
LITANY
LITAS
LITCHI
LITCHIS
LITE
LITED
LITENESS
LITER
LITERACY
LITERAL
LITERALLY
LITERALS
LITERARY
LITERATE
LITERATES
LITERATI
LITERATIM
LITERATO
LITERATOR
LITERATUS
LITEROSE
LITERS
LITES
LITEST
LITH
LITHARGE
LITHARGES
LITHATE
LITHATES
LITHE
LITHED
LITHELY
LITHEMIA
LITHEMIAS
LITHEMIC
LITHENESS
LITHER
LITHERLY
LITHES
LITHESOME
LITHEST
LITHIA
LITHIAS

LITHIASES
LITHIASIS
LITHIC
LITHIFIED
LITHIFIES
LITHIFY
LITHING
LITHISTID
LITHITE
LITHITES
LITHIUM
LITHIUMS
LITHO
LITHOCYST
LITHOED
LITHOES
LITHOID
LITHOIDAL
LITHOING
LITHOLOGY
LITHOPONE
LITHOPS
LITHOS
LITHOSOL
LITHOSOLS
LITHOTOME
LITHOTOMY
LITHOTYPE
LITHS
LITIGABLE
LITIGANT
LITIGANTS
LITIGATE
LITIGATED
LITIGATES
LITIGATOR
LITIGIOUS
LITING
LITMUS
LITMUSES
LITORAL
LITOTES
LITOTIC
LITRE
LITREAGE
LITREAGES
LITRES
LITS
LITTEN
LITTER
LITTERBAG
LITTERBUG
LITTERED
LITTERER
LITTERERS
LITTERIER
LITTERING
LITTERS
LITTERY
LITTLE
LITTLER
LITTLES
LITTLEST
LITTLIE
LITTLIES
LITTLIN
LITTLING
LITTLINGS
LITTLINS
LITTLISH
LITTORAL
LITTORALS
LITU
LITURGIC
LITURGICS
LITURGIES
LITURGISM
LITURGIST
LITURGY
LITUUS
LITUUSES
LIVABLE
LIVE
LIVEABLE
LIVEBLOG
LIVEBLOGS
LIVED
LIVEDO
LIVEDOS
LIVELIER
LIVELIEST
LIVELILY
LIVELOD
LIVELODS
LIVELONG
LIVELONGS
LIVELOOD
LIVELOODS
LIVELY
LIVEN
LIVENED
LIVENER
LIVENERS
LIVENESS
LIVENING
LIVENS
LIVER
LIVERED
LIVERIED
LIVERIES
LIVERING
LIVERINGS
LIVERISH
LIVERLEAF
LIVERLESS
LIVERS
LIVERWORT
LIVERY
LIVERYMAN
LIVERYMEN
LIVES
LIVEST
LIVESTOCK
LIVETRAP
LIVETRAPS
LIVEWARE
LIVEWARES
LIVEWELL
LIVEWELLS
LIVEYER
LIVEYERE
LIVEYERES
LIVEYERS
LIVID
LIVIDER
LIVIDEST
LIVIDITY
LIVIDLY
LIVIDNESS
LIVIER
LIVIERS
LIVING
LIVINGLY
LIVINGS
LIVOR
LIVORS
LIVRAISON
LIVRE
LIVRES
LIVYER
LIVYERS
LIXIVIA
LIXIVIAL
LIXIVIATE
LIXIVIOUS
LIXIVIUM
LIXIVIUMS
LIZARD
LIZARDS
LIZZIE
LIZZIES
LLAMA
LLAMAS
LLANERO
LLANEROS
LLANO
LLANOS
LO
LOACH
LOACHES
LOAD
LOADABLE
LOADED
LOADEN
LOADENED
LOADENING
LOADENS
LOADER
LOADERS
LOADING
LOADINGS
LOADS
LOADSPACE
LOADSTAR
LOADSTARS
LOADSTONE
LOAF
LOAFED
LOAFER
LOAFERISH
LOAFERS
LOAFING
LOAFINGS
LOAFS
LOAM
LOAMED
LOAMIER
LOAMIEST
LOAMINESS
LOAMING
LOAMLESS
LOAMS
LOAMY
LOAN
LOANABLE
LOANBACK
LOANBACKS
LOANED
LOANEE
LOANEES
LOANER
LOANERS
LOANING
LOANINGS
LOANS
LOANSHIFT
LOANWORD
LOANWORDS
LOAST
LOATH
LOATHE
LOATHED
LOATHER
LOATHERS
LOATHES
LOATHEST
LOATHFUL
LOATHING
LOATHINGS
LOATHLIER
LOATHLY
LOATHNESS
LOATHSOME
LOATHY
LOAVE
LOAVED
LOAVES
LOAVING
LOB
LOBAR

LOBATE
LOBATED
LOBATELY
LOBATION
LOBATIONS
LOBBED
LOBBER
LOBBERS
LOBBIED
LOBBIES
LOBBING
LOBBY
LOBBYER
LOBBYERS
LOBBYGOW
LOBBYGOWS
LOBBYING
LOBBYINGS
LOBBYISM
LOBBYISMS
LOBBYIST
LOBBYISTS
LOBE
LOBECTOMY
LOBED
LOBEFIN
LOBEFINS
LOBELESS
LOBELET
LOBELETS
LOBELIA
LOBELIAS
LOBELIKE
LOBELINE
LOBELINES
LOBES
LOBI
LOBING
LOBINGS
LOBIPED
LOBLOLLY
LOBO
LOBOLA
LOBOLAS
LOBOLO
LOBOLOS
LOBOS
LOBOSE
LOBOTOMY
LOBS
LOBSCOUSE
LOBSTER
LOBSTERED
LOBSTERER
LOBSTERS
LOBSTICK
LOBSTICKS
LOBTAIL
LOBTAILED
LOBTAILS
LOBULAR
LOBULARLY
LOBULATE
LOBULATED
LOBULE
LOBULES
LOBULI
LOBULOSE
LOBULUS
LOBUS
LOBWORM
LOBWORMS
LOCA
LOCAL
LOCALE
LOCALES
LOCALISE
LOCALISED
LOCALISER
LOCALISES
LOCALISM
LOCALISMS
LOCALIST
LOCALISTS
LOCALITE
LOCALITES
LOCALITY
LOCALIZE
LOCALIZED
LOCALIZER
LOCALIZES
LOCALLY
LOCALNESS
LOCALS
LOCATABLE
LOCATE
LOCATED
LOCATER
LOCATERS
LOCATES
LOCATING
LOCATION
LOCATIONS
LOCATIVE
LOCATIVES
LOCATOR
LOCATORS
LOCAVORE
LOCAVORES
LOCELLATE
LOCH
LOCHAN
LOCHANS
LOCHE
LOCHES
LOCHIA
LOCHIAL
LOCHIAS
LOCHS
LOCI
LOCIE
LOCIES
LOCIS
LOCK
LOCKABLE
LOCKAGE
LOCKAGES
LOCKAWAY
LOCKAWAYS
LOCKBOX
LOCKBOXES
LOCKDOWN
LOCKDOWNS
LOCKED
LOCKER
LOCKERS
LOCKET
LOCKETS
LOCKFAST
LOCKFUL
LOCKFULS
LOCKHOUSE
LOCKING
LOCKINGS
LOCKJAW
LOCKJAWS
LOCKLESS
LOCKMAKER
LOCKMAN
LOCKMEN
LOCKNUT
LOCKNUTS
LOCKOUT
LOCKOUTS
LOCKPICK
LOCKPICKS
LOCKRAM
LOCKRAMS
LOCKS
LOCKSET
LOCKSETS
LOCKSMAN
LOCKSMEN
LOCKSMITH
LOCKSTEP
LOCKSTEPS
LOCKUP
LOCKUPS
LOCO
LOCOED
LOCOES
LOCOFOCO
LOCOFOCOS
LOCOING
LOCOISM
LOCOISMS
LOCOMAN
LOCOMEN
LOCOMOTE
LOCOMOTED
LOCOMOTES
LOCOMOTOR
LOCOPLANT
LOCOS
LOCOWEED
LOCOWEEDS
LOCULAR
LOCULATE
LOCULATED
LOCULE
LOCULED
LOCULES
LOCULI
LOCULUS
LOCUM
LOCUMS
LOCUPLETE
LOCUS
LOCUST
LOCUSTA
LOCUSTAE
LOCUSTAL
LOCUSTED
LOCUSTING
LOCUSTS
LOCUTION
LOCUTIONS
LOCUTORY
LOD
LODE
LODEN
LODENS
LODES
LODESMAN
LODESMEN
LODESTAR
LODESTARS
LODESTONE
LODGE
LODGEABLE
LODGED
LODGEMENT
LODGEPOLE
LODGER
LODGERS
LODGES
LODGING
LODGINGS
LODGMENT
LODGMENTS
LODICULA
LODICULAE
LODICULE
LODICULES
LODS
LOERIE
LOERIES
LOESS
LOESSAL
LOESSES

L

L

LOESSIAL
LOESSIC
LOFT
LOFTED
LOFTER
LOFTERS
LOFTIER
LOFTIEST
LOFTILY
LOFTINESS
LOFTING
LOFTLESS
LOFTLIKE
LOFTS
LOFTSMAN
LOFTSMEN
LOFTY
LOG
LOGAN
LOGANIA
LOGANIAS
LOGANS
LOGAOEDIC
LOGARITHM
LOGBOARD
LOGBOARDS
LOGBOOK
LOGBOOKS
LOGE
LOGES
LOGGAT
LOGGATS
LOGGED
LOGGER
LOGGERS
LOGGETS
LOGGIA
LOGGIAS
LOGGIE
LOGGIER
LOGGIEST
LOGGING
LOGGINGS
LOGGISH
LOGGY
LOGIA
LOGIC
LOGICAL
LOGICALLY
LOGICIAN
LOGICIANS
LOGICISE
LOGICISED
LOGICISES
LOGICISM
LOGICISMS
LOGICIST
LOGICISTS
LOGICIZE
LOGICIZED
LOGICIZES
LOGICLESS
LOGICS
LOGIE
LOGIER
LOGIES
LOGIEST
LOGILY
LOGIN
LOGINESS
LOGINS
LOGION
LOGIONS
LOGISTIC
LOGISTICS
LOGJAM
LOGJAMMED
LOGJAMS
LOGJUICE
LOGJUICES
LOGLINE
LOGLINES
LOGLOG
LOGLOGS
LOGNORMAL
LOGO
LOGOED
LOGOFF
LOGOFFS
LOGOGRAM
LOGOGRAMS
LOGOGRAPH
LOGOGRIPH
LOGOI
LOGOMACH
LOGOMACHS
LOGOMACHY
LOGON
LOGONS
LOGOPEDIC
LOGOPHILE
LOGORRHEA
LOGOS
LOGOTHETE
LOGOTYPE
LOGOTYPES
LOGOTYPY
LOGOUT
LOGOUTS
LOGROLL
LOGROLLED
LOGROLLER
LOGROLLS
LOGS
LOGWAY
LOGWAYS
LOGWOOD
LOGWOODS
LOGY
LOHAN
LOHANS
LOIASES
LOIASIS
LOIASISES
LOID
LOIDED
LOIDING
LOIDS
LOIN
LOINCLOTH
LOINS
LOIPE
LOIPEN
LOIR
LOIRS
LOITER
LOITERED
LOITERER
LOITERERS
LOITERING
LOITERS
LOKE
LOKES
LOKSHEN
LOLIGO
LOLIGOS
LOLIUM
LOLIUMS
LOLL
LOLLED
LOLLER
LOLLERS
LOLLIES
LOLLING
LOLLINGLY
LOLLIPOP
LOLLIPOPS
LOLLOP
LOLLOPED
LOLLOPIER
LOLLOPING
LOLLOPS
LOLLOPY
LOLLS
LOLLY
LOLLYGAG
LOLLYGAGS
LOLLYPOP
LOLLYPOPS
LOLOG
LOLOGS
LOLZ
LOMA
LOMAS
LOMATA
LOME
LOMED
LOMEIN
LOMEINS
LOMENT
LOMENTA
LOMENTS
LOMENTUM
LOMENTUMS
LOMES
LOMING
LOMPISH
LONE
LONELIER
LONELIEST
LONELILY
LONELY
LONENESS
LONER
LONERS
LONESOME
LONESOMES
LONG
LONGA
LONGAEVAL
LONGAN
LONGANS
LONGAS
LONGBOARD
LONGBOAT
LONGBOATS
LONGBOW
LONGBOWS
LONGCASE
LONGCLOTH
LONGE
LONGED
LONGEING
LONGER
LONGERON
LONGERONS
LONGERS
LONGES
LONGEST
LONGEVAL
LONGEVITY
LONGEVOUS
LONGFORM
LONGHAIR
LONGHAIRS
LONGHAND
LONGHANDS
LONGHEAD
LONGHEADS
LONGHORN
LONGHORNS
LONGHOUSE
LONGICORN
LONGIES
LONGING
LONGINGLY
LONGINGS
LONGISH
LONGITUDE
LONGJUMP

LONGJUMPS
LONGLEAF
LONGLINE
LONGLINER
LONGLINES
LONGLIST
LONGLISTS
LONGLY
LONGNECK
LONGNECKS
LONGNESS
LONGS
LONGSHIP
LONGSHIPS
LONGSHORE
LONGSOME
LONGSPUR
LONGSPURS
LONGTIME
LONGUEUR
LONGUEURS
LONGWALL
LONGWALLS
LONGWAYS
LONGWISE
LONGWORM
LONGWORMS
LONICERA
LONICERAS
LOO
LOOBIER
LOOBIES
LOOBIEST
LOOBILY
LOOBY
LOOED
LOOEY
LOOEYS
LOOF
LOOFA
LOOFAH
LOOFAHS
LOOFAS
LOOFFUL
LOOFFULS
LOOFS
LOOGIE
LOOGIES
LOOIE
LOOIES
LOOING
LOOK
LOOKALIKE
LOOKDOWN
LOOKDOWNS
LOOKED
LOOKER
LOOKERS
LOOKIE
LOOKING
LOOKISM
LOOKISMS
LOOKIST
LOOKISTS
LOOKIT
LOOKOUT
LOOKOUTS
LOOKOVER
LOOKOVERS
LOOKS
LOOKSISM
LOOKSISMS
LOOKUP
LOOKUPS
LOOKY
LOOM
LOOMED
LOOMING
LOOMS
LOON
LOONEY
LOONEYS
LOONIE
LOONIER
LOONIES
LOONIEST
LOONILY
LOONINESS
LOONING
LOONINGS
LOONS
LOONY
LOOP
LOOPED
LOOPER
LOOPERS
LOOPHOLE
LOOPHOLED
LOOPHOLES
LOOPIER
LOOPIEST
LOOPILY
LOOPINESS
LOOPING
LOOPINGS
LOOPLIKE
LOOPS
LOOPY
LOOR
LOORD
LOORDS
LOOS
LOOSE
LOOSEBOX
LOOSED
LOOSELY
LOOSEN
LOOSENED
LOOSENER
LOOSENERS
LOOSENESS
LOOSENING
LOOSENS
LOOSER
LOOSES
LOOSEST
LOOSIE
LOOSIES
LOOSING
LOOSINGS
LOOT
LOOTED
LOOTEN
LOOTER
LOOTERS
LOOTING
LOOTINGS
LOOTS
LOOVES
LOP
LOPE
LOPED
LOPER
LOPERS
LOPES
LOPGRASS
LOPHODONT
LOPING
LOPINGLY
LOPOLITH
LOPOLITHS
LOPPED
LOPPER
LOPPERED
LOPPERING
LOPPERS
LOPPET
LOPPETS
LOPPIER
LOPPIES
LOPPIEST
LOPPING
LOPPINGS
LOPPY
LOPS
LOPSIDED
LOPSTICK
LOPSTICKS
LOQUACITY
LOQUAT
LOQUATS
LOQUITUR
LOR
LORAL
LORAN
LORANS
LORATE
LORAZEPAM
LORCHA
LORCHAS
LORD
LORDED
LORDING
LORDINGS
LORDKIN
LORDKINS
LORDLESS
LORDLIER
LORDLIEST
LORDLIKE
LORDLING
LORDLINGS
LORDLY
LORDOMA
LORDOMAS
LORDOSES
LORDOSIS
LORDOTIC
LORDS
LORDSHIP
LORDSHIPS
LORDY
LORE
LOREAL
LOREL
LORELS
LORES
LORETTE
LORETTES
LORGNETTE
LORGNON
LORGNONS
LORIC
LORICA
LORICAE
LORICAS
LORICATE
LORICATED
LORICATES
LORICS
LORIES
LORIKEET
LORIKEETS
LORIMER
LORIMERS
LORINER
LORINERS
LORING
LORINGS
LORIOT
LORIOTS
LORIS
LORISES
LORN
LORNER
LORNEST
LORNNESS
LORRELL
LORRELLS
LORRIES

L

LORRY
LORY
LOS
LOSABLE
LOSE
LOSED
LOSEL
LOSELS
LOSEN
LOSER
LOSERS
LOSES
LOSH
LOSING
LOSINGEST
LOSINGLY
LOSINGS
LOSLYF
LOSLYFS
LOSS
LOSSES
LOSSIER
LOSSIEST
LOSSLESS
LOSSMAKER
LOSSY
LOST
LOSTNESS
LOT
LOTA
LOTAH
LOTAHS
LOTAS
LOTE
LOTES
LOTH
LOTHARIO
LOTHARIOS
LOTHEFULL
LOTHER
LOTHEST
LOTHFULL
LOTHNESS
LOTHSOME
LOTI
LOTIC
LOTION
LOTIONS
LOTO
LOTOS
LOTOSES
LOTS
LOTSA
LOTTA
LOTTE
LOTTED
LOTTER
LOTTERIES
LOTTERS
LOTTERY
LOTTES
LOTTING
LOTTO
LOTTOS
LOTUS
LOTUSES
LOTUSLAND
LOU
LOUCHE
LOUCHELY
LOUCHER
LOUCHEST
LOUD
LOUDEN
LOUDENED
LOUDENING
LOUDENS
LOUDER
LOUDEST
LOUDISH
LOUDLIER
LOUDLIEST
LOUDLY
LOUDMOUTH
LOUDNESS
LOUED
LOUGH
LOUGHS
LOUIE
LOUIES
LOUING
LOUIS
LOUMA
LOUMAS
LOUN
LOUND
LOUNDED
LOUNDER
LOUNDERED
LOUNDERS
LOUNDING
LOUNDS
LOUNED
LOUNGE
LOUNGED
LOUNGER
LOUNGERS
LOUNGES
LOUNGEY
LOUNGIER
LOUNGIEST
LOUNGING
LOUNGINGS
LOUNGY
LOUNING
LOUNS
LOUP
LOUPE
LOUPED
LOUPEN
LOUPES
LOUPING
LOUPIT
LOUPS
LOUR
LOURE
LOURED
LOURES
LOURIE
LOURIER
LOURIES
LOURIEST
LOURING
LOURINGLY
LOURINGS
LOURS
LOURY
LOUS
LOUSE
LOUSED
LOUSER
LOUSERS
LOUSES
LOUSEWORT
LOUSIER
LOUSIEST
LOUSILY
LOUSINESS
LOUSING
LOUSINGS
LOUSY
LOUT
LOUTED
LOUTERIES
LOUTERY
LOUTING
LOUTISH
LOUTISHLY
LOUTS
LOUVAR
LOUVARS
LOUVER
LOUVERED
LOUVERS
LOUVRE
LOUVRED
LOUVRES
LOVABLE
LOVABLY
LOVAGE
LOVAGES
LOVAT
LOVATS
LOVE
LOVEABLE
LOVEABLY
LOVEBIRD
LOVEBIRDS
LOVEBITE
LOVEBITES
LOVEBUG
LOVEBUGS
LOVED
LOVEFEST
LOVEFESTS
LOVELESS
LOVELIER
LOVELIES
LOVELIEST
LOVELIGHT
LOVELILY
LOVELOCK
LOVELOCKS
LOVELORN
LOVELY
LOVEMAKER
LOVER
LOVERED
LOVERLESS
LOVERLY
LOVERS
LOVES
LOVESEAT
LOVESEATS
LOVESICK
LOVESOME
LOVEVINE
LOVEVINES
LOVEY
LOVEYS
LOVIE
LOVIER
LOVIES
LOVIEST
LOVING
LOVINGLY
LOVINGS
LOW
LOWAN
LOWANS
LOWBALL
LOWBALLED
LOWBALLS
LOWBORN
LOWBOY
LOWBOYS
LOWBRED
LOWBROW
LOWBROWED
LOWBROWS
LOWBUSH
LOWBUSHES
LOWDOWN
LOWDOWNS
LOWE
LOWED
LOWER
LOWERABLE
LOWERCASE
LOWERED

LOWERIER
LOWERIEST
LOWERING
LOWERINGS
LOWERMOST
LOWERS
LOWERY
LOWES
LOWEST
LOWING
LOWINGS
LOWISH
LOWLAND
LOWLANDER
LOWLANDS
LOWLIER
LOWLIEST
LOWLIFE
LOWLIFER
LOWLIFERS
LOWLIFES
LOWLIGHT
LOWLIGHTS
LOWLIHEAD
LOWLILY
LOWLINESS
LOWLIVES
LOWLY
LOWN
LOWND
LOWNDED
LOWNDING
LOWNDS
LOWNE
LOWNED
LOWNES
LOWNESS
LOWNESSES
LOWNING
LOWNS
LOWP
LOWPASS
LOWPED
LOWPING
LOWPS
LOWRIDER
LOWRIDERS
LOWRIE
LOWRIES
LOWRY
LOWS
LOWSE
LOWSED
LOWSENING
LOWSER
LOWSES
LOWSEST
LOWSING
LOWSIT
LOWT
LOWTED
LOWTING
LOWTS
LOWVELD
LOWVELDS
LOX
LOXED
LOXES
LOXING
LOXODROME
LOXODROMY
LOXYGEN
LOXYGENS
LOY
LOYAL
LOYALER
LOYALEST
LOYALISM
LOYALISMS
LOYALIST
LOYALISTS
LOYALLER
LOYALLEST
LOYALLY
LOYALNESS
LOYALTIES
LOYALTY
LOYS
LOZELL
LOZELLS
LOZEN
LOZENGE
LOZENGED
LOZENGES
LOZENGIER
LOZENGY
LOZENS
LUACH
LUAU
LUAUS
LUBBARD
LUBBARDS
LUBBER
LUBBERLY
LUBBERS
LUBE
LUBED
LUBES
LUBFISH
LUBFISHES
LUBING
LUBRA
LUBRAS
LUBRIC
LUBRICAL
LUBRICANT
LUBRICATE
LUBRICITY
LUBRICOUS
LUCARNE
LUCARNES
LUCE
LUCENCE
LUCENCES
LUCENCIES
LUCENCY
LUCENT
LUCENTLY
LUCERN
LUCERNE
LUCERNES
LUCERNS
LUCES
LUCHOT
LUCHOTH
LUCID
LUCIDER
LUCIDEST
LUCIDITY
LUCIDLY
LUCIDNESS
LUCIFER
LUCIFERIN
LUCIFERS
LUCIGEN
LUCIGENS
LUCITE
LUCITES
LUCK
LUCKED
LUCKEN
LUCKIE
LUCKIER
LUCKIES
LUCKIEST
LUCKILY
LUCKINESS
LUCKING
LUCKLESS
LUCKPENNY
LUCKS
LUCKY
LUCRATIVE
LUCRE
LUCRES
LUCTATION
LUCUBRATE
LUCULENT
LUCUMA
LUCUMAS
LUCUMO
LUCUMONES
LUCUMOS
LUD
LUDE
LUDERICK
LUDERICKS
LUDES
LUDIC
LUDICALLY
LUDICROUS
LUDO
LUDOS
LUDS
LUDSHIP
LUDSHIPS
LUES
LUETIC
LUETICS
LUFF
LUFFA
LUFFAS
LUFFED
LUFFING
LUFFS
LUG
LUGE
LUGED
LUGEING
LUGEINGS
LUGER
LUGERS
LUGES
LUGGABLE
LUGGABLES
LUGGAGE
LUGGAGES
LUGGED
LUGGER
LUGGERS
LUGGIE
LUGGIES
LUGGING
LUGHOLE
LUGHOLES
LUGING
LUGINGS
LUGS
LUGSAIL
LUGSAILS
LUGWORM
LUGWORMS
LUIT
LUITEN
LUKE
LUKEWARM
LULIBUB
LULIBUBS
LULL
LULLABIED
LULLABIES
LULLABY
LULLED
LULLER
LULLERS
LULLING
LULLINGLY
LULIS
LULU
LULUS

L

LULZ
LUM
LUMA
LUMAS
LUMBAGO
LUMBAGOS
LUMBANG
LUMBANGS
LUMBAR
LUMBARS
LUMBER
LUMBERED
LUMBERER
LUMBERERS
LUMBERING
LUMBERLY
LUMBERMAN
LUMBERMEN
LUMBERS
LUMBI
LUMBRICAL
LUMBRICI
LUMBRICUS
LUMBUS
LUMEN
LUMENAL
LUMENS
LUMINA
LUMINAIRE
LUMINAL
LUMINANCE
LUMINANT
LUMINANTS
LUMINARIA
LUMINARY
LUMINE
LUMINED
LUMINES
LUMINESCE
LUMINING
LUMINISM
LUMINISMS
LUMINIST
LUMINISTS
LUMINOUS
LUMME
LUMMIER
LUMMIEST
LUMMOX
LUMMOXES
LUMMY
LUMP
LUMPED
LUMPEN
LUMPENLY
LUMPENS
LUMPER
LUMPERS
LUMPFISH
LUMPIA
LUMPIAS
LUMPIER
LUMPIEST
LUMPILY
LUMPINESS
LUMPING
LUMPINGLY
LUMPISH
LUMPISHLY
LUMPKIN
LUMPKINS
LUMPS
LUMPY
LUMS
LUN
LUNA
LUNACIES
LUNACY
LUNANAUT
LUNANAUTS
LUNAR
LUNARIAN
LUNARIANS
LUNARIES
LUNARIST
LUNARISTS
LUNARNAUT
LUNARS
LUNARY
LUNAS
LUNATE
LUNATED
LUNATELY
LUNATES
LUNATIC
LUNATICAL
LUNATICS
LUNATION
LUNATIONS
LUNCH
LUNCHBOX
LUNCHED
LUNCHEON
LUNCHEONS
LUNCHER
LUNCHERS
LUNCHES
LUNCHING
LUNCHMEAT
LUNCHPAIL
LUNCHROOM
LUNCHTIME
LUNE
LUNES
LUNET
LUNETS
LUNETTE
LUNETTES
LUNG
LUNGAN
LUNGANS
LUNGE
LUNGED
LUNGEE
LUNGEES
LUNGEING
LUNGER
LUNGERS
LUNGES
LUNGFISH
LUNGFUL
LUNGFULS
LUNGI
LUNGIE
LUNGIES
LUNGING
LUNGIS
LUNGLESS
LUNGLIKE
LUNGS
LUNGWORM
LUNGWORMS
LUNGWORT
LUNGWORTS
LUNGYI
LUNGYIS
LUNIER
LUNIES
LUNIEST
LUNINESS
LUNISOLAR
LUNITIDAL
LUNK
LUNKER
LUNKERS
LUNKHEAD
LUNKHEADS
LUNKS
LUNS
LUNT
LUNTED
LUNTING
LUNTS
LUNULA
LUNULAE
LUNULAR
LUNULATE
LUNULATED
LUNULE
LUNULES
LUNY
LUNYIE
LUNYIES
LUPANAR
LUPANARS
LUPIN
LUPINE
LUPINES
LUPINS
LUPOID
LUPOUS
LUPPEN
LUPULIN
LUPULINE
LUPULINIC
LUPULINS
LUPUS
LUPUSES
LUR
LURCH
LURCHED
LURCHER
LURCHERS
LURCHES
LURCHING
LURDAN
LURDANE
LURDANES
LURDANS
LURDEN
LURDENS
LURE
LURED
LURER
LURERS
LURES
LUREX
LUREXES
LURGI
LURGIES
LURGIS
LURGY
LURID
LURIDER
LURIDEST
LURIDLY
LURIDNESS
LURING
LURINGLY
LURINGS
LURK
LURKED
LURKER
LURKERS
LURKING
LURKINGLY
LURKINGS
LURKS
LURRIES
LURRY
LURS
LURVE
LURVES
LUSCIOUS
LUSER
LUSERS
LUSH
LUSHED
LUSHER
LUSHERS

LUSHES
LUSHEST
LUSHIER
LUSHIES
LUSHIEST
LUSHING
LUSHLY
LUSHNESS
LUSHY
LUSK
LUSKED
LUSKING
LUSKISH
LUSKS
LUST
LUSTED
LUSTER
LUSTERED
LUSTERING
LUSTERS
LUSTFUL
LUSTFULLY
LUSTICK
LUSTIER
LUSTIEST
LUSTIHEAD
LUSTIHOOD
LUSTILY
LUSTINESS
LUSTING
LUSTIQUE
LUSTLESS
LUSTRA
LUSTRAL
LUSTRATE
LUSTRATED
LUSTRATES
LUSTRE
LUSTRED
LUSTRES
LUSTRINE
LUSTRINES
LUSTRING
LUSTRINGS
LUSTROUS
LUSTRUM
LUSTRUMS
LUSTS
LUSTY
LUSUS
LUSUSES
LUTANIST
LUTANISTS
LUTE
LUTEA
LUTEAL
LUTECIUM
LUTECIUMS
LUTED
LUTEFISK
LUTEFISKS
LUTEIN
LUTEINISE
LUTEINIZE
LUTEINS
LUTELIKE
LUTENIST
LUTENISTS
LUTEOLIN
LUTEOLINS
LUTEOLOUS
LUTEOUS
LUTER
LUTERS
LUTES
LUTESCENT
LUTETIUM
LUTETIUMS
LUTEUM
LUTFISK
LUTFISKS
LUTHERN
LUTHERNS
LUTHIER
LUTHIERS
LUTING
LUTINGS
LUTIST
LUTISTS
LUTITE
LUTITES
LUTTEN
LUTZ
LUTZES
LUV
LUVS
LUVVED
LUVVIE
LUVVIEDOM
LUVVIES
LUVVING
LUVVY
LUX
LUXATE
LUXATED
LUXATES
LUXATING
LUXATION
LUXATIONS
LUXE
LUXED
LUXER
LUXES
LUXEST
LUXING
LUXMETER
LUXMETERS
LUXURIANT
LUXURIATE
LUXURIES
LUXURIOUS
LUXURIST
LUXURISTS
LUXURY
LUZ
LUZERN
LUZERNS
LUZZES
LWEI
LWEIS
LYAM
LYAMS
LYARD
LYART
LYASE
LYASES
LYCAENID
LYCAENIDS
LYCEA
LYCEE
LYCEES
LYCEUM
LYCEUMS
LYCH
LYCHEE
LYCHEES
LYCHES
LYCHGATE
LYCHGATES
LYCHNIS
LYCHNISES
LYCOPENE
LYCOPENES
LYCOPOD
LYCOPODS
LYCOPSID
LYCOPSIDS
LYCRA
LYCRAS
LYDDITE
LYDDITES
LYE
LYES
LYFULL
LYING
LYINGLY
LYINGS
LYKEWAKE
LYKEWAKES
LYKEWALK
LYKEWALKS
LYM
LYME
LYMES
LYMITER
LYMITERS
LYMPH
LYMPHAD
LYMPHADS
LYMPHATIC
LYMPHOID
LYMPHOMA
LYMPHOMAS
LYMPHOUS
LYMPHS
LYMS
LYNAGE
LYNAGES
LYNCEAN
LYNCH
LYNCHED
LYNCHER
LYNCHERS
LYNCHES
LYNCHET
LYNCHETS
LYNCHING
LYNCHINGS
LYNCHPIN
LYNCHPINS
LYNE
LYNES
LYNX
LYNXES
LYNXLIKE
LYOLYSES
LYOLYSIS
LYOMEROUS
LYONNAISE
LYOPHIL
LYOPHILE
LYOPHILED
LYOPHILIC
LYOPHOBE
LYOPHOBIC
LYRA
LYRATE
LYRATED
LYRATELY
LYRE
LYREBIRD
LYREBIRDS
LYRES
LYRIC
LYRICAL
LYRICALLY
LYRICISE
LYRICISED
LYRICISES
LYRICISM
LYRICISMS
LYRICIST
LYRICISTS
LYRICIZE
LYRICIZED
LYRICIZES
LYRICON
LYRICONS
LYRICS
LYRIFORM

L

- LYRISM
- LYRISMS
- LYRIST
- LYRISTS
- LYSATE
- LYSATES
- LYSE
- LYSED
- LYSERGIC
- LYSERGIDE
- LYSES
- LYSIGENIC
- LYSIMETER
- LYSIN
- LYSINE
- LYSINES
- LYSING
- LYSINS
- LYSIS
- LYSOGEN
- LYSOGENIC
- LYSOGENS
- LYSOGENY
- LYSOL
- LYSOLS
- LYSOSOMAL
- LYSOSOME
- LYSOSOMES
- LYSOZYME
- LYSOZYMES
- LYSSA
- LYSSAS
- LYTE
- LYTED
- LYTES
- LYTHE
- LYTHES
- LYTHRUM
- LYTHRUMS
- LYTIC
- LYTICALLY
- LYTING
- LYTTA
- LYTTAE
- LYTTAS

MA
MAA
MAAED
MAAING
MAAR
MAARE
MAARS
MAAS
MAASES
MAATJES
MABE
MABELA
MABELAS
MABES
MAC
MACA
MACABER
MACABRE
MACABRELY
MACABRER
MACABREST
MACACO
MACACOS
MACADAM
MACADAMED
MACADAMIA
MACADAMS
MACAHUBA
MACAHUBAS
MACALLUM
MACALLUMS
MACAQUE
MACAQUES
MACARISE
MACARISED
MACARISES
MACARISM
MACARISMS
MACARIZE
MACARIZED
MACARIZES
MACARON
MACARONI
MACARONIC
MACARONIS
MACARONS
MACAROON
MACAROONS
MACAS
MACASSAR
MACASSARS
MACAW
MACAWS
MACCABAW
MACCABAWS
MACCABOY
MACCABOYS
MACCARONI
MACCHIA
MACCHIATO
MACCHIE
MACCOBOY
MACCOBOYS
MACE
MACED
MACEDOINE
MACER
MACERAL
MACERALS
MACERATE
MACERATED
MACERATER
MACERATES
MACERATOR
MACERS
MACES
MACH
MACHACA
MACHACAS
MACHAIR
MACHAIRS
MACHAN
MACHANS
MACHE
MACHER
MACHERS
MACHES
MACHETE
MACHETES
MACHI
MACHINATE
MACHINE
MACHINED
MACHINERY
MACHINES
MACHINIMA
MACHINING
MACHINIST
MACHISMO
MACHISMOS
MACHMETER
MACHO
MACHOISM
MACHOISMS
MACHOS
MACHREE
MACHREES
MACHS
MACHZOR
MACHZORIM
MACHZORS
MACING
MACINTOSH
MACK
MACKEREL
MACKERELS
MACKINAW
MACKINAWS
MACKLE
MACKLED
MACKLES
MACKLING
MACKS
MACLE
MACLED
MACLES
MACON
MACONS
MACOYA
MACOYAS
MACRAME
MACRAMES
MACRAMI
MACRAMIS
MACRO
MACROBIAN
MACROCODE
MACROCOPY
MACROCOSM
MACROCYST
MACROCYTE
MACRODOME
MACRODONT
MACROGLIA
MACROLIDE
MACROLOGY
MACROMERE
MACROMOLE
MACRON
MACRONS
MACROPOD
MACROPODS
MACROPSIA
MACROS
MACROTOUS
MACRURAL
MACRURAN
MACRURANS
MACRUROID
MACRUROUS
MACS
MACTATION
MACULA
MACULAE
MACULAR
MACULAS
MACULATE
MACULATED
MACULATES
MACULE
MACULED
MACULES
MACULING
MACULOSE
MACUMBA
MACUMBAS
MAD
MADAFU
MADAFUS
MADAM
MADAME
MADAMED
MADAMES
MADAMING
MADAMS
MADAROSES
MADAROSIS
MADBRAIN
MADBRAINS
MADCAP
MADCAPS
MADDED
MADDEN
MADDENED
MADDENING
MADDENS
MADDER
MADDERS
MADDEST
MADDING
MADDINGLY
MADDISH
MADDOCK
MADDOCKS
MADE
MADEFIED
MADEFIES
MADEFY
MADEFYING
MADEIRA

M

MADEIRAS
MADELEINE
MADERISE
MADERISED
MADERISES
MADERIZE
MADERIZED
MADERIZES
MADEUPPY
MADGE
MADGES
MADHOUSE
MADHOUSES
MADID
MADISON
MADISONS
MADLING
MADLINGS
MADLY
MADMAN
MADMEN
MADNESS
MADNESSES
MADONNA
MADONNAS
MADOQUA
MADOQUAS
MADRAS
MADRASA
MADRASAH
MADRASAHS
MADRASAS
MADRASES
MADRASSA
MADRASSAH
MADRASSAS
MADRE
MADREPORE
MADRES
MADRIGAL
MADRIGALS
MADRILENE
MADRONA
MADRONAS
MADRONE
MADRONES
MADRONO
MADRONOS
MADS
MADTOM
MADTOMS
MADURO
MADUROS
MADWOMAN
MADWOMEN
MADWORT
MADWORTS
MADZOON
MADZOONS
MAE
MAELID
MAELIDS
MAELSTROM
MAENAD
MAENADES
MAENADIC
MAENADISM
MAENADS
MAERL
MAERLS
MAES
MAESTOSO
MAESTOSOS
MAESTRI
MAESTRO
MAESTROS
MAFFIA
MAFFIAS
MAFFICK
MAFFICKED
MAFFICKER
MAFFICKS
MAFFLED
MAFFLIN
MAFFLING
MAFFLINGS
MAFFLINS
MAFIA
MAFIAS
MAFIC
MAFICS
MAFIOSI
MAFIOSO
MAFIOSOS
MAFTED
MAFTIR
MAFTIRS
MAG
MAGAININ
MAGAININS
MAGALOG
MAGALOGS
MAGALOGUE
MAGAZINE
MAGAZINES
MAGDALEN
MAGDALENE
MAGDALENS
MAGE
MAGENTA
MAGENTAS
MAGES
MAGESHIP
MAGESHIPS
MAGG
MAGGED
MAGGIE
MAGGIES
MAGGING
MAGGOT
MAGGOTIER
MAGGOTS
MAGGOTY
MAGGS
MAGI
MAGIAN
MAGIANISM
MAGIANS
MAGIC
MAGICAL
MAGICALLY
MAGICIAN
MAGICIANS
MAGICKED
MAGICKING
MAGICS
MAGILP
MAGILPS
MAGISM
MAGISMS
MAGISTER
MAGISTERS
MAGISTERY
MAGISTRAL
MAGLEV
MAGLEVS
MAGMA
MAGMAS
MAGMATA
MAGMATIC
MAGMATISM
MAGNALIUM
MAGNATE
MAGNATES
MAGNES
MAGNESES
MAGNESIA
MAGNESIAL
MAGNESIAN
MAGNESIAS
MAGNESIC
MAGNESITE
MAGNESIUM
MAGNET
MAGNETAR
MAGNETARS
MAGNETIC
MAGNETICS
MAGNETISE
MAGNETISM
MAGNETIST
MAGNETITE
MAGNETIZE
MAGNETO
MAGNETON
MAGNETONS
MAGNETOS
MAGNETRON
MAGNETS
MAGNIFIC
MAGNIFICO
MAGNIFIED
MAGNIFIER
MAGNIFIES
MAGNIFY
MAGNITUDE
MAGNOLIA
MAGNOLIAS
MAGNON
MAGNONS
MAGNOX
MAGNOXES
MAGNUM
MAGNUMS
MAGNUS
MAGOT
MAGOTS
MAGPIE
MAGPIES
MAGS
MAGSMAN
MAGSMEN
MAGUEY
MAGUEYS
MAGUS
MAGYAR
MAHA
MAHANT
MAHANTS
MAHARAJA
MAHARAJAH
MAHARAJAS
MAHARANEE
MAHARANI
MAHARANIS
MAHARISHI
MAHATMA
MAHATMAS
MAHEWU
MAHEWUS
MAHIMAHI
MAHIMAHIS
MAHJONG
MAHJONGG
MAHJONGGS
MAHJONGS
MAHLSTICK
MAHMAL
MAHMALS
MAHOE
MAHOES
MAHOGANY
MAHONIA
MAHONIAS
MAHOUT
MAHOUTS
MAHSEER
MAHSEERS
MAHSIR
MAHSIRS

MAHUA
MAHUANG
MAHUANGS
MAHUAS
MAHWA
MAHWAS
MAHZOR
MAHZORIM
MAHZORS
MAIASAUR
MAIASAURA
MAIASAURS
MAID
MAIDAN
MAIDANS
MAIDED
MAIDEN
MAIDENISH
MAIDENLY
MAIDENS
MAIDHOOD
MAIDHOODS
MAIDING
MAIDISH
MAIDISM
MAIDISMS
MAIDLESS
MAIDS
MAIEUTIC
MAIEUTICS
MAIGRE
MAIGRES
MAIHEM
MAIHEMS
MAIK
MAIKO
MAIKOS
MAIKS
MAIL
MAILABLE
MAILBAG
MAILBAGS
MAILBOAT
MAILBOATS
MAILBOX
MAILBOXES
MAILCAR
MAILCARS
MAILCOACH
MAILE
MAILED
MAILER
MAILERS
MAILES
MAILGRAM
MAILGRAMS
MAILING
MAILINGS
MAILL
MAILLESS
MAILLOT
MAILLOTS
MAILLS
MAILMAN
MAILMEN
MAILMERGE
MAILPOUCH
MAILROOM
MAILROOMS
MAILS
MAILSACK
MAILSACKS
MAILSHOT
MAILSHOTS
MAILVAN
MAILVANS
MAIM
MAIMED
MAIMER
MAIMERS
MAIMING
MAIMINGS
MAIMS
MAIN
MAINBOOM
MAINBOOMS
MAINBRACE
MAINDOOR
MAINDOORS
MAINED
MAINER
MAINEST
MAINFRAME
MAINING
MAINLAND
MAINLANDS
MAINLINE
MAINLINED
MAINLINER
MAINLINES
MAINLY
MAINMAST
MAINMASTS
MAINOR
MAINORS
MAINOUR
MAINOURS
MAINPRISE
MAINS
MAINSAIL
MAINSAILS
MAINSHEET
MAINSTAGE
MAINSTAY
MAINSTAYS
MAINTAIN
MAINTAINS
MAINTOP
MAINTOPS
MAINYARD
MAINYARDS
MAIOLICA
MAIOLICAS
MAIR
MAIRE
MAIREHAU
MAIREHAUS
MAIRES
MAIRS
MAISE
MAISES
MAIST
MAISTER
MAISTERED
MAISTERS
MAISTRIES
MAISTRING
MAISTRY
MAISTS
MAIZE
MAIZES
MAJAGUA
MAJAGUAS
MAJESTIC
MAJESTIES
MAJESTY
MAJLIS
MAJLISES
MAJOLICA
MAJOLICAS
MAJOR
MAJORAT
MAJORATS
MAJORDOMO
MAJORED
MAJORETTE
MAJORING
MAJORITY
MAJORLY
MAJORS
MAJORSHIP
MAJUSCULE
MAK
MAKABLE
MAKAR
MAKARS
MAKE
MAKEABLE
MAKEABLES
MAKEBATE
MAKEBATES
MAKEFAST
MAKEFASTS
MAKELESS
MAKEOVER
MAKEOVERS
MAKER
MAKEREADY
MAKERS
MAKES
MAKESHIFT
MAKEUP
MAKEUPS
MAKHANI
MAKHANIS
MAKI
MAKIMONO
MAKIMONOS
MAKING
MAKINGS
MAKIS
MAKO
MAKOS
MAKS
MAKUTA
MAKUTU
MAKUTUED
MAKUTUING
MAKUTUS
MAL
MALA
MALACCA
MALACCAS
MALACHITE
MALACIA
MALACIAS
MALADIES
MALADROIT
MALADY
MALAGUENA
MALAISE
MALAISES
MALAM
MALAMS
MALAMUTE
MALAMUTES
MALANDER
MALANDERS
MALANGA
MALANGAS
MALAPERT
MALAPERTS
MALAPROP
MALAPROPS
MALAR
MALARIA
MALARIAL
MALARIAN
MALARIAS
MALARIOUS
MALARKEY
MALARKEYS
MALARKIES
MALARKY
MALAROMA
MALAROMAS
MALARS
MALAS
MALATE
MALATES

M

MALATHION
MALAX
MALAXAGE
MALAXAGES
MALAXATE
MALAXATED
MALAXATES
MALAXATOR
MALAXED
MALAXES
MALAXING
MALE
MALEATE
MALEATES
MALEDICT
MALEDICTS
MALEFFECT
MALEFIC
MALEFICE
MALEFICES
MALEIC
MALEMIUT
MALEMIUTS
MALEMUTE
MALEMUTES
MALENESS
MALENGINE
MALES
MALFED
MALFORMED
MALGRADO
MALGRE
MALGRED
MALGRES
MALGRING
MALI
MALIBU
MALIC
MALICE
MALICED
MALICES
MALICHO
MALICHOS
MALICING
MALICIOUS
MALIGN
MALIGNANT
MALIGNED
MALIGNER
MALIGNERS
MALIGNING
MALIGNITY
MALIGNLY
MALIGNS
MALIHINI
MALIHINIS
MALIK
MALIKS
MALINE
MALINES
MALINGER
MALINGERS
MALINGERY
MALIS
MALISM
MALISMS
MALISON
MALISONS
MALIST
MALKIN
MALKINS
MALL
MALLAM
MALLAMS
MALLANDER
MALLARD
MALLARDS
MALLCORE
MALLCORES
MALLEABLE
MALLEABLY
MALLEATE
MALLEATED
MALLEATES
MALLECHO
MALLECHOS
MALLED
MALLEE
MALLEES
MALLEI
MALLEMUCK
MALLENDER
MALLEOLAR
MALLEOLI
MALLEOLUS
MALLET
MALLETS
MALLEUS
MALLEUSES
MALLING
MALLINGS
MALLOW
MALLOWS
MALLS
MALM
MALMAG
MALMAGS
MALMIER
MALMIEST
MALMS
MALMSEY
MALMSEYS
MALMSTONE
MALMY
MALODOR
MALODORS
MALODOUR
MALODOURS
MALONATE
MALONATES
MALONIC
MALOTI
MALPIGHIA
MALPOSED
MALS
MALSTICK
MALSTICKS
MALT
MALTALENT
MALTASE
MALTASES
MALTED
MALTEDS
MALTESE
MALTHA
MALTHAS
MALTIER
MALTIEST
MALTINESS
MALTING
MALTINGS
MALTIPOO
MALTIPOOS
MALTMAN
MALTMEN
MALTOL
MALTOLS
MALTOSE
MALTOSES
MALTREAT
MALTREATS
MALTS
MALTSTER
MALTSTERS
MALTWORM
MALTWORMS
MALTY
MALUS
MALUSES
MALVA
MALVAS
MALVASIA
MALVASIAN
MALVASIAS
MALVESIE
MALVESIES
MALVOISIE
MALWA
MALWARE
MALWARES
MALWAS
MAM
MAMA
MAMAGUY
MAMAGUYED
MAMAGUYS
MAMAKAU
MAMAKAUS
MAMAKO
MAMAKOS
MAMAKU
MAMAKUS
MAMALIGA
MAMALIGAS
MAMAS
MAMASAN
MAMASANS
MAMATEEK
MAMATEEKS
MAMBA
MAMBAS
MAMBO
MAMBOED
MAMBOES
MAMBOING
MAMBOS
MAMEE
MAMEES
MAMELON
MAMELONS
MAMELUCO
MAMELUCOS
MAMELUKE
MAMELUKES
MAMEY
MAMEYES
MAMEYS
MAMIE
MAMIES
MAMILLA
MAMILLAE
MAMILLAR
MAMILLARY
MAMILLATE
MAMLUK
MAMLUKS
MAMMA
MAMMAE
MAMMAL
MAMMALIAN
MAMMALITY
MAMMALOGY
MAMMALS
MAMMARIES
MAMMARY
MAMMAS
MAMMATE
MAMMATI
MAMMATUS
MAMMEE
MAMMEES
MAMMER
MAMMERED
MAMMERING
MAMMERS
MAMMET
MAMMETRY
MAMMETS
MAMMEY
MAMMEYS

MAMMIE
MAMMIES
MAMMIFER
MAMMIFERS
MAMMIFORM
MAMMILLA
MAMMILLAE
MAMMILLAR
MAMMITIS
MAMMOCK
MAMMOCKED
MAMMOCKS
MAMMOGRAM
MAMMON
MAMMONISH
MAMMONISM
MAMMONIST
MAMMONITE
MAMMONS
MAMMOTH
MAMMOTHS
MAMMY
MAMPARA
MAMPARAS
MAMPOER
MAMPOERS
MAMS
MAMSELLE
MAMSELLES
MAMZER
MAMZERIM
MAMZERS
MAN
MANA
MANACLE
MANACLED
MANACLES
MANACLING
MANAGE
MANAGED
MANAGER
MANAGERS
MANAGES
MANAGING
MANAIA
MANAIAS
MANAKIN
MANAKINS
MANANA
MANANAS
MANAS
MANAT
MANATEE
MANATEES
MANATI
MANATIS
MANATOID
MANATS
MANATU
MANATUS
MANAWA
MANAWAS
MANBAG
MANBAGS
MANBAND
MANBANDS
MANCALA
MANCALAS
MANCANDO
MANCHE
MANCHEGO
MANCHEGOS
MANCHES
MANCHET
MANCHETS
MANCIPATE
MANCIPLE
MANCIPLES
MANCUS
MANCUSES
MAND
MANDALA
MANDALAS
MANDALIC
MANDAMUS
MANDARIN
MANDARINE
MANDARINS
MANDATARY
MANDATE
MANDATED
MANDATES
MANDATING
MANDATOR
MANDATORS
MANDATORY
MANDI
MANDIBLE
MANDIBLES
MANDILION
MANDIOC
MANDIOCA
MANDIOCAS
MANDIOCCA
MANDIOCS
MANDIR
MANDIRA
MANDIRAS
MANDIRS
MANDIS
MANDOLA
MANDOLAS
MANDOLIN
MANDOLINE
MANDOLINS
MANDOM
MANDOMS
MANDORA
MANDORAS
MANDORLA
MANDORLAS
MANDRAKE
MANDRAKES
MANDREL
MANDRELS
MANDRIL
MANDRILL
MANDRILLS
MANDRILS
MANDUCATE
MANDYLION
MANE
MANEB
MANEBS
MANED
MANEGE
MANEGED
MANEGES
MANEGING
MANEH
MANEHS
MANELESS
MANENT
MANES
MANET
MANEUVER
MANEUVERS
MANFUL
MANFULLER
MANFULLY
MANG
MANGA
MANGABEY
MANGABEYS
MANGABIES
MANGABY
MANGAL
MANGALS
MANGANATE
MANGANESE
MANGANIC
MANGANIN
MANGANINS
MANGANITE
MANGANOUS
MANGAS
MANGE
MANGEAO
MANGEAOS
MANGED
MANGEL
MANGELS
MANGER
MANGERS
MANGES
MANGETOUT
MANGEY
MANGIER
MANGIEST
MANGILY
MANGINESS
MANGING
MANGLE
MANGLED
MANGLER
MANGLERS
MANGLES
MANGLING
MANGO
MANGOES
MANGOLD
MANGOLDS
MANGONEL
MANGONELS
MANGOS
MANGOSTAN
MANGOUSTE
MANGROVE
MANGROVES
MANGS
MANGULATE
MANGY
MANHANDLE
MANHATTAN
MANHOLE
MANHOLES
MANHOOD
MANHOODS
MANHUNT
MANHUNTER
MANHUNTS
MANI
MANIA
MANIAC
MANIACAL
MANIACS
MANIAS
MANIC
MANICALLY
MANICOTTI
MANICS
MANICURE
MANICURED
MANICURES
MANIES
MANIFEST
MANIFESTO
MANIFESTS
MANIFOLD
MANIFOLDS
MANIFORM
MANIHOC
MANIHOCS
MANIHOT
MANIHOTS
MANIKIN
MANIKINS
MANILA
MANILAS
MANILLA

MANILLAS
MANILLE
MANILLES
MANIOC
MANIOCA
MANIOCAS
MANIOCS
MANIPLE
MANIPLES
MANIPLIES
MANIPULAR
MANIS
MANISES
MANITO
MANITOS
MANITOU
MANITOUS
MANITU
MANITUS
MANJACK
MANJACKS
MANKIER
MANKIEST
MANKIND
MANKINDS
MANKINI
MANKINIS
MANKY
MANLESS
MANLIER
MANLIEST
MANLIKE
MANLIKELY
MANLILY
MANLINESS
MANLY
MANMADE
MANNA
MANNAN
MANNANS
MANNAS
MANNED
MANNEQUIN
MANNER
MANNERED
MANNERISM
MANNERIST
MANNERLY
MANNERS
MANNIKIN
MANNIKINS
MANNING
MANNISH
MANNISHLY
MANNITE
MANNITES
MANNITIC
MANNITOL
MANNITOLS
MANNOSE
MANNOSES
MANO
MANOAO
MANOAOS
MANOES
MANOEUVER
MANOEUVRE
MANOMETER
MANOMETRY
MANOR
MANORIAL
MANORS
MANOS
MANOSCOPY
MANPACK
MANPACKS
MANPOWER
MANPOWERS
MANQUE
MANQUES
MANRED
MANREDS
MANRENT
MANRENTS
MANRIDER
MANRIDERS
MANRIDING
MANROPE
MANROPES
MANS
MANSARD
MANSARDED
MANSARDS
MANSCAPE
MANSCAPED
MANSCAPES
MANSE
MANSES
MANSHIFT
MANSHIFTS
MANSION
MANSIONS
MANSLAYER
MANSONRY
MANSPLAIN
MANSPREAD
MANSUETE
MANSWORN
MANSWORNS
MANTA
MANTAS
MANTEAU
MANTEAUS
MANTEAUX
MANTEEL
MANTEELS
MANTEL
MANTELET
MANTELETS
MANTELS
MANTES
MANTIC
MANTICORA
MANTICORE
MANTID
MANTIDS
MANTIES
MANTILLA
MANTILLAS
MANTIS
MANTISES
MANTISSA
MANTISSAS
MANTLE
MANTLED
MANTLES
MANTLET
MANTLETS
MANTLING
MANTLINGS
MANTO
MANTOES
MANTOS
MANTRA
MANTRAM
MANTRAMS
MANTRAP
MANTRAPS
MANTRAS
MANTRIC
MANTUA
MANTUAS
MANTY
MANTYHOSE
MANUAL
MANUALLY
MANUALS
MANUARY
MANUBRIA
MANUBRIAL
MANUBRIUM
MANUCODE
MANUCODES
MANUHIRI
MANUHIRIS
MANUKA
MANUKAS
MANUL
MANULS
MANUMATIC
MANUMEA
MANUMEAS
MANUMIT
MANUMITS
MANURANCE
MANURE
MANURED
MANURER
MANURERS
MANURES
MANURIAL
MANURING
MANURINGS
MANUS
MANWARD
MANWARDS
MANWISE
MANY
MANYATA
MANYATAS
MANYATTA
MANYATTAS
MANYFOLD
MANYPLIES
MANZANITA
MANZELLO
MANZELLOS
MAOMAO
MAOMAOS
MAORMOR
MAORMORS
MAP
MAPAU
MAPAUS
MAPLE
MAPLELIKE
MAPLES
MAPLESS
MAPLIKE
MAPMAKER
MAPMAKERS
MAPMAKING
MAPPABLE
MAPPED
MAPPEMOND
MAPPER
MAPPERIES
MAPPERS
MAPPERY
MAPPING
MAPPINGS
MAPPIST
MAPPISTS
MAPS
MAPSTICK
MAPSTICKS
MAPWISE
MAQUETTE
MAQUETTES
MAQUI
MAQUILA
MAQUILAS
MAQUIS
MAQUISARD
MAR
MARA
MARABI
MARABIS
MARABOU
MARABOUS

MARABOUT
MARABOUTS
MARABUNTA
MARACA
MARACAS
MARAE
MARAES
MARAGING
MARAGINGS
MARAH
MARAHS
MARAKA
MARANATHA
MARANTA
MARANTAS
MARARI
MARARIS
MARAS
MARASCA
MARASCAS
MARASMIC
MARASMOID
MARASMUS
MARATHON
MARATHONS
MARAUD
MARAUDED
MARAUDER
MARAUDERS
MARAUDING
MARAUDS
MARAVEDI
MARAVEDIS
MARBELISE
MARBELIZE
MARBLE
MARBLED
MARBLEISE
MARBLEIZE
MARBLER
MARBLERS
MARBLES
MARBLIER
MARBLIEST
MARBLING
MARBLINGS
MARBLY
MARC
MARCASITE
MARCATO
MARCATOS
MARCEL
MARCELLA
MARCELLAS
MARCELLED
MARCELLER
MARCELS
MARCH
MARCHED
MARCHEN
MARCHER
MARCHERS
MARCHES
MARCHESA
MARCHESAS
MARCHESE
MARCHESI
MARCHING
MARCHLAND
MARCHLIKE
MARCHMAN
MARCHMEN
MARCHPANE
MARCONI
MARCONIED
MARCONIS
MARCS
MARD
MARDIED
MARDIER
MARDIES
MARDIEST
MARDY
MARDYING
MARE
MAREMMA
MAREMMAS
MAREMME
MARENGO
MARERO
MAREROS
MARES
MARESCHAL
MARG
MARGARIC
MARGARIN
MARGARINE
MARGARINS
MARGARITA
MARGARITE
MARGATE
MARGATES
MARGAY
MARGAYS
MARGE
MARGENT
MARGENTED
MARGENTS
MARGES
MARGIN
MARGINAL
MARGINALS
MARGINATE
MARGINED
MARGINING
MARGINS
MARGOSA
MARGOSAS
MARGRAVE
MARGRAVES
MARGS
MARIA
MARIACHI
MARIACHIS
MARIALITE
MARID
MARIDS
MARIES
MARIGOLD
MARIGOLDS
MARIGRAM
MARIGRAMS
MARIGRAPH
MARIHUANA
MARIJUANA
MARIMBA
MARIMBAS
MARIMBIST
MARINA
MARINADE
MARINADED
MARINADES
MARINARA
MARINARAS
MARINAS
MARINATE
MARINATED
MARINATES
MARINE
MARINER
MARINERA
MARINERAS
MARINERS
MARINES
MARINIERE
MARIPOSA
MARIPOSAS
MARISCHAL
MARISH
MARISHES
MARITAGE
MARITAGES
MARITAL
MARITALLY
MARITIME
MARJORAM
MARJORAMS
MARK
MARKA
MARKAS
MARKDOWN
MARKDOWNS
MARKED
MARKEDLY
MARKER
MARKERS
MARKET
MARKETED
MARKETEER
MARKETER
MARKETERS
MARKETING
MARKETISE
MARKETIZE
MARKETS
MARKHOOR
MARKHOORS
MARKHOR
MARKHORS
MARKING
MARKINGS
MARKKA
MARKKAA
MARKKAS
MARKMAN
MARKMEN
MARKS
MARKSMAN
MARKSMEN
MARKUP
MARKUPS
MARL
MARLE
MARLED
MARLES
MARLIER
MARLIEST
MARLIN
MARLINE
MARLINES
MARLING
MARLINGS
MARLINS
MARLITE
MARLITES
MARLITIC
MARLS
MARLSTONE
MARLY
MARM
MARMALADE
MARMALISE
MARMALIZE
MARMARISE
MARMARIZE
MARMELISE
MARMELIZE
MARMEM
MARMITE
MARMITES
MARMOREAL
MARMOREAN
MARMOSE
MARMOSES
MARMOSET
MARMOSETS
MARMOT
MARMOTS
MARMS
MAROCAIN

M

MAROCAINS
MARON
MARONS
MAROON
MAROONED
MAROONER
MAROONERS
MAROONING
MAROONS
MAROQUIN
MAROQUINS
MAROR
MARORS
MARPLOT
MARPLOTS
MARQUE
MARQUEE
MARQUEES
MARQUES
MARQUESS
MARQUETRY
MARQUIS
MARQUISE
MARQUISES
MARRA
MARRAM
MARRAMS
MARRANO
MARRANOS
MARRAS
MARRED
MARRELS
MARRER
MARRERS
MARRI
MARRIAGE
MARRIAGES
MARRIED
MARRIEDS
MARRIER
MARRIERS
MARRIES
MARRING
MARRIS
MARRON
MARRONS
MARROW
MARROWED
MARROWFAT
MARROWIER
MARROWING
MARROWISH
MARROWS
MARROWSKY
MARROWY
MARRUM
MARRUMS
MARRY
MARRYING
MARRYINGS
MARS
MARSALA
MARSALAS
MARSE
MARSEILLE
MARSES
MARSH
MARSHAL
MARSHALCY
MARSHALED
MARSHALER
MARSHALL
MARSHALLS
MARSHALS
MARSHBUCK
MARSHED
MARSHES
MARSHIER
MARSHIEST
MARSHLAND
MARSHLIKE
MARSHWORT
MARSHY
MARSPORT
MARSPORTS
MARSQUAKE
MARSUPIA
MARSUPIAL
MARSUPIAN
MARSUPIUM
MART
MARTAGON
MARTAGONS
MARTED
MARTEL
MARTELLED
MARTELLO
MARTELLOS
MARTELS
MARTEN
MARTENS
MARTEXT
MARTEXTS
MARTIAL
MARTIALLY
MARTIALS
MARTIAN
MARTIANS
MARTIN
MARTINET
MARTINETS
MARTING
MARTINGAL
MARTINI
MARTINIS
MARTINS
MARTLET
MARTLETS
MARTS
MARTYR
MARTYRDOM
MARTYRED
MARTYRIA
MARTYRIES
MARTYRING
MARTYRISE
MARTYRISH
MARTYRIUM
MARTYRIZE
MARTYRLY
MARTYRS
MARTYRY
MARVEL
MARVELED
MARVELER
MARVELERS
MARVELING
MARVELLED
MARVELLER
MARVELOUS
MARVELS
MARVER
MARVERED
MARVERING
MARVERS
MARVIER
MARVIEST
MARVY
MARXISANT
MARY
MARYBUD
MARYBUDS
MARYJANE
MARYJANES
MARZIPAN
MARZIPANS
MAS
MASA
MASALA
MASALAS
MASAS
MASCARA
MASCARAED
MASCARAS
MASCARON
MASCARONS
MASCLE
MASCLED
MASCLES
MASCON
MASCONS
MASCOT
MASCOTS
MASCULINE
MASCULIST
MASCULY
MASE
MASED
MASER
MASERS
MASES
MASH
MASHALLAH
MASHED
MASHER
MASHERS
MASHES
MASHGIACH
MASHGIAH
MASHGIHIM
MASHIACH
MASHIACHS
MASHIE
MASHIER
MASHIES
MASHIEST
MASHING
MASHINGS
MASHLAM
MASHLAMS
MASHLIM
MASHLIMS
MASHLIN
MASHLINS
MASHLOCH
MASHLOCHS
MASHLUM
MASHLUMS
MASHMAN
MASHMEN
MASHUA
MASHUAS
MASHUP
MASHUPS
MASHY
MASING
MASJID
MASJIDS
MASK
MASKABLE
MASKED
MASKEG
MASKEGS
MASKER
MASKERS
MASKING
MASKINGS
MASKLIKE
MASKS
MASLIN
MASLINS
MASOCHISM
MASOCHIST
MASON
MASONED
MASONIC
MASONING
MASONITE
MASONITES
MASONRIED

M

MASONRIES
MASONRY
MASONS
MASOOLAH
MASOOLAHS
MASQUE
MASQUER
MASQUERS
MASQUES
MASS
MASSA
MASSACRE
MASSACRED
MASSACRER
MASSACRES
MASSAGE
MASSAGED
MASSAGER
MASSAGERS
MASSAGES
MASSAGING
MASSAGIST
MASSAS
MASSCULT
MASSCULTS
MASSE
MASSED
MASSEDLY
MASSES
MASSETER
MASSETERS
MASSEUR
MASSEURS
MASSEUSE
MASSEUSES
MASSICOT
MASSICOTS
MASSIER
MASSIEST
MASSIF
MASSIFS
MASSINESS
MASSING
MASSIVE
MASSIVELY
MASSIVES
MASSLESS
MASSOOLA
MASSOOLAS
MASSTIGE
MASSTIGES
MASSY
MASSYMORE
MAST
MASTABA
MASTABAH
MASTABAHS
MASTABAS
MASTED
MASTER
MASTERATE
MASTERDOM
MASTERED
MASTERFUL
MASTERIES
MASTERING
MASTERLY
MASTERS
MASTERY
MASTFUL
MASTHEAD
MASTHEADS
MASTHOUSE
MASTIC
MASTICATE
MASTICH
MASTICHE
MASTICHES
MASTICHS
MASTICOT
MASTICOTS
MASTICS
MASTIER
MASTIEST
MASTIFF
MASTIFFS
MASTING
MASTITIC
MASTITIS
MASTIX
MASTIXES
MASTLESS
MASTLIKE
MASTODON
MASTODONS
MASTODONT
MASTOID
MASTOIDAL
MASTOIDS
MASTOPEXY
MASTS
MASTY
MASU
MASULA
MASULAS
MASURIUM
MASURIUMS
MASUS
MAT
MATACHIN
MATACHINA
MATACHINI
MATACHINS
MATADOR
MATADORA
MATADORAS
MATADORE
MATADORES
MATADORS
MATAGOURI
MATAI
MATAIS
MATAMATA
MATAMATAS
MATAMBALA
MATATA
MATATAS
MATATU
MATATUS
MATCH
MATCHA
MATCHABLE
MATCHAS
MATCHBOOK
MATCHBOX
MATCHED
MATCHER
MATCHERS
MATCHES
MATCHET
MATCHETS
MATCHING
MATCHLESS
MATCHLOCK
MATCHMADE
MATCHMAKE
MATCHMARK
MATCHPLAY
MATCHUP
MATCHUPS
MATCHWOOD
MATE
MATED
MATELASSE
MATELESS
MATELOT
MATELOTE
MATELOTES
MATELOTS
MATELOTTE
MATER
MATERIAL
MATERIALS
MATERIEL
MATERIELS
MATERNAL
MATERNITY
MATERS
MATES
MATESHIP
MATESHIPS
MATEY
MATEYNESS
MATEYS
MATFELLON
MATFELON
MATFELONS
MATGRASS
MATH
MATHESES
MATHESIS
MATHS
MATICO
MATICOS
MATIER
MATIES
MATIEST
MATILDA
MATILDAS
MATILY
MATIN
MATINAL
MATINEE
MATINEES
MATINESS
MATING
MATINGS
MATINS
MATIPO
MATIPOS
MATJES
MATLESS
MATLO
MATLOS
MATLOW
MATLOWS
MATOKE
MATOKES
MATOOKE
MATOOKES
MATRASS
MATRASSES
MATRES
MATRIARCH
MATRIC
MATRICE
MATRICES
MATRICIDE
MATRICS
MATRICULA
MATRILINY
MATRIMONY
MATRIX
MATRIXES
MATRON
MATRONAGE
MATRONAL
MATRONISE
MATRONIZE
MATRONLY
MATRONS
MATROSS
MATROSSES
MATS
MATSAH
MATSAHS
MATSURI
MATSURIS
MATSUTAKE
MATT

M

MATTAMORE
MATTE
MATTED
MATTEDLY
MATTER
MATTERED
MATTERFUL
MATTERIER
MATTERING
MATTERS
MATTERY
MATTES
MATTIE
MATTIES
MATTIFIED
MATTIFIES
MATTIFY
MATTIN
MATTING
MATTINGS
MATTINS
MATTOCK
MATTOCKS
MATTOID
MATTOIDS
MATTRASS
MATTRESS
MATTS
MATURABLE
MATURATE
MATURATED
MATURATES
MATURE
MATURED
MATURELY
MATURER
MATURERS
MATURES
MATUREST
MATURING
MATURITY
MATUTINAL
MATUTINE
MATWEED
MATWEEDS
MATY
MATZA
MATZAH
MATZAHS
MATZAS
MATZO
MATZOH
MATZOHS
MATZOON
MATZOONS
MATZOS
MATZOT
MATZOTH
MAUBIES
MAUBY
MAUD
MAUDLIN
MAUDLINLY
MAUDS
MAUGER
MAUGRE
MAUGRED
MAUGRES
MAUGRING
MAUL
MAULED
MAULER
MAULERS
MAULGRE
MAULGRED
MAULGRES
MAULGRING
MAULING
MAULINGS
MAULS
MAULSTICK
MAULVI
MAULVIS
MAUMET
MAUMETRY
MAUMETS
MAUN
MAUND
MAUNDED
MAUNDER
MAUNDERED
MAUNDERER
MAUNDERS
MAUNDIES
MAUNDING
MAUNDS
MAUNDY
MAUNGIER
MAUNGIEST
MAUNGY
MAUNNA
MAURI
MAURIS
MAUSIER
MAUSIEST
MAUSOLEA
MAUSOLEAN
MAUSOLEUM
MAUSY
MAUT
MAUTHER
MAUTHERS
MAUTS
MAUVAIS
MAUVAISE
MAUVE
MAUVEIN
MAUVEINE
MAUVEINES
MAUVEINS
MAUVER
MAUVES
MAUVEST
MAUVIN
MAUVINE
MAUVINES
MAUVINS
MAUZIER
MAUZIEST
MAUZY
MAVEN
MAVENS
MAVERICK
MAVERICKS
MAVIE
MAVIES
MAVIN
MAVINS
MAVIS
MAVISES
MAVOURNIN
MAW
MAWBOUND
MAWED
MAWGER
MAWING
MAWK
MAWKIER
MAWKIEST
MAWKIN
MAWKINS
MAWKISH
MAWKISHLY
MAWKS
MAWKY
MAWMET
MAWMETRY
MAWMETS
MAWN
MAWNS
MAWPUS
MAWPUSES
MAWR
MAWRS
MAWS
MAWSEED
MAWSEEDS
MAWTHER
MAWTHERS
MAX
MAXED
MAXES
MAXI
MAXIBOAT
MAXIBOATS
MAXICOAT
MAXICOATS
MAXIDRESS
MAXILLA
MAXILLAE
MAXILLAR
MAXILLARY
MAXILLAS
MAXILLULA
MAXIM
MAXIMA
MAXIMAL
MAXIMALLY
MAXIMALS
MAXIMAND
MAXIMANDS
MAXIMIN
MAXIMINS
MAXIMISE
MAXIMISED
MAXIMISER
MAXIMISES
MAXIMIST
MAXIMISTS
MAXIMITE
MAXIMITES
MAXIMIZE
MAXIMIZED
MAXIMIZER
MAXIMIZES
MAXIMS
MAXIMUM
MAXIMUMLY
MAXIMUMS
MAXIMUS
MAXIMUSES
MAXING
MAXIS
MAXIXE
MAXIXES
MAXWELL
MAXWELLS
MAY
MAYA
MAYAN
MAYAPPLE
MAYAPPLES
MAYAS
MAYBE
MAYBES
MAYBIRD
MAYBIRDS
MAYBUSH
MAYBUSHES
MAYDAY
MAYDAYS
MAYED
MAYEST
MAYFISH
MAYFISHES
MAYFLIES
MAYFLOWER
MAYFLY
MAYHAP
MAYHAPPEN

MAYHEM
MAYHEMS
MAYING
MAYINGS
MAYO
MAYOR
MAYORAL
MAYORALTY
MAYORESS
MAYORS
MAYORSHIP
MAYOS
MAYPOLE
MAYPOLES
MAYPOP
MAYPOPS
MAYS
MAYST
MAYSTER
MAYSTERS
MAYVIN
MAYVINS
MAYWEED
MAYWEEDS
MAZAEDIA
MAZAEDIUM
MAZARD
MAZARDS
MAZARINE
MAZARINES
MAZE
MAZED
MAZEDLY
MAZEDNESS
MAZEFUL
MAZELIKE
MAZELTOV
MAZEMENT
MAZEMENTS
MAZER
MAZERS
MAZES
MAZEY
MAZHBI
MAZHBIS
MAZIER
MAZIEST
MAZILY
MAZINESS
MAZING
MAZOURKA
MAZOURKAS
MAZOUT
MAZOUTS
MAZUMA
MAZUMAS
MAZURKA
MAZURKAS
MAZUT
MAZUTS
MAZY
MAZZARD
MAZZARDS
MBAQANGA
MBAQANGAS
MBIRA
MBIRAS
ME
MEACOCK
MEACOCKS
MEAD
MEADOW
MEADOWIER
MEADOWS
MEADOWY
MEADS
MEAGER
MEAGERER
MEAGEREST
MEAGERLY
MEAGRE
MEAGRELY
MEAGRER
MEAGRES
MEAGREST
MEAL
MEALED
MEALER
MEALERS
MEALIE
MEALIER
MEALIES
MEALIEST
MEALINESS
MEALING
MEALLESS
MEALS
MEALTIME
MEALTIMES
MEALWORM
MEALWORMS
MEALY
MEALYBUG
MEALYBUGS
MEAN
MEANDER
MEANDERED
MEANDERER
MEANDERS
MEANDRIAN
MEANDROUS
MEANE
MEANED
MEANER
MEANERS
MEANES
MEANEST
MEANIE
MEANIES
MEANING
MEANINGLY
MEANINGS
MEANLY
MEANNESS
MEANS
MEANT
MEANTIME
MEANTIMES
MEANWHILE
MEANY
MEARE
MEARES
MEARING
MEASE
MEASED
MEASES
MEASING
MEASLE
MEASLED
MEASLES
MEASLIER
MEASLIEST
MEASLING
MEASLY
MEASURE
MEASURED
MEASURER
MEASURERS
MEASURES
MEASURING
MEAT
MEATAL
MEATAXE
MEATAXES
MEATBALL
MEATBALLS
MEATED
MEATH
MEATHE
MEATHEAD
MEATHEADS
MEATHES
MEATHOOK
MEATHOOKS
MEATHS
MEATIER
MEATIEST
MEATILY
MEATINESS
MEATLESS
MEATLOAF
MEATMAN
MEATMEN
MEATS
MEATSPACE
MEATUS
MEATUSES
MEATY
MEAWES
MEAZEL
MEAZELS
MEBIBYTE
MEBIBYTES
MEBOS
MEBOSES
MECCA
MECCAS
MECH
MECHANIC
MECHANICS
MECHANISE
MECHANISM
MECHANIST
MECHANIZE
MECHITZA
MECHITZAS
MECHITZOT
MECHOUI
MECHOUIS
MECHS
MECK
MECKS
MECLIZINE
MECONATE
MECONATES
MECONIC
MECONIN
MECONINS
MECONIUM
MECONIUMS
MED
MEDACCA
MEDACCAS
MEDAILLON
MEDAKA
MEDAKAS
MEDAL
MEDALED
MEDALET
MEDALETS
MEDALING
MEDALIST
MEDALISTS
MEDALLED
MEDALLIC
MEDALLING
MEDALLION
MEDALLIST
MEDALPLAY
MEDALS
MEDCINAL
MEDDLE
MEDDLED
MEDDLER
MEDDLERS
MEDDLES
MEDDLING
MEDDLINGS
MEDEVAC
MEDEVACED

M

MEDEVACS
MEDFLIES
MEDFLY
MEDIA
MEDIACIES
MEDIACY
MEDIAD
MEDIAE
MEDIAEVAL
MEDIAL
MEDIALLY
MEDIALS
MEDIAN
MEDIANLY
MEDIANS
MEDIANT
MEDIANTS
MEDIAS
MEDIATE
MEDIATED
MEDIATELY
MEDIATES
MEDIATING
MEDIATION
MEDIATISE
MEDIATIVE
MEDIATIZE
MEDIATOR
MEDIATORS
MEDIATORY
MEDIATRIX
MEDIC
MEDICABLE
MEDICABLY
MEDICAID
MEDICAIDS
MEDICAL
MEDICALLY
MEDICALS
MEDICANT
MEDICANTS
MEDICARE
MEDICARES
MEDICATE
MEDICATED
MEDICATES
MEDICIDE
MEDICIDES
MEDICINAL
MEDICINE
MEDICINED
MEDICINER
MEDICINES
MEDICK
MEDICKS
MEDICO
MEDICOS
MEDICS
MEDIEVAL
MEDIEVALS
MEDIGAP
MEDIGAPS
MEDII
MEDINA
MEDINAS
MEDIOCRE
MEDITATE
MEDITATED
MEDITATES
MEDITATOR
MEDIUM
MEDIUMS
MEDIUS
MEDIUSES
MEDIVAC
MEDIVACED
MEDIVACS
MEDLAR
MEDLARS
MEDLE
MEDLED
MEDLES
MEDLEY
MEDLEYS
MEDLING
MEDRESA
MEDRESAS
MEDRESE
MEDRESES
MEDRESSEH
MEDS
MEDULLA
MEDULLAE
MEDULLAR
MEDULLARY
MEDULLAS
MEDULLATE
MEDUSA
MEDUSAE
MEDUSAL
MEDUSAN
MEDUSANS
MEDUSAS
MEDUSOID
MEDUSOIDS
MEE
MEED
MEEDS
MEEK
MEEKEN
MEEKENED
MEEKENING
MEEKENS
MEEKER
MEEKEST
MEEKLY
MEEKNESS
MEEMIE
MEEMIES
MEER
MEERCAT
MEERCATS
MEERED
MEERING
MEERKAT
MEERKATS
MEERS
MEES
MEET
MEETER
MEETERS
MEETEST
MEETING
MEETINGS
MEETLY
MEETNESS
MEETS
MEFF
MEFFS
MEG
MEGA
MEGABAR
MEGABARS
MEGABIT
MEGABITS
MEGABUCK
MEGABUCKS
MEGABYTE
MEGABYTES
MEGACITY
MEGACURIE
MEGACYCLE
MEGADEAL
MEGADEALS
MEGADEATH
MEGADOSE
MEGADOSES
MEGADYNE
MEGADYNES
MEGAFARAD
MEGAFAUNA
MEGAFLOP
MEGAFLOPS
MEGAFLORA
MEGAFOG
MEGAFOGS
MEGAGAUSS
MEGAHERTZ
MEGAHIT
MEGAHITS
MEGAJOULE
MEGALITH
MEGALITHS
MEGALITRE
MEGALODON
MEGALOPIC
MEGALOPS
MEGAMALL
MEGAMALLS
MEGAPHONE
MEGAPHYLL
MEGAPIXEL
MEGAPLEX
MEGAPOD
MEGAPODE
MEGAPODES
MEGAPODS
MEGAQUAKE
MEGARA
MEGARAD
MEGARADS
MEGARON
MEGARONS
MEGASCOPE
MEGASPORE
MEGASS
MEGASSE
MEGASSES
MEGASTAR
MEGASTARS
MEGASTORE
MEGASTORM
MEGATHERE
MEGATON
MEGATONIC
MEGATONS
MEGAVOLT
MEGAVOLTS
MEGAWATT
MEGAWATTS
MEGILLA
MEGILLAH
MEGILLAHS
MEGILLAS
MEGILLOTH
MEGILP
MEGILPH
MEGILPHS
MEGILPS
MEGOHM
MEGOHMS
MEGRIM
MEGRIMS
MEGS
MEH
MEHNDI
MEHNDIS
MEIBOMIAN
MEIKLE
MEIN
MEINED
MEINEY
MEINEYS
MEINIE
MEINIES
MEINING
MEINS
MEINT
MEINY
MEIOCYTE

MEIOCYTES
MEIOFAUNA
MEIONITE
MEIONITES
MEIOSES
MEIOSIS
MEIOSPORE
MEIOTIC
MEISHI
MEISHIS
MEISTER
MEISTERS
MEITH
MEITHS
MEJLIS
MEJLISES
MEKKA
MEKKAS
MEKOMETER
MEL
MELA
MELAENA
MELAENAS
MELALEUCA
MELAMDIM
MELAMED
MELAMINE
MELAMINES
MELAMPODE
MELANGE
MELANGES
MELANIAN
MELANIANS
MELANIC
MELANICS
MELANIN
MELANINS
MELANISE
MELANISED
MELANISES
MELANISM
MELANISMS
MELANIST
MELANISTS
MELANITE
MELANITES
MELANITIC
MELANIZE
MELANIZED
MELANIZES
MELANO
MELANOID
MELANOIDS
MELANOMA
MELANOMAS
MELANOS
MELANOSES
MELANOSIS
MELANOTIC
MELANOUS
MELANURIA
MELANURIC
MELAPHYRE
MELAS
MELASTOME
MELATONIN
MELBA
MELD
MELDED
MELDER
MELDERS
MELDING
MELDS
MELEE
MELEES
MELENA
MELENAS
MELIC
MELICK
MELICKS
MELICS
MELIK
MELIKS
MELILITE
MELILITES
MELILOT
MELILOTS
MELINITE
MELINITES
MELIORATE
MELIORISM
MELIORIST
MELIORITY
MELISMA
MELISMAS
MELISMATA
MELITTIN
MELITTINS
MELL
MELLAY
MELLAYS
MELLED
MELLIFIC
MELLING
MELLITE
MELLITES
MELLITIC
MELLOTRON
MELLOW
MELLOWED
MELLOWER
MELLOWEST
MELLOWIER
MELLOWING
MELLOWLY
MELLOWS
MELLOWY
MELLS
MELOCOTON
MELODEON
MELODEONS
MELODIA
MELODIAS
MELODIC
MELODICA
MELODICAS
MELODICS
MELODIES
MELODION
MELODIONS
MELODIOUS
MELODISE
MELODISED
MELODISER
MELODISES
MELODIST
MELODISTS
MELODIZE
MELODIZED
MELODIZER
MELODIZES
MELODRAMA
MELODRAME
MELODY
MELOID
MELOIDS
MELOMANIA
MELOMANIC
MELON
MELONGENE
MELONIER
MELONIEST
MELONS
MELONY
MELOXICAM
MELPHALAN
MELS
MELT
MELTABLE
MELTAGE
MELTAGES
MELTDOWN
MELTDOWNS
MELTED
MELTEMI
MELTEMIS
MELTER
MELTERS
MELTIER
MELTIEST
MELTING
MELTINGLY
MELTINGS
MELTITH
MELTITHS
MELTON
MELTONS
MELTS
MELTWATER
MELTY
MELUNGEON
MEM
MEMBER
MEMBERED
MEMBERS
MEMBRAL
MEMBRANAL
MEMBRANE
MEMBRANED
MEMBRANES
MEME
MEMENTO
MEMENTOES
MEMENTOS
MEMES
MEMETIC
MEMETICS
MEMO
MEMOIR
MEMOIRISM
MEMOIRIST
MEMOIRS
MEMORABLE
MEMORABLY
MEMORANDA
MEMORIAL
MEMORIALS
MEMORIES
MEMORISE
MEMORISED
MEMORISER
MEMORISES
MEMORITER
MEMORIZE
MEMORIZED
MEMORIZER
MEMORIZES
MEMORY
MEMOS
MEMS
MEMSAHIB
MEMSAHIBS
MEN
MENACE
MENACED
MENACER
MENACERS
MENACES
MENACING
MENAD
MENADIONE
MENADS
MENAGE
MENAGED
MENAGERIE
MENAGES
MENAGING
MENARCHE
MENARCHES
MENAZON

M

MENAZONS
MEND
MENDABLE
MENDACITY
MENDED
MENDER
MENDERS
MENDICANT
MENDICITY
MENDIGO
MENDIGOS
MENDING
MENDINGS
MENDS
MENE
MENED
MENEER
MENEERS
MENES
MENFOLK
MENFOLKS
MENG
MENGE
MENGED
MENGES
MENGING
MENGS
MENHADEN
MENHADENS
MENHIR
MENHIRS
MENIAL
MENIALLY
MENIALS
MENILITE
MENILITES
MENING
MENINGEAL
MENINGES
MENINX
MENISCAL
MENISCATE
MENISCI
MENISCOID
MENISCUS
MENO
MENOLOGY
MENOMINEE
MENOMINI
MENOMINIS
MENOPAUSE
MENOPOLIS
MENOPOME
MENOPOMES
MENORAH
MENORAHS
MENORRHEA
MENSA
MENSAE
MENSAL
MENSAS
MENSCH
MENSCHEN
MENSCHES
MENSCHIER
MENSCHY
MENSE
MENSED
MENSEFUL
MENSELESS
MENSES
MENSH
MENSHED
MENSHEN
MENSHES
MENSHING
MENSING
MENSTRUA
MENSTRUAL
MENSTRUUM
MENSUAL
MENSURAL
MENSWEAR
MENSWEARS
MENT
MENTA
MENTAL
MENTALESE
MENTALISM
MENTALIST
MENTALITY
MENTALLY
MENTATION
MENTEE
MENTEES
MENTHENE
MENTHENES
MENTHOL
MENTHOLS
MENTICIDE
MENTION
MENTIONED
MENTIONER
MENTIONS
MENTO
MENTOR
MENTORED
MENTORIAL
MENTORING
MENTORS
MENTOS
MENTUM
MENU
MENUDO
MENUDOS
MENUISIER
MENUS
MENYIE
MENYIES
MEOU
MEOUED
MEOUING
MEOUS
MEOW
MEOWED
MEOWING
MEOWS
MEPACRINE
MEPHITIC
MEPHITIS
MEPHITISM
MERANTI
MERANTIS
MERBROMIN
MERC
MERCADO
MERCADOS
MERCAPTAN
MERCAPTO
MERCAT
MERCATS
MERCENARY
MERCER
MERCERIES
MERCERISE
MERCERIZE
MERCERS
MERCERY
MERCES
MERCH
MERCHANT
MERCHANTS
MERCHES
MERCHET
MERCHETS
MERCHILD
MERCIABLE
MERCIES
MERCIFIDE
MERCIFIED
MERCIFIES
MERCIFUL
MERCIFY
MERCILESS
MERCS
MERCURATE
MERCURIAL
MERCURIC
MERCURIES
MERCURISE
MERCURIZE
MERCUROUS
MERCURY
MERCY
MERDE
MERDES
MERE
MERED
MEREL
MERELL
MERELLS
MERELS
MERELY
MERENGUE
MERENGUES
MEREOLOGY
MERER
MERES
MERESMAN
MERESMEN
MEREST
MERESTONE
MERFOLK
MERFOLKS
MERGANSER
MERGE
MERGED
MERGEE
MERGEES
MERGENCE
MERGENCES
MERGER
MERGERS
MERGES
MERGING
MERGINGS
MERGUEZ
MERI
MERICARP
MERICARPS
MERIDIAN
MERIDIANS
MERIL
MERILS
MERIMAKE
MERIMAKES
MERING
MERINGS
MERINGUE
MERINGUES
MERINO
MERINOS
MERIS
MERISES
MERISIS
MERISM
MERISMS
MERISTEM
MERISTEMS
MERISTIC
MERIT
MERITED
MERITING
MERITLESS
MERITS
MERK
MERKIN
MERKINS
MERKS
MERL

MERLE
MERLES
MERLIN
MERLING
MERLINGS
MERLINS
MERLON
MERLONS
MERLOT
MERLOTS
MERLS
MERMAID
MERMAIDEN
MERMAIDS
MERMAN
MERMEN
MEROCRINE
MEROGONY
MEROISTIC
MEROME
MEROMES
MERONYM
MERONYMS
MERONYMY
MEROPIA
MEROPIAS
MEROPIC
MEROPIDAN
MEROSOME
MEROSOMES
MEROZOITE
MERPEOPLE
MERRIE
MERRIER
MERRIES
MERRIEST
MERRILY
MERRIMENT
MERRINESS
MERRY
MERRYMAN
MERRYMEN
MERSALYL
MERSALYLS
MERSE
MERSES
MERSION
MERSIONS
MERYCISM
MERYCISMS
MES
MESA
MESAIL
MESAILS
MESAL
MESALLY
MESARAIC
MESARCH
MESAS
MESCAL
MESCALIN
MESCALINE
MESCALINS
MESCALISM
MESCALS
MESCLUM
MESCLUMS
MESCLUN
MESCLUNS
MESDAMES
MESE
MESEEMED
MESEEMETH
MESEEMS
MESEL
MESELED
MESELS
MESENTERA
MESENTERY
MESES
MESETA
MESETAS
MESH
MESHED
MESHES
MESHIER
MESHIEST
MESHING
MESHINGS
MESHUGA
MESHUGAAS
MESHUGAH
MESHUGAS
MESHUGGA
MESHUGGAH
MESHUGGE
MESHWORK
MESHWORKS
MESHY
MESIAD
MESIAL
MESIALLY
MESIAN
MESIC
MESICALLY
MESMERIC
MESMERISE
MESMERISM
MESMERIST
MESMERIZE
MESNALTY
MESNE
MESNES
MESOBLAST
MESOCARP
MESOCARPS
MESOCRANY
MESODERM
MESODERMS
MESOGLEA
MESOGLEAL
MESOGLEAS
MESOGLOEA
MESOLITE
MESOLITES
MESOMERE
MESOMERES
MESOMORPH
MESON
MESONIC
MESONS
MESOPAUSE
MESOPHILE
MESOPHYL
MESOPHYLL
MESOPHYLS
MESOPHYTE
MESOSAUR
MESOSAURS
MESOSCALE
MESOSOME
MESOSOMES
MESOTRON
MESOTRONS
MESOZOAN
MESOZOANS
MESOZOIC
MESPIL
MESPILS
MESPRISE
MESPRISES
MESPRIZE
MESPRIZES
MESQUIN
MESQUINE
MESQUIT
MESQUITE
MESQUITES
MESQUITS
MESS
MESSAGE
MESSAGED
MESSAGES
MESSAGING
MESSALINE
MESSAN
MESSANS
MESSED
MESSENGER
MESSES
MESSIAH
MESSIAHS
MESSIANIC
MESSIAS
MESSIASES
MESSIER
MESSIEST
MESSIEURS
MESSILY
MESSINESS
MESSING
MESSMAN
MESSMATE
MESSMATES
MESSMEN
MESSUAGE
MESSUAGES
MESSY
MESTEE
MESTEES
MESTER
MESTERS
MESTESO
MESTESOES
MESTESOS
MESTINO
MESTINOES
MESTINOS
MESTIZA
MESTIZAS
MESTIZO
MESTIZOES
MESTIZOS
MESTO
MESTOM
MESTOME
MESTOMES
MESTOMS
MESTRANOL
MET
META
METABASES
METABASIS
METABATIC
METABOLIC
METABOLY
METACARPI
METADATA
METADATAS
METAFILE
METAFILES
METAGE
METAGENIC
METAGES
METAIRIE
METAIRIES
METAL
METALED
METALHEAD
METALING
METALISE
METALISED
METALISES
METALIST
METALISTS
METALIZE
METALIZED
METALIZES
METALLED
METALLIC

M

METALLICS
METALLIKE
METALLINE
METALLING
METALLISE
METALLIST
METALLIZE
METALLOID
METALLY
METALMARK
METALS
METALWARE
METALWORK
METAMALE
METAMALES
METAMER
METAMERAL
METAMERE
METAMERES
METAMERIC
METAMERS
METAMICT
METANOIA
METANOIAS
METAPELET
METAPHASE
METAPHOR
METAPHORS
METAPLASM
METAPLOT
METARCHON
METASOMA
METASOMAS
METATAG
METATAGS
METATARSI
METATE
METATES
METAVERSE
METAXYLEM
METAYAGE
METAYAGES
METAYER
METAYERS
METAZOA
METAZOAL
METAZOAN
METAZOANS
METAZOIC
METAZOON
METCAST
METCASTS
METE
METED
METEOR
METEORIC
METEORISM
METEORIST
METEORITE
METEOROID
METEOROUS
METEORS
METEPA
METEPAS
METER
METERAGE
METERAGES
METERED
METERING
METERS
METES
METESTICK
METESTRUS
METEWAND
METEWANDS
METEYARD
METEYARDS
METFORMIN
METH
METHADON
METHADONE
METHADONS
METHANAL
METHANALS
METHANE
METHANES
METHANOIC
METHANOL
METHANOLS
METHANOYL
METHEGLIN
METHINK
METHINKS
METHO
METHOD
METHODIC
METHODISE
METHODISM
METHODIST
METHODIZE
METHODS
METHOS
METHOUGHT
METHOXIDE
METHOXIES
METHOXY
METHOXYL
METHOXYLS
METHS
METHYL
METHYLAL
METHYLALS
METHYLASE
METHYLATE
METHYLENE
METHYLIC
METHYLS
METHYSES
METHYSIS
METHYSTIC
METIC
METICA
METICAIS
METICAL
METICALS
METICAS
METICS
METIER
METIERS
METIF
METIFS
METING
METIS
METISSE
METISSES
METOL
METOLS
METONYM
METONYMIC
METONYMS
METONYMY
METOPAE
METOPE
METOPES
METOPIC
METOPISM
METOPISMS
METOPON
METOPONS
METOPRYL
METOPRYLS
METRALGIA
METRAZOL
METRAZOLS
METRE
METRED
METRES
METRIC
METRICAL
METRICATE
METRICIAN
METRICISE
METRICISM
METRICIST
METRICIZE
METRICS
METRIFIED
METRIFIER
METRIFIES
METRIFY
METRING
METRIST
METRISTS
METRITIS
METRO
METROLOGY
METRONOME
METROPLEX
METROS
METS
METTLE
METTLED
METTLES
METUMP
METUMPS
MEU
MEUNIERE
MEUS
MEUSE
MEUSED
MEUSES
MEUSING
MEVE
MEVED
MEVES
MEVING
MEVROU
MEVROUS
MEW
MEWED
MEWING
MEWL
MEWLED
MEWLER
MEWLERS
MEWLING
MEWLS
MEWS
MEWSED
MEWSES
MEWSING
MEYNT
MEZAIL
MEZAILS
MEZCAL
MEZCALINE
MEZCALS
MEZE
MEZEREON
MEZEREONS
MEZEREUM
MEZEREUMS
MEZES
MEZQUIT
MEZQUITE
MEZQUITES
MEZQUITS
MEZUZA
MEZUZAH
MEZUZAHS
MEZUZAS
MEZUZOT
MEZUZOTH
MEZZ
MEZZALUNA
MEZZANINE
MEZZE
MEZZES
MEZZO
MEZZOS

MEZZOTINT
MGANGA
MGANGAS
MHO
MHORR
MHORRS
MHOS
MI
MIAOU
MIAOUED
MIAOUING
MIAOUS
MIAOW
MIAOWED
MIAOWING
MIAOWS
MIASM
MIASMA
MIASMAL
MIASMAS
MIASMATA
MIASMATIC
MIASMIC
MIASMOUS
MIASMS
MIAUL
MIAULED
MIAULING
MIAULS
MIB
MIBS
MIBUNA
MIBUNAS
MIC
MICA
MICACEOUS
MICAS
MICATE
MICATED
MICATES
MICATING
MICAWBER
MICAWBERS
MICE
MICELL
MICELLA
MICELLAE
MICELLAR
MICELLAS
MICELLE
MICELLES
MICELLS
MICH
MICHAEL
MICHAELS
MICHE
MICHED
MICHER
MICHERS
MICHES
MICHIGAN
MICHIGANS
MICHING
MICHINGS
MICHT
MICHTS
MICK
MICKERIES
MICKERY
MICKEY
MICKEYED
MICKEYING
MICKEYS
MICKIES
MICKLE
MICKLER
MICKLES
MICKLEST
MICKS
MICKY
MICO
MICOS
MICRA
MICRIFIED
MICRIFIES
MICRIFY
MICRO
MICROBAR
MICROBARS
MICROBE
MICROBEAD
MICROBEAM
MICROBES
MICROBIAL
MICROBIAN
MICROBIC
MICROBLOG
MICROBREW
MICROBUS
MICROCAP
MICROCAR
MICROCARD
MICROCARS
MICROCHIP
MICROCODE
MICROCOPY
MICROCOSM
MICROCYTE
MICRODONT
MICRODOT
MICRODOTS
MICROFILM
MICROFINE
MICROFORM
MICROGLIA
MICROGRAM
MICROHM
MICROHMS
MICROINCH
MICROJET
MICROJETS
MICROLITE
MICROLITH
MICROLOAN
MICROLOGY
MICROLUX
MICROMERE
MICROMESH
MICROMHO
MICROMHOS
MICROMINI
MICROMOLE
MICROMORT
MICRON
MICRONISE
MICRONIZE
MICRONS
MICROPORE
MICROPSIA
MICROPUMP
MICROPYLE
MICROS
MICROSITE
MICROSOME
MICROTOME
MICROTOMY
MICROTONE
MICROTUBE
MICROVOLT
MICROWATT
MICROWAVE
MICROWIRE
MICRURGY
MICS
MICTION
MICTIONS
MICTURATE
MID
MIDAIR
MIDAIRS
MIDBAND
MIDBRAIN
MIDBRAINS
MIDCALF
MIDCALVES
MIDCAP
MIDCOURSE
MIDCULT
MIDCULTS
MIDDAY
MIDDAYS
MIDDEN
MIDDENS
MIDDEST
MIDDIE
MIDDIES
MIDDLE
MIDDLED
MIDDLEMAN
MIDDLEMEN
MIDDLER
MIDDLERS
MIDDLES
MIDDLING
MIDDLINGS
MIDDORSAL
MIDDY
MIDFIELD
MIDFIELDS
MIDGE
MIDGES
MIDGET
MIDGETS
MIDGIE
MIDGIER
MIDGIES
MIDGIEST
MIDGUT
MIDGUTS
MIDGY
MIDI
MIDIBUS
MIDIBUSES
MIDINETTE
MIDIRON
MIDIRONS
MIDIS
MIDISKIRT
MIDLAND
MIDLANDER
MIDLANDS
MIDLEG
MIDLEGS
MIDLIFE
MIDLIFER
MIDLIFERS
MIDLINE
MIDLINES
MIDLIST
MIDLISTS
MIDLIVES
MIDMONTH
MIDMONTHS
MIDMOST
MIDMOSTS
MIDNIGHT
MIDNIGHTS
MIDNOON
MIDNOONS
MIDPAY
MIDPOINT
MIDPOINTS
MIDRANGE
MIDRANGES
MIDRASH
MIDRASHIC
MIDRASHIM
MIDRASHOT
MIDRIB
MIDRIBS

MIDRIFF
MIDRIFFS
MIDS
MIDSEASON
MIDSHIP
MIDSHIPS
MIDSHORE
MIDSIZE
MIDSIZED
MIDSOLE
MIDSOLES
MIDSPACE
MIDSPACES
MIDST
MIDSTORY
MIDSTREAM
MIDSTS
MIDSUMMER
MIDTERM
MIDTERMS
MIDTHIGH
MIDTHIGHS
MIDTOWN
MIDTOWNS
MIDWATCH
MIDWATER
MIDWATERS
MIDWAY
MIDWAYS
MIDWEEK
MIDWEEKLY
MIDWEEKS
MIDWIFE
MIDWIFED
MIDWIFERY
MIDWIFES
MIDWIFING
MIDWINTER
MIDWIVE
MIDWIVED
MIDWIVES
MIDWIVING
MIDYEAR
MIDYEARS
MIELIE
MIELIES
MIEN
MIENS
MIEVE
MIEVED
MIEVES
MIEVING
MIFF
MIFFED
MIFFIER
MIFFIEST
MIFFILY
MIFFINESS
MIFFING
MIFFS
MIFFY
MIFTY
MIG
MIGAWD
MIGG
MIGGLE
MIGGLES
MIGGS
MIGHT
MIGHTEST
MIGHTFUL
MIGHTIER
MIGHTIEST
MIGHTILY
MIGHTS
MIGHTST
MIGHTY
MIGMATITE
MIGNON
MIGNONNE
MIGNONNES
MIGNONS
MIGRAINE
MIGRAINES
MIGRANT
MIGRANTS
MIGRATE
MIGRATED
MIGRATES
MIGRATING
MIGRATION
MIGRATOR
MIGRATORS
MIGRATORY
MIGS
MIHA
MIHAS
MIHI
MIHIED
MIHIING
MIHIS
MIHRAB
MIHRABS
MIJNHEER
MIJNHEERS
MIKADO
MIKADOS
MIKE
MIKED
MIKES
MIKING
MIKRA
MIKRON
MIKRONS
MIKVA
MIKVAH
MIKVAHS
MIKVAS
MIKVEH
MIKVEHS
MIKVOS
MIKVOT
MIKVOTH
MIL
MILADI
MILADIES
MILADIS
MILADY
MILAGE
MILAGES
MILCH
MILCHIG
MILCHIK
MILD
MILDED
MILDEN
MILDENED
MILDENING
MILDENS
MILDER
MILDEST
MILDEW
MILDEWED
MILDEWIER
MILDEWING
MILDEWS
MILDEWY
MILDING
MILDISH
MILDLY
MILDNESS
MILDS
MILE
MILEAGE
MILEAGES
MILEPOST
MILEPOSTS
MILER
MILERS
MILES
MILESIAN
MILESIMO
MILESIMOS
MILESTONE
MILF
MILFOIL
MILFOILS
MILFS
MILIA
MILIARIA
MILIARIAL
MILIARIAS
MILIARY
MILIEU
MILIEUS
MILIEUX
MILING
MILINGS
MILITANCE
MILITANCY
MILITANT
MILITANTS
MILITAR
MILITARIA
MILITARY
MILITATE
MILITATED
MILITATES
MILITIA
MILITIAS
MILIUM
MILK
MILKED
MILKEN
MILKER
MILKERS
MILKFISH
MILKIER
MILKIEST
MILKILY
MILKINESS
MILKING
MILKINGS
MILKLESS
MILKLIKE
MILKMAID
MILKMAIDS
MILKMAN
MILKMEN
MILKO
MILKOS
MILKS
MILKSHAKE
MILKSHED
MILKSHEDS
MILKSOP
MILKSOPPY
MILKSOPS
MILKTOAST
MILKWEED
MILKWEEDS
MILKWOOD
MILKWOODS
MILKWORT
MILKWORTS
MILKY
MILL
MILLABLE
MILLAGE
MILLAGES
MILLBOARD
MILLCAKE
MILLCAKES
MILLDAM
MILLDAMS
MILLE
MILLED
MILLENARY
MILLENNIA
MILLEPED

MILLEPEDE
MILLEPEDS
MILLEPORE
MILLER
MILLERITE
MILLERS
MILLES
MILLET
MILLETS
MILLHAND
MILLHANDS
MILLHOUSE
MILLIAMP
MILLIAMPS
MILLIARD
MILLIARDS
MILLIARE
MILLIARES
MILLIARY
MILLIBAR
MILLIBARS
MILLIE
MILLIEME
MILLIEMES
MILLIER
MILLIERS
MILLIES
MILLIGAL
MILLIGALS
MILLIGRAM
MILLILUX
MILLIME
MILLIMES
MILLIMHO
MILLIMHOS
MILLIMOLE
MILLINE
MILLINER
MILLINERS
MILLINERY
MILLINES
MILLING
MILLINGS
MILLIOHM
MILLIOHMS
MILLION
MILLIONS
MILLIONTH
MILLIPED
MILLIPEDE
MILLIPEDS
MILLIREM
MILLIREMS
MILLIVOLT
MILLIWATT
MILLOCRAT
MILLPOND
MILLPONDS
MILLRACE
MILLRACES
MILLRIND
MILLRINDS
MILLRUN
MILLRUNS
MILLS
MILLSCALE
MILLSTONE
MILLTAIL
MILLTAILS
MILLWHEEL
MILLWORK
MILLWORKS
MILNEB
MILNEBS
MILO
MILOMETER
MILOR
MILORD
MILORDS
MILORS
MILOS
MILPA
MILPAS
MILREIS
MILS
MILSEY
MILSEYS
MILT
MILTED
MILTER
MILTERS
MILTIER
MILTIEST
MILTING
MILTONIA
MILTONIAS
MILTS
MILTY
MILTZ
MILTZES
MILVINE
MIM
MIMBAR
MIMBARS
MIME
MIMED
MIMEO
MIMEOED
MIMEOING
MIMEOS
MIMER
MIMERS
MIMES
MIMESES
MIMESIS
MIMESISES
MIMESTER
MIMESTERS
MIMETIC
MIMETICAL
MIMETITE
MIMETITES
MIMIC
MIMICAL
MIMICKED
MIMICKER
MIMICKERS
MIMICKING
MIMICRIES
MIMICRY
MIMICS
MIMING
MIMIVIRUS
MIMMER
MIMMEST
MIMMICK
MIMMICKED
MIMMICKS
MIMOSA
MIMOSAE
MIMOSAS
MIMSEY
MIMSIER
MIMSIEST
MIMSY
MIMULUS
MIMULUSES
MINA
MINABLE
MINACIOUS
MINACITY
MINAE
MINAR
MINARET
MINARETED
MINARETS
MINARS
MINAS
MINATORY
MINBAR
MINBARS
MINCE
MINCED
MINCEMEAT
MINCER
MINCERS
MINCES
MINCEUR
MINCIER
MINCIEST
MINCING
MINCINGLY
MINCY
MIND
MINDED
MINDEDLY
MINDER
MINDERS
MINDFUCK
MINDFUCKS
MINDFUL
MINDFULLY
MINDING
MINDINGS
MINDLESS
MINDS
MINDSCAPE
MINDSET
MINDSETS
MINDSHARE
MINE
MINEABLE
MINED
MINEFIELD
MINELAYER
MINEOLA
MINEOLAS
MINER
MINERAL
MINERALS
MINERS
MINES
MINESHAFT
MINESTONE
MINETTE
MINETTES
MINEVER
MINEVERS
MING
MINGE
MINGED
MINGER
MINGERS
MINGES
MINGIER
MINGIEST
MINGILY
MINGINESS
MINGING
MINGLE
MINGLED
MINGLER
MINGLERS
MINGLES
MINGLING
MINGLINGS
MINGS
MINGY
MINI
MINIATE
MINIATED
MINIATES
MINIATING
MINIATION
MINIATURE
MINIBAR
MINIBARS
MINIBIKE
MINIBIKER
MINIBIKES

M

MINIBREAK
MINIBUS
MINIBUSES
MINICAB
MINICABS
MINICAM
MINICAMP
MINICAMPS
MINICAMS
MINICAR
MINICARS
MINICOM
MINICOMS
MINIDISC
MINIDISCS
MINIDISH
MINIDISK
MINIDISKS
MINIDRESS
MINIER
MINIEST
MINIFIED
MINIFIES
MINIFY
MINIFYING
MINIGOLF
MINIGOLFS
MINIKIN
MINIKINS
MINILAB
MINILABS
MINIM
MINIMA
MINIMAL
MINIMALLY
MINIMALS
MINIMART
MINIMARTS
MINIMAX
MINIMAXED
MINIMAXES
MINIMENT
MINIMENTS
MINIMILL
MINIMILLS
MINIMISE
MINIMISED
MINIMISER
MINIMISES
MINIMISM
MINIMISMS
MINIMIST
MINIMISTS
MINIMIZE
MINIMIZED
MINIMIZER
MINIMIZES
MINIMOTO
MINIMOTOS
MINIMS
MINIMUM
MINIMUMS
MINIMUS
MINIMUSES
MINING
MININGS
MINION
MINIONS
MINIPARK
MINIPARKS
MINIPILL
MINIPILLS
MINIRUGBY
MINIS
MINISCULE
MINISH
MINISHED
MINISHES
MINISHING
MINISKI
MINISKIRT
MINISKIS
MINISODE
MINISODES
MINISTATE
MINISTER
MINISTERS
MINISTRY
MINITOWER
MINITRACK
MINIUM
MINIUMS
MINIVAN
MINIVANS
MINIVER
MINIVERS
MINIVET
MINIVETS
MINK
MINKE
MINKES
MINKS
MINNEOLA
MINNEOLAS
MINNICK
MINNICKED
MINNICKS
MINNIE
MINNIES
MINNOCK
MINNOCKED
MINNOCKS
MINNOW
MINNOWS
MINNY
MINO
MINOR
MINORCA
MINORCAS
MINORED
MINORING
MINORITY
MINORS
MINORSHIP
MINOS
MINOTAUR
MINOXIDIL
MINSHUKU
MINSHUKUS
MINSTER
MINSTERS
MINSTREL
MINSTRELS
MINT
MINTAGE
MINTAGES
MINTED
MINTER
MINTERS
MINTIER
MINTIEST
MINTING
MINTLIKE
MINTS
MINTY
MINUEND
MINUENDS
MINUET
MINUETED
MINUETING
MINUETS
MINUS
MINUSCULE
MINUSES
MINUTE
MINUTED
MINUTELY
MINUTEMAN
MINUTEMEN
MINUTER
MINUTES
MINUTEST
MINUTIA
MINUTIAE
MINUTIAL
MINUTING
MINUTIOSE
MINX
MINXES
MINXISH
MINY
MINYAN
MINYANIM
MINYANS
MIOCENE
MIOMBO
MIOMBOS
MIOSES
MIOSIS
MIOSISES
MIOTIC
MIOTICS
MIPS
MIQUELET
MIQUELETS
MIR
MIRABELLE
MIRABILIA
MIRABILIS
MIRABLE
MIRACIDIA
MIRACLE
MIRACLES
MIRADOR
MIRADORS
MIRAGE
MIRAGES
MIRANDISE
MIRANDIZE
MIRBANE
MIRBANES
MIRCHI
MIRE
MIRED
MIREPOIX
MIRES
MIREX
MIREXES
MIRI
MIRID
MIRIDS
MIRIER
MIRIEST
MIRIFIC
MIRIFICAL
MIRIN
MIRINESS
MIRING
MIRINS
MIRITI
MIRITIS
MIRK
MIRKER
MIRKEST
MIRKIER
MIRKIEST
MIRKILY
MIRKINESS
MIRKS
MIRKY
MIRLIER
MIRLIEST
MIRLIGOES
MIRLITON
MIRLITONS
MIRLY
MIRO
MIROMIRO
MIROMIROS
MIROS

MIRROR
MIRRORED
MIRRORING
MIRRORS
MIRS
MIRTH
MIRTHFUL
MIRTHLESS
MIRTHS
MIRV
MIRVED
MIRVING
MIRVS
MIRY
MIRZA
MIRZAS
MIS
MISACT
MISACTED
MISACTING
MISACTS
MISADAPT
MISADAPTS
MISADD
MISADDED
MISADDING
MISADDS
MISADJUST
MISADVICE
MISADVISE
MISAGENT
MISAGENTS
MISAIM
MISAIMED
MISAIMING
MISAIMS
MISALIGN
MISALIGNS
MISALLEGE
MISALLIED
MISALLIES
MISALLOT
MISALLOTS
MISALLY
MISALTER
MISALTERS
MISANDRY
MISAPPLY
MISARRAY
MISARRAYS
MISASSAY
MISASSAYS
MISASSIGN
MISASSUME
MISATE
MISATONE
MISATONED
MISATONES
MISAUNTER
MISAVER
MISAVERS
MISAVISED
MISAWARD
MISAWARDS
MISBECAME
MISBECOME
MISBEGAN
MISBEGIN
MISBEGINS
MISBEGOT
MISBEGUN
MISBEHAVE
MISBELIEF
MISBESEEM
MISBESTOW
MISBIAS
MISBIASED
MISBIASES
MISBILL
MISBILLED
MISBILLS
MISBIND
MISBINDS
MISBIRTH
MISBIRTHS
MISBORN
MISBOUND
MISBRAND
MISBRANDS
MISBUILD
MISBUILDS
MISBUILT
MISBUTTON
MISCALL
MISCALLED
MISCALLER
MISCALLS
MISCARRY
MISCAST
MISCASTS
MISCEGEN
MISCEGENE
MISCEGENS
MISCEGINE
MISCH
MISCHANCE
MISCHANCY
MISCHARGE
MISCHIEF
MISCHIEFS
MISCHOICE
MISCHOOSE
MISCHOSE
MISCHOSEN
MISCIBLE
MISCITE
MISCITED
MISCITES
MISCITING
MISCLAIM
MISCLAIMS
MISCLASS
MISCODE
MISCODED
MISCODES
MISCODING
MISCOIN
MISCOINED
MISCOINS
MISCOLOR
MISCOLORS
MISCOLOUR
MISCOOK
MISCOOKED
MISCOOKS
MISCOPIED
MISCOPIES
MISCOPY
MISCOUNT
MISCOUNTS
MISCREANT
MISCREATE
MISCREDIT
MISCREED
MISCREEDS
MISCUE
MISCUED
MISCUEING
MISCUES
MISCUING
MISCUT
MISCUTS
MISDATE
MISDATED
MISDATES
MISDATING
MISDEAL
MISDEALER
MISDEALS
MISDEALT
MISDEED
MISDEEDS
MISDEEM
MISDEEMED
MISDEEMS
MISDEFINE
MISDEMEAN
MISDEMPT
MISDESERT
MISDIAL
MISDIALED
MISDIALS
MISDID
MISDIET
MISDIETED
MISDIETS
MISDIGHT
MISDIGHTS
MISDIRECT
MISDIVIDE
MISDO
MISDOER
MISDOERS
MISDOES
MISDOING
MISDOINGS
MISDONE
MISDONNE
MISDOUBT
MISDOUBTS
MISDRAW
MISDRAWN
MISDRAWS
MISDREAD
MISDREADS
MISDREW
MISDRIVE
MISDRIVEN
MISDRIVES
MISDROVE
MISE
MISEASE
MISEASES
MISEAT
MISEATEN
MISEATING
MISEATS
MISEDIT
MISEDITED
MISEDITS
MISEMPLOY
MISENROL
MISENROLL
MISENROLS
MISENTER
MISENTERS
MISENTRY
MISER
MISERABLE
MISERABLY
MISERE
MISERERE
MISERERES
MISERES
MISERIES
MISERLIER
MISERLY
MISERS
MISERY
MISES
MISESTEEM
MISEVENT
MISEVENTS
MISFAITH
MISFAITHS
MISFALL
MISFALLEN
MISFALLS
MISFALNE
MISFARE

MISFARED
MISFARES
MISFARING
MISFEASOR
MISFED
MISFEED
MISFEEDS
MISFEIGN
MISFEIGNS
MISFELL
MISFIELD
MISFIELDS
MISFILE
MISFILED
MISFILES
MISFILING
MISFIRE
MISFIRED
MISFIRES
MISFIRING
MISFIT
MISFITS
MISFITTED
MISFOCUS
MISFOLD
MISFOLDED
MISFOLDS
MISFORM
MISFORMED
MISFORMS
MISFRAME
MISFRAMED
MISFRAMES
MISGAGE
MISGAGED
MISGAGES
MISGAGING
MISGAUGE
MISGAUGED
MISGAUGES
MISGAVE
MISGENDER
MISGIVE
MISGIVEN
MISGIVES
MISGIVING
MISGO
MISGOES
MISGOING
MISGONE
MISGOTTEN
MISGOVERN
MISGRADE
MISGRADED
MISGRADES
MISGRAFF
MISGRAFT
MISGRAFTS
MISGREW
MISGROW
MISGROWN
MISGROWS
MISGROWTH
MISGUESS
MISGUGGLE
MISGUIDE
MISGUIDED
MISGUIDER
MISGUIDES
MISHANDLE
MISHANTER
MISHAP
MISHAPPED
MISHAPPEN
MISHAPS
MISHAPT
MISHEAR
MISHEARD
MISHEARS
MISHEGAAS
MISHEGOSS
MISHIT
MISHITS
MISHMASH
MISHMEE
MISHMEES
MISHMI
MISHMIS
MISHMOSH
MISHUGAS
MISINFER
MISINFERS
MISINFORM
MISINTEND
MISINTER
MISINTERS
MISJOIN
MISJOINED
MISJOINS
MISJUDGE
MISJUDGED
MISJUDGER
MISJUDGES
MISKAL
MISKALS
MISKEEP
MISKEEPS
MISKEN
MISKENNED
MISKENS
MISKENT
MISKEPT
MISKEY
MISKEYED
MISKEYING
MISKEYS
MISKICK
MISKICKED
MISKICKS
MISKNEW
MISKNOW
MISKNOWN
MISKNOWS
MISLABEL
MISLABELS
MISLABOR
MISLABORS
MISLABOUR
MISLAID
MISLAIN
MISLAY
MISLAYER
MISLAYERS
MISLAYING
MISLAYS
MISLEAD
MISLEADER
MISLEADS
MISLEARED
MISLEARN
MISLEARNS
MISLEARNT
MISLED
MISLEEKE
MISLEEKED
MISLEEKES
MISLETOE
MISLETOES
MISLIE
MISLIES
MISLIGHT
MISLIGHTS
MISLIKE
MISLIKED
MISLIKER
MISLIKERS
MISLIKES
MISLIKING
MISLIPPEN
MISLIT
MISLIVE
MISLIVED
MISLIVES
MISLIVING
MISLOCATE
MISLODGE
MISLODGED
MISLODGES
MISLUCK
MISLUCKED
MISLUCKS
MISLYING
MISMADE
MISMAKE
MISMAKES
MISMAKING
MISMANAGE
MISMARK
MISMARKED
MISMARKS
MISMARRY
MISMATCH
MISMATE
MISMATED
MISMATES
MISMATING
MISMEET
MISMEETS
MISMET
MISMETRE
MISMETRED
MISMETRES
MISMOVE
MISMOVED
MISMOVES
MISMOVING
MISNAME
MISNAMED
MISNAMES
MISNAMING
MISNOMER
MISNOMERS
MISNUMBER
MISO
MISOCLERE
MISOGAMIC
MISOGAMY
MISOGYNIC
MISOGYNY
MISOLOGY
MISONEISM
MISONEIST
MISORDER
MISORDERS
MISORIENT
MISOS
MISPAGE
MISPAGED
MISPAGES
MISPAGING
MISPAINT
MISPAINTS
MISPARSE
MISPARSED
MISPARSES
MISPART
MISPARTED
MISPARTS
MISPATCH
MISPEN
MISPENNED
MISPENS
MISPHRASE
MISPICKEL
MISPLACE
MISPLACED
MISPLACES
MISPLAN
MISPLANS
MISPLANT

MISPLANTS
MISPLAY
MISPLAYED
MISPLAYS
MISPLEAD
MISPLEADS
MISPLEASE
MISPLED
MISPOINT
MISPOINTS
MISPOISE
MISPOISED
MISPOISES
MISPRAISE
MISPRICE
MISPRICED
MISPRICES
MISPRINT
MISPRINTS
MISPRISE
MISPRISED
MISPRISES
MISPRIZE
MISPRIZED
MISPRIZER
MISPRIZES
MISPROUD
MISQUOTE
MISQUOTED
MISQUOTER
MISQUOTES
MISRAISE
MISRAISED
MISRAISES
MISRATE
MISRATED
MISRATES
MISRATING
MISREAD
MISREADS
MISRECKON
MISRECORD
MISREFER
MISREFERS
MISREGARD
MISRELATE
MISRELIED
MISRELIES
MISRELY
MISRENDER
MISREPORT
MISRHYMED
MISROUTE
MISROUTED
MISROUTES
MISRULE
MISRULED
MISRULES
MISRULING
MISS
MISSA
MISSABLE
MISSAE
MISSAID
MISSAL
MISSALS
MISSAW
MISSAY
MISSAYING
MISSAYS
MISSEAT
MISSEATED
MISSEATS
MISSED
MISSEE
MISSEEING
MISSEEM
MISSEEMED
MISSEEMS
MISSEEN
MISSEES
MISSEL
MISSELL
MISSELLS
MISSELS
MISSEND
MISSENDS
MISSENSE
MISSENSED
MISSENSES
MISSENT
MISSES
MISSET
MISSETS
MISSHAPE
MISSHAPED
MISSHAPEN
MISSHAPER
MISSHAPES
MISSHOD
MISSHOOD
MISSHOODS
MISSIER
MISSIES
MISSIEST
MISSILE
MISSILEER
MISSILERY
MISSILES
MISSILRY
MISSING
MISSINGLY
MISSION
MISSIONAL
MISSIONED
MISSIONER
MISSIONS
MISSIS
MISSISES
MISSISH
MISSIVE
MISSIVES
MISSOLD
MISSORT
MISSORTED
MISSORTS
MISSOUND
MISSOUNDS
MISSOUT
MISSOUTS
MISSPACE
MISSPACED
MISSPACES
MISSPEAK
MISSPEAKS
MISSPELL
MISSPELLS
MISSPELT
MISSPEND
MISSPENDS
MISSPENT
MISSPOKE
MISSPOKEN
MISSTAMP
MISSTAMPS
MISSTART
MISSTARTS
MISSTATE
MISSTATED
MISSTATES
MISSTEER
MISSTEERS
MISSTEP
MISSTEPS
MISSTOP
MISSTOPS
MISSTRIKE
MISSTRUCK
MISSTYLE
MISSTYLED
MISSTYLES
MISSUIT
MISSUITED
MISSUITS
MISSUS
MISSUSES
MISSY
MIST
MISTAKE
MISTAKEN
MISTAKER
MISTAKERS
MISTAKES
MISTAKING
MISTAL
MISTALS
MISTAUGHT
MISTBOW
MISTBOWS
MISTEACH
MISTED
MISTELL
MISTELLS
MISTEMPER
MISTEND
MISTENDED
MISTENDS
MISTER
MISTERED
MISTERIES
MISTERING
MISTERM
MISTERMED
MISTERMS
MISTERS
MISTERY
MISTEUK
MISTFUL
MISTHINK
MISTHINKS
MISTHREW
MISTHROW
MISTHROWN
MISTHROWS
MISTICO
MISTICOS
MISTIER
MISTIEST
MISTIGRIS
MISTILY
MISTIME
MISTIMED
MISTIMES
MISTIMING
MISTINESS
MISTING
MISTINGS
MISTITLE
MISTITLED
MISTITLES
MISTLE
MISTLED
MISTLES
MISTLETOE
MISTLING
MISTOLD
MISTOOK
MISTOUCH
MISTRACE
MISTRACED
MISTRACES
MISTRAIN
MISTRAINS
MISTRAL
MISTRALS
MISTREAT
MISTREATS
MISTRESS
MISTRIAL
MISTRIALS

M

MISTRUST
MISTRUSTS
MISTRUTH
MISTRUTHS
MISTRYST
MISTRYSTS
MISTS
MISTUNE
MISTUNED
MISTUNES
MISTUNING
MISTUTOR
MISTUTORS
MISTY
MISTYPE
MISTYPED
MISTYPES
MISTYPING
MISUNION
MISUNIONS
MISUSAGE
MISUSAGES
MISUSE
MISUSED
MISUSER
MISUSERS
MISUSES
MISUSING
MISUST
MISVALUE
MISVALUED
MISVALUES
MISWEEN
MISWEENED
MISWEENS
MISWEND
MISWENDS
MISWENT
MISWORD
MISWORDED
MISWORDS
MISWRIT
MISWRITE
MISWRITES
MISWROTE
MISYOKE
MISYOKED
MISYOKES
MISYOKING
MITCH
MITCHED
MITCHES
MITCHING
MITE
MITER
MITERED
MITERER
MITERERS
MITERING
MITERS
MITERWORT
MITES
MITHER
MITHERED
MITHERING
MITHERS
MITICIDAL
MITICIDE
MITICIDES
MITIER
MITIEST
MITIGABLE
MITIGANT
MITIGANTS
MITIGATE
MITIGATED
MITIGATES
MITIGATOR
MITIS
MITISES
MITOGEN
MITOGENIC
MITOGENS
MITOMYCIN
MITOSES
MITOSIS
MITOTIC
MITRAILLE
MITRAL
MITRE
MITRED
MITRES
MITREWORT
MITRIFORM
MITRING
MITSVAH
MITSVAHS
MITSVOTH
MITT
MITTEN
MITTENED
MITTENS
MITTIMUS
MITTS
MITUMBA
MITUMBAS
MITY
MITZVAH
MITZVAHS
MITZVOTH
MIURUS
MIURUSES
MIX
MIXABLE
MIXDOWN
MIXDOWNS
MIXED
MIXEDLY
MIXEDNESS
MIXEN
MIXENS
MIXER
MIXERS
MIXES
MIXIBLE
MIXIER
MIXIEST
MIXING
MIXINGS
MIXMASTER
MIXOLOGY
MIXT
MIXTAPE
MIXTAPES
MIXTE
MIXTION
MIXTIONS
MIXTURE
MIXTURES
MIXUP
MIXUPS
MIXY
MIZ
MIZEN
MIZENMAST
MIZENS
MIZMAZE
MIZMAZES
MIZUNA
MIZUNAS
MIZZ
MIZZEN
MIZZENS
MIZZES
MIZZLE
MIZZLED
MIZZLES
MIZZLIER
MIZZLIEST
MIZZLING
MIZZLINGS
MIZZLY
MIZZONITE
MIZZY
MM
MMM
MNA
MNAS
MNEME
MNEMES
MNEMIC
MNEMON
MNEMONIC
MNEMONICS
MNEMONIST
MNEMONS
MO
MOA
MOAI
MOAN
MOANED
MOANER
MOANERS
MOANFUL
MOANFULLY
MOANING
MOANINGLY
MOANINGS
MOANS
MOAS
MOAT
MOATED
MOATING
MOATLIKE
MOATS
MOB
MOBBED
MOBBER
MOBBERS
MOBBIE
MOBBIES
MOBBING
MOBBINGS
MOBBISH
MOBBISHLY
MOBBISM
MOBBISMS
MOBBLE
MOBBLED
MOBBLES
MOBBLING
MOBBY
MOBCAP
MOBCAPS
MOBCAST
MOBCASTED
MOBCASTS
MOBE
MOBES
MOBEY
MOBEYS
MOBIE
MOBIES
MOBILE
MOBILES
MOBILISE
MOBILISED
MOBILISER
MOBILISES
MOBILITY
MOBILIZE
MOBILIZED
MOBILIZER
MOBILIZES
MOBISODE
MOBISODES
MOBLE
MOBLED
MOBLES
MOBLING

MOBLOG
MOBLOGGER
MOBLOGS
MOBOCRACY
MOBOCRAT
MOBOCRATS
MOBS
MOBSMAN
MOBSMEN
MOBSTER
MOBSTERS
MOBY
MOC
MOCASSIN
MOCASSINS
MOCCASIN
MOCCASINS
MOCCIES
MOCH
MOCHA
MOCHAS
MOCHED
MOCHELL
MOCHELLS
MOCHI
MOCHIE
MOCHIER
MOCHIEST
MOCHILA
MOCHILAS
MOCHINESS
MOCHING
MOCHIS
MOCHS
MOCHY
MOCK
MOCKABLE
MOCKADO
MOCKADOES
MOCKAGE
MOCKAGES
MOCKED
MOCKER
MOCKERED
MOCKERIES
MOCKERING
MOCKERNUT
MOCKERS
MOCKERY
MOCKING
MOCKINGLY
MOCKINGS
MOCKNEY
MOCKNEYS
MOCKS
MOCKTAIL
MOCKTAILS
MOCKUP
MOCKUPS
MOCOCK
MOCOCKS
MOCS
MOCUCK
MOCUCKS
MOCUDDUM
MOCUDDUMS
MOD
MODAFINIL
MODAL
MODALISM
MODALISMS
MODALIST
MODALISTS
MODALITY
MODALLY
MODALS
MODDED
MODDER
MODDERS
MODDING
MODDINGS
MODE
MODEL
MODELED
MODELER
MODELERS
MODELING
MODELINGS
MODELIST
MODELISTS
MODELLED
MODELLER
MODELLERS
MODELLI
MODELLING
MODELLIST
MODELLO
MODELLOS
MODELS
MODEM
MODEMED
MODEMING
MODEMS
MODENA
MODENAS
MODER
MODERATE
MODERATED
MODERATES
MODERATO
MODERATOR
MODERATOS
MODERN
MODERNE
MODERNER
MODERNES
MODERNEST
MODERNISE
MODERNISM
MODERNIST
MODERNITY
MODERNIZE
MODERNLY
MODERNS
MODERS
MODES
MODEST
MODESTER
MODESTEST
MODESTIES
MODESTLY
MODESTY
MODGE
MODGED
MODGES
MODGING
MODI
MODICA
MODICUM
MODICUMS
MODIFIED
MODIFIER
MODIFIERS
MODIFIES
MODIFY
MODIFYING
MODII
MODILLION
MODIOLAR
MODIOLI
MODIOLUS
MODISH
MODISHLY
MODIST
MODISTE
MODISTES
MODISTS
MODIUS
MODIWORT
MODIWORTS
MODS
MODULAR
MODULARLY
MODULARS
MODULATE
MODULATED
MODULATES
MODULATOR
MODULE
MODULES
MODULI
MODULO
MODULUS
MODUS
MOE
MOELLON
MOELLONS
MOER
MOERED
MOERING
MOERS
MOES
MOFETTE
MOFETTES
MOFFETTE
MOFFETTES
MOFFIE
MOFFIES
MOFO
MOFOS
MOFUSSIL
MOFUSSILS
MOG
MOGGAN
MOGGANS
MOGGED
MOGGIE
MOGGIES
MOGGING
MOGGY
MOGHUL
MOGHULS
MOGS
MOGUL
MOGULED
MOGULS
MOHAIR
MOHAIRS
MOHALIM
MOHAWK
MOHAWKS
MOHEL
MOHELIM
MOHELS
MOHICAN
MOHICANS
MOHO
MOHOS
MOHR
MOHRS
MOHUA
MOHUAS
MOHUR
MOHURS
MOI
MOIDER
MOIDERED
MOIDERING
MOIDERS
MOIDORE
MOIDORES
MOIETIES
MOIETY
MOIL
MOILE
MOILED
MOILER
MOILERS
MOILES
MOILING

MOILINGLY
MOILS
MOINEAU
MOINEAUS
MOIRA
MOIRAI
MOIRE
MOIRES
MOISER
MOISERS
MOIST
MOISTED
MOISTEN
MOISTENED
MOISTENER
MOISTENS
MOISTER
MOISTEST
MOISTFUL
MOISTIFY
MOISTING
MOISTLY
MOISTNESS
MOISTS
MOISTURE
MOISTURES
MOIT
MOITHER
MOITHERED
MOITHERS
MOITS
MOJAHEDIN
MOJARRA
MOJARRAS
MOJITO
MOJITOS
MOJO
MOJOES
MOJOS
MOKADDAM
MOKADDAMS
MOKE
MOKES
MOKI
MOKIHI
MOKIHIS
MOKIS
MOKO
MOKOMOKO
MOKOMOKOS
MOKOPUNA
MOKOPUNAS
MOKORO
MOKOROS
MOKOS
MOKSHA
MOKSHAS
MOL
MOLA
MOLAL
MOLALITY
MOLAR
MOLARITY
MOLARS
MOLAS
MOLASSE
MOLASSES
MOLD
MOLDABLE
MOLDAVITE
MOLDBOARD
MOLDED
MOLDER
MOLDERED
MOLDERING
MOLDERS
MOLDIER
MOLDIEST
MOLDINESS
MOLDING
MOLDINGS
MOLDS
MOLDWARP
MOLDWARPS
MOLDY
MOLE
MOLECAST
MOLECASTS
MOLECULAR
MOLECULE
MOLECULES
MOLED
MOLEHILL
MOLEHILLS
MOLEHUNT
MOLEHUNTS
MOLELIKE
MOLES
MOLESKIN
MOLESKINS
MOLEST
MOLESTED
MOLESTER
MOLESTERS
MOLESTFUL
MOLESTING
MOLESTS
MOLIES
MOLIMEN
MOLIMENS
MOLINE
MOLINES
MOLINET
MOLINETS
MOLING
MOLL
MOLLA
MOLLAH
MOLLAHS
MOLLAS
MOLLIE
MOLLIES
MOLLIFIED
MOLLIFIER
MOLLIFIES
MOLLIFY
MOLLITIES
MOLLS
MOLLUSC
MOLLUSCA
MOLLUSCAN
MOLLUSCS
MOLLUSCUM
MOLLUSK
MOLLUSKAN
MOLLUSKS
MOLLY
MOLLYHAWK
MOLLYMAWK
MOLOCH
MOLOCHISE
MOLOCHIZE
MOLOCHS
MOLOSSI
MOLOSSUS
MOLS
MOLT
MOLTED
MOLTEN
MOLTENLY
MOLTER
MOLTERS
MOLTING
MOLTO
MOLTS
MOLY
MOLYBDATE
MOLYBDIC
MOLYBDOUS
MOLYS
MOM
MOME
MOMENT
MOMENTA
MOMENTANY
MOMENTARY
MOMENTLY
MOMENTO
MOMENTOES
MOMENTOS
MOMENTOUS
MOMENTS
MOMENTUM
MOMENTUMS
MOMES
MOMI
MOMISM
MOMISMS
MOMMA
MOMMAS
MOMMET
MOMMETS
MOMMIES
MOMMY
MOMOIR
MOMOIRS
MOMS
MOMSER
MOMSERS
MOMUS
MOMUSES
MOMZER
MOMZERIM
MOMZERS
MON
MONA
MONACHAL
MONACHISM
MONACHIST
MONACID
MONACIDIC
MONACIDS
MONACT
MONACTINE
MONACTS
MONAD
MONADAL
MONADES
MONADIC
MONADICAL
MONADISM
MONADISMS
MONADNOCK
MONADS
MONAL
MONALS
MONAMINE
MONAMINES
MONANDRY
MONARCH
MONARCHAL
MONARCHIC
MONARCHS
MONARCHY
MONARDA
MONARDAS
MONAS
MONASES
MONASTERY
MONASTIC
MONASTICS
MONATOMIC
MONAUL
MONAULS
MONAURAL
MONAXIAL
MONAXON
MONAXONIC
MONAXONS
MONAZITE

M

MONAZITES
MONDAIN
MONDAINE
MONDAINES
MONDAINS
MONDE
MONDES
MONDIAL
MONDO
MONDOS
MONECIAN
MONECIOUS
MONELLIN
MONELLINS
MONEME
MONEMES
MONER
MONERA
MONERAN
MONERANS
MONERGISM
MONERON
MONETARY
MONETH
MONETHS
MONETISE
MONETISED
MONETISES
MONETIZE
MONETIZED
MONETIZES
MONEY
MONEYBAG
MONEYBAGS
MONEYBELT
MONEYBOX
MONEYED
MONEYER
MONEYERS
MONEYLESS
MONEYMAN
MONEYMEN
MONEYS
MONEYWORT
MONG
MONGCORN
MONGCORNS
MONGED
MONGEESE
MONGER
MONGERED
MONGERIES
MONGERING
MONGERS
MONGERY
MONGO
MONGOE
MONGOES
MONGOL
MONGOLIAN
MONGOLISM
MONGOLOID
MONGOLS
MONGOOSE
MONGOOSES
MONGOS
MONGREL
MONGRELLY
MONGRELS
MONGS
MONGST
MONIAL
MONIALS
MONIC
MONICKER
MONICKERS
MONIE
MONIED
MONIES
MONIKER
MONIKERED
MONIKERS
MONILIA
MONILIAE
MONILIAL
MONILIAS
MONIMENT
MONIMENTS
MONIPLIES
MONISH
MONISHED
MONISHES
MONISHING
MONISM
MONISMS
MONIST
MONISTIC
MONISTS
MONITION
MONITIONS
MONITIVE
MONITOR
MONITORED
MONITORS
MONITORY
MONITRESS
MONK
MONKERIES
MONKERY
MONKEY
MONKEYED
MONKEYING
MONKEYISH
MONKEYISM
MONKEYPOD
MONKEYPOT
MONKEYPOX
MONKEYS
MONKFISH
MONKHOOD
MONKHOODS
MONKISH
MONKISHLY
MONKS
MONKSHOOD
MONO
MONOACID
MONOACIDS
MONOAMINE
MONOAO
MONOAOS
MONOBASIC
MONOBLOC
MONOBROW
MONOBROWS
MONOCARP
MONOCARPS
MONOCEROS
MONOCHORD
MONOCLE
MONOCLED
MONOCLES
MONOCLINE
MONOCOQUE
MONOCOT
MONOCOTS
MONOCOTYL
MONOCRACY
MONOCRAT
MONOCRATS
MONOCROP
MONOCROPS
MONOCULAR
MONOCYCLE
MONOCYTE
MONOCYTES
MONOCYTIC
MONODIC
MONODICAL
MONODIES
MONODIST
MONODISTS
MONODONT
MONODRAMA
MONODY
MONOECIES
MONOECISM
MONOECY
MONOESTER
MONOFIL
MONOFILS
MONOFUEL
MONOFUELS
MONOGAMIC
MONOGAMY
MONOGENIC
MONOGENY
MONOGERM
MONOGLOT
MONOGLOTS
MONOGONY
MONOGRAM
MONOGRAMS
MONOGRAPH
MONOGYNY
MONOHULL
MONOHULLS
MONOICOUS
MONOKINE
MONOKINES
MONOKINI
MONOKINIS
MONOLATER
MONOLATRY
MONOLAYER
MONOLINE
MONOLITH
MONOLITHS
MONOLOG
MONOLOGIC
MONOLOGS
MONOLOGUE
MONOLOGY
MONOMACHY
MONOMANIA
MONOMARK
MONOMARKS
MONOMER
MONOMERIC
MONOMERS
MONOMETER
MONOMIAL
MONOMIALS
MONOMODE
MONONYM
MONONYMS
MONOPHAGY
MONOPHASE
MONOPHONY
MONOPHYLY
MONOPITCH
MONOPLANE
MONOPLOID
MONOPOD
MONOPODE
MONOPODES
MONOPODIA
MONOPODS
MONOPODY
MONOPOLE
MONOPOLES
MONOPOLY
MONOPRINT
MONOPSONY
MONOPTERA
MONOPTOTE
MONOPULSE
MONORAIL
MONORAILS
MONORCHID

MONORHINE
MONORHYME
MONOS
MONOSEMIC
MONOSEMY
MONOSES
MONOSIES
MONOSIS
MONOSKI
MONOSKIED
MONOSKIER
MONOSKIS
MONOSOME
MONOSOMES
MONOSOMIC
MONOSOMY
MONOSTELE
MONOSTELY
MONOSTICH
MONOSTOME
MONOSTYLE
MONOSY
MONOTASK
MONOTASKS
MONOTINT
MONOTINTS
MONOTONE
MONOTONED
MONOTONES
MONOTONIC
MONOTONY
MONOTREME
MONOTROCH
MONOTYPE
MONOTYPES
MONOTYPIC
MONOVULAR
MONOXIDE
MONOXIDES
MONOXYLON
MONS
MONSIEUR
MONSIGNOR
MONSOON
MONSOONAL
MONSOONS
MONSTER
MONSTERA
MONSTERAS
MONSTERED
MONSTERS
MONSTROUS
MONTADALE
MONTAGE
MONTAGED
MONTAGES
MONTAGING
MONTAN
MONTANE
MONTANES
MONTANT
MONTANTO
MONTANTOS
MONTANTS
MONTARIA
MONTARIAS
MONTE
MONTEITH
MONTEITHS
MONTEM
MONTEMS
MONTERO
MONTEROS
MONTES
MONTH
MONTHLIES
MONTHLING
MONTHLONG
MONTHLY
MONTHS
MONTICLE
MONTICLES
MONTICULE
MONTIES
MONTRE
MONTRES
MONTURE
MONTURES
MONTY
MONUMENT
MONUMENTS
MONURON
MONURONS
MONY
MONYPLIES
MONZONITE
MOO
MOOBIES
MOOBS
MOOCH
MOOCHED
MOOCHER
MOOCHERS
MOOCHES
MOOCHING
MOOD
MOODIED
MOODIER
MOODIES
MOODIEST
MOODILY
MOODINESS
MOODS
MOODY
MOODYING
MOOED
MOOI
MOOING
MOOK
MOOKS
MOOKTAR
MOOKTARS
MOOL
MOOLA
MOOLAH
MOOLAHS
MOOLAS
MOOLED
MOOLEY
MOOLEYS
MOOLI
MOOLIES
MOOLING
MOOLIS
MOOLOO
MOOLOOS
MOOLS
MOOLVI
MOOLVIE
MOOLVIES
MOOLVIS
MOOLY
MOON
MOONBEAM
MOONBEAMS
MOONBLIND
MOONBOOTS
MOONBOW
MOONBOWS
MOONCAKE
MOONCAKES
MOONCALF
MOONCHILD
MOONCRAFT
MOONDOG
MOONDOGS
MOONDUST
MOONDUSTS
MOONED
MOONER
MOONERS
MOONEYE
MOONEYES
MOONFACE
MOONFACED
MOONFACES
MOONFISH
MOONG
MOONGATE
MOONGATES
MOONIER
MOONIES
MOONIEST
MOONILY
MOONINESS
MOONING
MOONISH
MOONISHLY
MOONLESS
MOONLET
MOONLETS
MOONLIGHT
MOONLIKE
MOONLIT
MOONPHASE
MOONPORT
MOONPORTS
MOONQUAKE
MOONRAKER
MOONRISE
MOONRISES
MOONROCK
MOONROCKS
MOONROOF
MOONROOFS
MOONS
MOONSAIL
MOONSAILS
MOONSCAPE
MOONSEED
MOONSEEDS
MOONSET
MOONSETS
MOONSHEE
MOONSHEES
MOONSHINE
MOONSHINY
MOONSHIP
MOONSHIPS
MOONSHOT
MOONSHOTS
MOONSTONE
MOONWALK
MOONWALKS
MOONWARD
MOONWARDS
MOONWORT
MOONWORTS
MOONY
MOOP
MOOPED
MOOPING
MOOPS
MOOR
MOORAGE
MOORAGES
MOORBURN
MOORBURNS
MOORCOCK
MOORCOCKS
MOORED
MOORFOWL
MOORFOWLS
MOORHEN
MOORHENS
MOORIER
MOORIEST
MOORILL
MOORILLS
MOORING

MOORINGS
MOORISH
MOORLAND
MOORLANDS
MOORLOG
MOORLOGS
MOORMAN
MOORMEN
MOORS
MOORVA
MOORVAS
MOORWORT
MOORWORTS
MOORY
MOOS
MOOSE
MOOSEBIRD
MOOSEHAIR
MOOSEHIDE
MOOSEWOOD
MOOSEYARD
MOOT
MOOTABLE
MOOTED
MOOTER
MOOTERS
MOOTEST
MOOTING
MOOTINGS
MOOTMAN
MOOTMEN
MOOTNESS
MOOTS
MOOVE
MOOVED
MOOVES
MOOVING
MOP
MOPANE
MOPANES
MOPANI
MOPANIS
MOPBOARD
MOPBOARDS
MOPE
MOPED
MOPEDS
MOPEHAWK
MOPEHAWKS
MOPER
MOPERIES
MOPERS
MOPERY
MOPES
MOPEY
MOPHEAD
MOPHEADS
MOPIER
MOPIEST
MOPILY
MOPINESS
MOPING
MOPINGLY
MOPISH
MOPISHLY
MOPOKE
MOPOKES
MOPPED
MOPPER
MOPPERS
MOPPET
MOPPETS
MOPPIER
MOPPIEST
MOPPING
MOPPY
MOPS
MOPSIES
MOPSTICK
MOPSTICKS
MOPSY
MOPUS
MOPUSES
MOPY
MOQUETTE
MOQUETTES
MOR
MORA
MORACEOUS
MORAE
MORAINAL
MORAINE
MORAINES
MORAINIC
MORAL
MORALE
MORALES
MORALISE
MORALISED
MORALISER
MORALISES
MORALISM
MORALISMS
MORALIST
MORALISTS
MORALITY
MORALIZE
MORALIZED
MORALIZER
MORALIZES
MORALL
MORALLED
MORALLER
MORALLERS
MORALLING
MORALLS
MORALLY
MORALS
MORAS
MORASS
MORASSES
MORASSIER
MORASSY
MORAT
MORATORIA
MORATORY
MORATS
MORAY
MORAYS
MORBID
MORBIDER
MORBIDEST
MORBIDITY
MORBIDLY
MORBIFIC
MORBILLI
MORBUS
MORBUSES
MORCEAU
MORCEAUX
MORCHA
MORCHAS
MORDACITY
MORDANCY
MORDANT
MORDANTED
MORDANTLY
MORDANTS
MORDENT
MORDENTS
MORE
MOREEN
MOREENS
MOREISH
MOREL
MORELLE
MORELLES
MORELLO
MORELLOS
MORELS
MORENDO
MORENDOS
MORENESS
MOREOVER
MOREPORK
MOREPORKS
MORES
MORESQUE
MORESQUES
MORGAN
MORGANITE
MORGANS
MORGAY
MORGAYS
MORGEN
MORGENS
MORGUE
MORGUES
MORIA
MORIAS
MORIBUND
MORICHE
MORICHES
MORION
MORIONS
MORISCO
MORISCOES
MORISCOS
MORISH
MORKIN
MORKINS
MORLING
MORLINGS
MORMAOR
MORMAORS
MORN
MORNAY
MORNAYS
MORNE
MORNED
MORNES
MORNING
MORNINGS
MORNS
MOROCCO
MOROCCOS
MORON
MORONIC
MORONISM
MORONISMS
MORONITY
MORONS
MOROSE
MOROSELY
MOROSER
MOROSEST
MOROSITY
MORPH
MORPHEAN
MORPHED
MORPHEME
MORPHEMES
MORPHEMIC
MORPHETIC
MORPHEW
MORPHEWS
MORPHIA
MORPHIAS
MORPHIC
MORPHIN
MORPHINE
MORPHINES
MORPHING
MORPHINGS
MORPHINIC
MORPHINS
MORPHO
MORPHOGEN
MORPHOS
MORPHOSES

MORPHOSIS
MORPHOTIC
MORPHS
MORRA
MORRAS
MORRELL
MORRELLS
MORRHUA
MORRHUAS
MORRICE
MORRICES
MORRION
MORRIONS
MORRIS
MORRISED
MORRISES
MORRISING
MORRO
MORROS
MORROW
MORROWS
MORS
MORSAL
MORSALS
MORSE
MORSEL
MORSELED
MORSELING
MORSELLED
MORSELS
MORSES
MORSURE
MORSURES
MORT
MORTAL
MORTALISE
MORTALITY
MORTALIZE
MORTALLY
MORTALS
MORTAR
MORTARED
MORTARIER
MORTARING
MORTARMAN
MORTARMEN
MORTARS
MORTARY
MORTBELL
MORTBELLS
MORTCLOTH
MORTGAGE
MORTGAGED
MORTGAGEE
MORTGAGER
MORTGAGES
MORTGAGOR
MORTICE
MORTICED
MORTICER
MORTICERS
MORTICES
MORTICIAN
MORTICING
MORTIFIC
MORTIFIED
MORTIFIER
MORTIFIES
MORTIFY
MORTISE
MORTISED
MORTISER
MORTISERS
MORTISES
MORTISING
MORTLING
MORTLINGS
MORTMAIN
MORTMAINS
MORTS
MORTSAFE
MORTSAFES
MORTUARY
MORULA
MORULAE
MORULAR
MORULAS
MORWONG
MORWONGS
MORYAH
MOS
MOSAIC
MOSAICISM
MOSAICIST
MOSAICKED
MOSAICS
MOSASAUR
MOSASAURI
MOSASAURS
MOSCATO
MOSCATOS
MOSCHATE
MOSCHATEL
MOSCOVIUM
MOSE
MOSED
MOSELLE
MOSELLES
MOSES
MOSEY
MOSEYED
MOSEYING
MOSEYS
MOSH
MOSHAV
MOSHAVIM
MOSHED
MOSHER
MOSHERS
MOSHES
MOSHING
MOSHINGS
MOSING
MOSK
MOSKONFYT
MOSKS
MOSLINGS
MOSQUE
MOSQUES
MOSQUITO
MOSQUITOS
MOSS
MOSSBACK
MOSSBACKS
MOSSED
MOSSER
MOSSERS
MOSSES
MOSSGROWN
MOSSIE
MOSSIER
MOSSIES
MOSSIEST
MOSSINESS
MOSSING
MOSSLAND
MOSSLANDS
MOSSLIKE
MOSSO
MOSSPLANT
MOSSY
MOST
MOSTE
MOSTEST
MOSTESTS
MOSTLY
MOSTS
MOSTWHAT
MOT
MOTE
MOTED
MOTEL
MOTELIER
MOTELIERS
MOTELS
MOTEN
MOTES
MOTET
MOTETS
MOTETT
MOTETTIST
MOTETTS
MOTEY
MOTEYS
MOTH
MOTHBALL
MOTHBALLS
MOTHED
MOTHER
MOTHERED
MOTHERESE
MOTHERIER
MOTHERING
MOTHERLY
MOTHERS
MOTHERY
MOTHIER
MOTHIEST
MOTHLIKE
MOTHPROOF
MOTHS
MOTHY
MOTI
MOTIER
MOTIEST
MOTIF
MOTIFIC
MOTIFS
MOTILE
MOTILES
MOTILITY
MOTION
MOTIONAL
MOTIONED
MOTIONER
MOTIONERS
MOTIONING
MOTIONIST
MOTIONS
MOTIS
MOTIVATE
MOTIVATED
MOTIVATES
MOTIVATOR
MOTIVE
MOTIVED
MOTIVES
MOTIVIC
MOTIVING
MOTIVITY
MOTLEY
MOTLEYER
MOTLEYEST
MOTLEYS
MOTLIER
MOTLIEST
MOTMOT
MOTMOTS
MOTOCROSS
MOTOR
MOTORABLE
MOTORAIL
MOTORAILS
MOTORBIKE
MOTORBOAT
MOTORBUS
MOTORCADE
MOTORCAR
MOTORCARS
MOTORDOM

MOTORDOMS
MOTORED
MOTORHOME
MOTORIAL
MOTORIC
MOTORICS
MOTORING
MOTORINGS
MOTORISE
MOTORISED
MOTORISES
MOTORIST
MOTORISTS
MOTORIUM
MOTORIUMS
MOTORIZE
MOTORIZED
MOTORIZES
MOTORLESS
MOTORMAN
MOTORMEN
MOTORS
MOTORSHIP
MOTORWAY
MOTORWAYS
MOTORY
MOTOSCAFI
MOTOSCAFO
MOTS
MOTSER
MOTSERS
MOTT
MOTTE
MOTTES
MOTTIER
MOTTIES
MOTTIEST
MOTTLE
MOTTLED
MOTTLER
MOTTLERS
MOTTLES
MOTTLING
MOTTLINGS
MOTTO
MOTTOED
MOTTOES
MOTTOS
MOTTS
MOTTY
MOTU
MOTUCA
MOTUCAS
MOTUS
MOTZA
MOTZAS
MOU
MOUCH
MOUCHARD
MOUCHARDS
MOUCHED
MOUCHER
MOUCHERS
MOUCHES
MOUCHING
MOUCHOIR
MOUCHOIRS
MOUDIWART
MOUDIWORT
MOUE
MOUES
MOUFFLON
MOUFFLONS
MOUFLON
MOUFLONS
MOUGHT
MOUILLE
MOUJIK
MOUJIKS
MOULAGE
MOULAGES
MOULD
MOULDABLE
MOULDED
MOULDER
MOULDERED
MOULDERS
MOULDIER
MOULDIEST
MOULDING
MOULDINGS
MOULDS
MOULDWARP
MOULDY
MOULIN
MOULINET
MOULINETS
MOULINS
MOULS
MOULT
MOULTED
MOULTEN
MOULTER
MOULTERS
MOULTING
MOULTINGS
MOULTS
MOUND
MOUNDBIRD
MOUNDED
MOUNDING
MOUNDS
MOUNSEER
MOUNSEERS
MOUNT
MOUNTABLE
MOUNTAIN
MOUNTAINS
MOUNTAINY
MOUNTANT
MOUNTANTS
MOUNTED
MOUNTER
MOUNTERS
MOUNTING
MOUNTINGS
MOUNTS
MOUP
MOUPED
MOUPING
MOUPS
MOURN
MOURNED
MOURNER
MOURNERS
MOURNFUL
MOURNING
MOURNINGS
MOURNIVAL
MOURNS
MOURVEDRE
MOUS
MOUSAKA
MOUSAKAS
MOUSE
MOUSEBIRD
MOUSED
MOUSEKIN
MOUSEKINS
MOUSELIKE
MOUSEMAT
MOUSEMATS
MOUSEOVER
MOUSEPAD
MOUSEPADS
MOUSER
MOUSERIES
MOUSERS
MOUSERY
MOUSES
MOUSETAIL
MOUSETRAP
MOUSEY
MOUSIE
MOUSIER
MOUSIES
MOUSIEST
MOUSILY
MOUSINESS
MOUSING
MOUSINGS
MOUSLE
MOUSLED
MOUSLES
MOUSLING
MOUSME
MOUSMEE
MOUSMEES
MOUSMES
MOUSSAKA
MOUSSAKAS
MOUSSE
MOUSSED
MOUSSES
MOUSSEUX
MOUSSING
MOUST
MOUSTACHE
MOUSTED
MOUSTING
MOUSTS
MOUSY
MOUTAN
MOUTANS
MOUTER
MOUTERED
MOUTERER
MOUTERERS
MOUTERING
MOUTERS
MOUTH
MOUTHABLE
MOUTHED
MOUTHER
MOUTHERS
MOUTHFEEL
MOUTHFUL
MOUTHFULS
MOUTHIER
MOUTHIEST
MOUTHILY
MOUTHING
MOUTHLESS
MOUTHLIKE
MOUTHPART
MOUTHS
MOUTHWASH
MOUTHY
MOUTON
MOUTONNEE
MOUTONS
MOVABLE
MOVABLES
MOVABLY
MOVANT
MOVANTS
MOVE
MOVEABLE
MOVEABLES
MOVEABLY
MOVED
MOVELESS
MOVEMENT
MOVEMENTS
MOVER
MOVERS
MOVES
MOVIE
MOVIEDOM
MOVIEDOMS

MOVIEGOER
MOVIELAND
MOVIEOKE
MOVIEOKES
MOVIEOLA
MOVIEOLAS
MOVIES
MOVING
MOVINGLY
MOVIOLA
MOVIOLAS
MOW
MOWA
MOWAS
MOWBURN
MOWBURNED
MOWBURNS
MOWBURNT
MOWDIE
MOWDIES
MOWED
MOWER
MOWERS
MOWING
MOWINGS
MOWN
MOWRA
MOWRAS
MOWS
MOXA
MOXAS
MOXIE
MOXIES
MOY
MOYA
MOYAS
MOYGASHEL
MOYITIES
MOYITY
MOYL
MOYLE
MOYLED
MOYLES
MOYLING
MOYLS
MOYS
MOZ
MOZE
MOZED
MOZES
MOZETTA
MOZETTAS
MOZETTE
MOZING
MOZO
MOZOS
MOZZ
MOZZES
MOZZETTA
MOZZETTAS
MOZZETTE
MOZZIE
MOZZIES
MOZZLE
MOZZLED
MOZZLES
MOZZLING
MPRET
MPRETS
MRIDAMGAM
MRIDANG
MRIDANGA
MRIDANGAM
MRIDANGAS
MRIDANGS
MU
MUCATE
MUCATES
MUCH
MUCHACHA
MUCHACHAS
MUCHACHO
MUCHACHOS
MUCHEL
MUCHELL
MUCHELLS
MUCHELS
MUCHES
MUCHLY
MUCHNESS
MUCHO
MUCIC
MUCID
MUCIDITY
MUCIDNESS
MUCIGEN
MUCIGENS
MUCILAGE
MUCILAGES
MUCIN
MUCINOGEN
MUCINOID
MUCINOUS
MUCINS
MUCK
MUCKAMUCK
MUCKED
MUCKENDER
MUCKER
MUCKERED
MUCKERING
MUCKERISH
MUCKERS
MUCKHEAP
MUCKHEAPS
MUCKIER
MUCKIEST
MUCKILY
MUCKINESS
MUCKING
MUCKLE
MUCKLER
MUCKLES
MUCKLEST
MUCKLUCK
MUCKLUCKS
MUCKRAKE
MUCKRAKED
MUCKRAKER
MUCKRAKES
MUCKS
MUCKSWEAT
MUCKWORM
MUCKWORMS
MUCKY
MUCKYMUCK
MUCLUC
MUCLUCS
MUCOID
MUCOIDAL
MUCOIDS
MUCOLYTIC
MUCOR
MUCORS
MUCOSA
MUCOSAE
MUCOSAL
MUCOSAS
MUCOSE
MUCOSITY
MUCOUS
MUCRO
MUCRONATE
MUCRONES
MUCROS
MUCULENT
MUCUS
MUCUSES
MUD
MUDBANK
MUDBANKS
MUDBATH
MUDBATHS
MUDBUG
MUDBUGS
MUDCAP
MUDCAPPED
MUDCAPS
MUDCAT
MUDCATS
MUDDED
MUDDER
MUDDERS
MUDDIED
MUDDIER
MUDDIES
MUDDIEST
MUDDILY
MUDDINESS
MUDDING
MUDDLE
MUDDLED
MUDDLER
MUDDLERS
MUDDLES
MUDDLIER
MUDDLIEST
MUDDLING
MUDDLINGS
MUDDLY
MUDDY
MUDDYING
MUDEJAR
MUDEJARES
MUDEYE
MUDEYES
MUDFISH
MUDFISHES
MUDFLAP
MUDFLAPS
MUDFLAT
MUDFLATS
MUDFLOW
MUDFLOWS
MUDGE
MUDGED
MUDGER
MUDGERS
MUDGES
MUDGING
MUDGUARD
MUDGUARDS
MUDHEN
MUDHENS
MUDHOLE
MUDHOLES
MUDHOOK
MUDHOOKS
MUDHOPPER
MUDIR
MUDIRIA
MUDIRIAS
MUDIRIEH
MUDIRIEHS
MUDIRS
MUDLARK
MUDLARKED
MUDLARKS
MUDLOGGER
MUDPACK
MUDPACKS
MUDPIE
MUDPIES
MUDPUPPY
MUDRA
MUDRAS
MUDROCK
MUDROCKS
MUDROOM
MUDROOMS

MUDS
MUDSCOW
MUDSCOWS
MUDSILL
MUDSILLS
MUDSLIDE
MUDSLIDES
MUDSLING
MUDSLINGS
MUDSLUNG
MUDSTONE
MUDSTONES
MUDWORT
MUDWORTS
MUEDDIN
MUEDDINS
MUENSTER
MUENSTERS
MUESLI
MUESLIS
MUEZZIN
MUEZZINS
MUFF
MUFFED
MUFFETTEE
MUFFIN
MUFFINEER
MUFFING
MUFFINS
MUFFISH
MUFFLE
MUFFLED
MUFFLER
MUFFLERED
MUFFLERS
MUFFLES
MUFFLING
MUFFS
MUFLON
MUFLONS
MUFTI
MUFTIS
MUG
MUGEARITE
MUGFUL
MUGFULS
MUGG
MUGGA
MUGGAR
MUGGARS
MUGGAS
MUGGED
MUGGEE
MUGGEES
MUGGER
MUGGERS
MUGGIER
MUGGIEST
MUGGILY
MUGGINESS
MUGGING
MUGGINGS
MUGGINS
MUGGINSES
MUGGISH
MUGGLE
MUGGLES
MUGGS
MUGGUR
MUGGURS
MUGGY
MUGHAL
MUGHALS
MUGS
MUGSHOT
MUGSHOTS
MUGWORT
MUGWORTS
MUGWUMP
MUGWUMPS
MUHLIES
MUHLY
MUID
MUIDS
MUIL
MUILS
MUIR
MUIRBURN
MUIRBURNS
MUIRS
MUIST
MUISTED
MUISTING
MUISTS
MUJAHEDIN
MUJAHIDIN
MUJIK
MUJIKS
MUKHTAR
MUKHTARS
MUKLUK
MUKLUKS
MUKTUK
MUKTUKS
MULATRESS
MULATTA
MULATTAS
MULATTO
MULATTOES
MULATTOS
MULBERRY
MULCH
MULCHED
MULCHES
MULCHING
MULCT
MULCTED
MULCTING
MULCTS
MULE
MULED
MULES
MULESED
MULESES
MULESING
MULESINGS
MULETA
MULETAS
MULETEER
MULETEERS
MULEY
MULEYS
MULGA
MULGAS
MULIE
MULIES
MULING
MULISH
MULISHLY
MULL
MULLA
MULLAH
MULLAHED
MULLAHING
MULLAHISM
MULLAHS
MULLARKY
MULLAS
MULLED
MULLEIN
MULLEINS
MULLEN
MULLENS
MULLER
MULLERED
MULLERIAN
MULLERING
MULLERS
MULLET
MULLETS
MULLEY
MULLEYS
MULLIGAN
MULLIGANS
MULLING
MULLION
MULLIONED
MULLIONS
MULLITE
MULLITES
MULLOCK
MULLOCKS
MULLOCKY
MULLOWAY
MULLOWAYS
MULLS
MULMUL
MULMULL
MULMULLS
MULMULS
MULSE
MULSES
MULSH
MULSHED
MULSHES
MULSHING
MULTEITY
MULTIAGE
MULTIATOM
MULTIBAND
MULTIBANK
MULTICAR
MULTICAST
MULTICELL
MULTICIDE
MULTICITY
MULTICOPY
MULTICORE
MULTICULT
MULTIDAY
MULTIDISC
MULTIDISK
MULTIDRUG
MULTIFID
MULTIFIL
MULTIFILS
MULTIFOIL
MULTIFOLD
MULTIFORM
MULTIGENE
MULTIGERM
MULTIGRID
MULTIGYM
MULTIGYMS
MULTIHUED
MULTIHULL
MULTIJET
MULTILANE
MULTILINE
MULTILOBE
MULTIMODE
MULTIPACK
MULTIPAGE
MULTIPARA
MULTIPART
MULTIPATH
MULTIPED
MULTIPEDE
MULTIPEDS
MULTIPION
MULTIPLE
MULTIPLES
MULTIPLET
MULTIPLEX
MULTIPLY
MULTIPOLE
MULTIPORT
MULTIRISK
MULTIROLE
MULTIROOM

MULTISITE
MULTISIZE
MULTISTEP
MULTITASK
MULTITIER
MULTITON
MULTITONE
MULTITOOL
MULTITUDE
MULTIUNIT
MULTIUSE
MULTIUSER
MULTIWALL
MULTIWAY
MULTIYEAR
MULTUM
MULTUMS
MULTURE
MULTURED
MULTURER
MULTURERS
MULTURES
MULTURING
MUM
MUMBLE
MUMBLED
MUMBLER
MUMBLERS
MUMBLES
MUMBLIER
MUMBLIEST
MUMBLING
MUMBLINGS
MUMBLY
MUMCHANCE
MUMM
MUMMED
MUMMER
MUMMERED
MUMMERIES
MUMMERING
MUMMERS
MUMMERY
MUMMIA
MUMMIAS
MUMMICHOG
MUMMIED
MUMMIES
MUMMIFIED
MUMMIFIES
MUMMIFORM
MUMMIFY
MUMMING
MUMMINGS
MUMMOCK
MUMMOCKS
MUMMS
MUMMY
MUMMYING
MUMP
MUMPED
MUMPER
MUMPERS
MUMPING
MUMPISH
MUMPISHLY
MUMPS
MUMPSIMUS
MUMS
MUMSIER
MUMSIES
MUMSIEST
MUMSINESS
MUMSY
MUMU
MUMUS
MUN
MUNCH
MUNCHABLE
MUNCHED
MUNCHER
MUNCHERS
MUNCHES
MUNCHIE
MUNCHIER
MUNCHIES
MUNCHIEST
MUNCHING
MUNCHKIN
MUNCHKINS
MUNCHY
MUNDANE
MUNDANELY
MUNDANER
MUNDANEST
MUNDANITY
MUNDIC
MUNDICS
MUNDIFIED
MUNDIFIES
MUNDIFY
MUNDUNGO
MUNDUNGOS
MUNDUNGUS
MUNG
MUNGA
MUNGAS
MUNGCORN
MUNGCORNS
MUNGE
MUNGED
MUNGES
MUNGING
MUNGO
MUNGOES
MUNGOOSE
MUNGOOSES
MUNGOS
MUNGS
MUNI
MUNICIPAL
MUNIFIED
MUNIFIES
MUNIFY
MUNIFYING
MUNIMENT
MUNIMENTS
MUNIS
MUNITE
MUNITED
MUNITES
MUNITING
MUNITION
MUNITIONS
MUNNION
MUNNIONS
MUNS
MUNSHI
MUNSHIS
MUNSTER
MUNSTERS
MUNT
MUNTED
MUNTER
MUNTERS
MUNTIN
MUNTINED
MUNTING
MUNTINGS
MUNTINS
MUNTJAC
MUNTJACS
MUNTJAK
MUNTJAKS
MUNTRIE
MUNTRIES
MUNTS
MUNTU
MUNTUS
MUON
MUONIC
MUONIUM
MUONIUMS
MUONS
MUPPET
MUPPETS
MUQADDAM
MUQADDAMS
MURA
MURAENA
MURAENAS
MURAENID
MURAENIDS
MURAGE
MURAGES
MURAL
MURALED
MURALIST
MURALISTS
MURALLED
MURALS
MURAS
MURDABAD
MURDER
MURDERED
MURDEREE
MURDEREES
MURDERER
MURDERERS
MURDERESS
MURDERING
MURDEROUS
MURDERS
MURE
MURED
MUREIN
MUREINS
MURENA
MURENAS
MURES
MUREX
MUREXES
MURGEON
MURGEONED
MURGEONS
MURIATE
MURIATED
MURIATES
MURIATIC
MURICATE
MURICATED
MURICES
MURID
MURIDS
MURIFORM
MURINE
MURINES
MURING
MURK
MURKED
MURKER
MURKEST
MURKIER
MURKIEST
MURKILY
MURKINESS
MURKING
MURKISH
MURKLY
MURKS
MURKSOME
MURKY
MURL
MURLAIN
MURLAINS
MURLAN
MURLANS
MURLED
MURLIER
MURLIEST

MURLIN
MURLING
MURLINS
MURLS
MURLY
MURMUR
MURMURED
MURMURER
MURMURERS
MURMURING
MURMUROUS
MURMURS
MURPHIES
MURPHY
MURR
MURRA
MURRAGH
MURRAGHS
MURRAIN
MURRAINED
MURRAINS
MURRAM
MURRAMS
MURRAS
MURRAY
MURRAYS
MURRE
MURREE
MURREES
MURRELET
MURRELETS
MURREN
MURRENS
MURRES
MURREY
MURREYS
MURRHA
MURRHAS
MURRHINE
MURRHINES
MURRI
MURRIES
MURRIN
MURRINE
MURRINES
MURRINS
MURRION
MURRIONS
MURRIS
MURRS
MURRY
MURSHID
MURSHIDS
MURTHER
MURTHERED
MURTHERER
MURTHERS
MURTI
MURTIS
MURVA
MURVAS
MUS
MUSACEOUS
MUSANG
MUSANGS
MUSAR
MUSARS
MUSCA
MUSCADEL
MUSCADELS
MUSCADET
MUSCADETS
MUSCADIN
MUSCADINE
MUSCADINS
MUSCAE
MUSCARINE
MUSCAT
MUSCATEL
MUSCATELS
MUSCATS
MUSCAVADO
MUSCID
MUSCIDS
MUSCLE
MUSCLED
MUSCLEMAN
MUSCLEMEN
MUSCLES
MUSCLEY
MUSCLIER
MUSCLIEST
MUSCLING
MUSCLINGS
MUSCLY
MUSCOID
MUSCOIDS
MUSCOLOGY
MUSCONE
MUSCONES
MUSCOSE
MUSCOVADO
MUSCOVITE
MUSCOVY
MUSCULAR
MUSCULOUS
MUSE
MUSED
MUSEFUL
MUSEFULLY
MUSEOLOGY
MUSER
MUSERS
MUSES
MUSET
MUSETS
MUSETTE
MUSETTES
MUSEUM
MUSEUMS
MUSH
MUSHA
MUSHED
MUSHER
MUSHERS
MUSHES
MUSHIE
MUSHIER
MUSHIES
MUSHIEST
MUSHILY
MUSHINESS
MUSHING
MUSHINGS
MUSHMOUTH
MUSHRAT
MUSHRATS
MUSHROOM
MUSHROOMS
MUSHROOMY
MUSHY
MUSIC
MUSICAL
MUSICALE
MUSICALES
MUSICALLY
MUSICALS
MUSICIAN
MUSICIANS
MUSICK
MUSICKED
MUSICKER
MUSICKERS
MUSICKING
MUSICKS
MUSICLESS
MUSICS
MUSIMON
MUSIMONS
MUSING
MUSINGLY
MUSINGS
MUSIT
MUSITS
MUSIVE
MUSJID
MUSJIDS
MUSK
MUSKED
MUSKEG
MUSKEGS
MUSKET
MUSKETEER
MUSKETOON
MUSKETRY
MUSKETS
MUSKIE
MUSKIER
MUSKIES
MUSKIEST
MUSKILY
MUSKINESS
MUSKING
MUSKIT
MUSKITS
MUSKLE
MUSKLES
MUSKMELON
MUSKONE
MUSKONES
MUSKOX
MUSKOXEN
MUSKRAT
MUSKRATS
MUSKROOT
MUSKROOTS
MUSKS
MUSKY
MUSLIN
MUSLINED
MUSLINET
MUSLINETS
MUSLINS
MUSMON
MUSMONS
MUSO
MUSOS
MUSPIKE
MUSPIKES
MUSQUASH
MUSROL
MUSROLS
MUSS
MUSSE
MUSSED
MUSSEL
MUSSELLED
MUSSELS
MUSSES
MUSSIER
MUSSIEST
MUSSILY
MUSSINESS
MUSSING
MUSSITATE
MUSSY
MUST
MUSTACHE
MUSTACHED
MUSTACHES
MUSTACHIO
MUSTANG
MUSTANGS
MUSTARD
MUSTARDS
MUSTARDY
MUSTED
MUSTEE
MUSTEES
MUSTELID

MUSTELIDS
MUSTELINE
MUSTER
MUSTERED
MUSTERER
MUSTERERS
MUSTERING
MUSTERS
MUSTH
MUSTHS
MUSTIER
MUSTIEST
MUSTILY
MUSTINESS
MUSTING
MUSTS
MUSTY
MUT
MUTABLE
MUTABLY
MUTAGEN
MUTAGENIC
MUTAGENS
MUTANDA
MUTANDUM
MUTANT
MUTANTS
MUTASE
MUTASES
MUTATE
MUTATED
MUTATES
MUTATING
MUTATION
MUTATIONS
MUTATIVE
MUTATOR
MUTATORS
MUTATORY
MUTCH
MUTCHED
MUTCHES
MUTCHING
MUTCHKIN
MUTCHKINS
MUTE
MUTED
MUTEDLY
MUTELY
MUTENESS
MUTER
MUTES
MUTEST
MUTHA
MUTHAS
MUTI
MUTICATE
MUTICOUS
MUTILATE
MUTILATED
MUTILATES
MUTILATOR
MUTINE
MUTINED
MUTINEER
MUTINEERS
MUTINES
MUTING
MUTINIED
MUTINIES
MUTINING
MUTINOUS
MUTINY
MUTINYING
MUTIS
MUTISM
MUTISMS
MUTON
MUTONS
MUTOSCOPE
MUTS
MUTT
MUTTER
MUTTERED
MUTTERER
MUTTERERS
MUTTERING
MUTTERS
MUTTON
MUTTONIER
MUTTONS
MUTTONY
MUTTS
MUTUAL
MUTUALISE
MUTUALISM
MUTUALIST
MUTUALITY
MUTUALIZE
MUTUALLY
MUTUALS
MUTUCA
MUTUCAS
MUTUEL
MUTUELS
MUTULAR
MUTULE
MUTULES
MUTUUM
MUTUUMS
MUUMUU
MUUMUUS
MUX
MUXED
MUXES
MUXING
MUZAK
MUZAKIER
MUZAKIEST
MUZAKS
MUZAKY
MUZHIK
MUZHIKS
MUZJIK
MUZJIKS
MUZZ
MUZZED
MUZZES
MUZZIER
MUZZIEST
MUZZILY
MUZZINESS
MUZZING
MUZZLE
MUZZLED
MUZZLER
MUZZLERS
MUZZLES
MUZZLING
MUZZY
MVULE
MVULES
MWAH
MWALIMU
MWALIMUS
MY
MYAL
MYALGIA
MYALGIAS
MYALGIC
MYALISM
MYALISMS
MYALIST
MYALISTS
MYALL
MYALLS
MYASES
MYASIS
MYC
MYCELE
MYCELES
MYCELIA
MYCELIAL
MYCELIAN
MYCELIUM
MYCELLA
MYCELLAS
MYCELOID
MYCETES
MYCETOMA
MYCETOMAS
MYCOBIONT
MYCOFLORA
MYCOLOGIC
MYCOLOGY
MYCOPHAGY
MYCOPHILE
MYCORHIZA
MYCOSES
MYCOSIS
MYCOTIC
MYCOTOXIN
MYCOVIRUS
MYCS
MYDRIASES
MYDRIASIS
MYDRIATIC
MYELIN
MYELINE
MYELINES
MYELINIC
MYELINS
MYELITES
MYELITIS
MYELOCYTE
MYELOGRAM
MYELOID
MYELOMA
MYELOMAS
MYELOMATA
MYELON
MYELONS
MYGALE
MYGALES
MYIASES
MYIASIS
MYIOPHILY
MYLAR
MYLARS
MYLODON
MYLODONS
MYLODONT
MYLODONTS
MYLOHYOID
MYLONITE
MYLONITES
MYLONITIC
MYNA
MYNAH
MYNAHS
MYNAS
MYNHEER
MYNHEERS
MYOBLAST
MYOBLASTS
MYOCARDIA
MYOCLONIC
MYOCLONUS
MYOFIBRIL
MYOGEN
MYOGENIC
MYOGENS
MYOGLOBIN
MYOGRAM
MYOGRAMS
MYOGRAPH
MYOGRAPHS
MYOGRAPHY
MYOID
MYOIDS

MYOLOGIC
MYOLOGIES
MYOLOGIST
MYOLOGY
MYOMA
MYOMANCY
MYOMANTIC
MYOMAS
MYOMATA
MYOMATOUS
MYOMERE
MYOMERES
MYONEURAL
MYOPATHIC
MYOPATHY
MYOPE
MYOPES
MYOPHILY
MYOPIA
MYOPIAS
MYOPIC
MYOPICS
MYOPIES
MYOPS
MYOPSES
MYOPY
MYOSCOPE
MYOSCOPES
MYOSES
MYOSIN
MYOSINS
MYOSIS
MYOSISES
MYOSITIS
MYOSOTE
MYOSOTES
MYOSOTIS
MYOSTATIN
MYOTIC
MYOTICS
MYOTOME
MYOTOMES
MYOTONIA
MYOTONIAS
MYOTONIC
MYOTUBE
MYOTUBES
MYRBANE
MYRBANES
MYRIAD
MYRIADS
MYRIADTH
MYRIADTHS
MYRIAPOD
MYRIAPODS
MYRICA
MYRICAS
MYRINGA
MYRINGAS
MYRIOPOD
MYRIOPODS
MYRIORAMA
MYRISTIC
MYRMECOID
MYRMIDON
MYRMIDONS
MYROBALAN
MYRRH
MYRRHIC
MYRRHIER
MYRRHIEST
MYRRHINE
MYRRHOL
MYRRHOLS
MYRRHS
MYRRHY
MYRTLE
MYRTLES
MYSELF
MYSID
MYSIDS
MYSOST
MYSOSTS
MYSPACE
MYSPACED
MYSPACES
MYSPACING
MYSTAGOG
MYSTAGOGS
MYSTAGOGY
MYSTERIES
MYSTERY
MYSTIC
MYSTICAL
MYSTICETE
MYSTICISM
MYSTICLY
MYSTICS
MYSTIFIED
MYSTIFIER
MYSTIFIES
MYSTIFY
MYSTIQUE
MYSTIQUES
MYTH
MYTHI
MYTHIC
MYTHICAL
MYTHICISE
MYTHICISM
MYTHICIST
MYTHICIZE
MYTHIER
MYTHIEST
MYTHISE
MYTHISED
MYTHISES
MYTHISING
MYTHISM
MYTHISMS
MYTHIST
MYTHISTS
MYTHIZE
MYTHIZED
MYTHIZES
MYTHIZING
MYTHMAKER
MYTHOI
MYTHOLOGY
MYTHOMANE
MYTHOPEIC
MYTHOPOET
MYTHOS
MYTHS
MYTHUS
MYTHY
MYTILOID
MYXAMEBA
MYXAMEBAE
MYXAMEBAS
MYXAMOEBA
MYXEDEMA
MYXEDEMAS
MYXEDEMIC
MYXO
MYXOCYTE
MYXOCYTES
MYXOEDEMA
MYXOID
MYXOMA
MYXOMAS
MYXOMATA
MYXOS
MYXOVIRAL
MYXOVIRUS
MZEE
MZEES
MZUNGU
MZUNGUS

N

NA
NAAM
NAAMS
NAAN
NAANS
NAARTJE
NAARTJES
NAARTJIE
NAARTJIES
NAB
NABBED
NABBER
NABBERS
NABBING
NABE
NABES
NABIS
NABK
NABKS
NABLA
NABLAS
NABOB
NABOBERY
NABOBESS
NABOBISH
NABOBISM
NABOBISMS
NABOBS
NABS
NACARAT
NACARATS
NACELLE
NACELLES
NACH
NACHAS
NACHE
NACHES
NACHO
NACHOS
NACHTMAAL
NACKET
NACKETS
NACRE
NACRED
NACREOUS
NACRES
NACRITE
NACRITES
NACROUS
NADA
NADAS
NADIR
NADIRAL
NADIRS
NADORS
NADS
NAE
NAEBODIES
NAEBODY
NAES
NAETHING
NAETHINGS
NAEVE
NAEVES
NAEVI
NAEVOID
NAEVUS
NAFF
NAFFED
NAFFER
NAFFEST
NAFFING
NAFFLY
NAFFNESS
NAFFS
NAG
NAGA
NAGANA
NAGANAS
NAGAPIE
NAGAPIES
NAGARI
NAGARIS
NAGAS
NAGGED
NAGGER
NAGGERS
NAGGIER
NAGGIEST
NAGGING
NAGGINGLY
NAGGINGS
NAGGY
NAGMAAL
NAGMAALS
NAGOR
NAGORS
NAGS
NAGWARE
NAGWARES
NAH
NAHAL
NAHALS
NAIAD
NAIADES
NAIADS
NAIANT
NAIF
NAIFER
NAIFEST
NAIFLY
NAIFNESS
NAIFS
NAIK
NAIKS
NAIL
NAILBITER
NAILBRUSH
NAILED
NAILER
NAILERIES
NAILERS
NAILERY
NAILFILE
NAILFILES
NAILFOLD
NAILFOLDS
NAILHEAD
NAILHEADS
NAILING
NAILINGS
NAILLESS
NAILS
NAILSET
NAILSETS
NAIN
NAINSELL
NAINSELLS
NAINSOOK
NAINSOOKS
NAIRA
NAIRAS
NAIRU
NAIRUS
NAISSANCE
NAISSANT
NAIVE
NAIVELY
NAIVENESS
NAIVER
NAIVES
NAIVEST
NAIVETE
NAIVETES
NAIVETIES
NAIVETY
NAIVIST
NAKED
NAKEDER
NAKEDEST
NAKEDLY
NAKEDNESS
NAKER
NAKERS
NAKFA
NAKFAS
NALA
NALAS
NALED
NALEDS
NALIDIXIC
NALLA
NALLAH
NALLAHS
NALLAS
NALOXONE
NALOXONES
NAM
NAMABLE
NAMASKAR
NAMASKARS
NAMASTE
NAMASTES
NAMAYCUSH
NAME
NAMEABLE
NAMECHECK
NAMED
NAMELESS
NAMELY
NAMEPLATE
NAMER
NAMERS
NAMES
NAMESAKE
NAMESAKES
NAMETAG
NAMETAGS
NAMETAPE
NAMETAPES
NAMING
NAMINGS
NAMMA
NAMS
NAMU
NAMUS
NAN
NANA
NANAS
NANCE

NANCES
NANCIER
NANCIES
NANCIEST
NANCIFIED
NANCY
NANDIN
NANDINA
NANDINAS
NANDINE
NANDINES
NANDINS
NANDOO
NANDOOS
NANDU
NANDUS
NANE
NANG
NANISM
NANISMS
NANITE
NANITES
NANKEEN
NANKEENS
NANKIN
NANKINS
NANNA
NANNAS
NANNIE
NANNIED
NANNIES
NANNY
NANNYGAI
NANNYGAIS
NANNYING
NANNYINGS
NANNYISH
NANO
NANOBE
NANOBEE
NANOBEES
NANOBES
NANOBOT
NANOBOTS
NANODOT
NANODOTS
NANOGRAM
NANOGRAMS
NANOGRASS
NANOMETER
NANOMETRE
NANOOK
NANOOKS
NANOPORE
NANOPORES
NANOS
NANOSCALE
NANOTECH
NANOTECHS
NANOTESLA
NANOTUBE
NANOTUBES
NANOWATT
NANOWATTS
NANOWIRE
NANOWIRES
NANOWORLD
NANS
NANUA
NANUAS
NAOI
NAOS
NAOSES
NAP
NAPA
NAPALM
NAPALMED
NAPALMING
NAPALMS
NAPAS
NAPE
NAPED
NAPERIES
NAPERY
NAPES
NAPHTHA
NAPHTHAS
NAPHTHENE
NAPHTHOL
NAPHTHOLS
NAPHTHOUS
NAPHTHYL
NAPHTHYLS
NAPHTOL
NAPHTOLS
NAPIFORM
NAPING
NAPKIN
NAPKINS
NAPLESS
NAPOLEON
NAPOLEONS
NAPOO
NAPOOED
NAPOOING
NAPOOS
NAPPA
NAPPAS
NAPPE
NAPPED
NAPPER
NAPPERS
NAPPES
NAPPIE
NAPPIER
NAPPIES
NAPPIEST
NAPPINESS
NAPPING
NAPPY
NAPRON
NAPRONS
NAPROXEN
NAPROXENS
NAPS
NARAS
NARASES
NARC
NARCEEN
NARCEENS
NARCEIN
NARCEINE
NARCEINES
NARCEINS
NARCISM
NARCISMS
NARCISSI
NARCISSUS
NARCIST
NARCISTIC
NARCISTS
NARCO
NARCOMA
NARCOMAS
NARCOMATA
NARCOS
NARCOSE
NARCOSES
NARCOSIS
NARCOTIC
NARCOTICS
NARCOTINE
NARCOTISE
NARCOTISM
NARCOTIST
NARCOTIZE
NARCS
NARD
NARDED
NARDINE
NARDING
NARDOO
NARDOOS
NARDS
NARE
NARES
NARGHILE
NARGHILES
NARGHILLY
NARGHILY
NARGILE
NARGILEH
NARGILEHS
NARGILES
NARGILIES
NARGILY
NARGUILEH
NARIAL
NARIC
NARICORN
NARICORNS
NARINE
NARIS
NARK
NARKED
NARKIER
NARKIEST
NARKING
NARKS
NARKY
NARQUOIS
NARRAS
NARRASES
NARRATE
NARRATED
NARRATER
NARRATERS
NARRATES
NARRATING
NARRATION
NARRATIVE
NARRATOR
NARRATORS
NARRATORY
NARRE
NARROW
NARROWED
NARROWER
NARROWEST
NARROWING
NARROWISH
NARROWLY
NARROWS
NARTHEX
NARTHEXES
NARTJIE
NARTJIES
NARWAL
NARWALS
NARWHAL
NARWHALE
NARWHALES
NARWHALS
NARY
NAS
NASAL
NASALISE
NASALISED
NASALISES
NASALISM
NASALISMS
NASALITY
NASALIZE
NASALIZED
NASALIZES
NASALLY
NASALS
NASARD
NASARDS
NASCENCE

NASCENCES
NASCENCY
NASCENT
NASEBERRY
NASHGAB
NASHGABS
NASHI
NASHIS
NASIAL
NASION
NASIONS
NASSELLA
NASTALIK
NASTALIKS
NASTIC
NASTIER
NASTIES
NASTIEST
NASTILY
NASTINESS
NASTY
NASUTE
NASUTES
NAT
NATAL
NATALITY
NATANT
NATANTLY
NATATION
NATATIONS
NATATORIA
NATATORY
NATCH
NATCHES
NATES
NATHELESS
NATHEMO
NATHEMORE
NATHLESS
NATIFORM
NATION
NATIONAL
NATIONALS
NATIONS
NATIS
NATIVE
NATIVELY
NATIVES
NATIVISM
NATIVISMS
NATIVIST
NATIVISTS
NATIVITY
NATRIUM
NATRIUMS
NATROLITE
NATRON
NATRONS
NATS
NATTER
NATTERED
NATTERER
NATTERERS
NATTERIER
NATTERING
NATTERS
NATTERY
NATTIER
NATTIEST
NATTILY
NATTINESS
NATTY
NATURA
NATURAE
NATURAL
NATURALLY
NATURALS
NATURE
NATURED
NATURES
NATURING
NATURISM
NATURISMS
NATURIST
NATURISTS
NAUCH
NAUCHES
NAUGAHYDE
NAUGHT
NAUGHTIER
NAUGHTIES
NAUGHTILY
NAUGHTS
NAUGHTY
NAUMACHIA
NAUMACHY
NAUNT
NAUNTS
NAUPLIAL
NAUPLII
NAUPLIOID
NAUPLIUS
NAUSEA
NAUSEANT
NAUSEANTS
NAUSEAS
NAUSEATE
NAUSEATED
NAUSEATES
NAUSEOUS
NAUTCH
NAUTCHES
NAUTIC
NAUTICAL
NAUTICS
NAUTILI
NAUTILOID
NAUTILUS
NAV
NAVAID
NAVAIDS
NAVAL
NAVALISM
NAVALISMS
NAVALLY
NAVAR
NAVARCH
NAVARCHS
NAVARCHY
NAVARHO
NAVARHOS
NAVARIN
NAVARINS
NAVARS
NAVE
NAVEL
NAVELS
NAVELWORT
NAVES
NAVETTE
NAVETTES
NAVEW
NAVEWS
NAVICERT
NAVICERTS
NAVICULA
NAVICULAR
NAVICULAS
NAVIES
NAVIGABLE
NAVIGABLY
NAVIGATE
NAVIGATED
NAVIGATES
NAVIGATOR
NAVS
NAVVIED
NAVVIES
NAVVY
NAVVYING
NAVY
NAW
NAWAB
NAWABS
NAY
NAYS
NAYSAID
NAYSAY
NAYSAYER
NAYSAYERS
NAYSAYING
NAYSAYS
NAYTHLES
NAYWARD
NAYWARDS
NAYWORD
NAYWORDS
NAZE
NAZES
NAZI
NAZIFIED
NAZIFIES
NAZIFY
NAZIFYING
NAZIR
NAZIRS
NAZIS
NDUJA
NDUJAS
NE
NEAFE
NEAFES
NEAFFE
NEAFFES
NEAL
NEALED
NEALING
NEALS
NEANIC
NEAP
NEAPED
NEAPING
NEAPS
NEAR
NEARBY
NEARED
NEARER
NEAREST
NEARING
NEARISH
NEARLIER
NEARLIEST
NEARLY
NEARNESS
NEARS
NEARSHORE
NEARSIDE
NEARSIDES
NEAT
NEATEN
NEATENED
NEATENING
NEATENS
NEATER
NEATEST
NEATH
NEATHERD
NEATHERDS
NEATLY
NEATNESS
NEATNIK
NEATNIKS
NEATS
NEB
NEBBED
NEBBICH
NEBBICHS
NEBBING
NEBBISH
NEBBISHE

NEBBISHER
NEBBISHES
NEBBISHY
NEBBUK
NEBBUKS
NEBECK
NEBECKS
NEBEK
NEBEKS
NEBEL
NEBELS
NEBENKERN
NEBISH
NEBISHES
NEBRIS
NEBRISES
NEBS
NEBULA
NEBULAE
NEBULAR
NEBULAS
NEBULE
NEBULES
NEBULISE
NEBULISED
NEBULISER
NEBULISES
NEBULIUM
NEBULIUMS
NEBULIZE
NEBULIZED
NEBULIZER
NEBULIZES
NEBULOSE
NEBULOUS
NEBULY
NECESSARY
NECESSITY
NECK
NECKATEE
NECKATEES
NECKBAND
NECKBANDS
NECKBEEF
NECKBEEFS
NECKCLOTH
NECKED
NECKER
NECKERS
NECKGEAR
NECKGEARS
NECKING
NECKINGS
NECKLACE
NECKLACED
NECKLACES
NECKLESS
NECKLET
NECKLETS
NECKLIKE
NECKLINE
NECKLINES
NECKPIECE
NECKS
NECKSHOT
NECKSHOTS
NECKTIE
NECKTIES
NECKVERSE
NECKWEAR
NECKWEARS
NECKWEED
NECKWEEDS
NECROLOGY
NECROPHIL
NECROPOLI
NECROPSY
NECROSE
NECROSED
NECROSES
NECROSING
NECROSIS
NECROTIC
NECROTISE
NECROTIZE
NECROTOMY
NECTAR
NECTAREAL
NECTAREAN
NECTARED
NECTARIAL
NECTARIED
NECTARIES
NECTARINE
NECTAROUS
NECTARS
NECTARY
NED
NEDDIER
NEDDIES
NEDDIEST
NEDDISH
NEDDY
NEDETTE
NEDETTES
NEDS
NEE
NEED
NEEDED
NEEDER
NEEDERS
NEEDFIRE
NEEDFIRES
NEEDFUL
NEEDFULLY
NEEDFULS
NEEDIER
NEEDIEST
NEEDILY
NEEDINESS
NEEDING
NEEDLE
NEEDLED
NEEDLEFUL
NEEDLER
NEEDLERS
NEEDLES
NEEDLESS
NEEDLIER
NEEDLIEST
NEEDLING
NEEDLINGS
NEEDLY
NEEDMENT
NEEDMENTS
NEEDS
NEEDY
NEELD
NEELDS
NEELE
NEELES
NEEM
NEEMB
NEEMBS
NEEMS
NEEP
NEEPS
NEESBERRY
NEESE
NEESED
NEESES
NEESING
NEEZE
NEEZED
NEEZES
NEEZING
NEF
NEFANDOUS
NEFARIOUS
NEFAST
NEFS
NEG
NEGATE
NEGATED
NEGATER
NEGATERS
NEGATES
NEGATING
NEGATION
NEGATIONS
NEGATIVE
NEGATIVED
NEGATIVES
NEGATON
NEGATONS
NEGATOR
NEGATORS
NEGATORY
NEGATRON
NEGATRONS
NEGLECT
NEGLECTED
NEGLECTER
NEGLECTOR
NEGLECTS
NEGLIGE
NEGLIGEE
NEGLIGEES
NEGLIGENT
NEGLIGES
NEGOCIANT
NEGOTIANT
NEGOTIATE
NEGRESS
NEGRESSES
NEGRITUDE
NEGRO
NEGROES
NEGROHEAD
NEGROID
NEGROIDAL
NEGROIDS
NEGROISM
NEGROISMS
NEGRONI
NEGRONIS
NEGROPHIL
NEGS
NEGUS
NEGUSES
NEIF
NEIFS
NEIGH
NEIGHBOR
NEIGHBORS
NEIGHBOUR
NEIGHED
NEIGHING
NEIGHINGS
NEIGHS
NEINEI
NEINEIS
NEIST
NEITHER
NEIVE
NEIVES
NEK
NEKS
NEKTON
NEKTONIC
NEKTONS
NELIES
NELIS
NELLIE
NELLIES
NELLY
NELSON
NELSONS
NELUMBIUM
NELUMBO

NELUMBOS
NEMA
NEMAS
NEMATIC
NEMATICS
NEMATODE
NEMATODES
NEMATOID
NEMERTEAN
NEMERTIAN
NEMERTINE
NEMESES
NEMESIA
NEMESIAS
NEMESIS
NEMN
NEMNED
NEMNING
NEMNS
NEMOPHILA
NEMORAL
NEMOROUS
NEMPT
NENE
NENES
NENNIGAI
NENNIGAIS
NENUPHAR
NENUPHARS
NEOBLAST
NEOBLASTS
NEOCON
NEOCONS
NEOCORTEX
NEODYMIUM
NEOGENE
NEOGOTHIC
NEOLITH
NEOLITHIC
NEOLITHS
NEOLOGIAN
NEOLOGIC
NEOLOGIES
NEOLOGISE
NEOLOGISM
NEOLOGIST
NEOLOGIZE
NEOLOGY
NEOMORPH
NEOMORPHS
NEOMYCIN
NEOMYCINS
NEON
NEONATAL
NEONATE
NEONATES
NEONED
NEONOMIAN
NEONS
NEOPAGAN
NEOPAGANS
NEOPHILE
NEOPHILES
NEOPHILIA
NEOPHOBE
NEOPHOBES
NEOPHOBIA
NEOPHOBIC
NEOPHYTE
NEOPHYTES
NEOPHYTIC
NEOPILINA
NEOPLASIA
NEOPLASM
NEOPLASMS
NEOPLASTY
NEOPRENE
NEOPRENES
NEOSOUL
NEOSOULS
NEOTEINIA
NEOTENIC
NEOTENIES
NEOTENOUS
NEOTENY
NEOTERIC
NEOTERICS
NEOTERISE
NEOTERISM
NEOTERIST
NEOTERIZE
NEOTOXIN
NEOTOXINS
NEOTROPIC
NEOTYPE
NEOTYPES
NEP
NEPENTHE
NEPENTHES
NEPER
NEPERS
NEPETA
NEPETAS
NEPHALISM
NEPHALIST
NEPHELINE
NEPHELITE
NEPHEW
NEPHEWS
NEPHOGRAM
NEPHOLOGY
NEPHRALGY
NEPHRIC
NEPHRIDIA
NEPHRISM
NEPHRISMS
NEPHRITE
NEPHRITES
NEPHRITIC
NEPHRITIS
NEPHROID
NEPHRON
NEPHRONS
NEPHROSES
NEPHROSIS
NEPHROTIC
NEPIONIC
NEPIT
NEPITS
NEPOTIC
NEPOTISM
NEPOTISMS
NEPOTIST
NEPOTISTS
NEPS
NEPTUNIUM
NERAL
NERALS
NERD
NERDIC
NERDICS
NERDIER
NERDIEST
NERDINESS
NERDISH
NERDS
NERDY
NEREID
NEREIDES
NEREIDS
NEREIS
NERINE
NERINES
NERITE
NERITES
NERITIC
NERK
NERKA
NERKAS
NERKS
NEROL
NEROLI
NEROLIS
NEROLS
NERTS
NERTZ
NERVAL
NERVATE
NERVATION
NERVATURE
NERVE
NERVED
NERVELESS
NERVELET
NERVELETS
NERVER
NERVERS
NERVES
NERVIER
NERVIEST
NERVILY
NERVINE
NERVINES
NERVINESS
NERVING
NERVINGS
NERVOSITY
NERVOUS
NERVOUSLY
NERVULAR
NERVULE
NERVULES
NERVURE
NERVURES
NERVY
NESCIENCE
NESCIENT
NESCIENTS
NESH
NESHER
NESHEST
NESHNESS
NESS
NESSES
NEST
NESTABLE
NESTED
NESTER
NESTERS
NESTFUL
NESTFULS
NESTING
NESTINGS
NESTLE
NESTLED
NESTLER
NESTLERS
NESTLES
NESTLIKE
NESTLING
NESTLINGS
NESTMATE
NESTMATES
NESTOR
NESTORS
NESTS
NET
NETBALL
NETBALLER
NETBALLS
NETBOOK
NETBOOKS
NETE
NETES
NETFUL
NETFULS
NETHEAD
NETHEADS
NETHELESS
NETHER

NETIZEN
NETIZENS
NETLESS
NETLIKE
NETMINDER
NETOP
NETOPS
NETROOT
NETROOTS
NETS
NETSPEAK
NETSPEAKS
NETSUKE
NETSUKES
NETSURF
NETSURFED
NETSURFER
NETSURFS
NETT
NETTABLE
NETTED
NETTER
NETTERS
NETTIE
NETTIER
NETTIES
NETTIEST
NETTING
NETTINGS
NETTLE
NETTLED
NETTLER
NETTLERS
NETTLES
NETTLIER
NETTLIEST
NETTLING
NETTLY
NETTS
NETTY
NETWORK
NETWORKED
NETWORKER
NETWORKS
NEUK
NEUKS
NEUM
NEUMATIC
NEUME
NEUMES
NEUMIC
NEUMS
NEURAL
NEURALGIA
NEURALGIC
NEURALLY
NEURATION
NEURAXON
NEURAXONS
NEURILITY
NEURINE
NEURINES
NEURISM
NEURISMS
NEURITE
NEURITES
NEURITIC
NEURITICS
NEURITIS
NEUROCHIP
NEUROCOEL
NEUROGLIA
NEUROGRAM
NEUROID
NEUROIDS
NEUROLOGY
NEUROMA
NEUROMAS
NEUROMAST
NEUROMATA
NEURON
NEURONAL
NEURONE
NEURONES
NEURONIC
NEURONS
NEUROPATH
NEUROPIL
NEUROPILS
NEUROSAL
NEUROSES
NEUROSIS
NEUROTIC
NEUROTICS
NEUROTOMY
NEURULA
NEURULAE
NEURULAR
NEURULAS
NEUSTIC
NEUSTICS
NEUSTON
NEUSTONIC
NEUSTONS
NEUTER
NEUTERED
NEUTERING
NEUTERS
NEUTRAL
NEUTRALLY
NEUTRALS
NEUTRETTO
NEUTRINO
NEUTRINOS
NEUTRON
NEUTRONIC
NEUTRONS
NEVE
NEVEL
NEVELLED
NEVELLING
NEVELS
NEVER
NEVERMIND
NEVERMORE
NEVES
NEVI
NEVOID
NEVUS
NEW
NEWB
NEWBIE
NEWBIES
NEWBORN
NEWBORNS
NEWBS
NEWCOME
NEWCOMER
NEWCOMERS
NEWED
NEWEL
NEWELL
NEWELLED
NEWELLS
NEWELS
NEWER
NEWEST
NEWFANGLE
NEWFOUND
NEWIE
NEWIES
NEWING
NEWISH
NEWISHLY
NEWLY
NEWLYWED
NEWLYWEDS
NEWMARKET
NEWMOWN
NEWNESS
NEWNESSES
NEWS
NEWSAGENT
NEWSBEAT
NEWSBEATS
NEWSBOY
NEWSBOYS
NEWSBREAK
NEWSCAST
NEWSCASTS
NEWSCLIP
NEWSCLIPS
NEWSDESK
NEWSDESKS
NEWSED
NEWSES
NEWSFEED
NEWSFEEDS
NEWSFLASH
NEWSGIRL
NEWSGIRLS
NEWSGROUP
NEWSHAWK
NEWSHAWKS
NEWSHOUND
NEWSIE
NEWSIER
NEWSIES
NEWSIEST
NEWSINESS
NEWSING
NEWSLESS
NEWSMAKER
NEWSMAN
NEWSMEN
NEWSPAPER
NEWSPEAK
NEWSPEAKS
NEWSPRINT
NEWSREEL
NEWSREELS
NEWSROOM
NEWSROOMS
NEWSSHEET
NEWSSTAND
NEWSTRADE
NEWSWIRE
NEWSWIRES
NEWSWOMAN
NEWSWOMEN
NEWSY
NEWT
NEWTON
NEWTONS
NEWTS
NEWWAVER
NEWWAVERS
NEXT
NEXTDOOR
NEXTLY
NEXTNESS
NEXTS
NEXUS
NEXUSES
NGAI
NGAIO
NGAIOS
NGANA
NGANAS
NGARARA
NGARARAS
NGATI
NGATIS
NGOMA
NGOMAS
NGULTRUM
NGULTRUMS
NGWEE
NGWEES
NHANDU

NHANDUS
NIACIN
NIACINS
NIAGARA
NIAGARAS
NIAISERIE
NIALAMIDE
NIB
NIBBED
NIBBING
NIBBLE
NIBBLED
NIBBLER
NIBBLERS
NIBBLES
NIBBLIES
NIBBLING
NIBBLINGS
NIBBLY
NIBLET
NIBLETS
NIBLICK
NIBLICKS
NIBLIKE
NIBS
NICAD
NICADS
NICCOLITE
NICE
NICEISH
NICELY
NICENESS
NICER
NICEST
NICETIES
NICETY
NICHE
NICHED
NICHER
NICHERED
NICHERING
NICHERS
NICHES
NICHING
NICHROME
NICHROMES
NICHT
NICHTS
NICISH
NICK
NICKAR
NICKARS
NICKED
NICKEL
NICKELED
NICKELIC
NICKELINE
NICKELING
NICKELISE
NICKELIZE
NICKELLED
NICKELOUS
NICKELS
NICKER
NICKERED
NICKERING
NICKERNUT
NICKERS
NICKING
NICKLE
NICKLED
NICKLES
NICKLING
NICKNACK
NICKNACKS
NICKNAME
NICKNAMED
NICKNAMER
NICKNAMES
NICKPOINT
NICKS
NICKSTICK
NICKUM
NICKUMS
NICOISE
NICOL
NICOLS
NICOMPOOP
NICOTIAN
NICOTIANA
NICOTIANS
NICOTIN
NICOTINE
NICOTINED
NICOTINES
NICOTINIC
NICOTINS
NICTATE
NICTATED
NICTATES
NICTATING
NICTATION
NICTITANT
NICTITATE
NID
NIDAL
NIDAMENTA
NIDATE
NIDATED
NIDATES
NIDATING
NIDATION
NIDATIONS
NIDDERING
NIDDICK
NIDDICKS
NIDE
NIDED
NIDERING
NIDERINGS
NIDERLING
NIDES
NIDGET
NIDGETED
NIDGETING
NIDGETS
NIDI
NIDIFIED
NIDIFIES
NIDIFY
NIDIFYING
NIDING
NIDINGS
NIDOR
NIDOROUS
NIDORS
NIDS
NIDUS
NIDUSES
NIE
NIECE
NIECES
NIED
NIEF
NIEFS
NIELLATED
NIELLI
NIELLIST
NIELLISTS
NIELLO
NIELLOED
NIELLUING
NIELLOS
NIENTE
NIES
NIEVE
NIEVEFUL
NIEVEFULS
NIEVES
NIFE
NIFES
NIFF
NIFFED
NIFFER
NIFFERED
NIFFERING
NIFFERS
NIFFIER
NIFFIEST
NIFFING
NIFFNAFF
NIFFNAFFS
NIFFS
NIFFY
NIFTIER
NIFTIES
NIFTIEST
NIFTILY
NIFTINESS
NIFTY
NIGELLA
NIGELLAS
NIGER
NIGERS
NIGGARD
NIGGARDED
NIGGARDLY
NIGGARDS
NIGGER
NIGGERDOM
NIGGERED
NIGGERIER
NIGGERING
NIGGERISH
NIGGERISM
NIGGERS
NIGGERY
NIGGLE
NIGGLED
NIGGLER
NIGGLERS
NIGGLES
NIGGLIER
NIGGLIEST
NIGGLING
NIGGLINGS
NIGGLY
NIGH
NIGHED
NIGHER
NIGHEST
NIGHING
NIGHLY
NIGHNESS
NIGHS
NIGHT
NIGHTBIRD
NIGHTCAP
NIGHTCAPS
NIGHTCLUB
NIGHTED
NIGHTFALL
NIGHTFIRE
NIGHTGEAR
NIGHTGLOW
NIGHTGOWN
NIGHTHAWK
NIGHTIE
NIGHTIES
NIGHTJAR
NIGHTJARS
NIGHTLESS
NIGHTLIFE
NIGHTLIKE
NIGHTLONG
NIGHTLY
NIGHTMARE
NIGHTMARY
NIGHTS
NIGHTSIDE

N

NIGHTSPOT
NIGHTTIDE
NIGHTTIME
NIGHTWARD
NIGHTWEAR
NIGHTY
NIGIRI
NIGIRIS
NIGRICANT
NIGRIFIED
NIGRIFIES
NIGRIFY
NIGRITUDE
NIGROSIN
NIGROSINE
NIGROSINS
NIHIL
NIHILISM
NIHILISMS
NIHILIST
NIHILISTS
NIHILITY
NIHILS
NIHONGA
NIHONGAS
NIHONIUM
NIHONIUMS
NIKAB
NIKABS
NIKAH
NIKAHS
NIKAU
NIKAUS
NIL
NILGAI
NILGAIS
NILGAU
NILGAUS
NILGHAI
NILGHAIS
NILGHAU
NILGHAUS
NILL
NILLED
NILLING
NILLS
NILPOTENT
NILS

NIM
NIMB
NIMBED
NIMBI
NIMBLE
NIMBLER
NIMBLESSE
NIMBLEST
NIMBLEWIT
NIMBLY
NIMBS
NIMBUS
NIMBUSED
NIMBUSES
NIMBYISM
NIMBYISMS
NIMBYNESS
NIMIETIES
NIMIETY
NIMIOUS
NIMMED
NIMMER
NIMMERS
NIMMING
NIMONIC
NIMPS
NIMROD
NIMRODS
NIMS
NINCOM
NINCOMS
NINCUM
NINCUMS
NINE
NINEBARK
NINEBARKS
NINEFOLD
NINEHOLES
NINEPENCE
NINEPENNY
NINEPIN
NINEPINS
NINER
NINERS
NINES
NINESCORE
NINETEEN
NINETEENS

NINETIES
NINETIETH
NINETY
NINHYDRIN
NINJA
NINJAS
NINJITSU
NINJITSUS
NINJUTSU
NINJUTSUS
NINNIES
NINNY
NINNYISH
NINON
NINONS
NINTH
NINTHLY
NINTHS
NIOBATE
NIOBATES
NIOBIC
NIOBITE
NIOBITES
NIOBIUM
NIOBIUMS
NIOBOUS
NIP
NIPA
NIPAS
NIPCHEESE
NIPPED
NIPPER
NIPPERED
NIPPERING
NIPPERKIN
NIPPERS
NIPPIER
NIPPIEST
NIPPILY
NIPPINESS
NIPPING
NIPPINGLY
NIPPLE
NIPPLED
NIPPLES
NIPPLING
NIPPY
NIPS

NIPTER
NIPTERS
NIQAAB
NIQAABS
NIQAB
NIQABS
NIRAMIAI
NIRAMIAIS
NIRL
NIRLED
NIRLIE
NIRLIER
NIRLIEST
NIRLING
NIRLIT
NIRLS
NIRLY
NIRVANA
NIRVANAS
NIRVANIC
NIS
NISBERRY
NISEI
NISEIS
NISGUL
NISGULS
NISH
NISHES
NISI
NISSE
NISSES
NISUS
NIT
NITCHIE
NITCHIES
NITE
NITER
NITERIE
NITERIES
NITERS
NITERY
NITES
NITHER
NITHERED
NITHERING
NITHERS
NITHING
NITHINGS

NITID
NITINOL
NITINOLS
NITON
NITONS
NITPICK
NITPICKED
NITPICKER
NITPICKS
NITPICKY
NITRAMINE
NITRATE
NITRATED
NITRATES
NITRATINE
NITRATING
NITRATION
NITRATOR
NITRATORS
NITRE
NITREOUS
NITRES
NITRIC
NITRID
NITRIDE
NITRIDED
NITRIDES
NITRIDING
NITRIDS
NITRIFIED
NITRIFIER
NITRIFIES
NITRIFY
NITRIL
NITRILE
NITRILES
NITRILS
NITRITE
NITRITES
NITRO
NITROGEN
NITROGENS
NITROLIC
NITROS
NITROSO
NITROSYL
NITROSYLS
NITROUS

N

NITROX
NITROXES
NITROXYL
NITROXYLS
NITRY
NITRYL
NITRYLS
NITS
NITTIER
NITTIEST
NITTY
NITWIT
NITWITS
NITWITTED
NIVAL
NIVATION
NIVATIONS
NIVEOUS
NIX
NIXE
NIXED
NIXER
NIXERS
NIXES
NIXIE
NIXIES
NIXING
NIXY
NIZAM
NIZAMATE
NIZAMATES
NIZAMS
NKOSI
NKOSIS
NO
NOAH
NOAHS
NOB
NOBBIER
NOBBIEST
NOBBILY
NOBBINESS
NOBBLE
NOBBLED
NOBBLER
NOBBLERS
NOBBLES
NOBBLING
NOBBUT
NOBBY
NOBELIUM
NOBELIUMS
NOBILESSE
NOBILIARY
NOBILITY
NOBLE
NOBLEMAN
NOBLEMEN
NOBLENESS
NOBLER
NOBLES
NOBLESSE
NOBLESSES
NOBLEST
NOBLY
NOBODIES
NOBODY
NOBS
NOCAKE
NOCAKES
NOCEBO
NOCEBOS
NOCENT
NOCENTLY
NOCENTS
NOCHEL
NOCHELED
NOCHELING
NOCHELLED
NOCHELS
NOCK
NOCKED
NOCKET
NOCKETS
NOCKING
NOCKS
NOCTILIO
NOCTILIOS
NOCTILUCA
NOCTUA
NOCTUARY
NOCTUAS
NOCTUID
NOCTUIDS
NOCTULE
NOCTULES
NOCTUOID
NOCTUOIDS
NOCTURIA
NOCTURIAS
NOCTURN
NOCTURNAL
NOCTURNE
NOCTURNES
NOCTURNS
NOCUOUS
NOCUOUSLY
NOD
NODAL
NODALISE
NODALISED
NODALISES
NODALITY
NODALIZE
NODALIZED
NODALIZES
NODALLY
NODATED
NODATION
NODATIONS
NODDED
NODDER
NODDERS
NODDIER
NODDIES
NODDIEST
NODDING
NODDINGLY
NODDINGS
NODDLE
NODDLED
NODDLES
NODDLING
NODDY
NODE
NODES
NODI
NODICAL
NODOSE
NODOSITY
NODOUS
NODS
NODULAR
NODULATED
NODULE
NODULED
NODULES
NODULOSE
NODULOUS
NODUS
NOEL
NOELS
NOES
NOESES
NOESIS
NOESISES
NOETIC
NOG
NOGAKU
NOGG
NOGGED
NOGGIN
NOGGING
NOGGINGS
NOGGINS
NOGGS
NOGOODNIK
NOGS
NOH
NOHOW
NOHOWISH
NOIL
NOILIER
NOILIES
NOILIEST
NOILS
NOILY
NOINT
NOINTED
NOINTER
NOINTERS
NOINTING
NOINTS
NOIR
NOIRISH
NOIRS
NOISE
NOISED
NOISEFUL
NOISELESS
NOISENIK
NOISENIKS
NOISES
NOISETTE
NOISETTES
NOISIER
NOISIEST
NOISILY
NOISINESS
NOISING
NOISOME
NOISOMELY
NOISY
NOLE
NOLES
NOLITION
NOLITIONS
NOLL
NOLLS
NOLO
NOLOS
NOM
NOMA
NOMAD
NOMADE
NOMADES
NOMADIC
NOMADIES
NOMADISE
NOMADISED
NOMADISES
NOMADISM
NOMADISMS
NOMADIZE
NOMADIZED
NOMADIZES
NOMADS
NOMADY
NOMARCH
NOMARCHS
NOMARCHY
NOMAS
NOMBLES
NOMBRIL
NOMBRILS
NOME
NOMEN
NOMENS
NOMES
NOMIC

NOMINA
NOMINABLE
NOMINAL
NOMINALLY
NOMINALS
NOMINATE
NOMINATED
NOMINATES
NOMINATOR
NOMINEE
NOMINEES
NOMISM
NOMISMS
NOMISTIC
NOMOCRACY
NOMOGENY
NOMOGRAM
NOMOGRAMS
NOMOGRAPH
NOMOI
NOMOLOGIC
NOMOLOGY
NOMOS
NOMOTHETE
NOMS
NON
NONA
NONACID
NONACIDIC
NONACIDS
NONACTING
NONACTION
NONACTIVE
NONACTOR
NONACTORS
NONADDICT
NONADULT
NONADULTS
NONAGE
NONAGED
NONAGES
NONAGON
NONAGONAL
NONAGONS
NONANE
NONANES
NONANIMAL
NONANOIC
NONANSWER
NONARABLE
NONARIES
NONART
NONARTIST
NONARTS
NONARY
NONAS
NONATOMIC
NONAUTHOR
NONAVIAN
NONBANK
NONBANKS
NONBASIC
NONBEING
NONBEINGS
NONBELIEF
NONBINARY
NONBITING
NONBLACK
NONBLACKS
NONBODIES
NONBODY
NONBONDED
NONBOOK
NONBOOKS
NONBRAND
NONBUYING
NONCAKING
NONCAMPUS
NONCAREER
NONCASH
NONCASUAL
NONCAUSAL
NONCE
NONCEREAL
NONCES
NONCHURCH
NONCLASS
NONCLING
NONCODING
NONCOITAL
NONCOKING
NONCOLA
NONCOLAS
NONCOLOR
NONCOLORS
NONCOLOUR
NONCOM
NONCOMBAT
NONCOMS
NONCONCUR
NONCORE
NONCOUNT
NONCOUNTY
NONCREDIT
NONCRIME
NONCRIMES
NONCRISES
NONCRISIS
NONCYCLIC
NONDAIRY
NONDANCE
NONDANCER
NONDANCES
NONDEALER
NONDEGREE
NONDEMAND
NONDESERT
NONDOCTOR
NONDOLLAR
NONDRIP
NONDRIVER
NONDRUG
NONDRYING
NONE
NONEDIBLE
NONEGO
NONEGOS
NONELECT
NONELECTS
NONELITE
NONEMPTY
NONENDING
NONENERGY
NONENTITY
NONENTRY
NONEQUAL
NONEQUALS
NONEROTIC
NONES
NONESUCH
NONET
NONETHNIC
NONETS
NONETTE
NONETTES
NONETTI
NONETTO
NONETTOS
NONEVENT
NONEVENTS
NONEXEMPT
NONEXOTIC
NONEXPERT
NONEXTANT
NONFACT
NONFACTOR
NONFACTS
NONFADING
NONFAMILY
NONFAN
NONFANS
NONFARM
NONFARMER
NONFAT
NONFATAL
NONFATTY
NONFEUDAL
NONFILIAL
NONFINAL
NONFINITE
NONFISCAL
NONFLUID
NONFLUIDS
NONFLYING
NONFOCAL
NONFOOD
NONFOODS
NONFORMAL
NONFOSSIL
NONFROZEN
NONFUEL
NONFUELS
NONFUNDED
NONG
NONGAME
NONGAY
NONGAYS
NONGHETTO
NONGLARE
NONGLARES
NONGLAZED
NONGLOSSY
NONGOLFER
NONGRADED
NONGREASY
NONGREEN
NONGROWTH
NONGS
NONGUEST
NONGUESTS
NONGUILT
NONGUILTS
NONHARDY
NONHEME
NONHERO
NONHEROES
NONHEROIC
NONHOME
NONHUMAN
NONHUMANS
NONHUNTER
NONI
NONIDEAL
NONILLION
NONIMAGE
NONIMAGES
NONIMMUNE
NONIMPACT
NONINERT
NONINJURY
NONINSECT
NONIONIC
NONIRON
NONIS
NONISSUE
NONISSUES
NONJOINER
NONJURIES
NONJURING
NONJUROR
NONJURORS
NONJURY
NONKIN
NONKINS
NONKOSHER
NONLABOR
NONLABOUR
NONLAWYER
NONLEADED
NONLEAFY

N

NONLEAGUE
NONLEGAL
NONLEGUME
NONLETHAL
NONLEVEL
NONLIABLE
NONLIFE
NONLINEAL
NONLINEAR
NONLIQUID
NONLIVES
NONLIVING
NONLOCAL
NONLOCALS
NONLOVING
NONLOYAL
NONLYRIC
NONMAJOR
NONMAJORS
NONMAN
NONMANUAL
NONMARKET
NONMATURE
NONMEAT
NONMEATS
NONMEMBER
NONMEN
NONMENTAL
NONMETAL
NONMETALS
NONMETRIC
NONMETRO
NONMOBILE
NONMODAL
NONMODERN
NONMONEY
NONMORAL
NONMORTAL
NONMOTILE
NONMOVING
NONMUSIC
NONMUSICS
NONMUTANT
NONMUTUAL
NONNASAL
NONNATIVE
NONNAVAL
NONNEURAL
NONNEWS
NONNIES
NONNOBLE
NONNORMAL
NONNOVEL
NONNOVELS
NONNY
NONOBESE
NONOHMIC
NONOILY
NONORAL
NONORALLY
NONOWNER
NONOWNERS
NONPAGAN
NONPAGANS
NONPAID
NONPAPAL
NONPAPIST
NONPAR
NONPAREIL
NONPARENT
NONPARITY
NONPAROUS
NONPARTY
NONPAST
NONPASTS
NONPAYING
NONPEAK
NONPEAKS
NONPERSON
NONPLANAR
NONPLAY
NONPLAYER
NONPLAYS
NONPLIANT
NONPLUS
NONPLUSED
NONPLUSES
NONPOETIC
NONPOINT
NONPOLAR
NONPOLICE
NONPOOR
NONPOORS
NONPOROUS
NONPOSTAL
NONPRINT
NONPROFIT
NONPROS
NONPROVEN
NONPUBLIC
NONQUOTA
NONRACIAL
NONRACISM
NONRANDOM
NONRATED
NONREADER
NONRETURN
NONRHOTIC
NONRIGID
NONRIOTER
NONRIVAL
NONRIVALS
NONROYAL
NONROYALS
NONRUBBER
NONRULING
NONRUN
NONRUNNER
NONRURAL
NONSACRED
NONSALINE
NONSCHOOL
NONSECRET
NONSECURE
NONSELF
NONSELVES
NONSENSE
NONSENSES
NONSERIAL
NONSEXIST
NONSEXUAL
NONSHRINK
NONSIGNER
NONSKATER
NONSKED
NONSKEDS
NONSKID
NONSKIER
NONSKIERS
NONSLIP
NONSMOKER
NONSOCIAL
NONSOLAR
NONSOLID
NONSOLIDS
NONSPEECH
NONSTAPLE
NONSTATE
NONSTATIC
NONSTEADY
NONSTICK
NONSTICKY
NONSTOP
NONSTOPS
NONSTORY
NONSTYLE
NONSTYLES
NONSUCH
NONSUCHES
NONSUGAR
NONSUGARS
NONSUIT
NONSUITED
NONSUITS
NONSYSTEM
NONTALKER
NONTARGET
NONTARIFF
NONTAX
NONTAXES
NONTHEISM
NONTHEIST
NONTIDAL
NONTITLE
NONTONAL
NONTONIC
NONTOXIC
NONTOXICS
NONTRAGIC
NONTRIBAL
NONTRUMP
NONTRUTH
NONTRUTHS
NONUNION
NONUNIONS
NONUNIQUE
NONUPLE
NONUPLES
NONUPLET
NONUPLETS
NONURBAN
NONURGENT
NONUSABLE
NONUSE
NONUSER
NONUSERS
NONUSES
NONUSING
NONVACANT
NONVALID
NONVECTOR
NONVENOUS
NONVERBAL
NONVESTED
NONVIABLE
NONVIEWER
NONVIRAL
NONVIRGIN
NONVIRILE
NONVISUAL
NONVITAL
NONVOCAL
NONVOCALS
NONVOTER
NONVOTERS
NONVOTING
NONWAGE
NONWAR
NONWARS
NONWHITE
NONWHITES
NONWINGED
NONWOODY
NONWOOL
NONWORD
NONWORDS
NONWORK
NONWORKER
NONWORKS
NONWOVEN
NONWOVENS
NONWRITER
NONYL
NONYLS
NONZERO
NOO
NOOB
NOOBS
NOODGE
NOODGED

NOODGES
NOODGING
NOODLE
NOODLED
NOODLEDOM
NOODLES
NOODLING
NOODLINGS
NOOGIE
NOOGIES
NOOIT
NOOK
NOOKIE
NOOKIER
NOOKIES
NOOKIEST
NOOKLIKE
NOOKS
NOOKY
NOOLOGIES
NOOLOGY
NOOMETRY
NOON
NOONDAY
NOONDAYS
NOONED
NOONER
NOONERS
NOONING
NOONINGS
NOONS
NOONTIDE
NOONTIDES
NOONTIME
NOONTIMES
NOOP
NOOPS
NOOSE
NOOSED
NOOSELIKE
NOOSER
NOOSERS
NOOSES
NOOSING
NOOSPHERE
NOOTROPIC
NOPAL
NOPALES
NOPALITO
NOPALITOS
NOPALS
NOPE
NOPLACE
NOR
NORDIC
NORDICITY
NORI
NORIA
NORIAS
NORIMON
NORIMONS
NORIS
NORITE
NORITES
NORITIC
NORK
NORKS
NORLAND
NORLANDS
NORM
NORMA
NORMAL
NORMALCY
NORMALISE
NORMALITY
NORMALIZE
NORMALLY
NORMALS
NORMAN
NORMANDE
NORMANDES
NORMANS
NORMAS
NORMATIVE
NORMCORE
NORMCORES
NORMED
NORMLESS
NORMS
NOROVIRUS
NORSEL
NORSELLED
NORSELLER
NORSELS
NORTENA
NORTENAS
NORTENO
NORTENOS
NORTH
NORTHEAST
NORTHED
NORTHER
NORTHERED
NORTHERLY
NORTHERN
NORTHERNS
NORTHERS
NORTHING
NORTHINGS
NORTHLAND
NORTHMOST
NORTHS
NORTHWARD
NORTHWEST
NORWARD
NORWARDS
NOS
NOSE
NOSEAN
NOSEANS
NOSEBAG
NOSEBAGS
NOSEBAND
NOSEBANDS
NOSEBLEED
NOSED
NOSEDIVE
NOSEDIVED
NOSEDIVES
NOSEDOVE
NOSEGAY
NOSEGAYS
NOSEGUARD
NOSELESS
NOSELIKE
NOSELITE
NOSELITES
NOSEPIECE
NOSER
NOSERS
NOSES
NOSEWHEEL
NOSEY
NOSEYS
NOSH
NOSHED
NOSHER
NOSHERIE
NOSHERIES
NOSHERS
NOSHERY
NOSHES
NOSHING
NOSIER
NOSIES
NOSIEST
NOSILY
NOSINESS
NOSING
NOSINGS
NOSODE
NOSODES
NOSOLOGIC
NOSOLOGY
NOSTALGIA
NOSTALGIC
NOSTOC
NOSTOCS
NOSTOI
NOSTOLOGY
NOSTOS
NOSTRIL
NOSTRILS
NOSTRO
NOSTRUM
NOSTRUMS
NOSY
NOT
NOTA
NOTABILIA
NOTABLE
NOTABLES
NOTABLY
NOTAEUM
NOTAEUMS
NOTAIRE
NOTAIRES
NOTAL
NOTANDA
NOTANDUM
NOTAPHILY
NOTARIAL
NOTARIES
NOTARISE
NOTARISED
NOTARISES
NOTARIZE
NOTARIZED
NOTARIZES
NOTARY
NOTATE
NOTATED
NOTATES
NOTATING
NOTATION
NOTATIONS
NOTATOR
NOTATORS
NOTCH
NOTCHBACK
NOTCHED
NOTCHEL
NOTCHELED
NOTCHELS
NOTCHER
NOTCHERS
NOTCHES
NOTCHIER
NOTCHIEST
NOTCHING
NOTCHINGS
NOTCHY
NOTE
NOTEBANDI
NOTEBOOK
NOTEBOOKS
NOTECARD
NOTECARDS
NOTECASE
NOTECASES
NOTED
NOTEDLY
NOTEDNESS
NOTELESS
NOTELET
NOTELETS
NOTEPAD
NOTEPADS
NOTEPAPER
NOTER

NOTERS
NOTES
NOTHER
NOTHING
NOTHINGS
NOTICE
NOTICED
NOTICER
NOTICERS
NOTICES
NOTICING
NOTIFIED
NOTIFIER
NOTIFIERS
NOTIFIES
NOTIFY
NOTIFYING
NOTING
NOTION
NOTIONAL
NOTIONIST
NOTIONS
NOTITIA
NOTITIAE
NOTITIAS
NOTOCHORD
NOTORIETY
NOTORIOUS
NOTORNIS
NOTOUR
NOTT
NOTTURNI
NOTTURNO
NOTUM
NOUGAT
NOUGATINE
NOUGATS
NOUGHT
NOUGHTIES
NOUGHTS
NOUL
NOULD
NOULDE
NOULE
NOULES
NOULS
NOUMENA
NOUMENAL
NOUMENON
NOUN
NOUNAL
NOUNALLY
NOUNIER
NOUNIEST
NOUNLESS
NOUNS
NOUNY
NOUP
NOUPS
NOURICE
NOURICES
NOURISH
NOURISHED
NOURISHER
NOURISHES
NOURITURE
NOURSLE
NOURSLED
NOURSLES
NOURSLING
NOUS
NOUSELL
NOUSELLED
NOUSELLS
NOUSES
NOUSLE
NOUSLED
NOUSLES
NOUSLING
NOUT
NOUVEAU
NOUVEAUX
NOUVELLE
NOUVELLES
NOVA
NOVAE
NOVALIA
NOVALIKE
NOVAS
NOVATE
NOVATED
NOVATES
NOVATING
NOVATION
NOVATIONS
NOVEL
NOVELDOM
NOVELDOMS
NOVELESE
NOVELESES
NOVELETTE
NOVELISE
NOVELISED
NOVELISER
NOVELISES
NOVELISH
NOVELISM
NOVELISMS
NOVELIST
NOVELISTS
NOVELIZE
NOVELIZED
NOVELIZER
NOVELIZES
NOVELLA
NOVELLAE
NOVELLAS
NOVELLE
NOVELLY
NOVELS
NOVELTIES
NOVELTY
NOVEMBER
NOVEMBERS
NOVENA
NOVENAE
NOVENARY
NOVENAS
NOVENNIAL
NOVERCAL
NOVERINT
NOVERINTS
NOVICE
NOVICES
NOVICHOK
NOVICHOKS
NOVICIATE
NOVITIATE
NOVITIES
NOVITY
NOVOCAINE
NOVODAMUS
NOVUM
NOVUMS
NOW
NOWADAYS
NOWAY
NOWAYS
NOWCAST
NOWCASTS
NOWED
NOWHENCE
NOWHERE
NOWHERES
NOWHITHER
NOWISE
NOWL
NOWLS
NOWN
NOWNESS
NOWNESSES
NOWS
NOWT
NOWTIER
NOWTIEST
NOWTS
NOWTY
NOWY
NOX
NOXAL
NOXES
NOXIOUS
NOXIOUSLY
NOY
NOYADE
NOYADES
NOYANCE
NOYANCES
NOYAU
NOYAUS
NOYAUX
NOYED
NOYES
NOYESES
NOYING
NOYOUS
NOYS
NOYSOME
NOZZER
NOZZERS
NOZZLE
NOZZLES
NTH
NU
NUANCE
NUANCED
NUANCES
NUANCING
NUB
NUBBED
NUBBER
NUBBERS
NUBBIER
NUBBIEST
NUBBIN
NUBBINESS
NUBBING
NUBBINGS
NUBBINS
NUBBLE
NUBBLED
NUBBLES
NUBBLIER
NUBBLIEST
NUBBLING
NUBBLY
NUBBY
NUBECULA
NUBECULAE
NUBIA
NUBIAS
NUBIFORM
NUBILE
NUBILITY
NUBILOSE
NUBILOUS
NUBS
NUBUCK
NUBUCKS
NUCELLAR
NUCELLI
NUCELLUS
NUCHA
NUCHAE
NUCHAL
NUCHALS
NUCLEAL
NUCLEAR
NUCLEASE
NUCLEASES

NUCLEATE
NUCLEATED
NUCLEATES
NUCLEATOR
NUCLEI
NUCLEIC
NUCLEIDE
NUCLEIDES
NUCLEIN
NUCLEINIC
NUCLEINS
NUCLEOID
NUCLEOIDS
NUCLEOLAR
NUCLEOLE
NUCLEOLES
NUCLEOLI
NUCLEOLUS
NUCLEON
NUCLEONIC
NUCLEONS
NUCLEUS
NUCLEUSES
NUCLIDE
NUCLIDES
NUCLIDIC
NUCULE
NUCULES
NUDATION
NUDATIONS
NUDDIES
NUDDY
NUDE
NUDELY
NUDENESS
NUDER
NUDES
NUDEST
NUDGE
NUDGED
NUDGER
NUDGERS
NUDGES
NUDGING
NUDICAUL
NUDIE
NUDIES
NUDISM
NUDISMS
NUDIST
NUDISTS
NUDITIES
NUDITY
NUDNICK
NUDNICKS
NUDNIK
NUDNIKS
NUDZH
NUDZHED
NUDZHES
NUDZHING
NUFF
NUFFIN
NUFFINS
NUFFS
NUG
NUGAE
NUGATORY
NUGGAR
NUGGARS
NUGGET
NUGGETED
NUGGETIER
NUGGETING
NUGGETS
NUGGETTED
NUGGETY
NUGS
NUISANCE
NUISANCER
NUISANCES
NUKE
NUKED
NUKES
NUKING
NULL
NULLA
NULLAH
NULLAHS
NULLAS
NULLED
NULLIFIED
NULLIFIER
NULLIFIES
NULLIFY
NULLING
NULLINGS
NULLIPARA
NULLIPORE
NULLITIES
NULLITY
NULLNESS
NULLS
NUMB
NUMBAT
NUMBATS
NUMBED
NUMBER
NUMBERED
NUMBERER
NUMBERERS
NUMBERING
NUMBERS
NUMBEST
NUMBFISH
NUMBHEAD
NUMBHEADS
NUMBING
NUMBINGLY
NUMBLES
NUMBLY
NUMBNESS
NUMBNUT
NUMBNUTS
NUMBS
NUMBSKULL
NUMCHUCK
NUMCHUCKS
NUMDAH
NUMDAHS
NUMEN
NUMERABLE
NUMERABLY
NUMERACY
NUMERAIRE
NUMERAL
NUMERALLY
NUMERALS
NUMERARY
NUMERATE
NUMERATED
NUMERATES
NUMERATOR
NUMERIC
NUMERICAL
NUMERICS
NUMEROUS
NUMINA
NUMINOUS
NUMMARY
NUMMIER
NUMMIEST
NUMMULAR
NUMMULARY
NUMMULINE
NUMMULITE
NUMMY
NUMNAH
NUMNAHS
NUMPKIN
NUMPKINS
NUMPTIES
NUMPTY
NUMSKULL
NUMSKULLS
NUN
NUNATAK
NUNATAKER
NUNATAKS
NUNCHAKU
NUNCHAKUS
NUNCHEON
NUNCHEONS
NUNCHUCK
NUNCHUCKS
NUNCHUK
NUNCHUKS
NUNCIO
NUNCIOS
NUNCLE
NUNCLES
NUNCUPATE
NUNDINAL
NUNDINALS
NUNDINE
NUNDINES
NUNHOOD
NUNHOODS
NUNLIKE
NUNNATION
NUNNERIES
NUNNERY
NUNNISH
NUNNY
NUNS
NUNSHIP
NUNSHIPS
NUPTIAL
NUPTIALLY
NUPTIALS
NUR
NURAGHE
NURAGHI
NURAGHIC
NURD
NURDIER
NURDIEST
NURDISH
NURDLE
NURDLED
NURDLES
NURDLING
NURDS
NURDY
NURHAG
NURHAGS
NURL
NURLED
NURLING
NURLS
NURR
NURRS
NURS
NURSE
NURSED
NURSELIKE
NURSELING
NURSEMAID
NURSER
NURSERIES
NURSERS
NURSERY
NURSES
NURSING
NURSINGS
NURSLE
NURSLED
NURSLES
NURSLING
NURSLINGS

N

NURTURAL
NURTURANT
NURTURE
NURTURED
NURTURER
NURTURERS
NURTURES
NURTURING
NUS
NUT
NUTANT
NUTARIAN
NUTARIANS
NUTATE
NUTATED
NUTATES
NUTATING
NUTATION
NUTATIONS
NUTBAR
NUTBARS
NUTBROWN
NUTBUTTER
NUTCASE
NUTCASES
NUTGALL
NUTGALLS
NUTGRASS
NUTHATCH
NUTHIN
NUTHOUSE
NUTHOUSES
NUTJOB
NUTJOBBER
NUTJOBS
NUTLET
NUTLETS
NUTLIKE
NUTLOAF
NUTLOAVES
NUTMEAL
NUTMEALS
NUTMEAT
NUTMEATS
NUTMEG
NUTMEGGED
NUTMEGGY
NUTMEGS
NUTPECKER
NUTPICK
NUTPICKS
NUTRIA
NUTRIAS
NUTRIENT
NUTRIENTS
NUTRIMENT
NUTRITION
NUTRITIVE
NUTS
NUTSEDGE
NUTSEDGES
NUTSHELL
NUTSHELLS
NUTSIER
NUTSIEST
NUTSO
NUTSOS
NUTSY
NUTTED
NUTTER
NUTTERIES
NUTTERS
NUTTERY
NUTTIER
NUTTIEST
NUTTILY
NUTTINESS
NUTTING
NUTTINGS
NUTTY
NUTWOOD
NUTWOODS
NUZZER
NUZZERS
NUZZLE
NUZZLED
NUZZLER
NUZZLERS
NUZZLES
NUZZLING
NY
NYAFF
NYAFFED
NYAFFING
NYAFFS
NYAH
NYALA
NYALAS
NYANZA
NYANZAS
NYAOPE
NYAOPES
NYAS
NYASES
NYBBLE
NYBBLES
NYCTALOPE
NYCTALOPS
NYE
NYED
NYES
NYING
NYLGHAI
NYLGHAIS
NYLGHAU
NYLGHAUS
NYLON
NYLONED
NYLONS
NYM
NYMPH
NYMPHA
NYMPHAE
NYMPHAEA
NYMPHAEAS
NYMPHAEUM
NYMPHAL
NYMPHALID
NYMPHEAN
NYMPHED
NYMPHET
NYMPHETIC
NYMPHETS
NYMPHETTE
NYMPHIC
NYMPHICAL
NYMPHING
NYMPHISH
NYMPHLIER
NYMPHLIKE
NYMPHLY
NYMPHO
NYMPHOS
NYMPHS
NYS
NYSSA
NYSSAS
NYSTAGMIC
NYSTAGMUS
NYSTATIN
NYSTATINS

O

OAF
OAFISH
OAFISHLY
OAFS
OAK
OAKED
OAKEN
OAKENSHAW
OAKER
OAKERS
OAKIER
OAKIES
OAKIEST
OAKINESS
OAKLEAF
OAKLEAVES
OAKLIKE
OAKLING
OAKLINGS
OAKMOSS
OAKMOSSES
OAKS
OAKUM
OAKUMS
OAKWOOD
OAKWOODS
OAKY
OANSHAGH
OANSHAGHS
OAR
OARAGE
OARAGES
OARED
OARFISH
OARFISHES
OARIER
OARIEST
OARING
OARLESS
OARLIKE
OARLOCK
OARLOCKS
OARS
OARSMAN
OARSMEN
OARSWOMAN
OARSWOMEN
OARWEED
OARWEEDS
OARY
OASES
OASIS
OAST
OASTHOUSE
OASTS
OAT
OATCAKE
OATCAKES
OATEN
OATER
OATERS
OATH
OATHABLE
OATHS
OATIER
OATIEST
OATLIKE
OATMEAL
OATMEALS
OATS
OATY
OAVES
OB
OBA
OBANG
OBANGS
OBAS
OBBLIGATI
OBBLIGATO
OBCONIC
OBCONICAL
OBCORDATE
OBDURACY
OBDURATE
OBDURATED
OBDURATES
OBDURE
OBDURED
OBDURES
OBDURING
OBE
OBEAH
OBEAHED
OBEAHING
OBEAHISM
OBEAHISMS
OBEAHS
OBECHE
OBECHES
OBEDIENCE
OBEDIENT
OBEISANCE
OBEISANT
OBEISM
OBEISMS
OBELI
OBELIA
OBELIAS
OBELION
OBELISCAL
OBELISE
OBELISED
OBELISES
OBELISING
OBELISK
OBELISKS
OBELISM
OBELISMS
OBELIZE
OBELIZED
OBELIZES
OBELIZING
OBELUS
OBENTO
OBENTOS
OBES
OBESE
OBESELY
OBESENESS
OBESER
OBESEST
OBESITIES
OBESITY
OBESOGEN
OBESOGENS
OBEY
OBEYABLE
OBEYED
OBEYER
OBEYERS
OBEYING
OBEYS
OBFUSCATE
OBI
OBIA
OBIAS
OBIED
OBIING
OBIISM
OBIISMS
OBIIT
OBIS
OBIT
OBITAL
OBITER
OBITS
OBITUAL
OBITUARY
OBJECT
OBJECTED
OBJECTIFY
OBJECTING
OBJECTION
OBJECTIVE
OBJECTOR
OBJECTORS
OBJECTS
OBJET
OBJETS
OBJURE
OBJURED
OBJURES
OBJURGATE
OBJURING
OBLAST
OBLASTI
OBLASTS
OBLATE
OBLATELY
OBLATES
OBLATION
OBLATIONS
OBLATORY
OBLIGABLE
OBLIGANT
OBLIGANTS
OBLIGATE
OBLIGATED
OBLIGATES
OBLIGATI
OBLIGATO
OBLIGATOR
OBLIGATOS
OBLIGE
OBLIGED
OBLIGEE
OBLIGEES
OBLIGER
OBLIGERS
OBLIGES
OBLIGING
OBLIGOR
OBLIGORS
OBLIQUE
OBLIQUED
OBLIQUELY
OBLIQUER
OBLIQUES
OBLIQUEST
OBLIQUID

O

OBLIQUING
OBLIQUITY
OBLIVION
OBLIVIONS
OBLIVIOUS
OBLONG
OBLONGLY
OBLONGS
OBLOQUIAL
OBLOQUIES
OBLOQUY
OBNOXIOUS
OBO
OBOE
OBOES
OBOIST
OBOISTS
OBOL
OBOLARY
OBOLE
OBOLES
OBOLI
OBOLS
OBOLUS
OBOS
OBOVATE
OBOVATELY
OBOVOID
OBREPTION
OBS
OBSCENE
OBSCENELY
OBSCENER
OBSCENEST
OBSCENITY
OBSCURANT
OBSCURE
OBSCURED
OBSCURELY
OBSCURER
OBSCURERS
OBSCURES
OBSCUREST
OBSCURING
OBSCURITY
OBSECRATE
OBSEQUENT
OBSEQUIAL
OBSEQUIE
OBSEQUIES
OBSEQUY
OBSERVANT
OBSERVE
OBSERVED
OBSERVER
OBSERVERS
OBSERVES
OBSERVING
OBSESS
OBSESSED
OBSESSES
OBSESSING
OBSESSION
OBSESSIVE
OBSESSOR
OBSESSORS
OBSIDIAN
OBSIDIANS
OBSIGN
OBSIGNATE
OBSIGNED
OBSIGNING
OBSIGNS
OBSOLESCE
OBSOLETE
OBSOLETED
OBSOLETES
OBSTACLE
OBSTACLES
OBSTETRIC
OBSTINACY
OBSTINATE
OBSTRUCT
OBSTRUCTS
OBSTRUENT
OBTAIN
OBTAINED
OBTAINER
OBTAINERS
OBTAINING
OBTAINS
OBTECT
OBTECTED
OBTEMPER
OBTEMPERS
OBTEND
OBTENDED
OBTENDING
OBTENDS
OBTENTION
OBTEST
OBTESTED
OBTESTING
OBTESTS
OBTRUDE
OBTRUDED
OBTRUDER
OBTRUDERS
OBTRUDES
OBTRUDING
OBTRUSION
OBTRUSIVE
OBTUND
OBTUNDED
OBTUNDENT
OBTUNDING
OBTUNDITY
OBTUNDS
OBTURATE
OBTURATED
OBTURATES
OBTURATOR
OBTUSE
OBTUSELY
OBTUSER
OBTUSEST
OBTUSITY
OBUMBRATE
OBVENTION
OBVERSE
OBVERSELY
OBVERSES
OBVERSION
OBVERT
OBVERTED
OBVERTING
OBVERTS
OBVIABLE
OBVIATE
OBVIATED
OBVIATES
OBVIATING
OBVIATION
OBVIATOR
OBVIATORS
OBVIOUS
OBVIOUSLY
OBVOLUTE
OBVOLUTED
OBVOLVENT
OBVS
OCA
OCARINA
OCARINAS
OCAS
OCCAM
OCCAMIES
OCCAMS
OCCAMY
OCCASION
OCCASIONS
OCCIDENT
OCCIDENTS
OCCIES
OCCIPITA
OCCIPITAL
OCCIPUT
OCCIPUTS
OCCLUDE
OCCLUDED
OCCLUDENT
OCCLUDER
OCCLUDERS
OCCLUDES
OCCLUDING
OCCLUSAL
OCCLUSION
OCCLUSIVE
OCCLUSOR
OCCLUSORS
OCCULT
OCCULTED
OCCULTER
OCCULTERS
OCCULTING
OCCULTISM
OCCULTIST
OCCULTLY
OCCULTS
OCCUPANCE
OCCUPANCY
OCCUPANT
OCCUPANTS
OCCUPATE
OCCUPATED
OCCUPATES
OCCUPIED
OCCUPIER
OCCUPIERS
OCCUPIES
OCCUPY
OCCUPYING
OCCUR
OCCURRED
OCCURRENT
OCCURRING
OCCURS
OCCY
OCEAN
OCEANARIA
OCEANAUT
OCEANAUTS
OCEANIC
OCEANID
OCEANIDES
OCEANIDS
OCEANS
OCEANSIDE
OCEANVIEW
OCEANWARD
OCELLAR
OCELLATE
OCELLATED
OCELLI
OCELLUS
OCELOID
OCELOT
OCELOTS
OCH
OCHE
OCHER
OCHERED
OCHERIER
OCHERIEST
OCHERING
OCHERISH
OCHEROID
OCHEROUS
OCHERS
OCHERY

O

OCHES
OCHIDORE
OCHIDORES
OCHLOCRAT
OCHONE
OCHRE
OCHREA
OCHREAE
OCHREAS
OCHREATE
OCHRED
OCHREOUS
OCHRES
OCHREY
OCHRIER
OCHRIEST
OCHRING
OCHROID
OCHROUS
OCHRY
OCICAT
OCICATS
OCKER
OCKERISM
OCKERISMS
OCKERS
OCKODOLS
OCOTILLO
OCOTILLOS
OCREA
OCREAE
OCREAS
OCREATE
OCTA
OCTACHORD
OCTAD
OCTADIC
OCTADS
OCTAGON
OCTAGONAL
OCTAGONS
OCTAHEDRA
OCTAL
OCTALS
OCTAMETER
OCTAN
OCTANE
OCTANES
OCTANGLE
OCTANGLES
OCTANOL
OCTANOLS
OCTANS
OCTANT
OCTANTAL
OCTANTS
OCTAPLA
OCTAPLAS
OCTAPLOID
OCTAPODIC
OCTAPODY
OCTARCHY
OCTAROON
OCTAROONS
OCTAS
OCTASTICH
OCTASTYLE
OCTAVAL
OCTAVE
OCTAVES
OCTAVO
OCTAVOS
OCTENNIAL
OCTET
OCTETS
OCTETT
OCTETTE
OCTETTES
OCTETTS
OCTILLION
OCTOFID
OCTOHEDRA
OCTONARII
OCTONARY
OCTOPI
OCTOPLOID
OCTOPOD
OCTOPODAN
OCTOPODES
OCTOPODS
OCTOPOID
OCTOPUS
OCTOPUSES
OCTOPUSH
OCTOROON
OCTOROONS
OCTOSTYLE
OCTOTHORP
OCTROI
OCTROIS
OCTUOR
OCTUORS
OCTUPLE
OCTUPLED
OCTUPLES
OCTUPLET
OCTUPLETS
OCTUPLEX
OCTUPLING
OCTUPLY
OCTYL
OCTYLS
OCULAR
OCULARIST
OCULARLY
OCULARS
OCULATE
OCULATED
OCULI
OCULIST
OCULISTS
OCULUS
OD
ODA
ODAH
ODAHS
ODAL
ODALIQUE
ODALIQUES
ODALISK
ODALISKS
ODALISQUE
ODALLER
ODALLERS
ODALS
ODAS
ODD
ODDBALL
ODDBALLS
ODDER
ODDEST
ODDISH
ODDITIES
ODDITY
ODDLY
ODDMENT
ODDMENTS
ODDNESS
ODDNESSES
ODDS
ODDSMAKER
ODDSMAN
ODDSMEN
ODE
ODEA
ODEON
ODEONS
ODES
ODEUM
ODEUMS
ODIC
ODIFEROUS
ODIOUS
ODIOUSLY
ODISM
ODISMS
ODIST
ODISTS
ODIUM
ODIUMS
ODOGRAPH
ODOGRAPHS
ODOMETER
ODOMETERS
ODOMETRY
ODONATA
ODONATE
ODONATES
ODONATIST
ODONTALGY
ODONTIC
ODONTIST
ODONTISTS
ODONTOID
ODONTOIDS
ODONTOMA
ODONTOMAS
ODOR
ODORANT
ODORANTS
ODORATE
ODORED
ODORFUL
ODORISE
ODORISED
ODORISER
ODORISERS
ODORISES
ODORISING
ODORIZE
ODORIZED
ODORIZER
ODORIZERS
ODORIZES
ODORIZING
ODORLESS
ODOROUS
ODOROUSLY
ODORS
ODOUR
ODOURED
ODOURFUL
ODOURLESS
ODOURS
ODS
ODSO
ODYL
ODYLE
ODYLES
ODYLISM
ODYLISMS
ODYLS
ODYSSEAN
ODYSSEY
ODYSSEYS
ODZOOKS
OE
OECIST
OECISTS
OECOLOGIC
OECOLOGY
OECUMENIC
OEDEMA
OEDEMAS
OEDEMATA
OEDIPAL
OEDIPALLY
OEDIPEAN
OEDOMETER
OEILLADE

OEILLADES
OENANTHIC
OENOLOGY
OENOMANCY
OENOMANIA
OENOMEL
OENOMELS
OENOMETER
OENOPHIL
OENOPHILE
OENOPHILS
OENOPHILY
OENOTHERA
OERLIKON
OERLIKONS
OERSTED
OERSTEDS
OES
OESOPHAGI
OESTRAL
OESTRIN
OESTRINS
OESTRIOL
OESTRIOLS
OESTROGEN
OESTRONE
OESTRONES
OESTROUS
OESTRUAL
OESTRUM
OESTRUMS
OESTRUS
OESTRUSES
OEUVRE
OEUVRES
OF
OFAY
OFAYS
OFF
OFFA
OFFAL
OFFALS
OFFBEAT
OFFBEATS
OFFCAST
OFFCASTS
OFFCUT
OFFCUTS
OFFED
OFFENCE
OFFENCES
OFFEND
OFFENDED
OFFENDER
OFFENDERS
OFFENDING
OFFENDS
OFFENSE
OFFENSES
OFFENSIVE
OFFER
OFFERABLE
OFFERED
OFFEREE
OFFEREES
OFFERER
OFFERERS
OFFERING
OFFERINGS
OFFEROR
OFFERORS
OFFERS
OFFERTORY
OFFHAND
OFFHANDED
OFFICE
OFFICER
OFFICERED
OFFICERS
OFFICES
OFFICIAL
OFFICIALS
OFFICIANT
OFFICIARY
OFFICIATE
OFFICINAL
OFFICIOUS
OFFIE
OFFIES
OFFING
OFFINGS
OFFISH
OFFISHLY
OFFKEY
OFFLINE
OFFLOAD
OFFLOADED
OFFLOADS
OFFPEAK
OFFPRINT
OFFPRINTS
OFFPUT
OFFPUTS
OFFRAMP
OFFRAMPS
OFFS
OFFSADDLE
OFFSCREEN
OFFSCUM
OFFSCUMS
OFFSEASON
OFFSET
OFFSETS
OFFSHOOT
OFFSHOOTS
OFFSHORE
OFFSHORED
OFFSHORES
OFFSIDE
OFFSIDER
OFFSIDERS
OFFSIDES
OFFSPRING
OFFSTAGE
OFFSTAGES
OFFTAKE
OFFTAKES
OFFTRACK
OFFY
OFLAG
OFLAGS
OFT
OFTEN
OFTENER
OFTENEST
OFTENNESS
OFTER
OFTEST
OFTTIMES
OGAM
OGAMIC
OGAMS
OGANESSON
OGDOAD
OGDOADS
OGEE
OGEED
OGEES
OGGIN
OGGINS
OGHAM
OGHAMIC
OGHAMIST
OGHAMISTS
OGHAMS
OGIVAL
OGIVE
OGIVES
OGLE
OGLED
OGLER
OGLERS
OGLES
OGLING
OGLINGS
OGMIC
OGRE
OGREISH
OGREISHLY
OGREISM
OGREISMS
OGRES
OGRESS
OGRESSES
OGRISH
OGRISHLY
OGRISM
OGRISMS
OH
OHED
OHIA
OHIAS
OHING
OHM
OHMAGE
OHMAGES
OHMIC
OHMICALLY
OHMMETER
OHMMETERS
OHMS
OHO
OHONE
OHS
OI
OIDIA
OIDIOID
OIDIUM
OIK
OIKIST
OIKISTS
OIKS
OIL
OILBIRD
OILBIRDS
OILCAMP
OILCAMPS
OILCAN
OILCANS
OILCLOTH
OILCLOTHS
OILCUP
OILCUPS
OILED
OILER
OILERIES
OILERS
OILERY
OILFIELD
OILFIELDS
OILFIRED
OILGAS
OILGASES
OILHOLE
OILHOLES
OILIER
OILIEST
OILILY
OILINESS
OILING
OILLET
OILLETS
OILMAN
OILMEN
OILNUT
OILNUTS
OILPAN
OILPANS
OILPAPER
OILPAPERS

OILPROOF
OILS
OILSEED
OILSEEDS
OILSKIN
OILSKINS
OILSTONE
OILSTONES
OILTIGHT
OILWAY
OILWAYS
OILY
OINK
OINKED
OINKING
OINKS
OINOLOGY
OINOMEL
OINOMELS
OINT
OINTED
OINTING
OINTMENT
OINTMENTS
OINTS
OIS
OITICICA
OITICICAS
OJIME
OJIMES
OK
OKA
OKAPI
OKAPIS
OKAS
OKAY
OKAYED
OKAYING
OKAYS
OKE
OKEH
OKEHS
OKES
OKEYDOKE
OKEYDOKEY
OKIMONO
OKIMONOS
OKRA
OKRAS
OKTA
OKTAS
OLD
OLDE
OLDEN
OLDENED
OLDENING
OLDENS
OLDER
OLDEST
OLDIE
OLDIES
OLDISH
OLDNESS
OLDNESSES
OLDS
OLDSQUAW
OLDSQUAWS
OLDSTER
OLDSTERS
OLDSTYLE
OLDSTYLES
OLDWIFE
OLDWIVES
OLDY
OLE
OLEA
OLEACEOUS
OLEANDER
OLEANDERS
OLEARIA
OLEARIAS
OLEASTER
OLEASTERS
OLEATE
OLEATES
OLECRANAL
OLECRANON
OLEFIANT
OLEFIN
OLEFINE
OLEFINES
OLEFINIC
OLEFINS
OLEIC
OLEIN
OLEINE
OLEINES
OLEINS
OLENT
OLEO
OLEOGRAPH
OLEORESIN
OLEOS
OLES
OLESTRA
OLESTRAS
OLEUM
OLEUMS
OLFACT
OLFACTED
OLFACTING
OLFACTION
OLFACTIVE
OLFACTORY
OLFACTS
OLIBANUM
OLIBANUMS
OLICOOK
OLICOOKS
OLID
OLIGAEMIA
OLIGAEMIC
OLIGARCH
OLIGARCHS
OLIGARCHY
OLIGEMIA
OLIGEMIAS
OLIGEMIC
OLIGIST
OLIGISTS
OLIGOCENE
OLIGOGENE
OLIGOMER
OLIGOMERS
OLIGOPOLY
OLIGURIA
OLIGURIAS
OLIGURIC
OLINGO
OLINGOS
OLINGUITO
OLIO
OLIOS
OLIPHANT
OLIPHANTS
OLITORIES
OLITORY
OLIVARY
OLIVE
OLIVENITE
OLIVER
OLIVERS
OLIVES
OLIVET
OLIVETS
OLIVEWOOD
OLIVINE
OLIVINES
OLIVINIC
OLLA
OLLAMH
OLLAMHS
OLLAS
OLLAV
OLLAVS
OLLER
OLLERS
OLLIE
OLLIED
OLLIEING
OLLIES
OLM
OLMS
OLOGIES
OLOGIST
OLOGISTS
OLOGOAN
OLOGOANED
OLOGOANS
OLOGY
OLOLIUQUI
OLOROSO
OLOROSOS
OLPAE
OLPE
OLPES
OLYCOOK
OLYCOOKS
OLYKOEK
OLYKOEKS
OLYMPIAD
OLYMPIADS
OLYMPICS
OM
OMA
OMADHAUN
OMADHAUNS
OMAS
OMASA
OMASAL
OMASUM
OMBER
OMBERS
OMBRE
OMBRELLA
OMBRELLAS
OMBRES
OMBROPHIL
OMBU
OMBUDSMAN
OMBUDSMEN
OMBUS
OMEGA
OMEGAS
OMELET
OMELETS
OMELETTE
OMELETTES
OMEN
OMENED
OMENING
OMENS
OMENTA
OMENTAL
OMENTUM
OMENTUMS
OMER
OMERS
OMERTA
OMERTAS
OMICRON
OMICRONS
OMIGOD
OMIKRON
OMIKRONS
OMINOUS
OMINOUSLY
OMISSIBLE
OMISSION
OMISSIONS

OMISSIVE
OMIT
OMITS
OMITTANCE
OMITTED
OMITTER
OMITTERS
OMITTING
OMLAH
OMLAHS
OMMATEA
OMMATEUM
OMMATIDIA
OMNEITIES
OMNEITY
OMNIANA
OMNIANAS
OMNIARCH
OMNIARCHS
OMNIBUS
OMNIBUSES
OMNIETIES
OMNIETY
OMNIFIC
OMNIFIED
OMNIFIES
OMNIFORM
OMNIFY
OMNIFYING
OMNIMODE
OMNIRANGE
OMNIUM
OMNIUMS
OMNIVORA
OMNIVORE
OMNIVORES
OMNIVORY
OMOHYOID
OMOHYOIDS
OMOPHAGIA
OMOPHAGIC
OMOPHAGY
OMOPHORIA
OMOPLATE
OMOPLATES
OMOV
OMOVS
OMPHACITE
OMPHALI
OMPHALIC
OMPHALOI
OMPHALOID
OMPHALOS
OMRAH
OMRAHS
OMS
ON
ONAGER
ONAGERS
ONAGRI
ONANISM
ONANISMS
ONANIST
ONANISTIC
ONANISTS
ONBEAT
ONBEATS
ONBOARD
ONBOARDED
ONBOARDS
ONCE
ONCER
ONCERS
ONCES
ONCET
ONCIDIUM
ONCIDIUMS
ONCOGEN
ONCOGENE
ONCOGENES
ONCOGENIC
ONCOGENS
ONCOLOGIC
ONCOLOGY
ONCOLYSES
ONCOLYSIS
ONCOLYTIC
ONCOME
ONCOMES
ONCOMETER
ONCOMICE
ONCOMING
ONCOMINGS
ONCOMOUSE
ONCOST
ONCOSTMAN
ONCOSTMEN
ONCOSTS
ONCOTOMY
ONCOVIRUS
ONCUS
ONDATRA
ONDATRAS
ONDINE
ONDINES
ONDING
ONDINGS
ONDOGRAM
ONDOGRAMS
ONDOGRAPH
ONE
ONEFOLD
ONEIRIC
ONELY
ONENESS
ONENESSES
ONER
ONERIER
ONERIEST
ONEROUS
ONEROUSLY
ONERS
ONERY
ONES
ONESELF
ONESIE
ONESIES
ONETIME
ONEYER
ONEYERS
ONEYRE
ONEYRES
ONFALL
ONFALLS
ONFLOW
ONFLOWS
ONGAONGA
ONGAONGAS
ONGOING
ONGOINGS
ONIE
ONION
ONIONED
ONIONIER
ONIONIEST
ONIONING
ONIONS
ONIONSKIN
ONIONY
ONIRIC
ONISCOID
ONIUM
ONIUMS
ONKUS
ONLAY
ONLAYS
ONLIEST
ONLINE
ONLINER
ONLINERS
ONLOAD
ONLOADED
ONLOADING
ONLOADS
ONLOOKER
ONLOOKERS
ONLOOKING
ONLY
ONNED
ONNING
ONO
ONOMAST
ONOMASTIC
ONOMASTS
ONOS
ONRUSH
ONRUSHES
ONRUSHING
ONS
ONSCREEN
ONSET
ONSETS
ONSETTER
ONSETTERS
ONSETTING
ONSHORE
ONSHORING
ONSIDE
ONSIDES
ONSLAUGHT
ONST
ONSTAGE
ONSTEAD
ONSTEADS
ONSTREAM
ONTIC
ONTICALLY
ONTO
ONTOGENIC
ONTOGENY
ONTOLOGIC
ONTOLOGY
ONUS
ONUSES
ONWARD
ONWARDLY
ONWARDS
ONY
ONYCHA
ONYCHAS
ONYCHIA
ONYCHIAS
ONYCHITE
ONYCHITES
ONYCHITIS
ONYCHIUM
ONYCHIUMS
ONYMOUS
ONYX
ONYXES
OO
OOBIT
OOBITS
OOCYST
OOCYSTS
OOCYTE
OOCYTES
OODLES
OODLINS
OOF
OOFIER
OOFIEST
OOFS
OOFTISH
OOFTISHES
OOFY
OOGAMETE
OOGAMETES
OOGAMIES
OOGAMOUS

OOGAMY
OOGENESES
OOGENESIS
OOGENETIC
OOGENIES
OOGENY
OOGONIA
OOGONIAL
OOGONIUM
OOGONIUMS
OOH
OOHED
OOHING
OOHINGS
OOHS
OOIDAL
OOLACHAN
OOLACHANS
OOLAKAN
OOLAKANS
OOLICHAN
OOLICHANS
OOLITE
OOLITES
OOLITH
OOLITHS
OOLITIC
OOLOGIC
OOLOGICAL
OOLOGIES
OOLOGIST
OOLOGISTS
OOLOGY
OOLONG
OOLONGS
OOM
OOMIAC
OOMIACK
OOMIACKS
OOMIACS
OOMIAK
OOMIAKS
OOMPAH
OOMPAHED
OOMPAHING
OOMPAHPAH
OOMPAHS
OOMPH
OOMPHS
OOMS
OOMYCETE
OOMYCETES
OON
OONS
OONT
OONTS
OOP
OOPED
OOPHORON
OOPHORONS
OOPHYTE
OOPHYTES
OOPHYTIC
OOPING
OOPS
OOR
OORALI
OORALIS
OORIAL
OORIALS
OORIE
OORIER
OORIEST
OOS
OOSE
OOSES
OOSIER
OOSIEST
OOSPERM
OOSPERMS
OOSPHERE
OOSPHERES
OOSPORE
OOSPORES
OOSPORIC
OOSPOROUS
OOSY
OOT
OOTHECA
OOTHECAE
OOTHECAL
OOTID
OOTIDS
OOTS
OOZE
OOZED
OOZES
OOZIER
OOZIEST
OOZILY
OOZINESS
OOZING
OOZY
OP
OPA
OPACIFIED
OPACIFIER
OPACIFIES
OPACIFY
OPACITIES
OPACITY
OPACOUS
OPAH
OPAHS
OPAL
OPALED
OPALESCE
OPALESCED
OPALESCES
OPALINE
OPALINES
OPALISED
OPALIZED
OPALS
OPAQUE
OPAQUED
OPAQUELY
OPAQUER
OPAQUES
OPAQUEST
OPAQUING
OPAS
OPCODE
OPCODES
OPE
OPED
OPEN
OPENABLE
OPENCAST
OPENED
OPENER
OPENERS
OPENEST
OPENING
OPENINGS
OPENLY
OPENNESS
OPENS
OPENSIDE
OPENSIDES
OPENWORK
OPENWORKS
OPEPE
OPEPES
OPERA
OPERABLE
OPERABLY
OPERAGOER
OPERAND
OPERANDS
OPERANT
OPERANTLY
OPERANTS
OPERAS
OPERATE
OPERATED
OPERATES
OPERATIC
OPERATICS
OPERATING
OPERATION
OPERATISE
OPERATIVE
OPERATIZE
OPERATOR
OPERATORS
OPERCELE
OPERCELES
OPERCULA
OPERCULAR
OPERCULE
OPERCULES
OPERCULUM
OPERETTA
OPERETTAS
OPERON
OPERONS
OPEROSE
OPEROSELY
OPEROSITY
OPES
OPGEFOK
OPHIDIAN
OPHIDIANS
OPHIOLITE
OPHIOLOGY
OPHITE
OPHITES
OPHITIC
OPHIURA
OPHIURAN
OPHIURANS
OPHIURAS
OPHIURID
OPHIURIDS
OPHIUROID
OPIATE
OPIATED
OPIATES
OPIATING
OPIFICER
OPIFICERS
OPINABLE
OPINE
OPINED
OPINES
OPING
OPINICUS
OPINING
OPINION
OPINIONED
OPINIONS
OPIOID
OPIOIDS
OPIUM
OPIUMISM
OPIUMISMS
OPIUMS
OPOBALSAM
OPODELDOC
OPOPANAX
OPORICE
OPORICES
OPOSSUM
OPOSSUMS
OPPIDAN
OPPIDANS
OPPILANT
OPPILATE
OPPILATED

OPPILATES
OPPO
OPPONENCY
OPPONENS
OPPONENT
OPPONENTS
OPPORTUNE
OPPOS
OPPOSABLE
OPPOSABLY
OPPOSE
OPPOSED
OPPOSER
OPPOSERS
OPPOSES
OPPOSING
OPPOSITE
OPPOSITES
OPPRESS
OPPRESSED
OPPRESSES
OPPRESSOR
OPPUGN
OPPUGNANT
OPPUGNED
OPPUGNER
OPPUGNERS
OPPUGNING
OPPUGNS
OPS
OPSIMATH
OPSIMATHS
OPSIMATHY
OPSIN
OPSINS
OPSOMANIA
OPSONIC
OPSONIFY
OPSONIN
OPSONINS
OPSONISE
OPSONISED
OPSONISES
OPSONIUM
OPSONIUMS
OPSONIZE
OPSONIZED
OPSONIZES
OPT
OPTANT
OPTANTS
OPTATIVE
OPTATIVES
OPTED
OPTER
OPTERS
OPTIC
OPTICAL
OPTICALLY
OPTICIAN
OPTICIANS
OPTICIST
OPTICISTS
OPTICS
OPTIMA
OPTIMAL
OPTIMALLY
OPTIMATE
OPTIMATES
OPTIME
OPTIMES
OPTIMISE
OPTIMISED
OPTIMISER
OPTIMISES
OPTIMISM
OPTIMISMS
OPTIMIST
OPTIMISTS
OPTIMIZE
OPTIMIZED
OPTIMIZER
OPTIMIZES
OPTIMUM
OPTIMUMS
OPTING
OPTION
OPTIONAL
OPTIONALS
OPTIONED
OPTIONEE
OPTIONEES
OPTIONING
OPTIONS
OPTOLOGY
OPTOMETER
OPTOMETRY
OPTOPHONE
OPTRONIC
OPTRONICS
OPTS
OPULENCE
OPULENCES
OPULENCY
OPULENT
OPULENTLY
OPULUS
OPULUSES
OPUNTIA
OPUNTIAS
OPUS
OPUSCLE
OPUSCLES
OPUSCULA
OPUSCULAR
OPUSCULE
OPUSCULES
OPUSCULUM
OPUSES
OQUASSA
OQUASSAS
OR
ORA
ORACH
ORACHE
ORACHES
ORACIES
ORACLE
ORACLED
ORACLES
ORACLING
ORACULAR
ORACULOUS
ORACY
ORAD
ORAGIOUS
ORAL
ORALISM
ORALISMS
ORALIST
ORALISTS
ORALITIES
ORALITY
ORALLY
ORALS
ORANG
ORANGE
ORANGEADE
ORANGER
ORANGERIE
ORANGERY
ORANGES
ORANGEST
ORANGEY
ORANGIER
ORANGIEST
ORANGISH
ORANGS
ORANGUTAN
ORANGY
ORANT
ORANTS
ORARIA
ORARIAN
ORARIANS
ORARION
ORARIONS
ORARIUM
ORATE
ORATED
ORATES
ORATING
ORATION
ORATIONS
ORATOR
ORATORIAL
ORATORIAN
ORATORIES
ORATORIO
ORATORIOS
ORATORS
ORATORY
ORATRESS
ORATRICES
ORATRIX
ORATRIXES
ORATURE
ORATURES
ORB
ORBED
ORBICULAR
ORBIER
ORBIEST
ORBING
ORBIT
ORBITA
ORBITAL
ORBITALLY
ORBITALS
ORBITAS
ORBITED
ORBITER
ORBITERS
ORBITIES
ORBITING
ORBITS
ORBITY
ORBLESS
ORBLIKE
ORBS
ORBY
ORC
ORCA
ORCAS
ORCEIN
ORCEINS
ORCHARD
ORCHARDS
ORCHAT
ORCHATS
ORCHEL
ORCHELLA
ORCHELLAS
ORCHELS
ORCHESES
ORCHESIS
ORCHESTIC
ORCHESTRA
ORCHID
ORCHIDIST
ORCHIDS
ORCHIL
ORCHILLA
ORCHILLAS
ORCHILS
ORCHIS
ORCHISES
ORCHITIC
ORCHITIS
ORCIN

ORCINE
ORCINES
ORCINOL
ORCINOLS
ORCINS
ORCS
ORD
ORDAIN
ORDAINED
ORDAINER
ORDAINERS
ORDAINING
ORDAINS
ORDALIAN
ORDALIUM
ORDALIUMS
ORDEAL
ORDEALS
ORDER
ORDERABLE
ORDERED
ORDERER
ORDERERS
ORDERING
ORDERINGS
ORDERLESS
ORDERLIES
ORDERLY
ORDERS
ORDINAIRE
ORDINAL
ORDINALLY
ORDINALS
ORDINANCE
ORDINAND
ORDINANDS
ORDINANT
ORDINANTS
ORDINAR
ORDINARS
ORDINARY
ORDINATE
ORDINATED
ORDINATES
ORDINEE
ORDINEES
ORDINES
ORDNANCE
ORDNANCES
ORDO
ORDOS
ORDS
ORDURE
ORDURES
ORDUROUS
ORE
OREAD
OREADES
OREADS
OREBODIES
OREBODY
ORECTIC
ORECTIVE
OREGANO
OREGANOS
OREIDE
OREIDES
OREODONT
OREODONTS
OREOLOGY
OREPEARCH
ORES
ORESTUNCK
OREWEED
OREWEEDS
OREXIN
OREXINS
OREXIS
OREXISES
ORF
ORFE
ORFES
ORFRAY
ORFRAYS
ORFS
ORG
ORGAN
ORGANA
ORGANDIE
ORGANDIES
ORGANDY
ORGANELLE
ORGANIC
ORGANICAL
ORGANICS
ORGANISE
ORGANISED
ORGANISER
ORGANISES
ORGANISM
ORGANISMS
ORGANIST
ORGANISTS
ORGANITY
ORGANIZE
ORGANIZED
ORGANIZER
ORGANIZES
ORGANON
ORGANONS
ORGANOSOL
ORGANOTIN
ORGANS
ORGANUM
ORGANUMS
ORGANZA
ORGANZAS
ORGANZINE
ORGASM
ORGASMED
ORGASMIC
ORGASMING
ORGASMS
ORGASTIC
ORGEAT
ORGEATS
ORGIA
ORGIAC
ORGIAS
ORGIAST
ORGIASTIC
ORGIASTS
ORGIC
ORGIES
ORGILLOUS
ORGONE
ORGONES
ORGS
ORGUE
ORGUES
ORGULOUS
ORGY
ORIBATID
ORIBATIDS
ORIBI
ORIBIS
ORICALCHE
ORICHALC
ORICHALCS
ORIEL
ORIELLED
ORIELS
ORIENCIES
ORIENCY
ORIENT
ORIENTAL
ORIENTALS
ORIENTATE
ORIENTED
ORIENTEER
ORIENTER
ORIENTERS
ORIENTING
ORIENTS
ORIFEX
ORIFEXES
ORIFICE
ORIFICES
ORIFICIAL
ORIFLAMME
ORIGAMI
ORIGAMIS
ORIGAN
ORIGANE
ORIGANES
ORIGANS
ORIGANUM
ORIGANUMS
ORIGIN
ORIGINAL
ORIGINALS
ORIGINARY
ORIGINATE
ORIGINS
ORIHOU
ORIHOUS
ORILLION
ORILLIONS
ORINASAL
ORINASALS
ORIOLE
ORIOLES
ORISHA
ORISHAS
ORISON
ORISONS
ORIXA
ORIXAS
ORLE
ORLEANS
ORLEANSES
ORLES
ORLISTAT
ORLISTATS
ORLON
ORLONS
ORLOP
ORLOPS
ORMER
ORMERS
ORMOLU
ORMOLUS
ORNAMENT
ORNAMENTS
ORNATE
ORNATELY
ORNATER
ORNATEST
ORNERIER
ORNERIEST
ORNERY
ORNIS
ORNISES
ORNITHES
ORNITHIC
ORNITHINE
ORNITHOID
OROGEN
OROGENIC
OROGENIES
OROGENS
OROGENY
OROGRAPHY
OROIDE
OROIDES
OROLOGIES
OROLOGIST
OROLOGY
OROMETER
OROMETERS

ORONASAL
OROPESA
OROPESAS
OROTUND
OROTUNDLY
ORPHAN
ORPHANAGE
ORPHANED
ORPHANING
ORPHANISM
ORPHANS
ORPHARION
ORPHIC
ORPHICAL
ORPHISM
ORPHISMS
ORPHREY
ORPHREYED
ORPHREYS
ORPIMENT
ORPIMENTS
ORPIN
ORPINE
ORPINES
ORPINS
ORRA
ORRAMAN
ORRAMEN
ORRERIES
ORRERY
ORRICE
ORRICES
ORRIS
ORRISES
ORRISROOT
ORS
ORSEILLE
ORSEILLES
ORSELLIC
ORT
ORTANIQUE
ORTHIAN
ORTHICON
ORTHICONS
ORTHO
ORTHOAXES
ORTHOAXIS
ORTHODOX
ORTHODOXY
ORTHOEPIC
ORTHOEPY
ORTHOPEDY
ORTHOPOD
ORTHOPODS
ORTHOPTER
ORTHOPTIC
ORTHOS
ORTHOSES
ORTHOSIS
ORTHOTIC
ORTHOTICS
ORTHOTIST
ORTHOTONE
ORTHROS
ORTHROSES
ORTOLAN
ORTOLANS
ORTS
ORVAL
ORVALS
ORYX
ORYXES
ORZO
ORZOS
OS
OSAR
OSCAR
OSCARS
OSCHEAL
OSCILLATE
OSCINE
OSCINES
OSCININE
OSCITANCE
OSCITANCY
OSCITANT
OSCITATE
OSCITATED
OSCITATES
OSCULA
OSCULANT
OSCULAR
OSCULATE
OSCULATED
OSCULATES
OSCULE
OSCULES
OSCULUM
OSE
OSES
OSETRA
OSETRAS
OSHAC
OSHACS
OSIER
OSIERED
OSIERIES
OSIERS
OSIERY
OSMATE
OSMATES
OSMATIC
OSMETERIA
OSMIATE
OSMIATES
OSMIC
OSMICALLY
OSMICS
OSMIOUS
OSMIUM
OSMIUMS
OSMOL
OSMOLAL
OSMOLAR
OSMOLE
OSMOLES
OSMOLS
OSMOMETER
OSMOMETRY
OSMOSE
OSMOSED
OSMOSES
OSMOSING
OSMOSIS
OSMOTIC
OSMOUS
OSMUND
OSMUNDA
OSMUNDAS
OSMUNDINE
OSMUNDS
OSNABURG
OSNABURGS
OSPREY
OSPREYS
OSSA
OSSARIUM
OSSARIUMS
OSSATURE
OSSATURES
OSSEIN
OSSEINS
OSSELET
OSSELETS
OSSEOUS
OSSEOUSLY
OSSETER
OSSETERS
OSSETRA
OSSETRAS
OSSIA
OSSIAS
OSSICLE
OSSICLES
OSSICULAR
OSSIFIC
OSSIFIED
OSSIFIER
OSSIFIERS
OSSIFIES
OSSIFRAGA
OSSIFRAGE
OSSIFY
OSSIFYING
OSSOBUCO
OSSOBUCOS
OSSUARIES
OSSUARY
OSTEAL
OSTEITIC
OSTEITIS
OSTENSIVE
OSTENSORY
OSTENT
OSTENTED
OSTENTING
OSTENTS
OSTEOCYTE
OSTEODERM
OSTEOGEN
OSTEOGENS
OSTEOGENY
OSTEOID
OSTEOIDS
OSTEOLOGY
OSTEOMA
OSTEOMAS
OSTEOMATA
OSTEOPATH
OSTEOSES
OSTEOSIS
OSTEOTOME
OSTEOTOMY
OSTIA
OSTIAL
OSTIARIES
OSTIARY
OSTIATE
OSTINATI
OSTINATO
OSTINATOS
OSTIOLAR
OSTIOLATE
OSTIOLE
OSTIOLES
OSTIUM
OSTLER
OSTLERESS
OSTLERS
OSTMARK
OSTMARKS
OSTOMATE
OSTOMATES
OSTOMIES
OSTOMY
OSTOSES
OSTOSIS
OSTOSISES
OSTRACA
OSTRACEAN
OSTRACISE
OSTRACISM
OSTRACIZE
OSTRACOD
OSTRACODE
OSTRACODS
OSTRACON
OSTRAKA
OSTRAKON
OSTREGER

O

OSTREGERS
OSTRICH
OSTRICHES
OTAKU
OTAKUS
OTALGIA
OTALGIAS
OTALGIC
OTALGIES
OTALGY
OTARID
OTARIES
OTARINE
OTARY
OTHER
OTHERED
OTHERING
OTHERNESS
OTHERS
OTHERWISE
OTIC
OTIOSE
OTIOSELY
OTIOSITY
OTITIC
OTITIDES
OTITIS
OTITISES
OTOCYST
OTOCYSTIC
OTOCYSTS
OTOLITH
OTOLITHIC
OTOLITHS
OTOLOGIC
OTOLOGIES
OTOLOGIST
OTOLOGY
OTOPLASTY
OTORRHOEA
OTOSCOPE
OTOSCOPES
OTOSCOPIC
OTOSCOPY
OTOTOXIC
OTTAR
OTTARS
OTTAVA
OTTAVAS
OTTAVINO
OTTAVINOS
OTTER
OTTERED
OTTERING
OTTERS
OTTO
OTTOMAN
OTTOMANS
OTTOS
OTTRELITE
OU
OUABAIN
OUABAINS
OUAKARI
OUAKARIS
OUBAAS
OUBAASES
OUBIT
OUBITS
OUBLIETTE
OUCH
OUCHED
OUCHES
OUCHING
OUCHT
OUCHTS
OUD
OUDS
OUENS
OUGHLIED
OUGHLIES
OUGHLY
OUGHLYING
OUGHT
OUGHTED
OUGHTING
OUGHTNESS
OUGHTS
OUGIYA
OUGIYAS
OUGLIE
OUGLIED
OUGLIEING
OUGLIES
OUGUIYA
OUGUIYAS
OUIJA
OUIJAS
OUISTITI
OUISTITIS
OUK
OUKS
OULACHON
OULACHONS
OULAKAN
OULAKANS
OULD
OULDER
OULDEST
OULK
OULKS
OULONG
OULONGS
OUMA
OUMAS
OUNCE
OUNCES
OUNDIER
OUNDIEST
OUNDY
OUP
OUPA
OUPAS
OUPED
OUPH
OUPHE
OUPHES
OUPHS
OUPING
OUPS
OUR
OURALI
OURALIS
OURANG
OURANGS
OURARI
OURARIS
OUREBI
OUREBIS
OURIE
OURIER
OURIEST
OURN
OUROBOROS
OUROLOGY
OUROSCOPY
OURS
OURSELF
OURSELVES
OUS
OUSEL
OUSELS
OUST
OUSTED
OUSTER
OUSTERS
OUSTING
OUSTITI
OUSTITIS
OUSTS
OUT
OUTA
OUTACT
OUTACTED
OUTACTING
OUTACTS
OUTADD
OUTADDED
OUTADDING
OUTADDS
OUTAGE
OUTAGES
OUTARGUE
OUTARGUED
OUTARGUES
OUTASIGHT
OUTASITE
OUTASK
OUTASKED
OUTASKING
OUTASKS
OUTATE
OUTBACK
OUTBACKER
OUTBACKS
OUTBAKE
OUTBAKED
OUTBAKES
OUTBAKING
OUTBAR
OUTBARK
OUTBARKED
OUTBARKS
OUTBARRED
OUTBARS
OUTBAWL
OUTBAWLED
OUTBAWLS
OUTBEAM
OUTBEAMED
OUTBEAMS
OUTBEG
OUTBEGGED
OUTBEGS
OUTBID
OUTBIDDEN
OUTBIDDER
OUTBIDS
OUTBITCH
OUTBLAZE
OUTBLAZED
OUTBLAZES
OUTBLEAT
OUTBLEATS
OUTBLESS
OUTBLOOM
OUTBLOOMS
OUTBLUFF
OUTBLUFFS
OUTBLUSH
OUTBOARD
OUTBOARDS
OUTBOAST
OUTBOASTS
OUTBOUGHT
OUTBOUND
OUTBOUNDS
OUTBOX
OUTBOXED
OUTBOXES
OUTBOXING
OUTBRAG
OUTBRAGS
OUTBRAVE
OUTBRAVED
OUTBRAVES
OUTBRAWL
OUTBRAWLS
OUTBRAZEN
OUTBREAK

OUTBREAKS	OUTCHEATS	OUTDATES	OUTEARN	OUTFIRE
OUTBRED	OUTCHID	OUTDATING	OUTEARNED	OUTFIRED
OUTBREED	OUTCHIDE	OUTDAZZLE	OUTEARNS	OUTFIRES
OUTBREEDS	OUTCHIDED	OUTDEBATE	OUTEAT	OUTFIRING
OUTBRIBE	OUTCHIDES	OUTDESIGN	OUTEATEN	OUTFISH
OUTBRIBED	OUTCITIES	OUTDID	OUTEATING	OUTFISHED
OUTBRIBES	OUTCITY	OUTDO	OUTEATS	OUTFISHES
OUTBROKE	OUTCLASS	OUTDODGE	OUTECHO	OUTFIT
OUTBROKEN	OUTCLIMB	OUTDODGED	OUTECHOED	OUTFITS
OUTBUILD	OUTCLIMBS	OUTDODGES	OUTECHOES	OUTFITTED
OUTBUILDS	OUTCLOMB	OUTDOER	OUTED	OUTFITTER
OUTBUILT	OUTCOACH	OUTDOERS	OUTEDGE	OUTFLANK
OUTBULGE	OUTCOME	OUTDOES	OUTEDGES	OUTFLANKS
OUTBULGED	OUTCOMES	OUTDOING	OUTER	OUTFLASH
OUTBULGES	OUTCOOK	OUTDONE	OUTERCOAT	OUTFLEW
OUTBULK	OUTCOOKED	OUTDOOR	OUTERMOST	OUTFLIES
OUTBULKED	OUTCOOKS	OUTDOORS	OUTERS	OUTFLING
OUTBULKS	OUTCOUNT	OUTDOORSY	OUTERWEAR	OUTFLINGS
OUTBULLY	OUTCOUNTS	OUTDRAG	OUTFABLE	OUTFLOAT
OUTBURN	OUTCRAFTY	OUTDRAGS	OUTFABLED	OUTFLOATS
OUTBURNED	OUTCRAWL	OUTDRANK	OUTFABLES	OUTFLOW
OUTBURNS	OUTCRAWLS	OUTDRAW	OUTFACE	OUTFLOWED
OUTBURNT	OUTCRIED	OUTDRAWN	OUTFACED	OUTFLOWN
OUTBURST	OUTCRIES	OUTDRAWS	OUTFACES	OUTFLOWS
OUTBURSTS	OUTCROP	OUTDREAM	OUTFACING	OUTFLUNG
OUTBUY	OUTCROPS	OUTDREAMS	OUTFALL	OUTFLUSH
OUTBUYING	OUTCROSS	OUTDREAMT	OUTFALLS	OUTFLY
OUTBUYS	OUTCROW	OUTDRESS	OUTFAST	OUTFLYING
OUTBY	OUTCROWD	OUTDREW	OUTFASTED	OUTFOOL
OUTBYE	OUTCROWDS	OUTDRINK	OUTFASTS	OUTFOOLED
OUTCALL	OUTCROWED	OUTDRINKS	OUTFAWN	OUTFOOLS
OUTCALLED	OUTCROWS	OUTDRIVE	OUTFAWNED	OUTFOOT
OUTCALLS	OUTCRY	OUTDRIVEN	OUTFAWNS	OUTFOOTED
OUTCAPER	OUTCRYING	OUTDRIVES	OUTFEAST	OUTFOOTS
OUTCAPERS	OUTCURSE	OUTDROP	OUTFEASTS	OUTFOUGHT
OUTCAST	OUTCURSED	OUTDROPS	OUTFEEL	OUTFOUND
OUTCASTE	OUTCURSES	OUTDROVE	OUTFEELS	OUTFOX
OUTCASTED	OUTCURVE	OUTDRUNK	OUTFELT	OUTFOXED
OUTCASTES	OUTCURVES	OUTDUEL	OUTFENCE	OUTFOXES
OUTCASTS	OUTDANCE	OUTDUELED	OUTFENCED	OUTFOXING
OUTCATCH	OUTDANCED	OUTDUELS	OUTFENCES	OUTFROWN
OUTCAUGHT	OUTDANCES	OUTDURE	OUTFIELD	OUTFROWNS
OUTCAVIL	OUTDARE	OUTDURED	OUTFIELDS	OUTFUMBLE
OUTCAVILS	OUTDARED	OUTDURES	OUTFIGHT	OUTGAIN
OUTCHARGE	OUTDARES	OUTDURING	OUTFIGHTS	OUTGAINED
OUTCHARM	OUTDARING	OUTDWELL	OUTFIGURE	OUTGAINS
OUTCHARMS	OUTDATE	OUTDWELLS	OUTFIND	OUTGALLOP
OUTCHEAT	OUTDATED	OUTDWELT	OUTFINDS	OUTGAMBLE

OUTGAS
OUTGASES
OUTGASSED
OUTGASSES
OUTGATE
OUTGATES
OUTGAVE
OUTGAZE
OUTGAZED
OUTGAZES
OUTGAZING
OUTGIVE
OUTGIVEN
OUTGIVES
OUTGIVING
OUTGLARE
OUTGLARED
OUTGLARES
OUTGLEAM
OUTGLEAMS
OUTGLOW
OUTGLOWED
OUTGLOWS
OUTGNAW
OUTGNAWED
OUTGNAWN
OUTGNAWS
OUTGO
OUTGOER
OUTGOERS
OUTGOES
OUTGOING
OUTGOINGS
OUTGONE
OUTGREW
OUTGRIN
OUTGRINS
OUTGROSS
OUTGROUP
OUTGROUPS
OUTGROW
OUTGROWN
OUTGROWS
OUTGROWTH
OUTGUARD
OUTGUARDS
OUTGUESS
OUTGUIDE
OUTGUIDED
OUTGUIDES
OUTGUN
OUTGUNNED
OUTGUNS
OUTGUSH
OUTGUSHED
OUTGUSHES
OUTHANDLE
OUTHARBOR
OUTHAUL
OUTHAULER
OUTHAULS
OUTHEAR
OUTHEARD
OUTHEARS
OUTHER
OUTHIRE
OUTHIRED
OUTHIRES
OUTHIRING
OUTHIT
OUTHITS
OUTHOMER
OUTHOMERS
OUTHOUSE
OUTHOUSES
OUTHOWL
OUTHOWLED
OUTHOWLS
OUTHUMOR
OUTHUMORS
OUTHUMOUR
OUTHUNT
OUTHUNTED
OUTHUNTS
OUTHUSTLE
OUTHYRE
OUTHYRED
OUTHYRES
OUTHYRING
OUTING
OUTINGS
OUTJEST
OUTJESTED
OUTJESTS
OUTJET
OUTJETS
OUTJINX
OUTJINXED
OUTJINXES
OUTJOCKEY
OUTJUGGLE
OUTJUMP
OUTJUMPED
OUTJUMPS
OUTJUT
OUTJUTS
OUTJUTTED
OUTKEEP
OUTKEEPS
OUTKEPT
OUTKICK
OUTKICKED
OUTKICKS
OUTKILL
OUTKILLED
OUTKILLS
OUTKISS
OUTKISSED
OUTKISSES
OUTLAID
OUTLAIN
OUTLAND
OUTLANDER
OUTLANDS
OUTLASH
OUTLASHED
OUTLASHES
OUTLAST
OUTLASTED
OUTLASTS
OUTLAUGH
OUTLAUGHS
OUTLAUNCE
OUTLAUNCH
OUTLAW
OUTLAWED
OUTLAWING
OUTLAWRY
OUTLAWS
OUTLAY
OUTLAYING
OUTLAYS
OUTLEAD
OUTLEADS
OUTLEAP
OUTLEAPED
OUTLEAPS
OUTLEAPT
OUTLEARN
OUTLEARNS
OUTLEARNT
OUTLED
OUTLER
OUTLERS
OUTLET
OUTLETS
OUTLIE
OUTLIED
OUTLIER
OUTLIERS
OUTLIES
OUTLINE
OUTLINEAR
OUTLINED
OUTLINER
OUTLINERS
OUTLINES
OUTLINING
OUTLIVE
OUTLIVED
OUTLIVER
OUTLIVERS
OUTLIVES
OUTLIVING
OUTLOOK
OUTLOOKED
OUTLOOKS
OUTLOVE
OUTLOVED
OUTLOVES
OUTLOVING
OUTLUSTER
OUTLUSTRE
OUTLYING
OUTMAN
OUTMANNED
OUTMANS
OUTMANTLE
OUTMARCH
OUTMASTER
OUTMATCH
OUTMODE
OUTMODED
OUTMODES
OUTMODING
OUTMOST
OUTMOVE
OUTMOVED
OUTMOVES
OUTMOVING
OUTMUSCLE
OUTNAME
OUTNAMED
OUTNAMES
OUTNAMING
OUTNESS
OUTNESSES
OUTNIGHT
OUTNIGHTS
OUTNUMBER
OUTOFFICE
OUTPACE
OUTPACED
OUTPACES
OUTPACING
OUTPAINT
OUTPAINTS
OUTPART
OUTPARTS
OUTPASS
OUTPASSED
OUTPASSES
OUTPEEP
OUTPEEPED
OUTPEEPS
OUTPEER
OUTPEERED
OUTPEERS
OUTPEOPLE
OUTPITCH
OUTPITIED
OUTPITIES
OUTPITY
OUTPLACE
OUTPLACED
OUTPLACER
OUTPLACES
OUTPLAN
OUTPLANS
OUTPLAY

O

OUTPLAYED
OUTPLAYS
OUTPLOD
OUTPLODS
OUTPLOT
OUTPLOTS
OUTPOINT
OUTPOINTS
OUTPOLL
OUTPOLLED
OUTPOLLS
OUTPORT
OUTPORTER
OUTPORTS
OUTPOST
OUTPOSTS
OUTPOUR
OUTPOURED
OUTPOURER
OUTPOURS
OUTPOWER
OUTPOWERS
OUTPRAY
OUTPRAYED
OUTPRAYS
OUTPREACH
OUTPREEN
OUTPREENS
OUTPRESS
OUTPRICE
OUTPRICED
OUTPRICES
OUTPRIZE
OUTPRIZED
OUTPRIZES
OUTPSYCH
OUTPSYCHS
OUTPULL
OUTPULLED
OUTPULLS
OUTPUNCH
OUTPUPIL
OUTPUPILS
OUTPURSUE
OUTPUSH
OUTPUSHED
OUTPUSHES
OUTPUT
OUTPUTS
OUTPUTTED
OUTQUOTE
OUTQUOTED
OUTQUOTES
OUTRACE
OUTRACED
OUTRACES
OUTRACING
OUTRAGE
OUTRAGED
OUTRAGES
OUTRAGING
OUTRAISE
OUTRAISED
OUTRAISES
OUTRAN
OUTRANCE
OUTRANCES
OUTRANG
OUTRANGE
OUTRANGED
OUTRANGES
OUTRANK
OUTRANKED
OUTRANKS
OUTRATE
OUTRATED
OUTRATES
OUTRATING
OUTRAVE
OUTRAVED
OUTRAVES
OUTRAVING
OUTRE
OUTREACH
OUTREAD
OUTREADS
OUTREASON
OUTRECKON
OUTRED
OUTREDDED
OUTREDDEN
OUTREDS
OUTREIGN
OUTREIGNS
OUTRELIEF
OUTREMER
OUTREMERS
OUTRIDDEN
OUTRIDE
OUTRIDER
OUTRIDERS
OUTRIDES
OUTRIDING
OUTRIG
OUTRIGGED
OUTRIGGER
OUTRIGHT
OUTRIGS
OUTRING
OUTRINGS
OUTRIVAL
OUTRIVALS
OUTRO
OUTROAR
OUTROARED
OUTROARS
OUTROCK
OUTROCKED
OUTROCKS
OUTRODE
OUTROLL
OUTROLLED
OUTROLLS
OUTROOP
OUTROOPER
OUTROOPS
OUTROOT
OUTROOTED
OUTROOTS
OUTROPE
OUTROPER
OUTROPERS
OUTROPES
OUTROS
OUTROW
OUTROWED
OUTROWING
OUTROWS
OUTRUN
OUTRUNG
OUTRUNNER
OUTRUNS
OUTRUSH
OUTRUSHED
OUTRUSHES
OUTS
OUTSAID
OUTSAIL
OUTSAILED
OUTSAILS
OUTSANG
OUTSAT
OUTSAVOR
OUTSAVORS
OUTSAVOUR
OUTSAW
OUTSAY
OUTSAYING
OUTSAYS
OUTSCHEME
OUTSCOLD
OUTSCOLDS
OUTSCOOP
OUTSCOOPS
OUTSCORE
OUTSCORED
OUTSCORES
OUTSCORN
OUTSCORNS
OUTSCREAM
OUTSEE
OUTSEEING
OUTSEEN
OUTSEES
OUTSELL
OUTSELLS
OUTSERT
OUTSERTS
OUTSERVE
OUTSERVED
OUTSERVES
OUTSET
OUTSETS
OUTSHAME
OUTSHAMED
OUTSHAMES
OUTSHINE
OUTSHINED
OUTSHINES
OUTSHONE
OUTSHOOT
OUTSHOOTS
OUTSHOT
OUTSHOTS
OUTSHOUT
OUTSHOUTS
OUTSIDE
OUTSIDER
OUTSIDERS
OUTSIDES
OUTSIGHT
OUTSIGHTS
OUTSIN
OUTSING
OUTSINGS
OUTSINNED
OUTSINS
OUTSIT
OUTSITS
OUTSIZE
OUTSIZED
OUTSIZES
OUTSKATE
OUTSKATED
OUTSKATES
OUTSKIRT
OUTSKIRTS
OUTSLEEP
OUTSLEEPS
OUTSLEPT
OUTSLICK
OUTSLICKS
OUTSMART
OUTSMARTS
OUTSMELL
OUTSMELLS
OUTSMELT
OUTSMILE
OUTSMILED
OUTSMILES
OUTSMOKE
OUTSMOKED
OUTSMOKES
OUTSNORE
OUTSNORED
OUTSNORES
OUTSOAR
OUTSOARED
OUTSOARS
OUTSOLD

O

OUTSOLE
OUTSOLES
OUTSOURCE
OUTSPAN
OUTSPANS
OUTSPEAK
OUTSPEAKS
OUTSPED
OUTSPEED
OUTSPEEDS
OUTSPELL
OUTSPELLS
OUTSPELT
OUTSPEND
OUTSPENDS
OUTSPENT
OUTSPOKE
OUTSPOKEN
OUTSPORT
OUTSPORTS
OUTSPRANG
OUTSPREAD
OUTSPRING
OUTSPRINT
OUTSPRUNG
OUTSTAND
OUTSTANDS
OUTSTARE
OUTSTARED
OUTSTARES
OUTSTART
OUTSTARTS
OUTSTATE
OUTSTATED
OUTSTATES
OUTSTAY
OUTSTAYED
OUTSTAYS
OUTSTEER
OUTSTEERS
OUTSTEP
OUTSTEPS
OUTSTOOD
OUTSTRAIN
OUTSTRIDE
OUTSTRIKE
OUTSTRIP
OUTSTRIPS
OUTSTRIVE
OUTSTRODE
OUTSTROKE
OUTSTROVE
OUTSTRUCK
OUTSTUDY
OUTSTUNT
OUTSTUNTS
OUTSULK
OUTSULKED
OUTSULKS
OUTSUM
OUTSUMMED
OUTSUMS
OUTSUNG
OUTSWAM
OUTSWARE
OUTSWEAR
OUTSWEARS
OUTSWEEP
OUTSWEEPS
OUTSWELL
OUTSWELLS
OUTSWEPT
OUTSWIM
OUTSWIMS
OUTSWING
OUTSWINGS
OUTSWORE
OUTSWORN
OUTSWUM
OUTSWUNG
OUTTA
OUTTAKE
OUTTAKEN
OUTTAKES
OUTTAKING
OUTTALK
OUTTALKED
OUTTALKS
OUTTASK
OUTTASKED
OUTTASKS
OUTTELL
OUTTELLS
OUTTHANK
OUTTHANKS
OUTTHIEVE
OUTTHINK
OUTTHINKS
OUTTHREW
OUTTHROB
OUTTHROBS
OUTTHROW
OUTTHROWN
OUTTHROWS
OUTTHRUST
OUTTOLD
OUTTONGUE
OUTTOOK
OUTTOP
OUTTOPPED
OUTTOPS
OUTTOWER
OUTTOWERS
OUTTRADE
OUTTRADED
OUTTRADES
OUTTRAVEL
OUTTRICK
OUTTRICKS
OUTTROT
OUTTROTS
OUTTRUMP
OUTTRUMPS
OUTTURN
OUTTURNS
OUTVALUE
OUTVALUED
OUTVALUES
OUTVAUNT
OUTVAUNTS
OUTVENOM
OUTVENOMS
OUTVIE
OUTVIED
OUTVIES
OUTVOICE
OUTVOICED
OUTVOICES
OUTVOTE
OUTVOTED
OUTVOTER
OUTVOTERS
OUTVOTES
OUTVOTING
OUTVYING
OUTWAIT
OUTWAITED
OUTWAITS
OUTWALK
OUTWALKED
OUTWALKS
OUTWAR
OUTWARD
OUTWARDLY
OUTWARDS
OUTWARRED
OUTWARS
OUTWASH
OUTWASHES
OUTWASTE
OUTWASTED
OUTWASTES
OUTWATCH
OUTWEAR
OUTWEARS
OUTWEARY
OUTWEED
OUTWEEDED
OUTWEEDS
OUTWEEP
OUTWEEPS
OUTWEIGH
OUTWEIGHS
OUTWELL
OUTWELLED
OUTWELLS
OUTWENT
OUTWEPT
OUTWHIRL
OUTWHIRLS
OUTWICK
OUTWICKED
OUTWICKS
OUTWILE
OUTWILED
OUTWILES
OUTWILING
OUTWILL
OUTWILLED
OUTWILLS
OUTWIN
OUTWIND
OUTWINDED
OUTWINDS
OUTWING
OUTWINGED
OUTWINGS
OUTWINS
OUTWISH
OUTWISHED
OUTWISHES
OUTWIT
OUTWITH
OUTWITS
OUTWITTED
OUTWON
OUTWORE
OUTWORK
OUTWORKED
OUTWORKER
OUTWORKS
OUTWORN
OUTWORTH
OUTWORTHS
OUTWOUND
OUTWREST
OUTWRESTS
OUTWRIT
OUTWRITE
OUTWRITES
OUTWROTE
OUTYELL
OUTYELLED
OUTYELLS
OUTYELP
OUTYELPED
OUTYELPS
OUTYIELD
OUTYIELDS
OUVERT
OUVERTE
OUVRAGE
OUVRAGES
OUVRIER
OUVRIERE
OUVRIERES
OUVRIERS
OUZEL
OUZELS
OUZO

OUZOS
OVA
OVAL
OVALBUMIN
OVALITIES
OVALITY
OVALLY
OVALNESS
OVALS
OVARIAL
OVARIAN
OVARIES
OVARIOLE
OVARIOLES
OVARIOUS
OVARITIS
OVARY
OVATE
OVATED
OVATELY
OVATES
OVATING
OVATION
OVATIONAL
OVATIONS
OVATOR
OVATORS
OVEL
OVELS
OVEN
OVENABLE
OVENBIRD
OVENBIRDS
OVENED
OVENING
OVENLIKE
OVENPROOF
OVENS
OVENWARE
OVENWARES
OVENWOOD
OVENWOODS
OVER
OVERABLE
OVERACT
OVERACTED
OVERACTS
OVERACUTE
OVERAGE
OVERAGED
OVERAGES
OVERALERT
OVERALL
OVERALLED
OVERALLS
OVERAPT
OVERARCH
OVERARM
OVERARMED
OVERARMS
OVERATE
OVERAWE
OVERAWED
OVERAWES
OVERAWING
OVERBAKE
OVERBAKED
OVERBAKES
OVERBANK
OVERBANKS
OVERBEAR
OVERBEARS
OVERBEAT
OVERBEATS
OVERBED
OVERBET
OVERBETS
OVERBID
OVERBIDS
OVERBIG
OVERBILL
OVERBILLS
OVERBITE
OVERBITES
OVERBLEW
OVERBLOW
OVERBLOWN
OVERBLOWS
OVERBOARD
OVERBOIL
OVERBOILS
OVERBOLD
OVERBOOK
OVERBOOKS
OVERBOOT
OVERBOOTS
OVERBORE
OVERBORN
OVERBORNE
OVERBOUND
OVERBRAKE
OVERBRED
OVERBREED
OVERBRIEF
OVERBRIM
OVERBRIMS
OVERBROAD
OVERBROW
OVERBROWS
OVERBUILD
OVERBUILT
OVERBULK
OVERBULKS
OVERBURN
OVERBURNS
OVERBURNT
OVERBUSY
OVERBUY
OVERBUYS
OVERBY
OVERCALL
OVERCALLS
OVERCAME
OVERCARRY
OVERCAST
OVERCASTS
OVERCATCH
OVERCHEAP
OVERCHECK
OVERCHILL
OVERCIVIL
OVERCLAD
OVERCLAIM
OVERCLASS
OVERCLEAN
OVERCLEAR
OVERCLOCK
OVERCLOSE
OVERCLOUD
OVERCLOY
OVERCLOYS
OVERCLUB
OVERCLUBS
OVERCOACH
OVERCOAT
OVERCOATS
OVERCOLD
OVERCOLOR
OVERCOME
OVERCOMER
OVERCOMES
OVERCOOK
OVERCOOKS
OVERCOOL
OVERCOOLS
OVERCOUNT
OVERCOVER
OVERCOY
OVERCRAM
OVERCRAMS
OVERCRAW
OVERCRAWS
OVERCROP
OVERCROPS
OVERCROW
OVERCROWD
OVERCROWS
OVERCURE
OVERCURED
OVERCURES
OVERCUT
OVERCUTS
OVERDARE
OVERDARED
OVERDARES
OVERDATED
OVERDEAR
OVERDECK
OVERDECKS
OVERDID
OVERDIGHT
OVERDO
OVERDOER
OVERDOERS
OVERDOES
OVERDOG
OVERDOGS
OVERDOING
OVERDONE
OVERDOSE
OVERDOSED
OVERDOSES
OVERDRAFT
OVERDRANK
OVERDRAW
OVERDRAWN
OVERDRAWS
OVERDRESS
OVERDREW
OVERDRIED
OVERDRIES
OVERDRINK
OVERDRIVE
OVERDROVE
OVERDRUNK
OVERDRY
OVERDUB
OVERDUBS
OVERDUE
OVERDUST
OVERDUSTS
OVERDYE
OVERDYED
OVERDYER
OVERDYERS
OVERDYES
OVEREAGER
OVEREASY
OVEREAT
OVEREATEN
OVEREATER
OVEREATS
OVERED
OVEREDIT
OVEREDITS
OVEREGG
OVEREGGED
OVEREGGS
OVEREMOTE
OVEREQUIP
OVEREXERT
OVEREYE
OVEREYED
OVEREYES
OVEREYING
OVERFALL
OVERFALLS
OVERFAR
OVERFAST
OVERFAT

O

OVERFAVOR
OVERFEAR
OVERFEARS
OVERFED
OVERFEED
OVERFEEDS
OVERFELL
OVERFILL
OVERFILLS
OVERFINE
OVERFISH
OVERFIT
OVERFLEW
OVERFLIES
OVERFLOOD
OVERFLOW
OVERFLOWN
OVERFLOWS
OVERFLUSH
OVERFLY
OVERFOCUS
OVERFOLD
OVERFOLDS
OVERFOND
OVERFOUL
OVERFRANK
OVERFREE
OVERFULL
OVERFUND
OVERFUNDS
OVERFUSSY
OVERGALL
OVERGALLS
OVERGANG
OVERGANGS
OVERGAVE
OVERGEAR
OVERGEARS
OVERGET
OVERGETS
OVERGILD
OVERGILDS
OVERGILT
OVERGIRD
OVERGIRDS
OVERGIRT
OVERGIVE
OVERGIVEN
OVERGIVES
OVERGLAD
OVERGLAZE
OVERGLOOM
OVERGO
OVERGOAD
OVERGOADS
OVERGOES
OVERGOING
OVERGONE
OVERGORGE
OVERGOT
OVERGRADE
OVERGRAIN
OVERGRASS
OVERGRAZE
OVERGREAT
OVERGREEN
OVERGREW
OVERGROW
OVERGROWN
OVERGROWS
OVERHAILE
OVERHAIR
OVERHAIRS
OVERHALE
OVERHALED
OVERHALES
OVERHAND
OVERHANDS
OVERHANG
OVERHANGS
OVERHAPPY
OVERHARD
OVERHASTE
OVERHASTY
OVERHATE
OVERHATED
OVERHATES
OVERHAUL
OVERHAULS
OVERHEAD
OVERHEADS
OVERHEAP
OVERHEAPS
OVERHEAR
OVERHEARD
OVERHEARS
OVERHEAT
OVERHEATS
OVERHELD
OVERHENT
OVERHENTS
OVERHIGH
OVERHIT
OVERHITS
OVERHOLD
OVERHOLDS
OVERHOLY
OVERHONOR
OVERHOPE
OVERHOPED
OVERHOPES
OVERHOT
OVERHUNG
OVERHUNT
OVERHUNTS
OVERHYPE
OVERHYPED
OVERHYPES
OVERIDLE
OVERING
OVERINKED
OVERISSUE
OVERJOY
OVERJOYED
OVERJOYS
OVERJUMP
OVERJUMPS
OVERJUST
OVERKEEN
OVERKEEP
OVERKEEPS
OVERKEPT
OVERKEST
OVERKILL
OVERKILLS
OVERKIND
OVERKING
OVERKINGS
OVERKNEE
OVERLABOR
OVERLADE
OVERLADED
OVERLADEN
OVERLADES
OVERLAID
OVERLAIN
OVERLAND
OVERLANDS
OVERLAP
OVERLAPS
OVERLARD
OVERLARDS
OVERLARGE
OVERLATE
OVERLAX
OVERLAY
OVERLAYS
OVERLEAF
OVERLEAP
OVERLEAPS
OVERLEAPT
OVERLEARN
OVERLEND
OVERLENDS
OVERLENT
OVERLET
OVERLETS
OVERLEWD
OVERLIE
OVERLIER
OVERLIERS
OVERLIES
OVERLIGHT
OVERLIT
OVERLIVE
OVERLIVED
OVERLIVES
OVERLOAD
OVERLOADS
OVERLOCK
OVERLOCKS
OVERLONG
OVERLOOK
OVERLOOKS
OVERLORD
OVERLORDS
OVERLOUD
OVERLOVE
OVERLOVED
OVERLOVES
OVERLUSH
OVERLUSTY
OVERLY
OVERLYING
OVERMAN
OVERMANS
OVERMANY
OVERMAST
OVERMASTS
OVERMATCH
OVERMEEK
OVERMELT
OVERMELTS
OVERMEN
OVERMERRY
OVERMILD
OVERMILK
OVERMILKS
OVERMINE
OVERMINED
OVERMINES
OVERMIX
OVERMIXED
OVERMIXES
OVERMOUNT
OVERMUCH
OVERNAME
OVERNAMED
OVERNAMES
OVERNEAR
OVERNEAT
OVERNET
OVERNETS
OVERNEW
OVERNICE
OVERNIGHT
OVERPACK
OVERPACKS
OVERPAGE
OVERPAID
OVERPAINT
OVERPART
OVERPARTS
OVERPASS
OVERPAST
OVERPAY
OVERPAYS
OVERPEDAL
OVERPEER
OVERPEERS

O

OVERPERCH
OVERPERT
OVERPITCH
OVERPLAID
OVERPLAN
OVERPLANS
OVERPLANT
OVERPLAST
OVERPLAY
OVERPLAYS
OVERPLIED
OVERPLIES
OVERPLOT
OVERPLOTS
OVERPLUS
OVERPLY
OVERPOISE
OVERPOST
OVERPOSTS
OVERPOWER
OVERPRESS
OVERPRICE
OVERPRINT
OVERPRIZE
OVERPROOF
OVERPROUD
OVERPUMP
OVERPUMPS
OVERQUICK
OVERRACK
OVERRACKS
OVERRAKE
OVERRAKED
OVERRAKES
OVERRAN
OVERRANK
OVERRANKS
OVERRASH
OVERRATE
OVERRATED
OVERRATES
OVERREACH
OVERREACT
OVERREAD
OVERREADS
OVERRED
OVERREDS
OVERREN
OVERRENS
OVERRICH
OVERRIDE
OVERRIDER
OVERRIDES
OVERRIFE
OVERRIGID
OVERRIPE
OVERRIPEN
OVERROAST
OVERRODE
OVERRUDE
OVERRUFF
OVERRUFFS
OVERRULE
OVERRULED
OVERRULER
OVERRULES
OVERRUN
OVERRUNS
OVERS
OVERSAD
OVERSAIL
OVERSAILS
OVERSALE
OVERSALES
OVERSALT
OVERSALTS
OVERSAUCE
OVERSAVE
OVERSAVED
OVERSAVES
OVERSAW
OVERSCALE
OVERSCORE
OVERSEA
OVERSEAS
OVERSEE
OVERSEED
OVERSEEDS
OVERSEEN
OVERSEER
OVERSEERS
OVERSEES
OVERSELL
OVERSELLS
OVERSET
OVERSETS
OVERSEW
OVERSEWED
OVERSEWN
OVERSEWS
OVERSEXED
OVERSHADE
OVERSHARE
OVERSHARP
OVERSHINE
OVERSHIRT
OVERSHOE
OVERSHOES
OVERSHONE
OVERSHOOT
OVERSHOT
OVERSHOTS
OVERSICK
OVERSIDE
OVERSIDES
OVERSIGHT
OVERSIZE
OVERSIZED
OVERSIZES
OVERSKATE
OVERSKIP
OVERSKIPS
OVERSKIRT
OVERSLEEP
OVERSLEPT
OVERSLIP
OVERSLIPS
OVERSLIPT
OVERSLOW
OVERSMAN
OVERSMEN
OVERSMOKE
OVERSOAK
OVERSOAKS
OVERSOFT
OVERSOLD
OVERSOON
OVERSOUL
OVERSOULS
OVERSOW
OVERSOWED
OVERSOWN
OVERSOWS
OVERSPEND
OVERSPENT
OVERSPICE
OVERSPILL
OVERSPILT
OVERSPIN
OVERSPINS
OVERSTAFF
OVERSTAIN
OVERSTAND
OVERSTANK
OVERSTARE
OVERSTATE
OVERSTAY
OVERSTAYS
OVERSTEER
OVERSTEP
OVERSTEPS
OVERSTINK
OVERSTIR
OVERSTIRS
OVERSTOCK
OVERSTOOD
OVERSTORY
OVERSTREW
OVERSTUDY
OVERSTUFF
OVERSTUNK
OVERSUDS
OVERSUP
OVERSUPS
OVERSURE
OVERSWAM
OVERSWAY
OVERSWAYS
OVERSWEAR
OVERSWEET
OVERSWELL
OVERSWIM
OVERSWIMS
OVERSWING
OVERSWORE
OVERSWORN
OVERSWUM
OVERSWUNG
OVERT
OVERTAKE
OVERTAKEN
OVERTAKES
OVERTALK
OVERTALKS
OVERTAME
OVERTART
OVERTASK
OVERTASKS
OVERTAX
OVERTAXED
OVERTAXES
OVERTEACH
OVERTEEM
OVERTEEMS
OVERTHICK
OVERTHIN
OVERTHINK
OVERTHINS
OVERTHREW
OVERTHROW
OVERTIGHT
OVERTIME
OVERTIMED
OVERTIMER
OVERTIMES
OVERTIMID
OVERTIP
OVERTIPS
OVERTIRE
OVERTIRED
OVERTIRES
OVERTLY
OVERTNESS
OVERTOIL
OVERTOILS
OVERTONE
OVERTONES
OVERTOOK
OVERTOP
OVERTOPS
OVERTOWER
OVERTRADE
OVERTRAIN
OVERTREAT
OVERTRICK
OVERTRIM
OVERTRIMS
OVERTRIP
OVERTRIPS
OVERTRUMP

OVERTRUST
OVERTURE
OVERTURED
OVERTURES
OVERTURN
OVERTURNS
OVERTYPE
OVERTYPED
OVERTYPES
OVERURGE
OVERURGED
OVERURGES
OVERUSE
OVERUSED
OVERUSES
OVERUSING
OVERVALUE
OVERVEIL
OVERVEILS
OVERVIEW
OVERVIEWS
OVERVIVID
OVERVOTE
OVERVOTED
OVERVOTES
OVERWARM
OVERWARMS
OVERWARY
OVERWASH
OVERWATCH
OVERWATER
OVERWEAK
OVERWEAR
OVERWEARS
OVERWEARY
OVERWEEN
OVERWEENS
OVERWEIGH
OVERWENT
OVERWET
OVERWETS
OVERWHELM
OVERWIDE
OVERWILY
OVERWIND
OVERWINDS
OVERWING
OVERWINGS
OVERWISE
OVERWORD
OVERWORDS
OVERWORE
OVERWORK
OVERWORKS
OVERWORN
OVERWOUND
OVERWRAP
OVERWRAPS
OVERWRAPT
OVERWREST
OVERWRITE
OVERWROTE
OVERYEAR
OVERYEARS
OVERZEAL
OVERZEALS
OVIBOS
OVIBOSES
OVIBOVINE
OVICIDAL
OVICIDE
OVICIDES
OVIDUCAL
OVIDUCT
OVIDUCTAL
OVIDUCTS
OVIFEROUS
OVIFORM
OVIGEROUS
OVINE
OVINES
OVIPARA
OVIPARITY
OVIPAROUS
OVIPOSIT
OVIPOSITS
OVIRAPTOR
OVISAC
OVISACS
OVIST
OVISTS
OVOID
OVOIDAL
OVOIDALS
OVOIDS
OVOLI
OVOLO
OVOLOS
OVONIC
OVONICS
OVOTESTES
OVOTESTIS
OVULAR
OVULARY
OVULATE
OVULATED
OVULATES
OVULATING
OVULATION
OVULATORY
OVULE
OVULES
OVUM
OW
OWCHE
OWCHES
OWE
OWED
OWELTIES
OWELTY
OWER
OWERBY
OWERLOUP
OWERLOUPS
OWES
OWIE
OWIES
OWING
OWL
OWLED
OWLER
OWLERIES
OWLERS
OWLERY
OWLET
OWLETS
OWLIER
OWLIEST
OWLING
OWLISH
OWLISHLY
OWLLIKE
OWLS
OWLY
OWN
OWNABLE
OWNED
OWNER
OWNERLESS
OWNERS
OWNERSHIP
OWNING
OWNS
OWNSOME
OWNSOMES
OWRE
OWRECAME
OWRECOME
OWRECOMES
OWRELAY
OWRELAYS
OWRES
OWREWORD
OWREWORDS
OWRIE
OWRIER
OWRIEST
OWSE
OWSEN
OWT
OWTS
OX
OXACILLIN
OXALATE
OXALATED
OXALATES
OXALATING
OXALIC
OXALIS
OXALISES
OXAZEPAM
OXAZEPAMS
OXAZINE
OXAZINES
OXAZOLE
OXAZOLES
OXBLOOD
OXBLOODS
OXBOW
OXBOWS
OXCART
OXCARTS
OXEN
OXER
OXERS
OXES
OXEYE
OXEYES
OXFORD
OXFORDS
OXGANG
OXGANGS
OXGATE
OXGATES
OXHEAD
OXHEADS
OXHEART
OXHEARTS
OXHERD
OXHERDS
OXHIDE
OXHIDES
OXIC
OXID
OXIDABLE
OXIDANT
OXIDANTS
OXIDASE
OXIDASES
OXIDASIC
OXIDATE
OXIDATED
OXIDATES
OXIDATING
OXIDATION
OXIDATIVE
OXIDE
OXIDES
OXIDIC
OXIDISE
OXIDISED
OXIDISER
OXIDISERS
OXIDISES
OXIDISING
OXIDIZE
OXIDIZED
OXIDIZER
OXIDIZERS
OXIDIZES

OXIDIZING
OXIDS
OXIES
OXIM
OXIME
OXIMES
OXIMETER
OXIMETERS
OXIMETRY
OXIMS
OXLAND
OXLANDS
OXLIKE
OXLIP
OXLIPS
OXO
OXONIUM
OXONIUMS
OXPECKER
OXPECKERS
OXSLIP
OXSLIPS
OXTAIL
OXTAILS
OXTER

OXTERED
OXTERING
OXTERS
OXTONGUE
OXTONGUES
OXY
OXYACID
OXYACIDS
OXYANION
OXYANIONS
OXYCODONE
OXYGEN
OXYGENASE
OXYGENATE
OXYGENIC
OXYGENISE
OXYGENIZE
OXYGENOUS
OXYGENS
OXYMEL
OXYMELS
OXYMORA
OXYMORON
OXYMORONS
OXYNTIC

OXYPHIL
OXYPHILE
OXYPHILES
OXYPHILIC
OXYPHILS
OXYSALT
OXYSALTS
OXYSOME
OXYSOMES
OXYTOCIC
OXYTOCICS
OXYTOCIN
OXYTOCINS
OXYTONE
OXYTONES
OXYTONIC
OXYTROPE
OXYTROPES
OY
OYE
OYER
OYERS
OYES
OYESES
OYESSES

OYEZ
OYEZES
OYS
OYSTER
OYSTERED
OYSTERER
OYSTERERS
OYSTERING
OYSTERMAN
OYSTERMEN
OYSTERS
OYSTRIGE
OYSTRIGES
OZAENA
OZAENAS
OZALID
OZALIDS
OZEKI
OZEKIS
OZOCERITE
OZOKERITE
OZONATE
OZONATED
OZONATES
OZONATING

OZONATION
OZONE
OZONES
OZONIC
OZONIDE
OZONIDES
OZONISE
OZONISED
OZONISER
OZONISERS
OZONISES
OZONISING
OZONIZE
OZONIZED
OZONIZER
OZONIZERS
OZONIZES
OZONIZING
OZONOUS
OZZIE
OZZIES

O

P

PA
PAAL
PAALS
PAAN
PAANS
PABLUM
PABLUMS
PABOUCHE
PABOUCHES
PABULAR
PABULOUS
PABULUM
PABULUMS
PAC
PACA
PACABLE
PACAS
PACATION
PACATIONS
PACE
PACED
PACEMAKER
PACEMAN
PACEMEN
PACER
PACERS
PACES
PACEWAY
PACEWAYS
PACEY
PACHA
PACHADOM
PACHADOMS
PACHAK
PACHAKS
PACHALIC
PACHALICS
PACHAS
PACHINKO
PACHINKOS
PACHISI
PACHISIS
PACHOULI
PACHOULIS
PACHUCO
PACHUCOS
PACHYDERM
PACHYTENE
PACIER
PACIEST
PACIFIC
PACIFICAE
PACIFICAL
PACIFIED
PACIFIER
PACIFIERS
PACIFIES
PACIFISM
PACIFISMS
PACIFIST
PACIFISTS
PACIFY
PACIFYING
PACING
PACINGS
PACK
PACKABLE
PACKAGE
PACKAGED
PACKAGER
PACKAGERS
PACKAGES
PACKAGING
PACKBOARD
PACKCLOTH
PACKED
PACKER
PACKERS
PACKET
PACKETED
PACKETING
PACKETISE
PACKETIZE
PACKETS
PACKFONG
PACKFONGS
PACKFRAME
PACKHORSE
PACKING
PACKINGS
PACKLY
PACKMAN
PACKMEN
PACKMULE
PACKMULES
PACKNESS
PACKS
PACKSACK
PACKSACKS
PACKSHEET
PACKSTAFF
PACKWAX
PACKWAXES
PACKWAY
PACKWAYS
PACO
PACOS
PACS
PACT
PACTA
PACTION
PACTIONAL
PACTIONED
PACTIONS
PACTS
PACTUM
PACY
PACZKI
PACZKIS
PAD
PADANG
PADANGS
PADAUK
PADAUKS
PADDED
PADDER
PADDERS
PADDIES
PADDING
PADDINGS
PADDLE
PADDLED
PADDLER
PADDLERS
PADDLES
PADDLING
PADDLINGS
PADDOCK
PADDOCKED
PADDOCKS
PADDY
PADDYWACK
PADELLA
PADELLAS
PADEMELON
PADERERO
PADEREROS
PADI
PADIS
PADISHAH
PADISHAHS
PADKOS
PADLE
PADLES
PADLOCK
PADLOCKED
PADLOCKS
PADMA
PADMAS
PADNAG
PADNAGS
PADOUK
PADOUKS
PADRE
PADRES
PADRI
PADRONA
PADRONAS
PADRONE
PADRONES
PADRONI
PADRONISM
PADS
PADSAW
PADSAWS
PADSHAH
PADSHAHS
PADUASOY
PADUASOYS
PADYMELON
PAEAN
PAEANISM
PAEANISMS
PAEANS
PAEDERAST
PAEDEUTIC
PAEDIATRY
PAEDO
PAEDOLOGY
PAEDOS
PAELLA
PAELLAS
PAENULA
PAENULAE
PAENULAS
PAEON
PAEONIC
PAEONICS
PAEONIES
PAEONS
PAEONY
PAESAN
PAESANI
PAESANO
PAESANOS
PAESANS
PAGAN
PAGANDOM
PAGANDOMS
PAGANISE

P

PAGANISED
PAGANISER
PAGANISES
PAGANISH
PAGANISM
PAGANISMS
PAGANIST
PAGANISTS
PAGANIZE
PAGANIZED
PAGANIZER
PAGANIZES
PAGANS
PAGE
PAGEANT
PAGEANTRY
PAGEANTS
PAGEBOY
PAGEBOYS
PAGED
PAGEFUL
PAGEFULS
PAGEHOOD
PAGEHOODS
PAGER
PAGERS
PAGES
PAGEVIEW
PAGEVIEWS
PAGINAL
PAGINATE
PAGINATED
PAGINATES
PAGING
PAGINGS
PAGLE
PAGLES
PAGOD
PAGODA
PAGODAS
PAGODITE
PAGODITES
PAGODS
PAGRI
PAGRIS
PAGURIAN
PAGURIANS
PAGURID
PAGURIDS
PAH
PAHAUTEA
PAHAUTEAS
PAHLAVI
PAHLAVIS
PAHOEHOE
PAHOEHOES
PAHS
PAID
PAIDEUTIC
PAIDLE
PAIDLES
PAIGLE
PAIGLES
PAIK
PAIKED
PAIKING
PAIKS
PAIL
PAILFUL
PAILFULS
PAILLARD
PAILLARDS
PAILLASSE
PAILLETTE
PAILLON
PAILLONS
PAILS
PAILSFUL
PAIN
PAINCH
PAINCHES
PAINED
PAINFUL
PAINFULLY
PAINIM
PAINIMS
PAINING
PAINLESS
PAINS
PAINT
PAINTABLE
PAINTBALL
PAINTBOX
PAINTED
PAINTER
PAINTERLY
PAINTERS
PAINTIER
PAINTIEST
PAINTING
PAINTINGS
PAINTPOT
PAINTPOTS
PAINTRESS
PAINTS
PAINTURE
PAINTURES
PAINTWORK
PAINTY
PAIOCK
PAIOCKE
PAIOCKES
PAIOCKS
PAIR
PAIRE
PAIRED
PAIRER
PAIRES
PAIREST
PAIRIAL
PAIRIALS
PAIRING
PAIRINGS
PAIRS
PAIRWISE
PAIS
PAISA
PAISAN
PAISANA
PAISANAS
PAISANO
PAISANOS
PAISANS
PAISAS
PAISE
PAISLEY
PAISLEYS
PAITRICK
PAITRICKS
PAJAMA
PAJAMAED
PAJAMAS
PAJOCK
PAJOCKE
PAJOCKES
PAJOCKS
PAK
PAKAHI
PAKAHIS
PAKAPOO
PAKAPOOS
PAKEHA
PAKEHAS
PAKFONG
PAKFONGS
PAKIHI
PAKIHIS
PAKKA
PAKOKO
PAKOKOS
PAKORA
PAKORAS
PAKS
PAKTHONG
PAKTHONGS
PAKTONG
PAKTONGS
PAL
PALABRA
PALABRAS
PALACE
PALACED
PALACES
PALACINKE
PALADIN
PALADINS
PALAEOSOL
PALAESTRA
PALAFITTE
PALAGI
PALAGIS
PALAIS
PALAMA
PALAMAE
PALAMATE
PALAMINO
PALAMINOS
PALAMPORE
PALANKEEN
PALANQUIN
PALAPA
PALAPAS
PALAS
PALASES
PALATABLE
PALATABLY
PALATAL
PALATALLY
PALATALS
PALATE
PALATED
PALATES
PALATIAL
PALATINE
PALATINES
PALATING
PALAVER
PALAVERED
PALAVERER
PALAVERS
PALAY
PALAYS
PALAZZI
PALAZZO
PALAZZOS
PALE
PALEA
PALEAE
PALEAL
PALEATE
PALEBUCK
PALEBUCKS
PALED
PALEFACE
PALEFACES
PALELY
PALEMPORE
PALENESS
PALEOCENE
PALEOCON
PALEOCONS
PALEOGENE
PALEOLITH
PALEOLOGY
PALEOSOL
PALEOSOLS
PALEOZOIC
PALER
PALES
PALEST

PALESTRA
PALESTRAE
PALESTRAL
PALESTRAS
PALET
PALETOT
PALETOTS
PALETS
PALETTE
PALETTES
PALEWAYS
PALEWISE
PALFREY
PALFREYED
PALFREYS
PALI
PALIER
PALIEST
PALIFORM
PALIKAR
PALIKARS
PALILALIA
PALILLOGY
PALIMONY
PALING
PALINGS
PALINKA
PALINKAS
PALINODE
PALINODES
PALINODY
PALINOPIA
PALIS
PALISADE
PALISADED
PALISADES
PALISADO
PALISH
PALKEE
PALKEES
PALKI
PALKIS
PALL
PALLA
PALLADIA
PALLADIC
PALLADIUM
PALLADOUS
PALLAE
PALLAH
PALLAHS
PALLASITE
PALLED
PALLET
PALLETED
PALLETING
PALLETISE
PALLETIZE
PALLETS
PALLETTE
PALLETTES
PALLIA
PALLIAL
PALLIARD
PALLIARDS
PALLIASSE
PALLIATE
PALLIATED
PALLIATES
PALLIATOR
PALLID
PALLIDER
PALLIDEST
PALLIDITY
PALLIDLY
PALLIED
PALLIER
PALLIES
PALLIEST
PALLING
PALLIUM
PALLIUMS
PALLONE
PALLONES
PALLOR
PALLORS
PALLS
PALLY
PALLYING
PALM
PALMAR
PALMARIAN
PALMARY
PALMATE
PALMATED
PALMATELY
PALMATION
PALMBALL
PALMBALLS
PALMED
PALMER
PALMERS
PALMETTE
PALMETTES
PALMETTO
PALMETTOS
PALMFUL
PALMFULS
PALMHOUSE
PALMIE
PALMIER
PALMIERS
PALMIES
PALMIEST
PALMIET
PALMIETS
PALMING
PALMIPED
PALMIPEDE
PALMIPEDS
PALMIST
PALMISTER
PALMISTRY
PALMISTS
PALMITATE
PALMITIC
PALMITIN
PALMITINS
PALMLIKE
PALMPRINT
PALMS
PALMTOP
PALMTOPS
PALMY
PALMYRA
PALMYRAS
PALOLO
PALOLOS
PALOMINO
PALOMINOS
PALOOKA
PALOOKAS
PALOVERDE
PALP
PALPABLE
PALPABLY
PALPAL
PALPATE
PALPATED
PALPATES
PALPATING
PALPATION
PALPATOR
PALPATORS
PALPATORY
PALPEBRA
PALPEBRAE
PALPEBRAL
PALPEBRAS
PALPED
PALPI
PALPING
PALPITANT
PALPITATE
PALPS
PALPUS
PALPUSES
PALS
PALSA
PALSAS
PALSGRAVE
PALSHIP
PALSHIPS
PALSIED
PALSIER
PALSIES
PALSIEST
PALSTAFF
PALSTAFFS
PALSTAVE
PALSTAVES
PALSY
PALSYING
PALSYLIKE
PALTER
PALTERED
PALTERER
PALTERERS
PALTERING
PALTERS
PALTRIER
PALTRIEST
PALTRILY
PALTRY
PALUDAL
PALUDIC
PALUDINAL
PALUDINE
PALUDISM
PALUDISMS
PALUDOSE
PALUDOUS
PALUSTRAL
PALY
PAM
PAMPA
PAMPAS
PAMPASES
PAMPEAN
PAMPEANS
PAMPER
PAMPERED
PAMPERER
PAMPERERS
PAMPERING
PAMPERO
PAMPEROS
PAMPERS
PAMPHLET
PAMPHLETS
PAMPHREY
PAMPHREYS
PAMPOEN
PAMPOENS
PAMPOOTIE
PAMS
PAN
PANACEA
PANACEAN
PANACEAS
PANACHAEA
PANACHE
PANACHES
PANADA
PANADAS
PANAMA
PANAMAS
PANARIES
PANARY
PANATELA

P

PANATELAS
PANATELLA
PANAX
PANAXES
PANBROIL
PANBROILS
PANCAKE
PANCAKED
PANCAKES
PANCAKING
PANCE
PANCES
PANCETTA
PANCETTAS
PANCHAX
PANCHAXES
PANCHAYAT
PANCHEON
PANCHEONS
PANCHION
PANCHIONS
PANCOSMIC
PANCRATIA
PANCRATIC
PANCREAS
PAND
PANDA
PANDAN
PANDANI
PANDANIS
PANDANS
PANDANUS
PANDAR
PANDARED
PANDARING
PANDARS
PANDAS
PANDATION
PANDECT
PANDECTS
PANDEMIA
PANDEMIAN
PANDEMIAS
PANDEMIC
PANDEMICS
PANDER
PANDERED
PANDERER
PANDERERS
PANDERESS
PANDERING
PANDERISM
PANDERLY
PANDEROUS
PANDERS
PANDIED
PANDIES
PANDIT
PANDITS
PANDOOR
PANDOORS
PANDORA
PANDORAS
PANDORE
PANDORES
PANDOUR
PANDOURS
PANDOWDY
PANDROP
PANDROPS
PANDS
PANDURA
PANDURAS
PANDURATE
PANDY
PANDYING
PANE
PANED
PANEER
PANEERS
PANEGOISM
PANEGYRIC
PANEGYRY
PANEITIES
PANEITY
PANEL
PANELED
PANELESS
PANELING
PANELINGS
PANELISED
PANELIST
PANELISTS
PANELIZED
PANELLED
PANELLING
PANELLIST
PANELS
PANES
PANETELA
PANETELAS
PANETELLA
PANETTONE
PANETTONI
PANFISH
PANFISHED
PANFISHES
PANFORTE
PANFORTES
PANFRIED
PANFRIES
PANFRY
PANFRYING
PANFUL
PANFULS
PANG
PANGA
PANGAMIC
PANGAMIES
PANGAMY
PANGAS
PANGED
PANGEN
PANGENE
PANGENES
PANGENS
PANGING
PANGLESS
PANGOLIN
PANGOLINS
PANGRAM
PANGRAMS
PANGS
PANHANDLE
PANHUMAN
PANIC
PANICALLY
PANICK
PANICKED
PANICKIER
PANICKING
PANICKS
PANICKY
PANICLE
PANICLED
PANICLES
PANICS
PANICUM
PANICUMS
PANIER
PANIERS
PANIM
PANIMS
PANING
PANINI
PANINIS
PANINO
PANISC
PANISCS
PANISK
PANISKS
PANISLAM
PANISLAMS
PANJANDRA
PANKO
PANKOS
PANLIKE
PANLOGISM
PANMICTIC
PANMIXES
PANMIXIA
PANMIXIAS
PANMIXIS
PANNAGE
PANNAGES
PANNE
PANNED
PANNELLED
PANNER
PANNERS
PANNES
PANNI
PANNICK
PANNICKS
PANNICLE
PANNICLES
PANNIER
PANNIERED
PANNIERS
PANNIKEL
PANNIKELL
PANNIKELS
PANNIKIN
PANNIKINS
PANNING
PANNINGS
PANNIST
PANNISTS
PANNOSE
PANNUS
PANNUSES
PANOCHA
PANOCHAS
PANOCHE
PANOCHES
PANOISTIC
PANOPLIED
PANOPLIES
PANOPLY
PANOPTIC
PANORAMA
PANORAMAS
PANORAMIC
PANPIPE
PANPIPES
PANS
PANSEXUAL
PANSIED
PANSIES
PANSOPHIC
PANSOPHY
PANSPERMY
PANSTICK
PANSTICKS
PANSY
PANT
PANTABLE
PANTABLES
PANTAGAMY
PANTALEON
PANTALET
PANTALETS
PANTALON
PANTALONE
PANTALONS
PANTALOON
PANTDRESS
PANTED
PANTER
PANTERS

PANTHEISM
PANTHEIST
PANTHENOL
PANTHEON
PANTHEONS
PANTHER
PANTHERS
PANTIE
PANTIES
PANTIHOSE
PANTILE
PANTILED
PANTILES
PANTILING
PANTINE
PANTINES
PANTING
PANTINGLY
PANTINGS
PANTLEG
PANTLEGS
PANTLER
PANTLERS
PANTO
PANTOFFLE
PANTOFLE
PANTOFLES
PANTOMIME
PANTON
PANTONS
PANTOS
PANTOUFLE
PANTOUM
PANTOUMS
PANTRIES
PANTROPIC
PANTRY
PANTRYMAN
PANTRYMEN
PANTS
PANTSUIT
PANTSUITS
PANTUN
PANTUNS
PANTY
PANTYHOSE
PANZER
PANZERS
PANZOOTIC
PAOLI
PAOLO
PAP
PAPA
PAPABLE
PAPACIES
PAPACY
PAPADAM
PAPADAMS
PAPADOM
PAPADOMS
PAPADUM
PAPADUMS
PAPAIN
PAPAINS
PAPAL
PAPALISE
PAPALISED
PAPALISES
PAPALISM
PAPALISMS
PAPALIST
PAPALISTS
PAPALIZE
PAPALIZED
PAPALIZES
PAPALLY
PAPARAZZI
PAPARAZZO
PAPAS
PAPASAN
PAPASANS
PAPAUMA
PAPAUMAS
PAPAVER
PAPAVERS
PAPAW
PAPAWS
PAPAYA
PAPAYAN
PAPAYAS
PAPE
PAPER
PAPERBACK
PAPERBARK
PAPERBOY
PAPERBOYS
PAPERCLIP
PAPERED
PAPERER
PAPERERS
PAPERGIRL
PAPERIER
PAPERIEST
PAPERING
PAPERINGS
PAPERLESS
PAPERS
PAPERWARE
PAPERWORK
PAPERY
PAPES
PAPETERIE
PAPHIAN
PAPHIANS
PAPILIO
PAPILIOS
PAPILLA
PAPILLAE
PAPILLAR
PAPILLARY
PAPILLATE
PAPILLOMA
PAPILLON
PAPILLONS
PAPILLOSE
PAPILLOTE
PAPILLOUS
PAPILLULE
PAPISH
PAPISHER
PAPISHERS
PAPISHES
PAPISM
PAPISMS
PAPIST
PAPISTIC
PAPISTRY
PAPISTS
PAPOOSE
PAPOOSES
PAPPADAM
PAPPADAMS
PAPPADOM
PAPPADOMS
PAPPADUM
PAPPADUMS
PAPPED
PAPPI
PAPPIER
PAPPIES
PAPPIEST
PAPPING
PAPPOOSE
PAPPOOSES
PAPPOSE
PAPPOUS
PAPPUS
PAPPUSES
PAPPY
PAPRICA
PAPRICAS
PAPRIKA
PAPRIKAS
PAPRIKASH
PAPS
PAPULA
PAPULAE
PAPULAR
PAPULAS
PAPULE
PAPULES
PAPULOSE
PAPULOUS
PAPYRAL
PAPYRI
PAPYRIAN
PAPYRINE
PAPYRUS
PAPYRUSES
PAR
PARA
PARABASES
PARABASIS
PARABEMA
PARABEN
PARABENS
PARABLAST
PARABLE
PARABLED
PARABLES
PARABLING
PARABOLA
PARABOLAE
PARABOLAS
PARABOLE
PARABOLES
PARABOLIC
PARABRAKE
PARACHOR
PARACHORS
PARACHUTE
PARACLETE
PARACME
PARACMES
PARACRINE
PARACUSES
PARACUSIS
PARADE
PARADED
PARADER
PARADERS
PARADES
PARADIGM
PARADIGMS
PARADING
PARADISAL
PARADISE
PARADISES
PARADISIC
PARADOR
PARADORES
PARADORS
PARADOS
PARADOSES
PARADOX
PARADOXAL
PARADOXER
PARADOXES
PARADOXY
PARADROP
PARADROPS
PARAE
PARAFFIN
PARAFFINE
PARAFFINS
PARAFFINY
PARAFFLE
PARAFFLES
PARAFLE
PARAFLES

P

PARAFOIL
PARAFOILS
PARAFORM
PARAFORMS
PARAGE
PARAGES
PARAGLIDE
PARAGOGE
PARAGOGES
PARAGOGIC
PARAGOGUE
PARAGON
PARAGONED
PARAGONS
PARAGRAM
PARAGRAMS
PARAGRAPH
PARAKEET
PARAKEETS
PARAKELIA
PARAKITE
PARAKITES
PARALALIA
PARALEGAL
PARALEXIA
PARALEXIC
PARALLAX
PARALLEL
PARALLELS
PARALOGIA
PARALOGUE
PARALOGY
PARALYSE
PARALYSED
PARALYSER
PARALYSES
PARALYSIS
PARALYTIC
PARALYZE
PARALYZED
PARALYZER
PARALYZES
PARAMATTA
PARAMECIA
PARAMEDIC
PARAMENT
PARAMENTA
PARAMENTS
PARAMESE
PARAMESES
PARAMETER
PARAMO
PARAMORPH
PARAMOS
PARAMOUNT
PARAMOUR
PARAMOURS
PARAMYLUM
PARANETE
PARANETES
PARANG
PARANGS
PARANOEA
PARANOEAS
PARANOEIC
PARANOIA
PARANOIAC
PARANOIAS
PARANOIC
PARANOICS
PARANOID
PARANOIDS
PARANYM
PARANYMPH
PARANYMS
PARAPARA
PARAPARAS
PARAPENTE
PARAPET
PARAPETED
PARAPETS
PARAPH
PARAPHED
PARAPHING
PARAPHS
PARAPODIA
PARAQUAT
PARAQUATS
PARAQUET
PARAQUETS
PARAQUITO
PARARHYME
PARAS
PARASAIL
PARASAILS
PARASANG
PARASANGS
PARASCEVE
PARASHAH
PARASHAHS
PARASHOT
PARASHOTH
PARASITE
PARASITES
PARASITIC
PARASOL
PARASOLED
PARASOLS
PARATAXES
PARATAXIS
PARATHA
PARATHAS
PARATHION
PARATONIC
PARATROOP
PARAVAIL
PARAVANE
PARAVANES
PARAVANT
PARAVANTS
PARAVAUNT
PARAWING
PARAWINGS
PARAXIAL
PARAZOA
PARAZOAN
PARAZOANS
PARAZOON
PARBAKE
PARBAKED
PARBAKES
PARBAKING
PARBOIL
PARBOILED
PARBOILS
PARBREAK
PARBREAKS
PARBUCKLE
PARCEL
PARCELED
PARCELING
PARCELLED
PARCELS
PARCENARY
PARCENER
PARCENERS
PARCH
PARCHED
PARCHEDLY
PARCHEESI
PARCHES
PARCHESI
PARCHESIS
PARCHING
PARCHISI
PARCHISIS
PARCHMENT
PARCIMONY
PARCLOSE
PARCLOSES
PARD
PARDAH
PARDAHS
PARDAL
PARDALE
PARDALES
PARDALIS
PARDALOTE
PARDALS
PARDED
PARDEE
PARDI
PARDIE
PARDINE
PARDNER
PARDNERS
PARDON
PARDONED
PARDONER
PARDONERS
PARDONING
PARDONS
PARDS
PARDY
PARE
PARECIOUS
PARECISM
PARECISMS
PARED
PAREGORIC
PAREIRA
PAREIRAS
PARELLA
PARELLAS
PARELLE
PARELLES
PAREN
PARENESES
PARENESIS
PARENS
PARENT
PARENTAGE
PARENTAL
PARENTED
PARENTING
PARENTS
PAREO
PAREOS
PARER
PARERA
PARERAS
PARERGA
PARERGON
PARERS
PARES
PARESES
PARESIS
PARETIC
PARETICS
PAREU
PAREUS
PAREV
PAREVE
PARFAIT
PARFAITS
PARFLECHE
PARFLESH
PARFOCAL
PARGANA
PARGANAS
PARGASITE
PARGE
PARGED
PARGES
PARGET
PARGETED
PARGETER
PARGETERS
PARGETING
PARGETS

P

PARGETTED
PARGETTER
PARGING
PARGINGS
PARGO
PARGOES
PARGOS
PARGYLINE
PARHELIA
PARHELIC
PARHELION
PARHYPATE
PARIAH
PARIAHS
PARIAL
PARIALS
PARIAN
PARIANS
PARIES
PARIETAL
PARIETALS
PARIETES
PARING
PARINGS
PARIS
PARISCHAN
PARISES
PARISH
PARISHAD
PARISHADS
PARISHEN
PARISHENS
PARISHES
PARISON
PARISONS
PARITIES
PARITOR
PARITORS
PARITY
PARK
PARKA
PARKADE
PARKADES
PARKAS
PARKED
PARKEE
PARKEES
PARKER
PARKERS
PARKETTE
PARKETTES
PARKI
PARKIE
PARKIER
PARKIES
PARKIEST
PARKIN
PARKING
PARKINGS
PARKINS
PARKIS
PARKISH
PARKLAND
PARKLANDS
PARKLIKE
PARKLY
PARKOUR
PARKOURS
PARKS
PARKWARD
PARKWARDS
PARKWAY
PARKWAYS
PARKY
PARLANCE
PARLANCES
PARLANDO
PARLANTE
PARLAY
PARLAYED
PARLAYING
PARLAYS
PARLE
PARLED
PARLEMENT
PARLES
PARLEY
PARLEYED
PARLEYER
PARLEYERS
PARLEYING
PARLEYS
PARLEYVOO
PARLIES
PARLING
PARLOR
PARLORS
PARLOUR
PARLOURS
PARLOUS
PARLOUSLY
PARLY
PARMA
PARMAS
PARMESAN
PARMESANS
PAROCHIAL
PAROCHIN
PAROCHINE
PAROCHINS
PARODIC
PARODICAL
PARODIED
PARODIES
PARODIST
PARODISTS
PARODOI
PARODOS
PARODY
PARODYING
PAROECISM
PAROEMIA
PAROEMIAC
PAROEMIAL
PAROEMIAS
PAROICOUS
PAROL
PAROLABLE
PAROLE
PAROLED
PAROLEE
PAROLEES
PAROLES
PAROLING
PAROLS
PARONYM
PARONYMIC
PARONYMS
PARONYMY
PAROQUET
PAROQUETS
PARORE
PARORES
PAROSMIA
PAROSMIAS
PAROTIC
PAROTID
PAROTIDES
PAROTIDS
PAROTIS
PAROTISES
PAROTITIC
PAROTITIS
PAROTOID
PAROTOIDS
PAROUS
PAROUSIA
PAROUSIAS
PAROXYSM
PAROXYSMS
PARP
PARPANE
PARPANES
PARPED
PARPEN
PARPEND
PARPENDS
PARPENS
PARPENT
PARPENTS
PARPING
PARPOINT
PARPOINTS
PARPS
PARQUET
PARQUETED
PARQUETRY
PARQUETS
PARR
PARRA
PARRAKEET
PARRAL
PARRALS
PARRAS
PARRED
PARREL
PARRELS
PARRHESIA
PARRICIDE
PARRIDGE
PARRIDGES
PARRIED
PARRIER
PARRIERS
PARRIES
PARRING
PARRITCH
PARROCK
PARROCKED
PARROCKS
PARROKET
PARROKETS
PARROQUET
PARROT
PARROTED
PARROTER
PARROTERS
PARROTIER
PARROTING
PARROTRY
PARROTS
PARROTY
PARRS
PARRY
PARRYING
PARS
PARSABLE
PARSE
PARSEC
PARSECS
PARSED
PARSER
PARSERS
PARSES
PARSIMONY
PARSING
PARSINGS
PARSLEY
PARSLEYED
PARSLEYS
PARSLIED
PARSNEP
PARSNEPS
PARSNIP
PARSNIPS
PARSON
PARSONAGE
PARSONIC
PARSONISH
PARSONS

PART
PARTAKE
PARTAKEN
PARTAKER
PARTAKERS
PARTAKES
PARTAKING
PARTAN
PARTANS
PARTED
PARTER
PARTERRE
PARTERRES
PARTERS
PARTI
PARTIAL
PARTIALLY
PARTIALS
PARTIBLE
PARTICLE
PARTICLES
PARTIED
PARTIER
PARTIERS
PARTIES
PARTIEST
PARTIM
PARTING
PARTINGS
PARTIS
PARTISAN
PARTISANS
PARTITA
PARTITAS
PARTITE
PARTITION
PARTITIVE
PARTITURA
PARTIZAN
PARTIZANS
PARTLET
PARTLETS
PARTLY
PARTNER
PARTNERED
PARTNERS
PARTON
PARTONS
PARTOOK
PARTRIDGE
PARTS
PARTURE
PARTURES
PARTWAY
PARTWORK
PARTWORKS
PARTY
PARTYER
PARTYERS
PARTYGOER
PARTYING
PARTYINGS
PARTYISM
PARTYISMS
PARULIDES
PARULIS
PARULISES
PARURA
PARURAS
PARURE
PARURES
PARURESES
PARURESIS
PARURETIC
PARVE
PARVENU
PARVENUE
PARVENUES
PARVENUS
PARVIS
PARVISE
PARVISES
PARVO
PARVOLIN
PARVOLINE
PARVOLINS
PARVOS
PAS
PASCAL
PASCALS
PASCHAL
PASCHALS
PASCUAL
PASCUALS
PASE
PASEAR
PASEARED
PASEARING
PASEARS
PASELA
PASELAS
PASEO
PASEOS
PASES
PASH
PASHA
PASHADOM
PASHADOMS
PASHALIC
PASHALICS
PASHALIK
PASHALIKS
PASHAS
PASHED
PASHES
PASHIM
PASHIMS
PASHING
PASHKA
PASHKAS
PASHM
PASHMINA
PASHMINAS
PASHMS
PASKA
PASKAS
PASKHA
PASKHAS
PASODOBLE
PASPALUM
PASPALUMS
PASPIES
PASPY
PASQUIL
PASQUILER
PASQUILS
PASS
PASSABLE
PASSABLY
PASSADE
PASSADES
PASSADO
PASSADOES
PASSADOS
PASSAGE
PASSAGED
PASSAGER
PASSAGES
PASSAGING
PASSALONG
PASSAMENT
PASSANT
PASSATA
PASSATAS
PASSBAND
PASSBANDS
PASSBOOK
PASSBOOKS
PASSCODE
PASSCODES
PASSE
PASSED
PASSEE
PASSEL
PASSELS
PASSEMENT
PASSENGER
PASSEPIED
PASSER
PASSERBY
PASSERINE
PASSERS
PASSERSBY
PASSES
PASSIBLE
PASSIBLY
PASSIM
PASSING
PASSINGLY
PASSINGS
PASSION
PASSIONAL
PASSIONED
PASSIONS
PASSIVATE
PASSIVE
PASSIVELY
PASSIVES
PASSIVISM
PASSIVIST
PASSIVITY
PASSKEY
PASSKEYS
PASSLESS
PASSMAN
PASSMEN
PASSMENT
PASSMENTS
PASSOUT
PASSOUTS
PASSOVER
PASSOVERS
PASSPORT
PASSPORTS
PASSUS
PASSUSES
PASSWORD
PASSWORDS
PAST
PASTA
PASTALIKE
PASTANCE
PASTANCES
PASTAS
PASTE
PASTED
PASTEDOWN
PASTEL
PASTELIKE
PASTELIST
PASTELS
PASTER
PASTERN
PASTERNS
PASTERS
PASTES
PASTEUP
PASTEUPS
PASTICCI
PASTICCIO
PASTICHE
PASTICHES
PASTIE
PASTIER
PASTIES
PASTIEST
PASTIL
PASTILLE
PASTILLES
PASTILS

PASTILY
PASTIME
PASTIMES
PASTINA
PASTINAS
PASTINESS
PASTING
PASTINGS
PASTIS
PASTISES
PASTITSIO
PASTITSO
PASTITSOS
PASTLESS
PASTNESS
PASTOR
PASTORAL
PASTORALE
PASTORALI
PASTORALS
PASTORATE
PASTORED
PASTORING
PASTORIUM
PASTORLY
PASTORS
PASTRAMI
PASTRAMIS
PASTRIES
PASTROMI
PASTROMIS
PASTRY
PASTS
PASTURAGE
PASTURAL
PASTURE
PASTURED
PASTURER
PASTURERS
PASTURES
PASTURING
PASTY
PAT
PATACA
PATACAS
PATAGIA
PATAGIAL
PATAGIUM
PATAKA
PATAKAS
PATAMAR
PATAMARS
PATBALL
PATBALLS
PATCH
PATCHABLE
PATCHED
PATCHER
PATCHERS
PATCHERY
PATCHES
PATCHIER
PATCHIEST
PATCHILY
PATCHING
PATCHINGS
PATCHOCKE
PATCHOULI
PATCHOULY
PATCHWORK
PATCHY
PATE
PATED
PATELLA
PATELLAE
PATELLAR
PATELLAS
PATELLATE
PATEN
PATENCIES
PATENCY
PATENS
PATENT
PATENTED
PATENTEE
PATENTEES
PATENTING
PATENTLY
PATENTOR
PATENTORS
PATENTS
PATER
PATERA
PATERAE
PATERCOVE
PATERERO
PATEREROS
PATERNAL
PATERNITY
PATERS
PATES
PATH
PATHED
PATHETIC
PATHETICS
PATHIC
PATHICS
PATHING
PATHLESS
PATHNAME
PATHNAMES
PATHOGEN
PATHOGENE
PATHOGENS
PATHOGENY
PATHOLOGY
PATHOS
PATHOSES
PATHS
PATHWAY
PATHWAYS
PATIBLE
PATIENCE
PATIENCES
PATIENT
PATIENTED
PATIENTER
PATIENTLY
PATIENTS
PATIKI
PATIKIS
PATIN
PATINA
PATINAE
PATINAED
PATINAS
PATINATE
PATINATED
PATINATES
PATINE
PATINED
PATINES
PATINING
PATINISE
PATINISED
PATINISES
PATINIZE
PATINIZED
PATINIZES
PATINS
PATIO
PATIOS
PATISSIER
PATKA
PATKAS
PATLY
PATNESS
PATNESSES
PATOIS
PATONCE
PATOOT
PATOOTIE
PATOOTIES
PATOOTS
PATRIAL
PATRIALS
PATRIARCH
PATRIATE
PATRIATED
PATRIATES
PATRICIAN
PATRICIDE
PATRICK
PATRICKS
PATRICO
PATRICOES
PATRICOS
PATRILINY
PATRIMONY
PATRIOT
PATRIOTIC
PATRIOTS
PATRISTIC
PATROL
PATROLLED
PATROLLER
PATROLMAN
PATROLMEN
PATROLOGY
PATROLS
PATRON
PATRONAGE
PATRONAL
PATRONESS
PATRONISE
PATRONIZE
PATRONLY
PATRONNE
PATRONNES
PATRONS
PATROON
PATROONS
PATS
PATSIES
PATSY
PATTAMAR
PATTAMARS
PATTE
PATTED
PATTEE
PATTEN
PATTENED
PATTENING
PATTENS
PATTER
PATTERED
PATTERER
PATTERERS
PATTERING
PATTERN
PATTERNED
PATTERNS
PATTERS
PATTES
PATTEST
PATTIE
PATTIES
PATTING
PATTLE
PATTLES
PATTRESS
PATTY
PATTYPAN
PATTYPANS
PATU
PATULENT
PATULIN
PATULINS
PATULOUS
PATUS

P

PATUTUKI
PATUTUKIS
PATY
PATZER
PATZERS
PAUA
PAUAS
PAUCAL
PAUCALS
PAUCITIES
PAUCITY
PAUGHTIER
PAUGHTY
PAUL
PAULDRON
PAULDRONS
PAULIN
PAULINS
PAULOWNIA
PAULS
PAUNCE
PAUNCES
PAUNCH
PAUNCHED
PAUNCHES
PAUNCHIER
PAUNCHING
PAUNCHY
PAUPER
PAUPERDOM
PAUPERED
PAUPERESS
PAUPERING
PAUPERISE
PAUPERISM
PAUPERIZE
PAUPERS
PAUPIETTE
PAURAQUE
PAURAQUES
PAUROPOD
PAUROPODS
PAUSAL
PAUSE
PAUSED
PAUSEFUL
PAUSELESS
PAUSER
PAUSERS
PAUSES
PAUSING
PAUSINGLY
PAUSINGS
PAV
PAVAGE
PAVAGES
PAVAN
PAVANE
PAVANES
PAVANS
PAVE
PAVED
PAVEED
PAVEMENT
PAVEMENTS
PAVEN
PAVENS
PAVER
PAVERS
PAVES
PAVID
PAVILION
PAVILIONS
PAVILLON
PAVILLONS
PAVIN
PAVING
PAVINGS
PAVINS
PAVIOR
PAVIORS
PAVIOUR
PAVIOURS
PAVIS
PAVISE
PAVISER
PAVISERS
PAVISES
PAVISSE
PAVISSES
PAVLOVA
PAVLOVAS
PAVONAZZO
PAVONE
PAVONES
PAVONIAN
PAVONINE
PAVS
PAW
PAWA
PAWAS
PAWAW
PAWAWED
PAWAWING
PAWAWS
PAWED
PAWER
PAWERS
PAWING
PAWK
PAWKIER
PAWKIEST
PAWKILY
PAWKINESS
PAWKS
PAWKY
PAWL
PAWLS
PAWN
PAWNABLE
PAWNAGE
PAWNAGES
PAWNCE
PAWNCES
PAWNED
PAWNEE
PAWNEES
PAWNER
PAWNERS
PAWNING
PAWNOR
PAWNORS
PAWNS
PAWNSHOP
PAWNSHOPS
PAWPAW
PAWPAWS
PAWS
PAX
PAXES
PAXIUBA
PAXIUBAS
PAXWAX
PAXWAXES
PAY
PAYABLE
PAYABLES
PAYABLY
PAYBACK
PAYBACKS
PAYCHECK
PAYCHECKS
PAYCHEQUE
PAYDAY
PAYDAYS
PAYDOWN
PAYDOWNS
PAYED
PAYEE
PAYEES
PAYER
PAYERS
PAYESS
PAYFONE
PAYFONES
PAYGRADE
PAYGRADES
PAYING
PAYINGS
PAYLIST
PAYLISTS
PAYLOAD
PAYLOADS
PAYMASTER
PAYMENT
PAYMENTS
PAYNIM
PAYNIMRY
PAYNIMS
PAYOFF
PAYOFFS
PAYOLA
PAYOLAS
PAYOR
PAYORS
PAYOUT
PAYOUTS
PAYPHONE
PAYPHONES
PAYROLL
PAYROLLS
PAYS
PAYSAGE
PAYSAGES
PAYSAGIST
PAYSD
PAYSLIP
PAYSLIPS
PAYWALL
PAYWALLS
PAZAZZ
PAZAZZES
PAZZAZZ
PAZZAZZES
PE
PEA
PEABERRY
PEABRAIN
PEABRAINS
PEACE
PEACEABLE
PEACEABLY
PEACED
PEACEFUL
PEACELESS
PEACENIK
PEACENIKS
PEACES
PEACETIME
PEACH
PEACHBLOW
PEACHED
PEACHER
PEACHERS
PEACHES
PEACHICK
PEACHICKS
PEACHIER
PEACHIEST
PEACHILY
PEACHING
PEACHY
PEACING
PEACOAT
PEACOATS
PEACOCK
PEACOCKED
PEACOCKS
PEACOCKY
PEACOD

PEACODS
PEAFOWL
PEAFOWLS
PEAG
PEAGE
PEAGES
PEAGS
PEAHEN
PEAHENS
PEAK
PEAKED
PEAKIER
PEAKIEST
PEAKINESS
PEAKING
PEAKINGS
PEAKISH
PEAKLESS
PEAKLIKE
PEAKS
PEAKY
PEAL
PEALED
PEALIKE
PEALING
PEALS
PEAN
PEANED
PEANING
PEANS
PEANUT
PEANUTS
PEANUTTY
PEAPOD
PEAPODS
PEAR
PEARCE
PEARCED
PEARCES
PEARCING
PEARE
PEARES
PEARL
PEARLASH
PEARLED
PEARLER
PEARLERS
PEARLIER
PEARLIES
PEARLIEST
PEARLIN
PEARLING
PEARLINGS
PEARLINS
PEARLISED
PEARLITE
PEARLITES
PEARLITIC
PEARLIZED
PEARLS
PEARLWARE
PEARLWORT
PEARLY
PEARMAIN
PEARMAINS
PEARS
PEARST
PEART
PEARTER
PEARTEST
PEARTLY
PEARTNESS
PEARWOOD
PEARWOODS
PEAS
PEASANT
PEASANTRY
PEASANTS
PEASANTY
PEASCOD
PEASCODS
PEASE
PEASECOD
PEASECODS
PEASED
PEASEN
PEASES
PEASING
PEASON
PEASOUPER
PEAT
PEATARIES
PEATARY
PEATERIES
PEATERY
PEATIER
PEATIEST
PEATLAND
PEATLANDS
PEATMAN
PEATMEN
PEATS
PEATSHIP
PEATSHIPS
PEATY
PEAVEY
PEAVEYS
PEAVIES
PEAVY
PEAZE
PEAZED
PEAZES
PEAZING
PEBA
PEBAS
PEBBLE
PEBBLED
PEBBLES
PEBBLIER
PEBBLIEST
PEBBLING
PEBBLINGS
PEBBLY
PEBIBYTE
PEBIBYTES
PEBRINE
PEBRINES
PEC
PECAN
PECANS
PECCABLE
PECCANCY
PECCANT
PECCANTLY
PECCARIES
PECCARY
PECCAVI
PECCAVIS
PECH
PECHAN
PECHANS
PECHED
PECHING
PECHS
PECK
PECKE
PECKED
PECKER
PECKERS
PECKES
PECKIER
PECKIEST
PECKING
PECKINGS
PECKISH
PECKISHLY
PECKS
PECKY
PECORINI
PECORINO
PECORINOS
PECS
PECTASE
PECTASES
PECTATE
PECTATES
PECTEN
PECTENS
PECTIC
PECTIN
PECTINAL
PECTINALS
PECTINATE
PECTINEAL
PECTINEI
PECTINES
PECTINEUS
PECTINOUS
PECTINS
PECTISE
PECTISED
PECTISES
PECTISING
PECTIZE
PECTIZED
PECTIZES
PECTIZING
PECTOLITE
PECTORAL
PECTORALS
PECTOSE
PECTOSES
PECULATE
PECULATED
PECULATES
PECULATOR
PECULIA
PECULIAR
PECULIARS
PECULIUM
PECUNIARY
PECUNIOUS
PED
PEDAGOG
PEDAGOGIC
PEDAGOGS
PEDAGOGUE
PEDAGOGY
PEDAL
PEDALBOAT
PEDALCAR
PEDALCARS
PEDALED
PEDALER
PEDALERS
PEDALFER
PEDALFERS
PEDALIER
PEDALIERS
PEDALING
PEDALLED
PEDALLER
PEDALLERS
PEDALLING
PEDALO
PEDALOES
PEDALOS
PEDALS
PEDANT
PEDANTIC
PEDANTISE
PEDANTISM
PEDANTIZE
PEDANTRY
PEDANTS
PEDATE
PEDATELY
PEDATIFID
PEDDER
PEDDERS

PEDDLE
PEDDLED
PEDDLER
PEDDLERS
PEDDLERY
PEDDLES
PEDDLING
PEDDLINGS
PEDERAST
PEDERASTS
PEDERASTY
PEDERERO
PEDEREROS
PEDES
PEDESES
PEDESIS
PEDESTAL
PEDESTALS
PEDETIC
PEDI
PEDIATRIC
PEDICAB
PEDICABS
PEDICEL
PEDICELS
PEDICLE
PEDICLED
PEDICLES
PEDICULAR
PEDICULI
PEDICULUS
PEDICURE
PEDICURED
PEDICURES
PEDIFORM
PEDIGREE
PEDIGREED
PEDIGREES
PEDIMENT
PEDIMENTS
PEDIPALP
PEDIPALPI
PEDIPALPS
PEDIS
PEDLAR
PEDLARIES
PEDLARS
PEDLARY

PEDLER
PEDLERIES
PEDLERS
PEDLERY
PEDOCAL
PEDOCALIC
PEDOCALS
PEDOGENIC
PEDOLOGIC
PEDOLOGY
PEDOMETER
PEDOPHILE
PEDORTHIC
PEDRAIL
PEDRAILS
PEDRERO
PEDREROES
PEDREROS
PEDRO
PEDROS
PEDS
PEDUNCLE
PEDUNCLED
PEDUNCLES
PEDWAY
PEDWAYS
PEE
PEEBEEN
PEEBEENS
PEECE
PEECES
PEED
PEEING
PEEK
PEEKABO
PEEKABOO
PEEKABOOS
PEEKABOS
PEEKAPOO
PEEKAPOOS
PEEKED
PEEKING
PEEKS
PEEL
PEELABLE
PEELED
PEELER
PEELERS

PEELING
PEELINGS
PEELS
PEEN
PEENED
PEENGE
PEENGED
PEENGEING
PEENGES
PEENGING
PEENING
PEENINGS
PEENS
PEEOY
PEEOYS
PEEP
PEEPBO
PEEPBOS
PEEPE
PEEPED
PEEPER
PEEPERS
PEEPES
PEEPHOLE
PEEPHOLES
PEEPING
PEEPS
PEEPSHOW
PEEPSHOWS
PEEPTOE
PEEPUL
PEEPULS
PEER
PEERAGE
PEERAGES
PEERED
PEERESS
PEERESSES
PEERIE
PEERIER
PEERIES
PEERIEST
PEERING
PEERLESS
PEERS
PEERY
PEES
PEESWEEP

PEESWEEPS
PEETWEET
PEETWEETS
PEEVE
PEEVED
PEEVER
PEEVERS
PEEVES
PEEVING
PEEVISH
PEEVISHLY
PEEWEE
PEEWEES
PEEWIT
PEEWITS
PEG
PEGASUS
PEGASUSES
PEGBOARD
PEGBOARDS
PEGBOX
PEGBOXES
PEGGED
PEGGIER
PEGGIES
PEGGIEST
PEGGING
PEGGINGS
PEGGY
PEGH
PEGHED
PEGHING
PEGHS
PEGLEGGED
PEGLESS
PEGLIKE
PEGMATITE
PEGS
PEGTOP
PEGTOPS
PEH
PEHS
PEIGNOIR
PEIGNOIRS
PEIN
PEINCT
PEINCTED
PEINCTING

PEINCTS
PEINED
PEINING
PEINS
PEIRASTIC
PEISE
PEISED
PEISES
PEISHWA
PEISHWAH
PEISHWAHS
PEISHWAS
PEISING
PEIZE
PEIZED
PEIZES
PEIZING
PEJORATE
PEJORATED
PEJORATES
PEKAN
PEKANS
PEKE
PEKEPOO
PEKEPOOS
PEKES
PEKIN
PEKINS
PEKOE
PEKOES
PEL
PELA
PELAGE
PELAGES
PELAGIAL
PELAGIALS
PELAGIAN
PELAGIANS
PELAGIC
PELAGICS
PELAS
PELAU
PELAUS
PELE
PELECYPOD
PELERINE
PELERINES
PELES

PELF
PELFS
PELHAM
PELHAMS
PELICAN
PELICANS
PELISSE
PELISSES
PELITE
PELITES
PELITIC
PELL
PELLACH
PELLACHS
PELLACK
PELLACKS
PELLAGRA
PELLAGRAS
PELLAGRIN
PELLED
PELLET
PELLETAL
PELLETED
PELLETIFY
PELLETING
PELLETISE
PELLETIZE
PELLETS
PELLICLE
PELLICLES
PELLING
PELLITORY
PELLMELL
PELLMELLS
PELLOCK
PELLOCKS
PELLS
PELLUCID
PELLUM
PELLUMS
PELMA
PELMANISM
PELMAS
PELMATIC
PELMET
PELMETS
PELOID
PELOIDS
PELOLOGY
PELON
PELONS
PELORIA
PELORIAN
PELORIAS
PELORIC
PELORIES
PELORISED
PELORISM
PELORISMS
PELORIZED
PELORUS
PELORUSES
PELORY
PELOTA
PELOTAS
PELOTON
PELOTONS
PELS
PELT
PELTA
PELTAE
PELTAS
PELTAST
PELTASTS
PELTATE
PELTATELY
PELTATION
PELTED
PELTER
PELTERED
PELTERING
PELTERS
PELTING
PELTINGLY
PELTINGS
PELTLESS
PELTRIES
PELTRY
PELTS
PELVES
PELVIC
PELVICS
PELVIFORM
PELVIS
PELVISES
PEMBINA
PEMBINAS
PEMBROKE
PEMBROKES
PEMICAN
PEMICANS
PEMMICAN
PEMMICANS
PEMOLINE
PEMOLINES
PEMPHIGI
PEMPHIGUS
PEMPHIX
PEMPHIXES
PEN
PENAL
PENALISE
PENALISED
PENALISES
PENALITY
PENALIZE
PENALIZED
PENALIZES
PENALLY
PENALTIES
PENALTY
PENANCE
PENANCED
PENANCES
PENANCING
PENANG
PENANGS
PENATES
PENCE
PENCEL
PENCELS
PENCES
PENCHANT
PENCHANTS
PENCIL
PENCILED
PENCILER
PENCILERS
PENCILING
PENCILLED
PENCILLER
PENCILS
PENCRAFT
PENCRAFTS
PEND
PENDANT
PENDANTLY
PENDANTS
PENDED
PENDENCY
PENDENT
PENDENTLY
PENDENTS
PENDICLE
PENDICLER
PENDICLES
PENDING
PENDRAGON
PENDS
PENDU
PENDULAR
PENDULATE
PENDULE
PENDULES
PENDULINE
PENDULOUS
PENDULUM
PENDULUMS
PENE
PENED
PENEPLAIN
PENEPLANE
PENES
PENETRANT
PENETRATE
PENFOLD
PENFOLDS
PENFRIEND
PENFUL
PENFULS
PENGO
PENGOS
PENGUIN
PENGUINRY
PENGUINS
PENHOLDER
PENI
PENIAL
PENICIL
PENICILLI
PENICILS
PENIE
PENIES
PENILE
PENILL
PENILLION
PENING
PENINSULA
PENIS
PENISES
PENISTONE
PENITENCE
PENITENCY
PENITENT
PENITENTS
PENK
PENKNIFE
PENKNIVES
PENKS
PENLIGHT
PENLIGHTS
PENLIKE
PENLITE
PENLITES
PENMAN
PENMEN
PENNA
PENNAE
PENNAL
PENNALISM
PENNALS
PENNAME
PENNAMES
PENNANT
PENNANTS
PENNATE
PENNATED
PENNATULA
PENNE
PENNED
PENNEECH
PENNEECHS
PENNEECK
PENNEECKS
PENNER
PENNERS
PENNES
PENNI
PENNIA
PENNIED

PENNIES
PENNIFORM
PENNILESS
PENNILL
PENNINE
PENNINES
PENNING
PENNINITE
PENNIS
PENNON
PENNONCEL
PENNONED
PENNONS
PENNY
PENNYBOY
PENNYBOYS
PENNYFEE
PENNYFEES
PENNYLAND
PENNYWISE
PENNYWORT
PENOCHE
PENOCHES
PENOLOGY
PENONCEL
PENONCELS
PENPOINT
PENPOINTS
PENPUSHER
PENS
PENSEE
PENSEES
PENSEL
PENSELS
PENSEROSO
PENSIL
PENSILE
PENSILITY
PENSILS
PENSION
PENSIONE
PENSIONED
PENSIONER
PENSIONES
PENSIONI
PENSIONS
PENSIVE
PENSIVELY
PENSTEMON
PENSTER
PENSTERS
PENSTOCK
PENSTOCKS
PENSUM
PENSUMS
PENT
PENTACLE
PENTACLES
PENTACT
PENTACTS
PENTAD
PENTADIC
PENTADS
PENTAGON
PENTAGONS
PENTAGRAM
PENTALOGY
PENTALPHA
PENTAMERY
PENTANE
PENTANES
PENTANGLE
PENTANOIC
PENTANOL
PENTANOLS
PENTAPODY
PENTARCH
PENTARCHS
PENTARCHY
PENTATHLA
PENTEL
PENTELS
PENTENE
PENTENES
PENTHIA
PENTHIAS
PENTHOUSE
PENTICE
PENTICED
PENTICES
PENTICING
PENTISE
PENTISED
PENTISES
PENTISING
PENTITI
PENTITO
PENTODE
PENTODES
PENTOMIC
PENTOSAN
PENTOSANE
PENTOSANS
PENTOSE
PENTOSES
PENTOSIDE
PENTOXIDE
PENTROOF
PENTROOFS
PENTS
PENTYL
PENTYLENE
PENTYLS
PENUCHE
PENUCHES
PENUCHI
PENUCHIS
PENUCHLE
PENUCHLES
PENUCKLE
PENUCKLES
PENULT
PENULTIMA
PENULTS
PENUMBRA
PENUMBRAE
PENUMBRAL
PENUMBRAS
PENURIES
PENURIOUS
PENURY
PENWIPER
PENWIPERS
PENWOMAN
PENWOMEN
PEON
PEONAGE
PEONAGES
PEONES
PEONIES
PEONISM
PEONISMS
PEONS
PEONY
PEOPLE
PEOPLED
PEOPLER
PEOPLERS
PEOPLES
PEOPLING
PEP
PEPERINO
PEPERINOS
PEPEROMIA
PEPERONI
PEPERONIS
PEPFUL
PEPINO
PEPINOS
PEPITA
PEPITAS
PEPLA
PEPLOS
PEPLOSES
PEPLUM
PEPLUMED
PEPLUMS
PEPLUS
PEPLUSES
PEPO
PEPONIDA
PEPONIDAS
PEPONIUM
PEPONIUMS
PEPOS
PEPPED
PEPPER
PEPPERBOX
PEPPERED
PEPPERER
PEPPERERS
PEPPERIER
PEPPERING
PEPPERONI
PEPPERS
PEPPERY
PEPPIER
PEPPIEST
PEPPILY
PEPPINESS
PEPPING
PEPPY
PEPS
PEPSI
PEPSIN
PEPSINATE
PEPSINE
PEPSINES
PEPSINS
PEPSIS
PEPTALK
PEPTALKED
PEPTALKS
PEPTIC
PEPTICITY
PEPTICS
PEPTID
PEPTIDASE
PEPTIDE
PEPTIDES
PEPTIDIC
PEPTIDS
PEPTISE
PEPTISED
PEPTISER
PEPTISERS
PEPTISES
PEPTISING
PEPTIZE
PEPTIZED
PEPTIZER
PEPTIZERS
PEPTIZES
PEPTIZING
PEPTONE
PEPTONES
PEPTONIC
PEPTONISE
PEPTONIZE
PEQUISTE
PEQUISTES
PER
PERACID
PERACIDS
PERACUTE
PERAEA
PERAEON
PERAEONS
PERAEOPOD
PERAI

P

PERAIS
PERBORATE
PERBORIC
PERC
PERCALE
PERCALES
PERCALINE
PERCASE
PERCE
PERCEABLE
PERCEANT
PERCED
PERCEIVE
PERCEIVED
PERCEIVER
PERCEIVES
PERCEN
PERCENT
PERCENTAL
PERCENTS
PERCEPT
PERCEPTS
PERCES
PERCH
PERCHANCE
PERCHED
PERCHER
PERCHERON
PERCHERS
PERCHERY
PERCHES
PERCHING
PERCHINGS
PERCID
PERCIDS
PERCIFORM
PERCINE
PERCINES
PERCING
PERCOCT
PERCOCTED
PERCOCTS
PERCOID
PERCOIDS
PERCOLATE
PERCOLIN
PERCOLINS
PERCS
PERCUSS
PERCUSSED
PERCUSSES
PERCUSSOR
PERDENDO
PERDIE
PERDITION
PERDU
PERDUE
PERDUES
PERDURE
PERDURED
PERDURES
PERDURING
PERDUS
PERDY
PERE
PEREA
PEREGAL
PEREGALS
PEREGRIN
PEREGRINE
PEREGRINS
PEREIA
PEREION
PEREIONS
PEREIOPOD
PEREIRA
PEREIRAS
PERENNATE
PERENNIAL
PERENNITY
PERENTIE
PERENTIES
PERENTY
PEREON
PEREONS
PEREOPOD
PEREOPODS
PERES
PERFAY
PERFECT
PERFECTA
PERFECTAS
PERFECTED
PERFECTER
PERFECTI
PERFECTLY
PERFECTO
PERFECTOR
PERFECTOS
PERFECTS
PERFERVID
PERFERVOR
PERFET
PERFIDIES
PERFIDY
PERFIN
PERFING
PERFINGS
PERFINS
PERFORANS
PERFORANT
PERFORATE
PERFORCE
PERFORM
PERFORMED
PERFORMER
PERFORMS
PERFUME
PERFUMED
PERFUMER
PERFUMERS
PERFUMERY
PERFUMES
PERFUMIER
PERFUMING
PERFUMY
PERFUSATE
PERFUSE
PERFUSED
PERFUSES
PERFUSING
PERFUSION
PERFUSIVE
PERGOLA
PERGOLAS
PERGUNNAH
PERHAPS
PERHAPSES
PERI
PERIAGUA
PERIAGUAS
PERIAKTOI
PERIAKTOS
PERIANTH
PERIANTHS
PERIAPSES
PERIAPSIS
PERIAPT
PERIAPTS
PERIBLAST
PERIBLEM
PERIBLEMS
PERIBOLI
PERIBOLOI
PERIBOLOS
PERIBOLUS
PERICARP
PERICARPS
PERICLASE
PERICLINE
PERICON
PERICONES
PERICOPAE
PERICOPAL
PERICOPE
PERICOPES
PERICOPIC
PERICYCLE
PERIDERM
PERIDERMS
PERIDIA
PERIDIAL
PERIDINIA
PERIDIUM
PERIDIUMS
PERIDOT
PERIDOTE
PERIDOTES
PERIDOTIC
PERIDOTS
PERIDROME
PERIGEAL
PERIGEAN
PERIGEE
PERIGEES
PERIGON
PERIGONE
PERIGONES
PERIGONIA
PERIGONS
PERIGYNY
PERIHELIA
PERIKARYA
PERIL
PERILED
PERILING
PERILLA
PERILLAS
PERILLED
PERILLING
PERILOUS
PERILS
PERILUNE
PERILUNES
PERILYMPH
PERIMETER
PERIMETRY
PERIMORPH
PERIMYSIA
PERINAEUM
PERINATAL
PERINEA
PERINEAL
PERINEUM
PERINEUMS
PERIOD
PERIODATE
PERIODED
PERIODIC
PERIODID
PERIODIDE
PERIODIDS
PERIODING
PERIODISE
PERIODIZE
PERIODS
PERIOST
PERIOSTEA
PERIOSTS
PERIOTIC
PERIOTICS
PERIPATUS
PERIPETIA
PERIPETY
PERIPHERY
PERIPLASM
PERIPLAST
PERIPLUS
PERIPROCT
PERIPTER

P

PERIPTERS
PERIPTERY
PERIQUE
PERIQUES
PERIS
PERISARC
PERISARCS
PERISCIAN
PERISCOPE
PERISH
PERISHED
PERISHER
PERISHERS
PERISHES
PERISHING
PERISPERM
PERISTOME
PERISTYLE
PERITI
PERITONEA
PERITRACK
PERITRICH
PERITUS
PERIWIG
PERIWIGS
PERJINK
PERJURE
PERJURED
PERJURER
PERJURERS
PERJURES
PERJURIES
PERJURING
PERJUROUS
PERJURY
PERK
PERKED
PERKIER
PERKIEST
PERKILY
PERKIN
PERKINESS
PERKING
PERKINS
PERKISH
PERKS
PERKY
PERLEMOEN
PERLITE
PERLITES
PERLITIC
PERLOUS
PERM
PERMABEAR
PERMABULL
PERMALINK
PERMALLOY
PERMANENT
PERMATAN
PERMATANS
PERMEABLE
PERMEABLY
PERMEANCE
PERMEANT
PERMEANTS
PERMEASE
PERMEASES
PERMEATE
PERMEATED
PERMEATES
PERMEATOR
PERMED
PERMIAN
PERMIE
PERMIES
PERMING
PERMIT
PERMITS
PERMITTED
PERMITTEE
PERMITTER
PERMS
PERMUTATE
PERMUTE
PERMUTED
PERMUTES
PERMUTING
PERN
PERNANCY
PERNED
PERNING
PERNIO
PERNIONES
PERNOD
PERNODS
PERNS
PEROG
PEROGEN
PEROGI
PEROGIE
PEROGIES
PEROGIS
PEROGS
PEROGY
PERONE
PERONEAL
PERONEI
PERONES
PERONEUS
PERORAL
PERORALLY
PERORATE
PERORATED
PERORATES
PERORATOR
PEROVSKIA
PEROXID
PEROXIDE
PEROXIDED
PEROXIDES
PEROXIDIC
PEROXIDS
PEROXO
PEROXY
PERP
PERPEND
PERPENDED
PERPENDS
PERPENT
PERPENTS
PERPETUAL
PERPLEX
PERPLEXED
PERPLEXER
PERPLEXES
PERPS
PERRADIAL
PERRADII
PERRADIUS
PERRIER
PERRIERS
PERRIES
PERRON
PERRONS
PERRUQUE
PERRUQUES
PERRY
PERSALT
PERSALTS
PERSANT
PERSAUNT
PERSE
PERSECUTE
PERSEITY
PERSELINE
PERSES
PERSEVERE
PERSICO
PERSICOS
PERSICOT
PERSICOTS
PERSIENNE
PERSIMMON
PERSING
PERSIST
PERSISTED
PERSISTER
PERSISTS
PERSON
PERSONA
PERSONAE
PERSONAGE
PERSONAL
PERSONALS
PERSONAS
PERSONATE
PERSONIFY
PERSONISE
PERSONIZE
PERSONNED
PERSONNEL
PERSONS
PERSPEX
PERSPEXES
PERSPIRE
PERSPIRED
PERSPIRES
PERSPIRY
PERST
PERSUADE
PERSUADED
PERSUADER
PERSUADES
PERSUE
PERSUED
PERSUES
PERSUING
PERSWADE
PERSWADED
PERSWADES
PERT
PERTAIN
PERTAINED
PERTAINS
PERTAKE
PERTAKEN
PERTAKES
PERTAKING
PERTER
PERTEST
PERTHITE
PERTHITES
PERTHITIC
PERTINENT
PERTLY
PERTNESS
PERTOOK
PERTS
PERTURB
PERTURBED
PERTURBER
PERTURBS
PERTUSATE
PERTUSE
PERTUSED
PERTUSION
PERTUSSAL
PERTUSSES
PERTUSSIS
PERUKE
PERUKED
PERUKES
PERUSABLE
PERUSAL
PERUSALS
PERUSE
PERUSED
PERUSER
PERUSERS
PERUSES

PERUSING
PERV
PERVADE
PERVADED
PERVADER
PERVADERS
PERVADES
PERVADING
PERVASION
PERVASIVE
PERVE
PERVED
PERVERSE
PERVERSER
PERVERT
PERVERTED
PERVERTER
PERVERTS
PERVES
PERVIATE
PERVIATED
PERVIATES
PERVICACY
PERVIER
PERVIEST
PERVING
PERVIOUS
PERVO
PERVOS
PERVS
PERVY
PES
PESADE
PESADES
PESANT
PESANTE
PESANTS
PESAUNT
PESAUNTS
PESETA
PESETAS
PESEWA
PESEWAS
PESHMERGA
PESHWA
PESHWAS
PESKIER
PESKIEST
PESKILY
PESKINESS
PESKY
PESO
PESOS
PESSARIES
PESSARY
PESSIMA
PESSIMAL
PESSIMISM
PESSIMIST
PESSIMUM
PEST
PESTER
PESTERED
PESTERER
PESTERERS
PESTERING
PESTEROUS
PESTERS
PESTFUL
PESTHOLE
PESTHOLES
PESTHOUSE
PESTICIDE
PESTIER
PESTIEST
PESTILENT
PESTLE
PESTLED
PESTLES
PESTLING
PESTO
PESTOLOGY
PESTOS
PESTS
PESTY
PET
PETABYTE
PETABYTES
PETAFLOP
PETAFLOPS
PETAHERTZ
PETAL
PETALED
PETALINE
PETALISM
PETALISMS
PETALLED
PETALLIKE
PETALODIC
PETALODY
PETALOID
PETALOUS
PETALS
PETAMETER
PETAMETRE
PETANQUE
PETANQUES
PETAR
PETARA
PETARAS
PETARD
PETARDS
PETARIES
PETARS
PETARY
PETASOS
PETASOSES
PETASUS
PETASUSES
PETAURINE
PETAURIST
PETCHARY
PETCOCK
PETCOCKS
PETECHIA
PETECHIAE
PETECHIAL
PETER
PETERED
PETERING
PETERMAN
PETERMEN
PETERS
PETERSHAM
PETHER
PETHERS
PETHIDINE
PETILLANT
PETIOLAR
PETIOLATE
PETIOLE
PETIOLED
PETIOLES
PETIOLULE
PETIT
PETITE
PETITES
PETITIO
PETITION
PETITIONS
PETITIOS
PETITORY
PETNAP
PETNAPER
PETNAPERS
PETNAPING
PETNAPPED
PETNAPPER
PETNAPS
PETRALE
PETRALES
PETRARIES
PETRARY
PETRE
PETREL
PETRELS
PETRES
PETRI
PETRICHOR
PETRIFIC
PETRIFIED
PETRIFIER
PETRIFIES
PETRIFY
PETROGENY
PETROGRAM
PETROL
PETROLAGE
PETROLEUM
PETROLEUR
PETROLIC
PETROLLED
PETROLOGY
PETROLS
PETRONEL
PETRONELS
PETROSAL
PETROSALS
PETROUS
PETS
PETSAI
PETSAIS
PETTABLE
PETTED
PETTEDLY
PETTER
PETTERS
PETTI
PETTICOAT
PETTIER
PETTIES
PETTIEST
PETTIFOG
PETTIFOGS
PETTILY
PETTINESS
PETTING
PETTINGS
PETTIS
PETTISH
PETTISHLY
PETTITOES
PETTLE
PETTLED
PETTLES
PETTLING
PETTO
PETTY
PETULANCE
PETULANCY
PETULANT
PETUNIA
PETUNIAS
PETUNTSE
PETUNTSES
PETUNTZE
PETUNTZES
PEW
PEWEE
PEWEES
PEWHOLDER
PEWIT
PEWITS
PEWS
PEWTER
PEWTERER
PEWTERERS
PEWTERIER
PEWTERS
PEWTERY

PEYOTE
PEYOTES
PEYOTISM
PEYOTISMS
PEYOTIST
PEYOTISTS
PEYOTL
PEYOTLS
PEYSE
PEYSED
PEYSES
PEYSING
PEYTRAL
PEYTRALS
PEYTREL
PEYTRELS
PEZANT
PEZANTS
PEZIZOID
PFENNIG
PFENNIGE
PFENNIGS
PFENNING
PFENNINGS
PFFT
PFUI
PHABLET
PHABLETS
PHACELIA
PHACELIAS
PHACOID
PHACOIDAL
PHACOLITE
PHACOLITH
PHAEIC
PHAEISM
PHAEISMS
PHAENOGAM
PHAETON
PHAETONS
PHAGE
PHAGEDENA
PHAGES
PHAGOCYTE
PHAGOSOME
PHALANGAL
PHALANGE
PHALANGER
PHALANGES
PHALANGID
PHALANX
PHALANXES
PHALAROPE
PHALLI
PHALLIC
PHALLIN
PHALLINS
PHALLISM
PHALLISMS
PHALLIST
PHALLISTS
PHALLOID
PHALLUS
PHALLUSES
PHANG
PHANGED
PHANGING
PHANGS
PHANSIGAR
PHANTASIM
PHANTASM
PHANTASMA
PHANTASMS
PHANTAST
PHANTASTS
PHANTASY
PHANTOM
PHANTOMS
PHANTOMY
PHANTOSME
PHARAOH
PHARAOHS
PHARAONIC
PHARE
PHARES
PHARISAIC
PHARISEE
PHARISEES
PHARM
PHARMA
PHARMACY
PHARMAS
PHARMED
PHARMER
PHARMERS
PHARMING
PHARMINGS
PHARMS
PHAROS
PHAROSES
PHARYNGAL
PHARYNGES
PHARYNX
PHARYNXES
PHASE
PHASEAL
PHASED
PHASEDOWN
PHASELESS
PHASEOLIN
PHASEOUT
PHASEOUTS
PHASER
PHASERS
PHASES
PHASIC
PHASING
PHASINGS
PHASIS
PHASMID
PHASMIDS
PHASOR
PHASORS
PHAT
PHATIC
PHATTER
PHATTEST
PHEASANT
PHEASANTS
PHEAZAR
PHEAZARS
PHEER
PHEERE
PHEERES
PHEERS
PHEESE
PHEESED
PHEESES
PHEESING
PHEEZE
PHEEZED
PHEEZES
PHEEZING
PHELLEM
PHELLEMS
PHELLOGEN
PHELLOID
PHELONIA
PHELONION
PHENACITE
PHENAKISM
PHENAKITE
PHENATE
PHENATES
PHENAZIN
PHENAZINE
PHENAZINS
PHENE
PHENES
PHENETIC
PHENETICS
PHENETOL
PHENETOLE
PHENETOLS
PHENGITE
PHENGITES
PHENIC
PHENIX
PHENIXES
PHENOBARB
PHENOCOPY
PHENOGAM
PHENOGAMS
PHENOL
PHENOLATE
PHENOLIC
PHENOLICS
PHENOLOGY
PHENOLS
PHENOM
PHENOME
PHENOMENA
PHENOMES
PHENOMS
PHENOTYPE
PHENOXIDE
PHENOXY
PHENYL
PHENYLENE
PHENYLIC
PHENYLS
PHENYTOIN
PHEON
PHEONS
PHERESES
PHERESIS
PHEROMONE
PHESE
PHESED
PHESES
PHESING
PHEW
PHI
PHIAL
PHIALLED
PHIALLING
PHIALS
PHILABEG
PHILABEGS
PHILAMOT
PHILAMOTS
PHILANDER
PHILATELY
PHILAVERY
PHILHORSE
PHILIBEG
PHILIBEGS
PHILIPPIC
PHILISTIA
PHILLABEG
PHILLIBEG
PHILOGYNY
PHILOLOGY
PHILOMATH
PHILOMEL
PHILOMELA
PHILOMELS
PHILOMOT
PHILOMOTS
PHILOPENA
PHILTER
PHILTERED
PHILTERS
PHILTRA
PHILTRE
PHILTRED
PHILTRES
PHILTRING
PHILTRUM
PHIMOSES

PHIMOSIS
PHIMOTIC
PHINNOCK
PHINNOCKS
PHIS
PHISH
PHISHED
PHISHER
PHISHERS
PHISHES
PHISHING
PHISHINGS
PHISNOMY
PHIZ
PHIZES
PHIZOG
PHIZOGS
PHIZZ
PHIZZES
PHLEBITIC
PHLEBITIS
PHLEGM
PHLEGMIER
PHLEGMON
PHLEGMONS
PHLEGMS
PHLEGMY
PHLOEM
PHLOEMS
PHLOMIS
PHLOMISES
PHLORIZIN
PHLOX
PHLOXES
PHLYCTENA
PHO
PHOBIA
PHOBIAS
PHOBIC
PHOBICS
PHOBISM
PHOBISMS
PHOBIST
PHOBISTS
PHOCA
PHOCAE
PHOCAS
PHOCINE
PHOCOMELY
PHOEBE
PHOEBES
PHOEBUS
PHOEBUSES
PHOENIX
PHOENIXES
PHOH
PHOLADES
PHOLAS
PHON
PHONAL
PHONATE
PHONATED
PHONATES
PHONATHON
PHONATING
PHONATION
PHONATORY
PHONE
PHONECAM
PHONECAMS
PHONECARD
PHONED
PHONEME
PHONEMES
PHONEMIC
PHONEMICS
PHONER
PHONERS
PHONES
PHONETIC
PHONETICS
PHONETISE
PHONETISM
PHONETIST
PHONETIZE
PHONEY
PHONEYED
PHONEYING
PHONEYS
PHONIC
PHONICS
PHONIED
PHONIER
PHONIES
PHONIEST
PHONILY
PHONINESS
PHONING
PHONMETER
PHONO
PHONOGRAM
PHONOLITE
PHONOLOGY
PHONON
PHONONS
PHONOPORE
PHONOS
PHONOTYPE
PHONOTYPY
PHONS
PHONY
PHONYING
PHOOEY
PHORATE
PHORATES
PHORESIES
PHORESY
PHORETIC
PHORMINX
PHORMIUM
PHORMIUMS
PHORONID
PHORONIDS
PHOS
PHOSGENE
PHOSGENES
PHOSPHATE
PHOSPHENE
PHOSPHID
PHOSPHIDE
PHOSPHIDS
PHOSPHIN
PHOSPHINE
PHOSPHINS
PHOSPHITE
PHOSPHOR
PHOSPHORE
PHOSPHORI
PHOSPHORS
PHOSSY
PHOT
PHOTIC
PHOTICS
PHOTINIA
PHOTINIAS
PHOTINO
PHOTINOS
PHOTISM
PHOTISMS
PHOTO
PHOTOBLOG
PHOTOBOMB
PHOTOCALL
PHOTOCARD
PHOTOCELL
PHOTOCOPY
PHOTODISK
PHOTOED
PHOTOFIT
PHOTOFITS
PHOTOG
PHOTOGEN
PHOTOGENE
PHOTOGENS
PHOTOGENY
PHOTOGRAM
PHOTOGS
PHOTOING
PHOTOLYSE
PHOTOLYZE
PHOTOMAP
PHOTOMAPS
PHOTOMASK
PHOTON
PHOTONIC
PHOTONICS
PHOTONS
PHOTOPHIL
PHOTOPIA
PHOTOPIAS
PHOTOPIC
PHOTOPLAY
PHOTOPSIA
PHOTOPSY
PHOTOS
PHOTOSCAN
PHOTOSET
PHOTOSETS
PHOTOSHOP
PHOTOSTAT
PHOTOTAXY
PHOTOTUBE
PHOTOTYPE
PHOTOTYPY
PHOTS
PHPHT
PHRASAL
PHRASALLY
PHRASE
PHRASED
PHRASEMAN
PHRASEMEN
PHRASER
PHRASERS
PHRASES
PHRASIER
PHRASIEST
PHRASING
PHRASINGS
PHRASY
PHRATRAL
PHRATRIC
PHRATRIES
PHRATRY
PHREAK
PHREAKED
PHREAKER
PHREAKERS
PHREAKING
PHREAKS
PHREATIC
PHRENESES
PHRENESIS
PHRENETIC
PHRENIC
PHRENICS
PHRENISM
PHRENISMS
PHRENITIC
PHRENITIS
PHRENSIED
PHRENSIES
PHRENSY
PHRENTICK
PHRYGANA
PHRYGANAS
PHT
PHTHALATE
PHTHALEIN
PHTHALIC

P

PHTHALIN
PHTHALINS
PHTHISES
PHTHISIC
PHTHISICS
PHTHISIS
PHUT
PHUTS
PHUTTED
PHUTTING
PHWOAH
PHWOAR
PHYCOCYAN
PHYCOLOGY
PHYLA
PHYLACTIC
PHYLAE
PHYLAR
PHYLARCH
PHYLARCHS
PHYLARCHY
PHYLAXIS
PHYLE
PHYLESES
PHYLESIS
PHYLETIC
PHYLETICS
PHYLIC
PHYLLARY
PHYLLID
PHYLLIDS
PHYLLITE
PHYLLITES
PHYLLITIC
PHYLLO
PHYLLODE
PHYLLODES
PHYLLODIA
PHYLLODY
PHYLLOID
PHYLLOIDS
PHYLLOME
PHYLLOMES
PHYLLOMIC
PHYLLOPOD
PHYLLOS
PHYLOGENY
PHYLON
PHYLUM
PHYSALIA
PHYSALIAS
PHYSALIS
PHYSED
PHYSEDS
PHYSES
PHYSETER
PHYSETERS
PHYSIATRY
PHYSIC
PHYSICAL
PHYSICALS
PHYSICIAN
PHYSICISM
PHYSICIST
PHYSICKED
PHYSICKY
PHYSICS
PHYSIO
PHYSIOS
PHYSIQUE
PHYSIQUED
PHYSIQUES
PHYSIS
PHYTANE
PHYTANES
PHYTIN
PHYTINS
PHYTOGENY
PHYTOID
PHYTOL
PHYTOLITH
PHYTOLOGY
PHYTOLS
PHYTON
PHYTONIC
PHYTONS
PHYTOSES
PHYTOSIS
PHYTOTOMY
PHYTOTRON
PI
PIA
PIACEVOLE
PIACULAR
PIAFFE
PIAFFED
PIAFFER
PIAFFERS
PIAFFES
PIAFFING
PIAL
PIAN
PIANETTE
PIANETTES
PIANI
PIANIC
PIANINO
PIANINOS
PIANISM
PIANISMS
PIANIST
PIANISTE
PIANISTES
PIANISTIC
PIANISTS
PIANO
PIANOLA
PIANOLAS
PIANOLESS
PIANOLIST
PIANOS
PIANS
PIARIST
PIARISTS
PIAS
PIASABA
PIASABAS
PIASAVA
PIASAVAS
PIASSABA
PIASSABAS
PIASSAVA
PIASSAVAS
PIASTER
PIASTERS
PIASTRE
PIASTRES
PIAZZA
PIAZZAS
PIAZZE
PIAZZIAN
PIBAL
PIBALS
PIBROCH
PIBROCHS
PIC
PICA
PICACHO
PICACHOS
PICADILLO
PICADOR
PICADORES
PICADORS
PICAL
PICAMAR
PICAMARS
PICANINNY
PICANTE
PICARA
PICARAS
PICARIAN
PICARIANS
PICARO
PICAROON
PICAROONS
PICAROS
PICAS
PICAYUNE
PICAYUNES
PICCADILL
PICCANIN
PICCANINS
PICCATA
PICCATAS
PICCIES
PICCOLO
PICCOLOS
PICCY
PICE
PICENE
PICENES
PICEOUS
PICHOLINE
PICHURIM
PICHURIMS
PICIFORM
PICINE
PICK
PICKABACK
PICKABLE
PICKADIL
PICKADILL
PICKADILS
PICKAPACK
PICKAROON
PICKAX
PICKAXE
PICKAXED
PICKAXES
PICKAXING
PICKBACK
PICKBACKS
PICKED
PICKEER
PICKEERED
PICKEERER
PICKEERS
PICKER
PICKEREL
PICKERELS
PICKERIES
PICKERS
PICKERY
PICKET
PICKETED
PICKETER
PICKETERS
PICKETING
PICKETS
PICKIER
PICKIEST
PICKILY
PICKIN
PICKINESS
PICKING
PICKINGS
PICKINS
PICKLE
PICKLED
PICKLER
PICKLERS
PICKLES
PICKLING
PICKLOCK
PICKLOCKS
PICKMAW
PICKMAWS
PICKNEY
PICKNEYS
PICKOFF

PICKOFFS
PICKPROOF
PICKS
PICKTHANK
PICKUP
PICKUPS
PICKWICK
PICKWICKS
PICKY
PICLORAM
PICLORAMS
PICNIC
PICNICKED
PICNICKER
PICNICKY
PICNICS
PICOCURIE
PICOFARAD
PICOGRAM
PICOGRAMS
PICOLIN
PICOLINE
PICOLINES
PICOLINIC
PICOLINS
PICOMETER
PICOMETRE
PICOMOLE
PICOMOLES
PICONG
PICONGS
PICOT
PICOTE
PICOTED
PICOTEE
PICOTEES
PICOTING
PICOTITE
PICOTITES
PICOTS
PICOWAVE
PICOWAVED
PICOWAVES
PICQUET
PICQUETED
PICQUETS
PICRA
PICRAS
PICRATE
PICRATED
PICRATES
PICRIC
PICRITE
PICRITES
PICRITIC
PICS
PICTARNIE
PICTOGRAM
PICTORIAL
PICTURAL
PICTURALS
PICTURE
PICTURED
PICTURES
PICTURING
PICTURISE
PICTURIZE
PICUL
PICULET
PICULETS
PICULS
PIDDLE
PIDDLED
PIDDLER
PIDDLERS
PIDDLES
PIDDLIER
PIDDLIEST
PIDDLING
PIDDLY
PIDDOCK
PIDDOCKS
PIDGEON
PIDGEONS
PIDGIN
PIDGINISE
PIDGINIZE
PIDGINS
PIE
PIEBALD
PIEBALDS
PIECE
PIECED
PIECELESS
PIECEMEAL
PIECEN
PIECENED
PIECENER
PIECENERS
PIECENING
PIECENS
PIECER
PIECERS
PIECES
PIECEWISE
PIECEWORK
PIECING
PIECINGS
PIECRUST
PIECRUSTS
PIED
PIEDFORT
PIEDFORTS
PIEDISH
PIEDISHES
PIEDMONT
PIEDMONTS
PIEDNESS
PIEFORT
PIEFORTS
PIEHOLE
PIEHOLES
PIEING
PIEINGS
PIEMAN
PIEMEN
PIEND
PIENDS
PIEPLANT
PIEPLANTS
PIEPOWDER
PIER
PIERAGE
PIERAGES
PIERCE
PIERCED
PIERCER
PIERCERS
PIERCES
PIERCING
PIERCINGS
PIERHEAD
PIERHEADS
PIERID
PIERIDINE
PIERIDS
PIERIS
PIERISES
PIEROG
PIEROGEN
PIEROGI
PIEROGIES
PIEROGS
PIERRETTE
PIERROT
PIERROTS
PIERS
PIERST
PIERT
PIERTS
PIES
PIET
PIETA
PIETAS
PIETIES
PIETISM
PIETISMS
PIETIST
PIETISTIC
PIETISTS
PIETS
PIETY
PIEZO
PIFFERARI
PIFFERARO
PIFFERO
PIFFEROS
PIFFLE
PIFFLED
PIFFLER
PIFFLERS
PIFFLES
PIFFLING
PIG
PIGBOAT
PIGBOATS
PIGEON
PIGEONED
PIGEONING
PIGEONITE
PIGEONRY
PIGEONS
PIGFACE
PIGFACES
PIGFEED
PIGFEEDS
PIGFISH
PIGFISHES
PIGGED
PIGGERIES
PIGGERY
PIGGIE
PIGGIER
PIGGIES
PIGGIEST
PIGGIN
PIGGINESS
PIGGING
PIGGINGS
PIGGINS
PIGGISH
PIGGISHLY
PIGGY
PIGGYBACK
PIGHEADED
PIGHT
PIGHTED
PIGHTING
PIGHTLE
PIGHTLES
PIGHTS
PIGLET
PIGLETS
PIGLIKE
PIGLING
PIGLINGS
PIGMAEAN
PIGMAN
PIGMEAN
PIGMEAT
PIGMEATS
PIGMEN
PIGMENT
PIGMENTAL
PIGMENTED
PIGMENTS
PIGMIES
PIGMOID
PIGMOIDS
PIGMY

PIGNERATE
PIGNOLI
PIGNOLIA
PIGNOLIAS
PIGNOLIS
PIGNORA
PIGNORATE
PIGNUS
PIGNUT
PIGNUTS
PIGOUT
PIGOUTS
PIGPEN
PIGPENS
PIGS
PIGSCONCE
PIGSKIN
PIGSKINS
PIGSNEY
PIGSNEYS
PIGSNIE
PIGSNIES
PIGSNY
PIGSTICK
PIGSTICKS
PIGSTIES
PIGSTUCK
PIGSTY
PIGSWILL
PIGSWILLS
PIGTAIL
PIGTAILED
PIGTAILS
PIGWASH
PIGWASHES
PIGWEED
PIGWEEDS
PIHOIHOI
PIHOIHOIS
PIING
PIKA
PIKAKE
PIKAKES
PIKAS
PIKAU
PIKAUS
PIKE
PIKED
PIKELET
PIKELETS
PIKELIKE
PIKEMAN
PIKEMEN
PIKEPERCH
PIKER
PIKERS
PIKES
PIKESTAFF
PIKEY
PIKEYS
PIKI
PIKING
PIKINGS
PIKIS
PIKUL
PIKULS
PILA
PILAE
PILAF
PILAFF
PILAFFS
PILAFS
PILAO
PILAOS
PILAR
PILASTER
PILASTERS
PILAU
PILAUS
PILAW
PILAWS
PILCH
PILCHARD
PILCHARDS
PILCHER
PILCHERS
PILCHES
PILCORN
PILCORNS
PILCROW
PILCROWS
PILE
PILEA
PILEAS
PILEATE
PILEATED
PILED
PILEI
PILELESS
PILEOUS
PILER
PILERS
PILES
PILEUM
PILEUP
PILEUPS
PILEUS
PILEWORK
PILEWORKS
PILEWORT
PILEWORTS
PILFER
PILFERAGE
PILFERED
PILFERER
PILFERERS
PILFERIES
PILFERING
PILFERS
PILFERY
PILGARLIC
PILGRIM
PILGRIMED
PILGRIMER
PILGRIMS
PILI
PILIER
PILIEST
PILIFORM
PILING
PILINGS
PILINUT
PILINUTS
PILIS
PILL
PILLAGE
PILLAGED
PILLAGER
PILLAGERS
PILLAGES
PILLAGING
PILLAR
PILLARED
PILLARING
PILLARIST
PILLARS
PILLAU
PILLAUS
PILLBOX
PILLBOXES
PILLBUG
PILLBUGS
PILLED
PILLHEAD
PILLHEADS
PILLICOCK
PILLIE
PILLIES
PILLING
PILLINGS
PILLION
PILLIONED
PILLIONS
PILLOCK
PILLOCKS
PILLORIED
PILLORIES
PILLORISE
PILLORIZE
PILLORY
PILLOW
PILLOWED
PILLOWIER
PILLOWING
PILLOWS
PILLOWY
PILLS
PILLWORM
PILLWORMS
PILLWORT
PILLWORTS
PILOMOTOR
PILONIDAL
PILOSE
PILOSITY
PILOT
PILOTAGE
PILOTAGES
PILOTED
PILOTFISH
PILOTING
PILOTINGS
PILOTIS
PILOTLESS
PILOTMAN
PILOTMEN
PILOTS
PILOUS
PILOW
PILOWS
PILSENER
PILSENERS
PILSNER
PILSNERS
PILULA
PILULAE
PILULAR
PILULAS
PILULE
PILULES
PILUM
PILUS
PILY
PIMA
PIMAS
PIMENT
PIMENTO
PIMENTON
PIMENTONS
PIMENTOS
PIMENTS
PIMIENTO
PIMIENTOS
PIMP
PIMPED
PIMPERNEL
PIMPING
PIMPINGS
PIMPLE
PIMPLED
PIMPLES
PIMPLIER
PIMPLIEST
PIMPLY
PIMPS
PIN
PINA
PINACEOUS
PINACOID
PINACOIDS

PINAFORE
PINAFORED
PINAFORES
PINAKOID
PINAKOIDS
PINANG
PINANGS
PINAS
PINASTER
PINASTERS
PINATA
PINATAS
PINBALL
PINBALLED
PINBALLS
PINBOARD
PINBOARDS
PINBONE
PINBONES
PINCASE
PINCASES
PINCER
PINCERED
PINCERING
PINCERS
PINCH
PINCHBECK
PINCHBUG
PINCHBUGS
PINCHCOCK
PINCHECK
PINCHECKS
PINCHED
PINCHER
PINCHERS
PINCHES
PINCHFIST
PINCHGUT
PINCHGUTS
PINCHING
PINCHINGS
PINCURL
PINCURLS
PINDAN
PINDANS
PINDAREE
PINDAREES
PINDARI
PINDARIS
PINDER
PINDERS
PINDLING
PINDOWN
PINDOWNS
PINE
PINEAL
PINEALS
PINEAPPLE
PINECONE
PINECONES
PINED
PINEDROPS
PINELAND
PINELANDS
PINELIKE
PINENE
PINENES
PINERIES
PINERY
PINES
PINESAP
PINESAPS
PINETA
PINETUM
PINEWOOD
PINEWOODS
PINEY
PINFALL
PINFALLS
PINFISH
PINFISHES
PINFOLD
PINFOLDED
PINFOLDS
PING
PINGED
PINGER
PINGERS
PINGING
PINGLE
PINGLED
PINGLER
PINGLERS
PINGLES
PINGLING
PINGO
PINGOES
PINGOS
PINGPONG
PINGPONGS
PINGRASS
PINGS
PINGUEFY
PINGUID
PINGUIN
PINGUINS
PINHEAD
PINHEADED
PINHEADS
PINHOLE
PINHOLES
PINHOOKER
PINIER
PINIES
PINIEST
PINING
PINION
PINIONED
PINIONING
PINIONS
PINITE
PINITES
PINITOL
PINITOLS
PINK
PINKED
PINKEN
PINKENED
PINKENING
PINKENS
PINKER
PINKERS
PINKERTON
PINKEST
PINKEY
PINKEYE
PINKEYES
PINKEYS
PINKIE
PINKIER
PINKIES
PINKIEST
PINKINESS
PINKING
PINKINGS
PINKISH
PINKLY
PINKNESS
PINKO
PINKOES
PINKOS
PINKROOT
PINKROOTS
PINKS
PINKY
PINLESS
PINNA
PINNACE
PINNACES
PINNACLE
PINNACLED
PINNACLES
PINNAE
PINNAL
PINNAS
PINNATE
PINNATED
PINNATELY
PINNATION
PINNED
PINNER
PINNERS
PINNET
PINNETS
PINNIE
PINNIES
PINNING
PINNINGS
PINNIPED
PINNIPEDE
PINNIPEDS
PINNOCK
PINNOCKS
PINNOED
PINNULA
PINNULAE
PINNULAR
PINNULAS
PINNULATE
PINNULE
PINNULES
PINNY
PINOCHLE
PINOCHLES
PINOCLE
PINOCLES
PINOCYTIC
PINOLE
PINOLES
PINON
PINONES
PINONS
PINOT
PINOTAGE
PINOTAGES
PINOTS
PINPOINT
PINPOINTS
PINPRICK
PINPRICKS
PINS
PINSCHER
PINSCHERS
PINSETTER
PINSPOT
PINSPOTS
PINSTRIPE
PINSWELL
PINSWELLS
PINT
PINTA
PINTABLE
PINTABLES
PINTADA
PINTADAS
PINTADERA
PINTADO
PINTADOES
PINTADOS
PINTAIL
PINTAILED
PINTAILS
PINTANO
PINTANOS
PINTAS
PINTLE
PINTLES
PINTO
PINTOES
PINTOS

PINTS
PINTSIZE
PINTSIZED
PINTUCK
PINTUCKED
PINTUCKS
PINUP
PINUPS
PINWALE
PINWALES
PINWEED
PINWEEDS
PINWHEEL
PINWHEELS
PINWORK
PINWORKS
PINWORM
PINWORMS
PINWRENCH
PINXIT
PINY
PINYIN
PINYINS
PINYON
PINYONS
PIOLET
PIOLETS
PION
PIONED
PIONEER
PIONEERED
PIONEERS
PIONER
PIONERS
PIONEY
PIONEYS
PIONIC
PIONIES
PIONING
PIONINGS
PIONS
PIONY
PIOPIO
PIOPIOS
PIOSITIES
PIOSITY
PIOTED
PIOUS
PIOUSLY
PIOUSNESS
PIOY
PIOYE
PIOYES
PIOYS
PIP
PIPA
PIPAGE
PIPAGES
PIPAL
PIPALS
PIPAS
PIPE
PIPEAGE
PIPEAGES
PIPECLAY
PIPECLAYS
PIPED
PIPEFISH
PIPEFUL
PIPEFULS
PIPELESS
PIPELIKE
PIPELINE
PIPELINED
PIPELINES
PIPER
PIPERIC
PIPERINE
PIPERINES
PIPERONAL
PIPERS
PIPES
PIPESTEM
PIPESTEMS
PIPESTONE
PIPET
PIPETS
PIPETTE
PIPETTED
PIPETTES
PIPETTING
PIPEWORK
PIPEWORKS
PIPEWORT
PIPEWORTS
PIPI
PIPIER
PIPIEST
PIPINESS
PIPING
PIPINGLY
PIPINGS
PIPIS
PIPISTREL
PIPIT
PIPITS
PIPKIN
PIPKINS
PIPLESS
PIPPED
PIPPIER
PIPPIEST
PIPPIN
PIPPING
PIPPINS
PIPPY
PIPS
PIPSQUEAK
PIPUL
PIPULS
PIPY
PIQUANCE
PIQUANCES
PIQUANCY
PIQUANT
PIQUANTLY
PIQUE
PIQUED
PIQUES
PIQUET
PIQUETED
PIQUETING
PIQUETS
PIQUILLO
PIQUILLOS
PIQUING
PIR
PIRACETAM
PIRACIES
PIRACY
PIRAGUA
PIRAGUAS
PIRAI
PIRAIS
PIRANA
PIRANAS
PIRANHA
PIRANHAS
PIRARUCU
PIRARUCUS
PIRATE
PIRATED
PIRATES
PIRATIC
PIRATICAL
PIRATING
PIRATINGS
PIRAYA
PIRAYAS
PIRIFORM
PIRL
PIRLICUE
PIRLICUED
PIRLICUES
PIRLS
PIRN
PIRNIE
PIRNIES
PIRNIT
PIRNS
PIROG
PIROGEN
PIROGHI
PIROGI
PIROGIES
PIROGUE
PIROGUES
PIROJKI
PIROPLASM
PIROQUE
PIROQUES
PIROSHKI
PIROUETTE
PIROZHKI
PIROZHOK
PIRS
PIS
PISCARIES
PISCARY
PISCATOR
PISCATORS
PISCATORY
PISCATRIX
PISCIFORM
PISCINA
PISCINAE
PISCINAL
PISCINAS
PISCINE
PISCINES
PISCIVORE
PISCO
PISCOS
PISE
PISES
PISH
PISHED
PISHEOG
PISHEOGS
PISHER
PISHERS
PISHES
PISHING
PISHOGE
PISHOGES
PISHOGUE
PISHOGUES
PISIFORM
PISIFORMS
PISKIES
PISKY
PISMIRE
PISMIRES
PISO
PISOLITE
PISOLITES
PISOLITH
PISOLITHS
PISOLITIC
PISOS
PISS
PISSANT
PISSANTS
PISSED
PISSER
PISSERS
PISSES
PISSHEAD
PISSHEADS
PISSHOLE

PISSHOLES
PISSIER
PISSIEST
PISSING
PISSOIR
PISSOIRS
PISSY
PISTACHE
PISTACHES
PISTACHIO
PISTAREEN
PISTE
PISTED
PISTES
PISTIL
PISTILLAR
PISTILS
PISTOL
PISTOLE
PISTOLED
PISTOLEER
PISTOLERO
PISTOLES
PISTOLET
PISTOLETS
PISTOLIER
PISTOLING
PISTOLLED
PISTOLS
PISTON
PISTONS
PISTOU
PISTOUS
PIT
PITA
PITAHAYA
PITAHAYAS
PITAPAT
PITAPATS
PITARA
PITARAH
PITARAHS
PITARAS
PITAS
PITAYA
PITAYAS
PITCH
PITCHBEND
PITCHED
PITCHER
PITCHERS
PITCHES
PITCHFORK
PITCHIER
PITCHIEST
PITCHILY
PITCHING
PITCHINGS
PITCHMAN
PITCHMEN
PITCHOUT
PITCHOUTS
PITCHPINE
PITCHPIPE
PITCHPOLE
PITCHY
PITEOUS
PITEOUSLY
PITFALL
PITFALLS
PITH
PITHBALL
PITHBALLS
PITHEAD
PITHEADS
PITHECOID
PITHED
PITHFUL
PITHIER
PITHIEST
PITHILY
PITHINESS
PITHING
PITHLESS
PITHLIKE
PITHOI
PITHOS
PITHS
PITHY
PITIABLE
PITIABLY
PITIED
PITIER
PITIERS
PITIES
PITIETH
PITIFUL
PITIFULLY
PITIKINS
PITILESS
PITLIKE
PITMAN
PITMANS
PITMEN
PITON
PITONS
PITOT
PITOTS
PITPROP
PITPROPS
PITS
PITSAW
PITSAWS
PITTA
PITTANCE
PITTANCES
PITTAS
PITTED
PITTEN
PITTER
PITTERED
PITTERING
PITTERS
PITTING
PITTINGS
PITTITE
PITTITES
PITUITA
PITUITARY
PITUITAS
PITUITE
PITUITES
PITUITRIN
PITURI
PITURIS
PITY
PITYING
PITYINGLY
PITYROID
PIU
PIUM
PIUMS
PIUPIU
PIUPIUS
PIVOT
PIVOTABLE
PIVOTAL
PIVOTALLY
PIVOTED
PIVOTER
PIVOTERS
PIVOTING
PIVOTINGS
PIVOTMAN
PIVOTMEN
PIVOTS
PIX
PIXEL
PIXELATE
PIXELATED
PIXELATES
PIXELLATE
PIXELS
PIXES
PIXIE
PIXIEISH
PIXIES
PIXILATE
PIXILATED
PIXILATES
PIXILLATE
PIXINESS
PIXY
PIXYISH
PIZAZZ
PIZAZZES
PIZAZZIER
PIZAZZY
PIZE
PIZED
PIZES
PIZING
PIZZA
PIZZAIOLA
PIZZALIKE
PIZZAS
PIZZAZ
PIZZAZES
PIZZAZZ
PIZZAZZES
PIZZAZZY
PIZZELLE
PIZZELLES
PIZZERIA
PIZZERIAS
PIZZICATI
PIZZICATO
PIZZLE
PIZZLES
PLAAS
PLAASES
PLACABLE
PLACABLY
PLACARD
PLACARDED
PLACARDS
PLACATE
PLACATED
PLACATER
PLACATERS
PLACATES
PLACATING
PLACATION
PLACATIVE
PLACATORY
PLACCAT
PLACCATE
PLACCATES
PLACCATS
PLACE
PLACEABLE
PLACEBO
PLACEBOES
PLACEBOS
PLACED
PLACEKICK
PLACELESS
PLACEMAN
PLACEMAT
PLACEMATS
PLACEMEN
PLACEMENT
PLACENTA
PLACENTAE
PLACENTAL
PLACENTAS
PLACER
PLACERS
PLACES
PLACET

P

PLACETS
PLACID
PLACIDER
PLACIDEST
PLACIDITY
PLACIDLY
PLACING
PLACINGS
PLACIT
PLACITA
PLACITORY
PLACITS
PLACITUM
PLACK
PLACKET
PLACKETS
PLACKLESS
PLACKS
PLACODERM
PLACOID
PLACOIDS
PLAFOND
PLAFONDS
PLAGAL
PLAGE
PLAGES
PLAGIARY
PLAGIUM
PLAGIUMS
PLAGUE
PLAGUED
PLAGUER
PLAGUERS
PLAGUES
PLAGUEY
PLAGUIER
PLAGUIEST
PLAGUILY
PLAGUING
PLAGUY
PLAICE
PLAICES
PLAID
PLAIDED
PLAIDING
PLAIDINGS
PLAIDMAN
PLAIDMEN
PLAIDS
PLAIN
PLAINANT
PLAINANTS
PLAINED
PLAINER
PLAINEST
PLAINFUL
PLAINING
PLAININGS
PLAINISH
PLAINLY
PLAINNESS
PLAINS
PLAINSMAN
PLAINSMEN
PLAINSONG
PLAINT
PLAINTEXT
PLAINTFUL
PLAINTIFF
PLAINTIVE
PLAINTS
PLAINWORK
PLAISTER
PLAISTERS
PLAIT
PLAITED
PLAITER
PLAITERS
PLAITING
PLAITINGS
PLAITS
PLAN
PLANAR
PLANARIA
PLANARIAN
PLANARIAS
PLANARITY
PLANATE
PLANATION
PLANCH
PLANCHE
PLANCHED
PLANCHES
PLANCHET
PLANCHETS
PLANCHING
PLANE
PLANED
PLANELOAD
PLANENESS
PLANER
PLANERS
PLANES
PLANESIDE
PLANET
PLANETARY
PLANETIC
PLANETOID
PLANETS
PLANFORM
PLANFORMS
PLANGENCY
PLANGENT
PLANIGRAM
PLANING
PLANISH
PLANISHED
PLANISHER
PLANISHES
PLANK
PLANKED
PLANKING
PLANKINGS
PLANKLIKE
PLANKS
PLANKTER
PLANKTERS
PLANKTIC
PLANKTON
PLANKTONS
PLANLESS
PLANNED
PLANNER
PLANNERS
PLANNING
PLANNINGS
PLANOGRAM
PLANOSOL
PLANOSOLS
PLANS
PLANT
PLANTA
PLANTABLE
PLANTAE
PLANTAGE
PLANTAGES
PLANTAIN
PLANTAINS
PLANTAR
PLANTAS
PLANTED
PLANTER
PLANTERS
PLANTING
PLANTINGS
PLANTLESS
PLANTLET
PLANTLETS
PLANTLIKE
PLANTLING
PLANTS
PLANTSMAN
PLANTSMEN
PLANTULE
PLANTULES
PLANULA
PLANULAE
PLANULAR
PLANULATE
PLANULOID
PLANURIA
PLANURIAS
PLANURIES
PLANURY
PLANXTIES
PLANXTY
PLAP
PLAPPED
PLAPPING
PLAPS
PLAQUE
PLAQUES
PLAQUETTE
PLASH
PLASHED
PLASHER
PLASHERS
PLASHES
PLASHET
PLASHETS
PLASHIER
PLASHIEST
PLASHING
PLASHINGS
PLASHY
PLASM
PLASMA
PLASMAGEL
PLASMAS
PLASMASOL
PLASMATIC
PLASMIC
PLASMID
PLASMIDS
PLASMIN
PLASMINS
PLASMODIA
PLASMOID
PLASMOIDS
PLASMON
PLASMONS
PLASMS
PLAST
PLASTE
PLASTER
PLASTERED
PLASTERER
PLASTERS
PLASTERY
PLASTIC
PLASTICKY
PLASTICLY
PLASTICS
PLASTID
PLASTIDS
PLASTIQUE
PLASTISOL
PLASTRAL
PLASTRON
PLASTRONS
PLASTRUM
PLASTRUMS
PLAT
PLATAN
PLATANE
PLATANES
PLATANNA
PLATANNAS
PLATANS
PLATBAND

PLATBANDS
PLATE
PLATEASM
PLATEASMS
PLATEAU
PLATEAUED
PLATEAUS
PLATEAUX
PLATED
PLATEFUL
PLATEFULS
PLATELESS
PLATELET
PLATELETS
PLATELIKE
PLATEMAN
PLATEMARK
PLATEMEN
PLATEN
PLATENS
PLATER
PLATERS
PLATES
PLATESFUL
PLATFORM
PLATFORMS
PLATIER
PLATIES
PLATIEST
PLATINA
PLATINAS
PLATING
PLATINGS
PLATINIC
PLATINISE
PLATINIZE
PLATINOID
PLATINOUS
PLATINUM
PLATINUMS
PLATITUDE
PLATONIC
PLATONICS
PLATONISM
PLATOON
PLATOONED
PLATOONS
PLATS

PLATT
PLATTED
PLATTER
PLATTERS
PLATTING
PLATTINGS
PLATY
PLATYFISH
PLATYPI
PLATYPUS
PLATYS
PLATYSMA
PLATYSMAS
PLAUDIT
PLAUDITE
PLAUDITS
PLAUSIBLE
PLAUSIBLY
PLAUSIVE
PLAUSTRAL
PLAY
PLAYA
PLAYABLE
PLAYACT
PLAYACTED
PLAYACTOR
PLAYACTS
PLAYAS
PLAYBACK
PLAYBACKS
PLAYBILL
PLAYBILLS
PLAYBOOK
PLAYBOOKS
PLAYBOY
PLAYBOYS
PLAYBUS
PLAYBUSES
PLAYDATE
PLAYDATES
PLAYDAY
PLAYDAYS
PLAYDOUGH
PLAYDOWN
PLAYDOWNS
PLAYED
PLAYER
PLAYERS

PLAYFIELD
PLAYFUL
PLAYFULLY
PLAYGIRL
PLAYGIRLS
PLAYGOER
PLAYGOERS
PLAYGOING
PLAYGROUP
PLAYHOUSE
PLAYING
PLAYINGS
PLAYLAND
PLAYLANDS
PLAYLESS
PLAYLET
PLAYLETS
PLAYLIKE
PLAYLIST
PLAYLISTS
PLAYMAKER
PLAYMATE
PLAYMATES
PLAYOFF
PLAYOFFS
PLAYPEN
PLAYPENS
PLAYROOM
PLAYROOMS
PLAYS
PLAYSET
PLAYSETS
PLAYSLIP
PLAYSLIPS
PLAYSOME
PLAYSUIT
PLAYSUITS
PLAYTHING
PLAYTIME
PLAYTIMES
PLAYWEAR
PLAYWEARS
PLAZA
PLAZAS
PLEA
PLEACH
PLEACHED
PLEACHES

PLEACHING
PLEAD
PLEADABLE
PLEADED
PLEADER
PLEADERS
PLEADING
PLEADINGS
PLEADS
PLEAED
PLEAING
PLEAS
PLEASABLE
PLEASANCE
PLEASANT
PLEASE
PLEASED
PLEASEDLY
PLEASEMAN
PLEASEMEN
PLEASER
PLEASERS
PLEASES
PLEASETH
PLEASING
PLEASINGS
PLEASURE
PLEASURED
PLEASURER
PLEASURES
PLEAT
PLEATED
PLEATER
PLEATERS
PLEATHER
PLEATHERS
PLEATING
PLEATINGS
PLEATLESS
PLEATS
PLEB
PLEBBIER
PLEBBIEST
PLEBBY
PLEBE
PLEBEAN
PLEBEIAN
PLEBEIANS

PLEBES
PLEBIFIED
PLEBIFIES
PLEBIFY
PLEBS
PLECTRA
PLECTRE
PLECTRES
PLECTRON
PLECTRONS
PLECTRUM
PLECTRUMS
PLED
PLEDGABLE
PLEDGE
PLEDGED
PLEDGEE
PLEDGEES
PLEDGEOR
PLEDGEORS
PLEDGER
PLEDGERS
PLEDGES
PLEDGET
PLEDGETS
PLEDGING
PLEDGOR
PLEDGORS
PLEIAD
PLEIADES
PLEIADS
PLEIOCENE
PLEIOMERY
PLEIOTAXY
PLENA
PLENARIES
PLENARILY
PLENARTY
PLENARY
PLENCH
PLENCHES
PLENILUNE
PLENIPO
PLENIPOES
PLENIPOS
PLENISH
PLENISHED
PLENISHER

P

PLENISHES
PLENISM
PLENISMS
PLENIST
PLENISTS
PLENITUDE
PLENTEOUS
PLENTIES
PLENTIFUL
PLENTY
PLENUM
PLENUMS
PLEON
PLEONAL
PLEONASM
PLEONASMS
PLEONAST
PLEONASTE
PLEONASTS
PLEONEXIA
PLEONIC
PLEONS
PLEOPOD
PLEOPODS
PLERION
PLERIONS
PLEROMA
PLEROMAS
PLEROME
PLEROMES
PLESH
PLESHES
PLESSOR
PLESSORS
PLETHORA
PLETHORAS
PLETHORIC
PLEUCH
PLEUCHED
PLEUCHING
PLEUCHS
PLEUGH
PLEUGHED
PLEUGHING
PLEUGHS
PLEURA
PLEURAE
PLEURAL
PLEURAS
PLEURISY
PLEURITIC
PLEURITIS
PLEURON
PLEURONIA
PLEUSTON
PLEUSTONS
PLEW
PLEWS
PLEX
PLEXAL
PLEXED
PLEXES
PLEXIFORM
PLEXING
PLEXOR
PLEXORS
PLEXURE
PLEXURES
PLEXUS
PLEXUSES
PLIABLE
PLIABLY
PLIANCIES
PLIANCY
PLIANT
PLIANTLY
PLICA
PLICAE
PLICAL
PLICAS
PLICATE
PLICATED
PLICATELY
PLICATES
PLICATING
PLICATION
PLICATURE
PLIE
PLIED
PLIER
PLIERS
PLIES
PLIGHT
PLIGHTED
PLIGHTER
PLIGHTERS
PLIGHTFUL
PLIGHTING
PLIGHTS
PLIM
PLIMMED
PLIMMING
PLIMS
PLIMSOL
PLIMSOLE
PLIMSOLES
PLIMSOLL
PLIMSOLLS
PLIMSOLS
PLING
PLINGED
PLINGING
PLINGS
PLINK
PLINKED
PLINKER
PLINKERS
PLINKIER
PLINKIEST
PLINKING
PLINKINGS
PLINKS
PLINKY
PLINTH
PLINTHS
PLIOCENE
PLIOFILM
PLIOFILMS
PLIOSAUR
PLIOSAURS
PLIOTRON
PLIOTRONS
PLISKIE
PLISKIER
PLISKIES
PLISKIEST
PLISKY
PLISSE
PLISSES
PLOAT
PLOATED
PLOATING
PLOATS
PLOD
PLODDED
PLODDER
PLODDERS
PLODDING
PLODDINGS
PLODGE
PLODGED
PLODGES
PLODGING
PLODS
PLOGGING
PLOGGINGS
PLOIDIES
PLOIDY
PLONG
PLONGD
PLONGE
PLONGED
PLONGES
PLONGING
PLONGS
PLONK
PLONKED
PLONKER
PLONKERS
PLONKIER
PLONKIEST
PLONKING
PLONKINGS
PLONKO
PLONKOS
PLONKS
PLONKY
PLOOK
PLOOKIE
PLOOKIER
PLOOKIEST
PLOOKS
PLOOKY
PLOP
PLOPPED
PLOPPING
PLOPS
PLOSION
PLOSIONS
PLOSIVE
PLOSIVES
PLOT
PLOTFUL
PLOTLESS
PLOTLINE
PLOTLINES
PLOTS
PLOTTAGE
PLOTTAGES
PLOTTED
PLOTTER
PLOTTERED
PLOTTERS
PLOTTIE
PLOTTIER
PLOTTIES
PLOTTIEST
PLOTTING
PLOTTINGS
PLOTTY
PLOTZ
PLOTZED
PLOTZES
PLOTZING
PLOUGH
PLOUGHBOY
PLOUGHED
PLOUGHER
PLOUGHERS
PLOUGHING
PLOUGHMAN
PLOUGHMEN
PLOUGHS
PLOUK
PLOUKIE
PLOUKIER
PLOUKIEST
PLOUKS
PLOUKY
PLOUTER
PLOUTERED
PLOUTERS
PLOVER
PLOVERIER
PLOVERS
PLOVERY
PLOW
PLOWABLE
PLOWBACK
PLOWBACKS

PLOWBOY
PLOWBOYS
PLOWED
PLOWER
PLOWERS
PLOWHEAD
PLOWHEADS
PLOWING
PLOWINGS
PLOWLAND
PLOWLANDS
PLOWMAN
PLOWMEN
PLOWS
PLOWSHARE
PLOWSTAFF
PLOWTAIL
PLOWTAILS
PLOWTER
PLOWTERED
PLOWTERS
PLOWWISE
PLOY
PLOYE
PLOYED
PLOYES
PLOYING
PLOYS
PLU
PLUCK
PLUCKED
PLUCKER
PLUCKERS
PLUCKIER
PLUCKIEST
PLUCKILY
PLUCKING
PLUCKS
PLUCKY
PLUE
PLUES
PLUFF
PLUFFED
PLUFFIER
PLUFFIEST
PLUFFING
PLUFFS
PLUFFY
PLUG
PLUGBOARD
PLUGGED
PLUGGER
PLUGGERS
PLUGGING
PLUGGINGS
PLUGHOLE
PLUGHOLES
PLUGLESS
PLUGOLA
PLUGOLAS
PLUGS
PLUGUGLY
PLUM
PLUMAGE
PLUMAGED
PLUMAGES
PLUMATE
PLUMB
PLUMBABLE
PLUMBAGO
PLUMBAGOS
PLUMBATE
PLUMBATES
PLUMBED
PLUMBEOUS
PLUMBER
PLUMBERS
PLUMBERY
PLUMBIC
PLUMBING
PLUMBINGS
PLUMBISM
PLUMBISMS
PLUMBITE
PLUMBITES
PLUMBLESS
PLUMBNESS
PLUMBOUS
PLUMBS
PLUMBUM
PLUMBUMS
PLUMCAKE
PLUMCAKES
PLUMCOT
PLUMCOTS
PLUMDAMAS
PLUME
PLUMED
PLUMELESS
PLUMELET
PLUMELETS
PLUMELIKE
PLUMERIA
PLUMERIAS
PLUMERIES
PLUMERY
PLUMES
PLUMIER
PLUMIEST
PLUMING
PLUMIPED
PLUMIPEDS
PLUMIST
PLUMISTS
PLUMLIKE
PLUMMER
PLUMMEST
PLUMMET
PLUMMETED
PLUMMETS
PLUMMIER
PLUMMIEST
PLUMMY
PLUMOSE
PLUMOSELY
PLUMOSITY
PLUMOUS
PLUMP
PLUMPED
PLUMPEN
PLUMPENED
PLUMPENS
PLUMPER
PLUMPERS
PLUMPEST
PLUMPIE
PLUMPIER
PLUMPIEST
PLUMPING
PLUMPISH
PLUMPLY
PLUMPNESS
PLUMPS
PLUMPY
PLUMS
PLUMULA
PLUMULAE
PLUMULAR
PLUMULATE
PLUMULE
PLUMULES
PLUMULOSE
PLUMY
PLUNDER
PLUNDERED
PLUNDERER
PLUNDERS
PLUNGE
PLUNGED
PLUNGER
PLUNGERS
PLUNGES
PLUNGING
PLUNGINGS
PLUNK
PLUNKED
PLUNKER
PLUNKERS
PLUNKIER
PLUNKIEST
PLUNKING
PLUNKS
PLUNKY
PLUOT
PLUOTS
PLURAL
PLURALISE
PLURALISM
PLURALIST
PLURALITY
PLURALIZE
PLURALLY
PLURALS
PLURIPARA
PLURISIE
PLURISIES
PLURRY
PLUS
PLUSAGE
PLUSAGES
PLUSED
PLUSES
PLUSH
PLUSHED
PLUSHER
PLUSHES
PLUSHEST
PLUSHIER
PLUSHIEST
PLUSHILY
PLUSHLY
PLUSHNESS
PLUSHY
PLUSING
PLUSSAGE
PLUSSAGES
PLUSSED
PLUSSES
PLUSSING
PLUTEAL
PLUTEI
PLUTEUS
PLUTEUSES
PLUTO
PLUTOCRAT
PLUTOED
PLUTOES
PLUTOID
PLUTOIDS
PLUTOING
PLUTOLOGY
PLUTON
PLUTONIAN
PLUTONIC
PLUTONISM
PLUTONIUM
PLUTONOMY
PLUTONS
PLUTOS
PLUVIAL
PLUVIALS
PLUVIAN
PLUVIANS
PLUVIOSE
PLUVIOUS
PLUVIUS
PLY
PLYER
PLYERS
PLYING

PLYINGLY
PLYWOOD
PLYWOODS
PNEUMA
PNEUMAS
PNEUMATIC
PNEUMONIA
PNEUMONIC
PO
POA
POACEOUS
POACH
POACHABLE
POACHED
POACHER
POACHERS
POACHES
POACHIER
POACHIEST
POACHING
POACHINGS
POACHY
POAKA
POAKAS
POAKE
POAKES
POAS
POBLANO
POBLANOS
POBOY
POBOYS
POCHARD
POCHARDS
POCHAY
POCHAYED
POCHAYING
POCHAYS
POCHETTE
POCHETTES
POCHOIR
POCHOIRS
POCK
POCKARD
POCKARDS
POCKED
POCKET
POCKETED
POCKETER
POCKETERS
POCKETFUL
POCKETING
POCKETS
POCKIER
POCKIES
POCKIEST
POCKILY
POCKING
POCKMANKY
POCKMARK
POCKMARKS
POCKPIT
POCKPITS
POCKS
POCKY
POCO
POCOSEN
POCOSENS
POCOSIN
POCOSINS
POCOSON
POCOSONS
POD
PODAGRA
PODAGRAL
PODAGRAS
PODAGRIC
PODAGROUS
PODAL
PODALIC
PODARGUS
PODCAST
PODCASTED
PODCASTER
PODCASTS
PODDED
PODDIE
PODDIER
PODDIES
PODDIEST
PODDING
PODDLE
PODDLED
PODDLES
PODDLING
PODDY
PODESTA
PODESTAS
PODEX
PODEXES
PODGE
PODGES
PODGIER
PODGIEST
PODGILY
PODGINESS
PODGY
PODIA
PODIAL
PODIATRIC
PODIATRY
PODITE
PODITES
PODITIC
PODIUM
PODIUMED
PODIUMING
PODIUMS
PODLEY
PODLEYS
PODLIKE
PODOCARP
PODOCARPS
PODOLOGY
PODOMERE
PODOMERES
PODS
PODSOL
PODSOLIC
PODSOLISE
PODSOLIZE
PODSOLS
PODUNK
PODUNKS
PODZOL
PODZOLIC
PODZOLISE
PODZOLIZE
PODZOLS
POECHORE
POECHORES
POEM
POEMATIC
POEMS
POENOLOGY
POEP
POEPED
POEPING
POEPOL
POEPOLS
POEPS
POESIED
POESIES
POESY
POESYING
POET
POETASTER
POETASTRY
POETESS
POETESSES
POETIC
POETICAL
POETICALS
POETICISE
POETICISM
POETICIZE
POETICS
POETICULE
POETISE
POETISED
POETISER
POETISERS
POETISES
POETISING
POETIZE
POETIZED
POETIZER
POETIZERS
POETIZES
POETIZING
POETLESS
POETLIKE
POETRESSE
POETRIES
POETRY
POETS
POETSHIP
POETSHIPS
POFFLE
POFFLES
POGEY
POGEYS
POGGE
POGGES
POGIES
POGO
POGOED
POGOER
POGOERS
POGOES
POGOING
POGONIA
POGONIAS
POGONIP
POGONIPS
POGOS
POGROM
POGROMED
POGROMING
POGROMIST
POGROMS
POGY
POH
POHED
POHING
POHIRI
POHIRIS
POHS
POI
POIGNADO
POIGNANCE
POIGNANCY
POIGNANT
POILU
POILUS
POINADO
POINADOES
POINCIANA
POIND
POINDED
POINDER
POINDERS
POINDING
POINDINGS
POINDS
POINT
POINTABLE
POINTE
POINTED
POINTEDLY
POINTEL

POINTELLE
POINTELS
POINTER
POINTERS
POINTES
POINTIER
POINTIEST
POINTILLE
POINTING
POINTINGS
POINTLESS
POINTLIKE
POINTMAN
POINTMEN
POINTS
POINTSMAN
POINTSMEN
POINTY
POIS
POISE
POISED
POISER
POISERS
POISES
POISHA
POISHAS
POISING
POISON
POISONED
POISONER
POISONERS
POISONING
POISONOUS
POISONS
POISSON
POISSONS
POITIN
POITINS
POITREL
POITRELS
POITRINE
POITRINES
POKABLE
POKAL
POKALS
POKE
POKEBERRY
POKED
POKEFUL
POKEFULS
POKELOGAN
POKER
POKERISH
POKEROOT
POKEROOTS
POKERS
POKERWORK
POKES
POKEWEED
POKEWEEDS
POKEY
POKEYS
POKIE
POKIER
POKIES
POKIEST
POKILY
POKINESS
POKING
POKY
POL
POLACCA
POLACCAS
POLACK
POLACKS
POLACRE
POLACRES
POLAR
POLARISE
POLARISED
POLARISER
POLARISES
POLARITY
POLARIZE
POLARIZED
POLARIZER
POLARIZES
POLARON
POLARONS
POLARS
POLDER
POLDERED
POLDERING
POLDERS
POLE
POLEAX
POLEAXE
POLEAXED
POLEAXES
POLEAXING
POLECAT
POLECATS
POLED
POLEIS
POLELESS
POLEMARCH
POLEMIC
POLEMICAL
POLEMICS
POLEMISE
POLEMISED
POLEMISES
POLEMIST
POLEMISTS
POLEMIZE
POLEMIZED
POLEMIZES
POLENTA
POLENTAS
POLER
POLERS
POLES
POLESTAR
POLESTARS
POLEWARD
POLEY
POLEYN
POLEYNS
POLEYS
POLIANITE
POLICE
POLICED
POLICEMAN
POLICEMEN
POLICER
POLICERS
POLICES
POLICIER
POLICIERS
POLICIES
POLICING
POLICINGS
POLICY
POLIES
POLING
POLINGS
POLIO
POLIOS
POLIS
POLISES
POLISH
POLISHED
POLISHER
POLISHERS
POLISHES
POLISHING
POLITBURO
POLITE
POLITELY
POLITER
POLITESSE
POLITEST
POLITIC
POLITICAL
POLITICK
POLITICKS
POLITICLY
POLITICO
POLITICOS
POLITICS
POLITIES
POLITIQUE
POLITY
POLJE
POLJES
POLK
POLKA
POLKAED
POLKAING
POLKAS
POLKED
POLKING
POLKS
POLL
POLLACK
POLLACKS
POLLAN
POLLANS
POLLARD
POLLARDED
POLLARDS
POLLAXE
POLLAXED
POLLAXES
POLLAXING
POLLED
POLLEE
POLLEES
POLLEN
POLLENATE
POLLENED
POLLENING
POLLENS
POLLENT
POLLER
POLLERS
POLLEX
POLLICAL
POLLICES
POLLICIE
POLLICIES
POLLICY
POLLIES
POLLINATE
POLLING
POLLINGS
POLLINIA
POLLINIC
POLLINISE
POLLINIUM
POLLINIZE
POLLIST
POLLISTS
POLLIWIG
POLLIWIGS
POLLIWOG
POLLIWOGS
POLLMAN
POLLMEN
POLLOCK
POLLOCKS
POLLS
POLLSTER
POLLSTERS
POLLTAKER
POLLUCITE
POLLUSION
POLLUTANT
POLLUTE
POLLUTED

P

POLLUTER
POLLUTERS
POLLUTES
POLLUTING
POLLUTION
POLLUTIVE
POLLY
POLLYANNA
POLLYWIG
POLLYWIGS
POLLYWOG
POLLYWOGS
POLO
POLOIDAL
POLOIST
POLOISTS
POLONAISE
POLONIE
POLONIES
POLONISE
POLONISED
POLONISES
POLONISM
POLONISMS
POLONIUM
POLONIUMS
POLONIZE
POLONIZED
POLONIZES
POLONY
POLOS
POLS
POLT
POLTED
POLTFEET
POLTFOOT
POLTING
POLTROON
POLTROONS
POLTS
POLVERINE
POLY
POLYACID
POLYACIDS
POLYACT
POLYADIC
POLYAMIDE
POLYAMINE
POLYAMORY
POLYANDRY
POLYANTHA
POLYANTHI
POLYARCH
POLYARCHY
POLYAXIAL
POLYAXON
POLYAXONS
POLYBAG
POLYBAGS
POLYBASIC
POLYBRID
POLYBRIDS
POLYCARPY
POLYCHETE
POLYCONIC
POLYCOT
POLYCOTS
POLYDEMIC
POLYDRUG
POLYENE
POLYENES
POLYENIC
POLYESTER
POLYGALA
POLYGALAS
POLYGAM
POLYGAMIC
POLYGAMS
POLYGAMY
POLYGENE
POLYGENES
POLYGENIC
POLYGENY
POLYGLOT
POLYGLOTS
POLYGLOTT
POLYGON
POLYGONAL
POLYGONS
POLYGONUM
POLYGONY
POLYGRAPH
POLYGYNE
POLYGYNY
POLYHEDRA
POLYIMIDE
POLYLEMMA
POLYMASTY
POLYMATH
POLYMATHS
POLYMATHY
POLYMER
POLYMERIC
POLYMERS
POLYMERY
POLYMORPH
POLYMYXIN
POLYNIA
POLYNIAS
POLYNYA
POLYNYAS
POLYNYI
POLYOL
POLYOLS
POLYOMA
POLYOMAS
POLYOMINO
POLYONYM
POLYONYMS
POLYONYMY
POLYP
POLYPARIA
POLYPARY
POLYPE
POLYPED
POLYPEDS
POLYPES
POLYPHAGY
POLYPHASE
POLYPHON
POLYPHONE
POLYPHONS
POLYPHONY
POLYPI
POLYPIDE
POLYPIDES
POLYPIDOM
POLYPILL
POLYPILLS
POLYPINE
POLYPITE
POLYPITES
POLYPLOID
POLYPNEA
POLYPNEAS
POLYPNEIC
POLYPOD
POLYPODS
POLYPODY
POLYPOID
POLYPORE
POLYPORES
POLYPOSES
POLYPOSIS
POLYPOUS
POLYPS
POLYPTYCH
POLYPUS
POLYPUSES
POLYS
POLYSEME
POLYSEMES
POLYSEMIC
POLYSEMY
POLYSOME
POLYSOMES
POLYSOMIC
POLYSOMY
POLYSTYLE
POLYTENE
POLYTENY
POLYTHENE
POLYTONAL
POLYTYPE
POLYTYPED
POLYTYPES
POLYTYPIC
POLYURIA
POLYURIAS
POLYURIC
POLYVINYL
POLYWATER
POLYZOA
POLYZOAN
POLYZOANS
POLYZOARY
POLYZOIC
POLYZONAL
POLYZOOID
POLYZOON
POM
POMACE
POMACEOUS
POMACES
POMADE
POMADED
POMADES
POMADING
POMANDER
POMANDERS
POMATO
POMATOES
POMATUM
POMATUMED
POMATUMS
POMBE
POMBES
POME
POMELIKE
POMELO
POMELOS
POMEROY
POMEROYS
POMES
POMFRET
POMFRETS
POMMEE
POMMEL
POMMELE
POMMELED
POMMELING
POMMELLED
POMMELS
POMMETTY
POMMIE
POMMIES
POMMY
POMO
POMOERIUM
POMOLOGY
POMOS
POMP
POMPADOUR
POMPANO
POMPANOS
POMPELO
POMPELOS
POMPEY
POMPEYED
POMPEYING

P

POMPEYS
POMPHOLYX
POMPIER
POMPIERS
POMPILID
POMPILIDS
POMPION
POMPIONS
POMPOM
POMPOMS
POMPON
POMPONS
POMPOON
POMPOONS
POMPOSITY
POMPOSO
POMPOUS
POMPOUSLY
POMPS
POMROY
POMROYS
POMS
POMWATER
POMWATERS
PONCE
PONCEAU
PONCEAUS
PONCEAUX
PONCED
PONCES
PONCEY
PONCHO
PONCHOED
PONCHOS
PONCIER
PONCIEST
PONCING
PONCY
POND
PONDAGE
PONDAGES
PONDED
PONDER
PONDERAL
PONDERATE
PONDERED
PONDERER
PONDERERS
PONDERING
PONDEROSA
PONDEROUS
PONDERS
PONDING
PONDOK
PONDOKKIE
PONDOKS
PONDS
PONDWEED
PONDWEEDS
PONE
PONENT
PONENTS
PONES
PONEY
PONEYS
PONG
PONGA
PONGAL
PONGALS
PONGAS
PONGED
PONGEE
PONGEES
PONGID
PONGIDS
PONGIER
PONGIEST
PONGING
PONGO
PONGOES
PONGOS
PONGS
PONGY
PONIARD
PONIARDED
PONIARDS
PONIED
PONIES
PONK
PONKED
PONKING
PONKS
PONS
PONT
PONTAGE
PONTAGES
PONTAL
PONTES
PONTIANAC
PONTIANAK
PONTIC
PONTIE
PONTIES
PONTIFEX
PONTIFF
PONTIFFS
PONTIFIC
PONTIFICE
PONTIFIED
PONTIFIES
PONTIFY
PONTIL
PONTILE
PONTILES
PONTILS
PONTINE
PONTLEVIS
PONTON
PONTONEER
PONTONIER
PONTONS
PONTOON
PONTOONED
PONTOONER
PONTOONS
PONTS
PONTY
PONY
PONYING
PONYSKIN
PONYSKINS
PONYTAIL
PONYTAILS
PONZU
PONZUS
POO
POOBAH
POOBAHS
POOCH
POOCHED
POOCHES
POOCHING
POOD
POODLE
POODLES
POODS
POOED
POOF
POOFIER
POOFIEST
POOFS
POOFTAH
POOFTAHS
POOFTER
POOFTERS
POOFY
POOGYE
POOGYES
POOH
POOHED
POOHING
POOHS
POOING
POOJA
POOJAH
POOJAHS
POOJAS
POOK
POOKA
POOKAS
POOKING
POOKIT
POOKS
POOL
POOLED
POOLER
POOLERS
POOLHALL
POOLHALLS
POOLING
POOLROOM
POOLROOMS
POOLS
POOLSIDE
POOLSIDES
POON
POONAC
POONACS
POONCE
POONCED
POONCES
POONCING
POONS
POONTANG
POONTANGS
POOP
POOPED
POOPER
POOPERS
POOPIER
POOPIEST
POOPING
POOPS
POOPY
POOR
POORBOX
POORBOXES
POORER
POOREST
POORHOUSE
POORI
POORIS
POORISH
POORLIER
POORLIEST
POORLY
POORMOUTH
POORNESS
POORT
POORTITH
POORTITHS
POORTS
POORWILL
POORWILLS
POOS
POOT
POOTED
POOTER
POOTERED
POOTERING
POOTERS
POOTING
POOTLE
POOTLED
POOTLES
POOTLING
POOTS
POOVE
POOVERIES
POOVERY

P

POOVES
POOVIER
POOVIEST
POOVY
POP
POPADUM
POPADUMS
POPCORN
POPCORNS
POPE
POPEDOM
POPEDOMS
POPEHOOD
POPEHOODS
POPELESS
POPELIKE
POPELING
POPELINGS
POPERA
POPERAS
POPERIES
POPERIN
POPERINS
POPERY
POPES
POPESEYE
POPESHIP
POPESHIPS
POPETTE
POPETTES
POPEYED
POPGUN
POPGUNS
POPINAC
POPINACK
POPINACKS
POPINACS
POPINJAY
POPINJAYS
POPISH
POPISHLY
POPJOY
POPJOYED
POPJOYING
POPJOYS
POPLAR
POPLARS
POPLIN
POPLINS
POPLITEAL
POPLITEI
POPLITEUS
POPLITIC
POPOUT
POPOUTS
POPOVER
POPOVERS
POPPA
POPPADOM
POPPADOMS
POPPADUM
POPPADUMS
POPPAS
POPPED
POPPER
POPPERING
POPPERS
POPPET
POPPETS
POPPIED
POPPIER
POPPIES
POPPIEST
POPPING
POPPISH
POPPIT
POPPITS
POPPLE
POPPLED
POPPLES
POPPLIER
POPPLIEST
POPPLING
POPPLY
POPPY
POPPYCOCK
POPPYHEAD
POPPYSEED
POPRIN
POPS
POPSICLE
POPSICLES
POPSIE
POPSIES
POPSOCK
POPSOCKS
POPSTER
POPSTERS
POPSTREL
POPSTRELS
POPSY
POPTASTIC
POPULACE
POPULACES
POPULAR
POPULARLY
POPULARS
POPULATE
POPULATED
POPULATES
POPULISM
POPULISMS
POPULIST
POPULISTS
POPULOUS
PORAE
PORAES
PORAL
PORANGI
PORBEAGLE
PORCELAIN
PORCH
PORCHED
PORCHES
PORCHETTA
PORCHLESS
PORCINE
PORCINI
PORCINIS
PORCINO
PORCUPINE
PORCUPINY
PORE
PORED
PORER
PORERS
PORES
PORGE
PORGED
PORGES
PORGIE
PORGIES
PORGING
PORGY
PORIER
PORIEST
PORIFER
PORIFERAL
PORIFERAN
PORIFERS
PORIN
PORINA
PORINAS
PORINESS
PORING
PORINS
PORISM
PORISMS
PORISTIC
PORK
PORKED
PORKER
PORKERS
PORKIER
PORKIES
PORKIEST
PORKINESS
PORKING
PORKLING
PORKLINGS
PORKPIE
PORKPIES
PORKS
PORKWOOD
PORKWOODS
PORKY
PORLOCK
PORLOCKED
PORLOCKS
PORN
PORNIER
PORNIEST
PORNO
PORNOMAG
PORNOMAGS
PORNOS
PORNS
PORNY
POROGAMIC
POROGAMY
POROMERIC
POROSCOPE
POROSCOPY
POROSE
POROSES
POROSIS
POROSITY
POROUS
POROUSLY
PORPESS
PORPESSE
PORPESSES
PORPHYRIA
PORPHYRIC
PORPHYRIN
PORPHYRIO
PORPHYRY
PORPOISE
PORPOISED
PORPOISES
PORPORATE
PORRECT
PORRECTED
PORRECTS
PORRENGER
PORRIDGE
PORRIDGES
PORRIDGY
PORRIGO
PORRIGOS
PORRINGER
PORT
PORTA
PORTABLE
PORTABLES
PORTABLY
PORTAGE
PORTAGED
PORTAGES
PORTAGING
PORTAGUE
PORTAGUES
PORTAL
PORTALED
PORTALS
PORTANCE
PORTANCES
PORTAPACK
PORTAPAK
PORTAPAKS

PORTAS
PORTASES
PORTATE
PORTATILE
PORTATIVE
PORTED
PORTEND
PORTENDED
PORTENDS
PORTENT
PORTENTS
PORTEOUS
PORTER
PORTERAGE
PORTERED
PORTERESS
PORTERING
PORTERLY
PORTERS
PORTESS
PORTESSE
PORTESSES
PORTFIRE
PORTFIRES
PORTFOLIO
PORTHOLE
PORTHOLES
PORTHORS
PORTHOS
PORTHOSES
PORTHOUSE
PORTICO
PORTICOED
PORTICOES
PORTICOS
PORTIER
PORTIERE
PORTIERED
PORTIERES
PORTIEST
PORTIGUE
PORTIGUES
PORTING
PORTION
PORTIONED
PORTIONER
PORTIONS
PORTLAND
PORTLANDS
PORTLAST
PORTLASTS
PORTLESS
PORTLIER
PORTLIEST
PORTLY
PORTMAN
PORTMEN
PORTOISE
PORTOISES
PORTOLAN
PORTOLANI
PORTOLANO
PORTOLANS
PORTOUS
PORTOUSES
PORTRAIT
PORTRAITS
PORTRAY
PORTRAYAL
PORTRAYED
PORTRAYER
PORTRAYS
PORTREEVE
PORTRESS
PORTS
PORTSIDE
PORTULACA
PORTULAN
PORTULANS
PORTY
PORWIGGLE
PORY
POS
POSABLE
POSADA
POSADAS
POSAUNE
POSAUNES
POSE
POSEABLE
POSED
POSER
POSERISH
POSERS
POSES
POSEUR
POSEURS
POSEUSE
POSEUSES
POSEY
POSH
POSHED
POSHER
POSHES
POSHEST
POSHING
POSHLY
POSHNESS
POSHO
POSHOS
POSHTEEN
POSHTEENS
POSIDRIVE
POSIER
POSIES
POSIEST
POSIGRADE
POSING
POSINGLY
POSINGS
POSIT
POSITED
POSITIF
POSITIFS
POSITING
POSITION
POSITIONS
POSITIVE
POSITIVER
POSITIVES
POSITON
POSITONS
POSITRON
POSITRONS
POSITS
POSNET
POSNETS
POSOLE
POSOLES
POSOLOGIC
POSOLOGY
POSS
POSSE
POSSED
POSSER
POSSERS
POSSES
POSSESS
POSSESSED
POSSESSES
POSSESSOR
POSSET
POSSETED
POSSETING
POSSETS
POSSIBLE
POSSIBLER
POSSIBLES
POSSIBLY
POSSIE
POSSIES
POSSING
POSSUM
POSSUMED
POSSUMING
POSSUMS
POST
POSTAGE
POSTAGES
POSTAL
POSTALLY
POSTALS
POSTANAL
POSTAXIAL
POSTBAG
POSTBAGS
POSTBASE
POSTBASES
POSTBOX
POSTBOXES
POSTBOY
POSTBOYS
POSTBURN
POSTBUS
POSTBUSES
POSTCARD
POSTCARDS
POSTCAVA
POSTCAVAE
POSTCAVAL
POSTCAVAS
POSTCODE
POSTCODED
POSTCODES
POSTCOUP
POSTCRASH
POSTDATE
POSTDATED
POSTDATES
POSTDIVE
POSTDOC
POSTDOCS
POSTDRUG
POSTED
POSTEEN
POSTEENS
POSTER
POSTERED
POSTERING
POSTERIOR
POSTERISE
POSTERITY
POSTERIZE
POSTERN
POSTERNS
POSTERS
POSTFACE
POSTFACES
POSTFACT
POSTFAULT
POSTFIRE
POSTFIX
POSTFIXAL
POSTFIXED
POSTFIXES
POSTFORM
POSTFORMS
POSTGAME
POSTGRAD
POSTGRADS
POSTHASTE
POSTHEAT
POSTHEATS
POSTHOLE
POSTHOLES
POSTHORSE
POSTHOUSE
POSTICAL
POSTICHE
POSTICHES

P

POSTICOUS
POSTIE
POSTIES
POSTIL
POSTILED
POSTILING
POSTILION
POSTILLED
POSTILLER
POSTILS
POSTIN
POSTING
POSTINGS
POSTINS
POSTIQUE
POSTIQUES
POSTLIKE
POSTLUDE
POSTLUDES
POSTMAN
POSTMARK
POSTMARKS
POSTMEN
POSTNASAL
POSTNATAL
POSTNATI
POSTOP
POSTOPS
POSTORAL
POSTPAID
POSTPONE
POSTPONED
POSTPONER
POSTPONES
POSTPOSE
POSTPOSED
POSTPOSES
POSTPUNK
POSTPUNKS
POSTRACE
POSTRIDER
POSTRIOT
POSTS
POSTSHOW
POSTSYNC
POSTSYNCS
POSTTAX
POSTTEEN
POSTTEENS
POSTTEST
POSTTESTS
POSTTRIAL
POSTTRUTH
POSTULANT
POSTULATA
POSTULATE
POSTURAL
POSTURE
POSTURED
POSTURER
POSTURERS
POSTURES
POSTURING
POSTURISE
POSTURIST
POSTURIZE
POSTVIRAL
POSTWAR
POSTWOMAN
POSTWOMEN
POSY
POT
POTABLE
POTABLES
POTAE
POTAES
POTAGE
POTAGER
POTAGERS
POTAGES
POTALE
POTALES
POTAMIC
POTASH
POTASHED
POTASHES
POTASHING
POTASS
POTASSA
POTASSAS
POTASSES
POTASSIC
POTASSIUM
POTATION
POTATIONS
POTATO
POTATOBUG
POTATOES
POTATORY
POTBELLY
POTBOIL
POTBOILED
POTBOILER
POTBOILS
POTBOUND
POTBOY
POTBOYS
POTCH
POTCHE
POTCHED
POTCHER
POTCHERS
POTCHES
POTCHING
POTE
POTED
POTEEN
POTEENS
POTENCE
POTENCES
POTENCIES
POTENCY
POTENT
POTENTATE
POTENTIAL
POTENTISE
POTENTIZE
POTENTLY
POTENTS
POTES
POTFUL
POTFULS
POTGUN
POTGUNS
POTHEAD
POTHEADS
POTHECARY
POTHEEN
POTHEENS
POTHER
POTHERB
POTHERBS
POTHERED
POTHERIER
POTHERING
POTHERS
POTHERY
POTHOLDER
POTHOLE
POTHOLED
POTHOLER
POTHOLERS
POTHOLES
POTHOLING
POTHOOK
POTHOOKS
POTHOS
POTHOSES
POTHOUSE
POTHOUSES
POTHUNTER
POTICARY
POTICHE
POTICHES
POTIN
POTING
POTINS
POTION
POTIONS
POTJIE
POTJIES
POTLACH
POTLACHE
POTLACHES
POTLATCH
POTLIKE
POTLINE
POTLINES
POTLUCK
POTLUCKS
POTMAN
POTMEN
POTOMETER
POTOO
POTOOS
POTOROO
POTOROOS
POTPIE
POTPIES
POTPOURRI
POTS
POTSHARD
POTSHARDS
POTSHARE
POTSHARES
POTSHERD
POTSHERDS
POTSHOP
POTSHOPS
POTSHOT
POTSHOTS
POTSIE
POTSIES
POTSTONE
POTSTONES
POTSY
POTT
POTTABLE
POTTAGE
POTTAGES
POTTED
POTTEEN
POTTEENS
POTTER
POTTERED
POTTERER
POTTERERS
POTTERIES
POTTERING
POTTERS
POTTERY
POTTIER
POTTIES
POTTIEST
POTTINESS
POTTING
POTTINGAR
POTTINGER
POTTLE
POTTLES
POTTO
POTTOS
POTTS
POTTY
POTWALLER
POTZER
POTZERS
POUCH
POUCHED
POUCHES

POUCHFUL
POUCHFULS
POUCHIER
POUCHIEST
POUCHING
POUCHLIKE
POUCHY
POUDER
POUDERS
POUDRE
POUDRES
POUF
POUFED
POUFF
POUFFE
POUFFED
POUFFES
POUFFIER
POUFFIEST
POUFFING
POUFFS
POUFFY
POUFING
POUFS
POUFTAH
POUFTAHS
POUFTER
POUFTERS
POUK
POUKE
POUKES
POUKING
POUKIT
POUKS
POULAINE
POULAINES
POULARD
POULARDE
POULARDES
POULARDS
POULDER
POULDERS
POULDRE
POULDRES
POULDRON
POULDRONS
POULE
POULES
POULP
POULPE
POULPES
POULPS
POULT
POULTER
POULTERER
POULTERS
POULTICE
POULTICED
POULTICES
POULTRIES
POULTRY
POULTS
POUNCE
POUNCED
POUNCER
POUNCERS
POUNCES
POUNCET
POUNCETS
POUNCHING
POUNCING
POUND
POUNDAGE
POUNDAGES
POUNDAL
POUNDALS
POUNDCAKE
POUNDED
POUNDER
POUNDERS
POUNDING
POUNDINGS
POUNDS
POUPE
POUPED
POUPES
POUPING
POUPT
POUR
POURABLE
POURBOIRE
POURED
POURER
POURERS
POURIE
POURIES
POURING
POURINGLY
POURINGS
POURPOINT
POURS
POURSEW
POURSEWED
POURSEWS
POURSUE
POURSUED
POURSUES
POURSUING
POURSUIT
POURSUITS
POURTRAY
POURTRAYD
POURTRAYS
POUSADA
POUSADAS
POUSOWDIE
POUSSE
POUSSES
POUSSETTE
POUSSIE
POUSSIES
POUSSIN
POUSSINS
POUT
POUTASSOU
POUTED
POUTER
POUTERS
POUTFUL
POUTHER
POUTHERED
POUTHERS
POUTIER
POUTIEST
POUTINE
POUTINES
POUTING
POUTINGLY
POUTINGS
POUTS
POUTY
POVERTIES
POVERTY
POW
POWAN
POWANS
POWDER
POWDERED
POWDERER
POWDERERS
POWDERIER
POWDERING
POWDERMAN
POWDERMEN
POWDERS
POWDERY
POWELLISE
POWELLITE
POWELLIZE
POWER
POWERBAND
POWERBOAT
POWERED
POWERFUL
POWERING
POWERLESS
POWERPLAY
POWERS
POWFAGGED
POWHIRI
POWHIRIS
POWIN
POWINS
POWN
POWND
POWNDED
POWNDING
POWNDS
POWNEY
POWNEYS
POWNIE
POWNIES
POWNS
POWNY
POWRE
POWRED
POWRES
POWRING
POWS
POWSOWDY
POWTER
POWTERED
POWTERING
POWTERS
POWWAW
POWWOW
POWWOWED
POWWOWING
POWWOWS
POX
POXED
POXES
POXIER
POXIEST
POXING
POXVIRUS
POXY
POYNANT
POYNT
POYNTED
POYNTING
POYNTS
POYOU
POYOUS
POYSE
POYSED
POYSES
POYSING
POYSON
POYSONED
POYSONING
POYSONS
POZ
POZIDRIVE
POZOLE
POZOLES
POZZ
POZZIES
POZZOLAN
POZZOLANA
POZZOLANS
POZZY
PRAAM
PRAAMS
PRABBLE
PRABBLES
PRACHARAK
PRACTIC
PRACTICAL
PRACTICE

PRACTICED
PRACTICER
PRACTICES
PRACTICK
PRACTICKS
PRACTICS
PRACTICUM
PRACTIQUE
PRACTISE
PRACTISED
PRACTISER
PRACTISES
PRACTIVE
PRACTOLOL
PRAD
PRADHAN
PRADHANS
PRADS
PRAEAMBLE
PRAECIPE
PRAECIPES
PRAECOCES
PRAEDIAL
PRAEDIALS
PRAEFECT
PRAEFECTS
PRAELECT
PRAELECTS
PRAELUDIA
PRAENOMEN
PRAESES
PRAESIDIA
PRAETOR
PRAETORS
PRAGMATIC
PRAHU
PRAHUS
PRAIRIE
PRAIRIED
PRAIRIES
PRAISE
PRAISEACH
PRAISED
PRAISEFUL
PRAISER
PRAISERS
PRAISES
PRAISING
PRAISINGS
PRAJNA
PRAJNAS
PRALINE
PRALINES
PRAM
PRAMS
PRANA
PRANAS
PRANAYAMA
PRANCE
PRANCED
PRANCER
PRANCERS
PRANCES
PRANCING
PRANCINGS
PRANCK
PRANCKE
PRANCKED
PRANCKES
PRANCKING
PRANCKS
PRANDIAL
PRANG
PRANGED
PRANGING
PRANGS
PRANK
PRANKED
PRANKFUL
PRANKIER
PRANKIEST
PRANKING
PRANKINGS
PRANKISH
PRANKLE
PRANKLED
PRANKLES
PRANKLING
PRANKS
PRANKSOME
PRANKSTER
PRANKY
PRAO
PRAOS
PRASE
PRASES
PRAT
PRATE
PRATED
PRATER
PRATERS
PRATES
PRATFALL
PRATFALLS
PRATFELL
PRATIE
PRATIES
PRATING
PRATINGLY
PRATINGS
PRATIQUE
PRATIQUES
PRATS
PRATT
PRATTED
PRATTING
PRATTLE
PRATTLED
PRATTLER
PRATTLERS
PRATTLES
PRATTLING
PRATTS
PRATY
PRAU
PRAUNCE
PRAUNCED
PRAUNCES
PRAUNCING
PRAUS
PRAVITIES
PRAVITY
PRAWLE
PRAWLES
PRAWLIN
PRAWLINS
PRAWN
PRAWNED
PRAWNER
PRAWNERS
PRAWNING
PRAWNS
PRAXES
PRAXIS
PRAXISES
PRAY
PRAYED
PRAYER
PRAYERFUL
PRAYERS
PRAYING
PRAYINGLY
PRAYINGS
PRAYS
PRE
PREABSORB
PREACCUSE
PREACE
PREACED
PREACES
PREACH
PREACHED
PREACHER
PREACHERS
PREACHES
PREACHIER
PREACHIFY
PREACHILY
PREACHING
PREACHY
PREACING
PREACT
PREACTED
PREACTING
PREACTS
PREADAMIC
PREADAPT
PREADAPTS
PREADJUST
PREADMIT
PREADMITS
PREADOPT
PREADOPTS
PREADULT
PREADULTS
PREAGED
PREALLOT
PREALLOTS
PREALTER
PREALTERS
PREAMBLE
PREAMBLED
PREAMBLES
PREAMP
PREAMPS
PREANAL
PREAPPLY
PREARM
PREARMED
PREARMING
PREARMS
PREASE
PREASED
PREASES
PREASING
PREASSE
PREASSED
PREASSES
PREASSIGN
PREASSING
PREASSURE
PREATOMIC
PREATTUNE
PREAUDIT
PREAUDITS
PREAVER
PREAVERS
PREAXIAL
PREBADE
PREBAKE
PREBAKED
PREBAKES
PREBAKING
PREBASAL
PREBATTLE
PREBEND
PREBENDAL
PREBENDS
PREBID
PREBIDDEN
PREBIDS
PREBILL
PREBILLED
PREBILLS
PREBIND
PREBINDS
PREBIOTIC
PREBIRTH
PREBIRTHS
PREBLESS

PREBOARD
PREBOARDS
PREBOIL
PREBOILED
PREBOILS
PREBOOK
PREBOOKED
PREBOOKS
PREBOOM
PREBORN
PREBOUGHT
PREBOUND
PREBUDGET
PREBUILD
PREBUILDS
PREBUILT
PREBUTTAL
PREBUY
PREBUYING
PREBUYS
PRECANCEL
PRECANCER
PRECARIAT
PRECAST
PRECASTS
PRECATIVE
PRECATORY
PRECAUDAL
PRECAVA
PRECAVAE
PRECAVAL
PRECAVALS
PRECEDE
PRECEDED
PRECEDENT
PRECEDES
PRECEDING
PRECEESE
PRECENSOR
PRECENT
PRECENTED
PRECENTOR
PRECENTS
PRECEPIT
PRECEPITS
PRECEPT
PRECEPTOR
PRECEPTS
PRECES
PRECESS
PRECESSED
PRECESSES
PRECHARGE
PRECHECK
PRECHECKS
PRECHILL
PRECHILLS
PRECHOOSE
PRECHOSE
PRECHOSEN
PRECIEUSE
PRECIEUX
PRECINCT
PRECINCTS
PRECIOUS
PRECIP
PRECIPE
PRECIPES
PRECIPICE
PRECIPS
PRECIS
PRECISE
PRECISED
PRECISELY
PRECISER
PRECISES
PRECISEST
PRECISIAN
PRECISING
PRECISION
PRECISIVE
PRECITED
PRECLEAN
PRECLEANS
PRECLEAR
PRECLEARS
PRECLUDE
PRECLUDED
PRECLUDES
PRECOCIAL
PRECOCITY
PRECODE
PRECODED
PRECODES
PRECODING
PRECOITAL
PRECONISE
PRECONIZE
PRECOOK
PRECOOKED
PRECOOKER
PRECOOKS
PRECOOL
PRECOOLED
PRECOOLS
PRECOUP
PRECRASH
PRECREASE
PRECRISIS
PRECURE
PRECURED
PRECURES
PRECURING
PRECURRER
PRECURSE
PRECURSED
PRECURSES
PRECURSOR
PRECUT
PRECUTS
PRECYCLE
PRECYCLED
PRECYCLES
PREDACITY
PREDATE
PREDATED
PREDATES
PREDATING
PREDATION
PREDATISM
PREDATIVE
PREDATOR
PREDATORS
PREDATORY
PREDAWN
PREDAWNS
PREDEATH
PREDEATHS
PREDEBATE
PREDEDUCT
PREDEFINE
PREDELLA
PREDELLAS
PREDELLE
PREDESIGN
PREDEVOTE
PREDIAL
PREDIALS
PREDICANT
PREDICATE
PREDICT
PREDICTED
PREDICTER
PREDICTOR
PREDICTS
PREDIED
PREDIES
PREDIGEST
PREDIKANT
PREDILECT
PREDINNER
PREDIVE
PREDOOM
PREDOOMED
PREDOOMS
PREDRAFT
PREDRAFTS
PREDRIED
PREDRIES
PREDRILL
PREDRILLS
PREDRY
PREDRYING
PREDUSK
PREDUSKS
PREDY
PREDYING
PREE
PREED
PREEDIT
PREEDITED
PREEDITS
PREEING
PREELECT
PREELECTS
PREEMIE
PREEMIES
PREEMPT
PREEMPTED
PREEMPTOR
PREEMPTS
PREEN
PREENACT
PREENACTS
PREENED
PREENER
PREENERS
PREENING
PREENS
PREERECT
PREERECTS
PREES
PREEVE
PREEVED
PREEVES
PREEVING
PREEXCITE
PREEXEMPT
PREEXILIC
PREEXIST
PREEXISTS
PREEXPOSE
PREFAB
PREFABBED
PREFABS
PREFACE
PREFACED
PREFACER
PREFACERS
PREFACES
PREFACIAL
PREFACING
PREFADE
PREFADED
PREFADES
PREFADING
PREFARD
PREFATORY
PREFECT
PREFECTS
PREFER
PREFERRED
PREFERRER
PREFERS
PREFEUDAL
PREFIGHT
PREFIGURE
PREFILE
PREFILED
PREFILES

P

PREFILING
PREFILLED
PREFIRE
PREFIRED
PREFIRES
PREFIRING
PREFIX
PREFIXAL
PREFIXED
PREFIXES
PREFIXING
PREFIXION
PREFLAME
PREFLIGHT
PREFOCUS
PREFORM
PREFORMAT
PREFORMED
PREFORMS
PREFRANK
PREFRANKS
PREFREEZE
PREFROZE
PREFROZEN
PREFUND
PREFUNDED
PREFUNDS
PREGAME
PREGAMED
PREGAMES
PREGAMING
PREGGERS
PREGGIER
PREGGIEST
PREGGO
PREGGY
PREGNABLE
PREGNANCE
PREGNANCY
PREGNANT
PREGROWTH
PREGUIDE
PREGUIDED
PREGUIDES
PREHAB
PREHABS
PREHALLUX
PREHANDLE
PREHARDEN
PREHEAT
PREHEATED
PREHEATER
PREHEATS
PREHEND
PREHENDED
PREHENDS
PREHENSOR
PREHIRING
PREHNITE
PREHNITES
PREHUMAN
PREHUMANS
PREIF
PREIFE
PREIFES
PREIFS
PREIMPOSE
PREINFORM
PREINSERT
PREINVITE
PREJINK
PREJUDGE
PREJUDGED
PREJUDGER
PREJUDGES
PREJUDICE
PREJUDIZE
PRELACIES
PRELACY
PRELATE
PRELATES
PRELATESS
PRELATIAL
PRELATIC
PRELATIES
PRELATION
PRELATISE
PRELATISH
PRELATISM
PRELATIST
PRELATIZE
PRELATURE
PRELATY
PRELAUNCH
PRELAW
PRELECT
PRELECTED
PRELECTOR
PRELECTS
PRELEGAL
PRELIFE
PRELIM
PRELIMIT
PRELIMITS
PRELIMS
PRELIVES
PRELOAD
PRELOADED
PRELOADS
PRELOCATE
PRELOVED
PRELUDE
PRELUDED
PRELUDER
PRELUDERS
PRELUDES
PRELUDI
PRELUDIAL
PRELUDING
PRELUDIO
PRELUDIOS
PRELUNCH
PRELUSION
PRELUSIVE
PRELUSORY
PREM
PREMADE
PREMAKE
PREMAKES
PREMAKING
PREMAN
PREMARKET
PREMATURE
PREMEAL
PREMED
PREMEDIC
PREMEDICS
PREMEDS
PREMEET
PREMEN
PREMERGER
PREMIA
PREMIE
PREMIER
PREMIERE
PREMIERED
PREMIERES
PREMIERS
PREMIES
PREMISE
PREMISED
PREMISES
PREMISING
PREMISS
PREMISSED
PREMISSES
PREMIUM
PREMIUMS
PREMIX
PREMIXED
PREMIXES
PREMIXING
PREMIXT
PREMODERN
PREMODIFY
PREMOLAR
PREMOLARS
PREMOLD
PREMOLDED
PREMOLDS
PREMOLT
PREMONISH
PREMORAL
PREMORSE
PREMOSAIC
PREMOTION
PREMOTOR
PREMOULD
PREMOULDS
PREMOULT
PREMOVE
PREMOVED
PREMOVES
PREMOVING
PREMS
PREMUNE
PREMY
PRENAME
PRENAMES
PRENASAL
PRENASALS
PRENATAL
PRENATALS
PRENEED
PRENOMEN
PRENOMENS
PRENOMINA
PRENOON
PRENOTIFY
PRENOTION
PRENT
PRENTED
PRENTICE
PRENTICED
PRENTICES
PRENTING
PRENTS
PRENUBILE
PRENUMBER
PRENUP
PRENUPS
PRENZIE
PREOBTAIN
PREOCCUPY
PREOCULAR
PREON
PREONS
PREOP
PREOPS
PREOPTION
PREORAL
PREORDAIN
PREORDER
PREORDERS
PREOWNED
PREP
PREPACK
PREPACKED
PREPACKS
PREPAID
PREPARE
PREPARED
PREPARER
PREPARERS
PREPARES
PREPARING
PREPASTE
PREPASTED
PREPASTES
PREPAVE

P

PREPAVED
PREPAVES
PREPAVING
PREPAY
PREPAYING
PREPAYS
PREPENSE
PREPENSED
PREPENSES
PREPILL
PREPLACE
PREPLACED
PREPLACES
PREPLAN
PREPLANS
PREPLANT
PREPOLLEX
PREPONE
PREPONED
PREPONES
PREPONING
PREPOSE
PREPOSED
PREPOSES
PREPOSING
PREPOSTOR
PREPOTENT
PREPPED
PREPPIE
PREPPIER
PREPPIES
PREPPIEST
PREPPILY
PREPPING
PREPPY
PREPREG
PREPREGS
PREPRESS
PREPRICE
PREPRICED
PREPRICES
PREPRINT
PREPRINTS
PREPS
PREPUBES
PREPUBIS
PREPUCE
PREPUCES
PREPUEBLO
PREPUNCH
PREPUPA
PREPUPAE
PREPUPAL
PREPUPAS
PREPUTIAL
PREQUEL
PREQUELS
PRERACE
PRERADIO
PRERECORD
PRERECTAL
PREREFORM
PRERENAL
PRERETURN
PREREVIEW
PRERINSE
PRERINSED
PRERINSES
PRERIOT
PREROCK
PRERUPT
PRESA
PRESAGE
PRESAGED
PRESAGER
PRESAGERS
PRESAGES
PRESAGING
PRESALE
PRESALES
PRESBYOPE
PRESBYOPY
PRESBYTE
PRESBYTER
PRESBYTES
PRESBYTIC
PRESCHOOL
PRESCIENT
PRESCIND
PRESCINDS
PRESCIOUS
PRESCORE
PRESCORED
PRESCORES
PRESCREEN
PRESCRIBE
PRESCRIPT
PRESCUTA
PRESCUTUM
PRESE
PRESEASON
PRESELECT
PRESELL
PRESELLS
PRESENCE
PRESENCES
PRESENILE
PRESENT
PRESENTED
PRESENTEE
PRESENTER
PRESENTLY
PRESENTS
PRESERVE
PRESERVED
PRESERVER
PRESERVES
PRESES
PRESET
PRESETS
PRESETTLE
PRESHAPE
PRESHAPED
PRESHAPES
PRESHIP
PRESHIPS
PRESHOW
PRESHOWED
PRESHOWN
PRESHOWS
PRESHRANK
PRESHRINK
PRESHRUNK
PRESIDE
PRESIDED
PRESIDENT
PRESIDER
PRESIDERS
PRESIDES
PRESIDIA
PRESIDIAL
PRESIDING
PRESIDIO
PRESIDIOS
PRESIDIUM
PRESIFT
PRESIFTED
PRESIFTS
PRESIGNAL
PRESLEEP
PRESLICE
PRESLICED
PRESLICES
PRESOAK
PRESOAKED
PRESOAKS
PRESOLD
PRESOLVE
PRESOLVED
PRESOLVES
PRESONG
PRESORT
PRESORTED
PRESORTS
PRESPLIT
PRESS
PRESSBACK
PRESSED
PRESSER
PRESSERS
PRESSES
PRESSFAT
PRESSFATS
PRESSFUL
PRESSFULS
PRESSGANG
PRESSIE
PRESSIES
PRESSING
PRESSINGS
PRESSION
PRESSIONS
PRESSMAN
PRESSMARK
PRESSMEN
PRESSOR
PRESSORS
PRESSROOM
PRESSRUN
PRESSRUNS
PRESSURE
PRESSURED
PRESSURES
PRESSWORK
PRESSY
PREST
PRESTAMP
PRESTAMPS
PRESTED
PRESTER
PRESTERNA
PRESTERS
PRESTIGE
PRESTIGES
PRESTING
PRESTO
PRESTORE
PRESTORED
PRESTORES
PRESTOS
PRESTRESS
PRESTRIKE
PRESTS
PRESUME
PRESUMED
PRESUMER
PRESUMERS
PRESUMES
PRESUMING
PRESUMMIT
PRESURVEY
PRETAPE
PRETAPED
PRETAPES
PRETAPING
PRETASTE
PRETASTED
PRETASTES
PRETAX
PRETEEN
PRETEENS
PRETELL
PRETELLS
PRETENCE
PRETENCES
PRETEND
PRETENDED
PRETENDER
PRETENDS
PRETENSE

P

PRETENSES
PRETERIST
PRETERIT
PRETERITE
PRETERITS
PRETERM
PRETERMIT
PRETERMS
PRETEST
PRETESTED
PRETESTS
PRETEXT
PRETEXTED
PRETEXTS
PRETOLD
PRETONIC
PRETOR
PRETORIAL
PRETORIAN
PRETORS
PRETRAIN
PRETRAINS
PRETRAVEL
PRETREAT
PRETREATS
PRETRIAL
PRETRIALS
PRETRIM
PRETRIMS
PRETTIED
PRETTIER
PRETTIES
PRETTIEST
PRETTIFY
PRETTILY
PRETTY
PRETTYING
PRETTYISH
PRETTYISM
PRETYPE
PRETYPED
PRETYPES
PRETYPING
PRETZEL
PRETZELS
PREUNION
PREUNIONS
PREUNITE
PREUNITED
PREUNITES
PREVAIL
PREVAILED
PREVAILER
PREVAILS
PREVALENT
PREVALUE
PREVALUED
PREVALUES
PREVE
PREVED
PREVENE
PREVENED
PREVENES
PREVENING
PREVENT
PREVENTED
PREVENTER
PREVENTS
PREVERB
PREVERBAL
PREVERBS
PREVES
PREVIABLE
PREVIEW
PREVIEWED
PREVIEWER
PREVIEWS
PREVING
PREVIOUS
PREVISE
PREVISED
PREVISES
PREVISING
PREVISION
PREVISIT
PREVISITS
PREVISOR
PREVISORS
PREVUE
PREVUED
PREVUES
PREVUING
PREWAR
PREWARM
PREWARMED
PREWARMS
PREWARN
PREWARNED
PREWARNS
PREWASH
PREWASHED
PREWASHES
PREWEANED
PREWEIGH
PREWEIGHS
PREWIRE
PREWIRED
PREWIRES
PREWIRING
PREWORK
PREWORKED
PREWORKS
PREWORN
PREWRAP
PREWRAPS
PREWRITE
PREWRITES
PREWROTE
PREWYN
PREWYNS
PREX
PREXES
PREXIE
PREXIES
PREXY
PREY
PREYED
PREYER
PREYERS
PREYFUL
PREYING
PREYS
PREZ
PREZES
PREZZIE
PREZZIES
PRIAL
PRIALS
PRIAPEAN
PRIAPI
PRIAPIC
PRIAPISM
PRIAPISMS
PRIAPUS
PRIAPUSES
PRIBBLE
PRIBBLES
PRICE
PRICEABLE
PRICED
PRICELESS
PRICER
PRICERS
PRICES
PRICEY
PRICIER
PRICIEST
PRICILY
PRICINESS
PRICING
PRICINGS
PRICK
PRICKED
PRICKER
PRICKERS
PRICKET
PRICKETS
PRICKIER
PRICKIEST
PRICKING
PRICKINGS
PRICKLE
PRICKLED
PRICKLES
PRICKLIER
PRICKLING
PRICKLY
PRICKS
PRICKWOOD
PRICKY
PRICY
PRIDE
PRIDED
PRIDEFUL
PRIDELESS
PRIDES
PRIDIAN
PRIDING
PRIED
PRIEDIEU
PRIEDIEUS
PRIEDIEUX
PRIEF
PRIEFE
PRIEFES
PRIEFS
PRIER
PRIERS
PRIES
PRIEST
PRIESTED
PRIESTESS
PRIESTING
PRIESTLY
PRIESTS
PRIEVE
PRIEVED
PRIEVES
PRIEVING
PRIG
PRIGGED
PRIGGER
PRIGGERS
PRIGGERY
PRIGGING
PRIGGINGS
PRIGGISH
PRIGGISM
PRIGGISMS
PRIGS
PRILL
PRILLED
PRILLING
PRILLS
PRIM
PRIMA
PRIMACIES
PRIMACY
PRIMAEVAL
PRIMAGE
PRIMAGES
PRIMAL
PRIMALITY
PRIMALLY
PRIMARIES
PRIMARILY
PRIMARY
PRIMAS
PRIMATAL
PRIMATALS

PRIMATE
PRIMATES
PRIMATIAL
PRIMATIC
PRIMAVERA
PRIME
PRIMED
PRIMELY
PRIMENESS
PRIMER
PRIMERO
PRIMEROS
PRIMERS
PRIMES
PRIMETIME
PRIMEUR
PRIMEURS
PRIMEVAL
PRIMI
PRIMINE
PRIMINES
PRIMING
PRIMINGS
PRIMIPARA
PRIMITIAE
PRIMITIAL
PRIMITIAS
PRIMITIVE
PRIMLY
PRIMMED
PRIMMER
PRIMMERS
PRIMMEST
PRIMMING
PRIMNESS
PRIMO
PRIMORDIA
PRIMOS
PRIMP
PRIMPED
PRIMPING
PRIMPS
PRIMROSE
PRIMROSED
PRIMROSES
PRIMROSY
PRIMS
PRIMSIE
PRIMSIER
PRIMSIEST
PRIMULA
PRIMULAS
PRIMULINE
PRIMUS
PRIMUSES
PRIMY
PRINCE
PRINCED
PRINCEDOM
PRINCEKIN
PRINCELET
PRINCELY
PRINCES
PRINCESS
PRINCESSE
PRINCING
PRINCIPAL
PRINCIPE
PRINCIPI
PRINCIPIA
PRINCIPLE
PRINCOCK
PRINCOCKS
PRINCOX
PRINCOXES
PRINK
PRINKED
PRINKER
PRINKERS
PRINKING
PRINKS
PRINT
PRINTABLE
PRINTED
PRINTER
PRINTERS
PRINTERY
PRINTHEAD
PRINTING
PRINTINGS
PRINTLESS
PRINTOUT
PRINTOUTS
PRINTS
PRION
PRIONS
PRIOR
PRIORATE
PRIORATES
PRIORESS
PRIORIES
PRIORITY
PRIORLY
PRIORS
PRIORSHIP
PRIORY
PRISAGE
PRISAGES
PRISE
PRISED
PRISER
PRISERE
PRISERES
PRISERS
PRISES
PRISING
PRISM
PRISMATIC
PRISMOID
PRISMOIDS
PRISMS
PRISMY
PRISON
PRISONED
PRISONER
PRISONERS
PRISONING
PRISONOUS
PRISONS
PRISS
PRISSED
PRISSES
PRISSIER
PRISSIES
PRISSIEST
PRISSILY
PRISSING
PRISSY
PRISTANE
PRISTANES
PRISTINE
PRITHEE
PRIVACIES
PRIVACY
PRIVADO
PRIVADOES
PRIVADOS
PRIVATE
PRIVATEER
PRIVATELY
PRIVATER
PRIVATES
PRIVATEST
PRIVATION
PRIVATISE
PRIVATISM
PRIVATIST
PRIVATIVE
PRIVATIZE
PRIVET
PRIVETS
PRIVIER
PRIVIES
PRIVIEST
PRIVILEGE
PRIVILY
PRIVITIES
PRIVITY
PRIVY
PRIZABLE
PRIZE
PRIZED
PRIZEMAN
PRIZEMEN
PRIZER
PRIZERS
PRIZES
PRIZING
PRO
PROA
PROACTION
PROACTIVE
PROAS
PROB
PROBABLE
PROBABLES
PROBABLY
PROBALL
PROBAND
PROBANDS
PROBANG
PROBANGS
PROBATE
PROBATED
PROBATES
PROBATING
PROBATION
PROBATIVE
PROBATORY
PROBE
PROBEABLE
PROBED
PROBER
PROBERS
PROBES
PROBING
PROBINGLY
PROBINGS
PROBIOTIC
PROBIT
PROBITIES
PROBITS
PROBITY
PROBLEM
PROBLEMS
PROBOSCIS
PROBS
PROCACITY
PROCAINE
PROCAINES
PROCAMBIA
PROCARP
PROCARPS
PROCARYON
PROCEDURE
PROCEED
PROCEEDED
PROCEEDER
PROCEEDS
PROCERITY
PROCESS
PROCESSED
PROCESSER
PROCESSES
PROCESSOR
PROCHAIN
PROCHEIN
PROCHOICE
PROCHURCH
PROCIDENT

PROCINCT
PROCINCTS
PROCLAIM
PROCLAIMS
PROCLISES
PROCLISIS
PROCLITIC
PROCLIVE
PROCONSUL
PROCREANT
PROCREATE
PROCTAL
PROCTITIS
PROCTODEA
PROCTOR
PROCTORED
PROCTORS
PROCURACY
PROCURAL
PROCURALS
PROCURE
PROCURED
PROCURER
PROCURERS
PROCURES
PROCURESS
PROCUREUR
PROCURING
PROCYONID
PROD
PRODDED
PRODDER
PRODDERS
PRODDING
PRODDINGS
PRODIGAL
PRODIGALS
PRODIGIES
PRODIGY
PRODITOR
PRODITORS
PRODITORY
PRODNOSE
PRODNOSED
PRODNOSES
PRODROMA
PRODROMAL
PRODROME
PRODROMES
PRODROMI
PRODROMIC
PRODROMUS
PRODRUG
PRODRUGS
PRODS
PRODUCE
PRODUCED
PRODUCER
PRODUCERS
PRODUCES
PRODUCING
PRODUCT
PRODUCTS
PROEM
PROEMBRYO
PROEMIAL
PROEMS
PROENZYME
PROESTRUS
PROETTE
PROETTES
PROF
PROFACE
PROFAMILY
PROFANE
PROFANED
PROFANELY
PROFANER
PROFANERS
PROFANES
PROFANING
PROFANITY
PROFESS
PROFESSED
PROFESSES
PROFESSOR
PROFFER
PROFFERED
PROFFERER
PROFFERS
PROFILE
PROFILED
PROFILER
PROFILERS
PROFILES
PROFILING
PROFILIST
PROFIT
PROFITED
PROFITEER
PROFITER
PROFITERS
PROFITING
PROFITS
PROFLUENT
PROFORMA
PROFORMAS
PROFOUND
PROFOUNDS
PROFS
PROFUSE
PROFUSELY
PROFUSER
PROFUSERS
PROFUSION
PROFUSIVE
PROG
PROGENIES
PROGENY
PROGERIA
PROGERIAS
PROGESTIN
PROGGED
PROGGER
PROGGERS
PROGGING
PROGGINS
PROGNOSE
PROGNOSED
PROGNOSES
PROGNOSIS
PROGRADE
PROGRADED
PROGRADES
PROGRAM
PROGRAMED
PROGRAMER
PROGRAMME
PROGRAMS
PROGRESS
PROGS
PROGUN
PROHIBIT
PROHIBITS
PROIGN
PROIGNED
PROIGNING
PROIGNS
PROIN
PROINE
PROINED
PROINES
PROINING
PROINS
PROJECT
PROJECTED
PROJECTOR
PROJECTS
PROJET
PROJETS
PROKARYON
PROKARYOT
PROKE
PROKED
PROKER
PROKERS
PROKES
PROKING
PROLABOR
PROLABOUR
PROLACTIN
PROLAMIN
PROLAMINE
PROLAMINS
PROLAN
PROLANS
PROLAPSE
PROLAPSED
PROLAPSES
PROLAPSUS
PROLATE
PROLATED
PROLATELY
PROLATES
PROLATING
PROLATION
PROLATIVE
PROLE
PROLED
PROLEG
PROLEGS
PROLEPSES
PROLEPSIS
PROLEPTIC
PROLER
PROLERS
PROLES
PROLETARY
PROLICIDE
PROLIFIC
PROLINE
PROLINES
PROLING
PROLIX
PROLIXITY
PROLIXLY
PROLL
PROLLED
PROLLER
PROLLERS
PROLLING
PROLLS
PROLLY
PROLOG
PROLOGED
PROLOGING
PROLOGISE
PROLOGIST
PROLOGIZE
PROLOGS
PROLOGUE
PROLOGUED
PROLOGUES
PROLONG
PROLONGE
PROLONGED
PROLONGER
PROLONGES
PROLONGS
PROLUSION
PROLUSORY
PROM
PROMACHOS
PROMENADE
PROMETAL
PROMETALS
PROMETRIC
PROMINE
PROMINENT
PROMINES

PROMISE
PROMISED
PROMISEE
PROMISEES
PROMISER
PROMISERS
PROMISES
PROMISING
PROMISOR
PROMISORS
PROMISSOR
PROMMER
PROMMERS
PROMO
PROMODERN
PROMOED
PROMOING
PROMOS
PROMOTE
PROMOTED
PROMOTER
PROMOTERS
PROMOTES
PROMOTING
PROMOTION
PROMOTIVE
PROMOTOR
PROMOTORS
PROMPT
PROMPTED
PROMPTER
PROMPTERS
PROMPTEST
PROMPTING
PROMPTLY
PROMPTS
PROMPTURE
PROMS
PROMULGE
PROMULGED
PROMULGES
PROMUSCES
PROMUSCIS
PRONAOI
PRONAOS
PRONATE
PRONATED
PRONATES
PRONATING
PRONATION
PRONATOR
PRONATORS
PRONE
PRONELY
PRONENESS
PRONEPHRA
PRONER
PRONES
PRONEST
PRONEUR
PRONEURS
PRONG
PRONGBUCK
PRONGED
PRONGHORN
PRONGING
PRONGS
PRONK
PRONKED
PRONKING
PRONKINGS
PRONKS
PRONOTA
PRONOTAL
PRONOTUM
PRONOUN
PRONOUNCE
PRONOUNS
PRONTO
PRONUCLEI
PRONUNCIO
PROO
PROOEMION
PROOEMIUM
PROOF
PROOFED
PROOFER
PROOFERS
PROOFING
PROOFINGS
PROOFLESS
PROOFREAD
PROOFROOM
PROOFS
PROOTIC
PROOTICS
PROP
PROPAGATE
PROPAGE
PROPAGED
PROPAGES
PROPAGING
PROPAGULA
PROPAGULE
PROPALE
PROPALED
PROPALES
PROPALING
PROPANE
PROPANES
PROPANOIC
PROPANOL
PROPANOLS
PROPANONE
PROPEL
PROPELLED
PROPELLER
PROPELLOR
PROPELS
PROPENAL
PROPENALS
PROPEND
PROPENDED
PROPENDS
PROPENE
PROPENES
PROPENOIC
PROPENOL
PROPENOLS
PROPENSE
PROPENYL
PROPENYLS
PROPER
PROPERDIN
PROPERER
PROPEREST
PROPERLY
PROPERS
PROPERTY
PROPHAGE
PROPHAGES
PROPHASE
PROPHASES
PROPHASIC
PROPHECY
PROPHESY
PROPHET
PROPHETIC
PROPHETS
PROPHYLL
PROPHYLLS
PROPINE
PROPINED
PROPINES
PROPINING
PROPIONIC
PROPJET
PROPJETS
PROPMAN
PROPMEN
PROPODEON
PROPODEUM
PROPOLIS
PROPONE
PROPONED
PROPONENT
PROPONES
PROPONING
PROPOSAL
PROPOSALS
PROPOSE
PROPOSED
PROPOSER
PROPOSERS
PROPOSES
PROPOSING
PROPOSITA
PROPOSITI
PROPOUND
PROPOUNDS
PROPPANT
PROPPANTS
PROPPED
PROPPING
PROPRETOR
PROPRIA
PROPRIETY
PROPRIUM
PROPS
PROPTOSES
PROPTOSIS
PROPULSOR
PROPYL
PROPYLA
PROPYLAEA
PROPYLENE
PROPYLIC
PROPYLITE
PROPYLON
PROPYLONS
PROPYLS
PROPYNE
PROPYNES
PRORATE
PRORATED
PRORATES
PRORATING
PRORATION
PRORE
PRORECTOR
PROREFORM
PRORES
PROROGATE
PROROGUE
PROROGUED
PROROGUES
PROS
PROSAIC
PROSAICAL
PROSAISM
PROSAISMS
PROSAIST
PROSAISTS
PROSATEUR
PROSCENIA
PROSCRIBE
PROSCRIPT
PROSE
PROSECCO
PROSECCOS
PROSECT
PROSECTED
PROSECTOR
PROSECTS
PROSECUTE
PROSED
PROSELIKE
PROSELYTE
PROSEMAN
PROSEMEN

P

PROSER
PROSERS
PROSES
PROSEUCHA
PROSEUCHE
PROSIER
PROSIEST
PROSIFIED
PROSIFIES
PROSIFY
PROSILY
PROSIMIAN
PROSINESS
PROSING
PROSINGS
PROSIT
PROSO
PROSOCIAL
PROSODIAL
PROSODIAN
PROSODIC
PROSODIES
PROSODIST
PROSODY
PROSOMA
PROSOMAL
PROSOMAS
PROSOMATA
PROSOPON
PROSOPONS
PROSOS
PROSPECT
PROSPECTS
PROSPER
PROSPERED
PROSPERS
PROSS
PROSSES
PROSSIE
PROSSIES
PROST
PROSTATE
PROSTATES
PROSTATIC
PROSTERNA
PROSTIE
PROSTIES
PROSTOMIA
PROSTRATE
PROSTYLE
PROSTYLES
PROSUMER
PROSUMERS
PROSY
PROTAMIN
PROTAMINE
PROTAMINS
PROTANDRY
PROTANOPE
PROTASES
PROTASIS
PROTATIC
PROTEA
PROTEAN
PROTEANS
PROTEAS
PROTEASE
PROTEASES
PROTECT
PROTECTED
PROTECTER
PROTECTOR
PROTECTS
PROTEGE
PROTEGEE
PROTEGEES
PROTEGES
PROTEI
PROTEID
PROTEIDE
PROTEIDES
PROTEIDS
PROTEIN
PROTEINIC
PROTEINS
PROTEND
PROTENDED
PROTENDS
PROTENSE
PROTENSES
PROTEOME
PROTEOMES
PROTEOMIC
PROTEOSE
PROTEOSES
PROTEST
PROTESTED
PROTESTER
PROTESTOR
PROTESTS
PROTEUS
PROTEUSES
PROTHALLI
PROTHESES
PROTHESIS
PROTHETIC
PROTHORAX
PROTHYL
PROTHYLS
PROTIST
PROTISTAN
PROTISTIC
PROTISTS
PROTIUM
PROTIUMS
PROTO
PROTOAVIS
PROTOCOL
PROTOCOLS
PROTODERM
PROTOGINE
PROTOGYNY
PROTON
PROTONATE
PROTONEMA
PROTONIC
PROTONS
PROTOPOD
PROTOPODS
PROTORE
PROTORES
PROTOSTAR
PROTOTYPE
PROTOXID
PROTOXIDE
PROTOXIDS
PROTOZOA
PROTOZOAL
PROTOZOAN
PROTOZOIC
PROTOZOON
PROTRACT
PROTRACTS
PROTRADE
PROTRUDE
PROTRUDED
PROTRUDES
PROTURAN
PROTURANS
PROTYL
PROTYLE
PROTYLES
PROTYLS
PROUD
PROUDER
PROUDEST
PROUDFUL
PROUDISH
PROUDLY
PROUDNESS
PROUL
PROULED
PROULER
PROULERS
PROULING
PROULS
PROUNION
PROUSTITE
PROVABLE
PROVABLY
PROVAND
PROVANDS
PROVANT
PROVANTED
PROVANTS
PROVE
PROVEABLE
PROVEABLY
PROVED
PROVEDOR
PROVEDORE
PROVEDORS
PROVEN
PROVEND
PROVENDER
PROVENDS
PROVENLY
PROVER
PROVERB
PROVERBED
PROVERBS
PROVERS
PROVES
PROVIANT
PROVIANTS
PROVIDE
PROVIDED
PROVIDENT
PROVIDER
PROVIDERS
PROVIDES
PROVIDING
PROVIDOR
PROVIDORS
PROVINCE
PROVINCES
PROVINE
PROVINED
PROVINES
PROVING
PROVINGS
PROVINING
PROVIRAL
PROVIRUS
PROVISION
PROVISO
PROVISOES
PROVISOR
PROVISORS
PROVISORY
PROVISOS
PROVOCANT
PROVOKE
PROVOKED
PROVOKER
PROVOKERS
PROVOKES
PROVOKING
PROVOLONE
PROVOST
PROVOSTRY
PROVOSTS
PROW
PROWAR
PROWER
PROWESS
PROWESSED
PROWESSES
PROWEST
PROWL

PROWLED
PROWLER
PROWLERS
PROWLING
PROWLINGS
PROWLS
PROWS
PROXEMIC
PROXEMICS
PROXIES
PROXIMAL
PROXIMATE
PROXIMITY
PROXIMO
PROXY
PROYN
PROYNE
PROYNED
PROYNES
PROYNING
PROYNS
PROZYMITE
PROZZIE
PROZZIES
PRUDE
PRUDENCE
PRUDENCES
PRUDENT
PRUDENTLY
PRUDERIES
PRUDERY
PRUDES
PRUDISH
PRUDISHLY
PRUH
PRUINA
PRUINAS
PRUINE
PRUINES
PRUINOSE
PRUNABLE
PRUNE
PRUNED
PRUNELLA
PRUNELLAS
PRUNELLE
PRUNELLES
PRUNELLO
PRUNELLOS
PRUNER
PRUNERS
PRUNES
PRUNEY
PRUNIER
PRUNIEST
PRUNING
PRUNINGS
PRUNT
PRUNTED
PRUNTS
PRUNUS
PRUNUSES
PRURIENCE
PRURIENCY
PRURIENT
PRURIGO
PRURIGOS
PRURITIC
PRURITUS
PRUSIK
PRUSIKED
PRUSIKING
PRUSIKS
PRUSSIAN
PRUSSIATE
PRUSSIC
PRUTA
PRUTAH
PRUTOT
PRUTOTH
PRY
PRYER
PRYERS
PRYING
PRYINGLY
PRYINGS
PRYS
PRYSE
PRYSED
PRYSES
PRYSING
PRYTANEA
PRYTANEUM
PRYTHEE
PSALM
PSALMBOOK
PSALMED
PSALMIC
PSALMING
PSALMIST
PSALMISTS
PSALMODIC
PSALMODY
PSALMS
PSALTER
PSALTERIA
PSALTERS
PSALTERY
PSALTRESS
PSALTRIES
PSALTRY
PSAMMITE
PSAMMITES
PSAMMITIC
PSAMMON
PSAMMONS
PSCHENT
PSCHENTS
PSELLISM
PSELLISMS
PSEPHISM
PSEPHISMS
PSEPHITE
PSEPHITES
PSEPHITIC
PSEUD
PSEUDAXES
PSEUDAXIS
PSEUDERY
PSEUDISH
PSEUDO
PSEUDONYM
PSEUDOPOD
PSEUDOS
PSEUDS
PSHAW
PSHAWED
PSHAWING
PSHAWS
PSI
PSILOCIN
PSILOCINS
PSILOSES
PSILOSIS
PSILOTIC
PSION
PSIONIC
PSIONICS
PSIONS
PSIS
PSOAE
PSOAI
PSOAS
PSOASES
PSOATIC
PSOCID
PSOCIDS
PSORA
PSORALEA
PSORALEAS
PSORALEN
PSORALENS
PSORAS
PSORIASES
PSORIASIS
PSORIATIC
PSORIC
PSST
PST
PSYCH
PSYCHE
PSYCHED
PSYCHES
PSYCHIC
PSYCHICAL
PSYCHICS
PSYCHING
PSYCHISM
PSYCHISMS
PSYCHIST
PSYCHISTS
PSYCHO
PSYCHOGAS
PSYCHOID
PSYCHOIDS
PSYCHOS
PSYCHOSES
PSYCHOSIS
PSYCHOTIC
PSYCHS
PSYLLA
PSYLLAS
PSYLLID
PSYLLIDS
PSYLLIUM
PSYLLIUMS
PSYOP
PSYOPS
PSYWAR
PSYWARS
PTARMIC
PTARMICS
PTARMIGAN
PTERIA
PTERIDINE
PTERIN
PTERINS
PTERION
PTEROIC
PTEROPOD
PTEROPODS
PTEROSAUR
PTERYGIA
PTERYGIAL
PTERYGIUM
PTERYGOID
PTERYLA
PTERYLAE
PTILOSES
PTILOSIS
PTISAN
PTISANS
PTOMAIN
PTOMAINE
PTOMAINES
PTOMAINIC
PTOMAINS
PTOOEY
PTOSES
PTOSIS
PTOTIC
PTUI
PTYALIN
PTYALINS
PTYALISE
PTYALISED
PTYALISES
PTYALISM
PTYALISMS
PTYALIZE

P

PTYALIZED
PTYALIZES
PTYXES
PTYXIS
PTYXISES
PUB
PUBBED
PUBBING
PUBBINGS
PUBCO
PUBCOS
PUBE
PUBERAL
PUBERTAL
PUBERTIES
PUBERTY
PUBES
PUBESCENT
PUBIC
PUBIS
PUBISES
PUBLIC
PUBLICAN
PUBLICANS
PUBLICISE
PUBLICIST
PUBLICITY
PUBLICIZE
PUBLICLY
PUBLICS
PUBLISH
PUBLISHED
PUBLISHER
PUBLISHES
PUBS
PUCAN
PUCANS
PUCCOON
PUCCOONS
PUCE
PUCELAGE
PUCELAGES
PUCELLE
PUCELLES
PUCER
PUCES
PUCEST
PUCK
PUCKA
PUCKED
PUCKER
PUCKERED
PUCKERER
PUCKERERS
PUCKERIER
PUCKERIES
PUCKERING
PUCKEROOD
PUCKERS
PUCKERY
PUCKFIST
PUCKFISTS
PUCKING
PUCKISH
PUCKISHLY
PUCKLE
PUCKLES
PUCKOUT
PUCKOUTS
PUCKS
PUCKSTER
PUCKSTERS
PUD
PUDDEN
PUDDENING
PUDDENS
PUDDER
PUDDERED
PUDDERING
PUDDERS
PUDDIER
PUDDIES
PUDDIEST
PUDDING
PUDDINGS
PUDDINGY
PUDDLE
PUDDLED
PUDDLER
PUDDLERS
PUDDLES
PUDDLIER
PUDDLIEST
PUDDLING
PUDDLINGS
PUDDLY
PUDDOCK
PUDDOCKS
PUDDY
PUDENCIES
PUDENCY
PUDENDA
PUDENDAL
PUDENDOUS
PUDENDUM
PUDENT
PUDEUR
PUDEURS
PUDGE
PUDGES
PUDGIER
PUDGIEST
PUDGILY
PUDGINESS
PUDGY
PUDIBUND
PUDIC
PUDICITY
PUDOR
PUDORS
PUDS
PUDSEY
PUDSIER
PUDSIES
PUDSIEST
PUDSY
PUDU
PUDUS
PUEBLO
PUEBLOS
PUER
PUERED
PUERILE
PUERILELY
PUERILISM
PUERILITY
PUERING
PUERPERA
PUERPERAE
PUERPERAL
PUERPERIA
PUERS
PUFF
PUFFA
PUFFBACK
PUFFBACKS
PUFFBALL
PUFFBALLS
PUFFBIRD
PUFFBIRDS
PUFFED
PUFFER
PUFFERIES
PUFFERS
PUFFERY
PUFFIER
PUFFIEST
PUFFILY
PUFFIN
PUFFINESS
PUFFING
PUFFINGLY
PUFFINGS
PUFFINS
PUFFS
PUFFY
PUFTALOON
PUG
PUGAREE
PUGAREES
PUGGAREE
PUGGAREES
PUGGED
PUGGERIES
PUGGERY
PUGGIE
PUGGIER
PUGGIES
PUGGIEST
PUGGINESS
PUGGING
PUGGINGS
PUGGISH
PUGGLE
PUGGLED
PUGGLES
PUGGLING
PUGGREE
PUGGREES
PUGGRIES
PUGGRY
PUGGY
PUGH
PUGIL
PUGILISM
PUGILISMS
PUGILIST
PUGILISTS
PUGILS
PUGMARK
PUGMARKS
PUGNACITY
PUGREE
PUGREES
PUGS
PUH
PUHA
PUHAS
PUIR
PUIRER
PUIREST
PUIRTITH
PUIRTITHS
PUISNE
PUISNES
PUISNY
PUISSANCE
PUISSANT
PUISSAUNT
PUJA
PUJAH
PUJAHS
PUJARI
PUJARIS
PUJAS
PUKA
PUKAS
PUKATEA
PUKATEAS
PUKE
PUKED
PUKEKO
PUKEKOS
PUKER
PUKERS
PUKES
PUKEY
PUKIER
PUKIEST
PUKING

P

PUKKA
PUKKAH
PUKU
PUKUS
PUKY
PUL
PULA
PULAO
PULAOS
PULAS
PULDRON
PULDRONS
PULE
PULED
PULER
PULERS
PULES
PULI
PULICENE
PULICIDE
PULICIDES
PULIER
PULIEST
PULIK
PULING
PULINGLY
PULINGS
PULIS
PULK
PULKA
PULKAS
PULKHA
PULKHAS
PULKS
PULL
PULLBACK
PULLBACKS
PULLED
PULLER
PULLERS
PULLET
PULLETS
PULLEY
PULLEYED
PULLEYING
PULLEYS
PULLI
PULLIES
PULLING
PULLMAN
PULLMANS
PULLORUM
PULLOUT
PULLOUTS
PULLOVER
PULLOVERS
PULLS
PULLULATE
PULLUP
PULLUPS
PULLUS
PULLY
PULMO
PULMONARY
PULMONATE
PULMONES
PULMONIC
PULMONICS
PULMOTOR
PULMOTORS
PULP
PULPAL
PULPALLY
PULPBOARD
PULPED
PULPER
PULPERS
PULPIER
PULPIEST
PULPIFIED
PULPIFIES
PULPIFY
PULPILY
PULPINESS
PULPING
PULPINGS
PULPIT
PULPITAL
PULPITED
PULPITEER
PULPITER
PULPITERS
PULPITRY
PULPITS
PULPITUM
PULPITUMS
PULPLESS
PULPMILL
PULPMILLS
PULPOUS
PULPS
PULPSTONE
PULPWOOD
PULPWOODS
PULPY
PULQUE
PULQUES
PULS
PULSANT
PULSAR
PULSARS
PULSATE
PULSATED
PULSATES
PULSATILE
PULSATING
PULSATION
PULSATIVE
PULSATOR
PULSATORS
PULSATORY
PULSE
PULSEBEAT
PULSED
PULSEJET
PULSEJETS
PULSELESS
PULSER
PULSERS
PULSES
PULSIDGE
PULSIDGES
PULSIFIC
PULSING
PULSION
PULSIONS
PULSOJET
PULSOJETS
PULTAN
PULTANS
PULTON
PULTONS
PULTOON
PULTOONS
PULTRUDE
PULTRUDED
PULTRUDES
PULTUN
PULTUNS
PULTURE
PULTURES
PULU
PULUS
PULVER
PULVERED
PULVERINE
PULVERING
PULVERISE
PULVERIZE
PULVEROUS
PULVERS
PULVIL
PULVILIO
PULVILIOS
PULVILLAR
PULVILLE
PULVILLED
PULVILLES
PULVILLI
PULVILLIO
PULVILLUS
PULVILS
PULVINAR
PULVINARS
PULVINATE
PULVINI
PULVINULE
PULVINUS
PULWAR
PULWARS
PULY
PUMA
PUMAS
PUMELO
PUMELOS
PUMICATE
PUMICATED
PUMICATES
PUMICE
PUMICED
PUMICEOUS
PUMICER
PUMICERS
PUMICES
PUMICING
PUMICITE
PUMICITES
PUMIE
PUMIES
PUMMEL
PUMMELED
PUMMELING
PUMMELLED
PUMMELO
PUMMELOS
PUMMELS
PUMP
PUMPABLE
PUMPED
PUMPER
PUMPERS
PUMPHOOD
PUMPHOODS
PUMPHOUSE
PUMPING
PUMPINGS
PUMPION
PUMPIONS
PUMPJACK
PUMPJACKS
PUMPKIN
PUMPKING
PUMPKINGS
PUMPKINS
PUMPLESS
PUMPLIKE
PUMPS
PUMY
PUN
PUNA
PUNAANI
PUNAANY
PUNALUA
PUNALUAN
PUNALUAS
PUNANI
PUNANY
PUNAS
PUNCE
PUNCED

PUNCES
PUNCH
PUNCHBAG
PUNCHBAGS
PUNCHBALL
PUNCHBOWL
PUNCHED
PUNCHEON
PUNCHEONS
PUNCHER
PUNCHERS
PUNCHES
PUNCHIER
PUNCHIEST
PUNCHILY
PUNCHING
PUNCHLESS
PUNCHLINE
PUNCHOUT
PUNCHOUTS
PUNCHY
PUNCING
PUNCTA
PUNCTATE
PUNCTATED
PUNCTATOR
PUNCTILIO
PUNCTO
PUNCTOS
PUNCTUAL
PUNCTUATE
PUNCTULE
PUNCTULES
PUNCTUM
PUNCTUMS
PUNCTURE
PUNCTURED
PUNCTURER
PUNCTURES
PUNDIT
PUNDITIC
PUNDITRY
PUNDITS
PUNDONOR
PUNG
PUNGA
PUNGAS
PUNGENCE
PUNGENCES
PUNGENCY
PUNGENT
PUNGENTLY
PUNGLE
PUNGLED
PUNGLES
PUNGLING
PUNGS
PUNIER
PUNIEST
PUNILY
PUNINESS
PUNISH
PUNISHED
PUNISHER
PUNISHERS
PUNISHES
PUNISHING
PUNITION
PUNITIONS
PUNITIVE
PUNITORY
PUNJI
PUNJIED
PUNJIES
PUNJIING
PUNJIS
PUNK
PUNKA
PUNKAH
PUNKAHS
PUNKAS
PUNKER
PUNKERS
PUNKEST
PUNKETTE
PUNKETTES
PUNKEY
PUNKEYS
PUNKIE
PUNKIER
PUNKIES
PUNKIEST
PUNKIN
PUNKINESS
PUNKINS
PUNKISH
PUNKS
PUNKY
PUNNED
PUNNER
PUNNERS
PUNNET
PUNNETS
PUNNIER
PUNNIEST
PUNNING
PUNNINGLY
PUNNINGS
PUNNY
PUNS
PUNSTER
PUNSTERS
PUNT
PUNTED
PUNTEE
PUNTEES
PUNTER
PUNTERS
PUNTIES
PUNTING
PUNTO
PUNTOS
PUNTS
PUNTSMAN
PUNTSMEN
PUNTY
PUNY
PUP
PUPA
PUPAE
PUPAL
PUPARIA
PUPARIAL
PUPARIUM
PUPAS
PUPATE
PUPATED
PUPATES
PUPATING
PUPATION
PUPATIONS
PUPFISH
PUPFISHES
PUPIL
PUPILAGE
PUPILAGES
PUPILAR
PUPILARY
PUPILLAGE
PUPILLAR
PUPILLARY
PUPILLATE
PUPILS
PUPILSHIP
PUPPED
PUPPET
PUPPETEER
PUPPETRY
PUPPETS
PUPPIED
PUPPIES
PUPPING
PUPPODUM
PUPPODUMS
PUPPY
PUPPYDOM
PUPPYDOMS
PUPPYHOOD
PUPPYING
PUPPYISH
PUPPYISM
PUPPYISMS
PUPPYLIKE
PUPS
PUPU
PUPUNHA
PUPUNHAS
PUPUS
PUR
PURANA
PURANAS
PURANIC
PURBLIND
PURCHASE
PURCHASED
PURCHASER
PURCHASES
PURDA
PURDAH
PURDAHED
PURDAHS
PURDAS
PURDONIUM
PURE
PUREBLOOD
PUREBRED
PUREBREDS
PURED
PUREE
PUREED
PUREEING
PUREES
PURELY
PURENESS
PURER
PURES
PUREST
PURFLE
PURFLED
PURFLER
PURFLERS
PURFLES
PURFLING
PURFLINGS
PURFLY
PURGATION
PURGATIVE
PURGATORY
PURGE
PURGEABLE
PURGED
PURGER
PURGERS
PURGES
PURGING
PURGINGS
PURI
PURIFIED
PURIFIER
PURIFIERS
PURIFIES
PURIFY
PURIFYING
PURIN
PURINE
PURINES
PURING
PURINS
PURIRI
PURIRIS

P

PURIS
PURISM
PURISMS
PURIST
PURISTIC
PURISTS
PURITAN
PURITANIC
PURITANS
PURITIES
PURITY
PURL
PURLED
PURLER
PURLERS
PURLICUE
PURLICUED
PURLICUES
PURLIEU
PURLIEUS
PURLIEUX
PURLIN
PURLINE
PURLINES
PURLING
PURLINGS
PURLINS
PURLOIN
PURLOINED
PURLOINER
PURLOINS
PURLS
PUROMYCIN
PURPIE
PURPIES
PURPLE
PURPLED
PURPLER
PURPLES
PURPLEST
PURPLIER
PURPLIEST
PURPLING
PURPLISH
PURPLY
PURPORT
PURPORTED
PURPORTS
PURPOSE
PURPOSED
PURPOSELY
PURPOSES
PURPOSING
PURPOSIVE
PURPURA
PURPURAS
PURPURE
PURPUREAL
PURPURES
PURPURIC
PURPURIN
PURPURINS
PURPY
PURR
PURRED
PURRING
PURRINGLY
PURRINGS
PURRS
PURS
PURSE
PURSED
PURSEFUL
PURSEFULS
PURSELIKE
PURSER
PURSERS
PURSES
PURSEW
PURSEWED
PURSEWING
PURSEWS
PURSIER
PURSIEST
PURSILY
PURSINESS
PURSING
PURSLAIN
PURSLAINS
PURSLANE
PURSLANES
PURSUABLE
PURSUAL
PURSUALS
PURSUANCE
PURSUANT
PURSUE
PURSUED
PURSUER
PURSUERS
PURSUES
PURSUING
PURSUINGS
PURSUIT
PURSUITS
PURSY
PURTIER
PURTIEST
PURTRAID
PURTRAYD
PURTY
PURULENCE
PURULENCY
PURULENT
PURVEY
PURVEYED
PURVEYING
PURVEYOR
PURVEYORS
PURVEYS
PURVIEW
PURVIEWS
PUS
PUSES
PUSH
PUSHBACK
PUSHBACKS
PUSHBALL
PUSHBALLS
PUSHBIKE
PUSHBIKES
PUSHCART
PUSHCARTS
PUSHCHAIR
PUSHDOWN
PUSHDOWNS
PUSHED
PUSHER
PUSHERS
PUSHES
PUSHFUL
PUSHFULLY
PUSHIER
PUSHIEST
PUSHILY
PUSHINESS
PUSHING
PUSHINGLY
PUSHOVER
PUSHOVERS
PUSHPIN
PUSHPINS
PUSHPIT
PUSHPITS
PUSHROD
PUSHRODS
PUSHUP
PUSHUPS
PUSHY
PUSLE
PUSLED
PUSLES
PUSLEY
PUSLEYS
PUSLIKE
PUSLING
PUSS
PUSSEL
PUSSELS
PUSSER
PUSSERS
PUSSES
PUSSIER
PUSSIES
PUSSIEST
PUSSLEY
PUSSLEYS
PUSSLIES
PUSSLIKE
PUSSLY
PUSSY
PUSSYCAT
PUSSYCATS
PUSSYFOOT
PUSSYTOES
PUSTULANT
PUSTULAR
PUSTULATE
PUSTULE
PUSTULED
PUSTULES
PUSTULOUS
PUT
PUTAMEN
PUTAMENS
PUTAMINA
PUTATIVE
PUTCHEON
PUTCHEONS
PUTCHER
PUTCHERS
PUTCHOCK
PUTCHOCKS
PUTCHUK
PUTCHUKS
PUTDOWN
PUTDOWNS
PUTEAL
PUTEALS
PUTELI
PUTELIS
PUTID
PUTLOCK
PUTLOCKS
PUTLOG
PUTLOGS
PUTOFF
PUTOFFS
PUTOIS
PUTON
PUTONGHUA
PUTONS
PUTOUT
PUTOUTS
PUTREFIED
PUTREFIER
PUTREFIES
PUTREFY
PUTRID
PUTRIDER
PUTRIDEST
PUTRIDITY
PUTRIDLY
PUTS
PUTSCH
PUTSCHES
PUTSCHIST
PUTT
PUTTED
PUTTEE

P

PUTTEES
PUTTEN
PUTTER
PUTTERED
PUTTERER
PUTTERERS
PUTTERING
PUTTERS
PUTTI
PUTTIE
PUTTIED
PUTTIER
PUTTIERS
PUTTIES
PUTTING
PUTTINGS
PUTTO
PUTTOCK
PUTTOCKS
PUTTS
PUTTY
PUTTYING
PUTTYLESS
PUTTYLIKE
PUTTYROOT
PUTURE
PUTURES
PUTZ
PUTZED
PUTZES
PUTZING
PUY
PUYS
PUZEL
PUZELS
PUZZEL
PUZZELS
PUZZLE
PUZZLED
PUZZLEDLY
PUZZLEDOM
PUZZLER
PUZZLERS
PUZZLES
PUZZLING
PUZZOLANA
PWN
PWNED
PWNING
PWNS
PYA
PYAEMIA
PYAEMIAS
PYAEMIC
PYAS
PYAT
PYATS
PYCNIC
PYCNIDIA
PYCNIDIAL
PYCNIDIUM
PYCNITE
PYCNITES
PYCNON
PYCNONS
PYCNOSES
PYCNOSIS
PYCNOSOME
PYCNOTIC
PYE
PYEBALD
PYEBALDS
PYEING
PYELITIC
PYELITIS
PYELOGRAM
PYEMIA
PYEMIAS
PYEMIC
PYENGADU
PYENGADUS
PYES
PYET
PYETS
PYGAL
PYGALS
PYGARG
PYGARGS
PYGARGUS
PYGIDIA
PYGIDIAL
PYGIDIUM
PYGMAEAN
PYGMEAN
PYGMIES
PYGMOID
PYGMOIDS
PYGMY
PYGMYISH
PYGMYISM
PYGMYISMS
PYGOSTYLE
PYIC
PYIN
PYINKADO
PYINKADOS
PYINS
PYJAMA
PYJAMAED
PYJAMAS
PYKNIC
PYKNICS
PYKNOSES
PYKNOSIS
PYKNOSOME
PYKNOTIC
PYLON
PYLONS
PYLORI
PYLORIC
PYLORUS
PYLORUSES
PYNE
PYNED
PYNES
PYNING
PYODERMA
PYODERMAS
PYODERMIC
PYOGENIC
PYOID
PYONER
PYONERS
PYONINGS
PYORRHEA
PYORRHEAL
PYORRHEAS
PYORRHEIC
PYORRHOEA
PYOSES
PYOSIS
PYOT
PYOTS
PYRACANTH
PYRAL
PYRALID
PYRALIDID
PYRALIDS
PYRALIS
PYRALISES
PYRAMID
PYRAMIDAL
PYRAMIDED
PYRAMIDES
PYRAMIDIA
PYRAMIDIC
PYRAMIDON
PYRAMIDS
PYRAMIS
PYRAMISES
PYRAN
PYRANOID
PYRANOSE
PYRANOSES
PYRANS
PYRAZOLE
PYRAZOLES
PYRE
PYRENE
PYRENEITE
PYRENES
PYRENOID
PYRENOIDS
PYRES
PYRETHRIN
PYRETHRUM
PYRETIC
PYREX
PYREXES
PYREXIA
PYREXIAL
PYREXIAS
PYREXIC
PYRIC
PYRIDIC
PYRIDINE
PYRIDINES
PYRIDOXAL
PYRIDOXIN
PYRIFORM
PYRITE
PYRITES
PYRITIC
PYRITICAL
PYRITISE
PYRITISED
PYRITISES
PYRITIZE
PYRITIZED
PYRITIZES
PYRITOUS
PYRO
PYROBORIC
PYROCERAM
PYROCLAST
PYROGEN
PYROGENIC
PYROGENS
PYROGIES
PYROGY
PYROHIES
PYROHY
PYROLA
PYROLAS
PYROLATER
PYROLATRY
PYROLISE
PYROLISED
PYROLISES
PYROLIZE
PYROLIZED
PYROLIZES
PYROLOGY
PYROLYSE
PYROLYSED
PYROLYSER
PYROLYSES
PYROLYSIS
PYROLYTIC
PYROLYZE
PYROLYZED
PYROLYZER
PYROLYZES
PYROMANCY
PYROMANIA
PYROMETER
PYROMETRY
PYRONE
PYRONES
PYRONIN

PYRONINE
PYRONINES
PYRONINS
PYROPE
PYROPES
PYROPHONE
PYROPUS
PYROPUSES
PYROS
PYROSCOPE
PYROSES
PYROSIS
PYROSISES
PYROSOME
PYROSOMES
PYROSTAT
PYROSTATS
PYROXENE
PYROXENES
PYROXENIC
PYROXYLE
PYROXYLES
PYROXYLIC
PYROXYLIN
PYRRHIC
PYRRHICS
PYRRHOUS
PYRROL
PYRROLE
PYRROLES
PYRROLIC
PYRROLS
PYRUVATE
PYRUVATES
PYRUVIC
PYSANKA
PYSANKY
PYTHIUM
PYTHIUMS
PYTHON
PYTHONESS
PYTHONIC
PYTHONS
PYURIA
PYURIAS
PYX
PYXED
PYXES
PYXIDES
PYXIDIA
PYXIDIUM
PYXIE
PYXIES
PYXING
PYXIS
PZAZZ
PZAZZES

P

Q

QABALA
QABALAH
QABALAHS
QABALAS
QABALISM
QABALISMS
QABALIST
QABALISTS
QADI
QADIS
QAID
QAIDS
QAIMAQAM
QAIMAQAMS
QAJAQ
QAJAQS
QALAMDAN
QALAMDANS
QAMUTIK
QAMUTIKS
QANAT
QANATS
QAPIK
QAPIKS
QASIDA
QASIDAS
QAT
QATS
QAWWAL
QAWWALI
QAWWALIS
QAWWALS
QI
QIBLA
QIBLAS
QIGONG
QIGONGS
QIN
QINDAR
QINDARKA
QINDARS
QINGHAOSU
QINS
QINTAR
QINTARKA
QINTARS
QIS
QIVIUT
QIVIUTS
QOPH
QOPHS
QORMA
QORMAS
QUA
QUAALUDE
QUAALUDES
QUACK
QUACKED
QUACKER
QUACKERS
QUACKERY
QUACKIER
QUACKIEST
QUACKING
QUACKISH
QUACKISM
QUACKISMS
QUACKLE
QUACKLED
QUACKLES
QUACKLING
QUACKS
QUACKY
QUAD
QUADDED
QUADDING
QUADDINGS
QUADPLAY
QUADPLAYS
QUADPLEX
QUADRANS
QUADRANT
QUADRANTS
QUADRAT
QUADRATE
QUADRATED
QUADRATES
QUADRATI
QUADRATIC
QUADRATS
QUADRATUS
QUADRELLA
QUADRIC
QUADRICEP
QUADRICS
QUADRIFID
QUADRIGA
QUADRIGAE
QUADRIGAS
QUADRILLE
QUADRIVIA
QUADROON
QUADROONS
QUADRUMAN
QUADRUPED
QUADRUPLE
QUADRUPLY
QUADS
QUAERE
QUAERED
QUAEREING
QUAERES
QUAERITUR
QUAESITUM
QUAESTOR
QUAESTORS
QUAFF
QUAFFABLE
QUAFFED
QUAFFER
QUAFFERS
QUAFFING
QUAFFS
QUAG
QUAGGA
QUAGGAS
QUAGGIER
QUAGGIEST
QUAGGY
QUAGMIRE
QUAGMIRED
QUAGMIRES
QUAGMIRY
QUAGS
QUAHAUG
QUAHAUGS
QUAHOG
QUAHOGS
QUAI
QUAICH
QUAICHES
QUAICHS
QUAIGH
QUAIGHS
QUAIL
QUAILED
QUAILING
QUAILINGS
QUAILS
QUAINT
QUAINTER
QUAINTEST
QUAINTLY
QUAIR
QUAIRS
QUAIS
QUAKE
QUAKED
QUAKER
QUAKERS
QUAKES
QUAKIER
QUAKIEST
QUAKILY
QUAKINESS
QUAKING
QUAKINGLY
QUAKINGS
QUAKY
QUALE
QUALIA
QUALIFIED
QUALIFIER
QUALIFIES
QUALIFY
QUALITIED
QUALITIES
QUALITY
QUALM
QUALMIER
QUALMIEST
QUALMING
QUALMINGS
QUALMISH
QUALMLESS
QUALMS
QUALMY
QUAMASH
QUAMASHES
QUANDANG
QUANDANGS
QUANDARY
QUANDONG
QUANDONGS
QUANGO
QUANGOS
QUANNET
QUANNETS
QUANT
QUANTA
QUANTAL
QUANTALLY
QUANTED
QUANTIC
QUANTICAL
QUANTICS
QUANTIFY
QUANTILE
QUANTILES
QUANTING

Q

QUANTISE
QUANTISED
QUANTISER
QUANTISES
QUANTITY
QUANTIZE
QUANTIZED
QUANTIZER
QUANTIZES
QUANTONG
QUANTONGS
QUANTS
QUANTUM
QUANTUMS
QUARE
QUARENDEN
QUARENDER
QUARER
QUAREST
QUARK
QUARKS
QUARREL
QUARRELED
QUARRELER
QUARRELS
QUARRIAN
QUARRIANS
QUARRIED
QUARRIER
QUARRIERS
QUARRIES
QUARRION
QUARRIONS
QUARRY
QUARRYING
QUARRYMAN
QUARRYMEN
QUART
QUARTAN
QUARTANS
QUARTE
QUARTER
QUARTERED
QUARTERER
QUARTERLY
QUARTERN
QUARTERNS
QUARTERS
QUARTES
QUARTET
QUARTETS
QUARTETT
QUARTETTE
QUARTETTI
QUARTETTO
QUARTETTS
QUARTIC
QUARTICS
QUARTIER
QUARTIERS
QUARTILE
QUARTILES
QUARTO
QUARTOS
QUARTS
QUARTZ
QUARTZES
QUARTZIER
QUARTZITE
QUARTZOSE
QUARTZOUS
QUARTZY
QUASAR
QUASARS
QUASH
QUASHED
QUASHEE
QUASHEES
QUASHER
QUASHERS
QUASHES
QUASHIE
QUASHIES
QUASHING
QUASI
QUASS
QUASSES
QUASSIA
QUASSIAS
QUASSIN
QUASSINS
QUAT
QUATCH
QUATCHED
QUATCHES
QUATCHING
QUATE
QUATES
QUATORZE
QUATORZES
QUATRAIN
QUATRAINS
QUATRE
QUATRES
QUATS
QUATTED
QUATTING
QUAVER
QUAVERED
QUAVERER
QUAVERERS
QUAVERIER
QUAVERING
QUAVERS
QUAVERY
QUAY
QUAYAGE
QUAYAGES
QUAYD
QUAYLIKE
QUAYS
QUAYSIDE
QUAYSIDES
QUAZZIER
QUAZZIEST
QUAZZY
QUBIT
QUBITS
QUBYTE
QUBYTES
QUEACH
QUEACHES
QUEACHIER
QUEACHY
QUEAN
QUEANS
QUEASIER
QUEASIEST
QUEASILY
QUEASY
QUEAZIER
QUEAZIEST
QUEAZY
QUEBEC
QUEBECS
QUEBRACHO
QUEECHIER
QUEECHY
QUEEN
QUEENCAKE
QUEENCUP
QUEENCUPS
QUEENDOM
QUEENDOMS
QUEENED
QUEENFISH
QUEENHOOD
QUEENIE
QUEENIER
QUEENIES
QUEENIEST
QUEENING
QUEENINGS
QUEENITE
QUEENITES
QUEENLESS
QUEENLET
QUEENLETS
QUEENLIER
QUEENLIKE
QUEENLY
QUEENS
QUEENSHIP
QUEENSIDE
QUEENY
QUEER
QUEERCORE
QUEERDOM
QUEERDOMS
QUEERED
QUEERER
QUEEREST
QUEERING
QUEERISH
QUEERITY
QUEERLY
QUEERNESS
QUEERS
QUEEST
QUEESTS
QUEINT
QUELCH
QUELCHED
QUELCHES
QUELCHING
QUELEA
QUELEAS
QUELL
QUELLABLE
QUELLED
QUELLER
QUELLERS
QUELLING
QUELLS
QUEME
QUEMED
QUEMES
QUEMING
QUENA
QUENAS
QUENCH
QUENCHED
QUENCHER
QUENCHERS
QUENCHES
QUENCHING
QUENELLE
QUENELLES
QUEP
QUERCETIC
QUERCETIN
QUERCETUM
QUERCINE
QUERCITIN
QUERIDA
QUERIDAS
QUERIED
QUERIER
QUERIERS
QUERIES
QUERIMONY
QUERIST
QUERISTS
QUERN
QUERNS
QUERULOUS
QUERY
QUERYING
QUERYINGS
QUEST

Q

QUESTANT
QUESTANTS
QUESTED
QUESTER
QUESTERS
QUESTING
QUESTINGS
QUESTION
QUESTIONS
QUESTOR
QUESTORS
QUESTRIST
QUESTS
QUETCH
QUETCHED
QUETCHES
QUETCHING
QUETHE
QUETHES
QUETHING
QUETSCH
QUETSCHES
QUETZAL
QUETZALES
QUETZALS
QUEUE
QUEUED
QUEUEING
QUEUEINGS
QUEUER
QUEUERS
QUEUES
QUEUING
QUEUINGS
QUEY
QUEYN
QUEYNIE
QUEYNIES
QUEYNS
QUEYS
QUEZAL
QUEZALES
QUEZALS
QUIBBLE
QUIBBLED
QUIBBLER
QUIBBLERS
QUIBBLES
QUIBBLING
QUIBLIN
QUIBLINS
QUICH
QUICHE
QUICHED
QUICHES
QUICHING
QUICK
QUICKBEAM
QUICKEN
QUICKENED
QUICKENER
QUICKENS
QUICKER
QUICKEST
QUICKFIRE
QUICKIE
QUICKIES
QUICKLIME
QUICKLY
QUICKNESS
QUICKS
QUICKSAND
QUICKSET
QUICKSETS
QUICKSTEP
QUICKY
QUID
QUIDAM
QUIDAMS
QUIDDANY
QUIDDIT
QUIDDITCH
QUIDDITS
QUIDDITY
QUIDDLE
QUIDDLED
QUIDDLER
QUIDDLERS
QUIDDLES
QUIDDLING
QUIDNUNC
QUIDNUNCS
QUIDS
QUIESCE
QUIESCED
QUIESCENT
QUIESCES
QUIESCING
QUIET
QUIETED
QUIETEN
QUIETENED
QUIETENER
QUIETENS
QUIETER
QUIETERS
QUIETEST
QUIETING
QUIETINGS
QUIETISM
QUIETISMS
QUIETIST
QUIETISTS
QUIETIVE
QUIETIVES
QUIETLY
QUIETNESS
QUIETS
QUIETSOME
QUIETUDE
QUIETUDES
QUIETUS
QUIETUSES
QUIFF
QUIFFED
QUIFFS
QUIGHT
QUIGHTED
QUIGHTING
QUIGHTS
QUILL
QUILLAI
QUILLAIA
QUILLAIAS
QUILLAIS
QUILLAJA
QUILLAJAS
QUILLBACK
QUILLED
QUILLET
QUILLETS
QUILLING
QUILLINGS
QUILLMAN
QUILLMEN
QUILLON
QUILLONS
QUILLOW
QUILLOWS
QUILLS
QUILLWORK
QUILLWORKS
QUILT
QUILTED
QUILTER
QUILTERS
QUILTING
QUILTINGS
QUILTS
QUIM
QUIMS
QUIN
QUINA
QUINARIES
QUINARY
QUINAS
QUINATE
QUINCE
QUINCES
QUINCHE
QUINCHED
QUINCHES
QUINCHING
QUINCUNX
QUINE
QUINELA
QUINELAS
QUINELLA
QUINELLAS
QUINES
QUINIC
QUINIDINE
QUINIE
QUINIELA
QUINIELAS
QUINIES
QUININ
QUININA
QUININAS
QUININE
QUININES
QUININS
QUINNAT
QUINNATS
QUINO
QUINOA
QUINOAS
QUINOID
QUINOIDAL
QUINOIDS
QUINOL
QUINOLIN
QUINOLINE
QUINOLINS
QUINOLONE
QUINOLS
QUINONE
QUINONES
QUINONOID
QUINOS
QUINQUINA
QUINS
QUINSIED
QUINSIES
QUINSY
QUINT
QUINTA
QUINTAIN
QUINTAINS
QUINTAL
QUINTALS
QUINTAN
QUINTANS
QUINTAR
QUINTARS
QUINTAS
QUINTE
QUINTES
QUINTET
QUINTETS
QUINTETT
QUINTETTE
QUINTETTI
QUINTETTO
QUINTETTS
QUINTIC
QUINTICS
QUINTILE
QUINTILES
QUINTIN

QUINTINS
QUINTROON
QUINTS
QUINTUPLE
QUINTUPLY
QUINZE
QUINZES
QUINZHEE
QUINZHEES
QUINZIE
QUINZIES
QUIP
QUIPO
QUIPOS
QUIPPED
QUIPPER
QUIPPERS
QUIPPIER
QUIPPIEST
QUIPPING
QUIPPISH
QUIPPU
QUIPPUS
QUIPPY
QUIPS
QUIPSTER
QUIPSTERS
QUIPU
QUIPUS
QUIRE
QUIRED
QUIRES
QUIRING
QUIRISTER
QUIRK
QUIRKED
QUIRKIER
QUIRKIEST
QUIRKILY
QUIRKING
QUIRKISH
QUIRKS
QUIRKY
QUIRT
QUIRTED
QUIRTING
QUIRTS
QUISLING
QUISLINGS
QUIST
QUISTS
QUIT
QUITCH
QUITCHED
QUITCHES
QUITCHING
QUITCLAIM
QUITE
QUITED
QUITES
QUITING
QUITRENT
QUITRENTS
QUITS
QUITTAL
QUITTALS
QUITTANCE
QUITTED
QUITTER
QUITTERS
QUITTING
QUITTOR
QUITTORS
QUIVER
QUIVERED
QUIVERER
QUIVERERS
QUIVERFUL
QUIVERIER
QUIVERING
QUIVERISH
QUIVERS
QUIVERY
QUIXOTE
QUIXOTES
QUIXOTIC
QUIXOTISM
QUIXOTRY
QUIZ
QUIZZED
QUIZZER
QUIZZERS
QUIZZERY
QUIZZES
QUIZZICAL
QUIZZIFY
QUIZZING
QUIZZINGS
QULLIQ
QULLIQS
QUOAD
QUOD
QUODDED
QUODDING
QUODLIBET
QUODLIN
QUODLINS
QUODS
QUOHOG
QUOHOGS
QUOIF
QUOIFED
QUOIFING
QUOIFS
QUOIN
QUOINED
QUOINING
QUOININGS
QUOINS
QUOIST
QUOISTS
QUOIT
QUOITED
QUOITER
QUOITERS
QUOITING
QUOITS
QUOKKA
QUOKKAS
QUOLL
QUOLLS
QUOMODO
QUOMODOS
QUONDAM
QUONK
QUONKED
QUONKING
QUONKS
QUOOKE
QUOP
QUOPPED
QUOPPING
QUOPS
QUORATE
QUORUM
QUORUMS
QUOTA
QUOTABLE
QUOTABLY
QUOTAS
QUOTATION
QUOTATIVE
QUOTE
QUOTED
QUOTER
QUOTERS
QUOTES
QUOTH
QUOTHA
QUOTIDIAN
QUOTIENT
QUOTIENTS
QUOTING
QUOTITION
QUOTUM
QUOTUMS
QURSH
QURSHES
QURUSH
QURUSHES
QUYTE
QUYTED
QUYTES
QUYTING
QWERTIES
QWERTY
QWERTYS

R

RABANNA
RABANNAS
RABASKA
RABASKAS
RABAT
RABATINE
RABATINES
RABATMENT
RABATO
RABATOES
RABATOS
RABATS
RABATTE
RABATTED
RABATTES
RABATTING
RABBET
RABBETED
RABBETING
RABBETS
RABBI
RABBIES
RABBIN
RABBINATE
RABBINIC
RABBINICS
RABBINISM
RABBINIST
RABBINITE
RABBINS
RABBIS
RABBIT
RABBITED
RABBITER
RABBITERS
RABBITIER
RABBITING
RABBITO
RABBITOH
RABBITOHS
RABBITOS
RABBITRY
RABBITS
RABBITY
RABBLE
RABBLED
RABBLER
RABBLERS
RABBLES
RABBLING
RABBLINGS
RABBONI
RABBONIS
RABI
RABIC
RABID
RABIDER
RABIDEST
RABIDITY
RABIDLY
RABIDNESS
RABIES
RABIETIC
RABIS
RABONA
RABONAS
RACA
RACAHOUT
RACAHOUTS
RACCAHOUT
RACCOON
RACCOONS
RACE
RACEABLE
RACECARD
RACECARDS
RACED
RACEGOER
RACEGOERS
RACEGOING
RACEHORSE
RACEMATE
RACEMATES
RACEME
RACEMED
RACEMES
RACEMIC
RACEMISE
RACEMISED
RACEMISES
RACEMISM
RACEMISMS
RACEMIZE
RACEMIZED
RACEMIZES
RACEMOID
RACEMOSE
RACEMOUS
RACEPATH
RACEPATHS
RACER
RACERS
RACES
RACETRACK
RACEWALK
RACEWALKS
RACEWAY
RACEWAYS
RACH
RACHE
RACHES
RACHET
RACHETED
RACHETING
RACHETS
RACHIAL
RACHIDES
RACHIDIAL
RACHIDIAN
RACHILLA
RACHILLAE
RACHILLAS
RACHIS
RACHISES
RACHITIC
RACHITIS
RACIAL
RACIALISE
RACIALISM
RACIALIST
RACIALIZE
RACIALLY
RACIATION
RACIER
RACIEST
RACILY
RACINESS
RACING
RACINGS
RACINO
RACINOS
RACISM
RACISMS
RACIST
RACISTS
RACK
RACKED
RACKER
RACKERS
RACKET
RACKETED
RACKETEER
RACKETER
RACKETERS
RACKETIER
RACKETING
RACKETRY
RACKETS
RACKETT
RACKETTS
RACKETY
RACKFUL
RACKFULS
RACKING
RACKINGLY
RACKINGS
RACKLE
RACKLES
RACKS
RACKWORK
RACKWORKS
RACLETTE
RACLETTES
RACLOIR
RACLOIRS
RACON
RACONS
RACONTEUR
RACOON
RACOONS
RACQUET
RACQUETED
RACQUETS
RACY
RAD
RADAR
RADARS
RADDED
RADDER
RADDEST
RADDING
RADDLE
RADDLED
RADDLEMAN
RADDLEMEN
RADDLES
RADDLING
RADDOCKE
RADDOCKES
RADE
RADGE
RADGER
RADGES
RADGEST
RADIABLE
RADIAL
RADIALE
RADIALIA
RADIALISE
RADIALITY

R

RADIALIZE
RADIALLY
RADIALS
RADIAN
RADIANCE
RADIANCES
RADIANCY
RADIANS
RADIANT
RADIANTLY
RADIANTS
RADIATA
RADIATAS
RADIATE
RADIATED
RADIATELY
RADIATES
RADIATING
RADIATION
RADIATIVE
RADIATOR
RADIATORS
RADIATORY
RADICAL
RADICALLY
RADICALS
RADICAND
RADICANDS
RADICANT
RADICATE
RADICATED
RADICATES
RADICCHIO
RADICEL
RADICELS
RADICES
RADICLE
RADICLES
RADICULAR
RADICULE
RADICULES
RADII
RADIO
RADIOED
RADIOES
RADIOGOLD
RADIOGRAM
RADIOING
RADIOLOGY
RADIOMAN
RADIOMEN
RADIONICS
RADIOS
RADIOTHON
RADISH
RADISHES
RADIUM
RADIUMS
RADIUS
RADIUSED
RADIUSES
RADIUSING
RADIX
RADIXES
RADOME
RADOMES
RADON
RADONS
RADS
RADULA
RADULAE
RADULAR
RADULAS
RADULATE
RADWASTE
RADWASTES
RAFALE
RAFALES
RAFF
RAFFIA
RAFFIAS
RAFFINATE
RAFFINOSE
RAFFISH
RAFFISHLY
RAFFLE
RAFFLED
RAFFLER
RAFFLERS
RAFFLES
RAFFLESIA
RAFFLING
RAFFS
RAFT
RAFTED
RAFTER
RAFTERED
RAFTERING
RAFTERS
RAFTING
RAFTINGS
RAFTMAN
RAFTMEN
RAFTS
RAFTSMAN
RAFTSMEN
RAG
RAGA
RAGAS
RAGBAG
RAGBAGS
RAGBOLT
RAGBOLTS
RAGDE
RAGDOLL
RAGDOLLS
RAGE
RAGED
RAGEE
RAGEES
RAGEFUL
RAGER
RAGERS
RAGES
RAGG
RAGGA
RAGGAS
RAGGED
RAGGEDER
RAGGEDEST
RAGGEDIER
RAGGEDLY
RAGGEDY
RAGGEE
RAGGEES
RAGGERIES
RAGGERY
RAGGIER
RAGGIES
RAGGIEST
RAGGING
RAGGINGS
RAGGLE
RAGGLED
RAGGLES
RAGGLING
RAGGS
RAGGY
RAGHEAD
RAGHEADS
RAGI
RAGING
RAGINGLY
RAGINGS
RAGINI
RAGINIS
RAGIS
RAGLAN
RAGLANS
RAGMAN
RAGMANS
RAGMEN
RAGMENT
RAGMENTS
RAGOUT
RAGOUTED
RAGOUTING
RAGOUTS
RAGPICKER
RAGS
RAGSTONE
RAGSTONES
RAGTAG
RAGTAGS
RAGTAIL
RAGTIME
RAGTIMER
RAGTIMERS
RAGTIMES
RAGTOP
RAGTOPS
RAGU
RAGULED
RAGULY
RAGUS
RAGWEED
RAGWEEDS
RAGWHEEL
RAGWHEELS
RAGWORK
RAGWORKS
RAGWORM
RAGWORMS
RAGWORT
RAGWORTS
RAH
RAHED
RAHING
RAHS
RAHUI
RAHUIS
RAI
RAIA
RAIAS
RAID
RAIDED
RAIDER
RAIDERS
RAIDING
RAIDINGS
RAIDS
RAIK
RAIKED
RAIKING
RAIKS
RAIL
RAILAGE
RAILAGES
RAILBED
RAILBEDS
RAILBIRD
RAILBIRDS
RAILBUS
RAILBUSES
RAILCAR
RAILCARD
RAILCARDS
RAILCARS
RAILE
RAILED
RAILER
RAILERS
RAILES
RAILHEAD
RAILHEADS
RAILING
RAILINGLY
RAILINGS
RAILLERY
RAILLESS

R

RAILLIES
RAILLY
RAILMAN
RAILMEN
RAILROAD
RAILROADS
RAILS
RAILWAY
RAILWAYS
RAILWOMAN
RAILWOMEN
RAIMENT
RAIMENTS
RAIN
RAINBAND
RAINBANDS
RAINBIRD
RAINBIRDS
RAINBOW
RAINBOWED
RAINBOWS
RAINBOWY
RAINCHECK
RAINCOAT
RAINCOATS
RAINDATE
RAINDATES
RAINDROP
RAINDROPS
RAINE
RAINED
RAINES
RAINFALL
RAINFALLS
RAINIER
RAINIEST
RAINILY
RAININESS
RAINING
RAINLESS
RAINMAKER
RAINOUT
RAINOUTS
RAINPROOF
RAINS
RAINSPOUT
RAINSTICK
RAINSTORM
RAINSUIT
RAINSUITS
RAINSWEPT
RAINTIGHT
RAINWASH
RAINWATER
RAINWEAR
RAINWEARS
RAINY
RAIRD
RAIRDS
RAIS
RAISABLE
RAISE
RAISEABLE
RAISED
RAISER
RAISERS
RAISES
RAISIN
RAISING
RAISINGS
RAISINIER
RAISINS
RAISINY
RAISONNE
RAIT
RAITA
RAITAS
RAITED
RAITING
RAITS
RAIYAT
RAIYATS
RAJ
RAJA
RAJAH
RAJAHS
RAJAHSHIP
RAJAS
RAJASHIP
RAJASHIPS
RAJES
RAKE
RAKED
RAKEE
RAKEES
RAKEHELL
RAKEHELLS
RAKEHELLY
RAKELIKE
RAKEOFF
RAKEOFFS
RAKER
RAKERIES
RAKERS
RAKERY
RAKES
RAKESHAME
RAKI
RAKIA
RAKIAS
RAKIJA
RAKIJAS
RAKING
RAKINGS
RAKIS
RAKISH
RAKISHLY
RAKSHAS
RAKSHASA
RAKSHASAS
RAKSHASES
RAKU
RAKUS
RALE
RALES
RALLIED
RALLIER
RALLIERS
RALLIES
RALLIFORM
RALLINE
RALLY
RALLYE
RALLYES
RALLYING
RALLYINGS
RALLYIST
RALLYISTS
RALPH
RALPHED
RALPHING
RALPHS
RAM
RAMADA
RAMADAS
RAMAKIN
RAMAKINS
RAMAL
RAMATE
RAMBLA
RAMBLAS
RAMBLE
RAMBLED
RAMBLER
RAMBLERS
RAMBLES
RAMBLING
RAMBLINGS
RAMBUTAN
RAMBUTANS
RAMCAT
RAMCATS
RAMEAL
RAMEE
RAMEES
RAMEKIN
RAMEKINS
RAMEN
RAMENS
RAMENTA
RAMENTUM
RAMEOUS
RAMEQUIN
RAMEQUINS
RAMET
RAMETS
RAMI
RAMIE
RAMIES
RAMIFIED
RAMIFIES
RAMIFORM
RAMIFY
RAMIFYING
RAMILIE
RAMILIES
RAMILLIE
RAMILLIES
RAMIN
RAMINS
RAMIS
RAMJET
RAMJETS
RAMMED
RAMMEL
RAMMELS
RAMMER
RAMMERS
RAMMIER
RAMMIES
RAMMIEST
RAMMING
RAMMISH
RAMMISHLY
RAMMLE
RAMMLES
RAMMY
RAMONA
RAMONAS
RAMOSE
RAMOSELY
RAMOSITY
RAMOUS
RAMOUSLY
RAMP
RAMPAGE
RAMPAGED
RAMPAGER
RAMPAGERS
RAMPAGES
RAMPAGING
RAMPANCY
RAMPANT
RAMPANTLY
RAMPART
RAMPARTED
RAMPARTS
RAMPAUGE
RAMPAUGED
RAMPAUGES
RAMPED
RAMPER
RAMPERS
RAMPICK
RAMPICKED
RAMPICKS
RAMPIKE
RAMPIKES
RAMPING
RAMPINGS

R

RAMPION
RAMPIONS
RAMPIRE
RAMPIRED
RAMPIRES
RAMPOLE
RAMPOLES
RAMPS
RAMPSMAN
RAMPSMEN
RAMROD
RAMRODDED
RAMRODS
RAMS
RAMSHORN
RAMSHORNS
RAMSON
RAMSONS
RAMSTAM
RAMTIL
RAMTILLA
RAMTILLAS
RAMTILS
RAMULAR
RAMULI
RAMULOSE
RAMULOUS
RAMULUS
RAMUS
RAN
RANA
RANARIAN
RANARIUM
RANARIUMS
RANAS
RANCE
RANCED
RANCEL
RANCELLED
RANCELS
RANCES
RANCH
RANCHED
RANCHER
RANCHERA
RANCHERAS
RANCHERIA
RANCHERIE
RANCHERO
RANCHEROS
RANCHERS
RANCHES
RANCHETTE
RANCHING
RANCHINGS
RANCHLAND
RANCHLESS
RANCHLIKE
RANCHMAN
RANCHMEN
RANCHO
RANCHOS
RANCID
RANCIDER
RANCIDEST
RANCIDITY
RANCIDLY
RANCING
RANCOR
RANCORED
RANCOROUS
RANCORS
RANCOUR
RANCOURED
RANCOURS
RAND
RANDAN
RANDANS
RANDED
RANDEM
RANDEMS
RANDIE
RANDIER
RANDIES
RANDIEST
RANDILY
RANDINESS
RANDING
RANDLORD
RANDLORDS
RANDOM
RANDOMISE
RANDOMIZE
RANDOMLY
RANDOMS
RANDON
RANDONS
RANDS
RANDY
RANEE
RANEES
RANG
RANGA
RANGAS
RANGATIRA
RANGE
RANGED
RANGELAND
RANGER
RANGERS
RANGES
RANGI
RANGIER
RANGIEST
RANGILY
RANGINESS
RANGING
RANGINGS
RANGIORA
RANGIORAS
RANGIS
RANGOLI
RANGOLIS
RANGS
RANGY
RANI
RANID
RANIDS
RANIFORM
RANINE
RANIS
RANK
RANKE
RANKED
RANKER
RANKERS
RANKES
RANKEST
RANKING
RANKINGS
RANKISH
RANKISM
RANKISMS
RANKIST
RANKISTS
RANKLE
RANKLED
RANKLES
RANKLESS
RANKLING
RANKLY
RANKNESS
RANKS
RANKSHIFT
RANPIKE
RANPIKES
RANSACK
RANSACKED
RANSACKER
RANSACKS
RANSEL
RANSELS
RANSHAKLE
RANSOM
RANSOMED
RANSOMER
RANSOMERS
RANSOMING
RANSOMS
RANT
RANTED
RANTER
RANTERISM
RANTERS
RANTING
RANTINGLY
RANTINGS
RANTIPOLE
RANTS
RANULA
RANULAR
RANULAS
RANUNCULI
RANZEL
RANZELMAN
RANZELMEN
RANZELS
RAOULIA
RAOULIAS
RAP
RAPACIOUS
RAPACITY
RAPE
RAPED
RAPER
RAPERS
RAPES
RAPESEED
RAPESEEDS
RAPHAE
RAPHANIA
RAPHANIAS
RAPHE
RAPHES
RAPHIA
RAPHIAS
RAPHIDE
RAPHIDES
RAPHIS
RAPID
RAPIDER
RAPIDEST
RAPIDITY
RAPIDLY
RAPIDNESS
RAPIDS
RAPIER
RAPIERED
RAPIERS
RAPINE
RAPINES
RAPING
RAPINI
RAPINIS
RAPIST
RAPISTS
RAPLOCH
RAPLOCHS
RAPPAREE
RAPPAREES
RAPPE
RAPPED
RAPPEE
RAPPEES
RAPPEL
RAPPELED
RAPPELING
RAPPELLED
RAPPELS
RAPPEN

R

RAPPER
RAPPERS
RAPPES
RAPPING
RAPPINGS
RAPPINI
RAPPORT
RAPPORTS
RAPS
RAPT
RAPTLY
RAPTNESS
RAPTOR
RAPTORIAL
RAPTORS
RAPTURE
RAPTURED
RAPTURES
RAPTURING
RAPTURISE
RAPTURIST
RAPTURIZE
RAPTUROUS
RARE
RAREBIT
RAREBITS
RARED
RAREE
RAREFIED
RAREFIER
RAREFIERS
RAREFIES
RAREFY
RAREFYING
RARELY
RARENESS
RARER
RARERIPE
RARERIPES
RARES
RAREST
RARIFIED
RARIFIES
RARIFY
RARIFYING
RARING
RARITIES
RARITY
RARK
RARKED
RARKING
RARKS
RAS
RASBORA
RASBORAS
RASCAILLE
RASCAL
RASCALDOM
RASCALISM
RASCALITY
RASCALLY
RASCALS
RASCASSE
RASCASSES
RASCHEL
RASCHELS
RASE
RASED
RASER
RASERS
RASES
RASH
RASHED
RASHER
RASHERS
RASHES
RASHEST
RASHIE
RASHIES
RASHING
RASHLIKE
RASHLY
RASHNESS
RASING
RASMALAI
RASMALAIS
RASORIAL
RASP
RASPATORY
RASPBERRY
RASPED
RASPER
RASPERS
RASPIER
RASPIEST
RASPINESS
RASPING
RASPINGLY
RASPINGS
RASPISH
RASPS
RASPY
RASSE
RASSES
RASSLE
RASSLED
RASSLER
RASSLERS
RASSLES
RASSLING
RAST
RASTA
RASTAFARI
RASTER
RASTERED
RASTERING
RASTERISE
RASTERIZE
RASTERS
RASTRUM
RASTRUMS
RASURE
RASURES
RAT
RATA
RATABLE
RATABLES
RATABLY
RATAFEE
RATAFEES
RATAFIA
RATAFIAS
RATAL
RATALS
RATAN
RATANIES
RATANS
RATANY
RATAPLAN
RATAPLANS
RATAS
RATATAT
RATATATS
RATBAG
RATBAGS
RATBITE
RATCH
RATCHED
RATCHES
RATCHET
RATCHETED
RATCHETS
RATCHING
RATE
RATEABLE
RATEABLES
RATEABLY
RATED
RATEEN
RATEENS
RATEL
RATELS
RATEMETER
RATEPAYER
RATER
RATERS
RATES
RATFINK
RATFINKS
RATFISH
RATFISHES
RATH
RATHA
RATHAS
RATHE
RATHER
RATHEREST
RATHERIPE
RATHERISH
RATHEST
RATHOLE
RATHOLES
RATHOUSE
RATHOUSES
RATHRIPE
RATHRIPES
RATHS
RATICIDE
RATICIDES
RATIFIED
RATIFIER
RATIFIERS
RATIFIES
RATIFY
RATIFYING
RATINE
RATINES
RATING
RATINGS
RATIO
RATION
RATIONAL
RATIONALE
RATIONALS
RATIONED
RATIONING
RATIONS
RATIOS
RATITE
RATITES
RATLIKE
RATLIN
RATLINE
RATLINES
RATLING
RATLINGS
RATLINS
RATO
RATOO
RATOON
RATOONED
RATOONER
RATOONERS
RATOONING
RATOONS
RATOOS
RATOS
RATPACK
RATPACKS
RATPROOF
RATS
RATSBANE
RATSBANES
RATTAIL
RATTAILED
RATTAILS
RATTAN
RATTANS
RATTED
RATTEEN

R

RATTEENS
RATTEN
RATTENED
RATTENER
RATTENERS
RATTENING
RATTENS
RATTER
RATTERIES
RATTERS
RATTERY
RATTIER
RATTIEST
RATTILY
RATTINESS
RATTING
RATTINGS
RATTISH
RATTLE
RATTLEBAG
RATTLEBOX
RATTLED
RATTLER
RATTLERS
RATTLES
RATTLIER
RATTLIEST
RATTLIN
RATTLINE
RATTLINES
RATTLING
RATTLINGS
RATTLINS
RATTLY
RATTON
RATTONS
RATTOON
RATTOONED
RATTOONS
RATTRAP
RATTRAPS
RATTY
RATU
RATUS
RAUCID
RAUCITIES
RAUCITY
RAUCLE

RAUCLER
RAUCLEST
RAUCOUS
RAUCOUSLY
RAUGHT
RAUN
RAUNCH
RAUNCHED
RAUNCHES
RAUNCHIER
RAUNCHILY
RAUNCHING
RAUNCHY
RAUNGE
RAUNGED
RAUNGES
RAUNGING
RAUNS
RAUPATU
RAUPATUS
RAUPO
RAUPOS
RAURIKI
RAURIKIS
RAUWOLFIA
RAV
RAVAGE
RAVAGED
RAVAGER
RAVAGERS
RAVAGES
RAVAGING
RAVE
RAVED
RAVEL
RAVELED
RAVELER
RAVELERS
RAVELIN
RAVELING
RAVELINGS
RAVELINS
RAVELLED
RAVELLER
RAVELLERS
RAVELLIER
RAVELLING
RAVELLY

RAVELMENT
RAVELS
RAVEN
RAVENED
RAVENER
RAVENERS
RAVENEST
RAVENING
RAVENINGS
RAVENLIKE
RAVENOUS
RAVENS
RAVER
RAVERS
RAVES
RAVEY
RAVIER
RAVIEST
RAVIGOTE
RAVIGOTES
RAVIGOTTE
RAVIN
RAVINE
RAVINED
RAVINES
RAVING
RAVINGLY
RAVINGS
RAVINING
RAVINS
RAVIOLI
RAVIOLIS
RAVISH
RAVISHED
RAVISHER
RAVISHERS
RAVISHES
RAVISHING
RAVS
RAW
RAWARU
RAWARUS
RAWBONE
RAWBONED
RAWER
RAWEST
RAWHEAD
RAWHEADS

RAWHIDE
RAWHIDED
RAWHIDES
RAWHIDING
RAWIN
RAWING
RAWINGS
RAWINS
RAWISH
RAWLY
RAWMAISH
RAWN
RAWNESS
RAWNESSES
RAWNS
RAWS
RAX
RAXED
RAXES
RAXING
RAY
RAYA
RAYAH
RAYAHS
RAYAS
RAYED
RAYGRASS
RAYING
RAYLE
RAYLED
RAYLES
RAYLESS
RAYLESSLY
RAYLET
RAYLETS
RAYLIKE
RAYLING
RAYNE
RAYNES
RAYON
RAYONS
RAYS
RAZE
RAZED
RAZEE
RAZEED
RAZEEING
RAZEES

RAZER
RAZERS
RAZES
RAZING
RAZMATAZ
RAZOO
RAZOOS
RAZOR
RAZORABLE
RAZORBACK
RAZORBILL
RAZORCLAM
RAZORED
RAZORFISH
RAZORING
RAZORS
RAZURE
RAZURES
RAZZ
RAZZBERRY
RAZZED
RAZZES
RAZZIA
RAZZIAS
RAZZING
RAZZINGS
RAZZLE
RAZZLES
RE
REABSORB
REABSORBS
REACCEDE
REACCEDED
REACCEDES
REACCENT
REACCENTS
REACCEPT
REACCEPTS
REACCLAIM
REACCUSE
REACCUSED
REACCUSES
REACH
REACHABLE
REACHED
REACHER
REACHERS
REACHES

REACHING
REACHLESS
REACQUIRE
REACT
REACTANCE
REACTANT
REACTANTS
REACTED
REACTING
REACTION
REACTIONS
REACTIVE
REACTOR
REACTORS
REACTS
REACTUATE
READ
READABLE
READABLY
READAPT
READAPTED
READAPTS
READD
READDED
READDICT
READDICTS
READDING
READDRESS
READDS
READER
READERLY
READERS
READIED
READIER
READIES
READIEST
READILY
READINESS
READING
READINGS
READJUST
READJUSTS
README
READMES
READMIT
READMITS
READOPT
READOPTED
READOPTS
READORN
READORNED
READORNS
READOUT
READOUTS
READS
READVANCE
READVISE
READVISED
READVISES
READY
READYING
READYMADE
REAEDIFY
REAEDIFYE
REAFFIRM
REAFFIRMS
REAFFIX
REAFFIXED
REAFFIXES
REAGENCY
REAGENT
REAGENTS
REAGIN
REAGINIC
REAGINS
REAIS
REAK
REAKED
REAKING
REAKS
REAL
REALER
REALES
REALEST
REALGAR
REALGARS
REALIA
REALIGN
REALIGNED
REALIGNS
REALISE
REALISED
REALISER
REALISERS
REALISES
REALISING
REALISM
REALISMS
REALIST
REALISTIC
REALISTS
REALITIES
REALITY
REALIZE
REALIZED
REALIZER
REALIZERS
REALIZES
REALIZING
REALLIE
REALLIED
REALLIES
REALLOT
REALLOTS
REALLY
REALLYING
REALM
REALMLESS
REALMS
REALNESS
REALO
REALOS
REALS
REALTER
REALTERED
REALTERS
REALTIE
REALTIES
REALTIME
REALTONE
REALTONES
REALTOR
REALTORS
REALTY
REAM
REAME
REAMED
REAMEND
REAMENDED
REAMENDS
REAMER
REAMERS
REAMES
REAMIER
REAMIEST
REAMING
REAMS
REAMY
REAN
REANALYSE
REANALYZE
REANIMATE
REANNEX
REANNEXED
REANNEXES
REANOINT
REANOINTS
REANS
REANSWER
REANSWERS
REAP
REAPABLE
REAPED
REAPER
REAPERS
REAPHOOK
REAPHOOKS
REAPING
REAPINGS
REAPPAREL
REAPPEAR
REAPPEARS
REAPPLIED
REAPPLIES
REAPPLY
REAPPOINT
REAPPROVE
REAPS
REAR
REARED
REARER
REARERS
REARGUARD
REARGUE
REARGUED
REARGUES
REARGUING
REARHORSE
REARING
REARINGS
REARISE
REARISEN
REARISES
REARISING
REARLY
REARM
REARMED
REARMICE
REARMING
REARMOST
REARMOUSE
REARMS
REAROSE
REAROUSAL
REAROUSE
REAROUSED
REAROUSES
REARRANGE
REARREST
REARRESTS
REARS
REARWARD
REARWARDS
REASCEND
REASCENDS
REASCENT
REASCENTS
REASON
REASONED
REASONER
REASONERS
REASONING
REASONS
REASSAIL
REASSAILS
REASSERT
REASSERTS
REASSESS
REASSIGN
REASSIGNS
REASSORT
REASSORTS
REASSUME
REASSUMED
REASSUMES
REASSURE
REASSURED
REASSURER
REASSURES
REAST

REASTED
REASTIER
REASTIEST
REASTING
REASTS
REASTY
REATA
REATAS
REATE
REATES
REATTACH
REATTACK
REATTACKS
REATTAIN
REATTAINS
REATTEMPT
REAVAIL
REAVAILED
REAVAILS
REAVE
REAVED
REAVER
REAVERS
REAVES
REAVING
REAVOW
REAVOWED
REAVOWING
REAVOWS
REAWAKE
REAWAKED
REAWAKEN
REAWAKENS
REAWAKES
REAWAKING
REAWOKE
REAWOKEN
REB
REBACK
REBACKED
REBACKING
REBACKS
REBADGE
REBADGED
REBADGES
REBADGING
REBAIT
REBAITED
REBAITING
REBAITS
REBALANCE
REBAPTISE
REBAPTISM
REBAPTIZE
REBAR
REBARS
REBASE
REBASED
REBASES
REBASING
REBATABLE
REBATE
REBATED
REBATER
REBATERS
REBATES
REBATING
REBATO
REBATOES
REBATOS
REBBE
REBBES
REBBETZIN
REBEC
REBECK
REBECKS
REBECS
REBEGAN
REBEGIN
REBEGINS
REBEGUN
REBEL
REBELDOM
REBELDOMS
REBELLED
REBELLER
REBELLERS
REBELLING
REBELLION
REBELLOW
REBELLOWS
REBELS
REBID
REBIDDEN
REBIDDING
REBIDS
REBILL
REBILLED
REBILLING
REBILLS
REBIND
REBINDING
REBINDS
REBIRTH
REBIRTHER
REBIRTHS
REBIT
REBITE
REBITES
REBITING
REBITTEN
REBLEND
REBLENDED
REBLENDS
REBLENT
REBLOCHON
REBLOOM
REBLOOMED
REBLOOMER
REBLOOMS
REBLOSSOM
REBOANT
REBOARD
REBOARDED
REBOARDS
REBOATION
REBODIED
REBODIES
REBODY
REBODYING
REBOIL
REBOILED
REBOILING
REBOILS
REBOOK
REBOOKED
REBOOKING
REBOOKS
REBOOT
REBOOTED
REBOOTING
REBOOTS
REBOP
REBOPS
REBORE
REBORED
REBORES
REBORING
REBORN
REBORROW
REBORROWS
REBOTTLE
REBOTTLED
REBOTTLES
REBOUGHT
REBOUND
REBOUNDED
REBOUNDER
REBOUNDS
REBOZO
REBOZOS
REBRACE
REBRACED
REBRACES
REBRACING
REBRANCH
REBRAND
REBRANDED
REBRANDS
REBRED
REBREED
REBREEDS
REBS
REBUFF
REBUFFED
REBUFFING
REBUFFS
REBUILD
REBUILDED
REBUILDS
REBUILT
REBUKABLE
REBUKE
REBUKED
REBUKEFUL
REBUKER
REBUKERS
REBUKES
REBUKING
REBURIAL
REBURIALS
REBURIED
REBURIES
REBURY
REBURYING
REBUS
REBUSES
REBUT
REBUTMENT
REBUTS
REBUTTAL
REBUTTALS
REBUTTED
REBUTTER
REBUTTERS
REBUTTING
REBUTTON
REBUTTONS
REBUY
REBUYING
REBUYS
REC
RECAL
RECALESCE
RECALL
RECALLED
RECALLER
RECALLERS
RECALLING
RECALLS
RECALMENT
RECALS
RECAMIER
RECAMIERS
RECANE
RECANED
RECANES
RECANING
RECANT
RECANTED
RECANTER
RECANTERS
RECANTING
RECANTS
RECAP
RECAPPED
RECAPPING
RECAPS
RECAPTION
RECAPTOR

RECAPTORS
RECAPTURE
RECARPET
RECARPETS
RECARRIED
RECARRIES
RECARRY
RECAST
RECASTING
RECASTS
RECATALOG
RECATCH
RECATCHES
RECAUGHT
RECAUTION
RECCE
RECCED
RECCEED
RECCEING
RECCES
RECCIED
RECCIES
RECCO
RECCOS
RECCY
RECCYING
RECEDE
RECEDED
RECEDES
RECEDING
RECEIPT
RECEIPTED
RECEIPTOR
RECEIPTS
RECEIVAL
RECEIVALS
RECEIVE
RECEIVED
RECEIVER
RECEIVERS
RECEIVES
RECEIVING
RECEMENT
RECEMENTS
RECENCIES
RECENCY
RECENSE
RECENSED
RECENSES
RECENSING
RECENSION
RECENSOR
RECENSORS
RECENT
RECENTER
RECENTEST
RECENTLY
RECENTRE
RECENTRED
RECENTRES
RECEPT
RECEPTION
RECEPTIVE
RECEPTOR
RECEPTORS
RECEPTS
RECERTIFY
RECESS
RECESSED
RECESSES
RECESSING
RECESSION
RECESSIVE
RECHANGE
RECHANGED
RECHANGES
RECHANNEL
RECHARGE
RECHARGED
RECHARGER
RECHARGES
RECHART
RECHARTED
RECHARTER
RECHARTS
RECHATE
RECHATES
RECHAUFFE
RECHEAT
RECHEATED
RECHEATS
RECHECK
RECHECKED
RECHECKS
RECHERCHE
RECHEW
RECHEWED
RECHEWING
RECHEWS
RECHIE
RECHIP
RECHIPPED
RECHIPS
RECHLESSE
RECHOOSE
RECHOOSES
RECHOSE
RECHOSEN
RECIPE
RECIPES
RECIPIENT
RECIRCLE
RECIRCLED
RECIRCLES
RECISION
RECISIONS
RECIT
RECITABLE
RECITAL
RECITALS
RECITE
RECITED
RECITER
RECITERS
RECITES
RECITING
RECITS
RECK
RECKAN
RECKANS
RECKED
RECKING
RECKLESS
RECKLING
RECKLINGS
RECKON
RECKONED
RECKONER
RECKONERS
RECKONING
RECKONS
RECKS
RECLAD
RECLADDED
RECLADS
RECLAIM
RECLAIMED
RECLAIMER
RECLAIMS
RECLAME
RECLAMES
RECLASP
RECLASPED
RECLASPS
RECLEAN
RECLEANED
RECLEANS
RECLIMB
RECLIMBED
RECLIMBS
RECLINATE
RECLINE
RECLINED
RECLINER
RECLINERS
RECLINES
RECLINING
RECLOSE
RECLOSED
RECLOSES
RECLOSING
RECLOTHE
RECLOTHED
RECLOTHES
RECLUSE
RECLUSELY
RECLUSES
RECLUSION
RECLUSIVE
RECLUSORY
RECOAL
RECOALED
RECOALING
RECOALS
RECOAT
RECOATED
RECOATING
RECOATS
RECOCK
RECOCKED
RECOCKING
RECOCKS
RECODE
RECODED
RECODES
RECODIFY
RECODING
RECOGNISE
RECOGNIZE
RECOIL
RECOILED
RECOILER
RECOILERS
RECOILING
RECOILS
RECOIN
RECOINAGE
RECOINED
RECOINING
RECOINS
RECOLLECT
RECOLLET
RECOLLETS
RECOLOR
RECOLORED
RECOLORS
RECOLOUR
RECOLOURS
RECOMB
RECOMBED
RECOMBINE
RECOMBING
RECOMBS
RECOMFORT
RECOMMEND
RECOMMIT
RECOMMITS
RECOMPACT
RECOMPILE
RECOMPOSE
RECOMPUTE
RECON
RECONCILE
RECONDITE
RECONDUCT
RECONFER
RECONFERS
RECONFINE
RECONFIRM
RECONNECT

RECONNED
RECONNING
RECONQUER
RECONS
RECONSIGN
RECONSOLE
RECONSULT
RECONTACT
RECONTOUR
RECONVENE
RECONVERT
RECONVEY
RECONVEYS
RECONVICT
RECOOK
RECOOKED
RECOOKING
RECOOKS
RECOPIED
RECOPIES
RECOPY
RECOPYING
RECORD
RECORDED
RECORDER
RECORDERS
RECORDING
RECORDIST
RECORDS
RECORK
RECORKED
RECORKING
RECORKS
RECOUNT
RECOUNTAL
RECOUNTED
RECOUNTER
RECOUNTS
RECOUP
RECOUPE
RECOUPED
RECOUPES
RECOUPING
RECOUPLE
RECOUPLED
RECOUPLES
RECOUPS
RECOURE
RECOURED
RECOURES
RECOURING
RECOURSE
RECOURSED
RECOURSES
RECOVER
RECOVERED
RECOVEREE
RECOVERER
RECOVEROR
RECOVERS
RECOVERY
RECOWER
RECOWERED
RECOWERS
RECOYLE
RECOYLED
RECOYLES
RECOYLING
RECRATE
RECRATED
RECRATES
RECRATING
RECREANCE
RECREANCY
RECREANT
RECREANTS
RECREATE
RECREATED
RECREATES
RECREATOR
RECREMENT
RECROSS
RECROSSED
RECROSSES
RECROWN
RECROWNED
RECROWNS
RECRUIT
RECRUITAL
RECRUITED
RECRUITER
RECRUITS
RECS
RECTA
RECTAL
RECTALLY
RECTANGLE
RECTI
RECTIFIED
RECTIFIER
RECTIFIES
RECTIFY
RECTION
RECTIONS
RECTITIC
RECTITIS
RECTITUDE
RECTO
RECTOCELE
RECTOR
RECTORAL
RECTORATE
RECTORESS
RECTORIAL
RECTORIES
RECTORS
RECTORY
RECTOS
RECTRESS
RECTRICES
RECTRIX
RECTUM
RECTUMS
RECTUS
RECUILE
RECUILED
RECUILES
RECUILING
RECULE
RECULED
RECULES
RECULING
RECUMBENT
RECUR
RECURE
RECURED
RECURES
RECURING
RECURRED
RECURRENT
RECURRING
RECURS
RECURSION
RECURSIVE
RECURVATE
RECURVE
RECURVED
RECURVES
RECURVING
RECUSAL
RECUSALS
RECUSANCE
RECUSANCY
RECUSANT
RECUSANTS
RECUSE
RECUSED
RECUSES
RECUSING
RECUT
RECUTS
RECUTTING
RECYCLATE
RECYCLE
RECYCLED
RECYCLER
RECYCLERS
RECYCLES
RECYCLING
RECYCLIST
RED
REDACT
REDACTED
REDACTING
REDACTION
REDACTOR
REDACTORS
REDACTS
REDAMAGE
REDAMAGED
REDAMAGES
REDAN
REDANS
REDARGUE
REDARGUED
REDARGUES
REDATE
REDATED
REDATES
REDATING
REDBACK
REDBACKS
REDBAIT
REDBAITED
REDBAITER
REDBAITS
REDBAY
REDBAYS
REDBELLY
REDBIRD
REDBIRDS
REDBONE
REDBONES
REDBREAST
REDBRICK
REDBRICKS
REDBUD
REDBUDS
REDBUG
REDBUGS
REDCAP
REDCAPS
REDCOAT
REDCOATS
REDD
REDDED
REDDEN
REDDENDA
REDDENDO
REDDENDOS
REDDENDUM
REDDENED
REDDENING
REDDENS
REDDER
REDDERS
REDDEST
REDDIER
REDDIEST
REDDING
REDDINGS
REDDISH
REDDISHLY
REDDLE
REDDLED
REDDLEMAN
REDDLEMEN
REDDLES
REDDLING
REDDS

R

REDDY
REDE
REDEAL
REDEALING
REDEALS
REDEALT
REDEAR
REDEARS
REDECIDE
REDECIDED
REDECIDES
REDECRAFT
REDED
REDEEM
REDEEMED
REDEEMER
REDEEMERS
REDEEMING
REDEEMS
REDEFEAT
REDEFEATS
REDEFECT
REDEFECTS
REDEFIED
REDEFIES
REDEFINE
REDEFINED
REDEFINES
REDEFY
REDEFYING
REDELESS
REDELIVER
REDEMAND
REDEMANDS
REDENIED
REDENIES
REDENY
REDENYING
REDEPLOY
REDEPLOYS
REDEPOSIT
REDES
REDESCEND
REDESIGN
REDESIGNS
REDEVELOP
REDEYE
REDEYES
REDFIN
REDFINS
REDFISH
REDFISHES
REDFOOT
REDFOOTS
REDHANDED
REDHEAD
REDHEADED
REDHEADS
REDHORSE
REDHORSES
REDIA
REDIAE
REDIAL
REDIALED
REDIALING
REDIALLED
REDIALS
REDIAS
REDICTATE
REDID
REDIGEST
REDIGESTS
REDIGRESS
REDING
REDINGOTE
REDIP
REDIPPED
REDIPPING
REDIPS
REDIPT
REDIRECT
REDIRECTS
REDISCUSS
REDISPLAY
REDISPOSE
REDISTIL
REDISTILL
REDISTILS
REDIVIDE
REDIVIDED
REDIVIDES
REDIVIVUS
REDIVORCE
REDLEG
REDLEGS
REDLINE
REDLINED
REDLINER
REDLINERS
REDLINES
REDLINING
REDLY
REDNECK
REDNECKED
REDNECKS
REDNESS
REDNESSES
REDO
REDOCK
REDOCKED
REDOCKING
REDOCKS
REDOES
REDOING
REDOLENCE
REDOLENCY
REDOLENT
REDON
REDONE
REDONNED
REDONNING
REDONS
REDOS
REDOUBLE
REDOUBLED
REDOUBLER
REDOUBLES
REDOUBT
REDOUBTED
REDOUBTS
REDOUND
REDOUNDED
REDOUNDS
REDOUT
REDOUTS
REDOWA
REDOWAS
REDOX
REDOXES
REDPOLL
REDPOLLS
REDRAFT
REDRAFTED
REDRAFTS
REDRAW
REDRAWER
REDRAWERS
REDRAWING
REDRAWN
REDRAWS
REDREAM
REDREAMED
REDREAMS
REDREAMT
REDRESS
REDRESSAL
REDRESSED
REDRESSER
REDRESSES
REDRESSOR
REDREW
REDRIED
REDRIES
REDRILL
REDRILLED
REDRILLS
REDRIVE
REDRIVEN
REDRIVES
REDRIVING
REDROOT
REDROOTS
REDROVE
REDRY
REDRYING
REDS
REDSEAR
REDSHANK
REDSHANKS
REDSHARE
REDSHIFT
REDSHIFTS
REDSHIRE
REDSHIRT
REDSHIRTS
REDSHORT
REDSKIN
REDSKINS
REDSTART
REDSTARTS
REDSTREAK
REDTAIL
REDTAILS
REDTOP
REDTOPS
REDUB
REDUBBED
REDUBBING
REDUBS
REDUCE
REDUCED
REDUCER
REDUCERS
REDUCES
REDUCIBLE
REDUCIBLY
REDUCING
REDUCTANT
REDUCTASE
REDUCTION
REDUCTIVE
REDUCTOR
REDUCTORS
REDUIT
REDUITS
REDUNDANT
REDUVIID
REDUVIIDS
REDUX
REDWARE
REDWARES
REDWATER
REDWATERS
REDWING
REDWINGS
REDWOOD
REDWOODS
REDYE
REDYED
REDYEING
REDYES
REE
REEARN
REEARNED
REEARNING
REEARNS
REEBOK
REEBOKS
REECH
REECHED

R

REECHES
REECHIE
REECHIER
REECHIEST
REECHING
REECHO
REECHOED
REECHOES
REECHOING
REECHY
REED
REEDBED
REEDBEDS
REEDBIRD
REEDBIRDS
REEDBUCK
REEDBUCKS
REEDE
REEDED
REEDEN
REEDER
REEDERS
REEDES
REEDIER
REEDIEST
REEDIFIED
REEDIFIES
REEDIFY
REEDILY
REEDINESS
REEDING
REEDINGS
REEDIT
REEDITED
REEDITING
REEDITION
REEDITS
REEDLIKE
REEDLING
REEDLINGS
REEDMAN
REEDMEN
REEDS
REEDSTOP
REEDSTOPS
REEDUCATE
REEDY
REEF
REEFABLE
REEFED
REEFER
REEFERS
REEFIER
REEFIEST
REEFING
REEFINGS
REEFPOINT
REEFS
REEFY
REEJECT
REEJECTED
REEJECTS
REEK
REEKED
REEKER
REEKERS
REEKIE
REEKIER
REEKIEST
REEKING
REEKINGLY
REEKS
REEKY
REEL
REELABLE
REELECT
REELECTED
REELECTS
REELED
REELER
REELERS
REELEVATE
REELING
REELINGLY
REELINGS
REELMAN
REELMEN
REELS
REEMBARK
REEMBARKS
REEMBODY
REEMBRACE
REEMERGE
REEMERGED
REEMERGES
REEMIT
REEMITS
REEMITTED
REEMPLOY
REEMPLOYS
REEN
REENACT
REENACTED
REENACTOR
REENACTS
REENDOW
REENDOWED
REENDOWS
REENFORCE
REENGAGE
REENGAGED
REENGAGES
REENGRAVE
REENJOY
REENJOYED
REENJOYS
REENLARGE
REENLIST
REENLISTS
REENROLL
REENROLLS
REENS
REENSLAVE
REENTER
REENTERED
REENTERS
REENTRANT
REENTRIES
REENTRY
REEQUIP
REEQUIPS
REERECT
REERECTED
REERECTS
REES
REEST
REESTED
REESTIER
REESTIEST
REESTING
REESTS
REESTY
REEVE
REEVED
REEVES
REEVESHIP
REEVING
REEVOKE
REEVOKED
REEVOKES
REEVOKING
REEXAMINE
REEXECUTE
REEXHIBIT
REEXPEL
REEXPELS
REEXPLAIN
REEXPLORE
REEXPORT
REEXPORTS
REEXPOSE
REEXPOSED
REEXPOSES
REEXPRESS
REF
REFACE
REFACED
REFACES
REFACING
REFALL
REFALLEN
REFALLING
REFALLS
REFASHION
REFASTEN
REFASTENS
REFECT
REFECTED
REFECTING
REFECTION
REFECTIVE
REFECTORY
REFECTS
REFED
REFEED
REFEEDING
REFEEDS
REFEEL
REFEELING
REFEELS
REFEL
REFELL
REFELLED
REFELLING
REFELS
REFELT
REFENCE
REFENCED
REFENCES
REFENCING
REFER
REFERABLE
REFEREE
REFEREED
REFEREES
REFERENCE
REFERENDA
REFERENT
REFERENTS
REFERRAL
REFERRALS
REFERRED
REFERRER
REFERRERS
REFERRING
REFERS
REFFED
REFFING
REFFINGS
REFFO
REFFOS
REFI
REFIGHT
REFIGHTS
REFIGURE
REFIGURED
REFIGURES
REFILE
REFILED
REFILES
REFILING
REFILL
REFILLED
REFILLING
REFILLS
REFILM
REFILMED
REFILMING
REFILMS
REFILTER

REFILTERS
REFINABLE
REFINANCE
REFIND
REFINDING
REFINDS
REFINE
REFINED
REFINEDLY
REFINER
REFINERS
REFINERY
REFINES
REFINING
REFININGS
REFINISH
REFIRE
REFIRED
REFIRES
REFIRING
REFIS
REFIT
REFITMENT
REFITS
REFITTED
REFITTING
REFIX
REFIXED
REFIXES
REFIXING
REFLAG
REFLAGGED
REFLAGS
REFLATE
REFLATED
REFLATES
REFLATING
REFLATION
REFLECT
REFLECTED
REFLECTER
REFLECTOR
REFLECTS
REFLET
REFLETS
REFLEW
REFLEX
REFLEXED
REFLEXES
REFLEXING
REFLEXION
REFLEXIVE
REFLEXLY
REFLIES
REFLOAT
REFLOATED
REFLOATS
REFLOOD
REFLOODED
REFLOODS
REFLOW
REFLOWED
REFLOWER
REFLOWERS
REFLOWING
REFLOWN
REFLOWS
REFLUENCE
REFLUENT
REFLUX
REFLUXED
REFLUXES
REFLUXING
REFLY
REFLYING
REFOCUS
REFOCUSED
REFOCUSES
REFOLD
REFOLDED
REFOLDING
REFOLDS
REFOOT
REFOOTED
REFOOTING
REFOOTS
REFOREST
REFORESTS
REFORGE
REFORGED
REFORGES
REFORGING
REFORM
REFORMADE
REFORMADO
REFORMAT
REFORMATE
REFORMATS
REFORMED
REFORMER
REFORMERS
REFORMING
REFORMISM
REFORMIST
REFORMS
REFORTIFY
REFOUGHT
REFOUND
REFOUNDED
REFOUNDER
REFOUNDS
REFRACT
REFRACTED
REFRACTOR
REFRACTS
REFRAIN
REFRAINED
REFRAINER
REFRAINS
REFRAME
REFRAMED
REFRAMES
REFRAMING
REFREEZE
REFREEZES
REFRESH
REFRESHED
REFRESHEN
REFRESHER
REFRESHES
REFRIED
REFRIES
REFRINGE
REFRINGED
REFRINGES
REFRONT
REFRONTED
REFRONTS
REFROZE
REFROZEN
REFRY
REFRYING
REFS
REFT
REFUEL
REFUELED
REFUELING
REFUELLED
REFUELS
REFUGE
REFUGED
REFUGEE
REFUGEES
REFUGES
REFUGIA
REFUGING
REFUGIUM
REFULGENT
REFUND
REFUNDED
REFUNDER
REFUNDERS
REFUNDING
REFUNDS
REFURB
REFURBED
REFURBING
REFURBISH
REFURBS
REFURNISH
REFUSABLE
REFUSAL
REFUSALS
REFUSE
REFUSED
REFUSENIK
REFUSER
REFUSERS
REFUSES
REFUSING
REFUSION
REFUSIONS
REFUSNIK
REFUSNIKS
REFUTABLE
REFUTABLY
REFUTAL
REFUTALS
REFUTE
REFUTED
REFUTER
REFUTERS
REFUTES
REFUTING
REG
REGAIN
REGAINED
REGAINER
REGAINERS
REGAINING
REGAINS
REGAL
REGALE
REGALED
REGALER
REGALERS
REGALES
REGALIA
REGALIAN
REGALIAS
REGALING
REGALISM
REGALISMS
REGALIST
REGALISTS
REGALITY
REGALLY
REGALNESS
REGALS
REGAR
REGARD
REGARDANT
REGARDED
REGARDER
REGARDERS
REGARDFUL
REGARDING
REGARDS
REGARS
REGATHER
REGATHERS
REGATTA
REGATTAS
REGAUGE
REGAUGED
REGAUGES
REGAUGING
REGAVE
REGEAR
REGEARED

R

REGEARING
REGEARS
REGELATE
REGELATED
REGELATES
REGENCE
REGENCES
REGENCIES
REGENCY
REGENT
REGENTAL
REGENTS
REGES
REGEST
REGESTED
REGESTING
REGESTS
REGGAE
REGGAES
REGGAETON
REGGO
REGGOS
REGICIDAL
REGICIDE
REGICIDES
REGIE
REGIES
REGIFT
REGIFTED
REGIFTER
REGIFTERS
REGIFTING
REGIFTS
REGILD
REGILDED
REGILDING
REGILDS
REGILT
REGIME
REGIMEN
REGIMENS
REGIMENT
REGIMENTS
REGIMES
REGIMINAL
REGINA
REGINAE
REGINAL
REGINAS
REGION
REGIONAL
REGIONALS
REGIONARY
REGIONS
REGISSEUR
REGISTER
REGISTERS
REGISTRAR
REGISTRY
REGIUS
REGIVE
REGIVEN
REGIVES
REGIVING
REGLAZE
REGLAZED
REGLAZES
REGLAZING
REGLET
REGLETS
REGLORIFY
REGLOSS
REGLOSSED
REGLOSSES
REGLOW
REGLOWED
REGLOWING
REGLOWS
REGLUE
REGLUED
REGLUES
REGLUING
REGMA
REGMAKER
REGMAKERS
REGMATA
REGNA
REGNAL
REGNANCY
REGNANT
REGNUM
REGO
REGOLITH
REGOLITHS
REGORGE
REGORGED
REGORGES
REGORGING
REGOS
REGOSOL
REGOSOLS
REGRADE
REGRADED
REGRADES
REGRADING
REGRAFT
REGRAFTED
REGRAFTS
REGRANT
REGRANTED
REGRANTS
REGRATE
REGRATED
REGRATER
REGRATERS
REGRATES
REGRATING
REGRATOR
REGRATORS
REGREDE
REGREDED
REGREDES
REGREDING
REGREEN
REGREENED
REGREENS
REGREET
REGREETED
REGREETS
REGRESS
REGRESSED
REGRESSES
REGRESSOR
REGRET
REGRETFUL
REGRETS
REGRETTED
REGRETTER
REGREW
REGRIND
REGRINDS
REGROOM
REGROOMED
REGROOMS
REGROOVE
REGROOVED
REGROOVES
REGROUND
REGROUP
REGROUPED
REGROUPS
REGROW
REGROWING
REGROWN
REGROWS
REGROWTH
REGROWTHS
REGS
REGUERDON
REGULA
REGULABLE
REGULAE
REGULAR
REGULARLY
REGULARS
REGULATE
REGULATED
REGULATES
REGULATOR
REGULI
REGULINE
REGULISE
REGULISED
REGULISES
REGULIZE
REGULIZED
REGULIZES
REGULO
REGULOS
REGULUS
REGULUSES
REGUR
REGURS
REH
REHAB
REHABBED
REHABBER
REHABBERS
REHABBING
REHABS
REHAMMER
REHAMMERS
REHANDLE
REHANDLED
REHANDLES
REHANG
REHANGED
REHANGING
REHANGS
REHARDEN
REHARDENS
REHASH
REHASHED
REHASHES
REHASHING
REHEAR
REHEARD
REHEARING
REHEARS
REHEARSAL
REHEARSE
REHEARSED
REHEARSER
REHEARSES
REHEAT
REHEATED
REHEATER
REHEATERS
REHEATING
REHEATS
REHEEL
REHEELED
REHEELING
REHEELS
REHEM
REHEMMED
REHEMMING
REHEMS
REHINGE
REHINGED
REHINGES
REHINGING
REHIRE
REHIRED
REHIRES
REHIRING
REHOBOAM
REHOBOAMS
REHOME
REHOMED

R

REHOMES
REHOMING
REHOMINGS
REHOUSE
REHOUSED
REHOUSES
REHOUSING
REHS
REHUNG
REHYDRATE
REI
REIF
REIFIED
REIFIER
REIFIERS
REIFIES
REIFS
REIFY
REIFYING
REIGN
REIGNED
REIGNING
REIGNITE
REIGNITED
REIGNITES
REIGNS
REIK
REIKI
REIKIS
REIKS
REILLUME
REILLUMED
REILLUMES
REIMAGE
REIMAGED
REIMAGES
REIMAGINE
REIMAGING
REIMBURSE
REIMMERSE
REIMPLANT
REIMPORT
REIMPORTS
REIMPOSE
REIMPOSED
REIMPOSES
REIN
REINCITE
REINCITED
REINCITES
REINCUR
REINCURS
REINDEER
REINDEERS
REINDEX
REINDEXED
REINDEXES
REINDICT
REINDICTS
REINDUCE
REINDUCED
REINDUCES
REINDUCT
REINDUCTS
REINED
REINETTE
REINETTES
REINFECT
REINFECTS
REINFLAME
REINFLATE
REINFORCE
REINFORM
REINFORMS
REINFUND
REINFUNDS
REINFUSE
REINFUSED
REINFUSES
REINHABIT
REINING
REINJECT
REINJECTS
REINJURE
REINJURED
REINJURES
REINJURY
REINK
REINKED
REINKING
REINKS
REINLESS
REINS
REINSERT
REINSERTS
REINSMAN
REINSMEN
REINSPECT
REINSPIRE
REINSTAL
REINSTALL
REINSTALS
REINSTATE
REINSURE
REINSURED
REINSURER
REINSURES
REINTER
REINTERS
REINVADE
REINVADED
REINVADES
REINVENT
REINVENTS
REINVEST
REINVESTS
REINVITE
REINVITED
REINVITES
REINVOKE
REINVOKED
REINVOKES
REINVOLVE
REIRD
REIRDS
REIS
REISES
REISHI
REISHIS
REISSUE
REISSUED
REISSUER
REISSUERS
REISSUES
REISSUING
REIST
REISTAFEL
REISTED
REISTING
REISTS
REITBOK
REITBOKS
REITER
REITERANT
REITERATE
REITERED
REITERING
REITERS
REIVE
REIVED
REIVER
REIVERS
REIVES
REIVING
REIVINGS
REJACKET
REJACKETS
REJECT
REJECTED
REJECTEE
REJECTEES
REJECTER
REJECTERS
REJECTING
REJECTION
REJECTIVE
REJECTOR
REJECTORS
REJECTS
REJIG
REJIGGED
REJIGGER
REJIGGERS
REJIGGING
REJIGS
REJOICE
REJOICED
REJOICER
REJOICERS
REJOICES
REJOICING
REJOIN
REJOINDER
REJOINED
REJOINING
REJOINS
REJON
REJONEO
REJONEOS
REJONES
REJOURN
REJOURNED
REJOURNS
REJUDGE
REJUDGED
REJUDGES
REJUDGING
REJUGGLE
REJUGGLED
REJUGGLES
REJUSTIFY
REKE
REKED
REKES
REKEY
REKEYED
REKEYING
REKEYS
REKINDLE
REKINDLED
REKINDLES
REKING
REKNIT
REKNITS
REKNITTED
REKNOT
REKNOTS
REKNOTTED
RELABEL
RELABELED
RELABELS
RELACE
RELACED
RELACES
RELACHE
RELACHES
RELACING
RELACQUER
RELAID
RELAND
RELANDED
RELANDING
RELANDS
RELAPSE
RELAPSED
RELAPSER
RELAPSERS
RELAPSES
RELAPSING
RELATA

RELATABLE
RELATE
RELATED
RELATEDLY
RELATER
RELATERS
RELATES
RELATING
RELATION
RELATIONS
RELATIVAL
RELATIVE
RELATIVES
RELATOR
RELATORS
RELATUM
RELAUNCH
RELAUNDER
RELAX
RELAXABLE
RELAXANT
RELAXANTS
RELAXED
RELAXEDLY
RELAXER
RELAXERS
RELAXES
RELAXIN
RELAXING
RELAXINS
RELAY
RELAYED
RELAYING
RELAYS
RELEARN
RELEARNED
RELEARNS
RELEARNT
RELEASE
RELEASED
RELEASEE
RELEASEES
RELEASER
RELEASERS
RELEASES
RELEASING
RELEASOR
RELEASORS
RELEGABLE
RELEGATE
RELEGATED
RELEGATES
RELEND
RELENDING
RELENDS
RELENT
RELENTED
RELENTING
RELENTS
RELET
RELETS
RELETTER
RELETTERS
RELETTING
RELEVANCE
RELEVANCY
RELEVANT
RELEVE
RELEVES
RELIABLE
RELIABLES
RELIABLY
RELIANCE
RELIANCES
RELIANT
RELIANTLY
RELIC
RELICENSE
RELICS
RELICT
RELICTION
RELICTS
RELIDE
RELIE
RELIED
RELIEF
RELIEFS
RELIER
RELIERS
RELIES
RELIEVE
RELIEVED
RELIEVER
RELIEVERS
RELIEVES
RELIEVING
RELIEVO
RELIEVOS
RELIGHT
RELIGHTED
RELIGHTS
RELIGIEUX
RELIGION
RELIGIONS
RELIGIOSE
RELIGIOSO
RELIGIOUS
RELINE
RELINED
RELINES
RELINING
RELINK
RELINKED
RELINKING
RELINKS
RELIQUARY
RELIQUE
RELIQUEFY
RELIQUES
RELIQUIAE
RELIQUIFY
RELISH
RELISHED
RELISHES
RELISHING
RELIST
RELISTED
RELISTEN
RELISTENS
RELISTING
RELISTS
RELIT
RELIVABLE
RELIVE
RELIVED
RELIVER
RELIVERED
RELIVERS
RELIVES
RELIVING
RELLENO
RELLENOS
RELLIE
RELLIES
RELLISH
RELLISHED
RELLISHES
RELLO
RELLOS
RELOAD
RELOADED
RELOADER
RELOADERS
RELOADING
RELOADS
RELOAN
RELOANED
RELOANING
RELOANS
RELOCATE
RELOCATED
RELOCATEE
RELOCATES
RELOCATOR
RELOCK
RELOCKED
RELOCKING
RELOCKS
RELOOK
RELOOKED
RELOOKING
RELOOKS
RELUCENT
RELUCT
RELUCTANT
RELUCTATE
RELUCTED
RELUCTING
RELUCTS
RELUME
RELUMED
RELUMES
RELUMINE
RELUMINED
RELUMINES
RELUMING
RELY
RELYING
REM
REMADE
REMADES
REMAIL
REMAILED
REMAILER
REMAILERS
REMAILING
REMAILS
REMAIN
REMAINDER
REMAINED
REMAINER
REMAINERS
REMAINING
REMAINS
REMAKE
REMAKER
REMAKERS
REMAKES
REMAKING
REMAN
REMAND
REMANDED
REMANDING
REMANDS
REMANENCE
REMANENCY
REMANENT
REMANENTS
REMANET
REMANETS
REMANIE
REMANIES
REMANNED
REMANNING
REMANS
REMAP
REMAPPED
REMAPPING
REMAPS
REMARK
REMARKED
REMARKER
REMARKERS
REMARKET
REMARKETS
REMARKING
REMARKS
REMARQUE
REMARQUED
REMARQUES

R

REMARRIED
REMARRIES
REMARRY
REMASTER
REMASTERS
REMATCH
REMATCHED
REMATCHES
REMATE
REMATED
REMATES
REMATING
REMBLAI
REMBLAIS
REMBLE
REMBLED
REMBLES
REMBLING
REMEAD
REMEADED
REMEADING
REMEADS
REMEASURE
REMEDE
REMEDED
REMEDES
REMEDIAL
REMEDIAT
REMEDIATE
REMEDIED
REMEDIES
REMEDING
REMEDY
REMEDYING
REMEET
REMEETING
REMEETS
REMEID
REMEIDED
REMEIDING
REMEIDS
REMELT
REMELTED
REMELTING
REMELTS
REMEMBER
REMEMBERS
REMEN
REMEND
REMENDED
REMENDING
REMENDS
REMENS
REMERCIED
REMERCIES
REMERCY
REMERGE
REMERGED
REMERGES
REMERGING
REMET
REMEX
REMIGATE
REMIGATED
REMIGATES
REMIGES
REMIGIAL
REMIGRATE
REMIND
REMINDED
REMINDER
REMINDERS
REMINDFUL
REMINDING
REMINDS
REMINISCE
REMINT
REMINTED
REMINTING
REMINTS
REMISE
REMISED
REMISES
REMISING
REMISS
REMISSION
REMISSIVE
REMISSLY
REMISSORY
REMIT
REMITMENT
REMITS
REMITTAL
REMITTALS
REMITTED
REMITTEE
REMITTEES
REMITTENT
REMITTER
REMITTERS
REMITTING
REMITTOR
REMITTORS
REMIX
REMIXED
REMIXER
REMIXERS
REMIXES
REMIXING
REMIXT
REMIXTURE
REMNANT
REMNANTAL
REMNANTS
REMODEL
REMODELED
REMODELER
REMODELS
REMODIFY
REMOISTEN
REMOLADE
REMOLADES
REMOLD
REMOLDED
REMOLDING
REMOLDS
REMONTANT
REMONTOIR
REMORA
REMORAS
REMORID
REMORSE
REMORSES
REMOTE
REMOTELY
REMOTER
REMOTES
REMOTEST
REMOTION
REMOTIONS
REMOUD
REMOULADE
REMOULD
REMOULDED
REMOULDS
REMOUNT
REMOUNTED
REMOUNTS
REMOVABLE
REMOVABLY
REMOVAL
REMOVALS
REMOVE
REMOVED
REMOVEDLY
REMOVER
REMOVERS
REMOVES
REMOVING
REMS
REMUAGE
REMUAGES
REMUDA
REMUDAS
REMUEUR
REMUEURS
REMURMUR
REMURMURS
REN
RENAGUE
RENAGUED
RENAGUES
RENAGUING
RENAIL
RENAILED
RENAILING
RENAILS
RENAL
RENAME
RENAMED
RENAMES
RENAMING
RENASCENT
RENATURE
RENATURED
RENATURES
RENAY
RENAYED
RENAYING
RENAYS
RENCONTRE
REND
RENDANG
RENDANGS
RENDED
RENDER
RENDERED
RENDERER
RENDERERS
RENDERING
RENDERS
RENDIBLE
RENDING
RENDITION
RENDS
RENDZINA
RENDZINAS
RENEAGUE
RENEAGUED
RENEAGUES
RENEGADE
RENEGADED
RENEGADES
RENEGADO
RENEGADOS
RENEGATE
RENEGATES
RENEGE
RENEGED
RENEGER
RENEGERS
RENEGES
RENEGING
RENEGUE
RENEGUED
RENEGUER
RENEGUERS
RENEGUES
RENEGUING
RENEST
RENESTED
RENESTING
RENESTS
RENEW
RENEWABLE
RENEWABLY
RENEWAL
RENEWALS
RENEWED
RENEWEDLY

RENEWER
RENEWERS
RENEWING
RENEWINGS
RENEWS
RENEY
RENEYED
RENEYING
RENEYS
RENFIERST
RENFORCE
RENFORCED
RENFORCES
RENFORST
RENGA
RENGAS
RENIED
RENIES
RENIFORM
RENIG
RENIGGED
RENIGGING
RENIGS
RENIN
RENINS
RENITENCE
RENITENCY
RENITENT
RENK
RENKER
RENKEST
RENMINBI
RENMINBIS
RENNASE
RENNASES
RENNE
RENNED
RENNES
RENNET
RENNETS
RENNIN
RENNING
RENNINGS
RENNINS
RENO
RENOGRAM
RENOGRAMS
RENOS

RENOTIFY
RENOUNCE
RENOUNCED
RENOUNCER
RENOUNCES
RENOVATE
RENOVATED
RENOVATES
RENOVATOR
RENOWN
RENOWNED
RENOWNER
RENOWNERS
RENOWNING
RENOWNS
RENS
RENT
RENTABLE
RENTAL
RENTALLER
RENTALS
RENTE
RENTED
RENTER
RENTERS
RENTES
RENTIER
RENTIERS
RENTING
RENTINGS
RENTS
RENUMBER
RENUMBERS
RENVERSE
RENVERSED
RENVERSES
RENVERST
RENVOI
RENVOIS
RENVOY
RENVOYS
RENY
RENYING
REO
REOBJECT
REOBJECTS
REOBSERVE
REOBTAIN

REOBTAINS
REOCCUPY
REOCCUR
REOCCURS
REOFFEND
REOFFENDS
REOFFER
REOFFERED
REOFFERS
REOIL
REOILED
REOILING
REOILS
REOPEN
REOPENED
REOPENER
REOPENERS
REOPENING
REOPENS
REOPERATE
REOPPOSE
REOPPOSED
REOPPOSES
REORDAIN
REORDAINS
REORDER
REORDERED
REORDERS
REORG
REORGED
REORGING
REORGS
REORIENT
REORIENTS
REOS
REOUTFIT
REOUTFITS
REOVIRUS
REOXIDISE
REOXIDIZE
REP
REPACIFY
REPACK
REPACKAGE
REPACKED
REPACKING
REPACKS
REPAID

REPAINT
REPAINTED
REPAINTS
REPAIR
REPAIRED
REPAIRER
REPAIRERS
REPAIRING
REPAIRMAN
REPAIRMEN
REPAIRS
REPAND
REPANDLY
REPANEL
REPANELED
REPANELS
REPAPER
REPAPERED
REPAPERS
REPARABLE
REPARABLY
REPARK
REPARKED
REPARKING
REPARKS
REPARTEE
REPARTEED
REPARTEES
REPASS
REPASSAGE
REPASSED
REPASSES
REPASSING
REPAST
REPASTED
REPASTING
REPASTS
REPASTURE
REPATCH
REPATCHED
REPATCHES
REPATTERN
REPAVE
REPAVED
REPAVES
REPAVING
REPAY
REPAYABLE

REPAYING
REPAYMENT
REPAYS
REPEAL
REPEALED
REPEALER
REPEALERS
REPEALING
REPEALS
REPEAT
REPEATED
REPEATER
REPEATERS
REPEATING
REPEATS
REPECHAGE
REPEG
REPEGGED
REPEGGING
REPEGS
REPEL
REPELLANT
REPELLED
REPELLENT
REPELLER
REPELLERS
REPELLING
REPELS
REPENT
REPENTANT
REPENTED
REPENTER
REPENTERS
REPENTING
REPENTS
REPEOPLE
REPEOPLED
REPEOPLES
REPERCUSS
REPEREPE
REPEREPES
REPERK
REPERKED
REPERKING
REPERKS
REPERTORY
REPERUSAL
REPERUSE

R

REPERUSED
REPERUSES
REPETEND
REPETENDS
REPHRASE
REPHRASED
REPHRASES
REPIGMENT
REPIN
REPINE
REPINED
REPINER
REPINERS
REPINES
REPINING
REPININGS
REPINNED
REPINNING
REPINS
REPIQUE
REPIQUED
REPIQUES
REPIQUING
REPLA
REPLACE
REPLACED
REPLACER
REPLACERS
REPLACES
REPLACING
REPLAN
REPLANNED
REPLANS
REPLANT
REPLANTED
REPLANTS
REPLASTER
REPLATE
REPLATED
REPLATES
REPLATING
REPLAY
REPLAYED
REPLAYING
REPLAYS
REPLEAD
REPLEADED
REPLEADER
REPLEADS
REPLED
REPLEDGE
REPLEDGED
REPLEDGES
REPLENISH
REPLETE
REPLETED
REPLETELY
REPLETES
REPLETING
REPLETION
REPLEVIED
REPLEVIES
REPLEVIN
REPLEVINS
REPLEVY
REPLICA
REPLICANT
REPLICAS
REPLICASE
REPLICATE
REPLICON
REPLICONS
REPLIED
REPLIER
REPLIERS
REPLIES
REPLOT
REPLOTS
REPLOTTED
REPLOUGH
REPLOUGHS
REPLOW
REPLOWED
REPLOWING
REPLOWS
REPLUM
REPLUMB
REPLUMBED
REPLUMBS
REPLUNGE
REPLUNGED
REPLUNGES
REPLY
REPLYING
REPO
REPOINT
REPOINTED
REPOINTS
REPOLISH
REPOLL
REPOLLED
REPOLLING
REPOLLS
REPOMAN
REPOMEN
REPONE
REPONED
REPONES
REPONING
REPORT
REPORTAGE
REPORTED
REPORTER
REPORTERS
REPORTING
REPORTS
REPOS
REPOSAL
REPOSALL
REPOSALLS
REPOSALS
REPOSE
REPOSED
REPOSEDLY
REPOSEFUL
REPOSER
REPOSERS
REPOSES
REPOSING
REPOSIT
REPOSITED
REPOSITOR
REPOSITS
REPOSSESS
REPOST
REPOSTED
REPOSTING
REPOSTS
REPOSURE
REPOSURES
REPOT
REPOTS
REPOTTED
REPOTTING
REPOUR
REPOURED
REPOURING
REPOURS
REPOUSSE
REPOUSSES
REPOWER
REPOWERED
REPOWERS
REPP
REPPED
REPPING
REPPINGS
REPPS
REPREEVE
REPREEVED
REPREEVES
REPREHEND
REPRESENT
REPRESS
REPRESSED
REPRESSER
REPRESSES
REPRESSOR
REPRICE
REPRICED
REPRICES
REPRICING
REPRIEFE
REPRIEFES
REPRIEVAL
REPRIEVE
REPRIEVED
REPRIEVER
REPRIEVES
REPRIMAND
REPRIME
REPRIMED
REPRIMES
REPRIMING
REPRINT
REPRINTED
REPRINTER
REPRINTS
REPRISAL
REPRISALS
REPRISE
REPRISED
REPRISES
REPRISING
REPRIVE
REPRIVED
REPRIVES
REPRIVING
REPRIZE
REPRIZED
REPRIZES
REPRIZING
REPRO
REPROACH
REPROBACY
REPROBATE
REPROBE
REPROBED
REPROBES
REPROBING
REPROCESS
REPRODUCE
REPROGRAM
REPROOF
REPROOFED
REPROOFS
REPROS
REPROVAL
REPROVALS
REPROVE
REPROVED
REPROVER
REPROVERS
REPROVES
REPROVING
REPRYVE
REPRYVED
REPRYVES
REPRYVING
REPS
REPTANT
REPTATION
REPTILE
REPTILES
REPTILIA
REPTILIAN
REPTILIUM
REPTILOID
REPUBLIC
REPUBLICS

REPUBLISH
REPUDIATE
REPUGN
REPUGNANT
REPUGNED
REPUGNING
REPUGNS
REPULP
REPULPED
REPULPING
REPULPS
REPULSE
REPULSED
REPULSER
REPULSERS
REPULSES
REPULSING
REPULSION
REPULSIVE
REPUMP
REPUMPED
REPUMPING
REPUMPS
REPUNIT
REPUNITS
REPURE
REPURED
REPURES
REPURIFY
REPURING
REPURPOSE
REPURSUE
REPURSUED
REPURSUES
REPUTABLE
REPUTABLY
REPUTE
REPUTED
REPUTEDLY
REPUTES
REPUTING
REPUTINGS
REQUALIFY
REQUERE
REQUERED
REQUERES
REQUERING
REQUEST
REQUESTED
REQUESTER
REQUESTOR
REQUESTS
REQUICKEN
REQUIEM
REQUIEMS
REQUIGHT
REQUIGHTS
REQUIN
REQUINS
REQUINTO
REQUINTOS
REQUIRE
REQUIRED
REQUIRER
REQUIRERS
REQUIRES
REQUIRING
REQUISITE
REQUIT
REQUITAL
REQUITALS
REQUITE
REQUITED
REQUITER
REQUITERS
REQUITES
REQUITING
REQUITS
REQUITTED
REQUOTE
REQUOTED
REQUOTES
REQUOTING
REQUOYLE
REQUOYLED
REQUOYLES
RERACK
RERACKED
RERACKING
RERACKS
RERADIATE
RERAIL
RERAILED
RERAILING
RERAILS
RERAISE
RERAISED
RERAISES
RERAISING
RERAN
REREAD
REREADING
REREADS
REREBRACE
RERECORD
RERECORDS
REREDOS
REREDOSES
REREDOSSE
RERELEASE
REREMAI
REREMAIS
REREMICE
REREMIND
REREMINDS
REREMOUSE
RERENT
RERENTED
RERENTING
RERENTS
REREPEAT
REREPEATS
REREVIEW
REREVIEWS
REREVISE
REREVISED
REREVISES
REREWARD
REREWARDS
RERIG
RERIGGED
RERIGGING
RERIGS
RERISE
RERISEN
RERISES
RERISING
REROLL
REROLLED
REROLLER
REROLLERS
REROLLING
REROLLS
REROOF
REROOFED
REROOFING
REROOFS
REROSE
REROUTE
REROUTED
REROUTES
REROUTING
RERUN
RERUNNING
RERUNS
RES
RESADDLE
RESADDLED
RESADDLES
RESAID
RESAIL
RESAILED
RESAILING
RESAILS
RESALABLE
RESALE
RESALES
RESALGAR
RESALGARS
RESALUTE
RESALUTED
RESALUTES
RESAMPLE
RESAMPLED
RESAMPLES
RESAT
RESAW
RESAWED
RESAWING
RESAWN
RESAWS
RESAY
RESAYING
RESAYS
RESCALE
RESCALED
RESCALES
RESCALING
RESCHOOL
RESCHOOLS
RESCIND
RESCINDED
RESCINDER
RESCINDS
RESCORE
RESCORED
RESCORES
RESCORING
RESCREEN
RESCREENS
RESCRIPT
RESCRIPTS
RESCUABLE
RESCUE
RESCUED
RESCUEE
RESCUEES
RESCUER
RESCUERS
RESCUES
RESCUING
RESCULPT
RESCULPTS
RESEAL
RESEALED
RESEALING
RESEALS
RESEARCH
RESEASON
RESEASONS
RESEAT
RESEATED
RESEATING
RESEATS
RESEAU
RESEAUS
RESEAUX
RESECT
RESECTED
RESECTING
RESECTION
RESECTS
RESECURE
RESECURED
RESECURES
RESEDA
RESEDAS
RESEE
RESEED
RESEEDED

RESEEDING
RESEEDS
RESEEING
RESEEK
RESEEKING
RESEEKS
RESEEN
RESEES
RESEIZE
RESEIZED
RESEIZES
RESEIZING
RESEIZURE
RESELECT
RESELECTS
RESELL
RESELLER
RESELLERS
RESELLING
RESELLS
RESEMBLE
RESEMBLED
RESEMBLER
RESEMBLES
RESEND
RESENDING
RESENDS
RESENT
RESENTED
RESENTER
RESENTERS
RESENTFUL
RESENTING
RESENTIVE
RESENTS
RESERPINE
RESERVE
RESERVED
RESERVER
RESERVERS
RESERVES
RESERVICE
RESERVING
RESERVIST
RESERVOIR
RESES
RESET
RESETS
RESETTED
RESETTER
RESETTERS
RESETTING
RESETTLE
RESETTLED
RESETTLES
RESEW
RESEWED
RESEWING
RESEWN
RESEWS
RESH
RESHAPE
RESHAPED
RESHAPER
RESHAPERS
RESHAPES
RESHAPING
RESHARPEN
RESHAVE
RESHAVED
RESHAVEN
RESHAVES
RESHAVING
RESHES
RESHINE
RESHINED
RESHINES
RESHINGLE
RESHINING
RESHIP
RESHIPPED
RESHIPPER
RESHIPS
RESHOD
RESHOE
RESHOED
RESHOEING
RESHOES
RESHONE
RESHOOT
RESHOOTS
RESHOT
RESHOW
RESHOWED
RESHOWER
RESHOWERS
RESHOWING
RESHOWN
RESHOWS
RESHUFFLE
RESIANCE
RESIANCES
RESIANT
RESIANTS
RESID
RESIDE
RESIDED
RESIDENCE
RESIDENCY
RESIDENT
RESIDENTS
RESIDER
RESIDERS
RESIDES
RESIDING
RESIDS
RESIDUA
RESIDUAL
RESIDUALS
RESIDUARY
RESIDUE
RESIDUES
RESIDUOUS
RESIDUUM
RESIDUUMS
RESIFT
RESIFTED
RESIFTING
RESIFTS
RESIGHT
RESIGHTED
RESIGHTS
RESIGN
RESIGNED
RESIGNER
RESIGNERS
RESIGNING
RESIGNS
RESILE
RESILED
RESILES
RESILIENT
RESILIN
RESILING
RESILINS
RESILVER
RESILVERS
RESIN
RESINATA
RESINATAS
RESINATE
RESINATED
RESINATES
RESINED
RESINER
RESINERS
RESINIER
RESINIEST
RESINIFY
RESINING
RESINISE
RESINISED
RESINISES
RESINIZE
RESINIZED
RESINIZES
RESINLIKE
RESINOID
RESINOIDS
RESINOSES
RESINOSIS
RESINOUS
RESINS
RESINY
RESIST
RESISTANT
RESISTED
RESISTENT
RESISTER
RESISTERS
RESISTING
RESISTIVE
RESISTOR
RESISTORS
RESISTS
RESIT
RESITE
RESITED
RESITES
RESITING
RESITS
RESITTING
RESITUATE
RESIZABLE
RESIZE
RESIZED
RESIZES
RESIZING
RESKETCH
RESKEW
RESKEWED
RESKEWING
RESKEWS
RESKILL
RESKILLED
RESKILLS
RESKIN
RESKINNED
RESKINS
RESKUE
RESKUED
RESKUES
RESKUING
RESLATE
RESLATED
RESLATES
RESLATING
RESMELT
RESMELTED
RESMELTS
RESMOOTH
RESMOOTHS
RESNATRON
RESOAK
RESOAKED
RESOAKING
RESOAKS
RESOD
RESODDED
RESODDING
RESODS
RESOFTEN
RESOFTENS
RESOJET
RESOJETS
RESOLD
RESOLDER
RESOLDERS
RESOLE
RESOLED

R

RESOLES
RESOLING
RESOLUBLE
RESOLUTE
RESOLUTER
RESOLUTES
RESOLVE
RESOLVED
RESOLVENT
RESOLVER
RESOLVERS
RESOLVES
RESOLVING
RESONANCE
RESONANT
RESONANTS
RESONATE
RESONATED
RESONATES
RESONATOR
RESORB
RESORBED
RESORBENT
RESORBING
RESORBS
RESORCIN
RESORCINS
RESORT
RESORTED
RESORTER
RESORTERS
RESORTING
RESORTS
RESOUGHT
RESOUND
RESOUNDED
RESOUNDS
RESOURCE
RESOURCED
RESOURCES
RESOW
RESOWED
RESOWING
RESOWN
RESOWS
RESPACE
RESPACED
RESPACES
RESPACING
RESPADE
RESPADED
RESPADES
RESPADING
RESPEAK
RESPEAKS
RESPECIFY
RESPECT
RESPECTED
RESPECTER
RESPECTS
RESPELL
RESPELLED
RESPELLS
RESPELT
RESPIRE
RESPIRED
RESPIRES
RESPIRING
RESPITE
RESPITED
RESPITES
RESPITING
RESPLEND
RESPLENDS
RESPLICE
RESPLICED
RESPLICES
RESPLIT
RESPLITS
RESPOKE
RESPOKEN
RESPOND
RESPONDED
RESPONDER
RESPONDS
RESPONSA
RESPONSE
RESPONSER
RESPONSES
RESPONSOR
RESPONSUM
RESPOOL
RESPOOLED
RESPOOLS
RESPOT
RESPOTS
RESPOTTED
RESPRANG
RESPRAY
RESPRAYED
RESPRAYS
RESPREAD
RESPREADS
RESPRING
RESPRINGS
RESPROUT
RESPROUTS
RESPRUNG
RESSALDAR
REST
RESTABLE
RESTABLED
RESTABLES
RESTACK
RESTACKED
RESTACKS
RESTAFF
RESTAFFED
RESTAFFS
RESTAGE
RESTAGED
RESTAGES
RESTAGING
RESTAMP
RESTAMPED
RESTAMPS
RESTART
RESTARTED
RESTARTER
RESTARTS
RESTATE
RESTATED
RESTATES
RESTATING
RESTATION
RESTED
RESTEM
RESTEMMED
RESTEMS
RESTER
RESTERS
RESTFUL
RESTFULLY
RESTIER
RESTIEST
RESTIFF
RESTIFORM
RESTING
RESTINGS
RESTITCH
RESTITUTE
RESTIVE
RESTIVELY
RESTLESS
RESTO
RESTOCK
RESTOCKED
RESTOCKS
RESTOKE
RESTOKED
RESTOKES
RESTOKING
RESTORAL
RESTORALS
RESTORE
RESTORED
RESTORER
RESTORERS
RESTORES
RESTORING
RESTOS
RESTRAIN
RESTRAINS
RESTRAINT
RESTRESS
RESTRETCH
RESTRICT
RESTRICTS
RESTRIKE
RESTRIKES
RESTRING
RESTRINGE
RESTRINGS
RESTRIVE
RESTRIVEN
RESTRIVES
RESTROOM
RESTROOMS
RESTROVE
RESTRUCK
RESTRUNG
RESTS
RESTUDIED
RESTUDIES
RESTUDY
RESTUFF
RESTUFFED
RESTUFFS
RESTUMP
RESTUMPED
RESTUMPS
RESTY
RESTYLE
RESTYLED
RESTYLES
RESTYLING
RESUBJECT
RESUBMIT
RESUBMITS
RESULT
RESULTANT
RESULTED
RESULTFUL
RESULTING
RESULTS
RESUMABLE
RESUME
RESUMED
RESUMER
RESUMERS
RESUMES
RESUMING
RESUMMON
RESUMMONS
RESUPINE
RESUPPLY
RESURFACE
RESURGE
RESURGED
RESURGENT
RESURGES
RESURGING
RESURRECT
RESURVEY
RESURVEYS
RESUS
RESUSES
RESUSPEND
RESUSSES
RESWALLOW

R

RETABLE
RETABLES
RETABLO
RETABLOS
RETACK
RETACKED
RETACKING
RETACKLE
RETACKLED
RETACKLES
RETACKS
RETAG
RETAGGED
RETAGGING
RETAGS
RETAIL
RETAILED
RETAILER
RETAILERS
RETAILING
RETAILOR
RETAILORS
RETAILS
RETAIN
RETAINED
RETAINER
RETAINERS
RETAINING
RETAINS
RETAKE
RETAKEN
RETAKER
RETAKERS
RETAKES
RETAKING
RETAKINGS
RETALIATE
RETALLIED
RETALLIES
RETALLY
RETAMA
RETAMAS
RETAPE
RETAPED
RETAPES
RETAPING
RETARD
RETARDANT
RETARDATE
RETARDED
RETARDER
RETARDERS
RETARDING
RETARDS
RETARGET
RETARGETS
RETASTE
RETASTED
RETASTES
RETASTING
RETAUGHT
RETAX
RETAXED
RETAXES
RETAXING
RETCH
RETCHED
RETCHES
RETCHING
RETCHINGS
RETCHLESS
RETE
RETEACH
RETEACHES
RETEAM
RETEAMED
RETEAMING
RETEAMS
RETEAR
RETEARING
RETEARS
RETELL
RETELLER
RETELLERS
RETELLING
RETELLS
RETEM
RETEMPER
RETEMPERS
RETEMS
RETENE
RETENES
RETENTION
RETENTIVE
RETEST
RETESTED
RETESTIFY
RETESTING
RETESTS
RETEXTURE
RETHINK
RETHINKER
RETHINKS
RETHOUGHT
RETHREAD
RETHREADS
RETIA
RETIAL
RETIARII
RETIARIUS
RETIARY
RETICELLA
RETICENCE
RETICENCY
RETICENT
RETICLE
RETICLES
RETICULA
RETICULAR
RETICULE
RETICULES
RETICULUM
RETIE
RETIED
RETIEING
RETIES
RETIFORM
RETIGHTEN
RETILE
RETILED
RETILES
RETILING
RETIME
RETIMED
RETIMES
RETIMING
RETINA
RETINAE
RETINAL
RETINALS
RETINAS
RETINE
RETINENE
RETINENES
RETINES
RETINITE
RETINITES
RETINITIS
RETINOIC
RETINOID
RETINOIDS
RETINOL
RETINOLS
RETINT
RETINTED
RETINTING
RETINTS
RETINUE
RETINUED
RETINUES
RETINULA
RETINULAE
RETINULAR
RETINULAS
RETIRACY
RETIRAL
RETIRALS
RETIRANT
RETIRANTS
RETIRE
RETIRED
RETIREDLY
RETIREE
RETIREES
RETIRER
RETIRERS
RETIRES
RETIRING
RETITLE
RETITLED
RETITLES
RETITLING
RETOLD
RETOOK
RETOOL
RETOOLED
RETOOLING
RETOOLS
RETORE
RETORN
RETORSION
RETORT
RETORTED
RETORTER
RETORTERS
RETORTING
RETORTION
RETORTIVE
RETORTS
RETOTAL
RETOTALED
RETOTALS
RETOUCH
RETOUCHED
RETOUCHER
RETOUCHES
RETOUR
RETOURED
RETOURING
RETOURS
RETOX
RETOXED
RETOXES
RETOXING
RETRACE
RETRACED
RETRACER
RETRACERS
RETRACES
RETRACING
RETRACK
RETRACKED
RETRACKS
RETRACT
RETRACTED
RETRACTOR
RETRACTS
RETRAICT
RETRAICTS
RETRAIN
RETRAINED
RETRAINEE
RETRAINS
RETRAIT
RETRAITE
RETRAITES
RETRAITS
RETRAITT
RETRAITTS

RETRAL
RETRALLY
RETRATE
RETRATED
RETRATES
RETRATING
RETREAD
RETREADED
RETREADS
RETREAT
RETREATED
RETREATER
RETREATS
RETREE
RETREES
RETRENCH
RETRIAL
RETRIALS
RETRIBUTE
RETRIED
RETRIES
RETRIEVAL
RETRIEVE
RETRIEVED
RETRIEVER
RETRIEVES
RETRIM
RETRIMMED
RETRIMS
RETRO
RETROACT
RETROACTS
RETROCEDE
RETROD
RETRODDEN
RETRODICT
RETROFIRE
RETROFIT
RETROFITS
RETROFLEX
RETROJECT
RETRONYM
RETRONYMS
RETROPACK
RETRORSE
RETROS
RETROUSSE
RETROVERT
RETRY
RETRYING
RETS
RETSINA
RETSINAS
RETTED
RETTERIES
RETTERY
RETTING
RETUND
RETUNDED
RETUNDING
RETUNDS
RETUNE
RETUNED
RETUNES
RETUNING
RETURF
RETURFED
RETURFING
RETURFS
RETURN
RETURNED
RETURNEE
RETURNEES
RETURNER
RETURNERS
RETURNIK
RETURNIKS
RETURNING
RETURNS
RETUSE
RETWEET
RETWEETED
RETWEETS
RETWIST
RETWISTED
RETWISTS
RETYING
RETYPE
RETYPED
RETYPES
RETYPING
REUNIFIED
REUNIFIES
REUNIFY
REUNION
REUNIONS
REUNITE
REUNITED
REUNITER
REUNITERS
REUNITES
REUNITING
REUPTAKE
REUPTAKEN
REUPTAKES
REUPTOOK
REURGE
REURGED
REURGES
REURGING
REUSABLE
REUSABLES
REUSE
REUSED
REUSES
REUSING
REUTILISE
REUTILIZE
REUTTER
REUTTERED
REUTTERS
REV
REVALENTA
REVALUATE
REVALUE
REVALUED
REVALUES
REVALUING
REVAMP
REVAMPED
REVAMPER
REVAMPERS
REVAMPING
REVAMPS
REVANCHE
REVANCHES
REVARNISH
REVEAL
REVEALED
REVEALER
REVEALERS
REVEALING
REVEALS
REVEHENT
REVEILLE
REVEILLES
REVEL
REVELATOR
REVELED
REVELER
REVELERS
REVELING
REVELLED
REVELLER
REVELLERS
REVELLING
REVELMENT
REVELRIES
REVELROUS
REVELRY
REVELS
REVENANT
REVENANTS
REVENGE
REVENGED
REVENGER
REVENGERS
REVENGES
REVENGING
REVENGIVE
REVENUAL
REVENUE
REVENUED
REVENUER
REVENUERS
REVENUES
REVERABLE
REVERB
REVERBED
REVERBING
REVERBS
REVERE
REVERED
REVERENCE
REVEREND
REVERENDS
REVERENT
REVERER
REVERERS
REVERES
REVERIE
REVERIES
REVERIFY
REVERING
REVERIST
REVERISTS
REVERS
REVERSAL
REVERSALS
REVERSE
REVERSED
REVERSELY
REVERSER
REVERSERS
REVERSES
REVERSI
REVERSING
REVERSION
REVERSIS
REVERSO
REVERSOS
REVERT
REVERTANT
REVERTED
REVERTER
REVERTERS
REVERTING
REVERTIVE
REVERTS
REVERY
REVEST
REVESTED
REVESTING
REVESTRY
REVESTS
REVET
REVETMENT
REVETS
REVETTED
REVETTING
REVEUR
REVEURS
REVEUSE
REVEUSES
REVIBRATE
REVICTUAL
REVIE
REVIED
REVIES
REVIEW

R

REVIEWAL
REVIEWALS
REVIEWED
REVIEWER
REVIEWERS
REVIEWING
REVIEWS
REVILE
REVILED
REVILER
REVILERS
REVILES
REVILING
REVILINGS
REVIOLATE
REVISABLE
REVISAL
REVISALS
REVISE
REVISED
REVISER
REVISERS
REVISES
REVISING
REVISION
REVISIONS
REVISIT
REVISITED
REVISITS
REVISOR
REVISORS
REVISORY
REVIVABLE
REVIVABLY
REVIVAL
REVIVALS
REVIVE
REVIVED
REVIVER
REVIVERS
REVIVES
REVIVIFY
REVIVING
REVIVINGS
REVIVOR
REVIVORS
REVOCABLE
REVOCABLY
REVOICE
REVOICED
REVOICES
REVOICING
REVOKABLE
REVOKABLY
REVOKE
REVOKED
REVOKER
REVOKERS
REVOKES
REVOKING
REVOLT
REVOLTED
REVOLTER
REVOLTERS
REVOLTING
REVOLTS
REVOLUTE
REVOLVE
REVOLVED
REVOLVER
REVOLVERS
REVOLVES
REVOLVING
REVOTE
REVOTED
REVOTES
REVOTING
REVS
REVUE
REVUES
REVUIST
REVUISTS
REVULSED
REVULSION
REVULSIVE
REVVED
REVVING
REVYING
REW
REWAKE
REWAKED
REWAKEN
REWAKENED
REWAKENS
REWAKES
REWAKING
REWAN
REWARD
REWARDED
REWARDER
REWARDERS
REWARDFUL
REWARDING
REWARDS
REWAREWA
REWAREWAS
REWARM
REWARMED
REWARMING
REWARMS
REWASH
REWASHED
REWASHES
REWASHING
REWATER
REWATERED
REWATERS
REWAX
REWAXED
REWAXES
REWAXING
REWEAR
REWEARING
REWEARS
REWEAVE
REWEAVED
REWEAVES
REWEAVING
REWED
REWEDDED
REWEDDING
REWEDS
REWEIGH
REWEIGHED
REWEIGHS
REWELD
REWELDED
REWELDING
REWELDS
REWET
REWETS
REWETTED
REWETTING
REWIDEN
REWIDENED
REWIDENS
REWILD
REWILDED
REWILDING
REWILDS
REWIN
REWIND
REWINDED
REWINDER
REWINDERS
REWINDING
REWINDS
REWINNING
REWINS
REWIRABLE
REWIRE
REWIRED
REWIRES
REWIRING
REWIRINGS
REWOKE
REWOKEN
REWON
REWORD
REWORDED
REWORDING
REWORDS
REWORE
REWORK
REWORKED
REWORKING
REWORKS
REWORN
REWOUND
REWOVE
REWOVEN
REWRAP
REWRAPPED
REWRAPS
REWRAPT
REWRITE
REWRITER
REWRITERS
REWRITES
REWRITING
REWRITTEN
REWROTE
REWROUGHT
REWS
REWTH
REWTHS
REX
REXES
REXINE
REXINES
REYNARD
REYNARDS
REZ
REZERO
REZEROED
REZEROES
REZEROING
REZEROS
REZES
REZONE
REZONED
REZONES
REZONING
REZONINGS
REZZES
RHABDOID
RHABDOIDS
RHABDOM
RHABDOMAL
RHABDOME
RHABDOMES
RHABDOMS
RHABDUS
RHABDUSES
RHACHIAL
RHACHIDES
RHACHILLA
RHACHIS
RHACHISES
RHACHITIS
RHAGADES
RHAMNOSE
RHAMNOSES
RHAMNUS
RHAMNUSES
RHAMPHOID
RHANJA
RHANJAS
RHAPHAE
RHAPHE

R

RHAPHES
RHAPHIDE
RHAPHIDES
RHAPHIS
RHAPONTIC
RHAPSODE
RHAPSODES
RHAPSODIC
RHAPSODY
RHATANIES
RHATANY
RHEA
RHEAS
RHEBOK
RHEBOKS
RHEMATIC
RHEME
RHEMES
RHENIUM
RHENIUMS
RHEOBASE
RHEOBASES
RHEOBASIC
RHEOCHORD
RHEOCORD
RHEOCORDS
RHEOLOGIC
RHEOLOGY
RHEOMETER
RHEOMETRY
RHEOPHIL
RHEOPHILE
RHEOSCOPE
RHEOSTAT
RHEOSTATS
RHEOTAXES
RHEOTAXIS
RHEOTOME
RHEOTOMES
RHEOTROPE
RHESUS
RHESUSES
RHETOR
RHETORIC
RHETORICS
RHETORISE
RHETORIZE
RHETORS
RHEUM
RHEUMATIC
RHEUMATIZ
RHEUMED
RHEUMIC
RHEUMIER
RHEUMIEST
RHEUMS
RHEUMY
RHEXES
RHEXIS
RHEXISES
RHIES
RHIGOLENE
RHIME
RHIMES
RHINAL
RHINE
RHINES
RHINITIC
RHINITIS
RHINO
RHINOCERI
RHINOLITH
RHINOLOGY
RHINOS
RHIPIDATE
RHIPIDION
RHIPIDIUM
RHIZIC
RHIZINE
RHIZINES
RHIZOBIA
RHIZOBIAL
RHIZOBIUM
RHIZOCARP
RHIZOCAUL
RHIZOID
RHIZOIDAL
RHIZOIDS
RHIZOMA
RHIZOMATA
RHIZOME
RHIZOMES
RHIZOMIC
RHIZOPI
RHIZOPOD
RHIZOPODS
RHIZOPUS
RHIZOTOMY
RHO
RHODAMIN
RHODAMINE
RHODAMINS
RHODANATE
RHODANIC
RHODANISE
RHODANIZE
RHODIC
RHODIE
RHODIES
RHODINAL
RHODINALS
RHODIUM
RHODIUMS
RHODOLITE
RHODONITE
RHODOPSIN
RHODORA
RHODORAS
RHODOUS
RHODY
RHOEADINE
RHOMB
RHOMBI
RHOMBIC
RHOMBICAL
RHOMBOI
RHOMBOID
RHOMBOIDS
RHOMBOS
RHOMBS
RHOMBUS
RHOMBUSES
RHONCHAL
RHONCHI
RHONCHIAL
RHONCHUS
RHONCUS
RHONCUSES
RHONE
RHONES
RHOPALIC
RHOPALISM
RHOS
RHOTACISE
RHOTACISM
RHOTACIST
RHOTACIZE
RHOTIC
RHOTICITY
RHUBARB
RHUBARBED
RHUBARBS
RHUBARBY
RHUMB
RHUMBA
RHUMBAED
RHUMBAING
RHUMBAS
RHUMBS
RHUS
RHUSES
RHY
RHYME
RHYMED
RHYMELESS
RHYMER
RHYMERS
RHYMES
RHYMESTER
RHYMING
RHYMIST
RHYMISTS
RHYNE
RHYNES
RHYOLITE
RHYOLITES
RHYOLITIC
RHYTA
RHYTHM
RHYTHMAL
RHYTHMED
RHYTHMI
RHYTHMIC
RHYTHMICS
RHYTHMISE
RHYTHMIST
RHYTHMIZE
RHYTHMS
RHYTHMUS
RHYTIDOME
RHYTINA
RHYTINAS
RHYTON
RHYTONS
RIA
RIAD
RIADS
RIAL
RIALS
RIALTO
RIALTOS
RIANCIES
RIANCY
RIANT
RIANTLY
RIAS
RIATA
RIATAS
RIB
RIBA
RIBALD
RIBALDER
RIBALDEST
RIBALDLY
RIBALDRY
RIBALDS
RIBAND
RIBANDS
RIBAS
RIBATTUTA
RIBAUD
RIBAUDRED
RIBAUDRY
RIBAUDS
RIBAVIRIN
RIBBAND
RIBBANDS
RIBBED
RIBBER
RIBBERS
RIBBIE
RIBBIER
RIBBIES
RIBBIEST
RIBBING
RIBBINGS
RIBBIT
RIBBITS
RIBBON
RIBBONED

RIBBONIER
RIBBONING
RIBBONRY
RIBBONS
RIBBONY
RIBBY
RIBCAGE
RIBCAGES
RIBES
RIBEYE
RIBEYES
RIBGRASS
RIBIBE
RIBIBES
RIBIBLE
RIBIBLES
RIBIER
RIBIERS
RIBLESS
RIBLET
RIBLETS
RIBLIKE
RIBOSE
RIBOSES
RIBOSOMAL
RIBOSOME
RIBOSOMES
RIBOZYMAL
RIBOZYME
RIBOZYMES
RIBS
RIBSTON
RIBSTONE
RIBSTONES
RIBSTONS
RIBULOSE
RIBULOSES
RIBWORK
RIBWORKS
RIBWORT
RIBWORTS
RICE
RICEBIRD
RICEBIRDS
RICED
RICEFIELD
RICEGRASS
RICER
RICERCAR
RICERCARE
RICERCARI
RICERCARS
RICERCATA
RICERS
RICES
RICEY
RICH
RICHED
RICHEN
RICHENED
RICHENING
RICHENS
RICHER
RICHES
RICHESSE
RICHESSES
RICHEST
RICHING
RICHLY
RICHNESS
RICHT
RICHTED
RICHTER
RICHTEST
RICHTING
RICHTS
RICHWEED
RICHWEEDS
RICIER
RICIEST
RICIN
RICING
RICINS
RICINUS
RICINUSES
RICK
RICKED
RICKER
RICKERS
RICKET
RICKETIER
RICKETILY
RICKETS
RICKETTY
RICKETY
RICKEY
RICKEYS
RICKING
RICKLE
RICKLES
RICKLIER
RICKLIEST
RICKLY
RICKRACK
RICKRACKS
RICKS
RICKSHA
RICKSHAS
RICKSHAW
RICKSHAWS
RICKSTAND
RICKSTICK
RICKYARD
RICKYARDS
RICOCHET
RICOCHETS
RICOTTA
RICOTTAS
RICRAC
RICRACS
RICTAL
RICTUS
RICTUSES
RICY
RID
RIDABLE
RIDDANCE
RIDDANCES
RIDDED
RIDDEN
RIDDER
RIDDERS
RIDDING
RIDDLE
RIDDLED
RIDDLER
RIDDLERS
RIDDLES
RIDDLING
RIDDLINGS
RIDE
RIDEABLE
RIDENT
RIDER
RIDERED
RIDERLESS
RIDERS
RIDERSHIP
RIDES
RIDGE
RIDGEBACK
RIDGED
RIDGEL
RIDGELIKE
RIDGELINE
RIDGELING
RIDGELS
RIDGEPOLE
RIDGER
RIDGERS
RIDGES
RIDGETOP
RIDGETOPS
RIDGETREE
RIDGEWAY
RIDGEWAYS
RIDGIER
RIDGIEST
RIDGIL
RIDGILS
RIDGING
RIDGINGS
RIDGLING
RIDGLINGS
RIDGY
RIDIC
RIDICULE
RIDICULED
RIDICULER
RIDICULES
RIDING
RIDINGS
RIDLEY
RIDLEYS
RIDOTTO
RIDOTTOS
RIDS
RIEL
RIELS
RIEM
RIEMPIE
RIEMPIES
RIEMS
RIESLING
RIESLINGS
RIEVE
RIEVED
RIEVER
RIEVERS
RIEVES
RIEVING
RIF
RIFAMPIN
RIFAMPINS
RIFAMYCIN
RIFE
RIFELY
RIFENESS
RIFER
RIFEST
RIFF
RIFFAGE
RIFFAGES
RIFFED
RIFFING
RIFFLE
RIFFLED
RIFFLER
RIFFLERS
RIFFLES
RIFFLING
RIFFOLA
RIFFOLAS
RIFFRAFF
RIFFRAFFS
RIFFS
RIFLE
RIFLEBIRD
RIFLED
RIFLEMAN
RIFLEMEN
RIFLER
RIFLERIES
RIFLERS
RIFLERY
RIFLES
RIFLING
RIFLINGS
RIFLIP
RIFLIPS

RIFS
RIFT
RIFTE
RIFTED
RIFTIER
RIFTIEST
RIFTING
RIFTLESS
RIFTS
RIFTY
RIG
RIGADOON
RIGADOONS
RIGATONI
RIGATONIS
RIGAUDON
RIGAUDONS
RIGG
RIGGALD
RIGGALDS
RIGGED
RIGGER
RIGGERS
RIGGING
RIGGINGS
RIGGISH
RIGGS
RIGHT
RIGHTABLE
RIGHTABLY
RIGHTED
RIGHTEN
RIGHTENED
RIGHTENS
RIGHTEOUS
RIGHTER
RIGHTERS
RIGHTEST
RIGHTFUL
RIGHTIER
RIGHTIES
RIGHTIEST
RIGHTING
RIGHTINGS
RIGHTISH
RIGHTISM
RIGHTISMS
RIGHTIST
RIGHTISTS
RIGHTLESS
RIGHTLY
RIGHTMOST
RIGHTNESS
RIGHTO
RIGHTS
RIGHTSIZE
RIGHTWARD
RIGHTY
RIGID
RIGIDER
RIGIDEST
RIGIDIFY
RIGIDISE
RIGIDISED
RIGIDISES
RIGIDITY
RIGIDIZE
RIGIDIZED
RIGIDIZES
RIGIDLY
RIGIDNESS
RIGIDS
RIGLIN
RIGLING
RIGLINGS
RIGLINS
RIGMAROLE
RIGOL
RIGOLL
RIGOLLS
RIGOLS
RIGOR
RIGORISM
RIGORISMS
RIGORIST
RIGORISTS
RIGOROUS
RIGORS
RIGOUR
RIGOURS
RIGOUT
RIGOUTS
RIGS
RIGSDALER
RIGWIDDIE
RIGWOODIE
RIJSTAFEL
RIKISHA
RIKISHAS
RIKISHI
RIKSHAW
RIKSHAWS
RILE
RILED
RILES
RILEY
RILIER
RILIEST
RILIEVI
RILIEVO
RILING
RILL
RILLE
RILLED
RILLES
RILLET
RILLETS
RILLETTES
RILLING
RILLMARK
RILLMARKS
RILLS
RIM
RIMA
RIMAE
RIMAYE
RIMAYES
RIME
RIMED
RIMELESS
RIMER
RIMERS
RIMES
RIMESTER
RIMESTERS
RIMFIRE
RIMFIRES
RIMIER
RIMIEST
RIMINESS
RIMING
RIMLAND
RIMLANDS
RIMLESS
RIMMED
RIMMER
RIMMERS
RIMMING
RIMMINGS
RIMOSE
RIMOSELY
RIMOSITY
RIMOUS
RIMPLE
RIMPLED
RIMPLES
RIMPLING
RIMROCK
RIMROCKS
RIMS
RIMSHOT
RIMSHOTS
RIMU
RIMUS
RIMY
RIN
RIND
RINDED
RINDIER
RINDIEST
RINDING
RINDLESS
RINDS
RINDY
RINE
RINES
RING
RINGBARK
RINGBARKS
RINGBIT
RINGBITS
RINGBOLT
RINGBOLTS
RINGBONE
RINGBONES
RINGDOVE
RINGDOVES
RINGED
RINGENT
RINGER
RINGERS
RINGETTE
RINGETTES
RINGGIT
RINGGITS
RINGHALS
RINGING
RINGINGLY
RINGINGS
RINGLESS
RINGLET
RINGLETED
RINGLETS
RINGLETY
RINGLIKE
RINGMAN
RINGMEN
RINGNECK
RINGNECKS
RINGS
RINGSIDE
RINGSIDER
RINGSIDES
RINGSTAND
RINGSTER
RINGSTERS
RINGTAIL
RINGTAILS
RINGTAW
RINGTAWS
RINGTONE
RINGTONES
RINGTOSS
RINGWAY
RINGWAYS
RINGWISE
RINGWOMB
RINGWOMBS
RINGWORK
RINGWORKS
RINGWORM
RINGWORMS
RINK
RINKED
RINKHALS
RINKING
RINKS
RINKSIDE
RINKSIDES
RINNING

R

RINS
RINSABLE
RINSE
RINSEABLE
RINSED
RINSER
RINSERS
RINSES
RINSIBLE
RINSING
RINSINGS
RIOJA
RIOJAS
RIOT
RIOTED
RIOTER
RIOTERS
RIOTING
RIOTINGS
RIOTISE
RIOTISES
RIOTIZE
RIOTIZES
RIOTOUS
RIOTOUSLY
RIOTRIES
RIOTRY
RIOTS
RIP
RIPARIAL
RIPARIALS
RIPARIAN
RIPARIANS
RIPCORD
RIPCORDS
RIPE
RIPECK
RIPECKS
RIPED
RIPELY
RIPEN
RIPENED
RIPENER
RIPENERS
RIPENESS
RIPENING
RIPENS
RIPER
RIPERS
RIPES
RIPEST
RIPIENI
RIPIENIST
RIPIENO
RIPIENOS
RIPING
RIPOFF
RIPOFFS
RIPOST
RIPOSTE
RIPOSTED
RIPOSTES
RIPOSTING
RIPOSTS
RIPP
RIPPABLE
RIPPED
RIPPER
RIPPERS
RIPPIER
RIPPIERS
RIPPING
RIPPINGLY
RIPPINGS
RIPPLE
RIPPLED
RIPPLER
RIPPLERS
RIPPLES
RIPPLET
RIPPLETS
RIPPLIER
RIPPLIEST
RIPPLING
RIPPLINGS
RIPPLY
RIPPS
RIPRAP
RIPRAPPED
RIPRAPS
RIPS
RIPSAW
RIPSAWED
RIPSAWING
RIPSAWN
RIPSAWS
RIPSTOP
RIPSTOPS
RIPT
RIPTIDE
RIPTIDES
RIRORIRO
RIRORIROS
RISALDAR
RISALDARS
RISE
RISEN
RISER
RISERS
RISES
RISHI
RISHIS
RISIBLE
RISIBLES
RISIBLY
RISING
RISINGS
RISK
RISKED
RISKER
RISKERS
RISKFUL
RISKIER
RISKIEST
RISKILY
RISKINESS
RISKING
RISKLESS
RISKS
RISKY
RISOLUTO
RISORII
RISORIUS
RISOTTO
RISOTTOS
RISP
RISPED
RISPETTI
RISPETTO
RISPING
RISPINGS
RISPS
RISQUE
RISQUES
RISSOLE
RISSOLES
RISTRA
RISTRAS
RISTRETTO
RISUS
RISUSES
RIT
RITARD
RITARDS
RITE
RITELESS
RITENUTO
RITENUTOS
RITES
RITONAVIR
RITORNEL
RITORNELL
RITORNELS
RITS
RITT
RITTED
RITTER
RITTERS
RITTING
RITTS
RITUAL
RITUALISE
RITUALISM
RITUALIST
RITUALIZE
RITUALLY
RITUALS
RITUXIMAB
RITZ
RITZES
RITZIER
RITZIEST
RITZILY
RITZINESS
RITZY
RIVA
RIVAGE
RIVAGES
RIVAL
RIVALED
RIVALESS
RIVALING
RIVALISE
RIVALISED
RIVALISES
RIVALITY
RIVALIZE
RIVALIZED
RIVALIZES
RIVALLED
RIVALLESS
RIVALLING
RIVALRIES
RIVALROUS
RIVALRY
RIVALS
RIVALSHIP
RIVAS
RIVE
RIVED
RIVEL
RIVELLED
RIVELLING
RIVELS
RIVEN
RIVER
RIVERAIN
RIVERAINS
RIVERBANK
RIVERBED
RIVERBEDS
RIVERBOAT
RIVERED
RIVERET
RIVERETS
RIVERHEAD
RIVERIER
RIVERIEST
RIVERINE
RIVERLESS
RIVERLIKE
RIVERMAN
RIVERMEN
RIVERS
RIVERSIDE
RIVERWALK
RIVERWARD
RIVERWAY
RIVERWAYS
RIVERWEED

RIVERY
RIVES
RIVET
RIVETED
RIVETER
RIVETERS
RIVETING
RIVETINGS
RIVETS
RIVETTED
RIVETTING
RIVIERA
RIVIERAS
RIVIERE
RIVIERES
RIVING
RIVLIN
RIVLINS
RIVO
RIVULET
RIVULETS
RIVULOSE
RIVULUS
RIVULUSES
RIYAL
RIYALS
RIZ
RIZA
RIZARD
RIZARDS
RIZAS
RIZZAR
RIZZARED
RIZZARING
RIZZARS
RIZZART
RIZZARTS
RIZZER
RIZZERED
RIZZERING
RIZZERS
RIZZOR
RIZZORED
RIZZORING
RIZZORS
ROACH
ROACHED
ROACHES
ROACHING
ROAD
ROADBED
ROADBEDS
ROADBLOCK
ROADCRAFT
ROADEO
ROADEOS
ROADHOG
ROADHOGS
ROADHOUSE
ROADIE
ROADIES
ROADING
ROADINGS
ROADKILL
ROADKILLS
ROADLESS
ROADMAN
ROADMEN
ROADS
ROADSHOW
ROADSHOWS
ROADSIDE
ROADSIDES
ROADSMAN
ROADSMEN
ROADSTEAD
ROADSTER
ROADSTERS
ROADWAY
ROADWAYS
ROADWORK
ROADWORKS
ROAM
ROAMED
ROAMER
ROAMERS
ROAMING
ROAMINGS
ROAMS
ROAN
ROANPIPE
ROANPIPES
ROANS
ROAR
ROARED
ROARER
ROARERS
ROARIE
ROARIER
ROARIEST
ROARING
ROARINGLY
ROARINGS
ROARMING
ROARS
ROARY
ROAST
ROASTED
ROASTER
ROASTERS
ROASTIE
ROASTIES
ROASTING
ROASTINGS
ROASTS
ROATE
ROATED
ROATES
ROATING
ROB
ROBALO
ROBALOS
ROBAND
ROBANDS
ROBATA
ROBATAS
ROBBED
ROBBER
ROBBERIES
ROBBERS
ROBBERY
ROBBIN
ROBBING
ROBBINS
ROBE
ROBED
ROBELIKE
ROBES
ROBIN
ROBING
ROBINGS
ROBINIA
ROBINIAS
ROBINS
ROBLE
ROBLES
ROBOCALL
ROBOCALLS
ROBORANT
ROBORANTS
ROBOT
ROBOTIC
ROBOTICS
ROBOTISE
ROBOTISED
ROBOTISES
ROBOTISM
ROBOTISMS
ROBOTIZE
ROBOTIZED
ROBOTIZES
ROBOTRIES
ROBOTRY
ROBOTS
ROBS
ROBURITE
ROBURITES
ROBUST
ROBUSTA
ROBUSTAS
ROBUSTER
ROBUSTEST
ROBUSTLY
ROC
ROCAILLE
ROCAILLES
ROCAMBOLE
ROCH
ROCHES
ROCHET
ROCHETS
ROCK
ROCKABIES
ROCKABLE
ROCKABY
ROCKABYE
ROCKABYES
ROCKAWAY
ROCKAWAYS
ROCKBOUND
ROCKBURST
ROCKCRESS
ROCKED
ROCKER
ROCKERIES
ROCKERS
ROCKERY
ROCKET
ROCKETED
ROCKETEER
ROCKETER
ROCKETERS
ROCKETING
ROCKETRY
ROCKETS
ROCKFALL
ROCKFALLS
ROCKFISH
ROCKHOUND
ROCKIER
ROCKIERS
ROCKIEST
ROCKILY
ROCKINESS
ROCKING
ROCKINGLY
ROCKINGS
ROCKLAY
ROCKLAYS
ROCKLESS
ROCKLIKE
ROCKLING
ROCKLINGS
ROCKOON
ROCKOONS
ROCKROSE
ROCKROSES
ROCKS
ROCKSHAFT
ROCKSLIDE
ROCKWATER
ROCKWEED
ROCKWEEDS
ROCKWOOL
ROCKWOOLS
ROCKWORK
ROCKWORKS
ROCKY
ROCOCO
ROCOCOS

R

ROCQUET
ROCQUETS
ROCS
ROD
RODDED
RODDING
RODDINGS
RODE
RODED
RODENT
RODENTIAL
RODENTS
RODEO
RODEOED
RODEOING
RODEOS
RODES
RODEWAY
RODEWAYS
RODFISHER
RODGERSIA
RODING
RODINGS
RODLESS
RODLIKE
RODMAN
RODMEN
RODNEY
RODNEYS
RODS
RODSMAN
RODSMEN
RODSTER
RODSTERS
ROE
ROEBUCK
ROEBUCKS
ROED
ROEMER
ROEMERS
ROENTGEN
ROENTGENS
ROES
ROESTI
ROESTIS
ROESTONE
ROESTONES
ROGALLO
ROGALLOS
ROGATION
ROGATIONS
ROGATORY
ROGER
ROGERED
ROGERING
ROGERINGS
ROGERS
ROGNON
ROGNONS
ROGUE
ROGUED
ROGUEING
ROGUER
ROGUERIES
ROGUERS
ROGUERY
ROGUES
ROGUESHIP
ROGUIER
ROGUIEST
ROGUING
ROGUISH
ROGUISHLY
ROGUY
ROHE
ROHES
ROID
ROIDS
ROIL
ROILED
ROILIER
ROILIEST
ROILING
ROILS
ROILY
ROIN
ROINED
ROINING
ROINISH
ROINS
ROIST
ROISTED
ROISTER
ROISTERED
ROISTERER
ROISTERS
ROISTING
ROISTS
ROJAK
ROJAKS
ROJI
ROJIS
ROK
ROKE
ROKED
ROKELAY
ROKELAYS
ROKER
ROKERS
ROKES
ROKIER
ROKIEST
ROKING
ROKKAKU
ROKS
ROKY
ROLAG
ROLAGS
ROLAMITE
ROLAMITES
ROLE
ROLES
ROLF
ROLFED
ROLFER
ROLFERS
ROLFING
ROLFINGS
ROLFS
ROLL
ROLLABLE
ROLLAWAY
ROLLAWAYS
ROLLBACK
ROLLBACKS
ROLLBAR
ROLLBARS
ROLLED
ROLLER
ROLLERS
ROLLICK
ROLLICKED
ROLLICKS
ROLLICKY
ROLLIE
ROLLIES
ROLLING
ROLLINGS
ROLLMOP
ROLLMOPS
ROLLNECK
ROLLNECKS
ROLLOCK
ROLLOCKS
ROLLOUT
ROLLOUTS
ROLLOVER
ROLLOVERS
ROLLS
ROLLTOP
ROLLUP
ROLLUPS
ROLLWAY
ROLLWAYS
ROM
ROMA
ROMAGE
ROMAGES
ROMAIKA
ROMAIKAS
ROMAINE
ROMAINES
ROMAJI
ROMAJIS
ROMAL
ROMALS
ROMAN
ROMANCE
ROMANCED
ROMANCER
ROMANCERS
ROMANCES
ROMANCING
ROMANESCO
ROMANISE
ROMANISED
ROMANISES
ROMANIZE
ROMANIZED
ROMANIZES
ROMANO
ROMANOS
ROMANS
ROMANTIC
ROMANTICS
ROMANZA
ROMANZAS
ROMAUNT
ROMAUNTS
ROMCOM
ROMCOMS
ROMELDALE
ROMEO
ROMEOS
ROMNEYA
ROMNEYAS
ROMP
ROMPED
ROMPER
ROMPERS
ROMPING
ROMPINGLY
ROMPISH
ROMPISHLY
ROMPS
ROMS
RONCADOR
RONCADORS
RONDACHE
RONDACHES
RONDAVEL
RONDAVELS
RONDE
RONDEAU
RONDEAUX
RONDEL
RONDELET
RONDELETS
RONDELLE
RONDELLES
RONDELS
RONDES
RONDINO
RONDINOS
RONDO
RONDOS
RONDURE
RONDURES
RONE
RONEO

RONEOED
RONEOING
RONEOS
RONEPIPE
RONEPIPES
RONES
RONG
RONGGENG
RONGGENGS
RONIN
RONINS
RONION
RONIONS
RONNE
RONNEL
RONNELS
RONNIE
RONNIES
RONNING
RONT
RONTE
RONTES
RONTGEN
RONTGENS
RONTS
RONYON
RONYONS
RONZ
RONZER
RONZERS
ROO
ROOD
ROODS
ROOF
ROOFED
ROOFER
ROOFERS
ROOFIE
ROOFIER
ROOFIES
ROOFIEST
ROOFING
ROOFINGS
ROOFLESS
ROOFLIKE
ROOFLINE
ROOFLINES
ROOFS
ROOFSCAPE
ROOFTOP
ROOFTOPS
ROOFTREE
ROOFTREES
ROOFY
ROOIBOS
ROOIBOSES
ROOIKAT
ROOIKATS
ROOINEK
ROOINEKS
ROOK
ROOKED
ROOKERIES
ROOKERY
ROOKIE
ROOKIER
ROOKIES
ROOKIEST
ROOKING
ROOKISH
ROOKS
ROOKY
ROOM
ROOMED
ROOMER
ROOMERS
ROOMETTE
ROOMETTES
ROOMFUL
ROOMFULS
ROOMIE
ROOMIER
ROOMIES
ROOMIEST
ROOMILY
ROOMINESS
ROOMING
ROOMMATE
ROOMMATES
ROOMS
ROOMSFUL
ROOMSOME
ROOMY
ROON
ROONS
ROOP
ROOPED
ROOPIER
ROOPIEST
ROOPING
ROOPIT
ROOPS
ROOPY
ROORBACH
ROORBACHS
ROORBACK
ROORBACKS
ROOS
ROOSA
ROOSAS
ROOSE
ROOSED
ROOSER
ROOSERS
ROOSES
ROOSING
ROOST
ROOSTED
ROOSTER
ROOSTERS
ROOSTING
ROOSTS
ROOT
ROOTAGE
ROOTAGES
ROOTBALL
ROOTBALLS
ROOTBOUND
ROOTCAP
ROOTCAPS
ROOTED
ROOTEDLY
ROOTER
ROOTERS
ROOTHOLD
ROOTHOLDS
ROOTIER
ROOTIES
ROOTIEST
ROOTINESS
ROOTING
ROOTINGS
ROOTKIT
ROOTKITS
ROOTLE
ROOTLED
ROOTLES
ROOTLESS
ROOTLET
ROOTLETS
ROOTLIKE
ROOTLING
ROOTS
ROOTSIER
ROOTSIEST
ROOTSTALK
ROOTSTOCK
ROOTSY
ROOTWORM
ROOTWORMS
ROOTY
ROPABLE
ROPE
ROPEABLE
ROPED
ROPELIKE
ROPER
ROPERIES
ROPERS
ROPERY
ROPES
ROPEWALK
ROPEWALKS
ROPEWAY
ROPEWAYS
ROPEWORK
ROPEWORKS
ROPEY
ROPIER
ROPIEST
ROPILY
ROPINESS
ROPING
ROPINGS
ROPY
ROQUE
ROQUEFORT
ROQUES
ROQUET
ROQUETED
ROQUETING
ROQUETS
ROQUETTE
ROQUETTES
RORAL
RORE
RORES
RORIC
RORID
RORIE
RORIER
RORIEST
RORQUAL
RORQUALS
RORT
RORTED
RORTER
RORTERS
RORTIER
RORTIEST
RORTING
RORTINGS
RORTS
RORTY
RORY
ROSACE
ROSACEA
ROSACEAS
ROSACEOUS
ROSACES
ROSAKER
ROSAKERS
ROSALIA
ROSALIAS
ROSANILIN
ROSARIA
ROSARIAN
ROSARIANS
ROSARIES
ROSARIUM
ROSARIUMS
ROSARY
ROSBIF
ROSBIFS
ROSCID
ROSCOE
ROSCOES
ROSE
ROSEAL
ROSEATE

R

ROSEATELY
ROSEBAY
ROSEBAYS
ROSEBED
ROSEBEDS
ROSEBOWL
ROSEBOWLS
ROSEBUD
ROSEBUDS
ROSEBUSH
ROSED
ROSEFINCH
ROSEFISH
ROSEHIP
ROSEHIPS
ROSELESS
ROSELIKE
ROSELLA
ROSELLAS
ROSELLE
ROSELLES
ROSEMARY
ROSEOLA
ROSEOLAR
ROSEOLAS
ROSERIES
ROSEROOT
ROSEROOTS
ROSERY
ROSES
ROSESLUG
ROSESLUGS
ROSET
ROSETED
ROSETING
ROSETS
ROSETTE
ROSETTED
ROSETTES
ROSETTING
ROSETTY
ROSETY
ROSEWATER
ROSEWOOD
ROSEWOODS
ROSHAMBO
ROSHAMBOS
ROSHI
ROSHIS
ROSIED
ROSIER
ROSIERE
ROSIERES
ROSIERS
ROSIES
ROSIEST
ROSILY
ROSIN
ROSINATE
ROSINATES
ROSINED
ROSINER
ROSINERS
ROSINESS
ROSING
ROSINIER
ROSINIEST
ROSINING
ROSINOL
ROSINOLS
ROSINOUS
ROSINS
ROSINWEED
ROSINY
ROSIT
ROSITED
ROSITING
ROSITS
ROSMARINE
ROSOGLIO
ROSOGLIOS
ROSOLIO
ROSOLIOS
ROSSER
ROSSERS
ROST
ROSTED
ROSTELLA
ROSTELLAR
ROSTELLUM
ROSTER
ROSTERED
ROSTERING
ROSTERS
ROSTI
ROSTING
ROSTIS
ROSTRA
ROSTRAL
ROSTRALLY
ROSTRATE
ROSTRATED
ROSTRUM
ROSTRUMS
ROSTS
ROSULA
ROSULAS
ROSULATE
ROSY
ROSYING
ROT
ROTA
ROTACHUTE
ROTAL
ROTAMETER
ROTAN
ROTANS
ROTAPLANE
ROTARIES
ROTARY
ROTAS
ROTATABLE
ROTATE
ROTATED
ROTATES
ROTATING
ROTATION
ROTATIONS
ROTATIVE
ROTATOR
ROTATORES
ROTATORS
ROTATORY
ROTAVATE
ROTAVATED
ROTAVATES
ROTAVATOR
ROTAVIRAL
ROTAVIRUS
ROTCH
ROTCHE
ROTCHES
ROTCHIE
ROTCHIES
ROTE
ROTED
ROTELY
ROTENONE
ROTENONES
ROTES
ROTGRASS
ROTGUT
ROTGUTS
ROTHER
ROTHERS
ROTI
ROTIFER
ROTIFERAL
ROTIFERAN
ROTIFERS
ROTIFORM
ROTING
ROTINI
ROTINIS
ROTIS
ROTL
ROTLS
ROTO
ROTOGRAPH
ROTOLI
ROTOLO
ROTOLOS
ROTON
ROTONS
ROTOR
ROTORS
ROTOS
ROTOSCOPE
ROTOTILL
ROTOTILLS
ROTOVATE
ROTOVATED
ROTOVATES
ROTOVATOR
ROTPROOF
ROTS
ROTTAN
ROTTANS
ROTTE
ROTTED
ROTTEN
ROTTENER
ROTTENEST
ROTTENLY
ROTTENS
ROTTER
ROTTERS
ROTTES
ROTTING
ROTULA
ROTULAE
ROTULAS
ROTUND
ROTUNDA
ROTUNDAS
ROTUNDATE
ROTUNDED
ROTUNDER
ROTUNDEST
ROTUNDING
ROTUNDITY
ROTUNDLY
ROTUNDS
ROTURIER
ROTURIERS
ROUBLE
ROUBLES
ROUCHE
ROUCHED
ROUCHES
ROUCHING
ROUCHINGS
ROUCOU
ROUCOUS
ROUE
ROUEN
ROUENS
ROUES
ROUGE
ROUGED
ROUGES
ROUGH
ROUGHAGE
ROUGHAGES
ROUGHBACK
ROUGHCAST
ROUGHDRY
ROUGHED
ROUGHEN
ROUGHENED

R

ROUGHENS
ROUGHER
ROUGHERS
ROUGHEST
ROUGHHEW
ROUGHHEWN
ROUGHHEWS
ROUGHIE
ROUGHIES
ROUGHING
ROUGHINGS
ROUGHISH
ROUGHLEG
ROUGHLEGS
ROUGHLY
ROUGHNECK
ROUGHNESS
ROUGHOUT
ROUGHOUTS
ROUGHS
ROUGHSHOD
ROUGHT
ROUGHY
ROUGING
ROUILLE
ROUILLES
ROUL
ROULADE
ROULADES
ROULE
ROULEAU
ROULEAUS
ROULEAUX
ROULES
ROULETTE
ROULETTED
ROULETTES
ROULS
ROUM
ROUMING
ROUMINGS
ROUMS
ROUNCE
ROUNCES
ROUNCEVAL
ROUNCIES
ROUNCY
ROUND
ROUNDARCH
ROUNDBALL
ROUNDED
ROUNDEDLY
ROUNDEL
ROUNDELAY
ROUNDELS
ROUNDER
ROUNDERS
ROUNDEST
ROUNDHAND
ROUNDHEEL
ROUNDING
ROUNDINGS
ROUNDISH
ROUNDLE
ROUNDLES
ROUNDLET
ROUNDLETS
ROUNDLY
ROUNDNESS
ROUNDS
ROUNDSMAN
ROUNDSMEN
ROUNDTRIP
ROUNDUP
ROUNDUPS
ROUNDURE
ROUNDURES
ROUNDWOOD
ROUNDWORM
ROUP
ROUPED
ROUPET
ROUPIER
ROUPIEST
ROUPILY
ROUPING
ROUPIT
ROUPS
ROUPY
ROUSABLE
ROUSANT
ROUSE
ROUSED
ROUSEMENT
ROUSER
ROUSERS
ROUSES
ROUSING
ROUSINGLY
ROUSSEAU
ROUSSEAUS
ROUSSETTE
ROUST
ROUSTED
ROUSTER
ROUSTERS
ROUSTING
ROUSTS
ROUT
ROUTE
ROUTED
ROUTEING
ROUTEMAN
ROUTEMEN
ROUTER
ROUTERS
ROUTES
ROUTEWAY
ROUTEWAYS
ROUTH
ROUTHIE
ROUTHIER
ROUTHIEST
ROUTHS
ROUTINE
ROUTINEER
ROUTINELY
ROUTINES
ROUTING
ROUTINGS
ROUTINISE
ROUTINISM
ROUTINIST
ROUTINIZE
ROUTOUS
ROUTOUSLY
ROUTS
ROUX
ROVE
ROVED
ROVEN
ROVER
ROVERS
ROVES
ROVING
ROVINGLY
ROVINGS
ROW
ROWABLE
ROWAN
ROWANS
ROWBOAT
ROWBOATS
ROWDEDOW
ROWDEDOWS
ROWDIER
ROWDIES
ROWDIEST
ROWDILY
ROWDINESS
ROWDY
ROWDYDOW
ROWDYDOWS
ROWDYISH
ROWDYISM
ROWDYISMS
ROWED
ROWEL
ROWELED
ROWELING
ROWELLED
ROWELLING
ROWELS
ROWEN
ROWENS
ROWER
ROWERS
ROWIE
ROWIES
ROWING
ROWINGS
ROWLOCK
ROWLOCKS
ROWME
ROWMES
ROWND
ROWNDED
ROWNDELL
ROWNDELLS
ROWNDING
ROWNDS
ROWOVER
ROWOVERS
ROWS
ROWT
ROWTED
ROWTH
ROWTHS
ROWTING
ROWTS
ROYAL
ROYALET
ROYALETS
ROYALISE
ROYALISED
ROYALISES
ROYALISM
ROYALISMS
ROYALIST
ROYALISTS
ROYALIZE
ROYALIZED
ROYALIZES
ROYALLER
ROYALLEST
ROYALLY
ROYALMAST
ROYALS
ROYALTIES
ROYALTY
ROYNE
ROYNED
ROYNES
ROYNING
ROYNISH
ROYST
ROYSTED
ROYSTER
ROYSTERED
ROYSTERER
ROYSTERS
ROYSTING
ROYSTS
ROZELLE
ROZELLES
ROZET
ROZETED
ROZETING
ROZETS
ROZIT

ROZITED
ROZITING
ROZITS
ROZZER
ROZZERS
RUANA
RUANAS
RUB
RUBABOO
RUBABOOS
RUBACE
RUBACES
RUBAI
RUBAIS
RUBAIYAT
RUBASSE
RUBASSES
RUBATI
RUBATO
RUBATOS
RUBBABOO
RUBBABOOS
RUBBED
RUBBER
RUBBERED
RUBBERIER
RUBBERING
RUBBERISE
RUBBERIZE
RUBBERS
RUBBERY
RUBBET
RUBBIDIES
RUBBIDY
RUBBIES
RUBBING
RUBBINGS
RUBBISH
RUBBISHED
RUBBISHES
RUBBISHLY
RUBBISHY
RUBBIT
RUBBITIES
RUBBITY
RUBBLE
RUBBLED
RUBBLES
RUBBLIER
RUBBLIEST
RUBBLING
RUBBLY
RUBBOARD
RUBBOARDS
RUBBY
RUBBYDUB
RUBBYDUBS
RUBDOWN
RUBDOWNS
RUBE
RUBEFIED
RUBEFIES
RUBEFY
RUBEFYING
RUBEL
RUBELLA
RUBELLAN
RUBELLANS
RUBELLAS
RUBELLITE
RUBELS
RUBEOLA
RUBEOLAR
RUBEOLAS
RUBES
RUBESCENT
RUBICELLE
RUBICON
RUBICONED
RUBICONS
RUBICUND
RUBIDIC
RUBIDIUM
RUBIDIUMS
RUBIED
RUBIER
RUBIES
RUBIEST
RUBIFIED
RUBIFIES
RUBIFY
RUBIFYING
RUBIGO
RUBIGOS
RUBIN
RUBINE
RUBINEOUS
RUBINES
RUBINS
RUBIOUS
RUBLE
RUBLES
RUBLI
RUBOFF
RUBOFFS
RUBOUT
RUBOUTS
RUBRIC
RUBRICAL
RUBRICATE
RUBRICIAN
RUBRICS
RUBS
RUBSTONE
RUBSTONES
RUBUS
RUBUSES
RUBY
RUBYING
RUBYLIKE
RUC
RUCHE
RUCHED
RUCHES
RUCHING
RUCHINGS
RUCK
RUCKED
RUCKING
RUCKLE
RUCKLED
RUCKLES
RUCKLING
RUCKMAN
RUCKMEN
RUCKS
RUCKSACK
RUCKSACKS
RUCKSEAT
RUCKSEATS
RUCKUS
RUCKUSES
RUCOLA
RUCOLAS
RUCS
RUCTATION
RUCTION
RUCTIONS
RUCTIOUS
RUD
RUDACEOUS
RUDAS
RUDASES
RUDBECKIA
RUDD
RUDDED
RUDDER
RUDDERS
RUDDIED
RUDDIER
RUDDIES
RUDDIEST
RUDDILY
RUDDINESS
RUDDING
RUDDLE
RUDDLED
RUDDLEMAN
RUDDLEMEN
RUDDLES
RUDDLING
RUDDOCK
RUDDOCKS
RUDDS
RUDDY
RUDDYING
RUDE
RUDELY
RUDENESS
RUDER
RUDERAL
RUDERALS
RUDERIES
RUDERY
RUDES
RUDESBIES
RUDESBY
RUDEST
RUDI
RUDIE
RUDIES
RUDIMENT
RUDIMENTS
RUDIS
RUDISH
RUDIST
RUDISTID
RUDISTIDS
RUDISTS
RUDS
RUDY
RUE
RUED
RUEDA
RUEDAS
RUEFUL
RUEFULLY
RUEING
RUEINGS
RUELLE
RUELLES
RUELLIA
RUELLIAS
RUER
RUERS
RUES
RUFESCENT
RUFF
RUFFE
RUFFED
RUFFES
RUFFIAN
RUFFIANED
RUFFIANLY
RUFFIANS
RUFFIN
RUFFING
RUFFINS
RUFFLE
RUFFLED
RUFFLER
RUFFLERS
RUFFLES
RUFFLIER
RUFFLIEST
RUFFLIKE
RUFFLING
RUFFLINGS
RUFFLY
RUFFS

RUFIYAA
RUFIYAAS
RUFOUS
RUFOUSES
RUG
RUGA
RUGAE
RUGAL
RUGALACH
RUGATE
RUGBIES
RUGBY
RUGELACH
RUGELACHS
RUGGED
RUGGEDER
RUGGEDEST
RUGGEDISE
RUGGEDIZE
RUGGEDLY
RUGGELACH
RUGGER
RUGGERS
RUGGIER
RUGGIEST
RUGGING
RUGGINGS
RUGGY
RUGLIKE
RUGOLA
RUGOLAS
RUGOSA
RUGOSAS
RUGOSE
RUGOSELY
RUGOSITY
RUGOUS
RUGRAT
RUGRATS
RUGS
RUGULOSE
RUIN
RUINABLE
RUINATE
RUINATED
RUINATES
RUINATING
RUINATION
RUINED
RUINER
RUINERS
RUING
RUINGS
RUINING
RUININGS
RUINOUS
RUINOUSLY
RUINS
RUKH
RUKHS
RULABLE
RULE
RULED
RULELESS
RULER
RULERED
RULERING
RULERS
RULERSHIP
RULES
RULESSE
RULIER
RULIEST
RULING
RULINGS
RULLION
RULLIONS
RULLOCK
RULLOCKS
RULY
RUM
RUMAKI
RUMAKIS
RUMAL
RUMALS
RUMBA
RUMBAED
RUMBAING
RUMBAS
RUMBELOW
RUMBELOWS
RUMBLE
RUMBLED
RUMBLER
RUMBLERS
RUMBLES
RUMBLIER
RUMBLIEST
RUMBLING
RUMBLINGS
RUMBLY
RUMBO
RUMBOS
RUMDUM
RUMDUMS
RUME
RUMEN
RUMENS
RUMES
RUMINA
RUMINAL
RUMINANT
RUMINANTS
RUMINATE
RUMINATED
RUMINATES
RUMINATOR
RUMKIN
RUMKINS
RUMLY
RUMMAGE
RUMMAGED
RUMMAGER
RUMMAGERS
RUMMAGES
RUMMAGING
RUMMER
RUMMERS
RUMMEST
RUMMIER
RUMMIES
RUMMIEST
RUMMILY
RUMMINESS
RUMMISH
RUMMISHED
RUMMISHES
RUMMY
RUMNESS
RUMNESSES
RUMOR
RUMORED
RUMORER
RUMORERS
RUMORING
RUMOROUS
RUMORS
RUMOUR
RUMOURED
RUMOURER
RUMOURERS
RUMOURING
RUMOURS
RUMP
RUMPED
RUMPIER
RUMPIES
RUMPIEST
RUMPING
RUMPLE
RUMPLED
RUMPLES
RUMPLESS
RUMPLIER
RUMPLIEST
RUMPLING
RUMPLY
RUMPO
RUMPOS
RUMPOT
RUMPOTS
RUMPS
RUMPUS
RUMPUSES
RUMPY
RUMRUNNER
RUMS
RUN
RUNABOUT
RUNABOUTS
RUNAGATE
RUNAGATES
RUNANGA
RUNANGAS
RUNAROUND
RUNAWAY
RUNAWAYS
RUNBACK
RUNBACKS
RUNCH
RUNCHES
RUNCIBLE
RUNCINATE
RUND
RUNDALE
RUNDALES
RUNDLE
RUNDLED
RUNDLES
RUNDLET
RUNDLETS
RUNDOWN
RUNDOWNS
RUNDS
RUNE
RUNECRAFT
RUNED
RUNELIKE
RUNES
RUNFLAT
RUNFLATS
RUNG
RUNGED
RUNGLESS
RUNGS
RUNIC
RUNKLE
RUNKLED
RUNKLES
RUNKLING
RUNLESS
RUNLET
RUNLETS
RUNNABLE
RUNNEL
RUNNELS
RUNNER
RUNNERS
RUNNET
RUNNETS
RUNNIER
RUNNIEST
RUNNINESS
RUNNING
RUNNINGLY
RUNNINGS
RUNNION
RUNNIONS
RUNNY
RUNOFF

R

RUNOFFS
RUNOUT
RUNOUTS
RUNOVER
RUNOVERS
RUNPROOF
RUNRIG
RUNRIGS
RUNROUND
RUNROUNDS
RUNS
RUNT
RUNTED
RUNTIER
RUNTIEST
RUNTINESS
RUNTISH
RUNTISHLY
RUNTS
RUNTY
RUNWAY
RUNWAYS
RUPEE
RUPEES
RUPIA
RUPIAH
RUPIAHS
RUPIAS
RUPTURE
RUPTURED
RUPTURES
RUPTURING
RURAL
RURALISE
RURALISED
RURALISES
RURALISM
RURALISMS
RURALIST
RURALISTS
RURALITE
RURALITES
RURALITY
RURALIZE
RURALIZED
RURALIZES
RURALLY
RURALNESS
RURALS
RURBAN
RURP
RURPS
RURU
RURUS
RUSA
RUSALKA
RUSALKAS
RUSAS
RUSCUS
RUSCUSES
RUSE
RUSES
RUSH
RUSHED
RUSHEE
RUSHEES
RUSHEN
RUSHER
RUSHERS
RUSHES
RUSHIER
RUSHIEST
RUSHINESS
RUSHING
RUSHINGS
RUSHLIGHT
RUSHLIKE
RUSHY
RUSINE
RUSK
RUSKS
RUSMA
RUSMAS
RUSSE
RUSSEL
RUSSELS
RUSSET
RUSSETED
RUSSETIER
RUSSETING
RUSSETS
RUSSETY
RUSSIA
RUSSIAS
RUSSIFIED
RUSSIFIES
RUSSIFY
RUSSULA
RUSSULAE
RUSSULAS
RUST
RUSTABLE
RUSTED
RUSTIC
RUSTICAL
RUSTICALS
RUSTICANA
RUSTICATE
RUSTICIAL
RUSTICISE
RUSTICISM
RUSTICITY
RUSTICIZE
RUSTICLY
RUSTICS
RUSTIER
RUSTIEST
RUSTILY
RUSTINESS
RUSTING
RUSTINGS
RUSTLE
RUSTLED
RUSTLER
RUSTLERS
RUSTLES
RUSTLESS
RUSTLING
RUSTLINGS
RUSTPROOF
RUSTRE
RUSTRED
RUSTRES
RUSTS
RUSTY
RUT
RUTABAGA
RUTABAGAS
RUTACEOUS
RUTH
RUTHENIC
RUTHENIUM
RUTHER
RUTHFUL
RUTHFULLY
RUTHLESS
RUTHS
RUTILANT
RUTILATED
RUTILE
RUTILES
RUTIN
RUTINS
RUTS
RUTTED
RUTTER
RUTTERS
RUTTIER
RUTTIEST
RUTTILY
RUTTINESS
RUTTING
RUTTINGS
RUTTISH
RUTTISHLY
RUTTY
RYA
RYAL
RYALS
RYAS
RYBAT
RYBATS
RYBAUDRYE
RYE
RYEBREAD
RYEBREADS
RYEFLOUR
RYEFLOURS
RYEGRASS
RYEPECK
RYEPECKS
RYES
RYFE
RYKE
RYKED
RYKES
RYKING
RYMME
RYMMED
RYMMES
RYMMING
RYND
RYNDS
RYOKAN
RYOKANS
RYOT
RYOTS
RYOTWARI
RYOTWARIS
RYPE
RYPECK
RYPECKS
RYPER
RYU
RYUS

S

SAAG
SAAGS
SAB
SABADILLA
SABAL
SABALS
SABATON
SABATONS
SABAYON
SABAYONS
SABBAT
SABBATH
SABBATHS
SABBATIC
SABBATICS
SABBATINE
SABBATISE
SABBATISM
SABBATIZE
SABBATS
SABBED
SABBING
SABBINGS
SABE
SABED
SABEING
SABELLA
SABELLAS
SABER
SABERED
SABERING
SABERLIKE
SABERS
SABES
SABHA
SABHAS
SABICU
SABICUS
SABIN
SABINE
SABINES
SABINS
SABIR
SABIRS
SABKHA
SABKHAH
SABKHAHS
SABKHAS
SABKHAT
SABKHATS
SABLE
SABLED
SABLEFISH
SABLER
SABLES
SABLEST
SABLING
SABOT
SABOTAGE
SABOTAGED
SABOTAGES
SABOTED
SABOTEUR
SABOTEURS
SABOTIER
SABOTIERS
SABOTS
SABRA
SABRAS
SABRE
SABRED
SABRELIKE
SABRES
SABREUR
SABREURS
SABREWING
SABRING
SABS
SABULINE
SABULOSE
SABULOUS
SABURRA
SABURRAL
SABURRAS
SAC
SACATON
SACATONS
SACBUT
SACBUTS
SACCADE
SACCADES
SACCADIC
SACCATE
SACCHARIC
SACCHARIN
SACCHARUM
SACCIFORM
SACCOI
SACCOS
SACCOSES
SACCULAR
SACCULATE
SACCULE
SACCULES
SACCULI
SACCULUS
SACELLA
SACELLUM
SACHEM
SACHEMDOM
SACHEMIC
SACHEMS
SACHET
SACHETED
SACHETS
SACK
SACKABLE
SACKAGE
SACKAGED
SACKAGES
SACKAGING
SACKBUT
SACKBUTS
SACKCLOTH
SACKED
SACKER
SACKERS
SACKFUL
SACKFULS
SACKING
SACKINGS
SACKLESS
SACKLIKE
SACKLOAD
SACKLOADS
SACKS
SACKSFUL
SACLESS
SACLIKE
SACQUE
SACQUES
SACRA
SACRAL
SACRALGIA
SACRALISE
SACRALITY
SACRALIZE
SACRALS
SACRAMENT
SACRARIA
SACRARIAL
SACRARIUM
SACRED
SACREDER
SACREDEST
SACREDLY
SACRIFICE
SACRIFIDE
SACRIFIED
SACRIFIES
SACRIFY
SACRILEGE
SACRING
SACRINGS
SACRIST
SACRISTAN
SACRISTS
SACRISTY
SACRUM
SACRUMS
SACS
SAD
SADDED
SADDEN
SADDENED
SADDENING
SADDENS
SADDER
SADDEST
SADDHU
SADDHUS
SADDIE
SADDIES
SADDING
SADDISH
SADDLE
SADDLEBAG
SADDLEBOW
SADDLED
SADDLER
SADDLERS
SADDLERY
SADDLES
SADDLING
SADDO
SADDOES
SADDOS
SADE
SADES
SADHANA
SADHANAS
SADHE
SADHES
SADHU
SADHUS
SADI
SADIRON
SADIRONS
SADIS
SADISM

SADISMS
SADIST
SADISTIC
SADISTS
SADLY
SADNESS
SADNESSES
SADO
SADOS
SADS
SADZA
SADZAS
SAE
SAECULA
SAECULUM
SAECULUMS
SAETER
SAETERS
SAFARI
SAFARIED
SAFARIING
SAFARIS
SAFARIST
SAFARISTS
SAFE
SAFED
SAFEGUARD
SAFELIGHT
SAFELY
SAFENESS
SAFER
SAFES
SAFEST
SAFETIED
SAFETIES
SAFETY
SAFETYING
SAFETYMAN
SAFETYMEN
SAFFIAN
SAFFIANS
SAFFLOWER
SAFFRON
SAFFRONED
SAFFRONS
SAFFRONY
SAFING
SAFRANIN
SAFRANINE
SAFRANINS
SAFROL
SAFROLE
SAFROLES
SAFROLS
SAFRONAL
SAFRONALS
SAFT
SAFTER
SAFTEST
SAG
SAGA
SAGACIOUS
SAGACITY
SAGAMAN
SAGAMEN
SAGAMORE
SAGAMORES
SAGANASH
SAGAPENUM
SAGAS
SAGATHIES
SAGATHY
SAGBUT
SAGBUTS
SAGE
SAGEBRUSH
SAGEHOOD
SAGEHOODS
SAGELY
SAGENE
SAGENES
SAGENESS
SAGENITE
SAGENITES
SAGENITIC
SAGER
SAGES
SAGEST
SAGGAR
SAGGARD
SAGGARDS
SAGGARED
SAGGARING
SAGGARS
SAGGED
SAGGER
SAGGERED
SAGGERING
SAGGERS
SAGGIER
SAGGIEST
SAGGING
SAGGINGS
SAGGY
SAGIER
SAGIEST
SAGINATE
SAGINATED
SAGINATES
SAGITTA
SAGITTAL
SAGITTARY
SAGITTAS
SAGITTATE
SAGO
SAGOIN
SAGOINS
SAGOS
SAGOUIN
SAGOUINS
SAGRADA
SAGS
SAGUARO
SAGUAROS
SAGUIN
SAGUINS
SAGUM
SAGY
SAHEB
SAHEBS
SAHIB
SAHIBA
SAHIBAH
SAHIBAHS
SAHIBAS
SAHIBS
SAHIWAL
SAHIWALS
SAHUARO
SAHUAROS
SAI
SAIBLING
SAIBLINGS
SAIC
SAICE
SAICES
SAICK
SAICKS
SAICS
SAID
SAIDEST
SAIDS
SAIDST
SAIGA
SAIGAS
SAIKEI
SAIKEIS
SAIKLESS
SAIL
SAILABLE
SAILBOARD
SAILBOAT
SAILBOATS
SAILCLOTH
SAILED
SAILER
SAILERS
SAILFISH
SAILING
SAILINGS
SAILLESS
SAILMAKER
SAILOR
SAILORING
SAILORLY
SAILORS
SAILPAST
SAILPASTS
SAILPLANE
SAILROOM
SAILROOMS
SAILS
SAIM
SAIMIN
SAIMINS
SAIMIRI
SAIMIRIS
SAIMS
SAIN
SAINE
SAINED
SAINFOIN
SAINFOINS
SAINING
SAINS
SAINT
SAINTDOM
SAINTDOMS
SAINTED
SAINTESS
SAINTFOIN
SAINTHOOD
SAINTING
SAINTISH
SAINTISM
SAINTISMS
SAINTLESS
SAINTLIER
SAINTLIKE
SAINTLILY
SAINTLING
SAINTLY
SAINTS
SAINTSHIP
SAIQUE
SAIQUES
SAIR
SAIRED
SAIRER
SAIREST
SAIRING
SAIRS
SAIS
SAIST
SAITH
SAITHE
SAITHES
SAITHS
SAIYID
SAIYIDS
SAJOU
SAJOUS
SAKAI
SAKAIS
SAKE
SAKER
SAKERET
SAKERETS
SAKERS
SAKES

S

SAKI
SAKIA
SAKIAS
SAKIEH
SAKIEHS
SAKIS
SAKIYEH
SAKIYEHS
SAKKOI
SAKKOS
SAKKOSES
SAKSAUL
SAKSAULS
SAKTI
SAKTIS
SAL
SALAAM
SALAAMED
SALAAMING
SALAAMS
SALABLE
SALABLY
SALACIOUS
SALACITY
SALAD
SALADANG
SALADANGS
SALADE
SALADES
SALADING
SALADINGS
SALADS
SALAL
SALALS
SALAMI
SALAMIS
SALAMON
SALAMONS
SALANGANE
SALARIAT
SALARIATS
SALARIED
SALARIES
SALARY
SALARYING
SALARYMAN
SALARYMEN
SALAT
SALATS
SALBAND
SALBANDS
SALCHOW
SALCHOWS
SALE
SALEABLE
SALEABLY
SALEP
SALEPS
SALERATUS
SALERING
SALERINGS
SALEROOM
SALEROOMS
SALES
SALESGIRL
SALESLADY
SALESMAN
SALESMEN
SALESROOM
SALET
SALETS
SALEWD
SALEYARD
SALEYARDS
SALFERN
SALFERNS
SALIAUNCE
SALIC
SALICES
SALICET
SALICETA
SALICETS
SALICETUM
SALICIN
SALICINE
SALICINES
SALICINS
SALICYLIC
SALIENCE
SALIENCES
SALIENCY
SALIENT
SALIENTLY
SALIENTS
SALIFIED
SALIFIES
SALIFY
SALIFYING
SALIGOT
SALIGOTS
SALIMETER
SALIMETRY
SALINA
SALINAS
SALINE
SALINES
SALINISE
SALINISED
SALINISES
SALINITY
SALINIZE
SALINIZED
SALINIZES
SALIVA
SALIVAL
SALIVARY
SALIVAS
SALIVATE
SALIVATED
SALIVATES
SALIVATOR
SALIX
SALL
SALLAD
SALLADS
SALLAL
SALLALS
SALLE
SALLEE
SALLEES
SALLES
SALLET
SALLETS
SALLIED
SALLIER
SALLIERS
SALLIES
SALLOW
SALLOWED
SALLOWER
SALLOWEST
SALLOWIER
SALLOWING
SALLOWISH
SALLOWLY
SALLOWS
SALLOWY
SALLY
SALLYING
SALLYPORT
SALMI
SALMIS
SALMON
SALMONET
SALMONETS
SALMONID
SALMONIDS
SALMONIER
SALMONOID
SALMONS
SALMONY
SALOL
SALOLS
SALOMETER
SALON
SALONS
SALOON
SALOONS
SALOOP
SALOOPS
SALOP
SALOPIAN
SALOPS
SALP
SALPA
SALPAE
SALPAS
SALPIAN
SALPIANS
SALPICON
SALPICONS
SALPID
SALPIDS
SALPIFORM
SALPINGES
SALPINX
SALPINXES
SALPS
SALS
SALSA
SALSAED
SALSAING
SALSAS
SALSE
SALSES
SALSIFIES
SALSIFY
SALSILLA
SALSILLAS
SALT
SALTANDO
SALTANDOS
SALTANT
SALTANTS
SALTATE
SALTATED
SALTATES
SALTATING
SALTATION
SALTATO
SALTATORY
SALTATOS
SALTBOX
SALTBOXES
SALTBUSH
SALTCAT
SALTCATS
SALTCHUCK
SALTED
SALTER
SALTERIES
SALTERN
SALTERNS
SALTERS
SALTERY
SALTEST
SALTFISH
SALTIE
SALTIER
SALTIERS
SALTIES
SALTIEST
SALTILY
SALTINE
SALTINES
SALTINESS
SALTING
SALTINGS
SALTIRE
SALTIRES

S

SALTISH
SALTISHLY
SALTLESS
SALTLIKE
SALTLY
SALTNESS
SALTO
SALTOED
SALTOING
SALTOS
SALTPAN
SALTPANS
SALTPETER
SALTPETRE
SALTS
SALTUS
SALTUSES
SALTWATER
SALTWORK
SALTWORKS
SALTWORT
SALTWORTS
SALTY
SALUBRITY
SALUE
SALUED
SALUES
SALUING
SALUKI
SALUKIS
SALURETIC
SALUT
SALUTARY
SALUTE
SALUTED
SALUTER
SALUTERS
SALUTES
SALUTING
SALVABLE
SALVABLY
SALVAGE
SALVAGED
SALVAGEE
SALVAGEES
SALVAGER
SALVAGERS
SALVAGES
SALVAGING
SALVARSAN
SALVATION
SALVATORY
SALVE
SALVED
SALVER
SALVERS
SALVES
SALVETE
SALVETES
SALVIA
SALVIAS
SALVIFIC
SALVING
SALVINGS
SALVO
SALVOED
SALVOES
SALVOING
SALVOR
SALVORS
SALVOS
SALWAR
SALWARS
SAM
SAMA
SAMAAN
SAMAANS
SAMADHI
SAMADHIS
SAMAN
SAMANS
SAMARA
SAMARAS
SAMARITAN
SAMARIUM
SAMARIUMS
SAMAS
SAMBA
SAMBAED
SAMBAING
SAMBAL
SAMBALS
SAMBAR
SAMBARS
SAMBAS
SAMBHAR
SAMBHARS
SAMBHUR
SAMBHURS
SAMBO
SAMBOES
SAMBOS
SAMBUCA
SAMBUCAS
SAMBUKE
SAMBUKES
SAMBUR
SAMBURS
SAME
SAMECH
SAMECHS
SAMEK
SAMEKH
SAMEKHS
SAMEKS
SAMEL
SAMELY
SAMEN
SAMENESS
SAMES
SAMEY
SAMEYNESS
SAMFOO
SAMFOOS
SAMFU
SAMFUS
SAMIEL
SAMIELS
SAMIER
SAMIEST
SAMISEN
SAMISENS
SAMITE
SAMITES
SAMITHI
SAMITHIS
SAMITI
SAMITIS
SAMIZDAT
SAMIZDATS
SAMLET
SAMLETS
SAMLOR
SAMLORS
SAMMED
SAMMIE
SAMMIES
SAMMING
SAMMY
SAMNITIS
SAMOSA
SAMOSAS
SAMOVAR
SAMOVARS
SAMOYED
SAMOYEDS
SAMP
SAMPAN
SAMPANS
SAMPHIRE
SAMPHIRES
SAMPI
SAMPIRE
SAMPIRES
SAMPIS
SAMPLE
SAMPLED
SAMPLER
SAMPLERS
SAMPLERY
SAMPLES
SAMPLING
SAMPLINGS
SAMPS
SAMS
SAMSARA
SAMSARAS
SAMSARIC
SAMSHOO
SAMSHOOS
SAMSHU
SAMSHUS
SAMSKARA
SAMSKARAS
SAMURAI
SAMURAIS
SAN
SANATIVE
SANATORIA
SANATORY
SANBENITO
SANCAI
SANCAIS
SANCHO
SANCHOS
SANCTA
SANCTIFY
SANCTION
SANCTIONS
SANCTITY
SANCTUARY
SANCTUM
SANCTUMS
SAND
SANDABLE
SANDAL
SANDALED
SANDALING
SANDALLED
SANDALS
SANDARAC
SANDARACH
SANDARACS
SANDBAG
SANDBAGS
SANDBANK
SANDBANKS
SANDBAR
SANDBARS
SANDBLAST
SANDBOX
SANDBOXES
SANDBOY
SANDBOYS
SANDBUR
SANDBURR
SANDBURRS
SANDBURS
SANDCRACK
SANDDAB
SANDDABS
SANDED
SANDEK
SANDEKS
SANDER
SANDERS
SANDERSES
SANDFISH
SANDFLIES
SANDFLY

S

SANDGLASS
SANDHEAP
SANDHEAPS
SANDHI
SANDHILL
SANDHILLS
SANDHIS
SANDHOG
SANDHOGS
SANDIER
SANDIEST
SANDINESS
SANDING
SANDINGS
SANDIVER
SANDIVERS
SANDLESS
SANDLIKE
SANDLING
SANDLINGS
SANDLOT
SANDLOTS
SANDMAN
SANDMEN
SANDPAPER
SANDPEEP
SANDPEEPS
SANDPILE
SANDPILES
SANDPIPER
SANDPIT
SANDPITS
SANDPUMP
SANDPUMPS
SANDS
SANDSHOE
SANDSHOES
SANDSOAP
SANDSOAPS
SANDSPIT
SANDSPITS
SANDSPOUT
SANDSPUR
SANDSPURS
SANDSTONE
SANDSTORM
SANDWICH
SANDWORM
SANDWORMS
SANDWORT
SANDWORTS
SANDY
SANDYISH
SANE
SANED
SANELY
SANENESS
SANER
SANES
SANEST
SANG
SANGA
SANGAR
SANGAREE
SANGAREES
SANGARS
SANGAS
SANGEET
SANGEETS
SANGER
SANGERS
SANGFROID
SANGH
SANGHA
SANGHAS
SANGHAT
SANGHATS
SANGHS
SANGLIER
SANGLIERS
SANGO
SANGOMA
SANGOMAS
SANGOS
SANGRAIL
SANGRAILS
SANGREAL
SANGREALS
SANGRIA
SANGRIAS
SANGS
SANGUIFY
SANGUINE
SANGUINED
SANGUINES
SANICLE
SANICLES
SANIDINE
SANIDINES
SANIES
SANIFIED
SANIFIES
SANIFY
SANIFYING
SANING
SANIOUS
SANITARIA
SANITARY
SANITATE
SANITATED
SANITATES
SANITIES
SANITISE
SANITISED
SANITISER
SANITISES
SANITIZE
SANITIZED
SANITIZER
SANITIZES
SANITORIA
SANITY
SANJAK
SANJAKS
SANK
SANKO
SANKOS
SANNIE
SANNIES
SANNOP
SANNOPS
SANNUP
SANNUPS
SANNYASI
SANNYASIN
SANNYASIS
SANPAN
SANPANS
SANPRO
SANPROS
SANS
SANSA
SANSAR
SANSARS
SANSAS
SANSEI
SANSEIS
SANSERIF
SANSERIFS
SANT
SANTAL
SANTALIC
SANTALIN
SANTALINS
SANTALOL
SANTALOLS
SANTALS
SANTERA
SANTERAS
SANTERIA
SANTERIAS
SANTERO
SANTEROS
SANTIM
SANTIMI
SANTIMS
SANTIMU
SANTIR
SANTIRS
SANTO
SANTOKU
SANTOKUS
SANTOL
SANTOLINA
SANTOLS
SANTON
SANTONICA
SANTONIN
SANTONINS
SANTONS
SANTOOR
SANTOORS
SANTOS
SANTOUR
SANTOURS
SANTS
SANTUR
SANTURS
SANYASI
SANYASIS
SAOLA
SAOLAS
SAOUARI
SAOUARIS
SAP
SAPAJOU
SAPAJOUS
SAPAN
SAPANS
SAPANWOOD
SAPEGO
SAPEGOES
SAPELE
SAPELES
SAPFUL
SAPHEAD
SAPHEADED
SAPHEADS
SAPHENA
SAPHENAE
SAPHENAS
SAPHENOUS
SAPID
SAPIDER
SAPIDEST
SAPIDITY
SAPIDLESS
SAPIDNESS
SAPIENCE
SAPIENCES
SAPIENCY
SAPIENS
SAPIENT
SAPIENTLY
SAPIENTS
SAPLESS
SAPLING
SAPLINGS
SAPODILLA
SAPOGENIN
SAPONARIA
SAPONATED
SAPONIFY
SAPONIN
SAPONINE
SAPONINES
SAPONINS
SAPONITE
SAPONITES
SAPOR

SAPORIFIC
SAPOROUS
SAPORS
SAPOTA
SAPOTAS
SAPOTE
SAPOTES
SAPOUR
SAPOURS
SAPPAN
SAPPANS
SAPPED
SAPPER
SAPPERS
SAPPHIC
SAPPHICS
SAPPHIRE
SAPPHIRED
SAPPHIRES
SAPPHISM
SAPPHISMS
SAPPHIST
SAPPHISTS
SAPPIER
SAPPIEST
SAPPILY
SAPPINESS
SAPPING
SAPPINGS
SAPPLE
SAPPLED
SAPPLES
SAPPLING
SAPPY
SAPRAEMIA
SAPRAEMIC
SAPREMIA
SAPREMIAS
SAPREMIC
SAPROBE
SAPROBES
SAPROBIAL
SAPROBIC
SAPROBITY
SAPROLITE
SAPROPEL
SAPROPELS
SAPROZOIC
SAPS
SAPSAGO
SAPSAGOS
SAPSUCKER
SAPUCAIA
SAPUCAIAS
SAPWOOD
SAPWOODS
SAR
SARABAND
SARABANDE
SARABANDS
SARAFAN
SARAFANS
SARAN
SARANGI
SARANGIS
SARANS
SARAPE
SARAPES
SARBACANE
SARCASM
SARCASMS
SARCASTIC
SARCENET
SARCENETS
SARCINA
SARCINAE
SARCINAS
SARCOCARP
SARCODE
SARCODES
SARCODIC
SARCOID
SARCOIDS
SARCOLOGY
SARCOMA
SARCOMAS
SARCOMATA
SARCOMERE
SARCONET
SARCONETS
SARCOPTIC
SARCOSOME
SARCOUS
SARD
SARDANA
SARDANAS
SARDAR
SARDARS
SARDEL
SARDELLE
SARDELLES
SARDELS
SARDINE
SARDINED
SARDINES
SARDINING
SARDIUS
SARDIUSES
SARDONIAN
SARDONIC
SARDONYX
SARDS
SARED
SAREE
SAREES
SARGASSA
SARGASSO
SARGASSOS
SARGASSUM
SARGE
SARGES
SARGO
SARGOS
SARGOSES
SARGUS
SARGUSES
SARI
SARIN
SARING
SARINS
SARIS
SARK
SARKIER
SARKIEST
SARKILY
SARKINESS
SARKING
SARKINGS
SARKS
SARKY
SARMENT
SARMENTA
SARMENTS
SARMENTUM
SARMIE
SARMIES
SARNEY
SARNEYS
SARNIE
SARNIES
SAROD
SARODE
SARODES
SARODIST
SARODISTS
SARODS
SARONG
SARONGS
SARONIC
SAROS
SAROSES
SARPANCH
SARRASIN
SARRASINS
SARRAZIN
SARRAZINS
SARS
SARSAR
SARSARS
SARSDEN
SARSDENS
SARSEN
SARSENET
SARSENETS
SARSENS
SARSNET
SARSNETS
SARTOR
SARTORIAL
SARTORIAN
SARTORII
SARTORIUS
SARTORS
SARUS
SARUSES
SASANQUA
SASANQUAS
SASARARA
SASARARAS
SASER
SASERS
SASH
SASHAY
SASHAYED
SASHAYING
SASHAYS
SASHED
SASHES
SASHIMI
SASHIMIS
SASHING
SASHLESS
SASIN
SASINE
SASINES
SASINS
SASKATOON
SASQUATCH
SASS
SASSABIES
SASSABY
SASSAFRAS
SASSARARA
SASSE
SASSED
SASSES
SASSIER
SASSIES
SASSIEST
SASSILY
SASSINESS
SASSING
SASSOLIN
SASSOLINS
SASSOLITE
SASSWOOD
SASSWOODS
SASSY
SASSYWOOD
SASTRA
SASTRAS
SASTRUGA
SASTRUGI
SAT
SATAI
SATAIS
SATANG
SATANGS
SATANIC
SATANICAL

S

SATANISM
SATANISMS
SATANIST
SATANISTS
SATANITY
SATARA
SATARAS
SATAY
SATAYS
SATCHEL
SATCHELED
SATCHELS
SATCOM
SATCOMS
SATE
SATED
SATEDNESS
SATEEN
SATEENS
SATELESS
SATELLES
SATELLITE
SATEM
SATES
SATI
SATIABLE
SATIABLY
SATIATE
SATIATED
SATIATES
SATIATING
SATIATION
SATIETIES
SATIETY
SATIN
SATINED
SATINET
SATINETS
SATINETTA
SATINETTE
SATING
SATINIER
SATINIEST
SATINING
SATINPOD
SATINPODS
SATINS
SATINWOOD
SATINY
SATIRE
SATIRES
SATIRIC
SATIRICAL
SATIRISE
SATIRISED
SATIRISER
SATIRISES
SATIRIST
SATIRISTS
SATIRIZE
SATIRIZED
SATIRIZER
SATIRIZES
SATIS
SATISFICE
SATISFIED
SATISFIER
SATISFIES
SATISFY
SATIVE
SATNAV
SATNAVS
SATORI
SATORIS
SATRAP
SATRAPAL
SATRAPIES
SATRAPS
SATRAPY
SATSANG
SATSANGS
SATSUMA
SATSUMAS
SATURABLE
SATURANT
SATURANTS
SATURATE
SATURATED
SATURATER
SATURATES
SATURATOR
SATURNIC
SATURNIID
SATURNINE
SATURNISM
SATURNIST
SATYR
SATYRA
SATYRAL
SATYRALS
SATYRAS
SATYRE
SATYRES
SATYRESS
SATYRIC
SATYRICAL
SATYRID
SATYRIDS
SATYRISK
SATYRISKS
SATYRLIKE
SATYRS
SAU
SAUBA
SAUBAS
SAUCE
SAUCEBOAT
SAUCEBOX
SAUCED
SAUCELESS
SAUCEPAN
SAUCEPANS
SAUCEPOT
SAUCEPOTS
SAUCER
SAUCERFUL
SAUCERS
SAUCES
SAUCH
SAUCHS
SAUCIER
SAUCIERS
SAUCIEST
SAUCILY
SAUCINESS
SAUCING
SAUCISSE
SAUCISSES
SAUCISSON
SAUCY
SAUFGARD
SAUFGARDS
SAUGER
SAUGERS
SAUGH
SAUGHS
SAUGHY
SAUL
SAULGE
SAULGES
SAULIE
SAULIES
SAULS
SAULT
SAULTS
SAUNA
SAUNAED
SAUNAING
SAUNAS
SAUNT
SAUNTED
SAUNTER
SAUNTERED
SAUNTERER
SAUNTERS
SAUNTING
SAUNTS
SAUREL
SAURELS
SAURIAN
SAURIANS
SAURIES
SAUROID
SAUROIDS
SAUROPOD
SAUROPODS
SAURY
SAUSAGE
SAUSAGES
SAUT
SAUTE
SAUTED
SAUTEED
SAUTEEING
SAUTEING
SAUTERNE
SAUTERNES
SAUTES
SAUTING
SAUTOIR
SAUTOIRE
SAUTOIRES
SAUTOIRS
SAUTS
SAV
SAVABLE
SAVAGE
SAVAGED
SAVAGEDOM
SAVAGELY
SAVAGER
SAVAGERY
SAVAGES
SAVAGEST
SAVAGING
SAVAGISM
SAVAGISMS
SAVANNA
SAVANNAH
SAVANNAHS
SAVANNAS
SAVANT
SAVANTE
SAVANTES
SAVANTS
SAVARIN
SAVARINS
SAVASANA
SAVASANAS
SAVATE
SAVATES
SAVE
SAVEABLE
SAVED
SAVEGARD
SAVEGARDS
SAVELOY
SAVELOYS
SAVER
SAVERS
SAVES
SAVEY
SAVEYED
SAVEYING
SAVEYS
SAVIN
SAVINE
SAVINES
SAVING
SAVINGLY

S

SAVINGS
SAVINS
SAVIOR
SAVIORS
SAVIOUR
SAVIOURS
SAVOR
SAVORED
SAVORER
SAVORERS
SAVORIER
SAVORIES
SAVORIEST
SAVORILY
SAVORING
SAVORLESS
SAVOROUS
SAVORS
SAVORY
SAVOUR
SAVOURED
SAVOURER
SAVOURERS
SAVOURIER
SAVOURIES
SAVOURILY
SAVOURING
SAVOURLY
SAVOURS
SAVOURY
SAVOY
SAVOYARD
SAVOYARDS
SAVOYS
SAVS
SAVVEY
SAVVEYED
SAVVEYING
SAVVEYS
SAVVIED
SAVVIER
SAVVIES
SAVVIEST
SAVVILY
SAVVINESS
SAVVY
SAVVYING
SAW
SAWAH
SAWAHS
SAWBILL
SAWBILLS
SAWBLADE
SAWBLADES
SAWBONES
SAWBUCK
SAWBUCKS
SAWDER
SAWDERED
SAWDERING
SAWDERS
SAWDUST
SAWDUSTED
SAWDUSTS
SAWDUSTY
SAWED
SAWER
SAWERS
SAWFISH
SAWFISHES
SAWFLIES
SAWFLY
SAWGRASS
SAWHORSE
SAWHORSES
SAWING
SAWINGS
SAWLIKE
SAWLOG
SAWLOGS
SAWMILL
SAWMILLER
SAWMILLS
SAWN
SAWNEY
SAWNEYS
SAWPIT
SAWPITS
SAWS
SAWSHARK
SAWSHARKS
SAWTEETH
SAWTIMBER
SAWTOOTH
SAWYER
SAWYERS
SAX
SAXATILE
SAXAUL
SAXAULS
SAXE
SAXES
SAXHORN
SAXHORNS
SAXICOLE
SAXIFRAGE
SAXIST
SAXISTS
SAXITOXIN
SAXMAN
SAXMEN
SAXONIES
SAXONITE
SAXONITES
SAXONY
SAXOPHONE
SAXTUBA
SAXTUBAS
SAY
SAYABLE
SAYABLES
SAYED
SAYEDS
SAYER
SAYERS
SAYEST
SAYID
SAYIDS
SAYING
SAYINGS
SAYNE
SAYON
SAYONARA
SAYONARAS
SAYONS
SAYS
SAYST
SAYYID
SAYYIDS
SAZ
SAZERAC
SAZERACS
SAZES
SAZHEN
SAZHENS
SAZZES
SBIRRI
SBIRRO
SCAB
SCABBARD
SCABBARDS
SCABBED
SCABBIER
SCABBIEST
SCABBILY
SCABBING
SCABBLE
SCABBLED
SCABBLES
SCABBLING
SCABBY
SCABIES
SCABIETIC
SCABIOSA
SCABIOSAS
SCABIOUS
SCABLAND
SCABLANDS
SCABLIKE
SCABRID
SCABROUS
SCABS
SCAD
SCADS
SCAFF
SCAFFED
SCAFFIE
SCAFFIER
SCAFFIES
SCAFFIEST
SCAFFING
SCAFFOLD
SCAFFOLDS
SCAFFS
SCAFFY
SCAG
SCAGGED
SCAGGING
SCAGLIA
SCAGLIAS
SCAGLIOLA
SCAGS
SCAIL
SCAILED
SCAILING
SCAILS
SCAITH
SCAITHED
SCAITHING
SCAITHS
SCALA
SCALABLE
SCALABLY
SCALADE
SCALADES
SCALADO
SCALADOS
SCALAE
SCALAGE
SCALAGES
SCALAR
SCALARE
SCALARES
SCALARS
SCALATION
SCALAWAG
SCALAWAGS
SCALD
SCALDED
SCALDER
SCALDERS
SCALDFISH
SCALDHEAD
SCALDIC
SCALDING
SCALDINGS
SCALDINI
SCALDINO
SCALDS
SCALDSHIP
SCALE
SCALEABLE
SCALEABLY
SCALED
SCALELESS
SCALELIKE
SCALENE
SCALENES
SCALENI
SCALENUS

S

SCALEPAN
SCALEPANS
SCALER
SCALERS
SCALES
SCALETAIL
SCALEUP
SCALEUPS
SCALEWORK
SCALIER
SCALIEST
SCALINESS
SCALING
SCALINGS
SCALL
SCALLAWAG
SCALLED
SCALLIES
SCALLION
SCALLIONS
SCALLOP
SCALLOPED
SCALLOPER
SCALLOPS
SCALLS
SCALLY
SCALLYWAG
SCALOGRAM
SCALP
SCALPED
SCALPEL
SCALPELS
SCALPER
SCALPERS
SCALPING
SCALPINGS
SCALPINS
SCALPLESS
SCALPRUM
SCALPRUMS
SCALPS
SCALY
SCAM
SCAMBLE
SCAMBLED
SCAMBLER
SCAMBLERS
SCAMBLES
SCAMBLING
SCAMEL
SCAMELS
SCAMMED
SCAMMER
SCAMMERS
SCAMMING
SCAMMONY
SCAMP
SCAMPED
SCAMPER
SCAMPERED
SCAMPERER
SCAMPERS
SCAMPI
SCAMPIES
SCAMPING
SCAMPINGS
SCAMPIS
SCAMPISH
SCAMPS
SCAMS
SCAMSTER
SCAMSTERS
SCAMTO
SCAMTOS
SCAN
SCAND
SCANDAL
SCANDALED
SCANDALS
SCANDENT
SCANDIA
SCANDIAS
SCANDIC
SCANDIUM
SCANDIUMS
SCANNABLE
SCANNED
SCANNER
SCANNERS
SCANNING
SCANNINGS
SCANS
SCANSION
SCANSIONS
SCANT
SCANTED
SCANTER
SCANTEST
SCANTIER
SCANTIES
SCANTIEST
SCANTILY
SCANTING
SCANTITY
SCANTLE
SCANTLED
SCANTLES
SCANTLING
SCANTLY
SCANTNESS
SCANTS
SCANTY
SCAPA
SCAPAED
SCAPAING
SCAPAS
SCAPE
SCAPED
SCAPEGOAT
SCAPELESS
SCAPEMENT
SCAPES
SCAPHOID
SCAPHOIDS
SCAPHOPOD
SCAPI
SCAPING
SCAPOLITE
SCAPOSE
SCAPPLE
SCAPPLED
SCAPPLES
SCAPPLING
SCAPULA
SCAPULAE
SCAPULAR
SCAPULARS
SCAPULARY
SCAPULAS
SCAPUS
SCAR
SCARAB
SCARABAEI
SCARABEE
SCARABEES
SCARABOID
SCARABS
SCARCE
SCARCELY
SCARCER
SCARCEST
SCARCITY
SCARE
SCARECROW
SCARED
SCAREDER
SCAREDEST
SCAREDIES
SCAREDY
SCAREHEAD
SCARER
SCARERS
SCARES
SCAREWARE
SCAREY
SCARF
SCARFED
SCARFER
SCARFERS
SCARFING
SCARFINGS
SCARFISH
SCARFPIN
SCARFPINS
SCARFS
SCARFSKIN
SCARFWISE
SCARIER
SCARIEST
SCARIFIED
SCARIFIER
SCARIFIES
SCARIFY
SCARILY
SCARINESS
SCARING
SCARIOSE
SCARIOUS
SCARLESS
SCARLET
SCARLETED
SCARLETS
SCARMOGE
SCARMOGES
SCARP
SCARPA
SCARPAED
SCARPAING
SCARPAS
SCARPED
SCARPER
SCARPERED
SCARPERS
SCARPETTI
SCARPETTO
SCARPH
SCARPHED
SCARPHING
SCARPHS
SCARPINES
SCARPING
SCARPINGS
SCARPS
SCARRE
SCARRED
SCARRES
SCARRIER
SCARRIEST
SCARRING
SCARRINGS
SCARRY
SCARS
SCART
SCARTED
SCARTH
SCARTHS
SCARTING
SCARTS
SCARVED
SCARVES
SCARY
SCAT
SCATBACK
SCATBACKS
SCATCH
SCATCHES
SCATH
SCATHE
SCATHED
SCATHEFUL

S

SCATHES
SCATHING
SCATHS
SCATOLE
SCATOLES
SCATOLOGY
SCATS
SCATT
SCATTED
SCATTER
SCATTERED
SCATTERER
SCATTERS
SCATTERY
SCATTIER
SCATTIEST
SCATTILY
SCATTING
SCATTINGS
SCATTS
SCATTY
SCAUD
SCAUDED
SCAUDING
SCAUDS
SCAUP
SCAUPED
SCAUPER
SCAUPERS
SCAUPING
SCAUPS
SCAUR
SCAURED
SCAURIES
SCAURING
SCAURS
SCAURY
SCAVAGE
SCAVAGED
SCAVAGER
SCAVAGERS
SCAVAGES
SCAVAGING
SCAVENGE
SCAVENGED
SCAVENGER
SCAVENGES
SCAW
SCAWS
SCAWTITE
SCAWTITES
SCAZON
SCAZONS
SCAZONTES
SCAZONTIC
SCEAT
SCEATS
SCEATT
SCEATTAS
SCEATTS
SCEDULE
SCEDULED
SCEDULES
SCEDULING
SCELERAT
SCELERATE
SCELERATS
SCENA
SCENARIES
SCENARIO
SCENARIOS
SCENARISE
SCENARIST
SCENARIZE
SCENARY
SCENAS
SCEND
SCENDED
SCENDING
SCENDS
SCENE
SCENED
SCENEMAN
SCENEMEN
SCENERIES
SCENERY
SCENES
SCENESTER
SCENIC
SCENICAL
SCENICS
SCENING
SCENT
SCENTED
SCENTFUL
SCENTING
SCENTINGS
SCENTLESS
SCENTS
SCEPSIS
SCEPSISES
SCEPTER
SCEPTERED
SCEPTERS
SCEPTIC
SCEPTICAL
SCEPTICS
SCEPTRAL
SCEPTRE
SCEPTRED
SCEPTRES
SCEPTRING
SCEPTRY
SCERNE
SCERNED
SCERNES
SCERNING
SCHANSE
SCHANSES
SCHANTZE
SCHANTZES
SCHANZE
SCHANZES
SCHAPPE
SCHAPPED
SCHAPPES
SCHAPSKA
SCHAPSKAS
SCHATCHEN
SCHAV
SCHAVS
SCHECHITA
SCHEDULAR
SCHEDULE
SCHEDULED
SCHEDULER
SCHEDULES
SCHEELITE
SCHELLIES
SCHELLUM
SCHELLUMS
SCHELLY
SCHELM
SCHELMS
SCHEMA
SCHEMAS
SCHEMATA
SCHEMATIC
SCHEME
SCHEMED
SCHEMER
SCHEMERS
SCHEMES
SCHEMIE
SCHEMIES
SCHEMING
SCHEMINGS
SCHERZI
SCHERZO
SCHERZOS
SCHIAVONE
SCHIEDAM
SCHIEDAMS
SCHILLER
SCHILLERS
SCHILLING
SCHIMMEL
SCHIMMELS
SCHISM
SCHISMA
SCHISMAS
SCHISMS
SCHIST
SCHISTOSE
SCHISTOUS
SCHISTS
SCHIZIER
SCHIZIEST
SCHIZO
SCHIZOID
SCHIZOIDS
SCHIZONT
SCHIZONTS
SCHIZOPOD
SCHIZOS
SCHIZY
SCHIZZIER
SCHIZZY
SCHLAGER
SCHLAGERS
SCHLEMIEL
SCHLEMIHL
SCHLEP
SCHLEPP
SCHLEPPED
SCHLEPPER
SCHLEPPS
SCHLEPPY
SCHLEPS
SCHLICH
SCHLICHS
SCHLIERE
SCHLIEREN
SCHLIERIC
SCHLOCK
SCHLOCKER
SCHLOCKEY
SCHLOCKS
SCHLOCKY
SCHLONG
SCHLONGS
SCHLOSS
SCHLOSSES
SCHLUB
SCHLUBS
SCHLUMP
SCHLUMPED
SCHLUMPS
SCHLUMPY
SCHMALTZ
SCHMALTZY
SCHMALZ
SCHMALZES
SCHMALZY
SCHMATTE
SCHMATTES
SCHMEAR
SCHMEARED
SCHMEARS
SCHMECK
SCHMECKED
SCHMECKER
SCHMECKS
SCHMEER
SCHMEERED
SCHMEERS
SCHMELZ
SCHMELZE
SCHMELZES
SCHMICK

S

SCHMICKER
SCHMO
SCHMOCK
SCHMOCKS
SCHMOE
SCHMOES
SCHMOOS
SCHMOOSE
SCHMOOSED
SCHMOOSES
SCHMOOZ
SCHMOOZE
SCHMOOZED
SCHMOOZER
SCHMOOZES
SCHMOOZY
SCHMOS
SCHMUCK
SCHMUCKED
SCHMUCKS
SCHMUCKY
SCHMUTTER
SCHMUTZ
SCHMUTZES
SCHNAPPER
SCHNAPPS
SCHNAPS
SCHNAPSES
SCHNAUZER
SCHNECKE
SCHNECKEN
SCHNEID
SCHNEIDS
SCHNELL
SCHNITZEL
SCHNOODLE
SCHNOOK
SCHNOOKS
SCHNORKEL
SCHNORR
SCHNORRED
SCHNORRER
SCHNORRS
SCHNOZ
SCHNOZES
SCHNOZZ
SCHNOZZES
SCHNOZZLE
SCHOLAR
SCHOLARCH
SCHOLARLY
SCHOLARS
SCHOLIA
SCHOLIAST
SCHOLION
SCHOLIUM
SCHOLIUMS
SCHOOL
SCHOOLBAG
SCHOOLBOY
SCHOOLDAY
SCHOOLE
SCHOOLED
SCHOOLER
SCHOOLERS
SCHOOLERY
SCHOOLES
SCHOOLIE
SCHOOLIES
SCHOOLING
SCHOOLKID
SCHOOLMAN
SCHOOLMEN
SCHOOLS
SCHOONER
SCHOONERS
SCHORL
SCHORLS
SCHOUT
SCHOUTS
SCHRIK
SCHRIKS
SCHROD
SCHRODS
SCHTICK
SCHTICKS
SCHTIK
SCHTIKS
SCHTOOK
SCHTOOKS
SCHTOOM
SCHTUCK
SCHTUCKS
SCHTUM
SCHTUP
SCHTUPPED
SCHTUPS
SCHUIT
SCHUITS
SCHUL
SCHULN
SCHULS
SCHUSS
SCHUSSED
SCHUSSER
SCHUSSERS
SCHUSSES
SCHUSSING
SCHUYT
SCHUYTS
SCHVARTZE
SCHVITZ
SCHVITZED
SCHVITZES
SCHWA
SCHWAG
SCHWAGS
SCHWARTZE
SCHWAS
SCIAENID
SCIAENIDS
SCIAENOID
SCIAMACHY
SCIARID
SCIARIDS
SCIATIC
SCIATICA
SCIATICAL
SCIATICAS
SCIATICS
SCIENCE
SCIENCED
SCIENCES
SCIENT
SCIENTER
SCIENTIAL
SCIENTISE
SCIENTISM
SCIENTIST
SCIENTIZE
SCILICET
SCILLA
SCILLAS
SCIMETAR
SCIMETARS
SCIMITAR
SCIMITARS
SCIMITER
SCIMITERS
SCINCOID
SCINCOIDS
SCINTILLA
SCIOLISM
SCIOLISMS
SCIOLIST
SCIOLISTS
SCIOLOUS
SCIOLTO
SCIOMACHY
SCIOMANCY
SCION
SCIONS
SCIOPHYTE
SCIOSOPHY
SCIROC
SCIROCCO
SCIROCCOS
SCIROCS
SCIRRHI
SCIRRHOID
SCIRRHOUS
SCIRRHUS
SCISSEL
SCISSELS
SCISSIL
SCISSILE
SCISSILS
SCISSION
SCISSIONS
SCISSOR
SCISSORED
SCISSORER
SCISSORS
SCISSURE
SCISSURES
SCIURID
SCIURIDS
SCIURINE
SCIURINES
SCIUROID
SCLAFF
SCLAFFED
SCLAFFER
SCLAFFERS
SCLAFFING
SCLAFFS
SCLATE
SCLATED
SCLATES
SCLATING
SCLAUNDER
SCLAVE
SCLAVES
SCLERA
SCLERAE
SCLERAL
SCLERAS
SCLERE
SCLEREID
SCLEREIDE
SCLEREIDS
SCLEREMA
SCLEREMAS
SCLERES
SCLERITE
SCLERITES
SCLERITIC
SCLERITIS
SCLEROID
SCLEROMA
SCLEROMAS
SCLEROSAL
SCLEROSE
SCLEROSED
SCLEROSES
SCLEROSIS
SCLEROTAL
SCLEROTIA
SCLEROTIC
SCLEROTIN
SCLEROUS
SCLIFF
SCLIFFS
SCLIM
SCLIMMED
SCLIMMING
SCLIMS
SCODIER
SCODIEST
SCODY

S

SCOFF
SCOFFED
SCOFFER
SCOFFERS
SCOFFING
SCOFFINGS
SCOFFLAW
SCOFFLAWS
SCOFFS
SCOG
SCOGGED
SCOGGING
SCOGS
SCOINSON
SCOINSONS
SCOLD
SCOLDABLE
SCOLDED
SCOLDER
SCOLDERS
SCOLDING
SCOLDINGS
SCOLDS
SCOLECES
SCOLECID
SCOLECIDS
SCOLECITE
SCOLECOID
SCOLEX
SCOLIA
SCOLICES
SCOLIOMA
SCOLIOMAS
SCOLION
SCOLIOSES
SCOLIOSIS
SCOLIOTIC
SCOLLOP
SCOLLOPED
SCOLLOPS
SCOLYTID
SCOLYTIDS
SCOLYTOID
SCOMBRID
SCOMBRIDS
SCOMBROID
SCOMFISH
SCONCE
SCONCED
SCONCES
SCONCHEON
SCONCING
SCONE
SCONES
SCONTION
SCONTIONS
SCOOBIES
SCOOBY
SCOOCH
SCOOCHED
SCOOCHES
SCOOCHING
SCOOG
SCOOGED
SCOOGING
SCOOGS
SCOOP
SCOOPABLE
SCOOPED
SCOOPER
SCOOPERS
SCOOPFUL
SCOOPFULS
SCOOPING
SCOOPINGS
SCOOPS
SCOOPSFUL
SCOOSH
SCOOSHED
SCOOSHES
SCOOSHING
SCOOT
SCOOTCH
SCOOTCHED
SCOOTCHES
SCOOTED
SCOOTER
SCOOTERED
SCOOTERS
SCOOTING
SCOOTS
SCOP
SCOPA
SCOPAE
SCOPAS
SCOPATE
SCOPE
SCOPED
SCOPELID
SCOPELIDS
SCOPELOID
SCOPES
SCOPING
SCOPOLINE
SCOPS
SCOPULA
SCOPULAE
SCOPULAS
SCOPULATE
SCORBUTIC
SCORCH
SCORCHED
SCORCHER
SCORCHERS
SCORCHES
SCORCHING
SCORDATO
SCORE
SCORECARD
SCORED
SCORELESS
SCORELINE
SCOREPAD
SCOREPADS
SCORER
SCORERS
SCORES
SCORIA
SCORIAC
SCORIAE
SCORIFIED
SCORIFIER
SCORIFIES
SCORIFY
SCORING
SCORINGS
SCORIOUS
SCORN
SCORNED
SCORNER
SCORNERS
SCORNFUL
SCORNING
SCORNINGS
SCORNS
SCORODITE
SCORPER
SCORPERS
SCORPIOID
SCORPION
SCORPIONS
SCORRENDO
SCORSE
SCORSED
SCORSER
SCORSERS
SCORSES
SCORSING
SCOT
SCOTCH
SCOTCHED
SCOTCHES
SCOTCHING
SCOTER
SCOTERS
SCOTIA
SCOTIAS
SCOTOMA
SCOTOMAS
SCOTOMATA
SCOTOMIA
SCOTOMIAS
SCOTOMIES
SCOTOMY
SCOTOPHIL
SCOTOPIA
SCOTOPIAS
SCOTOPIC
SCOTS
SCOTTIE
SCOTTIES
SCOUG
SCOUGED
SCOUGING
SCOUGS
SCOUNDREL
SCOUP
SCOUPED
SCOUPING
SCOUPS
SCOUR
SCOURED
SCOURER
SCOURERS
SCOURGE
SCOURGED
SCOURGER
SCOURGERS
SCOURGES
SCOURGING
SCOURIE
SCOURIES
SCOURING
SCOURINGS
SCOURS
SCOURSE
SCOURSED
SCOURSES
SCOURSING
SCOUSE
SCOUSER
SCOUSERS
SCOUSES
SCOUT
SCOUTED
SCOUTER
SCOUTERS
SCOUTH
SCOUTHER
SCOUTHERS
SCOUTHERY
SCOUTHS
SCOUTING
SCOUTINGS
SCOUTS
SCOW
SCOWDER
SCOWDERED
SCOWDERS
SCOWED
SCOWING
SCOWL
SCOWLED
SCOWLER
SCOWLERS
SCOWLING
SCOWLS
SCOWP
SCOWPED
SCOWPING

S

SCOWPS
SCOWRER
SCOWRERS
SCOWRIE
SCOWRIES
SCOWS
SCOWTH
SCOWTHER
SCOWTHERS
SCOWTHS
SCOZZA
SCOZZAS
SCRAB
SCRABBED
SCRABBING
SCRABBLE
SCRABBLED
SCRABBLER
SCRABBLES
SCRABBLY
SCRABS
SCRAE
SCRAES
SCRAG
SCRAGGED
SCRAGGIER
SCRAGGILY
SCRAGGING
SCRAGGLY
SCRAGGY
SCRAGS
SCRAICH
SCRAICHED
SCRAICHS
SCRAIGH
SCRAIGHED
SCRAIGHS
SCRAM
SCRAMB
SCRAMBED
SCRAMBING
SCRAMBLE
SCRAMBLED
SCRAMBLER
SCRAMBLES
SCRAMBS
SCRAMJET
SCRAMJETS
SCRAMMED
SCRAMMING
SCRAMS
SCRAN
SCRANCH
SCRANCHED
SCRANCHES
SCRANNEL
SCRANNELS
SCRANNIER
SCRANNY
SCRANS
SCRAP
SCRAPABLE
SCRAPBOOK
SCRAPE
SCRAPED
SCRAPEGUT
SCRAPER
SCRAPERS
SCRAPES
SCRAPHEAP
SCRAPIE
SCRAPIES
SCRAPING
SCRAPINGS
SCRAPPAGE
SCRAPPED
SCRAPPER
SCRAPPERS
SCRAPPIER
SCRAPPILY
SCRAPPING
SCRAPPLE
SCRAPPLES
SCRAPPY
SCRAPS
SCRAPYARD
SCRAT
SCRATCH
SCRATCHED
SCRATCHER
SCRATCHES
SCRATCHIE
SCRATCHY
SCRATS
SCRATTED
SCRATTING
SCRATTLE
SCRATTLED
SCRATTLES
SCRAUCH
SCRAUCHED
SCRAUCHS
SCRAUGH
SCRAUGHED
SCRAUGHS
SCRAVEL
SCRAVELED
SCRAVELS
SCRAW
SCRAWB
SCRAWBED
SCRAWBING
SCRAWBS
SCRAWL
SCRAWLED
SCRAWLER
SCRAWLERS
SCRAWLIER
SCRAWLING
SCRAWLS
SCRAWLY
SCRAWM
SCRAWMED
SCRAWMING
SCRAWMS
SCRAWNIER
SCRAWNILY
SCRAWNY
SCRAWP
SCRAWPED
SCRAWPING
SCRAWPS
SCRAWS
SCRAY
SCRAYE
SCRAYES
SCRAYS
SCREAK
SCREAKED
SCREAKIER
SCREAKING
SCREAKS
SCREAKY
SCREAM
SCREAMED
SCREAMER
SCREAMERS
SCREAMING
SCREAMO
SCREAMOS
SCREAMS
SCREE
SCREECH
SCREECHED
SCREECHER
SCREECHES
SCREECHY
SCREED
SCREEDED
SCREEDER
SCREEDERS
SCREEDING
SCREEDS
SCREEN
SCREENED
SCREENER
SCREENERS
SCREENFUL
SCREENIE
SCREENIES
SCREENING
SCREENS
SCREES
SCREET
SCREETED
SCREETING
SCREETS
SCREEVE
SCREEVED
SCREEVER
SCREEVERS
SCREEVES
SCREEVING
SCREICH
SCREICHED
SCREICHS
SCREIGH
SCREIGHED
SCREIGHS
SCREW
SCREWABLE
SCREWBALL
SCREWBEAN
SCREWED
SCREWER
SCREWERS
SCREWHEAD
SCREWIER
SCREWIEST
SCREWING
SCREWINGS
SCREWLIKE
SCREWS
SCREWTOP
SCREWTOPS
SCREWUP
SCREWUPS
SCREWWORM
SCREWY
SCRIBABLE
SCRIBAL
SCRIBBLE
SCRIBBLED
SCRIBBLER
SCRIBBLES
SCRIBBLY
SCRIBE
SCRIBED
SCRIBER
SCRIBERS
SCRIBES
SCRIBING
SCRIBINGS
SCRIBISM
SCRIBISMS
SCRIECH
SCRIECHED
SCRIECHS
SCRIED
SCRIENE
SCRIENES
SCRIES
SCRIEVE
SCRIEVED
SCRIEVES
SCRIEVING
SCRIGGLE
SCRIGGLED
SCRIGGLES
SCRIGGLY

S

SCRIKE
SCRIKED
SCRIKES
SCRIKING
SCRIM
SCRIMMAGE
SCRIMP
SCRIMPED
SCRIMPER
SCRIMPERS
SCRIMPIER
SCRIMPILY
SCRIMPING
SCRIMPIT
SCRIMPLY
SCRIMPS
SCRIMPY
SCRIMS
SCRIMSHAW
SCRIMURE
SCRIMURES
SCRINE
SCRINES
SCRIP
SCRIPPAGE
SCRIPS
SCRIPT
SCRIPTED
SCRIPTER
SCRIPTERS
SCRIPTING
SCRIPTORY
SCRIPTS
SCRIPTURE
SCRITCH
SCRITCHED
SCRITCHES
SCRIVE
SCRIVED
SCRIVENER
SCRIVES
SCRIVING
SCROB
SCROBBED
SCROBBING
SCROBBLE
SCROBBLED
SCROBBLES
SCROBE
SCROBES
SCROBS
SCROD
SCRODDLED
SCRODS
SCROFULA
SCROFULAS
SCROG
SCROGGIE
SCROGGIER
SCROGGIN
SCROGGINS
SCROGGY
SCROGS
SCROLL
SCROLLED
SCROLLER
SCROLLERS
SCROLLING
SCROLLS
SCROME
SCROMED
SCROMES
SCROMING
SCROOCH
SCROOCHED
SCROOCHES
SCROOGE
SCROOGED
SCROOGES
SCROOGING
SCROOP
SCROOPED
SCROOPING
SCROOPS
SCROOTCH
SCRORP
SCRORPS
SCROTA
SCROTAL
SCROTE
SCROTES
SCROTUM
SCROTUMS
SCROUGE
SCROUGED
SCROUGER
SCROUGERS
SCROUGES
SCROUGING
SCROUNGE
SCROUNGED
SCROUNGER
SCROUNGES
SCROUNGY
SCROW
SCROWDGE
SCROWDGED
SCROWDGES
SCROWL
SCROWLE
SCROWLED
SCROWLES
SCROWLING
SCROWLS
SCROWS
SCROYLE
SCROYLES
SCRUB
SCRUBBED
SCRUBBER
SCRUBBERS
SCRUBBIER
SCRUBBILY
SCRUBBING
SCRUBBY
SCRUBLAND
SCRUBS
SCRUFF
SCRUFFED
SCRUFFIER
SCRUFFILY
SCRUFFING
SCRUFFS
SCRUFFY
SCRUM
SCRUMDOWN
SCRUMMAGE
SCRUMMED
SCRUMMIE
SCRUMMIER
SCRUMMIES
SCRUMMING
SCRUMMY
SCRUMP
SCRUMPED
SCRUMPIES
SCRUMPING
SCRUMPLE
SCRUMPLED
SCRUMPLES
SCRUMPOX
SCRUMPS
SCRUMPY
SCRUMS
SCRUNCH
SCRUNCHED
SCRUNCHES
SCRUNCHIE
SCRUNCHIN
SCRUNCHY
SCRUNT
SCRUNTIER
SCRUNTS
SCRUNTY
SCRUPLE
SCRUPLED
SCRUPLER
SCRUPLERS
SCRUPLES
SCRUPLING
SCRUTABLE
SCRUTATOR
SCRUTINY
SCRUTO
SCRUTOIRE
SCRUTOS
SCRUZE
SCRUZED
SCRUZES
SCRUZING
SCRY
SCRYDE
SCRYER
SCRYERS
SCRYING
SCRYINGS
SCRYNE
SCRYNES
SCUBA
SCUBAED
SCUBAING
SCUBAS
SCUCHIN
SCUCHINS
SCUD
SCUDDALER
SCUDDED
SCUDDER
SCUDDERS
SCUDDING
SCUDDLE
SCUDDLED
SCUDDLES
SCUDDLING
SCUDI
SCUDLER
SCUDLERS
SCUDO
SCUDS
SCUFF
SCUFFED
SCUFFER
SCUFFERS
SCUFFING
SCUFFLE
SCUFFLED
SCUFFLER
SCUFFLERS
SCUFFLES
SCUFFLING
SCUFFS
SCUFT
SCUFTS
SCUG
SCUGGED
SCUGGING
SCUGS
SCUL
SCULCH
SCULCHES
SCULK
SCULKED
SCULKER
SCULKERS
SCULKING
SCULKS
SCULL
SCULLE
SCULLED
SCULLER

S

SCULLERS
SCULLERY
SCULLES
SCULLING
SCULLINGS
SCULLION
SCULLIONS
SCULLS
SCULP
SCULPED
SCULPIN
SCULPING
SCULPINS
SCULPS
SCULPSIT
SCULPT
SCULPTED
SCULPTING
SCULPTOR
SCULPTORS
SCULPTS
SCULPTURE
SCULS
SCULTCH
SCULTCHES
SCUM
SCUMBAG
SCUMBAGS
SCUMBALL
SCUMBALLS
SCUMBER
SCUMBERED
SCUMBERS
SCUMBLE
SCUMBLED
SCUMBLES
SCUMBLING
SCUMFISH
SCUMLESS
SCUMLIKE
SCUMMED
SCUMMER
SCUMMERS
SCUMMIER
SCUMMIEST
SCUMMILY
SCUMMING
SCUMMINGS
SCUMMY
SCUMS
SCUNCHEON
SCUNDERED
SCUNGE
SCUNGED
SCUNGES
SCUNGIER
SCUNGIEST
SCUNGILE
SCUNGILI
SCUNGILLE
SCUNGILLI
SCUNGING
SCUNGY
SCUNNER
SCUNNERED
SCUNNERS
SCUP
SCUPPAUG
SCUPPAUGS
SCUPPER
SCUPPERED
SCUPPERS
SCUPS
SCUR
SCURF
SCURFIER
SCURFIEST
SCURFS
SCURFY
SCURRED
SCURRIED
SCURRIER
SCURRIERS
SCURRIES
SCURRIL
SCURRILE
SCURRING
SCURRIOUR
SCURRY
SCURRYING
SCURS
SCURVIER
SCURVIES
SCURVIEST
SCURVILY
SCURVY
SCUSE
SCUSED
SCUSES
SCUSING
SCUT
SCUTA
SCUTAGE
SCUTAGES
SCUTAL
SCUTATE
SCUTATION
SCUTCH
SCUTCHED
SCUTCHEON
SCUTCHER
SCUTCHERS
SCUTCHES
SCUTCHING
SCUTE
SCUTELLA
SCUTELLAR
SCUTELLUM
SCUTES
SCUTIFORM
SCUTIGER
SCUTIGERS
SCUTS
SCUTTER
SCUTTERED
SCUTTERS
SCUTTLE
SCUTTLED
SCUTTLER
SCUTTLERS
SCUTTLES
SCUTTLING
SCUTUM
SCUTWORK
SCUTWORKS
SCUZZ
SCUZZBAG
SCUZZBAGS
SCUZZBALL
SCUZZES
SCUZZIER
SCUZZIEST
SCUZZY
SCYBALA
SCYBALOUS
SCYBALUM
SCYE
SCYES
SCYPHATE
SCYPHI
SCYPHUS
SCYTALE
SCYTALES
SCYTHE
SCYTHED
SCYTHEMAN
SCYTHEMEN
SCYTHER
SCYTHERS
SCYTHES
SCYTHING
SDAINE
SDAINED
SDAINES
SDAINING
SDAYN
SDAYNED
SDAYNING
SDAYNS
SDEIGN
SDEIGNE
SDEIGNED
SDEIGNES
SDEIGNING
SDEIGNS
SDEIN
SDEINED
SDEINING
SDEINS
SEA
SEABAG
SEABAGS
SEABANK
SEABANKS
SEABEACH
SEABED
SEABEDS
SEABIRD
SEABIRDS
SEABLITE
SEABLITES
SEABOARD
SEABOARDS
SEABOOT
SEABOOTS
SEABORNE
SEABOTTLE
SEABREAM
SEABREAMS
SEACOAST
SEACOASTS
SEACOCK
SEACOCKS
SEACRAFT
SEACRAFTS
SEACUNNY
SEADOG
SEADOGS
SEADROME
SEADROMES
SEAFARER
SEAFARERS
SEAFARING
SEAFLOOR
SEAFLOORS
SEAFOAM
SEAFOAMS
SEAFOLK
SEAFOLKS
SEAFOOD
SEAFOODS
SEAFOWL
SEAFOWLS
SEAFRONT
SEAFRONTS
SEAGIRT
SEAGOING
SEAGRASS
SEAGULL
SEAGULLS
SEAHAWK
SEAHAWKS
SEAHOG
SEAHOGS
SEAHORSE
SEAHORSES
SEAHOUND
SEAHOUNDS
SEAKALE
SEAKALES

S

SEAKINDLY
SEAL
SEALABLE
SEALANT
SEALANTS
SEALCH
SEALCHS
SEALED
SEALER
SEALERIES
SEALERS
SEALERY
SEALGH
SEALGHS
SEALIFT
SEALIFTED
SEALIFTS
SEALINE
SEALINES
SEALING
SEALINGS
SEALLIKE
SEALPOINT
SEALS
SEALSKIN
SEALSKINS
SEALWAX
SEALWAXES
SEALYHAM
SEALYHAMS
SEAM
SEAMAID
SEAMAIDS
SEAMAN
SEAMANLY
SEAMARK
SEAMARKS
SEAME
SEAMED
SEAMEN
SEAMER
SEAMERS
SEAMES
SEAMFREE
SEAMIER
SEAMIEST
SEAMINESS
SEAMING
SEAMINGS
SEAMLESS
SEAMLIKE
SEAMOUNT
SEAMOUNTS
SEAMS
SEAMSET
SEAMSETS
SEAMSTER
SEAMSTERS
SEAMY
SEAN
SEANCE
SEANCES
SEANED
SEANING
SEANNACHY
SEANS
SEAPIECE
SEAPIECES
SEAPLANE
SEAPLANES
SEAPORT
SEAPORTS
SEAQUAKE
SEAQUAKES
SEAQUARIA
SEAR
SEARAT
SEARATS
SEARCE
SEARCED
SEARCES
SEARCH
SEARCHED
SEARCHER
SEARCHERS
SEARCHES
SEARCHING
SEARCING
SEARE
SEARED
SEARER
SEAREST
SEARING
SEARINGLY
SEARINGS
SEARNESS
SEAROBIN
SEAROBINS
SEARS
SEAS
SEASCAPE
SEASCAPES
SEASCOUT
SEASCOUTS
SEASE
SEASED
SEASES
SEASHELL
SEASHELLS
SEASHORE
SEASHORES
SEASICK
SEASICKER
SEASIDE
SEASIDES
SEASING
SEASON
SEASONAL
SEASONALS
SEASONED
SEASONER
SEASONERS
SEASONING
SEASONS
SEASPEAK
SEASPEAKS
SEASTRAND
SEASURE
SEASURES
SEAT
SEATBACK
SEATBACKS
SEATBELT
SEATBELTS
SEATED
SEATER
SEATERS
SEATING
SEATINGS
SEATLESS
SEATMATE
SEATMATES
SEATRAIN
SEATRAINS
SEATROUT
SEATROUTS
SEATS
SEATWORK
SEATWORKS
SEAWALL
SEAWALLED
SEAWALLS
SEAWAN
SEAWANS
SEAWANT
SEAWANTS
SEAWARD
SEAWARDLY
SEAWARDS
SEAWARE
SEAWARES
SEAWATER
SEAWATERS
SEAWAY
SEAWAYS
SEAWEED
SEAWEEDS
SEAWEEDY
SEAWIFE
SEAWIVES
SEAWOMAN
SEAWOMEN
SEAWORM
SEAWORMS
SEAWORTHY
SEAZE
SEAZED
SEAZES
SEAZING
SEBACEOUS
SEBACIC
SEBASIC
SEBATE
SEBATES
SEBESTEN
SEBESTENS
SEBIFIC
SEBORRHEA
SEBUM
SEBUMS
SEBUNDIES
SEBUNDY
SEC
SECALOSE
SECALOSES
SECANT
SECANTLY
SECANTS
SECATEUR
SECATEURS
SECCO
SECCOS
SECEDE
SECEDED
SECEDER
SECEDERS
SECEDES
SECEDING
SECERN
SECERNED
SECERNENT
SECERNING
SECERNS
SECESH
SECESHER
SECESHERS
SECESHES
SECESSION
SECH
SECHS
SECKEL
SECKELS
SECKLE
SECKLES
SECLUDE
SECLUDED
SECLUDES
SECLUDING
SECLUSION
SECLUSIVE
SECO
SECODONT
SECODONTS
SECONAL
SECONALS
SECOND
SECONDARY
SECONDE
SECONDED
SECONDEE

SECONDEES
SECONDER
SECONDERS
SECONDES
SECONDI
SECONDING
SECONDLY
SECONDO
SECONDS
SECPAR
SECPARS
SECRECIES
SECRECY
SECRET
SECRETA
SECRETAGE
SECRETARY
SECRETE
SECRETED
SECRETER
SECRETES
SECRETEST
SECRETIN
SECRETING
SECRETINS
SECRETION
SECRETIVE
SECRETLY
SECRETOR
SECRETORS
SECRETORY
SECRETS
SECS
SECT
SECTARIAL
SECTARIAN
SECTARIES
SECTARY
SECTATOR
SECTATORS
SECTILE
SECTILITY
SECTION
SECTIONAL
SECTIONED
SECTIONS
SECTOR
SECTORAL
SECTORED
SECTORIAL
SECTORING
SECTORISE
SECTORIZE
SECTORS
SECTS
SECULA
SECULAR
SECULARLY
SECULARS
SECULUM
SECULUMS
SECUND
SECUNDINE
SECUNDLY
SECUNDUM
SECURABLE
SECURANCE
SECURE
SECURED
SECURELY
SECURER
SECURERS
SECURES
SECUREST
SECURING
SECURITAN
SECURITY
SED
SEDAN
SEDANS
SEDARIM
SEDATE
SEDATED
SEDATELY
SEDATER
SEDATES
SEDATEST
SEDATING
SEDATION
SEDATIONS
SEDATIVE
SEDATIVES
SEDENT
SEDENTARY
SEDER
SEDERS
SEDERUNT
SEDERUNTS
SEDES
SEDGE
SEDGED
SEDGELAND
SEDGES
SEDGIER
SEDGIEST
SEDGY
SEDILE
SEDILIA
SEDILIUM
SEDIMENT
SEDIMENTS
SEDITION
SEDITIONS
SEDITIOUS
SEDUCE
SEDUCED
SEDUCER
SEDUCERS
SEDUCES
SEDUCIBLE
SEDUCING
SEDUCINGS
SEDUCIVE
SEDUCTION
SEDUCTIVE
SEDUCTOR
SEDUCTORS
SEDULITY
SEDULOUS
SEDUM
SEDUMS
SEE
SEEABLE
SEECATCH
SEED
SEEDBED
SEEDBEDS
SEEDBOX
SEEDBOXES
SEEDCAKE
SEEDCAKES
SEEDCASE
SEEDCASES
SEEDEATER
SEEDED
SEEDER
SEEDERS
SEEDHEAD
SEEDHEADS
SEEDIER
SEEDIEST
SEEDILY
SEEDINESS
SEEDING
SEEDINGS
SEEDLESS
SEEDLIKE
SEEDLING
SEEDLINGS
SEEDLIP
SEEDLIPS
SEEDMAN
SEEDMEN
SEEDNESS
SEEDPOD
SEEDPODS
SEEDS
SEEDSMAN
SEEDSMEN
SEEDSTOCK
SEEDTIME
SEEDTIMES
SEEDY
SEEING
SEEINGS
SEEK
SEEKER
SEEKERS
SEEKING
SEEKS
SEEL
SEELD
SEELED
SEELIE
SEELIER
SEELIEST
SEELING
SEELINGS
SEELS
SEELY
SEEM
SEEMED
SEEMER
SEEMERS
SEEMING
SEEMINGLY
SEEMINGS
SEEMLESS
SEEMLIER
SEEMLIEST
SEEMLIHED
SEEMLY
SEEMLYHED
SEEMS
SEEN
SEEP
SEEPAGE
SEEPAGES
SEEPED
SEEPIER
SEEPIEST
SEEPING
SEEPS
SEEPY
SEER
SEERESS
SEERESSES
SEERS
SEES
SEESAW
SEESAWED
SEESAWING
SEESAWS
SEETHE
SEETHED
SEETHER
SEETHERS
SEETHES
SEETHING
SEETHINGS
SEEWING
SEEWINGS
SEFER
SEG
SEGAR
SEGARS
SEGETAL
SEGGAR
SEGGARS
SEGHOL

S

SEGHOLATE
SEGHOLS
SEGMENT
SEGMENTAL
SEGMENTED
SEGMENTS
SEGNI
SEGNO
SEGNOS
SEGO
SEGOL
SEGOLATE
SEGOLATES
SEGOLS
SEGOS
SEGREANT
SEGREGANT
SEGREGATE
SEGS
SEGUE
SEGUED
SEGUEING
SEGUES
SEGUGIO
SEGUGIOS
SEHRI
SEHRIS
SEI
SEICENTO
SEICENTOS
SEICHE
SEICHES
SEIDEL
SEIDELS
SEIF
SEIFS
SEIGNEUR
SEIGNEURS
SEIGNEURY
SEIGNIOR
SEIGNIORS
SEIGNIORY
SEIGNORAL
SEIGNORY
SEIK
SEIKER
SEIKEST
SEIL
SEILED
SEILING
SEILS
SEINE
SEINED
SEINER
SEINERS
SEINES
SEINING
SEININGS
SEIR
SEIRS
SEIS
SEISABLE
SEISE
SEISED
SEISER
SEISERS
SEISES
SEISIN
SEISING
SEISINGS
SEISINS
SEISM
SEISMAL
SEISMIC
SEISMICAL
SEISMISM
SEISMISMS
SEISMS
SEISOR
SEISORS
SEISURE
SEISURES
SEITAN
SEITANS
SEITEN
SEITENS
SEITIES
SEITY
SEIZA
SEIZABLE
SEIZAS
SEIZE
SEIZED
SEIZER
SEIZERS
SEIZES
SEIZIN
SEIZING
SEIZINGS
SEIZINS
SEIZOR
SEIZORS
SEIZURE
SEIZURES
SEJANT
SEJEANT
SEKOS
SEKOSES
SEKT
SEKTS
SEL
SELACHIAN
SELADANG
SELADANGS
SELAH
SELAHS
SELAMLIK
SELAMLIKS
SELCOUTH
SELD
SELDOM
SELDOMLY
SELDSEEN
SELDSHOWN
SELE
SELECT
SELECTA
SELECTAS
SELECTED
SELECTEE
SELECTEES
SELECTING
SELECTION
SELECTIVE
SELECTLY
SELECTMAN
SELECTMEN
SELECTOR
SELECTORS
SELECTS
SELENATE
SELENATES
SELENIAN
SELENIC
SELENIDE
SELENIDES
SELENIOUS
SELENITE
SELENITES
SELENITIC
SELENIUM
SELENIUMS
SELENOSES
SELENOSIS
SELENOUS
SELES
SELF
SELFDOM
SELFDOMS
SELFED
SELFHEAL
SELFHEALS
SELFHOOD
SELFHOODS
SELFIE
SELFIES
SELFING
SELFINGS
SELFISH
SELFISHLY
SELFISM
SELFISMS
SELFIST
SELFISTS
SELFLESS
SELFNESS
SELFS
SELFSAME
SELFWARD
SELFWARDS
SELICTAR
SELICTARS
SELKIE
SELKIES
SELL
SELLA
SELLABLE
SELLAE
SELLAS
SELLE
SELLER
SELLERS
SELLES
SELLING
SELLINGS
SELLOFF
SELLOFFS
SELLOTAPE
SELLOUT
SELLOUTS
SELLS
SELS
SELSYN
SELSYNS
SELTZER
SELTZERS
SELVA
SELVAGE
SELVAGED
SELVAGEE
SELVAGEES
SELVAGES
SELVAGING
SELVAS
SELVEDGE
SELVEDGED
SELVEDGES
SELVES
SEMAINIER
SEMANTEME
SEMANTIC
SEMANTICS
SEMANTIDE
SEMANTRA
SEMANTRON
SEMAPHORE
SEMATIC
SEMBLABLE
SEMBLABLY
SEMBLANCE
SEMBLANT
SEMBLANTS
SEMBLE
SEMBLED
SEMBLES
SEMBLING
SEME
SEMEE
SEMEED
SEMEIA

SEMEION
SEMEIOTIC
SEMEME
SEMEMES
SEMEMIC
SEMEN
SEMENS
SEMES
SEMESTER
SEMESTERS
SEMESTRAL
SEMI
SEMIANGLE
SEMIARID
SEMIBALD
SEMIBOLD
SEMIBOLDS
SEMIBREVE
SEMIBULL
SEMIBULLS
SEMICOLON
SEMICOMA
SEMICOMAS
SEMICURED
SEMIDEAF
SEMIDEIFY
SEMIDOME
SEMIDOMED
SEMIDOMES
SEMIDRIER
SEMIDRY
SEMIDWARF
SEMIE
SEMIERECT
SEMIES
SEMIFINAL
SEMIFIT
SEMIFLUID
SEMIGALA
SEMIGALAS
SEMIGLOBE
SEMIGLOSS
SEMIGROUP
SEMIHARD
SEMIHIGH
SEMIHOBO
SEMIHOBOS
SEMILLON
SEMILLONS
SEMILOG
SEMILUNAR
SEMILUNE
SEMILUNES
SEMIMAT
SEMIMATT
SEMIMATTE
SEMIMETAL
SEMIMICRO
SEMIMILD
SEMIMOIST
SEMIMUTE
SEMIMUTES
SEMINA
SEMINAL
SEMINALLY
SEMINAR
SEMINARS
SEMINARY
SEMINATE
SEMINATED
SEMINATES
SEMINOMA
SEMINOMAD
SEMINOMAS
SEMINUDE
SEMIOLOGY
SEMIOPEN
SEMIOSES
SEMIOSIS
SEMIOTIC
SEMIOTICS
SEMIOVAL
SEMIPED
SEMIPEDS
SEMIPIOUS
SEMIPLUME
SEMIPOLAR
SEMIPRO
SEMIPROS
SEMIRAW
SEMIRIGID
SEMIROUND
SEMIRURAL
SEMIS
SEMISES
SEMISOFT
SEMISOLID
SEMISOLUS
SEMISTIFF
SEMISWEET
SEMITAR
SEMITARS
SEMITAUR
SEMITAURS
SEMITIST
SEMITISTS
SEMITONAL
SEMITONE
SEMITONES
SEMITONIC
SEMITRUCK
SEMIURBAN
SEMIVOCAL
SEMIVOWEL
SEMIWATER
SEMIWILD
SEMIWORKS
SEMMIT
SEMMITS
SEMOLINA
SEMOLINAS
SEMPER
SEMPLE
SEMPLER
SEMPLEST
SEMPLICE
SEMPRE
SEMPSTER
SEMPSTERS
SEMSEM
SEMSEMS
SEMUNCIA
SEMUNCIAE
SEMUNCIAL
SEMUNCIAS
SEN
SENA
SENARIES
SENARII
SENARIUS
SENARY
SENAS
SENATE
SENATES
SENATOR
SENATORS
SEND
SENDABLE
SENDAL
SENDALS
SENDED
SENDER
SENDERS
SENDING
SENDINGS
SENDOFF
SENDOFFS
SENDS
SENDUP
SENDUPS
SENE
SENECA
SENECAS
SENECIO
SENECIOS
SENEGA
SENEGAS
SENES
SENESCE
SENESCED
SENESCENT
SENESCES
SENESCHAL
SENESCING
SENGI
SENGIS
SENGREEN
SENGREENS
SENHOR
SENHORA
SENHORAS
SENHORES
SENHORITA
SENHORS
SENILE
SENILELY
SENILES
SENILITY
SENIOR
SENIORITY
SENIORS
SENITI
SENITIS
SENNA
SENNACHIE
SENNAS
SENNET
SENNETS
SENNIGHT
SENNIGHTS
SENNIT
SENNITS
SENOPIA
SENOPIAS
SENOR
SENORA
SENORAS
SENORES
SENORITA
SENORITAS
SENORS
SENRYU
SENS
SENSA
SENSATE
SENSATED
SENSATELY
SENSATES
SENSATING
SENSATION
SENSE
SENSED
SENSEFUL
SENSEI
SENSEIS
SENSELESS
SENSES
SENSI
SENSIBLE
SENSIBLER
SENSIBLES
SENSIBLY
SENSILE
SENSILLA
SENSILLAE
SENSILLUM
SENSING
SENSINGS
SENSIS
SENSISM

S

SENSISMS
SENSIST
SENSISTS
SENSITISE
SENSITIVE
SENSITIZE
SENSOR
SENSORIA
SENSORIAL
SENSORILY
SENSORIUM
SENSORS
SENSORY
SENSUAL
SENSUALLY
SENSUM
SENSUOUS
SENT
SENTE
SENTED
SENTENCE
SENTENCED
SENTENCER
SENTENCES
SENTENTIA
SENTI
SENTIENCE
SENTIENCY
SENTIENT
SENTIENTS
SENTIMENT
SENTIMO
SENTIMOS
SENTINEL
SENTINELS
SENTING
SENTRIES
SENTRY
SENTS
SENVIES
SENVY
SENZA
SEPAD
SEPADDED
SEPADDING
SEPADS
SEPAL
SEPALED
SEPALINE
SEPALLED
SEPALODY
SEPALOID
SEPALOUS
SEPALS
SEPARABLE
SEPARABLY
SEPARATA
SEPARATE
SEPARATED
SEPARATES
SEPARATOR
SEPARATUM
SEPHEN
SEPHENS
SEPIA
SEPIAS
SEPIC
SEPIMENT
SEPIMENTS
SEPIOLITE
SEPIOST
SEPIOSTS
SEPIUM
SEPIUMS
SEPMAG
SEPOY
SEPOYS
SEPPUKU
SEPPUKUS
SEPS
SEPSES
SEPSIS
SEPT
SEPTA
SEPTAGE
SEPTAGES
SEPTAL
SEPTARIA
SEPTARIAN
SEPTARIUM
SEPTATE
SEPTATION
SEPTEMFID
SEPTEMVIR
SEPTENARY
SEPTENNIA
SEPTET
SEPTETS
SEPTETTE
SEPTETTES
SEPTIC
SEPTICAL
SEPTICITY
SEPTICS
SEPTIFORM
SEPTIMAL
SEPTIME
SEPTIMES
SEPTIMOLE
SEPTLEVA
SEPTLEVAS
SEPTORIA
SEPTORIAS
SEPTS
SEPTUM
SEPTUMS
SEPTUOR
SEPTUORS
SEPTUPLE
SEPTUPLED
SEPTUPLES
SEPTUPLET
SEPULCHER
SEPULCHRE
SEPULTURE
SEQUACITY
SEQUEL
SEQUELA
SEQUELAE
SEQUELISE
SEQUELIZE
SEQUELS
SEQUENCE
SEQUENCED
SEQUENCER
SEQUENCES
SEQUENCY
SEQUENT
SEQUENTLY
SEQUENTS
SEQUESTER
SEQUESTRA
SEQUIN
SEQUINED
SEQUINING
SEQUINNED
SEQUINS
SEQUITUR
SEQUITURS
SEQUOIA
SEQUOIAS
SER
SERA
SERAC
SERACS
SERAFILE
SERAFILES
SERAFIN
SERAFINS
SERAGLIO
SERAGLIOS
SERAI
SERAIL
SERAILS
SERAIS
SERAL
SERANG
SERANGS
SERAPE
SERAPES
SERAPH
SERAPHIC
SERAPHIM
SERAPHIMS
SERAPHIN
SERAPHINE
SERAPHINS
SERAPHS
SERASKIER
SERDAB
SERDABS
SERE
SERED
SEREIN
SEREINS
SERENADE
SERENADED
SERENADER
SERENADES
SERENATA
SERENATAS
SERENATE
SERENATED
SERENATES
SERENE
SERENED
SERENELY
SERENER
SERENES
SERENEST
SERENING
SERENITY
SERER
SERES
SEREST
SERF
SERFAGE
SERFAGES
SERFDOM
SERFDOMS
SERFHOOD
SERFHOODS
SERFISH
SERFLIKE
SERFS
SERFSHIP
SERFSHIPS
SERGE
SERGEANCY
SERGEANT
SERGEANTS
SERGEANTY
SERGED
SERGER
SERGERS
SERGES
SERGING
SERGINGS
SERIAL
SERIALISE
SERIALISM
SERIALIST
SERIALITY
SERIALIZE
SERIALLY
SERIALS
SERIATE
SERIATED
SERIATELY
SERIATES

S

SERIATIM
SERIATING
SERIATION
SERIC
SERICEOUS
SERICIN
SERICINS
SERICITE
SERICITES
SERICITIC
SERICON
SERICONS
SERIEMA
SERIEMAS
SERIES
SERIF
SERIFED
SERIFFED
SERIFS
SERIGRAPH
SERIN
SERINE
SERINES
SERINETTE
SERING
SERINGA
SERINGAS
SERINS
SERIOUS
SERIOUSLY
SERIPH
SERIPHS
SERJEANCY
SERJEANT
SERJEANTS
SERJEANTY
SERK
SERKALI
SERKALIS
SERKS
SERMON
SERMONED
SERMONEER
SERMONER
SERMONERS
SERMONET
SERMONETS
SERMONIC
SERMONING
SERMONISE
SERMONIZE
SERMONS
SEROGROUP
SEROLOGIC
SEROLOGY
SEROMA
SEROMAS
SERON
SERONS
SEROON
SEROONS
SEROPUS
SEROPUSES
SEROSA
SEROSAE
SEROSAL
SEROSAS
SEROSITY
SEROTINAL
SEROTINE
SEROTINES
SEROTINY
SEROTONIN
SEROTYPE
SEROTYPED
SEROTYPES
SEROTYPIC
SEROUS
SEROVAR
SEROVARS
SEROW
SEROWS
SERPENT
SERPENTRY
SERPENTS
SERPIGO
SERPIGOES
SERPIGOS
SERPULA
SERPULAE
SERPULAS
SERPULID
SERPULIDS
SERPULITE
SERR
SERRA
SERRAE
SERRAN
SERRANID
SERRANIDS
SERRANO
SERRANOID
SERRANOS
SERRANS
SERRAS
SERRATE
SERRATED
SERRATES
SERRATI
SERRATING
SERRATION
SERRATURE
SERRATUS
SERRE
SERRED
SERREFILE
SERRES
SERRICORN
SERRIED
SERRIEDLY
SERRIES
SERRIFORM
SERRING
SERRS
SERRULATE
SERRY
SERRYING
SERS
SERUEWE
SERUEWED
SERUEWES
SERUEWING
SERUM
SERUMAL
SERUMS
SERVABLE
SERVAL
SERVALS
SERVANT
SERVANTED
SERVANTRY
SERVANTS
SERVE
SERVEABLE
SERVED
SERVER
SERVERIES
SERVERS
SERVERY
SERVES
SERVEWARE
SERVEWE
SERVEWED
SERVEWES
SERVEWING
SERVICE
SERVICED
SERVICER
SERVICERS
SERVICES
SERVICING
SERVIENT
SERVIETTE
SERVILE
SERVILELY
SERVILES
SERVILISM
SERVILITY
SERVING
SERVINGS
SERVITOR
SERVITORS
SERVITUDE
SERVLET
SERVLETS
SERVO
SERVOS
SERVQUAL
SERVQUALS
SESAME
SESAMES
SESAMOID
SESAMOIDS
SESE
SESELI
SESELIS
SESEY
SESH
SESHES
SESS
SESSA
SESSED
SESSES
SESSILE
SESSILITY
SESSING
SESSION
SESSIONAL
SESSIONS
SESSPOOL
SESSPOOLS
SESTERCE
SESTERCES
SESTERTIA
SESTERTII
SESTET
SESTETS
SESTETT
SESTETTE
SESTETTES
SESTETTO
SESTETTOS
SESTETTS
SESTINA
SESTINAS
SESTINE
SESTINES
SESTON
SESTONS
SET
SETA
SETACEOUS
SETAE
SETAL
SETBACK
SETBACKS
SETENANT
SETENANTS
SETIFORM
SETLINE
SETLINES
SETNESS
SETNESSES
SETOFF
SETOFFS
SETON
SETONS
SETOSE
SETOUS
SETOUT

SETOUTS
SETS
SETSCREW
SETSCREWS
SETT
SETTEE
SETTEES
SETTER
SETTERED
SETTERING
SETTERS
SETTING
SETTINGS
SETTLE
SETTLED
SETTLER
SETTLERS
SETTLES
SETTLING
SETTLINGS
SETTLOR
SETTLORS
SETTS
SETUALE
SETUALES
SETULE
SETULES
SETULOSE
SETULOUS
SETUP
SETUPS
SETWALL
SETWALLS
SEV
SEVEN
SEVENFOLD
SEVENISH
SEVENS
SEVENTEEN
SEVENTH
SEVENTHLY
SEVENTHS
SEVENTIES
SEVENTY
SEVER
SEVERABLE
SEVERAL
SEVERALLY
SEVERALS
SEVERALTY
SEVERANCE
SEVERE
SEVERED
SEVERELY
SEVERER
SEVEREST
SEVERIES
SEVERING
SEVERITY
SEVERS
SEVERY
SEVICHE
SEVICHES
SEVRUGA
SEVRUGAS
SEVS
SEW
SEWABLE
SEWAGE
SEWAGES
SEWAN
SEWANS
SEWAR
SEWARS
SEWED
SEWEL
SEWELLEL
SEWELLELS
SEWELS
SEWEN
SEWENS
SEWER
SEWERAGE
SEWERAGES
SEWERED
SEWERING
SEWERINGS
SEWERLESS
SEWERLIKE
SEWERS
SEWIN
SEWING
SEWINGS
SEWINS
SEWN
SEWS
SEX
SEXAHOLIC
SEXCAPADE
SEXED
SEXENNIAL
SEXER
SEXERCISE
SEXERS
SEXES
SEXFID
SEXFOIL
SEXFOILS
SEXIER
SEXIEST
SEXILY
SEXINESS
SEXING
SEXINGS
SEXISM
SEXISMS
SEXIST
SEXISTS
SEXLESS
SEXLESSLY
SEXLINKED
SEXOLOGIC
SEXOLOGY
SEXPERT
SEXPERTS
SEXPOT
SEXPOTS
SEXT
SEXTAIN
SEXTAINS
SEXTAN
SEXTANS
SEXTANSES
SEXTANT
SEXTANTAL
SEXTANTS
SEXTARII
SEXTARIUS
SEXTED
SEXTET
SEXTETS
SEXTETT
SEXTETTE
SEXTETTES
SEXTETTS
SEXTILE
SEXTILES
SEXTING
SEXTINGS
SEXTO
SEXTOLET
SEXTOLETS
SEXTON
SEXTONESS
SEXTONS
SEXTOS
SEXTS
SEXTUOR
SEXTUORS
SEXTUPLE
SEXTUPLED
SEXTUPLES
SEXTUPLET
SEXTUPLY
SEXUAL
SEXUALISE
SEXUALISM
SEXUALIST
SEXUALITY
SEXUALIZE
SEXUALLY
SEXVALENT
SEXY
SEY
SEYEN
SEYENS
SEYS
SEYSURE
SEYSURES
SEZ
SFERICS
SFORZANDI
SFORZANDO
SFORZATI
SFORZATO
SFORZATOS
SFUMATO
SFUMATOS
SGRAFFITI
SGRAFFITO
SH
SHA
SHABASH
SHABBATOT
SHABBIER
SHABBIEST
SHABBILY
SHABBLE
SHABBLES
SHABBY
SHABRACK
SHABRACKS
SHACK
SHACKED
SHACKIER
SHACKIEST
SHACKING
SHACKLE
SHACKLED
SHACKLER
SHACKLERS
SHACKLES
SHACKLING
SHACKO
SHACKOES
SHACKOS
SHACKS
SHACKTOWN
SHACKY
SHAD
SHADBERRY
SHADBLOW
SHADBLOWS
SHADBUSH
SHADCHAN
SHADCHANS
SHADDOCK
SHADDOCKS
SHADDUP
SHADE
SHADED
SHADELESS
SHADER
SHADERS
SHADES
SHADFLIES
SHADFLY
SHADIER
SHADIEST
SHADILY

S

SHADINESS
SHADING
SHADINGS
SHADKHAN
SHADKHANS
SHADOOF
SHADOOFS
SHADOW
SHADOWBOX
SHADOWED
SHADOWER
SHADOWERS
SHADOWIER
SHADOWILY
SHADOWING
SHADOWS
SHADOWY
SHADRACH
SHADRACHS
SHADS
SHADUF
SHADUFS
SHADY
SHAFT
SHAFTED
SHAFTER
SHAFTERS
SHAFTING
SHAFTINGS
SHAFTLESS
SHAFTS
SHAG
SHAGBARK
SHAGBARKS
SHAGGABLE
SHAGGED
SHAGGER
SHAGGERS
SHAGGIER
SHAGGIEST
SHAGGILY
SHAGGING
SHAGGY
SHAGPILE
SHAGREEN
SHAGREENS
SHAGROON
SHAGROONS
SHAGS
SHAH
SHAHADA
SHAHADAH
SHAHADAHS
SHAHADAS
SHAHDOM
SHAHDOMS
SHAHEED
SHAHEEDS
SHAHID
SHAHIDS
SHAHS
SHAHTOOSH
SHAIKH
SHAIKHS
SHAIRD
SHAIRDS
SHAIRN
SHAIRNS
SHAITAN
SHAITANS
SHAKABLE
SHAKE
SHAKEABLE
SHAKED
SHAKEDOWN
SHAKEN
SHAKEOUT
SHAKEOUTS
SHAKER
SHAKERS
SHAKES
SHAKEUP
SHAKEUPS
SHAKIER
SHAKIEST
SHAKILY
SHAKINESS
SHAKING
SHAKINGS
SHAKO
SHAKOES
SHAKOS
SHAKT
SHAKUDO
SHAKUDOS
SHAKY
SHALE
SHALED
SHALELIKE
SHALES
SHALEY
SHALIER
SHALIEST
SHALING
SHALL
SHALLI
SHALLIS
SHALLON
SHALLONS
SHALLOON
SHALLOONS
SHALLOP
SHALLOPS
SHALLOT
SHALLOTS
SHALLOW
SHALLOWED
SHALLOWER
SHALLOWLY
SHALLOWS
SHALM
SHALMS
SHALOM
SHALOMS
SHALOT
SHALOTS
SHALT
SHALWAR
SHALWARS
SHALY
SHAM
SHAMA
SHAMABLE
SHAMABLY
SHAMAL
SHAMALS
SHAMAN
SHAMANIC
SHAMANISM
SHAMANIST
SHAMANS
SHAMAS
SHAMATEUR
SHAMBA
SHAMBAS
SHAMBLE
SHAMBLED
SHAMBLES
SHAMBLIER
SHAMBLING
SHAMBLY
SHAMBOLIC
SHAME
SHAMEABLE
SHAMEABLY
SHAMED
SHAMEFAST
SHAMEFUL
SHAMELESS
SHAMER
SHAMERS
SHAMES
SHAMIANA
SHAMIANAH
SHAMIANAS
SHAMINA
SHAMINAS
SHAMING
SHAMINGS
SHAMISEN
SHAMISENS
SHAMMAS
SHAMMASH
SHAMMASIM
SHAMMED
SHAMMER
SHAMMERS
SHAMMES
SHAMMIED
SHAMMIES
SHAMMING
SHAMMOS
SHAMMOSIM
SHAMMY
SHAMMYING
SHAMOIS
SHAMOISED
SHAMOISES
SHAMOS
SHAMOSIM
SHAMOY
SHAMOYED
SHAMOYING
SHAMOYS
SHAMPOO
SHAMPOOED
SHAMPOOER
SHAMPOOS
SHAMROCK
SHAMROCKS
SHAMS
SHAMUS
SHAMUSES
SHAN
SHANACHIE
SHAND
SHANDIES
SHANDRIES
SHANDRY
SHANDS
SHANDY
SHANGHAI
SHANGHAIS
SHANK
SHANKBONE
SHANKED
SHANKING
SHANKS
SHANNIES
SHANNY
SHANS
SHANTEY
SHANTEYS
SHANTI
SHANTIES
SHANTIH
SHANTIHS
SHANTIS
SHANTUNG
SHANTUNGS
SHANTY
SHANTYMAN
SHANTYMEN
SHAPABLE
SHAPE
SHAPEABLE
SHAPED
SHAPELESS
SHAPELIER
SHAPELY

S

SHAPEN
SHAPENED
SHAPENING
SHAPENS
SHAPER
SHAPERS
SHAPES
SHAPEUP
SHAPEUPS
SHAPEWEAR
SHAPING
SHAPINGS
SHAPS
SHARABLE
SHARD
SHARDED
SHARDS
SHARE
SHAREABLE
SHARECROP
SHARED
SHAREMAN
SHAREMEN
SHARER
SHARERS
SHARES
SHARESMAN
SHARESMEN
SHAREWARE
SHARIA
SHARIAH
SHARIAHS
SHARIAS
SHARIAT
SHARIATS
SHARIF
SHARIFIAN
SHARIFS
SHARING
SHARINGS
SHARK
SHARKED
SHARKER
SHARKERS
SHARKING
SHARKINGS
SHARKISH
SHARKLIKE
SHARKS
SHARKSKIN
SHARN
SHARNIER
SHARNIES
SHARNIEST
SHARNS
SHARNY
SHARON
SHARP
SHARPED
SHARPEN
SHARPENED
SHARPENER
SHARPENS
SHARPER
SHARPERS
SHARPEST
SHARPIE
SHARPIES
SHARPING
SHARPINGS
SHARPISH
SHARPLY
SHARPNESS
SHARPS
SHARPTAIL
SHARPY
SHASH
SHASHED
SHASHES
SHASHING
SHASHLICK
SHASHLIK
SHASHLIKS
SHASLIK
SHASLIKS
SHASTA
SHASTAS
SHASTER
SHASTERS
SHASTRA
SHASTRAS
SHAT
SHATOOSH
SHATTER
SHATTERED
SHATTERER
SHATTERS
SHATTERY
SHAUCHLE
SHAUCHLED
SHAUCHLES
SHAUCHLY
SHAUGH
SHAUGHS
SHAUL
SHAULED
SHAULING
SHAULS
SHAVABLE
SHAVASANA
SHAVE
SHAVEABLE
SHAVED
SHAVELING
SHAVEN
SHAVER
SHAVERS
SHAVES
SHAVETAIL
SHAVIE
SHAVIES
SHAVING
SHAVINGS
SHAW
SHAWARMA
SHAWARMAS
SHAWED
SHAWING
SHAWL
SHAWLED
SHAWLEY
SHAWLEYS
SHAWLIE
SHAWLIES
SHAWLING
SHAWLINGS
SHAWLLESS
SHAWLS
SHAWM
SHAWMS
SHAWN
SHAWS
SHAY
SHAYA
SHAYAS
SHAYKH
SHAYKHS
SHAYS
SHAZAM
SHCHI
SHCHIS
SHE
SHEA
SHEADING
SHEADINGS
SHEAF
SHEAFED
SHEAFIER
SHEAFIEST
SHEAFING
SHEAFLIKE
SHEAFS
SHEAFY
SHEAL
SHEALED
SHEALING
SHEALINGS
SHEALS
SHEAR
SHEARED
SHEARER
SHEARERS
SHEARING
SHEARINGS
SHEARLEG
SHEARLEGS
SHEARLING
SHEARMAN
SHEARMEN
SHEARS
SHEAS
SHEATFISH
SHEATH
SHEATHE
SHEATHED
SHEATHER
SHEATHERS
SHEATHES
SHEATHIER
SHEATHING
SHEATHS
SHEATHY
SHEAVE
SHEAVED
SHEAVES
SHEAVING
SHEBANG
SHEBANGS
SHEBEAN
SHEBEANS
SHEBEEN
SHEBEENED
SHEBEENER
SHEBEENS
SHECHITA
SHECHITAH
SHECHITAS
SHED
SHEDABLE
SHEDDABLE
SHEDDED
SHEDDER
SHEDDERS
SHEDDING
SHEDDINGS
SHEDFUL
SHEDFULS
SHEDHAND
SHEDHANDS
SHEDLIKE
SHEDLOAD
SHEDLOADS
SHEDS
SHEEL
SHEELED
SHEELING
SHEELS
SHEEN
SHEENED
SHEENEY
SHEENEYS
SHEENFUL
SHEENIE
SHEENIER
SHEENIES
SHEENIEST
SHEENING
SHEENS
SHEENY
SHEEP

S

SHEEPCOT
SHEEPCOTE
SHEEPCOTS
SHEEPDOG
SHEEPDOGS
SHEEPFOLD
SHEEPHEAD
SHEEPIER
SHEEPIEST
SHEEPISH
SHEEPLE
SHEEPLES
SHEEPLIKE
SHEEPMAN
SHEEPMEN
SHEEPO
SHEEPOS
SHEEPSKIN
SHEEPWALK
SHEEPY
SHEER
SHEERED
SHEERER
SHEEREST
SHEERING
SHEERLEG
SHEERLEGS
SHEERLY
SHEERNESS
SHEERS
SHEESH
SHEESHA
SHEESHAS
SHEET
SHEETED
SHEETER
SHEETERS
SHEETFED
SHEETIER
SHEETIEST
SHEETING
SHEETINGS
SHEETLESS
SHEETLIKE
SHEETROCK
SHEETS
SHEETY
SHEEVE
SHEEVES
SHEGETZ
SHEHITA
SHEHITAH
SHEHITAHS
SHEHITAS
SHEHNAI
SHEHNAIS
SHEIK
SHEIKDOM
SHEIKDOMS
SHEIKH
SHEIKHA
SHEIKHAS
SHEIKHDOM
SHEIKHS
SHEIKS
SHEILA
SHEILAS
SHEILING
SHEILINGS
SHEITAN
SHEITANS
SHEITEL
SHEITELS
SHEKALIM
SHEKEL
SHEKELIM
SHEKELS
SHELDDUCK
SHELDRAKE
SHELDUCK
SHELDUCKS
SHELF
SHELFED
SHELFFUL
SHELFFULS
SHELFIER
SHELFIEST
SHELFING
SHELFLIKE
SHELFROOM
SHELFS
SHELFY
SHELL
SHELLAC
SHELLACK
SHELLACKS
SHELLACS
SHELLBACK
SHELLBARK
SHELLDUCK
SHELLED
SHELLER
SHELLERS
SHELLFIRE
SHELLFISH
SHELLFUL
SHELLFULS
SHELLIER
SHELLIEST
SHELLING
SHELLINGS
SHELLS
SHELLWORK
SHELLY
SHELTA
SHELTAS
SHELTER
SHELTERED
SHELTERER
SHELTERS
SHELTERY
SHELTIE
SHELTIES
SHELTY
SHELVE
SHELVED
SHELVER
SHELVERS
SHELVES
SHELVIER
SHELVIEST
SHELVING
SHELVINGS
SHELVY
SHEMALE
SHEMALES
SHEMOZZLE
SHEN
SHENAI
SHENAIS
SHEND
SHENDING
SHENDS
SHENT
SHEOL
SHEOLS
SHEPHERD
SHEPHERDS
SHEQALIM
SHEQEL
SHEQELS
SHERANG
SHERANGS
SHERBERT
SHERBERTS
SHERBET
SHERBETS
SHERD
SHERDS
SHERE
SHEREEF
SHEREEFS
SHERIA
SHERIAS
SHERIAT
SHERIATS
SHERIF
SHERIFF
SHERIFFS
SHERIFIAN
SHERIFS
SHERLOCK
SHERLOCKS
SHERO
SHEROES
SHEROOT
SHEROOTS
SHERPA
SHERPAS
SHERRIED
SHERRIES
SHERRIS
SHERRISES
SHERRY
SHERWANI
SHERWANIS
SHES
SHET
SHETLAND
SHETLANDS
SHETS
SHETTING
SHEUCH
SHEUCHED
SHEUCHING
SHEUCHS
SHEUGH
SHEUGHED
SHEUGHING
SHEUGHS
SHEVA
SHEVAS
SHEW
SHEWBREAD
SHEWED
SHEWEL
SHEWELS
SHEWER
SHEWERS
SHEWING
SHEWN
SHEWS
SHH
SHHH
SHIAI
SHIAIS
SHIATSU
SHIATSUS
SHIATZU
SHIATZUS
SHIBAH
SHIBAHS
SHIBUICHI
SHICKER
SHICKERED
SHICKERS
SHICKSA
SHICKSAS
SHIDDER
SHIDDERS
SHIDDUCH
SHIED
SHIEL
SHIELD
SHIELDED
SHIELDER
SHIELDERS
SHIELDING
SHIELDS
SHIELED

S

SHIELING
SHIELINGS
SHIELS
SHIER
SHIERS
SHIES
SHIEST
SHIFT
SHIFTABLE
SHIFTED
SHIFTER
SHIFTERS
SHIFTIER
SHIFTIEST
SHIFTILY
SHIFTING
SHIFTINGS
SHIFTLESS
SHIFTS
SHIFTWORK
SHIFTY
SHIGELLA
SHIGELLAE
SHIGELLAS
SHIITAKE
SHIITAKES
SHIKAR
SHIKARA
SHIKARAS
SHIKAREE
SHIKAREES
SHIKARI
SHIKARIS
SHIKARRED
SHIKARS
SHIKKER
SHIKKERED
SHIKKERS
SHIKRA
SHIKRAS
SHIKSA
SHIKSAS
SHIKSE
SHIKSEH
SHIKSEHS
SHIKSES
SHILINGI
SHILINGIS
SHILL
SHILLABER
SHILLALA
SHILLALAH
SHILLALAS
SHILLED
SHILLELAH
SHILLING
SHILLINGS
SHILLS
SHILPIT
SHILY
SHIM
SHIMAAL
SHIMAALS
SHIMMED
SHIMMER
SHIMMERED
SHIMMERS
SHIMMERY
SHIMMEY
SHIMMEYS
SHIMMIED
SHIMMIES
SHIMMING
SHIMMY
SHIMMYING
SHIMOZZLE
SHIMS
SHIN
SHINBONE
SHINBONES
SHINDIES
SHINDIG
SHINDIGS
SHINDY
SHINDYS
SHINE
SHINED
SHINELESS
SHINER
SHINERS
SHINES
SHINESS
SHINESSES
SHINGLE
SHINGLED
SHINGLER
SHINGLERS
SHINGLES
SHINGLIER
SHINGLING
SHINGLY
SHINGUARD
SHINIER
SHINIES
SHINIEST
SHINILY
SHININESS
SHINING
SHININGLY
SHINJU
SHINJUS
SHINKIN
SHINKINS
SHINLEAF
SHINLEAFS
SHINNE
SHINNED
SHINNERY
SHINNES
SHINNEY
SHINNEYED
SHINNEYS
SHINNIED
SHINNIES
SHINNING
SHINNY
SHINNYING
SHINOLA
SHINOLAS
SHINS
SHINTIED
SHINTIES
SHINTY
SHINTYING
SHINY
SHIP
SHIPBOARD
SHIPBORNE
SHIPFUL
SHIPFULS
SHIPLAP
SHIPLAPS
SHIPLESS
SHIPLOAD
SHIPLOADS
SHIPMAN
SHIPMATE
SHIPMATES
SHIPMEN
SHIPMENT
SHIPMENTS
SHIPOWNER
SHIPPABLE
SHIPPED
SHIPPEN
SHIPPENS
SHIPPER
SHIPPERS
SHIPPIE
SHIPPIES
SHIPPING
SHIPPINGS
SHIPPO
SHIPPON
SHIPPONS
SHIPPOS
SHIPPOUND
SHIPS
SHIPSHAPE
SHIPSIDE
SHIPSIDES
SHIPTIME
SHIPTIMES
SHIPWAY
SHIPWAYS
SHIPWORM
SHIPWORMS
SHIPWRECK
SHIPYARD
SHIPYARDS
SHIR
SHIRALEE
SHIRALEES
SHIRAZ
SHIRAZES
SHIRE
SHIRED
SHIREMAN
SHIREMEN
SHIRES
SHIRETOWN
SHIRING
SHIRK
SHIRKED
SHIRKER
SHIRKERS
SHIRKING
SHIRKS
SHIRR
SHIRRA
SHIRRALEE
SHIRRAS
SHIRRED
SHIRRING
SHIRRINGS
SHIRRS
SHIRS
SHIRT
SHIRTBAND
SHIRTED
SHIRTIER
SHIRTIEST
SHIRTILY
SHIRTING
SHIRTINGS
SHIRTLESS
SHIRTLIKE
SHIRTS
SHIRTTAIL
SHIRTY
SHISH
SHISHA
SHISHAS
SHISO
SHISOS
SHIST
SHISTS
SHIT
SHITAKE
SHITAKES
SHITBAG
SHITBAGS
SHITCAN
SHITCANS
SHITE
SHITED
SHITES
SHITFACE
SHITFACED
SHITFACES

SHITHEAD
SHITHEADS
SHITHEEL
SHITHEELS
SHITHOLE
SHITHOLES
SHITHOUSE
SHITING
SHITLESS
SHITLIST
SHITLISTS
SHITLOAD
SHITLOADS
SHITS
SHITSTORM
SHITTAH
SHITTAHS
SHITTED
SHITTER
SHITTERS
SHITTIER
SHITTIEST
SHITTILY
SHITTIM
SHITTIMS
SHITTING
SHITTY
SHITWORK
SHITWORKS
SHITZU
SHITZUS
SHIUR
SHIURIM
SHIV
SHIVA
SHIVAH
SHIVAHS
SHIVAREE
SHIVAREED
SHIVAREES
SHIVAS
SHIVE
SHIVER
SHIVERED
SHIVERER
SHIVERERS
SHIVERIER
SHIVERING
SHIVERS
SHIVERY
SHIVES
SHIVITI
SHIVITIS
SHIVOO
SHIVOOS
SHIVS
SHIVVED
SHIVVING
SHIZZLE
SHIZZLES
SHKOTZIM
SHLEMIEHL
SHLEMIEL
SHLEMIELS
SHLEP
SHLEPP
SHLEPPED
SHLEPPER
SHLEPPERS
SHLEPPIER
SHLEPPING
SHLEPPS
SHLEPPY
SHLEPS
SHLIMAZEL
SHLOCK
SHLOCKIER
SHLOCKS
SHLOCKY
SHLONG
SHLONGS
SHLOSHIM
SHLOSHIMS
SHLUB
SHLUBS
SHLUMP
SHLUMPED
SHLUMPIER
SHLUMPING
SHLUMPS
SHLUMPY
SHMALTZ
SHMALTZES
SHMALTZY
SHMATTE
SHMATTES
SHMEAR
SHMEARED
SHMEARING
SHMEARS
SHMEER
SHMEERED
SHMEERING
SHMEERS
SHMEK
SHMEKS
SHMO
SHMOCK
SHMOCKS
SHMOE
SHMOES
SHMOOSE
SHMOOSED
SHMOOSES
SHMOOSING
SHMOOZE
SHMOOZED
SHMOOZER
SHMOOZERS
SHMOOZES
SHMOOZIER
SHMOOZING
SHMOOZY
SHMUCK
SHMUCKIER
SHMUCKS
SHMUCKY
SHNAPPS
SHNAPS
SHNOOK
SHNOOKS
SHNORRER
SHNORRERS
SHO
SHOAL
SHOALED
SHOALER
SHOALEST
SHOALIER
SHOALIEST
SHOALING
SHOALINGS
SHOALNESS
SHOALS
SHOALWISE
SHOALY
SHOAT
SHOATS
SHOCHET
SHOCHETIM
SHOCHETS
SHOCHU
SHOCHUS
SHOCK
SHOCKABLE
SHOCKED
SHOCKER
SHOCKERS
SHOCKING
SHOCKS
SHOD
SHODDEN
SHODDIER
SHODDIES
SHODDIEST
SHODDILY
SHODDY
SHODER
SHODERS
SHOE
SHOEBILL
SHOEBILLS
SHOEBLACK
SHOEBOX
SHOEBOXES
SHOEBRUSH
SHOED
SHOEHORN
SHOEHORNS
SHOEING
SHOEINGS
SHOELACE
SHOELACES
SHOELESS
SHOEMAKER
SHOEPAC
SHOEPACK
SHOEPACKS
SHOEPACS
SHOER
SHOERS
SHOES
SHOESHINE
SHOETREE
SHOETREES
SHOFAR
SHOFARS
SHOFROTH
SHOG
SHOGGED
SHOGGING
SHOGGLE
SHOGGLED
SHOGGLES
SHOGGLIER
SHOGGLING
SHOGGLY
SHOGI
SHOGIS
SHOGS
SHOGUN
SHOGUNAL
SHOGUNATE
SHOGUNS
SHOJI
SHOJIS
SHOJO
SHOLA
SHOLAS
SHOLOM
SHOLOMS
SHONE
SHONEEN
SHONEENS
SHONKIER
SHONKIEST
SHONKY
SHOO
SHOOED
SHOOFLIES
SHOOFLY
SHOOGIE
SHOOGIED
SHOOGIES
SHOOGLE
SHOOGLED
SHOOGLES
SHOOGLIER
SHOOGLING
SHOOGLY

S

SHOOING
SHOOK
SHOOKS
SHOOL
SHOOLE
SHOOLED
SHOOLES
SHOOLING
SHOOLS
SHOON
SHOORA
SHOORAS
SHOOS
SHOOSH
SHOOSHED
SHOOSHES
SHOOSHING
SHOOT
SHOOTABLE
SHOOTDOWN
SHOOTER
SHOOTERS
SHOOTIE
SHOOTIES
SHOOTING
SHOOTINGS
SHOOTIST
SHOOTISTS
SHOOTOUT
SHOOTOUTS
SHOOTS
SHOP
SHOPBOARD
SHOPBOT
SHOPBOTS
SHOPBOY
SHOPBOYS
SHOPE
SHOPFRONT
SHOPFUL
SHOPFULS
SHOPGIRL
SHOPGIRLS
SHOPHAR
SHOPHARS
SHOPHOUSE
SHOPHROTH
SHOPLESS
SHOPLIFT
SHOPLIFTS
SHOPMAN
SHOPMEN
SHOPPE
SHOPPED
SHOPPER
SHOPPERS
SHOPPES
SHOPPIER
SHOPPIES
SHOPPIEST
SHOPPING
SHOPPINGS
SHOPPY
SHOPS
SHOPTALK
SHOPTALKS
SHOPWOMAN
SHOPWOMEN
SHOPWORN
SHORAN
SHORANS
SHORE
SHOREBIRD
SHORED
SHOREFAST
SHORELESS
SHORELINE
SHOREMAN
SHOREMEN
SHORER
SHORERS
SHORES
SHORESIDE
SHORESMAN
SHORESMEN
SHOREWARD
SHOREWEED
SHORING
SHORINGS
SHORL
SHORLS
SHORN
SHORT
SHORTAGE
SHORTAGES
SHORTARM
SHORTARSE
SHORTCAKE
SHORTCUT
SHORTCUTS
SHORTED
SHORTEN
SHORTENED
SHORTENER
SHORTENS
SHORTER
SHORTEST
SHORTFALL
SHORTGOWN
SHORTHAIR
SHORTHAND
SHORTHEAD
SHORTHOLD
SHORTHORN
SHORTIA
SHORTIAS
SHORTIE
SHORTIES
SHORTING
SHORTISH
SHORTLIST
SHORTLY
SHORTNESS
SHORTS
SHORTSTOP
SHORTWAVE
SHORTY
SHOT
SHOTCRETE
SHOTE
SHOTES
SHOTFIRER
SHOTGUN
SHOTGUNS
SHOTHOLE
SHOTHOLES
SHOTMAKER
SHOTPROOF
SHOTS
SHOTT
SHOTTE
SHOTTED
SHOTTEN
SHOTTES
SHOTTING
SHOTTLE
SHOTTLES
SHOTTS
SHOUGH
SHOUGHS
SHOULD
SHOULDER
SHOULDERS
SHOULDEST
SHOULDST
SHOUSE
SHOUSES
SHOUT
SHOUTED
SHOUTER
SHOUTERS
SHOUTHER
SHOUTHERS
SHOUTIER
SHOUTIEST
SHOUTING
SHOUTINGS
SHOUTLINE
SHOUTOUT
SHOUTOUTS
SHOUTS
SHOUTY
SHOVE
SHOVED
SHOVEL
SHOVELED
SHOVELER
SHOVELERS
SHOVELFUL
SHOVELING
SHOVELLED
SHOVELLER
SHOVELS
SHOVER
SHOVERS
SHOVES
SHOVING
SHOVINGS
SHOW
SHOWABLE
SHOWBIZ
SHOWBIZZY
SHOWBOAT
SHOWBOATS
SHOWBOX
SHOWBOXES
SHOWBREAD
SHOWCASE
SHOWCASED
SHOWCASES
SHOWD
SHOWDED
SHOWDING
SHOWDOWN
SHOWDOWNS
SHOWDS
SHOWED
SHOWER
SHOWERED
SHOWERER
SHOWERERS
SHOWERFUL
SHOWERIER
SHOWERING
SHOWERS
SHOWERY
SHOWGHE
SHOWGHES
SHOWGIRL
SHOWGIRLS
SHOWGOER
SHOWGOERS
SHOWIER
SHOWIEST
SHOWILY
SHOWINESS
SHOWING
SHOWINGS
SHOWJUMP
SHOWJUMPS
SHOWMAN
SHOWMANCE
SHOWMANLY
SHOWMEN
SHOWN
SHOWOFF
SHOWOFFS
SHOWPIECE
SHOWPLACE
SHOWRING

S

SHOWRINGS
SHOWROOM
SHOWROOMS
SHOWS
SHOWTIME
SHOWTIMES
SHOWY
SHOWYARD
SHOWYARDS
SHOYU
SHOYUS
SHRADDHA
SHRADDHAS
SHRANK
SHRAPNEL
SHRAPNELS
SHRED
SHREDDED
SHREDDER
SHREDDERS
SHREDDIER
SHREDDING
SHREDDY
SHREDLESS
SHREDS
SHREEK
SHREEKED
SHREEKING
SHREEKS
SHREIK
SHREIKED
SHREIKING
SHREIKS
SHREW
SHREWD
SHREWDER
SHREWDEST
SHREWDIE
SHREWDIES
SHREWDLY
SHREWED
SHREWING
SHREWISH
SHREWLIKE
SHREWMICE
SHREWS
SHRI
SHRIECH
SHRIECHED
SHRIECHES
SHRIEK
SHRIEKED
SHRIEKER
SHRIEKERS
SHRIEKIER
SHRIEKING
SHRIEKS
SHRIEKY
SHRIEVAL
SHRIEVE
SHRIEVED
SHRIEVES
SHRIEVING
SHRIFT
SHRIFTS
SHRIGHT
SHRIGHTS
SHRIKE
SHRIKED
SHRIKES
SHRIKING
SHRILL
SHRILLED
SHRILLER
SHRILLEST
SHRILLIER
SHRILLING
SHRILLS
SHRILLY
SHRIMP
SHRIMPED
SHRIMPER
SHRIMPERS
SHRIMPIER
SHRIMPING
SHRIMPS
SHRIMPY
SHRINAL
SHRINE
SHRINED
SHRINES
SHRINING
SHRINK
SHRINKAGE
SHRINKER
SHRINKERS
SHRINKING
SHRINKS
SHRIS
SHRITCH
SHRITCHED
SHRITCHES
SHRIVE
SHRIVED
SHRIVEL
SHRIVELED
SHRIVELS
SHRIVEN
SHRIVER
SHRIVERS
SHRIVES
SHRIVING
SHRIVINGS
SHROFF
SHROFFAGE
SHROFFED
SHROFFING
SHROFFS
SHROOM
SHROOMED
SHROOMER
SHROOMERS
SHROOMING
SHROOMS
SHROUD
SHROUDED
SHROUDIER
SHROUDING
SHROUDS
SHROUDY
SHROVE
SHROVED
SHROVES
SHROVING
SHROW
SHROWD
SHROWED
SHROWING
SHROWS
SHRUB
SHRUBBED
SHRUBBERY
SHRUBBIER
SHRUBBING
SHRUBBY
SHRUBLAND
SHRUBLESS
SHRUBLIKE
SHRUBS
SHRUG
SHRUGGED
SHRUGGING
SHRUGS
SHRUNK
SHRUNKEN
SHTCHI
SHTCHIS
SHTETEL
SHTETELS
SHTETL
SHTETLACH
SHTETLS
SHTICK
SHTICKIER
SHTICKS
SHTICKY
SHTIK
SHTIKS
SHTOOK
SHTOOKS
SHTOOM
SHTOOMER
SHTOOMEST
SHTREIMEL
SHTUCK
SHTUCKS
SHTUM
SHTUMM
SHTUMMER
SHTUMMEST
SHTUP
SHTUPPED
SHTUPPING
SHTUPS
SHUBUNKIN
SHUCK
SHUCKED
SHUCKER
SHUCKERS
SHUCKING
SHUCKINGS
SHUCKS
SHUDDER
SHUDDERED
SHUDDERS
SHUDDERY
SHUFFLE
SHUFFLED
SHUFFLER
SHUFFLERS
SHUFFLES
SHUFFLING
SHUFTI
SHUFTIES
SHUFTIS
SHUFTY
SHUGGIES
SHUGGY
SHUL
SHULE
SHULED
SHULES
SHULING
SHULN
SHULS
SHUMAI
SHUN
SHUNLESS
SHUNNABLE
SHUNNED
SHUNNER
SHUNNERS
SHUNNING
SHUNPIKE
SHUNPIKED
SHUNPIKER
SHUNPIKES
SHUNS
SHUNT
SHUNTED
SHUNTER
SHUNTERS
SHUNTING
SHUNTINGS
SHUNTS
SHURA
SHURAS
SHURIKEN
SHURIKENS
SHUSH

S

SHUSHED
SHUSHER
SHUSHERS
SHUSHES
SHUSHING
SHUT
SHUTDOWN
SHUTDOWNS
SHUTE
SHUTED
SHUTES
SHUTEYE
SHUTEYES
SHUTING
SHUTOFF
SHUTOFFS
SHUTOUT
SHUTOUTS
SHUTS
SHUTTER
SHUTTERED
SHUTTERS
SHUTTING
SHUTTLE
SHUTTLED
SHUTTLER
SHUTTLERS
SHUTTLES
SHUTTLING
SHVARTZE
SHVARTZES
SHVITZ
SHVITZED
SHVITZES
SHVITZING
SHWA
SHWANPAN
SHWANPANS
SHWAS
SHWESHWE
SHWESHWES
SHY
SHYER
SHYERS
SHYEST
SHYING
SHYISH
SHYLOCK
SHYLOCKED
SHYLOCKS
SHYLY
SHYNESS
SHYNESSES
SHYPOO
SHYPOOS
SHYSTER
SHYSTERS
SI
SIAL
SIALIC
SIALID
SIALIDAN
SIALIDANS
SIALIDS
SIALOGRAM
SIALOID
SIALOLITH
SIALON
SIALONS
SIALS
SIAMANG
SIAMANGS
SIAMESE
SIAMESED
SIAMESES
SIAMESING
SIAMEZE
SIAMEZED
SIAMEZES
SIAMEZING
SIB
SIBB
SIBBS
SIBILANCE
SIBILANCY
SIBILANT
SIBILANTS
SIBILATE
SIBILATED
SIBILATES
SIBILATOR
SIBILOUS
SIBLING
SIBLINGS
SIBS
SIBSHIP
SIBSHIPS
SIBYL
SIBYLIC
SIBYLLIC
SIBYLLINE
SIBYLS
SIC
SICARIO
SICARIOS
SICCAN
SICCAR
SICCATIVE
SICCED
SICCING
SICCITIES
SICCITY
SICE
SICES
SICH
SICHT
SICHTED
SICHTING
SICHTS
SICILIANA
SICILIANE
SICILIANO
SICK
SICKBAY
SICKBAYS
SICKBED
SICKBEDS
SICKED
SICKEE
SICKEES
SICKEN
SICKENED
SICKENER
SICKENERS
SICKENING
SICKENS
SICKER
SICKERLY
SICKEST
SICKIE
SICKIES
SICKING
SICKISH
SICKISHLY
SICKLE
SICKLED
SICKLEMAN
SICKLEMEN
SICKLEMIA
SICKLEMIC
SICKLES
SICKLIED
SICKLIER
SICKLIES
SICKLIEST
SICKLILY
SICKLING
SICKLY
SICKLYING
SICKNESS
SICKNURSE
SICKO
SICKOS
SICKOUT
SICKOUTS
SICKROOM
SICKROOMS
SICKS
SICKY
SICLIKE
SICS
SIDA
SIDALCEA
SIDALCEAS
SIDAS
SIDDHA
SIDDHAS
SIDDHI
SIDDHIS
SIDDHUISM
SIDDUR
SIDDURIM
SIDDURS
SIDE
SIDEARM
SIDEARMED
SIDEARMER
SIDEARMS
SIDEBAND
SIDEBANDS
SIDEBAR
SIDEBARS
SIDEBOARD
SIDEBONE
SIDEBONES
SIDEBURN
SIDEBURNS
SIDECAR
SIDECARS
SIDECHAIR
SIDECHECK
SIDED
SIDEDLY
SIDEDNESS
SIDEDRESS
SIDEHILL
SIDEHILLS
SIDEKICK
SIDEKICKS
SIDELESS
SIDELIGHT
SIDELINE
SIDELINED
SIDELINER
SIDELINES
SIDELING
SIDELINGS
SIDELOCK
SIDELOCKS
SIDELONG
SIDEMAN
SIDEMEAT
SIDEMEATS
SIDEMEN
SIDENOTE
SIDENOTES
SIDEPATH
SIDEPATHS
SIDEPIECE
SIDER
SIDERAL
SIDERATE
SIDERATED
SIDERATES
SIDEREAL
SIDERITE
SIDERITES
SIDERITIC
SIDEROAD
SIDEROADS

S

SIDEROSES
SIDEROSIS
SIDEROTIC
SIDERS
SIDES
SIDESHOOT
SIDESHOW
SIDESHOWS
SIDESLIP
SIDESLIPS
SIDESMAN
SIDESMEN
SIDESPIN
SIDESPINS
SIDESPLIT
SIDESTEP
SIDESTEPS
SIDESWIPE
SIDETABLE
SIDETRACK
SIDEWALK
SIDEWALKS
SIDEWALL
SIDEWALLS
SIDEWARD
SIDEWARDS
SIDEWAY
SIDEWAYS
SIDEWHEEL
SIDEWISE
SIDH
SIDHA
SIDHAS
SIDHE
SIDHUISM
SIDHUISMS
SIDING
SIDINGS
SIDLE
SIDLED
SIDLER
SIDLERS
SIDLES
SIDLING
SIDLINGLY
SIECLE
SIECLES
SIEGE
SIEGED
SIEGER
SIEGERS
SIEGES
SIEGING
SIELD
SIEMENS
SIEMENSES
SIEN
SIENITE
SIENITES
SIENNA
SIENNAS
SIENS
SIENT
SIENTS
SIEROZEM
SIEROZEMS
SIERRA
SIERRAN
SIERRAS
SIES
SIESTA
SIESTAS
SIETH
SIETHS
SIEUR
SIEURS
SIEVE
SIEVED
SIEVELIKE
SIEVERT
SIEVERTS
SIEVES
SIEVING
SIF
SIFAKA
SIFAKAS
SIFFLE
SIFFLED
SIFFLES
SIFFLEUR
SIFFLEURS
SIFFLEUSE
SIFFLING
SIFREI
SIFT
SIFTED
SIFTER
SIFTERS
SIFTING
SIFTINGLY
SIFTINGS
SIFTS
SIG
SIGANID
SIGANIDS
SIGH
SIGHED
SIGHER
SIGHERS
SIGHFUL
SIGHING
SIGHINGLY
SIGHINGS
SIGHLESS
SIGHLIKE
SIGHS
SIGHT
SIGHTABLE
SIGHTED
SIGHTER
SIGHTERS
SIGHTING
SIGHTINGS
SIGHTLESS
SIGHTLIER
SIGHTLINE
SIGHTLY
SIGHTS
SIGHTSAW
SIGHTSEE
SIGHTSEEN
SIGHTSEER
SIGHTSEES
SIGHTSMAN
SIGHTSMEN
SIGIL
SIGILLARY
SIGILLATE
SIGILS
SIGISBEI
SIGISBEO
SIGLA
SIGLAS
SIGLOI
SIGLOS
SIGLUM
SIGMA
SIGMAS
SIGMATE
SIGMATED
SIGMATES
SIGMATIC
SIGMATING
SIGMATION
SIGMATISM
SIGMATRON
SIGMOID
SIGMOIDAL
SIGMOIDS
SIGN
SIGNA
SIGNABLE
SIGNAGE
SIGNAGES
SIGNAL
SIGNALED
SIGNALER
SIGNALERS
SIGNALING
SIGNALISE
SIGNALIZE
SIGNALLED
SIGNALLER
SIGNALLY
SIGNALMAN
SIGNALMEN
SIGNALS
SIGNARIES
SIGNARY
SIGNATORY
SIGNATURE
SIGNBOARD
SIGNED
SIGNEE
SIGNEES
SIGNER
SIGNERS
SIGNET
SIGNETED
SIGNETING
SIGNETS
SIGNEUR
SIGNEURIE
SIGNIEUR
SIGNIEURS
SIGNIFICS
SIGNIFIED
SIGNIFIER
SIGNIFIES
SIGNIFY
SIGNING
SIGNINGS
SIGNIOR
SIGNIORI
SIGNIORS
SIGNIORY
SIGNLESS
SIGNOR
SIGNORA
SIGNORAS
SIGNORE
SIGNORES
SIGNORI
SIGNORIA
SIGNORIAL
SIGNORIAS
SIGNORIES
SIGNORINA
SIGNORINE
SIGNORINI
SIGNORINO
SIGNORS
SIGNORY
SIGNPOST
SIGNPOSTS
SIGNS
SIGS
SIJO
SIJOS
SIK
SIKA
SIKAS
SIKE
SIKER
SIKES
SIKORSKY
SIKSIK
SIKSIKS
SILAGE
SILAGED

S

SILAGEING
SILAGES
SILAGING
SILANE
SILANES
SILASTIC
SILASTICS
SILD
SILDS
SILE
SILED
SILEN
SILENCE
SILENCED
SILENCER
SILENCERS
SILENCES
SILENCING
SILENE
SILENES
SILENI
SILENS
SILENT
SILENTER
SILENTEST
SILENTLY
SILENTS
SILENUS
SILER
SILERS
SILES
SILESIA
SILESIAS
SILEX
SILEXES
SILICA
SILICAS
SILICATE
SILICATED
SILICATES
SILICEOUS
SILICIC
SILICIDE
SILICIDES
SILICIFY
SILICIOUS
SILICIUM
SILICIUMS

SILICLE
SILICLES
SILICON
SILICONE
SILICONES
SILICONS
SILICOSES
SILICOSIS
SILICOTIC
SILICULA
SILICULAE
SILICULAS
SILICULE
SILICULES
SILING
SILIQUA
SILIQUAE
SILIQUAS
SILIQUE
SILIQUES
SILIQUOSE
SILIQUOUS
SILK
SILKALENE
SILKALINE
SILKED
SILKEN
SILKENED
SILKENING
SILKENS
SILKIE
SILKIER
SILKIES
SILKIEST
SILKILY
SILKINESS
SILKING
SILKLIKE
SILKOLINE
SILKS
SILKTAIL
SILKTAILS
SILKWEED
SILKWEEDS
SILKWORM
SILKWORMS
SILKY
SILL

SILLABUB
SILLABUBS
SILLADAR
SILLADARS
SILLER
SILLERS
SILLIBUB
SILLIBUBS
SILLIER
SILLIES
SILLIEST
SILLILY
SILLINESS
SILLOCK
SILLOCKS
SILLS
SILLY
SILO
SILOED
SILOING
SILOS
SILOXANE
SILOXANES
SILPHIA
SILPHIUM
SILPHIUMS
SILT
SILTATION
SILTED
SILTIER
SILTIEST
SILTING
SILTS
SILTSTONE
SILTY
SILURIAN
SILURID
SILURIDS
SILURIST
SILURISTS
SILUROID
SILUROIDS
SILVA
SILVAE
SILVAN
SILVANS
SILVAS
SILVATIC

SILVER
SILVERED
SILVERER
SILVERERS
SILVEREYE
SILVERIER
SILVERING
SILVERISE
SILVERIZE
SILVERLY
SILVERN
SILVERS
SILVERTIP
SILVERY
SILVEX
SILVEXES
SILVICAL
SILVICS
SILYMARIN
SIM
SIMA
SIMAR
SIMAROUBA
SIMARRE
SIMARRES
SIMARS
SIMARUBA
SIMARUBAS
SIMAS
SIMATIC
SIMAZINE
SIMAZINES
SIMBA
SIMBAS
SIMCHA
SIMCHAS
SIMI
SIMIAL
SIMIAN
SIMIANS
SIMILAR
SIMILARLY
SIMILE
SIMILES
SIMILISE
SIMILISED
SIMILISES
SIMILIZE

SIMILIZED
SIMILIZES
SIMILOR
SIMILORS
SIMIOID
SIMIOUS
SIMIS
SIMITAR
SIMITARS
SIMKIN
SIMKINS
SIMLIN
SIMLINS
SIMMER
SIMMERED
SIMMERING
SIMMERS
SIMNEL
SIMNELS
SIMOLEON
SIMOLEONS
SIMONIAC
SIMONIACS
SIMONIES
SIMONIOUS
SIMONISE
SIMONISED
SIMONISES
SIMONIST
SIMONISTS
SIMONIZE
SIMONIZED
SIMONIZES
SIMONY
SIMOOM
SIMOOMS
SIMOON
SIMOONS
SIMORG
SIMORGS
SIMP
SIMPAI
SIMPAIS
SIMPATICO
SIMPER
SIMPERED
SIMPERER
SIMPERERS

SIMPERING
SIMPERS
SIMPKIN
SIMPKINS
SIMPLE
SIMPLED
SIMPLER
SIMPLERS
SIMPLES
SIMPLESSE
SIMPLEST
SIMPLETON
SIMPLEX
SIMPLEXES
SIMPLICES
SIMPLICIA
SIMPLIFY
SIMPLING
SIMPLINGS
SIMPLISM
SIMPLISMS
SIMPLIST
SIMPLISTE
SIMPLISTS
SIMPLY
SIMPS
SIMS
SIMUL
SIMULACRA
SIMULACRE
SIMULANT
SIMULANTS
SIMULAR
SIMULARS
SIMULATE
SIMULATED
SIMULATES
SIMULATOR
SIMULCAST
SIMULIUM
SIMULIUMS
SIMULS
SIMURG
SIMURGH
SIMURGHS
SIMURGS
SIN
SINAPISM
SINAPISMS
SINCE
SINCERE
SINCERELY
SINCERER
SINCEREST
SINCERITY
SINCIPITA
SINCIPUT
SINCIPUTS
SIND
SINDED
SINDING
SINDINGS
SINDON
SINDONS
SINDS
SINE
SINECURE
SINECURES
SINED
SINES
SINEW
SINEWED
SINEWIER
SINEWIEST
SINEWING
SINEWLESS
SINEWS
SINEWY
SINFONIA
SINFONIAS
SINFONIE
SINFUL
SINFULLY
SING
SINGABLE
SINGALONG
SINGE
SINGED
SINGEING
SINGER
SINGERS
SINGES
SINGING
SINGINGLY
SINGINGS
SINGLE
SINGLED
SINGLEDOM
SINGLES
SINGLET
SINGLETON
SINGLETS
SINGLING
SINGLINGS
SINGLY
SINGS
SINGSONG
SINGSONGS
SINGSONGY
SINGSPIEL
SINGULAR
SINGULARS
SINGULARY
SINGULT
SINGULTS
SINGULTUS
SINH
SINHS
SINICAL
SINICISE
SINICISED
SINICISES
SINICIZE
SINICIZED
SINICIZES
SINING
SINISTER
SINISTRAL
SINK
SINKABLE
SINKAGE
SINKAGES
SINKER
SINKERS
SINKFUL
SINKFULS
SINKHOLE
SINKHOLES
SINKIER
SINKIEST
SINKING
SINKINGS
SINKS
SINKY
SINLESS
SINLESSLY
SINNED
SINNER
SINNERED
SINNERING
SINNERS
SINNET
SINNETS
SINNING
SINNINGIA
SINOLOGUE
SINOLOGY
SINOPIA
SINOPIAS
SINOPIE
SINOPIS
SINOPISES
SINOPITE
SINOPITES
SINS
SINSYNE
SINTER
SINTERED
SINTERIER
SINTERING
SINTERS
SINTERY
SINUATE
SINUATED
SINUATELY
SINUATES
SINUATING
SINUATION
SINUITIS
SINUOSE
SINUOSITY
SINUOUS
SINUOUSLY
SINUS
SINUSES
SINUSITIS
SINUSLIKE
SINUSOID
SINUSOIDS
SIP
SIPE
SIPED
SIPES
SIPHON
SIPHONAGE
SIPHONAL
SIPHONATE
SIPHONED
SIPHONET
SIPHONETS
SIPHONIC
SIPHONING
SIPHONS
SIPHUNCLE
SIPING
SIPPABLE
SIPPED
SIPPER
SIPPERS
SIPPET
SIPPETS
SIPPING
SIPPLE
SIPPLED
SIPPLES
SIPPLING
SIPPY
SIPS
SIR
SIRCAR
SIRCARS
SIRDAR
SIRDARS
SIRE
SIRED
SIREE
SIREES
SIREN
SIRENIAN
SIRENIANS
SIRENIC
SIRENISE
SIRENISED
SIRENISES
SIRENIZE
SIRENIZED
SIRENIZES
SIRENS
SIRES
SIRGANG

S

SIRGANGS
SIRI
SIRIASES
SIRIASIS
SIRIH
SIRIHS
SIRING
SIRINGS
SIRIS
SIRKAR
SIRKARS
SIRLOIN
SIRLOINS
SIRNAME
SIRNAMED
SIRNAMES
SIRNAMING
SIROC
SIROCCO
SIROCCOS
SIROCS
SIRONISE
SIRONISED
SIRONISES
SIRONIZE
SIRONIZED
SIRONIZES
SIROSET
SIRRA
SIRRAH
SIRRAHS
SIRRAS
SIRRED
SIRREE
SIRREES
SIRRING
SIRS
SIRTUIN
SIRTUINS
SIRUP
SIRUPED
SIRUPIER
SIRUPIEST
SIRUPING
SIRUPS
SIRUPY
SIRVENTE
SIRVENTES
SIS
SISAL
SISALS
SISERARY
SISES
SISKIN
SISKINS
SISS
SISSES
SISSIER
SISSIES
SISSIEST
SISSIFIED
SISSINESS
SISSOO
SISSOOS
SISSY
SISSYISH
SISSYNESS
SIST
SISTA
SISTAS
SISTED
SISTER
SISTERED
SISTERING
SISTERLY
SISTERS
SISTING
SISTRA
SISTROID
SISTRUM
SISTRUMS
SISTS
SIT
SITAR
SITARIST
SITARISTS
SITARS
SITATUNGA
SITCOM
SITCOMS
SITE
SITED
SITELLA
SITELLAS
SITES
SITFAST
SITFASTS
SITH
SITHE
SITHED
SITHEE
SITHEN
SITHENCE
SITHENS
SITHES
SITHING
SITING
SITINGS
SITIOLOGY
SITKA
SITKAMER
SITKAMERS
SITOLOGY
SITREP
SITREPS
SITS
SITTAR
SITTARS
SITTELLA
SITTELLAS
SITTEN
SITTER
SITTERS
SITTINE
SITTINES
SITTING
SITTINGS
SITUATE
SITUATED
SITUATES
SITUATING
SITUATION
SITULA
SITULAE
SITUP
SITUPS
SITUS
SITUSES
SITUTUNGA
SITZ
SITZKRIEG
SITZMARK
SITZMARKS
SIVER
SIVERS
SIWASH
SIWASHED
SIWASHES
SIWASHING
SIX
SIXAIN
SIXAINE
SIXAINES
SIXAINS
SIXER
SIXERS
SIXES
SIXFOLD
SIXISH
SIXMO
SIXMOS
SIXPENCE
SIXPENCES
SIXPENNY
SIXSCORE
SIXSCORES
SIXTE
SIXTEEN
SIXTEENER
SIXTEENMO
SIXTEENS
SIXTEENTH
SIXTES
SIXTH
SIXTHLY
SIXTHS
SIXTIES
SIXTIETH
SIXTIETHS
SIXTY
SIXTYFOLD
SIXTYISH
SIZABLE
SIZABLY
SIZAR
SIZARS
SIZARSHIP
SIZE
SIZEABLE
SIZEABLY
SIZED
SIZEISM
SIZEISMS
SIZEIST
SIZEISTS
SIZEL
SIZELS
SIZER
SIZERS
SIZES
SIZIER
SIZIEST
SIZINESS
SIZING
SIZINGS
SIZISM
SIZISMS
SIZIST
SIZISTS
SIZY
SIZZLE
SIZZLED
SIZZLER
SIZZLERS
SIZZLES
SIZZLING
SIZZLINGS
SJAMBOK
SJAMBOKED
SJAMBOKS
SJOE
SKA
SKAG
SKAGS
SKAIL
SKAILED
SKAILING
SKAILS
SKAITH
SKAITHED
SKAITHING
SKAITHS
SKALD
SKALDIC
SKALDS
SKALDSHIP
SKANGER
SKANGERS
SKANK
SKANKED

S

SKANKER
SKANKERS
SKANKIER
SKANKIEST
SKANKING
SKANKINGS
SKANKS
SKANKY
SKART
SKARTH
SKARTHS
SKARTS
SKAS
SKAT
SKATE
SKATED
SKATEPARK
SKATEPUNK
SKATER
SKATERS
SKATES
SKATING
SKATINGS
SKATOL
SKATOLE
SKATOLES
SKATOLS
SKATS
SKATT
SKATTS
SKAW
SKAWS
SKEAN
SKEANE
SKEANES
SKEANS
SKEAR
SKEARED
SKEARIER
SKEARIEST
SKEARING
SKEARS
SKEARY
SKED
SKEDADDLE
SKEDDED
SKEDDING
SKEDS
SKEE
SKEECHAN
SKEECHANS
SKEED
SKEEF
SKEEING
SKEELIER
SKEELIEST
SKEELY
SKEEN
SKEENS
SKEER
SKEERED
SKEERIER
SKEERIEST
SKEERING
SKEERS
SKEERY
SKEES
SKEESICKS
SKEET
SKEETER
SKEETERS
SKEETS
SKEEVIER
SKEEVIEST
SKEEVY
SKEG
SKEGG
SKEGGER
SKEGGERS
SKEGGS
SKEGS
SKEIGH
SKEIGHER
SKEIGHEST
SKEIN
SKEINED
SKEINING
SKEINS
SKELDER
SKELDERED
SKELDERS
SKELETAL
SKELETON
SKELETONS
SKELF
SKELFS
SKELL
SKELLIE
SKELLIED
SKELLIER
SKELLIES
SKELLIEST
SKELLOCH
SKELLOCHS
SKELLS
SKELLUM
SKELLUMS
SKELLY
SKELLYING
SKELM
SKELMS
SKELP
SKELPED
SKELPING
SKELPINGS
SKELPIT
SKELPS
SKELTER
SKELTERED
SKELTERS
SKELUM
SKELUMS
SKEN
SKENE
SKENES
SKENNED
SKENNING
SKENS
SKEO
SKEOES
SKEOS
SKEP
SKEPFUL
SKEPFULS
SKEPPED
SKEPPING
SKEPS
SKEPSIS
SKEPSISES
SKEPTIC
SKEPTICAL
SKEPTICS
SKER
SKERRED
SKERRICK
SKERRICKS
SKERRIES
SKERRING
SKERRY
SKERS
SKET
SKETCH
SKETCHED
SKETCHER
SKETCHERS
SKETCHES
SKETCHIER
SKETCHILY
SKETCHING
SKETCHPAD
SKETCHY
SKETS
SKETTED
SKETTING
SKEW
SKEWBACK
SKEWBACKS
SKEWBALD
SKEWBALDS
SKEWED
SKEWER
SKEWERED
SKEWERING
SKEWERS
SKEWEST
SKEWING
SKEWNESS
SKEWS
SKEWWHIFF
SKI
SKIABLE
SKIAGRAM
SKIAGRAMS
SKIAGRAPH
SKIAMACHY
SKIASCOPE
SKIASCOPY
SKIATRON
SKIATRONS
SKIBOB
SKIBOBBED
SKIBOBBER
SKIBOBS
SKID
SKIDDED
SKIDDER
SKIDDERS
SKIDDIER
SKIDDIEST
SKIDDING
SKIDDINGS
SKIDDOO
SKIDDOOED
SKIDDOOS
SKIDDY
SKIDLID
SKIDLIDS
SKIDMARK
SKIDMARKS
SKIDOO
SKIDOOED
SKIDOOER
SKIDOOERS
SKIDOOING
SKIDOOS
SKIDPAD
SKIDPADS
SKIDPAN
SKIDPANS
SKIDPROOF
SKIDS
SKIDWAY
SKIDWAYS
SKIED
SKIER
SKIERS
SKIES
SKIEY
SKIEYER
SKIEYEST
SKIFF
SKIFFED
SKIFFING
SKIFFLE
SKIFFLED
SKIFFLES
SKIFFLESS
SKIFFLING
SKIFFS
SKIING

S

SKIINGS
SKIJORER
SKIJORERS
SKIJORING
SKIJUMPER
SKIKJORER
SKILFUL
SKILFULL
SKILFULLY
SKILL
SKILLED
SKILLESS
SKILLET
SKILLETS
SKILLFUL
SKILLIER
SKILLIES
SKILLIEST
SKILLING
SKILLINGS
SKILLION
SKILLIONS
SKILLS
SKILLY
SKIM
SKIMBOARD
SKIMMED
SKIMMER
SKIMMERS
SKIMMIA
SKIMMIAS
SKIMMING
SKIMMINGS
SKIMO
SKIMOBILE
SKIMOS
SKIMP
SKIMPED
SKIMPIER
SKIMPIEST
SKIMPILY
SKIMPING
SKIMPS
SKIMPY
SKIMS
SKIN
SKINCARE
SKINCARES
SKINFLICK
SKINFLINT
SKINFOOD
SKINFOODS
SKINFUL
SKINFULS
SKINHEAD
SKINHEADS
SKINK
SKINKED
SKINKER
SKINKERS
SKINKING
SKINKS
SKINLESS
SKINLIKE
SKINNED
SKINNER
SKINNERS
SKINNIER
SKINNIES
SKINNIEST
SKINNING
SKINNY
SKINS
SKINSUIT
SKINSUITS
SKINT
SKINTER
SKINTEST
SKINTIGHT
SKIO
SKIOES
SKIORER
SKIORERS
SKIORING
SKIORINGS
SKIOS
SKIP
SKIPJACK
SKIPJACKS
SKIPLANE
SKIPLANES
SKIPPABLE
SKIPPED
SKIPPER
SKIPPERED
SKIPPERS
SKIPPET
SKIPPETS
SKIPPIER
SKIPPIEST
SKIPPING
SKIPPINGS
SKIPPY
SKIPS
SKIRL
SKIRLED
SKIRLING
SKIRLINGS
SKIRLS
SKIRMISH
SKIRR
SKIRRED
SKIRRET
SKIRRETS
SKIRRING
SKIRRS
SKIRT
SKIRTED
SKIRTER
SKIRTERS
SKIRTING
SKIRTINGS
SKIRTLESS
SKIRTLIKE
SKIRTS
SKIS
SKIT
SKITCH
SKITCHED
SKITCHES
SKITCHING
SKITE
SKITED
SKITES
SKITING
SKITS
SKITTER
SKITTERED
SKITTERS
SKITTERY
SKITTISH
SKITTLE
SKITTLED
SKITTLES
SKITTLING
SKIVE
SKIVED
SKIVER
SKIVERED
SKIVERING
SKIVERS
SKIVES
SKIVIE
SKIVIER
SKIVIEST
SKIVING
SKIVINGS
SKIVVIED
SKIVVIES
SKIVVY
SKIVVYING
SKIVY
SKIWEAR
SKIWEARS
SKLATE
SKLATED
SKLATES
SKLATING
SKLENT
SKLENTED
SKLENTING
SKLENTS
SKLIFF
SKLIFFED
SKLIFFING
SKLIFFS
SKLIM
SKLIMMED
SKLIMMING
SKLIMS
SKOAL
SKOALED
SKOALING
SKOALS
SKODIER
SKODIEST
SKODY
SKOFF
SKOFFED
SKOFFING
SKOFFS
SKOG
SKOGGED
SKOGGING
SKOGS
SKOKIAAN
SKOKIAANS
SKOL
SKOLED
SKOLIA
SKOLING
SKOLION
SKOLLED
SKOLLIE
SKOLLIES
SKOLLING
SKOLLY
SKOLS
SKOOKUM
SKOOKUMS
SKOOL
SKOOLS
SKOOSH
SKOOSHED
SKOOSHES
SKOOSHING
SKORDALIA
SKORT
SKORTS
SKOSH
SKOSHES
SKRAN
SKRANS
SKREEGH
SKREEGHED
SKREEGHS
SKREEN
SKREENS
SKREIGH
SKREIGHED
SKREIGHS
SKRIECH
SKRIECHED
SKRIECHS
SKRIED
SKRIEGH
SKRIEGHED
SKRIEGHS
SKRIES
SKRIK

SKRIKE
SKRIKED
SKRIKES
SKRIKING
SKRIKS
SKRIMMAGE
SKRIMP
SKRIMPED
SKRIMPING
SKRIMPS
SKRONK
SKRONKS
SKRUMP
SKRUMPED
SKRUMPING
SKRUMPS
SKRY
SKRYER
SKRYERS
SKRYING
SKUA
SKUAS
SKUDLER
SKUDLERS
SKUG
SKUGGED
SKUGGING
SKUGS
SKULK
SKULKED
SKULKER
SKULKERS
SKULKING
SKULKINGS
SKULKS
SKULL
SKULLCAP
SKULLCAPS
SKULLED
SKULLING
SKULLS
SKULPIN
SKULPINS
SKUMMER
SKUMMERED
SKUMMERS
SKUNK
SKUNKBIRD
SKUNKED
SKUNKIER
SKUNKIEST
SKUNKING
SKUNKS
SKUNKWEED
SKUNKY
SKURRIED
SKURRIES
SKURRY
SKURRYING
SKUTTLE
SKUTTLED
SKUTTLES
SKUTTLING
SKY
SKYBOARD
SKYBOARDS
SKYBORN
SKYBORNE
SKYBOX
SKYBOXES
SKYBRIDGE
SKYCAP
SKYCAPS
SKYCLAD
SKYDIVE
SKYDIVED
SKYDIVER
SKYDIVERS
SKYDIVES
SKYDIVING
SKYDOVE
SKYED
SKYER
SKYERS
SKYEY
SKYEYER
SKYEYEST
SKYF
SKYFED
SKYFING
SKYFS
SKYGLOW
SKYGLOWS
SKYHOME
SKYHOMES
SKYHOOK
SKYHOOKS
SKYIER
SKYIEST
SKYING
SKYISH
SKYJACK
SKYJACKED
SKYJACKER
SKYJACKS
SKYLAB
SKYLABS
SKYLARK
SKYLARKED
SKYLARKER
SKYLARKS
SKYLESS
SKYLIGHT
SKYLIGHTS
SKYLIKE
SKYLINE
SKYLINES
SKYLIT
SKYMAN
SKYMEN
SKYPHOI
SKYPHOS
SKYR
SKYRE
SKYRED
SKYRES
SKYRING
SKYRMION
SKYRMIONS
SKYROCKET
SKYRS
SKYSAIL
SKYSAILS
SKYSCAPE
SKYSCAPES
SKYSURF
SKYSURFED
SKYSURFER
SKYSURFS
SKYTE
SKYTED
SKYTES
SKYTING
SKYWALK
SKYWALKS
SKYWARD
SKYWARDS
SKYWATCH
SKYWAY
SKYWAYS
SKYWRITE
SKYWRITER
SKYWRITES
SKYWROTE
SLAB
SLABBED
SLABBER
SLABBERED
SLABBERER
SLABBERS
SLABBERY
SLABBIER
SLABBIES
SLABBIEST
SLABBING
SLABBINGS
SLABBY
SLABLIKE
SLABS
SLABSTONE
SLACK
SLACKED
SLACKEN
SLACKENED
SLACKENER
SLACKENS
SLACKER
SLACKERS
SLACKEST
SLACKING
SLACKLY
SLACKNESS
SLACKS
SLADANG
SLADANGS
SLADE
SLADES
SLAE
SLAES
SLAG
SLAGGED
SLAGGIER
SLAGGIEST
SLAGGING
SLAGGINGS
SLAGGY
SLAGHEAP
SLAGHEAPS
SLAGS
SLAHAL
SLAHALS
SLAID
SLAIDS
SLAIN
SLAINTE
SLAIRG
SLAIRGED
SLAIRGING
SLAIRGS
SLAISTER
SLAISTERS
SLAISTERY
SLAKABLE
SLAKE
SLAKEABLE
SLAKED
SLAKELESS
SLAKER
SLAKERS
SLAKES
SLAKING
SLALOM
SLALOMED
SLALOMER
SLALOMERS
SLALOMING
SLALOMIST
SLALOMS
SLAM
SLAMDANCE
SLAMMAKIN
SLAMMED
SLAMMER
SLAMMERS
SLAMMING
SLAMMINGS
SLAMS
SLANDER
SLANDERED
SLANDERER

S

SLANDERS
SLANE
SLANES
SLANG
SLANGED
SLANGER
SLANGERS
SLANGIER
SLANGIEST
SLANGILY
SLANGING
SLANGINGS
SLANGISH
SLANGS
SLANGUAGE
SLANGULAR
SLANGY
SLANK
SLANT
SLANTED
SLANTER
SLANTERS
SLANTIER
SLANTIEST
SLANTING
SLANTLY
SLANTS
SLANTWAYS
SLANTWISE
SLANTY
SLAP
SLAPDASH
SLAPHAPPY
SLAPHEAD
SLAPHEADS
SLAPJACK
SLAPJACKS
SLAPPED
SLAPPER
SLAPPERS
SLAPPING
SLAPPINGS
SLAPS
SLAPSHOT
SLAPSHOTS
SLAPSTICK
SLART
SLARTED
SLARTING
SLARTS
SLASH
SLASHED
SLASHER
SLASHERS
SLASHES
SLASHFEST
SLASHING
SLASHINGS
SLAT
SLATCH
SLATCHES
SLATE
SLATED
SLATELIKE
SLATER
SLATERS
SLATES
SLATEY
SLATHER
SLATHERED
SLATHERS
SLATIER
SLATIEST
SLATINESS
SLATING
SLATINGS
SLATS
SLATTED
SLATTER
SLATTERED
SLATTERN
SLATTERNS
SLATTERS
SLATTERY
SLATTING
SLATTINGS
SLATY
SLAUGHTER
SLAVE
SLAVED
SLAVER
SLAVERED
SLAVERER
SLAVERERS
SLAVERIES
SLAVERING
SLAVERS
SLAVERY
SLAVES
SLAVEY
SLAVEYS
SLAVING
SLAVISH
SLAVISHLY
SLAVOCRAT
SLAVOPHIL
SLAW
SLAWS
SLAY
SLAYABLE
SLAYED
SLAYER
SLAYERS
SLAYING
SLAYINGS
SLAYS
SLEAVE
SLEAVED
SLEAVES
SLEAVING
SLEAZE
SLEAZEBAG
SLEAZED
SLEAZES
SLEAZIER
SLEAZIEST
SLEAZILY
SLEAZING
SLEAZO
SLEAZOID
SLEAZOIDS
SLEAZOS
SLEAZY
SLEB
SLEBS
SLED
SLEDDED
SLEDDER
SLEDDERS
SLEDDING
SLEDDINGS
SLEDED
SLEDGE
SLEDGED
SLEDGER
SLEDGERS
SLEDGES
SLEDGING
SLEDGINGS
SLEDS
SLEE
SLEECH
SLEECHES
SLEECHIER
SLEECHY
SLEEK
SLEEKED
SLEEKEN
SLEEKENED
SLEEKENS
SLEEKER
SLEEKERS
SLEEKEST
SLEEKIER
SLEEKIEST
SLEEKING
SLEEKINGS
SLEEKIT
SLEEKLY
SLEEKNESS
SLEEKS
SLEEKY
SLEEP
SLEEPAWAY
SLEEPER
SLEEPERS
SLEEPERY
SLEEPIER
SLEEPIEST
SLEEPILY
SLEEPING
SLEEPINGS
SLEEPLESS
SLEEPLIKE
SLEEPOUT
SLEEPOUTS
SLEEPOVER
SLEEPRY
SLEEPS
SLEEPSUIT
SLEEPWALK
SLEEPWEAR
SLEEPY
SLEER
SLEEST
SLEET
SLEETED
SLEETIER
SLEETIEST
SLEETING
SLEETS
SLEETY
SLEEVE
SLEEVED
SLEEVEEN
SLEEVEENS
SLEEVELET
SLEEVER
SLEEVERS
SLEEVES
SLEEVING
SLEEVINGS
SLEEZIER
SLEEZIEST
SLEEZY
SLEIDED
SLEIGH
SLEIGHED
SLEIGHER
SLEIGHERS
SLEIGHING
SLEIGHS
SLEIGHT
SLEIGHTS
SLENDER
SLENDERER
SLENDERLY
SLENTER
SLENTERS
SLEPT
SLEUTH
SLEUTHED
SLEUTHING
SLEUTHS
SLEW
SLEWED
SLEWING
SLEWS
SLEY
SLEYS

S

SLICE
SLICEABLE
SLICED
SLICER
SLICERS
SLICES
SLICING
SLICINGS
SLICK
SLICKED
SLICKEN
SLICKENED
SLICKENER
SLICKENS
SLICKER
SLICKERED
SLICKERS
SLICKEST
SLICKING
SLICKINGS
SLICKLY
SLICKNESS
SLICKROCK
SLICKS
SLICKSTER
SLID
SLIDABLE
SLIDDEN
SLIDDER
SLIDDERED
SLIDDERS
SLIDDERY
SLIDE
SLIDED
SLIDER
SLIDERS
SLIDES
SLIDESHOW
SLIDEWAY
SLIDEWAYS
SLIDING
SLIDINGLY
SLIDINGS
SLIER
SLIEST
SLIEVE
SLIEVES
SLIGHT
SLIGHTED
SLIGHTER
SLIGHTERS
SLIGHTEST
SLIGHTING
SLIGHTISH
SLIGHTLY
SLIGHTS
SLILY
SLIM
SLIMDOWN
SLIMDOWNS
SLIME
SLIMEBAG
SLIMEBAGS
SLIMEBALL
SLIMED
SLIMES
SLIMIER
SLIMIEST
SLIMILY
SLIMINESS
SLIMING
SLIMLINE
SLIMLY
SLIMMED
SLIMMER
SLIMMERS
SLIMMEST
SLIMMING
SLIMMINGS
SLIMMISH
SLIMNESS
SLIMPSIER
SLIMPSY
SLIMS
SLIMSIER
SLIMSIEST
SLIMSY
SLIMY
SLING
SLINGBACK
SLINGER
SLINGERS
SLINGIER
SLINGIEST
SLINGING
SLINGS
SLINGSHOT
SLINGY
SLINK
SLINKED
SLINKER
SLINKERS
SLINKIER
SLINKIEST
SLINKILY
SLINKING
SLINKS
SLINKSKIN
SLINKWEED
SLINKY
SLINTER
SLINTERS
SLIOTAR
SLIOTARS
SLIP
SLIPCASE
SLIPCASED
SLIPCASES
SLIPCOVER
SLIPDRESS
SLIPE
SLIPED
SLIPES
SLIPFORM
SLIPFORMS
SLIPING
SLIPKNOT
SLIPKNOTS
SLIPLESS
SLIPNOOSE
SLIPOUT
SLIPOUTS
SLIPOVER
SLIPOVERS
SLIPPAGE
SLIPPAGES
SLIPPED
SLIPPER
SLIPPERED
SLIPPERS
SLIPPERY
SLIPPIER
SLIPPIEST
SLIPPILY
SLIPPING
SLIPPY
SLIPRAIL
SLIPRAILS
SLIPS
SLIPSHEET
SLIPSHOD
SLIPSLOP
SLIPSLOPS
SLIPSOLE
SLIPSOLES
SLIPT
SLIPUP
SLIPUPS
SLIPWARE
SLIPWARES
SLIPWAY
SLIPWAYS
SLISH
SLISHES
SLIT
SLITHER
SLITHERED
SLITHERS
SLITHERY
SLITLESS
SLITLIKE
SLITS
SLITTED
SLITTER
SLITTERS
SLITTIER
SLITTIEST
SLITTING
SLITTY
SLIVE
SLIVED
SLIVEN
SLIVER
SLIVERED
SLIVERER
SLIVERERS
SLIVERING
SLIVERS
SLIVES
SLIVING
SLIVOVIC
SLIVOVICA
SLIVOVITZ
SLIVOWITZ
SLOAN
SLOANS
SLOB
SLOBBED
SLOBBER
SLOBBERED
SLOBBERER
SLOBBERS
SLOBBERY
SLOBBIER
SLOBBIEST
SLOBBING
SLOBBISH
SLOBBY
SLOBLAND
SLOBLANDS
SLOBS
SLOCKEN
SLOCKENED
SLOCKENS
SLOE
SLOEBUSH
SLOES
SLOETHORN
SLOETREE
SLOETREES
SLOG
SLOGAN
SLOGANED
SLOGANEER
SLOGANISE
SLOGANIZE
SLOGANS
SLOGGED
SLOGGER
SLOGGERS
SLOGGING
SLOGS
SLOID
SLOIDS
SLOJD
SLOJDS
SLOKEN
SLOKENED
SLOKENING
SLOKENS

S

SLOMMOCK
SLOMMOCKS
SLOMO
SLOMOS
SLOOM
SLOOMED
SLOOMIER
SLOOMIEST
SLOOMING
SLOOMS
SLOOMY
SLOOP
SLOOPS
SLOOSH
SLOOSHED
SLOOSHES
SLOOSHING
SLOOT
SLOOTS
SLOP
SLOPE
SLOPED
SLOPER
SLOPERS
SLOPES
SLOPESIDE
SLOPEWISE
SLOPIER
SLOPIEST
SLOPING
SLOPINGLY
SLOPPED
SLOPPIER
SLOPPIEST
SLOPPILY
SLOPPING
SLOPPY
SLOPS
SLOPWORK
SLOPWORKS
SLOPY
SLORM
SLORMED
SLORMING
SLORMS
SLOSH
SLOSHED
SLOSHES
SLOSHIER
SLOSHIEST
SLOSHING
SLOSHINGS
SLOSHY
SLOT
SLOTBACK
SLOTBACKS
SLOTH
SLOTHED
SLOTHFUL
SLOTHING
SLOTHS
SLOTS
SLOTTED
SLOTTER
SLOTTERS
SLOTTING
SLOUCH
SLOUCHED
SLOUCHER
SLOUCHERS
SLOUCHES
SLOUCHIER
SLOUCHILY
SLOUCHING
SLOUCHY
SLOUGH
SLOUGHED
SLOUGHI
SLOUGHIER
SLOUGHING
SLOUGHIS
SLOUGHS
SLOUGHY
SLOVE
SLOVEN
SLOVENLY
SLOVENRY
SLOVENS
SLOW
SLOWBACK
SLOWBACKS
SLOWCOACH
SLOWDOWN
SLOWDOWNS
SLOWED
SLOWER
SLOWEST
SLOWING
SLOWINGS
SLOWISH
SLOWLY
SLOWNESS
SLOWPOKE
SLOWPOKES
SLOWS
SLOWWORM
SLOWWORMS
SLOYD
SLOYDS
SLUB
SLUBB
SLUBBED
SLUBBER
SLUBBERED
SLUBBERS
SLUBBEST
SLUBBIER
SLUBBIEST
SLUBBING
SLUBBINGS
SLUBBS
SLUBBY
SLUBS
SLUDGE
SLUDGED
SLUDGES
SLUDGIER
SLUDGIEST
SLUDGING
SLUDGY
SLUE
SLUED
SLUEING
SLUES
SLUFF
SLUFFED
SLUFFING
SLUFFS
SLUG
SLUGABED
SLUGABEDS
SLUGFEST
SLUGFESTS
SLUGGABED
SLUGGARD
SLUGGARDS
SLUGGED
SLUGGER
SLUGGERS
SLUGGING
SLUGGISH
SLUGHORN
SLUGHORNE
SLUGHORNS
SLUGLIKE
SLUGS
SLUICE
SLUICED
SLUICES
SLUICEWAY
SLUICIER
SLUICIEST
SLUICING
SLUICY
SLUING
SLUIT
SLUITS
SLUM
SLUMBER
SLUMBERED
SLUMBERER
SLUMBERS
SLUMBERY
SLUMBROUS
SLUMBRY
SLUMGUM
SLUMGUMS
SLUMISM
SLUMISMS
SLUMLORD
SLUMLORDS
SLUMMED
SLUMMER
SLUMMERS
SLUMMIER
SLUMMIEST
SLUMMING
SLUMMINGS
SLUMMOCK
SLUMMOCKS
SLUMMY
SLUMP
SLUMPED
SLUMPIER
SLUMPIEST
SLUMPING
SLUMPS
SLUMPY
SLUMS
SLUNG
SLUNGSHOT
SLUNK
SLUR
SLURB
SLURBAN
SLURBS
SLURP
SLURPED
SLURPER
SLURPERS
SLURPIER
SLURPIEST
SLURPING
SLURPS
SLURPY
SLURRED
SLURRIED
SLURRIES
SLURRING
SLURRY
SLURRYING
SLURS
SLURVE
SLURVES
SLUSE
SLUSES
SLUSH
SLUSHED
SLUSHES
SLUSHIER
SLUSHIES
SLUSHIEST
SLUSHILY
SLUSHING
SLUSHY
SLUT
SLUTCH
SLUTCHES
SLUTCHIER
SLUTCHY

S

SLUTS
SLUTTERY
SLUTTIER
SLUTTIEST
SLUTTILY
SLUTTISH
SLUTTY
SLY
SLYBOOTS
SLYER
SLYEST
SLYISH
SLYLY
SLYNESS
SLYNESSES
SLYPE
SLYPES
SMA
SMAAK
SMAAKED
SMAAKING
SMAAKS
SMACK
SMACKDOWN
SMACKED
SMACKER
SMACKEROO
SMACKERS
SMACKHEAD
SMACKING
SMACKINGS
SMACKS
SMAIK
SMAIKS
SMALL
SMALLAGE
SMALLAGES
SMALLBOY
SMALLBOYS
SMALLED
SMALLER
SMALLEST
SMALLING
SMALLISH
SMALLNESS
SMALLPOX
SMALLS
SMALLSAT
SMALLSATS
SMALLTIME
SMALM
SMALMED
SMALMIER
SMALMIEST
SMALMILY
SMALMING
SMALMS
SMALMY
SMALT
SMALTI
SMALTINE
SMALTINES
SMALTITE
SMALTITES
SMALTO
SMALTOS
SMALTS
SMARAGD
SMARAGDE
SMARAGDES
SMARAGDS
SMARM
SMARMED
SMARMIER
SMARMIEST
SMARMILY
SMARMING
SMARMS
SMARMY
SMART
SMARTARSE
SMARTASS
SMARTED
SMARTEN
SMARTENED
SMARTENS
SMARTER
SMARTEST
SMARTIE
SMARTIES
SMARTING
SMARTISH
SMARTLY
SMARTNESS
SMARTS
SMARTWEED
SMARTY
SMASH
SMASHABLE
SMASHED
SMASHER
SMASHEROO
SMASHERS
SMASHES
SMASHING
SMASHINGS
SMASHUP
SMASHUPS
SMATCH
SMATCHED
SMATCHES
SMATCHING
SMATTER
SMATTERED
SMATTERER
SMATTERS
SMAZE
SMAZES
SMEAR
SMEARCASE
SMEARED
SMEARER
SMEARERS
SMEARIER
SMEARIEST
SMEARILY
SMEARING
SMEARS
SMEARY
SMEATH
SMEATHS
SMECTIC
SMECTITE
SMECTITES
SMECTITIC
SMEDDUM
SMEDDUMS
SMEE
SMEECH
SMEECHED
SMEECHES
SMEECHING
SMEEK
SMEEKED
SMEEKING
SMEEKS
SMEES
SMEETH
SMEETHED
SMEETHING
SMEETHS
SMEGMA
SMEGMAS
SMEIK
SMEIKED
SMEIKING
SMEIKS
SMEKE
SMEKED
SMEKES
SMEKING
SMELL
SMELLABLE
SMELLED
SMELLER
SMELLERS
SMELLIER
SMELLIES
SMELLIEST
SMELLING
SMELLINGS
SMELLS
SMELLY
SMELT
SMELTED
SMELTER
SMELTERS
SMELTERY
SMELTING
SMELTINGS
SMELTS
SMERK
SMERKED
SMERKING
SMERKS
SMEUSE
SMEUSES
SMEW
SMEWS
SMICKER
SMICKERED
SMICKERS
SMICKET
SMICKETS
SMICKLY
SMIDDIED
SMIDDIES
SMIDDY
SMIDDYING
SMIDGE
SMIDGEN
SMIDGENS
SMIDGEON
SMIDGEONS
SMIDGES
SMIDGIN
SMIDGINS
SMIERCASE
SMIGHT
SMIGHTING
SMIGHTS
SMILAX
SMILAXES
SMILE
SMILED
SMILEFUL
SMILELESS
SMILER
SMILERS
SMILES
SMILET
SMILETS
SMILEY
SMILEYS
SMILIER
SMILIES
SMILIEST
SMILING
SMILINGLY
SMILINGS
SMILODON
SMILODONS
SMIR
SMIRCH
SMIRCHED
SMIRCHER
SMIRCHERS
SMIRCHES
SMIRCHING
SMIRK

S

SMIRKED
SMIRKER
SMIRKERS
SMIRKIER
SMIRKIEST
SMIRKILY
SMIRKING
SMIRKS
SMIRKY
SMIRR
SMIRRED
SMIRRIER
SMIRRIEST
SMIRRING
SMIRRS
SMIRRY
SMIRS
SMIRTING
SMIRTINGS
SMISHING
SMISHINGS
SMIT
SMITE
SMITER
SMITERS
SMITES
SMITH
SMITHED
SMITHERS
SMITHERY
SMITHIED
SMITHIES
SMITHING
SMITHINGS
SMITHS
SMITHY
SMITHYING
SMITING
SMITS
SMITTED
SMITTEN
SMITTING
SMITTLE
SMOCK
SMOCKED
SMOCKING
SMOCKINGS
SMOCKLIKE
SMOCKS
SMOG
SMOGGIER
SMOGGIEST
SMOGGY
SMOGLESS
SMOGS
SMOILE
SMOILED
SMOILES
SMOILING
SMOKABLE
SMOKE
SMOKEABLE
SMOKEBOX
SMOKEBUSH
SMOKED
SMOKEHO
SMOKEHOOD
SMOKEHOS
SMOKEJACK
SMOKELESS
SMOKELIKE
SMOKEPOT
SMOKEPOTS
SMOKER
SMOKERS
SMOKES
SMOKEY
SMOKEYS
SMOKIE
SMOKIER
SMOKIES
SMOKIEST
SMOKILY
SMOKINESS
SMOKING
SMOKINGS
SMOKO
SMOKOS
SMOKY
SMOLDER
SMOLDERED
SMOLDERS
SMOLT
SMOLTS
SMOOCH
SMOOCHED
SMOOCHER
SMOOCHERS
SMOOCHES
SMOOCHIER
SMOOCHING
SMOOCHY
SMOODGE
SMOODGED
SMOODGES
SMOODGING
SMOOGE
SMOOGED
SMOOGES
SMOOGING
SMOOR
SMOORED
SMOORING
SMOORS
SMOOSH
SMOOSHED
SMOOSHES
SMOOSHING
SMOOT
SMOOTED
SMOOTH
SMOOTHE
SMOOTHED
SMOOTHEN
SMOOTHENS
SMOOTHER
SMOOTHERS
SMOOTHES
SMOOTHEST
SMOOTHIE
SMOOTHIES
SMOOTHING
SMOOTHISH
SMOOTHLY
SMOOTHS
SMOOTHY
SMOOTING
SMOOTS
SMORBROD
SMORBRODS
SMORE
SMORED
SMORES
SMORG
SMORGS
SMORING
SMORZANDO
SMORZATO
SMOTE
SMOTHER
SMOTHERED
SMOTHERER
SMOTHERS
SMOTHERY
SMOUCH
SMOUCHED
SMOUCHES
SMOUCHING
SMOULDER
SMOULDERS
SMOULDRY
SMOUSE
SMOUSED
SMOUSER
SMOUSERS
SMOUSES
SMOUSING
SMOUT
SMOUTED
SMOUTING
SMOUTS
SMOWT
SMOWTS
SMOYLE
SMOYLED
SMOYLES
SMOYLING
SMRITI
SMRITIS
SMUDGE
SMUDGED
SMUDGEDLY
SMUDGER
SMUDGERS
SMUDGES
SMUDGIER
SMUDGIEST
SMUDGILY
SMUDGING
SMUDGINGS
SMUDGY
SMUG
SMUGGED
SMUGGER
SMUGGERY
SMUGGEST
SMUGGING
SMUGGLE
SMUGGLED
SMUGGLER
SMUGGLERS
SMUGGLES
SMUGGLING
SMUGLY
SMUGNESS
SMUGS
SMUR
SMURFING
SMURFINGS
SMURRED
SMURRIER
SMURRIEST
SMURRING
SMURRY
SMURS
SMUSH
SMUSHED
SMUSHES
SMUSHING
SMUT
SMUTCH
SMUTCHED
SMUTCHES
SMUTCHIER
SMUTCHING
SMUTCHY
SMUTS
SMUTTED
SMUTTIER
SMUTTIEST
SMUTTILY
SMUTTING
SMUTTY
SMYTRIE
SMYTRIES
SNAB
SNABBLE
SNABBLED
SNABBLES
SNABBLING

SNABS
SNACK
SNACKED
SNACKER
SNACKERS
SNACKETTE
SNACKIER
SNACKIEST
SNACKING
SNACKS
SNACKY
SNAFFLE
SNAFFLED
SNAFFLES
SNAFFLING
SNAFU
SNAFUED
SNAFUING
SNAFUS
SNAG
SNAGGED
SNAGGER
SNAGGERS
SNAGGIER
SNAGGIEST
SNAGGING
SNAGGLE
SNAGGLES
SNAGGY
SNAGLIKE
SNAGS
SNAIL
SNAILED
SNAILERY
SNAILFISH
SNAILIER
SNAILIEST
SNAILING
SNAILLIKE
SNAILS
SNAILY
SNAKE
SNAKEBIRD
SNAKEBIT
SNAKEBITE
SNAKED
SNAKEFISH
SNAKEHEAD
SNAKELIKE
SNAKEPIT
SNAKEPITS
SNAKEROOT
SNAKES
SNAKESKIN
SNAKEWEED
SNAKEWISE
SNAKEWOOD
SNAKEY
SNAKIER
SNAKIEST
SNAKILY
SNAKINESS
SNAKING
SNAKISH
SNAKY
SNAP
SNAPBACK
SNAPBACKS
SNAPHANCE
SNAPLESS
SNAPLINK
SNAPLINKS
SNAPPABLE
SNAPPED
SNAPPER
SNAPPERED
SNAPPERS
SNAPPIER
SNAPPIEST
SNAPPILY
SNAPPING
SNAPPINGS
SNAPPISH
SNAPPY
SNAPS
SNAPSHOT
SNAPSHOTS
SNAPTIN
SNAPTINS
SNAPWEED
SNAPWEEDS
SNAR
SNARE
SNARED
SNARELESS
SNARER
SNARERS
SNARES
SNARF
SNARFED
SNARFING
SNARFLE
SNARFLED
SNARFLES
SNARFLING
SNARFS
SNARIER
SNARIEST
SNARING
SNARINGS
SNARK
SNARKIER
SNARKIEST
SNARKILY
SNARKS
SNARKY
SNARL
SNARLED
SNARLER
SNARLERS
SNARLIER
SNARLIEST
SNARLING
SNARLINGS
SNARLS
SNARLY
SNARRED
SNARRING
SNARS
SNARY
SNASH
SNASHED
SNASHES
SNASHING
SNASTE
SNASTES
SNATCH
SNATCHED
SNATCHER
SNATCHERS
SNATCHES
SNATCHIER
SNATCHILY
SNATCHING
SNATCHY
SNATH
SNATHE
SNATHES
SNATHS
SNAW
SNAWED
SNAWING
SNAWS
SNAZZIER
SNAZZIEST
SNAZZILY
SNAZZY
SNEAD
SNEADS
SNEAK
SNEAKBOX
SNEAKED
SNEAKER
SNEAKERED
SNEAKERS
SNEAKEUP
SNEAKEUPS
SNEAKIER
SNEAKIEST
SNEAKILY
SNEAKING
SNEAKISH
SNEAKS
SNEAKSBY
SNEAKY
SNEAP
SNEAPED
SNEAPING
SNEAPS
SNEATH
SNEATHS
SNEB
SNEBBE
SNEBBED
SNEBBES
SNEBBING
SNEBS
SNECK
SNECKED
SNECKING
SNECKS
SNED
SNEDDED
SNEDDING
SNEDS
SNEE
SNEED
SNEEING
SNEER
SNEERED
SNEERER
SNEERERS
SNEERFUL
SNEERIER
SNEERIEST
SNEERING
SNEERINGS
SNEERS
SNEERY
SNEES
SNEESH
SNEESHAN
SNEESHANS
SNEESHED
SNEESHES
SNEESHIN
SNEESHING
SNEESHINS
SNEEZE
SNEEZED
SNEEZER
SNEEZERS
SNEEZES
SNEEZIER
SNEEZIEST
SNEEZING
SNEEZINGS
SNEEZY
SNELL
SNELLED
SNELLER
SNELLEST
SNELLING
SNELLS
SNELLY
SNIB
SNIBBED
SNIBBING
SNIBS
SNICK

S

SNICKED
SNICKER
SNICKERED
SNICKERER
SNICKERS
SNICKERY
SNICKET
SNICKETS
SNICKING
SNICKS
SNIDE
SNIDED
SNIDELY
SNIDENESS
SNIDER
SNIDES
SNIDEST
SNIDEY
SNIDIER
SNIDIEST
SNIDING
SNIES
SNIFF
SNIFFABLE
SNIFFED
SNIFFER
SNIFFERS
SNIFFIER
SNIFFIEST
SNIFFILY
SNIFFING
SNIFFINGS
SNIFFISH
SNIFFLE
SNIFFLED
SNIFFLER
SNIFFLERS
SNIFFLES
SNIFFLIER
SNIFFLING
SNIFFLY
SNIFFS
SNIFFY
SNIFT
SNIFTED
SNIFTER
SNIFTERED
SNIFTERS
SNIFTIER
SNIFTIEST
SNIFTING
SNIFTS
SNIFTY
SNIG
SNIGGED
SNIGGER
SNIGGERED
SNIGGERER
SNIGGERS
SNIGGING
SNIGGLE
SNIGGLED
SNIGGLER
SNIGGLERS
SNIGGLES
SNIGGLING
SNIGLET
SNIGLETS
SNIGS
SNIP
SNIPE
SNIPED
SNIPEFISH
SNIPELIKE
SNIPER
SNIPERS
SNIPES
SNIPIER
SNIPIEST
SNIPING
SNIPINGS
SNIPPED
SNIPPER
SNIPPERS
SNIPPET
SNIPPETS
SNIPPETY
SNIPPIER
SNIPPIEST
SNIPPILY
SNIPPING
SNIPPINGS
SNIPPY
SNIPS
SNIPY
SNIRT
SNIRTED
SNIRTING
SNIRTLE
SNIRTLED
SNIRTLES
SNIRTLING
SNIRTS
SNIT
SNITCH
SNITCHED
SNITCHER
SNITCHERS
SNITCHES
SNITCHIER
SNITCHING
SNITCHY
SNITS
SNITTIER
SNITTIEST
SNITTY
SNIVEL
SNIVELED
SNIVELER
SNIVELERS
SNIVELIER
SNIVELING
SNIVELLED
SNIVELLER
SNIVELLY
SNIVELS
SNIVELY
SNOB
SNOBBERY
SNOBBIER
SNOBBIEST
SNOBBILY
SNOBBISH
SNOBBISM
SNOBBISMS
SNOBBY
SNOBLING
SNOBLINGS
SNOBS
SNOCOACH
SNOD
SNODDED
SNODDER
SNODDEST
SNODDING
SNODDIT
SNODS
SNOEK
SNOEKS
SNOEP
SNOG
SNOGGED
SNOGGER
SNOGGERS
SNOGGING
SNOGS
SNOKE
SNOKED
SNOKES
SNOKING
SNOOD
SNOODED
SNOODING
SNOODS
SNOOK
SNOOKED
SNOOKER
SNOOKERED
SNOOKERS
SNOOKING
SNOOKS
SNOOL
SNOOLED
SNOOLING
SNOOLS
SNOOP
SNOOPED
SNOOPER
SNOOPERS
SNOOPIER
SNOOPIEST
SNOOPILY
SNOOPING
SNOOPS
SNOOPY
SNOOSE
SNOOSES
SNOOT
SNOOTED
SNOOTFUL
SNOOTFULS
SNOOTIER
SNOOTIEST
SNOOTILY
SNOOTING
SNOOTS
SNOOTY
SNOOZE
SNOOZED
SNOOZER
SNOOZERS
SNOOZES
SNOOZIER
SNOOZIEST
SNOOZING
SNOOZLE
SNOOZLED
SNOOZLES
SNOOZLING
SNOOZY
SNORE
SNORED
SNORER
SNORERS
SNORES
SNORING
SNORINGS
SNORKEL
SNORKELED
SNORKELER
SNORKELS
SNORT
SNORTED
SNORTER
SNORTERS
SNORTIER
SNORTIEST
SNORTING
SNORTINGS
SNORTS
SNORTY
SNOT
SNOTRAG
SNOTRAGS
SNOTS
SNOTTED
SNOTTER
SNOTTERED
SNOTTERS
SNOTTERY

SNOTTIE
SNOTTIER
SNOTTIES
SNOTTIEST
SNOTTILY
SNOTTING
SNOTTY
SNOUT
SNOUTED
SNOUTIER
SNOUTIEST
SNOUTING
SNOUTISH
SNOUTLESS
SNOUTLIKE
SNOUTS
SNOUTY
SNOW
SNOWBALL
SNOWBALLS
SNOWBANK
SNOWBANKS
SNOWBELL
SNOWBELLS
SNOWBELT
SNOWBELTS
SNOWBERRY
SNOWBIRD
SNOWBIRDS
SNOWBLINK
SNOWBOARD
SNOWBOOT
SNOWBOOTS
SNOWBOUND
SNOWBRUSH
SNOWBUSH
SNOWCAP
SNOWCAPS
SNOWCAT
SNOWCATS
SNOWCLONE
SNOWCOACH
SNOWDOME
SNOWDOMES
SNOWDRIFT
SNOWDROP
SNOWDROPS
SNOWED
SNOWFALL
SNOWFALLS
SNOWFIELD
SNOWFLAKE
SNOWFLEA
SNOWFLEAS
SNOWFLECK
SNOWFLICK
SNOWGLOBE
SNOWIER
SNOWIEST
SNOWILY
SNOWINESS
SNOWING
SNOWISH
SNOWK
SNOWKED
SNOWKING
SNOWKS
SNOWLAND
SNOWLANDS
SNOWLESS
SNOWLIKE
SNOWLINE
SNOWLINES
SNOWMAKER
SNOWMAN
SNOWMELT
SNOWMELTS
SNOWMEN
SNOWMOLD
SNOWMOLDS
SNOWMOULD
SNOWPACK
SNOWPACKS
SNOWPLOW
SNOWPLOWS
SNOWS
SNOWSCAPE
SNOWSHED
SNOWSHEDS
SNOWSHOE
SNOWSHOED
SNOWSHOER
SNOWSHOES
SNOWSLIDE
SNOWSLIP
SNOWSLIPS
SNOWSNAKE
SNOWSTORM
SNOWSUIT
SNOWSUITS
SNOWY
SNUB
SNUBBE
SNUBBED
SNUBBER
SNUBBERS
SNUBBES
SNUBBEST
SNUBBIER
SNUBBIEST
SNUBBING
SNUBBINGS
SNUBBISH
SNUBBY
SNUBFIN
SNUBNESS
SNUBS
SNUCK
SNUDGE
SNUDGED
SNUDGES
SNUDGING
SNUFF
SNUFFBOX
SNUFFED
SNUFFER
SNUFFERS
SNUFFIER
SNUFFIEST
SNUFFILY
SNUFFING
SNUFFINGS
SNUFFLE
SNUFFLED
SNUFFLER
SNUFFLERS
SNUFFLES
SNUFFLIER
SNUFFLING
SNUFFLY
SNUFFS
SNUFFY
SNUG
SNUGGED
SNUGGER
SNUGGERIE
SNUGGERY
SNUGGEST
SNUGGIES
SNUGGING
SNUGGLE
SNUGGLED
SNUGGLES
SNUGGLIER
SNUGGLING
SNUGGLY
SNUGLY
SNUGNESS
SNUGS
SNUSH
SNUSHED
SNUSHES
SNUSHING
SNUZZLE
SNUZZLED
SNUZZLES
SNUZZLING
SNY
SNYE
SNYES
SO
SOAK
SOAKAGE
SOAKAGES
SOAKAWAY
SOAKAWAYS
SOAKED
SOAKEN
SOAKER
SOAKERS
SOAKING
SOAKINGLY
SOAKINGS
SOAKS
SOAP
SOAPBARK
SOAPBARKS
SOAPBERRY
SOAPBOX
SOAPBOXED
SOAPBOXES
SOAPDISH
SOAPED
SOAPER
SOAPERS
SOAPFISH
SOAPIE
SOAPIER
SOAPIES
SOAPIEST
SOAPILY
SOAPINESS
SOAPING
SOAPLAND
SOAPLANDS
SOAPLESS
SOAPLIKE
SOAPROOT
SOAPROOTS
SOAPS
SOAPSTONE
SOAPSUDS
SOAPSUDSY
SOAPWORT
SOAPWORTS
SOAPY
SOAR
SOARAWAY
SOARE
SOARED
SOARER
SOARERS
SOARES
SOARING
SOARINGLY
SOARINGS
SOARS
SOAVE
SOAVES
SOB
SOBA
SOBAS
SOBBED
SOBBER
SOBBERS
SOBBING
SOBBINGLY
SOBBINGS
SOBEIT
SOBER

SOBERED
SOBERER
SOBEREST
SOBERING
SOBERISE
SOBERISED
SOBERISES
SOBERIZE
SOBERIZED
SOBERIZES
SOBERLY
SOBERNESS
SOBERS
SOBFUL
SOBOLE
SOBOLES
SOBRIETY
SOBRIQUET
SOBS
SOC
SOCA
SOCAGE
SOCAGER
SOCAGERS
SOCAGES
SOCAS
SOCCAGE
SOCCAGES
SOCCER
SOCCERS
SOCES
SOCIABLE
SOCIABLES
SOCIABLY
SOCIAL
SOCIALISE
SOCIALISM
SOCIALIST
SOCIALITE
SOCIALITY
SOCIALIZE
SOCIALLY
SOCIALS
SOCIATE
SOCIATES
SOCIATION
SOCIATIVE
SOCIETAL
SOCIETIES
SOCIETY
SOCIOGRAM
SOCIOLECT
SOCIOLOGY
SOCIOPATH
SOCK
SOCKED
SOCKET
SOCKETED
SOCKETING
SOCKETS
SOCKETTE
SOCKETTES
SOCKEYE
SOCKEYES
SOCKING
SOCKLESS
SOCKMAN
SOCKMEN
SOCKO
SOCKS
SOCLE
SOCLES
SOCMAN
SOCMEN
SOCS
SOD
SODA
SODAIC
SODAIN
SODAINE
SODALESS
SODALIST
SODALISTS
SODALITE
SODALITES
SODALITY
SODAMIDE
SODAMIDES
SODAS
SODBUSTER
SODDED
SODDEN
SODDENED
SODDENING
SODDENLY
SODDENS
SODDIE
SODDIER
SODDIES
SODDIEST
SODDING
SODDY
SODGER
SODGERED
SODGERING
SODGERS
SODIC
SODICITY
SODIUM
SODIUMS
SODOM
SODOMIES
SODOMISE
SODOMISED
SODOMISES
SODOMIST
SODOMISTS
SODOMITE
SODOMITES
SODOMITIC
SODOMIZE
SODOMIZED
SODOMIZES
SODOMS
SODOMY
SODS
SOEVER
SOFA
SOFABED
SOFABEDS
SOFAR
SOFARS
SOFAS
SOFFIONI
SOFFIT
SOFFITS
SOFT
SOFTA
SOFTAS
SOFTBACK
SOFTBACKS
SOFTBALL
SOFTBALLS
SOFTBOUND
SOFTCORE
SOFTCOVER
SOFTED
SOFTEN
SOFTENED
SOFTENER
SOFTENERS
SOFTENING
SOFTENS
SOFTER
SOFTEST
SOFTGOODS
SOFTHEAD
SOFTHEADS
SOFTIE
SOFTIES
SOFTING
SOFTISH
SOFTLING
SOFTLINGS
SOFTLY
SOFTNESS
SOFTPASTE
SOFTS
SOFTSCAPE
SOFTSHELL
SOFTWARE
SOFTWARES
SOFTWOOD
SOFTWOODS
SOFTY
SOG
SOGER
SOGERS
SOGGED
SOGGIER
SOGGIEST
SOGGILY
SOGGINESS
SOGGING
SOGGINGS
SOGGY
SOGS
SOH
SOHO
SOHS
SOHUR
SOHURS
SOIGNE
SOIGNEE
SOIL
SOILAGE
SOILAGES
SOILBORNE
SOILED
SOILIER
SOILIEST
SOILINESS
SOILING
SOILINGS
SOILLESS
SOILS
SOILURE
SOILURES
SOILY
SOIREE
SOIREES
SOJA
SOJAS
SOJOURN
SOJOURNED
SOJOURNER
SOJOURNS
SOJU
SOJUS
SOKAH
SOKAHS
SOKAIYA
SOKE
SOKEMAN
SOKEMANRY
SOKEMEN
SOKEN
SOKENS
SOKES
SOKOL
SOKOLS
SOL
SOLA
SOLACE
SOLACED
SOLACER
SOLACERS
SOLACES
SOLACING
SOLACIOUS

S

SOLAH
SOLAHS
SOLAN
SOLAND
SOLANDER
SOLANDERS
SOLANDS
SOLANIN
SOLANINE
SOLANINES
SOLANINS
SOLANO
SOLANOS
SOLANS
SOLANUM
SOLANUMS
SOLAR
SOLARIA
SOLARISE
SOLARISED
SOLARISES
SOLARISM
SOLARISMS
SOLARIST
SOLARISTS
SOLARIUM
SOLARIUMS
SOLARIZE
SOLARIZED
SOLARIZES
SOLARS
SOLAS
SOLATE
SOLATED
SOLATES
SOLATIA
SOLATING
SOLATION
SOLATIONS
SOLATIUM
SOLD
SOLDADO
SOLDADOES
SOLDADOS
SOLDAN
SOLDANS
SOLDE
SOLDER
SOLDERED
SOLDERER
SOLDERERS
SOLDERING
SOLDERS
SOLDES
SOLDI
SOLDIER
SOLDIERED
SOLDIERLY
SOLDIERS
SOLDIERY
SOLDO
SOLDS
SOLE
SOLECISE
SOLECISED
SOLECISES
SOLECISM
SOLECISMS
SOLECIST
SOLECISTS
SOLECIZE
SOLECIZED
SOLECIZES
SOLED
SOLEI
SOLEIN
SOLELESS
SOLELY
SOLEMN
SOLEMNER
SOLEMNESS
SOLEMNEST
SOLEMNIFY
SOLEMNISE
SOLEMNITY
SOLEMNIZE
SOLEMNLY
SOLENESS
SOLENETTE
SOLENODON
SOLENOID
SOLENOIDS
SOLEPLATE
SOLEPRINT
SOLER
SOLERA
SOLERAS
SOLERET
SOLERETS
SOLERS
SOLES
SOLEUS
SOLEUSES
SOLFATARA
SOLFEGE
SOLFEGES
SOLFEGGI
SOLFEGGIO
SOLFERINO
SOLGEL
SOLI
SOLICIT
SOLICITED
SOLICITOR
SOLICITS
SOLICITY
SOLID
SOLIDAGO
SOLIDAGOS
SOLIDARE
SOLIDARES
SOLIDARY
SOLIDATE
SOLIDATED
SOLIDATES
SOLIDER
SOLIDEST
SOLIDI
SOLIDIFY
SOLIDISH
SOLIDISM
SOLIDISMS
SOLIDIST
SOLIDISTS
SOLIDITY
SOLIDLY
SOLIDNESS
SOLIDS
SOLIDUM
SOLIDUMS
SOLIDUS
SOLILOQUY
SOLING
SOLION
SOLIONS
SOLIPED
SOLIPEDS
SOLIPSISM
SOLIPSIST
SOLIQUID
SOLIQUIDS
SOLITAIRE
SOLITARY
SOLITO
SOLITON
SOLITONS
SOLITUDE
SOLITUDES
SOLIVE
SOLIVES
SOLLAR
SOLLARED
SOLLARING
SOLLARS
SOLLER
SOLLERET
SOLLERETS
SOLLERS
SOLLICKER
SOLO
SOLOED
SOLOES
SOLOING
SOLOIST
SOLOISTIC
SOLOISTS
SOLON
SOLONCHAK
SOLONETS
SOLONETZ
SOLONS
SOLOS
SOLPUGID
SOLPUGIDS
SOLS
SOLSTICE
SOLSTICES
SOLUBLE
SOLUBLES
SOLUBLY
SOLUM
SOLUMS
SOLUNAR
SOLUS
SOLUSES
SOLUTAL
SOLUTE
SOLUTES
SOLUTION
SOLUTIONS
SOLUTIVE
SOLUTIVES
SOLVABLE
SOLVATE
SOLVATED
SOLVATES
SOLVATING
SOLVATION
SOLVE
SOLVED
SOLVENCY
SOLVENT
SOLVENTLY
SOLVENTS
SOLVER
SOLVERS
SOLVES
SOLVING
SOM
SOMA
SOMAN
SOMANS
SOMAS
SOMASCOPE
SOMATA
SOMATIC
SOMATISM
SOMATISMS
SOMATIST
SOMATISTS
SOMBER
SOMBERED
SOMBERER
SOMBEREST
SOMBERING
SOMBERLY
SOMBERS
SOMBRE
SOMBRED
SOMBRELY

S

SOMBRER
SOMBRERO
SOMBREROS
SOMBRES
SOMBREST
SOMBRING
SOMBROUS
SOME
SOMEBODY
SOMEDAY
SOMEDEAL
SOMEDEALS
SOMEDELE
SOMEGATE
SOMEHOW
SOMEONE
SOMEONES
SOMEPLACE
SOMERSET
SOMERSETS
SOMETHING
SOMETIME
SOMETIMES
SOMEWAY
SOMEWAYS
SOMEWHAT
SOMEWHATS
SOMEWHEN
SOMEWHERE
SOMEWHILE
SOMEWHY
SOMEWISE
SOMITAL
SOMITE
SOMITES
SOMITIC
SOMMELIER
SOMNIAL
SOMNIATE
SOMNIATED
SOMNIATES
SOMNIFIC
SOMNOLENT
SOMONI
SOMONIS
SOMS
SOMY
SON
SONANCE
SONANCES
SONANCIES
SONANCY
SONANT
SONANTAL
SONANTIC
SONANTS
SONAR
SONARMAN
SONARMEN
SONARS
SONATA
SONATAS
SONATINA
SONATINAS
SONATINE
SONCE
SONCES
SONDAGE
SONDAGES
SONDE
SONDELI
SONDELIS
SONDER
SONDERS
SONDES
SONE
SONERI
SONERIS
SONES
SONG
SONGBIRD
SONGBIRDS
SONGBOOK
SONGBOOKS
SONGCRAFT
SONGFEST
SONGFESTS
SONGFUL
SONGFULLY
SONGKOK
SONGKOKS
SONGLESS
SONGLIKE
SONGMAN
SONGMEN
SONGOLOLO
SONGS
SONGSHEET
SONGSMITH
SONGSTER
SONGSTERS
SONHOOD
SONHOODS
SONIC
SONICALLY
SONICATE
SONICATED
SONICATES
SONICATOR
SONICS
SONLESS
SONLIER
SONLIEST
SONLIKE
SONLY
SONNE
SONNES
SONNET
SONNETARY
SONNETED
SONNETEER
SONNETING
SONNETISE
SONNETIZE
SONNETS
SONNETTED
SONNIES
SONNY
SONOBUOY
SONOBUOYS
SONOGRAM
SONOGRAMS
SONOGRAPH
SONOMETER
SONORANT
SONORANTS
SONORITY
SONOROUS
SONOVOX
SONOVOXES
SONS
SONSE
SONSES
SONSHIP
SONSHIPS
SONSIE
SONSIER
SONSIEST
SONSY
SONTAG
SONTAGS
SONTIES
SOOCHONG
SOOCHONGS
SOOEY
SOOGEE
SOOGEED
SOOGEEING
SOOGEES
SOOGIE
SOOGIED
SOOGIEING
SOOGIES
SOOJEY
SOOJEYS
SOOK
SOOKED
SOOKIER
SOOKIEST
SOOKING
SOOKS
SOOKY
SOOL
SOOLE
SOOLED
SOOLER
SOOLERS
SOOLES
SOOLING
SOOLS
SOOM
SOOMED
SOOMING
SOOMS
SOON
SOONER
SOONERS
SOONEST
SOONISH
SOOP
SOOPED
SOOPING
SOOPINGS
SOOPS
SOOPSTAKE
SOOT
SOOTE
SOOTED
SOOTERKIN
SOOTES
SOOTFLAKE
SOOTH
SOOTHE
SOOTHED
SOOTHER
SOOTHERED
SOOTHERS
SOOTHES
SOOTHEST
SOOTHFAST
SOOTHFUL
SOOTHING
SOOTHINGS
SOOTHLICH
SOOTHLY
SOOTHS
SOOTHSAID
SOOTHSAY
SOOTHSAYS
SOOTIER
SOOTIEST
SOOTILY
SOOTINESS
SOOTING
SOOTINGS
SOOTLESS
SOOTS
SOOTY
SOP
SOPAPILLA
SOPH
SOPHERIC
SOPHERIM
SOPHIES
SOPHISM
SOPHISMS
SOPHIST
SOPHISTER
SOPHISTIC
SOPHISTRY

SOPHISTS
SOPHOMORE
SOPHS
SOPHY
SOPITE
SOPITED
SOPITES
SOPITING
SOPOR
SOPORIFIC
SOPOROSE
SOPOROUS
SOPORS
SOPPED
SOPPIER
SOPPIEST
SOPPILY
SOPPINESS
SOPPING
SOPPINGS
SOPPY
SOPRA
SOPRANI
SOPRANINI
SOPRANINO
SOPRANIST
SOPRANO
SOPRANOS
SOPS
SORA
SORAGE
SORAGES
SORAL
SORAS
SORB
SORBABLE
SORBARIA
SORBARIAS
SORBATE
SORBATES
SORBED
SORBENT
SORBENTS
SORBET
SORBETS
SORBIC
SORBING
SORBITAN
SORBITANS
SORBITE
SORBITES
SORBITIC
SORBITISE
SORBITIZE
SORBITOL
SORBITOLS
SORBO
SORBOSE
SORBOSES
SORBS
SORBUS
SORBUSES
SORCERER
SORCERERS
SORCERESS
SORCERIES
SORCEROUS
SORCERY
SORD
SORDA
SORDED
SORDES
SORDID
SORDIDER
SORDIDEST
SORDIDLY
SORDINE
SORDINES
SORDING
SORDINI
SORDINO
SORDO
SORDOR
SORDORS
SORDS
SORE
SORED
SOREDIA
SOREDIAL
SOREDIATE
SOREDIUM
SOREE
SOREES
SOREHEAD
SOREHEADS
SOREHON
SOREHONS
SOREL
SORELL
SORELLS
SORELS
SORELY
SORENESS
SORER
SORES
SOREST
SOREX
SOREXES
SORGHO
SORGHOS
SORGHUM
SORGHUMS
SORGO
SORGOS
SORI
SORICINE
SORICOID
SORING
SORINGS
SORITES
SORITIC
SORITICAL
SORN
SORNED
SORNER
SORNERS
SORNING
SORNINGS
SORNS
SOROBAN
SOROBANS
SOROCHE
SOROCHES
SORORAL
SORORALLY
SORORATE
SORORATES
SORORIAL
SORORISE
SORORISED
SORORISES
SORORITY
SORORIZE
SORORIZED
SORORIZES
SOROSES
SOROSIS
SOROSISES
SORPTION
SORPTIONS
SORPTIVE
SORRA
SORRAS
SORREL
SORRELS
SORRIER
SORRIEST
SORRILY
SORRINESS
SORROW
SORROWED
SORROWER
SORROWERS
SORROWFUL
SORROWING
SORROWS
SORRY
SORRYISH
SORT
SORTA
SORTABLE
SORTABLY
SORTAL
SORTALS
SORTANCE
SORTANCES
SORTATION
SORTED
SORTER
SORTERS
SORTES
SORTIE
SORTIED
SORTIEING
SORTIES
SORTILEGE
SORTILEGY
SORTING
SORTINGS
SORTITION
SORTMENT
SORTMENTS
SORTS
SORUS
SOS
SOSATIE
SOSATIES
SOSS
SOSSED
SOSSES
SOSSING
SOSSINGS
SOSTENUTI
SOSTENUTO
SOT
SOTERIAL
SOTH
SOTHS
SOTOL
SOTOLS
SOTS
SOTTED
SOTTEDLY
SOTTING
SOTTINGS
SOTTISH
SOTTISHLY
SOTTISIER
SOU
SOUARI
SOUARIS
SOUBISE
SOUBISES
SOUBRETTE
SOUCAR
SOUCARS
SOUCE
SOUCED
SOUCES
SOUCHONG
SOUCHONGS
SOUCING
SOUCT
SOUDAN
SOUDANS
SOUFFLE
SOUFFLED
SOUFFLEED
SOUFFLES
SOUGH

S

SOUGHED
SOUGHING
SOUGHS
SOUGHT
SOUK
SOUKED
SOUKING
SOUKOUS
SOUKOUSES
SOUKS
SOUL
SOULDAN
SOULDANS
SOULDIER
SOULDIERS
SOULED
SOULFUL
SOULFULLY
SOULLESS
SOULLIKE
SOULMATE
SOULMATES
SOULS
SOULSTER
SOULSTERS
SOUM
SOUMED
SOUMING
SOUMINGS
SOUMS
SOUND
SOUNDABLE
SOUNDBAR
SOUNDBARS
SOUNDBITE
SOUNDBOX
SOUNDCARD
SOUNDED
SOUNDER
SOUNDERS
SOUNDEST
SOUNDING
SOUNDINGS
SOUNDLESS
SOUNDLY
SOUNDMAN
SOUNDMEN
SOUNDNESS
SOUNDPOST
SOUNDS
SOUP
SOUPCON
SOUPCONS
SOUPED
SOUPER
SOUPERS
SOUPFIN
SOUPFINS
SOUPIER
SOUPIEST
SOUPILY
SOUPINESS
SOUPING
SOUPLE
SOUPLED
SOUPLES
SOUPLESS
SOUPLIKE
SOUPLING
SOUPS
SOUPSPOON
SOUPY
SOUR
SOURBALL
SOURBALLS
SOURCE
SOURCED
SOURCEFUL
SOURCES
SOURCING
SOURCINGS
SOURDINE
SOURDINES
SOURDOUGH
SOURED
SOURER
SOUREST
SOURGUM
SOURGUMS
SOURING
SOURINGS
SOURISH
SOURISHLY
SOURLY
SOURNESS
SOUROCK
SOUROCKS
SOURPUSS
SOURS
SOURSE
SOURSES
SOURSOP
SOURSOPS
SOURVELD
SOURVELDS
SOURWOOD
SOURWOODS
SOUS
SOUSE
SOUSED
SOUSER
SOUSERS
SOUSES
SOUSING
SOUSINGS
SOUSLIK
SOUSLIKS
SOUT
SOUTACHE
SOUTACHES
SOUTANE
SOUTANES
SOUTAR
SOUTARS
SOUTENEUR
SOUTER
SOUTERLY
SOUTERS
SOUTH
SOUTHEAST
SOUTHED
SOUTHER
SOUTHERED
SOUTHERLY
SOUTHERN
SOUTHERNS
SOUTHERS
SOUTHING
SOUTHINGS
SOUTHLAND
SOUTHMOST
SOUTHPAW
SOUTHPAWS
SOUTHRON
SOUTHRONS
SOUTHS
SOUTHSAID
SOUTHSAY
SOUTHSAYS
SOUTHWARD
SOUTHWEST
SOUTIE
SOUTIES
SOUTPIEL
SOUTPIELS
SOUTS
SOUVENIR
SOUVENIRS
SOUVLAKI
SOUVLAKIA
SOUVLAKIS
SOV
SOVENANCE
SOVEREIGN
SOVIET
SOVIETIC
SOVIETISE
SOVIETISM
SOVIETIST
SOVIETIZE
SOVIETS
SOVKHOZ
SOVKHOZES
SOVKHOZY
SOVRAN
SOVRANLY
SOVRANS
SOVRANTY
SOVS
SOW
SOWABLE
SOWANS
SOWAR
SOWARREE
SOWARREES
SOWARRIES
SOWARRY
SOWARS
SOWBACK
SOWBACKS
SOWBELLY
SOWBREAD
SOWBREADS
SOWBUG
SOWBUGS
SOWCAR
SOWCARS
SOWCE
SOWCED
SOWCES
SOWCING
SOWDER
SOWDERS
SOWED
SOWENS
SOWER
SOWERS
SOWF
SOWFED
SOWFF
SOWFFED
SOWFFING
SOWFFS
SOWFING
SOWFS
SOWING
SOWINGS
SOWL
SOWLE
SOWLED
SOWLES
SOWLING
SOWLS
SOWM
SOWMED
SOWMING
SOWMS
SOWN
SOWND
SOWNDED
SOWNDING
SOWNDS
SOWNE
SOWNES
SOWP
SOWPED
SOWPING
SOWPS
SOWS
SOWSE

SOWSED
SOWSES
SOWSING
SOWSSE
SOWSSED
SOWSSES
SOWSSING
SOWTER
SOWTERS
SOWTH
SOWTHED
SOWTHING
SOWTHS
SOX
SOY
SOYA
SOYAS
SOYBEAN
SOYBEANS
SOYBURGER
SOYLE
SOYLED
SOYLES
SOYLING
SOYMEAL
SOYMEALS
SOYMILK
SOYMILKS
SOYS
SOYUZ
SOYUZES
SOZ
SOZIN
SOZINE
SOZINES
SOZINS
SOZZLE
SOZZLED
SOZZLES
SOZZLIER
SOZZLIEST
SOZZLING
SOZZLY
SPA
SPACE
SPACEBAND
SPACED
SPACELAB
SPACELABS
SPACELESS
SPACEMAN
SPACEMEN
SPACEPORT
SPACER
SPACERS
SPACES
SPACESHIP
SPACESUIT
SPACETIME
SPACEWALK
SPACEWARD
SPACEY
SPACIAL
SPACIALLY
SPACIER
SPACIEST
SPACINESS
SPACING
SPACINGS
SPACIOUS
SPACKLE
SPACKLED
SPACKLES
SPACKLING
SPACY
SPADASSIN
SPADE
SPADED
SPADEFEET
SPADEFISH
SPADEFOOT
SPADEFUL
SPADEFULS
SPADELIKE
SPADEMAN
SPADEMEN
SPADER
SPADERS
SPADES
SPADESMAN
SPADESMEN
SPADEWORK
SPADGER
SPADGERS
SPADICES
SPADILLE
SPADILLES
SPADILLIO
SPADILLO
SPADILLOS
SPADING
SPADIX
SPADIXES
SPADO
SPADOES
SPADONES
SPADOS
SPADROON
SPADROONS
SPAE
SPAED
SPAEING
SPAEINGS
SPAEMAN
SPAEMEN
SPAER
SPAERS
SPAES
SPAETZLE
SPAETZLES
SPAEWIFE
SPAEWIVES
SPAG
SPAGERIC
SPAGGED
SPAGGING
SPAGHETTI
SPAGIRIC
SPAGIRIST
SPAGS
SPAGYRIC
SPAGYRICS
SPAGYRIST
SPAHEE
SPAHEES
SPAHI
SPAHIS
SPAIL
SPAILS
SPAIN
SPAINED
SPAING
SPAINGS
SPAINING
SPAINS
SPAIRGE
SPAIRGED
SPAIRGES
SPAIRGING
SPAIT
SPAITS
SPAKE
SPALD
SPALDEEN
SPALDEENS
SPALDS
SPALE
SPALES
SPALL
SPALLABLE
SPALLE
SPALLED
SPALLER
SPALLERS
SPALLES
SPALLING
SPALLINGS
SPALLS
SPALPEEN
SPALPEENS
SPALT
SPALTED
SPALTING
SPALTS
SPAM
SPAMBOT
SPAMBOTS
SPAMMED
SPAMMER
SPAMMERS
SPAMMIE
SPAMMIER
SPAMMIES
SPAMMIEST
SPAMMING
SPAMMINGS
SPAMMY
SPAMS
SPAN
SPANAEMIA
SPANAEMIC
SPANCEL
SPANCELED
SPANCELS
SPANDEX
SPANDEXED
SPANDEXES
SPANDREL
SPANDRELS
SPANDRIL
SPANDRILS
SPANE
SPANED
SPANES
SPANG
SPANGED
SPANGHEW
SPANGHEWS
SPANGING
SPANGLE
SPANGLED
SPANGLER
SPANGLERS
SPANGLES
SPANGLET
SPANGLETS
SPANGLIER
SPANGLING
SPANGLY
SPANGS
SPANIEL
SPANIELS
SPANING
SPANK
SPANKED
SPANKER
SPANKERS
SPANKING
SPANKINGS
SPANKS
SPANLESS
SPANNED
SPANNER
SPANNERS
SPANNING
SPANS
SPANSPEK
SPANSPEKS
SPANSULE
SPANSULES

S

SPANWORM
SPANWORMS
SPAR
SPARABLE
SPARABLES
SPARAXIS
SPARD
SPARE
SPAREABLE
SPARED
SPARELESS
SPARELY
SPARENESS
SPARER
SPARERIB
SPARERIBS
SPARERS
SPARES
SPAREST
SPARGE
SPARGED
SPARGER
SPARGERS
SPARGES
SPARGING
SPARID
SPARIDS
SPARING
SPARINGLY
SPARK
SPARKE
SPARKED
SPARKER
SPARKERS
SPARKES
SPARKIE
SPARKIER
SPARKIES
SPARKIEST
SPARKILY
SPARKING
SPARKISH
SPARKLE
SPARKLED
SPARKLER
SPARKLERS
SPARKLES
SPARKLESS
SPARKLET
SPARKLETS
SPARKLIER
SPARKLIES
SPARKLING
SPARKLY
SPARKPLUG
SPARKS
SPARKY
SPARLIKE
SPARLING
SPARLINGS
SPAROID
SPAROIDS
SPARRE
SPARRED
SPARRER
SPARRERS
SPARRES
SPARRIER
SPARRIEST
SPARRING
SPARRINGS
SPARROW
SPARROWS
SPARRY
SPARS
SPARSE
SPARSEDLY
SPARSELY
SPARSER
SPARSEST
SPARSITY
SPART
SPARTAN
SPARTANS
SPARTEINE
SPARTERIE
SPARTH
SPARTHE
SPARTHES
SPARTHS
SPARTICLE
SPARTINA
SPARTINAS
SPARTS
SPAS
SPASM
SPASMATIC
SPASMED
SPASMIC
SPASMING
SPASMODIC
SPASMS
SPASTIC
SPASTICS
SPAT
SPATE
SPATES
SPATFALL
SPATFALLS
SPATHAL
SPATHE
SPATHED
SPATHES
SPATHIC
SPATHOSE
SPATIAL
SPATIALLY
SPATLESE
SPATLESEN
SPATLESES
SPATS
SPATTED
SPATTEE
SPATTEES
SPATTER
SPATTERED
SPATTERS
SPATTING
SPATULA
SPATULAR
SPATULAS
SPATULATE
SPATULE
SPATULES
SPATZLE
SPATZLES
SPAUL
SPAULD
SPAULDS
SPAULS
SPAVIE
SPAVIES
SPAVIET
SPAVIN
SPAVINED
SPAVINS
SPAW
SPAWL
SPAWLED
SPAWLING
SPAWLS
SPAWN
SPAWNED
SPAWNER
SPAWNERS
SPAWNIER
SPAWNIEST
SPAWNING
SPAWNINGS
SPAWNS
SPAWNY
SPAWS
SPAY
SPAYAD
SPAYADS
SPAYD
SPAYDS
SPAYED
SPAYING
SPAYS
SPAZ
SPAZA
SPAZZ
SPAZZED
SPAZZES
SPAZZING
SPEAK
SPEAKABLE
SPEAKEASY
SPEAKER
SPEAKERS
SPEAKING
SPEAKINGS
SPEAKOUT
SPEAKOUTS
SPEAKS
SPEAL
SPEALS
SPEAN
SPEANED
SPEANING
SPEANS
SPEAR
SPEARED
SPEARER
SPEARERS
SPEARFISH
SPEARGUN
SPEARGUNS
SPEARHEAD
SPEARIER
SPEARIEST
SPEARING
SPEARINGS
SPEARLIKE
SPEARMAN
SPEARMEN
SPEARMINT
SPEARS
SPEARWORT
SPEARY
SPEAT
SPEATS
SPEC
SPECCED
SPECCIER
SPECCIES
SPECCIEST
SPECCING
SPECCY
SPECIAL
SPECIALER
SPECIALLY
SPECIALS
SPECIALTY
SPECIATE
SPECIATED
SPECIATES
SPECIE
SPECIES
SPECIFIC
SPECIFICS
SPECIFIED
SPECIFIER
SPECIFIES
SPECIFY
SPECIMEN
SPECIMENS
SPECIOUS
SPECK

SPECKED
SPECKIER
SPECKIES
SPECKIEST
SPECKING
SPECKLE
SPECKLED
SPECKLES
SPECKLESS
SPECKLING
SPECKS
SPECKY
SPECS
SPECT
SPECTACLE
SPECTATE
SPECTATED
SPECTATES
SPECTATOR
SPECTED
SPECTER
SPECTERS
SPECTING
SPECTRA
SPECTRAL
SPECTRE
SPECTRES
SPECTRIN
SPECTRINS
SPECTRUM
SPECTRUMS
SPECTS
SPECULA
SPECULAR
SPECULATE
SPECULUM
SPECULUMS
SPED
SPEECH
SPEECHED
SPEECHES
SPEECHFUL
SPEECHIFY
SPEECHING
SPEED
SPEEDBALL
SPEEDBOAT
SPEEDED
SPEEDER
SPEEDERS
SPEEDFUL
SPEEDIER
SPEEDIEST
SPEEDILY
SPEEDING
SPEEDINGS
SPEEDLESS
SPEEDO
SPEEDOS
SPEEDREAD
SPEEDS
SPEEDSTER
SPEEDUP
SPEEDUPS
SPEEDWALK
SPEEDWAY
SPEEDWAYS
SPEEDWELL
SPEEDY
SPEEL
SPEELED
SPEELER
SPEELERS
SPEELING
SPEELS
SPEER
SPEERED
SPEERING
SPEERINGS
SPEERS
SPEIL
SPEILED
SPEILING
SPEILS
SPEIR
SPEIRED
SPEIRING
SPEIRINGS
SPEIRS
SPEISE
SPEISES
SPEISS
SPEISSES
SPEK
SPEKBOOM
SPEKBOOMS
SPEKS
SPELAEAN
SPELD
SPELDED
SPELDER
SPELDERED
SPELDERS
SPELDIN
SPELDING
SPELDINGS
SPELDINS
SPELDRIN
SPELDRING
SPELDRINS
SPELDS
SPELEAN
SPELK
SPELKS
SPELL
SPELLABLE
SPELLBIND
SPELLDOWN
SPELLED
SPELLER
SPELLERS
SPELLFUL
SPELLICAN
SPELLING
SPELLINGS
SPELLS
SPELT
SPELTER
SPELTERS
SPELTS
SPELTZ
SPELTZES
SPELUNK
SPELUNKED
SPELUNKER
SPELUNKS
SPENCE
SPENCER
SPENCERS
SPENCES
SPEND
SPENDABLE
SPENDALL
SPENDALLS
SPENDER
SPENDERS
SPENDIER
SPENDIEST
SPENDING
SPENDINGS
SPENDS
SPENDY
SPENSE
SPENSES
SPENT
SPEOS
SPEOSES
SPERLING
SPERLINGS
SPERM
SPERMARIA
SPERMARY
SPERMATIA
SPERMATIC
SPERMATID
SPERMIC
SPERMINE
SPERMINES
SPERMOUS
SPERMS
SPERRE
SPERRED
SPERRES
SPERRING
SPERSE
SPERSED
SPERSES
SPERSING
SPERST
SPERTHE
SPERTHES
SPET
SPETCH
SPETCHED
SPETCHES
SPETCHING
SPETS
SPETSNAZ
SPETTING
SPETZNAZ
SPEUG
SPEUGS
SPEW
SPEWED
SPEWER
SPEWERS
SPEWIER
SPEWIEST
SPEWINESS
SPEWING
SPEWS
SPEWY
SPHACELUS
SPHAER
SPHAERE
SPHAERES
SPHAERITE
SPHAERS
SPHAGNOUS
SPHAGNUM
SPHAGNUMS
SPHAIREE
SPHAIREES
SPHEAR
SPHEARE
SPHEARES
SPHEARS
SPHENDONE
SPHENE
SPHENES
SPHENIC
SPHENODON
SPHENOID
SPHENOIDS
SPHERAL
SPHERE
SPHERED
SPHERES
SPHERIC
SPHERICAL
SPHERICS
SPHERIER
SPHERIEST
SPHERING
SPHEROID
SPHEROIDS
SPHERULAR
SPHERULE
SPHERULES
SPHERY

S

SPHINCTER
SPHINGES
SPHINGID
SPHINGIDS
SPHINX
SPHINXES
SPHYGMIC
SPHYGMOID
SPHYGMUS
SPHYNX
SPHYNXES
SPIAL
SPIALS
SPIC
SPICA
SPICAE
SPICAS
SPICATE
SPICATED
SPICCATO
SPICCATOS
SPICE
SPICEBUSH
SPICED
SPICELESS
SPICER
SPICERIES
SPICERS
SPICERY
SPICES
SPICEY
SPICIER
SPICIEST
SPICILEGE
SPICILY
SPICINESS
SPICING
SPICK
SPICKER
SPICKEST
SPICKNEL
SPICKNELS
SPICKS
SPICS
SPICULA
SPICULAE
SPICULAR
SPICULATE
SPICULE
SPICULES
SPICULUM
SPICY
SPIDE
SPIDER
SPIDERED
SPIDERIER
SPIDERING
SPIDERISH
SPIDERMAN
SPIDERMEN
SPIDERS
SPIDERWEB
SPIDERY
SPIDES
SPIE
SPIED
SPIEGEL
SPIEGELS
SPIEL
SPIELED
SPIELER
SPIELERS
SPIELING
SPIELS
SPIER
SPIERED
SPIERING
SPIERS
SPIES
SPIF
SPIFF
SPIFFED
SPIFFIED
SPIFFIER
SPIFFIES
SPIFFIEST
SPIFFILY
SPIFFING
SPIFFS
SPIFFY
SPIFFYING
SPIFS
SPIGHT
SPIGHTED
SPIGHTING
SPIGHTS
SPIGNEL
SPIGNELS
SPIGOT
SPIGOTS
SPIK
SPIKE
SPIKED
SPIKEFISH
SPIKELET
SPIKELETS
SPIKELIKE
SPIKENARD
SPIKER
SPIKERIES
SPIKERS
SPIKERY
SPIKES
SPIKEY
SPIKIER
SPIKIEST
SPIKILY
SPIKINESS
SPIKING
SPIKS
SPIKY
SPILE
SPILED
SPILES
SPILIKIN
SPILIKINS
SPILING
SPILINGS
SPILITE
SPILITES
SPILITIC
SPILL
SPILLABLE
SPILLAGE
SPILLAGES
SPILLED
SPILLER
SPILLERS
SPILLIKIN
SPILLING
SPILLINGS
SPILLOVER
SPILLS
SPILLWAY
SPILLWAYS
SPILOSITE
SPILT
SPILTH
SPILTHS
SPIM
SPIMMER
SPIMMERS
SPIMMING
SPIMMINGS
SPIMS
SPIN
SPINA
SPINACENE
SPINACH
SPINACHES
SPINACHY
SPINAE
SPINAGE
SPINAGES
SPINAL
SPINALLY
SPINALS
SPINAR
SPINARAMA
SPINARS
SPINAS
SPINATE
SPINDLE
SPINDLED
SPINDLER
SPINDLERS
SPINDLES
SPINDLIER
SPINDLING
SPINDLY
SPINDRIFT
SPINE
SPINED
SPINEL
SPINELESS
SPINELIKE
SPINELLE
SPINELLES
SPINELS
SPINES
SPINET
SPINETS
SPINETTE
SPINETTES
SPINIER
SPINIEST
SPINIFEX
SPINIFORM
SPININESS
SPINK
SPINKED
SPINKING
SPINKS
SPINLESS
SPINNAKER
SPINNER
SPINNERET
SPINNERS
SPINNERY
SPINNET
SPINNETS
SPINNEY
SPINNEYS
SPINNIER
SPINNIES
SPINNIEST
SPINNING
SPINNINGS
SPINNY
SPINODE
SPINODES
SPINOFF
SPINOFFS
SPINONE
SPINONI
SPINOR
SPINORS
SPINOSE
SPINOSELY
SPINOSITY
SPINOUS
SPINOUT
SPINOUTS
SPINS
SPINSTER
SPINSTERS
SPINTEXT
SPINTEXTS
SPINTO
SPINTOS

S

SPINULA
SPINULAE
SPINULATE
SPINULE
SPINULES
SPINULOSE
SPINULOUS
SPINY
SPIRACLE
SPIRACLES
SPIRACULA
SPIRAEA
SPIRAEAS
SPIRAL
SPIRALED
SPIRALING
SPIRALISM
SPIRALIST
SPIRALITY
SPIRALLED
SPIRALLY
SPIRALS
SPIRANT
SPIRANTS
SPIRASTER
SPIRATED
SPIRATION
SPIRE
SPIREA
SPIREAS
SPIRED
SPIRELESS
SPIRELET
SPIRELETS
SPIREM
SPIREME
SPIREMES
SPIREMS
SPIRES
SPIREWISE
SPIRIC
SPIRICS
SPIRIER
SPIRIEST
SPIRILLA
SPIRILLAR
SPIRILLUM
SPIRING
SPIRIT
SPIRITED
SPIRITFUL
SPIRITING
SPIRITISM
SPIRITIST
SPIRITOSO
SPIRITOUS
SPIRITS
SPIRITUAL
SPIRITUEL
SPIRITUS
SPIRITY
SPIRLING
SPIRLINGS
SPIROGRAM
SPIROGYRA
SPIROID
SPIRT
SPIRTED
SPIRTING
SPIRTLE
SPIRTLES
SPIRTS
SPIRULA
SPIRULAE
SPIRULAS
SPIRULINA
SPIRY
SPIT
SPITAL
SPITALS
SPITBALL
SPITBALLS
SPITCHER
SPITCHERS
SPITE
SPITED
SPITEFUL
SPITES
SPITFIRE
SPITFIRES
SPITING
SPITS
SPITTED
SPITTEN
SPITTER
SPITTERS
SPITTIER
SPITTIEST
SPITTING
SPITTINGS
SPITTLE
SPITTLES
SPITTLIER
SPITTLY
SPITTOON
SPITTOONS
SPITTY
SPITZ
SPITZES
SPIV
SPIVS
SPIVVERY
SPIVVIER
SPIVVIEST
SPIVVISH
SPIVVY
SPLAKE
SPLAKES
SPLASH
SPLASHED
SPLASHER
SPLASHERS
SPLASHES
SPLASHIER
SPLASHILY
SPLASHING
SPLASHY
SPLAT
SPLATCH
SPLATCHED
SPLATCHES
SPLATS
SPLATTED
SPLATTER
SPLATTERS
SPLATTING
SPLAY
SPLAYED
SPLAYFEET
SPLAYFOOT
SPLAYING
SPLAYS
SPLEEN
SPLEENFUL
SPLEENIER
SPLEENISH
SPLEENS
SPLEENY
SPLENDENT
SPLENDID
SPLENDOR
SPLENDORS
SPLENDOUR
SPLENETIC
SPLENIA
SPLENIAL
SPLENIC
SPLENII
SPLENITIS
SPLENIUM
SPLENIUMS
SPLENIUS
SPLENT
SPLENTS
SPLEUCHAN
SPLICE
SPLICED
SPLICER
SPLICERS
SPLICES
SPLICING
SPLICINGS
SPLIFF
SPLIFFS
SPLINE
SPLINED
SPLINES
SPLINING
SPLINT
SPLINTED
SPLINTER
SPLINTERS
SPLINTERY
SPLINTING
SPLINTS
SPLISH
SPLISHED
SPLISHES
SPLISHING
SPLIT
SPLITS
SPLITTED
SPLITTER
SPLITTERS
SPLITTING
SPLITTISM
SPLITTIST
SPLODGE
SPLODGED
SPLODGES
SPLODGIER
SPLODGILY
SPLODGING
SPLODGY
SPLOG
SPLOGS
SPLOOSH
SPLOOSHED
SPLOOSHES
SPLORE
SPLORES
SPLOSH
SPLOSHED
SPLOSHES
SPLOSHING
SPLOTCH
SPLOTCHED
SPLOTCHES
SPLOTCHY
SPLURGE
SPLURGED
SPLURGER
SPLURGERS
SPLURGES
SPLURGIER
SPLURGING
SPLURGY
SPLURT
SPLURTED
SPLURTING
SPLURTS
SPLUTTER
SPLUTTERS
SPLUTTERY
SPOD
SPODDIER
SPODDIEST
SPODDY
SPODE
SPODES

S

SPODIUM
SPODIUMS
SPODOGRAM
SPODOSOL
SPODOSOLS
SPODS
SPODUMENE
SPOFFISH
SPOFFY
SPOIL
SPOILABLE
SPOILAGE
SPOILAGES
SPOILED
SPOILER
SPOILERS
SPOILFIVE
SPOILFUL
SPOILING
SPOILS
SPOILSMAN
SPOILSMEN
SPOILT
SPOKE
SPOKED
SPOKEN
SPOKES
SPOKESMAN
SPOKESMEN
SPOKEWISE
SPOKING
SPOLIATE
SPOLIATED
SPOLIATES
SPOLIATOR
SPONDAIC
SPONDAICS
SPONDEE
SPONDEES
SPONDULIX
SPONDYL
SPONDYLS
SPONGE
SPONGEBAG
SPONGED
SPONGEING
SPONGEOUS
SPONGER
SPONGERS
SPONGES
SPONGIER
SPONGIEST
SPONGILY
SPONGIN
SPONGING
SPONGINS
SPONGIOSE
SPONGIOUS
SPONGOID
SPONGY
SPONSAL
SPONSALIA
SPONSIBLE
SPONSING
SPONSINGS
SPONSION
SPONSIONS
SPONSON
SPONSONS
SPONSOR
SPONSORED
SPONSORS
SPONTOON
SPONTOONS
SPOOF
SPOOFED
SPOOFER
SPOOFERS
SPOOFERY
SPOOFIER
SPOOFIEST
SPOOFING
SPOOFINGS
SPOOFS
SPOOFY
SPOOK
SPOOKED
SPOOKERY
SPOOKIER
SPOOKIEST
SPOOKILY
SPOOKING
SPOOKISH
SPOOKS
SPOOKY
SPOOL
SPOOLED
SPOOLER
SPOOLERS
SPOOLING
SPOOLINGS
SPOOLS
SPOOM
SPOOMED
SPOOMING
SPOOMS
SPOON
SPOONBAIT
SPOONBILL
SPOONED
SPOONER
SPOONERS
SPOONEY
SPOONEYS
SPOONFED
SPOONFUL
SPOONFULS
SPOONHOOK
SPOONIER
SPOONIES
SPOONIEST
SPOONILY
SPOONING
SPOONLIKE
SPOONS
SPOONSFUL
SPOONWAYS
SPOONWISE
SPOONWORM
SPOONY
SPOOR
SPOORED
SPOORER
SPOORERS
SPOORING
SPOORS
SPOOT
SPOOTS
SPORADIC
SPORAL
SPORANGIA
SPORE
SPORED
SPORELIKE
SPORES
SPORICIDE
SPORIDESM
SPORIDIA
SPORIDIAL
SPORIDIUM
SPORING
SPORK
SPORKS
SPOROCARP
SPOROCYST
SPOROCYTE
SPOROGENY
SPOROGONY
SPOROID
SPOROPHYL
SPOROZOA
SPOROZOAL
SPOROZOAN
SPOROZOIC
SPOROZOON
SPORRAN
SPORRANS
SPORT
SPORTABLE
SPORTANCE
SPORTBIKE
SPORTCOAT
SPORTED
SPORTER
SPORTERS
SPORTFUL
SPORTIER
SPORTIES
SPORTIEST
SPORTIF
SPORTIFS
SPORTILY
SPORTING
SPORTIVE
SPORTLESS
SPORTS
SPORTSMAN
SPORTSMEN
SPORTY
SPORULAR
SPORULATE
SPORULE
SPORULES
SPOSH
SPOSHES
SPOSHIER
SPOSHIEST
SPOSHY
SPOT
SPOTLESS
SPOTLIGHT
SPOTLIT
SPOTS
SPOTTABLE
SPOTTED
SPOTTER
SPOTTERS
SPOTTIE
SPOTTIER
SPOTTIES
SPOTTIEST
SPOTTILY
SPOTTING
SPOTTINGS
SPOTTY
SPOUSAGE
SPOUSAGES
SPOUSAL
SPOUSALLY
SPOUSALS
SPOUSE
SPOUSED
SPOUSES
SPOUSING
SPOUT
SPOUTED
SPOUTER
SPOUTERS
SPOUTIER
SPOUTIEST
SPOUTING
SPOUTINGS
SPOUTLESS
SPOUTS
SPOUTY
SPRACK
SPRACKLE
SPRACKLED
SPRACKLES
SPRAD

SPRADDLE
SPRADDLED
SPRADDLES
SPRAG
SPRAGGED
SPRAGGING
SPRAGS
SPRAID
SPRAIN
SPRAINED
SPRAINING
SPRAINS
SPRAINT
SPRAINTS
SPRANG
SPRANGLE
SPRANGLED
SPRANGLES
SPRANGS
SPRAT
SPRATS
SPRATTLE
SPRATTLED
SPRATTLES
SPRAUCHLE
SPRAUNCY
SPRAWL
SPRAWLED
SPRAWLER
SPRAWLERS
SPRAWLIER
SPRAWLING
SPRAWLS
SPRAWLY
SPRAY
SPRAYED
SPRAYER
SPRAYERS
SPRAYEY
SPRAYIER
SPRAYIEST
SPRAYING
SPRAYINGS
SPRAYS
SPREAD
SPREADER
SPREADERS
SPREADING
SPREADS
SPREAGH
SPREAGHS
SPREATHE
SPREATHED
SPREATHES
SPREAZE
SPREAZED
SPREAZES
SPREAZING
SPRECHERY
SPRECKLED
SPRED
SPREDD
SPREDDE
SPREDDEN
SPREDDES
SPREDDING
SPREDDS
SPREDS
SPREE
SPREED
SPREEING
SPREES
SPREETHE
SPREETHED
SPREETHES
SPREEZE
SPREEZED
SPREEZES
SPREEZING
SPREKELIA
SPRENT
SPRENTED
SPRENTING
SPRENTS
SPREW
SPREWS
SPRIER
SPRIEST
SPRIG
SPRIGGED
SPRIGGER
SPRIGGERS
SPRIGGIER
SPRIGGING
SPRIGGY
SPRIGHT
SPRIGHTED
SPRIGHTLY
SPRIGHTS
SPRIGS
SPRIGTAIL
SPRING
SPRINGAL
SPRINGALD
SPRINGALS
SPRINGBOK
SPRINGE
SPRINGED
SPRINGER
SPRINGERS
SPRINGES
SPRINGIER
SPRINGILY
SPRINGING
SPRINGLE
SPRINGLES
SPRINGLET
SPRINGS
SPRINGY
SPRINKLE
SPRINKLED
SPRINKLER
SPRINKLES
SPRINT
SPRINTED
SPRINTER
SPRINTERS
SPRINTING
SPRINTS
SPRIT
SPRITE
SPRITEFUL
SPRITELY
SPRITES
SPRITS
SPRITSAIL
SPRITZ
SPRITZED
SPRITZER
SPRITZERS
SPRITZES
SPRITZIER
SPRITZIG
SPRITZIGS
SPRITZING
SPRITZY
SPROCKET
SPROCKETS
SPROD
SPRODS
SPROG
SPROGLET
SPROGLETS
SPROGS
SPRONG
SPROUT
SPROUTED
SPROUTING
SPROUTS
SPRUCE
SPRUCED
SPRUCELY
SPRUCER
SPRUCES
SPRUCEST
SPRUCIER
SPRUCIEST
SPRUCING
SPRUCY
SPRUE
SPRUES
SPRUG
SPRUGS
SPRUIK
SPRUIKED
SPRUIKER
SPRUIKERS
SPRUIKING
SPRUIKS
SPRUIT
SPRUITS
SPRUNG
SPRUSH
SPRUSHED
SPRUSHES
SPRUSHING
SPRY
SPRYER
SPRYEST
SPRYLY
SPRYNESS
SPUD
SPUDDED
SPUDDER
SPUDDERS
SPUDDIER
SPUDDIEST
SPUDDING
SPUDDINGS
SPUDDLE
SPUDDLES
SPUDDY
SPUDGEL
SPUDGELS
SPUDS
SPUE
SPUED
SPUEING
SPUER
SPUERS
SPUES
SPUG
SPUGGIES
SPUGGY
SPUGS
SPUILZIE
SPUILZIED
SPUILZIES
SPUING
SPULE
SPULES
SPULYE
SPULYED
SPULYEING
SPULYES
SPULYIE
SPULYIED
SPULYIES
SPULZIE
SPULZIED
SPULZIES
SPUMANTE
SPUMANTES
SPUME
SPUMED
SPUMES
SPUMIER
SPUMIEST
SPUMING
SPUMONE

SPUMONES
SPUMONI
SPUMONIS
SPUMOUS
SPUMY
SPUN
SPUNGE
SPUNGES
SPUNK
SPUNKED
SPUNKIE
SPUNKIER
SPUNKIES
SPUNKIEST
SPUNKILY
SPUNKING
SPUNKS
SPUNKY
SPUNYARN
SPUNYARNS
SPUR
SPURDOG
SPURDOGS
SPURGALL
SPURGALLS
SPURGE
SPURGES
SPURIAE
SPURIOUS
SPURLESS
SPURLIKE
SPURLING
SPURLINGS
SPURN
SPURNE
SPURNED
SPURNER
SPURNERS
SPURNES
SPURNING
SPURNINGS
SPURNS
SPURRED
SPURRER
SPURRERS
SPURREY
SPURREYS
SPURRIER
SPURRIERS
SPURRIES
SPURRIEST
SPURRING
SPURRINGS
SPURRY
SPURS
SPURT
SPURTED
SPURTER
SPURTERS
SPURTING
SPURTLE
SPURTLES
SPURTS
SPURWAY
SPURWAYS
SPUTA
SPUTNIK
SPUTNIKS
SPUTTER
SPUTTERED
SPUTTERER
SPUTTERS
SPUTTERY
SPUTUM
SPUTUMS
SPY
SPYAL
SPYALS
SPYCAM
SPYCAMS
SPYGLASS
SPYHOLE
SPYHOLES
SPYING
SPYINGS
SPYMASTER
SPYPLANE
SPYPLANES
SPYRE
SPYRES
SPYWARE
SPYWARES
SQUAB
SQUABASH
SQUABBED
SQUABBER
SQUABBEST
SQUABBIER
SQUABBING
SQUABBISH
SQUABBLE
SQUABBLED
SQUABBLER
SQUABBLES
SQUABBY
SQUABS
SQUACCO
SQUACCOS
SQUAD
SQUADDED
SQUADDIE
SQUADDIES
SQUADDING
SQUADDY
SQUADOOSH
SQUADRON
SQUADRONE
SQUADRONS
SQUADS
SQUAIL
SQUAILED
SQUAILER
SQUAILERS
SQUAILING
SQUAILS
SQUALENE
SQUALENES
SQUALID
SQUALIDER
SQUALIDLY
SQUALL
SQUALLED
SQUALLER
SQUALLERS
SQUALLIER
SQUALLING
SQUALLISH
SQUALLS
SQUALLY
SQUALOID
SQUALOR
SQUALORS
SQUAMA
SQUAMAE
SQUAMATE
SQUAMATES
SQUAME
SQUAMELLA
SQUAMES
SQUAMOSAL
SQUAMOSE
SQUAMOUS
SQUAMULA
SQUAMULAS
SQUAMULE
SQUAMULES
SQUANDER
SQUANDERS
SQUARE
SQUARED
SQUARELY
SQUARER
SQUARERS
SQUARES
SQUAREST
SQUARIAL
SQUARIALS
SQUARING
SQUARINGS
SQUARISH
SQUARK
SQUARKS
SQUARROSE
SQUARSON
SQUARSONS
SQUASH
SQUASHED
SQUASHER
SQUASHERS
SQUASHES
SQUASHIER
SQUASHILY
SQUASHING
SQUASHY
SQUAT
SQUATLY
SQUATNESS
SQUATS
SQUATTED
SQUATTER
SQUATTERS
SQUATTEST
SQUATTIER
SQUATTILY
SQUATTING
SQUATTLE
SQUATTLED
SQUATTLES
SQUATTY
SQUAW
SQUAWBUSH
SQUAWFISH
SQUAWK
SQUAWKED
SQUAWKER
SQUAWKERS
SQUAWKIER
SQUAWKING
SQUAWKS
SQUAWKY
SQUAWMAN
SQUAWMEN
SQUAWROOT
SQUAWS
SQUEAK
SQUEAKED
SQUEAKER
SQUEAKERS
SQUEAKERY
SQUEAKIER
SQUEAKILY
SQUEAKING
SQUEAKS
SQUEAKY
SQUEAL
SQUEALED
SQUEALER
SQUEALERS
SQUEALING
SQUEALS
SQUEAMISH
SQUEEGEE
SQUEEGEED
SQUEEGEES
SQUEEZE
SQUEEZED
SQUEEZER
SQUEEZERS
SQUEEZES
SQUEEZIER

S

SQUEEZING
SQUEEZY
SQUEG
SQUEGGED
SQUEGGER
SQUEGGERS
SQUEGGING
SQUEGS
SQUELCH
SQUELCHED
SQUELCHER
SQUELCHES
SQUELCHY
SQUIB
SQUIBBED
SQUIBBER
SQUIBBERS
SQUIBBING
SQUIBS
SQUID
SQUIDDED
SQUIDDING
SQUIDGE
SQUIDGED
SQUIDGES
SQUIDGIER
SQUIDGING
SQUIDGY
SQUIDLIKE
SQUIDS
SQUIER
SQUIERS
SQUIFF
SQUIFFED
SQUIFFER
SQUIFFERS
SQUIFFIER
SQUIFFY
SQUIGGLE
SQUIGGLED
SQUIGGLER
SQUIGGLES
SQUIGGLY
SQUILGEE
SQUILGEED
SQUILGEES
SQUILL
SQUILLA
SQUILLAE
SQUILLAS
SQUILLION
SQUILLS
SQUINANCY
SQUINCH
SQUINCHED
SQUINCHES
SQUINIED
SQUINIES
SQUINNIED
SQUINNIER
SQUINNIES
SQUINNY
SQUINT
SQUINTED
SQUINTER
SQUINTERS
SQUINTEST
SQUINTIER
SQUINTING
SQUINTS
SQUINTY
SQUINY
SQUINYING
SQUIRAGE
SQUIRAGES
SQUIRALTY
SQUIRARCH
SQUIRE
SQUIREAGE
SQUIRED
SQUIREDOM
SQUIREEN
SQUIREENS
SQUIRELY
SQUIRES
SQUIRESS
SQUIRING
SQUIRISH
SQUIRL
SQUIRLS
SQUIRM
SQUIRMED
SQUIRMER
SQUIRMERS
SQUIRMIER
SQUIRMING
SQUIRMS
SQUIRMY
SQUIRR
SQUIRRED
SQUIRREL
SQUIRRELS
SQUIRRELY
SQUIRRING
SQUIRRS
SQUIRT
SQUIRTED
SQUIRTER
SQUIRTERS
SQUIRTING
SQUIRTS
SQUISH
SQUISHED
SQUISHES
SQUISHIER
SQUISHING
SQUISHY
SQUIT
SQUITCH
SQUITCHES
SQUITS
SQUITTERS
SQUIZ
SQUIZZES
SQUOOSH
SQUOOSHED
SQUOOSHES
SQUOOSHY
SQUUSH
SQUUSHED
SQUUSHES
SQUUSHING
SRADDHA
SRADDHAS
SRADHA
SRADHAS
SRI
SRIRACHA
SRIRACHAS
SRIS
ST
STAB
STABBED
STABBER
STABBERS
STABBING
STABBINGS
STABILATE
STABILE
STABILES
STABILISE
STABILITY
STABILIZE
STABLE
STABLEBOY
STABLED
STABLEMAN
STABLEMEN
STABLER
STABLERS
STABLES
STABLEST
STABLING
STABLINGS
STABLISH
STABLY
STABS
STACATION
STACCATI
STACCATO
STACCATOS
STACHYS
STACHYSES
STACK
STACKABLE
STACKED
STACKER
STACKERS
STACKET
STACKETS
STACKING
STACKINGS
STACKLESS
STACKROOM
STACKS
STACKUP
STACKUPS
STACKYARD
STACTE
STACTES
STADDA
STADDAS
STADDLE
STADDLES
STADE
STADES
STADIA
STADIAL
STADIALS
STADIAS
STADIUM
STADIUMS
STAFF
STAFFAGE
STAFFAGES
STAFFED
STAFFER
STAFFERS
STAFFING
STAFFINGS
STAFFMAN
STAFFMEN
STAFFROOM
STAFFS
STAG
STAGE
STAGEABLE
STAGED
STAGEFUL
STAGEFULS
STAGEHAND
STAGEHEAD
STAGELIKE
STAGER
STAGERIES
STAGERS
STAGERY
STAGES
STAGETTE
STAGETTES
STAGEY
STAGGARD
STAGGARDS
STAGGART
STAGGARTS
STAGGED
STAGGER
STAGGERED
STAGGERER
STAGGERS

S

STAGGERY
STAGGIE
STAGGIER
STAGGIES
STAGGIEST
STAGGING
STAGGY
STAGHORN
STAGHORNS
STAGHOUND
STAGIER
STAGIEST
STAGILY
STAGINESS
STAGING
STAGINGS
STAGNANCE
STAGNANCY
STAGNANT
STAGNATE
STAGNATED
STAGNATES
STAGS
STAGY
STAID
STAIDER
STAIDEST
STAIDLY
STAIDNESS
STAIG
STAIGS
STAIN
STAINABLE
STAINED
STAINER
STAINERS
STAINING
STAININGS
STAINLESS
STAINS
STAIR
STAIRCASE
STAIRED
STAIRFOOT
STAIRHEAD
STAIRLESS
STAIRLIFT
STAIRLIKE
STAIRS
STAIRSTEP
STAIRWAY
STAIRWAYS
STAIRWELL
STAIRWISE
STAIRWORK
STAITH
STAITHE
STAITHES
STAITHS
STAKE
STAKED
STAKEOUT
STAKEOUTS
STAKER
STAKERS
STAKES
STAKING
STALACTIC
STALAG
STALAGMA
STALAGMAS
STALAGS
STALE
STALED
STALELY
STALEMATE
STALENESS
STALER
STALES
STALEST
STALING
STALK
STALKED
STALKER
STALKERS
STALKIER
STALKIEST
STALKILY
STALKING
STALKINGS
STALKLESS
STALKLIKE
STALKO
STALKOES
STALKOS
STALKS
STALKY
STALL
STALLAGE
STALLAGES
STALLED
STALLING
STALLINGS
STALLION
STALLIONS
STALLMAN
STALLMEN
STALLS
STALWART
STALWARTS
STALWORTH
STAMEN
STAMENED
STAMENS
STAMINA
STAMINAL
STAMINAS
STAMINATE
STAMINEAL
STAMINODE
STAMINODY
STAMINOID
STAMMEL
STAMMELS
STAMMER
STAMMERED
STAMMERER
STAMMERS
STAMNOI
STAMNOS
STAMP
STAMPED
STAMPEDE
STAMPEDED
STAMPEDER
STAMPEDES
STAMPEDO
STAMPEDOS
STAMPER
STAMPERS
STAMPING
STAMPINGS
STAMPLESS
STAMPS
STANCE
STANCES
STANCH
STANCHED
STANCHEL
STANCHELS
STANCHER
STANCHERS
STANCHES
STANCHEST
STANCHING
STANCHION
STANCHLY
STANCK
STAND
STANDARD
STANDARDS
STANDAWAY
STANDBY
STANDBYS
STANDDOWN
STANDEE
STANDEES
STANDEN
STANDER
STANDERS
STANDFAST
STANDGALE
STANDING
STANDINGS
STANDISH
STANDOFF
STANDOFFS
STANDOUT
STANDOUTS
STANDOVER
STANDPAT
STANDPIPE
STANDS
STANDUP
STANDUPS
STANE
STANED
STANES
STANG
STANGED
STANGING
STANGS
STANHOPE
STANHOPES
STANIEL
STANIELS
STANINE
STANINES
STANING
STANK
STANKED
STANKING
STANKS
STANNARY
STANNATE
STANNATES
STANNATOR
STANNEL
STANNELS
STANNIC
STANNITE
STANNITES
STANNOUS
STANNUM
STANNUMS
STANOL
STANOLS
STANYEL
STANYELS
STANZA
STANZAED
STANZAIC
STANZAS
STANZE
STANZES
STANZO
STANZOES
STANZOS
STAP
STAPEDES
STAPEDIAL
STAPEDII
STAPEDIUS
STAPELIA
STAPELIAS
STAPES
STAPH
STAPHS
STAPLE
STAPLED

STAPLER
STAPLERS
STAPLES
STAPLING
STAPLINGS
STAPPED
STAPPING
STAPPLE
STAPPLES
STAPS
STAR
STARAGEN
STARAGENS
STARBOARD
STARBURST
STARCH
STARCHED
STARCHER
STARCHERS
STARCHES
STARCHIER
STARCHILY
STARCHING
STARCHY
STARDOM
STARDOMS
STARDRIFT
STARDUST
STARDUSTS
STARE
STARED
STARER
STARERS
STARES
STARETS
STARETSES
STARETZ
STARETZES
STARFISH
STARFRUIT
STARGAZE
STARGAZED
STARGAZER
STARGAZES
STARGAZEY
STARING
STARINGLY
STARINGS
STARK
STARKED
STARKEN
STARKENED
STARKENS
STARKER
STARKERS
STARKEST
STARKING
STARKLY
STARKNESS
STARKS
STARLESS
STARLET
STARLETS
STARLIGHT
STARLIKE
STARLING
STARLINGS
STARLIT
STARN
STARNED
STARNIE
STARNIES
STARNING
STARNOSE
STARNOSES
STARNS
STAROSTA
STAROSTAS
STAROSTY
STARR
STARRED
STARRIER
STARRIEST
STARRILY
STARRING
STARRINGS
STARRS
STARRY
STARS
STARSHINE
STARSHIP
STARSHIPS
STARSPOT
STARSPOTS
STARSTONE
START
STARTED
STARTER
STARTERS
STARTFUL
STARTING
STARTINGS
STARTISH
STARTLE
STARTLED
STARTLER
STARTLERS
STARTLES
STARTLIER
STARTLING
STARTLISH
STARTLY
STARTS
STARTSY
STARTUP
STARTUPS
STARVE
STARVED
STARVER
STARVERS
STARVES
STARVING
STARVINGS
STARWORT
STARWORTS
STASES
STASH
STASHED
STASHES
STASHIE
STASHIES
STASHING
STASIDION
STASIMA
STASIMON
STASIS
STAT
STATABLE
STATAL
STATANT
STATE
STATEABLE
STATED
STATEDLY
STATEHOOD
STATELESS
STATELET
STATELETS
STATELIER
STATELILY
STATELY
STATEMENT
STATER
STATEROOM
STATERS
STATES
STATESIDE
STATESMAN
STATESMEN
STATEWIDE
STATIC
STATICAL
STATICE
STATICES
STATICKY
STATICS
STATIM
STATIN
STATING
STATINS
STATION
STATIONAL
STATIONED
STATIONER
STATIONS
STATISM
STATISMS
STATIST
STATISTIC
STATISTS
STATIVE
STATIVES
STATOCYST
STATOLITH
STATOR
STATORS
STATS
STATTO
STATTOS
STATUA
STATUARY
STATUAS
STATUE
STATUED
STATUES
STATUETTE
STATURE
STATURED
STATURES
STATUS
STATUSES
STATUSIER
STATUSY
STATUTE
STATUTES
STATUTORY
STAUMREL
STAUMRELS
STAUN
STAUNCH
STAUNCHED
STAUNCHER
STAUNCHES
STAUNCHLY
STAUNING
STAUNS
STAVE
STAVED
STAVES
STAVING
STAVUDINE
STAW
STAWED
STAWING
STAWS
STAY
STAYAWAY
STAYAWAYS
STAYED
STAYER
STAYERS
STAYING
STAYLESS
STAYMAKER
STAYNE
STAYNED
STAYNES
STAYNING
STAYRE
STAYRES

STAYS
STAYSAIL
STAYSAILS
STEAD
STEADED
STEADFAST
STEADIED
STEADIER
STEADIERS
STEADIES
STEADIEST
STEADILY
STEADING
STEADINGS
STEADS
STEADY
STEADYING
STEAK
STEAKETTE
STEAKS
STEAL
STEALABLE
STEALAGE
STEALAGES
STEALE
STEALED
STEALER
STEALERS
STEALES
STEALING
STEALINGS
STEALS
STEALT
STEALTH
STEALTHED
STEALTHS
STEALTHY
STEAM
STEAMBOAT
STEAMED
STEAMER
STEAMERED
STEAMERS
STEAMIE
STEAMIER
STEAMIES
STEAMIEST
STEAMILY
STEAMING
STEAMINGS
STEAMPUNK
STEAMROLL
STEAMS
STEAMSHIP
STEAMY
STEAN
STEANE
STEANED
STEANES
STEANING
STEANINGS
STEANS
STEAPSIN
STEAPSINS
STEAR
STEARAGE
STEARAGES
STEARATE
STEARATES
STEARD
STEARE
STEARED
STEARES
STEARIC
STEARIN
STEARINE
STEARINES
STEARING
STEARINS
STEARS
STEARSMAN
STEARSMEN
STEATITE
STEATITES
STEATITIC
STEATOMA
STEATOMAS
STEATOSES
STEATOSIS
STED
STEDD
STEDDE
STEDDED
STEDDES
STEDDIED
STEDDIES
STEDDING
STEDDS
STEDDY
STEDDYING
STEDE
STEDED
STEDES
STEDFAST
STEDING
STEDS
STEED
STEEDED
STEEDIED
STEEDIES
STEEDING
STEEDLIKE
STEEDS
STEEDY
STEEDYING
STEEK
STEEKED
STEEKING
STEEKIT
STEEKS
STEEL
STEELBOW
STEELBOWS
STEELD
STEELED
STEELHEAD
STEELIE
STEELIER
STEELIES
STEELIEST
STEELING
STEELINGS
STEELMAN
STEELMEN
STEELS
STEELWARE
STEELWORK
STEELY
STEELYARD
STEEM
STEEMED
STEEMING
STEEMS
STEEN
STEENBOK
STEENBOKS
STEENBRAS
STEENBUCK
STEENED
STEENING
STEENINGS
STEENKIRK
STEENS
STEEP
STEEPED
STEEPEN
STEEPENED
STEEPENS
STEEPER
STEEPERS
STEEPEST
STEEPEUP
STEEPIER
STEEPIEST
STEEPING
STEEPISH
STEEPLE
STEEPLED
STEEPLES
STEEPLING
STEEPLY
STEEPNESS
STEEPS
STEEPUP
STEEPY
STEER
STEERABLE
STEERAGE
STEERAGES
STEERED
STEERER
STEERERS
STEERIER
STEERIES
STEERIEST
STEERING
STEERINGS
STEERLING
STEERS
STEERSMAN
STEERSMEN
STEERY
STEEVE
STEEVED
STEEVELY
STEEVER
STEEVES
STEEVEST
STEEVING
STEEVINGS
STEGNOSES
STEGNOSIS
STEGNOTIC
STEGODON
STEGODONS
STEGODONT
STEGOMYIA
STEGOSAUR
STEIL
STEILS
STEIN
STEINBOCK
STEINBOK
STEINBOKS
STEINED
STEINING
STEININGS
STEINKIRK
STEINS
STELA
STELAE
STELAI
STELAR
STELE
STELENE
STELES
STELIC
STELL
STELLA
STELLAR
STELLAS
STELLATE
STELLATED
STELLED
STELLERID
STELLIFY
STELLING
STELLIO
STELLION
STELLIONS

STELLITE
STELLITES
STELLS
STELLULAR
STEM
STEMBOK
STEMBOKS
STEMBUCK
STEMBUCKS
STEME
STEMED
STEMES
STEMHEAD
STEMHEADS
STEMING
STEMLESS
STEMLET
STEMLETS
STEMLIKE
STEMMA
STEMMAS
STEMMATA
STEMMATIC
STEMME
STEMMED
STEMMER
STEMMERS
STEMMERY
STEMMES
STEMMIER
STEMMIEST
STEMMING
STEMMINGS
STEMMY
STEMPEL
STEMPELS
STEMPLE
STEMPLES
STEMS
STEMSON
STEMSONS
STEMWARE
STEMWARES
STEN
STENCH
STENCHED
STENCHES
STENCHFUL
STENCHIER
STENCHING
STENCHY
STENCIL
STENCILED
STENCILER
STENCILS
STEND
STENDED
STENDING
STENDS
STENGAH
STENGAHS
STENLOCK
STENLOCKS
STENNED
STENNING
STENO
STENOBATH
STENOKIES
STENOKOUS
STENOKY
STENOPAIC
STENOS
STENOSED
STENOSES
STENOSING
STENOSIS
STENOTIC
STENOTYPE
STENOTYPY
STENS
STENT
STENTED
STENTING
STENTOR
STENTORS
STENTOUR
STENTOURS
STENTS
STEP
STEPBAIRN
STEPCHILD
STEPDAD
STEPDADS
STEPDAME
STEPDAMES
STEPHANE
STEPHANES
STEPLESS
STEPLIKE
STEPMOM
STEPMOMS
STEPNEY
STEPNEYS
STEPOVER
STEPOVERS
STEPPE
STEPPED
STEPPER
STEPPERS
STEPPES
STEPPING
STEPS
STEPSON
STEPSONS
STEPSTOOL
STEPT
STEPWISE
STERADIAN
STERANE
STERANES
STERCORAL
STERCULIA
STERE
STEREO
STEREOED
STEREOING
STEREOME
STEREOMES
STEREOS
STERES
STERIC
STERICAL
STERIGMA
STERIGMAS
STERILANT
STERILE
STERILELY
STERILISE
STERILITY
STERILIZE
STERLET
STERLETS
STERLING
STERLINGS
STERN
STERNA
STERNAGE
STERNAGES
STERNAL
STERNEBRA
STERNED
STERNER
STERNEST
STERNFAST
STERNING
STERNITE
STERNITES
STERNITIC
STERNLY
STERNMOST
STERNNESS
STERNPORT
STERNPOST
STERNS
STERNSON
STERNSONS
STERNUM
STERNUMS
STERNWARD
STERNWAY
STERNWAYS
STEROID
STEROIDAL
STEROIDS
STEROL
STEROLS
STERTOR
STERTORS
STERVE
STERVED
STERVES
STERVING
STET
STETS
STETSON
STETSONS
STETTED
STETTING
STEVEDORE
STEVEN
STEVENS
STEVIA
STEVIAS
STEW
STEWABLE
STEWARD
STEWARDED
STEWARDRY
STEWARDS
STEWARTRY
STEWBUM
STEWBUMS
STEWED
STEWER
STEWERS
STEWIER
STEWIEST
STEWING
STEWINGS
STEWPAN
STEWPANS
STEWPOND
STEWPONDS
STEWPOT
STEWPOTS
STEWS
STEWY
STEY
STEYER
STEYEST
STEYS
STHENIA
STHENIAS
STHENIC
STIBBLE
STIBBLER
STIBBLERS
STIBBLES
STIBIAL
STIBINE
STIBINES
STIBIUM
STIBIUMS
STIBNITE
STIBNITES
STICCADO
STICCADOS
STICCATO
STICCATOS
STICH

S

STICHARIA
STICHERA
STICHERON
STICHIC
STICHIDIA
STICHOI
STICHOS
STICHS
STICK
STICKABLE
STICKBALL
STICKED
STICKER
STICKERED
STICKERS
STICKFUL
STICKFULS
STICKIE
STICKIED
STICKIER
STICKIES
STICKIEST
STICKILY
STICKING
STICKINGS
STICKIT
STICKJAW
STICKJAWS
STICKLE
STICKLED
STICKLER
STICKLERS
STICKLES
STICKLIKE
STICKLING
STICKMAN
STICKMEN
STICKOUT
STICKOUTS
STICKPIN
STICKPINS
STICKS
STICKSEED
STICKUM
STICKUMS
STICKUP
STICKUPS
STICKWEED
STICKWORK
STICKY
STICKYING
STICTION
STICTIONS
STIDDIE
STIDDIED
STIDDIES
STIE
STIED
STIES
STIEVE
STIEVELY
STIEVER
STIEVEST
STIFF
STIFFED
STIFFEN
STIFFENED
STIFFENER
STIFFENS
STIFFER
STIFFEST
STIFFIE
STIFFIES
STIFFING
STIFFISH
STIFFLY
STIFFNESS
STIFFS
STIFFWARE
STIFFY
STIFLE
STIFLED
STIFLER
STIFLERS
STIFLES
STIFLING
STIFLINGS
STIGMA
STIGMAL
STIGMAS
STIGMATA
STIGMATIC
STIGME
STIGMES
STILB
STILBENE
STILBENES
STILBITE
STILBITES
STILBS
STILE
STILED
STILES
STILET
STILETS
STILETTO
STILETTOS
STILING
STILL
STILLAGE
STILLAGES
STILLBORN
STILLED
STILLER
STILLERS
STILLEST
STILLIER
STILLIEST
STILLING
STILLINGS
STILLION
STILLIONS
STILLMAN
STILLMEN
STILLNESS
STILLROOM
STILLS
STILLSON
STILLSONS
STILLY
STILT
STILTBIRD
STILTED
STILTEDLY
STILTER
STILTERS
STILTIER
STILTIEST
STILTING
STILTINGS
STILTISH
STILTLIKE
STILTS
STILTY
STIM
STIME
STIMED
STIMES
STIMIE
STIMIED
STIMIES
STIMING
STIMS
STIMULANT
STIMULATE
STIMULI
STIMULUS
STIMY
STIMYING
STING
STINGAREE
STINGBULL
STINGE
STINGED
STINGER
STINGERS
STINGES
STINGFISH
STINGIER
STINGIES
STINGIEST
STINGILY
STINGING
STINGINGS
STINGLESS
STINGO
STINGOS
STINGRAY
STINGRAYS
STINGS
STINGY
STINK
STINKARD
STINKARDS
STINKBIRD
STINKBUG
STINKBUGS
STINKER
STINKEROO
STINKERS
STINKHORN
STINKIER
STINKIEST
STINKING
STINKO
STINKPOT
STINKPOTS
STINKS
STINKWEED
STINKWOOD
STINKY
STINT
STINTED
STINTEDLY
STINTER
STINTERS
STINTIER
STINTIEST
STINTING
STINTINGS
STINTLESS
STINTS
STINTY
STIPA
STIPAS
STIPE
STIPED
STIPEL
STIPELS
STIPEND
STIPENDS
STIPES
STIPIFORM
STIPITATE
STIPITES
STIPPLE
STIPPLED
STIPPLER
STIPPLERS
STIPPLES
STIPPLING
STIPULAR
STIPULARY
STIPULATE
STIPULE
STIPULED
STIPULES
STIR
STIRABOUT
STIRE

STIRED
STIRES
STIRING
STIRK
STIRKS
STIRLESS
STIRP
STIRPES
STIRPS
STIRRA
STIRRABLE
STIRRAH
STIRRAHS
STIRRAS
STIRRE
STIRRED
STIRRER
STIRRERS
STIRRES
STIRRING
STIRRINGS
STIRRUP
STIRRUPS
STIRS
STISHIE
STISHIES
STITCH
STITCHED
STITCHER
STITCHERS
STITCHERY
STITCHES
STITCHING
STITHIED
STITHIES
STITHY
STITHYING
STIVE
STIVED
STIVER
STIVERS
STIVES
STIVIER
STIVIEST
STIVING
STIVY
STOA
STOAE
STOAI
STOAS
STOAT
STOATS
STOB
STOBBED
STOBBING
STOBIE
STOBS
STOCCADO
STOCCADOS
STOCCATA
STOCCATAS
STOCIOUS
STOCK
STOCKADE
STOCKADED
STOCKADES
STOCKAGE
STOCKAGES
STOCKCAR
STOCKCARS
STOCKED
STOCKER
STOCKERS
STOCKFISH
STOCKHORN
STOCKIER
STOCKIEST
STOCKILY
STOCKINET
STOCKING
STOCKINGS
STOCKISH
STOCKIST
STOCKISTS
STOCKLESS
STOCKLIST
STOCKLOCK
STOCKMAN
STOCKMEN
STOCKPILE
STOCKPOT
STOCKPOTS
STOCKROOM
STOCKS
STOCKTAKE
STOCKTOOK
STOCKWORK
STOCKY
STOCKYARD
STODGE
STODGED
STODGER
STODGERS
STODGES
STODGIER
STODGIEST
STODGILY
STODGING
STODGY
STOEP
STOEPS
STOGEY
STOGEYS
STOGIE
STOGIES
STOGY
STOIC
STOICAL
STOICALLY
STOICISM
STOICISMS
STOICS
STOIT
STOITED
STOITER
STOITERED
STOITERS
STOITING
STOITS
STOKE
STOKED
STOKEHOLD
STOKEHOLE
STOKER
STOKERS
STOKES
STOKESIA
STOKESIAS
STOKING
STOKVEL
STOKVELS
STOLE
STOLED
STOLEN
STOLES
STOLID
STOLIDER
STOLIDEST
STOLIDITY
STOLIDLY
STOLLEN
STOLLENS
STOLN
STOLON
STOLONATE
STOLONIC
STOLONS
STOLPORT
STOLPORTS
STOMA
STOMACH
STOMACHAL
STOMACHED
STOMACHER
STOMACHIC
STOMACHS
STOMACHY
STOMACK
STOMACKS
STOMAL
STOMAS
STOMATA
STOMATAL
STOMATE
STOMATES
STOMATIC
STOMATOUS
STOMIA
STOMIUM
STOMIUMS
STOMODAEA
STOMODEA
STOMODEAL
STOMODEUM
STOMP
STOMPED
STOMPER
STOMPERS
STOMPIE
STOMPIER
STOMPIES
STOMPIEST
STOMPING
STOMPS
STOMPY
STONABLE
STOND
STONDS
STONE
STONEABLE
STONEBOAT
STONECAST
STONECHAT
STONECROP
STONECUT
STONECUTS
STONED
STONEFISH
STONEFLY
STONEHAND
STONELESS
STONELIKE
STONEN
STONER
STONERAG
STONERAGS
STONERAW
STONERAWS
STONERN
STONERS
STONES
STONESHOT
STONEWALL
STONEWARE
STONEWASH
STONEWORK
STONEWORT
STONEY
STONG
STONIED
STONIER
STONIES
STONIEST
STONILY
STONINESS
STONING
STONINGS
STONISH
STONISHED
STONISHES

S

STONK
STONKED
STONKER
STONKERED
STONKERS
STONKING
STONKS
STONN
STONNE
STONNED
STONNES
STONNING
STONNS
STONY
STONYING
STOOD
STOODEN
STOOGE
STOOGED
STOOGES
STOOGING
STOOK
STOOKED
STOOKER
STOOKERS
STOOKIE
STOOKIES
STOOKING
STOOKINGS
STOOKS
STOOL
STOOLBALL
STOOLED
STOOLIE
STOOLIES
STOOLING
STOOLS
STOOLY
STOOP
STOOPBALL
STOOPE
STOOPED
STOOPER
STOOPERS
STOOPES
STOOPING
STOOPS
STOOR
STOORS
STOOSHIE
STOOSHIES
STOOZE
STOOZED
STOOZER
STOOZERS
STOOZES
STOOZING
STOOZINGS
STOP
STOPBAND
STOPBANDS
STOPBANK
STOPBANKS
STOPCOCK
STOPCOCKS
STOPE
STOPED
STOPER
STOPERS
STOPES
STOPGAP
STOPGAPS
STOPING
STOPINGS
STOPLESS
STOPLIGHT
STOPOFF
STOPOFFS
STOPOVER
STOPOVERS
STOPPABLE
STOPPAGE
STOPPAGES
STOPPED
STOPPER
STOPPERED
STOPPERS
STOPPING
STOPPINGS
STOPPLE
STOPPLED
STOPPLES
STOPPLING
STOPS
STOPT
STOPWATCH
STOPWORD
STOPWORDS
STORABLE
STORABLES
STORAGE
STORAGES
STORAX
STORAXES
STORE
STORECARD
STORED
STOREMAN
STOREMEN
STORER
STOREROOM
STORERS
STORES
STORESHIP
STOREWIDE
STOREY
STOREYED
STOREYS
STORGE
STORGES
STORIATED
STORIED
STORIES
STORIETTE
STORING
STORK
STORKS
STORM
STORMBIRD
STORMCOCK
STORMED
STORMER
STORMERS
STORMFUL
STORMIER
STORMIEST
STORMILY
STORMING
STORMINGS
STORMLESS
STORMLIKE
STORMS
STORMY
STORNELLI
STORNELLO
STORY
STORYBOOK
STORYETTE
STORYING
STORYINGS
STORYLESS
STORYLINE
STORYTIME
STOSS
STOSSES
STOT
STOTIN
STOTINKA
STOTINKAS
STOTINKI
STOTINOV
STOTINS
STOTIOUS
STOTS
STOTT
STOTTED
STOTTER
STOTTERED
STOTTERS
STOTTIE
STOTTIES
STOTTING
STOTTS
STOTTY
STOUN
STOUND
STOUNDED
STOUNDING
STOUNDS
STOUNING
STOUNS
STOUP
STOUPS
STOUR
STOURE
STOURES
STOURIE
STOURIER
STOURIEST
STOURS
STOURY
STOUSH
STOUSHED
STOUSHES
STOUSHIE
STOUSHIES
STOUSHING
STOUT
STOUTEN
STOUTENED
STOUTENS
STOUTER
STOUTEST
STOUTH
STOUTHS
STOUTISH
STOUTLY
STOUTNESS
STOUTS
STOVAINE
STOVAINES
STOVE
STOVED
STOVEPIPE
STOVER
STOVERS
STOVES
STOVETOP
STOVETOPS
STOVEWOOD
STOVIES
STOVING
STOVINGS
STOW
STOWABLE
STOWAGE
STOWAGES
STOWAWAY
STOWAWAYS
STOWDOWN
STOWDOWNS
STOWED
STOWER
STOWERS
STOWING
STOWINGS
STOWLINS
STOWN
STOWND
STOWNDED

STOWNDING
STOWNDS
STOWNLINS
STOWP
STOWPS
STOWRE
STOWRES
STOWS
STRABISM
STRABISMS
STRACK
STRAD
STRADDLE
STRADDLED
STRADDLER
STRADDLES
STRADIOT
STRADIOTS
STRADS
STRAE
STRAES
STRAFE
STRAFED
STRAFER
STRAFERS
STRAFES
STRAFF
STRAFFED
STRAFFING
STRAFFS
STRAFING
STRAFINGS
STRAG
STRAGGLE
STRAGGLED
STRAGGLER
STRAGGLES
STRAGGLY
STRAGS
STRAICHT
STRAIGHT
STRAIGHTS
STRAIK
STRAIKED
STRAIKING
STRAIKS
STRAIN
STRAINED
STRAINER
STRAINERS
STRAINING
STRAINS
STRAINT
STRAINTS
STRAIT
STRAITED
STRAITEN
STRAITENS
STRAITER
STRAITEST
STRAITING
STRAITLY
STRAITS
STRAK
STRAKE
STRAKED
STRAKES
STRAMACON
STRAMASH
STRAMAZON
STRAMMEL
STRAMMELS
STRAMONY
STRAMP
STRAMPED
STRAMPING
STRAMPS
STRAND
STRANDED
STRANDER
STRANDERS
STRANDING
STRANDS
STRANG
STRANGE
STRANGELY
STRANGER
STRANGERS
STRANGES
STRANGEST
STRANGLE
STRANGLED
STRANGLER
STRANGLES
STRANGURY
STRAP
STRAPHANG
STRAPHUNG
STRAPLESS
STRAPLIKE
STRAPLINE
STRAPPADO
STRAPPED
STRAPPER
STRAPPERS
STRAPPIER
STRAPPING
STRAPPY
STRAPS
STRAPWORT
STRASS
STRASSES
STRATA
STRATAGEM
STRATAL
STRATAS
STRATEGIC
STRATEGY
STRATH
STRATHS
STRATI
STRATIFY
STRATONIC
STRATOSE
STRATOUS
STRATUM
STRATUMS
STRATUS
STRATUSES
STRAUCHT
STRAUCHTS
STRAUGHT
STRAUGHTS
STRAUNGE
STRAVAGE
STRAVAGED
STRAVAGES
STRAVAIG
STRAVAIGS
STRAW
STRAWED
STRAWEN
STRAWHAT
STRAWIER
STRAWIEST
STRAWING
STRAWLESS
STRAWLIKE
STRAWN
STRAWS
STRAWWORM
STRAWY
STRAY
STRAYED
STRAYER
STRAYERS
STRAYING
STRAYINGS
STRAYLING
STRAYS
STRAYVE
STRAYVED
STRAYVES
STRAYVING
STREAK
STREAKED
STREAKER
STREAKERS
STREAKIER
STREAKILY
STREAKING
STREAKS
STREAKY
STREAM
STREAMBED
STREAMED
STREAMER
STREAMERS
STREAMIER
STREAMING
STREAMLET
STREAMS
STREAMY
STREEK
STREEKED
STREEKER
STREEKERS
STREEKING
STREEKS
STREEL
STREELED
STREELING
STREELS
STREET
STREETAGE
STREETBOY
STREETCAR
STREETED
STREETFUL
STREETIER
STREETING
STREETS
STREETY
STREIGHT
STREIGHTS
STREIGNE
STREIGNED
STREIGNES
STRELITZ
STRELITZI
STRENE
STRENES
STRENGTH
STRENGTHS
STRENUITY
STRENUOUS
STREP
STREPENT
STREPS
STRESS
STRESSED
STRESSES
STRESSFUL
STRESSIER
STRESSING
STRESSOR
STRESSORS
STRESSY
STRETCH
STRETCHED
STRETCHER
STRETCHES
STRETCHY
STRETTA
STRETTAS
STRETTE
STRETTI
STRETTO
STRETTOS
STREUSEL

S

STREUSELS
STREW
STREWAGE
STREWAGES
STREWED
STREWER
STREWERS
STREWING
STREWINGS
STREWMENT
STREWN
STREWS
STREWTH
STRIA
STRIAE
STRIATA
STRIATAL
STRIATE
STRIATED
STRIATES
STRIATING
STRIATION
STRIATUM
STRIATUMS
STRIATURE
STRICH
STRICHES
STRICK
STRICKEN
STRICKLE
STRICKLED
STRICKLES
STRICKS
STRICT
STRICTER
STRICTEST
STRICTION
STRICTISH
STRICTLY
STRICTURE
STRIDDEN
STRIDDLE
STRIDDLED
STRIDDLES
STRIDE
STRIDENCE
STRIDENCY
STRIDENT
STRIDER
STRIDERS
STRIDES
STRIDING
STRIDLING
STRIDOR
STRIDORS
STRIFE
STRIFEFUL
STRIFES
STRIFT
STRIFTS
STRIG
STRIGA
STRIGAE
STRIGATE
STRIGGED
STRIGGING
STRIGIL
STRIGILS
STRIGINE
STRIGOSE
STRIGS
STRIKABLE
STRIKE
STRIKEOUT
STRIKER
STRIKERS
STRIKES
STRIKING
STRIKINGS
STRIM
STRIMMED
STRIMMING
STRIMS
STRINE
STRINES
STRING
STRINGED
STRINGENT
STRINGER
STRINGERS
STRINGIER
STRINGILY
STRINGING
STRINGS
STRINGY
STRINKLE
STRINKLED
STRINKLES
STRIP
STRIPE
STRIPED
STRIPER
STRIPERS
STRIPES
STRIPEY
STRIPIER
STRIPIEST
STRIPING
STRIPINGS
STRIPLING
STRIPPED
STRIPPER
STRIPPERS
STRIPPING
STRIPS
STRIPT
STRIPY
STRIVE
STRIVED
STRIVEN
STRIVER
STRIVERS
STRIVES
STRIVING
STRIVINGS
STROAM
STROAMED
STROAMING
STROAMS
STROBE
STROBED
STROBES
STROBIC
STROBIL
STROBILA
STROBILAE
STROBILAR
STROBILE
STROBILES
STROBILI
STROBILS
STROBILUS
STROBING
STROBINGS
STRODDLE
STRODDLED
STRODDLES
STRODE
STRODLE
STRODLED
STRODLES
STRODLING
STROKABLE
STROKE
STROKED
STROKEN
STROKER
STROKERS
STROKES
STROKING
STROKINGS
STROLL
STROLLED
STROLLER
STROLLERS
STROLLING
STROLLS
STROMA
STROMAL
STROMATA
STROMATIC
STROMB
STROMBS
STROMBUS
STROND
STRONDS
STRONG
STRONGARM
STRONGBOX
STRONGER
STRONGEST
STRONGISH
STRONGLY
STRONGMAN
STRONGMEN
STRONGYL
STRONGYLE
STRONGYLS
STRONTIA
STRONTIAN
STRONTIAS
STRONTIC
STRONTIUM
STROOK
STROOKE
STROOKEN
STROOKES
STROP
STROPHE
STROPHES
STROPHIC
STROPHOID
STROPHULI
STROPPED
STROPPER
STROPPERS
STROPPIER
STROPPILY
STROPPING
STROPPY
STROPS
STROSSERS
STROUD
STROUDING
STROUDS
STROUP
STROUPACH
STROUPAN
STROUPANS
STROUPS
STROUT
STROUTED
STROUTING
STROUTS
STROVE
STROW
STROWED
STROWER
STROWERS
STROWING
STROWINGS
STROWN
STROWS
STROY
STROYED
STROYER
STROYERS
STROYING
STROYS
STRUCK

STRUCKEN
STRUCTURE
STRUDEL
STRUDELS
STRUGGLE
STRUGGLED
STRUGGLER
STRUGGLES
STRUM
STRUMA
STRUMAE
STRUMAS
STRUMATIC
STRUMITIS
STRUMMED
STRUMMEL
STRUMMELS
STRUMMER
STRUMMERS
STRUMMING
STRUMOSE
STRUMOUS
STRUMPET
STRUMPETS
STRUMS
STRUNG
STRUNT
STRUNTED
STRUNTING
STRUNTS
STRUT
STRUTS
STRUTTED
STRUTTER
STRUTTERS
STRUTTING
STRYCHNIA
STRYCHNIC
STUB
STUBBED
STUBBIE
STUBBIER
STUBBIES
STUBBIEST
STUBBILY
STUBBING
STUBBLE
STUBBLED
STUBBLES
STUBBLIER
STUBBLY
STUBBORN
STUBBORNS
STUBBY
STUBS
STUCCO
STUCCOED
STUCCOER
STUCCOERS
STUCCOES
STUCCOING
STUCCOS
STUCK
STUCKS
STUD
STUDBOOK
STUDBOOKS
STUDDED
STUDDEN
STUDDIE
STUDDIES
STUDDING
STUDDINGS
STUDDLE
STUDDLES
STUDE
STUDENT
STUDENTRY
STUDENTS
STUDENTY
STUDFARM
STUDFARMS
STUDFISH
STUDHORSE
STUDIED
STUDIEDLY
STUDIER
STUDIERS
STUDIES
STUDIO
STUDIOS
STUDIOUS
STUDLIER
STUDLIEST
STUDLIKE
STUDLY
STUDS
STUDWORK
STUDWORKS
STUDY
STUDYING
STUFF
STUFFED
STUFFER
STUFFERS
STUFFIER
STUFFIEST
STUFFILY
STUFFING
STUFFINGS
STUFFLESS
STUFFS
STUFFY
STUGGIER
STUGGIEST
STUGGY
STUIVER
STUIVERS
STUKKEND
STULL
STULLS
STULM
STULMS
STULTIFY
STUM
STUMBLE
STUMBLED
STUMBLER
STUMBLERS
STUMBLES
STUMBLIER
STUMBLING
STUMBLY
STUMER
STUMERS
STUMM
STUMMED
STUMMEL
STUMMELS
STUMMING
STUMP
STUMPAGE
STUMPAGES
STUMPED
STUMPER
STUMPERS
STUMPIER
STUMPIES
STUMPIEST
STUMPILY
STUMPING
STUMPINGS
STUMPS
STUMPWORK
STUMPY
STUMS
STUN
STUNG
STUNK
STUNKARD
STUNNED
STUNNER
STUNNERS
STUNNING
STUNNINGS
STUNS
STUNSAIL
STUNSAILS
STUNT
STUNTED
STUNTING
STUNTMAN
STUNTMEN
STUNTS
STUPA
STUPAS
STUPE
STUPED
STUPEFIED
STUPEFIER
STUPEFIES
STUPEFY
STUPENT
STUPES
STUPID
STUPIDER
STUPIDEST
STUPIDITY
STUPIDLY
STUPIDS
STUPING
STUPOR
STUPOROUS
STUPORS
STUPRATE
STUPRATED
STUPRATES
STURDIED
STURDIER
STURDIES
STURDIEST
STURDILY
STURDY
STURE
STURGEON
STURGEONS
STURMER
STURMERS
STURNINE
STURNOID
STURNUS
STURNUSES
STURT
STURTED
STURTING
STURTS
STUSHIE
STUSHIES
STUTTER
STUTTERED
STUTTERER
STUTTERS
STY
STYE
STYED
STYES
STYGIAN
STYING
STYLAR
STYLATE
STYLE
STYLEBOOK
STYLED
STYLEE
STYLEES
STYLELESS
STYLER
STYLERS
STYLES
STYLET

STYLETS
STYLI
STYLIE
STYLIER
STYLIEST
STYLIFORM
STYLING
STYLINGS
STYLISE
STYLISED
STYLISER
STYLISERS
STYLISES
STYLISH
STYLISHLY
STYLISING
STYLIST
STYLISTIC
STYLISTS
STYLITE
STYLITES
STYLITIC
STYLITISM
STYLIZE
STYLIZED
STYLIZER
STYLIZERS
STYLIZES
STYLIZING
STYLO
STYLOBATE
STYLOID
STYLOIDS
STYLOLITE
STYLOPES
STYLOPID
STYLOPIDS
STYLOPISE
STYLOPIZE
STYLOPS
STYLOS
STYLUS
STYLUSES
STYME
STYMED
STYMES
STYMIE
STYMIED
STYMIEING
STYMIES
STYMING
STYMY
STYMYING
STYPSIS
STYPSISES
STYPTIC
STYPTICAL
STYPTICS
STYRAX
STYRAXES
STYRE
STYRED
STYRENE
STYRENES
STYRES
STYRING
STYROFOAM
STYTE
STYTED
STYTES
STYTING
SUABILITY
SUABLE
SUABLY
SUASIBLE
SUASION
SUASIONS
SUASIVE
SUASIVELY
SUASORY
SUAVE
SUAVELY
SUAVENESS
SUAVER
SUAVEST
SUAVITIES
SUAVITY
SUB
SUBA
SUBABBOT
SUBABBOTS
SUBACID
SUBACIDLY
SUBACRID
SUBACT
SUBACTED
SUBACTING
SUBACTION
SUBACTS
SUBACUTE
SUBADAR
SUBADARS
SUBADULT
SUBADULTS
SUBAERIAL
SUBAGENCY
SUBAGENT
SUBAGENTS
SUBAH
SUBAHDAR
SUBAHDARS
SUBAHDARY
SUBAHS
SUBAHSHIP
SUBALAR
SUBALPINE
SUBALTERN
SUBAPICAL
SUBAQUA
SUBARCTIC
SUBAREA
SUBAREAS
SUBARID
SUBAS
SUBASTRAL
SUBATOM
SUBATOMIC
SUBATOMS
SUBAUDIO
SUBAURAL
SUBAXIAL
SUBBASAL
SUBBASE
SUBBASES
SUBBASIN
SUBBASINS
SUBBASS
SUBBASSES
SUBBED
SUBBIE
SUBBIES
SUBBING
SUBBINGS
SUBBLOCK
SUBBLOCKS
SUBBRANCH
SUBBREED
SUBBREEDS
SUBBUREAU
SUBBY
SUBCANTOR
SUBCASTE
SUBCASTES
SUBCAUDAL
SUBCAUSE
SUBCAUSES
SUBCAVITY
SUBCELL
SUBCELLAR
SUBCELLS
SUBCENTER
SUBCENTRE
SUBCHASER
SUBCHIEF
SUBCHIEFS
SUBCHORD
SUBCHORDS
SUBCLAIM
SUBCLAIMS
SUBCLAN
SUBCLANS
SUBCLASS
SUBCLAUSE
SUBCLERK
SUBCLERKS
SUBCLIMAX
SUBCODE
SUBCODES
SUBCOLONY
SUBCONSUL
SUBCOOL
SUBCOOLED
SUBCOOLS
SUBCORTEX
SUBCOSTA
SUBCOSTAE
SUBCOSTAL
SUBCOUNTY
SUBCRUST
SUBCRUSTS
SUBCULT
SUBCULTS
SUBCUTES
SUBCUTIS
SUBDEACON
SUBDEALER
SUBDEAN
SUBDEANS
SUBDEB
SUBDEBS
SUBDEPOT
SUBDEPOTS
SUBDEPUTY
SUBDERMAL
SUBDEW
SUBDEWED
SUBDEWING
SUBDEWS
SUBDIVIDE
SUBDOLOUS
SUBDORSAL
SUBDUABLE
SUBDUABLY
SUBDUAL
SUBDUALS
SUBDUCE
SUBDUCED
SUBDUCES
SUBDUCING
SUBDUCT
SUBDUCTED
SUBDUCTS
SUBDUE
SUBDUED
SUBDUEDLY
SUBDUER
SUBDUERS
SUBDUES
SUBDUING
SUBDUPLE
SUBDURAL
SUBDWARF
SUBDWARFS
SUBECHO
SUBECHOES
SUBEDAR
SUBEDARS
SUBEDIT
SUBEDITED
SUBEDITOR

S

SUBEDITS
SUBENTIRE
SUBENTRY
SUBEPOCH
SUBEPOCHS
SUBEQUAL
SUBER
SUBERATE
SUBERATES
SUBERECT
SUBEREOUS
SUBERIC
SUBERIN
SUBERINS
SUBERISE
SUBERISED
SUBERISES
SUBERIZE
SUBERIZED
SUBERIZES
SUBEROSE
SUBEROUS
SUBERS
SUBFAMILY
SUBFEU
SUBFEUED
SUBFEUING
SUBFEUS
SUBFIELD
SUBFIELDS
SUBFILE
SUBFILES
SUBFIX
SUBFIXES
SUBFLOOR
SUBFLOORS
SUBFLUID
SUBFOLDER
SUBFOSSIL
SUBFRAME
SUBFRAMES
SUBFUSC
SUBFUSCS
SUBFUSK
SUBFUSKS
SUBGENERA
SUBGENRE
SUBGENRES
SUBGENUS
SUBGOAL
SUBGOALS
SUBGRADE
SUBGRADES
SUBGRAPH
SUBGRAPHS
SUBGROUP
SUBGROUPS
SUBGUM
SUBGUMS
SUBHA
SUBHAS
SUBHEAD
SUBHEADS
SUBHEDRAL
SUBHUMAN
SUBHUMANS
SUBHUMID
SUBIDEA
SUBIDEAS
SUBIMAGO
SUBIMAGOS
SUBINCISE
SUBINDEX
SUBINFEUD
SUBITEM
SUBITEMS
SUBITISE
SUBITISED
SUBITISES
SUBITIZE
SUBITIZED
SUBITIZES
SUBITO
SUBJACENT
SUBJECT
SUBJECTED
SUBJECTS
SUBJOIN
SUBJOINED
SUBJOINS
SUBJUGATE
SUBLATE
SUBLATED
SUBLATES
SUBLATING
SUBLATION
SUBLEASE
SUBLEASED
SUBLEASES
SUBLESSEE
SUBLESSOR
SUBLET
SUBLETHAL
SUBLETS
SUBLETTER
SUBLEVEL
SUBLEVELS
SUBLIMATE
SUBLIME
SUBLIMED
SUBLIMELY
SUBLIMER
SUBLIMERS
SUBLIMES
SUBLIMEST
SUBLIMING
SUBLIMISE
SUBLIMIT
SUBLIMITS
SUBLIMITY
SUBLIMIZE
SUBLINE
SUBLINEAR
SUBLINES
SUBLOT
SUBLOTS
SUBLUNAR
SUBLUNARY
SUBLUNATE
SUBLUXATE
SUBMAN
SUBMARINE
SUBMARKET
SUBMATRIX
SUBMEN
SUBMENTA
SUBMENTAL
SUBMENTUM
SUBMENU
SUBMENUS
SUBMERGE
SUBMERGED
SUBMERGES
SUBMERSE
SUBMERSED
SUBMERSES
SUBMICRON
SUBMISS
SUBMISSLY
SUBMIT
SUBMITS
SUBMITTAL
SUBMITTED
SUBMITTER
SUBMUCOSA
SUBMUCOUS
SUBNASAL
SUBNET
SUBNETS
SUBNEURAL
SUBNICHE
SUBNICHES
SUBNIVEAL
SUBNIVEAN
SUBNODAL
SUBNORMAL
SUBNUCLEI
SUBOCEAN
SUBOCTAVE
SUBOCULAR
SUBOFFICE
SUBOPTIC
SUBORAL
SUBORDER
SUBORDERS
SUBORN
SUBORNED
SUBORNER
SUBORNERS
SUBORNING
SUBORNS
SUBOSCINE
SUBOVAL
SUBOVATE
SUBOXIDE
SUBOXIDES
SUBPANEL
SUBPANELS
SUBPAR
SUBPART
SUBPARTS
SUBPENA
SUBPENAED
SUBPENAS
SUBPERIOD
SUBPHASE
SUBPHASES
SUBPHYLA
SUBPHYLAR
SUBPHYLUM
SUBPLOT
SUBPLOTS
SUBPOENA
SUBPOENAS
SUBPOLAR
SUBPOTENT
SUBPRIME
SUBPRIMES
SUBPRIOR
SUBPRIORS
SUBPUBIC
SUBRACE
SUBRACES
SUBREGION
SUBRENT
SUBRENTED
SUBRENTS
SUBRING
SUBRINGS
SUBROGATE
SUBRULE
SUBRULES
SUBS
SUBSACRAL
SUBSALE
SUBSALES
SUBSAMPLE
SUBSCALE
SUBSCALES
SUBSCHEMA
SUBSCRIBE
SUBSCRIPT
SUBSEA
SUBSECIVE
SUBSECT
SUBSECTOR
SUBSECTS
SUBSELLIA
SUBSENSE
SUBSENSES

S

SUBSERE
SUBSERES
SUBSERIES
SUBSERVE
SUBSERVED
SUBSERVES
SUBSET
SUBSETS
SUBSHAFT
SUBSHAFTS
SUBSHELL
SUBSHELLS
SUBSHRUB
SUBSHRUBS
SUBSIDE
SUBSIDED
SUBSIDER
SUBSIDERS
SUBSIDES
SUBSIDIES
SUBSIDING
SUBSIDISE
SUBSIDIZE
SUBSIDY
SUBSIST
SUBSISTED
SUBSISTER
SUBSISTS
SUBSITE
SUBSITES
SUBSIZAR
SUBSIZARS
SUBSKILL
SUBSKILLS
SUBSOCIAL
SUBSOIL
SUBSOILED
SUBSOILER
SUBSOILS
SUBSOLAR
SUBSONG
SUBSONGS
SUBSONIC
SUBSPACE
SUBSPACES
SUBSTAGE
SUBSTAGES
SUBSTANCE
SUBSTATE
SUBSTATES
SUBSTORM
SUBSTORMS
SUBSTRACT
SUBSTRATA
SUBSTRATE
SUBSTRUCT
SUBSTYLAR
SUBSTYLE
SUBSTYLES
SUBSULTUS
SUBSUME
SUBSUMED
SUBSUMES
SUBSUMING
SUBSYSTEM
SUBTACK
SUBTACKS
SUBTALAR
SUBTASK
SUBTASKS
SUBTAXA
SUBTAXON
SUBTAXONS
SUBTEEN
SUBTEENS
SUBTENANT
SUBTEND
SUBTENDED
SUBTENDS
SUBTENSE
SUBTENSES
SUBTENURE
SUBTEST
SUBTESTS
SUBTEXT
SUBTEXTS
SUBTHEME
SUBTHEMES
SUBTIDAL
SUBTIL
SUBTILE
SUBTILELY
SUBTILER
SUBTILEST
SUBTILIN
SUBTILINS
SUBTILISE
SUBTILITY
SUBTILIZE
SUBTILTY
SUBTITLE
SUBTITLED
SUBTITLES
SUBTLE
SUBTLER
SUBTLEST
SUBTLETY
SUBTLY
SUBTONE
SUBTONES
SUBTONIC
SUBTONICS
SUBTOPIA
SUBTOPIAN
SUBTOPIAS
SUBTOPIC
SUBTOPICS
SUBTORRID
SUBTOTAL
SUBTOTALS
SUBTRACT
SUBTRACTS
SUBTRADE
SUBTRADES
SUBTREND
SUBTRENDS
SUBTRIBE
SUBTRIBES
SUBTRIST
SUBTROPIC
SUBTRUDE
SUBTRUDED
SUBTRUDES
SUBTUNIC
SUBTUNICS
SUBTWEET
SUBTWEETS
SUBTYPE
SUBTYPES
SUBUCULA
SUBUCULAS
SUBULATE
SUBUNIT
SUBUNITS
SUBURB
SUBURBAN
SUBURBANS
SUBURBED
SUBURBIA
SUBURBIAS
SUBURBS
SUBURSINE
SUBVASSAL
SUBVENE
SUBVENED
SUBVENES
SUBVENING
SUBVERSAL
SUBVERSE
SUBVERSED
SUBVERSES
SUBVERST
SUBVERT
SUBVERTED
SUBVERTER
SUBVERTS
SUBVICAR
SUBVICARS
SUBVIRAL
SUBVIRUS
SUBVISUAL
SUBVOCAL
SUBWARDEN
SUBWAY
SUBWAYED
SUBWAYING
SUBWAYS
SUBWOOFER
SUBWORLD
SUBWORLDS
SUBWRITER
SUBZERO
SUBZONAL
SUBZONE
SUBZONES
SUCCADE
SUCCADES
SUCCAH
SUCCAHS
SUCCEDENT
SUCCEED
SUCCEEDED
SUCCEEDER
SUCCEEDS
SUCCENTOR
SUCCES
SUCCESS
SUCCESSES
SUCCESSOR
SUCCI
SUCCINATE
SUCCINCT
SUCCINIC
SUCCINITE
SUCCINYL
SUCCINYLS
SUCCISE
SUCCOR
SUCCORED
SUCCORER
SUCCORERS
SUCCORIES
SUCCORING
SUCCORS
SUCCORY
SUCCOS
SUCCOSE
SUCCOT
SUCCOTASH
SUCCOTH
SUCCOUR
SUCCOURED
SUCCOURER
SUCCOURS
SUCCOUS
SUCCUBA
SUCCUBAE
SUCCUBAS
SUCCUBI
SUCCUBINE
SUCCUBOUS
SUCCUBUS
SUCCULENT
SUCCUMB
SUCCUMBED
SUCCUMBER
SUCCUMBS
SUCCURSAL
SUCCUS
SUCCUSS

SUCCUSSED
SUCCUSSES
SUCH
SUCHLIKE
SUCHLIKES
SUCHNESS
SUCHWISE
SUCK
SUCKED
SUCKEN
SUCKENER
SUCKENERS
SUCKENS
SUCKER
SUCKERED
SUCKERING
SUCKERS
SUCKET
SUCKETS
SUCKFISH
SUCKHOLE
SUCKHOLED
SUCKHOLES
SUCKIER
SUCKIEST
SUCKINESS
SUCKING
SUCKINGS
SUCKLE
SUCKLED
SUCKLER
SUCKLERS
SUCKLES
SUCKLESS
SUCKLING
SUCKLINGS
SUCKS
SUCKY
SUCRALOSE
SUCRASE
SUCRASES
SUCRE
SUCRES
SUCRIER
SUCRIERS
SUCROSE
SUCROSES
SUCTION
SUCTIONAL
SUCTIONED
SUCTIONS
SUCTORIAL
SUCTORIAN
SUCURUJU
SUCURUJUS
SUD
SUDAMEN
SUDAMENS
SUDAMINA
SUDAMINAL
SUDARIA
SUDARIES
SUDARIUM
SUDARY
SUDATE
SUDATED
SUDATES
SUDATING
SUDATION
SUDATIONS
SUDATORIA
SUDATORY
SUDD
SUDDEN
SUDDENLY
SUDDENS
SUDDENTY
SUDDER
SUDDERS
SUDDS
SUDOKU
SUDOKUS
SUDOR
SUDORAL
SUDORIFIC
SUDOROUS
SUDORS
SUDS
SUDSED
SUDSER
SUDSERS
SUDSES
SUDSIER
SUDSIEST
SUDSING
SUDSLESS
SUDSY
SUE
SUEABLE
SUED
SUEDE
SUEDED
SUEDELIKE
SUEDES
SUEDETTE
SUEDETTES
SUEDING
SUENT
SUER
SUERS
SUES
SUET
SUETE
SUETES
SUETIER
SUETIEST
SUETS
SUETTIER
SUETTIEST
SUETTY
SUETY
SUFFARI
SUFFARIS
SUFFECT
SUFFECTS
SUFFER
SUFFERED
SUFFERER
SUFFERERS
SUFFERING
SUFFERS
SUFFETE
SUFFETES
SUFFICE
SUFFICED
SUFFICER
SUFFICERS
SUFFICES
SUFFICING
SUFFIX
SUFFIXAL
SUFFIXED
SUFFIXES
SUFFIXING
SUFFIXION
SUFFLATE
SUFFLATED
SUFFLATES
SUFFOCATE
SUFFRAGAN
SUFFRAGE
SUFFRAGES
SUFFUSE
SUFFUSED
SUFFUSES
SUFFUSING
SUFFUSION
SUFFUSIVE
SUG
SUGAN
SUGANS
SUGAR
SUGARALLY
SUGARBUSH
SUGARCANE
SUGARCOAT
SUGARED
SUGARER
SUGARERS
SUGARIER
SUGARIEST
SUGARING
SUGARINGS
SUGARLESS
SUGARLIKE
SUGARLOAF
SUGARPLUM
SUGARS
SUGARY
SUGGED
SUGGEST
SUGGESTED
SUGGESTER
SUGGESTS
SUGGING
SUGGINGS
SUGH
SUGHED
SUGHING
SUGHS
SUGO
SUGOS
SUGS
SUHUR
SUHURS
SUI
SUICIDAL
SUICIDE
SUICIDED
SUICIDES
SUICIDING
SUID
SUIDIAN
SUIDIANS
SUIDS
SUILLINE
SUING
SUINGS
SUINT
SUINTS
SUIPLAP
SUIPLAPS
SUIT
SUITABLE
SUITABLY
SUITCASE
SUITCASES
SUITE
SUITED
SUITER
SUITERS
SUITES
SUITING
SUITINGS
SUITLIKE
SUITOR
SUITORED
SUITORING
SUITORS
SUITRESS
SUITS
SUIVANTE
SUIVANTES
SUIVEZ
SUJEE
SUJEES
SUK
SUKH
SUKHS
SUKIYAKI

S

SUKIYAKIS
SUKKAH
SUKKAHS
SUKKOS
SUKKOT
SUKKOTH
SUKS
SUKUK
SUKUKS
SULCAL
SULCALISE
SULCALIZE
SULCATE
SULCATED
SULCATION
SULCI
SULCUS
SULDAN
SULDANS
SULFA
SULFAS
SULFATASE
SULFATE
SULFATED
SULFATES
SULFATIC
SULFATING
SULFATION
SULFID
SULFIDE
SULFIDES
SULFIDS
SULFINYL
SULFINYLS
SULFITE
SULFITES
SULFITIC
SULFO
SULFONATE
SULFONE
SULFONES
SULFONIC
SULFONIUM
SULFONYL
SULFONYLS
SULFOXIDE
SULFUR
SULFURATE
SULFURED
SULFURET
SULFURETS
SULFURIC
SULFURIER
SULFURING
SULFURISE
SULFURIZE
SULFUROUS
SULFURS
SULFURY
SULFURYL
SULFURYLS
SULK
SULKED
SULKER
SULKERS
SULKIER
SULKIES
SULKIEST
SULKILY
SULKINESS
SULKING
SULKS
SULKY
SULLAGE
SULLAGES
SULLEN
SULLENER
SULLENEST
SULLENLY
SULLENS
SULLIABLE
SULLIED
SULLIES
SULLY
SULLYING
SULPH
SULPHA
SULPHAS
SULPHATE
SULPHATED
SULPHATES
SULPHATIC
SULPHID
SULPHIDE
SULPHIDES
SULPHIDS
SULPHINYL
SULPHITE
SULPHITES
SULPHITIC
SULPHONE
SULPHONES
SULPHONIC
SULPHONYL
SULPHS
SULPHUR
SULPHURED
SULPHURET
SULPHURIC
SULPHURS
SULPHURY
SULPHURYL
SULTAN
SULTANA
SULTANAS
SULTANATE
SULTANESS
SULTANIC
SULTANS
SULTRIER
SULTRIEST
SULTRILY
SULTRY
SULU
SULUS
SUM
SUMAC
SUMACH
SUMACHS
SUMACS
SUMATRA
SUMATRAS
SUMBITCH
SUMI
SUMIS
SUMLESS
SUMMA
SUMMABLE
SUMMAE
SUMMAND
SUMMANDS
SUMMAR
SUMMARIES
SUMMARILY
SUMMARISE
SUMMARIST
SUMMARIZE
SUMMARY
SUMMAS
SUMMAT
SUMMATE
SUMMATED
SUMMATES
SUMMATING
SUMMATION
SUMMATIVE
SUMMATS
SUMMED
SUMMER
SUMMERED
SUMMERIER
SUMMERING
SUMMERLY
SUMMERS
SUMMERSET
SUMMERY
SUMMING
SUMMINGS
SUMMIST
SUMMISTS
SUMMIT
SUMMITAL
SUMMITED
SUMMITEER
SUMMITING
SUMMITRY
SUMMITS
SUMMON
SUMMONED
SUMMONER
SUMMONERS
SUMMONING
SUMMONS
SUMMONSED
SUMMONSES
SUMO
SUMOIST
SUMOISTS
SUMOS
SUMOTORI
SUMOTORIS
SUMP
SUMPH
SUMPHISH
SUMPHS
SUMPIT
SUMPITAN
SUMPITANS
SUMPITS
SUMPS
SUMPSIMUS
SUMPTER
SUMPTERS
SUMPTUARY
SUMPTUOUS
SUMPWEED
SUMPWEEDS
SUMS
SUMY
SUN
SUNBACK
SUNBAKE
SUNBAKED
SUNBAKES
SUNBAKING
SUNBATH
SUNBATHE
SUNBATHED
SUNBATHER
SUNBATHES
SUNBATHS
SUNBEAM
SUNBEAMED
SUNBEAMS
SUNBEAMY
SUNBEAT
SUNBEATEN
SUNBED
SUNBEDS
SUNBELT
SUNBELTS
SUNBERRY
SUNBIRD
SUNBIRDS
SUNBLIND
SUNBLINDS
SUNBLOCK
SUNBLOCKS
SUNBONNET
SUNBOW

S

SUNBOWS
SUNBRIGHT
SUNBURN
SUNBURNED
SUNBURNS
SUNBURNT
SUNBURST
SUNBURSTS
SUNCARE
SUNCARES
SUNCHOKE
SUNCHOKES
SUNDAE
SUNDAES
SUNDARI
SUNDARIS
SUNDECK
SUNDECKS
SUNDER
SUNDERED
SUNDERER
SUNDERERS
SUNDERING
SUNDERS
SUNDEW
SUNDEWS
SUNDIAL
SUNDIALS
SUNDOG
SUNDOGS
SUNDOWN
SUNDOWNED
SUNDOWNER
SUNDOWNS
SUNDRA
SUNDRAS
SUNDRESS
SUNDRI
SUNDRIES
SUNDRILY
SUNDRIS
SUNDROPS
SUNDRY
SUNFAST
SUNFISH
SUNFISHES
SUNFLOWER
SUNG
SUNGAR
SUNGARS
SUNGAZER
SUNGAZERS
SUNGAZING
SUNGLASS
SUNGLOW
SUNGLOWS
SUNGREBE
SUNGREBES
SUNHAT
SUNHATS
SUNI
SUNIS
SUNK
SUNKEN
SUNKER
SUNKERS
SUNKET
SUNKETS
SUNKIE
SUNKIES
SUNKS
SUNLAMP
SUNLAMPS
SUNLAND
SUNLANDS
SUNLESS
SUNLESSLY
SUNLIGHT
SUNLIGHTS
SUNLIKE
SUNLIT
SUNN
SUNNA
SUNNAH
SUNNAHS
SUNNAS
SUNNED
SUNNIER
SUNNIES
SUNNIEST
SUNNILY
SUNNINESS
SUNNING
SUNNS
SUNNY
SUNPORCH
SUNPROOF
SUNRAY
SUNRAYS
SUNRISE
SUNRISES
SUNRISING
SUNROOF
SUNROOFS
SUNROOM
SUNROOMS
SUNS
SUNSCALD
SUNSCALDS
SUNSCREEN
SUNSEEKER
SUNSET
SUNSETS
SUNSETTED
SUNSHADE
SUNSHADES
SUNSHINE
SUNSHINES
SUNSHINY
SUNSPECS
SUNSPOT
SUNSPOTS
SUNSTAR
SUNSTARS
SUNSTONE
SUNSTONES
SUNSTROKE
SUNSTRUCK
SUNSUIT
SUNSUITS
SUNTAN
SUNTANNED
SUNTANS
SUNTRAP
SUNTRAPS
SUNUP
SUNUPS
SUNWARD
SUNWARDS
SUNWISE
SUP
SUPAWN
SUPAWNS
SUPE
SUPER
SUPERABLE
SUPERABLY
SUPERADD
SUPERADDS
SUPERATE
SUPERATED
SUPERATES
SUPERATOM
SUPERB
SUPERBAD
SUPERBANK
SUPERBER
SUPERBEST
SUPERBIKE
SUPERBITY
SUPERBLY
SUPERBOLD
SUPERBOMB
SUPERBRAT
SUPERBUG
SUPERBUGS
SUPERCAR
SUPERCARS
SUPERCEDE
SUPERCELL
SUPERCHIC
SUPERCITY
SUPERCLUB
SUPERCOIL
SUPERCOLD
SUPERCOOL
SUPERCOP
SUPERCOPS
SUPERCOW
SUPERCOWS
SUPERCUTE
SUPERED
SUPEREGO
SUPEREGOS
SUPERETTE
SUPERFAN
SUPERFANS
SUPERFARM
SUPERFAST
SUPERFINE
SUPERFIRM
SUPERFIT
SUPERFIX
SUPERFLUX
SUPERFLY
SUPERFOOD
SUPERFUND
SUPERFUSE
SUPERGENE
SUPERGLUE
SUPERGOOD
SUPERGUN
SUPERGUNS
SUPERHARD
SUPERHEAT
SUPERHERO
SUPERHET
SUPERHETS
SUPERHIGH
SUPERHIT
SUPERHITS
SUPERHIVE
SUPERHOT
SUPERHYPE
SUPERING
SUPERIOR
SUPERIORS
SUPERJET
SUPERJETS
SUPERJOCK
SUPERLAIN
SUPERLAY
SUPERLIE
SUPERLIES
SUPERLOAD
SUPERLONG
SUPERLOO
SUPERLOOS
SUPERMALE
SUPERMAN
SUPERMART
SUPERMAX
SUPERMEN
SUPERMIND
SUPERMINI
SUPERMOM
SUPERMOMS
SUPERMOON
SUPERMOTO
SUPERNAL

SUPERNATE
SUPERNOVA
SUPERPIMP
SUPERPLUS
SUPERPORT
SUPERPOSE
SUPERPRO
SUPERPROS
SUPERRACE
SUPERREAL
SUPERRICH
SUPERROAD
SUPERS
SUPERSAFE
SUPERSALE
SUPERSALT
SUPERSAUR
SUPERSEDE
SUPERSELL
SUPERSET
SUPERSETS
SUPERSEX
SUPERSHOW
SUPERSIZE
SUPERSOFT
SUPERSOLD
SUPERSPY
SUPERSTAR
SUPERSTUD
SUPERTAX
SUPERTHIN
SUPERTRAM
SUPERUSER
SUPERVENE
SUPERVISE
SUPERWAIF
SUPERWAVE
SUPERWEED
SUPERWIDE
SUPERWIFE
SUPES
SUPINATE
SUPINATED
SUPINATES
SUPINATOR
SUPINE
SUPINELY
SUPINES
SUPLEX
SUPLEXES
SUPPAWN
SUPPAWNS
SUPPEAGO
SUPPED
SUPPER
SUPPERED
SUPPERING
SUPPERS
SUPPING
SUPPLANT
SUPPLANTS
SUPPLE
SUPPLED
SUPPLELY
SUPPLER
SUPPLES
SUPPLEST
SUPPLIAL
SUPPLIALS
SUPPLIANT
SUPPLICAT
SUPPLIED
SUPPLIER
SUPPLIERS
SUPPLIES
SUPPLING
SUPPLY
SUPPLYING
SUPPORT
SUPPORTED
SUPPORTER
SUPPORTS
SUPPOSAL
SUPPOSALS
SUPPOSE
SUPPOSED
SUPPOSER
SUPPOSERS
SUPPOSES
SUPPOSING
SUPPRESS
SUPPURATE
SUPRA
SUPREMA
SUPREMACY
SUPREME
SUPREMELY
SUPREMER
SUPREMES
SUPREMEST
SUPREMITY
SUPREMO
SUPREMOS
SUPREMUM
SUPREMUMS
SUPS
SUQ
SUQS
SUR
SURA
SURAH
SURAHS
SURAL
SURAMIN
SURAMINS
SURANCE
SURANCES
SURAS
SURAT
SURATS
SURBAHAR
SURBAHARS
SURBASE
SURBASED
SURBASES
SURBATE
SURBATED
SURBATES
SURBATING
SURBED
SURBEDDED
SURBEDS
SURBET
SURCEASE
SURCEASED
SURCEASES
SURCHARGE
SURCINGLE
SURCOAT
SURCOATS
SURCULI
SURCULOSE
SURCULUS
SURD
SURDITIES
SURDITY
SURDS
SURE
SURED
SUREFIRE
SURELY
SURENESS
SURER
SURES
SUREST
SURETIED
SURETIES
SURETY
SURETYING
SURF
SURFABLE
SURFACE
SURFACED
SURFACER
SURFACERS
SURFACES
SURFACING
SURFBIRD
SURFBIRDS
SURFBOARD
SURFBOAT
SURFBOATS
SURFED
SURFEIT
SURFEITED
SURFEITER
SURFEITS
SURFER
SURFERS
SURFFISH
SURFICIAL
SURFIE
SURFIER
SURFIES
SURFIEST
SURFING
SURFINGS
SURFLIKE
SURFMAN
SURFMEN
SURFPERCH
SURFRIDE
SURFRIDER
SURFRIDES
SURFRODE
SURFS
SURFSIDE
SURFY
SURGE
SURGED
SURGEFUL
SURGELESS
SURGENT
SURGEON
SURGEONCY
SURGEONS
SURGER
SURGERIES
SURGERS
SURGERY
SURGES
SURGICAL
SURGIER
SURGIEST
SURGING
SURGINGS
SURGY
SURICATE
SURICATES
SURIMI
SURIMIS
SURING
SURLIER
SURLIEST
SURLILY
SURLINESS
SURLOIN
SURLOINS
SURLY
SURMASTER
SURMISAL
SURMISALS
SURMISE
SURMISED
SURMISER
SURMISERS
SURMISES
SURMISING
SURMOUNT
SURMOUNTS

S

SURMULLET
SURNAME
SURNAMED
SURNAMER
SURNAMERS
SURNAMES
SURNAMING
SURPASS
SURPASSED
SURPASSER
SURPASSES
SURPLICE
SURPLICED
SURPLICES
SURPLUS
SURPLUSED
SURPLUSES
SURPRINT
SURPRINTS
SURPRISAL
SURPRISE
SURPRISED
SURPRISER
SURPRISES
SURPRIZE
SURPRIZED
SURPRIZES
SURQUEDRY
SURQUEDY
SURRA
SURRAS
SURREAL
SURREALLY
SURREALS
SURREBUT
SURREBUTS
SURREINED
SURREJOIN
SURRENDER
SURRENDRY
SURREY
SURREYS
SURROGACY
SURROGATE
SURROUND
SURROUNDS
SURROYAL
SURROYALS
SURTAX
SURTAXED
SURTAXES
SURTAXING
SURTITLE
SURTITLES
SURTOUT
SURTOUTS
SURUCUCU
SURUCUCUS
SURVEIL
SURVEILED
SURVEILLE
SURVEILS
SURVEY
SURVEYAL
SURVEYALS
SURVEYED
SURVEYING
SURVEYOR
SURVEYORS
SURVEYS
SURVIEW
SURVIEWED
SURVIEWS
SURVIVAL
SURVIVALS
SURVIVE
SURVIVED
SURVIVER
SURVIVERS
SURVIVES
SURVIVING
SURVIVOR
SURVIVORS
SUS
SUSCEPTOR
SUSCITATE
SUSED
SUSES
SUSHI
SUSHIS
SUSING
SUSLIK
SUSLIKS
SUSPECT
SUSPECTED
SUSPECTER
SUSPECTS
SUSPENCE
SUSPEND
SUSPENDED
SUSPENDER
SUSPENDS
SUSPENS
SUSPENSE
SUSPENSER
SUSPENSES
SUSPENSOR
SUSPICION
SUSPIRE
SUSPIRED
SUSPIRES
SUSPIRING
SUSS
SUSSED
SUSSES
SUSSING
SUSTAIN
SUSTAINED
SUSTAINER
SUSTAINS
SUSTINENT
SUSU
SUSURRANT
SUSURRATE
SUSURROUS
SUSURRUS
SUSUS
SUTILE
SUTLER
SUTLERIES
SUTLERS
SUTLERY
SUTOR
SUTORIAL
SUTORIAN
SUTORS
SUTRA
SUTRAS
SUTTA
SUTTAS
SUTTEE
SUTTEEISM
SUTTEES
SUTTLE
SUTTLED
SUTTLES
SUTTLETIE
SUTTLING
SUTTLY
SUTURAL
SUTURALLY
SUTURE
SUTURED
SUTURES
SUTURING
SUZERAIN
SUZERAINS
SVARAJ
SVARAJES
SVASTIKA
SVASTIKAS
SVEDBERG
SVEDBERGS
SVELTE
SVELTELY
SVELTER
SVELTEST
SWAB
SWABBED
SWABBER
SWABBERS
SWABBIE
SWABBIES
SWABBING
SWABBY
SWABS
SWACHH
SWACK
SWACKED
SWACKING
SWACKS
SWAD
SWADDIE
SWADDIES
SWADDLE
SWADDLED
SWADDLER
SWADDLERS
SWADDLES
SWADDLING
SWADDY
SWADS
SWAG
SWAGE
SWAGED
SWAGER
SWAGERS
SWAGES
SWAGGED
SWAGGER
SWAGGERED
SWAGGERER
SWAGGERS
SWAGGIE
SWAGGIES
SWAGGING
SWAGING
SWAGMAN
SWAGMEN
SWAGS
SWAGSHOP
SWAGSHOPS
SWAGSMAN
SWAGSMEN
SWAIL
SWAILS
SWAIN
SWAINING
SWAININGS
SWAINISH
SWAINS
SWALE
SWALED
SWALES
SWALIER
SWALIEST
SWALING
SWALINGS
SWALLET
SWALLETS
SWALLIES
SWALLOW
SWALLOWED
SWALLOWER
SWALLOWS
SWALLY
SWALY
SWAM
SWAMI
SWAMIES

S

SWAMIS
SWAMP
SWAMPED
SWAMPER
SWAMPERS
SWAMPIER
SWAMPIEST
SWAMPING
SWAMPISH
SWAMPLAND
SWAMPLESS
SWAMPS
SWAMPY
SWAMY
SWAN
SWANG
SWANHERD
SWANHERDS
SWANK
SWANKED
SWANKER
SWANKERS
SWANKEST
SWANKEY
SWANKEYS
SWANKIE
SWANKIER
SWANKIES
SWANKIEST
SWANKILY
SWANKING
SWANKPOT
SWANKPOTS
SWANKS
SWANKY
SWANLIKE
SWANNED
SWANNERY
SWANNIE
SWANNIER
SWANNIES
SWANNIEST
SWANNING
SWANNINGS
SWANNY
SWANPAN
SWANPANS
SWANS
SWANSDOWN
SWANSKIN
SWANSKINS
SWANSONG
SWANSONGS
SWAP
SWAPFILE
SWAPFILES
SWAPPABLE
SWAPPED
SWAPPER
SWAPPERS
SWAPPING
SWAPPINGS
SWAPS
SWAPT
SWAPTION
SWAPTIONS
SWARAJ
SWARAJES
SWARAJISM
SWARAJIST
SWARD
SWARDED
SWARDIER
SWARDIEST
SWARDING
SWARDS
SWARDY
SWARE
SWARF
SWARFED
SWARFING
SWARFS
SWARM
SWARMED
SWARMER
SWARMERS
SWARMING
SWARMINGS
SWARMS
SWART
SWARTH
SWARTHIER
SWARTHILY
SWARTHS
SWARTHY
SWARTIER
SWARTIEST
SWARTNESS
SWARTY
SWARVE
SWARVED
SWARVES
SWARVING
SWASH
SWASHED
SWASHER
SWASHERS
SWASHES
SWASHIER
SWASHIEST
SWASHING
SWASHINGS
SWASHWORK
SWASHY
SWASTICA
SWASTICAS
SWASTIKA
SWASTIKAS
SWAT
SWATCH
SWATCHES
SWATH
SWATHABLE
SWATHE
SWATHED
SWATHER
SWATHERS
SWATHES
SWATHIER
SWATHIEST
SWATHING
SWATHINGS
SWATHS
SWATHY
SWATS
SWATTED
SWATTER
SWATTERED
SWATTERS
SWATTIER
SWATTIEST
SWATTING
SWATTINGS
SWATTY
SWAY
SWAYABLE
SWAYBACK
SWAYBACKS
SWAYED
SWAYER
SWAYERS
SWAYFUL
SWAYING
SWAYINGS
SWAYL
SWAYLED
SWAYLING
SWAYLINGS
SWAYLS
SWAYS
SWAZZLE
SWAZZLES
SWEAL
SWEALED
SWEALING
SWEALINGS
SWEALS
SWEAR
SWEARD
SWEARDS
SWEARER
SWEARERS
SWEARIER
SWEARIEST
SWEARING
SWEARINGS
SWEARS
SWEARWORD
SWEARY
SWEAT
SWEATBAND
SWEATBOX
SWEATED
SWEATER
SWEATERED
SWEATERS
SWEATIER
SWEATIEST
SWEATILY
SWEATING
SWEATINGS
SWEATLESS
SWEATS
SWEATSHOP
SWEATSUIT
SWEATY
SWEDE
SWEDES
SWEDGER
SWEDGERS
SWEE
SWEED
SWEEING
SWEEL
SWEELED
SWEELING
SWEELS
SWEENEY
SWEENEYS
SWEENIES
SWEENY
SWEEP
SWEEPBACK
SWEEPER
SWEEPERS
SWEEPIER
SWEEPIEST
SWEEPING
SWEEPINGS
SWEEPS
SWEEPY
SWEER
SWEERED
SWEERING
SWEERS
SWEERT
SWEES
SWEET
SWEETCORN
SWEETED
SWEETEN
SWEETENED
SWEETENER
SWEETENS
SWEETER
SWEETEST
SWEETFISH
SWEETIE
SWEETIES
SWEETING

SWEETINGS
SWEETISH
SWEETLIP
SWEETLIPS
SWEETLY
SWEETMAN
SWEETMEAL
SWEETMEAT
SWEETMEN
SWEETNESS
SWEETS
SWEETSHOP
SWEETSOP
SWEETSOPS
SWEETVELD
SWEETWOOD
SWEETY
SWEIR
SWEIRED
SWEIRER
SWEIREST
SWEIRING
SWEIRNESS
SWEIRS
SWEIRT
SWELCHIE
SWELCHIES
SWELL
SWELLDOM
SWELLDOMS
SWELLED
SWELLER
SWELLERS
SWELLEST
SWELLFISH
SWELLHEAD
SWELLING
SWELLINGS
SWELLISH
SWELLS
SWELT
SWELTED
SWELTER
SWELTERED
SWELTERS
SWELTING
SWELTRIER
SWELTRY
SWELTS
SWEPT
SWEPTBACK
SWEPTWING
SWERF
SWERFED
SWERFING
SWERFS
SWERVABLE
SWERVE
SWERVED
SWERVER
SWERVERS
SWERVES
SWERVING
SWERVINGS
SWEVEN
SWEVENS
SWEY
SWEYED
SWEYING
SWEYS
SWIDDEN
SWIDDENS
SWIES
SWIFT
SWIFTED
SWIFTER
SWIFTERS
SWIFTEST
SWIFTIE
SWIFTIES
SWIFTING
SWIFTLET
SWIFTLETS
SWIFTLY
SWIFTNESS
SWIFTS
SWIFTY
SWIG
SWIGGED
SWIGGER
SWIGGERS
SWIGGING
SWIGS
SWILE
SWILER
SWILERS
SWILES
SWILING
SWILINGS
SWILL
SWILLED
SWILLER
SWILLERS
SWILLING
SWILLINGS
SWILLS
SWIM
SWIMMABLE
SWIMMER
SWIMMERET
SWIMMERS
SWIMMIER
SWIMMIEST
SWIMMILY
SWIMMING
SWIMMINGS
SWIMMY
SWIMS
SWIMSUIT
SWIMSUITS
SWIMWEAR
SWIMWEARS
SWINDGE
SWINDGED
SWINDGES
SWINDGING
SWINDLE
SWINDLED
SWINDLER
SWINDLERS
SWINDLES
SWINDLING
SWINE
SWINEHERD
SWINEHOOD
SWINELIKE
SWINEPOX
SWINERIES
SWINERY
SWINES
SWING
SWINGARM
SWINGARMS
SWINGBEAT
SWINGBIN
SWINGBINS
SWINGBOAT
SWINGBY
SWINGBYS
SWINGE
SWINGED
SWINGEING
SWINGER
SWINGERS
SWINGES
SWINGIER
SWINGIEST
SWINGING
SWINGINGS
SWINGISM
SWINGISMS
SWINGLE
SWINGLED
SWINGLES
SWINGLING
SWINGMAN
SWINGMEN
SWINGS
SWINGTAIL
SWINGTREE
SWINGY
SWINISH
SWINISHLY
SWINK
SWINKED
SWINKER
SWINKERS
SWINKING
SWINKS
SWINNEY
SWINNEYS
SWIPE
SWIPED
SWIPER
SWIPERS
SWIPES
SWIPEY
SWIPIER
SWIPIEST
SWIPING
SWIPLE
SWIPLES
SWIPPLE
SWIPPLES
SWIRE
SWIRES
SWIRL
SWIRLED
SWIRLIER
SWIRLIEST
SWIRLING
SWIRLS
SWIRLY
SWISH
SWISHED
SWISHER
SWISHERS
SWISHES
SWISHEST
SWISHIER
SWISHIEST
SWISHING
SWISHINGS
SWISHY
SWISS
SWISSES
SWISSING
SWISSINGS
SWITCH
SWITCHED
SWITCHEL
SWITCHELS
SWITCHER
SWITCHERS
SWITCHES
SWITCHIER
SWITCHING
SWITCHMAN
SWITCHMEN
SWITCHY
SWITH
SWITHE
SWITHER
SWITHERED
SWITHERS
SWITHLY
SWITS
SWITSES
SWIVE
SWIVED

SWIVEL
SWIVELED
SWIVELING
SWIVELLED
SWIVELS
SWIVES
SWIVET
SWIVETS
SWIVING
SWIZ
SWIZZ
SWIZZED
SWIZZES
SWIZZING
SWIZZLE
SWIZZLED
SWIZZLER
SWIZZLERS
SWIZZLES
SWIZZLING
SWOB
SWOBBED
SWOBBER
SWOBBERS
SWOBBING
SWOBS
SWOFFER
SWOFFERS
SWOFFING
SWOFFINGS
SWOLE
SWOLER
SWOLEST
SWOLLEN
SWOLLENLY
SWOLN
SWOON
SWOONED
SWOONER
SWOONERS
SWOONIER
SWOONIEST
SWOONING
SWOONINGS
SWOONS
SWOONY
SWOOP
SWOOPED
SWOOPER
SWOOPERS
SWOOPIER
SWOOPIEST
SWOOPING
SWOOPS
SWOOPY
SWOOSH
SWOOSHED
SWOOSHES
SWOOSHING
SWOP
SWOPPABLE
SWOPPED
SWOPPER
SWOPPERS
SWOPPING
SWOPPINGS
SWOPS
SWOPT
SWORD
SWORDBILL
SWORDED
SWORDER
SWORDERS
SWORDFERN
SWORDFISH
SWORDING
SWORDLESS
SWORDLIKE
SWORDMAN
SWORDMEN
SWORDPLAY
SWORDS
SWORDSMAN
SWORDSMEN
SWORDTAIL
SWORE
SWORN
SWOT
SWOTS
SWOTTED
SWOTTER
SWOTTERS
SWOTTIER
SWOTTIEST
SWOTTING
SWOTTINGS
SWOTTY
SWOUN
SWOUND
SWOUNDED
SWOUNDING
SWOUNDS
SWOUNE
SWOUNED
SWOUNES
SWOUNING
SWOUNS
SWOWND
SWOWNDS
SWOWNE
SWOWNES
SWOZZLE
SWOZZLES
SWUM
SWUNG
SWY
SYBARITE
SYBARITES
SYBARITIC
SYBBE
SYBBES
SYBIL
SYBILS
SYBO
SYBOE
SYBOES
SYBOTIC
SYBOTISM
SYBOTISMS
SYBOW
SYBOWS
SYCAMINE
SYCAMINES
SYCAMORE
SYCAMORES
SYCE
SYCEE
SYCEES
SYCES
SYCOMORE
SYCOMORES
SYCON
SYCONIA
SYCONIUM
SYCONOID
SYCONS
SYCOPHANT
SYCOSES
SYCOSIS
SYE
SYED
SYEING
SYEN
SYENITE
SYENITES
SYENITIC
SYENS
SYES
SYKE
SYKER
SYKES
SYLI
SYLIS
SYLLABARY
SYLLABI
SYLLABIC
SYLLABICS
SYLLABIFY
SYLLABISE
SYLLABISM
SYLLABIZE
SYLLABLE
SYLLABLED
SYLLABLES
SYLLABUB
SYLLABUBS
SYLLABUS
SYLLEPSES
SYLLEPSIS
SYLLEPTIC
SYLLOGE
SYLLOGES
SYLLOGISE
SYLLOGISM
SYLLOGIST
SYLLOGIZE
SYLPH
SYLPHIC
SYLPHID
SYLPHIDE
SYLPHIDES
SYLPHIDS
SYLPHIER
SYLPHIEST
SYLPHINE
SYLPHISH
SYLPHLIKE
SYLPHS
SYLPHY
SYLVA
SYLVAE
SYLVAN
SYLVANER
SYLVANERS
SYLVANITE
SYLVANS
SYLVAS
SYLVATIC
SYLVIA
SYLVIAS
SYLVIINE
SYLVIN
SYLVINE
SYLVINES
SYLVINITE
SYLVINS
SYLVITE
SYLVITES
SYMAR
SYMARS
SYMBION
SYMBIONS
SYMBIONT
SYMBIONTS
SYMBIOSES
SYMBIOSIS
SYMBIOT
SYMBIOTE
SYMBIOTES
SYMBIOTIC
SYMBIOTS
SYMBOL
SYMBOLE
SYMBOLED
SYMBOLES
SYMBOLIC
SYMBOLICS
SYMBOLING
SYMBOLISE
SYMBOLISM

SYMBOLIST
SYMBOLIZE
SYMBOLLED
SYMBOLOGY
SYMBOLS
SYMITAR
SYMITARE
SYMITARES
SYMITARS
SYMMETRAL
SYMMETRIC
SYMMETRY
SYMPATHIN
SYMPATHY
SYMPATICO
SYMPATRIC
SYMPATRY
SYMPETALY
SYMPHILE
SYMPHILES
SYMPHILY
SYMPHONIC
SYMPHONY
SYMPHYSES
SYMPHYSIS
SYMPHYTIC
SYMPLAST
SYMPLASTS
SYMPLOCE
SYMPLOCES
SYMPODIA
SYMPODIAL
SYMPODIUM
SYMPOSIA
SYMPOSIAC
SYMPOSIAL
SYMPOSIUM
SYMPTOM
SYMPTOMS
SYMPTOSES
SYMPTOSIS
SYMPTOTIC
SYN
SYNAGOG
SYNAGOGAL
SYNAGOGS
SYNAGOGUE
SYNALEPHA
SYNANDRIA
SYNANGIA
SYNANGIUM
SYNANON
SYNANONS
SYNANTHIC
SYNANTHY
SYNAPHEA
SYNAPHEAS
SYNAPHEIA
SYNAPSE
SYNAPSED
SYNAPSES
SYNAPSID
SYNAPSIDS
SYNAPSING
SYNAPSIS
SYNAPTASE
SYNAPTE
SYNAPTES
SYNAPTIC
SYNARCHY
SYNASTRY
SYNAXARIA
SYNAXES
SYNAXIS
SYNBIOTIC
SYNC
SYNCARP
SYNCARPS
SYNCARPY
SYNCED
SYNCH
SYNCHED
SYNCHING
SYNCHRO
SYNCHRONY
SYNCHROS
SYNCHS
SYNCHYSES
SYNCHYSIS
SYNCING
SYNCLINAL
SYNCLINE
SYNCLINES
SYNCOM
SYNCOMS
SYNCOPAL
SYNCOPATE
SYNCOPE
SYNCOPES
SYNCOPIC
SYNCOPTIC
SYNCRETIC
SYNCS
SYNCYTIA
SYNCYTIAL
SYNCYTIUM
SYND
SYNDACTYL
SYNDED
SYNDESES
SYNDESIS
SYNDET
SYNDETIC
SYNDETON
SYNDETONS
SYNDETS
SYNDIC
SYNDICAL
SYNDICATE
SYNDICS
SYNDING
SYNDINGS
SYNDROME
SYNDROMES
SYNDROMIC
SYNDS
SYNE
SYNECHIA
SYNECHIAS
SYNECIOUS
SYNECTIC
SYNECTICS
SYNED
SYNEDRIA
SYNEDRIAL
SYNEDRION
SYNEDRIUM
SYNERESES
SYNERESIS
SYNERGIA
SYNERGIAS
SYNERGIC
SYNERGID
SYNERGIDS
SYNERGIES
SYNERGISE
SYNERGISM
SYNERGIST
SYNERGIZE
SYNERGY
SYNES
SYNESES
SYNESIS
SYNESISES
SYNFUEL
SYNFUELS
SYNGAMIC
SYNGAMIES
SYNGAMOUS
SYNGAMY
SYNGAS
SYNGASES
SYNGASSES
SYNGENEIC
SYNGENIC
SYNGRAPH
SYNGRAPHS
SYNING
SYNIZESES
SYNIZESIS
SYNKARYA
SYNKARYON
SYNOD
SYNODAL
SYNODALS
SYNODIC
SYNODICAL
SYNODS
SYNODSMAN
SYNODSMEN
SYNOECETE
SYNOECISE
SYNOECISM
SYNOECIZE
SYNOEKETE
SYNOICOUS
SYNONYM
SYNONYME
SYNONYMES
SYNONYMIC
SYNONYMS
SYNONYMY
SYNOPSES
SYNOPSIS
SYNOPSISE
SYNOPSIZE
SYNOPTIC
SYNOPTICS
SYNOPTIST
SYNOVIA
SYNOVIAL
SYNOVIAS
SYNOVITIC
SYNOVITIS
SYNROC
SYNROCS
SYNTACTIC
SYNTAGM
SYNTAGMA
SYNTAGMAS
SYNTAGMIC
SYNTAGMS
SYNTAN
SYNTANS
SYNTAX
SYNTAXES
SYNTECTIC
SYNTENIC
SYNTENIES
SYNTENY
SYNTEXIS
SYNTH
SYNTHASE
SYNTHASES
SYNTHESES
SYNTHESIS
SYNTHETIC
SYNTHON
SYNTHONS
SYNTHPOP
SYNTHPOPS
SYNTHRONI
SYNTHS
SYNTONE
SYNTONES
SYNTONIC
SYNTONIES
SYNTONIN
SYNTONINS
SYNTONISE

SYNTONIZE
SYNTONOUS
SYNTONY
SYNTYPE
SYNTYPES
SYNURA
SYNURAE
SYPE
SYPED
SYPES
SYPH
SYPHER
SYPHERED
SYPHERING
SYPHERS
SYPHILIS
SYPHILISE
SYPHILIZE
SYPHILOID
SYPHILOMA
SYPHON
SYPHONAGE
SYPHONAL
SYPHONED
SYPHONIC
SYPHONING
SYPHONS
SYPHS
SYPING
SYRAH
SYRAHS
SYREN
SYRENS
SYRETTE
SYRETTES
SYRINGA
SYRINGAS
SYRINGE
SYRINGEAL
SYRINGED
SYRINGES
SYRINGING
SYRINX
SYRINXES
SYRPHIAN
SYRPHIANS
SYRPHID
SYRPHIDS
SYRTES
SYRTIS
SYRUP
SYRUPED
SYRUPIER
SYRUPIEST
SYRUPING
SYRUPLIKE
SYRUPS
SYRUPY
SYSADMIN
SYSADMINS
SYSOP
SYSOPS
SYSSITIA
SYSSITIAS
SYSTALTIC
SYSTEM
SYSTEMED
SYSTEMIC
SYSTEMICS
SYSTEMISE
SYSTEMIZE
SYSTEMS
SYSTOLE
SYSTOLES
SYSTOLIC
SYSTYLE
SYSTYLES
SYTHE
SYTHES
SYVER
SYVERS
SYZYGAL
SYZYGETIC
SYZYGIAL
SYZYGIES
SYZYGY

T

TA
TAAL
TAALS
TAATA
TAATAS
TAB
TABANID
TABANIDS
TABARD
TABARDED
TABARDS
TABARET
TABARETS
TABASHEER
TABASHIR
TABASHIRS
TABBED
TABBIED
TABBIER
TABBIES
TABBIEST
TABBINET
TABBINETS
TABBING
TABBINGS
TABBIS
TABBISES
TABBOULEH
TABBOULI
TABBOULIS
TABBY
TABBYHOOD
TABBYING
TABEFIED
TABEFIES
TABEFY
TABEFYING
TABELLION
TABER
TABERD
TABERDAR
TABERDARS
TABERDS
TABERED
TABERING
TABERS
TABES
TABESCENT
TABETIC
TABETICS
TABI
TABID
TABINET
TABINETS
TABIS
TABLA
TABLAS
TABLATURE
TABLE
TABLEAU
TABLEAUS
TABLEAUX
TABLED
TABLEFUL
TABLEFULS
TABLELAND
TABLELESS
TABLEMAT
TABLEMATE
TABLEMATS
TABLES
TABLESFUL
TABLESIDE
TABLET
TABLETED
TABLETING
TABLETOP
TABLETOPS
TABLETS
TABLETTED
TABLEWARE
TABLEWISE
TABLIER
TABLIERS
TABLING
TABLINGS
TABLOID
TABLOIDS
TABLOIDY
TABOGGAN
TABOGGANS
TABOO
TABOOED
TABOOING
TABOOLEY
TABOOLEYS
TABOOS
TABOR
TABORED
TABORER
TABORERS
TABORET
TABORETS
TABORIN
TABORINE
TABORINES
TABORING
TABORINS
TABORS
TABOULEH
TABOULEHS
TABOULI
TABOULIS
TABOUR
TABOURED
TABOURER
TABOURERS
TABOURET
TABOURETS
TABOURIN
TABOURING
TABOURINS
TABOURS
TABRERE
TABRERES
TABRET
TABRETS
TABS
TABU
TABUED
TABUING
TABULA
TABULABLE
TABULAE
TABULAR
TABULARLY
TABULATE
TABULATED
TABULATES
TABULATOR
TABULI
TABULIS
TABUN
TABUNS
TABUS
TACAHOUT
TACAHOUTS
TACAMAHAC
TACAN
TACANS
TACE
TACES
TACET
TACH
TACHE
TACHES
TACHINA
TACHINID
TACHINIDS
TACHISM
TACHISME
TACHISMES
TACHISMS
TACHIST
TACHISTE
TACHISTES
TACHISTS
TACHO
TACHOGRAM
TACHOS
TACHS
TACHYLITE
TACHYLYTE
TACHYON
TACHYONIC
TACHYONS
TACHYPNEA
TACIT
TACITLY
TACITNESS
TACITURN
TACK
TACKBOARD
TACKED
TACKER
TACKERS
TACKET
TACKETIER
TACKETS
TACKETY
TACKEY
TACKIER
TACKIES
TACKIEST
TACKIFIED
TACKIFIER
TACKIFIES
TACKIFY
TACKILY
TACKINESS
TACKING
TACKINGS
TACKLE
TACKLED
TACKLER
TACKLERS
TACKLES
TACKLESS
TACKLING
TACKLINGS

T

TACKS
TACKSMAN
TACKSMEN
TACKY
TACMAHACK
TACNODE
TACNODES
TACO
TACONITE
TACONITES
TACOS
TACRINE
TACRINES
TACT
TACTFUL
TACTFULLY
TACTIC
TACTICAL
TACTICIAN
TACTICITY
TACTICS
TACTILE
TACTILELY
TACTILIST
TACTILITY
TACTION
TACTIONS
TACTISM
TACTISMS
TACTLESS
TACTS
TACTUAL
TACTUALLY
TAD
TADALAFIL
TADDIE
TADDIES
TADPOLE
TADPOLES
TADS
TAE
TAED
TAEDIUM
TAEDIUMS
TAEING
TAEKWONDO
TAEL
TAELS
TAENIA
TAENIAE
TAENIAS
TAENIASES
TAENIASIS
TAENIATE
TAENIOID
TAENITE
TAENITES
TAES
TAFFAREL
TAFFARELS
TAFFEREL
TAFFERELS
TAFFETA
TAFFETAS
TAFFETIER
TAFFETY
TAFFIA
TAFFIAS
TAFFIES
TAFFRAIL
TAFFRAILS
TAFFY
TAFIA
TAFIAS
TAG
TAGALONG
TAGALONGS
TAGAREEN
TAGAREENS
TAGBOARD
TAGBOARDS
TAGETES
TAGGANT
TAGGANTS
TAGGED
TAGGEE
TAGGEES
TAGGER
TAGGERS
TAGGIER
TAGGIEST
TAGGING
TAGGINGS
TAGGY
TAGHAIRM
TAGHAIRMS
TAGINE
TAGINES
TAGLESS
TAGLIKE
TAGLINE
TAGLINES
TAGLIONI
TAGLIONIS
TAGMA
TAGMATA
TAGMEME
TAGMEMES
TAGMEMIC
TAGMEMICS
TAGRAG
TAGRAGS
TAGS
TAGUAN
TAGUANS
TAHA
TAHAS
TAHINA
TAHINAS
TAHINI
TAHINIS
TAHR
TAHRS
TAHSIL
TAHSILDAR
TAHSILS
TAI
TAIAHA
TAIAHAS
TAIG
TAIGA
TAIGAS
TAIGLACH
TAIGLE
TAIGLED
TAIGLES
TAIGLING
TAIGS
TAIHOA
TAIHOAED
TAIHOAING
TAIHOAS
TAIKO
TAIKONAUT
TAIKOS
TAIL
TAILARD
TAILARDS
TAILBACK
TAILBACKS
TAILBOARD
TAILBONE
TAILBONES
TAILCOAT
TAILCOATS
TAILED
TAILENDER
TAILER
TAILERON
TAILERONS
TAILERS
TAILFAN
TAILFANS
TAILFIN
TAILFINS
TAILFLIES
TAILFLY
TAILGATE
TAILGATED
TAILGATER
TAILGATES
TAILHOOK
TAILHOOKS
TAILING
TAILINGS
TAILLAMP
TAILLAMPS
TAILLE
TAILLES
TAILLESS
TAILLEUR
TAILLEURS
TAILLIE
TAILLIES
TAILLIGHT
TAILLIKE
TAILOR
TAILORED
TAILORESS
TAILORING
TAILORS
TAILPIECE
TAILPIPE
TAILPIPED
TAILPIPES
TAILPLANE
TAILRACE
TAILRACES
TAILS
TAILSKID
TAILSKIDS
TAILSLIDE
TAILSPIN
TAILSPINS
TAILSPUN
TAILSTOCK
TAILWATER
TAILWHEEL
TAILWIND
TAILWINDS
TAILYE
TAILYES
TAILZIE
TAILZIES
TAIN
TAINS
TAINT
TAINTED
TAINTING
TAINTLESS
TAINTS
TAINTURE
TAINTURES
TAIPAN
TAIPANS
TAIRA
TAIRAS
TAIS
TAISCH
TAISCHES
TAISH
TAISHES
TAIT
TAITS
TAIVER
TAIVERED
TAIVERING
TAIVERS
TAIVERT
TAJ

TAJES
TAJINE
TAJINES
TAK
TAKA
TAKABLE
TAKAHE
TAKAHES
TAKAMAKA
TAKAMAKAS
TAKAS
TAKE
TAKEABLE
TAKEAWAY
TAKEAWAYS
TAKEDOWN
TAKEDOWNS
TAKEN
TAKEOFF
TAKEOFFS
TAKEOUT
TAKEOUTS
TAKEOVER
TAKEOVERS
TAKER
TAKERS
TAKES
TAKEUP
TAKEUPS
TAKHI
TAKHIS
TAKI
TAKIER
TAKIEST
TAKIN
TAKING
TAKINGLY
TAKINGS
TAKINS
TAKIS
TAKKIES
TAKKY
TAKS
TAKY
TALA
TALAK
TALAKS
TALANT
TALANTS
TALAPOIN
TALAPOINS
TALAQ
TALAQS
TALAR
TALARIA
TALARS
TALAS
TALAUNT
TALAUNTS
TALAYOT
TALAYOTS
TALBOT
TALBOTS
TALBOTYPE
TALC
TALCED
TALCIER
TALCIEST
TALCING
TALCKED
TALCKIER
TALCKIEST
TALCKING
TALCKY
TALCOSE
TALCOUS
TALCS
TALCUM
TALCUMED
TALCUMING
TALCUMS
TALCY
TALE
TALEA
TALEAE
TALEFUL
TALEGALLA
TALEGGIO
TALEGGIOS
TALENT
TALENTED
TALENTS
TALER
TALERS
TALES
TALESMAN
TALESMEN
TALEYSIM
TALI
TALIGRADE
TALION
TALIONIC
TALIONS
TALIPAT
TALIPATS
TALIPED
TALIPEDS
TALIPES
TALIPOT
TALIPOTS
TALISMAN
TALISMANS
TALK
TALKABLE
TALKATHON
TALKATIVE
TALKBACK
TALKBACKS
TALKBOX
TALKBOXES
TALKED
TALKER
TALKERS
TALKFEST
TALKFESTS
TALKIE
TALKIER
TALKIES
TALKIEST
TALKINESS
TALKING
TALKINGS
TALKS
TALKTIME
TALKTIMES
TALKY
TALL
TALLAGE
TALLAGED
TALLAGES
TALLAGING
TALLAISIM
TALLAT
TALLATS
TALLBOY
TALLBOYS
TALLENT
TALLENTS
TALLER
TALLEST
TALLET
TALLETS
TALLGRASS
TALLIABLE
TALLIATE
TALLIATED
TALLIATES
TALLIED
TALLIER
TALLIERS
TALLIES
TALLIS
TALLISES
TALLISH
TALLISIM
TALLIT
TALLITES
TALLITH
TALLITHES
TALLITHIM
TALLITHS
TALLITIM
TALLITOT
TALLITOTH
TALLITS
TALLNESS
TALLOL
TALLOLS
TALLOT
TALLOTS
TALLOW
TALLOWED
TALLOWIER
TALLOWING
TALLOWISH
TALLOWS
TALLOWY
TALLS
TALLY
TALLYHO
TALLYHOED
TALLYHOES
TALLYHOS
TALLYING
TALLYMAN
TALLYMEN
TALLYSHOP
TALMA
TALMAS
TALMUD
TALMUDIC
TALMUDISM
TALMUDS
TALON
TALONED
TALONS
TALOOKA
TALOOKAS
TALPA
TALPAE
TALPAS
TALUK
TALUKA
TALUKAS
TALUKDAR
TALUKDARS
TALUKS
TALUS
TALUSES
TALWEG
TALWEGS
TAM
TAMABLE
TAMAL
TAMALE
TAMALES
TAMALS
TAMANDU
TAMANDUA
TAMANDUAS
TAMANDUS
TAMANOIR
TAMANOIRS
TAMANU
TAMANUS
TAMARA
TAMARACK
TAMARACKS
TAMARAO
TAMARAOS

T

TAMARAS
TAMARAU
TAMARAUS
TAMARI
TAMARILLO
TAMARIN
TAMARIND
TAMARINDS
TAMARINS
TAMARIS
TAMARISK
TAMARISKS
TAMASHA
TAMASHAS
TAMBAC
TAMBACS
TAMBAK
TAMBAKS
TAMBALA
TAMBALAS
TAMBER
TAMBERS
TAMBOUR
TAMBOURA
TAMBOURAS
TAMBOURED
TAMBOURER
TAMBOURIN
TAMBOURS
TAMBUR
TAMBURA
TAMBURAS
TAMBURIN
TAMBURINS
TAMBURS
TAME
TAMEABLE
TAMED
TAMEIN
TAMEINS
TAMELESS
TAMELY
TAMENESS
TAMER
TAMERS
TAMES
TAMEST
TAMIN
TAMINE
TAMINES
TAMING
TAMINGS
TAMINS
TAMIS
TAMISE
TAMISES
TAMMAR
TAMMARS
TAMMIE
TAMMIED
TAMMIES
TAMMY
TAMMYING
TAMOXIFEN
TAMP
TAMPALA
TAMPALAS
TAMPAN
TAMPANS
TAMPED
TAMPER
TAMPERED
TAMPERER
TAMPERERS
TAMPERING
TAMPERS
TAMPING
TAMPINGS
TAMPION
TAMPIONS
TAMPON
TAMPONADE
TAMPONAGE
TAMPONED
TAMPONING
TAMPONS
TAMPS
TAMS
TAMWORTH
TAMWORTHS
TAN
TANA
TANADAR
TANADARS
TANAGER
TANAGERS
TANAGRA
TANAGRAS
TANAGRINE
TANAISTE
TANAISTES
TANALISED
TANALIZED
TANAS
TANBARK
TANBARKS
TANDEM
TANDEMS
TANDOOR
TANDOORI
TANDOORIS
TANDOORS
TANE
TANG
TANGA
TANGAS
TANGED
TANGELO
TANGELOS
TANGENCE
TANGENCES
TANGENCY
TANGENT
TANGENTAL
TANGENTS
TANGERINE
TANGHIN
TANGHININ
TANGHINS
TANGI
TANGIBLE
TANGIBLES
TANGIBLY
TANGIE
TANGIER
TANGIES
TANGIEST
TANGINESS
TANGING
TANGIS
TANGLE
TANGLED
TANGLER
TANGLERS
TANGLES
TANGLIER
TANGLIEST
TANGLING
TANGLINGS
TANGLY
TANGO
TANGOED
TANGOES
TANGOING
TANGOIST
TANGOISTS
TANGOLIKE
TANGOS
TANGRAM
TANGRAMS
TANGS
TANGUN
TANGUNS
TANGY
TANH
TANHS
TANIST
TANISTRY
TANISTS
TANIWHA
TANIWHAS
TANK
TANKA
TANKAGE
TANKAGES
TANKARD
TANKARDS
TANKAS
TANKED
TANKER
TANKERED
TANKERING
TANKERS
TANKFUL
TANKFULS
TANKIA
TANKIAS
TANKIES
TANKING
TANKINGS
TANKINI
TANKINIS
TANKLESS
TANKLIKE
TANKS
TANKSHIP
TANKSHIPS
TANKY
TANLING
TANLINGS
TANNA
TANNABLE
TANNAGE
TANNAGES
TANNAH
TANNAHS
TANNAS
TANNATE
TANNATES
TANNED
TANNER
TANNERIES
TANNERS
TANNERY
TANNEST
TANNIC
TANNIE
TANNIES
TANNIN
TANNING
TANNINGS
TANNINS
TANNISH
TANNOY
TANNOYED
TANNOYING
TANNOYS
TANOREXIC
TANREC
TANRECS
TANS
TANSIES
TANSY
TANTALATE
TANTALIC
TANTALISE
TANTALISM
TANTALITE
TANTALIZE
TANTALOUS

TANTALUM
TANTALUMS
TANTALUS
TANTARA
TANTARARA
TANTARAS
TANTI
TANTIES
TANTIVIES
TANTIVY
TANTO
TANTONIES
TANTONY
TANTOS
TANTRA
TANTRAS
TANTRIC
TANTRISM
TANTRISMS
TANTRIST
TANTRISTS
TANTRUM
TANTRUMS
TANTY
TANUKI
TANUKIS
TANYARD
TANYARDS
TANZANITE
TAO
TAONGA
TAONGAS
TAOS
TAP
TAPA
TAPACOLO
TAPACOLOS
TAPACULO
TAPACULOS
TAPADERA
TAPADERAS
TAPADERO
TAPADEROS
TAPALO
TAPALOS
TAPAS
TAPE
TAPEABLE
TAPED
TAPELESS
TAPELIKE
TAPELINE
TAPELINES
TAPEN
TAPENADE
TAPENADES
TAPER
TAPERED
TAPERER
TAPERERS
TAPERING
TAPERINGS
TAPERNESS
TAPERS
TAPERWISE
TAPES
TAPESTRY
TAPET
TAPETA
TAPETAL
TAPETED
TAPETI
TAPETING
TAPETIS
TAPETS
TAPETUM
TAPETUMS
TAPEWORM
TAPEWORMS
TAPHOLE
TAPHOLES
TAPHONOMY
TAPHOUSE
TAPHOUSES
TAPING
TAPINGS
TAPIOCA
TAPIOCAS
TAPIR
TAPIROID
TAPIROIDS
TAPIRS
TAPIS
TAPISES
TAPIST
TAPISTS
TAPLASH
TAPLASHES
TAPLESS
TAPPA
TAPPABLE
TAPPAS
TAPPED
TAPPER
TAPPERS
TAPPET
TAPPETS
TAPPICE
TAPPICED
TAPPICES
TAPPICING
TAPPING
TAPPINGS
TAPPIT
TAPROOM
TAPROOMS
TAPROOT
TAPROOTED
TAPROOTS
TAPS
TAPSMAN
TAPSMEN
TAPSTER
TAPSTERS
TAPSTRESS
TAPSTRIES
TAPSTRY
TAPU
TAPUED
TAPUING
TAPUS
TAQUERIA
TAQUERIAS
TAR
TARA
TARABISH
TARAIRE
TARAIRES
TARAKIHI
TARAKIHIS
TARAMA
TARAMAS
TARAMEA
TARAMEAS
TARAND
TARANDS
TARANTARA
TARANTAS
TARANTASS
TARANTISM
TARANTIST
TARANTULA
TARAS
TARAXACUM
TARBOGGIN
TARBOOSH
TARBOUCHE
TARBOUSH
TARBOY
TARBOYS
TARBUSH
TARBUSHES
TARCEL
TARCELS
TARDIED
TARDIER
TARDIES
TARDIEST
TARDILY
TARDINESS
TARDIVE
TARDO
TARDY
TARDYING
TARDYON
TARDYONS
TARE
TARED
TARES
TARGA
TARGAS
TARGE
TARGED
TARGES
TARGET
TARGETED
TARGETEER
TARGETING
TARGETS
TARGING
TARIFF
TARIFFED
TARIFFING
TARIFFS
TARING
TARINGS
TARLATAN
TARLATANS
TARLETAN
TARLETANS
TARMAC
TARMACKED
TARMACS
TARN
TARNAL
TARNALLY
TARNATION
TARNISH
TARNISHED
TARNISHER
TARNISHES
TARNS
TARO
TAROC
TAROCS
TAROK
TAROKS
TAROS
TAROT
TAROTS
TARP
TARPAN
TARPANS
TARPAPER
TARPAPERS
TARPAULIN
TARPON
TARPONS
TARPS
TARRAGON
TARRAGONS
TARRAS
TARRASES
TARRE
TARRED
TARRES
TARRIANCE
TARRIED
TARRIER
TARRIERS

T

TARRIES
TARRIEST
TARRINESS
TARRING
TARRINGS
TARROCK
TARROCKS
TARROW
TARROWED
TARROWING
TARROWS
TARRY
TARRYING
TARS
TARSAL
TARSALGIA
TARSALS
TARSEAL
TARSEALS
TARSEL
TARSELS
TARSI
TARSIA
TARSIAS
TARSIER
TARSIERS
TARSIOID
TARSIOIDS
TARSIPED
TARSIPEDS
TARSUS
TART
TARTAN
TARTANA
TARTANAS
TARTANE
TARTANED
TARTANES
TARTANRY
TARTANS
TARTAR
TARTARE
TARTARES
TARTARIC
TARTARISE
TARTARIZE
TARTARLY
TARTAROUS
TARTARS
TARTED
TARTER
TARTEST
TARTIER
TARTIEST
TARTILY
TARTINE
TARTINES
TARTINESS
TARTING
TARTISH
TARTISHLY
TARTLET
TARTLETS
TARTLY
TARTNESS
TARTRATE
TARTRATED
TARTRATES
TARTS
TARTUFE
TARTUFES
TARTUFFE
TARTUFFES
TARTUFI
TARTUFO
TARTUFOS
TARTY
TARWEED
TARWEEDS
TARWHINE
TARWHINES
TARZAN
TARZANS
TAS
TASAR
TASARS
TASBIH
TASBIHS
TASE
TASED
TASER
TASERED
TASERING
TASERS
TASES
TASH
TASHED
TASHES
TASHING
TASIMETER
TASIMETRY
TASING
TASK
TASKBAR
TASKBARS
TASKED
TASKER
TASKERS
TASKING
TASKINGS
TASKLESS
TASKS
TASKWORK
TASKWORKS
TASLET
TASLETS
TASS
TASSA
TASSAS
TASSE
TASSEL
TASSELED
TASSELIER
TASSELING
TASSELL
TASSELLED
TASSELLS
TASSELLY
TASSELS
TASSELY
TASSES
TASSET
TASSETS
TASSIE
TASSIES
TASSO
TASSOS
TASSWAGE
TASTABLE
TASTE
TASTEABLE
TASTED
TASTEFUL
TASTELESS
TASTER
TASTERS
TASTES
TASTEVIN
TASTEVINS
TASTIER
TASTIEST
TASTILY
TASTINESS
TASTING
TASTINGS
TASTY
TAT
TATAHASH
TATAMI
TATAMIS
TATAR
TATARS
TATE
TATER
TATERS
TATES
TATH
TATHATA
TATHATAS
TATHED
TATHING
TATHS
TATIE
TATIES
TATLER
TATLERS
TATOU
TATOUAY
TATOUAYS
TATOUS
TATS
TATSOI
TATSOIS
TATT
TATTED
TATTER
TATTERED
TATTERIER
TATTERING
TATTERS
TATTERY
TATTIE
TATTIER
TATTIES
TATTIEST
TATTILY
TATTINESS
TATTING
TATTINGS
TATTLE
TATTLED
TATTLER
TATTLERS
TATTLES
TATTLING
TATTLINGS
TATTOO
TATTOOED
TATTOOER
TATTOOERS
TATTOOING
TATTOOIST
TATTOOS
TATTOW
TATTOWED
TATTOWING
TATTOWS
TATTS
TATTY
TATU
TATUED
TATUING
TATUS
TAU
TAUBE
TAUBES
TAUGHT
TAUHINU
TAUHINUS
TAUHOU
TAUHOUS
TAUIWI
TAUIWIS
TAULD
TAUNT
TAUNTED
TAUNTER
TAUNTERS
TAUNTING
TAUNTINGS

TAUNTS
TAUON
TAUONS
TAUPATA
TAUPATAS
TAUPE
TAUPES
TAUPIE
TAUPIES
TAUREAN
TAURIC
TAURIFORM
TAURINE
TAURINES
TAUS
TAUT
TAUTAUG
TAUTAUGS
TAUTED
TAUTEN
TAUTENED
TAUTENING
TAUTENS
TAUTER
TAUTEST
TAUTING
TAUTIT
TAUTLY
TAUTNESS
TAUTOG
TAUTOGS
TAUTOLOGY
TAUTOMER
TAUTOMERS
TAUTONYM
TAUTONYMS
TAUTONYMY
TAUTS
TAV
TAVA
TAVAH
TAVAHS
TAVAS
TAVER
TAVERED
TAVERING
TAVERN
TAVERNA
TAVERNAS
TAVERNER
TAVERNERS
TAVERNS
TAVERS
TAVERT
TAVS
TAW
TAWA
TAWAI
TAWAIS
TAWAS
TAWDRIER
TAWDRIES
TAWDRIEST
TAWDRILY
TAWDRY
TAWED
TAWER
TAWERIES
TAWERS
TAWERY
TAWHAI
TAWHAIS
TAWHIRI
TAWHIRIS
TAWIE
TAWIER
TAWIEST
TAWING
TAWINGS
TAWNEY
TAWNEYS
TAWNIER
TAWNIES
TAWNIEST
TAWNILY
TAWNINESS
TAWNY
TAWPIE
TAWPIES
TAWS
TAWSE
TAWSED
TAWSES
TAWSING
TAWT
TAWTED
TAWTIE
TAWTIER
TAWTIEST
TAWTING
TAWTS
TAX
TAXA
TAXABLE
TAXABLES
TAXABLY
TAXACEOUS
TAXAMETER
TAXATION
TAXATIONS
TAXATIVE
TAXED
TAXEME
TAXEMES
TAXEMIC
TAXER
TAXERS
TAXES
TAXI
TAXIARCH
TAXIARCHS
TAXICAB
TAXICABS
TAXIDERMY
TAXIED
TAXIES
TAXIING
TAXIMAN
TAXIMEN
TAXIMETER
TAXING
TAXINGLY
TAXINGS
TAXIPLANE
TAXIS
TAXISES
TAXITE
TAXITES
TAXITIC
TAXIWAY
TAXIWAYS
TAXLESS
TAXMAN
TAXMEN
TAXOL
TAXOLS
TAXON
TAXONOMER
TAXONOMIC
TAXONOMY
TAXONS
TAXOR
TAXORS
TAXPAID
TAXPAYER
TAXPAYERS
TAXPAYING
TAXUS
TAXWISE
TAXYING
TAY
TAYASSUID
TAYBERRY
TAYRA
TAYRAS
TAYS
TAZZA
TAZZAS
TAZZE
TCHICK
TCHICKED
TCHICKING
TCHICKS
TCHOTCHKE
TE
TEA
TEABAG
TEABAGS
TEABERRY
TEABOARD
TEABOARDS
TEABOWL
TEABOWLS
TEABOX
TEABOXES
TEABREAD
TEABREADS
TEACAKE
TEACAKES
TEACART
TEACARTS
TEACH
TEACHABLE
TEACHABLY
TEACHER
TEACHERLY
TEACHERS
TEACHES
TEACHIE
TEACHING
TEACHINGS
TEACHLESS
TEACUP
TEACUPFUL
TEACUPS
TEAD
TEADE
TEADES
TEADS
TEAED
TEAGLE
TEAGLED
TEAGLES
TEAGLING
TEAHOUSE
TEAHOUSES
TEAING
TEAK
TEAKETTLE
TEAKS
TEAKWOOD
TEAKWOODS
TEAL
TEALIGHT
TEALIGHTS
TEALIKE
TEALS
TEAM
TEAMAKER
TEAMAKERS
TEAMED
TEAMER
TEAMERS
TEAMING
TEAMINGS
TEAMMATE
TEAMMATES
TEAMS
TEAMSTER
TEAMSTERS

T

TEAMWISE
TEAMWORK
TEAMWORKS
TEAPOT
TEAPOTS
TEAPOY
TEAPOYS
TEAR
TEARABLE
TEARAWAY
TEARAWAYS
TEARDOWN
TEARDOWNS
TEARDROP
TEARDROPS
TEARED
TEARER
TEARERS
TEARFUL
TEARFULLY
TEARGAS
TEARGASES
TEARIER
TEARIEST
TEARILY
TEARINESS
TEARING
TEARLESS
TEARLIKE
TEAROOM
TEAROOMS
TEARS
TEARSHEET
TEARSTAIN
TEARSTRIP
TEARY
TEAS
TEASABLE
TEASE
TEASED
TEASEL
TEASELED
TEASELER
TEASELERS
TEASELING
TEASELLED
TEASELLER
TEASELS
TEASER
TEASERS
TEASES
TEASHOP
TEASHOPS
TEASING
TEASINGLY
TEASINGS
TEASPOON
TEASPOONS
TEAT
TEATASTER
TEATED
TEATIME
TEATIMES
TEATS
TEAWARE
TEAWARES
TEAZE
TEAZED
TEAZEL
TEAZELED
TEAZELING
TEAZELLED
TEAZELS
TEAZES
TEAZING
TEAZLE
TEAZLED
TEAZLES
TEAZLING
TEBBAD
TEBBADS
TEBIBYTE
TEBIBYTES
TEC
TECH
TECHED
TECHIE
TECHIER
TECHIES
TECHIEST
TECHILY
TECHINESS
TECHNIC
TECHNICAL
TECHNICS
TECHNIKON
TECHNIQUE
TECHNO
TECHNOID
TECHNOIDS
TECHNOPOP
TECHNOS
TECHS
TECHY
TECKEL
TECKELS
TECS
TECTA
TECTAL
TECTIFORM
TECTITE
TECTITES
TECTONIC
TECTONICS
TECTONISM
TECTORIAL
TECTRICES
TECTRIX
TECTUM
TECTUMS
TED
TEDDED
TEDDER
TEDDERED
TEDDERING
TEDDERS
TEDDIE
TEDDIES
TEDDING
TEDDY
TEDIER
TEDIEST
TEDIOSITY
TEDIOUS
TEDIOUSLY
TEDISOME
TEDIUM
TEDIUMS
TEDS
TEDY
TEE
TEED
TEEING
TEEK
TEEL
TEELS
TEEM
TEEMED
TEEMER
TEEMERS
TEEMFUL
TEEMING
TEEMINGLY
TEEMLESS
TEEMS
TEEN
TEENAGE
TEENAGED
TEENAGER
TEENAGERS
TEENAGES
TEEND
TEENDED
TEENDING
TEENDOM
TEENDOMS
TEENDS
TEENE
TEENED
TEENER
TEENERS
TEENES
TEENFUL
TEENIER
TEENIEST
TEENING
TEENS
TEENSIER
TEENSIEST
TEENSY
TEENTIER
TEENTIEST
TEENTSIER
TEENTSY
TEENTY
TEENY
TEENYBOP
TEEPEE
TEEPEES
TEER
TEERED
TEERING
TEERS
TEES
TEETER
TEETERED
TEETERING
TEETERS
TEETH
TEETHE
TEETHED
TEETHER
TEETHERS
TEETHES
TEETHING
TEETHINGS
TEETHLESS
TEETOTAL
TEETOTALS
TEETOTUM
TEETOTUMS
TEEVEE
TEEVEES
TEF
TEFF
TEFFS
TEFILLAH
TEFILLIN
TEFLON
TEFLONS
TEFS
TEG
TEGG
TEGGS
TEGMEN
TEGMENTA
TEGMENTAL
TEGMENTUM
TEGMINA
TEGMINAL
TEGS
TEGU
TEGUA
TEGUAS
TEGUEXIN
TEGUEXINS
TEGULA
TEGULAE
TEGULAR
TEGULARLY

TEGULATED
TEGUMEN
TEGUMENT
TEGUMENTS
TEGUMINA
TEGUS
TEHR
TEHRS
TEHSIL
TEHSILDAR
TEHSILS
TEIGLACH
TEIID
TEIIDS
TEIL
TEILS
TEIN
TEIND
TEINDED
TEINDING
TEINDS
TEINS
TEKKIE
TEKKIES
TEKNONYMY
TEKTITE
TEKTITES
TEKTITIC
TEL
TELA
TELAE
TELAMON
TELAMONES
TELAMONS
TELARY
TELCO
TELCOS
TELD
TELE
TELECAST
TELECASTS
TELECHIR
TELECHIRS
TELECINE
TELECINES
TELECOM
TELECOMM
TELECOMMS
TELECOMS
TELECON
TELECONS
TELECOPY
TELEDU
TELEDUS
TELEFAX
TELEFAXED
TELEFAXES
TELEFILM
TELEFILMS
TELEGA
TELEGAS
TELEGENIC
TELEGONIC
TELEGONY
TELEGRAM
TELEGRAMS
TELEGRAPH
TELEMAN
TELEMARK
TELEMARKS
TELEMATIC
TELEMEN
TELEMETER
TELEMETRY
TELEOLOGY
TELEONOMY
TELEOSAUR
TELEOST
TELEOSTS
TELEPATH
TELEPATHS
TELEPATHY
TELEPHEME
TELEPHONE
TELEPHONY
TELEPHOTO
TELEPIC
TELEPICS
TELEPLAY
TELEPLAYS
TELEPOINT
TELEPORT
TELEPORTS
TELEPRINT
TELERAN
TELERANS
TELERGIC
TELERGIES
TELERGY
TELEROBOT
TELES
TELESALE
TELESALES
TELESCOPE
TELESCOPY
TELESEME
TELESEMES
TELESES
TELESHOP
TELESHOPS
TELESIS
TELESM
TELESMS
TELESTIC
TELESTICH
TELESTICS
TELETEX
TELETEXES
TELETEXT
TELETEXTS
TELETHON
TELETHONS
TELETRON
TELETRONS
TELETYPE
TELETYPED
TELETYPES
TELEVIEW
TELEVIEWS
TELEVISE
TELEVISED
TELEVISER
TELEVISES
TELEVISOR
TELEWORK
TELEWORKS
TELEX
TELEXED
TELEXES
TELEXING
TELFER
TELFERAGE
TELFERED
TELFERIC
TELFERING
TELFERS
TELFORD
TELFORDS
TELIA
TELIAL
TELIC
TELICALLY
TELICITY
TELIUM
TELL
TELLABLE
TELLAR
TELLARED
TELLARING
TELLARS
TELLEN
TELLENS
TELLER
TELLERED
TELLERING
TELLERS
TELLIES
TELLIN
TELLING
TELLINGLY
TELLINGS
TELLINOID
TELLINS
TELLS
TELLTALE
TELLTALES
TELLURAL
TELLURATE
TELLURIAN
TELLURIC
TELLURIDE
TELLURION
TELLURISE
TELLURITE
TELLURIUM
TELLURIZE
TELLUROUS
TELLUS
TELLUSES
TELLY
TELLYS
TELNET
TELNETED
TELNETING
TELNETS
TELNETTED
TELOGEN
TELOGENS
TELOI
TELOME
TELOMERE
TELOMERES
TELOMES
TELOMIC
TELOPHASE
TELOS
TELOTAXES
TELOTAXIS
TELPHER
TELPHERED
TELPHERIC
TELPHERS
TELS
TELSON
TELSONIC
TELSONS
TELT
TEMAZEPAM
TEMBLOR
TEMBLORES
TEMBLORS
TEME
TEMED
TEMENE
TEMENOS
TEMERITY
TEMEROUS
TEMES
TEMP
TEMPED
TEMPEH
TEMPEHS
TEMPER
TEMPERA
TEMPERAS
TEMPERATE
TEMPERED
TEMPERER
TEMPERERS
TEMPERING

TEMPERS
TEMPEST
TEMPESTED
TEMPESTS
TEMPI
TEMPING
TEMPINGS
TEMPLAR
TEMPLARS
TEMPLATE
TEMPLATES
TEMPLE
TEMPLED
TEMPLES
TEMPLET
TEMPLETS
TEMPO
TEMPORAL
TEMPORALS
TEMPORARY
TEMPORE
TEMPORISE
TEMPORIZE
TEMPOS
TEMPS
TEMPT
TEMPTABLE
TEMPTED
TEMPTER
TEMPTERS
TEMPTING
TEMPTINGS
TEMPTRESS
TEMPTS
TEMPURA
TEMPURAS
TEMS
TEMSE
TEMSED
TEMSES
TEMSING
TEMULENCE
TEMULENCY
TEMULENT
TEN
TENABLE
TENABLY
TENACE
TENACES
TENACIOUS
TENACITY
TENACULA
TENACULUM
TENAIL
TENAILLE
TENAILLES
TENAILLON
TENAILS
TENANCIES
TENANCY
TENANT
TENANTED
TENANTING
TENANTRY
TENANTS
TENCH
TENCHES
TEND
TENDANCE
TENDANCES
TENDED
TENDENCE
TENDENCES
TENDENCY
TENDENZ
TENDENZEN
TENDER
TENDERED
TENDERER
TENDERERS
TENDEREST
TENDERING
TENDERISE
TENDERIZE
TENDERLY
TENDERS
TENDING
TENDINOUS
TENDON
TENDONS
TENDRE
TENDRES
TENDRESSE
TENDRIL
TENDRILED
TENDRILLY
TENDRILS
TENDRON
TENDRONS
TENDS
TENDU
TENDUS
TENE
TENEBRAE
TENEBRIO
TENEBRIOS
TENEBRISM
TENEBRIST
TENEBRITY
TENEBROSE
TENEBROUS
TENEMENT
TENEMENTS
TENENDA
TENENDUM
TENENDUMS
TENES
TENESI
TENESMIC
TENESMUS
TENET
TENETS
TENFOLD
TENFOLDS
TENGE
TENGES
TENIA
TENIACIDE
TENIAE
TENIAFUGE
TENIAS
TENIASES
TENIASIS
TENIOID
TENNE
TENNER
TENNERS
TENNES
TENNESI
TENNIES
TENNIS
TENNISES
TENNIST
TENNISTS
TENNO
TENNOS
TENNY
TENON
TENONED
TENONER
TENONERS
TENONING
TENONS
TENOR
TENORINI
TENORINO
TENORIST
TENORISTS
TENORITE
TENORITES
TENORLESS
TENORMAN
TENORMEN
TENOROON
TENOROONS
TENORS
TENOTOMY
TENOUR
TENOURS
TENPENCE
TENPENCES
TENPENNY
TENPIN
TENPINNER
TENPINS
TENREC
TENRECS
TENS
TENSE
TENSED
TENSELESS
TENSELY
TENSENESS
TENSER
TENSES
TENSEST
TENSIBLE
TENSIBLY
TENSILE
TENSILELY
TENSILITY
TENSING
TENSION
TENSIONAL
TENSIONED
TENSIONER
TENSIONS
TENSITIES
TENSITY
TENSIVE
TENSON
TENSONS
TENSOR
TENSORIAL
TENSORS
TENT
TENTACLE
TENTACLED
TENTACLES
TENTACULA
TENTAGE
TENTAGES
TENTATION
TENTATIVE
TENTED
TENTER
TENTERED
TENTERING
TENTERS
TENTFUL
TENTFULS
TENTH
TENTHLY
TENTHS
TENTIE
TENTIER
TENTIEST
TENTIGO
TENTIGOS
TENTING
TENTINGS
TENTLESS
TENTLIKE
TENTMAKER
TENTORIA
TENTORIAL
TENTORIUM
TENTPOLE
TENTPOLES
TENTS

T

TENTWISE
TENTY
TENUE
TENUES
TENUIOUS
TENUIS
TENUITIES
TENUITY
TENUOUS
TENUOUSLY
TENURABLE
TENURE
TENURED
TENURES
TENURIAL
TENURING
TENUTI
TENUTO
TENUTOS
TENZON
TENZONS
TEOCALLI
TEOCALLIS
TEOPAN
TEOPANS
TEOSINTE
TEOSINTES
TEPA
TEPACHE
TEPACHES
TEPAL
TEPALS
TEPAS
TEPEE
TEPEES
TEPEFIED
TEPEFIES
TEPEFY
TEPEFYING
TEPHIGRAM
TEPHILLAH
TEPHILLIN
TEPHRA
TEPHRAS
TEPHRITE
TEPHRITES
TEPHRITIC
TEPHROITE
TEPID
TEPIDARIA
TEPIDER
TEPIDEST
TEPIDITY
TEPIDLY
TEPIDNESS
TEPOY
TEPOYS
TEQUILA
TEQUILAS
TEQUILLA
TEQUILLAS
TERABYTE
TERABYTES
TERAFLOP
TERAFLOPS
TERAGLIN
TERAGLINS
TERAHERTZ
TERAI
TERAIS
TERAKIHI
TERAKIHIS
TERAMETER
TERAOHM
TERAOHMS
TERAPH
TERAPHIM
TERAPHIMS
TERAS
TERATA
TERATISM
TERATISMS
TERATOGEN
TERATOID
TERATOMA
TERATOMAS
TERAWATT
TERAWATTS
TERBIA
TERBIAS
TERBIC
TERBIUM
TERBIUMS
TERCE
TERCEL
TERCELET
TERCELETS
TERCELS
TERCES
TERCET
TERCETS
TERCIO
TERCIOS
TEREBENE
TEREBENES
TEREBIC
TEREBINTH
TEREBRA
TEREBRAE
TEREBRANT
TEREBRAS
TEREBRATE
TEREDINES
TEREDO
TEREDOS
TEREFA
TEREFAH
TEREK
TEREKS
TERES
TERESES
TERETE
TERETES
TERF
TERFE
TERFES
TERFS
TERGA
TERGAL
TERGITE
TERGITES
TERGUM
TERIYAKI
TERIYAKIS
TERM
TERMAGANT
TERMED
TERMER
TERMERS
TERMINAL
TERMINALS
TERMINATE
TERMINER
TERMINERS
TERMING
TERMINI
TERMINISM
TERMINIST
TERMINUS
TERMITARY
TERMITE
TERMITES
TERMITIC
TERMLESS
TERMLIES
TERMLY
TERMOR
TERMORS
TERMS
TERMTIME
TERMTIMES
TERN
TERNAL
TERNARIES
TERNARY
TERNATE
TERNATELY
TERNE
TERNED
TERNES
TERNING
TERNION
TERNIONS
TERNS
TERPENE
TERPENES
TERPENIC
TERPENOID
TERPINE
TERPINEOL
TERPINES
TERPINOL
TERPINOLS
TERRA
TERRACE
TERRACED
TERRACES
TERRACING
TERRAE
TERRAFORM
TERRAIN
TERRAINS
TERRAMARA
TERRAMARE
TERRANE
TERRANES
TERRAPIN
TERRAPINS
TERRARIA
TERRARIUM
TERRAS
TERRASES
TERRASSE
TERRASSES
TERRAZZO
TERRAZZOS
TERREEN
TERREENS
TERRELLA
TERRELLAS
TERRENE
TERRENELY
TERRENES
TERRET
TERRETS
TERRIBLE
TERRIBLES
TERRIBLY
TERRICOLE
TERRIER
TERRIERS
TERRIES
TERRIFIC
TERRIFIED
TERRIFIER
TERRIFIES
TERRIFY
TERRINE
TERRINES
TERRIT
TERRITORY
TERRITS
TERROIR
TERROIRS
TERROR
TERRORFUL
TERRORISE
TERRORISM
TERRORIST
TERRORIZE

T

TERRORS
TERRY
TERSE
TERSELY
TERSENESS
TERSER
TERSEST
TERSION
TERSIONS
TERTIA
TERTIAL
TERTIALS
TERTIAN
TERTIANS
TERTIARY
TERTIAS
TERTIUM
TERTIUS
TERTIUSES
TERTS
TERVALENT
TERYLENE
TERYLENES
TERZETTA
TERZETTAS
TERZETTI
TERZETTO
TERZETTOS
TES
TESLA
TESLAS
TESSELATE
TESSELLA
TESSELLAE
TESSELLAR
TESSERA
TESSERACT
TESSERAE
TESSERAL
TESSITURA
TESSITURE
TEST
TESTA
TESTABLE
TESTACEAN
TESTACIES
TESTACY
TESTAE
TESTAMENT
TESTAMUR
TESTAMURS
TESTATA
TESTATE
TESTATES
TESTATION
TESTATOR
TESTATORS
TESTATRIX
TESTATUM
TESTATUMS
TESTCROSS
TESTE
TESTED
TESTEE
TESTEES
TESTER
TESTERN
TESTERNED
TESTERNS
TESTERS
TESTES
TESTICLE
TESTICLES
TESTIER
TESTIEST
TESTIFIED
TESTIFIER
TESTIFIES
TESTIFY
TESTILY
TESTIMONY
TESTINESS
TESTING
TESTINGS
TESTIS
TESTON
TESTONS
TESTOON
TESTOONS
TESTRIL
TESTRILL
TESTRILLS
TESTRILS
TESTS
TESTUDO
TESTUDOS
TESTY
TET
TETANAL
TETANIC
TETANICAL
TETANICS
TETANIES
TETANISE
TETANISED
TETANISES
TETANIZE
TETANIZED
TETANIZES
TETANOID
TETANUS
TETANUSES
TETANY
TETCHED
TETCHIER
TETCHIEST
TETCHILY
TETCHY
TETE
TETES
TETH
TETHER
TETHERED
TETHERING
TETHERS
TETHS
TETOTUM
TETOTUMS
TETRA
TETRACID
TETRACIDS
TETRACT
TETRACTS
TETRAD
TETRADIC
TETRADITE
TETRADS
TETRAGON
TETRAGONS
TETRAGRAM
TETRALOGY
TETRAMER
TETRAMERS
TETRAPLA
TETRAPLAS
TETRAPOD
TETRAPODS
TETRAPODY
TETRARCH
TETRARCHS
TETRARCHY
TETRAS
TETRAXON
TETRAXONS
TETRI
TETRIS
TETRODE
TETRODES
TETRONAL
TETRONALS
TETROSE
TETROSES
TETROXID
TETROXIDE
TETROXIDS
TETRYL
TETRYLS
TETS
TETTER
TETTERED
TETTERING
TETTEROUS
TETTERS
TETTIX
TETTIXES
TEUCH
TEUCHAT
TEUCHATS
TEUCHER
TEUCHEST
TEUCHTER
TEUCHTERS
TEUGH
TEUGHER
TEUGHEST
TEUGHLY
TEUTONISE
TEUTONIZE
TEVATRON
TEVATRONS
TEW
TEWART
TEWARTS
TEWED
TEWEL
TEWELS
TEWHIT
TEWHITS
TEWING
TEWIT
TEWITS
TEWS
TEX
TEXAS
TEXASES
TEXES
TEXT
TEXTBOOK
TEXTBOOKS
TEXTED
TEXTER
TEXTERS
TEXTILE
TEXTILES
TEXTING
TEXTINGS
TEXTISM
TEXTISMS
TEXTLESS
TEXTONYM
TEXTONYMS
TEXTORIAL
TEXTPHONE
TEXTS
TEXTSPEAK
TEXTUAL
TEXTUALLY
TEXTUARY
TEXTURAL
TEXTURE
TEXTURED
TEXTURES
TEXTURING
TEXTURISE
TEXTURIZE
TEXTUROUS
THACK
THACKED
THACKING
THACKS

THAE
THAGI
THAGIS
THAIM
THAIRM
THAIRMS
THALAMI
THALAMIC
THALAMUS
THALASSIC
THALE
THALER
THALERS
THALI
THALIAN
THALIS
THALLI
THALLIC
THALLINE
THALLINES
THALLIOUS
THALLIUM
THALLIUMS
THALLOID
THALLOUS
THALLUS
THALLUSES
THALWEG
THALWEGS
THAN
THANA
THANADAR
THANADARS
THANAGE
THANAGES
THANAH
THANAHS
THANAS
THANATISM
THANATIST
THANATOID
THANATOS
THANE
THANEDOM
THANEDOMS
THANEHOOD
THANES
THANESHIP
THANG
THANGKA
THANGKAS
THANGS
THANK
THANKED
THANKEE
THANKER
THANKERS
THANKFUL
THANKING
THANKINGS
THANKIT
THANKLESS
THANKS
THANKYOU
THANKYOUS
THANNA
THANNAH
THANNAHS
THANNAS
THANS
THANX
THAR
THARM
THARMS
THARS
THAT
THATAWAY
THATCH
THATCHED
THATCHER
THATCHERS
THATCHES
THATCHIER
THATCHING
THATCHT
THATCHY
THATNESS
THAUMATIN
THAW
THAWED
THAWER
THAWERS
THAWIER
THAWIEST
THAWING
THAWINGS
THAWLESS
THAWS
THAWY
THE
THEACEOUS
THEANDRIC
THEANINE
THEANINES
THEARCHIC
THEARCHY
THEATER
THEATERS
THEATRAL
THEATRE
THEATRES
THEATRIC
THEATRICS
THEAVE
THEAVES
THEBAINE
THEBAINES
THEBE
THEBES
THECA
THECAE
THECAL
THECATE
THECODONT
THEE
THEED
THEEING
THEEK
THEEKED
THEEKING
THEEKS
THEELIN
THEELINS
THEELOL
THEELOLS
THEES
THEFT
THEFTLESS
THEFTS
THEFTUOUS
THEGITHER
THEGN
THEGNLIER
THEGNLY
THEGNS
THEIC
THEICS
THEIN
THEINE
THEINES
THEINS
THEIR
THEIRS
THEIRSELF
THEISM
THEISMS
THEIST
THEISTIC
THEISTS
THELEMENT
THELF
THELITIS
THELVES
THELYTOKY
THEM
THEMA
THEMATA
THEMATIC
THEMATICS
THEMATISE
THEMATIZE
THEME
THEMED
THEMELESS
THEMES
THEMING
THEMSELF
THEN
THENABOUT
THENAGE
THENAGES
THENAL
THENAR
THENARS
THENCE
THENS
THEOCON
THEOCONS
THEOCRACY
THEOCRASY
THEOCRAT
THEOCRATS
THEODICY
THEOGONIC
THEOGONY
THEOLOG
THEOLOGER
THEOLOGIC
THEOLOGS
THEOLOGUE
THEOLOGY
THEOMACHY
THEOMANCY
THEOMANIA
THEONOMY
THEOPATHY
THEOPHAGY
THEOPHANY
THEORBIST
THEORBO
THEORBOS
THEOREM
THEOREMIC
THEOREMS
THEORETIC
THEORIC
THEORICS
THEORIES
THEORIQUE
THEORISE
THEORISED
THEORISER
THEORISES
THEORIST
THEORISTS
THEORIZE
THEORIZED
THEORIZER
THEORIZES
THEORY
THEOSOPH
THEOSOPHS
THEOSOPHY
THEOTOKOI
THEOTOKOS
THEOW
THEOWS
THERALITE
THERAPIES
THERAPISE

THERAPIST
THERAPIZE
THERAPSID
THERAPY
THERBLIG
THERBLIGS
THERE
THEREAT
THEREAWAY
THEREBY
THEREFOR
THEREFORE
THEREFROM
THEREIN
THEREINTO
THEREMIN
THEREMINS
THERENESS
THEREOF
THEREON
THEREOUT
THERES
THERETO
THEREUNTO
THEREUPON
THEREWITH
THERIAC
THERIACA
THERIACAL
THERIACAS
THERIACS
THERIAN
THERIANS
THERM
THERMAE
THERMAL
THERMALLY
THERMALS
THERME
THERMEL
THERMELS
THERMES
THERMETTE
THERMIC
THERMICAL
THERMIDOR
THERMION
THERMIONS
THERMIT
THERMITE
THERMITES
THERMITS
THERMOS
THERMOSES
THERMOSET
THERMOTIC
THERMS
THEROID
THEROLOGY
THEROPOD
THEROPODS
THESAURAL
THESAURI
THESAURUS
THESE
THESES
THESIS
THESP
THESPIAN
THESPIANS
THESPS
THETA
THETAS
THETCH
THETCHED
THETCHES
THETCHING
THETE
THETES
THETHER
THETIC
THETICAL
THETRI
THETRIS
THEURGIC
THEURGIES
THEURGIST
THEURGY
THEW
THEWED
THEWES
THEWIER
THEWIEST
THEWLESS
THEWS
THEWY
THEY
THIAMIN
THIAMINE
THIAMINES
THIAMINS
THIASUS
THIASUSES
THIAZIDE
THIAZIDES
THIAZIN
THIAZINE
THIAZINES
THIAZINS
THIAZOL
THIAZOLE
THIAZOLES
THIAZOLS
THIBET
THIBETS
THIBLE
THIBLES
THICK
THICKED
THICKEN
THICKENED
THICKENER
THICKENS
THICKER
THICKEST
THICKET
THICKETED
THICKETS
THICKETY
THICKHEAD
THICKIE
THICKIES
THICKING
THICKISH
THICKLEAF
THICKLY
THICKNESS
THICKO
THICKOES
THICKOS
THICKS
THICKSET
THICKSETS
THICKSKIN
THICKY
THIEF
THIEFLIKE
THIEVE
THIEVED
THIEVERY
THIEVES
THIEVING
THIEVINGS
THIEVISH
THIG
THIGGED
THIGGER
THIGGERS
THIGGING
THIGGINGS
THIGGIT
THIGH
THIGHBONE
THIGHED
THIGHS
THIGS
THILK
THILL
THILLER
THILLERS
THILLS
THIMBLE
THIMBLED
THIMBLES
THIMBLING
THIN
THINCLAD
THINCLADS
THINDOWN
THINDOWNS
THINE
THING
THINGAMY
THINGHOOD
THINGIER
THINGIES
THINGIEST
THINGNESS
THINGO
THINGOS
THINGS
THINGUMMY
THINGY
THINK
THINKABLE
THINKABLY
THINKER
THINKERS
THINKING
THINKINGS
THINKS
THINLY
THINNED
THINNER
THINNERS
THINNESS
THINNEST
THINNING
THINNINGS
THINNISH
THINS
THIO
THIOFURAN
THIOL
THIOLIC
THIOLS
THIONATE
THIONATES
THIONIC
THIONIN
THIONINE
THIONINES
THIONINS
THIONYL
THIONYLS
THIOPHEN
THIOPHENE
THIOPHENS
THIOPHIL
THIOTEPA
THIOTEPAS
THIOUREA
THIOUREAS
THIR
THIRAM
THIRAMS
THIRD
THIRDED
THIRDHAND
THIRDING

T

THIRDINGS
THIRDLY
THIRDS
THIRDSMAN
THIRDSMEN
THIRL
THIRLAGE
THIRLAGES
THIRLED
THIRLING
THIRLS
THIRST
THIRSTED
THIRSTER
THIRSTERS
THIRSTFUL
THIRSTIER
THIRSTILY
THIRSTING
THIRSTS
THIRSTY
THIRTEEN
THIRTEENS
THIRTIES
THIRTIETH
THIRTY
THIRTYISH
THIS
THISAWAY
THISNESS
THISTLE
THISTLES
THISTLIER
THISTLY
THITHER
THITHERTO
THIVEL
THIVELS
THLIPSES
THLIPSIS
THO
THOFT
THOFTS
THOLE
THOLED
THOLEIITE
THOLEPIN
THOLEPINS
THOLES
THOLI
THOLING
THOLOBATE
THOLOI
THOLOS
THOLUS
THON
THONDER
THONG
THONGED
THONGIER
THONGIEST
THONGING
THONGS
THONGY
THORACAL
THORACES
THORACIC
THORAX
THORAXES
THORIA
THORIAS
THORIC
THORITE
THORITES
THORIUM
THORIUMS
THORN
THORNBACK
THORNBILL
THORNBIRD
THORNBUSH
THORNED
THORNIER
THORNIEST
THORNILY
THORNING
THORNLESS
THORNLIKE
THORNS
THORNSET
THORNTAIL
THORNTREE
THORNY
THORO
THORON
THORONS
THOROUGH
THOROUGHS
THORP
THORPE
THORPES
THORPS
THOSE
THOTHER
THOU
THOUED
THOUGH
THOUGHT
THOUGHTED
THOUGHTEN
THOUGHTS
THOUING
THOUS
THOUSAND
THOUSANDS
THOWEL
THOWELS
THOWL
THOWLESS
THOWLS
THRAE
THRAIPING
THRALDOM
THRALDOMS
THRALL
THRALLDOM
THRALLED
THRALLING
THRALLS
THRANG
THRANGED
THRANGING
THRANGS
THRAPPLE
THRAPPLED
THRAPPLES
THRASH
THRASHED
THRASHER
THRASHERS
THRASHES
THRASHIER
THRASHING
THRASHY
THRASONIC
THRAVE
THRAVES
THRAW
THRAWARD
THRAWART
THRAWED
THRAWING
THRAWN
THRAWNLY
THRAWS
THREAD
THREADED
THREADEN
THREADER
THREADERS
THREADFIN
THREADIER
THREADING
THREADS
THREADY
THREAP
THREAPED
THREAPER
THREAPERS
THREAPING
THREAPIT
THREAPS
THREAT
THREATED
THREATEN
THREATENS
THREATFUL
THREATING
THREATS
THREAVE
THREAVES
THREE
THREEFOLD
THREENESS
THREEP
THREEPEAT
THREEPED
THREEPER
THREEPERS
THREEPING
THREEPIT
THREEPS
THREEQUEL
THREES
THREESOME
THRENE
THRENES
THRENETIC
THRENODE
THRENODES
THRENODIC
THRENODY
THRENOS
THRENOSES
THREONINE
THRESH
THRESHED
THRESHEL
THRESHELS
THRESHER
THRESHERS
THRESHES
THRESHING
THRESHOLD
THRETTIES
THRETTY
THREW
THRICE
THRID
THRIDACE
THRIDACES
THRIDDED
THRIDDING
THRIDS
THRIFT
THRIFTIER
THRIFTILY
THRIFTS
THRIFTY
THRILL
THRILLANT
THRILLED
THRILLER
THRILLERS
THRILLIER
THRILLING
THRILLS
THRILLY
THRIMSA
THRIMSAS

THRIP
THRIPS
THRIPSES
THRISSEL
THRISSELS
THRIST
THRISTED
THRISTING
THRISTLE
THRISTLES
THRISTS
THRISTY
THRIVE
THRIVED
THRIVEN
THRIVER
THRIVERS
THRIVES
THRIVING
THRIVINGS
THRO
THROAT
THROATED
THROATIER
THROATILY
THROATING
THROATS
THROATY
THROB
THROBBED
THROBBER
THROBBERS
THROBBING
THROBLESS
THROBS
THROE
THROED
THROEING
THROES
THROMBI
THROMBIN
THROMBINS
THROMBOSE
THROMBUS
THRONE
THRONED
THRONES
THRONG
THRONGED
THRONGFUL
THRONGING
THRONGS
THRONING
THRONNER
THRONNERS
THROPPLE
THROPPLED
THROPPLES
THROSTLE
THROSTLES
THROTTLE
THROTTLED
THROTTLER
THROTTLES
THROUGH
THROUGHLY
THROVE
THROW
THROWABLE
THROWAWAY
THROWBACK
THROWDOWN
THROWE
THROWER
THROWERS
THROWES
THROWING
THROWINGS
THROWN
THROWOVER
THROWS
THROWSTER
THRU
THRUM
THRUMMED
THRUMMER
THRUMMERS
THRUMMIER
THRUMMING
THRUMMY
THRUMS
THRUPENNY
THRUPUT
THRUPUTS
THRUSH
THRUSHES
THRUST
THRUSTED
THRUSTER
THRUSTERS
THRUSTFUL
THRUSTING
THRUSTOR
THRUSTORS
THRUSTS
THRUTCH
THRUTCHED
THRUTCHES
THRUWAY
THRUWAYS
THRYMSA
THRYMSAS
THUD
THUDDED
THUDDING
THUDDINGS
THUDS
THUG
THUGGEE
THUGGEES
THUGGERY
THUGGISH
THUGGISM
THUGGISMS
THUGGO
THUGGOS
THUGS
THUJA
THUJAS
THULIA
THULIAS
THULITE
THULITES
THULIUM
THULIUMS
THUMB
THUMBED
THUMBHOLE
THUMBIER
THUMBIEST
THUMBING
THUMBKIN
THUMBKINS
THUMBLESS
THUMBLIKE
THUMBLING
THUMBNAIL
THUMBNUT
THUMBNUTS
THUMBPOT
THUMBPOTS
THUMBS
THUMBTACK
THUMBY
THUMP
THUMPED
THUMPER
THUMPERS
THUMPING
THUMPS
THUNDER
THUNDERED
THUNDERER
THUNDERS
THUNDERY
THUNDROUS
THUNK
THUNKED
THUNKING
THUNKS
THURIBLE
THURIBLES
THURIFER
THURIFERS
THURIFIED
THURIFIES
THURIFY
THURL
THURLS
THUS
THUSES
THUSLY
THUSNESS
THUSWISE
THUYA
THUYAS
THWACK
THWACKED
THWACKER
THWACKERS
THWACKING
THWACKS
THWAITE
THWAITES
THWART
THWARTED
THWARTER
THWARTERS
THWARTING
THWARTLY
THWARTS
THY
THYINE
THYLACINE
THYLAKOID
THYLOSE
THYLOSES
THYLOSIS
THYME
THYMES
THYMEY
THYMI
THYMIC
THYMIDINE
THYMIER
THYMIEST
THYMINE
THYMINES
THYMOCYTE
THYMOL
THYMOLS
THYMOMA
THYMOMAS
THYMOMATA
THYMOSIN
THYMOSINS
THYMUS
THYMUSES
THYMY
THYRATRON
THYREOID
THYREOIDS
THYRISTOR
THYROID
THYROIDAL
THYROIDS
THYROXIN
THYROXINE
THYROXINS
THYRSE

T

THYRSES
THYRSI
THYRSOID
THYRSUS
THYSELF
TI
TIAN
TIANS
TIAR
TIARA
TIARAED
TIARAS
TIARS
TIBIA
TIBIAE
TIBIAL
TIBIALES
TIBIALIS
TIBIAS
TIC
TICAL
TICALS
TICCA
TICCED
TICCING
TICE
TICED
TICES
TICH
TICHES
TICHIER
TICHIEST
TICHY
TICING
TICK
TICKED
TICKEN
TICKENS
TICKER
TICKERS
TICKET
TICKETED
TICKETING
TICKETS
TICKEY
TICKEYS
TICKIES
TICKING
TICKINGS
TICKLACE
TICKLACES
TICKLE
TICKLEASS
TICKLED
TICKLER
TICKLERS
TICKLES
TICKLIER
TICKLIEST
TICKLING
TICKLINGS
TICKLISH
TICKLY
TICKS
TICKSEED
TICKSEEDS
TICKTACK
TICKTACKS
TICKTOCK
TICKTOCKS
TICKY
TICS
TICTAC
TICTACKED
TICTACS
TICTOC
TICTOCKED
TICTOCS
TID
TIDAL
TIDALLY
TIDBIT
TIDBITS
TIDDIER
TIDDIES
TIDDIEST
TIDDLE
TIDDLED
TIDDLER
TIDDLERS
TIDDLES
TIDDLEY
TIDDLEYS
TIDDLIER
TIDDLIES
TIDDLIEST
TIDDLING
TIDDLY
TIDDY
TIDE
TIDED
TIDELAND
TIDELANDS
TIDELESS
TIDELIKE
TIDELINE
TIDELINES
TIDEMARK
TIDEMARKS
TIDEMILL
TIDEMILLS
TIDERIP
TIDERIPS
TIDES
TIDESMAN
TIDESMEN
TIDEWATER
TIDEWAVE
TIDEWAVES
TIDEWAY
TIDEWAYS
TIDIED
TIDIER
TIDIERS
TIDIES
TIDIEST
TIDILY
TIDINESS
TIDING
TIDINGS
TIDIVATE
TIDIVATED
TIDIVATES
TIDS
TIDY
TIDYING
TIDYTIPS
TIE
TIEBACK
TIEBACKS
TIEBREAK
TIEBREAKS
TIECLASP
TIECLASPS
TIED
TIEING
TIELESS
TIEPIN
TIEPINS
TIER
TIERCE
TIERCED
TIERCEL
TIERCELET
TIERCELS
TIERCERON
TIERCES
TIERCET
TIERCETS
TIERED
TIERING
TIERS
TIES
TIETAC
TIETACK
TIETACKS
TIETACS
TIFF
TIFFANIES
TIFFANY
TIFFED
TIFFIN
TIFFINED
TIFFING
TIFFINGS
TIFFINING
TIFFINS
TIFFS
TIFO
TIFOS
TIFOSI
TIFOSO
TIFOSOS
TIFT
TIFTED
TIFTING
TIFTS
TIG
TIGE
TIGER
TIGEREYE
TIGEREYES
TIGERIER
TIGERIEST
TIGERISH
TIGERISM
TIGERISMS
TIGERLIER
TIGERLIKE
TIGERLY
TIGERS
TIGERWOOD
TIGERY
TIGES
TIGGED
TIGGER
TIGGERED
TIGGERING
TIGGERS
TIGGING
TIGHT
TIGHTASS
TIGHTEN
TIGHTENED
TIGHTENER
TIGHTENS
TIGHTER
TIGHTEST
TIGHTISH
TIGHTKNIT
TIGHTLY
TIGHTNESS
TIGHTROPE
TIGHTS
TIGHTWAD
TIGHTWADS
TIGHTWIRE
TIGLIC
TIGLON
TIGLONS
TIGNON
TIGNONS
TIGON
TIGONS
TIGRESS
TIGRESSES
TIGRIDIA
TIGRIDIAS
TIGRINE
TIGRISH

T

TIGRISHLY
TIGROID
TIGS
TIK
TIKA
TIKANGA
TIKANGAS
TIKAS
TIKE
TIKES
TIKI
TIKIED
TIKIING
TIKINAGAN
TIKIS
TIKKA
TIKKAS
TIKOLOSHE
TIKS
TIKTAALIK
TIL
TILAK
TILAKS
TILAPIA
TILAPIAS
TILBURIES
TILBURY
TILDE
TILDES
TILE
TILED
TILEFISH
TILELIKE
TILER
TILERIES
TILERS
TILERY
TILES
TILING
TILINGS
TILL
TILLABLE
TILLAGE
TILLAGES
TILLED
TILLER
TILLERED
TILLERING
TILLERMAN
TILLERMEN
TILLERS
TILLICUM
TILLICUMS
TILLIER
TILLIEST
TILLING
TILLINGS
TILLITE
TILLITES
TILLS
TILLY
TILS
TILT
TILTABLE
TILTED
TILTER
TILTERS
TILTH
TILTHS
TILTING
TILTINGS
TILTMETER
TILTROTOR
TILTS
TILTYARD
TILTYARDS
TIMARAU
TIMARAUS
TIMARIOT
TIMARIOTS
TIMBAL
TIMBALE
TIMBALES
TIMBALS
TIMBER
TIMBERED
TIMBERIER
TIMBERING
TIMBERMAN
TIMBERMEN
TIMBERS
TIMBERY
TIMBO
TIMBOS
TIMBRAL
TIMBRE
TIMBREL
TIMBRELS
TIMBRES
TIME
TIMEBOMB
TIMEBOMBS
TIMECARD
TIMECARDS
TIMED
TIMEFRAME
TIMELESS
TIMELIER
TIMELIEST
TIMELINE
TIMELINES
TIMELY
TIMENOGUY
TIMEOUS
TIMEOUSLY
TIMEOUT
TIMEOUTS
TIMEPASS
TIMEPIECE
TIMER
TIMERS
TIMES
TIMESAVER
TIMESCALE
TIMESHARE
TIMESHIFT
TIMESTAMP
TIMETABLE
TIMEWORK
TIMEWORKS
TIMEWORN
TIMID
TIMIDER
TIMIDEST
TIMIDITY
TIMIDLY
TIMIDNESS
TIMING
TIMINGS
TIMIST
TIMISTS
TIMOCRACY
TIMOLOL
TIMOLOLS
TIMON
TIMONEER
TIMONEERS
TIMONS
TIMOROUS
TIMORSOME
TIMOTHIES
TIMOTHY
TIMOUS
TIMOUSLY
TIMPANA
TIMPANAS
TIMPANI
TIMPANIST
TIMPANO
TIMPANUM
TIMPANUMS
TIMPS
TIN
TINA
TINAJA
TINAJAS
TINAMOU
TINAMOUS
TINAS
TINCAL
TINCALS
TINCHEL
TINCHELS
TINCT
TINCTED
TINCTING
TINCTS
TINCTURE
TINCTURED
TINCTURES
TIND
TINDAL
TINDALS
TINDED
TINDER
TINDERBOX
TINDERIER
TINDERS
TINDERY
TINDING
TINDS
TINE
TINEA
TINEAL
TINEAS
TINED
TINEID
TINEIDS
TINES
TINFOIL
TINFOILS
TINFUL
TINFULS
TING
TINGE
TINGED
TINGEING
TINGES
TINGING
TINGLE
TINGLED
TINGLER
TINGLERS
TINGLES
TINGLIER
TINGLIEST
TINGLING
TINGLINGS
TINGLISH
TINGLY
TINGS
TINGUAITE
TINHORN
TINHORNS
TINIER
TINIES
TINIEST
TINILY
TININESS
TINING
TINK
TINKED
TINKER
TINKERED
TINKERER
TINKERERS
TINKERING
TINKERMAN
TINKERMEN
TINKERS

TINKERTOY
TINKING
TINKLE
TINKLED
TINKLER
TINKLERS
TINKLES
TINKLIER
TINKLIEST
TINKLING
TINKLINGS
TINKLY
TINKS
TINLIKE
TINMAN
TINMEN
TINNED
TINNER
TINNERS
TINNIE
TINNIER
TINNIES
TINNIEST
TINNILY
TINNINESS
TINNING
TINNINGS
TINNITUS
TINNY
TINPLATE
TINPLATED
TINPLATES
TINPOT
TINPOTS
TINS
TINSEL
TINSELED
TINSELIER
TINSELING
TINSELLED
TINSELLY
TINSELRY
TINSELS
TINSELY
TINSEY
TINSEYS
TINSMITH
TINSMITHS
TINSNIPS
TINSTONE
TINSTONES
TINT
TINTACK
TINTACKS
TINTED
TINTER
TINTERS
TINTIER
TINTIEST
TINTINESS
TINTING
TINTINGS
TINTLESS
TINTOOKIE
TINTS
TINTY
TINTYPE
TINTYPES
TINWARE
TINWARES
TINWORK
TINWORKS
TINY
TIP
TIPCART
TIPCARTS
TIPCAT
TIPCATS
TIPI
TIPIS
TIPLESS
TIPOFF
TIPOFFS
TIPPABLE
TIPPED
TIPPEE
TIPPEES
TIPPER
TIPPERS
TIPPET
TIPPETS
TIPPIER
TIPPIEST
TIPPING
TIPPINGS
TIPPLE
TIPPLED
TIPPLER
TIPPLERS
TIPPLES
TIPPLING
TIPPY
TIPPYTOE
TIPPYTOED
TIPPYTOES
TIPS
TIPSHEET
TIPSHEETS
TIPSIER
TIPSIEST
TIPSIFIED
TIPSIFIES
TIPSIFY
TIPSILY
TIPSINESS
TIPSTAFF
TIPSTAFFS
TIPSTAVES
TIPSTER
TIPSTERS
TIPSTOCK
TIPSTOCKS
TIPSY
TIPT
TIPTOE
TIPTOED
TIPTOEING
TIPTOES
TIPTOP
TIPTOPS
TIPTRONIC
TIPULA
TIPULAS
TIPUNA
TIPUNAS
TIRADE
TIRADES
TIRAGE
TIRAGES
TIRAMISU
TIRAMISUS
TIRASSE
TIRASSES
TIRE
TIRED
TIREDER
TIREDEST
TIREDLY
TIREDNESS
TIRELESS
TIRELING
TIRELINGS
TIREMAKER
TIRES
TIRESOME
TIREWOMAN
TIREWOMEN
TIRING
TIRINGS
TIRITI
TIRITIS
TIRL
TIRLED
TIRLING
TIRLS
TIRO
TIROES
TIRONIC
TIROS
TIRR
TIRRED
TIRRING
TIRRIT
TIRRITS
TIRRIVEE
TIRRIVEES
TIRRIVIE
TIRRIVIES
TIRRS
TIS
TISANE
TISANES
TISICK
TISICKS
TISSUAL
TISSUE
TISSUED
TISSUES
TISSUEY
TISSUIER
TISSUIEST
TISSUING
TISSULAR
TISWAS
TISWASES
TIT
TITAN
TITANATE
TITANATES
TITANESS
TITANIA
TITANIAS
TITANIC
TITANIS
TITANISES
TITANISM
TITANISMS
TITANITE
TITANITES
TITANIUM
TITANIUMS
TITANOUS
TITANS
TITBIT
TITBITS
TITCH
TITCHES
TITCHIE
TITCHIER
TITCHIEST
TITCHY
TITE
TITELY
TITER
TITERS
TITFER
TITFERS
TITHABLE
TITHE
TITHED
TITHER
TITHERS
TITHES
TITHING
TITHINGS
TITHONIA
TITHONIAS
TITI
TITIAN
TITIANS

TITILLATE
TITIS
TITIVATE
TITIVATED
TITIVATES
TITIVATOR
TITLARK
TITLARKS
TITLE
TITLED
TITLELESS
TITLER
TITLERS
TITLES
TITLIKE
TITLING
TITLINGS
TITLIST
TITLISTS
TITMAN
TITMEN
TITMICE
TITMOSE
TITMOUSE
TITOKI
TITOKIS
TITRABLE
TITRANT
TITRANTS
TITRATE
TITRATED
TITRATES
TITRATING
TITRATION
TITRATOR
TITRATORS
TITRE
TITRES
TITS
TITTED
TITTER
TITTERED
TITTERER
TITTERERS
TITTERING
TITTERS
TITTIE
TITTIES
TITTING
TITTISH
TITTIVATE
TITTLE
TITTLEBAT
TITTLED
TITTLES
TITTLING
TITTUP
TITTUPED
TITTUPIER
TITTUPING
TITTUPPED
TITTUPPY
TITTUPS
TITTUPY
TITTY
TITUBANCY
TITUBANT
TITUBATE
TITUBATED
TITUBATES
TITULAR
TITULARLY
TITULARS
TITULARY
TITULE
TITULED
TITULES
TITULI
TITULING
TITULUS
TITUP
TITUPED
TITUPIER
TITUPIEST
TITUPING
TITUPPED
TITUPPING
TITUPS
TITUPY
TIVY
TIX
TIYIN
TIYINS
TIYN
TIYNS
TIZ
TIZES
TIZWAS
TIZWASES
TIZZ
TIZZES
TIZZIES
TIZZY
TJANTING
TJANTINGS
TMESES
TMESIS
TO
TOAD
TOADEATER
TOADFISH
TOADFLAX
TOADGRASS
TOADIED
TOADIES
TOADISH
TOADLESS
TOADLET
TOADLETS
TOADLIKE
TOADRUSH
TOADS
TOADSTONE
TOADSTOOL
TOADY
TOADYING
TOADYINGS
TOADYISH
TOADYISM
TOADYISMS
TOAST
TOASTED
TOASTER
TOASTERS
TOASTIE
TOASTIER
TOASTIES
TOASTIEST
TOASTING
TOASTINGS
TOASTS
TOASTY
TOAZE
TOAZED
TOAZES
TOAZING
TOBACCO
TOBACCOES
TOBACCOS
TOBIES
TOBOGGAN
TOBOGGANS
TOBOGGIN
TOBOGGINS
TOBY
TOC
TOCCATA
TOCCATAS
TOCCATE
TOCCATINA
TOCHER
TOCHERED
TOCHERING
TOCHERS
TOCK
TOCKED
TOCKIER
TOCKIEST
TOCKING
TOCKLEY
TOCKLEYS
TOCKS
TOCKY
TOCO
TOCOLOGY
TOCOS
TOCS
TOCSIN
TOCSINS
TOD
TODAY
TODAYS
TODDE
TODDED
TODDES
TODDIES
TODDING
TODDLE
TODDLED
TODDLER
TODDLERS
TODDLES
TODDLING
TODDY
TODGER
TODGERS
TODIES
TODS
TODY
TOE
TOEA
TOEAS
TOEBIE
TOEBIES
TOECAP
TOECAPS
TOECLIP
TOECLIPS
TOED
TOEHOLD
TOEHOLDS
TOEIER
TOEIEST
TOEING
TOELESS
TOELIKE
TOENAIL
TOENAILED
TOENAILS
TOEPIECE
TOEPIECES
TOEPLATE
TOEPLATES
TOERAG
TOERAGGER
TOERAGS
TOES
TOESHOE
TOESHOES
TOETOE
TOETOES
TOEY
TOFF
TOFFEE
TOFFEES
TOFFIER
TOFFIES
TOFFIEST
TOFFISH
TOFFS

TOFFY
TOFORE
TOFT
TOFTS
TOFU
TOFUS
TOFUTTI
TOFUTTIS
TOG
TOGA
TOGAE
TOGAED
TOGAS
TOGATE
TOGATED
TOGAVIRUS
TOGE
TOGED
TOGES
TOGETHER
TOGGED
TOGGER
TOGGERED
TOGGERIES
TOGGERING
TOGGERS
TOGGERY
TOGGING
TOGGLE
TOGGLED
TOGGLER
TOGGLERS
TOGGLES
TOGGLING
TOGROG
TOGROGS
TOGS
TOGUE
TOGUES
TOHEROA
TOHEROAS
TOHO
TOHOS
TOHUNGA
TOHUNGAS
TOIL
TOILE
TOILED
TOILER
TOILERS
TOILES
TOILET
TOILETED
TOILETING
TOILETRY
TOILETS
TOILETTE
TOILETTES
TOILFUL
TOILFULLY
TOILINET
TOILINETS
TOILING
TOILINGS
TOILLESS
TOILS
TOILSOME
TOILWORN
TOING
TOINGS
TOISE
TOISEACH
TOISEACHS
TOISECH
TOISECHS
TOISES
TOISON
TOISONS
TOIT
TOITED
TOITING
TOITOI
TOITOIS
TOITS
TOKAMAK
TOKAMAKS
TOKAY
TOKAYS
TOKE
TOKED
TOKEN
TOKENED
TOKENING
TOKENISM
TOKENISMS
TOKENS
TOKER
TOKERS
TOKES
TOKING
TOKO
TOKOLOGY
TOKOLOSHE
TOKOLOSHI
TOKOMAK
TOKOMAKS
TOKONOMA
TOKONOMAS
TOKOS
TOKOTOKO
TOKOTOKOS
TOKTOKKIE
TOLA
TOLAN
TOLANE
TOLANES
TOLANS
TOLAR
TOLARJEV
TOLARJI
TOLARS
TOLAS
TOLBOOTH
TOLBOOTHS
TOLD
TOLE
TOLED
TOLEDO
TOLEDOS
TOLERABLE
TOLERABLY
TOLERANCE
TOLERANT
TOLERATE
TOLERATED
TOLERATES
TOLERATOR
TOLES
TOLEWARE
TOLEWARES
TOLIDIN
TOLIDINE
TOLIDINES
TOLIDINS
TOLING
TOLINGS
TOLL
TOLLABLE
TOLLAGE
TOLLAGES
TOLLBAR
TOLLBARS
TOLLBOOTH
TOLLDISH
TOLLED
TOLLER
TOLLERS
TOLLEY
TOLLEYS
TOLLGATE
TOLLGATED
TOLLGATES
TOLLHOUSE
TOLLIE
TOLLIES
TOLLING
TOLLINGS
TOLLMAN
TOLLMEN
TOLLS
TOLLWAY
TOLLWAYS
TOLLY
TOLSEL
TOLSELS
TOLSEY
TOLSEYS
TOLT
TOLTER
TOLTERED
TOLTERING
TOLTERS
TOLTS
TOLU
TOLUATE
TOLUATES
TOLUENE
TOLUENES
TOLUIC
TOLUID
TOLUIDE
TOLUIDES
TOLUIDIDE
TOLUIDIN
TOLUIDINE
TOLUIDINS
TOLUIDS
TOLUOL
TOLUOLE
TOLUOLES
TOLUOLS
TOLUS
TOLUYL
TOLUYLS
TOLYL
TOLYLS
TOLZEY
TOLZEYS
TOM
TOMAHAWK
TOMAHAWKS
TOMALLEY
TOMALLEYS
TOMAN
TOMANS
TOMATILLO
TOMATO
TOMATOES
TOMATOEY
TOMATOIER
TOMB
TOMBAC
TOMBACK
TOMBACKS
TOMBACS
TOMBAK
TOMBAKS
TOMBAL
TOMBED
TOMBIC
TOMBING
TOMBLESS
TOMBLIKE
TOMBOC
TOMBOCS
TOMBOLA
TOMBOLAS
TOMBOLO
TOMBOLOS
TOMBOY

TOMBOYISH
TOMBOYS
TOMBS
TOMBSTONE
TOMCAT
TOMCATS
TOMCATTED
TOMCOD
TOMCODS
TOME
TOMENTA
TOMENTOSE
TOMENTOUS
TOMENTUM
TOMES
TOMFOOL
TOMFOOLED
TOMFOOLS
TOMIA
TOMIAL
TOMIUM
TOMMED
TOMMIED
TOMMIES
TOMMING
TOMMY
TOMMYCOD
TOMMYCODS
TOMMYING
TOMMYROT
TOMMYROTS
TOMO
TOMOGRAM
TOMOGRAMS
TOMOGRAPH
TOMORROW
TOMORROWS
TOMOS
TOMPION
TOMPIONS
TOMPON
TOMPONED
TOMPONING
TOMPONS
TOMPOT
TOMS
TOMTIT
TOMTITS
TON
TONAL
TONALITE
TONALITES
TONALITIC
TONALITY
TONALLY
TONANT
TONDI
TONDINI
TONDINO
TONDINOS
TONDO
TONDOS
TONE
TONEARM
TONEARMS
TONED
TONELESS
TONEME
TONEMES
TONEMIC
TONEPAD
TONEPADS
TONER
TONERS
TONES
TONETIC
TONETICS
TONETTE
TONETTES
TONEY
TONG
TONGA
TONGAS
TONGED
TONGER
TONGERS
TONGING
TONGMAN
TONGMEN
TONGS
TONGSTER
TONGSTERS
TONGUE
TONGUED
TONGUELET
TONGUES
TONGUING
TONGUINGS
TONIC
TONICALLY
TONICITY
TONICS
TONIER
TONIES
TONIEST
TONIFIED
TONIFIES
TONIFY
TONIFYING
TONIGHT
TONIGHTS
TONING
TONINGS
TONISH
TONISHLY
TONITE
TONITES
TONK
TONKA
TONKED
TONKER
TONKERS
TONKING
TONKS
TONLET
TONLETS
TONNAG
TONNAGE
TONNAGES
TONNAGS
TONNE
TONNEAU
TONNEAUS
TONNEAUX
TONNELL
TONNELLS
TONNER
TONNERS
TONNES
TONNISH
TONNISHLY
TONOMETER
TONOMETRY
TONOPLAST
TONS
TONSIL
TONSILAR
TONSILLAR
TONSILS
TONSOR
TONSORIAL
TONSORS
TONSURE
TONSURED
TONSURES
TONSURING
TONTINE
TONTINER
TONTINERS
TONTINES
TONUS
TONUSES
TONY
TOO
TOOART
TOOARTS
TOODLE
TOODLED
TOODLES
TOODLING
TOOK
TOOL
TOOLBAG
TOOLBAGS
TOOLBAR
TOOLBARS
TOOLBOX
TOOLBOXES
TOOLCASE
TOOLCASES
TOOLCHEST
TOOLED
TOOLER
TOOLERS
TOOLHEAD
TOOLHEADS
TOOLHOUSE
TOOLIE
TOOLIES
TOOLING
TOOLINGS
TOOLKIT
TOOLKITS
TOOLLESS
TOOLMAKER
TOOLMAN
TOOLMEN
TOOLPUSH
TOOLROOM
TOOLROOMS
TOOLS
TOOLSET
TOOLSETS
TOOLSHED
TOOLSHEDS
TOOLTIP
TOOLTIPS
TOOM
TOOMED
TOOMER
TOOMEST
TOOMING
TOOMS
TOON
TOONIE
TOONIES
TOONS
TOORIE
TOORIES
TOOSHIE
TOOSHIER
TOOSHIEST
TOOT
TOOTED
TOOTER
TOOTERS
TOOTH
TOOTHACHE
TOOTHCOMB
TOOTHED
TOOTHFISH
TOOTHFUL
TOOTHFULS
TOOTHIER
TOOTHIEST
TOOTHILY
TOOTHING
TOOTHINGS
TOOTHLESS
TOOTHLIKE

TOOTHPICK
TOOTHS
TOOTHSOME
TOOTHWASH
TOOTHWORT
TOOTHY
TOOTING
TOOTLE
TOOTLED
TOOTLER
TOOTLERS
TOOTLES
TOOTLING
TOOTS
TOOTSED
TOOTSES
TOOTSIE
TOOTSIES
TOOTSING
TOOTSY
TOP
TOPALGIA
TOPALGIAS
TOPARCH
TOPARCHS
TOPARCHY
TOPAZ
TOPAZES
TOPAZINE
TOPCOAT
TOPCOATS
TOPCROSS
TOPE
TOPECTOMY
TOPED
TOPEE
TOPEES
TOPEK
TOPEKS
TOPER
TOPERS
TOPES
TOPFLIGHT
TOPFUL
TOPFULL
TOPH
TOPHE
TOPHES
TOPHI
TOPHS
TOPHUS
TOPI
TOPIARIAN
TOPIARIES
TOPIARIST
TOPIARY
TOPIC
TOPICAL
TOPICALLY
TOPICALS
TOPICS
TOPING
TOPIS
TOPKICK
TOPKICKS
TOPKNOT
TOPKNOTS
TOPLESS
TOPLINE
TOPLINED
TOPLINER
TOPLINERS
TOPLINES
TOPLINING
TOPLOFTY
TOPMAKER
TOPMAKERS
TOPMAKING
TOPMAN
TOPMAST
TOPMASTS
TOPMEN
TOPMINNOW
TOPMOST
TOPNOTCH
TOPO
TOPOGRAPH
TOPOI
TOPOLOGIC
TOPOLOGY
TOPOMETRY
TOPONYM
TOPONYMAL
TOPONYMIC
TOPONYMS
TOPONYMY
TOPOS
TOPOTYPE
TOPOTYPES
TOPPED
TOPPER
TOPPERS
TOPPIER
TOPPIEST
TOPPING
TOPPINGLY
TOPPINGS
TOPPLE
TOPPLED
TOPPLES
TOPPLING
TOPPY
TOPRAIL
TOPRAILS
TOPS
TOPSAIL
TOPSAILS
TOPSCORE
TOPSCORED
TOPSCORES
TOPSIDE
TOPSIDER
TOPSIDERS
TOPSIDES
TOPSMAN
TOPSMEN
TOPSOIL
TOPSOILED
TOPSOILS
TOPSPIN
TOPSPINS
TOPSTITCH
TOPSTONE
TOPSTONES
TOPWATER
TOPWORK
TOPWORKED
TOPWORKS
TOQUE
TOQUES
TOQUET
TOQUETS
TOQUILLA
TOQUILLAS
TOR
TORA
TORAH
TORAHS
TORAN
TORANA
TORANAS
TORANS
TORAS
TORBANITE
TORC
TORCH
TORCHABLE
TORCHED
TORCHER
TORCHERE
TORCHERES
TORCHERS
TORCHES
TORCHIER
TORCHIERE
TORCHIERS
TORCHIEST
TORCHING
TORCHINGS
TORCHLIKE
TORCHLIT
TORCHON
TORCHONS
TORCHWOOD
TORCHY
TORCS
TORCULAR
TORCULARS
TORDION
TORDIONS
TORE
TOREADOR
TOREADORS
TORERO
TOREROS
TORES
TOREUTIC
TOREUTICS
TORGOCH
TORGOCHS
TORI
TORIC
TORICS
TORIES
TORII
TORMENT
TORMENTA
TORMENTED
TORMENTER
TORMENTIL
TORMENTOR
TORMENTS
TORMENTUM
TORMINA
TORMINAL
TORMINOUS
TORN
TORNADE
TORNADES
TORNADIC
TORNADO
TORNADOES
TORNADOS
TORNILLO
TORNILLOS
TORO
TOROID
TOROIDAL
TOROIDS
TOROS
TOROSE
TOROSITY
TOROT
TOROTH
TOROUS
TORPEDO
TORPEDOED
TORPEDOER
TORPEDOES
TORPEDOS
TORPEFIED
TORPEFIES
TORPEFY
TORPID
TORPIDITY
TORPIDLY
TORPIDS
TORPITUDE
TORPOR
TORPORS

T

TORQUATE
TORQUATED
TORQUE
TORQUED
TORQUER
TORQUERS
TORQUES
TORQUESES
TORQUEY
TORQUIER
TORQUIEST
TORQUING
TORR
TORREFIED
TORREFIES
TORREFY
TORRENT
TORRENTS
TORRET
TORRETS
TORRID
TORRIDER
TORRIDEST
TORRIDITY
TORRIDLY
TORRIFIED
TORRIFIES
TORRIFY
TORRS
TORS
TORSADE
TORSADES
TORSE
TORSEL
TORSELS
TORSES
TORSI
TORSION
TORSIONAL
TORSIONS
TORSIVE
TORSK
TORSKS
TORSO
TORSOS
TORT
TORTA
TORTAS
TORTE
TORTELLI
TORTELLIS
TORTEN
TORTES
TORTIE
TORTIES
TORTILE
TORTILITY
TORTILLA
TORTILLAS
TORTILLON
TORTIOUS
TORTIVE
TORTOISE
TORTOISES
TORTONI
TORTONIS
TORTRICES
TORTRICID
TORTRIX
TORTRIXES
TORTS
TORTUOUS
TORTURE
TORTURED
TORTURER
TORTURERS
TORTURES
TORTURING
TORTUROUS
TORULA
TORULAE
TORULAS
TORULI
TORULIN
TORULINS
TORULOSE
TORULOSES
TORULOSIS
TORULUS
TORUS
TORUSES
TORY
TOSA
TOSAS
TOSE
TOSED
TOSES
TOSH
TOSHACH
TOSHACHS
TOSHED
TOSHER
TOSHERS
TOSHES
TOSHIER
TOSHIEST
TOSHING
TOSHY
TOSING
TOSS
TOSSED
TOSSEN
TOSSER
TOSSERS
TOSSES
TOSSIER
TOSSIEST
TOSSILY
TOSSING
TOSSINGS
TOSSPOT
TOSSPOTS
TOSSUP
TOSSUPS
TOSSY
TOST
TOSTADA
TOSTADAS
TOSTADO
TOSTADOS
TOSTONE
TOSTONES
TOT
TOTABLE
TOTAL
TOTALED
TOTALING
TOTALISE
TOTALISED
TOTALISER
TOTALISES
TOTALISM
TOTALISMS
TOTALIST
TOTALISTS
TOTALITY
TOTALIZE
TOTALIZED
TOTALIZER
TOTALIZES
TOTALLED
TOTALLING
TOTALLY
TOTALS
TOTANUS
TOTANUSES
TOTAQUINE
TOTARA
TOTARAS
TOTE
TOTEABLE
TOTED
TOTEM
TOTEMIC
TOTEMISM
TOTEMISMS
TOTEMIST
TOTEMISTS
TOTEMITE
TOTEMITES
TOTEMS
TOTER
TOTERS
TOTES
TOTHER
TOTHERS
TOTIENT
TOTIENTS
TOTING
TOTITIVE
TOTITIVES
TOTS
TOTTED
TOTTER
TOTTERED
TOTTERER
TOTTERERS
TOTTERIER
TOTTERING
TOTTERS
TOTTERY
TOTTIE
TOTTIER
TOTTIES
TOTTIEST
TOTTING
TOTTINGS
TOTTRING
TOTTY
TOUCAN
TOUCANET
TOUCANETS
TOUCANS
TOUCH
TOUCHABLE
TOUCHABLY
TOUCHBACK
TOUCHDOWN
TOUCHE
TOUCHED
TOUCHER
TOUCHERS
TOUCHES
TOUCHHOLE
TOUCHIER
TOUCHIEST
TOUCHILY
TOUCHING
TOUCHINGS
TOUCHLESS
TOUCHLINE
TOUCHMARK
TOUCHPAD
TOUCHPADS
TOUCHTONE
TOUCHUP
TOUCHUPS
TOUCHWOOD
TOUCHY
TOUGH
TOUGHED
TOUGHEN
TOUGHENED
TOUGHENER
TOUGHENS
TOUGHER
TOUGHEST
TOUGHIE
TOUGHIES
TOUGHING

TOUGHISH
TOUGHLY
TOUGHNESS
TOUGHS
TOUGHY
TOUK
TOUKED
TOUKING
TOUKS
TOULADI
TOULADIS
TOUN
TOUNS
TOUPEE
TOUPEED
TOUPEES
TOUPET
TOUPETS
TOUPIE
TOUPIES
TOUR
TOURACO
TOURACOS
TOURED
TOURER
TOURERS
TOURIE
TOURIES
TOURING
TOURINGS
TOURISM
TOURISMS
TOURIST
TOURISTA
TOURISTAS
TOURISTED
TOURISTIC
TOURISTS
TOURISTY
TOURNEDOS
TOURNEY
TOURNEYED
TOURNEYER
TOURNEYS
TOURNURE
TOURNURES
TOURS
TOURTIERE
TOUSE
TOUSED
TOUSER
TOUSERS
TOUSES
TOUSIER
TOUSIEST
TOUSING
TOUSINGS
TOUSLE
TOUSLED
TOUSLES
TOUSLING
TOUSTIE
TOUSTIER
TOUSTIEST
TOUSY
TOUT
TOUTED
TOUTER
TOUTERS
TOUTIE
TOUTIER
TOUTIEST
TOUTING
TOUTON
TOUTONS
TOUTS
TOUZE
TOUZED
TOUZES
TOUZIER
TOUZIEST
TOUZING
TOUZLE
TOUZLED
TOUZLES
TOUZLING
TOUZY
TOVARICH
TOVARISCH
TOVARISH
TOW
TOWABLE
TOWAGE
TOWAGES
TOWARD
TOWARDLY
TOWARDS
TOWAWAY
TOWAWAYS
TOWBAR
TOWBARS
TOWBOAT
TOWBOATS
TOWED
TOWEL
TOWELED
TOWELETTE
TOWELHEAD
TOWELING
TOWELINGS
TOWELLED
TOWELLING
TOWELS
TOWER
TOWERED
TOWERIER
TOWERIEST
TOWERING
TOWERLESS
TOWERLIKE
TOWERS
TOWERY
TOWHEAD
TOWHEADED
TOWHEADS
TOWHEE
TOWHEES
TOWIE
TOWIER
TOWIES
TOWIEST
TOWING
TOWINGS
TOWKAY
TOWKAYS
TOWLINE
TOWLINES
TOWMON
TOWMOND
TOWMONDS
TOWMONS
TOWMONT
TOWMONTS
TOWN
TOWNEE
TOWNEES
TOWNFOLK
TOWNHALL
TOWNHOME
TOWNHOMES
TOWNHOUSE
TOWNIE
TOWNIER
TOWNIES
TOWNIEST
TOWNISH
TOWNLAND
TOWNLANDS
TOWNLESS
TOWNLET
TOWNLETS
TOWNLIER
TOWNLIEST
TOWNLING
TOWNLINGS
TOWNLY
TOWNS
TOWNSCAPE
TOWNSFOLK
TOWNSHIP
TOWNSHIPS
TOWNSITE
TOWNSITES
TOWNSKIP
TOWNSKIPS
TOWNSMAN
TOWNSMEN
TOWNWARD
TOWNWEAR
TOWNWEARS
TOWNY
TOWPATH
TOWPATHS
TOWPLANE
TOWPLANES
TOWROPE
TOWROPES
TOWS
TOWSACK
TOWSACKS
TOWSE
TOWSED
TOWSER
TOWSERS
TOWSES
TOWSIER
TOWSIEST
TOWSING
TOWSY
TOWT
TOWTED
TOWTING
TOWTS
TOWY
TOWZE
TOWZED
TOWZES
TOWZIER
TOWZIEST
TOWZING
TOWZY
TOXAEMIA
TOXAEMIAS
TOXAEMIC
TOXAPHENE
TOXEMIA
TOXEMIAS
TOXEMIC
TOXIC
TOXICAL
TOXICALLY
TOXICANT
TOXICANTS
TOXICITY
TOXICOSES
TOXICOSIS
TOXICS
TOXIGENIC
TOXIN
TOXINE
TOXINES
TOXINS
TOXOCARA
TOXOCARAL
TOXOCARAS
TOXOID
TOXOIDS
TOXOPHILY
TOY
TOYBOX

T

TOYBOXES
TOYCHEST
TOYCHESTS
TOYED
TOYER
TOYERS
TOYETIC
TOYING
TOYINGS
TOYISH
TOYISHLY
TOYLAND
TOYLANDS
TOYLESOME
TOYLESS
TOYLIKE
TOYLSOM
TOYMAN
TOYMEN
TOYO
TOYON
TOYONS
TOYOS
TOYS
TOYSHOP
TOYSHOPS
TOYSOME
TOYTOWN
TOYTOWNS
TOYWOMAN
TOYWOMEN
TOZE
TOZED
TOZES
TOZIE
TOZIES
TOZING
TRABEATE
TRABEATED
TRABECULA
TRABS
TRACE
TRACEABLE
TRACEABLY
TRACED
TRACELESS
TRACER
TRACERIED
TRACERIES
TRACERS
TRACERY
TRACES
TRACEUR
TRACEURS
TRACHEA
TRACHEAE
TRACHEAL
TRACHEARY
TRACHEAS
TRACHEATE
TRACHEID
TRACHEIDE
TRACHEIDS
TRACHEOLE
TRACHINUS
TRACHITIS
TRACHLE
TRACHLED
TRACHLES
TRACHLING
TRACHOMA
TRACHOMAS
TRACHYTE
TRACHYTES
TRACHYTIC
TRACING
TRACINGS
TRACK
TRACKABLE
TRACKAGE
TRACKAGES
TRACKBALL
TRACKBED
TRACKBEDS
TRACKED
TRACKER
TRACKERS
TRACKIE
TRACKIES
TRACKING
TRACKINGS
TRACKLESS
TRACKMAN
TRACKMEN
TRACKPAD
TRACKPADS
TRACKROAD
TRACKS
TRACKSIDE
TRACKSUIT
TRACKWAY
TRACKWAYS
TRACT
TRACTABLE
TRACTABLY
TRACTATE
TRACTATES
TRACTATOR
TRACTED
TRACTILE
TRACTING
TRACTION
TRACTIONS
TRACTIVE
TRACTOR
TRACTORS
TRACTRIX
TRACTS
TRACTUS
TRACTUSES
TRAD
TRADABLE
TRADE
TRADEABLE
TRADED
TRADEFUL
TRADELESS
TRADEMARK
TRADENAME
TRADEOFF
TRADEOFFS
TRADER
TRADERS
TRADES
TRADESMAN
TRADESMEN
TRADIE
TRADIES
TRADING
TRADINGS
TRADITION
TRADITIVE
TRADITOR
TRADITORS
TRADS
TRADUCE
TRADUCED
TRADUCER
TRADUCERS
TRADUCES
TRADUCIAN
TRADUCING
TRAFFIC
TRAFFICKY
TRAFFICS
TRAGAL
TRAGEDIAN
TRAGEDIES
TRAGEDY
TRAGELAPH
TRAGI
TRAGIC
TRAGICAL
TRAGICS
TRAGOPAN
TRAGOPANS
TRAGULE
TRAGULES
TRAGULINE
TRAGUS
TRAHISON
TRAHISONS
TRAIK
TRAIKED
TRAIKING
TRAIKIT
TRAIKS
TRAIL
TRAILABLE
TRAILED
TRAILER
TRAILERED
TRAILERS
TRAILHEAD
TRAILING
TRAILLESS
TRAILS
TRAILSIDE
TRAIN
TRAINABLE
TRAINBAND
TRAINED
TRAINEE
TRAINEES
TRAINER
TRAINERS
TRAINFUL
TRAINFULS
TRAINING
TRAININGS
TRAINLESS
TRAINLOAD
TRAINMAN
TRAINMEN
TRAINS
TRAINWAY
TRAINWAYS
TRAIPSE
TRAIPSED
TRAIPSES
TRAIPSING
TRAIT
TRAITOR
TRAITORLY
TRAITORS
TRAITRESS
TRAITS
TRAJECT
TRAJECTED
TRAJECTS
TRAM
TRAMCAR
TRAMCARS
TRAMEL
TRAMELED
TRAMELING
TRAMELL
TRAMELLED
TRAMELLS
TRAMELS
TRAMLESS
TRAMLINE
TRAMLINED
TRAMLINES
TRAMMED
TRAMMEL
TRAMMELED
TRAMMELER
TRAMMELS
TRAMMIE

T

TRAMMIES
TRAMMING
TRAMP
TRAMPED
TRAMPER
TRAMPERS
TRAMPET
TRAMPETS
TRAMPETTE
TRAMPIER
TRAMPIEST
TRAMPING
TRAMPINGS
TRAMPISH
TRAMPLE
TRAMPLED
TRAMPLER
TRAMPLERS
TRAMPLES
TRAMPLING
TRAMPOLIN
TRAMPS
TRAMPY
TRAMROAD
TRAMROADS
TRAMS
TRAMWAY
TRAMWAYS
TRANCE
TRANCED
TRANCEDLY
TRANCES
TRANCEY
TRANCHE
TRANCHES
TRANCHET
TRANCHETS
TRANCIER
TRANCIEST
TRANCING
TRANECT
TRANECTS
TRANGAM
TRANGAMS
TRANGLE
TRANGLES
TRANK
TRANKED

TRANKING
TRANKS
TRANKUM
TRANKUMS
TRANNIE
TRANNIES
TRANNY
TRANQ
TRANQS
TRANQUIL
TRANS
TRANSACT
TRANSACTS
TRANSAXLE
TRANSCEND
TRANSCODE
TRANSDUCE
TRANSE
TRANSECT
TRANSECTS
TRANSENNA
TRANSEPT
TRANSEPTS
TRANSES
TRANSEUNT
TRANSFARD
TRANSFECT
TRANSFER
TRANSFERS
TRANSFIX
TRANSFIXT
TRANSFORM
TRANSFUSE
TRANSGENE
TRANSHIP
TRANSHIPS
TRANSHUME
TRANSIENT
TRANSIRE
TRANSIRES
TRANSIT
TRANSITED
TRANSITS
TRANSLATE
TRANSMAN
TRANSMEN
TRANSMEW
TRANSMEWS

TRANSMIT
TRANSMITS
TRANSMOVE
TRANSMUTE
TRANSOM
TRANSOMED
TRANSOMS
TRANSONIC
TRANSPIRE
TRANSPORT
TRANSPOSE
TRANSSHIP
TRANSUDE
TRANSUDED
TRANSUDES
TRANSUME
TRANSUMED
TRANSUMES
TRANSUMPT
TRANSVEST
TRANT
TRANTED
TRANTER
TRANTERS
TRANTING
TRANTS
TRAP
TRAPAN
TRAPANNED
TRAPANNER
TRAPANS
TRAPBALL
TRAPBALLS
TRAPDOOR
TRAPDOORS
TRAPE
TRAPED
TRAPES
TRAPESED
TRAPESES
TRAPESING
TRAPEZE
TRAPEZED
TRAPEZES
TRAPEZIA
TRAPEZIAL
TRAPEZII
TRAPEZING

TRAPEZIST
TRAPEZIUM
TRAPEZIUS
TRAPEZOID
TRAPFALL
TRAPFALLS
TRAPING
TRAPLIKE
TRAPLINE
TRAPLINES
TRAPNEST
TRAPNESTS
TRAPPEAN
TRAPPED
TRAPPER
TRAPPERS
TRAPPIER
TRAPPIEST
TRAPPING
TRAPPINGS
TRAPPOSE
TRAPPOUS
TRAPPY
TRAPROCK
TRAPROCKS
TRAPS
TRAPSE
TRAPSED
TRAPSES
TRAPSING
TRAPT
TRAPUNTO
TRAPUNTOS
TRASH
TRASHCAN
TRASHCANS
TRASHED
TRASHER
TRASHERS
TRASHERY
TRASHES
TRASHIER
TRASHIEST
TRASHILY
TRASHING
TRASHMAN
TRASHMEN
TRASHTRIE

TRASHY
TRASS
TRASSES
TRAT
TRATS
TRATT
TRATTORIA
TRATTORIE
TRATTS
TRAUCHLE
TRAUCHLED
TRAUCHLES
TRAUMA
TRAUMAS
TRAUMATA
TRAUMATIC
TRAVAIL
TRAVAILED
TRAVAILS
TRAVE
TRAVEL
TRAVELED
TRAVELER
TRAVELERS
TRAVELING
TRAVELLED
TRAVELLER
TRAVELOG
TRAVELOGS
TRAVELS
TRAVERSAL
TRAVERSE
TRAVERSED
TRAVERSER
TRAVERSES
TRAVERTIN
TRAVES
TRAVESTY
TRAVIS
TRAVISES
TRAVOIS
TRAVOISE
TRAVOISES
TRAWL
TRAWLED
TRAWLER
TRAWLERS
TRAWLEY

T

TRAWLEYS
TRAWLING
TRAWLINGS
TRAWLNET
TRAWLNETS
TRAWLS
TRAY
TRAYBAKE
TRAYBAKES
TRAYBIT
TRAYBITS
TRAYCLOTH
TRAYF
TRAYFUL
TRAYFULS
TRAYNE
TRAYNED
TRAYNES
TRAYNING
TRAYS
TRAZODONE
TREACHER
TREACHERS
TREACHERY
TREACHOUR
TREACLE
TREACLED
TREACLES
TREACLIER
TREACLING
TREACLY
TREAD
TREADED
TREADER
TREADERS
TREADING
TREADINGS
TREADLE
TREADLED
TREADLER
TREADLERS
TREADLES
TREADLESS
TREADLING
TREADMILL
TREADS
TREAGUE
TREAGUES
TREASON
TREASONS
TREASURE
TREASURED
TREASURER
TREASURES
TREASURY
TREAT
TREATABLE
TREATED
TREATER
TREATERS
TREATIES
TREATING
TREATINGS
TREATISE
TREATISES
TREATMENT
TREATS
TREATY
TREBBIANO
TREBLE
TREBLED
TREBLES
TREBLIER
TREBLIEST
TREBLING
TREBLINGS
TREBLY
TREBUCHET
TREBUCKET
TRECENTO
TRECENTOS
TRECK
TRECKED
TRECKING
TRECKS
TREDDLE
TREDDLED
TREDDLES
TREDDLING
TREDILLE
TREDILLES
TREDRILLE
TREE
TREED
TREEHOUSE
TREEING
TREELAWN
TREELAWNS
TREELESS
TREELIKE
TREELINE
TREELINES
TREEN
TREENAIL
TREENAILS
TREENS
TREENWARE
TREES
TREESHIP
TREESHIPS
TREETOP
TREETOPS
TREEWARE
TREEWARES
TREEWAX
TREEWAXES
TREF
TREFA
TREFAH
TREFOIL
TREFOILED
TREFOILS
TREGETOUR
TREGGINGS
TREHALA
TREHALAS
TREHALOSE
TREIF
TREIFA
TREILLAGE
TREILLE
TREILLES
TREK
TREKKED
TREKKER
TREKKERS
TREKKING
TREKKINGS
TREKS
TRELLIS
TRELLISED
TRELLISES
TREM
TREMA
TREMAS
TREMATIC
TREMATODE
TREMATOID
TREMBLANT
TREMBLE
TREMBLED
TREMBLER
TREMBLERS
TREMBLES
TREMBLIER
TREMBLING
TREMBLOR
TREMBLORS
TREMBLY
TREMIE
TREMIES
TREMOLANT
TREMOLITE
TREMOLO
TREMOLOS
TREMOR
TREMORED
TREMORING
TREMOROUS
TREMORS
TREMS
TREMULANT
TREMULATE
TREMULOUS
TRENAIL
TRENAILS
TRENCH
TRENCHAND
TRENCHANT
TRENCHARD
TRENCHED
TRENCHER
TRENCHERS
TRENCHES
TRENCHING
TREND
TRENDED
TRENDIER
TRENDIES
TRENDIEST
TRENDIFY
TRENDILY
TRENDING
TRENDOID
TRENDOIDS
TRENDS
TRENDY
TRENDYISM
TRENISE
TRENISES
TRENTAL
TRENTALS
TREPAN
TREPANG
TREPANGS
TREPANNED
TREPANNER
TREPANS
TREPHINE
TREPHINED
TREPHINER
TREPHINES
TREPID
TREPIDANT
TREPONEMA
TREPONEME
TRES
TRESPASS
TRESS
TRESSED
TRESSEL
TRESSELS
TRESSES
TRESSIER
TRESSIEST
TRESSING
TRESSOUR
TRESSOURS
TRESSURE
TRESSURED
TRESSURES
TRESSY
TREST
TRESTLE
TRESTLES
TRESTS
TRET
TRETINOIN
TRETS
TREVALLY

TREVALLYS
TREVET
TREVETS
TREVIS
TREVISES
TREVISS
TREVISSES
TREW
TREWS
TREWSMAN
TREWSMEN
TREY
TREYBIT
TREYBITS
TREYF
TREYFA
TREYS
TREZ
TREZES
TRIABLE
TRIAC
TRIACID
TRIACIDS
TRIACS
TRIACT
TRIACTINE
TRIACTOR
TRIACTORS
TRIACTS
TRIAD
TRIADIC
TRIADICS
TRIADISM
TRIADISMS
TRIADIST
TRIADISTS
TRIADS
TRIAGE
TRIAGED
TRIAGES
TRIAGING
TRIAL
TRIALED
TRIALING
TRIALISM
TRIALISMS
TRIALIST
TRIALISTS
TRIALITY
TRIALLED
TRIALLING
TRIALLIST
TRIALOGUE
TRIALS
TRIALWARE
TRIANGLE
TRIANGLED
TRIANGLES
TRIAPSAL
TRIARCH
TRIARCHS
TRIARCHY
TRIASSIC
TRIATHLON
TRIATIC
TRIATICS
TRIATOMIC
TRIAXIAL
TRIAXIALS
TRIAXON
TRIAXONS
TRIAZIN
TRIAZINE
TRIAZINES
TRIAZINS
TRIAZOLE
TRIAZOLES
TRIAZOLIC
TRIBADE
TRIBADES
TRIBADIC
TRIBADIES
TRIBADISM
TRIBADY
TRIBAL
TRIBALISM
TRIBALIST
TRIBALLY
TRIBALS
TRIBASIC
TRIBBLE
TRIBBLES
TRIBE
TRIBELESS
TRIBES
TRIBESMAN
TRIBESMEN
TRIBLET
TRIBLETS
TRIBOLOGY
TRIBRACH
TRIBRACHS
TRIBULATE
TRIBUNAL
TRIBUNALS
TRIBUNARY
TRIBUNATE
TRIBUNE
TRIBUNES
TRIBUTARY
TRIBUTE
TRIBUTER
TRIBUTERS
TRIBUTES
TRICAR
TRICARS
TRICE
TRICED
TRICEP
TRICEPS
TRICEPSES
TRICERION
TRICES
TRICHINA
TRICHINAE
TRICHINAL
TRICHINAS
TRICHITE
TRICHITES
TRICHITIC
TRICHOID
TRICHOME
TRICHOMES
TRICHOMIC
TRICHORD
TRICHORDS
TRICHOSES
TRICHOSIS
TRICHROIC
TRICHROME
TRICING
TRICITIES
TRICITY
TRICK
TRICKED
TRICKER
TRICKERS
TRICKERY
TRICKIE
TRICKIER
TRICKIEST
TRICKILY
TRICKING
TRICKINGS
TRICKISH
TRICKLE
TRICKLED
TRICKLES
TRICKLESS
TRICKLET
TRICKLETS
TRICKLIER
TRICKLING
TRICKLY
TRICKS
TRICKSIER
TRICKSILY
TRICKSOME
TRICKSTER
TRICKSY
TRICKY
TRICLAD
TRICLADS
TRICLINIA
TRICLINIC
TRICLOSAN
TRICOLOR
TRICOLORS
TRICOLOUR
TRICORN
TRICORNE
TRICORNES
TRICORNS
TRICOT
TRICOTINE
TRICOTS
TRICROTIC
TRICTRAC
TRICTRACS
TRICUSPID
TRICYCLE
TRICYCLED
TRICYCLER
TRICYCLES
TRICYCLIC
TRIDACNA
TRIDACNAS
TRIDACTYL
TRIDARN
TRIDARNS
TRIDE
TRIDENT
TRIDENTAL
TRIDENTED
TRIDENTS
TRIDUAN
TRIDUUM
TRIDUUMS
TRIDYMITE
TRIE
TRIECIOUS
TRIED
TRIELLA
TRIELLAS
TRIENE
TRIENES
TRIENNIA
TRIENNIAL
TRIENNIUM
TRIENS
TRIENTES
TRIER
TRIERARCH
TRIERS
TRIES
TRIETERIC
TRIETHYL
TRIFACIAL
TRIFECTA
TRIFECTAS
TRIFF
TRIFFER
TRIFFEST
TRIFFIC
TRIFFID
TRIFFIDS
TRIFFIDY
TRIFID
TRIFLE
TRIFLED

T

TRIFLER
TRIFLERS
TRIFLES
TRIFLING
TRIFLINGS
TRIFOCAL
TRIFOCALS
TRIFOLD
TRIFOLIA
TRIFOLIES
TRIFOLIUM
TRIFOLY
TRIFORIA
TRIFORIAL
TRIFORIUM
TRIFORM
TRIFORMED
TRIG
TRIGAMIES
TRIGAMIST
TRIGAMOUS
TRIGAMY
TRIGEMINI
TRIGGED
TRIGGER
TRIGGERED
TRIGGERS
TRIGGEST
TRIGGING
TRIGLOT
TRIGLOTS
TRIGLY
TRIGLYPH
TRIGLYPHS
TRIGNESS
TRIGO
TRIGON
TRIGONAL
TRIGONIC
TRIGONOUS
TRIGONS
TRIGOS
TRIGRAM
TRIGRAMS
TRIGRAPH
TRIGRAPHS
TRIGS
TRIGYNIAN
TRIGYNOUS
TRIHEDRA
TRIHEDRAL
TRIHEDRON
TRIHYBRID
TRIHYDRIC
TRIJET
TRIJETS
TRIJUGATE
TRIJUGOUS
TRIKE
TRIKES
TRILBIED
TRILBIES
TRILBY
TRILBYS
TRILD
TRILEMMA
TRILEMMAS
TRILINEAR
TRILITH
TRILITHIC
TRILITHON
TRILITHS
TRILL
TRILLED
TRILLER
TRILLERS
TRILLING
TRILLINGS
TRILLION
TRILLIONS
TRILLIUM
TRILLIUMS
TRILLO
TRILLOES
TRILLS
TRILOBAL
TRILOBATE
TRILOBE
TRILOBED
TRILOBES
TRILOBITE
TRILOGIES
TRILOGY
TRIM
TRIMARAN
TRIMARANS
TRIMER
TRIMERIC
TRIMERISM
TRIMEROUS
TRIMERS
TRIMESTER
TRIMETER
TRIMETERS
TRIMETHYL
TRIMETRIC
TRIMIX
TRIMIXES
TRIMLY
TRIMMED
TRIMMER
TRIMMERS
TRIMMEST
TRIMMING
TRIMMINGS
TRIMNESS
TRIMORPH
TRIMORPHS
TRIMOTOR
TRIMOTORS
TRIMPHONE
TRIMPOT
TRIMPOTS
TRIMS
TRIMTAB
TRIMTABS
TRIN
TRINAL
TRINARY
TRINDLE
TRINDLED
TRINDLES
TRINDLING
TRINE
TRINED
TRINES
TRINGLE
TRINGLES
TRINING
TRINITIES
TRINITRIN
TRINITY
TRINKET
TRINKETED
TRINKETER
TRINKETRY
TRINKETS
TRINKUM
TRINKUMS
TRINODAL
TRINOMIAL
TRINS
TRIO
TRIODE
TRIODES
TRIOL
TRIOLEIN
TRIOLEINS
TRIOLET
TRIOLETS
TRIOLS
TRIONES
TRIONYM
TRIONYMAL
TRIONYMS
TRIOR
TRIORS
TRIOS
TRIOSE
TRIOSES
TRIOXID
TRIOXIDE
TRIOXIDES
TRIOXIDS
TRIOXYGEN
TRIP
TRIPACK
TRIPACKS
TRIPART
TRIPE
TRIPEDAL
TRIPERIES
TRIPERY
TRIPES
TRIPEY
TRIPHASE
TRIPHONE
TRIPHONES
TRIPIER
TRIPIEST
TRIPITAKA
TRIPLANE
TRIPLANES
TRIPLE
TRIPLED
TRIPLES
TRIPLET
TRIPLETS
TRIPLEX
TRIPLEXED
TRIPLEXES
TRIPLIED
TRIPLIES
TRIPLING
TRIPLINGS
TRIPLITE
TRIPLITES
TRIPLOID
TRIPLOIDS
TRIPLOIDY
TRIPLY
TRIPLYING
TRIPMAN
TRIPMEN
TRIPMETER
TRIPOD
TRIPODAL
TRIPODIC
TRIPODIES
TRIPODS
TRIPODY
TRIPOLI
TRIPOLIS
TRIPOS
TRIPOSES
TRIPPANT
TRIPPED
TRIPPER
TRIPPERS
TRIPPERY
TRIPPET
TRIPPETS
TRIPPIER
TRIPPIEST
TRIPPING
TRIPPINGS
TRIPPLE
TRIPPLED
TRIPPLER
TRIPPLERS

T

TRIPPLES
TRIPPLING
TRIPPY
TRIPS
TRIPSES
TRIPSIS
TRIPTAN
TRIPTANE
TRIPTANES
TRIPTANS
TRIPTOTE
TRIPTOTES
TRIPTYCA
TRIPTYCAS
TRIPTYCH
TRIPTYCHS
TRIPTYQUE
TRIPUDIA
TRIPUDIUM
TRIPWIRE
TRIPWIRES
TRIPY
TRIQUETRA
TRIRADIAL
TRIREME
TRIREMES
TRISAGION
TRISCELE
TRISCELES
TRISECT
TRISECTED
TRISECTOR
TRISECTS
TRISEME
TRISEMES
TRISEMIC
TRISERIAL
TRISHAW
TRISHAWS
TRISKELE
TRISKELES
TRISKELIA
TRISMIC
TRISMUS
TRISMUSES
TRISODIUM
TRISOME
TRISOMES
TRISOMIC
TRISOMICS
TRISOMIES
TRISOMY
TRIST
TRISTATE
TRISTE
TRISTESSE
TRISTEZA
TRISTEZAS
TRISTFUL
TRISTICH
TRISTICHS
TRISUL
TRISULA
TRISULAS
TRISULS
TRITANOPE
TRITE
TRITELY
TRITENESS
TRITER
TRITES
TRITEST
TRITHEISM
TRITHEIST
TRITHING
TRITHINGS
TRITIATE
TRITIATED
TRITIATES
TRITICAL
TRITICALE
TRITICISM
TRITICUM
TRITICUMS
TRITIDE
TRITIDES
TRITIUM
TRITIUMS
TRITOMA
TRITOMAS
TRITON
TRITONE
TRITONES
TRITONIA
TRITONIAS
TRITONS
TRITURATE
TRIUMPH
TRIUMPHAL
TRIUMPHED
TRIUMPHER
TRIUMPHS
TRIUMVIR
TRIUMVIRI
TRIUMVIRS
TRIUMVIRY
TRIUNE
TRIUNES
TRIUNITY
TRIVALENT
TRIVALVE
TRIVALVED
TRIVALVES
TRIVET
TRIVETS
TRIVIA
TRIVIAL
TRIVIALLY
TRIVIUM
TRIVIUMS
TRIWEEKLY
TRIZONAL
TRIZONE
TRIZONES
TROAD
TROADE
TROADES
TROADS
TROAK
TROAKED
TROAKING
TROAKS
TROAT
TROATED
TROATING
TROATS
TROCAR
TROCARS
TROCHAIC
TROCHAICS
TROCHAL
TROCHAR
TROCHARS
TROCHE
TROCHEE
TROCHEES
TROCHES
TROCHI
TROCHIL
TROCHILI
TROCHILIC
TROCHILS
TROCHILUS
TROCHISCI
TROCHISK
TROCHISKS
TROCHITE
TROCHITES
TROCHLEA
TROCHLEAE
TROCHLEAR
TROCHLEAS
TROCHOID
TROCHOIDS
TROCHUS
TROCHUSES
TROCK
TROCKED
TROCKEN
TROCKING
TROCKS
TROD
TRODDEN
TRODE
TRODES
TRODS
TROELIE
TROELIES
TROELY
TROFFER
TROFFERS
TROG
TROGGED
TROGGING
TROGGS
TROGON
TROGONS
TROGS
TROIKA
TROIKAS
TROILISM
TROILISMS
TROILIST
TROILISTS
TROILITE
TROILITES
TROILUS
TROILUSES
TROIS
TROJAN
TROJANS
TROKE
TROKED
TROKES
TROKING
TROLAND
TROLANDS
TROLL
TROLLED
TROLLER
TROLLERS
TROLLEY
TROLLEYED
TROLLEYS
TROLLIED
TROLLIES
TROLLING
TROLLINGS
TROLLISH
TROLLIUS
TROLLOP
TROLLOPED
TROLLOPEE
TROLLOPS
TROLLOPY
TROLLS
TROLLY
TROLLYING
TROMBONE
TROMBONES
TROMINO
TROMINOES
TROMINOS
TROMMEL
TROMMELS
TROMP
TROMPE
TROMPED
TROMPES
TROMPING

T

TROMPS
TRON
TRONA
TRONAS
TRONC
TRONCS
TRONE
TRONES
TRONK
TRONKS
TRONS
TROOLIE
TROOLIES
TROOP
TROOPED
TROOPER
TROOPERS
TROOPIAL
TROOPIALS
TROOPING
TROOPS
TROOPSHIP
TROOSTITE
TROOZ
TROP
TROPAEOLA
TROPARIA
TROPARION
TROPE
TROPED
TROPEOLIN
TROPES
TROPHESY
TROPHI
TROPHIC
TROPHIED
TROPHIES
TROPHY
TROPHYING
TROPIC
TROPICAL
TROPICALS
TROPICS
TROPIN
TROPINE
TROPINES
TROPING
TROPINS
TROPISM
TROPISMS
TROPIST
TROPISTIC
TROPISTS
TROPOLOGY
TROPONIN
TROPONINS
TROPPO
TROSSERS
TROT
TROTH
TROTHED
TROTHFUL
TROTHING
TROTHLESS
TROTHS
TROTLINE
TROTLINES
TROTS
TROTTED
TROTTER
TROTTERS
TROTTING
TROTTINGS
TROTTOIR
TROTTOIRS
TROTYL
TROTYLS
TROU
TROUBLE
TROUBLED
TROUBLER
TROUBLERS
TROUBLES
TROUBLING
TROUBLOUS
TROUCH
TROUCHES
TROUGH
TROUGHED
TROUGHING
TROUGHS
TROULE
TROULED
TROULES
TROULING
TROUNCE
TROUNCED
TROUNCER
TROUNCERS
TROUNCES
TROUNCING
TROUPE
TROUPED
TROUPER
TROUPERS
TROUPES
TROUPIAL
TROUPIALS
TROUPING
TROUSE
TROUSER
TROUSERED
TROUSERS
TROUSES
TROUSSEAU
TROUT
TROUTER
TROUTERS
TROUTFUL
TROUTIER
TROUTIEST
TROUTING
TROUTINGS
TROUTLESS
TROUTLET
TROUTLETS
TROUTLIKE
TROUTLING
TROUTS
TROUTY
TROUVERE
TROUVERES
TROUVEUR
TROUVEURS
TROVE
TROVER
TROVERS
TROVES
TROW
TROWED
TROWEL
TROWELED
TROWELER
TROWELERS
TROWELING
TROWELLED
TROWELLER
TROWELS
TROWING
TROWS
TROWSERS
TROWTH
TROWTHS
TROY
TROYS
TRUANCIES
TRUANCY
TRUANT
TRUANTED
TRUANTING
TRUANTLY
TRUANTRY
TRUANTS
TRUCAGE
TRUCAGES
TRUCE
TRUCED
TRUCELESS
TRUCES
TRUCHMAN
TRUCHMANS
TRUCHMEN
TRUCIAL
TRUCING
TRUCK
TRUCKABLE
TRUCKAGE
TRUCKAGES
TRUCKED
TRUCKER
TRUCKERS
TRUCKFUL
TRUCKFULS
TRUCKIE
TRUCKIES
TRUCKING
TRUCKINGS
TRUCKLE
TRUCKLED
TRUCKLER
TRUCKLERS
TRUCKLES
TRUCKLINE
TRUCKLING
TRUCKLOAD
TRUCKMAN
TRUCKMEN
TRUCKS
TRUCKSTOP
TRUCULENT
TRUDGE
TRUDGED
TRUDGEN
TRUDGENS
TRUDGEON
TRUDGEONS
TRUDGER
TRUDGERS
TRUDGES
TRUDGING
TRUDGINGS
TRUE
TRUEBLUE
TRUEBLUES
TRUEBORN
TRUEBRED
TRUED
TRUEING
TRUELOVE
TRUELOVES
TRUEMAN
TRUEMEN
TRUENESS
TRUEPENNY
TRUER
TRUES
TRUEST
TRUFFE
TRUFFES
TRUFFLE
TRUFFLED
TRUFFLES
TRUFFLING
TRUG
TRUGO
TRUGOS
TRUGS
TRUING
TRUISM
TRUISMS

T

TRUISTIC
TRULL
TRULLS
TRULY
TRUMEAU
TRUMEAUX
TRUMP
TRUMPED
TRUMPERY
TRUMPET
TRUMPETED
TRUMPETER
TRUMPETS
TRUMPING
TRUMPINGS
TRUMPLESS
TRUMPS
TRUNCAL
TRUNCATE
TRUNCATED
TRUNCATES
TRUNCHEON
TRUNDLE
TRUNDLED
TRUNDLER
TRUNDLERS
TRUNDLES
TRUNDLING
TRUNK
TRUNKED
TRUNKFISH
TRUNKFUL
TRUNKFULS
TRUNKING
TRUNKINGS
TRUNKLESS
TRUNKLIKE
TRUNKS
TRUNKWORK
TRUNNEL
TRUNNELS
TRUNNION
TRUNNIONS
TRUQUAGE
TRUQUAGES
TRUQUEUR
TRUQUEURS
TRUSS
TRUSSED
TRUSSER
TRUSSERS
TRUSSES
TRUSSING
TRUSSINGS
TRUST
TRUSTABLE
TRUSTED
TRUSTEE
TRUSTEED
TRUSTEES
TRUSTER
TRUSTERS
TRUSTFUL
TRUSTIER
TRUSTIES
TRUSTIEST
TRUSTILY
TRUSTING
TRUSTLESS
TRUSTOR
TRUSTORS
TRUSTS
TRUSTY
TRUTH
TRUTHER
TRUTHERS
TRUTHFUL
TRUTHIER
TRUTHIEST
TRUTHLESS
TRUTHLIKE
TRUTHS
TRUTHY
TRY
TRYE
TRYER
TRYERS
TRYING
TRYINGLY
TRYINGS
TRYKE
TRYKES
TRYMA
TRYMATA
TRYOUT
TRYOUTS
TRYP
TRYPAN
TRYPS
TRYPSIN
TRYPSINS
TRYPTIC
TRYSAIL
TRYSAILS
TRYST
TRYSTE
TRYSTED
TRYSTER
TRYSTERS
TRYSTES
TRYSTING
TRYSTS
TRYWORKS
TSADDIK
TSADDIKIM
TSADDIKS
TSADDIQ
TSADDIQIM
TSADDIQS
TSADE
TSADES
TSADI
TSADIK
TSADIKS
TSADIS
TSAMBA
TSAMBAS
TSANTSA
TSANTSAS
TSAR
TSARDOM
TSARDOMS
TSAREVICH
TSAREVNA
TSAREVNAS
TSARINA
TSARINAS
TSARISM
TSARISMS
TSARIST
TSARISTS
TSARITSA
TSARITSAS
TSARITZA
TSARITZAS
TSARS
TSATSKE
TSATSKES
TSESSEBE
TSESSEBES
TSETSE
TSETSES
TSIGANE
TSIGANES
TSIMMES
TSITSITH
TSK
TSKED
TSKING
TSKS
TSKTSK
TSKTSKED
TSKTSKING
TSKTSKS
TSOORIS
TSORES
TSORIS
TSORRISS
TSOTSI
TSOTSIS
TSOURIS
TSOURISES
TSUBA
TSUBAS
TSUBO
TSUBOS
TSUNAMI
TSUNAMIC
TSUNAMIS
TSURIS
TSURISES
TSUTSUMU
TSUTSUMUS
TUAN
TUANS
TUART
TUARTS
TUATARA
TUATARAS
TUATERA
TUATERAS
TUATH
TUATHS
TUATUA
TUATUAS
TUB
TUBA
TUBAE
TUBAGE
TUBAGES
TUBAIST
TUBAISTS
TUBAL
TUBAR
TUBAS
TUBATE
TUBBABLE
TUBBED
TUBBER
TUBBERS
TUBBIER
TUBBIEST
TUBBINESS
TUBBING
TUBBINGS
TUBBISH
TUBBY
TUBE
TUBECTOMY
TUBED
TUBEFUL
TUBEFULS
TUBELESS
TUBELIKE
TUBENOSE
TUBENOSES
TUBER
TUBERCLE
TUBERCLED
TUBERCLES
TUBERCULA
TUBERCULE
TUBEROID
TUBEROIDS
TUBEROSE
TUBEROSES
TUBEROUS
TUBERS
TUBES
TUBEWELL

TUBEWELLS
TUBEWORK
TUBEWORKS
TUBEWORM
TUBEWORMS
TUBFAST
TUBFASTS
TUBFISH
TUBFISHES
TUBFUL
TUBFULS
TUBICOLAR
TUBICOLE
TUBICOLES
TUBIFEX
TUBIFEXES
TUBIFICID
TUBIFORM
TUBING
TUBINGS
TUBIST
TUBISTS
TUBLIKE
TUBS
TUBULAR
TUBULARLY
TUBULARS
TUBULATE
TUBULATED
TUBULATES
TUBULATOR
TUBULE
TUBULES
TUBULIN
TUBULINS
TUBULOSE
TUBULOUS
TUBULURE
TUBULURES
TUCHIS
TUCHISES
TUCHUN
TUCHUNS
TUCHUS
TUCHUSES
TUCK
TUCKAHOE
TUCKAHOES
TUCKAMORE
TUCKBOX
TUCKBOXES
TUCKED
TUCKER
TUCKERBAG
TUCKERBOX
TUCKERED
TUCKERING
TUCKERS
TUCKET
TUCKETS
TUCKING
TUCKINGS
TUCKS
TUCKSHOP
TUCKSHOPS
TUCOTUCO
TUCOTUCOS
TUCUTUCO
TUCUTUCOS
TUCUTUCU
TUCUTUCUS
TUFA
TUFACEOUS
TUFAS
TUFF
TUFFE
TUFFES
TUFFET
TUFFETS
TUFFS
TUFOLI
TUFOLIS
TUFT
TUFTED
TUFTER
TUFTERS
TUFTIER
TUFTIEST
TUFTILY
TUFTING
TUFTINGS
TUFTS
TUFTY
TUG
TUGBOAT
TUGBOATS
TUGGED
TUGGER
TUGGERS
TUGGING
TUGGINGLY
TUGGINGS
TUGHRA
TUGHRAS
TUGHRIK
TUGHRIKS
TUGLESS
TUGRA
TUGRAS
TUGRIK
TUGRIKS
TUGS
TUI
TUILE
TUILES
TUILLE
TUILLES
TUILLETTE
TUILYIE
TUILYIED
TUILYIES
TUILZIE
TUILZIED
TUILZIES
TUINA
TUINAS
TUIS
TUISM
TUISMS
TUITION
TUITIONAL
TUITIONS
TUKTOO
TUKTOOS
TUKTU
TUKTUS
TULADI
TULADIS
TULAREMIA
TULAREMIC
TULBAN
TULBANS
TULCHAN
TULCHANS
TULE
TULES
TULIP
TULIPANT
TULIPANTS
TULIPLIKE
TULIPS
TULIPWOOD
TULLE
TULLES
TULLIBEE
TULLIBEES
TULPA
TULPAS
TULSI
TULSIS
TULWAR
TULWARS
TUM
TUMBLE
TUMBLEBUG
TUMBLED
TUMBLER
TUMBLERS
TUMBLES
TUMBLESET
TUMBLING
TUMBLINGS
TUMBREL
TUMBRELS
TUMBRIL
TUMBRILS
TUMEFIED
TUMEFIES
TUMEFY
TUMEFYING
TUMESCE
TUMESCED
TUMESCENT
TUMESCES
TUMESCING
TUMID
TUMIDITY
TUMIDLY
TUMIDNESS
TUMMIES
TUMMLER
TUMMLERS
TUMMY
TUMOR
TUMORAL
TUMORLIKE
TUMOROUS
TUMORS
TUMOUR
TUMOURS
TUMP
TUMPED
TUMPHIES
TUMPHY
TUMPIER
TUMPIEST
TUMPING
TUMPLINE
TUMPLINES
TUMPS
TUMPY
TUMS
TUMSHIE
TUMSHIES
TUMULAR
TUMULARY
TUMULI
TUMULOSE
TUMULOUS
TUMULT
TUMULTED
TUMULTING
TUMULTS
TUMULUS
TUMULUSES
TUN
TUNA
TUNABLE
TUNABLY
TUNAS
TUNBELLY
TUND
TUNDED
TUNDING
TUNDISH
TUNDISHES
TUNDRA
TUNDRAS
TUNDS
TUNDUN

TUNDUNS
TUNE
TUNEABLE
TUNEABLY
TUNEAGE
TUNEAGES
TUNED
TUNEFUL
TUNEFULLY
TUNELESS
TUNER
TUNERS
TUNES
TUNESMITH
TUNEUP
TUNEUPS
TUNG
TUNGS
TUNGSTATE
TUNGSTEN
TUNGSTENS
TUNGSTIC
TUNGSTITE
TUNGSTOUS
TUNIC
TUNICA
TUNICAE
TUNICATE
TUNICATED
TUNICATES
TUNICIN
TUNICINS
TUNICKED
TUNICLE
TUNICLES
TUNICS
TUNIER
TUNIEST
TUNING
TUNINGS
TUNKET
TUNKETS
TUNNAGE
TUNNAGES
TUNNED
TUNNEL
TUNNELED
TUNNELER

TUNNELERS
TUNNELING
TUNNELLED
TUNNELLER
TUNNELS
TUNNIES
TUNNING
TUNNINGS
TUNNY
TUNS
TUNY
TUP
TUPEK
TUPEKS
TUPELO
TUPELOS
TUPIK
TUPIKS
TUPLE
TUPLES
TUPPED
TUPPENCE
TUPPENCES
TUPPENNY
TUPPING
TUPPINGS
TUPS
TUPTOWING
TUPUNA
TUPUNAS
TUQUE
TUQUES
TURACIN
TURACINS
TURACO
TURACOS
TURACOU
TURACOUS
TURBAN
TURBAND
TURBANDS
TURBANED
TURBANNED
TURBANS
TURBANT
TURBANTS
TURBARIES
TURBARY

TURBETH
TURBETHS
TURBID
TURBIDITE
TURBIDITY
TURBIDLY
TURBINAL
TURBINALS
TURBINATE
TURBINE
TURBINED
TURBINES
TURBIT
TURBITH
TURBITHS
TURBITS
TURBO
TURBOCAR
TURBOCARS
TURBOFAN
TURBOFANS
TURBOJET
TURBOJETS
TURBOND
TURBONDS
TURBOPROP
TURBOS
TURBOT
TURBOTS
TURBULENT
TURCOPOLE
TURD
TURDINE
TURDION
TURDIONS
TURDOID
TURDS
TURDUCKEN
TUREEN
TUREENS
TURF
TURFED
TURFEN
TURFGRASS
TURFIER
TURFIEST
TURFINESS
TURFING

TURFINGS
TURFITE
TURFITES
TURFLESS
TURFLIKE
TURFMAN
TURFMEN
TURFS
TURFSKI
TURFSKIS
TURFY
TURGENCY
TURGENT
TURGENTLY
TURGID
TURGIDER
TURGIDEST
TURGIDITY
TURGIDLY
TURGITE
TURGITES
TURGOR
TURGORS
TURION
TURIONS
TURISTA
TURISTAS
TURK
TURKEY
TURKEYS
TURKIES
TURKIESES
TURKIS
TURKISES
TURKOIS
TURKOISES
TURKS
TURLOUGH
TURLOUGHS
TURM
TURME
TURMERIC
TURMERICS
TURMES
TURMOIL
TURMOILED
TURMOILS
TURMS

TURN
TURNABLE
TURNABOUT
TURNAGAIN
TURNBACK
TURNBACKS
TURNCOAT
TURNCOATS
TURNCOCK
TURNCOCKS
TURNDOWN
TURNDOWNS
TURNDUN
TURNDUNS
TURNED
TURNER
TURNERIES
TURNERS
TURNERY
TURNHALL
TURNHALLS
TURNING
TURNINGS
TURNIP
TURNIPED
TURNIPIER
TURNIPING
TURNIPS
TURNIPY
TURNKEY
TURNKEYS
TURNOFF
TURNOFFS
TURNON
TURNONS
TURNOUT
TURNOUTS
TURNOVER
TURNOVERS
TURNPIKE
TURNPIKES
TURNROUND
TURNS
TURNSKIN
TURNSKINS
TURNSOLE
TURNSOLES
TURNSPIT

T

TURNSPITS
TURNSTILE
TURNSTONE
TURNT
TURNTABLE
TURNUP
TURNUPS
TUROPHILE
TURPETH
TURPETHS
TURPITUDE
TURPS
TURQUOIS
TURQUOISE
TURR
TURRET
TURRETED
TURRETS
TURRIBANT
TURRICAL
TURRS
TURTLE
TURTLED
TURTLER
TURTLERS
TURTLES
TURTLING
TURTLINGS
TURVES
TUSCHE
TUSCHES
TUSH
TUSHED
TUSHERIES
TUSHERY
TUSHES
TUSHIE
TUSHIES
TUSHING
TUSHKAR
TUSHKARS
TUSHKER
TUSHKERS
TUSHY
TUSK
TUSKAR
TUSKARS
TUSKED
TUSKER
TUSKERS
TUSKIER
TUSKIEST
TUSKING
TUSKINGS
TUSKLESS
TUSKLIKE
TUSKS
TUSKY
TUSSAC
TUSSAH
TUSSAHS
TUSSAL
TUSSAR
TUSSARS
TUSSEH
TUSSEHS
TUSSER
TUSSERS
TUSSES
TUSSIS
TUSSISES
TUSSIVE
TUSSLE
TUSSLED
TUSSLES
TUSSLING
TUSSOCK
TUSSOCKED
TUSSOCKS
TUSSOCKY
TUSSOR
TUSSORE
TUSSORES
TUSSORS
TUSSUCK
TUSSUCKS
TUSSUR
TUSSURS
TUT
TUTANIA
TUTANIAS
TUTEE
TUTEES
TUTELAGE
TUTELAGES
TUTELAR
TUTELARS
TUTELARY
TUTENAG
TUTENAGS
TUTIORISM
TUTIORIST
TUTMAN
TUTMEN
TUTOR
TUTORAGE
TUTORAGES
TUTORED
TUTORESS
TUTORIAL
TUTORIALS
TUTORING
TUTORINGS
TUTORISE
TUTORISED
TUTORISES
TUTORISM
TUTORISMS
TUTORIZE
TUTORIZED
TUTORIZES
TUTORS
TUTORSHIP
TUTOYED
TUTOYER
TUTOYERED
TUTOYERS
TUTRESS
TUTRESSES
TUTRICES
TUTRIX
TUTRIXES
TUTS
TUTSAN
TUTSANS
TUTSED
TUTSES
TUTSING
TUTTED
TUTTI
TUTTIES
TUTTING
TUTTINGS
TUTTIS
TUTTY
TUTU
TUTUED
TUTUS
TUTWORK
TUTWORKER
TUTWORKS
TUX
TUXEDO
TUXEDOED
TUXEDOES
TUXEDOS
TUXES
TUYER
TUYERE
TUYERES
TUYERS
TUZZ
TUZZES
TWA
TWADDLE
TWADDLED
TWADDLER
TWADDLERS
TWADDLES
TWADDLIER
TWADDLING
TWADDLY
TWAE
TWAES
TWAFALD
TWAIN
TWAINS
TWAITE
TWAITES
TWAL
TWALPENNY
TWALS
TWANG
TWANGED
TWANGER
TWANGERS
TWANGIER
TWANGIEST
TWANGING
TWANGINGS
TWANGLE
TWANGLED
TWANGLER
TWANGLERS
TWANGLES
TWANGLING
TWANGS
TWANGY
TWANK
TWANKAY
TWANKAYS
TWANKED
TWANKIES
TWANKING
TWANKS
TWANKY
TWAS
TWASOME
TWASOMES
TWAT
TWATS
TWATTED
TWATTING
TWATTLE
TWATTLED
TWATTLER
TWATTLERS
TWATTLES
TWATTLING
TWAY
TWAYBLADE
TWAYS
TWEAK
TWEAKED
TWEAKER
TWEAKERS
TWEAKIER
TWEAKIEST
TWEAKING
TWEAKINGS
TWEAKS
TWEAKY
TWEE
TWEED
TWEEDIER
TWEEDIEST
TWEEDILY
TWEEDLE
TWEEDLED
TWEEDLER

TWEEDLERS
TWEEDLES
TWEEDLING
TWEEDS
TWEEDY
TWEEL
TWEELED
TWEELING
TWEELS
TWEELY
TWEEN
TWEENAGE
TWEENAGER
TWEENER
TWEENERS
TWEENESS
TWEENIE
TWEENIES
TWEENS
TWEENY
TWEEP
TWEEPLE
TWEEPS
TWEER
TWEERED
TWEERING
TWEERS
TWEEST
TWEET
TWEETABLE
TWEETED
TWEETER
TWEETERS
TWEETING
TWEETS
TWEETUP
TWEETUPS
TWEEZE
TWEEZED
TWEEZER
TWEEZERS
TWEEZES
TWEEZING
TWELFTH
TWELFTHLY
TWELFTHS
TWELVE
TWELVEMO
TWELVEMOS
TWELVES
TWENTIES
TWENTIETH
TWENTY
TWENTYISH
TWERK
TWERKED
TWERKING
TWERKINGS
TWERKS
TWERP
TWERPIER
TWERPIEST
TWERPS
TWERPY
TWIBIL
TWIBILL
TWIBILLS
TWIBILS
TWICE
TWICER
TWICERS
TWICHILD
TWIDDLE
TWIDDLED
TWIDDLER
TWIDDLERS
TWIDDLES
TWIDDLIER
TWIDDLING
TWIDDLY
TWIER
TWIERS
TWIFOLD
TWIFORKED
TWIFORMED
TWIG
TWIGGED
TWIGGEN
TWIGGER
TWIGGERS
TWIGGIER
TWIGGIEST
TWIGGING
TWIGGY
TWIGHT
TWIGHTED
TWIGHTING
TWIGHTS
TWIGLESS
TWIGLET
TWIGLETS
TWIGLIKE
TWIGLOO
TWIGLOOS
TWIGS
TWIGSOME
TWILIGHT
TWILIGHTS
TWILIT
TWILL
TWILLED
TWILLIES
TWILLING
TWILLINGS
TWILLS
TWILLY
TWILT
TWILTED
TWILTING
TWILTS
TWIN
TWINBERRY
TWINBORN
TWINE
TWINED
TWINER
TWINERS
TWINES
TWINGE
TWINGED
TWINGEING
TWINGES
TWINGING
TWINIER
TWINIEST
TWINIGHT
TWINING
TWININGLY
TWININGS
TWINJET
TWINJETS
TWINK
TWINKED
TWINKIE
TWINKIES
TWINKING
TWINKLE
TWINKLED
TWINKLER
TWINKLERS
TWINKLES
TWINKLIER
TWINKLING
TWINKLY
TWINKS
TWINKY
TWINLING
TWINLINGS
TWINNED
TWINNING
TWINNINGS
TWINS
TWINSET
TWINSETS
TWINSHIP
TWINSHIPS
TWINTER
TWINTERS
TWINY
TWIRE
TWIRED
TWIRES
TWIRING
TWIRL
TWIRLED
TWIRLER
TWIRLERS
TWIRLIER
TWIRLIEST
TWIRLING
TWIRLS
TWIRLY
TWIRP
TWIRPIER
TWIRPIEST
TWIRPS
TWIRPY
TWISCAR
TWISCARS
TWIST
TWISTABLE
TWISTED
TWISTER
TWISTERS
TWISTIER
TWISTIEST
TWISTING
TWISTINGS
TWISTOR
TWISTORS
TWISTS
TWISTY
TWIT
TWITCH
TWITCHED
TWITCHER
TWITCHERS
TWITCHES
TWITCHIER
TWITCHILY
TWITCHING
TWITCHY
TWITE
TWITES
TWITS
TWITTED
TWITTEN
TWITTENS
TWITTER
TWITTERED
TWITTERER
TWITTERS
TWITTERY
TWITTING
TWITTINGS
TWITTISH
TWIXT
TWIZZLE
TWIZZLED
TWIZZLES
TWIZZLING
TWO
TWOCCER
TWOCCERS
TWOCCING
TWOCCINGS
TWOCKER
TWOCKERS
TWOCKING
TWOCKINGS

T

TWOER
TWOERS
TWOFER
TWOFERS
TWOFOLD
TWOFOLDS
TWONESS
TWONESSES
TWONIE
TWONIES
TWOONIE
TWOONIES
TWOPENCE
TWOPENCES
TWOPENNY
TWOS
TWOSEATER
TWOSOME
TWOSOMES
TWOSTROKE
TWP
TWYER
TWYERE
TWYERES
TWYERS
TWYFOLD
TYCHISM
TYCHISMS
TYCOON
TYCOONATE
TYCOONERY
TYCOONS
TYDE
TYE
TYED
TYEE
TYEES
TYEING
TYER
TYERS
TYES
TYG
TYGS
TYIN
TYING
TYIYN
TYIYNS
TYKE
TYKES
TYKISH
TYLECTOMY
TYLER
TYLERS
TYLOPOD
TYLOPODS
TYLOSES
TYLOSIN
TYLOSINS
TYLOSIS
TYLOTE
TYLOTES
TYMBAL
TYMBALS
TYMP
TYMPAN
TYMPANA
TYMPANAL
TYMPANI
TYMPANIC
TYMPANICS
TYMPANIES
TYMPANIST
TYMPANO
TYMPANS
TYMPANUM
TYMPANUMS
TYMPANY
TYMPS
TYND
TYNDE
TYNE
TYNED
TYNES
TYNING
TYPABLE
TYPAL
TYPE
TYPEABLE
TYPEBAR
TYPEBARS
TYPECASE
TYPECASES
TYPECAST
TYPECASTS
TYPED
TYPEFACE
TYPEFACES
TYPES
TYPESET
TYPESETS
TYPESTYLE
TYPEWRITE
TYPEWROTE
TYPEY
TYPHLITIC
TYPHLITIS
TYPHOID
TYPHOIDAL
TYPHOIDIN
TYPHOIDS
TYPHON
TYPHONIAN
TYPHONIC
TYPHONS
TYPHOON
TYPHOONS
TYPHOSE
TYPHOUS
TYPHUS
TYPHUSES
TYPIC
TYPICAL
TYPICALLY
TYPIER
TYPIEST
TYPIFIED
TYPIFIER
TYPIFIERS
TYPIFIES
TYPIFY
TYPIFYING
TYPING
TYPINGS
TYPIST
TYPISTS
TYPO
TYPOGRAPH
TYPOLOGIC
TYPOLOGY
TYPOMANIA
TYPOS
TYPP
TYPPS
TYPTO
TYPTOED
TYPTOING
TYPTOS
TYPY
TYRAMINE
TYRAMINES
TYRAN
TYRANED
TYRANING
TYRANNE
TYRANNED
TYRANNES
TYRANNESS
TYRANNIC
TYRANNIES
TYRANNING
TYRANNIS
TYRANNISE
TYRANNIZE
TYRANNOUS
TYRANNY
TYRANS
TYRANT
TYRANTED
TYRANTING
TYRANTS
TYRE
TYRED
TYRELESS
TYREMAKER
TYRES
TYRING
TYRO
TYROCIDIN
TYROES
TYRONES
TYRONIC
TYROPITA
TYROPITAS
TYROPITTA
TYROS
TYROSINE
TYROSINES
TYSTIE
TYSTIES
TYTE
TYTHE
TYTHED
TYTHES
TYTHING
TZADDI
TZADDIK
TZADDIKIM
TZADDIKS
TZADDIQ
TZADDIQIM
TZADDIQS
TZADDIS
TZADIK
TZADIKS
TZAR
TZARDOM
TZARDOMS
TZAREVNA
TZAREVNAS
TZARINA
TZARINAS
TZARISM
TZARISMS
TZARIST
TZARISTS
TZARITZA
TZARITZAS
TZARS
TZATZIKI
TZATZIKIS
TZEDAKAH
TZEDAKAHS
TZETSE
TZETSES
TZETZE
TZETZES
TZIGANE
TZIGANES
TZIGANIES
TZIGANY
TZIMMES
TZITZIS
TZITZIT
TZITZITH
TZURIS
TZURISES

U

UAKARI
UAKARIS
UBEROUS
UBERTIES
UBERTY
UBIETIES
UBIETY
UBIQUE
UBIQUITIN
UBIQUITY
UBUNTU
UBUNTUS
UCKERS
UDAL
UDALLER
UDALLERS
UDALS
UDDER
UDDERED
UDDERFUL
UDDERFULS
UDDERLESS
UDDERS
UDO
UDOMETER
UDOMETERS
UDOMETRIC
UDOMETRY
UDON
UDONS
UDOS
UDS
UEY
UEYS
UFO
UFOLOGIES
UFOLOGIST
UFOLOGY
UFOS
UG
UGALI
UGALIS
UGGED
UGGING
UGH
UGHS
UGLIED
UGLIER
UGLIES
UGLIEST
UGLIFIED
UGLIFIER
UGLIFIERS
UGLIFIES
UGLIFY
UGLIFYING
UGLILY
UGLINESS
UGLY
UGLYING
UGS
UGSOME
UH
UHLAN
UHLANS
UHURU
UHURUS
UILLEAN
UILLEANN
UINTAHITE
UINTAITE
UINTAITES
UITLANDER
UJAMAA
UJAMAAS
UKASE
UKASES
UKE
UKELELE
UKELELES
UKES
UKULELE
UKULELES
ULAMA
ULAMAS
ULAN
ULANS
ULCER
ULCERATE
ULCERATED
ULCERATES
ULCERED
ULCERING
ULCEROUS
ULCERS
ULE
ULEMA
ULEMAS
ULES
ULEX
ULEXES
ULEXITE
ULEXITES
ULICES
ULICON
ULICONS
ULIGINOSE
ULIGINOUS
ULIKON
ULIKONS
ULITIS
ULITISES
ULLAGE
ULLAGED
ULLAGES
ULLAGING
ULLING
ULLINGS
ULMACEOUS
ULMIN
ULMINS
ULNA
ULNAD
ULNAE
ULNAR
ULNARE
ULNARIA
ULNAS
ULOSES
ULOSIS
ULOTRICHY
ULPAN
ULPANIM
ULSTER
ULSTERED
ULSTERS
ULTERIOR
ULTIMA
ULTIMACY
ULTIMAS
ULTIMATA
ULTIMATE
ULTIMATED
ULTIMATES
ULTIMATUM
ULTIMO
ULTION
ULTIONS
ULTISOL
ULTISOLS
ULTRA
ULTRACHIC
ULTRACOLD
ULTRACOOL
ULTRADRY
ULTRAFAST
ULTRAFINE
ULTRAHEAT
ULTRAHIGH
ULTRAHIP
ULTRAHOT
ULTRAISM
ULTRAISMS
ULTRAIST
ULTRAISTS
ULTRALEFT
ULTRALOW
ULTRAPOSH
ULTRAPURE
ULTRARARE
ULTRARED
ULTRAREDS
ULTRARICH
ULTRAS
ULTRASAFE
ULTRASLOW
ULTRASOFT
ULTRATHIN
ULTRATINY
ULTRAWIDE
ULU
ULULANT
ULULATE
ULULATED
ULULATES
ULULATING
ULULATION
ULUS
ULVA
ULVAS
ULYIE
ULYIES
ULZIE
ULZIES
UM
UMAMI
UMAMIS
UMANGITE
UMANGITES
UMBEL
UMBELED
UMBELLAR
UMBELLATE
UMBELLED
UMBELLET
UMBELLETS
UMBELLULE
UMBELS
UMBELULE
UMBELULES

U

UMBER
UMBERED
UMBERIER
UMBERIEST
UMBERING
UMBERS
UMBERY
UMBILICAL
UMBILICI
UMBILICUS
UMBLE
UMBLES
UMBO
UMBONAL
UMBONATE
UMBONES
UMBONIC
UMBOS
UMBRA
UMBRACULA
UMBRAE
UMBRAGE
UMBRAGED
UMBRAGES
UMBRAGING
UMBRAL
UMBRAS
UMBRATED
UMBRATIC
UMBRATILE
UMBRE
UMBREL
UMBRELLA
UMBRELLAS
UMBRELLO
UMBRELLOS
UMBRELS
UMBRERE
UMBRERES
UMBRES
UMBRETTE
UMBRETTES
UMBRIERE
UMBRIERES
UMBRIL
UMBRILS
UMBROSE
UMBROUS
UME
UMEBOSHI
UMEBOSHIS
UMES
UMFAZI
UMFAZIS
UMIAC
UMIACK
UMIACKS
UMIACS
UMIAK
UMIAKS
UMIAQ
UMIAQS
UMLAUT
UMLAUTED
UMLAUTING
UMLAUTS
UMLUNGU
UMLUNGUS
UMM
UMMA
UMMAH
UMMAHS
UMMAS
UMMED
UMMING
UMP
UMPED
UMPH
UMPHS
UMPIE
UMPIES
UMPING
UMPIRAGE
UMPIRAGES
UMPIRE
UMPIRED
UMPIRES
UMPIRING
UMPS
UMPTEEN
UMPTEENTH
UMPTIER
UMPTIEST
UMPTIETH
UMPTY
UMPY
UMQUHILE
UMRA
UMRAH
UMRAHS
UMRAS
UMS
UMTEENTH
UMU
UMUS
UMWELT
UMWELTS
UMWHILE
UN
UNABASHED
UNABATED
UNABATING
UNABETTED
UNABIDING
UNABJURED
UNABLE
UNABORTED
UNABRADED
UNABUSED
UNABUSIVE
UNACCRUED
UNACCUSED
UNACERBIC
UNACHING
UNACIDIC
UNACTABLE
UNACTED
UNACTIVE
UNACTIVED
UNACTIVES
UNADAPTED
UNADDED
UNADEPT
UNADEPTLY
UNADEPTS
UNADMIRED
UNADOPTED
UNADORED
UNADORNED
UNADULT
UNADVISED
UNAFRAID
UNAGED
UNAGEING
UNAGILE
UNAGING
UNAGREED
UNAI
UNAIDABLE
UNAIDED
UNAIDEDLY
UNAIMED
UNAIRED
UNAIS
UNAKIN
UNAKING
UNAKITE
UNAKITES
UNALARMED
UNALERTED
UNALIGNED
UNALIKE
UNALIST
UNALISTS
UNALIVE
UNALLAYED
UNALLEGED
UNALLIED
UNALLOWED
UNALLOYED
UNALTERED
UNAMASSED
UNAMAZED
UNAMENDED
UNAMERCED
UNAMIABLE
UNAMUSED
UNAMUSING
UNANCHOR
UNANCHORS
UNANELED
UNANIMITY
UNANIMOUS
UNANNEXED
UNANNOYED
UNANXIOUS
UNAPPAREL
UNAPPLIED
UNAPT
UNAPTLY
UNAPTNESS
UNARCHED
UNARGUED
UNARISEN
UNARM
UNARMED
UNARMING
UNARMORED
UNARMS
UNAROUSED
UNARRAYED
UNARTFUL
UNARY
UNASHAMED
UNASKED
UNASSAYED
UNASSUMED
UNASSURED
UNATONED
UNATTIRED
UNATTUNED
UNAU
UNAUDITED
UNAUS
UNAVENGED
UNAVERAGE
UNAVERTED
UNAVOIDED
UNAVOWED
UNAWAKE
UNAWAKED
UNAWARDED
UNAWARE
UNAWARELY
UNAWARES
UNAWED
UNAWESOME
UNAXED
UNBACKED
UNBAFFLED
UNBAG
UNBAGGED
UNBAGGING
UNBAGS
UNBAITED
UNBAKED
UNBALANCE
UNBALE
UNBALED
UNBALES

U

UNBALING
UNBAN
UNBANDAGE
UNBANDED
UNBANKED
UNBANNED
UNBANNING
UNBANS
UNBAPTISE
UNBAPTIZE
UNBAR
UNBARBED
UNBARE
UNBARED
UNBARES
UNBARING
UNBARK
UNBARKED
UNBARKING
UNBARKS
UNBARRED
UNBARRING
UNBARS
UNBASED
UNBASHFUL
UNBASTED
UNBATED
UNBATHED
UNBE
UNBEAR
UNBEARDED
UNBEARED
UNBEARING
UNBEARS
UNBEATEN
UNBED
UNBEDDED
UNBEDDING
UNBEDS
UNBEEN
UNBEGET
UNBEGETS
UNBEGGED
UNBEGOT
UNBEGUILE
UNBEGUN
UNBEING
UNBEINGS
UNBEKNOWN
UNBELIEF
UNBELIEFS
UNBELIEVE
UNBELOVED
UNBELT
UNBELTED
UNBELTING
UNBELTS
UNBEMUSED
UNBEND
UNBENDED
UNBENDING
UNBENDS
UNBENIGN
UNBENT
UNBEREFT
UNBERUFEN
UNBESEEM
UNBESEEMS
UNBESPEAK
UNBESPOKE
UNBIAS
UNBIASED
UNBIASES
UNBIASING
UNBIASSED
UNBIASSES
UNBID
UNBIDDEN
UNBIGOTED
UNBILLED
UNBIND
UNBINDING
UNBINDS
UNBISHOP
UNBISHOPS
UNBITT
UNBITTED
UNBITTEN
UNBITTER
UNBITTING
UNBITTS
UNBLAMED
UNBLENDED
UNBLENT
UNBLESS
UNBLESSED
UNBLESSES
UNBLEST
UNBLIND
UNBLINDED
UNBLINDS
UNBLOCK
UNBLOCKED
UNBLOCKS
UNBLOODED
UNBLOODY
UNBLOTTED
UNBLOWED
UNBLOWN
UNBLUNTED
UNBLURRED
UNBOARDED
UNBOBBED
UNBODIED
UNBODING
UNBOILED
UNBOLT
UNBOLTED
UNBOLTING
UNBOLTS
UNBONDED
UNBONE
UNBONED
UNBONES
UNBONING
UNBONNET
UNBONNETS
UNBOOKED
UNBOOKISH
UNBOOT
UNBOOTED
UNBOOTING
UNBOOTS
UNBORE
UNBORN
UNBORNE
UNBOSOM
UNBOSOMED
UNBOSOMER
UNBOSOMS
UNBOTTLE
UNBOTTLED
UNBOTTLES
UNBOUGHT
UNBOUNCY
UNBOUND
UNBOUNDED
UNBOWED
UNBOWING
UNBOX
UNBOXED
UNBOXES
UNBOXING
UNBRACE
UNBRACED
UNBRACES
UNBRACING
UNBRAID
UNBRAIDED
UNBRAIDS
UNBRAKE
UNBRAKED
UNBRAKES
UNBRAKING
UNBRANDED
UNBRASTE
UNBRED
UNBREECH
UNBRIDGED
UNBRIDLE
UNBRIDLED
UNBRIDLES
UNBRIEFED
UNBRIGHT
UNBRIZZED
UNBROILED
UNBROKE
UNBROKEN
UNBROWNED
UNBRUISED
UNBRUSED
UNBRUSHED
UNBUCKLE
UNBUCKLED
UNBUCKLES
UNBUDDED
UNBUDGING
UNBUILD
UNBUILDS
UNBUILT
UNBULKIER
UNBULKY
UNBUNDLE
UNBUNDLED
UNBUNDLER
UNBUNDLES
UNBURDEN
UNBURDENS
UNBURIED
UNBURIES
UNBURNED
UNBURNT
UNBURROW
UNBURROWS
UNBURTHEN
UNBURY
UNBURYING
UNBUSIED
UNBUSIER
UNBUSIES
UNBUSIEST
UNBUSTED
UNBUSY
UNBUSYING
UNBUTTON
UNBUTTONS
UNCAGE
UNCAGED
UNCAGES
UNCAGING
UNCAKE
UNCAKED
UNCAKES
UNCAKING
UNCALLED
UNCANDID
UNCANDLED
UNCANDOR
UNCANDORS
UNCANDOUR
UNCANNED
UNCANNIER
UNCANNILY
UNCANNY
UNCANONIC
UNCAP
UNCAPABLE
UNCAPE
UNCAPED
UNCAPES

UNCAPING
UNCAPPED
UNCAPPING
UNCAPS
UNCARDED
UNCARED
UNCAREFUL
UNCARING
UNCART
UNCARTED
UNCARTING
UNCARTS
UNCARVED
UNCASE
UNCASED
UNCASES
UNCASHED
UNCASING
UNCASKED
UNCAST
UNCASTED
UNCASTING
UNCASTS
UNCATCHY
UNCATE
UNCATERED
UNCAUGHT
UNCAUSED
UNCE
UNCEASING
UNCEDED
UNCERTAIN
UNCES
UNCESSANT
UNCHAIN
UNCHAINED
UNCHAINS
UNCHAIR
UNCHAIRED
UNCHAIRS
UNCHANCY
UNCHANGED
UNCHARGE
UNCHARGED
UNCHARGES
UNCHARIER
UNCHARITY
UNCHARM
UNCHARMED
UNCHARMS
UNCHARNEL
UNCHARRED
UNCHARTED
UNCHARY
UNCHASTE
UNCHASTER
UNCHECK
UNCHECKED
UNCHECKS
UNCHEERED
UNCHEWED
UNCHIC
UNCHICLY
UNCHILD
UNCHILDED
UNCHILDS
UNCHILLED
UNCHOKE
UNCHOKED
UNCHOKES
UNCHOKING
UNCHOSEN
UNCHRISOM
UNCHURCH
UNCI
UNCIA
UNCIAE
UNCIAL
UNCIALLY
UNCIALS
UNCIFORM
UNCIFORMS
UNCINAL
UNCINARIA
UNCINATE
UNCINATED
UNCINI
UNCINUS
UNCIPHER
UNCIPHERS
UNCITED
UNCIVIL
UNCIVILLY
UNCLAD
UNCLAIMED
UNCLAMP
UNCLAMPED
UNCLAMPS
UNCLARITY
UNCLASP
UNCLASPED
UNCLASPS
UNCLASSED
UNCLASSY
UNCLAWED
UNCLE
UNCLEAN
UNCLEANED
UNCLEANER
UNCLEANLY
UNCLEAR
UNCLEARED
UNCLEARER
UNCLEARLY
UNCLED
UNCLEFT
UNCLENCH
UNCLES
UNCLESHIP
UNCLEW
UNCLEWED
UNCLEWING
UNCLEWS
UNCLICHED
UNCLIMBED
UNCLINCH
UNCLING
UNCLIP
UNCLIPPED
UNCLIPS
UNCLIPT
UNCLOAK
UNCLOAKED
UNCLOAKS
UNCLOG
UNCLOGGED
UNCLOGS
UNCLONED
UNCLOSE
UNCLOSED
UNCLOSES
UNCLOSING
UNCLOTHE
UNCLOTHED
UNCLOTHES
UNCLOUD
UNCLOUDED
UNCLOUDS
UNCLOUDY
UNCLOVEN
UNCLOYED
UNCLOYING
UNCLUTCH
UNCLUTTER
UNCO
UNCOATED
UNCOATING
UNCOBBLED
UNCOCK
UNCOCKED
UNCOCKING
UNCOCKS
UNCODED
UNCOER
UNCOERCED
UNCOES
UNCOEST
UNCOFFIN
UNCOFFINS
UNCOIL
UNCOILED
UNCOILING
UNCOILS
UNCOINED
UNCOLORED
UNCOLT
UNCOLTED
UNCOLTING
UNCOLTS
UNCOMBED
UNCOMBINE
UNCOMELY
UNCOMFIER
UNCOMFY
UNCOMIC
UNCOMMON
UNCONCERN
UNCONFINE
UNCONFORM
UNCONFUSE
UNCONGEAL
UNCOOKED
UNCOOL
UNCOOLED
UNCOPE
UNCOPED
UNCOPES
UNCOPING
UNCORD
UNCORDED
UNCORDIAL
UNCORDING
UNCORDS
UNCORK
UNCORKED
UNCORKING
UNCORKS
UNCORRUPT
UNCOS
UNCOSTLY
UNCOUNTED
UNCOUPLE
UNCOUPLED
UNCOUPLER
UNCOUPLES
UNCOURTLY
UNCOUTH
UNCOUTHER
UNCOUTHLY
UNCOVER
UNCOVERED
UNCOVERS
UNCOWL
UNCOWLED
UNCOWLING
UNCOWLS
UNCOY
UNCOYNED
UNCRACKED
UNCRATE
UNCRATED
UNCRATES
UNCRATING
UNCRAZIER
UNCRAZY
UNCREASED
UNCREATE
UNCREATED
UNCREATES
UNCREWED

UNCROPPED
UNCROSS
UNCROSSED
UNCROSSES
UNCROWDED
UNCROWN
UNCROWNED
UNCROWNS
UNCRUDDED
UNCRUMPLE
UNCRUSHED
UNCTION
UNCTIONS
UNCTUOUS
UNCUFF
UNCUFFED
UNCUFFING
UNCUFFS
UNCULLED
UNCURABLE
UNCURABLY
UNCURB
UNCURBED
UNCURBING
UNCURBS
UNCURDLED
UNCURED
UNCURIOUS
UNCURL
UNCURLED
UNCURLING
UNCURLS
UNCURRENT
UNCURSE
UNCURSED
UNCURSES
UNCURSING
UNCURTAIN
UNCURVED
UNCUS
UNCUT
UNCUTE
UNCYNICAL
UNDAM
UNDAMAGED
UNDAMMED
UNDAMMING
UNDAMNED
UNDAMPED
UNDAMS
UNDARING
UNDASHED
UNDATABLE
UNDATE
UNDATED
UNDATES
UNDATING
UNDAUNTED
UNDAWNING
UNDAZZLE
UNDAZZLED
UNDAZZLES
UNDE
UNDEAD
UNDEAF
UNDEAFED
UNDEAFING
UNDEAFS
UNDEALT
UNDEAR
UNDEBASED
UNDEBATED
UNDECAGON
UNDECAYED
UNDECEIVE
UNDECENT
UNDECIDED
UNDECIMAL
UNDECK
UNDECKED
UNDECKING
UNDECKS
UNDEE
UNDEEDED
UNDEFACED
UNDEFIDE
UNDEFIED
UNDEFILED
UNDEFINED
UNDEIFIED
UNDEIFIES
UNDEIFY
UNDELAYED
UNDELETE
UNDELETED
UNDELETES
UNDELIGHT
UNDELUDED
UNDENIED
UNDENTED
UNDER
UNDERACT
UNDERACTS
UNDERAGE
UNDERAGED
UNDERAGES
UNDERARM
UNDERARMS
UNDERATE
UNDERBAKE
UNDERBEAR
UNDERBID
UNDERBIDS
UNDERBIT
UNDERBITE
UNDERBODY
UNDERBORE
UNDERBOSS
UNDERBRED
UNDERBRIM
UNDERBUD
UNDERBUDS
UNDERBUSH
UNDERBUY
UNDERBUYS
UNDERCARD
UNDERCART
UNDERCAST
UNDERCLAD
UNDERCLAY
UNDERCLUB
UNDERCOAT
UNDERCOOK
UNDERCOOL
UNDERCUT
UNDERCUTS
UNDERDAKS
UNDERDECK
UNDERDID
UNDERDO
UNDERDOER
UNDERDOES
UNDERDOG
UNDERDOGS
UNDERDONE
UNDERDOSE
UNDERDRAW
UNDERDREW
UNDEREAT
UNDEREATS
UNDERFED
UNDERFEED
UNDERFELT
UNDERFIRE
UNDERFISH
UNDERFLOW
UNDERFONG
UNDERFOOT
UNDERFUND
UNDERFUR
UNDERFURS
UNDERGIRD
UNDERGIRT
UNDERGO
UNDERGOD
UNDERGODS
UNDERGOER
UNDERGOES
UNDERGONE
UNDERGOWN
UNDERGRAD
UNDERHAIR
UNDERHAND
UNDERHEAT
UNDERHUNG
UNDERIVED
UNDERJAW
UNDERJAWS
UNDERKEEP
UNDERKEPT
UNDERKILL
UNDERKING
UNDERLAID
UNDERLAIN
UNDERLAP
UNDERLAPS
UNDERLAY
UNDERLAYS
UNDERLEAF
UNDERLET
UNDERLETS
UNDERLIE
UNDERLIER
UNDERLIES
UNDERLINE
UNDERLING
UNDERLIP
UNDERLIPS
UNDERLIT
UNDERLOAD
UNDERMAN
UNDERMANS
UNDERMEN
UNDERMINE
UNDERMOST
UNDERN
UNDERNOTE
UNDERNS
UNDERPAD
UNDERPADS
UNDERPAID
UNDERPART
UNDERPASS
UNDERPAY
UNDERPAYS
UNDERPEEP
UNDERPIN
UNDERPINS
UNDERPLAY
UNDERPLOT
UNDERPROP
UNDERRAN
UNDERRATE
UNDERRIPE
UNDERRUN
UNDERRUNS
UNDERSAID
UNDERSAY
UNDERSAYS
UNDERSEA
UNDERSEAL
UNDERSEAS
UNDERSELF
UNDERSELL
UNDERSET
UNDERSETS
UNDERSHOT
UNDERSIDE
UNDERSIGN
UNDERSIZE

U

UNDERSKY
UNDERSOIL
UNDERSOLD
UNDERSONG
UNDERSOW
UNDERSOWN
UNDERSOWS
UNDERSPIN
UNDERTAKE
UNDERTANE
UNDERTAX
UNDERTIME
UNDERTINT
UNDERTONE
UNDERTOOK
UNDERTOW
UNDERTOWS
UNDERUSE
UNDERUSED
UNDERUSES
UNDERVEST
UNDERVOTE
UNDERWAY
UNDERWEAR
UNDERWENT
UNDERWING
UNDERWIRE
UNDERWIT
UNDERWITS
UNDERWOOD
UNDERWOOL
UNDERWORK
UNDESERT
UNDESERTS
UNDESERVE
UNDESIRED
UNDEVOUT
UNDID
UNDIES
UNDIGHT
UNDIGHTS
UNDIGNIFY
UNDILUTED
UNDIMMED
UNDINE
UNDINES
UNDINISM
UNDINISMS
UNDINTED
UNDIPPED
UNDIVIDED
UNDIVINE
UNDO
UNDOABLE
UNDOCILE
UNDOCK
UNDOCKED
UNDOCKING
UNDOCKS
UNDOER
UNDOERS
UNDOES
UNDOING
UNDOINGS
UNDONE
UNDOOMED
UNDOS
UNDOTTED
UNDOUBLE
UNDOUBLED
UNDOUBLES
UNDOUBTED
UNDOWERED
UNDRAINED
UNDRAPE
UNDRAPED
UNDRAPES
UNDRAPING
UNDRAW
UNDRAWING
UNDRAWN
UNDRAWS
UNDREADED
UNDREAMED
UNDREAMT
UNDRESS
UNDRESSED
UNDRESSES
UNDREST
UNDREW
UNDRIED
UNDRILLED
UNDRIVEN
UNDROSSY
UNDROWNED
UNDRUNK
UNDUBBED
UNDUE
UNDUG
UNDULANCE
UNDULANCY
UNDULANT
UNDULAR
UNDULATE
UNDULATED
UNDULATES
UNDULATOR
UNDULLED
UNDULOSE
UNDULOUS
UNDULY
UNDUTEOUS
UNDUTIFUL
UNDY
UNDYED
UNDYING
UNDYINGLY
UNDYNAMIC
UNEAGER
UNEAGERLY
UNEARED
UNEARNED
UNEARTH
UNEARTHED
UNEARTHLY
UNEARTHS
UNEASE
UNEASES
UNEASIER
UNEASIEST
UNEASILY
UNEASY
UNEATABLE
UNEATEN
UNEATH
UNEATHES
UNEDGE
UNEDGED
UNEDGES
UNEDGING
UNEDIBLE
UNEDITED
UNEFFACED
UNELATED
UNELECTED
UNEMPTIED
UNENDED
UNENDING
UNENDOWED
UNENGAGED
UNENJOYED
UNENSURED
UNENTERED
UNENVIED
UNENVIOUS
UNENVYING
UNEQUABLE
UNEQUAL
UNEQUALED
UNEQUALLY
UNEQUALS
UNERASED
UNEROTIC
UNERRING
UNERUPTED
UNESPIED
UNESSAYED
UNESSENCE
UNETH
UNETHICAL
UNEVADED
UNEVEN
UNEVENER
UNEVENEST
UNEVENLY
UNEVOLVED
UNEXALTED
UNEXCITED
UNEXCUSED
UNEXOTIC
UNEXPERT
UNEXPIRED
UNEXPOSED
UNEXTINCT
UNEXTREME
UNEYED
UNFABLED
UNFACETED
UNFACT
UNFACTS
UNFADABLE
UNFADED
UNFADING
UNFAILING
UNFAIR
UNFAIRED
UNFAIRER
UNFAIREST
UNFAIRING
UNFAIRLY
UNFAIRS
UNFAITH
UNFAITHS
UNFAKED
UNFALLEN
UNFAMED
UNFAMOUS
UNFANCIED
UNFANCIER
UNFANCY
UNFANNED
UNFASTEN
UNFASTENS
UNFAULTY
UNFAVORED
UNFAZABLE
UNFAZED
UNFEARED
UNFEARFUL
UNFEARING
UNFED
UNFEED
UNFEELING
UNFEIGNED
UNFELLED
UNFELT
UNFELTED
UNFENCE
UNFENCED
UNFENCES
UNFENCING
UNFERTILE
UNFETTER
UNFETTERS
UNFEUDAL
UNFEUED
UNFIGURED
UNFILDE
UNFILED
UNFILIAL

U

UNFILLED
UNFILMED
UNFINE
UNFIRED
UNFIRM
UNFISHED
UNFIT
UNFITLY
UNFITNESS
UNFITS
UNFITTED
UNFITTER
UNFITTEST
UNFITTING
UNFIX
UNFIXED
UNFIXES
UNFIXING
UNFIXITY
UNFIXT
UNFLAPPED
UNFLASHY
UNFLAWED
UNFLEDGED
UNFLESH
UNFLESHED
UNFLESHES
UNFLESHLY
UNFLEXED
UNFLOORED
UNFLUSH
UNFLUSHED
UNFLUSHES
UNFLUTED
UNFLYABLE
UNFOCUSED
UNFOILED
UNFOLD
UNFOLDED
UNFOLDER
UNFOLDERS
UNFOLDING
UNFOLDS
UNFOLLOW
UNFOLLOWS
UNFOND
UNFONDLY
UNFOOL
UNFOOLED
UNFOOLING
UNFOOLS
UNFOOTED
UNFORBID
UNFORCED
UNFORGED
UNFORGOT
UNFORKED
UNFORM
UNFORMAL
UNFORMED
UNFORMING
UNFORMS
UNFORTUNE
UNFOUGHT
UNFOUND
UNFOUNDED
UNFRAMED
UNFRANKED
UNFRAUGHT
UNFREE
UNFREED
UNFREEDOM
UNFREEING
UNFREEMAN
UNFREEMEN
UNFREES
UNFREEZE
UNFREEZES
UNFRETTED
UNFRIEND
UNFRIENDS
UNFROCK
UNFROCKED
UNFROCKS
UNFROZE
UNFROZEN
UNFUELLED
UNFUMED
UNFUNDED
UNFUNNIER
UNFUNNILY
UNFUNNY
UNFURL
UNFURLED
UNFURLING
UNFURLS
UNFURNISH
UNFURRED
UNFUSED
UNFUSSED
UNFUSSIER
UNFUSSILY
UNFUSSY
UNGAG
UNGAGGED
UNGAGGING
UNGAGS
UNGAIN
UNGAINFUL
UNGAINLY
UNGALLANT
UNGALLED
UNGARBED
UNGARBLED
UNGATED
UNGAUGED
UNGAZED
UNGAZING
UNGEAR
UNGEARED
UNGEARING
UNGEARS
UNGELDED
UNGENIAL
UNGENTEEL
UNGENTLE
UNGENTLER
UNGENTLY
UNGENUINE
UNGERMANE
UNGET
UNGETS
UNGETTING
UNGHOSTED
UNGHOSTLY
UNGIFTED
UNGILD
UNGILDED
UNGILDING
UNGILDS
UNGILT
UNGIRD
UNGIRDED
UNGIRDING
UNGIRDS
UNGIRT
UNGIRTH
UNGIRTHED
UNGIRTHS
UNGIVING
UNGLAD
UNGLAZED
UNGLITZY
UNGLOSSED
UNGLOVE
UNGLOVED
UNGLOVES
UNGLOVING
UNGLUE
UNGLUED
UNGLUES
UNGLUING
UNGOD
UNGODDED
UNGODDING
UNGODLIER
UNGODLIKE
UNGODLILY
UNGODLY
UNGODS
UNGORD
UNGORED
UNGORGED
UNGOT
UNGOTTEN
UNGOWN
UNGOWNED
UNGOWNING
UNGOWNS
UNGRACED
UNGRADED
UNGRASSED
UNGRAVELY
UNGRAZED
UNGREASED
UNGREEDY
UNGREEN
UNGREENER
UNGROOMED
UNGROUND
UNGROUP
UNGROUPED
UNGROUPS
UNGROWN
UNGRUDGED
UNGUAL
UNGUARD
UNGUARDED
UNGUARDS
UNGUENT
UNGUENTA
UNGUENTS
UNGUENTUM
UNGUES
UNGUESSED
UNGUIDED
UNGUIFORM
UNGUILTY
UNGUINOUS
UNGUIS
UNGULA
UNGULAE
UNGULAR
UNGULATE
UNGULATES
UNGULED
UNGUM
UNGUMMED
UNGUMMING
UNGUMS
UNGYVE
UNGYVED
UNGYVES
UNGYVING
UNHABLE
UNHACKED
UNHAILED
UNHAIR
UNHAIRED
UNHAIRER
UNHAIRERS
UNHAIRING
UNHAIRS
UNHALLOW
UNHALLOWS
UNHALSED
UNHALVED
UNHAND
UNHANDED
UNHANDIER

U

UNHANDILY
UNHANDING
UNHANDLED
UNHANDS
UNHANDY
UNHANG
UNHANGED
UNHANGING
UNHANGS
UNHAPPEN
UNHAPPENS
UNHAPPIED
UNHAPPIER
UNHAPPIES
UNHAPPILY
UNHAPPY
UNHARBOUR
UNHARDIER
UNHARDY
UNHARMED
UNHARMFUL
UNHARMING
UNHARNESS
UNHARRIED
UNHASP
UNHASPED
UNHASPING
UNHASPS
UNHASTIER
UNHASTING
UNHASTY
UNHAT
UNHATCHED
UNHATS
UNHATTED
UNHATTING
UNHAUNTED
UNHEAD
UNHEADED
UNHEADING
UNHEADS
UNHEAL
UNHEALED
UNHEALING
UNHEALS
UNHEALTH
UNHEALTHS
UNHEALTHY
UNHEARD
UNHEARSE
UNHEARSED
UNHEARSES
UNHEART
UNHEARTED
UNHEARTS
UNHEATED
UNHEDGED
UNHEEDED
UNHEEDFUL
UNHEEDIER
UNHEEDILY
UNHEEDING
UNHEEDY
UNHELE
UNHELED
UNHELES
UNHELING
UNHELM
UNHELMED
UNHELMING
UNHELMS
UNHELPED
UNHELPFUL
UNHEMMED
UNHEPPEN
UNHEROIC
UNHERST
UNHEWN
UNHIDDEN
UNHINGE
UNHINGED
UNHINGES
UNHINGING
UNHIP
UNHIPPER
UNHIPPEST
UNHIRABLE
UNHIRED
UNHITCH
UNHITCHED
UNHITCHES
UNHIVE
UNHIVED
UNHIVES
UNHIVING
UNHOARD
UNHOARDED
UNHOARDS
UNHOLIER
UNHOLIEST
UNHOLILY
UNHOLPEN
UNHOLSTER
UNHOLY
UNHOMELY
UNHONEST
UNHONORED
UNHOOD
UNHOODED
UNHOODING
UNHOODS
UNHOOK
UNHOOKED
UNHOOKING
UNHOOKS
UNHOOP
UNHOOPED
UNHOOPING
UNHOOPS
UNHOPED
UNHOPEFUL
UNHORSE
UNHORSED
UNHORSES
UNHORSING
UNHOSTILE
UNHOUSE
UNHOUSED
UNHOUSES
UNHOUSING
UNHUMAN
UNHUMANLY
UNHUMBLED
UNHUNG
UNHUNTED
UNHURRIED
UNHURT
UNHURTFUL
UNHUSK
UNHUSKED
UNHUSKING
UNHUSKS
UNI
UNIALGAL
UNIAXIAL
UNIBODIES
UNIBODY
UNIBROW
UNIBROWS
UNICA
UNICED
UNICITIES
UNICITY
UNICOLOR
UNICOLOUR
UNICOM
UNICOMS
UNICORN
UNICORNS
UNICUM
UNICYCLE
UNICYCLED
UNICYCLES
UNIDEAED
UNIDEAL
UNIFACE
UNIFACES
UNIFIABLE
UNIFIC
UNIFIED
UNIFIER
UNIFIERS
UNIFIES
UNIFILAR
UNIFORM
UNIFORMED
UNIFORMER
UNIFORMLY
UNIFORMS
UNIFY
UNIFYING
UNIFYINGS
UNIGNITED
UNIJUGATE
UNILINEAL
UNILINEAR
UNILLUMED
UNILOBAR
UNILOBED
UNIMBUED
UNIMODAL
UNIMPEDED
UNIMPOSED
UNINCITED
UNINDEXED
UNINJURED
UNINSTAL
UNINSTALL
UNINSTALS
UNINSURED
UNINURED
UNINVITED
UNINVOKED
UNION
UNIONISE
UNIONISED
UNIONISER
UNIONISES
UNIONISM
UNIONISMS
UNIONIST
UNIONISTS
UNIONIZE
UNIONIZED
UNIONIZER
UNIONIZES
UNIONS
UNIPAROUS
UNIPED
UNIPEDS
UNIPLANAR
UNIPOD
UNIPODS
UNIPOLAR
UNIPOTENT
UNIQUE
UNIQUELY
UNIQUER
UNIQUES
UNIQUEST
UNIRAMOSE
UNIRAMOUS
UNIRONED
UNIRONIC
UNIS
UNISERIAL
UNISEX
UNISEXES
UNISEXUAL
UNISIZE

UNISON
UNISONAL
UNISONANT
UNISONOUS
UNISONS
UNISSUED
UNIT
UNITAGE
UNITAGES
UNITAL
UNITARD
UNITARDS
UNITARIAN
UNITARILY
UNITARITY
UNITARY
UNITE
UNITED
UNITEDLY
UNITER
UNITERS
UNITES
UNITIES
UNITING
UNITINGS
UNITION
UNITIONS
UNITISE
UNITISED
UNITISER
UNITISERS
UNITISES
UNITISING
UNITIVE
UNITIVELY
UNITIZE
UNITIZED
UNITIZER
UNITIZERS
UNITIZES
UNITIZING
UNITRUST
UNITRUSTS
UNITS
UNITY
UNIVALENT
UNIVALVE
UNIVALVED
UNIVALVES
UNIVERSAL
UNIVERSE
UNIVERSES
UNIVOCAL
UNIVOCALS
UNJADED
UNJAM
UNJAMMED
UNJAMMING
UNJAMS
UNJEALOUS
UNJOINED
UNJOINT
UNJOINTED
UNJOINTS
UNJOYFUL
UNJOYOUS
UNJUDGED
UNJUST
UNJUSTER
UNJUSTEST
UNJUSTLY
UNKED
UNKEELED
UNKEMPT
UNKEMPTLY
UNKEND
UNKENNED
UNKENNEL
UNKENNELS
UNKENT
UNKEPT
UNKET
UNKID
UNKIND
UNKINDER
UNKINDEST
UNKINDLED
UNKINDLY
UNKING
UNKINGED
UNKINGING
UNKINGLY
UNKINGS
UNKINK
UNKINKED
UNKINKING
UNKINKS
UNKISS
UNKISSED
UNKISSES
UNKISSING
UNKNELLED
UNKNIGHT
UNKNIGHTS
UNKNIT
UNKNITS
UNKNITTED
UNKNOT
UNKNOTS
UNKNOTTED
UNKNOWING
UNKNOWN
UNKNOWNS
UNKOSHER
UNLABELED
UNLABORED
UNLACE
UNLACED
UNLACES
UNLACING
UNLADE
UNLADED
UNLADEN
UNLADES
UNLADING
UNLADINGS
UNLAID
UNLASH
UNLASHED
UNLASHES
UNLASHING
UNLAST
UNLASTE
UNLATCH
UNLATCHED
UNLATCHES
UNLAW
UNLAWED
UNLAWFUL
UNLAWING
UNLAWS
UNLAY
UNLAYING
UNLAYS
UNLEAD
UNLEADED
UNLEADEDS
UNLEADING
UNLEADS
UNLEAL
UNLEARN
UNLEARNED
UNLEARNS
UNLEARNT
UNLEASED
UNLEASH
UNLEASHED
UNLEASHES
UNLED
UNLESS
UNLET
UNLETHAL
UNLETTED
UNLEVEL
UNLEVELED
UNLEVELS
UNLEVIED
UNLICH
UNLICKED
UNLID
UNLIDDED
UNLIDDING
UNLIDS
UNLIGHTED
UNLIKABLE
UNLIKE
UNLIKED
UNLIKELY
UNLIKES
UNLIMBER
UNLIMBERS
UNLIME
UNLIMED
UNLIMES
UNLIMING
UNLIMITED
UNLINE
UNLINEAL
UNLINED
UNLINES
UNLINING
UNLINK
UNLINKED
UNLINKING
UNLINKS
UNLISTED
UNLIT
UNLIVABLE
UNLIVE
UNLIVED
UNLIVELY
UNLIVES
UNLIVING
UNLOAD
UNLOADED
UNLOADER
UNLOADERS
UNLOADING
UNLOADS
UNLOBED
UNLOCATED
UNLOCK
UNLOCKED
UNLOCKING
UNLOCKS
UNLOGICAL
UNLOOKED
UNLOOSE
UNLOOSED
UNLOOSEN
UNLOOSENS
UNLOOSES
UNLOOSING
UNLOPPED
UNLORD
UNLORDED
UNLORDING
UNLORDLY
UNLORDS
UNLOSABLE
UNLOST
UNLOVABLE
UNLOVE
UNLOVED
UNLOVELY
UNLOVES
UNLOVING
UNLUCKIER
UNLUCKILY
UNLUCKY

UNLYRICAL
UNMACHO
UNMADE
UNMAILED
UNMAIMED
UNMAKABLE
UNMAKE
UNMAKER
UNMAKERS
UNMAKES
UNMAKING
UNMAKINGS
UNMAN
UNMANACLE
UNMANAGED
UNMANFUL
UNMANLIER
UNMANLIKE
UNMANLY
UNMANNED
UNMANNING
UNMANNISH
UNMANS
UNMANTLE
UNMANTLED
UNMANTLES
UNMANURED
UNMAPPED
UNMARD
UNMARKED
UNMARRED
UNMARRIED
UNMARRIES
UNMARRY
UNMASK
UNMASKED
UNMASKER
UNMASKERS
UNMASKING
UNMASKS
UNMATCHED
UNMATED
UNMATTED
UNMATURED
UNMEANING
UNMEANT
UNMEEK
UNMEET
UNMEETLY
UNMELLOW
UNMELTED
UNMENDED
UNMERITED
UNMERRIER
UNMERRY
UNMESH
UNMESHED
UNMESHES
UNMESHING
UNMET
UNMETED
UNMETERED
UNMEW
UNMEWED
UNMEWING
UNMEWS
UNMILKED
UNMILLED
UNMINDED
UNMINDFUL
UNMINED
UNMINGLE
UNMINGLED
UNMINGLES
UNMIRIER
UNMIRIEST
UNMIRY
UNMISSED
UNMITER
UNMITERED
UNMITERS
UNMITRE
UNMITRED
UNMITRES
UNMITRING
UNMIX
UNMIXABLE
UNMIXED
UNMIXEDLY
UNMIXES
UNMIXING
UNMIXT
UNMOANED
UNMODISH
UNMOLD
UNMOLDED
UNMOLDING
UNMOLDS
UNMOLTEN
UNMONEYED
UNMONIED
UNMOOR
UNMOORED
UNMOORING
UNMOORS
UNMORAL
UNMORALLY
UNMORTISE
UNMOTIVED
UNMOULD
UNMOULDED
UNMOULDS
UNMOUNT
UNMOUNTED
UNMOUNTS
UNMOURNED
UNMOVABLE
UNMOVABLY
UNMOVED
UNMOVEDLY
UNMOVING
UNMOWN
UNMUFFLE
UNMUFFLED
UNMUFFLES
UNMUSICAL
UNMUZZLE
UNMUZZLED
UNMUZZLES
UNNAIL
UNNAILED
UNNAILING
UNNAILS
UNNAMABLE
UNNAMED
UNNANELD
UNNATIVE
UNNATIVED
UNNATIVES
UNNATURAL
UNNEATH
UNNEEDED
UNNEEDFUL
UNNERVE
UNNERVED
UNNERVES
UNNERVING
UNNEST
UNNESTED
UNNESTING
UNNESTS
UNNETHES
UNNETTED
UNNOBLE
UNNOBLED
UNNOBLES
UNNOBLING
UNNOISIER
UNNOISY
UNNOTED
UNNOTICED
UNNUANCED
UNOAKED
UNOBEYED
UNOBVIOUS
UNOFFERED
UNOFTEN
UNOILED
UNOPEN
UNOPENED
UNOPPOSED
UNORDER
UNORDERED
UNORDERLY
UNORDERS
UNORNATE
UNOWED
UNOWNED
UNPACED
UNPACK
UNPACKED
UNPACKER
UNPACKERS
UNPACKING
UNPACKS
UNPADDED
UNPAGED
UNPAID
UNPAINED
UNPAINFUL
UNPAINT
UNPAINTED
UNPAINTS
UNPAIRED
UNPALSIED
UNPANEL
UNPANELS
UNPANGED
UNPANNEL
UNPANNELS
UNPAPER
UNPAPERED
UNPAPERS
UNPARED
UNPARTED
UNPARTIAL
UNPATCHED
UNPATHED
UNPAVED
UNPAY
UNPAYABLE
UNPAYING
UNPAYS
UNPEELED
UNPEERED
UNPEG
UNPEGGED
UNPEGGING
UNPEGS
UNPEN
UNPENNED
UNPENNIED
UNPENNING
UNPENS
UNPENT
UNPEOPLE
UNPEOPLED
UNPEOPLES
UNPERCH
UNPERCHED
UNPERCHES
UNPERFECT
UNPERPLEX
UNPERSON
UNPERSONS
UNPERVERT
UNPICK
UNPICKED
UNPICKING
UNPICKS

U

UNPIERCED
UNPILE
UNPILED
UNPILES
UNPILING
UNPILOTED
UNPIN
UNPINKED
UNPINKT
UNPINNED
UNPINNING
UNPINS
UNPITIED
UNPITIFUL
UNPITTED
UNPITYING
UNPLACE
UNPLACED
UNPLACES
UNPLACING
UNPLAGUED
UNPLAINED
UNPLAIT
UNPLAITED
UNPLAITS
UNPLANKED
UNPLANNED
UNPLANTED
UNPLAYED
UNPLEASED
UNPLEATED
UNPLEDGED
UNPLIABLE
UNPLIABLY
UNPLIANT
UNPLOWED
UNPLUCKED
UNPLUG
UNPLUGGED
UNPLUGS
UNPLUMB
UNPLUMBED
UNPLUMBS
UNPLUME
UNPLUMED
UNPLUMES
UNPLUMING
UNPOETIC
UNPOINTED
UNPOISED
UNPOISON
UNPOISONS
UNPOLICED
UNPOLISH
UNPOLITE
UNPOLITIC
UNPOLLED
UNPOPE
UNPOPED
UNPOPES
UNPOPING
UNPOPULAR
UNPOSED
UNPOSTED
UNPOTABLE
UNPOTTED
UNPOURED
UNPOWERED
UNPRAISE
UNPRAISED
UNPRAISES
UNPRAY
UNPRAYED
UNPRAYING
UNPRAYS
UNPREACH
UNPRECISE
UNPREDICT
UNPREPARE
UNPRESSED
UNPRETTY
UNPRICED
UNPRIEST
UNPRIESTS
UNPRIMED
UNPRINTED
UNPRISON
UNPRISONS
UNPRIZED
UNPROBED
UNPROP
UNPROPER
UNPROPPED
UNPROPS
UNPROVED
UNPROVEN
UNPROVIDE
UNPROVOKE
UNPRUNED
UNPUCKER
UNPUCKERS
UNPULLED
UNPURE
UNPURELY
UNPURGED
UNPURSE
UNPURSED
UNPURSES
UNPURSING
UNPURSUED
UNPUZZLE
UNPUZZLED
UNPUZZLES
UNQUAKING
UNQUALIFY
UNQUEEN
UNQUEENED
UNQUEENLY
UNQUEENS
UNQUELLED
UNQUIET
UNQUIETED
UNQUIETER
UNQUIETLY
UNQUIETS
UNQUOTE
UNQUOTED
UNQUOTES
UNQUOTING
UNRACED
UNRACKED
UNRAISED
UNRAKE
UNRAKED
UNRAKES
UNRAKING
UNRANKED
UNRATED
UNRAVAGED
UNRAVEL
UNRAVELED
UNRAVELS
UNRAZED
UNRAZORED
UNREACHED
UNREAD
UNREADIER
UNREADILY
UNREADY
UNREAL
UNREALISE
UNREALISM
UNREALITY
UNREALIZE
UNREALLY
UNREAPED
UNREASON
UNREASONS
UNREAVE
UNREAVED
UNREAVES
UNREAVING
UNREBATED
UNREBUKED
UNRECKED
UNRED
UNREDREST
UNREDUCED
UNREDY
UNREEL
UNREELED
UNREELER
UNREELERS
UNREELING
UNREELS
UNREEVE
UNREEVED
UNREEVES
UNREEVING
UNREFINED
UNREFUTED
UNREIN
UNREINED
UNREINING
UNREINS
UNRELATED
UNRELAXED
UNREMOVED
UNRENEWED
UNRENT
UNRENTED
UNREPAID
UNREPAIR
UNREPAIRS
UNRESERVE
UNREST
UNRESTED
UNRESTFUL
UNRESTING
UNRESTS
UNRETIRE
UNRETIRED
UNRETIRES
UNREVISED
UNREVOKED
UNRHYMED
UNRIBBED
UNRID
UNRIDABLE
UNRIDDEN
UNRIDDLE
UNRIDDLED
UNRIDDLER
UNRIDDLES
UNRIDGED
UNRIFLED
UNRIG
UNRIGGED
UNRIGGING
UNRIGHT
UNRIGHTED
UNRIGHTS
UNRIGS
UNRIMED
UNRINGED
UNRINSED
UNRIP
UNRIPE
UNRIPELY
UNRIPENED
UNRIPER
UNRIPEST
UNRIPPED
UNRIPPING
UNRIPS
UNRISEN
UNRIVALED
UNRIVEN
UNRIVET
UNRIVETED

UNRIVETS
UNROASTED
UNROBE
UNROBED
UNROBES
UNROBING
UNROLL
UNROLLED
UNROLLING
UNROLLS
UNROOF
UNROOFED
UNROOFING
UNROOFS
UNROOST
UNROOSTED
UNROOSTS
UNROOT
UNROOTED
UNROOTING
UNROOTS
UNROPE
UNROPED
UNROPES
UNROPING
UNROSINED
UNROTTED
UNROTTEN
UNROUGED
UNROUGH
UNROUND
UNROUNDED
UNROUNDS
UNROUSED
UNROVE
UNROVEN
UNROYAL
UNROYALLY
UNRUBBED
UNRUDE
UNRUFFE
UNRUFFLE
UNRUFFLED
UNRUFFLES
UNRULE
UNRULED
UNRULES
UNRULIER
UNRULIEST
UNRULY
UNRUMPLED
UNRUSHED
UNRUSTED
UNS
UNSADDLE
UNSADDLED
UNSADDLES
UNSAFF
UNSAFELY
UNSAFER
UNSAFEST
UNSAFETY
UNSAID
UNSAILED
UNSAINED
UNSAINT
UNSAINTED
UNSAINTLY
UNSAINTS
UNSALABLE
UNSALABLY
UNSALTED
UNSALUTED
UNSAMPLED
UNSAPPED
UNSASHED
UNSATABLE
UNSATED
UNSATIATE
UNSATING
UNSAVED
UNSAVORY
UNSAVOURY
UNSAW
UNSAWED
UNSAWN
UNSAY
UNSAYABLE
UNSAYING
UNSAYS
UNSCALE
UNSCALED
UNSCALES
UNSCALING
UNSCANNED
UNSCARIER
UNSCARRED
UNSCARY
UNSCATHED
UNSCENTED
UNSCOURED
UNSCREW
UNSCREWED
UNSCREWS
UNSCYTHED
UNSEAL
UNSEALED
UNSEALING
UNSEALS
UNSEAM
UNSEAMED
UNSEAMING
UNSEAMS
UNSEARED
UNSEASON
UNSEASONS
UNSEAT
UNSEATED
UNSEATING
UNSEATS
UNSECRET
UNSECRETS
UNSECULAR
UNSECURED
UNSEDUCED
UNSEE
UNSEEABLE
UNSEEDED
UNSEEING
UNSEEL
UNSEELED
UNSEELIE
UNSEELING
UNSEELS
UNSEEMING
UNSEEMLY
UNSEEN
UNSEENS
UNSEES
UNSEIZED
UNSELDOM
UNSELF
UNSELFED
UNSELFING
UNSELFISH
UNSELFS
UNSELL
UNSELLING
UNSELLS
UNSELVES
UNSENSE
UNSENSED
UNSENSES
UNSENSING
UNSENT
UNSERIOUS
UNSERVED
UNSET
UNSETS
UNSETTING
UNSETTLE
UNSETTLED
UNSETTLES
UNSEVERED
UNSEW
UNSEWED
UNSEWING
UNSEWN
UNSEWS
UNSEX
UNSEXED
UNSEXES
UNSEXIER
UNSEXIEST
UNSEXILY
UNSEXING
UNSEXIST
UNSEXUAL
UNSEXY
UNSHACKLE
UNSHADED
UNSHADOW
UNSHADOWS
UNSHAKED
UNSHAKEN
UNSHALE
UNSHALED
UNSHALES
UNSHALING
UNSHAMED
UNSHAPE
UNSHAPED
UNSHAPELY
UNSHAPEN
UNSHAPES
UNSHAPING
UNSHARED
UNSHARP
UNSHAVED
UNSHAVEN
UNSHEATHE
UNSHED
UNSHELL
UNSHELLED
UNSHELLS
UNSHENT
UNSHEWN
UNSHIFT
UNSHIFTED
UNSHIFTS
UNSHIP
UNSHIPPED
UNSHIPS
UNSHIRTED
UNSHOCKED
UNSHOD
UNSHOE
UNSHOED
UNSHOEING
UNSHOES
UNSHOOT
UNSHOOTED
UNSHOOTS
UNSHORN
UNSHOT
UNSHOTS
UNSHOTTED
UNSHOUT
UNSHOUTED
UNSHOUTS
UNSHOWIER
UNSHOWN
UNSHOWY
UNSHRIVED
UNSHRIVEN
UNSHROUD
UNSHROUDS
UNSHRUBD
UNSHRUNK
UNSHUNNED

UNSHUT
UNSHUTS
UNSHUTTER
UNSICKER
UNSICKLED
UNSIFTED
UNSIGHING
UNSIGHT
UNSIGHTED
UNSIGHTLY
UNSIGHTS
UNSIGNED
UNSILENT
UNSIMILAR
UNSINEW
UNSINEWED
UNSINEWS
UNSINFUL
UNSISTING
UNSIZABLE
UNSIZED
UNSKILFUL
UNSKILLED
UNSKIMMED
UNSKINNED
UNSLAIN
UNSLAKED
UNSLICED
UNSLICK
UNSLING
UNSLINGS
UNSLUICE
UNSLUICED
UNSLUICES
UNSLUNG
UNSMART
UNSMILING
UNSMITTEN
UNSMOKED
UNSMOOTH
UNSMOOTHS
UNSMOTE
UNSNAG
UNSNAGGED
UNSNAGS
UNSNAP
UNSNAPPED
UNSNAPS
UNSNARL
UNSNARLED
UNSNARLS
UNSNECK
UNSNECKED
UNSNECKS
UNSNUFFED
UNSOAKED
UNSOAPED
UNSOBER
UNSOBERED
UNSOBERLY
UNSOBERS
UNSOCIAL
UNSOCKET
UNSOCKETS
UNSOD
UNSODDEN
UNSOFT
UNSOILED
UNSOLACED
UNSOLD
UNSOLDER
UNSOLDERS
UNSOLEMN
UNSOLID
UNSOLIDLY
UNSOLVED
UNSONCY
UNSONSIE
UNSONSIER
UNSONSY
UNSOOTE
UNSOOTHED
UNSORTED
UNSOUGHT
UNSOUL
UNSOULED
UNSOULING
UNSOULS
UNSOUND
UNSOUNDED
UNSOUNDER
UNSOUNDLY
UNSOURCED
UNSOURED
UNSOWED
UNSOWN
UNSPAR
UNSPARED
UNSPARING
UNSPARRED
UNSPARS
UNSPEAK
UNSPEAKS
UNSPED
UNSPELL
UNSPELLED
UNSPELLS
UNSPENT
UNSPHERE
UNSPHERED
UNSPHERES
UNSPIDE
UNSPIED
UNSPILLED
UNSPILT
UNSPLIT
UNSPOILED
UNSPOILT
UNSPOKE
UNSPOKEN
UNSPOOL
UNSPOOLED
UNSPOOLS
UNSPOTTED
UNSPRAYED
UNSPRUNG
UNSPUN
UNSQUARED
UNSTABLE
UNSTABLER
UNSTABLY
UNSTACK
UNSTACKED
UNSTACKS
UNSTAGED
UNSTAID
UNSTAINED
UNSTALKED
UNSTAMPED
UNSTARCH
UNSTARRED
UNSTARRY
UNSTATE
UNSTATED
UNSTATES
UNSTATING
UNSTAYED
UNSTAYING
UNSTEADY
UNSTEEL
UNSTEELED
UNSTEELS
UNSTEMMED
UNSTEP
UNSTEPPED
UNSTEPS
UNSTERILE
UNSTICK
UNSTICKS
UNSTIFFEN
UNSTIFLED
UNSTILLED
UNSTINTED
UNSTIRRED
UNSTITCH
UNSTOCK
UNSTOCKED
UNSTOCKS
UNSTONED
UNSTOP
UNSTOPPED
UNSTOPPER
UNSTOPS
UNSTOW
UNSTOWED
UNSTOWING
UNSTOWS
UNSTRAP
UNSTRAPS
UNSTRESS
UNSTRING
UNSTRINGS
UNSTRIP
UNSTRIPED
UNSTRIPS
UNSTRUCK
UNSTRUNG
UNSTUCK
UNSTUDIED
UNSTUFFED
UNSTUFFY
UNSTUFT
UNSTUNG
UNSTYLISH
UNSUBDUED
UNSUBJECT
UNSUBTLE
UNSUBTLER
UNSUBTLY
UNSUCCESS
UNSUCKED
UNSUIT
UNSUITED
UNSUITING
UNSUITS
UNSULLIED
UNSUMMED
UNSUNG
UNSUNK
UNSUNNED
UNSUNNIER
UNSUNNY
UNSUPPLE
UNSURE
UNSURED
UNSURELY
UNSURER
UNSUREST
UNSUSPECT
UNSWADDLE
UNSWATHE
UNSWATHED
UNSWATHES
UNSWAYED
UNSWEAR
UNSWEARS
UNSWEET
UNSWEPT
UNSWOLLEN
UNSWORE
UNSWORN
UNTACK
UNTACKED
UNTACKING
UNTACKLE
UNTACKLED
UNTACKLES
UNTACKS
UNTACTFUL
UNTAGGED

UNTAILED
UNTAINTED
UNTAKEN
UNTAMABLE
UNTAMABLY
UNTAME
UNTAMED
UNTAMES
UNTAMING
UNTANGLE
UNTANGLED
UNTANGLES
UNTANNED
UNTAPPED
UNTARRED
UNTASTED
UNTAUGHT
UNTAX
UNTAXABLE
UNTAXED
UNTAXES
UNTAXING
UNTEACH
UNTEACHES
UNTEAM
UNTEAMED
UNTEAMING
UNTEAMS
UNTEMPER
UNTEMPERS
UNTEMPTED
UNTENABLE
UNTENABLY
UNTENANT
UNTENANTS
UNTENDED
UNTENDER
UNTENT
UNTENTED
UNTENTIER
UNTENTING
UNTENTS
UNTENTY
UNTENURED
UNTESTED
UNTETHER
UNTETHERS
UNTHANKED
UNTHATCH
UNTHAW
UNTHAWED
UNTHAWING
UNTHAWS
UNTHINK
UNTHINKS
UNTHOUGHT
UNTHREAD
UNTHREADS
UNTHRIFT
UNTHRIFTS
UNTHRIFTY
UNTHRONE
UNTHRONED
UNTHRONES
UNTIDIED
UNTIDIER
UNTIDIES
UNTIDIEST
UNTIDILY
UNTIDY
UNTIDYING
UNTIE
UNTIED
UNTIEING
UNTIES
UNTIL
UNTILE
UNTILED
UNTILES
UNTILING
UNTILLED
UNTILTED
UNTIMED
UNTIMELY
UNTIMEOUS
UNTIN
UNTINGED
UNTINNED
UNTINNING
UNTINS
UNTIPPED
UNTIRABLE
UNTIRED
UNTIRING
UNTITLED
UNTO
UNTOILING
UNTOLD
UNTOMB
UNTOMBED
UNTOMBING
UNTOMBS
UNTONED
UNTOOLED
UNTOOTHED
UNTORN
UNTOUCHED
UNTOWARD
UNTRACE
UNTRACED
UNTRACES
UNTRACING
UNTRACK
UNTRACKED
UNTRACKS
UNTRADED
UNTRAINED
UNTRAPPED
UNTREAD
UNTREADED
UNTREADS
UNTREATED
UNTRENDY
UNTRESSED
UNTRIDE
UNTRIED
UNTRIM
UNTRIMMED
UNTRIMS
UNTROD
UNTRODDEN
UNTRUE
UNTRUER
UNTRUEST
UNTRUISM
UNTRUISMS
UNTRULY
UNTRUSS
UNTRUSSED
UNTRUSSER
UNTRUSSES
UNTRUST
UNTRUSTED
UNTRUSTS
UNTRUSTY
UNTRUTH
UNTRUTHS
UNTUCK
UNTUCKED
UNTUCKING
UNTUCKS
UNTUFTED
UNTUMBLED
UNTUNABLE
UNTUNABLY
UNTUNE
UNTUNED
UNTUNEFUL
UNTUNES
UNTUNING
UNTURBID
UNTURF
UNTURFED
UNTURFING
UNTURFS
UNTURN
UNTURNED
UNTURNING
UNTURNS
UNTUTORED
UNTWILLED
UNTWINE
UNTWINED
UNTWINES
UNTWINING
UNTWIST
UNTWISTED
UNTWISTS
UNTYING
UNTYINGS
UNTYPABLE
UNTYPICAL
UNUNBIUM
UNUNBIUMS
UNUNITED
UNUNUNIUM
UNURGED
UNUSABLE
UNUSABLY
UNUSED
UNUSEFUL
UNUSHERED
UNUSUAL
UNUSUALLY
UNUTTERED
UNVAIL
UNVAILE
UNVAILED
UNVAILES
UNVAILING
UNVAILS
UNVALUED
UNVARIED
UNVARYING
UNVEIL
UNVEILED
UNVEILER
UNVEILERS
UNVEILING
UNVEILS
UNVEINED
UNVENTED
UNVERSED
UNVESTED
UNVETTED
UNVEXED
UNVEXT
UNVIABLE
UNVIEWED
UNVIRTUE
UNVIRTUES
UNVISITED
UNVISOR
UNVISORED
UNVISORS
UNVITAL
UNVIZARD
UNVIZARDS
UNVOCAL
UNVOICE
UNVOICED
UNVOICES
UNVOICING
UNVULGAR
UNWAGED
UNWAISTED
UNWAKED
UNWAKENED
UNWALLED
UNWANING

U

UNWANTED
UNWARDED
UNWARE
UNWARELY
UNWARES
UNWARIE
UNWARIER
UNWARIEST
UNWARILY
UNWARLIKE
UNWARMED
UNWARNED
UNWARPED
UNWARY
UNWASHED
UNWASHEDS
UNWASHEN
UNWASTED
UNWASTING
UNWATCHED
UNWATER
UNWATERED
UNWATERS
UNWATERY
UNWAXED
UNWAYED
UNWEAL
UNWEALS
UNWEANED
UNWEAPON
UNWEAPONS
UNWEARIED
UNWEARIER
UNWEARIES
UNWEARY
UNWEAVE
UNWEAVES
UNWEAVING
UNWEBBED
UNWED
UNWEDDED
UNWEEDED
UNWEENED
UNWEETING
UNWEIGHED
UNWEIGHT
UNWEIGHTS
UNWELCOME
UNWELDED
UNWELDY
UNWELL
UNWEPT
UNWET
UNWETTED
UNWHIPPED
UNWHIPT
UNWHITE
UNWIELDLY
UNWIELDY
UNWIFELY
UNWIGGED
UNWILFUL
UNWILL
UNWILLED
UNWILLING
UNWILLS
UNWIND
UNWINDER
UNWINDERS
UNWINDING
UNWINDS
UNWINGED
UNWINKING
UNWIPED
UNWIRE
UNWIRED
UNWIRES
UNWIRING
UNWISDOM
UNWISDOMS
UNWISE
UNWISELY
UNWISER
UNWISEST
UNWISH
UNWISHED
UNWISHES
UNWISHFUL
UNWISHING
UNWIST
UNWIT
UNWITCH
UNWITCHED
UNWITCHES
UNWITS
UNWITTED
UNWITTIER
UNWITTILY
UNWITTING
UNWITTY
UNWIVE
UNWIVED
UNWIVES
UNWIVING
UNWOMAN
UNWOMANED
UNWOMANLY
UNWOMANS
UNWON
UNWONT
UNWONTED
UNWOODED
UNWOOED
UNWORDED
UNWORK
UNWORKED
UNWORKING
UNWORKS
UNWORLDLY
UNWORMED
UNWORN
UNWORRIED
UNWORTH
UNWORTHS
UNWORTHY
UNWOUND
UNWOUNDED
UNWOVE
UNWOVEN
UNWRAP
UNWRAPPED
UNWRAPS
UNWREAKED
UNWREATHE
UNWRINKLE
UNWRITE
UNWRITES
UNWRITING
UNWRITTEN
UNWROTE
UNWROUGHT
UNWRUNG
UNYEANED
UNYIELDED
UNYOKE
UNYOKED
UNYOKES
UNYOKING
UNYOUNG
UNZEALOUS
UNZIP
UNZIPPED
UNZIPPING
UNZIPS
UNZONED
UP
UPADAISY
UPAITHRIC
UPALONG
UPALONGS
UPAS
UPASES
UPBEAR
UPBEARER
UPBEARERS
UPBEARING
UPBEARS
UPBEAT
UPBEATS
UPBIND
UPBINDING
UPBINDS
UPBLEW
UPBLOW
UPBLOWING
UPBLOWN
UPBLOWS
UPBOIL
UPBOILED
UPBOILING
UPBOILS
UPBORE
UPBORNE
UPBOUND
UPBOUNDEN
UPBOW
UPBOWS
UPBRAID
UPBRAIDED
UPBRAIDER
UPBRAIDS
UPBRAST
UPBRAY
UPBRAYED
UPBRAYING
UPBRAYS
UPBREAK
UPBREAKS
UPBRING
UPBRINGS
UPBROKE
UPBROKEN
UPBROUGHT
UPBUILD
UPBUILDER
UPBUILDS
UPBUILT
UPBURNING
UPBURST
UPBURSTS
UPBY
UPBYE
UPCAST
UPCASTING
UPCASTS
UPCATCH
UPCATCHES
UPCAUGHT
UPCHEER
UPCHEERED
UPCHEERS
UPCHUCK
UPCHUCKED
UPCHUCKS
UPCLIMB
UPCLIMBED
UPCLIMBS
UPCLOSE
UPCLOSED
UPCLOSES
UPCLOSING
UPCOAST
UPCOIL
UPCOILED
UPCOILING
UPCOILS
UPCOME
UPCOMES
UPCOMING
UPCOUNTRY

UPCOURT
UPCURL
UPCURLED
UPCURLING
UPCURLS
UPCURVE
UPCURVED
UPCURVES
UPCURVING
UPCYCLE
UPCYCLED
UPCYCLES
UPCYCLING
UPDART
UPDARTED
UPDARTING
UPDARTS
UPDATABLE
UPDATE
UPDATED
UPDATER
UPDATERS
UPDATES
UPDATING
UPDIVE
UPDIVED
UPDIVES
UPDIVING
UPDO
UPDOMING
UPDOMINGS
UPDOS
UPDOVE
UPDRAFT
UPDRAFTS
UPDRAG
UPDRAGGED
UPDRAGS
UPDRAUGHT
UPDRAW
UPDRAWING
UPDRAWN
UPDRAWS
UPDREW
UPDRIED
UPDRIES
UPDRY
UPDRYING
UPEND
UPENDED
UPENDING
UPENDS
UPFIELD
UPFILL
UPFILLED
UPFILLING
UPFILLS
UPFLING
UPFLINGS
UPFLOW
UPFLOWED
UPFLOWING
UPFLOWS
UPFLUNG
UPFOLD
UPFOLDED
UPFOLDING
UPFOLDS
UPFOLLOW
UPFOLLOWS
UPFRONT
UPFURL
UPFURLED
UPFURLING
UPFURLS
UPGANG
UPGANGS
UPGATHER
UPGATHERS
UPGAZE
UPGAZED
UPGAZES
UPGAZING
UPGIRD
UPGIRDED
UPGIRDING
UPGIRDS
UPGIRT
UPGIRTED
UPGIRTING
UPGIRTS
UPGO
UPGOES
UPGOING
UPGOINGS
UPGONE
UPGRADE
UPGRADED
UPGRADER
UPGRADERS
UPGRADES
UPGRADING
UPGREW
UPGROW
UPGROWING
UPGROWN
UPGROWS
UPGROWTH
UPGROWTHS
UPGUSH
UPGUSHED
UPGUSHES
UPGUSHING
UPHAND
UPHANG
UPHANGING
UPHANGS
UPHAUD
UPHAUDING
UPHAUDS
UPHEAP
UPHEAPED
UPHEAPING
UPHEAPS
UPHEAVAL
UPHEAVALS
UPHEAVE
UPHEAVED
UPHEAVER
UPHEAVERS
UPHEAVES
UPHEAVING
UPHELD
UPHILD
UPHILL
UPHILLS
UPHOARD
UPHOARDED
UPHOARDS
UPHOIST
UPHOISTED
UPHOISTS
UPHOLD
UPHOLDER
UPHOLDERS
UPHOLDING
UPHOLDS
UPHOLSTER
UPHOORD
UPHOORDED
UPHOORDS
UPHOVE
UPHROE
UPHROES
UPHUDDEN
UPHUNG
UPHURL
UPHURLED
UPHURLING
UPHURLS
UPJET
UPJETS
UPJETTED
UPJETTING
UPKEEP
UPKEEPS
UPKNIT
UPKNITS
UPKNITTED
UPLAID
UPLAND
UPLANDER
UPLANDERS
UPLANDISH
UPLANDS
UPLAY
UPLAYING
UPLAYS
UPLEAD
UPLEADING
UPLEADS
UPLEAN
UPLEANED
UPLEANING
UPLEANS
UPLEANT
UPLEAP
UPLEAPED
UPLEAPING
UPLEAPS
UPLEAPT
UPLED
UPLIFT
UPLIFTED
UPLIFTER
UPLIFTERS
UPLIFTING
UPLIFTS
UPLIGHT
UPLIGHTED
UPLIGHTER
UPLIGHTS
UPLINK
UPLINKED
UPLINKING
UPLINKS
UPLIT
UPLOAD
UPLOADED
UPLOADING
UPLOADS
UPLOCK
UPLOCKED
UPLOCKING
UPLOCKS
UPLOOK
UPLOOKED
UPLOOKING
UPLOOKS
UPLYING
UPMADE
UPMAKE
UPMAKER
UPMAKERS
UPMAKES
UPMAKING
UPMAKINGS
UPMANSHIP
UPMARKET
UPMARKETS
UPMOST
UPO
UPON
UPPED
UPPER
UPPERCASE
UPPERCUT
UPPERCUTS
UPPERMOST
UPPERPART

UPPERS
UPPILE
UPPILED
UPPILES
UPPILING
UPPING
UPPINGS
UPPISH
UPPISHLY
UPPITIER
UPPITIEST
UPPITY
UPPROP
UPPROPPED
UPPROPS
UPRAISE
UPRAISED
UPRAISER
UPRAISERS
UPRAISES
UPRAISING
UPRAN
UPRATE
UPRATED
UPRATES
UPRATING
UPREACH
UPREACHED
UPREACHES
UPREAR
UPREARED
UPREARING
UPREARS
UPREST
UPRESTS
UPRIGHT
UPRIGHTED
UPRIGHTLY
UPRIGHTS
UPRISAL
UPRISALS
UPRISE
UPRISEN
UPRISER
UPRISERS
UPRISES
UPRISING
UPRISINGS
UPRIST
UPRISTS
UPRIVER
UPRIVERS
UPROAR
UPROARED
UPROARING
UPROARS
UPROLL
UPROLLED
UPROLLING
UPROLLS
UPROOT
UPROOTAL
UPROOTALS
UPROOTED
UPROOTER
UPROOTERS
UPROOTING
UPROOTS
UPROSE
UPROUSE
UPROUSED
UPROUSES
UPROUSING
UPRUN
UPRUNNING
UPRUNS
UPRUSH
UPRUSHED
UPRUSHES
UPRUSHING
UPRYST
UPS
UPSADAISY
UPSCALE
UPSCALED
UPSCALES
UPSCALING
UPSEE
UPSEES
UPSELL
UPSELLING
UPSELLS
UPSEND
UPSENDING
UPSENDS
UPSENT
UPSET
UPSETS
UPSETTER
UPSETTERS
UPSETTING
UPSEY
UPSEYS
UPSHIFT
UPSHIFTED
UPSHIFTS
UPSHOOT
UPSHOOTS
UPSHOT
UPSHOTS
UPSIDE
UPSIDES
UPSIES
UPSILON
UPSILONS
UPSITTING
UPSIZE
UPSIZED
UPSIZES
UPSIZING
UPSKILL
UPSKILLED
UPSKILLS
UPSKIRT
UPSKIRTS
UPSLOPE
UPSLOPES
UPSOAR
UPSOARED
UPSOARING
UPSOARS
UPSOLD
UPSPAKE
UPSPEAK
UPSPEAKS
UPSPEAR
UPSPEARED
UPSPEARS
UPSPOKE
UPSPOKEN
UPSPRANG
UPSPRING
UPSPRINGS
UPSPRUNG
UPSTAGE
UPSTAGED
UPSTAGER
UPSTAGERS
UPSTAGES
UPSTAGING
UPSTAIR
UPSTAIRS
UPSTAND
UPSTANDS
UPSTARE
UPSTARED
UPSTARES
UPSTARING
UPSTART
UPSTARTED
UPSTARTS
UPSTATE
UPSTATER
UPSTATERS
UPSTATES
UPSTAY
UPSTAYED
UPSTAYING
UPSTAYS
UPSTEP
UPSTEPPED
UPSTEPS
UPSTIR
UPSTIRRED
UPSTIRS
UPSTOOD
UPSTREAM
UPSTREAMS
UPSTROKE
UPSTROKES
UPSURGE
UPSURGED
UPSURGES
UPSURGING
UPSWARM
UPSWARMED
UPSWARMS
UPSWAY
UPSWAYED
UPSWAYING
UPSWAYS
UPSWEEP
UPSWEEPS
UPSWELL
UPSWELLED
UPSWELLS
UPSWEPT
UPSWING
UPSWINGS
UPSWOLLEN
UPSWUNG
UPSY
UPTA
UPTAK
UPTAKE
UPTAKEN
UPTAKES
UPTAKING
UPTAKS
UPTALK
UPTALKED
UPTALKING
UPTALKS
UPTEAR
UPTEARING
UPTEARS
UPTEMPO
UPTEMPOS
UPTER
UPTHREW
UPTHROW
UPTHROWN
UPTHROWS
UPTHRUST
UPTHRUSTS
UPTHUNDER
UPTICK
UPTICKS
UPTIE
UPTIED
UPTIES
UPTIGHT
UPTIGHTER
UPTILT
UPTILTED
UPTILTING
UPTILTS
UPTIME
UPTIMES
UPTITLING

U

UPTOOK
UPTORE
UPTORN
UPTOSS
UPTOSSED
UPTOSSES
UPTOSSING
UPTOWN
UPTOWNER
UPTOWNERS
UPTOWNS
UPTRAIN
UPTRAINED
UPTRAINS
UPTREND
UPTRENDS
UPTRILLED
UPTURN
UPTURNED
UPTURNING
UPTURNS
UPTYING
UPVALUE
UPVALUED
UPVALUES
UPVALUING
UPVOTE
UPVOTED
UPVOTES
UPVOTING
UPWAFT
UPWAFTED
UPWAFTING
UPWAFTS
UPWARD
UPWARDLY
UPWARDS
UPWELL
UPWELLED
UPWELLING
UPWELLS
UPWENT
UPWHIRL
UPWHIRLED
UPWHIRLS
UPWIND
UPWINDING
UPWINDS
UPWOUND
UPWRAP
UPWRAPS
UPWROUGHT
UR
URACHI
URACHUS
URACHUSES
URACIL
URACILS
URAEI
URAEMIA
URAEMIAS
URAEMIC
URAEUS
URAEUSES
URALI
URALIS
URALITE
URALITES
URALITIC
URALITISE
URALITIZE
URANIA
URANIAN
URANIAS
URANIC
URANIDE
URANIDES
URANIN
URANINITE
URANINS
URANISCI
URANISCUS
URANISM
URANISMS
URANITE
URANITES
URANITIC
URANIUM
URANIUMS
URANOLOGY
URANOUS
URANYL
URANYLIC
URANYLS
URAO
URAOS
URARE
URARES
URARI
URARIS
URASE
URASES
URATE
URATES
URATIC
URB
URBAN
URBANE
URBANELY
URBANER
URBANEST
URBANISE
URBANISED
URBANISES
URBANISM
URBANISMS
URBANIST
URBANISTS
URBANITE
URBANITES
URBANITY
URBANIZE
URBANIZED
URBANIZES
URBEX
URBEXES
URBIA
URBIAS
URBS
URCEOLATE
URCEOLI
URCEOLUS
URCHIN
URCHINS
URD
URDE
URDEE
URDS
URDY
URE
UREA
UREAL
UREAS
UREASE
UREASES
UREDIA
UREDIAL
UREDINE
UREDINES
UREDINIA
UREDINIAL
UREDINIUM
UREDINOUS
UREDIUM
UREDO
UREDOS
UREDOSORI
UREIC
UREIDE
UREIDES
UREMIA
UREMIAS
UREMIC
URENA
URENAS
URENT
UREOTELIC
URES
URESES
URESIS
URETER
URETERAL
URETERIC
URETERS
URETHAN
URETHANE
URETHANED
URETHANES
URETHANS
URETHRA
URETHRAE
URETHRAL
URETHRAS
URETIC
URGE
URGED
URGENCE
URGENCES
URGENCIES
URGENCY
URGENT
URGENTLY
URGER
URGERS
URGES
URGING
URGINGLY
URGINGS
URIAL
URIALS
URIC
URICASE
URICASES
URIDINE
URIDINES
URIDYLIC
URINAL
URINALS
URINANT
URINARIES
URINARY
URINATE
URINATED
URINATES
URINATING
URINATION
URINATIVE
URINATOR
URINATORS
URINE
URINED
URINEMIA
URINEMIAS
URINEMIC
URINES
URINING
URINOLOGY
URINOSE
URINOUS
URITE
URITES
URMAN
URMANS
URN
URNAL
URNED
URNFIELD
URNFIELDS
URNFUL
URNFULS

URNING
URNINGS
URNLIKE
URNS
UROBILIN
UROBILINS
UROBORIC
UROBOROS
UROCHORD
UROCHORDS
UROCHROME
URODELAN
URODELANS
URODELE
URODELES
URODELOUS
UROGENOUS
UROGRAM
UROGRAMS
UROGRAPHY
UROKINASE
UROLAGNIA
UROLITH
UROLITHIC
UROLITHS
UROLOGIC
UROLOGIES
UROLOGIST
UROLOGY
UROMERE
UROMERES
UROPOD
UROPODAL
UROPODOUS
UROPODS
UROPYGIA
UROPYGIAL
UROPYGIUM
UROSCOPIC
UROSCOPY
UROSES
UROSIS
UROSOME
UROSOMES
UROSTEGE
UROSTEGES
UROSTOMY
UROSTYLE
UROSTYLES
URP
URPED
URPING
URPS
URSA
URSAE
URSID
URSIDS
URSIFORM
URSINE
URSON
URSONS
URTEXT
URTEXTE
URTEXTS
URTICA
URTICANT
URTICANTS
URTICARIA
URTICAS
URTICATE
URTICATED
URTICATES
URUBU
URUBUS
URUS
URUSES
URUSHIOL
URUSHIOLS
URVA
URVAS
US
USABILITY
USABLE
USABLY
USAGE
USAGER
USAGERS
USAGES
USANCE
USANCES
USAUNCE
USAUNCES
USE
USEABLE
USEABLY
USED
USEFUL
USEFULLY
USEFULS
USELESS
USELESSLY
USER
USERNAME
USERNAMES
USERS
USES
USHER
USHERED
USHERESS
USHERETTE
USHERING
USHERINGS
USHERS
USHERSHIP
USING
USNEA
USNEAS
USQUABAE
USQUABAES
USQUE
USQUEBAE
USQUEBAES
USQUES
USTION
USTIONS
USTULATE
USTULATED
USTULATES
USUAL
USUALLY
USUALNESS
USUALS
USUCAPION
USUCAPT
USUCAPTED
USUCAPTS
USUFRUCT
USUFRUCTS
USURE
USURED
USURER
USURERS
USURES
USURESS
USURESSES
USURIES
USURING
USURIOUS
USUROUS
USURP
USURPED
USURPEDLY
USURPER
USURPERS
USURPING
USURPINGS
USURPS
USURY
USWARD
USWARDS
UT
UTA
UTAS
UTASES
UTE
UTENSIL
UTENSILS
UTERI
UTERINE
UTERITIS
UTEROTOMY
UTERUS
UTERUSES
UTES
UTILE
UTILES
UTILIDOR
UTILIDORS
UTILISE
UTILISED
UTILISER
UTILISERS
UTILISES
UTILISING
UTILITIES
UTILITY
UTILIZE
UTILIZED
UTILIZER
UTILIZERS
UTILIZES
UTILIZING
UTIS
UTISES
UTMOST
UTMOSTS
UTOPIA
UTOPIAN
UTOPIANS
UTOPIAS
UTOPIAST
UTOPIASTS
UTOPISM
UTOPISMS
UTOPIST
UTOPISTIC
UTOPISTS
UTRICLE
UTRICLES
UTRICULAR
UTRICULI
UTRICULUS
UTS
UTTER
UTTERABLE
UTTERANCE
UTTERED
UTTERER
UTTERERS
UTTEREST
UTTERING
UTTERINGS
UTTERLESS
UTTERLY
UTTERMOST
UTTERNESS
UTTERS
UTU
UTUS
UVA
UVAE
UVAROVITE
UVAS
UVEA
UVEAL
UVEAS
UVEITIC
UVEITIS
UVEITISES
UVEOUS

U

UVULA

UVULA
UVULAE
UVULAR
UVULARLY
UVULARS
UVULAS
UVULITIS
UXORIAL
UXORIALLY
UXORICIDE
UXORIOUS

U

V

VAC
VACANCE
VACANCES
VACANCIES
VACANCY
VACANT
VACANTLY
VACATABLE
VACATE
VACATED
VACATES
VACATING
VACATION
VACATIONS
VACATUR
VACATURS
VACCINA
VACCINAL
VACCINAS
VACCINATE
VACCINE
VACCINEE
VACCINEES
VACCINES
VACCINIA
VACCINIAL
VACCINIAS
VACCINIUM
VACHERIN
VACHERINS
VACILLANT
VACILLATE
VACKED
VACKING
VACS
VACUA
VACUATE
VACUATED
VACUATES
VACUATING
VACUATION
VACUIST
VACUISTS
VACUITIES
VACUITY
VACUOLAR
VACUOLATE
VACUOLE
VACUOLES
VACUOUS
VACUOUSLY
VACUUM
VACUUMED
VACUUMING
VACUUMS
VADE
VADED
VADES
VADING
VADOSE
VAE
VAES
VAG
VAGABOND
VAGABONDS
VAGAL
VAGALLY
VAGARIES
VAGARIOUS
VAGARISH
VAGARY
VAGGED
VAGGING
VAGI
VAGILE
VAGILITY
VAGINA
VAGINAE
VAGINAL
VAGINALLY
VAGINANT
VAGINAS
VAGINATE
VAGINATED
VAGINITIS
VAGINOSES
VAGINOSIS
VAGINULA
VAGINULAE
VAGINULE
VAGINULES
VAGITUS
VAGITUSES
VAGOTOMY
VAGOTONIA
VAGOTONIC
VAGRANCY
VAGRANT
VAGRANTLY
VAGRANTS
VAGROM
VAGS
VAGUE
VAGUED
VAGUELY
VAGUENESS
VAGUER
VAGUES
VAGUEST
VAGUING
VAGUISH
VAGUS
VAHANA
VAHANAS
VAHINE
VAHINES
VAIL
VAILED
VAILING
VAILS
VAIN
VAINER
VAINESSE
VAINESSES
VAINEST
VAINGLORY
VAINLY
VAINNESS
VAIR
VAIRE
VAIRIER
VAIRIEST
VAIRS
VAIRY
VAIVODE
VAIVODES
VAJAZZLE
VAJAZZLED
VAJAZZLES
VAKAS
VAKASES
VAKASS
VAKASSES
VAKEEL
VAKEELS
VAKIL
VAKILS
VALANCE
VALANCED
VALANCES
VALANCING
VALE
VALENCE
VALENCES
VALENCIA
VALENCIAS
VALENCIES
VALENCY
VALENTINE
VALERATE
VALERATES
VALERIAN
VALERIANS
VALERIC
VALES
VALET
VALETA
VALETAS
VALETE
VALETED
VALETES
VALETING
VALETINGS
VALETS
VALGOID
VALGOUS
VALGUS
VALGUSES
VALI
VALIANCE
VALIANCES
VALIANCY
VALIANT
VALIANTLY
VALIANTS
VALID
VALIDATE
VALIDATED
VALIDATES
VALIDATOR
VALIDER
VALIDEST
VALIDITY
VALIDLY
VALIDNESS
VALINE
VALINES
VALIS
VALISE
VALISES
VALIUM
VALIUMS
VALKYR
VALKYRIE
VALKYRIES
VALKYRS
VALLAR
VALLARIES
VALLARS
VALLARY

V

VALLATE
VALLATION
VALLECULA
VALLEY
VALLEYED
VALLEYS
VALLHUND
VALLHUNDS
VALLONIA
VALLONIAS
VALLUM
VALLUMS
VALONEA
VALONEAS
VALONIA
VALONIAS
VALOR
VALORISE
VALORISED
VALORISES
VALORIZE
VALORIZED
VALORIZES
VALOROUS
VALORS
VALOUR
VALOURS
VALPROATE
VALPROIC
VALSE
VALSED
VALSES
VALSING
VALUABLE
VALUABLES
VALUABLY
VALUATE
VALUATED
VALUATES
VALUATING
VALUATION
VALUATOR
VALUATORS
VALUE
VALUED
VALUELESS
VALUER
VALUERS
VALUES
VALUING
VALUTA
VALUTAS
VALVAL
VALVAR
VALVASSOR
VALVATE
VALVE
VALVED
VALVELESS
VALVELET
VALVELETS
VALVELIKE
VALVES
VALVING
VALVULA
VALVULAE
VALVULAR
VALVULE
VALVULES
VAMBRACE
VAMBRACED
VAMBRACES
VAMOOSE
VAMOOSED
VAMOOSES
VAMOOSING
VAMOSE
VAMOSED
VAMOSES
VAMOSING
VAMP
VAMPED
VAMPER
VAMPERS
VAMPIER
VAMPIEST
VAMPING
VAMPINGS
VAMPIRE
VAMPIRED
VAMPIRES
VAMPIRIC
VAMPIRING
VAMPIRISE
VAMPIRISH
VAMPIRISM
VAMPIRIZE
VAMPISH
VAMPISHLY
VAMPLATE
VAMPLATES
VAMPS
VAMPY
VAN
VANADATE
VANADATES
VANADIATE
VANADIC
VANADIUM
VANADIUMS
VANADOUS
VANASPATI
VANDA
VANDAL
VANDALIC
VANDALISE
VANDALISH
VANDALISM
VANDALIZE
VANDALS
VANDAS
VANDYKE
VANDYKED
VANDYKES
VANDYKING
VANE
VANED
VANELESS
VANES
VANESSA
VANESSAS
VANESSID
VANESSIDS
VANG
VANGS
VANGUARD
VANGUARDS
VANILLA
VANILLAS
VANILLIC
VANILLIN
VANILLINS
VANISH
VANISHED
VANISHER
VANISHERS
VANISHES
VANISHING
VANITAS
VANITASES
VANITIED
VANITIES
VANITORY
VANITY
VANLIKE
VANLOAD
VANLOADS
VANMAN
VANMEN
VANNED
VANNER
VANNERS
VANNING
VANNINGS
VANPOOL
VANPOOLS
VANQUISH
VANS
VANT
VANTAGE
VANTAGED
VANTAGES
VANTAGING
VANTBRACE
VANTBRASS
VANTS
VANWARD
VAPE
VAPED
VAPER
VAPERS
VAPES
VAPID
VAPIDER
VAPIDEST
VAPIDITY
VAPIDLY
VAPIDNESS
VAPING
VAPINGS
VAPOR
VAPORABLE
VAPORED
VAPORER
VAPORERS
VAPORETTI
VAPORETTO
VAPORIER
VAPORIEST
VAPORIFIC
VAPORING
VAPORINGS
VAPORISE
VAPORISED
VAPORISER
VAPORISES
VAPORISH
VAPORIZE
VAPORIZED
VAPORIZER
VAPORIZES
VAPORLESS
VAPORLIKE
VAPOROUS
VAPORS
VAPORWARE
VAPORY
VAPOUR
VAPOURED
VAPOURER
VAPOURERS
VAPOURIER
VAPOURING
VAPOURISH
VAPOUROUS
VAPOURS
VAPOURY
VAPULATE
VAPULATED
VAPULATES
VAQUERO
VAQUEROS
VAR
VARA
VARACTOR
VARACTORS
VARAN
VARANS
VARAS
VARDIES

VARDY
VARE
VAREC
VARECH
VARECHS
VARECS
VARENYKY
VARES
VAREUSE
VAREUSES
VARGUENO
VARGUENOS
VARIA
VARIABLE
VARIABLES
VARIABLY
VARIANCE
VARIANCES
VARIANT
VARIANTS
VARIAS
VARIATE
VARIATED
VARIATES
VARIATING
VARIATION
VARIATIVE
VARICEAL
VARICELLA
VARICES
VARICOID
VARICOSE
VARICOSED
VARICOSES
VARICOSIS
VARIED
VARIEDLY
VARIEGATE
VARIER
VARIERS
VARIES
VARIETAL
VARIETALS
VARIETIES
VARIETY
VARIFOCAL
VARIFORM
VARIOLA
VARIOLAR
VARIOLAS
VARIOLATE
VARIOLE
VARIOLES
VARIOLITE
VARIOLOID
VARIOLOUS
VARIORUM
VARIORUMS
VARIOUS
VARIOUSLY
VARISCITE
VARISIZED
VARISTOR
VARISTORS
VARITYPE
VARITYPED
VARITYPES
VARIX
VARLET
VARLETESS
VARLETRY
VARLETS
VARLETTO
VARLETTOS
VARMENT
VARMENTS
VARMINT
VARMINTS
VARNA
VARNAS
VARNISH
VARNISHED
VARNISHER
VARNISHES
VARNISHY
VAROOM
VAROOMED
VAROOMING
VAROOMS
VARROA
VARROAS
VARS
VARSAL
VARSITIES
VARSITY
VARTABED
VARTABEDS
VARUS
VARUSES
VARVE
VARVED
VARVEL
VARVELLED
VARVELS
VARVES
VARY
VARYING
VARYINGLY
VARYINGS
VAS
VASA
VASAL
VASCULA
VASCULAR
VASCULUM
VASCULUMS
VASE
VASECTOMY
VASEFUL
VASEFULS
VASELIKE
VASELINE
VASELINED
VASELINES
VASES
VASIFORM
VASOMOTOR
VASOSPASM
VASOTOCIN
VASOTOMY
VASOVAGAL
VASSAIL
VASSAILS
VASSAL
VASSALAGE
VASSALESS
VASSALISE
VASSALIZE
VASSALLED
VASSALRY
VASSALS
VAST
VASTER
VASTEST
VASTIDITY
VASTIER
VASTIEST
VASTITIES
VASTITUDE
VASTITY
VASTLY
VASTNESS
VASTS
VASTY
VAT
VATABLE
VATFUL
VATFULS
VATIC
VATICAL
VATICIDE
VATICIDES
VATICINAL
VATMAN
VATMEN
VATS
VATTED
VATTER
VATTERS
VATTING
VATU
VATUS
VAU
VAUCH
VAUCHED
VAUCHES
VAUCHING
VAUDOO
VAUDOOS
VAUDOUX
VAULT
VAULTAGE
VAULTAGES
VAULTED
VAULTER
VAULTERS
VAULTIER
VAULTIEST
VAULTING
VAULTINGS
VAULTLIKE
VAULTS
VAULTY
VAUNCE
VAUNCED
VAUNCES
VAUNCING
VAUNT
VAUNTAGE
VAUNTAGES
VAUNTED
VAUNTER
VAUNTERS
VAUNTERY
VAUNTFUL
VAUNTIE
VAUNTIER
VAUNTIEST
VAUNTING
VAUNTINGS
VAUNTS
VAUNTY
VAURIEN
VAURIENS
VAUS
VAUT
VAUTE
VAUTED
VAUTES
VAUTING
VAUTS
VAV
VAVASOR
VAVASORS
VAVASORY
VAVASOUR
VAVASOURS
VAVASSOR
VAVASSORS
VAVS
VAW
VAWARD
VAWARDS
VAWNTIE
VAWNTIER
VAWNTIEST
VAWS
VAWTE
VAWTED
VAWTES

VAWTING
VAX
VAXES
VEAL
VEALE
VEALED
VEALER
VEALERS
VEALES
VEALIER
VEALIEST
VEALING
VEALS
VEALY
VECTOR
VECTORED
VECTORIAL
VECTORING
VECTORISE
VECTORIZE
VECTORS
VEDALIA
VEDALIAS
VEDETTE
VEDETTES
VEDUTA
VEDUTAS
VEDUTE
VEDUTISTA
VEDUTISTE
VEDUTISTI
VEE
VEEJAY
VEEJAYS
VEENA
VEENAS
VEEP
VEEPEE
VEEPEES
VEEPS
VEER
VEERED
VEERIES
VEERING
VEERINGLY
VEERINGS
VEERS
VEERY
VEES
VEG
VEGA
VEGAN
VEGANIC
VEGANISM
VEGANISMS
VEGANS
VEGAS
VEGELATE
VEGELATES
VEGEMITE
VEGEMITES
VEGES
VEGETABLE
VEGETABLY
VEGETAL
VEGETALLY
VEGETALS
VEGETANT
VEGETATE
VEGETATED
VEGETATES
VEGETE
VEGETIST
VEGETISTS
VEGETIVE
VEGETIVES
VEGGED
VEGGES
VEGGIE
VEGGIER
VEGGIES
VEGGIEST
VEGGING
VEGIE
VEGIER
VEGIES
VEGIEST
VEGO
VEGOS
VEHEMENCE
VEHEMENCY
VEHEMENT
VEHICLE
VEHICLES
VEHICULAR
VEHM
VEHME
VEHMIC
VEHMIQUE
VEIL
VEILED
VEILEDLY
VEILER
VEILERS
VEILIER
VEILIEST
VEILING
VEILINGS
VEILLESS
VEILLEUSE
VEILLIKE
VEILS
VEILY
VEIN
VEINAL
VEINED
VEINER
VEINERS
VEINIER
VEINIEST
VEINING
VEININGS
VEINLESS
VEINLET
VEINLETS
VEINLIKE
VEINOUS
VEINS
VEINSTONE
VEINSTUFF
VEINULE
VEINULES
VEINULET
VEINULETS
VEINY
VELA
VELAMEN
VELAMINA
VELAR
VELARIA
VELARIC
VELARISE
VELARISED
VELARISES
VELARIUM
VELARIZE
VELARIZED
VELARIZES
VELARS
VELATE
VELATED
VELATURA
VELATURAS
VELCRO
VELCROS
VELD
VELDS
VELDSKOEN
VELDT
VELDTS
VELE
VELES
VELETA
VELETAS
VELIGER
VELIGERS
VELITES
VELL
VELLEITY
VELLENAGE
VELLET
VELLETS
VELLICATE
VELLON
VELLONS
VELLS
VELLUM
VELLUMS
VELLUS
VELOCE
VELOCITY
VELODROME
VELOUR
VELOURS
VELOUTE
VELOUTES
VELOUTINE
VELSKOEN
VELSKOENS
VELUM
VELURE
VELURED
VELURES
VELURING
VELVERET
VELVERETS
VELVET
VELVETED
VELVETEEN
VELVETIER
VELVETING
VELVETS
VELVETY
VENA
VENAE
VENAL
VENALITY
VENALLY
VENATIC
VENATICAL
VENATION
VENATIONS
VENATOR
VENATORS
VEND
VENDABLE
VENDABLES
VENDACE
VENDACES
VENDAGE
VENDAGES
VENDANGE
VENDANGES
VENDED
VENDEE
VENDEES
VENDER
VENDERS
VENDETTA
VENDETTAS
VENDEUSE
VENDEUSES
VENDIBLE
VENDIBLES
VENDIBLY
VENDING
VENDINGS
VENDIS
VENDISES
VENDISS

VENDISSES
VENDITION
VENDOR
VENDORS
VENDS
VENDU
VENDUE
VENDUES
VENDUS
VENEER
VENEERED
VENEERER
VENEERERS
VENEERING
VENEERS
VENEFIC
VENEFICAL
VENENATE
VENENATED
VENENATES
VENENE
VENENES
VENENOSE
VENERABLE
VENERABLY
VENERATE
VENERATED
VENERATES
VENERATOR
VENEREAL
VENEREAN
VENEREANS
VENEREOUS
VENERER
VENERERS
VENERIES
VENERY
VENETIAN
VENETIANS
VENEWE
VENEWES
VENEY
VENEYS
VENGE
VENGEABLE
VENGEABLY
VENGEANCE
VENGED
VENGEFUL
VENGEMENT
VENGER
VENGERS
VENGES
VENGING
VENIAL
VENIALITY
VENIALLY
VENIDIUM
VENIDIUMS
VENIN
VENINE
VENINES
VENINS
VENIRE
VENIREMAN
VENIREMEN
VENIRES
VENISON
VENISONS
VENITE
VENITES
VENNEL
VENNELS
VENOGRAM
VENOGRAMS
VENOLOGY
VENOM
VENOMED
VENOMER
VENOMERS
VENOMING
VENOMLESS
VENOMOUS
VENOMS
VENOSE
VENOSITY
VENOUS
VENOUSLY
VENT
VENTAGE
VENTAGES
VENTAIL
VENTAILE
VENTAILES
VENTAILS
VENTANA
VENTANAS
VENTAYLE
VENTAYLES
VENTED
VENTER
VENTERS
VENTIDUCT
VENTIFACT
VENTIGE
VENTIGES
VENTIL
VENTILATE
VENTILS
VENTING
VENTINGS
VENTLESS
VENTOSE
VENTOSES
VENTOSITY
VENTOUSE
VENTOUSES
VENTRAL
VENTRALLY
VENTRALS
VENTRE
VENTRED
VENTRES
VENTRICLE
VENTRING
VENTRINGS
VENTROUS
VENTS
VENTURE
VENTURED
VENTURER
VENTURERS
VENTURES
VENTURI
VENTURING
VENTURIS
VENTUROUS
VENUE
VENUES
VENULAR
VENULE
VENULES
VENULOSE
VENULOUS
VENUS
VENUSES
VENVILLE
VENVILLES
VERA
VERACIOUS
VERACITY
VERANDA
VERANDAED
VERANDAH
VERANDAHS
VERANDAS
VERAPAMIL
VERATRIA
VERATRIAS
VERATRIN
VERATRINE
VERATRINS
VERATRUM
VERATRUMS
VERB
VERBAL
VERBALISE
VERBALISM
VERBALIST
VERBALITY
VERBALIZE
VERBALLED
VERBALLY
VERBALS
VERBARIAN
VERBASCUM
VERBATIM
VERBENA
VERBENAS
VERBERATE
VERBIAGE
VERBIAGES
VERBICIDE
VERBID
VERBIDS
VERBIFIED
VERBIFIES
VERBIFY
VERBILE
VERBILES
VERBING
VERBINGS
VERBLESS
VERBOSE
VERBOSELY
VERBOSER
VERBOSEST
VERBOSITY
VERBOTEN
VERBS
VERD
VERDANCY
VERDANT
VERDANTLY
VERDELHO
VERDELHOS
VERDERER
VERDERERS
VERDEROR
VERDERORS
VERDET
VERDETS
VERDICT
VERDICTS
VERDIGRIS
VERDIN
VERDINS
VERDIT
VERDITE
VERDITER
VERDITERS
VERDITES
VERDITS
VERDOY
VERDOYS
VERDURE
VERDURED
VERDURES
VERDUROUS
VERECUND
VERGE
VERGED
VERGENCE
VERGENCES
VERGENCY
VERGER
VERGERS
VERGES
VERGING
VERGLAS

V

VERGLASES
VERIDIC
VERIDICAL
VERIER
VERIEST
VERIFIED
VERIFIER
VERIFIERS
VERIFIES
VERIFY
VERIFYING
VERILY
VERISM
VERISMO
VERISMOS
VERISMS
VERIST
VERISTIC
VERISTS
VERITABLE
VERITABLY
VERITAS
VERITATES
VERITE
VERITES
VERITIES
VERITY
VERJUICE
VERJUICED
VERJUICES
VERJUS
VERJUSES
VERKLEMPT
VERKRAMP
VERLAN
VERLANS
VERLIG
VERLIGTE
VERLIGTES
VERMAL
VERMEIL
VERMEILED
VERMEILLE
VERMEILS
VERMELL
VERMELLS
VERMES
VERMIAN
VERMICIDE
VERMICULE
VERMIFORM
VERMIFUGE
VERMIL
VERMILIES
VERMILION
VERMILLED
VERMILS
VERMILY
VERMIN
VERMINATE
VERMINED
VERMINIER
VERMINOUS
VERMINS
VERMINY
VERMIS
VERMOULU
VERMOUTH
VERMOUTHS
VERMUTH
VERMUTHS
VERNACLE
VERNACLES
VERNAL
VERNALISE
VERNALITY
VERNALIZE
VERNALLY
VERNANT
VERNATION
VERNICLE
VERNICLES
VERNIER
VERNIERS
VERNIX
VERNIXES
VERONAL
VERONALS
VERONICA
VERONICAS
VERONIQUE
VERQUERE
VERQUERES
VERQUIRE
VERQUIRES
VERRA
VERREL
VERRELS
VERREY
VERRINE
VERRINES
VERRUCA
VERRUCAE
VERRUCAS
VERRUCOSE
VERRUCOUS
VERRUGA
VERRUGAS
VERRY
VERS
VERSAL
VERSALS
VERSANT
VERSANTS
VERSATILE
VERSE
VERSED
VERSELET
VERSELETS
VERSEMAN
VERSEMEN
VERSER
VERSERS
VERSES
VERSET
VERSETS
VERSICLE
VERSICLES
VERSIFIED
VERSIFIER
VERSIFIES
VERSIFORM
VERSIFY
VERSIN
VERSINE
VERSINES
VERSING
VERSINGS
VERSINS
VERSION
VERSIONAL
VERSIONED
VERSIONER
VERSIONS
VERSO
VERSOS
VERST
VERSTE
VERSTES
VERSTS
VERSUS
VERSUTE
VERT
VERTEBRA
VERTEBRAE
VERTEBRAL
VERTEBRAS
VERTED
VERTEX
VERTEXES
VERTICAL
VERTICALS
VERTICES
VERTICIL
VERTICILS
VERTICITY
VERTIGO
VERTIGOES
VERTIGOS
VERTING
VERTIPORT
VERTISOL
VERTISOLS
VERTS
VERTU
VERTUE
VERTUES
VERTUOUS
VERTUS
VERVAIN
VERVAINS
VERVE
VERVEL
VERVELLED
VERVELS
VERVEN
VERVENS
VERVES
VERVET
VERVETS
VERY
VESICA
VESICAE
VESICAL
VESICANT
VESICANTS
VESICAS
VESICATE
VESICATED
VESICATES
VESICLE
VESICLES
VESICULA
VESICULAE
VESICULAR
VESPA
VESPAS
VESPER
VESPERAL
VESPERALS
VESPERS
VESPIARY
VESPID
VESPIDS
VESPINE
VESPOID
VESSAIL
VESSAILS
VESSEL
VESSELED
VESSELS
VEST
VESTA
VESTAL
VESTALLY
VESTALS
VESTAS
VESTED
VESTEE
VESTEES
VESTIARY
VESTIBULA
VESTIBULE
VESTIGE
VESTIGES
VESTIGIA
VESTIGIAL
VESTIGIUM
VESTIMENT
VESTING

VESTINGS
VESTITURE
VESTLESS
VESTLIKE
VESTMENT
VESTMENTS
VESTRAL
VESTRIES
VESTRY
VESTRYMAN
VESTRYMEN
VESTS
VESTURAL
VESTURE
VESTURED
VESTURER
VESTURERS
VESTURES
VESTURING
VESUVIAN
VESUVIANS
VET
VETCH
VETCHES
VETCHIER
VETCHIEST
VETCHLING
VETCHY
VETERAN
VETERANS
VETIVER
VETIVERS
VETIVERT
VETIVERTS
VETKOEK
VETKOEKS
VETO
VETOED
VETOER
VETOERS
VETOES
VETOING
VETOLESS
VETS
VETTED
VETTER
VETTERS
VETTING
VETTINGS
VETTURA
VETTURAS
VETTURINI
VETTURINO
VEX
VEXATION
VEXATIONS
VEXATIOUS
VEXATORY
VEXED
VEXEDLY
VEXEDNESS
VEXER
VEXERS
VEXES
VEXIL
VEXILLA
VEXILLAR
VEXILLARY
VEXILLATE
VEXILLUM
VEXILS
VEXING
VEXINGLY
VEXINGS
VEXT
VEZIR
VEZIRS
VIA
VIABILITY
VIABLE
VIABLY
VIADUCT
VIADUCTS
VIAE
VIAL
VIALED
VIALFUL
VIALFULS
VIALING
VIALLED
VIALLING
VIALS
VIAMETER
VIAMETERS
VIAND
VIANDS
VIAS
VIATIC
VIATICA
VIATICAL
VIATICALS
VIATICUM
VIATICUMS
VIATOR
VIATORES
VIATORIAL
VIATORS
VIBE
VIBES
VIBEX
VIBEY
VIBICES
VIBIER
VIBIEST
VIBIST
VIBISTS
VIBRACULA
VIBRAHARP
VIBRANCE
VIBRANCES
VIBRANCY
VIBRANT
VIBRANTLY
VIBRANTS
VIBRATE
VIBRATED
VIBRATES
VIBRATILE
VIBRATING
VIBRATION
VIBRATIVE
VIBRATO
VIBRATOR
VIBRATORS
VIBRATORY
VIBRATOS
VIBRIO
VIBRIOID
VIBRION
VIBRIONIC
VIBRIONS
VIBRIOS
VIBRIOSES
VIBRIOSIS
VIBRISSA
VIBRISSAE
VIBRISSAL
VIBRONIC
VIBS
VIBURNUM
VIBURNUMS
VICAR
VICARAGE
VICARAGES
VICARATE
VICARATES
VICARESS
VICARIAL
VICARIANT
VICARIATE
VICARIES
VICARIOUS
VICARLIER
VICARLY
VICARS
VICARSHIP
VICARY
VICE
VICED
VICEGERAL
VICELESS
VICELIKE
VICENARY
VICENNIAL
VICEREGAL
VICEREINE
VICEROY
VICEROYS
VICES
VICESIMAL
VICHIES
VICHY
VICIATE
VICIATED
VICIATES
VICIATING
VICINAGE
VICINAGES
VICINAL
VICING
VICINITY
VICIOSITY
VICIOUS
VICIOUSLY
VICOMTE
VICOMTES
VICTIM
VICTIMISE
VICTIMIZE
VICTIMS
VICTOR
VICTORESS
VICTORIA
VICTORIAS
VICTORIES
VICTORINE
VICTORS
VICTORY
VICTRESS
VICTRIX
VICTRIXES
VICTROLA
VICTROLAS
VICTUAL
VICTUALED
VICTUALER
VICTUALS
VICUGNA
VICUGNAS
VICUNA
VICUNAS
VID
VIDALIA
VIDALIAS
VIDAME
VIDAMES
VIDE
VIDELICET
VIDENDA
VIDENDUM
VIDEO
VIDEOCAM
VIDEOCAMS
VIDEODISC
VIDEODISK
VIDEOED
VIDEOFIT
VIDEOFITS
VIDEOGRAM
VIDEOING

V

VIDEOLAND
VIDEOS
VIDEOTAPE
VIDEOTEX
VIDEOTEXT
VIDETTE
VIDETTES
VIDICON
VIDICONS
VIDIMUS
VIDIMUSES
VIDIOT
VIDIOTS
VIDS
VIDSCREEN
VIDUAGE
VIDUAGES
VIDUAL
VIDUITIES
VIDUITY
VIDUOUS
VIE
VIED
VIELLE
VIELLES
VIENNA
VIER
VIERS
VIES
VIEW
VIEWABLE
VIEWBOOK
VIEWBOOKS
VIEWDATA
VIEWDATAS
VIEWED
VIEWER
VIEWERS
VIEWIER
VIEWIEST
VIEWINESS
VIEWING
VIEWINGS
VIEWLESS
VIEWLY
VIEWPHONE
VIEWPOINT
VIEWPORT
VIEWPORTS
VIEWS
VIEWSHED
VIEWSHEDS
VIEWY
VIFDA
VIFDAS
VIFF
VIFFED
VIFFING
VIFFS
VIG
VIGA
VIGAS
VIGESIMAL
VIGIA
VIGIAS
VIGIL
VIGILANCE
VIGILANT
VIGILANTE
VIGILS
VIGNERON
VIGNERONS
VIGNETTE
VIGNETTED
VIGNETTER
VIGNETTES
VIGOR
VIGORISH
VIGORO
VIGOROS
VIGOROSO
VIGOROUS
VIGORS
VIGOUR
VIGOURS
VIGS
VIHARA
VIHARAS
VIHUELA
VIHUELAS
VIKING
VIKINGISM
VIKINGS
VILAYET
VILAYETS
VILD
VILDE
VILDLY
VILDNESS
VILE
VILELY
VILENESS
VILER
VILEST
VILIACO
VILIACOES
VILIACOS
VILIAGO
VILIAGOES
VILIAGOS
VILIFIED
VILIFIER
VILIFIERS
VILIFIES
VILIFY
VILIFYING
VILIPEND
VILIPENDS
VILL
VILLA
VILLADOM
VILLADOMS
VILLAE
VILLAGE
VILLAGER
VILLAGERS
VILLAGERY
VILLAGES
VILLAGEY
VILLAGIER
VILLAGIO
VILLAGIOS
VILLAGREE
VILLAIN
VILLAINS
VILLAINY
VILLAN
VILLANAGE
VILLANIES
VILLANOUS
VILLANS
VILLANY
VILLAR
VILLAS
VILLATIC
VILLEIN
VILLEINS
VILLENAGE
VILLI
VILLIACO
VILLIACOS
VILLIAGO
VILLIAGOS
VILLIFORM
VILLOSE
VILLOSITY
VILLOUS
VILLOUSLY
VILLS
VILLUS
VIM
VIMANA
VIMANAS
VIMEN
VIMINA
VIMINAL
VIMINEOUS
VIMS
VIN
VINA
VINACEOUS
VINAL
VINALS
VINAS
VINASSE
VINASSES
VINCA
VINCAS
VINCIBLE
VINCIBLY
VINCULA
VINCULAR
VINCULUM
VINCULUMS
VINDALOO
VINDALOOS
VINDEMIAL
VINDICATE
VINE
VINEAL
VINED
VINEGAR
VINEGARED
VINEGARS
VINEGARY
VINELESS
VINELIKE
VINER
VINERIES
VINERS
VINERY
VINES
VINEW
VINEWED
VINEWING
VINEWS
VINEYARD
VINEYARDS
VINIC
VINIER
VINIEST
VINIFERA
VINIFERAS
VINIFIED
VINIFIES
VINIFY
VINIFYING
VINING
VINO
VINOLENT
VINOLOGY
VINOS
VINOSITY
VINOUS
VINOUSLY
VINS
VINT
VINTAGE
VINTAGED
VINTAGER
VINTAGERS
VINTAGES
VINTAGING
VINTED
VINTING
VINTNER
VINTNERS
VINTRIES
VINTRY
VINTS

VINY
VINYL
VINYLIC
VINYLS
VIOL
VIOLA
VIOLABLE
VIOLABLY
VIOLAS
VIOLATE
VIOLATED
VIOLATER
VIOLATERS
VIOLATES
VIOLATING
VIOLATION
VIOLATIVE
VIOLATOR
VIOLATORS
VIOLD
VIOLENCE
VIOLENCES
VIOLENT
VIOLENTED
VIOLENTLY
VIOLENTS
VIOLER
VIOLERS
VIOLET
VIOLETS
VIOLIN
VIOLINIST
VIOLINS
VIOLIST
VIOLISTS
VIOLONE
VIOLONES
VIOLS
VIOMYCIN
VIOMYCINS
VIOSTEROL
VIPASSANA
VIPER
VIPERFISH
VIPERINE
VIPERISH
VIPERLIKE
VIPEROUS
VIPERS
VIRAEMIA
VIRAEMIAS
VIRAEMIC
VIRAGO
VIRAGOES
VIRAGOISH
VIRAGOS
VIRAL
VIRALITY
VIRALLY
VIRALS
VIRANDA
VIRANDAS
VIRANDO
VIRANDOS
VIRE
VIRED
VIRELAI
VIRELAIS
VIRELAY
VIRELAYS
VIREMENT
VIREMENTS
VIREMIA
VIREMIAS
VIREMIC
VIRENT
VIREO
VIREONINE
VIREOS
VIRES
VIRESCENT
VIRETOT
VIRETOTS
VIRGA
VIRGAE
VIRGAS
VIRGATE
VIRGATES
VIRGE
VIRGER
VIRGERS
VIRGES
VIRGIN
VIRGINAL
VIRGINALS
VIRGINED
VIRGINIA
VIRGINIAS
VIRGINING
VIRGINITY
VIRGINIUM
VIRGINLY
VIRGINS
VIRGULATE
VIRGULE
VIRGULES
VIRICIDAL
VIRICIDE
VIRICIDES
VIRID
VIRIDIAN
VIRIDIANS
VIRIDITE
VIRIDITES
VIRIDITY
VIRILE
VIRILELY
VIRILISE
VIRILISED
VIRILISES
VIRILISM
VIRILISMS
VIRILITY
VIRILIZE
VIRILIZED
VIRILIZES
VIRILOCAL
VIRING
VIRINO
VIRINOS
VIRION
VIRIONS
VIRL
VIRLS
VIROGENE
VIROGENES
VIROID
VIROIDS
VIROLOGIC
VIROLOGY
VIROSE
VIROSES
VIROSIS
VIROUS
VIRTU
VIRTUAL
VIRTUALLY
VIRTUE
VIRTUES
VIRTUOSA
VIRTUOSAS
VIRTUOSE
VIRTUOSI
VIRTUOSIC
VIRTUOSO
VIRTUOSOS
VIRTUOUS
VIRTUS
VIRUCIDAL
VIRUCIDE
VIRUCIDES
VIRULENCE
VIRULENCY
VIRULENT
VIRUS
VIRUSES
VIRUSLIKE
VIRUSOID
VIRUSOIDS
VIS
VISA
VISAED
VISAGE
VISAGED
VISAGES
VISAGIST
VISAGISTE
VISAGISTS
VISAING
VISARD
VISARDS
VISAS
VISCACHA
VISCACHAS
VISCARIA
VISCARIAS
VISCERA
VISCERAL
VISCERATE
VISCID
VISCIDITY
VISCIDLY
VISCIN
VISCINS
VISCOID
VISCOIDAL
VISCOSE
VISCOSES
VISCOSITY
VISCOUNT
VISCOUNTS
VISCOUNTY
VISCOUS
VISCOUSLY
VISCUM
VISCUMS
VISCUS
VISE
VISED
VISEED
VISEING
VISELIKE
VISES
VISHING
VISHINGS
VISIBLE
VISIBLES
VISIBLY
VISIE
VISIED
VISIEING
VISIER
VISIERS
VISIES
VISILE
VISILES
VISING
VISION
VISIONAL
VISIONARY
VISIONED
VISIONER
VISIONERS
VISIONING
VISIONIST
VISIONS
VISIT
VISITABLE
VISITANT
VISITANTS

V

VISITATOR
VISITE
VISITED
VISITEE
VISITEES
VISITER
VISITERS
VISITES
VISITING
VISITINGS
VISITOR
VISITORS
VISITRESS
VISITS
VISIVE
VISNE
VISNES
VISNOMIE
VISNOMIES
VISNOMY
VISON
VISONS
VISOR
VISORED
VISORING
VISORLESS
VISORS
VISTA
VISTAED
VISTAING
VISTAL
VISTALESS
VISTAS
VISTO
VISTOS
VISUAL
VISUALISE
VISUALIST
VISUALITY
VISUALIZE
VISUALLY
VISUALS
VITA
VITACEOUS
VITAE
VITAL
VITALISE
VITALISED
VITALISER
VITALISES
VITALISM
VITALISMS
VITALIST
VITALISTS
VITALITY
VITALIZE
VITALIZED
VITALIZER
VITALIZES
VITALLY
VITALNESS
VITALS
VITAMER
VITAMERS
VITAMIN
VITAMINE
VITAMINES
VITAMINIC
VITAMINS
VITAS
VITASCOPE
VITATIVE
VITE
VITELLARY
VITELLI
VITELLIN
VITELLINE
VITELLINS
VITELLUS
VITESSE
VITESSES
VITEX
VITEXES
VITIABLE
VITIATE
VITIATED
VITIATES
VITIATING
VITIATION
VITIATOR
VITIATORS
VITICETA
VITICETUM
VITICIDE
VITICIDES
VITILIGO
VITILIGOS
VITIOSITY
VITIOUS
VITRAGE
VITRAGES
VITRAIL
VITRAIN
VITRAINS
VITRAUX
VITREOUS
VITREUM
VITREUMS
VITRIC
VITRICS
VITRIFIED
VITRIFIES
VITRIFORM
VITRIFY
VITRINE
VITRINES
VITRIOL
VITRIOLED
VITRIOLIC
VITRIOLS
VITRO
VITTA
VITTAE
VITTATE
VITTLE
VITTLED
VITTLES
VITTLING
VITULAR
VITULINE
VIVA
VIVACE
VIVACES
VIVACIOUS
VIVACITY
VIVAED
VIVAING
VIVAMENTE
VIVANDIER
VIVARIA
VIVARIES
VIVARIUM
VIVARIUMS
VIVARY
VIVAS
VIVAT
VIVATS
VIVDA
VIVDAS
VIVE
VIVELY
VIVENCIES
VIVENCY
VIVER
VIVERRA
VIVERRAS
VIVERRID
VIVERRIDS
VIVERRINE
VIVERS
VIVES
VIVIANITE
VIVID
VIVIDER
VIVIDEST
VIVIDITY
VIVIDLY
VIVIDNESS
VIVIFIC
VIVIFIED
VIVIFIER
VIVIFIERS
VIVIFIES
VIVIFY
VIVIFYING
VIVIPARA
VIVIPARY
VIVISECT
VIVISECTS
VIVO
VIVRES
VIXEN
VIXENISH
VIXENLY
VIXENS
VIZAMENT
VIZAMENTS
VIZARD
VIZARDED
VIZARDING
VIZARDS
VIZCACHA
VIZCACHAS
VIZIED
VIZIER
VIZIERATE
VIZIERIAL
VIZIERS
VIZIES
VIZIR
VIZIRATE
VIZIRATES
VIZIRIAL
VIZIRS
VIZIRSHIP
VIZOR
VIZORED
VIZORING
VIZORLESS
VIZORS
VIZSLA
VIZSLAS
VIZY
VIZYING
VIZZIE
VIZZIED
VIZZIEING
VIZZIES
VLEI
VLEIS
VLIES
VLOG
VLOGGED
VLOGGER
VLOGGERS
VLOGGING
VLOGGINGS
VLOGS
VLY
VOAR
VOARS
VOCAB
VOCABLE
VOCABLES
VOCABLY
VOCABS
VOCABULAR
VOCAL
VOCALESE
VOCALESES

V

VOCALIC
VOCALICS
VOCALION
VOCALIONS
VOCALISE
VOCALISED
VOCALISER
VOCALISES
VOCALISM
VOCALISMS
VOCALIST
VOCALISTS
VOCALITY
VOCALIZE
VOCALIZED
VOCALIZER
VOCALIZES
VOCALLY
VOCALNESS
VOCALS
VOCATION
VOCATIONS
VOCATIVE
VOCATIVES
VOCES
VOCODER
VOCODERED
VOCODERS
VOCULAR
VOCULE
VOCULES
VODCAST
VODCASTED
VODCASTER
VODCASTS
VODDIES
VODDY
VODKA
VODKAS
VODOU
VODOUN
VODOUNS
VODOUS
VODUN
VODUNS
VOE
VOEMA
VOEMAS
VOERTSAK
VOERTSEK
VOES
VOETSAK
VOETSEK
VOG
VOGIE
VOGIER
VOGIEST
VOGS
VOGUE
VOGUED
VOGUEING
VOGUEINGS
VOGUER
VOGUERS
VOGUES
VOGUEY
VOGUIER
VOGUIEST
VOGUING
VOGUINGS
VOGUISH
VOGUISHLY
VOICE
VOICED
VOICEFUL
VOICELESS
VOICEMAIL
VOICEOVER
VOICER
VOICERS
VOICES
VOICING
VOICINGS
VOID
VOIDABLE
VOIDANCE
VOIDANCES
VOIDED
VOIDEE
VOIDEES
VOIDER
VOIDERS
VOIDING
VOIDINGS
VOIDNESS
VOIDS
VOILA
VOILE
VOILES
VOIP
VOIPS
VOISINAGE
VOITURE
VOITURES
VOITURIER
VOIVODE
VOIVODES
VOL
VOLA
VOLABLE
VOLAE
VOLAGE
VOLANT
VOLANTE
VOLANTES
VOLAR
VOLARIES
VOLARY
VOLATIC
VOLATICS
VOLATILE
VOLATILES
VOLCANIAN
VOLCANIC
VOLCANICS
VOLCANISE
VOLCANISM
VOLCANIST
VOLCANIZE
VOLCANO
VOLCANOES
VOLCANOS
VOLE
VOLED
VOLELIKE
VOLENS
VOLERIES
VOLERY
VOLES
VOLET
VOLETS
VOLING
VOLITANT
VOLITATE
VOLITATED
VOLITATES
VOLITIENT
VOLITION
VOLITIONS
VOLITIVE
VOLITIVES
VOLK
VOLKS
VOLKSLIED
VOLKSRAAD
VOLLEY
VOLLEYED
VOLLEYER
VOLLEYERS
VOLLEYING
VOLLEYS
VOLOST
VOLOSTS
VOLPINO
VOLPINOS
VOLPLANE
VOLPLANED
VOLPLANES
VOLS
VOLT
VOLTA
VOLTAGE
VOLTAGES
VOLTAIC
VOLTAISM
VOLTAISMS
VOLTE
VOLTED
VOLTES
VOLTI
VOLTIGEUR
VOLTING
VOLTINISM
VOLTIS
VOLTMETER
VOLTS
VOLUBIL
VOLUBLE
VOLUBLY
VOLUCRINE
VOLUME
VOLUMED
VOLUMES
VOLUMETER
VOLUMETRY
VOLUMINAL
VOLUMING
VOLUMISE
VOLUMISED
VOLUMISER
VOLUMISES
VOLUMIST
VOLUMISTS
VOLUMIZE
VOLUMIZED
VOLUMIZER
VOLUMIZES
VOLUNTARY
VOLUNTEER
VOLUSPA
VOLUSPAS
VOLUTE
VOLUTED
VOLUTES
VOLUTIN
VOLUTINS
VOLUTION
VOLUTIONS
VOLUTOID
VOLVA
VOLVAE
VOLVAS
VOLVATE
VOLVE
VOLVED
VOLVES
VOLVING
VOLVOX
VOLVOXES
VOLVULI
VOLVULUS
VOM
VOMER
VOMERINE
VOMERS
VOMICA
VOMICAE
VOMICAS
VOMIT
VOMITED

VOMITER
VOMITERS
VOMITIER
VOMITIEST
VOMITING
VOMITINGS
VOMITIVE
VOMITIVES
VOMITO
VOMITORIA
VOMITORY
VOMITOS
VOMITOUS
VOMITS
VOMITUS
VOMITUSES
VOMITY
VOMMED
VOMMING
VOMS
VONGOLE
VOODOO
VOODOOED
VOODOOING
VOODOOISM
VOODOOIST
VOODOOS
VOORKAMER
VOORSKOT
VOORSKOTS
VOR
VORACIOUS
VORACITY
VORAGO
VORAGOES
VORAGOS
VORANT
VORLAGE
VORLAGES
VORPAL
VORRED
VORRING
VORS
VORTEX
VORTEXES
VORTICAL
VORTICES
VORTICISM
VORTICIST
VORTICITY
VORTICOSE
VOSTRO
VOTABLE
VOTARESS
VOTARIES
VOTARIST
VOTARISTS
VOTARY
VOTE
VOTEABLE
VOTED
VOTEEN
VOTEENS
VOTELESS
VOTER
VOTERS
VOTES
VOTING
VOTINGS
VOTIVE
VOTIVELY
VOTIVES
VOTRESS
VOTRESSES
VOUCH
VOUCHED
VOUCHEE
VOUCHEES
VOUCHER
VOUCHERED
VOUCHERS
VOUCHES
VOUCHING
VOUCHSAFE
VOUDON
VOUDONS
VOUDOU
VOUDOUED
VOUDOUING
VOUDOUN
VOUDOUNS
VOUDOUS
VOUGE
VOUGES
VOULGE
VOULGES
VOULU
VOUSSOIR
VOUSSOIRS
VOUTSAFE
VOUTSAFED
VOUTSAFES
VOUVRAY
VOUVRAYS
VOW
VOWED
VOWEL
VOWELED
VOWELISE
VOWELISED
VOWELISES
VOWELIZE
VOWELIZED
VOWELIZES
VOWELLED
VOWELLESS
VOWELLIER
VOWELLING
VOWELLY
VOWELS
VOWER
VOWERS
VOWESS
VOWESSES
VOWING
VOWLESS
VOWS
VOX
VOXEL
VOXELS
VOYAGE
VOYAGED
VOYAGER
VOYAGERS
VOYAGES
VOYAGEUR
VOYAGEURS
VOYAGING
VOYAGINGS
VOYEUR
VOYEURISM
VOYEURS
VOZHD
VOZHDS
VRAIC
VRAICKER
VRAICKERS
VRAICKING
VRAICS
VRIL
VRILS
VROOM
VROOMED
VROOMING
VROOMS
VROT
VROU
VROUS
VROUW
VROUWS
VROW
VROWS
VRYSTATER
VUG
VUGG
VUGGIER
VUGGIEST
VUGGS
VUGGY
VUGH
VUGHIER
VUGHIEST
VUGHS
VUGHY
VUGS
VUGULAR
VULCAN
VULCANIAN
VULCANIC
VULCANISE
VULCANISM
VULCANIST
VULCANITE
VULCANIZE
VULCANS
VULGAR
VULGARER
VULGAREST
VULGARIAN
VULGARISE
VULGARISM
VULGARITY
VULGARIZE
VULGARLY
VULGARS
VULGATE
VULGATES
VULGO
VULGUS
VULGUSES
VULN
VULNED
VULNERARY
VULNERATE
VULNING
VULNS
VULPICIDE
VULPINE
VULPINISM
VULPINITE
VULSELLA
VULSELLAE
VULSELLUM
VULTURE
VULTURES
VULTURINE
VULTURISH
VULTURISM
VULTURN
VULTURNS
VULTUROUS
VULVA
VULVAE
VULVAL
VULVAR
VULVAS
VULVATE
VULVIFORM
VULVITIS
VUM
VUMMED
VUMMING
VUMS
VUTTIER
VUTTIEST
VUTTY
VUVUZELA
VUVUZELAS
VYING
VYINGLY
VYINGS

WAAC
WAACS
WAAH
WAB
WABAIN
WABAINS
WABBIT
WABBLE
WABBLED
WABBLER
WABBLERS
WABBLES
WABBLIER
WABBLIEST
WABBLING
WABBLY
WABOOM
WABOOMS
WABS
WABSTER
WABSTERS
WACK
WACKE
WACKED
WACKER
WACKERS
WACKES
WACKEST
WACKIER
WACKIEST
WACKILY
WACKINESS
WACKO
WACKOES
WACKOS
WACKS
WACKY
WACONDA
WACONDAS
WAD
WADABLE
WADD
WADDED
WADDER
WADDERS
WADDIE
WADDIED
WADDIES
WADDING
WADDINGS
WADDLE
WADDLED
WADDLER
WADDLERS
WADDLES
WADDLIER
WADDLIEST
WADDLING
WADDLY
WADDS
WADDY
WADDYING
WADE
WADEABLE
WADED
WADER
WADERS
WADES
WADGE
WADGES
WADI
WADIES
WADING
WADINGS
WADIS
WADMAAL
WADMAALS
WADMAL
WADMALS
WADMEL
WADMELS
WADMOL
WADMOLL
WADMOLLS
WADMOLS
WADS
WADSET
WADSETS
WADSETT
WADSETTED
WADSETTER
WADSETTS
WADT
WADTS
WADY
WAE
WAEFUL
WAENESS
WAENESSES
WAES
WAESOME
WAESUCK
WAESUCKS
WAFER
WAFERED
WAFERIER
WAFERIEST
WAFERING
WAFERS
WAFERY
WAFF
WAFFED
WAFFIE
WAFFIES
WAFFING
WAFFLE
WAFFLED
WAFFLER
WAFFLERS
WAFFLES
WAFFLIER
WAFFLIEST
WAFFLING
WAFFLINGS
WAFFLY
WAFFS
WAFT
WAFTAGE
WAFTAGES
WAFTED
WAFTER
WAFTERS
WAFTING
WAFTINGS
WAFTS
WAFTURE
WAFTURES
WAG
WAGE
WAGED
WAGELESS
WAGENBOOM
WAGER
WAGERED
WAGERER
WAGERERS
WAGERING
WAGERINGS
WAGERS
WAGES
WAGGA
WAGGAS
WAGGED
WAGGER
WAGGERIES
WAGGERS
WAGGERY
WAGGING
WAGGISH
WAGGISHLY
WAGGLE
WAGGLED
WAGGLER
WAGGLERS
WAGGLES
WAGGLIER
WAGGLIEST
WAGGLING
WAGGLY
WAGGON
WAGGONED
WAGGONER
WAGGONERS
WAGGONING
WAGGONS
WAGHALTER
WAGING
WAGMOIRE
WAGMOIRES
WAGON
WAGONAGE
WAGONAGES
WAGONED
WAGONER
WAGONERS
WAGONETTE
WAGONFUL
WAGONFULS
WAGONING
WAGONLESS
WAGONLOAD
WAGONS
WAGS
WAGSOME
WAGTAIL
WAGTAILS
WAGYU
WAGYUS
WAHCONDA
WAHCONDAS
WAHINE
WAHINES
WAHOO
WAHOOS
WAI
WAIATA
WAIATAS
WAID
WAIDE
WAIF

W

WAIFED
WAIFING
WAIFISH
WAIFLIKE
WAIFS
WAIFT
WAIFTS
WAIL
WAILED
WAILER
WAILERS
WAILFUL
WAILFULLY
WAILING
WAILINGLY
WAILINGS
WAILS
WAILSOME
WAIN
WAINAGE
WAINAGES
WAINED
WAINING
WAINS
WAINSCOT
WAINSCOTS
WAIR
WAIRED
WAIRING
WAIRS
WAIRSH
WAIRSHER
WAIRSHEST
WAIRUA
WAIRUAS
WAIS
WAIST
WAISTBAND
WAISTBELT
WAISTCOAT
WAISTED
WAISTER
WAISTERS
WAISTING
WAISTINGS
WAISTLESS
WAISTLINE
WAISTS
WAIT
WAITE
WAITED
WAITER
WAITERAGE
WAITERED
WAITERING
WAITERS
WAITES
WAITING
WAITINGLY
WAITINGS
WAITLIST
WAITLISTS
WAITRESS
WAITRON
WAITRONS
WAITS
WAITSTAFF
WAIVE
WAIVED
WAIVER
WAIVERS
WAIVES
WAIVING
WAIVODE
WAIVODES
WAIWODE
WAIWODES
WAKA
WAKAME
WAKAMES
WAKANDA
WAKANDAS
WAKANE
WAKANES
WAKAS
WAKE
WAKEBOARD
WAKED
WAKEFUL
WAKEFULLY
WAKELESS
WAKEMAN
WAKEMEN
WAKEN
WAKENED
WAKENER
WAKENERS
WAKENING
WAKENINGS
WAKENS
WAKER
WAKERIFE
WAKERS
WAKES
WAKF
WAKFS
WAKIKI
WAKIKIS
WAKING
WAKINGS
WALD
WALDFLUTE
WALDGRAVE
WALDHORN
WALDHORNS
WALDO
WALDOES
WALDOS
WALDRAPP
WALDRAPPS
WALDS
WALE
WALED
WALER
WALERS
WALES
WALI
WALIE
WALIER
WALIES
WALIEST
WALING
WALIS
WALISE
WALISES
WALK
WALKABLE
WALKABOUT
WALKATHON
WALKAWAY
WALKAWAYS
WALKED
WALKER
WALKERS
WALKIES
WALKING
WALKINGS
WALKMILL
WALKMILLS
WALKOUT
WALKOUTS
WALKOVER
WALKOVERS
WALKS
WALKUP
WALKUPS
WALKWAY
WALKWAYS
WALKYRIE
WALKYRIES
WALL
WALLA
WALLABA
WALLABAS
WALLABIES
WALLABY
WALLAH
WALLAHS
WALLAROO
WALLAROOS
WALLAS
WALLBOARD
WALLCHART
WALLED
WALLER
WALLERS
WALLET
WALLETS
WALLEY
WALLEYE
WALLEYED
WALLEYES
WALLEYS
WALLFISH
WALLIE
WALLIER
WALLIES
WALLIEST
WALLING
WALLINGS
WALLOP
WALLOPED
WALLOPER
WALLOPERS
WALLOPING
WALLOPS
WALLOW
WALLOWED
WALLOWER
WALLOWERS
WALLOWING
WALLOWS
WALLPAPER
WALLS
WALLSEND
WALLSENDS
WALLWORT
WALLWORTS
WALLY
WALLYBALL
WALLYDRAG
WALNUT
WALNUTS
WALRUS
WALRUSES
WALTIER
WALTIEST
WALTY
WALTZ
WALTZED
WALTZER
WALTZERS
WALTZES
WALTZING
WALTZINGS
WALTZLIKE
WALY
WAMBENGER
WAMBLE
WAMBLED
WAMBLES
WAMBLIER
WAMBLIEST
WAMBLING
WAMBLINGS
WAMBLY
WAME
WAMED
WAMEFOU
WAMEFOUS

W

WAMEFUL
WAMEFULS
WAMES
WAMMUL
WAMMULS
WAMMUS
WAMMUSES
WAMPEE
WAMPEES
WAMPISH
WAMPISHED
WAMPISHES
WAMPUM
WAMPUMS
WAMPUS
WAMPUSES
WAMUS
WAMUSES
WAN
WANCHANCY
WAND
WANDER
WANDERED
WANDERER
WANDERERS
WANDERING
WANDEROO
WANDEROOS
WANDERS
WANDLE
WANDLED
WANDLES
WANDLIKE
WANDLING
WANDOO
WANDOOS
WANDS
WANE
WANED
WANES
WANEY
WANG
WANGAN
WANGANS
WANGLE
WANGLED
WANGLER
WANGLERS
WANGLES
WANGLING
WANGLINGS
WANGS
WANGUN
WANGUNS
WANHOPE
WANHOPES
WANIER
WANIEST
WANIGAN
WANIGANS
WANING
WANINGS
WANION
WANIONS
WANK
WANKED
WANKER
WANKERS
WANKIER
WANKIEST
WANKING
WANKLE
WANKS
WANKSTA
WANKSTAS
WANKY
WANLE
WANLY
WANNA
WANNABE
WANNABEE
WANNABEES
WANNABES
WANNED
WANNEL
WANNER
WANNESS
WANNESSES
WANNEST
WANNIGAN
WANNIGANS
WANNING
WANNION
WANNIONS
WANNISH
WANS
WANT
WANTAGE
WANTAGES
WANTAWAY
WANTAWAYS
WANTED
WANTER
WANTERS
WANTHILL
WANTHILLS
WANTIES
WANTING
WANTON
WANTONED
WANTONER
WANTONERS
WANTONEST
WANTONING
WANTONISE
WANTONIZE
WANTONLY
WANTONS
WANTS
WANTY
WANWORDY
WANWORTH
WANWORTHS
WANY
WANZE
WANZED
WANZES
WANZING
WAP
WAPENSHAW
WAPENTAKE
WAPINSHAW
WAPITI
WAPITIS
WAPPED
WAPPEND
WAPPER
WAPPERED
WAPPERING
WAPPERS
WAPPING
WAPS
WAQF
WAQFS
WAR
WARAGI
WARAGIS
WARATAH
WARATAHS
WARB
WARBIER
WARBIEST
WARBIRD
WARBIRDS
WARBLE
WARBLED
WARBLER
WARBLERS
WARBLES
WARBLIER
WARBLIEST
WARBLING
WARBLINGS
WARBLY
WARBONNET
WARBOT
WARBOTS
WARBS
WARBY
WARCRAFT
WARCRAFTS
WARD
WARDCORN
WARDCORNS
WARDED
WARDEN
WARDENED
WARDENING
WARDENRY
WARDENS
WARDER
WARDERED
WARDERING
WARDERS
WARDIAN
WARDING
WARDINGS
WARDLESS
WARDMOTE
WARDMOTES
WARDOG
WARDOGS
WARDRESS
WARDROBE
WARDROBED
WARDROBER
WARDROBES
WARDROOM
WARDROOMS
WARDROP
WARDROPS
WARDS
WARDSHIP
WARDSHIPS
WARE
WARED
WAREHOU
WAREHOUS
WAREHOUSE
WARELESS
WAREROOM
WAREROOMS
WARES
WAREZ
WARFARE
WARFARED
WARFARER
WARFARERS
WARFARES
WARFARIN
WARFARING
WARFARINS
WARGAME
WARGAMED
WARGAMER
WARGAMERS
WARGAMES
WARGAMING
WARHABLE
WARHEAD
WARHEADS
WARHORSE
WARHORSES
WARIBASHI
WARIER
WARIEST
WARILY
WARIMENT
WARIMENTS
WARINESS

W

WARING
WARISON
WARISONS
WARK
WARKED
WARKING
WARKS
WARLESS
WARLIKE
WARLING
WARLINGS
WARLOCK
WARLOCKRY
WARLOCKS
WARLORD
WARLORDS
WARM
WARMAKER
WARMAKERS
WARMAN
WARMBLOOD
WARMED
WARMEN
WARMER
WARMERS
WARMEST
WARMING
WARMINGS
WARMISH
WARMIST
WARMISTS
WARMLY
WARMNESS
WARMONGER
WARMOUTH
WARMOUTHS
WARMS
WARMTH
WARMTHS
WARMUP
WARMUPS
WARN
WARNED
WARNER
WARNERS
WARNING
WARNINGLY
WARNINGS
WARNS
WARP
WARPAGE
WARPAGES
WARPAINT
WARPAINTS
WARPATH
WARPATHS
WARPED
WARPER
WARPERS
WARPING
WARPINGS
WARPLANE
WARPLANES
WARPOWER
WARPOWERS
WARPS
WARPWISE
WARRAGAL
WARRAGALS
WARRAGLE
WARRAGLES
WARRAGUL
WARRAGULS
WARRAN
WARRAND
WARRANDED
WARRANDS
WARRANED
WARRANING
WARRANS
WARRANT
WARRANTED
WARRANTEE
WARRANTER
WARRANTOR
WARRANTS
WARRANTY
WARRAY
WARRAYED
WARRAYING
WARRAYS
WARRE
WARRED
WARREN
WARRENER
WARRENERS
WARRENS
WARREY
WARREYED
WARREYING
WARREYS
WARRIGAL
WARRIGALS
WARRING
WARRIOR
WARRIORS
WARRISON
WARRISONS
WARS
WARSAW
WARSAWS
WARSHIP
WARSHIPS
WARSLE
WARSLED
WARSLER
WARSLERS
WARSLES
WARSLING
WARST
WARSTLE
WARSTLED
WARSTLER
WARSTLERS
WARSTLES
WARSTLING
WART
WARTED
WARTHOG
WARTHOGS
WARTIER
WARTIEST
WARTIME
WARTIMES
WARTLESS
WARTLIKE
WARTS
WARTWEED
WARTWEEDS
WARTWORT
WARTWORTS
WARTY
WARWOLF
WARWOLVES
WARWORK
WARWORKS
WARWORN
WARY
WARZONE
WARZONES
WAS
WASABI
WASABIS
WASE
WASES
WASH
WASHABLE
WASHABLES
WASHAWAY
WASHAWAYS
WASHBAG
WASHBAGS
WASHBALL
WASHBALLS
WASHBASIN
WASHBOARD
WASHBOWL
WASHBOWLS
WASHCLOTH
WASHDAY
WASHDAYS
WASHDOWN
WASHDOWNS
WASHED
WASHEN
WASHER
WASHERED
WASHERIES
WASHERING
WASHERMAN
WASHERMEN
WASHERS
WASHERY
WASHES
WASHFAST
WASHHAND
WASHHOUSE
WASHIER
WASHIEST
WASHILY
WASHIN
WASHINESS
WASHING
WASHINGS
WASHINS
WASHLAND
WASHLANDS
WASHOUT
WASHOUTS
WASHPOT
WASHPOTS
WASHRAG
WASHRAGS
WASHROOM
WASHROOMS
WASHSTAND
WASHTUB
WASHTUBS
WASHUP
WASHUPS
WASHWIPE
WASHWIPES
WASHWOMAN
WASHWOMEN
WASHY
WASM
WASMS
WASP
WASPIE
WASPIER
WASPIES
WASPIEST
WASPILY
WASPINESS
WASPISH
WASPISHLY
WASPLIKE
WASPNEST
WASPNESTS
WASPS
WASPY
WASSAIL
WASSAILED
WASSAILER
WASSAILRY
WASSAILS
WASSERMAN
WASSERMEN
WASSUP
WAST

W

WASTABLE
WASTAGE
WASTAGES
WASTE
WASTEBIN
WASTEBINS
WASTED
WASTEFUL
WASTEL
WASTELAND
WASTELOT
WASTELOTS
WASTELS
WASTENESS
WASTER
WASTERED
WASTERFUL
WASTERIE
WASTERIES
WASTERING
WASTERS
WASTERY
WASTES
WASTEWAY
WASTEWAYS
WASTEWEIR
WASTFULL
WASTING
WASTINGLY
WASTINGS
WASTNESS
WASTREL
WASTRELS
WASTRIE
WASTRIES
WASTRIFE
WASTRIFES
WASTRY
WASTS
WAT
WATAP
WATAPE
WATAPES
WATAPS
WATCH
WATCHA
WATCHABLE
WATCHBAND
WATCHBOX
WATCHCASE
WATCHCRY
WATCHDOG
WATCHDOGS
WATCHED
WATCHER
WATCHERS
WATCHES
WATCHET
WATCHETS
WATCHEYE
WATCHEYES
WATCHFUL
WATCHING
WATCHLIST
WATCHMAN
WATCHMEN
WATCHOUT
WATCHOUTS
WATCHWORD
WATE
WATER
WATERAGE
WATERAGES
WATERBED
WATERBEDS
WATERBIRD
WATERBUCK
WATERBUS
WATERDOG
WATERDOGS
WATERED
WATERER
WATERERS
WATERFALL
WATERFOWL
WATERGATE
WATERHEAD
WATERHEN
WATERHENS
WATERHOLE
WATERIER
WATERIEST
WATERILY
WATERING
WATERINGS
WATERISH
WATERJET
WATERJETS
WATERLEAF
WATERLESS
WATERLILY
WATERLINE
WATERLOG
WATERLOGS
WATERLOO
WATERLOOS
WATERMAN
WATERMARK
WATERMEN
WATERMILL
WATERPOX
WATERS
WATERSHED
WATERSIDE
WATERSKI
WATERSKIS
WATERWAY
WATERWAYS
WATERWEED
WATERWORK
WATERWORN
WATERY
WATERZOOI
WATS
WATT
WATTAGE
WATTAGES
WATTAPE
WATTAPES
WATTER
WATTEST
WATTHOUR
WATTHOURS
WATTLE
WATTLED
WATTLES
WATTLESS
WATTLING
WATTLINGS
WATTMETER
WATTS
WAUCHT
WAUCHTED
WAUCHTING
WAUCHTS
WAUFF
WAUFFED
WAUFFING
WAUFFS
WAUGH
WAUGHED
WAUGHING
WAUGHS
WAUGHT
WAUGHTED
WAUGHTING
WAUGHTS
WAUK
WAUKED
WAUKER
WAUKERS
WAUKING
WAUKMILL
WAUKMILLS
WAUKRIFE
WAUKS
WAUL
WAULED
WAULING
WAULINGS
WAULK
WAULKED
WAULKER
WAULKERS
WAULKING
WAULKMILL
WAULKS
WAULS
WAUR
WAURED
WAURING
WAURS
WAURST
WAVE
WAVEBAND
WAVEBANDS
WAVED
WAVEFORM
WAVEFORMS
WAVEFRONT
WAVEGUIDE
WAVELESS
WAVELET
WAVELETS
WAVELIKE
WAVELLITE
WAVEMETER
WAVEOFF
WAVEOFFS
WAVER
WAVERED
WAVERER
WAVERERS
WAVERIER
WAVERIEST
WAVERING
WAVERINGS
WAVEROUS
WAVERS
WAVERY
WAVES
WAVESHAPE
WAVESON
WAVESONS
WAVETABLE
WAVEY
WAVEYS
WAVICLE
WAVICLES
WAVIER
WAVIES
WAVIEST
WAVILY
WAVINESS
WAVING
WAVINGS
WAVY
WAW
WAWA
WAWAED
WAWAING
WAWAS
WAWE
WAWES
WAWL
WAWLED
WAWLING
WAWLINGS
WAWLS
WAWS

W

WAX
WAXABLE
WAXBERRY
WAXBILL
WAXBILLS
WAXCLOTH
WAXCLOTHS
WAXED
WAXEN
WAXER
WAXERS
WAXES
WAXEYE
WAXEYES
WAXFLOWER
WAXIER
WAXIEST
WAXILY
WAXINESS
WAXING
WAXINGS
WAXLIKE
WAXPLANT
WAXPLANTS
WAXWEED
WAXWEEDS
WAXWING
WAXWINGS
WAXWORK
WAXWORKER
WAXWORKS
WAXWORM
WAXWORMS
WAXY
WAY
WAYANG
WAYANGS
WAYBACK
WAYBACKS
WAYBILL
WAYBILLS
WAYBOARD
WAYBOARDS
WAYBREAD
WAYBREADS
WAYED
WAYFARE
WAYFARED
WAYFARER
WAYFARERS
WAYFARES
WAYFARING
WAYGOING
WAYGOINGS
WAYGONE
WAYGOOSE
WAYGOOSES
WAYING
WAYLAID
WAYLAY
WAYLAYER
WAYLAYERS
WAYLAYING
WAYLAYS
WAYLEAVE
WAYLEAVES
WAYLEGGO
WAYLESS
WAYMARK
WAYMARKED
WAYMARKS
WAYMENT
WAYMENTED
WAYMENTS
WAYPOINT
WAYPOINTS
WAYPOST
WAYPOSTS
WAYS
WAYSIDE
WAYSIDES
WAYWARD
WAYWARDLY
WAYWISER
WAYWISERS
WAYWODE
WAYWODES
WAYWORN
WAYZGOOSE
WAZ
WAZIR
WAZIRS
WAZOO
WAZOOS
WAZZ
WAZZED
WAZZES
WAZZING
WAZZOCK
WAZZOCKS
WE
WEAK
WEAKEN
WEAKENED
WEAKENER
WEAKENERS
WEAKENING
WEAKENS
WEAKER
WEAKEST
WEAKFISH
WEAKISH
WEAKISHLY
WEAKLIER
WEAKLIEST
WEAKLING
WEAKLINGS
WEAKLY
WEAKNESS
WEAKON
WEAKONS
WEAKSIDE
WEAKSIDES
WEAL
WEALD
WEALDS
WEALS
WEALSMAN
WEALSMEN
WEALTH
WEALTHIER
WEALTHILY
WEALTHS
WEALTHY
WEAMB
WEAMBS
WEAN
WEANED
WEANEL
WEANELS
WEANER
WEANERS
WEANING
WEANINGS
WEANLING
WEANLINGS
WEANS
WEAPON
WEAPONED
WEAPONEER
WEAPONING
WEAPONISE
WEAPONIZE
WEAPONRY
WEAPONS
WEAR
WEARABLE
WEARABLES
WEARED
WEARER
WEARERS
WEARIED
WEARIER
WEARIES
WEARIEST
WEARIFUL
WEARILESS
WEARILY
WEARINESS
WEARING
WEARINGLY
WEARINGS
WEARISH
WEARISOME
WEARPROOF
WEARS
WEARY
WEARYING
WEASAND
WEASANDS
WEASEL
WEASELED
WEASELER
WEASELERS
WEASELIER
WEASELING
WEASELLED
WEASELLER
WEASELLY
WEASELS
WEASELY
WEASON
WEASONS
WEATHER
WEATHERED
WEATHERER
WEATHERLY
WEATHERS
WEAVE
WEAVED
WEAVER
WEAVERS
WEAVES
WEAVING
WEAVINGS
WEAZAND
WEAZANDS
WEAZEN
WEAZENED
WEAZENING
WEAZENS
WEB
WEBAPP
WEBAPPS
WEBBED
WEBBIE
WEBBIER
WEBBIES
WEBBIEST
WEBBING
WEBBINGS
WEBBY
WEBCAM
WEBCAMS
WEBCAST
WEBCASTED
WEBCASTER
WEBCASTS
WEBCHAT
WEBCHATS
WEBER
WEBERS
WEBFED
WEBFEET
WEBFOOT
WEBFOOTED
WEBHEAD
WEBHEADS
WEBIFIED
WEBIFIES

W

WEBIFY
WEBIFYING
WEBINAR
WEBINARS
WEBISODE
WEBISODES
WEBLESS
WEBLIKE
WEBLISH
WEBLISHES
WEBLOG
WEBLOGGER
WEBLOGS
WEBMAIL
WEBMAILS
WEBMASTER
WEBPAGE
WEBPAGES
WEBRING
WEBRINGS
WEBS
WEBSITE
WEBSITES
WEBSPACE
WEBSPACES
WEBSTER
WEBSTERS
WEBWHEEL
WEBWHEELS
WEBWORK
WEBWORKS
WEBWORM
WEBWORMS
WEBZINE
WEBZINES
WECHT
WECHTED
WECHTING
WECHTS
WED
WEDDED
WEDDER
WEDDERED
WEDDERING
WEDDERS
WEDDING
WEDDINGS
WEDEL
WEDELED
WEDELING
WEDELN
WEDELNED
WEDELNING
WEDELNS
WEDELS
WEDGE
WEDGED
WEDGELIKE
WEDGES
WEDGEWISE
WEDGIE
WEDGIER
WEDGIES
WEDGIEST
WEDGING
WEDGINGS
WEDGY
WEDLOCK
WEDLOCKS
WEDS
WEE
WEED
WEEDBED
WEEDBEDS
WEEDED
WEEDER
WEEDERIES
WEEDERS
WEEDERY
WEEDHEAD
WEEDHEADS
WEEDICIDE
WEEDIER
WEEDIEST
WEEDILY
WEEDINESS
WEEDING
WEEDINGS
WEEDLESS
WEEDLIKE
WEEDLINE
WEEDLINES
WEEDS
WEEDY
WEEING
WEEJUNS
WEEK
WEEKDAY
WEEKDAYS
WEEKE
WEEKEND
WEEKENDED
WEEKENDER
WEEKENDS
WEEKES
WEEKLIES
WEEKLONG
WEEKLY
WEEKNIGHT
WEEKS
WEEL
WEELS
WEEM
WEEMS
WEEN
WEENED
WEENIE
WEENIER
WEENIES
WEENIEST
WEENING
WEENS
WEENSIER
WEENSIEST
WEENSY
WEENY
WEEP
WEEPER
WEEPERS
WEEPHOLE
WEEPHOLES
WEEPIE
WEEPIER
WEEPIES
WEEPIEST
WEEPILY
WEEPINESS
WEEPING
WEEPINGLY
WEEPINGS
WEEPS
WEEPY
WEER
WEES
WEEST
WEET
WEETE
WEETED
WEETEN
WEETER
WEETEST
WEETING
WEETINGLY
WEETLESS
WEETS
WEEVER
WEEVERS
WEEVIL
WEEVILED
WEEVILIER
WEEVILLED
WEEVILLY
WEEVILS
WEEVILY
WEEWEE
WEEWEED
WEEWEEING
WEEWEES
WEFT
WEFTAGE
WEFTAGES
WEFTE
WEFTED
WEFTES
WEFTING
WEFTS
WEFTWISE
WEID
WEIDS
WEIGELA
WEIGELAS
WEIGELIA
WEIGELIAS
WEIGH
WEIGHABLE
WEIGHAGE
WEIGHAGES
WEIGHED
WEIGHER
WEIGHERS
WEIGHING
WEIGHINGS
WEIGHMAN
WEIGHMEN
WEIGHS
WEIGHT
WEIGHTAGE
WEIGHTED
WEIGHTER
WEIGHTERS
WEIGHTIER
WEIGHTILY
WEIGHTING
WEIGHTS
WEIGHTY
WEIL
WEILS
WEINER
WEINERS
WEIR
WEIRD
WEIRDED
WEIRDER
WEIRDEST
WEIRDIE
WEIRDIES
WEIRDING
WEIRDLY
WEIRDNESS
WEIRDO
WEIRDOES
WEIRDOS
WEIRDS
WEIRDY
WEIRED
WEIRING
WEIRS
WEISE
WEISED
WEISES
WEISING
WEIZE
WEIZED
WEIZES
WEIZING
WEKA
WEKAS
WELAWAY
WELCH
WELCHED

WELCHER
WELCHERS
WELCHES
WELCHING
WELCOME
WELCOMED
WELCOMELY
WELCOMER
WELCOMERS
WELCOMES
WELCOMING
WELD
WELDABLE
WELDED
WELDER
WELDERS
WELDING
WELDINGS
WELDLESS
WELDMENT
WELDMENTS
WELDMESH
WELDOR
WELDORS
WELDS
WELFARE
WELFARES
WELFARISM
WELFARIST
WELFARITE
WELK
WELKE
WELKED
WELKES
WELKIN
WELKING
WELKINS
WELKS
WELKT
WELL
WELLADAY
WELLADAYS
WELLANEAR
WELLAWAY
WELLAWAYS
WELLBEING
WELLBORN
WELLCURB
WELLCURBS
WELLDOER
WELLDOERS
WELLED
WELLHEAD
WELLHEADS
WELLHOLE
WELLHOLES
WELLHOUSE
WELLIE
WELLIES
WELLING
WELLINGS
WELLNESS
WELLS
WELLSITE
WELLSITES
WELLY
WELS
WELSH
WELSHED
WELSHER
WELSHERS
WELSHES
WELSHING
WELT
WELTED
WELTER
WELTERED
WELTERING
WELTERS
WELTING
WELTINGS
WELTS
WEM
WEMB
WEMBS
WEMS
WEN
WENA
WENCH
WENCHED
WENCHER
WENCHERS
WENCHES
WENCHING
WEND
WENDED
WENDIGO
WENDIGOES
WENDIGOS
WENDING
WENDS
WENGE
WENGES
WENNIER
WENNIEST
WENNISH
WENNY
WENS
WENT
WENTS
WEPT
WERE
WEREGILD
WEREGILDS
WEREWOLF
WERGELD
WERGELDS
WERGELT
WERGELTS
WERGILD
WERGILDS
WERNERITE
WERO
WEROS
WERRIS
WERRISES
WERSH
WERSHER
WERSHEST
WERT
WERWOLF
WERWOLVES
WESAND
WESANDS
WESKIT
WESKITS
WESSAND
WESSANDS
WEST
WESTABOUT
WESTBOUND
WESTED
WESTER
WESTERED
WESTERING
WESTERLY
WESTERN
WESTERNER
WESTERNS
WESTERS
WESTIE
WESTIES
WESTING
WESTINGS
WESTLIN
WESTLINS
WESTMOST
WESTS
WESTWARD
WESTWARDS
WET
WETA
WETAS
WETBACK
WETBACKS
WETHER
WETHERS
WETLAND
WETLANDS
WETLY
WETNESS
WETNESSES
WETPROOF
WETS
WETSUIT
WETSUITS
WETTABLE
WETTED
WETTER
WETTERS
WETTEST
WETTIE
WETTIES
WETTING
WETTINGS
WETTISH
WETWARE
WETWARES
WEX
WEXE
WEXED
WEXES
WEXING
WEY
WEYARD
WEYS
WEYWARD
WEZAND
WEZANDS
WHA
WHACK
WHACKED
WHACKER
WHACKERS
WHACKIER
WHACKIEST
WHACKING
WHACKINGS
WHACKO
WHACKOES
WHACKOS
WHACKS
WHACKY
WHAE
WHAISLE
WHAISLED
WHAISLES
WHAISLING
WHAIZLE
WHAIZLED
WHAIZLES
WHAIZLING
WHAKAIRO
WHAKAIROS
WHAKAPAPA
WHALE
WHALEBACK
WHALEBOAT
WHALEBONE
WHALED
WHALELIKE
WHALEMAN
WHALEMEN
WHALER
WHALERIES
WHALERS
WHALERY
WHALES
WHALING
WHALINGS

W

WHALLY
WHAM
WHAMMED
WHAMMIES
WHAMMING
WHAMMO
WHAMMOS
WHAMMY
WHAMO
WHAMPLE
WHAMPLES
WHAMS
WHANAU
WHANAUS
WHANG
WHANGAM
WHANGAMS
WHANGED
WHANGEE
WHANGEES
WHANGING
WHANGS
WHAP
WHAPPED
WHAPPER
WHAPPERS
WHAPPING
WHAPS
WHARE
WHARENUI
WHARENUIS
WHAREPUNI
WHARES
WHARF
WHARFAGE
WHARFAGES
WHARFED
WHARFIE
WHARFIES
WHARFING
WHARFINGS
WHARFS
WHARVE
WHARVES
WHAT
WHATA
WHATAS
WHATCHA
WHATEN
WHATEVER
WHATEVS
WHATNA
WHATNESS
WHATNOT
WHATNOTS
WHATS
WHATSIS
WHATSISES
WHATSIT
WHATSITS
WHATSO
WHATTEN
WHAUP
WHAUPS
WHAUR
WHAURS
WHEAL
WHEALS
WHEAR
WHEARE
WHEAT
WHEATEAR
WHEATEARS
WHEATEN
WHEATENS
WHEATGERM
WHEATIER
WHEATIEST
WHEATLAND
WHEATLESS
WHEATLIKE
WHEATMEAL
WHEATS
WHEATWORM
WHEATY
WHEE
WHEECH
WHEECHED
WHEECHING
WHEECHS
WHEEDLE
WHEEDLED
WHEEDLER
WHEEDLERS
WHEEDLES
WHEEDLING
WHEEL
WHEELBASE
WHEELED
WHEELER
WHEELERS
WHEELIE
WHEELIER
WHEELIES
WHEELIEST
WHEELING
WHEELINGS
WHEELLESS
WHEELMAN
WHEELMEN
WHEELS
WHEELSMAN
WHEELSMEN
WHEELSPIN
WHEELWORK
WHEELY
WHEEN
WHEENGE
WHEENGED
WHEENGES
WHEENGING
WHEENS
WHEEP
WHEEPED
WHEEPING
WHEEPLE
WHEEPLED
WHEEPLES
WHEEPLING
WHEEPS
WHEESH
WHEESHED
WHEESHES
WHEESHING
WHEESHT
WHEESHTED
WHEESHTS
WHEEZE
WHEEZED
WHEEZER
WHEEZERS
WHEEZES
WHEEZIER
WHEEZIEST
WHEEZILY
WHEEZING
WHEEZINGS
WHEEZLE
WHEEZLED
WHEEZLES
WHEEZLING
WHEEZY
WHEFT
WHEFTS
WHELK
WHELKED
WHELKIER
WHELKIEST
WHELKS
WHELKY
WHELM
WHELMED
WHELMING
WHELMS
WHELP
WHELPED
WHELPING
WHELPLESS
WHELPS
WHEMMLE
WHEMMLED
WHEMMLES
WHEMMLING
WHEN
WHENAS
WHENCE
WHENCES
WHENCEVER
WHENEVER
WHENS
WHENUA
WHENUAS
WHENWE
WHENWES
WHERE
WHEREAS
WHEREASES
WHEREAT
WHEREBY
WHEREFOR
WHEREFORE
WHEREFORS
WHEREFROM
WHEREIN
WHEREINTO
WHERENESS
WHEREOF
WHEREON
WHEREOUT
WHERES
WHERESO
WHERETO
WHEREUNTO
WHEREUPON
WHEREVER
WHEREWITH
WHERRET
WHERRETED
WHERRETS
WHERRIED
WHERRIES
WHERRIT
WHERRITED
WHERRITS
WHERRY
WHERRYING
WHERRYMAN
WHERRYMEN
WHERVE
WHERVES
WHET
WHETHER
WHETS
WHETSTONE
WHETTED
WHETTER
WHETTERS
WHETTING
WHEUGH
WHEUGHED
WHEUGHING
WHEUGHS
WHEW
WHEWED
WHEWING
WHEWS
WHEY
WHEYEY
WHEYFACE
WHEYFACED

W

WHEYFACES
WHEYIER
WHEYIEST
WHEYISH
WHEYLIKE
WHEYS
WHICH
WHICHEVER
WHICKER
WHICKERED
WHICKERS
WHID
WHIDAH
WHIDAHS
WHIDDED
WHIDDER
WHIDDERED
WHIDDERS
WHIDDING
WHIDS
WHIFF
WHIFFED
WHIFFER
WHIFFERS
WHIFFET
WHIFFETS
WHIFFIER
WHIFFIEST
WHIFFING
WHIFFINGS
WHIFFLE
WHIFFLED
WHIFFLER
WHIFFLERS
WHIFFLERY
WHIFFLES
WHIFFLING
WHIFFS
WHIFFY
WHIFT
WHIFTS
WHIG
WHIGGED
WHIGGING
WHIGS
WHILE
WHILED
WHILERE
WHILES
WHILEVER
WHILING
WHILK
WHILLIED
WHILLIES
WHILLY
WHILLYING
WHILLYWHA
WHILOM
WHILST
WHIM
WHIMBERRY
WHIMBREL
WHIMBRELS
WHIMMED
WHIMMIER
WHIMMIEST
WHIMMING
WHIMMY
WHIMPER
WHIMPERED
WHIMPERER
WHIMPERS
WHIMPLE
WHIMPLED
WHIMPLES
WHIMPLING
WHIMS
WHIMSEY
WHIMSEYS
WHIMSICAL
WHIMSIED
WHIMSIER
WHIMSIES
WHIMSIEST
WHIMSILY
WHIMSY
WHIN
WHINBERRY
WHINCHAT
WHINCHATS
WHINE
WHINED
WHINER
WHINERS
WHINES
WHINEY
WHINGDING
WHINGE
WHINGED
WHINGEING
WHINGER
WHINGERS
WHINGES
WHINGIER
WHINGIEST
WHINGING
WHINGY
WHINIARD
WHINIARDS
WHINIER
WHINIEST
WHININESS
WHINING
WHININGLY
WHININGS
WHINNIED
WHINNIER
WHINNIES
WHINNIEST
WHINNY
WHINNYING
WHINS
WHINSTONE
WHINY
WHINYARD
WHINYARDS
WHIO
WHIOS
WHIP
WHIPBIRD
WHIPBIRDS
WHIPCAT
WHIPCATS
WHIPCORD
WHIPCORDS
WHIPCORDY
WHIPCRACK
WHIPJACK
WHIPJACKS
WHIPLASH
WHIPLESS
WHIPLIKE
WHIPPED
WHIPPER
WHIPPERS
WHIPPET
WHIPPETS
WHIPPIER
WHIPPIEST
WHIPPING
WHIPPINGS
WHIPPIT
WHIPPITS
WHIPPY
WHIPRAY
WHIPRAYS
WHIPS
WHIPSAW
WHIPSAWED
WHIPSAWN
WHIPSAWS
WHIPSNAKE
WHIPSTAFF
WHIPSTALL
WHIPSTER
WHIPSTERS
WHIPSTOCK
WHIPT
WHIPTAIL
WHIPTAILS
WHIPWORM
WHIPWORMS
WHIR
WHIRL
WHIRLBAT
WHIRLBATS
WHIRLED
WHIRLER
WHIRLERS
WHIRLIER
WHIRLIES
WHIRLIEST
WHIRLIGIG
WHIRLING
WHIRLINGS
WHIRLPOOL
WHIRLS
WHIRLWIND
WHIRLY
WHIRR
WHIRRA
WHIRRED
WHIRRET
WHIRRETED
WHIRRETS
WHIRRIED
WHIRRIER
WHIRRIES
WHIRRIEST
WHIRRING
WHIRRINGS
WHIRRS
WHIRRY
WHIRRYING
WHIRS
WHIRTLE
WHIRTLES
WHISH
WHISHED
WHISHES
WHISHING
WHISHT
WHISHTED
WHISHTING
WHISHTS
WHISK
WHISKED
WHISKER
WHISKERED
WHISKERS
WHISKERY
WHISKET
WHISKETS
WHISKEY
WHISKEYS
WHISKIES
WHISKING
WHISKS
WHISKY
WHISPER
WHISPERED
WHISPERER
WHISPERS
WHISPERY
WHISS
WHISSED
WHISSES
WHISSING
WHIST
WHISTED

WHISTING
WHISTLE
WHISTLED
WHISTLER
WHISTLERS
WHISTLES
WHISTLING
WHISTS
WHIT
WHITE
WHITEBAIT
WHITEBASS
WHITEBEAM
WHITECAP
WHITECAPS
WHITECOAT
WHITECOMB
WHITED
WHITEDAMP
WHITEFACE
WHITEFISH
WHITEFLY
WHITEHEAD
WHITELIST
WHITELY
WHITEN
WHITENED
WHITENER
WHITENERS
WHITENESS
WHITENING
WHITENS
WHITEOUT
WHITEOUTS
WHITEPOT
WHITEPOTS
WHITER
WHITES
WHITEST
WHITETAIL
WHITEWALL
WHITEWARE
WHITEWASH
WHITEWING
WHITEWOOD
WHITEY
WHITEYS
WHITHER
WHITHERED
WHITHERS
WHITIER
WHITIES
WHITIEST
WHITING
WHITINGS
WHITISH
WHITLING
WHITLINGS
WHITLOW
WHITLOWS
WHITRACK
WHITRACKS
WHITRET
WHITRETS
WHITRICK
WHITRICKS
WHITS
WHITSTER
WHITSTERS
WHITTAW
WHITTAWER
WHITTAWS
WHITTER
WHITTERED
WHITTERS
WHITTLE
WHITTLED
WHITTLER
WHITTLERS
WHITTLES
WHITTLING
WHITTRET
WHITTRETS
WHITY
WHIZ
WHIZBANG
WHIZBANGS
WHIZZ
WHIZZBANG
WHIZZED
WHIZZER
WHIZZERS
WHIZZES
WHIZZIER
WHIZZIEST
WHIZZING
WHIZZINGS
WHIZZO
WHIZZY
WHO
WHOA
WHODUNIT
WHODUNITS
WHODUNNIT
WHOEVER
WHOLE
WHOLEFOOD
WHOLEMEAL
WHOLENESS
WHOLES
WHOLESALE
WHOLESOME
WHOLISM
WHOLISMS
WHOLIST
WHOLISTIC
WHOLISTS
WHOLLY
WHOLPHIN
WHOLPHINS
WHOM
WHOMBLE
WHOMBLED
WHOMBLES
WHOMBLING
WHOMEVER
WHOMMLE
WHOMMLED
WHOMMLES
WHOMMLING
WHOMP
WHOMPED
WHOMPING
WHOMPS
WHOMSO
WHOOBUB
WHOOBUBS
WHOOF
WHOOFED
WHOOFING
WHOOFS
WHOOMP
WHOOMPH
WHOOMPHS
WHOOMPS
WHOONGA
WHOONGAS
WHOOP
WHOOPED
WHOOPEE
WHOOPEES
WHOOPER
WHOOPERS
WHOOPIE
WHOOPIES
WHOOPING
WHOOPINGS
WHOOPLA
WHOOPLAS
WHOOPS
WHOOPSIE
WHOOPSIES
WHOOSH
WHOOSHED
WHOOSHES
WHOOSHING
WHOOSIS
WHOOSISES
WHOOT
WHOOTED
WHOOTING
WHOOTS
WHOP
WHOPPED
WHOPPER
WHOPPERS
WHOPPING
WHOPPINGS
WHOPS
WHORE
WHORED
WHOREDOM
WHOREDOMS
WHORES
WHORESON
WHORESONS
WHORING
WHORINGS
WHORISH
WHORISHLY
WHORL
WHORLBAT
WHORLBATS
WHORLED
WHORLING
WHORLS
WHORT
WHORTLE
WHORTLES
WHORTS
WHOSE
WHOSESO
WHOSEVER
WHOSIS
WHOSISES
WHOSIT
WHOSITS
WHOSO
WHOSOEVER
WHOT
WHOW
WHOWED
WHOWING
WHOWS
WHUMMLE
WHUMMLED
WHUMMLES
WHUMMLING
WHUMP
WHUMPED
WHUMPING
WHUMPS
WHUNSTANE
WHUP
WHUPPED
WHUPPING
WHUPPINGS
WHUPS
WHY
WHYDA
WHYDAH
WHYDAHS
WHYDAS
WHYDUNIT
WHYDUNITS
WHYDUNNIT
WHYEVER
WHYS
WIBBLE
WIBBLED

W

WIBBLES
WIBBLING
WICCA
WICCAN
WICCANS
WICCAS
WICE
WICH
WICHES
WICK
WICKAPE
WICKAPES
WICKED
WICKEDER
WICKEDEST
WICKEDLY
WICKEDS
WICKEN
WICKENS
WICKER
WICKERED
WICKERS
WICKET
WICKETS
WICKIES
WICKING
WICKINGS
WICKIUP
WICKIUPS
WICKLESS
WICKS
WICKTHING
WICKY
WICKYUP
WICKYUPS
WICOPIES
WICOPY
WIDDER
WIDDERS
WIDDIE
WIDDIES
WIDDLE
WIDDLED
WIDDLES
WIDDLING
WIDDY
WIDE
WIDEAWAKE
WIDEBAND
WIDEBANDS
WIDEBODY
WIDELY
WIDEN
WIDENED
WIDENER
WIDENERS
WIDENESS
WIDENING
WIDENINGS
WIDENS
WIDEOUT
WIDEOUTS
WIDER
WIDES
WIDEST
WIDGEON
WIDGEONS
WIDGET
WIDGETS
WIDGIE
WIDGIES
WIDISH
WIDOW
WIDOWBIRD
WIDOWED
WIDOWER
WIDOWERED
WIDOWERS
WIDOWHOOD
WIDOWING
WIDOWMAN
WIDOWMEN
WIDOWS
WIDTH
WIDTHS
WIDTHWAY
WIDTHWAYS
WIDTHWISE
WIEL
WIELD
WIELDABLE
WIELDED
WIELDER
WIELDERS
WIELDIER
WIELDIEST
WIELDING
WIELDLESS
WIELDS
WIELDY
WIELS
WIENER
WIENERS
WIENIE
WIENIES
WIFE
WIFED
WIFEDOM
WIFEDOMS
WIFEHOOD
WIFEHOODS
WIFELESS
WIFELIER
WIFELIEST
WIFELIKE
WIFELY
WIFES
WIFEY
WIFEYS
WIFIE
WIFIES
WIFING
WIFTIER
WIFTIEST
WIFTY
WIG
WIGAN
WIGANS
WIGEON
WIGEONS
WIGGA
WIGGAS
WIGGED
WIGGER
WIGGERIES
WIGGERS
WIGGERY
WIGGIER
WIGGIEST
WIGGING
WIGGINGS
WIGGLE
WIGGLED
WIGGLER
WIGGLERS
WIGGLES
WIGGLIER
WIGGLIEST
WIGGLING
WIGGLY
WIGGY
WIGHT
WIGHTED
WIGHTING
WIGHTLY
WIGHTS
WIGLESS
WIGLET
WIGLETS
WIGLIKE
WIGMAKER
WIGMAKERS
WIGS
WIGWAG
WIGWAGGED
WIGWAGGER
WIGWAGS
WIGWAM
WIGWAMS
WIKI
WIKIALITY
WIKIS
WIKIUP
WIKIUPS
WILCO
WILD
WILDCARD
WILDCARDS
WILDCAT
WILDCATS
WILDED
WILDER
WILDERED
WILDERING
WILDERS
WILDEST
WILDFIRE
WILDFIRES
WILDFOWL
WILDFOWLS
WILDGRAVE
WILDING
WILDINGS
WILDISH
WILDLAND
WILDLANDS
WILDLIFE
WILDLIFES
WILDLING
WILDLINGS
WILDLY
WILDMAN
WILDMEN
WILDNESS
WILDS
WILDWOOD
WILDWOODS
WILE
WILED
WILEFUL
WILES
WILFUL
WILFULLY
WILGA
WILGAS
WILI
WILIER
WILIEST
WILILY
WILINESS
WILING
WILIS
WILJA
WILJAS
WILL
WILLABLE
WILLED
WILLEMITE
WILLER
WILLERS
WILLEST
WILLET
WILLETS
WILLEY
WILLEYED
WILLEYING
WILLEYS
WILLFUL
WILLFULLY
WILLIAM

WILLIAMS
WILLIE
WILLIED
WILLIES
WILLING
WILLINGER
WILLINGLY
WILLIWAU
WILLIWAUS
WILLIWAW
WILLIWAWS
WILLOW
WILLOWED
WILLOWER
WILLOWERS
WILLOWIER
WILLOWING
WILLOWISH
WILLOWS
WILLOWY
WILLPOWER
WILLS
WILLY
WILLYARD
WILLYART
WILLYING
WILLYWAW
WILLYWAWS
WILT
WILTED
WILTING
WILTJA
WILTJAS
WILTS
WILY
WIMBLE
WIMBLED
WIMBLES
WIMBLING
WIMBREL
WIMBRELS
WIMMIN
WIMP
WIMPED
WIMPIER
WIMPIEST
WIMPINESS
WIMPING
WIMPISH
WIMPISHLY
WIMPLE
WIMPLED
WIMPLES
WIMPLING
WIMPS
WIMPY
WIN
WINCE
WINCED
WINCER
WINCERS
WINCES
WINCEY
WINCEYS
WINCH
WINCHED
WINCHER
WINCHERS
WINCHES
WINCHING
WINCHMAN
WINCHMEN
WINCING
WINCINGLY
WINCINGS
WINCOPIPE
WIND
WINDABLE
WINDAC
WINDACS
WINDAGE
WINDAGES
WINDAS
WINDASES
WINDBAG
WINDBAGS
WINDBELL
WINDBELLS
WINDBILL
WINDBILLS
WINDBLAST
WINDBLOW
WINDBLOWN
WINDBLOWS
WINDBORNE
WINDBOUND
WINDBREAK
WINDBURN
WINDBURNS
WINDBURNT
WINDCHILL
WINDED
WINDER
WINDERS
WINDFALL
WINDFALLS
WINDFLAW
WINDFLAWS
WINDGALL
WINDGALLS
WINDGUN
WINDGUNS
WINDHOVER
WINDIER
WINDIEST
WINDIGO
WINDIGOES
WINDIGOS
WINDILY
WINDINESS
WINDING
WINDINGLY
WINDINGS
WINDLASS
WINDLE
WINDLED
WINDLES
WINDLESS
WINDLING
WINDLINGS
WINDLOAD
WINDLOADS
WINDMILL
WINDMILLS
WINDOCK
WINDOCKS
WINDORE
WINDORES
WINDOW
WINDOWED
WINDOWIER
WINDOWING
WINDOWS
WINDOWY
WINDPACK
WINDPACKS
WINDPIPE
WINDPIPES
WINDPROOF
WINDRING
WINDROW
WINDROWED
WINDROWER
WINDROWS
WINDS
WINDSAIL
WINDSAILS
WINDSES
WINDSHAKE
WINDSHIP
WINDSHIPS
WINDSLAB
WINDSLABS
WINDSOCK
WINDSOCKS
WINDSTORM
WINDSURF
WINDSURFS
WINDSWEPT
WINDTHROW
WINDTIGHT
WINDUP
WINDUPS
WINDWARD
WINDWARDS
WINDWAY
WINDWAYS
WINDY
WINE
WINEBERRY
WINED
WINEGLASS
WINELESS
WINEMAKER
WINEPRESS
WINERIES
WINERY
WINES
WINESAP
WINESAPS
WINESHOP
WINESHOPS
WINESKIN
WINESKINS
WINESOP
WINESOPS
WINEY
WING
WINGBACK
WINGBACKS
WINGBEAT
WINGBEATS
WINGBOW
WINGBOWS
WINGCHAIR
WINGDING
WINGDINGS
WINGE
WINGED
WINGEDLY
WINGEING
WINGER
WINGERS
WINGES
WINGIER
WINGIEST
WINGING
WINGLESS
WINGLET
WINGLETS
WINGLIKE
WINGMAN
WINGMEN
WINGNUT
WINGNUTS
WINGOVER
WINGOVERS
WINGS
WINGSPAN
WINGSPANS
WINGSUIT
WINGSUITS
WINGTIP
WINGTIPS
WINGY
WINIER
WINIEST
WINING
WINISH
WINK

W

WINKED
WINKER
WINKERS
WINKING
WINKINGLY
WINKINGS
WINKLE
WINKLED
WINKLER
WINKLERS
WINKLES
WINKLING
WINKS
WINLESS
WINN
WINNA
WINNABLE
WINNARD
WINNARDS
WINNED
WINNER
WINNERS
WINNING
WINNINGLY
WINNINGS
WINNLE
WINNLES
WINNOCK
WINNOCKS
WINNOW
WINNOWED
WINNOWER
WINNOWERS
WINNOWING
WINNOWS
WINNS
WINO
WINOES
WINOS
WINS
WINSEY
WINSEYS
WINSOME
WINSOMELY
WINSOMER
WINSOMEST
WINTER
WINTERED
WINTERER
WINTERERS
WINTERFED
WINTERIER
WINTERING
WINTERISE
WINTERISH
WINTERIZE
WINTERLY
WINTERS
WINTERY
WINTLE
WINTLED
WINTLES
WINTLING
WINTRIER
WINTRIEST
WINTRILY
WINTRY
WINY
WINZE
WINZES
WIPE
WIPEABLE
WIPED
WIPEOUT
WIPEOUTS
WIPER
WIPERS
WIPES
WIPING
WIPINGS
WIPPEN
WIPPENS
WIRABLE
WIRE
WIRED
WIREDRAW
WIREDRAWN
WIREDRAWS
WIREDREW
WIREFRAME
WIREGRASS
WIREHAIR
WIREHAIRS
WIRELESS
WIRELIKE
WIRELINE
WIRELINES
WIREMAN
WIREMEN
WIREPHOTO
WIRER
WIRERS
WIRES
WIRETAP
WIRETAPS
WIREWAY
WIREWAYS
WIREWORK
WIREWORKS
WIREWORM
WIREWORMS
WIREWOVE
WIRIER
WIRIEST
WIRILDA
WIRILDAS
WIRILY
WIRINESS
WIRING
WIRINGS
WIRRA
WIRRAH
WIRRAHS
WIRRICOW
WIRRICOWS
WIRY
WIS
WISARD
WISARDS
WISDOM
WISDOMS
WISE
WISEACRE
WISEACRES
WISEASS
WISEASSES
WISECRACK
WISED
WISEGUY
WISEGUYS
WISELIER
WISELIEST
WISELING
WISELINGS
WISELY
WISENESS
WISENT
WISENTS
WISER
WISES
WISEST
WISEWOMAN
WISEWOMEN
WISH
WISHA
WISHBONE
WISHBONES
WISHED
WISHER
WISHERS
WISHES
WISHFUL
WISHFULLY
WISHING
WISHINGS
WISHLESS
WISHT
WISING
WISKET
WISKETS
WISP
WISPED
WISPIER
WISPIEST
WISPILY
WISPINESS
WISPING
WISPISH
WISPLIKE
WISPS
WISPY
WISS
WISSED
WISSES
WISSING
WIST
WISTARIA
WISTARIAS
WISTED
WISTERIA
WISTERIAS
WISTFUL
WISTFULLY
WISTING
WISTITI
WISTITIS
WISTLY
WISTS
WIT
WITAN
WITANS
WITBLITS
WITCH
WITCHED
WITCHEN
WITCHENS
WITCHERY
WITCHES
WITCHETTY
WITCHHOOD
WITCHIER
WITCHIEST
WITCHING
WITCHINGS
WITCHKNOT
WITCHLIKE
WITCHWEED
WITCHY
WITE
WITED
WITELESS
WITES
WITGAT
WITGATS
WITH
WITHAL
WITHDRAW
WITHDRAWN
WITHDRAWS
WITHDREW
WITHE
WITHED
WITHER
WITHERED
WITHERER
WITHERERS
WITHERING
WITHERITE
WITHEROD
WITHERODS

W

WITHERS
WITHES
WITHHAULT
WITHHELD
WITHHOLD
WITHHOLDS
WITHIER
WITHIES
WITHIEST
WITHIN
WITHING
WITHINS
WITHOUT
WITHOUTEN
WITHOUTS
WITHS
WITHSTAND
WITHSTOOD
WITHWIND
WITHWINDS
WITHY
WITHYWIND
WITING
WITLESS
WITLESSLY
WITLING
WITLINGS
WITLOOF
WITLOOFS
WITNESS
WITNESSED
WITNESSER
WITNESSES
WITNEY
WITNEYS
WITS
WITTED
WITTER
WITTERED
WITTERING
WITTERS
WITTICISM
WITTIER
WITTIEST
WITTILY
WITTINESS
WITTING
WITTINGLY
WITTINGS
WITTOL
WITTOLLY
WITTOLS
WITTY
WITWALL
WITWALLS
WITWANTON
WIVE
WIVED
WIVEHOOD
WIVEHOODS
WIVER
WIVERN
WIVERNS
WIVERS
WIVES
WIVING
WIZ
WIZARD
WIZARDER
WIZARDEST
WIZARDLY
WIZARDRY
WIZARDS
WIZEN
WIZENED
WIZENER
WIZENEST
WIZENING
WIZENS
WIZES
WIZIER
WIZIERS
WIZZEN
WIZZENS
WIZZES
WO
WOAD
WOADED
WOADS
WOADWAX
WOADWAXEN
WOADWAXES
WOAH
WOALD
WOALDS
WOBBEGONG
WOBBLE
WOBBLED
WOBBLER
WOBBLERS
WOBBLES
WOBBLIER
WOBBLIES
WOBBLIEST
WOBBLING
WOBBLINGS
WOBBLY
WOBEGONE
WOCK
WOCKS
WODGE
WODGES
WOE
WOEBEGONE
WOEFUL
WOEFULLER
WOEFULLY
WOENESS
WOENESSES
WOES
WOESOME
WOF
WOFS
WOFUL
WOFULLER
WOFULLEST
WOFULLY
WOFULNESS
WOG
WOGGISH
WOGGLE
WOGGLES
WOGS
WOIWODE
WOIWODES
WOJUS
WOK
WOKE
WOKEN
WOKER
WOKEST
WOKKA
WOKS
WOLD
WOLDS
WOLF
WOLFBERRY
WOLFED
WOLFER
WOLFERS
WOLFFISH
WOLFHOUND
WOLFING
WOLFINGS
WOLFISH
WOLFISHLY
WOLFKIN
WOLFKINS
WOLFLIKE
WOLFLING
WOLFLINGS
WOLFRAM
WOLFRAMS
WOLFS
WOLFSBANE
WOLFSKIN
WOLFSKINS
WOLLIES
WOLLY
WOLVE
WOLVED
WOLVER
WOLVERENE
WOLVERINE
WOLVERS
WOLVES
WOLVING
WOLVINGS
WOLVISH
WOLVISHLY
WOMAN
WOMANED
WOMANHOOD
WOMANING
WOMANISE
WOMANISED
WOMANISER
WOMANISES
WOMANISH
WOMANISM
WOMANISMS
WOMANIST
WOMANISTS
WOMANIZE
WOMANIZED
WOMANIZER
WOMANIZES
WOMANKIND
WOMANLESS
WOMANLIER
WOMANLIKE
WOMANLY
WOMANNED
WOMANNESS
WOMANNING
WOMANS
WOMB
WOMBAT
WOMBATS
WOMBED
WOMBIER
WOMBIEST
WOMBING
WOMBLIKE
WOMBS
WOMBY
WOMEN
WOMENFOLK
WOMENKIND
WOMERA
WOMERAS
WOMMERA
WOMMERAS
WOMMIT
WOMMITS
WOMYN
WON
WONDER
WONDERED
WONDERER
WONDERERS
WONDERFUL
WONDERING
WONDERKID
WONDEROUS
WONDERS
WONDRED
WONDROUS
WONGA
WONGAS

W

WONGI
WONGIED
WONGIING
WONGIS
WONING
WONINGS
WONK
WONKERIES
WONKERY
WONKIER
WONKIEST
WONKILY
WONKINESS
WONKISH
WONKS
WONKY
WONNED
WONNER
WONNERS
WONNING
WONNINGS
WONS
WONT
WONTED
WONTEDLY
WONTING
WONTLESS
WONTON
WONTONS
WONTS
WOO
WOOABLE
WOOBUT
WOOBUTS
WOOD
WOODBIN
WOODBIND
WOODBINDS
WOODBINE
WOODBINES
WOODBINS
WOODBLOCK
WOODBORER
WOODBOX
WOODBOXES
WOODCHAT
WOODCHATS
WOODCHIP
WOODCHIPS
WOODCHOP
WOODCHOPS
WOODCHUCK
WOODCOCK
WOODCOCKS
WOODCRAFT
WOODCUT
WOODCUTS
WOODED
WOODEN
WOODENED
WOODENER
WOODENEST
WOODENING
WOODENLY
WOODENS
WOODENTOP
WOODFERN
WOODFERNS
WOODFREE
WOODGRAIN
WOODHEN
WOODHENS
WOODHOLE
WOODHOLES
WOODHORSE
WOODHOUSE
WOODIE
WOODIER
WOODIES
WOODIEST
WOODINESS
WOODING
WOODLAND
WOODLANDS
WOODLARK
WOODLARKS
WOODLESS
WOODLICE
WOODLORE
WOODLORES
WOODLOT
WOODLOTS
WOODLOUSE
WOODMAN
WOODMEAL
WOODMEALS
WOODMEN
WOODMICE
WOODMOUSE
WOODNESS
WOODNOTE
WOODNOTES
WOODPILE
WOODPILES
WOODPRINT
WOODRAT
WOODRATS
WOODREEVE
WOODROOF
WOODROOFS
WOODRUFF
WOODRUFFS
WOODRUSH
WOODS
WOODSCREW
WOODSHED
WOODSHEDS
WOODSHOCK
WOODSIA
WOODSIAS
WOODSIER
WOODSIEST
WOODSKIN
WOODSKINS
WOODSMAN
WOODSMEN
WOODSMOKE
WOODSPITE
WOODSTONE
WOODSTOVE
WOODSY
WOODTONE
WOODTONES
WOODWALE
WOODWALES
WOODWARD
WOODWARDS
WOODWASP
WOODWASPS
WOODWAX
WOODWAXEN
WOODWAXES
WOODWIND
WOODWINDS
WOODWORK
WOODWORKS
WOODWORM
WOODWORMS
WOODWOSE
WOODWOSES
WOODY
WOODYARD
WOODYARDS
WOOED
WOOER
WOOERS
WOOF
WOOFED
WOOFER
WOOFERS
WOOFIER
WOOFIEST
WOOFING
WOOFS
WOOFTAH
WOOFTAHS
WOOFTER
WOOFTERS
WOOFY
WOOHOO
WOOING
WOOINGLY
WOOINGS
WOOL
WOOLD
WOOLDED
WOOLDER
WOOLDERS
WOOLDING
WOOLDINGS
WOOLDS
WOOLED
WOOLEN
WOOLENS
WOOLER
WOOLERS
WOOLFAT
WOOLFATS
WOOLFELL
WOOLFELLS
WOOLHAT
WOOLHATS
WOOLIE
WOOLIER
WOOLIES
WOOLIEST
WOOLILY
WOOLINESS
WOOLLED
WOOLLEN
WOOLLENS
WOOLLIER
WOOLLIES
WOOLLIEST
WOOLLIKE
WOOLLILY
WOOLLY
WOOLMAN
WOOLMEN
WOOLPACK
WOOLPACKS
WOOLS
WOOLSACK
WOOLSACKS
WOOLSEY
WOOLSEYS
WOOLSHED
WOOLSHEDS
WOOLSKIN
WOOLSKINS
WOOLWARD
WOOLWORK
WOOLWORKS
WOOLY
WOOMERA
WOOMERANG
WOOMERAS
WOON
WOONED
WOONERF
WOONERFS
WOONING
WOONS
WOOPIE
WOOPIES
WOOPS
WOOPSED
WOOPSES
WOOPSING
WOOPY

W

WOORALI
WOORALIS
WOORARA
WOORARAS
WOORARI
WOORARIS
WOOS
WOOSE
WOOSEL
WOOSELL
WOOSELLS
WOOSELS
WOOSES
WOOSH
WOOSHED
WOOSHES
WOOSHING
WOOT
WOOTZ
WOOTZES
WOOZIER
WOOZIEST
WOOZILY
WOOZINESS
WOOZY
WOP
WOPPED
WOPPING
WOPS
WORCESTER
WORD
WORDAGE
WORDAGES
WORDBOOK
WORDBOOKS
WORDBOUND
WORDBREAK
WORDCOUNT
WORDED
WORDGAME
WORDGAMES
WORDIE
WORDIER
WORDIES
WORDIEST
WORDILY
WORDINESS
WORDING
WORDINGS
WORDISH
WORDLESS
WORDLORE
WORDLORES
WORDPLAY
WORDPLAYS
WORDS
WORDSMITH
WORDWRAP
WORDWRAPS
WORDY
WORE
WORK
WORKABLE
WORKABLY
WORKADAY
WORKADAYS
WORKBAG
WORKBAGS
WORKBENCH
WORKBOAT
WORKBOATS
WORKBOOK
WORKBOOKS
WORKBOOT
WORKBOOTS
WORKBOX
WORKBOXES
WORKDAY
WORKDAYS
WORKED
WORKER
WORKERIST
WORKERS
WORKFARE
WORKFARES
WORKFLOW
WORKFLOWS
WORKFOLK
WORKFOLKS
WORKFORCE
WORKFUL
WORKGIRL
WORKGIRLS
WORKGROUP
WORKHORSE
WORKHOUR
WORKHOURS
WORKHOUSE
WORKING
WORKINGS
WORKLESS
WORKLOAD
WORKLOADS
WORKMAN
WORKMANLY
WORKMATE
WORKMATES
WORKMEN
WORKOUT
WORKOUTS
WORKPIECE
WORKPLACE
WORKPRINT
WORKROOM
WORKROOMS
WORKS
WORKSAFE
WORKSHEET
WORKSHOP
WORKSHOPS
WORKSHY
WORKSITE
WORKSITES
WORKSOME
WORKSONG
WORKSONGS
WORKSPACE
WORKTABLE
WORKTOP
WORKTOPS
WORKUP
WORKUPS
WORKWEAR
WORKWEARS
WORKWEEK
WORKWEEKS
WORKWOMAN
WORKWOMEN
WORLD
WORLDBEAT
WORLDED
WORLDER
WORLDERS
WORLDIE
WORLDIES
WORLDLIER
WORLDLING
WORLDLY
WORLDS
WORLDVIEW
WORLDWIDE
WORM
WORMCAST
WORMCASTS
WORMED
WORMER
WORMERIES
WORMERS
WORMERY
WORMFLIES
WORMFLY
WORMGEAR
WORMGEARS
WORMHOLE
WORMHOLED
WORMHOLES
WORMIER
WORMIEST
WORMIL
WORMILS
WORMINESS
WORMING
WORMISH
WORMLIKE
WORMROOT
WORMROOTS
WORMS
WORMSEED
WORMSEEDS
WORMWHEEL
WORMWOOD
WORMWOODS
WORMY
WORN
WORNNESS
WORRAL
WORRALS
WORREL
WORRELS
WORRICOW
WORRICOWS
WORRIED
WORRIEDLY
WORRIER
WORRIERS
WORRIES
WORRIMENT
WORRISOME
WORRIT
WORRITED
WORRITING
WORRITS
WORRY
WORRYCOW
WORRYCOWS
WORRYGUTS
WORRYING
WORRYINGS
WORRYWART
WORSE
WORSED
WORSEN
WORSENED
WORSENESS
WORSENING
WORSENS
WORSER
WORSES
WORSET
WORSETS
WORSHIP
WORSHIPED
WORSHIPER
WORSHIPS
WORSING
WORST
WORSTED
WORSTEDS
WORSTING
WORSTS
WORT
WORTH
WORTHED
WORTHFUL
WORTHIED
WORTHIER
WORTHIES
WORTHIEST
WORTHILY
WORTHING

WORTHLESS
WORTHS
WORTHY
WORTHYING
WORTLE
WORTLES
WORTS
WOS
WOSBIRD
WOSBIRDS
WOST
WOT
WOTCHA
WOTCHER
WOTS
WOTTED
WOTTEST
WOTTETH
WOTTING
WOUBIT
WOUBITS
WOULD
WOULDEST
WOULDS
WOULDST
WOUND
WOUNDABLE
WOUNDED
WOUNDEDLY
WOUNDER
WOUNDERS
WOUNDIER
WOUNDIEST
WOUNDILY
WOUNDING
WOUNDINGS
WOUNDLESS
WOUNDS
WOUNDWORT
WOUNDY
WOURALI
WOURALIS
WOVE
WOVEN
WOVENS
WOW
WOWED
WOWEE
WOWF
WOWFER
WOWFEST
WOWING
WOWS
WOWSER
WOWSERS
WOX
WOXEN
WRACK
WRACKED
WRACKFUL
WRACKING
WRACKS
WRAITH
WRAITHS
WRANG
WRANGED
WRANGING
WRANGLE
WRANGLED
WRANGLER
WRANGLERS
WRANGLES
WRANGLING
WRANGS
WRAP
WRAPOVER
WRAPOVERS
WRAPPAGE
WRAPPAGES
WRAPPED
WRAPPER
WRAPPERED
WRAPPERS
WRAPPING
WRAPPINGS
WRAPROUND
WRAPS
WRAPT
WRASSE
WRASSES
WRASSLE
WRASSLED
WRASSLES
WRASSLING
WRAST
WRASTED
WRASTING
WRASTLE
WRASTLED
WRASTLES
WRASTLING
WRASTS
WRATE
WRATH
WRATHED
WRATHFUL
WRATHIER
WRATHIEST
WRATHILY
WRATHING
WRATHLESS
WRATHS
WRATHY
WRAWL
WRAWLED
WRAWLING
WRAWLS
WRAXLE
WRAXLED
WRAXLES
WRAXLING
WRAXLINGS
WREAK
WREAKED
WREAKER
WREAKERS
WREAKFUL
WREAKING
WREAKLESS
WREAKS
WREATH
WREATHE
WREATHED
WREATHEN
WREATHER
WREATHERS
WREATHES
WREATHIER
WREATHING
WREATHS
WREATHY
WRECK
WRECKAGE
WRECKAGES
WRECKED
WRECKER
WRECKERS
WRECKFISH
WRECKFUL
WRECKING
WRECKINGS
WRECKS
WREN
WRENCH
WRENCHED
WRENCHER
WRENCHERS
WRENCHES
WRENCHING
WRENS
WRENTIT
WRENTITS
WREST
WRESTED
WRESTER
WRESTERS
WRESTING
WRESTLE
WRESTLED
WRESTLER
WRESTLERS
WRESTLES
WRESTLING
WRESTS
WRETCH
WRETCHED
WRETCHES
WRETHE
WRETHED
WRETHES
WRETHING
WRICK
WRICKED
WRICKING
WRICKS
WRIED
WRIER
WRIES
WRIEST
WRIGGLE
WRIGGLED
WRIGGLER
WRIGGLERS
WRIGGLES
WRIGGLIER
WRIGGLING
WRIGGLY
WRIGHT
WRIGHTS
WRING
WRINGED
WRINGER
WRINGERS
WRINGING
WRINGS
WRINKLE
WRINKLED
WRINKLES
WRINKLIE
WRINKLIER
WRINKLIES
WRINKLING
WRINKLY
WRIST
WRISTBAND
WRISTED
WRISTER
WRISTERS
WRISTIER
WRISTIEST
WRISTING
WRISTLET
WRISTLETS
WRISTLOCK
WRISTS
WRISTY
WRIT
WRITABLE
WRITATIVE
WRITE
WRITEABLE
WRITEDOWN
WRITEOFF
WRITEOFFS
WRITER
WRITERESS
WRITERLY
WRITERS
WRITES
WRITHE

WRITHED
WRITHEN
WRITHER
WRITHERS
WRITHES
WRITHING
WRITHINGS
WRITHLED
WRITING
WRITINGS
WRITS
WRITTEN
WRIZLED
WROATH
WROATHS
WROKE
WROKEN
WRONG
WRONGDOER
WRONGED
WRONGER
WRONGERS
WRONGEST
WRONGFUL
WRONGING
WRONGLY
WRONGNESS
WRONGOUS
WRONGS
WROOT
WROOTED
WROOTING
WROOTS
WROTE
WROTH
WROTHFUL
WROUGHT
WRUNG
WRY
WRYBILL
WRYBILLS
WRYER
WRYEST
WRYING
WRYLY
WRYNECK
WRYNECKS
WRYNESS
WRYNESSES
WRYTHEN
WUD
WUDDED
WUDDIES
WUDDING
WUDDY
WUDJULA
WUDJULAS
WUDS
WUDU
WUDUS
WUKKAS
WULFENITE
WULL
WULLED
WULLING
WULLS
WUNNER
WUNNERS
WURLEY
WURLEYS
WURLIE
WURLIES
WURST
WURSTS
WURTZITE
WURTZITES
WURZEL
WURZELS
WUS
WUSES
WUSHU
WUSHUS
WUSS
WUSSES
WUSSIER
WUSSIES
WUSSIEST
WUSSY
WUTHER
WUTHERED
WUTHERING
WUTHERS
WUXIA
WUXIAS
WUZ
WUZZLE
WUZZLED
WUZZLES
WUZZLING
WYANDOTTE
WYCH
WYCHES
WYE
WYES
WYLE
WYLED
WYLES
WYLIECOAT
WYLING
WYN
WYND
WYNDS
WYNN
WYNNS
WYNS
WYSIWYG
WYTE
WYTED
WYTES
WYTING
WYVERN
WYVERNS

W

X

XANTHAM
XANTHAMS
XANTHAN
XANTHANS
XANTHATE
XANTHATES
XANTHEIN
XANTHEINS
XANTHENE
XANTHENES
XANTHIC
XANTHIN
XANTHINE
XANTHINES
XANTHINS
XANTHISM
XANTHISMS
XANTHOMA
XANTHOMAS
XANTHONE
XANTHONES
XANTHOUS
XANTHOXYL
XEBEC
XEBECS
XED
XENIA
XENIAL
XENIAS
XENIC
XENIUM
XENOBLAST
XENOCRYST
XENOGAMY
XENOGENIC
XENOGENY
XENOGRAFT
XENOLITH
XENOLITHS
XENOMANIA
XENOMENIA
XENON
XENONS
XENOPHILE
XENOPHOBE
XENOPHOBY
XENOPHYA
XENOPUS
XENOPUSES
XENOTIME
XENOTIMES
XENURINE
XENURINES
XERAFIN
XERAFINS
XERANSES
XERANSIS
XERANTIC
XERAPHIN
XERAPHINS
XERARCH
XERASIA
XERASIAS
XERIC
XERICALLY
XERISCAPE
XEROCHASY
XERODERMA
XEROMA
XEROMAS
XEROMATA
XEROMORPH
XEROPHAGY
XEROPHILE
XEROPHILY
XEROPHYTE
XEROSERE
XEROSERES
XEROSES
XEROSIS
XEROSTOMA
XEROTES
XEROTIC
XEROX
XEROXED
XEROXES
XEROXING
XERUS
XERUSES
XI
XIPHOID
XIPHOIDAL
XIPHOIDS
XIPHOPAGI
XIS
XOANA
XOANON
XRAY
XRAYS
XU
XYLAN
XYLANS
XYLEM
XYLEMS
XYLENE
XYLENES
XYLENOL
XYLENOLS
XYLIC
XYLIDIN
XYLIDINE
XYLIDINES
XYLIDINS
XYLITOL
XYLITOLS
XYLOCARP
XYLOCARPS
XYLOGEN
XYLOGENS
XYLOGRAPH
XYLOID
XYLOIDIN
XYLOIDINE
XYLOIDINS
XYLOL
XYLOLOGY
XYLOLS
XYLOMA
XYLOMAS
XYLOMATA
XYLOMETER
XYLONIC
XYLONITE
XYLONITES
XYLOPHAGE
XYLOPHONE
XYLORIMBA
XYLOSE
XYLOSES
XYLOTOMY
XYLYL
XYLYLS
XYST
XYSTER
XYSTERS
XYSTI
XYSTOI
XYSTOS
XYSTS
XYSTUS

Y

YA
YAAR
YAARS
YABA
YABAS
YABBA
YABBAS
YABBER
YABBERED
YABBERING
YABBERS
YABBIE
YABBIED
YABBIES
YABBY
YABBYING
YACCA
YACCAS
YACHT
YACHTED
YACHTER
YACHTERS
YACHTIE
YACHTIES
YACHTING
YACHTINGS
YACHTMAN
YACHTMEN
YACHTS
YACHTSMAN
YACHTSMEN
YACK
YACKA
YACKAS
YACKED
YACKER
YACKERS
YACKING
YACKS
YAD
YADS
YAE
YAFF
YAFFED
YAFFING
YAFFLE
YAFFLES
YAFFS
YAG
YAGE
YAGER
YAGERS
YAGES
YAGGER
YAGGERS
YAGI
YAGIS
YAGS
YAH
YAHOO
YAHOOISM
YAHOOISMS
YAHOOS
YAHRZEIT
YAHRZEITS
YAHS
YAIRD
YAIRDS
YAK
YAKHDAN
YAKHDANS
YAKIMONO
YAKIMONOS
YAKITORI
YAKITORIS
YAKKA
YAKKAS
YAKKED
YAKKER
YAKKERS
YAKKING
YAKOW
YAKOWS
YAKS
YAKUZA
YALD
YALE
YALES
YAM
YAMALKA
YAMALKAS
YAMEN
YAMENS
YAMMER
YAMMERED
YAMMERER
YAMMERERS
YAMMERING
YAMMERS
YAMPIES
YAMPY
YAMS
YAMULKA
YAMULKAS
YAMUN
YAMUNS
YANG
YANGS
YANK
YANKED
YANKEE
YANKEES
YANKER
YANKERS
YANKIE
YANKIES
YANKING
YANKS
YANQUI
YANQUIS
YANTRA
YANTRAS
YAOURT
YAOURTS
YAP
YAPOCK
YAPOCKS
YAPOK
YAPOKS
YAPON
YAPONS
YAPP
YAPPED
YAPPER
YAPPERS
YAPPIE
YAPPIER
YAPPIES
YAPPIEST
YAPPING
YAPPINGLY
YAPPINGS
YAPPS
YAPPY
YAPS
YAPSTER
YAPSTERS
YAQONA
YAQONAS
YAR
YARAK
YARAKS
YARCO
YARCOS
YARD
YARDAGE
YARDAGES
YARDANG
YARDANGS
YARDARM
YARDARMS
YARDBIRD
YARDBIRDS
YARDED
YARDER
YARDERS
YARDING
YARDINGS
YARDLAND
YARDLANDS
YARDLIGHT
YARDMAN
YARDMEN
YARDS
YARDSTICK
YARDWAND
YARDWANDS
YARDWORK
YARDWORKS
YARE
YARELY
YARER
YAREST
YARFA
YARFAS
YARK
YARKED
YARKING
YARKS
YARMELKE
YARMELKES
YARMULKA
YARMULKAS
YARMULKE
YARMULKES
YARN
YARNED
YARNER
YARNERS
YARNING
YARNS
YARPHA
YARPHAS
YARR
YARRAMAN
YARRAMANS
YARRAMEN
YARRAN
YARRANS
YARRED

Y

YARRING
YARROW
YARROWS
YARRS
YARTA
YARTAS
YARTO
YARTOS
YAS
YASHMAC
YASHMACS
YASHMAK
YASHMAKS
YASMAK
YASMAKS
YATAGAN
YATAGANS
YATAGHAN
YATAGHANS
YATE
YATES
YATTER
YATTERED
YATTERING
YATTERS
YAUD
YAUDS
YAULD
YAUP
YAUPED
YAUPER
YAUPERS
YAUPING
YAUPON
YAUPONS
YAUPS
YAUTIA
YAUTIAS
YAW
YAWED
YAWEY
YAWIER
YAWIEST
YAWING
YAWL
YAWLED
YAWLING
YAWLS
YAWMETER
YAWMETERS
YAWN
YAWNED
YAWNER
YAWNERS
YAWNIER
YAWNIEST
YAWNING
YAWNINGLY
YAWNINGS
YAWNS
YAWNSOME
YAWNY
YAWP
YAWPED
YAWPER
YAWPERS
YAWPING
YAWPINGS
YAWPS
YAWS
YAWY
YAY
YAYS
YBET
YBLENT
YBORE
YBOUND
YBOUNDEN
YBRENT
YCLAD
YCLED
YCLEEPE
YCLEEPED
YCLEEPES
YCLEEPING
YCLEPED
YCLEPT
YCOND
YDRAD
YDRED
YE
YEA
YEAD
YEADING
YEADS
YEAH
YEAHS
YEALDON
YEALDONS
YEALING
YEALINGS
YEALM
YEALMED
YEALMING
YEALMS
YEAN
YEANED
YEANING
YEANLING
YEANLINGS
YEANS
YEAR
YEARBOOK
YEARBOOKS
YEARD
YEARDED
YEARDING
YEARDS
YEAREND
YEARENDS
YEARLIES
YEARLING
YEARLINGS
YEARLONG
YEARLY
YEARN
YEARNED
YEARNER
YEARNERS
YEARNING
YEARNINGS
YEARNS
YEARS
YEAS
YEASAYER
YEASAYERS
YEAST
YEASTED
YEASTIER
YEASTIEST
YEASTILY
YEASTING
YEASTLESS
YEASTLIKE
YEASTS
YEASTY
YEBO
YECCH
YECCHS
YECH
YECHIER
YECHIEST
YECHS
YECHY
YEDE
YEDES
YEDING
YEED
YEEDING
YEEDS
YEELIN
YEELINS
YEESH
YEGG
YEGGMAN
YEGGMEN
YEGGS
YEH
YELD
YELDRING
YELDRINGS
YELDROCK
YELDROCKS
YELK
YELKS
YELL
YELLED
YELLER
YELLERS
YELLING
YELLINGS
YELLOCH
YELLOCHED
YELLOCHS
YELLOW
YELLOWED
YELLOWER
YELLOWEST
YELLOWFIN
YELLOWIER
YELLOWING
YELLOWISH
YELLOWLY
YELLOWS
YELLOWY
YELLS
YELM
YELMED
YELMING
YELMS
YELP
YELPED
YELPER
YELPERS
YELPING
YELPINGS
YELPS
YELT
YELTS
YEMMER
YEMMERS
YEN
YENNED
YENNING
YENS
YENTA
YENTAS
YENTE
YENTES
YEOMAN
YEOMANLY
YEOMANRY
YEOMEN
YEOW
YEP
YEPS
YER
YERBA
YERBAS
YERD
YERDED
YERDING
YERDS
YERK
YERKED
YERKING
YERKS
YERSINIA
YERSINIAE
YERSINIAS

YES
YESES
YESHIVA
YESHIVAH
YESHIVAHS
YESHIVAS
YESHIVOT
YESHIVOTH
YESK
YESKED
YESKING
YESKS
YESSED
YESSES
YESSING
YESSIR
YESSIREE
YESSUM
YEST
YESTER
YESTERDAY
YESTEREVE
YESTERN
YESTREEN
YESTREENS
YESTS
YESTY
YET
YETI
YETIS
YETT
YETTIE
YETTIES
YETTS
YEUK
YEUKED
YEUKIER
YEUKIEST
YEUKING
YEUKS
YEUKY
YEVE
YEVEN
YEVES
YEVING
YEW
YEWEN
YEWS
YEX
YEXED
YEXES
YEXING
YEZ
YFERE
YFERES
YGLAUNST
YGO
YGOE
YIBBLES
YICKER
YICKERED
YICKERING
YICKERS
YID
YIDAKI
YIDAKIS
YIDS
YIELD
YIELDABLE
YIELDED
YIELDER
YIELDERS
YIELDING
YIELDINGS
YIELDS
YIKE
YIKED
YIKES
YIKING
YIKKER
YIKKERED
YIKKERING
YIKKERS
YILL
YILLED
YILLING
YILLS
YIN
YINCE
YINDIE
YINDIES
YINGYANG
YINGYANGS
YINS
YIP
YIPE
YIPES
YIPPED
YIPPEE
YIPPER
YIPPERS
YIPPIE
YIPPIES
YIPPING
YIPPY
YIPS
YIRD
YIRDED
YIRDING
YIRDS
YIRK
YIRKED
YIRKING
YIRKS
YIRR
YIRRED
YIRRING
YIRRS
YIRTH
YIRTHS
YITE
YITES
YITIE
YITIES
YITTEN
YLEM
YLEMS
YLIKE
YLKE
YLKES
YMOLT
YMOLTEN
YMPE
YMPES
YMPING
YMPT
YNAMBU
YNAMBUS
YO
YOB
YOBBERIES
YOBBERY
YOBBIER
YOBBIEST
YOBBISH
YOBBISHLY
YOBBISM
YOBBISMS
YOBBO
YOBBOES
YOBBOS
YOBBY
YOBS
YOCK
YOCKED
YOCKING
YOCKS
YOD
YODE
YODEL
YODELED
YODELER
YODELERS
YODELING
YODELINGS
YODELLED
YODELLER
YODELLERS
YODELLING
YODELS
YODH
YODHS
YODLE
YODLED
YODLER
YODLERS
YODLES
YODLING
YODS
YOGA
YOGAS
YOGEE
YOGEES
YOGH
YOGHOURT
YOGHOURTS
YOGHS
YOGHURT
YOGHURTS
YOGI
YOGIC
YOGIN
YOGINI
YOGINIS
YOGINS
YOGIS
YOGISM
YOGISMS
YOGOURT
YOGOURTS
YOGURT
YOGURTS
YOHIMBE
YOHIMBES
YOHIMBINE
YOICK
YOICKED
YOICKING
YOICKS
YOICKSED
YOICKSES
YOICKSING
YOJAN
YOJANA
YOJANAS
YOJANS
YOK
YOKE
YOKED
YOKEL
YOKELESS
YOKELISH
YOKELS
YOKEMATE
YOKEMATES
YOKER
YOKERED
YOKERING
YOKERS
YOKES
YOKING
YOKINGS
YOKKED
YOKKING
YOKOZUNA
YOKOZUNAS
YOKS
YOKUL
YOLD
YOLDRING

Y

YOLDRINGS
YOLK
YOLKED
YOLKIER
YOLKIEST
YOLKLESS
YOLKS
YOLKY
YOM
YOMIM
YOMP
YOMPED
YOMPING
YOMPS
YON
YOND
YONDER
YONDERLY
YONDERS
YONI
YONIC
YONIS
YONKER
YONKERS
YONKS
YONNIE
YONNIES
YONT
YOOF
YOOFS
YOOP
YOOPS
YOPPER
YOPPERS
YORE
YORES
YORK
YORKED
YORKER
YORKERS
YORKIE
YORKIES
YORKING
YORKS
YORLING
YORLINGS
YORP
YORPED
YORPING
YORPS
YOTTABYTE
YOU
YOUK
YOUKED
YOUKING
YOUKS
YOUNG
YOUNGER
YOUNGERS
YOUNGEST
YOUNGISH
YOUNGLING
YOUNGLY
YOUNGNESS
YOUNGS
YOUNGSTER
YOUNGTH
YOUNGTHLY
YOUNGTHS
YOUNKER
YOUNKERS
YOUPON
YOUPONS
YOUR
YOURN
YOURS
YOURSELF
YOURT
YOURTS
YOUS
YOUSE
YOUTH
YOUTHEN
YOUTHENED
YOUTHENS
YOUTHFUL
YOUTHHEAD
YOUTHHOOD
YOUTHIER
YOUTHIEST
YOUTHLESS
YOUTHLY
YOUTHS
YOUTHSOME
YOUTHY
YOW
YOWE
YOWED
YOWES
YOWIE
YOWIES
YOWING
YOWL
YOWLED
YOWLER
YOWLERS
YOWLEY
YOWLEYS
YOWLING
YOWLINGS
YOWLS
YOWS
YOWZA
YPERITE
YPERITES
YPIGHT
YPLAST
YPLIGHT
YPSILOID
YPSILON
YPSILONS
YRAPT
YRAVISHED
YRENT
YRIVD
YRNEH
YRNEHS
YSAME
YSHEND
YSHENDING
YSHENDS
YSHENT
YSLAKED
YTOST
YTTERBIA
YTTERBIAS
YTTERBIC
YTTERBITE
YTTERBIUM
YTTERBOUS
YTTRIA
YTTRIAS
YTTRIC
YTTRIOUS
YTTRIUM
YTTRIUMS
YU
YUAN
YUANS
YUCA
YUCAS
YUCCA
YUCCAS
YUCCH
YUCH
YUCK
YUCKED
YUCKER
YUCKERS
YUCKIER
YUCKIEST
YUCKINESS
YUCKING
YUCKO
YUCKS
YUCKY
YUFT
YUFTS
YUG
YUGA
YUGARIE
YUGARIES
YUGAS
YUGS
YUK
YUKATA
YUKATAS
YUKE
YUKED
YUKES
YUKIER
YUKIEST
YUKING
YUKKED
YUKKIER
YUKKIEST
YUKKING
YUKKY
YUKO
YUKOS
YUKS
YUKY
YULAN
YULANS
YULE
YULES
YULETIDE
YULETIDES
YUM
YUMBERRY
YUMMIER
YUMMIES
YUMMIEST
YUMMINESS
YUMMO
YUMMY
YUMP
YUMPED
YUMPIE
YUMPIES
YUMPING
YUMPS
YUNX
YUNXES
YUP
YUPON
YUPONS
YUPPIE
YUPPIEDOM
YUPPIEISH
YUPPIES
YUPPIFIED
YUPPIFIES
YUPPIFY
YUPPY
YUPPYDOM
YUPPYDOMS
YUPS
YUPSTER
YUPSTERS
YURT
YURTA
YURTAS
YURTS
YUS
YUTZ
YUTZES
YUZU
YUZUS
YWIS
YWROKE

Z

ZA
ZABAIONE
ZABAIONES
ZABAJONE
ZABAJONES
ZABETA
ZABETAS
ZABRA
ZABRAS
ZABTIEH
ZABTIEHS
ZACATON
ZACATONS
ZACK
ZACKS
ZADDICK
ZADDICKS
ZADDIK
ZADDIKIM
ZADDIKS
ZAFFAR
ZAFFARS
ZAFFER
ZAFFERS
ZAFFIR
ZAFFIRS
ZAFFRE
ZAFFRES
ZAFTIG
ZAG
ZAGGED
ZAGGING
ZAGS
ZAIBATSU
ZAIBATSUS
ZAIDA
ZAIDAS
ZAIDEH
ZAIDEHS
ZAIDIES
ZAIDY
ZAIKAI
ZAIKAIS
ZAIRE
ZAIRES
ZAITECH
ZAITECHS
ZAKAT
ZAKATS
ZAKOUSKA
ZAKOUSKI
ZAKUSKA
ZAKUSKI
ZAMAN
ZAMANG
ZAMANGS
ZAMANS
ZAMARRA
ZAMARRAS
ZAMARRO
ZAMARROS
ZAMBO
ZAMBOMBA
ZAMBOMBAS
ZAMBOORAK
ZAMBOS
ZAMBUCK
ZAMBUCKS
ZAMBUK
ZAMBUKS
ZAMIA
ZAMIAS
ZAMINDAR
ZAMINDARI
ZAMINDARS
ZAMINDARY
ZAMOUSE
ZAMOUSES
ZAMPOGNA
ZAMPOGNAS
ZAMPONE
ZAMPONI
ZAMZAWED
ZANAMIVIR
ZANANA
ZANANAS
ZANDER
ZANDERS
ZANELLA
ZANELLAS
ZANIED
ZANIER
ZANIES
ZANIEST
ZANILY
ZANINESS
ZANJA
ZANJAS
ZANJERO
ZANJEROS
ZANTE
ZANTES
ZANTEWOOD
ZANTHOXYL
ZANY
ZANYING
ZANYISH
ZANYISM
ZANYISMS
ZANZA
ZANZAS
ZANZE
ZANZES
ZAP
ZAPATA
ZAPATEADO
ZAPATEO
ZAPATEOS
ZAPOTILLA
ZAPPED
ZAPPER
ZAPPERS
ZAPPIER
ZAPPIEST
ZAPPING
ZAPPY
ZAPS
ZAPTIAH
ZAPTIAHS
ZAPTIEH
ZAPTIEHS
ZARAPE
ZARAPES
ZARATITE
ZARATITES
ZAREBA
ZAREBAS
ZAREEBA
ZAREEBAS
ZARF
ZARFS
ZARI
ZARIBA
ZARIBAS
ZARIS
ZARNEC
ZARNECS
ZARNICH
ZARNICHS
ZARZUELA
ZARZUELAS
ZAS
ZASTRUGA
ZASTRUGI
ZATI
ZATIS
ZAX
ZAXES
ZAYIN
ZAYINS
ZAZEN
ZAZENS
ZE
ZEA
ZEAL
ZEALANT
ZEALANTS
ZEALFUL
ZEALLESS
ZEALOT
ZEALOTISM
ZEALOTRY
ZEALOTS
ZEALOUS
ZEALOUSLY
ZEALS
ZEAS
ZEATIN
ZEATINS
ZEBEC
ZEBECK
ZEBECKS
ZEBECS
ZEBRA
ZEBRAFISH
ZEBRAIC
ZEBRANO
ZEBRANOS
ZEBRAS
ZEBRASS
ZEBRASSES
ZEBRAWOOD
ZEBRINA
ZEBRINAS
ZEBRINE
ZEBRINES
ZEBRINNY
ZEBROID
ZEBRULA
ZEBRULAS
ZEBRULE
ZEBRULES
ZEBU
ZEBUB
ZEBUBS
ZEBUS
ZECCHIN
ZECCHINE
ZECCHINES
ZECCHINI

ZECCHINO
ZECCHINOS
ZECCHINS
ZECHIN
ZECHINS
ZED
ZEDA
ZEDAS
ZEDOARIES
ZEDOARY
ZEDS
ZEE
ZEES
ZEIN
ZEINS
ZEITGEBER
ZEITGEIST
ZEK
ZEKS
ZEL
ZELANT
ZELANTS
ZELATOR
ZELATORS
ZELATRICE
ZELATRIX
ZELKOVA
ZELKOVAS
ZELOSO
ZELOTYPIA
ZELS
ZEMINDAR
ZEMINDARI
ZEMINDARS
ZEMINDARY
ZEMSTVA
ZEMSTVO
ZEMSTVOS
ZEN
ZENAIDA
ZENAIDAS
ZENANA
ZENANAS
ZENDIK
ZENDIKS
ZENDO
ZENDOS
ZENITH
ZENITHAL
ZENITHS
ZENS
ZEOLITE
ZEOLITES
ZEOLITIC
ZEP
ZEPHYR
ZEPHYRS
ZEPPELIN
ZEPPELINS
ZEPPOLE
ZEPPOLES
ZEPPOLI
ZEPS
ZERDA
ZERDAS
ZEREBA
ZEREBAS
ZERIBA
ZERIBAS
ZERK
ZERKS
ZERO
ZEROED
ZEROES
ZEROING
ZEROS
ZEROTH
ZERUMBET
ZERUMBETS
ZEST
ZESTED
ZESTER
ZESTERS
ZESTFUL
ZESTFULLY
ZESTIER
ZESTIEST
ZESTILY
ZESTINESS
ZESTING
ZESTLESS
ZESTS
ZESTY
ZETA
ZETAS
ZETETIC
ZETETICS
ZETTABYTE
ZEUGMA
ZEUGMAS
ZEUGMATIC
ZEUXITE
ZEUXITES
ZEX
ZEXES
ZEZE
ZEZES
ZHO
ZHOMO
ZHOMOS
ZHOOSH
ZHOOSHED
ZHOOSHES
ZHOOSHING
ZHOS
ZIBELINE
ZIBELINES
ZIBELLINE
ZIBET
ZIBETH
ZIBETHS
ZIBETS
ZIFF
ZIFFIUS
ZIFFIUSES
ZIFFS
ZIG
ZIGAN
ZIGANKA
ZIGANKAS
ZIGANS
ZIGGED
ZIGGING
ZIGGURAT
ZIGGURATS
ZIGS
ZIGZAG
ZIGZAGGED
ZIGZAGGER
ZIGZAGGY
ZIGZAGS
ZIKKURAT
ZIKKURATS
ZIKURAT
ZIKURATS
ZILA
ZILAS
ZILCH
ZILCHES
ZILL
ZILLA
ZILLAH
ZILLAHS
ZILLAS
ZILLION
ZILLIONS
ZILLIONTH
ZILLS
ZIMB
ZIMBI
ZIMBIS
ZIMBS
ZIMOCCA
ZIMOCCAS
ZIN
ZINC
ZINCATE
ZINCATES
ZINCED
ZINCIC
ZINCIER
ZINCIEST
ZINCIFIED
ZINCIFIES
ZINCIFY
ZINCING
ZINCITE
ZINCITES
ZINCKED
ZINCKIER
ZINCKIEST
ZINCKIFY
ZINCKING
ZINCKY
ZINCO
ZINCODE
ZINCODES
ZINCOID
ZINCOS
ZINCOUS
ZINCS
ZINCY
ZINDABAD
ZINE
ZINEB
ZINEBS
ZINES
ZINFANDEL
ZING
ZINGANI
ZINGANO
ZINGARA
ZINGARE
ZINGARI
ZINGARO
ZINGED
ZINGEL
ZINGELS
ZINGER
ZINGERS
ZINGIBER
ZINGIBERS
ZINGIER
ZINGIEST
ZINGING
ZINGS
ZINGY
ZINKE
ZINKED
ZINKENITE
ZINKES
ZINKIER
ZINKIEST
ZINKIFIED
ZINKIFIES
ZINKIFY
ZINKING
ZINKY
ZINNIA
ZINNIAS
ZINS
ZIP
ZIPLESS
ZIPLINE
ZIPLINES
ZIPLOCK
ZIPLOCKED
ZIPLOCKS
ZIPOLA
ZIPOLAS

ZIPPED
ZIPPER
ZIPPERED
ZIPPERING
ZIPPERS
ZIPPIER
ZIPPIEST
ZIPPILY
ZIPPINESS
ZIPPING
ZIPPO
ZIPPOS
ZIPPY
ZIPS
ZIPTOP
ZIPWIRE
ZIPWIRES
ZIRAM
ZIRAMS
ZIRCALLOY
ZIRCALOY
ZIRCALOYS
ZIRCON
ZIRCONIA
ZIRCONIAS
ZIRCONIC
ZIRCONIUM
ZIRCONS
ZIT
ZITE
ZITHER
ZITHERIST
ZITHERN
ZITHERNS
ZITHERS
ZITI
ZITIS
ZITS
ZIZ
ZIZANIA
ZIZANIAS
ZIZEL
ZIZELS
ZIZIT
ZIZITH
ZIZYPHUS
ZIZZ
ZIZZED
ZIZZES
ZIZZING
ZIZZLE
ZIZZLED
ZIZZLES
ZIZZLING
ZLOTE
ZLOTIES
ZLOTY
ZLOTYCH
ZLOTYS
ZO
ZOA
ZOAEA
ZOAEAE
ZOAEAS
ZOARIA
ZOARIAL
ZOARIUM
ZOBO
ZOBOS
ZOBU
ZOBUS
ZOCALO
ZOCALOS
ZOCCO
ZOCCOLO
ZOCCOLOS
ZOCCOS
ZODIAC
ZODIACAL
ZODIACS
ZOEA
ZOEAE
ZOEAL
ZOEAS
ZOECHROME
ZOECIA
ZOECIUM
ZOEFORM
ZOETIC
ZOETROPE
ZOETROPES
ZOETROPIC
ZOFTIG
ZOIATRIA
ZOIATRIAS
ZOIATRICS
ZOIC
ZOISITE
ZOISITES
ZOISM
ZOISMS
ZOIST
ZOISTS
ZOL
ZOLPIDEM
ZOLPIDEMS
ZOLS
ZOMBI
ZOMBIE
ZOMBIES
ZOMBIFIED
ZOMBIFIES
ZOMBIFY
ZOMBIISM
ZOMBIISMS
ZOMBIS
ZOMBOID
ZOMBORUK
ZOMBORUKS
ZONA
ZONAE
ZONAL
ZONALLY
ZONARY
ZONATE
ZONATED
ZONATION
ZONATIONS
ZONDA
ZONDAS
ZONE
ZONED
ZONELESS
ZONER
ZONERS
ZONES
ZONETIME
ZONETIMES
ZONING
ZONINGS
ZONK
ZONKED
ZONKING
ZONKS
ZONOID
ZONOIDS
ZONULA
ZONULAE
ZONULAR
ZONULAS
ZONULE
ZONULES
ZONULET
ZONULETS
ZONURE
ZONURES
ZOO
ZOOBIOTIC
ZOOBLAST
ZOOBLASTS
ZOOCHORE
ZOOCHORES
ZOOCHORY
ZOOCYTIA
ZOOCYTIUM
ZOOEA
ZOOEAE
ZOOEAL
ZOOEAS
ZOOECIA
ZOOECIUM
ZOOEY
ZOOGAMETE
ZOOGAMIES
ZOOGAMOUS
ZOOGAMY
ZOOGENIC
ZOOGENIES
ZOOGENOUS
ZOOGENY
ZOOGLEA
ZOOGLEAE
ZOOGLEAL
ZOOGLEAS
ZOOGLOEA
ZOOGLOEAE
ZOOGLOEAL
ZOOGLOEAS
ZOOGLOEIC
ZOOGONIES
ZOOGONOUS
ZOOGONY
ZOOGRAFT
ZOOGRAFTS
ZOOGRAPHY
ZOOID
ZOOIDAL
ZOOIDS
ZOOIER
ZOOIEST
ZOOKEEPER
ZOOKS
ZOOLATER
ZOOLATERS
ZOOLATRIA
ZOOLATRY
ZOOLITE
ZOOLITES
ZOOLITH
ZOOLITHIC
ZOOLITHS
ZOOLITIC
ZOOLOGIC
ZOOLOGIES
ZOOLOGIST
ZOOLOGY
ZOOM
ZOOMABLE
ZOOMANCY
ZOOMANIA
ZOOMANIAS
ZOOMANTIC
ZOOMED
ZOOMETRIC
ZOOMETRY
ZOOMING
ZOOMORPH
ZOOMORPHS
ZOOMORPHY
ZOOMS
ZOON
ZOONAL
ZOONED
ZOONIC
ZOONING
ZOONITE
ZOONITES
ZOONITIC
ZOONOMIA
ZOONOMIAS

Z

ZOONOMIC
ZOONOMIES
ZOONOMIST
ZOONOMY
ZOONOSES
ZOONOSIS
ZOONOTIC
ZOONS
ZOOPATHY
ZOOPERAL
ZOOPERIES
ZOOPERIST
ZOOPERY
ZOOPHAGAN
ZOOPHAGY
ZOOPHILE
ZOOPHILES
ZOOPHILIA
ZOOPHILIC
ZOOPHILY
ZOOPHOBE
ZOOPHOBES
ZOOPHOBIA
ZOOPHORI
ZOOPHORIC
ZOOPHORUS
ZOOPHYTE
ZOOPHYTES
ZOOPHYTIC
ZOOPLASTY
ZOOS
ZOOSCOPIC
ZOOSCOPY
ZOOSPERM
ZOOSPERMS
ZOOSPORE
ZOOSPORES
ZOOSPORIC
ZOOSTEROL
ZOOT

ZOOTAXIES
ZOOTAXY
ZOOTECHNY
ZOOTHECIA
ZOOTHEISM
ZOOTHOME
ZOOTHOMES
ZOOTIER
ZOOTIEST
ZOOTOMIC
ZOOTOMIES
ZOOTOMIST
ZOOTOMY
ZOOTOXIC
ZOOTOXIN
ZOOTOXINS
ZOOTROPE
ZOOTROPES
ZOOTROPHY
ZOOTY
ZOOTYPE
ZOOTYPES
ZOOTYPIC
ZOOZOO
ZOOZOOS
ZOPILOTE
ZOPILOTES
ZOPPA
ZOPPO
ZORBING
ZORBINGS
ZORBONAUT
ZORGITE
ZORGITES
ZORI
ZORIL
ZORILLA
ZORILLAS
ZORILLE
ZORILLES

ZORILLO
ZORILLOS
ZORILS
ZORINO
ZORINOS
ZORIS
ZORRO
ZORROS
ZOS
ZOSTER
ZOSTERS
ZOUAVE
ZOUAVES
ZOUK
ZOUKS
ZOUNDS
ZOWEE
ZOWIE
ZOYSIA
ZOYSIAS
ZUCCHETTI
ZUCCHETTO
ZUCCHINI
ZUCCHINIS
ZUCHETTA
ZUCHETTAS
ZUCHETTO
ZUCHETTOS
ZUFFOLI
ZUFFOLO
ZUFOLI
ZUFOLO
ZUFOLOS
ZUGZWANG
ZUGZWANGS
ZULU
ZULUS
ZUMBOORUK
ZUPA
ZUPAN

ZUPANS
ZUPAS
ZUPPA
ZUPPAS
ZURF
ZURFS
ZUZ
ZUZIM
ZUZZIM
ZWANZIGER
ZWIEBACK
ZWIEBACKS
ZYDECO
ZYDECOS
ZYGA
ZYGAENID
ZYGAENOID
ZYGAL
ZYGANTRA
ZYGANTRUM
ZYGOCACTI
ZYGODONT
ZYGOID
ZYGOMA
ZYGOMAS
ZYGOMATA
ZYGOMATIC
ZYGON
ZYGOPHYTE
ZYGOSE
ZYGOSES
ZYGOSIS
ZYGOSITY
ZYGOSPERM
ZYGOSPORE
ZYGOTE
ZYGOTENE
ZYGOTENES
ZYGOTES
ZYGOTIC

ZYLONITE
ZYLONITES
ZYMASE
ZYMASES
ZYME
ZYMES
ZYMIC
ZYMITE
ZYMITES
ZYMOGEN
ZYMOGENE
ZYMOGENES
ZYMOGENIC
ZYMOGENS
ZYMOGRAM
ZYMOGRAMS
ZYMOID
ZYMOLOGIC
ZYMOLOGY
ZYMOLYSES
ZYMOLYSIS
ZYMOLYTIC
ZYMOME
ZYMOMES
ZYMOMETER
ZYMOSAN
ZYMOSANS
ZYMOSES
ZYMOSIS
ZYMOTIC
ZYMOTICS
ZYMURGIES
ZYMURGY
ZYTHUM
ZYTHUMS
ZYZZYVA
ZYZZYVAS
ZZZ
ZZZS

ten to fifteen letter words

A

AARDWOLVES
ABACTERIAL
ABACTINALLY
ABANDONEDLY
ABANDONEES
ABANDONERS
ABANDONING
ABANDONMENT
ABANDONMENTS
ABANDONWARE
ABANDONWARES
ABASEMENTS
ABASHMENTS
ABATEMENTS
ABBOTSHIPS
ABBREVIATE
ABBREVIATED
ABBREVIATES
ABBREVIATING
ABBREVIATION
ABBREVIATIONS
ABBREVIATOR
ABBREVIATORS
ABBREVIATORY
ABBREVIATURE
ABBREVIATURES
ABCOULOMBS
ABDICATING
ABDICATION
ABDICATIONS
ABDICATIVE
ABDICATORS
ABDOMINALLY
ABDOMINALS
ABDOMINOPLASTY
ABDOMINOUS
ABDUCENTES
ABDUCTIONS
ABDUCTORES
ABECEDARIAN
ABECEDARIANS
ABERDEVINE
ABERDEVINES
ABERNETHIES
ABERRANCES
ABERRANCIES
ABERRANTLY
ABERRATING
ABERRATION
ABERRATIONAL
ABERRATIONS
ABEYANCIES
ABHOMINABLE
ABHORRENCE
ABHORRENCES
ABHORRENCIES
ABHORRENCY
ABHORRENTLY
ABHORRINGS
ABIOGENESES
ABIOGENESIS
ABIOGENETIC
ABIOGENETICALLY
ABIOGENICALLY
ABIOGENIST
ABIOGENISTS
ABIOLOGICAL
ABIOTICALLY
ABIOTROPHIC
ABIOTROPHIES
ABIOTROPHY
ABIRRITANT
ABIRRITANTS
ABIRRITATE
ABIRRITATED
ABIRRITATES
ABIRRITATING
ABITURIENT
ABITURIENTS
ABJECTIONS
ABJECTNESS
ABJECTNESSES
ABJOINTING
ABJUNCTION
ABJUNCTIONS
ABJURATION
ABJURATIONS
ABLACTATION
ABLACTATIONS
ABLATITIOUS
ABLATIVELY
ABLUTIONARY
ABLUTOMANE
ABLUTOMANES
ABNEGATING
ABNEGATION
ABNEGATIONS
ABNEGATORS
ABNORMALISM
ABNORMALISMS
ABNORMALITIES
ABNORMALITY
ABNORMALLY
ABNORMITIES
ABODEMENTS
ABOLISHABLE
ABOLISHERS
ABOLISHING
ABOLISHMENT
ABOLISHMENTS
ABOLITIONAL
ABOLITIONARY
ABOLITIONISM
ABOLITIONISMS
ABOLITIONIST
ABOLITIONISTS
ABOLITIONS
ABOMINABLE
ABOMINABLENESS
ABOMINABLY
ABOMINATED
ABOMINATES
ABOMINATING
ABOMINATION
ABOMINATIONS
ABOMINATOR
ABOMINATORS
ABONDANCES
ABONNEMENT
ABONNEMENTS
ABORIGINAL
ABORIGINALISM
ABORIGINALISMS
ABORIGINALITIES
ABORIGINALITY
ABORIGINALLY
ABORIGINALS
ABORIGINES
ABORTICIDE
ABORTICIDES
ABORTIFACIENT
ABORTIFACIENTS
ABORTIONAL
ABORTIONIST
ABORTIONISTS
ABORTIVELY
ABORTIVENESS
ABORTIVENESSES
ABORTUARIES
ABOVEBOARD
ABOVEGROUND
ABRACADABRA
ABRACADABRAS
ABRANCHIAL
ABRANCHIATE
ABRASIVELY
ABRASIVENESS
ABRASIVENESSES
ABREACTING
ABREACTION
ABREACTIONS
ABREACTIVE
ABRIDGABLE
ABRIDGEABLE
ABRIDGEMENT
ABRIDGEMENTS
ABRIDGMENT
ABRIDGMENTS
ABROGATING
ABROGATION
ABROGATIONS
ABROGATIVE
ABROGATORS
ABRUPTIONS
ABRUPTNESS
ABRUPTNESSES
ABSCESSING
ABSCINDING
ABSCISSINS
ABSCISSION
ABSCISSIONS
ABSCONDENCE
ABSCONDENCES
ABSCONDERS
ABSCONDING
ABSCONDINGS
ABSEILINGS
ABSENTEEISM
ABSENTEEISMS
ABSENTMINDED
ABSENTMINDEDLY
ABSINTHIATED
ABSINTHISM
ABSINTHISMS
ABSOLUTELY
ABSOLUTENESS
ABSOLUTENESSES
ABSOLUTEST
ABSOLUTION
ABSOLUTIONS
ABSOLUTISE
ABSOLUTISED
ABSOLUTISES
ABSOLUTISING
ABSOLUTISM
ABSOLUTISMS
ABSOLUTIST
ABSOLUTISTIC
ABSOLUTISTS
ABSOLUTIVE

A

ABSOLUTIVES
ABSOLUTIZE
ABSOLUTIZED
ABSOLUTIZES
ABSOLUTIZING
ABSOLUTORY
ABSOLVABLE
ABSOLVENTS
ABSOLVITOR
ABSOLVITORS
ABSORBABILITIES
ABSORBABILITY
ABSORBABLE
ABSORBANCE
ABSORBANCES
ABSORBANCIES
ABSORBANCY
ABSORBANTS
ABSORBATES
ABSORBEDLY
ABSORBEFACIENT
ABSORBEFACIENTS
ABSORBENCIES
ABSORBENCY
ABSORBENTS
ABSORBINGLY
ABSORPTANCE
ABSORPTANCES
ABSORPTIOMETER
ABSORPTIOMETERS
ABSORPTION
ABSORPTIONS
ABSORPTIVE
ABSORPTIVENESS
ABSORPTIVITIES
ABSORPTIVITY
ABSQUATULATE
ABSQUATULATED
ABSQUATULATES
ABSQUATULATING
ABSTAINERS
ABSTAINING
ABSTEMIOUS
ABSTEMIOUSLY
ABSTEMIOUSNESS
ABSTENTION
ABSTENTIONISM
ABSTENTIONISMS
ABSTENTIONIST
ABSTENTIONISTS
ABSTENTIONS
ABSTENTIOUS
ABSTERGENT
ABSTERGENTS
ABSTERGING
ABSTERSION
ABSTERSIONS
ABSTERSIVE
ABSTERSIVES
ABSTINENCE
ABSTINENCES
ABSTINENCIES
ABSTINENCY
ABSTINENTLY
ABSTRACTABLE
ABSTRACTED
ABSTRACTEDLY
ABSTRACTEDNESS
ABSTRACTER
ABSTRACTERS
ABSTRACTEST
ABSTRACTING
ABSTRACTION
ABSTRACTIONAL
ABSTRACTIONISM
ABSTRACTIONISMS
ABSTRACTIONIST
ABSTRACTIONISTS
ABSTRACTIONS
ABSTRACTIVE
ABSTRACTIVELY
ABSTRACTIVES
ABSTRACTLY
ABSTRACTNESS
ABSTRACTNESSES
ABSTRACTOR
ABSTRACTORS
ABSTRICTED
ABSTRICTING
ABSTRICTION
ABSTRICTIONS
ABSTRUSELY
ABSTRUSENESS
ABSTRUSENESSES
ABSTRUSEST
ABSTRUSITIES
ABSTRUSITY
ABSURDISMS
ABSURDISTS
ABSURDITIES
ABSURDNESS
ABSURDNESSES
ABUNDANCES
ABUNDANCIES
ABUNDANTLY
ABUSIVENESS
ABUSIVENESSES
ABYSSOPELAGIC
ACADEMICAL
ACADEMICALISM
ACADEMICALISMS
ACADEMICALLY
ACADEMICALS
ACADEMICIAN
ACADEMICIANS
ACADEMICISM
ACADEMICISMS
ACADEMISMS
ACADEMISTS
ACALCULIAS
ACALEPHANS
ACANACEOUS
ACANTHACEOUS
ACANTHOCEPHALAN
ACANTHUSES
ACARICIDAL
ACARICIDES
ACARIDEANS
ACARIDIANS
ACARIDOMATIA
ACARIDOMATIUM
ACARODOMATIA
ACARODOMATIUM
ACAROLOGIES
ACAROLOGIST
ACAROLOGISTS
ACAROPHILIES
ACAROPHILY
ACARPELLOUS
ACARPELOUS
ACATALECTIC
ACATALECTICS
ACATALEPSIES
ACATALEPSY
ACATALEPTIC
ACATALEPTICS
ACATAMATHESIA
ACATAMATHESIAS
ACATHISIAS
ACAULESCENT
ACCEDENCES
ACCELERABLE
ACCELERANDO
ACCELERANDOS
ACCELERANT
ACCELERANTS
ACCELERATE
ACCELERATED
ACCELERATES
ACCELERATING
ACCELERATINGLY
ACCELERATION
ACCELERATIONS
ACCELERATIVE
ACCELERATOR
ACCELERATORS
ACCELERATORY
ACCELEROMETER
ACCELEROMETERS
ACCENSIONS
ACCENTLESS
ACCENTUALITIES
ACCENTUALITY
ACCENTUALLY
ACCENTUATE
ACCENTUATED
ACCENTUATES
ACCENTUATING
ACCENTUATION
ACCENTUATIONS
ACCEPTABILITIES
ACCEPTABILITY
ACCEPTABLE
ACCEPTABLENESS
ACCEPTABLY
ACCEPTANCE
ACCEPTANCES
ACCEPTANCIES
ACCEPTANCY
ACCEPTANTS
ACCEPTATION
ACCEPTATIONS
ACCEPTEDLY
ACCEPTILATION
ACCEPTILATIONS
ACCEPTINGLY
ACCEPTINGNESS
ACCEPTINGNESSES
ACCEPTIVITIES
ACCEPTIVITY
ACCESSARIES
ACCESSARILY
ACCESSARINESS
ACCESSARINESSES
ACCESSIBILITIES
ACCESSIBILITY
ACCESSIBLE
ACCESSIBLENESS
ACCESSIBLY
ACCESSIONAL
ACCESSIONED
ACCESSIONING
ACCESSIONS
ACCESSORIAL
ACCESSORIES
ACCESSORII
ACCESSORILY
ACCESSORINESS
ACCESSORINESSES
ACCESSORISE
ACCESSORISED
ACCESSORISES
ACCESSORISING
ACCESSORIUS
ACCESSORIZE
ACCESSORIZED
ACCESSORIZES
ACCESSORIZING
ACCIACCATURA
ACCIACCATURAS
ACCIACCATURE
ACCIDENCES
ACCIDENTAL
ACCIDENTALISM
ACCIDENTALISMS
ACCIDENTALITIES
ACCIDENTALITY
ACCIDENTALLY
ACCIDENTALNESS
ACCIDENTALS

ACCIDENTED
ACCIDENTLY
ACCIDENTOLOGIES
ACCIDENTOLOGY
ACCIPITERS
ACCIPITRAL
ACCIPITRINE
ACCIPITRINES
ACCLAIMERS
ACCLAIMING
ACCLAMATION
ACCLAMATIONS
ACCLAMATORY
ACCLIMATABLE
ACCLIMATATION
ACCLIMATATIONS
ACCLIMATED
ACCLIMATES
ACCLIMATING
ACCLIMATION
ACCLIMATIONS
ACCLIMATISABLE
ACCLIMATISATION
ACCLIMATISE
ACCLIMATISED
ACCLIMATISER
ACCLIMATISERS
ACCLIMATISES
ACCLIMATISING
ACCLIMATIZABLE
ACCLIMATIZATION
ACCLIMATIZE
ACCLIMATIZED
ACCLIMATIZER
ACCLIMATIZERS
ACCLIMATIZES
ACCLIMATIZING
ACCLIVITIES
ACCLIVITOUS
ACCOASTING
ACCOLADING
ACCOMMODABLE
ACCOMMODATE
ACCOMMODATED
ACCOMMODATES
ACCOMMODATING
ACCOMMODATINGLY
ACCOMMODATION
ACCOMMODATIONAL
ACCOMMODATIONS
ACCOMMODATIVE
ACCOMMODATOR
ACCOMMODATORS
ACCOMPANIED
ACCOMPANIER
ACCOMPANIERS
ACCOMPANIES
ACCOMPANIMENT
ACCOMPANIMENTS
ACCOMPANIST
ACCOMPANISTS
ACCOMPANYING
ACCOMPANYIST
ACCOMPANYISTS
ACCOMPLICE
ACCOMPLICES
ACCOMPLISH
ACCOMPLISHABLE
ACCOMPLISHED
ACCOMPLISHER
ACCOMPLISHERS
ACCOMPLISHES
ACCOMPLISHING
ACCOMPLISHMENT
ACCOMPLISHMENTS
ACCOMPTABLE
ACCOMPTANT
ACCOMPTANTS
ACCOMPTING
ACCORAGING
ACCORDABLE
ACCORDANCE
ACCORDANCES
ACCORDANCIES
ACCORDANCY
ACCORDANTLY
ACCORDINGLY
ACCORDIONIST
ACCORDIONISTS
ACCORDIONS
ACCOSTABLE
ACCOUCHEMENT
ACCOUCHEMENTS
ACCOUCHEUR
ACCOUCHEURS
ACCOUCHEUSE
ACCOUCHEUSES
ACCOUNTABILITY
ACCOUNTABLE
ACCOUNTABLENESS
ACCOUNTABLY
ACCOUNTANCIES
ACCOUNTANCY
ACCOUNTANT
ACCOUNTANTS
ACCOUNTANTSHIP
ACCOUNTANTSHIPS
ACCOUNTING
ACCOUNTINGS
ACCOUPLEMENT
ACCOUPLEMENTS
ACCOURAGED
ACCOURAGES
ACCOURAGING
ACCOURTING
ACCOUSTREMENT
ACCOUSTREMENTS
ACCOUTERED
ACCOUTERING
ACCOUTERMENT
ACCOUTERMENTS
ACCOUTREMENT
ACCOUTREMENTS
ACCOUTRING
ACCREDITABLE
ACCREDITATION
ACCREDITATIONS
ACCREDITED
ACCREDITING
ACCRESCENCE
ACCRESCENCES
ACCRESCENT
ACCRETIONARY
ACCRETIONS
ACCRUEMENT
ACCRUEMENTS
ACCUBATION
ACCUBATIONS
ACCULTURAL
ACCULTURATE
ACCULTURATED
ACCULTURATES
ACCULTURATING
ACCULTURATION
ACCULTURATIONAL
ACCULTURATIONS
ACCULTURATIVE
ACCUMBENCIES
ACCUMBENCY
ACCUMULABLE
ACCUMULATE
ACCUMULATED
ACCUMULATES
ACCUMULATING
ACCUMULATION
ACCUMULATIONS
ACCUMULATIVE
ACCUMULATIVELY
ACCUMULATOR
ACCUMULATORS
ACCURACIES
ACCURATELY
ACCURATENESS
ACCURATENESSES
ACCURSEDLY
ACCURSEDNESS
ACCURSEDNESSES
ACCUSATION
ACCUSATIONS
ACCUSATIVAL
ACCUSATIVE
ACCUSATIVELY
ACCUSATIVES
ACCUSATORIAL
ACCUSATORY
ACCUSEMENT
ACCUSEMENTS
ACCUSINGLY
ACCUSTOMARY
ACCUSTOMATION
ACCUSTOMATIONS
ACCUSTOMED
ACCUSTOMEDNESS
ACCUSTOMING
ACCUSTREMENT
ACCUSTREMENTS
ACEPHALOUS
ACERACEOUS
ACERBATING
ACERBICALLY
ACERBITIES
ACERVATELY
ACERVATION
ACERVATIONS
ACESCENCES
ACESCENCIES
ACETABULAR
ACETABULUM
ACETABULUMS
ACETALDEHYDE
ACETALDEHYDES
ACETAMIDES
ACETAMINOPHEN
ACETAMINOPHENS
ACETANILID
ACETANILIDE
ACETANILIDES
ACETANILIDS
ACETAZOLAMIDE
ACETAZOLAMIDES
ACETIFICATION
ACETIFICATIONS
ACETIFIERS
ACETIFYING
ACETOACETIC
ACETOMETER
ACETOMETERS
ACETONAEMIA
ACETONAEMIAS
ACETONEMIA
ACETONEMIAS
ACETONITRILE
ACETONITRILES
ACETONURIA
ACETONURIAS
ACETOPHENETIDIN
ACETYLATED
ACETYLATES
ACETYLATING
ACETYLATION
ACETYLATIONS
ACETYLATIVE
ACETYLCHOLINE
ACETYLCHOLINES
ACETYLENES
ACETYLENIC
ACETYLIDES
ACETYLSALICYLIC
ACHAENIUMS
ACHAENOCARP

ACHAENOCARPS
ACHALASIAS
ACHIEVABLE
ACHIEVEMENT
ACHIEVEMENTS
ACHINESSES
ACHLAMYDEOUS
ACHLORHYDRIA
ACHLORHYDRIAS
ACHLORHYDRIC
ACHONDRITE
ACHONDRITES
ACHONDRITIC
ACHONDROPLASIA
ACHONDROPLASIAS
ACHONDROPLASTIC
ACHROMATIC
ACHROMATICALLY
ACHROMATICITIES
ACHROMATICITY
ACHROMATIN
ACHROMATINS
ACHROMATISATION
ACHROMATISE
ACHROMATISED
ACHROMATISES
ACHROMATISING
ACHROMATISM
ACHROMATISMS
ACHROMATIZATION
ACHROMATIZE
ACHROMATIZED
ACHROMATIZES
ACHROMATIZING
ACHROMATOPSIA
ACHROMATOPSIAS
ACHROMATOUS
ACICLOVIRS
ACICULATED
ACIDANTHERA
ACIDANTHERAS
ACIDICALLY
ACIDIFIABLE
ACIDIFICATION
ACIDIFICATIONS
ACIDIFIERS
ACIDIFYING
ACIDIMETER
ACIDIMETERS
ACIDIMETRIC
ACIDIMETRICAL
ACIDIMETRICALLY
ACIDIMETRIES
ACIDIMETRY
ACIDNESSES
ACIDOMETER
ACIDOMETERS
ACIDOPHILE
ACIDOPHILES
ACIDOPHILIC
ACIDOPHILOUS
ACIDOPHILS
ACIDOPHILUS
ACIDOPHILUSES
ACIDULATED
ACIDULATES
ACIDULATING
ACIDULATION
ACIDULATIONS
ACIERATING
ACIERATION
ACIERATIONS
ACINACEOUS
ACINACIFORM
ACINETOBACTER
ACINETOBACTERS
ACKNOWLEDGE
ACKNOWLEDGEABLE
ACKNOWLEDGEABLY
ACKNOWLEDGED
ACKNOWLEDGEDLY
ACKNOWLEDGEMENT
ACKNOWLEDGER
ACKNOWLEDGERS
ACKNOWLEDGES
ACKNOWLEDGING
ACKNOWLEDGMENT
ACKNOWLEDGMENTS
ACOELOMATE
ACOELOMATES
ACOLOUTHIC
ACOLOUTHITE
ACOLOUTHITES
ACOLOUTHOS
ACOLOUTHOSES
ACONITINES
ACOTYLEDON
ACOTYLEDONOUS
ACOTYLEDONS
ACOUSTICAL
ACOUSTICALLY
ACOUSTICIAN
ACOUSTICIANS
ACQUAINTANCE
ACQUAINTANCES
ACQUAINTED
ACQUAINTING
ACQUIESCED
ACQUIESCENCE
ACQUIESCENCES
ACQUIESCENT
ACQUIESCENTLY
ACQUIESCENTS
ACQUIESCES
ACQUIESCING
ACQUIESCINGLY
ACQUIGHTING
ACQUIRABILITIES
ACQUIRABILITY
ACQUIRABLE
ACQUIREMENT
ACQUIREMENTS
ACQUISITION
ACQUISITIONAL
ACQUISITIONS
ACQUISITIVE
ACQUISITIVELY
ACQUISITIVENESS
ACQUISITOR
ACQUISITORS
ACQUITMENT
ACQUITMENTS
ACQUITTALS
ACQUITTANCE
ACQUITTANCED
ACQUITTANCES
ACQUITTANCING
ACQUITTERS
ACQUITTING
ACRIDITIES
ACRIDNESSES
ACRIFLAVIN
ACRIFLAVINE
ACRIFLAVINES
ACRIFLAVINS
ACRIMONIES
ACRIMONIOUS
ACRIMONIOUSLY
ACRIMONIOUSNESS
ACRITARCHS
ACROAMATIC
ACROAMATICAL
ACROBATICALLY
ACROBATICS
ACROBATISM
ACROBATISMS
ACROCARPOUS
ACROCENTRIC
ACROCENTRICS
ACROCYANOSES
ACROCYANOSIS
ACRODROMOUS
ACROGENOUS
ACROGENOUSLY
ACROLITHIC
ACROMEGALIC
ACROMEGALICS
ACROMEGALIES
ACROMEGALY
ACRONICALLY
ACRONYCALLY
ACRONYCHAL
ACRONYCHALLY
ACRONYMANIA
ACRONYMANIAS
ACRONYMICALLY
ACRONYMOUS
ACROPARESTHESIA
ACROPETALLY
ACROPHOBES
ACROPHOBIA
ACROPHOBIAS
ACROPHOBIC
ACROPHOBICS
ACROPHONETIC
ACROPHONIC
ACROPHONIES
ACROPOLISES
ACROSPIRES
ACROSTICAL
ACROSTICALLY
ACROTERIAL
ACROTERION
ACROTERIUM
ACRYLAMIDE
ACRYLAMIDES
ACRYLONITRILE
ACRYLONITRILES
ACTABILITIES
ACTABILITY
ACTINICALLY
ACTINIFORM
ACTINOBACILLI
ACTINOBACILLUS
ACTINOBIOLOGIES
ACTINOBIOLOGY
ACTINOCHEMISTRY
ACTINOLITE
ACTINOLITES
ACTINOMERE
ACTINOMERES
ACTINOMETER
ACTINOMETERS
ACTINOMETRIC
ACTINOMETRICAL
ACTINOMETRIES
ACTINOMETRY
ACTINOMORPHIC
ACTINOMORPHIES
ACTINOMORPHOUS
ACTINOMORPHY
ACTINOMYCES
ACTINOMYCETE
ACTINOMYCETES
ACTINOMYCETOUS
ACTINOMYCIN
ACTINOMYCINS
ACTINOMYCOSES
ACTINOMYCOSIS
ACTINOMYCOTIC
ACTINOPODS
ACTINOTHERAPIES
ACTINOTHERAPY
ACTINOURANIUM
ACTINOURANIUMS
ACTINOZOAN
ACTINOZOANS
ACTIONABLE
ACTIONABLY
ACTIONISTS

ACTIONLESS
ACTIVATING
ACTIVATION
ACTIVATIONS
ACTIVATORS
ACTIVENESS
ACTIVENESSES
ACTIVISING
ACTIVISTIC
ACTIVITIES
ACTIVIZING
ACTOMYOSIN
ACTOMYOSINS
ACTORLIEST
ACTRESSIER
ACTRESSIEST
ACTUALISATION
ACTUALISATIONS
ACTUALISED
ACTUALISES
ACTUALISING
ACTUALISTS
ACTUALITES
ACTUALITIES
ACTUALIZATION
ACTUALIZATIONS
ACTUALIZED
ACTUALIZES
ACTUALIZING
ACTUARIALLY
ACTUATIONS
ACUMINATED
ACUMINATES
ACUMINATING
ACUMINATION
ACUMINATIONS
ACUPRESSURE
ACUPRESSURES
ACUPUNCTURAL
ACUPUNCTURE
ACUPUNCTURES
ACUPUNCTURIST
ACUPUNCTURISTS
ACUTENESSES
ACYCLOVIRS
ACYLATIONS
ADACTYLOUS
ADAMANCIES
ADAMANTEAN
ADAMANTINE
ADAPTABILITIES
ADAPTABILITY
ADAPTABLENESS
ADAPTABLENESSES
ADAPTATION
ADAPTATIONAL
ADAPTATIONALLY
ADAPTATIONS
ADAPTATIVE
ADAPTEDNESS
ADAPTEDNESSES
ADAPTIVELY
ADAPTIVENESS
ADAPTIVENESSES
ADAPTIVITIES
ADAPTIVITY
ADAPTOGENIC
ADAPTOGENS
ADDERBEADS
ADDERSTONE
ADDERSTONES
ADDERWORTS
ADDICTEDNESS
ADDICTEDNESSES
ADDICTIONS
ADDICTIVENESS
ADDICTIVENESSES
ADDITAMENT
ADDITAMENTS
ADDITIONAL
ADDITIONALITIES
ADDITIONALITY
ADDITIONALLY
ADDITITIOUS
ADDITIVELY
ADDITIVITIES
ADDITIVITY
ADDLEMENTS
ADDLEPATED
ADDRESSABILITY
ADDRESSABLE
ADDRESSEES
ADDRESSERS
ADDRESSING
ADDRESSINGS
ADDRESSORS
ADDUCEABLE
ADDUCTIONS
ADELANTADO
ADELANTADOS
ADEMPTIONS
ADENECTOMIES
ADENECTOMY
ADENITISES
ADENOCARCINOMA
ADENOCARCINOMAS
ADENOHYPOPHYSES
ADENOHYPOPHYSIS
ADENOIDECTOMIES
ADENOIDECTOMY
ADENOMATOUS
ADENOPATHIES
ADENOPATHY
ADENOSINES
ADENOVIRAL
ADENOVIRUS
ADENOVIRUSES
ADENYLATES
ADEPTNESSES
ADEQUACIES
ADEQUATELY
ADEQUATENESS
ADEQUATENESSES
ADEQUATIVE
ADHERENCES
ADHERENTLY
ADHESIONAL
ADHESIVELY
ADHESIVENESS
ADHESIVENESSES
ADHIBITING
ADHIBITION
ADHIBITIONS
ADHOCRACIES
ADIABATICALLY
ADIABATICS
ADIACTINIC
ADIAPHORISM
ADIAPHORISMS
ADIAPHORIST
ADIAPHORISTIC
ADIAPHORISTS
ADIAPHORON
ADIAPHOROUS
ADIATHERMANCIES
ADIATHERMANCY
ADIATHERMANOUS
ADIATHERMIC
ADIPOCERES
ADIPOCEROUS
ADIPOCYTES
ADIPOSITIES
ADJACENCES
ADJACENCIES
ADJACENTLY
ADJECTIVAL
ADJECTIVALLY
ADJECTIVELY
ADJECTIVES
ADJOURNING
ADJOURNMENT
ADJOURNMENTS
ADJUDGEMENT
ADJUDGEMENTS
ADJUDGMENT
ADJUDGMENTS
ADJUDICATE
ADJUDICATED
ADJUDICATES
ADJUDICATING
ADJUDICATION
ADJUDICATIONS
ADJUDICATIVE
ADJUDICATOR
ADJUDICATORS
ADJUDICATORY
ADJUNCTION
ADJUNCTIONS
ADJUNCTIVE
ADJUNCTIVELY
ADJURATION
ADJURATIONS
ADJURATORY
ADJUSTABILITIES
ADJUSTABILITY
ADJUSTABLE
ADJUSTABLY
ADJUSTMENT
ADJUSTMENTAL
ADJUSTMENTS
ADJUTANCIES
ADJUVANCIES
ADMEASURED
ADMEASUREMENT
ADMEASUREMENTS
ADMEASURES
ADMEASURING
ADMINICLES
ADMINICULAR
ADMINICULATE
ADMINICULATED
ADMINICULATES
ADMINICULATING
ADMINISTER
ADMINISTERED
ADMINISTERING
ADMINISTERS
ADMINISTRABLE
ADMINISTRANT
ADMINISTRANTS
ADMINISTRATE
ADMINISTRATED
ADMINISTRATES
ADMINISTRATING
ADMINISTRATION
ADMINISTRATIONS
ADMINISTRATIVE
ADMINISTRATOR
ADMINISTRATORS
ADMINISTRATRIX
ADMIRABILITIES
ADMIRABILITY
ADMIRABLENESS
ADMIRABLENESSES
ADMIRALSHIP
ADMIRALSHIPS
ADMIRALTIES
ADMIRANCES
ADMIRATION
ADMIRATIONS
ADMIRATIVE
ADMIRAUNCE
ADMIRAUNCES
ADMIRINGLY
ADMISSIBILITIES
ADMISSIBILITY
ADMISSIBLE
ADMISSIBLENESS
ADMISSIONS
ADMITTABLE

A

ADMITTANCE
ADMITTANCES
ADMITTEDLY
ADMIXTURES
ADMONISHED
ADMONISHER
ADMONISHERS
ADMONISHES
ADMONISHING
ADMONISHINGLY
ADMONISHMENT
ADMONISHMENTS
ADMONITION
ADMONITIONS
ADMONITIVE
ADMONITORILY
ADMONITORS
ADMONITORY
ADNOMINALS
ADOLESCENCE
ADOLESCENCES
ADOLESCENT
ADOLESCENTLY
ADOLESCENTS
ADOPTABILITIES
ADOPTABILITY
ADOPTIANISM
ADOPTIANISMS
ADOPTIANIST
ADOPTIANISTS
ADOPTIONISM
ADOPTIONISMS
ADOPTIONIST
ADOPTIONISTS
ADOPTIVELY
ADORABILITIES
ADORABILITY
ADORABLENESS
ADORABLENESSES
ADORATIONS
ADORNMENTS
ADPRESSING
ADRENALECTOMIES
ADRENALECTOMY
ADRENALINE
ADRENALINES
ADRENALINS
ADRENALISED
ADRENALIZED
ADRENERGIC
ADRENERGICALLY
ADRENOCEPTOR
ADRENOCEPTORS
ADRENOCHROME
ADRENOCHROMES
ADRENOCORTICAL
ADRIAMYCIN
ADRIAMYCINS
ADROITNESS
ADROITNESSES
ADSCITITIOUS
ADSCITITIOUSLY
ADSCRIPTION
ADSCRIPTIONS
ADSORBABILITIES
ADSORBABILITY
ADSORBABLE
ADSORBATES
ADSORBENTS
ADSORPTION
ADSORPTIONS
ADSORPTIVE
ADULARESCENCE
ADULARESCENCES
ADULARESCENT
ADULATIONS
ADULTERANT
ADULTERANTS
ADULTERATE
ADULTERATED
ADULTERATES
ADULTERATING
ADULTERATION
ADULTERATIONS
ADULTERATOR
ADULTERATORS
ADULTERERS
ADULTERESS
ADULTERESSES
ADULTERIES
ADULTERINE
ADULTERINES
ADULTERISE
ADULTERISED
ADULTERISES
ADULTERISING
ADULTERIZE
ADULTERIZED
ADULTERIZES
ADULTERIZING
ADULTEROUS
ADULTEROUSLY
ADULTESCENT
ADULTESCENTS
ADULTHOODS
ADULTNESSES
ADULTRESSES
ADUMBRATED
ADUMBRATES
ADUMBRATING
ADUMBRATION
ADUMBRATIONS
ADUMBRATIVE
ADUMBRATIVELY
ADUNCITIES
ADVANCEMENT
ADVANCEMENTS
ADVANCINGLY
ADVANTAGEABLE
ADVANTAGED
ADVANTAGEOUS
ADVANTAGEOUSLY
ADVANTAGES
ADVANTAGING
ADVECTIONS
ADVENTITIA
ADVENTITIAL
ADVENTITIAS
ADVENTITIOUS
ADVENTITIOUSLY
ADVENTIVES
ADVENTURED
ADVENTUREFUL
ADVENTURER
ADVENTURERS
ADVENTURES
ADVENTURESOME
ADVENTURESS
ADVENTURESSES
ADVENTURING
ADVENTURINGS
ADVENTURISM
ADVENTURISMS
ADVENTURIST
ADVENTURISTIC
ADVENTURISTS
ADVENTUROUS
ADVENTUROUSLY
ADVENTUROUSNESS
ADVERBIALISE
ADVERBIALISED
ADVERBIALISES
ADVERBIALISING
ADVERBIALIZE
ADVERBIALIZED
ADVERBIALIZES
ADVERBIALIZING
ADVERBIALLY
ADVERBIALS
ADVERGAMING
ADVERGAMINGS
ADVERSARIA
ADVERSARIAL
ADVERSARIES
ADVERSARINESS
ADVERSARINESSES
ADVERSATIVE
ADVERSATIVELY
ADVERSATIVES
ADVERSENESS
ADVERSENESSES
ADVERSITIES
ADVERTENCE
ADVERTENCES
ADVERTENCIES
ADVERTENCY
ADVERTENTLY
ADVERTISED
ADVERTISEMENT
ADVERTISEMENTS
ADVERTISER
ADVERTISERS
ADVERTISES
ADVERTISING
ADVERTISINGS
ADVERTIZED
ADVERTIZEMENT
ADVERTIZEMENTS
ADVERTIZER
ADVERTIZERS
ADVERTIZES
ADVERTIZING
ADVERTIZINGS
ADVERTORIAL
ADVERTORIALS
ADVISABILITIES
ADVISABILITY
ADVISABLENESS
ADVISABLENESSES
ADVISATORY
ADVISEDNESS
ADVISEDNESSES
ADVISEMENT
ADVISEMENTS
ADVISERSHIP
ADVISERSHIPS
ADVISORATE
ADVISORATES
ADVISORIES
ADVOCACIES
ADVOCATING
ADVOCATION
ADVOCATIONS
ADVOCATIVE
ADVOCATORS
ADVOCATORY
ADVOUTRERS
ADVOUTRIES
AECIDIOSPORE
AECIDIOSPORES
AECIDOSPORE
AECIDOSPORES
AECIOSPORE
AECIOSPORES
AEDILESHIP
AEDILESHIPS
AEOLIPILES
AEOLIPYLES
AEOLOTROPIC
AEOLOTROPIES
AEOLOTROPY
AEPYORNISES
AERENCHYMA
AERENCHYMAS
AERENCHYMATOUS
AERIALISTS
AERIALITIES
AERIFICATION
AERIFICATIONS
AEROACOUSTICS

AEROBALLISTICS
AEROBATICS
AEROBICALLY
AEROBICISE
AEROBICISED
AEROBICISES
AEROBICISING
AEROBICIST
AEROBICISTS
AEROBICIZE
AEROBICIZED
AEROBICIZES
AEROBICIZING
AEROBIOLOGICAL
AEROBIOLOGIES
AEROBIOLOGIST
AEROBIOLOGISTS
AEROBIOLOGY
AEROBIONTS
AEROBIOSES
AEROBIOSIS
AEROBIOTIC
AEROBIOTICALLY
AEROBRAKED
AEROBRAKES
AEROBRAKING
AEROBRAKINGS
AEROBUSSES
AERODIGESTIVE
AERODONETICS
AERODROMES
AERODYNAMIC
AERODYNAMICAL
AERODYNAMICALLY
AERODYNAMICIST
AERODYNAMICISTS
AERODYNAMICS
AEROELASTIC
AEROELASTICIAN
AEROELASTICIANS
AEROELASTICITY
AEROEMBOLISM
AEROEMBOLISMS
AEROGENERATOR
AEROGENERATORS
AEROGRAMME
AEROGRAMMES
AEROGRAPHIES
AEROGRAPHS
AEROGRAPHY
AEROHYDROPLANE
AEROHYDROPLANES
AEROLITHOLOGIES
AEROLITHOLOGY
AEROLOGICAL
AEROLOGIES
AEROLOGIST
AEROLOGISTS
AEROMAGNETIC
AEROMANCIES
AEROMECHANIC
AEROMECHANICAL
AEROMECHANICS
AEROMEDICAL
AEROMEDICINE
AEROMEDICINES
AEROMETERS
AEROMETRIC
AEROMETRIES
AEROMODELLING
AEROMODELLINGS
AEROMOTORS
AERONAUTIC
AERONAUTICAL
AERONAUTICALLY
AERONAUTICS
AERONEUROSES
AERONEUROSIS
AERONOMERS
AERONOMICAL
AERONOMIES
AERONOMIST
AERONOMISTS
AEROPAUSES
AEROPHAGIA
AEROPHAGIAS
AEROPHAGIES
AEROPHOBES
AEROPHOBIA
AEROPHOBIAS
AEROPHOBIC
AEROPHONES
AEROPHORES
AEROPHYTES
AEROPLANES
AEROPLANKTON
AEROPLANKTONS
AEROPULSES
AEROSCOPES
AEROSHELLS
AEROSIDERITE
AEROSIDERITES
AEROSOLISATION
AEROSOLISATIONS
AEROSOLISE
AEROSOLISED
AEROSOLISES
AEROSOLISING
AEROSOLIZATION
AEROSOLIZATIONS
AEROSOLIZE
AEROSOLIZED
AEROSOLIZES
AEROSOLIZING
AEROSPACES
AEROSPHERE
AEROSPHERES
AEROSPIKES
AEROSTATIC
AEROSTATICAL
AEROSTATICS
AEROSTATION
AEROSTATIONS
AEROSTRUCTURE
AEROSTRUCTURES
AEROTACTIC
AEROTRAINS
AEROTROPIC
AEROTROPISM
AEROTROPISMS
AERUGINOUS
AESTHESIAS
AESTHESIOGEN
AESTHESIOGENIC
AESTHESIOGENS
AESTHETICAL
AESTHETICALLY
AESTHETICIAN
AESTHETICIANS
AESTHETICISE
AESTHETICISED
AESTHETICISES
AESTHETICISING
AESTHETICISM
AESTHETICISMS
AESTHETICIST
AESTHETICISTS
AESTHETICIZE
AESTHETICIZED
AESTHETICIZES
AESTHETICIZING
AESTHETICS
AESTIVATED
AESTIVATES
AESTIVATING
AESTIVATION
AESTIVATIONS
AESTIVATOR
AESTIVATORS
AETHEREALITIES
AETHEREALITY
AETHEREALLY
AETHRIOSCOPE
AETHRIOSCOPES
AETIOLOGICAL
AETIOLOGICALLY
AETIOLOGIES
AETIOLOGIST
AETIOLOGISTS
AFFABILITIES
AFFABILITY
AFFECTABILITIES
AFFECTABILITY
AFFECTABLE
AFFECTATION
AFFECTATIONS
AFFECTEDLY
AFFECTEDNESS
AFFECTEDNESSES
AFFECTINGLY
AFFECTIONAL
AFFECTIONALLY
AFFECTIONATE
AFFECTIONATELY
AFFECTIONED
AFFECTIONING
AFFECTIONLESS
AFFECTIONS
AFFECTIVELY
AFFECTIVENESS
AFFECTIVENESSES
AFFECTIVITIES
AFFECTIVITY
AFFECTLESS
AFFECTLESSNESS
AFFEERMENT
AFFEERMENTS
AFFENPINSCHER
AFFENPINSCHERS
AFFERENTLY
AFFETTUOSO
AFFIANCING
AFFICIONADO
AFFICIONADOS
AFFIDAVITS
AFFILIABLE
AFFILIATED
AFFILIATES
AFFILIATING
AFFILIATION
AFFILIATIONS
AFFINITIES
AFFINITIVE
AFFIRMABLE
AFFIRMANCE
AFFIRMANCES
AFFIRMANTS
AFFIRMATION
AFFIRMATIONS
AFFIRMATIVE
AFFIRMATIVELY
AFFIRMATIVES
AFFIRMATORY
AFFIRMINGLY
AFFIXATION
AFFIXATIONS
AFFIXMENTS
AFFIXTURES
AFFLATIONS
AFFLATUSES
AFFLICTERS
AFFLICTING
AFFLICTINGS
AFFLICTION
AFFLICTIONS
AFFLICTIVE
AFFLICTIVELY
AFFLUENCES
AFFLUENCIES
AFFLUENTIAL

A

AFFLUENTIALS
AFFLUENTLY
AFFLUENTNESS
AFFLUENTNESSES
AFFLUENZAS
AFFLUXIONS
AFFOORDING
AFFORCEMENT
AFFORCEMENTS
AFFORDABILITIES
AFFORDABILITY
AFFORDABLE
AFFORDABLY
AFFORESTABLE
AFFORESTATION
AFFORESTATIONS
AFFORESTED
AFFORESTING
AFFRANCHISE
AFFRANCHISED
AFFRANCHISEMENT
AFFRANCHISES
AFFRANCHISING
AFFRAPPING
AFFREIGHTMENT
AFFREIGHTMENTS
AFFRICATED
AFFRICATES
AFFRICATING
AFFRICATION
AFFRICATIONS
AFFRICATIVE
AFFRICATIVES
AFFRIGHTED
AFFRIGHTEDLY
AFFRIGHTEN
AFFRIGHTENED
AFFRIGHTENING
AFFRIGHTENS
AFFRIGHTFUL
AFFRIGHTING
AFFRIGHTMENT
AFFRIGHTMENTS
AFFRONTING
AFFRONTINGLY
AFFRONTINGS
AFFRONTIVE
AFICIONADA
AFICIONADAS
AFICIONADO
AFICIONADOS
AFLATOXINS
AFOREMENTIONED
AFORETHOUGHT
AFORETHOUGHTS
AFRORMOSIA
AFRORMOSIAS
AFTERBIRTH
AFTERBIRTHS
AFTERBODIES
AFTERBRAIN
AFTERBRAINS
AFTERBURNER
AFTERBURNERS
AFTERBURNING
AFTERBURNINGS
AFTERBURNS
AFTERCARES
AFTERCLAPS
AFTERDAMPS
AFTERDECKS
AFTEREFFECT
AFTEREFFECTS
AFTEREYEING
AFTEREYING
AFTERGAMES
AFTERGLOWS
AFTERGRASS
AFTERGRASSES
AFTERGROWTH
AFTERGROWTHS
AFTERGUARD
AFTERGUARDS
AFTERHEATS
AFTERIMAGE
AFTERIMAGES
AFTERLIFES
AFTERLIVES
AFTERMARKET
AFTERMARKETS
AFTERMASTS
AFTERMATHS
AFTERNOONS
AFTERPAINS
AFTERPARTIES
AFTERPARTY
AFTERPEAKS
AFTERPIECE
AFTERPIECES
AFTERSALES
AFTERSENSATION
AFTERSENSATIONS
AFTERSHAFT
AFTERSHAFTS
AFTERSHAVE
AFTERSHAVES
AFTERSHOCK
AFTERSHOCKS
AFTERSHOWS
AFTERSUPPER
AFTERSUPPERS
AFTERSWARM
AFTERSWARMS
AFTERTASTE
AFTERTASTES
AFTERTHOUGHT
AFTERTHOUGHTS
AFTERTIMES
AFTERTREATMENT
AFTERTREATMENTS
AFTERWARDS
AFTERWORDS
AFTERWORLD
AFTERWORLDS
AGALACTIAS
AGALMATOLITE
AGALMATOLITES
AGAMICALLY
AGAMOGENESES
AGAMOGENESIS
AGAMOGENETIC
AGAMOGONIES
AGAMOSPERMIES
AGAMOSPERMY
AGAPANTHUS
AGAPANTHUSES
AGARICACEOUS
AGATEWARES
AGATHODAIMON
AGATHODAIMONS
AGEDNESSES
AGELESSNESS
AGELESSNESSES
AGENDALESS
AGENTIVITIES
AGENTIVITY
AGFLATIONS
AGGIORNAMENTI
AGGIORNAMENTO
AGGIORNAMENTOS
AGGLOMERATE
AGGLOMERATED
AGGLOMERATES
AGGLOMERATING
AGGLOMERATION
AGGLOMERATIONS
AGGLOMERATIVE
AGGLUTINABILITY
AGGLUTINABLE
AGGLUTINANT
AGGLUTINANTS
AGGLUTINATE
AGGLUTINATED
AGGLUTINATES
AGGLUTINATING
AGGLUTINATION
AGGLUTINATIONS
AGGLUTINATIVE
AGGLUTININ
AGGLUTININS
AGGLUTINOGEN
AGGLUTINOGENIC
AGGLUTINOGENS
AGGRADATION
AGGRADATIONS
AGGRANDISE
AGGRANDISED
AGGRANDISEMENT
AGGRANDISEMENTS
AGGRANDISER
AGGRANDISERS
AGGRANDISES
AGGRANDISING
AGGRANDIZE
AGGRANDIZED
AGGRANDIZEMENT
AGGRANDIZEMENTS
AGGRANDIZER
AGGRANDIZERS
AGGRANDIZES
AGGRANDIZING
AGGRAVATED
AGGRAVATES
AGGRAVATING
AGGRAVATINGLY
AGGRAVATION
AGGRAVATIONS
AGGREGATED
AGGREGATELY
AGGREGATENESS
AGGREGATENESSES
AGGREGATES
AGGREGATING
AGGREGATION
AGGREGATIONAL
AGGREGATIONS
AGGREGATIVE
AGGREGATIVELY
AGGREGATOR
AGGREGATORS
AGGRESSING
AGGRESSION
AGGRESSIONS
AGGRESSIVE
AGGRESSIVELY
AGGRESSIVENESS
AGGRESSIVITIES
AGGRESSIVITY
AGGRESSORS
AGGRIEVEDLY
AGGRIEVEMENT
AGGRIEVEMENTS
AGGRIEVING
AGILENESSES
AGISTMENTS
AGITATEDLY
AGITATIONAL
AGITATIONS
AGNATICALLY
AGNOIOLOGIES
AGNOIOLOGY
AGNOLOTTIS
AGNOSTICISM
AGNOSTICISMS
AGONISEDLY
AGONISINGLY
AGONISTICAL
AGONISTICALLY
AGONISTICS
AGONIZEDLY

AGONIZINGLY
AGONOTHETES
AGORAPHOBE
AGORAPHOBES
AGORAPHOBIA
AGORAPHOBIAS
AGORAPHOBIC
AGORAPHOBICS
AGRAMMATICAL
AGRANULOCYTE
AGRANULOCYTES
AGRANULOCYTOSES
AGRANULOCYTOSIS
AGRANULOSES
AGRANULOSIS
AGRARIANISM
AGRARIANISMS
AGREEABILITIES
AGREEABILITY
AGREEABLENESS
AGREEABLENESSES
AGREEMENTS
AGREGATION
AGREGATIONS
AGRIBUSINESS
AGRIBUSINESSES
AGRIBUSINESSMAN
AGRIBUSINESSMEN
AGRICHEMICAL
AGRICHEMICALS
AGRICULTURAL
AGRICULTURALIST
AGRICULTURALLY
AGRICULTURE
AGRICULTURES
AGRICULTURIST
AGRICULTURISTS
AGRIFOODSTUFFS
AGRIMONIES
AGRIOLOGIES
AGRIPRODUCT
AGRIPRODUCTS
AGRITOURISM
AGRITOURISMS
AGRITOURIST
AGRITOURISTS
AGROBIOLOGICAL
AGROBIOLOGIES
AGROBIOLOGIST
AGROBIOLOGISTS
AGROBIOLOGY
AGROBUSINESS
AGROBUSINESSES
AGROCHEMICAL
AGROCHEMICALS
AGRODOLCES
AGROFORESTER
AGROFORESTERS
AGROFORESTRIES
AGROFORESTRY
AGROINDUSTRIAL
AGROINDUSTRIES
AGROINDUSTRY
AGROLOGICAL
AGROLOGIES
AGROLOGIST
AGROLOGISTS
AGRONOMIAL
AGRONOMICAL
AGRONOMICALLY
AGRONOMICS
AGRONOMIES
AGRONOMIST
AGRONOMISTS
AGROSTEMMA
AGROSTEMMAS
AGROSTEMMATA
AGROSTOLOGIC
AGROSTOLOGICAL
AGROSTOLOGIES
AGROSTOLOGIST
AGROSTOLOGISTS
AGROSTOLOGY
AGROTERRORISM
AGROTERRORISMS
AGROTOURISM
AGROTOURISMS
AGROTOURIST
AGROTOURISTS
AGRYPNOTIC
AGRYPNOTICS
AGTERSKOTS
AGUARDIENTE
AGUARDIENTES
AHISTORICAL
AHORSEBACK
AHURUHURUS
AICHMOPHOBIA
AICHMOPHOBIAS
AIGUILLETTE
AIGUILLETTES
AILANTHUSES
AILOUROPHILE
AILOUROPHILES
AILOUROPHILIA
AILOUROPHILIAS
AILOUROPHILIC
AILOUROPHOBE
AILOUROPHOBES
AILOUROPHOBIA
AILOUROPHOBIAS
AILOUROPHOBIC
AILUROPHILE
AILUROPHILES
AILUROPHILIA
AILUROPHILIAS
AILUROPHILIC
AILUROPHOBE
AILUROPHOBES
AILUROPHOBIA
AILUROPHOBIAS
AILUROPHOBIC
AIMLESSNESS
AIMLESSNESSES
AIRBALLING
AIRBOARDING
AIRBOARDINGS
AIRBRUSHED
AIRBRUSHES
AIRBRUSHING
AIRBURSTED
AIRBURSTING
AIRCOACHES
AIRCRAFTMAN
AIRCRAFTMEN
AIRCRAFTSMAN
AIRCRAFTSMEN
AIRCRAFTSWOMAN
AIRCRAFTSWOMEN
AIRCRAFTWOMAN
AIRCRAFTWOMEN
AIRDROPPED
AIRDROPPING
AIRFREIGHT
AIRFREIGHTED
AIRFREIGHTING
AIRFREIGHTS
AIRINESSES
AIRLESSNESS
AIRLESSNESSES
AIRLIFTING
AIRMAILING
AIRMANSHIP
AIRMANSHIPS
AIRPROOFED
AIRPROOFING
AIRSICKNESS
AIRSICKNESSES
AIRSTREAMS
AIRSTRIKES
AIRTIGHTNESS
AIRTIGHTNESSES
AIRWORTHIER
AIRWORTHIEST
AIRWORTHINESS
AIRWORTHINESSES
AITCHBONES
AKATHISIAS
AKOLOUTHOS
AKOLOUTHOSES
AKOLUTHOSES
ALABAMINES
ALABANDINE
ALABANDINES
ALABANDITE
ALABANDITES
ALABASTERS
ALABASTRINE
ALABLASTER
ALABLASTERS
ALACRITIES
ALACRITOUS
ALARMINGLY
ALBARELLOS
ALBATROSSES
ALBERTITES
ALBESCENCE
ALBESCENCES
ALBESPINES
ALBESPYNES
ALBINESSES
ALBINISTIC
ALBINOISMS
ALBITISING
ALBITIZING
ALBUGINEOUS
ALBUMBLATT
ALBUMBLATTER
ALBUMBLATTS
ALBUMENISE
ALBUMENISED
ALBUMENISES
ALBUMENISING
ALBUMENIZE
ALBUMENIZED
ALBUMENIZES
ALBUMENIZING
ALBUMINATE
ALBUMINATES
ALBUMINISE
ALBUMINISED
ALBUMINISES
ALBUMINISING
ALBUMINIZE
ALBUMINIZED
ALBUMINIZES
ALBUMINIZING
ALBUMINOID
ALBUMINOIDS
ALBUMINOUS
ALBUMINURIA
ALBUMINURIAS
ALBUMINURIC
ALBUTEROLS
ALCAICERIA
ALCAICERIAS
ALCARRAZAS
ALCATRASES
ALCHEMICAL
ALCHEMICALLY
ALCHEMISED
ALCHEMISES
ALCHEMISING
ALCHEMISTIC
ALCHEMISTICAL
ALCHEMISTS
ALCHEMIZED
ALCHEMIZES
ALCHEMIZING
ALCHERINGA

ALCHERINGAS
ALCOHOLICALLY
ALCOHOLICITIES
ALCOHOLICITY
ALCOHOLICS
ALCOHOLISATION
ALCOHOLISATIONS
ALCOHOLISE
ALCOHOLISED
ALCOHOLISES
ALCOHOLISING
ALCOHOLISM
ALCOHOLISMS
ALCOHOLIZATION
ALCOHOLIZATIONS
ALCOHOLIZE
ALCOHOLIZED
ALCOHOLIZES
ALCOHOLIZING
ALCOHOLOMETER
ALCOHOLOMETERS
ALCOHOLOMETRIES
ALCOHOLOMETRY
ALCYONARIAN
ALCYONARIANS
ALDERFLIES
ALDERMANIC
ALDERMANITIES
ALDERMANITY
ALDERMANLIER
ALDERMANLIEST
ALDERMANLIKE
ALDERMANLY
ALDERMANRIES
ALDERMANRY
ALDERMANSHIP
ALDERMANSHIPS
ALDERWOMAN
ALDERWOMEN
ALDOHEXOSE
ALDOHEXOSES
ALDOLISATION
ALDOLISATIONS
ALDOLIZATION
ALDOLIZATIONS
ALDOPENTOSE
ALDOPENTOSES
ALDOSTERONE

ALDOSTERONES
ALDOSTERONISM
ALDOSTERONISMS
ALEATORIES
ALEBENCHES
ALECTRYONS
ALEGGEAUNCE
ALEGGEAUNCES
ALEMBICATED
ALEMBICATION
ALEMBICATIONS
ALEMBROTHS
ALERTNESSES
ALEXANDERS
ALEXANDERSES
ALEXANDRINE
ALEXANDRINES
ALEXANDRITE
ALEXANDRITES
ALEXIPHARMAKON
ALEXIPHARMAKONS
ALEXIPHARMIC
ALEXIPHARMICS
ALEXITHYMIA
ALEXITHYMIAS
ALFILARIAS
ALFILERIAS
ALGAECIDES
ALGARROBAS
ALGARROBOS
ALGEBRAICAL
ALGEBRAICALLY
ALGEBRAIST
ALGEBRAISTS
ALGIDITIES
ALGIDNESSES
ALGOLAGNIA
ALGOLAGNIAC
ALGOLAGNIACS
ALGOLAGNIAS
ALGOLAGNIC
ALGOLAGNIST
ALGOLAGNISTS
ALGOLOGICAL
ALGOLOGICALLY
ALGOLOGIES
ALGOLOGIST
ALGOLOGISTS

ALGOMETERS
ALGOMETRIES
ALGOPHOBIA
ALGOPHOBIAS
ALGORISMIC
ALGORITHMIC
ALGORITHMICALLY
ALGORITHMS
ALIENABILITIES
ALIENABILITY
ALIENATING
ALIENATION
ALIENATIONS
ALIENATORS
ALIENNESSES
ALIGHTMENT
ALIGHTMENTS
ALIGNMENTS
ALIKENESSES
ALIMENTARY
ALIMENTATION
ALIMENTATIONS
ALIMENTATIVE
ALIMENTING
ALIMENTIVENESS
ALINEATION
ALINEATIONS
ALINEMENTS
ALISMACEOUS
ALITERACIES
ALITERATES
ALIVENESSES
ALIZARINES
ALKAHESTIC
ALKALESCENCE
ALKALESCENCES
ALKALESCENCIES
ALKALESCENCY
ALKALESCENT
ALKALIFIED
ALKALIFIES
ALKALIFYING
ALKALIMETER
ALKALIMETERS
ALKALIMETRIC
ALKALIMETRIES
ALKALIMETRY
ALKALINISATION

ALKALINISATIONS
ALKALINISE
ALKALINISED
ALKALINISES
ALKALINISING
ALKALINITIES
ALKALINITY
ALKALINIZATION
ALKALINIZATIONS
ALKALINIZE
ALKALINIZED
ALKALINIZES
ALKALINIZING
ALKALISABLE
ALKALISERS
ALKALISING
ALKALIZABLE
ALKALIZERS
ALKALIZING
ALKALOIDAL
ALKYLATING
ALKYLATION
ALKYLATIONS
ALLANTOIDAL
ALLANTOIDES
ALLANTOIDS
ALLANTOINS
ALLANTOISES
ALLARGANDO
ALLAYMENTS
ALLEGATION
ALLEGATIONS
ALLEGEANCE
ALLEGEANCES
ALLEGIANCE
ALLEGIANCES
ALLEGIANTS
ALLEGORICAL
ALLEGORICALLY
ALLEGORICALNESS
ALLEGORIES
ALLEGORISATION
ALLEGORISATIONS
ALLEGORISE
ALLEGORISED
ALLEGORISER
ALLEGORISERS
ALLEGORISES

ALLEGORISING
ALLEGORIST
ALLEGORISTS
ALLEGORIZATION
ALLEGORIZATIONS
ALLEGORIZE
ALLEGORIZED
ALLEGORIZER
ALLEGORIZERS
ALLEGORIZES
ALLEGORIZING
ALLEGRETTO
ALLEGRETTOS
ALLELOMORPH
ALLELOMORPHIC
ALLELOMORPHISM
ALLELOMORPHISMS
ALLELOMORPHS
ALLELOPATHIC
ALLELOPATHIES
ALLELOPATHY
ALLELUIAHS
ALLEMANDES
ALLERGENIC
ALLERGENICITIES
ALLERGENICITY
ALLERGISTS
ALLETHRINS
ALLEVIANTS
ALLEVIATED
ALLEVIATES
ALLEVIATING
ALLEVIATION
ALLEVIATIONS
ALLEVIATIVE
ALLEVIATOR
ALLEVIATORS
ALLEVIATORY
ALLHALLOND
ALLHALLOWEN
ALLHALLOWN
ALLHOLLOWN
ALLIACEOUS
ALLICHOLIES
ALLIGARTAS
ALLIGATING
ALLIGATION
ALLIGATIONS

ALLIGATORS
ALLINEATION
ALLINEATIONS
ALLITERATE
ALLITERATED
ALLITERATES
ALLITERATING
ALLITERATION
ALLITERATIONS
ALLITERATIVE
ALLITERATIVELY
ALLNIGHTER
ALLNIGHTERS
ALLOANTIBODIES
ALLOANTIBODY
ALLOANTIGEN
ALLOANTIGENS
ALLOCARPIES
ALLOCATABLE
ALLOCATING
ALLOCATION
ALLOCATIONS
ALLOCATORS
ALLOCHEIRIA
ALLOCHEIRIAS
ALLOCHIRIA
ALLOCHIRIAS
ALLOCHTHONOUS
ALLOCUTION
ALLOCUTIONS
ALLODYNIAS
ALLOGAMIES
ALLOGAMOUS
ALLOGENEIC
ALLOGRAFTED
ALLOGRAFTING
ALLOGRAFTS
ALLOGRAPHIC
ALLOGRAPHS
ALLOIOSTROPHOS
ALLOMERISM
ALLOMERISMS
ALLOMEROUS
ALLOMETRIC
ALLOMETRIES
ALLOMORPHIC
ALLOMORPHISM
ALLOMORPHISMS
ALLOMORPHS
ALLONYMOUS
ALLOPATHIC
ALLOPATHICALLY
ALLOPATHIES
ALLOPATHIST
ALLOPATHISTS
ALLOPATRIC
ALLOPATRICALLY
ALLOPATRIES
ALLOPHANES
ALLOPHONES
ALLOPHONIC
ALLOPLASMIC
ALLOPLASMS
ALLOPLASTIC
ALLOPOLYPLOID
ALLOPOLYPLOIDS
ALLOPOLYPLOIDY
ALLOPURINOL
ALLOPURINOLS
ALLOSAURUS
ALLOSAURUSES
ALLOSTERIC
ALLOSTERICALLY
ALLOSTERIES
ALLOTETRAPLOID
ALLOTETRAPLOIDS
ALLOTETRAPLOIDY
ALLOTHEISM
ALLOTHEISMS
ALLOTMENTS
ALLOTRIOMORPHIC
ALLOTROPES
ALLOTROPIC
ALLOTROPICALLY
ALLOTROPIES
ALLOTROPISM
ALLOTROPISMS
ALLOTROPOUS
ALLOTTERIES
ALLOTYPICALLY
ALLOTYPIES
ALLOWABILITIES
ALLOWABILITY
ALLOWABLENESS
ALLOWABLENESSES
ALLOWABLES
ALLOWANCED
ALLOWANCES
ALLOWANCING
ALLUREMENT
ALLUREMENTS
ALLURINGLY
ALLUSIVELY
ALLUSIVENESS
ALLUSIVENESSES
ALLWEATHER
ALLWEATHERS
ALLYCHOLLIES
ALLYCHOLLY
ALMACANTAR
ALMACANTARS
ALMANDINES
ALMANDITES
ALMIGHTIER
ALMIGHTIEST
ALMIGHTILY
ALMIGHTINESS
ALMIGHTINESSES
ALMONDIEST
ALMONDITES
ALMSGIVERS
ALMSGIVING
ALMSGIVINGS
ALMSHOUSES
ALMUCANTAR
ALMUCANTARS
ALOESWOODS
ALOGICALLY
ALONENESSES
ALONGSHORE
ALONGSHOREMAN
ALONGSHOREMEN
ALOOFNESSES
ALOPECOIDS
ALPARGATAS
ALPENGLOWS
ALPENHORNS
ALPENSTOCK
ALPENSTOCKS
ALPESTRINE
ALPHABETARIAN
ALPHABETARIANS
ALPHABETED
ALPHABETIC
ALPHABETICAL
ALPHABETICALLY
ALPHABETIFORM
ALPHABETING
ALPHABETISATION
ALPHABETISE
ALPHABETISED
ALPHABETISER
ALPHABETISERS
ALPHABETISES
ALPHABETISING
ALPHABETIZATION
ALPHABETIZE
ALPHABETIZED
ALPHABETIZER
ALPHABETIZERS
ALPHABETIZES
ALPHABETIZING
ALPHAMERIC
ALPHAMERICAL
ALPHAMERICALLY
ALPHAMETIC
ALPHAMETICS
ALPHANUMERIC
ALPHANUMERICAL
ALPHANUMERICS
ALPHASORTED
ALPHASORTING
ALPHASORTS
ALPHATESTED
ALPHATESTING
ALPHATESTS
ALPHOSISES
ALSTROEMERIA
ALSTROEMERIAS
ALTALTISSIMO
ALTALTISSIMOS
ALTARPIECE
ALTARPIECES
ALTAZIMUTH
ALTAZIMUTHS
ALTERABILITIES
ALTERABILITY
ALTERATION
ALTERATIONS
ALTERATIVE
ALTERATIVES
ALTERCATED
ALTERCATES
ALTERCATING
ALTERCATION
ALTERCATIONS
ALTERCATIVE
ALTERITIES
ALTERNANCE
ALTERNANCES
ALTERNANTS
ALTERNATED
ALTERNATELY
ALTERNATES
ALTERNATIM
ALTERNATING
ALTERNATION
ALTERNATIONS
ALTERNATIVE
ALTERNATIVELY
ALTERNATIVENESS
ALTERNATIVES
ALTERNATOR
ALTERNATORS
ALTIGRAPHS
ALTIMETERS
ALTIMETRICAL
ALTIMETRICALLY
ALTIMETRIES
ALTIPLANOS
ALTISONANT
ALTISSIMOS
ALTITONANT
ALTITUDINAL
ALTITUDINARIAN
ALTITUDINARIANS
ALTITUDINOUS
ALTOCUMULI
ALTOCUMULUS
ALTOGETHER
ALTOGETHERS
ALTORUFFLED
ALTOSTRATI
ALTOSTRATUS
ALTRICIALS
ALTRUISTIC
ALTRUISTICALLY
ALUMINATES
ALUMINIDES
ALUMINIFEROUS

ALUMINISED
ALUMINISES
ALUMINISING
ALUMINIUMS
ALUMINIZED
ALUMINIZES
ALUMINIZING
ALUMINOSILICATE
ALUMINOSITIES
ALUMINOSITY
ALUMINOTHERMIES
ALUMINOTHERMY
ALUMSTONES
ALVEOLARLY
ALVEOLATION
ALVEOLATIONS
ALVEOLITIS
ALVEOLITISES
ALYCOMPAINE
ALYCOMPAINES
AMAKWEREKWERE
AMALGAMATE
AMALGAMATED
AMALGAMATES
AMALGAMATING
AMALGAMATION
AMALGAMATIONS
AMALGAMATIVE
AMALGAMATOR
AMALGAMATORS
AMANTADINE
AMANTADINES
AMANUENSES
AMANUENSIS
AMARACUSES
AMARANTACEOUS
AMARANTHACEOUS
AMARANTHINE
AMARANTINE
AMARANTINS
AMARYLLIDACEOUS
AMARYLLIDS
AMARYLLISES
AMASSMENTS
AMATEURISH
AMATEURISHLY
AMATEURISHNESS
AMATEURISM
AMATEURISMS
AMATEURSHIP
AMATEURSHIPS
AMATIVENESS
AMATIVENESSES
AMATORIALLY
AMATORIOUS
AMAZEBALLS
AMAZEDNESS
AMAZEDNESSES
AMAZEMENTS
AMAZONIANS
AMAZONITES
AMAZONSTONE
AMAZONSTONES
AMBAGITORY
AMBASSADOR
AMBASSADORIAL
AMBASSADORS
AMBASSADORSHIP
AMBASSADORSHIPS
AMBASSADRESS
AMBASSADRESSES
AMBASSAGES
AMBERGRISES
AMBERJACKS
AMBIDENTATE
AMBIDEXTER
AMBIDEXTERITIES
AMBIDEXTERITY
AMBIDEXTEROUS
AMBIDEXTERS
AMBIDEXTROUS
AMBIDEXTROUSLY
AMBIGUITIES
AMBIGUOUSLY
AMBIGUOUSNESS
AMBIGUOUSNESSES
AMBILATERAL
AMBIOPHONIES
AMBIOPHONY
AMBISEXUAL
AMBISEXUALITIES
AMBISEXUALITY
AMBISEXUALS
AMBISONICS
AMBITIONED
AMBITIONING
AMBITIONLESS
AMBITIOUSLY
AMBITIOUSNESS
AMBITIOUSNESSES
AMBIVALENCE
AMBIVALENCES
AMBIVALENCIES
AMBIVALENCY
AMBIVALENT
AMBIVALENTLY
AMBIVERSION
AMBIVERSIONS
AMBLYGONITE
AMBLYGONITES
AMBLYOPIAS
AMBOCEPTOR
AMBOCEPTORS
AMBOSEXUAL
AMBROSIALLY
AMBROTYPES
AMBULACRAL
AMBULACRUM
AMBULANCEMAN
AMBULANCEMEN
AMBULANCES
AMBULANCEWOMAN
AMBULANCEWOMEN
AMBULATING
AMBULATION
AMBULATIONS
AMBULATORIES
AMBULATORILY
AMBULATORS
AMBULATORY
AMBULETTES
AMBUSCADED
AMBUSCADER
AMBUSCADERS
AMBUSCADES
AMBUSCADING
AMBUSCADOES
AMBUSCADOS
AMBUSHMENT
AMBUSHMENTS
AMEBOCYTES
AMELIORABLE
AMELIORANT
AMELIORANTS
AMELIORATE
AMELIORATED
AMELIORATES
AMELIORATING
AMELIORATION
AMELIORATIONS
AMELIORATIVE
AMELIORATOR
AMELIORATORS
AMELIORATORY
AMELOBLAST
AMELOBLASTS
AMELOGENESES
AMELOGENESIS
AMENABILITIES
AMENABILITY
AMENABLENESS
AMENABLENESSES
AMENAUNCES
AMENDATORY
AMENDMENTS
AMENORRHEA
AMENORRHEAS
AMENORRHEIC
AMENORRHOEA
AMENORRHOEAS
AMENTACEOUS
AMENTIFEROUS
AMERCEABLE
AMERCEMENT
AMERCEMENTS
AMERCIABLE
AMERCIAMENT
AMERCIAMENTS
AMERICIUMS
AMETABOLIC
AMETABOLISM
AMETABOLISMS
AMETABOLOUS
AMETHYSTINE
AMETROPIAS
AMIABILITIES
AMIABILITY
AMIABLENESS
AMIABLENESSES
AMIANTHINE
AMIANTHOID
AMIANTHOIDAL
AMIANTHUSES
AMIANTUSES
AMICABILITIES
AMICABILITY
AMICABLENESS
AMICABLENESSES
AMINOACETIC
AMINOACIDURIA
AMINOACIDURIAS
AMINOBENZOIC
AMINOBUTENE
AMINOBUTENES
AMINOPEPTIDASE
AMINOPEPTIDASES
AMINOPHENAZONE
AMINOPHENAZONES
AMINOPHENOL
AMINOPHENOLS
AMINOPHYLLINE
AMINOPHYLLINES
AMINOPTERIN
AMINOPTERINS
AMINOPYRINE
AMINOPYRINES
AMINOTOLUENE
AMINOTOLUENES
AMISSIBILITIES
AMISSIBILITY
AMITOTICALLY
AMITRIPTYLINE
AMITRIPTYLINES
AMITRYPTYLINE
AMITRYPTYLINES
AMMOCOETES
AMMONIACAL
AMMONIACUM
AMMONIACUMS
AMMONIATED
AMMONIATES
AMMONIATING
AMMONIATION
AMMONIATIONS
AMMONIFICATION
AMMONIFICATIONS
AMMONIFIED
AMMONIFIES
AMMONIFYING
AMMONOLYSES

AMMONOLYSIS
AMMOPHILOUS
AMMUNITION
AMMUNITIONED
AMMUNITIONING
AMMUNITIONS
AMNESTYING
AMNIOCENTESES
AMNIOCENTESIS
AMNIOTOMIES
AMOBARBITAL
AMOBARBITALS
AMOEBIASES
AMOEBIASIS
AMOEBIFORM
AMOEBOCYTE
AMOEBOCYTES
AMONTILLADO
AMONTILLADOS
AMORALISMS
AMORALISTS
AMORALITIES
AMOROSITIES
AMOROUSNESS
AMOROUSNESSES
AMORPHISMS
AMORPHOUSLY
AMORPHOUSNESS
AMORPHOUSNESSES
AMORTISABLE
AMORTISATION
AMORTISATIONS
AMORTISEMENT
AMORTISEMENTS
AMORTISING
AMORTIZABLE
AMORTIZATION
AMORTIZATIONS
AMORTIZEMENT
AMORTIZEMENTS
AMORTIZING
AMOURETTES
AMOXICILLIN
AMOXICILLINS
AMOXYCILLIN
AMOXYCILLINS
AMPACITIES
AMPELOGRAPHIES
AMPELOGRAPHY
AMPELOPSES
AMPELOPSIS
AMPELOPSISES
AMPEROMETRIC
AMPERSANDS
AMPERZANDS
AMPHETAMINE
AMPHETAMINES
AMPHIARTHROSES
AMPHIARTHROSIS
AMPHIASTER
AMPHIASTERS
AMPHIBIANS
AMPHIBIOTIC
AMPHIBIOUS
AMPHIBIOUSLY
AMPHIBIOUSNESS
AMPHIBLASTIC
AMPHIBLASTULA
AMPHIBLASTULAE
AMPHIBOLES
AMPHIBOLIC
AMPHIBOLIES
AMPHIBOLITE
AMPHIBOLITES
AMPHIBOLOGICAL
AMPHIBOLOGIES
AMPHIBOLOGY
AMPHIBOLOUS
AMPHIBRACH
AMPHIBRACHIC
AMPHIBRACHS
AMPHICHROIC
AMPHICHROMATIC
AMPHICOELOUS
AMPHICTYON
AMPHICTYONIC
AMPHICTYONIES
AMPHICTYONS
AMPHICTYONY
AMPHIDENTATE
AMPHIDIPLOID
AMPHIDIPLOIDIES
AMPHIDIPLOIDS
AMPHIDIPLOIDY
AMPHIGASTRIA
AMPHIGASTRIUM
AMPHIGORIC
AMPHIGORIES
AMPHIGOURI
AMPHIGOURIS
AMPHIMACER
AMPHIMACERS
AMPHIMICTIC
AMPHIMIXES
AMPHIMIXIS
AMPHIOXUSES
AMPHIPATHIC
AMPHIPHILE
AMPHIPHILES
AMPHIPHILIC
AMPHIPLOID
AMPHIPLOIDIES
AMPHIPLOIDS
AMPHIPLOIDY
AMPHIPODOUS
AMPHIPROSTYLAR
AMPHIPROSTYLE
AMPHIPROSTYLES
AMPHIPROTIC
AMPHISBAENA
AMPHISBAENAE
AMPHISBAENAS
AMPHISBAENIC
AMPHISCIAN
AMPHISCIANS
AMPHISTOMATAL
AMPHISTOMATIC
AMPHISTOMOUS
AMPHISTYLAR
AMPHISTYLARS
AMPHITHEATER
AMPHITHEATERS
AMPHITHEATRAL
AMPHITHEATRE
AMPHITHEATRES
AMPHITHEATRIC
AMPHITHEATRICAL
AMPHITHECIA
AMPHITHECIUM
AMPHITRICHA
AMPHITRICHOUS
AMPHITROPOUS
AMPHOLYTES
AMPHOTERIC
AMPICILLIN
AMPICILLINS
AMPLENESSES
AMPLEXICAUL
AMPLEXUSES
AMPLIATION
AMPLIATIONS
AMPLIATIVE
AMPLIDYNES
AMPLIFIABLE
AMPLIFICATION
AMPLIFICATIONS
AMPLIFIERS
AMPLIFYING
AMPLITUDES
AMPLOSOMES
AMPULLACEAL
AMPULLACEOUS
AMPULLOSITIES
AMPULLOSITY
AMPUTATING
AMPUTATION
AMPUTATIONS
AMPUTATORS
AMRITATTVA
AMRITATTVAS
AMSINCKIAS
AMUSEMENTS
AMUSINGNESS
AMUSINGNESSES
AMUSIVENESS
AMUSIVENESSES
AMYGDALACEOUS
AMYGDALATE
AMYGDALINE
AMYGDALINS
AMYGDALOID
AMYGDALOIDAL
AMYGDALOIDS
AMYLACEOUS
AMYLOBARBITONE
AMYLOBARBITONES
AMYLOIDOSES
AMYLOIDOSIS
AMYLOLYSES
AMYLOLYSIS
AMYLOLYTIC
AMYLOPECTIN
AMYLOPECTINS
AMYLOPLAST
AMYLOPLASTS
AMYLOPSINS
AMYOTONIAS
AMYOTROPHIC
AMYOTROPHIES
AMYOTROPHY
ANABANTIDS
ANABAPTISE
ANABAPTISED
ANABAPTISES
ANABAPTISING
ANABAPTISM
ANABAPTISMS
ANABAPTIST
ANABAPTISTIC
ANABAPTISTS
ANABAPTIZE
ANABAPTIZED
ANABAPTIZES
ANABAPTIZING
ANABLEPSES
ANABOLISMS
ANABOLITES
ANABOLITIC
ANABRANCHES
ANACARDIACEOUS
ANACARDIUM
ANACARDIUMS
ANACATHARSES
ANACATHARSIS
ANACATHARTIC
ANACATHARTICS
ANACHARISES
ANACHORISM
ANACHORISMS
ANACHRONIC
ANACHRONICAL
ANACHRONICALLY
ANACHRONISM
ANACHRONISMS
ANACHRONISTIC
ANACHRONOUS
ANACHRONOUSLY
ANACLASTIC
ANACOLUTHA
ANACOLUTHIA

ANACOLUTHIAS
ANACOLUTHIC
ANACOLUTHICALLY
ANACOLUTHON
ANACOLUTHONS
ANACOUSTIC
ANACREONTIC
ANACREONTICALLY
ANACREONTICS
ANACRUSTIC
ANADIPLOSES
ANADIPLOSIS
ANADROMOUS
ANADYOMENE
ANAEMICALLY
ANAEROBICALLY
ANAEROBIONT
ANAEROBIONTS
ANAEROBIOSES
ANAEROBIOSIS
ANAEROBIOTIC
ANAEROBIUM
ANAESTHESES
ANAESTHESIA
ANAESTHESIAS
ANAESTHESIOLOGY
ANAESTHESIS
ANAESTHETIC
ANAESTHETICALLY
ANAESTHETICS
ANAESTHETISE
ANAESTHETISED
ANAESTHETISES
ANAESTHETISING
ANAESTHETIST
ANAESTHETISTS
ANAESTHETIZE
ANAESTHETIZED
ANAESTHETIZES
ANAESTHETIZING
ANAGENESES
ANAGENESIS
ANAGLYPHIC
ANAGLYPHICAL
ANAGLYPHIES
ANAGLYPTIC
ANAGLYPTICAL
ANAGNORISES
ANAGNORISIS
ANAGOGICAL
ANAGOGICALLY
ANAGRAMMATIC
ANAGRAMMATICAL
ANAGRAMMATISE
ANAGRAMMATISED
ANAGRAMMATISES
ANAGRAMMATISING
ANAGRAMMATISM
ANAGRAMMATISMS
ANAGRAMMATIST
ANAGRAMMATISTS
ANAGRAMMATIZE
ANAGRAMMATIZED
ANAGRAMMATIZES
ANAGRAMMATIZING
ANAGRAMMED
ANAGRAMMER
ANAGRAMMERS
ANAGRAMMING
ANALEMMATA
ANALEMMATIC
ANALEPTICS
ANALGESIAS
ANALGESICS
ANALGETICS
ANALOGICAL
ANALOGICALLY
ANALOGISED
ANALOGISES
ANALOGISING
ANALOGISMS
ANALOGISTS
ANALOGIZED
ANALOGIZES
ANALOGIZING
ANALOGOUSLY
ANALOGOUSNESS
ANALOGOUSNESSES
ANALPHABET
ANALPHABETE
ANALPHABETES
ANALPHABETIC
ANALPHABETICS
ANALPHABETISM
ANALPHABETISMS
ANALPHABETS
ANALYSABILITIES
ANALYSABILITY
ANALYSABLE
ANALYSANDS
ANALYSATION
ANALYSATIONS
ANALYTICAL
ANALYTICALLY
ANALYTICITIES
ANALYTICITY
ANALYZABILITIES
ANALYZABILITY
ANALYZABLE
ANALYZATION
ANALYZATIONS
ANAMNESTIC
ANAMNESTICALLY
ANAMNIOTES
ANAMNIOTIC
ANAMORPHIC
ANAMORPHISM
ANAMORPHISMS
ANAMORPHOSCOPE
ANAMORPHOSCOPES
ANAMORPHOSES
ANAMORPHOSIS
ANAMORPHOUS
ANANDAMIDE
ANANDAMIDES
ANAPAESTIC
ANAPAESTICAL
ANAPESTICS
ANAPHORESES
ANAPHORESIS
ANAPHORICAL
ANAPHORICALLY
ANAPHRODISIA
ANAPHRODISIAC
ANAPHRODISIACS
ANAPHRODISIAS
ANAPHYLACTIC
ANAPHYLACTOID
ANAPHYLAXES
ANAPHYLAXIES
ANAPHYLAXIS
ANAPHYLAXY
ANAPLASIAS
ANAPLASMOSES
ANAPLASMOSIS
ANAPLASTIC
ANAPLASTIES
ANAPLEROSES
ANAPLEROSIS
ANAPLEROTIC
ANAPTYCTIC
ANAPTYCTICAL
ANARCHICAL
ANARCHICALLY
ANARCHISED
ANARCHISES
ANARCHISING
ANARCHISMS
ANARCHISTIC
ANARCHISTICALLY
ANARCHISTS
ANARCHIZED
ANARCHIZES
ANARCHIZING
ANARTHRIAS
ANARTHROUS
ANARTHROUSLY
ANARTHROUSNESS
ANASARCOUS
ANASTIGMAT
ANASTIGMATIC
ANASTIGMATISM
ANASTIGMATISMS
ANASTIGMATS
ANASTOMOSE
ANASTOMOSED
ANASTOMOSES
ANASTOMOSING
ANASTOMOSIS
ANASTOMOTIC
ANASTROPHE
ANASTROPHES
ANASTROZOLE
ANASTROZOLES
ANATHEMATA
ANATHEMATICAL
ANATHEMATICALS
ANATHEMATISE
ANATHEMATISED
ANATHEMATISES
ANATHEMATISING
ANATHEMATIZE
ANATHEMATIZED
ANATHEMATIZES
ANATHEMATIZING
ANATOMICAL
ANATOMICALLY
ANATOMISATION
ANATOMISATIONS
ANATOMISED
ANATOMISER
ANATOMISERS
ANATOMISES
ANATOMISING
ANATOMISTS
ANATOMIZATION
ANATOMIZATIONS
ANATOMIZED
ANATOMIZER
ANATOMIZERS
ANATOMIZES
ANATOMIZING
ANATROPIES
ANATROPOUS
ANCESTORED
ANCESTORIAL
ANCESTORING
ANCESTRALLY
ANCESTRALS
ANCESTRESS
ANCESTRESSES
ANCESTRIES
ANCHORAGES
ANCHORESSES
ANCHORETIC
ANCHORETICAL
ANCHORETTE
ANCHORETTES
ANCHORITES
ANCHORITIC
ANCHORITICAL
ANCHORITICALLY
ANCHORLESS
ANCHORPEOPLE
ANCHORPERSON
ANCHORPERSONS
ANCHORWOMAN
ANCHORWOMEN
ANCHOVETAS
ANCHOVETTA

ANCHOVETTAS
ANCHYLOSED
ANCHYLOSES
ANCHYLOSING
ANCHYLOSIS
ANCHYLOTIC
ANCIENTEST
ANCIENTNESS
ANCIENTNESSES
ANCIENTRIES
ANCILLARIES
ANCIPITOUS
ANCYLOSTOMIASES
ANCYLOSTOMIASIS
ANDALUSITE
ANDALUSITES
ANDANTINOS
ANDOUILLES
ANDOUILLETTE
ANDOUILLETTES
ANDRADITES
ANDROCENTRIC
ANDROCENTRISM
ANDROCENTRISMS
ANDROCEPHALOUS
ANDROCLINIA
ANDROCLINIUM
ANDRODIOECIOUS
ANDRODIOECISM
ANDRODIOECISMS
ANDROECIAL
ANDROECIUM
ANDROGENESES
ANDROGENESIS
ANDROGENETIC
ANDROGENIC
ANDROGENOUS
ANDROGYNES
ANDROGYNIES
ANDROGYNOPHORE
ANDROGYNOPHORES
ANDROGYNOUS
ANDROLOGIES
ANDROLOGIST
ANDROLOGISTS
ANDROMEDAS
ANDROMEDOTOXIN
ANDROMEDOTOXINS
ANDROMONOECIOUS
ANDROMONOECISM
ANDROMONOECISMS
ANDROPAUSE
ANDROPAUSES
ANDROPHORE
ANDROPHORES
ANDROSPHINGES
ANDROSPHINX
ANDROSPHINXES
ANDROSTERONE
ANDROSTERONES
ANECDOTAGE
ANECDOTAGES
ANECDOTALISM
ANECDOTALISMS
ANECDOTALIST
ANECDOTALISTS
ANECDOTALLY
ANECDOTICAL
ANECDOTICALLY
ANECDOTIST
ANECDOTISTS
ANELASTICITIES
ANELASTICITY
ANEMICALLY
ANEMOCHORE
ANEMOCHORES
ANEMOCHOROUS
ANEMOGRAMS
ANEMOGRAPH
ANEMOGRAPHIC
ANEMOGRAPHIES
ANEMOGRAPHS
ANEMOGRAPHY
ANEMOLOGIES
ANEMOMETER
ANEMOMETERS
ANEMOMETRIC
ANEMOMETRICAL
ANEMOMETRIES
ANEMOMETRY
ANEMOPHILIES
ANEMOPHILOUS
ANEMOPHILY
ANEMOPHOBIA
ANEMOPHOBIAS
ANEMOSCOPE
ANEMOSCOPES
ANENCEPHALIA
ANENCEPHALIAS
ANENCEPHALIC
ANENCEPHALIES
ANENCEPHALY
ANESTHESIA
ANESTHESIAS
ANESTHESIOLOGY
ANESTHETIC
ANESTHETICALLY
ANESTHETICS
ANESTHETISATION
ANESTHETISE
ANESTHETISED
ANESTHETISES
ANESTHETISING
ANESTHETIST
ANESTHETISTS
ANESTHETIZATION
ANESTHETIZE
ANESTHETIZED
ANESTHETIZES
ANESTHETIZING
ANEUPLOIDIES
ANEUPLOIDS
ANEUPLOIDY
ANEURISMAL
ANEURISMALLY
ANEURISMATIC
ANEURYSMAL
ANEURYSMALLY
ANEURYSMATIC
ANFRACTUOSITIES
ANFRACTUOSITY
ANFRACTUOUS
ANGASHORES
ANGELFISHES
ANGELHOODS
ANGELICALLY
ANGELOLATRIES
ANGELOLATRY
ANGELOLOGIES
ANGELOLOGIST
ANGELOLOGISTS
ANGELOLOGY
ANGELOPHANIES
ANGELOPHANY
ANGIOCARPOUS
ANGIOGENESES
ANGIOGENESIS
ANGIOGENIC
ANGIOGRAMS
ANGIOGRAPHIC
ANGIOGRAPHIES
ANGIOGRAPHY
ANGIOLOGIES
ANGIOMATOUS
ANGIOPLASTIES
ANGIOPLASTY
ANGIOSARCOMA
ANGIOSARCOMAS
ANGIOSARCOMATA
ANGIOSPERM
ANGIOSPERMAL
ANGIOSPERMOUS
ANGIOSPERMS
ANGIOSTOMATOUS
ANGIOSTOMOUS
ANGIOTENSIN
ANGIOTENSINS
ANGISHORES
ANGLEBERRIES
ANGLEBERRY
ANGLEDOZER
ANGLEDOZERS
ANGLERFISH
ANGLERFISHES
ANGLESITES
ANGLETWITCH
ANGLETWITCHES
ANGLEWORMS
ANGLICISATION
ANGLICISATIONS
ANGLICISED
ANGLICISES
ANGLICISING
ANGLICISMS
ANGLICISTS
ANGLICIZATION
ANGLICIZATIONS
ANGLICIZED
ANGLICIZES
ANGLICIZING
ANGLIFYING
ANGLISTICS
ANGLOMANIA
ANGLOMANIAC
ANGLOMANIACS
ANGLOMANIAS
ANGLOPHILE
ANGLOPHILES
ANGLOPHILIA
ANGLOPHILIAS
ANGLOPHILIC
ANGLOPHILS
ANGLOPHOBE
ANGLOPHOBES
ANGLOPHOBIA
ANGLOPHOBIAC
ANGLOPHOBIACS
ANGLOPHOBIAS
ANGLOPHOBIC
ANGLOPHONE
ANGLOPHONES
ANGLOPHONIC
ANGOPHORAS
ANGOSTURAS
ANGRINESSES
ANGUIFAUNA
ANGUIFAUNAE
ANGUIFAUNAS
ANGUILLIFORM
ANGUIPEDES
ANGUISHING
ANGULARITIES
ANGULARITY
ANGULARNESS
ANGULARNESSES
ANGULATING
ANGULATION
ANGULATIONS
ANGUSTIFOLIATE
ANGUSTIROSTRATE
ANGWANTIBO
ANGWANTIBOS
ANHARMONIC
ANHEDONIAS
ANHELATION
ANHELATIONS
ANHIDROSES
ANHIDROSIS
ANHIDROTIC
ANHIDROTICS

ANHUNGERED
ANHYDRASES
ANHYDRIDES
ANHYDRITES
ANICONISMS
ANICONISTS
ANILINCTUS
ANILINCTUSES
ANILINGUSES
ANIMADVERSION
ANIMADVERSIONS
ANIMADVERT
ANIMADVERTED
ANIMADVERTER
ANIMADVERTERS
ANIMADVERTING
ANIMADVERTS
ANIMALCULA
ANIMALCULAR
ANIMALCULE
ANIMALCULES
ANIMALCULISM
ANIMALCULISMS
ANIMALCULIST
ANIMALCULISTS
ANIMALCULUM
ANIMALIERS
ANIMALISATION
ANIMALISATIONS
ANIMALISED
ANIMALISES
ANIMALISING
ANIMALISMS
ANIMALISTIC
ANIMALISTS
ANIMALITIES
ANIMALIZATION
ANIMALIZATIONS
ANIMALIZED
ANIMALIZES
ANIMALIZING
ANIMALLIKE
ANIMATEDLY
ANIMATENESS
ANIMATENESSES
ANIMATEURS
ANIMATINGLY
ANIMATIONS
ANIMATISMS
ANIMATISTS
ANIMATRONIC
ANIMATRONICALLY
ANIMATRONICS
ANIMOSITIES
ANISEIKONIA
ANISEIKONIAS
ANISEIKONIC
ANISOCERCAL
ANISODACTYL
ANISODACTYLOUS
ANISODACTYLS
ANISOGAMIES
ANISOGAMOUS
ANISOMERIC
ANISOMEROUS
ANISOMETRIC
ANISOMETROPIA
ANISOMETROPIAS
ANISOMETROPIC
ANISOMORPHIC
ANISOPHYLLIES
ANISOPHYLLOUS
ANISOPHYLLY
ANISOTROPIC
ANISOTROPICALLY
ANISOTROPIES
ANISOTROPISM
ANISOTROPISMS
ANISOTROPY
ANKLEBONES
ANKYLOSAUR
ANKYLOSAURS
ANKYLOSAURUS
ANKYLOSAURUSES
ANKYLOSING
ANKYLOSTOMIASES
ANKYLOSTOMIASIS
ANNABERGITE
ANNABERGITES
ANNALISING
ANNALISTIC
ANNALIZING
ANNEALINGS
ANNELIDANS
ANNEXATION
ANNEXATIONAL
ANNEXATIONISM
ANNEXATIONISMS
ANNEXATIONIST
ANNEXATIONISTS
ANNEXATIONS
ANNEXMENTS
ANNIHILABLE
ANNIHILATE
ANNIHILATED
ANNIHILATES
ANNIHILATING
ANNIHILATION
ANNIHILATIONISM
ANNIHILATIONS
ANNIHILATIVE
ANNIHILATOR
ANNIHILATORS
ANNIHILATORY
ANNIVERSARIES
ANNIVERSARY
ANNOTATABLE
ANNOTATING
ANNOTATION
ANNOTATIONS
ANNOTATIVE
ANNOTATORS
ANNOUNCEMENT
ANNOUNCEMENTS
ANNOUNCERS
ANNOUNCING
ANNOYANCES
ANNOYINGLY
ANNUALISED
ANNUALISES
ANNUALISING
ANNUALIZED
ANNUALIZES
ANNUALIZING
ANNUITANTS
ANNUITISED
ANNUITISES
ANNUITISING
ANNUITIZED
ANNUITIZES
ANNUITIZING
ANNULARITIES
ANNULARITY
ANNULATION
ANNULATIONS
ANNULLABLE
ANNULMENTS
ANNUNCIATE
ANNUNCIATED
ANNUNCIATES
ANNUNCIATING
ANNUNCIATION
ANNUNCIATIONS
ANNUNCIATIVE
ANNUNCIATOR
ANNUNCIATORS
ANNUNCIATORY
ANNUNTIATE
ANNUNTIATED
ANNUNTIATES
ANNUNTIATING
ANODICALLY
ANODISATION
ANODISATIONS
ANODIZATION
ANODIZATIONS
ANODONTIAS
ANOESTROUS
ANOINTINGS
ANOINTMENT
ANOINTMENTS
ANOMALISTIC
ANOMALISTICAL
ANOMALISTICALLY
ANOMALOUSLY
ANOMALOUSNESS
ANOMALOUSNESSES
ANONACEOUS
ANONYMISED
ANONYMISES
ANONYMISING
ANONYMITIES
ANONYMIZED
ANONYMIZES
ANONYMIZING
ANONYMOUSLY
ANONYMOUSNESS
ANONYMOUSNESSES
ANOPHELINE
ANOPHELINES
ANORECTICS
ANOREXIGENIC
ANORTHITES
ANORTHITIC
ANORTHOSITE
ANORTHOSITES
ANORTHOSITIC
ANOTHERGUESS
ANOVULANTS
ANOVULATION
ANOVULATIONS
ANOVULATORY
ANOXAEMIAS
ANSAPHONES
ANSWERABILITIES
ANSWERABILITY
ANSWERABLE
ANSWERABLENESS
ANSWERABLY
ANSWERLESS
ANSWERPHONE
ANSWERPHONES
ANTAGONISABLE
ANTAGONISATION
ANTAGONISATIONS
ANTAGONISE
ANTAGONISED
ANTAGONISES
ANTAGONISING
ANTAGONISM
ANTAGONISMS
ANTAGONIST
ANTAGONISTIC
ANTAGONISTS
ANTAGONIZABLE
ANTAGONIZATION
ANTAGONIZATIONS
ANTAGONIZE
ANTAGONIZED
ANTAGONIZES
ANTAGONIZING
ANTALKALIES
ANTALKALINE
ANTALKALINES
ANTALKALIS
ANTAPHRODISIAC
ANTAPHRODISIACS
ANTARTHRITIC
ANTARTHRITICS
ANTASTHMATIC

ANTASTHMATICS
ANTEBELLUM
ANTECEDENCE
ANTECEDENCES
ANTECEDENT
ANTECEDENTLY
ANTECEDENTS
ANTECEDING
ANTECESSOR
ANTECESSORS
ANTECHAMBER
ANTECHAMBERS
ANTECHAPEL
ANTECHAPELS
ANTECHOIRS
ANTEDATING
ANTEDATINGS
ANTEDILUVIAL
ANTEDILUVIALLY
ANTEDILUVIAN
ANTEDILUVIANS
ANTEMERIDIAN
ANTEMORTEM
ANTEMUNDANE
ANTENATALLY
ANTENATALS
ANTENNIFEROUS
ANTENNIFORM
ANTENNULAR
ANTENNULES
ANTENUPTIAL
ANTENUPTIALS
ANTEORBITAL
ANTEPENDIA
ANTEPENDIUM
ANTEPENDIUMS
ANTEPENULT
ANTEPENULTIMA
ANTEPENULTIMAS
ANTEPENULTIMATE
ANTEPENULTS
ANTEPOSITION
ANTEPOSITIONS
ANTEPRANDIAL
ANTERIORITIES
ANTERIORITY
ANTERIORLY
ANTEROGRADE
ANTEVERSION
ANTEVERSIONS
ANTEVERTED
ANTEVERTING
ANTHELICES
ANTHELIONS
ANTHELIXES
ANTHELMINTHIC
ANTHELMINTHICS
ANTHELMINTIC
ANTHELMINTICS
ANTHEMISES
ANTHEMWISE
ANTHERIDIA
ANTHERIDIAL
ANTHERIDIUM
ANTHEROZOID
ANTHEROZOIDS
ANTHEROZOOID
ANTHEROZOOIDS
ANTHERSMUT
ANTHERSMUTS
ANTHOCARPOUS
ANTHOCARPS
ANTHOCHLORE
ANTHOCHLORES
ANTHOCYANIN
ANTHOCYANINS
ANTHOCYANS
ANTHOLOGICAL
ANTHOLOGIES
ANTHOLOGISE
ANTHOLOGISED
ANTHOLOGISER
ANTHOLOGISERS
ANTHOLOGISES
ANTHOLOGISING
ANTHOLOGIST
ANTHOLOGISTS
ANTHOLOGIZE
ANTHOLOGIZED
ANTHOLOGIZER
ANTHOLOGIZERS
ANTHOLOGIZES
ANTHOLOGIZING
ANTHOMANIA
ANTHOMANIAC
ANTHOMANIACS
ANTHOMANIAS
ANTHOPHILOUS
ANTHOPHORE
ANTHOPHORES
ANTHOPHYLLITE
ANTHOPHYLLITES
ANTHOTAXIES
ANTHOXANTHIN
ANTHOXANTHINS
ANTHOZOANS
ANTHRACENE
ANTHRACENES
ANTHRACITE
ANTHRACITES
ANTHRACITIC
ANTHRACNOSE
ANTHRACNOSES
ANTHRACOID
ANTHRACOSES
ANTHRACOSIS
ANTHRACYCLINE
ANTHRACYCLINES
ANTHRANILATE
ANTHRANILATES
ANTHRANILIC
ANTHRAQUINONE
ANTHRAQUINONES
ANTHROPICAL
ANTHROPOBIOLOGY
ANTHROPOCENTRIC
ANTHROPOGENESES
ANTHROPOGENESIS
ANTHROPOGENETIC
ANTHROPOGENIC
ANTHROPOGENIES
ANTHROPOGENY
ANTHROPOGONIES
ANTHROPOGONY
ANTHROPOGRAPHY
ANTHROPOID
ANTHROPOIDAL
ANTHROPOIDS
ANTHROPOLATRIES
ANTHROPOLATRY
ANTHROPOLOGICAL
ANTHROPOLOGIES
ANTHROPOLOGIST
ANTHROPOLOGISTS
ANTHROPOLOGY
ANTHROPOMETRIC
ANTHROPOMETRIES
ANTHROPOMETRIST
ANTHROPOMETRY
ANTHROPOMORPH
ANTHROPOMORPHIC
ANTHROPOMORPHS
ANTHROPOPATHIC
ANTHROPOPATHIES
ANTHROPOPATHISM
ANTHROPOPATHY
ANTHROPOPHAGI
ANTHROPOPHAGIC
ANTHROPOPHAGIES
ANTHROPOPHAGITE
ANTHROPOPHAGOUS
ANTHROPOPHAGUS
ANTHROPOPHAGY
ANTHROPOPHOBIA
ANTHROPOPHOBIAS
ANTHROPOPHOBIC
ANTHROPOPHOBICS
ANTHROPOPHUISM
ANTHROPOPHUISMS
ANTHROPOPHYTE
ANTHROPOPHYTES
ANTHROPOPSYCHIC
ANTHROPOSOPHIC
ANTHROPOSOPHIES
ANTHROPOSOPHIST
ANTHROPOSOPHY
ANTHROPOTOMIES
ANTHROPOTOMY
ANTHURIUMS
ANTIABORTION
ANTIABORTIONIST
ANTIACADEMIC
ANTIADITIS
ANTIADITISES
ANTIAGGRESSION
ANTIAIRCRAFT
ANTIAIRCRAFTS
ANTIALCOHOL
ANTIALCOHOLISM
ANTIALCOHOLISMS
ANTIALLERGENIC
ANTIANDROGEN
ANTIANDROGENS
ANTIANEMIA
ANTIANXIETY
ANTIAPARTHEID
ANTIAPHRODISIAC
ANTIARMOUR
ANTIARRHYTHMIC
ANTIARRHYTHMICS
ANTIARTHRITIC
ANTIARTHRITICS
ANTIARTHRITIS
ANTIASTHMA
ANTIASTHMATIC
ANTIASTHMATICS
ANTIAUTHORITY
ANTIAUXINS
ANTIBACCHII
ANTIBACCHIUS
ANTIBACKLASH
ANTIBACTERIAL
ANTIBACTERIALS
ANTIBALLISTIC
ANTIBARBARUS
ANTIBARBARUSES
ANTIBARYON
ANTIBARYONS
ANTIBILIOUS
ANTIBILLBOARD
ANTIBIOSES
ANTIBIOSIS
ANTIBIOTIC
ANTIBIOTICALLY
ANTIBIOTICS
ANTIBLACKISM
ANTIBLACKISMS
ANTIBODIES
ANTIBOURGEOIS
ANTIBOYCOTT
ANTIBURGLAR
ANTIBURGLARY
ANTIBUSERS
ANTIBUSINESS
ANTIBUSING
ANTICAKING
ANTICANCER
ANTICAPITALISM
ANTICAPITALISMS
ANTICAPITALIST

ANTICAPITALISTS
ANTICARCINOGEN
ANTICARCINOGENS
ANTICARIES
ANTICATALYST
ANTICATALYSTS
ANTICATHODE
ANTICATHODES
ANTICATHOLIC
ANTICELLULITE
ANTICENSORSHIP
ANTICHLORISTIC
ANTICHLORS
ANTICHOICE
ANTICHOICER
ANTICHOICERS
ANTICHOLESTEROL
ANTICHOLINERGIC
ANTICHRIST
ANTICHRISTIAN
ANTICHRISTIANLY
ANTICHRISTS
ANTICHTHONES
ANTICHURCH
ANTICIGARETTE
ANTICIPANT
ANTICIPANTS
ANTICIPATABLE
ANTICIPATE
ANTICIPATED
ANTICIPATES
ANTICIPATING
ANTICIPATION
ANTICIPATIONS
ANTICIPATIVE
ANTICIPATIVELY
ANTICIPATOR
ANTICIPATORILY
ANTICIPATORS
ANTICIPATORY
ANTICISING
ANTICIVISM
ANTICIVISMS
ANTICIZING
ANTICLASSICAL
ANTICLASTIC
ANTICLERICAL
ANTICLERICALISM
ANTICLERICALS
ANTICLIMACTIC
ANTICLIMACTICAL
ANTICLIMAX
ANTICLIMAXES
ANTICLINAL
ANTICLINALS
ANTICLINES
ANTICLINORIA
ANTICLINORIUM
ANTICLOCKWISE
ANTICLOTTING
ANTICOAGULANT
ANTICOAGULANTS
ANTICODONS
ANTICOINCIDENCE
ANTICOLLISION
ANTICOLONIAL
ANTICOLONIALISM
ANTICOLONIALIST
ANTICOLONIALS
ANTICOMMERCIAL
ANTICOMMUNISM
ANTICOMMUNISMS
ANTICOMMUNIST
ANTICOMMUNISTS
ANTICOMPETITIVE
ANTICONSUMER
ANTICONVULSANT
ANTICONVULSANTS
ANTICONVULSIVE
ANTICONVULSIVES
ANTICORPORATE
ANTICORROSION
ANTICORROSIONS
ANTICORROSIVE
ANTICORROSIVES
ANTICORRUPTION
ANTICREATIVE
ANTICRUELTY
ANTICULTURAL
ANTICYCLONE
ANTICYCLONES
ANTICYCLONIC
ANTIDANDRUFF
ANTIDAZZLE
ANTIDEFAMATION
ANTIDEMOCRATIC
ANTIDEPRESSANT
ANTIDEPRESSANTS
ANTIDEPRESSION
ANTIDERIVATIVE
ANTIDERIVATIVES
ANTIDESICCANT
ANTIDESICCANTS
ANTIDEVELOPMENT
ANTIDIABETIC
ANTIDIABETICS
ANTIDIARRHEAL
ANTIDIARRHEALS
ANTIDIARRHOEAL
ANTIDIARRHOEALS
ANTIDILUTION
ANTIDIURETIC
ANTIDIURETICS
ANTIDOGMATIC
ANTIDOTALLY
ANTIDOTING
ANTIDROMIC
ANTIDROMICALLY
ANTIDUMPING
ANTIDUMPINGS
ANTIECONOMIC
ANTIEDUCATIONAL
ANTIEGALITARIAN
ANTIELECTRON
ANTIELECTRONS
ANTIELITES
ANTIELITISM
ANTIELITISMS
ANTIELITIST
ANTIELITISTS
ANTIEMETIC
ANTIEMETICS
ANTIENTROPIC
ANTIEPILEPSY
ANTIEPILEPTIC
ANTIEPILEPTICS
ANTIEROTIC
ANTIESTROGEN
ANTIESTROGENS
ANTIEVOLUTION
ANTIEVOLUTIONS
ANTIFAMILY
ANTIFASCISM
ANTIFASCISMS
ANTIFASCIST
ANTIFASCISTS
ANTIFASHION
ANTIFASHIONABLE
ANTIFASHIONS
ANTIFATIGUE
ANTIFEBRILE
ANTIFEBRILES
ANTIFEDERALIST
ANTIFEDERALISTS
ANTIFEMALE
ANTIFEMININE
ANTIFEMINISM
ANTIFEMINISMS
ANTIFEMINIST
ANTIFEMINISTS
ANTIFERROMAGNET
ANTIFERTILITY
ANTIFILIBUSTER
ANTIFILIBUSTERS
ANTIFOAMING
ANTIFOGGING
ANTIFORECLOSURE
ANTIFOREIGN
ANTIFOREIGNER
ANTIFORMALIST
ANTIFOULING
ANTIFOULINGS
ANTIFREEZE
ANTIFREEZES
ANTIFRICTION
ANTIFUNGAL
ANTIFUNGALS
ANTIGAMBLING
ANTIGENICALLY
ANTIGENICITIES
ANTIGENICITY
ANTIGLOBULIN
ANTIGLOBULINS
ANTIGOVERNMENT
ANTIGRAVITIES
ANTIGRAVITY
ANTIGROPELOES
ANTIGROPELOS
ANTIGROWTH
ANTIGUERRILLA
ANTIHALATION
ANTIHALATIONS
ANTIHELICES
ANTIHELIXES
ANTIHELMINTHIC
ANTIHELMINTHICS
ANTIHEROES
ANTIHEROIC
ANTIHEROINE
ANTIHEROINES
ANTIHERPES
ANTIHIJACK
ANTIHISTAMINE
ANTIHISTAMINES
ANTIHISTAMINIC
ANTIHISTAMINICS
ANTIHISTORICAL
ANTIHOMOSEXUAL
ANTIHUMANISM
ANTIHUMANISMS
ANTIHUMANISTIC
ANTIHUNTER
ANTIHUNTERS
ANTIHUNTING
ANTIHYDROGEN
ANTIHYDROGENS
ANTIHYSTERIC
ANTIHYSTERICS
ANTIJACOBIN
ANTIJACOBINS
ANTIJAMMING
ANTIJAMMINGS
ANTIKICKBACK
ANTIKNOCKS
ANTILEGOMENA
ANTILEPROSY
ANTILEPTON
ANTILEPTONS
ANTILEUKEMIC
ANTILIBERAL
ANTILIBERALISM
ANTILIBERALISMS
ANTILIBERALS
ANTILIBERTARIAN
ANTILIFERS
ANTILITERATE
ANTILITTER
ANTILITTERING
ANTILOGARITHM
ANTILOGARITHMIC

ANTILOGARITHMS
ANTILOGICAL
ANTILOGIES
ANTILOGOUS
ANTILOPINE
ANTILYNCHING
ANTIMACASSAR
ANTIMACASSARS
ANTIMAGNETIC
ANTIMALARIA
ANTIMALARIAL
ANTIMALARIALS
ANTIMANAGEMENT
ANTIMARIJUANA
ANTIMARKET
ANTIMARKETEER
ANTIMARKETEERS
ANTIMASQUE
ANTIMASQUES
ANTIMATERIALISM
ANTIMATERIALIST
ANTIMATTER
ANTIMATTERS
ANTIMECHANIST
ANTIMECHANISTS
ANTIMERGER
ANTIMERISM
ANTIMERISMS
ANTIMETABOLE
ANTIMETABOLES
ANTIMETABOLIC
ANTIMETABOLITE
ANTIMETABOLITES
ANTIMETATHESES
ANTIMETATHESIS
ANTIMICROBIAL
ANTIMICROBIALS
ANTIMILITARISM
ANTIMILITARISMS
ANTIMILITARIST
ANTIMILITARISTS
ANTIMILITARY
ANTIMISSILE
ANTIMISSILES
ANTIMITOTIC
ANTIMITOTICS
ANTIMNEMONIC
ANTIMNEMONICS
ANTIMODERN
ANTIMODERNIST
ANTIMODERNISTS
ANTIMONARCHICAL
ANTIMONARCHIST
ANTIMONARCHISTS
ANTIMONATE
ANTIMONATES
ANTIMONIAL
ANTIMONIALS
ANTIMONIATE
ANTIMONIATES
ANTIMONIDE
ANTIMONIDES
ANTIMONIES
ANTIMONIOUS
ANTIMONITE
ANTIMONITES
ANTIMONOPOLIST
ANTIMONOPOLISTS
ANTIMONOPOLY
ANTIMONOUS
ANTIMONYLS
ANTIMOSQUITO
ANTIMUSICAL
ANTIMUSICS
ANTIMUTAGEN
ANTIMUTAGENS
ANTIMYCINS
ANTIMYCOTIC
ANTINARRATIVE
ANTINARRATIVES
ANTINATIONAL
ANTINATIONALIST
ANTINATURAL
ANTINATURE
ANTINAUSEA
ANTINEOPLASTIC
ANTINEOPLASTICS
ANTINEPHRITIC
ANTINEPHRITICS
ANTINEPOTISM
ANTINEUTRINO
ANTINEUTRINOS
ANTINEUTRON
ANTINEUTRONS
ANTINOISES
ANTINOMIAN
ANTINOMIANISM
ANTINOMIANISMS
ANTINOMIANS
ANTINOMICAL
ANTINOMICALLY
ANTINOMIES
ANTINOVELIST
ANTINOVELISTS
ANTINOVELS
ANTINUCLEAR
ANTINUCLEARIST
ANTINUCLEARISTS
ANTINUCLEON
ANTINUCLEONS
ANTINUKERS
ANTIOBESITY
ANTIOBSCENITY
ANTIODONTALGIC
ANTIODONTALGICS
ANTIOESTROGEN
ANTIOESTROGENS
ANTIOXIDANT
ANTIOXIDANTS
ANTIOZONANT
ANTIOZONANTS
ANTIPARALLEL
ANTIPARALLELS
ANTIPARASITIC
ANTIPARASITICS
ANTIPARTICLE
ANTIPARTICLES
ANTIPARTIES
ANTIPASTOS
ANTIPATHETIC
ANTIPATHETICAL
ANTIPATHIC
ANTIPATHIES
ANTIPATHIST
ANTIPATHISTS
ANTIPERIODIC
ANTIPERIODICS
ANTIPERISTALSES
ANTIPERISTALSIS
ANTIPERISTALTIC
ANTIPERISTASES
ANTIPERISTASIS
ANTIPERSONNEL
ANTIPERSPIRANT
ANTIPERSPIRANTS
ANTIPESTICIDE
ANTIPETALOUS
ANTIPHLOGISTIC
ANTIPHLOGISTICS
ANTIPHONAL
ANTIPHONALLY
ANTIPHONALS
ANTIPHONARIES
ANTIPHONARY
ANTIPHONER
ANTIPHONERS
ANTIPHONIC
ANTIPHONICAL
ANTIPHONICALLY
ANTIPHONIES
ANTIPHRASES
ANTIPHRASIS
ANTIPHRASTIC
ANTIPHRASTICAL
ANTIPIRACY
ANTIPLAGUE
ANTIPLAQUE
ANTIPLEASURE
ANTIPOACHING
ANTIPODALS
ANTIPODEAN
ANTIPODEANS
ANTIPOETIC
ANTIPOLICE
ANTIPOLITICAL
ANTIPOLITICS
ANTIPOLLUTION
ANTIPOLLUTIONS
ANTIPOPULAR
ANTIPORNOGRAPHY
ANTIPORTER
ANTIPORTERS
ANTIPOVERTY
ANTIPREDATOR
ANTIPRIESTLY
ANTIPROGRESSIVE
ANTIPROTON
ANTIPROTONS
ANTIPRURITIC
ANTIPRURITICS
ANTIPSYCHIATRY
ANTIPSYCHOTIC
ANTIPSYCHOTICS
ANTIPYRESES
ANTIPYRESIS
ANTIPYRETIC
ANTIPYRETICS
ANTIPYRINE
ANTIPYRINES
ANTIQUARIAN
ANTIQUARIANISM
ANTIQUARIANISMS
ANTIQUARIANS
ANTIQUARIES
ANTIQUARKS
ANTIQUATED
ANTIQUATEDNESS
ANTIQUATES
ANTIQUATING
ANTIQUATION
ANTIQUATIONS
ANTIQUENESS
ANTIQUENESSES
ANTIQUIEST
ANTIQUITARIAN
ANTIQUITARIANS
ANTIQUITIES
ANTIRABIES
ANTIRACHITIC
ANTIRACHITICS
ANTIRACISM
ANTIRACISMS
ANTIRACIST
ANTIRACISTS
ANTIRADARS
ANTIRADICAL
ANTIRADICALISM
ANTIRADICALISMS
ANTIRATIONAL
ANTIRATIONALISM
ANTIRATIONALIST
ANTIRATIONALITY
ANTIREALISM
ANTIREALISMS
ANTIREALIST
ANTIREALISTS
ANTIRECESSION
ANTIREFLECTION
ANTIREFLECTIVE
ANTIREFORM

ANTIREGULATORY
ANTIREJECTION
ANTIRELIGION
ANTIRELIGIONS
ANTIRELIGIOUS
ANTIREPUBLICAN
ANTIREPUBLICANS
ANTIRETROVIRAL
ANTIRETROVIRALS
ANTIRHEUMATIC
ANTIRHEUMATICS
ANTIRITUALISM
ANTIRITUALISMS
ANTIROMANTIC
ANTIROMANTICISM
ANTIROMANTICS
ANTIROYALIST
ANTIROYALISTS
ANTIRRHINUM
ANTIRRHINUMS
ANTISATELLITE
ANTISCIANS
ANTISCIENCE
ANTISCIENCES
ANTISCIENTIFIC
ANTISCORBUTIC
ANTISCORBUTICS
ANTISCRIPTURAL
ANTISECRECY
ANTISEGREGATION
ANTISEIZURE
ANTISENTIMENTAL
ANTISEPALOUS
ANTISEPARATIST
ANTISEPARATISTS
ANTISEPSES
ANTISEPSIS
ANTISEPTIC
ANTISEPTICALLY
ANTISEPTICISE
ANTISEPTICISED
ANTISEPTICISES
ANTISEPTICISING
ANTISEPTICISM
ANTISEPTICISMS
ANTISEPTICIZE
ANTISEPTICIZED
ANTISEPTICIZES
ANTISEPTICIZING
ANTISEPTICS
ANTISERUMS
ANTISEXIST
ANTISEXISTS
ANTISEXUAL
ANTISEXUALITIES
ANTISEXUALITY
ANTISEXUALS
ANTISHAKES
ANTISHOCKS
ANTISHOPLIFTING
ANTISLAVERY
ANTISMOKER
ANTISMOKERS
ANTISMOKING
ANTISMUGGLING
ANTISOCIAL
ANTISOCIALISM
ANTISOCIALISMS
ANTISOCIALIST
ANTISOCIALISTS
ANTISOCIALITIES
ANTISOCIALITY
ANTISOCIALLY
ANTISOCIALS
ANTISPASMODIC
ANTISPASMODICS
ANTISPASTIC
ANTISPASTICS
ANTISPASTS
ANTISPECULATION
ANTISPECULATIVE
ANTISPENDING
ANTISTATIC
ANTISTATICS
ANTISTORIES
ANTISTRESS
ANTISTRIKE
ANTISTROPHE
ANTISTROPHES
ANTISTROPHIC
ANTISTROPHON
ANTISTROPHONS
ANTISTUDENT
ANTISTYLES
ANTISUBMARINE
ANTISUBSIDY
ANTISUBVERSION
ANTISUBVERSIVE
ANTISUICIDE
ANTISYMMETRIC
ANTISYPHILITIC
ANTISYPHILITICS
ANTISYZYGIES
ANTISYZYGY
ANTITAKEOVER
ANTITARNISH
ANTITECHNOLOGY
ANTITERRORISM
ANTITERRORISMS
ANTITERRORIST
ANTITERRORISTS
ANTITHALIAN
ANTITHEISM
ANTITHEISMS
ANTITHEIST
ANTITHEISTIC
ANTITHEISTS
ANTITHEORETICAL
ANTITHESES
ANTITHESIS
ANTITHETIC
ANTITHETICAL
ANTITHETICALLY
ANTITHROMBIN
ANTITHROMBINS
ANTITHROMBOTIC
ANTITHROMBOTICS
ANTITHYROID
ANTITOBACCO
ANTITOXINS
ANTITRADES
ANTITRADITIONAL
ANTITRAGUS
ANTITRANSPIRANT
ANTITRINITARIAN
ANTITRUSTER
ANTITRUSTERS
ANTITUBERCULAR
ANTITUBERCULOUS
ANTITUMORAL
ANTITUMORS
ANTITUMOUR
ANTITUMOURAL
ANTITUSSIVE
ANTITUSSIVES
ANTITYPHOID
ANTITYPICAL
ANTITYPICALLY
ANTIUNIVERSITY
ANTIVAXERS
ANTIVAXXER
ANTIVAXXERS
ANTIVENENE
ANTIVENENES
ANTIVENINS
ANTIVENOMS
ANTIVIOLENCE
ANTIVIRALS
ANTIVIRUSES
ANTIVITAMIN
ANTIVITAMINS
ANTIVIVISECTION
ANTIWELFARE
ANTIWHALING
ANTIWORLDS
ANTIWRINKLE
ANTONINIANUS
ANTONINIANUSES
ANTONOMASIA
ANTONOMASIAS
ANTONOMASTIC
ANTONYMIES
ANTONYMOUS
ANTRORSELY
ANTSINESSES
ANUCLEATED
ANXIOLYTIC
ANXIOLYTICS
ANXIOUSNESS
ANXIOUSNESSES
ANYTHINGARIAN
ANYTHINGARIANS
ANYWHITHER
AORISTICALLY
AORTITISES
AORTOGRAPHIC
AORTOGRAPHIES
AORTOGRAPHY
APAGOGICAL
APAGOGICALLY
APARTHEIDS
APARTHOTEL
APARTHOTELS
APARTMENTAL
APARTMENTS
APARTNESSES
APATHATONS
APATHETICAL
APATHETICALLY
APATOSAURS
APATOSAURUS
APATOSAURUSES
APERIODICALLY
APERIODICITIES
APERIODICITY
APERITIVES
APERTNESSES
APFELSTRUDEL
APFELSTRUDELS
APHAERESES
APHAERESIS
APHAERETIC
APHANIPTEROUS
APHELANDRA
APHELANDRAS
APHELIOTROPIC
APHELIOTROPISM
APHELIOTROPISMS
APHETICALLY
APHETISING
APHETIZING
APHIDICIDE
APHIDICIDES
APHORISERS
APHORISING
APHORISTIC
APHORISTICALLY
APHORIZERS
APHORIZING
APHRODISIA
APHRODISIAC
APHRODISIACAL
APHRODISIACS
APHRODISIAS
APHRODITES
APICULTURAL
APICULTURE
APICULTURES
APICULTURIST
APICULTURISTS

APIOLOGIES
APISHNESSES
APITHERAPIES
APITHERAPY
APLACENTAL
APLANATICALLY
APLANATISM
APLANATISMS
APLANOGAMETE
APLANOGAMETES
APLANOSPORE
APLANOSPORES
APOAPSIDES
APOCALYPSE
APOCALYPSES
APOCALYPTIC
APOCALYPTICAL
APOCALYPTICALLY
APOCALYPTICISM
APOCALYPTICISMS
APOCALYPTISM
APOCALYPTISMS
APOCALYPTIST
APOCALYPTISTS
APOCARPIES
APOCARPOUS
APOCATASTASES
APOCATASTASIS
APOCHROMAT
APOCHROMATIC
APOCHROMATISM
APOCHROMATISMS
APOCHROMATS
APOCOPATED
APOCOPATES
APOCOPATING
APOCOPATION
APOCOPATIONS
APOCRYPHAL
APOCRYPHALLY
APOCRYPHALNESS
APOCRYPHON
APOCYNACEOUS
APOCYNTHION
APOCYNTHIONS
APODEICTIC
APODEICTICAL
APODEICTICALLY
APODICTICAL
APODICTICALLY
APODYTERIUM
APODYTERIUMS
APOENZYMES
APOGAMOUSLY
APOGEOTROPIC
APOGEOTROPISM
APOGEOTROPISMS
APOLAUSTIC
APOLAUSTICS
APOLIPOPROTEIN
APOLIPOPROTEINS
APOLITICAL
APOLITICALITIES
APOLITICALITY
APOLITICALLY
APOLITICISM
APOLITICISMS
APOLLONIAN
APOLLONICON
APOLLONICONS
APOLOGETIC
APOLOGETICAL
APOLOGETICALLY
APOLOGETICS
APOLOGISED
APOLOGISER
APOLOGISERS
APOLOGISES
APOLOGISING
APOLOGISTS
APOLOGIZED
APOLOGIZER
APOLOGIZERS
APOLOGIZES
APOLOGIZING
APOMICTICAL
APOMICTICALLY
APOMORPHIA
APOMORPHIAS
APOMORPHINE
APOMORPHINES
APONEUROSES
APONEUROSIS
APONEUROTIC
APOPEMPTIC
APOPEMPTICS
APOPHENIAS
APOPHLEGMATIC
APOPHLEGMATICS
APOPHONIES
APOPHTHEGM
APOPHTHEGMATIC
APOPHTHEGMATISE
APOPHTHEGMATIST
APOPHTHEGMATIZE
APOPHTHEGMS
APOPHYLLITE
APOPHYLLITES
APOPHYSATE
APOPHYSEAL
APOPHYSIAL
APOPLECTIC
APOPLECTICAL
APOPLECTICALLY
APOPLECTICS
APOPLEXIES
APOPLEXING
APOPROTEIN
APOPROTEINS
APOSEMATIC
APOSEMATICALLY
APOSIOPESES
APOSIOPESIS
APOSIOPETIC
APOSPORIES
APOSPOROUS
APOSTACIES
APOSTASIES
APOSTATICAL
APOSTATISE
APOSTATISED
APOSTATISES
APOSTATISING
APOSTATIZE
APOSTATIZED
APOSTATIZES
APOSTATIZING
APOSTILLES
APOSTLESHIP
APOSTLESHIPS
APOSTOLATE
APOSTOLATES
APOSTOLICAL
APOSTOLICALLY
APOSTOLICISM
APOSTOLICISMS
APOSTOLICITIES
APOSTOLICITY
APOSTOLISE
APOSTOLISED
APOSTOLISES
APOSTOLISING
APOSTOLIZE
APOSTOLIZED
APOSTOLIZES
APOSTOLIZING
APOSTROPHE
APOSTROPHES
APOSTROPHIC
APOSTROPHISE
APOSTROPHISED
APOSTROPHISES
APOSTROPHISING
APOSTROPHIZE
APOSTROPHIZED
APOSTROPHIZES
APOSTROPHIZING
APOSTROPHUS
APOSTROPHUSES
APOTHECARIES
APOTHECARY
APOTHECIAL
APOTHECIUM
APOTHEGMATIC
APOTHEGMATICAL
APOTHEGMATISE
APOTHEGMATISED
APOTHEGMATISES
APOTHEGMATISING
APOTHEGMATIST
APOTHEGMATISTS
APOTHEGMATIZE
APOTHEGMATIZED
APOTHEGMATIZES
APOTHEGMATIZING
APOTHEOSES
APOTHEOSIS
APOTHEOSISE
APOTHEOSISED
APOTHEOSISES
APOTHEOSISING
APOTHEOSIZE
APOTHEOSIZED
APOTHEOSIZES
APOTHEOSIZING
APOTROPAIC
APOTROPAICALLY
APOTROPAISM
APOTROPAISMS
APOTROPOUS
APPALLINGLY
APPALOOSAS
APPARATCHIK
APPARATCHIKI
APPARATCHIKS
APPARATUSES
APPARELING
APPARELLED
APPARELLING
APPARELMENT
APPARELMENTS
APPARENCIES
APPARENTLY
APPARENTNESS
APPARENTNESSES
APPARITION
APPARITIONAL
APPARITIONS
APPARITORS
APPARTEMENT
APPARTEMENTS
APPASSIONATO
APPEACHING
APPEACHMENT
APPEACHMENTS
APPEALABILITIES
APPEALABILITY
APPEALABLE
APPEALINGLY
APPEALINGNESS
APPEALINGNESSES
APPEARANCE
APPEARANCES
APPEASABLE
APPEASEMENT
APPEASEMENTS
APPEASINGLY
APPELLANTS
APPELLATION
APPELLATIONAL

A

APPELLATIONS
APPELLATIVE
APPELLATIVELY
APPELLATIVES
APPENDAGES
APPENDANTS
APPENDECTOMIES
APPENDECTOMY
APPENDENTS
APPENDICECTOMY
APPENDICES
APPENDICITIS
APPENDICITISES
APPENDICLE
APPENDICLES
APPENDICULAR
APPENDICULARIAN
APPENDICULATE
APPENDIXES
APPERCEIVE
APPERCEIVED
APPERCEIVES
APPERCEIVING
APPERCEPTION
APPERCEPTIONS
APPERCEPTIVE
APPERCIPIENT
APPERTAINANCE
APPERTAINANCES
APPERTAINED
APPERTAINING
APPERTAINMENT
APPERTAINMENTS
APPERTAINS
APPERTINENT
APPERTINENTS
APPETEEZEMENT
APPETEEZEMENTS
APPETENCES
APPETENCIES
APPETISEMENT
APPETISEMENTS
APPETISERS
APPETISING
APPETISINGLY
APPETITION
APPETITIONS
APPETITIVE
APPETIZERS
APPETIZING
APPETIZINGLY
APPLAUDABLE
APPLAUDABLY
APPLAUDERS
APPLAUDING
APPLAUDINGLY
APPLAUSIVE
APPLAUSIVELY
APPLECARTS
APPLEDRAIN
APPLEDRAINS
APPLEJACKS
APPLERINGIE
APPLERINGIES
APPLESAUCE
APPLESAUCES
APPLETINIS
APPLIANCES
APPLICABILITIES
APPLICABILITY
APPLICABLE
APPLICABLENESS
APPLICABLY
APPLICANTS
APPLICATION
APPLICATIONS
APPLICATIVE
APPLICATIVELY
APPLICATOR
APPLICATORS
APPLICATORY
APPLIQUEING
APPOGGIATURA
APPOGGIATURAS
APPOGGIATURE
APPOINTEES
APPOINTERS
APPOINTING
APPOINTIVE
APPOINTMENT
APPOINTMENTS
APPOINTORS
APPORTIONABLE
APPORTIONED
APPORTIONER
APPORTIONERS
APPORTIONING
APPORTIONMENT
APPORTIONMENTS
APPORTIONS
APPOSITELY
APPOSITENESS
APPOSITENESSES
APPOSITION
APPOSITIONAL
APPOSITIONS
APPOSITIVE
APPOSITIVELY
APPOSITIVES
APPRAISABLE
APPRAISALS
APPRAISEES
APPRAISEMENT
APPRAISEMENTS
APPRAISERS
APPRAISING
APPRAISINGLY
APPRAISIVE
APPRAISIVELY
APPRECIABLE
APPRECIABLY
APPRECIATE
APPRECIATED
APPRECIATES
APPRECIATING
APPRECIATION
APPRECIATIONS
APPRECIATIVE
APPRECIATIVELY
APPRECIATOR
APPRECIATORILY
APPRECIATORS
APPRECIATORY
APPREHENDED
APPREHENDING
APPREHENDS
APPREHENSIBLE
APPREHENSIBLY
APPREHENSION
APPREHENSIONS
APPREHENSIVE
APPREHENSIVELY
APPRENTICE
APPRENTICED
APPRENTICEHOOD
APPRENTICEHOODS
APPRENTICEMENT
APPRENTICEMENTS
APPRENTICES
APPRENTICESHIP
APPRENTICESHIPS
APPRENTICING
APPRESSING
APPRESSORIA
APPRESSORIUM
APPRISINGS
APPRIZINGS
APPROACHABILITY
APPROACHABLE
APPROACHED
APPROACHES
APPROACHING
APPROBATED
APPROBATES
APPROBATING
APPROBATION
APPROBATIONS
APPROBATIVE
APPROBATORY
APPROPINQUATE
APPROPINQUATED
APPROPINQUATES
APPROPINQUATING
APPROPINQUATION
APPROPINQUE
APPROPINQUED
APPROPINQUES
APPROPINQUING
APPROPINQUITIES
APPROPINQUITY
APPROPRIABLE
APPROPRIACIES
APPROPRIACY
APPROPRIATE
APPROPRIATED
APPROPRIATELY
APPROPRIATENESS
APPROPRIATES
APPROPRIATING
APPROPRIATION
APPROPRIATIONS
APPROPRIATIVE
APPROPRIATOR
APPROPRIATORS
APPROVABLE
APPROVABLY
APPROVANCE
APPROVANCES
APPROVINGLY
APPROXIMAL
APPROXIMATE
APPROXIMATED
APPROXIMATELY
APPROXIMATES
APPROXIMATING
APPROXIMATION
APPROXIMATIONS
APPROXIMATIVE
APPROXIMEETING
APPROXIMEETINGS
APPULSIVELY
APPURTENANCE
APPURTENANCES
APPURTENANT
APPURTENANTS
APRICATING
APRICATION
APRICATIONS
APRIORISMS
APRIORISTS
APRIORITIES
APSIDIOLES
APTERYGIAL
APTITUDINAL
APTITUDINALLY
AQUABATICS
AQUABOARDS
AQUACEUTICAL
AQUACEUTICALS
AQUACULTURAL
AQUACULTURE
AQUACULTURES
AQUACULTURIST
AQUACULTURISTS
AQUADROMES
AQUAEROBICS
AQUAFARMED
AQUAFARMING
AQUAFARMINGS
AQUAFITNESS

AQUAFITNESSES
AQUAFORTIS
AQUAFORTISES
AQUAFORTIST
AQUAFORTISTS
AQUALEATHER
AQUALEATHERS
AQUAMANALE
AQUAMANALES
AQUAMANILE
AQUAMANILES
AQUAMARINE
AQUAMARINES
AQUANAUTICS
AQUAPHOBES
AQUAPHOBIA
AQUAPHOBIAS
AQUAPHOBIC
AQUAPHOBICS
AQUAPLANED
AQUAPLANER
AQUAPLANERS
AQUAPLANES
AQUAPLANING
AQUAPLANINGS
AQUAPORINS
AQUARELLES
AQUARELLIST
AQUARELLISTS
AQUARIISTS
AQUAROBICS
AQUASCAPES
AQUATICALLY
AQUATINTAS
AQUATINTED
AQUATINTER
AQUATINTERS
AQUATINTING
AQUATINTIST
AQUATINTISTS
AQUICULTURAL
AQUICULTURE
AQUICULTURES
AQUICULTURIST
AQUICULTURISTS
AQUIFEROUS
AQUIFOLIACEOUS
AQUILEGIAS
AQUILINITIES
AQUILINITY
ARABESQUED
ARABESQUES
ARABICISATION
ARABICISATIONS
ARABICISED
ARABICISES
ARABICISING
ARABICIZATION
ARABICIZATIONS
ARABICIZED
ARABICIZES
ARABICIZING
ARABILITIES
ARABINOSES
ARABINOSIDE
ARABINOSIDES
ARABISATION
ARABISATIONS
ARABIZATION
ARABIZATIONS
ARACHIDONIC
ARACHNIDAN
ARACHNIDANS
ARACHNOIDAL
ARACHNOIDITIS
ARACHNOIDITISES
ARACHNOIDS
ARACHNOLOGICAL
ARACHNOLOGIES
ARACHNOLOGIST
ARACHNOLOGISTS
ARACHNOLOGY
ARACHNOPHOBE
ARACHNOPHOBES
ARACHNOPHOBIA
ARACHNOPHOBIAS
ARACHNOPHOBIC
ARACHNOPHOBICS
ARAEOMETER
ARAEOMETERS
ARAEOMETRIC
ARAEOMETRICAL
ARAEOMETRIES
ARAEOMETRY
ARAEOSTYLE
ARAEOSTYLES
ARAEOSYSTYLE
ARAEOSYSTYLES
ARAGONITES
ARAGONITIC
ARALIACEOUS
ARAUCARIAN
ARAUCARIAS
ARBALESTER
ARBALESTERS
ARBALISTER
ARBALISTERS
ARBITRABLE
ARBITRAGED
ARBITRAGER
ARBITRAGERS
ARBITRAGES
ARBITRAGEUR
ARBITRAGEURS
ARBITRAGING
ARBITRAMENT
ARBITRAMENTS
ARBITRARILY
ARBITRARINESS
ARBITRARINESSES
ARBITRATED
ARBITRATES
ARBITRATING
ARBITRATION
ARBITRATIONAL
ARBITRATIONS
ARBITRATIVE
ARBITRATOR
ARBITRATORS
ARBITRATRICES
ARBITRATRIX
ARBITRATRIXES
ARBITREMENT
ARBITREMENTS
ARBITRESSES
ARBITRIUMS
ARBLASTERS
ARBORACEOUS
ARBOREALLY
ARBORESCENCE
ARBORESCENCES
ARBORESCENT
ARBORETUMS
ARBORICULTURAL
ARBORICULTURE
ARBORICULTURES
ARBORICULTURIST
ARBORISATION
ARBORISATIONS
ARBORISING
ARBORIZATION
ARBORIZATIONS
ARBORIZING
ARBORVITAE
ARBORVITAES
ARBOVIRUSES
ARBUSCULAR
ARCANENESS
ARCANENESSES
ARCCOSINES
ARCHAEBACTERIA
ARCHAEBACTERIUM
ARCHAEOBOTANIES
ARCHAEOBOTANIST
ARCHAEOBOTANY
ARCHAEOLOGICAL
ARCHAEOLOGIES
ARCHAEOLOGIST
ARCHAEOLOGISTS
ARCHAEOLOGY
ARCHAEOMETRIC
ARCHAEOMETRIES
ARCHAEOMETRIST
ARCHAEOMETRISTS
ARCHAEOMETRY
ARCHAEOPTERYX
ARCHAEOPTERYXES
ARCHAEORNIS
ARCHAEORNISES
ARCHAEOZOOLOGY
ARCHAEZOOLOGIES
ARCHAEZOOLOGY
ARCHAICALLY
ARCHAICISM
ARCHAICISMS
ARCHAISERS
ARCHAISING
ARCHAISTIC
ARCHAIZERS
ARCHAIZING
ARCHANGELIC
ARCHANGELS
ARCHBISHOP
ARCHBISHOPRIC
ARCHBISHOPRICS
ARCHBISHOPS
ARCHDEACON
ARCHDEACONRIES
ARCHDEACONRY
ARCHDEACONS
ARCHDIOCESAN
ARCHDIOCESE
ARCHDIOCESES
ARCHDRUIDS
ARCHDUCHESS
ARCHDUCHESSES
ARCHDUCHIES
ARCHDUKEDOM
ARCHDUKEDOMS
ARCHEGONIA
ARCHEGONIAL
ARCHEGONIATE
ARCHEGONIATES
ARCHEGONIUM
ARCHENEMIES
ARCHENTERA
ARCHENTERIC
ARCHENTERON
ARCHENTERONS
ARCHEOASTRONOMY
ARCHEOBOTANIES
ARCHEOBOTANIST
ARCHEOBOTANISTS
ARCHEOBOTANY
ARCHEOLOGICAL
ARCHEOLOGICALLY
ARCHEOLOGIES
ARCHEOLOGIST
ARCHEOLOGISTS
ARCHEOLOGY
ARCHEOMAGNETISM
ARCHEOMETRIES
ARCHEOMETRY
ARCHEOZOOLOGIES
ARCHEOZOOLOGIST
ARCHEOZOOLOGY
ARCHERESSES
ARCHERFISH
ARCHERFISHES
ARCHESPORE

ARCHESPORES
ARCHESPORIA
ARCHESPORIAL
ARCHESPORIUM
ARCHETYPAL
ARCHETYPALLY
ARCHETYPES
ARCHETYPICAL
ARCHETYPICALLY
ARCHFIENDS
ARCHGENETHLIAC
ARCHGENETHLIACS
ARCHICARPS
ARCHIDIACONAL
ARCHIDIACONATE
ARCHIDIACONATES
ARCHIEPISCOPACY
ARCHIEPISCOPAL
ARCHIEPISCOPATE
ARCHILOWES
ARCHIMAGES
ARCHIMANDRITE
ARCHIMANDRITES
ARCHIPELAGIAN
ARCHIPELAGIC
ARCHIPELAGO
ARCHIPELAGOES
ARCHIPELAGOS
ARCHIPHONEME
ARCHIPHONEMES
ARCHIPLASM
ARCHIPLASMIC
ARCHIPLASMS
ARCHITECTED
ARCHITECTING
ARCHITECTONIC
ARCHITECTONICS
ARCHITECTS
ARCHITECTURAL
ARCHITECTURALLY
ARCHITECTURE
ARCHITECTURES
ARCHITRAVE
ARCHITRAVED
ARCHITRAVES
ARCHITYPES
ARCHIVISTS
ARCHIVOLTS

ARCHNESSES
ARCHOLOGIES
ARCHONSHIP
ARCHONSHIPS
ARCHONTATE
ARCHONTATES
ARCHOPLASM
ARCHOPLASMIC
ARCHOPLASMS
ARCHOSAURIAN
ARCHOSAURIANS
ARCHOSAURS
ARCHPRIEST
ARCHPRIESTHOOD
ARCHPRIESTHOODS
ARCHPRIESTS
ARCHPRIESTSHIP
ARCHPRIESTSHIPS
ARCHRIVALS
ARCHSTONES
ARCMINUTES
ARCOGRAPHS
ARCOLOGIES
ARCSECONDS
ARCTANGENT
ARCTANGENTS
ARCTICALLY
ARCTOPHILE
ARCTOPHILES
ARCTOPHILIA
ARCTOPHILIAS
ARCTOPHILIES
ARCTOPHILIST
ARCTOPHILISTS
ARCTOPHILS
ARCTOPHILY
ARCUATIONS
ARCUBALIST
ARCUBALISTS
ARDUOUSNESS
ARDUOUSNESSES
ARECOLINES
AREFACTION
AREFACTIONS
ARENACEOUS
ARENATIONS
ARENICOLOUS
AREOCENTRIC

AREOGRAPHIC
AREOGRAPHIES
AREOGRAPHY
AREOLATION
AREOLATIONS
AREOLOGIES
AREOMETERS
AREOMETRIES
AREOSTYLES
AREOSYSTILE
AREOSYSTILES
ARFVEDSONITE
ARFVEDSONITES
ARGENTIFEROUS
ARGENTINES
ARGENTITES
ARGILLACEOUS
ARGILLIFEROUS
ARGILLITES
ARGILLITIC
ARGONAUTIC
ARGUMENTATION
ARGUMENTATIONS
ARGUMENTATIVE
ARGUMENTATIVELY
ARGUMENTIVE
ARGUMENTUM
ARGUMENTUMS
ARGUTENESS
ARGUTENESSES
ARGYRODITE
ARGYRODITES
ARHATSHIPS
ARHYTHMIAS
ARIBOFLAVINOSES
ARIBOFLAVINOSIS
ARIDNESSES
ARISTOCRACIES
ARISTOCRACY
ARISTOCRAT
ARISTOCRATIC
ARISTOCRATICAL
ARISTOCRATISM
ARISTOCRATISMS
ARISTOCRATS
ARISTOLOCHIA
ARISTOLOCHIAS
ARISTOLOGIES

ARISTOLOGY
ARISTOTLES
ARITHMETIC
ARITHMETICAL
ARITHMETICALLY
ARITHMETICIAN
ARITHMETICIANS
ARITHMETICS
ARITHMOMANIA
ARITHMOMANIAS
ARITHMOMETER
ARITHMOMETERS
ARITHMOPHOBIA
ARITHMOPHOBIAS
ARMADILLOS
ARMAMENTARIA
ARMAMENTARIUM
ARMAMENTARIUMS
ARMATURING
ARMIGEROUS
ARMILLARIA
ARMILLARIAS
ARMIPOTENCE
ARMIPOTENCES
ARMIPOTENT
ARMISTICES
ARMLOCKING
ARMORIALLY
ARMOURLESS
AROMATASES
AROMATHERAPIES
AROMATHERAPIST
AROMATHERAPISTS
AROMATHERAPY
AROMATICALLY
AROMATICITIES
AROMATICITY
AROMATISATION
AROMATISATIONS
AROMATISED
AROMATISES
AROMATISING
AROMATIZATION
AROMATIZATIONS
AROMATIZED
AROMATIZES
AROMATIZING
ARPEGGIATE

ARPEGGIATED
ARPEGGIATES
ARPEGGIATING
ARPEGGIATION
ARPEGGIATIONS
ARPEGGIONE
ARPEGGIONES
ARPILLERAS
ARQUEBUSADE
ARQUEBUSADES
ARQUEBUSES
ARQUEBUSIER
ARQUEBUSIERS
ARRACACHAS
ARRAGONITE
ARRAGONITES
ARRAGONITIC
ARRAIGNERS
ARRAIGNING
ARRAIGNINGS
ARRAIGNMENT
ARRAIGNMENTS
ARRANGEABLE
ARRANGEMENT
ARRANGEMENTS
ARRAYMENTS
ARREARAGES
ARRESTABLE
ARRESTANTS
ARRESTATION
ARRESTATIONS
ARRESTINGLY
ARRESTMENT
ARRESTMENTS
ARRHENOTOKIES
ARRHENOTOKY
ARRHYTHMIA
ARRHYTHMIAS
ARRHYTHMIC
ARRIVANCES
ARRIVANCIES
ARRIVEDERCI
ARRIVISMES
ARRIVISTES
ARROGANCES
ARROGANCIES
ARROGANTLY
ARROGATING

ARROGATION
ARROGATIONS
ARROGATIVE
ARROGATORS
ARRONDISSEMENT
ARRONDISSEMENTS
ARROWGRASS
ARROWGRASSES
ARROWHEADS
ARROWROOTS
ARROWWOODS
ARROWWORMS
ARSENIATES
ARSENICALS
ARSENOPYRITE
ARSENOPYRITES
ARSMETRICK
ARSMETRICKS
ARSPHENAMINE
ARSPHENAMINES
ARTEFACTUAL
ARTEMISIAS
ARTEMISININ
ARTEMISININS
ARTERIALISATION
ARTERIALISE
ARTERIALISED
ARTERIALISES
ARTERIALISING
ARTERIALIZATION
ARTERIALIZE
ARTERIALIZED
ARTERIALIZES
ARTERIALIZING
ARTERIALLY
ARTERIOGRAM
ARTERIOGRAMS
ARTERIOGRAPHIC
ARTERIOGRAPHIES
ARTERIOGRAPHY
ARTERIOLAR
ARTERIOLES
ARTERIOTOMIES
ARTERIOTOMY
ARTERIOVENOUS
ARTERITIDES
ARTERITISES
ARTFULNESS
ARTFULNESSES
ARTHRALGIA
ARTHRALGIAS
ARTHRALGIC
ARTHRECTOMIES
ARTHRECTOMY
ARTHRITICALLY
ARTHRITICS
ARTHRITIDES
ARTHRITISES
ARTHRODESES
ARTHRODESIS
ARTHRODIAE
ARTHRODIAL
ARTHROGRAPHIES
ARTHROGRAPHY
ARTHROMERE
ARTHROMERES
ARTHROMERIC
ARTHROPATHIES
ARTHROPATHY
ARTHROPLASTIES
ARTHROPLASTY
ARTHROPODAL
ARTHROPODAN
ARTHROPODOUS
ARTHROPODS
ARTHROSCOPE
ARTHROSCOPES
ARTHROSCOPIC
ARTHROSCOPIES
ARTHROSCOPY
ARTHROSPORE
ARTHROSPORES
ARTHROSPORIC
ARTHROSPOROUS
ARTICHOKES
ARTICULABLE
ARTICULACIES
ARTICULACY
ARTICULATE
ARTICULATED
ARTICULATELY
ARTICULATENESS
ARTICULATES
ARTICULATING
ARTICULATION
ARTICULATIONS
ARTICULATIVE
ARTICULATOR
ARTICULATORS
ARTICULATORY
ARTIFACTUAL
ARTIFICERS
ARTIFICIAL
ARTIFICIALISE
ARTIFICIALISED
ARTIFICIALISES
ARTIFICIALISING
ARTIFICIALITIES
ARTIFICIALITY
ARTIFICIALIZE
ARTIFICIALIZED
ARTIFICIALIZES
ARTIFICIALIZING
ARTIFICIALLY
ARTIFICIALNESS
ARTILLERIES
ARTILLERIST
ARTILLERISTS
ARTILLERYMAN
ARTILLERYMEN
ARTINESSES
ARTIODACTYL
ARTIODACTYLOUS
ARTIODACTYLS
ARTISANSHIP
ARTISANSHIPS
ARTISTICAL
ARTISTICALLY
ARTISTRIES
ARTLESSNESS
ARTLESSNESSES
ARTMAKINGS
ARTOCARPUS
ARTOCARPUSES
ARTSINESSES
ARUNDINACEOUS
ARVICOLINE
ARYBALLOID
ARYBALLOSES
ARYTAENOID
ARYTAENOIDS
ARYTENOIDAL
ARYTENOIDS
ASAFETIDAS
ASAFOETIDA
ASAFOETIDAS
ASARABACCA
ASARABACCAS
ASBESTIFORM
ASBESTOSES
ASBESTOSIS
ASBESTUSES
ASCARIASES
ASCARIASIS
ASCENDABLE
ASCENDANCE
ASCENDANCES
ASCENDANCIES
ASCENDANCY
ASCENDANTLY
ASCENDANTS
ASCENDENCE
ASCENDENCES
ASCENDENCIES
ASCENDENCY
ASCENDENTS
ASCENDEURS
ASCENDIBLE
ASCENSIONAL
ASCENSIONIST
ASCENSIONISTS
ASCENSIONS
ASCERTAINABLE
ASCERTAINABLY
ASCERTAINED
ASCERTAINING
ASCERTAINMENT
ASCERTAINMENTS
ASCERTAINS
ASCETICALLY
ASCETICISM
ASCETICISMS
ASCITITIOUS
ASCLEPIADACEOUS
ASCLEPIADS
ASCLEPIASES
ASCOCARPIC
ASCOGONIUM
ASCOMYCETE
ASCOMYCETES
ASCOMYCETOUS
ASCORBATES
ASCOSPORES
ASCOSPORIC
ASCRIBABLE
ASCRIPTION
ASCRIPTIONS
ASCRIPTIVE
ASEPTICALLY
ASEPTICISE
ASEPTICISED
ASEPTICISES
ASEPTICISING
ASEPTICISM
ASEPTICISMS
ASEPTICIZE
ASEPTICIZED
ASEPTICIZES
ASEPTICIZING
ASEXUALITIES
ASEXUALITY
ASHAMEDNESS
ASHAMEDNESSES
ASHINESSES
ASHLARINGS
ASHLERINGS
ASHRAMITES
ASININITIES
ASKEWNESSES
ASPARAGINASE
ASPARAGINASES
ASPARAGINE
ASPARAGINES
ASPARAGUSES
ASPARTAMES
ASPARTATES
ASPECTABLE
ASPERATING
ASPERGATION
ASPERGATIONS
ASPERGILLA
ASPERGILLI
ASPERGILLOSES
ASPERGILLOSIS
ASPERGILLS
ASPERGILLUM
ASPERGILLUMS
ASPERGILLUS
ASPERITIES
ASPERSIONS

ASPERSIVELY
ASPERSOIRS
ASPERSORIA
ASPERSORIES
ASPERSORIUM
ASPERSORIUMS
ASPHALTERS
ASPHALTING
ASPHALTITE
ASPHALTITES
ASPHALTUMS
ASPHERICAL
ASPHETERISE
ASPHETERISED
ASPHETERISES
ASPHETERISING
ASPHETERISM
ASPHETERISMS
ASPHETERIZE
ASPHETERIZED
ASPHETERIZES
ASPHETERIZING
ASPHYXIANT
ASPHYXIANTS
ASPHYXIATE
ASPHYXIATED
ASPHYXIATES
ASPHYXIATING
ASPHYXIATION
ASPHYXIATIONS
ASPHYXIATOR
ASPHYXIATORS
ASPHYXYING
ASPIDISTRA
ASPIDISTRAS
ASPIRATING
ASPIRATION
ASPIRATIONAL
ASPIRATIONS
ASPIRATORS
ASPIRATORY
ASPIRINGLY
ASPIRINGNESS
ASPIRINGNESSES
ASPLANCHNIC
ASPLENIUMS
ASPORTATION
ASPORTATIONS
ASSAFETIDA
ASSAFETIDAS
ASSAFOETIDA
ASSAFOETIDAS
ASSAGAIING
ASSAILABLE
ASSAILANTS
ASSAILMENT
ASSAILMENTS
ASSASSINATE
ASSASSINATED
ASSASSINATES
ASSASSINATING
ASSASSINATION
ASSASSINATIONS
ASSASSINATOR
ASSASSINATORS
ASSAULTERS
ASSAULTING
ASSAULTIVE
ASSAULTIVELY
ASSAULTIVENESS
ASSEGAAIED
ASSEGAAIING
ASSEGAIING
ASSEMBLAGE
ASSEMBLAGES
ASSEMBLAGIST
ASSEMBLAGISTS
ASSEMBLANCE
ASSEMBLANCES
ASSEMBLAUNCE
ASSEMBLAUNCES
ASSEMBLERS
ASSEMBLIES
ASSEMBLING
ASSEMBLYMAN
ASSEMBLYMEN
ASSEMBLYWOMAN
ASSEMBLYWOMEN
ASSENTANEOUS
ASSENTATION
ASSENTATIONS
ASSENTATOR
ASSENTATORS
ASSENTIENT
ASSENTIENTS
ASSENTINGLY
ASSENTIVENESS
ASSENTIVENESSES
ASSERTABLE
ASSERTEDLY
ASSERTIBLE
ASSERTIONS
ASSERTIVELY
ASSERTIVENESS
ASSERTIVENESSES
ASSERTORIC
ASSESSABLE
ASSESSMENT
ASSESSMENTS
ASSESSORIAL
ASSESSORSHIP
ASSESSORSHIPS
ASSEVERATE
ASSEVERATED
ASSEVERATES
ASSEVERATING
ASSEVERATINGLY
ASSEVERATION
ASSEVERATIONS
ASSEVERATIVE
ASSEVERING
ASSIBILATE
ASSIBILATED
ASSIBILATES
ASSIBILATING
ASSIBILATION
ASSIBILATIONS
ASSIDUITIES
ASSIDUOUSLY
ASSIDUOUSNESS
ASSIDUOUSNESSES
ASSIGNABILITIES
ASSIGNABILITY
ASSIGNABLE
ASSIGNABLY
ASSIGNATION
ASSIGNATIONS
ASSIGNMENT
ASSIGNMENTS
ASSIMILABILITY
ASSIMILABLE
ASSIMILABLY
ASSIMILATE
ASSIMILATED
ASSIMILATES
ASSIMILATING
ASSIMILATION
ASSIMILATIONISM
ASSIMILATIONIST
ASSIMILATIONS
ASSIMILATIVE
ASSIMILATIVELY
ASSIMILATOR
ASSIMILATORS
ASSIMILATORY
ASSISTANCE
ASSISTANCES
ASSISTANTS
ASSISTANTSHIP
ASSISTANTSHIPS
ASSOCIABILITIES
ASSOCIABILITY
ASSOCIABLE
ASSOCIATED
ASSOCIATES
ASSOCIATESHIP
ASSOCIATESHIPS
ASSOCIATING
ASSOCIATION
ASSOCIATIONAL
ASSOCIATIONISM
ASSOCIATIONISMS
ASSOCIATIONIST
ASSOCIATIONISTS
ASSOCIATIONS
ASSOCIATIVE
ASSOCIATIVELY
ASSOCIATIVITIES
ASSOCIATIVITY
ASSOCIATOR
ASSOCIATORS
ASSOCIATORY
ASSOILMENT
ASSOILMENTS
ASSOILZIED
ASSOILZIEING
ASSOILZIES
ASSONANCES
ASSONANTAL
ASSONATING
ASSORTATIVE
ASSORTATIVELY
ASSORTEDNESS
ASSORTEDNESSES
ASSORTMENT
ASSORTMENTS
ASSUAGEMENT
ASSUAGEMENTS
ASSUAGINGS
ASSUBJUGATE
ASSUBJUGATED
ASSUBJUGATES
ASSUBJUGATING
ASSUEFACTION
ASSUEFACTIONS
ASSUETUDES
ASSUMABILITIES
ASSUMABILITY
ASSUMINGLY
ASSUMPSITS
ASSUMPTION
ASSUMPTIONS
ASSUMPTIVE
ASSUMPTIVELY
ASSURANCES
ASSUREDNESS
ASSUREDNESSES
ASSURGENCIES
ASSURGENCY
ASSYTHMENT
ASSYTHMENTS
ASTACOLOGICAL
ASTACOLOGIES
ASTACOLOGIST
ASTACOLOGISTS
ASTACOLOGY
ASTARBOARD
ASTATICALLY
ASTATICISM
ASTATICISMS
ASTEREOGNOSES
ASTEREOGNOSIS
ASTERIATED
ASTERIDIAN
ASTERIDIANS
ASTERISKED
ASTERISKING
ASTERISKLESS
ASTEROIDAL
ASTEROIDEAN

ASTEROIDEANS
ASTHENOPIA
ASTHENOPIAS
ASTHENOPIC
ASTHENOSPHERE
ASTHENOSPHERES
ASTHENOSPHERIC
ASTHMATICAL
ASTHMATICALLY
ASTHMATICS
ASTIGMATIC
ASTIGMATICALLY
ASTIGMATICS
ASTIGMATISM
ASTIGMATISMS
ASTOMATOUS
ASTONISHED
ASTONISHES
ASTONISHING
ASTONISHINGLY
ASTONISHMENT
ASTONISHMENTS
ASTOUNDING
ASTOUNDINGLY
ASTOUNDMENT
ASTOUNDMENTS
ASTRACHANS
ASTRAGALUS
ASTRAKHANS
ASTRANTIAS
ASTRAPHOBIA
ASTRAPHOBIAS
ASTRAPHOBIC
ASTRAPOPHOBIA
ASTRAPOPHOBIAS
ASTRICTING
ASTRICTION
ASTRICTIONS
ASTRICTIVE
ASTRICTIVELY
ASTRINGENCE
ASTRINGENCES
ASTRINGENCIES
ASTRINGENCY
ASTRINGENT
ASTRINGENTLY
ASTRINGENTS
ASTRINGERS
ASTRINGING
ASTROBIOLOGIES
ASTROBIOLOGIST
ASTROBIOLOGISTS
ASTROBIOLOGY
ASTROBLEME
ASTROBLEMES
ASTROBOTANIES
ASTROBOTANY
ASTROCHEMISTRY
ASTROCOMPASS
ASTROCOMPASSES
ASTROCYTES
ASTROCYTIC
ASTROCYTOMA
ASTROCYTOMAS
ASTROCYTOMATA
ASTRODOMES
ASTRODYNAMICIST
ASTRODYNAMICS
ASTROFELLS
ASTROGEOLOGIES
ASTROGEOLOGIST
ASTROGEOLOGISTS
ASTROGEOLOGY
ASTROHATCH
ASTROHATCHES
ASTROLABES
ASTROLATRIES
ASTROLATRY
ASTROLOGER
ASTROLOGERS
ASTROLOGIC
ASTROLOGICAL
ASTROLOGICALLY
ASTROLOGIES
ASTROLOGIST
ASTROLOGISTS
ASTROMETRIC
ASTROMETRICAL
ASTROMETRIES
ASTROMETRY
ASTRONAUTIC
ASTRONAUTICAL
ASTRONAUTICALLY
ASTRONAUTICS
ASTRONAUTS
ASTRONAVIGATION
ASTRONAVIGATOR
ASTRONAVIGATORS
ASTRONOMER
ASTRONOMERS
ASTRONOMIC
ASTRONOMICAL
ASTRONOMICALLY
ASTRONOMIES
ASTRONOMISE
ASTRONOMISED
ASTRONOMISES
ASTRONOMISING
ASTRONOMIZE
ASTRONOMIZED
ASTRONOMIZES
ASTRONOMIZING
ASTROPHELS
ASTROPHOBIA
ASTROPHOBIAS
ASTROPHOBIC
ASTROPHOTOGRAPH
ASTROPHYSICAL
ASTROPHYSICALLY
ASTROPHYSICIST
ASTROPHYSICISTS
ASTROPHYSICS
ASTROSPHERE
ASTROSPHERES
ASTROTOURISM
ASTROTOURISMS
ASTROTOURIST
ASTROTOURISTS
ASTROTURFER
ASTROTURFERS
ASTROTURFING
ASTROTURFINGS
ASTUCIOUSLY
ASTUCITIES
ASTUTENESS
ASTUTENESSES
ASYMMETRIC
ASYMMETRICAL
ASYMMETRICALLY
ASYMMETRIES
ASYMPTOMATIC
ASYMPTOTES
ASYMPTOTIC
ASYMPTOTICAL
ASYMPTOTICALLY
ASYNARTETE
ASYNARTETES
ASYNARTETIC
ASYNCHRONIES
ASYNCHRONISM
ASYNCHRONISMS
ASYNCHRONOUS
ASYNCHRONOUSLY
ASYNCHRONY
ASYNDETICALLY
ASYNDETONS
ASYNERGIAS
ASYNERGIES
ASYNTACTIC
ASYSTOLISM
ASYSTOLISMS
ATACAMITES
ATARACTICS
ATAVISTICALLY
ATCHIEVING
ATELECTASES
ATELECTASIS
ATELECTATIC
ATELEIOSES
ATELEIOSIS
ATHANASIES
ATHEISTICAL
ATHEISTICALLY
ATHEMATICALLY
ATHENAEUMS
ATHEOLOGICAL
ATHEOLOGIES
ATHEORETICAL
ATHERMANCIES
ATHERMANCY
ATHERMANOUS
ATHEROGENESES
ATHEROGENESIS
ATHEROGENIC
ATHEROMATA
ATHEROMATOUS
ATHEROSCLEROSES
ATHEROSCLEROSIS
ATHEROSCLEROTIC
ATHETISING
ATHETIZING
ATHLEISURE
ATHLEISURES
ATHLETICALLY
ATHLETICISM
ATHLETICISMS
ATHROCYTES
ATHROCYTOSES
ATHROCYTOSIS
ATHWARTSHIP
ATHWARTSHIPS
ATMOLOGIES
ATMOLOGIST
ATMOLOGISTS
ATMOLYSING
ATMOLYZING
ATMOMETERS
ATMOMETRIES
ATMOSPHERE
ATMOSPHERED
ATMOSPHERES
ATMOSPHERIC
ATMOSPHERICAL
ATMOSPHERICALLY
ATMOSPHERICS
ATOMICALLY
ATOMICITIES
ATOMISATION
ATOMISATIONS
ATOMISTICAL
ATOMISTICALLY
ATOMIZATION
ATOMIZATIONS
ATONALISMS
ATONALISTS
ATONALITIES
ATONEMENTS
ATONICITIES
ATORVASTATIN
ATORVASTATINS
ATRABILIAR
ATRABILIOUS
ATRABILIOUSNESS
ATRACURIUM
ATRACURIUMS
ATRAMENTAL
ATRAMENTOUS
ATROCIOUSLY
ATROCIOUSNESS
ATROCIOUSNESSES

ATROCITIES
ATROPHYING
ATTACHABLE
ATTACHMENT
ATTACHMENTS
ATTACKABLE
ATTAINABILITIES
ATTAINABILITY
ATTAINABLE
ATTAINABLENESS
ATTAINDERS
ATTAINMENT
ATTAINMENTS
ATTAINTING
ATTAINTMENT
ATTAINTMENTS
ATTAINTURE
ATTAINTURES
ATTEMPERED
ATTEMPERING
ATTEMPERMENT
ATTEMPERMENTS
ATTEMPTABILITY
ATTEMPTABLE
ATTEMPTERS
ATTEMPTING
ATTENDANCE
ATTENDANCES
ATTENDANCIES
ATTENDANCY
ATTENDANTS
ATTENDEMENT
ATTENDEMENTS
ATTENDINGS
ATTENDMENT
ATTENDMENTS
ATTENTIONAL
ATTENTIONS
ATTENTIVELY
ATTENTIVENESS
ATTENTIVENESSES
ATTENUANTS
ATTENUATED
ATTENUATES
ATTENUATING
ATTENUATION
ATTENUATIONS
ATTENUATOR
ATTENUATORS
ATTESTABLE
ATTESTANTS
ATTESTATION
ATTESTATIONS
ATTESTATIVE
ATTESTATOR
ATTESTATORS
ATTICISING
ATTICIZING
ATTIREMENT
ATTIREMENTS
ATTITUDINAL
ATTITUDINALLY
ATTITUDINARIAN
ATTITUDINARIANS
ATTITUDINISE
ATTITUDINISED
ATTITUDINISER
ATTITUDINISERS
ATTITUDINISES
ATTITUDINISING
ATTITUDINISINGS
ATTITUDINIZE
ATTITUDINIZED
ATTITUDINIZER
ATTITUDINIZERS
ATTITUDINIZES
ATTITUDINIZING
ATTITUDINIZINGS
ATTOLASERS
ATTOLLENTS
ATTOMETERS
ATTOMETRES
ATTOPHYSICS
ATTORNEYDOM
ATTORNEYDOMS
ATTORNEYED
ATTORNEYING
ATTORNEYISM
ATTORNEYISMS
ATTORNEYSHIP
ATTORNEYSHIPS
ATTORNMENT
ATTORNMENTS
ATTOSECOND
ATTOSECONDS
ATTOTESLAS
ATTRACTABLE
ATTRACTANCE
ATTRACTANCES
ATTRACTANCIES
ATTRACTANCY
ATTRACTANT
ATTRACTANTS
ATTRACTERS
ATTRACTING
ATTRACTINGLY
ATTRACTION
ATTRACTIONS
ATTRACTIVE
ATTRACTIVELY
ATTRACTIVENESS
ATTRACTORS
ATTRAHENTS
ATTRAPPING
ATTRIBUTABLE
ATTRIBUTED
ATTRIBUTER
ATTRIBUTERS
ATTRIBUTES
ATTRIBUTING
ATTRIBUTION
ATTRIBUTIONAL
ATTRIBUTIONS
ATTRIBUTIVE
ATTRIBUTIVELY
ATTRIBUTIVENESS
ATTRIBUTIVES
ATTRIBUTOR
ATTRIBUTORS
ATTRISTING
ATTRITIONAL
ATTRITIONS
ATTRITTING
ATTUITIONAL
ATTUITIONS
ATTUITIVELY
ATTUNEMENT
ATTUNEMENTS
ATYPICALITIES
ATYPICALITY
ATYPICALLY
AUBERGINES
AUBERGISTE
AUBERGISTES
AUBRIETIAS
AUCTIONARY
AUCTIONEER
AUCTIONEERED
AUCTIONEERING
AUCTIONEERS
AUCTIONING
AUDACIOUSLY
AUDACIOUSNESS
AUDACIOUSNESSES
AUDACITIES
AUDIBILITIES
AUDIBILITY
AUDIBLENESS
AUDIBLENESSES
AUDIENCIAS
AUDIOBOOKS
AUDIOCASSETTE
AUDIOCASSETTES
AUDIOGENIC
AUDIOGRAMS
AUDIOGRAPH
AUDIOGRAPHS
AUDIOLOGIC
AUDIOLOGICAL
AUDIOLOGICALLY
AUDIOLOGIES
AUDIOLOGIST
AUDIOLOGISTS
AUDIOMETER
AUDIOMETERS
AUDIOMETRIC
AUDIOMETRICALLY
AUDIOMETRICIAN
AUDIOMETRICIANS
AUDIOMETRIES
AUDIOMETRIST
AUDIOMETRISTS
AUDIOMETRY
AUDIOPHILE
AUDIOPHILES
AUDIOPHILS
AUDIOTAPED
AUDIOTAPES
AUDIOTAPING
AUDIOTYPING
AUDIOTYPINGS
AUDIOTYPIST
AUDIOTYPISTS
AUDIOVISUAL
AUDIOVISUALLY
AUDIOVISUALS
AUDIPHONES
AUDITIONED
AUDITIONER
AUDITIONERS
AUDITIONING
AUDITORIAL
AUDITORIES
AUDITORILY
AUDITORIUM
AUDITORIUMS
AUDITORSHIP
AUDITORSHIPS
AUDITRESSES
AUGMENTABLE
AUGMENTATION
AUGMENTATIONS
AUGMENTATIVE
AUGMENTATIVELY
AUGMENTATIVES
AUGMENTERS
AUGMENTING
AUGMENTORS
AUGURSHIPS
AUGUSTNESS
AUGUSTNESSES
AURALITIES
AUREATENESS
AUREATENESSES
AURICULARLY
AURICULARS
AURICULATE
AURICULATED
AURICULATELY
AURIFEROUS
AURISCOPES
AURISCOPIC
AUSCULTATE
AUSCULTATED
AUSCULTATES
AUSCULTATING
AUSCULTATION
AUSCULTATIONS
AUSCULTATIVE
AUSCULTATOR

AUSCULTATORS
AUSCULTATORY
AUSFORMING
AUSFORMINGS
AUSLANDERS
AUSPICATED
AUSPICATES
AUSPICATING
AUSPICIOUS
AUSPICIOUSLY
AUSPICIOUSNESS
AUSTENITES
AUSTENITIC
AUSTERENESS
AUSTERENESSES
AUSTERITIES
AUSTRALITE
AUSTRALITES
AUSTRINGER
AUSTRINGERS
AUTARCHICAL
AUTARCHIES
AUTARCHIST
AUTARCHISTS
AUTARKICAL
AUTARKISTS
AUTECOLOGIC
AUTECOLOGICAL
AUTECOLOGIES
AUTECOLOGY
AUTEURISMS
AUTEURISTS
AUTHENTICAL
AUTHENTICALLY
AUTHENTICATE
AUTHENTICATED
AUTHENTICATES
AUTHENTICATING
AUTHENTICATION
AUTHENTICATIONS
AUTHENTICATOR
AUTHENTICATORS
AUTHENTICITIES
AUTHENTICITY
AUTHIGENIC
AUTHORCRAFT
AUTHORCRAFTS
AUTHORESSES
AUTHORINGS
AUTHORISABLE
AUTHORISATION
AUTHORISATIONS
AUTHORISED
AUTHORISER
AUTHORISERS
AUTHORISES
AUTHORISING
AUTHORISMS
AUTHORITARIAN
AUTHORITARIANS
AUTHORITATIVE
AUTHORITATIVELY
AUTHORITIES
AUTHORIZABLE
AUTHORIZATION
AUTHORIZATIONS
AUTHORIZED
AUTHORIZER
AUTHORIZERS
AUTHORIZES
AUTHORIZING
AUTHORLESS
AUTHORSHIP
AUTHORSHIPS
AUTISTICALLY
AUTOALLOGAMIES
AUTOALLOGAMY
AUTOANTIBODIES
AUTOANTIBODY
AUTOBAHNEN
AUTOBIOGRAPHER
AUTOBIOGRAPHERS
AUTOBIOGRAPHIC
AUTOBIOGRAPHIES
AUTOBIOGRAPHY
AUTOBODIES
AUTOBUSSES
AUTOCATALYSE
AUTOCATALYSED
AUTOCATALYSES
AUTOCATALYSING
AUTOCATALYSIS
AUTOCATALYTIC
AUTOCATALYZE
AUTOCATALYZED
AUTOCATALYZES
AUTOCATALYZING
AUTOCEPHALIC
AUTOCEPHALIES
AUTOCEPHALOUS
AUTOCEPHALY
AUTOCHANGER
AUTOCHANGERS
AUTOCHTHON
AUTOCHTHONAL
AUTOCHTHONES
AUTOCHTHONIC
AUTOCHTHONIES
AUTOCHTHONISM
AUTOCHTHONISMS
AUTOCHTHONOUS
AUTOCHTHONOUSLY
AUTOCHTHONS
AUTOCHTHONY
AUTOCLAVED
AUTOCLAVES
AUTOCLAVING
AUTOCOMPLETE
AUTOCOMPLETES
AUTOCOPROPHAGY
AUTOCORRECT
AUTOCORRECTS
AUTOCORRELATION
AUTOCRACIES
AUTOCRATIC
AUTOCRATICAL
AUTOCRATICALLY
AUTOCRIMES
AUTOCRITIQUE
AUTOCRITIQUES
AUTOCROSSES
AUTOCUTIES
AUTOCYCLES
AUTODESTRUCT
AUTODESTRUCTED
AUTODESTRUCTING
AUTODESTRUCTIVE
AUTODESTRUCTS
AUTODIALED
AUTODIALING
AUTODIALLED
AUTODIALLING
AUTODIDACT
AUTODIDACTIC
AUTODIDACTICISM
AUTODIDACTS
AUTODROMES
AUTOECIOUS
AUTOECIOUSLY
AUTOECISMS
AUTOEROTIC
AUTOEROTICISM
AUTOEROTICISMS
AUTOEROTISM
AUTOEROTISMS
AUTOEXPOSURE
AUTOEXPOSURES
AUTOFLARES
AUTOFOCUSES
AUTOGAMIES
AUTOGAMOUS
AUTOGENESES
AUTOGENESIS
AUTOGENETIC
AUTOGENICS
AUTOGENIES
AUTOGENOUS
AUTOGENOUSLY
AUTOGRAFTED
AUTOGRAFTING
AUTOGRAFTS
AUTOGRAPHED
AUTOGRAPHIC
AUTOGRAPHICAL
AUTOGRAPHICALLY
AUTOGRAPHIES
AUTOGRAPHING
AUTOGRAPHS
AUTOGRAPHY
AUTOGRAVURE
AUTOGRAVURES
AUTOGUIDES
AUTOHYPNOSES
AUTOHYPNOSIS
AUTOHYPNOTIC
AUTOIMMUNE
AUTOIMMUNITIES
AUTOIMMUNITY
AUTOINFECTION
AUTOINFECTIONS
AUTOINOCULATION
AUTOIONISATION
AUTOIONISATIONS
AUTOIONIZATION
AUTOIONIZATIONS
AUTOJUMBLE
AUTOJUMBLES
AUTOKINESES
AUTOKINESIS
AUTOKINETIC
AUTOLATRIES
AUTOLOADED
AUTOLOADING
AUTOLOGIES
AUTOLOGOUS
AUTOLYSATE
AUTOLYSATES
AUTOLYSING
AUTOLYSINS
AUTOLYZATE
AUTOLYZATES
AUTOLYZING
AUTOMAGICALLY
AUTOMAKERS
AUTOMATABLE
AUTOMATICAL
AUTOMATICALLY
AUTOMATICITIES
AUTOMATICITY
AUTOMATICS
AUTOMATING
AUTOMATION
AUTOMATIONS
AUTOMATISATION
AUTOMATISATIONS
AUTOMATISE
AUTOMATISED
AUTOMATISES
AUTOMATISING
AUTOMATISM
AUTOMATISMS
AUTOMATIST
AUTOMATISTS
AUTOMATIZATION
AUTOMATIZATIONS
AUTOMATIZE
AUTOMATIZED
AUTOMATIZES
AUTOMATIZING
AUTOMATONS

A

AUTOMATOUS
AUTOMETERS
AUTOMOBILE
AUTOMOBILED
AUTOMOBILES
AUTOMOBILIA
AUTOMOBILING
AUTOMOBILISM
AUTOMOBILISMS
AUTOMOBILIST
AUTOMOBILISTS
AUTOMOBILITIES
AUTOMOBILITY
AUTOMORPHIC
AUTOMORPHICALLY
AUTOMORPHISM
AUTOMORPHISMS
AUTOMOTIVE
AUTONOMICAL
AUTONOMICALLY
AUTONOMICS
AUTONOMIES
AUTONOMIST
AUTONOMISTS
AUTONOMOUS
AUTONOMOUSLY
AUTONYMOUS
AUTOPHAGIA
AUTOPHAGIAS
AUTOPHAGIES
AUTOPHAGOUS
AUTOPHANOUS
AUTOPHOBIA
AUTOPHOBIAS
AUTOPHOBIES
AUTOPHONIES
AUTOPHYTES
AUTOPHYTIC
AUTOPHYTICALLY
AUTOPILOTS
AUTOPISTAS
AUTOPLASTIC
AUTOPLASTIES
AUTOPLASTY
AUTOPOINTS
AUTOPOLYPLOID
AUTOPOLYPLOIDS
AUTOPOLYPLOIDY
AUTOPSISTS
AUTOPSYING
AUTOPTICAL
AUTOPTICALLY
AUTORADIOGRAM
AUTORADIOGRAMS
AUTORADIOGRAPH
AUTORADIOGRAPHS
AUTORADIOGRAPHY
AUTOREPLIES
AUTOREVERSE
AUTOREVERSES
AUTORICKSHAW
AUTORICKSHAWS
AUTOROTATE
AUTOROTATED
AUTOROTATES
AUTOROTATING
AUTOROTATION
AUTOROTATIONS
AUTOROUTES
AUTOSAVING
AUTOSCHEDIASM
AUTOSCHEDIASMS
AUTOSCHEDIASTIC
AUTOSCHEDIAZE
AUTOSCHEDIAZED
AUTOSCHEDIAZES
AUTOSCHEDIAZING
AUTOSCOPIC
AUTOSCOPIES
AUTOSEXING
AUTOSEXINGS
AUTOSOMALLY
AUTOSPORES
AUTOSPORTS
AUTOSTABILITIES
AUTOSTABILITY
AUTOSTRADA
AUTOSTRADAS
AUTOSTRADE
AUTOSUGGEST
AUTOSUGGESTED
AUTOSUGGESTING
AUTOSUGGESTION
AUTOSUGGESTIONS
AUTOSUGGESTIVE
AUTOSUGGESTS
AUTOTELLER
AUTOTELLERS
AUTOTETRAPLOID
AUTOTETRAPLOIDS
AUTOTETRAPLOIDY
AUTOTHEISM
AUTOTHEISMS
AUTOTHEIST
AUTOTHEISTS
AUTOTIMERS
AUTOTOMIES
AUTOTOMISE
AUTOTOMISED
AUTOTOMISES
AUTOTOMISING
AUTOTOMIZE
AUTOTOMIZED
AUTOTOMIZES
AUTOTOMIZING
AUTOTOMOUS
AUTOTOXAEMIA
AUTOTOXAEMIAS
AUTOTOXEMIA
AUTOTOXEMIAS
AUTOTOXINS
AUTOTRANSFORMER
AUTOTRANSFUSION
AUTOTROPHIC
AUTOTROPHICALLY
AUTOTROPHIES
AUTOTROPHS
AUTOTROPHY
AUTOTYPIES
AUTOTYPING
AUTOTYPOGRAPHY
AUTOWINDER
AUTOWINDERS
AUTOWORKER
AUTOWORKERS
AUTOXIDATION
AUTOXIDATIONS
AUTUMNALLY
AUTUMNIEST
AUXANOMETER
AUXANOMETERS
AUXILIARIES
AUXOCHROME
AUXOCHROMES
AUXOMETERS
AUXOSPORES
AUXOTROPHIC
AUXOTROPHIES
AUXOTROPHS
AUXOTROPHY
AVAILABILITIES
AVAILABILITY
AVAILABLENESS
AVAILABLENESSES
AVAILINGLY
AVALANCHED
AVALANCHES
AVALANCHING
AVALEMENTS
AVANTURINE
AVANTURINES
AVARICIOUS
AVARICIOUSLY
AVARICIOUSNESS
AVASCULARITIES
AVASCULARITY
AVENACEOUS
AVENGEMENT
AVENGEMENTS
AVENGERESS
AVENGERESSES
AVENTAILES
AVENTURINE
AVENTURINES
AVENTURINS
AVERAGENESS
AVERAGENESSES
AVERAGINGS
AVERRUNCATE
AVERRUNCATED
AVERRUNCATES
AVERRUNCATING
AVERRUNCATION
AVERRUNCATIONS
AVERRUNCATOR
AVERRUNCATORS
AVERSENESS
AVERSENESSES
AVERSIVELY
AVERSIVENESS
AVERSIVENESSES
AVERTIMENT
AVERTIMENTS
AVGOLEMONO
AVGOLEMONOS
AVIANISING
AVIANIZING
AVIATRESSES
AVIATRICES
AVIATRIXES
AVICULTURE
AVICULTURES
AVICULTURIST
AVICULTURISTS
AVIDNESSES
AVISANDUMS
AVISEMENTS
AVITAMINOSES
AVITAMINOSIS
AVITAMINOTIC
AVIZANDUMS
AVOCATIONAL
AVOCATIONALLY
AVOCATIONS
AVOIDANCES
AVOIRDUPOIS
AVOIRDUPOISES
AVOPARCINS
AVOUCHABLE
AVOUCHMENT
AVOUCHMENTS
AVOUTERERS
AVOWABLENESS
AVOWABLENESSES
AVUNCULARITIES
AVUNCULARITY
AVUNCULARLY
AVUNCULATE
AVUNCULATES
AVVOGADORE
AVVOGADORES
AWAKENINGS
AWARENESSES
AWAYNESSES
AWELESSNESS
AWELESSNESSES
AWESOMENESS
AWESOMENESSES
AWESTRICKEN
AWESTRIKES

AWESTRIKING
AWFULNESSES
AWKWARDEST
AWKWARDISH
AWKWARDNESS
AWKWARDNESSES
AXENICALLY
AXEROPHTHOL
AXEROPHTHOLS
AXIALITIES
AXILLARIES
AXINOMANCIES
AXINOMANCY
AXIOLOGICAL
AXIOLOGICALLY
AXIOLOGIES
AXIOLOGIST
AXIOLOGISTS
AXIOMATICAL
AXIOMATICALLY
AXIOMATICS
AXIOMATISATION
AXIOMATISATIONS
AXIOMATISE
AXIOMATISED
AXIOMATISES
AXIOMATISING
AXIOMATIZATION
AXIOMATIZATIONS
AXIOMATIZE
AXIOMATIZED
AXIOMATIZES
AXIOMATIZING
AXISYMMETRIC
AXISYMMETRICAL
AXISYMMETRIES
AXISYMMETRY
AXOLEMMATA
AXONOMETRIC
AXONOMETRIES
AXONOMETRY
AXOPLASMIC
AYAHUASCAS
AYAHUASCOS
AYATOLLAHS
AYUNTAMIENTO
AYUNTAMIENTOS
AYURVEDICS
AZATHIOPRINE
AZATHIOPRINES
AZEDARACHS
AZEOTROPES
AZEOTROPIC
AZEOTROPIES
AZIDOTHYMIDINE
AZIDOTHYMIDINES
AZIMUTHALLY
AZOBENZENE
AZOBENZENES
AZOOSPERMIA
AZOOSPERMIAS
AZOOSPERMIC
AZOTAEMIAS
AZOTOBACTER
AZOTOBACTERS
AZYGOSPORE
AZYGOSPORES

A

B

B

BAALEBATIM
BABACOOTES
BABBITRIES
BABBITTING
BABBITTRIES
BABBLATIVE
BABBLEMENT
BABBLEMENTS
BABELESQUE
BABESIASES
BABESIASIS
BABESIOSES
BABESIOSIS
BABINGTONITE
BABINGTONITES
BABIROUSSA
BABIROUSSAS
BABIRUSSAS
BABOONERIES
BABYCCINOS
BABYDADDIES
BABYPROOFED
BABYPROOFING
BABYPROOFS
BABYSITTING
BACCALAUREAN
BACCALAUREATE
BACCALAUREATES
BACCHANALIA
BACCHANALIAN
BACCHANALIANISM
BACCHANALIANS
BACCHANALS
BACCHANTES
BACCIFEROUS
BACCIVOROUS
BACHARACHS
BACHELORDOM
BACHELORDOMS
BACHELORETTE
BACHELORETTES
BACHELORHOOD
BACHELORHOODS
BACHELORISM
BACHELORISMS
BACHELORSHIP
BACHELORSHIPS
BACILLAEMIA
BACILLAEMIAS
BACILLEMIA
BACILLEMIAS
BACILLICIDE
BACILLICIDES
BACILLIFORM
BACILLURIA
BACILLURIAS
BACITRACIN
BACITRACINS
BACKACTERS
BACKBENCHER
BACKBENCHERS
BACKBENCHES
BACKBITERS
BACKBITING
BACKBITINGS
BACKBITTEN
BACKBLOCKER
BACKBLOCKERS
BACKBLOCKS
BACKBOARDS
BACKBONELESS
BACKBREAKER
BACKBREAKERS
BACKBREAKING
BACKBURNED
BACKBURNING
BACKCASTING
BACKCHANNEL
BACKCHANNELS
BACKCHATTED
BACKCHATTING
BACKCHECKED
BACKCHECKING
BACKCHECKS
BACKCLOTHS
BACKCOMBED
BACKCOMBING
BACKCOUNTRIES
BACKCOUNTRY
BACKCOURTMAN
BACKCOURTMEN
BACKCOURTS
BACKCROSSED
BACKCROSSES
BACKCROSSING
BACKDATING
BACKDRAFTS
BACKDRAUGHT
BACKDRAUGHTS
BACKDROPPED
BACKDROPPING
BACKFIELDS
BACKFILLED
BACKFILLING
BACKFILLINGS
BACKFIRING
BACKFISCHES
BACKFITTED
BACKFITTING
BACKFITTINGS
BACKFLIPPED
BACKFLIPPING
BACKFLIPPINGS
BACKGAMMON
BACKGAMMONED
BACKGAMMONING
BACKGAMMONS
BACKGROUND
BACKGROUNDED
BACKGROUNDER
BACKGROUNDERS
BACKGROUNDING
BACKGROUNDS
BACKHANDED
BACKHANDEDLY
BACKHANDEDNESS
BACKHANDER
BACKHANDERS
BACKHANDING
BACKHAULED
BACKHAULING
BACKHOEING
BACKHOUSES
BACKLASHED
BACKLASHER
BACKLASHERS
BACKLASHES
BACKLASHING
BACKLIGHTED
BACKLIGHTING
BACKLIGHTS
BACKLINERS
BACKLISTED
BACKLISTING
BACKLOADED
BACKLOADING
BACKLOGGED
BACKLOGGING
BACKMARKER
BACKMARKERS
BACKPACKED
BACKPACKER
BACKPACKERS
BACKPACKING
BACKPACKINGS
BACKPEDALED
BACKPEDALING
BACKPEDALLED
BACKPEDALLING
BACKPEDALS
BACKPIECES
BACKPLANES
BACKPLATES
BACKRONYMS
BACKRUSHES
BACKSCATTER
BACKSCATTERED
BACKSCATTERING
BACKSCATTERINGS
BACKSCATTERS
BACKSCRATCH
BACKSCRATCHED
BACKSCRATCHER
BACKSCRATCHERS
BACKSCRATCHES
BACKSCRATCHING
BACKSCRATCHINGS
BACKSETTING
BACKSHEESH
BACKSHEESHED
BACKSHEESHES
BACKSHEESHING
BACKSHISHED
BACKSHISHES
BACKSHISHING
BACKSHORES
BACKSIGHTS
BACKSLAPPED
BACKSLAPPER
BACKSLAPPERS
BACKSLAPPING
BACKSLASHES
BACKSLIDDEN
BACKSLIDER
BACKSLIDERS
BACKSLIDES
BACKSLIDING
BACKSLIDINGS
BACKSPACED
BACKSPACER
BACKSPACERS
BACKSPACES
BACKSPACING
BACKSPEERED
BACKSPEERING
BACKSPEERS
BACKSPEIRED
BACKSPEIRING
BACKSPEIRS
BACKSPLASH

BACKSPLASHES
BACKSPLITS
BACKSTABBED
BACKSTABBER
BACKSTABBERS
BACKSTABBING
BACKSTABBINGS
BACKSTAGES
BACKSTAIRS
BACKSTALLED
BACKSTALLING
BACKSTALLS
BACKSTAMPED
BACKSTAMPING
BACKSTAMPS
BACKSTARTING
BACKSTARTINGS
BACKSTITCH
BACKSTITCHED
BACKSTITCHES
BACKSTITCHING
BACKSTOPPED
BACKSTOPPING
BACKSTORIES
BACKSTRAPS
BACKSTREET
BACKSTREETS
BACKSTRETCH
BACKSTRETCHES
BACKSTROKE
BACKSTROKED
BACKSTROKES
BACKSTROKING
BACKSWIMMER
BACKSWIMMERS
BACKSWINGS
BACKSWORDMAN
BACKSWORDMEN
BACKSWORDS
BACKSWORDSMAN
BACKSWORDSMEN
BACKTRACKED
BACKTRACKING
BACKTRACKINGS
BACKTRACKS
BACKVELDER
BACKVELDERS
BACKWARDATION
BACKWARDATIONS
BACKWARDLY
BACKWARDNESS
BACKWARDNESSES
BACKWASHED
BACKWASHES
BACKWASHING
BACKWATERS
BACKWINDED
BACKWINDING
BACKWOODSIER
BACKWOODSIEST
BACKWOODSMAN
BACKWOODSMEN
BACKWOODSY
BACKWORKER
BACKWORKERS
BACTERAEMIA
BACTERAEMIAS
BACTERAEMIC
BACTEREMIA
BACTEREMIAS
BACTEREMIC
BACTERIALLY
BACTERIALS
BACTERICIDAL
BACTERICIDALLY
BACTERICIDE
BACTERICIDES
BACTERIOCIN
BACTERIOCINS
BACTERIOID
BACTERIOIDS
BACTERIOLOGIC
BACTERIOLOGICAL
BACTERIOLOGIES
BACTERIOLOGIST
BACTERIOLOGISTS
BACTERIOLOGY
BACTERIOLYSES
BACTERIOLYSIN
BACTERIOLYSINS
BACTERIOLYSIS
BACTERIOLYTIC
BACTERIOPHAGE
BACTERIOPHAGES
BACTERIOPHAGIC
BACTERIOPHAGIES
BACTERIOPHAGOUS
BACTERIOPHAGY
BACTERIOSES
BACTERIOSIS
BACTERIOSTASES
BACTERIOSTASIS
BACTERIOSTAT
BACTERIOSTATIC
BACTERIOSTATS
BACTERIOTOXIN
BACTERIOTOXINS
BACTERISATION
BACTERISATIONS
BACTERISED
BACTERISES
BACTERISING
BACTERIURIA
BACTERIURIAS
BACTERIZATION
BACTERIZATIONS
BACTERIZED
BACTERIZES
BACTERIZING
BACTEROIDS
BACTERURIA
BACTERURIAS
BACULIFORM
BACULOVIRUS
BACULOVIRUSES
BADDELEYITE
BADDELEYITES
BADDERLOCK
BADDERLOCKS
BADGERLIER
BADGERLIEST
BADINAGING
BADINERIES
BADMINTONS
BADMOUTHED
BADMOUTHING
BAFFLEGABS
BAFFLEMENT
BAFFLEMENTS
BAFFLINGLY
BAGASSOSES
BAGASSOSIS
BAGATELLES
BAGGINESSES
BAGPIPINGS
BAGSWINGER
BAGSWINGERS
BAHUVRIHIS
BAIGNOIRES
BAILIESHIP
BAILIESHIPS
BAILIFFSHIP
BAILIFFSHIPS
BAILIWICKS
BAILLIAGES
BAILLIESHIP
BAILLIESHIPS
BAIRNLIEST
BAISEMAINS
BAITFISHES
BAJILLIONS
BAKEAPPLES
BAKEBOARDS
BAKEHOUSES
BAKESTONES
BAKHSHISHED
BAKHSHISHES
BAKHSHISHING
BAKSHEESHED
BAKSHEESHES
BAKSHEESHING
BAKSHISHED
BAKSHISHES
BAKSHISHING
BALACLAVAS
BALALAIKAS
BALANCEABLE
BALANCINGS
BALANITISES
BALAYAGING
BALBRIGGAN
BALBRIGGANS
BALBUTIENT
BALCONETTE
BALCONETTES
BALDACHINO
BALDACHINOS
BALDACHINS
BALDAQUINS
BALDERDASH
BALDERDASHES
BALDERLOCKS
BALDERLOCKSES
BALDHEADED
BALDICOOTS
BALDMONEYS
BALDNESSES
BALECTIONS
BALEFULNESS
BALEFULNESSES
BALIBUNTAL
BALIBUNTALS
BALKANISATION
BALKANISATIONS
BALKANISED
BALKANISES
BALKANISING
BALKANIZATION
BALKANIZATIONS
BALKANIZED
BALKANIZES
BALKANIZING
BALKINESSES
BALLABILES
BALLADEERED
BALLADEERING
BALLADEERS
BALLADINES
BALLADISTS
BALLADMONGER
BALLADMONGERS
BALLADRIES
BALLANTING
BALLANWRASSE
BALLANWRASSES
BALLASTERS
BALLASTING
BALLBREAKER
BALLBREAKERS
BALLCARRIER
BALLCARRIERS
BALLERINAS
BALLETICALLY
BALLETOMANE
BALLETOMANES
BALLETOMANIA
BALLETOMANIAS
BALLFIELDS
BALLFLOWER
BALLFLOWERS

B

B

BALLHANDLING
BALLHANDLINGS
BALLHAWKED
BALLHAWKING
BALLICATTER
BALLICATTERS
BALLISTICALLY
BALLISTICS
BALLISTITE
BALLISTITES
BALLISTOSPORE
BALLISTOSPORES
BALLOCKSED
BALLOCKSES
BALLOCKSING
BALLOONING
BALLOONINGS
BALLOONIST
BALLOONISTS
BALLOTINGS
BALLOTTEMENT
BALLOTTEMENTS
BALLPLAYER
BALLPLAYERS
BALLPOINTS
BALLSINESS
BALLSINESSES
BALLYHOOED
BALLYHOOING
BALLYRAGGED
BALLYRAGGING
BALMACAANS
BALMINESSES
BALMORALITIES
BALMORALITY
BALNEARIES
BALNEATION
BALNEATIONS
BALNEOLOGICAL
BALNEOLOGIES
BALNEOLOGIST
BALNEOLOGISTS
BALNEOLOGY
BALNEOTHERAPIES
BALNEOTHERAPY
BALSAMIEST
BALSAMIFEROUS
BALSAMINACEOUS
BALSAWOODS
BALTHASARS
BALTHAZARS
BALUSTERED
BALUSTRADE
BALUSTRADED
BALUSTRADES
BALZARINES
BAMBOOZLED
BAMBOOZLEMENT
BAMBOOZLEMENTS
BAMBOOZLER
BAMBOOZLERS
BAMBOOZLES
BAMBOOZLING
BANALISATION
BANALISATIONS
BANALISING
BANALITIES
BANALIZATION
BANALIZATIONS
BANALIZING
BANCASSURANCE
BANCASSURANCES
BANCASSURER
BANCASSURERS
BANDAGINGS
BANDALORES
BANDBRAKES
BANDEIRANTE
BANDEIRANTES
BANDELIERS
BANDERILLA
BANDERILLAS
BANDERILLERO
BANDERILLEROS
BANDEROLES
BANDERSNATCH
BANDERSNATCHES
BANDFISHES
BANDICOOTED
BANDICOOTING
BANDICOOTS
BANDINESSES
BANDITRIES
BANDLEADER
BANDLEADERS
BANDMASTER
BANDMASTERS
BANDOBASTS
BANDOBUSTS
BANDOLEERED
BANDOLEERS
BANDOLEONS
BANDOLEROS
BANDOLIERED
BANDOLIERS
BANDOLINED
BANDOLINES
BANDOLINING
BANDONEONS
BANDONIONS
BANDPASSES
BANDSAWING
BANDSHELLS
BANDSPREADING
BANDSPREADINGS
BANDSTANDS
BANDURISTS
BANDWAGONS
BANDWIDTHS
BANEBERRIES
BANEFULNESS
BANEFULNESSES
BANGBELLIES
BANGSRINGS
BANISHMENT
BANISHMENTS
BANISTERED
BANJOLELES
BANJULELES
BANKABILITIES
BANKABILITY
BANKERLIER
BANKERLIEST
BANKROLLED
BANKROLLER
BANKROLLERS
BANKROLLING
BANKRUPTCIES
BANKRUPTCY
BANKRUPTED
BANKRUPTING
BANNERALLS
BANNERETTE
BANNERETTES
BANNISTERS
BANQUETEER
BANQUETEERS
BANQUETERS
BANQUETING
BANQUETINGS
BANQUETTES
BANTAMWEIGHT
BANTAMWEIGHTS
BANTERINGLY
BANTERINGS
BANTINGISM
BANTINGISMS
BAPHOMETIC
BAPTISMALLY
BAPTISTERIES
BAPTISTERY
BAPTISTRIES
BARACHOISES
BARAESTHESIA
BARAESTHESIAS
BARAGOUINS
BARASINGAS
BARASINGHA
BARASINGHAS
BARATHRUMS
BARBARESQUE
BARBARIANISM
BARBARIANISMS
BARBARIANS
BARBARICALLY
BARBARISATION
BARBARISATIONS
BARBARISED
BARBARISES
BARBARISING
BARBARISMS
BARBARITIES
BARBARIZATION
BARBARIZATIONS
BARBARIZED
BARBARIZES
BARBARIZING
BARBAROUSLY
BARBAROUSNESS
BARBAROUSNESSES
BARBASCOES
BARBASTELLE
BARBASTELLES
BARBASTELS
BARBECUERS
BARBECUING
BARBELLATE
BARBEQUING
BARBERRIES
BARBERSHOP
BARBERSHOPS
BARBITONES
BARBITURATE
BARBITURATES
BARBITURIC
BARBOTINES
BARCAROLES
BARCAROLLE
BARCAROLLES
BARDOLATER
BARDOLATERS
BARDOLATRIES
BARDOLATROUS
BARDOLATRY
BAREBACKED
BAREBACKING
BAREBACKINGS
BAREFACEDLY
BAREFACEDNESS
BAREFACEDNESSES
BAREFOOTED
BAREHANDED
BAREHANDING
BAREHEADED
BARELEGGED
BARENESSES
BARESTHESIA
BARESTHESIAS
BARGAINERS
BARGAINING
BARGAININGS
BARGANDERS
BARGEBOARD
BARGEBOARDS
BARGEMASTER
BARGEMASTERS
BARGEPOLES
BARHOPPING
BARIATRICS
BARKANTINE

BARKANTINES
BARKEEPERS
BARKENTINE
BARKENTINES
BARLEYCORN
BARLEYCORNS
BARMBRACKS
BARMINESSES
BARMITSVAH
BARMITSVAHS
BARMITZVAH
BARMITZVAHS
BARNBOARDS
BARNBRACKS
BARNSBREAKING
BARNSBREAKINGS
BARNSTORMED
BARNSTORMER
BARNSTORMERS
BARNSTORMING
BARNSTORMINGS
BARNSTORMS
BAROCEPTOR
BAROCEPTORS
BARODYNAMICS
BAROGNOSES
BAROGNOSIS
BAROGRAPHIC
BAROGRAPHS
BAROMETERS
BAROMETRIC
BAROMETRICAL
BAROMETRICALLY
BAROMETRIES
BAROMETZES
BARONESSES
BARONETAGE
BARONETAGES
BARONETCIES
BARONETESS
BARONETESSES
BARONETICAL
BAROPHILES
BAROPHILIC
BAROPHORESES
BAROPHORESIS
BARORECEPTOR
BARORECEPTORS
BAROSCOPES
BAROSCOPIC
BAROTITISES
BAROTRAUMA
BAROTRAUMAS
BAROTRAUMATA
BARPERSONS
BARQUANTINE
BARQUANTINES
BARQUENTINE
BARQUENTINES
BARQUETTES
BARRACKERS
BARRACKING
BARRACKINGS
BARRACOONS
BARRACOUTA
BARRACOUTAS
BARRACUDAS
BARRAMUNDA
BARRAMUNDAS
BARRAMUNDI
BARRAMUNDIES
BARRAMUNDIS
BARRASWAYS
BARRATRIES
BARRATROUS
BARRATROUSLY
BARRELAGES
BARRELFULS
BARRELHEAD
BARRELHEADS
BARRELHOUSE
BARRELHOUSES
BARRELLING
BARRELSFUL
BARRENNESS
BARRENNESSES
BARRENWORT
BARRENWORTS
BARRETRIES
BARRETROUS
BARRETROUSLY
BARRETTERS
BARRICADED
BARRICADER
BARRICADERS
BARRICADES
BARRICADING
BARRICADOED
BARRICADOES
BARRICADOING
BARRICADOS
BARRIERING
BARRISTERIAL
BARRISTERS
BARRISTERSHIP
BARRISTERSHIPS
BARROWFULS
BARTENDERS
BARTENDING
BARTENDINGS
BARTIZANED
BARYCENTRE
BARYCENTRES
BARYCENTRIC
BARYSPHERE
BARYSPHERES
BASALTINES
BASALTWARE
BASALTWARES
BASEBALLER
BASEBALLERS
BASEBOARDS
BASEBURNER
BASEBURNERS
BASELESSLY
BASELESSNESS
BASELESSNESSES
BASELINERS
BASEMENTLESS
BASENESSES
BASEPLATES
BASERUNNER
BASERUNNERS
BASERUNNING
BASERUNNINGS
BASHAWISMS
BASHAWSHIP
BASHAWSHIPS
BASHFULLER
BASHFULLEST
BASHFULNESS
BASHFULNESSES
BASHIBAZOUK
BASHIBAZOUKS
BASICITIES
BASICRANIAL
BASIDIOCARP
BASIDIOCARPS
BASIDIOMYCETE
BASIDIOMYCETES
BASIDIOMYCETOUS
BASIDIOSPORE
BASIDIOSPORES
BASIDIOSPOROUS
BASIFICATION
BASIFICATIONS
BASILICONS
BASIPETALLY
BASKETBALL
BASKETBALLS
BASKETFULS
BASKETLIKE
BASKETRIES
BASKETSFUL
BASKETWEAVE
BASKETWEAVER
BASKETWEAVERS
BASKETWEAVES
BASKETWORK
BASKETWORKS
BASMITZVAH
BASMITZVAHS
BASOPHILES
BASOPHILIA
BASOPHILIAS
BASOPHILIC
BASSETTING
BASSNESSES
BASSOONIST
BASSOONISTS
BASTARDIES
BASTARDISATION
BASTARDISATIONS
BASTARDISE
BASTARDISED
BASTARDISES
BASTARDISING
BASTARDISM
BASTARDISMS
BASTARDIZATION
BASTARDIZATIONS
BASTARDIZE
BASTARDIZED
BASTARDIZES
BASTARDIZING
BASTARDLIER
BASTARDLIEST
BASTARDRIES
BASTINADED
BASTINADES
BASTINADING
BASTINADOED
BASTINADOES
BASTINADOING
BASTNAESITE
BASTNAESITES
BASTNASITE
BASTNASITES
BATFOWLERS
BATFOWLING
BATFOWLINGS
BATHETICALLY
BATHHOUSES
BATHMITSVAH
BATHMITSVAHS
BATHMITZVAH
BATHMITZVAHS
BATHMIZVAH
BATHMIZVAHS
BATHOCHROME
BATHOCHROMES
BATHOCHROMIC
BATHOLITES
BATHOLITHIC
BATHOLITHS
BATHOLITIC
BATHOMETER
BATHOMETERS
BATHOMETRIC
BATHOMETRICALLY
BATHOMETRIES
BATHOMETRY
BATHOPHILOUS
BATHOPHOBIA
BATHOPHOBIAS
BATHWATERS
BATHYBIUSES
BATHYGRAPHIC
BATHYGRAPHICAL
BATHYLIMNETIC

BATHYLITES
BATHYLITHIC
BATHYLITHS
BATHYLITIC
BATHYMETER
BATHYMETERS
BATHYMETRIC
BATHYMETRICAL
BATHYMETRICALLY
BATHYMETRIES
BATHYMETRY
BATHYPELAGIC
BATHYSCAPE
BATHYSCAPES
BATHYSCAPH
BATHYSCAPHE
BATHYSCAPHES
BATHYSCAPHS
BATHYSPHERE
BATHYSPHERES
BATMITZVAH
BATMITZVAHS
BATOLOGICAL
BATOLOGIES
BATOLOGIST
BATOLOGISTS
BATONNIERS
BATRACHIAN
BATRACHIANS
BATRACHOPHOBIA
BATRACHOPHOBIAS
BATRACHOPHOBIC
BATSMANSHIP
BATSMANSHIPS
BATTAILOUS
BATTALIONS
BATTEILANT
BATTELLING
BATTEMENTS
BATTENINGS
BATTERINGS
BATTILLING
BATTINESSES
BATTLEAXES
BATTLEBUSES
BATTLEBUSSES
BATTLEDOOR
BATTLEDOORS
BATTLEDORE
BATTLEDORES
BATTLEDRESS
BATTLEDRESSES
BATTLEFIELD
BATTLEFIELDS
BATTLEFRONT
BATTLEFRONTS
BATTLEGROUND
BATTLEGROUNDS
BATTLEMENT
BATTLEMENTED
BATTLEMENTS
BATTLEPIECE
BATTLEPIECES
BATTLEPLANE
BATTLEPLANES
BATTLESHIP
BATTLESHIPS
BATTLESPACE
BATTLESPACES
BATTLEWAGON
BATTLEWAGONS
BATTOLOGICAL
BATTOLOGIES
BAUDRICKES
BAUDRONSES
BAULKINESS
BAULKINESSES
BAULKINGLY
BAULKLINES
BAVARDAGES
BAVAROISES
BAWDINESSES
BAWDYHOUSE
BAWDYHOUSES
BAYBERRIES
BAYNODDIES
BAYONETING
BAYONETTED
BAYONETTING
BAZILLIONS
BEACHBALLS
BEACHCOMBED
BEACHCOMBER
BEACHCOMBERS
BEACHCOMBING
BEACHCOMBINGS
BEACHCOMBS
BEACHFRONT
BEACHFRONTS
BEACHGOERS
BEACHHEADS
BEACHWEARS
BEADBLASTED
BEADBLASTER
BEADBLASTERS
BEADBLASTING
BEADBLASTS
BEADHOUSES
BEADINESSES
BEADLEDOMS
BEADLEHOOD
BEADLEHOODS
BEADLESHIP
BEADLESHIPS
BEADSWOMAN
BEADSWOMEN
BEAKERFULS
BEAMINESSES
BEANFEASTS
BEANSPROUT
BEANSPROUTS
BEANSTALKS
BEARABILITIES
BEARABILITY
BEARABLENESS
BEARABLENESSES
BEARBAITING
BEARBAITINGS
BEARBERRIES
BEARDEDNESS
BEARDEDNESSES
BEARDLESSNESS
BEARDLESSNESSES
BEARDTONGUE
BEARDTONGUES
BEARGRASSES
BEARHUGGED
BEARHUGGING
BEARISHNESS
BEARISHNESSES
BEARNAISES
BEASTHOODS
BEASTLIEST
BEASTLINESS
BEASTLINESSES
BEATBOXERS
BEATBOXING
BEATBOXINGS
BEATIFICAL
BEATIFICALLY
BEATIFICATION
BEATIFICATIONS
BEATIFYING
BEATITUDES
BEAUJOLAIS
BEAUJOLAISES
BEAUMONTAGE
BEAUMONTAGES
BEAUMONTAGUE
BEAUMONTAGUES
BEAUTEOUSLY
BEAUTEOUSNESS
BEAUTEOUSNESSES
BEAUTICIAN
BEAUTICIANS
BEAUTIFICATION
BEAUTIFICATIONS
BEAUTIFIED
BEAUTIFIER
BEAUTIFIERS
BEAUTIFIES
BEAUTIFULLER
BEAUTIFULLEST
BEAUTIFULLY
BEAUTIFULNESS
BEAUTIFULNESSES
BEAUTIFYING
BEAVERBOARD
BEAVERBOARDS
BEBEERINES
BEBLOODING
BEBLUBBERED
BECARPETED
BECARPETING
BECCACCIAS
BECCAFICOS
BECHALKING
BECHANCING
BECHARMING
BECKONINGLY
BECKONINGS
BECLAMORED
BECLAMORING
BECLAMOURED
BECLAMOURING
BECLAMOURS
BECLASPING
BECLOAKING
BECLOGGING
BECLOTHING
BECLOUDING
BECLOWNING
BECOMINGLY
BECOMINGNESS
BECOMINGNESSES
BECOWARDED
BECOWARDING
BECQUERELS
BECRAWLING
BECROWDING
BECRUSTING
BECUDGELED
BECUDGELING
BECUDGELLED
BECUDGELLING
BEDABBLING
BEDAGGLING
BEDARKENED
BEDARKENING
BEDAZZLEMENT
BEDAZZLEMENTS
BEDAZZLING
BEDCHAMBER
BEDCHAMBERS
BEDCLOTHES
BEDCOVERING
BEDCOVERINGS
BEDEAFENED
BEDEAFENING
BEDEHOUSES
BEDELLSHIP
BEDELLSHIPS
BEDELSHIPS
BEDEVILING
BEDEVILLED
BEDEVILLING
BEDEVILMENT
BEDEVILMENTS
BEDFELLOWS
BEDIAPERED

BEDIAPERING
BEDIGHTING
BEDIMMINGS
BEDIMPLING
BEDIRTYING
BEDIZENING
BEDIZENMENT
BEDIZENMENTS
BEDLAMISMS
BEDLAMITES
BEDPRESSER
BEDPRESSERS
BEDRAGGLED
BEDRAGGLES
BEDRAGGLING
BEDRENCHED
BEDRENCHES
BEDRENCHING
BEDRIVELED
BEDRIVELING
BEDRIVELLED
BEDRIVELLING
BEDROPPING
BEDRUGGING
BEDSITTERS
BEDSITTING
BEDSPREADS
BEDSPRINGS
BEDWARFING
BEDWARMERS
BEDWETTERS
BEECHDROPS
BEECHMASTS
BEECHWOODS
BEEFBURGER
BEEFBURGERS
BEEFEATERS
BEEFINESSES
BEEFSTEAKS
BEEKEEPERS
BEEKEEPING
BEEKEEPINGS
BEERINESSES
BEESWAXING
BEESWINGED
BEETLEBRAIN
BEETLEBRAINED
BEETLEBRAINS
BEETLEHEAD
BEETLEHEADED
BEETLEHEADS
BEETMASTER
BEETMASTERS
BEETMISTER
BEETMISTERS
BEFINGERED
BEFINGERING
BEFITTINGLY
BEFLAGGING
BEFLECKING
BEFLOWERED
BEFLOWERING
BEFLUMMING
BEFOREHAND
BEFORETIME
BEFORTUNED
BEFORTUNES
BEFORTUNING
BEFOULMENT
BEFOULMENTS
BEFRETTING
BEFRIENDED
BEFRIENDER
BEFRIENDERS
BEFRIENDING
BEFRINGING
BEFUDDLEMENT
BEFUDDLEMENTS
BEFUDDLING
BEGGARDOMS
BEGGARHOOD
BEGGARHOODS
BEGGARLIER
BEGGARLIEST
BEGGARLINESS
BEGGARLINESSES
BEGGARWEED
BEGGARWEEDS
BEGINNINGLESS
BEGINNINGS
BEGIRDLING
BEGLADDING
BEGLAMORED
BEGLAMORING
BEGLAMOURED
BEGLAMOURING
BEGLAMOURS
BEGLERBEGS
BEGLOOMING
BEGRIMMING
BEGROANING
BEGRUDGERIES
BEGRUDGERS
BEGRUDGERY
BEGRUDGING
BEGRUDGINGLY
BEGUILEMENT
BEGUILEMENTS
BEGUILINGLY
BEGUINAGES
BEHAPPENED
BEHAPPENING
BEHAVIORAL
BEHAVIORALLY
BEHAVIORISM
BEHAVIORISMS
BEHAVIORIST
BEHAVIORISTIC
BEHAVIORISTS
BEHAVIOURAL
BEHAVIOURALLY
BEHAVIOURISM
BEHAVIOURISMS
BEHAVIOURIST
BEHAVIOURISTIC
BEHAVIOURISTS
BEHAVIOURS
BEHEADINGS
BEHIGHTING
BEHINDHAND
BEHOLDINGS
BEINGNESSES
BEINNESSES
BEJABERSES
BEJEEZUSES
BEJESUITED
BEJESUITING
BEJEWELING
BEJEWELLED
BEJEWELLING
BEJUMBLING
BEKNIGHTED
BEKNIGHTING
BEKNOTTING
BELABORING
BELABOURED
BELABOURING
BELAMOURES
BELATEDNESS
BELATEDNESSES
BELEAGUERED
BELEAGUERING
BELEAGUERMENT
BELEAGUERMENTS
BELEAGUERS
BELEMNITES
BELGICISMS
BELIEFLESS
BELIEVABILITIES
BELIEVABILITY
BELIEVABLE
BELIEVABLY
BELIEVINGLY
BELIEVINGS
BELIQUORED
BELIQUORING
BELITTLEMENT
BELITTLEMENTS
BELITTLERS
BELITTLING
BELITTLINGLY
BELLADONNA
BELLADONNAS
BELLAMOURE
BELLAMOURES
BELLARMINE
BELLARMINES
BELLETRISM
BELLETRISMS
BELLETRIST
BELLETRISTIC
BELLETRISTICAL
BELLETRISTS
BELLETTRIST
BELLETTRISTS
BELLFLOWER
BELLFLOWERS
BELLFOUNDER
BELLFOUNDERS
BELLFOUNDRIES
BELLFOUNDRY
BELLHANGER
BELLHANGERS
BELLIBONES
BELLICOSELY
BELLICOSITIES
BELLICOSITY
BELLIGERATI
BELLIGERENCE
BELLIGERENCES
BELLIGERENCIES
BELLIGERENCY
BELLIGERENT
BELLIGERENTLY
BELLIGERENTS
BELLOCKING
BELLOWINGS
BELLWETHER
BELLWETHERS
BELLYACHED
BELLYACHER
BELLYACHERS
BELLYACHES
BELLYACHING
BELLYACHINGS
BELLYBANDS
BELLYBOATS
BELLYBUTTON
BELLYBUTTONS
BELLYFLOPPED
BELLYFLOPPING
BELLYFLOPS
BELOMANCIES
BELONGINGNESS
BELONGINGNESSES
BELONGINGS
BELOWDECKS
BELOWGROUND
BELOWSTAIRS
BELSHAZZAR
BELSHAZZARS
BELTCOURSE
BELTCOURSES
BELVEDERES
BEMADAMING
BEMADDENED
BEMADDENING
BEMEDALING
BEMEDALLED
BEMEDALLING

BEMINGLING
BEMOANINGS
BEMONSTERED
BEMONSTERING
BEMONSTERS
BEMOUTHING
BEMUDDLING
BEMUFFLING
BEMURMURED
BEMURMURING
BEMUSEMENT
BEMUSEMENTS
BEMUZZLING
BENCHERSHIP
BENCHERSHIPS
BENCHLANDS
BENCHMARKED
BENCHMARKING
BENCHMARKINGS
BENCHMARKS
BENCHWARMER
BENCHWARMERS
BENDINESSES
BENEDICITE
BENEDICITES
BENEDICTION
BENEDICTIONAL
BENEDICTIONALS
BENEDICTIONS
BENEDICTIVE
BENEDICTORY
BENEDICTUS
BENEDICTUSES
BENEFACTED
BENEFACTING
BENEFACTION
BENEFACTIONS
BENEFACTOR
BENEFACTORS
BENEFACTORY
BENEFACTRESS
BENEFACTRESSES
BENEFICENCE
BENEFICENCES
BENEFICENT
BENEFICENTIAL
BENEFICENTLY
BENEFICIAL
BENEFICIALLY
BENEFICIALNESS
BENEFICIALS
BENEFICIARIES
BENEFICIARY
BENEFICIATE
BENEFICIATED
BENEFICIATES
BENEFICIATING
BENEFICIATION
BENEFICIATIONS
BENEFICING
BENEFITERS
BENEFITING
BENEFITTED
BENEFITTING
BENEPLACITO
BENEVOLENCE
BENEVOLENCES
BENEVOLENT
BENEVOLENTLY
BENEVOLENTNESS
BENGALINES
BENIGHTEDLY
BENIGHTEDNESS
BENIGHTEDNESSES
BENIGHTENED
BENIGHTENING
BENIGHTENINGS
BENIGHTENS
BENIGHTERS
BENIGHTING
BENIGHTINGS
BENIGHTMENT
BENIGHTMENTS
BENIGNANCIES
BENIGNANCY
BENIGNANTLY
BENIGNITIES
BENTGRASSES
BENTHOPELAGIC
BENTHOSCOPE
BENTHOSCOPES
BENTONITES
BENTONITIC
BENUMBEDNESS
BENUMBEDNESSES
BENUMBINGLY
BENUMBMENT
BENUMBMENTS
BENZALDEHYDE
BENZALDEHYDES
BENZANTHRACENE
BENZANTHRACENES
BENZENECARBONYL
BENZENOIDS
BENZIDINES
BENZIMIDAZOLE
BENZIMIDAZOLES
BENZOAPYRENE
BENZOAPYRENES
BENZOCAINE
BENZOCAINES
BENZODIAZEPINE
BENZODIAZEPINES
BENZOFURAN
BENZOFURANS
BENZOLINES
BENZOPHENONE
BENZOPHENONES
BENZOQUINONE
BENZOQUINONES
BENZPYRENE
BENZPYRENES
BENZYLIDINE
BENZYLIDINES
BEPAINTING
BEPEARLING
BEPEPPERED
BEPEPPERING
BEPESTERED
BEPESTERING
BEPIMPLING
BEPLASTERED
BEPLASTERING
BEPLASTERS
BEPOMMELLED
BEPOMMELLING
BEPOWDERED
BEPOWDERING
BEPRAISING
BEQUEATHABLE
BEQUEATHAL
BEQUEATHALS
BEQUEATHED
BEQUEATHER
BEQUEATHERS
BEQUEATHING
BEQUEATHMENT
BEQUEATHMENTS
BERASCALED
BERASCALING
BERBERIDACEOUS
BERBERINES
BERBERISES
BEREAVEMENT
BEREAVEMENTS
BERGAMASKO
BERGAMASKOS
BERGAMASKS
BERGANDERS
BERGOMASKS
BERGSCHRUND
BERGSCHRUNDS
BERIBBONED
BERKELIUMS
BERRYFRUIT
BERRYFRUITS
BERSAGLIERE
BERSAGLIERI
BERSERKERS
BERTILLONAGE
BERTILLONAGES
BERYLLIOSES
BERYLLIOSIS
BERYLLIUMS
BESAINTING
BESCATTERED
BESCATTERING
BESCATTERS
BESCORCHED
BESCORCHES
BESCORCHING
BESCOURING
BESCRAWLED
BESCRAWLING
BESCREENED
BESCREENING
BESCRIBBLE
BESCRIBBLED
BESCRIBBLES
BESCRIBBLING
BESEECHERS
BESEECHING
BESEECHINGLY
BESEECHINGNESS
BESEECHINGS
BESEEMINGLY
BESEEMINGNESS
BESEEMINGNESSES
BESEEMINGS
BESEEMLIER
BESEEMLIEST
BESETMENTS
BESHADOWED
BESHADOWING
BESHIVERED
BESHIVERING
BESHOUTING
BESHREWING
BESHROUDED
BESHROUDING
BESIEGEMENT
BESIEGEMENTS
BESIEGINGLY
BESIEGINGS
BESLAVERED
BESLAVERING
BESLOBBERED
BESLOBBERING
BESLOBBERS
BESLUBBERED
BESLUBBERING
BESLUBBERS
BESMEARERS
BESMEARING
BESMIRCHED
BESMIRCHES
BESMIRCHING
BESMOOTHED
BESMOOTHING
BESMUDGING
BESMUTCHED
BESMUTCHES
BESMUTCHING
BESMUTTING
BESOOTHING
BESOTTEDLY
BESOTTEDNESS
BESOTTEDNESSES
BESPANGLED
BESPANGLES

BESPANGLING
BESPATTERED
BESPATTERING
BESPATTERS
BESPEAKING
BESPECKLED
BESPECKLES
BESPECKLING
BESPECTACLED
BESPEEDING
BESPITTING
BESPORTING
BESPOTTEDNESS
BESPOTTEDNESSES
BESPOTTING
BESPOUSING
BESPOUTING
BESPREADING
BESPRINKLE
BESPRINKLED
BESPRINKLES
BESPRINKLING
BESTAINING
BESTARRING
BESTEADING
BESTIALISE
BESTIALISED
BESTIALISES
BESTIALISING
BESTIALISM
BESTIALISMS
BESTIALITIES
BESTIALITY
BESTIALIZE
BESTIALIZED
BESTIALIZES
BESTIALIZING
BESTIARIES
BESTICKING
BESTILLING
BESTIRRING
BESTORMING
BESTOWMENT
BESTOWMENTS
BESTRADDLE
BESTRADDLED
BESTRADDLES
BESTRADDLING
BESTRAUGHT
BESTREAKED
BESTREAKING
BESTREWING
BESTRIDABLE
BESTRIDDEN
BESTRIDING
BESTROWING
BESTSELLER
BESTSELLERDOM
BESTSELLERDOMS
BESTSELLERS
BESTSELLING
BESTUDDING
BESWARMING
BETACAROTENE
BETACAROTENES
BETACYANIN
BETACYANINS
BETATTERED
BETATTERING
BETHANKING
BETHANKITS
BETHINKING
BETHORNING
BETHRALLED
BETHRALLING
BETHUMBING
BETHUMPING
BETHWACKED
BETHWACKING
BETOKENING
BETREADING
BETRIMMING
BETROTHALS
BETROTHEDS
BETROTHING
BETROTHMENT
BETROTHMENTS
BETTERINGS
BETTERMENT
BETTERMENTS
BETTERMOST
BETTERNESS
BETTERNESSES
BETULACEOUS
BETWEENBRAIN
BETWEENBRAINS
BETWEENITIES
BETWEENITY
BETWEENNESS
BETWEENNESSES
BETWEENTIME
BETWEENTIMES
BETWEENWHILES
BEVELLINGS
BEVELMENTS
BEVOMITING
BEWAILINGLY
BEWAILINGS
BEWEARYING
BEWELTERED
BEWHISKERED
BEWILDERED
BEWILDEREDLY
BEWILDEREDNESS
BEWILDERING
BEWILDERINGLY
BEWILDERMENT
BEWILDERMENTS
BEWITCHERIES
BEWITCHERS
BEWITCHERY
BEWITCHING
BEWITCHINGLY
BEWITCHMENT
BEWITCHMENTS
BEWORRYING
BEWRAPPING
BHIKKHUNIS
BIANNUALLY
BIANNULATE
BIASNESSES
BIATHLETES
BIAURICULAR
BIAURICULATE
BIBLICALLY
BIBLICISMS
BIBLICISTS
BIBLIOGRAPHER
BIBLIOGRAPHERS
BIBLIOGRAPHIC
BIBLIOGRAPHICAL
BIBLIOGRAPHIES
BIBLIOGRAPHY
BIBLIOLATER
BIBLIOLATERS
BIBLIOLATRIES
BIBLIOLATRIST
BIBLIOLATRISTS
BIBLIOLATROUS
BIBLIOLATRY
BIBLIOLOGICAL
BIBLIOLOGIES
BIBLIOLOGIST
BIBLIOLOGISTS
BIBLIOLOGY
BIBLIOMANCIES
BIBLIOMANCY
BIBLIOMANE
BIBLIOMANES
BIBLIOMANIA
BIBLIOMANIAC
BIBLIOMANIACAL
BIBLIOMANIACS
BIBLIOMANIAS
BIBLIOPEGIC
BIBLIOPEGIES
BIBLIOPEGIST
BIBLIOPEGISTS
BIBLIOPEGY
BIBLIOPHAGIST
BIBLIOPHAGISTS
BIBLIOPHIL
BIBLIOPHILE
BIBLIOPHILES
BIBLIOPHILIC
BIBLIOPHILIES
BIBLIOPHILISM
BIBLIOPHILISMS
BIBLIOPHILIST
BIBLIOPHILISTIC
BIBLIOPHILISTS
BIBLIOPHILS
BIBLIOPHILY
BIBLIOPHOBIA
BIBLIOPHOBIAS
BIBLIOPOLE
BIBLIOPOLES
BIBLIOPOLIC
BIBLIOPOLICAL
BIBLIOPOLIES
BIBLIOPOLIST
BIBLIOPOLISTS
BIBLIOPOLY
BIBLIOTHECA
BIBLIOTHECAE
BIBLIOTHECAL
BIBLIOTHECARIES
BIBLIOTHECARY
BIBLIOTHECAS
BIBLIOTHERAPIES
BIBLIOTHERAPY
BIBLIOTICS
BIBLIOTIST
BIBLIOTISTS
BIBULOUSLY
BIBULOUSNESS
BIBULOUSNESSES
BICAMERALISM
BICAMERALISMS
BICAMERALIST
BICAMERALISTS
BICAPSULAR
BICARBONATE
BICARBONATES
BICARPELLARY
BICENTENARIES
BICENTENARY
BICENTENNIAL
BICENTENNIALS
BICEPHALOUS
BICHLORIDE
BICHLORIDES
BICHROMATE
BICHROMATED
BICHROMATES
BICKERINGS
BICOLLATERAL
BICOLOURED
BICOMPONENT
BICOMPONENTS
BICONCAVITIES
BICONCAVITY
BICONDITIONAL
BICONDITIONALS
BICONVEXITIES
BICONVEXITY
BICORNUATE
BICORPORATE
BICULTURAL
BICULTURALISM

B

BICULTURALISMS
BICUSPIDATE
BICUSPIDATES
BICYCLICAL
BICYCLISTS
BIDDABILITIES
BIDDABILITY
BIDDABLENESS
BIDDABLENESSES
BIDENTATED
BIDIALECTAL
BIDIALECTALISM
BIDIALECTALISMS
BIDIRECTIONAL
BIDIRECTIONALLY
BIDONVILLE
BIDONVILLES
BIENNIALLY
BIENSEANCE
BIENSEANCES
BIERKELLER
BIERKELLERS
BIERWURSTS
BIFACIALLY
BIFARIOUSLY
BIFIDITIES
BIFLAGELLATE
BIFOLIOLATE
BIFUNCTIONAL
BIFURCATED
BIFURCATES
BIFURCATING
BIFURCATION
BIFURCATIONS
BIGAMOUSLY
BIGARREAUS
BIGEMINIES
BIGFOOTING
BIGGETIEST
BIGGITIEST
BIGHEADEDLY
BIGHEADEDNESS
BIGHEADEDNESSES
BIGHEARTED
BIGHEARTEDLY
BIGHEARTEDNESS
BIGMOUTHED
BIGNONIACEOUS
BIGUANIDES
BIJECTIONS
BIJOUTERIE
BIJOUTERIES
BILATERALISM
BILATERALISMS
BILATERALLY
BILBERRIES
BILDUNGSROMAN
BILDUNGSROMANS
BILECTIONS
BILESTONES
BILGEWATER
BILGEWATERS
BILHARZIAL
BILHARZIAS
BILHARZIASES
BILHARZIASIS
BILHARZIOSES
BILHARZIOSIS
BILIMBINGS
BILINGUALISM
BILINGUALISMS
BILINGUALLY
BILINGUALS
BILINGUIST
BILINGUISTS
BILIOUSNESS
BILIOUSNESSES
BILIRUBINS
BILIVERDIN
BILIVERDINS
BILLABONGS
BILLBOARDED
BILLBOARDING
BILLBOARDS
BILLETINGS
BILLFISHES
BILLINGSGATE
BILLINGSGATES
BILLIONAIRE
BILLIONAIRES
BILLIONTHS
BILLOWIEST
BILLOWINESS
BILLOWINESSES
BILLOWINGS
BILLPOSTER
BILLPOSTERS
BILLPOSTING
BILLPOSTINGS
BILLSTICKER
BILLSTICKERS
BILLSTICKING
BILLSTICKINGS
BILLYCOCKS
BILOCATION
BILOCATIONS
BILOCULATE
BIMANUALLY
BIMATERNAL
BIMESTRIAL
BIMESTRIALLY
BIMETALLIC
BIMETALLICS
BIMETALLISM
BIMETALLISMS
BIMETALLIST
BIMETALLISTIC
BIMETALLISTS
BIMILLENARIES
BIMILLENARY
BIMILLENNIA
BIMILLENNIAL
BIMILLENNIALS
BIMILLENNIUM
BIMILLENNIUMS
BIMODALITIES
BIMODALITY
BIMOLECULAR
BIMOLECULARLY
BIMONTHLIES
BIMORPHEMIC
BINATIONAL
BINAURALLY
BINDINGNESS
BINDINGNESSES
BINOCULARITIES
BINOCULARITY
BINOCULARLY
BINOCULARS
BINOMIALLY
BINOMINALS
BINTURONGS
BINUCLEATE
BINUCLEATED
BIOACCUMULATE
BIOACCUMULATED
BIOACCUMULATES
BIOACCUMULATING
BIOACCUMULATION
BIOACOUSTICS
BIOACTIVITIES
BIOACTIVITY
BIOAERATION
BIOAERATIONS
BIOAERONAUTICS
BIOARCHAEOLOGY
BIOASSAYED
BIOASSAYING
BIOASTRONAUTICS
BIOASTRONOMIES
BIOASTRONOMY
BIOAVAILABILITY
BIOAVAILABLE
BIOBANKING
BIOBANKINGS
BIOCATALYST
BIOCATALYSTS
BIOCATALYTIC
BIOCELLATE
BIOCENOLOGIES
BIOCENOLOGY
BIOCENOSES
BIOCENOSIS
BIOCENOTIC
BIOCHEMICAL
BIOCHEMICALLY
BIOCHEMICALS
BIOCHEMIST
BIOCHEMISTRIES
BIOCHEMISTRY
BIOCHEMISTS
BIOCLASTIC
BIOCLIMATIC
BIOCLIMATOLOGY
BIOCOENOLOGIES
BIOCOENOLOGY
BIOCOENOSES
BIOCOENOSIS
BIOCOENOTIC
BIOCOMPATIBLE
BIOCOMPUTING
BIOCOMPUTINGS
BIOCONTROL
BIOCONTROLS
BIOCONVERSION
BIOCONVERSIONS
BIODEGRADABLE
BIODEGRADABLES
BIODEGRADATION
BIODEGRADATIONS
BIODEGRADE
BIODEGRADED
BIODEGRADES
BIODEGRADING
BIODESTRUCTIBLE
BIODIESELS
BIODIVERSE
BIODIVERSITIES
BIODIVERSITY
BIODYNAMIC
BIODYNAMICAL
BIODYNAMICS
BIOECOLOGICAL
BIOECOLOGICALLY
BIOECOLOGIES
BIOECOLOGIST
BIOECOLOGISTS
BIOECOLOGY
BIOELECTRIC
BIOELECTRICAL
BIOELECTRICITY
BIOENERGETIC
BIOENERGETICS
BIOENERGIES
BIOENGINEER
BIOENGINEERED
BIOENGINEERING
BIOENGINEERINGS
BIOENGINEERS
BIOETHANOL
BIOETHANOLS
BIOETHICAL
BIOETHICIST
BIOETHICISTS
BIOFEEDBACK
BIOFEEDBACKS
BIOFLAVONOID
BIOFLAVONOIDS
BIOFOULERS
BIOFOULING

BIOFOULINGS
BIOFUELLED
BIOGENESES
BIOGENESIS
BIOGENETIC
BIOGENETICAL
BIOGENETICALLY
BIOGENETICS
BIOGEOCHEMICAL
BIOGEOCHEMICALS
BIOGEOCHEMISTRY
BIOGEOGRAPHER
BIOGEOGRAPHERS
BIOGEOGRAPHIC
BIOGEOGRAPHICAL
BIOGEOGRAPHIES
BIOGEOGRAPHY
BIOGRAPHED
BIOGRAPHEE
BIOGRAPHEES
BIOGRAPHER
BIOGRAPHERS
BIOGRAPHIC
BIOGRAPHICAL
BIOGRAPHICALLY
BIOGRAPHIES
BIOGRAPHING
BIOGRAPHISE
BIOGRAPHISED
BIOGRAPHISES
BIOGRAPHISING
BIOGRAPHIZE
BIOGRAPHIZED
BIOGRAPHIZES
BIOGRAPHIZING
BIOHACKERS
BIOHAZARDOUS
BIOHAZARDS
BIOINDUSTRIES
BIOINDUSTRY
BIOINFORMATICS
BIOLOGICAL
BIOLOGICALLY
BIOLOGICALS
BIOLOGISMS
BIOLOGISTIC
BIOLOGISTS
BIOLUMINESCENCE
BIOLUMINESCENT
BIOMAGNETICS
BIOMARKERS
BIOMATERIAL
BIOMATERIALS
BIOMATHEMATICAL
BIOMATHEMATICS
BIOMECHANICAL
BIOMECHANICALLY
BIOMECHANICS
BIOMEDICAL
BIOMEDICINE
BIOMEDICINES
BIOMETEOROLOGY
BIOMETRICAL
BIOMETRICALLY
BIOMETRICIAN
BIOMETRICIANS
BIOMETRICS
BIOMETRIES
BIOMIMETIC
BIOMIMETICS
BIOMIMICRIES
BIOMIMICRY
BIOMININGS
BIOMOLECULAR
BIOMOLECULE
BIOMOLECULES
BIOMORPHIC
BIONOMICALLY
BIONOMISTS
BIOPARENTS
BIOPESTICIDAL
BIOPESTICIDE
BIOPESTICIDES
BIOPHILIAS
BIOPHYSICAL
BIOPHYSICALLY
BIOPHYSICIST
BIOPHYSICISTS
BIOPHYSICS
BIOPIRACIES
BIOPIRATES
BIOPLASMIC
BIOPLASTIC
BIOPLASTICS
BIOPOIESES
BIOPOIESIS
BIOPOLYMER
BIOPOLYMERS
BIOPRINTING
BIOPRINTINGS
BIOPRIVACIES
BIOPRIVACY
BIOPROSPECTING
BIOPROSPECTINGS
BIOPSYCHOLOGIES
BIOPSYCHOLOGY
BIOREACTOR
BIOREACTORS
BIOREAGENT
BIOREAGENTS
BIOREGIONAL
BIOREGIONALISM
BIOREGIONALISMS
BIOREGIONALIST
BIOREGIONALISTS
BIOREGIONS
BIOREMEDIATION
BIOREMEDIATIONS
BIORHYTHMIC
BIORHYTHMICALLY
BIORHYTHMICS
BIORHYTHMS
BIOSAFETIES
BIOSATELLITE
BIOSATELLITES
BIOSCIENCE
BIOSCIENCES
BIOSCIENTIFIC
BIOSCIENTIST
BIOSCIENTISTS
BIOSCOPIES
BIOSENSORS
BIOSOCIALLY
BIOSPHERES
BIOSPHERIC
BIOSTATICALLY
BIOSTATICS
BIOSTATISTICAL
BIOSTATISTICIAN
BIOSTATISTICS
BIOSTRATIGRAPHY
BIOSTROMES
BIOSURGERIES
BIOSURGERY
BIOSYNTHESES
BIOSYNTHESIS
BIOSYNTHETIC
BIOSYSTEMATIC
BIOSYSTEMATICS
BIOSYSTEMATIST
BIOSYSTEMATISTS
BIOTECHNICAL
BIOTECHNOLOGIES
BIOTECHNOLOGIST
BIOTECHNOLOGY
BIOTELEMETRIC
BIOTELEMETRIES
BIOTELEMETRY
BIOTERRORS
BIOTICALLY
BIOTURBATION
BIOTURBATIONS
BIOWEAPONS
BIPARENTAL
BIPARENTALLY
BIPARIETAL
BIPARTISAN
BIPARTISANISM
BIPARTISANISMS
BIPARTISANSHIP
BIPARTISANSHIPS
BIPARTITELY
BIPARTITION
BIPARTITIONS
BIPEDALISM
BIPEDALISMS
BIPEDALITIES
BIPEDALITY
BIPETALOUS
BIPINNARIA
BIPINNARIAS
BIPINNATELY
BIPOLARISATION
BIPOLARISATIONS
BIPOLARISE
BIPOLARISED
BIPOLARISES
BIPOLARISING
BIPOLARITIES
BIPOLARITY
BIPOLARIZATION
BIPOLARIZATIONS
BIPOLARIZE
BIPOLARIZED
BIPOLARIZES
BIPOLARIZING
BIPROPELLANT
BIPROPELLANTS
BIPYRAMIDAL
BIPYRAMIDS
BIQUADRATE
BIQUADRATES
BIQUADRATIC
BIQUADRATICS
BIQUARTERLY
BIQUINTILE
BIQUINTILES
BIRACIALISM
BIRACIALISMS
BIRACIALLY
BIRADICALS
BIRCHBARKS
BIRCHWOODS
BIRDBRAINED
BIRDBRAINS
BIRDDOGGED
BIRDDOGGING
BIRDDOGGINGS
BIRDHOUSES
BIRDLIMING
BIRDSFOOTS
BIRDWATCHED
BIRDWATCHER
BIRDWATCHERS
BIRDWATCHES
BIRDWATCHING
BIRDWATCHINGS
BIREFRINGENCE
BIREFRINGENCES
BIREFRINGENT
BIROSTRATE
BIRTHDATES
BIRTHMARKS
BIRTHNAMES
BIRTHNIGHT
BIRTHNIGHTS
BIRTHPLACE
BIRTHPLACES
BIRTHRATES
BIRTHRIGHT

BIRTHRIGHTS
BIRTHROOTS
BIRTHSTONE
BIRTHSTONES
BIRTHWORTS
BISCUITIER
BISCUITIEST
BISECTIONAL
BISECTIONALLY
BISECTIONS
BISECTRICES
BISEXUALISM
BISEXUALISMS
BISEXUALITIES
BISEXUALITY
BISEXUALLY
BISHOPBIRD
BISHOPBIRDS
BISHOPDOMS
BISHOPESSES
BISHOPRICS
BISHOPWEED
BISHOPWEEDS
BISMUTHINITE
BISMUTHINITES
BISMUTHOUS
BISOCIATION
BISOCIATIONS
BISOCIATIVE
BISPHENOLS
BISPHOSPHONATE
BISPHOSPHONATES
BISSEXTILE
BISSEXTILES
BISTOURIES
BISULFATES
BISULFIDES
BISULFITES
BISULPHATE
BISULPHATES
BISULPHIDE
BISULPHIDES
BISULPHITE
BISULPHITES
BISYMMETRIC
BISYMMETRICAL
BISYMMETRICALLY
BISYMMETRIES
BISYMMETRY
BITARTRATE
BITARTRATES
BITCHERIES
BITCHFESTS
BITCHINESS
BITCHINESSES
BITEPLATES
BITMAPPING
BITONALITIES
BITONALITY
BITSTREAMS
BITTERBARK
BITTERBARKS
BITTERBRUSH
BITTERBRUSHES
BITTERCRESS
BITTERCRESSES
BITTERLING
BITTERLINGS
BITTERNESS
BITTERNESSES
BITTERNUTS
BITTERROOT
BITTERROOTS
BITTERSWEET
BITTERSWEETLY
BITTERSWEETNESS
BITTERSWEETS
BITTERWEED
BITTERWEEDS
BITTERWOOD
BITTERWOODS
BITTINESSES
BITUMINATE
BITUMINATED
BITUMINATES
BITUMINATING
BITUMINISATION
BITUMINISATIONS
BITUMINISE
BITUMINISED
BITUMINISES
BITUMINISING
BITUMINIZATION
BITUMINIZATIONS
BITUMINIZE
BITUMINIZED
BITUMINIZES
BITUMINIZING
BITUMINOUS
BIUNIQUENESS
BIUNIQUENESSES
BIVALENCES
BIVALENCIES
BIVALVULAR
BIVARIANTS
BIVARIATES
BIVOUACKED
BIVOUACKING
BIWEEKLIES
BIZARRENESS
BIZARRENESSES
BIZARRERIE
BIZARRERIES
BLABBERING
BLABBERMOUTH
BLABBERMOUTHS
BLACKAMOOR
BLACKAMOORS
BLACKBALLED
BLACKBALLING
BLACKBALLINGS
BLACKBALLS
BLACKBANDS
BLACKBERRIED
BLACKBERRIES
BLACKBERRY
BLACKBERRYING
BLACKBERRYINGS
BLACKBIRDED
BLACKBIRDER
BLACKBIRDERS
BLACKBIRDING
BLACKBIRDINGS
BLACKBIRDS
BLACKBOARD
BLACKBOARDS
BLACKBODIES
BLACKBUCKS
BLACKBUTTS
BLACKCOCKS
BLACKCURRANT
BLACKCURRANTS
BLACKDAMPS
BLACKENERS
BLACKENING
BLACKENINGS
BLACKFACED
BLACKFACES
BLACKFELLA
BLACKFELLAS
BLACKFISHES
BLACKFLIES
BLACKGAMES
BLACKGUARD
BLACKGUARDED
BLACKGUARDING
BLACKGUARDISM
BLACKGUARDISMS
BLACKGUARDLIER
BLACKGUARDLIEST
BLACKGUARDLY
BLACKGUARDS
BLACKHANDER
BLACKHANDERS
BLACKHEADED
BLACKHEADS
BLACKHEART
BLACKHEARTS
BLACKISHLY
BLACKJACKED
BLACKJACKING
BLACKJACKS
BLACKLANDS
BLACKLEADED
BLACKLEADING
BLACKLEADS
BLACKLEGGED
BLACKLEGGING
BLACKLISTED
BLACKLISTER
BLACKLISTERS
BLACKLISTING
BLACKLISTINGS
BLACKLISTS
BLACKMAILED
BLACKMAILER
BLACKMAILERS
BLACKMAILING
BLACKMAILS
BLACKNESSES
BLACKPOLLS
BLACKSMITH
BLACKSMITHING
BLACKSMITHINGS
BLACKSMITHS
BLACKSNAKE
BLACKSNAKES
BLACKSPOTS
BLACKSTRAP
BLACKSTRAPS
BLACKTAILS
BLACKTHORN
BLACKTHORNS
BLACKTOPPED
BLACKTOPPING
BLACKWASHED
BLACKWASHES
BLACKWASHING
BLACKWATER
BLACKWATERS
BLACKWOODS
BLADDERIER
BLADDERIEST
BLADDERLIKE
BLADDERNOSE
BLADDERNOSES
BLADDERNUT
BLADDERNUTS
BLADDERWORT
BLADDERWORTS
BLADDERWRACK
BLADDERWRACKS
BLADEWORKS
BLAEBERRIES
BLAMABLENESS
BLAMABLENESSES
BLAMEABLENESS
BLAMEABLENESSES
BLAMEFULLY
BLAMEFULNESS
BLAMEFULNESSES
BLAMELESSLY
BLAMELESSNESS
BLAMELESSNESSES
BLAMESTORM
BLAMESTORMED
BLAMESTORMING
BLAMESTORMINGS
BLAMESTORMS
BLAMEWORTHIER

BLAMEWORTHIEST
BLAMEWORTHINESS
BLAMEWORTHY
BLANCHISSEUSE
BLANCHISSEUSES
BLANCMANGE
BLANCMANGES
BLANDISHED
BLANDISHER
BLANDISHERS
BLANDISHES
BLANDISHING
BLANDISHMENT
BLANDISHMENTS
BLANDNESSES
BLANKETFLOWER
BLANKETFLOWERS
BLANKETIES
BLANKETING
BLANKETINGS
BLANKETLIKE
BLANKETWEED
BLANKETWEEDS
BLANKNESSES
BLANQUETTE
BLANQUETTES
BLARNEYING
BLASPHEMED
BLASPHEMER
BLASPHEMERS
BLASPHEMES
BLASPHEMIES
BLASPHEMING
BLASPHEMOUS
BLASPHEMOUSLY
BLASPHEMOUSNESS
BLASTEMATA
BLASTEMATIC
BLASTHOLES
BLASTMENTS
BLASTOCHYLE
BLASTOCHYLES
BLASTOCOEL
BLASTOCOELE
BLASTOCOELES
BLASTOCOELIC
BLASTOCOELS
BLASTOCYST
BLASTOCYSTS
BLASTODERM
BLASTODERMIC
BLASTODERMS
BLASTODISC
BLASTODISCS
BLASTOGENESES
BLASTOGENESIS
BLASTOGENETIC
BLASTOGENIC
BLASTOMATA
BLASTOMERE
BLASTOMERES
BLASTOMERIC
BLASTOMYCOSES
BLASTOMYCOSIS
BLASTOPORAL
BLASTOPORE
BLASTOPORES
BLASTOPORIC
BLASTOPORS
BLASTOSPHERE
BLASTOSPHERES
BLASTOSPORE
BLASTOSPORES
BLASTULATION
BLASTULATIONS
BLATANCIES
BLATHERERS
BLATHERING
BLATHERINGS
BLATHERSKITE
BLATHERSKITES
BLATTERING
BLAXPLOITATION
BLAXPLOITATIONS
BLAZONINGS
BLAZONRIES
BLEACHABLE
BLEACHERIES
BLEACHERITE
BLEACHERITES
BLEACHINGS
BLEAKNESSES
BLEARINESS
BLEARINESSES
BLEMISHERS
BLEMISHING
BLEMISHMENT
BLEMISHMENTS
BLENNIOIDS
BLENNORRHEA
BLENNORRHEAS
BLENNORRHOEA
BLENNORRHOEAS
BLEOMYCINS
BLEPHARISM
BLEPHARISMS
BLEPHARITIC
BLEPHARITIS
BLEPHARITISES
BLEPHAROPLAST
BLEPHAROPLASTS
BLEPHAROPLASTY
BLEPHAROSPASM
BLEPHAROSPASMS
BLESSEDEST
BLESSEDNESS
BLESSEDNESSES
BLETHERANSKATE
BLETHERANSKATES
BLETHERATION
BLETHERATIONS
BLETHERERS
BLETHERING
BLETHERINGS
BLETHERSKATE
BLETHERSKATES
BLIGHTINGLY
BLIGHTINGS
BLIMPERIES
BLIMPISHLY
BLIMPISHNESS
BLIMPISHNESSES
BLINDFISHES
BLINDFOLDED
BLINDFOLDING
BLINDFOLDS
BLINDINGLY
BLINDNESSES
BLINDSIDED
BLINDSIDES
BLINDSIDING
BLINDSIGHT
BLINDSIGHTS
BLINDSTOREY
BLINDSTOREYS
BLINDSTORIES
BLINDSTORY
BLINDWORMS
BLINGLISHES
BLINKERING
BLISSFULLY
BLISSFULNESS
BLISSFULNESSES
BLISTERIER
BLISTERIEST
BLISTERING
BLISTERINGLY
BLITHENESS
BLITHENESSES
BLITHERING
BLITHESOME
BLITHESOMELY
BLITHESOMENESS
BLITZKRIEG
BLITZKRIEGS
BLIZZARDED
BLIZZARDIER
BLIZZARDIEST
BLIZZARDING
BLIZZARDLY
BLOATEDNESS
BLOATEDNESSES
BLOATWARES
BLOCKADERS
BLOCKADING
BLOCKBOARD
BLOCKBOARDS
BLOCKBUSTED
BLOCKBUSTER
BLOCKBUSTERS
BLOCKBUSTING
BLOCKBUSTINGS
BLOCKBUSTS
BLOCKCHAIN
BLOCKCHAINS
BLOCKHEADED
BLOCKHEADEDLY
BLOCKHEADEDNESS
BLOCKHEADS
BLOCKHOLES
BLOCKHOUSE
BLOCKHOUSES
BLOCKINESS
BLOCKINESSES
BLOCKISHLY
BLOCKISHNESS
BLOCKISHNESSES
BLOCKSHIPS
BLOCKWORKS
BLOGGERATI
BLOGJACKING
BLOGJACKINGS
BLOGOSPHERE
BLOGOSPHERES
BLOGSTREAM
BLOGSTREAMS
BLOKARTING
BLOKARTINGS
BLOKEISHNESS
BLOKEISHNESSES
BLOKISHNESS
BLOKISHNESSES
BLONDENESS
BLONDENESSES
BLONDINING
BLONDNESSES
BLOODBATHS
BLOODCURDLING
BLOODCURDLINGLY
BLOODGUILT
BLOODGUILTIER
BLOODGUILTIEST
BLOODGUILTINESS
BLOODGUILTS
BLOODGUILTY
BLOODHOUND
BLOODHOUNDS
BLOODINESS
BLOODINESSES
BLOODLESSLY
BLOODLESSNESS
BLOODLESSNESSES
BLOODLETTER
BLOODLETTERS
BLOODLETTING
BLOODLETTINGS
BLOODLINES
BLOODLUSTS
BLOODMOBILE
BLOODMOBILES

B

BLOODROOTS
BLOODSHEDS
BLOODSPRENT
BLOODSTAIN
BLOODSTAINED
BLOODSTAINS
BLOODSTOCK
BLOODSTOCKS
BLOODSTONE
BLOODSTONES
BLOODSTREAM
BLOODSTREAMS
BLOODSUCKER
BLOODSUCKERS
BLOODSUCKING
BLOODTHIRSTIER
BLOODTHIRSTIEST
BLOODTHIRSTILY
BLOODTHIRSTY
BLOODWOODS
BLOODWORMS
BLOODWORTS
BLOOMERIES
BLOQUISTES
BLOSSOMIER
BLOSSOMIEST
BLOSSOMING
BLOSSOMINGS
BLOSSOMLESS
BLOTCHIEST
BLOTCHINESS
BLOTCHINESSES
BLOTCHINGS
BLOTTESQUE
BLOTTESQUES
BLOVIATING
BLOVIATION
BLOVIATIONS
BLOWFISHES
BLOWINESSES
BLOWSINESS
BLOWSINESSES
BLOWTORCHED
BLOWTORCHES
BLOWTORCHING
BLOWZINESS
BLOWZINESSES
BLUBBERERS
BLUBBERIER
BLUBBERIEST
BLUBBERING
BLUDGEONED
BLUDGEONER
BLUDGEONERS
BLUDGEONING
BLUEBEARDS
BLUEBERRIES
BLUEBLOODS
BLUEBONNET
BLUEBONNETS
BLUEBOTTLE
BLUEBOTTLES
BLUEBREAST
BLUEBREASTS
BLUEBUSHES
BLUEFISHES
BLUEGRASSES
BLUEISHNESS
BLUEISHNESSES
BLUEJACKET
BLUEJACKETS
BLUEJACKING
BLUEJACKINGS
BLUELINERS
BLUEMOUTHS
BLUENESSES
BLUEPOINTS
BLUEPRINTED
BLUEPRINTING
BLUEPRINTS
BLUESHIFTED
BLUESHIFTS
BLUESNARFING
BLUESNARFINGS
BLUESTOCKING
BLUESTOCKINGS
BLUESTONES
BLUETHROAT
BLUETHROATS
BLUETONGUE
BLUETONGUES
BLUFFNESSES
BLUISHNESS
BLUISHNESSES
BLUNDERBUSS
BLUNDERBUSSES
BLUNDERERS
BLUNDERING
BLUNDERINGLY
BLUNDERINGS
BLUNTHEADS
BLUNTNESSES
BLURREDNESS
BLURREDNESSES
BLURRINESS
BLURRINESSES
BLURRINGLY
BLUSHINGLY
BLUSHLESSLY
BLUSTERERS
BLUSTERIER
BLUSTERIEST
BLUSTERING
BLUSTERINGLY
BLUSTERINGS
BLUSTEROUS
BLUSTEROUSLY
BLUTWURSTS
BOARDINGHOUSE
BOARDINGHOUSES
BOARDROOMS
BOARDSAILING
BOARDSAILINGS
BOARDSAILOR
BOARDSAILORS
BOARDWALKS
BOARFISHES
BOARHOUNDS
BOARISHNESS
BOARISHNESSES
BOASTFULLY
BOASTFULNESS
BOASTFULNESSES
BOASTINGLY
BOATBUILDER
BOATBUILDERS
BOATBUILDING
BOATBUILDINGS
BOATHOUSES
BOATLIFTED
BOATLIFTING
BOATSWAINS
BOBBEJAANS
BOBBITTING
BOBBLEHEAD
BOBBLEHEADS
BOBBYSOCKS
BOBBYSOXER
BOBBYSOXERS
BOBSLEDDED
BOBSLEDDER
BOBSLEDDERS
BOBSLEDDING
BOBSLEDDINGS
BOBSLEIGHED
BOBSLEIGHING
BOBSLEIGHINGS
BOBSLEIGHS
BOBTAILING
BOBWEIGHTS
BOCCONCINI
BODACIOUSLY
BODDHISATTVA
BODDHISATTVAS
BODEGUEROS
BODHISATTVA
BODHISATTVAS
BODYBOARDED
BODYBOARDING
BODYBOARDINGS
BODYBOARDS
BODYBUILDER
BODYBUILDERS
BODYBUILDING
BODYBUILDINGS
BODYBUILDS
BODYCHECKED
BODYCHECKING
BODYCHECKS
BODYGUARDED
BODYGUARDING
BODYGUARDS
BODYSHAPER
BODYSHAPERS
BODYSHELLS
BODYSNATCHER
BODYSNATCHERS
BODYSURFED
BODYSURFER
BODYSURFERS
BODYSURFING
BODYSURFINGS
BODYWASHES
BODYWORKER
BODYWORKERS
BOEREMUSIEK
BOEREMUSIEKS
BOEREWORSES
BOFFINIEST
BOGGINESSES
BOGTROTTER
BOGTROTTERS
BOGTROTTING
BOGTROTTINGS
BOGUSNESSES
BOHEMIANISM
BOHEMIANISMS
BOILERMAKER
BOILERMAKERS
BOILERMAKING
BOILERMAKINGS
BOILERPLATE
BOILERPLATED
BOILERPLATES
BOILERPLATING
BOILERSUIT
BOILERSUITS
BOISTEROUS
BOISTEROUSLY
BOISTEROUSNESS
BOKMAKIERIE
BOKMAKIERIES
BOLDFACING
BOLDNESSES
BOLECTIONS
BOLIVIANOS
BOLLETRIES
BOLLOCKING
BOLLOCKINGS
BOLLOCKSED
BOLLOCKSES
BOLLOCKSING
BOLOGNESES
BOLOGRAPHS
BOLOMETERS
BOLOMETRIC
BOLOMETRICALLY
BOLOMETRIES
BOLSHEVIKI
BOLSHEVIKS

BOLSHEVISE
BOLSHEVISED
BOLSHEVISES
BOLSHEVISING
BOLSHEVISM
BOLSHEVISMS
BOLSHEVIZE
BOLSHEVIZED
BOLSHEVIZES
BOLSHEVIZING
BOLSTERERS
BOLSTERING
BOLSTERINGS
BOMBACACEOUS
BOMBARDERS
BOMBARDIER
BOMBARDIERS
BOMBARDING
BOMBARDMENT
BOMBARDMENTS
BOMBARDONS
BOMBASINES
BOMBASTERS
BOMBASTICALLY
BOMBASTING
BOMBAZINES
BOMBILATED
BOMBILATES
BOMBILATING
BOMBILATION
BOMBILATIONS
BOMBINATED
BOMBINATES
BOMBINATING
BOMBINATION
BOMBINATIONS
BOMBPROOFED
BOMBPROOFING
BOMBPROOFS
BOMBSHELLS
BOMBSIGHTS
BONAMIASES
BONAMIASIS
BONASSUSES
BONBONNIERE
BONBONNIERES
BONDHOLDER
BONDHOLDERS
BONDMANSHIP
BONDMANSHIPS
BONDSERVANT
BONDSERVANTS
BONDSTONES
BONDSWOMAN
BONDSWOMEN
BONEBLACKS
BONEFISHES
BONEFISHING
BONEFISHINGS
BONEHEADED
BONEHEADEDNESS
BONESETTER
BONESETTERS
BONESHAKER
BONESHAKERS
BONHOMMIES
BONILASSES
BONINESSES
BONKBUSTER
BONKBUSTERS
BONNIBELLS
BONNILASSE
BONNILASSES
BONNINESSES
BONNYCLABBER
BONNYCLABBERS
BOOBIALLAS
BOOBOISIES
BOOGALOOED
BOOGALOOING
BOOKBINDER
BOOKBINDERIES
BOOKBINDERS
BOOKBINDERY
BOOKBINDING
BOOKBINDINGS
BOOKCROSSING
BOOKCROSSINGS
BOOKENDING
BOOKISHNESS
BOOKISHNESSES
BOOKKEEPER
BOOKKEEPERS
BOOKKEEPING
BOOKKEEPINGS
BOOKLIGHTS
BOOKMAKERS
BOOKMAKING
BOOKMAKINGS
BOOKMARKED
BOOKMARKER
BOOKMARKERS
BOOKMARKING
BOOKMOBILE
BOOKMOBILES
BOOKPLATES
BOOKSELLER
BOOKSELLERS
BOOKSELLING
BOOKSELLINGS
BOOKSHELVES
BOOKSTALLS
BOOKSTANDS
BOOKSTORES
BOOMERANGED
BOOMERANGING
BOOMERANGS
BOOMSLANGS
BOOMSTICKS
BOONDOGGLE
BOONDOGGLED
BOONDOGGLER
BOONDOGGLERS
BOONDOGGLES
BOONDOGGLING
BOONGARIES
BOORISHNESS
BOORISHNESSES
BOOSTERISH
BOOSTERISM
BOOSTERISMS
BOOTBLACKS
BOOTLEGGED
BOOTLEGGER
BOOTLEGGERS
BOOTLEGGING
BOOTLEGGINGS
BOOTLESSLY
BOOTLESSNESS
BOOTLESSNESSES
BOOTLICKED
BOOTLICKER
BOOTLICKERS
BOOTLICKING
BOOTLICKINGS
BOOTLOADER
BOOTLOADERS
BOOTMAKERS
BOOTMAKING
BOOTMAKINGS
BOOTSTRAPPED
BOOTSTRAPPING
BOOTSTRAPS
BOOTYLICIOUS
BOOZEHOUND
BOOZEHOUNDS
BOOZINESSES
BORAGINACEOUS
BORBORYGMAL
BORBORYGMI
BORBORYGMIC
BORBORYGMUS
BORDEREAUX
BORDERLAND
BORDERLANDS
BORDERLESS
BORDERLINE
BORDERLINES
BORDRAGING
BORDRAGINGS
BORESCOPES
BORGHETTOS
BORINGNESS
BORINGNESSES
BOROHYDRIDE
BOROHYDRIDES
BOROSILICATE
BOROSILICATES
BORROWINGS
BOSBERAADS
BOSCHVARKS
BOSCHVELDS
BOSKINESSES
BOSSINESSES
BOSSNAPPING
BOSSNAPPINGS
BOSSYBOOTS
BOTANICALLY
BOTANICALS
BOTANISERS
BOTANISING
BOTANIZERS
BOTANIZING
BOTANOMANCIES
BOTANOMANCY
BOTCHERIES
BOTCHINESS
BOTCHINESSES
BOTHERATION
BOTHERATIONS
BOTHERSOME
BOTRYOIDAL
BOTRYTISES
BOTTLEBRUSH
BOTTLEBRUSHES
BOTTLEFULS
BOTTLENECK
BOTTLENECKED
BOTTLENECKING
BOTTLENECKS
BOTTLENOSE
BOTTLENOSES
BOTTOMINGS
BOTTOMLAND
BOTTOMLANDS
BOTTOMLESS
BOTTOMLESSLY
BOTTOMLESSNESS
BOTTOMMOST
BOTTOMNESS
BOTTOMNESSES
BOTTOMRIES
BOTULINUMS
BOTULINUSES
BOUGAINVILIA
BOUGAINVILIAS
BOUGAINVILLAEA
BOUGAINVILLAEAS
BOUGAINVILLEA
BOUGAINVILLEAS
BOUILLABAISSE
BOUILLABAISSES
BOUILLOTTE
BOUILLOTTES
BOULDERERS
BOULDERIER
BOULDERIEST
BOULDERING
BOULDERINGS
BOULEVARDIER

B

BOULEVARDIERS
BOULEVARDS
BOULEVERSEMENT
BOULEVERSEMENTS
BOULLEWORK
BOULLEWORKS
BOUNCEDOWN
BOUNCEDOWNS
BOUNCINESS
BOUNCINESSES
BOUNCINGLY
BOUNDARIES
BOUNDEDNESS
BOUNDEDNESSES
BOUNDERISH
BOUNDLESSLY
BOUNDLESSNESS
BOUNDLESSNESSES
BOUNDNESSES
BOUNTEOUSLY
BOUNTEOUSNESS
BOUNTEOUSNESSES
BOUNTIFULLY
BOUNTIFULNESS
BOUNTIFULNESSES
BOUNTYHEDS
BOUQUETIERE
BOUQUETIERES
BOURASQUES
BOURBONISM
BOURBONISMS
BOURGEOISE
BOURGEOISES
BOURGEOISIE
BOURGEOISIES
BOURGEOISIFIED
BOURGEOISIFIES
BOURGEOISIFY
BOURGEOISIFYING
BOURGEONED
BOURGEONING
BOURGUIGNON
BOURGUIGNONNE
BOURGUIGNONNES
BOURGUIGNONS
BOUSINGKEN
BOUSINGKENS
BOUSTROPHEDON
BOUSTROPHEDONIC
BOUSTROPHEDONS
BOUTIQUIER
BOUTIQUIEST
BOUTONNIERE
BOUTONNIERES
BOUVARDIAS
BOVINITIES
BOWDLERISATION
BOWDLERISATIONS
BOWDLERISE
BOWDLERISED
BOWDLERISER
BOWDLERISERS
BOWDLERISES
BOWDLERISING
BOWDLERISM
BOWDLERISMS
BOWDLERIZATION
BOWDLERIZATIONS
BOWDLERIZE
BOWDLERIZED
BOWDLERIZER
BOWDLERIZERS
BOWDLERIZES
BOWDLERIZING
BOWERBIRDS
BOWERWOMAN
BOWERWOMEN
BOWHUNTERS
BOWHUNTING
BOWHUNTINGS
BOWLINGUAL
BOWLINGUALS
BOWSTRINGED
BOWSTRINGING
BOWSTRINGS
BOXBERRIES
BOXERCISES
BOXHAULING
BOXINESSES
BOXKEEPERS
BOXWALLAHS
BOYCOTTERS
BOYCOTTING
BOYFRIENDS
BOYISHNESS
BOYISHNESSES
BOYSENBERRIES
BOYSENBERRY
BRAAIVLEIS
BRAAIVLEISES
BRABBLEMENT
BRABBLEMENTS
BRACHIATED
BRACHIATES
BRACHIATING
BRACHIATION
BRACHIATIONS
BRACHIATOR
BRACHIATORS
BRACHIOCEPHALIC
BRACHIOPOD
BRACHIOPODS
BRACHIOSAURUS
BRACHIOSAURUSES
BRACHISTOCHRONE
BRACHYAXES
BRACHYAXIS
BRACHYCEPHAL
BRACHYCEPHALIC
BRACHYCEPHALICS
BRACHYCEPHALIES
BRACHYCEPHALISM
BRACHYCEPHALOUS
BRACHYCEPHALS
BRACHYCEPHALY
BRACHYCEROUS
BRACHYDACTYL
BRACHYDACTYLIC
BRACHYDACTYLIES
BRACHYDACTYLISM
BRACHYDACTYLOUS
BRACHYDACTYLY
BRACHYDIAGONAL
BRACHYDIAGONALS
BRACHYDOME
BRACHYDOMES
BRACHYGRAPHIES
BRACHYGRAPHY
BRACHYLOGIES
BRACHYLOGOUS
BRACHYLOGY
BRACHYODONT
BRACHYPINAKOID
BRACHYPINAKOIDS
BRACHYPRISM
BRACHYPRISMS
BRACHYPTERISM
BRACHYPTERISMS
BRACHYPTEROUS
BRACHYTHERAPIES
BRACHYTHERAPY
BRACHYURAL
BRACHYURAN
BRACHYURANS
BRACHYUROUS
BRACKETING
BRACKETINGS
BRACKISHNESS
BRACKISHNESSES
BRACTEATES
BRACTEOLATE
BRACTEOLES
BRADYCARDIA
BRADYCARDIAC
BRADYCARDIAS
BRADYKINESIA
BRADYKINESIAS
BRADYKININ
BRADYKININS
BRADYPEPTIC
BRADYPEPTICS
BRADYSEISM
BRADYSEISMS
BRAGADISME
BRAGADISMES
BRAGGADOCIO
BRAGGADOCIOS
BRAGGADOCIOUS
BRAGGARTISM
BRAGGARTISMS
BRAGGARTLIER
BRAGGARTLIEST
BRAGGARTLY
BRAGGINGLY
BRAHMANISM
BRAHMANISMS
BRAHMANIST
BRAHMANISTS
BRAHMINISM
BRAHMINISMS
BRAHMINIST
BRAHMINISTS
BRAILLEWRITER
BRAILLEWRITERS
BRAILLISTS
BRAINBOXES
BRAINCASES
BRAINCHILD
BRAINCHILDREN
BRAINFARTS
BRAINFOODS
BRAININESS
BRAININESSES
BRAINLESSLY
BRAINLESSNESS
BRAINLESSNESSES
BRAINPOWER
BRAINPOWERS
BRAINSICKLY
BRAINSICKNESS
BRAINSICKNESSES
BRAINSTEMS
BRAINSTORM
BRAINSTORMED
BRAINSTORMER
BRAINSTORMERS
BRAINSTORMING
BRAINSTORMINGS
BRAINSTORMS
BRAINTEASER
BRAINTEASERS
BRAINWASHED
BRAINWASHER
BRAINWASHERS
BRAINWASHES
BRAINWASHING
BRAINWASHINGS
BRAINWAVES
BRAINWORKS
BRAMBLIEST
BRAMBLINGS
BRANCHERIES
BRANCHIATE
BRANCHIEST
BRANCHINGS
BRANCHIOPOD
BRANCHIOPODS
BRANCHIOSTEGAL
BRANCHLESS
BRANCHLETS

BRANCHLIKE
BRANCHLINE
BRANCHLINES
BRANDERING
BRANDISHED
BRANDISHER
BRANDISHERS
BRANDISHES
BRANDISHING
BRANDLINGS
BRANDRETHS
BRANFULNESS
BRANFULNESSES
BRANGLINGS
BRANKURSINE
BRANKURSINES
BRANNIGANS
BRASHINESS
BRASHINESSES
BRASHNESSES
BRASILEINS
BRASSBOUND
BRASSERIES
BRASSFOUNDER
BRASSFOUNDERS
BRASSFOUNDING
BRASSFOUNDINGS
BRASSICACEOUS
BRASSIERES
BRASSINESS
BRASSINESSES
BRASSWARES
BRATPACKER
BRATPACKERS
BRATTICING
BRATTICINGS
BRATTINESS
BRATTINESSES
BRATTISHED
BRATTISHES
BRATTISHING
BRATTISHINGS
BRATTLINGS
BRATWURSTS
BRAUNCHING
BRAUNSCHWEIGER
BRAUNSCHWEIGERS
BRAVADOING
BRAVENESSES
BRAVISSIMO
BRAWNINESS
BRAWNINESSES
BRAZENNESS
BRAZENNESSES
BRAZENRIES
BRAZIERIES
BRAZILEINS
BRAZILWOOD
BRAZILWOODS
BREADBASKET
BREADBASKETS
BREADBERRIES
BREADBERRY
BREADBOARD
BREADBOARDED
BREADBOARDING
BREADBOARDS
BREADBOXES
BREADCRUMB
BREADCRUMBED
BREADCRUMBING
BREADCRUMBS
BREADFRUIT
BREADFRUITS
BREADHEADS
BREADKNIFE
BREADKNIVES
BREADLINES
BREADROOMS
BREADROOTS
BREADSTICK
BREADSTICKS
BREADSTUFF
BREADSTUFFS
BREADTHWAYS
BREADTHWISE
BREADWINNER
BREADWINNERS
BREADWINNING
BREADWINNINGS
BREAKABLENESS
BREAKABLENESSES
BREAKABLES
BREAKAWAYS
BREAKBEATS
BREAKDANCE
BREAKDANCED
BREAKDANCER
BREAKDANCERS
BREAKDANCES
BREAKDANCING
BREAKDANCINGS
BREAKDOWNS
BREAKEVENS
BREAKFASTED
BREAKFASTER
BREAKFASTERS
BREAKFASTING
BREAKFASTS
BREAKFRONT
BREAKFRONTS
BREAKPOINT
BREAKPOINTS
BREAKTHROUGH
BREAKTHROUGHS
BREAKTIMES
BREAKWALLS
BREAKWATER
BREAKWATERS
BREASTBONE
BREASTBONES
BREASTFEED
BREASTFEEDING
BREASTFEEDINGS
BREASTFEEDS
BREASTPINS
BREASTPLATE
BREASTPLATES
BREASTPLOUGH
BREASTPLOUGHS
BREASTRAIL
BREASTRAILS
BREASTSTROKE
BREASTSTROKER
BREASTSTROKERS
BREASTSTROKES
BREASTSUMMER
BREASTSUMMERS
BREASTWORK
BREASTWORKS
BREATHABILITIES
BREATHABILITY
BREATHABLE
BREATHALYSE
BREATHALYSED
BREATHALYSER
BREATHALYSERS
BREATHALYSES
BREATHALYSING
BREATHALYZE
BREATHALYZED
BREATHALYZER
BREATHALYZERS
BREATHALYZES
BREATHALYZING
BREATHARIAN
BREATHARIANISM
BREATHARIANISMS
BREATHARIANS
BREATHIEST
BREATHINESS
BREATHINESSES
BREATHINGS
BREATHLESS
BREATHLESSLY
BREATHLESSNESS
BREATHTAKING
BREATHTAKINGLY
BRECCIATED
BRECCIATES
BRECCIATING
BRECCIATION
BRECCIATIONS
BREECHBLOCK
BREECHBLOCKS
BREECHCLOTH
BREECHCLOTHS
BREECHCLOUT
BREECHCLOUTS
BREECHINGS
BREECHLESS
BREECHLOADER
BREECHLOADERS
BREEZELESS
BREEZEWAYS
BREEZINESS
BREEZINESSES
BREMSSTRAHLUNG
BREMSSTRAHLUNGS
BRESSUMMER
BRESSUMMERS
BRETASCHES
BRETTICING
BREUNNERITE
BREUNNERITES
BREVETCIES
BREVETTING
BREVIARIES
BREVIPENNATE
BREWHOUSES
BREWMASTER
BREWMASTERS
BRIARROOTS
BRIARWOODS
BRICABRACS
BRICKCLAYS
BRICKEARTH
BRICKEARTHS
BRICKFIELD
BRICKFIELDER
BRICKFIELDERS
BRICKFIELDS
BRICKKILNS
BRICKLAYER
BRICKLAYERS
BRICKLAYING
BRICKLAYINGS
BRICKMAKER
BRICKMAKERS
BRICKMAKING
BRICKMAKINGS
BRICKSHAPED
BRICKWALLS
BRICKWORKS
BRICKYARDS
BRICOLAGES
BRICOLEURS
BRIDECAKES
BRIDEGROOM
BRIDEGROOMS
BRIDEMAIDEN
BRIDEMAIDENS
BRIDEMAIDS
BRIDESMAID
BRIDESMAIDS
BRIDEWEALTH
BRIDEWEALTHS
BRIDEWELLS
BRIDEZILLA
BRIDEZILLAS

BRIDGEABLE
BRIDGEBOARD
BRIDGEBOARDS
BRIDGEHEAD
BRIDGEHEADS
BRIDGELESS
BRIDGELIKE
BRIDGEWORK
BRIDGEWORKS
BRIDLEWAYS
BRIDLEWISE
BRIEFCASES
BRIEFNESSES
BRIERROOTS
BRIERWOODS
BRIGADIERS
BRIGANDAGE
BRIGANDAGES
BRIGANDINE
BRIGANDINES
BRIGANDRIES
BRIGANTINE
BRIGANTINES
BRIGHTENED
BRIGHTENER
BRIGHTENERS
BRIGHTENING
BRIGHTNESS
BRIGHTNESSES
BRIGHTSOME
BRIGHTWORK
BRIGHTWORKS
BRILLIANCE
BRILLIANCES
BRILLIANCIES
BRILLIANCY
BRILLIANTE
BRILLIANTED
BRILLIANTINE
BRILLIANTINED
BRILLIANTINES
BRILLIANTING
BRILLIANTLY
BRILLIANTNESS
BRILLIANTNESSES
BRILLIANTS
BRIMFULLNESS
BRIMFULLNESSES
BRIMFULNESS
BRIMFULNESSES
BRIMSTONES
BRIMSTONIER
BRIMSTONIEST
BRINELLING
BRINELLINGS
BRINGDOWNS
BRININESSES
BRINJARRIES
BRINKMANSHIP
BRINKMANSHIPS
BRINKSMANSHIP
BRINKSMANSHIPS
BRIOLETTES
BRIQUETTED
BRIQUETTES
BRIQUETTING
BRISKENING
BRISKNESSES
BRISTLECONE
BRISTLECONES
BRISTLELIKE
BRISTLETAIL
BRISTLETAILS
BRISTLIEST
BRISTLINESS
BRISTLINESSES
BRITANNIAS
BRITSCHKAS
BRITTANIAS
BRITTLENESS
BRITTLENESSES
BROADBANDS
BROADBEANS
BROADBILLS
BROADBRIMS
BROADBRUSH
BROADCASTED
BROADCASTER
BROADCASTERS
BROADCASTING
BROADCASTINGS
BROADCASTS
BROADCLOTH
BROADCLOTHS
BROADENERS
BROADENING
BROADLEAVED
BROADLEAVES
BROADLINES
BROADLOOMS
BROADNESSES
BROADPIECE
BROADPIECES
BROADSCALE
BROADSHEET
BROADSHEETS
BROADSIDED
BROADSIDES
BROADSIDING
BROADSWORD
BROADSWORDS
BROADTAILS
BROBDINGNAGIAN
BROCATELLE
BROCATELLES
BROCCOLINI
BROCCOLINIS
BROCHETTES
BROGUERIES
BROIDERERS
BROIDERIES
BROIDERING
BROIDERINGS
BROKENHEARTED
BROKENHEARTEDLY
BROKENNESS
BROKENNESSES
BROKERAGES
BROKERINGS
BROMEGRASS
BROMEGRASSES
BROMELAINS
BROMELIACEOUS
BROMELIADS
BROMEOSINS
BROMHIDROSES
BROMHIDROSIS
BROMIDROSES
BROMIDROSIS
BROMINATED
BROMINATES
BROMINATING
BROMINATION
BROMINATIONS
BROMINISMS
BROMOCRIPTINE
BROMOCRIPTINES
BROMOFORMS
BROMOURACIL
BROMOURACILS
BRONCHIALLY
BRONCHIECTASES
BRONCHIECTASIS
BRONCHIOLAR
BRONCHIOLE
BRONCHIOLES
BRONCHIOLITIS
BRONCHIOLITISES
BRONCHITIC
BRONCHITICS
BRONCHITIS
BRONCHITISES
BRONCHODILATOR
BRONCHODILATORS
BRONCHOGENIC
BRONCHOGRAPHIES
BRONCHOGRAPHY
BRONCHOSCOPE
BRONCHOSCOPES
BRONCHOSCOPIC
BRONCHOSCOPICAL
BRONCHOSCOPIES
BRONCHOSCOPIST
BRONCHOSCOPISTS
BRONCHOSCOPY
BRONCHOSPASM
BRONCHOSPASMS
BRONCHOSPASTIC
BRONCOBUSTER
BRONCOBUSTERS
BRONDYRONS
BRONTOBYTE
BRONTOBYTES
BRONTOSAUR
BRONTOSAURS
BRONTOSAURUS
BRONTOSAURUSES
BRONZIFIED
BRONZIFIES
BRONZIFYING
BROODINESS
BROODINESSES
BROODINGLY
BROODMARES
BROOKLIMES
BROOKWEEDS
BROOMBALLER
BROOMBALLERS
BROOMBALLS
BROOMCORNS
BROOMRAPES
BROOMSTAFF
BROOMSTAFFS
BROOMSTICK
BROOMSTICKS
BROTHERHOOD
BROTHERHOODS
BROTHERING
BROTHERLIER
BROTHERLIEST
BROTHERLIKE
BROTHERLINESS
BROTHERLINESSES
BROUGHTASES
BROWALLIAS
BROWBEATEN
BROWBEATER
BROWBEATERS
BROWBEATING
BROWBEATINGS
BROWNFIELD
BROWNFIELDS
BROWNNESSES
BROWNNOSED
BROWNNOSER
BROWNNOSERS
BROWNNOSES
BROWNNOSING
BROWNSHIRT
BROWNSHIRTS
BROWNSTONE
BROWNSTONES
BROWRIDGES
BROWSABLES
BRUCELLOSES
BRUCELLOSIS
BRUGMANSIA
BRUGMANSIAS
BRUMMAGEMS
BRUSCHETTA

BRUSCHETTAS
BRUSCHETTE
BRUSHABILITIES
BRUSHABILITY
BRUSHBACKS
BRUSHFIRES
BRUSHLANDS
BRUSHMARKS
BRUSHSTROKE
BRUSHSTROKES
BRUSHWHEEL
BRUSHWHEELS
BRUSHWOODS
BRUSHWORKS
BRUSQUENESS
BRUSQUENESSES
BRUSQUERIE
BRUSQUERIES
BRUTALISATION
BRUTALISATIONS
BRUTALISED
BRUTALISES
BRUTALISING
BRUTALISMS
BRUTALISTS
BRUTALITIES
BRUTALIZATION
BRUTALIZATIONS
BRUTALIZED
BRUTALIZES
BRUTALIZING
BRUTENESSES
BRUTIFYING
BRUTISHNESS
BRUTISHNESSES
BRYOLOGICAL
BRYOLOGIES
BRYOLOGIST
BRYOLOGISTS
BRYOPHYLLUM
BRYOPHYLLUMS
BRYOPHYTES
BRYOPHYTIC
BUBBLEGUMS
BUBBLEHEAD
BUBBLEHEADED
BUBBLEHEADS
BUBONOCELE
BUBONOCELES
BUCCANEERED
BUCCANEERING
BUCCANEERINGS
BUCCANEERISH
BUCCANEERS
BUCCANIERED
BUCCANIERING
BUCCANIERS
BUCCINATOR
BUCCINATORS
BUCCINATORY
BUCELLASES
BUCENTAURS
BUCKBOARDS
BUCKBRUSHES
BUCKETFULS
BUCKETINGS
BUCKETSFUL
BUCKHOUNDS
BUCKJUMPER
BUCKJUMPERS
BUCKJUMPING
BUCKJUMPINGS
BUCKLERING
BUCKRAMING
BUCKSHISHED
BUCKSHISHES
BUCKSHISHING
BUCKSKINNED
BUCKTHORNS
BUCKTOOTHED
BUCKWHEATS
BUCKYBALLS
BUCKYTUBES
BUCOLICALLY
BUDGERIGAR
BUDGERIGARS
BUDGETEERS
BUDGETINGS
BUDTENDERS
BUFFALOBERRIES
BUFFALOBERRY
BUFFALOFISH
BUFFALOFISHES
BUFFALOING
BUFFERINGS
BUFFETINGS
BUFFLEHEAD
BUFFLEHEADS
BUFFOONERIES
BUFFOONERY
BUFFOONISH
BUFOTALINS
BUFOTENINE
BUFOTENINES
BUGGINESSES
BUGLEWEEDS
BUHRSTONES
BUILDDOWNS
BUIRDLIEST
BULBIFEROUS
BULBOSITIES
BULBOUSNESS
BULBOUSNESSES
BULGINESSES
BULKHEADED
BULKINESSES
BULLBAITING
BULLBAITINGS
BULLBRIERS
BULLDOGGED
BULLDOGGER
BULLDOGGERS
BULLDOGGING
BULLDOGGINGS
BULLDOZERS
BULLDOZING
BULLETINED
BULLETINING
BULLETPROOF
BULLETPROOFED
BULLETPROOFING
BULLETPROOFS
BULLETRIES
BULLETWOOD
BULLETWOODS
BULLFIGHTER
BULLFIGHTERS
BULLFIGHTING
BULLFIGHTINGS
BULLFIGHTS
BULLFINCHES
BULLHEADED
BULLHEADEDLY
BULLHEADEDNESS
BULLIONIST
BULLIONISTS
BULLISHNESS
BULLISHNESSES
BULLMASTIFF
BULLMASTIFFS
BULLNECKED
BULLOCKIER
BULLOCKIES
BULLOCKIEST
BULLOCKING
BULLROARER
BULLROARERS
BULLRUSHES
BULLSHITTED
BULLSHITTER
BULLSHITTERS
BULLSHITTING
BULLSHITTINGS
BULLSNAKES
BULLTERRIER
BULLTERRIERS
BULLWADDIE
BULLWADDIES
BULLWHACKED
BULLWHACKING
BULLWHACKS
BULLWHIPPED
BULLWHIPPING
BULLYCIDES
BULLYRAGGED
BULLYRAGGING
BULRUSHIER
BULRUSHIEST
BULWADDEES
BULWADDIES
BULWARKING
BUMBAILIFF
BUMBAILIFFS
BUMBERSHOOT
BUMBERSHOOTS
BUMBLEBEES
BUMBLEBERRIES
BUMBLEBERRY
BUMBLEDOMS
BUMBLINGLY
BUMFREEZER
BUMFREEZERS
BUMFUZZLED
BUMFUZZLES
BUMFUZZLING
BUMMALOTIS
BUMPINESSES
BUMPKINISH
BUMPKINLIER
BUMPKINLIEST
BUMPOLOGIES
BUMPSADAISY
BUMPTIOUSLY
BUMPTIOUSNESS
BUMPTIOUSNESSES
BUMSUCKERS
BUMSUCKING
BUMSUCKINGS
BUNBURYING
BUNCHBERRIES
BUNCHBERRY
BUNCHGRASS
BUNCHGRASSES
BUNCHINESS
BUNCHINESSES
BUNDOBUSTS
BUNGALOIDS
BUNGLESOME
BUNGLINGLY
BUNKHOUSES
BUOYANCIES
BUOYANTNESS
BUOYANTNESSES
BUPIVACAINE
BUPIVACAINES
BUPRENORPHINE
BUPRENORPHINES
BUPRESTIDS
BUPROPIONS
BURDENSOME
BUREAUCRACIES
BUREAUCRACY
BUREAUCRAT
BUREAUCRATESE
BUREAUCRATESES
BUREAUCRATIC
BUREAUCRATISE
BUREAUCRATISED
BUREAUCRATISES
BUREAUCRATISING

BUREAUCRATISM
BUREAUCRATISMS
BUREAUCRATIST
BUREAUCRATISTS
BUREAUCRATIZE
BUREAUCRATIZED
BUREAUCRATIZES
BUREAUCRATIZING
BUREAUCRATS
BURGEONING
BURGLARIES
BURGLARING
BURGLARIOUS
BURGLARIOUSLY
BURGLARISE
BURGLARISED
BURGLARISES
BURGLARISING
BURGLARIZE
BURGLARIZED
BURGLARIZES
BURGLARIZING
BURGLARPROOF
BURGOMASTER
BURGOMASTERS
BURGUNDIES
BURLADEROS
BURLESQUED
BURLESQUELY
BURLESQUER
BURLESQUERS
BURLESQUES
BURLESQUING
BURLEYCUES
BURLINESSES
BURNETTISE
BURNETTISED
BURNETTISES
BURNETTISING
BURNETTIZE
BURNETTIZED
BURNETTIZES
BURNETTIZING
BURNISHABLE
BURNISHERS
BURNISHING
BURNISHINGS
BURNISHMENT
BURNISHMENTS
BURRAMUNDI
BURRAMUNDIS
BURRAMYSES
BURRAWANGS
BURRFISHES
BURROWSTOWN
BURROWSTOWNS
BURRSTONES
BURSARSHIP
BURSARSHIPS
BURSERACEOUS
BURSICULATE
BURSITISES
BURTHENING
BURTHENSOME
BUSHBABIES
BUSHBASHING
BUSHBASHINGS
BUSHCRAFTS
BUSHELFULS
BUSHELLERS
BUSHELLING
BUSHELLINGS
BUSHELWOMAN
BUSHELWOMEN
BUSHFIGHTING
BUSHFIGHTINGS
BUSHHAMMER
BUSHHAMMERS
BUSHINESSES
BUSHMANSHIP
BUSHMANSHIPS
BUSHMASTER
BUSHMASTERS
BUSHRANGER
BUSHRANGERS
BUSHRANGING
BUSHRANGINGS
BUSHWALKED
BUSHWALKER
BUSHWALKERS
BUSHWALKING
BUSHWALKINGS
BUSHWHACKED
BUSHWHACKER
BUSHWHACKERS
BUSHWHACKING
BUSHWHACKINGS
BUSHWHACKS
BUSINESSES
BUSINESSIER
BUSINESSIEST
BUSINESSLIKE
BUSINESSMAN
BUSINESSMEN
BUSINESSPEOPLE
BUSINESSPERSON
BUSINESSPERSONS
BUSINESSWOMAN
BUSINESSWOMEN
BUSTICATED
BUSTICATES
BUSTICATING
BUSTINESSES
BUSTLINGLY
BUSYBODIED
BUSYBODIES
BUSYBODYING
BUSYBODYINGS
BUSYNESSES
BUTADIENES
BUTCHERBIRD
BUTCHERBIRDS
BUTCHERERS
BUTCHERIES
BUTCHERING
BUTCHERINGS
BUTCHERLIER
BUTCHERLIEST
BUTCHNESSES
BUTENEDIOIC
BUTEONINES
BUTLERAGES
BUTLERSHIP
BUTLERSHIPS
BUTTERBALL
BUTTERBALLS
BUTTERBURS
BUTTERCREAM
BUTTERCREAMS
BUTTERCUPS
BUTTERDOCK
BUTTERDOCKS
BUTTERFATS
BUTTERFINGERED
BUTTERFINGERS
BUTTERFISH
BUTTERFISHES
BUTTERFLIED
BUTTERFLIES
BUTTERFLYER
BUTTERFLYERS
BUTTERFLYFISH
BUTTERFLYFISHES
BUTTERFLYING
BUTTERIEST
BUTTERINES
BUTTERINESS
BUTTERINESSES
BUTTERLESS
BUTTERMILK
BUTTERMILKS
BUTTERNUTS
BUTTERSCOTCH
BUTTERSCOTCHES
BUTTERWEED
BUTTERWEEDS
BUTTERWORT
BUTTERWORTS
BUTTINSKIES
BUTTINSKIS
BUTTOCKING
BUTTONBALL
BUTTONBALLS
BUTTONBUSH
BUTTONBUSHES
BUTTONHELD
BUTTONHOLD
BUTTONHOLDING
BUTTONHOLDS
BUTTONHOLE
BUTTONHOLED
BUTTONHOLER
BUTTONHOLERS
BUTTONHOLES
BUTTONHOLING
BUTTONHOOK
BUTTONHOOKED
BUTTONHOOKING
BUTTONHOOKS
BUTTONIEST
BUTTONLESS
BUTTONMOULD
BUTTONMOULDS
BUTTONWOOD
BUTTONWOODS
BUTTRESSED
BUTTRESSES
BUTTRESSING
BUTTSTOCKS
BUTYLATING
BUTYLATION
BUTYLATIONS
BUTYRACEOUS
BUTYRALDEHYDE
BUTYRALDEHYDES
BUTYROPHENONE
BUTYROPHENONES
BUXOMNESSES
BUZZKILLER
BUZZKILLERS
BYPRODUCTS
BYSSACEOUS
BYSSINOSES
BYSSINOSIS
BYSTANDERS
BYTOWNITES

C

CABALETTAS
CABALISTIC
CABALISTICAL
CABALLEROS
CABBAGETOWN
CABBAGETOWNS
CABBAGEWORM
CABBAGEWORMS
CABBAGIEST
CABBALISMS
CABBALISTIC
CABBALISTICAL
CABBALISTS
CABDRIVERS
CABINETMAKER
CABINETMAKERS
CABINETMAKING
CABINETMAKINGS
CABINETRIES
CABINETWORK
CABINETWORKS
CABINMATES
CABLECASTED
CABLECASTING
CABLECASTS
CABLEGRAMS
CABLEVISION
CABLEVISIONS
CABRIOLETS
CACAFUEGOS
CACCIATORA
CACCIATORE
CACHAEMIAS
CACHECTICAL
CACHINNATE
CACHINNATED
CACHINNATES
CACHINNATING
CACHINNATION
CACHINNATIONS
CACHINNATORY
CACHOLONGS
CACIQUISMS
CACKERMANDER
CACKERMANDERS
CACKLEBERRIES
CACKLEBERRY
CACODAEMON
CACODAEMONS
CACODEMONIC
CACODEMONS
CACODOXIES
CACOEPISTIC
CACOGASTRIC
CACOGENICS
CACOGRAPHER
CACOGRAPHERS
CACOGRAPHIC
CACOGRAPHICAL
CACOGRAPHIES
CACOGRAPHY
CACOLOGIES
CACOMISTLE
CACOMISTLES
CACOMIXLES
CACONYMIES
CACOPHONIC
CACOPHONICAL
CACOPHONICALLY
CACOPHONIES
CACOPHONIOUS
CACOPHONOUS
CACOPHONOUSLY
CACOTOPIAN
CACOTOPIAS
CACOTROPHIES
CACOTROPHY
CACTACEOUS
CACTOBLASTES
CACTOBLASTIS
CACUMINALS
CACUMINOUS
CADASTRALLY
CADAVERINE
CADAVERINES
CADAVEROUS
CADAVEROUSLY
CADAVEROUSNESS
CADDISFLIES
CADDISHNESS
CADDISHNESSES
CADDISWORM
CADDISWORMS
CADETSHIPS
CADUCITIES
CAECILIANS
CAECITISES
CAENOGENESES
CAENOGENESIS
CAENOGENETIC
CAESALPINOID
CAESAREANS
CAESARIANS
CAESARISMS
CAESAROPAPISM
CAESAROPAPISMS
CAESPITOSE
CAESPITOSELY
CAFETERIAS
CAFETIERES
CAFETORIUM
CAFETORIUMS
CAFFEINATED
CAFFEINISM
CAFFEINISMS
CAGEYNESSES
CAGINESSES
CAGMAGGING
CAGYNESSES
CAILLEACHS
CAILLIACHS
CAINOGENESES
CAINOGENESIS
CAINOGENETIC
CAIRNGORMS
CAJOLEMENT
CAJOLEMENTS
CAJOLERIES
CAJOLINGLY
CAKEWALKED
CAKEWALKER
CAKEWALKERS
CAKEWALKING
CAKINESSES
CALABASHES
CALABOGUSES
CALABOOSES
CALABRESES
CALAMANCOES
CALAMANCOS
CALAMANDER
CALAMANDERS
CALAMARIES
CALAMINING
CALAMITIES
CALAMITOUS
CALAMITOUSLY
CALAMITOUSNESS
CALAMONDIN
CALAMONDINS
CALANDRIAS
CALAVANCES
CALAVERITE
CALAVERITES
CALCAREOUS
CALCAREOUSLY
CALCARIFEROUS
CALCARIFORM
CALCEAMENTA
CALCEAMENTUM
CALCEATING
CALCEDONIES
CALCEDONIO
CALCEDONIOS
CALCEIFORM
CALCEOLARIA
CALCEOLARIAS
CALCEOLATE
CALCICOLES
CALCICOLOUS
CALCIFEROL
CALCIFEROLS
CALCIFEROUS
CALCIFICATION
CALCIFICATIONS
CALCIFUGAL
CALCIFUGES
CALCIFUGOUS
CALCIFYING
CALCIGEROUS
CALCIMINED
CALCIMINES
CALCIMINING
CALCINABLE
CALCINATION
CALCINATIONS
CALCINOSES
CALCINOSIS
CALCITONIN
CALCITONINS
CALCSINTER
CALCSINTERS
CALCULABILITIES
CALCULABILITY
CALCULABLE
CALCULABLY
CALCULATED
CALCULATEDLY
CALCULATEDNESS
CALCULATES
CALCULATING
CALCULATINGLY
CALCULATION
CALCULATIONAL
CALCULATIONS
CALCULATIVE
CALCULATOR
CALCULATORS
CALCULUSES
CALEFACIENT

C

CALEFACIENTS
CALEFACTION
CALEFACTIONS
CALEFACTIVE
CALEFACTOR
CALEFACTORIES
CALEFACTORS
CALEFACTORY
CALEMBOURS
CALENDARED
CALENDARER
CALENDARERS
CALENDARING
CALENDARISATION
CALENDARISE
CALENDARISED
CALENDARISES
CALENDARISING
CALENDARIST
CALENDARISTS
CALENDARIZATION
CALENDARIZE
CALENDARIZED
CALENDARIZES
CALENDARIZING
CALENDERED
CALENDERER
CALENDERERS
CALENDERING
CALENDERINGS
CALENDRERS
CALENDRICAL
CALENDRIES
CALENDULAS
CALENTURES
CALESCENCE
CALESCENCES
CALFDOZERS
CALIATOURS
CALIBRATED
CALIBRATER
CALIBRATERS
CALIBRATES
CALIBRATING
CALIBRATION
CALIBRATIONS
CALIBRATOR
CALIBRATORS
CALIDITIES
CALIFORNIUM
CALIFORNIUMS
CALIGINOSITIES
CALIGINOSITY
CALIGINOUS
CALIMOCHOS
CALIOLOGIES
CALIPASHES
CALIPERING
CALIPHATES
CALISTHENIC
CALISTHENICS
CALLBOARDS
CALLIATURE
CALLIATURES
CALLIDITIES
CALLIGRAMME
CALLIGRAMMES
CALLIGRAMS
CALLIGRAPHER
CALLIGRAPHERS
CALLIGRAPHIC
CALLIGRAPHICAL
CALLIGRAPHIES
CALLIGRAPHIST
CALLIGRAPHISTS
CALLIGRAPHY
CALLIOPSIS
CALLIPASHES
CALLIPERED
CALLIPERING
CALLIPYGEAN
CALLIPYGIAN
CALLIPYGOUS
CALLISTEMON
CALLISTEMONS
CALLISTHENIC
CALLISTHENICS
CALLITHUMP
CALLITHUMPIAN
CALLITHUMPS
CALLOSITIES
CALLOUSING
CALLOUSNESS
CALLOUSNESSES
CALLOWNESS
CALLOWNESSES
CALMATIVES
CALMNESSES
CALMODULIN
CALMODULINS
CALMSTANES
CALMSTONES
CALORESCENCE
CALORESCENCES
CALORESCENT
CALORICALLY
CALORICITIES
CALORICITY
CALORIFICALLY
CALORIFICATION
CALORIFICATIONS
CALORIFIER
CALORIFIERS
CALORIMETER
CALORIMETERS
CALORIMETRIC
CALORIMETRICAL
CALORIMETRIES
CALORIMETRY
CALORISING
CALORIZING
CALOTYPIST
CALOTYPISTS
CALUMNIABLE
CALUMNIATE
CALUMNIATED
CALUMNIATES
CALUMNIATING
CALUMNIATION
CALUMNIATIONS
CALUMNIATOR
CALUMNIATORS
CALUMNIATORY
CALUMNIOUS
CALUMNIOUSLY
CALUMNYING
CALVADOSES
CALVARIUMS
CALYCANTHEMIES
CALYCANTHEMY
CALYCANTHUS
CALYCANTHUSES
CALYCIFORM
CALYCOIDEOUS
CALYCULATE
CALYPSONIAN
CALYPSONIANS
CALYPTERAS
CALYPTRATE
CALYPTROGEN
CALYPTROGENS
CAMANACHDS
CAMARADERIE
CAMARADERIES
CAMARILLAS
CAMBERINGS
CAMBISTRIES
CAMCORDERS
CAMCORDING
CAMELBACKS
CAMELEOPARD
CAMELEOPARDS
CAMELHAIRS
CAMELOPARD
CAMELOPARDS
CAMERAPERSON
CAMERAPERSONS
CAMERAPHONE
CAMERAPHONES
CAMERATION
CAMERATIONS
CAMERAWOMAN
CAMERAWOMEN
CAMERAWORK
CAMERAWORKS
CAMERLENGO
CAMERLENGOS
CAMERLINGO
CAMERLINGOS
CAMIKNICKERS
CAMIKNICKS
CAMISADOES
CAMORRISTA
CAMORRISTI
CAMORRISTS
CAMOUFLAGE
CAMOUFLAGEABLE
CAMOUFLAGED
CAMOUFLAGES
CAMOUFLAGIC
CAMOUFLAGING
CAMOUFLETS
CAMOUFLEUR
CAMOUFLEURS
CAMPAIGNED
CAMPAIGNER
CAMPAIGNERS
CAMPAIGNING
CAMPANEROS
CAMPANIFORM
CAMPANILES
CAMPANISTS
CAMPANOLOGER
CAMPANOLOGERS
CAMPANOLOGICAL
CAMPANOLOGIES
CAMPANOLOGIST
CAMPANOLOGISTS
CAMPANOLOGY
CAMPANULACEOUS
CAMPANULAR
CAMPANULAS
CAMPANULATE
CAMPCRAFTS
CAMPEADORS
CAMPESINOS
CAMPESTRAL
CAMPESTRIAN
CAMPGROUND
CAMPGROUNDS
CAMPHORACEOUS
CAMPHORATE
CAMPHORATED
CAMPHORATES
CAMPHORATING
CAMPIMETRIES
CAMPIMETRY
CAMPINESSES
CAMPNESSES
CAMPODEIDS
CAMPODEIFORM
CAMPSHIRTS
CAMPSTOOLS
CAMPYLOBACTER
CAMPYLOBACTERS
CAMPYLOTROPOUS
CAMSTEERIE
CAMWHORING
CANALBOATS
CANALICULAR

CANALICULATE
CANALICULATED
CANALICULI
CANALICULUS
CANALISATION
CANALISATIONS
CANALISING
CANALIZATION
CANALIZATIONS
CANALIZING
CANCELABLE
CANCELATION
CANCELATIONS
CANCELBOTS
CANCELEERED
CANCELEERING
CANCELEERS
CANCELIERED
CANCELIERING
CANCELIERS
CANCELLABLE
CANCELLARIAL
CANCELLARIAN
CANCELLARIATE
CANCELLARIATES
CANCELLATE
CANCELLATED
CANCELLATION
CANCELLATIONS
CANCELLERS
CANCELLING
CANCELLOUS
CANCERATED
CANCERATES
CANCERATING
CANCERATION
CANCERATIONS
CANCEROPHOBIA
CANCEROPHOBIAS
CANCEROUSLY
CANCERPHOBIA
CANCERPHOBIAS
CANCIONERO
CANCIONEROS
CANCRIFORM
CANCRIZANS
CANDELABRA
CANDELABRAS
CANDELABRUM
CANDELABRUMS
CANDELILLA
CANDELILLAS
CANDESCENCE
CANDESCENCES
CANDESCENT
CANDESCENTLY
CANDIDACIES
CANDIDATES
CANDIDATESHIP
CANDIDATESHIPS
CANDIDATURE
CANDIDATURES
CANDIDIASES
CANDIDIASIS
CANDIDNESS
CANDIDNESSES
CANDLEBERRIES
CANDLEBERRY
CANDLEFISH
CANDLEFISHES
CANDLEHOLDER
CANDLEHOLDERS
CANDLELIGHT
CANDLELIGHTED
CANDLELIGHTER
CANDLELIGHTERS
CANDLELIGHTS
CANDLENUTS
CANDLEPINS
CANDLEPOWER
CANDLEPOWERS
CANDLESNUFFER
CANDLESNUFFERS
CANDLESTICK
CANDLESTICKS
CANDLEWICK
CANDLEWICKS
CANDLEWOOD
CANDLEWOODS
CANDYFLOSS
CANDYFLOSSES
CANDYGRAMS
CANDYTUFTS
CANEBRAKES
CANEFRUITS
CANEPHORAS
CANEPHORES
CANEPHORUS
CANEPHORUSES
CANESCENCE
CANESCENCES
CANINITIES
CANISTERED
CANISTERING
CANISTERISATION
CANISTERISE
CANISTERISED
CANISTERISES
CANISTERISING
CANISTERIZATION
CANISTERIZE
CANISTERIZED
CANISTERIZES
CANISTERIZING
CANKEREDLY
CANKEREDNESS
CANKEREDNESSES
CANKERIEST
CANKERWORM
CANKERWORMS
CANNABINOID
CANNABINOIDS
CANNABINOL
CANNABINOLS
CANNABISES
CANNELLINI
CANNELLINIS
CANNELLONI
CANNELURES
CANNIBALISATION
CANNIBALISE
CANNIBALISED
CANNIBALISES
CANNIBALISING
CANNIBALISM
CANNIBALISMS
CANNIBALISTIC
CANNIBALIZATION
CANNIBALIZE
CANNIBALIZED
CANNIBALIZES
CANNIBALIZING
CANNIBALLY
CANNINESSES
CANNISTERS
CANNONADED
CANNONADES
CANNONADING
CANNONBALL
CANNONBALLED
CANNONBALLING
CANNONBALLS
CANNONEERS
CANNONIERS
CANNONRIES
CANNULATED
CANNULATES
CANNULATING
CANNULATION
CANNULATIONS
CANOEWOODS
CANONESSES
CANONICALLY
CANONICALS
CANONICATE
CANONICATES
CANONICITIES
CANONICITY
CANONISATION
CANONISATIONS
CANONISERS
CANONISING
CANONISTIC
CANONIZATION
CANONIZATIONS
CANONIZERS
CANONIZING
CANOODLERS
CANOODLING
CANOPHILIA
CANOPHILIAS
CANOPHILIST
CANOPHILISTS
CANOPHOBIA
CANOPHOBIAS
CANOROUSLY
CANOROUSNESS
CANOROUSNESSES
CANTABANKS
CANTABILES
CANTALOUPE
CANTALOUPES
CANTALOUPS
CANTANKEROUS
CANTANKEROUSLY
CANTATRICE
CANTATRICES
CANTATRICI
CANTERBURIES
CANTERBURY
CANTERBURYS
CANTHARIDAL
CANTHARIDES
CANTHARIDIAN
CANTHARIDIC
CANTHARIDIN
CANTHARIDINS
CANTHARIDS
CANTHAXANTHIN
CANTHAXANTHINE
CANTHAXANTHINES
CANTHAXANTHINS
CANTHITISES
CANTICOING
CANTICOYED
CANTICOYING
CANTILENAS
CANTILEVER
CANTILEVERED
CANTILEVERING
CANTILEVERS
CANTILLATE
CANTILLATED
CANTILLATES
CANTILLATING
CANTILLATION
CANTILLATIONS
CANTILLATORY
CANTINESSES
CANTONISATION
CANTONISATIONS
CANTONISED
CANTONISES
CANTONISING
CANTONIZATION
CANTONIZATIONS
CANTONIZED
CANTONIZES
CANTONIZING
CANTONMENT

CANTONMENTS
CANULATING
CANULATION
CANULATIONS
CANVASBACK
CANVASBACKS
CANVASLIKE
CANVASSERS
CANVASSING
CANVASSINGS
CANYONEERS
CANYONINGS
CANZONETTA
CANZONETTAS
CANZONETTE
CAOUTCHOUC
CAOUTCHOUCS
CAPABILITIES
CAPABILITY
CAPABLENESS
CAPABLENESSES
CAPACIOUSLY
CAPACIOUSNESS
CAPACIOUSNESSES
CAPACITANCE
CAPACITANCES
CAPACITATE
CAPACITATED
CAPACITATES
CAPACITATING
CAPACITATION
CAPACITATIONS
CAPACITIES
CAPACITIVE
CAPACITIVELY
CAPACITORS
CAPARISONED
CAPARISONING
CAPARISONS
CAPELLINES
CAPELLINIS
CAPELLMEISTER
CAPELLMEISTERS
CAPERCAILLIE
CAPERCAILLIES
CAPERCAILZIE
CAPERCAILZIES
CAPERINGLY
CAPERNOITED
CAPERNOITIE
CAPERNOITIES
CAPERNOITY
CAPICOLLAS
CAPICOLLOS
CAPILLACEOUS
CAPILLAIRE
CAPILLAIRES
CAPILLARIES
CAPILLARITIES
CAPILLARITY
CAPILLITIA
CAPILLITIUM
CAPITALISATION
CAPITALISATIONS
CAPITALISE
CAPITALISED
CAPITALISES
CAPITALISING
CAPITALISM
CAPITALISMS
CAPITALIST
CAPITALISTIC
CAPITALISTS
CAPITALIZATION
CAPITALIZATIONS
CAPITALIZE
CAPITALIZED
CAPITALIZES
CAPITALIZING
CAPITATION
CAPITATIONS
CAPITATIVE
CAPITELLUM
CAPITOLIAN
CAPITOLINE
CAPITULANT
CAPITULANTS
CAPITULARIES
CAPITULARLY
CAPITULARS
CAPITULARY
CAPITULATE
CAPITULATED
CAPITULATES
CAPITULATING
CAPITULATION
CAPITULATIONS
CAPITULATOR
CAPITULATORS
CAPITULATORY
CAPNOMANCIES
CAPNOMANCY
CAPOCCHIAS
CAPODASTRO
CAPODASTROS
CAPONIERES
CAPONISING
CAPONIZING
CAPOTASTOS
CAPPARIDACEOUS
CAPPELLETTI
CAPPERNOITIES
CAPPERNOITY
CAPPUCCINI
CAPPUCCINO
CAPPUCCINOS
CAPREOLATE
CAPRICCIOS
CAPRICCIOSO
CAPRICIOUS
CAPRICIOUSLY
CAPRICIOUSNESS
CAPRIFICATION
CAPRIFICATIONS
CAPRIFOILS
CAPRIFOLES
CAPRIFOLIACEOUS
CAPRIFYING
CAPRIOLING
CAPROLACTAM
CAPROLACTAMS
CAPRYLATES
CAPSAICINS
CAPSIZABLE
CAPSOMERES
CAPSULATED
CAPSULATION
CAPSULATIONS
CAPSULISED
CAPSULISES
CAPSULISING
CAPSULIZED
CAPSULIZES
CAPSULIZING
CAPTAINCIES
CAPTAINING
CAPTAINRIES
CAPTAINSHIP
CAPTAINSHIPS
CAPTIONING
CAPTIONLESS
CAPTIOUSLY
CAPTIOUSNESS
CAPTIOUSNESSES
CAPTIVANCE
CAPTIVANCES
CAPTIVATED
CAPTIVATES
CAPTIVATING
CAPTIVATINGLY
CAPTIVATION
CAPTIVATIONS
CAPTIVATOR
CAPTIVATORS
CAPTIVAUNCE
CAPTIVAUNCES
CAPTIVITIES
CAPTOPRILS
CARABINEER
CARABINEERS
CARABINERO
CARABINEROS
CARABINERS
CARABINIER
CARABINIERE
CARABINIERI
CARABINIERS
CARACOLERS
CARACOLING
CARACOLLED
CARACOLLING
CARAGEENAN
CARAGEENANS
CARAMBOLAS
CARAMBOLED
CARAMBOLES
CARAMBOLING
CARAMELISATION
CARAMELISATIONS
CARAMELISE
CARAMELISED
CARAMELISES
CARAMELISING
CARAMELIZATION
CARAMELIZATIONS
CARAMELIZE
CARAMELIZED
CARAMELIZES
CARAMELIZING
CARAMELLED
CARAMELLING
CARANGOIDS
CARAPACIAL
CARAVANCES
CARAVANEER
CARAVANEERS
CARAVANERS
CARAVANETTE
CARAVANETTES
CARAVANING
CARAVANINGS
CARAVANNED
CARAVANNER
CARAVANNERS
CARAVANNING
CARAVANNINGS
CARAVANSARAI
CARAVANSARAIS
CARAVANSARIES
CARAVANSARY
CARAVANSERAI
CARAVANSERAIS
CARAVELLES
CARBACHOLS
CARBAMATES
CARBAMAZEPINE
CARBAMAZEPINES
CARBAMIDES
CARBAMIDINE
CARBAMIDINES
CARBAMOYLS
CARBANIONS
CARBAZOLES
CARBIDOPAS
CARBIMAZOLE
CARBIMAZOLES
CARBINEERS
CARBINIERS
CARBOCYCLIC
CARBOHYDRASE

CARBOHYDRASES
CARBOHYDRATE
CARBOHYDRATES
CARBOLATED
CARBOLISED
CARBOLISES
CARBOLISING
CARBOLIZED
CARBOLIZES
CARBOLIZING
CARBONACEOUS
CARBONADES
CARBONADOED
CARBONADOES
CARBONADOING
CARBONADOS
CARBONARAS
CARBONATED
CARBONATES
CARBONATING
CARBONATION
CARBONATIONS
CARBONATITE
CARBONATITES
CARBONETTE
CARBONETTES
CARBONIFEROUS
CARBONISATION
CARBONISATIONS
CARBONISED
CARBONISER
CARBONISERS
CARBONISES
CARBONISING
CARBONIUMS
CARBONIZATION
CARBONIZATIONS
CARBONIZED
CARBONIZER
CARBONIZERS
CARBONIZES
CARBONIZING
CARBONLESS
CARBONNADE
CARBONNADES
CARBONYLATE
CARBONYLATED
CARBONYLATES
CARBONYLATING
CARBONYLATION
CARBONYLATIONS
CARBONYLIC
CARBOREXIC
CARBOREXICS
CARBOXYLASE
CARBOXYLASES
CARBOXYLATE
CARBOXYLATED
CARBOXYLATES
CARBOXYLATING
CARBOXYLATION
CARBOXYLATIONS
CARBOXYLIC
CARBUNCLED
CARBUNCLES
CARBUNCULAR
CARBURATED
CARBURATES
CARBURATING
CARBURATION
CARBURATIONS
CARBURETED
CARBURETER
CARBURETERS
CARBURETING
CARBURETION
CARBURETIONS
CARBURETOR
CARBURETORS
CARBURETTED
CARBURETTER
CARBURETTERS
CARBURETTING
CARBURETTOR
CARBURETTORS
CARBURISATION
CARBURISATIONS
CARBURISED
CARBURISES
CARBURISING
CARBURIZATION
CARBURIZATIONS
CARBURIZED
CARBURIZES
CARBURIZING
CARBYLAMINE
CARBYLAMINES
CARCASSING
CARCINOGEN
CARCINOGENESES
CARCINOGENESIS
CARCINOGENIC
CARCINOGENICITY
CARCINOGENS
CARCINOIDS
CARCINOLOGICAL
CARCINOLOGIES
CARCINOLOGIST
CARCINOLOGISTS
CARCINOLOGY
CARCINOMAS
CARCINOMATA
CARCINOMATOID
CARCINOMATOSES
CARCINOMATOSIS
CARCINOMATOUS
CARCINOSARCOMA
CARCINOSARCOMAS
CARCINOSES
CARCINOSIS
CARDAMINES
CARDBOARDIER
CARDBOARDIEST
CARDBOARDS
CARDBOARDY
CARDCASTLE
CARDCASTLES
CARDHOLDER
CARDHOLDERS
CARDIALGIA
CARDIALGIAS
CARDIALGIC
CARDIALGIES
CARDIGANED
CARDINALATE
CARDINALATES
CARDINALATIAL
CARDINALITIAL
CARDINALITIES
CARDINALITY
CARDINALLY
CARDINALSHIP
CARDINALSHIPS
CARDIOCENTESES
CARDIOCENTESIS
CARDIOGENIC
CARDIOGRAM
CARDIOGRAMS
CARDIOGRAPH
CARDIOGRAPHER
CARDIOGRAPHERS
CARDIOGRAPHIC
CARDIOGRAPHICAL
CARDIOGRAPHIES
CARDIOGRAPHS
CARDIOGRAPHY
CARDIOLOGICAL
CARDIOLOGIES
CARDIOLOGIST
CARDIOLOGISTS
CARDIOLOGY
CARDIOMEGALIES
CARDIOMEGALY
CARDIOMOTOR
CARDIOMYOPATHY
CARDIOPATHIES
CARDIOPATHY
CARDIOPLEGIA
CARDIOPLEGIAS
CARDIOPULMONARY
CARDIOTHORACIC
CARDIOTONIC
CARDIOTONICS
CARDIOVASCULAR
CARDITISES
CARDOPHAGI
CARDOPHAGUS
CARDPHONES
CARDPLAYER
CARDPLAYERS
CARDPUNCHES
CARDSHARPER
CARDSHARPERS
CARDSHARPING
CARDSHARPINGS
CARDSHARPS
CARDUACEOUS
CAREENAGES
CAREERISMS
CAREERISTS
CAREFREENESS
CAREFREENESSES
CAREFULLER
CAREFULLEST
CAREFULNESS
CAREFULNESSES
CAREGIVERS
CAREGIVING
CAREGIVINGS
CARELESSLY
CARELESSNESS
CARELESSNESSES
CARESSINGLY
CARESSINGS
CARESSIVELY
CARETAKERS
CARETAKING
CARETAKINGS
CAREWORKER
CAREWORKERS
CARFUFFLED
CARFUFFLES
CARFUFFLING
CARHOPPING
CARHOPPINGS
CARICATURA
CARICATURAL
CARICATURAS
CARICATURE
CARICATURED
CARICATURES
CARICATURING
CARICATURIST
CARICATURISTS
CARILLONED
CARILLONING
CARILLONIST
CARILLONISTS
CARILLONNED
CARILLONNEUR
CARILLONNEURS
CARILLONNING
CARIOGENIC
CARIOSITIES
CARIOUSNESS
CARIOUSNESSES
CARJACKERS
CARJACKING
CARJACKINGS
CARMAGNOLE

CARMAGNOLES
CARMELITES
CARMINATIVE
CARMINATIVES
CARNAHUBAS
CARNALISED
CARNALISES
CARNALISING
CARNALISMS
CARNALISTS
CARNALITIES
CARNALIZED
CARNALIZES
CARNALIZING
CARNALLING
CARNALLITE
CARNALLITES
CARNAPTIOUS
CARNAROLIS
CARNASSIAL
CARNASSIALS
CARNATIONED
CARNATIONS
CARNELIANS
CARNIFEXES
CARNIFICATION
CARNIFICATIONS
CARNIFICIAL
CARNIFYING
CARNITINES
CARNIVALESQUE
CARNIVORES
CARNIVORIES
CARNIVOROUS
CARNIVOROUSLY
CARNIVOROUSNESS
CARNOSAURS
CARNOSITIES
CARNOTITES
CAROLLINGS
CAROMELLED
CAROMELLING
CAROTENOID
CAROTENOIDS
CAROTINOID
CAROTINOIDS
CAROUSINGLY
CAROUSINGS
CARPACCIOS
CARPELLARY
CARPELLATE
CARPELLATES
CARPENTARIA
CARPENTARIAS
CARPENTERED
CARPENTERING
CARPENTERS
CARPENTRIES
CARPETBAGGED
CARPETBAGGER
CARPETBAGGERIES
CARPETBAGGERS
CARPETBAGGERY
CARPETBAGGING
CARPETBAGGINGS
CARPETBAGS
CARPETINGS
CARPETLIKE
CARPETMONGER
CARPETMONGERS
CARPETWEED
CARPETWEEDS
CARPHOLOGIES
CARPHOLOGY
CARPOGONIA
CARPOGONIAL
CARPOGONIUM
CARPOLOGICAL
CARPOLOGIES
CARPOLOGIST
CARPOLOGISTS
CARPOMETACARPI
CARPOMETACARPUS
CARPOOLERS
CARPOOLING
CARPOOLINGS
CARPOPHAGOUS
CARPOPHORE
CARPOPHORES
CARPOSPORE
CARPOSPORES
CARRAGEENAN
CARRAGEENANS
CARRAGEENIN
CARRAGEENINS
CARRAGEENS
CARRAGHEEN
CARRAGHEENAN
CARRAGHEENANS
CARRAGHEENIN
CARRAGHEENINS
CARRAGHEENS
CARREFOURS
CARRIAGEABLE
CARRIAGEWAY
CARRIAGEWAYS
CARRITCHES
CARRIWITCHET
CARRIWITCHETS
CARRONADES
CARROTIEST
CARROTTOPPED
CARROTTOPS
CARROUSELS
CARRYBACKS
CARRYFORWARD
CARRYFORWARDS
CARRYOVERS
CARRYTALES
CARSHARING
CARSHARINGS
CARSICKNESS
CARSICKNESSES
CARTELISATION
CARTELISATIONS
CARTELISED
CARTELISES
CARTELISING
CARTELISMS
CARTELISTS
CARTELIZATION
CARTELIZATIONS
CARTELIZED
CARTELIZES
CARTELIZING
CARTHAMINE
CARTHAMINES
CARTHORSES
CARTILAGES
CARTILAGINOUS
CARTOGRAMS
CARTOGRAPHER
CARTOGRAPHERS
CARTOGRAPHIC
CARTOGRAPHICAL
CARTOGRAPHIES
CARTOGRAPHY
CARTOLOGICAL
CARTOLOGIES
CARTOMANCIES
CARTOMANCY
CARTONAGES
CARTONNAGE
CARTONNAGES
CARTOONIER
CARTOONIEST
CARTOONING
CARTOONINGS
CARTOONISH
CARTOONISHLY
CARTOONIST
CARTOONISTS
CARTOONLIKE
CARTOPHILE
CARTOPHILES
CARTOPHILIC
CARTOPHILIES
CARTOPHILIST
CARTOPHILISTS
CARTOPHILY
CARTOPPERS
CARTOUCHES
CARTRIDGES
CARTULARIES
CARTWHEELED
CARTWHEELER
CARTWHEELERS
CARTWHEELING
CARTWHEELS
CARTWRIGHT
CARTWRIGHTS
CARUNCULAR
CARUNCULATE
CARUNCULATED
CARUNCULOUS
CARVACROLS
CARYATIDAL
CARYATIDEAN
CARYATIDES
CARYATIDIC
CARYOPSIDES
CARYOPTERIS
CARYOPTERISES
CASCADURAS
CASCARILLA
CASCARILLAS
CASEATIONS
CASEBEARER
CASEBEARERS
CASEINATES
CASEINOGEN
CASEINOGENS
CASEMAKERS
CASEMENTED
CASEVACING
CASEWORKER
CASEWORKERS
CASHIERERS
CASHIERING
CASHIERINGS
CASHIERMENT
CASHIERMENTS
CASHMOBBING
CASHMOBBINGS
CASHPOINTS
CASHSPIELS
CASINGHEAD
CASINGHEADS
CASKSTANDS
CASSAREEPS
CASSATIONS
CASSEROLED
CASSEROLES
CASSEROLING
CASSIMERES
CASSINGLES
CASSIOPEIUM
CASSIOPEIUMS
CASSITERITE
CASSITERITES
CASSOLETTE
CASSOLETTES
CASSONADES
CASSOULETS
CASSOWARIES
CASSUMUNAR
CASSUMUNARS
CASTABILITIES
CASTABILITY
CASTANOSPERMINE

CASTELLANS
CASTELLATED
CASTELLATION
CASTELLATIONS
CASTELLUMS
CASTIGATED
CASTIGATES
CASTIGATING
CASTIGATION
CASTIGATIONS
CASTIGATOR
CASTIGATORS
CASTIGATORY
CASTOREUMS
CASTRAMETATION
CASTRAMETATIONS
CASTRATERS
CASTRATING
CASTRATION
CASTRATIONS
CASTRATORS
CASTRATORY
CASUALISATION
CASUALISATIONS
CASUALISED
CASUALISES
CASUALISING
CASUALISMS
CASUALIZATION
CASUALIZATIONS
CASUALIZED
CASUALIZES
CASUALIZING
CASUALNESS
CASUALNESSES
CASUALTIES
CASUARINAS
CASUISTICAL
CASUISTICALLY
CASUISTRIES
CATABOLICALLY
CATABOLISE
CATABOLISED
CATABOLISES
CATABOLISING
CATABOLISM
CATABOLISMS
CATABOLITE
CATABOLITES
CATABOLIZE
CATABOLIZED
CATABOLIZES
CATABOLIZING
CATACAUSTIC
CATACAUSTICS
CATACHRESES
CATACHRESIS
CATACHRESTIC
CATACHRESTICAL
CATACLASES
CATACLASIS
CATACLASMIC
CATACLASMS
CATACLASTIC
CATACLINAL
CATACLYSMAL
CATACLYSMIC
CATACLYSMICALLY
CATACLYSMS
CATACOUSTICS
CATACUMBAL
CATADIOPTRIC
CATADIOPTRICAL
CATADROMOUS
CATAFALCOES
CATAFALQUE
CATAFALQUES
CATALECTIC
CATALECTICS
CATALEPSIES
CATALEPTIC
CATALEPTICALLY
CATALEPTICS
CATALLACTIC
CATALLACTICALLY
CATALLACTICS
CATALOGERS
CATALOGING
CATALOGISE
CATALOGISED
CATALOGISES
CATALOGISING
CATALOGIZE
CATALOGIZED
CATALOGIZES
CATALOGIZING
CATALOGNES
CATALOGUED
CATALOGUER
CATALOGUERS
CATALOGUES
CATALOGUING
CATALOGUISE
CATALOGUISED
CATALOGUISES
CATALOGUISING
CATALOGUIST
CATALOGUISTS
CATALOGUIZE
CATALOGUIZED
CATALOGUIZES
CATALOGUIZING
CATALYSERS
CATALYSING
CATALYTICAL
CATALYTICALLY
CATALYZERS
CATALYZING
CATAMARANS
CATAMENIAL
CATAMOUNTAIN
CATAMOUNTAINS
CATAMOUNTS
CATANANCHE
CATANANCHES
CATAPHONIC
CATAPHONICS
CATAPHORAS
CATAPHORESES
CATAPHORESIS
CATAPHORETIC
CATAPHORIC
CATAPHORICALLY
CATAPHRACT
CATAPHRACTIC
CATAPHRACTS
CATAPHYLLARY
CATAPHYLLS
CATAPHYSICAL
CATAPLASIA
CATAPLASIAS
CATAPLASMS
CATAPLASTIC
CATAPLECTIC
CATAPLEXIES
CATAPULTED
CATAPULTIC
CATAPULTIER
CATAPULTIERS
CATAPULTING
CATARACTOUS
CATARHINES
CATARRHALLY
CATARRHINE
CATARRHINES
CATARRHOUS
CATASTASES
CATASTASIS
CATASTROPHE
CATASTROPHES
CATASTROPHIC
CATASTROPHISM
CATASTROPHISMS
CATASTROPHIST
CATASTROPHISTS
CATATONIAS
CATATONICALLY
CATATONICS
CATATONIES
CATCALLERS
CATCALLING
CATCHCRIES
CATCHFLIES
CATCHINESS
CATCHINESSES
CATCHLINES
CATCHMENTS
CATCHPENNIES
CATCHPENNY
CATCHPHRASE
CATCHPHRASES
CATCHPOLES
CATCHPOLLS
CATCHWATER
CATCHWATERS
CATCHWEEDS
CATCHWEIGHT
CATCHWORDS
CATECHESES
CATECHESIS
CATECHESISES
CATECHETIC
CATECHETICAL
CATECHETICALLY
CATECHETICS
CATECHISATION
CATECHISATIONS
CATECHISED
CATECHISER
CATECHISERS
CATECHISES
CATECHISING
CATECHISINGS
CATECHISMAL
CATECHISMS
CATECHISTIC
CATECHISTICAL
CATECHISTICALLY
CATECHISTS
CATECHIZATION
CATECHIZATIONS
CATECHIZED
CATECHIZER
CATECHIZERS
CATECHIZES
CATECHIZING
CATECHIZINGS
CATECHOLAMINE
CATECHOLAMINES
CATECHUMEN
CATECHUMENAL
CATECHUMENATE
CATECHUMENATES
CATECHUMENICAL
CATECHUMENISM
CATECHUMENISMS
CATECHUMENS
CATECHUMENSHIP
CATECHUMENSHIPS
CATEGOREMATIC
CATEGORIAL
CATEGORIALLY
CATEGORICAL
CATEGORICALLY
CATEGORICALNESS
CATEGORIES
CATEGORISATION
CATEGORISATIONS
CATEGORISE
CATEGORISED

CATEGORISES
CATEGORISING
CATEGORIST
CATEGORISTS
CATEGORIZATION
CATEGORIZATIONS
CATEGORIZE
CATEGORIZED
CATEGORIZES
CATEGORIZING
CATENACCIO
CATENACCIOS
CATENARIAN
CATENARIES
CATENATING
CATENATION
CATENATIONS
CATENULATE
CATERCORNER
CATERCORNERED
CATERESSES
CATERPILLAR
CATERPILLARS
CATERWAULED
CATERWAULER
CATERWAULERS
CATERWAULING
CATERWAULINGS
CATERWAULS
CATFACINGS
CATFISHING
CATHARISED
CATHARISES
CATHARISING
CATHARIZED
CATHARIZES
CATHARIZING
CATHARTICAL
CATHARTICALLY
CATHARTICS
CATHECTING
CATHEDRALS
CATHEDRATIC
CATHEPSINS
CATHETERISATION
CATHETERISE
CATHETERISED
CATHETERISES
CATHETERISING
CATHETERISM
CATHETERISMS
CATHETERIZATION
CATHETERIZE
CATHETERIZED
CATHETERIZES
CATHETERIZING
CATHETOMETER
CATHETOMETERS
CATHETUSES
CATHINONES
CATHIODERMIE
CATHIODERMIES
CATHODALLY
CATHODICAL
CATHODICALLY
CATHODOGRAPH
CATHODOGRAPHER
CATHODOGRAPHERS
CATHODOGRAPHIES
CATHODOGRAPHS
CATHODOGRAPHY
CATHOLICALLY
CATHOLICATE
CATHOLICATES
CATHOLICISATION
CATHOLICISE
CATHOLICISED
CATHOLICISES
CATHOLICISING
CATHOLICISM
CATHOLICISMS
CATHOLICITIES
CATHOLICITY
CATHOLICIZATION
CATHOLICIZE
CATHOLICIZED
CATHOLICIZES
CATHOLICIZING
CATHOLICLY
CATHOLICOI
CATHOLICON
CATHOLICONS
CATHOLICOS
CATHOLICOSES
CATHOLYTES
CATIONICALLY
CATLINITES
CATNAPPERS
CATNAPPING
CATOPTRICAL
CATOPTRICS
CATTINESSES
CATTISHNESS
CATTISHNESSES
CAUCHEMARS
CAUCUSSING
CAUCUSSINGS
CAUDATIONS
CAUDILLISMO
CAUDILLISMOS
CAULESCENT
CAULICOLOUS
CAULICULATE
CAULICULUS
CAULICULUSES
CAULIFLORIES
CAULIFLOROUS
CAULIFLORY
CAULIFLOWER
CAULIFLOWERET
CAULIFLOWERETS
CAULIFLOWERS
CAULIGENOUS
CAUMSTANES
CAUMSTONES
CAUSABILITIES
CAUSABILITY
CAUSALGIAS
CAUSALITIES
CAUSATIONAL
CAUSATIONISM
CAUSATIONISMS
CAUSATIONIST
CAUSATIONISTS
CAUSATIONS
CAUSATIVELY
CAUSATIVENESS
CAUSATIVENESSES
CAUSATIVES
CAUSELESSLY
CAUSELESSNESS
CAUSELESSNESSES
CAUSEWAYED
CAUSEWAYING
CAUSTICALLY
CAUSTICITIES
CAUSTICITY
CAUSTICNESS
CAUSTICNESSES
CAUTERANTS
CAUTERISATION
CAUTERISATIONS
CAUTERISED
CAUTERISES
CAUTERISING
CAUTERISMS
CAUTERIZATION
CAUTERIZATIONS
CAUTERIZED
CAUTERIZES
CAUTERIZING
CAUTIONARY
CAUTIONERS
CAUTIONING
CAUTIONRIES
CAUTIOUSLY
CAUTIOUSNESS
CAUTIOUSNESSES
CAVALCADED
CAVALCADES
CAVALCADING
CAVALIERED
CAVALIERING
CAVALIERISH
CAVALIERISM
CAVALIERISMS
CAVALIERLY
CAVALLETTI
CAVALRYMAN
CAVALRYMEN
CAVEFISHES
CAVENDISHES
CAVERNICOLOUS
CAVERNOUSLY
CAVERNULOUS
CAVILLATION
CAVILLATIONS
CAVILLINGS
CAVITATING
CAVITATION
CAVITATIONS
CAVORTINGS
CEANOTHUSES
CEASEFIRES
CEASELESSLY
CEASELESSNESS
CEASELESSNESSES
CEBADILLAS
CECUTIENCIES
CECUTIENCY
CEDARBIRDS
CEDARWOODS
CEDRELACEOUS
CEILOMETER
CEILOMETERS
CELANDINES
CELEBRANTS
CELEBRATED
CELEBRATEDNESS
CELEBRATES
CELEBRATING
CELEBRATION
CELEBRATIONS
CELEBRATIVE
CELEBRATOR
CELEBRATORS
CELEBRATORY
CELEBREALITIES
CELEBREALITY
CELEBRITIES
CELEBUTANTE
CELEBUTANTES
CELECOXIBS
CELERITIES
CELERYLIKE
CELESTIALLY
CELESTIALS
CELESTINES
CELESTITES
CELIBACIES
CELIBATARIAN
CELIBATARIANS
CELLARAGES
CELLARETTE
CELLARETTES
CELLARISTS
CELLARWAYS
CELLBLOCKS
CELLENTANI
CELLENTANIS

CELLIFEROUS
CELLOBIOSE
CELLOBIOSES
CELLOIDINS
CELLOPHANE
CELLOPHANES
CELLPHONES
CELLULARITIES
CELLULARITY
CELLULASES
CELLULATED
CELLULIFEROUS
CELLULITES
CELLULITIS
CELLULITISES
CELLULOIDS
CELLULOLYTIC
CELLULOSES
CELLULOSIC
CELLULOSICS
CELSITUDES
CEMBALISTS
CEMENTATION
CEMENTATIONS
CEMENTATORY
CEMENTITES
CEMENTITIOUS
CEMETERIES
CENESTHESES
CENESTHESIA
CENESTHESIAS
CENESTHESIS
CENESTHETIC
CENOBITICAL
CENOGENESES
CENOGENESIS
CENOGENETIC
CENOGENETICALLY
CENOSPECIES
CENOTAPHIC
CENSORABLE
CENSORIOUS
CENSORIOUSLY
CENSORIOUSNESS
CENSORSHIP
CENSORSHIPS
CENSURABILITIES
CENSURABILITY
CENSURABLE
CENSURABLENESS
CENSURABLY
CENTAUREAS
CENTAURIAN
CENTAURIES
CENTENARIAN
CENTENARIANISM
CENTENARIANISMS
CENTENARIANS
CENTENARIES
CENTENIERS
CENTENNIAL
CENTENNIALLY
CENTENNIALS
CENTERBOARD
CENTERBOARDS
CENTEREDNESS
CENTEREDNESSES
CENTERFOLD
CENTERFOLDS
CENTERINGS
CENTERLESS
CENTERLINE
CENTERLINES
CENTERPIECE
CENTERPIECES
CENTESIMAL
CENTESIMALLY
CENTESIMALS
CENTESIMOS
CENTIGRADE
CENTIGRADES
CENTIGRAMME
CENTIGRAMMES
CENTIGRAMS
CENTILITER
CENTILITERS
CENTILITRE
CENTILITRES
CENTILLION
CENTILLIONS
CENTILLIONTH
CENTILLIONTHS
CENTIMETER
CENTIMETERS
CENTIMETRE
CENTIMETRES
CENTIMETRIC
CENTIMORGAN
CENTIMORGANS
CENTINELLS
CENTIPEDES
CENTIPOISE
CENTIPOISES
CENTONATES
CENTONELLS
CENTONISTS
CENTRALEST
CENTRALISATION
CENTRALISATIONS
CENTRALISE
CENTRALISED
CENTRALISER
CENTRALISERS
CENTRALISES
CENTRALISING
CENTRALISM
CENTRALISMS
CENTRALIST
CENTRALISTIC
CENTRALISTS
CENTRALITIES
CENTRALITY
CENTRALIZATION
CENTRALIZATIONS
CENTRALIZE
CENTRALIZED
CENTRALIZER
CENTRALIZERS
CENTRALIZES
CENTRALIZING
CENTREBOARD
CENTREBOARDS
CENTREDNESS
CENTREDNESSES
CENTREFOLD
CENTREFOLDS
CENTREINGS
CENTRELESS
CENTRELINE
CENTRELINES
CENTREPIECE
CENTREPIECES
CENTRICALLY
CENTRICALNESS
CENTRICALNESSES
CENTRICITIES
CENTRICITY
CENTRIFUGAL
CENTRIFUGALISE
CENTRIFUGALISED
CENTRIFUGALISES
CENTRIFUGALIZE
CENTRIFUGALIZED
CENTRIFUGALIZES
CENTRIFUGALLY
CENTRIFUGALS
CENTRIFUGATION
CENTRIFUGATIONS
CENTRIFUGE
CENTRIFUGED
CENTRIFUGENCE
CENTRIFUGENCES
CENTRIFUGES
CENTRIFUGING
CENTRIOLES
CENTRIPETAL
CENTRIPETALISM
CENTRIPETALISMS
CENTRIPETALLY
CENTROBARIC
CENTROCLINAL
CENTROIDAL
CENTROLECITHAL
CENTROMERE
CENTROMERES
CENTROMERIC
CENTROSOME
CENTROSOMES
CENTROSOMIC
CENTROSPHERE
CENTROSPHERES
CENTROSYMMETRIC
CENTUMVIRATE
CENTUMVIRATES
CENTUMVIRI
CENTUMVIRS
CENTUPLICATE
CENTUPLICATED
CENTUPLICATES
CENTUPLICATING
CENTUPLICATION
CENTUPLICATIONS
CENTUPLING
CENTURIATION
CENTURIATIONS
CENTURIATOR
CENTURIATORS
CENTURIONS
CEPHALAGRA
CEPHALAGRAS
CEPHALALGIA
CEPHALALGIAS
CEPHALALGIC
CEPHALALGICS
CEPHALEXIN
CEPHALEXINS
CEPHALICALLY
CEPHALISATION
CEPHALISATIONS
CEPHALITIS
CEPHALITISES
CEPHALIZATION
CEPHALIZATIONS
CEPHALOCELE
CEPHALOCELES
CEPHALOCHORDATE
CEPHALOMETER
CEPHALOMETERS
CEPHALOMETRIC
CEPHALOMETRIES
CEPHALOMETRY
CEPHALOPOD
CEPHALOPODAN
CEPHALOPODANS
CEPHALOPODIC
CEPHALOPODOUS
CEPHALOPODS
CEPHALORIDINE
CEPHALORIDINES
CEPHALOSPORIN
CEPHALOSPORINS
CEPHALOTHIN
CEPHALOTHINS
CEPHALOTHORACES
CEPHALOTHORACIC
CEPHALOTHORAX
CEPHALOTHORAXES
CEPHALOTOMIES
CEPHALOTOMY
CERAMICIST

C

CERAMICISTS
CERAMOGRAPHIES
CERAMOGRAPHY
CERARGYRITE
CERARGYRITES
CERASTIUMS
CERATITISES
CERATODUSES
CERATOPSIAN
CERATOPSIANS
CERATOPSID
CERATOPSIDS
CERAUNOGRAPH
CERAUNOGRAPHS
CERCARIANS
CERCOPITHECID
CERCOPITHECIDS
CERCOPITHECOID
CERCOPITHECOIDS
CEREALISTS
CEREBELLAR
CEREBELLIC
CEREBELLOUS
CEREBELLUM
CEREBELLUMS
CEREBRALISM
CEREBRALISMS
CEREBRALIST
CEREBRALISTS
CEREBRALLY
CEREBRATED
CEREBRATES
CEREBRATING
CEREBRATION
CEREBRATIONS
CEREBRIFORM
CEREBRITIS
CEREBRITISES
CEREBROSIDE
CEREBROSIDES
CEREBROSPINAL
CEREBROTONIA
CEREBROTONIAS
CEREBROTONIC
CEREBROTONICS
CEREBROVASCULAR
CERECLOTHS
CEREMONIAL
CEREMONIALISM
CEREMONIALISMS
CEREMONIALIST
CEREMONIALISTS
CEREMONIALLY
CEREMONIALS
CEREMONIES
CEREMONIOUS
CEREMONIOUSLY
CEREMONIOUSNESS
CERIFEROUS
CEROGRAPHIC
CEROGRAPHICAL
CEROGRAPHIES
CEROGRAPHIST
CEROGRAPHISTS
CEROGRAPHS
CEROGRAPHY
CEROMANCIES
CEROPLASTIC
CEROPLASTICS
CERTAINEST
CERTAINTIES
CERTIFIABLE
CERTIFIABLY
CERTIFICATE
CERTIFICATED
CERTIFICATES
CERTIFICATING
CERTIFICATION
CERTIFICATIONS
CERTIFICATORIES
CERTIFICATORY
CERTIFIERS
CERTIFYING
CERTIORARI
CERTIORARIS
CERTITUDES
CERULOPLASMIN
CERULOPLASMINS
CERUMINOUS
CERUSSITES
CERVELASES
CERVICITIS
CERVICITISES
CERVICOGRAPHIES
CERVICOGRAPHY
CESAREVICH
CESAREVICHES
CESAREVITCH
CESAREVITCHES
CESAREVNAS
CESAREWICH
CESAREWICHES
CESAREWITCH
CESAREWITCHES
CESPITOSELY
CESSATIONS
CESSIONARIES
CESSIONARY
CESTOIDEAN
CESTOIDEANS
CETEOSAURUS
CETEOSAURUSES
CETOLOGICAL
CETOLOGIES
CETOLOGIST
CETOLOGISTS
CETRIMIDES
CETUXIMABS
CEVADILLAS
CEYLANITES
CEYLONITES
CHABAZITES
CHACONINES
CHAENOMELES
CHAENOMELESES
CHAETIFEROUS
CHAETODONS
CHAETOGNATH
CHAETOGNATHS
CHAETOPODS
CHAFFERERS
CHAFFERIES
CHAFFERING
CHAFFINCHES
CHAFFINGLY
CHAGRINING
CHAGRINNED
CHAGRINNING
CHAINBRAKE
CHAINBRAKES
CHAINFALLS
CHAINPLATE
CHAINPLATES
CHAINSAWED
CHAINSAWING
CHAINSHOTS
CHAINSTITCH
CHAINSTITCHES
CHAINWHEEL
CHAINWHEELS
CHAINWORKS
CHAIRBACKS
CHAIRBORNE
CHAIRBOUND
CHAIRLIFTS
CHAIRMANED
CHAIRMANING
CHAIRMANNED
CHAIRMANNING
CHAIRMANSHIP
CHAIRMANSHIPS
CHAIRPERSON
CHAIRPERSONS
CHAIRWARMER
CHAIRWARMERS
CHAIRWOMAN
CHAIRWOMEN
CHAISELESS
CHAKALAKAS
CHALANNING
CHALAZIONS
CHALAZOGAMIC
CHALAZOGAMIES
CHALAZOGAMY
CHALCANTHITE
CHALCANTHITES
CHALCEDONIC
CHALCEDONIES
CHALCEDONY
CHALCEDONYX
CHALCEDONYXES
CHALCOCITE
CHALCOCITES
CHALCOGENIDE
CHALCOGENIDES
CHALCOGENS
CHALCOGRAPHER
CHALCOGRAPHERS
CHALCOGRAPHIC
CHALCOGRAPHICAL
CHALCOGRAPHIES
CHALCOGRAPHIST
CHALCOGRAPHISTS
CHALCOGRAPHY
CHALCOLITHIC
CHALCOPYRITE
CHALCOPYRITES
CHALICOTHERE
CHALICOTHERES
CHALKBOARD
CHALKBOARDS
CHALKFACES
CHALKINESS
CHALKINESSES
CHALKLANDS
CHALKMARKS
CHALKSTONE
CHALKSTONES
CHALKSTRIPE
CHALKSTRIPES
CHALLENGEABLE
CHALLENGED
CHALLENGER
CHALLENGERS
CHALLENGES
CHALLENGING
CHALLENGINGLY
CHALUMEAUS
CHALUMEAUX
CHALYBEATE
CHALYBEATES
CHALYBITES
CHAMAELEON
CHAMAELEONS
CHAMAEPHYTE
CHAMAEPHYTES
CHAMBERERS
CHAMBERHAND
CHAMBERHANDS
CHAMBERING
CHAMBERINGS
CHAMBERLAIN
CHAMBERLAINS
CHAMBERLAINSHIP
CHAMBERMAID
CHAMBERMAIDS
CHAMBERPOT
CHAMBERPOTS
CHAMBRANLE
CHAMBRANLES

CHAMELEONIC
CHAMELEONLIKE
CHAMELEONS
CHAMFERERS
CHAMFERING
CHAMFRAINS
CHAMOISING
CHAMOMILES
CHAMPAGNES
CHAMPAIGNS
CHAMPERTIES
CHAMPERTOUS
CHAMPIGNON
CHAMPIGNONS
CHAMPIONED
CHAMPIONESS
CHAMPIONESSES
CHAMPIONING
CHAMPIONSHIP
CHAMPIONSHIPS
CHAMPLEVES
CHANCELESS
CHANCELLERIES
CHANCELLERY
CHANCELLOR
CHANCELLORIES
CHANCELLORS
CHANCELLORSHIP
CHANCELLORSHIPS
CHANCELLORY
CHANCERIES
CHANCINESS
CHANCINESSES
CHANCROIDAL
CHANCROIDS
CHANDELIER
CHANDELIERED
CHANDELIERS
CHANDELLED
CHANDELLES
CHANDELLING
CHANDLERIES
CHANDLERING
CHANDLERINGS
CHANDLERLY
CHANGEABILITIES
CHANGEABILITY
CHANGEABLE
CHANGEABLENESS
CHANGEABLY
CHANGEAROUND
CHANGEAROUNDS
CHANGEFULLY
CHANGEFULNESS
CHANGEFULNESSES
CHANGELESS
CHANGELESSLY
CHANGELESSNESS
CHANGELING
CHANGELINGS
CHANGEOVER
CHANGEOVERS
CHANGEROUND
CHANGEROUNDS
CHANNELERS
CHANNELING
CHANNELISATION
CHANNELISATIONS
CHANNELISE
CHANNELISED
CHANNELISES
CHANNELISING
CHANNELIZATION
CHANNELIZATIONS
CHANNELIZE
CHANNELIZED
CHANNELIZES
CHANNELIZING
CHANNELLED
CHANNELLER
CHANNELLERS
CHANNELLING
CHANSONETTE
CHANSONETTES
CHANSONNIER
CHANSONNIERS
CHANTARELLE
CHANTARELLES
CHANTECLER
CHANTECLERS
CHANTERELLE
CHANTERELLES
CHANTEUSES
CHANTICLEER
CHANTICLEERS
CHANTINGLY
CHANTRESSES
CHANUKIAHS
CHAOLOGIES
CHAOLOGIST
CHAOLOGISTS
CHAOTICALLY
CHAPARAJOS
CHAPAREJOS
CHAPARRALS
CHAPATTIES
CHAPELRIES
CHAPERONAGE
CHAPERONAGES
CHAPERONED
CHAPERONES
CHAPERONING
CHAPFALLEN
CHAPLAINCIES
CHAPLAINCY
CHAPLAINRIES
CHAPLAINRY
CHAPLAINSHIP
CHAPLAINSHIPS
CHAPMANSHIP
CHAPMANSHIPS
CHAPPESSES
CHAPRASSIES
CHAPRASSIS
CHAPSTICKS
CHAPTALISATION
CHAPTALISATIONS
CHAPTALISE
CHAPTALISED
CHAPTALISES
CHAPTALISING
CHAPTALIZATION
CHAPTALIZATIONS
CHAPTALIZE
CHAPTALIZED
CHAPTALIZES
CHAPTALIZING
CHAPTERHOUSE
CHAPTERHOUSES
CHAPTERING
CHARABANCS
CHARACINOID
CHARACTERED
CHARACTERFUL
CHARACTERIES
CHARACTERING
CHARACTERISABLE
CHARACTERISE
CHARACTERISED
CHARACTERISER
CHARACTERISERS
CHARACTERISES
CHARACTERISING
CHARACTERISM
CHARACTERISMS
CHARACTERISTIC
CHARACTERISTICS
CHARACTERIZABLE
CHARACTERIZE
CHARACTERIZED
CHARACTERIZER
CHARACTERIZERS
CHARACTERIZES
CHARACTERIZING
CHARACTERLESS
CHARACTEROLOGY
CHARACTERS
CHARACTERY
CHARBROILED
CHARBROILER
CHARBROILERS
CHARBROILING
CHARBROILS
CHARCOALED
CHARCOALIER
CHARCOALIEST
CHARCOALING
CHARCUTERIE
CHARCUTERIES
CHARDONNAY
CHARDONNAYS
CHARGEABILITIES
CHARGEABILITY
CHARGEABLE
CHARGEABLENESS
CHARGEABLY
CHARGEBACK
CHARGEBACKS
CHARGEHAND
CHARGEHANDS
CHARGELESS
CHARGESHEET
CHARGESHEETS
CHARGRILLED
CHARGRILLING
CHARGRILLS
CHARINESSES
CHARIOTEER
CHARIOTEERED
CHARIOTEERING
CHARIOTEERS
CHARIOTING
CHARISMATA
CHARISMATIC
CHARISMATICS
CHARITABLE
CHARITABLENESS
CHARITABLY
CHARIVARIED
CHARIVARIING
CHARIVARIS
CHARLADIES
CHARLATANIC
CHARLATANICAL
CHARLATANISM
CHARLATANISMS
CHARLATANISTIC
CHARLATANRIES
CHARLATANRY
CHARLATANS
CHARLESTON
CHARLESTONED
CHARLESTONING
CHARLESTONS
CHARLOTTES
CHARMEUSES
CHARMINGER
CHARMINGEST
CHARMINGLY
CHARMLESSLY
CHARMONIUM
CHAROSETHS
CHARREADAS
CHARTACEOUS
CHARTERERS
CHARTERING
CHARTERPARTIES
CHARTERPARTY
CHARTHOUSE
CHARTHOUSES

C

CHARTOGRAPHER
CHARTOGRAPHERS
CHARTOGRAPHIC
CHARTOGRAPHICAL
CHARTOGRAPHIES
CHARTOGRAPHY
CHARTREUSE
CHARTREUSES
CHARTULARIES
CHARTULARY
CHASEPORTS
CHASMOGAMIC
CHASMOGAMIES
CHASMOGAMOUS
CHASMOGAMY
CHASSEPOTS
CHASTENERS
CHASTENESS
CHASTENESSES
CHASTENING
CHASTENINGLY
CHASTENMENT
CHASTENMENTS
CHASTISABLE
CHASTISEMENT
CHASTISEMENTS
CHASTISERS
CHASTISING
CHASTITIES
CHATEAUBRIAND
CHATEAUBRIANDS
CHATELAINE
CHATELAINES
CHATELAINS
CHATOYANCE
CHATOYANCES
CHATOYANCIES
CHATOYANCY
CHATOYANTS
CHATTERATI
CHATTERBOX
CHATTERBOXES
CHATTERERS
CHATTERIER
CHATTERIEST
CHATTERING
CHATTERINGS
CHATTINESS
CHATTINESSES
CHAUDFROID
CHAUDFROIDS
CHAUFFEURED
CHAUFFEURING
CHAUFFEURS
CHAUFFEUSE
CHAUFFEUSED
CHAUFFEUSES
CHAUFFEUSING
CHAULMOOGRA
CHAULMOOGRAS
CHAULMUGRA
CHAULMUGRAS
CHAUNTRESS
CHAUNTRESSES
CHAUNTRIES
CHAUSSURES
CHAUTAUQUA
CHAUTAUQUAS
CHAUVINISM
CHAUVINISMS
CHAUVINIST
CHAUVINISTIC
CHAUVINISTS
CHAVENDERS
CHAVTASTIC
CHAWBACONS
CHEAPENERS
CHEAPENING
CHEAPISHLY
CHEAPJACKS
CHEAPNESSES
CHEAPSHOTS
CHEAPSKATE
CHEAPSKATES
CHEATERIES
CHEATINGLY
CHECHAKOES
CHECHAQUOS
CHECKBOOKS
CHECKBOXES
CHECKCLERK
CHECKCLERKS
CHECKERBERRIES
CHECKERBERRY
CHECKERBLOOM
CHECKERBLOOMS
CHECKERBOARD
CHECKERBOARDS
CHECKERING
CHECKLATON
CHECKLATONS
CHECKLISTED
CHECKLISTING
CHECKLISTS
CHECKMARKED
CHECKMARKING
CHECKMARKS
CHECKMATED
CHECKMATES
CHECKMATING
CHECKPOINT
CHECKPOINTS
CHECKRAILS
CHECKREINS
CHECKROOMS
CHECKROWED
CHECKROWING
CHECKSTOPS
CHECKWEIGHER
CHECKWEIGHERS
CHEDDARIER
CHEDDARIEST
CHEECHAKOES
CHEECHAKOS
CHEECHALKO
CHEECHALKOES
CHEECHALKOS
CHEEKBONES
CHEEKINESS
CHEEKINESSES
CHEEKPIECE
CHEEKPIECES
CHEEKPOUCH
CHEEKPOUCHES
CHEEKTEETH
CHEEKTOOTH
CHEERFULLER
CHEERFULLEST
CHEERFULLY
CHEERFULNESS
CHEERFULNESSES
CHEERINESS
CHEERINESSES
CHEERINGLY
CHEERISHNESS
CHEERISHNESSES
CHEERLEADER
CHEERLEADERS
CHEERLEADING
CHEERLEADS
CHEERLESSLY
CHEERLESSNESS
CHEERLESSNESSES
CHEESEBOARD
CHEESEBOARDS
CHEESEBURGER
CHEESEBURGERS
CHEESECAKE
CHEESECAKES
CHEESECLOTH
CHEESECLOTHS
CHEESECUTTER
CHEESECUTTERS
CHEESEHOPPER
CHEESEHOPPERS
CHEESELIKE
CHEESEMITE
CHEESEMITES
CHEESEMONGER
CHEESEMONGERS
CHEESEPARER
CHEESEPARERS
CHEESEPARING
CHEESEPARINGS
CHEESEPRESS
CHEESEPRESSES
CHEESESTEAK
CHEESESTEAKS
CHEESETASTER
CHEESETASTERS
CHEESEVATS
CHEESEWIRE
CHEESEWIRES
CHEESEWOOD
CHEESEWOODS
CHEESEWRING
CHEESEWRINGS
CHEESINESS
CHEESINESSES
CHEILITISES
CHEIROMANCER
CHEIROMANCERS
CHEIROMANCIES
CHEIROMANCY
CHELASHIPS
CHELATABLE
CHELATIONS
CHELICERAE
CHELICERAL
CHELICERATE
CHELICERATES
CHELIFEROUS
CHELONIANS
CHELUVIATION
CHELUVIATIONS
CHEMAUTOTROPH
CHEMAUTOTROPHIC
CHEMAUTOTROPHS
CHEMIATRIC
CHEMICALLY
CHEMICKING
CHEMICKINGS
CHEMICOPHYSICAL
CHEMIOSMOSES
CHEMIOSMOSIS
CHEMIOSMOTIC
CHEMISETTE
CHEMISETTES
CHEMISORBED
CHEMISORBING
CHEMISORBS
CHEMISORPTION
CHEMISORPTIONS
CHEMISTRIES
CHEMITYPES
CHEMITYPIES
CHEMOATTRACTANT
CHEMOAUTOTROPH
CHEMOAUTOTROPHS
CHEMOAUTOTROPHY
CHEMOAUTROPH
CHEMOAUTROPHS
CHEMOCEPTOR
CHEMOCEPTORS
CHEMOKINES
CHEMOKINESES
CHEMOKINESIS
CHEMOLITHOTROPH
CHEMONASTIES
CHEMONASTY

CHEMOPREVENTION
CHEMOPSYCHIATRY
CHEMORECEPTION
CHEMORECEPTIONS
CHEMORECEPTIVE
CHEMORECEPTOR
CHEMORECEPTORS
CHEMOSMOSES
CHEMOSMOSIS
CHEMOSMOTIC
CHEMOSORBED
CHEMOSORBING
CHEMOSORBS
CHEMOSPHERE
CHEMOSPHERES
CHEMOSPHERIC
CHEMOSTATS
CHEMOSURGERIES
CHEMOSURGERY
CHEMOSURGICAL
CHEMOSYNTHESES
CHEMOSYNTHESIS
CHEMOSYNTHETIC
CHEMOTACTIC
CHEMOTACTICALLY
CHEMOTAXES
CHEMOTAXIS
CHEMOTAXISES
CHEMOTAXONOMIC
CHEMOTAXONOMIES
CHEMOTAXONOMIST
CHEMOTAXONOMY
CHEMOTHERAPIES
CHEMOTHERAPIST
CHEMOTHERAPISTS
CHEMOTHERAPY
CHEMOTROPIC
CHEMOTROPICALLY
CHEMOTROPISM
CHEMOTROPISMS
CHEMPADUKS
CHEMTRAILS
CHEMURGICAL
CHEMURGIES
CHENOPODIACEOUS
CHEONGSAMS
CHEQUEBOOK
CHEQUEBOOKS
CHEQUERBOARD
CHEQUERBOARDS
CHEQUERING
CHEQUERWISE
CHEQUERWORK
CHEQUERWORKS
CHERALITES
CHERIMOYAS
CHERIMOYER
CHERIMOYERS
CHERISHABLE
CHERISHERS
CHERISHING
CHERISHINGLY
CHERISHMENT
CHERISHMENTS
CHERMOULAS
CHERNOZEMIC
CHERNOZEMS
CHERRYLIKE
CHERRYSTONE
CHERRYSTONES
CHERSONESE
CHERSONESES
CHERUBICAL
CHERUBICALLY
CHERUBIMIC
CHERUBLIKE
CHERVONETS
CHESSBOARD
CHESSBOARDS
CHESSBOXING
CHESSBOXINGS
CHESSPIECE
CHESSPIECES
CHESSPLAYER
CHESSPLAYERS
CHESSYLITE
CHESSYLITES
CHESTERFIELD
CHESTERFIELDS
CHESTINESS
CHESTINESSES
CHEVALIERS
CHEVELURES
CHEVESAILE
CHEVESAILES
CHEVISANCE
CHEVISANCES
CHEVRETTES
CHEVROTAIN
CHEVROTAINS
CHEVROTINS
CHEWINESSES
CHIACKINGS
CHIAREZZAS
CHIAROSCURISM
CHIAROSCURISMS
CHIAROSCURIST
CHIAROSCURISTS
CHIAROSCURO
CHIAROSCUROS
CHIASMATIC
CHIASTOLITE
CHIASTOLITES
CHIBOUQUES
CHICALOTES
CHICANERIES
CHICANINGS
CHICCORIES
CHICKABIDDIES
CHICKABIDDY
CHICKADEES
CHICKAREES
CHICKENHEARTED
CHICKENING
CHICKENPOX
CHICKENPOXES
CHICKENSHIT
CHICKENSHITS
CHICKLINGS
CHICKORIES
CHICKWEEDS
CHICNESSES
CHIEFERIES
CHIEFESSES
CHIEFLINGS
CHIEFSHIPS
CHIEFTAINCIES
CHIEFTAINCY
CHIEFTAINESS
CHIEFTAINESSES
CHIEFTAINRIES
CHIEFTAINRY
CHIEFTAINS
CHIEFTAINSHIP
CHIEFTAINSHIPS
CHIFFCHAFF
CHIFFCHAFFS
CHIFFONADE
CHIFFONADES
CHIFFONIER
CHIFFONIERS
CHIFFONNIER
CHIFFONNIERS
CHIFFONNIEST
CHIFFOROBE
CHIFFOROBES
CHIHUAHUAS
CHILBLAINED
CHILBLAINS
CHILDBEARING
CHILDBEARINGS
CHILDBIRTH
CHILDBIRTHS
CHILDCARES
CHILDCROWING
CHILDCROWINGS
CHILDERMAS
CHILDERMASES
CHILDHOODS
CHILDISHLY
CHILDISHNESS
CHILDISHNESSES
CHILDLESSNESS
CHILDLESSNESSES
CHILDLIEST
CHILDLIKENESS
CHILDLIKENESSES
CHILDMINDER
CHILDMINDERS
CHILDMINDING
CHILDMINDINGS
CHILDNESSES
CHILDPROOF
CHILDPROOFED
CHILDPROOFING
CHILDPROOFS
CHILDRENSWEAR
CHILDRENSWEARS
CHILIAGONS
CHILIAHEDRA
CHILIAHEDRON
CHILIAHEDRONS
CHILIARCHIES
CHILIARCHS
CHILIARCHY
CHILIASTIC
CHILLAXING
CHILLINESS
CHILLINESSES
CHILLINGLY
CHILLNESSES
CHILOPODAN
CHILOPODANS
CHILOPODOUS
CHILTEPINS
CHIMAERISM
CHIMAERISMS
CHIMERICAL
CHIMERICALLY
CHIMERICALNESS
CHIMERISMS
CHIMICHANGA
CHIMICHANGAS
CHIMNEYBOARD
CHIMNEYBOARDS
CHIMNEYBREAST
CHIMNEYBREASTS
CHIMNEYING
CHIMNEYLIKE
CHIMNEYPIECE
CHIMNEYPIECES
CHIMNEYPOT
CHIMNEYPOTS
CHIMPANZEE
CHIMPANZEES
CHINABERRIES
CHINABERRY
CHINACHINA
CHINACHINAS
CHINAROOTS
CHINAWARES
CHINCAPINS
CHINCHERINCHEE
CHINCHERINCHEES
CHINCHIEST
CHINCHILLA
CHINCHILLAS
CHINCOUGHS
CHINKAPINS
CHINKERINCHEE

C

CHINKERINCHEES
CHINOISERIE
CHINOISERIES
CHINOVNIKS
CHINQUAPIN
CHINQUAPINS
CHINSTRAPS
CHINTZIEST
CHINWAGGED
CHINWAGGING
CHIONODOXA
CHIONODOXAS
CHIPBOARDS
CHIPMAKERS
CHIPOCHIAS
CHIPOLATAS
CHIPPEREST
CHIPPERING
CHIPPINESS
CHIPPINESSES
CHIQUICHIQUI
CHIQUICHIQUIS
CHIRAGRICAL
CHIRALITIES
CHIRIMOYAS
CHIROGNOMIES
CHIROGNOMIST
CHIROGNOMISTS
CHIROGNOMY
CHIROGRAPH
CHIROGRAPHER
CHIROGRAPHERS
CHIROGRAPHIC
CHIROGRAPHICAL
CHIROGRAPHIES
CHIROGRAPHIST
CHIROGRAPHISTS
CHIROGRAPHS
CHIROGRAPHY
CHIROLOGIES
CHIROLOGIST
CHIROLOGISTS
CHIROMANCER
CHIROMANCERS
CHIROMANCIES
CHIROMANCY
CHIROMANTIC
CHIROMANTICAL
CHIRONOMER
CHIRONOMERS
CHIRONOMIC
CHIRONOMID
CHIRONOMIDS
CHIRONOMIES
CHIROPODIAL
CHIROPODIES
CHIROPODIST
CHIROPODISTS
CHIROPRACTIC
CHIROPRACTICS
CHIROPRACTOR
CHIROPRACTORS
CHIROPTERAN
CHIROPTERANS
CHIROPTEROUS
CHIROPTERS
CHIRPINESS
CHIRPINESSES
CHIRRUPERS
CHIRRUPIER
CHIRRUPIEST
CHIRRUPING
CHIRURGEON
CHIRURGEONLY
CHIRURGEONS
CHIRURGERIES
CHIRURGERY
CHIRURGICAL
CHISELLERS
CHISELLING
CHISELLINGS
CHITARRONE
CHITARRONI
CHITCHATTED
CHITCHATTING
CHITTAGONG
CHITTAGONGS
CHITTERING
CHITTERINGS
CHITTERLING
CHITTERLINGS
CHIVALRESQUE
CHIVALRIES
CHIVALROUS
CHIVALROUSLY
CHIVALROUSNESS
CHIVAREEING
CHIVARIING
CHIWEENIES
CHIYOGAMIS
CHLAMYDATE
CHLAMYDEOUS
CHLAMYDIAE
CHLAMYDIAL
CHLAMYDIAS
CHLAMYDOMONADES
CHLAMYDOMONAS
CHLAMYDOSPORE
CHLAMYDOSPORES
CHLOANTHITE
CHLOANTHITES
CHLOASMATA
CHLORACETIC
CHLORACNES
CHLORALISM
CHLORALISMS
CHLORALOSE
CHLORALOSED
CHLORALOSES
CHLORAMBUCIL
CHLORAMBUCILS
CHLORAMINE
CHLORAMINES
CHLORAMPHENICOL
CHLORARGYRITE
CHLORARGYRITES
CHLORDANES
CHLORELLAS
CHLORENCHYMA
CHLORENCHYMAS
CHLORHEXIDINE
CHLORHEXIDINES
CHLORIDATE
CHLORIDATED
CHLORIDATES
CHLORIDATING
CHLORIDISE
CHLORIDISED
CHLORIDISES
CHLORIDISING
CHLORIDIZE
CHLORIDIZED
CHLORIDIZES
CHLORIDIZING
CHLORIMETER
CHLORIMETERS
CHLORIMETRIC
CHLORIMETRIES
CHLORIMETRY
CHLORINATE
CHLORINATED
CHLORINATES
CHLORINATING
CHLORINATION
CHLORINATIONS
CHLORINATOR
CHLORINATORS
CHLORINISE
CHLORINISED
CHLORINISES
CHLORINISING
CHLORINITIES
CHLORINITY
CHLORINIZE
CHLORINIZED
CHLORINIZES
CHLORINIZING
CHLORITISATION
CHLORITISATIONS
CHLORITIZATION
CHLORITIZATIONS
CHLOROACETIC
CHLOROARGYRITE
CHLOROBENZENE
CHLOROBENZENES
CHLOROBROMIDE
CHLOROBROMIDES
CHLOROCALCITE
CHLOROCALCITES
CHLOROCRUORIN
CHLOROCRUORINS
CHLORODYNE
CHLORODYNES
CHLOROETHENE
CHLOROETHENES
CHLOROETHYLENE
CHLOROETHYLENES
CHLOROFORM
CHLOROFORMED
CHLOROFORMER
CHLOROFORMERS
CHLOROFORMING
CHLOROFORMIST
CHLOROFORMISTS
CHLOROFORMS
CHLOROHYDRIN
CHLOROHYDRINS
CHLOROMETER
CHLOROMETERS
CHLOROMETHANE
CHLOROMETHANES
CHLOROMETRIC
CHLOROMETRIES
CHLOROMETRY
CHLOROPHYL
CHLOROPHYLL
CHLOROPHYLLOID
CHLOROPHYLLOUS
CHLOROPHYLLS
CHLOROPHYLS
CHLOROPHYTUM
CHLOROPHYTUMS
CHLOROPICRIN
CHLOROPICRINS
CHLOROPLAST
CHLOROPLASTAL
CHLOROPLASTIC
CHLOROPLASTS
CHLOROPRENE
CHLOROPRENES
CHLOROQUIN
CHLOROQUINE
CHLOROQUINES
CHLOROQUINS
CHLOROSISES
CHLOROTHIAZIDE
CHLOROTHIAZIDES
CHLORPICRIN
CHLORPICRINS
CHLORPROMAZINE
CHLORPROMAZINES
CHLORPROPAMIDE
CHLORPROPAMIDES
CHLORTHALIDONE
CHLORTHALIDONES
CHOANOCYTE
CHOANOCYTES
CHOCAHOLIC
CHOCAHOLICS
CHOCKABLOCK

CHOCKSTONE
CHOCKSTONES
CHOCOHOLIC
CHOCOHOLICS
CHOCOLATES
CHOCOLATEY
CHOCOLATIER
CHOCOLATIERS
CHOCOLATIEST
CHOICENESS
CHOICENESSES
CHOIRGIRLS
CHOIRMASTER
CHOIRMASTERS
CHOIRSCREEN
CHOIRSCREENS
CHOIRSTALL
CHOIRSTALLS
CHOKEBERRIES
CHOKEBERRY
CHOKEBORES
CHOKECHERRIES
CHOKECHERRY
CHOKECOILS
CHOKEDAMPS
CHOKEHOLDS
CHOLAEMIAS
CHOLAGOGIC
CHOLAGOGUE
CHOLAGOGUES
CHOLANGIOGRAM
CHOLANGIOGRAMS
CHOLANGIOGRAPHY
CHOLECALCIFEROL
CHOLECYSTECTOMY
CHOLECYSTITIDES
CHOLECYSTITIS
CHOLECYSTITISES
CHOLECYSTOKININ
CHOLECYSTOSTOMY
CHOLECYSTOTOMY
CHOLECYSTS
CHOLELITHIASES
CHOLELITHIASIS
CHOLELITHS
CHOLERICALLY
CHOLERICLY
CHOLESTASES
CHOLESTASIS
CHOLESTATIC
CHOLESTERATE
CHOLESTERATES
CHOLESTERIC
CHOLESTERIN
CHOLESTERINS
CHOLESTEROL
CHOLESTEROLEMIA
CHOLESTEROLS
CHOLESTYRAMINE
CHOLESTYRAMINES
CHOLIAMBIC
CHOLIAMBICS
CHOLINERGIC
CHOLINERGICALLY
CHOLINESTERASE
CHOLINESTERASES
CHOMOPHYTE
CHOMOPHYTES
CHONDRICHTHYAN
CHONDRICHTHYANS
CHONDRIFICATION
CHONDRIFIED
CHONDRIFIES
CHONDRIFYING
CHONDRIOSOMAL
CHONDRIOSOME
CHONDRIOSOMES
CHONDRITES
CHONDRITIC
CHONDRITIS
CHONDRITISES
CHONDROBLAST
CHONDROBLASTS
CHONDROCRANIA
CHONDROCRANIUM
CHONDROCRANIUMS
CHONDROCYTE
CHONDROCYTES
CHONDROGENESES
CHONDROGENESIS
CHONDROITIN
CHONDROITINS
CHONDROMAS
CHONDROMATA
CHONDROMATOSES
CHONDROMATOSIS
CHONDROMATOUS
CHONDROPHORE
CHONDROPHORES
CHONDROPHORINE
CHONDROPHORINES
CHONDROSAMINE
CHONDROSAMINES
CHONDROSKELETON
CHONDROSTIAN
CHONDROSTIANS
CHONDRULES
CHOPFALLEN
CHOPHOUSES
CHOPLOGICS
CHOPPERING
CHOPPINESS
CHOPPINESSES
CHOPSOCKIES
CHOPSTICKS
CHORAGUSES
CHORALISTS
CHORDAMESODERM
CHORDAMESODERMS
CHORDOPHONE
CHORDOPHONES
CHORDOPHONIC
CHORDOTOMIES
CHORDOTOMY
CHOREGRAPH
CHOREGRAPHED
CHOREGRAPHER
CHOREGRAPHERS
CHOREGRAPHIC
CHOREGRAPHIES
CHOREGRAPHING
CHOREGRAPHS
CHOREGRAPHY
CHOREGUSES
CHOREIFORM
CHOREODRAMA
CHOREODRAMAS
CHOREOGRAPH
CHOREOGRAPHED
CHOREOGRAPHER
CHOREOGRAPHERS
CHOREOGRAPHIC
CHOREOGRAPHIES
CHOREOGRAPHING
CHOREOGRAPHS
CHOREOGRAPHY
CHOREOLOGIES
CHOREOLOGIST
CHOREOLOGISTS
CHOREOLOGY
CHOREPISCOPAL
CHORIAMBIC
CHORIAMBICS
CHORIAMBUS
CHORIAMBUSES
CHORIOALLANTOIC
CHORIOALLANTOIS
CHORIOCARCINOMA
CHORISATION
CHORISATIONS
CHORISTERS
CHORIZATION
CHORIZATIONS
CHORIZONTIST
CHORIZONTISTS
CHORIZONTS
CHOROGRAPHER
CHOROGRAPHERS
CHOROGRAPHIC
CHOROGRAPHICAL
CHOROGRAPHIES
CHOROGRAPHY
CHOROIDITIS
CHOROIDITISES
CHOROLOGICAL
CHOROLOGIES
CHOROLOGIST
CHOROLOGISTS
CHOROPLETH
CHOROPLETHS
CHORUSMASTER
CHORUSMASTERS
CHORUSSING
CHOUCROUTE
CHOUCROUTES
CHOULTRIES
CHOUNTERED
CHOUNTERING
CHOWDERHEAD
CHOWDERHEADED
CHOWDERHEADS
CHOWDERING
CHOWHOUNDS
CHOWKIDARS
CHREMATIST
CHREMATISTIC
CHREMATISTICS
CHREMATISTS
CHRESTOMATHIC
CHRESTOMATHICAL
CHRESTOMATHIES
CHRESTOMATHY
CHRISMATION
CHRISMATIONS
CHRISMATORIES
CHRISMATORY
CHRISTCROSS
CHRISTCROSSES
CHRISTENED
CHRISTENER
CHRISTENERS
CHRISTENING
CHRISTENINGS
CHRISTIANIA
CHRISTIANIAS
CHRISTOPHANIES
CHRISTOPHANY
CHROMAFFIN
CHROMAKEYS
CHROMATICALLY
CHROMATICISM
CHROMATICISMS
CHROMATICITIES
CHROMATICITY
CHROMATICNESS
CHROMATICNESSES
CHROMATICS
CHROMATIDS
CHROMATINIC
CHROMATINS
CHROMATIST
CHROMATISTS
CHROMATOGRAM
CHROMATOGRAMS
CHROMATOGRAPH
CHROMATOGRAPHED
CHROMATOGRAPHER
CHROMATOGRAPHIC
CHROMATOGRAPHS
CHROMATOGRAPHY

CHROMATOID
CHROMATOLOGIES
CHROMATOLOGIST
CHROMATOLOGISTS
CHROMATOLOGY
CHROMATOLYSES
CHROMATOLYSIS
CHROMATOLYTIC
CHROMATOPHORE
CHROMATOPHORES
CHROMATOPHORIC
CHROMATOPHOROUS
CHROMATOPSIA
CHROMATOPSIAS
CHROMATOSPHERE
CHROMATOSPHERES
CHROMATYPE
CHROMATYPES
CHROMIDIUM
CHROMINANCE
CHROMINANCES
CHROMISING
CHROMIZING
CHROMOCENTER
CHROMOCENTERS
CHROMOCENTRE
CHROMOCENTRES
CHROMODYNAMICS
CHROMOGENIC
CHROMOGENS
CHROMOGRAM
CHROMOGRAMS
CHROMOLIES
CHROMOMERE
CHROMOMERES
CHROMOMERIC
CHROMONEMA
CHROMONEMAL
CHROMONEMATA
CHROMONEMATIC
CHROMONEMIC
CHROMOPHIL
CHROMOPHILIC
CHROMOPHILS
CHROMOPHOBE
CHROMOPHOBES
CHROMOPHORE
CHROMOPHORES
CHROMOPHORIC
CHROMOPHOROUS
CHROMOPLAST
CHROMOPLASTS
CHROMOPROTEIN
CHROMOPROTEINS
CHROMOSCOPE
CHROMOSCOPES
CHROMOSOMAL
CHROMOSOMALLY
CHROMOSOME
CHROMOSOMES
CHROMOSPHERE
CHROMOSPHERES
CHROMOSPHERIC
CHROMOTHERAPIES
CHROMOTHERAPY
CHROMOTYPE
CHROMOTYPES
CHROMOXYLOGRAPH
CHRONAXIES
CHRONICALLY
CHRONICITIES
CHRONICITY
CHRONICLED
CHRONICLER
CHRONICLERS
CHRONICLES
CHRONICLING
CHRONOBIOLOGIC
CHRONOBIOLOGIES
CHRONOBIOLOGIST
CHRONOBIOLOGY
CHRONOGRAM
CHRONOGRAMMATIC
CHRONOGRAMS
CHRONOGRAPH
CHRONOGRAPHER
CHRONOGRAPHERS
CHRONOGRAPHIC
CHRONOGRAPHIES
CHRONOGRAPHS
CHRONOGRAPHY
CHRONOLOGER
CHRONOLOGERS
CHRONOLOGIC
CHRONOLOGICAL
CHRONOLOGICALLY
CHRONOLOGIES
CHRONOLOGISE
CHRONOLOGISED
CHRONOLOGISES
CHRONOLOGISING
CHRONOLOGIST
CHRONOLOGISTS
CHRONOLOGIZE
CHRONOLOGIZED
CHRONOLOGIZES
CHRONOLOGIZING
CHRONOLOGY
CHRONOMETER
CHRONOMETERS
CHRONOMETRIC
CHRONOMETRICAL
CHRONOMETRIES
CHRONOMETRY
CHRONOSCOPE
CHRONOSCOPES
CHRONOSCOPIC
CHRONOTHERAPIES
CHRONOTHERAPY
CHRONOTRON
CHRONOTRONS
CHRYSALIDAL
CHRYSALIDES
CHRYSALIDS
CHRYSALISES
CHRYSANTHEMUM
CHRYSANTHEMUMS
CHRYSANTHS
CHRYSAROBIN
CHRYSAROBINS
CHRYSOBERYL
CHRYSOBERYLS
CHRYSOCOLLA
CHRYSOCOLLAS
CHRYSOCRACIES
CHRYSOCRACY
CHRYSOLITE
CHRYSOLITES
CHRYSOLITIC
CHRYSOMELID
CHRYSOMELIDS
CHRYSOPHAN
CHRYSOPHANS
CHRYSOPHILITE
CHRYSOPHILITES
CHRYSOPHYTE
CHRYSOPHYTES
CHRYSOPRASE
CHRYSOPRASES
CHRYSOTILE
CHRYSOTILES
CHUBBINESS
CHUBBINESSES
CHUCKAWALLA
CHUCKAWALLAS
CHUCKHOLES
CHUCKLEHEAD
CHUCKLEHEADED
CHUCKLEHEADS
CHUCKLESOME
CHUCKLINGLY
CHUCKLINGS
CHUCKWALLA
CHUCKWALLAS
CHUFFINESS
CHUFFINESSES
CHUGALUGGED
CHUGALUGGING
CHUMMINESS
CHUMMINESSES
CHUNDERING
CHUNDEROUS
CHUNKINESS
CHUNKINESSES
CHUNNERING
CHUNTERING
CHUPATTIES
CHUPRASSIES
CHURCHGOER
CHURCHGOERS
CHURCHGOING
CHURCHGOINGS
CHURCHIANITIES
CHURCHIANITY
CHURCHIEST
CHURCHINGS
CHURCHISMS
CHURCHLESS
CHURCHLIER
CHURCHLIEST
CHURCHLINESS
CHURCHLINESSES
CHURCHMANLIER
CHURCHMANLIEST
CHURCHMANLY
CHURCHMANSHIP
CHURCHMANSHIPS
CHURCHPEOPLE
CHURCHWARD
CHURCHWARDEN
CHURCHWARDENS
CHURCHWARDS
CHURCHWAYS
CHURCHWOMAN
CHURCHWOMEN
CHURCHYARD
CHURCHYARDS
CHURLISHLY
CHURLISHNESS
CHURLISHNESSES
CHURNALISM
CHURNALISMS
CHURNMILKS
CHURRIGUERESCO
CHURRIGUERESQUE
CHYLACEOUS
CHYLIFEROUS
CHYLIFICATION
CHYLIFICATIONS
CHYLIFYING
CHYLOMICRON
CHYLOMICRONS
CHYMIFEROUS
CHYMIFICATION
CHYMIFICATIONS
CHYMIFYING
CHYMISTRIES
CHYMOTRYPSIN
CHYMOTRYPSINS
CHYMOTRYPTIC
CIBACHROME
CIBACHROMES
CICADELLID
CICADELLIDS
CICATRICES
CICATRICHULE
CICATRICHULES
CICATRICIAL
CICATRICLE
CICATRICLES

CICATRICOSE
CICATRICULA
CICATRICULAS
CICATRISANT
CICATRISATION
CICATRISATIONS
CICATRISED
CICATRISER
CICATRISERS
CICATRISES
CICATRISING
CICATRIXES
CICATRIZANT
CICATRIZATION
CICATRIZATIONS
CICATRIZED
CICATRIZER
CICATRIZERS
CICATRIZES
CICATRIZING
CICERONEING
CICHORACEOUS
CICINNUSES
CICISBEISM
CICISBEISMS
CICLATOUNS
CICLOSPORIN
CICLOSPORINS
CIGARETTES
CIGARILLOS
CIGUATERAS
CIGUATOXIN
CIGUATOXINS
CILIATIONS
CIMETIDINE
CIMETIDINES
CINCHONACEOUS
CINCHONIDINE
CINCHONIDINES
CINCHONINE
CINCHONINES
CINCHONINIC
CINCHONISATION
CINCHONISATIONS
CINCHONISE
CINCHONISED
CINCHONISES
CINCHONISING
CINCHONISM
CINCHONISMS
CINCHONIZATION
CINCHONIZATIONS
CINCHONIZE
CINCHONIZED
CINCHONIZES
CINCHONIZING
CINCINNATE
CINCINNUSES
CINCTURING
CINDERIEST
CINEANGIOGRAPHY
CINEMAGOER
CINEMAGOERS
CINEMATHEQUE
CINEMATHEQUES
CINEMATICALLY
CINEMATISE
CINEMATISED
CINEMATISES
CINEMATISING
CINEMATIZE
CINEMATIZED
CINEMATIZES
CINEMATIZING
CINEMATOGRAPH
CINEMATOGRAPHED
CINEMATOGRAPHER
CINEMATOGRAPHIC
CINEMATOGRAPHS
CINEMATOGRAPHY
CINEMICROGRAPHY
CINEPHILES
CINEPLEXES
CINERARIAS
CINERARIUM
CINERARIUMS
CINERATION
CINERATIONS
CINERATORS
CINERITIOUS
CINGULATED
CINNABARIC
CINNABARINE
CINNAMONIC
CINNAMONIER
CINNAMONIEST
CINNARIZINE
CINNARIZINES
CINQUECENTIST
CINQUECENTISTS
CINQUECENTO
CINQUECENTOS
CINQUEFOIL
CINQUEFOILS
CIPHERINGS
CIPHERTEXT
CIPHERTEXTS
CIPOLLINOS
CIPROFLOXACIN
CIPROFLOXACINS
CIRCASSIAN
CIRCASSIANS
CIRCASSIENNE
CIRCASSIENNES
CIRCENSIAL
CIRCENSIAN
CIRCINATELY
CIRCUITEER
CIRCUITEERED
CIRCUITEERING
CIRCUITEERS
CIRCUITIES
CIRCUITING
CIRCUITOUS
CIRCUITOUSLY
CIRCUITOUSNESS
CIRCUITRIES
CIRCULABLE
CIRCULARISATION
CIRCULARISE
CIRCULARISED
CIRCULARISER
CIRCULARISERS
CIRCULARISES
CIRCULARISING
CIRCULARITIES
CIRCULARITY
CIRCULARIZATION
CIRCULARIZE
CIRCULARIZED
CIRCULARIZER
CIRCULARIZERS
CIRCULARIZES
CIRCULARIZING
CIRCULARLY
CIRCULARNESS
CIRCULARNESSES
CIRCULATABLE
CIRCULATED
CIRCULATES
CIRCULATING
CIRCULATINGS
CIRCULATION
CIRCULATIONS
CIRCULATIVE
CIRCULATOR
CIRCULATORS
CIRCULATORY
CIRCUMAMBAGES
CIRCUMAMBAGIOUS
CIRCUMAMBIENCE
CIRCUMAMBIENCES
CIRCUMAMBIENCY
CIRCUMAMBIENT
CIRCUMAMBIENTLY
CIRCUMAMBULATE
CIRCUMAMBULATED
CIRCUMAMBULATES
CIRCUMAMBULATOR
CIRCUMBENDIBUS
CIRCUMCENTER
CIRCUMCENTERS
CIRCUMCENTRE
CIRCUMCENTRES
CIRCUMCIRCLE
CIRCUMCIRCLES
CIRCUMCISE
CIRCUMCISED
CIRCUMCISER
CIRCUMCISERS
CIRCUMCISES
CIRCUMCISING
CIRCUMCISION
CIRCUMCISIONS
CIRCUMDUCE
CIRCUMDUCED
CIRCUMDUCES
CIRCUMDUCING
CIRCUMDUCT
CIRCUMDUCTED
CIRCUMDUCTING
CIRCUMDUCTION
CIRCUMDUCTIONS
CIRCUMDUCTORY
CIRCUMDUCTS
CIRCUMFERENCE
CIRCUMFERENCES
CIRCUMFERENTIAL
CIRCUMFERENTOR
CIRCUMFERENTORS
CIRCUMFLECT
CIRCUMFLECTED
CIRCUMFLECTING
CIRCUMFLECTS
CIRCUMFLEX
CIRCUMFLEXES
CIRCUMFLEXION
CIRCUMFLEXIONS
CIRCUMFLUENCE
CIRCUMFLUENCES
CIRCUMFLUENT
CIRCUMFLUOUS
CIRCUMFORANEAN
CIRCUMFORANEOUS
CIRCUMFUSE
CIRCUMFUSED
CIRCUMFUSES
CIRCUMFUSILE
CIRCUMFUSING
CIRCUMFUSION
CIRCUMFUSIONS
CIRCUMGYRATE
CIRCUMGYRATED
CIRCUMGYRATES
CIRCUMGYRATING
CIRCUMGYRATION
CIRCUMGYRATIONS
CIRCUMGYRATORY
CIRCUMINCESSION
CIRCUMINSESSION
CIRCUMJACENCIES
CIRCUMJACENCY
CIRCUMJACENT
CIRCUMLITTORAL
CIRCUMLOCUTE
CIRCUMLOCUTED
CIRCUMLOCUTES
CIRCUMLOCUTING
CIRCUMLOCUTION
CIRCUMLOCUTIONS

CIRCUMLOCUTORY
CIRCUMLUNAR
CIRCUMMURE
CIRCUMMURED
CIRCUMMURES
CIRCUMMURING
CIRCUMNAVIGABLE
CIRCUMNAVIGATE
CIRCUMNAVIGATED
CIRCUMNAVIGATES
CIRCUMNAVIGATOR
CIRCUMNUTATE
CIRCUMNUTATED
CIRCUMNUTATES
CIRCUMNUTATING
CIRCUMNUTATION
CIRCUMNUTATIONS
CIRCUMNUTATORY
CIRCUMPOLAR
CIRCUMPOSE
CIRCUMPOSED
CIRCUMPOSES
CIRCUMPOSING
CIRCUMPOSITION
CIRCUMPOSITIONS
CIRCUMROTATE
CIRCUMROTATED
CIRCUMROTATES
CIRCUMROTATING
CIRCUMSCISSILE
CIRCUMSCRIBABLE
CIRCUMSCRIBE
CIRCUMSCRIBED
CIRCUMSCRIBER
CIRCUMSCRIBERS
CIRCUMSCRIBES
CIRCUMSCRIBING
CIRCUMSCRIPTION
CIRCUMSCRIPTIVE
CIRCUMSOLAR
CIRCUMSPECT
CIRCUMSPECTION
CIRCUMSPECTIONS
CIRCUMSPECTIVE
CIRCUMSPECTLY
CIRCUMSPECTNESS
CIRCUMSTANCE
CIRCUMSTANCED
CIRCUMSTANCES
CIRCUMSTANCING
CIRCUMSTANTIAL
CIRCUMSTANTIALS
CIRCUMSTANTIATE
CIRCUMSTELLAR
CIRCUMVALLATE
CIRCUMVALLATED
CIRCUMVALLATES
CIRCUMVALLATING
CIRCUMVALLATION
CIRCUMVENT
CIRCUMVENTED
CIRCUMVENTER
CIRCUMVENTERS
CIRCUMVENTING
CIRCUMVENTION
CIRCUMVENTIONS
CIRCUMVENTIVE
CIRCUMVENTOR
CIRCUMVENTORS
CIRCUMVENTS
CIRCUMVOLUTION
CIRCUMVOLUTIONS
CIRCUMVOLUTORY
CIRCUMVOLVE
CIRCUMVOLVED
CIRCUMVOLVES
CIRCUMVOLVING
CIRCUSIEST
CIRCUSSIER
CIRCUSSIEST
CIRRHIPEDE
CIRRHIPEDES
CIRRHOTICS
CIRRIGRADE
CIRRIPEDES
CIRROCUMULI
CIRROCUMULUS
CIRROSTRATI
CIRROSTRATIVE
CIRROSTRATUS
CISGENDERED
CISMONTANE
CISPLATINS
CISPONTINE
CISTACEOUS
CITATIONAL
CITHARISTIC
CITHARISTS
CITIFICATION
CITIFICATIONS
CITIZENESS
CITIZENESSES
CITIZENISE
CITIZENISED
CITIZENISES
CITIZENISING
CITIZENIZE
CITIZENIZED
CITIZENIZES
CITIZENIZING
CITIZENLIER
CITIZENLIEST
CITIZENRIES
CITIZENSHIP
CITIZENSHIPS
CITRICULTURE
CITRICULTURES
CITRICULTURIST
CITRICULTURISTS
CITRONELLA
CITRONELLAL
CITRONELLALS
CITRONELLAS
CITRONELLOL
CITRONELLOLS
CITRULLINE
CITRULLINES
CITRUSIEST
CITRUSSIER
CITRUSSIEST
CITYFICATION
CITYFICATIONS
CITYSCAPES
CIVILIANISATION
CIVILIANISE
CIVILIANISED
CIVILIANISES
CIVILIANISING
CIVILIANIZATION
CIVILIANIZE
CIVILIANIZED
CIVILIANIZES
CIVILIANIZING
CIVILISABLE
CIVILISATION
CIVILISATIONAL
CIVILISATIONS
CIVILISERS
CIVILISING
CIVILITIES
CIVILIZABLE
CIVILIZATION
CIVILIZATIONAL
CIVILIZATIONS
CIVILIZERS
CIVILIZING
CIVILNESSES
CLABBERING
CLACKBOXES
CLACKDISHES
CLADISTICALLY
CLADISTICS
CLADOCERAN
CLADOCERANS
CLADOGENESES
CLADOGENESIS
CLADOGENETIC
CLADOGRAMS
CLADOPHYLL
CLADOPHYLLS
CLADOSPORIA
CLADOSPORIUM
CLAIRAUDIENCE
CLAIRAUDIENCES
CLAIRAUDIENT
CLAIRAUDIENTLY
CLAIRAUDIENTS
CLAIRCOLLE
CLAIRCOLLES
CLAIRSCHACH
CLAIRSCHACHS
CLAIRVOYANCE
CLAIRVOYANCES
CLAIRVOYANCIES
CLAIRVOYANCY
CLAIRVOYANT
CLAIRVOYANTLY
CLAIRVOYANTS
CLAMANCIES
CLAMATORIAL
CLAMBERERS
CLAMBERING
CLAMJAMFRIES
CLAMJAMFRY
CLAMJAMPHRIE
CLAMJAMPHRIES
CLAMMINESS
CLAMMINESSES
CLAMOROUSLY
CLAMOROUSNESS
CLAMOROUSNESSES
CLAMOURERS
CLAMOURING
CLAMPDOWNS
CLAMPERING
CLAMSHELLS
CLANDESTINE
CLANDESTINELY
CLANDESTINENESS
CLANDESTINITIES
CLANDESTINITY
CLANGBOXES
CLANGORING
CLANGOROUS
CLANGOROUSLY
CLANGOURED
CLANGOURING
CLANJAMFRAY
CLANJAMFRAYS
CLANKINGLY
CLANNISHLY
CLANNISHNESS
CLANNISHNESSES
CLANSWOMAN
CLANSWOMEN
CLAPBOARDED
CLAPBOARDING
CLAPBOARDS
CLAPBREADS
CLAPDISHES
CLAPOMETER
CLAPOMETERS
CLAPPERBOARD
CLAPPERBOARDS
CLAPPERBOY
CLAPPERBOYS
CLAPPERCLAW
CLAPPERCLAWED
CLAPPERCLAWER
CLAPPERCLAWERS

CLAPPERCLAWING
CLAPPERCLAWS
CLAPPERING
CLAPPERINGS
CLAPTRAPPERIES
CLAPTRAPPERY
CLARABELLA
CLARABELLAS
CLARENDONS
CLARIBELLA
CLARIBELLAS
CLARICHORD
CLARICHORDS
CLARIFICATION
CLARIFICATIONS
CLARIFIERS
CLARIFYING
CLARINETIST
CLARINETISTS
CLARINETTIST
CLARINETTISTS
CLARIONETS
CLARIONING
CLARTHEADS
CLASHINGLY
CLASSICALISM
CLASSICALISMS
CLASSICALIST
CLASSICALISTS
CLASSICALITIES
CLASSICALITY
CLASSICALLY
CLASSICALNESS
CLASSICALNESSES
CLASSICALS
CLASSICISE
CLASSICISED
CLASSICISES
CLASSICISING
CLASSICISM
CLASSICISMS
CLASSICIST
CLASSICISTIC
CLASSICISTS
CLASSICIZE
CLASSICIZED
CLASSICIZES
CLASSICIZING
CLASSIFIABLE
CLASSIFICATION
CLASSIFICATIONS
CLASSIFICATORY
CLASSIFIED
CLASSIFIEDS
CLASSIFIER
CLASSIFIERS
CLASSIFIES
CLASSIFYING
CLASSINESS
CLASSINESSES
CLASSLESSNESS
CLASSLESSNESSES
CLASSMATES
CLASSROOMS
CLASSWORKS
CLATHRATES
CLATTERERS
CLATTERIER
CLATTERIEST
CLATTERING
CLATTERINGLY
CLAUCHTING
CLAUDICATION
CLAUDICATIONS
CLAUGHTING
CLAUSTRATION
CLAUSTRATIONS
CLAUSTROPHILIA
CLAUSTROPHILIAS
CLAUSTROPHOBE
CLAUSTROPHOBES
CLAUSTROPHOBIA
CLAUSTROPHOBIAS
CLAUSTROPHOBIC
CLAVATIONS
CLAVECINIST
CLAVECINISTS
CLAVICEMBALO
CLAVICEMBALOS
CLAVICHORD
CLAVICHORDIST
CLAVICHORDISTS
CLAVICHORDS
CLAVICORNS
CLAVICULAE
CLAVICULAR
CLAVICULATE
CLAVICYTHERIA
CLAVICYTHERIUM
CLAVIERIST
CLAVIERISTIC
CLAVIERISTS
CLAVIGEROUS
CLAWHAMMER
CLAWHAMMERS
CLAYMATION
CLAYMATIONS
CLAYSTONES
CLAYTONIAS
CLEANABILITIES
CLEANABILITY
CLEANHANDED
CLEANLIEST
CLEANLINESS
CLEANLINESSES
CLEANNESSES
CLEANSABLE
CLEANSINGS
CLEANSKINS
CLEANTECHS
CLEARANCES
CLEARCOLED
CLEARCOLES
CLEARCOLING
CLEARCUTTING
CLEARCUTTINGS
CLEARHEADED
CLEARHEADEDLY
CLEARHEADEDNESS
CLEARINGHOUSE
CLEARINGHOUSES
CLEARNESSES
CLEARSKINS
CLEARSTORIED
CLEARSTORIES
CLEARSTORY
CLEARWEEDS
CLEARWINGS
CLEAVABILITIES
CLEAVABILITY
CLEAVABLENESS
CLEAVABLENESSES
CLEISTOGAMIC
CLEISTOGAMIES
CLEISTOGAMOUS
CLEISTOGAMOUSLY
CLEISTOGAMY
CLEMATISES
CLEMENCIES
CLEMENTINE
CLEMENTINES
CLENBUTEROL
CLENBUTEROLS
CLEOPATRAS
CLEPSYDRAE
CLEPSYDRAS
CLEPTOCRACIES
CLEPTOCRACY
CLEPTOMANIA
CLEPTOMANIAC
CLEPTOMANIACS
CLEPTOMANIAS
CLERESTORIED
CLERESTORIES
CLERESTORY
CLERGIABLE
CLERGYABLE
CLERGYWOMAN
CLERGYWOMEN
CLERICALISM
CLERICALISMS
CLERICALIST
CLERICALISTS
CLERICALLY
CLERICATES
CLERICITIES
CLERKESSES
CLERKLIEST
CLERKLINESS
CLERKLINESSES
CLERKLINGS
CLERKSHIPS
CLEROMANCIES
CLEROMANCY
CLERUCHIAL
CLERUCHIAS
CLERUCHIES
CLEVERALITIES
CLEVERALITY
CLEVERDICK
CLEVERDICKS
CLEVERNESS
CLEVERNESSES
CLIANTHUSES
CLICKBAITS
CLICKETING
CLICKJACKING
CLICKJACKINGS
CLICKSTREAM
CLICKSTREAMS
CLICKTIVISM
CLICKTIVISMS
CLICKWRAPS
CLIENTAGES
CLIENTELES
CLIENTLESS
CLIENTSHIP
CLIENTSHIPS
CLIFFHANGER
CLIFFHANGERS
CLIFFHANGING
CLIFFHANGINGS
CLIFFHANGS
CLIFFSIDES
CLIMACTERIC
CLIMACTERICAL
CLIMACTERICALLY
CLIMACTERICS
CLIMACTICAL
CLIMACTICALLY
CLIMATICAL
CLIMATICALLY
CLIMATISED
CLIMATISES
CLIMATISING
CLIMATIZED
CLIMATIZES
CLIMATIZING
CLIMATOGRAPHIES
CLIMATOGRAPHY
CLIMATOLOGIC
CLIMATOLOGICAL
CLIMATOLOGIES
CLIMATOLOGIST
CLIMATOLOGISTS
CLIMATOLOGY
CLIMATURES
CLIMAXLESS
CLIMBDOWNS
CLINANDRIA

C

CLINANDRIUM
CLINCHINGLY
CLINDAMYCIN
CLINDAMYCINS
CLINGFILMS
CLINGFISHES
CLINGINESS
CLINGINESSES
CLINGINGLY
CLINGINGNESS
CLINGINGNESSES
CLINGSTONE
CLINGSTONES
CLINGWRAPS
CLINICALLY
CLINICALNESS
CLINICALNESSES
CLINICIANS
CLINKERING
CLINKSTONE
CLINKSTONES
CLINOCHLORE
CLINOCHLORES
CLINODIAGONAL
CLINODIAGONALS
CLINOMETER
CLINOMETERS
CLINOMETRIC
CLINOMETRICAL
CLINOMETRIES
CLINOMETRY
CLINOPINACOID
CLINOPINACOIDS
CLINOPINAKOID
CLINOPINAKOIDS
CLINOPYROXENE
CLINOPYROXENES
CLINOSTATS
CLINQUANTS
CLINTONIAS
CLIOMETRIC
CLIOMETRICAL
CLIOMETRICIAN
CLIOMETRICIANS
CLIOMETRICS
CLIOMETRIES
CLIPBOARDS
CLIPSHEARS
CLIPSHEETS
CLIQUINESS
CLIQUINESSES
CLIQUISHLY
CLIQUISHNESS
CLIQUISHNESSES
CLISHMACLAVER
CLISHMACLAVERS
CLISTOGAMIES
CLISTOGAMY
CLITICISED
CLITICISES
CLITICISING
CLITICIZED
CLITICIZES
CLITICIZING
CLITORECTOMIES
CLITORECTOMY
CLITORIDECTOMY
CLITORIDES
CLITORISES
CLITTERING
CLOACALINE
CLOACITISES
CLOAKROOMS
CLOBBERING
CLOCKFACES
CLOCKMAKER
CLOCKMAKERS
CLOCKWORKS
CLODDISHLY
CLODDISHNESS
CLODDISHNESSES
CLODHOPPER
CLODHOPPERS
CLODHOPPING
CLOFIBRATE
CLOFIBRATES
CLOGDANCES
CLOGGINESS
CLOGGINESSES
CLOGMAKERS
CLOISONNAGE
CLOISONNAGES
CLOISONNES
CLOISTERED
CLOISTERER
CLOISTERERS
CLOISTERING
CLOISTRESS
CLOISTRESSES
CLOMIPHENE
CLOMIPHENES
CLONAZEPAM
CLONAZEPAMS
CLONICITIES
CLONIDINES
CLOSEDOWNS
CLOSEFISTED
CLOSEHEADS
CLOSEMOUTHED
CLOSENESSES
CLOSESTOOL
CLOSESTOOLS
CLOSETFULS
CLOSTRIDIA
CLOSTRIDIAL
CLOSTRIDIAN
CLOSTRIDIUM
CLOSTRIDIUMS
CLOTHBOUND
CLOTHESHORSE
CLOTHESHORSES
CLOTHESLINE
CLOTHESLINED
CLOTHESLINES
CLOTHESLINING
CLOTHESPIN
CLOTHESPINS
CLOTHESPRESS
CLOTHESPRESSES
CLOTTERING
CLOTTINESS
CLOTTINESSES
CLOUDBERRIES
CLOUDBERRY
CLOUDBURST
CLOUDBURSTS
CLOUDINESS
CLOUDINESSES
CLOUDLANDS
CLOUDLESSLY
CLOUDLESSNESS
CLOUDLESSNESSES
CLOUDSCAPE
CLOUDSCAPES
CLOUDTOWNS
CLOVERGRASS
CLOVERGRASSES
CLOVERIEST
CLOVERLEAF
CLOVERLEAFS
CLOVERLEAVES
CLOVERLIKE
CLOWNERIES
CLOWNFISHES
CLOWNISHLY
CLOWNISHNESS
CLOWNISHNESSES
CLOXACILLIN
CLOXACILLINS
CLOZAPINES
CLUBABILITIES
CLUBABILITY
CLUBBABILITIES
CLUBBABILITY
CLUBBINESS
CLUBBINESSES
CLUBFOOTED
CLUBHAULED
CLUBHAULING
CLUBHOUSES
CLUBMANSHIP
CLUBMANSHIPS
CLUBMASTER
CLUBMASTERS
CLUBMOSSES
CLUBRUSHES
CLUMPERING
CLUMPINESS
CLUMPINESSES
CLUMSINESS
CLUMSINESSES
CLUSTERIER
CLUSTERIEST
CLUSTERING
CLUSTERINGLY
CLUTCHIEST
CLUTTERIER
CLUTTERIEST
CLUTTERING
CLYPEIFORM
CNIDARIANS
CNIDOBLAST
CNIDOBLASTS
COACERVATE
COACERVATED
COACERVATES
COACERVATING
COACERVATION
COACERVATIONS
COACHBUILDER
COACHBUILDERS
COACHBUILDING
COACHBUILDINGS
COACHBUILT
COACHLINES
COACHLOADS
COACHROOFS
COACHWHIPS
COACHWOODS
COACHWORKS
COACTIVELY
COACTIVITIES
COACTIVITY
COADAPTATION
COADAPTATIONS
COADJACENCIES
COADJACENCY
COADJACENT
COADJACENTS
COADJUTANT
COADJUTANTS
COADJUTORS
COADJUTORSHIP
COADJUTORSHIPS
COADJUTRESS
COADJUTRESSES
COADJUTRICES
COADJUTRIX
COADJUTRIXES
COADMIRING
COADMITTED
COADMITTING
COADUNATED
COADUNATES
COADUNATING
COADUNATION
COADUNATIONS
COADUNATIVE
COAGENCIES
COAGULABILITIES

COAGULABILITY
COAGULABLE
COAGULANTS
COAGULASES
COAGULATED
COAGULATES
COAGULATING
COAGULATION
COAGULATIONS
COAGULATIVE
COAGULATOR
COAGULATORS
COAGULATORY
COALESCENCE
COALESCENCES
COALESCENT
COALESCING
COALFIELDS
COALFISHES
COALHOUSES
COALIFICATION
COALIFICATIONS
COALIFYING
COALITIONAL
COALITIONER
COALITIONERS
COALITIONISM
COALITIONISMS
COALITIONIST
COALITIONISTS
COALITIONS
COALMASTER
COALMASTERS
COALMINERS
COANCHORED
COANCHORING
COANNEXING
COAPPEARED
COAPPEARING
COAPTATION
COAPTATIONS
COARCTATED
COARCTATES
COARCTATING
COARCTATION
COARCTATIONS
COARSENESS
COARSENESSES
COARSENING
COASSISTED
COASSISTING
COASSUMING
COASTEERING
COASTEERINGS
COASTGUARD
COASTGUARDMAN
COASTGUARDMEN
COASTGUARDS
COASTGUARDSMAN
COASTGUARDSMEN
COASTLANDS
COASTLINES
COASTWARDS
COATDRESSES
COATIMUNDI
COATIMUNDIS
COATSTANDS
COATTENDED
COATTENDING
COATTESTED
COATTESTING
COAUTHORED
COAUTHORING
COAUTHORSHIP
COAUTHORSHIPS
COBALAMINS
COBALTIFEROUS
COBALTINES
COBALTITES
COBBLERIES
COBBLESTONE
COBBLESTONED
COBBLESTONES
COBBLESTONING
COBELLIGERENT
COBELLIGERENTS
COBWEBBERIES
COBWEBBERY
COBWEBBIER
COBWEBBIEST
COBWEBBING
COCAINISATION
COCAINISATIONS
COCAINISED
COCAINISES
COCAINISING
COCAINISMS
COCAINISTS
COCAINIZATION
COCAINIZATIONS
COCAINIZED
COCAINIZES
COCAINIZING
COCAPTAINED
COCAPTAINING
COCAPTAINS
COCARBOXYLASE
COCARBOXYLASES
COCARCINOGEN
COCARCINOGENIC
COCARCINOGENS
COCATALYST
COCATALYSTS
COCCIDIANS
COCCIDIOSES
COCCIDIOSIS
COCCIDIOSTAT
COCCIDIOSTATS
COCCIFEROUS
COCCINEOUS
COCCOLITES
COCCOLITHS
COCHAIRING
COCHAIRMAN
COCHAIRMANSHIP
COCHAIRMANSHIPS
COCHAIRMEN
COCHAIRPERSON
COCHAIRPERSONS
COCHAIRWOMAN
COCHAIRWOMEN
COCHAMPION
COCHAMPIONS
COCHINEALS
COCHLEARES
COCHLEARIFORM
COCHLEATED
COCKABULLIES
COCKABULLY
COCKALEEKIE
COCKALEEKIES
COCKALORUM
COCKALORUMS
COCKAMAMIE
COCKAMAMIER
COCKAMAMIEST
COCKATEELS
COCKATIELS
COCKATRICE
COCKATRICES
COCKBILLED
COCKBILLING
COCKCHAFER
COCKCHAFERS
COCKCROWING
COCKCROWINGS
COCKERNONIES
COCKERNONY
COCKEYEDLY
COCKEYEDNESS
COCKEYEDNESSES
COCKFIGHTING
COCKFIGHTINGS
COCKFIGHTS
COCKHORSES
COCKIELEEKIE
COCKIELEEKIES
COCKINESSES
COCKLEBOAT
COCKLEBOATS
COCKLEBURS
COCKLEERTS
COCKLESHELL
COCKLESHELLS
COCKMATCHES
COCKNEYDOM
COCKNEYDOMS
COCKNEYFICATION
COCKNEYFIED
COCKNEYFIES
COCKNEYFYING
COCKNEYISH
COCKNEYISM
COCKNEYISMS
COCKNIFICATION
COCKNIFICATIONS
COCKNIFIED
COCKNIFIES
COCKNIFYING
COCKROACHES
COCKSCOMBS
COCKSFOOTS
COCKSINESS
COCKSINESSES
COCKSUCKER
COCKSUCKERS
COCKSURELY
COCKSURENESS
COCKSURENESSES
COCKSWAINED
COCKSWAINING
COCKSWAINS
COCKTAILED
COCKTAILING
COCKTEASER
COCKTEASERS
COCKTHROWING
COCKTHROWINGS
COCKYLEEKIES
COCKYLEEKY
COCOMPOSER
COCOMPOSERS
COCONSCIOUS
COCONSCIOUSES
COCONSCIOUSNESS
COCONSPIRATOR
COCONSPIRATORS
COCONUTTIER
COCONUTTIEST
COCOONERIES
COCOONINGS
COCOUNSELED
COCOUNSELING
COCOUNSELLED
COCOUNSELLING
COCOUNSELS
COCOZELLES
COCREATING
COCREATORS
COCULTIVATE
COCULTIVATED
COCULTIVATES
COCULTIVATING
COCULTIVATION
COCULTIVATIONS
COCULTURED
COCULTURES
COCULTURING
COCURATING
COCURATORS

COCURRICULAR
COCUSWOODS
CODEBREAKER
CODEBREAKERS
CODECLINATION
CODECLINATIONS
CODEFENDANT
CODEFENDANTS
CODEPENDENCE
CODEPENDENCES
CODEPENDENCIES
CODEPENDENCY
CODEPENDENT
CODEPENDENTS
CODERIVING
CODESIGNED
CODESIGNING
CODETERMINATION
CODEVELOPED
CODEVELOPER
CODEVELOPERS
CODEVELOPING
CODEVELOPS
CODICILLARY
CODICOLOGICAL
CODICOLOGIES
CODICOLOGY
CODIFIABILITIES
CODIFIABILITY
CODIFIABLE
CODIFICATION
CODIFICATIONS
CODIRECTED
CODIRECTING
CODIRECTION
CODIRECTIONS
CODIRECTOR
CODIRECTORS
CODISCOVER
CODISCOVERED
CODISCOVERER
CODISCOVERERS
CODISCOVERING
CODISCOVERS
CODOLOGIES
CODOMINANCE
CODOMINANCES
CODOMINANT
CODOMINANTS
CODSWALLOP
CODSWALLOPS
COECILIANS
COEDUCATION
COEDUCATIONAL
COEDUCATIONALLY
COEDUCATIONS
COEFFICIENT
COEFFICIENTS
COELACANTH
COELACANTHIC
COELACANTHS
COELANAGLYPHIC
COELENTERA
COELENTERATE
COELENTERATES
COELENTERIC
COELENTERON
COELENTERONS
COELIOSCOPIES
COELIOSCOPY
COELOMATES
COELOMATIC
COELOSTATS
COELUROSAUR
COELUROSAURS
COEMBODIED
COEMBODIES
COEMBODYING
COEMPLOYED
COEMPLOYING
COEMPTIONS
COENACTING
COENAESTHESES
COENAESTHESIA
COENAESTHESIAS
COENAESTHESIS
COENAMORED
COENAMORING
COENAMOURED
COENAMOURING
COENAMOURS
COENDURING
COENENCHYMA
COENENCHYMAS
COENENCHYMATA
COENENCHYME
COENENCHYMES
COENESTHESES
COENESTHESIA
COENESTHESIAS
COENESTHESIS
COENESTHETIC
COENOBITES
COENOBITIC
COENOBITICAL
COENOBITISM
COENOBITISMS
COENOCYTES
COENOCYTIC
COENOSARCS
COENOSPECIES
COENOSTEUM
COENOSTEUMS
COENZYMATIC
COENZYMATICALLY
COEQUALITIES
COEQUALITY
COEQUALNESS
COEQUALNESSES
COEQUATING
COERCIMETER
COERCIMETERS
COERCIONIST
COERCIONISTS
COERCIVELY
COERCIVENESS
COERCIVENESSES
COERCIVITIES
COERCIVITY
COERECTING
COESSENTIAL
COESSENTIALITY
COESSENTIALLY
COESSENTIALNESS
COETANEOUS
COETANEOUSLY
COETANEOUSNESS
COETERNALLY
COETERNITIES
COETERNITY
COEVALITIES
COEVOLUTION
COEVOLUTIONARY
COEVOLUTIONS
COEVOLVING
COEXECUTOR
COEXECUTORS
COEXECUTRICES
COEXECUTRIX
COEXECUTRIXES
COEXERTING
COEXISTENCE
COEXISTENCES
COEXISTENT
COEXISTING
COEXTENDED
COEXTENDING
COEXTENSION
COEXTENSIONS
COEXTENSIVE
COEXTENSIVELY
COFAVORITE
COFAVORITES
COFEATURED
COFEATURES
COFEATURING
COFFEEHOUSE
COFFEEHOUSES
COFFEEMAKER
COFFEEMAKERS
COFFEEPOTS
COFFERDAMS
COFFINITES
COFINANCED
COFINANCES
COFINANCING
COFOUNDERS
COFOUNDING
COFUNCTION
COFUNCTIONS
COGENERATION
COGENERATIONS
COGENERATOR
COGENERATORS
COGITATING
COGITATINGLY
COGITATION
COGITATIONS
COGITATIVE
COGITATIVELY
COGITATIVENESS
COGITATORS
COGNATENESS
COGNATENESSES
COGNATIONS
COGNISABLE
COGNISABLY
COGNISANCE
COGNISANCES
COGNITIONAL
COGNITIONS
COGNITIVELY
COGNITIVISM
COGNITIVISMS
COGNITIVITIES
COGNITIVITY
COGNIZABLE
COGNIZABLY
COGNIZANCE
COGNIZANCES
COGNOMINAL
COGNOMINALLY
COGNOMINATE
COGNOMINATED
COGNOMINATES
COGNOMINATING
COGNOMINATION
COGNOMINATIONS
COGNOSCENTE
COGNOSCENTI
COGNOSCIBLE
COGNOSCING
COHABITANT
COHABITANTS
COHABITATION
COHABITATIONS
COHABITEES
COHABITERS
COHABITING
COHABITORS
COHEIRESSES
COHERENCES
COHERENCIES
COHERENTLY
COHERITORS
COHESIBILITIES
COHESIBILITY
COHESIONLESS
COHESIVELY
COHESIVENESS

COHESIVENESSES
COHIBITING
COHIBITION
COHIBITIONS
COHIBITIVE
COHOBATING
COHOMOLOGICAL
COHOMOLOGIES
COHOMOLOGY
COHORTATIVE
COHORTATIVES
COHOSTESSED
COHOSTESSES
COHOSTESSING
COHOUSINGS
COHYPONYMS
COIFFEUSES
COIFFURING
COILABILITIES
COILABILITY
COINCIDENCE
COINCIDENCES
COINCIDENCIES
COINCIDENCY
COINCIDENT
COINCIDENTAL
COINCIDENTALLY
COINCIDENTLY
COINCIDING
COINFECTED
COINFECTING
COINFERRED
COINFERRING
COINHERENCE
COINHERENCES
COINHERING
COINHERITANCE
COINHERITANCES
COINHERITOR
COINHERITORS
COINSTANTANEITY
COINSTANTANEOUS
COINSURANCE
COINSURANCES
COINSURERS
COINSURING
COINTERRED
COINTERRING
COINTREAUS
COINVENTED
COINVENTING
COINVENTOR
COINVENTORS
COINVESTED
COINVESTIGATOR
COINVESTIGATORS
COINVESTING
COINVESTOR
COINVESTORS
COKULORISES
COLATITUDE
COLATITUDES
COLCANNONS
COLCHICINE
COLCHICINES
COLCHICUMS
COLCOTHARS
COLDBLOODS
COLDCOCKED
COLDCOCKING
COLDHEARTED
COLDHEARTEDLY
COLDHEARTEDNESS
COLDHOUSES
COLDNESSES
COLECTOMIES
COLEMANITE
COLEMANITES
COLEOPTERA
COLEOPTERAL
COLEOPTERAN
COLEOPTERANS
COLEOPTERIST
COLEOPTERISTS
COLEOPTERON
COLEOPTERONS
COLEOPTEROUS
COLEOPTERS
COLEOPTILE
COLEOPTILES
COLEORHIZA
COLEORHIZAE
COLEORRHIZA
COLEORRHIZAE
COLESTIPOL
COLESTIPOLS
COLICKIEST
COLICROOTS
COLICWEEDS
COLINEARITIES
COLINEARITY
COLIPHAGES
COLLABORATE
COLLABORATED
COLLABORATES
COLLABORATING
COLLABORATION
COLLABORATIONS
COLLABORATIVE
COLLABORATIVELY
COLLABORATIVES
COLLABORATOR
COLLABORATORS
COLLAGENASE
COLLAGENASES
COLLAGENIC
COLLAGENOUS
COLLAGISTS
COLLAPSABILITY
COLLAPSABLE
COLLAPSARS
COLLAPSIBILITY
COLLAPSIBLE
COLLAPSING
COLLARBONE
COLLARBONES
COLLARETTE
COLLARETTES
COLLARLESS
COLLARSTUD
COLLARSTUDS
COLLATABLE
COLLATERAL
COLLATERALISE
COLLATERALISED
COLLATERALISES
COLLATERALISING
COLLATERALITIES
COLLATERALITY
COLLATERALIZE
COLLATERALIZED
COLLATERALIZES
COLLATERALIZING
COLLATERALLY
COLLATERALS
COLLATIONS
COLLEAGUED
COLLEAGUES
COLLEAGUESHIP
COLLEAGUESHIPS
COLLEAGUING
COLLECTABLE
COLLECTABLES
COLLECTANEA
COLLECTEDLY
COLLECTEDNESS
COLLECTEDNESSES
COLLECTIBLE
COLLECTIBLES
COLLECTING
COLLECTINGS
COLLECTION
COLLECTIONS
COLLECTIVE
COLLECTIVELY
COLLECTIVENESS
COLLECTIVES
COLLECTIVISE
COLLECTIVISED
COLLECTIVISES
COLLECTIVISING
COLLECTIVISM
COLLECTIVISMS
COLLECTIVIST
COLLECTIVISTIC
COLLECTIVISTS
COLLECTIVITIES
COLLECTIVITY
COLLECTIVIZE
COLLECTIVIZED
COLLECTIVIZES
COLLECTIVIZING
COLLECTORATE
COLLECTORATES
COLLECTORS
COLLECTORSHIP
COLLECTORSHIPS
COLLEGIALISM
COLLEGIALISMS
COLLEGIALITIES
COLLEGIALITY
COLLEGIALLY
COLLEGIANER
COLLEGIANERS
COLLEGIANS
COLLEGIATE
COLLEGIATELY
COLLEGIATES
COLLEGIUMS
COLLEMBOLAN
COLLEMBOLANS
COLLEMBOLOUS
COLLENCHYMA
COLLENCHYMAS
COLLENCHYMATA
COLLENCHYMATOUS
COLLETERIAL
COLLICULUS
COLLIERIES
COLLIESHANGIE
COLLIESHANGIES
COLLIGATED
COLLIGATES
COLLIGATING
COLLIGATION
COLLIGATIONS
COLLIGATIVE
COLLIMATED
COLLIMATES
COLLIMATING
COLLIMATION
COLLIMATIONS
COLLIMATOR
COLLIMATORS
COLLINEARITIES
COLLINEARITY
COLLINEARLY
COLLINSIAS
COLLIQUABLE
COLLIQUANT
COLLIQUATE
COLLIQUATED
COLLIQUATES
COLLIQUATING
COLLIQUATION
COLLIQUATIONS
COLLIQUATIVE
COLLIQUESCENCE
COLLIQUESCENCES
COLLISIONAL

COLLISIONALLY
COLLISIONS
COLLOCATED
COLLOCATES
COLLOCATING
COLLOCATION
COLLOCATIONAL
COLLOCATIONS
COLLOCUTOR
COLLOCUTORS
COLLOCUTORY
COLLODIONS
COLLODIUMS
COLLOGUING
COLLOIDALITIES
COLLOIDALITY
COLLOIDALLY
COLLOQUIAL
COLLOQUIALISM
COLLOQUIALISMS
COLLOQUIALIST
COLLOQUIALISTS
COLLOQUIALITIES
COLLOQUIALITY
COLLOQUIALLY
COLLOQUIALNESS
COLLOQUIALS
COLLOQUIED
COLLOQUIES
COLLOQUING
COLLOQUISE
COLLOQUISED
COLLOQUISES
COLLOQUISING
COLLOQUIST
COLLOQUISTS
COLLOQUIUM
COLLOQUIUMS
COLLOQUIZE
COLLOQUIZED
COLLOQUIZES
COLLOQUIZING
COLLOQUYING
COLLOTYPES
COLLOTYPIC
COLLOTYPIES
COLLUCTATION
COLLUCTATIONS
COLLUSIONS
COLLUSIVELY
COLLUVIUMS
COLLYRIUMS
COLLYWOBBLES
COLOBOMATA
COLOCATING
COLOCYNTHS
COLOGARITHM
COLOGARITHMS
COLOMBARDS
COLONELCIES
COLONELLING
COLONELLINGS
COLONELSHIP
COLONELSHIPS
COLONIALISE
COLONIALISED
COLONIALISES
COLONIALISING
COLONIALISM
COLONIALISMS
COLONIALIST
COLONIALISTIC
COLONIALISTS
COLONIALIZE
COLONIALIZED
COLONIALIZES
COLONIALIZING
COLONIALLY
COLONIALNESS
COLONIALNESSES
COLONISABLE
COLONISATION
COLONISATIONIST
COLONISATIONS
COLONISERS
COLONISING
COLONITISES
COLONIZABLE
COLONIZATION
COLONIZATIONIST
COLONIZATIONS
COLONIZERS
COLONIZING
COLONNADED
COLONNADES
COLONOSCOPE
COLONOSCOPES
COLONOSCOPIES
COLONOSCOPY
COLOPHONIES
COLOQUINTIDA
COLOQUINTIDAS
COLORABILITIES
COLORABILITY
COLORABLENESS
COLORABLENESSES
COLORATION
COLORATIONS
COLORATURA
COLORATURAS
COLORATURE
COLORATURES
COLORBREED
COLORBREEDING
COLORBREEDS
COLORCASTED
COLORCASTING
COLORCASTS
COLORECTAL
COLORFASTNESS
COLORFASTNESSES
COLORFULLY
COLORFULNESS
COLORFULNESSES
COLORIMETER
COLORIMETERS
COLORIMETRIC
COLORIMETRICAL
COLORIMETRIES
COLORIMETRY
COLORISATION
COLORISATIONS
COLORISERS
COLORISING
COLORISTIC
COLORISTICALLY
COLORIZATION
COLORIZATIONS
COLORIZERS
COLORIZING
COLORLESSLY
COLORLESSNESS
COLORLESSNESSES
COLORPOINT
COLORPOINTS
COLORWASHED
COLORWASHES
COLORWASHING
COLOSSALLY
COLOSSEUMS
COLOSSUSES
COLOSTOMIES
COLOSTROUS
COLOSTRUMS
COLOTOMIES
COLOURABILITIES
COLOURABILITY
COLOURABLE
COLOURABLENESS
COLOURABLY
COLOURANTS
COLOURATION
COLOURATIONS
COLOURBRED
COLOURBREED
COLOURBREEDING
COLOURBREEDS
COLOURCAST
COLOURCASTED
COLOURCASTING
COLOURCASTS
COLOURFAST
COLOURFASTNESS
COLOURFULLY
COLOURFULNESS
COLOURFULNESSES
COLOURIEST
COLOURINGS
COLOURISATION
COLOURISATIONS
COLOURISED
COLOURISER
COLOURISERS
COLOURISES
COLOURISING
COLOURISMS
COLOURISTIC
COLOURISTICALLY
COLOURISTS
COLOURIZATION
COLOURIZATIONS
COLOURIZED
COLOURIZER
COLOURIZERS
COLOURIZES
COLOURIZING
COLOURLESS
COLOURLESSLY
COLOURLESSNESS
COLOURPOINT
COLOURPOINTS
COLOURWASH
COLOURWASHED
COLOURWASHES
COLOURWASHING
COLOURWAYS
COLPITISES
COLPORTAGE
COLPORTAGES
COLPORTEUR
COLPORTEURS
COLPOSCOPE
COLPOSCOPES
COLPOSCOPICAL
COLPOSCOPICALLY
COLPOSCOPIES
COLPOSCOPY
COLPOTOMIES
COLTISHNESS
COLTISHNESSES
COLTSFOOTS
COLUBRIADS
COLUBRIFORM
COLUMBARIA
COLUMBARIES
COLUMBARIUM
COLUMBATES
COLUMBINES
COLUMBITES
COLUMBIUMS
COLUMELLAE
COLUMELLAR
COLUMNARITIES
COLUMNARITY
COLUMNATED
COLUMNIATED
COLUMNIATION
COLUMNIATIONS
COLUMNISTIC
COLUMNISTS

COMANAGEMENT
COMANAGEMENTS
COMANAGERS
COMANAGING
COMANCHERO
COMANCHEROS
COMATOSELY
COMATULIDS
COMBATABLE
COMBATANTS
COMBATIVELY
COMBATIVENESS
COMBATIVENESSES
COMBATTING
COMBINABILITIES
COMBINABILITY
COMBINABLE
COMBINATION
COMBINATIONAL
COMBINATIONS
COMBINATIVE
COMBINATORIAL
COMBINATORIALLY
COMBINATORICS
COMBINATORY
COMBININGS
COMBRETUMS
COMBURGESS
COMBURGESSES
COMBUSTIBILITY
COMBUSTIBLE
COMBUSTIBLENESS
COMBUSTIBLES
COMBUSTIBLY
COMBUSTING
COMBUSTION
COMBUSTIONS
COMBUSTIOUS
COMBUSTIVE
COMBUSTIVES
COMBUSTORS
COMEDDLING
COMEDICALLY
COMEDIENNE
COMEDIENNES
COMEDIETTA
COMEDIETTAS
COMEDOGENIC
COMELINESS
COMELINESSES
COMESTIBLE
COMESTIBLES
COMETOGRAPHIES
COMETOGRAPHY
COMETOLOGIES
COMETOLOGY
COMEUPPANCE
COMEUPPANCES
COMFINESSES
COMFITURES
COMFORTABLE
COMFORTABLENESS
COMFORTABLY
COMFORTERS
COMFORTING
COMFORTINGLY
COMFORTLESS
COMFORTLESSLY
COMFORTLESSNESS
COMICALITIES
COMICALITY
COMICALNESS
COMICALNESSES
COMINGLING
COMITADJIS
COMITATIVE
COMITATIVES
COMITATUSES
COMMANDABLE
COMMANDANT
COMMANDANTS
COMMANDANTSHIP
COMMANDANTSHIPS
COMMANDEER
COMMANDEERED
COMMANDEERING
COMMANDEERS
COMMANDERIES
COMMANDERS
COMMANDERSHIP
COMMANDERSHIPS
COMMANDERY
COMMANDING
COMMANDINGLY
COMMANDMENT
COMMANDMENTS
COMMANDOES
COMMEASURABLE
COMMEASURE
COMMEASURED
COMMEASURES
COMMEASURING
COMMEMORABLE
COMMEMORATE
COMMEMORATED
COMMEMORATES
COMMEMORATING
COMMEMORATION
COMMEMORATIONAL
COMMEMORATIONS
COMMEMORATIVE
COMMEMORATIVELY
COMMEMORATIVES
COMMEMORATOR
COMMEMORATORS
COMMEMORATORY
COMMENCEMENT
COMMENCEMENTS
COMMENCERS
COMMENCING
COMMENDABLE
COMMENDABLENESS
COMMENDABLY
COMMENDAMS
COMMENDATION
COMMENDATIONS
COMMENDATOR
COMMENDATORS
COMMENDATORY
COMMENDERS
COMMENDING
COMMENSALISM
COMMENSALISMS
COMMENSALITIES
COMMENSALITY
COMMENSALLY
COMMENSALS
COMMENSURABLE
COMMENSURABLY
COMMENSURATE
COMMENSURATELY
COMMENSURATION
COMMENSURATIONS
COMMENTARIAL
COMMENTARIAT
COMMENTARIATS
COMMENTARIES
COMMENTARY
COMMENTATE
COMMENTATED
COMMENTATES
COMMENTATING
COMMENTATION
COMMENTATIONS
COMMENTATOR
COMMENTATORIAL
COMMENTATORS
COMMENTERS
COMMENTING
COMMENTORS
COMMERCIAL
COMMERCIALESE
COMMERCIALESES
COMMERCIALISE
COMMERCIALISED
COMMERCIALISES
COMMERCIALISING
COMMERCIALISM
COMMERCIALISMS
COMMERCIALIST
COMMERCIALISTIC
COMMERCIALISTS
COMMERCIALITIES
COMMERCIALITY
COMMERCIALIZE
COMMERCIALIZED
COMMERCIALIZES
COMMERCIALIZING
COMMERCIALLY
COMMERCIALS
COMMERCING
COMMERGING
COMMINATED
COMMINATES
COMMINATING
COMMINATION
COMMINATIONS
COMMINATIVE
COMMINATORY
COMMINGLED
COMMINGLES
COMMINGLING
COMMINUTED
COMMINUTES
COMMINUTING
COMMINUTION
COMMINUTIONS
COMMISERABLE
COMMISERATE
COMMISERATED
COMMISERATES
COMMISERATING
COMMISERATINGLY
COMMISERATION
COMMISERATIONS
COMMISERATIVE
COMMISERATIVELY
COMMISERATOR
COMMISERATORS
COMMISSAIRE
COMMISSAIRES
COMMISSARIAL
COMMISSARIAT
COMMISSARIATS
COMMISSARIES
COMMISSARS
COMMISSARY
COMMISSARYSHIP
COMMISSARYSHIPS
COMMISSION
COMMISSIONAIRE
COMMISSIONAIRES
COMMISSIONAL
COMMISSIONARY
COMMISSIONED
COMMISSIONER
COMMISSIONERS
COMMISSIONING
COMMISSIONS
COMMISSURAL
COMMISSURE
COMMISSURES
COMMITMENT
COMMITMENTS
COMMITTABLE
COMMITTALS
COMMITTEEMAN
COMMITTEEMEN
COMMITTEES
COMMITTEESHIP

C

COMMITTEESHIPS
COMMITTEEWOMAN
COMMITTEEWOMEN
COMMITTERS
COMMITTING
COMMIXTION
COMMIXTIONS
COMMIXTURE
COMMIXTURES
COMMODIFICATION
COMMODIFIED
COMMODIFIES
COMMODIFYING
COMMODIOUS
COMMODIOUSLY
COMMODIOUSNESS
COMMODITIES
COMMODITISE
COMMODITISED
COMMODITISES
COMMODITISING
COMMODITIZE
COMMODITIZED
COMMODITIZES
COMMODITIZING
COMMODORES
COMMONABLE
COMMONAGES
COMMONALITIES
COMMONALITY
COMMONALTIES
COMMONALTY
COMMONHOLD
COMMONHOLDS
COMMONINGS
COMMONNESS
COMMONNESSES
COMMONPLACE
COMMONPLACED
COMMONPLACENESS
COMMONPLACES
COMMONPLACING
COMMONSENSE
COMMONSENSIBLE
COMMONSENSICAL
COMMONWEAL
COMMONWEALS
COMMONWEALTH
COMMONWEALTHS
COMMORANTS
COMMORIENTES
COMMOTIONAL
COMMOTIONS
COMMUNALISATION
COMMUNALISE
COMMUNALISED
COMMUNALISER
COMMUNALISERS
COMMUNALISES
COMMUNALISING
COMMUNALISM
COMMUNALISMS
COMMUNALIST
COMMUNALISTIC
COMMUNALISTS
COMMUNALITIES
COMMUNALITY
COMMUNALIZATION
COMMUNALIZE
COMMUNALIZED
COMMUNALIZER
COMMUNALIZERS
COMMUNALIZES
COMMUNALIZING
COMMUNALLY
COMMUNARDS
COMMUNAUTAIRE
COMMUNAUTAIRES
COMMUNICABILITY
COMMUNICABLE
COMMUNICABLY
COMMUNICANT
COMMUNICANTS
COMMUNICATE
COMMUNICATED
COMMUNICATEE
COMMUNICATEES
COMMUNICATES
COMMUNICATING
COMMUNICATION
COMMUNICATIONAL
COMMUNICATIONS
COMMUNICATIVE
COMMUNICATIVELY
COMMUNICATOR
COMMUNICATORS
COMMUNICATORY
COMMUNINGS
COMMUNIONAL
COMMUNIONALLY
COMMUNIONS
COMMUNIQUE
COMMUNIQUES
COMMUNISATION
COMMUNISATIONS
COMMUNISED
COMMUNISES
COMMUNISING
COMMUNISMS
COMMUNISTIC
COMMUNISTICALLY
COMMUNISTS
COMMUNITAIRE
COMMUNITAIRES
COMMUNITARIAN
COMMUNITARIANS
COMMUNITIES
COMMUNIZATION
COMMUNIZATIONS
COMMUNIZED
COMMUNIZES
COMMUNIZING
COMMUTABILITIES
COMMUTABILITY
COMMUTABLE
COMMUTABLENESS
COMMUTATED
COMMUTATES
COMMUTATING
COMMUTATION
COMMUTATIONS
COMMUTATIVE
COMMUTATIVELY
COMMUTATIVITIES
COMMUTATIVITY
COMMUTATOR
COMMUTATORS
COMMUTINGS
COMONOMERS
COMORBIDITIES
COMORBIDITY
COMPACTEDLY
COMPACTEDNESS
COMPACTEDNESSES
COMPACTERS
COMPACTEST
COMPACTIBLE
COMPACTIFIED
COMPACTIFIES
COMPACTIFY
COMPACTIFYING
COMPACTING
COMPACTION
COMPACTIONS
COMPACTNESS
COMPACTNESSES
COMPACTORS
COMPACTURE
COMPACTURES
COMPAGINATE
COMPAGINATED
COMPAGINATES
COMPAGINATING
COMPAGINATION
COMPAGINATIONS
COMPANDERS
COMPANDING
COMPANDORS
COMPANIABLE
COMPANIONABLE
COMPANIONABLY
COMPANIONATE
COMPANIONED
COMPANIONHOOD
COMPANIONHOODS
COMPANIONING
COMPANIONLESS
COMPANIONS
COMPANIONSHIP
COMPANIONSHIPS
COMPANIONWAY
COMPANIONWAYS
COMPANYING
COMPARABILITIES
COMPARABILITY
COMPARABLE
COMPARABLENESS
COMPARABLY
COMPARATIST
COMPARATISTS
COMPARATIVE
COMPARATIVELY
COMPARATIVENESS
COMPARATIVES
COMPARATIVIST
COMPARATIVISTS
COMPARATOR
COMPARATORS
COMPARISON
COMPARISONS
COMPARTING
COMPARTMENT
COMPARTMENTAL
COMPARTMENTALLY
COMPARTMENTED
COMPARTMENTING
COMPARTMENTS
COMPASSABLE
COMPASSING
COMPASSINGS
COMPASSION
COMPASSIONABLE
COMPASSIONATE
COMPASSIONATED
COMPASSIONATELY
COMPASSIONATES
COMPASSIONATING
COMPASSIONED
COMPASSIONING
COMPASSIONLESS
COMPASSIONS
COMPATIBILITIES
COMPATIBILITY
COMPATIBLE
COMPATIBLENESS
COMPATIBLES
COMPATIBLY
COMPATRIOT
COMPATRIOTIC
COMPATRIOTISM
COMPATRIOTISMS
COMPATRIOTS
COMPEARANCE
COMPEARANCES
COMPEARANT
COMPEARANTS
COMPEARING
COMPEERING
COMPELLABLE
COMPELLABLY

COMPELLATION
COMPELLATIONS
COMPELLATIVE
COMPELLATIVES
COMPELLERS
COMPELLING
COMPELLINGLY
COMPENDIOUS
COMPENDIOUSLY
COMPENDIOUSNESS
COMPENDIUM
COMPENDIUMS
COMPENSABILITY
COMPENSABLE
COMPENSATE
COMPENSATED
COMPENSATES
COMPENSATING
COMPENSATION
COMPENSATIONAL
COMPENSATIONS
COMPENSATIVE
COMPENSATOR
COMPENSATORS
COMPENSATORY
COMPESCING
COMPETENCE
COMPETENCES
COMPETENCIES
COMPETENCY
COMPETENTLY
COMPETENTNESS
COMPETENTNESSES
COMPETITION
COMPETITIONS
COMPETITIVE
COMPETITIVELY
COMPETITIVENESS
COMPETITOR
COMPETITORS
COMPILATION
COMPILATIONS
COMPILATOR
COMPILATORS
COMPILATORY
COMPILEMENT
COMPILEMENTS
COMPLACENCE
COMPLACENCES
COMPLACENCIES
COMPLACENCY
COMPLACENT
COMPLACENTLY
COMPLAINANT
COMPLAINANTS
COMPLAINED
COMPLAINER
COMPLAINERS
COMPLAINING
COMPLAININGLY
COMPLAININGS
COMPLAINTS
COMPLAISANCE
COMPLAISANCES
COMPLAISANT
COMPLAISANTLY
COMPLANATE
COMPLANATION
COMPLANATIONS
COMPLEATED
COMPLEATING
COMPLECTED
COMPLECTING
COMPLEMENT
COMPLEMENTAL
COMPLEMENTALLY
COMPLEMENTARIES
COMPLEMENTARILY
COMPLEMENTARITY
COMPLEMENTARY
COMPLEMENTATION
COMPLEMENTED
COMPLEMENTING
COMPLEMENTISER
COMPLEMENTISERS
COMPLEMENTIZER
COMPLEMENTIZERS
COMPLEMENTS
COMPLETABLE
COMPLETEDNESS
COMPLETEDNESSES
COMPLETELY
COMPLETENESS
COMPLETENESSES
COMPLETERS
COMPLETEST
COMPLETING
COMPLETION
COMPLETIONS
COMPLETIST
COMPLETISTS
COMPLETIVE
COMPLETORIES
COMPLETORY
COMPLEXATION
COMPLEXATIONS
COMPLEXEDNESS
COMPLEXEDNESSES
COMPLEXEST
COMPLEXIFIED
COMPLEXIFIES
COMPLEXIFY
COMPLEXIFYING
COMPLEXING
COMPLEXION
COMPLEXIONAL
COMPLEXIONED
COMPLEXIONLESS
COMPLEXIONS
COMPLEXITIES
COMPLEXITY
COMPLEXNESS
COMPLEXNESSES
COMPLEXOMETRIC
COMPLEXONE
COMPLEXONES
COMPLEXUSES
COMPLIABLE
COMPLIABLENESS
COMPLIABLY
COMPLIANCE
COMPLIANCES
COMPLIANCIES
COMPLIANCY
COMPLIANTLY
COMPLIANTNESS
COMPLIANTNESSES
COMPLICACIES
COMPLICACY
COMPLICANT
COMPLICATE
COMPLICATED
COMPLICATEDLY
COMPLICATEDNESS
COMPLICATES
COMPLICATING
COMPLICATION
COMPLICATIONS
COMPLICATIVE
COMPLICITIES
COMPLICITLY
COMPLICITOUS
COMPLICITY
COMPLIMENT
COMPLIMENTAL
COMPLIMENTARILY
COMPLIMENTARY
COMPLIMENTED
COMPLIMENTER
COMPLIMENTERS
COMPLIMENTING
COMPLIMENTS
COMPLISHED
COMPLISHES
COMPLISHING
COMPLOTTED
COMPLOTTER
COMPLOTTERS
COMPLOTTING
COMPLUVIUM
COMPLUVIUMS
COMPONENCIES
COMPONENCY
COMPONENTAL
COMPONENTIAL
COMPONENTS
COMPORTANCE
COMPORTANCES
COMPORTING
COMPORTMENT
COMPORTMENTS
COMPOSEDLY
COMPOSEDNESS
COMPOSEDNESSES
COMPOSITED
COMPOSITELY
COMPOSITENESS
COMPOSITENESSES
COMPOSITES
COMPOSITING
COMPOSITION
COMPOSITIONAL
COMPOSITIONALLY
COMPOSITIONS
COMPOSITIVE
COMPOSITOR
COMPOSITORIAL
COMPOSITORS
COMPOSITOUS
COMPOSSIBILITY
COMPOSSIBLE
COMPOSTABLE
COMPOSTERS
COMPOSTING
COMPOSTINGS
COMPOSTURE
COMPOSTURED
COMPOSTURES
COMPOSTURING
COMPOSURES
COMPOTATION
COMPOTATIONS
COMPOTATIONSHIP
COMPOTATOR
COMPOTATORS
COMPOTATORY
COMPOTIERS
COMPOUNDABLE
COMPOUNDED
COMPOUNDER
COMPOUNDERS
COMPOUNDING
COMPOUNDINGS
COMPRADORE
COMPRADORES
COMPRADORS
COMPREHEND
COMPREHENDED
COMPREHENDIBLE
COMPREHENDING
COMPREHENDS
COMPREHENSIBLE
COMPREHENSIBLY
COMPREHENSION
COMPREHENSIONS
COMPREHENSIVE
COMPREHENSIVELY
COMPREHENSIVES
COMPREHENSIVISE
COMPREHENSIVIZE

COMPRESSED
COMPRESSEDLY
COMPRESSES
COMPRESSIBILITY
COMPRESSIBLE
COMPRESSIBLY
COMPRESSING
COMPRESSION
COMPRESSIONAL
COMPRESSIONS
COMPRESSIVE
COMPRESSIVELY
COMPRESSOR
COMPRESSORS
COMPRESSURE
COMPRESSURES
COMPRIMARIO
COMPRIMARIOS
COMPRINTED
COMPRINTING
COMPRISABLE
COMPRISALS
COMPRISING
COMPRIZING
COMPROMISE
COMPROMISED
COMPROMISER
COMPROMISERS
COMPROMISES
COMPROMISING
COMPROMISINGLY
COMPROVINCIAL
COMPTROLLED
COMPTROLLER
COMPTROLLERS
COMPTROLLERSHIP
COMPTROLLING
COMPTROLLS
COMPULSATIVE
COMPULSATORY
COMPULSING
COMPULSION
COMPULSIONIST
COMPULSIONISTS
COMPULSIONS
COMPULSITOR
COMPULSITORS
COMPULSIVE
COMPULSIVELY
COMPULSIVENESS
COMPULSIVES
COMPULSIVITIES
COMPULSIVITY
COMPULSORIES
COMPULSORILY
COMPULSORINESS
COMPULSORY
COMPUNCTION
COMPUNCTIONS
COMPUNCTIOUS
COMPUNCTIOUSLY
COMPURGATION
COMPURGATIONS
COMPURGATOR
COMPURGATORIAL
COMPURGATORS
COMPURGATORY
COMPURSION
COMPURSIONS
COMPUTABILITIES
COMPUTABILITY
COMPUTABLE
COMPUTANTS
COMPUTATION
COMPUTATIONAL
COMPUTATIONALLY
COMPUTATIONS
COMPUTATIVE
COMPUTATOR
COMPUTATORS
COMPUTERATE
COMPUTERDOM
COMPUTERDOMS
COMPUTERESE
COMPUTERESES
COMPUTERISABLE
COMPUTERISATION
COMPUTERISE
COMPUTERISED
COMPUTERISES
COMPUTERISING
COMPUTERIST
COMPUTERISTS
COMPUTERITIS
COMPUTERITISES
COMPUTERIZABLE
COMPUTERIZATION
COMPUTERIZE
COMPUTERIZED
COMPUTERIZES
COMPUTERIZING
COMPUTERLESS
COMPUTERLIKE
COMPUTERNIK
COMPUTERNIKS
COMPUTERPHOBE
COMPUTERPHOBES
COMPUTERPHOBIA
COMPUTERPHOBIAS
COMPUTERPHOBIC
COMPUTERPHOBICS
COMPUTINGS
COMPUTISTS
COMRADELIER
COMRADELIEST
COMRADELINESS
COMRADELINESSES
COMRADERIES
COMRADESHIP
COMRADESHIPS
COMSTOCKER
COMSTOCKERIES
COMSTOCKERS
COMSTOCKERY
COMSTOCKISM
COMSTOCKISMS
CONACREISM
CONACREISMS
CONATIONAL
CONCANAVALIN
CONCANAVALINS
CONCATENATE
CONCATENATED
CONCATENATES
CONCATENATING
CONCATENATION
CONCATENATIONS
CONCAVENESS
CONCAVENESSES
CONCAVITIES
CONCEALABLE
CONCEALERS
CONCEALING
CONCEALINGLY
CONCEALMENT
CONCEALMENTS
CONCEDEDLY
CONCEITEDLY
CONCEITEDNESS
CONCEITEDNESSES
CONCEITFUL
CONCEITING
CONCEITLESS
CONCEIVABILITY
CONCEIVABLE
CONCEIVABLENESS
CONCEIVABLY
CONCEIVERS
CONCEIVING
CONCELEBRANT
CONCELEBRANTS
CONCELEBRATE
CONCELEBRATED
CONCELEBRATES
CONCELEBRATING
CONCELEBRATION
CONCELEBRATIONS
CONCENTERED
CONCENTERING
CONCENTERS
CONCENTRATE
CONCENTRATED
CONCENTRATEDLY
CONCENTRATES
CONCENTRATING
CONCENTRATION
CONCENTRATIONS
CONCENTRATIVE
CONCENTRATIVELY
CONCENTRATOR
CONCENTRATORS
CONCENTRED
CONCENTRES
CONCENTRIC
CONCENTRICAL
CONCENTRICALLY
CONCENTRICITIES
CONCENTRICITY
CONCENTRING
CONCEPTACLE
CONCEPTACLES
CONCEPTION
CONCEPTIONAL
CONCEPTIONS
CONCEPTIOUS
CONCEPTIVE
CONCEPTUAL
CONCEPTUALISE
CONCEPTUALISED
CONCEPTUALISER
CONCEPTUALISERS
CONCEPTUALISES
CONCEPTUALISING
CONCEPTUALISM
CONCEPTUALISMS
CONCEPTUALIST
CONCEPTUALISTIC
CONCEPTUALISTS
CONCEPTUALITIES
CONCEPTUALITY
CONCEPTUALIZE
CONCEPTUALIZED
CONCEPTUALIZER
CONCEPTUALIZERS
CONCEPTUALIZES
CONCEPTUALIZING
CONCEPTUALLY
CONCEPTUSES
CONCERNANCIES
CONCERNANCY
CONCERNEDLY
CONCERNEDNESS
CONCERNEDNESSES
CONCERNING
CONCERNMENT
CONCERNMENTS
CONCERTANTE
CONCERTANTES
CONCERTANTI
CONCERTEDLY
CONCERTEDNESS
CONCERTEDNESSES
CONCERTGOER
CONCERTGOERS
CONCERTGOING
CONCERTGOINGS
CONCERTINA
CONCERTINAED
CONCERTINAING
CONCERTINAS

CONCERTING
CONCERTINI
CONCERTINIST
CONCERTINISTS
CONCERTINO
CONCERTINOS
CONCERTISE
CONCERTISED
CONCERTISES
CONCERTISING
CONCERTIZE
CONCERTIZED
CONCERTIZES
CONCERTIZING
CONCERTMASTER
CONCERTMASTERS
CONCERTMEISTER
CONCERTMEISTERS
CONCERTMISTRESS
CONCERTSTUCK
CONCERTSTUCKS
CONCESSIBLE
CONCESSION
CONCESSIONAIRE
CONCESSIONAIRES
CONCESSIONAL
CONCESSIONARIES
CONCESSIONARY
CONCESSIONER
CONCESSIONERS
CONCESSIONIST
CONCESSIONISTS
CONCESSIONNAIRE
CONCESSIONS
CONCESSIVE
CONCESSIVELY
CONCETTISM
CONCETTISMS
CONCETTIST
CONCETTISTS
CONCHIFEROUS
CONCHIFORM
CONCHIGLIE
CONCHIOLIN
CONCHIOLINS
CONCHITISES
CONCHOIDAL
CONCHOIDALLY
CONCHOLOGICAL
CONCHOLOGIES
CONCHOLOGIST
CONCHOLOGISTS
CONCHOLOGY
CONCIERGES
CONCILIABLE
CONCILIARLY
CONCILIARY
CONCILIATE
CONCILIATED
CONCILIATES
CONCILIATING
CONCILIATION
CONCILIATIONS
CONCILIATIVE
CONCILIATOR
CONCILIATORILY
CONCILIATORS
CONCILIATORY
CONCINNITIES
CONCINNITY
CONCINNOUS
CONCIPIENCIES
CONCIPIENCY
CONCIPIENT
CONCISENESS
CONCISENESSES
CONCISIONS
CONCLAMATION
CONCLAMATIONS
CONCLAVISM
CONCLAVISMS
CONCLAVIST
CONCLAVISTS
CONCLUDERS
CONCLUDING
CONCLUSION
CONCLUSIONARY
CONCLUSIONS
CONCLUSIVE
CONCLUSIVELY
CONCLUSIVENESS
CONCLUSORY
CONCOCTERS
CONCOCTING
CONCOCTION
CONCOCTIONS
CONCOCTIVE
CONCOCTORS
CONCOLORATE
CONCOLOROUS
CONCOMITANCE
CONCOMITANCES
CONCOMITANCIES
CONCOMITANCY
CONCOMITANT
CONCOMITANTLY
CONCOMITANTS
CONCORDANCE
CONCORDANCES
CONCORDANT
CONCORDANTLY
CONCORDATS
CONCORDIAL
CONCORDING
CONCORPORATE
CONCORPORATED
CONCORPORATES
CONCORPORATING
CONCOURSES
CONCREATED
CONCREATES
CONCREATING
CONCREMATION
CONCREMATIONS
CONCRESCENCE
CONCRESCENCES
CONCRESCENT
CONCRETELY
CONCRETENESS
CONCRETENESSES
CONCRETING
CONCRETION
CONCRETIONARY
CONCRETIONS
CONCRETISATION
CONCRETISATIONS
CONCRETISE
CONCRETISED
CONCRETISES
CONCRETISING
CONCRETISM
CONCRETISMS
CONCRETIST
CONCRETISTS
CONCRETIVE
CONCRETIVELY
CONCRETIZATION
CONCRETIZATIONS
CONCRETIZE
CONCRETIZED
CONCRETIZES
CONCRETIZING
CONCREWING
CONCUBINAGE
CONCUBINAGES
CONCUBINARIES
CONCUBINARY
CONCUBINES
CONCUBITANCIES
CONCUBITANCY
CONCUBITANT
CONCUBITANTS
CONCUPISCENCE
CONCUPISCENCES
CONCUPISCENT
CONCUPISCIBLE
CONCURRENCE
CONCURRENCES
CONCURRENCIES
CONCURRENCY
CONCURRENT
CONCURRENTLY
CONCURRENTS
CONCURRING
CONCURRINGLY
CONCUSSING
CONCUSSION
CONCUSSIONS
CONCUSSIVE
CONCYCLICALLY
CONDEMNABLE
CONDEMNABLY
CONDEMNATION
CONDEMNATIONS
CONDEMNATORY
CONDEMNERS
CONDEMNING
CONDEMNINGLY
CONDEMNORS
CONDENSABILITY
CONDENSABLE
CONDENSATE
CONDENSATED
CONDENSATES
CONDENSATING
CONDENSATION
CONDENSATIONAL
CONDENSATIONS
CONDENSERIES
CONDENSERS
CONDENSERY
CONDENSIBILITY
CONDENSIBLE
CONDENSING
CONDESCEND
CONDESCENDED
CONDESCENDENCE
CONDESCENDENCES
CONDESCENDING
CONDESCENDINGLY
CONDESCENDS
CONDESCENSION
CONDESCENSIONS
CONDIDDLED
CONDIDDLES
CONDIDDLING
CONDIGNNESS
CONDIGNNESSES
CONDIMENTAL
CONDIMENTED
CONDIMENTING
CONDIMENTS
CONDISCIPLE
CONDISCIPLES
CONDITIONABLE
CONDITIONAL
CONDITIONALITY
CONDITIONALLY
CONDITIONALS
CONDITIONATE
CONDITIONATED
CONDITIONATES
CONDITIONATING
CONDITIONED
CONDITIONER
CONDITIONERS
CONDITIONING
CONDITIONINGS
CONDITIONS
CONDOLATORY

CONDOLEMENT
CONDOLEMENTS
CONDOLENCE
CONDOLENCES
CONDOLINGLY
CONDOMINIA
CONDOMINIUM
CONDOMINIUMS
CONDONABLE
CONDONATION
CONDONATIONS
CONDOTTIERE
CONDOTTIERI
CONDUCEMENT
CONDUCEMENTS
CONDUCIBLE
CONDUCINGLY
CONDUCIVENESS
CONDUCIVENESSES
CONDUCTANCE
CONDUCTANCES
CONDUCTIBILITY
CONDUCTIBLE
CONDUCTIMETRIC
CONDUCTING
CONDUCTIOMETRIC
CONDUCTION
CONDUCTIONAL
CONDUCTIONS
CONDUCTIVE
CONDUCTIVELY
CONDUCTIVITIES
CONDUCTIVITY
CONDUCTOMETRIC
CONDUCTORIAL
CONDUCTORS
CONDUCTORSHIP
CONDUCTORSHIPS
CONDUCTRESS
CONDUCTRESSES
CONDUPLICATE
CONDUPLICATION
CONDUPLICATIONS
CONDYLOMAS
CONDYLOMATA
CONDYLOMATOUS
CONEFLOWER
CONEFLOWERS
CONFABBING
CONFABULAR
CONFABULATE
CONFABULATED
CONFABULATES
CONFABULATING
CONFABULATION
CONFABULATIONS
CONFABULATOR
CONFABULATORS
CONFABULATORY
CONFARREATE
CONFARREATION
CONFARREATIONS
CONFECTING
CONFECTION
CONFECTIONARIES
CONFECTIONARY
CONFECTIONER
CONFECTIONERIES
CONFECTIONERS
CONFECTIONERY
CONFECTIONS
CONFEDERACIES
CONFEDERACY
CONFEDERAL
CONFEDERATE
CONFEDERATED
CONFEDERATES
CONFEDERATING
CONFEDERATION
CONFEDERATIONS
CONFEDERATIVE
CONFERENCE
CONFERENCES
CONFERENCIER
CONFERENCIERS
CONFERENCING
CONFERENCINGS
CONFERENTIAL
CONFERMENT
CONFERMENTS
CONFERRABLE
CONFERRALS
CONFERREES
CONFERRENCE
CONFERRENCES
CONFERRERS
CONFERRING
CONFERVOID
CONFERVOIDS
CONFESSABLE
CONFESSANT
CONFESSANTS
CONFESSEDLY
CONFESSING
CONFESSION
CONFESSIONAL
CONFESSIONALISM
CONFESSIONALIST
CONFESSIONALLY
CONFESSIONALS
CONFESSIONARIES
CONFESSIONARY
CONFESSIONS
CONFESSORESS
CONFESSORESSES
CONFESSORS
CONFESSORSHIP
CONFESSORSHIPS
CONFIDANTE
CONFIDANTES
CONFIDANTS
CONFIDENCE
CONFIDENCES
CONFIDENCIES
CONFIDENCY
CONFIDENTIAL
CONFIDENTIALITY
CONFIDENTIALLY
CONFIDENTLY
CONFIDENTS
CONFIDINGLY
CONFIDINGNESS
CONFIDINGNESSES
CONFIGURATE
CONFIGURATED
CONFIGURATES
CONFIGURATING
CONFIGURATION
CONFIGURATIONAL
CONFIGURATIONS
CONFIGURATIVE
CONFIGURATOR
CONFIGURATORS
CONFIGURED
CONFIGURES
CONFIGURING
CONFINABLE
CONFINEABLE
CONFINEDLY
CONFINEDNESS
CONFINEDNESSES
CONFINELESS
CONFINEMENT
CONFINEMENTS
CONFIRMABILITY
CONFIRMABLE
CONFIRMAND
CONFIRMANDS
CONFIRMATION
CONFIRMATIONAL
CONFIRMATIONS
CONFIRMATIVE
CONFIRMATOR
CONFIRMATORS
CONFIRMATORY
CONFIRMEDLY
CONFIRMEDNESS
CONFIRMEDNESSES
CONFIRMEES
CONFIRMERS
CONFIRMING
CONFIRMINGS
CONFIRMORS
CONFISCABLE
CONFISCATABLE
CONFISCATE
CONFISCATED
CONFISCATES
CONFISCATING
CONFISCATION
CONFISCATIONS
CONFISCATOR
CONFISCATORS
CONFISCATORY
CONFISERIE
CONFISERIES
CONFISEURS
CONFITEORS
CONFITURES
CONFLAGRANT
CONFLAGRATE
CONFLAGRATED
CONFLAGRATES
CONFLAGRATING
CONFLAGRATION
CONFLAGRATIONS
CONFLAGRATIVE
CONFLATING
CONFLATION
CONFLATIONS
CONFLICTED
CONFLICTFUL
CONFLICTING
CONFLICTINGLY
CONFLICTION
CONFLICTIONS
CONFLICTIVE
CONFLICTORY
CONFLICTUAL
CONFLUENCE
CONFLUENCES
CONFLUENTLY
CONFLUENTS
CONFOCALLY
CONFORMABILITY
CONFORMABLE
CONFORMABLENESS
CONFORMABLY
CONFORMANCE
CONFORMANCES
CONFORMATION
CONFORMATIONAL
CONFORMATIONS
CONFORMERS
CONFORMING
CONFORMINGLY
CONFORMISM
CONFORMISMS
CONFORMIST
CONFORMISTS
CONFORMITIES
CONFORMITY
CONFOUNDABLE
CONFOUNDED
CONFOUNDEDLY
CONFOUNDEDNESS
CONFOUNDER
CONFOUNDERS
CONFOUNDING
CONFOUNDINGLY

CONFRATERNAL
CONFRATERNITIES
CONFRATERNITY
CONFRERIES
CONFRONTAL
CONFRONTALS
CONFRONTATION
CONFRONTATIONAL
CONFRONTATIONS
CONFRONTED
CONFRONTER
CONFRONTERS
CONFRONTING
CONFRONTMENT
CONFRONTMENTS
CONFUSABILITIES
CONFUSABILITY
CONFUSABLE
CONFUSABLES
CONFUSEDLY
CONFUSEDNESS
CONFUSEDNESSES
CONFUSIBLE
CONFUSIBLES
CONFUSINGLY
CONFUSIONAL
CONFUSIONS
CONFUTABLE
CONFUTATION
CONFUTATIONS
CONFUTATIVE
CONFUTEMENT
CONFUTEMENTS
CONGEALABLE
CONGEALABLENESS
CONGEALERS
CONGEALING
CONGEALMENT
CONGEALMENTS
CONGELATION
CONGELATIONS
CONGENERIC
CONGENERICAL
CONGENERICS
CONGENEROUS
CONGENETIC
CONGENIALITIES
CONGENIALITY
CONGENIALLY
CONGENIALNESS
CONGENIALNESSES
CONGENITAL
CONGENITALLY
CONGENITALNESS
CONGESTIBLE
CONGESTING
CONGESTION
CONGESTIONS
CONGESTIVE
CONGIARIES
CONGLOBATE
CONGLOBATED
CONGLOBATES
CONGLOBATING
CONGLOBATION
CONGLOBATIONS
CONGLOBING
CONGLOBULATE
CONGLOBULATED
CONGLOBULATES
CONGLOBULATING
CONGLOBULATION
CONGLOBULATIONS
CONGLOMERATE
CONGLOMERATED
CONGLOMERATES
CONGLOMERATEUR
CONGLOMERATEURS
CONGLOMERATIC
CONGLOMERATING
CONGLOMERATION
CONGLOMERATIONS
CONGLOMERATIVE
CONGLOMERATOR
CONGLOMERATORS
CONGLUTINANT
CONGLUTINATE
CONGLUTINATED
CONGLUTINATES
CONGLUTINATING
CONGLUTINATION
CONGLUTINATIONS
CONGLUTINATIVE
CONGLUTINATOR
CONGLUTINATORS
CONGRATTERS
CONGRATULABLE
CONGRATULANT
CONGRATULANTS
CONGRATULATE
CONGRATULATED
CONGRATULATES
CONGRATULATING
CONGRATULATION
CONGRATULATIONS
CONGRATULATIVE
CONGRATULATOR
CONGRATULATORS
CONGRATULATORY
CONGREEING
CONGREETED
CONGREETING
CONGREGANT
CONGREGANTS
CONGREGATE
CONGREGATED
CONGREGATES
CONGREGATING
CONGREGATION
CONGREGATIONAL
CONGREGATIONS
CONGREGATIVE
CONGREGATOR
CONGREGATORS
CONGRESSED
CONGRESSES
CONGRESSING
CONGRESSIONAL
CONGRESSIONALLY
CONGRESSMAN
CONGRESSMEN
CONGRESSPEOPLE
CONGRESSPERSON
CONGRESSPERSONS
CONGRESSWOMAN
CONGRESSWOMEN
CONGRUENCE
CONGRUENCES
CONGRUENCIES
CONGRUENCY
CONGRUENTLY
CONGRUITIES
CONGRUOUSLY
CONGRUOUSNESS
CONGRUOUSNESSES
CONICITIES
CONIDIOPHORE
CONIDIOPHORES
CONIDIOPHOROUS
CONIDIOSPORE
CONIDIOSPORES
CONIFEROUS
CONIOLOGIES
CONIROSTRAL
CONJECTING
CONJECTURABLE
CONJECTURABLY
CONJECTURAL
CONJECTURALLY
CONJECTURE
CONJECTURED
CONJECTURER
CONJECTURERS
CONJECTURES
CONJECTURING
CONJOINERS
CONJOINING
CONJOINTLY
CONJUGABLE
CONJUGALITIES
CONJUGALITY
CONJUGALLY
CONJUGANTS
CONJUGATED
CONJUGATELY
CONJUGATENESS
CONJUGATENESSES
CONJUGATES
CONJUGATING
CONJUGATINGS
CONJUGATION
CONJUGATIONAL
CONJUGATIONALLY
CONJUGATIONS
CONJUGATIVE
CONJUGATOR
CONJUGATORS
CONJUNCTION
CONJUNCTIONAL
CONJUNCTIONALLY
CONJUNCTIONS
CONJUNCTIVA
CONJUNCTIVAE
CONJUNCTIVAL
CONJUNCTIVAS
CONJUNCTIVE
CONJUNCTIVELY
CONJUNCTIVENESS
CONJUNCTIVES
CONJUNCTIVITIS
CONJUNCTLY
CONJUNCTURAL
CONJUNCTURE
CONJUNCTURES
CONJURATION
CONJURATIONS
CONJURATOR
CONJURATORS
CONJUREMENT
CONJUREMENTS
CONJURINGS
CONLANGERS
CONNASCENCE
CONNASCENCES
CONNASCENCIES
CONNASCENCY
CONNASCENT
CONNATENESS
CONNATENESSES
CONNATIONS
CONNATURAL
CONNATURALISE
CONNATURALISED
CONNATURALISES
CONNATURALISING
CONNATURALITIES
CONNATURALITY
CONNATURALIZE
CONNATURALIZED
CONNATURALIZES
CONNATURALIZING
CONNATURALLY
CONNATURALNESS
CONNATURES
CONNECTABLE
CONNECTEDLY
CONNECTEDNESS
CONNECTEDNESSES
CONNECTERS
CONNECTIBLE

CONNECTING
CONNECTION
CONNECTIONAL
CONNECTIONISM
CONNECTIONISMS
CONNECTIONS
CONNECTIVE
CONNECTIVELY
CONNECTIVES
CONNECTIVITIES
CONNECTIVITY
CONNECTORS
CONNEXIONAL
CONNEXIONS
CONNIPTION
CONNIPTIONS
CONNIVANCE
CONNIVANCES
CONNIVANCIES
CONNIVANCY
CONNIVENCE
CONNIVENCES
CONNIVENCIES
CONNIVENCY
CONNIVENTLY
CONNIVERIES
CONNIVINGLY
CONNIVINGS
CONNOISSEUR
CONNOISSEURS
CONNOISSEURSHIP
CONNOTATED
CONNOTATES
CONNOTATING
CONNOTATION
CONNOTATIONAL
CONNOTATIONS
CONNOTATIVE
CONNOTATIVELY
CONNOTIVELY
CONNUBIALISM
CONNUBIALISMS
CONNUBIALITIES
CONNUBIALITY
CONNUBIALLY
CONNUMERATE
CONNUMERATED
CONNUMERATES
CONNUMERATING
CONNUMERATION
CONNUMERATIONS
CONOIDALLY
CONOIDICAL
CONOMINEES
CONOSCENTE
CONOSCENTI
CONQUERABILITY
CONQUERABLE
CONQUERABLENESS
CONQUERERS
CONQUERESS
CONQUERESSES
CONQUERING
CONQUERINGLY
CONQUERORS
CONQUISTADOR
CONQUISTADORES
CONQUISTADORS
CONSANGUINE
CONSANGUINEOUS
CONSANGUINITIES
CONSANGUINITY
CONSCIENCE
CONSCIENCELESS
CONSCIENCES
CONSCIENTIOUS
CONSCIENTIOUSLY
CONSCIENTISE
CONSCIENTISED
CONSCIENTISES
CONSCIENTISING
CONSCIENTIZE
CONSCIENTIZED
CONSCIENTIZES
CONSCIENTIZING
CONSCIONABILITY
CONSCIONABLE
CONSCIONABLY
CONSCIOUSES
CONSCIOUSLY
CONSCIOUSNESS
CONSCIOUSNESSES
CONSCRIBED
CONSCRIBES
CONSCRIBING
CONSCRIPTED
CONSCRIPTING
CONSCRIPTION
CONSCRIPTIONAL
CONSCRIPTIONIST
CONSCRIPTIONS
CONSCRIPTS
CONSECRATE
CONSECRATED
CONSECRATEDNESS
CONSECRATES
CONSECRATING
CONSECRATION
CONSECRATIONS
CONSECRATIVE
CONSECRATOR
CONSECRATORS
CONSECRATORY
CONSECTANEOUS
CONSECTARIES
CONSECTARY
CONSECUTION
CONSECUTIONS
CONSECUTIVE
CONSECUTIVELY
CONSECUTIVENESS
CONSENESCENCE
CONSENESCENCES
CONSENESCENCIES
CONSENESCENCY
CONSENSION
CONSENSIONS
CONSENSUAL
CONSENSUALLY
CONSENSUSES
CONSENTANEITIES
CONSENTANEITY
CONSENTANEOUS
CONSENTANEOUSLY
CONSENTERS
CONSENTIENCE
CONSENTIENCES
CONSENTIENT
CONSENTING
CONSENTINGLY
CONSEQUENCE
CONSEQUENCED
CONSEQUENCES
CONSEQUENCING
CONSEQUENT
CONSEQUENTIAL
CONSEQUENTIALLY
CONSEQUENTLY
CONSEQUENTS
CONSERVABLE
CONSERVANCIES
CONSERVANCY
CONSERVANT
CONSERVATION
CONSERVATIONAL
CONSERVATIONIST
CONSERVATIONS
CONSERVATISE
CONSERVATISED
CONSERVATISES
CONSERVATISING
CONSERVATISM
CONSERVATISMS
CONSERVATIVE
CONSERVATIVELY
CONSERVATIVES
CONSERVATIZE
CONSERVATIZED
CONSERVATIZES
CONSERVATIZING
CONSERVATOIRE
CONSERVATOIRES
CONSERVATOR
CONSERVATORIA
CONSERVATORIAL
CONSERVATORIES
CONSERVATORIUM
CONSERVATORIUMS
CONSERVATORS
CONSERVATORSHIP
CONSERVATORY
CONSERVATRICES
CONSERVATRIX
CONSERVATRIXES
CONSERVERS
CONSERVING
CONSIDERABLE
CONSIDERABLES
CONSIDERABLY
CONSIDERANCE
CONSIDERANCES
CONSIDERATE
CONSIDERATELY
CONSIDERATENESS
CONSIDERATION
CONSIDERATIONS
CONSIDERATIVE
CONSIDERATIVELY
CONSIDERED
CONSIDERER
CONSIDERERS
CONSIDERING
CONSIDERINGLY
CONSIGLIERE
CONSIGLIERES
CONSIGLIERI
CONSIGNABLE
CONSIGNATION
CONSIGNATIONS
CONSIGNATORIES
CONSIGNATORY
CONSIGNEES
CONSIGNERS
CONSIGNIFIED
CONSIGNIFIES
CONSIGNIFY
CONSIGNIFYING
CONSIGNING
CONSIGNMENT
CONSIGNMENTS
CONSIGNORS
CONSILIENCE
CONSILIENCES
CONSILIENT
CONSIMILAR
CONSIMILARITIES
CONSIMILARITY
CONSIMILITIES
CONSIMILITUDE
CONSIMILITUDES
CONSIMILITY
CONSISTENCE
CONSISTENCES
CONSISTENCIES
CONSISTENCY
CONSISTENT
CONSISTENTLY
CONSISTING
CONSISTORIAL
CONSISTORIAN

CONSISTORIES
CONSISTORY
CONSOCIATE
CONSOCIATED
CONSOCIATES
CONSOCIATING
CONSOCIATION
CONSOCIATIONAL
CONSOCIATIONS
CONSOLABLE
CONSOLATED
CONSOLATES
CONSOLATING
CONSOLATION
CONSOLATIONS
CONSOLATORIES
CONSOLATORY
CONSOLATRICES
CONSOLATRIX
CONSOLATRIXES
CONSOLEMENT
CONSOLEMENTS
CONSOLIDATE
CONSOLIDATED
CONSOLIDATES
CONSOLIDATING
CONSOLIDATION
CONSOLIDATIONS
CONSOLIDATIVE
CONSOLIDATOR
CONSOLIDATORS
CONSOLINGLY
CONSONANCE
CONSONANCES
CONSONANCIES
CONSONANCY
CONSONANTAL
CONSONANTALLY
CONSONANTLY
CONSONANTS
CONSORTABLE
CONSORTERS
CONSORTIAL
CONSORTING
CONSORTISM
CONSORTISMS
CONSORTIUM
CONSORTIUMS
CONSPECIFIC
CONSPECIFICS
CONSPECTUITIES
CONSPECTUITY
CONSPECTUS
CONSPECTUSES
CONSPICUITIES
CONSPICUITY
CONSPICUOUS
CONSPICUOUSLY
CONSPICUOUSNESS
CONSPIRACIES
CONSPIRACY
CONSPIRANT
CONSPIRANTS
CONSPIRATION
CONSPIRATIONAL
CONSPIRATIONS
CONSPIRATOR
CONSPIRATORIAL
CONSPIRATORS
CONSPIRATORY
CONSPIRATRESS
CONSPIRATRESSES
CONSPIRERS
CONSPIRING
CONSPIRINGLY
CONSPURCATION
CONSPURCATIONS
CONSTABLES
CONSTABLESHIP
CONSTABLESHIPS
CONSTABLEWICK
CONSTABLEWICKS
CONSTABULARIES
CONSTABULARY
CONSTANCIES
CONSTANTAN
CONSTANTANS
CONSTANTLY
CONSTATATION
CONSTATATIONS
CONSTATING
CONSTATIVE
CONSTATIVES
CONSTELLATE
CONSTELLATED
CONSTELLATES
CONSTELLATING
CONSTELLATION
CONSTELLATIONAL
CONSTELLATIONS
CONSTELLATORY
CONSTERING
CONSTERNATE
CONSTERNATED
CONSTERNATES
CONSTERNATING
CONSTERNATION
CONSTERNATIONS
CONSTIPATE
CONSTIPATED
CONSTIPATES
CONSTIPATING
CONSTIPATION
CONSTIPATIONS
CONSTITUENCIES
CONSTITUENCY
CONSTITUENT
CONSTITUENTLY
CONSTITUENTS
CONSTITUTE
CONSTITUTED
CONSTITUTER
CONSTITUTERS
CONSTITUTES
CONSTITUTING
CONSTITUTION
CONSTITUTIONAL
CONSTITUTIONALS
CONSTITUTIONIST
CONSTITUTIONS
CONSTITUTIVE
CONSTITUTIVELY
CONSTITUTOR
CONSTITUTORS
CONSTRAINABLE
CONSTRAINED
CONSTRAINEDLY
CONSTRAINER
CONSTRAINERS
CONSTRAINING
CONSTRAINS
CONSTRAINT
CONSTRAINTS
CONSTRICTED
CONSTRICTING
CONSTRICTION
CONSTRICTIONS
CONSTRICTIVE
CONSTRICTIVELY
CONSTRICTOR
CONSTRICTORS
CONSTRICTS
CONSTRINGE
CONSTRINGED
CONSTRINGENCE
CONSTRINGENCES
CONSTRINGENCIES
CONSTRINGENCY
CONSTRINGENT
CONSTRINGES
CONSTRINGING
CONSTRUABILITY
CONSTRUABLE
CONSTRUALS
CONSTRUCTABLE
CONSTRUCTED
CONSTRUCTER
CONSTRUCTERS
CONSTRUCTIBLE
CONSTRUCTING
CONSTRUCTION
CONSTRUCTIONAL
CONSTRUCTIONISM
CONSTRUCTIONIST
CONSTRUCTIONS
CONSTRUCTIVE
CONSTRUCTIVELY
CONSTRUCTIVISM
CONSTRUCTIVISMS
CONSTRUCTIVIST
CONSTRUCTIVISTS
CONSTRUCTOR
CONSTRUCTORS
CONSTRUCTS
CONSTRUCTURE
CONSTRUCTURES
CONSTRUERS
CONSTRUING
CONSTUPRATE
CONSTUPRATED
CONSTUPRATES
CONSTUPRATING
CONSTUPRATION
CONSTUPRATIONS
CONSUBSIST
CONSUBSISTED
CONSUBSISTING
CONSUBSISTS
CONSUBSTANTIAL
CONSUBSTANTIATE
CONSUETUDE
CONSUETUDES
CONSUETUDINARY
CONSULAGES
CONSULATES
CONSULSHIP
CONSULSHIPS
CONSULTABLE
CONSULTANCIES
CONSULTANCY
CONSULTANT
CONSULTANTS
CONSULTANTSHIP
CONSULTANTSHIPS
CONSULTATION
CONSULTATIONS
CONSULTATIVE
CONSULTATIVELY
CONSULTATORY
CONSULTEES
CONSULTERS
CONSULTING
CONSULTINGS
CONSULTIVE
CONSULTORS
CONSULTORY
CONSUMABLE
CONSUMABLES
CONSUMEDLY
CONSUMERISM
CONSUMERISMS
CONSUMERIST
CONSUMERISTIC
CONSUMERISTS
CONSUMERSHIP
CONSUMERSHIPS
CONSUMINGLY
CONSUMINGS
CONSUMMATE
CONSUMMATED

CONSUMMATELY
CONSUMMATES
CONSUMMATING
CONSUMMATION
CONSUMMATIONS
CONSUMMATIVE
CONSUMMATOR
CONSUMMATORS
CONSUMMATORY
CONSUMPTION
CONSUMPTIONS
CONSUMPTIVE
CONSUMPTIVELY
CONSUMPTIVENESS
CONSUMPTIVES
CONSUMPTIVITIES
CONSUMPTIVITY
CONTABESCENCE
CONTABESCENCES
CONTABESCENT
CONTACTABLE
CONTACTEES
CONTACTING
CONTACTLESS
CONTACTORS
CONTACTUAL
CONTACTUALLY
CONTADINAS
CONTADINOS
CONTAGIONIST
CONTAGIONISTS
CONTAGIONS
CONTAGIOUS
CONTAGIOUSLY
CONTAGIOUSNESS
CONTAINABLE
CONTAINERBOARD
CONTAINERBOARDS
CONTAINERISE
CONTAINERISED
CONTAINERISES
CONTAINERISING
CONTAINERIZE
CONTAINERIZED
CONTAINERIZES
CONTAINERIZING
CONTAINERLESS
CONTAINERPORT
CONTAINERPORTS
CONTAINERS
CONTAINERSHIP
CONTAINERSHIPS
CONTAINING
CONTAINMENT
CONTAINMENTS
CONTAMINABLE
CONTAMINANT
CONTAMINANTS
CONTAMINATE
CONTAMINATED
CONTAMINATES
CONTAMINATING
CONTAMINATION
CONTAMINATIONS
CONTAMINATIVE
CONTAMINATOR
CONTAMINATORS
CONTANGOED
CONTANGOES
CONTANGOING
CONTEMNERS
CONTEMNIBLE
CONTEMNIBLY
CONTEMNING
CONTEMNORS
CONTEMPERATION
CONTEMPERATIONS
CONTEMPERATURE
CONTEMPERATURES
CONTEMPERED
CONTEMPERING
CONTEMPERS
CONTEMPLABLE
CONTEMPLANT
CONTEMPLANTS
CONTEMPLATE
CONTEMPLATED
CONTEMPLATES
CONTEMPLATING
CONTEMPLATION
CONTEMPLATIONS
CONTEMPLATIST
CONTEMPLATISTS
CONTEMPLATIVE
CONTEMPLATIVELY
CONTEMPLATIVES
CONTEMPLATOR
CONTEMPLATORS
CONTEMPORANEAN
CONTEMPORANEANS
CONTEMPORANEITY
CONTEMPORANEOUS
CONTEMPORARIES
CONTEMPORARILY
CONTEMPORARY
CONTEMPORISE
CONTEMPORISED
CONTEMPORISES
CONTEMPORISING
CONTEMPORIZE
CONTEMPORIZED
CONTEMPORIZES
CONTEMPORIZING
CONTEMPTIBILITY
CONTEMPTIBLE
CONTEMPTIBLY
CONTEMPTUOUS
CONTEMPTUOUSLY
CONTENDENT
CONTENDENTS
CONTENDERS
CONTENDING
CONTENDINGLY
CONTENDINGS
CONTENEMENT
CONTENEMENTS
CONTENTATION
CONTENTATIONS
CONTENTEDLY
CONTENTEDNESS
CONTENTEDNESSES
CONTENTING
CONTENTION
CONTENTIONS
CONTENTIOUS
CONTENTIOUSLY
CONTENTIOUSNESS
CONTENTLESS
CONTENTMENT
CONTENTMENTS
CONTERMINAL
CONTERMINALLY
CONTERMINANT
CONTERMINATE
CONTERMINOUS
CONTERMINOUSLY
CONTESSERATION
CONTESSERATIONS
CONTESTABILITY
CONTESTABLE
CONTESTABLENESS
CONTESTABLY
CONTESTANT
CONTESTANTS
CONTESTATION
CONTESTATIONS
CONTESTERS
CONTESTING
CONTESTINGLY
CONTEXTLESS
CONTEXTUAL
CONTEXTUALISE
CONTEXTUALISED
CONTEXTUALISES
CONTEXTUALISING
CONTEXTUALIZE
CONTEXTUALIZED
CONTEXTUALIZES
CONTEXTUALIZING
CONTEXTUALLY
CONTEXTURAL
CONTEXTURE
CONTEXTURES
CONTIGNATION
CONTIGNATIONS
CONTIGUITIES
CONTIGUITY
CONTIGUOUS
CONTIGUOUSLY
CONTIGUOUSNESS
CONTINENCE
CONTINENCES
CONTINENCIES
CONTINENCY
CONTINENTAL
CONTINENTALISM
CONTINENTALISMS
CONTINENTALIST
CONTINENTALISTS
CONTINENTALLY
CONTINENTALS
CONTINENTLY
CONTINENTS
CONTINGENCE
CONTINGENCES
CONTINGENCIES
CONTINGENCY
CONTINGENT
CONTINGENTLY
CONTINGENTS
CONTINUABLE
CONTINUALITIES
CONTINUALITY
CONTINUALLY
CONTINUALNESS
CONTINUALNESSES
CONTINUANCE
CONTINUANCES
CONTINUANT
CONTINUANTS
CONTINUATE
CONTINUATION
CONTINUATIONS
CONTINUATIVE
CONTINUATIVELY
CONTINUATIVES
CONTINUATOR
CONTINUATORS
CONTINUEDLY
CONTINUEDNESS
CONTINUEDNESSES
CONTINUERS
CONTINUING
CONTINUINGLY
CONTINUITIES
CONTINUITY
CONTINUOUS
CONTINUOUSLY
CONTINUOUSNESS
CONTINUUMS
CONTORNIATE
CONTORNIATES
CONTORTEDLY
CONTORTEDNESS
CONTORTEDNESSES
CONTORTING
CONTORTION
CONTORTIONAL
CONTORTIONATE
CONTORTIONED

CONTORTIONISM
CONTORTIONISMS
CONTORTIONIST
CONTORTIONISTIC
CONTORTIONISTS
CONTORTIONS
CONTORTIVE
CONTOURING
CONTRABAND
CONTRABANDISM
CONTRABANDISMS
CONTRABANDIST
CONTRABANDISTS
CONTRABANDS
CONTRABASS
CONTRABASSES
CONTRABASSI
CONTRABASSIST
CONTRABASSISTS
CONTRABASSO
CONTRABASSOON
CONTRABASSOONS
CONTRABASSOS
CONTRABBASSI
CONTRABBASSO
CONTRABBASSOS
CONTRACEPTION
CONTRACEPTIONS
CONTRACEPTIVE
CONTRACEPTIVES
CONTRACLOCKWISE
CONTRACTABILITY
CONTRACTABLE
CONTRACTABLY
CONTRACTED
CONTRACTEDLY
CONTRACTEDNESS
CONTRACTIBILITY
CONTRACTIBLE
CONTRACTIBLY
CONTRACTILE
CONTRACTILITIES
CONTRACTILITY
CONTRACTING
CONTRACTION
CONTRACTIONAL
CONTRACTIONARY
CONTRACTIONS
CONTRACTIVE
CONTRACTIVELY
CONTRACTIVENESS
CONTRACTOR
CONTRACTORS
CONTRACTUAL
CONTRACTUALLY
CONTRACTURAL
CONTRACTURE
CONTRACTURES
CONTRACYCLICAL
CONTRADANCE
CONTRADANCES
CONTRADICT
CONTRADICTABLE
CONTRADICTED
CONTRADICTER
CONTRADICTERS
CONTRADICTING
CONTRADICTION
CONTRADICTIONS
CONTRADICTIOUS
CONTRADICTIVE
CONTRADICTIVELY
CONTRADICTOR
CONTRADICTORIES
CONTRADICTORILY
CONTRADICTORS
CONTRADICTORY
CONTRADICTS
CONTRAFAGOTTI
CONTRAFAGOTTO
CONTRAFAGOTTOS
CONTRAFLOW
CONTRAFLOWS
CONTRAGESTION
CONTRAGESTIONS
CONTRAGESTIVE
CONTRAGESTIVES
CONTRAHENT
CONTRAHENTS
CONTRAINDICANT
CONTRAINDICANTS
CONTRAINDICATE
CONTRAINDICATED
CONTRAINDICATES
CONTRALATERAL
CONTRALTOS
CONTRANATANT
CONTRAOCTAVE
CONTRAOCTAVES
CONTRAPLEX
CONTRAPOSITION
CONTRAPOSITIONS
CONTRAPOSITIVE
CONTRAPOSITIVES
CONTRAPPOSTO
CONTRAPPOSTOS
CONTRAPROP
CONTRAPROPELLER
CONTRAPROPS
CONTRAPTION
CONTRAPTIONS
CONTRAPUNTAL
CONTRAPUNTALIST
CONTRAPUNTALLY
CONTRAPUNTIST
CONTRAPUNTISTS
CONTRARIAN
CONTRARIANS
CONTRARIED
CONTRARIES
CONTRARIETIES
CONTRARIETY
CONTRARILY
CONTRARINESS
CONTRARINESSES
CONTRARIOUS
CONTRARIOUSLY
CONTRARIOUSNESS
CONTRARIWISE
CONTRARYING
CONTRASEXUAL
CONTRASEXUALS
CONTRASTABLE
CONTRASTABLY
CONTRASTED
CONTRASTIER
CONTRASTIEST
CONTRASTING
CONTRASTINGLY
CONTRASTIVE
CONTRASTIVELY
CONTRATERRENE
CONTRAVALLATION
CONTRAVENE
CONTRAVENED
CONTRAVENER
CONTRAVENERS
CONTRAVENES
CONTRAVENING
CONTRAVENTION
CONTRAVENTIONS
CONTRAYERVA
CONTRAYERVAS
CONTRECOUP
CONTRECOUPS
CONTREDANCE
CONTREDANCES
CONTREDANSE
CONTREDANSES
CONTRETEMPS
CONTRIBUTABLE
CONTRIBUTARIES
CONTRIBUTARY
CONTRIBUTE
CONTRIBUTED
CONTRIBUTES
CONTRIBUTING
CONTRIBUTION
CONTRIBUTIONS
CONTRIBUTIVE
CONTRIBUTIVELY
CONTRIBUTOR
CONTRIBUTORIES
CONTRIBUTORS
CONTRIBUTORY
CONTRISTATION
CONTRISTATIONS
CONTRISTED
CONTRISTING
CONTRITELY
CONTRITENESS
CONTRITENESSES
CONTRITION
CONTRITIONS
CONTRITURATE
CONTRITURATED
CONTRITURATES
CONTRITURATING
CONTRIVABLE
CONTRIVANCE
CONTRIVANCES
CONTRIVEMENT
CONTRIVEMENTS
CONTRIVERS
CONTRIVING
CONTROLLABILITY
CONTROLLABLE
CONTROLLABLY
CONTROLLED
CONTROLLER
CONTROLLERS
CONTROLLERSHIP
CONTROLLERSHIPS
CONTROLLING
CONTROLMENT
CONTROLMENTS
CONTROULED
CONTROULING
CONTROVERSE
CONTROVERSES
CONTROVERSIAL
CONTROVERSIALLY
CONTROVERSIES
CONTROVERSY
CONTROVERT
CONTROVERTED
CONTROVERTER
CONTROVERTERS
CONTROVERTIBLE
CONTROVERTIBLY
CONTROVERTING
CONTROVERTIST
CONTROVERTISTS
CONTROVERTS
CONTUBERNAL
CONTUBERNYAL
CONTUMACIES
CONTUMACIOUS
CONTUMACIOUSLY
CONTUMACITIES
CONTUMACITY
CONTUMELIES
CONTUMELIOUS
CONTUMELIOUSLY
CONTUNDING
CONTUSIONED
CONTUSIONS
CONUNDRUMS
CONURBATION
CONURBATIONS

CONVALESCE
CONVALESCED
CONVALESCENCE
CONVALESCENCES
CONVALESCENCIES
CONVALESCENCY
CONVALESCENT
CONVALESCENTLY
CONVALESCENTS
CONVALESCES
CONVALESCING
CONVECTING
CONVECTION
CONVECTIONAL
CONVECTIONS
CONVECTIVE
CONVECTORS
CONVENABLE
CONVENANCE
CONVENANCES
CONVENERSHIP
CONVENERSHIPS
CONVENIENCE
CONVENIENCES
CONVENIENCIES
CONVENIENCY
CONVENIENT
CONVENIENTLY
CONVENINGS
CONVENORSHIP
CONVENORSHIPS
CONVENTICLE
CONVENTICLED
CONVENTICLER
CONVENTICLERS
CONVENTICLES
CONVENTICLING
CONVENTING
CONVENTION
CONVENTIONAL
CONVENTIONALISE
CONVENTIONALISM
CONVENTIONALIST
CONVENTIONALITY
CONVENTIONALIZE
CONVENTIONALLY
CONVENTIONALS
CONVENTIONARY
CONVENTIONEER
CONVENTIONEERS
CONVENTIONER
CONVENTIONERS
CONVENTIONIST
CONVENTIONISTS
CONVENTIONS
CONVENTUAL
CONVENTUALLY
CONVENTUALS
CONVERGENCE
CONVERGENCES
CONVERGENCIES
CONVERGENCY
CONVERGENT
CONVERGING
CONVERSABLE
CONVERSABLENESS
CONVERSABLY
CONVERSANCE
CONVERSANCES
CONVERSANCIES
CONVERSANCY
CONVERSANT
CONVERSANTLY
CONVERSATION
CONVERSATIONAL
CONVERSATIONISM
CONVERSATIONIST
CONVERSATIONS
CONVERSATIVE
CONVERSAZIONE
CONVERSAZIONES
CONVERSAZIONI
CONVERSELY
CONVERSERS
CONVERSING
CONVERSION
CONVERSIONAL
CONVERSIONARY
CONVERSIONS
CONVERTAPLANE
CONVERTAPLANES
CONVERTEND
CONVERTENDS
CONVERTERS
CONVERTIBILITY
CONVERTIBLE
CONVERTIBLENESS
CONVERTIBLES
CONVERTIBLY
CONVERTING
CONVERTIPLANE
CONVERTIPLANES
CONVERTITE
CONVERTITES
CONVERTIVE
CONVERTOPLANE
CONVERTOPLANES
CONVERTORS
CONVEXEDLY
CONVEXITIES
CONVEXNESS
CONVEXNESSES
CONVEYABLE
CONVEYANCE
CONVEYANCER
CONVEYANCERS
CONVEYANCES
CONVEYANCING
CONVEYANCINGS
CONVEYORISATION
CONVEYORISE
CONVEYORISED
CONVEYORISES
CONVEYORISING
CONVEYORIZATION
CONVEYORIZE
CONVEYORIZED
CONVEYORIZES
CONVEYORIZING
CONVICINITIES
CONVICINITY
CONVICTABLE
CONVICTIBLE
CONVICTING
CONVICTION
CONVICTIONAL
CONVICTIONS
CONVICTISM
CONVICTISMS
CONVICTIVE
CONVICTIVELY
CONVINCEMENT
CONVINCEMENTS
CONVINCERS
CONVINCIBLE
CONVINCING
CONVINCINGLY
CONVINCINGNESS
CONVIVIALIST
CONVIVIALISTS
CONVIVIALITIES
CONVIVIALITY
CONVIVIALLY
CONVOCATED
CONVOCATES
CONVOCATING
CONVOCATION
CONVOCATIONAL
CONVOCATIONIST
CONVOCATIONISTS
CONVOCATIONS
CONVOCATIVE
CONVOCATOR
CONVOCATORS
CONVOLUTED
CONVOLUTEDLY
CONVOLUTEDNESS
CONVOLUTELY
CONVOLUTES
CONVOLUTING
CONVOLUTION
CONVOLUTIONAL
CONVOLUTIONARY
CONVOLUTIONS
CONVOLVING
CONVOLVULACEOUS
CONVOLVULI
CONVOLVULUS
CONVOLVULUSES
CONVULSANT
CONVULSANTS
CONVULSIBLE
CONVULSING
CONVULSION
CONVULSIONAL
CONVULSIONARIES
CONVULSIONARY
CONVULSIONIST
CONVULSIONISTS
CONVULSIONS
CONVULSIVE
CONVULSIVELY
CONVULSIVENESS
COOKHOUSES
COOKSHACKS
COOKSTOVES
COOLHEADED
COOLHOUSES
COOLINGNESS
COOLINGNESSES
COOLNESSES
COOMCEILED
COONHOUNDS
COOPERAGES
COOPERATED
COOPERATES
COOPERATING
COOPERATION
COOPERATIONIST
COOPERATIONISTS
COOPERATIONS
COOPERATIVE
COOPERATIVELY
COOPERATIVENESS
COOPERATIVES
COOPERATIVITIES
COOPERATIVITY
COOPERATOR
COOPERATORS
COOPERINGS
COOPTATION
COOPTATIONS
COOPTATIVE
COORDINANCE
COORDINANCES
COORDINATE
COORDINATED
COORDINATELY
COORDINATENESS
COORDINATES
COORDINATING
COORDINATION
COORDINATIONS
COORDINATIVE
COORDINATOR
COORDINATORS
COPARCENARIES
COPARCENARY
COPARCENER
COPARCENERIES

COPARCENERS
COPARCENERY
COPARCENIES
COPARENTED
COPARENTING
COPARTNERED
COPARTNERIES
COPARTNERING
COPARTNERS
COPARTNERSHIP
COPARTNERSHIPS
COPARTNERY
COPATRIOTS
COPAYMENTS
COPERNICIUM
COPERNICIUMS
COPESETTIC
COPESTONES
COPILOTING
COPINGSTONE
COPINGSTONES
COPIOUSNESS
COPIOUSNESSES
COPLAINTIFF
COPLAINTIFFS
COPLANARITIES
COPLANARITY
COPLOTTING
COPLOTTINGS
COPOLYMERIC
COPOLYMERISE
COPOLYMERISED
COPOLYMERISES
COPOLYMERISING
COPOLYMERIZE
COPOLYMERIZED
COPOLYMERIZES
COPOLYMERIZING
COPOLYMERS
COPPERASES
COPPERHEAD
COPPERHEADS
COPPERIEST
COPPERINGS
COPPERPLATE
COPPERPLATES
COPPERSKIN
COPPERSKINS
COPPERSMITH
COPPERSMITHS
COPPERWORK
COPPERWORKS
COPPERWORM
COPPERWORMS
COPPICINGS
COPRAEMIAS
COPRESENCE
COPRESENCES
COPRESENTED
COPRESENTING
COPRESENTS
COPRESIDENT
COPRESIDENTS
COPRINCIPAL
COPRINCIPALS
COPRISONER
COPRISONERS
COPROCESSING
COPROCESSINGS
COPROCESSOR
COPROCESSORS
COPRODUCED
COPRODUCER
COPRODUCERS
COPRODUCES
COPRODUCING
COPRODUCTION
COPRODUCTIONS
COPRODUCTS
COPROLALIA
COPROLALIAC
COPROLALIAS
COPROLITES
COPROLITHS
COPROLITIC
COPROLOGIES
COPROMOTER
COPROMOTERS
COPROPHAGAN
COPROPHAGANS
COPROPHAGIC
COPROPHAGIES
COPROPHAGIST
COPROPHAGISTS
COPROPHAGOUS
COPROPHAGY
COPROPHILIA
COPROPHILIAC
COPROPHILIACS
COPROPHILIAS
COPROPHILIC
COPROPHILOUS
COPROPRIETOR
COPROPRIETORS
COPROSPERITIES
COPROSPERITY
COPROSTEROL
COPROSTEROLS
COPSEWOODS
COPUBLISHED
COPUBLISHER
COPUBLISHERS
COPUBLISHES
COPUBLISHING
COPULATING
COPULATION
COPULATIONS
COPULATIVE
COPULATIVELY
COPULATIVES
COPULATORY
COPURIFIED
COPURIFIES
COPURIFYING
COPYCATTED
COPYCATTING
COPYEDITED
COPYEDITING
COPYFIGHTS
COPYGRAPHS
COPYHOLDER
COPYHOLDERS
COPYLEFTED
COPYLEFTING
COPYREADER
COPYREADERS
COPYREADING
COPYREADINGS
COPYRIGHTABLE
COPYRIGHTED
COPYRIGHTER
COPYRIGHTERS
COPYRIGHTING
COPYRIGHTS
COPYTAKERS
COPYWRITER
COPYWRITERS
COPYWRITING
COPYWRITINGS
COQUELICOT
COQUELICOTS
COQUETRIES
COQUETTING
COQUETTISH
COQUETTISHLY
COQUETTISHNESS
COQUIMBITE
COQUIMBITES
CORACIIFORM
CORADICATE
CORALBELLS
CORALBERRIES
CORALBERRY
CORALLACEOUS
CORALLIFEROUS
CORALLIFORM
CORALLIGENOUS
CORALLINES
CORALLITES
CORALLOIDAL
CORALLOIDS
CORALROOTS
CORALWORTS
CORBEILLES
CORBELINGS
CORBELLING
CORBELLINGS
CORBICULAE
CORBICULATE
CORDECTOMIES
CORDECTOMY
CORDELLING
CORDGRASSES
CORDIALISE
CORDIALISED
CORDIALISES
CORDIALISING
CORDIALITIES
CORDIALITY
CORDIALIZE
CORDIALIZED
CORDIALIZES
CORDIALIZING
CORDIALNESS
CORDIALNESSES
CORDIERITE
CORDIERITES
CORDILLERA
CORDILLERAN
CORDILLERAS
CORDLESSES
CORDOCENTESES
CORDOCENTESIS
CORDONNETS
CORDOTOMIES
CORDUROYED
CORDUROYING
CORDWAINER
CORDWAINERIES
CORDWAINERS
CORDWAINERY
CORDYLINES
CORECIPIENT
CORECIPIENTS
COREDEEMED
COREDEEMING
COREFERENTIAL
COREGONINE
CORELATING
CORELATION
CORELATIONS
CORELATIVE
CORELATIVES
CORELIGIONIST
CORELIGIONISTS
COREOPSISES
COREPRESSOR
COREPRESSORS
COREQUISITE
COREQUISITES
CORESEARCHER
CORESEARCHERS
CORESIDENT
CORESIDENTIAL
CORESIDENTS
CORESPONDENT
CORESPONDENTS
CORFHOUSES
CORIACEOUS
CORIANDERS

CORINTHIANISE
CORINTHIANISED
CORINTHIANISES
CORINTHIANISING
CORINTHIANIZE
CORINTHIANIZED
CORINTHIANIZES
CORINTHIANIZING
CORIVALLED
CORIVALLING
CORIVALRIES
CORIVALSHIP
CORIVALSHIPS
CORKBOARDS
CORKBORERS
CORKINESSES
CORKSCREWED
CORKSCREWING
CORKSCREWS
CORMOPHYTE
CORMOPHYTES
CORMOPHYTIC
CORMORANTS
CORNACEOUS
CORNBORERS
CORNBRAIDED
CORNBRAIDING
CORNBRAIDS
CORNBRANDIES
CORNBRANDY
CORNBRASHES
CORNBREADS
CORNCOCKLE
CORNCOCKLES
CORNCRAKES
CORNEITISES
CORNELIANS
CORNEMUSES
CORNERBACK
CORNERBACKS
CORNERINGS
CORNERSTONE
CORNERSTONES
CORNERWAYS
CORNERWISE
CORNETCIES
CORNETISTS
CORNETTINI
CORNETTINO
CORNETTINOS
CORNETTIST
CORNETTISTS
CORNFIELDS
CORNFLAKES
CORNFLOURS
CORNFLOWER
CORNFLOWERS
CORNHUSKER
CORNHUSKERS
CORNHUSKING
CORNHUSKINGS
CORNICHONS
CORNICINGS
CORNICULATE
CORNICULUM
CORNICULUMS
CORNIFEROUS
CORNIFICATION
CORNIFICATIONS
CORNIFYING
CORNIGEROUS
CORNINESSES
CORNOPEANS
CORNROWING
CORNSTALKS
CORNSTARCH
CORNSTARCHES
CORNSTONES
CORNUCOPIA
CORNUCOPIAN
CORNUCOPIAS
COROLLACEOUS
COROLLARIES
COROLLIFLORAL
COROLLIFLOROUS
COROLLIFORM
COROMANDEL
COROMANDELS
CORONAGRAPH
CORONAGRAPHS
CORONARIES
CORONATING
CORONATION
CORONATIONS
CORONAVIRUS
CORONAVIRUSES
CORONERSHIP
CORONERSHIPS
CORONOGRAPH
CORONOGRAPHS
COROTATING
COROTATION
COROTATIONS
CORPORALES
CORPORALITIES
CORPORALITY
CORPORALLY
CORPORALSHIP
CORPORALSHIPS
CORPORASES
CORPORATELY
CORPORATENESS
CORPORATENESSES
CORPORATES
CORPORATION
CORPORATIONS
CORPORATISE
CORPORATISED
CORPORATISES
CORPORATISING
CORPORATISM
CORPORATISMS
CORPORATIST
CORPORATISTS
CORPORATIVE
CORPORATIVISM
CORPORATIVISMS
CORPORATIZE
CORPORATIZED
CORPORATIZES
CORPORATIZING
CORPORATOR
CORPORATORS
CORPOREALISE
CORPOREALISED
CORPOREALISES
CORPOREALISING
CORPOREALISM
CORPOREALISMS
CORPOREALIST
CORPOREALISTS
CORPOREALITIES
CORPOREALITY
CORPOREALIZE
CORPOREALIZED
CORPOREALIZES
CORPOREALIZING
CORPOREALLY
CORPOREALNESS
CORPOREALNESSES
CORPOREITIES
CORPOREITY
CORPORIFICATION
CORPORIFIED
CORPORIFIES
CORPORIFYING
CORPOSANTS
CORPSELIKE
CORPULENCE
CORPULENCES
CORPULENCIES
CORPULENCY
CORPULENTLY
CORPUSCLES
CORPUSCULAR
CORPUSCULARIAN
CORPUSCULARIANS
CORPUSCULARITY
CORPUSCULE
CORPUSCULES
CORRALLING
CORRASIONS
CORRECTABLE
CORRECTEST
CORRECTIBLE
CORRECTING
CORRECTION
CORRECTIONAL
CORRECTIONER
CORRECTIONERS
CORRECTIONS
CORRECTITUDE
CORRECTITUDES
CORRECTIVE
CORRECTIVELY
CORRECTIVES
CORRECTNESS
CORRECTNESSES
CORRECTORS
CORRECTORY
CORREGIDOR
CORREGIDORS
CORRELATABLE
CORRELATED
CORRELATES
CORRELATING
CORRELATION
CORRELATIONAL
CORRELATIONS
CORRELATIVE
CORRELATIVELY
CORRELATIVENESS
CORRELATIVES
CORRELATIVITIES
CORRELATIVITY
CORRELATOR
CORRELATORS
CORRELIGIONIST
CORRELIGIONISTS
CORREPTION
CORREPTIONS
CORRESPOND
CORRESPONDED
CORRESPONDENCE
CORRESPONDENCES
CORRESPONDENCY
CORRESPONDENT
CORRESPONDENTLY
CORRESPONDENTS
CORRESPONDING
CORRESPONDINGLY
CORRESPONDS
CORRESPONSIVE
CORRIGENDA
CORRIGENDUM
CORRIGENTS
CORRIGIBILITIES
CORRIGIBILITY
CORRIGIBLE
CORRIGIBLY
CORRIVALLED
CORRIVALLING
CORRIVALRIES
CORRIVALRY
CORRIVALSHIP
CORRIVALSHIPS
CORROBORABLE
CORROBORANT
CORROBORATE
CORROBORATED

CORROBORATES
CORROBORATING
CORROBORATION
CORROBORATIONS
CORROBORATIVE
CORROBORATIVELY
CORROBORATIVES
CORROBORATOR
CORROBORATORS
CORROBORATORY
CORROBOREE
CORROBOREED
CORROBOREEING
CORROBOREES
CORRODANTS
CORRODENTS
CORRODIBILITIES
CORRODIBILITY
CORRODIBLE
CORROSIBILITIES
CORROSIBILITY
CORROSIBLE
CORROSIONS
CORROSIVELY
CORROSIVENESS
CORROSIVENESSES
CORROSIVES
CORRUGATED
CORRUGATES
CORRUGATING
CORRUGATION
CORRUGATIONS
CORRUGATOR
CORRUGATORS
CORRUPTERS
CORRUPTEST
CORRUPTIBILITY
CORRUPTIBLE
CORRUPTIBLENESS
CORRUPTIBLY
CORRUPTING
CORRUPTION
CORRUPTIONIST
CORRUPTIONISTS
CORRUPTIONS
CORRUPTIVE
CORRUPTIVELY
CORRUPTNESS
CORRUPTNESSES
CORRUPTORS
CORSELETTE
CORSELETTES
CORSETIERE
CORSETIERES
CORSETIERS
CORSETRIES
CORTICALLY
CORTICATED
CORTICATION
CORTICATIONS
CORTICOIDS
CORTICOLOUS
CORTICOSTEROID
CORTICOSTEROIDS
CORTICOSTERONE
CORTICOSTERONES
CORTICOTROPHIC
CORTICOTROPHIN
CORTICOTROPHINS
CORTICOTROPIC
CORTICOTROPIN
CORTICOTROPINS
CORTISONES
CORUSCATED
CORUSCATES
CORUSCATING
CORUSCATION
CORUSCATIONS
CORVETTING
CORYBANTES
CORYBANTIC
CORYBANTISM
CORYBANTISMS
CORYDALINE
CORYDALINES
CORYDALISES
CORYLOPSES
CORYLOPSIS
CORYMBOSELY
CORYNEBACTERIA
CORYNEBACTERIAL
CORYNEBACTERIUM
CORYNEFORM
CORYPHAEUS
CORYPHENES
COSCINOMANCIES
COSCINOMANCY
COSCRIPTED
COSCRIPTING
COSEISMALS
COSEISMICS
COSENTIENT
COSHERINGS
COSIGNATORIES
COSIGNATORY
COSIGNIFICATIVE
COSINESSES
COSMECEUTICAL
COSMECEUTICALS
COSMETICAL
COSMETICALLY
COSMETICIAN
COSMETICIANS
COSMETICISE
COSMETICISED
COSMETICISES
COSMETICISING
COSMETICISM
COSMETICISMS
COSMETICIZE
COSMETICIZED
COSMETICIZES
COSMETICIZING
COSMETICOLOGIES
COSMETICOLOGY
COSMETOLOGIES
COSMETOLOGIST
COSMETOLOGISTS
COSMETOLOGY
COSMICALLY
COSMOCHEMICAL
COSMOCHEMIST
COSMOCHEMISTRY
COSMOCHEMISTS
COSMOCRATIC
COSMOCRATS
COSMODROME
COSMODROMES
COSMOGENIC
COSMOGENIES
COSMOGONAL
COSMOGONIC
COSMOGONICAL
COSMOGONIES
COSMOGONIST
COSMOGONISTS
COSMOGRAPHER
COSMOGRAPHERS
COSMOGRAPHIC
COSMOGRAPHICAL
COSMOGRAPHIES
COSMOGRAPHIST
COSMOGRAPHISTS
COSMOGRAPHY
COSMOLATRIES
COSMOLATRY
COSMOLINED
COSMOLINES
COSMOLINING
COSMOLOGIC
COSMOLOGICAL
COSMOLOGICALLY
COSMOLOGIES
COSMOLOGIST
COSMOLOGISTS
COSMONAUTICS
COSMONAUTS
COSMOPLASTIC
COSMOPOLIS
COSMOPOLISES
COSMOPOLITAN
COSMOPOLITANISM
COSMOPOLITANS
COSMOPOLITE
COSMOPOLITES
COSMOPOLITIC
COSMOPOLITICAL
COSMOPOLITICS
COSMOPOLITISM
COSMOPOLITISMS
COSMORAMAS
COSMORAMIC
COSMOSPHERE
COSMOSPHERES
COSMOTHEISM
COSMOTHEISMS
COSMOTHETIC
COSMOTHETICAL
COSMOTRONS
COSPONSORED
COSPONSORING
COSPONSORS
COSPONSORSHIP
COSPONSORSHIPS
COSSETTING
COSTALGIAS
COSTARDMONGER
COSTARDMONGERS
COSTARRING
COSTEANING
COSTEANINGS
COSTERMONGER
COSTERMONGERS
COSTIVENESS
COSTIVENESSES
COSTLESSLY
COSTLINESS
COSTLINESSES
COSTMARIES
COSTOTOMIES
COSTUMERIES
COSTUMIERS
COSTUMINGS
COSURFACTANT
COSURFACTANTS
COTANGENTIAL
COTANGENTS
COTELETTES
COTEMPORANEOUS
COTEMPORARY
COTENANCIES
COTERMINOUS
COTERMINOUSLY
COTILLIONS
COTONEASTER
COTONEASTERS
COTRANSDUCE
COTRANSDUCED
COTRANSDUCES
COTRANSDUCING
COTRANSDUCTION
COTRANSDUCTIONS
COTRANSFER
COTRANSFERS
COTRANSPORT
COTRANSPORTED
COTRANSPORTING
COTRANSPORTS
COTRUSTEES
COTTABUSES

COTTAGIEST
COTTAGINGS
COTTERLESS
COTTIERISM
COTTIERISMS
COTTONADES
COTTONIEST
COTTONMOUTH
COTTONMOUTHS
COTTONOCRACIES
COTTONOCRACY
COTTONSEED
COTTONSEEDS
COTTONTAIL
COTTONTAILS
COTTONWEED
COTTONWEEDS
COTTONWOOD
COTTONWOODS
COTURNIXES
COTYLEDONAL
COTYLEDONARY
COTYLEDONOID
COTYLEDONOUS
COTYLEDONS
COTYLIFORM
COTYLOIDAL
COTYLOIDALS
COTYLOSAUR
COTYLOSAURS
COUCHETTES
COUCHSURFING
COUCHSURFINGS
COULIBIACA
COULIBIACAS
COULIBIACS
COULOMBMETER
COULOMBMETERS
COULOMETER
COULOMETERS
COULOMETRIC
COULOMETRICALLY
COULOMETRIES
COULOMETRY
COUMARILIC
COUMARONES
COUNCILLOR
COUNCILLORS
COUNCILLORSHIP
COUNCILLORSHIPS
COUNCILMAN
COUNCILMANIC
COUNCILMEN
COUNCILORS
COUNCILORSHIP
COUNCILORSHIPS
COUNCILWOMAN
COUNCILWOMEN
COUNSELABLE
COUNSELEES
COUNSELING
COUNSELINGS
COUNSELLABLE
COUNSELLED
COUNSELLEE
COUNSELLEES
COUNSELLING
COUNSELLINGS
COUNSELLOR
COUNSELLORS
COUNSELLORSHIP
COUNSELLORSHIPS
COUNSELORS
COUNSELORSHIP
COUNSELORSHIPS
COUNTABILITIES
COUNTABILITY
COUNTBACKS
COUNTDOWNS
COUNTENANCE
COUNTENANCED
COUNTENANCER
COUNTENANCERS
COUNTENANCES
COUNTENANCING
COUNTERACT
COUNTERACTED
COUNTERACTING
COUNTERACTION
COUNTERACTIONS
COUNTERACTIVE
COUNTERACTIVELY
COUNTERACTS
COUNTERAGENT
COUNTERAGENTS
COUNTERARGUE
COUNTERARGUED
COUNTERARGUES
COUNTERARGUING
COUNTERARGUMENT
COUNTERASSAULT
COUNTERASSAULTS
COUNTERATTACK
COUNTERATTACKED
COUNTERATTACKER
COUNTERATTACKS
COUNTERBALANCE
COUNTERBALANCED
COUNTERBALANCES
COUNTERBASE
COUNTERBASES
COUNTERBID
COUNTERBIDDER
COUNTERBIDDERS
COUNTERBIDS
COUNTERBLAST
COUNTERBLASTS
COUNTERBLOCKADE
COUNTERBLOW
COUNTERBLOWS
COUNTERBLUFF
COUNTERBLUFFS
COUNTERBOND
COUNTERBONDS
COUNTERBORE
COUNTERBORED
COUNTERBORES
COUNTERBORING
COUNTERBRACE
COUNTERBRACED
COUNTERBRACES
COUNTERBRACING
COUNTERBUFF
COUNTERBUFFED
COUNTERBUFFING
COUNTERBUFFS
COUNTERCAMPAIGN
COUNTERCHANGE
COUNTERCHANGED
COUNTERCHANGES
COUNTERCHANGING
COUNTERCHARGE
COUNTERCHARGED
COUNTERCHARGES
COUNTERCHARGING
COUNTERCHARM
COUNTERCHARMED
COUNTERCHARMING
COUNTERCHARMS
COUNTERCHECK
COUNTERCHECKED
COUNTERCHECKING
COUNTERCHECKS
COUNTERCLAIM
COUNTERCLAIMANT
COUNTERCLAIMED
COUNTERCLAIMING
COUNTERCLAIMS
COUNTERCOUP
COUNTERCOUPS
COUNTERCRIES
COUNTERCRY
COUNTERCULTURAL
COUNTERCULTURE
COUNTERCULTURES
COUNTERCURRENT
COUNTERCURRENTS
COUNTERCYCLICAL
COUNTERDEMAND
COUNTERDEMANDS
COUNTERDRAW
COUNTERDRAWING
COUNTERDRAWN
COUNTERDRAWS
COUNTERDREW
COUNTEREFFORT
COUNTEREFFORTS
COUNTEREVIDENCE
COUNTEREXAMPLE
COUNTEREXAMPLES
COUNTERFACTUAL
COUNTERFACTUALS
COUNTERFECT
COUNTERFEISANCE
COUNTERFEIT
COUNTERFEITED
COUNTERFEITER
COUNTERFEITERS
COUNTERFEITING
COUNTERFEITINGS
COUNTERFEITLY
COUNTERFEITS
COUNTERFESAUNCE
COUNTERFIRE
COUNTERFIRES
COUNTERFLOW
COUNTERFLOWS
COUNTERFOIL
COUNTERFOILS
COUNTERFORCE
COUNTERFORCES
COUNTERFORT
COUNTERFORTS
COUNTERGLOW
COUNTERGLOWS
COUNTERGUERILLA
COUNTERIMAGE
COUNTERIMAGES
COUNTERING
COUNTERINSTANCE
COUNTERION
COUNTERIONS
COUNTERIRRITANT
COUNTERLIGHT
COUNTERLIGHTS
COUNTERMAN
COUNTERMAND
COUNTERMANDABLE
COUNTERMANDED
COUNTERMANDING
COUNTERMANDS
COUNTERMARCH
COUNTERMARCHED
COUNTERMARCHES
COUNTERMARCHING
COUNTERMARK
COUNTERMARKS
COUNTERMEASURE
COUNTERMEASURES
COUNTERMELODIES
COUNTERMELODY
COUNTERMEMO
COUNTERMEMOS
COUNTERMEN
COUNTERMINE
COUNTERMINED
COUNTERMINES
COUNTERMINING
COUNTERMOTION
COUNTERMOTIONS

COUNTERMOVE
COUNTERMOVED
COUNTERMOVEMENT
COUNTERMOVES
COUNTERMOVING
COUNTERMURE
COUNTERMURED
COUNTERMURES
COUNTERMURING
COUNTERMYTH
COUNTERMYTHS
COUNTEROFFER
COUNTEROFFERS
COUNTERORDER
COUNTERORDERED
COUNTERORDERING
COUNTERORDERS
COUNTERPACE
COUNTERPACES
COUNTERPANE
COUNTERPANES
COUNTERPART
COUNTERPARTIES
COUNTERPARTS
COUNTERPARTY
COUNTERPEISE
COUNTERPEISED
COUNTERPEISES
COUNTERPEISING
COUNTERPETITION
COUNTERPICKET
COUNTERPICKETED
COUNTERPICKETS
COUNTERPLAN
COUNTERPLANNED
COUNTERPLANNING
COUNTERPLANS
COUNTERPLAY
COUNTERPLAYED
COUNTERPLAYER
COUNTERPLAYERS
COUNTERPLAYING
COUNTERPLAYS
COUNTERPLEA
COUNTERPLEAD
COUNTERPLEADED
COUNTERPLEADING
COUNTERPLEADS
COUNTERPLEAS
COUNTERPLED
COUNTERPLOT
COUNTERPLOTS
COUNTERPLOTTED
COUNTERPLOTTING
COUNTERPLOY
COUNTERPLOYS
COUNTERPOINT
COUNTERPOINTED
COUNTERPOINTING
COUNTERPOINTS
COUNTERPOISE
COUNTERPOISED
COUNTERPOISES
COUNTERPOISING
COUNTERPOSE
COUNTERPOSED
COUNTERPOSES
COUNTERPOSING
COUNTERPOWER
COUNTERPOWERS
COUNTERPRESSURE
COUNTERPROJECT
COUNTERPROJECTS
COUNTERPROOF
COUNTERPROOFS
COUNTERPROPOSAL
COUNTERPROTEST
COUNTERPROTESTS
COUNTERPUNCH
COUNTERPUNCHED
COUNTERPUNCHER
COUNTERPUNCHERS
COUNTERPUNCHES
COUNTERPUNCHING
COUNTERQUESTION
COUNTERRAID
COUNTERRAIDED
COUNTERRAIDING
COUNTERRAIDS
COUNTERRALLIED
COUNTERRALLIES
COUNTERRALLY
COUNTERRALLYING
COUNTERREACTION
COUNTERREFORM
COUNTERREFORMED
COUNTERREFORMER
COUNTERREFORMS
COUNTERRESPONSE
COUNTERSANK
COUNTERSCARP
COUNTERSCARPS
COUNTERSEAL
COUNTERSEALED
COUNTERSEALING
COUNTERSEALS
COUNTERSHADING
COUNTERSHADINGS
COUNTERSHAFT
COUNTERSHAFTS
COUNTERSHOT
COUNTERSHOTS
COUNTERSIGN
COUNTERSIGNED
COUNTERSIGNING
COUNTERSIGNS
COUNTERSINK
COUNTERSINKING
COUNTERSINKS
COUNTERSNIPER
COUNTERSNIPERS
COUNTERSPELL
COUNTERSPELLS
COUNTERSPIES
COUNTERSPY
COUNTERSPYING
COUNTERSPYINGS
COUNTERSTAIN
COUNTERSTAINED
COUNTERSTAINING
COUNTERSTAINS
COUNTERSTATE
COUNTERSTATED
COUNTERSTATES
COUNTERSTATING
COUNTERSTEP
COUNTERSTEPS
COUNTERSTRATEGY
COUNTERSTREAM
COUNTERSTREAMS
COUNTERSTRICKEN
COUNTERSTRIKE
COUNTERSTRIKES
COUNTERSTRIKING
COUNTERSTROKE
COUNTERSTROKES
COUNTERSTRUCK
COUNTERSTYLE
COUNTERSTYLES
COUNTERSUBJECT
COUNTERSUBJECTS
COUNTERSUE
COUNTERSUED
COUNTERSUES
COUNTERSUING
COUNTERSUIT
COUNTERSUITS
COUNTERSUNK
COUNTERTACTIC
COUNTERTACTICS
COUNTERTENDENCY
COUNTERTENOR
COUNTERTENORS
COUNTERTERROR
COUNTERTERRORS
COUNTERTHREAT
COUNTERTHREATS
COUNTERTHRUST
COUNTERTHRUSTS
COUNTERTOP
COUNTERTOPS
COUNTERTRADE
COUNTERTRADED
COUNTERTRADES
COUNTERTRADING
COUNTERTREND
COUNTERTRENDS
COUNTERTYPE
COUNTERTYPES
COUNTERVAIL
COUNTERVAILABLE
COUNTERVAILED
COUNTERVAILING
COUNTERVAILS
COUNTERVIEW
COUNTERVIEWS
COUNTERVIOLENCE
COUNTERWEIGH
COUNTERWEIGHED
COUNTERWEIGHING
COUNTERWEIGHS
COUNTERWEIGHT
COUNTERWEIGHTED
COUNTERWEIGHTS
COUNTERWORD
COUNTERWORDS
COUNTERWORK
COUNTERWORKED
COUNTERWORKER
COUNTERWORKERS
COUNTERWORKING
COUNTERWORKS
COUNTERWORLD
COUNTERWORLDS
COUNTESSES
COUNTINGHOUSE
COUNTINGHOUSES
COUNTLESSLY
COUNTLINES
COUNTRIFIED
COUNTROLLED
COUNTROLLING
COUNTRYFIED
COUNTRYISH
COUNTRYMAN
COUNTRYMEN
COUNTRYSEAT
COUNTRYSEATS
COUNTRYSIDE
COUNTRYSIDES
COUNTRYWIDE
COUNTRYWOMAN
COUNTRYWOMEN
COUNTSHIPS
COUPLEDOMS
COUPLEMENT
COUPLEMENTS
COUPONINGS
COURAGEFUL
COURAGEOUS
COURAGEOUSLY
COURAGEOUSNESS
COURANTOES
COURBARILS
COURBETTES
COURGETTES
COURIERING
COURSEBOOK
COURSEBOOKS
COURSEWARE

C

COURSEWARES
COURSEWORK
COURSEWORKS
COURTCRAFT
COURTCRAFTS
COURTEOUSLY
COURTEOUSNESS
COURTEOUSNESSES
COURTESANS
COURTESIED
COURTESIES
COURTESYING
COURTEZANS
COURTHOUSE
COURTHOUSES
COURTIERISM
COURTIERISMS
COURTIERLIKE
COURTIERLY
COURTLIEST
COURTLINESS
COURTLINESSES
COURTLINGS
COURTROOMS
COURTSHIPS
COURTSIDES
COURTYARDS
COUSCOUSES
COUSCOUSOU
COUSCOUSOUS
COUSINAGES
COUSINHOOD
COUSINHOODS
COUSINRIES
COUSINSHIP
COUSINSHIPS
COUTURIERE
COUTURIERES
COUTURIERS
COVALENCES
COVALENCIES
COVALENTLY
COVARIANCE
COVARIANCES
COVARIANTS
COVARIATES
COVARIATION
COVARIATIONS
COVELLINES
COVELLITES
COVENANTAL
COVENANTALLY
COVENANTED
COVENANTEE
COVENANTEES
COVENANTER
COVENANTERS
COVENANTING
COVENANTOR
COVENANTORS
COVERALLED
COVERMOUNT
COVERMOUNTED
COVERMOUNTING
COVERMOUNTS
COVERSINES
COVERSLIPS
COVERTNESS
COVERTNESSES
COVERTURES
COVETINGLY
COVETIVENESS
COVETIVENESSES
COVETOUSLY
COVETOUSNESS
COVETOUSNESSES
COWARDICES
COWARDLIER
COWARDLIEST
COWARDLINESS
COWARDLINESSES
COWARDRIES
COWARDSHIP
COWARDSHIPS
COWBERRIES
COWBOYINGS
COWCATCHER
COWCATCHERS
COWERINGLY
COWFEEDERS
COWFETERIA
COWFETERIAS
COWGRASSES
COWLSTAFFS
COWLSTAVES
COWPUNCHER
COWPUNCHERS
COXCOMBICAL
COXCOMBICALITY
COXCOMBICALLY
COXCOMBRIES
COXCOMICAL
COXINESSES
COXSWAINED
COXSWAINING
COYISHNESS
COYISHNESSES
COYOTILLOS
COZINESSES
CRABAPPLES
CRABBEDNESS
CRABBEDNESSES
CRABBINESS
CRABBINESSES
CRABEATERS
CRABGRASSES
CRABSTICKS
CRACKAJACK
CRACKAJACKS
CRACKBACKS
CRACKBERRIES
CRACKBERRY
CRACKBRAIN
CRACKBRAINED
CRACKBRAINS
CRACKDOWNS
CRACKERJACK
CRACKERJACKS
CRACKHEADS
CRACKLEWARE
CRACKLEWARES
CRACKLIEST
CRACKLINGS
CRACOVIENNE
CRACOVIENNES
CRADLESONG
CRADLESONGS
CRADLEWALK
CRADLEWALKS
CRAFTINESS
CRAFTINESSES
CRAFTMANSHIP
CRAFTMANSHIPS
CRAFTSMANLIKE
CRAFTSMANLY
CRAFTSMANSHIP
CRAFTSMANSHIPS
CRAFTSPEOPLE
CRAFTSPERSON
CRAFTSPERSONS
CRAFTSWOMAN
CRAFTSWOMEN
CRAFTWORKS
CRAGGEDNESS
CRAGGEDNESSES
CRAGGINESS
CRAGGINESSES
CRAIGFLUKE
CRAIGFLUKES
CRAKEBERRIES
CRAKEBERRY
CRAMBOCLINK
CRAMBOCLINKS
CRAMOISIES
CRAMPBARKS
CRAMPFISHES
CRAMPONING
CRAMPONNED
CRAMPONNING
CRAMPONNINGS
CRANACHANS
CRANBERRIES
CRANEFLIES
CRANESBILL
CRANESBILLS
CRANIECTOMIES
CRANIECTOMY
CRANIOCEREBRAL
CRANIOFACIAL
CRANIOGNOMIES
CRANIOGNOMY
CRANIOLOGICAL
CRANIOLOGICALLY
CRANIOLOGIES
CRANIOLOGIST
CRANIOLOGISTS
CRANIOLOGY
CRANIOMETER
CRANIOMETERS
CRANIOMETRIC
CRANIOMETRICAL
CRANIOMETRIES
CRANIOMETRIST
CRANIOMETRISTS
CRANIOMETRY
CRANIOPAGI
CRANIOPAGUS
CRANIOSACRAL
CRANIOSCOPIES
CRANIOSCOPIST
CRANIOSCOPISTS
CRANIOSCOPY
CRANIOTOMIES
CRANIOTOMY
CRANKBAITS
CRANKCASES
CRANKHANDLE
CRANKHANDLES
CRANKINESS
CRANKINESSES
CRANKNESSES
CRANKSHAFT
CRANKSHAFTS
CRANREUCHS
CRAPEHANGER
CRAPEHANGERS
CRAPEHANGING
CRAPEHANGINGS
CRAPSHOOTER
CRAPSHOOTERS
CRAPSHOOTS
CRAPULENCE
CRAPULENCES
CRAPULENTLY
CRAPULOSITIES
CRAPULOSITY
CRAPULOUSLY
CRAPULOUSNESS
CRAPULOUSNESSES
CRAQUELURE
CRAQUELURES
CRASHINGLY
CRASHWORTHIER
CRASHWORTHIEST
CRASHWORTHINESS
CRASHWORTHY
CRASSAMENTA
CRASSAMENTUM
CRASSITUDE
CRASSITUDES

CRASSNESSES
CRASSULACEAN
CRASSULACEOUS
CRATERIFORM
CRATERINGS
CRATERLESS
CRATERLETS
CRATERLIKE
CRAUNCHABLE
CRAUNCHIER
CRAUNCHIEST
CRAUNCHINESS
CRAUNCHINESSES
CRAUNCHING
CRAVATTING
CRAVENNESS
CRAVENNESSES
CRAWDADDIES
CRAWFISHED
CRAWFISHES
CRAWFISHING
CRAWLINGLY
CRAYFISHES
CRAYONISTS
CRAZINESSES
CRAZYWEEDS
CREAKINESS
CREAKINESSES
CREAKINGLY
CREAMERIES
CREAMINESS
CREAMINESSES
CREAMPUFFS
CREAMWARES
CREASELESS
CREASOTING
CREATIANISM
CREATIANISMS
CREATININE
CREATININES
CREATIONAL
CREATIONISM
CREATIONISMS
CREATIONIST
CREATIONISTIC
CREATIONISTS
CREATIVELY
CREATIVENESS
CREATIVENESSES
CREATIVITIES
CREATIVITY
CREATORSHIP
CREATORSHIPS
CREATRESSES
CREATRIXES
CREATUREHOOD
CREATUREHOODS
CREATURELINESS
CREATURELY
CREATURESHIP
CREATURESHIPS
CREDENTIAL
CREDENTIALED
CREDENTIALING
CREDENTIALINGS
CREDENTIALISM
CREDENTIALISMS
CREDENTIALLED
CREDENTIALLING
CREDENTIALLINGS
CREDENTIALS
CREDIBILITIES
CREDIBILITY
CREDIBLENESS
CREDIBLENESSES
CREDITABILITIES
CREDITABILITY
CREDITABLE
CREDITABLENESS
CREDITABLY
CREDITLESS
CREDITORSHIP
CREDITORSHIPS
CREDITWORTHIER
CREDITWORTHIEST
CREDITWORTHY
CREDULITIES
CREDULOUSLY
CREDULOUSNESS
CREDULOUSNESSES
CREEKSIDES
CREEPINESS
CREEPINESSES
CREEPINGLY
CREEPMOUSE
CREEPMOUSES
CREESHIEST
CREMAILLERE
CREMAILLERES
CREMASTERS
CREMATIONISM
CREMATIONISMS
CREMATIONIST
CREMATIONISTS
CREMATIONS
CREMATORIA
CREMATORIAL
CREMATORIES
CREMATORIUM
CREMATORIUMS
CREMOCARPS
CRENATIONS
CRENATURES
CRENELATED
CRENELATES
CRENELATING
CRENELATION
CRENELATIONS
CRENELLATE
CRENELLATED
CRENELLATES
CRENELLATING
CRENELLATION
CRENELLATIONS
CRENELLING
CRENULATED
CRENULATION
CRENULATIONS
CREOLISATION
CREOLISATIONS
CREOLISING
CREOLIZATION
CREOLIZATIONS
CREOLIZING
CREOPHAGIES
CREOPHAGOUS
CREOSOTING
CREPEHANGER
CREPEHANGERS
CREPEHANGING
CREPEHANGINGS
CREPINESSES
CREPITATED
CREPITATES
CREPITATING
CREPITATION
CREPITATIONS
CREPITATIVE
CREPITUSES
CREPOLINES
CREPUSCLES
CREPUSCULAR
CREPUSCULE
CREPUSCULES
CREPUSCULOUS
CRESCENDOED
CRESCENDOES
CRESCENDOING
CRESCENDOS
CRESCENTADE
CRESCENTADES
CRESCENTED
CRESCENTIC
CRESCIVELY
CRESCOGRAPH
CRESCOGRAPHS
CRESTFALLEN
CRESTFALLENLY
CRESTFALLENNESS
CRETACEOUS
CRETACEOUSES
CRETACEOUSLY
CRETINISED
CRETINISES
CRETINISING
CRETINISMS
CRETINIZED
CRETINIZES
CRETINIZING
CRETINOIDS
CREVASSING
CREWELISTS
CREWELLERIES
CREWELLERY
CREWELLING
CREWELLINGS
CREWELWORK
CREWELWORKS
CRIBRATION
CRIBRATIONS
CRIBRIFORM
CRICKETERS
CRICKETING
CRICKETINGS
CRIMEWAVES
CRIMINALESE
CRIMINALESES
CRIMINALISATION
CRIMINALISE
CRIMINALISED
CRIMINALISES
CRIMINALISING
CRIMINALIST
CRIMINALISTICS
CRIMINALISTS
CRIMINALITIES
CRIMINALITY
CRIMINALIZATION
CRIMINALIZE
CRIMINALIZED
CRIMINALIZES
CRIMINALIZING
CRIMINALLY
CRIMINATED
CRIMINATES
CRIMINATING
CRIMINATION
CRIMINATIONS
CRIMINATIVE
CRIMINATOR
CRIMINATORS
CRIMINATORY
CRIMINOGENIC
CRIMINOLOGIC
CRIMINOLOGICAL
CRIMINOLOGIES
CRIMINOLOGIST
CRIMINOLOGISTS
CRIMINOLOGY
CRIMINOUSNESS
CRIMINOUSNESSES
CRIMSONING
CRIMSONNESS
CRIMSONNESSES
CRINGELING
CRINGELINGS
CRINGEWORTHIER
CRINGEWORTHIEST
CRINGEWORTHY
CRINGINGLY

C

C

CRINICULTURAL
CRINIGEROUS
CRINKLEROOT
CRINKLEROOTS
CRINKLIEST
CRINOIDEAN
CRINOIDEANS
CRINOLETTE
CRINOLETTES
CRINOLINED
CRINOLINES
CRIPPLEDOM
CRIPPLEDOMS
CRIPPLEWARE
CRIPPLEWARES
CRIPPLINGLY
CRIPPLINGS
CRISPATION
CRISPATIONS
CRISPATURE
CRISPATURES
CRISPBREAD
CRISPBREADS
CRISPENING
CRISPHEADS
CRISPINESS
CRISPINESSES
CRISPNESSES
CRISSCROSS
CRISSCROSSED
CRISSCROSSES
CRISSCROSSING
CRISTIFORM
CRISTOBALITE
CRISTOBALITES
CRITERIONS
CRITERIUMS
CRITHIDIAL
CRITHOMANCIES
CRITHOMANCY
CRITICALITIES
CRITICALITY
CRITICALLY
CRITICALNESS
CRITICALNESSES
CRITICASTER
CRITICASTERS
CRITICISABLE
CRITICISED
CRITICISER
CRITICISERS
CRITICISES
CRITICISING
CRITICISINGLY
CRITICISMS
CRITICIZABLE
CRITICIZED
CRITICIZER
CRITICIZERS
CRITICIZES
CRITICIZING
CRITICIZINGLY
CRITIQUING
CROAKINESS
CROAKINESSES
CROCHETERS
CROCHETING
CROCHETINGS
CROCIDOLITE
CROCIDOLITES
CROCKERIES
CROCODILES
CROCODILIAN
CROCODILIANS
CROCOISITE
CROCOISITES
CROCOSMIAS
CROISSANTS
CROKINOLES
CROOKBACKED
CROOKBACKS
CROOKEDEST
CROOKEDNESS
CROOKEDNESSES
CROOKERIES
CROOKNECKS
CROPDUSTER
CROPDUSTERS
CROPDUSTING
CROPDUSTINGS
CROQUANTES
CROQUETING
CROQUETTES
CROQUIGNOLE
CROQUIGNOLES
CROREPATIS
CROSSABILITIES
CROSSABILITY
CROSSANDRA
CROSSANDRAS
CROSSBANDED
CROSSBANDING
CROSSBANDINGS
CROSSBANDS
CROSSBARRED
CROSSBARRING
CROSSBARRINGS
CROSSBEAMS
CROSSBEARER
CROSSBEARERS
CROSSBENCH
CROSSBENCHER
CROSSBENCHERS
CROSSBENCHES
CROSSBILLS
CROSSBIRTH
CROSSBIRTHS
CROSSBITES
CROSSBITING
CROSSBITTEN
CROSSBONES
CROSSBOWER
CROSSBOWERS
CROSSBOWMAN
CROSSBOWMEN
CROSSBREDS
CROSSBREED
CROSSBREEDING
CROSSBREEDINGS
CROSSBREEDS
CROSSBUCKS
CROSSCHECK
CROSSCHECKED
CROSSCHECKING
CROSSCHECKS
CROSSCLAIM
CROSSCLAIMS
CROSSCOURT
CROSSCURRENT
CROSSCURRENTS
CROSSCUTTING
CROSSCUTTINGS
CROSSETTES
CROSSFALLS
CROSSFIELD
CROSSFIRES
CROSSFISHES
CROSSHAIRS
CROSSHATCH
CROSSHATCHED
CROSSHATCHES
CROSSHATCHING
CROSSHATCHINGS
CROSSHEADS
CROSSJACKS
CROSSLIGHT
CROSSLIGHTS
CROSSLINGUISTIC
CROSSNESSES
CROSSOPTERYGIAN
CROSSOVERS
CROSSPATCH
CROSSPATCHES
CROSSPIECE
CROSSPIECES
CROSSROADS
CROSSRUFFED
CROSSRUFFING
CROSSRUFFS
CROSSTALKS
CROSSTREES
CROSSWALKS
CROSSWINDS
CROSSWIRES
CROSSWORDS
CROSSWORTS
CROTALARIA
CROTALARIAS
CROTALISMS
CROTCHETED
CROTCHETEER
CROTCHETEERS
CROTCHETIER
CROTCHETIEST
CROTCHETINESS
CROTCHETINESSES
CROTONALDEHYDE
CROTONALDEHYDES
CROTONBUGS
CROUPINESS
CROUPINESSES
CROUSTADES
CROWBARRED
CROWBARRING
CROWBERRIES
CROWDEDNESS
CROWDEDNESSES
CROWDFUNDED
CROWDFUNDING
CROWDFUNDINGS
CROWDFUNDS
CROWDSOURCE
CROWDSOURCED
CROWDSOURCES
CROWDSOURCING
CROWDSOURCINGS
CROWKEEPER
CROWKEEPERS
CROWNLANDS
CROWNPIECE
CROWNPIECES
CROWNWORKS
CROWSTEPPED
CRUCIATELY
CRUCIFEROUS
CRUCIFIERS
CRUCIFIXES
CRUCIFIXION
CRUCIFIXIONS
CRUCIFORMLY
CRUCIFORMS
CRUCIFYING
CRUCIVERBAL
CRUCIVERBALISM
CRUCIVERBALISMS
CRUCIVERBALIST
CRUCIVERBALISTS
CRUDENESSES
CRUELNESSES
CRUISERWEIGHT
CRUISERWEIGHTS
CRUISEWAYS
CRUISEWEAR
CRUISEWEARS
CRUMBCLOTH
CRUMBCLOTHS
CRUMBLIEST
CRUMBLINESS
CRUMBLINESSES
CRUMBLINGS

CRUMMINESS
CRUMMINESSES
CRUMPLIEST
CRUMPLINGS
CRUNCHABLE
CRUNCHIEST
CRUNCHINESS
CRUNCHINESSES
CRUNCHINGS
CRUSHABILITIES
CRUSHABILITY
CRUSHINGLY
CRUSHPROOF
CRUSTACEAN
CRUSTACEANS
CRUSTACEOUS
CRUSTATION
CRUSTATIONS
CRUSTINESS
CRUSTINESSES
CRUTCHINGS
CRYMOTHERAPIES
CRYMOTHERAPY
CRYOBIOLOGICAL
CRYOBIOLOGIES
CRYOBIOLOGIST
CRYOBIOLOGISTS
CRYOBIOLOGY
CRYOCABLES
CRYOCONITE
CRYOCONITES
CRYOGENICALLY
CRYOGENICS
CRYOGENIES
CRYOGLOBULIN
CRYOGLOBULINS
CRYOHYDRATE
CRYOHYDRATES
CRYOMETERS
CRYOMETRIC
CRYOMETRIES
CRYONICALLY
CRYOPHILIC
CRYOPHORUS
CRYOPHORUSES
CRYOPHYSICS
CRYOPHYTES
CRYOPLANKTON
CRYOPLANKTONS
CRYOPRECIPITATE
CRYOPRESERVE
CRYOPRESERVED
CRYOPRESERVES
CRYOPRESERVING
CRYOPROBES
CRYOPROTECTANT
CRYOPROTECTANTS
CRYOPROTECTIVE
CRYOSCOPES
CRYOSCOPIC
CRYOSCOPIES
CRYOSTATIC
CRYOSURGEON
CRYOSURGEONS
CRYOSURGERIES
CRYOSURGERY
CRYOSURGICAL
CRYOTHERAPIES
CRYOTHERAPY
CRYPTAESTHESIA
CRYPTAESTHESIAS
CRYPTAESTHETIC
CRYPTANALYSES
CRYPTANALYSIS
CRYPTANALYST
CRYPTANALYSTS
CRYPTANALYTIC
CRYPTANALYTICAL
CRYPTARITHM
CRYPTARITHMS
CRYPTESTHESIA
CRYPTESTHESIAS
CRYPTESTHETIC
CRYPTICALLY
CRYPTOBIONT
CRYPTOBIONTS
CRYPTOBIOSES
CRYPTOBIOSIS
CRYPTOCLASTIC
CRYPTOCOCCAL
CRYPTOCOCCI
CRYPTOCOCCOSES
CRYPTOCOCCOSIS
CRYPTOCOCCUS
CRYPTOCURRENCY
CRYPTOGAMIAN
CRYPTOGAMIC
CRYPTOGAMIES
CRYPTOGAMIST
CRYPTOGAMISTS
CRYPTOGAMOUS
CRYPTOGAMS
CRYPTOGAMY
CRYPTOGENIC
CRYPTOGRAM
CRYPTOGRAMS
CRYPTOGRAPH
CRYPTOGRAPHER
CRYPTOGRAPHERS
CRYPTOGRAPHIC
CRYPTOGRAPHICAL
CRYPTOGRAPHIES
CRYPTOGRAPHIST
CRYPTOGRAPHISTS
CRYPTOGRAPHS
CRYPTOGRAPHY
CRYPTOLOGIC
CRYPTOLOGICAL
CRYPTOLOGIES
CRYPTOLOGIST
CRYPTOLOGISTS
CRYPTOLOGY
CRYPTOMERIA
CRYPTOMERIAS
CRYPTOMETER
CRYPTOMETERS
CRYPTOMNESIA
CRYPTOMNESIAS
CRYPTOMNESIC
CRYPTONYMOUS
CRYPTONYMS
CRYPTOPHYTE
CRYPTOPHYTES
CRYPTOPHYTIC
CRYPTORCHID
CRYPTORCHIDISM
CRYPTORCHIDISMS
CRYPTORCHIDS
CRYPTORCHISM
CRYPTORCHISMS
CRYPTOSPORIDIA
CRYPTOSPORIDIUM
CRYPTOZOIC
CRYPTOZOITE
CRYPTOZOITES
CRYPTOZOOLOGIES
CRYPTOZOOLOGIST
CRYPTOZOOLOGY
CRYSTALISABLE
CRYSTALISATION
CRYSTALISATIONS
CRYSTALISE
CRYSTALISED
CRYSTALISER
CRYSTALISERS
CRYSTALISES
CRYSTALISING
CRYSTALIZABLE
CRYSTALIZATION
CRYSTALIZATIONS
CRYSTALIZE
CRYSTALIZED
CRYSTALIZER
CRYSTALIZERS
CRYSTALIZES
CRYSTALIZING
CRYSTALLINE
CRYSTALLINES
CRYSTALLINITIES
CRYSTALLINITY
CRYSTALLISABLE
CRYSTALLISATION
CRYSTALLISE
CRYSTALLISED
CRYSTALLISER
CRYSTALLISERS
CRYSTALLISES
CRYSTALLISING
CRYSTALLITE
CRYSTALLITES
CRYSTALLITIC
CRYSTALLITIS
CRYSTALLITISES
CRYSTALLIZABLE
CRYSTALLIZATION
CRYSTALLIZE
CRYSTALLIZED
CRYSTALLIZER
CRYSTALLIZERS
CRYSTALLIZES
CRYSTALLIZING
CRYSTALLOGRAPHY
CRYSTALLOID
CRYSTALLOIDAL
CRYSTALLOIDS
CRYSTALLOMANCY
CTENOPHORAN
CTENOPHORANS
CTENOPHORE
CTENOPHORES
CUADRILLAS
CUBANELLES
CUBBYHOLES
CUBICALNESS
CUBICALNESSES
CUBICITIES
CUBISTICALLY
CUCKOLDING
CUCKOLDISE
CUCKOLDISED
CUCKOLDISES
CUCKOLDISING
CUCKOLDIZE
CUCKOLDIZED
CUCKOLDIZES
CUCKOLDIZING
CUCKOLDOMS
CUCKOLDRIES
CUCKOOFLOWER
CUCKOOFLOWERS
CUCKOOPINT
CUCKOOPINTS
CUCULIFORM
CUCULLATED
CUCULLATELY
CUCUMIFORM
CUCURBITACEOUS
CUCURBITAL
CUDDLESOME
CUDGELINGS
CUDGELLERS
CUDGELLING
CUDGELLINGS
CUFFUFFLES
CUIRASSIER
CUIRASSIERS
CUIRASSING
CUISINARTS
CUISINIERS
CULICIFORM

CULINARIAN
CULINARIANS
CULINARILY
CULLENDERS
CULMIFEROUS
CULMINATED
CULMINATES
CULMINATING
CULMINATION
CULMINATIONS
CULPABILITIES
CULPABILITY
CULPABLENESS
CULPABLENESSES
CULTISHNESS
CULTISHNESSES
CULTIVABILITIES
CULTIVABILITY
CULTIVABLE
CULTIVATABLE
CULTIVATED
CULTIVATES
CULTIVATING
CULTIVATION
CULTIVATIONS
CULTIVATOR
CULTIVATORS
CULTRIFORM
CULTURABLE
CULTURALLY
CULTURELESS
CULTURISTS
CULVERINEER
CULVERINEERS
CULVERTAGE
CULVERTAGES
CULVERTAILED
CULVERTING
CUMBERBUND
CUMBERBUNDS
CUMBERLESS
CUMBERMENT
CUMBERMENTS
CUMBERSOME
CUMBERSOMELY
CUMBERSOMENESS
CUMBRANCES
CUMBROUSLY
CUMBROUSNESS
CUMBROUSNESSES
CUMMERBUND
CUMMERBUNDS
CUMMINGTONITE
CUMMINGTONITES
CUMULATELY
CUMULATING
CUMULATION
CUMULATIONS
CUMULATIVE
CUMULATIVELY
CUMULATIVENESS
CUMULIFORM
CUMULOCIRRI
CUMULOCIRRUS
CUMULONIMBI
CUMULONIMBUS
CUMULONIMBUSES
CUMULOSTRATI
CUMULOSTRATUS
CUNCTATION
CUNCTATIONS
CUNCTATIOUS
CUNCTATIVE
CUNCTATORS
CUNCTATORY
CUNEIFORMS
CUNNILINCTUS
CUNNILINCTUSES
CUNNILINGUS
CUNNILINGUSES
CUNNINGEST
CUNNINGNESS
CUNNINGNESSES
CUPBEARERS
CUPBOARDED
CUPBOARDING
CUPELLATION
CUPELLATIONS
CUPFERRONS
CUPHOLDERS
CUPIDINOUS
CUPIDITIES
CUPRAMMONIUM
CUPRAMMONIUMS
CUPRESSUSES
CUPRIFEROUS
CUPRONICKEL
CUPRONICKELS
CUPULIFEROUS
CURABILITIES
CURABILITY
CURABLENESS
CURABLENESSES
CURANDERAS
CURANDEROS
CURARISATION
CURARISATIONS
CURARISING
CURARIZATION
CURARIZATIONS
CURARIZING
CURATESHIP
CURATESHIPS
CURATIVELY
CURATIVENESS
CURATIVENESSES
CURATORIAL
CURATORSHIP
CURATORSHIPS
CURATRIXES
CURBSTONES
CURCUMINES
CURDINESSES
CURETTAGES
CURETTEMENT
CURETTEMENTS
CURFUFFLED
CURFUFFLES
CURFUFFLING
CURIALISMS
CURIALISTIC
CURIALISTS
CURIETHERAPIES
CURIETHERAPY
CURIOSITIES
CURIOUSEST
CURIOUSNESS
CURIOUSNESSES
CURLICUING
CURLIEWURLIE
CURLIEWURLIES
CURLINESSES
CURLPAPERS
CURMUDGEON
CURMUDGEONLIER
CURMUDGEONLIEST
CURMUDGEONLY
CURMUDGEONS
CURMURRING
CURMURRINGS
CURNAPTIOUS
CURRAJONGS
CURRANTIER
CURRANTIEST
CURRAWONGS
CURREJONGS
CURRENCIES
CURRENTNESS
CURRENTNESSES
CURRICULAR
CURRICULUM
CURRICULUMS
CURRIERIES
CURRIJONGS
CURRISHNESS
CURRISHNESSES
CURRYCOMBED
CURRYCOMBING
CURRYCOMBS
CURSEDNESS
CURSEDNESSES
CURSELARIE
CURSIVENESS
CURSIVENESSES
CURSORINESS
CURSORINESSES
CURSTNESSES
CURTAILERS
CURTAILING
CURTAILMENT
CURTAILMENTS
CURTAINING
CURTAINLESS
CURTALAXES
CURTATIONS
CURTILAGES
CURTNESSES
CURTSEYING
CURVACEOUS
CURVACEOUSLY
CURVACEOUSNESS
CURVACIOUS
CURVACIOUSLY
CURVACIOUSNESS
CURVATIONS
CURVATURES
CURVEBALLED
CURVEBALLING
CURVEBALLS
CURVEDNESS
CURVEDNESSES
CURVETTING
CURVICAUDATE
CURVICOSTATE
CURVIFOLIATE
CURVILINEAL
CURVILINEALLY
CURVILINEAR
CURVILINEARITY
CURVILINEARLY
CURVINESSES
CURVIROSTRAL
CUSHINESSES
CUSHIONETS
CUSHIONIER
CUSHIONIEST
CUSHIONING
CUSHIONINGS
CUSHIONLESS
CUSPIDATED
CUSPIDATION
CUSPIDATIONS
CUSPIDORES
CUSSEDNESS
CUSSEDNESSES
CUSTARDIER
CUSTARDIEST
CUSTODIANS
CUSTODIANSHIP
CUSTODIANSHIPS
CUSTODIERS
CUSTOMABLE
CUSTOMARIES
CUSTOMARILY
CUSTOMARINESS
CUSTOMARINESSES
CUSTOMHOUSE
CUSTOMHOUSES
CUSTOMISATION
CUSTOMISATIONS

CUSTOMISED
CUSTOMISER
CUSTOMISERS
CUSTOMISES
CUSTOMISING
CUSTOMIZATION
CUSTOMIZATIONS
CUSTOMIZED
CUSTOMIZER
CUSTOMIZERS
CUSTOMIZES
CUSTOMIZING
CUSTOMSHOUSE
CUSTOMSHOUSES
CUSTUMARIES
CUTABILITIES
CUTABILITY
CUTANEOUSLY
CUTCHERIES
CUTCHERRIES
CUTENESSES
CUTGRASSES
CUTINISATION
CUTINISATIONS
CUTINISING
CUTINIZATION
CUTINIZATIONS
CUTINIZING
CUTTHROATS
CUTTLEBONE
CUTTLEBONES
CUTTLEFISH
CUTTLEFISHES
CYANAMIDES
CYANIDATION
CYANIDATIONS
CYANIDINGS
CYANOACETYLENE
CYANOACETYLENES
CYANOACRYLATE
CYANOACRYLATES
CYANOBACTERIA
CYANOBACTERIUM
CYANOCOBALAMIN
CYANOCOBALAMINE
CYANOCOBALAMINS
CYANOETHYLATE
CYANOETHYLATED
CYANOETHYLATES
CYANOETHYLATING
CYANOETHYLATION
CYANOGENAMIDE
CYANOGENAMIDES
CYANOGENESES
CYANOGENESIS
CYANOGENETIC
CYANOGENIC
CYANOHYDRIN
CYANOHYDRINS
CYANOMETER
CYANOMETERS
CYANOPHYTE
CYANOPHYTES
CYANOTYPES
CYANURATES
CYATHIFORM
CYBERATHLETE
CYBERATHLETES
CYBERATHLETICS
CYBERATTACK
CYBERATTACKS
CYBERBULLIES
CYBERBULLY
CYBERBULLYING
CYBERBULLYINGS
CYBERCAFES
CYBERCASTS
CYBERCHONDRIA
CYBERCHONDRIAC
CYBERCHONDRIACS
CYBERCHONDRIAS
CYBERCRIME
CYBERCRIMES
CYBERCRIMINAL
CYBERCRIMINALS
CYBERNATED
CYBERNATES
CYBERNATING
CYBERNATION
CYBERNATIONS
CYBERNAUTS
CYBERNETIC
CYBERNETICAL
CYBERNETICALLY
CYBERNETICIAN
CYBERNETICIANS
CYBERNETICIST
CYBERNETICISTS
CYBERNETICS
CYBERPHOBIA
CYBERPHOBIAS
CYBERPHOBIC
CYBERPORNS
CYBERPUNKS
CYBERSECURITIES
CYBERSECURITY
CYBERSEXES
CYBERSPACE
CYBERSPACES
CYBERSQUATTER
CYBERSQUATTERS
CYBERSQUATTING
CYBERSQUATTINGS
CYBERSTALKER
CYBERSTALKERS
CYBERSTALKING
CYBERSTALKINGS
CYBERTERRORISM
CYBERTERRORISMS
CYBERTERRORIST
CYBERTERRORISTS
CYBRARIANS
CYCADACEOUS
CYCADEOIDS
CYCADOPHYTE
CYCADOPHYTES
CYCLAMATES
CYCLANDELATE
CYCLANDELATES
CYCLANTHACEOUS
CYCLAZOCINE
CYCLAZOCINES
CYCLEPATHS
CYCLICALITIES
CYCLICALITY
CYCLICALLY
CYCLICISMS
CYCLICITIES
CYCLISATION
CYCLISATIONS
CYCLIZATION
CYCLIZATIONS
CYCLIZINES
CYCLOADDITION
CYCLOADDITIONS
CYCLOALIPHATIC
CYCLOALKANE
CYCLOALKANES
CYCLOBARBITONE
CYCLOBARBITONES
CYCLODEXTRIN
CYCLODEXTRINS
CYCLODIALYSES
CYCLODIALYSIS
CYCLODIENE
CYCLODIENES
CYCLOGENESES
CYCLOGENESIS
CYCLOGIROS
CYCLOGRAPH
CYCLOGRAPHIC
CYCLOGRAPHS
CYCLOHEXANE
CYCLOHEXANES
CYCLOHEXANONE
CYCLOHEXANONES
CYCLOHEXIMIDE
CYCLOHEXIMIDES
CYCLOHEXYLAMINE
CYCLOIDALLY
CYCLOIDIAN
CYCLOIDIANS
CYCLOLITHS
CYCLOMETER
CYCLOMETERS
CYCLOMETRIES
CYCLOMETRY
CYCLONICAL
CYCLONICALLY
CYCLONITES
CYCLOOLEFIN
CYCLOOLEFINIC
CYCLOOLEFINS
CYCLOPAEDIA
CYCLOPAEDIAS
CYCLOPAEDIC
CYCLOPAEDIST
CYCLOPAEDISTS
CYCLOPARAFFIN
CYCLOPARAFFINS
CYCLOPEDIA
CYCLOPEDIAS
CYCLOPEDIC
CYCLOPEDIST
CYCLOPEDISTS
CYCLOPENTADIENE
CYCLOPENTANE
CYCLOPENTANES
CYCLOPENTOLATE
CYCLOPENTOLATES
CYCLOPLEGIA
CYCLOPLEGIAS
CYCLOPLEGIC
CYCLOPROPANE
CYCLOPROPANES
CYCLORAMAS
CYCLORAMIC
CYCLOSERINE
CYCLOSERINES
CYCLOSPERMOUS
CYCLOSPORIN
CYCLOSPORINE
CYCLOSPORINES
CYCLOSPORINS
CYCLOSTOMATE
CYCLOSTOMATOUS
CYCLOSTOME
CYCLOSTOMES
CYCLOSTOMOUS
CYCLOSTYLE
CYCLOSTYLED
CYCLOSTYLES
CYCLOSTYLING
CYCLOTHYME
CYCLOTHYMES
CYCLOTHYMIA
CYCLOTHYMIAC
CYCLOTHYMIACS
CYCLOTHYMIAS
CYCLOTHYMIC
CYCLOTHYMICS
CYCLOTOMIC
CYCLOTRONS
CYLINDERED
CYLINDERING
CYLINDRACEOUS
CYLINDRICAL
CYLINDRICALITY
CYLINDRICALLY
CYLINDRICALNESS

CYLINDRICITIES
CYLINDRICITY
CYLINDRIFORM
CYLINDRITE
CYLINDRITES
CYLINDROID
CYLINDROIDS
CYMAGRAPHS
CYMBALEERS
CYMBALISTS
CYMBIDIUMS
CYMIFEROUS
CYMOGRAPHIC
CYMOGRAPHS
CYMOPHANES
CYMOPHANOUS
CYMOTRICHIES
CYMOTRICHOUS
CYMOTRICHY
CYNGHANEDD
CYNGHANEDDS
CYNICALNESS
CYNICALNESSES
CYNOMOLGUS
CYNOMOLGUSES
CYNOPHILIA
CYNOPHILIAS
CYNOPHILIST
CYNOPHILISTS
CYNOPHOBIA
CYNOPHOBIAS
CYNOPODOUS
CYPERACEOUS
CYPRINODONT
CYPRINODONTS
CYPRINOIDS
CYPRIPEDIA
CYPRIPEDIUM
CYPRIPEDIUMS
CYPROHEPTADINE
CYPROHEPTADINES
CYPROTERONE
CYPROTERONES
CYSTEAMINE
CYSTEAMINES
CYSTECTOMIES
CYSTECTOMY
CYSTICERCI
CYSTICERCOID
CYSTICERCOIDS
CYSTICERCOSES
CYSTICERCOSIS
CYSTICERCUS
CYSTIDEANS
CYSTINOSES
CYSTINOSIS
CYSTINURIA
CYSTINURIAS
CYSTITIDES
CYSTITISES
CYSTOCARPIC
CYSTOCARPS
CYSTOCELES
CYSTOGENOUS
CYSTOGRAPHIES
CYSTOGRAPHY
CYSTOLITHIASES
CYSTOLITHIASIS
CYSTOLITHS
CYSTOSCOPE
CYSTOSCOPES
CYSTOSCOPIC
CYSTOSCOPIES
CYSTOSCOPY
CYSTOSTOMIES
CYSTOSTOMY
CYSTOTOMIES
CYTOCHALASIN
CYTOCHALASINS
CYTOCHEMICAL
CYTOCHEMISTRIES
CYTOCHEMISTRY
CYTOCHROME
CYTOCHROMES
CYTODIAGNOSES
CYTODIAGNOSIS
CYTOGENESES
CYTOGENESIS
CYTOGENETIC
CYTOGENETICAL
CYTOGENETICALLY
CYTOGENETICIST
CYTOGENETICISTS
CYTOGENETICS
CYTOGENIES
CYTOKINESES
CYTOKINESIS
CYTOKINETIC
CYTOKININS
CYTOLOGICAL
CYTOLOGICALLY
CYTOLOGIES
CYTOLOGIST
CYTOLOGISTS
CYTOLYSINS
CYTOMEGALIC
CYTOMEGALOVIRUS
CYTOMEMBRANE
CYTOMEMBRANES
CYTOMETERS
CYTOMETRIC
CYTOMETRIES
CYTOPATHIC
CYTOPATHIES
CYTOPATHOGENIC
CYTOPATHOLOGIES
CYTOPATHOLOGY
CYTOPENIAS
CYTOPHILIC
CYTOPHOTOMETRIC
CYTOPHOTOMETRY
CYTOPLASMIC
CYTOPLASMICALLY
CYTOPLASMS
CYTOPLASTIC
CYTOPLASTS
CYTOSKELETAL
CYTOSKELETON
CYTOSKELETONS
CYTOSTATIC
CYTOSTATICALLY
CYTOSTATICS
CYTOTAXONOMIC
CYTOTAXONOMIES
CYTOTAXONOMIST
CYTOTAXONOMISTS
CYTOTAXONOMY
CYTOTECHNOLOGY
CYTOTOXICITIES
CYTOTOXICITY
CYTOTOXINS
CZAREVICHES
CZAREVITCH
CZAREVITCHES

D

DABBLINGLY
DACHSHUNDS
DACOITAGES
DACQUOISES
DACTYLICALLY
DACTYLIOGRAPHY
DACTYLIOLOGIES
DACTYLIOLOGY
DACTYLIOMANCIES
DACTYLIOMANCY
DACTYLISTS
DACTYLOGRAM
DACTYLOGRAMS
DACTYLOGRAPHER
DACTYLOGRAPHERS
DACTYLOGRAPHIC
DACTYLOGRAPHIES
DACTYLOGRAPHY
DACTYLOLOGIES
DACTYLOLOGY
DACTYLOSCOPIES
DACTYLOSCOPY
DAFFADOWNDILLY
DAFFINESSES
DAFFODILLIES
DAFFODILLY
DAFTNESSES
DAGGERBOARD
DAGGERBOARDS
DAGGERLIKE
DAGUERREAN
DAGUERREOTYPE
DAGUERREOTYPED
DAGUERREOTYPER
DAGUERREOTYPERS
DAGUERREOTYPES
DAGUERREOTYPIES
DAGUERREOTYPING
DAGUERREOTYPIST
DAGUERREOTYPY
DAHABEEAHS
DAHABEEYAH
DAHABEEYAHS
DAHABIYAHS
DAHABIYEHS
DAILINESSES
DAILYNESSES
DAINTINESS
DAINTINESSES
DAIRYMAIDS
DAISYWHEEL
DAISYWHEELS
DALLIANCES
DALMATIANS
DALTONIANS
DALTONISMS
DAMAGEABILITIES
DAMAGEABILITY
DAMAGEABLE
DAMAGINGLY
DAMASCEENE
DAMASCEENED
DAMASCEENES
DAMASCEENING
DAMASCENED
DAMASCENES
DAMASCENING
DAMASCENINGS
DAMASKEENED
DAMASKEENING
DAMASKEENS
DAMASKINED
DAMASKINING
DAMASQUINED
DAMASQUINING
DAMASQUINS
DAMINOZIDE
DAMINOZIDES
DAMNABILITIES
DAMNABILITY
DAMNABLENESS
DAMNABLENESSES
DAMNATIONS
DAMNEDESTS
DAMNIFICATION
DAMNIFICATIONS
DAMNIFYING
DAMOISELLE
DAMOISELLES
DAMPCOURSE
DAMPCOURSES
DAMPISHNESS
DAMPISHNESSES
DAMPNESSES
DAMSELFISH
DAMSELFISHES
DAMSELFLIES
DANCECORES
DANCEHALLS
DANCEWEARS
DANDELIONS
DANDIFICATION
DANDIFICATIONS
DANDIFYING
DANDIPRATS
DANDRUFFIER
DANDRUFFIEST
DANDYFUNKS
DANDYISHLY
DANDYPRATS
DANGERLESS
DANGEROUSLY
DANGEROUSNESS
DANGEROUSNESSES
DANGLINGLY
DANKNESSES
DANNEBROGS
DANTHONIAS
DAPPERLING
DAPPERLINGS
DAPPERNESS
DAPPERNESSES
DAREDEVILRIES
DAREDEVILRY
DAREDEVILS
DAREDEVILTRIES
DAREDEVILTRY
DARINGNESS
DARINGNESSES
DARKNESSES
DARLINGNESS
DARLINGNESSES
DARMSTADTIUM
DARMSTADTIUMS
DARNATIONS
DARNEDESTS
DARRAIGNED
DARRAIGNES
DARRAIGNING
DARRAIGNMENT
DARRAIGNMENTS
DARRAINING
DARRAYNING
DARTBOARDS
DARTITISES
DASHBOARDS
DASHLIGHTS
DASTARDIES
DASTARDLIER
DASTARDLIEST
DASTARDLINESS
DASTARDLINESSES
DASTARDNESS
DASTARDNESSES
DASYMETERS
DASYPAEDAL
DASYPHYLLOUS
DATABASING
DATABUSSES
DATAGLOVES
DATAMATION
DATAMATIONS
DATAVEILLANCE
DATAVEILLANCES
DATEDNESSES
DATELINING
DAUGHTERBOARD
DAUGHTERBOARDS
DAUGHTERHOOD
DAUGHTERHOODS
DAUGHTERLESS
DAUGHTERLIER
DAUGHTERLIEST
DAUGHTERLINESS
DAUGHTERLING
DAUGHTERLINGS
DAUGHTERLY
DAUNDERING
DAUNOMYCIN
DAUNOMYCINS
DAUNORUBICIN
DAUNORUBICINS
DAUNTINGLY
DAUNTLESSLY
DAUNTLESSNESS
DAUNTLESSNESSES
DAUNTONING
DAUPHINESS
DAUPHINESSES
DAVENPORTS
DAWDLINGLY
DAWSONITES
DAYCATIONS
DAYCENTRES
DAYDREAMED
DAYDREAMER
DAYDREAMERS
DAYDREAMIER
DAYDREAMIEST
DAYDREAMING
DAYDREAMINGS
DAYDREAMLIKE
DAYFLOWERS
DAYLIGHTED
DAYLIGHTING
DAYLIGHTINGS
DAYSAILERS
DAYSAILING
DAYSAILORS
DAYSPRINGS

D

DAYWORKERS
DAZEDNESSES
DAZZLEMENT
DAZZLEMENTS
DAZZLINGLY
DEACIDIFICATION
DEACIDIFIED
DEACIDIFIES
DEACIDIFYING
DEACONESSES
DEACONHOOD
DEACONHOODS
DEACONRIES
DEACONSHIP
DEACONSHIPS
DEACTIVATE
DEACTIVATED
DEACTIVATES
DEACTIVATING
DEACTIVATION
DEACTIVATIONS
DEACTIVATOR
DEACTIVATORS
DEADENINGLY
DEADENINGS
DEADHEADED
DEADHEADING
DEADHOUSES
DEADLIFTED
DEADLIFTING
DEADLIGHTS
DEADLINESS
DEADLINESSES
DEADLINING
DEADLOCKED
DEADLOCKING
DEADNESSES
DEADPANNED
DEADPANNER
DEADPANNERS
DEADPANNING
DEADSTOCKS
DEADSTROKE
DEADWATERS
DEADWEIGHT
DEADWEIGHTS
DEAERATING
DEAERATION
DEAERATIONS
DEAERATORS
DEAFENINGLY
DEAFENINGS
DEAFNESSES
DEALATIONS
DEALBATION
DEALBATIONS
DEALBREAKER
DEALBREAKERS
DEALERSHIP
DEALERSHIPS
DEALFISHES
DEALIGNING
DEALMAKERS
DEAMBULATORIES
DEAMBULATORY
DEAMINASES
DEAMINATED
DEAMINATES
DEAMINATING
DEAMINATION
DEAMINATIONS
DEAMINISATION
DEAMINISATIONS
DEAMINISED
DEAMINISES
DEAMINISING
DEAMINIZATION
DEAMINIZATIONS
DEAMINIZED
DEAMINIZES
DEAMINIZING
DEARBOUGHT
DEARNESSES
DEARTICULATE
DEARTICULATED
DEARTICULATES
DEARTICULATING
DEASPIRATE
DEASPIRATED
DEASPIRATES
DEASPIRATING
DEASPIRATION
DEASPIRATIONS
DEATHBLOWS
DEATHLESSLY
DEATHLESSNESS
DEATHLESSNESSES
DEATHLIEST
DEATHLINESS
DEATHLINESSES
DEATHTRAPS
DEATHWARDS
DEATHWATCH
DEATHWATCHES
DEATTRIBUTE
DEATTRIBUTED
DEATTRIBUTES
DEATTRIBUTING
DEBAGGINGS
DEBARCATION
DEBARCATIONS
DEBARKATION
DEBARKATIONS
DEBARMENTS
DEBARRASSED
DEBARRASSES
DEBARRASSING
DEBASEDNESS
DEBASEDNESSES
DEBASEMENT
DEBASEMENTS
DEBASINGLY
DEBATEABLE
DEBATEMENT
DEBATEMENTS
DEBATINGLY
DEBAUCHEDLY
DEBAUCHEDNESS
DEBAUCHEDNESSES
DEBAUCHEES
DEBAUCHERIES
DEBAUCHERS
DEBAUCHERY
DEBAUCHING
DEBAUCHMENT
DEBAUCHMENTS
DEBEARDING
DEBENTURED
DEBENTURES
DEBILITATE
DEBILITATED
DEBILITATES
DEBILITATING
DEBILITATION
DEBILITATIONS
DEBILITATIVE
DEBILITIES
DEBONAIRLY
DEBONAIRNESS
DEBONAIRNESSES
DEBONNAIRE
DEBOUCHING
DEBOUCHMENT
DEBOUCHMENTS
DEBOUCHURE
DEBOUCHURES
DEBRIDEMENT
DEBRIDEMENTS
DEBRIEFERS
DEBRIEFING
DEBRIEFINGS
DEBRUISING
DEBUGGINGS
DEBUTANTES
DECACHORDS
DECADENCES
DECADENCIES
DECADENTLY
DECAFFEINATE
DECAFFEINATED
DECAFFEINATES
DECAFFEINATING
DECAGONALLY
DECAGRAMME
DECAGRAMMES
DECAGYNIAN
DECAGYNOUS
DECAHEDRAL
DECAHEDRON
DECAHEDRONS
DECAHYDRATE
DECAHYDRATES
DECALCIFICATION
DECALCIFIED
DECALCIFIER
DECALCIFIERS
DECALCIFIES
DECALCIFYING
DECALCOMANIA
DECALCOMANIAS
DECALESCENCE
DECALESCENCES
DECALESCENT
DECALITERS
DECALITRES
DECALOGIST
DECALOGISTS
DECALOGUES
DECAMERONIC
DECAMEROUS
DECAMETERS
DECAMETHONIUM
DECAMETHONIUMS
DECAMETRES
DECAMETRIC
DECAMPMENT
DECAMPMENTS
DECANDRIAN
DECANDROUS
DECANEDIOIC
DECANICALLY
DECANTATED
DECANTATES
DECANTATING
DECANTATION
DECANTATIONS
DECAPITALISE
DECAPITALISED
DECAPITALISES
DECAPITALISING
DECAPITALIZE
DECAPITALIZED
DECAPITALIZES
DECAPITALIZING
DECAPITATE
DECAPITATED
DECAPITATES
DECAPITATING
DECAPITATION
DECAPITATIONS
DECAPITATOR
DECAPITATORS
DECAPODANS
DECAPODOUS
DECAPSULATE
DECAPSULATED
DECAPSULATES
DECAPSULATING
DECAPSULATION
DECAPSULATIONS

DECARBONATE
DECARBONATED
DECARBONATES
DECARBONATING
DECARBONATION
DECARBONATIONS
DECARBONATOR
DECARBONATORS
DECARBONISATION
DECARBONISE
DECARBONISED
DECARBONISER
DECARBONISERS
DECARBONISES
DECARBONISING
DECARBONIZATION
DECARBONIZE
DECARBONIZED
DECARBONIZER
DECARBONIZERS
DECARBONIZES
DECARBONIZING
DECARBOXYLASE
DECARBOXYLASES
DECARBOXYLATE
DECARBOXYLATED
DECARBOXYLATES
DECARBOXYLATING
DECARBOXYLATION
DECARBURATION
DECARBURATIONS
DECARBURISATION
DECARBURISE
DECARBURISED
DECARBURISES
DECARBURISING
DECARBURIZATION
DECARBURIZE
DECARBURIZED
DECARBURIZES
DECARBURIZING
DECARTELISE
DECARTELISED
DECARTELISES
DECARTELISING
DECARTELIZE
DECARTELIZED
DECARTELIZES
DECARTELIZING
DECASTERES
DECASTICHS
DECASTYLES
DECASUALISATION
DECASUALISE
DECASUALISED
DECASUALISES
DECASUALISING
DECASUALIZATION
DECASUALIZE
DECASUALIZED
DECASUALIZES
DECASUALIZING
DECASYLLABIC
DECASYLLABICS
DECASYLLABLE
DECASYLLABLES
DECATHLETE
DECATHLETES
DECATHLONS
DECAUDATED
DECAUDATES
DECAUDATING
DECEITFULLY
DECEITFULNESS
DECEITFULNESSES
DECEIVABILITIES
DECEIVABILITY
DECEIVABLE
DECEIVABLENESS
DECEIVABLY
DECEIVINGLY
DECEIVINGS
DECELERATE
DECELERATED
DECELERATES
DECELERATING
DECELERATION
DECELERATIONS
DECELERATOR
DECELERATORS
DECELEROMETER
DECELEROMETERS
DECELERONS
DECEMVIRAL
DECEMVIRATE
DECEMVIRATES
DECENARIES
DECENNARIES
DECENNIALLY
DECENNIALS
DECENNIUMS
DECENNOVAL
DECENTERED
DECENTERING
DECENTERINGS
DECENTNESS
DECENTNESSES
DECENTRALISE
DECENTRALISED
DECENTRALISES
DECENTRALISING
DECENTRALIST
DECENTRALISTS
DECENTRALIZE
DECENTRALIZED
DECENTRALIZES
DECENTRALIZING
DECENTRING
DECEPTIBILITIES
DECEPTIBILITY
DECEPTIBLE
DECEPTIONAL
DECEPTIONS
DECEPTIOUS
DECEPTIVELY
DECEPTIVENESS
DECEPTIVENESSES
DECEREBRATE
DECEREBRATED
DECEREBRATES
DECEREBRATING
DECEREBRATION
DECEREBRATIONS
DECEREBRISE
DECEREBRISED
DECEREBRISES
DECEREBRISING
DECEREBRIZE
DECEREBRIZED
DECEREBRIZES
DECEREBRIZING
DECERTIFICATION
DECERTIFIED
DECERTIFIES
DECERTIFYING
DECESSIONS
DECHEANCES
DECHLORINATE
DECHLORINATED
DECHLORINATES
DECHLORINATING
DECHLORINATION
DECHLORINATIONS
DECHRISTIANISE
DECHRISTIANISED
DECHRISTIANISES
DECHRISTIANIZE
DECHRISTIANIZED
DECHRISTIANIZES
DECIDABILITIES
DECIDABILITY
DECIDEDNESS
DECIDEDNESSES
DECIDUOUSLY
DECIDUOUSNESS
DECIDUOUSNESSES
DECIGRAMME
DECIGRAMMES
DECILITERS
DECILITRES
DECILLIONS
DECILLIONTH
DECILLIONTHS
DECIMALISATION
DECIMALISATIONS
DECIMALISE
DECIMALISED
DECIMALISES
DECIMALISING
DECIMALISM
DECIMALISMS
DECIMALIST
DECIMALISTS
DECIMALIZATION
DECIMALIZATIONS
DECIMALIZE
DECIMALIZED
DECIMALIZES
DECIMALIZING
DECIMATING
DECIMATION
DECIMATIONS
DECIMATORS
DECIMETERS
DECIMETRES
DECIMETRIC
DECINORMAL
DECIPHERABILITY
DECIPHERABLE
DECIPHERED
DECIPHERER
DECIPHERERS
DECIPHERING
DECIPHERMENT
DECIPHERMENTS
DECISIONAL
DECISIONED
DECISIONING
DECISIVELY
DECISIVENESS
DECISIVENESSES
DECISTERES
DECITIZENISE
DECITIZENISED
DECITIZENISES
DECITIZENISING
DECITIZENIZE
DECITIZENIZED
DECITIZENIZES
DECITIZENIZING
DECIVILISE
DECIVILISED
DECIVILISES
DECIVILISING
DECIVILIZE
DECIVILIZED
DECIVILIZES
DECIVILIZING
DECKCHAIRS
DECKHOUSES
DECLAIMANT
DECLAIMANTS
DECLAIMERS
DECLAIMING
DECLAIMINGS
DECLAMATION
DECLAMATIONS
DECLAMATORILY
DECLAMATORY
DECLARABLE

DECLARANTS
DECLARATION
DECLARATIONS
DECLARATIVE
DECLARATIVELY
DECLARATOR
DECLARATORILY
DECLARATORS
DECLARATORY
DECLAREDLY
DECLASSIFIABLE
DECLASSIFIED
DECLASSIFIES
DECLASSIFY
DECLASSIFYING
DECLASSING
DECLENSION
DECLENSIONAL
DECLENSIONALLY
DECLENSIONS
DECLINABLE
DECLINANTS
DECLINATION
DECLINATIONAL
DECLINATIONS
DECLINATOR
DECLINATORIES
DECLINATORS
DECLINATORY
DECLINATURE
DECLINATURES
DECLINISTS
DECLINOMETER
DECLINOMETERS
DECLIVITIES
DECLIVITOUS
DECLUTCHED
DECLUTCHES
DECLUTCHING
DECLUTTERED
DECLUTTERING
DECLUTTERS
DECOCTIBLE
DECOCTIONS
DECOCTURES
DECOHERENCE
DECOHERENCES
DECOHERERS

DECOLLATED
DECOLLATES
DECOLLATING
DECOLLATION
DECOLLATIONS
DECOLLATOR
DECOLLATORS
DECOLLETAGE
DECOLLETAGES
DECOLLETES
DECOLONISATION
DECOLONISATIONS
DECOLONISE
DECOLONISED
DECOLONISES
DECOLONISING
DECOLONIZATION
DECOLONIZATIONS
DECOLONIZE
DECOLONIZED
DECOLONIZES
DECOLONIZING
DECOLORANT
DECOLORANTS
DECOLORATE
DECOLORATED
DECOLORATES
DECOLORATING
DECOLORATION
DECOLORATIONS
DECOLORING
DECOLORISATION
DECOLORISATIONS
DECOLORISE
DECOLORISED
DECOLORISER
DECOLORISERS
DECOLORISES
DECOLORISING
DECOLORIZATION
DECOLORIZATIONS
DECOLORIZE
DECOLORIZED
DECOLORIZER
DECOLORIZERS
DECOLORIZES
DECOLORIZING
DECOLOURED

DECOLOURING
DECOLOURISATION
DECOLOURISE
DECOLOURISED
DECOLOURISES
DECOLOURISING
DECOLOURIZATION
DECOLOURIZE
DECOLOURIZED
DECOLOURIZES
DECOLOURIZING
DECOMMISSION
DECOMMISSIONED
DECOMMISSIONER
DECOMMISSIONERS
DECOMMISSIONING
DECOMMISSIONS
DECOMMITTED
DECOMMITTING
DECOMMUNISATION
DECOMMUNISE
DECOMMUNISED
DECOMMUNISES
DECOMMUNISING
DECOMMUNIZATION
DECOMMUNIZE
DECOMMUNIZED
DECOMMUNIZES
DECOMMUNIZING
DECOMPENSATE
DECOMPENSATED
DECOMPENSATES
DECOMPENSATING
DECOMPENSATION
DECOMPENSATIONS
DECOMPOSABILITY
DECOMPOSABLE
DECOMPOSED
DECOMPOSER
DECOMPOSERS
DECOMPOSES
DECOMPOSING
DECOMPOSITE
DECOMPOSITES
DECOMPOSITION
DECOMPOSITIONS
DECOMPOUND
DECOMPOUNDABLE

DECOMPOUNDED
DECOMPOUNDING
DECOMPOUNDS
DECOMPRESS
DECOMPRESSED
DECOMPRESSES
DECOMPRESSING
DECOMPRESSION
DECOMPRESSIONS
DECOMPRESSIVE
DECOMPRESSOR
DECOMPRESSORS
DECONCENTRATE
DECONCENTRATED
DECONCENTRATES
DECONCENTRATING
DECONCENTRATION
DECONDITION
DECONDITIONED
DECONDITIONING
DECONDITIONS
DECONGESTANT
DECONGESTANTS
DECONGESTED
DECONGESTING
DECONGESTION
DECONGESTIONS
DECONGESTIVE
DECONGESTS
DECONSECRATE
DECONSECRATED
DECONSECRATES
DECONSECRATING
DECONSECRATION
DECONSECRATIONS
DECONSTRUCT
DECONSTRUCTED
DECONSTRUCTING
DECONSTRUCTION
DECONSTRUCTIONS
DECONSTRUCTIVE
DECONSTRUCTOR
DECONSTRUCTORS
DECONSTRUCTS
DECONTAMINANT
DECONTAMINANTS
DECONTAMINATE
DECONTAMINATED

DECONTAMINATES
DECONTAMINATING
DECONTAMINATION
DECONTAMINATIVE
DECONTAMINATOR
DECONTAMINATORS
DECONTEXTUALISE
DECONTEXTUALIZE
DECONTROLLED
DECONTROLLING
DECONTROLS
DECORATING
DECORATINGS
DECORATION
DECORATIONS
DECORATIVE
DECORATIVELY
DECORATIVENESS
DECORATORS
DECOROUSLY
DECOROUSNESS
DECOROUSNESSES
DECORTICATE
DECORTICATED
DECORTICATES
DECORTICATING
DECORTICATION
DECORTICATIONS
DECORTICATOR
DECORTICATORS
DECOUPAGED
DECOUPAGES
DECOUPAGING
DECOUPLERS
DECOUPLING
DECOUPLINGS
DECRASSIFIED
DECRASSIFIES
DECRASSIFY
DECRASSIFYING
DECREASING
DECREASINGLY
DECREASINGS
DECREEABLE
DECREMENTAL
DECREMENTED
DECREMENTING
DECREMENTS

DECREPITATE
DECREPITATED
DECREPITATES
DECREPITATING
DECREPITATION
DECREPITATIONS
DECREPITLY
DECREPITNESS
DECREPITNESSES
DECREPITUDE
DECREPITUDES
DECRESCENCE
DECRESCENCES
DECRESCENDO
DECRESCENDOS
DECRESCENT
DECRETALIST
DECRETALISTS
DECRETISTS
DECRIMINALISE
DECRIMINALISED
DECRIMINALISES
DECRIMINALISING
DECRIMINALIZE
DECRIMINALIZED
DECRIMINALIZES
DECRIMINALIZING
DECROWNING
DECRUSTATION
DECRUSTATIONS
DECRYPTING
DECRYPTION
DECRYPTIONS
DECUMBENCE
DECUMBENCES
DECUMBENCIES
DECUMBENCY
DECUMBENTLY
DECUMBITURE
DECUMBITURES
DECUMULATION
DECUMULATIONS
DECURIONATE
DECURIONATES
DECURRENCIES
DECURRENCY
DECURRENTLY
DECURSIONS
DECURSIVELY
DECURVATION
DECURVATIONS
DECUSSATED
DECUSSATELY
DECUSSATES
DECUSSATING
DECUSSATION
DECUSSATIONS
DEDICATEDLY
DEDICATEES
DEDICATING
DEDICATION
DEDICATIONAL
DEDICATIONS
DEDICATIVE
DEDICATORIAL
DEDICATORS
DEDICATORY
DEDIFFERENTIATE
DEDRAMATISE
DEDRAMATISED
DEDRAMATISES
DEDRAMATISING
DEDRAMATIZE
DEDRAMATIZED
DEDRAMATIZES
DEDRAMATIZING
DEDUCEMENT
DEDUCEMENTS
DEDUCIBILITIES
DEDUCIBILITY
DEDUCIBLENESS
DEDUCIBLENESSES
DEDUCTIBILITIES
DEDUCTIBILITY
DEDUCTIBLE
DEDUCTIBLES
DEDUCTIONS
DEDUCTIVELY
DEDUPLICATE
DEDUPLICATED
DEDUPLICATES
DEDUPLICATING
DEDUPLICATION
DEDUPLICATIONS
DEEJAYINGS
DEEMSTERSHIP
DEEMSTERSHIPS
DEEPENINGS
DEEPFREEZE
DEEPFREEZES
DEEPFREEZING
DEEPFROZEN
DEEPNESSES
DEEPWATERMAN
DEEPWATERMEN
DEERBERRIES
DEERGRASSES
DEERHOUNDS
DEERSTALKER
DEERSTALKERS
DEERSTALKING
DEERSTALKINGS
DEFACEABLE
DEFACEMENT
DEFACEMENTS
DEFACINGLY
DEFAECATED
DEFAECATES
DEFAECATING
DEFAECATION
DEFAECATIONS
DEFAECATOR
DEFAECATORS
DEFALCATED
DEFALCATES
DEFALCATING
DEFALCATION
DEFALCATIONS
DEFALCATOR
DEFALCATORS
DEFAMATION
DEFAMATIONS
DEFAMATORILY
DEFAMATORY
DEFAULTERS
DEFAULTING
DEFEASANCE
DEFEASANCED
DEFEASANCES
DEFEASIBILITIES
DEFEASIBILITY
DEFEASIBLE
DEFEASIBLENESS
DEFEATISMS
DEFEATISTS
DEFEATURED
DEFEATURES
DEFEATURING
DEFECATING
DEFECATION
DEFECATIONS
DEFECATORS
DEFECTIBILITIES
DEFECTIBILITY
DEFECTIBLE
DEFECTIONIST
DEFECTIONISTS
DEFECTIONS
DEFECTIVELY
DEFECTIVENESS
DEFECTIVENESSES
DEFECTIVES
DEFEMINISATION
DEFEMINISATIONS
DEFEMINISE
DEFEMINISED
DEFEMINISES
DEFEMINISING
DEFEMINIZATION
DEFEMINIZATIONS
DEFEMINIZE
DEFEMINIZED
DEFEMINIZES
DEFEMINIZING
DEFENCELESS
DEFENCELESSLY
DEFENCELESSNESS
DEFENCEMAN
DEFENCEMEN
DEFENDABLE
DEFENDANTS
DEFENESTRATE
DEFENESTRATED
DEFENESTRATES
DEFENESTRATING
DEFENESTRATION
DEFENESTRATIONS
DEFENSATIVE
DEFENSATIVES
DEFENSELESS
DEFENSELESSLY
DEFENSELESSNESS
DEFENSEMAN
DEFENSEMEN
DEFENSIBILITIES
DEFENSIBILITY
DEFENSIBLE
DEFENSIBLENESS
DEFENSIBLY
DEFENSIVELY
DEFENSIVENESS
DEFENSIVENESSES
DEFENSIVES
DEFERENCES
DEFERENTIAL
DEFERENTIALLY
DEFERMENTS
DEFERRABLE
DEFERRABLES
DEFERVESCENCE
DEFERVESCENCES
DEFERVESCENCIES
DEFERVESCENCY
DEFEUDALISE
DEFEUDALISED
DEFEUDALISES
DEFEUDALISING
DEFEUDALIZE
DEFEUDALIZED
DEFEUDALIZES
DEFEUDALIZING
DEFIANTNESS
DEFIANTNESSES
DEFIBRILLATE
DEFIBRILLATED
DEFIBRILLATES
DEFIBRILLATING
DEFIBRILLATION
DEFIBRILLATIONS
DEFIBRILLATOR
DEFIBRILLATORS
DEFIBRINATE
DEFIBRINATED
DEFIBRINATES
DEFIBRINATING
DEFIBRINATION
DEFIBRINATIONS
DEFIBRINISE
DEFIBRINISED
DEFIBRINISES

DEFIBRINISING
DEFIBRINIZE
DEFIBRINIZED
DEFIBRINIZES
DEFIBRINIZING
DEFICIENCE
DEFICIENCES
DEFICIENCIES
DEFICIENCY
DEFICIENTLY
DEFICIENTNESS
DEFICIENTNESSES
DEFICIENTS
DEFILADING
DEFILEMENT
DEFILEMENTS
DEFILIATION
DEFILIATIONS
DEFINABILITIES
DEFINABILITY
DEFINEMENT
DEFINEMENTS
DEFINIENDA
DEFINIENDUM
DEFINIENTIA
DEFINITELY
DEFINITENESS
DEFINITENESSES
DEFINITION
DEFINITIONAL
DEFINITIONS
DEFINITISE
DEFINITISED
DEFINITISES
DEFINITISING
DEFINITIVE
DEFINITIVELY
DEFINITIVENESS
DEFINITIVES
DEFINITIZE
DEFINITIZED
DEFINITIZES
DEFINITIZING
DEFINITUDE
DEFINITUDES
DEFLAGRABILITY
DEFLAGRABLE
DEFLAGRATE
DEFLAGRATED
DEFLAGRATES
DEFLAGRATING
DEFLAGRATION
DEFLAGRATIONS
DEFLAGRATOR
DEFLAGRATORS
DEFLATIONARY
DEFLATIONIST
DEFLATIONISTS
DEFLATIONS
DEFLECTABLE
DEFLECTING
DEFLECTION
DEFLECTIONAL
DEFLECTIONS
DEFLECTIVE
DEFLECTORS
DEFLEXIONAL
DEFLEXIONS
DEFLEXURES
DEFLOCCULANT
DEFLOCCULANTS
DEFLOCCULATE
DEFLOCCULATED
DEFLOCCULATES
DEFLOCCULATING
DEFLOCCULATION
DEFLOCCULATIONS
DEFLORATED
DEFLORATES
DEFLORATING
DEFLORATION
DEFLORATIONS
DEFLOWERED
DEFLOWERER
DEFLOWERERS
DEFLOWERING
DEFLUXIONS
DEFOCUSING
DEFOCUSSED
DEFOCUSSES
DEFOCUSSING
DEFOLIANTS
DEFOLIATED
DEFOLIATES
DEFOLIATING
DEFOLIATION
DEFOLIATIONS
DEFOLIATOR
DEFOLIATORS
DEFORCEMENT
DEFORCEMENTS
DEFORCIANT
DEFORCIANTS
DEFORCIATION
DEFORCIATIONS
DEFORESTATION
DEFORESTATIONS
DEFORESTED
DEFORESTER
DEFORESTERS
DEFORESTING
DEFORMABILITIES
DEFORMABILITY
DEFORMABLE
DEFORMALISE
DEFORMALISED
DEFORMALISES
DEFORMALISING
DEFORMALIZE
DEFORMALIZED
DEFORMALIZES
DEFORMALIZING
DEFORMATION
DEFORMATIONAL
DEFORMATIONS
DEFORMATIVE
DEFORMEDLY
DEFORMEDNESS
DEFORMEDNESSES
DEFORMITIES
DEFRAGGERS
DEFRAGGING
DEFRAGGINGS
DEFRAGMENT
DEFRAGMENTED
DEFRAGMENTING
DEFRAGMENTS
DEFRAUDATION
DEFRAUDATIONS
DEFRAUDERS
DEFRAUDING
DEFRAUDMENT
DEFRAUDMENTS
DEFRAYABLE
DEFRAYMENT
DEFRAYMENTS
DEFREEZING
DEFRIENDED
DEFRIENDING
DEFROCKING
DEFROSTERS
DEFROSTING
DEFROSTINGS
DEFTNESSES
DEFUELLING
DEFUNCTION
DEFUNCTIONS
DEFUNCTIVE
DEFUNCTNESS
DEFUNCTNESSES
DEGARNISHED
DEGARNISHES
DEGARNISHING
DEGAUSSERS
DEGAUSSING
DEGAUSSINGS
DEGEARINGS
DEGENDERED
DEGENDERING
DEGENERACIES
DEGENERACY
DEGENERATE
DEGENERATED
DEGENERATELY
DEGENERATENESS
DEGENERATES
DEGENERATING
DEGENERATION
DEGENERATIONIST
DEGENERATIONS
DEGENERATIVE
DEGENEROUS
DEGLACIATED
DEGLACIATION
DEGLACIATIONS
DEGLAMORISATION
DEGLAMORISE
DEGLAMORISED
DEGLAMORISES
DEGLAMORISING
DEGLAMORIZATION
DEGLAMORIZE
DEGLAMORIZED
DEGLAMORIZES
DEGLAMORIZING
DEGLUTINATE
DEGLUTINATED
DEGLUTINATES
DEGLUTINATING
DEGLUTINATION
DEGLUTINATIONS
DEGLUTITION
DEGLUTITIONS
DEGLUTITIVE
DEGLUTITORY
DEGRADABILITIES
DEGRADABILITY
DEGRADABLE
DEGRADATION
DEGRADATIONS
DEGRADATIVE
DEGRADEDLY
DEGRADINGLY
DEGRADINGNESS
DEGRADINGNESSES
DEGRANULATION
DEGRANULATIONS
DEGREASANT
DEGREASANTS
DEGREASERS
DEGREASING
DEGREASINGS
DEGREELESS
DEGRESSION
DEGRESSIONS
DEGRESSIVE
DEGRESSIVELY
DEGRINGOLADE
DEGRINGOLADED
DEGRINGOLADES
DEGRINGOLADING
DEGRINGOLER
DEGRINGOLERED
DEGRINGOLERING
DEGRINGOLERS
DEGUSTATED
DEGUSTATES
DEGUSTATING
DEGUSTATION
DEGUSTATIONS

DEGUSTATORY
DEHISCENCE
DEHISCENCES
DEHORTATION
DEHORTATIONS
DEHORTATIVE
DEHORTATORY
DEHUMANISATION
DEHUMANISATIONS
DEHUMANISE
DEHUMANISED
DEHUMANISES
DEHUMANISING
DEHUMANIZATION
DEHUMANIZATIONS
DEHUMANIZE
DEHUMANIZED
DEHUMANIZES
DEHUMANIZING
DEHUMIDIFIED
DEHUMIDIFIER
DEHUMIDIFIERS
DEHUMIDIFIES
DEHUMIDIFY
DEHUMIDIFYING
DEHYDRATED
DEHYDRATER
DEHYDRATERS
DEHYDRATES
DEHYDRATING
DEHYDRATION
DEHYDRATIONS
DEHYDRATOR
DEHYDRATORS
DEHYDROGENASE
DEHYDROGENASES
DEHYDROGENATE
DEHYDROGENATED
DEHYDROGENATES
DEHYDROGENATING
DEHYDROGENATION
DEHYDROGENISE
DEHYDROGENISED
DEHYDROGENISES
DEHYDROGENISING
DEHYDROGENIZE
DEHYDROGENIZED
DEHYDROGENIZES
DEHYDROGENIZING
DEHYDRORETINOL
DEHYDRORETINOLS
DEHYPNOTISATION
DEHYPNOTISE
DEHYPNOTISED
DEHYPNOTISES
DEHYPNOTISING
DEHYPNOTIZATION
DEHYPNOTIZE
DEHYPNOTIZED
DEHYPNOTIZES
DEHYPNOTIZING
DEICTICALLY
DEIFICATION
DEIFICATIONS
DEINDEXATION
DEINDEXATIONS
DEINDEXING
DEINDIVIDUATION
DEINDUSTRIALISE
DEINDUSTRIALIZE
DEINONYCHUS
DEINONYCHUSES
DEINOSAURS
DEINOTHERE
DEINOTHERES
DEINOTHERIA
DEINOTHERIUM
DEINOTHERIUMS
DEIONISATION
DEIONISATIONS
DEIONISERS
DEIONISING
DEIONIZATION
DEIONIZATIONS
DEIONIZERS
DEIONIZING
DEIPNOSOPHIST
DEIPNOSOPHISTS
DEISTICALLY
DEJECTEDLY
DEJECTEDNESS
DEJECTEDNESSES
DEJECTIONS
DEKALITERS
DEKALITRES
DEKALOGIES
DEKAMETERS
DEKAMETRES
DEKAMETRIC
DELAMINATE
DELAMINATED
DELAMINATES
DELAMINATING
DELAMINATION
DELAMINATIONS
DELAPSIONS
DELASSEMENT
DELASSEMENTS
DELAYERING
DELAYERINGS
DELAYINGLY
DELECTABILITIES
DELECTABILITY
DELECTABLE
DELECTABLENESS
DELECTABLES
DELECTABLY
DELECTATED
DELECTATES
DELECTATING
DELECTATION
DELECTATIONS
DELEGACIES
DELEGATEES
DELEGATING
DELEGATION
DELEGATIONS
DELEGATORS
DELEGITIMATION
DELEGITIMATIONS
DELEGITIMISE
DELEGITIMISED
DELEGITIMISES
DELEGITIMISING
DELEGITIMIZE
DELEGITIMIZED
DELEGITIMIZES
DELEGITIMIZING
DELETERIOUS
DELETERIOUSLY
DELETERIOUSNESS
DELEVERAGE
DELEVERAGED
DELEVERAGES
DELEVERAGING
DELEVERAGINGS
DELFTWARES
DELIBATING
DELIBATION
DELIBATIONS
DELIBERATE
DELIBERATED
DELIBERATELY
DELIBERATENESS
DELIBERATES
DELIBERATING
DELIBERATION
DELIBERATIONS
DELIBERATIVE
DELIBERATIVELY
DELIBERATOR
DELIBERATORS
DELICACIES
DELICATELY
DELICATENESS
DELICATENESSES
DELICATESSEN
DELICATESSENS
DELICIOUSLY
DELICIOUSNESS
DELICIOUSNESSES
DELIGATION
DELIGATIONS
DELIGHTEDLY
DELIGHTEDNESS
DELIGHTEDNESSES
DELIGHTERS
DELIGHTFUL
DELIGHTFULLY
DELIGHTFULNESS
DELIGHTING
DELIGHTLESS
DELIGHTSOME
DELIMITATE
DELIMITATED
DELIMITATES
DELIMITATING
DELIMITATION
DELIMITATIONS
DELIMITATIVE
DELIMITERS
DELIMITING
DELINEABLE
DELINEATED
DELINEATES
DELINEATING
DELINEATION
DELINEATIONS
DELINEATIVE
DELINEATOR
DELINEATORS
DELINEAVIT
DELINQUENCIES
DELINQUENCY
DELINQUENT
DELINQUENTLY
DELINQUENTS
DELIQUESCE
DELIQUESCED
DELIQUESCENCE
DELIQUESCENCES
DELIQUESCENT
DELIQUESCES
DELIQUESCING
DELIQUIUMS
DELIRATION
DELIRATIONS
DELIRIFACIENT
DELIRIFACIENTS
DELIRIOUSLY
DELIRIOUSNESS
DELIRIOUSNESSES
DELITESCENCE
DELITESCENCES
DELITESCENT
DELIVERABILITY
DELIVERABLE
DELIVERABLES
DELIVERANCE
DELIVERANCES
DELIVERERS
DELIVERIES
DELIVERING
DELIVERYMAN
DELIVERYMEN
DELOCALISATION
DELOCALISATIONS
DELOCALISE
DELOCALISED
DELOCALISES

DELOCALISING
DELOCALIZATION
DELOCALIZATIONS
DELOCALIZE
DELOCALIZED
DELOCALIZES
DELOCALIZING
DELPHICALLY
DELPHINIUM
DELPHINIUMS
DELPHINOID
DELPHINOIDS
DELTIOLOGIES
DELTIOLOGIST
DELTIOLOGISTS
DELTIOLOGY
DELTOIDEUS
DELUDINGLY
DELUNDUNGS
DELUSIONAL
DELUSIONARY
DELUSIONIST
DELUSIONISTS
DELUSIVELY
DELUSIVENESS
DELUSIVENESSES
DELUSTERED
DELUSTERING
DELUSTRANT
DELUSTRANTS
DELUSTRING
DEMAGNETISATION
DEMAGNETISE
DEMAGNETISED
DEMAGNETISER
DEMAGNETISERS
DEMAGNETISES
DEMAGNETISING
DEMAGNETIZATION
DEMAGNETIZE
DEMAGNETIZED
DEMAGNETIZER
DEMAGNETIZERS
DEMAGNETIZES
DEMAGNETIZING
DEMAGOGICAL
DEMAGOGICALLY
DEMAGOGIES
DEMAGOGING
DEMAGOGISM
DEMAGOGISMS
DEMAGOGUED
DEMAGOGUERIES
DEMAGOGUERY
DEMAGOGUES
DEMAGOGUING
DEMAGOGUISM
DEMAGOGUISMS
DEMANDABLE
DEMANDANTS
DEMANDINGLY
DEMANDINGNESS
DEMANDINGNESSES
DEMANNINGS
DEMANTOIDS
DEMARCATED
DEMARCATES
DEMARCATING
DEMARCATION
DEMARCATIONS
DEMARCATOR
DEMARCATORS
DEMARKATION
DEMARKATIONS
DEMARKETED
DEMARKETING
DEMATERIALISE
DEMATERIALISED
DEMATERIALISES
DEMATERIALISING
DEMATERIALIZE
DEMATERIALIZED
DEMATERIALIZES
DEMATERIALIZING
DEMEANOURS
DEMEASNURE
DEMEASNURES
DEMENTATED
DEMENTATES
DEMENTATING
DEMENTEDLY
DEMENTEDNESS
DEMENTEDNESSES
DEMERGERED
DEMERGERING
DEMERITING
DEMERITORIOUS
DEMERITORIOUSLY
DEMERSIONS
DEMIBASTION
DEMIBASTIONS
DEMICANTON
DEMICANTONS
DEMIGODDESS
DEMIGODDESSES
DEMIGRATION
DEMIGRATIONS
DEMILITARISE
DEMILITARISED
DEMILITARISES
DEMILITARISING
DEMILITARIZE
DEMILITARIZED
DEMILITARIZES
DEMILITARIZING
DEMIMONDAINE
DEMIMONDAINES
DEMIMONDES
DEMINERALISE
DEMINERALISED
DEMINERALISER
DEMINERALISERS
DEMINERALISES
DEMINERALISING
DEMINERALIZE
DEMINERALIZED
DEMINERALIZER
DEMINERALIZERS
DEMINERALIZES
DEMINERALIZING
DEMIPIQUES
DEMIRELIEF
DEMIRELIEFS
DEMIREPDOM
DEMIREPDOMS
DEMISEMIQUAVER
DEMISEMIQUAVERS
DEMISSIONS
DEMISTINGS
DEMITASSES
DEMIURGEOUS
DEMIURGICAL
DEMIURGICALLY
DEMIURGUSES
DEMIVEGGES
DEMIVIERGE
DEMIVIERGES
DEMIVOLTES
DEMIWORLDS
DEMOBILISATION
DEMOBILISATIONS
DEMOBILISE
DEMOBILISED
DEMOBILISES
DEMOBILISING
DEMOBILIZATION
DEMOBILIZATIONS
DEMOBILIZE
DEMOBILIZED
DEMOBILIZES
DEMOBILIZING
DEMOCRACIES
DEMOCRATIC
DEMOCRATICAL
DEMOCRATICALLY
DEMOCRATIES
DEMOCRATIFIABLE
DEMOCRATISATION
DEMOCRATISE
DEMOCRATISED
DEMOCRATISER
DEMOCRATISERS
DEMOCRATISES
DEMOCRATISING
DEMOCRATIST
DEMOCRATISTS
DEMOCRATIZATION
DEMOCRATIZE
DEMOCRATIZED
DEMOCRATIZER
DEMOCRATIZERS
DEMOCRATIZES
DEMOCRATIZING
DEMODULATE
DEMODULATED
DEMODULATES
DEMODULATING
DEMODULATION
DEMODULATIONS
DEMODULATOR
DEMODULATORS
DEMOGRAPHER
DEMOGRAPHERS
DEMOGRAPHIC
DEMOGRAPHICAL
DEMOGRAPHICALLY
DEMOGRAPHICS
DEMOGRAPHIES
DEMOGRAPHIST
DEMOGRAPHISTS
DEMOGRAPHY
DEMOISELLE
DEMOISELLES
DEMOLISHED
DEMOLISHER
DEMOLISHERS
DEMOLISHES
DEMOLISHING
DEMOLISHMENT
DEMOLISHMENTS
DEMOLITION
DEMOLITIONIST
DEMOLITIONISTS
DEMOLITIONS
DEMOLOGIES
DEMONESSES
DEMONETARISE
DEMONETARISED
DEMONETARISES
DEMONETARISING
DEMONETARIZE
DEMONETARIZED
DEMONETARIZES
DEMONETARIZING
DEMONETISATION
DEMONETISATIONS
DEMONETISE
DEMONETISED
DEMONETISES
DEMONETISING
DEMONETIZATION
DEMONETIZATIONS
DEMONETIZE
DEMONETIZED
DEMONETIZES
DEMONETIZING
DEMONIACAL
DEMONIACALLY
DEMONIACISM
DEMONIACISMS

DEMONIANISM
DEMONIANISMS
DEMONICALLY
DEMONISATION
DEMONISATIONS
DEMONISING
DEMONIZATION
DEMONIZATIONS
DEMONIZING
DEMONOCRACIES
DEMONOCRACY
DEMONOLATER
DEMONOLATERS
DEMONOLATRIES
DEMONOLATRY
DEMONOLOGIC
DEMONOLOGICAL
DEMONOLOGIES
DEMONOLOGIST
DEMONOLOGISTS
DEMONOLOGY
DEMONOMANIA
DEMONOMANIAS
DEMONSTRABILITY
DEMONSTRABLE
DEMONSTRABLY
DEMONSTRATE
DEMONSTRATED
DEMONSTRATES
DEMONSTRATING
DEMONSTRATION
DEMONSTRATIONAL
DEMONSTRATIONS
DEMONSTRATIVE
DEMONSTRATIVELY
DEMONSTRATIVES
DEMONSTRATOR
DEMONSTRATORS
DEMONSTRATORY
DEMORALISATION
DEMORALISATIONS
DEMORALISE
DEMORALISED
DEMORALISER
DEMORALISERS
DEMORALISES
DEMORALISING
DEMORALISINGLY
DEMORALIZATION
DEMORALIZATIONS
DEMORALIZE
DEMORALIZED
DEMORALIZER
DEMORALIZERS
DEMORALIZES
DEMORALIZING
DEMORALIZINGLY
DEMOSCENES
DEMOTICIST
DEMOTICISTS
DEMOTIVATE
DEMOTIVATED
DEMOTIVATES
DEMOTIVATING
DEMOTIVATION
DEMOTIVATIONS
DEMOUNTABLE
DEMOUNTING
DEMULCENTS
DEMULSIFICATION
DEMULSIFIED
DEMULSIFIER
DEMULSIFIERS
DEMULSIFIES
DEMULSIFYING
DEMULTIPLEXER
DEMULTIPLEXERS
DEMURENESS
DEMURENESSES
DEMURRABLE
DEMURRAGES
DEMUTUALISATION
DEMUTUALISE
DEMUTUALISED
DEMUTUALISES
DEMUTUALISING
DEMUTUALIZATION
DEMUTUALIZE
DEMUTUALIZED
DEMUTUALIZES
DEMUTUALIZING
DEMYELINATE
DEMYELINATED
DEMYELINATES
DEMYELINATING
DEMYELINATION
DEMYELINATIONS
DEMYSTIFICATION
DEMYSTIFIED
DEMYSTIFIES
DEMYSTIFYING
DEMYTHIFICATION
DEMYTHIFIED
DEMYTHIFIES
DEMYTHIFYING
DEMYTHOLOGISE
DEMYTHOLOGISED
DEMYTHOLOGISER
DEMYTHOLOGISERS
DEMYTHOLOGISES
DEMYTHOLOGISING
DEMYTHOLOGIZE
DEMYTHOLOGIZED
DEMYTHOLOGIZER
DEMYTHOLOGIZERS
DEMYTHOLOGIZES
DEMYTHOLOGIZING
DENATIONALISE
DENATIONALISED
DENATIONALISES
DENATIONALISING
DENATIONALIZE
DENATIONALIZED
DENATIONALIZES
DENATIONALIZING
DENATURALISE
DENATURALISED
DENATURALISES
DENATURALISING
DENATURALIZE
DENATURALIZED
DENATURALIZES
DENATURALIZING
DENATURANT
DENATURANTS
DENATURATION
DENATURATIONS
DENATURING
DENATURISE
DENATURISED
DENATURISES
DENATURISING
DENATURIZE
DENATURIZED
DENATURIZES
DENATURIZING
DENAZIFICATION
DENAZIFICATIONS
DENAZIFIED
DENAZIFIES
DENAZIFYING
DENDRACHATE
DENDRACHATES
DENDRIFORM
DENDRIMERS
DENDRITICAL
DENDRITICALLY
DENDROBIUM
DENDROBIUMS
DENDROGLYPH
DENDROGLYPHS
DENDROGRAM
DENDROGRAMS
DENDROIDAL
DENDROLATRIES
DENDROLATRY
DENDROLOGIC
DENDROLOGICAL
DENDROLOGIES
DENDROLOGIST
DENDROLOGISTS
DENDROLOGOUS
DENDROLOGY
DENDROMETER
DENDROMETERS
DENDROPHIS
DENDROPHISES
DENEGATION
DENEGATIONS
DENERVATED
DENERVATES
DENERVATING
DENERVATION
DENERVATIONS
DENIABILITIES
DENIABILITY
DENIALISTS
DENIGRATED
DENIGRATES
DENIGRATING
DENIGRATION
DENIGRATIONS
DENIGRATIVE
DENIGRATOR
DENIGRATORS
DENIGRATORY
DENISATION
DENISATIONS
DENITRATED
DENITRATES
DENITRATING
DENITRATION
DENITRATIONS
DENITRIFICATION
DENITRIFICATOR
DENITRIFICATORS
DENITRIFIED
DENITRIFIER
DENITRIFIERS
DENITRIFIES
DENITRIFYING
DENIZATION
DENIZATIONS
DENIZENING
DENIZENSHIP
DENIZENSHIPS
DENOMINABLE
DENOMINATE
DENOMINATED
DENOMINATES
DENOMINATING
DENOMINATION
DENOMINATIONAL
DENOMINATIONS
DENOMINATIVE
DENOMINATIVELY
DENOMINATIVES
DENOMINATOR
DENOMINATORS
DENOTATING
DENOTATION
DENOTATIONS
DENOTATIVE
DENOTATIVELY
DENOTEMENT
DENOTEMENTS
DENOUEMENT
DENOUEMENTS
DENOUNCEMENT
DENOUNCEMENTS

DENOUNCERS
DENOUNCING
DENSENESSES
DENSIFICATION
DENSIFICATIONS
DENSIFIERS
DENSIFYING
DENSIMETER
DENSIMETERS
DENSIMETRIC
DENSIMETRIES
DENSIMETRY
DENSITOMETER
DENSITOMETERS
DENSITOMETRIC
DENSITOMETRIES
DENSITOMETRY
DENTALISED
DENTALISES
DENTALISING
DENTALITIES
DENTALIUMS
DENTALIZED
DENTALIZES
DENTALIZING
DENTATIONS
DENTICARES
DENTICULATE
DENTICULATED
DENTICULATELY
DENTICULATION
DENTICULATIONS
DENTIFRICE
DENTIFRICES
DENTIGEROUS
DENTILABIAL
DENTILINGUAL
DENTILINGUALS
DENTIROSTRAL
DENTISTRIES
DENTITIONS
DENTURISMS
DENTURISTS
DENUCLEARISE
DENUCLEARISED
DENUCLEARISES
DENUCLEARISING
DENUCLEARIZE
DENUCLEARIZED
DENUCLEARIZES
DENUCLEARIZING
DENUDATING
DENUDATION
DENUDATIONS
DENUDEMENT
DENUDEMENTS
DENUMERABILITY
DENUMERABLE
DENUMERABLY
DENUNCIATE
DENUNCIATED
DENUNCIATES
DENUNCIATING
DENUNCIATION
DENUNCIATIONS
DENUNCIATIVE
DENUNCIATOR
DENUNCIATORS
DENUNCIATORY
DEOBSTRUENT
DEOBSTRUENTS
DEODORANTS
DEODORISATION
DEODORISATIONS
DEODORISED
DEODORISER
DEODORISERS
DEODORISES
DEODORISING
DEODORIZATION
DEODORIZATIONS
DEODORIZED
DEODORIZER
DEODORIZERS
DEODORIZES
DEODORIZING
DEONTOLOGICAL
DEONTOLOGIES
DEONTOLOGIST
DEONTOLOGISTS
DEONTOLOGY
DEOPPILATE
DEOPPILATED
DEOPPILATES
DEOPPILATING
DEOPPILATION
DEOPPILATIONS
DEOPPILATIVE
DEOPPILATIVES
DEORBITING
DEOXIDATED
DEOXIDATES
DEOXIDATING
DEOXIDATION
DEOXIDATIONS
DEOXIDISATION
DEOXIDISATIONS
DEOXIDISED
DEOXIDISER
DEOXIDISERS
DEOXIDISES
DEOXIDISING
DEOXIDIZATION
DEOXIDIZATIONS
DEOXIDIZED
DEOXIDIZER
DEOXIDIZERS
DEOXIDIZES
DEOXIDIZING
DEOXYCORTONE
DEOXYCORTONES
DEOXYGENATE
DEOXYGENATED
DEOXYGENATES
DEOXYGENATING
DEOXYGENATION
DEOXYGENATIONS
DEOXYGENISE
DEOXYGENISED
DEOXYGENISES
DEOXYGENISING
DEOXYGENIZE
DEOXYGENIZED
DEOXYGENIZES
DEOXYGENIZING
DEOXYRIBOSE
DEOXYRIBOSES
DEPAINTING
DEPANNEURS
DEPARTEMENT
DEPARTEMENTS
DEPARTINGS
DEPARTMENT
DEPARTMENTAL
DEPARTMENTALISE
DEPARTMENTALISM
DEPARTMENTALIZE
DEPARTMENTALLY
DEPARTMENTS
DEPARTURES
DEPASTURED
DEPASTURES
DEPASTURING
DEPAUPERATE
DEPAUPERATED
DEPAUPERATES
DEPAUPERATING
DEPAUPERISE
DEPAUPERISED
DEPAUPERISES
DEPAUPERISING
DEPAUPERIZE
DEPAUPERIZED
DEPAUPERIZES
DEPAUPERIZING
DEPEINCTED
DEPEINCTING
DEPENDABILITIES
DEPENDABILITY
DEPENDABLE
DEPENDABLENESS
DEPENDABLY
DEPENDANCE
DEPENDANCES
DEPENDANCIES
DEPENDANCY
DEPENDANTS
DEPENDENCE
DEPENDENCES
DEPENDENCIES
DEPENDENCY
DEPENDENTLY
DEPENDENTS
DEPENDINGLY
DEPEOPLING
DEPERSONALISE
DEPERSONALISED
DEPERSONALISES
DEPERSONALISING
DEPERSONALIZE
DEPERSONALIZED
DEPERSONALIZES
DEPERSONALIZING
DEPHLEGMATE
DEPHLEGMATED
DEPHLEGMATES
DEPHLEGMATING
DEPHLEGMATION
DEPHLEGMATIONS
DEPHLEGMATOR
DEPHLEGMATORS
DEPHLOGISTICATE
DEPHOSPHORYLATE
DEPICTIONS
DEPICTURED
DEPICTURES
DEPICTURING
DEPIGMENTATION
DEPIGMENTATIONS
DEPIGMENTED
DEPIGMENTING
DEPIGMENTS
DEPILATING
DEPILATION
DEPILATIONS
DEPILATORIES
DEPILATORS
DEPILATORY
DEPLENISHED
DEPLENISHES
DEPLENISHING
DEPLETABLE
DEPLETIONS
DEPLORABILITIES
DEPLORABILITY
DEPLORABLE
DEPLORABLENESS
DEPLORABLY
DEPLORATION
DEPLORATIONS
DEPLORINGLY
DEPLOYABLE
DEPLOYMENT
DEPLOYMENTS
DEPLUMATION
DEPLUMATIONS
DEPOLARISATION
DEPOLARISATIONS
DEPOLARISE
DEPOLARISED

DEPOLARISER
DEPOLARISERS
DEPOLARISES
DEPOLARISING
DEPOLARIZATION
DEPOLARIZATIONS
DEPOLARIZE
DEPOLARIZED
DEPOLARIZER
DEPOLARIZERS
DEPOLARIZES
DEPOLARIZING
DEPOLISHED
DEPOLISHES
DEPOLISHING
DEPOLITICISE
DEPOLITICISED
DEPOLITICISES
DEPOLITICISING
DEPOLITICIZE
DEPOLITICIZED
DEPOLITICIZES
DEPOLITICIZING
DEPOLYMERISE
DEPOLYMERISED
DEPOLYMERISES
DEPOLYMERISING
DEPOLYMERIZE
DEPOLYMERIZED
DEPOLYMERIZES
DEPOLYMERIZING
DEPOPULATE
DEPOPULATED
DEPOPULATES
DEPOPULATING
DEPOPULATION
DEPOPULATIONS
DEPOPULATOR
DEPOPULATORS
DEPORTABLE
DEPORTATION
DEPORTATIONS
DEPORTMENT
DEPORTMENTS
DEPOSITARIES
DEPOSITARY
DEPOSITATION
DEPOSITATIONS
DEPOSITING
DEPOSITION
DEPOSITIONAL
DEPOSITIONS
DEPOSITIVE
DEPOSITORIES
DEPOSITORS
DEPOSITORY
DEPRAVATION
DEPRAVATIONS
DEPRAVEDLY
DEPRAVEDNESS
DEPRAVEDNESSES
DEPRAVEMENT
DEPRAVEMENTS
DEPRAVINGLY
DEPRAVITIES
DEPRECABLE
DEPRECATED
DEPRECATES
DEPRECATING
DEPRECATINGLY
DEPRECATION
DEPRECATIONS
DEPRECATIVE
DEPRECATIVELY
DEPRECATOR
DEPRECATORILY
DEPRECATORS
DEPRECATORY
DEPRECIABLE
DEPRECIATE
DEPRECIATED
DEPRECIATES
DEPRECIATING
DEPRECIATINGLY
DEPRECIATION
DEPRECIATIONS
DEPRECIATIVE
DEPRECIATOR
DEPRECIATORS
DEPRECIATORY
DEPREDATED
DEPREDATES
DEPREDATING
DEPREDATION
DEPREDATIONS
DEPREDATOR
DEPREDATORS
DEPREDATORY
DEPREHENDED
DEPREHENDING
DEPREHENDS
DEPRESSANT
DEPRESSANTS
DEPRESSIBLE
DEPRESSING
DEPRESSINGLY
DEPRESSION
DEPRESSIONS
DEPRESSIVE
DEPRESSIVELY
DEPRESSIVENESS
DEPRESSIVES
DEPRESSOMOTOR
DEPRESSOMOTORS
DEPRESSORS
DEPRESSURISE
DEPRESSURISED
DEPRESSURISES
DEPRESSURISING
DEPRESSURIZE
DEPRESSURIZED
DEPRESSURIZES
DEPRESSURIZING
DEPRIVABLE
DEPRIVATION
DEPRIVATIONS
DEPRIVATIVE
DEPRIVEMENT
DEPRIVEMENTS
DEPROGRAMED
DEPROGRAMING
DEPROGRAMME
DEPROGRAMMED
DEPROGRAMMER
DEPROGRAMMERS
DEPROGRAMMES
DEPROGRAMMING
DEPROGRAMS
DEPURATING
DEPURATION
DEPURATIONS
DEPURATIVE
DEPURATIVES
DEPURATORS
DEPURATORY
DEPUTATION
DEPUTATIONS
DEPUTISATION
DEPUTISATIONS
DEPUTISING
DEPUTIZATION
DEPUTIZATIONS
DEPUTIZING
DEQUEUEING
DERACIALISE
DERACIALISED
DERACIALISES
DERACIALISING
DERACIALIZE
DERACIALIZED
DERACIALIZES
DERACIALIZING
DERACINATE
DERACINATED
DERACINATES
DERACINATING
DERACINATION
DERACINATIONS
DERAIGNING
DERAIGNMENT
DERAIGNMENTS
DERAILLEUR
DERAILLEURS
DERAILMENT
DERAILMENTS
DERANGEMENT
DERANGEMENTS
DERATIONED
DERATIONING
DEREALISATION
DEREALISATIONS
DEREALIZATION
DEREALIZATIONS
DERECOGNISE
DERECOGNISED
DERECOGNISES
DERECOGNISING
DERECOGNITION
DERECOGNITIONS
DERECOGNIZE
DERECOGNIZED
DERECOGNIZES
DERECOGNIZING
DEREGISTER
DEREGISTERED
DEREGISTERING
DEREGISTERS
DEREGISTRATION
DEREGISTRATIONS
DEREGULATE
DEREGULATED
DEREGULATES
DEREGULATING
DEREGULATION
DEREGULATIONS
DEREGULATOR
DEREGULATORS
DEREGULATORY
DERELICTION
DERELICTIONS
DERELIGIONISE
DERELIGIONISED
DERELIGIONISES
DERELIGIONISING
DERELIGIONIZE
DERELIGIONIZED
DERELIGIONIZES
DERELIGIONIZING
DEREPRESSED
DEREPRESSES
DEREPRESSING
DEREPRESSION
DEREPRESSIONS
DEREQUISITION
DEREQUISITIONED
DEREQUISITIONS
DERESTRICT
DERESTRICTED
DERESTRICTING
DERESTRICTION
DERESTRICTIONS
DERESTRICTS
DERIDINGLY
DERISIVELY
DERISIVENESS
DERISIVENESSES
DERIVATING
DERIVATION
DERIVATIONAL
DERIVATIONIST

D

DERIVATIONISTS
DERIVATIONS
DERIVATISATION
DERIVATISATIONS
DERIVATISE
DERIVATISED
DERIVATISES
DERIVATISING
DERIVATIVE
DERIVATIVELY
DERIVATIVENESS
DERIVATIVES
DERIVATIZATION
DERIVATIZATIONS
DERIVATIZE
DERIVATIZED
DERIVATIZES
DERIVATIZING
DERMABRASION
DERMABRASIONS
DERMAPLANING
DERMAPLANINGS
DERMAPTERAN
DERMAPTERANS
DERMATITIDES
DERMATITIS
DERMATITISES
DERMATOGEN
DERMATOGENS
DERMATOGLYPHIC
DERMATOGLYPHICS
DERMATOGRAPHIA
DERMATOGRAPHIAS
DERMATOGRAPHIC
DERMATOGRAPHIES
DERMATOGRAPHY
DERMATOLOGIC
DERMATOLOGICAL
DERMATOLOGIES
DERMATOLOGIST
DERMATOLOGISTS
DERMATOLOGY
DERMATOMAL
DERMATOMES
DERMATOMIC
DERMATOMYOSITIS
DERMATOPHYTE
DERMATOPHYTES
DERMATOPHYTIC
DERMATOPHYTOSES
DERMATOPHYTOSIS
DERMATOPLASTIC
DERMATOPLASTIES
DERMATOPLASTY
DERMATOSES
DERMATOSIS
DERMESTIDS
DERMOGRAPHIES
DERMOGRAPHY
DEROGATELY
DEROGATING
DEROGATION
DEROGATIONS
DEROGATIVE
DEROGATIVELY
DEROGATORILY
DEROGATORINESS
DEROGATORY
DERRICKING
DERRINGERS
DESACRALISATION
DESACRALISE
DESACRALISED
DESACRALISES
DESACRALISING
DESACRALIZATION
DESACRALIZE
DESACRALIZED
DESACRALIZES
DESACRALIZING
DESAGREMENT
DESAGREMENTS
DESALINATE
DESALINATED
DESALINATES
DESALINATING
DESALINATION
DESALINATIONS
DESALINATOR
DESALINATORS
DESALINISATION
DESALINISATIONS
DESALINISE
DESALINISED
DESALINISES
DESALINISING
DESALINIZATION
DESALINIZATIONS
DESALINIZE
DESALINIZED
DESALINIZES
DESALINIZING
DESALTINGS
DESATURATE
DESATURATED
DESATURATES
DESATURATING
DESATURATION
DESATURATIONS
DESCANTERS
DESCANTING
DESCENDABLE
DESCENDANT
DESCENDANTS
DESCENDENT
DESCENDENTS
DESCENDERS
DESCENDEUR
DESCENDEURS
DESCENDIBLE
DESCENDING
DESCENDINGS
DESCENSION
DESCENSIONAL
DESCENSIONS
DESCHOOLED
DESCHOOLER
DESCHOOLERS
DESCHOOLING
DESCHOOLINGS
DESCRAMBLE
DESCRAMBLED
DESCRAMBLER
DESCRAMBLERS
DESCRAMBLES
DESCRAMBLING
DESCRIBABLE
DESCRIBERS
DESCRIBING
DESCRIPTION
DESCRIPTIONS
DESCRIPTIVE
DESCRIPTIVELY
DESCRIPTIVENESS
DESCRIPTIVISM
DESCRIPTIVISMS
DESCRIPTIVIST
DESCRIPTOR
DESCRIPTORS
DESCRIVING
DESECRATED
DESECRATER
DESECRATERS
DESECRATES
DESECRATING
DESECRATION
DESECRATIONS
DESECRATOR
DESECRATORS
DESEGREGATE
DESEGREGATED
DESEGREGATES
DESEGREGATING
DESEGREGATION
DESEGREGATIONS
DESELECTED
DESELECTING
DESELECTION
DESELECTIONS
DESENSITISATION
DESENSITISE
DESENSITISED
DESENSITISER
DESENSITISERS
DESENSITISES
DESENSITISING
DESENSITIZATION
DESENSITIZE
DESENSITIZED
DESENSITIZER
DESENSITIZERS
DESENSITIZES
DESENSITIZING
DESERPIDINE
DESERPIDINES
DESERTIFICATION
DESERTIFIED
DESERTIFIES
DESERTIFYING
DESERTIONS
DESERTISATION
DESERTISATIONS
DESERTIZATION
DESERTIZATIONS
DESERTLESS
DESERVEDLY
DESERVEDNESS
DESERVEDNESSES
DESERVINGLY
DESERVINGNESS
DESERVINGNESSES
DESERVINGS
DESEXUALISATION
DESEXUALISE
DESEXUALISED
DESEXUALISES
DESEXUALISING
DESEXUALIZATION
DESEXUALIZE
DESEXUALIZED
DESEXUALIZES
DESEXUALIZING
DESHABILLE
DESHABILLES
DESICCANTS
DESICCATED
DESICCATES
DESICCATING
DESICCATION
DESICCATIONS
DESICCATIVE
DESICCATIVES
DESICCATOR
DESICCATORS
DESIDERATA
DESIDERATE
DESIDERATED
DESIDERATES
DESIDERATING
DESIDERATION
DESIDERATIONS
DESIDERATIVE
DESIDERATIVES
DESIDERATUM
DESIDERIUM
DESIDERIUMS
DESIGNABLE
DESIGNATED
DESIGNATES
DESIGNATING

DESIGNATION
DESIGNATIONS
DESIGNATIVE
DESIGNATOR
DESIGNATORS
DESIGNATORY
DESIGNEDLY
DESIGNINGLY
DESIGNINGS
DESIGNLESS
DESIGNMENT
DESIGNMENTS
DESILVERED
DESILVERING
DESILVERISATION
DESILVERISE
DESILVERISED
DESILVERISES
DESILVERISING
DESILVERIZATION
DESILVERIZE
DESILVERIZED
DESILVERIZES
DESILVERIZING
DESINENCES
DESINENTIAL
DESIPIENCE
DESIPIENCES
DESIPRAMINE
DESIPRAMINES
DESIRABILITIES
DESIRABILITY
DESIRABLENESS
DESIRABLENESSES
DESIRABLES
DESIRELESS
DESIROUSLY
DESIROUSNESS
DESIROUSNESSES
DESISTANCE
DESISTANCES
DESISTENCE
DESISTENCES
DESKILLING
DESKILLINGS
DESMODIUMS
DESMODROMIC
DESMOSOMAL
DESMOSOMES
DESNOODING
DESOBLIGEANTE
DESOBLIGEANTES
DESOLATELY
DESOLATENESS
DESOLATENESSES
DESOLATERS
DESOLATING
DESOLATINGLY
DESOLATION
DESOLATIONS
DESOLATORS
DESOLATORY
DESORIENTE
DESORPTION
DESORPTIONS
DESOXYRIBOSE
DESOXYRIBOSES
DESPAIRERS
DESPAIRFUL
DESPAIRING
DESPAIRINGLY
DESPATCHED
DESPATCHER
DESPATCHERS
DESPATCHES
DESPATCHING
DESPERADOES
DESPERADOS
DESPERATELY
DESPERATENESS
DESPERATENESSES
DESPERATION
DESPERATIONS
DESPICABILITIES
DESPICABILITY
DESPICABLE
DESPICABLENESS
DESPICABLY
DESPIRITUALISE
DESPIRITUALISED
DESPIRITUALISES
DESPIRITUALIZE
DESPIRITUALIZED
DESPIRITUALIZES
DESPISABLE
DESPISEDNESS
DESPISEDNESSES
DESPISEMENT
DESPISEMENTS
DESPISINGLY
DESPITEFUL
DESPITEFULLY
DESPITEFULNESS
DESPITEOUS
DESPITEOUSLY
DESPITEOUSNESS
DESPOILERS
DESPOILING
DESPOILINGS
DESPOILMENT
DESPOILMENTS
DESPOLIATION
DESPOLIATIONS
DESPONDENCE
DESPONDENCES
DESPONDENCIES
DESPONDENCY
DESPONDENT
DESPONDENTLY
DESPONDING
DESPONDINGLY
DESPONDINGS
DESPOTATES
DESPOTICAL
DESPOTICALLY
DESPOTICALNESS
DESPOTISMS
DESPOTOCRACIES
DESPOTOCRACY
DESPUMATED
DESPUMATES
DESPUMATING
DESPUMATION
DESPUMATIONS
DESQUAMATE
DESQUAMATED
DESQUAMATES
DESQUAMATING
DESQUAMATION
DESQUAMATIONS
DESQUAMATIVE
DESQUAMATORIES
DESQUAMATORY
DESSERTSPOON
DESSERTSPOONFUL
DESSERTSPOONS
DESSIATINE
DESSIATINES
DESSIGNMENT
DESSIGNMENTS
DESSYATINE
DESSYATINES
DESSYATINS
DESTABILISATION
DESTABILISE
DESTABILISED
DESTABILISER
DESTABILISERS
DESTABILISES
DESTABILISING
DESTABILIZATION
DESTABILIZE
DESTABILIZED
DESTABILIZER
DESTABILIZERS
DESTABILIZES
DESTABILIZING
DESTAINING
DESTEMPERED
DESTEMPERING
DESTEMPERS
DESTINATED
DESTINATES
DESTINATING
DESTINATION
DESTINATIONS
DESTITUTED
DESTITUTENESS
DESTITUTENESSES
DESTITUTES
DESTITUTING
DESTITUTION
DESTITUTIONS
DESTOCKING
DESTREAMED
DESTREAMING
DESTRESSED
DESTRESSES
DESTRESSING
DESTROYABLE
DESTROYERS
DESTROYING
DESTRUCTED
DESTRUCTIBILITY
DESTRUCTIBLE
DESTRUCTING
DESTRUCTION
DESTRUCTIONAL
DESTRUCTIONIST
DESTRUCTIONISTS
DESTRUCTIONS
DESTRUCTIVE
DESTRUCTIVELY
DESTRUCTIVENESS
DESTRUCTIVES
DESTRUCTIVISM
DESTRUCTIVISMS
DESTRUCTIVIST
DESTRUCTIVISTS
DESTRUCTIVITIES
DESTRUCTIVITY
DESTRUCTOR
DESTRUCTORS
DESTRUCTOS
DESUETUDES
DESUGARING
DESULFURATE
DESULFURATED
DESULFURATES
DESULFURATING
DESULFURATION
DESULFURATIONS
DESULFURED
DESULFURING
DESULFURISATION
DESULFURISE
DESULFURISED
DESULFURISER
DESULFURISERS
DESULFURISES
DESULFURISING
DESULFURIZATION
DESULFURIZE
DESULFURIZED
DESULFURIZER
DESULFURIZERS
DESULFURIZES
DESULFURIZING
DESULPHURATE
DESULPHURATED

D

DESULPHURATES
DESULPHURATING
DESULPHURATION
DESULPHURATIONS
DESULPHURED
DESULPHURING
DESULPHURISE
DESULPHURISED
DESULPHURISER
DESULPHURISERS
DESULPHURISES
DESULPHURISING
DESULPHURIZE
DESULPHURIZED
DESULPHURIZER
DESULPHURIZERS
DESULPHURIZES
DESULPHURIZING
DESULPHURS
DESULTORILY
DESULTORINESS
DESULTORINESSES
DETACHABILITIES
DETACHABILITY
DETACHABLE
DETACHABLY
DETACHEDLY
DETACHEDNESS
DETACHEDNESSES
DETACHMENT
DETACHMENTS
DETAILEDLY
DETAILEDNESS
DETAILEDNESSES
DETAILINGS
DETAINABLE
DETAINMENT
DETAINMENTS
DETANGLERS
DETANGLING
DETASSELED
DETASSELING
DETASSELLED
DETASSELLING
DETECTABILITIES
DETECTABILITY
DETECTABLE
DETECTIBLE
DETECTIONS
DETECTIVELIKE
DETECTIVES
DETECTIVIST
DETECTIVISTS
DETECTOPHONE
DETECTOPHONES
DETECTORIST
DETECTORISTS
DETENTIONS
DETENTISTS
DETERGENCE
DETERGENCES
DETERGENCIES
DETERGENCY
DETERGENTS
DETERIORATE
DETERIORATED
DETERIORATES
DETERIORATING
DETERIORATION
DETERIORATIONS
DETERIORATIVE
DETERIORISM
DETERIORISMS
DETERIORITIES
DETERIORITY
DETERMENTS
DETERMINABILITY
DETERMINABLE
DETERMINABLY
DETERMINACIES
DETERMINACY
DETERMINANT
DETERMINANTAL
DETERMINANTS
DETERMINATE
DETERMINATED
DETERMINATELY
DETERMINATENESS
DETERMINATES
DETERMINATING
DETERMINATION
DETERMINATIONS
DETERMINATIVE
DETERMINATIVELY
DETERMINATIVES
DETERMINATOR
DETERMINATORS
DETERMINED
DETERMINEDLY
DETERMINEDNESS
DETERMINER
DETERMINERS
DETERMINES
DETERMINING
DETERMINISM
DETERMINISMS
DETERMINIST
DETERMINISTIC
DETERMINISTS
DETERRABILITIES
DETERRABILITY
DETERRABLE
DETERRENCE
DETERRENCES
DETERRENTLY
DETERRENTS
DETERSIONS
DETERSIVES
DETESTABILITIES
DETESTABILITY
DETESTABLE
DETESTABLENESS
DETESTABLY
DETESTATION
DETESTATIONS
DETHATCHED
DETHATCHES
DETHATCHING
DETHRONEMENT
DETHRONEMENTS
DETHRONERS
DETHRONING
DETHRONINGS
DETHRONISE
DETHRONISED
DETHRONISES
DETHRONISING
DETHRONIZE
DETHRONIZED
DETHRONIZES
DETHRONIZING
DETONABILITIES
DETONABILITY
DETONATABLE
DETONATING
DETONATION
DETONATIONS
DETONATIVE
DETONATORS
DETORSIONS
DETORTIONS
DETOXICANT
DETOXICANTS
DETOXICATE
DETOXICATED
DETOXICATES
DETOXICATING
DETOXICATION
DETOXICATIONS
DETOXIFICATION
DETOXIFICATIONS
DETOXIFIED
DETOXIFIES
DETOXIFYING
DETRACTING
DETRACTINGLY
DETRACTINGS
DETRACTION
DETRACTIONS
DETRACTIVE
DETRACTIVELY
DETRACTORS
DETRACTORY
DETRACTRESS
DETRACTRESSES
DETRAINING
DETRAINMENT
DETRAINMENTS
DETRAQUEES
DETRIBALISATION
DETRIBALISE
DETRIBALISED
DETRIBALISES
DETRIBALISING
DETRIBALIZATION
DETRIBALIZE
DETRIBALIZED
DETRIBALIZES
DETRIBALIZING
DETRIMENTAL
DETRIMENTALLY
DETRIMENTALS
DETRIMENTS
DETRITIONS
DETRITOVORE
DETRITOVORES
DETRUNCATE
DETRUNCATED
DETRUNCATES
DETRUNCATING
DETRUNCATION
DETRUNCATIONS
DETRUSIONS
DETUMESCENCE
DETUMESCENCES
DETUMESCENT
DEUTERAGONIST
DEUTERAGONISTS
DEUTERANOMALIES
DEUTERANOMALOUS
DEUTERANOMALY
DEUTERANOPE
DEUTERANOPES
DEUTERANOPIA
DEUTERANOPIAS
DEUTERANOPIC
DEUTERATED
DEUTERATES
DEUTERATING
DEUTERATION
DEUTERATIONS
DEUTERIDES
DEUTERIUMS
DEUTEROGAMIES
DEUTEROGAMIST
DEUTEROGAMISTS
DEUTEROGAMY
DEUTEROPLASM
DEUTEROPLASMS
DEUTEROSCOPIC
DEUTEROSCOPIES
DEUTEROSCOPY
DEUTEROSTOME
DEUTEROSTOMES
DEUTEROTOKIES
DEUTEROTOKY
DEUTOPLASM
DEUTOPLASMIC
DEUTOPLASMS
DEUTOPLASTIC

DEVALORISATION
DEVALORISATIONS
DEVALORISE
DEVALORISED
DEVALORISES
DEVALORISING
DEVALORIZATION
DEVALORIZATIONS
DEVALORIZE
DEVALORIZED
DEVALORIZES
DEVALORIZING
DEVALUATED
DEVALUATES
DEVALUATING
DEVALUATION
DEVALUATIONS
DEVANAGARI
DEVANAGARIS
DEVASTATED
DEVASTATES
DEVASTATING
DEVASTATINGLY
DEVASTATION
DEVASTATIONS
DEVASTATIVE
DEVASTATOR
DEVASTATORS
DEVASTAVIT
DEVASTAVITS
DEVELOPABLE
DEVELOPERS
DEVELOPING
DEVELOPMENT
DEVELOPMENTAL
DEVELOPMENTALLY
DEVELOPMENTS
DEVELOPPES
DEVERBATIVE
DEVERBATIVES
DEVIANCIES
DEVIATIONISM
DEVIATIONISMS
DEVIATIONIST
DEVIATIONISTS
DEVIATIONS
DEVILESSES
DEVILFISHES
DEVILISHLY
DEVILISHNESS
DEVILISHNESSES
DEVILMENTS
DEVILSHIPS
DEVILTRIES
DEVILWOODS
DEVIOUSNESS
DEVIOUSNESSES
DEVITALISATION
DEVITALISATIONS
DEVITALISE
DEVITALISED
DEVITALISES
DEVITALISING
DEVITALIZATION
DEVITALIZATIONS
DEVITALIZE
DEVITALIZED
DEVITALIZES
DEVITALIZING
DEVITRIFICATION
DEVITRIFIED
DEVITRIFIES
DEVITRIFYING
DEVOCALISE
DEVOCALISED
DEVOCALISES
DEVOCALISING
DEVOCALIZE
DEVOCALIZED
DEVOCALIZES
DEVOCALIZING
DEVOICINGS
DEVOLUTION
DEVOLUTIONARY
DEVOLUTIONIST
DEVOLUTIONISTS
DEVOLUTIONS
DEVOLVEMENT
DEVOLVEMENTS
DEVONPORTS
DEVOTEDNESS
DEVOTEDNESSES
DEVOTEMENT
DEVOTEMENTS
DEVOTIONAL
DEVOTIONALIST
DEVOTIONALISTS
DEVOTIONALITIES
DEVOTIONALITY
DEVOTIONALLY
DEVOTIONALNESS
DEVOTIONALS
DEVOTIONIST
DEVOTIONISTS
DEVOURINGLY
DEVOURMENT
DEVOURMENTS
DEVOUTNESS
DEVOUTNESSES
DEVVELLING
DEWATERERS
DEWATERING
DEWATERINGS
DEWBERRIES
DEWINESSES
DEXAMETHASONE
DEXAMETHASONES
DEXAMPHETAMINE
DEXAMPHETAMINES
DEXIOTROPIC
DEXTERITIES
DEXTEROUSLY
DEXTEROUSNESS
DEXTEROUSNESSES
DEXTERWISE
DEXTRALITIES
DEXTRALITY
DEXTRANASE
DEXTRANASES
DEXTROCARDIA
DEXTROCARDIAC
DEXTROCARDIACS
DEXTROCARDIAS
DEXTROGLUCOSE
DEXTROGLUCOSES
DEXTROGYRATE
DEXTROGYRE
DEXTROROTARY
DEXTROROTATION
DEXTROROTATIONS
DEXTROROTATORY
DEXTRORSAL
DEXTRORSELY
DEXTROUSLY
DEXTROUSNESS
DEXTROUSNESSES
DEZINCKING
DHARMSALAS
DHARMSHALA
DHARMSHALAS
DIABETICAL
DIABETOGENIC
DIABETOLOGIST
DIABETOLOGISTS
DIABLERIES
DIABOLICAL
DIABOLICALLY
DIABOLICALNESS
DIABOLISED
DIABOLISES
DIABOLISING
DIABOLISMS
DIABOLISTS
DIABOLIZED
DIABOLIZES
DIABOLIZING
DIABOLOGIES
DIABOLOLOGIES
DIABOLOLOGY
DIACATHOLICON
DIACATHOLICONS
DIACAUSTIC
DIACAUSTICS
DIACHRONIC
DIACHRONICALLY
DIACHRONIES
DIACHRONISM
DIACHRONISMS
DIACHRONISTIC
DIACHRONOUS
DIACHYLONS
DIACHYLUMS
DIACODIONS
DIACODIUMS
DIACONATES
DIACONICON
DIACONICONS
DIACOUSTIC
DIACOUSTICS
DIACRITICAL
DIACRITICALLY
DIACRITICS
DIACTINISM
DIACTINISMS
DIADELPHOUS
DIADOCHIES
DIADROMOUS
DIAGENESES
DIAGENESIS
DIAGENETIC
DIAGENETICALLY
DIAGEOTROPIC
DIAGEOTROPISM
DIAGEOTROPISMS
DIAGNOSABILITY
DIAGNOSABLE
DIAGNOSEABLE
DIAGNOSING
DIAGNOSTIC
DIAGNOSTICAL
DIAGNOSTICALLY
DIAGNOSTICIAN
DIAGNOSTICIANS
DIAGNOSTICS
DIAGOMETER
DIAGOMETERS
DIAGONALISABLE
DIAGONALISATION
DIAGONALISE
DIAGONALISED
DIAGONALISES
DIAGONALISING
DIAGONALIZABLE
DIAGONALIZATION
DIAGONALIZE
DIAGONALIZED
DIAGONALIZES
DIAGONALIZING
DIAGONALLY
DIAGRAMING
DIAGRAMMABLE
DIAGRAMMATIC
DIAGRAMMATICAL
DIAGRAMMED
DIAGRAMMING
DIAGRAPHIC
DIAHELIOTROPIC
DIAHELIOTROPISM
DIAKINESES
DIAKINESIS

DIALECTALLY
DIALECTICAL
DIALECTICALLY
DIALECTICIAN
DIALECTICIANS
DIALECTICISM
DIALECTICISMS
DIALECTICS
DIALECTOLOGICAL
DIALECTOLOGIES
DIALECTOLOGIST
DIALECTOLOGISTS
DIALECTOLOGY
DIALLAGOID
DIALOGICAL
DIALOGICALLY
DIALOGISED
DIALOGISES
DIALOGISING
DIALOGISMS
DIALOGISTIC
DIALOGISTICAL
DIALOGISTS
DIALOGITES
DIALOGIZED
DIALOGIZES
DIALOGIZING
DIALOGUERS
DIALOGUING
DIALYPETALOUS
DIALYSABILITIES
DIALYSABILITY
DIALYSABLE
DIALYSATES
DIALYSATION
DIALYSATIONS
DIALYTICALLY
DIALYZABILITIES
DIALYZABILITY
DIALYZABLE
DIALYZATES
DIALYZATION
DIALYZATIONS
DIAMAGNETIC
DIAMAGNETICALLY
DIAMAGNETISM
DIAMAGNETISMS
DIAMAGNETS
DIAMANTIFEROUS
DIAMANTINE
DIAMETRALLY
DIAMETRICAL
DIAMETRICALLY
DIAMONDBACK
DIAMONDBACKS
DIAMONDIFEROUS
DIAMONDING
DIAMORPHINE
DIAMORPHINES
DIANTHUSES
DIAPASONAL
DIAPASONIC
DIAPAUSING
DIAPEDESES
DIAPEDESIS
DIAPEDETIC
DIAPERINGS
DIAPHANEITIES
DIAPHANEITY
DIAPHANOMETER
DIAPHANOMETERS
DIAPHANOUS
DIAPHANOUSLY
DIAPHANOUSNESS
DIAPHONIES
DIAPHORASE
DIAPHORASES
DIAPHORESES
DIAPHORESIS
DIAPHORETIC
DIAPHORETICS
DIAPHOTOTROPIC
DIAPHOTOTROPIES
DIAPHOTOTROPISM
DIAPHOTOTROPY
DIAPHRAGMAL
DIAPHRAGMATIC
DIAPHRAGMATITIS
DIAPHRAGMED
DIAPHRAGMING
DIAPHRAGMITIS
DIAPHRAGMITISES
DIAPHRAGMS
DIAPHYSEAL
DIAPHYSIAL
DIAPIRISMS
DIAPOPHYSES
DIAPOPHYSIAL
DIAPOPHYSIS
DIAPOSITIVE
DIAPOSITIVES
DIAPYETICS
DIARCHICAL
DIARRHETIC
DIARRHOEAL
DIARRHOEAS
DIARRHOEIC
DIARTHRODIAL
DIARTHROSES
DIARTHROSIS
DIASCORDIUM
DIASCORDIUMS
DIASKEUAST
DIASKEUASTS
DIASTALSES
DIASTALSIS
DIASTALTIC
DIASTEMATA
DIASTEMATIC
DIASTEREOISOMER
DIASTEREOMER
DIASTEREOMERIC
DIASTEREOMERS
DIASTROPHIC
DIASTROPHICALLY
DIASTROPHISM
DIASTROPHISMS
DIATESSARON
DIATESSARONS
DIATHERMACIES
DIATHERMACY
DIATHERMAL
DIATHERMANCIES
DIATHERMANCY
DIATHERMANEITY
DIATHERMANOUS
DIATHERMIA
DIATHERMIAS
DIATHERMIC
DIATHERMIES
DIATHERMOUS
DIATOMACEOUS
DIATOMICITIES
DIATOMICITY
DIATOMISTS
DIATOMITES
DIATONICALLY
DIATONICISM
DIATONICISMS
DIATRETUMS
DIATRIBIST
DIATRIBISTS
DIATROPISM
DIATROPISMS
DIAZEUCTIC
DIAZOMETHANE
DIAZOMETHANES
DIAZONIUMS
DIAZOTISATION
DIAZOTISATIONS
DIAZOTISED
DIAZOTISES
DIAZOTISING
DIAZOTIZATION
DIAZOTIZATIONS
DIAZOTIZED
DIAZOTIZES
DIAZOTIZING
DIBASICITIES
DIBASICITY
DIBENZOFURAN
DIBENZOFURANS
DIBRANCHIATE
DIBRANCHIATES
DIBROMIDES
DICACITIES
DICACODYLS
DICARBOXYLIC
DICARPELLARY
DICASTERIES
DICENTRICS
DICEPHALISM
DICEPHALISMS
DICEPHALOUS
DICHASIALLY
DICHLAMYDEOUS
DICHLORACETIC
DICHLORIDE
DICHLORIDES
DICHLOROBENZENE
DICHLOROETHANE
DICHLOROETHANES
DICHLOROMETHANE
DICHLORVOS
DICHLORVOSES
DICHOGAMIC
DICHOGAMIES
DICHOGAMOUS
DICHONDRAS
DICHOTICALLY
DICHOTOMIC
DICHOTOMIES
DICHOTOMISATION
DICHOTOMISE
DICHOTOMISED
DICHOTOMISES
DICHOTOMISING
DICHOTOMIST
DICHOTOMISTS
DICHOTOMIZATION
DICHOTOMIZE
DICHOTOMIZED
DICHOTOMIZES
DICHOTOMIZING
DICHOTOMOUS
DICHOTOMOUSLY
DICHOTOMOUSNESS
DICHROISCOPE
DICHROISCOPES
DICHROISCOPIC
DICHROISMS
DICHROITES
DICHROITIC
DICHROMATE
DICHROMATES
DICHROMATIC
DICHROMATICISM
DICHROMATICISMS
DICHROMATICS
DICHROMATISM
DICHROMATISMS
DICHROMATS
DICHROMISM
DICHROMISMS
DICHROOSCOPE
DICHROOSCOPES
DICHROOSCOPIC
DICHROSCOPE
DICHROSCOPES
DICHROSCOPIC

DICKCISSEL
DICKCISSELS
DICKEYBIRD
DICKEYBIRDS
DICKYBIRDS
DICLINISMS
DICOTYLEDON
DICOTYLEDONOUS
DICOTYLEDONS
DICOUMARIN
DICOUMARINS
DICOUMAROL
DICOUMAROLS
DICROTISMS
DICTATIONAL
DICTATIONS
DICTATORIAL
DICTATORIALLY
DICTATORIALNESS
DICTATORSHIP
DICTATORSHIPS
DICTATRESS
DICTATRESSES
DICTATRICES
DICTATRIXES
DICTATURES
DICTIONALLY
DICTIONARIES
DICTIONARY
DICTYOGENS
DICTYOPTERAN
DICTYOPTERANS
DICTYOSOME
DICTYOSOMES
DICTYOSTELE
DICTYOSTELES
DICUMAROLS
DICYNODONT
DICYNODONTS
DIDACTICAL
DIDACTICALLY
DIDACTICISM
DIDACTICISMS
DIDACTYLISM
DIDACTYLISMS
DIDACTYLOUS
DIDASCALIC
DIDELPHIAN
DIDELPHIDS
DIDELPHINE
DIDELPHOUS
DIDGERIDOO
DIDGERIDOOS
DIDJERIDOO
DIDJERIDOOS
DIDJERIDUS
DIDRACHMAS
DIDYNAMIAN
DIDYNAMIES
DIDYNAMOUS
DIECIOUSLY
DIECIOUSNESS
DIECIOUSNESSES
DIEFFENBACHIA
DIEFFENBACHIAS
DIELECTRIC
DIELECTRICALLY
DIELECTRICS
DIENCEPHALA
DIENCEPHALIC
DIENCEPHALON
DIENCEPHALONS
DIESELINGS
DIESELISATION
DIESELISATIONS
DIESELISED
DIESELISES
DIESELISING
DIESELIZATION
DIESELIZATIONS
DIESELIZED
DIESELIZES
DIESELIZING
DIESELLING
DIESELLINGS
DIESINKERS
DIESTRUSES
DIETARIANS
DIETETICAL
DIETETICALLY
DIETHYLAMIDE
DIETHYLAMIDES
DIETHYLAMINE
DIETHYLAMINES
DIETHYLENE
DIETHYLENES
DIETICIANS
DIETITIANS
DIEZEUGMENON
DIEZEUGMENONS
DIFFARREATION
DIFFARREATIONS
DIFFERENCE
DIFFERENCED
DIFFERENCES
DIFFERENCIED
DIFFERENCIES
DIFFERENCING
DIFFERENCY
DIFFERENCYING
DIFFERENTIA
DIFFERENTIABLE
DIFFERENTIAE
DIFFERENTIAL
DIFFERENTIALLY
DIFFERENTIALS
DIFFERENTIATE
DIFFERENTIATED
DIFFERENTIATES
DIFFERENTIATING
DIFFERENTIATION
DIFFERENTIATOR
DIFFERENTIATORS
DIFFERENTLY
DIFFERENTNESS
DIFFERENTNESSES
DIFFICULTIES
DIFFICULTLY
DIFFICULTY
DIFFIDENCE
DIFFIDENCES
DIFFIDENTLY
DIFFORMITIES
DIFFORMITY
DIFFRACTED
DIFFRACTING
DIFFRACTION
DIFFRACTIONS
DIFFRACTIVE
DIFFRACTIVELY
DIFFRACTIVENESS
DIFFRACTOMETER
DIFFRACTOMETERS
DIFFRACTOMETRIC
DIFFRACTOMETRY
DIFFRANGIBILITY
DIFFRANGIBLE
DIFFUSEDLY
DIFFUSEDNESS
DIFFUSEDNESSES
DIFFUSENESS
DIFFUSENESSES
DIFFUSIBILITIES
DIFFUSIBILITY
DIFFUSIBLE
DIFFUSIBLENESS
DIFFUSIONAL
DIFFUSIONISM
DIFFUSIONISMS
DIFFUSIONIST
DIFFUSIONISTS
DIFFUSIONS
DIFFUSIVELY
DIFFUSIVENESS
DIFFUSIVENESSES
DIFFUSIVITIES
DIFFUSIVITY
DIFUNCTIONAL
DIFUNCTIONALS
DIGASTRICS
DIGESTANTS
DIGESTEDLY
DIGESTIBILITIES
DIGESTIBILITY
DIGESTIBLE
DIGESTIBLENESS
DIGESTIBLY
DIGESTIONAL
DIGESTIONS
DIGESTIVELY
DIGESTIVES
DIGITALINS
DIGITALISATION
DIGITALISATIONS
DIGITALISE
DIGITALISED
DIGITALISES
DIGITALISING
DIGITALISM
DIGITALISMS
DIGITALIZATION
DIGITALIZATIONS
DIGITALIZE
DIGITALIZED
DIGITALIZES
DIGITALIZING
DIGITATELY
DIGITATION
DIGITATIONS
DIGITIFORM
DIGITIGRADE
DIGITIGRADES
DIGITISATION
DIGITISATIONS
DIGITISERS
DIGITISING
DIGITIZATION
DIGITIZATIONS
DIGITIZERS
DIGITIZING
DIGITONINS
DIGITORIUM
DIGITORIUMS
DIGITOXIGENIN
DIGITOXIGENINS
DIGITOXINS
DIGLADIATE
DIGLADIATED
DIGLADIATES
DIGLADIATING
DIGLADIATION
DIGLADIATIONS
DIGLADIATOR
DIGLADIATORS
DIGLOSSIAS
DIGLYCERIDE
DIGLYCERIDES
DIGNIFICATION
DIGNIFICATIONS
DIGNIFIEDLY
DIGNIFIEDNESS
DIGNIFIEDNESSES
DIGNIFYING
DIGNITARIES
DIGONEUTIC
DIGONEUTISM
DIGONEUTISMS
DIGRAPHICALLY
DIGRESSERS
DIGRESSING

D

DIGRESSION
DIGRESSIONAL
DIGRESSIONARY
DIGRESSIONS
DIGRESSIVE
DIGRESSIVELY
DIGRESSIVENESS
DIHYBRIDISM
DIHYBRIDISMS
DIHYDROCODEINE
DIHYDROCODEINES
DIHYDROGEN
DIJUDICATE
DIJUDICATED
DIJUDICATES
DIJUDICATING
DIJUDICATION
DIJUDICATIONS
DILACERATE
DILACERATED
DILACERATES
DILACERATING
DILACERATION
DILACERATIONS
DILAPIDATE
DILAPIDATED
DILAPIDATES
DILAPIDATING
DILAPIDATION
DILAPIDATIONS
DILAPIDATOR
DILAPIDATORS
DILATABILITIES
DILATABILITY
DILATABLENESS
DILATABLENESSES
DILATANCIES
DILATATION
DILATATIONAL
DILATATIONS
DILATATORS
DILATOMETER
DILATOMETERS
DILATOMETRIC
DILATOMETRIES
DILATOMETRY
DILATORILY
DILATORINESS
DILATORINESSES
DILEMMATIC
DILETTANTE
DILETTANTEISH
DILETTANTEISM
DILETTANTEISMS
DILETTANTES
DILETTANTI
DILETTANTISH
DILETTANTISM
DILETTANTISMS
DILIGENCES
DILIGENTLY
DILLYDALLIED
DILLYDALLIES
DILLYDALLY
DILLYDALLYING
DILTIAZEMS
DILUCIDATE
DILUCIDATED
DILUCIDATES
DILUCIDATING
DILUCIDATION
DILUCIDATIONS
DILUTABLES
DILUTENESS
DILUTENESSES
DILUTIONARY
DILUVIALISM
DILUVIALISMS
DILUVIALIST
DILUVIALISTS
DIMENHYDRINATE
DIMENHYDRINATES
DIMENSIONAL
DIMENSIONALITY
DIMENSIONALLY
DIMENSIONED
DIMENSIONING
DIMENSIONLESS
DIMENSIONS
DIMERCAPROL
DIMERCAPROLS
DIMERISATION
DIMERISATIONS
DIMERISING
DIMERIZATION
DIMERIZATIONS
DIMERIZING
DIMETHOATE
DIMETHOATES
DIMETHYLAMINE
DIMETHYLAMINES
DIMETHYLANILINE
DIMIDIATED
DIMIDIATES
DIMIDIATING
DIMIDIATION
DIMIDIATIONS
DIMINISHABLE
DIMINISHED
DIMINISHES
DIMINISHING
DIMINISHINGLY
DIMINISHINGS
DIMINISHMENT
DIMINISHMENTS
DIMINUENDO
DIMINUENDOES
DIMINUENDOS
DIMINUTION
DIMINUTIONS
DIMINUTIVAL
DIMINUTIVE
DIMINUTIVELY
DIMINUTIVENESS
DIMINUTIVES
DIMORPHISM
DIMORPHISMS
DIMORPHOUS
DIMPLEMENT
DIMPLEMENTS
DINANDERIE
DINANDERIES
DINARCHIES
DINGDONGED
DINGDONGING
DINGINESSES
DINGLEBERRIES
DINGLEBERRY
DINITROBENZENE
DINITROBENZENES
DINITROGEN
DINITROPHENOL
DINITROPHENOLS
DINNERLESS
DINNERTIME
DINNERTIMES
DINNERWARE
DINNERWARES
DINOCERASES
DINOFLAGELLATE
DINOFLAGELLATES
DINOMANIAS
DINOSAURIAN
DINOSAURIC
DINOTHERES
DINOTHERIA
DINOTHERIUM
DINOTHERIUMS
DINOTURBATION
DINOTURBATIONS
DINUCLEOTIDE
DINUCLEOTIDES
DIOECIOUSLY
DIOECIOUSNESS
DIOECIOUSNESSES
DIOESTRUSES
DIOICOUSLY
DIOICOUSNESS
DIOICOUSNESSES
DIOPHYSITE
DIOPHYSITES
DIOPTOMETER
DIOPTOMETERS
DIOPTOMETRIES
DIOPTOMETRY
DIOPTRICAL
DIOPTRICALLY
DIORISTICAL
DIORISTICALLY
DIORTHOSES
DIORTHOSIS
DIORTHOTIC
DIOSCOREACEOUS
DIOSGENINS
DIOTHELETE
DIOTHELETES
DIOTHELETIC
DIOTHELETICAL
DIOTHELISM
DIOTHELISMS
DIOTHELITE
DIOTHELITES
DIOXONITRIC
DIPEPTIDASE
DIPEPTIDASES
DIPEPTIDES
DIPETALOUS
DIPHENHYDRAMINE
DIPHENYLAMINE
DIPHENYLAMINES
DIPHENYLENE
DIPHENYLENIMINE
DIPHENYLKETONE
DIPHENYLKETONES
DIPHOSGENE
DIPHOSGENES
DIPHOSPHATE
DIPHOSPHATES
DIPHTHERIA
DIPHTHERIAL
DIPHTHERIAS
DIPHTHERIC
DIPHTHERITIC
DIPHTHERITIS
DIPHTHERITISES
DIPHTHEROID
DIPHTHEROIDS
DIPHTHONGAL
DIPHTHONGALLY
DIPHTHONGED
DIPHTHONGIC
DIPHTHONGING
DIPHTHONGISE
DIPHTHONGISED
DIPHTHONGISES
DIPHTHONGISING
DIPHTHONGIZE
DIPHTHONGIZED
DIPHTHONGIZES
DIPHTHONGIZING
DIPHTHONGS
DIPHYCERCAL
DIPHYLETIC
DIPHYLLOUS
DIPHYODONT
DIPHYODONTS
DIPHYSITES
DIPHYSITISM
DIPHYSITISMS
DIPLEIDOSCOPE

DIPLEIDOSCOPES
DIPLOBIONT
DIPLOBIONTIC
DIPLOBIONTS
DIPLOBLASTIC
DIPLOCARDIAC
DIPLOCOCCAL
DIPLOCOCCI
DIPLOCOCCIC
DIPLOCOCCUS
DIPLODOCUS
DIPLODOCUSES
DIPLOGENESES
DIPLOGENESIS
DIPLOIDIES
DIPLOMACIES
DIPLOMAING
DIPLOMATED
DIPLOMATES
DIPLOMATESE
DIPLOMATESES
DIPLOMATIC
DIPLOMATICAL
DIPLOMATICALLY
DIPLOMATICS
DIPLOMATING
DIPLOMATISE
DIPLOMATISED
DIPLOMATISES
DIPLOMATISING
DIPLOMATIST
DIPLOMATISTS
DIPLOMATIZE
DIPLOMATIZED
DIPLOMATIZES
DIPLOMATIZING
DIPLOMATOLOGIES
DIPLOMATOLOGY
DIPLONEMAS
DIPLOPHASE
DIPLOPHASES
DIPLOSPEAK
DIPLOSPEAKS
DIPLOSTEMONOUS
DIPLOTENES
DIPNETTING
DIPPERFULS
DIPPINESSES
DIPRIONIDIAN
DIPROPELLANT
DIPROPELLANTS
DIPROTODON
DIPROTODONS
DIPROTODONT
DIPROTODONTID
DIPROTODONTIDS
DIPROTODONTS
DIPSOMANIA
DIPSOMANIAC
DIPSOMANIACAL
DIPSOMANIACS
DIPSOMANIAS
DIPSWITCHES
DIPTERISTS
DIPTEROCARP
DIPTEROCARPOUS
DIPTEROCARPS
DIPTEROSES
DIRECTEDNESS
DIRECTEDNESSES
DIRECTIONAL
DIRECTIONALITY
DIRECTIONLESS
DIRECTIONS
DIRECTIVES
DIRECTIVITIES
DIRECTIVITY
DIRECTNESS
DIRECTNESSES
DIRECTORATE
DIRECTORATES
DIRECTORIAL
DIRECTORIALLY
DIRECTORIES
DIRECTORSHIP
DIRECTORSHIPS
DIRECTRESS
DIRECTRESSES
DIRECTRICE
DIRECTRICES
DIRECTRIXES
DIREFULNESS
DIREFULNESSES
DIREMPTING
DIREMPTION
DIREMPTIONS
DIRENESSES
DIRIGIBILITIES
DIRIGIBILITY
DIRIGIBLES
DIRIGISMES
DIRTINESSES
DISABILITIES
DISABILITY
DISABLEMENT
DISABLEMENTS
DISABLISMS
DISABLISTS
DISABUSALS
DISABUSING
DISACCHARID
DISACCHARIDASE
DISACCHARIDASES
DISACCHARIDE
DISACCHARIDES
DISACCHARIDS
DISACCOMMODATE
DISACCOMMODATED
DISACCOMMODATES
DISACCORDANT
DISACCORDED
DISACCORDING
DISACCORDS
DISACCREDIT
DISACCREDITED
DISACCREDITING
DISACCREDITS
DISACCUSTOM
DISACCUSTOMED
DISACCUSTOMING
DISACCUSTOMS
DISACKNOWLEDGE
DISACKNOWLEDGED
DISACKNOWLEDGES
DISADORNED
DISADORNING
DISADVANCE
DISADVANCED
DISADVANCES
DISADVANCING
DISADVANTAGE
DISADVANTAGED
DISADVANTAGEOUS
DISADVANTAGES
DISADVANTAGING
DISADVENTURE
DISADVENTURES
DISADVENTUROUS
DISAFFECTED
DISAFFECTEDLY
DISAFFECTEDNESS
DISAFFECTING
DISAFFECTION
DISAFFECTIONATE
DISAFFECTIONS
DISAFFECTS
DISAFFILIATE
DISAFFILIATED
DISAFFILIATES
DISAFFILIATING
DISAFFILIATION
DISAFFILIATIONS
DISAFFIRMANCE
DISAFFIRMANCES
DISAFFIRMATION
DISAFFIRMATIONS
DISAFFIRMED
DISAFFIRMING
DISAFFIRMS
DISAFFOREST
DISAFFORESTED
DISAFFORESTING
DISAFFORESTMENT
DISAFFORESTS
DISAGGREGATE
DISAGGREGATED
DISAGGREGATES
DISAGGREGATING
DISAGGREGATION
DISAGGREGATIONS
DISAGGREGATIVE
DISAGREEABILITY
DISAGREEABLE
DISAGREEABLES
DISAGREEABLY
DISAGREEING
DISAGREEMENT
DISAGREEMENTS
DISALLOWABLE
DISALLOWANCE
DISALLOWANCES
DISALLOWED
DISALLOWING
DISALLYING
DISAMBIGUATE
DISAMBIGUATED
DISAMBIGUATES
DISAMBIGUATING
DISAMBIGUATION
DISAMBIGUATIONS
DISAMENITIES
DISAMENITY
DISANALOGIES
DISANALOGOUS
DISANALOGY
DISANCHORED
DISANCHORING
DISANCHORS
DISANIMATE
DISANIMATED
DISANIMATES
DISANIMATING
DISANNEXED
DISANNEXES
DISANNEXING
DISANNULLED
DISANNULLER
DISANNULLERS
DISANNULLING
DISANNULLINGS
DISANNULMENT
DISANNULMENTS
DISANOINTED
DISANOINTING
DISANOINTS
DISAPPAREL
DISAPPARELLED
DISAPPARELLING
DISAPPARELS
DISAPPEARANCE
DISAPPEARANCES
DISAPPEARED
DISAPPEARING
DISAPPEARS
DISAPPLICATION
DISAPPLICATIONS
DISAPPLIED
DISAPPLIES
DISAPPLYING
DISAPPOINT

D

DISAPPOINTED
DISAPPOINTEDLY
DISAPPOINTING
DISAPPOINTINGLY
DISAPPOINTMENT
DISAPPOINTMENTS
DISAPPOINTS
DISAPPROBATION
DISAPPROBATIONS
DISAPPROBATIVE
DISAPPROBATORY
DISAPPROPRIATE
DISAPPROPRIATED
DISAPPROPRIATES
DISAPPROVAL
DISAPPROVALS
DISAPPROVE
DISAPPROVED
DISAPPROVER
DISAPPROVERS
DISAPPROVES
DISAPPROVING
DISAPPROVINGLY
DISARMAMENT
DISARMAMENTS
DISARMINGLY
DISARRANGE
DISARRANGED
DISARRANGEMENT
DISARRANGEMENTS
DISARRANGES
DISARRANGING
DISARRAYED
DISARRAYING
DISARTICULATE
DISARTICULATED
DISARTICULATES
DISARTICULATING
DISARTICULATION
DISARTICULATOR
DISARTICULATORS
DISASSEMBLE
DISASSEMBLED
DISASSEMBLER
DISASSEMBLERS
DISASSEMBLES
DISASSEMBLIES
DISASSEMBLING
DISASSEMBLY
DISASSIMILATE
DISASSIMILATED
DISASSIMILATES
DISASSIMILATING
DISASSIMILATION
DISASSIMILATIVE
DISASSOCIATE
DISASSOCIATED
DISASSOCIATES
DISASSOCIATING
DISASSOCIATION
DISASSOCIATIONS
DISASTROUS
DISASTROUSLY
DISATTIRED
DISATTIRES
DISATTIRING
DISATTRIBUTION
DISATTRIBUTIONS
DISATTUNED
DISATTUNES
DISATTUNING
DISAUTHORISE
DISAUTHORISED
DISAUTHORISES
DISAUTHORISING
DISAUTHORIZE
DISAUTHORIZED
DISAUTHORIZES
DISAUTHORIZING
DISAVAUNCE
DISAVAUNCED
DISAVAUNCES
DISAVAUNCING
DISAVENTROUS
DISAVENTURE
DISAVENTURES
DISAVOUCHED
DISAVOUCHES
DISAVOUCHING
DISAVOWABLE
DISAVOWALS
DISAVOWEDLY
DISAVOWERS
DISAVOWING
DISBANDING
DISBANDMENT
DISBANDMENTS
DISBARKING
DISBARMENT
DISBARMENTS
DISBARRING
DISBELIEFS
DISBELIEVE
DISBELIEVED
DISBELIEVER
DISBELIEVERS
DISBELIEVES
DISBELIEVING
DISBELIEVINGLY
DISBENCHED
DISBENCHES
DISBENCHING
DISBENEFIT
DISBENEFITS
DISBOSOMED
DISBOSOMING
DISBOWELED
DISBOWELING
DISBOWELLED
DISBOWELLING
DISBRANCHED
DISBRANCHES
DISBRANCHING
DISBUDDING
DISBURDENED
DISBURDENING
DISBURDENMENT
DISBURDENMENTS
DISBURDENS
DISBURSABLE
DISBURSALS
DISBURSEMENT
DISBURSEMENTS
DISBURSERS
DISBURSING
DISBURTHEN
DISBURTHENED
DISBURTHENING
DISBURTHENS
DISCALCEATE
DISCALCEATES
DISCANDERING
DISCANDERINGS
DISCANDIED
DISCANDIES
DISCANDYING
DISCANDYINGS
DISCANTERS
DISCANTING
DISCAPACITATE
DISCAPACITATED
DISCAPACITATES
DISCAPACITATING
DISCARDABLE
DISCARDERS
DISCARDING
DISCARDMENT
DISCARDMENTS
DISCARNATE
DISCEPTATION
DISCEPTATIONS
DISCEPTATIOUS
DISCEPTATOR
DISCEPTATORIAL
DISCEPTATORS
DISCEPTING
DISCERNABLE
DISCERNABLY
DISCERNERS
DISCERNIBLE
DISCERNIBLY
DISCERNING
DISCERNINGLY
DISCERNMENT
DISCERNMENTS
DISCERPIBILITY
DISCERPIBLE
DISCERPING
DISCERPTIBLE
DISCERPTION
DISCERPTIONS
DISCERPTIVE
DISCHARGEABLE
DISCHARGED
DISCHARGEE
DISCHARGEES
DISCHARGER
DISCHARGERS
DISCHARGES
DISCHARGING
DISCHUFFED
DISCHURCHED
DISCHURCHES
DISCHURCHING
DISCIPLESHIP
DISCIPLESHIPS
DISCIPLINABLE
DISCIPLINAL
DISCIPLINANT
DISCIPLINANTS
DISCIPLINARIAN
DISCIPLINARIANS
DISCIPLINARILY
DISCIPLINARITY
DISCIPLINARIUM
DISCIPLINARIUMS
DISCIPLINARY
DISCIPLINE
DISCIPLINED
DISCIPLINER
DISCIPLINERS
DISCIPLINES
DISCIPLING
DISCIPLINING
DISCIPULAR
DISCISSION
DISCISSIONS
DISCLAIMED
DISCLAIMER
DISCLAIMERS
DISCLAIMING
DISCLAMATION
DISCLAMATIONS
DISCLIMAXES
DISCLOSERS
DISCLOSING
DISCLOSURE
DISCLOSURES
DISCOBOLOS
DISCOBOLUS
DISCOBOLUSES
DISCOGRAPHER
DISCOGRAPHERS
DISCOGRAPHIC
DISCOGRAPHICAL
DISCOGRAPHIES
DISCOGRAPHY
DISCOLOGIES
DISCOLOGIST
DISCOLOGISTS

DISCOLORATION
DISCOLORATIONS
DISCOLORED
DISCOLORING
DISCOLORMENT
DISCOLORMENTS
DISCOLOURATION
DISCOLOURATIONS
DISCOLOURED
DISCOLOURING
DISCOLOURMENT
DISCOLOURMENTS
DISCOLOURS
DISCOMBOBERATE
DISCOMBOBERATED
DISCOMBOBERATES
DISCOMBOBULATE
DISCOMBOBULATED
DISCOMBOBULATES
DISCOMEDUSAN
DISCOMEDUSANS
DISCOMFITED
DISCOMFITER
DISCOMFITERS
DISCOMFITING
DISCOMFITS
DISCOMFITURE
DISCOMFITURES
DISCOMFORT
DISCOMFORTABLE
DISCOMFORTED
DISCOMFORTING
DISCOMFORTS
DISCOMMEND
DISCOMMENDABLE
DISCOMMENDATION
DISCOMMENDED
DISCOMMENDING
DISCOMMENDS
DISCOMMISSION
DISCOMMISSIONED
DISCOMMISSIONS
DISCOMMODE
DISCOMMODED
DISCOMMODES
DISCOMMODING
DISCOMMODIOUS
DISCOMMODIOUSLY
DISCOMMODITIES
DISCOMMODITY
DISCOMMONED
DISCOMMONING
DISCOMMONS
DISCOMMUNITIES
DISCOMMUNITY
DISCOMPOSE
DISCOMPOSED
DISCOMPOSEDLY
DISCOMPOSES
DISCOMPOSING
DISCOMPOSINGLY
DISCOMPOSURE
DISCOMPOSURES
DISCOMYCETE
DISCOMYCETES
DISCOMYCETOUS
DISCONCERT
DISCONCERTED
DISCONCERTEDLY
DISCONCERTING
DISCONCERTINGLY
DISCONCERTION
DISCONCERTIONS
DISCONCERTMENT
DISCONCERTMENTS
DISCONCERTS
DISCONFIRM
DISCONFIRMATION
DISCONFIRMED
DISCONFIRMING
DISCONFIRMS
DISCONFORMABLE
DISCONFORMITIES
DISCONFORMITY
DISCONNECT
DISCONNECTED
DISCONNECTEDLY
DISCONNECTER
DISCONNECTERS
DISCONNECTING
DISCONNECTION
DISCONNECTIONS
DISCONNECTIVE
DISCONNECTS
DISCONNEXION
DISCONNEXIONS
DISCONSENT
DISCONSENTED
DISCONSENTING
DISCONSENTS
DISCONSOLATE
DISCONSOLATELY
DISCONSOLATION
DISCONSOLATIONS
DISCONTENT
DISCONTENTED
DISCONTENTEDLY
DISCONTENTFUL
DISCONTENTING
DISCONTENTMENT
DISCONTENTMENTS
DISCONTENTS
DISCONTIGUITIES
DISCONTIGUITY
DISCONTIGUOUS
DISCONTINUANCE
DISCONTINUANCES
DISCONTINUATION
DISCONTINUE
DISCONTINUED
DISCONTINUER
DISCONTINUERS
DISCONTINUES
DISCONTINUING
DISCONTINUITIES
DISCONTINUITY
DISCONTINUOUS
DISCONTINUOUSLY
DISCOPHILE
DISCOPHILES
DISCOPHORAN
DISCOPHORANS
DISCOPHOROUS
DISCORDANCE
DISCORDANCES
DISCORDANCIES
DISCORDANCY
DISCORDANT
DISCORDANTLY
DISCORDFUL
DISCORDING
DISCORPORATE
DISCORPORATED
DISCORPORATES
DISCORPORATING
DISCOTHEQUE
DISCOTHEQUES
DISCOUNSEL
DISCOUNSELLED
DISCOUNSELLING
DISCOUNSELS
DISCOUNTABLE
DISCOUNTED
DISCOUNTENANCE
DISCOUNTENANCED
DISCOUNTENANCES
DISCOUNTER
DISCOUNTERS
DISCOUNTING
DISCOURAGE
DISCOURAGEABLE
DISCOURAGED
DISCOURAGEMENT
DISCOURAGEMENTS
DISCOURAGER
DISCOURAGERS
DISCOURAGES
DISCOURAGING
DISCOURAGINGLY
DISCOURING
DISCOURSAL
DISCOURSED
DISCOURSER
DISCOURSERS
DISCOURSES
DISCOURSING
DISCOURSIVE
DISCOURTEISE
DISCOURTEOUS
DISCOURTEOUSLY
DISCOURTESIES
DISCOURTESY
DISCOVERABLE
DISCOVERED
DISCOVERER
DISCOVERERS
DISCOVERIES
DISCOVERING
DISCOVERTURE
DISCOVERTURES
DISCREDITABLE
DISCREDITABLY
DISCREDITED
DISCREDITING
DISCREDITS
DISCREETER
DISCREETEST
DISCREETLY
DISCREETNESS
DISCREETNESSES
DISCREPANCE
DISCREPANCES
DISCREPANCIES
DISCREPANCY
DISCREPANT
DISCREPANTLY
DISCRETELY
DISCRETENESS
DISCRETENESSES
DISCRETEST
DISCRETION
DISCRETIONAL
DISCRETIONALLY
DISCRETIONARILY
DISCRETIONARY
DISCRETIONS
DISCRETIVE
DISCRETIVELY
DISCRETIVES
DISCRIMINABLE
DISCRIMINABLY
DISCRIMINANT
DISCRIMINANTS
DISCRIMINATE
DISCRIMINATED
DISCRIMINATELY
DISCRIMINATES
DISCRIMINATING
DISCRIMINATION
DISCRIMINATIONS
DISCRIMINATIVE
DISCRIMINATOR
DISCRIMINATORS
DISCRIMINATORY
DISCROWNED
DISCROWNING
DISCULPATE
DISCULPATED
DISCULPATES
DISCULPATING

DISCUMBERED
DISCUMBERING
DISCUMBERS
DISCURSION
DISCURSIONS
DISCURSIST
DISCURSISTS
DISCURSIVE
DISCURSIVELY
DISCURSIVENESS
DISCURSORY
DISCURSUSES
DISCUSSABLE
DISCUSSANT
DISCUSSANTS
DISCUSSERS
DISCUSSIBLE
DISCUSSING
DISCUSSION
DISCUSSIONAL
DISCUSSIONS
DISCUSSIVE
DISCUSSIVES
DISCUTIENT
DISCUTIENTS
DISDAINFUL
DISDAINFULLY
DISDAINFULNESS
DISDAINING
DISEASEDNESS
DISEASEDNESSES
DISEASEFUL
DISECONOMIES
DISECONOMY
DISEMBARKATION
DISEMBARKATIONS
DISEMBARKED
DISEMBARKING
DISEMBARKMENT
DISEMBARKMENTS
DISEMBARKS
DISEMBARRASS
DISEMBARRASSED
DISEMBARRASSES
DISEMBARRASSING
DISEMBELLISH
DISEMBELLISHED
DISEMBELLISHES
DISEMBELLISHING
DISEMBITTER
DISEMBITTERED
DISEMBITTERING
DISEMBITTERS
DISEMBODIED
DISEMBODIES
DISEMBODIMENT
DISEMBODIMENTS
DISEMBODYING
DISEMBOGUE
DISEMBOGUED
DISEMBOGUEMENT
DISEMBOGUEMENTS
DISEMBOGUES
DISEMBOGUING
DISEMBOSOM
DISEMBOSOMED
DISEMBOSOMING
DISEMBOSOMS
DISEMBOWEL
DISEMBOWELED
DISEMBOWELING
DISEMBOWELLED
DISEMBOWELLING
DISEMBOWELMENT
DISEMBOWELMENTS
DISEMBOWELS
DISEMBRANGLE
DISEMBRANGLED
DISEMBRANGLES
DISEMBRANGLING
DISEMBROIL
DISEMBROILED
DISEMBROILING
DISEMBROILS
DISEMBURDEN
DISEMBURDENED
DISEMBURDENING
DISEMBURDENS
DISEMPLOYED
DISEMPLOYING
DISEMPLOYMENT
DISEMPLOYMENTS
DISEMPLOYS
DISEMPOWER
DISEMPOWERED
DISEMPOWERING
DISEMPOWERMENT
DISEMPOWERMENTS
DISEMPOWERS
DISEMVOWEL
DISEMVOWELLED
DISEMVOWELLING
DISEMVOWELS
DISENABLED
DISENABLEMENT
DISENABLEMENTS
DISENABLES
DISENABLING
DISENCHAIN
DISENCHAINED
DISENCHAINING
DISENCHAINS
DISENCHANT
DISENCHANTED
DISENCHANTER
DISENCHANTERS
DISENCHANTING
DISENCHANTINGLY
DISENCHANTMENT
DISENCHANTMENTS
DISENCHANTRESS
DISENCHANTS
DISENCLOSE
DISENCLOSED
DISENCLOSES
DISENCLOSING
DISENCUMBER
DISENCUMBERED
DISENCUMBERING
DISENCUMBERMENT
DISENCUMBERS
DISENCUMBRANCE
DISENCUMBRANCES
DISENDOWED
DISENDOWER
DISENDOWERS
DISENDOWING
DISENDOWMENT
DISENDOWMENTS
DISENFRANCHISE
DISENFRANCHISED
DISENFRANCHISES
DISENGAGED
DISENGAGEDNESS
DISENGAGEMENT
DISENGAGEMENTS
DISENGAGES
DISENGAGING
DISENNOBLE
DISENNOBLED
DISENNOBLES
DISENNOBLING
DISENROLLED
DISENROLLING
DISENROLLINGS
DISENSHROUD
DISENSHROUDED
DISENSHROUDING
DISENSHROUDS
DISENSLAVE
DISENSLAVED
DISENSLAVES
DISENSLAVING
DISENTAILED
DISENTAILING
DISENTAILMENT
DISENTAILMENTS
DISENTAILS
DISENTANGLE
DISENTANGLED
DISENTANGLEMENT
DISENTANGLES
DISENTANGLING
DISENTHRAL
DISENTHRALL
DISENTHRALLED
DISENTHRALLING
DISENTHRALLMENT
DISENTHRALLS
DISENTHRALMENT
DISENTHRALMENTS
DISENTHRALS
DISENTHRONE
DISENTHRONED
DISENTHRONES
DISENTHRONING
DISENTITLE
DISENTITLED
DISENTITLES
DISENTITLING
DISENTOMBED
DISENTOMBING
DISENTOMBS
DISENTRAIL
DISENTRAILED
DISENTRAILING
DISENTRAILS
DISENTRAIN
DISENTRAINED
DISENTRAINING
DISENTRAINMENT
DISENTRAINMENTS
DISENTRAINS
DISENTRANCE
DISENTRANCED
DISENTRANCEMENT
DISENTRANCES
DISENTRANCING
DISENTRAYLE
DISENTRAYLED
DISENTRAYLES
DISENTRAYLING
DISENTWINE
DISENTWINED
DISENTWINES
DISENTWINING
DISENVELOP
DISENVELOPED
DISENVELOPING
DISENVELOPS
DISENVIRON
DISENVIRONED
DISENVIRONING
DISENVIRONS
DISEPALOUS
DISEQUILIBRATE
DISEQUILIBRATED
DISEQUILIBRATES
DISEQUILIBRIA
DISEQUILIBRIUM
DISEQUILIBRIUMS
DISESPOUSE
DISESPOUSED
DISESPOUSES
DISESPOUSING
DISESTABLISH
DISESTABLISHED
DISESTABLISHES
DISESTABLISHING
DISESTEEMED

DISESTEEMING
DISESTEEMS
DISESTIMATION
DISESTIMATIONS
DISFAVORED
DISFAVORING
DISFAVOURED
DISFAVOURER
DISFAVOURERS
DISFAVOURING
DISFAVOURS
DISFEATURE
DISFEATURED
DISFEATUREMENT
DISFEATUREMENTS
DISFEATURES
DISFEATURING
DISFELLOWSHIP
DISFELLOWSHIPED
DISFELLOWSHIPS
DISFIGURATION
DISFIGURATIONS
DISFIGURED
DISFIGUREMENT
DISFIGUREMENTS
DISFIGURER
DISFIGURERS
DISFIGURES
DISFIGURING
DISFLESHED
DISFLESHES
DISFLESHING
DISFLUENCIES
DISFLUENCY
DISFORESTATION
DISFORESTATIONS
DISFORESTED
DISFORESTING
DISFORESTS
DISFORMING
DISFRANCHISE
DISFRANCHISED
DISFRANCHISES
DISFRANCHISING
DISFROCKED
DISFROCKING
DISFUNCTION
DISFUNCTIONAL
DISFUNCTIONS
DISFURNISH
DISFURNISHED
DISFURNISHES
DISFURNISHING
DISFURNISHMENT
DISFURNISHMENTS
DISGARNISH
DISGARNISHED
DISGARNISHES
DISGARNISHING
DISGARRISON
DISGARRISONED
DISGARRISONING
DISGARRISONS
DISGAVELLED
DISGAVELLING
DISGAVELLINGS
DISGESTING
DISGESTION
DISGESTIONS
DISGLORIFIED
DISGLORIFIES
DISGLORIFY
DISGLORIFYING
DISGORGEMENT
DISGORGEMENTS
DISGORGERS
DISGORGING
DISGOSPELLING
DISGOWNING
DISGRACEFUL
DISGRACEFULLY
DISGRACEFULNESS
DISGRACERS
DISGRACING
DISGRACIOUS
DISGRADATION
DISGRADATIONS
DISGRADING
DISGREGATION
DISGREGATIONS
DISGRUNTLE
DISGRUNTLED
DISGRUNTLEMENT
DISGRUNTLEMENTS
DISGRUNTLES
DISGRUNTLING
DISGUISABLE
DISGUISEDLY
DISGUISEDNESS
DISGUISEDNESSES
DISGUISELESS
DISGUISEMENT
DISGUISEMENTS
DISGUISERS
DISGUISING
DISGUISINGS
DISGUSTEDLY
DISGUSTEDNESS
DISGUSTEDNESSES
DISGUSTFUL
DISGUSTFULLY
DISGUSTFULNESS
DISGUSTING
DISGUSTINGLY
DISGUSTINGNESS
DISHABILITATE
DISHABILITATED
DISHABILITATES
DISHABILITATING
DISHABILITATION
DISHABILLE
DISHABILLES
DISHABITED
DISHABITING
DISHABLING
DISHALLOWED
DISHALLOWING
DISHALLOWS
DISHARMONIC
DISHARMONIES
DISHARMONIOUS
DISHARMONIOUSLY
DISHARMONISE
DISHARMONISED
DISHARMONISES
DISHARMONISING
DISHARMONIZE
DISHARMONIZED
DISHARMONIZES
DISHARMONIZING
DISHARMONY
DISHCLOTHS
DISHCLOUTS
DISHDASHAS
DISHDASHES
DISHEARTEN
DISHEARTENED
DISHEARTENING
DISHEARTENINGLY
DISHEARTENMENT
DISHEARTENMENTS
DISHEARTENS
DISHELMING
DISHERISON
DISHERISONS
DISHERITED
DISHERITING
DISHERITOR
DISHERITORS
DISHEVELED
DISHEVELING
DISHEVELLED
DISHEVELLING
DISHEVELMENT
DISHEVELMENTS
DISHOARDED
DISHOARDING
DISHONESTIES
DISHONESTLY
DISHONESTY
DISHONORABLE
DISHONORABLY
DISHONORARY
DISHONORED
DISHONORER
DISHONORERS
DISHONORING
DISHONOURABLE
DISHONOURABLY
DISHONOURED
DISHONOURER
DISHONOURERS
DISHONOURING
DISHONOURS
DISHORNING
DISHORSING
DISHOUSING
DISHTOWELS
DISHUMOURED
DISHUMOURING
DISHUMOURS
DISHWASHER
DISHWASHERS
DISHWATERS
DISILLUDED
DISILLUDES
DISILLUDING
DISILLUMINATE
DISILLUMINATED
DISILLUMINATES
DISILLUMINATING
DISILLUSION
DISILLUSIONARY
DISILLUSIONED
DISILLUSIONING
DISILLUSIONISE
DISILLUSIONISED
DISILLUSIONISES
DISILLUSIONIZE
DISILLUSIONIZED
DISILLUSIONIZES
DISILLUSIONMENT
DISILLUSIONS
DISILLUSIVE
DISIMAGINE
DISIMAGINED
DISIMAGINES
DISIMAGINING
DISIMMURED
DISIMMURES
DISIMMURING
DISIMPASSIONED
DISIMPRISON
DISIMPRISONED
DISIMPRISONING
DISIMPRISONMENT
DISIMPRISONS
DISIMPROVE
DISIMPROVED
DISIMPROVES
DISIMPROVING
DISINCARCERATE
DISINCARCERATED
DISINCARCERATES
DISINCENTIVE
DISINCENTIVES
DISINCLINATION
DISINCLINATIONS
DISINCLINE
DISINCLINED

D

DISINCLINES
DISINCLINING
DISINCLOSE
DISINCLOSED
DISINCLOSES
DISINCLOSING
DISINCORPORATE
DISINCORPORATED
DISINCORPORATES
DISINFECTANT
DISINFECTANTS
DISINFECTED
DISINFECTING
DISINFECTION
DISINFECTIONS
DISINFECTOR
DISINFECTORS
DISINFECTS
DISINFESTANT
DISINFESTANTS
DISINFESTATION
DISINFESTATIONS
DISINFESTED
DISINFESTING
DISINFESTS
DISINFLATION
DISINFLATIONARY
DISINFLATIONS
DISINFORMATION
DISINFORMATIONS
DISINFORMED
DISINFORMING
DISINFORMS
DISINGENUITIES
DISINGENUITY
DISINGENUOUS
DISINGENUOUSLY
DISINHERISON
DISINHERISONS
DISINHERIT
DISINHERITANCE
DISINHERITANCES
DISINHERITED
DISINHERITING
DISINHERITS
DISINHIBIT
DISINHIBITED
DISINHIBITING
DISINHIBITION
DISINHIBITIONS
DISINHIBITORY
DISINHIBITS
DISINHUMED
DISINHUMES
DISINHUMING
DISINTEGRABLE
DISINTEGRATE
DISINTEGRATED
DISINTEGRATES
DISINTEGRATING
DISINTEGRATION
DISINTEGRATIONS
DISINTEGRATIVE
DISINTEGRATOR
DISINTEGRATORS
DISINTEREST
DISINTERESTED
DISINTERESTEDLY
DISINTERESTING
DISINTERESTS
DISINTERMENT
DISINTERMENTS
DISINTERRED
DISINTERRING
DISINTHRAL
DISINTHRALLED
DISINTHRALLING
DISINTHRALLINGS
DISINTHRALS
DISINTOXICATE
DISINTOXICATED
DISINTOXICATES
DISINTOXICATING
DISINTOXICATION
DISINTRICATE
DISINTRICATED
DISINTRICATES
DISINTRICATING
DISINURING
DISINVENTED
DISINVENTING
DISINVENTS
DISINVESTED
DISINVESTING
DISINVESTITURE
DISINVESTITURES
DISINVESTMENT
DISINVESTMENTS
DISINVESTS
DISINVIGORATE
DISINVIGORATED
DISINVIGORATES
DISINVIGORATING
DISINVITED
DISINVITES
DISINVITING
DISINVOLVE
DISINVOLVED
DISINVOLVES
DISINVOLVING
DISJECTING
DISJECTION
DISJECTIONS
DISJOINABLE
DISJOINING
DISJOINTED
DISJOINTEDLY
DISJOINTEDNESS
DISJOINTING
DISJUNCTION
DISJUNCTIONS
DISJUNCTIVE
DISJUNCTIVELY
DISJUNCTIVES
DISJUNCTOR
DISJUNCTORS
DISJUNCTURE
DISJUNCTURES
DISLEAFING
DISLEAVING
DISLIKABLE
DISLIKEABLE
DISLIKEFUL
DISLIKENED
DISLIKENESS
DISLIKENESSES
DISLIKENING
DISLIMBING
DISLIMNING
DISLINKING
DISLOADING
DISLOCATED
DISLOCATEDLY
DISLOCATES
DISLOCATING
DISLOCATION
DISLOCATIONS
DISLODGEMENT
DISLODGEMENTS
DISLODGING
DISLODGMENT
DISLODGMENTS
DISLOIGNED
DISLOIGNING
DISLOYALLY
DISLOYALTIES
DISLOYALTY
DISLUSTRED
DISLUSTRES
DISLUSTRING
DISMALITIES
DISMALLEST
DISMALNESS
DISMALNESSES
DISMANNING
DISMANTLED
DISMANTLEMENT
DISMANTLEMENTS
DISMANTLER
DISMANTLERS
DISMANTLES
DISMANTLING
DISMANTLINGS
DISMASKING
DISMASTING
DISMASTMENT
DISMASTMENTS
DISMAYEDNESS
DISMAYEDNESSES
DISMAYFULLY
DISMAYINGLY
DISMAYLING
DISMEMBERED
DISMEMBERER
DISMEMBERERS
DISMEMBERING
DISMEMBERMENT
DISMEMBERMENTS
DISMEMBERS
DISMISSALS
DISMISSIBLE
DISMISSING
DISMISSION
DISMISSIONS
DISMISSIVE
DISMISSIVELY
DISMISSORY
DISMOUNTABLE
DISMOUNTED
DISMOUNTING
DISMUTATION
DISMUTATIONS
DISNATURALISE
DISNATURALISED
DISNATURALISES
DISNATURALISING
DISNATURALIZE
DISNATURALIZED
DISNATURALIZES
DISNATURALIZING
DISNATURED
DISNATURES
DISNATURING
DISNESTING
DISOBEDIENCE
DISOBEDIENCES
DISOBEDIENT
DISOBEDIENTLY
DISOBEYERS
DISOBEYING
DISOBLIGATION
DISOBLIGATIONS
DISOBLIGATORY
DISOBLIGED
DISOBLIGEMENT
DISOBLIGEMENTS
DISOBLIGES
DISOBLIGING
DISOBLIGINGLY
DISOBLIGINGNESS
DISOPERATION
DISOPERATIONS
DISORDERED
DISORDEREDLY
DISORDEREDNESS
DISORDERING
DISORDERLIES
DISORDERLINESS
DISORDERLY
DISORDINATE

DISORDINATELY
DISORGANIC
DISORGANISATION
DISORGANISE
DISORGANISED
DISORGANISER
DISORGANISERS
DISORGANISES
DISORGANISING
DISORGANIZATION
DISORGANIZE
DISORGANIZED
DISORGANIZER
DISORGANIZERS
DISORGANIZES
DISORGANIZING
DISORIENTATE
DISORIENTATED
DISORIENTATES
DISORIENTATING
DISORIENTATION
DISORIENTATIONS
DISORIENTED
DISORIENTING
DISORIENTS
DISOWNMENT
DISOWNMENTS
DISPARAGED
DISPARAGEMENT
DISPARAGEMENTS
DISPARAGER
DISPARAGERS
DISPARAGES
DISPARAGING
DISPARAGINGLY
DISPARATELY
DISPARATENESS
DISPARATENESSES
DISPARATES
DISPARITIES
DISPARKING
DISPARTING
DISPASSION
DISPASSIONATE
DISPASSIONATELY
DISPASSIONS
DISPATCHED
DISPATCHER
DISPATCHERS
DISPATCHES
DISPATCHFUL
DISPATCHING
DISPATHIES
DISPAUPERED
DISPAUPERING
DISPAUPERISE
DISPAUPERISED
DISPAUPERISES
DISPAUPERISING
DISPAUPERIZE
DISPAUPERIZED
DISPAUPERIZES
DISPAUPERIZING
DISPAUPERS
DISPELLERS
DISPELLING
DISPENCING
DISPENDING
DISPENSABILITY
DISPENSABLE
DISPENSABLENESS
DISPENSABLY
DISPENSARIES
DISPENSARY
DISPENSATION
DISPENSATIONAL
DISPENSATIONS
DISPENSATIVE
DISPENSATIVELY
DISPENSATOR
DISPENSATORIES
DISPENSATORILY
DISPENSATORS
DISPENSATORY
DISPENSERS
DISPENSING
DISPEOPLED
DISPEOPLES
DISPEOPLING
DISPERMOUS
DISPERSALS
DISPERSANT
DISPERSANTS
DISPERSEDLY
DISPERSEDNESS
DISPERSEDNESSES
DISPERSERS
DISPERSIBLE
DISPERSING
DISPERSION
DISPERSIONS
DISPERSIVE
DISPERSIVELY
DISPERSIVENESS
DISPERSOID
DISPERSOIDS
DISPIRITED
DISPIRITEDLY
DISPIRITEDNESS
DISPIRITING
DISPIRITINGLY
DISPIRITMENT
DISPIRITMENTS
DISPITEOUS
DISPITEOUSLY
DISPITEOUSNESS
DISPLACEABLE
DISPLACEMENT
DISPLACEMENTS
DISPLACERS
DISPLACING
DISPLANTATION
DISPLANTATIONS
DISPLANTED
DISPLANTING
DISPLAYABLE
DISPLAYERS
DISPLAYING
DISPLEASANCE
DISPLEASANCES
DISPLEASANT
DISPLEASANTED
DISPLEASANTING
DISPLEASANTS
DISPLEASED
DISPLEASEDLY
DISPLEASEDNESS
DISPLEASES
DISPLEASING
DISPLEASINGLY
DISPLEASINGNESS
DISPLEASURE
DISPLEASURED
DISPLEASURES
DISPLEASURING
DISPLENISH
DISPLENISHED
DISPLENISHES
DISPLENISHING
DISPLENISHMENT
DISPLENISHMENTS
DISPLODING
DISPLOSION
DISPLOSIONS
DISPLUMING
DISPONDAIC
DISPONDEES
DISPONGING
DISPORTING
DISPORTMENT
DISPORTMENTS
DISPOSABILITIES
DISPOSABILITY
DISPOSABLE
DISPOSABLENESS
DISPOSABLES
DISPOSEDLY
DISPOSINGLY
DISPOSINGS
DISPOSITION
DISPOSITIONAL
DISPOSITIONED
DISPOSITIONS
DISPOSITIVE
DISPOSITIVELY
DISPOSITIVES
DISPOSITOR
DISPOSITORS
DISPOSSESS
DISPOSSESSED
DISPOSSESSES
DISPOSSESSING
DISPOSSESSION
DISPOSSESSIONS
DISPOSSESSOR
DISPOSSESSORS
DISPOSSESSORY
DISPOSTING
DISPOSURES
DISPRAISED
DISPRAISER
DISPRAISERS
DISPRAISES
DISPRAISING
DISPRAISINGLY
DISPREADING
DISPREDDEN
DISPREDDING
DISPRINCED
DISPRISONED
DISPRISONING
DISPRISONS
DISPRIVACIED
DISPRIVILEGE
DISPRIVILEGED
DISPRIVILEGES
DISPRIVILEGING
DISPRIZING
DISPROFESS
DISPROFESSED
DISPROFESSES
DISPROFESSING
DISPROFITED
DISPROFITING
DISPROFITS
DISPROOVED
DISPROOVES
DISPROOVING
DISPROPERTIED
DISPROPERTIES
DISPROPERTY
DISPROPERTYING
DISPROPORTION
DISPROPORTIONAL
DISPROPORTIONED
DISPROPORTIONS
DISPROPRIATE
DISPROPRIATED
DISPROPRIATES
DISPROPRIATING
DISPROVABLE
DISPROVALS
DISPROVERS
DISPROVIDE
DISPROVIDED
DISPROVIDES
DISPROVIDING
DISPROVING
DISPUNGING
DISPURSING

D

D

DISPURVEYANCE
DISPURVEYANCES
DISPURVEYED
DISPURVEYING
DISPURVEYS
DISPUTABILITIES
DISPUTABILITY
DISPUTABLE
DISPUTABLENESS
DISPUTABLY
DISPUTANTS
DISPUTATION
DISPUTATIONS
DISPUTATIOUS
DISPUTATIOUSLY
DISPUTATIVE
DISPUTATIVELY
DISPUTATIVENESS
DISQUALIFIABLE
DISQUALIFIED
DISQUALIFIER
DISQUALIFIERS
DISQUALIFIES
DISQUALIFY
DISQUALIFYING
DISQUANTITIED
DISQUANTITIES
DISQUANTITY
DISQUANTITYING
DISQUIETED
DISQUIETEDLY
DISQUIETEDNESS
DISQUIETEN
DISQUIETENED
DISQUIETENING
DISQUIETENS
DISQUIETFUL
DISQUIETING
DISQUIETINGLY
DISQUIETIVE
DISQUIETLY
DISQUIETNESS
DISQUIETNESSES
DISQUIETOUS
DISQUIETUDE
DISQUIETUDES
DISQUISITION
DISQUISITIONAL
DISQUISITIONARY
DISQUISITIONS
DISQUISITIVE
DISQUISITORY
DISRANKING
DISREGARDED
DISREGARDER
DISREGARDERS
DISREGARDFUL
DISREGARDFULLY
DISREGARDING
DISREGARDS
DISRELATED
DISRELATION
DISRELATIONS
DISRELISHED
DISRELISHES
DISRELISHING
DISREMEMBER
DISREMEMBERED
DISREMEMBERING
DISREMEMBERS
DISREPAIRS
DISREPUTABILITY
DISREPUTABLE
DISREPUTABLY
DISREPUTATION
DISREPUTATIONS
DISREPUTES
DISRESPECT
DISRESPECTABLE
DISRESPECTED
DISRESPECTFUL
DISRESPECTFULLY
DISRESPECTING
DISRESPECTS
DISROBEMENT
DISROBEMENTS
DISROOTING
DISRUPTERS
DISRUPTING
DISRUPTION
DISRUPTIONS
DISRUPTIVE
DISRUPTIVELY
DISRUPTIVENESS
DISRUPTORS
DISSATISFACTION
DISSATISFACTORY
DISSATISFIED
DISSATISFIEDLY
DISSATISFIES
DISSATISFY
DISSATISFYING
DISSAVINGS
DISSEATING
DISSECTIBLE
DISSECTING
DISSECTINGS
DISSECTION
DISSECTIONS
DISSECTIVE
DISSECTORS
DISSEISEES
DISSEISING
DISSEISINS
DISSEISORS
DISSEIZEES
DISSEIZING
DISSEIZINS
DISSEIZORS
DISSELBOOM
DISSELBOOMS
DISSEMBLANCE
DISSEMBLANCES
DISSEMBLED
DISSEMBLER
DISSEMBLERS
DISSEMBLES
DISSEMBLIES
DISSEMBLING
DISSEMBLINGLY
DISSEMBLINGS
DISSEMINATE
DISSEMINATED
DISSEMINATES
DISSEMINATING
DISSEMINATION
DISSEMINATIONS
DISSEMINATIVE
DISSEMINATOR
DISSEMINATORS
DISSEMINULE
DISSEMINULES
DISSENSION
DISSENSIONS
DISSENSUSES
DISSENTERISH
DISSENTERISM
DISSENTERISMS
DISSENTERS
DISSENTIENCE
DISSENTIENCES
DISSENTIENCIES
DISSENTIENCY
DISSENTIENT
DISSENTIENTLY
DISSENTIENTS
DISSENTING
DISSENTINGLY
DISSENTION
DISSENTIONS
DISSENTIOUS
DISSEPIMENT
DISSEPIMENTAL
DISSEPIMENTS
DISSERTATE
DISSERTATED
DISSERTATES
DISSERTATING
DISSERTATION
DISSERTATIONAL
DISSERTATIONIST
DISSERTATIONS
DISSERTATIVE
DISSERTATOR
DISSERTATORS
DISSERTING
DISSERVICE
DISSERVICEABLE
DISSERVICES
DISSERVING
DISSEVERANCE
DISSEVERANCES
DISSEVERATION
DISSEVERATIONS
DISSEVERED
DISSEVERING
DISSEVERMENT
DISSEVERMENTS
DISSHEATHE
DISSHEATHED
DISSHEATHES
DISSHEATHING
DISSHIVERED
DISSHIVERING
DISSHIVERS
DISSIDENCE
DISSIDENCES
DISSIDENTLY
DISSIDENTS
DISSILIENCE
DISSILIENCES
DISSILIENT
DISSIMILAR
DISSIMILARITIES
DISSIMILARITY
DISSIMILARLY
DISSIMILARS
DISSIMILATE
DISSIMILATED
DISSIMILATES
DISSIMILATING
DISSIMILATION
DISSIMILATIONS
DISSIMILATIVE
DISSIMILATORY
DISSIMILES
DISSIMILITUDE
DISSIMILITUDES
DISSIMULATE
DISSIMULATED
DISSIMULATES
DISSIMULATING
DISSIMULATION
DISSIMULATIONS
DISSIMULATIVE
DISSIMULATOR
DISSIMULATORS
DISSIPABLE
DISSIPATED
DISSIPATEDLY
DISSIPATEDNESS
DISSIPATER
DISSIPATERS
DISSIPATES
DISSIPATING
DISSIPATION
DISSIPATIONS
DISSIPATIVE
DISSIPATOR
DISSIPATORS

DISSOCIABILITY
DISSOCIABLE
DISSOCIABLENESS
DISSOCIABLY
DISSOCIALISE
DISSOCIALISED
DISSOCIALISES
DISSOCIALISING
DISSOCIALITIES
DISSOCIALITY
DISSOCIALIZE
DISSOCIALIZED
DISSOCIALIZES
DISSOCIALIZING
DISSOCIATE
DISSOCIATED
DISSOCIATES
DISSOCIATING
DISSOCIATION
DISSOCIATIONS
DISSOCIATIVE
DISSOLUBILITIES
DISSOLUBILITY
DISSOLUBLE
DISSOLUBLENESS
DISSOLUTELY
DISSOLUTENESS
DISSOLUTENESSES
DISSOLUTES
DISSOLUTION
DISSOLUTIONISM
DISSOLUTIONISMS
DISSOLUTIONIST
DISSOLUTIONISTS
DISSOLUTIONS
DISSOLUTIVE
DISSOLVABILITY
DISSOLVABLE
DISSOLVABLENESS
DISSOLVENT
DISSOLVENTS
DISSOLVERS
DISSOLVING
DISSOLVINGS
DISSONANCE
DISSONANCES
DISSONANCIES
DISSONANCY
DISSONANTLY
DISSUADABLE
DISSUADERS
DISSUADING
DISSUASION
DISSUASIONS
DISSUASIVE
DISSUASIVELY
DISSUASIVENESS
DISSUASIVES
DISSUASORIES
DISSUASORY
DISSUNDERED
DISSUNDERING
DISSUNDERS
DISSYLLABIC
DISSYLLABIFIED
DISSYLLABIFIES
DISSYLLABIFY
DISSYLLABIFYING
DISSYLLABISM
DISSYLLABISMS
DISSYLLABLE
DISSYLLABLES
DISSYMMETRIC
DISSYMMETRICAL
DISSYMMETRIES
DISSYMMETRY
DISTAINING
DISTANCELESS
DISTANCING
DISTANTNESS
DISTANTNESSES
DISTASTEFUL
DISTASTEFULLY
DISTASTEFULNESS
DISTASTING
DISTELFINK
DISTELFINKS
DISTEMPERATE
DISTEMPERATURE
DISTEMPERATURES
DISTEMPERED
DISTEMPERING
DISTEMPERS
DISTENDERS
DISTENDING
DISTENSIBILITY
DISTENSIBLE
DISTENSILE
DISTENSION
DISTENSIONS
DISTENSIVE
DISTENTION
DISTENTIONS
DISTHRONED
DISTHRONES
DISTHRONING
DISTHRONISE
DISTHRONISED
DISTHRONISES
DISTHRONISING
DISTHRONIZE
DISTHRONIZED
DISTHRONIZES
DISTHRONIZING
DISTICHOUS
DISTICHOUSLY
DISTILLABLE
DISTILLAND
DISTILLANDS
DISTILLATE
DISTILLATES
DISTILLATION
DISTILLATIONS
DISTILLATORY
DISTILLERIES
DISTILLERS
DISTILLERY
DISTILLING
DISTILLINGS
DISTILMENT
DISTILMENTS
DISTINCTER
DISTINCTEST
DISTINCTION
DISTINCTIONS
DISTINCTIVE
DISTINCTIVELY
DISTINCTIVENESS
DISTINCTIVES
DISTINCTLY
DISTINCTNESS
DISTINCTNESSES
DISTINCTURE
DISTINCTURES
DISTINGUEE
DISTINGUISH
DISTINGUISHABLE
DISTINGUISHABLY
DISTINGUISHED
DISTINGUISHER
DISTINGUISHERS
DISTINGUISHES
DISTINGUISHING
DISTINGUISHMENT
DISTORTEDLY
DISTORTEDNESS
DISTORTEDNESSES
DISTORTERS
DISTORTING
DISTORTION
DISTORTIONAL
DISTORTIONS
DISTORTIVE
DISTRACTABLE
DISTRACTED
DISTRACTEDLY
DISTRACTEDNESS
DISTRACTER
DISTRACTERS
DISTRACTIBILITY
DISTRACTIBLE
DISTRACTING
DISTRACTINGLY
DISTRACTION
DISTRACTIONS
DISTRACTIVE
DISTRACTIVELY
DISTRACTOR
DISTRACTORS
DISTRAINABLE
DISTRAINED
DISTRAINEE
DISTRAINEES
DISTRAINER
DISTRAINERS
DISTRAINING
DISTRAINMENT
DISTRAINMENTS
DISTRAINOR
DISTRAINORS
DISTRAINTS
DISTRAUGHT
DISTRAUGHTLY
DISTRESSED
DISTRESSER
DISTRESSERS
DISTRESSES
DISTRESSFUL
DISTRESSFULLY
DISTRESSFULNESS
DISTRESSING
DISTRESSINGLY
DISTRESSINGS
DISTRIBUEND
DISTRIBUENDS
DISTRIBUTABLE
DISTRIBUTARIES
DISTRIBUTARY
DISTRIBUTE
DISTRIBUTED
DISTRIBUTEE
DISTRIBUTEES
DISTRIBUTER
DISTRIBUTERS
DISTRIBUTES
DISTRIBUTING
DISTRIBUTION
DISTRIBUTIONAL
DISTRIBUTIONS
DISTRIBUTIVE
DISTRIBUTIVELY
DISTRIBUTIVES
DISTRIBUTIVITY
DISTRIBUTOR
DISTRIBUTORS
DISTRIBUTORSHIP
DISTRICTED
DISTRICTING
DISTRINGAS
DISTRINGASES
DISTROUBLE
DISTROUBLED
DISTROUBLES
DISTROUBLING
DISTRUSTED
DISTRUSTER
DISTRUSTERS
DISTRUSTFUL
DISTRUSTFULLY
DISTRUSTFULNESS

D

DISTRUSTING
DISTRUSTLESS
DISTURBANCE
DISTURBANCES
DISTURBANT
DISTURBANTS
DISTURBATIVE
DISTURBERS
DISTURBING
DISTURBINGLY
DISUBSTITUTED
DISULFATES
DISULFIDES
DISULFIRAM
DISULFIRAMS
DISULFOTON
DISULFOTONS
DISULPHATE
DISULPHATES
DISULPHIDE
DISULPHIDES
DISULPHURET
DISULPHURETS
DISULPHURIC
DISUNIONIST
DISUNIONISTS
DISUNITERS
DISUNITIES
DISUNITING
DISUTILITIES
DISUTILITY
DISVALUING
DISVOUCHED
DISVOUCHES
DISVOUCHING
DISWORSHIP
DISWORSHIPED
DISWORSHIPING
DISWORSHIPPED
DISWORSHIPPING
DISWORSHIPS
DISYLLABIC
DISYLLABIFIED
DISYLLABIFIES
DISYLLABIFY
DISYLLABIFYING
DISYLLABISM
DISYLLABISMS
DISYLLABLE
DISYLLABLES
DITCHDIGGER
DITCHDIGGERS
DITCHWATER
DITCHWATERS
DITHEISTIC
DITHEISTICAL
DITHELETES
DITHELETIC
DITHELETICAL
DITHELETISM
DITHELETISMS
DITHELISMS
DITHELITISM
DITHELITISMS
DITHERIEST
DITHERINGS
DITHIOCARBAMATE
DITHIOCARBAMIC
DITHIONATE
DITHIONATES
DITHIONITE
DITHIONITES
DITHIONOUS
DITHYRAMBIC
DITHYRAMBICALLY
DITHYRAMBIST
DITHYRAMBISTS
DITHYRAMBS
DITRANSITIVE
DITRANSITIVES
DITRIGLYPH
DITRIGLYPHIC
DITRIGLYPHS
DITROCHEAN
DITROCHEES
DITSINESSES
DITTANDERS
DITTOGRAPHIC
DITTOGRAPHIES
DITTOGRAPHY
DITTOLOGIES
DITZINESSES
DIURETICALLY
DIURETICALNESS
DIURNALIST
DIURNALISTS
DIUTURNITIES
DIUTURNITY
DIVAGATING
DIVAGATION
DIVAGATIONS
DIVALENCES
DIVALENCIES
DIVARICATE
DIVARICATED
DIVARICATELY
DIVARICATES
DIVARICATING
DIVARICATINGLY
DIVARICATION
DIVARICATIONS
DIVARICATOR
DIVARICATORS
DIVEBOMBED
DIVEBOMBING
DIVELLICATE
DIVELLICATED
DIVELLICATES
DIVELLICATING
DIVERGEMENT
DIVERGEMENTS
DIVERGENCE
DIVERGENCES
DIVERGENCIES
DIVERGENCY
DIVERGENTLY
DIVERGINGLY
DIVERSENESS
DIVERSENESSES
DIVERSIFIABLE
DIVERSIFICATION
DIVERSIFIED
DIVERSIFIER
DIVERSIFIERS
DIVERSIFIES
DIVERSIFORM
DIVERSIFYING
DIVERSIONAL
DIVERSIONARY
DIVERSIONIST
DIVERSIONISTS
DIVERSIONS
DIVERSITIES
DIVERTIBILITIES
DIVERTIBILITY
DIVERTIBLE
DIVERTICULA
DIVERTICULAR
DIVERTICULATE
DIVERTICULATED
DIVERTICULITIS
DIVERTICULOSES
DIVERTICULOSIS
DIVERTICULUM
DIVERTIMENTI
DIVERTIMENTO
DIVERTIMENTOS
DIVERTINGLY
DIVERTISEMENT
DIVERTISEMENTS
DIVERTISSEMENT
DIVERTISSEMENTS
DIVESTIBLE
DIVESTITURE
DIVESTITURES
DIVESTMENT
DIVESTMENTS
DIVESTURES
DIVIDEDNESS
DIVIDEDNESSES
DIVIDENDLESS
DIVINATION
DIVINATIONS
DIVINATORIAL
DIVINATORS
DIVINATORY
DIVINENESS
DIVINENESSES
DIVINERESS
DIVINERESSES
DIVINIFIED
DIVINIFIES
DIVINIFYING
DIVINISATION
DIVINISATIONS
DIVINISING
DIVINITIES
DIVINIZATION
DIVINIZATIONS
DIVINIZING
DIVISIBILITIES
DIVISIBILITY
DIVISIBLENESS
DIVISIBLENESSES
DIVISIONAL
DIVISIONALLY
DIVISIONARY
DIVISIONISM
DIVISIONISMS
DIVISIONIST
DIVISIONISTS
DIVISIVELY
DIVISIVENESS
DIVISIVENESSES
DIVORCEABLE
DIVORCEMENT
DIVORCEMENTS
DIVULGATED
DIVULGATER
DIVULGATERS
DIVULGATES
DIVULGATING
DIVULGATION
DIVULGATIONS
DIVULGATOR
DIVULGATORS
DIVULGEMENT
DIVULGEMENTS
DIVULGENCE
DIVULGENCES
DIVULSIONS
DIZENMENTS
DIZZINESSES
DIZZYINGLY
DJELLABAHS
DOBSONFLIES
DOCENTSHIP
DOCENTSHIPS
DOCHMIACAL
DOCHMIUSES
DOCIBILITIES
DOCIBILITY
DOCIBLENESS
DOCIBLENESSES
DOCILITIES
DOCIMASIES
DOCIMASTIC
DOCIMOLOGIES
DOCIMOLOGY
DOCKISATION

DOCKISATIONS
DOCKIZATION
DOCKIZATIONS
DOCKMASTER
DOCKMASTERS
DOCKWALLOPER
DOCKWALLOPERS
DOCKWORKER
DOCKWORKERS
DOCQUETING
DOCTORANDS
DOCTORATED
DOCTORATES
DOCTORATING
DOCTORESSES
DOCTORINGS
DOCTORLESS
DOCTORSHIP
DOCTORSHIPS
DOCTRESSES
DOCTRINAIRE
DOCTRINAIRES
DOCTRINAIRISM
DOCTRINAIRISMS
DOCTRINALITIES
DOCTRINALITY
DOCTRINALLY
DOCTRINARIAN
DOCTRINARIANISM
DOCTRINARIANS
DOCTRINARISM
DOCTRINARISMS
DOCTRINISM
DOCTRINISMS
DOCTRINIST
DOCTRINISTS
DOCUDRAMAS
DOCUMENTABLE
DOCUMENTAL
DOCUMENTALIST
DOCUMENTALISTS
DOCUMENTARIAN
DOCUMENTARIANS
DOCUMENTARIES
DOCUMENTARILY
DOCUMENTARISE
DOCUMENTARISED
DOCUMENTARISES
DOCUMENTARISING
DOCUMENTARIST
DOCUMENTARISTS
DOCUMENTARIZE
DOCUMENTARIZED
DOCUMENTARIZES
DOCUMENTARIZING
DOCUMENTARY
DOCUMENTATION
DOCUMENTATIONAL
DOCUMENTATIONS
DOCUMENTED
DOCUMENTER
DOCUMENTERS
DOCUMENTING
DODDERIEST
DODDIPOLLS
DODDYPOLLS
DODECAGONAL
DODECAGONS
DODECAGYNIAN
DODECAGYNOUS
DODECAHEDRA
DODECAHEDRAL
DODECAHEDRON
DODECAHEDRONS
DODECANDROUS
DODECANOIC
DODECAPHONIC
DODECAPHONIES
DODECAPHONISM
DODECAPHONISMS
DODECAPHONIST
DODECAPHONISTS
DODECAPHONY
DODECASTYLE
DODECASTYLES
DODECASYLLABIC
DODECASYLLABLE
DODECASYLLABLES
DODGEBALLS
DODGINESSES
DOGARESSAS
DOGBERRIES
DOGBERRYISM
DOGBERRYISMS
DOGCATCHER
DOGCATCHERS
DOGFIGHTING
DOGFIGHTINGS
DOGGEDNESS
DOGGEDNESSES
DOGGINESSES
DOGGISHNESS
DOGGISHNESSES
DOGGONEDER
DOGGONEDEST
DOGLEGGING
DOGMATICAL
DOGMATICALLY
DOGMATICALNESS
DOGMATISATION
DOGMATISATIONS
DOGMATISED
DOGMATISER
DOGMATISERS
DOGMATISES
DOGMATISING
DOGMATISMS
DOGMATISTS
DOGMATIZATION
DOGMATIZATIONS
DOGMATIZED
DOGMATIZER
DOGMATIZERS
DOGMATIZES
DOGMATIZING
DOGMATOLOGIES
DOGMATOLOGY
DOGNAPINGS
DOGNAPPERS
DOGNAPPING
DOGNAPPINGS
DOGROBBERS
DOGSBODIED
DOGSBODIES
DOGSBODYING
DOGSBODYINGS
DOGSLEDDED
DOGSLEDDER
DOGSLEDDERS
DOGSLEDDING
DOGSLEDDINGS
DOGTROTTED
DOGTROTTING
DOGWATCHES
DOLABRIFORM
DOLCELATTE
DOLCELATTES
DOLCEMENTE
DOLEFULLER
DOLEFULLEST
DOLEFULNESS
DOLEFULNESSES
DOLESOMELY
DOLICHOCEPHAL
DOLICHOCEPHALIC
DOLICHOCEPHALS
DOLICHOCEPHALY
DOLICHOSAURUS
DOLICHOSAURUSES
DOLICHOSES
DOLICHURUS
DOLICHURUSES
DOLLARBIRD
DOLLARBIRDS
DOLLARFISH
DOLLARFISHES
DOLLARISATION
DOLLARISATIONS
DOLLARISED
DOLLARISES
DOLLARISING
DOLLARIZATION
DOLLARIZATIONS
DOLLARIZED
DOLLARIZES
DOLLARIZING
DOLLARLESS
DOLLAROCRACIES
DOLLAROCRACY
DOLLARSHIP
DOLLARSHIPS
DOLLHOUSES
DOLLINESSES
DOLLISHNESS
DOLLISHNESSES
DOLLYBIRDS
DOLOMITISATION
DOLOMITISATIONS
DOLOMITISE
DOLOMITISED
DOLOMITISES
DOLOMITISING
DOLOMITIZATION
DOLOMITIZATIONS
DOLOMITIZE
DOLOMITIZED
DOLOMITIZES
DOLOMITIZING
DOLORIFEROUS
DOLORIMETRIES
DOLORIMETRY
DOLOROUSLY
DOLOROUSNESS
DOLOROUSNESSES
DOLOSTONES
DOLPHINARIA
DOLPHINARIUM
DOLPHINARIUMS
DOLPHINETS
DOLPHINFISH
DOLPHINFISHES
DOLTISHNESS
DOLTISHNESSES
DOMESTICABLE
DOMESTICAL
DOMESTICALLY
DOMESTICATE
DOMESTICATED
DOMESTICATES
DOMESTICATING
DOMESTICATION
DOMESTICATIONS
DOMESTICATIVE
DOMESTICATOR
DOMESTICATORS
DOMESTICISE
DOMESTICISED
DOMESTICISES
DOMESTICISING
DOMESTICITIES
DOMESTICITY
DOMESTICIZE
DOMESTICIZED
DOMESTICIZES
DOMESTICIZING
DOMESTIQUE
DOMESTIQUES
DOMICILIARY
DOMICILIATE
DOMICILIATED

DOMICILIATES
DOMICILIATING
DOMICILIATION
DOMICILIATIONS
DOMICILING
DOMINANCES
DOMINANCIES
DOMINANTLY
DOMINATING
DOMINATINGLY
DOMINATION
DOMINATIONS
DOMINATIVE
DOMINATORS
DOMINATRICES
DOMINATRIX
DOMINATRIXES
DOMINEERED
DOMINEERING
DOMINEERINGLY
DOMINEERINGNESS
DOMINICKER
DOMINICKERS
DOMINIQUES
DONATARIES
DONATISTIC
DONATISTICAL
DONATORIES
DONENESSES
DONEPEZILS
DONKEYWORK
DONKEYWORKS
DONNICKERS
DONNISHNESS
DONNISHNESSES
DONNYBROOK
DONNYBROOKS
DONORSHIPS
DOODLEBUGS
DOOHICKEYS
DOOHICKIES
DOOMSAYERS
DOOMSAYING
DOOMSAYINGS
DOOMSDAYER
DOOMSDAYERS
DOOMWATCHED
DOOMWATCHER
DOOMWATCHERS
DOOMWATCHES
DOOMWATCHING
DOOMWATCHINGS
DOORFRAMES
DOORKEEPER
DOORKEEPERS
DOORKNOCKED
DOORKNOCKER
DOORKNOCKERS
DOORKNOCKING
DOORKNOCKS
DOORNBOOMS
DOORPLATES
DOORSTEPPED
DOORSTEPPER
DOORSTEPPERS
DOORSTEPPING
DOORSTEPPINGS
DOORSTONES
DOPAMINERGIC
DOPESHEETS
DOPEYNESSES
DOPINESSES
DOPPELGANGER
DOPPELGANGERS
DOPPLERITE
DOPPLERITES
DORBEETLES
DORKINESSES
DORMANCIES
DORMITIONS
DORMITIVES
DORMITORIES
DORONICUMS
DORSIBRANCHIATE
DORSIFEROUS
DORSIFIXED
DORSIFLEXED
DORSIFLEXES
DORSIFLEXING
DORSIFLEXION
DORSIFLEXIONS
DORSIGRADE
DORSIVENTRAL
DORSIVENTRALITY
DORSIVENTRALLY
DORSOLATERAL
DORSOLUMBAR
DORSOVENTRAL
DORSOVENTRALITY
DORSOVENTRALLY
DORTINESSES
DOSEMETERS
DOSIMETERS
DOSIMETRIC
DOSIMETRICIAN
DOSIMETRICIANS
DOSIMETRIES
DOSIMETRIST
DOSIMETRISTS
DOSIOLOGIES
DOSOLOGIES
DOSSHOUSES
DOTARDLIER
DOTARDLIEST
DOTCOMMERS
DOTTINESSES
DOUBLEHEADER
DOUBLEHEADERS
DOUBLENESS
DOUBLENESSES
DOUBLESPEAK
DOUBLESPEAKER
DOUBLESPEAKERS
DOUBLESPEAKS
DOUBLETHINK
DOUBLETHINKS
DOUBLETONS
DOUBLETREE
DOUBLETREES
DOUBTFULLY
DOUBTFULNESS
DOUBTFULNESSES
DOUBTINGLY
DOUBTLESSLY
DOUBTLESSNESS
DOUBTLESSNESSES
DOUCENESSES
DOUCEPERES
DOUCHEBAGS
DOUGHBALLS
DOUGHFACED
DOUGHFACES
DOUGHINESS
DOUGHINESSES
DOUGHNUTLIKE
DOUGHNUTTED
DOUGHNUTTING
DOUGHNUTTINGS
DOUGHTIEST
DOUGHTINESS
DOUGHTINESSES
DOULOCRACIES
DOULOCRACY
DOUPPIONIS
DOURNESSES
DOUROUCOULI
DOUROUCOULIS
DOVEISHNESS
DOVEISHNESSES
DOVETAILED
DOVETAILING
DOVETAILINGS
DOVISHNESS
DOVISHNESSES
DOWDINESSES
DOWELLINGS
DOWFNESSES
DOWITCHERS
DOWNBURSTS
DOWNCOMERS
DOWNCRYING
DOWNDRAFTS
DOWNDRAUGHT
DOWNDRAUGHTS
DOWNFALLEN
DOWNFORCES
DOWNGRADED
DOWNGRADES
DOWNGRADING
DOWNHEARTED
DOWNHEARTEDLY
DOWNHEARTEDNESS
DOWNHILLER
DOWNHILLERS
DOWNINESSES
DOWNLIGHTER
DOWNLIGHTERS
DOWNLIGHTS
DOWNLINKED
DOWNLINKING
DOWNLOADABLE
DOWNLOADED
DOWNLOADING
DOWNLOADINGS
DOWNLOOKED
DOWNPLAYED
DOWNPLAYING
DOWNRATING
DOWNREGULATION
DOWNREGULATIONS
DOWNRIGHTLY
DOWNRIGHTNESS
DOWNRIGHTNESSES
DOWNRUSHES
DOWNSCALED
DOWNSCALES
DOWNSCALING
DOWNSHIFTED
DOWNSHIFTER
DOWNSHIFTERS
DOWNSHIFTING
DOWNSHIFTINGS
DOWNSHIFTS
DOWNSIZERS
DOWNSIZING
DOWNSIZINGS
DOWNSLIDES
DOWNSLOPES
DOWNSPOUTS
DOWNSTAGES
DOWNSTAIRS
DOWNSTAIRSES
DOWNSTATER
DOWNSTATERS
DOWNSTATES
DOWNSTREAM
DOWNSTROKE
DOWNSTROKES
DOWNSWINGS
DOWNTHROWS
DOWNTOWNER
DOWNTOWNERS
DOWNTRENDED
DOWNTRENDING
DOWNTRENDS
DOWNTRODDEN
DOWNTURNED
DOWNVOTING
DOWNWARDLY
DOWNWARDNESS

DOWNWARDNESSES
DOWNWASHES
DOWNZONING
DOXOGRAPHER
DOXOGRAPHERS
DOXOGRAPHIC
DOXOGRAPHIES
DOXOGRAPHY
DOXOLOGICAL
DOXOLOGICALLY
DOXOLOGIES
DOXORUBICIN
DOXORUBICINS
DOXYCYCLINE
DOXYCYCLINES
DOZINESSES
DRABBINESS
DRABBINESSES
DRABBLINGS
DRABNESSES
DRACONIANISM
DRACONIANISMS
DRACONICALLY
DRACONISMS
DRACONITES
DRACONTIASES
DRACONTIASIS
DRACUNCULIASES
DRACUNCULIASIS
DRACUNCULUS
DRACUNCULUSES
DRAFTINESS
DRAFTINESSES
DRAFTSMANSHIP
DRAFTSMANSHIPS
DRAFTSPERSON
DRAFTSPERSONS
DRAFTSWOMAN
DRAFTSWOMEN
DRAGGINGLY
DRAGGLETAILED
DRAGHOUNDS
DRAGONESSES
DRAGONFLIES
DRAGONHEAD
DRAGONHEADS
DRAGONISED
DRAGONISES
DRAGONISING
DRAGONISMS
DRAGONIZED
DRAGONIZES
DRAGONIZING
DRAGONLIKE
DRAGONNADE
DRAGONNADED
DRAGONNADES
DRAGONNADING
DRAGONROOT
DRAGONROOTS
DRAGOONAGE
DRAGOONAGES
DRAGOONING
DRAGSTRIPS
DRAGSVILLE
DRAGSVILLES
DRAINBOARD
DRAINBOARDS
DRAINLAYER
DRAINLAYERS
DRAINPIPES
DRAKESTONE
DRAKESTONES
DRAMATICAL
DRAMATICALLY
DRAMATICISM
DRAMATICISMS
DRAMATISABLE
DRAMATISATION
DRAMATISATIONS
DRAMATISED
DRAMATISER
DRAMATISERS
DRAMATISES
DRAMATISING
DRAMATISTS
DRAMATIZABLE
DRAMATIZATION
DRAMATIZATIONS
DRAMATIZED
DRAMATIZER
DRAMATIZERS
DRAMATIZES
DRAMATIZING
DRAMATURGE
DRAMATURGES
DRAMATURGIC
DRAMATURGICAL
DRAMATURGICALLY
DRAMATURGIES
DRAMATURGIST
DRAMATURGISTS
DRAMATURGS
DRAMATURGY
DRAPABILITIES
DRAPABILITY
DRAPEABILITIES
DRAPEABILITY
DRAPERYING
DRASTICALLY
DRATCHELLS
DRAUGHTBOARD
DRAUGHTBOARDS
DRAUGHTERS
DRAUGHTIER
DRAUGHTIEST
DRAUGHTILY
DRAUGHTINESS
DRAUGHTINESSES
DRAUGHTING
DRAUGHTMAN
DRAUGHTMEN
DRAUGHTPROOF
DRAUGHTPROOFED
DRAUGHTPROOFING
DRAUGHTPROOFS
DRAUGHTSMAN
DRAUGHTSMANSHIP
DRAUGHTSMEN
DRAUGHTSPERSON
DRAUGHTSPERSONS
DRAUGHTSWOMAN
DRAUGHTSWOMEN
DRAWBRIDGE
DRAWBRIDGES
DRAWERFULS
DRAWKNIVES
DRAWLINGLY
DRAWLINGNESS
DRAWLINGNESSES
DRAWNWORKS
DRAWPLATES
DRAWSHAVES
DRAWSTRING
DRAWSTRINGS
DRAYHORSES
DREADFULLY
DREADFULNESS
DREADFULNESSES
DREADLESSLY
DREADLESSNESS
DREADLESSNESSES
DREADLOCKED
DREADLOCKS
DREADNAUGHT
DREADNAUGHTS
DREADNOUGHT
DREADNOUGHTS
DREAMBOATS
DREAMERIES
DREAMFULLY
DREAMFULNESS
DREAMFULNESSES
DREAMHOLES
DREAMINESS
DREAMINESSES
DREAMINGLY
DREAMLANDS
DREAMLESSLY
DREAMLESSNESS
DREAMLESSNESSES
DREAMTIMES
DREAMWHILE
DREAMWHILES
DREAMWORLD
DREAMWORLDS
DREARIHEAD
DREARIHEADS
DREARIHOOD
DREARIHOODS
DREARIMENT
DREARIMENTS
DREARINESS
DREARINESSES
DREARISOME
DRECKSILLS
DREGGINESS
DREGGINESSES
DREIKANTER
DREIKANTERS
DRENCHINGS
DREPANIUMS
DRERIHEADS
DRESSGUARD
DRESSGUARDS
DRESSINESS
DRESSINESSES
DRESSMAKER
DRESSMAKERS
DRESSMAKES
DRESSMAKING
DRESSMAKINGS
DRIBBLIEST
DRIBBLINGS
DRICKSIEST
DRIFTINGLY
DRIFTWOODS
DRILLABILITIES
DRILLABILITY
DRILLHOLES
DRILLMASTER
DRILLMASTERS
DRILLSHIPS
DRILLSTOCK
DRILLSTOCKS
DRINKABILITIES
DRINKABILITY
DRINKABLENESS
DRINKABLENESSES
DRINKABLES
DRIPSTONES
DRIVABILITIES
DRIVABILITY
DRIVEABILITIES
DRIVEABILITY
DRIVELINES
DRIVELLERS
DRIVELLING
DRIVENNESS
DRIVENNESSES
DRIVERLESS
DRIVESHAFT
DRIVESHAFTS
DRIVETHROUGH
DRIVETHROUGHS
DRIVETRAIN
DRIVETRAINS
DRIZZLIEST
DRIZZLINGLY
DROICHIEST

D

DROLLERIES
DROLLNESSES
DROMEDARES
DROMEDARIES
DROMOPHOBIA
DROMOPHOBIAS
DRONISHNESS
DRONISHNESSES
DRONKVERDRIET
DROOLWORTHIER
DROOLWORTHIEST
DROOLWORTHY
DROOPINESS
DROOPINESSES
DROOPINGLY
DROPCLOTHS
DROPFORGED
DROPFORGES
DROPFORGING
DROPKICKER
DROPKICKERS
DROPLIGHTS
DROPPERFUL
DROPPERFULS
DROPPERSFUL
DROPSICALLY
DROPSONDES
DROPSTONES
DROSERACEOUS
DROSOMETER
DROSOMETERS
DROSOPHILA
DROSOPHILAE
DROSOPHILAS
DROSSINESS
DROSSINESSES
DROUGHTIER
DROUGHTIEST
DROUGHTINESS
DROUGHTINESSES
DROUTHIEST
DROUTHINESS
DROUTHINESSES
DROWSIHEAD
DROWSIHEADS
DROWSIHEDS
DROWSINESS
DROWSINESSES

DRUCKENNESS
DRUCKENNESSES
DRUDGERIES
DRUDGINGLY
DRUGMAKERS
DRUGSTORES
DRUIDESSES
DRUMBEATER
DRUMBEATERS
DRUMBEATING
DRUMBEATINGS
DRUMBLEDOR
DRUMBLEDORS
DRUMBLEDRANE
DRUMBLEDRANES
DRUMFISHES
DRUMSTICKS
DRUNKALOGUE
DRUNKALOGUES
DRUNKATHON
DRUNKATHONS
DRUNKENNESS
DRUNKENNESSES
DRUNKOMETER
DRUNKOMETERS
DRUPACEOUS
DRYASDUSTS
DRYBEATING
DRYOPITHECINE
DRYOPITHECINES
DRYSALTERIES
DRYSALTERS
DRYSALTERY
DRYWALLERS
DRYWALLING
DRYWALLINGS
DUALISTICALLY
DUATHLETES
DUBIOSITIES
DUBIOUSNESS
DUBIOUSNESSES
DUBITANCIES
DUBITATING
DUBITATION
DUBITATIONS
DUBITATIVE
DUBITATIVELY
DUCHESSING

DUCKBOARDS
DUCKSHOVED
DUCKSHOVER
DUCKSHOVERS
DUCKSHOVES
DUCKSHOVING
DUCKSHOVINGS
DUCKWALKED
DUCKWALKING
DUCTILENESS
DUCTILENESSES
DUCTILITIES
DUDENESSES
DUENNASHIP
DUENNASHIPS
DUFFERDOMS
DUFFERISMS
DUIKERBOKS
DUKKERIPEN
DUKKERIPENS
DULCAMARAS
DULCETNESS
DULCETNESSES
DULCIFICATION
DULCIFICATIONS
DULCIFLUOUS
DULCIFYING
DULCILOQUIES
DULCILOQUY
DULCIMORES
DULCITUDES
DULLNESSES
DULLSVILLE
DULLSVILLES
DULOCRACIES
DUMBFOUNDED
DUMBFOUNDER
DUMBFOUNDERED
DUMBFOUNDERING
DUMBFOUNDERS
DUMBFOUNDING
DUMBFOUNDS
DUMBLEDORE
DUMBLEDORES
DUMBNESSES
DUMBSIZING
DUMBSTRICKEN
DUMBSTRUCK

DUMBWAITER
DUMBWAITERS
DUMFOUNDED
DUMFOUNDER
DUMFOUNDERED
DUMFOUNDERING
DUMFOUNDERS
DUMFOUNDING
DUMMELHEAD
DUMMELHEADS
DUMMINESSES
DUMORTIERITE
DUMORTIERITES
DUMOSITIES
DUMPINESSES
DUMPISHNESS
DUMPISHNESSES
DUMPTRUCKS
DUNDERFUNK
DUNDERFUNKS
DUNDERHEAD
DUNDERHEADED
DUNDERHEADISM
DUNDERHEADISMS
DUNDERHEADS
DUNDERPATE
DUNDERPATES
DUNDREARIES
DUNGEONERS
DUNGEONING
DUNIEWASSAL
DUNIEWASSALS
DUNIWASSAL
DUNIWASSALS
DUNNIEWASSAL
DUNNIEWASSALS
DUODECENNIAL
DUODECILLION
DUODECILLIONS
DUODECIMAL
DUODECIMALLY
DUODECIMALS
DUODECIMOS
DUODENECTOMIES
DUODENECTOMY
DUODENITIS
DUODENITISES
DUOPOLISTIC

DUOPOLISTS
DUOPSONIES
DUPABILITIES
DUPABILITY
DUPLEXINGS
DUPLEXITIES
DUPLICABILITIES
DUPLICABILITY
DUPLICABLE
DUPLICANDS
DUPLICATED
DUPLICATELY
DUPLICATES
DUPLICATING
DUPLICATION
DUPLICATIONS
DUPLICATIVE
DUPLICATOR
DUPLICATORS
DUPLICATURE
DUPLICATURES
DUPLICIDENT
DUPLICITIES
DUPLICITOUS
DUPLICITOUSLY
DURABILITIES
DURABILITY
DURABLENESS
DURABLENESSES
DURALUMINIUM
DURALUMINIUMS
DURALUMINS
DURATIONAL
DURCHKOMPONIERT
DURCHKOMPONIRT
DURICRUSTS
DUROMETERS
DUSKINESSES
DUSKISHNESS
DUSKISHNESSES
DUSKNESSES
DUSTCLOTHS
DUSTCOVERS
DUSTINESSES
DUSTSHEETS
DUSTSTORMS
DUTEOUSNESS
DUTEOUSNESSES

DUTIABILITIES
DUTIABILITY
DUTIFULNESS
DUTIFULNESSES
DUUMVIRATE
DUUMVIRATES
DWARFISHLY
DWARFISHNESS
DWARFISHNESSES
DWARFNESSES
DWINDLEMENT
DWINDLEMENTS
DYADICALLY
DYARCHICAL
DYEABILITIES
DYEABILITY
DYINGNESSES
DYNAMETERS
DYNAMICALLY
DYNAMICIST
DYNAMICISTS
DYNAMISING
DYNAMISTIC
DYNAMITARD
DYNAMITARDS
DYNAMITERS
DYNAMITING
DYNAMIZING
DYNAMOELECTRIC
DYNAMOGENESES
DYNAMOGENESIS
DYNAMOGENIES
DYNAMOGENY
DYNAMOGRAPH
DYNAMOGRAPHS
DYNAMOMETER
DYNAMOMETERS
DYNAMOMETRIC
DYNAMOMETRICAL
DYNAMOMETRIES
DYNAMOMETRY
DYNAMOTORS
DYNASTICAL
DYNASTICALLY
DYNASTICISM
DYNASTICISMS
DYNORPHINS
DYOPHYSITE
DYOPHYSITES
DYOTHELETE
DYOTHELETES
DYOTHELETIC
DYOTHELETICAL
DYOTHELETISM
DYOTHELETISMS
DYOTHELISM
DYOTHELISMS
DYOTHELITE
DYOTHELITES
DYOTHELITIC
DYOTHELITICAL
DYSAESTHESIA
DYSAESTHESIAS
DYSAESTHETIC
DYSARTHRIA
DYSARTHRIAS
DYSBINDINS
DYSCALCULIA
DYSCALCULIAS
DYSCHROIAS
DYSCRASIAS
DYSCRASITE
DYSCRASITES
DYSENTERIC
DYSENTERIES
DYSFUNCTION
DYSFUNCTIONAL
DYSFUNCTIONS
DYSGENESES
DYSGENESIS
DYSGRAPHIA
DYSGRAPHIAS
DYSGRAPHIC
DYSGRAPHICS
DYSHARMONIC
DYSKINESIA
DYSKINESIAS
DYSKINETIC
DYSLECTICS
DYSLOGISTIC
DYSLOGISTICALLY
DYSMENORRHEA
DYSMENORRHEAL
DYSMENORRHEAS
DYSMENORRHEIC
DYSMENORRHOEA
DYSMENORRHOEAL
DYSMENORRHOEAS
DYSMENORRHOEIC
DYSMORPHIC
DYSMORPHOPHOBIA
DYSMORPHOPHOBIC
DYSPAREUNIA
DYSPAREUNIAS
DYSPATHETIC
DYSPATHIES
DYSPEPSIAS
DYSPEPSIES
DYSPEPTICAL
DYSPEPTICALLY
DYSPEPTICS
DYSPHAGIAS
DYSPHAGIES
DYSPHASIAS
DYSPHASICS
DYSPHEMISM
DYSPHEMISMS
DYSPHEMISTIC
DYSPHONIAS
DYSPHORIAS
DYSPLASIAS
DYSPLASTIC
DYSPRACTIC
DYSPRAXIAS
DYSPROSIUM
DYSPROSIUMS
DYSRHYTHMIA
DYSRHYTHMIAS
DYSRHYTHMIC
DYSRHYTHMICS
DYSSYNERGIA
DYSSYNERGIAS
DYSSYNERGIC
DYSSYNERGIES
DYSSYNERGY
DYSTELEOLOGICAL
DYSTELEOLOGIES
DYSTELEOLOGIST
DYSTELEOLOGISTS
DYSTELEOLOGY
DYSTHESIAS
DYSTHYMIAC
DYSTHYMIACS
DYSTHYMIAS
DYSTHYMICS
DYSTOPIANS
DYSTROPHIA
DYSTROPHIAS
DYSTROPHIC
DYSTROPHIES
DYSTROPHIN
DYSTROPHINS
DZIGGETAIS

E

EAGERNESSES
EAGLEHAWKS
EAGLESTONE
EAGLESTONES
EAGLEWOODS
EARBASHERS
EARBASHING
EARBASHINGS
EARLIERISE
EARLIERISED
EARLIERISES
EARLIERISING
EARLIERIZE
EARLIERIZED
EARLIERIZES
EARLIERIZING
EARLINESSES
EARLYWOODS
EARMARKING
EARNESTNESS
EARNESTNESSES
EARSPLITTING
EARTHBOUND
EARTHENWARE
EARTHENWARES
EARTHFALLS
EARTHFLAXES
EARTHINESS
EARTHINESSES
EARTHLIEST
EARTHLIGHT
EARTHLIGHTS
EARTHLINESS
EARTHLINESSES
EARTHLINGS
EARTHMOVER
EARTHMOVERS
EARTHMOVING
EARTHMOVINGS
EARTHQUAKE
EARTHQUAKED
EARTHQUAKES
EARTHQUAKING
EARTHRISES
EARTHSHAKER
EARTHSHAKERS
EARTHSHAKING
EARTHSHAKINGLY
EARTHSHATTERING
EARTHSHINE
EARTHSHINES
EARTHSTARS
EARTHWARDS
EARTHWAXES
EARTHWOLVES
EARTHWOMAN
EARTHWOMEN
EARTHWORKS
EARTHWORMS
EARWIGGIER
EARWIGGIEST
EARWIGGING
EARWIGGINGS
EARWITNESS
EARWITNESSES
EASEFULNESS
EASEFULNESSES
EASINESSES
EASSELGATE
EASSELWARD
EASTERLIES
EASTERLING
EASTERLINGS
EASTERMOST
EASTERNERS
EASTERNMOST
EASTWARDLY
EASYGOINGNESS
EASYGOINGNESSES
EAVESDRIPS
EAVESDROPPED
EAVESDROPPER
EAVESDROPPERS
EAVESDROPPING
EAVESDROPPINGS
EAVESDROPS
EAVESTROUGH
EAVESTROUGHS
EBIONISING
EBIONITISM
EBIONITISMS
EBIONIZING
EBOULEMENT
EBOULEMENTS
EBRACTEATE
EBRACTEOLATE
EBRILLADES
EBRIOSITIES
EBULLIENCE
EBULLIENCES
EBULLIENCIES
EBULLIENCY
EBULLIENTLY
EBULLIOMETER
EBULLIOMETERS
EBULLIOMETRIES
EBULLIOMETRY
EBULLIOSCOPE
EBULLIOSCOPES
EBULLIOSCOPIC
EBULLIOSCOPICAL
EBULLIOSCOPIES
EBULLIOSCOPY
EBULLITION
EBULLITIONS
EBURNATION
EBURNATIONS
EBURNIFICATION
EBURNIFICATIONS
ECARDINATE
ECBLASTESES
ECBLASTESIS
ECCALEOBION
ECCALEOBIONS
ECCENTRICAL
ECCENTRICALLY
ECCENTRICITIES
ECCENTRICITY
ECCENTRICS
ECCHYMOSED
ECCHYMOSES
ECCHYMOSIS
ECCHYMOTIC
ECCLESIARCH
ECCLESIARCHS
ECCLESIAST
ECCLESIASTIC
ECCLESIASTICAL
ECCLESIASTICISM
ECCLESIASTICS
ECCLESIASTS
ECCLESIOLATER
ECCLESIOLATERS
ECCLESIOLATRIES
ECCLESIOLATRY
ECCLESIOLOGICAL
ECCLESIOLOGIES
ECCLESIOLOGIST
ECCLESIOLOGISTS
ECCLESIOLOGY
ECCOPROTIC
ECCOPROTICS
ECCREMOCARPUS
ECCREMOCARPUSES
ECCRINOLOGIES
ECCRINOLOGY
ECDYSIASTS
ECHELONING
ECHEVERIAS
ECHIDNINES
ECHINACEAS
ECHINOCOCCI
ECHINOCOCCOSES
ECHINOCOCCOSIS
ECHINOCOCCUS
ECHINODERM
ECHINODERMAL
ECHINODERMATOUS
ECHINODERMS
ECHIUROIDS
ECHOCARDIOGRAM
ECHOCARDIOGRAMS
ECHOGRAPHIES
ECHOGRAPHS
ECHOGRAPHY
ECHOICALLY
ECHOLALIAS
ECHOLOCATION
ECHOLOCATIONS
ECHOPRAXES
ECHOPRAXIA
ECHOPRAXIAS
ECHOPRAXIS
ECHOVIRUSES
ECLAIRCISSEMENT
ECLAMPSIAS
ECLAMPSIES
ECLECTICALLY
ECLECTICISM
ECLECTICISMS
ECLIPSISES
ECLIPTICALLY
ECOCATASTROPHE
ECOCATASTROPHES
ECOCENTRIC
ECOCLIMATE
ECOCLIMATES
ECOFEMINISM
ECOFEMINISMS
ECOFEMINIST
ECOFEMINISTS
ECOFRIENDLIER
ECOFRIENDLIEST
ECOFRIENDLY
ECOLOGICAL
ECOLOGICALLY
ECOLOGISTS
ECOMMERCES
ECOMOVEMENT
ECOMOVEMENTS

ECOMUSEUMS
ECONOBOXES
ECONOMETER
ECONOMETERS
ECONOMETRIC
ECONOMETRICAL
ECONOMETRICALLY
ECONOMETRICIAN
ECONOMETRICIANS
ECONOMETRICS
ECONOMETRIST
ECONOMETRISTS
ECONOMICAL
ECONOMICALLY
ECONOMISATION
ECONOMISATIONS
ECONOMISED
ECONOMISER
ECONOMISERS
ECONOMISES
ECONOMISING
ECONOMISMS
ECONOMISTIC
ECONOMISTS
ECONOMIZATION
ECONOMIZATIONS
ECONOMIZED
ECONOMIZER
ECONOMIZERS
ECONOMIZES
ECONOMIZING
ECOPHOBIAS
ECOPHYSIOLOGIES
ECOPHYSIOLOGY
ECOREGIONS
ECOSPECIES
ECOSPECIFIC
ECOSPHERES
ECOSSAISES
ECOSYSTEMS
ECOTARIANISM
ECOTARIANISMS
ECOTARIANS
ECOTECTURE
ECOTECTURES
ECOTERRORISM
ECOTERRORISMS
ECOTERRORIST
ECOTERRORISTS
ECOTOURING
ECOTOURISM
ECOTOURISMS
ECOTOURIST
ECOTOURISTS
ECOTOXICOLOGIES
ECOTOXICOLOGIST
ECOTOXICOLOGY
ECOTYPICALLY
ECPHONESES
ECPHONESIS
ECPHRACTIC
ECPHRACTICS
ECRITOIRES
ECSTASISED
ECSTASISES
ECSTASISING
ECSTASIZED
ECSTASIZES
ECSTASIZING
ECSTASYING
ECSTATICALLY
ECTHLIPSES
ECTHLIPSIS
ECTOBLASTIC
ECTOBLASTS
ECTOCRINES
ECTODERMAL
ECTODERMIC
ECTOENZYME
ECTOENZYMES
ECTOGENESES
ECTOGENESIS
ECTOGENETIC
ECTOGENICALLY
ECTOGENIES
ECTOGENOUS
ECTOMORPHIC
ECTOMORPHIES
ECTOMORPHS
ECTOMORPHY
ECTOMYCORRHIZA
ECTOMYCORRHIZAE
ECTOMYCORRHIZAS
ECTOPARASITE
ECTOPARASITES
ECTOPARASITIC
ECTOPHYTES
ECTOPHYTIC
ECTOPICALLY
ECTOPLASMIC
ECTOPLASMS
ECTOPLASTIC
ECTOPROCTS
ECTOSARCOUS
ECTOTHERMIC
ECTOTHERMS
ECTOTROPHIC
ECTROPIONS
ECTROPIUMS
ECTYPOGRAPHIES
ECTYPOGRAPHY
ECUMENICAL
ECUMENICALISM
ECUMENICALISMS
ECUMENICALLY
ECUMENICISM
ECUMENICISMS
ECUMENICIST
ECUMENICISTS
ECUMENICITIES
ECUMENICITY
ECUMENISMS
ECUMENISTS
ECZEMATOUS
EDACIOUSLY
EDACIOUSNESS
EDACIOUSNESSES
EDAPHICALLY
EDAPHOLOGIES
EDAPHOLOGY
EDELWEISSES
EDENTULATE
EDENTULOUS
EDGINESSES
EDIBILITIES
EDIBLENESS
EDIBLENESSES
EDIFICATION
EDIFICATIONS
EDIFICATORY
EDIFYINGLY
EDITIONING
EDITORIALISE
EDITORIALISED
EDITORIALISER
EDITORIALISERS
EDITORIALISES
EDITORIALISING
EDITORIALIST
EDITORIALISTS
EDITORIALIZE
EDITORIALIZED
EDITORIALIZER
EDITORIALIZERS
EDITORIALIZES
EDITORIALIZING
EDITORIALLY
EDITORIALS
EDITORSHIP
EDITORSHIPS
EDITRESSES
EDRIOPHTHALMIAN
EDRIOPHTHALMIC
EDRIOPHTHALMOUS
EDUCABILITIES
EDUCABILITY
EDUCATABILITIES
EDUCATABILITY
EDUCATABLE
EDUCATEDNESS
EDUCATEDNESSES
EDUCATIONAL
EDUCATIONALIST
EDUCATIONALISTS
EDUCATIONALLY
EDUCATIONESE
EDUCATIONESES
EDUCATIONIST
EDUCATIONISTS
EDUCATIONS
EDUCEMENTS
EDULCORANT
EDULCORATE
EDULCORATED
EDULCORATES
EDULCORATING
EDULCORATION
EDULCORATIONS
EDULCORATIVE
EDULCORATOR
EDULCORATORS
EDUTAINMENT
EDUTAINMENTS
EELGRASSES
EERINESSES
EFFACEABLE
EFFACEMENT
EFFACEMENTS
EFFECTIBLE
EFFECTIVELY
EFFECTIVENESS
EFFECTIVENESSES
EFFECTIVES
EFFECTIVITIES
EFFECTIVITY
EFFECTLESS
EFFECTUALITIES
EFFECTUALITY
EFFECTUALLY
EFFECTUALNESS
EFFECTUALNESSES
EFFECTUATE
EFFECTUATED
EFFECTUATES
EFFECTUATING
EFFECTUATION
EFFECTUATIONS
EFFEMINACIES
EFFEMINACY
EFFEMINATE
EFFEMINATED
EFFEMINATELY
EFFEMINATENESS
EFFEMINATES
EFFEMINATING
EFFEMINISE
EFFEMINISED
EFFEMINISES
EFFEMINISING
EFFEMINIZE
EFFEMINIZED
EFFEMINIZES
EFFEMINIZING
EFFERENCES
EFFERENTLY
EFFERVESCE
EFFERVESCED
EFFERVESCENCE
EFFERVESCENCES
EFFERVESCENCIES

E

E

EFFERVESCENCY
EFFERVESCENT
EFFERVESCENTLY
EFFERVESCES
EFFERVESCIBLE
EFFERVESCING
EFFERVESCINGLY
EFFETENESS
EFFETENESSES
EFFICACIES
EFFICACIOUS
EFFICACIOUSLY
EFFICACIOUSNESS
EFFICACITIES
EFFICACITY
EFFICIENCE
EFFICIENCES
EFFICIENCIES
EFFICIENCY
EFFICIENTLY
EFFICIENTS
EFFIERCING
EFFIGURATE
EFFIGURATION
EFFIGURATIONS
EFFLEURAGE
EFFLEURAGED
EFFLEURAGES
EFFLEURAGING
EFFLORESCE
EFFLORESCED
EFFLORESCENCE
EFFLORESCENCES
EFFLORESCENT
EFFLORESCES
EFFLORESCING
EFFLUENCES
EFFLUVIUMS
EFFLUXIONS
EFFORTFULLY
EFFORTFULNESS
EFFORTFULNESSES
EFFORTLESS
EFFORTLESSLY
EFFORTLESSNESS
EFFRONTERIES
EFFRONTERY
EFFULGENCE
EFFULGENCES
EFFULGENTLY
EFFUSIOMETER
EFFUSIOMETERS
EFFUSIVELY
EFFUSIVENESS
EFFUSIVENESSES
EGALITARIAN
EGALITARIANISM
EGALITARIANISMS
EGALITARIANS
EGAREMENTS
EGGBEATERS
EGGHEADEDNESS
EGGHEADEDNESSES
EGLANDULAR
EGLANDULOSE
EGLANTINES
EGOCENTRIC
EGOCENTRICAL
EGOCENTRICALLY
EGOCENTRICITIES
EGOCENTRICITY
EGOCENTRICS
EGOCENTRISM
EGOCENTRISMS
EGOISTICAL
EGOISTICALLY
EGOMANIACAL
EGOMANIACALLY
EGOMANIACS
EGOSURFING
EGOTHEISMS
EGOTISTICAL
EGOTISTICALLY
EGREGIOUSLY
EGREGIOUSNESS
EGREGIOUSNESSES
EGRESSIONS
EGRESSIVES
EGURGITATE
EGURGITATED
EGURGITATES
EGURGITATING
EICOSANOID
EICOSANOIDS
EIDERDOWNS
EIDETICALLY
EIDOGRAPHS
EIGENFREQUENCY
EIGENFUNCTION
EIGENFUNCTIONS
EIGENMODES
EIGENTONES
EIGENVALUE
EIGENVALUES
EIGENVECTOR
EIGENVECTORS
EIGHTBALLS
EIGHTEENMO
EIGHTEENMOS
EIGHTEENTH
EIGHTEENTHLY
EIGHTEENTHS
EIGHTFOILS
EIGHTIETHS
EIGHTPENCE
EIGHTPENCES
EIGHTPENNY
EIGHTSCORE
EIGHTSCORES
EIGHTSOMES
EINSTEINIUM
EINSTEINIUMS
EIRENICALLY
EIRENICONS
EISTEDDFOD
EISTEDDFODAU
EISTEDDFODIC
EISTEDDFODS
EJACULATED
EJACULATES
EJACULATING
EJACULATION
EJACULATIONS
EJACULATIVE
EJACULATOR
EJACULATORS
EJACULATORY
EJECTAMENTA
EJECTIVELY
EJECTMENTS
EKISTICIAN
EKISTICIANS
ELABORATED
ELABORATELY
ELABORATENESS
ELABORATENESSES
ELABORATES
ELABORATING
ELABORATION
ELABORATIONS
ELABORATIVE
ELABORATOR
ELABORATORIES
ELABORATORS
ELABORATORY
ELAEAGNUSES
ELAEOLITES
ELAEOPTENE
ELAEOPTENES
ELAIOSOMES
ELASMOBRANCH
ELASMOBRANCHS
ELASMOSAUR
ELASMOSAURS
ELASTANCES
ELASTICALLY
ELASTICATE
ELASTICATED
ELASTICATES
ELASTICATING
ELASTICATION
ELASTICATIONS
ELASTICISE
ELASTICISED
ELASTICISES
ELASTICISING
ELASTICITIES
ELASTICITY
ELASTICIZE
ELASTICIZED
ELASTICIZES
ELASTICIZING
ELASTICNESS
ELASTICNESSES
ELASTOMERIC
ELASTOMERS
ELATEDNESS
ELATEDNESSES
ELATERITES
ELATERIUMS
ELBOWROOMS
ELDERBERRIES
ELDERBERRY
ELDERCARES
ELDERFLOWER
ELDERFLOWERS
ELDERLINESS
ELDERLINESSES
ELDERSHIPS
ELECAMPANE
ELECAMPANES
ELECTABILITIES
ELECTABILITY
ELECTIONEER
ELECTIONEERED
ELECTIONEERER
ELECTIONEERERS
ELECTIONEERING
ELECTIONEERINGS
ELECTIONEERS
ELECTIVELY
ELECTIVENESS
ELECTIVENESSES
ELECTIVITIES
ELECTIVITY
ELECTORALLY
ELECTORATE
ELECTORATES
ELECTORESS
ELECTORESSES
ELECTORIAL
ELECTORIALLY
ELECTORSHIP
ELECTORSHIPS
ELECTRESSES
ELECTRICAL
ELECTRICALLY
ELECTRICALS
ELECTRICIAN
ELECTRICIANS
ELECTRICITIES
ELECTRICITY
ELECTRIFIABLE
ELECTRIFICATION
ELECTRIFIED
ELECTRIFIER
ELECTRIFIERS
ELECTRIFIES
ELECTRIFYING
ELECTRIFYINGLY

ELECTRISATION
ELECTRISATIONS
ELECTRISED
ELECTRISES
ELECTRISING
ELECTRIZATION
ELECTRIZATIONS
ELECTRIZED
ELECTRIZES
ELECTRIZING
ELECTROACOUSTIC
ELECTROACTIVE
ELECTROACTIVITY
ELECTROANALYSES
ELECTROANALYSIS
ELECTROANALYTIC
ELECTROBIOLOGY
ELECTROCAUTERY
ELECTROCEMENT
ELECTROCEMENTS
ELECTROCHEMIC
ELECTROCHEMICAL
ELECTROCHEMIST
ELECTROCHEMISTS
ELECTROCLASH
ELECTROCLASHES
ELECTROCULTURE
ELECTROCULTURES
ELECTROCUTE
ELECTROCUTED
ELECTROCUTES
ELECTROCUTING
ELECTROCUTION
ELECTROCUTIONS
ELECTROCYTE
ELECTROCYTES
ELECTRODEPOSIT
ELECTRODEPOSITS
ELECTRODERMAL
ELECTRODES
ELECTRODIALYSES
ELECTRODIALYSIS
ELECTRODIALYTIC
ELECTRODYNAMIC
ELECTRODYNAMICS
ELECTROFISHING
ELECTROFISHINGS
ELECTROFLUOR
ELECTROFLUORS
ELECTROFORM
ELECTROFORMED
ELECTROFORMING
ELECTROFORMINGS
ELECTROFORMS
ELECTROGEN
ELECTROGENESES
ELECTROGENESIS
ELECTROGENIC
ELECTROGENS
ELECTROGILDING
ELECTROGILDINGS
ELECTROGRAM
ELECTROGRAMS
ELECTROGRAPH
ELECTROGRAPHIC
ELECTROGRAPHIES
ELECTROGRAPHS
ELECTROGRAPHY
ELECTROING
ELECTROJET
ELECTROJETS
ELECTROKINETIC
ELECTROKINETICS
ELECTROLESS
ELECTROLIER
ELECTROLIERS
ELECTROLOGIES
ELECTROLOGIST
ELECTROLOGISTS
ELECTROLOGY
ELECTROLYSATION
ELECTROLYSE
ELECTROLYSED
ELECTROLYSER
ELECTROLYSERS
ELECTROLYSES
ELECTROLYSING
ELECTROLYSIS
ELECTROLYTE
ELECTROLYTES
ELECTROLYTIC
ELECTROLYTICS
ELECTROLYZATION
ELECTROLYZE
ELECTROLYZED
ELECTROLYZER
ELECTROLYZERS
ELECTROLYZES
ELECTROLYZING
ELECTROMAGNET
ELECTROMAGNETIC
ELECTROMAGNETS
ELECTROMER
ELECTROMERIC
ELECTROMERISM
ELECTROMERISMS
ELECTROMERS
ELECTROMETER
ELECTROMETERS
ELECTROMETRIC
ELECTROMETRICAL
ELECTROMETRIES
ELECTROMETRY
ELECTROMOTANCE
ELECTROMOTANCES
ELECTROMOTIVE
ELECTROMOTOR
ELECTROMOTORS
ELECTROMYOGRAM
ELECTROMYOGRAMS
ELECTROMYOGRAPH
ELECTRONEGATIVE
ELECTRONIC
ELECTRONICA
ELECTRONICALLY
ELECTRONICAS
ELECTRONICS
ELECTRONVOLT
ELECTRONVOLTS
ELECTROOSMOSES
ELECTROOSMOSIS
ELECTROOSMOTIC
ELECTROPHILE
ELECTROPHILES
ELECTROPHILIC
ELECTROPHONE
ELECTROPHONES
ELECTROPHONIC
ELECTROPHORESE
ELECTROPHORESED
ELECTROPHORESES
ELECTROPHORESIS
ELECTROPHORETIC
ELECTROPHORI
ELECTROPHORUS
ELECTROPHORUSES
ELECTROPLATE
ELECTROPLATED
ELECTROPLATER
ELECTROPLATERS
ELECTROPLATES
ELECTROPLATING
ELECTROPLATINGS
ELECTROPOLAR
ELECTROPOP
ELECTROPOPS
ELECTROPOSITIVE
ELECTROPUNCTURE
ELECTRORECEPTOR
ELECTRORHEOLOGY
ELECTROSCOPE
ELECTROSCOPES
ELECTROSCOPIC
ELECTROSHOCK
ELECTROSHOCKS
ELECTROSONDE
ELECTROSONDES
ELECTROSTATIC
ELECTROSTATICS
ELECTROSURGERY
ELECTROSURGICAL
ELECTROTECHNICS
ELECTROTHERAPY
ELECTROTHERMAL
ELECTROTHERMIC
ELECTROTHERMICS
ELECTROTHERMIES
ELECTROTHERMY
ELECTROTINT
ELECTROTINTS
ELECTROTONIC
ELECTROTONUS
ELECTROTONUSES
ELECTROTYPE
ELECTROTYPED
ELECTROTYPER
ELECTROTYPERS
ELECTROTYPES
ELECTROTYPIC
ELECTROTYPIES
ELECTROTYPING
ELECTROTYPIST
ELECTROTYPISTS
ELECTROTYPY
ELECTROVALENCE
ELECTROVALENCES
ELECTROVALENCY
ELECTROVALENT
ELECTROVALENTLY
ELECTROWEAK
ELECTROWINNING
ELECTROWINNINGS
ELECTUARIES
ELEDOISINS
ELEEMOSYNARY
ELEGANCIES
ELEGIACALLY
ELEMENTALISM
ELEMENTALISMS
ELEMENTALLY
ELEMENTALS
ELEMENTARILY
ELEMENTARINESS
ELEMENTARY
ELEOPTENES
ELEPHANTIASES
ELEPHANTIASIC
ELEPHANTIASIS
ELEPHANTINE
ELEPHANTOID
ELEPIDOTES
ELEUTHERARCH
ELEUTHERARCHS
ELEUTHERIAN
ELEUTHEROCOCCI
ELEUTHEROCOCCUS
ELEUTHERODACTYL
ELEUTHEROMANIA
ELEUTHEROMANIAS
ELEUTHEROPHOBIA
ELEUTHEROPHOBIC
ELEVATIONAL
ELEVATIONS
ELEVENTHLY
ELFISHNESS
ELFISHNESSES
ELICITABLE
ELICITATION
ELICITATIONS
ELIGIBILITIES

ELIGIBILITY
ELIMINABILITIES
ELIMINABILITY
ELIMINABLE
ELIMINANTS
ELIMINATED
ELIMINATES
ELIMINATING
ELIMINATION
ELIMINATIONS
ELIMINATIVE
ELIMINATIVISM
ELIMINATIVISMS
ELIMINATOR
ELIMINATORS
ELIMINATORY
ELLIPSOGRAPH
ELLIPSOGRAPHS
ELLIPSOIDAL
ELLIPSOIDS
ELLIPTICAL
ELLIPTICALLY
ELLIPTICALNESS
ELLIPTICALS
ELLIPTICITIES
ELLIPTICITY
ELOCUTIONARY
ELOCUTIONIST
ELOCUTIONISTS
ELOCUTIONS
ELOIGNMENT
ELOIGNMENTS
ELOINMENTS
ELONGATING
ELONGATION
ELONGATIONS
ELOPEMENTS
ELOQUENCES
ELOQUENTLY
ELSEWHITHER
ELUCIDATED
ELUCIDATES
ELUCIDATING
ELUCIDATION
ELUCIDATIONS
ELUCIDATIVE
ELUCIDATOR
ELUCIDATORS
ELUCIDATORY
ELUCUBRATE
ELUCUBRATED
ELUCUBRATES
ELUCUBRATING
ELUCUBRATION
ELUCUBRATIONS
ELUSIVENESS
ELUSIVENESSES
ELUSORINESS
ELUSORINESSES
ELUTRIATED
ELUTRIATES
ELUTRIATING
ELUTRIATION
ELUTRIATIONS
ELUTRIATOR
ELUTRIATORS
ELUVIATING
ELUVIATION
ELUVIATIONS
ELVISHNESS
ELVISHNESSES
ELYTRIFORM
ELYTRIGEROUS
EMACIATING
EMACIATION
EMACIATIONS
EMALANGENI
EMANATIONAL
EMANATIONS
EMANATISTS
EMANCIPATE
EMANCIPATED
EMANCIPATES
EMANCIPATING
EMANCIPATION
EMANCIPATIONIST
EMANCIPATIONS
EMANCIPATIVE
EMANCIPATOR
EMANCIPATORS
EMANCIPATORY
EMANCIPIST
EMANCIPISTS
EMARGINATE
EMARGINATED
EMARGINATELY
EMARGINATES
EMARGINATING
EMARGINATION
EMARGINATIONS
EMASCULATE
EMASCULATED
EMASCULATES
EMASCULATING
EMASCULATION
EMASCULATIONS
EMASCULATIVE
EMASCULATOR
EMASCULATORS
EMASCULATORY
EMBALLINGS
EMBALMINGS
EMBALMMENT
EMBALMMENTS
EMBANKMENT
EMBANKMENTS
EMBARCADERO
EMBARCADEROS
EMBARCATION
EMBARCATIONS
EMBARGOING
EMBARKATION
EMBARKATIONS
EMBARKMENT
EMBARKMENTS
EMBARQUEMENT
EMBARQUEMENTS
EMBARRASSABLE
EMBARRASSED
EMBARRASSEDLY
EMBARRASSES
EMBARRASSING
EMBARRASSINGLY
EMBARRASSMENT
EMBARRASSMENTS
EMBARRINGS
EMBASEMENT
EMBASEMENTS
EMBASSADES
EMBASSADOR
EMBASSADORS
EMBASSAGES
EMBATTLEMENT
EMBATTLEMENTS
EMBATTLING
EMBAYMENTS
EMBEDDINGS
EMBEDMENTS
EMBELLISHED
EMBELLISHER
EMBELLISHERS
EMBELLISHES
EMBELLISHING
EMBELLISHINGLY
EMBELLISHMENT
EMBELLISHMENTS
EMBEZZLEMENT
EMBEZZLEMENTS
EMBEZZLERS
EMBEZZLING
EMBIGGENED
EMBIGGENING
EMBITTERED
EMBITTERER
EMBITTERERS
EMBITTERING
EMBITTERINGS
EMBITTERMENT
EMBITTERMENTS
EMBLAZONED
EMBLAZONER
EMBLAZONERS
EMBLAZONING
EMBLAZONMENT
EMBLAZONMENTS
EMBLAZONRIES
EMBLAZONRY
EMBLEMATIC
EMBLEMATICAL
EMBLEMATICALLY
EMBLEMATISE
EMBLEMATISED
EMBLEMATISES
EMBLEMATISING
EMBLEMATIST
EMBLEMATISTS
EMBLEMATIZE
EMBLEMATIZED
EMBLEMATIZES
EMBLEMATIZING
EMBLEMENTS
EMBLEMISED
EMBLEMISES
EMBLEMISING
EMBLEMIZED
EMBLEMIZES
EMBLEMIZING
EMBLOOMING
EMBLOSSOMED
EMBLOSSOMING
EMBLOSSOMS
EMBODIMENT
EMBODIMENTS
EMBOITEMENT
EMBOITEMENTS
EMBOLDENED
EMBOLDENER
EMBOLDENERS
EMBOLDENING
EMBOLECTOMIES
EMBOLECTOMY
EMBOLISATION
EMBOLISATIONS
EMBOLISING
EMBOLISMAL
EMBOLISMIC
EMBOLIZATION
EMBOLIZATIONS
EMBOLIZING
EMBONPOINT
EMBONPOINTS
EMBORDERED
EMBORDERING
EMBOSCATAS
EMBOSOMING
EMBOSSABLE
EMBOSSINGS
EMBOSSMENT
EMBOSSMENTS
EMBOTHRIUM
EMBOTHRIUMS
EMBOUCHURE
EMBOUCHURES
EMBOUNDING
EMBOURGEOISE
EMBOURGEOISED
EMBOURGEOISES
EMBOURGEOISING
EMBOWELING
EMBOWELLED

E

EMBOWELLING
EMBOWELMENT
EMBOWELMENTS
EMBOWERING
EMBOWERMENT
EMBOWERMENTS
EMBOWMENTS
EMBRACEABLE
EMBRACEMENT
EMBRACEMENTS
EMBRACEORS
EMBRACERIES
EMBRACINGLY
EMBRACINGNESS
EMBRACINGNESSES
EMBRAIDING
EMBRANCHMENT
EMBRANCHMENTS
EMBRANGLED
EMBRANGLEMENT
EMBRANGLEMENTS
EMBRANGLES
EMBRANGLING
EMBRASURED
EMBRASURES
EMBRAZURES
EMBREADING
EMBREATHED
EMBREATHES
EMBREATHING
EMBRITTLED
EMBRITTLEMENT
EMBRITTLEMENTS
EMBRITTLES
EMBRITTLING
EMBROCATED
EMBROCATES
EMBROCATING
EMBROCATION
EMBROCATIONS
EMBROGLIOS
EMBROIDERED
EMBROIDERER
EMBROIDERERS
EMBROIDERIES
EMBROIDERING
EMBROIDERS
EMBROIDERY
EMBROILERS
EMBROILING
EMBROILMENT
EMBROILMENTS
EMBROWNING
EMBRUEMENT
EMBRUEMENTS
EMBRYECTOMIES
EMBRYECTOMY
EMBRYOGENESES
EMBRYOGENESIS
EMBRYOGENETIC
EMBRYOGENIC
EMBRYOGENIES
EMBRYOGENY
EMBRYOLOGIC
EMBRYOLOGICAL
EMBRYOLOGICALLY
EMBRYOLOGIES
EMBRYOLOGIST
EMBRYOLOGISTS
EMBRYOLOGY
EMBRYONATE
EMBRYONATED
EMBRYONICALLY
EMBRYOPHYTE
EMBRYOPHYTES
EMBRYOTICALLY
EMBRYOTOMIES
EMBRYOTOMY
EMBRYULCIA
EMBRYULCIAS
EMENDATING
EMENDATION
EMENDATIONS
EMENDATORS
EMENDATORY
EMERGENCES
EMERGENCIES
EMERGENTLY
EMETICALLY
EMETOPHOBIA
EMETOPHOBIAS
EMICATIONS
EMIGRATING
EMIGRATION
EMIGRATIONAL
EMIGRATIONIST
EMIGRATIONISTS
EMIGRATIONS
EMIGRATORY
EMINENCIES
EMINENTIAL
EMISSARIES
EMISSIVITIES
EMISSIVITY
EMITTANCES
EMMARBLING
EMMENAGOGIC
EMMENAGOGUE
EMMENAGOGUES
EMMENOLOGIES
EMMENOLOGY
EMMETROPES
EMMETROPIA
EMMETROPIAS
EMMETROPIC
EMOLLESCENCE
EMOLLESCENCES
EMOLLIATED
EMOLLIATES
EMOLLIATING
EMOLLIENCE
EMOLLIENCES
EMOLLIENTS
EMOLLITION
EMOLLITIONS
EMOLUMENTAL
EMOLUMENTARY
EMOLUMENTS
EMOTIONABLE
EMOTIONALISE
EMOTIONALISED
EMOTIONALISES
EMOTIONALISING
EMOTIONALISM
EMOTIONALISMS
EMOTIONALIST
EMOTIONALISTIC
EMOTIONALISTS
EMOTIONALITIES
EMOTIONALITY
EMOTIONALIZE
EMOTIONALIZED
EMOTIONALIZES
EMOTIONALIZING
EMOTIONALLY
EMOTIONLESS
EMOTIONLESSLY
EMOTIONLESSNESS
EMOTIVENESS
EMOTIVENESSES
EMOTIVISMS
EMOTIVITIES
EMPACKETED
EMPACKETING
EMPALEMENT
EMPALEMENTS
EMPANELING
EMPANELLED
EMPANELLING
EMPANELMENT
EMPANELMENTS
EMPANOPLIED
EMPANOPLIES
EMPANOPLYING
EMPARADISE
EMPARADISED
EMPARADISES
EMPARADISING
EMPARLAUNCE
EMPARLAUNCES
EMPASSIONATE
EMPASSIONED
EMPATHETIC
EMPATHETICALLY
EMPATHICALLY
EMPATHISED
EMPATHISES
EMPATHISING
EMPATHISTS
EMPATHIZED
EMPATHIZES
EMPATHIZING
EMPATRONED
EMPATRONING
EMPEACHING
EMPENNAGES
EMPEOPLING
EMPERISHED
EMPERISHES
EMPERISHING
EMPERISING
EMPERIZING
EMPERORSHIP
EMPERORSHIPS
EMPHASISED
EMPHASISES
EMPHASISING
EMPHASIZED
EMPHASIZES
EMPHASIZING
EMPHATICAL
EMPHATICALLY
EMPHATICALNESS
EMPHRACTIC
EMPHRACTICS
EMPHYSEMAS
EMPHYSEMATOUS
EMPHYSEMIC
EMPHYSEMICS
EMPHYTEUSES
EMPHYTEUSIS
EMPHYTEUTIC
EMPIECEMENT
EMPIECEMENTS
EMPIERCING
EMPIGHTING
EMPIRICALLY
EMPIRICALNESS
EMPIRICALNESSES
EMPIRICALS
EMPIRICISM
EMPIRICISMS
EMPIRICIST
EMPIRICISTS
EMPIRICUTIC
EMPLACEMENT
EMPLACEMENTS
EMPLASTERED
EMPLASTERING
EMPLASTERS
EMPLASTICS
EMPLASTRON
EMPLASTRONS
EMPLASTRUM
EMPLASTRUMS
EMPLEACHED
EMPLEACHES
EMPLEACHING
EMPLECTIONS
EMPLECTUMS

EMPLONGING
EMPLOYABILITIES
EMPLOYABILITY
EMPLOYABLE
EMPLOYABLES
EMPLOYMENT
EMPLOYMENTS
EMPOISONED
EMPOISONING
EMPOISONMENT
EMPOISONMENTS
EMPOLDERED
EMPOLDERING
EMPOVERISH
EMPOVERISHED
EMPOVERISHER
EMPOVERISHERS
EMPOVERISHES
EMPOVERISHING
EMPOVERISHMENT
EMPOVERISHMENTS
EMPOWERING
EMPOWERMENT
EMPOWERMENTS
EMPRESSEMENT
EMPRESSEMENTS
EMPTINESSES
EMPURPLING
EMPYREUMATA
EMPYREUMATIC
EMPYREUMATICAL
EMPYREUMATISE
EMPYREUMATISED
EMPYREUMATISES
EMPYREUMATISING
EMPYREUMATIZE
EMPYREUMATIZED
EMPYREUMATIZES
EMPYREUMATIZING
EMULATIONS
EMULATIVELY
EMULATRESS
EMULATRESSES
EMULGENCES
EMULOUSNESS
EMULOUSNESSES
EMULSIFIABLE
EMULSIFICATION
EMULSIFICATIONS
EMULSIFIED
EMULSIFIER
EMULSIFIERS
EMULSIFIES
EMULSIFYING
EMULSIONISE
EMULSIONISED
EMULSIONISES
EMULSIONISING
EMULSIONIZE
EMULSIONIZED
EMULSIONIZES
EMULSIONIZING
EMULSOIDAL
EMUNCTIONS
EMUNCTORIES
ENABLEMENT
ENABLEMENTS
ENACTMENTS
ENALAPRILS
ENAMELINGS
ENAMELISTS
ENAMELLERS
ENAMELLING
ENAMELLINGS
ENAMELLIST
ENAMELLISTS
ENAMELWARE
ENAMELWARES
ENAMELWORK
ENAMELWORKS
ENAMORADOS
ENAMOURING
ENANTHEMAS
ENANTIODROMIA
ENANTIODROMIAS
ENANTIODROMIC
ENANTIOMER
ENANTIOMERIC
ENANTIOMERS
ENANTIOMORPH
ENANTIOMORPHIC
ENANTIOMORPHIES
ENANTIOMORPHISM
ENANTIOMORPHOUS
ENANTIOMORPHS
ENANTIOMORPHY
ENANTIOPATHIES
ENANTIOPATHY
ENANTIOSES
ENANTIOSIS
ENANTIOSTYLIES
ENANTIOSTYLOUS
ENANTIOSTYLY
ENANTIOTROPIC
ENANTIOTROPIES
ENANTIOTROPY
ENARRATION
ENARRATIONS
ENARTHRODIAL
ENARTHROSES
ENARTHROSIS
ENCAMPMENT
ENCAMPMENTS
ENCANTHISES
ENCAPSULATE
ENCAPSULATED
ENCAPSULATES
ENCAPSULATING
ENCAPSULATION
ENCAPSULATIONS
ENCAPSULED
ENCAPSULES
ENCAPSULING
ENCARNALISE
ENCARNALISED
ENCARNALISES
ENCARNALISING
ENCARNALIZE
ENCARNALIZED
ENCARNALIZES
ENCARNALIZING
ENCARPUSES
ENCASEMENT
ENCASEMENTS
ENCASHABLE
ENCASHMENT
ENCASHMENTS
ENCAUSTICALLY
ENCAUSTICS
ENCEPHALALGIA
ENCEPHALALGIAS
ENCEPHALIC
ENCEPHALIN
ENCEPHALINE
ENCEPHALINES
ENCEPHALINS
ENCEPHALITIC
ENCEPHALITIDES
ENCEPHALITIS
ENCEPHALITISES
ENCEPHALITOGEN
ENCEPHALITOGENS
ENCEPHALOCELE
ENCEPHALOCELES
ENCEPHALOGRAM
ENCEPHALOGRAMS
ENCEPHALOGRAPH
ENCEPHALOGRAPHS
ENCEPHALOGRAPHY
ENCEPHALOID
ENCEPHALOMA
ENCEPHALOMAS
ENCEPHALOMATA
ENCEPHALON
ENCEPHALONS
ENCEPHALOPATHIC
ENCEPHALOPATHY
ENCEPHALOTOMIES
ENCEPHALOTOMY
ENCEPHALOUS
ENCHAINING
ENCHAINMENT
ENCHAINMENTS
ENCHANTERS
ENCHANTING
ENCHANTINGLY
ENCHANTMENT
ENCHANTMENTS
ENCHANTRESS
ENCHANTRESSES
ENCHARGING
ENCHARMING
ENCHEASONS
ENCHEERING
ENCHEIRIDIA
ENCHEIRIDION
ENCHEIRIDIONS
ENCHILADAS
ENCHIRIDIA
ENCHIRIDION
ENCHIRIDIONS
ENCHONDROMA
ENCHONDROMAS
ENCHONDROMATA
ENCHONDROMATOUS
ENCINCTURE
ENCINCTURED
ENCINCTURES
ENCINCTURING
ENCIPHERED
ENCIPHERER
ENCIPHERERS
ENCIPHERING
ENCIPHERMENT
ENCIPHERMENTS
ENCIRCLEMENT
ENCIRCLEMENTS
ENCIRCLING
ENCLASPING
ENCLITICALLY
ENCLOISTER
ENCLOISTERED
ENCLOISTERING
ENCLOISTERS
ENCLOSABLE
ENCLOSURES
ENCLOTHING
ENCLOUDING
ENCODEMENT
ENCODEMENTS
ENCOIGNURE
ENCOIGNURES
ENCOLOURED
ENCOLOURING
ENCOLPIONS
ENCOLPIUMS
ENCOMENDERO
ENCOMENDEROS
ENCOMIASTIC
ENCOMIASTICAL
ENCOMIASTICALLY
ENCOMIASTS
ENCOMIENDA
ENCOMIENDAS
ENCOMPASSED
ENCOMPASSES
ENCOMPASSING
ENCOMPASSMENT
ENCOMPASSMENTS
ENCOPRESES

ENCOPRESIS
ENCOPRETIC
ENCOUNTERED
ENCOUNTERER
ENCOUNTERERS
ENCOUNTERING
ENCOUNTERS
ENCOURAGED
ENCOURAGEMENT
ENCOURAGEMENTS
ENCOURAGER
ENCOURAGERS
ENCOURAGES
ENCOURAGING
ENCOURAGINGLY
ENCOURAGINGS
ENCRADLING
ENCREASING
ENCRIMSONED
ENCRIMSONING
ENCRIMSONS
ENCRINITAL
ENCRINITES
ENCRINITIC
ENCROACHED
ENCROACHER
ENCROACHERS
ENCROACHES
ENCROACHING
ENCROACHINGLY
ENCROACHMENT
ENCROACHMENTS
ENCRUSTATION
ENCRUSTATIONS
ENCRUSTING
ENCRUSTMENT
ENCRUSTMENTS
ENCRYPTING
ENCRYPTION
ENCRYPTIONS
ENCULTURATE
ENCULTURATED
ENCULTURATES
ENCULTURATING
ENCULTURATION
ENCULTURATIONS
ENCULTURATIVE
ENCUMBERED
ENCUMBERING
ENCUMBERINGLY
ENCUMBERMENT
ENCUMBERMENTS
ENCUMBRANCE
ENCUMBRANCER
ENCUMBRANCERS
ENCUMBRANCES
ENCURTAINED
ENCURTAINING
ENCURTAINS
ENCYCLICAL
ENCYCLICALS
ENCYCLOPAEDIA
ENCYCLOPAEDIAS
ENCYCLOPAEDIC
ENCYCLOPAEDICAL
ENCYCLOPAEDISM
ENCYCLOPAEDISMS
ENCYCLOPAEDIST
ENCYCLOPAEDISTS
ENCYCLOPEDIA
ENCYCLOPEDIAN
ENCYCLOPEDIAS
ENCYCLOPEDIC
ENCYCLOPEDICAL
ENCYCLOPEDISM
ENCYCLOPEDISMS
ENCYCLOPEDIST
ENCYCLOPEDISTS
ENCYSTATION
ENCYSTATIONS
ENCYSTMENT
ENCYSTMENTS
ENDAMAGEMENT
ENDAMAGEMENTS
ENDAMAGING
ENDAMOEBAE
ENDAMOEBAS
ENDAMOEBIC
ENDANGERED
ENDANGERER
ENDANGERERS
ENDANGERING
ENDANGERMENT
ENDANGERMENTS
ENDARCHIES
ENDARTERECTOMY
ENDEARINGLY
ENDEARINGNESS
ENDEARINGNESSES
ENDEARMENT
ENDEARMENTS
ENDEAVORED
ENDEAVORER
ENDEAVORERS
ENDEAVORING
ENDEAVOURED
ENDEAVOURER
ENDEAVOURERS
ENDEAVOURING
ENDEAVOURMENT
ENDEAVOURMENTS
ENDEAVOURS
ENDECAGONS
ENDEIXISES
ENDEMICALLY
ENDEMICITIES
ENDEMICITY
ENDEMIOLOGIES
ENDEMIOLOGY
ENDENIZENED
ENDENIZENING
ENDENIZENS
ENDERGONIC
ENDERMATIC
ENDERMICAL
ENDLESSNESS
ENDLESSNESSES
ENDOBIOTIC
ENDOBLASTIC
ENDOBLASTS
ENDOCARDIA
ENDOCARDIAC
ENDOCARDIAL
ENDOCARDITIC
ENDOCARDITIDES
ENDOCARDITIS
ENDOCARDITISES
ENDOCARDIUM
ENDOCARPAL
ENDOCARPIC
ENDOCENTRIC
ENDOCHONDRAL
ENDOCHYLOUS
ENDOCRANIA
ENDOCRANIAL
ENDOCRANIUM
ENDOCRINAL
ENDOCRINES
ENDOCRINIC
ENDOCRINOLOGIC
ENDOCRINOLOGIES
ENDOCRINOLOGIST
ENDOCRINOLOGY
ENDOCRINOPATHIC
ENDOCRINOPATHY
ENDOCRINOUS
ENDOCRITIC
ENDOCUTICLE
ENDOCUTICLES
ENDOCYTOSES
ENDOCYTOSIS
ENDOCYTOTIC
ENDODERMAL
ENDODERMIC
ENDODERMIS
ENDODERMISES
ENDODONTAL
ENDODONTIC
ENDODONTICALLY
ENDODONTICS
ENDODONTIST
ENDODONTISTS
ENDOENZYME
ENDOENZYMES
ENDOGAMIES
ENDOGAMOUS
ENDOGENIES
ENDOGENOUS
ENDOGENOUSLY
ENDOLITHIC
ENDOLYMPHATIC
ENDOLYMPHS
ENDOMETRIA
ENDOMETRIAL
ENDOMETRIOSES
ENDOMETRIOSIS
ENDOMETRITIS
ENDOMETRITISES
ENDOMETRIUM
ENDOMITOSES
ENDOMITOSIS
ENDOMITOTIC
ENDOMIXISES
ENDOMORPHIC
ENDOMORPHIES
ENDOMORPHISM
ENDOMORPHISMS
ENDOMORPHS
ENDOMORPHY
ENDOMYCORRHIZA
ENDONEURIA
ENDONEURIUM
ENDONUCLEASE
ENDONUCLEASES
ENDONUCLEOLYTIC
ENDOPARASITE
ENDOPARASITES
ENDOPARASITIC
ENDOPARASITISM
ENDOPARASITISMS
ENDOPEPTIDASE
ENDOPEPTIDASES
ENDOPEROXIDE
ENDOPEROXIDES
ENDOPHAGIES
ENDOPHAGOUS
ENDOPHITIC
ENDOPHYLLOUS
ENDOPHYTES
ENDOPHYTIC
ENDOPHYTICALLY
ENDOPLASMIC
ENDOPLASMS
ENDOPLASTIC
ENDOPLEURA
ENDOPLEURAS
ENDOPODITE
ENDOPODITES
ENDOPOLYPLOID
ENDOPOLYPLOIDY
ENDOPROCTS
ENDORADIOSONDE
ENDORADIOSONDES
ENDORHIZAL
ENDORPHINS
ENDORSABLE
ENDORSATION
ENDORSATIONS
ENDORSEMENT
ENDORSEMENTS

ENDOSCOPES
ENDOSCOPIC
ENDOSCOPICALLY
ENDOSCOPIES
ENDOSCOPIST
ENDOSCOPISTS
ENDOSKELETAL
ENDOSKELETON
ENDOSKELETONS
ENDOSMOMETER
ENDOSMOMETERS
ENDOSMOMETRIC
ENDOSMOSES
ENDOSMOSIS
ENDOSMOTIC
ENDOSMOTICALLY
ENDOSPERMIC
ENDOSPERMS
ENDOSPORES
ENDOSPOROUS
ENDOSTEALLY
ENDOSTOSES
ENDOSTOSIS
ENDOSTYLES
ENDOSULFAN
ENDOSULFANS
ENDOSYMBIONT
ENDOSYMBIONTS
ENDOSYMBIOSES
ENDOSYMBIOSIS
ENDOSYMBIOTIC
ENDOTHECIA
ENDOTHECIAL
ENDOTHECIUM
ENDOTHELIA
ENDOTHELIAL
ENDOTHELIOID
ENDOTHELIOMA
ENDOTHELIOMAS
ENDOTHELIOMATA
ENDOTHELIUM
ENDOTHERMAL
ENDOTHERMIC
ENDOTHERMICALLY
ENDOTHERMIES
ENDOTHERMISM
ENDOTHERMISMS
ENDOTHERMS
ENDOTHERMY
ENDOTOXINS
ENDOTRACHEAL
ENDOTROPHIC
ENDOWMENTS
ENDPLAYING
ENDUNGEONED
ENDUNGEONING
ENDUNGEONS
ENDURABILITIES
ENDURABILITY
ENDURABLENESS
ENDURABLENESSES
ENDURANCES
ENDURINGLY
ENDURINGNESS
ENDURINGNESSES
ENERGETICAL
ENERGETICALLY
ENERGETICS
ENERGISATION
ENERGISATIONS
ENERGISERS
ENERGISING
ENERGIZATION
ENERGIZATIONS
ENERGIZERS
ENERGIZING
ENERGUMENS
ENERVATING
ENERVATION
ENERVATIONS
ENERVATIVE
ENERVATORS
ENFACEMENT
ENFACEMENTS
ENFEEBLEMENT
ENFEEBLEMENTS
ENFEEBLERS
ENFEEBLING
ENFELONING
ENFEOFFING
ENFEOFFMENT
ENFEOFFMENTS
ENFESTERED
ENFETTERED
ENFETTERING
ENFEVERING
ENFIERCING
ENFILADING
ENFLESHING
ENFLEURAGE
ENFLEURAGES
ENFLOWERED
ENFLOWERING
ENFOLDMENT
ENFOLDMENTS
ENFORCEABILITY
ENFORCEABLE
ENFORCEDLY
ENFORCEMENT
ENFORCEMENTS
ENFORESTED
ENFORESTING
ENFOULDERED
ENFRAMEMENT
ENFRAMEMENTS
ENFRANCHISE
ENFRANCHISED
ENFRANCHISEMENT
ENFRANCHISER
ENFRANCHISERS
ENFRANCHISES
ENFRANCHISING
ENFREEDOMED
ENFREEDOMING
ENFREEDOMS
ENFREEZING
ENGAGEMENT
ENGAGEMENTS
ENGAGINGLY
ENGAGINGNESS
ENGAGINGNESSES
ENGARLANDED
ENGARLANDING
ENGARLANDS
ENGARRISON
ENGARRISONED
ENGARRISONING
ENGARRISONS
ENGENDERED
ENGENDERER
ENGENDERERS
ENGENDERING
ENGENDERMENT
ENGENDERMENTS
ENGENDRURE
ENGENDRURES
ENGENDURES
ENGINEERED
ENGINEERING
ENGINEERINGS
ENGINERIES
ENGIRDLING
ENGLACIALLY
ENGLISHING
ENGLOOMING
ENGLUTTING
ENGORGEMENT
ENGORGEMENTS
ENGOUEMENT
ENGOUEMENTS
ENGOUMENTS
ENGRAFFING
ENGRAFTATION
ENGRAFTATIONS
ENGRAFTING
ENGRAFTMENT
ENGRAFTMENTS
ENGRAILING
ENGRAILMENT
ENGRAILMENTS
ENGRAINEDLY
ENGRAINEDNESS
ENGRAINEDNESSES
ENGRAINERS
ENGRAINING
ENGRAMMATIC
ENGRASPING
ENGRAVERIES
ENGRAVINGS
ENGRENAGES
ENGRIEVING
ENGROOVING
ENGROSSEDLY
ENGROSSERS
ENGROSSING
ENGROSSINGLY
ENGROSSMENT
ENGROSSMENTS
ENGUARDING
ENGULFMENT
ENGULFMENTS
ENGULPHING
ENGYSCOPES
ENHANCEMENT
ENHANCEMENTS
ENHARMONIC
ENHARMONICAL
ENHARMONICALLY
ENHEARSING
ENHEARTENED
ENHEARTENING
ENHEARTENS
ENHUNGERED
ENHUNGERING
ENHYDRITES
ENHYDRITIC
ENHYDROSES
ENHYPOSTASIA
ENHYPOSTASIAS
ENHYPOSTATIC
ENHYPOSTATISE
ENHYPOSTATISED
ENHYPOSTATISES
ENHYPOSTATISING
ENHYPOSTATIZE
ENHYPOSTATIZED
ENHYPOSTATIZES
ENHYPOSTATIZING
ENIGMATICAL
ENIGMATICALLY
ENIGMATISE
ENIGMATISED
ENIGMATISES
ENIGMATISING
ENIGMATIST
ENIGMATISTS
ENIGMATIZE
ENIGMATIZED
ENIGMATIZES
ENIGMATIZING
ENIGMATOGRAPHY
ENJAMBEMENT
ENJAMBEMENTS
ENJAMBMENT
ENJAMBMENTS
ENJOINDERS
ENJOINMENT
ENJOINMENTS
ENJOYABLENESS
ENJOYABLENESSES

ENJOYMENTS
ENKEPHALIN
ENKEPHALINE
ENKEPHALINES
ENKEPHALINS
ENKERNELLED
ENKERNELLING
ENKINDLERS
ENKINDLING
ENLACEMENT
ENLACEMENTS
ENLARGEABLE
ENLARGEDLY
ENLARGEDNESS
ENLARGEDNESSES
ENLARGEMENT
ENLARGEMENTS
ENLARGENED
ENLARGENING
ENLEVEMENT
ENLEVEMENTS
ENLIGHTENED
ENLIGHTENER
ENLIGHTENERS
ENLIGHTENING
ENLIGHTENMENT
ENLIGHTENMENTS
ENLIGHTENS
ENLIGHTING
ENLISTMENT
ENLISTMENTS
ENLIVENERS
ENLIVENING
ENLIVENMENT
ENLIVENMENTS
ENLUMINING
ENMESHMENT
ENMESHMENTS
ENNEAGONAL
ENNEAGRAMS
ENNEAHEDRA
ENNEAHEDRAL
ENNEAHEDRON
ENNEAHEDRONS
ENNEANDRIAN
ENNEANDROUS
ENNEASTYLE
ENNEATHLON
ENNEATHLONS
ENNOBLEMENT
ENNOBLEMENTS
ENOKIDAKES
ENOKITAKES
ENOLOGICAL
ENOLOGISTS
ENORMITIES
ENORMOUSLY
ENORMOUSNESS
ENORMOUSNESSES
ENOUNCEMENT
ENOUNCEMENTS
ENPHYTOTIC
ENQUEUEING
ENQUIRATION
ENQUIRATIONS
ENRAGEMENT
ENRAGEMENTS
ENRANCKLED
ENRANCKLES
ENRANCKLING
ENRAPTURED
ENRAPTURES
ENRAPTURING
ENRAUNGING
ENRAVISHED
ENRAVISHES
ENRAVISHING
ENREGIMENT
ENREGIMENTED
ENREGIMENTING
ENREGIMENTS
ENREGISTER
ENREGISTERED
ENREGISTERING
ENREGISTERS
ENRHEUMING
ENRICHMENT
ENRICHMENTS
ENROLLMENT
ENROLLMENTS
ENROLMENTS
ENROUGHING
ENROUNDING
ENSAMPLING
ENSANGUINATED
ENSANGUINE
ENSANGUINED
ENSANGUINES
ENSANGUINING
ENSCHEDULE
ENSCHEDULED
ENSCHEDULES
ENSCHEDULING
ENSCONCING
ENSCROLLED
ENSCROLLING
ENSEPULCHRE
ENSEPULCHRED
ENSEPULCHRES
ENSEPULCHRING
ENSERFMENT
ENSERFMENTS
ENSHEATHED
ENSHEATHES
ENSHEATHING
ENSHELLING
ENSHELTERED
ENSHELTERING
ENSHELTERS
ENSHIELDED
ENSHIELDING
ENSHRINEES
ENSHRINEMENT
ENSHRINEMENTS
ENSHRINING
ENSHROUDED
ENSHROUDING
ENSIGNCIES
ENSIGNSHIP
ENSIGNSHIPS
ENSILABILITIES
ENSILABILITY
ENSILAGEING
ENSILAGING
ENSLAVEMENT
ENSLAVEMENTS
ENSNAREMENT
ENSNAREMENTS
ENSNARLING
ENSORCELED
ENSORCELING
ENSORCELLED
ENSORCELLING
ENSORCELLMENT
ENSORCELLMENTS
ENSORCELLS
ENSOULMENT
ENSOULMENTS
ENSPHERING
ENSTAMPING
ENSTATITES
ENSTEEPING
ENSTRUCTURED
ENSWATHEMENT
ENSWATHEMENTS
ENSWATHING
ENSWEEPING
ENTABLATURE
ENTABLATURES
ENTABLEMENT
ENTABLEMENTS
ENTAILMENT
ENTAILMENTS
ENTAMOEBAE
ENTAMOEBAS
ENTANGLEMENT
ENTANGLEMENTS
ENTANGLERS
ENTANGLING
ENTELECHIES
ENTELLUSES
ENTENDERED
ENTENDERING
ENTERCHAUNGE
ENTERCHAUNGED
ENTERCHAUNGES
ENTERCHAUNGING
ENTERDEALE
ENTERDEALED
ENTERDEALES
ENTERDEALING
ENTERECTOMIES
ENTERECTOMY
ENTERITIDES
ENTERITISES
ENTEROBACTERIA
ENTEROBACTERIAL
ENTEROBACTERIUM
ENTEROBIASES
ENTEROBIASIS
ENTEROCELE
ENTEROCELES
ENTEROCENTESES
ENTEROCENTESIS
ENTEROCOCCAL
ENTEROCOCCI
ENTEROCOCCUS
ENTEROCOEL
ENTEROCOELE
ENTEROCOELES
ENTEROCOELIC
ENTEROCOELOUS
ENTEROCOELS
ENTEROCOLITIDES
ENTEROCOLITIS
ENTEROCOLITISES
ENTEROGASTRONE
ENTEROGASTRONES
ENTEROHEPATITIS
ENTEROKINASE
ENTEROKINASES
ENTEROLITH
ENTEROLITHS
ENTEROPATHIES
ENTEROPATHY
ENTEROPNEUST
ENTEROPNEUSTAL
ENTEROPNEUSTS
ENTEROPTOSES
ENTEROPTOSIS
ENTEROSTOMAL
ENTEROSTOMIES
ENTEROSTOMY
ENTEROTOMIES
ENTEROTOMY
ENTEROTOXIN
ENTEROTOXINS
ENTEROVIRAL
ENTEROVIRUS
ENTEROVIRUSES
ENTERPRISE
ENTERPRISED
ENTERPRISER
ENTERPRISERS
ENTERPRISES
ENTERPRISING
ENTERPRISINGLY
ENTERTAINED
ENTERTAINER
ENTERTAINERS

ENTERTAINING
ENTERTAININGLY
ENTERTAININGS
ENTERTAINMENT
ENTERTAINMENTS
ENTERTAINS
ENTERTAKEN
ENTERTAKES
ENTERTAKING
ENTERTISSUED
ENTHALPIES
ENTHRALDOM
ENTHRALDOMS
ENTHRALLED
ENTHRALLER
ENTHRALLERS
ENTHRALLING
ENTHRALLMENT
ENTHRALLMENTS
ENTHRALMENT
ENTHRALMENTS
ENTHRONEMENT
ENTHRONEMENTS
ENTHRONING
ENTHRONISATION
ENTHRONISATIONS
ENTHRONISE
ENTHRONISED
ENTHRONISES
ENTHRONISING
ENTHRONIZATION
ENTHRONIZATIONS
ENTHRONIZE
ENTHRONIZED
ENTHRONIZES
ENTHRONIZING
ENTHUSIASM
ENTHUSIASMS
ENTHUSIAST
ENTHUSIASTIC
ENTHUSIASTICAL
ENTHUSIASTS
ENTHYMEMATIC
ENTHYMEMATICAL
ENTHYMEMES
ENTICEABLE
ENTICEMENT
ENTICEMENTS
ENTICINGLY
ENTICINGNESS
ENTICINGNESSES
ENTIRENESS
ENTIRENESSES
ENTIRETIES
ENTITATIVE
ENTITLEMENT
ENTITLEMENTS
ENTOBLASTIC
ENTOBLASTS
ENTODERMAL
ENTODERMIC
ENTOILMENT
ENTOILMENTS
ENTOMBMENT
ENTOMBMENTS
ENTOMOFAUNA
ENTOMOFAUNAE
ENTOMOFAUNAS
ENTOMOLOGIC
ENTOMOLOGICAL
ENTOMOLOGICALLY
ENTOMOLOGIES
ENTOMOLOGISE
ENTOMOLOGISED
ENTOMOLOGISES
ENTOMOLOGISING
ENTOMOLOGIST
ENTOMOLOGISTS
ENTOMOLOGIZE
ENTOMOLOGIZED
ENTOMOLOGIZES
ENTOMOLOGIZING
ENTOMOLOGY
ENTOMOPHAGIES
ENTOMOPHAGOUS
ENTOMOPHAGY
ENTOMOPHILIES
ENTOMOPHILOUS
ENTOMOPHILY
ENTOMOSTRACAN
ENTOMOSTRACANS
ENTOMOSTRACOUS
ENTOPHYTAL
ENTOPHYTES
ENTOPHYTIC
ENTOPHYTOUS
ENTOPLASTRA
ENTOPLASTRAL
ENTOPLASTRON
ENTOPROCTS
ENTOURAGES
ENTRAILING
ENTRAINEMENT
ENTRAINEMENTS
ENTRAINERS
ENTRAINING
ENTRAINMENT
ENTRAINMENTS
ENTRAMMELED
ENTRAMMELING
ENTRAMMELLED
ENTRAMMELLING
ENTRAMMELS
ENTRANCEMENT
ENTRANCEMENTS
ENTRANCEWAY
ENTRANCEWAYS
ENTRANCING
ENTRANCINGLY
ENTRAPMENT
ENTRAPMENTS
ENTRAPPERS
ENTRAPPING
ENTREASURE
ENTREASURED
ENTREASURES
ENTREASURING
ENTREATABLE
ENTREATIES
ENTREATING
ENTREATINGLY
ENTREATINGS
ENTREATIVE
ENTREATMENT
ENTREATMENTS
ENTRECHATS
ENTRECOTES
ENTREMESSE
ENTREMESSES
ENTRENCHED
ENTRENCHER
ENTRENCHERS
ENTRENCHES
ENTRENCHING
ENTRENCHMENT
ENTRENCHMENTS
ENTREPRENEUR
ENTREPRENEURIAL
ENTREPRENEURS
ENTREPRENEUSE
ENTREPRENEUSES
ENTROPICALLY
ENTROPIONS
ENTROPIUMS
ENTRUSTING
ENTRUSTMENT
ENTRUSTMENTS
ENTWINEMENT
ENTWINEMENTS
ENTWISTING
ENUCLEATED
ENUCLEATES
ENUCLEATING
ENUCLEATION
ENUCLEATIONS
ENUMERABILITIES
ENUMERABILITY
ENUMERABLE
ENUMERATED
ENUMERATES
ENUMERATING
ENUMERATION
ENUMERATIONS
ENUMERATIVE
ENUMERATOR
ENUMERATORS
ENUNCIABLE
ENUNCIATED
ENUNCIATES
ENUNCIATING
ENUNCIATION
ENUNCIATIONS
ENUNCIATIVE
ENUNCIATIVELY
ENUNCIATOR
ENUNCIATORS
ENUNCIATORY
ENUREDNESS
ENUREDNESSES
ENUREMENTS
ENURESISES
ENVASSALLED
ENVASSALLING
ENVAULTING
ENVEIGLING
ENVELOPERS
ENVELOPING
ENVELOPMENT
ENVELOPMENTS
ENVENOMING
ENVENOMISATION
ENVENOMISATIONS
ENVENOMIZATION
ENVENOMIZATIONS
ENVERMEILED
ENVERMEILING
ENVERMEILS
ENVIABLENESS
ENVIABLENESSES
ENVIOUSNESS
ENVIOUSNESSES
ENVIRONICS
ENVIRONING
ENVIRONMENT
ENVIRONMENTAL
ENVIRONMENTALLY
ENVIRONMENTS
ENVISAGEMENT
ENVISAGEMENTS
ENVISAGING
ENVISIONED
ENVISIONING
ENVOYSHIPS
ENWALLOWED
ENWALLOWING
ENWHEELING
ENWRAPMENT
ENWRAPMENTS
ENWRAPPING
ENWRAPPINGS
ENWREATHED
ENWREATHES
ENWREATHING
ENZOOTICALLY
ENZYMATICALLY
ENZYMICALLY
ENZYMOLOGICAL
ENZYMOLOGIES
ENZYMOLOGIST
ENZYMOLOGISTS

ENZYMOLOGY
ENZYMOLYSES
ENZYMOLYSIS
ENZYMOLYTIC
EOHIPPUSES
EOSINOPHIL
EOSINOPHILE
EOSINOPHILES
EOSINOPHILIA
EOSINOPHILIAS
EOSINOPHILIC
EOSINOPHILOUS
EOSINOPHILS
EPAGOMENAL
EPANADIPLOSES
EPANADIPLOSIS
EPANALEPSES
EPANALEPSIS
EPANALEPTIC
EPANAPHORA
EPANAPHORAL
EPANAPHORAS
EPANODOSES
EPANORTHOSES
EPANORTHOSIS
EPANORTHOTIC
EPARCHATES
EPAULEMENT
EPAULEMENTS
EPAULETTED
EPAULETTES
EPEIROGENESES
EPEIROGENESIS
EPEIROGENETIC
EPEIROGENIC
EPEIROGENICALLY
EPEIROGENIES
EPEIROGENY
EPENCEPHALA
EPENCEPHALIC
EPENCEPHALON
EPENCEPHALONS
EPENTHESES
EPENTHESIS
EPENTHETIC
EPEOLATRIES
EPEXEGESES
EPEXEGESIS
EPEXEGETIC
EPEXEGETICAL
EPEXEGETICALLY
EPHEBOPHILE
EPHEBOPHILES
EPHEBOPHILIA
EPHEBOPHILIAS
EPHEDRINES
EPHEMERALITIES
EPHEMERALITY
EPHEMERALLY
EPHEMERALNESS
EPHEMERALNESSES
EPHEMERALS
EPHEMERIDES
EPHEMERIDIAN
EPHEMERIDS
EPHEMERIST
EPHEMERISTS
EPHEMERONS
EPHEMEROPTERAN
EPHEMEROPTERANS
EPHEMEROUS
EPHORALTIES
EPIBLASTIC
EPICALYCES
EPICALYXES
EPICANTHIC
EPICANTHUS
EPICARDIAC
EPICARDIAL
EPICARDIUM
EPICARDIUMS
EPICEDIANS
EPICENISMS
EPICENTERS
EPICENTRAL
EPICENTRES
EPICENTRUM
EPICHEIREMA
EPICHEIREMAS
EPICHEIREMATA
EPICHLOROHYDRIN
EPICONDYLE
EPICONDYLES
EPICONDYLITIS
EPICONDYLITISES
EPICONTINENTAL
EPICRANIUM
EPICRANIUMS
EPICUREANISM
EPICUREANISMS
EPICUREANS
EPICURISED
EPICURISES
EPICURISING
EPICURISMS
EPICURIZED
EPICURIZES
EPICURIZING
EPICUTICLE
EPICUTICLES
EPICUTICULAR
EPICYCLICAL
EPICYCLOID
EPICYCLOIDAL
EPICYCLOIDS
EPIDEICTIC
EPIDEICTICAL
EPIDEMICAL
EPIDEMICALLY
EPIDEMICITIES
EPIDEMICITY
EPIDEMIOLOGIC
EPIDEMIOLOGICAL
EPIDEMIOLOGIES
EPIDEMIOLOGIST
EPIDEMIOLOGISTS
EPIDEMIOLOGY
EPIDENDRONE
EPIDENDRONES
EPIDENDRUM
EPIDENDRUMS
EPIDERMISES
EPIDERMOID
EPIDERMOLYSES
EPIDERMOLYSIS
EPIDIASCOPE
EPIDIASCOPES
EPIDIDYMAL
EPIDIDYMIDES
EPIDIDYMIS
EPIDIDYMITIS
EPIDIDYMITISES
EPIDIORITE
EPIDIORITES
EPIDOSITES
EPIDOTISATION
EPIDOTISATIONS
EPIDOTISED
EPIDOTIZATION
EPIDOTIZATIONS
EPIDOTIZED
EPIGASTRIA
EPIGASTRIAL
EPIGASTRIC
EPIGASTRIUM
EPIGENESES
EPIGENESIS
EPIGENESIST
EPIGENESISTS
EPIGENETIC
EPIGENETICALLY
EPIGENETICIST
EPIGENETICISTS
EPIGENETICS
EPIGENISTS
EPIGENOMES
EPIGLOTTAL
EPIGLOTTIC
EPIGLOTTIDES
EPIGLOTTIS
EPIGLOTTISES
EPIGNATHOUS
EPIGONISMS
EPIGRAMMATIC
EPIGRAMMATICAL
EPIGRAMMATISE
EPIGRAMMATISED
EPIGRAMMATISER
EPIGRAMMATISERS
EPIGRAMMATISES
EPIGRAMMATISING
EPIGRAMMATISM
EPIGRAMMATISMS
EPIGRAMMATIST
EPIGRAMMATISTS
EPIGRAMMATIZE
EPIGRAMMATIZED
EPIGRAMMATIZER
EPIGRAMMATIZERS
EPIGRAMMATIZES
EPIGRAMMATIZING
EPIGRAPHED
EPIGRAPHER
EPIGRAPHERS
EPIGRAPHIC
EPIGRAPHICAL
EPIGRAPHICALLY
EPIGRAPHIES
EPIGRAPHING
EPIGRAPHIST
EPIGRAPHISTS
EPILATIONS
EPILEPSIES
EPILEPTICAL
EPILEPTICALLY
EPILEPTICS
EPILEPTIFORM
EPILEPTOGENIC
EPILEPTOID
EPILIMNION
EPILIMNIONS
EPILOBIUMS
EPILOGISED
EPILOGISES
EPILOGISING
EPILOGISTIC
EPILOGISTS
EPILOGIZED
EPILOGIZES
EPILOGIZING
EPILOGUING
EPILOGUISE
EPILOGUISED
EPILOGUISES
EPILOGUISING
EPILOGUIZE
EPILOGUIZED
EPILOGUIZES
EPILOGUIZING
EPIMELETIC
EPIMERASES
EPIMERISED
EPIMERISES
EPIMERISING
EPIMERISMS
EPIMERIZED
EPIMERIZES
EPIMERIZING
EPIMORPHIC
EPIMORPHOSES

EPIMORPHOSIS
EPINASTICALLY
EPINASTIES
EPINEPHRIN
EPINEPHRINE
EPINEPHRINES
EPINEPHRINS
EPINEURIAL
EPINEURIUM
EPINEURIUMS
EPINICIONS
EPINIKIANS
EPINIKIONS
EPIPELAGIC
EPIPETALOUS
EPIPHANIES
EPIPHANOUS
EPIPHENOMENA
EPIPHENOMENAL
EPIPHENOMENALLY
EPIPHENOMENON
EPIPHONEMA
EPIPHONEMAS
EPIPHRAGMS
EPIPHYLLOUS
EPIPHYSEAL
EPIPHYSIAL
EPIPHYTICAL
EPIPHYTICALLY
EPIPHYTISM
EPIPHYTISMS
EPIPHYTOLOGIES
EPIPHYTOLOGY
EPIPHYTOTIC
EPIPHYTOTICS
EPIPLASTRA
EPIPLASTRAL
EPIPLASTRON
EPIPOLISMS
EPIROGENETIC
EPIROGENIC
EPIROGENIES
EPIRRHEMAS
EPIRRHEMATA
EPIRRHEMATIC
EPISCOPACIES
EPISCOPACY
EPISCOPALIAN
EPISCOPALIANISM
EPISCOPALIANS
EPISCOPALISM
EPISCOPALISMS
EPISCOPALLY
EPISCOPANT
EPISCOPANTS
EPISCOPATE
EPISCOPATED
EPISCOPATES
EPISCOPATING
EPISCOPIES
EPISCOPISE
EPISCOPISED
EPISCOPISES
EPISCOPISING
EPISCOPIZE
EPISCOPIZED
EPISCOPIZES
EPISCOPIZING
EPISEMATIC
EPISEPALOUS
EPISIOTOMIES
EPISIOTOMY
EPISODICAL
EPISODICALLY
EPISOMALLY
EPISPASTIC
EPISPASTICS
EPISTASIES
EPISTAXISES
EPISTEMICALLY
EPISTEMICS
EPISTEMOLOGICAL
EPISTEMOLOGIES
EPISTEMOLOGIST
EPISTEMOLOGISTS
EPISTEMOLOGY
EPISTERNAL
EPISTERNUM
EPISTERNUMS
EPISTILBITE
EPISTILBITES
EPISTOLARIAN
EPISTOLARIANS
EPISTOLARIES
EPISTOLARY
EPISTOLATORY
EPISTOLERS
EPISTOLETS
EPISTOLICAL
EPISTOLISE
EPISTOLISED
EPISTOLISES
EPISTOLISING
EPISTOLIST
EPISTOLISTS
EPISTOLIZE
EPISTOLIZED
EPISTOLIZES
EPISTOLIZING
EPISTOLOGRAPHY
EPISTROPHE
EPISTROPHES
EPITAPHERS
EPITAPHIAL
EPITAPHIAN
EPITAPHING
EPITAPHIST
EPITAPHISTS
EPITAXIALLY
EPITHALAMIA
EPITHALAMIC
EPITHALAMION
EPITHALAMIUM
EPITHALAMIUMS
EPITHELIAL
EPITHELIALISE
EPITHELIALISED
EPITHELIALISES
EPITHELIALISING
EPITHELIALIZE
EPITHELIALIZED
EPITHELIALIZES
EPITHELIALIZING
EPITHELIOID
EPITHELIOMA
EPITHELIOMAS
EPITHELIOMATA
EPITHELIOMATOUS
EPITHELISATION
EPITHELISATIONS
EPITHELISE
EPITHELISED
EPITHELISES
EPITHELISING
EPITHELIUM
EPITHELIUMS
EPITHELIZATION
EPITHELIZATIONS
EPITHELIZE
EPITHELIZED
EPITHELIZES
EPITHELIZING
EPITHEMATA
EPITHERMAL
EPITHETICAL
EPITHETICALLY
EPITHETING
EPITHETONS
EPITHYMETIC
EPITOMICAL
EPITOMISATION
EPITOMISATIONS
EPITOMISED
EPITOMISER
EPITOMISERS
EPITOMISES
EPITOMISING
EPITOMISTS
EPITOMIZATION
EPITOMIZATIONS
EPITOMIZED
EPITOMIZER
EPITOMIZERS
EPITOMIZES
EPITOMIZING
EPITRACHELION
EPITRACHELIONS
EPITROCHOID
EPITROCHOIDS
EPIZEUXISES
EPIZOOTICALLY
EPIZOOTICS
EPIZOOTIES
EPIZOOTIOLOGIC
EPIZOOTIOLOGIES
EPIZOOTIOLOGY
EPONYCHIUM
EPONYCHIUMS
EPONYMOUSLY
EPOXIDATION
EPOXIDATIONS
EPOXIDISED
EPOXIDISES
EPOXIDISING
EPOXIDIZED
EPOXIDIZES
EPOXIDIZING
EPROUVETTE
EPROUVETTES
EPULATIONS
EPURATIONS
EQUABILITIES
EQUABILITY
EQUABLENESS
EQUABLENESSES
EQUALISATION
EQUALISATIONS
EQUALISERS
EQUALISING
EQUALITARIAN
EQUALITARIANISM
EQUALITARIANS
EQUALITIES
EQUALIZATION
EQUALIZATIONS
EQUALIZERS
EQUALIZING
EQUALNESSES
EQUANIMITIES
EQUANIMITY
EQUANIMOUS
EQUANIMOUSLY
EQUATABILITIES
EQUATABILITY
EQUATIONAL
EQUATIONALLY
EQUATORIAL
EQUATORIALLY
EQUATORIALS
EQUATORWARD
EQUESTRIAN
EQUESTRIANISM
EQUESTRIANISMS
EQUESTRIANS
EQUESTRIENNE
EQUESTRIENNES
EQUIANGULAR
EQUIANGULARITY
EQUIBALANCE
EQUIBALANCED

EQUIBALANCES
EQUIBALANCING
EQUICALORIC
EQUIDIFFERENT
EQUIDISTANCE
EQUIDISTANCES
EQUIDISTANT
EQUIDISTANTLY
EQUIFINALLY
EQUILATERAL
EQUILATERALLY
EQUILATERALS
EQUILIBRANT
EQUILIBRANTS
EQUILIBRATE
EQUILIBRATED
EQUILIBRATES
EQUILIBRATING
EQUILIBRATION
EQUILIBRATIONS
EQUILIBRATOR
EQUILIBRATORS
EQUILIBRATORY
EQUILIBRIA
EQUILIBRIST
EQUILIBRISTIC
EQUILIBRISTS
EQUILIBRITIES
EQUILIBRITY
EQUILIBRIUM
EQUILIBRIUMS
EQUIMOLECULAR
EQUIMULTIPLE
EQUIMULTIPLES
EQUINITIES
EQUINOCTIAL
EQUINOCTIALLY
EQUINOCTIALS
EQUINUMEROUS
EQUIPAGING
EQUIPARATE
EQUIPARATED
EQUIPARATES
EQUIPARATING
EQUIPARATION
EQUIPARATIONS
EQUIPARTITION
EQUIPARTITIONS
EQUIPMENTS
EQUIPOISED
EQUIPOISES
EQUIPOISING
EQUIPOLLENCE
EQUIPOLLENCES
EQUIPOLLENCIES
EQUIPOLLENCY
EQUIPOLLENT
EQUIPOLLENTLY
EQUIPOLLENTS
EQUIPONDERANCE
EQUIPONDERANCES
EQUIPONDERANCY
EQUIPONDERANT
EQUIPONDERATE
EQUIPONDERATED
EQUIPONDERATES
EQUIPONDERATING
EQUIPOTENT
EQUIPOTENTIAL
EQUIPOTENTIALS
EQUIPROBABILITY
EQUIPROBABLE
EQUISETACEOUS
EQUISETIFORM
EQUISETUMS
EQUITABILITIES
EQUITABILITY
EQUITABLENESS
EQUITABLENESSES
EQUITATION
EQUITATIONS
EQUIVALENCE
EQUIVALENCES
EQUIVALENCIES
EQUIVALENCY
EQUIVALENT
EQUIVALENTLY
EQUIVALENTS
EQUIVOCACIES
EQUIVOCACY
EQUIVOCALITIES
EQUIVOCALITY
EQUIVOCALLY
EQUIVOCALNESS
EQUIVOCALNESSES
EQUIVOCATE
EQUIVOCATED
EQUIVOCATES
EQUIVOCATING
EQUIVOCATINGLY
EQUIVOCATION
EQUIVOCATIONS
EQUIVOCATOR
EQUIVOCATORS
EQUIVOCATORY
EQUIVOQUES
ERADIATING
ERADIATION
ERADIATIONS
ERADICABLE
ERADICABLY
ERADICANTS
ERADICATED
ERADICATES
ERADICATING
ERADICATION
ERADICATIONS
ERADICATIVE
ERADICATOR
ERADICATORS
ERASABILITIES
ERASABILITY
ERASEMENTS
ERECTILITIES
ERECTILITY
ERECTNESSES
EREMACAUSES
EREMACAUSIS
EREMITICAL
EREMITISMS
EREMURUSES
ERETHISMIC
ERETHISTIC
ERGASTOPLASM
ERGASTOPLASMIC
ERGASTOPLASMS
ERGATANDROMORPH
ERGATANERS
ERGATIVITIES
ERGATIVITY
ERGATOCRACIES
ERGATOCRACY
ERGATOGYNE
ERGATOGYNES
ERGATOMORPH
ERGATOMORPHIC
ERGATOMORPHS
ERGODICITIES
ERGODICITY
ERGOGRAPHS
ERGOMANIAC
ERGOMANIACS
ERGOMANIAS
ERGOMETERS
ERGOMETRIC
ERGOMETRIES
ERGONOMICALLY
ERGONOMICS
ERGONOMIST
ERGONOMISTS
ERGONOVINE
ERGONOVINES
ERGOPHOBIA
ERGOPHOBIAS
ERGOSTEROL
ERGOSTEROLS
ERGOTAMINE
ERGOTAMINES
ERGOTISING
ERGOTIZING
ERICACEOUS
ERINACEOUS
ERIOMETERS
ERIOPHOROUS
ERIOPHORUM
ERIOPHORUMS
ERIOPHYIDS
ERIOSTEMON
ERIOSTEMONS
ERISTICALLY
ERODIBILITIES
ERODIBILITY
EROGENEITIES
EROGENEITY
EROSIONALLY
EROSIVENESS
EROSIVENESSES
EROSIVITIES
EROTICALLY
EROTICISATION
EROTICISATIONS
EROTICISED
EROTICISES
EROTICISING
EROTICISMS
EROTICISTS
EROTICIZATION
EROTICIZATIONS
EROTICIZED
EROTICIZES
EROTICIZING
EROTISATION
EROTISATIONS
EROTIZATION
EROTIZATIONS
EROTOGENIC
EROTOGENOUS
EROTOLOGICAL
EROTOLOGIES
EROTOLOGIST
EROTOLOGISTS
EROTOMANIA
EROTOMANIAC
EROTOMANIACS
EROTOMANIAS
EROTOPHOBIA
EROTOPHOBIAS
ERRANTRIES
ERRATICALLY
ERRATICISM
ERRATICISMS
ERRONEOUSLY
ERRONEOUSNESS
ERRONEOUSNESSES
ERUBESCENCE
ERUBESCENCES
ERUBESCENCIES
ERUBESCENCY
ERUBESCENT
ERUBESCITE
ERUBESCITES
ERUCTATING
ERUCTATION
ERUCTATIONS
ERUCTATIVE
ERUDITENESS
ERUDITENESSES
ERUDITIONS
ERUPTIONAL
ERUPTIVELY

ERUPTIVENESS
ERUPTIVENESSES
ERUPTIVITIES
ERUPTIVITY
ERVALENTAS
ERYSIPELAS
ERYSIPELASES
ERYSIPELATOUS
ERYSIPELOID
ERYSIPELOIDS
ERYTHEMATIC
ERYTHEMATOUS
ERYTHORBATE
ERYTHORBATES
ERYTHORBIC
ERYTHRAEMIA
ERYTHRAEMIAS
ERYTHREMIA
ERYTHREMIAS
ERYTHRINAS
ERYTHRISMAL
ERYTHRISMS
ERYTHRISTIC
ERYTHRITES
ERYTHRITIC
ERYTHRITOL
ERYTHRITOLS
ERYTHROBLAST
ERYTHROBLASTIC
ERYTHROBLASTS
ERYTHROCYTE
ERYTHROCYTES
ERYTHROCYTIC
ERYTHROMELALGIA
ERYTHROMYCIN
ERYTHROMYCINS
ERYTHRONIUM
ERYTHRONIUMS
ERYTHROPENIA
ERYTHROPENIAS
ERYTHROPHOBIA
ERYTHROPHOBIAS
ERYTHROPOIESES
ERYTHROPOIESIS
ERYTHROPOIETIC
ERYTHROPOIETIN
ERYTHROPOIETINS
ERYTHROPSIA
ERYTHROPSIAS
ERYTHROSIN
ERYTHROSINE
ERYTHROSINES
ERYTHROSINS
ESCABECHES
ESCADRILLE
ESCADRILLES
ESCALADERS
ESCALADING
ESCALADOES
ESCALATING
ESCALATION
ESCALATIONS
ESCALATORS
ESCALATORY
ESCALLONIA
ESCALLONIAS
ESCALLOPED
ESCALLOPING
ESCALOPING
ESCAMOTAGE
ESCAMOTAGES
ESCAPADOES
ESCAPELESS
ESCAPEMENT
ESCAPEMENTS
ESCAPOLOGIES
ESCAPOLOGIST
ESCAPOLOGISTS
ESCAPOLOGY
ESCARMOUCHE
ESCARMOUCHES
ESCARPMENT
ESCARPMENTS
ESCHAROTIC
ESCHAROTICS
ESCHATOLOGIC
ESCHATOLOGICAL
ESCHATOLOGIES
ESCHATOLOGIST
ESCHATOLOGISTS
ESCHATOLOGY
ESCHEATABLE
ESCHEATAGE
ESCHEATAGES
ESCHEATING
ESCHEATMENT
ESCHEATMENTS
ESCHEATORS
ESCHSCHOLTZIA
ESCHSCHOLTZIAS
ESCHSCHOLZIA
ESCHSCHOLZIAS
ESCLANDRES
ESCOPETTES
ESCORTAGES
ESCRIBANOS
ESCRITOIRE
ESCRITOIRES
ESCRITORIAL
ESCUTCHEON
ESCUTCHEONED
ESCUTCHEONS
ESEMPLASIES
ESEMPLASTIC
ESEMPLASTICALLY
ESOPHAGEAL
ESOPHAGITIDES
ESOPHAGITIS
ESOPHAGITISES
ESOPHAGOSCOPE
ESOPHAGOSCOPES
ESOPHAGOSCOPIES
ESOPHAGOSCOPY
ESOPHAGUSES
ESOTERICALLY
ESOTERICAS
ESOTERICISM
ESOTERICISMS
ESOTERICIST
ESOTERICISTS
ESOTERISMS
ESOTROPIAS
ESPADRILLE
ESPADRILLES
ESPAGNOLES
ESPAGNOLETTE
ESPAGNOLETTES
ESPALIERED
ESPALIERING
ESPECIALLY
ESPERANCES
ESPIEGLERIE
ESPIEGLERIES
ESPIONAGES
ESPLANADES
ESPRESSIVO
ESQUIRESSES
ESSAYETTES
ESSAYISTIC
ESSENTIALISE
ESSENTIALISED
ESSENTIALISES
ESSENTIALISING
ESSENTIALISM
ESSENTIALISMS
ESSENTIALIST
ESSENTIALISTS
ESSENTIALITIES
ESSENTIALITY
ESSENTIALIZE
ESSENTIALIZED
ESSENTIALIZES
ESSENTIALIZING
ESSENTIALLY
ESSENTIALNESS
ESSENTIALNESSES
ESSENTIALS
ESTABLISHABLE
ESTABLISHED
ESTABLISHER
ESTABLISHERS
ESTABLISHES
ESTABLISHING
ESTABLISHMENT
ESTABLISHMENTS
ESTAFETTES
ESTAMINETS
ESTANCIERO
ESTANCIEROS
ESTATESMAN
ESTATESMEN
ESTERIFICATION
ESTERIFICATIONS
ESTERIFIED
ESTERIFIES
ESTERIFYING
ESTERISATION
ESTERISATIONS
ESTERIZATION
ESTERIZATIONS
ESTHESIOGEN
ESTHESIOGENS
ESTHESISES
ESTHETICAL
ESTHETICALLY
ESTHETICIAN
ESTHETICIANS
ESTHETICISM
ESTHETICISMS
ESTIMABLENESS
ESTIMABLENESSES
ESTIMATING
ESTIMATION
ESTIMATIONS
ESTIMATIVE
ESTIMATORS
ESTIPULATE
ESTIVATING
ESTIVATION
ESTIVATIONS
ESTIVATORS
ESTOPPAGES
ESTRADIOLS
ESTRAMAZONE
ESTRAMAZONES
ESTRANGEDNESS
ESTRANGEDNESSES
ESTRANGELO
ESTRANGELOS
ESTRANGEMENT
ESTRANGEMENTS
ESTRANGERS
ESTRANGHELO
ESTRANGHELOS
ESTRANGING
ESTRAPADES
ESTREATING
ESTREPEMENT
ESTREPEMENTS
ESTRIBUTOR
ESTRIBUTORS
ESTRILDIDS
ESTROGENIC
ESTROGENICALLY
ESURIENCES
ESURIENCIES
ESURIENTLY
ETEPIMELETIC
ETERNALISATION
ETERNALISATIONS

ETERNALISE
ETERNALISED
ETERNALISES
ETERNALISING
ETERNALIST
ETERNALISTS
ETERNALITIES
ETERNALITY
ETERNALIZATION
ETERNALIZATIONS
ETERNALIZE
ETERNALIZED
ETERNALIZES
ETERNALIZING
ETERNALNESS
ETERNALNESSES
ETERNISATION
ETERNISATIONS
ETERNISING
ETERNITIES
ETERNIZATION
ETERNIZATIONS
ETERNIZING
ETHAMBUTOL
ETHAMBUTOLS
ETHANEDIOIC
ETHANEDIOL
ETHANEDIOLS
ETHANOATES
ETHANOLAMINE
ETHANOLAMINES
ETHEOSTOMINE
ETHEREALISATION
ETHEREALISE
ETHEREALISED
ETHEREALISES
ETHEREALISING
ETHEREALITIES
ETHEREALITY
ETHEREALIZATION
ETHEREALIZE
ETHEREALIZED
ETHEREALIZES
ETHEREALIZING
ETHEREALLY
ETHEREALNESS
ETHEREALNESSES
ETHERIFICATION
ETHERIFICATIONS
ETHERIFIED
ETHERIFIES
ETHERIFYING
ETHERISATION
ETHERISATIONS
ETHERISERS
ETHERISING
ETHERIZATION
ETHERIZATIONS
ETHERIZERS
ETHERIZING
ETHEROMANIA
ETHEROMANIAC
ETHEROMANIACS
ETHEROMANIAS
ETHICALITIES
ETHICALITY
ETHICALNESS
ETHICALNESSES
ETHICISING
ETHICIZING
ETHIONAMIDE
ETHIONAMIDES
ETHIONINES
ETHNARCHIES
ETHNICALLY
ETHNICISMS
ETHNICITIES
ETHNOBIOLOGIES
ETHNOBIOLOGY
ETHNOBOTANICAL
ETHNOBOTANIES
ETHNOBOTANIST
ETHNOBOTANISTS
ETHNOBOTANY
ETHNOCENTRIC
ETHNOCENTRICITY
ETHNOCENTRISM
ETHNOCENTRISMS
ETHNOCIDES
ETHNOGENIC
ETHNOGENIES
ETHNOGENIST
ETHNOGENISTS
ETHNOGRAPHER
ETHNOGRAPHERS
ETHNOGRAPHIC
ETHNOGRAPHICA
ETHNOGRAPHICAL
ETHNOGRAPHIES
ETHNOGRAPHY
ETHNOHISTORIAN
ETHNOHISTORIANS
ETHNOHISTORIC
ETHNOHISTORICAL
ETHNOHISTORIES
ETHNOHISTORY
ETHNOLINGUIST
ETHNOLINGUISTIC
ETHNOLINGUISTS
ETHNOLOGIC
ETHNOLOGICAL
ETHNOLOGICALLY
ETHNOLOGIES
ETHNOLOGIST
ETHNOLOGISTS
ETHNOMEDICINE
ETHNOMEDICINES
ETHNOMUSICOLOGY
ETHNOSCIENCE
ETHNOSCIENCES
ETHOLOGICAL
ETHOLOGICALLY
ETHOLOGIES
ETHOLOGIST
ETHOLOGISTS
ETHOXYETHANE
ETHOXYETHANES
ETHYLAMINE
ETHYLAMINES
ETHYLATING
ETHYLATION
ETHYLATIONS
ETHYLBENZENE
ETHYLBENZENES
ETIOLATING
ETIOLATION
ETIOLATIONS
ETIOLOGICAL
ETIOLOGICALLY
ETIOLOGIES
ETIOLOGIST
ETIOLOGISTS
ETIQUETTES
ETONOGESTREL
ETONOGESTRELS
ETOURDERIE
ETOURDERIES
ETRANGERES
ETYMOLOGICA
ETYMOLOGICAL
ETYMOLOGICALLY
ETYMOLOGICON
ETYMOLOGICUM
ETYMOLOGIES
ETYMOLOGISE
ETYMOLOGISED
ETYMOLOGISES
ETYMOLOGISING
ETYMOLOGIST
ETYMOLOGISTS
ETYMOLOGIZE
ETYMOLOGIZED
ETYMOLOGIZES
ETYMOLOGIZING
EUBACTERIA
EUBACTERIUM
EUCALYPTOL
EUCALYPTOLE
EUCALYPTOLES
EUCALYPTOLS
EUCALYPTUS
EUCALYPTUSES
EUCARYOTES
EUCARYOTIC
EUCHARISES
EUCHARISTIC
EUCHLORINE
EUCHLORINES
EUCHLORINS
EUCHOLOGIA
EUCHOLOGIES
EUCHOLOGION
EUCHROMATIC
EUCHROMATIN
EUCHROMATINS
EUCRYPHIAS
EUDAEMONIA
EUDAEMONIAS
EUDAEMONIC
EUDAEMONICS
EUDAEMONIES
EUDAEMONISM
EUDAEMONISMS
EUDAEMONIST
EUDAEMONISTIC
EUDAEMONISTICAL
EUDAEMONISTS
EUDAIMONISM
EUDAIMONISMS
EUDEMONIAS
EUDEMONICS
EUDEMONISM
EUDEMONISMS
EUDEMONIST
EUDEMONISTIC
EUDEMONISTICAL
EUDEMONISTS
EUDIALYTES
EUDICOTYLEDON
EUDICOTYLEDONS
EUDIOMETER
EUDIOMETERS
EUDIOMETRIC
EUDIOMETRICAL
EUDIOMETRICALLY
EUDIOMETRIES
EUDIOMETRY
EUGENECIST
EUGENECISTS
EUGENICALLY
EUGENICIST
EUGENICISTS
EUGEOSYNCLINAL
EUGEOSYNCLINE
EUGEOSYNCLINES
EUGLENOIDS
EUGLOBULIN
EUGLOBULINS
EUHARMONIC
EUHEMERISE
EUHEMERISED
EUHEMERISES
EUHEMERISING
EUHEMERISM
EUHEMERISMS
EUHEMERIST
EUHEMERISTIC
EUHEMERISTS
EUHEMERIZE
EUHEMERIZED

E

EUHEMERIZES
EUHEMERIZING
EUKARYOTES
EUKARYOTIC
EULOGISERS
EULOGISING
EULOGISTIC
EULOGISTICAL
EULOGISTICALLY
EULOGIZERS
EULOGIZING
EUMELANINS
EUNUCHISED
EUNUCHISES
EUNUCHISING
EUNUCHISMS
EUNUCHIZED
EUNUCHIZES
EUNUCHIZING
EUNUCHOIDISM
EUNUCHOIDISMS
EUNUCHOIDS
EUONYMUSES
EUPATORIUM
EUPATORIUMS
EUPATRIDAE
EUPEPTICITIES
EUPEPTICITY
EUPHAUSIACEAN
EUPHAUSIACEANS
EUPHAUSIDS
EUPHAUSIID
EUPHAUSIIDS
EUPHEMISED
EUPHEMISER
EUPHEMISERS
EUPHEMISES
EUPHEMISING
EUPHEMISMS
EUPHEMISTIC
EUPHEMISTICALLY
EUPHEMISTS
EUPHEMIZED
EUPHEMIZER
EUPHEMIZERS
EUPHEMIZES
EUPHEMIZING
EUPHONICAL
EUPHONICALLY
EUPHONIOUS
EUPHONIOUSLY
EUPHONIOUSNESS
EUPHONISED
EUPHONISES
EUPHONISING
EUPHONISMS
EUPHONIUMS
EUPHONIZED
EUPHONIZES
EUPHONIZING
EUPHORBIACEOUS
EUPHORBIAS
EUPHORBIUM
EUPHORBIUMS
EUPHORIANT
EUPHORIANTS
EUPHORICALLY
EUPHRASIAS
EUPHRASIES
EUPHUISING
EUPHUISTIC
EUPHUISTICAL
EUPHUISTICALLY
EUPHUIZING
EUPLASTICS
EUPLOIDIES
EURHYTHMIC
EURHYTHMICAL
EURHYTHMICS
EURHYTHMIES
EURHYTHMIST
EURHYTHMISTS
EUROCHEQUE
EUROCHEQUES
EUROCREDIT
EUROCREDITS
EUROCREEPS
EUROCURRENCIES
EUROCURRENCY
EURODEPOSIT
EURODEPOSITS
EURODOLLAR
EURODOLLARS
EUROMARKET
EUROMARKETS
EUROPHILES
EUROPHILIA
EUROPHILIAS
EUROPHOBIA
EUROPHOBIAS
EUROPHOBIC
EUROTERMINAL
EUROTERMINALS
EURYBATHIC
EURYHALINE
EURYOECIOUS
EURYPTERID
EURYPTERIDS
EURYPTEROID
EURYPTEROIDS
EURYTHERMAL
EURYTHERMIC
EURYTHERMOUS
EURYTHERMS
EURYTHMICAL
EURYTHMICS
EURYTHMIES
EURYTHMIST
EURYTHMISTS
EUSPORANGIATE
EUSTATICALLY
EUSTRESSES
EUTECTOIDS
EUTHANASED
EUTHANASES
EUTHANASIA
EUTHANASIAS
EUTHANASIAST
EUTHANASIASTS
EUTHANASIC
EUTHANASIES
EUTHANASING
EUTHANATISE
EUTHANATISED
EUTHANATISES
EUTHANATISING
EUTHANATIZE
EUTHANATIZED
EUTHANATIZES
EUTHANATIZING
EUTHANAZED
EUTHANAZES
EUTHANAZING
EUTHANISED
EUTHANISES
EUTHANISING
EUTHANIZED
EUTHANIZES
EUTHANIZING
EUTHENISTS
EUTHERIANS
EUTHYROIDS
EUTRAPELIA
EUTRAPELIAS
EUTRAPELIES
EUTROPHICATION
EUTROPHICATIONS
EUTROPHIES
EVACUATING
EVACUATION
EVACUATIONS
EVACUATIVE
EVACUATIVES
EVACUATORS
EVAGATIONS
EVAGINATED
EVAGINATES
EVAGINATING
EVAGINATION
EVAGINATIONS
EVALUATING
EVALUATION
EVALUATIONS
EVALUATIVE
EVALUATORS
EVANESCENCE
EVANESCENCES
EVANESCENT
EVANESCENTLY
EVANESCING
EVANGELARIUM
EVANGELARIUMS
EVANGELIAR
EVANGELIARIES
EVANGELIARION
EVANGELIARIONS
EVANGELIARIUM
EVANGELIARIUMS
EVANGELIARS
EVANGELIARY
EVANGELICAL
EVANGELICALISM
EVANGELICALISMS
EVANGELICALLY
EVANGELICALNESS
EVANGELICALS
EVANGELICISM
EVANGELICISMS
EVANGELIES
EVANGELISATION
EVANGELISATIONS
EVANGELISE
EVANGELISED
EVANGELISER
EVANGELISERS
EVANGELISES
EVANGELISING
EVANGELISM
EVANGELISMS
EVANGELIST
EVANGELISTARIES
EVANGELISTARION
EVANGELISTARY
EVANGELISTIC
EVANGELISTS
EVANGELIZATION
EVANGELIZATIONS
EVANGELIZE
EVANGELIZED
EVANGELIZER
EVANGELIZERS
EVANGELIZES
EVANGELIZING
EVANISHING
EVANISHMENT
EVANISHMENTS
EVANITIONS
EVAPORABILITIES
EVAPORABILITY
EVAPORABLE
EVAPORATED
EVAPORATES
EVAPORATING
EVAPORATION
EVAPORATIONS
EVAPORATIVE
EVAPORATOR
EVAPORATORS
EVAPORIMETER
EVAPORIMETERS

EVAPORITES
EVAPORITIC
EVAPOROGRAPH
EVAPOROGRAPHS
EVAPOROMETER
EVAPOROMETERS
EVASIVENESS
EVASIVENESSES
EVECTIONAL
EVENEMENTS
EVENHANDED
EVENHANDEDLY
EVENHANDEDNESS
EVENNESSES
EVENTFULLY
EVENTFULNESS
EVENTFULNESSES
EVENTRATED
EVENTRATES
EVENTRATING
EVENTRATION
EVENTRATIONS
EVENTUALISE
EVENTUALISED
EVENTUALISES
EVENTUALISING
EVENTUALITIES
EVENTUALITY
EVENTUALIZE
EVENTUALIZED
EVENTUALIZES
EVENTUALIZING
EVENTUALLY
EVENTUATED
EVENTUATES
EVENTUATING
EVENTUATION
EVENTUATIONS
EVERBLOOMING
EVERDURING
EVERGLADES
EVERGREENS
EVERLASTING
EVERLASTINGLY
EVERLASTINGNESS
EVERLASTINGS
EVERYDAYNESS
EVERYDAYNESSES
EVERYPLACE
EVERYTHING
EVERYWHENCE
EVERYWHERE
EVERYWHITHER
EVERYWOMAN
EVERYWOMEN
EVIDENCING
EVIDENTIAL
EVIDENTIALLY
EVIDENTIARY
EVILDOINGS
EVILNESSES
EVINCEMENT
EVINCEMENTS
EVISCERATE
EVISCERATED
EVISCERATES
EVISCERATING
EVISCERATION
EVISCERATIONS
EVISCERATOR
EVISCERATORS
EVITATIONS
EVITERNALLY
EVITERNITIES
EVITERNITY
EVOCATIONS
EVOCATIVELY
EVOCATIVENESS
EVOCATIVENESSES
EVOLUTIONAL
EVOLUTIONARILY
EVOLUTIONARY
EVOLUTIONISM
EVOLUTIONISMS
EVOLUTIONIST
EVOLUTIONISTIC
EVOLUTIONISTS
EVOLUTIONS
EVOLVEMENT
EVOLVEMENTS
EVONYMUSES
EVULGATING
EXACERBATE
EXACERBATED
EXACERBATES
EXACERBATING
EXACERBATION
EXACERBATIONS
EXACERBESCENCE
EXACERBESCENCES
EXACTINGLY
EXACTINGNESS
EXACTINGNESSES
EXACTITUDE
EXACTITUDES
EXACTMENTS
EXACTNESSES
EXACTRESSES
EXAGGERATE
EXAGGERATED
EXAGGERATEDLY
EXAGGERATEDNESS
EXAGGERATES
EXAGGERATING
EXAGGERATINGLY
EXAGGERATION
EXAGGERATIONS
EXAGGERATIVE
EXAGGERATOR
EXAGGERATORS
EXAGGERATORY
EXAHERTZES
EXALBUMINOUS
EXALTATION
EXALTATIONS
EXALTEDNESS
EXALTEDNESSES
EXAMINABILITIES
EXAMINABILITY
EXAMINABLE
EXAMINANTS
EXAMINATES
EXAMINATION
EXAMINATIONAL
EXAMINATIONS
EXAMINATOR
EXAMINATORS
EXAMINERSHIP
EXAMINERSHIPS
EXANIMATION
EXANIMATIONS
EXANTHEMAS
EXANTHEMATA
EXANTHEMATIC
EXANTHEMATOUS
EXARATIONS
EXARCHATES
EXARCHISTS
EXASPERATE
EXASPERATED
EXASPERATEDLY
EXASPERATER
EXASPERATERS
EXASPERATES
EXASPERATING
EXASPERATINGLY
EXASPERATION
EXASPERATIONS
EXASPERATIVE
EXASPERATOR
EXASPERATORS
EXCAMBIONS
EXCAMBIUMS
EXCARNATED
EXCARNATES
EXCARNATING
EXCARNATION
EXCARNATIONS
EXCAVATING
EXCAVATION
EXCAVATIONAL
EXCAVATIONS
EXCAVATORS
EXCEEDABLE
EXCEEDINGLY
EXCELLENCE
EXCELLENCES
EXCELLENCIES
EXCELLENCY
EXCELLENTLY
EXCELSIORS
EXCENTRICS
EXCEPTANTS
EXCEPTIONABLE
EXCEPTIONABLY
EXCEPTIONAL
EXCEPTIONALISM
EXCEPTIONALISMS
EXCEPTIONALITY
EXCEPTIONALLY
EXCEPTIONALNESS
EXCEPTIONALS
EXCEPTIONS
EXCEPTIOUS
EXCEPTLESS
EXCERPTERS
EXCERPTIBLE
EXCERPTING
EXCERPTINGS
EXCERPTION
EXCERPTIONS
EXCERPTORS
EXCESSIVELY
EXCESSIVENESS
EXCESSIVENESSES
EXCHANGEABILITY
EXCHANGEABLE
EXCHANGEABLY
EXCHANGERS
EXCHANGING
EXCHEQUERED
EXCHEQUERING
EXCHEQUERS
EXCIPIENTS
EXCISIONAL
EXCITABILITIES
EXCITABILITY
EXCITABLENESS
EXCITABLENESSES
EXCITANCIES
EXCITATION
EXCITATIONS
EXCITATIVE
EXCITATORY
EXCITEDNESS
EXCITEDNESSES
EXCITEMENT
EXCITEMENTS
EXCITINGLY
EXCLAIMERS
EXCLAIMING
EXCLAMATION
EXCLAMATIONAL
EXCLAMATIONS
EXCLAMATIVE
EXCLAMATIVES
EXCLAMATORILY
EXCLAMATORY
EXCLAUSTRATION
EXCLAUSTRATIONS

E

EXCLOSURES
EXCLUDABILITIES
EXCLUDABILITY
EXCLUDABLE
EXCLUDIBLE
EXCLUSIONARY
EXCLUSIONISM
EXCLUSIONISMS
EXCLUSIONIST
EXCLUSIONISTS
EXCLUSIONS
EXCLUSIVELY
EXCLUSIVENESS
EXCLUSIVENESSES
EXCLUSIVES
EXCLUSIVISM
EXCLUSIVISMS
EXCLUSIVIST
EXCLUSIVISTS
EXCLUSIVITIES
EXCLUSIVITY
EXCOGITABLE
EXCOGITATE
EXCOGITATED
EXCOGITATES
EXCOGITATING
EXCOGITATION
EXCOGITATIONS
EXCOGITATIVE
EXCOGITATOR
EXCOGITATORS
EXCOMMUNICABLE
EXCOMMUNICATE
EXCOMMUNICATED
EXCOMMUNICATES
EXCOMMUNICATING
EXCOMMUNICATION
EXCOMMUNICATIVE
EXCOMMUNICATOR
EXCOMMUNICATORS
EXCOMMUNICATORY
EXCOMMUNION
EXCOMMUNIONS
EXCORIATED
EXCORIATES
EXCORIATING
EXCORIATION
EXCORIATIONS
EXCORTICATE
EXCORTICATED
EXCORTICATES
EXCORTICATING
EXCORTICATION
EXCORTICATIONS
EXCREMENTA
EXCREMENTAL
EXCREMENTITIAL
EXCREMENTITIOUS
EXCREMENTS
EXCREMENTUM
EXCRESCENCE
EXCRESCENCES
EXCRESCENCIES
EXCRESCENCY
EXCRESCENT
EXCRESCENTIAL
EXCRESCENTLY
EXCRETIONS
EXCRETORIES
EXCRUCIATE
EXCRUCIATED
EXCRUCIATES
EXCRUCIATING
EXCRUCIATINGLY
EXCRUCIATION
EXCRUCIATIONS
EXCULPABLE
EXCULPATED
EXCULPATES
EXCULPATING
EXCULPATION
EXCULPATIONS
EXCULPATORY
EXCURSIONED
EXCURSIONING
EXCURSIONISE
EXCURSIONISED
EXCURSIONISES
EXCURSIONISING
EXCURSIONIST
EXCURSIONISTS
EXCURSIONIZE
EXCURSIONIZED
EXCURSIONIZES
EXCURSIONIZING
EXCURSIONS
EXCURSIVELY
EXCURSIVENESS
EXCURSIVENESSES
EXCURSUSES
EXCUSABLENESS
EXCUSABLENESSES
EXCUSATORY
EXECRABLENESS
EXECRABLENESSES
EXECRATING
EXECRATION
EXECRATIONS
EXECRATIVE
EXECRATIVELY
EXECRATORS
EXECRATORY
EXECUTABLE
EXECUTABLES
EXECUTANCIES
EXECUTANCY
EXECUTANTS
EXECUTARIES
EXECUTIONER
EXECUTIONERS
EXECUTIONS
EXECUTIVELY
EXECUTIVES
EXECUTORIAL
EXECUTORSHIP
EXECUTORSHIPS
EXECUTRESS
EXECUTRESSES
EXECUTRICES
EXECUTRIES
EXECUTRIXES
EXEGETICAL
EXEGETICALLY
EXEGETISTS
EXEMPLARILY
EXEMPLARINESS
EXEMPLARINESSES
EXEMPLARITIES
EXEMPLARITY
EXEMPLIFIABLE
EXEMPLIFICATION
EXEMPLIFICATIVE
EXEMPLIFIED
EXEMPLIFIER
EXEMPLIFIERS
EXEMPLIFIES
EXEMPLIFYING
EXEMPTIONS
EXENTERATE
EXENTERATED
EXENTERATES
EXENTERATING
EXENTERATION
EXENTERATIONS
EXEQUATURS
EXERCISABLE
EXERCISERS
EXERCISING
EXERCITATION
EXERCITATIONS
EXERCYCLES
EXERGAMING
EXERGAMINGS
EXERTAINMENT
EXERTAINMENTS
EXFILTRATE
EXFILTRATED
EXFILTRATES
EXFILTRATING
EXFOLIANTS
EXFOLIATED
EXFOLIATES
EXFOLIATING
EXFOLIATION
EXFOLIATIONS
EXFOLIATIVE
EXFOLIATOR
EXFOLIATORS
EXHALATION
EXHALATIONS
EXHAUSTEDLY
EXHAUSTERS
EXHAUSTIBILITY
EXHAUSTIBLE
EXHAUSTING
EXHAUSTINGLY
EXHAUSTION
EXHAUSTIONS
EXHAUSTIVE
EXHAUSTIVELY
EXHAUSTIVENESS
EXHAUSTIVITIES
EXHAUSTIVITY
EXHAUSTLESS
EXHAUSTLESSLY
EXHAUSTLESSNESS
EXHEREDATE
EXHEREDATED
EXHEREDATES
EXHEREDATING
EXHEREDATION
EXHEREDATIONS
EXHIBITERS
EXHIBITING
EXHIBITION
EXHIBITIONER
EXHIBITIONERS
EXHIBITIONISM
EXHIBITIONISMS
EXHIBITIONIST
EXHIBITIONISTIC
EXHIBITIONISTS
EXHIBITIONS
EXHIBITIVE
EXHIBITIVELY
EXHIBITORS
EXHIBITORY
EXHILARANT
EXHILARANTS
EXHILARATE
EXHILARATED
EXHILARATES
EXHILARATING
EXHILARATINGLY
EXHILARATION
EXHILARATIONS
EXHILARATIVE
EXHILARATOR
EXHILARATORS
EXHILARATORY
EXHORTATION
EXHORTATIONS
EXHORTATIVE
EXHORTATORY
EXHUMATING
EXHUMATION
EXHUMATIONS
EXIGENCIES
EXIGUITIES
EXIGUOUSLY

EXIGUOUSNESS
EXIGUOUSNESSES
EXILEMENTS
EXIMIOUSLY
EXISTENCES
EXISTENTIAL
EXISTENTIALISM
EXISTENTIALISMS
EXISTENTIALIST
EXISTENTIALISTS
EXISTENTIALLY
EXISTENTIALS
EXOBIOLOGICAL
EXOBIOLOGIES
EXOBIOLOGIST
EXOBIOLOGISTS
EXOBIOLOGY
EXOCENTRIC
EXOCUTICLE
EXOCUTICLES
EXOCYTOSED
EXOCYTOSES
EXOCYTOSING
EXOCYTOSIS
EXOCYTOTIC
EXODERMISES
EXODONTIAS
EXODONTICS
EXODONTIST
EXODONTISTS
EXOENZYMES
EXOERYTHROCYTIC
EXOGENETIC
EXOGENISMS
EXOGENOUSLY
EXONERATED
EXONERATES
EXONERATING
EXONERATION
EXONERATIONS
EXONERATIVE
EXONERATOR
EXONERATORS
EXONUCLEASE
EXONUCLEASES
EXONUMISTS
EXOPARASITE
EXOPARASITES
EXOPARASITIC
EXOPEPTIDASE
EXOPEPTIDASES
EXOPHAGIES
EXOPHAGOUS
EXOPHTHALMIA
EXOPHTHALMIAS
EXOPHTHALMIC
EXOPHTHALMOS
EXOPHTHALMOSES
EXOPHTHALMUS
EXOPHTHALMUSES
EXOPLANETS
EXOPODITES
EXOPODITIC
EXORABILITIES
EXORABILITY
EXORATIONS
EXORBITANCE
EXORBITANCES
EXORBITANCIES
EXORBITANCY
EXORBITANT
EXORBITANTLY
EXORBITATE
EXORBITATED
EXORBITATES
EXORBITATING
EXORCISERS
EXORCISING
EXORCISTIC
EXORCISTICAL
EXORCIZERS
EXORCIZING
EXOSKELETAL
EXOSKELETON
EXOSKELETONS
EXOSPHERES
EXOSPHERIC
EXOSPHERICAL
EXOSPORIUM
EXOSPOROUS
EXOTERICAL
EXOTERICALLY
EXOTERICISM
EXOTERICISMS
EXOTHERMAL
EXOTHERMALLY
EXOTHERMIC
EXOTHERMICALLY
EXOTHERMICITIES
EXOTHERMICITY
EXOTICALLY
EXOTICISED
EXOTICISES
EXOTICISING
EXOTICISMS
EXOTICISTS
EXOTICIZED
EXOTICIZES
EXOTICIZING
EXOTICNESS
EXOTICNESSES
EXOTROPIAS
EXPANDABILITIES
EXPANDABILITY
EXPANDABLE
EXPANSIBILITIES
EXPANSIBILITY
EXPANSIBLE
EXPANSIBLY
EXPANSIONAL
EXPANSIONARY
EXPANSIONISM
EXPANSIONISMS
EXPANSIONIST
EXPANSIONISTIC
EXPANSIONISTS
EXPANSIONS
EXPANSIVELY
EXPANSIVENESS
EXPANSIVENESSES
EXPANSIVITIES
EXPANSIVITY
EXPATIATED
EXPATIATES
EXPATIATING
EXPATIATION
EXPATIATIONS
EXPATIATIVE
EXPATIATOR
EXPATIATORS
EXPATIATORY
EXPATRIATE
EXPATRIATED
EXPATRIATES
EXPATRIATING
EXPATRIATION
EXPATRIATIONS
EXPATRIATISM
EXPATRIATISMS
EXPECTABLE
EXPECTABLY
EXPECTANCE
EXPECTANCES
EXPECTANCIES
EXPECTANCY
EXPECTANTLY
EXPECTANTS
EXPECTATION
EXPECTATIONAL
EXPECTATIONS
EXPECTATIVE
EXPECTATIVES
EXPECTEDLY
EXPECTEDNESS
EXPECTEDNESSES
EXPECTINGLY
EXPECTINGS
EXPECTORANT
EXPECTORANTS
EXPECTORATE
EXPECTORATED
EXPECTORATES
EXPECTORATING
EXPECTORATION
EXPECTORATIONS
EXPECTORATIVE
EXPECTORATIVES
EXPECTORATOR
EXPECTORATORS
EXPEDIENCE
EXPEDIENCES
EXPEDIENCIES
EXPEDIENCY
EXPEDIENTIAL
EXPEDIENTIALLY
EXPEDIENTLY
EXPEDIENTS
EXPEDITATE
EXPEDITATED
EXPEDITATES
EXPEDITATING
EXPEDITATION
EXPEDITATIONS
EXPEDITELY
EXPEDITERS
EXPEDITING
EXPEDITION
EXPEDITIONARY
EXPEDITIONS
EXPEDITIOUS
EXPEDITIOUSLY
EXPEDITIOUSNESS
EXPEDITIVE
EXPEDITORS
EXPELLABLE
EXPELLANTS
EXPELLENTS
EXPENDABILITIES
EXPENDABILITY
EXPENDABLE
EXPENDABLES
EXPENDABLY
EXPENDITURE
EXPENDITURES
EXPENSIVELY
EXPENSIVENESS
EXPENSIVENESSES
EXPERIENCE
EXPERIENCEABLE
EXPERIENCED
EXPERIENCELESS
EXPERIENCER
EXPERIENCERS
EXPERIENCES
EXPERIENCING
EXPERIENTIAL
EXPERIENTIALISM
EXPERIENTIALIST
EXPERIENTIALLY
EXPERIMENT
EXPERIMENTAL
EXPERIMENTALISE
EXPERIMENTALISM
EXPERIMENTALIST
EXPERIMENTALIZE
EXPERIMENTALLY
EXPERIMENTATION
EXPERIMENTATIVE
EXPERIMENTED
EXPERIMENTER

EXPERIMENTERS
EXPERIMENTING
EXPERIMENTIST
EXPERIMENTISTS
EXPERIMENTS
EXPERTISED
EXPERTISES
EXPERTISING
EXPERTISMS
EXPERTIZED
EXPERTIZES
EXPERTIZING
EXPERTNESS
EXPERTNESSES
EXPIATIONS
EXPIRATION
EXPIRATIONS
EXPIRATORY
EXPISCATED
EXPISCATES
EXPISCATING
EXPISCATION
EXPISCATIONS
EXPISCATORY
EXPLAINABLE
EXPLAINERS
EXPLAINING
EXPLANATION
EXPLANATIONS
EXPLANATIVE
EXPLANATIVELY
EXPLANATORILY
EXPLANATORY
EXPLANTATION
EXPLANTATIONS
EXPLANTING
EXPLETIVELY
EXPLETIVES
EXPLICABLE
EXPLICABLY
EXPLICATED
EXPLICATES
EXPLICATING
EXPLICATION
EXPLICATIONS
EXPLICATIVE
EXPLICATIVELY
EXPLICATOR
EXPLICATORS
EXPLICATORY
EXPLICITLY
EXPLICITNESS
EXPLICITNESSES
EXPLOITABLE
EXPLOITAGE
EXPLOITAGES
EXPLOITATION
EXPLOITATIONS
EXPLOITATIVE
EXPLOITATIVELY
EXPLOITERS
EXPLOITING
EXPLOITIVE
EXPLORATION
EXPLORATIONAL
EXPLORATIONIST
EXPLORATIONISTS
EXPLORATIONS
EXPLORATIVE
EXPLORATIVELY
EXPLORATORY
EXPLOSIBLE
EXPLOSIONS
EXPLOSIVELY
EXPLOSIVENESS
EXPLOSIVENESSES
EXPLOSIVES
EXPONENTIAL
EXPONENTIALLY
EXPONENTIALS
EXPONENTIATION
EXPONENTIATIONS
EXPORTABILITIES
EXPORTABILITY
EXPORTABLE
EXPORTATION
EXPORTATIONS
EXPOSEDNESS
EXPOSEDNESSES
EXPOSITING
EXPOSITION
EXPOSITIONAL
EXPOSITIONS
EXPOSITIVE
EXPOSITIVELY
EXPOSITORILY
EXPOSITORS
EXPOSITORY
EXPOSITRESS
EXPOSITRESSES
EXPOSTULATE
EXPOSTULATED
EXPOSTULATES
EXPOSTULATING
EXPOSTULATINGLY
EXPOSTULATION
EXPOSTULATIONS
EXPOSTULATIVE
EXPOSTULATOR
EXPOSTULATORS
EXPOSTULATORY
EXPOSTURES
EXPOUNDERS
EXPOUNDING
EXPRESSAGE
EXPRESSAGES
EXPRESSERS
EXPRESSIBLE
EXPRESSING
EXPRESSION
EXPRESSIONAL
EXPRESSIONISM
EXPRESSIONISMS
EXPRESSIONIST
EXPRESSIONISTIC
EXPRESSIONISTS
EXPRESSIONLESS
EXPRESSIONS
EXPRESSIVE
EXPRESSIVELY
EXPRESSIVENESS
EXPRESSIVITIES
EXPRESSIVITY
EXPRESSMAN
EXPRESSMEN
EXPRESSNESS
EXPRESSNESSES
EXPRESSURE
EXPRESSURES
EXPRESSWAY
EXPRESSWAYS
EXPROBRATE
EXPROBRATED
EXPROBRATES
EXPROBRATING
EXPROBRATION
EXPROBRATIONS
EXPROBRATIVE
EXPROBRATORY
EXPROMISSION
EXPROMISSIONS
EXPROMISSOR
EXPROMISSORS
EXPROPRIABLE
EXPROPRIATE
EXPROPRIATED
EXPROPRIATES
EXPROPRIATING
EXPROPRIATION
EXPROPRIATIONS
EXPROPRIATOR
EXPROPRIATORS
EXPUGNABLE
EXPUGNATION
EXPUGNATIONS
EXPULSIONS
EXPUNCTING
EXPUNCTION
EXPUNCTIONS
EXPURGATED
EXPURGATES
EXPURGATING
EXPURGATION
EXPURGATIONS
EXPURGATOR
EXPURGATORIAL
EXPURGATORS
EXPURGATORY
EXQUISITELY
EXQUISITENESS
EXQUISITENESSES
EXQUISITES
EXSANGUINATE
EXSANGUINATED
EXSANGUINATES
EXSANGUINATING
EXSANGUINATION
EXSANGUINATIONS
EXSANGUINE
EXSANGUINED
EXSANGUINEOUS
EXSANGUINITIES
EXSANGUINITY
EXSANGUINOUS
EXSCINDING
EXSECTIONS
EXSERTIONS
EXSICCANTS
EXSICCATED
EXSICCATES
EXSICCATING
EXSICCATION
EXSICCATIONS
EXSICCATIVE
EXSICCATOR
EXSICCATORS
EXSOLUTION
EXSOLUTIONS
EXSTIPULATE
EXSTROPHIES
EXSUFFLATE
EXSUFFLATED
EXSUFFLATES
EXSUFFLATING
EXSUFFLATION
EXSUFFLATIONS
EXSUFFLICATE
EXTEMPORAL
EXTEMPORALLY
EXTEMPORANEITY
EXTEMPORANEOUS
EXTEMPORARILY
EXTEMPORARINESS
EXTEMPORARY
EXTEMPORES
EXTEMPORISATION
EXTEMPORISE
EXTEMPORISED
EXTEMPORISER
EXTEMPORISERS
EXTEMPORISES
EXTEMPORISING
EXTEMPORIZATION
EXTEMPORIZE
EXTEMPORIZED
EXTEMPORIZER
EXTEMPORIZERS
EXTEMPORIZES
EXTEMPORIZING
EXTENDABILITIES

EXTENDABILITY
EXTENDABLE
EXTENDEDLY
EXTENDEDNESS
EXTENDEDNESSES
EXTENDIBILITIES
EXTENDIBILITY
EXTENDIBLE
EXTENSIBILITIES
EXTENSIBILITY
EXTENSIBLE
EXTENSIBLENESS
EXTENSIFICATION
EXTENSIMETER
EXTENSIMETERS
EXTENSIONAL
EXTENSIONALISM
EXTENSIONALISMS
EXTENSIONALITY
EXTENSIONALLY
EXTENSIONIST
EXTENSIONISTS
EXTENSIONS
EXTENSITIES
EXTENSIVELY
EXTENSIVENESS
EXTENSIVENESSES
EXTENSIVISATION
EXTENSIVIZATION
EXTENSOMETER
EXTENSOMETERS
EXTENUATED
EXTENUATES
EXTENUATING
EXTENUATINGLY
EXTENUATINGS
EXTENUATION
EXTENUATIONS
EXTENUATIVE
EXTENUATIVES
EXTENUATOR
EXTENUATORS
EXTENUATORY
EXTERIORISATION
EXTERIORISE
EXTERIORISED
EXTERIORISES
EXTERIORISING
EXTERIORITIES
EXTERIORITY
EXTERIORIZATION
EXTERIORIZE
EXTERIORIZED
EXTERIORIZES
EXTERIORIZING
EXTERIORLY
EXTERMINABLE
EXTERMINATE
EXTERMINATED
EXTERMINATES
EXTERMINATING
EXTERMINATION
EXTERMINATIONS
EXTERMINATIVE
EXTERMINATOR
EXTERMINATORS
EXTERMINATORY
EXTERMINED
EXTERMINES
EXTERMINING
EXTERNALISATION
EXTERNALISE
EXTERNALISED
EXTERNALISES
EXTERNALISING
EXTERNALISM
EXTERNALISMS
EXTERNALIST
EXTERNALISTS
EXTERNALITIES
EXTERNALITY
EXTERNALIZATION
EXTERNALIZE
EXTERNALIZED
EXTERNALIZES
EXTERNALIZING
EXTERNALLY
EXTERNSHIP
EXTERNSHIPS
EXTEROCEPTIVE
EXTEROCEPTOR
EXTEROCEPTORS
EXTERRITORIAL
EXTERRITORIALLY
EXTINCTING
EXTINCTION
EXTINCTIONS
EXTINCTIVE
EXTINCTURE
EXTINCTURES
EXTINGUISH
EXTINGUISHABLE
EXTINGUISHANT
EXTINGUISHANTS
EXTINGUISHED
EXTINGUISHER
EXTINGUISHERS
EXTINGUISHES
EXTINGUISHING
EXTINGUISHMENT
EXTINGUISHMENTS
EXTIRPABLE
EXTIRPATED
EXTIRPATES
EXTIRPATING
EXTIRPATION
EXTIRPATIONS
EXTIRPATIVE
EXTIRPATOR
EXTIRPATORS
EXTIRPATORY
EXTOLLINGLY
EXTOLMENTS
EXTORSIVELY
EXTORTIONARY
EXTORTIONATE
EXTORTIONATELY
EXTORTIONER
EXTORTIONERS
EXTORTIONIST
EXTORTIONISTS
EXTORTIONS
EXTRABOLDS
EXTRACANONICAL
EXTRACELLULAR
EXTRACELLULARLY
EXTRACORPOREAL
EXTRACRANIAL
EXTRACTABILITY
EXTRACTABLE
EXTRACTANT
EXTRACTANTS
EXTRACTIBLE
EXTRACTING
EXTRACTION
EXTRACTIONS
EXTRACTIVE
EXTRACTIVELY
EXTRACTIVES
EXTRACTORS
EXTRACURRICULAR
EXTRADITABLE
EXTRADITED
EXTRADITES
EXTRADITING
EXTRADITION
EXTRADITIONS
EXTRADOSES
EXTRADOTAL
EXTRADURAL
EXTRADURALS
EXTRAEMBRYONIC
EXTRAFLORAL
EXTRAFORANEOUS
EXTRAGALACTIC
EXTRAHEPATIC
EXTRAJUDICIAL
EXTRAJUDICIALLY
EXTRALEGAL
EXTRALEGALLY
EXTRALIMITAL
EXTRALIMITARY
EXTRALINGUISTIC
EXTRALITERARY
EXTRALITIES
EXTRALOGICAL
EXTRAMARITAL
EXTRAMARITALLY
EXTRAMETRICAL
EXTRAMUNDANE
EXTRAMURAL
EXTRAMURALLY
EXTRAMUSICAL
EXTRANEITIES
EXTRANEITY
EXTRANEOUS
EXTRANEOUSLY
EXTRANEOUSNESS
EXTRANUCLEAR
EXTRAORDINAIRE
EXTRAORDINARIES
EXTRAORDINARILY
EXTRAORDINARY
EXTRAPOLATE
EXTRAPOLATED
EXTRAPOLATES
EXTRAPOLATING
EXTRAPOLATION
EXTRAPOLATIONS
EXTRAPOLATIVE
EXTRAPOLATOR
EXTRAPOLATORS
EXTRAPOLATORY
EXTRAPOSED
EXTRAPOSES
EXTRAPOSING
EXTRAPOSITION
EXTRAPOSITIONS
EXTRAPYRAMIDAL
EXTRASENSORY
EXTRASOLAR
EXTRASYSTOLE
EXTRASYSTOLES
EXTRATEXTUAL
EXTRATROPICAL
EXTRAUTERINE
EXTRAVAGANCE
EXTRAVAGANCES
EXTRAVAGANCIES
EXTRAVAGANCY
EXTRAVAGANT
EXTRAVAGANTLY
EXTRAVAGANZA
EXTRAVAGANZAS
EXTRAVAGATE
EXTRAVAGATED
EXTRAVAGATES
EXTRAVAGATING
EXTRAVAGATION
EXTRAVAGATIONS
EXTRAVASATE
EXTRAVASATED
EXTRAVASATES
EXTRAVASATING
EXTRAVASATION
EXTRAVASATIONS
EXTRAVASCULAR
EXTRAVEHICULAR
EXTRAVERSION
EXTRAVERSIONS

EXTRAVERSIVE
EXTRAVERSIVELY
EXTRAVERTED
EXTRAVERTING
EXTRAVERTLY
EXTRAVERTS
EXTREATING
EXTREMENESS
EXTREMENESSES
EXTREMISMS
EXTREMISTS
EXTREMITIES
EXTREMOPHILE
EXTREMOPHILES
EXTRICABLE
EXTRICATED
EXTRICATES
EXTRICATING
EXTRICATION
EXTRICATIONS
EXTRINSICAL
EXTRINSICALITY
EXTRINSICALLY
EXTRINSICALS
EXTROPIANS
EXTROVERSION
EXTROVERSIONS
EXTROVERSIVE
EXTROVERSIVELY
EXTROVERTED
EXTROVERTING
EXTROVERTLY
EXTROVERTS
EXTRUDABILITIES
EXTRUDABILITY
EXTRUDABLE
EXTRUSIBLE
EXTRUSIONS
EXTUBATING
EXUBERANCE
EXUBERANCES
EXUBERANCIES
EXUBERANCY
EXUBERANTLY
EXUBERATED
EXUBERATES
EXUBERATING
EXUDATIONS
EXULCERATE
EXULCERATED
EXULCERATES
EXULCERATING
EXULCERATION
EXULCERATIONS
EXULTANCES
EXULTANCIES
EXULTANTLY
EXULTATION
EXULTATIONS
EXULTINGLY
EXURBANITE
EXURBANITES
EXUVIATING
EXUVIATION
EXUVIATIONS
EYEBALLING
EYEBRIGHTS
EYEBROWING
EYEBROWLESS
EYEDNESSES
EYEDROPPER
EYEDROPPERS
EYEGLASSES
EYELETEERS
EYELETTING
EYEOPENERS
EYEPATCHES
EYEPOPPERS
EYESHADOWS
EYESTRAINS
EYESTRINGS
EYEWITNESS
EYEWITNESSED
EYEWITNESSES
EYEWITNESSING

F

FABRICANTS
FABRICATED
FABRICATES
FABRICATING
FABRICATION
FABRICATIONS
FABRICATIVE
FABRICATOR
FABRICATORS
FABRICKING
FABRICKINGS
FABULATING
FABULATORS
FABULISING
FABULISTIC
FABULIZING
FABULOSITIES
FABULOSITY
FABULOUSLY
FABULOUSNESS
FABULOUSNESSES
FACEBOOKED
FACEBOOKING
FACECLOTHS
FACELESSNESS
FACELESSNESSES
FACELIFTED
FACELIFTING
FACEPALMED
FACEPALMING
FACEPLANTED
FACEPLANTING
FACEPLANTS
FACEPLATES
FACEPRINTS
FACETIMING
FACETIOUSLY
FACETIOUSNESS
FACETIOUSNESSES
FACEWORKER
FACEWORKERS
FACIALISTS
FACILENESS
FACILENESSES
FACILITATE
FACILITATED
FACILITATES
FACILITATING
FACILITATION
FACILITATIONS
FACILITATIVE
FACILITATOR
FACILITATORS
FACILITATORY
FACILITIES
FACINERIOUS
FACINOROUS
FACINOROUSNESS
FACSIMILED
FACSIMILEING
FACSIMILES
FACSIMILIST
FACSIMILISTS
FACTICITIES
FACTIONALISE
FACTIONALISED
FACTIONALISES
FACTIONALISING
FACTIONALISM
FACTIONALISMS
FACTIONALIST
FACTIONALISTS
FACTIONALIZE
FACTIONALIZED
FACTIONALIZES
FACTIONALIZING
FACTIONALLY
FACTIONARIES
FACTIONARY
FACTIONIST
FACTIONISTS
FACTIOUSLY
FACTIOUSNESS
FACTIOUSNESSES
FACTITIOUS
FACTITIOUSLY
FACTITIOUSNESS
FACTITIVELY
FACTORABILITIES
FACTORABILITY
FACTORABLE
FACTORAGES
FACTORIALLY
FACTORIALS
FACTORINGS
FACTORISATION
FACTORISATIONS
FACTORISED
FACTORISES
FACTORISING
FACTORIZATION
FACTORIZATIONS
FACTORIZED
FACTORIZES
FACTORIZING
FACTORSHIP
FACTORSHIPS
FACTORYLIKE
FACTSHEETS
FACTUALISM
FACTUALISMS
FACTUALIST
FACTUALISTIC
FACTUALISTS
FACTUALITIES
FACTUALITY
FACTUALNESS
FACTUALNESSES
FACULTATIVE
FACULTATIVELY
FACUNDITIES
FADDINESSES
FADDISHNESS
FADDISHNESSES
FADEDNESSES
FADELESSLY
FADOMETERS
FAGGOTIEST
FAGGOTINGS
FAGGOTRIES
FAGOTTISTS
FAINEANCES
FAINEANCIES
FAINEANTISE
FAINEANTISES
FAINNESSES
FAINTHEARTED
FAINTHEARTEDLY
FAINTINGLY
FAINTISHNESS
FAINTISHNESSES
FAINTNESSES
FAIRGROUND
FAIRGROUNDS
FAIRLEADER
FAIRLEADERS
FAIRNESSES
FAIRNITICKLE
FAIRNITICKLES
FAIRNITICLE
FAIRNITICLES
FAIRNYTICKLE
FAIRNYTICKLES
FAIRNYTICLE
FAIRNYTICLES
FAIRYFLOSS
FAIRYFLOSSES
FAIRYHOODS
FAIRYLANDS
FAITHCURES
FAITHFULLY
FAITHFULNESS
FAITHFULNESSES
FAITHLESSLY
FAITHLESSNESS
FAITHLESSNESSES
FAITHWORTHIER
FAITHWORTHIEST
FAITHWORTHINESS
FAITHWORTHY
FALANGISMS
FALANGISTS
FALCATIONS
FALCONIFORM
FALCONOIDS
FALCONRIES
FALDERALED
FALDERALING
FALDISTORIES
FALDISTORY
FALDSTOOLS
FALLACIOUS
FALLACIOUSLY
FALLACIOUSNESS
FALLALERIES
FALLALISHLY
FALLBOARDS
FALLFISHES
FALLIBILISM
FALLIBILISMS
FALLIBILIST
FALLIBILISTS
FALLIBILITIES
FALLIBILITY
FALLIBLENESS
FALLIBLENESSES
FALLOWNESS
FALLOWNESSES
FALSEFACES
FALSEHOODS
FALSENESSES
FALSEWORKS
FALSIDICAL
FALSIFIABILITY
FALSIFIABLE
FALSIFICATION
FALSIFICATIONS
FALSIFIERS
FALSIFYING
FALTERINGLY

FALTERINGS
FAMILIARISATION
FAMILIARISE
FAMILIARISED
FAMILIARISER
FAMILIARISERS
FAMILIARISES
FAMILIARISING
FAMILIARITIES
FAMILIARITY
FAMILIARIZATION
FAMILIARIZE
FAMILIARIZED
FAMILIARIZER
FAMILIARIZERS
FAMILIARIZES
FAMILIARIZING
FAMILIARLY
FAMILIARNESS
FAMILIARNESSES
FAMILISTIC
FAMISHMENT
FAMISHMENTS
FAMOUSNESS
FAMOUSNESSES
FANATICALLY
FANATICALNESS
FANATICALNESSES
FANATICISATION
FANATICISATIONS
FANATICISE
FANATICISED
FANATICISES
FANATICISING
FANATICISM
FANATICISMS
FANATICIZATION
FANATICIZATIONS
FANATICIZE
FANATICIZED
FANATICIZES
FANATICIZING
FANCIFULLY
FANCIFULNESS
FANCIFULNESSES
FANCIFYING
FANCINESSES
FANCYWORKS
FANDABIDOZI
FANDANGLES
FANDANGOES
FANFARADES
FANFARONADE
FANFARONADED
FANFARONADES
FANFARONADING
FANFARONAS
FANFOLDING
FANTABULOUS
FANTASISED
FANTASISER
FANTASISERS
FANTASISES
FANTASISING
FANTASISTS
FANTASIZED
FANTASIZER
FANTASIZERS
FANTASIZES
FANTASIZING
FANTASMALLY
FANTASMICALLY
FANTASQUES
FANTASTICAL
FANTASTICALITY
FANTASTICALLY
FANTASTICALNESS
FANTASTICATE
FANTASTICATED
FANTASTICATES
FANTASTICATING
FANTASTICATION
FANTASTICATIONS
FANTASTICISM
FANTASTICISMS
FANTASTICO
FANTASTICOES
FANTASTICS
FANTASTRIES
FANTASYING
FANTASYLAND
FANTASYLANDS
FANTOCCINI
FARADISATION
FARADISATIONS
FARADISERS
FARADISING
FARADIZATION
FARADIZATIONS
FARADIZERS
FARADIZING
FARANDINES
FARANDOLES
FARAWAYNESS
FARAWAYNESSES
FARBOROUGH
FARBOROUGHS
FARCEMEATS
FARCICALITIES
FARCICALITY
FARCICALLY
FARCICALNESS
FARCICALNESSES
FARCIFYING
FAREWELLED
FAREWELLING
FARFETCHEDNESS
FARINACEOUS
FARINOSELY
FARKLEBERRIES
FARKLEBERRY
FARMERESSES
FARMERETTE
FARMERETTES
FARMHOUSES
FARMSTEADS
FARMWORKER
FARMWORKERS
FARNARKELED
FARNARKELING
FARNARKELINGS
FARNARKELS
FARRAGINOUS
FARRANDINE
FARRANDINES
FARRIERIES
FARROWINGS
FARSIGHTED
FARSIGHTEDLY
FARSIGHTEDNESS
FARTHERMORE
FARTHERMOST
FARTHINGALE
FARTHINGALES
FARTHINGLAND
FARTHINGLANDS
FARTHINGLESS
FARTHINGSWORTH
FARTHINGSWORTHS
FASCIATELY
FASCIATION
FASCIATIONS
FASCICULAR
FASCICULARLY
FASCICULATE
FASCICULATED
FASCICULATELY
FASCICULATION
FASCICULATIONS
FASCICULES
FASCICULUS
FASCIITISES
FASCINATED
FASCINATEDLY
FASCINATES
FASCINATING
FASCINATINGLY
FASCINATION
FASCINATIONS
FASCINATIVE
FASCINATOR
FASCINATORS
FASCIOLIASES
FASCIOLIASIS
FASCISTICALLY
FASCITISES
FASHIONABILITY
FASHIONABLE
FASHIONABLENESS
FASHIONABLES
FASHIONABLY
FASHIONERS
FASHIONIER
FASHIONIEST
FASHIONING
FASHIONIST
FASHIONISTA
FASHIONISTAS
FASHIONISTS
FASHIONMONGER
FASHIONMONGERS
FASHIONMONGING
FASHIOUSNESS
FASHIOUSNESSES
FASTBALLER
FASTBALLERS
FASTENINGS
FASTIDIOUS
FASTIDIOUSLY
FASTIDIOUSNESS
FASTIGIATE
FASTIGIATED
FASTIGIUMS
FASTNESSES
FATALISTIC
FATALISTICALLY
FATALITIES
FATALNESSES
FATBRAINED
FATEFULNESS
FATEFULNESSES
FATHEADEDLY
FATHEADEDNESS
FATHEADEDNESSES
FATHERHOOD
FATHERHOODS
FATHERINGS
FATHERLAND
FATHERLANDS
FATHERLESS
FATHERLESSNESS
FATHERLIER
FATHERLIEST
FATHERLIKE
FATHERLINESS
FATHERLINESSES
FATHERSHIP
FATHERSHIPS
FATHOMABLE
FATHOMETER
FATHOMETERS
FATHOMLESS
FATHOMLESSLY
FATHOMLESSNESS
FATIDICALLY
FATIGABILITIES
FATIGABILITY
FATIGABLENESS
FATIGABLENESSES
FATIGATING

FATIGUABLE
FATIGUABLENESS
FATIGUELESS
FATIGUINGLY
FATISCENCE
FATISCENCES
FATSHEDERA
FATSHEDERAS
FATTENABLE
FATTENINGS
FATTINESSES
FATUOUSNESS
FATUOUSNESSES
FAUCETRIES
FAULCHIONS
FAULTFINDER
FAULTFINDERS
FAULTFINDING
FAULTFINDINGS
FAULTINESS
FAULTINESSES
FAULTLESSLY
FAULTLESSNESS
FAULTLESSNESSES
FAULTLINES
FAUNISTICALLY
FAUXBOURDON
FAUXBOURDONS
FAUXMANCES
FAVORABLENESS
FAVORABLENESSES
FAVOREDNESS
FAVOREDNESSES
FAVORINGLY
FAVORITISM
FAVORITISMS
FAVOURABLE
FAVOURABLENESS
FAVOURABLY
FAVOUREDNESS
FAVOUREDNESSES
FAVOURINGLY
FAVOURITES
FAVOURITISM
FAVOURITISMS
FAVOURLESS
FAWNINGNESS
FAWNINGNESSES
FAZENDEIRO
FAZENDEIROS
FEARFULLER
FEARFULLEST
FEARFULNESS
FEARFULNESSES
FEARLESSLY
FEARLESSNESS
FEARLESSNESSES
FEARMONGER
FEARMONGERING
FEARMONGERINGS
FEARMONGERS
FEARNAUGHT
FEARNAUGHTS
FEARNOUGHT
FEARNOUGHTS
FEARSOMELY
FEARSOMENESS
FEARSOMENESSES
FEASIBILITIES
FEASIBILITY
FEASIBLENESS
FEASIBLENESSES
FEATEOUSLY
FEATHERBED
FEATHERBEDDED
FEATHERBEDDING
FEATHERBEDDINGS
FEATHERBEDS
FEATHERBRAIN
FEATHERBRAINED
FEATHERBRAINS
FEATHEREDGE
FEATHEREDGED
FEATHEREDGES
FEATHEREDGING
FEATHERHEAD
FEATHERHEADED
FEATHERHEADS
FEATHERIER
FEATHERIEST
FEATHERINESS
FEATHERINESSES
FEATHERING
FEATHERINGS
FEATHERLESS
FEATHERLIGHT
FEATHERSTITCH
FEATHERSTITCHED
FEATHERSTITCHES
FEATHERWEIGHT
FEATHERWEIGHTS
FEATLINESS
FEATLINESSES
FEATURELESS
FEATURELESSNESS
FEATURETTE
FEATURETTES
FEBRICITIES
FEBRICULAS
FEBRICULES
FEBRIFACIENT
FEBRIFACIENTS
FEBRIFEROUS
FEBRIFUGAL
FEBRIFUGES
FEBRILITIES
FECKLESSLY
FECKLESSNESS
FECKLESSNESSES
FECULENCES
FECULENCIES
FECUNDATED
FECUNDATES
FECUNDATING
FECUNDATION
FECUNDATIONS
FECUNDATOR
FECUNDATORS
FECUNDATORY
FECUNDITIES
FEDERACIES
FEDERALESE
FEDERALESES
FEDERALISATION
FEDERALISATIONS
FEDERALISE
FEDERALISED
FEDERALISES
FEDERALISING
FEDERALISM
FEDERALISMS
FEDERALIST
FEDERALISTIC
FEDERALISTS
FEDERALIZATION
FEDERALIZATIONS
FEDERALIZE
FEDERALIZED
FEDERALIZES
FEDERALIZING
FEDERARIES
FEDERATING
FEDERATION
FEDERATIONS
FEDERATIVE
FEDERATIVELY
FEDERATORS
FEEBLEMINDED
FEEBLEMINDEDLY
FEEBLENESS
FEEBLENESSES
FEEDGRAINS
FEEDINGSTUFF
FEEDINGSTUFFS
FEEDSTOCKS
FEEDSTUFFS
FEEDTHROUGH
FEEDTHROUGHS
FEEDWATERS
FEELINGLESS
FEELINGNESS
FEELINGNESSES
FEIGNEDNESS
FEIGNEDNESSES
FEIGNINGLY
FEISTINESS
FEISTINESSES
FELDSCHARS
FELDSCHERS
FELDSPATHIC
FELDSPATHOID
FELDSPATHOIDS
FELDSPATHOSE
FELDSPATHS
FELICITATE
FELICITATED
FELICITATES
FELICITATING
FELICITATION
FELICITATIONS
FELICITATOR
FELICITATORS
FELICITIES
FELICITOUS
FELICITOUSLY
FELICITOUSNESS
FELINENESS
FELINENESSES
FELINITIES
FELLATIONS
FELLATRICES
FELLATRIXES
FELLFIELDS
FELLMONGER
FELLMONGERED
FELLMONGERIES
FELLMONGERING
FELLMONGERINGS
FELLMONGERS
FELLMONGERY
FELLNESSES
FELLOWSHIP
FELLOWSHIPED
FELLOWSHIPING
FELLOWSHIPPED
FELLOWSHIPPING
FELLOWSHIPS
FELLWALKER
FELLWALKERS
FELONIOUSLY
FELONIOUSNESS
FELONIOUSNESSES
FELQUISTES
FELSPATHIC
FELSPATHOID
FELSPATHOIDS
FELSPATHOSE
FEMALENESS
FEMALENESSES
FEMALITIES
FEMETARIES
FEMINACIES
FEMINALITIES
FEMINALITY
FEMINEITIES
FEMINILITIES
FEMINILITY
FEMININELY
FEMININENESS
FEMININENESSES

FEMININISM
FEMININISMS
FEMININITIES
FEMININITY
FEMINISATION
FEMINISATIONS
FEMINISING
FEMINISTIC
FEMINITIES
FEMINIZATION
FEMINIZATIONS
FEMINIZING
FEMTOSECOND
FEMTOSECONDS
FENCELESSNESS
FENCELESSNESSES
FENCELINES
FENCEWIRES
FENDERLESS
FENESTELLA
FENESTELLAE
FENESTELLAS
FENESTRALS
FENESTRATE
FENESTRATED
FENESTRATES
FENESTRATING
FENESTRATION
FENESTRATIONS
FENNELFLOWER
FENNELFLOWERS
FENUGREEKS
FEOFFMENTS
FERACITIES
FERETORIES
FERMENTABILITY
FERMENTABLE
FERMENTATION
FERMENTATIONS
FERMENTATIVE
FERMENTATIVELY
FERMENTERS
FERMENTESCIBLE
FERMENTING
FERMENTITIOUS
FERMENTIVE
FERMENTORS
FERNALLIES
FERNITICKLE
FERNITICKLES
FERNITICLE
FERNITICLES
FERNTICKLE
FERNTICKLED
FERNTICKLES
FERNTICLED
FERNTICLES
FERNYTICKLE
FERNYTICKLES
FERNYTICLE
FERNYTICLES
FEROCIOUSLY
FEROCIOUSNESS
FEROCIOUSNESSES
FEROCITIES
FERRANDINE
FERRANDINES
FERREDOXIN
FERREDOXINS
FERRELLING
FERRETIEST
FERRETINGS
FERRICYANIC
FERRICYANIDE
FERRICYANIDES
FERRICYANOGEN
FERRICYANOGENS
FERRIFEROUS
FERRIMAGNET
FERRIMAGNETIC
FERRIMAGNETISM
FERRIMAGNETISMS
FERRIMAGNETS
FERROCENES
FERROCHROME
FERROCHROMES
FERROCHROMIUM
FERROCHROMIUMS
FERROCONCRETE
FERROCONCRETES
FERROCYANIC
FERROCYANIDE
FERROCYANIDES
FERROCYANOGEN
FERROCYANOGENS
FERROELECTRIC
FERROELECTRICS
FERROGRAMS
FERROGRAPHIES
FERROGRAPHY
FERROMAGNESIAN
FERROMAGNET
FERROMAGNETIC
FERROMAGNETISM
FERROMAGNETISMS
FERROMAGNETS
FERROMANGANESE
FERROMANGANESES
FERROMOLYBDENUM
FERRONICKEL
FERRONICKELS
FERRONIERE
FERRONIERES
FERRONNIERE
FERRONNIERES
FERROPRUSSIATE
FERROPRUSSIATES
FERROSILICON
FERROSILICONS
FERROSOFERRIC
FERROTYPED
FERROTYPES
FERROTYPING
FERRUGINEOUS
FERRUGINOUS
FERRYBOATS
FERTIGATED
FERTIGATES
FERTIGATING
FERTIGATION
FERTIGATIONS
FERTILENESS
FERTILENESSES
FERTILISABLE
FERTILISATION
FERTILISATIONS
FERTILISED
FERTILISER
FERTILISERS
FERTILISES
FERTILISING
FERTILITIES
FERTILIZABLE
FERTILIZATION
FERTILIZATIONS
FERTILIZED
FERTILIZER
FERTILIZERS
FERTILIZES
FERTILIZING
FERULACEOUS
FERVENCIES
FERVENTEST
FERVENTNESS
FERVENTNESSES
FERVESCENT
FERVIDITIES
FERVIDNESS
FERVIDNESSES
FESCENNINE
FESTILOGIES
FESTINATED
FESTINATELY
FESTINATES
FESTINATING
FESTINATION
FESTINATIONS
FESTIVALGOER
FESTIVALGOERS
FESTIVENESS
FESTIVENESSES
FESTIVITIES
FESTOLOGIES
FESTOONERIES
FESTOONERY
FESTOONING
FESTSCHRIFT
FESTSCHRIFTEN
FESTSCHRIFTS
FETCHINGLY
FETICHISED
FETICHISES
FETICHISING
FETICHISMS
FETICHISTIC
FETICHISTS
FETICHIZED
FETICHIZES
FETICHIZING
FETIDITIES
FETIDNESSES
FETIPAROUS
FETISHISATION
FETISHISATIONS
FETISHISED
FETISHISES
FETISHISING
FETISHISMS
FETISHISTIC
FETISHISTICALLY
FETISHISTS
FETISHIZATION
FETISHIZATIONS
FETISHIZED
FETISHIZES
FETISHIZING
FETOLOGIES
FETOLOGIST
FETOLOGISTS
FETOPROTEIN
FETOPROTEINS
FETOSCOPES
FETOSCOPIES
FETTERLESS
FETTERLOCK
FETTERLOCKS
FETTUCCINE
FETTUCCINES
FETTUCCINI
FETTUCCINIS
FETTUCINES
FETTUCINIS
FEUDALISATION
FEUDALISATIONS
FEUDALISED
FEUDALISES
FEUDALISING
FEUDALISMS
FEUDALISTIC
FEUDALISTS
FEUDALITIES
FEUDALIZATION
FEUDALIZATIONS
FEUDALIZED
FEUDALIZES
FEUDALIZING
FEUDATORIES
FEUILLETES
FEUILLETON
FEUILLETONISM

FEUILLETONISMS
FEUILLETONIST
FEUILLETONISTIC
FEUILLETONISTS
FEUILLETONS
FEVERISHLY
FEVERISHNESS
FEVERISHNESSES
FEVEROUSLY
FEVERROOTS
FEVERWEEDS
FEVERWORTS
FIANCAILLES
FIANCHETTI
FIANCHETTO
FIANCHETTOED
FIANCHETTOES
FIANCHETTOING
FIANCHETTOS
FIBERBOARD
FIBERBOARDS
FIBERFILLS
FIBERGLASS
FIBERGLASSED
FIBERGLASSES
FIBERGLASSING
FIBERISATION
FIBERISATIONS
FIBERISING
FIBERIZATION
FIBERIZATIONS
FIBERIZING
FIBERSCOPE
FIBERSCOPES
FIBREBOARD
FIBREBOARDS
FIBREFILLS
FIBREGLASS
FIBREGLASSED
FIBREGLASSES
FIBREGLASSING
FIBREOPTIC
FIBRESCOPE
FIBRESCOPES
FIBRILLARY
FIBRILLATE
FIBRILLATED
FIBRILLATES
FIBRILLATING
FIBRILLATION
FIBRILLATIONS
FIBRILLIFORM
FIBRILLINS
FIBRILLOSE
FIBRILLOUS
FIBRINOGEN
FIBRINOGENIC
FIBRINOGENOUS
FIBRINOGENS
FIBRINOIDS
FIBRINOLYSES
FIBRINOLYSIN
FIBRINOLYSINS
FIBRINOLYSIS
FIBRINOLYTIC
FIBRINOPEPTIDE
FIBRINOPEPTIDES
FIBROBLAST
FIBROBLASTIC
FIBROBLASTS
FIBROCARTILAGE
FIBROCARTILAGES
FIBROCEMENT
FIBROCEMENTS
FIBROCYSTIC
FIBROCYTES
FIBROLINES
FIBROLITES
FIBROMATOUS
FIBROMYALGIA
FIBROMYALGIAS
FIBRONECTIN
FIBRONECTINS
FIBROSARCOMA
FIBROSARCOMAS
FIBROSARCOMATA
FIBROSITIS
FIBROSITISES
FIBROUSNESS
FIBROUSNESSES
FIBROVASCULAR
FICKLENESS
FICKLENESSES
FICTIONALISE
FICTIONALISED
FICTIONALISES
FICTIONALISING
FICTIONALITIES
FICTIONALITY
FICTIONALIZE
FICTIONALIZED
FICTIONALIZES
FICTIONALIZING
FICTIONALLY
FICTIONEER
FICTIONEERING
FICTIONEERINGS
FICTIONEERS
FICTIONISATION
FICTIONISATIONS
FICTIONISE
FICTIONISED
FICTIONISES
FICTIONISING
FICTIONIST
FICTIONISTS
FICTIONIZATION
FICTIONIZATIONS
FICTIONIZE
FICTIONIZED
FICTIONIZES
FICTIONIZING
FICTITIOUS
FICTITIOUSLY
FICTITIOUSNESS
FICTIVENESS
FICTIVENESSES
FIDDIOUSED
FIDDIOUSES
FIDDIOUSING
FIDDLEBACK
FIDDLEBACKS
FIDDLEDEDEE
FIDDLEDEEDEE
FIDDLEHEAD
FIDDLEHEADS
FIDDLENECK
FIDDLENECKS
FIDDLESTICK
FIDDLESTICKS
FIDDLEWOOD
FIDDLEWOODS
FIDEICOMMISSA
FIDEICOMMISSARY
FIDEICOMMISSUM
FIDELISMOS
FIDELISTAS
FIDELITIES
FIDGETIEST
FIDGETINESS
FIDGETINESSES
FIDGETINGLY
FIDUCIALLY
FIDUCIARIES
FIDUCIARILY
FIELDBOOTS
FIELDCRAFT
FIELDCRAFTS
FIELDFARES
FIELDMOUSE
FIELDPIECE
FIELDPIECES
FIELDSTONE
FIELDSTONES
FIELDSTRIP
FIELDSTRIPPED
FIELDSTRIPPING
FIELDSTRIPS
FIELDVOLES
FIELDWARDS
FIELDWORKER
FIELDWORKERS
FIELDWORKS
FIENDISHLY
FIENDISHNESS
FIENDISHNESSES
FIERCENESS
FIERCENESSES
FIERINESSES
FIFTEENERS
FIFTEENTHLY
FIFTEENTHS
FIGHTBACKS
FIGURABILITIES
FIGURABILITY
FIGURANTES
FIGURATELY
FIGURATION
FIGURATIONS
FIGURATIVE
FIGURATIVELY
FIGURATIVENESS
FIGUREHEAD
FIGUREHEADS
FIGURELESS
FIGUREWORK
FIGUREWORKS
FILAGGRINS
FILAGREEING
FILAMENTARY
FILAMENTOUS
FILARIASES
FILARIASIS
FILATORIES
FILCHINGLY
FILEFISHES
FILIALNESS
FILIALNESSES
FILIATIONS
FILIBUSTER
FILIBUSTERED
FILIBUSTERER
FILIBUSTERERS
FILIBUSTERING
FILIBUSTERINGS
FILIBUSTERISM
FILIBUSTERISMS
FILIBUSTEROUS
FILIBUSTERS
FILICINEAN
FILIGRAINS
FILIGRANES
FILIGREEING
FILIOPIETISTIC
FILIPENDULOUS
FILLAGREED
FILLAGREEING
FILLAGREES
FILLESTERS
FILLIPEENS
FILLISTERS
FILMGOINGS
FILMICALLY
FILMINESSES
FILMMAKERS
FILMMAKING
FILMMAKINGS
FILMOGRAPHIES
FILMOGRAPHY
FILMSETTER

FILMSETTERS
FILMSETTING
FILMSETTINGS
FILMSTRIPS
FILOPLUMES
FILOPODIUM
FILOSELLES
FILOVIRUSES
FILTERABILITIES
FILTERABILITY
FILTERABLE
FILTERABLENESS
FILTHINESS
FILTHINESSES
FILTRABILITIES
FILTRABILITY
FILTRABLENESS
FILTRABLENESSES
FILTRATABLE
FILTRATING
FILTRATION
FILTRATIONS
FIMBRIATED
FIMBRIATES
FIMBRIATING
FIMBRIATION
FIMBRIATIONS
FIMBRILLATE
FIMICOLOUS
FINABLENESS
FINABLENESSES
FINAGLINGS
FINALISATION
FINALISATIONS
FINALISERS
FINALISING
FINALISTIC
FINALITIES
FINALIZATION
FINALIZATIONS
FINALIZERS
FINALIZING
FINANCIALIST
FINANCIALISTS
FINANCIALLY
FINANCIALS
FINANCIERED
FINANCIERING
FINANCIERS
FINANCINGS
FINEABLENESS
FINEABLENESSES
FINENESSES
FINESSINGS
FINGERBOARD
FINGERBOARDS
FINGERBOWL
FINGERBOWLS
FINGERBREADTH
FINGERBREADTHS
FINGERGLASS
FINGERGLASSES
FINGERGUARD
FINGERGUARDS
FINGERHOLD
FINGERHOLDS
FINGERHOLE
FINGERHOLES
FINGERINGS
FINGERLESS
FINGERLIKE
FINGERLING
FINGERLINGS
FINGERMARK
FINGERMARKS
FINGERNAIL
FINGERNAILS
FINGERPICK
FINGERPICKED
FINGERPICKING
FINGERPICKINGS
FINGERPICKS
FINGERPLATE
FINGERPLATES
FINGERPOST
FINGERPOSTS
FINGERPRINT
FINGERPRINTED
FINGERPRINTING
FINGERPRINTINGS
FINGERPRINTS
FINGERSTALL
FINGERSTALLS
FINGERTIPS
FINICALITIES
FINICALITY
FINICALNESS
FINICALNESSES
FINICKETIER
FINICKETIEST
FINICKIEST
FINICKINESS
FINICKINESSES
FINICKINGS
FINISHINGS
FINITENESS
FINITENESSES
FINNICKIER
FINNICKIEST
FINNOCHIOS
FINOCCHIOS
FIORATURAE
FIREBALLER
FIREBALLERS
FIREBALLING
FIREBOARDS
FIREBOMBED
FIREBOMBER
FIREBOMBERS
FIREBOMBING
FIREBOMBINGS
FIREBRANDS
FIREBREAKS
FIREBRICKS
FIREBUSHES
FIRECRACKER
FIRECRACKERS
FIRECRESTS
FIREDRAGON
FIREDRAGONS
FIREDRAKES
FIREFANGED
FIREFANGING
FIREFIGHTER
FIREFIGHTERS
FIREFIGHTING
FIREFIGHTINGS
FIREFIGHTS
FIREFLOATS
FIREFLOODS
FIREGUARDS
FIREHOUSES
FIRELIGHTER
FIRELIGHTERS
FIRELIGHTS
FIREPLACED
FIREPLACES
FIREPOWERS
FIREPROOFED
FIREPROOFING
FIREPROOFINGS
FIREPROOFS
FIRESCAPED
FIRESCAPES
FIRESCAPING
FIRESCAPINGS
FIRESCREEN
FIRESCREENS
FIRESTONES
FIRESTORMS
FIRETHORNS
FIRETRUCKS
FIREWALLED
FIREWALLING
FIREWARDEN
FIREWARDENS
FIREWATERS
FIRMAMENTAL
FIRMAMENTS
FIRMNESSES
FIRSTBORNS
FIRSTFRUITS
FIRSTLINGS
FIRSTNESSES
FISCALISTS
FISHABILITIES
FISHABILITY
FISHBURGER
FISHBURGERS
FISHERFOLK
FISHERWOMAN
FISHERWOMEN
FISHFINGER
FISHFINGERS
FISHIFYING
FISHINESSES
FISHMONGER
FISHMONGERS
FISHPLATES
FISHTAILED
FISHTAILING
FISHWIFELIER
FISHWIFELIEST
FISHWIFELY
FISHYBACKS
FISSICOSTATE
FISSILINGUAL
FISSILITIES
FISSIONABILITY
FISSIONABLE
FISSIONABLES
FISSIONING
FISSIPALMATE
FISSIPARISM
FISSIPARISMS
FISSIPARITIES
FISSIPARITY
FISSIPAROUS
FISSIPAROUSLY
FISSIPAROUSNESS
FISSIPEDAL
FISSIPEDES
FISSIROSTRAL
FISTFIGHTS
FISTICUFFED
FISTICUFFING
FISTICUFFS
FITFULNESS
FITFULNESSES
FITTINGNESS
FITTINGNESSES
FIVEFINGER
FIVEFINGERS
FIVEPENCES
FIXEDNESSES
FIXTURELESS
FIZGIGGING
FIZZENLESS
FIZZINESSES
FLABBERGAST
FLABBERGASTED
FLABBERGASTING
FLABBERGASTS
FLABBINESS
FLABBINESSES
FLABELLATE
FLABELLATION
FLABELLATIONS
FLABELLIFORM
FLACCIDEST

FLACCIDITIES
FLACCIDITY
FLACCIDNESS
FLACCIDNESSES
FLACKERIES
FLACKERING
FLACKETING
FLAFFERING
FLAGELLANT
FLAGELLANTISM
FLAGELLANTISMS
FLAGELLANTS
FLAGELLATE
FLAGELLATED
FLAGELLATES
FLAGELLATING
FLAGELLATION
FLAGELLATIONS
FLAGELLATOR
FLAGELLATORS
FLAGELLATORY
FLAGELLIFEROUS
FLAGELLIFORM
FLAGELLINS
FLAGELLOMANIA
FLAGELLOMANIAC
FLAGELLOMANIACS
FLAGELLOMANIAS
FLAGELLUMS
FLAGEOLETS
FLAGGINESS
FLAGGINESSES
FLAGGINGLY
FLAGITATED
FLAGITATES
FLAGITATING
FLAGITATION
FLAGITATIONS
FLAGITIOUS
FLAGITIOUSLY
FLAGITIOUSNESS
FLAGRANCES
FLAGRANCIES
FLAGRANTLY
FLAGRANTNESS
FLAGRANTNESSES
FLAGSTAFFS
FLAGSTAVES

FLAGSTICKS
FLAGSTONES
FLAKINESSES
FLAMBEEING
FLAMBOYANCE
FLAMBOYANCES
FLAMBOYANCIES
FLAMBOYANCY
FLAMBOYANT
FLAMBOYANTE
FLAMBOYANTES
FLAMBOYANTLY
FLAMBOYANTS
FLAMEPROOF
FLAMEPROOFED
FLAMEPROOFER
FLAMEPROOFERS
FLAMEPROOFING
FLAMEPROOFS
FLAMETHROWER
FLAMETHROWERS
FLAMINGOES
FLAMINICAL
FLAMMABILITIES
FLAMMABILITY
FLAMMABLES
FLAMMIFEROUS
FLAMMULATED
FLAMMULATION
FLAMMULATIONS
FLANCHINGS
FLANCONADE
FLANCONADES
FLANGELESS
FLANKERING
FLANNELBOARD
FLANNELBOARDS
FLANNELETS
FLANNELETTE
FLANNELETTES
FLANNELGRAPH
FLANNELGRAPHS
FLANNELING
FLANNELLED
FLANNELLIER
FLANNELLIEST
FLANNELLING
FLANNELMOUTHED

FLAPDOODLE
FLAPDOODLES
FLAPPERHOOD
FLAPPERHOODS
FLAPPERISH
FLAPTRACKS
FLAREBACKS
FLASHBACKED
FLASHBACKING
FLASHBACKS
FLASHBANGS
FLASHBOARD
FLASHBOARDS
FLASHBULBS
FLASHCARDS
FLASHCUBES
FLASHFORWARD
FLASHFORWARDS
FLASHINESS
FLASHINESSES
FLASHLAMPS
FLASHLIGHT
FLASHLIGHTS
FLASHMOBBING
FLASHMOBBINGS
FLASHOVERS
FLASHPACKER
FLASHPACKERS
FLASHPOINT
FLASHPOINTS
FLASHTUBES
FLATBREADS
FLATFISHES
FLATFOOTED
FLATFOOTING
FLATLANDER
FLATLANDERS
FLATLINERS
FLATLINING
FLATNESSES
FLATPICKED
FLATPICKING
FLATSCREEN
FLATSCREENS
FLATSHARES
FLATTENERS
FLATTENING
FLATTERABLE

FLATTERERS
FLATTERIES
FLATTERING
FLATTERINGLY
FLATTEROUS
FLATTEROUSLY
FLATULENCE
FLATULENCES
FLATULENCIES
FLATULENCY
FLATULENTLY
FLATWASHES
FLATWATERS
FLAUGHTERED
FLAUGHTERING
FLAUGHTERS
FLAUGHTING
FLAUNCHING
FLAUNCHINGS
FLAUNTIEST
FLAUNTINESS
FLAUNTINESSES
FLAUNTINGLY
FLAVANONES
FLAVESCENT
FLAVIVIRUS
FLAVIVIRUSES
FLAVONOIDS
FLAVOPROTEIN
FLAVOPROTEINS
FLAVOPURPURIN
FLAVOPURPURINS
FLAVORFULLY
FLAVORIEST
FLAVORINGS
FLAVORISTS
FLAVORLESS
FLAVORSOME
FLAVOURDYNAMICS
FLAVOURERS
FLAVOURFUL
FLAVOURFULLY
FLAVOURIER
FLAVOURIEST
FLAVOURING
FLAVOURINGS
FLAVOURIST
FLAVOURISTS

FLAVOURLESS
FLAVOURSOME
FLAWLESSLY
FLAWLESSNESS
FLAWLESSNESSES
FLEAHOPPER
FLEAHOPPERS
FLECHETTES
FLECKERING
FLECTIONAL
FLECTIONLESS
FLEDGELING
FLEDGELINGS
FLEDGLINGS
FLEECELESS
FLEECHINGS
FLEECHMENT
FLEECHMENTS
FLEECINESS
FLEECINESSES
FLEERINGLY
FLEETINGLY
FLEETINGNESS
FLEETINGNESSES
FLEETNESSES
FLEHMENING
FLEMISHING
FLEROVIUMS
FLESHHOODS
FLESHINESS
FLESHINESSES
FLESHLIEST
FLESHLINESS
FLESHLINESSES
FLESHLINGS
FLESHMENTS
FLESHMONGER
FLESHMONGERS
FLESHWORMS
FLETCHINGS
FLEURETTES
FLEXECUTIVE
FLEXECUTIVES
FLEXIBILITIES
FLEXIBILITY
FLEXIBLENESS
FLEXIBLENESSES
FLEXICURITIES

F

FLEXICURITY
FLEXIHOURS
FLEXIONLESS
FLEXITARIAN
FLEXITARIANISM
FLEXITARIANISMS
FLEXITARIANS
FLEXITIMES
FLEXOGRAPHIC
FLEXOGRAPHICS
FLEXOGRAPHY
FLEXTIMERS
FLEXUOUSLY
FLIBBERTIGIBBET
FLICHTERED
FLICHTERING
FLICKERIER
FLICKERIEST
FLICKERING
FLICKERINGLY
FLICKERTAIL
FLICKERTAILS
FLIGHTIEST
FLIGHTINESS
FLIGHTINESSES
FLIGHTLESS
FLIMFLAMMED
FLIMFLAMMER
FLIMFLAMMERIES
FLIMFLAMMERS
FLIMFLAMMERY
FLIMFLAMMING
FLIMSINESS
FLIMSINESSES
FLINCHINGLY
FLINCHINGS
FLINDERING
FLINDERSIA
FLINDERSIAS
FLINTHEADS
FLINTIFIED
FLINTIFIES
FLINTIFYING
FLINTINESS
FLINTINESSES
FLINTLOCKS
FLIPBOARDS
FLIPCHARTS

FLIPFLOPPED
FLIPFLOPPING
FLIPPANCIES
FLIPPANTLY
FLIPPANTNESS
FLIPPANTNESSES
FLIRTATION
FLIRTATIONS
FLIRTATIOUS
FLIRTATIOUSLY
FLIRTATIOUSNESS
FLIRTINGLY
FLITTERING
FLITTERMICE
FLITTERMOUSE
FLOATABILITIES
FLOATABILITY
FLOATATION
FLOATATIONS
FLOATBASES
FLOATINGLY
FLOATPLANE
FLOATPLANES
FLOCCILLATION
FLOCCILLATIONS
FLOCCULANT
FLOCCULANTS
FLOCCULATE
FLOCCULATED
FLOCCULATES
FLOCCULATING
FLOCCULATION
FLOCCULATIONS
FLOCCULATOR
FLOCCULATORS
FLOCCULENCE
FLOCCULENCES
FLOCCULENCIES
FLOCCULENCY
FLOCCULENT
FLOCCULENTLY
FLOODGATES
FLOODLIGHT
FLOODLIGHTED
FLOODLIGHTING
FLOODLIGHTINGS
FLOODLIGHTS
FLOODMARKS

FLOODPLAIN
FLOODPLAINS
FLOODTIDES
FLOODWALLS
FLOODWATER
FLOODWATERS
FLOORBOARD
FLOORBOARDS
FLOORCLOTH
FLOORCLOTHS
FLOORDROBE
FLOORDROBES
FLOORHEADS
FLOORSHOWS
FLOORWALKER
FLOORWALKERS
FLOPHOUSES
FLOPPINESS
FLOPPINESSES
FLOPTICALS
FLORENTINE
FLORENTINES
FLORESCENCE
FLORESCENCES
FLORESCENT
FLORIATION
FLORIATIONS
FLORIBUNDA
FLORIBUNDAS
FLORICANES
FLORICULTURAL
FLORICULTURE
FLORICULTURES
FLORICULTURIST
FLORICULTURISTS
FLORIDEANS
FLORIDEOUS
FLORIDITIES
FLORIDNESS
FLORIDNESSES
FLORIFEROUS
FLORIFEROUSNESS
FLORIGENIC
FLORILEGIA
FLORILEGIUM
FLORISTICALLY
FLORISTICS
FLORISTRIES

FLOSCULOUS
FLOTATIONS
FLOUNCIEST
FLOUNCINGS
FLOUNDERED
FLOUNDERING
FLOURISHED
FLOURISHER
FLOURISHERS
FLOURISHES
FLOURISHIER
FLOURISHIEST
FLOURISHING
FLOURISHINGLY
FLOUTINGLY
FLOUTINGSTOCK
FLOUTINGSTOCKS
FLOWCHARTING
FLOWCHARTINGS
FLOWCHARTS
FLOWERAGES
FLOWERBEDS
FLOWERETTE
FLOWERETTES
FLOWERHORN
FLOWERIEST
FLOWERINESS
FLOWERINESSES
FLOWERINGS
FLOWERLESS
FLOWERLIKE
FLOWERPOTS
FLOWINGNESS
FLOWINGNESSES
FLOWMETERS
FLOWSTONES
FLUCTUATED
FLUCTUATES
FLUCTUATING
FLUCTUATION
FLUCTUATIONAL
FLUCTUATIONS
FLUEGELHORN
FLUEGELHORNS
FLUENTNESS
FLUENTNESSES
FLUFFBALLS
FLUFFINESS

FLUFFINESSES
FLUGELHORN
FLUGELHORNIST
FLUGELHORNISTS
FLUGELHORNS
FLUIDEXTRACT
FLUIDEXTRACTS
FLUIDIFIED
FLUIDIFIES
FLUIDIFYING
FLUIDISATION
FLUIDISATIONS
FLUIDISERS
FLUIDISING
FLUIDITIES
FLUIDIZATION
FLUIDIZATIONS
FLUIDIZERS
FLUIDIZING
FLUIDNESSES
FLUKINESSES
FLUMMERIES
FLUMMOXING
FLUNITRAZEPAM
FLUNITRAZEPAMS
FLUNKEYDOM
FLUNKEYDOMS
FLUNKEYISH
FLUNKEYISM
FLUNKEYISMS
FLUNKYISMS
FLUORAPATITE
FLUORAPATITES
FLUORESCED
FLUORESCEIN
FLUORESCEINE
FLUORESCEINES
FLUORESCEINS
FLUORESCENCE
FLUORESCENCES
FLUORESCENT
FLUORESCENTS
FLUORESCER
FLUORESCERS
FLUORESCES
FLUORESCING
FLUORIDATE
FLUORIDATED

FLUORIDATES
FLUORIDATING
FLUORIDATION
FLUORIDATIONS
FLUORIDISE
FLUORIDISED
FLUORIDISES
FLUORIDISING
FLUORIDIZE
FLUORIDIZED
FLUORIDIZES
FLUORIDIZING
FLUORIMETER
FLUORIMETERS
FLUORIMETRIC
FLUORIMETRIES
FLUORIMETRY
FLUORINATE
FLUORINATED
FLUORINATES
FLUORINATING
FLUORINATION
FLUORINATIONS
FLUOROACETATE
FLUOROACETATES
FLUOROCARBON
FLUOROCARBONS
FLUOROCHROME
FLUOROCHROMES
FLUOROGRAPHIC
FLUOROGRAPHIES
FLUOROGRAPHY
FLUOROMETER
FLUOROMETERS
FLUOROMETRIC
FLUOROMETRIES
FLUOROMETRY
FLUOROPHORE
FLUOROPHORES
FLUOROPHOSPHATE
FLUOROSCOPE
FLUOROSCOPED
FLUOROSCOPES
FLUOROSCOPIC
FLUOROSCOPIES
FLUOROSCOPING
FLUOROSCOPIST
FLUOROSCOPISTS
FLUOROSCOPY
FLUOROTYPE
FLUOROTYPES
FLUOROURACIL
FLUOROURACILS
FLUORSPARS
FLUOXETINE
FLUOXETINES
FLUPHENAZINE
FLUPHENAZINES
FLUSHNESSES
FLUSHWORKS
FLUSTEREDLY
FLUSTERIER
FLUSTERIEST
FLUSTERING
FLUSTERMENT
FLUSTERMENTS
FLUSTRATED
FLUSTRATES
FLUSTRATING
FLUSTRATION
FLUSTRATIONS
FLUTEMOUTH
FLUTEMOUTHS
FLUTTERBOARD
FLUTTERBOARDS
FLUTTERERS
FLUTTERIER
FLUTTERIEST
FLUTTERING
FLUTTERINGLY
FLUTTERINGS
FLUVIALIST
FLUVIALISTS
FLUVIATILE
FLUVIOMARINE
FLUVOXAMINE
FLUVOXAMINES
FLUXIONALLY
FLUXIONARY
FLUXIONIST
FLUXIONISTS
FLUXMETERS
FLYBLOWING
FLYBRIDGES
FLYCATCHER
FLYCATCHERS
FLYFISHERS
FLYPITCHER
FLYPITCHERS
FLYPITCHES
FLYPOSTERS
FLYPOSTING
FLYPOSTINGS
FLYRODDERS
FLYSCREENS
FLYSPECKED
FLYSPECKING
FLYSTRIKES
FLYSWATTER
FLYSWATTERS
FLYWEIGHTS
FOAMFLOWER
FOAMFLOWERS
FOAMINESSES
FOCALISATION
FOCALISATIONS
FOCALISING
FOCALIZATION
FOCALIZATIONS
FOCALIZING
FOCIMETERS
FOCOMETERS
FODDERINGS
FOEDERATUS
FOETATIONS
FOETICIDAL
FOETICIDES
FOETIDNESS
FOETIDNESSES
FOETIPAROUS
FOETOSCOPIES
FOETOSCOPY
FOGGINESSES
FOGRAMITES
FOGRAMITIES
FOILSWOMAN
FOILSWOMEN
FOISONLESS
FOLIACEOUS
FOLIATIONS
FOLIATURES
FOLKINESSES
FOLKISHNESS
FOLKISHNESSES
FOLKLORISH
FOLKLORIST
FOLKLORISTIC
FOLKLORISTS
FOLKSINESS
FOLKSINESSES
FOLKSINGER
FOLKSINGERS
FOLKSINGING
FOLKSINGINGS
FOLKSONOMIES
FOLKSONOMY
FOLKTRONICA
FOLKTRONICAS
FOLLICULAR
FOLLICULATE
FOLLICULATED
FOLLICULIN
FOLLICULINS
FOLLICULITIS
FOLLICULITISES
FOLLICULOSE
FOLLICULOUS
FOLLOWABLE
FOLLOWERSHIP
FOLLOWERSHIPS
FOLLOWINGS
FOLLOWSHIP
FOLLOWSHIPS
FOMENTATION
FOMENTATIONS
FONCTIONNAIRE
FONCTIONNAIRES
FONDLINGLY
FONDNESSES
FONTANELLE
FONTANELLES
FONTICULUS
FONTINALIS
FONTINALISES
FOODLESSNESS
FOODLESSNESSES
FOODSTUFFS
FOOLBEGGED
FOOLFISHES
FOOLHARDIER
FOOLHARDIEST
FOOLHARDILY
FOOLHARDINESS
FOOLHARDINESSES
FOOLHARDISE
FOOLHARDISES
FOOLHARDIZE
FOOLHARDIZES
FOOLISHEST
FOOLISHNESS
FOOLISHNESSES
FOOTBALLENE
FOOTBALLENES
FOOTBALLER
FOOTBALLERS
FOOTBALLING
FOOTBALLIST
FOOTBALLISTS
FOOTBOARDS
FOOTBRAKES
FOOTBREADTH
FOOTBREADTHS
FOOTBRIDGE
FOOTBRIDGES
FOOTCLOTHS
FOOTDRAGGER
FOOTDRAGGERS
FOOTDRAGGING
FOOTDRAGGINGS
FOOTFAULTED
FOOTFAULTING
FOOTFAULTS
FOOTGUARDS
FOOTLAMBERT
FOOTLAMBERTS
FOOTLESSLY
FOOTLESSNESS
FOOTLESSNESSES
FOOTLIGHTS
FOOTLOCKER
FOOTLOCKERS
FOOTNOTING
FOOTPLATEMAN
FOOTPLATEMEN
FOOTPLATES
FOOTPLATEWOMAN
FOOTPLATEWOMEN
FOOTPRINTS
FOOTSLOGGED
FOOTSLOGGER

FOOTSLOGGERS
FOOTSLOGGING
FOOTSLOGGINGS
FOOTSORENESS
FOOTSORENESSES
FOOTSTALKS
FOOTSTALLS
FOOTSTOCKS
FOOTSTONES
FOOTSTOOLED
FOOTSTOOLS
FOOTWEARIER
FOOTWEARIEST
FOPPISHNESS
FOPPISHNESSES
FORAMINATED
FORAMINIFER
FORAMINIFERA
FORAMINIFERAL
FORAMINIFERAN
FORAMINIFERANS
FORAMINIFEROUS
FORAMINIFERS
FORAMINOUS
FORBEARANCE
FORBEARANCES
FORBEARANT
FORBEARERS
FORBEARING
FORBEARINGLY
FORBIDDALS
FORBIDDANCE
FORBIDDANCES
FORBIDDENLY
FORBIDDERS
FORBIDDING
FORBIDDINGLY
FORBIDDINGNESS
FORBIDDINGS
FORCEDNESS
FORCEDNESSES
FORCEFULLY
FORCEFULNESS
FORCEFULNESSES
FORCEMEATS
FORCEPSLIKE
FORCIBILITIES
FORCIBILITY
FORCIBLENESS
FORCIBLENESSES
FORCIPATED
FORCIPATION
FORCIPATIONS
FOREARMING
FOREBITTER
FOREBITTERS
FOREBODEMENT
FOREBODEMENTS
FOREBODERS
FOREBODIES
FOREBODING
FOREBODINGLY
FOREBODINGNESS
FOREBODINGS
FOREBRAINS
FORECABINS
FORECADDIE
FORECADDIES
FORECARRIAGE
FORECARRIAGES
FORECASTABLE
FORECASTED
FORECASTER
FORECASTERS
FORECASTING
FORECASTINGS
FORECASTLE
FORECASTLES
FORECHECKED
FORECHECKER
FORECHECKERS
FORECHECKING
FORECHECKS
FORECHOSEN
FORECLOSABLE
FORECLOSED
FORECLOSES
FORECLOSING
FORECLOSURE
FORECLOSURES
FORECLOTHS
FORECOURSE
FORECOURSES
FORECOURTS
FOREDAMNED
FOREDATING
FOREDOOMED
FOREDOOMING
FOREFATHER
FOREFATHERLY
FOREFATHERS
FOREFEELING
FOREFEELINGLY
FOREFENDED
FOREFENDING
FOREFINGER
FOREFINGERS
FOREFRONTS
FOREGATHER
FOREGATHERED
FOREGATHERING
FOREGATHERS
FOREGLEAMS
FOREGOINGS
FOREGONENESS
FOREGONENESSES
FOREGROUND
FOREGROUNDED
FOREGROUNDING
FOREGROUNDS
FOREHANDED
FOREHANDEDLY
FOREHANDEDNESS
FOREHANDING
FOREHENTING
FOREHOOVES
FOREIGNERS
FOREIGNISM
FOREIGNISMS
FOREIGNNESS
FOREIGNNESSES
FOREJUDGED
FOREJUDGEMENT
FOREJUDGEMENTS
FOREJUDGES
FOREJUDGING
FOREJUDGMENT
FOREJUDGMENTS
FOREKNOWABLE
FOREKNOWING
FOREKNOWINGLY
FOREKNOWLEDGE
FOREKNOWLEDGES
FORELADIES
FORELAYING
FORELENDING
FORELIFTED
FORELIFTING
FORELOCKED
FORELOCKING
FOREMANSHIP
FOREMANSHIPS
FOREMASTMAN
FOREMASTMEN
FOREMEANING
FOREMENTIONED
FOREMOTHER
FOREMOTHERS
FORENIGHTS
FORENSICALITIES
FORENSICALITY
FORENSICALLY
FOREORDAIN
FOREORDAINED
FOREORDAINING
FOREORDAINMENT
FOREORDAINMENTS
FOREORDAINS
FOREORDINATION
FOREORDINATIONS
FOREPASSED
FOREPAYMENT
FOREPAYMENTS
FOREPLANNED
FOREPLANNING
FOREPOINTED
FOREPOINTING
FOREPOINTS
FOREQUARTER
FOREQUARTERS
FOREREACHED
FOREREACHES
FOREREACHING
FOREREADING
FOREREADINGS
FORERUNNER
FORERUNNERS
FORERUNNING
FORESAYING
FORESEEABILITY
FORESEEABLE
FORESEEING
FORESEEINGLY
FORESHADOW
FORESHADOWED
FORESHADOWER
FORESHADOWERS
FORESHADOWING
FORESHADOWINGS
FORESHADOWS
FORESHANKS
FORESHEETS
FORESHEWED
FORESHEWING
FORESHOCKS
FORESHORES
FORESHORTEN
FORESHORTENED
FORESHORTENING
FORESHORTENINGS
FORESHORTENS
FORESHOWED
FORESHOWING
FORESIGHTED
FORESIGHTEDLY
FORESIGHTEDNESS
FORESIGHTFUL
FORESIGHTLESS
FORESIGHTS
FORESIGNIFIED
FORESIGNIFIES
FORESIGNIFY
FORESIGNIFYING
FORESKIRTS
FORESLACKED
FORESLACKING
FORESLACKS
FORESLOWED
FORESLOWING
FORESPEAKING
FORESPEAKS
FORESPENDING
FORESPENDS
FORESPOKEN
FORESTAGES
FORESTAIRS
FORESTALLED
FORESTALLER
FORESTALLERS
FORESTALLING

FORESTALLINGS
FORESTALLMENT
FORESTALLMENTS
FORESTALLS
FORESTALMENT
FORESTALMENTS
FORESTATION
FORESTATIONS
FORESTAYSAIL
FORESTAYSAILS
FORESTLAND
FORESTLANDS
FORESTLESS
FORESTRIES
FORESWEARING
FORESWEARS
FORETASTED
FORETASTES
FORETASTING
FORETAUGHT
FORETEACHES
FORETEACHING
FORETELLER
FORETELLERS
FORETELLING
FORETHINKER
FORETHINKERS
FORETHINKING
FORETHINKS
FORETHOUGHT
FORETHOUGHTFUL
FORETHOUGHTS
FORETOKENED
FORETOKENING
FORETOKENINGS
FORETOKENS
FORETOPMAN
FORETOPMAST
FORETOPMASTS
FORETOPMEN
FORETRIANGLE
FORETRIANGLES
FOREVERMORE
FOREVERNESS
FOREVERNESSES
FOREVOUCHED
FOREWARDED
FOREWARDING
FOREWARNED
FOREWARNER
FOREWARNERS
FOREWARNING
FOREWARNINGLY
FOREWARNINGS
FOREWEIGHED
FOREWEIGHING
FOREWEIGHS
FORFAIRING
FORFAITERS
FORFAITING
FORFAITINGS
FORFEITABLE
FORFEITERS
FORFEITING
FORFEITURE
FORFEITURES
FORFENDING
FORFEUCHEN
FORFICULATE
FORFOUGHEN
FORFOUGHTEN
FORGATHERED
FORGATHERING
FORGATHERS
FORGEABILITIES
FORGEABILITY
FORGETFULLY
FORGETFULNESS
FORGETFULNESSES
FORGETTABLE
FORGETTERIES
FORGETTERS
FORGETTERY
FORGETTING
FORGETTINGLY
FORGETTINGS
FORGIVABLE
FORGIVABLY
FORGIVENESS
FORGIVENESSES
FORGIVINGLY
FORGIVINGNESS
FORGIVINGNESSES
FORGOTTENNESS
FORGOTTENNESSES
FORHAILING
FORHENTING
FORHOOIEING
FORINSECAL
FORISFAMILIATE
FORISFAMILIATED
FORISFAMILIATES
FORJUDGING
FORJUDGMENT
FORJUDGMENTS
FORKEDNESS
FORKEDNESSES
FORKINESSES
FORKLIFTED
FORKLIFTING
FORLENDING
FORLORNEST
FORLORNNESS
FORLORNNESSES
FORMABILITIES
FORMABILITY
FORMALDEHYDE
FORMALDEHYDES
FORMALINES
FORMALISABLE
FORMALISATION
FORMALISATIONS
FORMALISED
FORMALISER
FORMALISERS
FORMALISES
FORMALISING
FORMALISMS
FORMALISTIC
FORMALISTICALLY
FORMALISTS
FORMALITER
FORMALITIES
FORMALIZABLE
FORMALIZATION
FORMALIZATIONS
FORMALIZED
FORMALIZER
FORMALIZERS
FORMALIZES
FORMALIZING
FORMALNESS
FORMALNESSES
FORMAMIDES
FORMATIONAL
FORMATIONS
FORMATIVELY
FORMATIVENESS
FORMATIVENESSES
FORMATIVES
FORMATTERS
FORMATTING
FORMATTINGS
FORMFITTING
FORMICARIA
FORMICARIES
FORMICARIUM
FORMICATED
FORMICATES
FORMICATING
FORMICATION
FORMICATIONS
FORMIDABILITIES
FORMIDABILITY
FORMIDABLE
FORMIDABLENESS
FORMIDABLY
FORMLESSLY
FORMLESSNESS
FORMLESSNESSES
FORMULAICALLY
FORMULARIES
FORMULARISATION
FORMULARISE
FORMULARISED
FORMULARISER
FORMULARISERS
FORMULARISES
FORMULARISING
FORMULARISTIC
FORMULARIZATION
FORMULARIZE
FORMULARIZED
FORMULARIZER
FORMULARIZERS
FORMULARIZES
FORMULARIZING
FORMULATED
FORMULATES
FORMULATING
FORMULATION
FORMULATIONS
FORMULATOR
FORMULATORS
FORMULISED
FORMULISES
FORMULISING
FORMULISMS
FORMULISTIC
FORMULISTS
FORMULIZED
FORMULIZES
FORMULIZING
FORNICATED
FORNICATES
FORNICATING
FORNICATION
FORNICATIONS
FORNICATOR
FORNICATORS
FORNICATRESS
FORNICATRESSES
FORSAKENLY
FORSAKENNESS
FORSAKENNESSES
FORSAKINGS
FORSLACKED
FORSLACKING
FORSLOEING
FORSLOWING
FORSPEAKING
FORSPENDING
FORSTERITE
FORSTERITES
FORSWEARER
FORSWEARERS
FORSWEARING
FORSWINKED
FORSWINKING
FORSWORNNESS
FORSWORNNESSES
FORSYTHIAS
FORTALICES
FORTEPIANIST
FORTEPIANISTS
FORTEPIANO
FORTEPIANOS
FORTHCOMES
FORTHCOMING
FORTHCOMINGNESS

FORTHGOING
FORTHGOINGS
FORTHINKING
FORTHOUGHT
FORTHRIGHT
FORTHRIGHTLY
FORTHRIGHTNESS
FORTHRIGHTS
FORTIFIABLE
FORTIFICATION
FORTIFICATIONS
FORTIFIERS
FORTIFYING
FORTIFYINGLY
FORTILAGES
FORTISSIMI
FORTISSIMO
FORTISSIMOS
FORTISSISSIMO
FORTITUDES
FORTITUDINOUS
FORTNIGHTLIES
FORTNIGHTLY
FORTNIGHTS
FORTRESSED
FORTRESSES
FORTRESSING
FORTRESSLIKE
FORTUITIES
FORTUITISM
FORTUITISMS
FORTUITIST
FORTUITISTS
FORTUITOUS
FORTUITOUSLY
FORTUITOUSNESS
FORTUNATELY
FORTUNATENESS
FORTUNATENESSES
FORTUNATES
FORTUNELESS
FORTUNISED
FORTUNISES
FORTUNISING
FORTUNIZED
FORTUNIZES
FORTUNIZING
FORWANDERED
FORWANDERING
FORWANDERS
FORWARDERS
FORWARDEST
FORWARDING
FORWARDINGS
FORWARDNESS
FORWARDNESSES
FORWARNING
FORWASTING
FORWEARIED
FORWEARIES
FORWEARYING
FOSCARNETS
FOSSICKERS
FOSSICKING
FOSSICKINGS
FOSSILIFEROUS
FOSSILISABLE
FOSSILISATION
FOSSILISATIONS
FOSSILISED
FOSSILISES
FOSSILISING
FOSSILIZABLE
FOSSILIZATION
FOSSILIZATIONS
FOSSILIZED
FOSSILIZES
FOSSILIZING
FOSTERAGES
FOSTERINGS
FOSTERLING
FOSTERLINGS
FOSTRESSES
FOTHERGILLA
FOTHERGILLAS
FOUDROYANT
FOUGHTIEST
FOULBROODS
FOULDERING
FOULMOUTHED
FOULNESSES
FOUNDATION
FOUNDATIONAL
FOUNDATIONALLY
FOUNDATIONARY
FOUNDATIONER
FOUNDATIONERS
FOUNDATIONLESS
FOUNDATIONS
FOUNDERING
FOUNDEROUS
FOUNDLINGS
FOUNDRESSES
FOUNTAINED
FOUNTAINHEAD
FOUNTAINHEADS
FOUNTAINING
FOUNTAINLESS
FOURCHETTE
FOURCHETTES
FOURDRINIER
FOURDRINIERS
FOURFOLDNESS
FOURFOLDNESSES
FOURPENCES
FOURPENNIES
FOURPLEXES
FOURRAGERE
FOURRAGERES
FOURSCORTH
FOURSQUARE
FOURSQUARELY
FOURSQUARENESS
FOURTEENER
FOURTEENERS
FOURTEENTH
FOURTEENTHLY
FOURTEENTHS
FOVEOLATED
FOXBERRIES
FOXHUNTERS
FOXHUNTING
FOXHUNTINGS
FOXINESSES
FOXTROTTED
FOXTROTTING
FOZINESSES
FRABJOUSLY
FRACTALITIES
FRACTALITY
FRACTIONAL
FRACTIONALISE
FRACTIONALISED
FRACTIONALISES
FRACTIONALISING
FRACTIONALISM
FRACTIONALISMS
FRACTIONALIST
FRACTIONALISTS
FRACTIONALIZE
FRACTIONALIZED
FRACTIONALIZES
FRACTIONALIZING
FRACTIONALLY
FRACTIONARY
FRACTIONATE
FRACTIONATED
FRACTIONATES
FRACTIONATING
FRACTIONATION
FRACTIONATIONS
FRACTIONATOR
FRACTIONATORS
FRACTIONED
FRACTIONING
FRACTIONISATION
FRACTIONISE
FRACTIONISED
FRACTIONISES
FRACTIONISING
FRACTIONIZATION
FRACTIONIZE
FRACTIONIZED
FRACTIONIZES
FRACTIONIZING
FRACTIONLET
FRACTIONLETS
FRACTIOUSLY
FRACTIOUSNESS
FRACTIOUSNESSES
FRACTOCUMULI
FRACTOCUMULUS
FRACTOGRAPHIES
FRACTOGRAPHY
FRACTOSTRATI
FRACTOSTRATUS
FRACTURABLE
FRACTURERS
FRACTURING
FRAGILENESS
FRAGILENESSES
FRAGILITIES
FRAGMENTAL
FRAGMENTALLY
FRAGMENTARILY
FRAGMENTARINESS
FRAGMENTARY
FRAGMENTATE
FRAGMENTATED
FRAGMENTATES
FRAGMENTATING
FRAGMENTATION
FRAGMENTATIONS
FRAGMENTED
FRAGMENTING
FRAGMENTISE
FRAGMENTISED
FRAGMENTISES
FRAGMENTISING
FRAGMENTIZE
FRAGMENTIZED
FRAGMENTIZES
FRAGMENTIZING
FRAGRANCED
FRAGRANCES
FRAGRANCIES
FRAGRANCING
FRAGRANTLY
FRAGRANTNESS
FRAGRANTNESSES
FRAICHEURS
FRAILNESSES
FRAMBESIAS
FRAMBOESIA
FRAMBOESIAS
FRAMBOISES
FRAMESHIFT
FRAMESHIFTS
FRAMEWORKS
FRANCHISED
FRANCHISEE
FRANCHISEES
FRANCHISEMENT
FRANCHISEMENTS
FRANCHISER
FRANCHISERS
FRANCHISES
FRANCHISING
FRANCHISOR
FRANCHISORS

FRANCISATION
FRANCISATIONS
FRANCISING
FRANCIZATION
FRANCIZATIONS
FRANCIZING
FRANCOLINS
FRANCOMANIA
FRANCOMANIAS
FRANCOPHIL
FRANCOPHILE
FRANCOPHILES
FRANCOPHILS
FRANCOPHOBE
FRANCOPHOBES
FRANCOPHOBIA
FRANCOPHOBIAS
FRANCOPHONE
FRANCOPHONES
FRANGIBILITIES
FRANGIBILITY
FRANGIBLENESS
FRANGIBLENESSES
FRANGIPANE
FRANGIPANES
FRANGIPANI
FRANGIPANIS
FRANGIPANNI
FRANKALMOIGN
FRANKALMOIGNS
FRANKFORTS
FRANKFURTER
FRANKFURTERS
FRANKFURTS
FRANKINCENSE
FRANKINCENSES
FRANKLINITE
FRANKLINITES
FRANKNESSES
FRANKPLEDGE
FRANKPLEDGES
FRANSERIAS
FRANTICALLY
FRANTICNESS
FRANTICNESSES
FRATCHETIER
FRATCHETIEST
FRATCHIEST
FRATERNALISM
FRATERNALISMS
FRATERNALLY
FRATERNISATION
FRATERNISATIONS
FRATERNISE
FRATERNISED
FRATERNISER
FRATERNISERS
FRATERNISES
FRATERNISING
FRATERNITIES
FRATERNITY
FRATERNIZATION
FRATERNIZATIONS
FRATERNIZE
FRATERNIZED
FRATERNIZER
FRATERNIZERS
FRATERNIZES
FRATERNIZING
FRATRICIDAL
FRATRICIDE
FRATRICIDES
FRAUDFULLY
FRAUDSTERS
FRAUDULENCE
FRAUDULENCES
FRAUDULENCIES
FRAUDULENCY
FRAUDULENT
FRAUDULENTLY
FRAUDULENTNESS
FRAUGHTAGE
FRAUGHTAGES
FRAUGHTEST
FRAUGHTING
FRAXINELLA
FRAXINELLAS
FREAKERIES
FREAKINESS
FREAKINESSES
FREAKISHLY
FREAKISHNESS
FREAKISHNESSES
FRECKLIEST
FRECKLINGS
FREEBASERS
FREEBASING
FREEBOARDS
FREEBOOTED
FREEBOOTER
FREEBOOTERIES
FREEBOOTERS
FREEBOOTERY
FREEBOOTIES
FREEBOOTING
FREEBOOTINGS
FREECOOLING
FREECOOLINGS
FREECYCLED
FREECYCLES
FREECYCLING
FREEDIVERS
FREEDIVING
FREEDIVINGS
FREEDWOMAN
FREEDWOMEN
FREEGANISM
FREEGANISMS
FREEHANDED
FREEHANDEDLY
FREEHANDEDNESS
FREEHEARTED
FREEHEARTEDLY
FREEHOLDER
FREEHOLDERS
FREELANCED
FREELANCER
FREELANCERS
FREELANCES
FREELANCING
FREELOADED
FREELOADER
FREELOADERS
FREELOADING
FREELOADINGS
FREEMARTIN
FREEMARTINS
FREEMASONIC
FREEMASONRIES
FREEMASONRY
FREEMASONS
FREENESSES
FREEPHONES
FREESHEETS
FREESTANDING
FREESTONES
FREESTYLED
FREESTYLER
FREESTYLERS
FREESTYLES
FREESTYLING
FREESTYLINGS
FREETHINKER
FREETHINKERS
FREETHINKING
FREETHINKINGS
FREEWHEELED
FREEWHEELER
FREEWHEELERS
FREEWHEELING
FREEWHEELINGLY
FREEWHEELINGS
FREEWHEELS
FREEWRITES
FREEWRITING
FREEWRITINGS
FREEWRITTEN
FREEZINGLY
FREIGHTAGE
FREIGHTAGES
FREIGHTERS
FREIGHTING
FREIGHTLESS
FREMESCENCE
FREMESCENCES
FREMESCENT
FREMITUSES
FRENCHIFICATION
FRENCHIFIED
FRENCHIFIES
FRENCHIFYING
FRENETICAL
FRENETICALLY
FRENETICISM
FRENETICISMS
FRENETICNESS
FRENETICNESSES
FRENZIEDLY
FREQUENCES
FREQUENCIES
FREQUENTABLE
FREQUENTATION
FREQUENTATIONS
FREQUENTATIVE
FREQUENTATIVES
FREQUENTED
FREQUENTER
FREQUENTERS
FREQUENTEST
FREQUENTING
FREQUENTLY
FREQUENTNESS
FREQUENTNESSES
FRESCOINGS
FRESCOISTS
FRESHENERS
FRESHENING
FRESHERDOM
FRESHERDOMS
FRESHMANSHIP
FRESHMANSHIPS
FRESHNESSES
FRESHWATER
FRESHWATERS
FRETBOARDS
FRETFULNESS
FRETFULNESSES
FRIABILITIES
FRIABILITY
FRIABLENESS
FRIABLENESSES
FRIARBIRDS
FRICANDEAU
FRICANDEAUS
FRICANDEAUX
FRICANDOES
FRICASSEED
FRICASSEEING
FRICASSEES
FRICATIVES
FRICTIONAL
FRICTIONALLY
FRICTIONLESS
FRICTIONLESSLY
FRIEDCAKES
FRIENDINGS
FRIENDLESS
FRIENDLESSNESS
FRIENDLIER
FRIENDLIES

FRIENDLIEST
FRIENDLILY
FRIENDLINESS
FRIENDLINESSES
FRIENDSHIP
FRIENDSHIPS
FRIEZELIKE
FRIGATOONS
FRIGHTENED
FRIGHTENER
FRIGHTENERS
FRIGHTENING
FRIGHTENINGLY
FRIGHTFULLY
FRIGHTFULNESS
FRIGHTFULNESSES
FRIGHTSOME
FRIGIDARIA
FRIGIDARIUM
FRIGIDITIES
FRIGIDNESS
FRIGIDNESSES
FRIGORIFIC
FRIGORIFICO
FRIGORIFICOS
FRIKKADELS
FRILLERIES
FRILLINESS
FRILLINESSES
FRINGELESS
FRINGELIKE
FRINGILLACEOUS
FRINGILLID
FRINGILLIFORM
FRINGILLINE
FRIPONNERIE
FRIPONNERIES
FRIPPERERS
FRIPPERIES
FRISKINESS
FRISKINESSES
FRISKINGLY
FRITHBORHS
FRITHSOKEN
FRITHSOKENS
FRITHSTOOL
FRITHSTOOLS
FRITILLARIA
FRITILLARIAS
FRITILLARIES
FRITILLARY
FRITTERERS
FRITTERING
FRIVOLITIES
FRIVOLLERS
FRIVOLLING
FRIVOLOUSLY
FRIVOLOUSNESS
FRIVOLOUSNESSES
FRIZZINESS
FRIZZINESSES
FRIZZLIEST
FRIZZLINESS
FRIZZLINESSES
FROGFISHES
FROGGERIES
FROGHOPPER
FROGHOPPERS
FROGMARCHED
FROGMARCHES
FROGMARCHING
FROGMOUTHS
FROGSPAWNS
FROLICKERS
FROLICKIER
FROLICKIEST
FROLICKING
FROLICSOME
FROLICSOMELY
FROLICSOMENESS
FROMENTIES
FRONDESCENCE
FRONDESCENCES
FRONDESCENT
FRONDIFEROUS
FRONTAGERS
FRONTALITIES
FRONTALITY
FRONTBENCHER
FRONTBENCHERS
FRONTCOURT
FRONTCOURTS
FRONTENISES
FRONTIERED
FRONTIERING
FRONTIERSMAN
FRONTIERSMEN
FRONTIERSWOMAN
FRONTIERSWOMEN
FRONTISPIECE
FRONTISPIECED
FRONTISPIECES
FRONTISPIECING
FRONTLESSLY
FRONTLINES
FRONTLISTS
FRONTOGENESES
FRONTOGENESIS
FRONTOGENETIC
FRONTOLYSES
FRONTOLYSIS
FRONTPAGED
FRONTPAGES
FRONTPAGING
FRONTRUNNER
FRONTRUNNERS
FRONTRUNNING
FRONTRUNNINGS
FRONTWARDS
FROSTBITES
FROSTBITING
FROSTBITINGS
FROSTBITTEN
FROSTBOUND
FROSTFISHES
FROSTINESS
FROSTINESSES
FROSTLINES
FROSTWORKS
FROTHERIES
FROTHINESS
FROTHINESSES
FROUGHIEST
FROUZINESS
FROUZINESSES
FROWARDNESS
FROWARDNESSES
FROWNINGLY
FROWSINESS
FROWSINESSES
FROWSTIEST
FROWSTINESS
FROWSTINESSES
FROWZINESS
FROWZINESSES
FROZENNESS
FROZENNESSES
FRUCTIFEROUS
FRUCTIFEROUSLY
FRUCTIFICATION
FRUCTIFICATIONS
FRUCTIFIED
FRUCTIFIER
FRUCTIFIERS
FRUCTIFIES
FRUCTIFYING
FRUCTIVOROUS
FRUCTUARIES
FRUCTUATED
FRUCTUATES
FRUCTUATING
FRUCTUATION
FRUCTUATIONS
FRUCTUOUSLY
FRUCTUOUSNESS
FRUCTUOUSNESSES
FRUGALISTA
FRUGALISTAS
FRUGALISTS
FRUGALITIES
FRUGALNESS
FRUGALNESSES
FRUGIFEROUS
FRUGIVORES
FRUGIVOROUS
FRUITARIAN
FRUITARIANISM
FRUITARIANISMS
FRUITARIANS
FRUITCAKES
FRUITERERS
FRUITERESS
FRUITERESSES
FRUITERIES
FRUITFULLER
FRUITFULLEST
FRUITFULLY
FRUITFULNESS
FRUITFULNESSES
FRUITINESS
FRUITINESSES
FRUITLESSLY
FRUITLESSNESS
FRUITLESSNESSES
FRUITWOODS
FRUITWORMS
FRUMENTACEOUS
FRUMENTARIOUS
FRUMENTATION
FRUMENTATIONS
FRUMENTIES
FRUMPINESS
FRUMPINESSES
FRUMPISHLY
FRUMPISHNESS
FRUMPISHNESSES
FRUSEMIDES
FRUSTRATED
FRUSTRATER
FRUSTRATERS
FRUSTRATES
FRUSTRATING
FRUSTRATINGLY
FRUSTRATION
FRUSTRATIONS
FRUTESCENCE
FRUTESCENCES
FRUTESCENT
FRUTIFYING
FUCIVOROUS
FUCOXANTHIN
FUCOXANTHINS
FUGACIOUSLY
FUGACIOUSNESS
FUGACIOUSNESSES
FUGACITIES
FUGGINESSES
FUGITATION
FUGITATIONS
FUGITIVELY
FUGITIVENESS
FUGITIVENESSES
FUGITOMETER
FUGITOMETERS
FULFILLERS
FULFILLING
FULFILLINGS
FULFILLMENT
FULFILLMENTS
FULFILMENT

FULFILMENTS
FULGENCIES
FULGURATED
FULGURATES
FULGURATING
FULGURATION
FULGURATIONS
FULGURITES
FULIGINOSITIES
FULIGINOSITY
FULIGINOUS
FULIGINOUSLY
FULIGINOUSNESS
FULLBLOODS
FULLERENES
FULLERIDES
FULLERITES
FULLMOUTHED
FULLNESSES
FULMINANTS
FULMINATED
FULMINATES
FULMINATING
FULMINATION
FULMINATIONS
FULMINATOR
FULMINATORS
FULMINATORY
FULMINEOUS
FULSOMENESS
FULSOMENESSES
FUMATORIES
FUMATORIUM
FUMATORIUMS
FUMBLINGLY
FUMBLINGNESS
FUMBLINGNESSES
FUMIGATING
FUMIGATION
FUMIGATIONS
FUMIGATORS
FUMIGATORY
FUMITORIES
FUMOSITIES
FUNAMBULATE
FUNAMBULATED
FUNAMBULATES
FUNAMBULATING
FUNAMBULATION
FUNAMBULATIONS
FUNAMBULATOR
FUNAMBULATORS
FUNAMBULATORY
FUNAMBULISM
FUNAMBULISMS
FUNAMBULIST
FUNAMBULISTS
FUNCTIONAL
FUNCTIONALISM
FUNCTIONALISMS
FUNCTIONALIST
FUNCTIONALISTIC
FUNCTIONALISTS
FUNCTIONALITIES
FUNCTIONALITY
FUNCTIONALLY
FUNCTIONALS
FUNCTIONARIES
FUNCTIONARY
FUNCTIONATE
FUNCTIONATED
FUNCTIONATES
FUNCTIONATING
FUNCTIONED
FUNCTIONING
FUNCTIONLESS
FUNDAMENTAL
FUNDAMENTALISM
FUNDAMENTALISMS
FUNDAMENTALIST
FUNDAMENTALISTS
FUNDAMENTALITY
FUNDAMENTALLY
FUNDAMENTALNESS
FUNDAMENTALS
FUNDAMENTS
FUNDHOLDER
FUNDHOLDERS
FUNDHOLDING
FUNDHOLDINGS
FUNDRAISED
FUNDRAISER
FUNDRAISERS
FUNDRAISES
FUNDRAISING
FUNDRAISINGS
FUNEREALLY
FUNGIBILITIES
FUNGIBILITY
FUNGICIDAL
FUNGICIDALLY
FUNGICIDES
FUNGISTATIC
FUNGISTATICALLY
FUNGISTATS
FUNGOSITIES
FUNICULARS
FUNICULATE
FUNKINESSES
FUNNELFORM
FUNNELLING
FUNNINESSES
FURACIOUSNESS
FURACIOUSNESSES
FURACITIES
FURALDEHYDE
FURALDEHYDES
FURANOSIDE
FURANOSIDES
FURAZOLIDONE
FURAZOLIDONES
FURBEARERS
FURBELOWED
FURBELOWING
FURBISHERS
FURBISHING
FURCATIONS
FURCIFEROUS
FURFURACEOUS
FURFURACEOUSLY
FURFURALDEHYDE
FURFURALDEHYDES
FURFUROLES
FURIOSITIES
FURIOUSNESS
FURIOUSNESSES
FURLOUGHED
FURLOUGHING
FURMENTIES
FURNIMENTS
FURNISHERS
FURNISHING
FURNISHINGS
FURNISHMENT
FURNISHMENTS
FURNITURES
FUROSEMIDE
FUROSEMIDES
FURRIERIES
FURRINESSES
FURROWIEST
FURROWLESS
FURSHLUGGINER
FURTHCOMING
FURTHCOMINGS
FURTHERANCE
FURTHERANCES
FURTHERERS
FURTHERING
FURTHERMORE
FURTHERMOST
FURTHERSOME
FURTIVENESS
FURTIVENESSES
FURUNCULAR
FURUNCULOSES
FURUNCULOSIS
FURUNCULOUS
FUSHIONLESS
FUSIBILITIES
FUSIBILITY
FUSIBLENESS
FUSIBLENESSES
FUSILLADED
FUSILLADES
FUSILLADING
FUSILLATION
FUSILLATIONS
FUSIONISMS
FUSIONISTS
FUSIONLESS
FUSSBUDGET
FUSSBUDGETIER
FUSSBUDGETIEST
FUSSBUDGETS
FUSSBUDGETY
FUSSINESSES
FUSTANELLA
FUSTANELLAS
FUSTANELLE
FUSTANELLES
FUSTIANISE
FUSTIANISED
FUSTIANISES
FUSTIANISING
FUSTIANIST
FUSTIANISTS
FUSTIANIZE
FUSTIANIZED
FUSTIANIZES
FUSTIANIZING
FUSTIGATED
FUSTIGATES
FUSTIGATING
FUSTIGATION
FUSTIGATIONS
FUSTIGATOR
FUSTIGATORS
FUSTIGATORY
FUSTILARIAN
FUSTILARIANS
FUSTILIRIAN
FUSTILIRIANS
FUSTILLIRIAN
FUSTILLIRIANS
FUSTINESSES
FUSULINIDS
FUTILENESS
FUTILENESSES
FUTILITARIAN
FUTILITARIANISM
FUTILITARIANS
FUTILITIES
FUTURELESS
FUTURELESSNESS
FUTURISTIC
FUTURISTICALLY
FUTURISTICS
FUTURITIES
FUTURITION
FUTURITIONS
FUTUROLOGICAL
FUTUROLOGIES
FUTUROLOGIST
FUTUROLOGISTS
FUTUROLOGY
FUZZINESSES

G

GABAPENTIN
GABAPENTINS
GABARDINES
GABBINESSES
GABBLEMENT
GABBLEMENTS
GABBROITIC
GABERDINES
GABERLUNZIE
GABERLUNZIES
GABIONADES
GABIONAGES
GABIONNADE
GABIONNADES
GADGETEERS
GADGETIEST
GADGETRIES
GADOLINITE
GADOLINITES
GADOLINIUM
GADOLINIUMS
GADROONING
GADROONINGS
GADZOOKERIES
GADZOOKERY
GAELICISED
GAELICISES
GAELICISING
GAELICISMS
GAELICIZED
GAELICIZES
GAELICIZING
GAILLARDIA
GAILLARDIAS
GAINFULNESS
GAINFULNESSES
GAINGIVING
GAINGIVINGS
GAINLESSNESS
GAINLESSNESSES
GAINLINESS
GAINLINESSES
GAINSAYERS
GAINSAYING
GAINSAYINGS
GAINSHARING
GAINSHARINGS
GAINSTRIVE
GAINSTRIVED
GAINSTRIVEN
GAINSTRIVES
GAINSTRIVING
GAINSTROVE
GAITERLESS
GALABIYAHS
GALACTAGOGUE
GALACTAGOGUES
GALACTICOS
GALACTOMETER
GALACTOMETERS
GALACTOMETRIES
GALACTOMETRY
GALACTOPHOROUS
GALACTOPOIESES
GALACTOPOIESIS
GALACTOPOIETIC
GALACTOPOIETICS
GALACTORRHEA
GALACTORRHEAS
GALACTORRHOEA
GALACTORRHOEAS
GALACTOSAEMIA
GALACTOSAEMIAS
GALACTOSAEMIC
GALACTOSAMINE
GALACTOSAMINES
GALACTOSEMIA
GALACTOSEMIAS
GALACTOSEMIC
GALACTOSES
GALACTOSIDASE
GALACTOSIDASES
GALACTOSIDE
GALACTOSIDES
GALACTOSYL
GALACTOSYLS
GALANTAMINE
GALANTAMINES
GALANTINES
GALAVANTED
GALAVANTING
GALDRAGONS
GALENGALES
GALENICALS
GALEOPITHECINE
GALEOPITHECOID
GALIMATIAS
GALIMATIASES
GALINGALES
GALIONGEES
GALIVANTED
GALIVANTING
GALLABEAHS
GALLABIAHS
GALLABIEHS
GALLABIYAH
GALLABIYAHS
GALLABIYAS
GALLABIYEH
GALLABIYEHS
GALLAMINES
GALLANTEST
GALLANTING
GALLANTNESS
GALLANTNESSES
GALLANTRIES
GALLBLADDER
GALLBLADDERS
GALLEASSES
GALLERISTS
GALLERYGOER
GALLERYGOERS
GALLERYING
GALLERYITE
GALLERYITES
GALLIAMBIC
GALLIAMBICS
GALLIARDISE
GALLIARDISES
GALLIASSES
GALLICISATION
GALLICISATIONS
GALLICISED
GALLICISES
GALLICISING
GALLICISMS
GALLICIZATION
GALLICIZATIONS
GALLICIZED
GALLICIZES
GALLICIZING
GALLIGASKINS
GALLIMAUFRIES
GALLIMAUFRY
GALLINACEAN
GALLINACEANS
GALLINACEOUS
GALLINAZOS
GALLINIPPER
GALLINIPPERS
GALLINULES
GALLISISED
GALLISISES
GALLISISING
GALLISIZED
GALLISIZES
GALLISIZING
GALLIVANTED
GALLIVANTING
GALLIVANTS
GALLIWASPS
GALLOGLASS
GALLOGLASSES
GALLONAGES
GALLOPADED
GALLOPADES
GALLOPADING
GALLOWGLASS
GALLOWGLASSES
GALLOWSNESS
GALLOWSNESSES
GALLSICKNESS
GALLSICKNESSES
GALLSTONES
GALLUMPHED
GALLUMPHING
GALLYGASKINS
GALRAVAGED
GALRAVAGES
GALRAVAGING
GALRAVITCH
GALRAVITCHED
GALRAVITCHES
GALRAVITCHING
GALUMPHERS
GALUMPHING
GALVANICAL
GALVANICALLY
GALVANISATION
GALVANISATIONS
GALVANISED
GALVANISER
GALVANISERS
GALVANISES
GALVANISING
GALVANISMS
GALVANISTS
GALVANIZATION
GALVANIZATIONS
GALVANIZED
GALVANIZER
GALVANIZERS
GALVANIZES
GALVANIZING
GALVANOMETER
GALVANOMETERS
GALVANOMETRIC
GALVANOMETRICAL
GALVANOMETRIES
GALVANOMETRY

GALVANOPLASTIC
GALVANOPLASTIES
GALVANOPLASTY
GALVANOSCOPE
GALVANOSCOPES
GALVANOSCOPIC
GALVANOSCOPIES
GALVANOSCOPY
GALVANOTROPIC
GALVANOTROPISM
GALVANOTROPISMS
GAMAHUCHED
GAMAHUCHES
GAMAHUCHING
GAMARUCHED
GAMARUCHES
GAMARUCHING
GAMBADOING
GAMBOLLING
GAMEBREAKER
GAMEBREAKERS
GAMEFISHES
GAMEKEEPER
GAMEKEEPERS
GAMEKEEPING
GAMEKEEPINGS
GAMENESSES
GAMESMANSHIP
GAMESMANSHIPS
GAMESOMELY
GAMESOMENESS
GAMESOMENESSES
GAMETANGIA
GAMETANGIAL
GAMETANGIUM
GAMETICALLY
GAMETOCYTE
GAMETOCYTES
GAMETOGENESES
GAMETOGENESIS
GAMETOGENIC
GAMETOGENIES
GAMETOGENOUS
GAMETOGENY
GAMETOPHORE
GAMETOPHORES
GAMETOPHORIC
GAMETOPHYTE
GAMETOPHYTES
GAMETOPHYTIC
GAMEYNESSES
GAMIFICATION
GAMIFICATIONS
GAMINERIES
GAMINESQUE
GAMINESSES
GAMMERSTANG
GAMMERSTANGS
GAMMOCKING
GAMMONINGS
GAMOGENESES
GAMOGENESIS
GAMOGENETIC
GAMOGENETICAL
GAMOGENETICALLY
GAMOPETALOUS
GAMOPHYLLOUS
GAMOSEPALOUS
GAMOTROPIC
GAMOTROPISM
GAMOTROPISMS
GAMYNESSES
GANDERISMS
GANGBANGED
GANGBANGER
GANGBANGERS
GANGBANGING
GANGBOARDS
GANGBUSTER
GANGBUSTERS
GANGBUSTING
GANGBUSTINGS
GANGLIATED
GANGLIFORM
GANGLIONATED
GANGLIONIC
GANGLIOSIDE
GANGLIOSIDES
GANGMASTER
GANGMASTERS
GANGPLANKS
GANGRENING
GANGRENOUS
GANGSHAGGED
GANGSHAGGING
GANGSTERDOM
GANGSTERDOMS
GANGSTERISH
GANGSTERISM
GANGSTERISMS
GANGSTERLAND
GANGSTERLANDS
GANNETRIES
GANNISTERS
GANTELOPES
GANTLETING
GAOLBREAKING
GAOLBREAKS
GAOLBROKEN
GAOLERESSES
GARAGISTES
GARBAGEMAN
GARBAGEMEN
GARBAGIEST
GARBOLOGIES
GARBOLOGIST
GARBOLOGISTS
GARBURATOR
GARBURATORS
GARDENFULS
GARDENINGS
GARDENLESS
GARDEROBES
GARGANTUAN
GARGANTUAS
GARGARISED
GARGARISES
GARGARISING
GARGARISMS
GARGARIZED
GARGARIZES
GARGARIZING
GARGOYLISM
GARGOYLISMS
GARIBALDIS
GARISHNESS
GARISHNESSES
GARLANDAGE
GARLANDAGES
GARLANDING
GARLANDLESS
GARLANDRIES
GARLICKIER
GARLICKIEST
GARLICKING
GARMENTING
GARMENTLESS
GARMENTURE
GARMENTURES
GARNETIFEROUS
GARNIERITE
GARNIERITES
GARNISHEED
GARNISHEEING
GARNISHEEMENT
GARNISHEEMENTS
GARNISHEES
GARNISHERS
GARNISHING
GARNISHINGS
GARNISHMENT
GARNISHMENTS
GARNISHORS
GARNISHRIES
GARNITURES
GAROTTINGS
GARRETEERS
GARRISONED
GARRISONING
GARROTTERS
GARROTTING
GARROTTINGS
GARRULITIES
GARRULOUSLY
GARRULOUSNESS
GARRULOUSNESSES
GARRYOWENS
GASBAGGING
GASCONADED
GASCONADER
GASCONADERS
GASCONADES
GASCONADING
GASCONISMS
GASEOUSNESS
GASEOUSNESSES
GASHLINESS
GASHLINESSES
GASHOLDERS
GASIFIABLE
GASIFICATION
GASIFICATIONS
GASLIGHTED
GASLIGHTING
GASOMETERS
GASOMETRIC
GASOMETRICAL
GASOMETRIES
GASPEREAUS
GASPEREAUX
GASPINESSES
GASSINESSES
GASTEROPOD
GASTEROPODOUS
GASTEROPODS
GASTHAUSER
GASTHAUSES
GASTIGHTNESS
GASTIGHTNESSES
GASTNESSES
GASTRAEUMS
GASTRALGIA
GASTRALGIAS
GASTRALGIC
GASTRECTOMIES
GASTRECTOMY
GASTRITIDES
GASTRITISES
GASTROCNEMII
GASTROCNEMIUS
GASTROCOLIC
GASTRODUODENAL
GASTROENTERIC
GASTROENTERITIC
GASTROENTERITIS
GASTROLITH
GASTROLITHS
GASTROLOGER
GASTROLOGERS
GASTROLOGICAL
GASTROLOGIES
GASTROLOGIST
GASTROLOGISTS
GASTROLOGY
GASTROMANCIES
GASTROMANCY
GASTRONOME
GASTRONOMER
GASTRONOMERS
GASTRONOMES

G

G

GASTRONOMIC
GASTRONOMICAL
GASTRONOMICALLY
GASTRONOMICS
GASTRONOMIES
GASTRONOMIST
GASTRONOMISTS
GASTRONOMY
GASTROPODAN
GASTROPODANS
GASTROPODOUS
GASTROPODS
GASTROPORN
GASTROPORNS
GASTROPUBS
GASTROSCOPE
GASTROSCOPES
GASTROSCOPIC
GASTROSCOPIES
GASTROSCOPIST
GASTROSCOPISTS
GASTROSCOPY
GASTROSOPH
GASTROSOPHER
GASTROSOPHERS
GASTROSOPHIES
GASTROSOPHS
GASTROSOPHY
GASTROSTOMIES
GASTROSTOMY
GASTROTOMIES
GASTROTOMY
GASTROTRICH
GASTROTRICHS
GASTROVASCULAR
GASTRULATE
GASTRULATED
GASTRULATES
GASTRULATING
GASTRULATION
GASTRULATIONS
GATECRASHED
GATECRASHER
GATECRASHERS
GATECRASHES
GATECRASHING
GATEHOUSES
GATEKEEPER
GATEKEEPERS
GATEKEEPING
GATEKEEPINGS
GATHERABLE
GATHERINGS
GAUCHENESS
GAUCHENESSES
GAUCHERIES
GAUDEAMUSES
GAUDINESSES
GAUFFERING
GAUFFERINGS
GAULEITERS
GAULTHERIA
GAULTHERIAS
GAUNTLETED
GAUNTLETING
GAUNTNESSES
GAUSSMETER
GAUSSMETERS
GAUZINESSES
GAVELKINDS
GAWKIHOODS
GAWKINESSES
GAWKISHNESS
GAWKISHNESSES
GAYCATIONS
GAZEHOUNDS
GAZETTEERED
GAZETTEERING
GAZETTEERISH
GAZETTEERS
GAZILLIONAIRE
GAZILLIONAIRES
GAZILLIONS
GAZUMPINGS
GAZUNDERED
GAZUNDERER
GAZUNDERERS
GAZUNDERING
GEALOUSIES
GEANTICLINAL
GEANTICLINE
GEANTICLINES
GEARCHANGE
GEARCHANGES
GEARSHIFTS
GEARSTICKS
GEARWHEELS
GEEKINESSES
GEEKSPEAKS
GEFUFFLING
GEGENSCHEIN
GEGENSCHEINS
GEHLENITES
GEITONOGAMIES
GEITONOGAMOUS
GEITONOGAMY
GELANDESPRUNG
GELANDESPRUNGS
GELATINATE
GELATINATED
GELATINATES
GELATINATING
GELATINATION
GELATINATIONS
GELATINISATION
GELATINISATIONS
GELATINISE
GELATINISED
GELATINISER
GELATINISERS
GELATINISES
GELATINISING
GELATINIZATION
GELATINIZATIONS
GELATINIZE
GELATINIZED
GELATINIZER
GELATINIZERS
GELATINIZES
GELATINIZING
GELATINOID
GELATINOIDS
GELATINOUS
GELATINOUSLY
GELATINOUSNESS
GELIDITIES
GELIDNESSES
GELIGNITES
GELLIFLOWRE
GELLIFLOWRES
GELSEMINES
GELSEMININE
GELSEMININES
GELSEMIUMS
GEMEINSCHAFT
GEMEINSCHAFTEN
GEMEINSCHAFTS
GEMFIBROZIL
GEMFIBROZILS
GEMINATELY
GEMINATING
GEMINATION
GEMINATIONS
GEMMACEOUS
GEMMATIONS
GEMMIFEROUS
GEMMINESSES
GEMMIPAROUS
GEMMIPAROUSLY
GEMMOLOGICAL
GEMMOLOGIES
GEMMOLOGIST
GEMMOLOGISTS
GEMMULATION
GEMMULATIONS
GEMOLOGICAL
GEMOLOGIES
GEMOLOGIST
GEMOLOGISTS
GEMUTLICHKEIT
GEMUTLICHKEITS
GENDARMERIE
GENDARMERIES
GENDARMERY
GENDERISED
GENDERISES
GENDERISING
GENDERIZED
GENDERIZES
GENDERIZING
GENDERLESS
GENDERQUEER
GENDERQUEERS
GENEALOGIC
GENEALOGICAL
GENEALOGICALLY
GENEALOGIES
GENEALOGISE
GENEALOGISED
GENEALOGISES
GENEALOGISING
GENEALOGIST
GENEALOGISTS
GENEALOGIZE
GENEALOGIZED
GENEALOGIZES
GENEALOGIZING
GENECOLOGIES
GENECOLOGY
GENERALATE
GENERALATES
GENERALCIES
GENERALISABLE
GENERALISATION
GENERALISATIONS
GENERALISE
GENERALISED
GENERALISER
GENERALISERS
GENERALISES
GENERALISING
GENERALISM
GENERALISMS
GENERALISSIMO
GENERALISSIMOS
GENERALIST
GENERALISTS
GENERALITIES
GENERALITY
GENERALIZABLE
GENERALIZATION
GENERALIZATIONS
GENERALIZE
GENERALIZED
GENERALIZER
GENERALIZERS
GENERALIZES
GENERALIZING
GENERALLED
GENERALLING
GENERALNESS
GENERALNESSES
GENERALSHIP
GENERALSHIPS
GENERATING
GENERATION
GENERATIONAL
GENERATIONALLY
GENERATIONISM
GENERATIONISMS

GENERATIONS
GENERATIVE
GENERATORS
GENERATRICES
GENERATRIX
GENERICALLY
GENERICNESS
GENERICNESSES
GENEROSITIES
GENEROSITY
GENEROUSLY
GENEROUSNESS
GENEROUSNESSES
GENETHLIAC
GENETHLIACAL
GENETHLIACALLY
GENETHLIACON
GENETHLIACONS
GENETHLIACS
GENETHLIALOGIC
GENETHLIALOGIES
GENETHLIALOGY
GENETICALLY
GENETICIST
GENETICISTS
GENETOTROPHIC
GENETRICES
GENETRIXES
GENEVRETTE
GENEVRETTES
GENIALISED
GENIALISES
GENIALISING
GENIALITIES
GENIALIZED
GENIALIZES
GENIALIZING
GENIALNESS
GENIALNESSES
GENICULATE
GENICULATED
GENICULATELY
GENICULATES
GENICULATING
GENICULATION
GENICULATIONS
GENISTEINS
GENITALIAL
GENITIVALLY
GENITIVELY
GENITOURINARY
GENITRICES
GENITRIXES
GENLOCKING
GENLOCKINGS
GENOCIDAIRE
GENOCIDAIRES
GENOPHOBIA
GENOPHOBIAS
GENOTYPICAL
GENOTYPICALLY
GENOTYPICITIES
GENOTYPICITY
GENOTYPING
GENOUILLERE
GENOUILLERES
GENSDARMES
GENTAMICIN
GENTAMICINS
GENTEELEST
GENTEELISE
GENTEELISED
GENTEELISES
GENTEELISH
GENTEELISING
GENTEELISM
GENTEELISMS
GENTEELIZE
GENTEELIZED
GENTEELIZES
GENTEELIZING
GENTEELNESS
GENTEELNESSES
GENTIANACEOUS
GENTIANELLA
GENTIANELLAS
GENTILESSE
GENTILESSES
GENTILHOMME
GENTILISED
GENTILISES
GENTILISING
GENTILISMS
GENTILITIAL
GENTILITIAN
GENTILITIES
GENTILITIOUS
GENTILIZED
GENTILIZES
GENTILIZING
GENTILSHOMMES
GENTLEFOLK
GENTLEFOLKS
GENTLEHOOD
GENTLEHOODS
GENTLEMANHOOD
GENTLEMANHOODS
GENTLEMANLIER
GENTLEMANLIEST
GENTLEMANLIKE
GENTLEMANLINESS
GENTLEMANLY
GENTLEMANSHIP
GENTLEMANSHIPS
GENTLENESS
GENTLENESSE
GENTLENESSES
GENTLEPERSON
GENTLEPERSONS
GENTLEWOMAN
GENTLEWOMANLIER
GENTLEWOMANLY
GENTLEWOMEN
GENTRIFICATION
GENTRIFICATIONS
GENTRIFIED
GENTRIFIER
GENTRIFIERS
GENTRIFIES
GENTRIFYING
GENUFLECTED
GENUFLECTING
GENUFLECTION
GENUFLECTIONS
GENUFLECTOR
GENUFLECTORS
GENUFLECTS
GENUFLEXION
GENUFLEXIONS
GENUINENESS
GENUINENESSES
GEOBOTANIC
GEOBOTANICAL
GEOBOTANIES
GEOBOTANIST
GEOBOTANISTS
GEOCACHERS
GEOCACHING
GEOCACHINGS
GEOCARPIES
GEOCENTRIC
GEOCENTRICAL
GEOCENTRICALLY
GEOCENTRICISM
GEOCENTRICISMS
GEOCHEMICAL
GEOCHEMICALLY
GEOCHEMIST
GEOCHEMISTRIES
GEOCHEMISTRY
GEOCHEMISTS
GEOCHRONOLOGIC
GEOCHRONOLOGIES
GEOCHRONOLOGIST
GEOCHRONOLOGY
GEOCORONAE
GEOCORONAS
GEODEMOGRAPHICS
GEODESICAL
GEODESISTS
GEODETICAL
GEODETICALLY
GEODYNAMIC
GEODYNAMICAL
GEODYNAMICIST
GEODYNAMICISTS
GEODYNAMICS
GEOENGINEERING
GEOENGINEERINGS
GEOGNOSIES
GEOGNOSTIC
GEOGNOSTICAL
GEOGNOSTICALLY
GEOGRAPHER
GEOGRAPHERS
GEOGRAPHIC
GEOGRAPHICAL
GEOGRAPHICALLY
GEOGRAPHIES
GEOHYDROLOGIC
GEOHYDROLOGIES
GEOHYDROLOGIST
GEOHYDROLOGISTS
GEOHYDROLOGY
GEOLATRIES
GEOLINGUISTICS
GEOLOCATION
GEOLOCATIONS
GEOLOGIANS
GEOLOGICAL
GEOLOGICALLY
GEOLOGISED
GEOLOGISES
GEOLOGISING
GEOLOGISTS
GEOLOGIZED
GEOLOGIZES
GEOLOGIZING
GEOMAGNETIC
GEOMAGNETICALLY
GEOMAGNETISM
GEOMAGNETISMS
GEOMAGNETIST
GEOMAGNETISTS
GEOMANCERS
GEOMANCIES
GEOMECHANICS
GEOMEDICAL
GEOMEDICINE
GEOMEDICINES
GEOMETRICAL
GEOMETRICALLY
GEOMETRICIAN
GEOMETRICIANS
GEOMETRICS
GEOMETRIDS
GEOMETRIES
GEOMETRISATION
GEOMETRISATIONS
GEOMETRISE
GEOMETRISED
GEOMETRISES
GEOMETRISING
GEOMETRIST
GEOMETRISTS
GEOMETRIZATION
GEOMETRIZATIONS
GEOMETRIZE
GEOMETRIZED
GEOMETRIZES

GEOMETRIZING
GEOMORPHIC
GEOMORPHOGENIC
GEOMORPHOGENIES
GEOMORPHOGENIST
GEOMORPHOGENY
GEOMORPHOLOGIC
GEOMORPHOLOGIES
GEOMORPHOLOGIST
GEOMORPHOLOGY
GEOPHAGIAS
GEOPHAGIES
GEOPHAGISM
GEOPHAGISMS
GEOPHAGIST
GEOPHAGISTS
GEOPHAGOUS
GEOPHILOUS
GEOPHYSICAL
GEOPHYSICALLY
GEOPHYSICIST
GEOPHYSICISTS
GEOPHYSICS
GEOPOLITICAL
GEOPOLITICALLY
GEOPOLITICIAN
GEOPOLITICIANS
GEOPOLITICS
GEOPONICAL
GEOPRESSURED
GEORGETTES
GEOSCIENCE
GEOSCIENCES
GEOSCIENTIFIC
GEOSCIENTIST
GEOSCIENTISTS
GEOSPATIAL
GEOSPHERES
GEOSTATICS
GEOSTATIONARY
GEOSTRATEGIC
GEOSTRATEGICAL
GEOSTRATEGIES
GEOSTRATEGIST
GEOSTRATEGISTS
GEOSTRATEGY
GEOSTROPHIC
GEOSTROPHICALLY
GEOSYNCHRONOUS
GEOSYNCLINAL
GEOSYNCLINE
GEOSYNCLINES
GEOTACTICAL
GEOTACTICALLY
GEOTAGGING
GEOTECHNIC
GEOTECHNICAL
GEOTECHNICS
GEOTECHNOLOGIES
GEOTECHNOLOGY
GEOTECTONIC
GEOTECTONICALLY
GEOTECTONICS
GEOTEXTILE
GEOTEXTILES
GEOTHERMAL
GEOTHERMALLY
GEOTHERMIC
GEOTHERMOMETER
GEOTHERMOMETERS
GEOTROPICALLY
GEOTROPISM
GEOTROPISMS
GERANIACEOUS
GERATOLOGICAL
GERATOLOGIES
GERATOLOGIST
GERATOLOGISTS
GERATOLOGY
GERFALCONS
GERIATRICIAN
GERIATRICIANS
GERIATRICS
GERIATRIST
GERIATRISTS
GERMANDERS
GERMANENESS
GERMANENESSES
GERMANISATION
GERMANISATIONS
GERMANISED
GERMANISES
GERMANISING
GERMANITES
GERMANIUMS
GERMANIZATION
GERMANIZATIONS
GERMANIZED
GERMANIZES
GERMANIZING
GERMICIDAL
GERMICIDES
GERMINABILITIES
GERMINABILITY
GERMINABLE
GERMINALLY
GERMINATED
GERMINATES
GERMINATING
GERMINATION
GERMINATIONS
GERMINATIVE
GERMINATOR
GERMINATORS
GERMINESSES
GERMPLASMS
GERONTOCRACIES
GERONTOCRACY
GERONTOCRAT
GERONTOCRATIC
GERONTOCRATS
GERONTOLOGIC
GERONTOLOGICAL
GERONTOLOGIES
GERONTOLOGIST
GERONTOLOGISTS
GERONTOLOGY
GERONTOMORPHIC
GERONTOPHIL
GERONTOPHILE
GERONTOPHILES
GERONTOPHILIA
GERONTOPHILIAS
GERONTOPHILS
GERONTOPHOBE
GERONTOPHOBES
GERONTOPHOBIA
GERONTOPHOBIAS
GERRYMANDER
GERRYMANDERED
GERRYMANDERER
GERRYMANDERERS
GERRYMANDERING
GERRYMANDERINGS
GERRYMANDERS
GERUNDIVAL
GERUNDIVELY
GERUNDIVES
GESELLSCHAFT
GESELLSCHAFTEN
GESELLSCHAFTS
GESNERIADS
GESSAMINES
GESTALTISM
GESTALTISMS
GESTALTIST
GESTALTISTS
GESTATIONAL
GESTATIONS
GESTATORIAL
GESTICULANT
GESTICULATE
GESTICULATED
GESTICULATES
GESTICULATING
GESTICULATION
GESTICULATIONS
GESTICULATIVE
GESTICULATOR
GESTICULATORS
GESTICULATORY
GESTURALLY
GESUNDHEIT
GETTERINGS
GEWURZTRAMINER
GEWURZTRAMINERS
GEYSERITES
GHASTFULLY
GHASTLIEST
GHASTLINESS
GHASTLINESSES
GHASTNESSES
GHETTOISATION
GHETTOISATIONS
GHETTOISED
GHETTOISES
GHETTOISING
GHETTOIZATION
GHETTOIZATIONS
GHETTOIZED
GHETTOIZES
GHETTOIZING
GHOSTLIEST
GHOSTLINESS
GHOSTLINESSES
GHOSTWRITE
GHOSTWRITER
GHOSTWRITERS
GHOSTWRITES
GHOSTWRITING
GHOSTWRITTEN
GHOSTWROTE
GHOULISHLY
GHOULISHNESS
GHOULISHNESSES
GIANTESSES
GIANTHOODS
GIANTLIEST
GIANTSHIPS
GIARDIASES
GIARDIASIS
GIBBERELLIC
GIBBERELLIN
GIBBERELLINS
GIBBERINGS
GIBBERISHES
GIBBETTING
GIBBOSITIES
GIBBOUSNESS
GIBBOUSNESSES
GIDDINESSES
GIFTEDNESS
GIFTEDNESSES
GIFTWRAPPED
GIFTWRAPPING
GIFTWRAPPINGS
GIGACYCLES
GIGAHERTZES
GIGANTESQUE
GIGANTICALLY
GIGANTICIDE
GIGANTICIDES
GIGANTICNESS
GIGANTICNESSES
GIGANTISMS
GIGANTOLOGIES
GIGANTOLOGY
GIGANTOMACHIA
GIGANTOMACHIAS
GIGANTOMACHIES

G

GIGANTOMACHY
GIGGLESOME
GIGGLINGLY
GIGMANITIES
GILDSWOMAN
GILDSWOMEN
GILLFLIRTS
GILLIFLOWER
GILLIFLOWERS
GILLNETTED
GILLNETTER
GILLNETTERS
GILLNETTING
GILLRAVAGE
GILLRAVAGED
GILLRAVAGES
GILLRAVAGING
GILLRAVITCH
GILLRAVITCHED
GILLRAVITCHES
GILLRAVITCHING
GILLYFLOWER
GILLYFLOWERS
GILRAVAGED
GILRAVAGER
GILRAVAGERS
GILRAVAGES
GILRAVAGING
GILRAVITCH
GILRAVITCHED
GILRAVITCHES
GILRAVITCHING
GILSONITES
GIMBALLING
GIMCRACKERIES
GIMCRACKERY
GIMMICKIER
GIMMICKIEST
GIMMICKING
GIMMICKRIES
GINGELLIES
GINGERADES
GINGERBREAD
GINGERBREADED
GINGERBREADIER
GINGERBREADIEST
GINGERBREADS
GINGERBREADY
GINGERIEST
GINGERLIER
GINGERLIEST
GINGERLINESS
GINGERLINESSES
GINGERROOT
GINGERROOTS
GINGERSNAP
GINGERSNAPS
GINGIVECTOMIES
GINGIVECTOMY
GINGIVITIS
GINGIVITISES
GINGLIMOID
GIPSYHOODS
GIPSYWORTS
GIRANDOLAS
GIRANDOLES
GIRDLECAKE
GIRDLECAKES
GIRDLESCONE
GIRDLESCONES
GIRDLESTEAD
GIRDLESTEADS
GIRLFRIEND
GIRLFRIENDS
GIRLISHNESS
GIRLISHNESSES
GIRTHLINES
GISMOLOGIES
GITTARONES
GITTERNING
GIVENNESSES
GIZMOLOGIES
GLABRESCENT
GLABROUSNESS
GLABROUSNESSES
GLACIALIST
GLACIALISTS
GLACIATING
GLACIATION
GLACIATIONS
GLACIOLOGIC
GLACIOLOGICAL
GLACIOLOGIES
GLACIOLOGIST
GLACIOLOGISTS
GLACIOLOGY
GLADDENERS
GLADDENING
GLADFULNESS
GLADFULNESSES
GLADIATORIAL
GLADIATORIAN
GLADIATORS
GLADIATORSHIP
GLADIATORSHIPS
GLADIATORY
GLADIOLUSES
GLADNESSES
GLADSOMELY
GLADSOMENESS
GLADSOMENESSES
GLADSOMEST
GLADSTONES
GLADWRAPPED
GLADWRAPPING
GLAIKETNESS
GLAIKETNESSES
GLAIKITNESS
GLAIKITNESSES
GLAIRINESS
GLAIRINESSES
GLAMORISATION
GLAMORISATIONS
GLAMORISED
GLAMORISER
GLAMORISERS
GLAMORISES
GLAMORISING
GLAMORIZATION
GLAMORIZATIONS
GLAMORIZED
GLAMORIZER
GLAMORIZERS
GLAMORIZES
GLAMORIZING
GLAMOROUSLY
GLAMOROUSNESS
GLAMOROUSNESSES
GLAMOURING
GLAMOURISE
GLAMOURISED
GLAMOURISES
GLAMOURISING
GLAMOURIZE
GLAMOURIZED
GLAMOURIZES
GLAMOURIZING
GLAMOURLESS
GLAMOUROUS
GLAMOUROUSLY
GLAMOUROUSNESS
GLAMOURPUSS
GLAMOURPUSSES
GLANCINGLY
GLANDEROUS
GLANDIFEROUS
GLANDIFORM
GLANDULARLY
GLANDULIFEROUS
GLANDULOUS
GLANDULOUSLY
GLARINESSES
GLARINGNESS
GLARINGNESSES
GLASNOSTIAN
GLASNOSTIC
GLASSBLOWER
GLASSBLOWERS
GLASSBLOWING
GLASSBLOWINGS
GLASSCLOTH
GLASSCLOTHS
GLASSCUTTER
GLASSCUTTERS
GLASSHOUSE
GLASSHOUSES
GLASSIFIED
GLASSIFIES
GLASSIFYING
GLASSINESS
GLASSINESSES
GLASSMAKER
GLASSMAKERS
GLASSMAKING
GLASSMAKINGS
GLASSPAPER
GLASSPAPERED
GLASSPAPERING
GLASSPAPERS
GLASSWARES
GLASSWORKER
GLASSWORKERS
GLASSWORKS
GLASSWORMS
GLASSWORTS
GLASSYHEADED
GLAUBERITE
GLAUBERITES
GLAUCESCENCE
GLAUCESCENCES
GLAUCESCENT
GLAUCOMATOUS
GLAUCONITE
GLAUCONITES
GLAUCONITIC
GLAUCOUSLY
GLAUCOUSNESS
GLAUCOUSNESSES
GLAZIERIES
GLAZINESSES
GLEAMINGLY
GLEEFULNESS
GLEEFULNESSES
GLEEMAIDEN
GLEEMAIDENS
GLEGNESSES
GLEISATION
GLEISATIONS
GLEIZATION
GLEIZATIONS
GLENDOVEER
GLENDOVEERS
GLENGARRIES
GLIBNESSES
GLIDEPATHS
GLIMMERIER
GLIMMERIEST
GLIMMERING
GLIMMERINGLY
GLIMMERINGS
GLIOBLASTOMA
GLIOBLASTOMAS
GLIOBLASTOMATA
GLIOMATOSES
GLIOMATOSIS
GLIOMATOUS
GLISSADERS
GLISSADING
GLISSANDOS
GLISTENING

G

GLISTENINGLY
GLISTERING
GLISTERINGLY
GLITCHIEST
GLITTERAND
GLITTERATI
GLITTERIER
GLITTERIEST
GLITTERING
GLITTERINGLY
GLITTERINGS
GLITZINESS
GLITZINESSES
GLOATINGLY
GLOBALISATION
GLOBALISATIONS
GLOBALISED
GLOBALISES
GLOBALISING
GLOBALISMS
GLOBALISTS
GLOBALIZATION
GLOBALIZATIONS
GLOBALIZED
GLOBALIZES
GLOBALIZING
GLOBEFISHES
GLOBEFLOWER
GLOBEFLOWERS
GLOBESITIES
GLOBETROTS
GLOBETROTTED
GLOBETROTTER
GLOBETROTTERS
GLOBETROTTING
GLOBETROTTINGS
GLOBIGERINA
GLOBIGERINAE
GLOBIGERINAS
GLOBOSENESS
GLOBOSENESSES
GLOBOSITIES
GLOBULARITIES
GLOBULARITY
GLOBULARLY
GLOBULARNESS
GLOBULARNESSES
GLOBULIFEROUS
GLOBULITES
GLOCHIDIATE
GLOCHIDIUM
GLOCKENSPIEL
GLOCKENSPIELS
GLOMERATED
GLOMERATES
GLOMERATING
GLOMERATION
GLOMERATIONS
GLOMERULAR
GLOMERULATE
GLOMERULES
GLOMERULUS
GLOOMFULLY
GLOOMINESS
GLOOMINESSES
GLOOMSTERS
GLORIFIABLE
GLORIFICATION
GLORIFICATIONS
GLORIFIERS
GLORIFYING
GLORIOUSLY
GLORIOUSNESS
GLORIOUSNESSES
GLOSSARIAL
GLOSSARIALLY
GLOSSARIES
GLOSSARIST
GLOSSARISTS
GLOSSATORS
GLOSSECTOMIES
GLOSSECTOMY
GLOSSEMATICS
GLOSSINESS
GLOSSINESSES
GLOSSINGLY
GLOSSITISES
GLOSSODYNIA
GLOSSODYNIAS
GLOSSOGRAPHER
GLOSSOGRAPHERS
GLOSSOGRAPHICAL
GLOSSOGRAPHIES
GLOSSOGRAPHY
GLOSSOLALIA
GLOSSOLALIAS
GLOSSOLALIST
GLOSSOLALISTS
GLOSSOLARYNGEAL
GLOSSOLOGICAL
GLOSSOLOGIES
GLOSSOLOGIST
GLOSSOLOGISTS
GLOSSOLOGY
GLOTTIDEAN
GLOTTOGONIC
GLOTTOLOGIES
GLOTTOLOGY
GLOVEBOXES
GLOWERINGLY
GLOWSTICKS
GLUCINIUMS
GLUCOCORTICOID
GLUCOCORTICOIDS
GLUCOKINASE
GLUCOKINASES
GLUCONATES
GLUCONEOGENESES
GLUCONEOGENESIS
GLUCONEOGENIC
GLUCOPHORE
GLUCOPHORES
GLUCOPROTEIN
GLUCOPROTEINS
GLUCOSAMINE
GLUCOSAMINES
GLUCOSIDAL
GLUCOSIDASE
GLUCOSIDASES
GLUCOSIDES
GLUCOSIDIC
GLUCOSURIA
GLUCOSURIAS
GLUCOSURIC
GLUCURONIC
GLUCURONIDASE
GLUCURONIDASES
GLUCURONIDE
GLUCURONIDES
GLUEYNESSES
GLUINESSES
GLUMACEOUS
GLUMIFEROUS
GLUMNESSES
GLUTAMATES
GLUTAMINASE
GLUTAMINASES
GLUTAMINES
GLUTAMINIC
GLUTARALDEHYDE
GLUTARALDEHYDES
GLUTATHIONE
GLUTATHIONES
GLUTETHIMIDE
GLUTETHIMIDES
GLUTINOSITIES
GLUTINOSITY
GLUTINOUSLY
GLUTINOUSNESS
GLUTINOUSNESSES
GLUTTINGLY
GLUTTONIES
GLUTTONISE
GLUTTONISED
GLUTTONISES
GLUTTONISH
GLUTTONISING
GLUTTONIZE
GLUTTONIZED
GLUTTONIZES
GLUTTONIZING
GLUTTONOUS
GLUTTONOUSLY
GLUTTONOUSNESS
GLYCAEMIAS
GLYCATIONS
GLYCERALDEHYDE
GLYCERALDEHYDES
GLYCERIDES
GLYCERIDIC
GLYCERINATE
GLYCERINATED
GLYCERINATES
GLYCERINATING
GLYCERINES
GLYCOCOLLS
GLYCOGENESES
GLYCOGENESIS
GLYCOGENETIC
GLYCOGENIC
GLYCOGENOLYSES
GLYCOGENOLYSIS
GLYCOGENOLYTIC
GLYCOLIPID
GLYCOLIPIDS
GLYCOLYSES
GLYCOLYSIS
GLYCOLYTIC
GLYCONEOGENESES
GLYCONEOGENESIS
GLYCOPEPTIDE
GLYCOPEPTIDES
GLYCOPHYTE
GLYCOPHYTES
GLYCOPHYTIC
GLYCOPROTEIN
GLYCOPROTEINS
GLYCOSIDASE
GLYCOSIDASES
GLYCOSIDES
GLYCOSIDIC
GLYCOSIDICALLY
GLYCOSURIA
GLYCOSURIAS
GLYCOSURIC
GLYCOSYLATE
GLYCOSYLATED
GLYCOSYLATES
GLYCOSYLATING
GLYCOSYLATION
GLYCOSYLATIONS
GLYOXALINE
GLYOXALINES
GLYPHOGRAPH
GLYPHOGRAPHER
GLYPHOGRAPHERS
GLYPHOGRAPHIC
GLYPHOGRAPHICAL
GLYPHOGRAPHIES
GLYPHOGRAPHS
GLYPHOGRAPHY
GLYPHOSATE
GLYPHOSATES
GLYPTODONT
GLYPTODONTS
GLYPTOGRAPHER
GLYPTOGRAPHERS
GLYPTOGRAPHIC
GLYPTOGRAPHICAL
GLYPTOGRAPHIES

GLYPTOGRAPHY
GLYPTOTHECA
GLYPTOTHECAE
GMELINITES
GNAPHALIUM
GNAPHALIUMS
GNASHINGLY
GNATCATCHER
GNATCATCHERS
GNATHONICAL
GNATHONICALLY
GNATHOSTOMATOUS
GNATHOSTOME
GNATHOSTOMES
GNEISSITIC
GNETOPHYTE
GNETOPHYTES
GNOMICALLY
GNOMONICAL
GNOMONICALLY
GNOMONOLOGIES
GNOMONOLOGY
GNOSEOLOGIES
GNOSEOLOGY
GNOSIOLOGIES
GNOSIOLOGY
GNOSTICALLY
GNOSTICISM
GNOSTICISMS
GNOTOBIOLOGICAL
GNOTOBIOLOGIES
GNOTOBIOLOGY
GNOTOBIOSES
GNOTOBIOSIS
GNOTOBIOTE
GNOTOBIOTES
GNOTOBIOTIC
GNOTOBIOTICALLY
GNOTOBIOTICS
GOALKEEPER
GOALKEEPERS
GOALKEEPING
GOALKEEPINGS
GOALKICKER
GOALKICKERS
GOALKICKING
GOALKICKINGS
GOALMOUTHS
GOALSCORER
GOALSCORERS
GOALTENDER
GOALTENDERS
GOALTENDING
GOALTENDINGS
GOATFISHES
GOATISHNESS
GOATISHNESSES
GOATSBEARD
GOATSBEARDS
GOATSUCKER
GOATSUCKERS
GOBBELINES
GOBBLEDEGOOK
GOBBLEDEGOOKS
GOBBLEDYGOOK
GOBBLEDYGOOKS
GOBSMACKED
GOBSTOPPER
GOBSTOPPERS
GOCHUJANGS
GODAMNDEST
GODCHILDREN
GODDAMMING
GODDAMNDEST
GODDAMNEDEST
GODDAMNING
GODDAUGHTER
GODDAUGHTERS
GODDESSHOOD
GODDESSHOODS
GODFATHERED
GODFATHERING
GODFATHERS
GODFORSAKEN
GODLESSNESS
GODLESSNESSES
GODLIKENESS
GODLIKENESSES
GODLINESSES
GODMOTHERED
GODMOTHERING
GODMOTHERS
GODPARENTS
GODROONING
GODROONINGS
GOFFERINGS
GOGGLEBOXES
GOITROGENIC
GOITROGENICITY
GOITROGENS
GOLDARNING
GOLDBEATER
GOLDBEATERS
GOLDBRICKED
GOLDBRICKING
GOLDBRICKS
GOLDCRESTS
GOLDENBERRIES
GOLDENBERRY
GOLDENEYES
GOLDENNESS
GOLDENNESSES
GOLDENRODS
GOLDENSEAL
GOLDENSEALS
GOLDFIELDS
GOLDFINCHES
GOLDFINNIES
GOLDFISHES
GOLDILOCKS
GOLDILOCKSES
GOLDMINERS
GOLDSINNIES
GOLDSMITHERIES
GOLDSMITHERY
GOLDSMITHRIES
GOLDSMITHRY
GOLDSMITHS
GOLDSPINKS
GOLDSTICKS
GOLDSTONES
GOLDTHREAD
GOLDTHREADS
GOLIARDERIES
GOLIARDERY
GOLIARDIES
GOLIATHISE
GOLIATHISED
GOLIATHISES
GOLIATHISING
GOLIATHIZE
GOLIATHIZED
GOLIATHIZES
GOLIATHIZING
GOLLIWOGGS
GOLOMYNKAS
GOLOPTIOUS
GOLUPTIOUS
GOMBEENISM
GOMBEENISMS
GONADECTOMIES
GONADECTOMISED
GONADECTOMIZED
GONADECTOMY
GONADOTROPHIC
GONADOTROPHIN
GONADOTROPHINS
GONADOTROPIC
GONADOTROPIN
GONADOTROPINS
GONDOLIERS
GONENESSES
GONFALONIER
GONFALONIERS
GONGORISTIC
GONIATITES
GONIATITOID
GONIATITOIDS
GONIMOBLAST
GONIMOBLASTS
GONIOMETER
GONIOMETERS
GONIOMETRIC
GONIOMETRICAL
GONIOMETRICALLY
GONIOMETRIES
GONIOMETRY
GONIOSCOPE
GONIOSCOPES
GONOCOCCAL
GONOCOCCIC
GONOCOCCOID
GONOCOCCUS
GONOPHORES
GONOPHORIC
GONOPHOROUS
GONORRHEAL
GONORRHEAS
GONORRHEIC
GONORRHOEA
GONORRHOEAL
GONORRHOEAS
GONORRHOEIC
GOODFELLAS
GOODFELLOW
GOODFELLOWS
GOODFELLOWSHIP
GOODFELLOWSHIPS
GOODINESSES
GOODLIHEAD
GOODLIHEADS
GOODLINESS
GOODLINESSES
GOODLYHEAD
GOODLYHEADS
GOODNESSES
GOODNIGHTS
GOODWILLED
GOOEYNESSES
GOOFINESSES
GOOGLEWHACK
GOOGLEWHACKS
GOOGOLPLEX
GOOGOLPLEXES
GOOINESSES
GOONEYBIRD
GOONEYBIRDS
GOOPINESSES
GOOSANDERS
GOOSEBERRIES
GOOSEBERRY
GOOSEFISHES
GOOSEFLESH
GOOSEFLESHES
GOOSEFOOTS
GOOSEGRASS
GOOSEGRASSES
GOOSEHERDS
GOOSENECKED
GOOSENECKS
GOOSINESSES
GOPHERWOOD
GOPHERWOODS
GORBELLIES
GORBLIMEYS
GORBLIMIES
GOREHOUNDS
GORGEOUSLY
GORGEOUSNESS
GORGEOUSNESSES

GORGONEION
GORGONIANS
GORGONISED
GORGONISES
GORGONISING
GORGONIZED
GORGONIZES
GORGONIZING
GORILLAGRAM
GORILLAGRAMS
GORINESSES
GORMANDISE
GORMANDISED
GORMANDISER
GORMANDISERS
GORMANDISES
GORMANDISING
GORMANDISINGS
GORMANDISM
GORMANDISMS
GORMANDIZE
GORMANDIZED
GORMANDIZER
GORMANDIZERS
GORMANDIZES
GORMANDIZING
GORMANDIZINGS
GOSLARITES
GOSPELISED
GOSPELISES
GOSPELISING
GOSPELIZED
GOSPELIZES
GOSPELIZING
GOSPELLERS
GOSPELLIER
GOSPELLIEST
GOSPELLING
GOSPELLINGS
GOSPELLISE
GOSPELLISED
GOSPELLISES
GOSPELLISING
GOSPELLIZE
GOSPELLIZED
GOSPELLIZES
GOSPELLIZING
GOSSAMERIER
GOSSAMERIEST
GOSSIPIEST
GOSSIPINGLY
GOSSIPINGS
GOSSIPMONGER
GOSSIPMONGERS
GOSSIPPERS
GOSSIPPING
GOSSIPRIES
GOTHICALLY
GOTHICISED
GOTHICISES
GOTHICISING
GOTHICISMS
GOTHICIZED
GOTHICIZES
GOTHICIZING
GOURDINESS
GOURDINESSES
GOURMANDISE
GOURMANDISED
GOURMANDISES
GOURMANDISING
GOURMANDISM
GOURMANDISMS
GOURMANDIZE
GOURMANDIZED
GOURMANDIZES
GOURMANDIZING
GOUTINESSES
GOUVERNANTE
GOUVERNANTES
GOVERNABILITIES
GOVERNABILITY
GOVERNABLE
GOVERNABLENESS
GOVERNALLS
GOVERNANCE
GOVERNANCES
GOVERNANTE
GOVERNANTES
GOVERNESSED
GOVERNESSES
GOVERNESSIER
GOVERNESSIEST
GOVERNESSING
GOVERNESSY
GOVERNMENT
GOVERNMENTAL
GOVERNMENTALISE
GOVERNMENTALISM
GOVERNMENTALIST
GOVERNMENTALIZE
GOVERNMENTALLY
GOVERNMENTESE
GOVERNMENTESES
GOVERNMENTS
GOVERNORATE
GOVERNORATES
GOVERNORSHIP
GOVERNORSHIPS
GOWDSPINKS
GOWPENFULS
GRACEFULLER
GRACEFULLEST
GRACEFULLY
GRACEFULNESS
GRACEFULNESSES
GRACELESSLY
GRACELESSNESS
GRACELESSNESSES
GRACILENESS
GRACILENESSES
GRACILITIES
GRACIOSITIES
GRACIOSITY
GRACIOUSLY
GRACIOUSNESS
GRACIOUSNESSES
GRADABILITIES
GRADABILITY
GRADABLENESS
GRADABLENESSES
GRADATIONAL
GRADATIONALLY
GRADATIONED
GRADATIONS
GRADATORIES
GRADDANING
GRADELIEST
GRADIENTER
GRADIENTERS
GRADIOMETER
GRADIOMETERS
GRADUALISM
GRADUALISMS
GRADUALIST
GRADUALISTIC
GRADUALISTS
GRADUALITIES
GRADUALITY
GRADUALNESS
GRADUALNESSES
GRADUATESHIP
GRADUATESHIPS
GRADUATING
GRADUATION
GRADUATIONS
GRADUATORS
GRAECISING
GRAECIZING
GRAFFITIED
GRAFFITIING
GRAFFITING
GRAFFITIST
GRAFFITISTS
GRAINFIELD
GRAINFIELDS
GRAININESS
GRAININESSES
GRALLATORIAL
GRALLOCHED
GRALLOCHING
GRAMERCIES
GRAMICIDIN
GRAMICIDINS
GRAMINACEOUS
GRAMINEOUS
GRAMINICOLOUS
GRAMINIVOROUS
GRAMINOLOGIES
GRAMINOLOGY
GRAMMALOGUE
GRAMMALOGUES
GRAMMARIAN
GRAMMARIANS
GRAMMARLESS
GRAMMATICAL
GRAMMATICALITY
GRAMMATICALLY
GRAMMATICALNESS
GRAMMATICASTER
GRAMMATICASTERS
GRAMMATICISE
GRAMMATICISED
GRAMMATICISES
GRAMMATICISING
GRAMMATICISM
GRAMMATICISMS
GRAMMATICIZE
GRAMMATICIZED
GRAMMATICIZES
GRAMMATICIZING
GRAMMATIST
GRAMMATISTS
GRAMMATOLOGIES
GRAMMATOLOGIST
GRAMMATOLOGISTS
GRAMMATOLOGY
GRAMOPHONE
GRAMOPHONES
GRAMOPHONIC
GRAMOPHONICALLY
GRAMOPHONIES
GRAMOPHONIST
GRAMOPHONISTS
GRAMOPHONY
GRANADILLA
GRANADILLAS
GRANDADDIES
GRANDAUNTS
GRANDBABIES
GRANDCHILD
GRANDCHILDREN
GRANDDADDIES
GRANDDADDY
GRANDDAUGHTER
GRANDDAUGHTERS
GRANDEESHIP
GRANDEESHIPS
GRANDFATHER
GRANDFATHERED
GRANDFATHERING
GRANDFATHERLIER
GRANDFATHERLY
GRANDFATHERS
GRANDIFLORA
GRANDIFLORAS
GRANDILOQUENCE
GRANDILOQUENCES
GRANDILOQUENT
GRANDILOQUENTLY

GRANDILOQUOUS
GRANDIOSELY
GRANDIOSENESS
GRANDIOSENESSES
GRANDIOSITIES
GRANDIOSITY
GRANDMAMAS
GRANDMAMMA
GRANDMAMMAS
GRANDMASTER
GRANDMASTERS
GRANDMOTHER
GRANDMOTHERLIER
GRANDMOTHERLY
GRANDMOTHERS
GRANDNEPHEW
GRANDNEPHEWS
GRANDNESSES
GRANDNIECE
GRANDNIECES
GRANDPAPAS
GRANDPARENT
GRANDPARENTAL
GRANDPARENTHOOD
GRANDPARENTS
GRANDSIRES
GRANDSTAND
GRANDSTANDED
GRANDSTANDER
GRANDSTANDERS
GRANDSTANDING
GRANDSTANDINGS
GRANDSTANDS
GRANDSTOOD
GRANDUNCLE
GRANDUNCLES
GRANGERISATION
GRANGERISATIONS
GRANGERISE
GRANGERISED
GRANGERISER
GRANGERISERS
GRANGERISES
GRANGERISING
GRANGERISM
GRANGERISMS
GRANGERIZATION
GRANGERIZATIONS
GRANGERIZE
GRANGERIZED
GRANGERIZER
GRANGERIZERS
GRANGERIZES
GRANGERIZING
GRANITELIKE
GRANITEWARE
GRANITEWARES
GRANITIFICATION
GRANITIFORM
GRANITISATION
GRANITISATIONS
GRANITISED
GRANITISES
GRANITISING
GRANITITES
GRANITIZATION
GRANITIZATIONS
GRANITIZED
GRANITIZES
GRANITIZING
GRANITOIDS
GRANIVORES
GRANIVOROUS
GRANNIEING
GRANODIORITE
GRANODIORITES
GRANODIORITIC
GRANOLITHIC
GRANOLITHICS
GRANOLITHS
GRANOPHYRE
GRANOPHYRES
GRANOPHYRIC
GRANTSMANSHIP
GRANTSMANSHIPS
GRANULARITIES
GRANULARITY
GRANULARLY
GRANULATED
GRANULATER
GRANULATERS
GRANULATES
GRANULATING
GRANULATION
GRANULATIONS
GRANULATIVE
GRANULATOR
GRANULATORS
GRANULIFEROUS
GRANULIFORM
GRANULITES
GRANULITIC
GRANULITISATION
GRANULITIZATION
GRANULOCYTE
GRANULOCYTES
GRANULOCYTIC
GRANULOMAS
GRANULOMATA
GRANULOMATOUS
GRANULOSES
GRANULOSIS
GRAPEFRUIT
GRAPEFRUITS
GRAPELOUSE
GRAPESEEDS
GRAPESHOTS
GRAPESTONE
GRAPESTONES
GRAPETREES
GRAPEVINES
GRAPHEMICALLY
GRAPHEMICS
GRAPHICACIES
GRAPHICACY
GRAPHICALLY
GRAPHICALNESS
GRAPHICALNESSES
GRAPHICNESS
GRAPHICNESSES
GRAPHITISABLE
GRAPHITISATION
GRAPHITISATIONS
GRAPHITISE
GRAPHITISED
GRAPHITISES
GRAPHITISING
GRAPHITIZABLE
GRAPHITIZATION
GRAPHITIZATIONS
GRAPHITIZE
GRAPHITIZED
GRAPHITIZES
GRAPHITIZING
GRAPHITOID
GRAPHOLECT
GRAPHOLECTS
GRAPHOLOGIC
GRAPHOLOGICAL
GRAPHOLOGIES
GRAPHOLOGIST
GRAPHOLOGISTS
GRAPHOLOGY
GRAPHOMANIA
GRAPHOMANIAS
GRAPHOMOTOR
GRAPHOPHOBIA
GRAPHOPHOBIAS
GRAPINESSES
GRAPLEMENT
GRAPLEMENTS
GRAPPLINGS
GRAPTOLITE
GRAPTOLITES
GRAPTOLITIC
GRASPINGLY
GRASPINGNESS
GRASPINGNESSES
GRASSBIRDS
GRASSFINCH
GRASSFINCHES
GRASSHOOKS
GRASSHOPPER
GRASSHOPPERS
GRASSINESS
GRASSINESSES
GRASSLANDS
GRASSPLOTS
GRASSQUITS
GRASSROOTS
GRASSWRACK
GRASSWRACKS
GRATEFULLER
GRATEFULLEST
GRATEFULLY
GRATEFULNESS
GRATEFULNESSES
GRATICULATION
GRATICULATIONS
GRATICULES
GRATIFICATION
GRATIFICATIONS
GRATIFIERS
GRATIFYING
GRATIFYINGLY
GRATILLITIES
GRATILLITY
GRATINATED
GRATINATES
GRATINATING
GRATINEEING
GRATITUDES
GRATUITIES
GRATUITOUS
GRATUITOUSLY
GRATUITOUSNESS
GRATULATED
GRATULATES
GRATULATING
GRATULATION
GRATULATIONS
GRATULATORY
GRAUNCHERS
GRAUNCHING
GRAVADLAXES
GRAVEDIGGER
GRAVEDIGGERS
GRAVELLIER
GRAVELLIEST
GRAVELLING
GRAVENESSES
GRAVEOLENT
GRAVEROBBER
GRAVEROBBERS
GRAVESIDES
GRAVESITES
GRAVESTONE
GRAVESTONES
GRAVEYARDS
GRAVIDITIES
GRAVIDNESS
GRAVIDNESSES
GRAVIMETER
GRAVIMETERS
GRAVIMETRIC
GRAVIMETRICAL
GRAVIMETRICALLY
GRAVIMETRIES
GRAVIMETRY
GRAVIPERCEPTION

GRAVITASES
GRAVITATED
GRAVITATER
GRAVITATERS
GRAVITATES
GRAVITATING
GRAVITATION
GRAVITATIONAL
GRAVITATIONALLY
GRAVITATIONS
GRAVITATIVE
GRAVITINOS
GRAVITOMETER
GRAVITOMETERS
GRAYBEARDED
GRAYBEARDS
GRAYFISHES
GRAYHEADED
GRAYHOUNDS
GRAYLISTED
GRAYLISTING
GRAYNESSES
GRAYSTONES
GRAYWACKES
GRAYWATERS
GRAYWETHER
GRAYWETHERS
GREASEBALL
GREASEBALLS
GREASEBAND
GREASEBANDS
GREASEBUSH
GREASEBUSHES
GREASELESS
GREASEPAINT
GREASEPAINTS
GREASEPROOF
GREASEPROOFS
GREASEWOOD
GREASEWOODS
GREASINESS
GREASINESSES
GREATCOATED
GREATCOATS
GREATENING
GREATHEARTED
GREATHEARTEDLY
GREATNESSES
GRECIANISE
GRECIANISED
GRECIANISES
GRECIANISING
GRECIANIZE
GRECIANIZED
GRECIANIZES
GRECIANIZING
GREEDHEADS
GREEDINESS
GREEDINESSES
GREENBACKER
GREENBACKERS
GREENBACKISM
GREENBACKISMS
GREENBACKS
GREENBELTS
GREENBONES
GREENBOTTLE
GREENBOTTLES
GREENBRIER
GREENBRIERS
GREENCLOTH
GREENCLOTHS
GREENERIES
GREENFIELD
GREENFIELDS
GREENFINCH
GREENFINCHES
GREENFLIES
GREENGAGES
GREENGROCER
GREENGROCERIES
GREENGROCERS
GREENGROCERY
GREENHANDS
GREENHEADS
GREENHEART
GREENHEARTS
GREENHORNS
GREENHOUSE
GREENHOUSES
GREENISHNESS
GREENISHNESSES
GREENKEEPER
GREENKEEPERS
GREENLIGHT
GREENLIGHTED
GREENLIGHTING
GREENLIGHTS
GREENLINGS
GREENMAILED
GREENMAILER
GREENMAILERS
GREENMAILING
GREENMAILS
GREENNESSES
GREENOCKITE
GREENOCKITES
GREENROOMS
GREENSANDS
GREENSHANK
GREENSHANKS
GREENSICKNESS
GREENSICKNESSES
GREENSKEEPER
GREENSKEEPERS
GREENSOMES
GREENSPEAK
GREENSPEAKS
GREENSTICK
GREENSTONE
GREENSTONES
GREENSTUFF
GREENSTUFFS
GREENSWARD
GREENSWARDS
GREENWASHED
GREENWASHES
GREENWASHING
GREENWASHINGS
GREENWEEDS
GREENWINGS
GREENWOODS
GREGARIANISM
GREGARIANISMS
GREGARINES
GREGARINIAN
GREGARIOUS
GREGARIOUSLY
GREGARIOUSNESS
GREISENISATION
GREISENISATIONS
GREISENISE
GREISENISED
GREISENISES
GREISENISING
GREISENIZATION
GREISENIZATIONS
GREISENIZE
GREISENIZED
GREISENIZES
GREISENIZING
GREMOLATAS
GRENADIERS
GRENADILLA
GRENADILLAS
GRENADINES
GRESSORIAL
GRESSORIOUS
GREVILLEAS
GREWHOUNDS
GREWSOMEST
GREYBEARDED
GREYBEARDS
GREYHEADED
GREYHOUNDS
GREYLISTED
GREYLISTING
GREYNESSES
GREYSCALES
GREYSTONES
GREYWACKES
GREYWETHER
GREYWETHERS
GRIDDLEBREAD
GRIDDLEBREADS
GRIDDLECAKE
GRIDDLECAKES
GRIDIRONED
GRIDIRONING
GRIDLOCKED
GRIDLOCKING
GRIEVANCES
GRIEVINGLY
GRIEVOUSLY
GRIEVOUSNESS
GRIEVOUSNESSES
GRIFFINISH
GRIFFINISM
GRIFFINISMS
GRILLERIES
GRILLROOMS
GRILLSTEAK
GRILLSTEAKS
GRILLWORKS
GRIMACINGLY
GRIMALKINS
GRIMINESSES
GRIMLOOKED
GRIMNESSES
GRINDELIAS
GRINDERIES
GRINDHOUSE
GRINDHOUSES
GRINDINGLY
GRINDSTONE
GRINDSTONES
GRINNINGLY
GRIPPINGLY
GRISAILLES
GRISEOFULVIN
GRISEOFULVINS
GRISLINESS
GRISLINESSES
GRISTLIEST
GRISTLINESS
GRISTLINESSES
GRISTMILLS
GRITSTONES
GRITTINESS
GRITTINESSES
GRIVATIONS
GRIZZLIEST
GROANINGLY
GROATSWORTH
GROATSWORTHS
GROCETERIA
GROCETERIAS
GROGGERIES
GROGGINESS
GROGGINESSES
GROMMETING
GROOVELESS
GROOVELIKE
GROOVINESS
GROOVINESSES
GROSGRAINS
GROSSIERETE
GROSSIERETES
GROSSNESSES
GROSSULARITE

GROSSULARITES
GROSSULARS
GROTESQUELY
GROTESQUENESS
GROTESQUENESSES
GROTESQUER
GROTESQUERIE
GROTESQUERIES
GROTESQUERY
GROTESQUES
GROTESQUEST
GROTTINESS
GROTTINESSES
GROUCHIEST
GROUCHINESS
GROUCHINESSES
GROUNDAGES
GROUNDBAIT
GROUNDBAITED
GROUNDBAITING
GROUNDBAITS
GROUNDBREAKER
GROUNDBREAKERS
GROUNDBREAKING
GROUNDBREAKINGS
GROUNDBURST
GROUNDBURSTS
GROUNDEDLY
GROUNDFISH
GROUNDFISHES
GROUNDHOGS
GROUNDINGS
GROUNDLESS
GROUNDLESSLY
GROUNDLESSNESS
GROUNDLING
GROUNDLINGS
GROUNDMASS
GROUNDMASSES
GROUNDNUTS
GROUNDOUTS
GROUNDPLOT
GROUNDPLOTS
GROUNDPROX
GROUNDPROXES
GROUNDSELL
GROUNDSELLS
GROUNDSELS
GROUNDSHARE
GROUNDSHARED
GROUNDSHARES
GROUNDSHARING
GROUNDSHEET
GROUNDSHEETS
GROUNDSILL
GROUNDSILLS
GROUNDSKEEPER
GROUNDSKEEPERS
GROUNDSMAN
GROUNDSMEN
GROUNDSPEED
GROUNDSPEEDS
GROUNDSWELL
GROUNDSWELLS
GROUNDWATER
GROUNDWATERS
GROUNDWOOD
GROUNDWOODS
GROUNDWORK
GROUNDWORKS
GROUPTHINK
GROUPTHINKS
GROUPUSCULE
GROUPUSCULES
GROUPWARES
GROUPWORKS
GROUSELIKE
GROVELINGLY
GROVELINGS
GROVELLERS
GROVELLING
GROVELLINGLY
GROVELLINGS
GROWLERIES
GROWLINESS
GROWLINESSES
GROWLINGLY
GROWTHIEST
GROWTHINESS
GROWTHINESSES
GROWTHISTS
GRUBBINESS
GRUBBINESSES
GRUBSTAKED
GRUBSTAKER
GRUBSTAKERS
GRUBSTAKES
GRUBSTAKING
GRUBSTREET
GRUDGELESS
GRUDGINGLY
GRUELINGLY
GRUELLINGLY
GRUELLINGS
GRUESOMELY
GRUESOMENESS
GRUESOMENESSES
GRUESOMEST
GRUFFNESSES
GRUMBLIEST
GRUMBLINGLY
GRUMBLINGS
GRUMMETING
GRUMNESSES
GRUMPINESS
GRUMPINESSES
GRUMPISHLY
GRUMPISHNESS
GRUMPISHNESSES
GRUNTINGLY
GUACAMOLES
GUACHAMOLE
GUACHAMOLES
GUACHAROES
GUANABANAS
GUANAZOLOS
GUANETHIDINE
GUANETHIDINES
GUANIDINES
GUANIFEROUS
GUANOSINES
GUARANTEED
GUARANTEEING
GUARANTEES
GUARANTIED
GUARANTIES
GUARANTORS
GUARANTYING
GUARDEDNESS
GUARDEDNESSES
GUARDHOUSE
GUARDHOUSES
GUARDIANSHIP
GUARDIANSHIPS
GUARDRAILS
GUARDROOMS
GUARDSHIPS
GUARISHING
GUAYABERAS
GUBERNACULA
GUBERNACULAR
GUBERNACULUM
GUBERNATION
GUBERNATIONS
GUBERNATOR
GUBERNATORIAL
GUBERNATORS
GUBERNIYAS
GUDGEONING
GUERDONERS
GUERDONING
GUERILLAISM
GUERILLAISMS
GUERRILLAISM
GUERRILLAISMS
GUERRILLAS
GUERRILLERO
GUERRILLEROS
GUESSINGLY
GUESSTIMATE
GUESSTIMATED
GUESSTIMATES
GUESSTIMATING
GUESSWORKS
GUESTBOOKS
GUESTENING
GUESTHOUSE
GUESTHOUSES
GUESTIMATE
GUESTIMATED
GUESTIMATES
GUESTIMATING
GUIDEBOOKS
GUIDELINES
GUIDEPOSTS
GUIDESHIPS
GUIDEWORDS
GUIDWILLIE
GUILDHALLS
GUILDSHIPS
GUILDSWOMAN
GUILDSWOMEN
GUILEFULLY
GUILEFULNESS
GUILEFULNESSES
GUILELESSLY
GUILELESSNESS
GUILELESSNESSES
GUILLEMETS
GUILLEMOTS
GUILLOCHED
GUILLOCHES
GUILLOCHING
GUILLOTINE
GUILLOTINED
GUILLOTINER
GUILLOTINERS
GUILLOTINES
GUILLOTINING
GUILTINESS
GUILTINESSES
GUILTLESSLY
GUILTLESSNESS
GUILTLESSNESSES
GUITARFISH
GUITARFISHES
GUITARISTS
GULLIBILITIES
GULLIBILITY
GULOSITIES
GUMMIFEROUS
GUMMINESSES
GUMMOSITIES
GUMSHIELDS
GUMSHOEING
GUMSUCKERS
GUNCOTTONS
GUNFIGHTER
GUNFIGHTERS
GUNFIGHTING
GUNFIGHTINGS
GUNKHOLING
GUNMANSHIP
GUNMANSHIPS
GUNNERSHIP
GUNNERSHIPS
GUNNYSACKS
GUNPOWDERIER
GUNPOWDERIEST
GUNPOWDERS

G

GUNPOWDERY
GUNRUNNERS
GUNRUNNING
GUNRUNNINGS
GUNSLINGER
GUNSLINGERS
GUNSLINGING
GUNSLINGINGS
GUNSMITHING
GUNSMITHINGS
GURGITATION
GURGITATIONS
GUSHINESSES
GUSSETINGS
GUSTATIONS
GUSTATORILY
GUSTINESSES
GUTBUCKETS
GUTLESSNESS
GUTLESSNESSES
GUTSINESSES
GUTTATIONS
GUTTERBLOOD
GUTTERBLOODS
GUTTERIEST
GUTTERINGS
GUTTERSNIPE
GUTTERSNIPES
GUTTERSNIPISH
GUTTIFEROUS
GUTTURALISATION
GUTTURALISE
GUTTURALISED
GUTTURALISES
GUTTURALISING
GUTTURALISM
GUTTURALISMS
GUTTURALITIES
GUTTURALITY
GUTTURALIZATION
GUTTURALIZE
GUTTURALIZED
GUTTURALIZES
GUTTURALIZING
GUTTURALLY
GUTTURALNESS
GUTTURALNESSES
GYMNASIARCH
GYMNASIARCHS
GYMNASIAST
GYMNASIASTS
GYMNASIUMS
GYMNASTICAL
GYMNASTICALLY
GYMNASTICS
GYMNORHINAL
GYMNOSOPHIES
GYMNOSOPHIST
GYMNOSOPHISTS
GYMNOSOPHS
GYMNOSOPHY
GYMNOSPERM
GYMNOSPERMIES
GYMNOSPERMOUS
GYMNOSPERMS
GYMNOSPERMY
GYNAECEUMS
GYNAECOCRACIES
GYNAECOCRACY
GYNAECOCRATIC
GYNAECOLOGIC
GYNAECOLOGICAL
GYNAECOLOGIES
GYNAECOLOGIST
GYNAECOLOGISTS
GYNAECOLOGY
GYNAECOMAST
GYNAECOMASTIA
GYNAECOMASTIAS
GYNAECOMASTIES
GYNAECOMASTS
GYNAECOMASTY
GYNANDRIES
GYNANDRISM
GYNANDRISMS
GYNANDROMORPH
GYNANDROMORPHIC
GYNANDROMORPHS
GYNANDROMORPHY
GYNANDROUS
GYNARCHIES
GYNECOCRACIES
GYNECOCRACY
GYNECOCRATIC
GYNECOLOGIC
GYNECOLOGICAL
GYNECOLOGIES
GYNECOLOGIST
GYNECOLOGISTS
GYNECOLOGY
GYNECOMASTIA
GYNECOMASTIAS
GYNIATRICS
GYNIATRIES
GYNIOLATRIES
GYNIOLATRY
GYNOCRACIES
GYNOCRATIC
GYNODIOECIOUS
GYNODIOECISM
GYNODIOECISMS
GYNOGENESES
GYNOGENESIS
GYNOGENETIC
GYNOMONOECIOUS
GYNOMONOECISM
GYNOMONOECISMS
GYNOPHOBES
GYNOPHOBIA
GYNOPHOBIAS
GYNOPHOBIC
GYNOPHOBICS
GYNOPHORES
GYNOPHORIC
GYNOSTEMIA
GYNOSTEMIUM
GYPSIFEROUS
GYPSOPHILA
GYPSOPHILAS
GYPSYHOODS
GYPSYWORTS
GYRATIONAL
GYRFALCONS
GYROCOMPASS
GYROCOMPASSES
GYROCOPTER
GYROCOPTERS
GYROFREQUENCIES
GYROFREQUENCY
GYROMAGNETIC
GYROMAGNETISM
GYROMAGNETISMS
GYROMANCIES
GYROPILOTS
GYROPLANES
GYROSCOPES
GYROSCOPIC
GYROSCOPICALLY
GYROSCOPICS
GYROSTABILISER
GYROSTABILISERS
GYROSTABILIZER
GYROSTABILIZERS
GYROSTATIC
GYROSTATICALLY
GYROSTATICS
GYROVAGUES

HAANEPOOTS
HABERDASHER
HABERDASHERIES
HABERDASHERS
HABERDASHERY
HABERDINES
HABERGEONS
HABILATORY
HABILIMENT
HABILIMENTS
HABILITATE
HABILITATED
HABILITATES
HABILITATING
HABILITATION
HABILITATIONS
HABILITATOR
HABILITATORS
HABITABILITIES
HABITABILITY
HABITABLENESS
HABITABLENESSES
HABITATION
HABITATIONAL
HABITATIONS
HABITAUNCE
HABITAUNCES
HABITUALLY
HABITUALNESS
HABITUALNESSES
HABITUATED
HABITUATES
HABITUATING
HABITUATION
HABITUATIONS
HABITUDINAL
HACENDADOS
HACIENDADO
HACIENDADOS
HACKAMORES
HACKBERRIES
HACKBUTEER
HACKBUTEERS
HACKBUTTER
HACKBUTTERS
HACKERAZZI
HACKERAZZIS
HACKERAZZO
HACKMATACK
HACKMATACKS
HACKNEYING
HACKNEYISM
HACKNEYISMS
HACKNEYMAN
HACKNEYMEN
HACKSAWING
HACKTIVISM
HACKTIVISMS
HACKTIVIST
HACKTIVISTS
HACQUETONS
HADROSAURS
HADROSAURUS
HADROSAURUSES
HAECCEITIES
HAEMACHROME
HAEMACHROMES
HAEMACYTOMETER
HAEMACYTOMETERS
HAEMAGGLUTINATE
HAEMAGGLUTININ
HAEMAGGLUTININS
HAEMAGOGUE
HAEMAGOGUES
HAEMANGIOMA
HAEMANGIOMAS
HAEMANGIOMATA
HAEMATEINS
HAEMATEMESES
HAEMATEMESIS
HAEMATINIC
HAEMATINICS
HAEMATITES
HAEMATITIC
HAEMATOBLAST
HAEMATOBLASTIC
HAEMATOBLASTS
HAEMATOCELE
HAEMATOCELES
HAEMATOCRIT
HAEMATOCRITS
HAEMATOCRYAL
HAEMATOGENESES
HAEMATOGENESIS
HAEMATOGENETIC
HAEMATOGENIC
HAEMATOGENOUS
HAEMATOLOGIC
HAEMATOLOGICAL
HAEMATOLOGIES
HAEMATOLOGIST
HAEMATOLOGISTS
HAEMATOLOGY
HAEMATOLYSES
HAEMATOLYSIS
HAEMATOMAS
HAEMATOMATA
HAEMATOPHAGOUS
HAEMATOPOIESES
HAEMATOPOIESIS
HAEMATOPOIETIC
HAEMATOSES
HAEMATOSIS
HAEMATOTHERMAL
HAEMATOXYLIC
HAEMATOXYLIN
HAEMATOXYLINS
HAEMATOXYLON
HAEMATOXYLONS
HAEMATOZOA
HAEMATOZOON
HAEMATURIA
HAEMATURIAS
HAEMATURIC
HAEMOCHROME
HAEMOCHROMES
HAEMOCOELS
HAEMOCONIA
HAEMOCONIAS
HAEMOCYANIN
HAEMOCYANINS
HAEMOCYTES
HAEMOCYTOMETER
HAEMOCYTOMETERS
HAEMODIALYSER
HAEMODIALYSERS
HAEMODIALYSES
HAEMODIALYSIS
HAEMODIALYZER
HAEMODIALYZERS
HAEMODILUTION
HAEMODILUTIONS
HAEMODYNAMIC
HAEMODYNAMICS
HAEMOFLAGELLATE
HAEMOGLOBIN
HAEMOGLOBINS
HAEMOGLOBINURIA
HAEMOGLOBINURIC
HAEMOLYMPH
HAEMOLYMPHS
HAEMOLYSED
HAEMOLYSES
HAEMOLYSIN
HAEMOLYSING
HAEMOLYSINS
HAEMOLYSIS
HAEMOLYTIC
HAEMOLYZED
HAEMOLYZES
HAEMOLYZING
HAEMOPHILE
HAEMOPHILES
HAEMOPHILIA
HAEMOPHILIAC
HAEMOPHILIACS
HAEMOPHILIAS
HAEMOPHILIC
HAEMOPHILIOID
HAEMOPHOBIA
HAEMOPHOBIAS
HAEMOPOIESES
HAEMOPOIESIS
HAEMOPOIETIC
HAEMOPROTEIN
HAEMOPROTEINS
HAEMOPTYSES
HAEMOPTYSIS
HAEMORRHAGE
HAEMORRHAGED
HAEMORRHAGES
HAEMORRHAGIC
HAEMORRHAGING
HAEMORRHAGINGS
HAEMORRHOID
HAEMORRHOIDAL
HAEMORRHOIDS
HAEMOSIDERIN
HAEMOSIDERINS
HAEMOSTASES
HAEMOSTASIA
HAEMOSTASIAS
HAEMOSTASIS
HAEMOSTATIC
HAEMOSTATICS
HAEMOSTATS
HAEMOTOXIC
HAEMOTOXIN
HAEMOTOXINS
HAGBERRIES
HAGBUTEERS
HAGBUTTERS
HAGGADICAL
HAGGADISTIC
HAGGADISTS
HAGGARDNESS
HAGGARDNESSES
HAGGISHNESS
HAGGISHNESSES
HAGIARCHIES

HAGIOCRACIES
HAGIOCRACY
HAGIOGRAPHER
HAGIOGRAPHERS
HAGIOGRAPHIC
HAGIOGRAPHICAL
HAGIOGRAPHIES
HAGIOGRAPHIST
HAGIOGRAPHISTS
HAGIOGRAPHY
HAGIOLATER
HAGIOLATERS
HAGIOLATRIES
HAGIOLATROUS
HAGIOLATRY
HAGIOLOGIC
HAGIOLOGICAL
HAGIOLOGIES
HAGIOLOGIST
HAGIOLOGISTS
HAGIOSCOPE
HAGIOSCOPES
HAGIOSCOPIC
HAILSTONES
HAILSTORMS
HAIRBRAINED
HAIRBREADTH
HAIRBREADTHS
HAIRBRUSHES
HAIRCLOTHS
HAIRCUTTER
HAIRCUTTERS
HAIRCUTTING
HAIRCUTTINGS
HAIRDRESSER
HAIRDRESSERS
HAIRDRESSING
HAIRDRESSINGS
HAIRDRIERS
HAIRDRYERS
HAIRINESSES
HAIRLESSES
HAIRLESSNESS
HAIRLESSNESSES
HAIRPIECES
HAIRSBREADTH
HAIRSBREADTHS
HAIRSPLITTER
HAIRSPLITTERS
HAIRSPLITTING
HAIRSPLITTINGS
HAIRSPRAYS
HAIRSPRING
HAIRSPRINGS
HAIRSTREAK
HAIRSTREAKS
HAIRSTYLES
HAIRSTYLING
HAIRSTYLINGS
HAIRSTYLIST
HAIRSTYLISTS
HAIRWEAVING
HAIRWEAVINGS
HAIRYBACKS
HALACHISTS
HALAKHISTS
HALBERDIER
HALBERDIERS
HALCYONIAN
HALENESSES
HALFENDEALE
HALFENDEALES
HALFHEARTED
HALFHEARTEDLY
HALFHEARTEDNESS
HALFNESSES
HALFPENNIES
HALFPENNYWORTH
HALFPENNYWORTHS
HALFSERIOUSLY
HALFTRACKS
HALFWITTED
HALFWITTEDLY
HALFWITTEDNESS
HALIEUTICS
HALIPLANKTON
HALIPLANKTONS
HALLALLING
HALLEFLINTA
HALLEFLINTAS
HALLELUIAH
HALLELUIAHS
HALLELUJAH
HALLELUJAHS
HALLMARKED
HALLMARKING
HALLOWEDNESS
HALLOWEDNESSES
HALLOYSITE
HALLOYSITES
HALLSTANDS
HALLUCINANT
HALLUCINANTS
HALLUCINATE
HALLUCINATED
HALLUCINATES
HALLUCINATING
HALLUCINATION
HALLUCINATIONAL
HALLUCINATIONS
HALLUCINATIVE
HALLUCINATOR
HALLUCINATORS
HALLUCINATORY
HALLUCINOGEN
HALLUCINOGENIC
HALLUCINOGENICS
HALLUCINOGENS
HALLUCINOSES
HALLUCINOSIS
HALOBIONTIC
HALOBIONTS
HALOBIOTIC
HALOCARBON
HALOCARBONS
HALOCLINES
HALOGENATE
HALOGENATED
HALOGENATES
HALOGENATING
HALOGENATION
HALOGENATIONS
HALOGENOID
HALOGENOUS
HALOGETONS
HALOMORPHIC
HALOPERIDOL
HALOPERIDOLS
HALOPHILES
HALOPHILIC
HALOPHILIES
HALOPHILOUS
HALOPHOBES
HALOPHYTES
HALOPHYTIC
HALOPHYTISM
HALOPHYTISMS
HALOTHANES
HALTERBREAK
HALTERBREAKING
HALTERBREAKS
HALTERBROKE
HALTERBROKEN
HALTERNECK
HALTERNECKS
HALTINGNESS
HALTINGNESSES
HAMADRYADES
HAMADRYADS
HAMADRYASES
HAMAMELIDACEOUS
HAMAMELISES
HAMANTASCH
HAMANTASCHEN
HAMARTHRITIS
HAMARTHRITISES
HAMARTIOLOGIES
HAMARTIOLOGY
HAMBURGERS
HAMESUCKEN
HAMESUCKENS
HAMFATTERED
HAMFATTERING
HAMFATTERS
HAMMERCLOTH
HAMMERCLOTHS
HAMMERHEAD
HAMMERHEADED
HAMMERHEADS
HAMMERINGS
HAMMERKOPS
HAMMERLESS
HAMMERLOCK
HAMMERLOCKS
HAMMERSTONE
HAMMERSTONES
HAMMERTOES
HAMMINESSES
HAMPEREDNESS
HAMPEREDNESSES
HAMSHACKLE
HAMSHACKLED
HAMSHACKLES
HAMSHACKLING
HAMSTRINGED
HAMSTRINGING
HAMSTRINGS
HANDBAGGED
HANDBAGGING
HANDBAGGINGS
HANDBALLED
HANDBALLER
HANDBALLERS
HANDBALLING
HANDBARROW
HANDBARROWS
HANDBASKET
HANDBASKETS
HANDBRAKES
HANDBREADTH
HANDBREADTHS
HANDCLASPS
HANDCRAFTED
HANDCRAFTING
HANDCRAFTS
HANDCRAFTSMAN
HANDCRAFTSMEN
HANDCUFFED
HANDCUFFING
HANDEDNESS
HANDEDNESSES
HANDFASTED
HANDFASTING
HANDFASTINGS
HANDFEEDING
HANDGLASSES
HANDICAPPED
HANDICAPPER
HANDICAPPERS
HANDICAPPING
HANDICRAFT
HANDICRAFTER
HANDICRAFTERS
HANDICRAFTS
HANDICRAFTSMAN
HANDICRAFTSMEN
HANDICUFFS
HANDINESSES
HANDIWORKS
HANDKERCHER

HANDKERCHERS
HANDKERCHIEF
HANDKERCHIEFS
HANDKERCHIEVES
HANDLANGER
HANDLANGERS
HANDLEABLE
HANDLEBARS
HANDLELESS
HANDLINERS
HANDMAIDEN
HANDMAIDENS
HANDPASSED
HANDPASSES
HANDPASSING
HANDPHONES
HANDPICKED
HANDPICKING
HANDPRESSES
HANDPRINTS
HANDSBREADTH
HANDSBREADTHS
HANDSELING
HANDSELLED
HANDSELLING
HANDSHAKES
HANDSHAKING
HANDSHAKINGS
HANDSOMELY
HANDSOMENESS
HANDSOMENESSES
HANDSOMEST
HANDSPIKES
HANDSPRING
HANDSPRINGS
HANDSTAFFS
HANDSTAMPED
HANDSTAMPING
HANDSTAMPS
HANDSTANDS
HANDSTAVES
HANDSTROKE
HANDSTROKES
HANDSTURNS
HANDTOWELS
HANDWHEELS
HANDWORKED
HANDWORKER
HANDWORKERS
HANDWRINGER
HANDWRINGERS
HANDWRITES
HANDWRITING
HANDWRITINGS
HANDWRITTEN
HANDWROUGHT
HANDYPERSON
HANDYPERSONS
HANDYWORKS
HANGABILITIES
HANGABILITY
HANGARAGES
HANKERINGS
HANSARDISE
HANSARDISED
HANSARDISES
HANSARDISING
HANSARDIZE
HANSARDIZED
HANSARDIZES
HANSARDIZING
HANSELLING
HANTAVIRUS
HANTAVIRUSES
HAPAXANTHIC
HAPAXANTHOUS
HAPHAZARDLY
HAPHAZARDNESS
HAPHAZARDNESSES
HAPHAZARDRIES
HAPHAZARDRY
HAPHAZARDS
HAPHTARAHS
HAPHTAROTH
HAPLESSNESS
HAPLESSNESSES
HAPLOBIONT
HAPLOBIONTIC
HAPLOBIONTS
HAPLOGRAPHIES
HAPLOGRAPHY
HAPLOIDIES
HAPLOLOGIC
HAPLOLOGIES
HAPLOSTEMONOUS
HAPLOTYPES
HAPPENCHANCE
HAPPENCHANCES
HAPPENINGS
HAPPENSTANCE
HAPPENSTANCES
HAPPINESSES
HAPTOGLOBIN
HAPTOGLOBINS
HAPTOTROPIC
HAPTOTROPISM
HAPTOTROPISMS
HARAMZADAS
HARAMZADIS
HARANGUERS
HARANGUING
HARASSEDLY
HARASSINGLY
HARASSINGS
HARASSMENT
HARASSMENTS
HARBINGERED
HARBINGERING
HARBINGERS
HARBORAGES
HARBORFULS
HARBORLESS
HARBORMASTER
HARBORMASTERS
HARBORSIDE
HARBOURAGE
HARBOURAGES
HARBOURERS
HARBOURFUL
HARBOURFULS
HARBOURING
HARBOURLESS
HARBOURSIDE
HARBOURSIDES
HARDBACKED
HARDBOARDS
HARDBODIES
HARDBOUNDS
HARDCOVERS
HARDENINGS
HARDFISTED
HARDGRASSES
HARDHANDED
HARDHANDEDNESS
HARDHEADED
HARDHEADEDLY
HARDHEADEDNESS
HARDHEARTED
HARDHEARTEDLY
HARDHEARTEDNESS
HARDIHEADS
HARDIHOODS
HARDIMENTS
HARDINESSES
HARDINGGRASS
HARDINGGRASSES
HARDLINERS
HARDMOUTHED
HARDNESSES
HARDSCAPES
HARDSCRABBLE
HARDSCRABBLES
HARDSTANDING
HARDSTANDINGS
HARDSTANDS
HARDWAREMAN
HARDWAREMEN
HARDWIRING
HARDWORKING
HAREBRAINED
HARELIPPED
HARESTAILS
HARIOLATED
HARIOLATES
HARIOLATING
HARIOLATION
HARIOLATIONS
HARLEQUINADE
HARLEQUINADES
HARLEQUINED
HARLEQUINING
HARLEQUINS
HARLOTRIES
HARMALINES
HARMATTANS
HARMDOINGS
HARMFULNESS
HARMFULNESSES
HARMLESSLY
HARMLESSNESS
HARMLESSNESSES
HARMOLODIC
HARMOLODICS
HARMONICAL
HARMONICALLY
HARMONICAS
HARMONICHORD
HARMONICHORDS
HARMONICIST
HARMONICISTS
HARMONICON
HARMONICONS
HARMONIOUS
HARMONIOUSLY
HARMONIOUSNESS
HARMONIPHON
HARMONIPHONE
HARMONIPHONES
HARMONIPHONS
HARMONISABLE
HARMONISATION
HARMONISATIONS
HARMONISED
HARMONISER
HARMONISERS
HARMONISES
HARMONISING
HARMONISTIC
HARMONISTICALLY
HARMONISTS
HARMONIUMIST
HARMONIUMISTS
HARMONIUMS
HARMONIZABLE
HARMONIZATION
HARMONIZATIONS
HARMONIZED
HARMONIZER
HARMONIZERS
HARMONIZES
HARMONIZING
HARMONOGRAM
HARMONOGRAMS
HARMONOGRAPH
HARMONOGRAPHS
HARMONOMETER
HARMONOMETERS
HARMOSTIES
HARMOTOMES
HARNESSERS

HARNESSING
HARNESSLESS
HARPOONEER
HARPOONEERS
HARPOONERS
HARPOONING
HARPSICHORD
HARPSICHORDIST
HARPSICHORDISTS
HARPSICHORDS
HARQUEBUSE
HARQUEBUSES
HARQUEBUSIER
HARQUEBUSIERS
HARQUEBUSS
HARQUEBUSSES
HARROWINGLY
HARROWINGS
HARROWMENT
HARROWMENTS
HARRUMPHED
HARRUMPHING
HARSHENING
HARSHNESSES
HARTBEESES
HARTBEESTS
HARTEBEEST
HARTEBEESTS
HARTSHORNS
HARUMPHING
HARUSPICAL
HARUSPICATE
HARUSPICATED
HARUSPICATES
HARUSPICATING
HARUSPICATION
HARUSPICATIONS
HARUSPICES
HARUSPICIES
HARVESTABLE
HARVESTERS
HARVESTING
HARVESTINGS
HARVESTLESS
HARVESTMAN
HARVESTMEN
HARVESTTIME
HARVESTTIMES
HASENPFEFFER
HASENPFEFFERS
HASHEESHES
HASSOCKIER
HASSOCKIEST
HASTEFULLY
HASTINESSES
HATBRUSHES
HATCHABILITIES
HATCHABILITY
HATCHBACKS
HATCHELING
HATCHELLED
HATCHELLER
HATCHELLERS
HATCHELLING
HATCHERIES
HATCHETIER
HATCHETIEST
HATCHETTITE
HATCHETTITES
HATCHLINGS
HATCHMENTS
HATEFULNESS
HATEFULNESSES
HATELESSNESS
HATELESSNESSES
HATEWORTHIER
HATEWORTHIEST
HATEWORTHY
HATINATORS
HATLESSNESS
HATLESSNESSES
HAUBERGEON
HAUBERGEONS
HAUGHTIEST
HAUGHTINESS
HAUGHTINESSES
HAUNTINGLY
HAUSFRAUEN
HAUSSMANNISE
HAUSSMANNISED
HAUSSMANNISES
HAUSSMANNISING
HAUSSMANNIZE
HAUSSMANNIZED
HAUSSMANNIZES
HAUSSMANNIZING
HAUSTELLATE
HAUSTELLUM
HAUSTORIAL
HAUSTORIUM
HAVERSACKS
HAVERSINES
HAWFINCHES
HAWKISHNESS
HAWKISHNESSES
HAWKSBEARD
HAWKSBEARDS
HAWKSBILLS
HAWSEHOLES
HAWSEPIPES
HAWTHORNIER
HAWTHORNIEST
HAYCATIONS
HAYMAKINGS
HAZARDABLE
HAZARDIZES
HAZARDOUSLY
HAZARDOUSNESS
HAZARDOUSNESSES
HAZARDRIES
HAZELWOODS
HAZINESSES
HEADACHIER
HEADACHIEST
HEADBANGED
HEADBANGING
HEADBANGINGS
HEADBOARDS
HEADBOROUGH
HEADBOROUGHS
HEADCHAIRS
HEADCHEESE
HEADCHEESES
HEADCLOTHS
HEADCOUNTS
HEADDRESSES
HEADFISHES
HEADFOREMOST
HEADFRAMES
HEADGUARDS
HEADHUNTED
HEADHUNTER
HEADHUNTERS
HEADHUNTING
HEADHUNTINGS
HEADINESSES
HEADLEASES
HEADLESSNESS
HEADLESSNESSES
HEADLIGHTS
HEADLINERS
HEADLINING
HEADMASTER
HEADMASTERLIER
HEADMASTERLIEST
HEADMASTERLY
HEADMASTERS
HEADMASTERSHIP
HEADMASTERSHIPS
HEADMISTRESS
HEADMISTRESSES
HEADMISTRESSIER
HEADMISTRESSY
HEADPEACES
HEADPHONES
HEADPIECES
HEADQUARTER
HEADQUARTERED
HEADQUARTERING
HEADQUARTERS
HEADREACHED
HEADREACHES
HEADREACHING
HEADSCARVES
HEADSHAKES
HEADSHEETS
HEADSHRINKER
HEADSHRINKERS
HEADSPACES
HEADSPRING
HEADSPRINGS
HEADSQUARE
HEADSQUARES
HEADSTALLS
HEADSTANDS
HEADSTICKS
HEADSTOCKS
HEADSTONES
HEADSTREAM
HEADSTREAMS
HEADSTRONG
HEADSTRONGLY
HEADSTRONGNESS
HEADTEACHER
HEADTEACHERS
HEADWAITER
HEADWAITERS
HEADWATERS
HEADWORKER
HEADWORKERS
HEALTHCARE
HEALTHCARES
HEALTHFULLY
HEALTHFULNESS
HEALTHFULNESSES
HEALTHIEST
HEALTHINESS
HEALTHINESSES
HEALTHISMS
HEALTHLESS
HEALTHLESSNESS
HEALTHSOME
HEAPSTEADS
HEARKENERS
HEARKENING
HEARTACHES
HEARTBEATS
HEARTBREAK
HEARTBREAKER
HEARTBREAKERS
HEARTBREAKING
HEARTBREAKINGLY
HEARTBREAKS
HEARTBROKE
HEARTBROKEN
HEARTBROKENLY
HEARTBROKENNESS
HEARTBURNING
HEARTBURNINGS
HEARTBURNS
HEARTENERS
HEARTENING
HEARTENINGLY
HEARTHRUGS
HEARTHSTONE
HEARTHSTONES
HEARTIKINS
HEARTINESS
HEARTINESSES
HEARTLANDS

HEARTLESSLY
HEARTLESSNESS
HEARTLESSNESSES
HEARTLINGS
HEARTRENDING
HEARTRENDINGLY
HEARTSEASE
HEARTSEASES
HEARTSEEDS
HEARTSICKNESS
HEARTSICKNESSES
HEARTSINKS
HEARTSOMELY
HEARTSOMENESS
HEARTSOMENESSES
HEARTSORES
HEARTSTRING
HEARTSTRINGS
HEARTTHROB
HEARTTHROBS
HEARTWARMING
HEARTWATER
HEARTWATERS
HEARTWOODS
HEARTWORMS
HEATEDNESS
HEATEDNESSES
HEATHBERRIES
HEATHBERRY
HEATHBIRDS
HEATHCOCKS
HEATHENDOM
HEATHENDOMS
HEATHENESSE
HEATHENESSES
HEATHENISE
HEATHENISED
HEATHENISES
HEATHENISH
HEATHENISHLY
HEATHENISHNESS
HEATHENISING
HEATHENISM
HEATHENISMS
HEATHENIZE
HEATHENIZED
HEATHENIZES
HEATHENIZING
HEATHENNESS
HEATHENNESSES
HEATHENRIES
HEATHERIER
HEATHERIEST
HEATHFOWLS
HEATHLANDS
HEATSTROKE
HEATSTROKES
HEAVENLIER
HEAVENLIEST
HEAVENLINESS
HEAVENLINESSES
HEAVENWARD
HEAVENWARDS
HEAVINESSES
HEAVYHEARTED
HEAVYHEARTEDLY
HEAVYWEIGHT
HEAVYWEIGHTS
HEBDOMADAL
HEBDOMADALLY
HEBDOMADAR
HEBDOMADARIES
HEBDOMADARS
HEBDOMADARY
HEBDOMADER
HEBDOMADERS
HEBEPHRENIA
HEBEPHRENIAC
HEBEPHRENIACS
HEBEPHRENIAS
HEBEPHRENIC
HEBEPHRENICS
HEBETATING
HEBETATION
HEBETATIONS
HEBETATIVE
HEBETUDINOSITY
HEBETUDINOUS
HEBRAISATION
HEBRAISATIONS
HEBRAISING
HEBRAIZATION
HEBRAIZATIONS
HEBRAIZING
HECKELPHONE
HECKELPHONES
HECOGENINS
HECTICALLY
HECTOCOTYLI
HECTOCOTYLUS
HECTOGRAMME
HECTOGRAMMES
HECTOGRAMS
HECTOGRAPH
HECTOGRAPHED
HECTOGRAPHIC
HECTOGRAPHIES
HECTOGRAPHING
HECTOGRAPHS
HECTOGRAPHY
HECTOLITER
HECTOLITERS
HECTOLITRE
HECTOLITRES
HECTOMETER
HECTOMETERS
HECTOMETRE
HECTOMETRES
HECTORINGLY
HECTORINGS
HECTORISMS
HECTORSHIP
HECTORSHIPS
HECTOSTERE
HECTOSTERES
HEDGEBILLS
HEDGEHOPPED
HEDGEHOPPER
HEDGEHOPPERS
HEDGEHOPPING
HEDGEHOPPINGS
HEDONICALLY
HEDONISTIC
HEDONISTICALLY
HEDYPHANES
HEDYSARUMS
HEEDFULNESS
HEEDFULNESSES
HEEDINESSES
HEEDLESSLY
HEEDLESSNESS
HEEDLESSNESSES
HEELPIECES
HEELPLATES
HEFTINESSES
HEGEMONIAL
HEGEMONICAL
HEGEMONIES
HEGEMONISM
HEGEMONISMS
HEGEMONIST
HEGEMONISTS
HEGUMENIES
HEGUMENOSES
HEIGHTENED
HEIGHTENER
HEIGHTENERS
HEIGHTENING
HEIGHTISMS
HEINOUSNESS
HEINOUSNESSES
HEKTOGRAMS
HELDENTENOR
HELDENTENORS
HELIACALLY
HELIANTHEMUM
HELIANTHEMUMS
HELIANTHUS
HELIANTHUSES
HELIBUSSES
HELICHRYSUM
HELICHRYSUMS
HELICITIES
HELICLINES
HELICOGRAPH
HELICOGRAPHS
HELICOIDAL
HELICOIDALLY
HELICONIAS
HELICOPTED
HELICOPTER
HELICOPTERED
HELICOPTERING
HELICOPTERS
HELICOPTING
HELICTITES
HELIDROMES
HELILIFTED
HELILIFTING
HELIOCENTRIC
HELIOCENTRICISM
HELIOCENTRICITY
HELIOCHROME
HELIOCHROMES
HELIOCHROMIC
HELIOCHROMIES
HELIOCHROMY
HELIOGRAMS
HELIOGRAPH
HELIOGRAPHED
HELIOGRAPHER
HELIOGRAPHERS
HELIOGRAPHIC
HELIOGRAPHICAL
HELIOGRAPHIES
HELIOGRAPHING
HELIOGRAPHS
HELIOGRAPHY
HELIOGRAVURE
HELIOGRAVURES
HELIOLATER
HELIOLATERS
HELIOLATRIES
HELIOLATROUS
HELIOLATRY
HELIOLITHIC
HELIOLOGIES
HELIOMETER
HELIOMETERS
HELIOMETRIC
HELIOMETRICAL
HELIOMETRICALLY
HELIOMETRIES
HELIOMETRY
HELIOPAUSE
HELIOPAUSES
HELIOPHILOUS
HELIOPHOBIC
HELIOPHYTE
HELIOPHYTES
HELIOSCIOPHYTE
HELIOSCIOPHYTES
HELIOSCOPE
HELIOSCOPES
HELIOSCOPIC
HELIOSPHERE
HELIOSPHERES
HELIOSTATIC
HELIOSTATS
HELIOTACTIC

HELIOTAXES
HELIOTAXIS
HELIOTHERAPIES
HELIOTHERAPY
HELIOTROPE
HELIOTROPES
HELIOTROPIC
HELIOTROPICAL
HELIOTROPICALLY
HELIOTROPIES
HELIOTROPIN
HELIOTROPINS
HELIOTROPISM
HELIOTROPISMS
HELIOTROPY
HELIOTYPED
HELIOTYPES
HELIOTYPIC
HELIOTYPIES
HELIOTYPING
HELIOZOANS
HELIPILOTS
HELISKIING
HELISKIINGS
HELISPHERIC
HELISPHERICAL
HELLACIOUS
HELLACIOUSLY
HELLBENDER
HELLBENDERS
HELLBROTHS
HELLDIVERS
HELLEBORES
HELLEBORINE
HELLEBORINES
HELLENISATION
HELLENISATIONS
HELLENISED
HELLENISES
HELLENISING
HELLENIZATION
HELLENIZATIONS
HELLENIZED
HELLENIZES
HELLENIZING
HELLGRAMITE
HELLGRAMITES
HELLGRAMMITE
HELLGRAMMITES
HELLHOUNDS
HELLISHNESS
HELLISHNESSES
HELLSCAPES
HELMETINGS
HELMETLIKE
HELMINTHIASES
HELMINTHIASIS
HELMINTHIC
HELMINTHICS
HELMINTHOID
HELMINTHOLOGIC
HELMINTHOLOGIES
HELMINTHOLOGIST
HELMINTHOLOGY
HELMINTHOUS
HELMSMANSHIP
HELMSMANSHIPS
HELOPHYTES
HELPFULNESS
HELPFULNESSES
HELPLESSLY
HELPLESSNESS
HELPLESSNESSES
HELVETIUMS
HEMACHROME
HEMACHROMES
HEMACYTOMETER
HEMACYTOMETERS
HEMAGGLUTINATE
HEMAGGLUTINATED
HEMAGGLUTINATES
HEMAGGLUTININ
HEMAGGLUTININS
HEMAGOGUES
HEMANGIOMA
HEMANGIOMAS
HEMANGIOMATA
HEMATEMESES
HEMATEMESIS
HEMATINICS
HEMATOBLAST
HEMATOBLASTIC
HEMATOBLASTS
HEMATOCELE
HEMATOCELES
HEMATOCRIT
HEMATOCRITS
HEMATOCRYAL
HEMATOGENESES
HEMATOGENESIS
HEMATOGENETIC
HEMATOGENIC
HEMATOGENOUS
HEMATOLOGIC
HEMATOLOGICAL
HEMATOLOGIES
HEMATOLOGIST
HEMATOLOGISTS
HEMATOLOGY
HEMATOLYSES
HEMATOLYSIS
HEMATOMATA
HEMATOPHAGOUS
HEMATOPOIESES
HEMATOPOIESIS
HEMATOPOIETIC
HEMATOPORPHYRIN
HEMATOTHERMAL
HEMATOXYLIN
HEMATOXYLINS
HEMATOZOON
HEMATURIAS
HEMELYTRAL
HEMELYTRON
HEMELYTRUM
HEMERALOPIA
HEMERALOPIAS
HEMERALOPIC
HEMEROCALLIS
HEMEROCALLISES
HEMERYTHRIN
HEMERYTHRINS
HEMIACETAL
HEMIACETALS
HEMIALGIAS
HEMIANOPIA
HEMIANOPIAS
HEMIANOPIC
HEMIANOPSIA
HEMIANOPSIAS
HEMIANOPTIC
HEMICELLULOSE
HEMICELLULOSES
HEMICHORDATE
HEMICHORDATES
HEMICRANIA
HEMICRANIAS
HEMICRYPTOPHYTE
HEMICRYSTALLINE
HEMICYCLES
HEMICYCLIC
HEMIELYTRA
HEMIELYTRAL
HEMIELYTRON
HEMIHEDRAL
HEMIHEDRIES
HEMIHEDRISM
HEMIHEDRISMS
HEMIHEDRON
HEMIHEDRONS
HEMIHYDRATE
HEMIHYDRATED
HEMIHYDRATES
HEMIMETABOLOUS
HEMIMORPHIC
HEMIMORPHIES
HEMIMORPHISM
HEMIMORPHISMS
HEMIMORPHITE
HEMIMORPHITES
HEMIMORPHY
HEMIONUSES
HEMIOPSIAS
HEMIPARASITE
HEMIPARASITES
HEMIPARASITIC
HEMIPLEGIA
HEMIPLEGIAS
HEMIPLEGIC
HEMIPLEGICS
HEMIPTERAL
HEMIPTERAN
HEMIPTERANS
HEMIPTERON
HEMIPTERONS
HEMIPTEROUS
HEMISPACES
HEMISPHERE
HEMISPHERES
HEMISPHERIC
HEMISPHERICAL
HEMISPHEROID
HEMISPHEROIDAL
HEMISPHEROIDS
HEMISTICHAL
HEMISTICHS
HEMITERPENE
HEMITERPENES
HEMITROPAL
HEMITROPES
HEMITROPIC
HEMITROPIES
HEMITROPISM
HEMITROPISMS
HEMITROPOUS
HEMIZYGOUS
HEMOCHROMATOSES
HEMOCHROMATOSIS
HEMOCHROME
HEMOCHROMES
HEMOCONIAS
HEMOCYANIN
HEMOCYANINS
HEMOCYTOMETER
HEMOCYTOMETERS
HEMODIALYSES
HEMODIALYSIS
HEMODIALYZER
HEMODIALYZERS
HEMODILUTION
HEMODILUTIONS
HEMODYNAMIC
HEMODYNAMICALLY
HEMODYNAMICS
HEMOFLAGELLATE
HEMOFLAGELLATES
HEMOGLOBIN
HEMOGLOBINS
HEMOGLOBINURIA
HEMOGLOBINURIAS
HEMOGLOBINURIC
HEMOLYMPHS
HEMOLYSING
HEMOLYSINS
HEMOLYZING
HEMOPHILES
HEMOPHILIA
HEMOPHILIAC
HEMOPHILIACS
HEMOPHILIAS

HEMOPHILIC
HEMOPHILICS
HEMOPHILIOID
HEMOPOIESES
HEMOPOIESIS
HEMOPOIETIC
HEMOPROTEIN
HEMOPROTEINS
HEMOPTYSES
HEMOPTYSIS
HEMORRHAGE
HEMORRHAGED
HEMORRHAGES
HEMORRHAGIC
HEMORRHAGING
HEMORRHAGINGS
HEMORRHOID
HEMORRHOIDAL
HEMORRHOIDALS
HEMORRHOIDS
HEMOSIDERIN
HEMOSIDERINS
HEMOSTASES
HEMOSTASIA
HEMOSTASIAS
HEMOSTASIS
HEMOSTATIC
HEMOSTATICS
HEMOTOXINS
HEMSTITCHED
HEMSTITCHER
HEMSTITCHERS
HEMSTITCHES
HEMSTITCHING
HENCEFORTH
HENCEFORWARD
HENCEFORWARDS
HENCHPERSON
HENCHPERSONS
HENCHWOMAN
HENCHWOMEN
HENDECAGON
HENDECAGONAL
HENDECAGONS
HENDECAHEDRA
HENDECAHEDRON
HENDECAHEDRONS
HENDECASYLLABIC
HENDECASYLLABLE
HENDIADYSES
HENOTHEISM
HENOTHEISMS
HENOTHEIST
HENOTHEISTIC
HENOTHEISTS
HENPECKERIES
HENPECKERY
HENPECKING
HEORTOLOGICAL
HEORTOLOGIES
HEORTOLOGIST
HEORTOLOGISTS
HEORTOLOGY
HEPARINISED
HEPARINIZED
HEPARINOID
HEPATECTOMIES
HEPATECTOMISED
HEPATECTOMIZED
HEPATECTOMY
HEPATICOLOGICAL
HEPATICOLOGIES
HEPATICOLOGIST
HEPATICOLOGISTS
HEPATICOLOGY
HEPATISATION
HEPATISATIONS
HEPATISING
HEPATITIDES
HEPATITISES
HEPATIZATION
HEPATIZATIONS
HEPATIZING
HEPATOCELLULAR
HEPATOCYTE
HEPATOCYTES
HEPATOGENOUS
HEPATOLOGIES
HEPATOLOGIST
HEPATOLOGISTS
HEPATOLOGY
HEPATOMATA
HEPATOMEGALIES
HEPATOMEGALY
HEPATOPANCREAS
HEPATOSCOPIES
HEPATOSCOPY
HEPATOTOXIC
HEPATOTOXICITY
HEPHTHEMIMER
HEPHTHEMIMERAL
HEPHTHEMIMERS
HEPTACHLOR
HEPTACHLORS
HEPTACHORD
HEPTACHORDS
HEPTADECANOIC
HEPTAGLOTS
HEPTAGONAL
HEPTAGYNOUS
HEPTAHEDRA
HEPTAHEDRAL
HEPTAHEDRON
HEPTAHEDRONS
HEPTAMEROUS
HEPTAMETER
HEPTAMETERS
HEPTAMETRICAL
HEPTANDROUS
HEPTANGULAR
HEPTAPODIC
HEPTAPODIES
HEPTARCHAL
HEPTARCHIC
HEPTARCHIES
HEPTARCHIST
HEPTARCHISTS
HEPTASTICH
HEPTASTICHS
HEPTASYLLABIC
HEPTATHLETE
HEPTATHLETES
HEPTATHLON
HEPTATHLONS
HEPTATONIC
HEPTAVALENT
HERALDICALLY
HERALDISTS
HERALDRIES
HERALDSHIP
HERALDSHIPS
HERBACEOUS
HERBACEOUSLY
HERBALISMS
HERBALISTS
HERBARIANS
HERBARIUMS
HERBICIDAL
HERBICIDALLY
HERBICIDES
HERBIVORES
HERBIVORIES
HERBIVOROUS
HERBIVOROUSLY
HERBIVOROUSNESS
HERBOLOGIES
HERBORISATION
HERBORISATIONS
HERBORISED
HERBORISES
HERBORISING
HERBORISTS
HERBORIZATION
HERBORIZATIONS
HERBORIZED
HERBORIZES
HERBORIZING
HERCOGAMIES
HERCOGAMOUS
HERCULESES
HERCYNITES
HEREABOUTS
HEREAFTERS
HEREDITABILITY
HEREDITABLE
HEREDITABLY
HEREDITAMENT
HEREDITAMENTS
HEREDITARIAN
HEREDITARIANISM
HEREDITARIANIST
HEREDITARIANS
HEREDITARILY
HEREDITARINESS
HEREDITARY
HEREDITIES
HEREDITIST
HEREDITISTS
HEREINABOVE
HEREINAFTER
HEREINBEFORE
HEREINBELOW
HERENESSES
HERESIARCH
HERESIARCHS
HERESIOGRAPHER
HERESIOGRAPHERS
HERESIOGRAPHIES
HERESIOGRAPHY
HERESIOLOGIES
HERESIOLOGIST
HERESIOLOGISTS
HERESIOLOGY
HERESTHETIC
HERESTHETICAL
HERESTHETICIAN
HERESTHETICIANS
HERESTHETICS
HERETICALLY
HERETICATE
HERETICATED
HERETICATES
HERETICATING
HERETOFORE
HERETOFORES
HERETRICES
HERETRIXES
HERIOTABLE
HERITABILITIES
HERITABILITY
HERITRESSES
HERITRICES
HERITRIXES
HERKOGAMIES
HERMANDADS
HERMAPHRODITE
HERMAPHRODITES
HERMAPHRODITIC
HERMAPHRODITISM
HERMATYPIC
HERMENEUTIC
HERMENEUTICAL
HERMENEUTICALLY
HERMENEUTICS
HERMENEUTIST
HERMENEUTISTS
HERMETICAL
HERMETICALLY
HERMETICISM
HERMETICISMS

H

HERMETICITIES
HERMETICITY
HERMETISMS
HERMETISTS
HERMITAGES
HERMITESSES
HERMITICAL
HERMITICALLY
HERMITISMS
HERMITRIES
HERNIATING
HERNIATION
HERNIATIONS
HERNIORRHAPHIES
HERNIORRHAPHY
HERNIOTOMIES
HERNIOTOMY
HEROICALLY
HEROICALNESS
HEROICALNESSES
HEROICISED
HEROICISES
HEROICISING
HEROICIZED
HEROICIZES
HEROICIZING
HEROICNESS
HEROICNESSES
HEROICOMIC
HEROICOMICAL
HEROINISMS
HERONSHAWS
HERPESVIRUS
HERPESVIRUSES
HERPETOFAUNA
HERPETOFAUNAE
HERPETOFAUNAS
HERPETOLOGIC
HERPETOLOGICAL
HERPETOLOGIES
HERPETOLOGIST
HERPETOLOGISTS
HERPETOLOGY
HERRENVOLK
HERRENVOLKS
HERRIMENTS
HERRINGBONE
HERRINGBONED
HERRINGBONES
HERRINGBONING
HERRINGERS
HERRYMENTS
HERSTORIES
HESITANCES
HESITANCIES
HESITANTLY
HESITATERS
HESITATING
HESITATINGLY
HESITATION
HESITATIONS
HESITATIVE
HESITATORS
HESITATORY
HESPERIDIA
HESPERIDIN
HESPERIDINS
HESPERIDIUM
HESSONITES
HETAERISMIC
HETAERISMS
HETAERISTIC
HETAERISTS
HETAIRISMIC
HETAIRISMS
HETAIRISTIC
HETAIRISTS
HETERARCHIES
HETERARCHY
HETERAUXESES
HETERAUXESIS
HETEROAROMATIC
HETEROATOM
HETEROATOMS
HETEROAUXIN
HETEROAUXINS
HETEROBLASTIC
HETEROBLASTIES
HETEROBLASTY
HETEROCARPOUS
HETEROCERCAL
HETEROCERCALITY
HETEROCERCIES
HETEROCERCY
HETEROCHROMATIC
HETEROCHROMATIN
HETEROCHROMOUS
HETEROCHRONIC
HETEROCHRONIES
HETEROCHRONISM
HETEROCHRONISMS
HETEROCHRONOUS
HETEROCHRONY
HETEROCLITE
HETEROCLITES
HETEROCLITIC
HETEROCLITOUS
HETEROCONT
HETEROCONTS
HETEROCYCLE
HETEROCYCLES
HETEROCYCLIC
HETEROCYCLICS
HETEROCYST
HETEROCYSTOUS
HETEROCYSTS
HETERODACTYL
HETERODACTYLOUS
HETERODACTYLS
HETERODONT
HETERODOXIES
HETERODOXY
HETERODUPLEX
HETERODUPLEXES
HETERODYNE
HETERODYNED
HETERODYNES
HETERODYNING
HETEROECIOUS
HETEROECISM
HETEROECISMS
HETEROFLEXIBLE
HETEROFLEXIBLES
HETEROGAMETE
HETEROGAMETES
HETEROGAMETIC
HETEROGAMETIES
HETEROGAMETY
HETEROGAMIES
HETEROGAMOUS
HETEROGAMY
HETEROGENEITIES
HETEROGENEITY
HETEROGENEOUS
HETEROGENEOUSLY
HETEROGENESES
HETEROGENESIS
HETEROGENETIC
HETEROGENIC
HETEROGENIES
HETEROGENOUS
HETEROGENY
HETEROGONIC
HETEROGONIES
HETEROGONOUS
HETEROGONOUSLY
HETEROGONY
HETEROGRAFT
HETEROGRAFTS
HETEROGRAPHIC
HETEROGRAPHICAL
HETEROGRAPHIES
HETEROGRAPHY
HETEROGYNOUS
HETEROKARYON
HETEROKARYONS
HETEROKARYOSES
HETEROKARYOSIS
HETEROKARYOTIC
HETEROKONT
HETEROKONTAN
HETEROKONTS
HETEROLECITHAL
HETEROLOGIES
HETEROLOGOUS
HETEROLOGOUSLY
HETEROLOGY
HETEROLYSES
HETEROLYSIS
HETEROLYTIC
HETEROMEROUS
HETEROMORPHIC
HETEROMORPHIES
HETEROMORPHISM
HETEROMORPHISMS
HETEROMORPHOUS
HETEROMORPHY
HETERONOMIES
HETERONOMOUS
HETERONOMOUSLY
HETERONOMY
HETERONORMATIVE
HETERONYMOUS
HETERONYMOUSLY
HETERONYMS
HETEROOUSIAN
HETEROOUSIANS
HETEROPHIL
HETEROPHILE
HETEROPHILES
HETEROPHILS
HETEROPHONIES
HETEROPHONY
HETEROPHYLLIES
HETEROPHYLLOUS
HETEROPHYLLY
HETEROPLASIA
HETEROPLASIAS
HETEROPLASTIC
HETEROPLASTIES
HETEROPLASTY
HETEROPLOID
HETEROPLOIDIES
HETEROPLOIDS
HETEROPLOIDY
HETEROPODS
HETEROPOLAR
HETEROPOLARITY
HETEROPTERAN
HETEROPTERANS
HETEROPTEROUS
HETEROSCEDASTIC
HETEROSCIAN
HETEROSCIANS
HETEROSEXISM
HETEROSEXISMS
HETEROSEXIST
HETEROSEXISTS
HETEROSEXUAL
HETEROSEXUALITY
HETEROSEXUALLY
HETEROSEXUALS
HETEROSOCIAL
HETEROSOCIALITY
HETEROSOMATOUS
HETEROSPECIFIC
HETEROSPECIFICS
HETEROSPORIES
HETEROSPOROUS
HETEROSPORY

HETEROSTROPHIC
HETEROSTROPHIES
HETEROSTROPHY
HETEROSTYLED
HETEROSTYLIES
HETEROSTYLISM
HETEROSTYLISMS
HETEROSTYLOUS
HETEROSTYLY
HETEROTACTIC
HETEROTACTOUS
HETEROTAXES
HETEROTAXIA
HETEROTAXIAS
HETEROTAXIC
HETEROTAXIES
HETEROTAXIS
HETEROTAXY
HETEROTHALLIC
HETEROTHALLIES
HETEROTHALLISM
HETEROTHALLISMS
HETEROTHALLY
HETEROTHERMAL
HETEROTOPIA
HETEROTOPIAS
HETEROTOPIC
HETEROTOPIES
HETEROTOPOUS
HETEROTOPY
HETEROTROPH
HETEROTROPHIC
HETEROTROPHIES
HETEROTROPHS
HETEROTROPHY
HETEROTYPIC
HETEROTYPICAL
HETEROUSIAN
HETEROUSIANS
HETEROZYGOSES
HETEROZYGOSIS
HETEROZYGOSITY
HETEROZYGOTE
HETEROZYGOTES
HETEROZYGOUS
HETHERWARD
HETMANATES
HETMANSHIP
HETMANSHIPS
HEULANDITE
HEULANDITES
HEURISTICALLY
HEURISTICS
HEXACHLORETHANE
HEXACHLORIDE
HEXACHLORIDES
HEXACHLOROPHANE
HEXACHLOROPHENE
HEXACHORDS
HEXACOSANOIC
HEXACTINAL
HEXACTINELLID
HEXACTINELLIDS
HEXADACTYLIC
HEXADACTYLOUS
HEXADECANE
HEXADECANES
HEXADECANOIC
HEXADECIMAL
HEXADECIMALS
HEXADECYLS
HEXAEMERIC
HEXAEMERON
HEXAEMERONS
HEXAFLUORIDE
HEXAFLUORIDES
HEXAGONALLY
HEXAGRAMMOID
HEXAGRAMMOIDS
HEXAGYNIAN
HEXAGYNOUS
HEXAHEDRAL
HEXAHEDRON
HEXAHEDRONS
HEXAHEMERIC
HEXAHEMERON
HEXAHEMERONS
HEXAHYDRATE
HEXAHYDRATED
HEXAHYDRATES
HEXAMERISM
HEXAMERISMS
HEXAMEROUS
HEXAMETERS
HEXAMETHONIUM
HEXAMETHONIUMS
HEXAMETRAL
HEXAMETRIC
HEXAMETRICAL
HEXAMETRISE
HEXAMETRISED
HEXAMETRISES
HEXAMETRISING
HEXAMETRIST
HEXAMETRISTS
HEXAMETRIZE
HEXAMETRIZED
HEXAMETRIZES
HEXAMETRIZING
HEXANDRIAN
HEXANDROUS
HEXANGULAR
HEXAPLARIAN
HEXAPLARIC
HEXAPLOIDIES
HEXAPLOIDS
HEXAPLOIDY
HEXAPODIES
HEXARCHIES
HEXASTICHAL
HEXASTICHIC
HEXASTICHON
HEXASTICHONS
HEXASTICHS
HEXASTYLES
HEXATEUCHAL
HEXATHLONS
HEXAVALENT
HEXOBARBITAL
HEXOBARBITALS
HEXOKINASE
HEXOKINASES
HEXOSAMINIDASE
HEXOSAMINIDASES
HEXYLRESORCINOL
HIBAKUSHAS
HIBERNACLE
HIBERNACLES
HIBERNACULA
HIBERNACULUM
HIBERNATED
HIBERNATES
HIBERNATING
HIBERNATION
HIBERNATIONS
HIBERNATOR
HIBERNATORS
HIBERNICISATION
HIBERNICISE
HIBERNICISED
HIBERNICISES
HIBERNICISING
HIBERNICIZATION
HIBERNICIZE
HIBERNICIZED
HIBERNICIZES
HIBERNICIZING
HIBERNISATION
HIBERNISATIONS
HIBERNISED
HIBERNISES
HIBERNISING
HIBERNIZATION
HIBERNIZATIONS
HIBERNIZED
HIBERNIZES
HIBERNIZING
HIBISCUSES
HICCOUGHED
HICCOUGHING
HICCUPIEST
HICCUPPING
HIDALGOISH
HIDALGOISM
HIDALGOISMS
HIDDENITES
HIDDENMOST
HIDDENNESS
HIDDENNESSES
HIDEOSITIES
HIDEOUSNESS
HIDEOUSNESSES
HIERACIUMS
HIERACOSPHINGES
HIERACOSPHINX
HIERACOSPHINXES
HIERARCHAL
HIERARCHIC
HIERARCHICAL
HIERARCHICALLY
HIERARCHIES
HIERARCHISE
HIERARCHISED
HIERARCHISES
HIERARCHISING
HIERARCHISM
HIERARCHISMS
HIERARCHIZE
HIERARCHIZED
HIERARCHIZES
HIERARCHIZING
HIERATICAL
HIERATICALLY
HIERATICAS
HIEROCRACIES
HIEROCRACY
HIEROCRATIC
HIEROCRATICAL
HIEROCRATS
HIERODULES
HIERODULIC
HIEROGLYPH
HIEROGLYPHED
HIEROGLYPHIC
HIEROGLYPHICAL
HIEROGLYPHICS
HIEROGLYPHING
HIEROGLYPHIST
HIEROGLYPHISTS
HIEROGLYPHS
HIEROGRAMMAT
HIEROGRAMMATE
HIEROGRAMMATES
HIEROGRAMMATIC
HIEROGRAMMATIST
HIEROGRAMMATS
HIEROGRAMS
HIEROGRAPH
HIEROGRAPHER
HIEROGRAPHERS
HIEROGRAPHIC
HIEROGRAPHICAL
HIEROGRAPHIES
HIEROGRAPHS
HIEROGRAPHY
HIEROLATRIES
HIEROLATRY
HIEROLOGIC
HIEROLOGICAL
HIEROLOGIES

H

HIEROLOGIST
HIEROLOGISTS
HIEROMANCIES
HIEROMANCY
HIEROPHANT
HIEROPHANTIC
HIEROPHANTS
HIEROPHOBIA
HIEROPHOBIAS
HIEROPHOBIC
HIEROPHOBICS
HIEROSCOPIES
HIEROSCOPY
HIERURGICAL
HIERURGIES
HIGHBALLED
HIGHBALLING
HIGHBINDER
HIGHBINDERS
HIGHBLOODED
HIGHBROWED
HIGHBROWISM
HIGHBROWISMS
HIGHBUSHES
HIGHCHAIRS
HIGHERMOST
HIGHFALUTIN
HIGHFALUTING
HIGHFALUTINGS
HIGHFALUTINS
HIGHFLIERS
HIGHFLYERS
HIGHJACKED
HIGHJACKER
HIGHJACKERS
HIGHJACKING
HIGHJACKINGS
HIGHLANDER
HIGHLANDERS
HIGHLIGHTED
HIGHLIGHTER
HIGHLIGHTERS
HIGHLIGHTING
HIGHLIGHTS
HIGHNESSES
HIGHTAILED
HIGHTAILING
HIGHWAYMAN
HIGHWAYMEN
HIGHWROUGHT
HIJACKINGS
HILARIOUSLY
HILARIOUSNESS
HILARIOUSNESSES
HILARITIES
HILLBILLIES
HILLCRESTS
HILLINESSES
HILLOCKIER
HILLOCKIEST
HILLSLOPES
HILLWALKER
HILLWALKERS
HILLWALKING
HILLWALKINGS
HINDBERRIES
HINDBRAINS
HINDCASTED
HINDCASTING
HINDERANCE
HINDERANCES
HINDERINGLY
HINDERINGS
HINDERLAND
HINDERLANDS
HINDERLANS
HINDERLINGS
HINDERLINS
HINDERMOST
HINDFOREMOST
HINDQUARTER
HINDQUARTERS
HINDRANCES
HINDSHANKS
HINDSIGHTS
HINTERLAND
HINTERLANDS
HIPPEASTRUM
HIPPEASTRUMS
HIPPIATRIC
HIPPIATRICS
HIPPIATRIES
HIPPIATRIST
HIPPIATRISTS
HIPPIEDOMS
HIPPIENESS
HIPPIENESSES
HIPPINESSES
HIPPOCAMPAL
HIPPOCAMPI
HIPPOCAMPUS
HIPPOCENTAUR
HIPPOCENTAURS
HIPPOCRASES
HIPPOCREPIAN
HIPPOCREPIANS
HIPPODAMES
HIPPODAMIST
HIPPODAMISTS
HIPPODAMOUS
HIPPODROME
HIPPODROMES
HIPPODROMIC
HIPPOGRIFF
HIPPOGRIFFS
HIPPOGRYPH
HIPPOGRYPHS
HIPPOLOGIES
HIPPOLOGIST
HIPPOLOGISTS
HIPPOMANES
HIPPOPHAGIES
HIPPOPHAGIST
HIPPOPHAGISTS
HIPPOPHAGOUS
HIPPOPHAGY
HIPPOPHILE
HIPPOPHILES
HIPPOPHOBE
HIPPOPHOBES
HIPPOPOTAMI
HIPPOPOTAMIAN
HIPPOPOTAMIC
HIPPOPOTAMUS
HIPPOPOTAMUSES
HIPPURITES
HIPPURITIC
HIPSTERISM
HIPSTERISMS
HIRCOCERVUS
HIRCOCERVUSES
HIRCOSITIES
HIRSELLING
HIRSELLINGS
HIRSUTENESS
HIRSUTENESSES
HIRSUTISMS
HIRUDINEAN
HIRUDINEANS
HIRUDINOID
HIRUDINOUS
HISPANICISE
HISPANICISED
HISPANICISES
HISPANICISING
HISPANICISM
HISPANICISMS
HISPANICIZE
HISPANICIZED
HISPANICIZES
HISPANICIZING
HISPANIDAD
HISPANIDADS
HISPANIOLISE
HISPANIOLISED
HISPANIOLISES
HISPANIOLISING
HISPANIOLIZE
HISPANIOLIZED
HISPANIOLIZES
HISPANIOLIZING
HISPANISMS
HISPIDITIES
HISTAMINASE
HISTAMINASES
HISTAMINERGIC
HISTAMINES
HISTAMINIC
HISTIDINES
HISTIOCYTE
HISTIOCYTES
HISTIOCYTIC
HISTIOLOGIES
HISTIOLOGY
HISTIOPHOROID
HISTOBLAST
HISTOBLASTS
HISTOCHEMICAL
HISTOCHEMICALLY
HISTOCHEMIST
HISTOCHEMISTRY
HISTOCHEMISTS
HISTOCOMPATIBLE
HISTOGENESES
HISTOGENESIS
HISTOGENETIC
HISTOGENIC
HISTOGENICALLY
HISTOGENIES
HISTOGRAMS
HISTOLOGIC
HISTOLOGICAL
HISTOLOGICALLY
HISTOLOGIES
HISTOLOGIST
HISTOLOGISTS
HISTOLYSES
HISTOLYSIS
HISTOLYTIC
HISTOLYTICALLY
HISTOPATHOLOGIC
HISTOPATHOLOGY
HISTOPHYSIOLOGY
HISTOPLASMOSES
HISTOPLASMOSIS
HISTORIANS
HISTORIATED
HISTORICAL
HISTORICALLY
HISTORICALNESS
HISTORICISE
HISTORICISED
HISTORICISES
HISTORICISING
HISTORICISM
HISTORICISMS
HISTORICIST
HISTORICISTS
HISTORICITIES
HISTORICITY
HISTORICIZE
HISTORICIZED
HISTORICIZES
HISTORICIZING
HISTORIETTE
HISTORIETTES
HISTORIFIED
HISTORIFIES
HISTORIFYING
HISTORIOGRAPHER

HISTORIOGRAPHIC
HISTORIOGRAPHY
HISTORIOLOGIES
HISTORIOLOGY
HISTORISMS
HISTORYING
HISTRIONIC
HISTRIONICAL
HISTRIONICALLY
HISTRIONICISM
HISTRIONICISMS
HISTRIONICS
HISTRIONISM
HISTRIONISMS
HITCHHIKED
HITCHHIKER
HITCHHIKERS
HITCHHIKES
HITCHHIKING
HITCHHIKINGS
HITHERMOST
HITHERSIDE
HITHERSIDES
HITHERWARD
HITHERWARDS
HOACTZINES
HOARFROSTS
HOARHOUNDS
HOARINESSES
HOARSENESS
HOARSENESSES
HOARSENING
HOBBITRIES
HOBBLEBUSH
HOBBLEBUSHES
HOBBLEDEHOY
HOBBLEDEHOYDOM
HOBBLEDEHOYDOMS
HOBBLEDEHOYHOOD
HOBBLEDEHOYISH
HOBBLEDEHOYISM
HOBBLEDEHOYISMS
HOBBLEDEHOYS
HOBBLINGLY
HOBBYHORSE
HOBBYHORSED
HOBBYHORSES
HOBBYHORSING
HOBGOBLINISM
HOBGOBLINISMS
HOBGOBLINRIES
HOBGOBLINRY
HOBGOBLINS
HOBJOBBERS
HOBJOBBING
HOBJOBBINGS
HOBNAILING
HOBNOBBERS
HOBNOBBIER
HOBNOBBIEST
HOBNOBBING
HOCHMAGANDIES
HOCHMAGANDY
HODGEPODGE
HODGEPODGES
HODMANDODS
HODOGRAPHIC
HODOGRAPHS
HODOMETERS
HODOMETRIES
HODOSCOPES
HOGGISHNESS
HOGGISHNESSES
HOIDENISHNESS
HOIDENISHNESSES
HOJATOLESLAM
HOJATOLESLAMS
HOJATOLISLAM
HOJATOLISLAMS
HOKEYNESSES
HOKEYPOKEY
HOKEYPOKEYS
HOKINESSES
HOKYPOKIES
HOLARCHIES
HOLDERBATS
HOLDERSHIP
HOLDERSHIPS
HOLIDAYERS
HOLIDAYING
HOLIDAYMAKER
HOLIDAYMAKERS
HOLINESSES
HOLISTICALLY
HOLLANDAISE
HOLLANDAISES
HOLLOWARES
HOLLOWNESS
HOLLOWNESSES
HOLLOWWARE
HOLLOWWARES
HOLLYHOCKS
HOLOBENTHIC
HOLOBLASTIC
HOLOBLASTICALLY
HOLOCAINES
HOLOCAUSTAL
HOLOCAUSTIC
HOLOCAUSTS
HOLOCRYSTALLINE
HOLODISCUS
HOLODISCUSES
HOLOENZYME
HOLOENZYMES
HOLOGAMIES
HOLOGRAPHED
HOLOGRAPHER
HOLOGRAPHERS
HOLOGRAPHIC
HOLOGRAPHICALLY
HOLOGRAPHIES
HOLOGRAPHING
HOLOGRAPHS
HOLOGRAPHY
HOLOGYNIES
HOLOHEDRAL
HOLOHEDRISM
HOLOHEDRISMS
HOLOHEDRON
HOLOHEDRONS
HOLOMETABOLIC
HOLOMETABOLISM
HOLOMETABOLISMS
HOLOMETABOLOUS
HOLOMORPHIC
HOLOPHOTAL
HOLOPHOTES
HOLOPHRASE
HOLOPHRASES
HOLOPHRASTIC
HOLOPHYTES
HOLOPHYTIC
HOLOPHYTISM
HOLOPHYTISMS
HOLOPLANKTON
HOLOPLANKTONS
HOLOSTERIC
HOLOTHURIAN
HOLOTHURIANS
HOLSTERING
HOLYSTONED
HOLYSTONES
HOLYSTONING
HOMALOGRAPHIC
HOMALOIDAL
HOMEBIRTHS
HOMEBODIES
HOMEBUYERS
HOMECOMERS
HOMECOMING
HOMECOMINGS
HOMECRAFTS
HOMELESSNESS
HOMELESSNESSES
HOMELINESS
HOMELINESSES
HOMEMAKERS
HOMEMAKING
HOMEMAKINGS
HOMEOBOXES
HOMEOMERIC
HOMEOMERIES
HOMEOMEROUS
HOMEOMORPH
HOMEOMORPHIC
HOMEOMORPHIES
HOMEOMORPHISM
HOMEOMORPHISMS
HOMEOMORPHOUS
HOMEOMORPHS
HOMEOMORPHY
HOMEOPATHIC
HOMEOPATHICALLY
HOMEOPATHIES
HOMEOPATHIST
HOMEOPATHISTS
HOMEOPATHS
HOMEOPATHY
HOMEOSTASES
HOMEOSTASIS
HOMEOSTATIC
HOMEOTELEUTON
HOMEOTELEUTONS
HOMEOTHERM
HOMEOTHERMAL
HOMEOTHERMIC
HOMEOTHERMIES
HOMEOTHERMISM
HOMEOTHERMISMS
HOMEOTHERMOUS
HOMEOTHERMS
HOMEOTHERMY
HOMEOTYPIC
HOMEOTYPICAL
HOMEOWNERS
HOMEOWNERSHIP
HOMEOWNERSHIPS
HOMEPLACES
HOMEPORTED
HOMEPORTING
HOMESCHOOL
HOMESCHOOLED
HOMESCHOOLER
HOMESCHOOLERS
HOMESCHOOLING
HOMESCHOOLS
HOMESCREETCH
HOMESCREETCHES
HOMESHORING
HOMESHORINGS
HOMESICKNESS
HOMESICKNESSES
HOMESOURCING
HOMESOURCINGS
HOMESTALLS
HOMESTANDS
HOMESTEADED
HOMESTEADER
HOMESTEADERS
HOMESTEADING
HOMESTEADINGS
HOMESTEADS
HOMESTRETCH
HOMESTRETCHES
HOMEWORKER
HOMEWORKERS
HOMEWORKING
HOMEWORKINGS
HOMEYNESSES
HOMICIDALLY

H

HOMILETICAL
HOMILETICALLY
HOMILETICS
HOMINESSES
HOMINISATION
HOMINISATIONS
HOMINISING
HOMINIZATION
HOMINIZATIONS
HOMINIZING
HOMOBLASTIC
HOMOBLASTIES
HOMOBLASTY
HOMOCENTRIC
HOMOCENTRICALLY
HOMOCERCAL
HOMOCERCIES
HOMOCHLAMYDEOUS
HOMOCHROMATIC
HOMOCHROMATISM
HOMOCHROMATISMS
HOMOCHROMIES
HOMOCHROMOUS
HOMOCHROMY
HOMOCYCLIC
HOMOCYSTEINE
HOMOCYSTEINES
HOMOEOMERIC
HOMOEOMERIES
HOMOEOMEROUS
HOMOEOMERY
HOMOEOMORPH
HOMOEOMORPHIC
HOMOEOMORPHIES
HOMOEOMORPHISM
HOMOEOMORPHISMS
HOMOEOMORPHOUS
HOMOEOMORPHS
HOMOEOMORPHY
HOMOEOPATH
HOMOEOPATHIC
HOMOEOPATHIES
HOMOEOPATHIST
HOMOEOPATHISTS
HOMOEOPATHS
HOMOEOPATHY
HOMOEOSTASES
HOMOEOSTASIS
HOMOEOSTATIC
HOMOEOTELEUTON
HOMOEOTELEUTONS
HOMOEOTHERM
HOMOEOTHERMAL
HOMOEOTHERMIC
HOMOEOTHERMOUS
HOMOEOTHERMS
HOMOEOTYPIC
HOMOEOTYPICAL
HOMOEROTIC
HOMOEROTICISM
HOMOEROTICISMS
HOMOEROTISM
HOMOEROTISMS
HOMOGAMETIC
HOMOGAMIES
HOMOGAMOUS
HOMOGENATE
HOMOGENATES
HOMOGENEITIES
HOMOGENEITY
HOMOGENEOUS
HOMOGENEOUSLY
HOMOGENEOUSNESS
HOMOGENESES
HOMOGENESIS
HOMOGENETIC
HOMOGENETICAL
HOMOGENIES
HOMOGENISATION
HOMOGENISATIONS
HOMOGENISE
HOMOGENISED
HOMOGENISER
HOMOGENISERS
HOMOGENISES
HOMOGENISING
HOMOGENIZATION
HOMOGENIZATIONS
HOMOGENIZE
HOMOGENIZED
HOMOGENIZER
HOMOGENIZERS
HOMOGENIZES
HOMOGENIZING
HOMOGENOUS
HOMOGONIES
HOMOGONOUS
HOMOGONOUSLY
HOMOGRAFTS
HOMOGRAPHIC
HOMOGRAPHIES
HOMOGRAPHS
HOMOGRAPHY
HOMOIOMEROUS
HOMOIOTHERM
HOMOIOTHERMAL
HOMOIOTHERMIC
HOMOIOTHERMIES
HOMOIOTHERMS
HOMOIOTHERMY
HOMOIOUSIAN
HOMOIOUSIANS
HOMOLOGATE
HOMOLOGATED
HOMOLOGATES
HOMOLOGATING
HOMOLOGATION
HOMOLOGATIONS
HOMOLOGICAL
HOMOLOGICALLY
HOMOLOGIES
HOMOLOGISE
HOMOLOGISED
HOMOLOGISER
HOMOLOGISERS
HOMOLOGISES
HOMOLOGISING
HOMOLOGIZE
HOMOLOGIZED
HOMOLOGIZER
HOMOLOGIZERS
HOMOLOGIZES
HOMOLOGIZING
HOMOLOGOUMENA
HOMOLOGOUS
HOMOLOGRAPHIC
HOMOLOGUES
HOMOLOGUMENA
HOMOLOSINE
HOMOMORPHIC
HOMOMORPHIES
HOMOMORPHISM
HOMOMORPHISMS
HOMOMORPHOSES
HOMOMORPHOSIS
HOMOMORPHOUS
HOMOMORPHS
HOMOMORPHY
HOMONUCLEAR
HOMONYMIES
HOMONYMITIES
HOMONYMITY
HOMONYMOUS
HOMONYMOUSLY
HOMOOUSIAN
HOMOOUSIANS
HOMOPHILES
HOMOPHOBES
HOMOPHOBIA
HOMOPHOBIAS
HOMOPHOBIC
HOMOPHONES
HOMOPHONIC
HOMOPHONICALLY
HOMOPHONIES
HOMOPHONOUS
HOMOPHYLIES
HOMOPHYLLIC
HOMOPLASIES
HOMOPLASMIES
HOMOPLASMY
HOMOPLASTIC
HOMOPLASTICALLY
HOMOPLASTIES
HOMOPLASTY
HOMOPOLARITIES
HOMOPOLARITY
HOMOPOLYMER
HOMOPOLYMERIC
HOMOPOLYMERS
HOMOPTERAN
HOMOPTERANS
HOMOPTEROUS
HOMORGANIC
HOMOSCEDASTIC
HOMOSEXUAL
HOMOSEXUALISM
HOMOSEXUALISMS
HOMOSEXUALIST
HOMOSEXUALISTS
HOMOSEXUALITIES
HOMOSEXUALITY
HOMOSEXUALLY
HOMOSEXUALS
HOMOSOCIAL
HOMOSOCIALITIES
HOMOSOCIALITY
HOMOSPORIES
HOMOSPOROUS
HOMOSTYLIES
HOMOTAXIAL
HOMOTAXIALLY
HOMOTHALLIC
HOMOTHALLIES
HOMOTHALLISM
HOMOTHALLISMS
HOMOTHALLY
HOMOTHERMAL
HOMOTHERMIC
HOMOTHERMIES
HOMOTHERMOUS
HOMOTHERMY
HOMOTONIES
HOMOTONOUS
HOMOTRANSPLANT
HOMOTRANSPLANTS
HOMOTYPIES
HOMOUSIANS
HOMOZYGOSES
HOMOZYGOSIS
HOMOZYGOSITIES
HOMOZYGOSITY
HOMOZYGOTE
HOMOZYGOTES
HOMOZYGOTIC
HOMOZYGOUS
HOMOZYGOUSLY
HOMUNCULAR
HOMUNCULES
HOMUNCULUS
HONESTNESS
HONESTNESSES
HONEYBELLS
HONEYBUNCH
HONEYBUNCHES
HONEYCOMBED
HONEYCOMBING
HONEYCOMBINGS
HONEYCOMBS
HONEYCREEPER

HONEYCREEPERS
HONEYDEWED
HONEYEATER
HONEYEATERS
HONEYGUIDE
HONEYGUIDES
HONEYMONTH
HONEYMONTHED
HONEYMONTHING
HONEYMONTHS
HONEYMOONED
HONEYMOONER
HONEYMOONERS
HONEYMOONING
HONEYMOONS
HONEYSUCKER
HONEYSUCKERS
HONEYSUCKLE
HONEYSUCKLED
HONEYSUCKLES
HONEYTRAPS
HONORABILITIES
HONORABILITY
HONORABLENESS
HONORABLENESSES
HONORARIES
HONORARILY
HONORARIUM
HONORARIUMS
HONORIFICAL
HONORIFICALLY
HONORIFICS
HONOURABILITIES
HONOURABILITY
HONOURABLE
HONOURABLENESS
HONOURABLY
HONOURLESS
HOODEDNESS
HOODEDNESSES
HOODLUMISH
HOODLUMISM
HOODLUMISMS
HOODOOISMS
HOODWINKED
HOODWINKER
HOODWINKERS
HOODWINKING
HOOFPRINTS
HOOKCHECKS
HOOKEDNESS
HOOKEDNESSES
HOOLACHANS
HOOLIGANISM
HOOLIGANISMS
HOOPSKIRTS
HOOTANANNIE
HOOTANANNIES
HOOTANANNY
HOOTENANNIE
HOOTENANNIES
HOOTENANNY
HOOTNANNIE
HOOTNANNIES
HOOVERINGS
HOPEFULNESS
HOPEFULNESSES
HOPELESSLY
HOPELESSNESS
HOPELESSNESSES
HOPLOLOGIES
HOPLOLOGIST
HOPLOLOGISTS
HOPPERCARS
HOPPINESSES
HOPSACKING
HOPSACKINGS
HOPSCOTCHED
HOPSCOTCHES
HOPSCOTCHING
HOREHOUNDS
HORIATIKIS
HORIZONLESS
HORIZONTAL
HORIZONTALITIES
HORIZONTALITY
HORIZONTALLY
HORIZONTALNESS
HORIZONTALS
HORMOGONIA
HORMOGONIUM
HORMONALLY
HORMONELIKE
HORNBLENDE
HORNBLENDES
HORNBLENDIC
HORNEDNESS
HORNEDNESSES
HORNFELSES
HORNFISHES
HORNINESSES
HORNLESSNESS
HORNLESSNESSES
HORNSTONES
HORNSWOGGLE
HORNSWOGGLED
HORNSWOGGLES
HORNSWOGGLING
HORNWRACKS
HORNYHEADS
HORNYWINKS
HOROGRAPHER
HOROGRAPHERS
HOROGRAPHIES
HOROGRAPHY
HOROLOGERS
HOROLOGICAL
HOROLOGIES
HOROLOGION
HOROLOGIONS
HOROLOGIST
HOROLOGISTS
HOROLOGIUM
HOROMETRICAL
HOROMETRIES
HOROSCOPES
HOROSCOPIC
HOROSCOPIES
HOROSCOPIST
HOROSCOPISTS
HORRENDOUS
HORRENDOUSLY
HORRENDOUSNESS
HORRIBLENESS
HORRIBLENESSES
HORRIDNESS
HORRIDNESSES
HORRIFICALLY
HORRIFICATION
HORRIFICATIONS
HORRIFYING
HORRIFYINGLY
HORRIPILANT
HORRIPILATE
HORRIPILATED
HORRIPILATES
HORRIPILATING
HORRIPILATION
HORRIPILATIONS
HORRISONANT
HORRISONOUS
HORSEBACKS
HORSEBEANS
HORSEBOXES
HORSEFEATHERS
HORSEFLESH
HORSEFLESHES
HORSEFLIES
HORSEHAIRS
HORSEHEADS
HORSEHIDES
HORSELAUGH
HORSELAUGHS
HORSELEECH
HORSELEECHES
HORSEMANSHIP
HORSEMANSHIPS
HORSEMEATS
HORSEMINTS
HORSEPLAYER
HORSEPLAYERS
HORSEPLAYS
HORSEPONDS
HORSEPOWER
HORSEPOWERS
HORSEPOXES
HORSERACES
HORSERADISH
HORSERADISHES
HORSESHITS
HORSESHOED
HORSESHOEING
HORSESHOEINGS
HORSESHOER
HORSESHOERS
HORSESHOES
HORSETAILS
HORSEWEEDS
HORSEWHIPPED
HORSEWHIPPER
HORSEWHIPPERS
HORSEWHIPPING
HORSEWHIPS
HORSEWOMAN
HORSEWOMEN
HORSINESSES
HORTATIONS
HORTATIVELY
HORTATORILY
HORTENSIAS
HORTICULTURAL
HORTICULTURALLY
HORTICULTURE
HORTICULTURES
HORTICULTURIST
HORTICULTURISTS
HOSANNAING
HOSPITABLE
HOSPITABLENESS
HOSPITABLY
HOSPITAGES
HOSPITALER
HOSPITALERS
HOSPITALES
HOSPITALISATION
HOSPITALISE
HOSPITALISED
HOSPITALISES
HOSPITALISING
HOSPITALIST
HOSPITALISTS
HOSPITALITIES
HOSPITALITY
HOSPITALIZATION
HOSPITALIZE
HOSPITALIZED
HOSPITALIZES
HOSPITALIZING
HOSPITALLER
HOSPITALLERS
HOSTELINGS
HOSTELLERS
HOSTELLING
HOSTELLINGS
HOSTELRIES
HOSTESSING
HOSTILITIES
HOTCHPOTCH
HOTCHPOTCHES
HOTDOGGERS

H

HOTDOGGING
HOTELLINGS
HOTFOOTING
HOTHEADEDLY
HOTHEADEDNESS
HOTHEADEDNESSES
HOTHOUSING
HOTHOUSINGS
HOTPRESSED
HOTPRESSES
HOTPRESSING
HOTTENTOTS
HOUGHMAGANDIE
HOUGHMAGANDIES
HOUNDFISHES
HOURGLASSES
HOURPLATES
HOUSEBOATER
HOUSEBOATERS
HOUSEBOATS
HOUSEBOUND
HOUSEBREAK
HOUSEBREAKER
HOUSEBREAKERS
HOUSEBREAKING
HOUSEBREAKINGS
HOUSEBREAKS
HOUSEBROKE
HOUSEBROKEN
HOUSECARLS
HOUSECLEAN
HOUSECLEANED
HOUSECLEANING
HOUSECLEANINGS
HOUSECLEANS
HOUSECOATS
HOUSECRAFT
HOUSECRAFTS
HOUSEDRESS
HOUSEDRESSES
HOUSEFATHER
HOUSEFATHERS
HOUSEFLIES
HOUSEFRONT
HOUSEFRONTS
HOUSEGUEST
HOUSEGUESTS
HOUSEHOLDER
HOUSEHOLDERS
HOUSEHOLDERSHIP
HOUSEHOLDS
HOUSEHUSBAND
HOUSEHUSBANDS
HOUSEKEEPER
HOUSEKEEPERS
HOUSEKEEPING
HOUSEKEEPINGS
HOUSEKEEPS
HOUSELEEKS
HOUSELESSNESS
HOUSELESSNESSES
HOUSELIGHTS
HOUSELINES
HOUSELINGS
HOUSELLING
HOUSELLINGS
HOUSEMAIDS
HOUSEMASTER
HOUSEMASTERS
HOUSEMATES
HOUSEMISTRESS
HOUSEMISTRESSES
HOUSEMOTHER
HOUSEMOTHERS
HOUSEPAINTER
HOUSEPAINTERS
HOUSEPARENT
HOUSEPARENTS
HOUSEPERSON
HOUSEPERSONS
HOUSEPLANT
HOUSEPLANTS
HOUSEROOMS
HOUSESITTING
HOUSEWARES
HOUSEWARMING
HOUSEWARMINGS
HOUSEWIFELIER
HOUSEWIFELIEST
HOUSEWIFELINESS
HOUSEWIFELY
HOUSEWIFERIES
HOUSEWIFERY
HOUSEWIFESHIP
HOUSEWIFESHIPS
HOUSEWIFESKEP
HOUSEWIFESKEPS
HOUSEWIFEY
HOUSEWIFIER
HOUSEWIFIEST
HOUSEWIVES
HOUSEWORKER
HOUSEWORKERS
HOUSEWORKS
HOUSEWRAPS
HOUSTONIAS
HOVERBOARD
HOVERBOARDS
HOVERCRAFT
HOVERCRAFTS
HOVERFLIES
HOVERINGLY
HOVERPORTS
HOVERTRAIN
HOVERTRAINS
HOWLROUNDS
HOWSOMDEVER
HOWSOMEVER
HOWTOWDIES
HOYDENHOOD
HOYDENHOODS
HOYDENISHNESS
HOYDENISHNESSES
HOYDENISMS
HUBRISTICALLY
HUCKABACKS
HUCKLEBERRIES
HUCKLEBERRY
HUCKLEBERRYING
HUCKLEBERRYINGS
HUCKLEBONE
HUCKLEBONES
HUCKSTERAGE
HUCKSTERAGES
HUCKSTERED
HUCKSTERESS
HUCKSTERESSES
HUCKSTERIES
HUCKSTERING
HUCKSTERISM
HUCKSTERISMS
HUCKSTRESS
HUCKSTRESSES
HUDIBRASTIC
HUFFINESSES
HUFFISHNESS
HUFFISHNESSES
HUGENESSES
HUGEOUSNESS
HUGEOUSNESSES
HULLABALLOO
HULLABALLOOS
HULLABALOO
HULLABALOOS
HUMANENESS
HUMANENESSES
HUMANHOODS
HUMANISATION
HUMANISATIONS
HUMANISERS
HUMANISING
HUMANISTIC
HUMANISTICALLY
HUMANITARIAN
HUMANITARIANISM
HUMANITARIANIST
HUMANITARIANS
HUMANITIES
HUMANIZATION
HUMANIZATIONS
HUMANIZERS
HUMANIZING
HUMANKINDS
HUMANNESSES
HUMBLEBEES
HUMBLEBRAG
HUMBLEBRAGGED
HUMBLEBRAGGING
HUMBLEBRAGS
HUMBLENESS
HUMBLENESSES
HUMBLESSES
HUMBLINGLY
HUMBUCKERS
HUMBUGGABLE
HUMBUGGERIES
HUMBUGGERS
HUMBUGGERY
HUMBUGGING
HUMDINGERS
HUMDRUMNESS
HUMDRUMNESSES
HUMDUDGEON
HUMDUDGEONS
HUMDURGEON
HUMDURGEONS
HUMECTANTS
HUMECTATED
HUMECTATES
HUMECTATING
HUMECTATION
HUMECTATIONS
HUMECTIVES
HUMGRUFFIAN
HUMGRUFFIANS
HUMGRUFFIN
HUMGRUFFINS
HUMICOLOUS
HUMIDIFICATION
HUMIDIFICATIONS
HUMIDIFIED
HUMIDIFIER
HUMIDIFIERS
HUMIDIFIES
HUMIDIFYING
HUMIDISTAT
HUMIDISTATS
HUMIDITIES
HUMIDNESSES
HUMIFICATION
HUMIFICATIONS
HUMILIATED
HUMILIATES
HUMILIATING
HUMILIATINGLY
HUMILIATION
HUMILIATIONS
HUMILIATIVE
HUMILIATOR
HUMILIATORS
HUMILIATORY
HUMILITIES
HUMMELLERS
HUMMELLING
HUMMELLINGS
HUMMINGBIRD
HUMMINGBIRDS
HUMMOCKIER
HUMMOCKIEST
HUMMOCKING

HUMORALISM
HUMORALISMS
HUMORALIST
HUMORALISTS
HUMORESQUE
HUMORESQUES
HUMORISTIC
HUMORLESSLY
HUMORLESSNESS
HUMORLESSNESSES
HUMOROUSLY
HUMOROUSNESS
HUMOROUSNESSES
HUMORSOMENESS
HUMORSOMENESSES
HUMOURLESS
HUMOURLESSLY
HUMOURLESSNESS
HUMOURSOME
HUMOURSOMENESS
HUMPBACKED
HUMPINESSES
HUNCHBACKED
HUNCHBACKS
HUNDREDERS
HUNDREDFOLD
HUNDREDFOLDS
HUNDREDORS
HUNDREDTHS
HUNDREDWEIGHT
HUNDREDWEIGHTS
HUNGERINGLY
HUNGRINESS
HUNGRINESSES
HUNTIEGOWK
HUNTIEGOWKED
HUNTIEGOWKING
HUNTIEGOWKS
HUNTRESSES
HUNTSMANSHIP
HUNTSMANSHIPS
HUPAITHRIC
HURLBARROW
HURLBARROWS
HURRICANES
HURRICANOES
HURRIEDNESS
HURRIEDNESSES

HURRYINGLY
HURTFULNESS
HURTFULNESSES
HURTLEBERRIES
HURTLEBERRY
HURTLESSLY
HURTLESSNESS
HURTLESSNESSES
HUSBANDAGE
HUSBANDAGES
HUSBANDERS
HUSBANDING
HUSBANDLAND
HUSBANDLANDS
HUSBANDLESS
HUSBANDLIER
HUSBANDLIEST
HUSBANDLIKE
HUSBANDMAN
HUSBANDMEN
HUSBANDRIES
HUSHABYING
HUSHPUPPIES
HUSKINESSES
HYACINTHINE
HYALINISATION
HYALINISATIONS
HYALINISED
HYALINISES
HYALINISING
HYALINIZATION
HYALINIZATIONS
HYALINIZED
HYALINIZES
HYALINIZING
HYALOMELAN
HYALOMELANE
HYALOMELANES
HYALOMELANS
HYALONEMAS
HYALOPHANE
HYALOPHANES
HYALOPLASM
HYALOPLASMIC
HYALOPLASMS
HYALURONIC
HYALURONIDASE
HYALURONIDASES

HYBRIDISABLE
HYBRIDISATION
HYBRIDISATIONS
HYBRIDISED
HYBRIDISER
HYBRIDISERS
HYBRIDISES
HYBRIDISING
HYBRIDISMS
HYBRIDISTS
HYBRIDITIES
HYBRIDIZABLE
HYBRIDIZATION
HYBRIDIZATIONS
HYBRIDIZED
HYBRIDIZER
HYBRIDIZERS
HYBRIDIZES
HYBRIDIZING
HYBRIDOMAS
HYBRIDOMATA
HYDANTOINS
HYDATHODES
HYDATIDIFORM
HYDNOCARPATE
HYDNOCARPATES
HYDNOCARPIC
HYDRAEMIAS
HYDRAGOGUE
HYDRAGOGUES
HYDRALAZINE
HYDRALAZINES
HYDRANGEAS
HYDRARGYRAL
HYDRARGYRIA
HYDRARGYRIAS
HYDRARGYRIC
HYDRARGYRISM
HYDRARGYRISMS
HYDRARGYRUM
HYDRARGYRUMS
HYDRARTHROSES
HYDRARTHROSIS
HYDRASTINE
HYDRASTINES
HYDRASTININE
HYDRASTININES
HYDRASTISES

HYDRATIONS
HYDRAULICALLY
HYDRAULICKED
HYDRAULICKING
HYDRAULICKINGS
HYDRAULICS
HYDRAZIDES
HYDRAZINES
HYDRICALLY
HYDROACOUSTICS
HYDROBIOLOGICAL
HYDROBIOLOGIES
HYDROBIOLOGIST
HYDROBIOLOGISTS
HYDROBIOLOGY
HYDROBROMIC
HYDROCARBON
HYDROCARBONS
HYDROCASTS
HYDROCELES
HYDROCELLULOSE
HYDROCELLULOSES
HYDROCEPHALI
HYDROCEPHALIC
HYDROCEPHALICS
HYDROCEPHALIES
HYDROCEPHALOID
HYDROCEPHALOUS
HYDROCEPHALUS
HYDROCEPHALUSES
HYDROCEPHALY
HYDROCHLORIC
HYDROCHLORIDE
HYDROCHLORIDES
HYDROCHORE
HYDROCHORES
HYDROCHORIC
HYDROCODONE
HYDROCODONES
HYDROCOLLOID
HYDROCOLLOIDAL
HYDROCOLLOIDS
HYDROCORAL
HYDROCORALLINE
HYDROCORALLINES
HYDROCORALS
HYDROCORTISONE
HYDROCORTISONES

HYDROCRACK
HYDROCRACKED
HYDROCRACKER
HYDROCRACKERS
HYDROCRACKING
HYDROCRACKINGS
HYDROCRACKS
HYDROCYANIC
HYDRODYNAMIC
HYDRODYNAMICAL
HYDRODYNAMICIST
HYDRODYNAMICS
HYDROELASTIC
HYDROELECTRIC
HYDROEXTRACTOR
HYDROEXTRACTORS
HYDROFLUORIC
HYDROFOILS
HYDROFORMING
HYDROFORMINGS
HYDROGENASE
HYDROGENASES
HYDROGENATE
HYDROGENATED
HYDROGENATES
HYDROGENATING
HYDROGENATION
HYDROGENATIONS
HYDROGENATOR
HYDROGENATORS
HYDROGENISATION
HYDROGENISE
HYDROGENISED
HYDROGENISES
HYDROGENISING
HYDROGENIZATION
HYDROGENIZE
HYDROGENIZED
HYDROGENIZES
HYDROGENIZING
HYDROGENOLYSES
HYDROGENOLYSIS
HYDROGENOUS
HYDROGEOLOGICAL
HYDROGEOLOGIES
HYDROGEOLOGIST
HYDROGEOLOGISTS
HYDROGEOLOGY

HYDROGRAPH
HYDROGRAPHER
HYDROGRAPHERS
HYDROGRAPHIC
HYDROGRAPHICAL
HYDROGRAPHIES
HYDROGRAPHS
HYDROGRAPHY
HYDROKINETIC
HYDROKINETICAL
HYDROKINETICS
HYDROLASES
HYDROLOGIC
HYDROLOGICAL
HYDROLOGICALLY
HYDROLOGIES
HYDROLOGIST
HYDROLOGISTS
HYDROLYSABLE
HYDROLYSATE
HYDROLYSATES
HYDROLYSATION
HYDROLYSATIONS
HYDROLYSED
HYDROLYSER
HYDROLYSERS
HYDROLYSES
HYDROLYSING
HYDROLYSIS
HYDROLYTES
HYDROLYTIC
HYDROLYTICALLY
HYDROLYZABLE
HYDROLYZATE
HYDROLYZATES
HYDROLYZATION
HYDROLYZATIONS
HYDROLYZED
HYDROLYZER
HYDROLYZERS
HYDROLYZES
HYDROLYZING
HYDROMAGNETIC
HYDROMAGNETICS
HYDROMANCER
HYDROMANCERS
HYDROMANCIES
HYDROMANCY
HYDROMANIA
HYDROMANIAS
HYDROMANTIC
HYDROMECHANICAL
HYDROMECHANICS
HYDROMEDUSA
HYDROMEDUSAE
HYDROMEDUSAN
HYDROMEDUSANS
HYDROMEDUSAS
HYDROMEDUSOID
HYDROMEDUSOIDS
HYDROMETALLURGY
HYDROMETEOR
HYDROMETEORS
HYDROMETER
HYDROMETERS
HYDROMETRIC
HYDROMETRICAL
HYDROMETRICALLY
HYDROMETRIES
HYDROMETRY
HYDROMORPHIC
HYDRONAUTS
HYDRONEPHROSES
HYDRONEPHROSIS
HYDRONEPHROTIC
HYDRONICALLY
HYDRONIUMS
HYDROPATHIC
HYDROPATHICAL
HYDROPATHICALLY
HYDROPATHICS
HYDROPATHIES
HYDROPATHIST
HYDROPATHISTS
HYDROPATHS
HYDROPATHY
HYDROPEROXIDE
HYDROPEROXIDES
HYDROPHANE
HYDROPHANES
HYDROPHANOUS
HYDROPHILE
HYDROPHILES
HYDROPHILIC
HYDROPHILICITY
HYDROPHILIES
HYDROPHILITE
HYDROPHILITES
HYDROPHILOUS
HYDROPHILY
HYDROPHOBIA
HYDROPHOBIAS
HYDROPHOBIC
HYDROPHOBICITY
HYDROPHOBOUS
HYDROPHONE
HYDROPHONES
HYDROPHYTE
HYDROPHYTES
HYDROPHYTIC
HYDROPHYTON
HYDROPHYTONS
HYDROPHYTOUS
HYDROPLANE
HYDROPLANED
HYDROPLANES
HYDROPLANING
HYDROPNEUMATIC
HYDROPOLYP
HYDROPOLYPS
HYDROPONIC
HYDROPONICALLY
HYDROPONICS
HYDROPOWER
HYDROPOWERS
HYDROPSIES
HYDROPULTS
HYDROQUINOL
HYDROQUINOLS
HYDROQUINONE
HYDROQUINONES
HYDROSCOPE
HYDROSCOPES
HYDROSCOPIC
HYDROSCOPICAL
HYDROSERES
HYDROSOLIC
HYDROSOMAL
HYDROSOMATA
HYDROSOMATOUS
HYDROSOMES
HYDROSPACE
HYDROSPACES
HYDROSPHERE
HYDROSPHERES
HYDROSPHERIC
HYDROSTATIC
HYDROSTATICAL
HYDROSTATICALLY
HYDROSTATICS
HYDROSTATS
HYDROSULPHATE
HYDROSULPHATES
HYDROSULPHIDE
HYDROSULPHIDES
HYDROSULPHITE
HYDROSULPHITES
HYDROSULPHURIC
HYDROSULPHUROUS
HYDROTACTIC
HYDROTAXES
HYDROTAXIS
HYDROTHECA
HYDROTHECAE
HYDROTHERAPIC
HYDROTHERAPIES
HYDROTHERAPIST
HYDROTHERAPISTS
HYDROTHERAPY
HYDROTHERMAL
HYDROTHERMALLY
HYDROTHORACES
HYDROTHORACIC
HYDROTHORAX
HYDROTHORAXES
HYDROTROPIC
HYDROTROPICALLY
HYDROTROPISM
HYDROTROPISMS
HYDROVANES
HYDROXIDES
HYDROXIUMS
HYDROXONIUM
HYDROXONIUMS
HYDROXYACETIC
HYDROXYAPATITE
HYDROXYAPATITES
HYDROXYBUTYRATE
HYDROXYCITRIC
HYDROXYLAMINE
HYDROXYLAMINES
HYDROXYLAPATITE
HYDROXYLASE
HYDROXYLASES
HYDROXYLATE
HYDROXYLATED
HYDROXYLATES
HYDROXYLATING
HYDROXYLATION
HYDROXYLATIONS
HYDROXYLIC
HYDROXYPROLINE
HYDROXYPROLINES
HYDROXYUREA
HYDROXYUREAS
HYDROXYZINE
HYDROXYZINES
HYDROZINCITE
HYDROZINCITES
HYDROZOANS
HYETOGRAPH
HYETOGRAPHIC
HYETOGRAPHICAL
HYETOGRAPHIES
HYETOGRAPHS
HYETOGRAPHY
HYETOLOGIES
HYETOMETER
HYETOMETERS
HYETOMETROGRAPH
HYGIENICALLY
HYGIENISTS
HYGRISTORS
HYGROCHASIES
HYGROCHASTIC
HYGROCHASY
HYGRODEIKS
HYGROGRAPH
HYGROGRAPHIC
HYGROGRAPHICAL
HYGROGRAPHS
HYGROLOGIES
HYGROMETER
HYGROMETERS
HYGROMETRIC
HYGROMETRICAL
HYGROMETRICALLY
HYGROMETRIES
HYGROMETRY
HYGROPHILE

HYGROPHILES
HYGROPHILOUS
HYGROPHOBE
HYGROPHOBES
HYGROPHYTE
HYGROPHYTES
HYGROPHYTIC
HYGROSCOPE
HYGROSCOPES
HYGROSCOPIC
HYGROSCOPICAL
HYGROSCOPICALLY
HYGROSCOPICITY
HYGROSTATS
HYLOGENESES
HYLOGENESIS
HYLOMORPHIC
HYLOMORPHISM
HYLOMORPHISMS
HYLOPATHISM
HYLOPATHISMS
HYLOPATHIST
HYLOPATHISTS
HYLOPHAGOUS
HYLOPHYTES
HYLOTHEISM
HYLOTHEISMS
HYLOTHEIST
HYLOTHEISTS
HYLOTOMOUS
HYLOZOICAL
HYLOZOISMS
HYLOZOISTIC
HYLOZOISTICALLY
HYLOZOISTS
HYMENAEANS
HYMENEALLY
HYMENOPHORE
HYMENOPHORES
HYMENOPLASTIES
HYMENOPLASTY
HYMENOPTERA
HYMENOPTERAN
HYMENOPTERANS
HYMENOPTERON
HYMENOPTERONS
HYMENOPTEROUS
HYMNODICAL
HYMNODISTS
HYMNOGRAPHER
HYMNOGRAPHERS
HYMNOGRAPHIES
HYMNOGRAPHY
HYMNOLOGIC
HYMNOLOGICAL
HYMNOLOGIES
HYMNOLOGIST
HYMNOLOGISTS
HYOPLASTRA
HYOPLASTRAL
HYOPLASTRON
HYOSCYAMINE
HYOSCYAMINES
HYOSCYAMUS
HYOSCYAMUSES
HYPABYSSAL
HYPABYSSALLY
HYPAESTHESIA
HYPAESTHESIAS
HYPAESTHESIC
HYPAETHRAL
HYPAETHRON
HYPAETHRONS
HYPALGESIA
HYPALGESIAS
HYPALGESIC
HYPALLACTIC
HYPALLAGES
HYPANTHIAL
HYPANTHIUM
HYPERACIDITIES
HYPERACIDITY
HYPERACTION
HYPERACTIONS
HYPERACTIVE
HYPERACTIVES
HYPERACTIVITIES
HYPERACTIVITY
HYPERACUITIES
HYPERACUITY
HYPERACUSES
HYPERACUSIS
HYPERACUTE
HYPERACUTENESS
HYPERADRENALISM
HYPERAEMIA
HYPERAEMIAS
HYPERAEMIC
HYPERAESTHESIA
HYPERAESTHESIAS
HYPERAESTHESIC
HYPERAESTHETIC
HYPERAGGRESSIVE
HYPERALERT
HYPERALGESIA
HYPERALGESIAS
HYPERALGESIC
HYPERAROUSAL
HYPERAROUSALS
HYPERAWARE
HYPERAWARENESS
HYPERBARIC
HYPERBARICALLY
HYPERBATIC
HYPERBATICALLY
HYPERBATON
HYPERBATONS
HYPERBOLAE
HYPERBOLAEON
HYPERBOLAEONS
HYPERBOLAS
HYPERBOLES
HYPERBOLIC
HYPERBOLICAL
HYPERBOLICALLY
HYPERBOLISE
HYPERBOLISED
HYPERBOLISES
HYPERBOLISING
HYPERBOLISM
HYPERBOLISMS
HYPERBOLIST
HYPERBOLISTS
HYPERBOLIZE
HYPERBOLIZED
HYPERBOLIZES
HYPERBOLIZING
HYPERBOLOID
HYPERBOLOIDAL
HYPERBOLOIDS
HYPERBOREAN
HYPERBOREANS
HYPERCALCAEMIA
HYPERCALCAEMIAS
HYPERCALCAEMIC
HYPERCALCEMIA
HYPERCALCEMIAS
HYPERCALCEMIC
HYPERCAPNIA
HYPERCAPNIAS
HYPERCAPNIC
HYPERCARBIA
HYPERCARBIAS
HYPERCATABOLISM
HYPERCATALECTIC
HYPERCATALEXES
HYPERCATALEXIS
HYPERCAUTIOUS
HYPERCHARGE
HYPERCHARGED
HYPERCHARGES
HYPERCHARGING
HYPERCIVILISED
HYPERCIVILIZED
HYPERCOAGULABLE
HYPERCOLOUR
HYPERCOLOURS
HYPERCOMPLEX
HYPERCONSCIOUS
HYPERCORRECT
HYPERCORRECTION
HYPERCORRECTLY
HYPERCRITIC
HYPERCRITICAL
HYPERCRITICALLY
HYPERCRITICISE
HYPERCRITICISED
HYPERCRITICISES
HYPERCRITICISM
HYPERCRITICISMS
HYPERCRITICIZE
HYPERCRITICIZED
HYPERCRITICIZES
HYPERCRITICS
HYPERCUBES
HYPERDACTYL
HYPERDACTYLIES
HYPERDACTYLY
HYPERDORIAN
HYPERDULIA
HYPERDULIAS
HYPERDULIC
HYPERDULICAL
HYPEREFFICIENT
HYPEREMESES
HYPEREMESIS
HYPEREMETIC
HYPEREMIAS
HYPEREMOTIONAL
HYPERENDEMIC
HYPERENERGETIC
HYPERESTHESIA
HYPERESTHESIAS
HYPERESTHETIC
HYPEREUTECTIC
HYPEREUTECTOID
HYPEREXCITABLE
HYPEREXCITED
HYPEREXCITEMENT
HYPEREXCRETION
HYPEREXCRETIONS
HYPEREXTEND
HYPEREXTENDED
HYPEREXTENDING
HYPEREXTENDS
HYPEREXTENSION
HYPEREXTENSIONS
HYPERFASTIDIOUS
HYPERFOCAL
HYPERFUNCTION
HYPERFUNCTIONAL
HYPERFUNCTIONS
HYPERGAMIES
HYPERGAMOUS
HYPERGEOMETRIC
HYPERGLYCAEMIA
HYPERGLYCAEMIAS
HYPERGLYCAEMIC
HYPERGLYCEMIA
HYPERGLYCEMIAS
HYPERGLYCEMIC
HYPERGOLIC
HYPERGOLICALLY
HYPERHIDROSES
HYPERHIDROSIS
HYPERICINS
HYPERICUMS
HYPERIDROSES
HYPERIDROSIS
HYPERIMMUNE

H

HYPERIMMUNISE
HYPERIMMUNISED
HYPERIMMUNISES
HYPERIMMUNISING
HYPERIMMUNIZE
HYPERIMMUNIZED
HYPERIMMUNIZES
HYPERIMMUNIZING
HYPERINFLATED
HYPERINFLATION
HYPERINFLATIONS
HYPERINOSES
HYPERINOSIS
HYPERINOTIC
HYPERINSULINISM
HYPERINTENSE
HYPERINVOLUTION
HYPERIRRITABLE
HYPERKERATOSES
HYPERKERATOSIS
HYPERKERATOTIC
HYPERKINESES
HYPERKINESIA
HYPERKINESIAS
HYPERKINESIS
HYPERKINETIC
HYPERLINKED
HYPERLINKING
HYPERLINKS
HYPERLIPEMIA
HYPERLIPEMIAS
HYPERLIPEMIC
HYPERLIPIDAEMIA
HYPERLIPIDEMIA
HYPERLIPIDEMIAS
HYPERLYDIAN
HYPERMANIA
HYPERMANIAS
HYPERMANIC
HYPERMARKET
HYPERMARKETS
HYPERMARTS
HYPERMASCULINE
HYPERMEDIA
HYPERMEDIAS
HYPERMETABOLIC
HYPERMETABOLISM
HYPERMETER
HYPERMETERS
HYPERMETRIC
HYPERMETRICAL
HYPERMETROPIA
HYPERMETROPIAS
HYPERMETROPIC
HYPERMETROPICAL
HYPERMETROPIES
HYPERMETROPY
HYPERMILING
HYPERMILINGS
HYPERMNESIA
HYPERMNESIAS
HYPERMNESIC
HYPERMOBILITIES
HYPERMOBILITY
HYPERMODERN
HYPERMODERNISM
HYPERMODERNISMS
HYPERMODERNIST
HYPERMODERNISTS
HYPERMUTABILITY
HYPERMUTABLE
HYPERNATRAEMIA
HYPERNATRAEMIAS
HYPERNOVAE
HYPERNOVAS
HYPERNYMIES
HYPEROPIAS
HYPEROREXIA
HYPEROREXIAS
HYPEROSMIA
HYPEROSMIAS
HYPEROSTOSES
HYPEROSTOSIS
HYPEROSTOSISES
HYPEROSTOTIC
HYPEROXIDE
HYPEROXIDES
HYPERPARASITE
HYPERPARASITES
HYPERPARASITIC
HYPERPARASITISM
HYPERPHAGIA
HYPERPHAGIAS
HYPERPHAGIC
HYPERPHRYGIAN
HYPERPHYSICAL
HYPERPHYSICALLY
HYPERPIGMENTED
HYPERPITUITARY
HYPERPLANE
HYPERPLANES
HYPERPLASIA
HYPERPLASIAS
HYPERPLASTIC
HYPERPLOID
HYPERPLOIDIES
HYPERPLOIDS
HYPERPLOIDY
HYPERPNEAS
HYPERPNEIC
HYPERPNOEA
HYPERPNOEAS
HYPERPOLARISE
HYPERPOLARISED
HYPERPOLARISES
HYPERPOLARISING
HYPERPOLARIZE
HYPERPOLARIZED
HYPERPOLARIZES
HYPERPOLARIZING
HYPERPOWER
HYPERPOWERS
HYPERPRODUCER
HYPERPRODUCERS
HYPERPRODUCTION
HYPERPROSEXIA
HYPERPROSEXIAS
HYPERPYRETIC
HYPERPYREXIA
HYPERPYREXIAL
HYPERPYREXIAS
HYPERRATIONAL
HYPERREACTIVE
HYPERREACTIVITY
HYPERREACTOR
HYPERREACTORS
HYPERREALISM
HYPERREALISMS
HYPERREALIST
HYPERREALISTIC
HYPERREALISTS
HYPERREALITIES
HYPERREALITY
HYPERREALS
HYPERRESPONSIVE
HYPERROMANTIC
HYPERROMANTICS
HYPERSALINE
HYPERSALINITIES
HYPERSALINITY
HYPERSALIVATION
HYPERSARCOMA
HYPERSARCOMAS
HYPERSARCOMATA
HYPERSARCOSES
HYPERSARCOSIS
HYPERSECRETION
HYPERSECRETIONS
HYPERSENSITISE
HYPERSENSITISED
HYPERSENSITISES
HYPERSENSITIVE
HYPERSENSITIZE
HYPERSENSITIZED
HYPERSENSITIZES
HYPERSENSUAL
HYPERSEXUAL
HYPERSEXUALITY
HYPERSOMNIA
HYPERSOMNIAS
HYPERSOMNOLENCE
HYPERSONIC
HYPERSONICALLY
HYPERSONICS
HYPERSPACE
HYPERSPACES
HYPERSPATIAL
HYPERSTATIC
HYPERSTHENE
HYPERSTHENES
HYPERSTHENIA
HYPERSTHENIAS
HYPERSTHENIC
HYPERSTHENITE
HYPERSTHENITES
HYPERSTIMULATE
HYPERSTIMULATED
HYPERSTIMULATES
HYPERSTRESS
HYPERSTRESSES
HYPERSURFACE
HYPERSURFACES
HYPERTENSE
HYPERTENSION
HYPERTENSIONS
HYPERTENSIVE
HYPERTENSIVES
HYPERTEXTS
HYPERTHERMAL
HYPERTHERMIA
HYPERTHERMIAS
HYPERTHERMIC
HYPERTHERMIES
HYPERTHERMY
HYPERTHYMIA
HYPERTHYMIAS
HYPERTHYROID
HYPERTHYROIDISM
HYPERTHYROIDS
HYPERTONIA
HYPERTONIAS
HYPERTONIC
HYPERTONICITIES
HYPERTONICITY
HYPERTROPHIC
HYPERTROPHICAL
HYPERTROPHIED
HYPERTROPHIES
HYPERTROPHOUS
HYPERTROPHY
HYPERTROPHYING
HYPERTYPICAL
HYPERURBANISM
HYPERURBANISMS
HYPERURICAEMIA
HYPERURICAEMIAS
HYPERURICEMIA
HYPERURICEMIAS
HYPERVELOCITIES
HYPERVELOCITY
HYPERVENTILATE
HYPERVENTILATED
HYPERVENTILATES
HYPERVIGILANCE
HYPERVIGILANCES
HYPERVIGILANT
HYPERVIRULENT
HYPERVISCOSITY
HYPESTHESIA
HYPESTHESIAS

HYPESTHESIC
HYPHENATED
HYPHENATES
HYPHENATING
HYPHENATION
HYPHENATIONS
HYPHENISATION
HYPHENISATIONS
HYPHENISED
HYPHENISES
HYPHENISING
HYPHENISMS
HYPHENIZATION
HYPHENIZATIONS
HYPHENIZED
HYPHENIZES
HYPHENIZING
HYPHENLESS
HYPNAGOGIC
HYPNOANALYSES
HYPNOANALYSIS
HYPNOANALYTIC
HYPNOBIRTHING
HYPNOBIRTHINGS
HYPNOGENESES
HYPNOGENESIS
HYPNOGENETIC
HYPNOGENIC
HYPNOGENIES
HYPNOGENOUS
HYPNOGOGIC
HYPNOIDISE
HYPNOIDISED
HYPNOIDISES
HYPNOIDISING
HYPNOIDIZE
HYPNOIDIZED
HYPNOIDIZES
HYPNOIDIZING
HYPNOLOGIC
HYPNOLOGICAL
HYPNOLOGIES
HYPNOLOGIST
HYPNOLOGISTS
HYPNOPAEDIA
HYPNOPAEDIAS
HYPNOPHOBIA
HYPNOPHOBIAS
HYPNOPOMPIC
HYPNOTHERAPIES
HYPNOTHERAPIST
HYPNOTHERAPISTS
HYPNOTHERAPY
HYPNOTICALLY
HYPNOTISABILITY
HYPNOTISABLE
HYPNOTISATION
HYPNOTISATIONS
HYPNOTISED
HYPNOTISER
HYPNOTISERS
HYPNOTISES
HYPNOTISING
HYPNOTISMS
HYPNOTISTIC
HYPNOTISTS
HYPNOTIZABILITY
HYPNOTIZABLE
HYPNOTIZATION
HYPNOTIZATIONS
HYPNOTIZED
HYPNOTIZER
HYPNOTIZERS
HYPNOTIZES
HYPNOTIZING
HYPOACIDITIES
HYPOACIDITY
HYPOAEOLIAN
HYPOALLERGENIC
HYPOBLASTIC
HYPOBLASTS
HYPOCALCAEMIA
HYPOCALCAEMIAS
HYPOCALCAEMIC
HYPOCALCEMIA
HYPOCALCEMIAS
HYPOCALCEMIC
HYPOCAUSTS
HYPOCENTER
HYPOCENTERS
HYPOCENTRAL
HYPOCENTRE
HYPOCENTRES
HYPOCHLORITE
HYPOCHLORITES
HYPOCHLOROUS
HYPOCHONDRIA
HYPOCHONDRIAC
HYPOCHONDRIACAL
HYPOCHONDRIACS
HYPOCHONDRIAS
HYPOCHONDRIASES
HYPOCHONDRIASIS
HYPOCHONDRIASM
HYPOCHONDRIASMS
HYPOCHONDRIAST
HYPOCHONDRIASTS
HYPOCHONDRIUM
HYPOCORISM
HYPOCORISMA
HYPOCORISMAS
HYPOCORISMS
HYPOCORISTIC
HYPOCORISTICAL
HYPOCOTYLOUS
HYPOCOTYLS
HYPOCRISIES
HYPOCRITES
HYPOCRITIC
HYPOCRITICAL
HYPOCRITICALLY
HYPOCRYSTALLINE
HYPOCYCLOID
HYPOCYCLOIDAL
HYPOCYCLOIDS
HYPODERMAL
HYPODERMAS
HYPODERMIC
HYPODERMICALLY
HYPODERMICS
HYPODERMIS
HYPODERMISES
HYPODIPLOID
HYPODIPLOIDIES
HYPODIPLOIDY
HYPODORIAN
HYPOEUTECTIC
HYPOEUTECTOID
HYPOGAEOUS
HYPOGASTRIA
HYPOGASTRIC
HYPOGASTRIUM
HYPOGENOUS
HYPOGLOSSAL
HYPOGLOSSALS
HYPOGLYCAEMIA
HYPOGLYCAEMIAS
HYPOGLYCAEMIC
HYPOGLYCEMIA
HYPOGLYCEMIAS
HYPOGLYCEMIC
HYPOGLYCEMICS
HYPOGNATHISM
HYPOGNATHISMS
HYPOGNATHOUS
HYPOGYNIES
HYPOGYNOUS
HYPOKALEMIA
HYPOKALEMIAS
HYPOKALEMIC
HYPOLIMNIA
HYPOLIMNION
HYPOLIMNIONS
HYPOLYDIAN
HYPOMAGNESAEMIA
HYPOMAGNESEMIA
HYPOMAGNESEMIAS
HYPOMANIAS
HYPOMANICS
HYPOMENORRHEA
HYPOMENORRHEAS
HYPOMENORRHOEA
HYPOMENORRHOEAS
HYPOMIXOLYDIAN
HYPOMORPHIC
HYPOMORPHS
HYPONASTIC
HYPONASTICALLY
HYPONASTIES
HYPONATRAEMIA
HYPONATRAEMIAS
HYPONITRITE
HYPONITRITES
HYPONITROUS
HYPONYMIES
HYPOPHARYNGES
HYPOPHARYNX
HYPOPHARYNXES
HYPOPHOSPHATE
HYPOPHOSPHATES
HYPOPHOSPHITE
HYPOPHOSPHITES
HYPOPHOSPHORIC
HYPOPHOSPHOROUS
HYPOPHRYGIAN
HYPOPHYGES
HYPOPHYSEAL
HYPOPHYSECTOMY
HYPOPHYSES
HYPOPHYSIAL
HYPOPHYSIS
HYPOPITUITARISM
HYPOPITUITARY
HYPOPLASIA
HYPOPLASIAS
HYPOPLASTIC
HYPOPLASTIES
HYPOPLASTRA
HYPOPLASTRON
HYPOPLASTY
HYPOPLOIDIES
HYPOPLOIDS
HYPOPLOIDY
HYPOPNOEAS
HYPOSENSITISE
HYPOSENSITISED
HYPOSENSITISES
HYPOSENSITISING
HYPOSENSITIZE
HYPOSENSITIZED
HYPOSENSITIZES
HYPOSENSITIZING
HYPOSPADIAS
HYPOSPADIASES
HYPOSTASES
HYPOSTASIS
HYPOSTASISATION
HYPOSTASISE
HYPOSTASISED
HYPOSTASISES
HYPOSTASISING
HYPOSTASIZATION
HYPOSTASIZE
HYPOSTASIZED
HYPOSTASIZES
HYPOSTASIZING
HYPOSTATIC
HYPOSTATICAL
HYPOSTATICALLY
HYPOSTATISATION

HYPOSTATISE
HYPOSTATISED
HYPOSTATISES
HYPOSTATISING
HYPOSTATIZATION
HYPOSTATIZE
HYPOSTATIZED
HYPOSTATIZES
HYPOSTATIZING
HYPOSTHENIA
HYPOSTHENIAS
HYPOSTHENIC
HYPOSTOMES
HYPOSTRESS
HYPOSTRESSES
HYPOSTROPHE
HYPOSTROPHES
HYPOSTYLES
HYPOSULPHATE
HYPOSULPHATES
HYPOSULPHITE
HYPOSULPHITES
HYPOSULPHURIC
HYPOSULPHUROUS
HYPOTACTIC
HYPOTENSION
HYPOTENSIONS
HYPOTENSIVE
HYPOTENSIVES
HYPOTENUSE
HYPOTENUSES
HYPOTHALAMI
HYPOTHALAMIC
HYPOTHALAMUS
HYPOTHECAE
HYPOTHECARY
HYPOTHECATE
HYPOTHECATED
HYPOTHECATES
HYPOTHECATING
HYPOTHECATION
HYPOTHECATIONS
HYPOTHECATOR
HYPOTHECATORS
HYPOTHENUSE
HYPOTHENUSES
HYPOTHERMAL
HYPOTHERMIA
HYPOTHERMIAS
HYPOTHERMIC
HYPOTHESES
HYPOTHESIS
HYPOTHESISE
HYPOTHESISED
HYPOTHESISER
HYPOTHESISERS
HYPOTHESISES
HYPOTHESISING
HYPOTHESIST
HYPOTHESISTS
HYPOTHESIZE
HYPOTHESIZED
HYPOTHESIZER
HYPOTHESIZERS
HYPOTHESIZES
HYPOTHESIZING
HYPOTHETIC
HYPOTHETICAL
HYPOTHETICALLY
HYPOTHETISE
HYPOTHETISED
HYPOTHETISES
HYPOTHETISING
HYPOTHETIZE
HYPOTHETIZED
HYPOTHETIZES
HYPOTHETIZING
HYPOTHYMIA
HYPOTHYMIAS
HYPOTHYROID
HYPOTHYROIDISM
HYPOTHYROIDISMS
HYPOTHYROIDS
HYPOTONIAS
HYPOTONICITIES
HYPOTONICITY
HYPOTROCHOID
HYPOTROCHOIDS
HYPOTYPOSES
HYPOTYPOSIS
HYPOVENTILATION
HYPOXAEMIA
HYPOXAEMIAS
HYPOXAEMIC
HYPOXANTHINE
HYPOXANTHINES
HYPOXEMIAS
HYPSOCHROME
HYPSOCHROMES
HYPSOCHROMIC
HYPSOGRAPHIC
HYPSOGRAPHICAL
HYPSOGRAPHIES
HYPSOGRAPHY
HYPSOMETER
HYPSOMETERS
HYPSOMETRIC
HYPSOMETRICAL
HYPSOMETRICALLY
HYPSOMETRIES
HYPSOMETRIST
HYPSOMETRISTS
HYPSOMETRY
HYPSOPHOBE
HYPSOPHOBES
HYPSOPHOBIA
HYPSOPHOBIAS
HYPSOPHYLL
HYPSOPHYLLARY
HYPSOPHYLLS
HYRACOIDEAN
HYRACOIDEANS
HYSTERANTHOUS
HYSTERECTOMIES
HYSTERECTOMISE
HYSTERECTOMISED
HYSTERECTOMISES
HYSTERECTOMIZE
HYSTERECTOMIZED
HYSTERECTOMIZES
HYSTERECTOMY
HYSTERESES
HYSTERESIAL
HYSTERESIS
HYSTERETIC
HYSTERETICALLY
HYSTERICAL
HYSTERICALLY
HYSTERICKY
HYSTERITIS
HYSTERITISES
HYSTEROGENIC
HYSTEROGENIES
HYSTEROGENY
HYSTEROIDAL
HYSTEROMANIA
HYSTEROMANIAS
HYSTEROTOMIES
HYSTEROTOMY
HYSTRICOMORPH
HYSTRICOMORPHIC
HYSTRICOMORPHS

I

IAMBICALLY
IAMBOGRAPHER
IAMBOGRAPHERS
IATROCHEMICAL
IATROCHEMIST
IATROCHEMISTRY
IATROCHEMISTS
IATROGENIC
IATROGENICALLY
IATROGENICITIES
IATROGENICITY
IATROGENIES
IBUPROFENS
ICEBOATERS
ICEBOATING
ICEBOATINGS
ICEBREAKER
ICEBREAKERS
ICEBREAKING
ICEFISHING
ICHNEUMONS
ICHNOFOSSIL
ICHNOFOSSILS
ICHNOGRAPHIC
ICHNOGRAPHICAL
ICHNOGRAPHIES
ICHNOGRAPHY
ICHNOLITES
ICHNOLOGICAL
ICHNOLOGIES
ICHTHYOCOLLA
ICHTHYOCOLLAS
ICHTHYODORULITE
ICHTHYODORYLITE
ICHTHYOFAUNA
ICHTHYOFAUNAE
ICHTHYOFAUNAL
ICHTHYOFAUNAS
ICHTHYOIDAL
ICHTHYOIDS
ICHTHYOLATRIES
ICHTHYOLATROUS
ICHTHYOLATRY
ICHTHYOLITE
ICHTHYOLITES
ICHTHYOLITIC
ICHTHYOLOGIC
ICHTHYOLOGICAL
ICHTHYOLOGIES
ICHTHYOLOGIST
ICHTHYOLOGISTS
ICHTHYOLOGY
ICHTHYOPHAGIES
ICHTHYOPHAGIST
ICHTHYOPHAGISTS
ICHTHYOPHAGOUS
ICHTHYOPHAGY
ICHTHYOPSID
ICHTHYOPSIDAN
ICHTHYOPSIDANS
ICHTHYOPSIDS
ICHTHYORNIS
ICHTHYORNISES
ICHTHYOSAUR
ICHTHYOSAURI
ICHTHYOSAURIAN
ICHTHYOSAURIANS
ICHTHYOSAURS
ICHTHYOSAURUS
ICHTHYOSAURUSES
ICHTHYOSES
ICHTHYOSIS
ICHTHYOTIC
ICKINESSES
ICONICALLY
ICONICITIES
ICONIFYING
ICONOCLASM
ICONOCLASMS
ICONOCLAST
ICONOCLASTIC
ICONOCLASTS
ICONOGRAPHER
ICONOGRAPHERS
ICONOGRAPHIC
ICONOGRAPHICAL
ICONOGRAPHIES
ICONOGRAPHY
ICONOLATER
ICONOLATERS
ICONOLATRIES
ICONOLATROUS
ICONOLATRY
ICONOLOGICAL
ICONOLOGIES
ICONOLOGIST
ICONOLOGISTS
ICONOMACHIES
ICONOMACHIST
ICONOMACHISTS
ICONOMACHY
ICONOMATIC
ICONOMATICISM
ICONOMATICISMS
ICONOMETER
ICONOMETERS
ICONOMETRIES
ICONOMETRY
ICONOPHILISM
ICONOPHILISMS
ICONOPHILIST
ICONOPHILISTS
ICONOSCOPE
ICONOSCOPES
ICONOSTASES
ICONOSTASIS
ICOSAHEDRA
ICOSAHEDRAL
ICOSAHEDRON
ICOSAHEDRONS
ICOSANDRIAN
ICOSANDROUS
ICOSITETRAHEDRA
ICTERICALS
ICTERITIOUS
IDEALISATION
IDEALISATIONS
IDEALISERS
IDEALISING
IDEALISTIC
IDEALISTICALLY
IDEALITIES
IDEALIZATION
IDEALIZATIONS
IDEALIZERS
IDEALIZING
IDEALNESSES
IDEALOGIES
IDEALOGUES
IDEATIONAL
IDEATIONALLY
IDEMPOTENCIES
IDEMPOTENCY
IDEMPOTENT
IDEMPOTENTS
IDENTICALLY
IDENTICALNESS
IDENTICALNESSES
IDENTIFIABLE
IDENTIFIABLY
IDENTIFICATION
IDENTIFICATIONS
IDENTIFIED
IDENTIFIER
IDENTIFIERS
IDENTIFIES
IDENTIFYING
IDENTIKITS
IDENTITIES
IDEOGRAMIC
IDEOGRAMMATIC
IDEOGRAMMIC
IDEOGRAPHIC
IDEOGRAPHICAL
IDEOGRAPHICALLY
IDEOGRAPHIES
IDEOGRAPHS
IDEOGRAPHY
IDEOLOGICAL
IDEOLOGICALLY
IDEOLOGIES
IDEOLOGISE
IDEOLOGISED
IDEOLOGISES
IDEOLOGISING
IDEOLOGIST
IDEOLOGISTS
IDEOLOGIZE
IDEOLOGIZED
IDEOLOGIZES
IDEOLOGIZING
IDEOLOGUES
IDEOPHONES
IDEOPOLISES
IDEOPRAXIST
IDEOPRAXISTS
IDIOBLASTIC
IDIOBLASTS
IDIOGLOSSIA
IDIOGLOSSIAS
IDIOGRAPHIC
IDIOGRAPHS
IDIOLECTAL
IDIOLECTIC
IDIOMATICAL
IDIOMATICALLY
IDIOMATICALNESS
IDIOMATICNESS
IDIOMATICNESSES
IDIOMORPHIC
IDIOMORPHICALLY
IDIOMORPHISM
IDIOMORPHISMS
IDIOPATHIC
IDIOPATHICALLY
IDIOPATHIES
IDIOPHONES
IDIOPHONIC
IDIOPLASMATIC
IDIOPLASMIC

I

I

IDIOPLASMS
IDIORHYTHMIC
IDIORRHYTHMIC
IDIOSYNCRASIES
IDIOSYNCRASY
IDIOSYNCRATIC
IDIOSYNCRATICAL
IDIOTHERMOUS
IDIOTICALLY
IDIOTICALNESS
IDIOTICALNESSES
IDIOTICONS
IDLENESSES
IDOLATRESS
IDOLATRESSES
IDOLATRIES
IDOLATRISE
IDOLATRISED
IDOLATRISER
IDOLATRISERS
IDOLATRISES
IDOLATRISING
IDOLATRIZE
IDOLATRIZED
IDOLATRIZER
IDOLATRIZERS
IDOLATRIZES
IDOLATRIZING
IDOLATROUS
IDOLATROUSLY
IDOLATROUSNESS
IDOLISATION
IDOLISATIONS
IDOLIZATION
IDOLIZATIONS
IDOLOCLAST
IDOLOCLASTS
IDONEITIES
IDOXURIDINE
IDOXURIDINES
IDYLLICALLY
IFFINESSES
IGNESCENTS
IGNIMBRITE
IGNIMBRITES
IGNIPOTENT
IGNITABILITIES
IGNITABILITY
IGNITIBILITIES
IGNITIBILITY
IGNOBILITIES
IGNOBILITY
IGNOBLENESS
IGNOBLENESSES
IGNOMINIES
IGNOMINIOUS
IGNOMINIOUSLY
IGNOMINIOUSNESS
IGNORAMUSES
IGNORANCES
IGNORANTLY
IGNORANTNESS
IGNORANTNESSES
IGNORATION
IGNORATIONS
IGUANODONS
ILEOSTOMIES
ILLAQUEABLE
ILLAQUEATE
ILLAQUEATED
ILLAQUEATES
ILLAQUEATING
ILLAQUEATION
ILLAQUEATIONS
ILLATIVELY
ILLAUDABLE
ILLAUDABLY
ILLAWARRAS
ILLEGALISATION
ILLEGALISATIONS
ILLEGALISE
ILLEGALISED
ILLEGALISES
ILLEGALISING
ILLEGALITIES
ILLEGALITY
ILLEGALIZATION
ILLEGALIZATIONS
ILLEGALIZE
ILLEGALIZED
ILLEGALIZES
ILLEGALIZING
ILLEGIBILITIES
ILLEGIBILITY
ILLEGIBLENESS
ILLEGIBLENESSES
ILLEGITIMACIES
ILLEGITIMACY
ILLEGITIMATE
ILLEGITIMATED
ILLEGITIMATELY
ILLEGITIMATES
ILLEGITIMATING
ILLEGITIMATION
ILLEGITIMATIONS
ILLIBERALISE
ILLIBERALISED
ILLIBERALISES
ILLIBERALISING
ILLIBERALISM
ILLIBERALISMS
ILLIBERALITIES
ILLIBERALITY
ILLIBERALIZE
ILLIBERALIZED
ILLIBERALIZES
ILLIBERALIZING
ILLIBERALLY
ILLIBERALNESS
ILLIBERALNESSES
ILLICITNESS
ILLICITNESSES
ILLIMITABILITY
ILLIMITABLE
ILLIMITABLENESS
ILLIMITABLY
ILLIMITATION
ILLIMITATIONS
ILLIQUATION
ILLIQUATIONS
ILLIQUIDITIES
ILLIQUIDITY
ILLITERACIES
ILLITERACY
ILLITERATE
ILLITERATELY
ILLITERATENESS
ILLITERATES
ILLOCUTION
ILLOCUTIONARY
ILLOCUTIONS
ILLOGICALITIES
ILLOGICALITY
ILLOGICALLY
ILLOGICALNESS
ILLOGICALNESSES
ILLUMINABLE
ILLUMINANCE
ILLUMINANCES
ILLUMINANT
ILLUMINANTS
ILLUMINATE
ILLUMINATED
ILLUMINATES
ILLUMINATI
ILLUMINATING
ILLUMINATINGLY
ILLUMINATION
ILLUMINATIONAL
ILLUMINATIONS
ILLUMINATIVE
ILLUMINATO
ILLUMINATOR
ILLUMINATORS
ILLUMINERS
ILLUMINING
ILLUMINISM
ILLUMINISMS
ILLUMINIST
ILLUMINISTS
ILLUSIONAL
ILLUSIONARY
ILLUSIONED
ILLUSIONISM
ILLUSIONISMS
ILLUSIONIST
ILLUSIONISTIC
ILLUSIONISTS
ILLUSIVELY
ILLUSIVENESS
ILLUSIVENESSES
ILLUSORILY
ILLUSORINESS
ILLUSORINESSES
ILLUSTRATABLE
ILLUSTRATE
ILLUSTRATED
ILLUSTRATEDS
ILLUSTRATES
ILLUSTRATING
ILLUSTRATION
ILLUSTRATIONAL
ILLUSTRATIONS
ILLUSTRATIVE
ILLUSTRATIVELY
ILLUSTRATOR
ILLUSTRATORS
ILLUSTRATORY
ILLUSTRIOUS
ILLUSTRIOUSLY
ILLUSTRIOUSNESS
ILLUSTRISSIMO
ILLUVIATED
ILLUVIATES
ILLUVIATING
ILLUVIATION
ILLUVIATIONS
IMAGINABLE
IMAGINABLENESS
IMAGINABLY
IMAGINARIES
IMAGINARILY
IMAGINARINESS
IMAGINARINESSES
IMAGINATION
IMAGINATIONAL
IMAGINATIONS
IMAGINATIVE
IMAGINATIVELY
IMAGINATIVENESS
IMAGINEERED
IMAGINEERING
IMAGINEERS
IMAGININGS
IMAGINISTS
IMAGISTICALLY
IMBALANCED
IMBALANCES
IMBECILELY
IMBECILICALLY
IMBECILITIES
IMBECILITY
IMBIBITION
IMBIBITIONAL
IMBIBITIONS
IMBITTERED
IMBITTERING
IMBOLDENED
IMBOLDENING
IMBORDERED

IMBORDERING
IMBOSOMING
IMBOWERING
IMBRANGLED
IMBRANGLES
IMBRANGLING
IMBRICATED
IMBRICATELY
IMBRICATES
IMBRICATING
IMBRICATION
IMBRICATIONS
IMBROCCATA
IMBROCCATAS
IMBROGLIOS
IMBROWNING
IMBRUEMENT
IMBRUEMENTS
IMBUEMENTS
IMIDAZOLES
IMINAZOLES
IMINOUREAS
IMIPRAMINE
IMIPRAMINES
IMITABILITIES
IMITABILITY
IMITABLENESS
IMITABLENESSES
IMITANCIES
IMITATIONAL
IMITATIONS
IMITATIVELY
IMITATIVENESS
IMITATIVENESSES
IMMACULACIES
IMMACULACY
IMMACULATE
IMMACULATELY
IMMACULATENESS
IMMANACLED
IMMANACLES
IMMANACLING
IMMANATION
IMMANATIONS
IMMANENCES
IMMANENCIES
IMMANENTAL
IMMANENTISM
IMMANENTISMS
IMMANENTIST
IMMANENTISTIC
IMMANENTISTS
IMMANENTLY
IMMANITIES
IMMANTLING
IMMARCESCIBLE
IMMARGINATE
IMMATERIAL
IMMATERIALISE
IMMATERIALISED
IMMATERIALISES
IMMATERIALISING
IMMATERIALISM
IMMATERIALISMS
IMMATERIALIST
IMMATERIALISTS
IMMATERIALITIES
IMMATERIALITY
IMMATERIALIZE
IMMATERIALIZED
IMMATERIALIZES
IMMATERIALIZING
IMMATERIALLY
IMMATERIALNESS
IMMATURELY
IMMATURENESS
IMMATURENESSES
IMMATUREST
IMMATURITIES
IMMATURITY
IMMEASURABILITY
IMMEASURABLE
IMMEASURABLY
IMMEASURED
IMMEDIACIES
IMMEDIATELY
IMMEDIATENESS
IMMEDIATENESSES
IMMEDIATISM
IMMEDIATISMS
IMMEDICABLE
IMMEDICABLENESS
IMMEDICABLY
IMMEMORIAL
IMMEMORIALLY
IMMENSENESS
IMMENSENESSES
IMMENSITIES
IMMENSURABILITY
IMMENSURABLE
IMMERGENCE
IMMERGENCES
IMMERITOUS
IMMERSIBLE
IMMERSIONISM
IMMERSIONISMS
IMMERSIONIST
IMMERSIONISTS
IMMERSIONS
IMMETHODICAL
IMMETHODICALLY
IMMIGRANCIES
IMMIGRANCY
IMMIGRANTS
IMMIGRATED
IMMIGRATES
IMMIGRATING
IMMIGRATION
IMMIGRATIONAL
IMMIGRATIONS
IMMIGRATOR
IMMIGRATORS
IMMIGRATORY
IMMINENCES
IMMINENCIES
IMMINENTLY
IMMINENTNESS
IMMINENTNESSES
IMMINGLING
IMMINUTION
IMMINUTIONS
IMMISCIBILITIES
IMMISCIBILITY
IMMISCIBLE
IMMISCIBLY
IMMISERATION
IMMISERATIONS
IMMISERISATION
IMMISERISATIONS
IMMISERISE
IMMISERISED
IMMISERISES
IMMISERISING
IMMISERIZATION
IMMISERIZATIONS
IMMISERIZE
IMMISERIZED
IMMISERIZES
IMMISERIZING
IMMISSIONS
IMMITIGABILITY
IMMITIGABLE
IMMITIGABLY
IMMITTANCE
IMMITTANCES
IMMIXTURES
IMMOBILISATION
IMMOBILISATIONS
IMMOBILISE
IMMOBILISED
IMMOBILISER
IMMOBILISERS
IMMOBILISES
IMMOBILISING
IMMOBILISM
IMMOBILISMS
IMMOBILITIES
IMMOBILITY
IMMOBILIZATION
IMMOBILIZATIONS
IMMOBILIZE
IMMOBILIZED
IMMOBILIZER
IMMOBILIZERS
IMMOBILIZES
IMMOBILIZING
IMMODERACIES
IMMODERACY
IMMODERATE
IMMODERATELY
IMMODERATENESS
IMMODERATION
IMMODERATIONS
IMMODESTER
IMMODESTEST
IMMODESTIES
IMMODESTLY
IMMOLATING
IMMOLATION
IMMOLATIONS
IMMOLATORS
IMMOMENTOUS
IMMORALISM
IMMORALISMS
IMMORALIST
IMMORALISTS
IMMORALITIES
IMMORALITY
IMMORTALISATION
IMMORTALISE
IMMORTALISED
IMMORTALISER
IMMORTALISERS
IMMORTALISES
IMMORTALISING
IMMORTALITIES
IMMORTALITY
IMMORTALIZATION
IMMORTALIZE
IMMORTALIZED
IMMORTALIZER
IMMORTALIZERS
IMMORTALIZES
IMMORTALIZING
IMMORTALLY
IMMORTELLE
IMMORTELLES
IMMOTILITIES
IMMOTILITY
IMMOVABILITIES
IMMOVABILITY
IMMOVABLENESS
IMMOVABLENESSES
IMMOVABLES
IMMOVEABILITIES
IMMOVEABILITY
IMMOVEABLE
IMMOVEABLENESS
IMMOVEABLES
IMMOVEABLY
IMMUNIFACIENT
IMMUNISATION
IMMUNISATIONS
IMMUNISERS
IMMUNISING
IMMUNITIES
IMMUNIZATION
IMMUNIZATIONS
IMMUNIZERS
IMMUNIZING

IMMUNOASSAY
IMMUNOASSAYABLE
IMMUNOASSAYIST
IMMUNOASSAYISTS
IMMUNOASSAYS
IMMUNOBLOT
IMMUNOBLOTS
IMMUNOBLOTTING
IMMUNOBLOTTINGS
IMMUNOCHEMICAL
IMMUNOCHEMIST
IMMUNOCHEMISTRY
IMMUNOCHEMISTS
IMMUNOCOMPETENT
IMMUNOCOMPLEX
IMMUNOCOMPLEXES
IMMUNODEFICIENT
IMMUNODIAGNOSES
IMMUNODIAGNOSIS
IMMUNODIFFUSION
IMMUNOGENESES
IMMUNOGENESIS
IMMUNOGENETIC
IMMUNOGENETICAL
IMMUNOGENETICS
IMMUNOGENIC
IMMUNOGENICALLY
IMMUNOGENICITY
IMMUNOGENS
IMMUNOGLOBULIN
IMMUNOGLOBULINS
IMMUNOLOGIC
IMMUNOLOGICAL
IMMUNOLOGICALLY
IMMUNOLOGIES
IMMUNOLOGIST
IMMUNOLOGISTS
IMMUNOLOGY
IMMUNOMODULATOR
IMMUNOPATHOLOGY
IMMUNOPHORESES
IMMUNOPHORESIS
IMMUNOREACTION
IMMUNOREACTIONS
IMMUNOREACTIVE
IMMUNOSORBENT
IMMUNOSORBENTS
IMMUNOSTIMULANT
IMMUNOSUPPRESS
IMMUNOTHERAPIES
IMMUNOTHERAPY
IMMUNOTOXIC
IMMUNOTOXIN
IMMUNOTOXINS
IMMUREMENT
IMMUREMENTS
IMMUTABILITIES
IMMUTABILITY
IMMUTABLENESS
IMMUTABLENESSES
IMPACTIONS
IMPACTITES
IMPAINTING
IMPAIRABLE
IMPAIRINGS
IMPAIRMENT
IMPAIRMENTS
IMPALEMENT
IMPALEMENTS
IMPALPABILITIES
IMPALPABILITY
IMPALPABLE
IMPALPABLY
IMPALUDISM
IMPALUDISMS
IMPANATION
IMPANATIONS
IMPANELING
IMPANELLED
IMPANELLING
IMPANELMENT
IMPANELMENTS
IMPANNELLED
IMPANNELLING
IMPARADISE
IMPARADISED
IMPARADISES
IMPARADISING
IMPARIDIGITATE
IMPARIPINNATE
IMPARISYLLABIC
IMPARITIES
IMPARKATION
IMPARKATIONS
IMPARLANCE
IMPARLANCES
IMPARTABLE
IMPARTATION
IMPARTATIONS
IMPARTIALITIES
IMPARTIALITY
IMPARTIALLY
IMPARTIALNESS
IMPARTIALNESSES
IMPARTIBILITIES
IMPARTIBILITY
IMPARTIBLE
IMPARTIBLY
IMPARTMENT
IMPARTMENTS
IMPASSABILITIES
IMPASSABILITY
IMPASSABLE
IMPASSABLENESS
IMPASSABLY
IMPASSIBILITIES
IMPASSIBILITY
IMPASSIBLE
IMPASSIBLENESS
IMPASSIBLY
IMPASSIONATE
IMPASSIONED
IMPASSIONEDLY
IMPASSIONEDNESS
IMPASSIONING
IMPASSIONS
IMPASSIVELY
IMPASSIVENESS
IMPASSIVENESSES
IMPASSIVITIES
IMPASSIVITY
IMPASTATION
IMPASTATIONS
IMPATIENCE
IMPATIENCES
IMPATIENTLY
IMPEACHABILITY
IMPEACHABLE
IMPEACHERS
IMPEACHING
IMPEACHMENT
IMPEACHMENTS
IMPEARLING
IMPECCABILITIES
IMPECCABILITY
IMPECCABLE
IMPECCABLY
IMPECCANCIES
IMPECCANCY
IMPECUNIOSITIES
IMPECUNIOSITY
IMPECUNIOUS
IMPECUNIOUSLY
IMPECUNIOUSNESS
IMPEDANCES
IMPEDIMENT
IMPEDIMENTA
IMPEDIMENTAL
IMPEDIMENTARY
IMPEDIMENTS
IMPEDINGLY
IMPEDITIVE
IMPELLENTS
IMPENDENCE
IMPENDENCES
IMPENDENCIES
IMPENDENCY
IMPENETRABILITY
IMPENETRABLE
IMPENETRABLY
IMPENETRATE
IMPENETRATED
IMPENETRATES
IMPENETRATING
IMPENETRATION
IMPENETRATIONS
IMPENITENCE
IMPENITENCES
IMPENITENCIES
IMPENITENCY
IMPENITENT
IMPENITENTLY
IMPENITENTNESS
IMPENITENTS
IMPERATIVAL
IMPERATIVE
IMPERATIVELY
IMPERATIVENESS
IMPERATIVES
IMPERATORIAL
IMPERATORIALLY
IMPERATORS
IMPERATORSHIP
IMPERATORSHIPS
IMPERCEABLE
IMPERCEIVABLE
IMPERCEPTIBLE
IMPERCEPTIBLY
IMPERCEPTION
IMPERCEPTIONS
IMPERCEPTIVE
IMPERCEPTIVELY
IMPERCEPTIVITY
IMPERCIPIENCE
IMPERCIPIENCES
IMPERCIPIENT
IMPERCIPIENTLY
IMPERFECTER
IMPERFECTEST
IMPERFECTIBLE
IMPERFECTION
IMPERFECTIONS
IMPERFECTIVE
IMPERFECTIVELY
IMPERFECTIVES
IMPERFECTLY
IMPERFECTNESS
IMPERFECTNESSES
IMPERFECTS
IMPERFORABLE
IMPERFORATE
IMPERFORATED
IMPERFORATION
IMPERFORATIONS
IMPERIALISE
IMPERIALISED
IMPERIALISES
IMPERIALISING
IMPERIALISM
IMPERIALISMS
IMPERIALIST
IMPERIALISTIC
IMPERIALISTS
IMPERIALITIES
IMPERIALITY
IMPERIALIZE
IMPERIALIZED
IMPERIALIZES
IMPERIALIZING
IMPERIALLY

IMPERIALNESS
IMPERIALNESSES
IMPERILING
IMPERILLED
IMPERILLING
IMPERILMENT
IMPERILMENTS
IMPERIOUSLY
IMPERIOUSNESS
IMPERIOUSNESSES
IMPERISHABILITY
IMPERISHABLE
IMPERISHABLES
IMPERISHABLY
IMPERMANENCE
IMPERMANENCES
IMPERMANENCIES
IMPERMANENCY
IMPERMANENT
IMPERMANENTLY
IMPERMEABILITY
IMPERMEABLE
IMPERMEABLENESS
IMPERMEABLY
IMPERMISSIBLE
IMPERMISSIBLY
IMPERSCRIPTIBLE
IMPERSEVERANT
IMPERSISTENT
IMPERSONAL
IMPERSONALISE
IMPERSONALISED
IMPERSONALISES
IMPERSONALISING
IMPERSONALITIES
IMPERSONALITY
IMPERSONALIZE
IMPERSONALIZED
IMPERSONALIZES
IMPERSONALIZING
IMPERSONALLY
IMPERSONATE
IMPERSONATED
IMPERSONATES
IMPERSONATING
IMPERSONATION
IMPERSONATIONS
IMPERSONATOR
IMPERSONATORS
IMPERTINENCE
IMPERTINENCES
IMPERTINENCIES
IMPERTINENCY
IMPERTINENT
IMPERTINENTLY
IMPERTURBABLE
IMPERTURBABLY
IMPERTURBATION
IMPERTURBATIONS
IMPERVIABILITY
IMPERVIABLE
IMPERVIABLENESS
IMPERVIOUS
IMPERVIOUSLY
IMPERVIOUSNESS
IMPETICOSSED
IMPETICOSSES
IMPETICOSSING
IMPETIGINES
IMPETIGINOUS
IMPETRATED
IMPETRATES
IMPETRATING
IMPETRATION
IMPETRATIONS
IMPETRATIVE
IMPETRATOR
IMPETRATORS
IMPETRATORY
IMPETUOSITIES
IMPETUOSITY
IMPETUOUSLY
IMPETUOUSNESS
IMPETUOUSNESSES
IMPICTURED
IMPIERCEABLE
IMPIGNORATE
IMPIGNORATED
IMPIGNORATES
IMPIGNORATING
IMPIGNORATION
IMPIGNORATIONS
IMPINGEMENT
IMPINGEMENTS
IMPIOUSNESS
IMPIOUSNESSES
IMPISHNESS
IMPISHNESSES
IMPLACABILITIES
IMPLACABILITY
IMPLACABLE
IMPLACABLENESS
IMPLACABLY
IMPLACENTAL
IMPLANTABLE
IMPLANTATION
IMPLANTATIONS
IMPLANTERS
IMPLANTING
IMPLAUSIBILITY
IMPLAUSIBLE
IMPLAUSIBLENESS
IMPLAUSIBLY
IMPLEACHED
IMPLEACHES
IMPLEACHING
IMPLEADABLE
IMPLEADERS
IMPLEADING
IMPLEDGING
IMPLEMENTAL
IMPLEMENTATION
IMPLEMENTATIONS
IMPLEMENTED
IMPLEMENTER
IMPLEMENTERS
IMPLEMENTING
IMPLEMENTOR
IMPLEMENTORS
IMPLEMENTS
IMPLETIONS
IMPLEXIONS
IMPLEXUOUS
IMPLICATED
IMPLICATES
IMPLICATING
IMPLICATION
IMPLICATIONAL
IMPLICATIONS
IMPLICATIVE
IMPLICATIVELY
IMPLICATIVENESS
IMPLICATURE
IMPLICATURES
IMPLICITIES
IMPLICITLY
IMPLICITNESS
IMPLICITNESSES
IMPLODENTS
IMPLORATION
IMPLORATIONS
IMPLORATOR
IMPLORATORS
IMPLORATORY
IMPLORINGLY
IMPLOSIONS
IMPLOSIVELY
IMPLOSIVES
IMPLUNGING
IMPOCKETED
IMPOCKETING
IMPOLDERED
IMPOLDERING
IMPOLICIES
IMPOLITELY
IMPOLITENESS
IMPOLITENESSES
IMPOLITEST
IMPOLITICAL
IMPOLITICALLY
IMPOLITICLY
IMPOLITICNESS
IMPOLITICNESSES
IMPONDERABILIA
IMPONDERABILITY
IMPONDERABLE
IMPONDERABLES
IMPONDERABLY
IMPONDEROUS
IMPORTABILITIES
IMPORTABILITY
IMPORTABLE
IMPORTANCE
IMPORTANCES
IMPORTANCIES
IMPORTANCY
IMPORTANTLY
IMPORTATION
IMPORTATIONS
IMPORTINGS
IMPORTUNACIES
IMPORTUNACY
IMPORTUNATE
IMPORTUNATELY
IMPORTUNATENESS
IMPORTUNED
IMPORTUNELY
IMPORTUNER
IMPORTUNERS
IMPORTUNES
IMPORTUNING
IMPORTUNINGS
IMPORTUNITIES
IMPORTUNITY
IMPOSINGLY
IMPOSINGNESS
IMPOSINGNESSES
IMPOSITION
IMPOSITIONS
IMPOSSIBILISM
IMPOSSIBILISMS
IMPOSSIBILIST
IMPOSSIBILISTS
IMPOSSIBILITIES
IMPOSSIBILITY
IMPOSSIBLE
IMPOSSIBLENESS
IMPOSSIBLES
IMPOSSIBLY
IMPOSTHUMATE
IMPOSTHUMATED
IMPOSTHUMATES
IMPOSTHUMATING
IMPOSTHUMATION
IMPOSTHUMATIONS
IMPOSTHUME
IMPOSTHUMED
IMPOSTHUMES
IMPOSTOROUS
IMPOSTROUS
IMPOSTUMATE
IMPOSTUMATED
IMPOSTUMATES
IMPOSTUMATING
IMPOSTUMATION
IMPOSTUMATIONS
IMPOSTUMED
IMPOSTUMES
IMPOSTURES
IMPOSTUROUS

IMPOTENCES
IMPOTENCIES
IMPOTENTLY
IMPOTENTNESS
IMPOTENTNESSES
IMPOUNDABLE
IMPOUNDAGE
IMPOUNDAGES
IMPOUNDERS
IMPOUNDING
IMPOUNDMENT
IMPOUNDMENTS
IMPOVERISH
IMPOVERISHED
IMPOVERISHER
IMPOVERISHERS
IMPOVERISHES
IMPOVERISHING
IMPOVERISHMENT
IMPOVERISHMENTS
IMPOWERING
IMPRACTICABLE
IMPRACTICABLY
IMPRACTICAL
IMPRACTICALITY
IMPRACTICALLY
IMPRACTICALNESS
IMPRECATED
IMPRECATES
IMPRECATING
IMPRECATION
IMPRECATIONS
IMPRECATORY
IMPRECISELY
IMPRECISENESS
IMPRECISENESSES
IMPRECISION
IMPRECISIONS
IMPREDICATIVE
IMPREGNABILITY
IMPREGNABLE
IMPREGNABLENESS
IMPREGNABLY
IMPREGNANT
IMPREGNANTS
IMPREGNATABLE
IMPREGNATE
IMPREGNATED
IMPREGNATES
IMPREGNATING
IMPREGNATION
IMPREGNATIONS
IMPREGNATOR
IMPREGNATORS
IMPREGNING
IMPRESARIO
IMPRESARIOS
IMPRESCRIPTIBLE
IMPRESCRIPTIBLY
IMPRESSERS
IMPRESSIBILITY
IMPRESSIBLE
IMPRESSING
IMPRESSION
IMPRESSIONABLE
IMPRESSIONAL
IMPRESSIONALLY
IMPRESSIONISM
IMPRESSIONISMS
IMPRESSIONIST
IMPRESSIONISTIC
IMPRESSIONISTS
IMPRESSIONS
IMPRESSIVE
IMPRESSIVELY
IMPRESSIVENESS
IMPRESSMENT
IMPRESSMENTS
IMPRESSURE
IMPRESSURES
IMPRIMATUR
IMPRIMATURS
IMPRINTERS
IMPRINTING
IMPRINTINGS
IMPRISONABLE
IMPRISONED
IMPRISONER
IMPRISONERS
IMPRISONING
IMPRISONMENT
IMPRISONMENTS
IMPROBABILITIES
IMPROBABILITY
IMPROBABLE
IMPROBABLENESS
IMPROBABLY
IMPROBATION
IMPROBATIONS
IMPROBITIES
IMPROMPTUS
IMPROPERER
IMPROPEREST
IMPROPERLY
IMPROPERNESS
IMPROPERNESSES
IMPROPRIATE
IMPROPRIATED
IMPROPRIATES
IMPROPRIATING
IMPROPRIATION
IMPROPRIATIONS
IMPROPRIATOR
IMPROPRIATORS
IMPROPRIETIES
IMPROPRIETY
IMPROVABILITIES
IMPROVABILITY
IMPROVABLE
IMPROVABLENESS
IMPROVABLY
IMPROVEMENT
IMPROVEMENTS
IMPROVIDENCE
IMPROVIDENCES
IMPROVIDENT
IMPROVIDENTLY
IMPROVINGLY
IMPROVISATE
IMPROVISATED
IMPROVISATES
IMPROVISATING
IMPROVISATION
IMPROVISATIONAL
IMPROVISATIONS
IMPROVISATOR
IMPROVISATORE
IMPROVISATORES
IMPROVISATORI
IMPROVISATORIAL
IMPROVISATORS
IMPROVISATORY
IMPROVISATRICE
IMPROVISATRICES
IMPROVISATRIX
IMPROVISATRIXES
IMPROVISED
IMPROVISER
IMPROVISERS
IMPROVISES
IMPROVISING
IMPROVISOR
IMPROVISORS
IMPROVVISATORE
IMPROVVISATORES
IMPROVVISATRICE
IMPRUDENCE
IMPRUDENCES
IMPRUDENTLY
IMPSONITES
IMPUDENCES
IMPUDENCIES
IMPUDENTLY
IMPUDENTNESS
IMPUDENTNESSES
IMPUDICITIES
IMPUDICITY
IMPUGNABLE
IMPUGNATION
IMPUGNATIONS
IMPUGNMENT
IMPUGNMENTS
IMPUISSANCE
IMPUISSANCES
IMPUISSANT
IMPULSIONS
IMPULSIVELY
IMPULSIVENESS
IMPULSIVENESSES
IMPULSIVITIES
IMPULSIVITY
IMPUNDULUS
IMPUNITIES
IMPURENESS
IMPURENESSES
IMPURITIES
IMPURPLING
IMPUTABILITIES
IMPUTABILITY
IMPUTABLENESS
IMPUTABLENESSES
IMPUTATION
IMPUTATIONS
IMPUTATIVE
IMPUTATIVELY
INABILITIES
INABSTINENCE
INABSTINENCES
INACCESSIBILITY
INACCESSIBLE
INACCESSIBLY
INACCURACIES
INACCURACY
INACCURATE
INACCURATELY
INACCURATENESS
INACTIVATE
INACTIVATED
INACTIVATES
INACTIVATING
INACTIVATION
INACTIVATIONS
INACTIVELY
INACTIVENESS
INACTIVENESSES
INACTIVITIES
INACTIVITY
INADAPTABLE
INADAPTATION
INADAPTATIONS
INADAPTIVE
INADEQUACIES
INADEQUACY
INADEQUATE
INADEQUATELY
INADEQUATENESS
INADEQUATES
INADMISSIBILITY
INADMISSIBLE
INADMISSIBLY
INADVERTENCE
INADVERTENCES
INADVERTENCIES
INADVERTENCY
INADVERTENT
INADVERTENTLY
INADVISABILITY
INADVISABLE
INADVISABLENESS
INADVISABLY

INALIENABILITY
INALIENABLE
INALIENABLENESS
INALIENABLY
INALTERABILITY
INALTERABLE
INALTERABLENESS
INALTERABLY
INAMORATAS
INAMORATOS
INANENESSES
INANIMATELY
INANIMATENESS
INANIMATENESSES
INANIMATION
INANIMATIONS
INANITIONS
INAPPARENT
INAPPARENTLY
INAPPEASABLE
INAPPELLABLE
INAPPETENCE
INAPPETENCES
INAPPETENCIES
INAPPETENCY
INAPPETENT
INAPPLICABILITY
INAPPLICABLE
INAPPLICABLY
INAPPOSITE
INAPPOSITELY
INAPPOSITENESS
INAPPRECIABLE
INAPPRECIABLY
INAPPRECIATION
INAPPRECIATIONS
INAPPRECIATIVE
INAPPREHENSIBLE
INAPPREHENSION
INAPPREHENSIONS
INAPPREHENSIVE
INAPPROACHABLE
INAPPROACHABLY
INAPPROPRIATE
INAPPROPRIATELY
INAPTITUDE
INAPTITUDES
INAPTNESSES
INARGUABLE
INARGUABLY
INARTICULACIES
INARTICULACY
INARTICULATE
INARTICULATELY
INARTICULATES
INARTICULATION
INARTICULATIONS
INARTIFICIAL
INARTIFICIALLY
INARTISTIC
INARTISTICALLY
INATTENTION
INATTENTIONS
INATTENTIVE
INATTENTIVELY
INATTENTIVENESS
INAUDIBILITIES
INAUDIBILITY
INAUDIBLENESS
INAUDIBLENESSES
INAUGURALS
INAUGURATE
INAUGURATED
INAUGURATES
INAUGURATING
INAUGURATION
INAUGURATIONS
INAUGURATOR
INAUGURATORS
INAUGURATORY
INAURATING
INAUSPICIOUS
INAUSPICIOUSLY
INAUTHENTIC
INAUTHENTICITY
INBOUNDING
INBREATHED
INBREATHES
INBREATHING
INBREEDERS
INBREEDING
INBREEDINGS
INBRINGING
INBRINGINGS
INBURSTING
INCALCULABILITY
INCALCULABLE
INCALCULABLY
INCALESCENCE
INCALESCENCES
INCALESCENT
INCANDESCE
INCANDESCED
INCANDESCENCE
INCANDESCENCES
INCANDESCENCIES
INCANDESCENCY
INCANDESCENT
INCANDESCENTLY
INCANDESCENTS
INCANDESCES
INCANDESCING
INCANTATION
INCANTATIONAL
INCANTATIONS
INCANTATOR
INCANTATORS
INCANTATORY
INCAPABILITIES
INCAPABILITY
INCAPABLENESS
INCAPABLENESSES
INCAPABLES
INCAPACIOUS
INCAPACIOUSNESS
INCAPACITANT
INCAPACITANTS
INCAPACITATE
INCAPACITATED
INCAPACITATES
INCAPACITATING
INCAPACITATION
INCAPACITATIONS
INCAPACITIES
INCAPACITY
INCAPSULATE
INCAPSULATED
INCAPSULATES
INCAPSULATING
INCAPSULATION
INCAPSULATIONS
INCARCERATE
INCARCERATED
INCARCERATES
INCARCERATING
INCARCERATION
INCARCERATIONS
INCARCERATOR
INCARCERATORS
INCARDINATE
INCARDINATED
INCARDINATES
INCARDINATING
INCARDINATION
INCARDINATIONS
INCARNADINE
INCARNADINED
INCARNADINES
INCARNADINING
INCARNATED
INCARNATES
INCARNATING
INCARNATION
INCARNATIONS
INCARVILLEA
INCARVILLEAS
INCASEMENT
INCASEMENTS
INCATENATE
INCATENATED
INCATENATES
INCATENATING
INCATENATION
INCATENATIONS
INCAUTIONS
INCAUTIOUS
INCAUTIOUSLY
INCAUTIOUSNESS
INCEDINGLY
INCENDIARIES
INCENDIARISM
INCENDIARISMS
INCENDIARY
INCENDIVITIES
INCENDIVITY
INCENSATION
INCENSATIONS
INCENSEMENT
INCENSEMENTS
INCENSORIES
INCENTIVELY
INCENTIVES
INCENTIVISATION
INCENTIVISE
INCENTIVISED
INCENTIVISES
INCENTIVISING
INCENTIVIZATION
INCENTIVIZE
INCENTIVIZED
INCENTIVIZES
INCENTIVIZING
INCEPTIONS
INCEPTIVELY
INCEPTIVES
INCERTAINTIES
INCERTAINTY
INCERTITUDE
INCERTITUDES
INCESSANCIES
INCESSANCY
INCESSANTLY
INCESSANTNESS
INCESSANTNESSES
INCESTUOUS
INCESTUOUSLY
INCESTUOUSNESS
INCHARITABLE
INCHOATELY
INCHOATENESS
INCHOATENESSES
INCHOATING
INCHOATION
INCHOATIONS
INCHOATIVE
INCHOATIVELY
INCHOATIVES
INCIDENCES
INCIDENTAL
INCIDENTALLY
INCIDENTALNESS
INCIDENTALS
INCINERATE
INCINERATED
INCINERATES
INCINERATING
INCINERATION
INCINERATIONS
INCINERATOR
INCINERATORS

INCIPIENCE
INCIPIENCES
INCIPIENCIES
INCIPIENCY
INCIPIENTLY
INCISIFORM
INCISIVELY
INCISIVENESS
INCISIVENESSES
INCISORIAL
INCITATION
INCITATIONS
INCITATIVE
INCITATIVES
INCITEMENT
INCITEMENTS
INCITINGLY
INCIVILITIES
INCIVILITY
INCLASPING
INCLEMENCIES
INCLEMENCY
INCLEMENTLY
INCLEMENTNESS
INCLEMENTNESSES
INCLINABLE
INCLINABLENESS
INCLINATION
INCLINATIONAL
INCLINATIONS
INCLINATORIA
INCLINATORIUM
INCLINATORY
INCLININGS
INCLINOMETER
INCLINOMETERS
INCLIPPING
INCLOSABLE
INCLOSURES
INCLUDABLE
INCLUDEDNESS
INCLUDEDNESSES
INCLUDIBLE
INCLUSIONS
INCLUSIVELY
INCLUSIVENESS
INCLUSIVENESSES
INCLUSIVITIES
INCLUSIVITY
INCOAGULABLE
INCOERCIBLE
INCOGITABILITY
INCOGITABLE
INCOGITANCIES
INCOGITANCY
INCOGITANT
INCOGITATIVE
INCOGNISABLE
INCOGNISANCE
INCOGNISANCES
INCOGNISANT
INCOGNITAS
INCOGNITOS
INCOGNIZABLE
INCOGNIZANCE
INCOGNIZANCES
INCOGNIZANT
INCOHERENCE
INCOHERENCES
INCOHERENCIES
INCOHERENCY
INCOHERENT
INCOHERENTLY
INCOHERENTNESS
INCOHESIVE
INCOMBUSTIBLE
INCOMBUSTIBLES
INCOMBUSTIBLY
INCOMMENSURABLE
INCOMMENSURABLY
INCOMMENSURATE
INCOMMISCIBLE
INCOMMODED
INCOMMODES
INCOMMODING
INCOMMODIOUS
INCOMMODIOUSLY
INCOMMODITIES
INCOMMODITY
INCOMMUNICABLE
INCOMMUNICABLY
INCOMMUNICADO
INCOMMUNICATIVE
INCOMMUTABILITY
INCOMMUTABLE
INCOMMUTABLY
INCOMPARABILITY
INCOMPARABLE
INCOMPARABLY
INCOMPARED
INCOMPATIBILITY
INCOMPATIBLE
INCOMPATIBLES
INCOMPATIBLY
INCOMPETENCE
INCOMPETENCES
INCOMPETENCIES
INCOMPETENCY
INCOMPETENT
INCOMPETENTLY
INCOMPETENTS
INCOMPLETE
INCOMPLETELY
INCOMPLETENESS
INCOMPLETION
INCOMPLETIONS
INCOMPLIANCE
INCOMPLIANCES
INCOMPLIANCIES
INCOMPLIANCY
INCOMPLIANT
INCOMPLIANTLY
INCOMPOSED
INCOMPOSITE
INCOMPOSSIBLE
INCOMPREHENSION
INCOMPREHENSIVE
INCOMPRESSIBLE
INCOMPRESSIBLY
INCOMPUTABILITY
INCOMPUTABLE
INCOMPUTABLY
INCOMUNICADO
INCONCEIVABLE
INCONCEIVABLES
INCONCEIVABLY
INCONCINNITIES
INCONCINNITY
INCONCINNOUS
INCONCLUSION
INCONCLUSIONS
INCONCLUSIVE
INCONCLUSIVELY
INCONDENSABLE
INCONDENSIBLE
INCONDITELY
INCONFORMITIES
INCONFORMITY
INCONGRUENCE
INCONGRUENCES
INCONGRUENT
INCONGRUENTLY
INCONGRUITIES
INCONGRUITY
INCONGRUOUS
INCONGRUOUSLY
INCONGRUOUSNESS
INCONSCIENT
INCONSCIENTLY
INCONSCIONABLE
INCONSCIOUS
INCONSECUTIVE
INCONSECUTIVELY
INCONSEQUENCE
INCONSEQUENCES
INCONSEQUENT
INCONSEQUENTIAL
INCONSEQUENTLY
INCONSIDERABLE
INCONSIDERABLY
INCONSIDERATE
INCONSIDERATELY
INCONSIDERATION
INCONSISTENCE
INCONSISTENCES
INCONSISTENCIES
INCONSISTENCY
INCONSISTENT
INCONSISTENTLY
INCONSOLABILITY
INCONSOLABLE
INCONSOLABLY
INCONSONANCE
INCONSONANCES
INCONSONANT
INCONSONANTLY
INCONSPICUOUS
INCONSPICUOUSLY
INCONSTANCIES
INCONSTANCY
INCONSTANT
INCONSTANTLY
INCONSTRUABLE
INCONSUMABLE
INCONSUMABLY
INCONTESTABLE
INCONTESTABLY
INCONTIGUOUS
INCONTIGUOUSLY
INCONTINENCE
INCONTINENCES
INCONTINENCIES
INCONTINENCY
INCONTINENT
INCONTINENTLY
INCONTROLLABLE
INCONTROLLABLY
INCONVENIENCE
INCONVENIENCED
INCONVENIENCES
INCONVENIENCIES
INCONVENIENCING
INCONVENIENCY
INCONVENIENT
INCONVENIENTLY
INCONVERSABLE
INCONVERSANT
INCONVERTIBLE
INCONVERTIBLY
INCONVINCIBLE
INCONVINCIBLY
INCOORDINATE
INCOORDINATION
INCOORDINATIONS
INCORONATE
INCORONATED
INCORONATION
INCORONATIONS
INCORPORABLE
INCORPORAL
INCORPORALL
INCORPORATE
INCORPORATED
INCORPORATES
INCORPORATING
INCORPORATION
INCORPORATIONS
INCORPORATIVE
INCORPORATOR
INCORPORATORS

INCORPOREAL
INCORPOREALITY
INCORPOREALLY
INCORPOREITIES
INCORPOREITY
INCORPSING
INCORRECTLY
INCORRECTNESS
INCORRECTNESSES
INCORRIGIBILITY
INCORRIGIBLE
INCORRIGIBLES
INCORRIGIBLY
INCORRODIBLE
INCORROSIBLE
INCORRUPTED
INCORRUPTIBLE
INCORRUPTIBLES
INCORRUPTIBLY
INCORRUPTION
INCORRUPTIONS
INCORRUPTIVE
INCORRUPTLY
INCORRUPTNESS
INCORRUPTNESSES
INCRASSATE
INCRASSATED
INCRASSATES
INCRASSATING
INCRASSATION
INCRASSATIONS
INCRASSATIVE
INCRASSATIVES
INCREASABLE
INCREASEDLY
INCREASEFUL
INCREASERS
INCREASING
INCREASINGLY
INCREASINGS
INCREATELY
INCREDIBILITIES
INCREDIBILITY
INCREDIBLE
INCREDIBLENESS
INCREDIBLY
INCREDULITIES
INCREDULITY
INCREDULOUS
INCREDULOUSLY
INCREDULOUSNESS
INCREMATED
INCREMATES
INCREMATING
INCREMATION
INCREMATIONS
INCREMENTAL
INCREMENTALISM
INCREMENTALISMS
INCREMENTALIST
INCREMENTALISTS
INCREMENTALLY
INCREMENTALS
INCREMENTED
INCREMENTING
INCREMENTS
INCRESCENT
INCRETIONARY
INCRETIONS
INCRIMINATE
INCRIMINATED
INCRIMINATES
INCRIMINATING
INCRIMINATION
INCRIMINATIONS
INCRIMINATOR
INCRIMINATORS
INCRIMINATORY
INCROSSBRED
INCROSSBREDS
INCROSSBREED
INCROSSBREEDING
INCROSSBREEDS
INCROSSING
INCRUSTANT
INCRUSTANTS
INCRUSTATION
INCRUSTATIONS
INCRUSTING
INCRUSTMENT
INCRUSTMENTS
INCUBATING
INCUBATION
INCUBATIONAL
INCUBATIONS
INCUBATIVE
INCUBATORS
INCUBATORY
INCULCATED
INCULCATES
INCULCATING
INCULCATION
INCULCATIONS
INCULCATIVE
INCULCATOR
INCULCATORS
INCULCATORY
INCULPABILITIES
INCULPABILITY
INCULPABLE
INCULPABLENESS
INCULPABLY
INCULPATED
INCULPATES
INCULPATING
INCULPATION
INCULPATIONS
INCULPATIVE
INCULPATORY
INCUMBENCIES
INCUMBENCY
INCUMBENTLY
INCUMBENTS
INCUMBERED
INCUMBERING
INCUMBERINGLY
INCUMBRANCE
INCUMBRANCER
INCUMBRANCERS
INCUMBRANCES
INCUNABLES
INCUNABULA
INCUNABULAR
INCUNABULIST
INCUNABULISTS
INCUNABULUM
INCURABILITIES
INCURABILITY
INCURABLENESS
INCURABLENESSES
INCURABLES
INCURIOSITIES
INCURIOSITY
INCURIOUSLY
INCURIOUSNESS
INCURIOUSNESSES
INCURRABLE
INCURRENCE
INCURRENCES
INCURSIONS
INCURVATED
INCURVATES
INCURVATING
INCURVATION
INCURVATIONS
INCURVATURE
INCURVATURES
INCURVITIES
INDAGATING
INDAGATION
INDAGATIONS
INDAGATIVE
INDAGATORS
INDAGATORY
INDAPAMIDE
INDAPAMIDES
INDEBTEDNESS
INDEBTEDNESSES
INDECENCIES
INDECENTER
INDECENTEST
INDECENTLY
INDECIDUATE
INDECIDUOUS
INDECIPHERABLE
INDECIPHERABLY
INDECISION
INDECISIONS
INDECISIVE
INDECISIVELY
INDECISIVENESS
INDECLINABLE
INDECLINABLY
INDECOMPOSABLE
INDECOROUS
INDECOROUSLY
INDECOROUSNESS
INDECORUMS
INDEFATIGABLE
INDEFATIGABLY
INDEFEASIBILITY
INDEFEASIBLE
INDEFEASIBLY
INDEFECTIBILITY
INDEFECTIBLE
INDEFECTIBLY
INDEFENSIBILITY
INDEFENSIBLE
INDEFENSIBLY
INDEFINABILITY
INDEFINABLE
INDEFINABLENESS
INDEFINABLES
INDEFINABLY
INDEFINITE
INDEFINITELY
INDEFINITENESS
INDEFINITES
INDEHISCENCE
INDEHISCENCES
INDEHISCENT
INDELIBILITIES
INDELIBILITY
INDELIBLENESS
INDELIBLENESSES
INDELICACIES
INDELICACY
INDELICATE
INDELICATELY
INDELICATENESS
INDEMNIFICATION
INDEMNIFIED
INDEMNIFIER
INDEMNIFIERS
INDEMNIFIES
INDEMNIFYING
INDEMNITIES
INDEMONSTRABLE
INDEMONSTRABLY
INDENTATION
INDENTATIONS
INDENTIONS
INDENTURED
INDENTURES
INDENTURESHIP
INDENTURESHIPS
INDENTURING
INDEPENDENCE
INDEPENDENCES
INDEPENDENCIES

INDEPENDENCY
INDEPENDENT
INDEPENDENTLY
INDEPENDENTS
INDESCRIBABLE
INDESCRIBABLES
INDESCRIBABLY
INDESIGNATE
INDESTRUCTIBLE
INDESTRUCTIBLY
INDETECTABLE
INDETECTIBLE
INDETERMINABLE
INDETERMINABLY
INDETERMINACIES
INDETERMINACY
INDETERMINATE
INDETERMINATELY
INDETERMINATION
INDETERMINED
INDETERMINISM
INDETERMINISMS
INDETERMINIST
INDETERMINISTIC
INDETERMINISTS
INDEXATION
INDEXATIONS
INDEXICALS
INDEXTERITIES
INDEXTERITY
INDEXTROUS
INDICATABLE
INDICATING
INDICATION
INDICATIONAL
INDICATIONS
INDICATIVE
INDICATIVELY
INDICATIVES
INDICATORS
INDICATORY
INDICOLITE
INDICOLITES
INDICTABLE
INDICTABLY
INDICTIONAL
INDICTIONS
INDICTMENT
INDICTMENTS
INDIFFERENCE
INDIFFERENCES
INDIFFERENCIES
INDIFFERENCY
INDIFFERENT
INDIFFERENTISM
INDIFFERENTISMS
INDIFFERENTIST
INDIFFERENTISTS
INDIFFERENTLY
INDIFFERENTS
INDIGENCES
INDIGENCIES
INDIGENISATION
INDIGENISATIONS
INDIGENISE
INDIGENISED
INDIGENISES
INDIGENISING
INDIGENITIES
INDIGENITY
INDIGENIZATION
INDIGENIZATIONS
INDIGENIZE
INDIGENIZED
INDIGENIZES
INDIGENIZING
INDIGENOUS
INDIGENOUSLY
INDIGENOUSNESS
INDIGENTLY
INDIGESTED
INDIGESTIBILITY
INDIGESTIBLE
INDIGESTIBLES
INDIGESTIBLY
INDIGESTING
INDIGESTION
INDIGESTIONS
INDIGESTIVE
INDIGNANCE
INDIGNANCES
INDIGNANTLY
INDIGNATION
INDIGNATIONS
INDIGNIFIED
INDIGNIFIES
INDIGNIFYING
INDIGNITIES
INDIGOLITE
INDIGOLITES
INDIGOTINS
INDINAVIRS
INDIRECTION
INDIRECTIONS
INDIRECTLY
INDIRECTNESS
INDIRECTNESSES
INDIRUBINS
INDISCERNIBLE
INDISCERNIBLY
INDISCERPTIBLE
INDISCIPLINABLE
INDISCIPLINE
INDISCIPLINED
INDISCIPLINES
INDISCOVERABLE
INDISCREET
INDISCREETER
INDISCREETEST
INDISCREETLY
INDISCREETNESS
INDISCRETE
INDISCRETELY
INDISCRETENESS
INDISCRETION
INDISCRETIONARY
INDISCRETIONS
INDISCRIMINATE
INDISPENSABLE
INDISPENSABLES
INDISPENSABLY
INDISPOSED
INDISPOSEDNESS
INDISPOSES
INDISPOSING
INDISPOSITION
INDISPOSITIONS
INDISPUTABILITY
INDISPUTABLE
INDISPUTABLY
INDISSOCIABLE
INDISSOCIABLY
INDISSOLUBILITY
INDISSOLUBLE
INDISSOLUBLY
INDISSOLVABLE
INDISSUADABLE
INDISSUADABLY
INDISTINCT
INDISTINCTION
INDISTINCTIONS
INDISTINCTIVE
INDISTINCTIVELY
INDISTINCTLY
INDISTINCTNESS
INDISTRIBUTABLE
INDITEMENT
INDITEMENTS
INDIVERTIBLE
INDIVERTIBLY
INDIVIDABLE
INDIVIDUAL
INDIVIDUALISE
INDIVIDUALISED
INDIVIDUALISER
INDIVIDUALISERS
INDIVIDUALISES
INDIVIDUALISING
INDIVIDUALISM
INDIVIDUALISMS
INDIVIDUALIST
INDIVIDUALISTIC
INDIVIDUALISTS
INDIVIDUALITIES
INDIVIDUALITY
INDIVIDUALIZE
INDIVIDUALIZED
INDIVIDUALIZER
INDIVIDUALIZERS
INDIVIDUALIZES
INDIVIDUALIZING
INDIVIDUALLY
INDIVIDUALS
INDIVIDUATE
INDIVIDUATED
INDIVIDUATES
INDIVIDUATING
INDIVIDUATION
INDIVIDUATIONS
INDIVIDUATOR
INDIVIDUATORS
INDIVIDUUM
INDIVISIBILITY
INDIVISIBLE
INDIVISIBLENESS
INDIVISIBLES
INDIVISIBLY
INDOCILITIES
INDOCILITY
INDOCTRINATE
INDOCTRINATED
INDOCTRINATES
INDOCTRINATING
INDOCTRINATION
INDOCTRINATIONS
INDOCTRINATOR
INDOCTRINATORS
INDOLEACETIC
INDOLEBUTYRIC
INDOLENCES
INDOLENCIES
INDOLENTLY
INDOMETACIN
INDOMETACINS
INDOMETHACIN
INDOMETHACINS
INDOMITABILITY
INDOMITABLE
INDOMITABLENESS
INDOMITABLY
INDOPHENOL
INDOPHENOLS
INDORSABLE
INDORSATION
INDORSATIONS
INDORSEMENT
INDORSEMENTS
INDRAUGHTS
INDRENCHED
INDRENCHES
INDRENCHING
INDUBITABILITY
INDUBITABLE
INDUBITABLENESS
INDUBITABLY
INDUCEMENT
INDUCEMENTS
INDUCIBILITIES
INDUCIBILITY
INDUCTANCE

INDUCTANCES
INDUCTILITIES
INDUCTILITY
INDUCTIONAL
INDUCTIONS
INDUCTIVELY
INDUCTIVENESS
INDUCTIVENESSES
INDUCTIVITIES
INDUCTIVITY
INDULGENCE
INDULGENCED
INDULGENCES
INDULGENCIES
INDULGENCING
INDULGENCY
INDULGENTLY
INDULGINGLY
INDUMENTUM
INDUMENTUMS
INDUPLICATE
INDUPLICATED
INDUPLICATION
INDUPLICATIONS
INDURATING
INDURATION
INDURATIONS
INDURATIVE
INDUSTRIAL
INDUSTRIALISE
INDUSTRIALISED
INDUSTRIALISES
INDUSTRIALISING
INDUSTRIALISM
INDUSTRIALISMS
INDUSTRIALIST
INDUSTRIALISTS
INDUSTRIALIZE
INDUSTRIALIZED
INDUSTRIALIZES
INDUSTRIALIZING
INDUSTRIALLY
INDUSTRIALS
INDUSTRIES
INDUSTRIOUS
INDUSTRIOUSLY
INDUSTRIOUSNESS
INDUSTRYWIDE
INDWELLERS
INDWELLING
INDWELLINGS
INEARTHING
INEBRIANTS
INEBRIATED
INEBRIATES
INEBRIATING
INEBRIATION
INEBRIATIONS
INEBRIETIES
INEDIBILITIES
INEDIBILITY
INEDUCABILITIES
INEDUCABILITY
INEDUCABLE
INEFFABILITIES
INEFFABILITY
INEFFABLENESS
INEFFABLENESSES
INEFFACEABILITY
INEFFACEABLE
INEFFACEABLY
INEFFECTIVE
INEFFECTIVELY
INEFFECTIVENESS
INEFFECTUAL
INEFFECTUALITY
INEFFECTUALLY
INEFFECTUALNESS
INEFFICACIES
INEFFICACIOUS
INEFFICACIOUSLY
INEFFICACITIES
INEFFICACITY
INEFFICACY
INEFFICIENCIES
INEFFICIENCY
INEFFICIENT
INEFFICIENTLY
INEFFICIENTS
INEGALITARIAN
INEGALITARIANS
INELABORATE
INELABORATED
INELABORATELY
INELABORATES
INELABORATING
INELASTICALLY
INELASTICITIES
INELASTICITY
INELEGANCE
INELEGANCES
INELEGANCIES
INELEGANCY
INELEGANTLY
INELIGIBILITIES
INELIGIBILITY
INELIGIBLE
INELIGIBLENESS
INELIGIBLES
INELIGIBLY
INELOQUENCE
INELOQUENCES
INELOQUENT
INELOQUENTLY
INELUCTABILITY
INELUCTABLE
INELUCTABLY
INELUDIBILITIES
INELUDIBILITY
INELUDIBLE
INELUDIBLY
INENARRABLE
INEPTITUDE
INEPTITUDES
INEPTNESSES
INEQUALITIES
INEQUALITY
INEQUATION
INEQUATIONS
INEQUIPOTENT
INEQUITABLE
INEQUITABLENESS
INEQUITABLY
INEQUITIES
INEQUIVALVE
INEQUIVALVED
INERADICABILITY
INERADICABLE
INERADICABLY
INERASABLE
INERASABLY
INERASIBLE
INERASIBLY
INERRABILITIES
INERRABILITY
INERRABLENESS
INERRABLENESSES
INERRANCIES
INERTIALLY
INERTNESSES
INESCAPABLE
INESCAPABLY
INESCULENT
INESCUTCHEON
INESCUTCHEONS
INESSENTIAL
INESSENTIALITY
INESSENTIALS
INESTIMABILITY
INESTIMABLE
INESTIMABLENESS
INESTIMABLY
INEVITABILITIES
INEVITABILITY
INEVITABLE
INEVITABLENESS
INEVITABLES
INEVITABLY
INEXACTITUDE
INEXACTITUDES
INEXACTNESS
INEXACTNESSES
INEXCITABLE
INEXCUSABILITY
INEXCUSABLE
INEXCUSABLENESS
INEXCUSABLY
INEXECRABLE
INEXECUTABLE
INEXECUTION
INEXECUTIONS
INEXHAUSTED
INEXHAUSTIBLE
INEXHAUSTIBLY
INEXHAUSTIVE
INEXISTANT
INEXISTENCE
INEXISTENCES
INEXISTENCIES
INEXISTENCY
INEXISTENT
INEXORABILITIES
INEXORABILITY
INEXORABLE
INEXORABLENESS
INEXORABLY
INEXPANSIBLE
INEXPECTANCIES
INEXPECTANCY
INEXPECTANT
INEXPECTATION
INEXPECTATIONS
INEXPEDIENCE
INEXPEDIENCES
INEXPEDIENCIES
INEXPEDIENCY
INEXPEDIENT
INEXPEDIENTLY
INEXPENSIVE
INEXPENSIVELY
INEXPENSIVENESS
INEXPERIENCE
INEXPERIENCED
INEXPERIENCES
INEXPERTLY
INEXPERTNESS
INEXPERTNESSES
INEXPIABLE
INEXPIABLENESS
INEXPIABLY
INEXPLAINABLE
INEXPLAINABLY
INEXPLICABILITY
INEXPLICABLE
INEXPLICABLY
INEXPLICIT
INEXPLICITLY
INEXPLICITNESS
INEXPRESSIBLE
INEXPRESSIBLES
INEXPRESSIBLY
INEXPRESSIVE
INEXPRESSIVELY
INEXPUGNABILITY
INEXPUGNABLE
INEXPUGNABLY
INEXPUNGIBLE
INEXTENDED
INEXTENSIBILITY
INEXTENSIBLE

INEXTENSION
INEXTENSIONS
INEXTIRPABLE
INEXTRICABILITY
INEXTRICABLE
INEXTRICABLY
INFALLIBILISM
INFALLIBILISMS
INFALLIBILIST
INFALLIBILISTS
INFALLIBILITIES
INFALLIBILITY
INFALLIBLE
INFALLIBLENESS
INFALLIBLES
INFALLIBLY
INFAMISING
INFAMIZING
INFAMONISE
INFAMONISED
INFAMONISES
INFAMONISING
INFAMONIZE
INFAMONIZED
INFAMONIZES
INFAMONIZING
INFAMOUSLY
INFAMOUSNESS
INFAMOUSNESSES
INFANGTHIEF
INFANGTHIEFS
INFANTEERS
INFANTHOOD
INFANTHOODS
INFANTICIDAL
INFANTICIDE
INFANTICIDES
INFANTILISATION
INFANTILISE
INFANTILISED
INFANTILISES
INFANTILISING
INFANTILISM
INFANTILISMS
INFANTILITIES
INFANTILITY
INFANTILIZATION
INFANTILIZE
INFANTILIZED
INFANTILIZES
INFANTILIZING
INFANTRIES
INFANTRYMAN
INFANTRYMEN
INFARCTION
INFARCTIONS
INFATUATED
INFATUATEDLY
INFATUATES
INFATUATING
INFATUATION
INFATUATIONS
INFEASIBILITIES
INFEASIBILITY
INFEASIBLE
INFEASIBLENESS
INFECTANTS
INFECTIONS
INFECTIOUS
INFECTIOUSLY
INFECTIOUSNESS
INFECTIVELY
INFECTIVENESS
INFECTIVENESSES
INFECTIVITIES
INFECTIVITY
INFECUNDITIES
INFECUNDITY
INFEFTMENT
INFEFTMENTS
INFELICITIES
INFELICITOUS
INFELICITOUSLY
INFELICITY
INFEOFFING
INFERENCES
INFERENCING
INFERENCINGS
INFERENTIAL
INFERENTIALLY
INFERIORITIES
INFERIORITY
INFERIORLY
INFERNALITIES
INFERNALITY
INFERNALLY
INFERRABLE
INFERRIBLE
INFERTILELY
INFERTILITIES
INFERTILITY
INFESTANTS
INFESTATION
INFESTATIONS
INFEUDATION
INFEUDATIONS
INFIBULATE
INFIBULATED
INFIBULATES
INFIBULATING
INFIBULATION
INFIBULATIONS
INFIDELITIES
INFIDELITY
INFIELDERS
INFIELDSMAN
INFIELDSMEN
INFIGHTERS
INFIGHTING
INFIGHTINGS
INFILLINGS
INFILTRATE
INFILTRATED
INFILTRATES
INFILTRATING
INFILTRATION
INFILTRATIONS
INFILTRATIVE
INFILTRATOR
INFILTRATORS
INFINITANT
INFINITARY
INFINITATE
INFINITATED
INFINITATES
INFINITATING
INFINITELY
INFINITENESS
INFINITENESSES
INFINITESIMAL
INFINITESIMALLY
INFINITESIMALS
INFINITIES
INFINITIVAL
INFINITIVALLY
INFINITIVE
INFINITIVELY
INFINITIVES
INFINITUDE
INFINITUDES
INFIRMARER
INFIRMARERS
INFIRMARIAN
INFIRMARIANS
INFIRMARIES
INFIRMITIES
INFIRMNESS
INFIRMNESSES
INFIXATION
INFIXATIONS
INFLAMABLE
INFLAMINGLY
INFLAMMABILITY
INFLAMMABLE
INFLAMMABLENESS
INFLAMMABLES
INFLAMMABLY
INFLAMMATION
INFLAMMATIONS
INFLAMMATORILY
INFLAMMATORY
INFLATABLE
INFLATABLES
INFLATEDLY
INFLATEDNESS
INFLATEDNESSES
INFLATINGLY
INFLATIONARY
INFLATIONISM
INFLATIONISMS
INFLATIONIST
INFLATIONISTS
INFLATIONS
INFLATUSES
INFLECTABLE
INFLECTEDNESS
INFLECTEDNESSES
INFLECTING
INFLECTION
INFLECTIONAL
INFLECTIONALLY
INFLECTIONLESS
INFLECTIONS
INFLECTIVE
INFLECTORS
INFLEXIBILITIES
INFLEXIBILITY
INFLEXIBLE
INFLEXIBLENESS
INFLEXIBLY
INFLEXIONAL
INFLEXIONALLY
INFLEXIONLESS
INFLEXIONS
INFLEXURES
INFLICTABLE
INFLICTERS
INFLICTING
INFLICTION
INFLICTIONS
INFLICTIVE
INFLICTORS
INFLORESCENCE
INFLORESCENCES
INFLORESCENT
INFLOWINGS
INFLUENCEABLE
INFLUENCED
INFLUENCER
INFLUENCERS
INFLUENCES
INFLUENCING
INFLUENTIAL
INFLUENTIALLY
INFLUENTIALS
INFLUENZAL
INFLUENZAS
INFLUXIONS
INFOGRAPHIC
INFOGRAPHICS
INFOLDINGS
INFOLDMENT
INFOLDMENTS
INFOMANIAS
INFOMERCIAL
INFOMERCIALS
INFOPRENEURIAL
INFORMABLE
INFORMALITIES
INFORMALITY

INFORMALLY
INFORMANTS
INFORMATICIAN
INFORMATICIANS
INFORMATICS
INFORMATION
INFORMATIONAL
INFORMATIONALLY
INFORMATIONS
INFORMATISATION
INFORMATISE
INFORMATISED
INFORMATISES
INFORMATISING
INFORMATIVE
INFORMATIVELY
INFORMATIVENESS
INFORMATIZATION
INFORMATIZE
INFORMATIZED
INFORMATIZES
INFORMATIZING
INFORMATORILY
INFORMATORY
INFORMEDLY
INFORMIDABLE
INFORMINGLY
INFORTUNES
INFOSPHERE
INFOSPHERES
INFOTAINMENT
INFOTAINMENTS
INFRACOSTAL
INFRACTING
INFRACTION
INFRACTIONS
INFRACTORS
INFRAGRANT
INFRAHUMAN
INFRAHUMANS
INFRALAPSARIAN
INFRALAPSARIANS
INFRAMAXILLARY
INFRANGIBILITY
INFRANGIBLE
INFRANGIBLENESS
INFRANGIBLY
INFRAORBITAL
INFRAPOSED
INFRAPOSITION
INFRAPOSITIONS
INFRASONIC
INFRASOUND
INFRASOUNDS
INFRASPECIFIC
INFRASTRUCTURAL
INFRASTRUCTURE
INFRASTRUCTURES
INFREQUENCE
INFREQUENCES
INFREQUENCIES
INFREQUENCY
INFREQUENT
INFREQUENTLY
INFRINGEMENT
INFRINGEMENTS
INFRINGERS
INFRINGING
INFRUCTUOUS
INFRUCTUOUSLY
INFUNDIBULA
INFUNDIBULAR
INFUNDIBULATE
INFUNDIBULIFORM
INFUNDIBULUM
INFURIATED
INFURIATELY
INFURIATES
INFURIATING
INFURIATINGLY
INFURIATION
INFURIATIONS
INFUSCATED
INFUSIBILITIES
INFUSIBILITY
INFUSIBLENESS
INFUSIBLENESSES
INFUSIONISM
INFUSIONISMS
INFUSIONIST
INFUSIONISTS
INFUSORIAL
INFUSORIAN
INFUSORIANS
INFUSORIES
INGATHERED
INGATHERER
INGATHERERS
INGATHERING
INGATHERINGS
INGEMINATE
INGEMINATED
INGEMINATES
INGEMINATING
INGEMINATION
INGEMINATIONS
INGENERATE
INGENERATED
INGENERATES
INGENERATING
INGENERATION
INGENERATIONS
INGENIOUSLY
INGENIOUSNESS
INGENIOUSNESSES
INGENUITIES
INGENUOUSLY
INGENUOUSNESS
INGENUOUSNESSES
INGESTIBLE
INGESTIONS
INGLENEUKS
INGLENOOKS
INGLORIOUS
INGLORIOUSLY
INGLORIOUSNESS
INGRAFTATION
INGRAFTATIONS
INGRAFTING
INGRAFTMENT
INGRAFTMENTS
INGRAINEDLY
INGRAINEDNESS
INGRAINEDNESSES
INGRAINERS
INGRAINING
INGRATEFUL
INGRATIATE
INGRATIATED
INGRATIATES
INGRATIATING
INGRATIATINGLY
INGRATIATION
INGRATIATIONS
INGRATIATORY
INGRATITUDE
INGRATITUDES
INGRAVESCENCE
INGRAVESCENCES
INGRAVESCENT
INGREDIENT
INGREDIENTS
INGRESSION
INGRESSIONS
INGRESSIVE
INGRESSIVENESS
INGRESSIVES
INGROOVING
INGROSSING
INGROUNDED
INGROUNDING
INGROWNNESS
INGROWNNESSES
INGULFMENT
INGULFMENTS
INGULPHING
INGURGITATE
INGURGITATED
INGURGITATES
INGURGITATING
INGURGITATION
INGURGITATIONS
INHABITABILITY
INHABITABLE
INHABITANCE
INHABITANCES
INHABITANCIES
INHABITANCY
INHABITANT
INHABITANTS
INHABITATION
INHABITATIONS
INHABITERS
INHABITING
INHABITIVENESS
INHABITORS
INHABITRESS
INHABITRESSES
INHALATION
INHALATIONAL
INHALATIONS
INHALATORIUM
INHALATORIUMS
INHALATORS
INHARMONIC
INHARMONICAL
INHARMONICITIES
INHARMONICITY
INHARMONIES
INHARMONIOUS
INHARMONIOUSLY
INHAUSTING
INHEARSING
INHERENCES
INHERENCIES
INHERENTLY
INHERITABILITY
INHERITABLE
INHERITABLENESS
INHERITABLY
INHERITANCE
INHERITANCES
INHERITING
INHERITORS
INHERITRESS
INHERITRESSES
INHERITRICES
INHERITRIX
INHERITRIXES
INHIBITABLE
INHIBITEDLY
INHIBITERS
INHIBITING
INHIBITION
INHIBITIONS
INHIBITIVE
INHIBITORS
INHIBITORY
INHOLDINGS
INHOMOGENEITIES
INHOMOGENEITY
INHOMOGENEOUS
INHOSPITABLE
INHOSPITABLY
INHOSPITALITIES
INHOSPITALITY
INHUMANELY
INHUMANEST
INHUMANITIES
INHUMANITY

INHUMANNESS
INHUMANNESSES
INHUMATING
INHUMATION
INHUMATIONS
INIMICALITIES
INIMICALITY
INIMICALLY
INIMICALNESS
INIMICALNESSES
INIMICITIOUS
INIMITABILITIES
INIMITABILITY
INIMITABLE
INIMITABLENESS
INIMITABLY
INIQUITIES
INIQUITOUS
INIQUITOUSLY
INIQUITOUSNESS
INITIALERS
INITIALING
INITIALISATION
INITIALISATIONS
INITIALISE
INITIALISED
INITIALISES
INITIALISING
INITIALISM
INITIALISMS
INITIALIZATION
INITIALIZATIONS
INITIALIZE
INITIALIZED
INITIALIZES
INITIALIZING
INITIALLED
INITIALLER
INITIALLERS
INITIALLING
INITIALNESS
INITIALNESSES
INITIATING
INITIATION
INITIATIONS
INITIATIVE
INITIATIVELY
INITIATIVES
INITIATORIES
INITIATORS
INITIATORY
INITIATRESS
INITIATRESSES
INITIATRICES
INITIATRIX
INITIATRIXES
INJECTABLE
INJECTABLES
INJECTANTS
INJECTIONS
INJELLYING
INJOINTING
INJUDICIAL
INJUDICIALLY
INJUDICIOUS
INJUDICIOUSLY
INJUDICIOUSNESS
INJUNCTING
INJUNCTION
INJUNCTIONS
INJUNCTIVE
INJUNCTIVELY
INJURIOUSLY
INJURIOUSNESS
INJURIOUSNESSES
INJUSTICES
INKBERRIES
INKHOLDERS
INKINESSES
INMARRIAGE
INMARRIAGES
INMIGRANTS
INNATENESS
INNATENESSES
INNAVIGABLE
INNAVIGABLY
INNERMOSTS
INNERNESSES
INNERSOLES
INNERSPRING
INNERVATED
INNERVATES
INNERVATING
INNERVATION
INNERVATIONS
INNERWEARS
INNKEEPERS
INNOCENCES
INNOCENCIES
INNOCENTER
INNOCENTEST
INNOCENTLY
INNOCUITIES
INNOCUOUSLY
INNOCUOUSNESS
INNOCUOUSNESSES
INNOMINABLE
INNOMINABLES
INNOMINATE
INNOVATING
INNOVATION
INNOVATIONAL
INNOVATIONIST
INNOVATIONISTS
INNOVATIONS
INNOVATIVE
INNOVATIVELY
INNOVATIVENESS
INNOVATORS
INNOVATORY
INNOXIOUSLY
INNOXIOUSNESS
INNOXIOUSNESSES
INNUENDOED
INNUENDOES
INNUENDOING
INNUMERABILITY
INNUMERABLE
INNUMERABLENESS
INNUMERABLY
INNUMERACIES
INNUMERACY
INNUMERATE
INNUMERATES
INNUMEROUS
INNUTRIENT
INNUTRITION
INNUTRITIONS
INNUTRITIOUS
INOBEDIENCE
INOBEDIENCES
INOBEDIENT
INOBEDIENTLY
INOBSERVABLE
INOBSERVANCE
INOBSERVANCES
INOBSERVANT
INOBSERVANTLY
INOBSERVATION
INOBSERVATIONS
INOBTRUSIVE
INOBTRUSIVELY
INOBTRUSIVENESS
INOCCUPATION
INOCCUPATIONS
INOCULABILITIES
INOCULABILITY
INOCULABLE
INOCULANTS
INOCULATED
INOCULATES
INOCULATING
INOCULATION
INOCULATIONS
INOCULATIVE
INOCULATOR
INOCULATORS
INOCULATORY
INODOROUSLY
INODOROUSNESS
INODOROUSNESSES
INOFFENSIVE
INOFFENSIVELY
INOFFENSIVENESS
INOFFICIOUS
INOFFICIOUSLY
INOFFICIOUSNESS
INOPERABILITIES
INOPERABILITY
INOPERABLE
INOPERABLENESS
INOPERABLY
INOPERATIVE
INOPERATIVENESS
INOPERCULATE
INOPERCULATES
INOPPORTUNE
INOPPORTUNELY
INOPPORTUNENESS
INOPPORTUNITIES
INOPPORTUNITY
INORDINACIES
INORDINACY
INORDINATE
INORDINATELY
INORDINATENESS
INORDINATION
INORDINATIONS
INORGANICALLY
INORGANICS
INORGANISATION
INORGANISATIONS
INORGANISED
INORGANIZATION
INORGANIZATIONS
INORGANIZED
INOSCULATE
INOSCULATED
INOSCULATES
INOSCULATING
INOSCULATION
INOSCULATIONS
INOSILICATE
INOSILICATES
INPATIENTS
INPAYMENTS
INPOURINGS
INQUIETING
INQUIETUDE
INQUIETUDES
INQUILINES
INQUILINIC
INQUILINICS
INQUILINISM
INQUILINISMS
INQUILINITIES
INQUILINITY
INQUILINOUS
INQUINATED
INQUINATES
INQUINATING
INQUINATION
INQUINATIONS
INQUIRATION
INQUIRATIONS
INQUIRENDO
INQUIRENDOS
INQUIRINGLY
INQUISITION
INQUISITIONAL

INQUISITIONIST
INQUISITIONISTS
INQUISITIONS
INQUISITIVE
INQUISITIVELY
INQUISITIVENESS
INQUISITOR
INQUISITORIAL
INQUISITORIALLY
INQUISITORS
INQUISITRESS
INQUISITRESSES
INQUISITURIENT
INRUSHINGS
INSALIVATE
INSALIVATED
INSALIVATES
INSALIVATING
INSALIVATION
INSALIVATIONS
INSALUBRIOUS
INSALUBRIOUSLY
INSALUBRITIES
INSALUBRITY
INSALUTARY
INSANENESS
INSANENESSES
INSANITARINESS
INSANITARY
INSANITATION
INSANITATIONS
INSANITIES
INSATIABILITIES
INSATIABILITY
INSATIABLE
INSATIABLENESS
INSATIABLY
INSATIATELY
INSATIATENESS
INSATIATENESSES
INSATIETIES
INSCIENCES
INSCONCING
INSCRIBABLE
INSCRIBABLENESS
INSCRIBERS
INSCRIBING
INSCRIPTION
INSCRIPTIONAL
INSCRIPTIONS
INSCRIPTIVE
INSCRIPTIVELY
INSCROLLED
INSCROLLING
INSCRUTABILITY
INSCRUTABLE
INSCRUTABLENESS
INSCRUTABLY
INSCULPING
INSCULPTURE
INSCULPTURED
INSCULPTURES
INSCULPTURING
INSECTARIA
INSECTARIES
INSECTARIUM
INSECTARIUMS
INSECTICIDAL
INSECTICIDALLY
INSECTICIDE
INSECTICIDES
INSECTIFORM
INSECTIFUGE
INSECTIFUGES
INSECTIONS
INSECTIVORE
INSECTIVORES
INSECTIVOROUS
INSECTOLOGIES
INSECTOLOGIST
INSECTOLOGISTS
INSECTOLOGY
INSECURELY
INSECURENESS
INSECURENESSES
INSECUREST
INSECURITIES
INSECURITY
INSELBERGE
INSELBERGS
INSEMINATE
INSEMINATED
INSEMINATES
INSEMINATING
INSEMINATION
INSEMINATIONS
INSEMINATOR
INSEMINATORS
INSENSATELY
INSENSATENESS
INSENSATENESSES
INSENSIBILITIES
INSENSIBILITY
INSENSIBLE
INSENSIBLENESS
INSENSIBLY
INSENSITIVE
INSENSITIVELY
INSENSITIVENESS
INSENSITIVITIES
INSENSITIVITY
INSENSUOUS
INSENTIENCE
INSENTIENCES
INSENTIENCIES
INSENTIENCY
INSENTIENT
INSEPARABILITY
INSEPARABLE
INSEPARABLENESS
INSEPARABLES
INSEPARABLY
INSEPARATE
INSERTABLE
INSERTIONAL
INSERTIONS
INSESSORIAL
INSEVERABLE
INSHEATHED
INSHEATHES
INSHEATHING
INSHELLING
INSHELTERED
INSHELTERING
INSHELTERS
INSHIPPING
INSHRINEMENT
INSHRINEMENTS
INSHRINING
INSIDIOUSLY
INSIDIOUSNESS
INSIDIOUSNESSES
INSIGHTFUL
INSIGHTFULLY
INSIGNIFICANCE
INSIGNIFICANCES
INSIGNIFICANCY
INSIGNIFICANT
INSIGNIFICANTLY
INSIGNIFICATIVE
INSINCERELY
INSINCERER
INSINCEREST
INSINCERITIES
INSINCERITY
INSINEWING
INSINUATED
INSINUATES
INSINUATING
INSINUATINGLY
INSINUATION
INSINUATIONS
INSINUATIVE
INSINUATOR
INSINUATORS
INSINUATORY
INSIPIDEST
INSIPIDITIES
INSIPIDITY
INSIPIDNESS
INSIPIDNESSES
INSIPIENCE
INSIPIENCES
INSIPIENTLY
INSISTENCE
INSISTENCES
INSISTENCIES
INSISTENCY
INSISTENTLY
INSISTINGLY
INSNAREMENT
INSNAREMENTS
INSOBRIETIES
INSOBRIETY
INSOCIABILITIES
INSOCIABILITY
INSOCIABLE
INSOCIABLY
INSOLATING
INSOLATION
INSOLATIONS
INSOLENCES
INSOLENTLY
INSOLIDITIES
INSOLIDITY
INSOLUBILISE
INSOLUBILISED
INSOLUBILISES
INSOLUBILISING
INSOLUBILITIES
INSOLUBILITY
INSOLUBILIZE
INSOLUBILIZED
INSOLUBILIZES
INSOLUBILIZING
INSOLUBLENESS
INSOLUBLENESSES
INSOLUBLES
INSOLVABILITIES
INSOLVABILITY
INSOLVABLE
INSOLVABLY
INSOLVENCIES
INSOLVENCY
INSOLVENTS
INSOMNIACS
INSOMNIOUS
INSOMNOLENCE
INSOMNOLENCES
INSOUCIANCE
INSOUCIANCES
INSOUCIANT
INSOUCIANTLY
INSOULMENT
INSOULMENTS
INSOURCING
INSOURCINGS
INSPANNING
INSPECTABLE
INSPECTING
INSPECTINGLY
INSPECTION
INSPECTIONAL
INSPECTIONS
INSPECTIVE
INSPECTORAL
INSPECTORATE
INSPECTORATES
INSPECTORIAL
INSPECTORS

INSPECTORSHIP
INSPECTORSHIPS
INSPHERING
INSPIRABLE
INSPIRATION
INSPIRATIONAL
INSPIRATIONALLY
INSPIRATIONISM
INSPIRATIONISMS
INSPIRATIONIST
INSPIRATIONISTS
INSPIRATIONS
INSPIRATIVE
INSPIRATOR
INSPIRATORS
INSPIRATORY
INSPIRINGLY
INSPIRITED
INSPIRITER
INSPIRITERS
INSPIRITING
INSPIRITINGLY
INSPIRITMENT
INSPIRITMENTS
INSPISSATE
INSPISSATED
INSPISSATES
INSPISSATING
INSPISSATION
INSPISSATIONS
INSPISSATOR
INSPISSATORS
INSTABILITIES
INSTABILITY
INSTAGRAMMED
INSTAGRAMMING
INSTAGRAMS
INSTALLANT
INSTALLANTS
INSTALLATION
INSTALLATIONS
INSTALLERS
INSTALLING
INSTALLMENT
INSTALLMENTS
INSTALMENT
INSTALMENTS
INSTANCIES
INSTANCING
INSTANTANEITIES
INSTANTANEITY
INSTANTANEOUS
INSTANTANEOUSLY
INSTANTIAL
INSTANTIATE
INSTANTIATED
INSTANTIATES
INSTANTIATING
INSTANTIATION
INSTANTIATIONS
INSTANTNESS
INSTANTNESSES
INSTARRING
INSTATEMENT
INSTATEMENTS
INSTAURATION
INSTAURATIONS
INSTAURATOR
INSTAURATORS
INSTIGATED
INSTIGATES
INSTIGATING
INSTIGATINGLY
INSTIGATION
INSTIGATIONS
INSTIGATIVE
INSTIGATOR
INSTIGATORS
INSTILLATION
INSTILLATIONS
INSTILLERS
INSTILLING
INSTILLMENT
INSTILLMENTS
INSTILMENT
INSTILMENTS
INSTINCTIVE
INSTINCTIVELY
INSTINCTIVITIES
INSTINCTIVITY
INSTINCTUAL
INSTINCTUALLY
INSTITORIAL
INSTITUTED
INSTITUTER
INSTITUTERS
INSTITUTES
INSTITUTING
INSTITUTION
INSTITUTIONAL
INSTITUTIONALLY
INSTITUTIONARY
INSTITUTIONS
INSTITUTIST
INSTITUTISTS
INSTITUTIVE
INSTITUTIVELY
INSTITUTOR
INSTITUTORS
INSTREAMING
INSTREAMINGS
INSTRESSED
INSTRESSES
INSTRESSING
INSTRUCTED
INSTRUCTIBLE
INSTRUCTING
INSTRUCTION
INSTRUCTIONAL
INSTRUCTIONS
INSTRUCTIVE
INSTRUCTIVELY
INSTRUCTIVENESS
INSTRUCTOR
INSTRUCTORS
INSTRUCTORSHIP
INSTRUCTORSHIPS
INSTRUCTRESS
INSTRUCTRESSES
INSTRUMENT
INSTRUMENTAL
INSTRUMENTALISM
INSTRUMENTALIST
INSTRUMENTALITY
INSTRUMENTALLY
INSTRUMENTALS
INSTRUMENTATION
INSTRUMENTED
INSTRUMENTING
INSTRUMENTS
INSUBJECTION
INSUBJECTIONS
INSUBORDINATE
INSUBORDINATELY
INSUBORDINATES
INSUBORDINATION
INSUBSTANTIAL
INSUBSTANTIALLY
INSUFFERABLE
INSUFFERABLY
INSUFFICIENCE
INSUFFICIENCES
INSUFFICIENCIES
INSUFFICIENCY
INSUFFICIENT
INSUFFICIENTLY
INSUFFLATE
INSUFFLATED
INSUFFLATES
INSUFFLATING
INSUFFLATION
INSUFFLATIONS
INSUFFLATOR
INSUFFLATORS
INSULARISM
INSULARISMS
INSULARITIES
INSULARITY
INSULATING
INSULATION
INSULATIONS
INSULATORS
INSULINASE
INSULINASES
INSULSITIES
INSULTABLE
INSULTINGLY
INSULTMENT
INSULTMENTS
INSUPERABILITY
INSUPERABLE
INSUPERABLENESS
INSUPERABLY
INSUPPORTABLE
INSUPPORTABLY
INSUPPRESSIBLE
INSUPPRESSIBLY
INSURABILITIES
INSURABILITY
INSURANCER
INSURANCERS
INSURANCES
INSURGENCE
INSURGENCES
INSURGENCIES
INSURGENCY
INSURGENTLY
INSURGENTS
INSURMOUNTABLE
INSURMOUNTABLY
INSURRECTION
INSURRECTIONAL
INSURRECTIONARY
INSURRECTIONISM
INSURRECTIONIST
INSURRECTIONS
INSUSCEPTIBLE
INSUSCEPTIBLY
INSUSCEPTIVE
INSUSCEPTIVELY
INSWATHING
INSWINGERS
INTACTNESS
INTACTNESSES
INTAGLIATED
INTAGLIOED
INTAGLIOES
INTAGLIOING
INTANGIBILITIES
INTANGIBILITY
INTANGIBLE
INTANGIBLENESS
INTANGIBLES
INTANGIBLY
INTEGRABILITIES
INTEGRABILITY
INTEGRABLE
INTEGRALITIES
INTEGRALITY
INTEGRALLY
INTEGRANDS
INTEGRANTS
INTEGRATED
INTEGRATES
INTEGRATING
INTEGRATION
INTEGRATIONIST
INTEGRATIONISTS
INTEGRATIONS
INTEGRATIVE

INTEGRATOR
INTEGRATORS
INTEGRITIES
INTEGUMENT
INTEGUMENTAL
INTEGUMENTARY
INTEGUMENTS
INTELLECTED
INTELLECTION
INTELLECTIONS
INTELLECTIVE
INTELLECTIVELY
INTELLECTS
INTELLECTUAL
INTELLECTUALISE
INTELLECTUALISM
INTELLECTUALIST
INTELLECTUALITY
INTELLECTUALIZE
INTELLECTUALLY
INTELLECTUALS
INTELLIGENCE
INTELLIGENCER
INTELLIGENCERS
INTELLIGENCES
INTELLIGENT
INTELLIGENTIAL
INTELLIGENTLY
INTELLIGENTSIA
INTELLIGENTSIAS
INTELLIGENTZIA
INTELLIGENTZIAS
INTELLIGIBILITY
INTELLIGIBLE
INTELLIGIBLY
INTEMERATE
INTEMERATELY
INTEMERATENESS
INTEMPERANCE
INTEMPERANCES
INTEMPERANT
INTEMPERANTS
INTEMPERATE
INTEMPERATELY
INTEMPERATENESS
INTEMPESTIVE
INTEMPESTIVELY
INTEMPESTIVITY

INTENDANCE
INTENDANCES
INTENDANCIES
INTENDANCY
INTENDANTS
INTENDEDLY
INTENDERED
INTENDERING
INTENDMENT
INTENDMENTS
INTENERATE
INTENERATED
INTENERATES
INTENERATING
INTENERATION
INTENERATIONS
INTENSATED
INTENSATES
INTENSATING
INTENSATIVE
INTENSATIVES
INTENSENESS
INTENSENESSES
INTENSIFICATION
INTENSIFIED
INTENSIFIER
INTENSIFIERS
INTENSIFIES
INTENSIFYING
INTENSIONAL
INTENSIONALITY
INTENSIONALLY
INTENSIONS
INTENSITIES
INTENSITIVE
INTENSITIVES
INTENSIVELY
INTENSIVENESS
INTENSIVENESSES
INTENSIVES
INTENTIONAL
INTENTIONALITY
INTENTIONALLY
INTENTIONED
INTENTIONS
INTENTNESS
INTENTNESSES
INTERABANG

INTERABANGS
INTERACTANT
INTERACTANTS
INTERACTED
INTERACTING
INTERACTION
INTERACTIONAL
INTERACTIONISM
INTERACTIONISMS
INTERACTIONIST
INTERACTIONISTS
INTERACTIONS
INTERACTIVE
INTERACTIVELY
INTERACTIVITIES
INTERACTIVITY
INTERAGENCY
INTERALLELIC
INTERALLIED
INTERAMBULACRA
INTERAMBULACRAL
INTERAMBULACRUM
INTERANIMATION
INTERANIMATIONS
INTERANNUAL
INTERARCHED
INTERARCHES
INTERARCHING
INTERATOMIC
INTERBASIN
INTERBEDDED
INTERBEDDING
INTERBEDDINGS
INTERBEHAVIOR
INTERBEHAVIORAL
INTERBEHAVIORS
INTERBEHAVIOUR
INTERBEHAVIOURS
INTERBLEND
INTERBLENDED
INTERBLENDING
INTERBLENDS
INTERBOROUGH
INTERBRAIN
INTERBRAINS
INTERBRANCH
INTERBREED
INTERBREEDING

INTERBREEDINGS
INTERBREEDS
INTERBROKER
INTERCALAR
INTERCALARILY
INTERCALARY
INTERCALATE
INTERCALATED
INTERCALATES
INTERCALATING
INTERCALATION
INTERCALATIONS
INTERCALATIVE
INTERCAMPUS
INTERCASTE
INTERCEDED
INTERCEDENT
INTERCEDER
INTERCEDERS
INTERCEDES
INTERCEDING
INTERCELLULAR
INTERCENSAL
INTERCEPTED
INTERCEPTER
INTERCEPTERS
INTERCEPTING
INTERCEPTION
INTERCEPTIONS
INTERCEPTIVE
INTERCEPTOR
INTERCEPTORS
INTERCEPTS
INTERCESSION
INTERCESSIONAL
INTERCESSIONS
INTERCESSOR
INTERCESSORIAL
INTERCESSORS
INTERCESSORY
INTERCHAIN
INTERCHAINED
INTERCHAINING
INTERCHAINS
INTERCHANGE
INTERCHANGEABLE
INTERCHANGEABLY
INTERCHANGED

INTERCHANGEMENT
INTERCHANGER
INTERCHANGERS
INTERCHANGES
INTERCHANGING
INTERCHANNEL
INTERCHAPTER
INTERCHAPTERS
INTERCHURCH
INTERCIPIENT
INTERCIPIENTS
INTERCLASS
INTERCLAVICLE
INTERCLAVICLES
INTERCLAVICULAR
INTERCLUDE
INTERCLUDED
INTERCLUDES
INTERCLUDING
INTERCLUSION
INTERCLUSIONS
INTERCLUSTER
INTERCOASTAL
INTERCOLLEGIATE
INTERCOLLINE
INTERCOLONIAL
INTERCOLONIALLY
INTERCOLUMNAR
INTERCOMMUNAL
INTERCOMMUNE
INTERCOMMUNED
INTERCOMMUNES
INTERCOMMUNING
INTERCOMMUNION
INTERCOMMUNIONS
INTERCOMMUNITY
INTERCOMPANY
INTERCOMPARE
INTERCOMPARED
INTERCOMPARES
INTERCOMPARING
INTERCOMPARISON
INTERCONNECT
INTERCONNECTED
INTERCONNECTING
INTERCONNECTION
INTERCONNECTOR
INTERCONNECTORS

INTERCONNECTS
INTERCONNEXION
INTERCONNEXIONS
INTERCONVERSION
INTERCONVERT
INTERCONVERTED
INTERCONVERTING
INTERCONVERTS
INTERCOOLED
INTERCOOLER
INTERCOOLERS
INTERCOOLING
INTERCOOLS
INTERCORPORATE
INTERCORRELATE
INTERCORRELATED
INTERCORRELATES
INTERCORTICAL
INTERCOSTAL
INTERCOSTALLY
INTERCOSTALS
INTERCOUNTRY
INTERCOUNTY
INTERCOUPLE
INTERCOURSE
INTERCOURSES
INTERCRATER
INTERCROPPED
INTERCROPPING
INTERCROPS
INTERCROSS
INTERCROSSED
INTERCROSSES
INTERCROSSING
INTERCRURAL
INTERCULTURAL
INTERCULTURALLY
INTERCULTURE
INTERCULTURES
INTERCURRENCE
INTERCURRENCES
INTERCURRENT
INTERCURRENTLY
INTERCURRENTS
INTERCUTTING
INTERDASHED
INTERDASHES
INTERDASHING

INTERDEALER
INTERDEALERS
INTERDEALING
INTERDEALS
INTERDEALT
INTERDENTAL
INTERDENTALLY
INTERDEPEND
INTERDEPENDED
INTERDEPENDENCE
INTERDEPENDENCY
INTERDEPENDENT
INTERDEPENDING
INTERDEPENDS
INTERDIALECTAL
INTERDICTED
INTERDICTING
INTERDICTION
INTERDICTIONS
INTERDICTIVE
INTERDICTIVELY
INTERDICTOR
INTERDICTORS
INTERDICTORY
INTERDICTS
INTERDIFFUSE
INTERDIFFUSED
INTERDIFFUSES
INTERDIFFUSING
INTERDIFFUSION
INTERDIFFUSIONS
INTERDIGITAL
INTERDIGITATE
INTERDIGITATED
INTERDIGITATES
INTERDIGITATING
INTERDIGITATION
INTERDINED
INTERDINES
INTERDINING
INTERDISTRICT
INTERDIVISIONAL
INTERDOMINION
INTERELECTRODE
INTERELECTRON
INTERELECTRONIC
INTEREPIDEMIC
INTERESSED

INTERESSES
INTERESSING
INTERESTED
INTERESTEDLY
INTERESTEDNESS
INTERESTING
INTERESTINGLY
INTERESTINGNESS
INTERETHNIC
INTERFACED
INTERFACES
INTERFACIAL
INTERFACIALLY
INTERFACING
INTERFACINGS
INTERFACULTY
INTERFAITH
INTERFAMILIAL
INTERFAMILY
INTERFASCICULAR
INTERFEMORAL
INTERFERED
INTERFERENCE
INTERFERENCES
INTERFERENTIAL
INTERFERER
INTERFERERS
INTERFERES
INTERFERING
INTERFERINGLY
INTERFEROGRAM
INTERFEROGRAMS
INTERFEROMETER
INTERFEROMETERS
INTERFEROMETRIC
INTERFEROMETRY
INTERFERON
INTERFERONS
INTERFERTILE
INTERFERTILITY
INTERFIBER
INTERFIBRE
INTERFILED
INTERFILES
INTERFILING
INTERFLOWED
INTERFLOWING
INTERFLOWS

INTERFLUENCE
INTERFLUENCES
INTERFLUENT
INTERFLUOUS
INTERFLUVE
INTERFLUVES
INTERFLUVIAL
INTERFOLDED
INTERFOLDING
INTERFOLDS
INTERFOLIATE
INTERFOLIATED
INTERFOLIATES
INTERFOLIATING
INTERFRATERNITY
INTERFRETTED
INTERFRONTAL
INTERFUSED
INTERFUSES
INTERFUSING
INTERFUSION
INTERFUSIONS
INTERGALACTIC
INTERGENERATION
INTERGENERIC
INTERGLACIAL
INTERGLACIALS
INTERGRADATION
INTERGRADATIONS
INTERGRADE
INTERGRADED
INTERGRADES
INTERGRADIENT
INTERGRADING
INTERGRAFT
INTERGRAFTED
INTERGRAFTING
INTERGRAFTS
INTERGRANULAR
INTERGROUP
INTERGROUPS
INTERGROWING
INTERGROWN
INTERGROWS
INTERGROWTH
INTERGROWTHS
INTERINDIVIDUAL
INTERINDUSTRY

INTERINFLUENCE
INTERINFLUENCED
INTERINFLUENCES
INTERINVOLVE
INTERINVOLVED
INTERINVOLVES
INTERINVOLVING
INTERIONIC
INTERIORISATION
INTERIORISE
INTERIORISED
INTERIORISES
INTERIORISING
INTERIORITIES
INTERIORITY
INTERIORIZATION
INTERIORIZE
INTERIORIZED
INTERIORIZES
INTERIORIZING
INTERIORLY
INTERISLAND
INTERJACENCIES
INTERJACENCY
INTERJACENT
INTERJACULATE
INTERJACULATED
INTERJACULATES
INTERJACULATING
INTERJACULATORY
INTERJECTED
INTERJECTING
INTERJECTION
INTERJECTIONAL
INTERJECTIONARY
INTERJECTIONS
INTERJECTOR
INTERJECTORS
INTERJECTORY
INTERJECTS
INTERJECTURAL
INTERJOINED
INTERJOINING
INTERJOINS
INTERKINESES
INTERKINESIS
INTERKNITS
INTERKNITTED

INTERKNITTING
INTERKNOTS
INTERKNOTTED
INTERKNOTTING
INTERLACED
INTERLACEDLY
INTERLACEMENT
INTERLACEMENTS
INTERLACES
INTERLACING
INTERLACUSTRINE
INTERLAMINAR
INTERLAMINATE
INTERLAMINATED
INTERLAMINATES
INTERLAMINATING
INTERLAMINATION
INTERLAPPED
INTERLAPPING
INTERLARDED
INTERLARDING
INTERLARDS
INTERLAYER
INTERLAYERED
INTERLAYERING
INTERLAYERINGS
INTERLAYERS
INTERLAYING
INTERLEAVE
INTERLEAVED
INTERLEAVES
INTERLEAVING
INTERLENDING
INTERLENDS
INTERLEUKIN
INTERLEUKINS
INTERLIBRARY
INTERLINEAL
INTERLINEALLY
INTERLINEAR
INTERLINEARLY
INTERLINEARS
INTERLINEATE
INTERLINEATED
INTERLINEATES
INTERLINEATING
INTERLINEATION
INTERLINEATIONS
INTERLINED
INTERLINER
INTERLINERS
INTERLINES
INTERLINGUA
INTERLINGUAL
INTERLINGUALLY
INTERLINGUAS
INTERLINING
INTERLININGS
INTERLINKED
INTERLINKING
INTERLINKS
INTERLOANS
INTERLOBULAR
INTERLOCAL
INTERLOCATION
INTERLOCATIONS
INTERLOCKED
INTERLOCKER
INTERLOCKERS
INTERLOCKING
INTERLOCKS
INTERLOCUTION
INTERLOCUTIONS
INTERLOCUTOR
INTERLOCUTORILY
INTERLOCUTORS
INTERLOCUTORY
INTERLOCUTRESS
INTERLOCUTRICE
INTERLOCUTRICES
INTERLOCUTRIX
INTERLOCUTRIXES
INTERLOOPED
INTERLOOPING
INTERLOOPS
INTERLOPED
INTERLOPER
INTERLOPERS
INTERLOPES
INTERLOPING
INTERLUDED
INTERLUDES
INTERLUDIAL
INTERLUDING
INTERLUNAR
INTERLUNARY
INTERLUNATION
INTERLUNATIONS
INTERMARGINAL
INTERMARRIAGE
INTERMARRIAGES
INTERMARRIED
INTERMARRIES
INTERMARRY
INTERMARRYING
INTERMATTED
INTERMATTING
INTERMAXILLA
INTERMAXILLAE
INTERMAXILLARY
INTERMEDDLE
INTERMEDDLED
INTERMEDDLER
INTERMEDDLERS
INTERMEDDLES
INTERMEDDLING
INTERMEDIA
INTERMEDIACIES
INTERMEDIACY
INTERMEDIAL
INTERMEDIARIES
INTERMEDIARY
INTERMEDIATE
INTERMEDIATED
INTERMEDIATELY
INTERMEDIATES
INTERMEDIATING
INTERMEDIATION
INTERMEDIATIONS
INTERMEDIATOR
INTERMEDIATORS
INTERMEDIATORY
INTERMEDIN
INTERMEDINS
INTERMEDIUM
INTERMEDIUMS
INTERMEMBRANE
INTERMENSTRUAL
INTERMENTS
INTERMESHED
INTERMESHES
INTERMESHING
INTERMETALLIC
INTERMETALLICS
INTERMEZZI
INTERMEZZO
INTERMEZZOS
INTERMIGRATION
INTERMIGRATIONS
INTERMINABILITY
INTERMINABLE
INTERMINABLY
INTERMINGLE
INTERMINGLED
INTERMINGLES
INTERMINGLING
INTERMISSION
INTERMISSIONS
INTERMISSIVE
INTERMITOTIC
INTERMITTED
INTERMITTENCE
INTERMITTENCES
INTERMITTENCIES
INTERMITTENCY
INTERMITTENT
INTERMITTENTLY
INTERMITTER
INTERMITTERS
INTERMITTING
INTERMITTINGLY
INTERMITTOR
INTERMITTORS
INTERMIXED
INTERMIXES
INTERMIXING
INTERMIXTURE
INTERMIXTURES
INTERMODAL
INTERMODULATION
INTERMOLECULAR
INTERMONTANE
INTERMOUNTAIN
INTERMUNDANE
INTERMURED
INTERMURES
INTERMURING
INTERMUSCULAR
INTERNALISATION
INTERNALISE
INTERNALISED
INTERNALISES
INTERNALISING
INTERNALITIES
INTERNALITY
INTERNALIZATION
INTERNALIZE
INTERNALIZED
INTERNALIZES
INTERNALIZING
INTERNALLY
INTERNALNESS
INTERNALNESSES
INTERNATIONAL
INTERNATIONALLY
INTERNATIONALS
INTERNECINE
INTERNECIVE
INTERNEURAL
INTERNEURON
INTERNEURONAL
INTERNEURONS
INTERNISTS
INTERNMENT
INTERNMENTS
INTERNODAL
INTERNODES
INTERNODIAL
INTERNSHIP
INTERNSHIPS
INTERNUCLEAR
INTERNUCLEON
INTERNUCLEONIC
INTERNUCLEOTIDE
INTERNUNCIAL
INTERNUNCIO
INTERNUNCIOS
INTEROBSERVER
INTEROCEAN
INTEROCEANIC
INTEROCEPTION
INTEROCEPTIONS
INTEROCEPTIVE
INTEROCEPTOR
INTEROCEPTORS
INTEROCULAR
INTEROFFICE
INTEROPERABLE
INTEROPERATIVE
INTERORBITAL

INTERORGAN
INTEROSCULANT
INTEROSCULATE
INTEROSCULATED
INTEROSCULATES
INTEROSCULATING
INTEROSCULATION
INTEROSSEAL
INTEROSSEOUS
INTERPAGED
INTERPAGES
INTERPAGING
INTERPANDEMIC
INTERPARIETAL
INTERPARISH
INTERPAROCHIAL
INTERPAROXYSMAL
INTERPARTICLE
INTERPARTY
INTERPELLANT
INTERPELLANTS
INTERPELLATE
INTERPELLATED
INTERPELLATES
INTERPELLATING
INTERPELLATION
INTERPELLATIONS
INTERPELLATOR
INTERPELLATORS
INTERPENETRABLE
INTERPENETRANT
INTERPENETRATE
INTERPENETRATED
INTERPENETRATES
INTERPERCEPTUAL
INTERPERMEATE
INTERPERMEATED
INTERPERMEATES
INTERPERMEATING
INTERPERSONAL
INTERPERSONALLY
INTERPETIOLAR
INTERPHALANGEAL
INTERPHASE
INTERPHASES
INTERPHONE
INTERPHONES
INTERPILASTER
INTERPILASTERS
INTERPLANETARY
INTERPLANT
INTERPLANTED
INTERPLANTING
INTERPLANTS
INTERPLAYED
INTERPLAYING
INTERPLAYS
INTERPLEAD
INTERPLEADED
INTERPLEADER
INTERPLEADERS
INTERPLEADING
INTERPLEADS
INTERPLEURAL
INTERPLUVIAL
INTERPLUVIALS
INTERPOINT
INTERPOINTS
INTERPOLABLE
INTERPOLAR
INTERPOLATE
INTERPOLATED
INTERPOLATER
INTERPOLATERS
INTERPOLATES
INTERPOLATING
INTERPOLATION
INTERPOLATIONS
INTERPOLATIVE
INTERPOLATOR
INTERPOLATORS
INTERPONED
INTERPONES
INTERPONING
INTERPOPULATION
INTERPOSABLE
INTERPOSAL
INTERPOSALS
INTERPOSED
INTERPOSER
INTERPOSERS
INTERPOSES
INTERPOSING
INTERPOSITION
INTERPOSITIONS
INTERPRETABLE
INTERPRETABLY
INTERPRETATE
INTERPRETATED
INTERPRETATES
INTERPRETATING
INTERPRETATION
INTERPRETATIONS
INTERPRETATIVE
INTERPRETED
INTERPRETER
INTERPRETERS
INTERPRETERSHIP
INTERPRETESS
INTERPRETESSES
INTERPRETING
INTERPRETIVE
INTERPRETIVELY
INTERPRETRESS
INTERPRETRESSES
INTERPRETS
INTERPROVINCIAL
INTERPROXIMAL
INTERPSYCHIC
INTERPUNCTION
INTERPUNCTIONS
INTERPUNCTUATE
INTERPUNCTUATED
INTERPUNCTUATES
INTERPUPILLARY
INTERQUARTILE
INTERRACIAL
INTERRACIALLY
INTERRADIAL
INTERRADIALLY
INTERRADII
INTERRADIUS
INTERRADIUSES
INTERRAILED
INTERRAILER
INTERRAILERS
INTERRAILING
INTERRAILS
INTERRAMAL
INTERREGAL
INTERREGES
INTERREGIONAL
INTERREGNA
INTERREGNAL
INTERREGNUM
INTERREGNUMS
INTERRELATE
INTERRELATED
INTERRELATEDLY
INTERRELATES
INTERRELATING
INTERRELATION
INTERRELATIONS
INTERRELIGIOUS
INTERRENAL
INTERROBANG
INTERROBANGS
INTERROGABLE
INTERROGANT
INTERROGANTS
INTERROGATE
INTERROGATED
INTERROGATEE
INTERROGATEES
INTERROGATES
INTERROGATING
INTERROGATINGLY
INTERROGATION
INTERROGATIONAL
INTERROGATIONS
INTERROGATIVE
INTERROGATIVELY
INTERROGATIVES
INTERROGATOR
INTERROGATORIES
INTERROGATORILY
INTERROGATORS
INTERROGATORY
INTERROGEE
INTERROGEES
INTERRUPTED
INTERRUPTEDLY
INTERRUPTER
INTERRUPTERS
INTERRUPTIBLE
INTERRUPTING
INTERRUPTION
INTERRUPTIONS
INTERRUPTIVE
INTERRUPTIVELY
INTERRUPTOR
INTERRUPTORS
INTERRUPTS
INTERSCAPULAR
INTERSCHOLASTIC
INTERSCHOOL
INTERSCRIBE
INTERSCRIBED
INTERSCRIBES
INTERSCRIBING
INTERSECTED
INTERSECTING
INTERSECTION
INTERSECTIONAL
INTERSECTIONS
INTERSECTS
INTERSEGMENT
INTERSEGMENTAL
INTERSEGMENTS
INTERSENSORY
INTERSEPTAL
INTERSERTAL
INTERSERTED
INTERSERTING
INTERSERTS
INTERSERVICE
INTERSESSION
INTERSESSIONS
INTERSEXES
INTERSEXUAL
INTERSEXUALISM
INTERSEXUALISMS
INTERSEXUALITY
INTERSEXUALLY
INTERSEXUALS
INTERSIDEREAL
INTERSOCIETAL
INTERSOCIETY
INTERSPACE
INTERSPACED
INTERSPACES
INTERSPACING
INTERSPATIAL
INTERSPATIALLY
INTERSPECIES
INTERSPECIFIC
INTERSPERSAL
INTERSPERSALS
INTERSPERSE
INTERSPERSED

INTERSPERSEDLY
INTERSPERSES
INTERSPERSING
INTERSPERSION
INTERSPERSIONS
INTERSPINAL
INTERSPINOUS
INTERSTADIAL
INTERSTADIALS
INTERSTAGE
INTERSTATE
INTERSTATES
INTERSTATION
INTERSTELLAR
INTERSTELLARY
INTERSTERILE
INTERSTERILITY
INTERSTICE
INTERSTICES
INTERSTIMULUS
INTERSTITIAL
INTERSTITIALLY
INTERSTITIALS
INTERSTRAIN
INTERSTRAND
INTERSTRATIFIED
INTERSTRATIFIES
INTERSTRATIFY
INTERSUBJECTIVE
INTERSYSTEM
INTERTANGLE
INTERTANGLED
INTERTANGLEMENT
INTERTANGLES
INTERTANGLING
INTERTARSAL
INTERTENTACULAR
INTERTERMINAL
INTERTERMS
INTERTEXTS
INTERTEXTUAL
INTERTEXTUALITY
INTERTEXTUALLY
INTERTEXTURE
INTERTEXTURES
INTERTIDAL
INTERTIDALLY
INTERTILLAGE
INTERTILLAGES
INTERTILLED
INTERTILLING
INTERTILLS
INTERTISSUED
INTERTRAFFIC
INTERTRAFFICS
INTERTRIAL
INTERTRIBAL
INTERTRIGO
INTERTRIGOS
INTERTROOP
INTERTROPICAL
INTERTWINE
INTERTWINED
INTERTWINEMENT
INTERTWINEMENTS
INTERTWINES
INTERTWINING
INTERTWININGLY
INTERTWININGS
INTERTWIST
INTERTWISTED
INTERTWISTING
INTERTWISTINGLY
INTERTWISTS
INTERUNION
INTERUNIONS
INTERUNIVERSITY
INTERURBAN
INTERVALES
INTERVALLEY
INTERVALLIC
INTERVALLUM
INTERVALLUMS
INTERVALOMETER
INTERVALOMETERS
INTERVARSITY
INTERVEINED
INTERVEINING
INTERVEINS
INTERVENED
INTERVENER
INTERVENERS
INTERVENES
INTERVENIENT
INTERVENING
INTERVENOR
INTERVENORS
INTERVENTION
INTERVENTIONAL
INTERVENTIONISM
INTERVENTIONIST
INTERVENTIONS
INTERVENTOR
INTERVENTORS
INTERVERTEBRAL
INTERVIEWED
INTERVIEWEE
INTERVIEWEES
INTERVIEWER
INTERVIEWERS
INTERVIEWING
INTERVIEWS
INTERVILLAGE
INTERVISIBILITY
INTERVISIBLE
INTERVISITATION
INTERVITAL
INTERVOCALIC
INTERVOLVE
INTERVOLVED
INTERVOLVES
INTERVOLVING
INTERWEAVE
INTERWEAVED
INTERWEAVEMENT
INTERWEAVEMENTS
INTERWEAVER
INTERWEAVERS
INTERWEAVES
INTERWEAVING
INTERWINDING
INTERWINDS
INTERWORKED
INTERWORKING
INTERWORKINGS
INTERWORKS
INTERWOUND
INTERWOVEN
INTERWREATHE
INTERWREATHED
INTERWREATHES
INTERWREATHING
INTERWROUGHT
INTERZONAL
INTERZONES
INTESTACIES
INTESTATES
INTESTINAL
INTESTINALLY
INTESTINES
INTHRALLED
INTHRALLING
INTHRONING
INTIFADAHS
INTIFADEHS
INTIMACIES
INTIMATELY
INTIMATENESS
INTIMATENESSES
INTIMATERS
INTIMATING
INTIMATION
INTIMATIONS
INTIMIDATE
INTIMIDATED
INTIMIDATES
INTIMIDATING
INTIMIDATINGLY
INTIMIDATION
INTIMIDATIONS
INTIMIDATOR
INTIMIDATORS
INTIMIDATORY
INTIMISTES
INTIMITIES
INTINCTION
INTINCTIONS
INTITULING
INTOLERABILITY
INTOLERABLE
INTOLERABLENESS
INTOLERABLY
INTOLERANCE
INTOLERANCES
INTOLERANT
INTOLERANTLY
INTOLERANTNESS
INTOLERANTS
INTOLERATION
INTOLERATIONS
INTONATING
INTONATION
INTONATIONAL
INTONATIONS
INTONATORS
INTONINGLY
INTORSIONS
INTORTIONS
INTOXICABLE
INTOXICANT
INTOXICANTS
INTOXICATE
INTOXICATED
INTOXICATEDLY
INTOXICATES
INTOXICATING
INTOXICATINGLY
INTOXICATION
INTOXICATIONS
INTOXICATIVE
INTOXICATOR
INTOXICATORS
INTOXIMETER
INTOXIMETERS
INTRACAPSULAR
INTRACARDIAC
INTRACARDIAL
INTRACARDIALLY
INTRACAVITARY
INTRACELLULAR
INTRACELLULARLY
INTRACEREBRAL
INTRACEREBRALLY
INTRACOMPANY
INTRACRANIAL
INTRACRANIALLY
INTRACTABILITY
INTRACTABLE
INTRACTABLENESS
INTRACTABLY
INTRACUTANEOUS
INTRADERMAL
INTRADERMALLY
INTRADERMIC
INTRADERMICALLY
INTRADOSES
INTRAFALLOPIAN
INTRAFASCICULAR
INTRAGALACTIC
INTRAGENIC

INTRAMEDULLARY
INTRAMERCURIAL
INTRAMOLECULAR
INTRAMUNDANE
INTRAMURAL
INTRAMURALLY
INTRAMURALS
INTRAMUSCULAR
INTRAMUSCULARLY
INTRANASAL
INTRANASALLY
INTRANATIONAL
INTRANSIGEANCE
INTRANSIGEANCES
INTRANSIGEANT
INTRANSIGEANTLY
INTRANSIGEANTS
INTRANSIGENCE
INTRANSIGENCES
INTRANSIGENCIES
INTRANSIGENCY
INTRANSIGENT
INTRANSIGENTISM
INTRANSIGENTIST
INTRANSIGENTLY
INTRANSIGENTS
INTRANSITIVE
INTRANSITIVELY
INTRANSITIVES
INTRANSITIVITY
INTRANSMISSIBLE
INTRANSMUTABLE
INTRANUCLEAR
INTRAOCULAR
INTRAOCULARLY
INTRAPARIETAL
INTRAPARTUM
INTRAPERITONEAL
INTRAPERSONAL
INTRAPETIOLAR
INTRAPLATE
INTRAPOPULATION
INTRAPRENEUR
INTRAPRENEURIAL
INTRAPRENEURS
INTRAPSYCHIC
INTRASEXUAL
INTRASPECIES
INTRASPECIFIC
INTRASTATE
INTRATELLURIC
INTRATHECAL
INTRATHECALLY
INTRATHORACIC
INTRAUTERINE
INTRAVASATION
INTRAVASATIONS
INTRAVASCULAR
INTRAVASCULARLY
INTRAVENOUS
INTRAVENOUSLY
INTRAVERSABLE
INTRAVITAL
INTRAVITALLY
INTRAVITAM
INTRAZONAL
INTREATFULL
INTREATING
INTREATINGLY
INTREATMENT
INTREATMENTS
INTRENCHANT
INTRENCHED
INTRENCHER
INTRENCHERS
INTRENCHES
INTRENCHING
INTRENCHMENT
INTRENCHMENTS
INTREPIDITIES
INTREPIDITY
INTREPIDLY
INTREPIDNESS
INTREPIDNESSES
INTRICACIES
INTRICATELY
INTRICATENESS
INTRICATENESSES
INTRIGANTE
INTRIGANTES
INTRIGANTS
INTRIGUANT
INTRIGUANTE
INTRIGUANTES
INTRIGUANTS
INTRIGUERS
INTRIGUING
INTRIGUINGLY
INTRINSICAL
INTRINSICALITY
INTRINSICALLY
INTRINSICALNESS
INTRINSICATE
INTRODUCED
INTRODUCER
INTRODUCERS
INTRODUCES
INTRODUCIBLE
INTRODUCING
INTRODUCTION
INTRODUCTIONS
INTRODUCTIVE
INTRODUCTORILY
INTRODUCTORY
INTROFYING
INTROGRESSANT
INTROGRESSANTS
INTROGRESSION
INTROGRESSIONS
INTROGRESSIVE
INTROITUSES
INTROJECTED
INTROJECTING
INTROJECTION
INTROJECTIONS
INTROJECTIVE
INTROJECTS
INTROMISSIBLE
INTROMISSION
INTROMISSIONS
INTROMISSIVE
INTROMITTED
INTROMITTENT
INTROMITTER
INTROMITTERS
INTROMITTING
INTRORSELY
INTROSPECT
INTROSPECTED
INTROSPECTING
INTROSPECTION
INTROSPECTIONAL
INTROSPECTIONS
INTROSPECTIVE
INTROSPECTIVELY
INTROSPECTS
INTROSUSCEPTION
INTROVERSIBLE
INTROVERSION
INTROVERSIONS
INTROVERSIVE
INTROVERSIVELY
INTROVERTED
INTROVERTING
INTROVERTIVE
INTROVERTS
INTRUDINGLY
INTRUSIONAL
INTRUSIONIST
INTRUSIONISTS
INTRUSIONS
INTRUSIVELY
INTRUSIVENESS
INTRUSIVENESSES
INTRUSIVES
INTRUSTING
INTRUSTMENT
INTRUSTMENTS
INTUBATING
INTUBATION
INTUBATIONS
INTUITABLE
INTUITIONAL
INTUITIONALISM
INTUITIONALISMS
INTUITIONALIST
INTUITIONALISTS
INTUITIONALLY
INTUITIONISM
INTUITIONISMS
INTUITIONIST
INTUITIONISTS
INTUITIONS
INTUITIVELY
INTUITIVENESS
INTUITIVENESSES
INTUITIVISM
INTUITIVISMS
INTUMESCED
INTUMESCENCE
INTUMESCENCES
INTUMESCENCIES
INTUMESCENCY
INTUMESCENT
INTUMESCES
INTUMESCING
INTURBIDATE
INTURBIDATED
INTURBIDATES
INTURBIDATING
INTUSSUSCEPT
INTUSSUSCEPTED
INTUSSUSCEPTING
INTUSSUSCEPTION
INTUSSUSCEPTIVE
INTUSSUSCEPTS
INTWINEMENT
INTWINEMENTS
INTWISTING
INUMBRATED
INUMBRATES
INUMBRATING
INUNCTIONS
INUNDATING
INUNDATION
INUNDATIONS
INUNDATORS
INUNDATORY
INURBANELY
INURBANITIES
INURBANITY
INUREDNESS
INUREDNESSES
INUREMENTS
INURNMENTS
INUSITATION
INUSITATIONS
INUTILITIES
INUTTERABLE
INVAGINABLE
INVAGINATE
INVAGINATED
INVAGINATES
INVAGINATING
INVAGINATION
INVAGINATIONS
INVALIDATE
INVALIDATED
INVALIDATES
INVALIDATING

INVALIDATION
INVALIDATIONS
INVALIDATOR
INVALIDATORS
INVALIDEST
INVALIDHOOD
INVALIDHOODS
INVALIDING
INVALIDINGS
INVALIDISM
INVALIDISMS
INVALIDITIES
INVALIDITY
INVALIDNESS
INVALIDNESSES
INVALUABLE
INVALUABLENESS
INVALUABLY
INVARIABILITIES
INVARIABILITY
INVARIABLE
INVARIABLENESS
INVARIABLES
INVARIABLY
INVARIANCE
INVARIANCES
INVARIANCIES
INVARIANCY
INVARIANTS
INVASIVELY
INVASIVENESS
INVASIVENESSES
INVEAGLING
INVECTIVELY
INVECTIVENESS
INVECTIVENESSES
INVECTIVES
INVEIGHERS
INVEIGHING
INVEIGLEMENT
INVEIGLEMENTS
INVEIGLERS
INVEIGLING
INVENDIBILITIES
INVENDIBILITY
INVENDIBLE
INVENTABLE
INVENTIBLE
INVENTIONAL
INVENTIONLESS
INVENTIONS
INVENTIVELY
INVENTIVENESS
INVENTIVENESSES
INVENTORIABLE
INVENTORIAL
INVENTORIALLY
INVENTORIED
INVENTORIES
INVENTORYING
INVENTRESS
INVENTRESSES
INVERACITIES
INVERACITY
INVERITIES
INVERNESSES
INVERSIONS
INVERTASES
INVERTEBRAL
INVERTEBRATE
INVERTEBRATES
INVERTEDLY
INVERTIBILITIES
INVERTIBILITY
INVERTIBLE
INVESTABLE
INVESTIBLE
INVESTIGABLE
INVESTIGATE
INVESTIGATED
INVESTIGATES
INVESTIGATING
INVESTIGATION
INVESTIGATIONAL
INVESTIGATIONS
INVESTIGATIVE
INVESTIGATOR
INVESTIGATORS
INVESTIGATORY
INVESTITIVE
INVESTITURE
INVESTITURES
INVESTMENT
INVESTMENTS
INVETERACIES
INVETERACY
INVETERATE
INVETERATELY
INVETERATENESS
INVIABILITIES
INVIABILITY
INVIABLENESS
INVIABLENESSES
INVIDIOUSLY
INVIDIOUSNESS
INVIDIOUSNESSES
INVIGILATE
INVIGILATED
INVIGILATES
INVIGILATING
INVIGILATION
INVIGILATIONS
INVIGILATOR
INVIGILATORS
INVIGORANT
INVIGORANTS
INVIGORATE
INVIGORATED
INVIGORATES
INVIGORATING
INVIGORATINGLY
INVIGORATION
INVIGORATIONS
INVIGORATIVE
INVIGORATIVELY
INVIGORATOR
INVIGORATORS
INVINCIBILITIES
INVINCIBILITY
INVINCIBLE
INVINCIBLENESS
INVINCIBLY
INVIOLABILITIES
INVIOLABILITY
INVIOLABLE
INVIOLABLENESS
INVIOLABLY
INVIOLACIES
INVIOLATED
INVIOLATELY
INVIOLATENESS
INVIOLATENESSES
INVISIBILITIES
INVISIBILITY
INVISIBLENESS
INVISIBLENESSES
INVISIBLES
INVITATION
INVITATIONAL
INVITATIONALS
INVITATIONS
INVITATORIES
INVITATORY
INVITEMENT
INVITEMENTS
INVITINGLY
INVITINGNESS
INVITINGNESSES
INVOCATING
INVOCATION
INVOCATIONAL
INVOCATIONS
INVOCATIVE
INVOCATORS
INVOCATORY
INVOICINGS
INVOLUCELLA
INVOLUCELLATE
INVOLUCELLATED
INVOLUCELLUM
INVOLUCELS
INVOLUCRAL
INVOLUCRATE
INVOLUCRES
INVOLUCRUM
INVOLUNTARILY
INVOLUNTARINESS
INVOLUNTARY
INVOLUTEDLY
INVOLUTELY
INVOLUTING
INVOLUTION
INVOLUTIONAL
INVOLUTIONS
INVOLVEDLY
INVOLVEMENT
INVOLVEMENTS
INVULNERABILITY
INVULNERABLE
INVULNERABLY
INVULTUATION
INVULTUATIONS
INWARDNESS
INWARDNESSES
INWORKINGS
INWRAPMENT
INWRAPMENTS
INWRAPPING
INWRAPPINGS
INWREATHED
INWREATHES
INWREATHING
IODINATING
IODINATION
IODINATIONS
IODISATION
IODISATIONS
IODIZATION
IODIZATIONS
IODOMETRIC
IODOMETRICAL
IODOMETRICALLY
IODOMETRIES
IONICITIES
IONISATION
IONISATIONS
IONIZATION
IONIZATIONS
IONOPAUSES
IONOPHORES
IONOPHORESES
IONOPHORESIS
IONOSONDES
IONOSPHERE
IONOSPHERES
IONOSPHERIC
IONOSPHERICALLY
IONOTROPIC
IONOTROPIES
IONTOPHORESES
IONTOPHORESIS
IONTOPHORETIC
IPECACUANHA
IPECACUANHAS
IPRATROPIUM
IPRATROPIUMS
IPRINDOLES
IPRONIAZID
IPRONIAZIDS
IPSELATERAL

IPSILATERAL
IPSILATERALLY
IRACUNDITIES
IRACUNDITY
IRACUNDULOUS
IRASCIBILITIES
IRASCIBILITY
IRASCIBLENESS
IRASCIBLENESSES
IRATENESSES
IREFULNESS
IREFULNESSES
IRENICALLY
IRENICISMS
IRENOLOGIES
IRIDACEOUS
IRIDECTOMIES
IRIDECTOMY
IRIDESCENCE
IRIDESCENCES
IRIDESCENT
IRIDESCENTLY
IRIDISATION
IRIDISATIONS
IRIDIZATION
IRIDIZATIONS
IRIDOCYTES
IRIDOLOGIES
IRIDOLOGIST
IRIDOLOGISTS
IRIDOSMINE
IRIDOSMINES
IRIDOSMIUM
IRIDOSMIUMS
IRIDOTOMIES
IRISATIONS
IRKSOMENESS
IRKSOMENESSES
IRONFISTED
IRONHANDED
IRONHEARTED
IRONICALLY
IRONICALNESS
IRONICALNESSES
IRONMASTER
IRONMASTERS
IRONMONGER
IRONMONGERIES
IRONMONGERS
IRONMONGERY
IRONNESSES
IRONSMITHS
IRONSTONES
IRONWORKER
IRONWORKERS
IRRADIANCE
IRRADIANCES
IRRADIANCIES
IRRADIANCY
IRRADIATED
IRRADIATES
IRRADIATING
IRRADIATION
IRRADIATIONS
IRRADIATIVE
IRRADIATOR
IRRADIATORS
IRRADICABLE
IRRADICABLY
IRRADICATE
IRRADICATED
IRRADICATES
IRRADICATING
IRRATIONAL
IRRATIONALISE
IRRATIONALISED
IRRATIONALISES
IRRATIONALISING
IRRATIONALISM
IRRATIONALISMS
IRRATIONALIST
IRRATIONALISTIC
IRRATIONALISTS
IRRATIONALITIES
IRRATIONALITY
IRRATIONALIZE
IRRATIONALIZED
IRRATIONALIZES
IRRATIONALIZING
IRRATIONALLY
IRRATIONALNESS
IRRATIONALS
IRREALISABLE
IRREALITIES
IRREALIZABLE
IRREBUTTABLE
IRRECEPTIVE
IRRECIPROCAL
IRRECIPROCITIES
IRRECIPROCITY
IRRECLAIMABLE
IRRECLAIMABLY
IRRECOGNISABLE
IRRECOGNITION
IRRECOGNITIONS
IRRECOGNIZABLE
IRRECONCILABLE
IRRECONCILABLES
IRRECONCILABLY
IRRECONCILED
IRRECONCILEMENT
IRRECOVERABLE
IRRECOVERABLY
IRRECUSABLE
IRRECUSABLY
IRREDEEMABILITY
IRREDEEMABLE
IRREDEEMABLES
IRREDEEMABLY
IRREDENTAS
IRREDENTISM
IRREDENTISMS
IRREDENTIST
IRREDENTISTS
IRREDUCIBILITY
IRREDUCIBLE
IRREDUCIBLENESS
IRREDUCIBLY
IRREDUCTIBILITY
IRREDUCTION
IRREDUCTIONS
IRREFLECTION
IRREFLECTIONS
IRREFLECTIVE
IRREFLEXION
IRREFLEXIONS
IRREFLEXIVE
IRREFORMABILITY
IRREFORMABLE
IRREFORMABLY
IRREFRAGABILITY
IRREFRAGABLE
IRREFRAGABLY
IRREFRANGIBLE
IRREFRANGIBLY
IRREFUTABILITY
IRREFUTABLE
IRREFUTABLENESS
IRREFUTABLY
IRREGARDLESS
IRREGULARITIES
IRREGULARITY
IRREGULARLY
IRREGULARS
IRRELATION
IRRELATIONS
IRRELATIVE
IRRELATIVELY
IRRELATIVENESS
IRRELEVANCE
IRRELEVANCES
IRRELEVANCIES
IRRELEVANCY
IRRELEVANT
IRRELEVANTLY
IRRELIEVABLE
IRRELIGION
IRRELIGIONIST
IRRELIGIONISTS
IRRELIGIONS
IRRELIGIOUS
IRRELIGIOUSLY
IRRELIGIOUSNESS
IRREMEABLE
IRREMEABLY
IRREMEDIABLE
IRREMEDIABLY
IRREMISSIBILITY
IRREMISSIBLE
IRREMISSIBLY
IRREMISSION
IRREMISSIONS
IRREMISSIVE
IRREMOVABILITY
IRREMOVABLE
IRREMOVABLENESS
IRREMOVABLY
IRRENOWNED
IRREPAIRABLE
IRREPARABILITY
IRREPARABLE
IRREPARABLENESS
IRREPARABLY
IRREPEALABILITY
IRREPEALABLE
IRREPEALABLY
IRREPLACEABLE
IRREPLACEABLY
IRREPLEVIABLE
IRREPLEVISABLE
IRREPREHENSIBLE
IRREPREHENSIBLY
IRREPRESSIBLE
IRREPRESSIBLY
IRREPROACHABLE
IRREPROACHABLY
IRREPRODUCIBLE
IRREPROVABLE
IRREPROVABLY
IRRESISTANCE
IRRESISTANCES
IRRESISTIBILITY
IRRESISTIBLE
IRRESISTIBLY
IRRESOLUBILITY
IRRESOLUBLE
IRRESOLUBLY
IRRESOLUTE
IRRESOLUTELY
IRRESOLUTENESS
IRRESOLUTION
IRRESOLUTIONS
IRRESOLVABILITY
IRRESOLVABLE
IRRESOLVABLY
IRRESPECTIVE
IRRESPECTIVELY
IRRESPIRABLE
IRRESPONSIBLE
IRRESPONSIBLES
IRRESPONSIBLY
IRRESPONSIVE
IRRESPONSIVELY
IRRESTRAINABLE
IRRESUSCITABLE
IRRESUSCITABLY
IRRETENTION
IRRETENTIONS
IRRETENTIVE
IRRETENTIVENESS

IRRETRIEVABLE
IRRETRIEVABLY
IRREVERENCE
IRREVERENCES
IRREVERENT
IRREVERENTIAL
IRREVERENTLY
IRREVERSIBILITY
IRREVERSIBLE
IRREVERSIBLY
IRREVOCABILITY
IRREVOCABLE
IRREVOCABLENESS
IRREVOCABLY
IRRIDENTAS
IRRIGATING
IRRIGATION
IRRIGATIONAL
IRRIGATIONS
IRRIGATIVE
IRRIGATORS
IRRITABILITIES
IRRITABILITY
IRRITABLENESS
IRRITABLENESSES
IRRITANCIES
IRRITATEDLY
IRRITATING
IRRITATINGLY
IRRITATION
IRRITATIONS
IRRITATIVE
IRRITATORS
IRROTATIONAL
IRRUPTIONS
IRRUPTIVELY
IRUKANDJIS
ISABELLINE
ISABELLINES
ISALLOBARIC
ISALLOBARS
ISAPOSTOLIC
ISCHAEMIAS
ISCHURETIC
ISCHURETICS
ISEIKONIAS
ISENTROPIC
ISENTROPICALLY
ISINGLASSES
ISLOMANIAS
ISMATICALNESS
ISMATICALNESSES
ISOAGGLUTININ
ISOAGGLUTININS
ISOALLOXAZINE
ISOALLOXAZINES
ISOAMINILE
ISOAMINILES
ISOANTIBODIES
ISOANTIBODY
ISOANTIGEN
ISOANTIGENIC
ISOANTIGENS
ISOBARISMS
ISOBAROMETRIC
ISOBILATERAL
ISOBUTANES
ISOBUTENES
ISOBUTYLENE
ISOBUTYLENES
ISOCALORIC
ISOCARBOXAZID
ISOCARBOXAZIDS
ISOCHASMIC
ISOCHEIMAL
ISOCHEIMALS
ISOCHEIMENAL
ISOCHEIMENALS
ISOCHEIMIC
ISOCHIMALS
ISOCHROMATIC
ISOCHROMOSOME
ISOCHROMOSOMES
ISOCHRONAL
ISOCHRONALLY
ISOCHRONES
ISOCHRONISE
ISOCHRONISED
ISOCHRONISES
ISOCHRONISING
ISOCHRONISM
ISOCHRONISMS
ISOCHRONIZE
ISOCHRONIZED
ISOCHRONIZES
ISOCHRONIZING
ISOCHRONOUS
ISOCHRONOUSLY
ISOCHROOUS
ISOCLINALS
ISOCLINICS
ISOCRACIES
ISOCRYMALS
ISOCYANATE
ISOCYANATES
ISOCYANIDE
ISOCYANIDES
ISODIAMETRIC
ISODIAMETRICAL
ISODIAPHERE
ISODIAPHERES
ISODIMORPHIC
ISODIMORPHISM
ISODIMORPHISMS
ISODIMORPHOUS
ISODONTALS
ISODYNAMIC
ISODYNAMICS
ISOELECTRIC
ISOELECTRONIC
ISOENZYMATIC
ISOENZYMES
ISOENZYMIC
ISOFLAVONE
ISOFLAVONES
ISOGAMETES
ISOGAMETIC
ISOGENETIC
ISOGEOTHERM
ISOGEOTHERMAL
ISOGEOTHERMALS
ISOGEOTHERMIC
ISOGEOTHERMICS
ISOGEOTHERMS
ISOGLOSSAL
ISOGLOSSES
ISOGLOSSIC
ISOGLOTTAL
ISOGLOTTIC
ISOGRAFTED
ISOGRAFTING
ISOHYETALS
ISOIMMUNISATION
ISOIMMUNIZATION
ISOKINETIC
ISOKONTANS
ISOLABILITIES
ISOLABILITY
ISOLATABLE
ISOLATIONISM
ISOLATIONISMS
ISOLATIONIST
ISOLATIONISTS
ISOLATIONS
ISOLECITHAL
ISOLEUCINE
ISOLEUCINES
ISOMAGNETIC
ISOMAGNETICS
ISOMERASES
ISOMERISATION
ISOMERISATIONS
ISOMERISED
ISOMERISES
ISOMERISING
ISOMERISMS
ISOMERIZATION
ISOMERIZATIONS
ISOMERIZED
ISOMERIZES
ISOMERIZING
ISOMETRICAL
ISOMETRICALLY
ISOMETRICS
ISOMETRIES
ISOMETROPIA
ISOMETROPIAS
ISOMORPHIC
ISOMORPHICALLY
ISOMORPHISM
ISOMORPHISMS
ISOMORPHOUS
ISONIAZIDE
ISONIAZIDES
ISONIAZIDS
ISONITRILE
ISONITRILES
ISOOCTANES
ISOPACHYTE
ISOPACHYTES
ISOPERIMETER
ISOPERIMETERS
ISOPERIMETRICAL
ISOPERIMETRIES
ISOPERIMETRY
ISOPIESTIC
ISOPIESTICALLY
ISOPLETHIC
ISOPLUVIAL
ISOPLUVIALS
ISOPOLITIES
ISOPRENALINE
ISOPRENALINES
ISOPRENOID
ISOPRENOIDS
ISOPROPYLS
ISOPROTERENOL
ISOPROTERENOLS
ISOPTERANS
ISOPTEROUS
ISOPYCNALS
ISOPYCNICS
ISORHYTHMIC
ISOSEISMAL
ISOSEISMALS
ISOSEISMIC
ISOSEISMICS
ISOSMOTICALLY
ISOSPONDYLOUS
ISOSPORIES
ISOSPOROUS
ISOSTACIES
ISOSTASIES
ISOSTATICALLY
ISOSTEMONOUS
ISOSTHENURIA
ISOSTHENURIAS
ISOTENISCOPE
ISOTENISCOPES
ISOTHERALS
ISOTHERMAL
ISOTHERMALLY
ISOTHERMALS
ISOTONICALLY
ISOTONICITIES
ISOTONICITY
ISOTOPICALLY
ISOTRETINOIN
ISOTRETINOINS
ISOTROPICALLY

ISOTROPIES
ISOTROPISM
ISOTROPISMS
ISOTROPOUS
ISOXSUPRINE
ISOXSUPRINES
ISPAGHULAS
ITACOLUMITE
ITACOLUMITES
ITALIANATE
ITALIANATED
ITALIANATES
ITALIANATING
ITALIANISE
ITALIANISED
ITALIANISES
ITALIANISING
ITALIANIZE
ITALIANIZED
ITALIANIZES
ITALIANIZING
ITALICISATION
ITALICISATIONS
ITALICISED
ITALICISES
ITALICISING
ITALICIZATION
ITALICIZATIONS
ITALICIZED
ITALICIZES
ITALICIZING
ITCHINESSES
ITEMISATION
ITEMISATIONS
ITEMIZATION
ITEMIZATIONS
ITERATIONS
ITERATIVELY
ITERATIVENESS
ITERATIVENESSES
ITEROPARITIES
ITEROPARITY
ITEROPAROUS
ITHYPHALLI
ITHYPHALLIC
ITHYPHALLICS
ITHYPHALLUS
ITHYPHALLUSES
ITINERACIES
ITINERANCIES
ITINERANCY
ITINERANTLY
ITINERANTS
ITINERARIES
ITINERATED
ITINERATES
ITINERATING
ITINERATION
ITINERATIONS
IVERMECTIN
IVERMECTINS
IVORYBILLS
IVORYWOODS
IZVESTIYAS

J

JABBERINGLY
JABBERINGS
JABBERWOCK
JABBERWOCKIES
JABBERWOCKS
JABBERWOCKY
JABORANDIS
JABOTICABA
JABOTICABAS
JACARANDAS
JACKALLING
JACKALOPES
JACKANAPES
JACKANAPESES
JACKAROOED
JACKAROOING
JACKASSERIES
JACKASSERY
JACKBOOTED
JACKBOOTING
JACKEROOED
JACKEROOING
JACKETLESS
JACKFISHES
JACKFRUITS
JACKHAMMER
JACKHAMMERED
JACKHAMMERING
JACKHAMMERS
JACKKNIFED
JACKKNIFES
JACKKNIFING
JACKKNIVES
JACKLIGHTED
JACKLIGHTING
JACKLIGHTS
JACKPLANES
JACKPOTTED
JACKPOTTING
JACKRABBIT
JACKRABBITS
JACKROLLED
JACKROLLING
JACKSCREWS
JACKSHAFTS
JACKSMELTS
JACKSMITHS
JACKSNIPES
JACKSTAFFS
JACKSTAVES
JACKSTONES
JACKSTRAWS
JACQUERIES
JACTATIONS
JACTITATION
JACTITATIONS
JACULATING
JACULATION
JACULATIONS
JACULATORS
JACULATORY
JADEDNESSES
JADISHNESS
JADISHNESSES
JAGDWURSTS
JAGGEDNESS
JAGGEDNESSES
JAGGHERIES
JAGHIRDARS
JAGUARONDI
JAGUARONDIS
JAGUARUNDI
JAGUARUNDIS
JAILBREAKER
JAILBREAKERS
JAILBREAKING
JAILBREAKS
JAILBROKEN
JAILERESSES
JAILHOUSES
JAILORESSES
JALOALLOFANE
JALOALLOFANES
JAMAHIRIYA
JAMAHIRIYAS
JAMBALAYAS
JAMBOKKING
JAMBOLANAS
JAMBUSTERS
JANISARIES
JANISSARIES
JANITORIAL
JANITORSHIP
JANITORSHIPS
JANITRESSES
JANITRIXES
JANIZARIAN
JANIZARIES
JANNEYINGS
JAPANISING
JAPANIZING
JAPONAISERIE
JAPONAISERIES
JARDINIERE
JARDINIERES
JARGONEERS
JARGONELLE
JARGONELLES
JARGONIEST
JARGONISATION
JARGONISATIONS
JARGONISED
JARGONISES
JARGONISING
JARGONISTIC
JARGONISTS
JARGONIZATION
JARGONIZATIONS
JARGONIZED
JARGONIZES
JARGONIZING
JARLSBERGS
JAROVISING
JAROVIZING
JASMONATES
JASPERIEST
JASPERISED
JASPERISES
JASPERISING
JASPERIZED
JASPERIZES
JASPERIZING
JASPERWARE
JASPERWARES
JASPIDEOUS
JASPILITES
JAUNDICING
JAUNTINESS
JAUNTINESSES
JAUNTINGLY
JAVELINING
JAWBATIONS
JAWBONINGS
JAWBREAKER
JAWBREAKERS
JAWBREAKING
JAWBREAKINGLY
JAWCRUSHER
JAWCRUSHERS
JAYHAWKERS
JAYWALKERS
JAYWALKING
JAYWALKINGS
JAZZINESSES
JEALOUSEST
JEALOUSHOOD
JEALOUSHOODS
JEALOUSIES
JEALOUSING
JEALOUSNESS
JEALOUSNESSES
JEANSWEARS
JEISTIECOR
JEISTIECORS
JEJUNENESS
JEJUNENESSES
JEJUNITIES
JEJUNOSTOMIES
JEJUNOSTOMY
JELLIFICATION
JELLIFICATIONS
JELLIFYING
JELLYBEANS
JELLYFISHES
JELLYGRAPH
JELLYGRAPHED
JELLYGRAPHING
JELLYGRAPHS
JELLYROLLS
JEMMINESSES
JENNETINGS
JEOPARDERS
JEOPARDIED
JEOPARDIES
JEOPARDING
JEOPARDISE
JEOPARDISED
JEOPARDISES
JEOPARDISING
JEOPARDIZE
JEOPARDIZED
JEOPARDIZES
JEOPARDIZING
JEOPARDOUS
JEOPARDOUSLY
JEOPARDYING
JEQUERITIES
JEQUIRITIES
JERFALCONS
JERKINESSES
JERKINHEAD
JERKINHEADS
JERKWATERS
JERRYMANDER
JERRYMANDERED
JERRYMANDERING
JERRYMANDERS
JESSAMINES
JESSERANTS
JESUITICAL

J

JESUITICALLY
JESUITISMS
JESUITRIES
JETSTREAMS
JETTATURAS
JETTINESSES
JETTISONABLE
JETTISONED
JETTISONING
JEWELFISHES
JEWELLERIES
JEWELWEEDS
JICKAJOGGED
JICKAJOGGING
JICKAJOGGINGS
JIGAJIGGED
JIGAJIGGING
JIGAJOGGED
JIGAJOGGING
JIGAMAREES
JIGGERMAST
JIGGERMASTS
JIGGUMBOBS
JILLFLIRTS
JIMPNESSES
JIMSONWEED
JIMSONWEEDS
JINGOISTIC
JINGOISTICALLY
JINRICKSHA
JINRICKSHAS
JINRICKSHAW
JINRICKSHAWS
JINRIKISHA
JINRIKISHAS
JINRIKSHAS
JITTERBUGGED
JITTERBUGGING
JITTERBUGS
JITTERIEST
JITTERINESS
JITTERINESSES
JOBCENTRES
JOBERNOWLS
JOBHOLDERS
JOBLESSNESS
JOBLESSNESSES
JOBSEEKERS
JOBSWORTHS
JOCKEYISMS
JOCKEYSHIP
JOCKEYSHIPS
JOCKSTRAPS
JOCKTELEGS
JOCOSENESS
JOCOSENESSES
JOCOSERIOUS
JOCOSITIES
JOCULARITIES
JOCULARITY
JOCULATORS
JOCUNDITIES
JOCUNDNESS
JOCUNDNESSES
JOGTROTTED
JOGTROTTING
JOHANNESES
JOHNNYCAKE
JOHNNYCAKES
JOHNSONGRASS
JOHNSONGRASSES
JOINTEDNESS
JOINTEDNESSES
JOINTNESSES
JOINTRESSES
JOINTURESS
JOINTURESSES
JOINTURING
JOINTWEEDS
JOINTWORMS
JOKESMITHS
JOKINESSES
JOLIOTIUMS
JOLLEYINGS
JOLLIFICATION
JOLLIFICATIONS
JOLLIFYING
JOLLIMENTS
JOLLINESSES
JOLLYBOATS
JOLLYHEADS
JOLTERHEAD
JOLTERHEADS
JONNYCAKES
JOSEPHINITE
JOSEPHINITES
JOSTLEMENT
JOSTLEMENTS
JOUISANCES
JOURNALESE
JOURNALESES
JOURNALING
JOURNALINGS
JOURNALISATION
JOURNALISATIONS
JOURNALISE
JOURNALISED
JOURNALISER
JOURNALISERS
JOURNALISES
JOURNALISING
JOURNALISM
JOURNALISMS
JOURNALIST
JOURNALISTIC
JOURNALISTS
JOURNALIZATION
JOURNALIZATIONS
JOURNALIZE
JOURNALIZED
JOURNALIZER
JOURNALIZERS
JOURNALIZES
JOURNALIZING
JOURNALLED
JOURNALLING
JOURNALLINGS
JOURNEYERS
JOURNEYING
JOURNEYMAN
JOURNEYMEN
JOURNEYWORK
JOURNEYWORKS
JOUYSAUNCE
JOUYSAUNCES
JOVIALITIES
JOVIALNESS
JOVIALNESSES
JOVIALTIES
JOVYSAUNCE
JOVYSAUNCES
JOWLINESSES
JOYFULLEST
JOYFULNESS
JOYFULNESSES
JOYLESSNESS
JOYLESSNESSES
JOYOUSNESS
JOYOUSNESSES
JOYPOPPERS
JOYPOPPING
JOYRIDINGS
JUBILANCES
JUBILANCIES
JUBILANTLY
JUBILARIAN
JUBILARIANS
JUBILATING
JUBILATION
JUBILATIONS
JUDDERIEST
JUDGEMENTAL
JUDGEMENTALLY
JUDGEMENTS
JUDGESHIPS
JUDGMATICAL
JUDGMATICALLY
JUDGMENTAL
JUDGMENTALLY
JUDICATION
JUDICATIONS
JUDICATIVE
JUDICATORIAL
JUDICATORIES
JUDICATORS
JUDICATORY
JUDICATURE
JUDICATURES
JUDICIALLY
JUDICIARIES
JUDICIARILY
JUDICIOUSLY
JUDICIOUSNESS
JUDICIOUSNESSES
JUGGERNAUT
JUGGERNAUTS
JUGGLERIES
JUGGLINGLY
JUGLANDACEOUS
JUGULATING
JUGULATION
JUGULATIONS
JUICEHEADS
JUICINESSES
JULIENNING
JUMBLINGLY
JUMBOISING
JUMBOIZING
JUMHOURIYA
JUMHOURIYAS
JUMPINESSES
JUNCACEOUS
JUNCTIONAL
JUNEATINGS
JUNGLEGYMS
JUNGLELIKE
JUNIORATES
JUNIORITIES
JUNKERDOMS
JUNKETEERED
JUNKETEERING
JUNKETEERS
JUNKETINGS
JUNKETTERS
JUNKETTING
JUNKINESSES
JURIDICALLY
JURISCONSULT
JURISCONSULTS
JURISDICTION
JURISDICTIONAL
JURISDICTIONS
JURISDICTIVE
JURISPRUDENCE
JURISPRUDENCES
JURISPRUDENT
JURISPRUDENTIAL
JURISPRUDENTS
JURISTICAL
JURISTICALLY
JUSTICESHIP
JUSTICESHIPS
JUSTICIABILITY
JUSTICIABLE
JUSTICIALISM
JUSTICIALISMS
JUSTICIARIES
JUSTICIARS
JUSTICIARSHIP
JUSTICIARSHIPS

JUSTICIARY
JUSTIFIABILITY
JUSTIFIABLE
JUSTIFIABLENESS
JUSTIFIABLY
JUSTIFICATION
JUSTIFICATIONS
JUSTIFICATIVE
JUSTIFICATOR
JUSTIFICATORS
JUSTIFICATORY
JUSTIFIERS
JUSTIFYING
JUSTNESSES
JUVENESCENCE
JUVENESCENCES
JUVENESCENT
JUVENILELY
JUVENILENESS
JUVENILENESSES
JUVENILITIES
JUVENILITY
JUXTAPOSED
JUXTAPOSES
JUXTAPOSING
JUXTAPOSITION
JUXTAPOSITIONAL
JUXTAPOSITIONS

K

KABALISTIC
KABARAGOYA
KABARAGOYAS
KABBALISMS
KABBALISTIC
KABBALISTS
KABELJOUWS
KACHUMBERS
KADAITCHAS
KAFFEEKLATSCH
KAFFEEKLATSCHES
KAFFIRBOOM
KAFFIRBOOMS
KAHIKATEAS
KAHIKATOAS
KAIKAWAKAS
KAIKOMAKOS
KAILYAIRDS
KAINOGENESES
KAINOGENESIS
KAINOGENETIC
KAIROMONES
KAISERDOMS
KAISERISMS
KAISERSHIP
KAISERSHIPS
KAKISTOCRACIES
KAKISTOCRACY
KALAMKARIS
KALANCHOES
KALASHNIKOV
KALASHNIKOVS
KALEIDOPHONE
KALEIDOPHONES
KALEIDOSCOPE
KALEIDOSCOPES
KALEIDOSCOPIC
KALENDARED
KALENDARING
KALIPHATES
KALLIKREIN
KALLIKREINS
KALLITYPES
KALSOMINED
KALSOMINES
KALSOMINING
KAMELAUKION
KAMELAUKIONS
KAMERADING
KANAMYCINS
KANGAROOED
KANGAROOING
KANTIKOYED
KANTIKOYING
KAOLINISED
KAOLINISES
KAOLINISING
KAOLINITES
KAOLINITIC
KAOLINIZED
KAOLINIZES
KAOLINIZING
KAOLINOSES
KAOLINOSIS
KAPELLMEISTER
KAPELLMEISTERS
KARABINERS
KARANGAING
KARATEISTS
KARMICALLY
KARSTIFICATION
KARSTIFICATIONS
KARSTIFIED
KARSTIFIES
KARSTIFYING
KARUHIRUHI
KARUHIRUHIS
KARYOGAMIC
KARYOGAMIES
KARYOGRAMS
KARYOKINESES
KARYOKINESIS
KARYOKINETIC
KARYOLOGIC
KARYOLOGICAL
KARYOLOGIES
KARYOLOGIST
KARYOLOGISTS
KARYOLYMPH
KARYOLYMPHS
KARYOLYSES
KARYOLYSIS
KARYOLYTIC
KARYOMAPPING
KARYOMAPPINGS
KARYOPLASM
KARYOPLASMIC
KARYOPLASMS
KARYOSOMES
KARYOTYPED
KARYOTYPES
KARYOTYPIC
KARYOTYPICAL
KARYOTYPICALLY
KARYOTYPING
KATABOLICALLY
KATABOLISM
KATABOLISMS
KATABOTHRON
KATABOTHRONS
KATADROMOUS
KATATHERMOMETER
KATAVOTHRON
KATAVOTHRONS
KATHAKALIS
KATHAREVOUSA
KATHAREVOUSAS
KATHAROMETER
KATHAROMETERS
KATZENJAMMER
KATZENJAMMERS
KAWANATANGA
KAWANATANGAS
KAZATSKIES
KAZILLIONS
KEELHALING
KEELHAULED
KEELHAULING
KEELHAULINGS
KEELIVINES
KEELYVINES
KEENNESSES
KEEPERLESS
KEEPERSHIP
KEEPERSHIPS
KEEPSAKIER
KEEPSAKIEST
KEESHONDEN
KEFUFFLING
KEKERENGUS
KELPFISHES
KELYPHITIC
KENNELLING
KENNETTING
KENOGENESES
KENOGENESIS
KENOGENETIC
KENOGENETICALLY
KENOPHOBIA
KENOPHOBIAS
KENOTICIST
KENOTICISTS
KENSPECKLE
KENTLEDGES
KERATECTOMIES
KERATECTOMY
KERATINISATION
KERATINISATIONS
KERATINISE
KERATINISED
KERATINISES
KERATINISING
KERATINIZATION
KERATINIZATIONS
KERATINIZE
KERATINIZED
KERATINIZES
KERATINIZING
KERATINOPHILIC
KERATINOUS
KERATITIDES
KERATITISES
KERATOGENOUS
KERATOMATA
KERATOMETER
KERATOMETERS
KERATOPHYRE
KERATOPHYRES
KERATOPLASTIC
KERATOPLASTIES
KERATOPLASTY
KERATOTOMIES
KERATOTOMY
KERAUNOGRAPH
KERAUNOGRAPHS
KERBLOOEYS
KERBSTONES
KERCHIEFED
KERCHIEFING
KERCHIEVES
KERFUFFLED
KERFUFFLES
KERFUFFLING
KERMESITES
KERNELLIER
KERNELLIEST
KERNELLING
KERNICTERUS
KERNICTERUSES
KERNMANTEL
KERPLUNKED
KERPLUNKING
KERSANTITE
KERSANTITES
KERSEYMERE
KERSEYMERES
KERYGMATIC
KETCHUPIER
KETCHUPIEST
KETOACIDOSES

KETOACIDOSIS
KETOGENESES
KETOGENESIS
KETONAEMIA
KETONAEMIAS
KETONEMIAS
KETONURIAS
KETOSTEROID
KETOSTEROIDS
KETTLEBELL
KETTLEBELLS
KETTLEDRUM
KETTLEDRUMMER
KETTLEDRUMMERS
KETTLEDRUMS
KETTLEFULS
KETTLESTITCH
KETTLESTITCHES
KEYBOARDED
KEYBOARDER
KEYBOARDERS
KEYBOARDING
KEYBOARDINGS
KEYBOARDIST
KEYBOARDISTS
KEYBUTTONS
KEYLOGGERS
KEYLOGGING
KEYLOGGINGS
KEYPRESSES
KEYPUNCHED
KEYPUNCHER
KEYPUNCHERS
KEYPUNCHES
KEYPUNCHING
KEYSTONING
KEYSTROKED
KEYSTROKES
KEYSTROKING
KEYSTROKINGS
KEYWORKERS
KHALIFATES
KHANSAMAHS
KHEDIVATES
KHEDIVIATE
KHEDIVIATES
KHIDMUTGAR
KHIDMUTGARS
KHITMUTGAR
KHITMUTGARS
KHUSKHUSES
KIBBITZERS
KIBBITZING
KIBBUTZNIK
KIBBUTZNIKS
KICKABOUTS
KICKAROUND
KICKAROUNDS
KICKBOARDS
KICKBOXERS
KICKBOXING
KICKBOXINGS
KICKFLIPPED
KICKFLIPPING
KICKPLATES
KICKSHAWSES
KICKSORTER
KICKSORTERS
KICKSTANDS
KICKSTARTED
KICKSTARTING
KICKSTARTS
KIDDIEWINK
KIDDIEWINKIE
KIDDIEWINKIES
KIDDIEWINKS
KIDDISHNESS
KIDDISHNESSES
KIDDYWINKS
KIDNAPINGS
KIDNAPPEES
KIDNAPPERS
KIDNAPPING
KIDNAPPINGS
KIDNEYLIKE
KIDOLOGIES
KIDOLOGIST
KIDOLOGISTS
KIESELGUHR
KIESELGUHRS
KIESELGURS
KIESERITES
KILDERKINS
KILLIFISHES
KILLIKINICK
KILLIKINICKS
KILOCALORIE
KILOCALORIES
KILOCURIES
KILOCYCLES
KILOGAUSSES
KILOGRAMME
KILOGRAMMES
KILOHERTZES
KILOJOULES
KILOLITERS
KILOLITRES
KILOMETERS
KILOMETRES
KILOMETRIC
KILOMETRICAL
KILOPARSEC
KILOPARSECS
KILOPASCAL
KILOPASCALS
KILOTONNES
KIMBERLITE
KIMBERLITES
KINAESTHESES
KINAESTHESIA
KINAESTHESIAS
KINAESTHESIS
KINAESTHETIC
KINDERGARTEN
KINDERGARTENER
KINDERGARTENERS
KINDERGARTENS
KINDERGARTNER
KINDERGARTNERS
KINDERSPIEL
KINDERSPIELS
KINDHEARTED
KINDHEARTEDLY
KINDHEARTEDNESS
KINDLESSLY
KINDLINESS
KINDLINESSES
KINDNESSES
KINDREDNESS
KINDREDNESSES
KINDREDSHIP
KINDREDSHIPS
KINEMATICAL
KINEMATICALLY
KINEMATICS
KINEMATOGRAPH
KINEMATOGRAPHER
KINEMATOGRAPHIC
KINEMATOGRAPHS
KINEMATOGRAPHY
KINESCOPED
KINESCOPES
KINESCOPING
KINESIATRIC
KINESIATRICS
KINESIOLOGIES
KINESIOLOGIST
KINESIOLOGISTS
KINESIOLOGY
KINESIPATH
KINESIPATHIC
KINESIPATHIES
KINESIPATHIST
KINESIPATHISTS
KINESIPATHS
KINESIPATHY
KINESITHERAPIES
KINESITHERAPY
KINESTHESES
KINESTHESIA
KINESTHESIAS
KINESTHESIS
KINESTHETIC
KINESTHETICALLY
KINETHEODOLITE
KINETHEODOLITES
KINETICALLY
KINETICIST
KINETICISTS
KINETOCHORE
KINETOCHORES
KINETOGRAPH
KINETOGRAPHS
KINETONUCLEI
KINETONUCLEUS
KINETONUCLEUSES
KINETOPLAST
KINETOPLASTS
KINETOSCOPE
KINETOSCOPES
KINETOSOME
KINETOSOMES
KINGCRAFTS
KINGDOMLESS
KINGFISHER
KINGFISHERS
KINGFISHES
KINGLIHOOD
KINGLIHOODS
KINGLINESS
KINGLINESSES
KINGMAKERS
KINGSNAKES
KINKINESSES
KINNIKINIC
KINNIKINICK
KINNIKINICKS
KINNIKINICS
KINNIKINNICK
KINNIKINNICKS
KINTLEDGES
KIRBIGRIPS
KIRKYAIRDS
KIRSCHWASSER
KIRSCHWASSERS
KISSAGRAMS
KISSOGRAMS
KISSPEPTIN
KISSPEPTINS
KITCHENALIA
KITCHENALIAS
KITCHENDOM
KITCHENDOMS
KITCHENERS
KITCHENETS
KITCHENETTE
KITCHENETTES
KITCHENING
KITCHENMAID
KITCHENMAIDS
KITCHENWARE
KITCHENWARES
KITEBOARDS
KITESURFER
KITESURFERS
KITESURFING
KITESURFINGS
KITSCHIEST
KITSCHIFIED
KITSCHIFIES

K

KITSCHIFYING
KITSCHNESS
KITSCHNESSES
KITTENIEST
KITTENISHLY
KITTENISHNESS
KITTENISHNESSES
KITTIWAKES
KIWIFRUITS
KIWISPORTS
KLANGFARBE
KLANGFARBES
KLEBSIELLA
KLEBSIELLAS
KLEINHUISIE
KLEINHUISIES
KLENDUSITIES
KLENDUSITY
KLEPHTISMS
KLEPTOCRACIES
KLEPTOCRACY
KLEPTOCRATIC
KLEPTOMANIA
KLEPTOMANIAC
KLEPTOMANIACS
KLEPTOMANIAS
KLETTERSCHUH
KLETTERSCHUHE
KLINOSTATS
KLIPSPRINGER
KLIPSPRINGERS
KLONDIKERS
KLONDIKING
KLONDYKERS
KLONDYKING
KLOOCHMANS
KLOOTCHMAN
KLOOTCHMANS
KLOOTCHMEN
KLUTZINESS
KLUTZINESSES
KNACKERIES
KNACKERING
KNACKINESS
KNACKINESSES
KNACKWURST
KNACKWURSTS
KNAGGINESS
KNAGGINESSES
KNAPSACKED
KNAVESHIPS
KNAVISHNESS
KNAVISHNESSES
KNEEBOARDED
KNEEBOARDING
KNEEBOARDS
KNEECAPPED
KNEECAPPING
KNEECAPPINGS
KNEEPIECES
KNEVELLING
KNICKERBOCKER
KNICKERBOCKERS
KNICKKNACK
KNICKKNACKS
KNICKPOINT
KNICKPOINTS
KNIFEPOINT
KNIFEPOINTS
KNIFERESTS
KNIGHTAGES
KNIGHTHEAD
KNIGHTHEADS
KNIGHTHOOD
KNIGHTHOODS
KNIGHTLESS
KNIGHTLIER
KNIGHTLIEST
KNIGHTLINESS
KNIGHTLINESSES
KNIPHOFIAS
KNOBBINESS
KNOBBINESSES
KNOBBLIEST
KNOBKERRIE
KNOBKERRIES
KNOBSTICKS
KNOCKABOUT
KNOCKABOUTS
KNOCKBACKS
KNOCKDOWNS
KNOCKWURST
KNOCKWURSTS
KNOTGRASSES
KNOTTINESS
KNOTTINESSES
KNOWABLENESS
KNOWABLENESSES
KNOWINGEST
KNOWINGNESS
KNOWINGNESSES
KNOWLEDGABILITY
KNOWLEDGABLE
KNOWLEDGABLY
KNOWLEDGEABLE
KNOWLEDGEABLY
KNOWLEDGED
KNOWLEDGES
KNOWLEDGING
KNUBBLIEST
KNUCKLEBALL
KNUCKLEBALLER
KNUCKLEBALLERS
KNUCKLEBALLS
KNUCKLEBONE
KNUCKLEBONES
KNUCKLEDUSTER
KNUCKLEDUSTERS
KNUCKLEHEAD
KNUCKLEHEADED
KNUCKLEHEADS
KNUCKLIEST
KOEKSISTER
KOEKSISTERS
KOHLRABIES
KOHUTUHUTU
KOHUTUHUTUS
KOLINSKIES
KOLKHOZNIK
KOLKHOZNIKI
KOLKHOZNIKS
KOMONDOROCK
KOMONDOROK
KOMPROMATS
KONIMETERS
KONIOLOGIES
KONISCOPES
KOOKABURRA
KOOKABURRAS
KOOKINESSES
KOTAHITANGA
KOTAHITANGAS
KOTTABOSES
KOTUKUTUKU
KOTUKUTUKUS
KOULIBIACA
KOULIBIACAS
KOURBASHED
KOURBASHES
KOURBASHING
KOUSKOUSES
KOWHAIWHAI
KOWHAIWHAIS
KRAKOWIAKS
KRAUTROCKS
KREASOTING
KREMLINOLOGIES
KREMLINOLOGIST
KREMLINOLOGISTS
KREMLINOLOGY
KREOSOTING
KRIEGSPIEL
KRIEGSPIELS
KRIEGSSPIEL
KRIEGSSPIELS
KROMESKIES
KRUGERRAND
KRUGERRANDS
KRUMMHORNS
KRYOMETERS
KRYPTONITE
KRYPTONITES
KUMARAHOUS
KUMMERBUND
KUMMERBUNDS
KUNDALINIS
KURBASHING
KURCHATOVIUM
KURCHATOVIUMS
KURDAITCHA
KURDAITCHAS
KURFUFFLED
KURFUFFLES
KURFUFFLING
KURRAJONGS
KURTOSISES
KVETCHIEST
KVETCHINESS
KVETCHINESSES
KVETCHINGS
KWASHIORKOR
KWASHIORKORS
KYANISATION
KYANISATIONS
KYANIZATION
KYANIZATIONS
KYMOGRAPHIC
KYMOGRAPHIES
KYMOGRAPHS
KYMOGRAPHY

L

LABANOTATION
LABANOTATIONS
LABDACISMS
LABEFACTATION
LABEFACTATIONS
LABEFACTION
LABEFACTIONS
LABELLABLE
LABELLINGS
LABELLISTS
LABELMATES
LABIALISATION
LABIALISATIONS
LABIALISED
LABIALISES
LABIALISING
LABIALISMS
LABIALITIES
LABIALIZATION
LABIALIZATIONS
LABIALIZED
LABIALIZES
LABIALIZING
LABILITIES
LABIODENTAL
LABIODENTALS
LABIONASAL
LABIONASALS
LABIOVELAR
LABIOVELARS
LABORATORIES
LABORATORY
LABOREDNESS
LABOREDNESSES
LABORINGLY
LABORIOUSLY
LABORIOUSNESS
LABORIOUSNESSES
LABORSAVING
LABOUREDLY
LABOUREDNESS
LABOUREDNESSES
LABOURINGLY
LABOURISMS
LABOURISTS
LABOURITES
LABOURSAVING
LABOURSOME
LABRADOODLE
LABRADOODLES
LABRADORESCENT
LABRADORITE
LABRADORITES
LABYRINTHAL
LABYRINTHIAN
LABYRINTHIC
LABYRINTHICAL
LABYRINTHICALLY
LABYRINTHINE
LABYRINTHITIS
LABYRINTHITISES
LABYRINTHODONT
LABYRINTHODONTS
LABYRINTHS
LACCOLITES
LACCOLITHIC
LACCOLITHS
LACCOLITIC
LACEMAKERS
LACEMAKING
LACEMAKINGS
LACERABILITIES
LACERABILITY
LACERATING
LACERATION
LACERATIONS
LACERATIVE
LACERTIANS
LACERTILIAN
LACERTILIANS
LACERTINES
LACHRYMALS
LACHRYMARIES
LACHRYMARY
LACHRYMATION
LACHRYMATIONS
LACHRYMATOR
LACHRYMATORIES
LACHRYMATORS
LACHRYMATORY
LACHRYMOSE
LACHRYMOSELY
LACHRYMOSITIES
LACHRYMOSITY
LACINESSES
LACINIATED
LACINIATION
LACINIATIONS
LACKADAISICAL
LACKADAISICALLY
LACKADAISY
LACKLUSTER
LACKLUSTERS
LACKLUSTRE
LACKLUSTRES
LACONICALLY
LACONICISM
LACONICISMS
LACQUERERS
LACQUERING
LACQUERINGS
LACQUERWARE
LACQUERWARES
LACQUERWORK
LACQUERWORKS
LACQUEYING
LACRIMARIES
LACRIMATION
LACRIMATIONS
LACRIMATOR
LACRIMATORS
LACRIMATORY
LACRYMATOR
LACRYMATORS
LACRYMATORY
LACTALBUMIN
LACTALBUMINS
LACTARIANS
LACTATIONAL
LACTATIONALLY
LACTATIONS
LACTESCENCE
LACTESCENCES
LACTESCENT
LACTIFEROUS
LACTIFEROUSNESS
LACTIFLUOUS
LACTIVISMS
LACTIVISTS
LACTOBACILLI
LACTOBACILLUS
LACTOFLAVIN
LACTOFLAVINS
LACTOGENIC
LACTOGLOBULIN
LACTOGLOBULINS
LACTOMETER
LACTOMETERS
LACTOPROTEIN
LACTOPROTEINS
LACTOSCOPE
LACTOSCOPES
LACTOSURIA
LACTOSURIAS
LACTOVEGETARIAN
LACTULOSES
LACUNOSITIES
LACUNOSITY
LACUSTRINE
LADDERIEST
LADDERLIKE
LADDERPROOF
LADDISHNESS
LADDISHNESSES
LADIESWEAR
LADIESWEARS
LADYFINGER
LADYFINGERS
LADYFISHES
LADYLIKENESS
LADYLIKENESSES
LADYNESSES
LAEOTROPIC
LAEVIGATED
LAEVIGATES
LAEVIGATING
LAEVOGYRATE
LAEVOROTARY
LAEVOROTATION
LAEVOROTATIONS
LAEVOROTATORY
LAEVULOSES
LAGENIFORM
LAGERPHONE
LAGERPHONES
LAGGARDLIER
LAGGARDLIEST
LAGGARDNESS
LAGGARDNESSES
LAGNIAPPES
LAGOMORPHIC
LAGOMORPHOUS
LAGOMORPHS
LAICISATION
LAICISATIONS
LAICIZATION
LAICIZATIONS
LAIRDLIEST
LAIRDSHIPS
LAKEFRONTS
LAKESHORES
LALAPALOOZA
LALAPALOOZAS
LALLAPALOOZA
LALLAPALOOZAS
LALLATIONS
LALLYGAGGED
LALLYGAGGING
LAMASERAIS
LAMASERIES

LAMBASTING
LAMBDACISM
LAMBDACISMS
LAMBDOIDAL
LAMBENCIES
LAMBITIVES
LAMBREQUIN
LAMBREQUINS
LAMBRUSCOS
LAMBSWOOLS
LAMEBRAINED
LAMEBRAINS
LAMELLARLY
LAMELLATED
LAMELLATELY
LAMELLATION
LAMELLATIONS
LAMELLIBRANCH
LAMELLIBRANCHS
LAMELLICORN
LAMELLICORNS
LAMELLIFORM
LAMELLIROSTRAL
LAMELLIROSTRATE
LAMELLOSITIES
LAMELLOSITY
LAMENESSES
LAMENTABLE
LAMENTABLENESS
LAMENTABLY
LAMENTATION
LAMENTATIONS
LAMENTEDLY
LAMENTINGLY
LAMENTINGS
LAMESTREAM
LAMESTREAMS
LAMINARIAN
LAMINARIANS
LAMINARIAS
LAMINARINS
LAMINARISE
LAMINARISED
LAMINARISES
LAMINARISING
LAMINARIZE
LAMINARIZED
LAMINARIZES
LAMINARIZING
LAMINATING
LAMINATION
LAMINATIONS
LAMINATORS
LAMINECTOMIES
LAMINECTOMY
LAMINGTONS
LAMINITISES
LAMMERGEIER
LAMMERGEIERS
LAMMERGEYER
LAMMERGEYERS
LAMPADARIES
LAMPADEDROMIES
LAMPADEDROMY
LAMPADEPHORIA
LAMPADEPHORIAS
LAMPADISTS
LAMPADOMANCIES
LAMPADOMANCY
LAMPBLACKED
LAMPBLACKING
LAMPBLACKS
LAMPHOLDER
LAMPHOLDERS
LAMPLIGHTER
LAMPLIGHTERS
LAMPLIGHTS
LAMPOONERIES
LAMPOONERS
LAMPOONERY
LAMPOONING
LAMPOONIST
LAMPOONISTS
LAMPROPHYRE
LAMPROPHYRES
LAMPROPHYRIC
LAMPSHADES
LAMPSHELLS
LAMPSTANDS
LANCEJACKS
LANCEOLATE
LANCEOLATED
LANCEOLATELY
LANCEWOODS
LANCINATED
LANCINATES
LANCINATING
LANCINATION
LANCINATIONS
LANDAMMANN
LANDAMMANNS
LANDAMMANS
LANDAULETS
LANDAULETTE
LANDAULETTES
LANDBOARDING
LANDBOARDINGS
LANDBOARDS
LANDDAMNED
LANDDAMNES
LANDDAMNING
LANDDROSES
LANDDROSTS
LANDFILLED
LANDFILLING
LANDFILLINGS
LANDFORCES
LANDGRAVATE
LANDGRAVATES
LANDGRAVES
LANDGRAVIATE
LANDGRAVIATES
LANDGRAVINE
LANDGRAVINES
LANDHOLDER
LANDHOLDERS
LANDHOLDING
LANDHOLDINGS
LANDLADIES
LANDLESSNESS
LANDLESSNESSES
LANDLOCKED
LANDLOPERS
LANDLORDISM
LANDLORDISMS
LANDLUBBER
LANDLUBBERLY
LANDLUBBERS
LANDLUBBING
LANDMARKED
LANDMARKING
LANDMASSES
LANDMINING
LANDMININGS
LANDOWNERS
LANDOWNERSHIP
LANDOWNERSHIPS
LANDOWNING
LANDOWNINGS
LANDSCAPED
LANDSCAPER
LANDSCAPERS
LANDSCAPES
LANDSCAPING
LANDSCAPINGS
LANDSCAPIST
LANDSCAPISTS
LANDSHARKS
LANDSKIPPED
LANDSKIPPING
LANDSKNECHT
LANDSKNECHTS
LANDSLIDDEN
LANDSLIDES
LANDSLIDING
LANDWAITER
LANDWAITERS
LANDWASHES
LANGBEINITE
LANGBEINITES
LANGLAUFER
LANGLAUFERS
LANGOSTINO
LANGOSTINOS
LANGOUSTES
LANGOUSTINE
LANGOUSTINES
LANGRIDGES
LANGSPIELS
LANGUAGELESS
LANGUAGING
LANGUESCENT
LANGUETTES
LANGUIDNESS
LANGUIDNESSES
LANGUISHED
LANGUISHER
LANGUISHERS
LANGUISHES
LANGUISHING
LANGUISHINGLY
LANGUISHINGS
LANGUISHMENT
LANGUISHMENTS
LANGUOROUS
LANGUOROUSLY
LANGUOROUSNESS
LANIFEROUS
LANIGEROUS
LANKINESSES
LANKNESSES
LANOSITIES
LANSQUENET
LANSQUENETS
LANTERLOOS
LANTERNING
LANTERNIST
LANTERNISTS
LANTHANIDE
LANTHANIDES
LANTHANONS
LANTHANUMS
LANUGINOSE
LANUGINOUS
LANUGINOUSNESS
LANZKNECHT
LANZKNECHTS
LAODICEANS
LAPAROSCOPE
LAPAROSCOPES
LAPAROSCOPIC
LAPAROSCOPIES
LAPAROSCOPIST
LAPAROSCOPISTS
LAPAROSCOPY
LAPAROTOMIES
LAPAROTOMY
LAPIDARIAN
LAPIDARIES
LAPIDARIST
LAPIDARISTS
LAPIDATING
LAPIDATION
LAPIDATIONS
LAPIDESCENCE
LAPIDESCENCES
LAPIDESCENT
LAPIDICOLOUS
LAPIDIFICATION
LAPIDIFICATIONS

LAPIDIFIED
LAPIDIFIES
LAPIDIFYING
LAPILLIFORM
LAPSTRAKES
LAPSTREAKS
LARCENISTS
LARCENOUSLY
LARCHWOODS
LARDACEOUS
LARDALITES
LARGEHEARTED
LARGEMOUTH
LARGEMOUTHS
LARGENESSES
LARGHETTOS
LARGITIONS
LARKINESSES
LARKISHNESS
LARKISHNESSES
LARRIKINISM
LARRIKINISMS
LARVACEOUS
LARVICIDAL
LARVICIDED
LARVICIDES
LARVICIDING
LARVIKITES
LARVIPAROUS
LARYNGEALLY
LARYNGEALS
LARYNGECTOMEE
LARYNGECTOMEES
LARYNGECTOMIES
LARYNGECTOMISED
LARYNGECTOMIZED
LARYNGECTOMY
LARYNGISMUS
LARYNGISMUSES
LARYNGITIC
LARYNGITIDES
LARYNGITIS
LARYNGITISES
LARYNGOLOGIC
LARYNGOLOGICAL
LARYNGOLOGIES
LARYNGOLOGIST
LARYNGOLOGISTS
LARYNGOLOGY
LARYNGOPHONIES
LARYNGOPHONY
LARYNGOSCOPE
LARYNGOSCOPES
LARYNGOSCOPIC
LARYNGOSCOPIES
LARYNGOSCOPIST
LARYNGOSCOPISTS
LARYNGOSCOPY
LARYNGOSPASM
LARYNGOSPASMS
LARYNGOTOMIES
LARYNGOTOMY
LASCIVIOUS
LASCIVIOUSLY
LASCIVIOUSNESS
LASERDISCS
LASERDISKS
LASERWORTS
LASSITUDES
LASTINGNESS
LASTINGNESSES
LATCHSTRING
LATCHSTRINGS
LATECOMERS
LATEENRIGGED
LATENESSES
LATENSIFICATION
LATERALING
LATERALISATION
LATERALISATIONS
LATERALISE
LATERALISED
LATERALISES
LATERALISING
LATERALITIES
LATERALITY
LATERALIZATION
LATERALIZATIONS
LATERALIZE
LATERALIZED
LATERALIZES
LATERALIZING
LATERALLED
LATERALLING
LATERBORNS
LATERIGRADE
LATERISATION
LATERISATIONS
LATERISING
LATERITIOUS
LATERIZATION
LATERIZATIONS
LATERIZING
LATEROVERSION
LATEROVERSIONS
LATESCENCE
LATESCENCES
LATHERIEST
LATHYRISMS
LATHYRITIC
LATHYRUSES
LATICIFEROUS
LATICIFERS
LATICLAVES
LATIFUNDIA
LATIFUNDIO
LATIFUNDIOS
LATIFUNDIUM
LATIMERIAS
LATINISATION
LATINISATIONS
LATINISING
LATINITIES
LATINIZATION
LATINIZATIONS
LATINIZING
LATIROSTRAL
LATIROSTRATE
LATISEPTATE
LATITANCIES
LATITATION
LATITATIONS
LATITUDINAL
LATITUDINALLY
LATITUDINARIAN
LATITUDINARIANS
LATITUDINOUS
LATRATIONS
LATROCINIA
LATROCINIES
LATROCINIUM
LATTERMATH
LATTERMATHS
LATTERMOST
LATTICEWORK
LATTICEWORKS
LATTICINGS
LATTICINIO
LAUDABILITIES
LAUDABILITY
LAUDABLENESS
LAUDABLENESSES
LAUDATIONS
LAUDATIVES
LAUDATORIES
LAUGHABLENESS
LAUGHABLENESSES
LAUGHINGLY
LAUGHINGSTOCK
LAUGHINGSTOCKS
LAUGHLINES
LAUGHWORTHIER
LAUGHWORTHIEST
LAUGHWORTHY
LAUNCEGAYE
LAUNCEGAYES
LAUNCHINGS
LAUNCHPADS
LAUNDERERS
LAUNDERETTE
LAUNDERETTES
LAUNDERING
LAUNDERINGS
LAUNDRESSES
LAUNDRETTE
LAUNDRETTES
LAUNDRYMAN
LAUNDRYMEN
LAUNDRYWOMAN
LAUNDRYWOMEN
LAURACEOUS
LAURDALITE
LAURDALITES
LAUREATESHIP
LAUREATESHIPS
LAUREATING
LAUREATION
LAUREATIONS
LAURELLING
LAURUSTINE
LAURUSTINES
LAURUSTINUS
LAURUSTINUSES
LAURVIKITE
LAURVIKITES
LAVALIERES
LAVALLIERE
LAVALLIERES
LAVATIONAL
LAVATORIAL
LAVATORIES
LAVENDERED
LAVENDERING
LAVERBREAD
LAVERBREADS
LAVEROCKED
LAVEROCKING
LAVISHMENT
LAVISHMENTS
LAVISHNESS
LAVISHNESSES
LAVOLTAING
LAWBREAKER
LAWBREAKERS
LAWBREAKING
LAWBREAKINGS
LAWFULNESS
LAWFULNESSES
LAWGIVINGS
LAWLESSNESS
LAWLESSNESSES
LAWMAKINGS
LAWMONGERS
LAWNMOWERS
LAWRENCIUM
LAWRENCIUMS
LAWYERINGS
LAWYERLIER
LAWYERLIEST
LAWYERLIKE
LAXATIVENESS
LAXATIVENESSES
LAYBACKING
LAYMANISED
LAYMANISES
LAYMANISING
LAYMANIZED
LAYMANIZES
LAYMANIZING
LAYPERSONS

LAZARETTES
LAZARETTOS
LAZINESSES
LEACHABILITIES
LEACHABILITY
LEADENNESS
LEADENNESSES
LEADERBOARD
LEADERBOARDS
LEADERENES
LEADERETTE
LEADERETTES
LEADERLESS
LEADERSHIP
LEADERSHIPS
LEADPLANTS
LEADSCREWS
LEAFCUTTER
LEAFCUTTERS
LEAFHOPPER
LEAFHOPPERS
LEAFINESSES
LEAFLESSNESS
LEAFLESSNESSES
LEAFLETEER
LEAFLETEERS
LEAFLETERS
LEAFLETING
LEAFLETTED
LEAFLETTING
LEAFSTALKS
LEAGUERING
LEAKINESSES
LEANNESSES
LEAPFROGGED
LEAPFROGGING
LEARINESSES
LEARNABILITIES
LEARNABILITY
LEARNEDNESS
LEARNEDNESSES
LEASEBACKS
LEASEHOLDER
LEASEHOLDERS
LEASEHOLDS
LEASTAWAYS
LEATHERBACK
LEATHERBACKS
LEATHERBOUND
LEATHERETTE
LEATHERETTES
LEATHERGOODS
LEATHERHEAD
LEATHERHEADS
LEATHERIER
LEATHERIEST
LEATHERINESS
LEATHERINESSES
LEATHERING
LEATHERINGS
LEATHERJACKET
LEATHERJACKETS
LEATHERLEAF
LEATHERLEAFS
LEATHERLEAVES
LEATHERLIKE
LEATHERNECK
LEATHERNECKS
LEATHERWOOD
LEATHERWOODS
LEATHERWORK
LEATHERWORKS
LEAVENINGS
LEBENSRAUM
LEBENSRAUMS
LECHEROUSLY
LECHEROUSNESS
LECHEROUSNESSES
LECITHINASE
LECITHINASES
LECTIONARIES
LECTIONARY
LECTISTERNIA
LECTISTERNIUM
LECTISTERNIUMS
LECTORATES
LECTORSHIP
LECTORSHIPS
LECTOTYPES
LECTRESSES
LECTURESHIP
LECTURESHIPS
LECYTHIDACEOUS
LECYTHISES
LEDERHOSEN
LEECHCRAFT
LEECHCRAFTS
LEERINESSES
LEETSPEAKS
LEFTWARDLY
LEGALISATION
LEGALISATIONS
LEGALISERS
LEGALISING
LEGALISTIC
LEGALISTICALLY
LEGALITIES
LEGALIZATION
LEGALIZATIONS
LEGALIZERS
LEGALIZING
LEGATARIES
LEGATESHIP
LEGATESHIPS
LEGATIONARY
LEGATISSIMO
LEGATORIAL
LEGENDARIES
LEGENDARILY
LEGENDISED
LEGENDISES
LEGENDISING
LEGENDISTS
LEGENDIZED
LEGENDIZES
LEGENDIZING
LEGENDRIES
LEGERDEMAIN
LEGERDEMAINIST
LEGERDEMAINISTS
LEGERDEMAINS
LEGERITIES
LEGGINESSES
LEGIBILITIES
LEGIBILITY
LEGIBLENESS
LEGIBLENESSES
LEGIONARIES
LEGIONELLA
LEGIONELLAE
LEGIONELLAS
LEGIONNAIRE
LEGIONNAIRES
LEGISLATED
LEGISLATES
LEGISLATING
LEGISLATION
LEGISLATIONS
LEGISLATIVE
LEGISLATIVELY
LEGISLATIVES
LEGISLATOR
LEGISLATORIAL
LEGISLATORS
LEGISLATORSHIP
LEGISLATORSHIPS
LEGISLATRESS
LEGISLATRESSES
LEGISLATURE
LEGISLATURES
LEGITIMACIES
LEGITIMACY
LEGITIMATE
LEGITIMATED
LEGITIMATELY
LEGITIMATENESS
LEGITIMATES
LEGITIMATING
LEGITIMATION
LEGITIMATIONS
LEGITIMATISE
LEGITIMATISED
LEGITIMATISES
LEGITIMATISING
LEGITIMATIZE
LEGITIMATIZED
LEGITIMATIZES
LEGITIMATIZING
LEGITIMATOR
LEGITIMATORS
LEGITIMISATION
LEGITIMISATIONS
LEGITIMISE
LEGITIMISED
LEGITIMISER
LEGITIMISERS
LEGITIMISES
LEGITIMISING
LEGITIMISM
LEGITIMISMS
LEGITIMIST
LEGITIMISTIC
LEGITIMISTS
LEGITIMIZATION
LEGITIMIZATIONS
LEGITIMIZE
LEGITIMIZED
LEGITIMIZER
LEGITIMIZERS
LEGITIMIZES
LEGITIMIZING
LEGLESSNESS
LEGLESSNESSES
LEGUMINOUS
LEGWARMERS
LEIOMYOMAS
LEIOMYOMATA
LEIOTRICHIES
LEIOTRICHOUS
LEIOTRICHY
LEISHMANIA
LEISHMANIAE
LEISHMANIAL
LEISHMANIAS
LEISHMANIASES
LEISHMANIASIS
LEISHMANIOSES
LEISHMANIOSIS
LEISTERING
LEISURABLE
LEISURABLY
LEISURELIER
LEISURELIEST
LEISURELINESS
LEISURELINESSES
LEISUREWEAR
LEISUREWEARS
LEITMOTIFS
LEITMOTIVS
LEMMATISATION
LEMMATISATIONS
LEMMATISED
LEMMATISES
LEMMATISING
LEMMATIZATION
LEMMATIZATIONS
LEMMATIZED
LEMMATIZES
LEMMATIZING
LEMMINGLIKE

LEMNISCATE
LEMNISCATES
LEMONFISHES
LEMONGRASS
LEMONGRASSES
LEMONWOODS
LENGTHENED
LENGTHENER
LENGTHENERS
LENGTHENING
LENGTHIEST
LENGTHINESS
LENGTHINESSES
LENGTHSMAN
LENGTHSMEN
LENGTHWAYS
LENGTHWISE
LENIENCIES
LENITIVELY
LENOCINIUM
LENOCINIUMS
LENTAMENTE
LENTICELLATE
LENTICULAR
LENTICULARLY
LENTICULARS
LENTICULES
LENTIGINES
LENTIGINOSE
LENTIGINOUS
LENTISSIMO
LENTIVIRUS
LENTIVIRUSES
LEONTIASES
LEONTIASIS
LEONTOPODIUM
LEONTOPODIUMS
LEOPARDESS
LEOPARDESSES
LEOPARDSKIN
LEOPARDSKINS
LEPIDODENDROID
LEPIDODENDROIDS
LEPIDOLITE
LEPIDOLITES
LEPIDOMELANE
LEPIDOMELANES
LEPIDOPTERA
LEPIDOPTERAN
LEPIDOPTERANS
LEPIDOPTERIST
LEPIDOPTERISTS
LEPIDOPTEROLOGY
LEPIDOPTERON
LEPIDOPTERONS
LEPIDOPTEROUS
LEPIDOSIREN
LEPIDOSIRENS
LEPRECHAUN
LEPRECHAUNISH
LEPRECHAUNS
LEPRECHAWN
LEPRECHAWNS
LEPROMATOUS
LEPROSARIA
LEPROSARIUM
LEPROSARIUMS
LEPROSERIE
LEPROSERIES
LEPROSITIES
LEPROUSNESS
LEPROUSNESSES
LEPTOCEPHALI
LEPTOCEPHALIC
LEPTOCEPHALOUS
LEPTOCEPHALUS
LEPTOCERCAL
LEPTODACTYL
LEPTODACTYLOUS
LEPTODACTYLS
LEPTOKURTIC
LEPTOPHOSES
LEPTOPHYLLOUS
LEPTORRHINE
LEPTOSOMATIC
LEPTOSOMES
LEPTOSOMIC
LEPTOSPIRAL
LEPTOSPIRE
LEPTOSPIRES
LEPTOSPIROSES
LEPTOSPIROSIS
LEPTOTENES
LESBIANISM
LESBIANISMS
LESPEDEZAS
LESSEESHIP
LESSEESHIPS
LESSENINGS
LESSONINGS
LETHALITIES
LETHARGICAL
LETHARGICALLY
LETHARGIED
LETHARGIES
LETHARGISE
LETHARGISED
LETHARGISES
LETHARGISING
LETHARGIZE
LETHARGIZED
LETHARGIZES
LETHARGIZING
LETHIFEROUS
LETROZOLES
LETTERBOXED
LETTERBOXES
LETTERBOXING
LETTERBOXINGS
LETTERFORM
LETTERFORMS
LETTERHEAD
LETTERHEADS
LETTERINGS
LETTERLESS
LETTERPRESS
LETTERPRESSES
LETTERSETS
LETTERSPACING
LETTERSPACINGS
LEUCAEMIAS
LEUCAEMOGEN
LEUCAEMOGENESES
LEUCAEMOGENESIS
LEUCAEMOGENIC
LEUCAEMOGENS
LEUCHAEMIA
LEUCHAEMIAS
LEUCITOHEDRA
LEUCITOHEDRON
LEUCITOHEDRONS
LEUCOBLAST
LEUCOBLASTS
LEUCOCIDIN
LEUCOCIDINS
LEUCOCRATIC
LEUCOCYTES
LEUCOCYTHAEMIA
LEUCOCYTHAEMIAS
LEUCOCYTIC
LEUCOCYTOLYSES
LEUCOCYTOLYSIS
LEUCOCYTOPENIA
LEUCOCYTOPENIAS
LEUCOCYTOSES
LEUCOCYTOSIS
LEUCOCYTOTIC
LEUCODEPLETED
LEUCODERMA
LEUCODERMAL
LEUCODERMAS
LEUCODERMIA
LEUCODERMIAS
LEUCODERMIC
LEUCOMAINE
LEUCOMAINES
LEUCOPENIA
LEUCOPENIAS
LEUCOPENIC
LEUCOPLAKIA
LEUCOPLAKIAS
LEUCOPLAKIC
LEUCOPLAST
LEUCOPLASTID
LEUCOPLASTIDS
LEUCOPLASTS
LEUCOPOIESES
LEUCOPOIESIS
LEUCOPOIETIC
LEUCORRHOEA
LEUCORRHOEAL
LEUCORRHOEAS
LEUCOTOMES
LEUCOTOMIES
LEUKAEMIAS
LEUKAEMOGEN
LEUKAEMOGENESES
LEUKAEMOGENESIS
LEUKAEMOGENIC
LEUKAEMOGENS
LEUKEMOGEN
LEUKEMOGENESES
LEUKEMOGENESIS
LEUKEMOGENIC
LEUKEMOGENS
LEUKOBLAST
LEUKOBLASTS
LEUKOCIDIN
LEUKOCIDINS
LEUKOCYTES
LEUKOCYTIC
LEUKOCYTOLYSES
LEUKOCYTOLYSIS
LEUKOCYTOPENIA
LEUKOCYTOPENIAS
LEUKOCYTOSES
LEUKOCYTOSIS
LEUKOCYTOTIC
LEUKODEPLETED
LEUKODERMA
LEUKODERMAL
LEUKODERMAS
LEUKODERMIC
LEUKODYSTROPHY
LEUKOPENIA
LEUKOPENIAS
LEUKOPENIC
LEUKOPLAKIA
LEUKOPLAKIAS
LEUKOPLAKIC
LEUKOPOIESES
LEUKOPOIESIS
LEUKOPOIETIC
LEUKORRHEA
LEUKORRHEAL
LEUKORRHEAS
LEUKOTOMES
LEUKOTOMIES
LEUKOTRIENE
LEUKOTRIENES
LEVANTINES
LEVELHEADED
LEVELHEADEDNESS
LEVELLINGS
LEVELNESSES
LEVERAGING
LEVIATHANS
LEVIGATING
LEVIGATION
LEVIGATIONS

LEVIGATORS
LEVIRATICAL
LEVIRATION
LEVIRATIONS
LEVITATING
LEVITATION
LEVITATIONAL
LEVITATIONS
LEVITATORS
LEVITICALLY
LEVOROTARY
LEVOROTATORY
LEWDNESSES
LEXICALISATION
LEXICALISATIONS
LEXICALISE
LEXICALISED
LEXICALISES
LEXICALISING
LEXICALITIES
LEXICALITY
LEXICALIZATION
LEXICALIZATIONS
LEXICALIZE
LEXICALIZED
LEXICALIZES
LEXICALIZING
LEXICOGRAPHER
LEXICOGRAPHERS
LEXICOGRAPHIC
LEXICOGRAPHICAL
LEXICOGRAPHIES
LEXICOGRAPHIST
LEXICOGRAPHISTS
LEXICOGRAPHY
LEXICOLOGICAL
LEXICOLOGICALLY
LEXICOLOGIES
LEXICOLOGIST
LEXICOLOGISTS
LEXICOLOGY
LEXIGRAPHIC
LEXIGRAPHICAL
LEXIGRAPHIES
LEXIGRAPHY
LEYLANDIIS
LHERZOLITE
LHERZOLITES
LIABILITIES
LIABLENESS
LIABLENESSES
LIBATIONAL
LIBATIONARY
LIBECCHIOS
LIBELLANTS
LIBELLINGS
LIBELLOUSLY
LIBELOUSLY
LIBERALISATION
LIBERALISATIONS
LIBERALISE
LIBERALISED
LIBERALISER
LIBERALISERS
LIBERALISES
LIBERALISING
LIBERALISM
LIBERALISMS
LIBERALIST
LIBERALISTIC
LIBERALISTS
LIBERALITIES
LIBERALITY
LIBERALIZATION
LIBERALIZATIONS
LIBERALIZE
LIBERALIZED
LIBERALIZER
LIBERALIZERS
LIBERALIZES
LIBERALIZING
LIBERALNESS
LIBERALNESSES
LIBERATING
LIBERATION
LIBERATIONISM
LIBERATIONISMS
LIBERATIONIST
LIBERATIONISTS
LIBERATIONS
LIBERATORS
LIBERATORY
LIBERTARIAN
LIBERTARIANISM
LIBERTARIANISMS
LIBERTARIANS
LIBERTICIDAL
LIBERTICIDE
LIBERTICIDES
LIBERTINAGE
LIBERTINAGES
LIBERTINES
LIBERTINISM
LIBERTINISMS
LIBIDINALLY
LIBIDINIST
LIBIDINISTS
LIBIDINOSITIES
LIBIDINOSITY
LIBIDINOUS
LIBIDINOUSLY
LIBIDINOUSNESS
LIBRAIRIES
LIBRARIANS
LIBRARIANSHIP
LIBRARIANSHIPS
LIBRATIONAL
LIBRATIONS
LIBRETTIST
LIBRETTISTS
LICENSABLE
LICENSURES
LICENTIATE
LICENTIATES
LICENTIATESHIP
LICENTIATESHIPS
LICENTIATION
LICENTIATIONS
LICENTIOUS
LICENTIOUSLY
LICENTIOUSNESS
LICHANOSES
LICHENISMS
LICHENISTS
LICHENOLOGICAL
LICHENOLOGIES
LICHENOLOGIST
LICHENOLOGISTS
LICHENOLOGY
LICHTLYING
LICITNESSES
LICKERISHLY
LICKERISHNESS
LICKERISHNESSES
LICKPENNIES
LICKSPITTLE
LICKSPITTLES
LIDOCAINES
LIEBFRAUMILCH
LIEBFRAUMILCHS
LIENHOLDER
LIENHOLDERS
LIENTERIES
LIEUTENANCIES
LIEUTENANCY
LIEUTENANT
LIEUTENANTRIES
LIEUTENANTRY
LIEUTENANTS
LIEUTENANTSHIP
LIEUTENANTSHIPS
LIFEBLOODS
LIFEBOATMAN
LIFEBOATMEN
LIFEGUARDED
LIFEGUARDING
LIFEGUARDS
LIFEHACKED
LIFEHACKER
LIFEHACKERS
LIFEHACKING
LIFELESSLY
LIFELESSNESS
LIFELESSNESSES
LIFELIKENESS
LIFELIKENESSES
LIFEMANSHIP
LIFEMANSHIPS
LIFESAVERS
LIFESAVING
LIFESAVINGS
LIFESTYLER
LIFESTYLERS
LIFESTYLES
LIFEWORLDS
LIGAMENTAL
LIGAMENTARY
LIGAMENTOUS
LIGATURING
LIGHTBULBS
LIGHTENERS
LIGHTENING
LIGHTENINGS
LIGHTERAGE
LIGHTERAGES
LIGHTERING
LIGHTERMAN
LIGHTERMEN
LIGHTFACED
LIGHTFACES
LIGHTFASTNESS
LIGHTFASTNESSES
LIGHTHEARTED
LIGHTHEARTEDLY
LIGHTHOUSE
LIGHTHOUSEMAN
LIGHTHOUSEMEN
LIGHTHOUSES
LIGHTLYING
LIGHTNESSES
LIGHTNINGED
LIGHTNINGS
LIGHTPLANE
LIGHTPLANES
LIGHTPROOF
LIGHTSHIPS
LIGHTSOMELY
LIGHTSOMENESS
LIGHTSOMENESSES
LIGHTTIGHT
LIGHTWEIGHT
LIGHTWEIGHTS
LIGHTWOODS
LIGNICOLOUS
LIGNIFICATION
LIGNIFICATIONS
LIGNIFYING
LIGNIPERDOUS
LIGNIVOROUS
LIGNOCAINE
LIGNOCAINES
LIGNOCELLULOSE
LIGNOCELLULOSES
LIGNOCELLULOSIC
LIGNOSULFONATE
LIGNOSULFONATES
LIGULIFLORAL
LIGUSTRUMS
LIKABILITIES
LIKABILITY

LIKABLENESS
LIKABLENESSES
LIKEABILITIES
LIKEABILITY
LIKEABLENESS
LIKEABLENESSES
LIKELIHOOD
LIKELIHOODS
LIKELINESS
LIKELINESSES
LIKENESSES
LILANGENIS
LILIACEOUS
LILLIPUTIAN
LILLIPUTIANS
LILTINGNESS
LILTINGNESSES
LIMACIFORM
LIMACOLOGIES
LIMACOLOGIST
LIMACOLOGISTS
LIMACOLOGY
LIMBERNESS
LIMBERNESSES
LIMBURGITE
LIMBURGITES
LIMELIGHTED
LIMELIGHTER
LIMELIGHTERS
LIMELIGHTING
LIMELIGHTS
LIMERENCES
LIMESCALES
LIMESTONES
LIMEWASHES
LIMEWATERS
LIMICOLINE
LIMICOLOUS
LIMINESSES
LIMITABLENESS
LIMITABLENESSES
LIMITARIAN
LIMITARIANS
LIMITATION
LIMITATIONAL
LIMITATIONS
LIMITATIVE
LIMITEDNESS

LIMITEDNESSES
LIMITINGLY
LIMITLESSLY
LIMITLESSNESS
LIMITLESSNESSES
LIMITROPHE
LIMIVOROUS
LIMNOLOGIC
LIMNOLOGICAL
LIMNOLOGICALLY
LIMNOLOGIES
LIMNOLOGIST
LIMNOLOGISTS
LIMNOPHILOUS
LIMOUSINES
LIMPIDITIES
LIMPIDNESS
LIMPIDNESSES
LIMPNESSES
LINCOMYCIN
LINCOMYCINS
LINCRUSTAS
LINEALITIES
LINEAMENTAL
LINEAMENTS
LINEARISATION
LINEARISATIONS
LINEARISED
LINEARISES
LINEARISING
LINEARITIES
LINEARIZATION
LINEARIZATIONS
LINEARIZED
LINEARIZES
LINEARIZING
LINEATIONS
LINEBACKER
LINEBACKERS
LINEBACKING
LINEBACKINGS
LINEBREEDING
LINEBREEDINGS
LINECASTER
LINECASTERS
LINECASTING
LINECASTINGS
LINENFOLDS

LINEOLATED
LINERBOARD
LINERBOARDS
LINESCORES
LINGBERRIES
LINGERINGLY
LINGERINGS
LINGONBERRIES
LINGONBERRY
LINGUIFORM
LINGUISTER
LINGUISTERS
LINGUISTIC
LINGUISTICAL
LINGUISTICALLY
LINGUISTICIAN
LINGUISTICIANS
LINGUISTICS
LINGUISTRIES
LINGUISTRY
LINGULATED
LINISHINGS
LINKSLANDS
LINOLEATES
LINOTYPERS
LINOTYPING
LINTSTOCKS
LINTWHITES
LIONCELLES
LIONFISHES
LIONHEARTED
LIONHEARTEDNESS
LIONISATION
LIONISATIONS
LIONIZATION
LIONIZATIONS
LIPECTOMIES
LIPGLOSSES
LIPIDOPLAST
LIPIDOPLASTS
LIPOCHROME
LIPOCHROMES
LIPODYSTROPHIES
LIPODYSTROPHY
LIPOGENESES
LIPOGENESIS
LIPOGRAMMATIC
LIPOGRAMMATISM

LIPOGRAMMATISMS
LIPOGRAMMATIST
LIPOGRAMMATISTS
LIPOGRAPHIES
LIPOGRAPHY
LIPOMATOSES
LIPOMATOSIS
LIPOMATOUS
LIPOPHILIC
LIPOPLASTS
LIPOPROTEIN
LIPOPROTEINS
LIPOSCULPTURE
LIPOSCULPTURES
LIPOSUCKED
LIPOSUCKING
LIPOSUCTION
LIPOSUCTIONS
LIPOTROPIC
LIPOTROPIES
LIPOTROPIN
LIPOTROPINS
LIPPINESSES
LIPPITUDES
LIPREADERS
LIPREADING
LIPREADINGS
LIPSTICKED
LIPSTICKING
LIQUATIONS
LIQUEFACIENT
LIQUEFACIENTS
LIQUEFACTION
LIQUEFACTIONS
LIQUEFACTIVE
LIQUEFIABLE
LIQUEFIERS
LIQUEFYING
LIQUESCENCE
LIQUESCENCES
LIQUESCENCIES
LIQUESCENCY
LIQUESCENT
LIQUESCING
LIQUEURING
LIQUIDAMBAR
LIQUIDAMBARS
LIQUIDATED

LIQUIDATES
LIQUIDATING
LIQUIDATION
LIQUIDATIONISM
LIQUIDATIONISMS
LIQUIDATIONIST
LIQUIDATIONISTS
LIQUIDATIONS
LIQUIDATOR
LIQUIDATORS
LIQUIDIEST
LIQUIDISED
LIQUIDISER
LIQUIDISERS
LIQUIDISES
LIQUIDISING
LIQUIDITIES
LIQUIDIZED
LIQUIDIZER
LIQUIDIZERS
LIQUIDIZES
LIQUIDIZING
LIQUIDNESS
LIQUIDNESSES
LIQUIDUSES
LIQUIFACTION
LIQUIFACTIONS
LIQUIFACTIVE
LIQUIFIABLE
LIQUIFIERS
LIQUIFYING
LIQUORICES
LIQUORISHLY
LIQUORISHNESS
LIQUORISHNESSES
LIRIODENDRA
LIRIODENDRON
LIRIODENDRONS
LISSENCEPHALOUS
LISSOMENESS
LISSOMENESSES
LISSOMNESS
LISSOMNESSES
LISSOTRICHOUS
LISTENABILITIES
LISTENABILITY
LISTENABLE
LISTENERSHIP

LISTENERSHIPS
LISTENINGS
LISTERIOSES
LISTERIOSIS
LISTLESSLY
LISTLESSNESS
LISTLESSNESSES
LITENESSES
LITERACIES
LITERALISATION
LITERALISATIONS
LITERALISE
LITERALISED
LITERALISER
LITERALISERS
LITERALISES
LITERALISING
LITERALISM
LITERALISMS
LITERALIST
LITERALISTIC
LITERALISTS
LITERALITIES
LITERALITY
LITERALIZATION
LITERALIZATIONS
LITERALIZE
LITERALIZED
LITERALIZER
LITERALIZERS
LITERALIZES
LITERALIZING
LITERALNESS
LITERALNESSES
LITERARILY
LITERARINESS
LITERARINESSES
LITERARYISM
LITERARYISMS
LITERATELY
LITERATENESS
LITERATENESSES
LITERATION
LITERATIONS
LITERATORS
LITERATURE
LITERATURED
LITERATURES
LITEROSITIES
LITEROSITY
LITHENESSES
LITHESOMENESS
LITHESOMENESSES
LITHIFICATION
LITHIFICATIONS
LITHIFYING
LITHISTIDS
LITHOCHROMATIC
LITHOCHROMATICS
LITHOCHROMIES
LITHOCHROMY
LITHOCLAST
LITHOCLASTS
LITHOCYSTS
LITHODOMOUS
LITHOGENOUS
LITHOGLYPH
LITHOGLYPHS
LITHOGRAPH
LITHOGRAPHED
LITHOGRAPHER
LITHOGRAPHERS
LITHOGRAPHIC
LITHOGRAPHICAL
LITHOGRAPHIES
LITHOGRAPHING
LITHOGRAPHS
LITHOGRAPHY
LITHOLAPAXIES
LITHOLAPAXY
LITHOLATRIES
LITHOLATROUS
LITHOLATRY
LITHOLOGIC
LITHOLOGICAL
LITHOLOGICALLY
LITHOLOGIES
LITHOLOGIST
LITHOLOGISTS
LITHOMANCIES
LITHOMANCY
LITHOMARGE
LITHOMARGES
LITHOMETEOR
LITHOMETEORS
LITHONTHRYPTIC
LITHONTHRYPTICS
LITHONTRIPTIC
LITHONTRIPTICS
LITHONTRIPTIST
LITHONTRIPTISTS
LITHONTRIPTOR
LITHONTRIPTORS
LITHOPHAGOUS
LITHOPHANE
LITHOPHANES
LITHOPHILOUS
LITHOPHYSA
LITHOPHYSAE
LITHOPHYSE
LITHOPHYSES
LITHOPHYTE
LITHOPHYTES
LITHOPHYTIC
LITHOPONES
LITHOPRINT
LITHOPRINTS
LITHOSPERMUM
LITHOSPERMUMS
LITHOSPHERE
LITHOSPHERES
LITHOSPHERIC
LITHOSTATIC
LITHOTOMES
LITHOTOMIC
LITHOTOMICAL
LITHOTOMIES
LITHOTOMIST
LITHOTOMISTS
LITHOTOMOUS
LITHOTRIPSIES
LITHOTRIPSY
LITHOTRIPTER
LITHOTRIPTERS
LITHOTRIPTIC
LITHOTRIPTICS
LITHOTRIPTIST
LITHOTRIPTISTS
LITHOTRIPTOR
LITHOTRIPTORS
LITHOTRITE
LITHOTRITES
LITHOTRITIC
LITHOTRITICS
LITHOTRITIES
LITHOTRITISE
LITHOTRITISED
LITHOTRITISES
LITHOTRITISING
LITHOTRITIST
LITHOTRITISTS
LITHOTRITIZE
LITHOTRITIZED
LITHOTRITIZES
LITHOTRITIZING
LITHOTRITOR
LITHOTRITORS
LITHOTRITY
LITHOTYPES
LITIGATING
LITIGATION
LITIGATIONS
LITIGATORS
LITIGIOUSLY
LITIGIOUSNESS
LITIGIOUSNESSES
LITTERATEUR
LITTERATEURS
LITTERBAGS
LITTERBUGS
LITTERIEST
LITTERMATE
LITTERMATES
LITTLENECK
LITTLENECKS
LITTLENESS
LITTLENESSES
LITTLEWORTH
LITURGICAL
LITURGICALLY
LITURGIOLOGIES
LITURGIOLOGIST
LITURGIOLOGISTS
LITURGIOLOGY
LITURGISMS
LITURGISTIC
LITURGISTS
LIVABILITIES
LIVABILITY
LIVABLENESS
LIVABLENESSES
LIVEABILITIES
LIVEABILITY
LIVEABLENESS
LIVEABLENESSES
LIVEBLOGGED
LIVEBLOGGER
LIVEBLOGGERS
LIVEBLOGGING
LIVEBLOGGINGS
LIVELIHEAD
LIVELIHEADS
LIVELIHOOD
LIVELIHOODS
LIVELINESS
LIVELINESSES
LIVENESSES
LIVERISHLY
LIVERISHNESS
LIVERISHNESSES
LIVERLEAVES
LIVERMORIUM
LIVERMORIUMS
LIVERWORTS
LIVERWURST
LIVERWURSTS
LIVESTOCKS
LIVESTREAM
LIVESTREAMED
LIVESTREAMING
LIVESTREAMS
LIVETRAPPED
LIVETRAPPING
LIVIDITIES
LIVIDNESSES
LIVINGNESS
LIVINGNESSES
LIVRAISONS
LIXIVIATED
LIXIVIATES
LIXIVIATING
LIXIVIATION
LIXIVIATIONS
LOADMASTER
LOADMASTERS
LOADSAMONEY
LOADSAMONEYS
LOADSAMONIES
LOADSPACES
LOADSTONES

LOAMINESSES
LOANSHIFTS
LOATHEDNESS
LOATHEDNESSES
LOATHFULNESS
LOATHFULNESSES
LOATHINGLY
LOATHLIEST
LOATHLINESS
LOATHLINESSES
LOATHNESSES
LOATHSOMELY
LOATHSOMENESS
LOATHSOMENESSES
LOBECTOMIES
LOBLOLLIES
LOBOTOMIES
LOBOTOMISE
LOBOTOMISED
LOBOTOMISES
LOBOTOMISING
LOBOTOMIZE
LOBOTOMIZED
LOBOTOMIZES
LOBOTOMIZING
LOBSCOUSES
LOBSTERERS
LOBSTERING
LOBSTERINGS
LOBSTERLIKE
LOBSTERMAN
LOBSTERMEN
LOBTAILING
LOBTAILINGS
LOBULATION
LOBULATIONS
LOCALISABILITY
LOCALISABLE
LOCALISATION
LOCALISATIONS
LOCALISERS
LOCALISING
LOCALISTIC
LOCALITIES
LOCALIZABILITY
LOCALIZABLE
LOCALIZATION
LOCALIZATIONS
LOCALIZERS
LOCALIZING
LOCALNESSES
LOCATEABLE
LOCATIONAL
LOCATIONALLY
LOCKHOUSES
LOCKKEEPER
LOCKKEEPERS
LOCKMAKERS
LOCKSMITHERIES
LOCKSMITHERY
LOCKSMITHING
LOCKSMITHINGS
LOCKSMITHS
LOCKSTITCH
LOCKSTITCHED
LOCKSTITCHES
LOCKSTITCHING
LOCOMOBILE
LOCOMOBILES
LOCOMOBILITIES
LOCOMOBILITY
LOCOMOTING
LOCOMOTION
LOCOMOTIONS
LOCOMOTIVE
LOCOMOTIVELY
LOCOMOTIVENESS
LOCOMOTIVES
LOCOMOTIVITIES
LOCOMOTIVITY
LOCOMOTORS
LOCOMOTORY
LOCOPLANTS
LOCORESTIVE
LOCULAMENT
LOCULAMENTS
LOCULATION
LOCULATIONS
LOCULICIDAL
LOCUTIONARY
LOCUTORIES
LODESTONES
LODGEMENTS
LODGEPOLES
LOFTINESSES
LOGAGRAPHIA
LOGAGRAPHIAS
LOGANBERRIES
LOGANBERRY
LOGANIACEOUS
LOGAOEDICS
LOGARITHMIC
LOGARITHMICAL
LOGARITHMICALLY
LOGARITHMS
LOGGERHEAD
LOGGERHEADED
LOGGERHEADS
LOGICALITIES
LOGICALITY
LOGICALNESS
LOGICALNESSES
LOGICISING
LOGICIZING
LOGINESSES
LOGISTICAL
LOGISTICALLY
LOGISTICIAN
LOGISTICIANS
LOGJAMMING
LOGJAMMINGS
LOGNORMALITIES
LOGNORMALITY
LOGNORMALLY
LOGOCENTRISM
LOGOCENTRISMS
LOGODAEDALIC
LOGODAEDALIES
LOGODAEDALUS
LOGODAEDALUSES
LOGODAEDALY
LOGOGRAMMATIC
LOGOGRAPHER
LOGOGRAPHERS
LOGOGRAPHIC
LOGOGRAPHICAL
LOGOGRAPHICALLY
LOGOGRAPHIES
LOGOGRAPHS
LOGOGRAPHY
LOGOGRIPHIC
LOGOGRIPHS
LOGOMACHIES
LOGOMACHIST
LOGOMACHISTS
LOGOPAEDIC
LOGOPAEDICS
LOGOPEDICS
LOGOPHILES
LOGORRHEAS
LOGORRHEIC
LOGORRHOEA
LOGORRHOEAS
LOGOTHETES
LOGOTYPIES
LOGROLLERS
LOGROLLING
LOGROLLINGS
LOINCLOTHS
LOITERINGLY
LOITERINGS
LOLLAPALOOSA
LOLLAPALOOSAS
LOLLAPALOOZA
LOLLAPALOOZAS
LOLLOPIEST
LOLLYGAGGED
LOLLYGAGGING
LOMENTACEOUS
LONELINESS
LONELINESSES
LONENESSES
LONESOMELY
LONESOMENESS
LONESOMENESSES
LONGAEVOUS
LONGANIMITIES
LONGANIMITY
LONGANIMOUS
LONGBOARDS
LONGBOWMAN
LONGBOWMEN
LONGCLOTHS
LONGEVITIES
LONGHAIRED
LONGHEADED
LONGHEADEDNESS
LONGHOUSES
LONGICAUDATE
LONGICORNS
LONGINQUITIES
LONGINQUITY
LONGIPENNATE
LONGIROSTRAL
LONGITUDES
LONGITUDINAL
LONGITUDINALLY
LONGJUMPED
LONGJUMPING
LONGLEAVES
LONGLINERS
LONGLISTED
LONGLISTING
LONGNESSES
LONGPRIMER
LONGPRIMERS
LONGSHOREMAN
LONGSHOREMEN
LONGSHORING
LONGSHORINGS
LONGSIGHTED
LONGSIGHTEDNESS
LONGSOMELY
LONGSOMENESS
LONGSOMENESSES
LONGWEARING
LOOKALIKES
LOONINESSES
LOOPHOLING
LOOPINESSES
LOOSEBOXES
LOOSENESSES
LOOSENINGS
LOOSESTRIFE
LOOSESTRIFES
LOOYENWORK
LOOYENWORKS
LOPGRASSES
LOPHOBRANCH
LOPHOBRANCHIATE
LOPHOBRANCHS
LOPHOPHORATE
LOPHOPHORE
LOPHOPHORES
LOPSIDEDLY
LOPSIDEDNESS
LOPSIDEDNESSES
LOQUACIOUS
LOQUACIOUSLY
LOQUACIOUSNESS

LOQUACITIES
LORAZEPAMS
LORDLINESS
LORDLINESSES
LORDOLATRIES
LORDOLATRY
LORGNETTES
LORICATING
LORICATION
LORICATIONS
LORNNESSES
LOSABLENESS
LOSABLENESSES
LOSSMAKERS
LOSSMAKING
LOSTNESSES
LOTHNESSES
LOTUSLANDS
LOUDHAILER
LOUDHAILERS
LOUDMOUTHED
LOUDMOUTHS
LOUDNESSES
LOUDSPEAKER
LOUDSPEAKERS
LOUNDERING
LOUNDERINGS
LOUNGEWEAR
LOUNGEWEARS
LOUNGINGLY
LOUSEWORTS
LOUSINESSES
LOUTISHNESS
LOUTISHNESSES
LOVABILITIES
LOVABILITY
LOVABLENESS
LOVABLENESSES
LOVASTATIN
LOVASTATINS
LOVEABILITIES
LOVEABILITY
LOVEABLENESS
LOVEABLENESSES
LOVELESSLY
LOVELESSNESS
LOVELESSNESSES
LOVELIGHTS
LOVELIHEAD
LOVELIHEADS
LOVELINESS
LOVELINESSES
LOVELORNNESS
LOVELORNNESSES
LOVEMAKERS
LOVEMAKING
LOVEMAKINGS
LOVESICKNESS
LOVESICKNESSES
LOVESTRUCK
LOVEWORTHIER
LOVEWORTHIES
LOVEWORTHIEST
LOVEWORTHY
LOVINGNESS
LOVINGNESSES
LOWBALLING
LOWBALLINGS
LOWBROWISM
LOWBROWISMS
LOWERCASED
LOWERCASES
LOWERCASING
LOWERCLASSMAN
LOWERCLASSMEN
LOWERINGLY
LOWLANDERS
LOWLIGHTED
LOWLIGHTING
LOWLIHEADS
LOWLINESSES
LOWSENINGS
LOXODROMES
LOXODROMIC
LOXODROMICAL
LOXODROMICALLY
LOXODROMICS
LOXODROMIES
LOYALNESSES
LOZENGIEST
LUBBERLIER
LUBBERLIEST
LUBBERLINESS
LUBBERLINESSES
LUBRICANTS
LUBRICATED
LUBRICATES
LUBRICATING
LUBRICATION
LUBRICATIONAL
LUBRICATIONS
LUBRICATIVE
LUBRICATOR
LUBRICATORS
LUBRICIOUS
LUBRICIOUSLY
LUBRICITIES
LUBRICOUSLY
LUBRITORIA
LUBRITORIUM
LUBRITORIUMS
LUCIDITIES
LUCIDNESSES
LUCIFERASE
LUCIFERASES
LUCIFERINS
LUCIFEROUS
LUCIFUGOUS
LUCKENBOOTH
LUCKENBOOTHS
LUCKENGOWAN
LUCKENGOWANS
LUCKINESSES
LUCKLESSLY
LUCKLESSNESS
LUCKLESSNESSES
LUCKPENNIES
LUCRATIVELY
LUCRATIVENESS
LUCRATIVENESSES
LUCTATIONS
LUCUBRATED
LUCUBRATES
LUCUBRATING
LUCUBRATION
LUCUBRATIONS
LUCUBRATOR
LUCUBRATORS
LUCULENTLY
LUDICROUSLY
LUDICROUSNESS
LUDICROUSNESSES
LUETICALLY
LUFTMENSCH
LUFTMENSCHEN
LUGUBRIOUS
LUGUBRIOUSLY
LUGUBRIOUSNESS
LUKEWARMISH
LUKEWARMLY
LUKEWARMNESS
LUKEWARMNESSES
LUKEWARMTH
LUKEWARMTHS
LULLABYING
LUMBAGINOUS
LUMBERINGLY
LUMBERINGNESS
LUMBERINGNESSES
LUMBERINGS
LUMBERJACK
LUMBERJACKET
LUMBERJACKETS
LUMBERJACKS
LUMBERSOME
LUMBERSOMENESS
LUMBERYARD
LUMBERYARDS
LUMBOSACRAL
LUMBRICALES
LUMBRICALIS
LUMBRICALISES
LUMBRICALS
LUMBRICIFORM
LUMBRICOID
LUMBRICUSES
LUMINAIRES
LUMINANCES
LUMINARIAS
LUMINARIES
LUMINARISM
LUMINARISMS
LUMINARIST
LUMINARISTS
LUMINATION
LUMINATIONS
LUMINESCED
LUMINESCENCE
LUMINESCENCES
LUMINESCENT
LUMINESCES
LUMINESCING
LUMINIFEROUS
LUMINOSITIES
LUMINOSITY
LUMINOUSLY
LUMINOUSNESS
LUMINOUSNESSES
LUMISTEROL
LUMISTEROLS
LUMPECTOMIES
LUMPECTOMY
LUMPFISHES
LUMPINESSES
LUMPISHNESS
LUMPISHNESSES
LUMPSUCKER
LUMPSUCKERS
LUNARNAUTS
LUNATICALLY
LUNCHBOXES
LUNCHBREAK
LUNCHBREAKS
LUNCHEONED
LUNCHEONETTE
LUNCHEONETTES
LUNCHEONING
LUNCHMEATS
LUNCHPAILS
LUNCHROOMS
LUNCHTIMES
LUNGFISHES
LUNINESSES
LUNKHEADED
LURIDNESSES
LUSCIOUSLY
LUSCIOUSNESS
LUSCIOUSNESSES
LUSHNESSES
LUSKISHNESS
LUSKISHNESSES
LUSTERLESS
LUSTERWARE
LUSTERWARES
LUSTFULNESS
LUSTFULNESSES
LUSTIHEADS
LUSTIHOODS
LUSTINESSES
LUSTRATING

LUSTRATION
LUSTRATIONS
LUSTRATIVE
LUSTRELESS
LUSTREWARE
LUSTREWARES
LUSTROUSLY
LUSTROUSNESS
LUSTROUSNESSES
LUTEINISATION
LUTEINISATIONS
LUTEINISED
LUTEINISES
LUTEINISING
LUTEINIZATION
LUTEINIZATIONS
LUTEINIZED
LUTEINIZES
LUTEINIZING
LUTEOTROPHIC
LUTEOTROPHIN
LUTEOTROPHINS
LUTEOTROPIC
LUTEOTROPIN
LUTEOTROPINS
LUTESTRING
LUTESTRINGS
LUVVIEDOMS
LUXULIANITE
LUXULIANITES
LUXULLIANITE
LUXULLIANITES
LUXULYANITE
LUXULYANITES
LUXURIANCE
LUXURIANCES
LUXURIANCIES
LUXURIANCY
LUXURIANTLY
LUXURIATED
LUXURIATES
LUXURIATING
LUXURIATION
LUXURIATIONS
LUXURIOUSLY
LUXURIOUSNESS
LUXURIOUSNESSES
LYCANTHROPE
LYCANTHROPES
LYCANTHROPIC
LYCANTHROPIES
LYCANTHROPIST
LYCANTHROPISTS
LYCANTHROPY
LYCHNOSCOPE
LYCHNOSCOPES
LYCOPODIUM
LYCOPODIUMS
LYMPHADENITIS
LYMPHADENITISES
LYMPHADENOPATHY
LYMPHANGIAL
LYMPHANGIOGRAM
LYMPHANGIOGRAMS
LYMPHANGIOMA
LYMPHANGIOMAS
LYMPHANGIOMATA
LYMPHANGITIC
LYMPHANGITIDES
LYMPHANGITIS
LYMPHANGITISES
LYMPHATICALLY
LYMPHATICS
LYMPHOADENOMA
LYMPHOADENOMAS
LYMPHOADENOMATA
LYMPHOBLAST
LYMPHOBLASTIC
LYMPHOBLASTS
LYMPHOCYTE
LYMPHOCYTES
LYMPHOCYTIC
LYMPHOCYTOPENIA
LYMPHOCYTOSES
LYMPHOCYTOSIS
LYMPHOCYTOTIC
LYMPHOGRAM
LYMPHOGRAMS
LYMPHOGRANULOMA
LYMPHOGRAPHIC
LYMPHOGRAPHIES
LYMPHOGRAPHY
LYMPHOKINE
LYMPHOKINES
LYMPHOMATA
LYMPHOMATOID
LYMPHOMATOSES
LYMPHOMATOSIS
LYMPHOMATOUS
LYMPHOPENIA
LYMPHOPENIAS
LYMPHOPOIESES
LYMPHOPOIESIS
LYMPHOPOIETIC
LYMPHOSARCOMA
LYMPHOSARCOMAS
LYMPHOSARCOMATA
LYMPHOTROPHIC
LYOPHILISATION
LYOPHILISATIONS
LYOPHILISE
LYOPHILISED
LYOPHILISER
LYOPHILISERS
LYOPHILISES
LYOPHILISING
LYOPHILIZATION
LYOPHILIZATIONS
LYOPHILIZE
LYOPHILIZED
LYOPHILIZER
LYOPHILIZERS
LYOPHILIZES
LYOPHILIZING
LYOSORPTION
LYOSORPTIONS
LYRICALNESS
LYRICALNESSES
LYRICISING
LYRICIZING
LYSERGIDES
LYSIGENETIC
LYSIGENOUS
LYSIMETERS
LYSIMETRIC
LYSOGENICITIES
LYSOGENICITY
LYSOGENIES
LYSOGENISATION
LYSOGENISATIONS
LYSOGENISE
LYSOGENISED
LYSOGENISES
LYSOGENISING
LYSOGENIZATION
LYSOGENIZATIONS
LYSOGENIZE
LYSOGENIZED
LYSOGENIZES
LYSOGENIZING
LYSOLECITHIN
LYSOLECITHINS
LYTHRACEOUS

M

MACABERESQUE
MACADAMIAS
MACADAMISATION
MACADAMISATIONS
MACADAMISE
MACADAMISED
MACADAMISER
MACADAMISERS
MACADAMISES
MACADAMISING
MACADAMIZATION
MACADAMIZATIONS
MACADAMIZE
MACADAMIZED
MACADAMIZER
MACADAMIZERS
MACADAMIZES
MACADAMIZING
MACARISING
MACARIZING
MACARONICALLY
MACARONICS
MACARONIES
MACCARONIES
MACCARONIS
MACCHERONCINI
MACCHERONCINIS
MACCHIATOS
MACEBEARER
MACEBEARERS
MACEDOINES
MACERANDUBA
MACERANDUBAS
MACERATERS
MACERATING
MACERATION
MACERATIONS
MACERATIVE
MACERATORS
MACHAIRODONT
MACHAIRODONTS
MACHIAVELIAN
MACHIAVELIANS
MACHIAVELLIAN
MACHIAVELLIANS
MACHICOLATE
MACHICOLATED
MACHICOLATES
MACHICOLATING
MACHICOLATION
MACHICOLATIONS
MACHINABILITIES
MACHINABILITY
MACHINABLE
MACHINATED
MACHINATES
MACHINATING
MACHINATION
MACHINATIONS
MACHINATOR
MACHINATORS
MACHINEABILITY
MACHINEABLE
MACHINEGUN
MACHINEGUNNED
MACHINEGUNNING
MACHINEGUNS
MACHINELESS
MACHINELIKE
MACHINEMAN
MACHINEMEN
MACHINERIES
MACHINIMAS
MACHININGS
MACHINISTS
MACHMETERS
MACHTPOLITIK
MACHTPOLITIKS
MACINTOSHES
MACKINTOSH
MACKINTOSHES
MACONOCHIE
MACONOCHIES
MACRENCEPHALIA
MACRENCEPHALIAS
MACRENCEPHALIES
MACRENCEPHALY
MACROAGGREGATE
MACROAGGREGATED
MACROAGGREGATES
MACROBIOTA
MACROBIOTAS
MACROBIOTE
MACROBIOTES
MACROBIOTIC
MACROBIOTICS
MACROCARPA
MACROCARPAS
MACROCEPHALIA
MACROCEPHALIAS
MACROCEPHALIC
MACROCEPHALIES
MACROCEPHALOUS
MACROCEPHALY
MACROCLIMATE
MACROCLIMATES
MACROCLIMATIC
MACROCODES
MACROCOPIES
MACROCOSMIC
MACROCOSMICALLY
MACROCOSMS
MACROCYCLE
MACROCYCLES
MACROCYCLIC
MACROCYSTS
MACROCYTES
MACROCYTIC
MACROCYTOSES
MACROCYTOSIS
MACRODACTYL
MACRODACTYLIC
MACRODACTYLIES
MACRODACTYLOUS
MACRODACTYLS
MACRODACTYLY
MACRODIAGONAL
MACRODIAGONALS
MACRODOMES
MACROECONOMIC
MACROECONOMICS
MACROEVOLUTION
MACROEVOLUTIONS
MACROFAUNA
MACROFAUNAE
MACROFAUNAS
MACROFLORA
MACROFLORAE
MACROFLORAS
MACROFOSSIL
MACROFOSSILS
MACROGAMETE
MACROGAMETES
MACROGLIAS
MACROGLOBULIN
MACROGLOBULINS
MACROGRAPH
MACROGRAPHIC
MACROGRAPHS
MACROLIDES
MACROLOGIES
MACROMARKETING
MACROMARKETINGS
MACROMERES
MACROMOLECULAR
MACROMOLECULE
MACROMOLECULES
MACROMOLES
MACROMUTATION
MACROMUTATIONS
MACRONUCLEAR
MACRONUCLEI
MACRONUCLEUS
MACRONUCLEUSES
MACRONUTRIENT
MACRONUTRIENTS
MACROPHAGE
MACROPHAGES
MACROPHAGIC
MACROPHAGOUS
MACROPHOTOGRAPH
MACROPHYLA
MACROPHYLUM
MACROPHYSICS
MACROPHYTE
MACROPHYTES
MACROPHYTIC
MACROPINACOID
MACROPINACOIDS
MACROPINAKOID
MACROPINAKOIDS
MACROPRISM
MACROPRISMS
MACROPRUDENTIAL
MACROPSIAS
MACROPTEROUS
MACROSCALE
MACROSCALES
MACROSCOPIC
MACROSCOPICALLY
MACROSOCIOLOGY
MACROSPORANGIA
MACROSPORANGIUM
MACROSPORE
MACROSPORES
MACROSTRUCTURAL
MACROSTRUCTURE
MACROSTRUCTURES
MACROZAMIA
MACROZAMIAS
MACTATIONS
MACULATING
MACULATION
MACULATIONS
MACULATURE
MACULATURES
MADBRAINED
MADDENINGLY
MADDENINGNESS
MADDENINGNESSES

MADEFACTION
MADEFACTIONS
MADELEINES
MADEMOISELLE
MADEMOISELLES
MADERISATION
MADERISATIONS
MADERISING
MADERIZATION
MADERIZATIONS
MADERIZING
MADONNAISH
MADONNAWISE
MADRASSAHS
MADREPORAL
MADREPORES
MADREPORIAN
MADREPORIANS
MADREPORIC
MADREPORITE
MADREPORITES
MADREPORITIC
MADRIGALESQUE
MADRIGALIAN
MADRIGALIST
MADRIGALISTS
MADRILENES
MAELSTROMS
MAENADICALLY
MAENADISMS
MAFFICKERS
MAFFICKING
MAFFICKINGS
MAGALOGUES
MAGAZINIST
MAGAZINISTS
MAGDALENES
MAGGOTIEST
MAGGOTORIA
MAGGOTORIUM
MAGIANISMS
MAGISTERIAL
MAGISTERIALLY
MAGISTERIALNESS
MAGISTERIES
MAGISTERIUM
MAGISTERIUMS
MAGISTRACIES
MAGISTRACY
MAGISTRALITIES
MAGISTRALITY
MAGISTRALLY
MAGISTRALS
MAGISTRAND
MAGISTRANDS
MAGISTRATE
MAGISTRATES
MAGISTRATESHIP
MAGISTRATESHIPS
MAGISTRATIC
MAGISTRATICAL
MAGISTRATICALLY
MAGISTRATURE
MAGISTRATURES
MAGMATISMS
MAGNALIUMS
MAGNANIMITIES
MAGNANIMITY
MAGNANIMOUS
MAGNANIMOUSLY
MAGNANIMOUSNESS
MAGNATESHIP
MAGNATESHIPS
MAGNESITES
MAGNESIUMS
MAGNESSTONE
MAGNESSTONES
MAGNETICAL
MAGNETICALLY
MAGNETICIAN
MAGNETICIANS
MAGNETISABLE
MAGNETISATION
MAGNETISATIONS
MAGNETISED
MAGNETISER
MAGNETISERS
MAGNETISES
MAGNETISING
MAGNETISMS
MAGNETISTS
MAGNETITES
MAGNETITIC
MAGNETIZABLE
MAGNETIZATION
MAGNETIZATIONS
MAGNETIZED
MAGNETIZER
MAGNETIZERS
MAGNETIZES
MAGNETIZING
MAGNETOCHEMICAL
MAGNETOELECTRIC
MAGNETOGRAPH
MAGNETOGRAPHS
MAGNETOMETER
MAGNETOMETERS
MAGNETOMETRIC
MAGNETOMETRIES
MAGNETOMETRY
MAGNETOMOTIVE
MAGNETOPAUSE
MAGNETOPAUSES
MAGNETOSPHERE
MAGNETOSPHERES
MAGNETOSPHERIC
MAGNETOSTATIC
MAGNETOSTATICS
MAGNETRONS
MAGNIFIABLE
MAGNIFICAL
MAGNIFICALLY
MAGNIFICAT
MAGNIFICATION
MAGNIFICATIONS
MAGNIFICATS
MAGNIFICENCE
MAGNIFICENCES
MAGNIFICENT
MAGNIFICENTLY
MAGNIFICENTNESS
MAGNIFICOES
MAGNIFICOS
MAGNIFIERS
MAGNIFYING
MAGNILOQUENCE
MAGNILOQUENCES
MAGNILOQUENT
MAGNILOQUENTLY
MAGNITUDES
MAGNITUDINOUS
MAGNOLIACEOUS
MAHARAJAHS
MAHARANEES
MAHARISHIS
MAHATMAISM
MAHATMAISMS
MAHLSTICKS
MAHOGANIES
MAIASAURAS
MAIDENHAIR
MAIDENHAIRS
MAIDENHEAD
MAIDENHEADS
MAIDENHOOD
MAIDENHOODS
MAIDENLIER
MAIDENLIEST
MAIDENLIKE
MAIDENLINESS
MAIDENLINESSES
MAIDENWEED
MAIDENWEEDS
MAIDISHNESS
MAIDISHNESSES
MAIDSERVANT
MAIDSERVANTS
MAIEUTICAL
MAILABILITIES
MAILABILITY
MAILCOACHES
MAILGRAMMED
MAILGRAMMING
MAILMERGED
MAILMERGES
MAILMERGING
MAILPOUCHES
MAILSHOTTED
MAILSHOTTING
MAIMEDNESS
MAIMEDNESSES
MAINBRACES
MAINFRAMES
MAINLANDER
MAINLANDERS
MAINLINERS
MAINLINING
MAINLININGS
MAINPERNOR
MAINPERNORS
MAINPRISED
MAINPRISES
MAINPRISING
MAINSHEETS
MAINSPRING
MAINSPRINGS
MAINSTAGES
MAINSTREAM
MAINSTREAMED
MAINSTREAMING
MAINSTREAMINGS
MAINSTREAMS
MAINSTREETING
MAINSTREETINGS
MAINTAINABILITY
MAINTAINABLE
MAINTAINED
MAINTAINER
MAINTAINERS
MAINTAINING
MAINTENANCE
MAINTENANCED
MAINTENANCES
MAINTENANCING
MAINTOPMAST
MAINTOPMASTS
MAINTOPSAIL
MAINTOPSAILS
MAISONETTE
MAISONETTES
MAISONNETTE
MAISONNETTES
MAISTERDOME
MAISTERDOMES
MAISTERING
MAISTRINGS
MAJESTICAL
MAJESTICALLY
MAJESTICALNESS
MAJESTICNESS
MAJESTICNESSES
MAJOLICAWARE
MAJOLICAWARES
MAJORDOMOS
MAJORETTES
MAJORETTING
MAJORETTINGS
MAJORITAIRE
MAJORITAIRES
MAJORITARIAN

M

MAJORITARIANISM
MAJORITARIANS
MAJORITIES
MAJORSHIPS
MAJUSCULAR
MAJUSCULES
MAKEREADIES
MAKESHIFTS
MAKEWEIGHT
MAKEWEIGHTS
MAKUNOUCHI
MAKUNOUCHIS
MALABSORPTION
MALABSORPTIONS
MALACHITES
MALACOLOGICAL
MALACOLOGIES
MALACOLOGIST
MALACOLOGISTS
MALACOLOGY
MALACOPHILIES
MALACOPHILOUS
MALACOPHILY
MALACOPHYLLOUS
MALACOPTERYGIAN
MALACOSTRACAN
MALACOSTRACANS
MALACOSTRACOUS
MALADAPTATION
MALADAPTATIONS
MALADAPTED
MALADAPTIVE
MALADAPTIVELY
MALADDRESS
MALADDRESSES
MALADJUSTED
MALADJUSTIVE
MALADJUSTMENT
MALADJUSTMENTS
MALADMINISTER
MALADMINISTERED
MALADMINISTERS
MALADROITLY
MALADROITNESS
MALADROITNESSES
MALADROITS
MALAGUENAS
MALAGUETTA
MALAGUETTAS
MALAKATOONE
MALAKATOONES
MALAPERTLY
MALAPERTNESS
MALAPERTNESSES
MALAPPORTIONED
MALAPPROPRIATE
MALAPPROPRIATED
MALAPPROPRIATES
MALAPROPIAN
MALAPROPISM
MALAPROPISMS
MALAPROPIST
MALAPROPISTS
MALAPROPOS
MALARIOLOGIES
MALARIOLOGIST
MALARIOLOGISTS
MALARIOLOGY
MALASSIMILATION
MALATHIONS
MALAXATING
MALAXATION
MALAXATIONS
MALAXATORS
MALCONFORMATION
MALCONTENT
MALCONTENTED
MALCONTENTEDLY
MALCONTENTS
MALDEPLOYMENT
MALDEPLOYMENTS
MALDISTRIBUTION
MALEDICENT
MALEDICTED
MALEDICTING
MALEDICTION
MALEDICTIONS
MALEDICTIVE
MALEDICTORY
MALEFACTION
MALEFACTIONS
MALEFACTOR
MALEFACTORS
MALEFACTORY
MALEFACTRESS
MALEFACTRESSES
MALEFFECTS
MALEFICALLY
MALEFICENCE
MALEFICENCES
MALEFICENT
MALEFICIAL
MALENESSES
MALENGINES
MALENTENDU
MALENTENDUS
MALEVOLENCE
MALEVOLENCES
MALEVOLENT
MALEVOLENTLY
MALFEASANCE
MALFEASANCES
MALFEASANT
MALFEASANTS
MALFORMATION
MALFORMATIONS
MALFUNCTION
MALFUNCTIONED
MALFUNCTIONING
MALFUNCTIONINGS
MALFUNCTIONS
MALICIOUSLY
MALICIOUSNESS
MALICIOUSNESSES
MALIGNANCE
MALIGNANCES
MALIGNANCIES
MALIGNANCY
MALIGNANTLY
MALIGNANTS
MALIGNITIES
MALIGNMENT
MALIGNMENTS
MALIMPRINTED
MALIMPRINTING
MALIMPRINTINGS
MALINGERED
MALINGERER
MALINGERERS
MALINGERIES
MALINGERING
MALLANDERS
MALLEABILITIES
MALLEABILITY
MALLEABLENESS
MALLEABLENESSES
MALLEATING
MALLEATION
MALLEATIONS
MALLEIFORM
MALLEMAROKING
MALLEMAROKINGS
MALLEMUCKS
MALLENDERS
MALLEOLUSES
MALLOPHAGOUS
MALLOWPUFF
MALLOWPUFFS
MALMSTONES
MALNOURISHED
MALNUTRITION
MALNUTRITIONS
MALOCCLUDED
MALOCCLUSION
MALOCCLUSIONS
MALODOROUS
MALODOROUSLY
MALODOROUSNESS
MALOLACTIC
MALONYLUREA
MALONYLUREAS
MALPIGHIACEOUS
MALPIGHIAS
MALPOSITION
MALPOSITIONS
MALPRACTICE
MALPRACTICES
MALPRACTITIONER
MALPRESENTATION
MALTALENTS
MALTINESSES
MALTODEXTRIN
MALTODEXTRINS
MALTREATED
MALTREATER
MALTREATERS
MALTREATING
MALTREATMENT
MALTREATMENTS
MALVACEOUS
MALVERSATION
MALVERSATIONS
MALVOISIES
MAMAGUYING
MAMILLATED
MAMILLATION
MAMILLATIONS
MAMILLIFORM
MAMMALIANS
MAMMALIFEROUS
MAMMALITIES
MAMMALOGICAL
MAMMALOGIES
MAMMALOGIST
MAMMALOGISTS
MAMMAPLASTIES
MAMMAPLASTY
MAMMECTOMIES
MAMMECTOMY
MAMMETRIES
MAMMIFEROUS
MAMMILLARIA
MAMMILLARIAS
MAMMILLARY
MAMMILLATE
MAMMILLATED
MAMMILLATION
MAMMILLATIONS
MAMMILLIFORM
MAMMITIDES
MAMMOCKING
MAMMOGENIC
MAMMOGRAMS
MAMMOGRAPH
MAMMOGRAPHIC
MAMMOGRAPHIES
MAMMOGRAPHS
MAMMOGRAPHY
MAMMONISMS
MAMMONISTIC
MAMMONISTS
MAMMONITES
MAMMOPLASTIES
MAMMOPLASTY
MANAGEABILITIES
MANAGEABILITY
MANAGEABLE
MANAGEABLENESS
MANAGEABLY
MANAGEMENT

MANAGEMENTAL
MANAGEMENTS
MANAGERESS
MANAGERESSES
MANAGERIAL
MANAGERIALISM
MANAGERIALISMS
MANAGERIALIST
MANAGERIALISTS
MANAGERIALLY
MANAGERSHIP
MANAGERSHIPS
MANCHESTER
MANCHESTERS
MANCHINEEL
MANCHINEELS
MANCIPATED
MANCIPATES
MANCIPATING
MANCIPATION
MANCIPATIONS
MANCIPATORY
MANDAMUSED
MANDAMUSES
MANDAMUSING
MANDARINATE
MANDARINATES
MANDARINES
MANDARINIC
MANDARINISM
MANDARINISMS
MANDATARIES
MANDATORIES
MANDATORILY
MANDIBULAR
MANDIBULATE
MANDIBULATED
MANDIBULATES
MANDILIONS
MANDIOCCAS
MANDOLINES
MANDOLINIST
MANDOLINISTS
MANDRAGORA
MANDRAGORAS
MANDUCABLE
MANDUCATED
MANDUCATES
MANDUCATING
MANDUCATION
MANDUCATIONS
MANDUCATORY
MANDYLIONS
MANEUVERABILITY
MANEUVERABLE
MANEUVERED
MANEUVERER
MANEUVERERS
MANEUVERING
MANEUVERINGS
MANFULLEST
MANFULNESS
MANFULNESSES
MANGABEIRA
MANGABEIRAS
MANGALSUTRA
MANGALSUTRAS
MANGANATES
MANGANESES
MANGANESIAN
MANGANIFEROUS
MANGANITES
MANGELWURZEL
MANGELWURZELS
MANGEMANGE
MANGEMANGES
MANGETOUTS
MANGINESSES
MANGOLDWURZEL
MANGOLDWURZELS
MANGOSTANS
MANGOSTEEN
MANGOSTEENS
MANGOUSTES
MANGULATED
MANGULATES
MANGULATING
MANHANDLED
MANHANDLES
MANHANDLING
MANHATTANS
MANHUNTERS
MANIACALLY
MANICOTTIS
MANICURING
MANICURIST
MANICURISTS
MANIFESTABLE
MANIFESTANT
MANIFESTANTS
MANIFESTATION
MANIFESTATIONAL
MANIFESTATIONS
MANIFESTATIVE
MANIFESTED
MANIFESTER
MANIFESTERS
MANIFESTIBLE
MANIFESTING
MANIFESTLY
MANIFESTNESS
MANIFESTNESSES
MANIFESTOED
MANIFESTOES
MANIFESTOING
MANIFESTOS
MANIFOLDED
MANIFOLDER
MANIFOLDERS
MANIFOLDING
MANIFOLDLY
MANIFOLDNESS
MANIFOLDNESSES
MANIPULABILITY
MANIPULABLE
MANIPULARS
MANIPULATABLE
MANIPULATE
MANIPULATED
MANIPULATES
MANIPULATING
MANIPULATION
MANIPULATIONS
MANIPULATIVE
MANIPULATIVELY
MANIPULATIVES
MANIPULATOR
MANIPULATORS
MANIPULATORY
MANLINESSES
MANNEQUINS
MANNERISMS
MANNERISTIC
MANNERISTICAL
MANNERISTICALLY
MANNERISTS
MANNERLESS
MANNERLESSNESS
MANNERLIER
MANNERLIEST
MANNERLINESS
MANNERLINESSES
MANNIFEROUS
MANNISHNESS
MANNISHNESSES
MANOEUVERED
MANOEUVERING
MANOEUVERS
MANOEUVRABILITY
MANOEUVRABLE
MANOEUVRED
MANOEUVRER
MANOEUVRERS
MANOEUVRES
MANOEUVRING
MANOEUVRINGS
MANOMETERS
MANOMETRIC
MANOMETRICAL
MANOMETRICALLY
MANOMETRIES
MANORIALISM
MANORIALISMS
MANOSCOPIES
MANRIKIGUSARI
MANRIKIGUSARIS
MANSCAPING
MANSCAPINGS
MANSERVANT
MANSIONARIES
MANSIONARY
MANSLAUGHTER
MANSLAUGHTERS
MANSLAYERS
MANSONRIES
MANSPLAINED
MANSPLAINING
MANSPLAININGS
MANSPLAINS
MANSPREADING
MANSPREADINGS
MANSPREADS
MANSUETUDE
MANSUETUDES
MANTELLETTA
MANTELLETTAS
MANTELPIECE
MANTELPIECES
MANTELSHELF
MANTELSHELVES
MANTELTREE
MANTELTREES
MANTICALLY
MANTICORAS
MANTICORES
MANTLETREE
MANTLETREES
MANTYHOSES
MANUBRIUMS
MANUFACTORIES
MANUFACTORY
MANUFACTURABLE
MANUFACTURAL
MANUFACTURE
MANUFACTURED
MANUFACTURER
MANUFACTURERS
MANUFACTURES
MANUFACTURING
MANUFACTURINGS
MANUMISSION
MANUMISSIONS
MANUMITTED
MANUMITTER
MANUMITTERS
MANUMITTING
MANURANCES
MANUSCRIPT
MANUSCRIPTS
MANZANILLA
MANZANILLAS
MANZANITAS
MAPMAKINGS
MAPPEMONDS
MAQUILADORA
MAQUILADORAS
MAQUILLAGE
MAQUILLAGES
MAQUISARDS
MARABUNTAS

MARANATHAS
MARASCHINO
MARASCHINOS
MARASMUSES
MARATHONER
MARATHONERS
MARATHONING
MARATHONINGS
MARAUDINGS
MARBELISED
MARBELISES
MARBELISING
MARBELIZED
MARBELIZES
MARBELIZING
MARBLEISED
MARBLEISES
MARBLEISING
MARBLEIZED
MARBLEIZES
MARBLEIZING
MARBLEWOOD
MARBLEWOODS
MARCANTANT
MARCANTANTS
MARCASITES
MARCASITICAL
MARCATISSIMO
MARCELLERS
MARCELLING
MARCESCENCE
MARCESCENCES
MARCESCENT
MARCESCIBLE
MARCHANTIA
MARCHANTIAS
MARCHIONESS
MARCHIONESSES
MARCHLANDS
MARCHPANES
MARCONIGRAM
MARCONIGRAMS
MARCONIGRAPH
MARCONIGRAPHED
MARCONIGRAPHING
MARCONIGRAPHS
MARCONIING
MARESCHALS
MARGARINES
MARGARITAS
MARGARITES
MARGARITIC
MARGARITIFEROUS
MARGENTING
MARGHERITA
MARGHERITAS
MARGINALIA
MARGINALISATION
MARGINALISE
MARGINALISED
MARGINALISES
MARGINALISING
MARGINALISM
MARGINALISMS
MARGINALIST
MARGINALISTS
MARGINALITIES
MARGINALITY
MARGINALIZATION
MARGINALIZE
MARGINALIZED
MARGINALIZES
MARGINALIZING
MARGINALLY
MARGINATED
MARGINATES
MARGINATING
MARGINATION
MARGINATIONS
MARGRAVATE
MARGRAVATES
MARGRAVIAL
MARGRAVIATE
MARGRAVIATES
MARGRAVINE
MARGRAVINES
MARGUERITA
MARGUERITAS
MARGUERITE
MARGUERITES
MARIALITES
MARICULTURE
MARICULTURES
MARICULTURIST
MARICULTURISTS
MARIGRAPHS
MARIHUANAS
MARIJUANAS
MARIMBAPHONE
MARIMBAPHONES
MARIMBISTS
MARINADING
MARINATING
MARINATION
MARINATIONS
MARIONBERRIES
MARIONBERRY
MARIONETTE
MARIONETTES
MARISCHALLED
MARISCHALLING
MARISCHALS
MARIVAUDAGE
MARIVAUDAGES
MARKEDNESS
MARKEDNESSES
MARKETABILITIES
MARKETABILITY
MARKETABLE
MARKETABLENESS
MARKETABLY
MARKETEERS
MARKETINGS
MARKETISATION
MARKETISATIONS
MARKETISED
MARKETISES
MARKETISING
MARKETIZATION
MARKETIZATIONS
MARKETIZED
MARKETIZES
MARKETIZING
MARKETPLACE
MARKETPLACES
MARKSMANSHIP
MARKSMANSHIPS
MARKSWOMAN
MARKSWOMEN
MARLACIOUS
MARLINESPIKE
MARLINESPIKES
MARLINGSPIKE
MARLINGSPIKES
MARLINSPIKE
MARLINSPIKES
MARLSTONES
MARMALADES
MARMALISED
MARMALISES
MARMALISING
MARMALIZED
MARMALIZES
MARMALIZING
MARMARISED
MARMARISES
MARMARISING
MARMARIZED
MARMARIZES
MARMARIZING
MARMAROSES
MARMAROSIS
MARMELISED
MARMELISES
MARMELISING
MARMELIZED
MARMELIZES
MARMELIZING
MARMOREALLY
MAROONINGS
MARPRELATE
MARPRELATED
MARPRELATES
MARPRELATING
MARQUESSATE
MARQUESSATES
MARQUESSES
MARQUETERIE
MARQUETERIES
MARQUETRIES
MARQUISATE
MARQUISATES
MARQUISETTE
MARQUISETTES
MARRIAGEABILITY
MARRIAGEABLE
MARROWBONE
MARROWBONES
MARROWFATS
MARROWIEST
MARROWLESS
MARROWSKIED
MARROWSKIES
MARROWSKYING
MARSEILLES
MARSHALCIES
MARSHALERS
MARSHALING
MARSHALLED
MARSHALLER
MARSHALLERS
MARSHALLING
MARSHALLINGS
MARSHALSHIP
MARSHALSHIPS
MARSHBUCKS
MARSHELDER
MARSHELDERS
MARSHINESS
MARSHINESSES
MARSHLANDER
MARSHLANDERS
MARSHLANDS
MARSHLOCKS
MARSHLOCKSES
MARSHMALLOW
MARSHMALLOWIER
MARSHMALLOWIEST
MARSHMALLOWS
MARSHMALLOWY
MARSHWORTS
MARSIPOBRANCH
MARSIPOBRANCHS
MARSQUAKES
MARSUPIALIAN
MARSUPIALIANS
MARSUPIALS
MARSUPIANS
MARTELLANDO
MARTELLANDOS
MARTELLATO
MARTELLATOS
MARTELLING
MARTENSITE
MARTENSITES
MARTENSITIC
MARTENSITICALLY
MARTIALISM
MARTIALISMS
MARTIALIST

MARTIALISTS
MARTIALNESS
MARTIALNESSES
MARTINETISH
MARTINETISM
MARTINETISMS
MARTINGALE
MARTINGALES
MARTINGALS
MARTYRDOMS
MARTYRISATION
MARTYRISATIONS
MARTYRISED
MARTYRISES
MARTYRISING
MARTYRIZATION
MARTYRIZATIONS
MARTYRIZED
MARTYRIZES
MARTYRIZING
MARTYROLOGIC
MARTYROLOGICAL
MARTYROLOGIES
MARTYROLOGIST
MARTYROLOGISTS
MARTYROLOGY
MARVELLERS
MARVELLING
MARVELLOUS
MARVELLOUSLY
MARVELLOUSNESS
MARVELOUSLY
MARVELOUSNESS
MARVELOUSNESSES
MARZIPANNED
MARZIPANNING
MASCARAING
MASCARPONE
MASCARPONES
MASCULINELY
MASCULINENESS
MASCULINENESSES
MASCULINES
MASCULINISATION
MASCULINISE
MASCULINISED
MASCULINISES
MASCULINISING
MASCULINIST
MASCULINISTS
MASCULINITIES
MASCULINITY
MASCULINIZATION
MASCULINIZE
MASCULINIZED
MASCULINIZES
MASCULINIZING
MASCULISTS
MASHGICHIM
MASKALLONGE
MASKALLONGES
MASKALONGE
MASKALONGES
MASKANONGE
MASKANONGES
MASKINONGE
MASKINONGES
MASKIROVKA
MASKIROVKAS
MASOCHISMS
MASOCHISTIC
MASOCHISTICALLY
MASOCHISTS
MASONICALLY
MASQUERADE
MASQUERADED
MASQUERADER
MASQUERADERS
MASQUERADES
MASQUERADING
MASSACRERS
MASSACRING
MASSAGISTS
MASSARANDUBA
MASSARANDUBAS
MASSASAUGA
MASSASAUGAS
MASSERANDUBA
MASSERANDUBAS
MASSETERIC
MASSIFICATION
MASSIFICATIONS
MASSINESSES
MASSIVENESS
MASSIVENESSES
MASSOTHERAPIES
MASSOTHERAPIST
MASSOTHERAPISTS
MASSOTHERAPY
MASSPRIEST
MASSPRIESTS
MASSYMORES
MASTECTOMIES
MASTECTOMY
MASTERATES
MASTERCLASS
MASTERCLASSES
MASTERDOMS
MASTERFULLY
MASTERFULNESS
MASTERFULNESSES
MASTERHOOD
MASTERHOODS
MASTERINGS
MASTERLESS
MASTERLIER
MASTERLIEST
MASTERLINESS
MASTERLINESSES
MASTERMIND
MASTERMINDED
MASTERMINDING
MASTERMINDS
MASTERPIECE
MASTERPIECES
MASTERSHIP
MASTERSHIPS
MASTERSINGER
MASTERSINGERS
MASTERSTROKE
MASTERSTROKES
MASTERWORK
MASTERWORKS
MASTERWORT
MASTERWORTS
MASTHEADED
MASTHEADING
MASTHOUSES
MASTICABLE
MASTICATED
MASTICATES
MASTICATING
MASTICATION
MASTICATIONS
MASTICATOR
MASTICATORIES
MASTICATORS
MASTICATORY
MASTIGOPHORAN
MASTIGOPHORANS
MASTIGOPHORE
MASTIGOPHORES
MASTIGOPHORIC
MASTIGOPHOROUS
MASTITIDES
MASTITISES
MASTODONIC
MASTODONTIC
MASTODONTS
MASTODYNIA
MASTODYNIAS
MASTOIDECTOMIES
MASTOIDECTOMY
MASTOIDITIDES
MASTOIDITIS
MASTOIDITISES
MASTOPEXIES
MASTURBATE
MASTURBATED
MASTURBATES
MASTURBATING
MASTURBATION
MASTURBATIONS
MASTURBATOR
MASTURBATORS
MASTURBATORY
MATACHINAS
MATAGOURIS
MATCHBOARD
MATCHBOARDING
MATCHBOARDINGS
MATCHBOARDS
MATCHBOOKS
MATCHBOXES
MATCHLESSLY
MATCHLESSNESS
MATCHLESSNESSES
MATCHLOCKS
MATCHMAKER
MATCHMAKERS
MATCHMAKES
MATCHMAKING
MATCHMAKINGS
MATCHMARKED
MATCHMARKING
MATCHMARKS
MATCHPLAYS
MATCHSTICK
MATCHSTICKS
MATCHWOODS
MATELASSES
MATELLASSE
MATELLASSES
MATELOTTES
MATERFAMILIAS
MATERFAMILIASES
MATERIALISATION
MATERIALISE
MATERIALISED
MATERIALISER
MATERIALISERS
MATERIALISES
MATERIALISING
MATERIALISM
MATERIALISMS
MATERIALIST
MATERIALISTIC
MATERIALISTICAL
MATERIALISTS
MATERIALITIES
MATERIALITY
MATERIALIZATION
MATERIALIZE
MATERIALIZED
MATERIALIZER
MATERIALIZERS
MATERIALIZES
MATERIALIZING
MATERIALLY
MATERIALNESS
MATERIALNESSES
MATERNALISM
MATERNALISMS
MATERNALISTIC
MATERNALLY
MATERNITIES
MATEYNESSES
MATFELLONS
MATGRASSES
MATHEMATIC

M

MATHEMATICAL
MATHEMATICALLY
MATHEMATICIAN
MATHEMATICIANS
MATHEMATICISE
MATHEMATICISED
MATHEMATICISES
MATHEMATICISING
MATHEMATICISM
MATHEMATICISMS
MATHEMATICIZE
MATHEMATICIZED
MATHEMATICIZES
MATHEMATICIZING
MATHEMATICS
MATHEMATISATION
MATHEMATISE
MATHEMATISED
MATHEMATISES
MATHEMATISING
MATHEMATIZATION
MATHEMATIZE
MATHEMATIZED
MATHEMATIZES
MATHEMATIZING
MATINESSES
MATRESFAMILIAS
MATRIARCHAL
MATRIARCHALISM
MATRIARCHALISMS
MATRIARCHATE
MATRIARCHATES
MATRIARCHIC
MATRIARCHIES
MATRIARCHS
MATRIARCHY
MATRICIDAL
MATRICIDES
MATRICLINIC
MATRICLINOUS
MATRICULANT
MATRICULANTS
MATRICULAR
MATRICULAS
MATRICULATE
MATRICULATED
MATRICULATES
MATRICULATING
MATRICULATION
MATRICULATIONS
MATRICULATOR
MATRICULATORS
MATRICULATORY
MATRIFOCAL
MATRIFOCALITIES
MATRIFOCALITY
MATRILINEAL
MATRILINEALLY
MATRILINEAR
MATRILINIES
MATRILOCAL
MATRILOCALITIES
MATRILOCALITY
MATRILOCALLY
MATRIMONIAL
MATRIMONIALLY
MATRIMONIES
MATRIOSHKA
MATRIOSHKAS
MATRIOSHKI
MATROCLINAL
MATROCLINIC
MATROCLINIES
MATROCLINOUS
MATROCLINY
MATRONAGES
MATRONHOOD
MATRONHOODS
MATRONISED
MATRONISES
MATRONISING
MATRONIZED
MATRONIZES
MATRONIZING
MATRONLIER
MATRONLIEST
MATRONLINESS
MATRONLINESSES
MATRONSHIP
MATRONSHIPS
MATRONYMIC
MATRONYMICS
MATROYSHKA
MATROYSHKAS
MATRYOSHKA
MATRYOSHKAS
MATRYOSHKI
MATSUTAKES
MATTAMORES
MATTERIEST
MATTERLESS
MATTIFYING
MATTRASSES
MATTRESSES
MATURATING
MATURATION
MATURATIONAL
MATURATIONS
MATURATIVE
MATURENESS
MATURENESSES
MATURITIES
MATUTINALLY
MAUDLINISM
MAUDLINISMS
MAUDLINNESS
MAUDLINNESSES
MAULSTICKS
MAUMETRIES
MAUNDERERS
MAUNDERING
MAUNDERINGS
MAUSOLEUMS
MAVERICKED
MAVERICKING
MAVOURNEEN
MAVOURNEENS
MAVOURNINS
MAWKISHNESS
MAWKISHNESSES
MAWMETRIES
MAXIDRESSES
MAXILLARIES
MAXILLIPED
MAXILLIPEDARY
MAXILLIPEDE
MAXILLIPEDES
MAXILLIPEDS
MAXILLOFACIAL
MAXILLULAE
MAXIMALIST
MAXIMALISTS
MAXIMAPHILIES
MAXIMAPHILY
MAXIMATION
MAXIMATIONS
MAXIMISATION
MAXIMISATIONS
MAXIMISERS
MAXIMISING
MAXIMIZATION
MAXIMIZATIONS
MAXIMIZERS
MAXIMIZING
MAYFLOWERS
MAYONNAISE
MAYONNAISES
MAYORALTIES
MAYORESSES
MAYORSHIPS
MAYSTERDOME
MAYSTERDOMES
MAZARINADE
MAZARINADES
MAZEDNESSES
MAZINESSES
MEADOWIEST
MEADOWLAND
MEADOWLANDS
MEADOWLARK
MEADOWLARKS
MEADOWSWEET
MEADOWSWEETS
MEAGERNESS
MEAGERNESSES
MEAGRENESS
MEAGRENESSES
MEALINESSES
MEALYMOUTHED
MEANDERERS
MEANDERING
MEANDERINGLY
MEANDERINGS
MEANINGFUL
MEANINGFULLY
MEANINGFULNESS
MEANINGLESS
MEANINGLESSLY
MEANINGLESSNESS
MEANNESSES
MEANWHILES
MEASLINESS
MEASLINESSES
MEASURABILITIES
MEASURABILITY
MEASURABLE
MEASURABLENESS
MEASURABLY
MEASUREDLY
MEASUREDNESS
MEASUREDNESSES
MEASURELESS
MEASURELESSLY
MEASURELESSNESS
MEASUREMENT
MEASUREMENTS
MEASURINGS
MEATINESSES
MEATLOAVES
MEATPACKER
MEATPACKERS
MEATPACKING
MEATPACKINGS
MEATSCREEN
MEATSCREENS
MEATSPACES
MECAMYLAMINE
MECAMYLAMINES
MECHANICAL
MECHANICALISM
MECHANICALISMS
MECHANICALLY
MECHANICALNESS
MECHANICALS
MECHANICIAN
MECHANICIANS
MECHANISABLE
MECHANISATION
MECHANISATIONS
MECHANISED
MECHANISER
MECHANISERS
MECHANISES
MECHANISING
MECHANISMS
MECHANISTIC
MECHANISTICALLY
MECHANISTS
MECHANIZABLE
MECHANIZATION

M

MECHANIZATIONS
MECHANIZED
MECHANIZER
MECHANIZERS
MECHANIZES
MECHANIZING
MECHANOCHEMICAL
MECHANOMORPHISM
MECHANORECEPTOR
MECHANOTHERAPY
MECHATRONIC
MECHATRONICS
MECLIZINES
MECONOPSES
MECONOPSIS
MEDAILLONS
MEDALLIONED
MEDALLIONING
MEDALLIONS
MEDALLISTS
MEDALPLAYS
MEDDLESOME
MEDDLESOMELY
MEDDLESOMENESS
MEDDLINGLY
MEDEVACING
MEDEVACKED
MEDEVACKING
MEDIAEVALISM
MEDIAEVALISMS
MEDIAEVALIST
MEDIAEVALISTIC
MEDIAEVALISTS
MEDIAEVALLY
MEDIAEVALS
MEDIAGENIC
MEDIASTINA
MEDIASTINAL
MEDIASTINUM
MEDIATENESS
MEDIATENESSES
MEDIATIONAL
MEDIATIONS
MEDIATISATION
MEDIATISATIONS
MEDIATISED
MEDIATISES
MEDIATISING
MEDIATIZATION
MEDIATIZATIONS
MEDIATIZED
MEDIATIZES
MEDIATIZING
MEDIATORIAL
MEDIATORIALLY
MEDIATORSHIP
MEDIATORSHIPS
MEDIATRESS
MEDIATRESSES
MEDIATRICES
MEDIATRIXES
MEDICALISATION
MEDICALISATIONS
MEDICALISE
MEDICALISED
MEDICALISES
MEDICALISING
MEDICALIZATION
MEDICALIZATIONS
MEDICALIZE
MEDICALIZED
MEDICALIZES
MEDICALIZING
MEDICAMENT
MEDICAMENTAL
MEDICAMENTALLY
MEDICAMENTARY
MEDICAMENTED
MEDICAMENTING
MEDICAMENTOUS
MEDICAMENTS
MEDICASTER
MEDICASTERS
MEDICATING
MEDICATION
MEDICATIONS
MEDICATIVE
MEDICINABLE
MEDICINALLY
MEDICINALS
MEDICINERS
MEDICINING
MEDICOLEGAL
MEDIEVALISM
MEDIEVALISMS
MEDIEVALIST
MEDIEVALISTIC
MEDIEVALISTS
MEDIEVALLY
MEDIOCRACIES
MEDIOCRACY
MEDIOCRITIES
MEDIOCRITY
MEDITATING
MEDITATION
MEDITATIONS
MEDITATIVE
MEDITATIVELY
MEDITATIVENESS
MEDITATORS
MEDITERRANEAN
MEDIUMISTIC
MEDIUMSHIP
MEDIUMSHIPS
MEDIVACING
MEDIVACKED
MEDIVACKING
MEDRESSEHS
MEDULLATED
MEDULLOBLASTOMA
MEDUSIFORM
MEEKNESSES
MEERSCHAUM
MEERSCHAUMS
MEETINGHOUSE
MEETINGHOUSES
MEETNESSES
MEFLOQUINE
MEFLOQUINES
MEGACEPHALIC
MEGACEPHALIES
MEGACEPHALOUS
MEGACEPHALY
MEGACHURCH
MEGACHURCHES
MEGACITIES
MEGACORPORATION
MEGACURIES
MEGACYCLES
MEGADEATHS
MEGAFARADS
MEGAFAUNAE
MEGAFAUNAL
MEGAFAUNAS
MEGAFLORAE
MEGAFLORAS
MEGAGAMETE
MEGAGAMETES
MEGAGAMETOPHYTE
MEGAGAUSSES
MEGAHERBIVORE
MEGAHERBIVORES
MEGAHERTZES
MEGAJOULES
MEGAKARYOCYTE
MEGAKARYOCYTES
MEGAKARYOCYTIC
MEGALITHIC
MEGALITRES
MEGALOBLAST
MEGALOBLASTIC
MEGALOBLASTS
MEGALOCARDIA
MEGALOCARDIAS
MEGALOCEPHALIC
MEGALOCEPHALIES
MEGALOCEPHALOUS
MEGALOCEPHALY
MEGALODONS
MEGALOMANIA
MEGALOMANIAC
MEGALOMANIACAL
MEGALOMANIACS
MEGALOMANIAS
MEGALOMANIC
MEGALOPOLIS
MEGALOPOLISES
MEGALOPOLITAN
MEGALOPOLITANS
MEGALOPSES
MEGALOSAUR
MEGALOSAURI
MEGALOSAURIAN
MEGALOSAURIANS
MEGALOSAURS
MEGALOSAURUS
MEGANEWTON
MEGANEWTONS
MEGAPARSEC
MEGAPARSECS
MEGAPHONED
MEGAPHONES
MEGAPHONIC
MEGAPHONICALLY
MEGAPHONING
MEGAPHYLLS
MEGAPIXELS
MEGAPLEXES
MEGAPROJECT
MEGAPROJECTS
MEGAQUAKES
MEGASCOPES
MEGASCOPIC
MEGASCOPICALLY
MEGASPORANGIA
MEGASPORANGIUM
MEGASPORES
MEGASPORIC
MEGASPOROPHYLL
MEGASPOROPHYLLS
MEGASTORES
MEGASTORMS
MEGASTRUCTURE
MEGASTRUCTURES
MEGATECHNOLOGY
MEGATHERES
MEGATHERIAN
MEGATHRUST
MEGATONNAGE
MEGATONNAGES
MEGAVERTEBRATE
MEGAVERTEBRATES
MEGAVITAMIN
MEGAVITAMINS
MEIOFAUNAE
MEIOFAUNAL
MEIOFAUNAS
MEIOSPORES
MEIOTICALLY
MEITNERIUM
MEITNERIUMS
MEKOMETERS
MELACONITE
MELACONITES
MELALEUCAS
MELAMPODES
MELANAEMIA
MELANAEMIAS
MELANCHOLIA
MELANCHOLIAC

M

MELANCHOLIACS
MELANCHOLIAE
MELANCHOLIAS
MELANCHOLIC
MELANCHOLICALLY
MELANCHOLICS
MELANCHOLIES
MELANCHOLILY
MELANCHOLINESS
MELANCHOLIOUS
MELANCHOLY
MELANISATION
MELANISATIONS
MELANISING
MELANISTIC
MELANIZATION
MELANIZATIONS
MELANIZING
MELANOBLAST
MELANOBLASTS
MELANOCHROI
MELANOCHROIC
MELANOCHROOUS
MELANOCYTE
MELANOCYTES
MELANOGENESES
MELANOGENESIS
MELANOMATA
MELANOPHORE
MELANOPHORES
MELANOSITIES
MELANOSITY
MELANOSOME
MELANOSOMES
MELANOTROPIN
MELANOTROPINS
MELANTERITE
MELANTERITES
MELANURIAS
MELAPHYRES
MELASTOMACEOUS
MELASTOMES
MELATONINS
MELIACEOUS
MELICOTTON
MELICOTTONS
MELIORABLE
MELIORATED
MELIORATES
MELIORATING
MELIORATION
MELIORATIONS
MELIORATIVE
MELIORATIVES
MELIORATOR
MELIORATORS
MELIORISMS
MELIORISTIC
MELIORISTS
MELIORITIES
MELIPHAGOUS
MELISMATIC
MELLIFEROUS
MELLIFICATION
MELLIFICATIONS
MELLIFLUENCE
MELLIFLUENCES
MELLIFLUENT
MELLIFLUENTLY
MELLIFLUOUS
MELLIFLUOUSLY
MELLIFLUOUSNESS
MELLIPHAGOUS
MELLIVOROUS
MELLOPHONE
MELLOPHONES
MELLOTRONS
MELLOWIEST
MELLOWNESS
MELLOWNESSES
MELLOWSPEAK
MELLOWSPEAKS
MELOCOTONS
MELOCOTOON
MELOCOTOONS
MELODICALLY
MELODIOUSLY
MELODIOUSNESS
MELODIOUSNESSES
MELODISERS
MELODISING
MELODIZERS
MELODIZING
MELODRAMAS
MELODRAMATIC
MELODRAMATICS
MELODRAMATISE
MELODRAMATISED
MELODRAMATISES
MELODRAMATISING
MELODRAMATIST
MELODRAMATISTS
MELODRAMATIZE
MELODRAMATIZED
MELODRAMATIZES
MELODRAMATIZING
MELODRAMES
MELOMANIAC
MELOMANIACS
MELOMANIAS
MELONGENES
MELOXICAMS
MELPHALANS
MELTABILITIES
MELTABILITY
MELTINGNESS
MELTINGNESSES
MELTWATERS
MELUNGEONS
MEMBERLESS
MEMBERSHIP
MEMBERSHIPS
MEMBRANACEOUS
MEMBRANEOUS
MEMBRANOUS
MEMBRANOUSLY
MEMOIRISMS
MEMOIRISTS
MEMORABILE
MEMORABILIA
MEMORABILITIES
MEMORABILITY
MEMORABLENESS
MEMORABLENESSES
MEMORANDUM
MEMORANDUMS
MEMORATIVE
MEMORIALISATION
MEMORIALISE
MEMORIALISED
MEMORIALISER
MEMORIALISERS
MEMORIALISES
MEMORIALISING
MEMORIALIST
MEMORIALISTS
MEMORIALIZATION
MEMORIALIZE
MEMORIALIZED
MEMORIALIZER
MEMORIALIZERS
MEMORIALIZES
MEMORIALIZING
MEMORIALLY
MEMORISABLE
MEMORISATION
MEMORISATIONS
MEMORISERS
MEMORISING
MEMORIZABLE
MEMORIZATION
MEMORIZATIONS
MEMORIZERS
MEMORIZING
MEMORIZINGS
MENACINGLY
MENADIONES
MENAGERIES
MENAQUINONE
MENAQUINONES
MENARCHEAL
MENARCHIAL
MENDACIOUS
MENDACIOUSLY
MENDACIOUSNESS
MENDACITIES
MENDELEVIUM
MENDELEVIUMS
MENDICANCIES
MENDICANCY
MENDICANTS
MENDICITIES
MENINGIOMA
MENINGIOMAS
MENINGIOMATA
MENINGITIC
MENINGITIDES
MENINGITIS
MENINGITISES
MENINGOCELE
MENINGOCELES
MENINGOCOCCAL
MENINGOCOCCI
MENINGOCOCCIC
MENINGOCOCCUS
MENISCECTOMIES
MENISCECTOMY
MENISCUSES
MENISPERMACEOUS
MENISPERMUM
MENISPERMUMS
MENOLOGIES
MENOMINEES
MENOPAUSAL
MENOPAUSES
MENOPAUSIC
MENOPOLISES
MENORRHAGIA
MENORRHAGIAS
MENORRHAGIC
MENORRHEAS
MENORRHOEA
MENORRHOEAS
MENSCHIEST
MENSERVANTS
MENSTRUALLY
MENSTRUATE
MENSTRUATED
MENSTRUATES
MENSTRUATING
MENSTRUATION
MENSTRUATIONS
MENSTRUOUS
MENSTRUUMS
MENSURABILITIES
MENSURABILITY
MENSURABLE
MENSURATION
MENSURATIONAL
MENSURATIONS
MENSURATIVE
MENTALESES
MENTALISMS
MENTALISTIC
MENTALISTICALLY
MENTALISTS
MENTALITIES
MENTATIONS
MENTHACEOUS
MENTHOLATED

MENTICIDES
MENTIONABLE
MENTIONERS
MENTIONING
MENTONNIERE
MENTONNIERES
MENTORINGS
MENTORSHIP
MENTORSHIPS
MENUISIERS
MEPACRINES
MEPERIDINE
MEPERIDINES
MEPHITICAL
MEPHITICALLY
MEPHITISES
MEPHITISMS
MEPROBAMATE
MEPROBAMATES
MERBROMINS
MERCANTILE
MERCANTILISM
MERCANTILISMS
MERCANTILIST
MERCANTILISTIC
MERCANTILISTS
MERCAPTANS
MERCAPTIDE
MERCAPTIDES
MERCAPTOPURINE
MERCAPTOPURINES
MERCENARIES
MERCENARILY
MERCENARINESS
MERCENARINESSES
MERCENARISM
MERCENARISMS
MERCERISATION
MERCERISATIONS
MERCERISED
MERCERISER
MERCERISERS
MERCERISES
MERCERISING
MERCERIZATION
MERCERIZATIONS
MERCERIZED
MERCERIZER
MERCERIZERS
MERCERIZES
MERCERIZING
MERCHANDISE
MERCHANDISED
MERCHANDISER
MERCHANDISERS
MERCHANDISES
MERCHANDISING
MERCHANDISINGS
MERCHANDIZE
MERCHANDIZED
MERCHANDIZER
MERCHANDIZERS
MERCHANDIZES
MERCHANDIZING
MERCHANDIZINGS
MERCHANTABILITY
MERCHANTABLE
MERCHANTED
MERCHANTING
MERCHANTINGS
MERCHANTLIKE
MERCHANTMAN
MERCHANTMEN
MERCHANTRIES
MERCHANTRY
MERCHILDREN
MERCIFULLY
MERCIFULNESS
MERCIFULNESSES
MERCIFYING
MERCILESSLY
MERCILESSNESS
MERCILESSNESSES
MERCURATED
MERCURATES
MERCURATING
MERCURATION
MERCURATIONS
MERCURIALISE
MERCURIALISED
MERCURIALISES
MERCURIALISING
MERCURIALISM
MERCURIALISMS
MERCURIALIST
MERCURIALISTS
MERCURIALITIES
MERCURIALITY
MERCURIALIZE
MERCURIALIZED
MERCURIALIZES
MERCURIALIZING
MERCURIALLY
MERCURIALNESS
MERCURIALNESSES
MERCURIALS
MERCURISED
MERCURISES
MERCURISING
MERCURIZED
MERCURIZES
MERCURIZING
MERDIVOROUS
MEREOLOGICAL
MEREOLOGIES
MERESTONES
MERETRICIOUS
MERETRICIOUSLY
MERGANSERS
MERIDIONAL
MERIDIONALITIES
MERIDIONALITY
MERIDIONALLY
MERIDIONALS
MERISTEMATIC
MERISTICALLY
MERITOCRACIES
MERITOCRACY
MERITOCRAT
MERITOCRATIC
MERITOCRATS
MERITORIOUS
MERITORIOUSLY
MERITORIOUSNESS
MERMAIDENS
MEROBLASTIC
MEROBLASTICALLY
MEROGENESES
MEROGENESIS
MEROGENETIC
MEROGONIES
MEROMORPHIC
MEROMYOSIN
MEROMYOSINS
MERONYMIES
MEROPIDANS
MEROPLANKTON
MEROPLANKTONS
MEROZOITES
MERPEOPLES
MERRIMENTS
MERRINESSES
MERRYMAKER
MERRYMAKERS
MERRYMAKING
MERRYMAKINGS
MERRYTHOUGHT
MERRYTHOUGHTS
MERVEILLEUSE
MERVEILLEUSES
MERVEILLEUX
MERVEILLEUXES
MESALLIANCE
MESALLIANCES
MESATICEPHALIC
MESATICEPHALIES
MESATICEPHALOUS
MESATICEPHALY
MESCALINES
MESCALISMS
MESDEMOISELLES
MESENCEPHALA
MESENCEPHALIC
MESENCEPHALON
MESENCEPHALONS
MESENCHYMAL
MESENCHYMATOUS
MESENCHYME
MESENCHYMES
MESENTERIAL
MESENTERIC
MESENTERIES
MESENTERITIS
MESENTERITISES
MESENTERON
MESENTERONIC
MESHUGAASEN
MESHUGASEN
MESHUGGENAH
MESHUGGENAHS
MESHUGGENEH
MESHUGGENEHS
MESHUGGENER
MESHUGGENERS
MESITYLENE
MESITYLENES
MESMERICAL
MESMERICALLY
MESMERISATION
MESMERISATIONS
MESMERISED
MESMERISER
MESMERISERS
MESMERISES
MESMERISING
MESMERISMS
MESMERISTS
MESMERIZATION
MESMERIZATIONS
MESMERIZED
MESMERIZER
MESMERIZERS
MESMERIZES
MESMERIZING
MESNALTIES
MESOAMERICAN
MESOBENTHOS
MESOBENTHOSES
MESOBLASTIC
MESOBLASTS
MESOCEPHALIC
MESOCEPHALICS
MESOCEPHALIES
MESOCEPHALISM
MESOCEPHALISMS
MESOCEPHALOUS
MESOCEPHALY
MESOCRANIES
MESOCRATIC
MESOCYCLONE
MESOCYCLONES
MESODERMAL
MESODERMIC
MESOGASTRIA
MESOGASTRIC
MESOGASTRIUM
MESOGLOEAS
MESOGNATHIES
MESOGNATHISM
MESOGNATHISMS

M

MESOGNATHOUS
MESOGNATHY
MESOHIPPUS
MESOHIPPUSES
MESOKURTIC
MESOMERISM
MESOMERISMS
MESOMORPHIC
MESOMORPHIES
MESOMORPHISM
MESOMORPHISMS
MESOMORPHOUS
MESOMORPHS
MESOMORPHY
MESONEPHRIC
MESONEPHROI
MESONEPHROS
MESONEPHROSES
MESOPAUSES
MESOPELAGIC
MESOPHILES
MESOPHILIC
MESOPHYLLIC
MESOPHYLLOUS
MESOPHYLLS
MESOPHYTES
MESOPHYTIC
MESOSCAPHE
MESOSCAPHES
MESOSPHERE
MESOSPHERES
MESOSPHERIC
MESOTHELIA
MESOTHELIAL
MESOTHELIOMA
MESOTHELIOMAS
MESOTHELIOMATA
MESOTHELIUM
MESOTHELIUMS
MESOTHERAPIES
MESOTHERAPY
MESOTHORACES
MESOTHORACIC
MESOTHORAX
MESOTHORAXES
MESOTHORIUM
MESOTHORIUMS
MESOTROPHIC
MESQUINERIE
MESQUINERIES
MESSAGINGS
MESSALINES
MESSEIGNEURS
MESSENGERED
MESSENGERING
MESSENGERS
MESSIAHSHIP
MESSIAHSHIPS
MESSIANICALLY
MESSIANISM
MESSIANISMS
MESSINESSES
MESTRANOLS
METABISULPHITE
METABISULPHITES
METABOLICALLY
METABOLIES
METABOLISABLE
METABOLISE
METABOLISED
METABOLISES
METABOLISING
METABOLISM
METABOLISMS
METABOLITE
METABOLITES
METABOLIZABLE
METABOLIZE
METABOLIZED
METABOLIZES
METABOLIZING
METABOLOME
METABOLOMES
METABOLOMICS
METABOTROPIC
METACARPAL
METACARPALS
METACARPUS
METACENTER
METACENTERS
METACENTRE
METACENTRES
METACENTRIC
METACENTRICS
METACERCARIA
METACERCARIAE
METACERCARIAL
METACERCARIAS
METACHROMATIC
METACHROMATISM
METACHROMATISMS
METACHRONISM
METACHRONISMS
METACHROSES
METACHROSIS
METACINNABARITE
METACOGNITION
METACOGNITIONS
METACOMPUTER
METACOMPUTERS
METACOMPUTING
METACOMPUTINGS
METAETHICAL
METAETHICS
METAFEMALE
METAFEMALES
METAFICTION
METAFICTIONAL
METAFICTIONIST
METAFICTIONISTS
METAFICTIONS
METAGALACTIC
METAGALAXIES
METAGALAXY
METAGENESES
METAGENESIS
METAGENETIC
METAGENETICALLY
METAGNATHISM
METAGNATHISMS
METAGNATHOUS
METAGRABOLISE
METAGRABOLISED
METAGRABOLISES
METAGRABOLISING
METAGRABOLIZE
METAGRABOLIZED
METAGRABOLIZES
METAGRABOLIZING
METAGROBOLISE
METAGROBOLISED
METAGROBOLISES
METAGROBOLISING
METAGROBOLIZE
METAGROBOLIZED
METAGROBOLIZES
METAGROBOLIZING
METALANGUAGE
METALANGUAGES
METALDEHYDE
METALDEHYDES
METALEPSES
METALEPSIS
METALEPTIC
METALEPTICAL
METALHEADS
METALINGUISTIC
METALINGUISTICS
METALISATION
METALISATIONS
METALISING
METALIZATION
METALIZATIONS
METALIZING
METALLICALLY
METALLIDING
METALLIDINGS
METALLIFEROUS
METALLINGS
METALLISATION
METALLISATIONS
METALLISED
METALLISES
METALLISING
METALLISTS
METALLIZATION
METALLIZATIONS
METALLIZED
METALLIZES
METALLIZING
METALLOCENE
METALLOCENES
METALLOGENETIC
METALLOGENIC
METALLOGENIES
METALLOGENY
METALLOGRAPHER
METALLOGRAPHERS
METALLOGRAPHIC
METALLOGRAPHIES
METALLOGRAPHIST
METALLOGRAPHY
METALLOIDAL
METALLOIDS
METALLOPHONE
METALLOPHONES
METALLURGIC
METALLURGICAL
METALLURGICALLY
METALLURGIES
METALLURGIST
METALLURGISTS
METALLURGY
METALMARKS
METALSMITH
METALSMITHS
METALWARES
METALWORKER
METALWORKERS
METALWORKING
METALWORKINGS
METALWORKS
METAMATERIAL
METAMATERIALS
METAMATHEMATICS
METAMERICALLY
METAMERISM
METAMERISMS
METAMICTISATION
METAMICTIZATION
METAMORPHIC
METAMORPHICALLY
METAMORPHISM
METAMORPHISMS
METAMORPHIST
METAMORPHISTS
METAMORPHOSE
METAMORPHOSED
METAMORPHOSES
METAMORPHOSING
METAMORPHOSIS
METAMORPHOUS
METANALYSES
METANALYSIS
METANARRATIVE
METANARRATIVES
METANEPHRIC
METANEPHROI
METANEPHROS
METAPERIODIC

METAPHASES
METAPHORIC
METAPHORICAL
METAPHORICALLY
METAPHORIST
METAPHORISTS
METAPHOSPHATE
METAPHOSPHATES
METAPHOSPHORIC
METAPHRASE
METAPHRASED
METAPHRASES
METAPHRASING
METAPHRASIS
METAPHRAST
METAPHRASTIC
METAPHRASTICAL
METAPHRASTS
METAPHYSIC
METAPHYSICAL
METAPHYSICALLY
METAPHYSICIAN
METAPHYSICIANS
METAPHYSICISE
METAPHYSICISED
METAPHYSICISES
METAPHYSICISING
METAPHYSICIST
METAPHYSICISTS
METAPHYSICIZE
METAPHYSICIZED
METAPHYSICIZES
METAPHYSICIZING
METAPHYSICS
METAPLASES
METAPLASIA
METAPLASIAS
METAPLASIS
METAPLASMIC
METAPLASMS
METAPLASTIC
METAPOLITICAL
METAPOLITICS
METAPROTEIN
METAPROTEINS
METAPSYCHIC
METAPSYCHICAL
METAPSYCHICS
METAPSYCHOLOGY
METARCHONS
METASEQUOIA
METASEQUOIAS
METASILICATE
METASILICATES
METASILICIC
METASOMATA
METASOMATIC
METASOMATISM
METASOMATISMS
METASOMATOSES
METASOMATOSIS
METASTABILITIES
METASTABILITY
METASTABLE
METASTABLES
METASTABLY
METASTASES
METASTASIS
METASTASISE
METASTASISED
METASTASISES
METASTASISING
METASTASIZE
METASTASIZED
METASTASIZES
METASTASIZING
METASTATIC
METASTATICALLY
METATARSAL
METATARSALS
METATARSUS
METATHEORETICAL
METATHEORIES
METATHEORY
METATHERIAN
METATHERIANS
METATHESES
METATHESIS
METATHESISE
METATHESISED
METATHESISES
METATHESISING
METATHESIZE
METATHESIZED
METATHESIZES
METATHESIZING
METATHETIC
METATHETICAL
METATHETICALLY
METATHORACES
METATHORACIC
METATHORAX
METATHORAXES
METATUNGSTIC
METAVANADIC
METAVERSES
METAXYLEMS
METECDYSES
METECDYSIS
METEMPIRIC
METEMPIRICAL
METEMPIRICALLY
METEMPIRICISM
METEMPIRICISMS
METEMPIRICIST
METEMPIRICISTS
METEMPIRICS
METEMPSYCHOSES
METEMPSYCHOSIS
METEMPSYCHOSIST
METENCEPHALA
METENCEPHALIC
METENCEPHALON
METENCEPHALONS
METEORICALLY
METEORISMS
METEORISTS
METEORITAL
METEORITES
METEORITIC
METEORITICAL
METEORITICIST
METEORITICISTS
METEORITICS
METEOROGRAM
METEOROGRAMS
METEOROGRAPH
METEOROGRAPHIC
METEOROGRAPHS
METEOROIDAL
METEOROIDS
METEOROLITE
METEOROLITES
METEOROLOGIC
METEOROLOGICAL
METEOROLOGIES
METEOROLOGIST
METEOROLOGISTS
METEOROLOGY
METERSTICK
METERSTICKS
METESTICKS
METESTROUS
METESTRUSES
METFORMINS
METHACRYLATE
METHACRYLATES
METHACRYLIC
METHADONES
METHAEMOGLOBIN
METHAEMOGLOBINS
METHAMPHETAMINE
METHANAMIDE
METHANAMIDES
METHANATION
METHANATIONS
METHANOMETER
METHANOMETERS
METHANOYLS
METHAQUALONE
METHAQUALONES
METHEDRINE
METHEDRINES
METHEGLINS
METHEMOGLOBIN
METHEMOGLOBINS
METHENAMINE
METHENAMINES
METHICILLIN
METHICILLINS
METHINKETH
METHIONINE
METHIONINES
METHODICAL
METHODICALLY
METHODICALNESS
METHODISATION
METHODISATIONS
METHODISED
METHODISER
METHODISERS
METHODISES
METHODISING
METHODISMS
METHODISTIC
METHODISTS
METHODIZATION
METHODIZATIONS
METHODIZED
METHODIZER
METHODIZERS
METHODIZES
METHODIZING
METHODOLOGICAL
METHODOLOGIES
METHODOLOGIST
METHODOLOGISTS
METHODOLOGY
METHOMANIA
METHOMANIAS
METHOTREXATE
METHOTREXATES
METHOXIDES
METHOXYBENZENE
METHOXYBENZENES
METHOXYCHLOR
METHOXYCHLORS
METHOXYFLURANE
METHOXYFLURANES
METHYLAMINE
METHYLAMINES
METHYLASES
METHYLATED
METHYLATES
METHYLATING
METHYLATION
METHYLATIONS
METHYLATOR
METHYLATORS
METHYLCELLULOSE
METHYLDOPA
METHYLDOPAS
METHYLENES
METHYLMERCURIES
METHYLMERCURY
METHYLPHENIDATE
METHYLPHENOL
METHYLPHENOLS
METHYLTHIONINE
METHYLTHIONINES

METHYLXANTHINE
METHYLXANTHINES
METHYSERGIDE
METHYSERGIDES
METICULOSITIES
METICULOSITY
METICULOUS
METICULOUSLY
METICULOUSNESS
METOCLOPRAMIDE
METOCLOPRAMIDES
METOESTROUS
METOESTRUS
METOESTRUSES
METONYMICAL
METONYMICALLY
METONYMIES
METOPOSCOPIC
METOPOSCOPICAL
METOPOSCOPIES
METOPOSCOPIST
METOPOSCOPISTS
METOPOSCOPY
METRALGIAS
METRESTICK
METRESTICKS
METRICALLY
METRICATED
METRICATES
METRICATING
METRICATION
METRICATIONS
METRICIANS
METRICISED
METRICISES
METRICISING
METRICISMS
METRICISTS
METRICIZED
METRICIZES
METRICIZING
METRIFICATION
METRIFICATIONS
METRIFIERS
METRIFONATE
METRIFONATES
METRIFYING
METRITISES
METROLOGIC
METROLOGICAL
METROLOGICALLY
METROLOGIES
METROLOGIST
METROLOGISTS
METROMANIA
METROMANIAS
METRONIDAZOLE
METRONIDAZOLES
METRONOMES
METRONOMIC
METRONOMICAL
METRONOMICALLY
METRONYMIC
METRONYMICS
METROPLEXES
METROPOLIS
METROPOLISES
METROPOLITAN
METROPOLITANATE
METROPOLITANISE
METROPOLITANISM
METROPOLITANIZE
METROPOLITANS
METROPOLITICAL
METRORRHAGIA
METRORRHAGIAS
METROSEXUAL
METROSEXUALS
METROSTYLE
METROSTYLES
METTLESOME
METTLESOMENESS
MEZCALINES
MEZZALUNAS
MEZZANINES
MEZZOTINTED
MEZZOTINTER
MEZZOTINTERS
MEZZOTINTING
MEZZOTINTO
MEZZOTINTOS
MEZZOTINTS
MIAROLITIC
MIASMATICAL
MIASMATOUS
MIASMICALLY
MICRIFYING
MICROAEROPHILE
MICROAEROPHILES
MICROAEROPHILIC
MICROAGGRESSION
MICROAMPERE
MICROAMPERES
MICROANALYSES
MICROANALYSIS
MICROANALYST
MICROANALYSTS
MICROANALYTIC
MICROANALYTICAL
MICROANATOMICAL
MICROANATOMIES
MICROANATOMY
MICROARRAY
MICROARRAYS
MICROBALANCE
MICROBALANCES
MICROBAROGRAPH
MICROBAROGRAPHS
MICROBEADS
MICROBEAMS
MICROBIOLOGIC
MICROBIOLOGICAL
MICROBIOLOGIES
MICROBIOLOGIST
MICROBIOLOGISTS
MICROBIOLOGY
MICROBIOME
MICROBIOMES
MICROBIOTA
MICROBIOTAS
MICROBLOGGER
MICROBLOGGERS
MICROBLOGGING
MICROBLOGGINGS
MICROBLOGS
MICROBREWER
MICROBREWERIES
MICROBREWERS
MICROBREWERY
MICROBREWING
MICROBREWINGS
MICROBREWS
MICROBUBBLES
MICROBURST
MICROBURSTS
MICROBUSES
MICROBUSSES
MICROCAPSULE
MICROCAPSULES
MICROCARDS
MICROCASSETTE
MICROCASSETTES
MICROCELEBRITY
MICROCEPHAL
MICROCEPHALIC
MICROCEPHALICS
MICROCEPHALIES
MICROCEPHALOUS
MICROCEPHALS
MICROCEPHALY
MICROCHEMICAL
MICROCHEMISTRY
MICROCHIPPED
MICROCHIPPING
MICROCHIPS
MICROCIRCUIT
MICROCIRCUITRY
MICROCIRCUITS
MICROCLIMATE
MICROCLIMATES
MICROCLIMATIC
MICROCLINE
MICROCLINES
MICROCOCCAL
MICROCOCCI
MICROCOCCUS
MICROCODES
MICROCOMPONENT
MICROCOMPONENTS
MICROCOMPUTER
MICROCOMPUTERS
MICROCOMPUTING
MICROCOMPUTINGS
MICROCOPIED
MICROCOPIES
MICROCOPYING
MICROCOPYINGS
MICROCOSMIC
MICROCOSMICAL
MICROCOSMICALLY
MICROCOSMOS
MICROCOSMOSES
MICROCOSMS
MICROCRACK
MICROCRACKED
MICROCRACKING
MICROCRACKINGS
MICROCRACKS
MICROCRYSTAL
MICROCRYSTALS
MICROCULTURAL
MICROCULTURE
MICROCULTURES
MICROCURIE
MICROCURIES
MICROCYTES
MICROCYTIC
MICRODETECTION
MICRODETECTIONS
MICRODETECTOR
MICRODETECTORS
MICRODISSECTION
MICRODONTOUS
MICRODRIVE
MICRODRIVES
MICRODRONE
MICRODRONES
MICROEARTHQUAKE
MICROECONOMIC
MICROECONOMICS
MICROELECTRODE
MICROELECTRODES
MICROELECTRONIC
MICROELEMENT
MICROELEMENTS
MICROEVOLUTION
MICROEVOLUTIONS
MICROFARAD
MICROFARADS
MICROFAUNA
MICROFAUNAE
MICROFAUNAL
MICROFAUNAS
MICROFELSITIC
MICROFIBER
MICROFIBERS
MICROFIBRE
MICROFIBRES
MICROFIBRIL
MICROFIBRILLAR

MICROFIBRILS
MICROFICHE
MICROFICHES
MICROFILAMENT
MICROFILAMENTS
MICROFILARIA
MICROFILARIAE
MICROFILARIAL
MICROFILING
MICROFILINGS
MICROFILMABLE
MICROFILMED
MICROFILMER
MICROFILMERS
MICROFILMING
MICROFILMS
MICROFILTER
MICROFILTERS
MICROFLOPPIES
MICROFLOPPY
MICROFLORA
MICROFLORAE
MICROFLORAL
MICROFLORAS
MICROFORMS
MICROFOSSIL
MICROFOSSILS
MICROFUNGI
MICROFUNGUS
MICROFUNGUSES
MICROGAMETE
MICROGAMETES
MICROGAMETOCYTE
MICROGENERATION
MICROGLIAS
MICROGRAMS
MICROGRANITE
MICROGRANITES
MICROGRANITIC
MICROGRAPH
MICROGRAPHED
MICROGRAPHER
MICROGRAPHERS
MICROGRAPHIC
MICROGRAPHICS
MICROGRAPHIES
MICROGRAPHING
MICROGRAPHS
MICROGRAPHY
MICROGRAVITIES
MICROGRAVITY
MICROGREENS
MICROGROOVE
MICROGROOVES
MICROHABITAT
MICROHABITATS
MICROIMAGE
MICROIMAGES
MICROINCHES
MICROINJECT
MICROINJECTED
MICROINJECTING
MICROINJECTION
MICROINJECTIONS
MICROINJECTS
MICROLIGHT
MICROLIGHTING
MICROLIGHTINGS
MICROLIGHTS
MICROLITER
MICROLITERS
MICROLITES
MICROLITHIC
MICROLITHS
MICROLITIC
MICROLITRE
MICROLITRES
MICROLOANS
MICROLOGIC
MICROLOGICAL
MICROLOGICALLY
MICROLOGIES
MICROLOGIST
MICROLOGISTS
MICROLUCES
MICROLUXES
MICROMANAGE
MICROMANAGED
MICROMANAGEMENT
MICROMANAGER
MICROMANAGERS
MICROMANAGES
MICROMANAGING
MICROMARKETING
MICROMARKETINGS
MICROMERES
MICROMESHES
MICROMETEORITE
MICROMETEORITES
MICROMETEORITIC
MICROMETEOROID
MICROMETEOROIDS
MICROMETER
MICROMETERS
MICROMETHOD
MICROMETHODS
MICROMETRE
MICROMETRES
MICROMETRIC
MICROMETRICAL
MICROMETRIES
MICROMETRY
MICROMICROCURIE
MICROMICROFARAD
MICROMILLIMETRE
MICROMINIATURE
MICROMINIS
MICROMOLAR
MICROMOLES
MICROMORPHOLOGY
MICROMORTS
MICRONATION
MICRONATIONS
MICRONEEDLE
MICRONEEDLES
MICRONISATION
MICRONISATIONS
MICRONISED
MICRONISES
MICRONISING
MICRONIZATION
MICRONIZATIONS
MICRONIZED
MICRONIZES
MICRONIZING
MICRONUCLEI
MICRONUCLEUS
MICRONUCLEUSES
MICRONUTRIENT
MICRONUTRIENTS
MICROORGANISM
MICROORGANISMS
MICROPARASITE
MICROPARASITES
MICROPARASITIC
MICROPARTICLE
MICROPARTICLES
MICROPARTIES
MICROPARTY
MICROPAYMENT
MICROPAYMENTS
MICROPEGMATITE
MICROPEGMATITES
MICROPEGMATITIC
MICROPHAGE
MICROPHAGES
MICROPHAGOUS
MICROPHONE
MICROPHONES
MICROPHONIC
MICROPHONICS
MICROPHOTOGRAPH
MICROPHOTOMETER
MICROPHOTOMETRY
MICROPHYLL
MICROPHYLLOUS
MICROPHYLLS
MICROPHYSICAL
MICROPHYSICALLY
MICROPHYSICIST
MICROPHYSICISTS
MICROPHYSICS
MICROPHYTE
MICROPHYTES
MICROPHYTIC
MICROPIPET
MICROPIPETS
MICROPIPETTE
MICROPIPETTES
MICROPLANKTON
MICROPLANKTONS
MICROPLASTIC
MICROPLASTICS
MICROPOLIS
MICROPOLISES
MICROPORES
MICROPOROSITIES
MICROPOROSITY
MICROPOROUS
MICROPOWER
MICROPOWERS
MICROPRINT
MICROPRINTED
MICROPRINTING
MICROPRINTINGS
MICROPRINTS
MICROPRISM
MICROPRISMS
MICROPROBE
MICROPROBES
MICROPROCESSING
MICROPROCESSOR
MICROPROCESSORS
MICROPROGRAM
MICROPROGRAMS
MICROPROJECTION
MICROPROJECTOR
MICROPROJECTORS
MICROPSIAS
MICROPTEROUS
MICROPUBLISHER
MICROPUBLISHERS
MICROPUBLISHING
MICROPULSATION
MICROPULSATIONS
MICROPUMPS
MICROPUNCTURE
MICROPUNCTURES
MICROPYLAR
MICROPYLES
MICROPYROMETER
MICROPYROMETERS
MICROQUAKE
MICROQUAKES
MICRORADIOGRAPH
MICROREADER
MICROREADERS
MICROSATELLITE
MICROSATELLITES
MICROSCALE
MICROSCALES
MICROSCOPE
MICROSCOPES
MICROSCOPIC
MICROSCOPICAL
MICROSCOPICALLY
MICROSCOPIES
MICROSCOPIST
MICROSCOPISTS
MICROSCOPY

M

MICROSECOND
MICROSECONDS
MICROSEISM
MICROSEISMIC
MICROSEISMICAL
MICROSEISMICITY
MICROSEISMS
MICROSITES
MICROSKIRT
MICROSKIRTS
MICROSLEEP
MICROSLEEPS
MICROSMATIC
MICROSOMAL
MICROSOMES
MICROSPECIES
MICROSPHERE
MICROSPHERES
MICROSPHERICAL
MICROSPORANGIA
MICROSPORANGIUM
MICROSPORE
MICROSPORES
MICROSPORIC
MICROSPORIDIAN
MICROSPOROCYTE
MICROSPOROCYTES
MICROSPOROPHYLL
MICROSPOROUS
MICROSTATE
MICROSTATES
MICROSTOMATOUS
MICROSTOMOUS
MICROSTRUCTURAL
MICROSTRUCTURE
MICROSTRUCTURES
MICROSURGEON
MICROSURGEONS
MICROSURGERIES
MICROSURGERY
MICROSURGICAL
MICROSWITCH
MICROSWITCHES
MICROTECHNIC
MICROTECHNICS
MICROTECHNIQUE
MICROTECHNIQUES
MICROTECHNOLOGY
MICROTOMES
MICROTOMIC
MICROTOMICAL
MICROTOMIES
MICROTOMIST
MICROTOMISTS
MICROTONAL
MICROTONALITIES
MICROTONALITY
MICROTONALLY
MICROTONES
MICROTUBES
MICROTUBULAR
MICROTUBULE
MICROTUBULES
MICROTUNNELLING
MICROVASCULAR
MICROVILLAR
MICROVILLI
MICROVILLOUS
MICROVILLUS
MICROVOLTS
MICROWATTS
MICROWAVABLE
MICROWAVEABLE
MICROWAVED
MICROWAVES
MICROWAVING
MICROWIRES
MICROWORLD
MICROWORLDS
MICROWRITER
MICROWRITERS
MICRURGIES
MICTURATED
MICTURATES
MICTURATING
MICTURITION
MICTURITIONS
MIDDELMANNETJIE
MIDDELSKOT
MIDDELSKOTS
MIDDENSTEAD
MIDDENSTEADS
MIDDLEBREAKER
MIDDLEBREAKERS
MIDDLEBROW
MIDDLEBROWED
MIDDLEBROWISM
MIDDLEBROWISMS
MIDDLEBROWS
MIDDLEBUSTER
MIDDLEBUSTERS
MIDDLEMOST
MIDDLEWARE
MIDDLEWARES
MIDDLEWEIGHT
MIDDLEWEIGHTS
MIDDLINGLY
MIDFIELDER
MIDFIELDERS
MIDIBUSSES
MIDINETTES
MIDISKIRTS
MIDLANDERS
MIDLATITUDE
MIDLATITUDES
MIDLITTORAL
MIDLITTORALS
MIDNIGHTLY
MIDRASHOTH
MIDSAGITTAL
MIDSECTION
MIDSECTIONS
MIDSHIPMAN
MIDSHIPMATE
MIDSHIPMATES
MIDSHIPMEN
MIDSTORIES
MIDSTREAMS
MIDSUMMERS
MIDWATCHES
MIDWESTERN
MIDWIFERIES
MIDWINTERS
MIFEPRISTONE
MIFEPRISTONES
MIFFINESSES
MIGHTINESS
MIGHTINESSES
MIGMATITES
MIGNONETTE
MIGNONETTES
MIGRAINEUR
MIGRAINEURS
MIGRAINOUS
MIGRATIONAL
MIGRATIONIST
MIGRATIONISTS
MIGRATIONS
MILDEWIEST
MILDNESSES
MILEOMETER
MILEOMETERS
MILESTONES
MILITANCES
MILITANCIES
MILITANTLY
MILITANTNESS
MILITANTNESSES
MILITARIES
MILITARILY
MILITARISATION
MILITARISATIONS
MILITARISE
MILITARISED
MILITARISES
MILITARISING
MILITARISM
MILITARISMS
MILITARIST
MILITARISTIC
MILITARISTS
MILITARIZATION
MILITARIZATIONS
MILITARIZE
MILITARIZED
MILITARIZES
MILITARIZING
MILITATING
MILITATION
MILITATIONS
MILITIAMAN
MILITIAMEN
MILKFISHES
MILKINESSES
MILKSHAKES
MILKSOPISM
MILKSOPISMS
MILKSOPPIER
MILKSOPPIEST
MILKSOPPING
MILKTOASTS
MILLBOARDS
MILLEFEUILLE
MILLEFEUILLES
MILLEFIORI
MILLEFIORIS
MILLEFLEUR
MILLEFLEURS
MILLENARIAN
MILLENARIANISM
MILLENARIANISMS
MILLENARIANS
MILLENARIES
MILLENARISM
MILLENARISMS
MILLENNIAL
MILLENNIALISM
MILLENNIALISMS
MILLENNIALIST
MILLENNIALISTS
MILLENNIALLY
MILLENNIALS
MILLENNIANISM
MILLENNIANISMS
MILLENNIARISM
MILLENNIARISMS
MILLENNIUM
MILLENNIUMS
MILLEPEDES
MILLEPORES
MILLERITES
MILLESIMAL
MILLESIMALLY
MILLESIMALS
MILLHOUSES
MILLIAMPERE
MILLIAMPERES
MILLIARIES
MILLICURIE
MILLICURIES
MILLIDEGREE
MILLIDEGREES
MILLIGRAMME
MILLIGRAMMES
MILLIGRAMS
MILLIHENRIES
MILLIHENRY
MILLIHENRYS
MILLILAMBERT
MILLILAMBERTS

MILLILITER
MILLILITERS
MILLILITRE
MILLILITRES
MILLILUCES
MILLILUXES
MILLIMETER
MILLIMETERS
MILLIMETRE
MILLIMETRES
MILLIMICRON
MILLIMICRONS
MILLIMOLAR
MILLIMOLES
MILLINERIES
MILLIONAIRE
MILLIONAIRES
MILLIONAIRESS
MILLIONAIRESSES
MILLIONARY
MILLIONFOLD
MILLIONNAIRE
MILLIONNAIRES
MILLIONNAIRESS
MILLIONTHS
MILLIOSMOL
MILLIOSMOLS
MILLIPEDES
MILLIPROBE
MILLIPROBES
MILLIRADIAN
MILLIRADIANS
MILLIROENTGEN
MILLIROENTGENS
MILLISECOND
MILLISECONDS
MILLISIEVERT
MILLISIEVERTS
MILLIVOLTS
MILLIWATTS
MILLOCRACIES
MILLOCRACY
MILLOCRATS
MILLSCALES
MILLSTONES
MILLSTREAM
MILLSTREAMS
MILLWHEELS
MILLWRIGHT
MILLWRIGHTS
MILOMETERS
MILQUETOAST
MILQUETOASTS
MIMEOGRAPH
MIMEOGRAPHED
MIMEOGRAPHING
MIMEOGRAPHS
MIMETICALLY
MIMIVIRUSES
MIMMICKING
MIMOGRAPHER
MIMOGRAPHERS
MIMOGRAPHIES
MIMOGRAPHY
MIMOSACEOUS
MINACIOUSLY
MINACITIES
MINATORIAL
MINATORIALLY
MINATORILY
MINAUDERIE
MINAUDERIES
MINAUDIERE
MINAUDIERES
MINCEMEATS
MINDBLOWER
MINDBLOWERS
MINDEDNESS
MINDEDNESSES
MINDFULNESS
MINDFULNESSES
MINDLESSLY
MINDLESSNESS
MINDLESSNESSES
MINDSCAPES
MINDSHARES
MINEFIELDS
MINEHUNTER
MINEHUNTERS
MINELAYERS
MINELAYING
MINELAYINGS
MINERALISABLE
MINERALISATION
MINERALISATIONS
MINERALISE
MINERALISED
MINERALISER
MINERALISERS
MINERALISES
MINERALISING
MINERALIST
MINERALISTS
MINERALIZABLE
MINERALIZATION
MINERALIZATIONS
MINERALIZE
MINERALIZED
MINERALIZER
MINERALIZERS
MINERALIZES
MINERALIZING
MINERALOGIC
MINERALOGICAL
MINERALOGICALLY
MINERALOGIES
MINERALOGISE
MINERALOGISED
MINERALOGISES
MINERALOGISING
MINERALOGIST
MINERALOGISTS
MINERALOGIZE
MINERALOGIZED
MINERALOGIZES
MINERALOGIZING
MINERALOGY
MINESHAFTS
MINESTONES
MINESTRONE
MINESTRONES
MINESWEEPER
MINESWEEPERS
MINESWEEPING
MINESWEEPINGS
MINEWORKER
MINEWORKERS
MINGIMINGI
MINGIMINGIS
MINGINESSES
MINGLEMENT
MINGLEMENTS
MINGLINGLY
MINIATIONS
MINIATURED
MINIATURES
MINIATURING
MINIATURISATION
MINIATURISE
MINIATURISED
MINIATURISES
MINIATURISING
MINIATURIST
MINIATURISTIC
MINIATURISTS
MINIATURIZATION
MINIATURIZE
MINIATURIZED
MINIATURIZES
MINIATURIZING
MINIBIKERS
MINIBREAKS
MINIBUDGET
MINIBUDGETS
MINIBUSSES
MINICABBING
MINICABBINGS
MINICALCULATOR
MINICALCULATORS
MINICASSETTE
MINICASSETTES
MINICOMPUTER
MINICOMPUTERS
MINICOURSE
MINICOURSES
MINIDISHES
MINIDRESSES
MINIFICATION
MINIFICATIONS
MINIFLOPPIES
MINIFLOPPY
MINIMALISM
MINIMALISMS
MINIMALIST
MINIMALISTIC
MINIMALISTS
MINIMARKET
MINIMARKETS
MINIMAXING
MINIMISATION
MINIMISATIONS
MINIMISERS
MINIMISING
MINIMIZATION
MINIMIZATIONS
MINIMIZERS
MINIMIZING
MINIRUGBIES
MINISCHOOL
MINISCHOOLS
MINISCULES
MINISERIES
MINISKIRTED
MINISKIRTS
MINISTATES
MINISTERED
MINISTERIA
MINISTERIAL
MINISTERIALIST
MINISTERIALISTS
MINISTERIALLY
MINISTERING
MINISTERIUM
MINISTERSHIP
MINISTERSHIPS
MINISTRANT
MINISTRANTS
MINISTRATION
MINISTRATIONS
MINISTRATIVE
MINISTRESS
MINISTRESSES
MINISTRIES
MINISTROKE
MINISTROKES
MINISYSTEM
MINISYSTEMS
MINITOWERS
MINITRACKS
MINIVOLLEY
MINIVOLLEYS
MINNESINGER
MINNESINGERS
MINNICKING
MINNOCKING
MINORITAIRE
MINORITAIRES
MINORITIES
MINORSHIPS
MINOXIDILS

MINSTRELSIES
MINSTRELSY
MINUSCULAR
MINUSCULES
MINUTENESS
MINUTENESSES
MIRABELLES
MIRABILISES
MIRACIDIAL
MIRACIDIUM
MIRACULOUS
MIRACULOUSLY
MIRACULOUSNESS
MIRANDISED
MIRANDISES
MIRANDISING
MIRANDIZED
MIRANDIZES
MIRANDIZING
MIRIFICALLY
MIRINESSES
MIRKINESSES
MIRRORINGS
MIRRORLIKE
MIRRORWISE
MIRTHFULLY
MIRTHFULNESS
MIRTHFULNESSES
MIRTHLESSLY
MIRTHLESSNESS
MIRTHLESSNESSES
MISACCEPTATION
MISACCEPTATIONS
MISADAPTED
MISADAPTING
MISADDRESS
MISADDRESSED
MISADDRESSES
MISADDRESSING
MISADJUSTED
MISADJUSTING
MISADJUSTS
MISADVENTURE
MISADVENTURED
MISADVENTURER
MISADVENTURERS
MISADVENTURES
MISADVENTUROUS
MISADVERTENCE
MISADVERTENCES
MISADVICES
MISADVISED
MISADVISEDLY
MISADVISEDNESS
MISADVISES
MISADVISING
MISALIGNED
MISALIGNING
MISALIGNMENT
MISALIGNMENTS
MISALLEGED
MISALLEGES
MISALLEGING
MISALLIANCE
MISALLIANCES
MISALLOCATE
MISALLOCATED
MISALLOCATES
MISALLOCATING
MISALLOCATION
MISALLOCATIONS
MISALLOTMENT
MISALLOTMENTS
MISALLOTTED
MISALLOTTING
MISALLYING
MISALTERED
MISALTERING
MISANALYSES
MISANALYSIS
MISANDRIES
MISANDRIST
MISANDRISTS
MISANDROUS
MISANTHROPE
MISANTHROPES
MISANTHROPIC
MISANTHROPICAL
MISANTHROPIES
MISANTHROPIST
MISANTHROPISTS
MISANTHROPOS
MISANTHROPOSES
MISANTHROPY
MISAPPLICATION
MISAPPLICATIONS
MISAPPLIED
MISAPPLIES
MISAPPLYING
MISAPPRAISAL
MISAPPRAISALS
MISAPPRECIATE
MISAPPRECIATED
MISAPPRECIATES
MISAPPRECIATING
MISAPPRECIATION
MISAPPRECIATIVE
MISAPPREHEND
MISAPPREHENDED
MISAPPREHENDING
MISAPPREHENDS
MISAPPREHENSION
MISAPPREHENSIVE
MISAPPROPRIATE
MISAPPROPRIATED
MISAPPROPRIATES
MISARRANGE
MISARRANGED
MISARRANGEMENT
MISARRANGEMENTS
MISARRANGES
MISARRANGING
MISARTICULATE
MISARTICULATED
MISARTICULATES
MISARTICULATING
MISASSAYED
MISASSAYING
MISASSEMBLE
MISASSEMBLED
MISASSEMBLES
MISASSEMBLING
MISASSIGNED
MISASSIGNING
MISASSIGNS
MISASSUMED
MISASSUMES
MISASSUMING
MISASSUMPTION
MISASSUMPTIONS
MISATONING
MISATTRIBUTE
MISATTRIBUTED
MISATTRIBUTES
MISATTRIBUTING
MISATTRIBUTION
MISATTRIBUTIONS
MISAUNTERS
MISAVERRED
MISAVERRING
MISAWARDED
MISAWARDING
MISBALANCE
MISBALANCED
MISBALANCES
MISBALANCING
MISBECOMES
MISBECOMING
MISBECOMINGNESS
MISBEGINNING
MISBEGOTTEN
MISBEHAVED
MISBEHAVER
MISBEHAVERS
MISBEHAVES
MISBEHAVING
MISBEHAVIOR
MISBEHAVIORS
MISBEHAVIOUR
MISBEHAVIOURS
MISBELIEFS
MISBELIEVE
MISBELIEVED
MISBELIEVER
MISBELIEVERS
MISBELIEVES
MISBELIEVING
MISBESEEMED
MISBESEEMING
MISBESEEMS
MISBESTOWAL
MISBESTOWALS
MISBESTOWED
MISBESTOWING
MISBESTOWS
MISBIASING
MISBIASSED
MISBIASSES
MISBIASSING
MISBILLING
MISBINDING
MISBRANDED
MISBRANDING
MISBUILDING
MISBUTTONED
MISBUTTONING
MISBUTTONS
MISCALCULATE
MISCALCULATED
MISCALCULATES
MISCALCULATING
MISCALCULATION
MISCALCULATIONS
MISCALCULATOR
MISCALCULATORS
MISCALLERS
MISCALLING
MISCANTHUS
MISCANTHUSES
MISCAPTION
MISCAPTIONED
MISCAPTIONING
MISCAPTIONS
MISCARRIAGE
MISCARRIAGES
MISCARRIED
MISCARRIES
MISCARRYING
MISCASTING
MISCATALOG
MISCATALOGED
MISCATALOGING
MISCATALOGS
MISCEGENATE
MISCEGENATED
MISCEGENATES
MISCEGENATING
MISCEGENATION
MISCEGENATIONAL
MISCEGENATIONS
MISCEGENATOR
MISCEGENATORS
MISCEGENES
MISCEGENETIC
MISCEGENIST
MISCEGENISTS
MISCEGINES
MISCELLANARIAN
MISCELLANARIANS
MISCELLANEA

MISCELLANEOUS
MISCELLANEOUSLY
MISCELLANIES
MISCELLANIST
MISCELLANISTS
MISCELLANY
MISCHALLENGE
MISCHALLENGES
MISCHANCED
MISCHANCEFUL
MISCHANCES
MISCHANCIER
MISCHANCIEST
MISCHANCING
MISCHANNEL
MISCHANNELED
MISCHANNELING
MISCHANNELLED
MISCHANNELLING
MISCHANNELS
MISCHANTER
MISCHANTERS
MISCHARACTERISE
MISCHARACTERIZE
MISCHARGED
MISCHARGES
MISCHARGING
MISCHIEFED
MISCHIEFING
MISCHIEVOUS
MISCHIEVOUSLY
MISCHIEVOUSNESS
MISCHMETAL
MISCHMETALS
MISCHOICES
MISCHOOSES
MISCHOOSING
MISCIBILITIES
MISCIBILITY
MISCITATION
MISCITATIONS
MISCLAIMED
MISCLAIMING
MISCLASSED
MISCLASSES
MISCLASSIFIED
MISCLASSIFIES
MISCLASSIFY
MISCLASSIFYING
MISCLASSING
MISCOINING
MISCOLORED
MISCOLORING
MISCOLOURED
MISCOLOURING
MISCOLOURS
MISCOMPREHEND
MISCOMPREHENDED
MISCOMPREHENDS
MISCOMPUTATION
MISCOMPUTATIONS
MISCOMPUTE
MISCOMPUTED
MISCOMPUTES
MISCOMPUTING
MISCONCEIT
MISCONCEITED
MISCONCEITING
MISCONCEITS
MISCONCEIVE
MISCONCEIVED
MISCONCEIVER
MISCONCEIVERS
MISCONCEIVES
MISCONCEIVING
MISCONCEPTION
MISCONCEPTIONS
MISCONDUCT
MISCONDUCTED
MISCONDUCTING
MISCONDUCTS
MISCONJECTURE
MISCONJECTURED
MISCONJECTURES
MISCONJECTURING
MISCONNECT
MISCONNECTED
MISCONNECTING
MISCONNECTION
MISCONNECTIONS
MISCONNECTS
MISCONSTER
MISCONSTERED
MISCONSTERING
MISCONSTERS
MISCONSTRUCT
MISCONSTRUCTED
MISCONSTRUCTING
MISCONSTRUCTION
MISCONSTRUCTS
MISCONSTRUE
MISCONSTRUED
MISCONSTRUES
MISCONSTRUING
MISCONTENT
MISCONTENTED
MISCONTENTING
MISCONTENTMENT
MISCONTENTMENTS
MISCONTENTS
MISCOOKING
MISCOPYING
MISCORRECT
MISCORRECTED
MISCORRECTING
MISCORRECTION
MISCORRECTIONS
MISCORRECTS
MISCORRELATION
MISCORRELATIONS
MISCOUNSEL
MISCOUNSELLED
MISCOUNSELLING
MISCOUNSELLINGS
MISCOUNSELS
MISCOUNTED
MISCOUNTING
MISCREANCE
MISCREANCES
MISCREANCIES
MISCREANCY
MISCREANTS
MISCREATED
MISCREATES
MISCREATING
MISCREATION
MISCREATIONS
MISCREATIVE
MISCREATOR
MISCREATORS
MISCREAUNCE
MISCREAUNCES
MISCREDITED
MISCREDITING
MISCREDITS
MISCUTTING
MISDEALERS
MISDEALING
MISDEEMFUL
MISDEEMING
MISDEEMINGS
MISDEFINED
MISDEFINES
MISDEFINING
MISDEMEANANT
MISDEMEANANTS
MISDEMEANED
MISDEMEANING
MISDEMEANOR
MISDEMEANORS
MISDEMEANOUR
MISDEMEANOURS
MISDEMEANS
MISDESCRIBE
MISDESCRIBED
MISDESCRIBES
MISDESCRIBING
MISDESCRIPTION
MISDESCRIPTIONS
MISDESERTS
MISDEVELOP
MISDEVELOPED
MISDEVELOPING
MISDEVELOPS
MISDEVOTION
MISDEVOTIONS
MISDIAGNOSE
MISDIAGNOSED
MISDIAGNOSES
MISDIAGNOSING
MISDIAGNOSIS
MISDIALING
MISDIALLED
MISDIALLING
MISDIETING
MISDIGHTED
MISDIGHTING
MISDIRECTED
MISDIRECTING
MISDIRECTION
MISDIRECTIONS
MISDIRECTS
MISDISTRIBUTION
MISDIVIDED
MISDIVIDES
MISDIVIDING
MISDIVISION
MISDIVISIONS
MISDOUBTED
MISDOUBTFUL
MISDOUBTING
MISDRAWING
MISDRAWINGS
MISDREADED
MISDREADING
MISDRIVING
MISEDITING
MISEDUCATE
MISEDUCATED
MISEDUCATES
MISEDUCATING
MISEDUCATION
MISEDUCATIONS
MISEMPHASES
MISEMPHASIS
MISEMPHASISE
MISEMPHASISED
MISEMPHASISES
MISEMPHASISING
MISEMPHASIZE
MISEMPHASIZED
MISEMPHASIZES
MISEMPHASIZING
MISEMPLOYED
MISEMPLOYING
MISEMPLOYMENT
MISEMPLOYMENTS
MISEMPLOYS
MISENROLLED
MISENROLLING
MISENROLLS
MISENTERED
MISENTERING
MISENTREAT
MISENTREATED
MISENTREATING
MISENTREATS
MISENTRIES
MISERABILISM
MISERABILISMS

M

MISERABILIST
MISERABILISTS
MISERABLENESS
MISERABLENESSES
MISERABLES
MISERABLISM
MISERABLISMS
MISERABLIST
MISERABLISTS
MISERICORD
MISERICORDE
MISERICORDES
MISERICORDS
MISERLIEST
MISERLINESS
MISERLINESSES
MISESTEEMED
MISESTEEMING
MISESTEEMS
MISESTIMATE
MISESTIMATED
MISESTIMATES
MISESTIMATING
MISESTIMATION
MISESTIMATIONS
MISEVALUATE
MISEVALUATED
MISEVALUATES
MISEVALUATING
MISEVALUATION
MISEVALUATIONS
MISFALLING
MISFARINGS
MISFEASANCE
MISFEASANCES
MISFEASORS
MISFEATURE
MISFEATURED
MISFEATURES
MISFEATURING
MISFEEDING
MISFEIGNED
MISFEIGNING
MISFIELDED
MISFIELDING
MISFITTING
MISFOCUSED
MISFOCUSES
MISFOCUSING
MISFOCUSSED
MISFOCUSSES
MISFOCUSSING
MISFOLDING
MISFORMATION
MISFORMATIONS
MISFORMING
MISFORTUNE
MISFORTUNED
MISFORTUNES
MISFRAMING
MISFUNCTION
MISFUNCTIONED
MISFUNCTIONING
MISFUNCTIONS
MISGAUGING
MISGENDERED
MISGENDERING
MISGENDERS
MISGIVINGS
MISGOVERNANCE
MISGOVERNANCES
MISGOVERNAUNCE
MISGOVERNAUNCES
MISGOVERNED
MISGOVERNING
MISGOVERNMENT
MISGOVERNMENTS
MISGOVERNOR
MISGOVERNORS
MISGOVERNS
MISGRADING
MISGRAFTED
MISGRAFTING
MISGROWING
MISGROWTHS
MISGUESSED
MISGUESSES
MISGUESSING
MISGUGGLED
MISGUGGLES
MISGUGGLING
MISGUIDANCE
MISGUIDANCES
MISGUIDEDLY
MISGUIDEDNESS
MISGUIDEDNESSES
MISGUIDERS
MISGUIDING
MISHALLOWED
MISHANDLED
MISHANDLES
MISHANDLING
MISHANDLINGS
MISHANTERS
MISHAPPENED
MISHAPPENING
MISHAPPENS
MISHAPPING
MISHEARING
MISHEGAASEN
MISHGUGGLE
MISHGUGGLED
MISHGUGGLES
MISHGUGGLING
MISHITTING
MISHMASHES
MISHMOSHES
MISHUGASES
MISIDENTIFIED
MISIDENTIFIES
MISIDENTIFY
MISIDENTIFYING
MISIMPRESSION
MISIMPRESSIONS
MISIMPROVE
MISIMPROVED
MISIMPROVEMENT
MISIMPROVEMENTS
MISIMPROVES
MISIMPROVING
MISINFERRED
MISINFERRING
MISINFORMANT
MISINFORMANTS
MISINFORMATION
MISINFORMATIONS
MISINFORMED
MISINFORMER
MISINFORMERS
MISINFORMING
MISINFORMS
MISINSTRUCT
MISINSTRUCTED
MISINSTRUCTING
MISINSTRUCTION
MISINSTRUCTIONS
MISINSTRUCTS
MISINTELLIGENCE
MISINTENDED
MISINTENDING
MISINTENDS
MISINTERPRET
MISINTERPRETED
MISINTERPRETER
MISINTERPRETERS
MISINTERPRETING
MISINTERPRETS
MISINTERRED
MISINTERRING
MISJOINDER
MISJOINDERS
MISJOINING
MISJUDGEMENT
MISJUDGEMENTS
MISJUDGERS
MISJUDGING
MISJUDGMENT
MISJUDGMENTS
MISKEEPING
MISKENNING
MISKICKING
MISKNOWING
MISKNOWLEDGE
MISKNOWLEDGES
MISLABELED
MISLABELING
MISLABELLED
MISLABELLING
MISLABORED
MISLABORING
MISLABOURED
MISLABOURING
MISLABOURS
MISLEADERS
MISLEADING
MISLEADINGLY
MISLEARNED
MISLEARNING
MISLEEKING
MISLIGHTED
MISLIGHTING
MISLIKINGS
MISLIPPENED
MISLIPPENING
MISLIPPENS
MISLOCATED
MISLOCATES
MISLOCATING
MISLOCATION
MISLOCATIONS
MISLODGING
MISLUCKING
MISMANAGED
MISMANAGEMENT
MISMANAGEMENTS
MISMANAGER
MISMANAGERS
MISMANAGES
MISMANAGING
MISMANNERS
MISMARKING
MISMARRIAGE
MISMARRIAGES
MISMARRIED
MISMARRIES
MISMARRYING
MISMATCHED
MISMATCHES
MISMATCHING
MISMATCHMENT
MISMATCHMENTS
MISMATINGS
MISMEASURE
MISMEASURED
MISMEASUREMENT
MISMEASUREMENTS
MISMEASURES
MISMEASURING
MISMEETING
MISMETRING
MISNOMERED
MISNOMERING
MISNUMBERED
MISNUMBERING
MISNUMBERS
MISOBSERVANCE
MISOBSERVANCES
MISOBSERVE
MISOBSERVED
MISOBSERVES

MISOBSERVING
MISOCAPNIC
MISOGAMIES
MISOGAMIST
MISOGAMISTS
MISOGYNIES
MISOGYNIST
MISOGYNISTIC
MISOGYNISTICAL
MISOGYNISTS
MISOGYNOUS
MISOLOGIES
MISOLOGIST
MISOLOGISTS
MISONEISMS
MISONEISTIC
MISONEISTS
MISORDERED
MISORDERING
MISORIENTATION
MISORIENTATIONS
MISORIENTED
MISORIENTING
MISORIENTS
MISPACKAGE
MISPACKAGED
MISPACKAGES
MISPACKAGING
MISPAINTED
MISPAINTING
MISPARSING
MISPARTING
MISPATCHED
MISPATCHES
MISPATCHING
MISPENNING
MISPERCEIVE
MISPERCEIVED
MISPERCEIVES
MISPERCEIVING
MISPERCEPTION
MISPERCEPTIONS
MISPERSUADE
MISPERSUADED
MISPERSUADES
MISPERSUADING
MISPERSUASION
MISPERSUASIONS
MISPHRASED
MISPHRASES
MISPHRASING
MISPICKELS
MISPLACEMENT
MISPLACEMENTS
MISPLACING
MISPLANNED
MISPLANNING
MISPLANTED
MISPLANTING
MISPLAYING
MISPLEADED
MISPLEADING
MISPLEADINGS
MISPLEASED
MISPLEASES
MISPLEASING
MISPOINTED
MISPOINTING
MISPOISING
MISPOSITION
MISPOSITIONED
MISPOSITIONING
MISPOSITIONS
MISPRAISED
MISPRAISES
MISPRAISING
MISPRICING
MISPRINTED
MISPRINTING
MISPRISING
MISPRISION
MISPRISIONS
MISPRIZERS
MISPRIZING
MISPROGRAM
MISPROGRAMED
MISPROGRAMING
MISPROGRAMMED
MISPROGRAMMING
MISPROGRAMS
MISPRONOUNCE
MISPRONOUNCED
MISPRONOUNCES
MISPRONOUNCING
MISPROPORTION
MISPROPORTIONED
MISPROPORTIONS
MISPUNCTUATE
MISPUNCTUATED
MISPUNCTUATES
MISPUNCTUATING
MISPUNCTUATION
MISPUNCTUATIONS
MISQUOTATION
MISQUOTATIONS
MISQUOTERS
MISQUOTING
MISRAISING
MISREADING
MISREADINGS
MISRECKONED
MISRECKONING
MISRECKONINGS
MISRECKONS
MISRECOLLECTION
MISRECORDED
MISRECORDING
MISRECORDS
MISREFERENCE
MISREFERENCED
MISREFERENCES
MISREFERENCING
MISREFERRED
MISREFERRING
MISREGARDED
MISREGARDING
MISREGARDS
MISREGISTER
MISREGISTERED
MISREGISTERING
MISREGISTERS
MISREGISTRATION
MISRELATED
MISRELATES
MISRELATING
MISRELATION
MISRELATIONS
MISRELYING
MISREMEMBER
MISREMEMBERED
MISREMEMBERING
MISREMEMBERS
MISRENDERED
MISRENDERING
MISRENDERS
MISREPORTED
MISREPORTER
MISREPORTERS
MISREPORTING
MISREPORTS
MISREPRESENT
MISREPRESENTED
MISREPRESENTER
MISREPRESENTERS
MISREPRESENTING
MISREPRESENTS
MISROUTEING
MISROUTING
MISSAYINGS
MISSEATING
MISSEEMING
MISSEEMINGS
MISSELLING
MISSELLINGS
MISSENDING
MISSENSING
MISSETTING
MISSHAPENLY
MISSHAPENNESS
MISSHAPENNESSES
MISSHAPERS
MISSHAPING
MISSHEATHED
MISSILEERS
MISSILEMAN
MISSILEMEN
MISSILERIES
MISSILRIES
MISSIOLOGIES
MISSIOLOGY
MISSIONARIES
MISSIONARISE
MISSIONARISED
MISSIONARISES
MISSIONARISING
MISSIONARIZE
MISSIONARIZED
MISSIONARIZES
MISSIONARIZING
MISSIONARY
MISSIONERS
MISSIONING
MISSIONISATION
MISSIONISATIONS
MISSIONISE
MISSIONISED
MISSIONISER
MISSIONISERS
MISSIONISES
MISSIONISING
MISSIONIZATION
MISSIONIZATIONS
MISSIONIZE
MISSIONIZED
MISSIONIZER
MISSIONIZERS
MISSIONIZES
MISSIONIZING
MISSISHNESS
MISSISHNESSES
MISSORTING
MISSOUNDED
MISSOUNDING
MISSPACING
MISSPEAKING
MISSPELLED
MISSPELLING
MISSPELLINGS
MISSPENDER
MISSPENDERS
MISSPENDING
MISSTAMPED
MISSTAMPING
MISSTARTED
MISSTARTING
MISSTATEMENT
MISSTATEMENTS
MISSTATING
MISSTEERED
MISSTEERING
MISSTEPPED
MISSTEPPING
MISSTOPPED
MISSTOPPING
MISSTRICKEN
MISSTRIKES
MISSTRIKING
MISSTYLING
MISSUITING
MISSUMMATION

MISSUMMATIONS
MISTAKABLE
MISTAKABLY
MISTAKEABLE
MISTAKEABLY
MISTAKENLY
MISTAKENNESS
MISTAKENNESSES
MISTAKINGS
MISTEACHES
MISTEACHING
MISTELLING
MISTEMPERED
MISTEMPERING
MISTEMPERS
MISTENDING
MISTERMING
MISTHINKING
MISTHOUGHT
MISTHOUGHTS
MISTHROWING
MISTIGRISES
MISTIMINGS
MISTINESSES
MISTITLING
MISTLETOES
MISTOUCHED
MISTOUCHES
MISTOUCHING
MISTRACING
MISTRAINED
MISTRAINING
MISTRANSCRIBE
MISTRANSCRIBED
MISTRANSCRIBES
MISTRANSCRIBING
MISTRANSLATE
MISTRANSLATED
MISTRANSLATES
MISTRANSLATING
MISTRANSLATION
MISTRANSLATIONS
MISTRAYNED
MISTREADING
MISTREADINGS
MISTREATED
MISTREATING
MISTREATMENT
MISTREATMENTS
MISTRESSED
MISTRESSES
MISTRESSING
MISTRESSLESS
MISTRESSLIER
MISTRESSLIEST
MISTRESSLY
MISTRUSTED
MISTRUSTER
MISTRUSTERS
MISTRUSTFUL
MISTRUSTFULLY
MISTRUSTFULNESS
MISTRUSTING
MISTRUSTINGLY
MISTRUSTLESS
MISTRYSTED
MISTRYSTING
MISTUTORED
MISTUTORING
MISUNDERSTAND
MISUNDERSTANDS
MISUNDERSTOOD
MISUTILISATION
MISUTILISATIONS
MISUTILIZATION
MISUTILIZATIONS
MISVALUING
MISVENTURE
MISVENTURES
MISVENTUROUS
MISVOCALISATION
MISVOCALIZATION
MISWANDRED
MISWEENING
MISWENDING
MISWORDING
MISWORDINGS
MISWORSHIP
MISWORSHIPPED
MISWORSHIPPING
MISWORSHIPPINGS
MISWORSHIPS
MISWRITING
MISWRITTEN
MITERWORTS
MITHRADATIC
MITHRIDATE
MITHRIDATES
MITHRIDATIC
MITHRIDATISE
MITHRIDATISED
MITHRIDATISES
MITHRIDATISING
MITHRIDATISM
MITHRIDATISMS
MITHRIDATIZE
MITHRIDATIZED
MITHRIDATIZES
MITHRIDATIZING
MITIGATING
MITIGATION
MITIGATIONS
MITIGATIVE
MITIGATIVES
MITIGATORS
MITIGATORY
MITOCHONDRIA
MITOCHONDRIAL
MITOCHONDRION
MITOGENETIC
MITOGENICITIES
MITOGENICITY
MITOMYCINS
MITOTICALLY
MITRAILLES
MITRAILLEUR
MITRAILLEURS
MITRAILLEUSE
MITRAILLEUSES
MITREWORTS
MITTIMUSES
MIXABILITIES
MIXABILITY
MIXEDNESSES
MIXMASTERS
MIXOBARBARIC
MIXOLOGIES
MIXOLOGIST
MIXOLOGISTS
MIXOLYDIAN
MIXOTROPHIC
MIZENMASTS
MIZZENMAST
MIZZENMASTS
MIZZONITES
MNEMONICAL
MNEMONICALLY
MNEMONISTS
MNEMOTECHNIC
MNEMOTECHNICS
MNEMOTECHNIST
MNEMOTECHNISTS
MOBCASTING
MOBCASTINGS
MOBILISABLE
MOBILISATION
MOBILISATIONS
MOBILISERS
MOBILISING
MOBILITIES
MOBILIZABLE
MOBILIZATION
MOBILIZATIONS
MOBILIZERS
MOBILIZING
MOBLOGGERS
MOBOCRACIES
MOBOCRATIC
MOBOCRATICAL
MOCHINESSES
MOCKERNUTS
MOCKINGBIRD
MOCKINGBIRDS
MOCKUMENTARIES
MOCKUMENTARY
MODAFINILS
MODALISTIC
MODALITIES
MODELLINGS
MODELLISTS
MODERATELY
MODERATENESS
MODERATENESSES
MODERATING
MODERATION
MODERATIONS
MODERATISM
MODERATISMS
MODERATORS
MODERATORSHIP
MODERATORSHIPS
MODERATRICES
MODERATRIX
MODERATRIXES
MODERNISATION
MODERNISATIONS
MODERNISED
MODERNISER
MODERNISERS
MODERNISES
MODERNISING
MODERNISMS
MODERNISTIC
MODERNISTICALLY
MODERNISTS
MODERNITIES
MODERNIZATION
MODERNIZATIONS
MODERNIZED
MODERNIZER
MODERNIZERS
MODERNIZES
MODERNIZING
MODERNNESS
MODERNNESSES
MODIFIABILITIES
MODIFIABILITY
MODIFIABLE
MODIFIABLENESS
MODIFICATION
MODIFICATIONS
MODIFICATIVE
MODIFICATORY
MODILLIONS
MODISHNESS
MODISHNESSES
MODULABILITIES
MODULABILITY
MODULARISED
MODULARITIES
MODULARITY
MODULARIZED
MODULATING
MODULATION
MODULATIONS
MODULATIVE
MODULATORS
MODULATORY
MOISTENERS
MOISTENING

MOISTIFIED
MOISTIFIES
MOISTIFYING
MOISTNESSES
MOISTURELESS
MOISTURISE
MOISTURISED
MOISTURISER
MOISTURISERS
MOISTURISES
MOISTURISING
MOISTURIZE
MOISTURIZED
MOISTURIZER
MOISTURIZERS
MOISTURIZES
MOISTURIZING
MOITHERING
MOLALITIES
MOLARITIES
MOLASSESES
MOLDABILITIES
MOLDABILITY
MOLDAVITES
MOLDBOARDS
MOLDINESSES
MOLECATCHER
MOLECATCHERS
MOLECULARITIES
MOLECULARITY
MOLECULARLY
MOLENDINAR
MOLENDINARIES
MOLENDINARS
MOLENDINARY
MOLESTATION
MOLESTATIONS
MOLIMINOUS
MOLLIFIABLE
MOLLIFICATION
MOLLIFICATIONS
MOLLIFIERS
MOLLIFYING
MOLLITIOUS
MOLLUSCANS
MOLLUSCICIDAL
MOLLUSCICIDE
MOLLUSCICIDES
MOLLUSCOID
MOLLUSCOIDAL
MOLLUSCOIDS
MOLLUSCOUS
MOLLUSKANS
MOLLYCODDLE
MOLLYCODDLED
MOLLYCODDLER
MOLLYCODDLERS
MOLLYCODDLES
MOLLYCODDLING
MOLLYCODDLINGS
MOLLYHAWKS
MOLLYMAWKS
MOLOCHISED
MOLOCHISES
MOLOCHISING
MOLOCHIZED
MOLOCHIZES
MOLOCHIZING
MOLYBDATES
MOLYBDENITE
MOLYBDENITES
MOLYBDENOSES
MOLYBDENOSIS
MOLYBDENOUS
MOLYBDENUM
MOLYBDENUMS
MOLYBDOSES
MOLYBDOSIS
MOMENTANEOUS
MOMENTARILY
MOMENTARINESS
MOMENTARINESSES
MOMENTOUSLY
MOMENTOUSNESS
MOMENTOUSNESSES
MOMPRENEUR
MOMPRENEURS
MONACHISMS
MONACHISTS
MONACTINAL
MONACTINES
MONADELPHOUS
MONADICALLY
MONADIFORM
MONADISTIC
MONADNOCKS
MONADOLOGIES
MONADOLOGY
MONANDRIES
MONANDROUS
MONANTHOUS
MONARCHALLY
MONARCHIAL
MONARCHICAL
MONARCHICALLY
MONARCHIES
MONARCHISE
MONARCHISED
MONARCHISES
MONARCHISING
MONARCHISM
MONARCHISMS
MONARCHIST
MONARCHISTIC
MONARCHISTS
MONARCHIZE
MONARCHIZED
MONARCHIZES
MONARCHIZING
MONASTERIAL
MONASTERIES
MONASTICAL
MONASTICALLY
MONASTICISM
MONASTICISMS
MONAURALLY
MONCHIQUITE
MONCHIQUITES
MONDEGREEN
MONDEGREENS
MONECIOUSLY
MONERGISMS
MONESTROUS
MONETARILY
MONETARISM
MONETARISMS
MONETARIST
MONETARISTS
MONETISATION
MONETISATIONS
MONETISING
MONETIZATION
MONETIZATIONS
MONETIZING
MONEYBELTS
MONEYBOXES
MONEYCHANGER
MONEYCHANGERS
MONEYGRUBBING
MONEYGRUBBINGS
MONEYLENDER
MONEYLENDERS
MONEYLENDING
MONEYLENDINGS
MONEYMAKER
MONEYMAKERS
MONEYMAKING
MONEYMAKINGS
MONEYSPINNING
MONEYWORTS
MONGERINGS
MONGOLISMS
MONGOLOIDS
MONGRELISATION
MONGRELISATIONS
MONGRELISE
MONGRELISED
MONGRELISER
MONGRELISERS
MONGRELISES
MONGRELISING
MONGRELISM
MONGRELISMS
MONGRELIZATION
MONGRELIZATIONS
MONGRELIZE
MONGRELIZED
MONGRELIZER
MONGRELIZERS
MONGRELIZES
MONGRELIZING
MONGRELLIER
MONGRELLIEST
MONILIASES
MONILIASIS
MONILIFORM
MONISTICAL
MONISTICALLY
MONITORIAL
MONITORIALLY
MONITORIES
MONITORING
MONITORINGS
MONITORSHIP
MONITORSHIPS
MONITRESSES
MONKEYGLAND
MONKEYISMS
MONKEYPODS
MONKEYPOTS
MONKEYPOXES
MONKEYSHINE
MONKEYSHINES
MONKFISHES
MONKISHNESS
MONKISHNESSES
MONKSHOODS
MONOACIDIC
MONOAMINERGIC
MONOAMINES
MONOATOMIC
MONOBLEPSES
MONOBLEPSIS
MONOCARBOXYLIC
MONOCARDIAN
MONOCARDIANS
MONOCARPELLARY
MONOCARPIC
MONOCARPOUS
MONOCEROSES
MONOCEROUS
MONOCHASIA
MONOCHASIAL
MONOCHASIUM
MONOCHLAMYDEOUS
MONOCHLORIDE
MONOCHLORIDES
MONOCHORDS
MONOCHROIC
MONOCHROICS
MONOCHROMASIES
MONOCHROMASY
MONOCHROMAT
MONOCHROMATE
MONOCHROMATES
MONOCHROMATIC
MONOCHROMATICS
MONOCHROMATISM
MONOCHROMATISMS
MONOCHROMATOR

MONOCHROMATORS
MONOCHROMATS
MONOCHROME
MONOCHROMES
MONOCHROMIC
MONOCHROMICAL
MONOCHROMIES
MONOCHROMIST
MONOCHROMISTS
MONOCHROMY
MONOCLINAL
MONOCLINALLY
MONOCLINALS
MONOCLINES
MONOCLINIC
MONOCLINISM
MONOCLINISMS
MONOCLINOUS
MONOCLONAL
MONOCLONALS
MONOCOQUES
MONOCOTYLEDON
MONOCOTYLEDONS
MONOCOTYLS
MONOCRACIES
MONOCRATIC
MONOCROPPED
MONOCROPPING
MONOCRYSTAL
MONOCRYSTALLINE
MONOCRYSTALS
MONOCULARLY
MONOCULARS
MONOCULOUS
MONOCULTURAL
MONOCULTURE
MONOCULTURES
MONOCYCLES
MONOCYCLIC
MONOCYTOID
MONODACTYLOUS
MONODELPHIAN
MONODELPHIANS
MONODELPHIC
MONODELPHOUS
MONODICALLY
MONODISPERSE
MONODRAMAS
MONODRAMATIC
MONOECIOUS
MONOECIOUSLY
MONOECISMS
MONOESTERS
MONOFILAMENT
MONOFILAMENTS
MONOGAMIES
MONOGAMIST
MONOGAMISTIC
MONOGAMISTS
MONOGAMOUS
MONOGAMOUSLY
MONOGAMOUSNESS
MONOGASTRIC
MONOGENEAN
MONOGENEANS
MONOGENESES
MONOGENESIS
MONOGENETIC
MONOGENICALLY
MONOGENIES
MONOGENISM
MONOGENISMS
MONOGENIST
MONOGENISTIC
MONOGENISTS
MONOGENOUS
MONOGLYCERIDE
MONOGLYCERIDES
MONOGONIES
MONOGRAMED
MONOGRAMING
MONOGRAMMATIC
MONOGRAMMED
MONOGRAMMER
MONOGRAMMERS
MONOGRAMMING
MONOGRAPHED
MONOGRAPHER
MONOGRAPHERS
MONOGRAPHIC
MONOGRAPHICAL
MONOGRAPHICALLY
MONOGRAPHIES
MONOGRAPHING
MONOGRAPHIST
MONOGRAPHISTS
MONOGRAPHS
MONOGRAPHY
MONOGYNIAN
MONOGYNIES
MONOGYNIST
MONOGYNISTS
MONOGYNOUS
MONOHYBRID
MONOHYBRIDS
MONOHYDRATE
MONOHYDRATED
MONOHYDRATES
MONOHYDRIC
MONOHYDROGEN
MONOHYDROXY
MONOICOUSLY
MONOLATERS
MONOLATRIES
MONOLATRIST
MONOLATRISTS
MONOLATROUS
MONOLAYERS
MONOLINGUAL
MONOLINGUALISM
MONOLINGUALISMS
MONOLINGUALS
MONOLINGUIST
MONOLINGUISTS
MONOLITHIC
MONOLITHICALLY
MONOLOGGED
MONOLOGGING
MONOLOGICAL
MONOLOGIES
MONOLOGISE
MONOLOGISED
MONOLOGISES
MONOLOGISING
MONOLOGIST
MONOLOGISTS
MONOLOGIZE
MONOLOGIZED
MONOLOGIZES
MONOLOGIZING
MONOLOGUED
MONOLOGUES
MONOLOGUING
MONOLOGUISE
MONOLOGUISED
MONOLOGUISES
MONOLOGUISING
MONOLOGUIST
MONOLOGUISTS
MONOLOGUIZE
MONOLOGUIZED
MONOLOGUIZES
MONOLOGUIZING
MONOMACHIA
MONOMACHIAS
MONOMACHIES
MONOMANIAC
MONOMANIACAL
MONOMANIACALLY
MONOMANIACS
MONOMANIAS
MONOMEROUS
MONOMETALLIC
MONOMETALLISM
MONOMETALLISMS
MONOMETALLIST
MONOMETALLISTS
MONOMETERS
MONOMETRIC
MONOMETRICAL
MONOMOLECULAR
MONOMOLECULARLY
MONOMORPHEMIC
MONOMORPHIC
MONOMORPHISM
MONOMORPHISMS
MONOMORPHOUS
MONOMYARIAN
MONOMYARIANS
MONONUCLEAR
MONONUCLEARS
MONONUCLEATE
MONONUCLEATED
MONONUCLEOSES
MONONUCLEOSIS
MONONUCLEOTIDE
MONONUCLEOTIDES
MONOPETALOUS
MONOPHAGIES
MONOPHAGOUS
MONOPHASES
MONOPHASIC
MONOPHOBIA
MONOPHOBIAS
MONOPHOBIC
MONOPHOBICS
MONOPHONIC
MONOPHONICALLY
MONOPHONIES
MONOPHOSPHATE
MONOPHOSPHATES
MONOPHTHONG
MONOPHTHONGAL
MONOPHTHONGISE
MONOPHTHONGISED
MONOPHTHONGISES
MONOPHTHONGIZE
MONOPHTHONGIZED
MONOPHTHONGIZES
MONOPHTHONGS
MONOPHYLETIC
MONOPHYLIES
MONOPHYLLOUS
MONOPHYODONT
MONOPHYODONTS
MONOPHYSITE
MONOPHYSITES
MONOPHYSITIC
MONOPHYSITISM
MONOPHYSITISMS
MONOPITCHES
MONOPLANES
MONOPLEGIA
MONOPLEGIAS
MONOPLEGIC
MONOPLEGICS
MONOPLOIDS
MONOPODIAL
MONOPODIALLY
MONOPODIAS
MONOPODIES
MONOPODIUM
MONOPOLIES
MONOPOLISATION
MONOPOLISATIONS
MONOPOLISE
MONOPOLISED
MONOPOLISER
MONOPOLISERS
MONOPOLISES

MONOPOLISING
MONOPOLISM
MONOPOLISMS
MONOPOLIST
MONOPOLISTIC
MONOPOLISTS
MONOPOLIZATION
MONOPOLIZATIONS
MONOPOLIZE
MONOPOLIZED
MONOPOLIZER
MONOPOLIZERS
MONOPOLIZES
MONOPOLIZING
MONOPRINTS
MONOPRIONIDIAN
MONOPROPELLANT
MONOPROPELLANTS
MONOPSONIES
MONOPSONIST
MONOPSONISTIC
MONOPSONISTS
MONOPTERAL
MONOPTEROI
MONOPTERON
MONOPTEROS
MONOPTEROSES
MONOPTOTES
MONOPULSES
MONORCHIDISM
MONORCHIDISMS
MONORCHIDS
MONORCHISM
MONORCHISMS
MONORHINAL
MONORHINES
MONORHYMED
MONORHYMES
MONOSACCHARIDE
MONOSACCHARIDES
MONOSATURATED
MONOSEMIES
MONOSEPALOUS
MONOSKIERS
MONOSKIING
MONOSKIINGS
MONOSODIUM
MONOSOMICS
MONOSOMIES
MONOSPACED
MONOSPECIFIC
MONOSPECIFICITY
MONOSPERMAL
MONOSPERMOUS
MONOSTABLE
MONOSTELES
MONOSTELIC
MONOSTELIES
MONOSTICHIC
MONOSTICHOUS
MONOSTICHS
MONOSTOMOUS
MONOSTROPHE
MONOSTROPHES
MONOSTROPHIC
MONOSTROPHICS
MONOSTYLAR
MONOSTYLOUS
MONOSYLLABIC
MONOSYLLABICITY
MONOSYLLABISM
MONOSYLLABISMS
MONOSYLLABLE
MONOSYLLABLES
MONOSYMMETRIC
MONOSYMMETRICAL
MONOSYMMETRIES
MONOSYMMETRY
MONOSYNAPTIC
MONOTASKED
MONOTASKING
MONOTASKINGS
MONOTELEPHONE
MONOTELEPHONES
MONOTERPENE
MONOTERPENES
MONOTHALAMIC
MONOTHALAMOUS
MONOTHECAL
MONOTHECOUS
MONOTHEISM
MONOTHEISMS
MONOTHEIST
MONOTHEISTIC
MONOTHEISTICAL
MONOTHEISTS
MONOTHELETE
MONOTHELETES
MONOTHELETIC
MONOTHELETICAL
MONOTHELETISM
MONOTHELETISMS
MONOTHELISM
MONOTHELISMS
MONOTHELITE
MONOTHELITES
MONOTHELITISM
MONOTHELITISMS
MONOTHERAPIES
MONOTHERAPY
MONOTOCOUS
MONOTONICALLY
MONOTONICITIES
MONOTONICITY
MONOTONIES
MONOTONING
MONOTONISE
MONOTONISED
MONOTONISES
MONOTONISING
MONOTONIZE
MONOTONIZED
MONOTONIZES
MONOTONIZING
MONOTONOUS
MONOTONOUSLY
MONOTONOUSNESS
MONOTREMATOUS
MONOTREMES
MONOTRICHIC
MONOTRICHOUS
MONOTROCHS
MONOUNSATURATE
MONOUNSATURATED
MONOUNSATURATES
MONOVALENCE
MONOVALENCES
MONOVALENCIES
MONOVALENCY
MONOVALENT
MONOXYLONS
MONOXYLOUS
MONOZYGOTIC
MONOZYGOUS
MONSEIGNEUR
MONSEIGNEURS
MONSIGNORI
MONSIGNORIAL
MONSIGNORS
MONSTERING
MONSTERINGS
MONSTRANCE
MONSTRANCES
MONSTROSITIES
MONSTROSITY
MONSTROUSLY
MONSTROUSNESS
MONSTROUSNESSES
MONSTRUOSITIES
MONSTRUOSITY
MONSTRUOUS
MONTADALES
MONTAGNARD
MONTAGNARDS
MONTBRETIA
MONTBRETIAS
MONTELIMAR
MONTELIMARS
MONTGOLFIER
MONTGOLFIERS
MONTHLINGS
MONTICELLITE
MONTICELLITES
MONTICOLOUS
MONTICULATE
MONTICULES
MONTICULOUS
MONTICULUS
MONTICULUSES
MONTMORILLONITE
MONUMENTAL
MONUMENTALISE
MONUMENTALISED
MONUMENTALISES
MONUMENTALISING
MONUMENTALITIES
MONUMENTALITY
MONUMENTALIZE
MONUMENTALIZED
MONUMENTALIZES
MONUMENTALIZING
MONUMENTALLY
MONUMENTED
MONUMENTING
MONZONITES
MONZONITIC
MOODINESSES
MOONCALVES
MOONCHILDREN
MOONCRAFTS
MOONFISHES
MOONFLOWER
MOONFLOWERS
MOONINESSES
MOONLIGHTED
MOONLIGHTER
MOONLIGHTERS
MOONLIGHTING
MOONLIGHTINGS
MOONLIGHTS
MOONPHASES
MOONQUAKES
MOONRAKERS
MOONRAKING
MOONRAKINGS
MOONSCAPES
MOONSHINED
MOONSHINER
MOONSHINERS
MOONSHINES
MOONSHINIER
MOONSHINIEST
MOONSHINING
MOONSHININGS
MOONSTONES
MOONSTRICKEN
MOONSTRIKE
MOONSTRIKES
MOONSTRUCK
MOONWALKED
MOONWALKER
MOONWALKERS
MOONWALKING
MOORBUZZARD
MOORBUZZARDS
MOOSEBIRDS
MOOSEHAIRS
MOOSEHIDES
MOOSEWOODS
MOOSEYARDS

MOOTNESSES
MOPINESSES
MOPISHNESS
MOPISHNESSES
MORALISATION
MORALISATIONS
MORALISERS
MORALISING
MORALISINGS
MORALISTIC
MORALISTICALLY
MORALITIES
MORALIZATION
MORALIZATIONS
MORALIZERS
MORALIZING
MORALIZINGS
MORASSIEST
MORATORIUM
MORATORIUMS
MORBIDEZZA
MORBIDEZZAS
MORBIDITIES
MORBIDNESS
MORBIDNESSES
MORBIFEROUS
MORBIFICALLY
MORBILLIFORM
MORBILLIVIRUS
MORBILLIVIRUSES
MORBILLOUS
MORDACIOUS
MORDACIOUSLY
MORDACIOUSNESS
MORDACITIES
MORDANCIES
MORDANTING
MORENESSES
MORGANATIC
MORGANATICALLY
MORGANITES
MORGELLONS
MORGENSTERN
MORGENSTERNS
MORIBUNDITIES
MORIBUNDITY
MORIBUNDLY
MORIGERATE
MORIGERATED
MORIGERATES
MORIGERATING
MORIGERATION
MORIGERATIONS
MORIGEROUS
MORONICALLY
MORONITIES
MOROSENESS
MOROSENESSES
MOROSITIES
MORPHACTIN
MORPHACTINS
MORPHALLAXES
MORPHALLAXIS
MORPHEMICALLY
MORPHEMICS
MORPHINISM
MORPHINISMS
MORPHINOMANIA
MORPHINOMANIAC
MORPHINOMANIACS
MORPHINOMANIAS
MORPHOGENESES
MORPHOGENESIS
MORPHOGENETIC
MORPHOGENIC
MORPHOGENIES
MORPHOGENS
MORPHOGENY
MORPHOGRAPHER
MORPHOGRAPHERS
MORPHOGRAPHIES
MORPHOGRAPHY
MORPHOLINE
MORPHOLINES
MORPHOLINO
MORPHOLINOS
MORPHOLOGIC
MORPHOLOGICAL
MORPHOLOGICALLY
MORPHOLOGIES
MORPHOLOGIST
MORPHOLOGISTS
MORPHOLOGY
MORPHOMETRIC
MORPHOMETRICS
MORPHOMETRIES
MORPHOMETRY
MORPHOPHONEME
MORPHOPHONEMES
MORPHOPHONEMIC
MORPHOPHONEMICS
MORPHOPHONOLOGY
MORPHOSYNTAX
MORPHOSYNTAXES
MORPHOTROPIC
MORPHOTROPIES
MORPHOTROPY
MORSELLING
MORSELLINGS
MORTADELLA
MORTADELLAS
MORTADELLE
MORTALISED
MORTALISES
MORTALISING
MORTALITIES
MORTALIZED
MORTALIZES
MORTALIZING
MORTARBOARD
MORTARBOARDS
MORTARIEST
MORTARLESS
MORTCLOTHS
MORTGAGEABLE
MORTGAGEES
MORTGAGERS
MORTGAGING
MORTGAGORS
MORTICIANS
MORTIFEROUS
MORTIFEROUSNESS
MORTIFICATION
MORTIFICATIONS
MORTIFIERS
MORTIFYING
MORTIFYINGLY
MORTIFYINGS
MORTUARIES
MORULATION
MORULATIONS
MOSAICALLY
MOSAICISMS
MOSAICISTS
MOSAICKING
MOSAICKINGS
MOSAICLIKE
MOSASAURUS
MOSBOLLETJIE
MOSBOLLETJIES
MOSCHATELS
MOSCHIFEROUS
MOSCOVIUMS
MOSKONFYTS
MOSQUITOES
MOSQUITOEY
MOSQUITOFISH
MOSQUITOFISHES
MOSQUITOIER
MOSQUITOIEST
MOSSBACKED
MOSSBLUITER
MOSSBLUITERS
MOSSBUNKER
MOSSBUNKERS
MOSSINESSES
MOSSPLANTS
MOSSTROOPER
MOSSTROOPERS
MOTETTISTS
MOTHBALLED
MOTHBALLING
MOTHERBOARD
MOTHERBOARDS
MOTHERCRAFT
MOTHERCRAFTS
MOTHERESES
MOTHERFUCKER
MOTHERFUCKERS
MOTHERFUCKING
MOTHERHOOD
MOTHERHOODS
MOTHERHOUSE
MOTHERHOUSES
MOTHERIEST
MOTHERINGS
MOTHERLAND
MOTHERLANDS
MOTHERLESS
MOTHERLESSNESS
MOTHERLIER
MOTHERLIEST
MOTHERLINESS
MOTHERLINESSES
MOTHERWORT
MOTHERWORTS
MOTHPROOFED
MOTHPROOFER
MOTHPROOFERS
MOTHPROOFING
MOTHPROOFS
MOTILITIES
MOTIONISTS
MOTIONLESS
MOTIONLESSLY
MOTIONLESSNESS
MOTIVATING
MOTIVATION
MOTIVATIONAL
MOTIVATIONALLY
MOTIVATIONS
MOTIVATIVE
MOTIVATORS
MOTIVELESS
MOTIVELESSLY
MOTIVELESSNESS
MOTIVITIES
MOTOCROSSES
MOTONEURON
MOTONEURONAL
MOTONEURONS
MOTORBICYCLE
MOTORBICYCLES
MOTORBIKED
MOTORBIKES
MOTORBIKING
MOTORBOATED
MOTORBOATER
MOTORBOATERS
MOTORBOATING
MOTORBOATINGS
MOTORBOATS
MOTORBUSES
MOTORBUSSES
MOTORCADED
MOTORCADES
MOTORCADING
MOTORCOACH
MOTORCOACHES
MOTORCYCLE

MOTORCYCLED
MOTORCYCLES
MOTORCYCLING
MOTORCYCLINGS
MOTORCYCLIST
MOTORCYCLISTS
MOTORHOMES
MOTORICALLY
MOTORISATION
MOTORISATIONS
MOTORISING
MOTORIZATION
MOTORIZATIONS
MOTORIZING
MOTORMOUTH
MOTORMOUTHS
MOTORSHIPS
MOTORTRUCK
MOTORTRUCKS
MOTOSCAFOS
MOUCHARABIES
MOUCHARABY
MOUDIEWART
MOUDIEWARTS
MOUDIEWORT
MOUDIEWORTS
MOUDIWARTS
MOUDIWORTS
MOULDABILITIES
MOULDABILITY
MOULDBOARD
MOULDBOARDS
MOULDERING
MOULDINESS
MOULDINESSES
MOULDWARPS
MOULDYWARP
MOULDYWARPS
MOUNDBIRDS
MOUNTAINBOARD
MOUNTAINBOARDER
MOUNTAINBOARDS
MOUNTAINED
MOUNTAINEER
MOUNTAINEERED
MOUNTAINEERING
MOUNTAINEERINGS
MOUNTAINEERS
MOUNTAINIER
MOUNTAINIEST
MOUNTAINOUS
MOUNTAINOUSLY
MOUNTAINOUSNESS
MOUNTAINSIDE
MOUNTAINSIDES
MOUNTAINTOP
MOUNTAINTOPS
MOUNTEBANK
MOUNTEBANKED
MOUNTEBANKERIES
MOUNTEBANKERY
MOUNTEBANKING
MOUNTEBANKINGS
MOUNTEBANKISM
MOUNTEBANKISMS
MOUNTEBANKS
MOUNTENANCE
MOUNTENANCES
MOUNTENAUNCE
MOUNTENAUNCES
MOURNFULLER
MOURNFULLEST
MOURNFULLY
MOURNFULNESS
MOURNFULNESSES
MOURNINGLY
MOURNIVALS
MOURVEDRES
MOUSEBIRDS
MOUSEOVERS
MOUSEPIECE
MOUSEPIECES
MOUSETAILS
MOUSETRAPPED
MOUSETRAPPING
MOUSETRAPPINGS
MOUSETRAPS
MOUSINESSES
MOUSQUETAIRE
MOUSQUETAIRES
MOUSSELIKE
MOUSSELINE
MOUSSELINES
MOUSTACHED
MOUSTACHES
MOUSTACHIAL
MOUSTACHIO
MOUSTACHIOED
MOUSTACHIOS
MOUTHBREATHER
MOUTHBREATHERS
MOUTHBREEDER
MOUTHBREEDERS
MOUTHBROODER
MOUTHBROODERS
MOUTHFEELS
MOUTHPARTS
MOUTHPIECE
MOUTHPIECES
MOUTHWASHES
MOUTHWATERING
MOUTHWATERINGLY
MOUVEMENTE
MOVABILITIES
MOVABILITY
MOVABLENESS
MOVABLENESSES
MOVEABILITIES
MOVEABILITY
MOVEABLENESS
MOVEABLENESSES
MOVELESSLY
MOVELESSNESS
MOVELESSNESSES
MOVIEGOERS
MOVIEGOING
MOVIEGOINGS
MOVIELANDS
MOVIEMAKER
MOVIEMAKERS
MOVIEMAKING
MOVIEMAKINGS
MOWBURNING
MOWBURNINGS
MOWDIEWART
MOWDIEWARTS
MOWDIEWORT
MOWDIEWORTS
MOXIBUSTION
MOXIBUSTIONS
MOYGASHELS
MOZZARELLA
MOZZARELLAS
MRIDAMGAMS
MRIDANGAMS
MUCEDINOUS
MUCHNESSES
MUCIDITIES
MUCIDNESSES
MUCIFEROUS
MUCILAGINOUS
MUCILAGINOUSLY
MUCINOGENS
MUCKAMUCKED
MUCKAMUCKING
MUCKAMUCKS
MUCKENDERS
MUCKINESSES
MUCKRAKERS
MUCKRAKING
MUCKRAKINGS
MUCKSPREAD
MUCKSPREADER
MUCKSPREADERS
MUCKSPREADING
MUCKSPREADS
MUCKSWEATS
MUCKYMUCKS
MUCOCUTANEOUS
MUCOLYTICS
MUCOMEMBRANOUS
MUCOPEPTIDE
MUCOPEPTIDES
MUCOPROTEIN
MUCOPROTEINS
MUCOPURULENT
MUCOSANGUINEOUS
MUCOSITIES
MUCOVISCIDOSES
MUCOVISCIDOSIS
MUCRONATED
MUCRONATION
MUCRONATIONS
MUDCAPPING
MUDCAPPINGS
MUDDINESSES
MUDDLEDNESS
MUDDLEDNESSES
MUDDLEHEAD
MUDDLEHEADED
MUDDLEHEADEDLY
MUDDLEHEADS
MUDDLEMENT
MUDDLEMENTS
MUDDLINGLY
MUDHOPPERS
MUDLARKING
MUDLOGGERS
MUDLOGGING
MUDLOGGINGS
MUDPUPPIES
MUDSKIPPER
MUDSKIPPERS
MUDSLINGER
MUDSLINGERS
MUDSLINGING
MUDSLINGINGS
MUFFETTEES
MUFFINEERS
MUGEARITES
MUGGINESSES
MUGWUMPERIES
MUGWUMPERY
MUGWUMPISH
MUGWUMPISM
MUGWUMPISMS
MUJAHEDDIN
MUJAHEDEEN
MUJAHIDEEN
MUKHABARAT
MUKHABARATS
MULATRESSES
MULATTRESS
MULATTRESSES
MULBERRIES
MULIEBRITIES
MULIEBRITY
MULISHNESS
MULISHNESSES
MULLAHISMS
MULLARKIES
MULLIGATAWNIES
MULLIGATAWNY
MULLIGRUBS
MULLIONING
MULLOCKIER
MULLOCKIEST
MULTANGULAR
MULTANIMOUS
MULTARTICULATE

M

MULTEITIES
MULTIACCESS
MULTIACCESSES
MULTIAGENCY
MULTIANGULAR
MULTIARMED
MULTIARTICULATE
MULTIAUTHOR
MULTIAXIAL
MULTIBARREL
MULTIBARRELED
MULTIBARRELLED
MULTIBARRELS
MULTIBILLION
MULTIBLADED
MULTIBRANCHED
MULTIBUILDING
MULTICAMERATE
MULTICAMPUS
MULTICAPITATE
MULTICARBON
MULTICASTS
MULTICAULINE
MULTICAUSAL
MULTICELLED
MULTICELLULAR
MULTICENTER
MULTICENTRAL
MULTICENTRE
MULTICENTRIC
MULTICHAIN
MULTICHAMBERED
MULTICHANNEL
MULTICHARACTER
MULTICIDES
MULTICIPITAL
MULTICLIENT
MULTICOATED
MULTICOLOR
MULTICOLORED
MULTICOLORS
MULTICOLOUR
MULTICOLOURED
MULTICOLOURS
MULTICOLUMN
MULTICOMPONENT
MULTICONDUCTOR
MULTICOPIES
MULTICOSTATE
MULTICOUNTY
MULTICOURSE
MULTICULTI
MULTICULTIS
MULTICULTURAL
MULTICULTURALLY
MULTICURIE
MULTICURRENCIES
MULTICURRENCY
MULTICUSPID
MULTICUSPIDATE
MULTICUSPIDS
MULTICYCLE
MULTICYCLES
MULTICYLINDER
MULTIDENTATE
MULTIDIALECTAL
MULTIDIGITATE
MULTIDISCIPLINE
MULTIDIVISIONAL
MULTIDOMAIN
MULTIELECTRODE
MULTIELEMENT
MULTIEMPLOYER
MULTIEMPLOYERS
MULTIENGINE
MULTIENGINED
MULTIENZYME
MULTIETHNIC
MULTIETHNICS
MULTIFACED
MULTIFACETED
MULTIFACTOR
MULTIFACTORIAL
MULTIFAMILIES
MULTIFAMILY
MULTIFARIOUS
MULTIFARIOUSLY
MULTIFIDLY
MULTIFIDOUS
MULTIFILAMENT
MULTIFILAMENTS
MULTIFLASH
MULTIFLORA
MULTIFLORAS
MULTIFLOROUS
MULTIFOCAL
MULTIFOCALS
MULTIFOILS
MULTIFOLIATE
MULTIFOLIOLATE
MULTIFORMITIES
MULTIFORMITY
MULTIFORMS
MULTIFREQUENCY
MULTIFUNCTION
MULTIFUNCTIONAL
MULTIGENES
MULTIGENIC
MULTIGRADE
MULTIGRADES
MULTIGRAIN
MULTIGRAVIDA
MULTIGRAVIDAE
MULTIGRAVIDAS
MULTIGROUP
MULTIHEADED
MULTIHOSPITAL
MULTIHULLS
MULTIJUGATE
MULTIJUGOUS
MULTILANES
MULTILATERAL
MULTILATERALISM
MULTILATERALIST
MULTILATERALLY
MULTILAYER
MULTILAYERED
MULTILAYERS
MULTILEVEL
MULTILEVELED
MULTILEVELLED
MULTILINEAL
MULTILINEAR
MULTILINES
MULTILINGUAL
MULTILINGUALISM
MULTILINGUALLY
MULTILINGUIST
MULTILINGUISTS
MULTILOBATE
MULTILOBED
MULTILOBES
MULTILOBULAR
MULTILOBULATE
MULTILOCATIONAL
MULTILOCULAR
MULTILOCULATE
MULTILOQUENCE
MULTILOQUENCES
MULTILOQUENT
MULTILOQUIES
MULTILOQUOUS
MULTILOQUY
MULTIMANNED
MULTIMEDIA
MULTIMEDIAS
MULTIMEGATON
MULTIMEGAWATT
MULTIMEGAWATTS
MULTIMEMBER
MULTIMETALLIC
MULTIMETER
MULTIMETERS
MULTIMILLENNIAL
MULTIMILLION
MULTIMODAL
MULTIMODES
MULTIMOLECULAR
MULTINATION
MULTINATIONAL
MULTINATIONALS
MULTINOMIAL
MULTINOMIALS
MULTINOMINAL
MULTINUCLEAR
MULTINUCLEATE
MULTINUCLEATED
MULTINUCLEOLAR
MULTINUCLEOLATE
MULTIORGASMIC
MULTIPACKS
MULTIPANED
MULTIPARAE
MULTIPARAMETER
MULTIPARAS
MULTIPARITIES
MULTIPARITY
MULTIPAROUS
MULTIPARTICLE
MULTIPARTITE
MULTIPARTY
MULTIPARTYISM
MULTIPARTYISMS
MULTIPEDES
MULTIPHASE
MULTIPHASIC
MULTIPHOTON
MULTIPICTURE
MULTIPIECE
MULTIPISTON
MULTIPLANE
MULTIPLANES
MULTIPLANT
MULTIPLAYER
MULTIPLAYERS
MULTIPLETS
MULTIPLEXED
MULTIPLEXER
MULTIPLEXERS
MULTIPLEXES
MULTIPLEXING
MULTIPLEXINGS
MULTIPLEXOR
MULTIPLEXORS
MULTIPLIABLE
MULTIPLICABLE
MULTIPLICAND
MULTIPLICANDS
MULTIPLICATE
MULTIPLICATES
MULTIPLICATION
MULTIPLICATIONS
MULTIPLICATIVE
MULTIPLICATOR
MULTIPLICATORS
MULTIPLICITIES
MULTIPLICITY
MULTIPLIED
MULTIPLIER
MULTIPLIERS
MULTIPLIES
MULTIPLYING
MULTIPOINT
MULTIPOLAR
MULTIPOLARITIES
MULTIPOLARITY
MULTIPOLES
MULTIPOTENT
MULTIPOTENTIAL
MULTIPOWER

MULTIPRESENCE
MULTIPRESENCES
MULTIPRESENT
MULTIPROBLEM
MULTIPROCESSING
MULTIPROCESSOR
MULTIPROCESSORS
MULTIPRODUCT
MULTIPRONGED
MULTIPURPOSE
MULTIRACIAL
MULTIRACIALISM
MULTIRACIALISMS
MULTIRACIALLY
MULTIRAMIFIED
MULTIRANGE
MULTIREGIONAL
MULTIRELIGIOUS
MULTIROOMED
MULTISCIENCE
MULTISCIENCES
MULTISCREEN
MULTISCREENS
MULTISENSE
MULTISENSORY
MULTISEPTATE
MULTISERIAL
MULTISERIATE
MULTISERVICE
MULTISIDED
MULTISKILL
MULTISKILLED
MULTISKILLING
MULTISKILLINGS
MULTISKILLS
MULTISONANT
MULTISOURCE
MULTISPECIES
MULTISPECTRAL
MULTISPEED
MULTISPIRAL
MULTISPORT
MULTISTAGE
MULTISTANDARD
MULTISTATE
MULTISTEMMED
MULTISTOREY
MULTISTOREYS
MULTISTORIED
MULTISTORIES
MULTISTORY
MULTISTRANDED
MULTISTRIKE
MULTISTRIKES
MULTISULCATE
MULTISYLLABIC
MULTISYSTEM
MULTITALENTED
MULTITASKED
MULTITASKING
MULTITASKINGS
MULTITASKS
MULTITERMINAL
MULTITHREADING
MULTITHREADINGS
MULTITIERED
MULTITONED
MULTITONES
MULTITOOLS
MULTITOWERED
MULTITRACK
MULTITRACKED
MULTITRACKING
MULTITRACKS
MULTITRILLION
MULTITRILLIONS
MULTITUDES
MULTITUDINARY
MULTITUDINOUS
MULTITUDINOUSLY
MULTIUNION
MULTIUTILITIES
MULTIUTILITY
MULTIVALENCE
MULTIVALENCES
MULTIVALENCIES
MULTIVALENCY
MULTIVALENT
MULTIVALENTS
MULTIVARIABLE
MULTIVARIATE
MULTIVARIOUS
MULTIVERSE
MULTIVERSES
MULTIVERSITIES
MULTIVERSITY
MULTIVIBRATOR
MULTIVIBRATORS
MULTIVIOUS
MULTIVITAMIN
MULTIVITAMINS
MULTIVOCAL
MULTIVOCALS
MULTIVOLTINE
MULTIVOLUME
MULTIWARHEAD
MULTIWAVELENGTH
MULTIWINDOW
MULTIWINDOWS
MULTOCULAR
MULTUNGULATE
MULTUNGULATES
MUMBLEMENT
MUMBLEMENTS
MUMBLETYPEG
MUMBLETYPEGS
MUMBLINGLY
MUMCHANCES
MUMMERINGS
MUMMICHOGS
MUMMIFICATION
MUMMIFICATIONS
MUMMIFORMS
MUMMIFYING
MUMPISHNESS
MUMPISHNESSES
MUMPRENEUR
MUMPRENEURS
MUMPSIMUSES
MUMSINESSES
MUNCHABLES
MUNDANENESS
MUNDANENESSES
MUNDANITIES
MUNDIFICATION
MUNDIFICATIONS
MUNDIFICATIVE
MUNDIFICATIVES
MUNDIFYING
MUNDUNGUSES
MUNICIPALISE
MUNICIPALISED
MUNICIPALISES
MUNICIPALISING
MUNICIPALISM
MUNICIPALISMS
MUNICIPALIST
MUNICIPALISTS
MUNICIPALITIES
MUNICIPALITY
MUNICIPALIZE
MUNICIPALIZED
MUNICIPALIZES
MUNICIPALIZING
MUNICIPALLY
MUNICIPALS
MUNIFICENCE
MUNIFICENCES
MUNIFICENT
MUNIFICENTLY
MUNIFICENTNESS
MUNIFIENCE
MUNIFIENCES
MUNITIONED
MUNITIONEER
MUNITIONEERS
MUNITIONER
MUNITIONERS
MUNITIONETTE
MUNITIONETTES
MUNITIONING
MURDERABILIA
MURDERBALL
MURDERBALLS
MURDERESSES
MURDEROUSLY
MURDEROUSNESS
MURDEROUSNESSES
MURGEONING
MURKINESSES
MURMURATION
MURMURATIONS
MURMURINGLY
MURMURINGS
MURMUROUSLY
MURTHERERS
MURTHERING
MUSCADELLE
MUSCADELLES
MUSCADINES
MUSCARDINE
MUSCARDINES
MUSCARINES
MUSCARINIC
MUSCATORIA
MUSCATORIUM
MUSCAVADOS
MUSCOLOGIES
MUSCOVADOS
MUSCOVITES
MUSCULARITIES
MUSCULARITY
MUSCULARLY
MUSCULATION
MUSCULATIONS
MUSCULATURE
MUSCULATURES
MUSCULOSKELETAL
MUSEOLOGICAL
MUSEOLOGIES
MUSEOLOGIST
MUSEOLOGISTS
MUSHINESSES
MUSHMOUTHS
MUSHROOMED
MUSHROOMER
MUSHROOMERS
MUSHROOMIER
MUSHROOMIEST
MUSHROOMING
MUSHROOMINGS
MUSICALISATION
MUSICALISATIONS
MUSICALISE
MUSICALISED
MUSICALISES
MUSICALISING
MUSICALITIES
MUSICALITY
MUSICALIZATION
MUSICALIZATIONS
MUSICALIZE
MUSICALIZED
MUSICALIZES
MUSICALIZING
MUSICALNESS
MUSICALNESSES
MUSICIANER
MUSICIANERS
MUSICIANLIER

MUSICIANLIEST
MUSICIANLY
MUSICIANSHIP
MUSICIANSHIPS
MUSICOLOGICAL
MUSICOLOGICALLY
MUSICOLOGIES
MUSICOLOGIST
MUSICOLOGISTS
MUSICOLOGY
MUSICOTHERAPIES
MUSICOTHERAPY
MUSKELLUNGE
MUSKELLUNGES
MUSKETEERS
MUSKETOONS
MUSKETRIES
MUSKINESSES
MUSKMELONS
MUSQUASHES
MUSQUETOON
MUSQUETOONS
MUSSELCRACKER
MUSSELCRACKERS
MUSSINESSES
MUSSITATED
MUSSITATES
MUSSITATING
MUSSITATION
MUSSITATIONS
MUSTACHIOED
MUSTACHIOS
MUSTARDIER
MUSTARDIEST
MUSTELINES
MUSTINESSES
MUTABILITIES
MUTABILITY
MUTABLENESS
MUTABLENESSES
MUTAGENESES
MUTAGENESIS
MUTAGENICALLY
MUTAGENICITIES
MUTAGENICITY
MUTAGENISE
MUTAGENISED
MUTAGENISES
MUTAGENISING
MUTAGENIZE
MUTAGENIZED
MUTAGENIZES
MUTAGENIZING
MUTATIONAL
MUTATIONALLY
MUTATIONIST
MUTATIONISTS
MUTENESSES
MUTESSARIF
MUTESSARIFAT
MUTESSARIFATS
MUTESSARIFS
MUTILATING
MUTILATION
MUTILATIONS
MUTILATIVE
MUTILATORS
MUTINEERED
MUTINEERING
MUTINOUSLY
MUTINOUSNESS
MUTINOUSNESSES
MUTOSCOPES
MUTTERATION
MUTTERATIONS
MUTTERINGLY
MUTTERINGS
MUTTONBIRD
MUTTONBIRDER
MUTTONBIRDERS
MUTTONBIRDS
MUTTONCHOPS
MUTTONFISH
MUTTONFISHES
MUTTONHEAD
MUTTONHEADED
MUTTONHEADS
MUTTONIEST
MUTUALISATION
MUTUALISATIONS
MUTUALISED
MUTUALISES
MUTUALISING
MUTUALISMS
MUTUALISTIC
MUTUALISTS
MUTUALITIES
MUTUALIZATION
MUTUALIZATIONS
MUTUALIZED
MUTUALIZES
MUTUALIZING
MUTUALNESS
MUTUALNESSES
MUZZINESSES
MYASTHENIA
MYASTHENIAS
MYASTHENIC
MYASTHENICS
MYCETOLOGIES
MYCETOLOGY
MYCETOMATA
MYCETOMATOUS
MYCETOPHAGOUS
MYCETOZOAN
MYCETOZOANS
MYCOBACTERIA
MYCOBACTERIAL
MYCOBACTERIUM
MYCOBIONTS
MYCODOMATIA
MYCODOMATIUM
MYCOFLORAE
MYCOFLORAS
MYCOLOGICAL
MYCOLOGICALLY
MYCOLOGIES
MYCOLOGIST
MYCOLOGISTS
MYCOPHAGIES
MYCOPHAGIST
MYCOPHAGISTS
MYCOPHAGOUS
MYCOPHILES
MYCOPLASMA
MYCOPLASMAL
MYCOPLASMAS
MYCOPLASMATA
MYCOPLASMOSES
MYCOPLASMOSIS
MYCORHIZAE
MYCORHIZAL
MYCORHIZAS
MYCORRHIZA
MYCORRHIZAE
MYCORRHIZAL
MYCORRHIZAS
MYCOTOXICOLOGY
MYCOTOXICOSES
MYCOTOXICOSIS
MYCOTOXINS
MYCOTOXOLOGIES
MYCOTOXOLOGY
MYCOTROPHIC
MYCOVIRUSES
MYDRIATICS
MYELENCEPHALA
MYELENCEPHALIC
MYELENCEPHALON
MYELENCEPHALONS
MYELINATED
MYELITIDES
MYELITISES
MYELOBLAST
MYELOBLASTIC
MYELOBLASTS
MYELOCYTES
MYELOCYTIC
MYELOFIBROSES
MYELOFIBROSIS
MYELOFIBROTIC
MYELOGENOUS
MYELOGRAMS
MYELOGRAPHIES
MYELOGRAPHY
MYELOMATOID
MYELOMATOUS
MYELOPATHIC
MYELOPATHIES
MYELOPATHY
MYIOPHILIES
MYIOPHILOUS
MYLOHYOIDS
MYLONITISATION
MYLONITISATIONS
MYLONITISE
MYLONITISED
MYLONITISES
MYLONITISING
MYLONITIZATION
MYLONITIZATIONS
MYLONITIZE
MYLONITIZED
MYLONITIZES
MYLONITIZING
MYOBLASTIC
MYOCARDIAL
MYOCARDIOGRAPH
MYOCARDIOGRAPHS
MYOCARDIOPATHY
MYOCARDITIS
MYOCARDITISES
MYOCARDIUM
MYOCLONUSES
MYOELECTRIC
MYOELECTRICAL
MYOFIBRILLAR
MYOFIBRILS
MYOFILAMENT
MYOFILAMENTS
MYOGLOBINS
MYOGRAPHIC
MYOGRAPHICAL
MYOGRAPHICALLY
MYOGRAPHIES
MYOGRAPHIST
MYOGRAPHISTS
MYOINOSITOL
MYOINOSITOLS
MYOLOGICAL
MYOLOGISTS
MYOMANCIES
MYOMECTOMIES
MYOMECTOMY
MYOPATHIES
MYOPHILIES
MYOPHILOUS
MYOPICALLY
MYOSITISES
MYOSOTISES
MYOSTATINS
MYRIADFOLD
MYRIADFOLDS
MYRIAPODAN
MYRIAPODOUS
MYRINGITIS
MYRINGITISES
MYRINGOSCOPE
MYRINGOSCOPES
MYRINGOTOMIES

MYRINGOTOMY
MYRIORAMAS
MYRIOSCOPE
MYRIOSCOPES
MYRISTICIVOROUS
MYRMECOCHORIES
MYRMECOCHORY
MYRMECOLOGIC
MYRMECOLOGICAL
MYRMECOLOGIES
MYRMECOLOGIST
MYRMECOLOGISTS
MYRMECOLOGY
MYRMECOPHAGOUS
MYRMECOPHILE
MYRMECOPHILES
MYRMECOPHILIES
MYRMECOPHILOUS
MYRMECOPHILY
MYRMIDONES
MYRMIDONIAN
MYROBALANS
MYRTACEOUS
MYSOPHOBIA
MYSOPHOBIAS
MYSTAGOGIC
MYSTAGOGICAL
MYSTAGOGICALLY
MYSTAGOGIES
MYSTAGOGUE
MYSTAGOGUES
MYSTAGOGUS
MYSTAGOGUSES
MYSTERIOUS
MYSTERIOUSLY
MYSTERIOUSNESS
MYSTICALLY
MYSTICALNESS
MYSTICALNESSES
MYSTICETES
MYSTICISMS
MYSTIFICATION
MYSTIFICATIONS
MYSTIFIERS
MYSTIFYING
MYSTIFYINGLY
MYTHICALLY
MYTHICISATION
MYTHICISATIONS
MYTHICISED
MYTHICISER
MYTHICISERS
MYTHICISES
MYTHICISING
MYTHICISMS
MYTHICISTS
MYTHICIZATION
MYTHICIZATIONS
MYTHICIZED
MYTHICIZER
MYTHICIZERS
MYTHICIZES
MYTHICIZING
MYTHMAKERS
MYTHMAKING
MYTHMAKINGS
MYTHOGENESES
MYTHOGENESIS
MYTHOGRAPHER
MYTHOGRAPHERS
MYTHOGRAPHIES
MYTHOGRAPHY
MYTHOLOGER
MYTHOLOGERS
MYTHOLOGIAN
MYTHOLOGIANS
MYTHOLOGIC
MYTHOLOGICAL
MYTHOLOGICALLY
MYTHOLOGIES
MYTHOLOGISATION
MYTHOLOGISE
MYTHOLOGISED
MYTHOLOGISER
MYTHOLOGISERS
MYTHOLOGISES
MYTHOLOGISING
MYTHOLOGIST
MYTHOLOGISTS
MYTHOLOGIZATION
MYTHOLOGIZE
MYTHOLOGIZED
MYTHOLOGIZER
MYTHOLOGIZERS
MYTHOLOGIZES
MYTHOLOGIZING
MYTHOMANES
MYTHOMANIA
MYTHOMANIAC
MYTHOMANIACS
MYTHOMANIAS
MYTHOPOEIA
MYTHOPOEIAS
MYTHOPOEIC
MYTHOPOEISM
MYTHOPOEISMS
MYTHOPOEIST
MYTHOPOEISTS
MYTHOPOESES
MYTHOPOESIS
MYTHOPOETIC
MYTHOPOETICAL
MYTHOPOETS
MYTILIFORM
MYXAMOEBAE
MYXAMOEBAS
MYXEDEMATOUS
MYXOEDEMAS
MYXOEDEMATOUS
MYXOEDEMIC
MYXOMATOSES
MYXOMATOSIS
MYXOMATOUS
MYXOMYCETE
MYXOMYCETES
MYXOMYCETOUS
MYXOVIRUSES

M

N

NABOBERIES
NABOBESSES
NACHTMAALS
NAFFNESSES
NAIFNESSES
NAILBITERS
NAILBRUSHES
NAISSANCES
NAIVENESSES
NAKEDNESSES
NALBUPHINE
NALBUPHINES
NALORPHINE
NALORPHINES
NALTREXONE
NALTREXONES
NAMAYCUSHES
NAMECHECKED
NAMECHECKING
NAMECHECKS
NAMELESSLY
NAMELESSNESS
NAMELESSNESSES
NAMEPLATES
NAMEWORTHIER
NAMEWORTHIEST
NAMEWORTHY
NANDROLONE
NANDROLONES
NANISATION
NANISATIONS
NANIZATION
NANIZATIONS
NANNOPLANKTON
NANNOPLANKTONS
NANOGRAMME
NANOGRAMMES
NANOGRASSES
NANOMATERIAL
NANOMATERIALS
NANOMETERS
NANOMETRES
NANOPARTICLE
NANOPARTICLES
NANOPHYSICS
NANOPLANKTON
NANOPLANKTONS
NANOPUBLISHING
NANOPUBLISHINGS
NANOSECOND
NANOSECONDS
NANOTECHNOLOGY
NANOTESLAS
NANOWORLDS
NAPHTHALENE
NAPHTHALENES
NAPHTHALIC
NAPHTHALIN
NAPHTHALINE
NAPHTHALINES
NAPHTHALINS
NAPHTHALISE
NAPHTHALISED
NAPHTHALISES
NAPHTHALISING
NAPHTHALIZE
NAPHTHALIZED
NAPHTHALIZES
NAPHTHALIZING
NAPHTHENES
NAPHTHENIC
NAPHTHYLAMINE
NAPHTHYLAMINES
NAPOLEONITE
NAPOLEONITES
NAPPINESSES
NAPRAPATHIES
NAPRAPATHY
NARCISSISM
NARCISSISMS
NARCISSIST
NARCISSISTIC
NARCISSISTS
NARCISSUSES
NARCOANALYSES
NARCOANALYSIS
NARCOCATHARSES
NARCOCATHARSIS
NARCOHYPNOSES
NARCOHYPNOSIS
NARCOLEPSIES
NARCOLEPSY
NARCOLEPTIC
NARCOLEPTICS
NARCOSYNTHESES
NARCOSYNTHESIS
NARCOTERRORISM
NARCOTERRORISMS
NARCOTERRORIST
NARCOTERRORISTS
NARCOTICALLY
NARCOTINES
NARCOTISATION
NARCOTISATIONS
NARCOTISED
NARCOTISES
NARCOTISING
NARCOTISMS
NARCOTISTS
NARCOTIZATION
NARCOTIZATIONS
NARCOTIZED
NARCOTIZES
NARCOTIZING
NARGHILIES
NARGHILLIES
NARGUILEHS
NARRATABLE
NARRATIONAL
NARRATIONS
NARRATIVELY
NARRATIVES
NARRATOLOGICAL
NARRATOLOGIES
NARRATOLOGIST
NARRATOLOGISTS
NARRATOLOGY
NARROWBAND
NARROWBANDS
NARROWCAST
NARROWCASTED
NARROWCASTING
NARROWCASTINGS
NARROWCASTS
NARROWINGS
NARROWNESS
NARROWNESSES
NASALISATION
NASALISATIONS
NASALISING
NASALITIES
NASALIZATION
NASALIZATIONS
NASALIZING
NASCENCIES
NASEBERRIES
NASOFRONTAL
NASOGASTRIC
NASOLACRYMAL
NASOPHARYNGEAL
NASOPHARYNGES
NASOPHARYNX
NASOPHARYNXES
NASTINESSES
NASTURTIUM
NASTURTIUMS
NATALITIAL
NATALITIES
NATATIONAL
NATATORIAL
NATATORIUM
NATATORIUMS
NATHELESSE
NATIONALISATION
NATIONALISE
NATIONALISED
NATIONALISER
NATIONALISERS
NATIONALISES
NATIONALISING
NATIONALISM
NATIONALISMS
NATIONALIST
NATIONALISTIC
NATIONALISTS
NATIONALITIES
NATIONALITY
NATIONALIZATION
NATIONALIZE
NATIONALIZED
NATIONALIZER
NATIONALIZERS
NATIONALIZES
NATIONALIZING
NATIONALLY
NATIONHOOD
NATIONHOODS
NATIONLESS
NATIONWIDE
NATIVENESS
NATIVENESSES
NATIVISTIC
NATIVITIES
NATRIURESES
NATRIURESIS
NATRIURESISES
NATRIURETIC
NATRIURETICS
NATROLITES
NATTERIEST
NATTERJACK
NATTERJACKS
NATTINESSES
NATURALISATION
NATURALISATIONS
NATURALISE
NATURALISED
NATURALISES
NATURALISING
NATURALISM

NATURALISMS
NATURALIST
NATURALISTIC
NATURALISTS
NATURALIZATION
NATURALIZATIONS
NATURALIZE
NATURALIZED
NATURALIZES
NATURALIZING
NATURALNESS
NATURALNESSES
NATURISTIC
NATUROPATH
NATUROPATHIC
NATUROPATHIES
NATUROPATHS
NATUROPATHY
NAUGAHYDES
NAUGHTIEST
NAUGHTINESS
NAUGHTINESSES
NAUMACHIAE
NAUMACHIAS
NAUMACHIES
NAUPLIIFORM
NAUSEATING
NAUSEATINGLY
NAUSEATION
NAUSEATIONS
NAUSEATIVE
NAUSEOUSLY
NAUSEOUSNESS
NAUSEOUSNESSES
NAUTICALLY
NAUTILOIDS
NAUTILUSES
NAVARCHIES
NAVELWORTS
NAVICULARE
NAVICULARES
NAVICULARS
NAVIGABILITIES
NAVIGABILITY
NAVIGABLENESS
NAVIGABLENESSES
NAVIGATING
NAVIGATION
NAVIGATIONAL
NAVIGATIONALLY
NAVIGATIONS
NAVIGATORS
NAYSAYINGS
NAZIFICATION
NAZIFICATIONS
NEANDERTAL
NEANDERTALER
NEANDERTALERS
NEANDERTALS
NEANDERTHAL
NEANDERTHALER
NEANDERTHALERS
NEANDERTHALOID
NEANDERTHALS
NEAPOLITAN
NEAPOLITANS
NEARNESSES
NEARSHORED
NEARSHORES
NEARSHORING
NEARSIGHTED
NEARSIGHTEDLY
NEARSIGHTEDNESS
NEARTHROSES
NEARTHROSIS
NEATNESSES
NEBBISHERS
NEBBISHIER
NEBBISHIEST
NEBENKERNS
NEBUCHADNEZZAR
NEBUCHADNEZZARS
NEBULISATION
NEBULISATIONS
NEBULISERS
NEBULISING
NEBULIZATION
NEBULIZATIONS
NEBULIZERS
NEBULIZING
NEBULOSITIES
NEBULOSITY
NEBULOUSLY
NEBULOUSNESS
NEBULOUSNESSES
NECESSAIRE
NECESSAIRES
NECESSARIAN
NECESSARIANISM
NECESSARIANISMS
NECESSARIANS
NECESSARIES
NECESSARILY
NECESSARINESS
NECESSARINESSES
NECESSITARIAN
NECESSITARIANS
NECESSITATE
NECESSITATED
NECESSITATES
NECESSITATING
NECESSITATION
NECESSITATIONS
NECESSITATIVE
NECESSITIED
NECESSITIES
NECESSITOUS
NECESSITOUSLY
NECESSITOUSNESS
NECKCLOTHS
NECKERCHIEF
NECKERCHIEFS
NECKERCHIEVES
NECKLACING
NECKLACINGS
NECKPIECES
NECKVERSES
NECROBIOSES
NECROBIOSIS
NECROBIOTIC
NECROGRAPHER
NECROGRAPHERS
NECROLATER
NECROLATERS
NECROLATRIES
NECROLATRY
NECROLOGIC
NECROLOGICAL
NECROLOGIES
NECROLOGIST
NECROLOGISTS
NECROMANCER
NECROMANCERS
NECROMANCIES
NECROMANCY
NECROMANIA
NECROMANIAC
NECROMANIACS
NECROMANIAS
NECROMANTIC
NECROMANTICAL
NECROMANTICALLY
NECROPHAGOUS
NECROPHILE
NECROPHILES
NECROPHILIA
NECROPHILIAC
NECROPHILIACS
NECROPHILIAS
NECROPHILIC
NECROPHILIES
NECROPHILISM
NECROPHILISMS
NECROPHILOUS
NECROPHILS
NECROPHILY
NECROPHOBE
NECROPHOBES
NECROPHOBIA
NECROPHOBIAS
NECROPHOBIC
NECROPHOROUS
NECROPOLEIS
NECROPOLES
NECROPOLIS
NECROPOLISES
NECROPSIED
NECROPSIES
NECROPSYING
NECROSCOPIC
NECROSCOPICAL
NECROSCOPIES
NECROSCOPY
NECROTISED
NECROTISES
NECROTISING
NECROTIZED
NECROTIZES
NECROTIZING
NECROTOMIES
NECROTROPH
NECROTROPHIC
NECROTROPHS
NECTAREOUS
NECTAREOUSNESS
NECTARIFEROUS
NECTARINES
NECTARIVOROUS
NECTOCALYCES
NECTOCALYX
NEEDCESSITIES
NEEDCESSITY
NEEDFULNESS
NEEDFULNESSES
NEEDINESSES
NEEDLECORD
NEEDLECORDS
NEEDLECRAFT
NEEDLECRAFTS
NEEDLEFISH
NEEDLEFISHES
NEEDLEFULS
NEEDLELESS
NEEDLELIKE
NEEDLEPOINT
NEEDLEPOINTED
NEEDLEPOINTING
NEEDLEPOINTS
NEEDLESSLY
NEEDLESSNESS
NEEDLESSNESSES
NEEDLESTICK
NEEDLESTICKS
NEEDLEWOMAN
NEEDLEWOMEN
NEEDLEWORK
NEEDLEWORKER
NEEDLEWORKERS
NEEDLEWORKS
NEESBERRIES
NEFARIOUSLY
NEFARIOUSNESS
NEFARIOUSNESSES
NEGATIONAL
NEGATIONIST
NEGATIONISTS
NEGATIVELY
NEGATIVENESS
NEGATIVENESSES
NEGATIVING

NEGATIVISM
NEGATIVISMS
NEGATIVIST
NEGATIVISTIC
NEGATIVISTS
NEGATIVITIES
NEGATIVITY
NEGLECTABLE
NEGLECTEDNESS
NEGLECTEDNESSES
NEGLECTERS
NEGLECTFUL
NEGLECTFULLY
NEGLECTFULNESS
NEGLECTING
NEGLECTINGLY
NEGLECTION
NEGLECTIONS
NEGLECTIVE
NEGLECTORS
NEGLIGEABLE
NEGLIGENCE
NEGLIGENCES
NEGLIGENTLY
NEGLIGIBILITIES
NEGLIGIBILITY
NEGLIGIBLE
NEGLIGIBLENESS
NEGLIGIBLY
NEGOCIANTS
NEGOTIABILITIES
NEGOTIABILITY
NEGOTIABLE
NEGOTIANTS
NEGOTIATED
NEGOTIATES
NEGOTIATING
NEGOTIATION
NEGOTIATIONS
NEGOTIATOR
NEGOTIATORS
NEGOTIATORY
NEGOTIATRESS
NEGOTIATRESSES
NEGOTIATRICES
NEGOTIATRIX
NEGOTIATRIXES
NEGRITUDES
NEGROHEADS
NEGROPHILE
NEGROPHILES
NEGROPHILISM
NEGROPHILISMS
NEGROPHILIST
NEGROPHILISTS
NEGROPHILS
NEGROPHOBE
NEGROPHOBES
NEGROPHOBIA
NEGROPHOBIAS
NEIGHBORED
NEIGHBORHOOD
NEIGHBORHOODS
NEIGHBORING
NEIGHBORLESS
NEIGHBORLIER
NEIGHBORLIEST
NEIGHBORLINESS
NEIGHBORLY
NEIGHBOURED
NEIGHBOURHOOD
NEIGHBOURHOODS
NEIGHBOURING
NEIGHBOURLESS
NEIGHBOURLIER
NEIGHBOURLIEST
NEIGHBOURLINESS
NEIGHBOURLY
NEIGHBOURS
NELUMBIUMS
NEMATHELMINTH
NEMATHELMINTHIC
NEMATHELMINTHS
NEMATICIDAL
NEMATICIDE
NEMATICIDES
NEMATOBLAST
NEMATOBLASTS
NEMATOCIDAL
NEMATOCIDE
NEMATOCIDES
NEMATOCYST
NEMATOCYSTIC
NEMATOCYSTS
NEMATODIRIASES
NEMATODIRIASIS
NEMATODIRUS
NEMATODIRUSES
NEMATOLOGICAL
NEMATOLOGIES
NEMATOLOGIST
NEMATOLOGISTS
NEMATOLOGY
NEMATOPHORE
NEMATOPHORES
NEMERTEANS
NEMERTIANS
NEMERTINES
NEMOPHILAS
NEOANTHROPIC
NEOARSPHENAMINE
NEOCAPITALISM
NEOCAPITALISMS
NEOCAPITALIST
NEOCAPITALISTS
NEOCLASSIC
NEOCLASSICAL
NEOCLASSICISM
NEOCLASSICISMS
NEOCLASSICIST
NEOCLASSICISTS
NEOCOLONIAL
NEOCOLONIALISM
NEOCOLONIALISMS
NEOCOLONIALIST
NEOCOLONIALISTS
NEOCONSERVATISM
NEOCONSERVATIVE
NEOCORTEXES
NEOCORTICAL
NEOCORTICES
NEODYMIUMS
NEOGENESES
NEOGENESIS
NEOGENETIC
NEOGOTHICS
NEOGRAMMARIAN
NEOGRAMMARIANS
NEOLIBERAL
NEOLIBERALISM
NEOLIBERALISMS
NEOLIBERALS
NEOLITHICS
NEOLOGIANS
NEOLOGICAL
NEOLOGICALLY
NEOLOGISED
NEOLOGISES
NEOLOGISING
NEOLOGISMS
NEOLOGISTIC
NEOLOGISTICAL
NEOLOGISTICALLY
NEOLOGISTS
NEOLOGIZED
NEOLOGIZES
NEOLOGIZING
NEONATALLY
NEONATICIDE
NEONATICIDES
NEONATOLOGIES
NEONATOLOGIST
NEONATOLOGISTS
NEONATOLOGY
NEONOMIANISM
NEONOMIANISMS
NEONOMIANS
NEOORTHODOX
NEOORTHODOXIES
NEOORTHODOXY
NEOPAGANISE
NEOPAGANISED
NEOPAGANISES
NEOPAGANISING
NEOPAGANISM
NEOPAGANISMS
NEOPAGANIZE
NEOPAGANIZED
NEOPAGANIZES
NEOPAGANIZING
NEOPHILIAC
NEOPHILIACS
NEOPHILIAS
NEOPHOBIAS
NEOPILINAS
NEOPLASIAS
NEOPLASTIC
NEOPLASTICISM
NEOPLASTICISMS
NEOPLASTICIST
NEOPLASTICISTS
NEOPLASTIES
NEOREALISM
NEOREALISMS
NEOREALIST
NEOREALISTIC
NEOREALISTS
NEOSTIGMINE
NEOSTIGMINES
NEOTEINIAS
NEOTERICAL
NEOTERICALLY
NEOTERICALS
NEOTERISED
NEOTERISES
NEOTERISING
NEOTERISMS
NEOTERISTS
NEOTERIZED
NEOTERIZES
NEOTERIZING
NEOTROPICS
NEOVITALISM
NEOVITALISMS
NEOVITALIST
NEOVITALISTS
NEPENTHEAN
NEPHALISMS
NEPHALISTS
NEPHELINES
NEPHELINIC
NEPHELINITE
NEPHELINITES
NEPHELINITIC
NEPHELITES
NEPHELOMETER
NEPHELOMETERS
NEPHELOMETRIC
NEPHELOMETRIES
NEPHELOMETRY
NEPHOGRAMS
NEPHOGRAPH
NEPHOGRAPHS
NEPHOLOGIC
NEPHOLOGICAL
NEPHOLOGIES
NEPHOLOGIST
NEPHOLOGISTS
NEPHOSCOPE
NEPHOSCOPES

NEPHRALGIA
NEPHRALGIAS
NEPHRALGIC
NEPHRALGIES
NEPHRECTOMIES
NEPHRECTOMISE
NEPHRECTOMISED
NEPHRECTOMISES
NEPHRECTOMISING
NEPHRECTOMIZE
NEPHRECTOMIZED
NEPHRECTOMIZES
NEPHRECTOMIZING
NEPHRECTOMY
NEPHRIDIAL
NEPHRIDIUM
NEPHRITICAL
NEPHRITICS
NEPHRITIDES
NEPHRITISES
NEPHROBLASTOMA
NEPHROBLASTOMAS
NEPHROLEPIS
NEPHROLEPISES
NEPHROLOGICAL
NEPHROLOGIES
NEPHROLOGIST
NEPHROLOGISTS
NEPHROLOGY
NEPHROPATHIC
NEPHROPATHIES
NEPHROPATHY
NEPHROPEXIES
NEPHROPEXY
NEPHROPTOSES
NEPHROPTOSIS
NEPHROSCOPE
NEPHROSCOPES
NEPHROSCOPIES
NEPHROSCOPY
NEPHROSTOME
NEPHROSTOMES
NEPHROTICS
NEPHROTOMIES
NEPHROTOMY
NEPHROTOXIC
NEPHROTOXICITY
NEPOTISTIC
NEPTUNIUMS
NERDINESSES
NERVATIONS
NERVATURES
NERVELESSLY
NERVELESSNESS
NERVELESSNESSES
NERVINESSES
NERVOSITIES
NERVOUSNESS
NERVOUSNESSES
NERVURATION
NERVURATIONS
NESCIENCES
NESHNESSES
NESSELRODE
NESSELRODES
NETBALLERS
NETHERLINGS
NETHERMORE
NETHERMORES
NETHERMOST
NETHERSTOCK
NETHERSTOCKS
NETHERWARD
NETHERWARDS
NETHERWORLD
NETHERWORLDS
NETIQUETTE
NETIQUETTES
NETMINDERS
NETSURFERS
NETSURFING
NETSURFINGS
NETTLELIKE
NETTLESOME
NETWORKERS
NETWORKING
NETWORKINGS
NEURALGIAS
NEURAMINIC
NEURAMINIDASE
NEURAMINIDASES
NEURASTHENIA
NEURASTHENIAC
NEURASTHENIACS
NEURASTHENIAS
NEURASTHENIC
NEURASTHENICS
NEURATIONS
NEURECTOMIES
NEURECTOMY
NEURILEMMA
NEURILEMMAL
NEURILEMMAS
NEURILITIES
NEURITIDES
NEURITISES
NEUROACTIVE
NEUROANATOMIC
NEUROANATOMICAL
NEUROANATOMIES
NEUROANATOMIST
NEUROANATOMISTS
NEUROANATOMY
NEUROBIOLOGICAL
NEUROBIOLOGIES
NEUROBIOLOGIST
NEUROBIOLOGISTS
NEUROBIOLOGY
NEUROBLAST
NEUROBLASTOMA
NEUROBLASTOMAS
NEUROBLASTOMATA
NEUROBLASTS
NEUROCHEMICAL
NEUROCHEMICALS
NEUROCHEMIST
NEUROCHEMISTRY
NEUROCHEMISTS
NEUROCHIPS
NEUROCOELE
NEUROCOELES
NEUROCOELS
NEUROCOGNITIVE
NEUROCOMPUTER
NEUROCOMPUTERS
NEUROCOMPUTING
NEUROCOMPUTINGS
NEURODIVERSITY
NEUROECTODERMAL
NEUROENDOCRINE
NEUROETHOLOGIES
NEUROETHOLOGY
NEUROFEEDBACK
NEUROFEEDBACKS
NEUROFIBRIL
NEUROFIBRILAR
NEUROFIBRILLAR
NEUROFIBRILLARY
NEUROFIBRILS
NEUROFIBROMA
NEUROFIBROMAS
NEUROFIBROMATA
NEUROGENESES
NEUROGENESIS
NEUROGENIC
NEUROGENICALLY
NEUROGLIAL
NEUROGLIAS
NEUROGRAMS
NEUROHORMONAL
NEUROHORMONE
NEUROHORMONES
NEUROHUMOR
NEUROHUMORAL
NEUROHUMORS
NEUROHUMOUR
NEUROHUMOURS
NEUROHYPNOLOGY
NEUROHYPOPHYSES
NEUROHYPOPHYSIS
NEUROLEMMA
NEUROLEMMAS
NEUROLEPTIC
NEUROLEPTICS
NEUROLINGUIST
NEUROLINGUISTIC
NEUROLINGUISTS
NEUROLOGIC
NEUROLOGICAL
NEUROLOGICALLY
NEUROLOGIES
NEUROLOGIST
NEUROLOGISTS
NEUROLYSES
NEUROLYSIS
NEUROMARKETING
NEUROMARKETINGS
NEUROMASTS
NEUROMATOUS
NEUROMOTOR
NEUROMUSCULAR
NEUROPATHIC
NEUROPATHICAL
NEUROPATHICALLY
NEUROPATHIES
NEUROPATHIST
NEUROPATHISTS
NEUROPATHOLOGIC
NEUROPATHOLOGY
NEUROPATHS
NEUROPATHY
NEUROPEPTIDE
NEUROPEPTIDES
NEUROPHYSIOLOGY
NEUROPLASM
NEUROPLASMS
NEUROPSYCHIATRY
NEUROPSYCHOLOGY
NEUROPTERA
NEUROPTERAN
NEUROPTERANS
NEUROPTERIST
NEUROPTERISTS
NEUROPTERON
NEUROPTERONS
NEUROPTEROUS
NEURORADIOLOGY
NEUROSCIENCE
NEUROSCIENCES
NEUROSCIENTIFIC
NEUROSCIENTIST
NEUROSCIENTISTS
NEUROSECRETION
NEUROSECRETIONS
NEUROSECRETORY
NEUROSENSORY
NEUROSPORA
NEUROSPORAS
NEUROSURGEON
NEUROSURGEONS
NEUROSURGERIES
NEUROSURGERY
NEUROSURGICAL
NEUROSURGICALLY
NEUROSYPHILIS
NEUROSYPHILISES
NEUROTICALLY
NEUROTICISM
NEUROTICISMS
NEUROTOMIES

NEUROTOMIST
NEUROTOMISTS
NEUROTOXIC
NEUROTOXICITIES
NEUROTOXICITY
NEUROTOXIN
NEUROTOXINS
NEUROTROPHIC
NEUROTROPHIES
NEUROTROPHY
NEUROTROPIC
NEUROTYPICAL
NEUROVASCULAR
NEURULATION
NEURULATIONS
NEURYPNOLOGIES
NEURYPNOLOGY
NEUTERINGS
NEUTRALISATION
NEUTRALISATIONS
NEUTRALISE
NEUTRALISED
NEUTRALISER
NEUTRALISERS
NEUTRALISES
NEUTRALISING
NEUTRALISM
NEUTRALISMS
NEUTRALIST
NEUTRALISTIC
NEUTRALISTS
NEUTRALITIES
NEUTRALITY
NEUTRALIZATION
NEUTRALIZATIONS
NEUTRALIZE
NEUTRALIZED
NEUTRALIZER
NEUTRALIZERS
NEUTRALIZES
NEUTRALIZING
NEUTRALNESS
NEUTRALNESSES
NEUTRETTOS
NEUTRINOLESS
NEUTROPENIA
NEUTROPENIAS
NEUTROPHIL
NEUTROPHILE
NEUTROPHILES
NEUTROPHILIC
NEUTROPHILS
NEVERMINDS
NEVERTHELESS
NEVERTHEMORE
NEWFANGLED
NEWFANGLEDLY
NEWFANGLEDNESS
NEWFANGLENESS
NEWFANGLENESSES
NEWFANGLES
NEWISHNESS
NEWISHNESSES
NEWMARKETS
NEWSAGENCIES
NEWSAGENCY
NEWSAGENTS
NEWSBREAKS
NEWSCASTER
NEWSCASTERS
NEWSCASTING
NEWSCASTINGS
NEWSDEALER
NEWSDEALERS
NEWSFLASHES
NEWSGROUPS
NEWSHOUNDS
NEWSINESSES
NEWSLETTER
NEWSLETTERS
NEWSMAGAZINE
NEWSMAGAZINES
NEWSMAKERS
NEWSMONGER
NEWSMONGERS
NEWSPAPERDOM
NEWSPAPERDOMS
NEWSPAPERED
NEWSPAPERING
NEWSPAPERISM
NEWSPAPERISMS
NEWSPAPERMAN
NEWSPAPERMEN
NEWSPAPERS
NEWSPAPERWOMAN
NEWSPAPERWOMEN
NEWSPEOPLE
NEWSPERSON
NEWSPERSONS
NEWSPRINTS
NEWSREADER
NEWSREADERS
NEWSSHEETS
NEWSSTANDS
NEWSTRADES
NEWSWEEKLIES
NEWSWEEKLY
NEWSWORTHIER
NEWSWORTHIEST
NEWSWORTHINESS
NEWSWORTHY
NEWSWRITING
NEWSWRITINGS
NEXTNESSES
NIACINAMIDE
NIACINAMIDES
NIAISERIES
NIALAMIDES
NIBBLINGLY
NICCOLITES
NICENESSES
NICKELIFEROUS
NICKELINES
NICKELISED
NICKELISES
NICKELISING
NICKELIZED
NICKELIZES
NICKELIZING
NICKELLING
NICKELODEON
NICKELODEONS
NICKERNUTS
NICKNAMERS
NICKNAMING
NICKPOINTS
NICKSTICKS
NICKUMPOOP
NICKUMPOOPS
NICOMPOOPS
NICOTIANAS
NICOTINAMIDE
NICOTINAMIDES
NICOTINISM
NICOTINISMS
NICROSILAL
NICROSILALS
NICTATIONS
NICTITATED
NICTITATES
NICTITATING
NICTITATION
NICTITATIONS
NIDAMENTAL
NIDAMENTUM
NIDDERINGS
NIDDERLING
NIDDERLINGS
NIDERLINGS
NIDICOLOUS
NIDIFICATE
NIDIFICATED
NIDIFICATES
NIDIFICATING
NIDIFICATION
NIDIFICATIONS
NIDIFUGOUS
NIDULATION
NIDULATIONS
NIFEDIPINE
NIFEDIPINES
NIFFNAFFED
NIFFNAFFING
NIFTINESSES
NIGGARDING
NIGGARDISE
NIGGARDISES
NIGGARDIZE
NIGGARDIZES
NIGGARDLIER
NIGGARDLIEST
NIGGARDLINESS
NIGGARDLINESSES
NIGGERDOMS
NIGGERHEAD
NIGGERHEADS
NIGGERIEST
NIGGERISMS
NIGGERLING
NIGGERLINGS
NIGGLINGLY
NIGHNESSES
NIGHTBIRDS
NIGHTBLIND
NIGHTCLASS
NIGHTCLASSES
NIGHTCLOTHES
NIGHTCLUBBED
NIGHTCLUBBER
NIGHTCLUBBERS
NIGHTCLUBBING
NIGHTCLUBBINGS
NIGHTCLUBS
NIGHTDRESS
NIGHTDRESSES
NIGHTFALLS
NIGHTFARING
NIGHTFIRES
NIGHTGEARS
NIGHTGLOWS
NIGHTGOWNS
NIGHTHAWKS
NIGHTINGALE
NIGHTINGALES
NIGHTLIFES
NIGHTLIVES
NIGHTMARES
NIGHTMARIER
NIGHTMARIEST
NIGHTMARISH
NIGHTMARISHLY
NIGHTMARISHNESS
NIGHTPIECE
NIGHTPIECES
NIGHTRIDER
NIGHTRIDERS
NIGHTRIDING
NIGHTRIDINGS
NIGHTSCOPE
NIGHTSCOPES
NIGHTSHADE
NIGHTSHADES
NIGHTSHIRT
NIGHTSHIRTS
NIGHTSIDES
NIGHTSPOTS
NIGHTSTAND
NIGHTSTANDS
NIGHTSTICK
NIGHTSTICKS

N

NIGHTTIDES
NIGHTTIMES
NIGHTWALKER
NIGHTWALKERS
NIGHTWATCHMAN
NIGHTWATCHMEN
NIGHTWEARS
NIGRESCENCE
NIGRESCENCES
NIGRESCENT
NIGRIFYING
NIGRITUDES
NIGROMANCIES
NIGROMANCY
NIGROSINES
NIHILISTIC
NIHILITIES
NIKETHAMIDE
NIKETHAMIDES
NILPOTENTS
NIMBLENESS
NIMBLENESSES
NIMBLESSES
NIMBLEWITS
NIMBLEWITTED
NIMBOSTRATI
NIMBOSTRATUS
NIMBYNESSES
NINCOMPOOP
NINCOMPOOPERIES
NINCOMPOOPERY
NINCOMPOOPS
NINEPENCES
NINEPENNIES
NINESCORES
NINETEENTH
NINETEENTHLIES
NINETEENTHLY
NINETEENTHS
NINETIETHS
NINHYDRINS
NINNYHAMMER
NINNYHAMMERS
NIPCHEESES
NIPPERKINS
NIPPINESSES
NIPPLEWORT
NIPPLEWORTS
NISBERRIES
NITPICKERS
NITPICKIER
NITPICKIEST
NITPICKING
NITPICKINGS
NITRAMINES
NITRANILINE
NITRANILINES
NITRATINES
NITRATIONS
NITRAZEPAM
NITRAZEPAMS
NITRIDINGS
NITRIFIABLE
NITRIFICATION
NITRIFICATIONS
NITRIFIERS
NITRIFYING
NITROBACTERIA
NITROBACTERIUM
NITROBENZENE
NITROBENZENES
NITROCELLULOSE
NITROCELLULOSES
NITROCHLOROFORM
NITROCOTTON
NITROCOTTONS
NITROFURAN
NITROFURANS
NITROGELATIN
NITROGELATINE
NITROGELATINES
NITROGELATINS
NITROGENASE
NITROGENASES
NITROGENISATION
NITROGENISE
NITROGENISED
NITROGENISES
NITROGENISING
NITROGENIZATION
NITROGENIZE
NITROGENIZED
NITROGENIZES
NITROGENIZING
NITROGENOUS
NITROGLYCERIN
NITROGLYCERINE
NITROGLYCERINES
NITROGLYCERINS
NITROMETER
NITROMETERS
NITROMETHANE
NITROMETHANES
NITROMETRIC
NITROPARAFFIN
NITROPARAFFINS
NITROPHILOUS
NITROSAMINE
NITROSAMINES
NITROSATION
NITROSATIONS
NITROTOLUENE
NITROTOLUENES
NITWITTEDNESS
NITWITTEDNESSES
NITWITTERIES
NITWITTERY
NOBBINESSES
NOBILESSES
NOBILITATE
NOBILITATED
NOBILITATES
NOBILITATING
NOBILITATION
NOBILITATIONS
NOBILITIES
NOBLENESSES
NOBLEWOMAN
NOBLEWOMEN
NOCHELLING
NOCICEPTIVE
NOCICEPTOR
NOCICEPTORS
NOCIRECEPTOR
NOCIRECEPTORS
NOCTAMBULATION
NOCTAMBULATIONS
NOCTAMBULISM
NOCTAMBULISMS
NOCTAMBULIST
NOCTAMBULISTS
NOCTILUCAE
NOCTILUCAS
NOCTILUCENCE
NOCTILUCENCES
NOCTILUCENT
NOCTILUCOUS
NOCTIVAGANT
NOCTIVAGANTS
NOCTIVAGATION
NOCTIVAGATIONS
NOCTIVAGOUS
NOCTUARIES
NOCTURNALITIES
NOCTURNALITY
NOCTURNALLY
NOCTURNALS
NOCUOUSNESS
NOCUOUSNESSES
NODALISING
NODALITIES
NODALIZING
NODOSITIES
NODULATION
NODULATIONS
NOEMATICAL
NOEMATICALLY
NOGOODNIKS
NOISELESSLY
NOISELESSNESS
NOISELESSNESSES
NOISEMAKER
NOISEMAKERS
NOISEMAKING
NOISEMAKINGS
NOISINESSES
NOISOMENESS
NOISOMENESSES
NOMADICALLY
NOMADISATION
NOMADISATIONS
NOMADISING
NOMADIZATION
NOMADIZATIONS
NOMADIZING
NOMARCHIES
NOMENCLATIVE
NOMENCLATOR
NOMENCLATORIAL
NOMENCLATORS
NOMENCLATURAL
NOMENCLATURE
NOMENCLATURES
NOMENKLATURA
NOMENKLATURAS
NOMINALISATION
NOMINALISATIONS
NOMINALISE
NOMINALISED
NOMINALISES
NOMINALISING
NOMINALISM
NOMINALISMS
NOMINALIST
NOMINALISTIC
NOMINALISTS
NOMINALIZATION
NOMINALIZATIONS
NOMINALIZE
NOMINALIZED
NOMINALIZES
NOMINALIZING
NOMINATELY
NOMINATING
NOMINATION
NOMINATIONS
NOMINATIVAL
NOMINATIVALLY
NOMINATIVE
NOMINATIVELY
NOMINATIVES
NOMINATORS
NOMOCRACIES
NOMOGENIES
NOMOGRAPHER
NOMOGRAPHERS
NOMOGRAPHIC
NOMOGRAPHICAL
NOMOGRAPHICALLY
NOMOGRAPHIES
NOMOGRAPHS
NOMOGRAPHY
NOMOLOGICAL
NOMOLOGICALLY
NOMOLOGIES
NOMOLOGIST
NOMOLOGISTS
NOMOTHETES
NOMOTHETIC
NOMOTHETICAL

NONABRASIVE
NONABSORBABLE
NONABSORBENT
NONABSORPTIVE
NONABSTRACT
NONACADEMIC
NONACADEMICS
NONACCEPTANCE
NONACCEPTANCES
NONACCIDENTAL
NONACCOUNTABLE
NONACCREDITED
NONACCRUAL
NONACHIEVEMENT
NONACHIEVEMENTS
NONACQUISITIVE
NONACTINGS
NONACTIONS
NONACTIVATED
NONADAPTIVE
NONADDICTIVE
NONADDICTS
NONADDITIVE
NONADDITIVITIES
NONADDITIVITY
NONADHESIVE
NONADIABATIC
NONADJACENT
NONADMIRER
NONADMIRERS
NONADMISSION
NONADMISSIONS
NONAESTHETIC
NONAFFILIATED
NONAFFLUENT
NONAGENARIAN
NONAGENARIANS
NONAGESIMAL
NONAGESIMALS
NONAGGRESSION
NONAGGRESSIONS
NONAGGRESSIVE
NONAGRICULTURAL
NONALCOHOLIC
NONALGEBRAIC
NONALIGNED
NONALIGNMENT
NONALIGNMENTS
NONALLELIC
NONALLERGENIC
NONALLERGIC
NONALPHABETIC
NONALUMINIUM
NONALUMINUM
NONAMBIGUOUS
NONANALYTIC
NONANATOMIC
NONANSWERED
NONANSWERING
NONANSWERS
NONANTAGONISTIC
NONANTIBIOTIC
NONANTIBIOTICS
NONANTIGENIC
NONAPPEARANCE
NONAPPEARANCES
NONAQUATIC
NONAQUEOUS
NONARBITRARY
NONARCHITECT
NONARCHITECTS
NONARCHITECTURE
NONARGUMENT
NONARGUMENTS
NONARISTOCRATIC
NONAROMATIC
NONAROMATICS
NONARRIVAL
NONARRIVALS
NONARTISTIC
NONARTISTS
NONASCETIC
NONASCETICS
NONASPIRIN
NONASSERTIVE
NONASSOCIATED
NONASTRONOMICAL
NONATHLETE
NONATHLETES
NONATHLETIC
NONATTACHED
NONATTACHMENT
NONATTACHMENTS
NONATTENDANCE
NONATTENDANCES
NONATTENDER
NONATTENDERS
NONATTRIBUTABLE
NONAUDITORY
NONAUTHORS
NONAUTOMATED
NONAUTOMATIC
NONAUTOMOTIVE
NONAUTONOMOUS
NONAVAILABILITY
NONBACTERIAL
NONBANKING
NONBARBITURATE
NONBARBITURATES
NONBEARING
NONBEHAVIORAL
NONBEHAVIOURAL
NONBELIEFS
NONBELIEVER
NONBELIEVERS
NONBELLIGERENCY
NONBELLIGERENT
NONBELLIGERENTS
NONBETTING
NONBINDING
NONBIOGRAPHICAL
NONBIOLOGICAL
NONBIOLOGICALLY
NONBIOLOGIST
NONBIOLOGISTS
NONBONDING
NONBOTANIST
NONBOTANISTS
NONBREAKABLE
NONBREATHING
NONBREEDER
NONBREEDERS
NONBREEDING
NONBROADCAST
NONBUILDING
NONBURNABLE
NONBUSINESS
NONCABINET
NONCALLABLE
NONCALORIC
NONCANCELABLE
NONCANCELLABLE
NONCANCEROUS
NONCANDIDACIES
NONCANDIDACY
NONCANDIDATE
NONCANDIDATES
NONCAPITAL
NONCAPITALIST
NONCAPITALISTS
NONCARBOHYDRATE
NONCARCINOGEN
NONCARCINOGENIC
NONCARCINOGENS
NONCARDIAC
NONCARRIER
NONCARRIERS
NONCELEBRATION
NONCELEBRATIONS
NONCELEBRITIES
NONCELEBRITY
NONCELLULAR
NONCELLULOSIC
NONCELLULOSICS
NONCENTRAL
NONCERTIFICATED
NONCERTIFIED
NONCHALANCE
NONCHALANCES
NONCHALANT
NONCHALANTLY
NONCHARACTER
NONCHARACTERS
NONCHARISMATIC
NONCHARISMATICS
NONCHAUVINIST
NONCHAUVINISTS
NONCHEMICAL
NONCHEMICALS
NONCHROMOSOMAL
NONCHURCHED
NONCHURCHES
NONCHURCHGOER
NONCHURCHGOERS
NONCHURCHING
NONCIRCULAR
NONCIRCULATING
NONCITIZEN
NONCITIZENS
NONCLANDESTINE
NONCLASSES
NONCLASSICAL
NONCLASSIFIED
NONCLASSROOM
NONCLERICAL
NONCLINICAL
NONCLOGGING
NONCOERCIVE
NONCOGNITIVE
NONCOGNITIVISM
NONCOGNITIVISMS
NONCOHERENT
NONCOINCIDENCE
NONCOINCIDENCES
NONCOLLECTOR
NONCOLLECTORS
NONCOLLEGE
NONCOLLEGIATE
NONCOLLINEAR
NONCOLORED
NONCOLORFAST
NONCOLOURED
NONCOLOURFAST
NONCOLOURS
NONCOMBATANT
NONCOMBATANTS
NONCOMBATIVE
NONCOMBUSTIBLE
NONCOMBUSTIBLES
NONCOMMERCIAL
NONCOMMISSIONED
NONCOMMITMENT
NONCOMMITMENTS
NONCOMMITTAL
NONCOMMITTALLY
NONCOMMITTALS
NONCOMMITTED
NONCOMMUNICANT
NONCOMMUNICANTS
NONCOMMUNIST
NONCOMMUNISTS
NONCOMMUNITY
NONCOMMUTATIVE
NONCOMPARABLE
NONCOMPATIBLE
NONCOMPETITION
NONCOMPETITIONS
NONCOMPETITIVE
NONCOMPETITOR
NONCOMPETITORS

NONCOMPLETION
NONCOMPLETIONS
NONCOMPLEX
NONCOMPLIANCE
NONCOMPLIANCES
NONCOMPLICATED
NONCOMPLYING
NONCOMPLYINGS
NONCOMPOSER
NONCOMPOSERS
NONCOMPOUND
NONCOMPRESSIBLE
NONCOMPUTER
NONCOMPUTERISED
NONCOMPUTERIZED
NONCONCEPTUAL
NONCONCERN
NONCONCERNS
NONCONCLUSION
NONCONCLUSIONS
NONCONCURRED
NONCONCURRENCE
NONCONCURRENCES
NONCONCURRENT
NONCONCURRING
NONCONCURS
NONCONDENSABLE
NONCONDITIONED
NONCONDUCTING
NONCONDUCTION
NONCONDUCTIONS
NONCONDUCTIVE
NONCONDUCTOR
NONCONDUCTORS
NONCONFERENCE
NONCONFIDENCE
NONCONFIDENCES
NONCONFIDENTIAL
NONCONFLICTING
NONCONFORM
NONCONFORMANCE
NONCONFORMANCES
NONCONFORMED
NONCONFORMER
NONCONFORMERS
NONCONFORMING
NONCONFORMINGS
NONCONFORMISM
NONCONFORMISMS
NONCONFORMIST
NONCONFORMISTS
NONCONFORMITIES
NONCONFORMITY
NONCONFORMS
NONCONGRUENT
NONCONJUGATED
NONCONNECTION
NONCONNECTIONS
NONCONSCIOUS
NONCONSECUTIVE
NONCONSENSUAL
NONCONSERVATION
NONCONSERVATIVE
NONCONSOLIDATED
NONCONSTANT
NONCONSTRUCTION
NONCONSTRUCTIVE
NONCONSUMER
NONCONSUMERS
NONCONSUMING
NONCONSUMPTION
NONCONSUMPTIONS
NONCONSUMPTIVE
NONCONTACT
NONCONTACTS
NONCONTAGIOUS
NONCONTEMPORARY
NONCONTIGUOUS
NONCONTINGENT
NONCONTINUOUS
NONCONTRACT
NONCONTRACTUAL
NONCONTRIBUTING
NONCONTRIBUTORY
NONCONTROLLABLE
NONCONTROLLED
NONCONTROLLING
NONCONVENTIONAL
NONCONVERTIBLE
NONCOOPERATION
NONCOOPERATIONS
NONCOOPERATIVE
NONCOOPERATOR
NONCOOPFRATORS
NONCOPLANAR
NONCORPORATE
NONCORRELATION
NONCORRELATIONS
NONCORRODIBLE
NONCORRODING
NONCORROSIVE
NONCOUNTRIES
NONCOUNTRY
NONCOVERAGE
NONCOVERAGES
NONCREATIVE
NONCREATIVITIES
NONCREATIVITY
NONCREDENTIALED
NONCRIMINAL
NONCRIMINALS
NONCRITICAL
NONCROSSOVER
NONCROSSOVERS
NONCRUSHABLE
NONCRYSTALLINE
NONCULINARY
NONCULTIVATED
NONCULTIVATION
NONCULTIVATIONS
NONCULTURAL
NONCUMULATIVE
NONCURRENT
NONCUSTODIAL
NONCUSTOMER
NONCUSTOMERS
NONCYCLICAL
NONDANCERS
NONDEALERS
NONDECEPTIVE
NONDECISION
NONDECISIONS
NONDECREASING
NONDEDUCTIBLE
NONDEDUCTIVE
NONDEFENCE
NONDEFENSE
NONDEFERRABLE
NONDEFORMING
NONDEGENERATE
NONDEGRADABLE
NONDELEGATE
NONDELEGATES
NONDELIBERATE
NONDELINQUENT
NONDELINQUENTS
NONDELIVERIES
NONDELIVERY
NONDEMANDING
NONDEMANDS
NONDEMOCRATIC
NONDEPARTMENTAL
NONDEPENDENT
NONDEPENDENTS
NONDEPLETABLE
NONDEPLETING
NONDEPOSITION
NONDEPOSITIONS
NONDEPRESSED
NONDERIVATIVE
NONDESCRIPT
NONDESCRIPTIVE
NONDESCRIPTLY
NONDESCRIPTNESS
NONDESCRIPTS
NONDESTRUCTIVE
NONDETACHABLE
NONDEVELOPMENT
NONDEVELOPMENTS
NONDEVIANT
NONDIABETIC
NONDIABETICS
NONDIALYSABLE
NONDIALYZABLE
NONDIAPAUSING
NONDIDACTIC
NONDIFFUSIBLE
NONDIMENSIONAL
NONDIPLOMATIC
NONDIRECTED
NONDIRECTIONAL
NONDIRECTIVE
NONDISABLED
NONDISCLOSURE
NONDISCLOSURES
NONDISCOUNT
NONDISCURSIVE
NONDISJUNCTION
NONDISJUNCTIONS
NONDISPERSIVE
NONDISRUPTIVE
NONDISTINCTIVE
NONDIVERGENT
NONDIVERSIFIED
NONDIVIDING
NONDOCTORS
NONDOCTRINAIRE
NONDOCUMENTARY
NONDOGMATIC
NONDOMESTIC
NONDOMICILED
NONDOMINANT
NONDORMANT
NONDRAMATIC
NONDRINKER
NONDRINKERS
NONDRINKING
NONDRIVERS
NONDURABLE
NONDURABLES
NONEARNING
NONECONOMIC
NONECONOMIST
NONECONOMISTS
NONEDIBLES
NONEDITORIAL
NONEDUCATION
NONEDUCATIONAL
NONEFFECTIVE
NONEFFECTIVES
NONELASTIC
NONELECTED
NONELECTION
NONELECTIONS
NONELECTIVE
NONELECTRIC
NONELECTRICAL
NONELECTRICALS
NONELECTRICS
NONELECTROLYTE
NONELECTROLYTES
NONELECTRONIC
NONELEMENTARY
NONEMERGENCIES
NONEMERGENCY
NONEMOTIONAL
NONEMPHATIC
NONEMPIRICAL
NONEMPLOYEE
NONEMPLOYEES

NONEMPLOYMENT
NONEMPLOYMENTS
NONENCAPSULATED
NONENFORCEMENT
NONENFORCEMENTS
NONENGAGEMENT
NONENGAGEMENTS
NONENGINEERING
NONENTITIES
NONENTRIES
NONENZYMATIC
NONENZYMIC
NONEQUILIBRIA
NONEQUILIBRIUM
NONEQUILIBRIUMS
NONEQUIVALENCE
NONEQUIVALENCES
NONEQUIVALENT
NONESSENTIAL
NONESSENTIALS
NONESTABLISHED
NONESTERIFIED
NONESUCHES
NONETHELESS
NONETHICAL
NONETHNICS
NONEVALUATIVE
NONEVIDENCE
NONEVIDENCES
NONEXCLUSIVE
NONEXECUTIVE
NONEXECUTIVES
NONEXEMPTS
NONEXISTENCE
NONEXISTENCES
NONEXISTENT
NONEXISTENTIAL
NONEXISTENTS
NONEXPENDABLE
NONEXPERIMENTAL
NONEXPERTS
NONEXPLANATORY
NONEXPLOITATION
NONEXPLOITATIVE
NONEXPLOITIVE
NONEXPLOSIVE
NONEXPOSED
NONFACTORS
NONFACTUAL
NONFACULTIES
NONFACULTY
NONFAMILIAL
NONFAMILIES
NONFARMERS
NONFATTENING
NONFEASANCE
NONFEASANCES
NONFEDERAL
NONFEDERATED
NONFEEDING
NONFEMINIST
NONFEMINISTS
NONFERROUS
NONFICTION
NONFICTIONAL
NONFICTIONALLY
NONFICTIONS
NONFIGURATIVE
NONFILAMENTOUS
NONFILTERABLE
NONFINANCIAL
NONFISSIONABLE
NONFLAMMABILITY
NONFLAMMABLE
NONFLOWERING
NONFLUENCIES
NONFLUENCY
NONFLUORESCENT
NONFORFEITABLE
NONFORFEITURE
NONFORFEITURES
NONFREEZING
NONFRIVOLOUS
NONFULFILLMENT
NONFULFILLMENTS
NONFULFILMENT
NONFULFILMENTS
NONFUNCTIONAL
NONFUNCTIONING
NONGASEOUS
NONGENETIC
NONGENITAL
NONGEOMETRICAL
NONGLAMOROUS
NONGOLFERS
NONGONOCOCCAL
NONGOVERNMENT
NONGOVERNMENTAL
NONGRADUATE
NONGRADUATES
NONGRAMMATICAL
NONGRANULAR
NONGREGARIOUS
NONGROWING
NONGROWTHS
NONHAEMOLYTIC
NONHALOGENATED
NONHANDICAPPED
NONHAPPENING
NONHAPPENINGS
NONHARMONIC
NONHAZARDOUS
NONHEMOLYTIC
NONHEREDITARY
NONHIERARCHICAL
NONHISTONE
NONHISTORICAL
NONHOMOGENEITY
NONHOMOGENEOUS
NONHOMOLOGOUS
NONHOMOSEXUAL
NONHOMOSEXUALS
NONHORMONAL
NONHOSPITAL
NONHOSPITALISED
NONHOSPITALIZED
NONHOSTILE
NONHOUSING
NONHUNTERS
NONHUNTING
NONHYGROSCOPIC
NONHYSTERICAL
NONIDENTICAL
NONIDENTITIES
NONIDENTITY
NONIDEOLOGICAL
NONILLIONS
NONILLIONTH
NONILLIONTHS
NONIMITATIVE
NONIMMIGRANT
NONIMMIGRANTS
NONIMPACTS
NONIMPLICATION
NONIMPLICATIONS
NONIMPORTATION
NONIMPORTATIONS
NONINCLUSION
NONINCLUSIONS
NONINCREASING
NONINCUMBENT
NONINCUMBENTS
NONINDEPENDENCE
NONINDICTABLE
NONINDIGENOUS
NONINDIVIDUAL
NONINDIVIDUALS
NONINDUCTIVE
NONINDUSTRIAL
NONINDUSTRY
NONINFECTED
NONINFECTIOUS
NONINFECTIVE
NONINFESTED
NONINFLAMMABLE
NONINFLAMMATORY
NONINFLATIONARY
NONINFLECTIONAL
NONINFLUENCE
NONINFLUENCES
NONINFORMATION
NONINFORMATIONS
NONINFRINGEMENT
NONINITIAL
NONINITIATE
NONINITIATES
NONINSECTICIDAL
NONINSECTS
NONINSTALLMENT
NONINSTALLMENTS
NONINSTALMENT
NONINSTRUMENTAL
NONINSURANCE
NONINSURANCES
NONINSURED
NONINTEGRAL
NONINTEGRATED
NONINTELLECTUAL
NONINTERACTING
NONINTERACTIVE
NONINTERCOURSE
NONINTERCOURSES
NONINTEREST
NONINTERFERENCE
NONINTERSECTING
NONINTERVENTION
NONINTIMIDATING
NONINTOXICANT
NONINTOXICANTS
NONINTOXICATING
NONINTRUSIVE
NONINTUITIVE
NONINVASIVE
NONINVOLVED
NONINVOLVEMENT
NONINVOLVEMENTS
NONIONISING
NONIONIZING
NONIRRADIATED
NONIRRIGATED
NONIRRITANT
NONIRRITANTS
NONIRRITATING
NONJOINDER
NONJOINDERS
NONJOINERS
NONJUDGEMENTAL
NONJUDGMENTAL
NONJUDICIAL
NONJUSTICIABLE
NONKOSHERS
NONLADDERING
NONLANDOWNER
NONLANDOWNERS
NONLANGUAGE
NONLANGUAGES
NONLAWYERS
NONLEGUMES
NONLEGUMINOUS
NONLEXICAL
NONLIBRARIAN
NONLIBRARIANS
NONLIBRARY
NONLINEARITIES
NONLINEARITY
NONLINGUISTIC
NONLIQUIDS
NONLITERAL
NONLITERARY
NONLITERATE

NONLITERATES
NONLIVINGS
NONLOGICAL
NONLOGICALLY
NONLUMINOUS
NONMAGNETIC
NONMAINSTREAM
NONMALICIOUS
NONMALIGNANT
NONMALLEABLE
NONMANAGEMENT
NONMANAGERIAL
NONMANDATORY
NONMARITAL
NONMARKETS
NONMATERIAL
NONMATHEMATICAL
NONMATRICULATED
NONMEANINGFUL
NONMEASURABLE
NONMECHANICAL
NONMECHANISTIC
NONMEDICAL
NONMEETING
NONMEETINGS
NONMEMBERS
NONMEMBERSHIP
NONMEMBERSHIPS
NONMERCURIAL
NONMETALLIC
NONMETAMERIC
NONMETAPHORICAL
NONMETRICAL
NONMETROPOLITAN
NONMICROBIAL
NONMIGRANT
NONMIGRANTS
NONMIGRATORY
NONMILITANT
NONMILITANTS
NONMILITARY
NONMIMETIC
NONMINORITIES
NONMINORITY
NONMODERNS
NONMOLECULAR
NONMONETARIST
NONMONETARISTS
NONMONETARY
NONMONOGAMOUS
NONMORTALS
NONMOTILITIES
NONMOTILITY
NONMOTORISED
NONMOTORIZED
NONMUNICIPAL
NONMUSICAL
NONMUSICALS
NONMUSICIAN
NONMUSICIANS
NONMUTANTS
NONMYELINATED
NONMYSTICAL
NONNARRATIVE
NONNATIONAL
NONNATIONALS
NONNATIVES
NONNATURAL
NONNECESSITIES
NONNECESSITY
NONNEGATIVE
NONNEGLIGENT
NONNEGOTIABLE
NONNEGOTIABLES
NONNETWORK
NONNITROGENOUS
NONNORMATIVE
NONNUCLEAR
NONNUCLEATED
NONNUMERICAL
NONNUTRITIOUS
NONNUTRITIVE
NONOBJECTIVE
NONOBJECTIVISM
NONOBJECTIVISMS
NONOBJECTIVIST
NONOBJECTIVISTS
NONOBJECTIVITY
NONOBSCENE
NONOBSERVANCE
NONOBSERVANCES
NONOBSERVANT
NONOBVIOUS
NONOBVIOUSES
NONOCCUPATIONAL
NONOCCURRENCE
NONOCCURRENCES
NONOFFICIAL
NONOFFICIALS
NONOPERATIC
NONOPERATING
NONOPERATIONAL
NONOPERATIVE
NONOPTIMAL
NONORGANIC
NONORGASMIC
NONORTHODOX
NONOVERLAPPING
NONOXIDISING
NONOXIDIZING
NONPAPISTS
NONPARALLEL
NONPARAMETRIC
NONPARASITIC
NONPAREILS
NONPARENTS
NONPARITIES
NONPARTICIPANT
NONPARTICIPANTS
NONPARTIES
NONPARTISAN
NONPARTISANSHIP
NONPARTIZAN
NONPARTIZANSHIP
NONPASSERINE
NONPASSIVE
NONPATHOGENIC
NONPAYMENT
NONPAYMENTS
NONPECUNIARY
NONPERFORMANCE
NONPERFORMANCES
NONPERFORMER
NONPERFORMERS
NONPERFORMING
NONPERISHABLE
NONPERISHABLES
NONPERMANENT
NONPERMISSIVE
NONPERSISTENT
NONPERSONAL
NONPERSONS
NONPETROLEUM
NONPHILOSOPHER
NONPHILOSOPHERS
NONPHONEMIC
NONPHONETIC
NONPHOSPHATE
NONPHOTOGRAPHIC
NONPHYSICAL
NONPHYSICIAN
NONPHYSICIANS
NONPLASTIC
NONPLASTICS
NONPLAYERS
NONPLAYING
NONPLUSING
NONPLUSSED
NONPLUSSES
NONPLUSSING
NONPOISONOUS
NONPOLARISABLE
NONPOLARIZABLE
NONPOLITICAL
NONPOLITICALLY
NONPOLITICIAN
NONPOLITICIANS
NONPOLLUTING
NONPOPULAR
NONPORTABLE
NONPOSSESSION
NONPOSSESSIONS
NONPRACTICAL
NONPRACTICING
NONPRACTISING
NONPREGNANT
NONPREHENSILE
NONPRESCRIPTION
NONPRINTING
NONPROBLEM
NONPROBLEMS
NONPRODUCING
NONPRODUCTIVE
NONPRODUCTIVITY
NONPROFESSIONAL
NONPROFESSORIAL
NONPROFITS
NONPROGRAM
NONPROGRAMMER
NONPROGRAMMERS
NONPROGRESSIVE
NONPROPRIETARY
NONPROSSED
NONPROSSES
NONPROSSING
NONPROTEIN
NONPSYCHIATRIC
NONPSYCHIATRIST
NONPSYCHOTIC
NONPUNITIVE
NONPURPOSIVE
NONQUANTIFIABLE
NONQUANTITATIVE
NONRACIALLY
NONRACISMS
NONRADIOACTIVE
NONRAILROAD
NONRANDOMNESS
NONRANDOMNESSES
NONRATIONAL
NONREACTIVE
NONREACTOR
NONREACTORS
NONREADERS
NONREADING
NONREADINGS
NONREALISTIC
NONRECEIPT
NONRECEIPTS
NONRECIPROCAL
NONRECOGNITION
NONRECOGNITIONS
NONRECOMBINANT
NONRECOMBINANTS
NONRECOURSE
NONRECOVERABLE
NONRECURRENT
NONRECURRING
NONRECYCLABLE
NONRECYCLABLES
NONREDUCING
NONREDUNDANT
NONREFILLABLE
NONREFLECTING
NONREFLECTIVE
NONREFLEXIVE
NONREFUNDABLE
NONREGIMENTAL
NONREGULATED
NONREGULATION

N

NONREIGNING
NONRELATIVE
NONRELATIVES
NONRELATIVISTIC
NONRELEVANT
NONRELIGIOUS
NONRENEWABLE
NONRENEWAL
NONRENEWALS
NONREPAYABLE
NONREPRODUCTIVE
NONRESIDENCE
NONRESIDENCES
NONRESIDENCIES
NONRESIDENCY
NONRESIDENT
NONRESIDENTIAL
NONRESIDENTS
NONRESISTANCE
NONRESISTANCES
NONRESISTANT
NONRESISTANTS
NONRESONANT
NONRESPONDENT
NONRESPONDENTS
NONRESPONDER
NONRESPONDERS
NONRESPONSE
NONRESPONSES
NONRESPONSIVE
NONRESTRICTED
NONRESTRICTIVE
NONRETRACTILE
NONRETROACTIVE
NONRETURNABLE
NONRETURNABLES
NONREUSABLE
NONREVERSIBLE
NONRHOTICITIES
NONRHOTICITY
NONRIOTERS
NONRIOTING
NONROTATING
NONROUTINE
NONRUMINANT
NONRUMINANTS
NONRUNNERS
NONSALABLE
NONSALEABLE
NONSAPONIFIABLE
NONSCHEDULED
NONSCIENCE
NONSCIENCES
NONSCIENTIFIC
NONSCIENTIST
NONSCIENTISTS
NONSEASONAL
NONSECRETOR
NONSECRETORS
NONSECRETORY
NONSECRETS
NONSECTARIAN
NONSEDIMENTABLE
NONSEGREGATED
NONSEGREGATION
NONSEGREGATIONS
NONSELECTED
NONSELECTIVE
NONSENSATIONAL
NONSENSICAL
NONSENSICALITY
NONSENSICALLY
NONSENSICALNESS
NONSENSITIVE
NONSENSUOUS
NONSENTENCE
NONSENTENCES
NONSEPTATE
NONSEQUENTIAL
NONSERIALS
NONSERIOUS
NONSHRINKABLE
NONSIGNERS
NONSIGNIFICANT
NONSIGNIFICANTS
NONSIMULTANEOUS
NONSINKABLE
NONSINUSOIDAL
NONSKATERS
NONSKELETAL
NONSKILLED
NONSMOKERS
NONSMOKING
NONSOCIALIST
NONSOCIALISTS
NONSOLUTION
NONSOLUTIONS
NONSOLVENT
NONSPATIAL
NONSPEAKER
NONSPEAKERS
NONSPEAKING
NONSPECIALIST
NONSPECIALISTS
NONSPECIFIC
NONSPECIFICALLY
NONSPECIFICITY
NONSPECTACULAR
NONSPECTRAL
NONSPECULAR
NONSPECULATIVE
NONSPEECHES
NONSPHERICAL
NONSPORTING
NONSTAINING
NONSTANDARD
NONSTAPLES
NONSTARTER
NONSTARTERS
NONSTATIONARY
NONSTATISTICAL
NONSTATIVE
NONSTATIVES
NONSTATUTORY
NONSTELLAR
NONSTEROID
NONSTEROIDAL
NONSTEROIDS
NONSTORIES
NONSTRATEGIC
NONSTRIATED
NONSTRIKING
NONSTRUCTURAL
NONSTRUCTURED
NONSTUDENT
NONSTUDENTS
NONSUBJECT
NONSUBJECTIVE
NONSUBJECTS
NONSUBSIDISED
NONSUBSIDIZED
NONSUCCESS
NONSUCCESSES
NONSUITING
NONSUPERVISORY
NONSUPPORT
NONSUPPORTS
NONSURGICAL
NONSWIMMER
NONSWIMMERS
NONSYLLABIC
NONSYLLABICS
NONSYMBOLIC
NONSYMMETRIC
NONSYMMETRICAL
NONSYNCHRONOUS
NONSYSTEMATIC
NONSYSTEMIC
NONSYSTEMS
NONTACTICAL
NONTALKERS
NONTAXABLE
NONTEACHING
NONTECHNICAL
NONTEMPORAL
NONTENURED
NONTERMINAL
NONTERMINALS
NONTERMINATING
NONTEXTUAL
NONTHEATRICAL
NONTHEISMS
NONTHEISTIC
NONTHEISTS
NONTHEOLOGICAL
NONTHEORETICAL
NONTHERAPEUTIC
NONTHERMAL
NONTHINKING
NONTHINKINGS
NONTHREATENING
NONTOBACCO
NONTOTALITARIAN
NONTRADING
NONTRADITIONAL
NONTRANSFERABLE
NONTRANSITIVE
NONTREATMENT
NONTREATMENTS
NONTRIVIAL
NONTROPICAL
NONTURBULENT
NONTYPICAL
NONUNANIMOUS
NONUNIFORM
NONUNIFORMITIES
NONUNIFORMITY
NONUNIONISED
NONUNIONISM
NONUNIONISMS
NONUNIONIST
NONUNIONISTS
NONUNIONIZED
NONUNIQUENESS
NONUNIQUENESSES
NONUNIVERSAL
NONUNIVERSITY
NONUTILITARIAN
NONUTILITIES
NONUTILITY
NONUTOPIAN
NONVALIDITIES
NONVALIDITY
NONVANISHING
NONVASCULAR
NONVECTORS
NONVEGETARIAN
NONVEGETARIANS
NONVENEREAL
NONVENOMOUS
NONVERBALLY
NONVETERAN
NONVETERANS
NONVIEWERS
NONVINTAGE
NONVINTAGES
NONVIOLENCE
NONVIOLENCES
NONVIOLENT
NONVIOLENTLY
NONVIRGINS
NONVISCOUS
NONVOCATIONAL
NONVOLATILE
NONVOLCANIC
NONVOLUNTARY
NONWINNING
NONWORKERS
NONWORKING
NONWRITERS

NONYELLOWING
NOODLEDOMS
NOOGENESES
NOOGENESIS
NOOMETRIES
NOOSPHERES
NOOTROPICS
NORADRENALIN
NORADRENALINE
NORADRENALINES
NORADRENALINS
NORADRENERGIC
NORDICITIES
NOREPINEPHRINE
NOREPINEPHRINES
NORETHINDRONE
NORETHINDRONES
NORETHISTERONE
NORETHISTERONES
NORMALCIES
NORMALISABLE
NORMALISATION
NORMALISATIONS
NORMALISED
NORMALISER
NORMALISERS
NORMALISES
NORMALISING
NORMALITIES
NORMALIZABLE
NORMALIZATION
NORMALIZATIONS
NORMALIZED
NORMALIZER
NORMALIZERS
NORMALIZES
NORMALIZING
NORMATIVELY
NORMATIVENESS
NORMATIVENESSES
NORMOGLYCAEMIA
NORMOGLYCAEMIAS
NORMOGLYCAEMIC
NORMOGLYCEMIA
NORMOGLYCEMIAS
NORMOGLYCEMIC
NORMOTENSION
NORMOTENSIONS
NORMOTENSIVE
NORMOTENSIVES
NORMOTHERMIA
NORMOTHERMIAS
NORMOTHERMIC
NOROVIRUSES
NORSELLERS
NORSELLING
NORTHBOUND
NORTHCOUNTRYMAN
NORTHCOUNTRYMEN
NORTHEASTER
NORTHEASTERLIES
NORTHEASTERLY
NORTHEASTERN
NORTHEASTERS
NORTHEASTS
NORTHEASTWARD
NORTHEASTWARDLY
NORTHEASTWARDS
NORTHERING
NORTHERLIES
NORTHERLINESS
NORTHERLINESSES
NORTHERMOST
NORTHERNER
NORTHERNERS
NORTHERNISE
NORTHERNISED
NORTHERNISES
NORTHERNISING
NORTHERNISM
NORTHERNISMS
NORTHERNIZE
NORTHERNIZED
NORTHERNIZES
NORTHERNIZING
NORTHERNMOST
NORTHLANDS
NORTHWARDLY
NORTHWARDS
NORTHWESTER
NORTHWESTERLIES
NORTHWESTERLY
NORTHWESTERN
NORTHWESTERS
NORTHWESTS
NORTHWESTWARD
NORTHWESTWARDLY
NORTHWESTWARDS
NORTRIPTYLINE
NORTRIPTYLINES
NOSEBANDED
NOSEBLEEDING
NOSEBLEEDINGS
NOSEBLEEDS
NOSEDIVING
NOSEGUARDS
NOSEPIECES
NOSEWHEELS
NOSINESSES
NOSOCOMIAL
NOSOGRAPHER
NOSOGRAPHERS
NOSOGRAPHIC
NOSOGRAPHIES
NOSOGRAPHY
NOSOLOGICAL
NOSOLOGICALLY
NOSOLOGIES
NOSOLOGIST
NOSOLOGISTS
NOSOPHOBIA
NOSOPHOBIAS
NOSTALGIAS
NOSTALGICALLY
NOSTALGICS
NOSTALGIST
NOSTALGISTS
NOSTOLOGIC
NOSTOLOGICAL
NOSTOLOGIES
NOSTOMANIA
NOSTOMANIAS
NOSTOPATHIES
NOSTOPATHY
NOSTRADAMIC
NOTABILITIES
NOTABILITY
NOTABLENESS
NOTABLENESSES
NOTAPHILIC
NOTAPHILIES
NOTAPHILISM
NOTAPHILISMS
NOTAPHILIST
NOTAPHILISTS
NOTARIALLY
NOTARISATION
NOTARISATIONS
NOTARISING
NOTARIZATION
NOTARIZATIONS
NOTARIZING
NOTARYSHIP
NOTARYSHIPS
NOTATIONAL
NOTCHBACKS
NOTCHELING
NOTCHELLED
NOTCHELLING
NOTEBANDIS
NOTEDNESSES
NOTEPAPERS
NOTEWORTHIER
NOTEWORTHIEST
NOTEWORTHILY
NOTEWORTHINESS
NOTEWORTHY
NOTHINGARIAN
NOTHINGARIANISM
NOTHINGARIANS
NOTHINGISM
NOTHINGISMS
NOTHINGNESS
NOTHINGNESSES
NOTICEABILITIES
NOTICEABILITY
NOTICEABLE
NOTICEABLY
NOTICEBOARD
NOTICEBOARDS
NOTIFIABLE
NOTIFICATION
NOTIFICATIONS
NOTIONALIST
NOTIONALISTS
NOTIONALITIES
NOTIONALITY
NOTIONALLY
NOTIONISTS
NOTOCHORDAL
NOTOCHORDS
NOTODONTID
NOTODONTIDS
NOTONECTAL
NOTORIETIES
NOTORIOUSLY
NOTORIOUSNESS
NOTORIOUSNESSES
NOTORNISES
NOTOTHERIUM
NOTOTHERIUMS
NOTOUNGULATE
NOTOUNGULATES
NOTUNGULATE
NOTUNGULATES
NOTWITHSTANDING
NOTWORKING
NOTWORKINGS
NOUGATINES
NOUMENALISM
NOUMENALISMS
NOUMENALIST
NOUMENALISTS
NOUMENALITIES
NOUMENALITY
NOUMENALLY
NOURISHABLE
NOURISHERS
NOURISHING
NOURISHINGLY
NOURISHMENT
NOURISHMENTS
NOURITURES
NOURRITURE
NOURRITURES
NOUSELLING
NOVACULITE
NOVACULITES
NOVELETTES
NOVELETTISH
NOVELETTIST
NOVELETTISTS
NOVELISATION
NOVELISATIONS
NOVELISERS
NOVELISING
NOVELISTIC
NOVELISTICALLY
NOVELIZATION
NOVELIZATIONS

NOVELIZERS
NOVELIZING
NOVEMDECILLION
NOVEMDECILLIONS
NOVENARIES
NOVICEHOOD
NOVICEHOODS
NOVICESHIP
NOVICESHIPS
NOVICIATES
NOVITIATES
NOVOBIOCIN
NOVOBIOCINS
NOVOCAINES
NOVOCENTENARIES
NOVOCENTENARY
NOVODAMUSES
NOWCASTING
NOWCASTINGS
NOXIOUSNESS
NOXIOUSNESSES
NUBBINESSES
NUBIFEROUS
NUBIGENOUS
NUBILITIES
NUCIFEROUS
NUCIVOROUS
NUCLEARISATION
NUCLEARISATIONS
NUCLEARISE
NUCLEARISED
NUCLEARISES
NUCLEARISING
NUCLEARIZATION
NUCLEARIZATIONS
NUCLEARIZE
NUCLEARIZED
NUCLEARIZES
NUCLEARIZING
NUCLEATING
NUCLEATION
NUCLEATIONS
NUCLEATORS
NUCLEOCAPSID
NUCLEOCAPSIDS
NUCLEOLATE
NUCLEOLATED
NUCLEONICALLY
NUCLEONICS
NUCLEOPHILE
NUCLEOPHILES
NUCLEOPHILIC
NUCLEOPHILICITY
NUCLEOPLASM
NUCLEOPLASMATIC
NUCLEOPLASMIC
NUCLEOPLASMS
NUCLEOPROTEIN
NUCLEOPROTEINS
NUCLEOSIDE
NUCLEOSIDES
NUCLEOSOMAL
NUCLEOSOME
NUCLEOSOMES
NUCLEOSYNTHESES
NUCLEOSYNTHESIS
NUCLEOSYNTHETIC
NUCLEOTIDASE
NUCLEOTIDASES
NUCLEOTIDE
NUCLEOTIDES
NUDENESSES
NUDIBRANCH
NUDIBRANCHIATE
NUDIBRANCHIATES
NUDIBRANCHS
NUDICAUDATE
NUDICAULOUS
NUGATORINESS
NUGATORINESSES
NUGGETIEST
NUGGETTING
NUISANCERS
NULLIFICATION
NULLIFICATIONS
NULLIFIDIAN
NULLIFIDIANS
NULLIFIERS
NULLIFYING
NULLIPARAE
NULLIPARAS
NULLIPARITIES
NULLIPARITY
NULLIPAROUS
NULLIPORES
NULLNESSES
NUMBERABLE
NUMBERINGS
NUMBERLESS
NUMBERLESSLY
NUMBERLESSNESS
NUMBERPLATE
NUMBERPLATES
NUMBFISHES
NUMBNESSES
NUMBNUTSES
NUMBSKULLED
NUMBSKULLS
NUMERABILITIES
NUMERABILITY
NUMERACIES
NUMERAIRES
NUMERATING
NUMERATION
NUMERATIONS
NUMERATIVE
NUMERATORS
NUMERICALLY
NUMEROLOGICAL
NUMEROLOGIES
NUMEROLOGIST
NUMEROLOGISTS
NUMEROLOGY
NUMEROSITIES
NUMEROSITY
NUMEROUSLY
NUMEROUSNESS
NUMEROUSNESSES
NUMINOUSES
NUMINOUSNESS
NUMINOUSNESSES
NUMISMATIC
NUMISMATICALLY
NUMISMATICS
NUMISMATIST
NUMISMATISTS
NUMISMATOLOGIES
NUMISMATOLOGIST
NUMISMATOLOGY
NUMMULATED
NUMMULATION
NUMMULATIONS
NUMMULINES
NUMMULITES
NUMMULITIC
NUMSKULLED
NUNCIATURE
NUNCIATURES
NUNCUPATED
NUNCUPATES
NUNCUPATING
NUNCUPATION
NUNCUPATIONS
NUNCUPATIVE
NUNCUPATORY
NUNNATIONS
NUNNISHNESS
NUNNISHNESSES
NUPTIALITIES
NUPTIALITY
NURSEHOUND
NURSEHOUNDS
NURSELINGS
NURSEMAIDED
NURSEMAIDING
NURSEMAIDS
NURSERYMAID
NURSERYMAIDS
NURSERYMAN
NURSERYMEN
NURTURABLE
NURTURANCE
NURTURANCES
NUTATIONAL
NUTBUTTERS
NUTCRACKER
NUTCRACKERS
NUTGRASSES
NUTHATCHES
NUTJOBBERS
NUTMEGGIER
NUTMEGGIEST
NUTMEGGING
NUTPECKERS
NUTRACEUTICAL
NUTRACEUTICALS
NUTRIGENETICS
NUTRIGENOMICS
NUTRIMENTAL
NUTRIMENTS
NUTRITIONAL
NUTRITIONALLY
NUTRITIONARY
NUTRITIONIST
NUTRITIONISTS
NUTRITIONS
NUTRITIOUS
NUTRITIOUSLY
NUTRITIOUSNESS
NUTRITIVELY
NUTRITIVES
NUTTINESSES
NYCHTHEMERAL
NYCHTHEMERON
NYCHTHEMERONS
NYCTAGINACEOUS
NYCTALOPES
NYCTALOPIA
NYCTALOPIAS
NYCTALOPIC
NYCTANTHOUS
NYCTINASTIC
NYCTINASTIES
NYCTINASTY
NYCTITROPIC
NYCTITROPISM
NYCTITROPISMS
NYCTOPHOBIA
NYCTOPHOBIAS
NYCTOPHOBIC
NYMPHAEACEOUS
NYMPHAEUMS
NYMPHALIDS
NYMPHETTES
NYMPHLIEST
NYMPHOLEPSIES
NYMPHOLEPSY
NYMPHOLEPT
NYMPHOLEPTIC
NYMPHOLEPTS
NYMPHOMANIA
NYMPHOMANIAC
NYMPHOMANIACAL
NYMPHOMANIACS
NYMPHOMANIAS
NYSTAGMOID
NYSTAGMUSES

N

O

OAFISHNESS
OAFISHNESSES
OAKENSHAWS
OAKINESSES
OARSMANSHIP
OARSMANSHIPS
OASTHOUSES
OBBLIGATOS
OBCOMPRESSED
OBDURACIES
OBDURATELY
OBDURATENESS
OBDURATENESSES
OBDURATING
OBDURATION
OBDURATIONS
OBEDIENCES
OBEDIENTIAL
OBEDIENTIARIES
OBEDIENTIARY
OBEDIENTLY
OBEISANCES
OBEISANTLY
OBELISCOID
OBELISKOID
OBESENESSES
OBESOGENIC
OBFUSCATED
OBFUSCATES
OBFUSCATING
OBFUSCATION
OBFUSCATIONS
OBFUSCATORY
OBITUARIES
OBITUARIST
OBITUARISTS
OBJECTIFICATION
OBJECTIFIED
OBJECTIFIES
OBJECTIFYING
OBJECTIONABLE
OBJECTIONABLY
OBJECTIONS
OBJECTIVAL
OBJECTIVATE
OBJECTIVATED
OBJECTIVATES
OBJECTIVATING
OBJECTIVATION
OBJECTIVATIONS
OBJECTIVELY
OBJECTIVENESS
OBJECTIVENESSES
OBJECTIVES
OBJECTIVISE
OBJECTIVISED
OBJECTIVISES
OBJECTIVISING
OBJECTIVISM
OBJECTIVISMS
OBJECTIVIST
OBJECTIVISTIC
OBJECTIVISTS
OBJECTIVITIES
OBJECTIVITY
OBJECTIVIZE
OBJECTIVIZED
OBJECTIVIZES
OBJECTIVIZING
OBJECTLESS
OBJECTLESSNESS
OBJURATION
OBJURATIONS
OBJURGATED
OBJURGATES
OBJURGATING
OBJURGATION
OBJURGATIONS
OBJURGATIVE
OBJURGATOR
OBJURGATORS
OBJURGATORY
OBLANCEOLATE
OBLATENESS
OBLATENESSES
OBLATIONAL
OBLIGATELY
OBLIGATING
OBLIGATION
OBLIGATIONAL
OBLIGATIONS
OBLIGATIVE
OBLIGATORILY
OBLIGATORINESS
OBLIGATORS
OBLIGATORY
OBLIGEMENT
OBLIGEMENTS
OBLIGINGLY
OBLIGINGNESS
OBLIGINGNESSES
OBLIQUATION
OBLIQUATIONS
OBLIQUENESS
OBLIQUENESSES
OBLIQUITIES
OBLIQUITOUS
OBLITERATE
OBLITERATED
OBLITERATES
OBLITERATING
OBLITERATION
OBLITERATIONS
OBLITERATIVE
OBLITERATOR
OBLITERATORS
OBLIVIOUSLY
OBLIVIOUSNESS
OBLIVIOUSNESSES
OBLIVISCENCE
OBLIVISCENCES
OBMUTESCENCE
OBMUTESCENCES
OBMUTESCENT
OBNOXIOUSLY
OBNOXIOUSNESS
OBNOXIOUSNESSES
OBNUBILATE
OBNUBILATED
OBNUBILATES
OBNUBILATING
OBNUBILATION
OBNUBILATIONS
OBREPTIONS
OBREPTITIOUS
OBSCENENESS
OBSCENENESSES
OBSCENITIES
OBSCURANTIC
OBSCURANTISM
OBSCURANTISMS
OBSCURANTIST
OBSCURANTISTS
OBSCURANTS
OBSCURATION
OBSCURATIONS
OBSCUREMENT
OBSCUREMENTS
OBSCURENESS
OBSCURENESSES
OBSCURITIES
OBSECRATED
OBSECRATES
OBSECRATING
OBSECRATION
OBSECRATIONS
OBSEQUIOUS
OBSEQUIOUSLY
OBSEQUIOUSNESS
OBSERVABILITIES
OBSERVABILITY
OBSERVABLE
OBSERVABLENESS
OBSERVABLES
OBSERVABLY
OBSERVANCE
OBSERVANCES
OBSERVANCIES
OBSERVANCY
OBSERVANTLY
OBSERVANTS
OBSERVATION
OBSERVATIONAL
OBSERVATIONALLY
OBSERVATIONS
OBSERVATIVE
OBSERVATOR
OBSERVATORIES
OBSERVATORS
OBSERVATORY
OBSERVINGLY
OBSESSIONAL
OBSESSIONALLY
OBSESSIONIST
OBSESSIONISTS
OBSESSIONS
OBSESSIVELY
OBSESSIVENESS
OBSESSIVENESSES
OBSESSIVES
OBSIDIONAL
OBSIDIONARY
OBSIGNATED
OBSIGNATES
OBSIGNATING
OBSIGNATION
OBSIGNATIONS
OBSIGNATORY
OBSOLESCED
OBSOLESCENCE
OBSOLESCENCES
OBSOLESCENT
OBSOLESCENTLY
OBSOLESCES
OBSOLESCING
OBSOLETELY
OBSOLETENESS
OBSOLETENESSES
OBSOLETING
OBSOLETION

OBSOLETIONS
OBSOLETISM
OBSOLETISMS
OBSTETRICAL
OBSTETRICALLY
OBSTETRICIAN
OBSTETRICIANS
OBSTETRICS
OBSTINACIES
OBSTINATELY
OBSTINATENESS
OBSTINATENESSES
OBSTIPATION
OBSTIPATIONS
OBSTREPERATE
OBSTREPERATED
OBSTREPERATES
OBSTREPERATING
OBSTREPEROUS
OBSTREPEROUSLY
OBSTRICTION
OBSTRICTIONS
OBSTROPALOUS
OBSTROPULOUS
OBSTRUCTED
OBSTRUCTER
OBSTRUCTERS
OBSTRUCTING
OBSTRUCTINGLY
OBSTRUCTION
OBSTRUCTIONAL
OBSTRUCTIONALLY
OBSTRUCTIONISM
OBSTRUCTIONISMS
OBSTRUCTIONIST
OBSTRUCTIONISTS
OBSTRUCTIONS
OBSTRUCTIVE
OBSTRUCTIVELY
OBSTRUCTIVENESS
OBSTRUCTIVES
OBSTRUCTOR
OBSTRUCTORS
OBSTRUENTS
OBTAINABILITIES
OBTAINABILITY
OBTAINABLE
OBTAINMENT
OBTAINMENTS
OBTEMPERATE
OBTEMPERATED
OBTEMPERATES
OBTEMPERATING
OBTEMPERED
OBTEMPERING
OBTENTIONS
OBTESTATION
OBTESTATIONS
OBTRUDINGS
OBTRUNCATE
OBTRUNCATED
OBTRUNCATES
OBTRUNCATING
OBTRUSIONS
OBTRUSIVELY
OBTRUSIVENESS
OBTRUSIVENESSES
OBTUNDENTS
OBTUNDITIES
OBTURATING
OBTURATION
OBTURATIONS
OBTURATORS
OBTUSENESS
OBTUSENESSES
OBTUSITIES
OBUMBRATED
OBUMBRATES
OBUMBRATING
OBUMBRATION
OBUMBRATIONS
OBVENTIONS
OBVERSIONS
OBVIATIONS
OBVIOUSNESS
OBVIOUSNESSES
OBVOLUTION
OBVOLUTIONS
OBVOLUTIVE
OCCASIONAL
OCCASIONALISM
OCCASIONALISMS
OCCASIONALIST
OCCASIONALISTS
OCCASIONALITIES
OCCASIONALITY
OCCASIONALLY
OCCASIONED
OCCASIONER
OCCASIONERS
OCCASIONING
OCCIDENTAL
OCCIDENTALISE
OCCIDENTALISED
OCCIDENTALISES
OCCIDENTALISING
OCCIDENTALISM
OCCIDENTALISMS
OCCIDENTALIST
OCCIDENTALISTS
OCCIDENTALIZE
OCCIDENTALIZED
OCCIDENTALIZES
OCCIDENTALIZING
OCCIDENTALLY
OCCIDENTALS
OCCIPITALLY
OCCIPITALS
OCCLUDENTS
OCCLUSIONS
OCCLUSIVENESS
OCCLUSIVENESSES
OCCLUSIVES
OCCULTATION
OCCULTATIONS
OCCULTISMS
OCCULTISTS
OCCULTNESS
OCCULTNESSES
OCCUPANCES
OCCUPANCIES
OCCUPATING
OCCUPATION
OCCUPATIONAL
OCCUPATIONALLY
OCCUPATIONS
OCCUPATIVE
OCCURRENCE
OCCURRENCES
OCCURRENTS
OCEANARIUM
OCEANARIUMS
OCEANFRONT
OCEANFRONTS
OCEANGOING
OCEANOGRAPHER
OCEANOGRAPHERS
OCEANOGRAPHIC
OCEANOGRAPHICAL
OCEANOGRAPHIES
OCEANOGRAPHY
OCEANOLOGICAL
OCEANOLOGIES
OCEANOLOGIST
OCEANOLOGISTS
OCEANOLOGY
OCELLATION
OCELLATIONS
OCHLOCRACIES
OCHLOCRACY
OCHLOCRATIC
OCHLOCRATICAL
OCHLOCRATICALLY
OCHLOCRATS
OCHLOPHOBIA
OCHLOPHOBIAC
OCHLOPHOBIACS
OCHLOPHOBIAS
OCHLOPHOBIC
OCHLOPHOBICS
OCHRACEOUS
OCHROLEUCOUS
OCTACHORDAL
OCTACHORDS
OCTAGONALLY
OCTAHEDRAL
OCTAHEDRALLY
OCTAHEDRITE
OCTAHEDRITES
OCTAHEDRON
OCTAHEDRONS
OCTAMEROUS
OCTAMETERS
OCTANDRIAN
OCTANDROUS
OCTANEDIOIC
OCTANGULAR
OCTAPEPTIDE
OCTAPEPTIDES
OCTAPLOIDIES
OCTAPLOIDS
OCTAPLOIDY
OCTAPODIES
OCTARCHIES
OCTASTICHON
OCTASTICHONS
OCTASTICHOUS
OCTASTICHS
OCTASTROPHIC
OCTASTYLES
OCTAVALENT
OCTENNIALLY
OCTILLIONS
OCTILLIONTH
OCTILLIONTHS
OCTINGENARIES
OCTINGENARY
OCTINGENTENARY
OCTOCENTENARIES
OCTOCENTENARY
OCTODECILLION
OCTODECILLIONS
OCTODECIMO
OCTODECIMOS
OCTOGENARIAN
OCTOGENARIANS
OCTOGENARIES
OCTOGENARY
OCTOGYNOUS
OCTOHEDRON
OCTOHEDRONS
OCTONARIAN
OCTONARIANS
OCTONARIES
OCTONARIUS
OCTONOCULAR
OCTOPETALOUS
OCTOPLOIDS
OCTOPODANS
OCTOPODOUS
OCTOPUSHER
OCTOPUSHERS
OCTOPUSHES
OCTOSEPALOUS
OCTOSTICHOUS
OCTOSTYLES
OCTOSYLLABIC
OCTOSYLLABICS
OCTOSYLLABLE
OCTOSYLLABLES

OCTOTHORPS
OCTUPLICATE
OCTUPLICATES
OCULARISTS
OCULOMOTOR
ODALISQUES
ODDSMAKERS
ODIOUSNESS
ODIOUSNESSES
ODOMETRIES
ODONATISTS
ODONATOLOGIES
ODONATOLOGIST
ODONATOLOGISTS
ODONATOLOGY
ODONTALGIA
ODONTALGIAS
ODONTALGIC
ODONTALGIES
ODONTOBLAST
ODONTOBLASTIC
ODONTOBLASTS
ODONTOCETE
ODONTOCETES
ODONTOGENIC
ODONTOGENIES
ODONTOGENY
ODONTOGLOSSUM
ODONTOGLOSSUMS
ODONTOGRAPH
ODONTOGRAPHIES
ODONTOGRAPHS
ODONTOGRAPHY
ODONTOLITE
ODONTOLITES
ODONTOLOGIC
ODONTOLOGICAL
ODONTOLOGIES
ODONTOLOGIST
ODONTOLOGISTS
ODONTOLOGY
ODONTOMATA
ODONTOMATOUS
ODONTOPHOBIA
ODONTOPHOBIAS
ODONTOPHORAL
ODONTOPHORAN
ODONTOPHORANS
ODONTOPHORE
ODONTOPHORES
ODONTOPHOROUS
ODONTORHYNCHOUS
ODONTORNITHES
ODONTOSTOMATOUS
ODORIFEROUS
ODORIFEROUSLY
ODORIFEROUSNESS
ODORIMETRIES
ODORIMETRY
ODORIPHORE
ODORIPHORES
ODOROUSNESS
ODOROUSNESSES
OECOLOGICAL
OECOLOGICALLY
OECOLOGIES
OECOLOGIST
OECOLOGISTS
OECUMENICAL
OECUMENICALLY
OEDEMATOSE
OEDEMATOUS
OEDOMETERS
OENOLOGICAL
OENOLOGIES
OENOLOGIST
OENOLOGISTS
OENOMANCIES
OENOMANIAS
OENOMETERS
OENOPHILES
OENOPHILIES
OENOPHILIST
OENOPHILISTS
OENOTHERAS
OESOPHAGEAL
OESOPHAGITIS
OESOPHAGITISES
OESOPHAGOSCOPE
OESOPHAGOSCOPES
OESOPHAGOSCOPY
OESOPHAGUS
OESOPHAGUSES
OESTRADIOL
OESTRADIOLS
OESTROGENIC
OESTROGENICALLY
OESTROGENS
OFFENCEFUL
OFFENCELESS
OFFENDEDLY
OFFENDRESS
OFFENDRESSES
OFFENSELESS
OFFENSIVELY
OFFENSIVENESS
OFFENSIVENESSES
OFFENSIVES
OFFERTORIES
OFFHANDEDLY
OFFHANDEDNESS
OFFHANDEDNESSES
OFFICEHOLDER
OFFICEHOLDERS
OFFICERING
OFFICIALDOM
OFFICIALDOMS
OFFICIALESE
OFFICIALESES
OFFICIALISM
OFFICIALISMS
OFFICIALITIES
OFFICIALITY
OFFICIALLY
OFFICIALTIES
OFFICIALTY
OFFICIANTS
OFFICIARIES
OFFICIATED
OFFICIATES
OFFICIATING
OFFICIATION
OFFICIATIONS
OFFICIATOR
OFFICIATORS
OFFICINALLY
OFFICINALS
OFFICIOUSLY
OFFICIOUSNESS
OFFICIOUSNESSES
OFFISHNESS
OFFISHNESSES
OFFLOADING
OFFPRINTED
OFFPRINTING
OFFSADDLED
OFFSADDLES
OFFSADDLING
OFFSCOURING
OFFSCOURINGS
OFFSEASONS
OFFSETABLE
OFFSETTING
OFFSETTINGS
OFFSHORING
OFFSHORINGS
OFFSPRINGS
OFTENNESSES
OFTENTIMES
OGANESSONS
OILINESSES
OINOLOGIES
OLDFANGLED
OLEAGINOUS
OLEAGINOUSLY
OLEAGINOUSNESS
OLEANDOMYCIN
OLEANDOMYCINS
OLECRANONS
OLEIFEROUS
OLEOGRAPHIC
OLEOGRAPHIES
OLEOGRAPHS
OLEOGRAPHY
OLEOMARGARIN
OLEOMARGARINE
OLEOMARGARINES
OLEOMARGARINS
OLEOPHILIC
OLEORESINOUS
OLEORESINS
OLERACEOUS
OLFACTIBLE
OLFACTIONS
OLFACTOLOGIES
OLFACTOLOGIST
OLFACTOLOGISTS
OLFACTOLOGY
OLFACTOMETER
OLFACTOMETERS
OLFACTOMETRIES
OLFACTOMETRY
OLFACTORIES
OLFACTRONICS
OLIGAEMIAS
OLIGARCHAL
OLIGARCHIC
OLIGARCHICAL
OLIGARCHICALLY
OLIGARCHIES
OLIGOCHAETE
OLIGOCHAETES
OLIGOCHROME
OLIGOCHROMES
OLIGOCLASE
OLIGOCLASES
OLIGOCYTHAEMIA
OLIGOCYTHAEMIAS
OLIGODENDROCYTE
OLIGODENDROGLIA
OLIGOGENES
OLIGOMERIC
OLIGOMERISATION
OLIGOMERIZATION
OLIGOMEROUS
OLIGONUCLEOTIDE
OLIGOPEPTIDE
OLIGOPEPTIDES
OLIGOPHAGIES
OLIGOPHAGOUS
OLIGOPHAGY
OLIGOPOLIES
OLIGOPOLISTIC
OLIGOPSONIES
OLIGOPSONISTIC
OLIGOPSONY
OLIGOSACCHARIDE
OLIGOSPERMIA
OLIGOSPERMIAS
OLIGOTROPHIC
OLIGOTROPHIES
OLIGOTROPHY
OLIGURESES
OLIGURESIS
OLIGURETIC
OLINGUITOS
OLIVACEOUS
OLIVENITES
OLIVEWOODS
OLIVINITIC

OLOGOANING
OLOLIUQUIS
OMBROGENOUS
OMBROMETER
OMBROMETERS
OMBROPHILE
OMBROPHILES
OMBROPHILOUS
OMBROPHILS
OMBROPHOBE
OMBROPHOBES
OMBROPHOBOUS
OMBUDSMANSHIP
OMBUDSMANSHIPS
OMINOUSNESS
OMINOUSNESSES
OMISSIVENESS
OMISSIVENESSES
OMITTANCES
OMMATIDIAL
OMMATIDIUM
OMMATOPHORE
OMMATOPHORES
OMMATOPHOROUS
OMNIBENEVOLENCE
OMNIBENEVOLENT
OMNIBUSSES
OMNICOMPETENCE
OMNICOMPETENCES
OMNICOMPETENT
OMNIDIRECTIONAL
OMNIFARIOUS
OMNIFARIOUSLY
OMNIFARIOUSNESS
OMNIFEROUS
OMNIFICENCE
OMNIFICENCES
OMNIFICENT
OMNIFORMITIES
OMNIFORMITY
OMNIGENOUS
OMNIPARITIES
OMNIPARITY
OMNIPAROUS
OMNIPATIENT
OMNIPOTENCE
OMNIPOTENCES
OMNIPOTENCIES
OMNIPOTENCY
OMNIPOTENT
OMNIPOTENTLY
OMNIPOTENTS
OMNIPRESENCE
OMNIPRESENCES
OMNIPRESENT
OMNIRANGES
OMNISCIENCE
OMNISCIENCES
OMNISCIENT
OMNISCIENTLY
OMNISHAMBLES
OMNIVORIES
OMNIVOROUS
OMNIVOROUSLY
OMNIVOROUSNESS
OMOPHAGIAS
OMOPHAGIES
OMOPHAGOUS
OMOPHORION
OMOPLATOSCOPIES
OMOPLATOSCOPY
OMPHACITES
OMPHALOMANCIES
OMPHALOMANCY
OMPHALOSKEPSES
OMPHALOSKEPSIS
ONAGRACEOUS
ONBOARDING
ONBOARDINGS
ONCHOCERCIASES
ONCHOCERCIASIS
ONCOGENESES
ONCOGENESIS
ONCOGENETICIST
ONCOGENETICISTS
ONCOGENICITIES
ONCOGENICITY
ONCOGENOUS
ONCOLOGICAL
ONCOLOGIES
ONCOLOGIST
ONCOLOGISTS
ONCOLYTICS
ONCOMETERS
ONCORNAVIRUS
ONCORNAVIRUSES
ONCOTOMIES
ONCOVIRUSES
ONDOGRAPHS
ONEIRICALLY
ONEIROCRITIC
ONEIROCRITICAL
ONEIROCRITICISM
ONEIROCRITICS
ONEIRODYNIA
ONEIRODYNIAS
ONEIROLOGIES
ONEIROLOGY
ONEIROMANCER
ONEIROMANCERS
ONEIROMANCIES
ONEIROMANCY
ONEIROSCOPIES
ONEIROSCOPIST
ONEIROSCOPISTS
ONEIROSCOPY
ONEROUSNESS
ONEROUSNESSES
ONGOINGNESS
ONGOINGNESSES
ONIONSKINS
ONOCENTAUR
ONOCENTAURS
ONOMASIOLOGIES
ONOMASIOLOGY
ONOMASTICALLY
ONOMASTICIAN
ONOMASTICIANS
ONOMASTICON
ONOMASTICONS
ONOMASTICS
ONOMATOLOGIES
ONOMATOLOGIST
ONOMATOLOGISTS
ONOMATOLOGY
ONOMATOPOEIA
ONOMATOPOEIAS
ONOMATOPOEIC
ONOMATOPOESES
ONOMATOPOESIS
ONOMATOPOETIC
ONOMATOPOIESES
ONOMATOPOIESIS
ONSETTINGS
ONSHORINGS
ONSLAUGHTS
ONTOGENESES
ONTOGENESIS
ONTOGENETIC
ONTOGENETICALLY
ONTOGENICALLY
ONTOGENIES
ONTOLOGICAL
ONTOLOGICALLY
ONTOLOGIES
ONTOLOGIST
ONTOLOGISTS
ONYCHITISES
ONYCHOCRYPTOSES
ONYCHOCRYPTOSIS
ONYCHOMANCIES
ONYCHOMANCY
ONYCHOPHAGIES
ONYCHOPHAGIST
ONYCHOPHAGISTS
ONYCHOPHAGY
ONYCHOPHORAN
ONYCHOPHORANS
OOGAMOUSLY
OOJAMAFLIP
OOJAMAFLIPS
OOMPAHPAHS
OOPHORECTOMIES
OOPHORECTOMISE
OOPHORECTOMISED
OOPHORECTOMISES
OOPHORECTOMIZE
OOPHORECTOMIZED
OOPHORECTOMIZES
OOPHORECTOMY
OOPHORITIC
OOPHORITIS
OOPHORITISES
OOZINESSES
OPACIFIERS
OPACIFYING
OPALESCENCE
OPALESCENCES
OPALESCENT
OPALESCENTLY
OPALESCING
OPAQUENESS
OPAQUENESSES
OPEIDOSCOPE
OPEIDOSCOPES
OPENABILITIES
OPENABILITY
OPENHANDED
OPENHANDEDLY
OPENHANDEDNESS
OPENHEARTED
OPENHEARTEDLY
OPENHEARTEDNESS
OPENMOUTHED
OPENMOUTHEDLY
OPENMOUTHEDNESS
OPENNESSES
OPERABILITIES
OPERABILITY
OPERAGOERS
OPERAGOING
OPERAGOINGS
OPERATICALLY
OPERATIONAL
OPERATIONALISM
OPERATIONALISMS
OPERATIONALIST
OPERATIONALISTS
OPERATIONALLY
OPERATIONISM
OPERATIONISMS
OPERATIONIST
OPERATIONISTS
OPERATIONS
OPERATISED
OPERATISES
OPERATISING
OPERATIVELY
OPERATIVENESS
OPERATIVENESSES
OPERATIVES
OPERATIVITIES
OPERATIVITY
OPERATIZED
OPERATIZES
OPERATIZING
OPERATORLESS
OPERCULARS
OPERCULATE
OPERCULATED

OPERCULUMS
OPERETTIST
OPERETTISTS
OPEROSENESS
OPEROSENESSES
OPEROSITIES
OPHICALCITE
OPHICALCITES
OPHICLEIDE
OPHICLEIDES
OPHIDIARIA
OPHIDIARIUM
OPHIDIARIUMS
OPHIOLATER
OPHIOLATERS
OPHIOLATRIES
OPHIOLATROUS
OPHIOLATRY
OPHIOLITES
OPHIOLITIC
OPHIOLOGIC
OPHIOLOGICAL
OPHIOLOGIES
OPHIOLOGIST
OPHIOLOGISTS
OPHIOMORPH
OPHIOMORPHIC
OPHIOMORPHOUS
OPHIOMORPHS
OPHIOPHAGOUS
OPHIOPHILIST
OPHIOPHILISTS
OPHIUROIDS
OPHTHALMIA
OPHTHALMIAS
OPHTHALMIC
OPHTHALMIST
OPHTHALMISTS
OPHTHALMITIS
OPHTHALMITISES
OPHTHALMOLOGIC
OPHTHALMOLOGIES
OPHTHALMOLOGIST
OPHTHALMOLOGY
OPHTHALMOMETER
OPHTHALMOMETERS
OPHTHALMOMETRY
OPHTHALMOPHOBIA
OPHTHALMOPLEGIA
OPHTHALMOSCOPE
OPHTHALMOSCOPES
OPHTHALMOSCOPIC
OPHTHALMOSCOPY
OPINICUSES
OPINIONATE
OPINIONATED
OPINIONATEDLY
OPINIONATEDNESS
OPINIONATELY
OPINIONATES
OPINIONATING
OPINIONATIVE
OPINIONATIVELY
OPINIONATOR
OPINIONATORS
OPINIONIST
OPINIONISTS
OPISOMETER
OPISOMETERS
OPISTHOBRANCH
OPISTHOBRANCHS
OPISTHOCOELIAN
OPISTHOCOELOUS
OPISTHODOMOI
OPISTHODOMOS
OPISTHOGLOSSAL
OPISTHOGNATHISM
OPISTHOGNATHOUS
OPISTHOGRAPH
OPISTHOGRAPHIC
OPISTHOGRAPHIES
OPISTHOGRAPHS
OPISTHOGRAPHY
OPISTHOSOMA
OPISTHOSOMATA
OPISTHOTONIC
OPISTHOTONOS
OPISTHOTONOSES
OPOBALSAMS
OPODELDOCS
OPOPANAXES
OPOTHERAPIES
OPOTHERAPY
OPPIGNERATE
OPPIGNERATED
OPPIGNERATES
OPPIGNERATING
OPPIGNERATION
OPPIGNERATIONS
OPPIGNORATE
OPPIGNORATED
OPPIGNORATES
OPPIGNORATING
OPPIGNORATION
OPPIGNORATIONS
OPPILATING
OPPILATION
OPPILATIONS
OPPILATIVE
OPPONENCIES
OPPORTUNELY
OPPORTUNENESS
OPPORTUNENESSES
OPPORTUNISM
OPPORTUNISMS
OPPORTUNIST
OPPORTUNISTIC
OPPORTUNISTS
OPPORTUNITIES
OPPORTUNITY
OPPOSABILITIES
OPPOSABILITY
OPPOSELESS
OPPOSINGLY
OPPOSITELY
OPPOSITENESS
OPPOSITENESSES
OPPOSITION
OPPOSITIONAL
OPPOSITIONIST
OPPOSITIONISTS
OPPOSITIONLESS
OPPOSITIONS
OPPOSITIVE
OPPRESSING
OPPRESSINGLY
OPPRESSION
OPPRESSIONS
OPPRESSIVE
OPPRESSIVELY
OPPRESSIVENESS
OPPRESSORS
OPPROBRIOUS
OPPROBRIOUSLY
OPPROBRIOUSNESS
OPPROBRIUM
OPPROBRIUMS
OPPUGNANCIES
OPPUGNANCY
OPPUGNANTLY
OPPUGNANTS
OPSIMATHIES
OPSIOMETER
OPSIOMETERS
OPSOMANIAC
OPSOMANIACS
OPSOMANIAS
OPSONIFICATION
OPSONIFICATIONS
OPSONIFIED
OPSONIFIES
OPSONIFYING
OPSONISATION
OPSONISATIONS
OPSONISING
OPSONIZATION
OPSONIZATIONS
OPSONIZING
OPTATIVELY
OPTIMALISATION
OPTIMALISATIONS
OPTIMALISE
OPTIMALISED
OPTIMALISES
OPTIMALISING
OPTIMALITIES
OPTIMALITY
OPTIMALIZATION
OPTIMALIZATIONS
OPTIMALIZE
OPTIMALIZED
OPTIMALIZES
OPTIMALIZING
OPTIMISATION
OPTIMISATIONS
OPTIMISERS
OPTIMISING
OPTIMISTIC
OPTIMISTICAL
OPTIMISTICALLY
OPTIMIZATION
OPTIMIZATIONS
OPTIMIZERS
OPTIMIZING
OPTIONALITIES
OPTIONALITY
OPTIONALLY
OPTOACOUSTIC
OPTOELECTRONIC
OPTOELECTRONICS
OPTOKINETIC
OPTOLOGIES
OPTOLOGIST
OPTOLOGISTS
OPTOMETERS
OPTOMETRIC
OPTOMETRICAL
OPTOMETRIES
OPTOMETRIST
OPTOMETRISTS
OPTOPHONES
OPULENCIES
ORACULARITIES
ORACULARITY
ORACULARLY
ORACULARNESS
ORACULARNESSES
ORACULOUSLY
ORACULOUSNESS
ORACULOUSNESSES
ORANGEADES
ORANGERIES
ORANGEWOOD
ORANGEWOODS
ORANGUTANS
ORATORIANS
ORATORICAL
ORATORICALLY
ORATRESSES
ORBICULARES
ORBICULARIS
ORBICULARITIES
ORBICULARITY
ORBICULARLY
ORBICULATE
ORBICULATED
ORCHARDING
ORCHARDINGS
ORCHARDIST
ORCHARDISTS

O

ORCHARDMAN
ORCHARDMEN
ORCHESOGRAPHIES
ORCHESOGRAPHY
ORCHESTICS
ORCHESTRAL
ORCHESTRALIST
ORCHESTRALISTS
ORCHESTRALLY
ORCHESTRAS
ORCHESTRATE
ORCHESTRATED
ORCHESTRATER
ORCHESTRATERS
ORCHESTRATES
ORCHESTRATING
ORCHESTRATION
ORCHESTRATIONAL
ORCHESTRATIONS
ORCHESTRATOR
ORCHESTRATORS
ORCHESTRIC
ORCHESTRINA
ORCHESTRINAS
ORCHESTRION
ORCHESTRIONS
ORCHIDACEOUS
ORCHIDECTOMIES
ORCHIDECTOMY
ORCHIDEOUS
ORCHIDISTS
ORCHIDLIKE
ORCHIDOLOGIES
ORCHIDOLOGIST
ORCHIDOLOGISTS
ORCHIDOLOGY
ORCHIDOMANIA
ORCHIDOMANIAC
ORCHIDOMANIACS
ORCHIDOMANIAS
ORCHIECTOMIES
ORCHIECTOMY
ORCHITISES
ORDAINABLE
ORDAINMENT
ORDAINMENTS
ORDERLINESS
ORDERLINESSES
ORDINAIRES
ORDINANCES
ORDINARIER
ORDINARIES
ORDINARIEST
ORDINARILY
ORDINARINESS
ORDINARINESSES
ORDINATELY
ORDINATING
ORDINATION
ORDINATIONS
ORDONNANCE
ORDONNANCES
ORECCHIETTE
ORECCHIETTES
ORECCHIETTI
OREOGRAPHIC
OREOGRAPHICAL
OREOGRAPHICALLY
OREOGRAPHIES
OREOGRAPHY
OREOLOGICAL
OREOLOGIES
OREOLOGIST
OREOLOGISTS
OREPEARCHED
OREPEARCHES
OREPEARCHING
ORGANELLES
ORGANICALLY
ORGANICISM
ORGANICISMS
ORGANICIST
ORGANICISTIC
ORGANICISTS
ORGANICITIES
ORGANICITY
ORGANISABILITY
ORGANISABLE
ORGANISATION
ORGANISATIONAL
ORGANISATIONS
ORGANISERS
ORGANISING
ORGANISINGS
ORGANISMAL
ORGANISMALLY
ORGANISMIC
ORGANISMICALLY
ORGANISTRUM
ORGANISTRUMS
ORGANITIES
ORGANIZABILITY
ORGANIZABLE
ORGANIZATION
ORGANIZATIONAL
ORGANIZATIONS
ORGANIZERS
ORGANIZING
ORGANIZINGS
ORGANOCHLORINE
ORGANOCHLORINES
ORGANOGENESES
ORGANOGENESIS
ORGANOGENETIC
ORGANOGENIES
ORGANOGENY
ORGANOGRAM
ORGANOGRAMS
ORGANOGRAPHIC
ORGANOGRAPHICAL
ORGANOGRAPHIES
ORGANOGRAPHIST
ORGANOGRAPHISTS
ORGANOGRAPHY
ORGANOLEPTIC
ORGANOLOGICAL
ORGANOLOGIES
ORGANOLOGIST
ORGANOLOGISTS
ORGANOLOGY
ORGANOMERCURIAL
ORGANOMETALLIC
ORGANOMETALLICS
ORGANOPHOSPHATE
ORGANOSOLS
ORGANOTHERAPIES
ORGANOTHERAPY
ORGANZINES
ORGASMICALLY
ORGASTICALLY
ORGIASTICALLY
ORICALCHES
ORICHALCEOUS
ORIENTALISE
ORIENTALISED
ORIENTALISES
ORIENTALISING
ORIENTALISM
ORIENTALISMS
ORIENTALIST
ORIENTALISTS
ORIENTALITIES
ORIENTALITY
ORIENTALIZE
ORIENTALIZED
ORIENTALIZES
ORIENTALIZING
ORIENTALLY
ORIENTATED
ORIENTATES
ORIENTATING
ORIENTATION
ORIENTATIONAL
ORIENTATIONALLY
ORIENTATIONS
ORIENTATOR
ORIENTATORS
ORIENTEERED
ORIENTEERING
ORIENTEERINGS
ORIENTEERS
ORIFLAMMES
ORIGINALITIES
ORIGINALITY
ORIGINALLY
ORIGINATED
ORIGINATES
ORIGINATING
ORIGINATION
ORIGINATIONS
ORIGINATIVE
ORIGINATIVELY
ORIGINATOR
ORIGINATORS
ORINASALLY
ORISMOLOGICAL
ORISMOLOGIES
ORISMOLOGY
ORNAMENTAL
ORNAMENTALLY
ORNAMENTALS
ORNAMENTATION
ORNAMENTATIONS
ORNAMENTED
ORNAMENTER
ORNAMENTERS
ORNAMENTING
ORNAMENTIST
ORNAMENTISTS
ORNATENESS
ORNATENESSES
ORNERINESS
ORNERINESSES
ORNITHICHNITE
ORNITHICHNITES
ORNITHINES
ORNITHISCHIAN
ORNITHISCHIANS
ORNITHODELPHIAN
ORNITHODELPHIC
ORNITHODELPHOUS
ORNITHOGALUM
ORNITHOGALUMS
ORNITHOLOGIC
ORNITHOLOGICAL
ORNITHOLOGIES
ORNITHOLOGIST
ORNITHOLOGISTS
ORNITHOLOGY
ORNITHOMANCIES
ORNITHOMANCY
ORNITHOMANTIC
ORNITHOMORPH
ORNITHOMORPHIC
ORNITHOMORPHS
ORNITHOPHILIES
ORNITHOPHILOUS
ORNITHOPHILY
ORNITHOPHOBIA
ORNITHOPHOBIAS
ORNITHOPOD
ORNITHOPODS
ORNITHOPTER
ORNITHOPTERS
ORNITHORHYNCHUS
ORNITHOSAUR
ORNITHOSAURS
ORNITHOSCOPIES
ORNITHOSCOPY
ORNITHOSES

ORNITHOSIS
OROBANCHACEOUS
OROGENESES
OROGENESIS
OROGENETIC
OROGENETICALLY
OROGENICALLY
OROGRAPHER
OROGRAPHERS
OROGRAPHIC
OROGRAPHICAL
OROGRAPHICALLY
OROGRAPHIES
OROLOGICAL
OROLOGICALLY
OROLOGISTS
OROMAXILLARY
OROPHARYNGEAL
OROPHARYNGES
OROPHARYNX
OROPHARYNXES
OROROTUNDITIES
OROROTUNDITY
OROTUNDITIES
OROTUNDITY
ORPHANAGES
ORPHANHOOD
ORPHANHOODS
ORPHANISMS
ORPHARIONS
ORPHEOREON
ORPHEOREONS
ORPHICALLY
ORRISROOTS
ORTANIQUES
ORTHOBORATE
ORTHOBORATES
ORTHOBORIC
ORTHOCAINE
ORTHOCAINES
ORTHOCENTER
ORTHOCENTERS
ORTHOCENTRE
ORTHOCENTRES
ORTHOCEPHALIC
ORTHOCEPHALIES
ORTHOCEPHALOUS
ORTHOCEPHALY
ORTHOCHROMATIC
ORTHOCHROMATISM
ORTHOCLASE
ORTHOCLASES
ORTHOCLASTIC
ORTHOCOUSINS
ORTHODIAGONAL
ORTHODIAGONALS
ORTHODONTIA
ORTHODONTIAS
ORTHODONTIC
ORTHODONTICALLY
ORTHODONTICS
ORTHODONTIST
ORTHODONTISTS
ORTHODOXES
ORTHODOXIES
ORTHODOXLY
ORTHODROMIC
ORTHODROMICS
ORTHODROMIES
ORTHODROMY
ORTHOEPICAL
ORTHOEPICALLY
ORTHOEPIES
ORTHOEPIST
ORTHOEPISTS
ORTHOGENESES
ORTHOGENESIS
ORTHOGENETIC
ORTHOGENIC
ORTHOGENICALLY
ORTHOGENICS
ORTHOGNATHIC
ORTHOGNATHIES
ORTHOGNATHISM
ORTHOGNATHISMS
ORTHOGNATHOUS
ORTHOGNATHY
ORTHOGONAL
ORTHOGONALISE
ORTHOGONALISED
ORTHOGONALISES
ORTHOGONALISING
ORTHOGONALITIES
ORTHOGONALITY
ORTHOGONALIZE
ORTHOGONALIZED
ORTHOGONALIZES
ORTHOGONALIZING
ORTHOGONALLY
ORTHOGRADE
ORTHOGRAPH
ORTHOGRAPHER
ORTHOGRAPHERS
ORTHOGRAPHIC
ORTHOGRAPHICAL
ORTHOGRAPHIES
ORTHOGRAPHIST
ORTHOGRAPHISTS
ORTHOGRAPHS
ORTHOGRAPHY
ORTHOHYDROGEN
ORTHOHYDROGENS
ORTHOMOLECULAR
ORTHOMORPHIC
ORTHONORMAL
ORTHOPAEDIC
ORTHOPAEDICAL
ORTHOPAEDICALLY
ORTHOPAEDICS
ORTHOPAEDIES
ORTHOPAEDIST
ORTHOPAEDISTS
ORTHOPAEDY
ORTHOPEDIA
ORTHOPEDIAS
ORTHOPEDIC
ORTHOPEDICAL
ORTHOPEDICALLY
ORTHOPEDICS
ORTHOPEDIES
ORTHOPEDIST
ORTHOPEDISTS
ORTHOPHOSPHATE
ORTHOPHOSPHATES
ORTHOPHOSPHORIC
ORTHOPHYRE
ORTHOPHYRES
ORTHOPHYRIC
ORTHOPINAKOID
ORTHOPINAKOIDS
ORTHOPNOEA
ORTHOPNOEAS
ORTHOPRAXES
ORTHOPRAXIES
ORTHOPRAXIS
ORTHOPRAXY
ORTHOPRISM
ORTHOPRISMS
ORTHOPSYCHIATRY
ORTHOPTERA
ORTHOPTERAN
ORTHOPTERANS
ORTHOPTERIST
ORTHOPTERISTS
ORTHOPTEROID
ORTHOPTEROIDS
ORTHOPTEROLOGY
ORTHOPTERON
ORTHOPTEROUS
ORTHOPTERS
ORTHOPTICS
ORTHOPTIST
ORTHOPTISTS
ORTHOPYROXENE
ORTHOPYROXENES
ORTHOREXIA
ORTHOREXIAS
ORTHORHOMBIC
ORTHOSCOPE
ORTHOSCOPES
ORTHOSCOPIC
ORTHOSILICATE
ORTHOSILICATES
ORTHOSILICIC
ORTHOSTATIC
ORTHOSTICHIES
ORTHOSTICHOUS
ORTHOSTICHY
ORTHOTISTS
ORTHOTONES
ORTHOTONESES
ORTHOTONESIS
ORTHOTONIC
ORTHOTOPIC
ORTHOTROPIC
ORTHOTROPIES
ORTHOTROPISM
ORTHOTROPISMS
ORTHOTROPOUS
ORTHOTROPY
ORTHOTUNGSTIC
ORTHOVANADIC
ORYCTOLOGIES
ORYCTOLOGY
OSCILLATED
OSCILLATES
OSCILLATING
OSCILLATION
OSCILLATIONAL
OSCILLATIONS
OSCILLATIVE
OSCILLATOR
OSCILLATORS
OSCILLATORY
OSCILLOGRAM
OSCILLOGRAMS
OSCILLOGRAPH
OSCILLOGRAPHIC
OSCILLOGRAPHIES
OSCILLOGRAPHS
OSCILLOGRAPHY
OSCILLOSCOPE
OSCILLOSCOPES
OSCILLOSCOPIC
OSCITANCES
OSCITANCIES
OSCITANTLY
OSCITATING
OSCITATION
OSCITATIONS
OSCULATING
OSCULATION
OSCULATIONS
OSCULATORIES
OSCULATORY
OSMETERIUM
OSMIDROSES
OSMIDROSIS
OSMIRIDIUM
OSMIRIDIUMS
OSMOLALITIES
OSMOLALITY
OSMOLARITIES
OSMOLARITY
OSMOMETERS
OSMOMETRIC
OSMOMETRICALLY
OSMOMETRIES
OSMOREGULATION
OSMOREGULATIONS

OSMOREGULATORY
OSMOTICALLY
OSMUNDINES
OSSIFEROUS
OSSIFICATION
OSSIFICATIONS
OSSIFRAGAS
OSSIFRAGES
OSSIVOROUS
OSTEICHTHYAN
OSTEICHTHYANS
OSTEITIDES
OSTEITISES
OSTENSIBILITIES
OSTENSIBILITY
OSTENSIBLE
OSTENSIBLY
OSTENSIVELY
OSTENSORIA
OSTENSORIES
OSTENSORIUM
OSTENTATION
OSTENTATIONS
OSTENTATIOUS
OSTENTATIOUSLY
OSTEOARTHRITIC
OSTEOARTHRITICS
OSTEOARTHRITIS
OSTEOARTHROSES
OSTEOARTHROSIS
OSTEOBLAST
OSTEOBLASTIC
OSTEOBLASTS
OSTEOCLASES
OSTEOCLASIS
OSTEOCLAST
OSTEOCLASTIC
OSTEOCLASTS
OSTEOCOLLA
OSTEOCOLLAS
OSTEOCYTES
OSTEODERMAL
OSTEODERMATOUS
OSTEODERMIC
OSTEODERMOUS
OSTEODERMS
OSTEOFIBROSES
OSTEOFIBROSIS
OSTEOGENESES
OSTEOGENESIS
OSTEOGENETIC
OSTEOGENIC
OSTEOGENIES
OSTEOGENOUS
OSTEOGRAPHIES
OSTEOGRAPHY
OSTEOLOGICAL
OSTEOLOGICALLY
OSTEOLOGIES
OSTEOLOGIST
OSTEOLOGISTS
OSTEOMALACIA
OSTEOMALACIAL
OSTEOMALACIAS
OSTEOMALACIC
OSTEOMYELITIS
OSTEOMYELITISES
OSTEOPATHIC
OSTEOPATHICALLY
OSTEOPATHIES
OSTEOPATHIST
OSTEOPATHISTS
OSTEOPATHS
OSTEOPATHY
OSTEOPETROSES
OSTEOPETROSIS
OSTEOPHYTE
OSTEOPHYTES
OSTEOPHYTIC
OSTEOPLASTIC
OSTEOPLASTIES
OSTEOPLASTY
OSTEOPOROSES
OSTEOPOROSIS
OSTEOPOROTIC
OSTEOSARCOMA
OSTEOSARCOMAS
OSTEOSARCOMATA
OSTEOSISES
OSTEOTOMES
OSTEOTOMIES
OSTLERESSES
OSTRACEANS
OSTRACEOUS
OSTRACISABLE
OSTRACISED
OSTRACISER
OSTRACISERS
OSTRACISES
OSTRACISING
OSTRACISMS
OSTRACIZABLE
OSTRACIZED
OSTRACIZER
OSTRACIZERS
OSTRACIZES
OSTRACIZING
OSTRACODAN
OSTRACODERM
OSTRACODERMS
OSTRACODES
OSTRACODOUS
OSTREACEOUS
OSTREICULTURE
OSTREICULTURES
OSTREICULTURIST
OSTREOPHAGE
OSTREOPHAGES
OSTREOPHAGIES
OSTREOPHAGOUS
OSTREOPHAGY
OSTRICHISM
OSTRICHISMS
OSTRICHLIKE
OTHERGATES
OTHERGUESS
OTHERNESSES
OTHERWHERE
OTHERWHILE
OTHERWHILES
OTHERWORLD
OTHERWORLDISH
OTHERWORLDLIER
OTHERWORLDLIEST
OTHERWORLDLY
OTHERWORLDS
OTIOSENESS
OTIOSENESSES
OTIOSITIES
OTOLARYNGOLOGY
OTOLOGICAL
OTOLOGISTS
OTOPLASTIES
OTORRHOEAS
OTOSCLEROSES
OTOSCLEROSIS
OTOSCOPIES
OTOTOXICITIES
OTOTOXICITY
OTTERHOUND
OTTERHOUNDS
OTTRELITES
OUANANICHE
OUANANICHES
OUBLIETTES
OUGHTLINGS
OUGHTNESSES
OUROBOROSES
OUROLOGIES
OUROSCOPIES
OUTACHIEVE
OUTACHIEVED
OUTACHIEVES
OUTACHIEVING
OUTARGUING
OUTBACKERS
OUTBALANCE
OUTBALANCED
OUTBALANCES
OUTBALANCING
OUTBARGAIN
OUTBARGAINED
OUTBARGAINING
OUTBARGAINS
OUTBARKING
OUTBARRING
OUTBAWLING
OUTBEAMING
OUTBEGGING
OUTBIDDERS
OUTBIDDING
OUTBITCHED
OUTBITCHES
OUTBITCHING
OUTBLAZING
OUTBLEATED
OUTBLEATING
OUTBLESSED
OUTBLESSES
OUTBLESSING
OUTBLOOMED
OUTBLOOMING
OUTBLUFFED
OUTBLUFFING
OUTBLUSHED
OUTBLUSHES
OUTBLUSHING
OUTBLUSTER
OUTBLUSTERED
OUTBLUSTERING
OUTBLUSTERS
OUTBOASTED
OUTBOASTING
OUTBRAGGED
OUTBRAGGING
OUTBRAVING
OUTBRAWLED
OUTBRAWLING
OUTBRAZENED
OUTBRAZENING
OUTBRAZENS
OUTBREAKING
OUTBREATHE
OUTBREATHED
OUTBREATHES
OUTBREATHING
OUTBREEDING
OUTBREEDINGS
OUTBRIBING
OUTBUILDING
OUTBUILDINGS
OUTBULGING
OUTBULKING
OUTBULLIED
OUTBULLIES
OUTBULLYING
OUTBURNING
OUTBURSTING
OUTCALLING
OUTCAPERED
OUTCAPERING
OUTCASTEING
OUTCASTING
OUTCATCHES
OUTCATCHING
OUTCAVILED
OUTCAVILING
OUTCAVILLED
OUTCAVILLING
OUTCHARGED

O

OUTCHARGES
OUTCHARGING
OUTCHARMED
OUTCHARMING
OUTCHEATED
OUTCHEATING
OUTCHIDDEN
OUTCHIDING
OUTCLASSED
OUTCLASSES
OUTCLASSING
OUTCLIMBED
OUTCLIMBING
OUTCOACHED
OUTCOACHES
OUTCOACHING
OUTCOMPETE
OUTCOMPETED
OUTCOMPETES
OUTCOMPETING
OUTCOOKING
OUTCOUNTED
OUTCOUNTING
OUTCRAFTIED
OUTCRAFTIES
OUTCRAFTYING
OUTCRAWLED
OUTCRAWLING
OUTCROPPED
OUTCROPPING
OUTCROPPINGS
OUTCROSSED
OUTCROSSES
OUTCROSSING
OUTCROSSINGS
OUTCROWDED
OUTCROWDING
OUTCROWING
OUTCURSING
OUTDACIOUS
OUTDANCING
OUTDATEDLY
OUTDATEDNESS
OUTDATEDNESSES
OUTDAZZLED
OUTDAZZLES
OUTDAZZLING
OUTDEBATED
OUTDEBATES
OUTDEBATING
OUTDELIVER
OUTDELIVERED
OUTDELIVERING
OUTDELIVERS
OUTDESIGNED
OUTDESIGNING
OUTDESIGNS
OUTDISTANCE
OUTDISTANCED
OUTDISTANCES
OUTDISTANCING
OUTDODGING
OUTDOORSIER
OUTDOORSIEST
OUTDOORSMAN
OUTDOORSMANSHIP
OUTDOORSMEN
OUTDRAGGED
OUTDRAGGING
OUTDRAWING
OUTDREAMED
OUTDREAMING
OUTDRESSED
OUTDRESSES
OUTDRESSING
OUTDRINKING
OUTDRIVING
OUTDROPPED
OUTDROPPING
OUTDUELING
OUTDUELLED
OUTDUELLING
OUTDWELLED
OUTDWELLING
OUTEARNING
OUTECHOING
OUTERCOATS
OUTERCOURSE
OUTERCOURSES
OUTERWEARS
OUTFABLING
OUTFANGTHIEF
OUTFANGTHIEVES
OUTFASTING
OUTFAWNING
OUTFEASTED
OUTFEASTING
OUTFEELING
OUTFENCING
OUTFIELDER
OUTFIELDERS
OUTFIGHTING
OUTFIGHTINGS
OUTFIGURED
OUTFIGURES
OUTFIGURING
OUTFINDING
OUTFISHING
OUTFITTERS
OUTFITTING
OUTFITTINGS
OUTFLANKED
OUTFLANKING
OUTFLASHED
OUTFLASHES
OUTFLASHING
OUTFLINGING
OUTFLOATED
OUTFLOATING
OUTFLOWING
OUTFLOWINGS
OUTFLUSHED
OUTFLUSHES
OUTFLUSHING
OUTFOOLING
OUTFOOTING
OUTFROWNED
OUTFROWNING
OUTFUMBLED
OUTFUMBLES
OUTFUMBLING
OUTGAINING
OUTGALLOPED
OUTGALLOPING
OUTGALLOPS
OUTGAMBLED
OUTGAMBLES
OUTGAMBLING
OUTGASSING
OUTGASSINGS
OUTGENERAL
OUTGENERALED
OUTGENERALING
OUTGENERALLED
OUTGENERALLING
OUTGENERALS
OUTGIVINGS
OUTGLARING
OUTGLEAMED
OUTGLEAMING
OUTGLITTER
OUTGLITTERED
OUTGLITTERING
OUTGLITTERS
OUTGLOWING
OUTGNAWING
OUTGOINGNESS
OUTGOINGNESSES
OUTGRINNED
OUTGRINNING
OUTGROSSED
OUTGROSSES
OUTGROSSING
OUTGROWING
OUTGROWTHS
OUTGUESSED
OUTGUESSES
OUTGUESSING
OUTGUIDING
OUTGUNNING
OUTGUSHING
OUTHANDLED
OUTHANDLES
OUTHANDLING
OUTHARBORS
OUTHAULERS
OUTHEARING
OUTHITTING
OUTHOMERED
OUTHOMERING
OUTHOWLING
OUTHUMORED
OUTHUMORING
OUTHUMOURED
OUTHUMOURING
OUTHUMOURS
OUTHUNTING
OUTHUSTLED
OUTHUSTLES
OUTHUSTLING
OUTINTRIGUE
OUTINTRIGUED
OUTINTRIGUES
OUTINTRIGUING
OUTJESTING
OUTJETTING
OUTJETTINGS
OUTJINXING
OUTJOCKEYED
OUTJOCKEYING
OUTJOCKEYS
OUTJUGGLED
OUTJUGGLES
OUTJUGGLING
OUTJUMPING
OUTJUTTING
OUTJUTTINGS
OUTKEEPING
OUTKICKING
OUTKILLING
OUTKISSING
OUTLANDERS
OUTLANDISH
OUTLANDISHLY
OUTLANDISHNESS
OUTLASHING
OUTLASTING
OUTLAUGHED
OUTLAUGHING
OUTLAUNCED
OUTLAUNCES
OUTLAUNCHED
OUTLAUNCHES
OUTLAUNCHING
OUTLAUNCING
OUTLAWRIES
OUTLEADING
OUTLEAPING
OUTLEARNED
OUTLEARNING
OUTLODGING
OUTLODGINGS
OUTLOOKING
OUTLUSTERED
OUTLUSTERING
OUTLUSTERS
OUTLUSTRED
OUTLUSTRES
OUTLUSTRING
OUTMANEUVER

O

OUTMANEUVERED
OUTMANEUVERING
OUTMANEUVERS
OUTMANIPULATE
OUTMANIPULATED
OUTMANIPULATES
OUTMANIPULATING
OUTMANNING
OUTMANOEUVRE
OUTMANOEUVRED
OUTMANOEUVRES
OUTMANOEUVRING
OUTMANTLED
OUTMANTLES
OUTMANTLING
OUTMARCHED
OUTMARCHES
OUTMARCHING
OUTMARRIAGE
OUTMARRIAGES
OUTMASTERED
OUTMASTERING
OUTMASTERS
OUTMATCHED
OUTMATCHES
OUTMATCHING
OUTMEASURE
OUTMEASURED
OUTMEASURES
OUTMEASURING
OUTMODEDLY
OUTMODEDNESS
OUTMODEDNESSES
OUTMUSCLED
OUTMUSCLES
OUTMUSCLING
OUTNIGHTED
OUTNIGHTING
OUTNUMBERED
OUTNUMBERING
OUTNUMBERS
OUTOFFICES
OUTORGANISE
OUTORGANISED
OUTORGANISES
OUTORGANISING
OUTORGANIZE
OUTORGANIZED
OUTORGANIZES
OUTORGANIZING
OUTPAINTED
OUTPAINTING
OUTPASSING
OUTPASSION
OUTPASSIONED
OUTPASSIONING
OUTPASSIONS
OUTPATIENT
OUTPATIENTS
OUTPEEPING
OUTPEERING
OUTPEOPLED
OUTPEOPLES
OUTPEOPLING
OUTPERFORM
OUTPERFORMED
OUTPERFORMING
OUTPERFORMS
OUTPITCHED
OUTPITCHES
OUTPITCHING
OUTPITYING
OUTPLACEMENT
OUTPLACEMENTS
OUTPLACERS
OUTPLACING
OUTPLANNED
OUTPLANNING
OUTPLAYING
OUTPLODDED
OUTPLODDING
OUTPLOTTED
OUTPLOTTING
OUTPOINTED
OUTPOINTING
OUTPOLITICK
OUTPOLITICKED
OUTPOLITICKING
OUTPOLITICKS
OUTPOLLING
OUTPOPULATE
OUTPOPULATED
OUTPOPULATES
OUTPOPULATING
OUTPORTERS
OUTPOURERS
OUTPOURING
OUTPOURINGS
OUTPOWERED
OUTPOWERING
OUTPRAYING
OUTPREACHED
OUTPREACHES
OUTPREACHING
OUTPREENED
OUTPREENING
OUTPRESSED
OUTPRESSES
OUTPRESSING
OUTPRICING
OUTPRIZING
OUTPRODUCE
OUTPRODUCED
OUTPRODUCES
OUTPRODUCING
OUTPROMISE
OUTPROMISED
OUTPROMISES
OUTPROMISING
OUTPSYCHED
OUTPSYCHING
OUTPULLING
OUTPUNCHED
OUTPUNCHES
OUTPUNCHING
OUTPURSUED
OUTPURSUES
OUTPURSUING
OUTPUSHING
OUTPUTTING
OUTQUARTERS
OUTQUOTING
OUTRAGEOUS
OUTRAGEOUSLY
OUTRAGEOUSNESS
OUTRAISING
OUTRANGING
OUTRANKING
OUTREACHED
OUTREACHES
OUTREACHING
OUTREADING
OUTREASONED
OUTREASONING
OUTREASONS
OUTREBOUND
OUTREBOUNDED
OUTREBOUNDING
OUTREBOUNDS
OUTRECKONED
OUTRECKONING
OUTRECKONS
OUTRECUIDANCE
OUTRECUIDANCES
OUTREDDENED
OUTREDDENING
OUTREDDENS
OUTREDDING
OUTREDDINGS
OUTREIGNED
OUTREIGNING
OUTRELIEFS
OUTREPRODUCE
OUTREPRODUCED
OUTREPRODUCES
OUTREPRODUCING
OUTRIDINGS
OUTRIGGERS
OUTRIGGING
OUTRIGGINGS
OUTRIGHTLY
OUTRINGING
OUTRIVALED
OUTRIVALING
OUTRIVALLED
OUTRIVALLING
OUTROARING
OUTROCKING
OUTROLLING
OUTROOPERS
OUTROOTING
OUTRUNNERS
OUTRUNNING
OUTRUSHING
OUTSAILING
OUTSAVORED
OUTSAVORING
OUTSAVOURED
OUTSAVOURING
OUTSAVOURS
OUTSCHEMED
OUTSCHEMES
OUTSCHEMING
OUTSCOLDED
OUTSCOLDING
OUTSCOOPED
OUTSCOOPING
OUTSCORING
OUTSCORNED
OUTSCORNING
OUTSCREAMED
OUTSCREAMING
OUTSCREAMS
OUTSELLING
OUTSERVING
OUTSETTING
OUTSETTINGS
OUTSETTLEMENT
OUTSETTLEMENTS
OUTSHAMING
OUTSHINING
OUTSHOOTING
OUTSHOUTED
OUTSHOUTING
OUTSIDERNESS
OUTSIDERNESSES
OUTSINGING
OUTSINNING
OUTSITTING
OUTSKATING
OUTSLEEPING
OUTSLICKED
OUTSLICKING
OUTSMARTED
OUTSMARTING
OUTSMELLED
OUTSMELLING
OUTSMILING
OUTSMOKING
OUTSNORING
OUTSOARING
OUTSOURCED
OUTSOURCES
OUTSOURCING
OUTSOURCINGS
OUTSPANNED
OUTSPANNING
OUTSPARKLE
OUTSPARKLED
OUTSPARKLES

OUTSPARKLING
OUTSPEAKING
OUTSPECKLE
OUTSPECKLES
OUTSPEEDED
OUTSPEEDING
OUTSPELLED
OUTSPELLING
OUTSPENDING
OUTSPOKENLY
OUTSPOKENNESS
OUTSPOKENNESSES
OUTSPORTED
OUTSPORTING
OUTSPREADING
OUTSPREADS
OUTSPRINGING
OUTSPRINGS
OUTSPRINTED
OUTSPRINTING
OUTSPRINTS
OUTSTANDING
OUTSTANDINGLY
OUTSTARING
OUTSTARTED
OUTSTARTING
OUTSTATING
OUTSTATION
OUTSTATIONS
OUTSTAYING
OUTSTEERED
OUTSTEERING
OUTSTEPPED
OUTSTEPPING
OUTSTRAINED
OUTSTRAINING
OUTSTRAINS
OUTSTRETCH
OUTSTRETCHED
OUTSTRETCHES
OUTSTRETCHING
OUTSTRIDDEN
OUTSTRIDED
OUTSTRIDES
OUTSTRIDING
OUTSTRIKES
OUTSTRIKING
OUTSTRIPPED
OUTSTRIPPING
OUTSTRIVEN
OUTSTRIVES
OUTSTRIVING
OUTSTROKES
OUTSTUDIED
OUTSTUDIES
OUTSTUDYING
OUTSTUNTED
OUTSTUNTING
OUTSULKING
OUTSUMMING
OUTSWEARING
OUTSWEEPING
OUTSWEETEN
OUTSWEETENED
OUTSWEETENING
OUTSWEETENS
OUTSWELLED
OUTSWELLING
OUTSWIMMING
OUTSWINGER
OUTSWINGERS
OUTSWINGING
OUTSWOLLEN
OUTTALKING
OUTTASKING
OUTTELLING
OUTTHANKED
OUTTHANKING
OUTTHIEVED
OUTTHIEVES
OUTTHIEVING
OUTTHINKING
OUTTHOUGHT
OUTTHROBBED
OUTTHROBBING
OUTTHROWING
OUTTHRUSTED
OUTTHRUSTING
OUTTHRUSTS
OUTTONGUED
OUTTONGUES
OUTTONGUING
OUTTOPPING
OUTTOWERED
OUTTOWERING
OUTTRADING
OUTTRAVELED
OUTTRAVELING
OUTTRAVELLED
OUTTRAVELLING
OUTTRAVELS
OUTTRICKED
OUTTRICKING
OUTTROTTED
OUTTROTTING
OUTTRUMPED
OUTTRUMPING
OUTVALUING
OUTVAUNTED
OUTVAUNTING
OUTVENOMED
OUTVENOMING
OUTVILLAIN
OUTVILLAINED
OUTVILLAINING
OUTVILLAINS
OUTVOICING
OUTWAITING
OUTWALKING
OUTWARDNESS
OUTWARDNESSES
OUTWARRING
OUTWASTING
OUTWATCHED
OUTWATCHES
OUTWATCHING
OUTWEARIED
OUTWEARIES
OUTWEARING
OUTWEARYING
OUTWEEDING
OUTWEEPING
OUTWEIGHED
OUTWEIGHING
OUTWELLING
OUTWHIRLED
OUTWHIRLING
OUTWICKING
OUTWILLING
OUTWINDING
OUTWINGING
OUTWINNING
OUTWISHING
OUTWITTING
OUTWORKERS
OUTWORKING
OUTWORTHED
OUTWORTHING
OUTWRESTED
OUTWRESTING
OUTWRESTLE
OUTWRESTLED
OUTWRESTLES
OUTWRESTLING
OUTWRITING
OUTWRITTEN
OUTWROUGHT
OUTYELLING
OUTYELPING
OUTYIELDED
OUTYIELDING
OUVIRANDRA
OUVIRANDRAS
OVALBUMINS
OVALNESSES
OVARIECTOMIES
OVARIECTOMISED
OVARIECTOMIZED
OVARIECTOMY
OVARIOTOMIES
OVARIOTOMIST
OVARIOTOMISTS
OVARIOTOMY
OVARITIDES
OVARITISES
OVERABOUND
OVERABOUNDED
OVERABOUNDING
OVERABOUNDS
OVERABSTRACT
OVERABUNDANCE
OVERABUNDANCES
OVERABUNDANT
OVERACCENTUATE
OVERACCENTUATED
OVERACCENTUATES
OVERACHIEVE
OVERACHIEVED
OVERACHIEVEMENT
OVERACHIEVER
OVERACHIEVERS
OVERACHIEVES
OVERACHIEVING
OVERACTING
OVERACTION
OVERACTIONS
OVERACTIVE
OVERACTIVITIES
OVERACTIVITY
OVERADJUSTMENT
OVERADJUSTMENTS
OVERADVERTISE
OVERADVERTISED
OVERADVERTISES
OVERADVERTISING
OVERADVERTIZE
OVERADVERTIZED
OVERADVERTIZES
OVERADVERTIZING
OVERAGGRESSIVE
OVERAMBITIOUS
OVERAMPLIFIED
OVERANALYSE
OVERANALYSED
OVERANALYSES
OVERANALYSING
OVERANALYSIS
OVERANALYTICAL
OVERANALYZE
OVERANALYZED
OVERANALYZES
OVERANALYZING
OVERANXIETIES
OVERANXIETY
OVERANXIOUS
OVERAPPLICATION
OVERARCHED
OVERARCHES
OVERARCHING
OVERARMING
OVERAROUSAL
OVERAROUSALS
OVERARRANGE
OVERARRANGED
OVERARRANGES
OVERARRANGING
OVERARTICULATE
OVERARTICULATED
OVERARTICULATES
OVERASSERT

O

OVERASSERTED
OVERASSERTING
OVERASSERTION
OVERASSERTIONS
OVERASSERTIVE
OVERASSERTS
OVERASSESSMENT
OVERASSESSMENTS
OVERATTENTION
OVERATTENTIONS
OVERATTENTIVE
OVERBAKING
OVERBALANCE
OVERBALANCED
OVERBALANCES
OVERBALANCING
OVERBEARING
OVERBEARINGLY
OVERBEARINGNESS
OVERBEATEN
OVERBEATING
OVERBEJEWELED
OVERBEJEWELLED
OVERBETTED
OVERBETTING
OVERBETTINGS
OVERBIDDEN
OVERBIDDER
OVERBIDDERS
OVERBIDDING
OVERBIDDINGS
OVERBILLED
OVERBILLING
OVERBLANKET
OVERBLANKETS
OVERBLEACH
OVERBLEACHED
OVERBLEACHES
OVERBLEACHING
OVERBLOUSE
OVERBLOUSES
OVERBLOWING
OVERBOILED
OVERBOILING
OVERBOLDLY
OVERBOOKED
OVERBOOKING
OVERBOOKINGS
OVERBORROW
OVERBORROWED
OVERBORROWING
OVERBORROWS
OVERBOUGHT
OVERBOUNDED
OVERBOUNDING
OVERBOUNDS
OVERBRAKED
OVERBRAKES
OVERBRAKING
OVERBREATHING
OVERBREATHINGS
OVERBREEDING
OVERBREEDS
OVERBRIDGE
OVERBRIDGED
OVERBRIDGES
OVERBRIDGING
OVERBRIEFED
OVERBRIEFING
OVERBRIEFS
OVERBRIGHT
OVERBRIMMED
OVERBRIMMING
OVERBROWED
OVERBROWING
OVERBROWSE
OVERBROWSED
OVERBROWSES
OVERBROWSING
OVERBRUTAL
OVERBUILDING
OVERBUILDS
OVERBULKED
OVERBULKING
OVERBURDEN
OVERBURDENED
OVERBURDENING
OVERBURDENS
OVERBURDENSOME
OVERBURNED
OVERBURNING
OVERBURTHEN
OVERBURTHENED
OVERBURTHENING
OVERBURTHENS
OVERBUSIED
OVERBUSIES
OVERBUSYING
OVERBUYING
OVERCALLED
OVERCALLING
OVERCANOPIED
OVERCANOPIES
OVERCANOPY
OVERCANOPYING
OVERCAPACITIES
OVERCAPACITY
OVERCAPITALISE
OVERCAPITALISED
OVERCAPITALISES
OVERCAPITALIZE
OVERCAPITALIZED
OVERCAPITALIZES
OVERCAREFUL
OVERCARRIED
OVERCARRIES
OVERCARRYING
OVERCASTED
OVERCASTING
OVERCASTINGS
OVERCATCHES
OVERCATCHING
OVERCAUGHT
OVERCAUTION
OVERCAUTIONS
OVERCAUTIOUS
OVERCAUTIOUSLY
OVERCENTRALISE
OVERCENTRALISED
OVERCENTRALISES
OVERCENTRALIZE
OVERCENTRALIZED
OVERCENTRALIZES
OVERCHARGE
OVERCHARGED
OVERCHARGES
OVERCHARGING
OVERCHARGINGS
OVERCHECKS
OVERCHILLED
OVERCHILLING
OVERCHILLS
OVERCIVILISED
OVERCIVILIZED
OVERCLAIMED
OVERCLAIMING
OVERCLAIMS
OVERCLASSES
OVERCLASSIFIED
OVERCLASSIFIES
OVERCLASSIFY
OVERCLASSIFYING
OVERCLEANED
OVERCLEANING
OVERCLEANS
OVERCLEARED
OVERCLEARING
OVERCLEARS
OVERCLEVER
OVERCLOCKED
OVERCLOCKER
OVERCLOCKERS
OVERCLOCKING
OVERCLOCKINGS
OVERCLOCKS
OVERCLOUDED
OVERCLOUDING
OVERCLOUDS
OVERCLOYED
OVERCLOYING
OVERCLUBBED
OVERCLUBBING
OVERCOACHED
OVERCOACHES
OVERCOACHING
OVERCOATING
OVERCOATINGS
OVERCOLORED
OVERCOLORING
OVERCOLORS
OVERCOLOUR
OVERCOLOURED
OVERCOLOURING
OVERCOLOURS
OVERCOMERS
OVERCOMING
OVERCOMMIT
OVERCOMMITMENT
OVERCOMMITMENTS
OVERCOMMITS
OVERCOMMITTED
OVERCOMMITTING
OVERCOMMUNICATE
OVERCOMPENSATE
OVERCOMPENSATED
OVERCOMPENSATES
OVERCOMPLEX
OVERCOMPLIANCE
OVERCOMPLIANCES
OVERCOMPLICATE
OVERCOMPLICATED
OVERCOMPLICATES
OVERCOMPRESS
OVERCOMPRESSED
OVERCOMPRESSES
OVERCOMPRESSING
OVERCONCERN
OVERCONCERNED
OVERCONCERNING
OVERCONCERNS
OVERCONFIDENCE
OVERCONFIDENCES
OVERCONFIDENT
OVERCONFIDENTLY
OVERCONSCIOUS
OVERCONSTRUCT
OVERCONSTRUCTED
OVERCONSTRUCTS
OVERCONSUME
OVERCONSUMED
OVERCONSUMES
OVERCONSUMING
OVERCONSUMPTION
OVERCONTROL
OVERCONTROLLED
OVERCONTROLLING
OVERCONTROLS
OVERCOOKED
OVERCOOKING
OVERCOOLED
OVERCOOLING
OVERCORRECT
OVERCORRECTED
OVERCORRECTING
OVERCORRECTION
OVERCORRECTIONS
OVERCORRECTS
OVERCOUNTED
OVERCOUNTING
OVERCOUNTS

OVERCOVERED
OVERCOVERING
OVERCOVERS
OVERCRAMMED
OVERCRAMMING
OVERCRAMMINGS
OVERCRAWED
OVERCRAWING
OVERCREDULITIES
OVERCREDULITY
OVERCREDULOUS
OVERCRITICAL
OVERCROPPED
OVERCROPPING
OVERCROWDED
OVERCROWDING
OVERCROWDINGS
OVERCROWDS
OVERCROWED
OVERCROWING
OVERCULTIVATION
OVERCURING
OVERCUTTING
OVERCUTTINGS
OVERDARING
OVERDECKED
OVERDECKING
OVERDECORATE
OVERDECORATED
OVERDECORATES
OVERDECORATING
OVERDECORATION
OVERDECORATIONS
OVERDEEPENING
OVERDELICATE
OVERDEMANDING
OVERDEPENDENCE
OVERDEPENDENCES
OVERDEPENDENT
OVERDESIGN
OVERDESIGNED
OVERDESIGNING
OVERDESIGNS
OVERDETERMINED
OVERDEVELOP
OVERDEVELOPED
OVERDEVELOPING
OVERDEVELOPMENT
OVERDEVELOPS
OVERDEVIATE
OVERDEVIATED
OVERDEVIATES
OVERDEVIATING
OVERDIAGNOSES
OVERDIAGNOSIS
OVERDILUTED
OVERDIRECT
OVERDIRECTED
OVERDIRECTING
OVERDIRECTS
OVERDISCOUNT
OVERDISCOUNTED
OVERDISCOUNTING
OVERDISCOUNTS
OVERDIVERSITIES
OVERDIVERSITY
OVERDOCUMENT
OVERDOCUMENTED
OVERDOCUMENTING
OVERDOCUMENTS
OVERDOMINANCE
OVERDOMINANCES
OVERDOMINANT
OVERDOSAGE
OVERDOSAGES
OVERDOSING
OVERDRAFTS
OVERDRAMATIC
OVERDRAMATISE
OVERDRAMATISED
OVERDRAMATISES
OVERDRAMATISING
OVERDRAMATIZE
OVERDRAMATIZED
OVERDRAMATIZES
OVERDRAMATIZING
OVERDRAUGHT
OVERDRAUGHTS
OVERDRAWING
OVERDRESSED
OVERDRESSES
OVERDRESSING
OVERDRINKING
OVERDRINKS
OVERDRIVEN
OVERDRIVES
OVERDRIVING
OVERDRYING
OVERDUBBED
OVERDUBBING
OVERDUSTED
OVERDUSTING
OVERDYEING
OVEREAGERNESS
OVEREAGERNESSES
OVEREARNEST
OVEREASIER
OVEREASIEST
OVEREATERS
OVEREATING
OVEREATINGS
OVEREDITED
OVEREDITING
OVEREDUCATE
OVEREDUCATED
OVEREDUCATES
OVEREDUCATING
OVEREDUCATION
OVEREDUCATIONS
OVEREFFUSIVE
OVEREGGING
OVERELABORATE
OVERELABORATED
OVERELABORATES
OVERELABORATING
OVERELABORATION
OVEREMBELLISH
OVEREMBELLISHED
OVEREMBELLISHES
OVEREMOTED
OVEREMOTES
OVEREMOTING
OVEREMOTIONAL
OVEREMPHASES
OVEREMPHASIS
OVEREMPHASISE
OVEREMPHASISED
OVEREMPHASISES
OVEREMPHASISING
OVEREMPHASIZE
OVEREMPHASIZED
OVEREMPHASIZES
OVEREMPHASIZING
OVEREMPHATIC
OVEREMPLOYMENT
OVEREMPLOYMENTS
OVERENAMORED
OVERENAMOURED
OVERENCOURAGE
OVERENCOURAGED
OVERENCOURAGES
OVERENCOURAGING
OVERENERGETIC
OVERENGINEER
OVERENGINEERED
OVERENGINEERING
OVERENGINEERS
OVERENROLLED
OVERENTERTAINED
OVERENTHUSIASM
OVERENTHUSIASMS
OVEREQUIPPED
OVEREQUIPPING
OVEREQUIPS
OVERESTIMATE
OVERESTIMATED
OVERESTIMATES
OVERESTIMATING
OVERESTIMATION
OVERESTIMATIONS
OVEREVALUATION
OVEREVALUATIONS
OVEREXAGGERATE
OVEREXAGGERATED
OVEREXAGGERATES
OVEREXCITABLE
OVEREXCITE
OVEREXCITED
OVEREXCITEMENT
OVEREXCITEMENTS
OVEREXCITES
OVEREXCITING
OVEREXERCISE
OVEREXERCISED
OVEREXERCISES
OVEREXERCISING
OVEREXERTED
OVEREXERTING
OVEREXERTION
OVEREXERTIONS
OVEREXERTS
OVEREXPAND
OVEREXPANDED
OVEREXPANDING
OVEREXPANDS
OVEREXPANSION
OVEREXPANSIONS
OVEREXPECTATION
OVEREXPLAIN
OVEREXPLAINED
OVEREXPLAINING
OVEREXPLAINS
OVEREXPLICIT
OVEREXPLOIT
OVEREXPLOITED
OVEREXPLOITING
OVEREXPLOITS
OVEREXPOSE
OVEREXPOSED
OVEREXPOSES
OVEREXPOSING
OVEREXPOSURE
OVEREXPOSURES
OVEREXTEND
OVEREXTENDED
OVEREXTENDING
OVEREXTENDS
OVEREXTENSION
OVEREXTENSIONS
OVEREXTRACTION
OVEREXTRACTIONS
OVEREXTRAVAGANT
OVEREXUBERANT
OVEREYEING
OVERFACILE
OVERFALLEN
OVERFALLING
OVERFAMILIAR
OVERFAMILIARITY
OVERFASTIDIOUS
OVERFATIGUE
OVERFATIGUED
OVERFATIGUES
OVERFATIGUING
OVERFAVORED
OVERFAVORING
OVERFAVORS
OVERFAVOUR
OVERFAVOURED
OVERFAVOURING

O

OVERFAVOURS
OVERFEARED
OVERFEARING
OVERFEEDING
OVERFEEDINGS
OVERFERTILISE
OVERFERTILISED
OVERFERTILISES
OVERFERTILISING
OVERFERTILIZE
OVERFERTILIZED
OVERFERTILIZES
OVERFERTILIZING
OVERFILLED
OVERFILLING
OVERFINENESS
OVERFINENESSES
OVERFINISHED
OVERFISHED
OVERFISHES
OVERFISHING
OVERFISHINGS
OVERFLIGHT
OVERFLIGHTS
OVERFLOODED
OVERFLOODING
OVERFLOODS
OVERFLOURISH
OVERFLOURISHED
OVERFLOURISHES
OVERFLOURISHING
OVERFLOWED
OVERFLOWING
OVERFLOWINGLY
OVERFLOWINGS
OVERFLUSHES
OVERFLYING
OVERFOCUSED
OVERFOCUSES
OVERFOCUSING
OVERFOCUSSED
OVERFOCUSSES
OVERFOCUSSING
OVERFOLDED
OVERFOLDING
OVERFONDLY
OVERFONDNESS
OVERFONDNESSES
OVERFORWARD
OVERFORWARDNESS
OVERFRAUGHT
OVERFREEDOM
OVERFREEDOMS
OVERFREELY
OVERFREIGHT
OVERFREIGHTING
OVERFREIGHTS
OVERFULFIL
OVERFULFILL
OVERFULFILLED
OVERFULFILLING
OVERFULFILLS
OVERFULFILS
OVERFULLNESS
OVERFULLNESSES
OVERFULNESS
OVERFULNESSES
OVERFUNDED
OVERFUNDING
OVERFUNDINGS
OVERFUSSIER
OVERFUSSIEST
OVERGALLED
OVERGALLING
OVERGANGING
OVERGARMENT
OVERGARMENTS
OVERGEARED
OVERGEARING
OVERGENERALISE
OVERGENERALISED
OVERGENERALISES
OVERGENERALIZE
OVERGENERALIZED
OVERGENERALIZES
OVERGENEROSITY
OVERGENEROUS
OVERGENEROUSLY
OVERGETTING
OVERGILDED
OVERGILDING
OVERGIRDED
OVERGIRDING
OVERGIVING
OVERGLAMORISE
OVERGLAMORISED
OVERGLAMORISES
OVERGLAMORISING
OVERGLAMORIZE
OVERGLAMORIZED
OVERGLAMORIZES
OVERGLAMORIZING
OVERGLANCE
OVERGLANCED
OVERGLANCES
OVERGLANCING
OVERGLAZED
OVERGLAZES
OVERGLAZING
OVERGLOOMED
OVERGLOOMING
OVERGLOOMS
OVERGOADED
OVERGOADING
OVERGOINGS
OVERGORGED
OVERGORGES
OVERGORGING
OVERGOVERN
OVERGOVERNED
OVERGOVERNING
OVERGOVERNS
OVERGRADED
OVERGRADES
OVERGRADING
OVERGRAINED
OVERGRAINER
OVERGRAINERS
OVERGRAINING
OVERGRAINS
OVERGRASSED
OVERGRASSES
OVERGRASSING
OVERGRAZED
OVERGRAZES
OVERGRAZING
OVERGRAZINGS
OVERGREEDIER
OVERGREEDIEST
OVERGREEDY
OVERGREENED
OVERGREENING
OVERGREENS
OVERGROUND
OVERGROWING
OVERGROWTH
OVERGROWTHS
OVERHAILED
OVERHAILES
OVERHAILING
OVERHALING
OVERHANDED
OVERHANDING
OVERHANDLE
OVERHANDLED
OVERHANDLES
OVERHANDLING
OVERHANGING
OVERHAPPIER
OVERHAPPIEST
OVERHARVEST
OVERHARVESTED
OVERHARVESTING
OVERHARVESTS
OVERHASTES
OVERHASTILY
OVERHASTINESS
OVERHASTINESSES
OVERHATING
OVERHAULED
OVERHAULING
OVERHEAPED
OVERHEAPING
OVERHEARING
OVERHEATED
OVERHEATING
OVERHEATINGS
OVERHENTING
OVERHITTING
OVERHOLDING
OVERHOLIER
OVERHOLIEST
OVERHOMOGENISE
OVERHOMOGENISED
OVERHOMOGENISES
OVERHOMOGENIZE
OVERHOMOGENIZED
OVERHOMOGENIZES
OVERHONORED
OVERHONORING
OVERHONORS
OVERHONOUR
OVERHONOURED
OVERHONOURING
OVERHONOURS
OVERHOPING
OVERHUNTED
OVERHUNTING
OVERHUNTINGS
OVERHYPING
OVERIDEALISE
OVERIDEALISED
OVERIDEALISES
OVERIDEALISING
OVERIDEALIZE
OVERIDEALIZED
OVERIDEALIZES
OVERIDEALIZING
OVERIDENTIFIED
OVERIDENTIFIES
OVERIDENTIFY
OVERIDENTIFYING
OVERIMAGINATIVE
OVERIMPRESS
OVERIMPRESSED
OVERIMPRESSES
OVERIMPRESSING
OVERINCLINED
OVERINDULGE
OVERINDULGED
OVERINDULGENCE
OVERINDULGENCES
OVERINDULGENT
OVERINDULGES
OVERINDULGING
OVERINFLATE
OVERINFLATED
OVERINFLATES
OVERINFLATING
OVERINFLATION
OVERINFLATIONS
OVERINFORM
OVERINFORMED
OVERINFORMING
OVERINFORMS
OVERINGENIOUS
OVERINGENUITIES
OVERINGENUITY
OVERINSISTENT
OVERINSURANCE

OVERINSURANCES
OVERINSURE
OVERINSURED
OVERINSURES
OVERINSURING
OVERINTENSE
OVERINTENSITIES
OVERINTENSITY
OVERINVESTMENT
OVERINVESTMENTS
OVERISSUANCE
OVERISSUANCES
OVERISSUED
OVERISSUES
OVERISSUING
OVERJOYING
OVERJUMPED
OVERJUMPING
OVERKEEPING
OVERKILLED
OVERKILLING
OVERKINDNESS
OVERKINDNESSES
OVERLABORED
OVERLABORING
OVERLABORS
OVERLABOUR
OVERLABOURED
OVERLABOURING
OVERLABOURS
OVERLADING
OVERLANDED
OVERLANDER
OVERLANDERS
OVERLANDING
OVERLAPPED
OVERLAPPING
OVERLARDED
OVERLARDING
OVERLAUNCH
OVERLAUNCHED
OVERLAUNCHES
OVERLAUNCHING
OVERLAVISH
OVERLAYING
OVERLAYINGS
OVERLEAPED
OVERLEAPING
OVERLEARNED
OVERLEARNING
OVERLEARNS
OVERLEARNT
OVERLEATHER
OVERLEATHERS
OVERLEAVEN
OVERLEAVENED
OVERLEAVENING
OVERLEAVENS
OVERLENDING
OVERLENGTH
OVERLENGTHEN
OVERLENGTHENED
OVERLENGTHENING
OVERLENGTHENS
OVERLENGTHS
OVERLETTING
OVERLEVERAGED
OVERLIGHTED
OVERLIGHTING
OVERLIGHTS
OVERLITERAL
OVERLITERARY
OVERLIVING
OVERLOADED
OVERLOADING
OVERLOCKED
OVERLOCKER
OVERLOCKERS
OVERLOCKING
OVERLOCKINGS
OVERLOOKED
OVERLOOKER
OVERLOOKERS
OVERLOOKING
OVERLORDED
OVERLORDING
OVERLORDSHIP
OVERLORDSHIPS
OVERLOVING
OVERMANAGE
OVERMANAGED
OVERMANAGES
OVERMANAGING
OVERMANIES
OVERMANNED
OVERMANNERED
OVERMANNING
OVERMANNINGS
OVERMANTEL
OVERMANTELS
OVERMASTED
OVERMASTER
OVERMASTERED
OVERMASTERING
OVERMASTERS
OVERMASTING
OVERMATCHED
OVERMATCHES
OVERMATCHING
OVERMATTER
OVERMATTERS
OVERMATURE
OVERMATURITIES
OVERMATURITY
OVERMEASURE
OVERMEASURED
OVERMEASURES
OVERMEASURING
OVERMEDICATE
OVERMEDICATED
OVERMEDICATES
OVERMEDICATING
OVERMEDICATION
OVERMEDICATIONS
OVERMELTED
OVERMELTING
OVERMERRIER
OVERMERRIEST
OVERMIGHTIER
OVERMIGHTIEST
OVERMIGHTY
OVERMILKED
OVERMILKING
OVERMINING
OVERMIXING
OVERMODEST
OVERMODESTLY
OVERMOUNTED
OVERMOUNTING
OVERMOUNTS
OVERMUCHES
OVERMULTIPLIED
OVERMULTIPLIES
OVERMULTIPLY
OVERMULTIPLYING
OVERMULTITUDE
OVERMULTITUDED
OVERMULTITUDES
OVERMULTITUDING
OVERMUSCLED
OVERNAMING
OVERNETTED
OVERNETTING
OVERNETTINGS
OVERNICELY
OVERNICENESS
OVERNICENESSES
OVERNIGHTED
OVERNIGHTER
OVERNIGHTERS
OVERNIGHTING
OVERNIGHTS
OVERNOURISH
OVERNOURISHED
OVERNOURISHES
OVERNOURISHING
OVERNUTRITION
OVERNUTRITIONS
OVEROBVIOUS
OVEROFFICE
OVEROFFICED
OVEROFFICES
OVEROFFICING
OVEROPERATE
OVEROPERATED
OVEROPERATES
OVEROPERATING
OVEROPINIONATED
OVEROPTIMISM
OVEROPTIMISMS
OVEROPTIMIST
OVEROPTIMISTIC
OVEROPTIMISTS
OVERORCHESTRATE
OVERORGANISE
OVERORGANISED
OVERORGANISES
OVERORGANISING
OVERORGANIZE
OVERORGANIZED
OVERORGANIZES
OVERORGANIZING
OVERORNAMENT
OVERORNAMENTED
OVERORNAMENTING
OVERORNAMENTS
OVERPACKAGE
OVERPACKAGED
OVERPACKAGES
OVERPACKAGING
OVERPACKED
OVERPACKING
OVERPAINTED
OVERPAINTING
OVERPAINTS
OVERPARTED
OVERPARTICULAR
OVERPARTING
OVERPASSED
OVERPASSES
OVERPASSING
OVERPAYING
OVERPAYMENT
OVERPAYMENTS
OVERPEDALED
OVERPEDALING
OVERPEDALLED
OVERPEDALLING
OVERPEDALLINGS
OVERPEDALS
OVERPEERED
OVERPEERING
OVERPEOPLE
OVERPEOPLED
OVERPEOPLES
OVERPEOPLING
OVERPERCHED
OVERPERCHES
OVERPERCHING
OVERPERSUADE
OVERPERSUADED
OVERPERSUADES
OVERPERSUADING
OVERPERSUASION
OVERPERSUASIONS
OVERPESSIMISTIC
OVERPICTURE
OVERPICTURED
OVERPICTURES
OVERPICTURING

OVERPITCHED
OVERPITCHES
OVERPITCHING
OVERPLACED
OVERPLAIDED
OVERPLAIDS
OVERPLANNED
OVERPLANNING
OVERPLANNINGS
OVERPLANTED
OVERPLANTING
OVERPLANTS
OVERPLAYED
OVERPLAYING
OVERPLOTTED
OVERPLOTTING
OVERPLOTTINGS
OVERPLUSES
OVERPLUSSES
OVERPLYING
OVERPOISED
OVERPOISES
OVERPOISING
OVERPOPULATE
OVERPOPULATED
OVERPOPULATES
OVERPOPULATING
OVERPOPULATION
OVERPOPULATIONS
OVERPOSTED
OVERPOSTING
OVERPOTENT
OVERPOWERED
OVERPOWERING
OVERPOWERINGLY
OVERPOWERS
OVERPRAISE
OVERPRAISED
OVERPRAISES
OVERPRAISING
OVERPRECISE
OVERPREPARATION
OVERPREPARE
OVERPREPARED
OVERPREPARES
OVERPREPARING
OVERPRESCRIBE
OVERPRESCRIBED
OVERPRESCRIBES
OVERPRESCRIBING
OVERPRESSED
OVERPRESSES
OVERPRESSING
OVERPRESSURE
OVERPRESSURES
OVERPRICED
OVERPRICES
OVERPRICING
OVERPRINTED
OVERPRINTING
OVERPRINTS
OVERPRIVILEGED
OVERPRIZED
OVERPRIZES
OVERPRIZING
OVERPROCESS
OVERPROCESSED
OVERPROCESSES
OVERPROCESSING
OVERPRODUCE
OVERPRODUCED
OVERPRODUCES
OVERPRODUCING
OVERPRODUCTION
OVERPRODUCTIONS
OVERPROGRAM
OVERPROGRAMED
OVERPROGRAMING
OVERPROGRAMMED
OVERPROGRAMMING
OVERPROGRAMS
OVERPROMISE
OVERPROMISED
OVERPROMISES
OVERPROMISING
OVERPROMOTE
OVERPROMOTED
OVERPROMOTES
OVERPROMOTING
OVERPROOFS
OVERPROPORTION
OVERPROPORTIONS
OVERPROTECT
OVERPROTECTED
OVERPROTECTING
OVERPROTECTION
OVERPROTECTIONS
OVERPROTECTIVE
OVERPROTECTS
OVERPUMPED
OVERPUMPING
OVERQUALIFIED
OVERRACKED
OVERRACKING
OVERRAKING
OVERRANKED
OVERRANKING
OVERRASHLY
OVERRASHNESS
OVERRASHNESSES
OVERRATING
OVERRAUGHT
OVERREACHED
OVERREACHER
OVERREACHERS
OVERREACHES
OVERREACHING
OVERREACTED
OVERREACTING
OVERREACTION
OVERREACTIONS
OVERREACTS
OVERREADING
OVERRECKON
OVERRECKONED
OVERRECKONING
OVERRECKONS
OVERREDDED
OVERREDDING
OVERREFINE
OVERREFINED
OVERREFINEMENT
OVERREFINEMENTS
OVERREFINES
OVERREFINING
OVERREGULATE
OVERREGULATED
OVERREGULATES
OVERREGULATING
OVERREGULATION
OVERREGULATIONS
OVERRELIANCE
OVERRELIANCES
OVERRENNING
OVERREPORT
OVERREPORTED
OVERREPORTING
OVERREPORTS
OVERREPRESENTED
OVERRESPOND
OVERRESPONDED
OVERRESPONDING
OVERRESPONDS
OVERRIDDEN
OVERRIDERS
OVERRIDING
OVERRIPENED
OVERRIPENESS
OVERRIPENESSES
OVERRIPENING
OVERRIPENS
OVERROASTED
OVERROASTING
OVERROASTS
OVERRUFFED
OVERRUFFING
OVERRULERS
OVERRULING
OVERRULINGS
OVERRUNNER
OVERRUNNERS
OVERRUNNING
OVERSAILED
OVERSAILING
OVERSALTED
OVERSALTING
OVERSANGUINE
OVERSATURATE
OVERSATURATED
OVERSATURATES
OVERSATURATING
OVERSATURATION
OVERSATURATIONS
OVERSAUCED
OVERSAUCES
OVERSAUCING
OVERSAVING
OVERSCALED
OVERSCHUTCHT
OVERSCORED
OVERSCORES
OVERSCORING
OVERSCRUPULOUS
OVERSCUTCHED
OVERSECRETION
OVERSECRETIONS
OVERSEEDED
OVERSEEDING
OVERSEEING
OVERSELLING
OVERSENSITIVE
OVERSENSITIVITY
OVERSERIOUS
OVERSERIOUSLY
OVERSERVICE
OVERSERVICED
OVERSERVICES
OVERSERVICING
OVERSETTING
OVERSEWING
OVERSHADED
OVERSHADES
OVERSHADING
OVERSHADOW
OVERSHADOWED
OVERSHADOWING
OVERSHADOWS
OVERSHARED
OVERSHARES
OVERSHARING
OVERSHINES
OVERSHINING
OVERSHIRTS
OVERSHOOTING
OVERSHOOTS
OVERSHOWER
OVERSHOWERED
OVERSHOWERING
OVERSHOWERS
OVERSIGHTS
OVERSIMPLE
OVERSIMPLIFIED
OVERSIMPLIFIES
OVERSIMPLIFY
OVERSIMPLIFYING
OVERSIMPLISTIC
OVERSIMPLY
OVERSIZING
OVERSKATED
OVERSKATES

O

OVERSKATING
OVERSKIPPED
OVERSKIPPING
OVERSKIRTS
OVERSLAUGH
OVERSLAUGHED
OVERSLAUGHING
OVERSLAUGHS
OVERSLEEPING
OVERSLEEPS
OVERSLEEVE
OVERSLEEVES
OVERSLIPPED
OVERSLIPPING
OVERSMOKED
OVERSMOKES
OVERSMOKING
OVERSOAKED
OVERSOAKING
OVERSOLICITOUS
OVERSOWING
OVERSPECIALISE
OVERSPECIALISED
OVERSPECIALISES
OVERSPECIALIZE
OVERSPECIALIZED
OVERSPECIALIZES
OVERSPECULATE
OVERSPECULATED
OVERSPECULATES
OVERSPECULATING
OVERSPECULATION
OVERSPENDER
OVERSPENDERS
OVERSPENDING
OVERSPENDINGS
OVERSPENDS
OVERSPICED
OVERSPICES
OVERSPICING
OVERSPILLED
OVERSPILLING
OVERSPILLS
OVERSPREAD
OVERSPREADING
OVERSPREADS
OVERSTABILITIES
OVERSTABILITY
OVERSTAFFED
OVERSTAFFING
OVERSTAFFINGS
OVERSTAFFS
OVERSTAINED
OVERSTAINING
OVERSTAINS
OVERSTANDING
OVERSTANDS
OVERSTARED
OVERSTARES
OVERSTARING
OVERSTATED
OVERSTATEMENT
OVERSTATEMENTS
OVERSTATES
OVERSTATING
OVERSTAYED
OVERSTAYER
OVERSTAYERS
OVERSTAYING
OVERSTEERED
OVERSTEERING
OVERSTEERS
OVERSTEPPED
OVERSTEPPING
OVERSTIMULATE
OVERSTIMULATED
OVERSTIMULATES
OVERSTIMULATING
OVERSTIMULATION
OVERSTINKING
OVERSTINKS
OVERSTIRRED
OVERSTIRRING
OVERSTOCKED
OVERSTOCKING
OVERSTOCKS
OVERSTOREY
OVERSTOREYS
OVERSTORIES
OVERSTRAIN
OVERSTRAINED
OVERSTRAINING
OVERSTRAINS
OVERSTRESS
OVERSTRESSED
OVERSTRESSES
OVERSTRESSING
OVERSTRETCH
OVERSTRETCHED
OVERSTRETCHES
OVERSTRETCHING
OVERSTREWED
OVERSTREWING
OVERSTREWN
OVERSTREWS
OVERSTRIDDEN
OVERSTRIDE
OVERSTRIDES
OVERSTRIDING
OVERSTRIKE
OVERSTRIKES
OVERSTRIKING
OVERSTRODE
OVERSTRONG
OVERSTROOKE
OVERSTRUCK
OVERSTRUCTURED
OVERSTRUNG
OVERSTUDIED
OVERSTUDIES
OVERSTUDYING
OVERSTUFFED
OVERSTUFFING
OVERSTUFFS
OVERSUBSCRIBE
OVERSUBSCRIBED
OVERSUBSCRIBES
OVERSUBSCRIBING
OVERSUBTLE
OVERSUBTLETIES
OVERSUBTLETY
OVERSUDSED
OVERSUDSES
OVERSUDSING
OVERSUPPED
OVERSUPPING
OVERSUPPLIED
OVERSUPPLIES
OVERSUPPLY
OVERSUPPLYING
OVERSUSPICIOUS
OVERSWAYED
OVERSWAYING
OVERSWEARING
OVERSWEARS
OVERSWEETEN
OVERSWEETENED
OVERSWEETENING
OVERSWEETENS
OVERSWEETNESS
OVERSWEETNESSES
OVERSWELLED
OVERSWELLING
OVERSWELLS
OVERSWIMMING
OVERSWINGING
OVERSWINGS
OVERSWOLLEN
OVERTAKING
OVERTAKINGS
OVERTALKATIVE
OVERTALKED
OVERTALKING
OVERTASKED
OVERTASKING
OVERTAUGHT
OVERTAXATION
OVERTAXATIONS
OVERTAXING
OVERTEACHES
OVERTEACHING
OVERTEDIOUS
OVERTEEMED
OVERTEEMING
OVERTHINKING
OVERTHINKS
OVERTHINNED
OVERTHINNING
OVERTHOUGHT
OVERTHROWER
OVERTHROWERS
OVERTHROWING
OVERTHROWN
OVERTHROWS
OVERTHRUST
OVERTHRUSTS
OVERTHWART
OVERTHWARTED
OVERTHWARTING
OVERTHWARTS
OVERTIGHTEN
OVERTIGHTENED
OVERTIGHTENING
OVERTIGHTENS
OVERTIMELY
OVERTIMERS
OVERTIMING
OVERTIPPED
OVERTIPPING
OVERTIRING
OVERTNESSES
OVERTOILED
OVERTOILING
OVERTOPPED
OVERTOPPING
OVERTOPPINGS
OVERTOWERED
OVERTOWERING
OVERTOWERS
OVERTRADED
OVERTRADES
OVERTRADING
OVERTRADINGS
OVERTRAINED
OVERTRAINING
OVERTRAINS
OVERTREATED
OVERTREATING
OVERTREATMENT
OVERTREATMENTS
OVERTREATS
OVERTRICKS
OVERTRIMMED
OVERTRIMMING
OVERTRIPPED
OVERTRIPPING
OVERTRUMPED
OVERTRUMPING
OVERTRUMPS
OVERTRUSTED
OVERTRUSTING
OVERTRUSTS
OVERTURING
OVERTURNED
OVERTURNER
OVERTURNERS
OVERTURNING
OVERTYPING
OVERURGING
OVERUTILISATION

OVERUTILISE
OVERUTILISED
OVERUTILISES
OVERUTILISING
OVERUTILIZATION
OVERUTILIZE
OVERUTILIZED
OVERUTILIZES
OVERUTILIZING
OVERVALUATION
OVERVALUATIONS
OVERVALUED
OVERVALUES
OVERVALUING
OVERVEILED
OVERVEILING
OVERVIOLENT
OVERVOLTAGE
OVERVOLTAGES
OVERVOTING
OVERWARIER
OVERWARIEST
OVERWARMED
OVERWARMING
OVERWASHES
OVERWATCHED
OVERWATCHES
OVERWATCHING
OVERWATERED
OVERWATERING
OVERWATERS
OVERWEARIED
OVERWEARIES
OVERWEARING
OVERWEARYING
OVERWEATHER
OVERWEATHERED
OVERWEATHERING
OVERWEATHERS
OVERWEENED
OVERWEENING
OVERWEENINGLY
OVERWEENINGNESS
OVERWEENINGS
OVERWEIGHED
OVERWEIGHING
OVERWEIGHS
OVERWEIGHT
OVERWEIGHTED
OVERWEIGHTING
OVERWEIGHTS
OVERWETTED
OVERWETTING
OVERWHELMED
OVERWHELMING
OVERWHELMINGLY
OVERWHELMINGS
OVERWHELMS
OVERWILIER
OVERWILIEST
OVERWINDED
OVERWINDING
OVERWINGED
OVERWINGING
OVERWINTER
OVERWINTERED
OVERWINTERING
OVERWINTERS
OVERWISELY
OVERWITHHELD
OVERWITHHOLD
OVERWITHHOLDING
OVERWITHHOLDS
OVERWORKED
OVERWORKING
OVERWRAPPED
OVERWRAPPING
OVERWRESTED
OVERWRESTING
OVERWRESTLE
OVERWRESTLED
OVERWRESTLES
OVERWRESTLING
OVERWRESTS
OVERWRITES
OVERWRITING
OVERWRITTEN
OVERWROUGHT
OVERYEARED
OVERYEARING
OVERZEALOUS
OVERZEALOUSLY
OVERZEALOUSNESS
OVIPARITIES
OVIPAROUSLY
OVIPOSITED
OVIPOSITING
OVIPOSITION
OVIPOSITIONAL
OVIPOSITIONS
OVIPOSITOR
OVIPOSITORS
OVIRAPTORS
OVOVIVIPARITIES
OVOVIVIPARITY
OVOVIVIPAROUS
OVOVIVIPAROUSLY
OVULATIONS
OVULIFEROUS
OWERLOUPEN
OWERLOUPING
OWERLOUPIT
OWLISHNESS
OWLISHNESSES
OWNERSHIPS
OWRECOMING
OXACILLINS
OXALACETATE
OXALACETATES
OXALOACETATE
OXALOACETATES
OXALOACETIC
OXIDATIONAL
OXIDATIONS
OXIDATIVELY
OXIDIMETRIC
OXIDIMETRIES
OXIDIMETRY
OXIDISABLE
OXIDISATION
OXIDISATIONS
OXIDIZABLE
OXIDIZATION
OXIDIZATIONS
OXIDOREDUCTASE
OXIDOREDUCTASES
OXIMETRIES
OXYACETYLENE
OXYACETYLENES
OXYCEPHALIC
OXYCEPHALIES
OXYCEPHALOUS
OXYCEPHALY
OXYCODONES
OXYGENASES
OXYGENATED
OXYGENATES
OXYGENATING
OXYGENATION
OXYGENATIONS
OXYGENATOR
OXYGENATORS
OXYGENISED
OXYGENISER
OXYGENISERS
OXYGENISES
OXYGENISING
OXYGENIZED
OXYGENIZER
OXYGENIZERS
OXYGENIZES
OXYGENIZING
OXYGENLESS
OXYHAEMOGLOBIN
OXYHAEMOGLOBINS
OXYHEMOGLOBIN
OXYHEMOGLOBINS
OXYHYDROGEN
OXYHYDROGENS
OXYMORONIC
OXYMORONICALLY
OXYPHENBUTAZONE
OXYRHYNCHUS
OXYRHYNCHUSES
OXYSULPHIDE
OXYSULPHIDES
OXYTETRACYCLINE
OXYURIASES
OXYURIASIS
OYSTERCATCHER
OYSTERCATCHERS
OYSTERINGS
OZOCERITES
OZOKERITES
OZONATIONS
OZONIFEROUS
OZONISATION
OZONISATIONS
OZONIZATION
OZONIZATIONS
OZONOLYSES
OZONOLYSIS
OZONOSPHERE
OZONOSPHERES

O

P

PACEMAKERS
PACEMAKING
PACEMAKINGS
PACESETTER
PACESETTERS
PACESETTING
PACESETTINGS
PACHYCARPOUS
PACHYDACTYL
PACHYDACTYLOUS
PACHYDERMAL
PACHYDERMATOUS
PACHYDERMIA
PACHYDERMIAS
PACHYDERMIC
PACHYDERMOUS
PACHYDERMS
PACHYMENINGITIS
PACHYMETER
PACHYMETERS
PACHYSANDRA
PACHYSANDRAS
PACHYTENES
PACIFIABLE
PACIFICALLY
PACIFICATE
PACIFICATED
PACIFICATES
PACIFICATING
PACIFICATION
PACIFICATIONS
PACIFICATOR
PACIFICATORS
PACIFICATORY
PACIFICISM
PACIFICISMS
PACIFICIST
PACIFICISTS
PACIFISTIC
PACIFISTICALLY
PACKABILITIES
PACKABILITY
PACKAGINGS
PACKBOARDS
PACKCLOTHS
PACKETISED
PACKETISES
PACKETISING
PACKETIZED
PACKETIZES
PACKETIZING
PACKFRAMES
PACKHORSES
PACKINGHOUSE
PACKINGHOUSES
PACKNESSES
PACKSADDLE
PACKSADDLES
PACKSHEETS
PACKSTAFFS
PACKTHREAD
PACKTHREADS
PACLITAXEL
PACLITAXELS
PACTIONING
PADDLEBALL
PADDLEBALLS
PADDLEBOARD
PADDLEBOARDS
PADDLEBOAT
PADDLEBOATS
PADDLEFISH
PADDLEFISHES
PADDOCKING
PADDYMELON
PADDYMELONS
PADDYWACKED
PADDYWACKING
PADDYWACKS
PADDYWHACK
PADDYWHACKS
PADEMELONS
PADEREROES
PADLOCKING
PADRONISMS
PADYMELONS
PAEDAGOGIC
PAEDAGOGUE
PAEDAGOGUES
PAEDERASTIC
PAEDERASTIES
PAEDERASTS
PAEDERASTY
PAEDEUTICS
PAEDIATRIC
PAEDIATRICIAN
PAEDIATRICIANS
PAEDIATRICS
PAEDIATRIES
PAEDIATRIST
PAEDIATRISTS
PAEDOBAPTISM
PAEDOBAPTISMS
PAEDOBAPTIST
PAEDOBAPTISTS
PAEDODONTIC
PAEDODONTICS
PAEDOGENESES
PAEDOGENESIS
PAEDOGENETIC
PAEDOGENIC
PAEDOLOGICAL
PAEDOLOGIES
PAEDOLOGIST
PAEDOLOGISTS
PAEDOMORPHIC
PAEDOMORPHISM
PAEDOMORPHISMS
PAEDOMORPHOSES
PAEDOMORPHOSIS
PAEDOPHILE
PAEDOPHILES
PAEDOPHILIA
PAEDOPHILIAC
PAEDOPHILIACS
PAEDOPHILIAS
PAEDOPHILIC
PAEDOPHILICS
PAEDOTRIBE
PAEDOTRIBES
PAEDOTROPHIES
PAEDOTROPHY
PAGANISATION
PAGANISATIONS
PAGANISERS
PAGANISING
PAGANISTIC
PAGANISTICALLY
PAGANIZATION
PAGANIZATIONS
PAGANIZERS
PAGANIZING
PAGEANTRIES
PAGINATING
PAGINATION
PAGINATIONS
PAIDEUTICS
PAILLASSES
PAILLETTES
PAINFULLER
PAINFULLEST
PAINFULNESS
PAINFULNESSES
PAINKILLER
PAINKILLERS
PAINKILLING
PAINLESSLY
PAINLESSNESS
PAINLESSNESSES
PAINSTAKER
PAINSTAKERS
PAINSTAKING
PAINSTAKINGLY
PAINSTAKINGNESS
PAINSTAKINGS
PAINTBALLING
PAINTBALLINGS
PAINTBALLS
PAINTBOXES
PAINTBRUSH
PAINTBRUSHES
PAINTERLINESS
PAINTERLINESSES
PAINTINESS
PAINTINESSES
PAINTRESSES
PAINTWORKS
PAKIRIKIRI
PAKIRIKIRIS
PALACINKES
PALAEANTHROPIC
PALAEBIOLOGIES
PALAEBIOLOGIST
PALAEBIOLOGISTS
PALAEBIOLOGY
PALAEETHNOLOGY
PALAEOANTHROPIC
PALAEOBIOLOGIC
PALAEOBIOLOGIES
PALAEOBIOLOGIST
PALAEOBIOLOGY
PALAEOBOTANIC
PALAEOBOTANICAL
PALAEOBOTANIES
PALAEOBOTANIST
PALAEOBOTANISTS
PALAEOBOTANY
PALAEOCLIMATE
PALAEOCLIMATES
PALAEOCLIMATIC
PALAEOCRYSTIC
PALAEOCURRENT
PALAEOCURRENTS
PALAEOECOLOGIC
PALAEOECOLOGIES
PALAEOECOLOGIST
PALAEOECOLOGY
PALAEOETHNOLOGY
PALAEOGAEA
PALAEOGAEAS

P

PALAEOGEOGRAPHY
PALAEOGRAPHER
PALAEOGRAPHERS
PALAEOGRAPHIC
PALAEOGRAPHICAL
PALAEOGRAPHIES
PALAEOGRAPHIST
PALAEOGRAPHISTS
PALAEOGRAPHY
PALAEOLIMNOLOGY
PALAEOLITH
PALAEOLITHIC
PALAEOLITHS
PALAEOLOGIES
PALAEOLOGY
PALAEOMAGNETIC
PALAEOMAGNETISM
PALAEOMAGNETIST
PALAEONTOGRAPHY
PALAEONTOLOGIES
PALAEONTOLOGIST
PALAEONTOLOGY
PALAEOPATHOLOGY
PALAEOPEDOLOGY
PALAEOPHYTOLOGY
PALAEOSOLS
PALAEOTYPE
PALAEOTYPES
PALAEOTYPIC
PALAEOZOOLOGIES
PALAEOZOOLOGIST
PALAEOZOOLOGY
PALAESTRAE
PALAESTRAL
PALAESTRAS
PALAESTRIC
PALAESTRICAL
PALAFITTES
PALAGONITE
PALAGONITES
PALAMPORES
PALANKEENS
PALANQUINS
PALATABILITIES
PALATABILITY
PALATABLENESS
PALATABLENESSES
PALATALISATION
PALATALISATIONS
PALATALISE
PALATALISED
PALATALISES
PALATALISING
PALATALIZATION
PALATALIZATIONS
PALATALIZE
PALATALIZED
PALATALIZES
PALATALIZING
PALATIALLY
PALATIALNESS
PALATIALNESSES
PALATINATE
PALATINATES
PALAVERERS
PALAVERING
PALEACEOUS
PALEMPORES
PALENESSES
PALEOBIOLOGIC
PALEOBIOLOGICAL
PALEOBIOLOGIES
PALEOBIOLOGIST
PALEOBIOLOGISTS
PALEOBIOLOGY
PALEOBOTANIC
PALEOBOTANICAL
PALEOBOTANIES
PALEOBOTANIST
PALEOBOTANISTS
PALEOBOTANY
PALEOECOLOGIC
PALEOECOLOGICAL
PALEOECOLOGIES
PALEOECOLOGIST
PALEOECOLOGISTS
PALEOECOLOGY
PALEOGEOGRAPHIC
PALEOGEOGRAPHY
PALEOGRAPHER
PALEOGRAPHERS
PALEOGRAPHIC
PALEOGRAPHICAL
PALEOGRAPHIES
PALEOGRAPHY
PALEOLITHIC
PALEOLITHS
PALEOLOGIES
PALEOMAGNETIC
PALEOMAGNETISM
PALEOMAGNETISMS
PALEOMAGNETIST
PALEOMAGNETISTS
PALEONTOLOGIC
PALEONTOLOGICAL
PALEONTOLOGIES
PALEONTOLOGIST
PALEONTOLOGISTS
PALEONTOLOGY
PALEOPATHOLOGY
PALEOZOOLOGICAL
PALEOZOOLOGIES
PALEOZOOLOGIST
PALEOZOOLOGISTS
PALEOZOOLOGY
PALFRENIER
PALFRENIERS
PALIFICATION
PALIFICATIONS
PALILALIAS
PALILLOGIES
PALIMONIES
PALIMPSEST
PALIMPSESTS
PALINDROME
PALINDROMES
PALINDROMIC
PALINDROMICAL
PALINDROMIST
PALINDROMISTS
PALINGENESES
PALINGENESIA
PALINGENESIAS
PALINGENESIES
PALINGENESIS
PALINGENESIST
PALINGENESISTS
PALINGENESY
PALINGENETIC
PALINGENETICAL
PALINODIES
PALINOPIAS
PALINOPSIA
PALINOPSIAS
PALISADING
PALISADOED
PALISADOES
PALISADOING
PALISANDER
PALISANDERS
PALLADIOUS
PALLADIUMS
PALLASITES
PALLBEARER
PALLBEARERS
PALLESCENCE
PALLESCENCES
PALLESCENT
PALLETISATION
PALLETISATIONS
PALLETISED
PALLETISER
PALLETISERS
PALLETISES
PALLETISING
PALLETIZATION
PALLETIZATIONS
PALLETIZED
PALLETIZER
PALLETIZERS
PALLETIZES
PALLETIZING
PALLIAMENT
PALLIAMENTS
PALLIASSES
PALLIATING
PALLIATION
PALLIATIONS
PALLIATIVE
PALLIATIVELY
PALLIATIVES
PALLIATORS
PALLIATORY
PALLIDITIES
PALLIDNESS
PALLIDNESSES
PALMACEOUS
PALMATIFID
PALMATIONS
PALMATIPARTITE
PALMATISECT
PALMCORDER
PALMCORDERS
PALMERWORM
PALMERWORMS
PALMETTOES
PALMHOUSES
PALMIFICATION
PALMIFICATIONS
PALMIPEDES
PALMISTERS
PALMISTRIES
PALMITATES
PALMPRINTS
PALOVERDES
PALPABILITIES
PALPABILITY
PALPABLENESS
PALPABLENESSES
PALPATIONS
PALPEBRATE
PALPEBRATED
PALPEBRATES
PALPEBRATING
PALPITATED
PALPITATES
PALPITATING
PALPITATION
PALPITATIONS
PALSGRAVES
PALSGRAVINE
PALSGRAVINES
PALTRINESS
PALTRINESSES
PALUDAMENT
PALUDAMENTA
PALUDAMENTS
PALUDAMENTUM
PALUDAMENTUMS
PALUDICOLOUS
PALUDINOUS
PALUSTRIAN
PALUSTRINE
PALYNOLOGIC
PALYNOLOGICAL
PALYNOLOGICALLY
PALYNOLOGIES
PALYNOLOGIST
PALYNOLOGISTS
PALYNOLOGY

P

PAMPELMOOSE
PAMPELMOOSES
PAMPELMOUSE
PAMPELMOUSES
PAMPEREDNESS
PAMPEREDNESSES
PAMPERINGS
PAMPHLETED
PAMPHLETEER
PAMPHLETEERED
PAMPHLETEERING
PAMPHLETEERINGS
PAMPHLETEERS
PAMPHLETING
PAMPOOTIES
PANACHAEAS
PANAESTHESIA
PANAESTHESIAS
PANAESTHETISM
PANAESTHETISMS
PANARITIUM
PANARITIUMS
PANARTHRITIS
PANARTHRITISES
PANATELLAS
PANBROILED
PANBROILING
PANCHAYATS
PANCHROMATIC
PANCHROMATISM
PANCHROMATISMS
PANCOSMISM
PANCOSMISMS
PANCRATIAN
PANCRATIAST
PANCRATIASTS
PANCRATIST
PANCRATISTS
PANCRATIUM
PANCRATIUMS
PANCREASES
PANCREATECTOMY
PANCREATIC
PANCREATIN
PANCREATINS
PANCREATITIDES
PANCREATITIS
PANCREATITISES
PANCREOZYMIN
PANCREOZYMINS
PANCYTOPENIA
PANCYTOPENIAS
PANDAEMONIUM
PANDAEMONIUMS
PANDANACEOUS
PANDANUSES
PANDATIONS
PANDECTIST
PANDECTISTS
PANDEMONIAC
PANDEMONIACAL
PANDEMONIAN
PANDEMONIANS
PANDEMONIC
PANDEMONIUM
PANDEMONIUMS
PANDERESSES
PANDERINGS
PANDERISMS
PANDERMITE
PANDERMITES
PANDICULATION
PANDICULATIONS
PANDOWDIES
PANDURATED
PANDURIFORM
PANEGOISMS
PANEGYRICA
PANEGYRICAL
PANEGYRICALLY
PANEGYRICON
PANEGYRICS
PANEGYRIES
PANEGYRISE
PANEGYRISED
PANEGYRISES
PANEGYRISING
PANEGYRIST
PANEGYRISTS
PANEGYRIZE
PANEGYRIZED
PANEGYRIZES
PANEGYRIZING
PANELLINGS
PANELLISED
PANELLISTS
PANELLIZED
PANENTHEISM
PANENTHEISMS
PANENTHEIST
PANENTHEISTS
PANESTHESIA
PANESTHESIAS
PANETELLAS
PANETTONES
PANFISHING
PANFISHINGS
PANGENESES
PANGENESIS
PANGENETIC
PANGENETICALLY
PANGRAMMATIST
PANGRAMMATISTS
PANHANDLED
PANHANDLER
PANHANDLERS
PANHANDLES
PANHANDLING
PANHARMONICON
PANHARMONICONS
PANHELLENIC
PANHELLENION
PANHELLENIONS
PANHELLENIUM
PANHELLENIUMS
PANICKIEST
PANICMONGER
PANICMONGERS
PANICULATE
PANICULATED
PANICULATELY
PANIDIOMORPHIC
PANIFICATION
PANIFICATIONS
PANISLAMIST
PANJANDARUM
PANJANDARUMS
PANJANDRUM
PANJANDRUMS
PANLEUCOPENIA
PANLEUCOPENIAS
PANLEUKOPENIA
PANLEUKOPENIAS
PANLOGISMS
PANMIXISES
PANNICULUS
PANNICULUSES
PANNIKELLS
PANOMPHAEAN
PANOPHOBIA
PANOPHOBIAS
PANOPHTHALMIA
PANOPHTHALMIAS
PANOPHTHALMITIS
PANOPTICAL
PANOPTICALLY
PANOPTICON
PANOPTICONS
PANORAMICALLY
PANPHARMACON
PANPHARMACONS
PANPSYCHISM
PANPSYCHISMS
PANPSYCHIST
PANPSYCHISTIC
PANPSYCHISTS
PANRADIOMETER
PANRADIOMETERS
PANSEXUALISM
PANSEXUALISMS
PANSEXUALIST
PANSEXUALISTS
PANSEXUALITIES
PANSEXUALITY
PANSEXUALS
PANSOPHICAL
PANSOPHICALLY
PANSOPHIES
PANSOPHISM
PANSOPHISMS
PANSOPHIST
PANSOPHISTS
PANSPERMATIC
PANSPERMATISM
PANSPERMATISMS
PANSPERMATIST
PANSPERMATISTS
PANSPERMIA
PANSPERMIAS
PANSPERMIC
PANSPERMIES
PANSPERMISM
PANSPERMISMS
PANSPERMIST
PANSPERMISTS
PANTAGAMIES
PANTAGRAPH
PANTAGRAPHS
PANTALEONS
PANTALETTED
PANTALETTES
PANTALONES
PANTALOONED
PANTALOONERIES
PANTALOONERY
PANTALOONS
PANTDRESSES
PANTECHNICON
PANTECHNICONS
PANTHEISMS
PANTHEISTIC
PANTHEISTICAL
PANTHEISTICALLY
PANTHEISTS
PANTHENOLS
PANTHEOLOGIES
PANTHEOLOGIST
PANTHEOLOGISTS
PANTHEOLOGY
PANTHERESS
PANTHERESSES
PANTHERINE
PANTHERISH
PANTIHOSES
PANTILINGS
PANTISOCRACIES
PANTISOCRACY
PANTISOCRAT
PANTISOCRATIC
PANTISOCRATICAL
PANTISOCRATIST
PANTISOCRATISTS
PANTISOCRATS
PANTOFFLES
PANTOGRAPH
PANTOGRAPHER
PANTOGRAPHERS
PANTOGRAPHIC
PANTOGRAPHICAL
PANTOGRAPHIES

PANTOGRAPHS
PANTOGRAPHY
PANTOMIMED
PANTOMIMES
PANTOMIMIC
PANTOMIMICAL
PANTOMIMICALLY
PANTOMIMING
PANTOMIMIST
PANTOMIMISTS
PANTOPHAGIES
PANTOPHAGIST
PANTOPHAGISTS
PANTOPHAGOUS
PANTOPHAGY
PANTOPHOBIA
PANTOPHOBIAS
PANTOPRAGMATIC
PANTOPRAGMATICS
PANTOSCOPE
PANTOSCOPES
PANTOSCOPIC
PANTOTHENATE
PANTOTHENATES
PANTOTHENIC
PANTOUFLES
PANTROPICAL
PANTRYMAID
PANTRYMAIDS
PANTSUITED
PANTYHOSES
PANTYWAIST
PANTYWAISTS
PANZEROTTI
PANZEROTTO
PANZEROTTOS
PANZOOTICS
PAPALISING
PAPALIZING
PAPAPRELATIST
PAPAPRELATISTS
PAPAVERACEOUS
PAPAVERINE
PAPAVERINES
PAPAVEROUS
PAPERBACKED
PAPERBACKER
PAPERBACKERS
PAPERBACKING
PAPERBACKS
PAPERBARKS
PAPERBOARD
PAPERBOARDS
PAPERBOUND
PAPERBOUNDS
PAPERCLIPS
PAPERGIRLS
PAPERHANGER
PAPERHANGERS
PAPERHANGING
PAPERHANGINGS
PAPERINESS
PAPERINESSES
PAPERKNIFE
PAPERKNIVES
PAPERMAKER
PAPERMAKERS
PAPERMAKING
PAPERMAKINGS
PAPERWARES
PAPERWEIGHT
PAPERWEIGHTS
PAPERWORKS
PAPETERIES
PAPILIONACEOUS
PAPILLATED
PAPILLIFEROUS
PAPILLIFORM
PAPILLITIS
PAPILLITISES
PAPILLOMAS
PAPILLOMATA
PAPILLOMATOSES
PAPILLOMATOSIS
PAPILLOMATOUS
PAPILLOMAVIRUS
PAPILLOTES
PAPILLULATE
PAPILLULES
PAPISTICAL
PAPISTICALLY
PAPISTRIES
PAPOVAVIRUS
PAPOVAVIRUSES
PAPPARDELLE
PAPPARDELLES
PAPRIKASES
PAPRIKASHES
PAPULATION
PAPULATIONS
PAPULIFEROUS
PAPYRACEOUS
PAPYROLOGICAL
PAPYROLOGIES
PAPYROLOGIST
PAPYROLOGISTS
PAPYROLOGY
PARABAPTISM
PARABAPTISMS
PARABEMATA
PARABEMATIC
PARABIOSES
PARABIOSIS
PARABIOTIC
PARABIOTICALLY
PARABLASTIC
PARABLASTS
PARABLEPSES
PARABLEPSIES
PARABLEPSIS
PARABLEPSY
PARABLEPTIC
PARABOLANUS
PARABOLANUSES
PARABOLICAL
PARABOLICALLY
PARABOLISATION
PARABOLISATIONS
PARABOLISE
PARABOLISED
PARABOLISES
PARABOLISING
PARABOLIST
PARABOLISTS
PARABOLIZATION
PARABOLIZATIONS
PARABOLIZE
PARABOLIZED
PARABOLIZES
PARABOLIZING
PARABOLOID
PARABOLOIDAL
PARABOLOIDS
PARABRAKES
PARACASEIN
PARACASEINS
PARACENTESES
PARACENTESIS
PARACETAMOL
PARACETAMOLS
PARACHRONISM
PARACHRONISMS
PARACHUTED
PARACHUTES
PARACHUTIC
PARACHUTING
PARACHUTINGS
PARACHUTIST
PARACHUTISTS
PARACLETES
PARACROSTIC
PARACROSTICS
PARACYANOGEN
PARACYANOGENS
PARADIDDLE
PARADIDDLED
PARADIDDLES
PARADIDDLING
PARADIGMATIC
PARADIGMATICAL
PARADISAIC
PARADISAICAL
PARADISAICALLY
PARADISEAN
PARADISIAC
PARADISIACAL
PARADISIACALLY
PARADISIAL
PARADISIAN
PARADISICAL
PARADOCTOR
PARADOCTORS
PARADOXERS
PARADOXICAL
PARADOXICALITY
PARADOXICALLY
PARADOXICALNESS
PARADOXIDIAN
PARADOXIES
PARADOXIST
PARADOXISTS
PARADOXOLOGIES
PARADOXOLOGY
PARADOXURE
PARADOXURES
PARADOXURINE
PARADOXURINES
PARADROPPED
PARADROPPING
PARAENESES
PARAENESIS
PARAENETIC
PARAENETICAL
PARAESTHESIA
PARAESTHESIAS
PARAESTHETIC
PARAFFINED
PARAFFINES
PARAFFINIC
PARAFFINIER
PARAFFINIEST
PARAFFINING
PARAFFINOID
PARAGENESES
PARAGENESIA
PARAGENESIAS
PARAGENESIS
PARAGENETIC
PARAGENETICALLY
PARAGLIDED
PARAGLIDER
PARAGLIDERS
PARAGLIDES
PARAGLIDING
PARAGLIDINGS
PARAGLOSSA
PARAGLOSSAE
PARAGLOSSAL
PARAGLOSSATE
PARAGNATHISM
PARAGNATHISMS
PARAGNATHOUS
PARAGNOSES
PARAGNOSIS
PARAGOGICAL
PARAGOGICALLY
PARAGOGUES
PARAGONING
PARAGONITE
PARAGONITES

PARAGRAMMATIST
PARAGRAMMATISTS
PARAGRAPHED
PARAGRAPHER
PARAGRAPHERS
PARAGRAPHIA
PARAGRAPHIAS
PARAGRAPHIC
PARAGRAPHICAL
PARAGRAPHICALLY
PARAGRAPHING
PARAGRAPHIST
PARAGRAPHISTS
PARAGRAPHS
PARAHELIOTROPIC
PARAHYDROGEN
PARAHYDROGENS
PARAINFLUENZA
PARAINFLUENZAS
PARAJOURNALISM
PARAJOURNALISMS
PARAKEELYA
PARAKEELYAS
PARAKELIAS
PARAKITING
PARAKITINGS
PARALALIAS
PARALANGUAGE
PARALANGUAGES
PARALDEHYDE
PARALDEHYDES
PARALEGALS
PARALEIPOMENA
PARALEIPOMENON
PARALEIPSES
PARALEIPSIS
PARALEXIAS
PARALIMNION
PARALIMNIONS
PARALINGUISTIC
PARALINGUISTICS
PARALIPOMENA
PARALIPOMENON
PARALIPSES
PARALIPSIS
PARALLACTIC
PARALLACTICAL
PARALLACTICALLY
PARALLAXES
PARALLELED
PARALLELEPIPED
PARALLELEPIPEDA
PARALLELEPIPEDS
PARALLELING
PARALLELINGS
PARALLELISE
PARALLELISED
PARALLELISES
PARALLELISING
PARALLELISM
PARALLELISMS
PARALLELIST
PARALLELISTIC
PARALLELISTS
PARALLELIZE
PARALLELIZED
PARALLELIZES
PARALLELIZING
PARALLELLED
PARALLELLING
PARALLELLY
PARALLELOGRAM
PARALLELOGRAMS
PARALLELOPIPED
PARALLELOPIPEDA
PARALLELOPIPEDS
PARALLELWISE
PARALOGIAS
PARALOGIES
PARALOGISE
PARALOGISED
PARALOGISES
PARALOGISING
PARALOGISM
PARALOGISMS
PARALOGIST
PARALOGISTIC
PARALOGISTS
PARALOGIZE
PARALOGIZED
PARALOGIZES
PARALOGIZING
PARALOGUES
PARALYMPIC
PARALYMPICS
PARALYSATION
PARALYSATIONS
PARALYSERS
PARALYSING
PARALYSINGLY
PARALYTICALLY
PARALYTICS
PARALYZATION
PARALYZATIONS
PARALYZERS
PARALYZING
PARALYZINGLY
PARAMAECIA
PARAMAECIUM
PARAMAGNET
PARAMAGNETIC
PARAMAGNETISM
PARAMAGNETISMS
PARAMAGNETS
PARAMASTOID
PARAMASTOIDS
PARAMATTAS
PARAMECIUM
PARAMECIUMS
PARAMEDICAL
PARAMEDICALS
PARAMEDICO
PARAMEDICOS
PARAMEDICS
PARAMENSTRUA
PARAMENSTRUUM
PARAMENSTRUUMS
PARAMETERISE
PARAMETERISED
PARAMETERISES
PARAMETERISING
PARAMETERIZE
PARAMETERIZED
PARAMETERIZES
PARAMETERIZING
PARAMETERS
PARAMETRAL
PARAMETRIC
PARAMETRICAL
PARAMETRICALLY
PARAMETRISATION
PARAMETRISE
PARAMETRISED
PARAMETRISES
PARAMETRISING
PARAMETRIZATION
PARAMETRIZE
PARAMETRIZED
PARAMETRIZES
PARAMETRIZING
PARAMILITARIES
PARAMILITARY
PARAMNESIA
PARAMNESIAS
PARAMOECIA
PARAMOECIUM
PARAMORPHIC
PARAMORPHINE
PARAMORPHINES
PARAMORPHISM
PARAMORPHISMS
PARAMORPHOUS
PARAMORPHS
PARAMOUNCIES
PARAMOUNCY
PARAMOUNTCIES
PARAMOUNTCY
PARAMOUNTLY
PARAMOUNTS
PARAMYLUMS
PARAMYXOVIRUS
PARAMYXOVIRUSES
PARANEPHRIC
PARANEPHROS
PARANEPHROSES
PARANOEICS
PARANOIACS
PARANOICALLY
PARANOIDAL
PARANORMAL
PARANORMALITIES
PARANORMALITY
PARANORMALLY
PARANORMALS
PARANTHELIA
PARANTHELION
PARANTHROPUS
PARANTHROPUSES
PARANYMPHS
PARAPARESES
PARAPARESIS
PARAPARETIC
PARAPENTES
PARAPENTING
PARAPENTINGS
PARAPERIODIC
PARAPHASIA
PARAPHASIAS
PARAPHASIC
PARAPHERNALIA
PARAPHILIA
PARAPHILIAC
PARAPHILIACS
PARAPHILIAS
PARAPHIMOSES
PARAPHIMOSIS
PARAPHONIA
PARAPHONIAS
PARAPHONIC
PARAPHRASABLE
PARAPHRASE
PARAPHRASED
PARAPHRASER
PARAPHRASERS
PARAPHRASES
PARAPHRASING
PARAPHRAST
PARAPHRASTIC
PARAPHRASTICAL
PARAPHRASTS
PARAPHRAXES
PARAPHRAXIA
PARAPHRAXIAS
PARAPHRAXIS
PARAPHRENIA
PARAPHRENIAS
PARAPHYSATE
PARAPHYSES
PARAPHYSIS
PARAPINEAL
PARAPLANNER
PARAPLANNERS
PARAPLEGIA
PARAPLEGIAS
PARAPLEGIC
PARAPLEGICS
PARAPODIAL
PARAPODIUM
PARAPOPHYSES
PARAPOPHYSIAL

P

PARAPOPHYSIS
PARAPRAXES
PARAPRAXIS
PARAPRAXISES
PARAPSYCHIC
PARAPSYCHICAL
PARAPSYCHISM
PARAPSYCHISMS
PARAPSYCHOLOGY
PARAPSYCHOSES
PARAPSYCHOSIS
PARAQUADRATE
PARAQUADRATES
PARAQUITOS
PARARHYMES
PARAROSANILINE
PARAROSANILINES
PARARTHRIA
PARARTHRIAS
PARASAILED
PARASAILING
PARASAILINGS
PARASCENDER
PARASCENDERS
PARASCENDING
PARASCENDINGS
PARASCENIA
PARASCENIUM
PARASCEVES
PARASCIENCE
PARASCIENCES
PARASELENAE
PARASELENE
PARASELENIC
PARASEXUAL
PARASEXUALITIES
PARASEXUALITY
PARASHIOTH
PARASITAEMIA
PARASITAEMIAS
PARASITICAL
PARASITICALLY
PARASITICALNESS
PARASITICIDAL
PARASITICIDE
PARASITICIDES
PARASITISATION
PARASITISATIONS
PARASITISE
PARASITISED
PARASITISES
PARASITISING
PARASITISM
PARASITISMS
PARASITIZATION
PARASITIZATIONS
PARASITIZE
PARASITIZED
PARASITIZES
PARASITIZING
PARASITOID
PARASITOIDS
PARASITOLOGIC
PARASITOLOGICAL
PARASITOLOGIES
PARASITOLOGIST
PARASITOLOGISTS
PARASITOLOGY
PARASITOSES
PARASITOSIS
PARASKIING
PARASKIINGS
PARASOMNIA
PARASOMNIAS
PARASPHENOID
PARASPHENOIDS
PARASTATAL
PARASTATALS
PARASTICHIES
PARASTICHOUS
PARASTICHY
PARASUICIDE
PARASUICIDES
PARASYMBIONT
PARASYMBIONTS
PARASYMBIOSES
PARASYMBIOSIS
PARASYMBIOTIC
PARASYMPATHETIC
PARASYNAPSES
PARASYNAPSIS
PARASYNAPTIC
PARASYNTHESES
PARASYNTHESIS
PARASYNTHETA
PARASYNTHETIC
PARASYNTHETON
PARATACTIC
PARATACTICAL
PARATACTICALLY
PARATANIWHA
PARATANIWHAS
PARATHESES
PARATHESIS
PARATHIONS
PARATHORMONE
PARATHORMONES
PARATHYROID
PARATHYROIDS
PARATROOPER
PARATROOPERS
PARATROOPS
PARATUNGSTIC
PARATYPHOID
PARATYPHOIDS
PARAWALKER
PARAWALKERS
PARBOILING
PARBREAKED
PARBREAKING
PARBUCKLED
PARBUCKLES
PARBUCKLING
PARCELLING
PARCELWISE
PARCENARIES
PARCHEDNESS
PARCHEDNESSES
PARCHEESIS
PARCHMENTIER
PARCHMENTIEST
PARCHMENTISE
PARCHMENTISED
PARCHMENTISES
PARCHMENTISING
PARCHMENTIZE
PARCHMENTIZED
PARCHMENTIZES
PARCHMENTIZING
PARCHMENTS
PARCHMENTY
PARCIMONIES
PARDALISES
PARDALOTES
PARDONABLE
PARDONABLENESS
PARDONABLY
PARDONINGS
PARDONLESS
PAREGORICS
PAREIDOLIA
PAREIDOLIAS
PARENCEPHALA
PARENCEPHALON
PARENCHYMA
PARENCHYMAL
PARENCHYMAS
PARENCHYMATA
PARENCHYMATOUS
PARENTAGES
PARENTALLY
PARENTERAL
PARENTERALLY
PARENTHESES
PARENTHESIS
PARENTHESISE
PARENTHESISED
PARENTHESISES
PARENTHESISING
PARENTHESIZE
PARENTHESIZED
PARENTHESIZES
PARENTHESIZING
PARENTHETIC
PARENTHETICAL
PARENTHETICALLY
PARENTHOOD
PARENTHOODS
PARENTINGS
PARENTLESS
PARESTHESIA
PARESTHESIAS
PARESTHETIC
PARFLECHES
PARFLESHES
PARFOCALISE
PARFOCALISED
PARFOCALISES
PARFOCALISING
PARFOCALITIES
PARFOCALITY
PARFOCALIZE
PARFOCALIZED
PARFOCALIZES
PARFOCALIZING
PARGASITES
PARGETINGS
PARGETTERS
PARGETTING
PARGETTINGS
PARGYLINES
PARHELIACAL
PARHELIONS
PARHYPATES
PARIPINNATE
PARISCHANE
PARISCHANES
PARISCHANS
PARISHIONER
PARISHIONERS
PARISYLLABIC
PARKINSONIAN
PARKINSONIANS
PARKINSONISM
PARKINSONISMS
PARKLEAVES
PARLEMENTS
PARLEYVOOED
PARLEYVOOING
PARLEYVOOS
PARLIAMENT
PARLIAMENTARIAN
PARLIAMENTARILY
PARLIAMENTARISM
PARLIAMENTARY
PARLIAMENTING
PARLIAMENTINGS
PARLIAMENTS
PARLOURMAID
PARLOURMAIDS
PARLOUSNESS
PARLOUSNESSES
PARMACITIE
PARMACITIES
PARMIGIANA
PARMIGIANO
PARMIGIANOS
PAROCCIPITAL
PAROCCIPITALS
PAROCHIALISE

PAROCHIALISED
PAROCHIALISES
PAROCHIALISING
PAROCHIALISM
PAROCHIALISMS
PAROCHIALITIES
PAROCHIALITY
PAROCHIALIZE
PAROCHIALIZED
PAROCHIALIZES
PAROCHIALIZING
PAROCHIALLY
PAROCHINES
PARODISTIC
PAROECIOUS
PAROECISMS
PAROEMIACS
PAROEMIOGRAPHER
PAROEMIOGRAPHY
PAROEMIOLOGIES
PAROEMIOLOGY
PARONOMASIA
PARONOMASIAS
PARONOMASIES
PARONOMASTIC
PARONOMASTICAL
PARONOMASY
PARONYCHIA
PARONYCHIAL
PARONYCHIAS
PARONYMIES
PARONYMOUS
PARONYMOUSLY
PAROTIDITIC
PAROTIDITIS
PAROTIDITISES
PAROTITIDES
PAROTITISES
PAROXETINE
PAROXETINES
PAROXYSMAL
PAROXYSMALLY
PAROXYSMIC
PAROXYTONE
PAROXYTONES
PAROXYTONIC
PARQUETING
PARQUETRIES
PARQUETTED
PARQUETTING
PARRAKEETS
PARRAMATTA
PARRAMATTAS
PARRHESIAS
PARRICIDAL
PARRICIDES
PARRITCHES
PARROCKING
PARROQUETS
PARROTFISH
PARROTFISHES
PARROTIEST
PARROTRIES
PARSIMONIES
PARSIMONIOUS
PARSIMONIOUSLY
PARSONAGES
PARSONICAL
PARTAKINGS
PARTHENOCARPIC
PARTHENOCARPIES
PARTHENOCARPOUS
PARTHENOCARPY
PARTHENOGENESES
PARTHENOGENESIS
PARTHENOGENETIC
PARTHENOSPORE
PARTHENOSPORES
PARTIALISE
PARTIALISED
PARTIALISES
PARTIALISING
PARTIALISM
PARTIALISMS
PARTIALIST
PARTIALISTS
PARTIALITIES
PARTIALITY
PARTIALIZE
PARTIALIZED
PARTIALIZES
PARTIALIZING
PARTIALLED
PARTIALLING
PARTIALNESS
PARTIALNESSES
PARTIBILITIES
PARTIBILITY
PARTICIPABLE
PARTICIPANT
PARTICIPANTLY
PARTICIPANTS
PARTICIPATE
PARTICIPATED
PARTICIPATES
PARTICIPATING
PARTICIPATION
PARTICIPATIONAL
PARTICIPATIONS
PARTICIPATIVE
PARTICIPATOR
PARTICIPATORS
PARTICIPATORY
PARTICIPIAL
PARTICIPIALLY
PARTICIPIALS
PARTICIPLE
PARTICIPLES
PARTICLEBOARD
PARTICLEBOARDS
PARTICOLORED
PARTICOLOURED
PARTICULAR
PARTICULARISE
PARTICULARISED
PARTICULARISER
PARTICULARISERS
PARTICULARISES
PARTICULARISING
PARTICULARISM
PARTICULARISMS
PARTICULARIST
PARTICULARISTIC
PARTICULARISTS
PARTICULARITIES
PARTICULARITY
PARTICULARIZE
PARTICULARIZED
PARTICULARIZER
PARTICULARIZERS
PARTICULARIZES
PARTICULARIZING
PARTICULARLY
PARTICULARNESS
PARTICULARS
PARTICULATE
PARTICULATES
PARTISANLY
PARTISANSHIP
PARTISANSHIPS
PARTITIONED
PARTITIONER
PARTITIONERS
PARTITIONING
PARTITIONIST
PARTITIONISTS
PARTITIONMENT
PARTITIONMENTS
PARTITIONS
PARTITIVELY
PARTITIVES
PARTITURAS
PARTIZANLY
PARTIZANSHIP
PARTIZANSHIPS
PARTNERING
PARTNERINGS
PARTNERLESS
PARTNERSHIP
PARTNERSHIPS
PARTRIDGEBERRY
PARTRIDGES
PARTURIENCIES
PARTURIENCY
PARTURIENT
PARTURIENTS
PARTURIFACIENT
PARTURIFACIENTS
PARTURITION
PARTURITIONS
PARTYGOERS
PARURETICS
PARVANIMITIES
PARVANIMITY
PARVIFOLIATE
PARVOLINES
PARVOVIRUS
PARVOVIRUSES
PASIGRAPHIC
PASIGRAPHICAL
PASIGRAPHIES
PASIGRAPHY
PASODOBLES
PASQUEFLOWER
PASQUEFLOWERS
PASQUILANT
PASQUILANTS
PASQUILERS
PASQUILLED
PASQUILLING
PASQUINADE
PASQUINADED
PASQUINADER
PASQUINADERS
PASQUINADES
PASQUINADING
PASSABLENESS
PASSABLENESSES
PASSACAGLIA
PASSACAGLIAS
PASSAGEWAY
PASSAGEWAYS
PASSAGEWORK
PASSAGEWORKS
PASSALONGS
PASSAMENTED
PASSAMENTING
PASSAMENTS
PASSAMEZZO
PASSAMEZZOS
PASSEMEASURE
PASSEMEASURES
PASSEMENTED
PASSEMENTERIE
PASSEMENTERIES
PASSEMENTING
PASSEMENTS
PASSENGERS
PASSEPIEDS
PASSERIFORM
PASSERINES
PASSIBILITIES
PASSIBILITY
PASSIBLENESS
PASSIBLENESSES
PASSIFLORA
PASSIFLORACEOUS
PASSIFLORAS
PASSIMETER
PASSIMETERS

PASSIONALS
PASSIONARIES
PASSIONARY
PASSIONATE
PASSIONATED
PASSIONATELY
PASSIONATENESS
PASSIONATES
PASSIONATING
PASSIONFLOWER
PASSIONFLOWERS
PASSIONING
PASSIONLESS
PASSIONLESSLY
PASSIONLESSNESS
PASSIVATED
PASSIVATES
PASSIVATING
PASSIVATION
PASSIVATIONS
PASSIVENESS
PASSIVENESSES
PASSIVISMS
PASSIVISTS
PASSIVITIES
PASSMENTED
PASSMENTING
PASSPORTED
PASSPORTING
PASTEBOARD
PASTEBOARDS
PASTEDOWNS
PASTELISTS
PASTELLIST
PASTELLISTS
PASTEURELLA
PASTEURELLAE
PASTEURELLAS
PASTEURISATION
PASTEURISATIONS
PASTEURISE
PASTEURISED
PASTEURISER
PASTEURISERS
PASTEURISES
PASTEURISING
PASTEURISM
PASTEURISMS
PASTEURIZATION
PASTEURIZATIONS
PASTEURIZE
PASTEURIZED
PASTEURIZER
PASTEURIZERS
PASTEURIZES
PASTEURIZING
PASTICCIOS
PASTICHEUR
PASTICHEURS
PASTINESSES
PASTITSIOS
PASTNESSES
PASTORALES
PASTORALISM
PASTORALISMS
PASTORALIST
PASTORALISTS
PASTORALLY
PASTORALNESS
PASTORALNESSES
PASTORATES
PASTORIUMS
PASTORLIER
PASTORLIEST
PASTORSHIP
PASTORSHIPS
PASTOURELLE
PASTOURELLES
PASTRYCOOK
PASTRYCOOKS
PASTURABLE
PASTURAGES
PASTURELAND
PASTURELANDS
PASTURELESS
PATAPHYSICS
PATCHBOARD
PATCHBOARDS
PATCHCOCKE
PATCHCOCKES
PATCHERIES
PATCHINESS
PATCHINESSES
PATCHOCKES
PATCHOULIES
PATCHOULIS
PATCHWORKED
PATCHWORKING
PATCHWORKS
PATELLECTOMIES
PATELLECTOMY
PATELLIFORM
PATENTABILITIES
PATENTABILITY
PATENTABLE
PATERCOVES
PATEREROES
PATERFAMILIAS
PATERFAMILIASES
PATERNALISM
PATERNALISMS
PATERNALIST
PATERNALISTIC
PATERNALISTS
PATERNALLY
PATERNITIES
PATERNOSTER
PATERNOSTERS
PATHBREAKING
PATHETICAL
PATHETICALLY
PATHFINDER
PATHFINDERS
PATHFINDING
PATHFINDINGS
PATHLESSNESS
PATHLESSNESSES
PATHOBIOLOGIES
PATHOBIOLOGY
PATHOGENES
PATHOGENESES
PATHOGENESIS
PATHOGENETIC
PATHOGENIC
PATHOGENICITIES
PATHOGENICITY
PATHOGENIES
PATHOGENOUS
PATHOGNOMIES
PATHOGNOMONIC
PATHOGNOMY
PATHOGRAPHIES
PATHOGRAPHY
PATHOLOGIC
PATHOLOGICAL
PATHOLOGICALLY
PATHOLOGIES
PATHOLOGISE
PATHOLOGISED
PATHOLOGISES
PATHOLOGISING
PATHOLOGIST
PATHOLOGISTS
PATHOLOGIZE
PATHOLOGIZED
PATHOLOGIZES
PATHOLOGIZING
PATHOPHOBIA
PATHOPHOBIAS
PATHOPHYSIOLOGY
PATIBULARY
PATIENTEST
PATIENTING
PATINATING
PATINATION
PATINATIONS
PATINISING
PATINIZING
PATISSERIE
PATISSERIES
PATISSIERS
PATRESFAMILIAS
PATRIALISATION
PATRIALISATIONS
PATRIALISE
PATRIALISED
PATRIALISES
PATRIALISING
PATRIALISM
PATRIALISMS
PATRIALITIES
PATRIALITY
PATRIALIZATION
PATRIALIZATIONS
PATRIALIZE
PATRIALIZED
PATRIALIZES
PATRIALIZING
PATRIARCHAL
PATRIARCHALISM
PATRIARCHALISMS
PATRIARCHALLY
PATRIARCHATE
PATRIARCHATES
PATRIARCHIES
PATRIARCHISM
PATRIARCHISMS
PATRIARCHS
PATRIARCHY
PATRIATING
PATRIATION
PATRIATIONS
PATRICIANLY
PATRICIANS
PATRICIATE
PATRICIATES
PATRICIDAL
PATRICIDES
PATRICLINIC
PATRICLINOUS
PATRIFOCAL
PATRIFOCALITIES
PATRIFOCALITY
PATRILINEAGE
PATRILINEAGES
PATRILINEAL
PATRILINEALLY
PATRILINEAR
PATRILINEARLY
PATRILINIES
PATRILOCAL
PATRILOCALLY
PATRIMONIAL
PATRIMONIALLY
PATRIMONIES
PATRIOTICALLY
PATRIOTISM
PATRIOTISMS
PATRISTICAL
PATRISTICALLY
PATRISTICISM
PATRISTICISMS
PATRISTICS
PATROCLINAL
PATROCLINIC
PATROCLINIES
PATROCLINOUS
PATROCLINY
PATROLLERS
PATROLLING

P

PATROLOGICAL
PATROLOGIES
PATROLOGIST
PATROLOGISTS
PATROLWOMAN
PATROLWOMEN
PATRONAGED
PATRONAGES
PATRONAGING
PATRONESSES
PATRONISATION
PATRONISATIONS
PATRONISED
PATRONISER
PATRONISERS
PATRONISES
PATRONISING
PATRONISINGLY
PATRONIZATION
PATRONIZATIONS
PATRONIZED
PATRONIZER
PATRONIZERS
PATRONIZES
PATRONIZING
PATRONIZINGLY
PATRONLESS
PATRONLIER
PATRONLIEST
PATRONYMIC
PATRONYMICS
PATROONSHIP
PATROONSHIPS
PATTERNING
PATTERNINGS
PATTERNLESS
PATTRESSES
PATULOUSLY
PATULOUSNESS
PATULOUSNESSES
PAUCILOQUENT
PAUGHTIEST
PAULOWNIAS
PAUNCHIEST
PAUNCHINESS
PAUNCHINESSES
PAUPERDOMS
PAUPERESSES
PAUPERISATION
PAUPERISATIONS
PAUPERISED
PAUPERISES
PAUPERISING
PAUPERISMS
PAUPERIZATION
PAUPERIZATIONS
PAUPERIZED
PAUPERIZES
PAUPERIZING
PAUPIETTES
PAUSEFULLY
PAUSELESSLY
PAVEMENTED
PAVEMENTING
PAVILIONED
PAVILIONING
PAVONAZZOS
PAWKINESSES
PAWNBROKER
PAWNBROKERS
PAWNBROKING
PAWNBROKINGS
PAWNTICKET
PAWNTICKETS
PAYCHEQUES
PAYMASTERS
PAYNIMRIES
PAYSAGISTS
PEABERRIES
PEACEABLENESS
PEACEABLENESSES
PEACEFULLER
PEACEFULLEST
PEACEFULLY
PEACEFULNESS
PEACEFULNESSES
PEACEKEEPER
PEACEKEEPERS
PEACEKEEPING
PEACEKEEPINGS
PEACELESSNESS
PEACELESSNESSES
PEACEMAKER
PEACEMAKERS
PEACEMAKING
PEACEMAKINGS
PEACETIMES
PEACHBLOWS
PEACHERINO
PEACHERINOS
PEACHINESS
PEACHINESSES
PEACOCKERIES
PEACOCKERY
PEACOCKIER
PEACOCKIEST
PEACOCKING
PEACOCKISH
PEAKEDNESS
PEAKEDNESSES
PEAKINESSES
PEANUTTIER
PEANUTTIEST
PEARLASHES
PEARLESCENCE
PEARLESCENCES
PEARLESCENT
PEARLINESS
PEARLINESSES
PEARLWARES
PEARLWORTS
PEARMONGER
PEARMONGERS
PEARTNESSES
PEASANTIER
PEASANTIEST
PEASANTRIES
PEASHOOTER
PEASHOOTERS
PEASOUPERS
PEBBLEDASH
PEBBLEDASHED
PEBBLEDASHES
PEBBLEDASHING
PEBBLEWEAVE
PEBBLEWEAVES
PECCABILITIES
PECCABILITY
PECCADILLO
PECCADILLOES
PECCADILLOS
PECCANCIES
PECKERWOOD
PECKERWOODS
PECKISHNESS
PECKISHNESSES
PECTINACEOUS
PECTINATED
PECTINATELY
PECTINATION
PECTINATIONS
PECTINESTERASE
PECTINESTERASES
PECTINEUSES
PECTISABLE
PECTISATION
PECTISATIONS
PECTIZABLE
PECTIZATION
PECTIZATIONS
PECTOLITES
PECTORALLY
PECTORILOQUIES
PECTORILOQUY
PECULATING
PECULATION
PECULATIONS
PECULATORS
PECULIARISE
PECULIARISED
PECULIARISES
PECULIARISING
PECULIARITIES
PECULIARITY
PECULIARIZE
PECULIARIZED
PECULIARIZES
PECULIARIZING
PECULIARLY
PECUNIARILY
PEDAGOGICAL
PEDAGOGICALLY
PEDAGOGICS
PEDAGOGIES
PEDAGOGISM
PEDAGOGISMS
PEDAGOGUED
PEDAGOGUERIES
PEDAGOGUERY
PEDAGOGUES
PEDAGOGUING
PEDAGOGUISH
PEDAGOGUISHNESS
PEDAGOGUISM
PEDAGOGUISMS
PEDALBOATS
PEDALLINGS
PEDANTICAL
PEDANTICALLY
PEDANTICISE
PEDANTICISED
PEDANTICISES
PEDANTICISING
PEDANTICISM
PEDANTICISMS
PEDANTICIZE
PEDANTICIZED
PEDANTICIZES
PEDANTICIZING
PEDANTISED
PEDANTISES
PEDANTISING
PEDANTISMS
PEDANTIZED
PEDANTIZES
PEDANTIZING
PEDANTOCRACIES
PEDANTOCRACY
PEDANTOCRAT
PEDANTOCRATIC
PEDANTOCRATS
PEDANTRIES
PEDDLERIES
PEDERASTIC
PEDERASTIES
PEDEREROES
PEDESTALED
PEDESTALING
PEDESTALLED
PEDESTALLING
PEDESTRIAN
PEDESTRIANISE
PEDESTRIANISED
PEDESTRIANISES
PEDESTRIANISING
PEDESTRIANISM
PEDESTRIANISMS
PEDESTRIANIZE
PEDESTRIANIZED
PEDESTRIANIZES

P

PEDESTRIANIZING
PEDESTRIANS
PEDETENTOUS
PEDIATRICIAN
PEDIATRICIANS
PEDIATRICS
PEDIATRIST
PEDIATRISTS
PEDICELLARIA
PEDICELLARIAE
PEDICELLATE
PEDICULATE
PEDICULATED
PEDICULATES
PEDICULATION
PEDICULATIONS
PEDICULOSES
PEDICULOSIS
PEDICULOUS
PEDICURING
PEDICURIST
PEDICURISTS
PEDIMENTAL
PEDIMENTED
PEDIPALPUS
PEDOGENESES
PEDOGENESIS
PEDOGENETIC
PEDOLOGICAL
PEDOLOGIES
PEDOLOGIST
PEDOLOGISTS
PEDOMETERS
PEDOPHILES
PEDOPHILIA
PEDOPHILIAC
PEDOPHILIACS
PEDOPHILIAS
PEDOPHILIC
PEDOPHILICS
PEDUNCULAR
PEDUNCULATE
PEDUNCULATED
PEDUNCULATION
PEDUNCULATIONS
PEELGARLIC
PEELGARLICS
PEERLESSLY
PEERLESSNESS
PEERLESSNESSES
PEEVISHNESS
PEEVISHNESSES
PEGMATITES
PEGMATITIC
PEIRASTICALLY
PEJORATING
PEJORATION
PEJORATIONS
PEJORATIVE
PEJORATIVELY
PEJORATIVES
PELARGONIC
PELARGONIUM
PELARGONIUMS
PELECYPODS
PELLAGRINS
PELLAGROUS
PELLETIFIED
PELLETIFIES
PELLETIFYING
PELLETISATION
PELLETISATIONS
PELLETISED
PELLETISER
PELLETISERS
PELLETISES
PELLETISING
PELLETIZATION
PELLETIZATIONS
PELLETIZED
PELLETIZER
PELLETIZERS
PELLETIZES
PELLETIZING
PELLICULAR
PELLITORIES
PELLUCIDITIES
PELLUCIDITY
PELLUCIDLY
PELLUCIDNESS
PELLUCIDNESSES
PELMANISMS
PELOLOGIES
PELOTHERAPIES
PELOTHERAPY
PELTATIONS
PELTMONGER
PELTMONGERS
PELVIMETER
PELVIMETERS
PELVIMETRIES
PELVIMETRY
PELYCOSAUR
PELYCOSAURS
PEMPHIGOID
PEMPHIGOIDS
PEMPHIGOUS
PEMPHIGUSES
PENALISATION
PENALISATIONS
PENALISING
PENALITIES
PENALIZATION
PENALIZATIONS
PENALIZING
PENANNULAR
PENCILINGS
PENCILLERS
PENCILLING
PENCILLINGS
PENDENCIES
PENDENTIVE
PENDENTIVES
PENDICLERS
PENDRAGONS
PENDRAGONSHIP
PENDRAGONSHIPS
PENDULATED
PENDULATES
PENDULATING
PENDULOSITIES
PENDULOSITY
PENDULOUSLY
PENDULOUSNESS
PENDULOUSNESSES
PENELOPISE
PENELOPISED
PENELOPISES
PENELOPISING
PENELOPIZE
PENELOPIZED
PENELOPIZES
PENELOPIZING
PENEPLAINS
PENEPLANATION
PENEPLANATIONS
PENEPLANES
PENETRABILITIES
PENETRABILITY
PENETRABLE
PENETRABLENESS
PENETRABLY
PENETRALIA
PENETRALIAN
PENETRANCE
PENETRANCES
PENETRANCIES
PENETRANCY
PENETRANTS
PENETRATED
PENETRATES
PENETRATING
PENETRATINGLY
PENETRATION
PENETRATIONS
PENETRATIVE
PENETRATIVELY
PENETRATIVENESS
PENETRATOR
PENETRATORS
PENETROMETER
PENETROMETERS
PENFRIENDS
PENGUINERIES
PENGUINERY
PENGUINRIES
PENHOLDERS
PENICILLAMINE
PENICILLAMINES
PENICILLATE
PENICILLATELY
PENICILLATION
PENICILLATIONS
PENICILLIA
PENICILLIFORM
PENICILLIN
PENICILLINASE
PENICILLINASES
PENICILLINS
PENICILLIUM
PENICILLIUMS
PENICILLUS
PENINSULAR
PENINSULARITIES
PENINSULARITY
PENINSULAS
PENINSULATE
PENINSULATED
PENINSULATES
PENINSULATING
PENISTONES
PENITENCES
PENITENCIES
PENITENTIAL
PENITENTIALLY
PENITENTIALS
PENITENTIARIES
PENITENTIARY
PENITENTLY
PENMANSHIP
PENMANSHIPS
PENNACEOUS
PENNALISMS
PENNATULACEOUS
PENNATULAE
PENNATULAS
PENNILESSLY
PENNILESSNESS
PENNILESSNESSES
PENNILLION
PENNINITES
PENNONCELLE
PENNONCELLES
PENNONCELS
PENNYCRESS
PENNYCRESSES
PENNYLANDS
PENNYROYAL
PENNYROYALS
PENNYWEIGHT
PENNYWEIGHTS
PENNYWHISTLE
PENNYWHISTLES
PENNYWINKLE
PENNYWINKLES
PENNYWORTH
PENNYWORTHS
PENNYWORTS
PENOLOGICAL
PENOLOGICALLY

PENOLOGIES
PENOLOGIST
PENOLOGISTS
PENONCELLE
PENONCELLES
PENPUSHERS
PENPUSHING
PENPUSHINGS
PENSEROSOS
PENSIEROSO
PENSILENESS
PENSILENESSES
PENSILITIES
PENSIONABLE
PENSIONARIES
PENSIONARY
PENSIONEER
PENSIONERS
PENSIONING
PENSIONLESS
PENSIONNAT
PENSIONNATS
PENSIVENESS
PENSIVENESSES
PENSTEMONS
PENTABARBITAL
PENTABARBITALS
PENTACHORD
PENTACHORDS
PENTACRINOID
PENTACRINOIDS
PENTACTINAL
PENTACYCLIC
PENTADACTYL
PENTADACTYLE
PENTADACTYLES
PENTADACTYLIC
PENTADACTYLIES
PENTADACTYLISM
PENTADACTYLISMS
PENTADACTYLOUS
PENTADACTYLS
PENTADACTYLY
PENTADELPHOUS
PENTAGONAL
PENTAGONALLY
PENTAGONALS
PENTAGRAMS
PENTAGRAPH
PENTAGRAPHS
PENTAGYNIAN
PENTAGYNOUS
PENTAHEDRA
PENTAHEDRAL
PENTAHEDRON
PENTAHEDRONS
PENTAHYDRATE
PENTAHYDRATES
PENTALOGIES
PENTALPHAS
PENTAMERIES
PENTAMERISM
PENTAMERISMS
PENTAMEROUS
PENTAMETER
PENTAMETERS
PENTAMIDINE
PENTAMIDINES
PENTANDRIAN
PENTANDROUS
PENTANGLES
PENTANGULAR
PENTAPEPTIDE
PENTAPEPTIDES
PENTAPLOID
PENTAPLOIDIES
PENTAPLOIDS
PENTAPLOIDY
PENTAPODIC
PENTAPODIES
PENTAPOLIS
PENTAPOLISES
PENTAPOLITAN
PENTAPRISM
PENTAPRISMS
PENTAQUARK
PENTAQUARKS
PENTARCHICAL
PENTARCHIES
PENTASTICH
PENTASTICHOUS
PENTASTICHS
PENTASTYLE
PENTASTYLES
PENTASYLLABIC
PENTATEUCHAL
PENTATHLETE
PENTATHLETES
PENTATHLON
PENTATHLONS
PENTATHLUM
PENTATHLUMS
PENTATOMIC
PENTATONIC
PENTAVALENCE
PENTAVALENCES
PENTAVALENCIES
PENTAVALENCY
PENTAVALENT
PENTAZOCINE
PENTAZOCINES
PENTECONTER
PENTECONTERS
PENTETERIC
PENTHEMIMER
PENTHEMIMERAL
PENTHEMIMERS
PENTHOUSED
PENTHOUSES
PENTHOUSING
PENTIMENTI
PENTIMENTO
PENTLANDITE
PENTLANDITES
PENTOBARBITAL
PENTOBARBITALS
PENTOBARBITONE
PENTOBARBITONES
PENTOSANES
PENTOSIDES
PENTOXIDES
PENTSTEMON
PENTSTEMONS
PENTYLENES
PENULTIMAS
PENULTIMATE
PENULTIMATELY
PENULTIMATES
PENUMBROUS
PENURIOUSLY
PENURIOUSNESS
PENURIOUSNESSES
PEOPLEHOOD
PEOPLEHOODS
PEOPLELESS
PEPEROMIAS
PEPPERBOXES
PEPPERCORN
PEPPERCORNIER
PEPPERCORNIEST
PEPPERCORNS
PEPPERCORNY
PEPPERGRASS
PEPPERGRASSES
PEPPERIDGE
PEPPERIDGES
PEPPERIEST
PEPPERINESS
PEPPERINESSES
PEPPERINGS
PEPPERMILL
PEPPERMILLS
PEPPERMINT
PEPPERMINTIER
PEPPERMINTIEST
PEPPERMINTS
PEPPERMINTY
PEPPERONIS
PEPPERTREE
PEPPERTREES
PEPPERWORT
PEPPERWORTS
PEPPINESSES
PEPSINATED
PEPSINATES
PEPSINATING
PEPSINOGEN
PEPSINOGENS
PEPTALKING
PEPTICITIES
PEPTIDASES
PEPTIDOGLYCAN
PEPTIDOGLYCANS
PEPTISABLE
PEPTISATION
PEPTISATIONS
PEPTIZABLE
PEPTIZATION
PEPTIZATIONS
PEPTONISATION
PEPTONISATIONS
PEPTONISED
PEPTONISER
PEPTONISERS
PEPTONISES
PEPTONISING
PEPTONIZATION
PEPTONIZATIONS
PEPTONIZED
PEPTONIZER
PEPTONIZERS
PEPTONIZES
PEPTONIZING
PERACIDITIES
PERACIDITY
PERADVENTURE
PERADVENTURES
PERAEOPODS
PERAMBULATE
PERAMBULATED
PERAMBULATES
PERAMBULATING
PERAMBULATION
PERAMBULATIONS
PERAMBULATOR
PERAMBULATORS
PERAMBULATORY
PERBORATES
PERCALINES
PERCEIVABILITY
PERCEIVABLE
PERCEIVABLY
PERCEIVERS
PERCEIVING
PERCEIVINGS
PERCENTAGE
PERCENTAGES
PERCENTILE
PERCENTILES
PERCEPTIBILITY
PERCEPTIBLE
PERCEPTIBLY
PERCEPTION
PERCEPTIONAL
PERCEPTIONS
PERCEPTIVE
PERCEPTIVELY
PERCEPTIVENESS
PERCEPTIVITIES
PERCEPTIVITY

PERCEPTUAL
PERCEPTUALLY
PERCHERIES
PERCHERONS
PERCHLORATE
PERCHLORATES
PERCHLORIC
PERCHLORIDE
PERCHLORIDES
PERCHLOROETHENE
PERCIFORMS
PERCIPIENCE
PERCIPIENCES
PERCIPIENCIES
PERCIPIENCY
PERCIPIENT
PERCIPIENTLY
PERCIPIENTS
PERCOCTING
PERCOIDEAN
PERCOIDEANS
PERCOLABLE
PERCOLATED
PERCOLATES
PERCOLATING
PERCOLATION
PERCOLATIONS
PERCOLATIVE
PERCOLATOR
PERCOLATORS
PERCURRENT
PERCURSORY
PERCUSSANT
PERCUSSING
PERCUSSION
PERCUSSIONAL
PERCUSSIONIST
PERCUSSIONISTS
PERCUSSIONS
PERCUSSIVE
PERCUSSIVELY
PERCUSSIVENESS
PERCUSSORS
PERCUTANEOUS
PERCUTANEOUSLY
PERCUTIENT
PERCUTIENTS
PERDENDOSI
PERDITIONABLE
PERDITIONS
PERDUELLION
PERDUELLIONS
PERDURABILITIES
PERDURABILITY
PERDURABLE
PERDURABLY
PERDURANCE
PERDURANCES
PERDURATION
PERDURATIONS
PEREGRINATE
PEREGRINATED
PEREGRINATES
PEREGRINATING
PEREGRINATION
PEREGRINATIONS
PEREGRINATOR
PEREGRINATORS
PEREGRINATORY
PEREGRINES
PEREGRINITIES
PEREGRINITY
PEREIOPODS
PEREMPTORILY
PEREMPTORINESS
PEREMPTORY
PERENNATED
PERENNATES
PERENNATING
PERENNATION
PERENNATIONS
PERENNIALITIES
PERENNIALITY
PERENNIALLY
PERENNIALS
PERENNIBRANCH
PERENNIBRANCHS
PERENNITIES
PERESTROIKA
PERESTROIKAS
PERFECTATION
PERFECTATIONS
PERFECTERS
PERFECTEST
PERFECTIBILIAN
PERFECTIBILIANS
PERFECTIBILISM
PERFECTIBILISMS
PERFECTIBILIST
PERFECTIBILISTS
PERFECTIBILITY
PERFECTIBLE
PERFECTING
PERFECTION
PERFECTIONATE
PERFECTIONATED
PERFECTIONATES
PERFECTIONATING
PERFECTIONISM
PERFECTIONISMS
PERFECTIONIST
PERFECTIONISTIC
PERFECTIONISTS
PERFECTIONS
PERFECTIVE
PERFECTIVELY
PERFECTIVENESS
PERFECTIVES
PERFECTIVITIES
PERFECTIVITY
PERFECTNESS
PERFECTNESSES
PERFECTORS
PERFERVIDITIES
PERFERVIDITY
PERFERVIDLY
PERFERVIDNESS
PERFERVIDNESSES
PERFERVORS
PERFERVOUR
PERFERVOURS
PERFICIENT
PERFICIENTS
PERFIDIOUS
PERFIDIOUSLY
PERFIDIOUSNESS
PERFLUOROCARBON
PERFOLIATE
PERFOLIATION
PERFOLIATIONS
PERFORABLE
PERFORANSES
PERFORATED
PERFORATES
PERFORATING
PERFORATION
PERFORATIONS
PERFORATIVE
PERFORATOR
PERFORATORS
PERFORATORY
PERFORATUS
PERFORATUSES
PERFORMABILITY
PERFORMABLE
PERFORMANCE
PERFORMANCES
PERFORMATIVE
PERFORMATIVELY
PERFORMATIVES
PERFORMATORY
PERFORMERS
PERFORMING
PERFORMINGS
PERFUMELESS
PERFUMERIES
PERFUMIERS
PERFUMIEST
PERFUNCTORILY
PERFUNCTORINESS
PERFUNCTORY
PERFUSATES
PERFUSIONIST
PERFUSIONISTS
PERFUSIONS
PERGAMENEOUS
PERGAMENTACEOUS
PERGUNNAHS
PERIASTRON
PERIASTRONS
PERIBLASTS
PERICARDIA
PERICARDIAC
PERICARDIAL
PERICARDIAN
PERICARDITIC
PERICARDITIDES
PERICARDITIS
PERICARDITISES
PERICARDIUM
PERICARDIUMS
PERICARPIAL
PERICARPIC
PERICENTER
PERICENTERS
PERICENTRAL
PERICENTRE
PERICENTRES
PERICENTRIC
PERICHAETIA
PERICHAETIAL
PERICHAETIUM
PERICHONDRAL
PERICHONDRIA
PERICHONDRIAL
PERICHONDRIUM
PERICHORESES
PERICHORESIS
PERICHYLOUS
PERICLASES
PERICLASTIC
PERICLINAL
PERICLINES
PERICLITATE
PERICLITATED
PERICLITATES
PERICLITATING
PERICRANIA
PERICRANIAL
PERICRANIUM
PERICRANIUMS
PERICULOUS
PERICYCLES
PERICYCLIC
PERICYNTHIA
PERICYNTHION
PERICYNTHIONS
PERIDERMAL
PERIDERMIC
PERIDESMIA
PERIDESMIUM
PERIDINIAN
PERIDINIANS
PERIDINIUM
PERIDINIUMS
PERIDOTITE
PERIDOTITES
PERIDOTITIC
PERIDROMES
PERIEGESES

P

PERIEGESIS
PERIGASTRIC
PERIGASTRITIS
PERIGASTRITISES
PERIGENESES
PERIGENESIS
PERIGLACIAL
PERIGONIAL
PERIGONIUM
PERIGYNIES
PERIGYNOUS
PERIHELIAL
PERIHELION
PERIHEPATIC
PERIHEPATITIS
PERIHEPATITISES
PERIKARYAL
PERIKARYON
PERILOUSLY
PERILOUSNESS
PERILOUSNESSES
PERILYMPHS
PERIMENOPAUSAL
PERIMENOPAUSE
PERIMENOPAUSES
PERIMETERS
PERIMETRAL
PERIMETRIC
PERIMETRICAL
PERIMETRICALLY
PERIMETRIES
PERIMORPHIC
PERIMORPHISM
PERIMORPHISMS
PERIMORPHOUS
PERIMORPHS
PERIMYSIUM
PERINAEUMS
PERINATALLY
PERINEPHRIA
PERINEPHRIC
PERINEPHRITIS
PERINEPHRITISES
PERINEPHRIUM
PERINEURAL
PERINEURIA
PERINEURIAL
PERINEURITIC
PERINEURITIS
PERINEURITISES
PERINEURIUM
PERIODATES
PERIODICAL
PERIODICALIST
PERIODICALISTS
PERIODICALLY
PERIODICALS
PERIODICITIES
PERIODICITY
PERIODIDES
PERIODISATION
PERIODISATIONS
PERIODISED
PERIODISES
PERIODISING
PERIODIZATION
PERIODIZATIONS
PERIODIZED
PERIODIZES
PERIODIZING
PERIODONTAL
PERIODONTALLY
PERIODONTIA
PERIODONTIAS
PERIODONTIC
PERIODONTICALLY
PERIODONTICS
PERIODONTIST
PERIODONTISTS
PERIODONTITIS
PERIODONTITISES
PERIODONTOLOGY
PERIONYCHIA
PERIONYCHIUM
PERIOSTEAL
PERIOSTEUM
PERIOSTITIC
PERIOSTITIDES
PERIOSTITIS
PERIOSTITISES
PERIOSTRACUM
PERIOSTRACUMS
PERIPATETIC
PERIPATETICAL
PERIPATETICALLY
PERIPATETICISM
PERIPATETICISMS
PERIPATETICS
PERIPATUSES
PERIPETEIA
PERIPETEIAN
PERIPETEIAS
PERIPETIAN
PERIPETIAS
PERIPETIES
PERIPHERAL
PERIPHERALITIES
PERIPHERALITY
PERIPHERALLY
PERIPHERALS
PERIPHERIC
PERIPHERICAL
PERIPHERIES
PERIPHONIC
PERIPHRASE
PERIPHRASED
PERIPHRASES
PERIPHRASING
PERIPHRASIS
PERIPHRASTIC
PERIPHRASTICAL
PERIPHYTIC
PERIPHYTON
PERIPHYTONS
PERIPLASMS
PERIPLASTS
PERIPLUSES
PERIPROCTS
PERIPTERAL
PERIPTERIES
PERISARCAL
PERISARCOUS
PERISCIANS
PERISCOPES
PERISCOPIC
PERISCOPICALLY
PERISELENIA
PERISELENIUM
PERISHABILITIES
PERISHABILITY
PERISHABLE
PERISHABLENESS
PERISHABLES
PERISHABLY
PERISHINGLY
PERISPERMAL
PERISPERMIC
PERISPERMS
PERISPOMENA
PERISPOMENON
PERISPOMENONS
PERISSODACTYL
PERISSODACTYLE
PERISSODACTYLES
PERISSODACTYLIC
PERISSODACTYLS
PERISSOLOGIES
PERISSOLOGY
PERISSOSYLLABIC
PERISTALITH
PERISTALITHS
PERISTALSES
PERISTALSIS
PERISTALTIC
PERISTALTICALLY
PERISTERITE
PERISTERITES
PERISTERONIC
PERISTOMAL
PERISTOMATIC
PERISTOMES
PERISTOMIAL
PERISTREPHIC
PERISTYLAR
PERISTYLES
PERITECTIC
PERITECTICS
PERITHECIA
PERITHECIAL
PERITHECIUM
PERITONAEA
PERITONAEAL
PERITONAEUM
PERITONAEUMS
PERITONEAL
PERITONEALLY
PERITONEOSCOPY
PERITONEUM
PERITONEUMS
PERITONITIC
PERITONITIS
PERITONITISES
PERITRACKS
PERITRICHA
PERITRICHOUS
PERITRICHOUSLY
PERITRICHS
PERITYPHLITIS
PERITYPHLITISES
PERIVITELLINE
PERIWIGGED
PERIWIGGING
PERIWINKLE
PERIWINKLES
PERJINKETY
PERJINKITIES
PERJINKITY
PERJURIOUS
PERJURIOUSLY
PERKINESSES
PERLEMOENS
PERLOCUTION
PERLOCUTIONARY
PERLOCUTIONS
PERLUSTRATE
PERLUSTRATED
PERLUSTRATES
PERLUSTRATING
PERLUSTRATION
PERLUSTRATIONS
PERMABEARS
PERMABULLS
PERMACULTURE
PERMACULTURES
PERMAFROST
PERMAFROSTS
PERMALINKS
PERMALLOYS
PERMANENCE
PERMANENCES
PERMANENCIES
PERMANENCY
PERMANENTLY
PERMANENTNESS
PERMANENTNESSES
PERMANENTS
PERMANGANATE
PERMANGANATES
PERMANGANIC
PERMEABILITIES

P

PERMEABILITY
PERMEABLENESS
PERMEABLENESSES
PERMEAMETER
PERMEAMETERS
PERMEANCES
PERMEATING
PERMEATION
PERMEATIONS
PERMEATIVE
PERMEATORS
PERMETHRIN
PERMETHRINS
PERMILLAGE
PERMILLAGES
PERMISSIBILITY
PERMISSIBLE
PERMISSIBLENESS
PERMISSIBLY
PERMISSION
PERMISSIONS
PERMISSIVE
PERMISSIVELY
PERMISSIVENESS
PERMITTANCE
PERMITTANCES
PERMITTEES
PERMITTERS
PERMITTING
PERMITTIVITIES
PERMITTIVITY
PERMUTABILITIES
PERMUTABILITY
PERMUTABLE
PERMUTABLENESS
PERMUTABLY
PERMUTATED
PERMUTATES
PERMUTATING
PERMUTATION
PERMUTATIONAL
PERMUTATIONS
PERNANCIES
PERNICIOUS
PERNICIOUSLY
PERNICIOUSNESS
PERNICKETIER
PERNICKETIEST
PERNICKETINESS
PERNICKETY
PERNOCTATE
PERNOCTATED
PERNOCTATES
PERNOCTATING
PERNOCTATION
PERNOCTATIONS
PERONEUSES
PERORATING
PERORATION
PERORATIONAL
PERORATIONS
PERORATORS
PEROVSKIAS
PEROVSKITE
PEROVSKITES
PEROXIDASE
PEROXIDASES
PEROXIDATION
PEROXIDATIONS
PEROXIDING
PEROXIDISE
PEROXIDISED
PEROXIDISES
PEROXIDISING
PEROXIDIZE
PEROXIDIZED
PEROXIDIZES
PEROXIDIZING
PEROXISOMAL
PEROXISOME
PEROXISOMES
PEROXYSULPHURIC
PERPENDICULAR
PERPENDICULARLY
PERPENDICULARS
PERPENDING
PERPETRABLE
PERPETRATE
PERPETRATED
PERPETRATES
PERPETRATING
PERPETRATION
PERPETRATIONS
PERPETRATOR
PERPETRATORS
PERPETUABLE
PERPETUALISM
PERPETUALISMS
PERPETUALIST
PERPETUALISTS
PERPETUALITIES
PERPETUALITY
PERPETUALLY
PERPETUALS
PERPETUANCE
PERPETUANCES
PERPETUATE
PERPETUATED
PERPETUATES
PERPETUATING
PERPETUATION
PERPETUATIONS
PERPETUATOR
PERPETUATORS
PERPETUITIES
PERPETUITY
PERPHENAZINE
PERPHENAZINES
PERPLEXEDLY
PERPLEXEDNESS
PERPLEXEDNESSES
PERPLEXERS
PERPLEXING
PERPLEXINGLY
PERPLEXITIES
PERPLEXITY
PERQUISITE
PERQUISITES
PERQUISITION
PERQUISITIONS
PERQUISITOR
PERQUISITORS
PERRUQUIER
PERRUQUIERS
PERSCRUTATION
PERSCRUTATIONS
PERSECUTED
PERSECUTEE
PERSECUTEES
PERSECUTES
PERSECUTING
PERSECUTION
PERSECUTIONS
PERSECUTIVE
PERSECUTOR
PERSECUTORS
PERSECUTORY
PERSEITIES
PERSELINES
PERSEVERANCE
PERSEVERANCES
PERSEVERANT
PERSEVERATE
PERSEVERATED
PERSEVERATES
PERSEVERATING
PERSEVERATION
PERSEVERATIONS
PERSEVERATIVE
PERSEVERATOR
PERSEVERATORS
PERSEVERED
PERSEVERES
PERSEVERING
PERSEVERINGLY
PERSICARIA
PERSICARIAS
PERSIENNES
PERSIFLAGE
PERSIFLAGES
PERSIFLEUR
PERSIFLEURS
PERSIMMONS
PERSISTENCE
PERSISTENCES
PERSISTENCIES
PERSISTENCY
PERSISTENT
PERSISTENTLY
PERSISTENTS
PERSISTERS
PERSISTING
PERSISTINGLY
PERSISTIVE
PERSNICKETIER
PERSNICKETIEST
PERSNICKETINESS
PERSNICKETY
PERSONABLE
PERSONABLENESS
PERSONABLY
PERSONAGES
PERSONALIA
PERSONALISATION
PERSONALISE
PERSONALISED
PERSONALISES
PERSONALISING
PERSONALISM
PERSONALISMS
PERSONALIST
PERSONALISTIC
PERSONALISTS
PERSONALITIES
PERSONALITY
PERSONALIZATION
PERSONALIZE
PERSONALIZED
PERSONALIZES
PERSONALIZING
PERSONALLY
PERSONALTIES
PERSONALTY
PERSONATED
PERSONATES
PERSONATING
PERSONATINGS
PERSONATION
PERSONATIONS
PERSONATIVE
PERSONATOR
PERSONATORS
PERSONHOOD
PERSONHOODS
PERSONIFIABLE
PERSONIFICATION
PERSONIFIED
PERSONIFIER
PERSONIFIERS
PERSONIFIES
PERSONIFYING
PERSONISED
PERSONISES
PERSONISING
PERSONIZED
PERSONIZES
PERSONIZING
PERSONNELS
PERSONPOWER
PERSONPOWERS

PERSPECTIVAL
PERSPECTIVE
PERSPECTIVELY
PERSPECTIVES
PERSPECTIVISM
PERSPECTIVISMS
PERSPECTIVIST
PERSPECTIVISTS
PERSPICACIOUS
PERSPICACIOUSLY
PERSPICACITIES
PERSPICACITY
PERSPICUITIES
PERSPICUITY
PERSPICUOUS
PERSPICUOUSLY
PERSPICUOUSNESS
PERSPIRABLE
PERSPIRATE
PERSPIRATED
PERSPIRATES
PERSPIRATING
PERSPIRATION
PERSPIRATIONS
PERSPIRATORY
PERSPIRIER
PERSPIRIEST
PERSPIRING
PERSPIRINGLY
PERSTRINGE
PERSTRINGED
PERSTRINGES
PERSTRINGING
PERSUADABILITY
PERSUADABLE
PERSUADERS
PERSUADING
PERSUASIBILITY
PERSUASIBLE
PERSUASION
PERSUASIONS
PERSUASIVE
PERSUASIVELY
PERSUASIVENESS
PERSUASIVES
PERSUASORY
PERSULFATE
PERSULFATES
PERSULFURIC
PERSULPHATE
PERSULPHATES
PERSULPHURIC
PERSWADING
PERTAINING
PERTINACIOUS
PERTINACIOUSLY
PERTINACITIES
PERTINACITY
PERTINENCE
PERTINENCES
PERTINENCIES
PERTINENCY
PERTINENTLY
PERTINENTS
PERTNESSES
PERTURBABLE
PERTURBABLY
PERTURBANCE
PERTURBANCES
PERTURBANT
PERTURBANTS
PERTURBATE
PERTURBATED
PERTURBATES
PERTURBATING
PERTURBATION
PERTURBATIONAL
PERTURBATIONS
PERTURBATIVE
PERTURBATOR
PERTURBATORIES
PERTURBATORS
PERTURBATORY
PERTURBEDLY
PERTURBERS
PERTURBING
PERTURBINGLY
PERTUSIONS
PERTUSSISES
PERVASIONS
PERVASIVELY
PERVASIVENESS
PERVASIVENESSES
PERVERSELY
PERVERSENESS
PERVERSENESSES
PERVERSEST
PERVERSION
PERVERSIONS
PERVERSITIES
PERVERSITY
PERVERSIVE
PERVERTEDLY
PERVERTEDNESS
PERVERTEDNESSES
PERVERTERS
PERVERTIBLE
PERVERTING
PERVIATING
PERVICACIES
PERVICACIOUS
PERVICACITIES
PERVICACITY
PERVIOUSLY
PERVIOUSNESS
PERVIOUSNESSES
PESCATARIAN
PESCATARIANS
PESCETARIAN
PESCETARIANS
PESHMERGAS
PESKINESSES
PESSIMISMS
PESSIMISTIC
PESSIMISTICAL
PESSIMISTICALLY
PESSIMISTS
PESTERINGLY
PESTERMENT
PESTERMENTS
PESTHOUSES
PESTICIDAL
PESTICIDES
PESTIFEROUS
PESTIFEROUSLY
PESTIFEROUSNESS
PESTILENCE
PESTILENCES
PESTILENTIAL
PESTILENTIALLY
PESTILENTLY
PESTOLOGICAL
PESTOLOGIES
PESTOLOGIST
PESTOLOGISTS
PETAHERTZES
PETALIFEROUS
PETALODIES
PETALOMANIA
PETALOMANIAS
PETAMETERS
PETAMETRES
PETAURINES
PETAURISTS
PETCHARIES
PETERSHAMS
PETHIDINES
PETIOLATED
PETIOLULES
PETITENESS
PETITENESSES
PETITIONARY
PETITIONED
PETITIONER
PETITIONERS
PETITIONING
PETITIONINGS
PETITIONIST
PETITIONISTS
PETNAPINGS
PETNAPPERS
PETNAPPING
PETNAPPINGS
PETRICHORS
PETRIFACTION
PETRIFACTIONS
PETRIFACTIVE
PETRIFICATION
PETRIFICATIONS
PETRIFIERS
PETRIFYING
PETRISSAGE
PETRISSAGES
PETROCHEMICAL
PETROCHEMICALLY
PETROCHEMICALS
PETROCHEMIST
PETROCHEMISTRY
PETROCHEMISTS
PETROCURRENCIES
PETROCURRENCY
PETRODOLLAR
PETRODOLLARS
PETRODROME
PETRODROMES
PETROGENESES
PETROGENESIS
PETROGENETIC
PETROGENIES
PETROGLYPH
PETROGLYPHIC
PETROGLYPHIES
PETROGLYPHS
PETROGLYPHY
PETROGRAMS
PETROGRAPHER
PETROGRAPHERS
PETROGRAPHIC
PETROGRAPHICAL
PETROGRAPHIES
PETROGRAPHY
PETROLAGES
PETROLATUM
PETROLATUMS
PETROLEOUS
PETROLEUMS
PETROLEURS
PETROLEUSE
PETROLEUSES
PETROLHEAD
PETROLHEADS
PETROLIFEROUS
PETROLLING
PETROLOGIC
PETROLOGICAL
PETROLOGICALLY
PETROLOGIES
PETROLOGIST
PETROLOGISTS
PETROMONEY
PETROMONEYS
PETROMONIES
PETRONELLA
PETRONELLAS
PETROPHYSICAL
PETROPHYSICIST
PETROPHYSICISTS
PETROPHYSICS
PETROPOUNDS
PETROSTATE

P

PETROSTATES
PETTEDNESS
PETTEDNESSES
PETTICHAPS
PETTICHAPSES
PETTICOATED
PETTICOATS
PETTIFOGGED
PETTIFOGGER
PETTIFOGGERIES
PETTIFOGGERS
PETTIFOGGERY
PETTIFOGGING
PETTIFOGGINGS
PETTINESSES
PETTISHNESS
PETTISHNESSES
PETULANCES
PETULANCIES
PETULANTLY
PEWHOLDERS
PEWTERIEST
PHACOLITES
PHACOLITHS
PHAELONION
PHAELONIONS
PHAENOGAMIC
PHAENOGAMOUS
PHAENOGAMS
PHAENOLOGIES
PHAENOLOGY
PHAENOMENA
PHAENOMENON
PHAENOTYPE
PHAENOTYPED
PHAENOTYPES
PHAENOTYPING
PHAEOMELANIN
PHAEOMELANINS
PHAGEDAENA
PHAGEDAENAS
PHAGEDAENIC
PHAGEDENAS
PHAGEDENIC
PHAGOCYTES
PHAGOCYTIC
PHAGOCYTICAL
PHAGOCYTISE
PHAGOCYTISED
PHAGOCYTISES
PHAGOCYTISING
PHAGOCYTISM
PHAGOCYTISMS
PHAGOCYTIZE
PHAGOCYTIZED
PHAGOCYTIZES
PHAGOCYTIZING
PHAGOCYTOSE
PHAGOCYTOSED
PHAGOCYTOSES
PHAGOCYTOSING
PHAGOCYTOSIS
PHAGOCYTOTIC
PHAGOMANIA
PHAGOMANIAC
PHAGOMANIACS
PHAGOMANIAS
PHAGOPHOBIA
PHAGOPHOBIAS
PHAGOSOMES
PHALANGEAL
PHALANGERS
PHALANGIDS
PHALANGIST
PHALANGISTS
PHALANSTERIAN
PHALANSTERIANS
PHALANSTERIES
PHALANSTERISM
PHALANSTERISMS
PHALANSTERIST
PHALANSTERISTS
PHALANSTERY
PHALAROPES
PHALLICALLY
PHALLICISM
PHALLICISMS
PHALLICIST
PHALLICISTS
PHALLOCENTRIC
PHALLOCENTRISM
PHALLOCENTRISMS
PHALLOCRAT
PHALLOCRATIC
PHALLOCRATS
PHALLOIDIN
PHALLOIDINS
PHANEROGAM
PHANEROGAMIC
PHANEROGAMOUS
PHANEROGAMS
PHANEROPHYTE
PHANEROPHYTES
PHANSIGARS
PHANTASIAST
PHANTASIASTS
PHANTASIED
PHANTASIES
PHANTASIME
PHANTASIMES
PHANTASIMS
PHANTASMAGORIA
PHANTASMAGORIAL
PHANTASMAGORIAS
PHANTASMAGORIC
PHANTASMAGORIES
PHANTASMAGORY
PHANTASMAL
PHANTASMALIAN
PHANTASMALITIES
PHANTASMALITY
PHANTASMALLY
PHANTASMATA
PHANTASMIC
PHANTASMICAL
PHANTASMICALLY
PHANTASTIC
PHANTASTICS
PHANTASTRIES
PHANTASTRY
PHANTASYING
PHANTOMATIC
PHANTOMISH
PHANTOMLIKE
PHANTOSMES
PHARISAICAL
PHARISAICALLY
PHARISAICALNESS
PHARISAISM
PHARISAISMS
PHARISEEISM
PHARISEEISMS
PHARMACEUTIC
PHARMACEUTICAL
PHARMACEUTICALS
PHARMACEUTICS
PHARMACEUTIST
PHARMACEUTISTS
PHARMACIES
PHARMACIST
PHARMACISTS
PHARMACODYNAMIC
PHARMACOGENOMIC
PHARMACOGNOSIES
PHARMACOGNOSIST
PHARMACOGNOSTIC
PHARMACOGNOSY
PHARMACOKINETIC
PHARMACOLOGIC
PHARMACOLOGICAL
PHARMACOLOGIES
PHARMACOLOGIST
PHARMACOLOGISTS
PHARMACOLOGY
PHARMACOPEIA
PHARMACOPEIAL
PHARMACOPEIAS
PHARMACOPOEIA
PHARMACOPOEIAL
PHARMACOPOEIAN
PHARMACOPOEIANS
PHARMACOPOEIAS
PHARMACOPOEIC
PHARMACOPOEIST
PHARMACOPOEISTS
PHARMACOPOLIST
PHARMACOPOLISTS
PHARMACOTHERAPY
PHARYNGALS
PHARYNGEAL
PHARYNGEALS
PHARYNGITIC
PHARYNGITIDES
PHARYNGITIS
PHARYNGITISES
PHARYNGOLOGICAL
PHARYNGOLOGIES
PHARYNGOLOGIST
PHARYNGOLOGISTS
PHARYNGOLOGY
PHARYNGOSCOPE
PHARYNGOSCOPES
PHARYNGOSCOPIC
PHARYNGOSCOPIES
PHARYNGOSCOPY
PHARYNGOTOMIES
PHARYNGOTOMY
PHASCOGALE
PHASCOGALES
PHASEDOWNS
PHASEOLINS
PHATICALLY
PHEASANTRIES
PHEASANTRY
PHELLODERM
PHELLODERMAL
PHELLODERMS
PHELLOGENETIC
PHELLOGENIC
PHELLOGENS
PHELLOPLASTIC
PHELLOPLASTICS
PHELONIONS
PHENACAINE
PHENACAINES
PHENACETIN
PHENACETINS
PHENACITES
PHENAKISMS
PHENAKISTOSCOPE
PHENAKITES
PHENANTHRENE
PHENANTHRENES
PHENARSAZINE
PHENARSAZINES
PHENAZINES
PHENCYCLIDINE
PHENCYCLIDINES
PHENETICIST
PHENETICISTS
PHENETIDINE
PHENETIDINES
PHENETOLES
PHENFORMIN
PHENFORMINS
PHENGOPHOBIA
PHENGOPHOBIAS
PHENMETRAZINE
PHENMETRAZINES
PHENOBARBITAL

P

PHENOBARBITALS
PHENOBARBITONE
PHENOBARBITONES
PHENOBARBS
PHENOCOPIES
PHENOCRYST
PHENOCRYSTIC
PHENOCRYSTS
PHENOLATED
PHENOLATES
PHENOLATING
PHENOLOGICAL
PHENOLOGICALLY
PHENOLOGIES
PHENOLOGIST
PHENOLOGISTS
PHENOLPHTHALEIN
PHENOMENAL
PHENOMENALISE
PHENOMENALISED
PHENOMENALISES
PHENOMENALISING
PHENOMENALISM
PHENOMENALISMS
PHENOMENALIST
PHENOMENALISTIC
PHENOMENALISTS
PHENOMENALITIES
PHENOMENALITY
PHENOMENALIZE
PHENOMENALIZED
PHENOMENALIZES
PHENOMENALIZING
PHENOMENALLY
PHENOMENAS
PHENOMENISE
PHENOMENISED
PHENOMENISES
PHENOMENISING
PHENOMENISM
PHENOMENISMS
PHENOMENIST
PHENOMENISTS
PHENOMENIZE
PHENOMENIZED
PHENOMENIZES
PHENOMENIZING
PHENOMENOLOGIES
PHENOMENOLOGIST
PHENOMENOLOGY
PHENOMENON
PHENOMENONS
PHENOTHIAZINE
PHENOTHIAZINES
PHENOTYPED
PHENOTYPES
PHENOTYPIC
PHENOTYPICAL
PHENOTYPICALLY
PHENOTYPING
PHENOXIDES
PHENTOLAMINE
PHENTOLAMINES
PHENYLALANIN
PHENYLALANINE
PHENYLALANINES
PHENYLALANINS
PHENYLAMINE
PHENYLAMINES
PHENYLBUTAZONE
PHENYLBUTAZONES
PHENYLENES
PHENYLEPHRINE
PHENYLEPHRINES
PHENYLKETONURIA
PHENYLKETONURIC
PHENYLMETHYL
PHENYLMETHYLS
PHENYLTHIOUREA
PHENYLTHIOUREAS
PHENYTOINS
PHEROMONAL
PHEROMONES
PHIALIFORM
PHILADELPHUS
PHILADELPHUSES
PHILANDERED
PHILANDERER
PHILANDERERS
PHILANDERING
PHILANDERINGS
PHILANDERS
PHILANTHROPE
PHILANTHROPES
PHILANTHROPIC
PHILANTHROPICAL
PHILANTHROPIES
PHILANTHROPIST
PHILANTHROPISTS
PHILANTHROPOID
PHILANTHROPOIDS
PHILANTHROPY
PHILATELIC
PHILATELICALLY
PHILATELIES
PHILATELIST
PHILATELISTS
PHILAVERIES
PHILHARMONIC
PHILHARMONICS
PHILHELLENE
PHILHELLENES
PHILHELLENIC
PHILHELLENISM
PHILHELLENISMS
PHILHELLENIST
PHILHELLENISTS
PHILHORSES
PHILIPPICS
PHILIPPINA
PHILIPPINAS
PHILIPPINE
PHILIPPINES
PHILISTIAS
PHILISTINE
PHILISTINES
PHILISTINISM
PHILISTINISMS
PHILLABEGS
PHILLIBEGS
PHILLIPSITE
PHILLIPSITES
PHILLUMENIES
PHILLUMENIST
PHILLUMENISTS
PHILLUMENY
PHILODENDRA
PHILODENDRON
PHILODENDRONS
PHILOGYNIES
PHILOGYNIST
PHILOGYNISTS
PHILOGYNOUS
PHILOLOGER
PHILOLOGERS
PHILOLOGIAN
PHILOLOGIANS
PHILOLOGIC
PHILOLOGICAL
PHILOLOGICALLY
PHILOLOGIES
PHILOLOGIST
PHILOLOGISTS
PHILOLOGUE
PHILOLOGUES
PHILOMATHIC
PHILOMATHICAL
PHILOMATHIES
PHILOMATHS
PHILOMATHY
PHILOMELAS
PHILOPENAS
PHILOPOENA
PHILOPOENAS
PHILOSOPHASTER
PHILOSOPHASTERS
PHILOSOPHE
PHILOSOPHER
PHILOSOPHERESS
PHILOSOPHERS
PHILOSOPHES
PHILOSOPHESS
PHILOSOPHESSES
PHILOSOPHIC
PHILOSOPHICAL
PHILOSOPHICALLY
PHILOSOPHIES
PHILOSOPHISE
PHILOSOPHISED
PHILOSOPHISER
PHILOSOPHISERS
PHILOSOPHISES
PHILOSOPHISING
PHILOSOPHISINGS
PHILOSOPHISM
PHILOSOPHISMS
PHILOSOPHIST
PHILOSOPHISTIC
PHILOSOPHISTS
PHILOSOPHIZE
PHILOSOPHIZED
PHILOSOPHIZER
PHILOSOPHIZERS
PHILOSOPHIZES
PHILOSOPHIZING
PHILOSOPHIZINGS
PHILOSOPHY
PHILOXENIA
PHILOXENIAS
PHILTERING
PHISNOMIES
PHLEBECTOMIES
PHLEBECTOMY
PHLEBITIDES
PHLEBITISES
PHLEBOGRAM
PHLEBOGRAMS
PHLEBOGRAPHIC
PHLEBOGRAPHIES
PHLEBOGRAPHY
PHLEBOLITE
PHLEBOLITES
PHLEBOLOGIES
PHLEBOLOGY
PHLEBOSCLEROSES
PHLEBOSCLEROSIS
PHLEBOTOMIC
PHLEBOTOMICAL
PHLEBOTOMIES
PHLEBOTOMISE
PHLEBOTOMISED
PHLEBOTOMISES
PHLEBOTOMISING
PHLEBOTOMIST
PHLEBOTOMISTS
PHLEBOTOMIZE
PHLEBOTOMIZED
PHLEBOTOMIZES
PHLEBOTOMIZING
PHLEBOTOMY
PHLEGMAGOGIC
PHLEGMAGOGICS
PHLEGMAGOGUE
PHLEGMAGOGUES
PHLEGMASIA
PHLEGMASIAS
PHLEGMATIC
PHLEGMATICAL
PHLEGMATICALLY
PHLEGMATICNESS

PHLEGMIEST
PHLEGMONIC
PHLEGMONOID
PHLEGMONOUS
PHLOGISTIC
PHLOGISTICATE
PHLOGISTICATED
PHLOGISTICATES
PHLOGISTICATING
PHLOGISTON
PHLOGISTONS
PHLOGOPITE
PHLOGOPITES
PHLORIZINS
PHLYCTAENA
PHLYCTAENAE
PHLYCTENAE
PHOCOMELIA
PHOCOMELIAS
PHOCOMELIC
PHOCOMELIES
PHOENIXISM
PHOENIXISMS
PHOENIXLIKE
PHOLIDOSES
PHOLIDOSIS
PHONASTHENIA
PHONASTHENIAS
PHONATHONS
PHONATIONS
PHONAUTOGRAPH
PHONAUTOGRAPHIC
PHONAUTOGRAPHS
PHONECARDS
PHONEMATIC
PHONEMATICALLY
PHONEMICALLY
PHONEMICISATION
PHONEMICISE
PHONEMICISED
PHONEMICISES
PHONEMICISING
PHONEMICIST
PHONEMICISTS
PHONEMICIZATION
PHONEMICIZE
PHONEMICIZED
PHONEMICIZES
PHONEMICIZING
PHONENDOSCOPE
PHONENDOSCOPES
PHONETICAL
PHONETICALLY
PHONETICIAN
PHONETICIANS
PHONETICISATION
PHONETICISE
PHONETICISED
PHONETICISES
PHONETICISING
PHONETICISM
PHONETICISMS
PHONETICIST
PHONETICISTS
PHONETICIZATION
PHONETICIZE
PHONETICIZED
PHONETICIZES
PHONETICIZING
PHONETISATION
PHONETISATIONS
PHONETISED
PHONETISES
PHONETISING
PHONETISMS
PHONETISTS
PHONETIZATION
PHONETIZATIONS
PHONETIZED
PHONETIZES
PHONETIZING
PHONEYNESS
PHONEYNESSES
PHONICALLY
PHONINESSES
PHONMETERS
PHONOCAMPTIC
PHONOCAMPTICS
PHONOCARDIOGRAM
PHONOCHEMISTRY
PHONOFIDDLE
PHONOFIDDLES
PHONOGRAMIC
PHONOGRAMICALLY
PHONOGRAMMIC
PHONOGRAMS
PHONOGRAPH
PHONOGRAPHER
PHONOGRAPHERS
PHONOGRAPHIC
PHONOGRAPHIES
PHONOGRAPHIST
PHONOGRAPHISTS
PHONOGRAPHS
PHONOGRAPHY
PHONOLITES
PHONOLITIC
PHONOLOGIC
PHONOLOGICAL
PHONOLOGICALLY
PHONOLOGIES
PHONOLOGIST
PHONOLOGISTS
PHONOMETER
PHONOMETERS
PHONOMETRIC
PHONOMETRICAL
PHONOPHOBIA
PHONOPHOBIAS
PHONOPHORE
PHONOPHORES
PHONOPORES
PHONOSCOPE
PHONOSCOPES
PHONOTACTIC
PHONOTACTICS
PHONOTYPED
PHONOTYPER
PHONOTYPERS
PHONOTYPES
PHONOTYPIC
PHONOTYPICAL
PHONOTYPIES
PHONOTYPING
PHONOTYPIST
PHONOTYPISTS
PHORMINGES
PHOSGENITE
PHOSGENITES
PHOSPHATASE
PHOSPHATASES
PHOSPHATED
PHOSPHATES
PHOSPHATIC
PHOSPHATIDE
PHOSPHATIDES
PHOSPHATIDIC
PHOSPHATIDYL
PHOSPHATIDYLS
PHOSPHATING
PHOSPHATISATION
PHOSPHATISE
PHOSPHATISED
PHOSPHATISES
PHOSPHATISING
PHOSPHATIZATION
PHOSPHATIZE
PHOSPHATIZED
PHOSPHATIZES
PHOSPHATIZING
PHOSPHATURIA
PHOSPHATURIAS
PHOSPHATURIC
PHOSPHENES
PHOSPHIDES
PHOSPHINES
PHOSPHITES
PHOSPHOCREATIN
PHOSPHOCREATINE
PHOSPHOCREATINS
PHOSPHOKINASE
PHOSPHOKINASES
PHOSPHOLIPASE
PHOSPHOLIPASES
PHOSPHOLIPID
PHOSPHOLIPIDS
PHOSPHONIC
PHOSPHONIUM
PHOSPHONIUMS
PHOSPHOPROTEIN
PHOSPHOPROTEINS
PHOSPHORATE
PHOSPHORATED
PHOSPHORATES
PHOSPHORATING
PHOSPHORES
PHOSPHORESCE
PHOSPHORESCED
PHOSPHORESCENCE
PHOSPHORESCENT
PHOSPHORESCES
PHOSPHORESCING
PHOSPHORET
PHOSPHORETS
PHOSPHORETTED
PHOSPHORIC
PHOSPHORISE
PHOSPHORISED
PHOSPHORISES
PHOSPHORISING
PHOSPHORISM
PHOSPHORISMS
PHOSPHORITE
PHOSPHORITES
PHOSPHORITIC
PHOSPHORIZE
PHOSPHORIZED
PHOSPHORIZES
PHOSPHORIZING
PHOSPHOROLYSES
PHOSPHOROLYSIS
PHOSPHOROLYTIC
PHOSPHOROSCOPE
PHOSPHOROSCOPES
PHOSPHOROUS
PHOSPHORUS
PHOSPHORUSES
PHOSPHORYL
PHOSPHORYLASE
PHOSPHORYLASES
PHOSPHORYLATE
PHOSPHORYLATED
PHOSPHORYLATES
PHOSPHORYLATING
PHOSPHORYLATION
PHOSPHORYLATIVE
PHOSPHORYLS
PHOSPHURET
PHOSPHURETS
PHOSPHURETTED
PHOTICALLY
PHOTOACTINIC
PHOTOACTIVE
PHOTOAUTOTROPH
PHOTOAUTOTROPHS
PHOTOBATHIC
PHOTOBIOLOGIC
PHOTOBIOLOGICAL
PHOTOBIOLOGIES
PHOTOBIOLOGIST

PHOTOBIOLOGISTS
PHOTOBIOLOGY
PHOTOBLOGGED
PHOTOBLOGGING
PHOTOBLOGS
PHOTOBOMBED
PHOTOBOMBING
PHOTOBOMBS
PHOTOCALLS
PHOTOCARDS
PHOTOCATALYSES
PHOTOCATALYSIS
PHOTOCATALYTIC
PHOTOCATHODE
PHOTOCATHODES
PHOTOCELLS
PHOTOCHEMICAL
PHOTOCHEMICALLY
PHOTOCHEMIST
PHOTOCHEMISTRY
PHOTOCHEMISTS
PHOTOCHROMIC
PHOTOCHROMICS
PHOTOCHROMIES
PHOTOCHROMISM
PHOTOCHROMISMS
PHOTOCHROMY
PHOTOCOMPOSE
PHOTOCOMPOSED
PHOTOCOMPOSER
PHOTOCOMPOSERS
PHOTOCOMPOSES
PHOTOCOMPOSING
PHOTOCONDUCTING
PHOTOCONDUCTION
PHOTOCONDUCTIVE
PHOTOCONDUCTOR
PHOTOCONDUCTORS
PHOTOCOPIABLE
PHOTOCOPIED
PHOTOCOPIER
PHOTOCOPIERS
PHOTOCOPIES
PHOTOCOPYING
PHOTOCOPYINGS
PHOTOCURRENT
PHOTOCURRENTS
PHOTODEGRADABLE
PHOTODETECTOR
PHOTODETECTORS
PHOTODIODE
PHOTODIODES
PHOTODISKS
PHOTODISSOCIATE
PHOTODUPLICATE
PHOTODUPLICATED
PHOTODUPLICATES
PHOTODYNAMIC
PHOTODYNAMICS
PHOTOELASTIC
PHOTOELASTICITY
PHOTOELECTRIC
PHOTOELECTRICAL
PHOTOELECTRODE
PHOTOELECTRODES
PHOTOELECTRON
PHOTOELECTRONIC
PHOTOELECTRONS
PHOTOEMISSION
PHOTOEMISSIONS
PHOTOEMISSIVE
PHOTOENGRAVE
PHOTOENGRAVED
PHOTOENGRAVER
PHOTOENGRAVERS
PHOTOENGRAVES
PHOTOENGRAVING
PHOTOENGRAVINGS
PHOTOEXCITATION
PHOTOEXCITED
PHOTOFINISHER
PHOTOFINISHERS
PHOTOFINISHING
PHOTOFINISHINGS
PHOTOFISSION
PHOTOFISSIONS
PHOTOFLASH
PHOTOFLASHES
PHOTOFLOOD
PHOTOFLOODS
PHOTOFLUOROGRAM
PHOTOGELATIN
PHOTOGELATINE
PHOTOGENES
PHOTOGENIC
PHOTOGENICALLY
PHOTOGENIES
PHOTOGEOLOGIC
PHOTOGEOLOGICAL
PHOTOGEOLOGIES
PHOTOGEOLOGIST
PHOTOGEOLOGISTS
PHOTOGEOLOGY
PHOTOGLYPH
PHOTOGLYPHIC
PHOTOGLYPHIES
PHOTOGLYPHS
PHOTOGLYPHY
PHOTOGRAMMETRIC
PHOTOGRAMMETRY
PHOTOGRAMS
PHOTOGRAPH
PHOTOGRAPHED
PHOTOGRAPHER
PHOTOGRAPHERS
PHOTOGRAPHIC
PHOTOGRAPHICAL
PHOTOGRAPHIES
PHOTOGRAPHING
PHOTOGRAPHIST
PHOTOGRAPHISTS
PHOTOGRAPHS
PHOTOGRAPHY
PHOTOGRAVURE
PHOTOGRAVURES
PHOTOINDUCED
PHOTOINDUCTION
PHOTOINDUCTIONS
PHOTOINDUCTIVE
PHOTOIONISATION
PHOTOIONISE
PHOTOIONISED
PHOTOIONISES
PHOTOIONISING
PHOTOIONIZATION
PHOTOIONIZE
PHOTOIONIZED
PHOTOIONIZES
PHOTOIONIZING
PHOTOJOURNALISM
PHOTOJOURNALIST
PHOTOKINESES
PHOTOKINESIS
PHOTOKINETIC
PHOTOLITHO
PHOTOLITHOGRAPH
PHOTOLITHOS
PHOTOLUMINESCE
PHOTOLUMINESCED
PHOTOLUMINESCES
PHOTOLYSABLE
PHOTOLYSED
PHOTOLYSES
PHOTOLYSING
PHOTOLYSIS
PHOTOLYTIC
PHOTOLYTICALLY
PHOTOLYZABLE
PHOTOLYZED
PHOTOLYZES
PHOTOLYZING
PHOTOMACHINE
PHOTOMACHINES
PHOTOMACROGRAPH
PHOTOMAPPED
PHOTOMAPPING
PHOTOMASKS
PHOTOMECHANICAL
PHOTOMETER
PHOTOMETERS
PHOTOMETRIC
PHOTOMETRICALLY
PHOTOMETRIES
PHOTOMETRIST
PHOTOMETRISTS
PHOTOMETRY
PHOTOMICROGRAPH
PHOTOMONTAGE
PHOTOMONTAGES
PHOTOMOSAIC
PHOTOMOSAICS
PHOTOMULTIPLIER
PHOTOMURAL
PHOTOMURALS
PHOTONASTIC
PHOTONASTIES
PHOTONASTY
PHOTONEGATIVE
PHOTONEUTRON
PHOTONEUTRONS
PHOTONOVEL
PHOTONOVELS
PHOTONUCLEAR
PHOTOOXIDATION
PHOTOOXIDATIONS
PHOTOOXIDATIVE
PHOTOOXIDISE
PHOTOOXIDISED
PHOTOOXIDISES
PHOTOOXIDISING
PHOTOOXIDIZE
PHOTOOXIDIZED
PHOTOOXIDIZES
PHOTOOXIDIZING
PHOTOPERIOD
PHOTOPERIODIC
PHOTOPERIODISM
PHOTOPERIODISMS
PHOTOPERIODS
PHOTOPHASE
PHOTOPHASES
PHOTOPHILIC
PHOTOPHILIES
PHOTOPHILOUS
PHOTOPHILS
PHOTOPHILY
PHOTOPHOBE
PHOTOPHOBES
PHOTOPHOBIA
PHOTOPHOBIAS
PHOTOPHOBIC
PHOTOPHONE
PHOTOPHONES
PHOTOPHONIC
PHOTOPHONIES
PHOTOPHONY
PHOTOPHORE
PHOTOPHORES
PHOTOPHORESES
PHOTOPHORESIS
PHOTOPLAYS
PHOTOPOLYMER
PHOTOPOLYMERS
PHOTOPOSITIVE
PHOTOPRODUCT
PHOTOPRODUCTION
PHOTOPRODUCTS
PHOTOPSIAS
PHOTOPSIES
PHOTOREACTION

PHOTOREACTIONS
PHOTOREACTIVE
PHOTOREALISM
PHOTOREALISMS
PHOTOREALIST
PHOTOREALISTIC
PHOTOREALISTS
PHOTORECEPTION
PHOTORECEPTIONS
PHOTORECEPTIVE
PHOTORECEPTOR
PHOTORECEPTORS
PHOTOREDUCE
PHOTOREDUCED
PHOTOREDUCES
PHOTOREDUCING
PHOTOREDUCTION
PHOTOREDUCTIONS
PHOTOREFRACTIVE
PHOTORESIST
PHOTORESISTS
PHOTOSCANNED
PHOTOSCANNING
PHOTOSCANS
PHOTOSENSITISE
PHOTOSENSITISED
PHOTOSENSITISER
PHOTOSENSITISES
PHOTOSENSITIVE
PHOTOSENSITIZE
PHOTOSENSITIZED
PHOTOSENSITIZER
PHOTOSENSITIZES
PHOTOSENSOR
PHOTOSENSORS
PHOTOSETTER
PHOTOSETTERS
PHOTOSETTING
PHOTOSETTINGS
PHOTOSHOOT
PHOTOSHOOTS
PHOTOSHOPPED
PHOTOSHOPPING
PHOTOSHOPS
PHOTOSPHERE
PHOTOSPHERES
PHOTOSPHERIC
PHOTOSTATED
PHOTOSTATIC
PHOTOSTATING
PHOTOSTATS
PHOTOSTATTED
PHOTOSTATTING
PHOTOSYNTHATE
PHOTOSYNTHATES
PHOTOSYNTHESES
PHOTOSYNTHESIS
PHOTOSYNTHESISE
PHOTOSYNTHESIZE
PHOTOSYNTHETIC
PHOTOSYSTEM
PHOTOSYSTEMS
PHOTOTACTIC
PHOTOTACTICALLY
PHOTOTAXES
PHOTOTAXIES
PHOTOTAXIS
PHOTOTELEGRAM
PHOTOTELEGRAMS
PHOTOTELEGRAPH
PHOTOTELEGRAPHS
PHOTOTELEGRAPHY
PHOTOTHERAPIES
PHOTOTHERAPY
PHOTOTHERMAL
PHOTOTHERMALLY
PHOTOTHERMIC
PHOTOTONIC
PHOTOTONUS
PHOTOTONUSES
PHOTOTOPOGRAPHY
PHOTOTOXIC
PHOTOTOXICITIES
PHOTOTOXICITY
PHOTOTRANSISTOR
PHOTOTROPE
PHOTOTROPES
PHOTOTROPH
PHOTOTROPHIC
PHOTOTROPHS
PHOTOTROPIC
PHOTOTROPICALLY
PHOTOTROPIES
PHOTOTROPISM
PHOTOTROPISMS
PHOTOTROPY
PHOTOTUBES
PHOTOTYPED
PHOTOTYPES
PHOTOTYPESET
PHOTOTYPESETS
PHOTOTYPESETTER
PHOTOTYPIC
PHOTOTYPICALLY
PHOTOTYPIES
PHOTOTYPING
PHOTOTYPOGRAPHY
PHOTOVOLTAIC
PHOTOVOLTAICS
PHOTOXYLOGRAPHY
PHOTOZINCOGRAPH
PHRAGMOPLAST
PHRAGMOPLASTS
PHRASELESS
PHRASEMAKER
PHRASEMAKERS
PHRASEMAKING
PHRASEMAKINGS
PHRASEMONGER
PHRASEMONGERING
PHRASEMONGERS
PHRASEOGRAM
PHRASEOGRAMS
PHRASEOGRAPH
PHRASEOGRAPHIC
PHRASEOGRAPHIES
PHRASEOGRAPHS
PHRASEOGRAPHY
PHRASEOLOGIC
PHRASEOLOGICAL
PHRASEOLOGIES
PHRASEOLOGIST
PHRASEOLOGISTS
PHRASEOLOGY
PHREAKINGS
PHREATOPHYTE
PHREATOPHYTES
PHREATOPHYTIC
PHRENESIAC
PHRENETICAL
PHRENETICALLY
PHRENETICNESS
PHRENETICNESSES
PHRENETICS
PHRENITIDES
PHRENITISES
PHRENOLOGIC
PHRENOLOGICAL
PHRENOLOGICALLY
PHRENOLOGIES
PHRENOLOGISE
PHRENOLOGISED
PHRENOLOGISES
PHRENOLOGISING
PHRENOLOGIST
PHRENOLOGISTS
PHRENOLOGIZE
PHRENOLOGIZED
PHRENOLOGIZES
PHRENOLOGIZING
PHRENOLOGY
PHRENSICAL
PHRENSYING
PHRONTISTERIES
PHRONTISTERY
PHTHALATES
PHTHALEINS
PHTHALOCYANIN
PHTHALOCYANINE
PHTHALOCYANINES
PHTHALOCYANINS
PHTHIRIASES
PHTHIRIASIS
PHTHISICAL
PHTHISICKY
PHYCOBILIN
PHYCOBILINS
PHYCOBIONT
PHYCOBIONTS
PHYCOCYANIN
PHYCOCYANINS
PHYCOCYANS
PHYCOERYTHRIN
PHYCOERYTHRINS
PHYCOLOGICAL
PHYCOLOGIES
PHYCOLOGIST
PHYCOLOGISTS
PHYCOMYCETE
PHYCOMYCETES
PHYCOMYCETOUS
PHYCOPHAEIN
PHYCOPHAEINS
PHYCOXANTHIN
PHYCOXANTHINS
PHYLACTERIC
PHYLACTERICAL
PHYLACTERIES
PHYLACTERY
PHYLARCHIES
PHYLAXISES
PHYLESISES
PHYLETICALLY
PHYLLARIES
PHYLLOCLAD
PHYLLOCLADE
PHYLLOCLADES
PHYLLOCLADS
PHYLLODIAL
PHYLLODIES
PHYLLODIUM
PHYLLOMANIA
PHYLLOMANIAS
PHYLLOPHAGOUS
PHYLLOPLANE
PHYLLOPLANES
PHYLLOPODS
PHYLLOQUINONE
PHYLLOQUINONES
PHYLLOSILICATE
PHYLLOSILICATES
PHYLLOSPHERE
PHYLLOSPHERES
PHYLLOTACTIC
PHYLLOTACTICAL
PHYLLOTAXES
PHYLLOTAXIES
PHYLLOTAXIS
PHYLLOTAXY
PHYLLOXERA
PHYLLOXERAE
PHYLLOXERAS
PHYLOGENESES
PHYLOGENESIS
PHYLOGENETIC
PHYLOGENIC
PHYLOGENIES
PHYSALISES
PHYSHARMONICA
PHYSHARMONICAS

PHYSIATRIC
PHYSIATRICAL
PHYSIATRICS
PHYSIATRIES
PHYSIATRIST
PHYSIATRISTS
PHYSICALISM
PHYSICALISMS
PHYSICALIST
PHYSICALISTIC
PHYSICALISTS
PHYSICALITIES
PHYSICALITY
PHYSICALLY
PHYSICALNESS
PHYSICALNESSES
PHYSICIANCIES
PHYSICIANCY
PHYSICIANER
PHYSICIANERS
PHYSICIANS
PHYSICIANSHIP
PHYSICIANSHIPS
PHYSICISMS
PHYSICISTS
PHYSICKING
PHYSICOCHEMICAL
PHYSIOCRACIES
PHYSIOCRACY
PHYSIOCRAT
PHYSIOCRATIC
PHYSIOCRATS
PHYSIOGNOMIC
PHYSIOGNOMICAL
PHYSIOGNOMIES
PHYSIOGNOMIST
PHYSIOGNOMISTS
PHYSIOGNOMY
PHYSIOGRAPHER
PHYSIOGRAPHERS
PHYSIOGRAPHIC
PHYSIOGRAPHICAL
PHYSIOGRAPHIES
PHYSIOGRAPHY
PHYSIOLATER
PHYSIOLATERS
PHYSIOLATRIES
PHYSIOLATRY
PHYSIOLOGIC
PHYSIOLOGICAL
PHYSIOLOGICALLY
PHYSIOLOGIES
PHYSIOLOGIST
PHYSIOLOGISTS
PHYSIOLOGUS
PHYSIOLOGUSES
PHYSIOLOGY
PHYSIOPATHOLOGY
PHYSIOTHERAPIES
PHYSIOTHERAPIST
PHYSIOTHERAPY
PHYSITHEISM
PHYSITHEISMS
PHYSITHEISTIC
PHYSOCLISTOUS
PHYSOSTIGMIN
PHYSOSTIGMINE
PHYSOSTIGMINES
PHYSOSTIGMINS
PHYSOSTOMOUS
PHYTOALEXIN
PHYTOALEXINS
PHYTOBENTHOS
PHYTOBENTHOSES
PHYTOCHEMICAL
PHYTOCHEMICALLY
PHYTOCHEMICALS
PHYTOCHEMIST
PHYTOCHEMISTRY
PHYTOCHEMISTS
PHYTOCHROME
PHYTOCHROMES
PHYTOESTROGEN
PHYTOESTROGENS
PHYTOFLAGELLATE
PHYTOGENESES
PHYTOGENESIS
PHYTOGENETIC
PHYTOGENETICAL
PHYTOGENIC
PHYTOGENIES
PHYTOGEOGRAPHER
PHYTOGEOGRAPHIC
PHYTOGEOGRAPHY
PHYTOGRAPHER
PHYTOGRAPHERS
PHYTOGRAPHIC
PHYTOGRAPHIES
PHYTOGRAPHY
PHYTOHORMONE
PHYTOHORMONES
PHYTOLITHS
PHYTOLOGICAL
PHYTOLOGICALLY
PHYTOLOGIES
PHYTOLOGIST
PHYTOLOGISTS
PHYTONADIONE
PHYTONADIONES
PHYTOPATHOGEN
PHYTOPATHOGENIC
PHYTOPATHOGENS
PHYTOPATHOLOGY
PHYTOPHAGIC
PHYTOPHAGIES
PHYTOPHAGOUS
PHYTOPHAGY
PHYTOPLANKTER
PHYTOPLANKTERS
PHYTOPLANKTON
PHYTOPLANKTONIC
PHYTOPLANKTONS
PHYTOSANITARY
PHYTOSOCIOLOGY
PHYTOSTEROL
PHYTOSTEROLS
PHYTOTHERAPIES
PHYTOTHERAPY
PHYTOTOMIES
PHYTOTOMIST
PHYTOTOMISTS
PHYTOTOXIC
PHYTOTOXICITIES
PHYTOTOXICITY
PHYTOTOXIN
PHYTOTOXINS
PHYTOTRONS
PIACULARITIES
PIACULARITY
PIANISSIMI
PIANISSIMO
PIANISSIMOS
PIANISSISSIMO
PIANISTICALLY
PIANOFORTE
PIANOFORTES
PIANOLISTS
PICADILLOS
PICANINNIES
PICARESQUE
PICARESQUES
PICAROONED
PICAROONING
PICAYUNISH
PICAYUNISHLY
PICAYUNISHNESS
PICCADILLIES
PICCADILLO
PICCADILLOES
PICCADILLOS
PICCADILLS
PICCADILLY
PICCALILLI
PICCALILLIS
PICCANINNIES
PICCANINNY
PICCOLOIST
PICCOLOISTS
PICHICIAGO
PICHICIAGOS
PICHICIEGO
PICHICIEGOS
PICHOLINES
PICKABACKED
PICKABACKING
PICKABACKS
PICKADILLIES
PICKADILLO
PICKADILLOES
PICKADILLOS
PICKADILLS
PICKADILLY
PICKANINNIES
PICKANINNY
PICKAPACKED
PICKAPACKING
PICKAPACKS
PICKAROONS
PICKBACKED
PICKBACKING
PICKEDNESS
PICKEDNESSES
PICKEERERS
PICKEERING
PICKELHAUBE
PICKELHAUBES
PICKERELWEED
PICKERELWEEDS
PICKETBOAT
PICKETBOATS
PICKETINGS
PICKINESSES
PICKPOCKET
PICKPOCKETED
PICKPOCKETING
PICKPOCKETS
PICKTHANKS
PICNICKERS
PICNICKIER
PICNICKIEST
PICNICKING
PICOCURIES
PICOFARADS
PICOMETERS
PICOMETRES
PICORNAVIRUS
PICORNAVIRUSES
PICOSECOND
PICOSECONDS
PICOWAVING
PICQUETING
PICROCARMINE
PICROCARMINES
PICROTOXIN
PICROTOXINS
PICTARNIES
PICTOGRAMS
PICTOGRAPH
PICTOGRAPHIC
PICTOGRAPHIES
PICTOGRAPHS
PICTOGRAPHY
PICTORIALISE
PICTORIALISED
PICTORIALISES
PICTORIALISING
PICTORIALISM
PICTORIALISMS
PICTORIALIST
PICTORIALISTS

P

PICTORIALIZE
PICTORIALIZED
PICTORIALIZES
PICTORIALIZING
PICTORIALLY
PICTORIALNESS
PICTORIALNESSES
PICTORIALS
PICTORICAL
PICTORICALLY
PICTUREGOER
PICTUREGOERS
PICTUREPHONE
PICTUREPHONES
PICTURESQUE
PICTURESQUELY
PICTURESQUENESS
PICTURISATION
PICTURISATIONS
PICTURISED
PICTURISES
PICTURISING
PICTURIZATION
PICTURIZATIONS
PICTURIZED
PICTURIZES
PICTURIZING
PIDDLINGLY
PIDGINISATION
PIDGINISATIONS
PIDGINISED
PIDGINISES
PIDGINISING
PIDGINIZATION
PIDGINIZATIONS
PIDGINIZED
PIDGINIZES
PIDGINIZING
PIECEMEALED
PIECEMEALING
PIECEMEALS
PIECEWORKER
PIECEWORKERS
PIECEWORKS
PIEDMONTITE
PIEDMONTITES
PIEDNESSES
PIEMONTITE
PIEMONTITES
PIEPOWDERS
PIERCEABLE
PIERCINGLY
PIERCINGNESS
PIERCINGNESSES
PIERRETTES
PIETISTICAL
PIETISTICALLY
PIEZOCHEMISTRY
PIEZOELECTRIC
PIEZOMAGNETIC
PIEZOMAGNETISM
PIEZOMAGNETISMS
PIEZOMETER
PIEZOMETERS
PIEZOMETRIC
PIEZOMETRICALLY
PIEZOMETRIES
PIEZOMETRY
PIFFERAROS
PIGEONHOLE
PIGEONHOLED
PIGEONHOLER
PIGEONHOLERS
PIGEONHOLES
PIGEONHOLING
PIGEONITES
PIGEONRIES
PIGEONWING
PIGEONWINGS
PIGGINESSES
PIGGISHNESS
PIGGISHNESSES
PIGGYBACKED
PIGGYBACKING
PIGGYBACKS
PIGHEADEDLY
PIGHEADEDNESS
PIGHEADEDNESSES
PIGMENTARY
PIGMENTATION
PIGMENTATIONS
PIGMENTING
PIGMENTOSA
PIGMENTOSAS
PIGNERATED
PIGNERATES
PIGNERATING
PIGNERATION
PIGNERATIONS
PIGNORATED
PIGNORATES
PIGNORATING
PIGNORATION
PIGNORATIONS
PIGSCONCES
PIGSTICKED
PIGSTICKER
PIGSTICKERS
PIGSTICKING
PIGSTICKINGS
PIKEPERCHES
PIKESTAFFS
PIKESTAVES
PILASTERED
PILEORHIZA
PILEORHIZAS
PILFERABLE
PILFERAGES
PILFERINGLY
PILFERINGS
PILFERPROOF
PILGARLICK
PILGARLICKS
PILGARLICKY
PILGARLICS
PILGRIMAGE
PILGRIMAGED
PILGRIMAGER
PILGRIMAGERS
PILGRIMAGES
PILGRIMAGING
PILGRIMERS
PILGRIMING
PILGRIMISE
PILGRIMISED
PILGRIMISES
PILGRIMISING
PILGRIMIZE
PILGRIMIZED
PILGRIMIZES
PILGRIMIZING
PILIFEROUS
PILLAGINGS
PILLARISTS
PILLARLESS
PILLICOCKS
PILLIONING
PILLIONIST
PILLIONISTS
PILLIWINKS
PILLORISED
PILLORISES
PILLORISING
PILLORIZED
PILLORIZES
PILLORIZING
PILLORYING
PILLOWCASE
PILLOWCASES
PILLOWIEST
PILLOWSLIP
PILLOWSLIPS
PILNIEWINKS
PILOCARPIN
PILOCARPINE
PILOCARPINES
PILOCARPINS
PILOSITIES
PILOTFISHES
PILOTHOUSE
PILOTHOUSES
PIMPERNELS
PIMPLINESS
PIMPLINESSES
PIMPMOBILE
PIMPMOBILES
PINACOIDAL
PINACOTHECA
PINACOTHECAE
PINAKOIDAL
PINAKOTHEK
PINAKOTHEKS
PINBALLING
PINCERLIKE
PINCHBECKS
PINCHCOCKS
PINCHCOMMONS
PINCHCOMMONSES
PINCHFISTS
PINCHINGLY
PINCHPENNIES
PINCHPENNY
PINCHPOINT
PINCHPOINTS
PINCUSHION
PINCUSHIONS
PINEALECTOMIES
PINEALECTOMISE
PINEALECTOMISED
PINEALECTOMISES
PINEALECTOMIZE
PINEALECTOMIZED
PINEALECTOMIZES
PINEALECTOMY
PINEAPPLES
PINFEATHER
PINFEATHERS
PINFOLDING
PINGRASSES
PINGUEFIED
PINGUEFIES
PINGUEFYING
PINGUIDITIES
PINGUIDITY
PINGUITUDE
PINGUITUDES
PINHEADEDNESS
PINHEADEDNESSES
PINHOOKERS
PINKERTONS
PINKINESSES
PINKISHNESS
PINKISHNESSES
PINKNESSES
PINNACLING
PINNATIFID
PINNATIFIDLY
PINNATIONS
PINNATIPARTITE
PINNATIPED
PINNATISECT
PINNIEWINKLE
PINNIEWINKLES
PINNIPEDES
PINNIPEDIAN
PINNIPEDIANS
PINNULATED
PINNYWINKLE
PINNYWINKLES
PINOCYTOSES

PINOCYTOSIS
PINOCYTOTIC
PINOCYTOTICALLY
PINPOINTED
PINPOINTING
PINPRICKED
PINPRICKING
PINSETTERS
PINSPOTTED
PINSPOTTER
PINSPOTTERS
PINSPOTTING
PINSTRIPED
PINSTRIPES
PINTADERAS
PINTUCKING
PINTUCKINGS
PINWHEELED
PINWHEELING
PINWRENCHES
PIONEERING
PIOUSNESSES
PIPECLAYED
PIPECLAYING
PIPEFISHES
PIPEFITTER
PIPEFITTERS
PIPEFITTING
PIPEFITTINGS
PIPELINING
PIPELININGS
PIPERACEOUS
PIPERAZINE
PIPERAZINES
PIPERIDINE
PIPERIDINES
PIPERONALS
PIPESTONES
PIPINESSES
PIPISTRELLE
PIPISTRELLES
PIPISTRELS
PIPIWHARAUROA
PIPIWHARAUROAS
PIPSISSEWA
PIPSISSEWAS
PIPSQUEAKS
PIQUANCIES
PIQUANTNESS
PIQUANTNESSES
PIRACETAMS
PIRATICALLY
PIRLICUING
PIROPLASMA
PIROPLASMATA
PIROPLASMS
PIROUETTED
PIROUETTER
PIROUETTERS
PIROUETTES
PIROUETTING
PISCATORIAL
PISCATORIALLY
PISCATRIXES
PISCICOLOUS
PISCICULTURAL
PISCICULTURALLY
PISCICULTURE
PISCICULTURES
PISCICULTURIST
PISCICULTURISTS
PISCIFAUNA
PISCIFAUNAE
PISCIFAUNAS
PISCIVORES
PISCIVOROUS
PISSASPHALT
PISSASPHALTS
PISTACHIOS
PISTAREENS
PISTILLARY
PISTILLATE
PISTILLODE
PISTILLODES
PISTOLEERS
PISTOLEROS
PISTOLIERS
PISTOLLING
PITAPATTED
PITAPATTING
PITCHBENDS
PITCHBLENDE
PITCHBLENDES
PITCHERFUL
PITCHERFULS
PITCHERSFUL
PITCHFORKED
PITCHFORKING
PITCHFORKS
PITCHINESS
PITCHINESSES
PITCHOMETER
PITCHOMETERS
PITCHPERSON
PITCHPERSONS
PITCHPINES
PITCHPIPES
PITCHPOLED
PITCHPOLES
PITCHPOLING
PITCHSTONE
PITCHSTONES
PITCHWOMAN
PITCHWOMEN
PITEOUSNESS
PITEOUSNESSES
PITHECANTHROPI
PITHECANTHROPUS
PITHECOIDS
PITHINESSES
PITIABLENESS
PITIABLENESSES
PITIFULLER
PITIFULLEST
PITIFULNESS
PITIFULNESSES
PITILESSLY
PITILESSNESS
PITILESSNESSES
PITTOSPORUM
PITTOSPORUMS
PITUITARIES
PITUITRINS
PITYRIASES
PITYRIASIS
PITYROSPORUM
PITYROSPORUMS
PIWAKAWAKA
PIWAKAWAKAS
PIXELATING
PIXELATION
PIXELATIONS
PIXELLATED
PIXELLATES
PIXELLATING
PIXELLATION
PIXELLATIONS
PIXILATING
PIXILATION
PIXILATIONS
PIXILLATED
PIXILLATES
PIXILLATING
PIXILLATION
PIXILLATIONS
PIXINESSES
PIZAZZIEST
PIZZAZZIER
PIZZAZZIEST
PIZZICATOS
PLACABILITIES
PLACABILITY
PLACABLENESS
PLACABLENESSES
PLACARDING
PLACATINGLY
PLACATIONS
PLACEHOLDER
PLACEHOLDERS
PLACEKICKED
PLACEKICKER
PLACEKICKERS
PLACEKICKING
PLACEKICKS
PLACELESSLY
PLACEMENTS
PLACENTALS
PLACENTATE
PLACENTATION
PLACENTATIONS
PLACENTIFORM
PLACENTOLOGIES
PLACENTOLOGY
PLACIDITIES
PLACIDNESS
PLACIDNESSES
PLACODERMS
PLAGIARIES
PLAGIARISE
PLAGIARISED
PLAGIARISER
PLAGIARISERS
PLAGIARISES
PLAGIARISING
PLAGIARISM
PLAGIARISMS
PLAGIARIST
PLAGIARISTIC
PLAGIARISTS
PLAGIARIZE
PLAGIARIZED
PLAGIARIZER
PLAGIARIZERS
PLAGIARIZES
PLAGIARIZING
PLAGIOCEPHALIES
PLAGIOCEPHALY
PLAGIOCLASE
PLAGIOCLASES
PLAGIOCLASTIC
PLAGIOCLIMAX
PLAGIOCLIMAXES
PLAGIOSTOMATOUS
PLAGIOSTOME
PLAGIOSTOMES
PLAGIOSTOMOUS
PLAGIOTROPIC
PLAGIOTROPISM
PLAGIOTROPISMS
PLAGIOTROPOUS
PLAGUELIKE
PLAGUESOME
PLAINCHANT
PLAINCHANTS
PLAINCLOTHES
PLAINCLOTHESMAN
PLAINCLOTHESMEN
PLAINNESSES
PLAINSONGS
PLAINSPOKEN
PLAINSPOKENNESS
PLAINSTANES
PLAINSTONES
PLAINTEXTS
PLAINTIFFS
PLAINTIVELY
PLAINTIVENESS
PLAINTIVENESSES
PLAINTLESS
PLAINWORKS

PLAISTERED
PLAISTERING
PLANARIANS
PLANARITIES
PLANATIONS
PLANCHETTE
PLANCHETTES
PLANELOADS
PLANENESSES
PLANESIDES
PLANETARIA
PLANETARIES
PLANETARIUM
PLANETARIUMS
PLANETESIMAL
PLANETESIMALS
PLANETICAL
PLANETLIKE
PLANETOIDAL
PLANETOIDS
PLANETOLOGICAL
PLANETOLOGIES
PLANETOLOGIST
PLANETOLOGISTS
PLANETOLOGY
PLANETWIDE
PLANGENCIES
PLANGENTLY
PLANIGRAMS
PLANIGRAPH
PLANIGRAPHIES
PLANIGRAPHS
PLANIGRAPHY
PLANIMETER
PLANIMETERS
PLANIMETRIC
PLANIMETRICAL
PLANIMETRICALLY
PLANIMETRIES
PLANIMETRY
PLANISHERS
PLANISHING
PLANISPHERE
PLANISPHERES
PLANISPHERIC
PLANKTONIC
PLANLESSLY
PLANLESSNESS
PLANLESSNESSES
PLANOBLAST
PLANOBLASTS
PLANOCONVEX
PLANOGAMETE
PLANOGAMETES
PLANOGRAMS
PLANOGRAPHIC
PLANOGRAPHIES
PLANOGRAPHY
PLANOMETER
PLANOMETERS
PLANOMETRIC
PLANOMETRICALLY
PLANOMETRIES
PLANOMETRY
PLANTAGINACEOUS
PLANTATION
PLANTATIONS
PLANTIGRADE
PLANTIGRADES
PLANTLINGS
PLANTOCRACIES
PLANTOCRACY
PLANTSWOMAN
PLANTSWOMEN
PLANULIFORM
PLAQUETTES
PLASMAGELS
PLASMAGENE
PLASMAGENES
PLASMAGENIC
PLASMALEMMA
PLASMALEMMAS
PLASMAPHERESES
PLASMAPHERESIS
PLASMASOLS
PLASMATICAL
PLASMINOGEN
PLASMINOGENS
PLASMODESM
PLASMODESMA
PLASMODESMAS
PLASMODESMATA
PLASMODESMS
PLASMODIAL
PLASMODIUM
PLASMOGAMIES
PLASMOGAMY
PLASMOLYSE
PLASMOLYSED
PLASMOLYSES
PLASMOLYSING
PLASMOLYSIS
PLASMOLYTIC
PLASMOLYTICALLY
PLASMOLYZE
PLASMOLYZED
PLASMOLYZES
PLASMOLYZING
PLASMOSOMA
PLASMOSOMATA
PLASMOSOME
PLASMOSOMES
PLASTERBOARD
PLASTERBOARDS
PLASTERERS
PLASTERIER
PLASTERIEST
PLASTERINESS
PLASTERINESSES
PLASTERING
PLASTERINGS
PLASTERSTONE
PLASTERSTONES
PLASTERWORK
PLASTERWORKS
PLASTICALLY
PLASTICATED
PLASTICENE
PLASTICENES
PLASTICINE
PLASTICINES
PLASTICISATION
PLASTICISATIONS
PLASTICISE
PLASTICISED
PLASTICISER
PLASTICISERS
PLASTICISES
PLASTICISING
PLASTICITIES
PLASTICITY
PLASTICIZATION
PLASTICIZATIONS
PLASTICIZE
PLASTICIZED
PLASTICIZER
PLASTICIZERS
PLASTICIZES
PLASTICIZING
PLASTICKIER
PLASTICKIEST
PLASTIDIAL
PLASTIDULE
PLASTIDULES
PLASTILINA
PLASTILINAS
PLASTINATION
PLASTINATIONS
PLASTIQUES
PLASTISOLS
PLASTOCYANIN
PLASTOCYANINS
PLASTOGAMIES
PLASTOGAMY
PLASTOMETER
PLASTOMETERS
PLASTOMETRIC
PLASTOMETRIES
PLASTOMETRY
PLASTOQUINONE
PLASTOQUINONES
PLATANACEOUS
PLATEAUING
PLATEGLASS
PLATEGLASSES
PLATELAYER
PLATELAYERS
PLATELAYING
PLATELAYINGS
PLATEMAKER
PLATEMAKERS
PLATEMAKING
PLATEMAKINGS
PLATEMARKED
PLATEMARKING
PLATEMARKS
PLATERESQUE
PLATFORMED
PLATFORMER
PLATFORMERS
PLATFORMING
PLATFORMINGS
PLATINIFEROUS
PLATINIRIDIUM
PLATINIRIDIUMS
PLATINISATION
PLATINISATIONS
PLATINISED
PLATINISES
PLATINISING
PLATINIZATION
PLATINIZATIONS
PLATINIZED
PLATINIZES
PLATINIZING
PLATINOCYANIC
PLATINOCYANIDE
PLATINOCYANIDES
PLATINOIDS
PLATINOTYPE
PLATINOTYPES
PLATITUDES
PLATITUDINAL
PLATITUDINARIAN
PLATITUDINISE
PLATITUDINISED
PLATITUDINISER
PLATITUDINISERS
PLATITUDINISES
PLATITUDINISING
PLATITUDINIZE
PLATITUDINIZED
PLATITUDINIZER
PLATITUDINIZERS
PLATITUDINIZES
PLATITUDINIZING
PLATITUDINOUS
PLATITUDINOUSLY
PLATONICALLY
PLATONISMS
PLATOONING
PLATTELAND
PLATTELANDS
PLATTERFUL
PLATTERFULS
PLATTERSFUL
PLATYCEPHALIC
PLATYCEPHALOUS
PLATYFISHES
PLATYHELMINTH

PLATYHELMINTHIC
PLATYHELMINTHS
PLATYKURTIC
PLATYPUSES
PLATYRRHINE
PLATYRRHINES
PLATYRRHINIAN
PLATYRRHINIANS
PLAUDITORY
PLAUSIBILITIES
PLAUSIBILITY
PLAUSIBLENESS
PLAUSIBLENESSES
PLAYABILITIES
PLAYABILITY
PLAYACTING
PLAYACTINGS
PLAYACTORS
PLAYBUSSES
PLAYDOUGHS
PLAYFELLOW
PLAYFELLOWS
PLAYFIELDS
PLAYFULNESS
PLAYFULNESSES
PLAYGOINGS
PLAYGROUND
PLAYGROUNDS
PLAYGROUPS
PLAYHOUSES
PLAYLEADER
PLAYLEADERS
PLAYLISTED
PLAYLISTING
PLAYMAKERS
PLAYMAKING
PLAYMAKINGS
PLAYREADER
PLAYREADERS
PLAYSCHOOL
PLAYSCHOOLS
PLAYTHINGS
PLAYWRIGHT
PLAYWRIGHTING
PLAYWRIGHTINGS
PLAYWRIGHTS
PLAYWRITING
PLAYWRITINGS
PLEADINGLY
PLEASANCES
PLEASANTER
PLEASANTEST
PLEASANTLY
PLEASANTNESS
PLEASANTNESSES
PLEASANTRIES
PLEASANTRY
PLEASINGLY
PLEASINGNESS
PLEASINGNESSES
PLEASURABILITY
PLEASURABLE
PLEASURABLENESS
PLEASURABLY
PLEASUREFUL
PLEASURELESS
PLEASURERS
PLEASURING
PLEBEIANISE
PLEBEIANISED
PLEBEIANISES
PLEBEIANISING
PLEBEIANISM
PLEBEIANISMS
PLEBEIANIZE
PLEBEIANIZED
PLEBEIANIZES
PLEBEIANIZING
PLEBEIANLY
PLEBIFICATION
PLEBIFICATIONS
PLEBIFYING
PLEBISCITARY
PLEBISCITE
PLEBISCITES
PLECOPTERAN
PLECOPTERANS
PLECOPTEROUS
PLECTOGNATH
PLECTOGNATHIC
PLECTOGNATHOUS
PLECTOGNATHS
PLECTOPTEROUS
PLEDGEABLE
PLEINAIRISM
PLEINAIRISMS
PLEINAIRIST
PLEINAIRISTS
PLEIOCHASIA
PLEIOCHASIUM
PLEIOMERIES
PLEIOMEROUS
PLEIOTAXIES
PLEIOTROPIC
PLEIOTROPIES
PLEIOTROPISM
PLEIOTROPISMS
PLEIOTROPY
PLENARTIES
PLENILUNAR
PLENILUNES
PLENIPOTENCE
PLENIPOTENCES
PLENIPOTENCIES
PLENIPOTENCY
PLENIPOTENT
PLENIPOTENTIAL
PLENIPOTENTIARY
PLENISHERS
PLENISHING
PLENISHINGS
PLENISHMENT
PLENISHMENTS
PLENITUDES
PLENITUDINOUS
PLENTEOUSLY
PLENTEOUSNESS
PLENTEOUSNESSES
PLENTIFULLY
PLENTIFULNESS
PLENTIFULNESSES
PLENTITUDE
PLENTITUDES
PLEOCHROIC
PLEOCHROISM
PLEOCHROISMS
PLEOMORPHIC
PLEOMORPHIES
PLEOMORPHISM
PLEOMORPHISMS
PLEOMORPHOUS
PLEOMORPHY
PLEONASTES
PLEONASTIC
PLEONASTICAL
PLEONASTICALLY
PLEONECTIC
PLEONEXIAS
PLEROCERCOID
PLEROCERCOIDS
PLEROMATIC
PLEROPHORIA
PLEROPHORIAS
PLEROPHORIES
PLEROPHORY
PLESIOSAUR
PLESIOSAURIAN
PLESIOSAURIANS
PLESIOSAURS
PLESSIMETER
PLESSIMETERS
PLESSIMETRIC
PLESSIMETRIES
PLESSIMETRY
PLETHORICAL
PLETHORICALLY
PLETHYSMOGRAM
PLETHYSMOGRAMS
PLETHYSMOGRAPH
PLETHYSMOGRAPHS
PLETHYSMOGRAPHY
PLEURAPOPHYSES
PLEURAPOPHYSIS
PLEURISIES
PLEURITICAL
PLEURITICS
PLEURITISES
PLEUROCARPOUS
PLEUROCENTESES
PLEUROCENTESIS
PLEURODONT
PLEURODONTS
PLEURODYNIA
PLEURODYNIAS
PLEURONIAS
PLEUROPNEUMONIA
PLEUROTOMIES
PLEUROTOMY
PLEUSTONIC
PLEXIGLASS
PLEXIGLASSES
PLEXIMETER
PLEXIMETERS
PLEXIMETRIC
PLEXIMETRIES
PLEXIMETRY
PLIABILITIES
PLIABILITY
PLIABLENESS
PLIABLENESSES
PLIANTNESS
PLIANTNESSES
PLICATENESS
PLICATENESSES
PLICATIONS
PLICATURES
PLODDINGLY
PLODDINGNESS
PLODDINGNESSES
PLOTLESSNESS
PLOTLESSNESSES
PLOTTERING
PLOTTINGLY
PLOUGHABLE
PLOUGHBACK
PLOUGHBACKS
PLOUGHBOYS
PLOUGHGATE
PLOUGHGATES
PLOUGHHEAD
PLOUGHHEADS
PLOUGHINGS
PLOUGHLAND
PLOUGHLANDS
PLOUGHMANSHIP
PLOUGHMANSHIPS
PLOUGHSHARE
PLOUGHSHARES
PLOUGHSTAFF
PLOUGHSTAFFS
PLOUGHTAIL
PLOUGHTAILS
PLOUGHWISE
PLOUGHWRIGHT
PLOUGHWRIGHTS
PLOUTERING
PLOVERIEST
PLOWMANSHIP
PLOWMANSHIPS
PLOWSHARES

P

PLOWSTAFFS
PLOWTERING
PLOWWRIGHT
PLOWWRIGHTS
PLUCKINESS
PLUCKINESSES
PLUGBOARDS
PLUGUGLIES
PLUMASSIER
PLUMASSIERS
PLUMBAGINACEOUS
PLUMBAGINOUS
PLUMBERIES
PLUMBIFEROUS
PLUMBISOLVENCY
PLUMBISOLVENT
PLUMBNESSES
PLUMBOSOLVENCY
PLUMBOSOLVENT
PLUMDAMASES
PLUMIGEROUS
PLUMMETING
PLUMOSITIES
PLUMPENING
PLUMPNESSES
PLUMULACEOUS
PLUMULARIAN
PLUMULARIANS
PLUNDERABLE
PLUNDERAGE
PLUNDERAGES
PLUNDERERS
PLUNDERING
PLUNDEROUS
PLUPERFECT
PLUPERFECTS
PLURALISATION
PLURALISATIONS
PLURALISED
PLURALISER
PLURALISERS
PLURALISES
PLURALISING
PLURALISMS
PLURALISTIC
PLURALISTICALLY
PLURALISTS
PLURALITIES
PLURALIZATION
PLURALIZATIONS
PLURALIZED
PLURALIZER
PLURALIZERS
PLURALIZES
PLURALIZING
PLURILITERAL
PLURILOCULAR
PLURIPARAE
PLURIPARAS
PLURIPOTENT
PLURIPRESENCE
PLURIPRESENCES
PLURISERIAL
PLURISERIATE
PLUSHINESS
PLUSHINESSES
PLUSHNESSES
PLUTOCRACIES
PLUTOCRACY
PLUTOCRATIC
PLUTOCRATICAL
PLUTOCRATICALLY
PLUTOCRATS
PLUTOLATRIES
PLUTOLATRY
PLUTOLOGIES
PLUTOLOGIST
PLUTOLOGISTS
PLUTONISMS
PLUTONIUMS
PLUTONOMIES
PLUTONOMIST
PLUTONOMISTS
PLUVIOMETER
PLUVIOMETERS
PLUVIOMETRIC
PLUVIOMETRICAL
PLUVIOMETRIES
PLUVIOMETRY
PLYOMETRIC
PLYOMETRICS
PNEUMATHODE
PNEUMATHODES
PNEUMATICAL
PNEUMATICALLY
PNEUMATICITIES
PNEUMATICITY
PNEUMATICS
PNEUMATOLOGICAL
PNEUMATOLOGIES
PNEUMATOLOGIST
PNEUMATOLOGISTS
PNEUMATOLOGY
PNEUMATOLYSES
PNEUMATOLYSIS
PNEUMATOLYTIC
PNEUMATOMETER
PNEUMATOMETERS
PNEUMATOMETRIES
PNEUMATOMETRY
PNEUMATOPHORE
PNEUMATOPHORES
PNEUMECTOMIES
PNEUMECTOMY
PNEUMOBACILLI
PNEUMOBACILLUS
PNEUMOCOCCAL
PNEUMOCOCCI
PNEUMOCOCCUS
PNEUMOCONIOSES
PNEUMOCONIOSIS
PNEUMOCONIOTIC
PNEUMOCONIOTICS
PNEUMOCYSTIS
PNEUMOCYSTISES
PNEUMODYNAMICS
PNEUMOGASTRIC
PNEUMOGASTRICS
PNEUMOGRAM
PNEUMOGRAMS
PNEUMOGRAPH
PNEUMOGRAPHS
PNEUMOKONIOSES
PNEUMOKONIOSIS
PNEUMONECTOMIES
PNEUMONECTOMY
PNEUMONIAS
PNEUMONICS
PNEUMONITIDES
PNEUMONITIS
PNEUMONITISES
PNEUMONOLOGIES
PNEUMONOLOGIST
PNEUMONOLOGISTS
PNEUMONOLOGY
PNEUMOTHORACES
PNEUMOTHORAX
PNEUMOTHORAXES
POACHINESS
POACHINESSES
POCKETABLE
POCKETBIKE
POCKETBIKES
POCKETBOOK
POCKETBOOKS
POCKETFULS
POCKETKNIFE
POCKETKNIVES
POCKETLESS
POCKETPHONE
POCKETPHONES
POCKETSFUL
POCKMANKIES
POCKMANTIE
POCKMANTIES
POCKMARKED
POCKMARKING
POCKPITTED
POCOCURANTE
POCOCURANTEISM
POCOCURANTEISMS
POCOCURANTES
POCOCURANTISM
POCOCURANTISMS
POCOCURANTIST
POCOCURANTISTS
POCULIFORM
PODAGRICAL
PODARGUSES
PODCASTERS
PODCASTING
PODCASTINGS
PODGINESSES
PODIATRIES
PODIATRIST
PODIATRISTS
PODOCONIOSES
PODOCONIOSIS
PODOLOGIES
PODOLOGIST
PODOLOGISTS
PODOPHTHALMOUS
PODOPHYLIN
PODOPHYLINS
PODOPHYLLI
PODOPHYLLIN
PODOPHYLLINS
PODOPHYLLUM
PODOPHYLLUMS
PODOSPHERE
PODOSPHERES
PODSOLISATION
PODSOLISATIONS
PODSOLISED
PODSOLISES
PODSOLISING
PODSOLIZATION
PODSOLIZATIONS
PODSOLIZED
PODSOLIZES
PODSOLIZING
PODZOLISATION
PODZOLISATIONS
PODZOLISED
PODZOLISES
PODZOLISING
PODZOLIZATION
PODZOLIZATIONS
PODZOLIZED
PODZOLIZES
PODZOLIZING
POENOLOGIES
POETASTERIES
POETASTERING
POETASTERINGS
POETASTERS
POETASTERY
POETASTRIES
POETICALLY
POETICALNESS
POETICALNESSES
POETICISED
POETICISES
POETICISING
POETICISMS
POETICIZED
POETICIZES
POETICIZING
POETICULES
POETRESSES

P

POGONOPHORAN
POGONOPHORANS
POGONOTOMIES
POGONOTOMY
POGROMISTS
POHUTUKAWA
POHUTUKAWAS
POIGNADOES
POIGNANCES
POIGNANCIES
POIGNANTLY
POIKILITIC
POIKILOCYTE
POIKILOCYTES
POIKILOTHERM
POIKILOTHERMAL
POIKILOTHERMIC
POIKILOTHERMIES
POIKILOTHERMISM
POIKILOTHERMS
POIKILOTHERMY
POINCIANAS
POINSETTIA
POINSETTIAS
POINTEDNESS
POINTEDNESSES
POINTELLES
POINTILLES
POINTILLISM
POINTILLISME
POINTILLISMES
POINTILLISMS
POINTILLIST
POINTILLISTE
POINTILLISTES
POINTILLISTIC
POINTILLISTS
POINTLESSLY
POINTLESSNESS
POINTLESSNESSES
POISONABLE
POISONINGS
POISONOUSLY
POISONOUSNESS
POISONOUSNESSES
POISONWOOD
POISONWOODS
POKEBERRIES
POKELOGANS
POKERISHLY
POKERWORKS
POKINESSES
POLARIMETER
POLARIMETERS
POLARIMETRIC
POLARIMETRIES
POLARIMETRY
POLARISABILITY
POLARISABLE
POLARISATION
POLARISATIONS
POLARISCOPE
POLARISCOPES
POLARISCOPIC
POLARISERS
POLARISING
POLARITIES
POLARIZABILITY
POLARIZABLE
POLARIZATION
POLARIZATIONS
POLARIZERS
POLARIZING
POLAROGRAM
POLAROGRAMS
POLAROGRAPH
POLAROGRAPHIC
POLAROGRAPHIES
POLAROGRAPHS
POLAROGRAPHY
POLEMARCHS
POLEMICALLY
POLEMICISE
POLEMICISED
POLEMICISES
POLEMICISING
POLEMICIST
POLEMICISTS
POLEMICIZE
POLEMICIZED
POLEMICIZES
POLEMICIZING
POLEMISING
POLEMIZING
POLEMONIACEOUS
POLEMONIUM
POLEMONIUMS
POLIANITES
POLICEWOMAN
POLICEWOMEN
POLICYHOLDER
POLICYHOLDERS
POLICYMAKER
POLICYMAKERS
POLIOMYELITIDES
POLIOMYELITIS
POLIOMYELITISES
POLIORCETIC
POLIORCETICS
POLIOVIRUS
POLIOVIRUSES
POLISHABLE
POLISHINGS
POLISHMENT
POLISHMENTS
POLITBUROS
POLITENESS
POLITENESSES
POLITESSES
POLITICALISE
POLITICALISED
POLITICALISES
POLITICALISING
POLITICALIZE
POLITICALIZED
POLITICALIZES
POLITICALIZING
POLITICALLY
POLITICASTER
POLITICASTERS
POLITICIAN
POLITICIANS
POLITICISATION
POLITICISATIONS
POLITICISE
POLITICISED
POLITICISES
POLITICISING
POLITICIZATION
POLITICIZATIONS
POLITICIZE
POLITICIZED
POLITICIZES
POLITICIZING
POLITICKED
POLITICKER
POLITICKERS
POLITICKING
POLITICKINGS
POLITICOES
POLITIQUES
POLLARDING
POLLENATED
POLLENATES
POLLENATING
POLLENIFEROUS
POLLENISER
POLLENISERS
POLLENIZER
POLLENIZERS
POLLENOSES
POLLENOSIS
POLLICITATION
POLLICITATIONS
POLLINATED
POLLINATES
POLLINATING
POLLINATION
POLLINATIONS
POLLINATOR
POLLINATORS
POLLINIFEROUS
POLLINISED
POLLINISER
POLLINISERS
POLLINISES
POLLINISING
POLLINIZED
POLLINIZER
POLLINIZERS
POLLINIZES
POLLINIZING
POLLINOSES
POLLINOSIS
POLLTAKERS
POLLUCITES
POLLUSIONS
POLLUTANTS
POLLUTEDLY
POLLUTEDNESS
POLLUTEDNESSES
POLLUTIONS
POLLYANNAISH
POLLYANNAISM
POLLYANNAISMS
POLLYANNAS
POLLYANNISH
POLONAISES
POLONISING
POLONIZING
POLTERGEIST
POLTERGEISTS
POLTROONERIES
POLTROONERY
POLVERINES
POLYACRYLAMIDE
POLYACRYLAMIDES
POLYACTINAL
POLYACTINE
POLYACTINES
POLYADELPHOUS
POLYALCOHOL
POLYALCOHOLS
POLYAMIDES
POLYAMINES
POLYAMORIES
POLYAMOROUS
POLYANDRIES
POLYANDROUS
POLYANTHAS
POLYANTHUS
POLYANTHUSES
POLYARCHIES
POLYARTHRITIDES
POLYARTHRITIS
POLYARTHRITISES
POLYATOMIC
POLYAXIALS
POLYAXONIC
POLYBAGGED
POLYBAGGING
POLYBASITE
POLYBASITES
POLYBUTADIENE
POLYBUTADIENES
POLYCARBONATE
POLYCARBONATES
POLYCARBOXYLATE
POLYCARBOXYLIC
POLYCARPELLARY

P

POLYCARPIC
POLYCARPIES
POLYCARPOUS
POLYCENTRIC
POLYCENTRICS
POLYCENTRISM
POLYCENTRISMS
POLYCHAETE
POLYCHAETES
POLYCHAETOUS
POLYCHASIA
POLYCHASIUM
POLYCHETES
POLYCHETOUS
POLYCHLORINATED
POLYCHLOROPRENE
POLYCHOTOMIES
POLYCHOTOMOUS
POLYCHOTOMY
POLYCHREST
POLYCHRESTS
POLYCHROIC
POLYCHROISM
POLYCHROISMS
POLYCHROMATIC
POLYCHROMATISM
POLYCHROMATISMS
POLYCHROME
POLYCHROMED
POLYCHROMES
POLYCHROMIC
POLYCHROMIES
POLYCHROMING
POLYCHROMOUS
POLYCHROMY
POLYCISTRONIC
POLYCLINIC
POLYCLINICS
POLYCLONAL
POLYCLONALS
POLYCOTTON
POLYCOTTONS
POLYCOTYLEDON
POLYCOTYLEDONS
POLYCROTIC
POLYCROTISM
POLYCROTISMS
POLYCRYSTAL
POLYCRYSTALLINE
POLYCRYSTALS
POLYCULTURE
POLYCULTURES
POLYCYCLIC
POLYCYCLICS
POLYCYSTIC
POLYCYTHAEMIA
POLYCYTHAEMIAS
POLYCYTHEMIA
POLYCYTHEMIAS
POLYCYTHEMIC
POLYDACTYL
POLYDACTYLIES
POLYDACTYLISM
POLYDACTYLISMS
POLYDACTYLOUS
POLYDACTYLS
POLYDACTYLY
POLYDAEMONISM
POLYDAEMONISMS
POLYDEMONISM
POLYDEMONISMS
POLYDIPSIA
POLYDIPSIAS
POLYDIPSIC
POLYDISPERSE
POLYDISPERSITY
POLYELECTROLYTE
POLYEMBRYONATE
POLYEMBRYONIC
POLYEMBRYONIES
POLYEMBRYONY
POLYESTERS
POLYESTROUS
POLYETHENE
POLYETHENES
POLYETHYLENE
POLYETHYLENES
POLYGALACEOUS
POLYGAMIES
POLYGAMISE
POLYGAMISED
POLYGAMISES
POLYGAMISING
POLYGAMIST
POLYGAMISTS
POLYGAMIZE
POLYGAMIZED
POLYGAMIZES
POLYGAMIZING
POLYGAMOUS
POLYGAMOUSLY
POLYGENESES
POLYGENESIS
POLYGENETIC
POLYGENETICALLY
POLYGENIES
POLYGENISM
POLYGENISMS
POLYGENIST
POLYGENISTS
POLYGENOUS
POLYGLOTISM
POLYGLOTISMS
POLYGLOTTAL
POLYGLOTTIC
POLYGLOTTISM
POLYGLOTTISMS
POLYGLOTTOUS
POLYGLOTTS
POLYGONACEOUS
POLYGONALLY
POLYGONATUM
POLYGONATUMS
POLYGONIES
POLYGONUMS
POLYGRAPHED
POLYGRAPHER
POLYGRAPHERS
POLYGRAPHIC
POLYGRAPHICALLY
POLYGRAPHIES
POLYGRAPHING
POLYGRAPHIST
POLYGRAPHISTS
POLYGRAPHS
POLYGRAPHY
POLYGYNIAN
POLYGYNIES
POLYGYNIST
POLYGYNISTS
POLYGYNOUS
POLYHALITE
POLYHALITES
POLYHEDRAL
POLYHEDRIC
POLYHEDRON
POLYHEDRONS
POLYHEDROSES
POLYHEDROSIS
POLYHISTOR
POLYHISTORIAN
POLYHISTORIANS
POLYHISTORIC
POLYHISTORIES
POLYHISTORS
POLYHISTORY
POLYHYBRID
POLYHYBRIDS
POLYHYDRIC
POLYHYDROXY
POLYIMIDES
POLYISOPRENE
POLYISOPRENES
POLYLEMMAS
POLYLINGUAL
POLYLYSINE
POLYLYSINES
POLYMASTIA
POLYMASTIAS
POLYMASTIC
POLYMASTICS
POLYMASTIES
POLYMASTISM
POLYMASTISMS
POLYMATHIC
POLYMATHIES
POLYMERASE
POLYMERASES
POLYMERIDE
POLYMERIDES
POLYMERIES
POLYMERISATION
POLYMERISATIONS
POLYMERISE
POLYMERISED
POLYMERISES
POLYMERISING
POLYMERISM
POLYMERISMS
POLYMERIZATION
POLYMERIZATIONS
POLYMERIZE
POLYMERIZED
POLYMERIZES
POLYMERIZING
POLYMEROUS
POLYMORPHIC
POLYMORPHICALLY
POLYMORPHISM
POLYMORPHISMS
POLYMORPHOUS
POLYMORPHOUSLY
POLYMORPHS
POLYMYOSITIS
POLYMYOSITISES
POLYMYXINS
POLYNEURITIDES
POLYNEURITIS
POLYNEURITISES
POLYNOMIAL
POLYNOMIALISM
POLYNOMIALISMS
POLYNOMIALS
POLYNUCLEAR
POLYNUCLEATE
POLYNUCLEOTIDE
POLYNUCLEOTIDES
POLYOLEFIN
POLYOLEFINS
POLYOMINOES
POLYOMINOS
POLYONYMIC
POLYONYMIES
POLYONYMOUS
POLYPARIES
POLYPARIUM
POLYPEPTIDE
POLYPEPTIDES
POLYPEPTIDIC
POLYPETALOUS
POLYPHAGIA
POLYPHAGIAS
POLYPHAGIES
POLYPHAGOUS
POLYPHARMACIES
POLYPHARMACY
POLYPHASIC
POLYPHENOL
POLYPHENOLIC
POLYPHENOLS

POLYPHLOESBOEAN
POLYPHLOISBIC
POLYPHONES
POLYPHONIC
POLYPHONICALLY
POLYPHONIES
POLYPHONIST
POLYPHONISTS
POLYPHONOUS
POLYPHONOUSLY
POLYPHOSPHORIC
POLYPHYLETIC
POLYPHYLLOUS
POLYPHYODONT
POLYPIDOMS
POLYPLOIDAL
POLYPLOIDIC
POLYPLOIDIES
POLYPLOIDS
POLYPLOIDY
POLYPODIES
POLYPODOUS
POLYPROPENE
POLYPROPENES
POLYPROPYLENE
POLYPROPYLENES
POLYPROTODONT
POLYPROTODONTS
POLYPTYCHS
POLYRHYTHM
POLYRHYTHMIC
POLYRHYTHMS
POLYRIBOSOMAL
POLYRIBOSOME
POLYRIBOSOMES
POLYSACCHARIDE
POLYSACCHARIDES
POLYSACCHAROSE
POLYSACCHAROSES
POLYSEMANT
POLYSEMANTS
POLYSEMIES
POLYSEMOUS
POLYSEPALOUS
POLYSILOXANE
POLYSILOXANES
POLYSOMICS
POLYSOMIES
POLYSORBATE
POLYSORBATES
POLYSTICHOUS
POLYSTYLAR
POLYSTYLES
POLYSTYRENE
POLYSTYRENES
POLYSULFIDE
POLYSULFIDES
POLYSULPHIDE
POLYSULPHIDES
POLYSYLLABIC
POLYSYLLABICAL
POLYSYLLABICISM
POLYSYLLABISM
POLYSYLLABISMS
POLYSYLLABLE
POLYSYLLABLES
POLYSYLLOGISM
POLYSYLLOGISMS
POLYSYNAPTIC
POLYSYNDETON
POLYSYNDETONS
POLYSYNTHESES
POLYSYNTHESIS
POLYSYNTHESISM
POLYSYNTHESISMS
POLYSYNTHETIC
POLYSYNTHETICAL
POLYSYNTHETISM
POLYSYNTHETISMS
POLYTECHNIC
POLYTECHNICAL
POLYTECHNICS
POLYTENIES
POLYTHALAMOUS
POLYTHEISM
POLYTHEISMS
POLYTHEIST
POLYTHEISTIC
POLYTHEISTICAL
POLYTHEISTS
POLYTHENES
POLYTOCOUS
POLYTONALISM
POLYTONALISMS
POLYTONALIST
POLYTONALISTS
POLYTONALITIES
POLYTONALITY
POLYTONALLY
POLYTROPHIC
POLYTUNNEL
POLYTUNNELS
POLYTYPICAL
POLYTYPING
POLYUNSATURATE
POLYUNSATURATED
POLYUNSATURATES
POLYURETHAN
POLYURETHANE
POLYURETHANES
POLYURETHANS
POLYVALENCE
POLYVALENCES
POLYVALENCIES
POLYVALENCY
POLYVALENT
POLYVINYLIDENE
POLYVINYLIDENES
POLYVINYLS
POLYWATERS
POLYZOARIA
POLYZOARIAL
POLYZOARIES
POLYZOARIUM
POMATUMING
POMEGRANATE
POMEGRANATES
POMICULTURE
POMICULTURES
POMIFEROUS
POMMELLING
POMOERIUMS
POMOLOGICAL
POMOLOGICALLY
POMOLOGIES
POMOLOGIST
POMOLOGISTS
POMOSEXUAL
POMOSEXUALS
POMPADOURED
POMPADOURS
POMPELMOOSE
POMPELMOOSES
POMPELMOUS
POMPELMOUSE
POMPELMOUSES
POMPHOLYGOUS
POMPHOLYXES
POMPOSITIES
POMPOUSNESS
POMPOUSNESSES
PONDERABILITIES
PONDERABILITY
PONDERABLE
PONDERABLES
PONDERABLY
PONDERANCE
PONDERANCES
PONDERANCIES
PONDERANCY
PONDERATED
PONDERATES
PONDERATING
PONDERATION
PONDERATIONS
PONDERINGLY
PONDERMENT
PONDERMENTS
PONDEROSAS
PONDEROSITIES
PONDEROSITY
PONDEROUSLY
PONDEROUSNESS
PONDEROUSNESSES
PONDOKKIES
PONEROLOGIES
PONEROLOGY
PONIARDING
PONTIANACS
PONTIANAKS
PONTICELLO
PONTICELLOS
PONTIFICAL
PONTIFICALITIES
PONTIFICALITY
PONTIFICALLY
PONTIFICALS
PONTIFICATE
PONTIFICATED
PONTIFICATES
PONTIFICATING
PONTIFICATION
PONTIFICATIONS
PONTIFICATOR
PONTIFICATORS
PONTIFICES
PONTIFYING
PONTLEVISES
PONTONEERS
PONTONIERS
PONTONNIER
PONTONNIERS
PONTOONERS
PONTOONING
PONYTAILED
POORHOUSES
POORMOUTHED
POORMOUTHING
POORMOUTHS
POORNESSES
POPLINETTE
POPLINETTES
POPMOBILITIES
POPMOBILITY
POPPERINGS
POPPYCOCKS
POPPYHEADS
POPULARISATION
POPULARISATIONS
POPULARISE
POPULARISED
POPULARISER
POPULARISERS
POPULARISES
POPULARISING
POPULARIST
POPULARITIES
POPULARITY
POPULARIZATION
POPULARIZATIONS
POPULARIZE
POPULARIZED
POPULARIZER
POPULARIZERS
POPULARIZES
POPULARIZING
POPULATING
POPULATION
POPULATIONAL
POPULATIONS

POPULISTIC
POPULOUSLY
POPULOUSNESS
POPULOUSNESSES
PORBEAGLES
PORCELAINEOUS
PORCELAINISE
PORCELAINISED
PORCELAINISES
PORCELAINISING
PORCELAINIZE
PORCELAINIZED
PORCELAINIZES
PORCELAINIZING
PORCELAINLIKE
PORCELAINOUS
PORCELAINS
PORCELANEOUS
PORCELLANEOUS
PORCELLANISE
PORCELLANISED
PORCELLANISES
PORCELLANISING
PORCELLANITE
PORCELLANITES
PORCELLANIZE
PORCELLANIZED
PORCELLANIZES
PORCELLANIZING
PORCELLANOUS
PORCHETTAS
PORCUPINES
PORCUPINIER
PORCUPINIEST
PORCUPINISH
PORIFERANS
PORIFEROUS
PORINESSES
PORISMATIC
PORISMATICAL
PORISTICAL
PORKINESSES
PORLOCKING
PORNIFICATION
PORNIFICATIONS
PORNOCRACIES
PORNOCRACY
PORNOGRAPHER
PORNOGRAPHERS
PORNOGRAPHIC
PORNOGRAPHIES
PORNOGRAPHY
PORNOTOPIA
PORNOTOPIAN
PORNOTOPIAS
POROGAMIES
POROMERICS
POROSCOPES
POROSCOPIC
POROSCOPIES
POROSITIES
POROUSNESS
POROUSNESSES
PORPENTINE
PORPENTINES
PORPHYRIAS
PORPHYRIES
PORPHYRINS
PORPHYRIOS
PORPHYRITE
PORPHYRITES
PORPHYRITIC
PORPHYROGENITE
PORPHYROGENITES
PORPHYROID
PORPHYROIDS
PORPHYROPSIN
PORPHYROPSINS
PORPHYROUS
PORPOISING
PORRACEOUS
PORRECTING
PORRECTION
PORRECTIONS
PORRENGERS
PORRIDGIER
PORRIDGIEST
PORRIGINOUS
PORRINGERS
PORTABELLA
PORTABELLAS
PORTABELLO
PORTABELLOS
PORTABILITIES
PORTABILITY
PORTAMENTI
PORTAMENTO
PORTAPACKS
PORTATIVES
PORTCULLIS
PORTCULLISED
PORTCULLISES
PORTCULLISING
PORTENDING
PORTENTOUS
PORTENTOUSLY
PORTENTOUSNESS
PORTEOUSES
PORTERAGES
PORTERESSES
PORTERHOUSE
PORTERHOUSES
PORTFOLIOS
PORTHORSES
PORTHOUSES
PORTIONERS
PORTIONING
PORTIONIST
PORTIONISTS
PORTIONLESS
PORTLINESS
PORTLINESSES
PORTMANTEAU
PORTMANTEAUS
PORTMANTEAUX
PORTMANTLE
PORTMANTLES
PORTMANTUA
PORTMANTUAS
PORTOBELLO
PORTOBELLOS
PORTOLANOS
PORTRAITED
PORTRAITING
PORTRAITIST
PORTRAITISTS
PORTRAITURE
PORTRAITURES
PORTRAYABLE
PORTRAYALS
PORTRAYERS
PORTRAYING
PORTREEVES
PORTRESSES
PORTULACACEOUS
PORTULACAS
PORWIGGLES
POSHNESSES
POSITIONAL
POSITIONALLY
POSITIONED
POSITIONING
POSITIONINGS
POSITIVELY
POSITIVENESS
POSITIVENESSES
POSITIVEST
POSITIVISM
POSITIVISMS
POSITIVIST
POSITIVISTIC
POSITIVISTS
POSITIVITIES
POSITIVITY
POSITRONIUM
POSITRONIUMS
POSOLOGICAL
POSOLOGIES
POSSESSABLE
POSSESSEDLY
POSSESSEDNESS
POSSESSEDNESSES
POSSESSING
POSSESSION
POSSESSIONAL
POSSESSIONARY
POSSESSIONATE
POSSESSIONATES
POSSESSIONED
POSSESSIONLESS
POSSESSIONS
POSSESSIVE
POSSESSIVELY
POSSESSIVENESS
POSSESSIVES
POSSESSORS
POSSESSORSHIP
POSSESSORSHIPS
POSSESSORY
POSSIBILISM
POSSIBILISMS
POSSIBILIST
POSSIBILISTS
POSSIBILITIES
POSSIBILITY
POSSIBLEST
POSTABORTION
POSTACCIDENT
POSTADOLESCENT
POSTADOLESCENTS
POSTAMPUTATION
POSTAPOCALYPTIC
POSTARREST
POSTATOMIC
POSTATTACK
POSTBELLUM
POSTBIBLICAL
POSTBOURGEOIS
POSTBUSSES
POSTCAPITALIST
POSTCARDED
POSTCARDING
POSTCARDLIKE
POSTCLASSIC
POSTCLASSICAL
POSTCODING
POSTCOITAL
POSTCOLLEGE
POSTCOLLEGIATE
POSTCOLONIAL
POSTCONCEPTION
POSTCONCERT
POSTCONQUEST
POSTCONSONANTAL
POSTCONVENTION
POSTCOPULATORY
POSTCORONARY
POSTCRANIAL
POSTCRANIALLY
POSTCRISIS
POSTDATING
POSTDEADLINE
POSTDEBATE
POSTDEBUTANTE
POSTDELIVERY
POSTDEPRESSION
POSTDEVALUATION
POSTDILUVIAL
POSTDILUVIAN
POSTDILUVIANS

POSTDIVESTITURE
POSTDIVORCE
POSTDOCTORAL
POSTDOCTORALS
POSTDOCTORATE
POSTDOCTORATES
POSTEDITING
POSTEDITINGS
POSTELECTION
POSTEMBRYONAL
POSTEMBRYONIC
POSTEMERGENCE
POSTEMERGENCY
POSTEPILEPTIC
POSTERIORITIES
POSTERIORITY
POSTERIORLY
POSTERIORS
POSTERISATION
POSTERISATIONS
POSTERISED
POSTERISES
POSTERISING
POSTERITIES
POSTERIZATION
POSTERIZATIONS
POSTERIZED
POSTERIZES
POSTERIZING
POSTEROLATERAL
POSTERUPTIVE
POSTEXERCISE
POSTEXILIAN
POSTEXILIC
POSTEXPERIENCE
POSTEXPOSURE
POSTFEMINISM
POSTFEMINISMS
POSTFEMINIST
POSTFEMINISTS
POSTFIXING
POSTFLIGHT
POSTFORMED
POSTFORMING
POSTFRACTURE
POSTFREEZE
POSTGANGLIONIC
POSTGLACIAL
POSTGRADUATE
POSTGRADUATES
POSTGRADUATION
POSTGRADUATIONS
POSTHARVEST
POSTHASTES
POSTHEATED
POSTHEATING
POSTHEMORRHAGIC
POSTHOLDER
POSTHOLDERS
POSTHOLIDAY
POSTHOLOCAUST
POSTHORSES
POSTHOSPITAL
POSTHOUSES
POSTHUMOUS
POSTHUMOUSLY
POSTHUMOUSNESS
POSTHYPNOTIC
POSTILIONS
POSTILLATE
POSTILLATED
POSTILLATES
POSTILLATING
POSTILLATION
POSTILLATIONS
POSTILLATOR
POSTILLATORS
POSTILLERS
POSTILLING
POSTILLION
POSTILLIONS
POSTIMPACT
POSTIMPERIAL
POSTINAUGURAL
POSTINDUSTRIAL
POSTINFECTION
POSTINJECTION
POSTINOCULATION
POSTIRRADIATION
POSTISCHEMIC
POSTISOLATION
POSTLANDING
POSTLAPSARIAN
POSTLAUNCH
POSTLIBERATION
POSTLIMINARY
POSTLIMINIA
POSTLIMINIARY
POSTLIMINIES
POSTLIMINIOUS
POSTLIMINIUM
POSTLIMINOUS
POSTLIMINY
POSTLITERATE
POSTMARITAL
POSTMARKED
POSTMARKING
POSTMASTECTOMY
POSTMASTER
POSTMASTERS
POSTMASTERSHIP
POSTMASTERSHIPS
POSTMATING
POSTMEDIEVAL
POSTMENOPAUSAL
POSTMENSTRUAL
POSTMERIDIAN
POSTMIDNIGHT
POSTMILLENARIAN
POSTMILLENNIAL
POSTMISTRESS
POSTMISTRESSES
POSTMODERN
POSTMODERNISM
POSTMODERNISMS
POSTMODERNIST
POSTMODERNISTS
POSTMODERNS
POSTMODIFIED
POSTMODIFIES
POSTMODIFY
POSTMODIFYING
POSTMORTEM
POSTMORTEMS
POSTNATALLY
POSTNEONATAL
POSTNUPTIAL
POSTOCULAR
POSTOCULARS
POSTOPERATIVE
POSTOPERATIVELY
POSTORBITAL
POSTORGASMIC
POSTPARTUM
POSTPERSON
POSTPERSONS
POSTPOLLINATION
POSTPONABLE
POSTPONEMENT
POSTPONEMENTS
POSTPONENCE
POSTPONENCES
POSTPONERS
POSTPONING
POSTPOSING
POSTPOSITION
POSTPOSITIONAL
POSTPOSITIONS
POSTPOSITIVE
POSTPOSITIVELY
POSTPOSITIVES
POSTPRANDIAL
POSTPRIMARY
POSTPRISON
POSTPRODUCTION
POSTPRODUCTIONS
POSTPUBERTIES
POSTPUBERTY
POSTPUBESCENT
POSTPUBESCENTS
POSTRECESSION
POSTRETIREMENT
POSTRIDERS
POSTROMANTIC
POSTROMANTICS
POSTSCENIUM
POSTSCENIUMS
POSTSCRIPT
POSTSCRIPTS
POSTSEASON
POSTSEASONS
POSTSECONDARY
POSTSTIMULATION
POSTSTIMULATORY
POSTSTIMULUS
POSTSTRIKE
POSTSURGICAL
POSTSYNAPTIC
POSTSYNCED
POSTSYNCHRONISE
POSTSYNCHRONIZE
POSTSYNCING
POSTTENSION
POSTTENSIONED
POSTTENSIONING
POSTTENSIONS
POSTTRANSFUSION
POSTTRAUMATIC
POSTTREATMENT
POSTTREATMENTS
POSTULANCIES
POSTULANCY
POSTULANTS
POSTULANTSHIP
POSTULANTSHIPS
POSTULATED
POSTULATES
POSTULATING
POSTULATION
POSTULATIONAL
POSTULATIONALLY
POSTULATIONS
POSTULATOR
POSTULATORS
POSTULATORY
POSTULATUM
POSTURINGS
POSTURISED
POSTURISES
POSTURISING
POSTURISTS
POSTURIZED
POSTURIZES
POSTURIZING
POSTVACCINAL
POSTVACCINATION
POSTVAGOTOMY
POSTVASECTOMY
POSTVOCALIC
POSTWEANING
POSTWORKSHOP
POTABILITIES
POTABILITY
POTABLENESS
POTABLENESSES
POTAMOGETON
POTAMOGETONS
POTAMOLOGICAL
POTAMOLOGIES
POTAMOLOGIST

POTAMOLOGISTS
POTAMOLOGY
POTASSIUMS
POTATOBUGS
POTBELLIED
POTBELLIES
POTBOILERS
POTBOILING
POTBOILINGS
POTENTIATES
POTENTIALITIES
POTENTIALITY
POTENTIALLY
POTENTIALS
POTENTIARIES
POTENTIARY
POTENTIATE
POTENTIATED
POTENTIATES
POTENTIATING
POTENTIATION
POTENTIATIONS
POTENTIATOR
POTENTIATORS
POTENTILLA
POTENTILLAS
POTENTIOMETER
POTENTIOMETERS
POTENTIOMETRIC
POTENTIOMETRIES
POTENTIOMETRY
POTENTISED
POTENTISES
POTENTISING
POTENTIZED
POTENTIZES
POTENTIZING
POTENTNESS
POTENTNESSES
POTHECARIES
POTHERIEST
POTHOLDERS
POTHOLINGS
POTHUNTERS
POTHUNTING
POTHUNTINGS
POTICARIES
POTICHOMANIA
POTICHOMANIAS
POTLATCHED
POTLATCHES
POTLATCHING
POTOMETERS
POTPOURRIS
POTSHOTTING
POTSHOTTINGS
POTTERINGLY
POTTERINGS
POTTINESSES
POTTINGARS
POTTINGERS
POTTYMOUTH
POTTYMOUTHS
POTWALLERS
POULTERERS
POULTICING
POULTROONE
POULTROONES
POULTRYMAN
POULTRYMEN
POUNDCAKES
POURBOIRES
POURPARLER
POURPARLERS
POURPOINTS
POURSEWING
POURTRAHED
POURTRAICT
POURTRAICTS
POURTRAYED
POURTRAYING
POUSOWDIES
POUSSETTED
POUSSETTES
POUSSETTING
POUTASSOUS
POUTHERING
POWDERIEST
POWDERINGS
POWDERLESS
POWDERLIKE
POWELLISED
POWELLISES
POWELLISING
POWELLITES
POWELLIZED
POWELLIZES
POWELLIZING
POWERBANDS
POWERBOATING
POWERBOATINGS
POWERBOATS
POWERFULLY
POWERFULNESS
POWERFULNESSES
POWERHOUSE
POWERHOUSES
POWERLESSLY
POWERLESSNESS
POWERLESSNESSES
POWERLIFTER
POWERLIFTERS
POWERLIFTING
POWERLIFTINGS
POWERPLAYS
POWERTRAIN
POWERTRAINS
POWSOWDIES
POXVIRUSES
POZZOLANAS
POZZOLANIC
POZZUOLANA
POZZUOLANAS
PRACHARAKS
PRACTICABILITY
PRACTICABLE
PRACTICABLENESS
PRACTICABLY
PRACTICALISM
PRACTICALISMS
PRACTICALIST
PRACTICALISTS
PRACTICALITIES
PRACTICALITY
PRACTICALLY
PRACTICALNESS
PRACTICALNESSES
PRACTICALS
PRACTICERS
PRACTICIAN
PRACTICIANS
PRACTICING
PRACTICKED
PRACTICKING
PRACTICUMS
PRACTIQUES
PRACTISANT
PRACTISANTS
PRACTISERS
PRACTISING
PRACTITIONER
PRACTITIONERS
PRACTOLOLS
PRAEAMBLES
PRAECOCIAL
PRAECORDIAL
PRAEDIALITIES
PRAEDIALITY
PRAEFECTORIAL
PRAELECTED
PRAELECTING
PRAELUDIUM
PRAEMUNIRE
PRAEMUNIRES
PRAENOMENS
PRAENOMINA
PRAENOMINAL
PRAENOMINALLY
PRAEPOSTOR
PRAEPOSTORS
PRAESIDIUM
PRAESIDIUMS
PRAETORIAL
PRAETORIAN
PRAETORIANS
PRAETORIUM
PRAETORIUMS
PRAETORSHIP
PRAETORSHIPS
PRAGMATICAL
PRAGMATICALITY
PRAGMATICALLY
PRAGMATICALNESS
PRAGMATICISM
PRAGMATICISMS
PRAGMATICIST
PRAGMATICISTS
PRAGMATICS
PRAGMATISATION
PRAGMATISATIONS
PRAGMATISE
PRAGMATISED
PRAGMATISER
PRAGMATISERS
PRAGMATISES
PRAGMATISING
PRAGMATISM
PRAGMATISMS
PRAGMATIST
PRAGMATISTIC
PRAGMATISTS
PRAGMATIZATION
PRAGMATIZATIONS
PRAGMATIZE
PRAGMATIZED
PRAGMATIZER
PRAGMATIZERS
PRAGMATIZES
PRAGMATIZING
PRAISEACHS
PRAISELESS
PRAISEWORTHIER
PRAISEWORTHIEST
PRAISEWORTHILY
PRAISEWORTHY
PRAISINGLY
PRALLTRILLER
PRALLTRILLERS
PRANAYAMAS
PRANCINGLY
PRANDIALLY
PRANKINGLY
PRANKISHLY
PRANKISHNESS
PRANKISHNESSES
PRANKSTERS
PRASEODYMIUM
PRASEODYMIUMS
PRATFALLEN
PRATFALLING
PRATINCOLE
PRATINCOLES
PRATTLEBOX
PRATTLEBOXES
PRATTLEMENT
PRATTLEMENTS
PRATTLINGLY
PRAXEOLOGICAL
PRAXEOLOGIES
PRAXEOLOGY

P

PRAXINOSCOPE
PRAXINOSCOPES
PRAYERFULLY
PRAYERFULNESS
PRAYERFULNESSES
PRAYERLESS
PRAYERLESSLY
PRAYERLESSNESS
PREABSORBED
PREABSORBING
PREABSORBS
PREACCUSED
PREACCUSES
PREACCUSING
PREACHABLE
PREACHERSHIP
PREACHERSHIPS
PREACHIEST
PREACHIFIED
PREACHIFIES
PREACHIFYING
PREACHIFYINGS
PREACHINESS
PREACHINESSES
PREACHINGLY
PREACHINGS
PREACHMENT
PREACHMENTS
PREACQUAINT
PREACQUAINTANCE
PREACQUAINTED
PREACQUAINTING
PREACQUAINTS
PREACQUISITION
PREADAMITE
PREADAMITES
PREADAPTATION
PREADAPTATIONS
PREADAPTED
PREADAPTING
PREADAPTIVE
PREADJUSTED
PREADJUSTING
PREADJUSTS
PREADMISSION
PREADMISSIONS
PREADMITTED
PREADMITTING
PREADMONISH
PREADMONISHED
PREADMONISHES
PREADMONISHING
PREADMONITION
PREADMONITIONS
PREADOLESCENCE
PREADOLESCENCES
PREADOLESCENT
PREADOLESCENTS
PREADOPTED
PREADOPTING
PREAGRICULTURAL
PREALLOTTED
PREALLOTTING
PREALTERED
PREALTERING
PREAMBLING
PREAMBULARY
PREAMBULATE
PREAMBULATED
PREAMBULATES
PREAMBULATING
PREAMBULATORY
PREAMPLIFIER
PREAMPLIFIERS
PREANAESTHETIC
PREANAESTHETICS
PREANESTHETIC
PREANNOUNCE
PREANNOUNCED
PREANNOUNCES
PREANNOUNCING
PREAPPLIED
PREAPPLIES
PREAPPLYING
PREAPPOINT
PREAPPOINTED
PREAPPOINTING
PREAPPOINTS
PREAPPROVE
PREAPPROVED
PREAPPROVES
PREAPPROVING
PREARRANGE
PREARRANGED
PREARRANGEMENT
PREARRANGEMENTS
PREARRANGES
PREARRANGING
PREASSEMBLED
PREASSIGNED
PREASSIGNING
PREASSIGNS
PREASSURANCE
PREASSURANCES
PREASSURED
PREASSURES
PREASSURING
PREATTUNED
PREATTUNES
PREATTUNING
PREAUDIENCE
PREAUDIENCES
PREAVERRED
PREAVERRING
PREAXIALLY
PREBENDARIES
PREBENDARY
PREBIBLICAL
PREBIDDING
PREBIDDINGS
PREBILLING
PREBINDING
PREBIOLOGIC
PREBIOLOGICAL
PREBIOTICS
PREBLESSED
PREBLESSES
PREBLESSING
PREBOARDED
PREBOARDING
PREBOILING
PREBOOKING
PREBREAKFAST
PREBUDGETS
PREBUILDING
PREBUTTALS
PRECALCULI
PRECALCULUS
PRECALCULUSES
PRECANCELED
PRECANCELING
PRECANCELLATION
PRECANCELLED
PRECANCELLING
PRECANCELS
PRECANCEROUS
PRECANCERS
PRECAPITALIST
PRECARIATS
PRECARIOUS
PRECARIOUSLY
PRECARIOUSNESS
PRECASTING
PRECAUTION
PRECAUTIONAL
PRECAUTIONARY
PRECAUTIONED
PRECAUTIONING
PRECAUTIONS
PRECAUTIOUS
PRECEDENCE
PRECEDENCES
PRECEDENCIES
PRECEDENCY
PRECEDENTED
PRECEDENTIAL
PRECEDENTIALLY
PRECEDENTLY
PRECEDENTS
PRECENSORED
PRECENSORING
PRECENSORS
PRECENTING
PRECENTORIAL
PRECENTORS
PRECENTORSHIP
PRECENTORSHIPS
PRECENTRESS
PRECENTRESSES
PRECENTRICES
PRECENTRIX
PRECENTRIXES
PRECEPTIAL
PRECEPTIVE
PRECEPTIVELY
PRECEPTORAL
PRECEPTORATE
PRECEPTORATES
PRECEPTORIAL
PRECEPTORIALS
PRECEPTORIES
PRECEPTORS
PRECEPTORSHIP
PRECEPTORSHIPS
PRECEPTORY
PRECEPTRESS
PRECEPTRESSES
PRECESSING
PRECESSION
PRECESSIONAL
PRECESSIONALLY
PRECESSIONS
PRECHARGED
PRECHARGES
PRECHARGING
PRECHECKED
PRECHECKING
PRECHILLED
PRECHILLING
PRECHOOSES
PRECHOOSING
PRECHRISTIAN
PRECIEUSES
PRECIOSITIES
PRECIOSITY
PRECIOUSES
PRECIOUSLY
PRECIOUSNESS
PRECIOUSNESSES
PRECIPICED
PRECIPICES
PRECIPITABILITY
PRECIPITABLE
PRECIPITANCE
PRECIPITANCES
PRECIPITANCIES
PRECIPITANCY
PRECIPITANT
PRECIPITANTLY
PRECIPITANTNESS
PRECIPITANTS
PRECIPITATE
PRECIPITATED
PRECIPITATELY
PRECIPITATENESS
PRECIPITATES
PRECIPITATING
PRECIPITATION
PRECIPITATIONS
PRECIPITATIVE

PRECIPITATOR
PRECIPITATORS
PRECIPITIN
PRECIPITINOGEN
PRECIPITINOGENS
PRECIPITINS
PRECIPITOUS
PRECIPITOUSLY
PRECIPITOUSNESS
PRECISENESS
PRECISENESSES
PRECISIANISM
PRECISIANISMS
PRECISIANIST
PRECISIANISTS
PRECISIANS
PRECISIONISM
PRECISIONISMS
PRECISIONIST
PRECISIONISTS
PRECISIONS
PRECLASSICAL
PRECLEANED
PRECLEANING
PRECLEARANCE
PRECLEARANCES
PRECLEARED
PRECLEARING
PRECLINICAL
PRECLINICALLY
PRECLUDABLE
PRECLUDING
PRECLUSION
PRECLUSIONS
PRECLUSIVE
PRECLUSIVELY
PRECOCIALS
PRECOCIOUS
PRECOCIOUSLY
PRECOCIOUSNESS
PRECOCITIES
PRECOGNISANT
PRECOGNISE
PRECOGNISED
PRECOGNISES
PRECOGNISING
PRECOGNITION
PRECOGNITIONS
PRECOGNITIVE
PRECOGNIZANT
PRECOGNIZE
PRECOGNIZED
PRECOGNIZES
PRECOGNIZING
PRECOGNOSCE
PRECOGNOSCED
PRECOGNOSCES
PRECOGNOSCING
PRECOLLEGE
PRECOLLEGIATE
PRECOLONIAL
PRECOMBUSTION
PRECOMBUSTIONS
PRECOMMITMENT
PRECOMMITMENTS
PRECOMPETITIVE
PRECOMPOSE
PRECOMPOSED
PRECOMPOSES
PRECOMPOSING
PRECOMPUTE
PRECOMPUTED
PRECOMPUTER
PRECOMPUTES
PRECOMPUTING
PRECONCEIT
PRECONCEITED
PRECONCEITING
PRECONCEITS
PRECONCEIVE
PRECONCEIVED
PRECONCEIVES
PRECONCEIVING
PRECONCEPTION
PRECONCEPTIONS
PRECONCERT
PRECONCERTED
PRECONCERTEDLY
PRECONCERTING
PRECONCERTS
PRECONCILIAR
PRECONDEMN
PRECONDEMNED
PRECONDEMNING
PRECONDEMNS
PRECONDITION
PRECONDITIONED
PRECONDITIONING
PRECONDITIONS
PRECONISATION
PRECONISATIONS
PRECONISED
PRECONISES
PRECONISING
PRECONIZATION
PRECONIZATIONS
PRECONIZED
PRECONIZES
PRECONIZING
PRECONQUEST
PRECONSCIOUS
PRECONSCIOUSES
PRECONSCIOUSLY
PRECONSONANTAL
PRECONSTRUCT
PRECONSTRUCTED
PRECONSTRUCTING
PRECONSTRUCTION
PRECONSTRUCTS
PRECONSUME
PRECONSUMED
PRECONSUMES
PRECONSUMING
PRECONTACT
PRECONTACTS
PRECONTRACT
PRECONTRACTED
PRECONTRACTING
PRECONTRACTS
PRECONVENTION
PRECONVICTION
PRECONVICTIONS
PRECOOKERS
PRECOOKING
PRECOOLING
PRECOPULATORY
PRECORDIAL
PRECREASED
PRECREASES
PRECREASING
PRECRITICAL
PRECURRERS
PRECURSING
PRECURSIVE
PRECURSORS
PRECURSORY
PRECUTTING
PRECYCLING
PREDACEOUS
PREDACEOUSNESS
PREDACIOUS
PREDACIOUSNESS
PREDACITIES
PREDATIONS
PREDATISMS
PREDATORILY
PREDATORINESS
PREDATORINESSES
PREDECEASE
PREDECEASED
PREDECEASES
PREDECEASING
PREDECESSOR
PREDECESSORS
PREDEDUCTED
PREDEDUCTING
PREDEDUCTS
PREDEFINED
PREDEFINES
PREDEFINING
PREDEFINITION
PREDEFINITIONS
PREDELIVERIES
PREDELIVERY
PREDENTARY
PREDENTATE
PREDEPARTURE
PREDEPOSIT
PREDEPOSITED
PREDEPOSITING
PREDEPOSITS
PREDESIGNATE
PREDESIGNATED
PREDESIGNATES
PREDESIGNATING
PREDESIGNATION
PREDESIGNATIONS
PREDESIGNATORY
PREDESIGNED
PREDESIGNING
PREDESIGNS
PREDESTINABLE
PREDESTINARIAN
PREDESTINARIANS
PREDESTINATE
PREDESTINATED
PREDESTINATES
PREDESTINATING
PREDESTINATION
PREDESTINATIONS
PREDESTINATIVE
PREDESTINATOR
PREDESTINATORS
PREDESTINE
PREDESTINED
PREDESTINES
PREDESTINIES
PREDESTINING
PREDESTINY
PREDETERMINABLE
PREDETERMINATE
PREDETERMINE
PREDETERMINED
PREDETERMINER
PREDETERMINERS
PREDETERMINES
PREDETERMINING
PREDETERMINISM
PREDETERMINISMS
PREDEVALUATION
PREDEVELOP
PREDEVELOPED
PREDEVELOPING
PREDEVELOPMENT
PREDEVELOPMENTS
PREDEVELOPS
PREDEVOTED
PREDEVOTES
PREDEVOTING
PREDIABETES
PREDIABETESES
PREDIABETIC
PREDIABETICS
PREDIALITIES
PREDIALITY
PREDICABILITIES
PREDICABILITY
PREDICABLE
PREDICABLENESS
PREDICABLES

PREDICAMENT
PREDICAMENTAL
PREDICAMENTS
PREDICANTS
PREDICATED
PREDICATES
PREDICATING
PREDICATION
PREDICATIONS
PREDICATIVE
PREDICATIVELY
PREDICATOR
PREDICATORS
PREDICATORY
PREDICTABILITY
PREDICTABLE
PREDICTABLENESS
PREDICTABLY
PREDICTERS
PREDICTING
PREDICTION
PREDICTIONS
PREDICTIVE
PREDICTIVELY
PREDICTORS
PREDIGESTED
PREDIGESTING
PREDIGESTION
PREDIGESTIONS
PREDIGESTS
PREDIKANTS
PREDILECTED
PREDILECTION
PREDILECTIONS
PREDINNERS
PREDISCHARGE
PREDISCOVERIES
PREDISCOVERY
PREDISPOSAL
PREDISPOSALS
PREDISPOSE
PREDISPOSED
PREDISPOSES
PREDISPOSING
PREDISPOSITION
PREDISPOSITIONS
PREDNISOLONE
PREDNISOLONES
PREDNISONE
PREDNISONES
PREDOCTORAL
PREDOMINANCE
PREDOMINANCES
PREDOMINANCIES
PREDOMINANCY
PREDOMINANT
PREDOMINANTLY
PREDOMINATE
PREDOMINATED
PREDOMINATELY
PREDOMINATES
PREDOMINATING
PREDOMINATION
PREDOMINATIONS
PREDOMINATOR
PREDOMINATORS
PREDOOMING
PREDRILLED
PREDRILLING
PREDYNASTIC
PREECLAMPSIA
PREECLAMPSIAS
PREECLAMPTIC
PREEDITING
PREELECTED
PREELECTING
PREELECTION
PREELECTRIC
PREEMBARGO
PREEMERGENCE
PREEMERGENT
PREEMINENCE
PREEMINENCES
PREEMINENT
PREEMINENTLY
PREEMPLOYMENT
PREEMPTING
PREEMPTION
PREEMPTIONS
PREEMPTIVE
PREEMPTIVELY
PREEMPTORS
PREENACTED
PREENACTING
PREENROLLMENT
PREERECTED
PREERECTING
PREESTABLISH
PREESTABLISHED
PREESTABLISHES
PREESTABLISHING
PREETHICAL
PREEXCITED
PREEXCITES
PREEXCITING
PREEXEMPTED
PREEXEMPTING
PREEXEMPTS
PREEXISTED
PREEXISTENCE
PREEXISTENCES
PREEXISTENT
PREEXISTING
PREEXPERIMENT
PREEXPOSED
PREEXPOSES
PREEXPOSING
PREFABBING
PREFABRICATE
PREFABRICATED
PREFABRICATES
PREFABRICATING
PREFABRICATION
PREFABRICATIONS
PREFABRICATOR
PREFABRICATORS
PREFASCIST
PREFATORIAL
PREFATORIALLY
PREFATORILY
PREFECTORIAL
PREFECTSHIP
PREFECTSHIPS
PREFECTURAL
PREFECTURE
PREFECTURES
PREFERABILITIES
PREFERABILITY
PREFERABLE
PREFERABLENESS
PREFERABLY
PREFERENCE
PREFERENCES
PREFERENTIAL
PREFERENTIALISM
PREFERENTIALIST
PREFERENTIALITY
PREFERENTIALLY
PREFERMENT
PREFERMENTS
PREFERRABLE
PREFERRERS
PREFERRING
PREFIGURATE
PREFIGURATED
PREFIGURATES
PREFIGURATING
PREFIGURATION
PREFIGURATIONS
PREFIGURATIVE
PREFIGURATIVELY
PREFIGURED
PREFIGUREMENT
PREFIGUREMENTS
PREFIGURES
PREFIGURING
PREFINANCE
PREFINANCED
PREFINANCES
PREFINANCING
PREFINANCINGS
PREFIXALLY
PREFIXIONS
PREFIXTURE
PREFIXTURES
PREFLIGHTED
PREFLIGHTING
PREFLIGHTS
PREFLORATION
PREFLORATIONS
PREFOCUSED
PREFOCUSES
PREFOCUSING
PREFOCUSSED
PREFOCUSSES
PREFOCUSSING
PREFOLIATION
PREFOLIATIONS
PREFORMATION
PREFORMATIONISM
PREFORMATIONIST
PREFORMATIONS
PREFORMATIVE
PREFORMATIVES
PREFORMATS
PREFORMATTED
PREFORMATTING
PREFORMING
PREFORMULATE
PREFORMULATED
PREFORMULATES
PREFORMULATING
PREFRANKED
PREFRANKING
PREFREEZES
PREFREEZING
PREFRESHMAN
PREFRESHMEN
PREFRONTAL
PREFRONTALS
PREFULGENT
PREFUNDING
PREGANGLIONIC
PREGENITAL
PREGLACIAL
PREGNABILITIES
PREGNABILITY
PREGNANCES
PREGNANCIES
PREGNANTLY
PREGNENOLONE
PREGNENOLONES
PREGROWTHS
PREGUIDING
PREGUSTATION
PREGUSTATIONS
PREHALLUCES
PREHANDLED
PREHANDLES
PREHANDLING
PREHARDENED
PREHARDENING
PREHARDENS
PREHARVEST
PREHARVESTS
PREHEADACHE
PREHEATERS
PREHEATING
PREHEMINENCE
PREHEMINENCES

PREHENDING
PREHENSIBLE
PREHENSILE
PREHENSILITIES
PREHENSILITY
PREHENSION
PREHENSIONS
PREHENSIVE
PREHENSORIAL
PREHENSORS
PREHENSORY
PREHISTORIAN
PREHISTORIANS
PREHISTORIC
PREHISTORICAL
PREHISTORICALLY
PREHISTORIES
PREHISTORY
PREHOLIDAY
PREHOMINID
PREHOMINIDS
PREIGNITION
PREIGNITIONS
PREIMPLANTATION
PREIMPOSED
PREIMPOSES
PREIMPOSING
PREINAUGURAL
PREINDUCTION
PREINDUSTRIAL
PREINFORMED
PREINFORMING
PREINFORMS
PREINSERTED
PREINSERTING
PREINSERTS
PREINTERVIEW
PREINTERVIEWED
PREINTERVIEWING
PREINTERVIEWS
PREINVASION
PREINVITED
PREINVITES
PREINVITING
PREJUDGEMENT
PREJUDGEMENTS
PREJUDGERS
PREJUDGING
PREJUDGMENT
PREJUDGMENTS
PREJUDICANT
PREJUDICATE
PREJUDICATED
PREJUDICATES
PREJUDICATING
PREJUDICATION
PREJUDICATIONS
PREJUDICATIVE
PREJUDICED
PREJUDICES
PREJUDICIAL
PREJUDICIALLY
PREJUDICIALNESS
PREJUDICING
PREJUDIZES
PREKINDERGARTEN
PRELAPSARIAN
PRELATESHIP
PRELATESHIPS
PRELATESSES
PRELATICAL
PRELATICALLY
PRELATIONS
PRELATISED
PRELATISES
PRELATISING
PRELATISMS
PRELATISTS
PRELATIZED
PRELATIZES
PRELATIZING
PRELATURES
PRELAUNCHED
PRELAUNCHES
PRELAUNCHING
PRELECTING
PRELECTION
PRELECTIONS
PRELECTORS
PRELEXICAL
PRELIBATION
PRELIBATIONS
PRELIMINARIES
PRELIMINARILY
PRELIMINARY
PRELIMITED
PRELIMITING
PRELINGUAL
PRELINGUALLY
PRELITERACIES
PRELITERACY
PRELITERARY
PRELITERATE
PRELITERATES
PRELOADING
PRELOCATED
PRELOCATES
PRELOCATING
PRELOGICAL
PRELUDIOUS
PRELUNCHEON
PRELUNCHEONS
PRELUSIONS
PRELUSIVELY
PRELUSORILY
PREMALIGNANT
PREMANDIBULAR
PREMANDIBULARS
PREMANUFACTURE
PREMANUFACTURED
PREMANUFACTURES
PREMARITAL
PREMARITALLY
PREMARKETED
PREMARKETING
PREMARKETS
PREMARRIAGE
PREMATURELY
PREMATURENESS
PREMATURENESSES
PREMATURES
PREMATURITIES
PREMATURITY
PREMAXILLA
PREMAXILLAE
PREMAXILLARIES
PREMAXILLARY
PREMAXILLAS
PREMEASURE
PREMEASURED
PREMEASURES
PREMEASURING
PREMEDICAL
PREMEDICALLY
PREMEDICATE
PREMEDICATED
PREMEDICATES
PREMEDICATING
PREMEDICATION
PREMEDICATIONS
PREMEDIEVAL
PREMEDITATE
PREMEDITATED
PREMEDITATEDLY
PREMEDITATES
PREMEDITATING
PREMEDITATION
PREMEDITATIONS
PREMEDITATIVE
PREMEDITATOR
PREMEDITATORS
PREMEIOTIC
PREMENOPAUSAL
PREMENSTRUAL
PREMENSTRUALLY
PREMIERING
PREMIERSHIP
PREMIERSHIPS
PREMIGRATION
PREMILLENARIAN
PREMILLENARIANS
PREMILLENNIAL
PREMILLENNIALLY
PREMILLENNIALS
PREMISSING
PREMODIFICATION
PREMODIFIED
PREMODIFIES
PREMODIFYING
PREMOISTEN
PREMOISTENED
PREMOISTENING
PREMOISTENS
PREMOLDING
PREMONISHED
PREMONISHES
PREMONISHING
PREMONISHMENT
PREMONISHMENTS
PREMONITION
PREMONITIONS
PREMONITIVE
PREMONITOR
PREMONITORILY
PREMONITORS
PREMONITORY
PREMOTIONS
PREMOULDED
PREMOULDING
PREMOVEMENT
PREMOVEMENTS
PREMUNITION
PREMUNITIONS
PREMYCOTIC
PRENATALLY
PRENEGOTIATE
PRENEGOTIATED
PRENEGOTIATES
PRENEGOTIATING
PRENEGOTIATION
PRENEGOTIATIONS
PRENOMINAL
PRENOMINALLY
PRENOMINATE
PRENOMINATED
PRENOMINATES
PRENOMINATING
PRENOMINATION
PRENOMINATIONS
PRENOTIFICATION
PRENOTIFIED
PRENOTIFIES
PRENOTIFYING
PRENOTIONS
PRENTICESHIP
PRENTICESHIPS
PRENTICING
PRENUMBERED
PRENUMBERING
PRENUMBERS
PRENUPTIAL
PRENUPTIALS
PREOBTAINED
PREOBTAINING
PREOBTAINS
PREOCCUPANCIES
PREOCCUPANCY
PREOCCUPANT
PREOCCUPANTS
PREOCCUPATE

PREOCCUPATED
PREOCCUPATES
PREOCCUPATING
PREOCCUPATION
PREOCCUPATIONS
PREOCCUPIED
PREOCCUPIES
PREOCCUPYING
PREOCULARS
PREOPENING
PREOPERATIONAL
PREOPERATIVE
PREOPERATIVELY
PREOPTIONS
PREORDAINED
PREORDAINING
PREORDAINMENT
PREORDAINMENTS
PREORDAINS
PREORDERED
PREORDERING
PREORDINANCE
PREORDINANCES
PREORDINATION
PREORDINATIONS
PREOVULATORY
PREPACKAGE
PREPACKAGED
PREPACKAGES
PREPACKAGING
PREPACKING
PREPARATION
PREPARATIONS
PREPARATIVE
PREPARATIVELY
PREPARATIVES
PREPARATOR
PREPARATORILY
PREPARATORS
PREPARATORY
PREPAREDLY
PREPAREDNESS
PREPAREDNESSES
PREPASTING
PREPATELLAR
PREPAYABLE
PREPAYMENT
PREPAYMENTS
PREPENSELY
PREPENSING
PREPENSIVE
PREPERFORMANCE
PREPLACING
PREPLANNED
PREPLANNING
PREPLANTING
PREPOLLENCE
PREPOLLENCES
PREPOLLENCIES
PREPOLLENCY
PREPOLLENT
PREPOLLICES
PREPONDERANCE
PREPONDERANCES
PREPONDERANCIES
PREPONDERANCY
PREPONDERANT
PREPONDERANTLY
PREPONDERATE
PREPONDERATED
PREPONDERATELY
PREPONDERATES
PREPONDERATING
PREPONDERATION
PREPONDERATIONS
PREPORTION
PREPORTIONED
PREPORTIONING
PREPORTIONS
PREPOSITION
PREPOSITIONAL
PREPOSITIONALLY
PREPOSITIONS
PREPOSITIVE
PREPOSITIVELY
PREPOSITIVES
PREPOSITOR
PREPOSITORS
PREPOSSESS
PREPOSSESSED
PREPOSSESSES
PREPOSSESSING
PREPOSSESSINGLY
PREPOSSESSION
PREPOSSESSIONS
PREPOSTEROUS
PREPOSTEROUSLY
PREPOSTORS
PREPOTENCE
PREPOTENCES
PREPOTENCIES
PREPOTENCY
PREPOTENTLY
PREPPINESS
PREPPINESSES
PREPRANDIAL
PREPREPARED
PREPRESIDENTIAL
PREPRESSES
PREPRICING
PREPRIMARIES
PREPRIMARY
PREPRINTED
PREPRINTING
PREPROCESS
PREPROCESSED
PREPROCESSES
PREPROCESSING
PREPROCESSOR
PREPROCESSORS
PREPRODUCTION
PREPRODUCTIONS
PREPROFESSIONAL
PREPROGRAM
PREPROGRAMED
PREPROGRAMING
PREPROGRAMMED
PREPROGRAMMING
PREPROGRAMMINGS
PREPROGRAMS
PREPSYCHEDELIC
PREPUBERAL
PREPUBERTAL
PREPUBERTIES
PREPUBERTY
PREPUBESCENCE
PREPUBESCENCES
PREPUBESCENT
PREPUBESCENTS
PREPUBLICATION
PREPUBLICATIONS
PREPUNCHED
PREPUNCHES
PREPUNCHING
PREPUNCTUAL
PREPURCHASE
PREPURCHASED
PREPURCHASES
PREPURCHASING
PREQUALIFIED
PREQUALIFIES
PREQUALIFY
PREQUALIFYING
PREREADING
PRERECESSION
PRERECORDED
PRERECORDING
PRERECORDS
PREREGISTER
PREREGISTERED
PREREGISTERING
PREREGISTERS
PREREGISTRATION
PREREHEARSAL
PREREHEARSALS
PRERELEASE
PRERELEASED
PRERELEASES
PRERELEASING
PREREQUIRE
PREREQUIRED
PREREQUIRES
PREREQUIRING
PREREQUISITE
PREREQUISITES
PRERETIREMENT
PREREVIEWED
PREREVIEWING
PREREVIEWS
PREREVISIONIST
PREREVOLUTION
PRERINSING
PREROGATIVE
PREROGATIVED
PREROGATIVELY
PREROGATIVES
PREROMANTIC
PREROMANTICS
PRESAGEFUL
PRESAGEFULLY
PRESAGEMENT
PRESAGEMENTS
PRESANCTIFIED
PRESANCTIFIES
PRESANCTIFY
PRESANCTIFYING
PRESBYACOUSES
PRESBYACOUSIS
PRESBYACUSES
PRESBYACUSIS
PRESBYCOUSES
PRESBYCOUSIS
PRESBYCUSES
PRESBYCUSIS
PRESBYOPES
PRESBYOPIA
PRESBYOPIAS
PRESBYOPIC
PRESBYOPICS
PRESBYOPIES
PRESBYTERAL
PRESBYTERATE
PRESBYTERATES
PRESBYTERIAL
PRESBYTERIALLY
PRESBYTERIALS
PRESBYTERIAN
PRESBYTERIANISE
PRESBYTERIANISM
PRESBYTERIANIZE
PRESBYTERIANS
PRESBYTERIES
PRESBYTERS
PRESBYTERSHIP
PRESBYTERSHIPS
PRESBYTERY
PRESBYTISM
PRESBYTISMS
PRESCHEDULE
PRESCHEDULED
PRESCHEDULES
PRESCHEDULING
PRESCHOOLER
PRESCHOOLERS
PRESCHOOLS
PRESCIENCE
PRESCIENCES
PRESCIENTIFIC
PRESCIENTLY
PRESCINDED

P

PRESCINDENT
PRESCINDING
PRESCISSION
PRESCISSIONS
PRESCORING
PRESCREENED
PRESCREENING
PRESCREENS
PRESCRIBED
PRESCRIBER
PRESCRIBERS
PRESCRIBES
PRESCRIBING
PRESCRIBINGS
PRESCRIPTIBLE
PRESCRIPTION
PRESCRIPTIONS
PRESCRIPTIVE
PRESCRIPTIVELY
PRESCRIPTIVISM
PRESCRIPTIVISMS
PRESCRIPTIVIST
PRESCRIPTIVISTS
PRESCRIPTS
PRESEASONS
PRESELECTED
PRESELECTING
PRESELECTION
PRESELECTIONS
PRESELECTOR
PRESELECTORS
PRESELECTS
PRESELLING
PRESENSION
PRESENSIONS
PRESENTABILITY
PRESENTABLE
PRESENTABLENESS
PRESENTABLY
PRESENTATION
PRESENTATIONAL
PRESENTATIONISM
PRESENTATIONIST
PRESENTATIONS
PRESENTATIVE
PRESENTEEISM
PRESENTEEISMS
PRESENTEES
PRESENTENCE
PRESENTENCED
PRESENTENCES
PRESENTENCING
PRESENTERS
PRESENTIAL
PRESENTIALITIES
PRESENTIALITY
PRESENTIALLY
PRESENTIENT
PRESENTIMENT
PRESENTIMENTAL
PRESENTIMENTS
PRESENTING
PRESENTISM
PRESENTISMS
PRESENTIST
PRESENTISTS
PRESENTIVE
PRESENTIVENESS
PRESENTIVES
PRESENTMENT
PRESENTMENTS
PRESENTNESS
PRESENTNESSES
PRESERVABILITY
PRESERVABLE
PRESERVABLY
PRESERVATION
PRESERVATIONIST
PRESERVATIONS
PRESERVATIVE
PRESERVATIVES
PRESERVATORIES
PRESERVATORY
PRESERVERS
PRESERVICE
PRESERVING
PRESETTING
PRESETTLED
PRESETTLEMENT
PRESETTLES
PRESETTLING
PRESHAPING
PRESHIPPED
PRESHIPPING
PRESHOWING
PRESHRINKING
PRESHRINKS
PRESHRUNKEN
PRESIDENCIES
PRESIDENCY
PRESIDENTESS
PRESIDENTESSES
PRESIDENTIAL
PRESIDENTIALLY
PRESIDENTS
PRESIDENTSHIP
PRESIDENTSHIPS
PRESIDIARY
PRESIDIUMS
PRESIFTING
PRESIGNALED
PRESIGNALING
PRESIGNALLED
PRESIGNALLING
PRESIGNALS
PRESIGNIFIED
PRESIGNIFIES
PRESIGNIFY
PRESIGNIFYING
PRESLAUGHTER
PRESLICING
PRESOAKING
PRESOLVING
PRESORTING
PRESPECIFIED
PRESPECIFIES
PRESPECIFY
PRESPECIFYING
PRESSBOARD
PRESSBOARDS
PRESSGANGS
PRESSINGLY
PRESSINGNESS
PRESSINGNESSES
PRESSMARKS
PRESSROOMS
PRESSURELESS
PRESSURING
PRESSURISATION
PRESSURISATIONS
PRESSURISE
PRESSURISED
PRESSURISER
PRESSURISERS
PRESSURISES
PRESSURISING
PRESSURIZATION
PRESSURIZATIONS
PRESSURIZE
PRESSURIZED
PRESSURIZER
PRESSURIZERS
PRESSURIZES
PRESSURIZING
PRESSWOMAN
PRESSWOMEN
PRESSWORKS
PRESTAMPED
PRESTAMPING
PRESTATION
PRESTATIONS
PRESTERILISE
PRESTERILISED
PRESTERILISES
PRESTERILISING
PRESTERILIZE
PRESTERILIZED
PRESTERILIZES
PRESTERILIZING
PRESTERNUM
PRESTERNUMS
PRESTIDIGITATOR
PRESTIGEFUL
PRESTIGIATOR
PRESTIGIATORS
PRESTIGIOUS
PRESTIGIOUSLY
PRESTIGIOUSNESS
PRESTISSIMO
PRESTISSIMOS
PRESTORAGE
PRESTORING
PRESTRESSED
PRESTRESSES
PRESTRESSING
PRESTRICTION
PRESTRICTIONS
PRESTRUCTURE
PRESTRUCTURED
PRESTRUCTURES
PRESTRUCTURING
PRESUMABLE
PRESUMABLY
PRESUMEDLY
PRESUMINGLY
PRESUMMITS
PRESUMPTION
PRESUMPTIONS
PRESUMPTIVE
PRESUMPTIVELY
PRESUMPTIVENESS
PRESUMPTUOUS
PRESUMPTUOUSLY
PRESUPPOSE
PRESUPPOSED
PRESUPPOSES
PRESUPPOSING
PRESUPPOSITION
PRESUPPOSITIONS
PRESURGERY
PRESURMISE
PRESURMISES
PRESURVEYED
PRESURVEYING
PRESURVEYS
PRESWEETEN
PRESWEETENED
PRESWEETENING
PRESWEETENS
PRESYMPTOMATIC
PRESYNAPTIC
PRESYNAPTICALLY
PRETASTING
PRETELEVISION
PRETELLING
PRETENCELESS
PRETENDANT
PRETENDANTS
PRETENDEDLY
PRETENDENT
PRETENDENTS
PRETENDERS
PRETENDERSHIP
PRETENDERSHIPS
PRETENDING
PRETENDINGLY
PRETENSELESS
PRETENSION
PRETENSIONED
PRETENSIONING

P

PRETENSIONLESS
PRETENSIONS
PRETENSIVE
PRETENTIOUS
PRETENTIOUSLY
PRETENTIOUSNESS
PRETERHUMAN
PRETERISTS
PRETERITENESS
PRETERITENESSES
PRETERITES
PRETERITION
PRETERITIONS
PRETERITIVE
PRETERMINAL
PRETERMINATION
PRETERMINATIONS
PRETERMISSION
PRETERMISSIONS
PRETERMITS
PRETERMITTED
PRETERMITTER
PRETERMITTERS
PRETERMITTING
PRETERNATURAL
PRETERNATURALLY
PRETERPERFECT
PRETERPERFECTS
PRETESTING
PRETEXTING
PRETEXTINGS
PRETHEATER
PRETHEATRE
PRETORIANS
PRETORSHIP
PRETORSHIPS
PRETOURNAMENT
PRETRAINED
PRETRAINING
PRETREATED
PRETREATING
PRETREATMENT
PRETREATMENTS
PRETRIMMED
PRETRIMMING
PRETTIFICATION
PRETTIFICATIONS
PRETTIFIED
PRETTIFIER
PRETTIFIERS
PRETTIFIES
PRETTIFYING
PRETTINESS
PRETTINESSES
PRETTYISMS
PRETZELLED
PRETZELLING
PREUNIFICATION
PREUNITING
PREUNIVERSITY
PREVAILERS
PREVAILING
PREVAILINGLY
PREVAILMENT
PREVAILMENTS
PREVALENCE
PREVALENCES
PREVALENCIES
PREVALENCY
PREVALENTLY
PREVALENTNESS
PREVALENTNESSES
PREVALENTS
PREVALUING
PREVARICATE
PREVARICATED
PREVARICATES
PREVARICATING
PREVARICATION
PREVARICATIONS
PREVARICATOR
PREVARICATORS
PREVENANCIES
PREVENANCY
PREVENIENCE
PREVENIENCES
PREVENIENT
PREVENIENTLY
PREVENTABILITY
PREVENTABLE
PREVENTABLY
PREVENTATIVE
PREVENTATIVES
PREVENTERS
PREVENTIBILITY
PREVENTIBLE
PREVENTIBLY
PREVENTING
PREVENTION
PREVENTIONS
PREVENTIVE
PREVENTIVELY
PREVENTIVENESS
PREVENTIVES
PREVIEWERS
PREVIEWING
PREVIOUSLY
PREVIOUSNESS
PREVIOUSNESSES
PREVISIONAL
PREVISIONARY
PREVISIONED
PREVISIONING
PREVISIONS
PREVISITED
PREVISITING
PREVOCALIC
PREVOCALICALLY
PREVOCATIONAL
PREWARMING
PREWARNING
PREWASHING
PREWEANING
PREWEIGHED
PREWEIGHING
PREWORKING
PREWRAPPED
PREWRAPPING
PREWRITING
PREWRITINGS
PREWRITTEN
PRICELESSLY
PRICELESSNESS
PRICELESSNESSES
PRICINESSES
PRICKLIEST
PRICKLINESS
PRICKLINESSES
PRICKLINGS
PRICKWOODS
PRIDEFULLY
PRIDEFULNESS
PRIDEFULNESSES
PRIESTCRAFT
PRIESTCRAFTS
PRIESTESSES
PRIESTHOOD
PRIESTHOODS
PRIESTLIER
PRIESTLIEST
PRIESTLIKE
PRIESTLINESS
PRIESTLINESSES
PRIESTLING
PRIESTLINGS
PRIESTSHIP
PRIESTSHIPS
PRIGGERIES
PRIGGISHLY
PRIGGISHNESS
PRIGGISHNESSES
PRIMAEVALLY
PRIMALITIES
PRIMAQUINE
PRIMAQUINES
PRIMARINESS
PRIMARINESSES
PRIMATESHIP
PRIMATESHIPS
PRIMATIALS
PRIMATICAL
PRIMATOLOGICAL
PRIMATOLOGIES
PRIMATOLOGIST
PRIMATOLOGISTS
PRIMATOLOGY
PRIMAVERAS
PRIMENESSES
PRIMEVALLY
PRIMIGENIAL
PRIMIGRAVIDA
PRIMIGRAVIDAE
PRIMIGRAVIDAS
PRIMIPARAE
PRIMIPARAS
PRIMIPARITIES
PRIMIPARITY
PRIMIPAROUS
PRIMITIVELY
PRIMITIVENESS
PRIMITIVENESSES
PRIMITIVES
PRIMITIVISM
PRIMITIVISMS
PRIMITIVIST
PRIMITIVISTIC
PRIMITIVISTS
PRIMITIVITIES
PRIMITIVITY
PRIMNESSES
PRIMOGENIAL
PRIMOGENIT
PRIMOGENITAL
PRIMOGENITARY
PRIMOGENITIVE
PRIMOGENITIVES
PRIMOGENITOR
PRIMOGENITORS
PRIMOGENITRICES
PRIMOGENITRIX
PRIMOGENITRIXES
PRIMOGENITS
PRIMOGENITURE
PRIMOGENITURES
PRIMORDIAL
PRIMORDIALISM
PRIMORDIALISMS
PRIMORDIALITIES
PRIMORDIALITY
PRIMORDIALLY
PRIMORDIALS
PRIMORDIUM
PRIMROSIER
PRIMROSIEST
PRIMROSING
PRIMULACEOUS
PRIMULINES
PRINCEDOMS
PRINCEHOOD
PRINCEHOODS
PRINCEKINS
PRINCELETS
PRINCELIER
PRINCELIEST
PRINCELIKE
PRINCELINESS
PRINCELINESSES
PRINCELING
PRINCELINGS
PRINCESHIP

P

PRINCESHIPS
PRINCESSES
PRINCESSLIER
PRINCESSLIEST
PRINCESSLY
PRINCIFIED
PRINCIPALITIES
PRINCIPALITY
PRINCIPALLY
PRINCIPALNESS
PRINCIPALNESSES
PRINCIPALS
PRINCIPALSHIP
PRINCIPALSHIPS
PRINCIPATE
PRINCIPATES
PRINCIPIAL
PRINCIPIUM
PRINCIPLED
PRINCIPLES
PRINCIPLING
PRINTABILITIES
PRINTABILITY
PRINTABLENESS
PRINTABLENESSES
PRINTERIES
PRINTHEADS
PRINTMAKER
PRINTMAKERS
PRINTMAKING
PRINTMAKINGS
PRINTWHEEL
PRINTWHEELS
PRINTWORKS
PRIORESSES
PRIORITIES
PRIORITISATION
PRIORITISATIONS
PRIORITISE
PRIORITISED
PRIORITISES
PRIORITISING
PRIORITIZATION
PRIORITIZATIONS
PRIORITIZE
PRIORITIZED
PRIORITIZES
PRIORITIZING
PRIORSHIPS
PRISMATICAL
PRISMATICALLY
PRISMATOID
PRISMATOIDAL
PRISMATOIDS
PRISMOIDAL
PRISONMENT
PRISONMENTS
PRISSINESS
PRISSINESSES
PRISTINELY
PRIVATDOCENT
PRIVATDOCENTS
PRIVATDOZENT
PRIVATDOZENTS
PRIVATEERED
PRIVATEERING
PRIVATEERINGS
PRIVATEERS
PRIVATEERSMAN
PRIVATEERSMEN
PRIVATENESS
PRIVATENESSES
PRIVATIONS
PRIVATISATION
PRIVATISATIONS
PRIVATISED
PRIVATISER
PRIVATISERS
PRIVATISES
PRIVATISING
PRIVATISMS
PRIVATISTS
PRIVATIVELY
PRIVATIVES
PRIVATIZATION
PRIVATIZATIONS
PRIVATIZED
PRIVATIZER
PRIVATIZERS
PRIVATIZES
PRIVATIZING
PRIVILEGED
PRIVILEGES
PRIVILEGING
PRIZEFIGHT
PRIZEFIGHTER
PRIZEFIGHTERS
PRIZEFIGHTING
PRIZEFIGHTINGS
PRIZEFIGHTS
PRIZEWINNER
PRIZEWINNERS
PRIZEWINNING
PRIZEWOMAN
PRIZEWOMEN
PROABORTION
PROACTIONS
PROAIRESES
PROAIRESIS
PROBABILIORISM
PROBABILIORISMS
PROBABILIORIST
PROBABILIORISTS
PROBABILISM
PROBABILISMS
PROBABILIST
PROBABILISTIC
PROBABILISTS
PROBABILITIES
PROBABILITY
PROBATIONAL
PROBATIONALLY
PROBATIONARIES
PROBATIONARY
PROBATIONER
PROBATIONERS
PROBATIONERSHIP
PROBATIONS
PROBATIVELY
PROBENECID
PROBENECIDS
PROBIOTICS
PROBLEMATIC
PROBLEMATICAL
PROBLEMATICALLY
PROBLEMATICS
PROBLEMIST
PROBLEMISTS
PROBOSCIDEAN
PROBOSCIDEANS
PROBOSCIDES
PROBOSCIDIAN
PROBOSCIDIANS
PROBOSCISES
PROBOULEUTIC
PROBUSINESS
PROCACIOUS
PROCACITIES
PROCAMBIAL
PROCAMBIUM
PROCAMBIUMS
PROCAPITALIST
PROCARBAZINE
PROCARBAZINES
PROCARYONS
PROCARYOTE
PROCARYOTES
PROCARYOTIC
PROCATHEDRAL
PROCATHEDRALS
PROCEDURAL
PROCEDURALLY
PROCEDURALS
PROCEDURES
PROCEEDERS
PROCEEDING
PROCEEDINGS
PROCELEUSMATIC
PROCELEUSMATICS
PROCELLARIAN
PROCELLARIANS
PROCEPHALIC
PROCERCOID
PROCERCOIDS
PROCEREBRA
PROCEREBRAL
PROCEREBRUM
PROCEREBRUMS
PROCERITIES
PROCESSABILITY
PROCESSABLE
PROCESSERS
PROCESSIBILITY
PROCESSIBLE
PROCESSING
PROCESSINGS
PROCESSION
PROCESSIONAL
PROCESSIONALIST
PROCESSIONALLY
PROCESSIONALS
PROCESSIONARIES
PROCESSIONARY
PROCESSIONED
PROCESSIONER
PROCESSIONERS
PROCESSIONING
PROCESSIONINGS
PROCESSIONS
PROCESSORS
PROCESSUAL
PROCHRONISM
PROCHRONISMS
PROCIDENCE
PROCIDENCES
PROCLAIMANT
PROCLAIMANTS
PROCLAIMED
PROCLAIMER
PROCLAIMERS
PROCLAIMING
PROCLAMATION
PROCLAMATIONS
PROCLAMATORY
PROCLITICS
PROCLIVITIES
PROCLIVITY
PROCOELOUS
PROCONSULAR
PROCONSULATE
PROCONSULATES
PROCONSULS
PROCONSULSHIP
PROCONSULSHIPS
PROCRASTINATE
PROCRASTINATED
PROCRASTINATES
PROCRASTINATING
PROCRASTINATION
PROCRASTINATIVE
PROCRASTINATOR
PROCRASTINATORS
PROCRASTINATORY
PROCREANTS
PROCREATED
PROCREATES
PROCREATING
PROCREATION
PROCREATIONAL
PROCREATIONS

PROCREATIVE
PROCREATIVENESS
PROCREATOR
PROCREATORS
PROCRUSTEAN
PROCRYPSES
PROCRYPSIS
PROCRYPTIC
PROCRYPTICALLY
PROCTALGIA
PROCTALGIAS
PROCTITIDES
PROCTITISES
PROCTODAEA
PROCTODAEAL
PROCTODAEUM
PROCTODAEUMS
PROCTODEAL
PROCTODEUM
PROCTODEUMS
PROCTOLOGIC
PROCTOLOGICAL
PROCTOLOGIES
PROCTOLOGIST
PROCTOLOGISTS
PROCTOLOGY
PROCTORAGE
PROCTORAGES
PROCTORIAL
PROCTORIALLY
PROCTORING
PROCTORISE
PROCTORISED
PROCTORISES
PROCTORISING
PROCTORIZE
PROCTORIZED
PROCTORIZES
PROCTORIZING
PROCTORSHIP
PROCTORSHIPS
PROCTOSCOPE
PROCTOSCOPES
PROCTOSCOPIC
PROCTOSCOPIES
PROCTOSCOPY
PROCUMBENT
PROCURABLE
PROCURACIES
PROCURANCE
PROCURANCES
PROCURATION
PROCURATIONS
PROCURATOR
PROCURATORIAL
PROCURATORIES
PROCURATORS
PROCURATORSHIP
PROCURATORSHIPS
PROCURATORY
PROCUREMENT
PROCUREMENTS
PROCURESSES
PROCUREURS
PROCURINGS
PROCYONIDS
PRODIGALISE
PRODIGALISED
PRODIGALISES
PRODIGALISING
PRODIGALITIES
PRODIGALITY
PRODIGALIZE
PRODIGALIZED
PRODIGALIZES
PRODIGALIZING
PRODIGALLY
PRODIGIOSITIES
PRODIGIOSITY
PRODIGIOUS
PRODIGIOUSLY
PRODIGIOUSNESS
PRODITORIOUS
PRODNOSING
PRODROMATA
PRODUCEMENT
PRODUCEMENTS
PRODUCIBILITIES
PRODUCIBILITY
PRODUCIBLE
PRODUCTIBILITY
PRODUCTILE
PRODUCTION
PRODUCTIONAL
PRODUCTIONS
PRODUCTIVE
PRODUCTIVELY
PRODUCTIVENESS
PRODUCTIVITIES
PRODUCTIVITY
PROEMBRYOS
PROENZYMES
PROESTRUSES
PROFANATION
PROFANATIONS
PROFANATORY
PROFANENESS
PROFANENESSES
PROFANITIES
PROFASCIST
PROFECTITIOUS
PROFEMINIST
PROFESSEDLY
PROFESSING
PROFESSION
PROFESSIONAL
PROFESSIONALISE
PROFESSIONALISM
PROFESSIONALIST
PROFESSIONALIZE
PROFESSIONALLY
PROFESSIONALS
PROFESSIONS
PROFESSORATE
PROFESSORATES
PROFESSORESS
PROFESSORESSES
PROFESSORIAL
PROFESSORIALLY
PROFESSORIAT
PROFESSORIATE
PROFESSORIATES
PROFESSORIATS
PROFESSORS
PROFESSORSHIP
PROFESSORSHIPS
PROFFERERS
PROFFERING
PROFICIENCE
PROFICIENCES
PROFICIENCIES
PROFICIENCY
PROFICIENT
PROFICIENTLY
PROFICIENTS
PROFILINGS
PROFILISTS
PROFITABILITIES
PROFITABILITY
PROFITABLE
PROFITABLENESS
PROFITABLY
PROFITEERED
PROFITEERING
PROFITEERINGS
PROFITEERS
PROFITEROLE
PROFITEROLES
PROFITINGS
PROFITLESS
PROFITLESSLY
PROFITWISE
PROFLIGACIES
PROFLIGACY
PROFLIGATE
PROFLIGATELY
PROFLIGATES
PROFLUENCE
PROFLUENCES
PROFOUNDER
PROFOUNDEST
PROFOUNDLY
PROFOUNDNESS
PROFOUNDNESSES
PROFULGENT
PROFUNDITIES
PROFUNDITY
PROFUSENESS
PROFUSENESSES
PROFUSIONS
PROGENITIVE
PROGENITIVENESS
PROGENITOR
PROGENITORIAL
PROGENITORS
PROGENITORSHIP
PROGENITORSHIPS
PROGENITRESS
PROGENITRESSES
PROGENITRICES
PROGENITRIX
PROGENITRIXES
PROGENITURE
PROGENITURES
PROGESTATIONAL
PROGESTERONE
PROGESTERONES
PROGESTINS
PROGESTOGEN
PROGESTOGENIC
PROGESTOGENS
PROGGINSES
PROGLOTTIC
PROGLOTTID
PROGLOTTIDEAN
PROGLOTTIDES
PROGLOTTIDS
PROGLOTTIS
PROGNATHIC
PROGNATHISM
PROGNATHISMS
PROGNATHOUS
PROGNOSING
PROGNOSTIC
PROGNOSTICATE
PROGNOSTICATED
PROGNOSTICATES
PROGNOSTICATING
PROGNOSTICATION
PROGNOSTICATIVE
PROGNOSTICATOR
PROGNOSTICATORS
PROGNOSTICS
PROGRADATION
PROGRADATIONS
PROGRADING
PROGRAMABLE
PROGRAMERS
PROGRAMING
PROGRAMINGS
PROGRAMMABILITY
PROGRAMMABLE
PROGRAMMABLES
PROGRAMMATIC
PROGRAMMED
PROGRAMMER
PROGRAMMERS
PROGRAMMES
PROGRAMMING
PROGRAMMINGS

P

PROGRESSED
PROGRESSES
PROGRESSING
PROGRESSION
PROGRESSIONAL
PROGRESSIONALLY
PROGRESSIONARY
PROGRESSIONISM
PROGRESSIONISMS
PROGRESSIONIST
PROGRESSIONISTS
PROGRESSIONS
PROGRESSISM
PROGRESSISMS
PROGRESSIST
PROGRESSISTS
PROGRESSIVE
PROGRESSIVELY
PROGRESSIVENESS
PROGRESSIVES
PROGRESSIVISM
PROGRESSIVISMS
PROGRESSIVIST
PROGRESSIVISTIC
PROGRESSIVISTS
PROGRESSIVITIES
PROGRESSIVITY
PROGYMNASIA
PROGYMNASIUM
PROGYMNASIUMS
PROHIBITED
PROHIBITER
PROHIBITERS
PROHIBITING
PROHIBITION
PROHIBITIONARY
PROHIBITIONISM
PROHIBITIONISMS
PROHIBITIONIST
PROHIBITIONISTS
PROHIBITIONS
PROHIBITIVE
PROHIBITIVELY
PROHIBITIVENESS
PROHIBITOR
PROHIBITORS
PROHIBITORY
PROINSULIN
PROINSULINS
PROJECTABLE
PROJECTILE
PROJECTILES
PROJECTING
PROJECTINGS
PROJECTION
PROJECTIONAL
PROJECTIONIST
PROJECTIONISTS
PROJECTIONS
PROJECTISATION
PROJECTISATIONS
PROJECTIVE
PROJECTIVELY
PROJECTIVITIES
PROJECTIVITY
PROJECTIZATION
PROJECTIZATIONS
PROJECTMENT
PROJECTMENTS
PROJECTORS
PROJECTURE
PROJECTURES
PROKARYONS
PROKARYOTE
PROKARYOTES
PROKARYOTIC
PROKARYOTS
PROLACTINS
PROLAMINES
PROLAPSING
PROLAPSUSES
PROLATENESS
PROLATENESSES
PROLATIONS
PROLEGOMENA
PROLEGOMENAL
PROLEGOMENARY
PROLEGOMENON
PROLEGOMENOUS
PROLEPTICAL
PROLEPTICALLY
PROLETARIAN
PROLETARIANISE
PROLETARIANISED
PROLETARIANISES
PROLETARIANISM
PROLETARIANISMS
PROLETARIANIZE
PROLETARIANIZED
PROLETARIANIZES
PROLETARIANNESS
PROLETARIANS
PROLETARIAT
PROLETARIATE
PROLETARIATES
PROLETARIATS
PROLETARIES
PROLICIDAL
PROLICIDES
PROLIFERATE
PROLIFERATED
PROLIFERATES
PROLIFERATING
PROLIFERATION
PROLIFERATIONS
PROLIFERATIVE
PROLIFEROUS
PROLIFEROUSLY
PROLIFICACIES
PROLIFICACY
PROLIFICAL
PROLIFICALLY
PROLIFICATION
PROLIFICATIONS
PROLIFICITIES
PROLIFICITY
PROLIFICNESS
PROLIFICNESSES
PROLIXIOUS
PROLIXITIES
PROLIXNESS
PROLIXNESSES
PROLOCUTION
PROLOCUTIONS
PROLOCUTOR
PROLOCUTORS
PROLOCUTORSHIP
PROLOCUTORSHIPS
PROLOCUTRICES
PROLOCUTRIX
PROLOCUTRIXES
PROLOGISED
PROLOGISES
PROLOGISING
PROLOGISTS
PROLOGIZED
PROLOGIZES
PROLOGIZING
PROLOGUING
PROLOGUISE
PROLOGUISED
PROLOGUISES
PROLOGUISING
PROLOGUIZE
PROLOGUIZED
PROLOGUIZES
PROLOGUIZING
PROLONGABLE
PROLONGATE
PROLONGATED
PROLONGATES
PROLONGATING
PROLONGATION
PROLONGATIONS
PROLONGERS
PROLONGING
PROLONGMENT
PROLONGMENTS
PROLUSIONS
PROMACHOSES
PROMENADED
PROMENADER
PROMENADERS
PROMENADES
PROMENADING
PROMETHAZINE
PROMETHAZINES
PROMETHEUM
PROMETHEUMS
PROMETHIUM
PROMETHIUMS
PROMILITARY
PROMINENCE
PROMINENCES
PROMINENCIES
PROMINENCY
PROMINENTLY
PROMINENTNESS
PROMINENTNESSES
PROMINENTS
PROMISCUITIES
PROMISCUITY
PROMISCUOUS
PROMISCUOUSLY
PROMISCUOUSNESS
PROMISEFUL
PROMISELESS
PROMISINGLY
PROMISSIVE
PROMISSORILY
PROMISSORS
PROMISSORY
PROMONARCHIST
PROMONTORIES
PROMONTORY
PROMOTABILITIES
PROMOTABILITY
PROMOTABLE
PROMOTIONAL
PROMOTIONS
PROMOTIVENESS
PROMOTIVENESSES
PROMPTBOOK
PROMPTBOOKS
PROMPTINGS
PROMPTITUDE
PROMPTITUDES
PROMPTNESS
PROMPTNESSES
PROMPTUARIES
PROMPTUARY
PROMPTURES
PROMULGATE
PROMULGATED
PROMULGATES
PROMULGATING
PROMULGATION
PROMULGATIONS
PROMULGATOR
PROMULGATORS
PROMULGING
PROMUSCIDATE
PROMUSCIDES
PROMYCELIA
PROMYCELIAL
PROMYCELIUM
PRONATIONS
PRONATORES
PRONENESSES
PRONEPHRIC

P

PRONEPHROI
PRONEPHROS
PRONEPHROSES
PRONGBUCKS
PRONGHORNS
PRONOMINAL
PRONOMINALISE
PRONOMINALISED
PRONOMINALISES
PRONOMINALISING
PRONOMINALIZE
PRONOMINALIZED
PRONOMINALIZES
PRONOMINALIZING
PRONOMINALLY
PRONOUNCEABLE
PRONOUNCED
PRONOUNCEDLY
PRONOUNCEMENT
PRONOUNCEMENTS
PRONOUNCER
PRONOUNCERS
PRONOUNCES
PRONOUNCING
PRONOUNCINGS
PRONUCLEAR
PRONUCLEARIST
PRONUCLEARISTS
PRONUCLEUS
PRONUCLEUSES
PRONUNCIAMENTO
PRONUNCIAMENTOS
PRONUNCIATION
PRONUNCIATIONAL
PRONUNCIATIONS
PRONUNCIOS
PROOEMIONS
PROOEMIUMS
PROOFREADER
PROOFREADERS
PROOFREADING
PROOFREADINGS
PROOFREADS
PROOFROOMS
PROPAEDEUTIC
PROPAEDEUTICAL
PROPAEDEUTICS
PROPAGABILITIES
PROPAGABILITY
PROPAGABLE
PROPAGABLENESS
PROPAGANDA
PROPAGANDAS
PROPAGANDISE
PROPAGANDISED
PROPAGANDISER
PROPAGANDISERS
PROPAGANDISES
PROPAGANDISING
PROPAGANDISM
PROPAGANDISMS
PROPAGANDIST
PROPAGANDISTIC
PROPAGANDISTS
PROPAGANDIZE
PROPAGANDIZED
PROPAGANDIZER
PROPAGANDIZERS
PROPAGANDIZES
PROPAGANDIZING
PROPAGATED
PROPAGATES
PROPAGATING
PROPAGATION
PROPAGATIONAL
PROPAGATIONS
PROPAGATIVE
PROPAGATOR
PROPAGATORS
PROPAGULES
PROPAGULUM
PROPANEDIOIC
PROPANONES
PROPAROXYTONE
PROPAROXYTONES
PROPELLANT
PROPELLANTS
PROPELLENT
PROPELLENTS
PROPELLERS
PROPELLING
PROPELLINGS
PROPELLORS
PROPELMENT
PROPELMENTS
PROPENDENT
PROPENDING
PROPENSELY
PROPENSENESS
PROPENSENESSES
PROPENSION
PROPENSIONS
PROPENSITIES
PROPENSITY
PROPENSIVE
PROPERDINS
PROPERISPOMENA
PROPERISPOMENON
PROPERNESS
PROPERNESSES
PROPERTIED
PROPERTIES
PROPERTYING
PROPERTYLESS
PROPHECIES
PROPHESIABLE
PROPHESIED
PROPHESIER
PROPHESIERS
PROPHESIES
PROPHESYING
PROPHESYINGS
PROPHETESS
PROPHETESSES
PROPHETHOOD
PROPHETHOODS
PROPHETICAL
PROPHETICALLY
PROPHETICISM
PROPHETICISMS
PROPHETISM
PROPHETISMS
PROPHETSHIP
PROPHETSHIPS
PROPHYLACTIC
PROPHYLACTICS
PROPHYLAXES
PROPHYLAXIS
PROPINQUITIES
PROPINQUITY
PROPIONATE
PROPIONATES
PROPITIABLE
PROPITIATE
PROPITIATED
PROPITIATES
PROPITIATING
PROPITIATION
PROPITIATIONS
PROPITIATIOUS
PROPITIATIVE
PROPITIATOR
PROPITIATORIES
PROPITIATORILY
PROPITIATORS
PROPITIATORY
PROPITIOUS
PROPITIOUSLY
PROPITIOUSNESS
PROPLASTID
PROPLASTIDS
PROPODEONS
PROPODEUMS
PROPOLISES
PROPONENTS
PROPORTION
PROPORTIONABLE
PROPORTIONABLY
PROPORTIONAL
PROPORTIONALITY
PROPORTIONALLY
PROPORTIONALS
PROPORTIONATE
PROPORTIONATED
PROPORTIONATELY
PROPORTIONATES
PROPORTIONATING
PROPORTIONED
PROPORTIONING
PROPORTIONINGS
PROPORTIONLESS
PROPORTIONMENT
PROPORTIONMENTS
PROPORTIONS
PROPOSABLE
PROPOSITAE
PROPOSITION
PROPOSITIONAL
PROPOSITIONALLY
PROPOSITIONED
PROPOSITIONING
PROPOSITIONS
PROPOSITUS
PROPOUNDED
PROPOUNDER
PROPOUNDERS
PROPOUNDING
PROPOXYPHENE
PROPOXYPHENES
PROPRAETOR
PROPRAETORIAL
PROPRAETORIAN
PROPRAETORS
PROPRANOLOL
PROPRANOLOLS
PROPRETORS
PROPRIETARIES
PROPRIETARILY
PROPRIETARY
PROPRIETIES
PROPRIETOR
PROPRIETORIAL
PROPRIETORIALLY
PROPRIETORS
PROPRIETORSHIP
PROPRIETORSHIPS
PROPRIETRESS
PROPRIETRESSES
PROPRIETRICES
PROPRIETRIX
PROPRIETRIXES
PROPRIOCEPTION
PROPRIOCEPTIONS
PROPRIOCEPTIVE
PROPRIOCEPTOR
PROPRIOCEPTORS
PROPROCTOR
PROPROCTORS
PROPUGNATION
PROPUGNATIONS
PROPULSION
PROPULSIONS
PROPULSIVE
PROPULSORS
PROPULSORY
PROPYLAEUM
PROPYLAMINE
PROPYLAMINES
PROPYLENES
PROPYLITES

PROPYLITISATION
PROPYLITISE
PROPYLITISED
PROPYLITISES
PROPYLITISING
PROPYLITIZATION
PROPYLITIZE
PROPYLITIZED
PROPYLITIZES
PROPYLITIZING
PRORATABLE
PRORATIONS
PRORECTORS
PROROGATED
PROROGATES
PROROGATING
PROROGATION
PROROGATIONS
PROROGUING
PROSAICALLY
PROSAICALNESS
PROSAICALNESSES
PROSAICISM
PROSAICISMS
PROSAICNESS
PROSAICNESSES
PROSATEURS
PROSAUROPOD
PROSAUROPODS
PROSCENIUM
PROSCENIUMS
PROSCIUTTI
PROSCIUTTO
PROSCIUTTOS
PROSCRIBED
PROSCRIBER
PROSCRIBERS
PROSCRIBES
PROSCRIBING
PROSCRIPTION
PROSCRIPTIONS
PROSCRIPTIVE
PROSCRIPTIVELY
PROSCRIPTS
PROSECTING
PROSECTORIAL
PROSECTORS
PROSECTORSHIP
PROSECTORSHIPS
PROSECUTABLE
PROSECUTED
PROSECUTES
PROSECUTING
PROSECUTION
PROSECUTIONS
PROSECUTOR
PROSECUTORIAL
PROSECUTORS
PROSECUTRICES
PROSECUTRIX
PROSECUTRIXES
PROSELYTED
PROSELYTES
PROSELYTIC
PROSELYTING
PROSELYTISATION
PROSELYTISE
PROSELYTISED
PROSELYTISER
PROSELYTISERS
PROSELYTISES
PROSELYTISING
PROSELYTISM
PROSELYTISMS
PROSELYTIZATION
PROSELYTIZE
PROSELYTIZED
PROSELYTIZER
PROSELYTIZERS
PROSELYTIZES
PROSELYTIZING
PROSEMINAR
PROSEMINARS
PROSENCEPHALA
PROSENCEPHALIC
PROSENCEPHALON
PROSENCHYMA
PROSENCHYMAS
PROSENCHYMATA
PROSENCHYMATOUS
PROSEUCHAE
PROSIFYING
PROSILIENCIES
PROSILIENCY
PROSILIENT
PROSIMIANS
PROSINESSES
PROSLAMBANOMENE
PROSLAVERY
PROSOBRANCH
PROSOBRANCHS
PROSODIANS
PROSODICAL
PROSODICALLY
PROSODISTS
PROSOPAGNOSIA
PROSOPAGNOSIAS
PROSOPOGRAPHER
PROSOPOGRAPHERS
PROSOPOGRAPHIES
PROSOPOGRAPHY
PROSOPOPEIA
PROSOPOPEIAL
PROSOPOPEIAS
PROSOPOPOEIA
PROSOPOPOEIAL
PROSOPOPOEIAS
PROSPECTED
PROSPECTING
PROSPECTINGS
PROSPECTION
PROSPECTIONS
PROSPECTIVE
PROSPECTIVELY
PROSPECTIVENESS
PROSPECTIVES
PROSPECTLESS
PROSPECTOR
PROSPECTORS
PROSPECTUS
PROSPECTUSES
PROSPERING
PROSPERITIES
PROSPERITY
PROSPEROUS
PROSPEROUSLY
PROSPEROUSNESS
PROSTACYCLIN
PROSTACYCLINS
PROSTAGLANDIN
PROSTAGLANDINS
PROSTANTHERA
PROSTANTHERAS
PROSTATECTOMIES
PROSTATECTOMY
PROSTATISM
PROSTATISMS
PROSTATITIS
PROSTATITISES
PROSTERNUM
PROSTERNUMS
PROSTHESES
PROSTHESIS
PROSTHETIC
PROSTHETICALLY
PROSTHETICS
PROSTHETIST
PROSTHETISTS
PROSTHODONTIA
PROSTHODONTIAS
PROSTHODONTICS
PROSTHODONTIST
PROSTHODONTISTS
PROSTITUTE
PROSTITUTED
PROSTITUTES
PROSTITUTING
PROSTITUTION
PROSTITUTIONS
PROSTITUTOR
PROSTITUTORS
PROSTOMIAL
PROSTOMIUM
PROSTRATED
PROSTRATES
PROSTRATING
PROSTRATION
PROSTRATIONS
PROSYLLOGISM
PROSYLLOGISMS
PROTACTINIUM
PROTACTINIUMS
PROTAGONISM
PROTAGONISMS
PROTAGONIST
PROTAGONISTS
PROTAMINES
PROTANDRIES
PROTANDROUS
PROTANOMALIES
PROTANOMALOUS
PROTANOMALY
PROTANOPES
PROTANOPIA
PROTANOPIAS
PROTANOPIC
PROTEACEOUS
PROTECTANT
PROTECTANTS
PROTECTERS
PROTECTING
PROTECTINGLY
PROTECTION
PROTECTIONISM
PROTECTIONISMS
PROTECTIONIST
PROTECTIONISTS
PROTECTIONS
PROTECTIVE
PROTECTIVELY
PROTECTIVENESS
PROTECTIVES
PROTECTORAL
PROTECTORATE
PROTECTORATES
PROTECTORIAL
PROTECTORIES
PROTECTORLESS
PROTECTORS
PROTECTORSHIP
PROTECTORSHIPS
PROTECTORY
PROTECTRESS
PROTECTRESSES
PROTECTRICES
PROTECTRIX
PROTECTRIXES
PROTEIFORM
PROTEINACEOUS
PROTEINASE
PROTEINASES
PROTEINOUS
PROTEINURIA
PROTEINURIAS
PROTENDING
PROTENSION
PROTENSIONS
PROTENSITIES
PROTENSITY
PROTENSIVE

PROTENSIVELY
PROTEOCLASTIC
PROTEOGLYCAN
PROTEOGLYCANS
PROTEOLYSE
PROTEOLYSED
PROTEOLYSES
PROTEOLYSING
PROTEOLYSIS
PROTEOLYTIC
PROTEOLYTICALLY
PROTEOMICS
PROTERANDRIES
PROTERANDROUS
PROTERANDRY
PROTEROGYNIES
PROTEROGYNOUS
PROTEROGYNY
PROTERVITIES
PROTERVITY
PROTESTANT
PROTESTANTS
PROTESTATION
PROTESTATIONS
PROTESTERS
PROTESTING
PROTESTINGLY
PROTESTORS
PROTHALAMIA
PROTHALAMION
PROTHALAMIUM
PROTHALLIA
PROTHALLIAL
PROTHALLIC
PROTHALLIUM
PROTHALLOID
PROTHALLUS
PROTHALLUSES
PROTHETICALLY
PROTHONOTARIAL
PROTHONOTARIAT
PROTHONOTARIATS
PROTHONOTARIES
PROTHONOTARY
PROTHORACES
PROTHORACIC
PROTHORAXES
PROTHROMBIN
PROTHROMBINS
PROTISTANS
PROTISTOLOGIES
PROTISTOLOGIST
PROTISTOLOGISTS
PROTISTOLOGY
PROTOACTINIUM
PROTOACTINIUMS
PROTOAVISES
PROTOCHORDATE
PROTOCHORDATES
PROTOCOCCAL
PROTOCOLED
PROTOCOLIC
PROTOCOLING
PROTOCOLISE
PROTOCOLISED
PROTOCOLISES
PROTOCOLISING
PROTOCOLIST
PROTOCOLISTS
PROTOCOLIZE
PROTOCOLIZED
PROTOCOLIZES
PROTOCOLIZING
PROTOCOLLED
PROTOCOLLING
PROTOCTIST
PROTOCTISTS
PROTODERMS
PROTOGALAXIES
PROTOGALAXY
PROTOGENIC
PROTOGINES
PROTOGYNIES
PROTOGYNOUS
PROTOHISTORIAN
PROTOHISTORIANS
PROTOHISTORIC
PROTOHISTORIES
PROTOHISTORY
PROTOHUMAN
PROTOHUMANS
PROTOLANGUAGE
PROTOLANGUAGES
PROTOLITHIC
PROTOMARTYR
PROTOMARTYRS
PROTOMORPHIC
PROTONATED
PROTONATES
PROTONATING
PROTONATION
PROTONATIONS
PROTONEMAL
PROTONEMATA
PROTONEMATAL
PROTONOTARIAL
PROTONOTARIAT
PROTONOTARIATS
PROTONOTARIES
PROTONOTARY
PROTOPATHIC
PROTOPATHIES
PROTOPATHY
PROTOPHILIC
PROTOPHLOEM
PROTOPHLOEMS
PROTOPHYTE
PROTOPHYTES
PROTOPHYTIC
PROTOPLANET
PROTOPLANETARY
PROTOPLANETS
PROTOPLASM
PROTOPLASMAL
PROTOPLASMATIC
PROTOPLASMIC
PROTOPLASMS
PROTOPLAST
PROTOPLASTIC
PROTOPLASTS
PROTOPORPHYRIN
PROTOPORPHYRINS
PROTOSPATAIRE
PROTOSPATAIRES
PROTOSPATHAIRE
PROTOSPATHAIRES
PROTOSPATHARIUS
PROTOSTARS
PROTOSTELE
PROTOSTELES
PROTOSTELIC
PROTOSTOME
PROTOSTOMES
PROTOTHERIAN
PROTOTHERIANS
PROTOTROPH
PROTOTROPHIC
PROTOTROPHIES
PROTOTROPHS
PROTOTROPHY
PROTOTYPAL
PROTOTYPED
PROTOTYPES
PROTOTYPIC
PROTOTYPICAL
PROTOTYPICALLY
PROTOTYPING
PROTOXIDES
PROTOXYLEM
PROTOXYLEMS
PROTOZOANS
PROTOZOOLOGICAL
PROTOZOOLOGIES
PROTOZOOLOGIST
PROTOZOOLOGISTS
PROTOZOOLOGY
PROTOZOONS
PROTRACTED
PROTRACTEDLY
PROTRACTEDNESS
PROTRACTIBLE
PROTRACTILE
PROTRACTING
PROTRACTION
PROTRACTIONS
PROTRACTIVE
PROTRACTOR
PROTRACTORS
PROTREPTIC
PROTREPTICAL
PROTREPTICS
PROTRUDABLE
PROTRUDENT
PROTRUDING
PROTRUSIBLE
PROTRUSILE
PROTRUSION
PROTRUSIONS
PROTRUSIVE
PROTRUSIVELY
PROTRUSIVENESS
PROTUBERANCE
PROTUBERANCES
PROTUBERANCIES
PROTUBERANCY
PROTUBERANT
PROTUBERANTLY
PROTUBERATE
PROTUBERATED
PROTUBERATES
PROTUBERATING
PROTUBERATION
PROTUBERATIONS
PROUDHEARTED
PROUDNESSES
PROUSTITES
PROVABILITIES
PROVABILITY
PROVABLENESS
PROVABLENESSES
PROVANTING
PROVASCULAR
PROVEABILITIES
PROVEABILITY
PROVECTION
PROVECTIONS
PROVEDITOR
PROVEDITORE
PROVEDITORES
PROVEDITORS
PROVEDORES
PROVENANCE
PROVENANCES
PROVENDERED
PROVENDERING
PROVENDERS
PROVENIENCE
PROVENIENCES
PROVENTRICULAR
PROVENTRICULI
PROVENTRICULUS
PROVERBIAL
PROVERBIALISE
PROVERBIALISED
PROVERBIALISES
PROVERBIALISING
PROVERBIALISM
PROVERBIALISMS
PROVERBIALIST
PROVERBIALISTS

PROVERBIALIZE
PROVERBIALIZED
PROVERBIALIZES
PROVERBIALIZING
PROVERBIALLY
PROVERBING
PROVIDABLE
PROVIDENCE
PROVIDENCES
PROVIDENTIAL
PROVIDENTIALLY
PROVIDENTLY
PROVINCEWIDE
PROVINCIAL
PROVINCIALISE
PROVINCIALISED
PROVINCIALISES
PROVINCIALISING
PROVINCIALISM
PROVINCIALISMS
PROVINCIALIST
PROVINCIALISTS
PROVINCIALITIES
PROVINCIALITY
PROVINCIALIZE
PROVINCIALIZED
PROVINCIALIZES
PROVINCIALIZING
PROVINCIALLY
PROVINCIALS
PROVIRUSES
PROVISIONAL
PROVISIONALLY
PROVISIONALS
PROVISIONARIES
PROVISIONARY
PROVISIONED
PROVISIONER
PROVISIONERS
PROVISIONING
PROVISIONS
PROVISORILY
PROVITAMIN
PROVITAMINS
PROVOCABLE
PROVOCANTS
PROVOCATEUR
PROVOCATEURS
PROVOCATION
PROVOCATIONS
PROVOCATIVE
PROVOCATIVELY
PROVOCATIVENESS
PROVOCATIVES
PROVOCATOR
PROVOCATORS
PROVOCATORY
PROVOKABLE
PROVOKEMENT
PROVOKEMENTS
PROVOKINGLY
PROVOLONES
PROVOSTRIES
PROVOSTSHIP
PROVOSTSHIPS
PROWLINGLY
PROXIMALLY
PROXIMATELY
PROXIMATENESS
PROXIMATENESSES
PROXIMATION
PROXIMATIONS
PROXIMITIES
PROZYMITES
PRUDENTIAL
PRUDENTIALISM
PRUDENTIALISMS
PRUDENTIALIST
PRUDENTIALISTS
PRUDENTIALITIES
PRUDENTIALITY
PRUDENTIALLY
PRUDENTIALS
PRUDISHNESS
PRUDISHNESSES
PRURIENCES
PRURIENCIES
PRURIENTLY
PRURIGINOUS
PRURITUSES
PRUSSIANISATION
PRUSSIANISE
PRUSSIANISED
PRUSSIANISES
PRUSSIANISING
PRUSSIANIZATION
PRUSSIANIZE
PRUSSIANIZED
PRUSSIANIZES
PRUSSIANIZING
PRUSSIATES
PSALIGRAPHIES
PSALIGRAPHY
PSALMBOOKS
PSALMODICAL
PSALMODIES
PSALMODISE
PSALMODISED
PSALMODISES
PSALMODISING
PSALMODIST
PSALMODISTS
PSALMODIZE
PSALMODIZED
PSALMODIZES
PSALMODIZING
PSALTERIAN
PSALTERIES
PSALTERIUM
PSALTRESSES
PSAMMOPHIL
PSAMMOPHILE
PSAMMOPHILES
PSAMMOPHILOUS
PSAMMOPHILS
PSAMMOPHYTE
PSAMMOPHYTES
PSAMMOPHYTIC
PSELLISMUS
PSELLISMUSES
PSEPHOANALYSES
PSEPHOANALYSIS
PSEPHOLOGICAL
PSEPHOLOGICALLY
PSEPHOLOGIES
PSEPHOLOGIST
PSEPHOLOGISTS
PSEPHOLOGY
PSEUDAESTHESIA
PSEUDAESTHESIAS
PSEUDARTHROSES
PSEUDARTHROSIS
PSEUDEPIGRAPH
PSEUDEPIGRAPHA
PSEUDEPIGRAPHIC
PSEUDEPIGRAPHON
PSEUDEPIGRAPHS
PSEUDEPIGRAPHY
PSEUDERIES
PSEUDIMAGINES
PSEUDIMAGO
PSEUDIMAGOES
PSEUDIMAGOS
PSEUDOACID
PSEUDOACIDS
PSEUDOALLELE
PSEUDOALLELES
PSEUDOARTHROSES
PSEUDOARTHROSIS
PSEUDOBULB
PSEUDOBULBS
PSEUDOCARP
PSEUDOCARPOUS
PSEUDOCARPS
PSEUDOCIDE
PSEUDOCIDES
PSEUDOCLASSIC
PSEUDOCLASSICS
PSEUDOCODE
PSEUDOCODES
PSEUDOCOEL
PSEUDOCOELOMATE
PSEUDOCOELS
PSEUDOCYESES
PSEUDOCYESIS
PSEUDOEPHEDRINE
PSEUDOGRAPH
PSEUDOGRAPHIES
PSEUDOGRAPHS
PSEUDOGRAPHY
PSEUDOLOGIA
PSEUDOLOGIAS
PSEUDOLOGIES
PSEUDOLOGUE
PSEUDOLOGUES
PSEUDOLOGY
PSEUDOMARTYR
PSEUDOMARTYRS
PSEUDOMEMBRANE
PSEUDOMEMBRANES
PSEUDOMONAD
PSEUDOMONADES
PSEUDOMONADS
PSEUDOMONAS
PSEUDOMORPH
PSEUDOMORPHIC
PSEUDOMORPHISM
PSEUDOMORPHISMS
PSEUDOMORPHOUS
PSEUDOMORPHS
PSEUDOMUTUALITY
PSEUDONYMITIES
PSEUDONYMITY
PSEUDONYMOUS
PSEUDONYMOUSLY
PSEUDONYMS
PSEUDOPODAL
PSEUDOPODIA
PSEUDOPODIAL
PSEUDOPODIUM
PSEUDOPODS
PSEUDOPREGNANCY
PSEUDOPREGNANT
PSEUDORANDOM
PSEUDOSCALAR
PSEUDOSCALARS
PSEUDOSCIENCE
PSEUDOSCIENCES
PSEUDOSCIENTIST
PSEUDOSCOPE
PSEUDOSCOPES
PSEUDOSCORPION
PSEUDOSCORPIONS
PSEUDOSOLUTION
PSEUDOSOLUTIONS
PSEUDOSYMMETRY
PSEUDOVECTOR
PSEUDOVECTORS
PSILANTHROPIC
PSILANTHROPIES
PSILANTHROPISM
PSILANTHROPISMS
PSILANTHROPIST
PSILANTHROPISTS
PSILANTHROPY
PSILOCYBIN
PSILOCYBINS
PSILOMELANE
PSILOMELANES
PSILOPHYTE

PSILOPHYTES
PSILOPHYTIC
PSITTACINE
PSITTACINES
PSITTACOSES
PSITTACOSIS
PSITTACOTIC
PSORIATICS
PSYCHAGOGUE
PSYCHAGOGUES
PSYCHASTHENIA
PSYCHASTHENIAS
PSYCHASTHENIC
PSYCHASTHENICS
PSYCHEDELIA
PSYCHEDELIAS
PSYCHEDELIC
PSYCHEDELICALLY
PSYCHEDELICS
PSYCHIATER
PSYCHIATERS
PSYCHIATRIC
PSYCHIATRICAL
PSYCHIATRICALLY
PSYCHIATRIES
PSYCHIATRIST
PSYCHIATRISTS
PSYCHIATRY
PSYCHICALLY
PSYCHICISM
PSYCHICISMS
PSYCHICIST
PSYCHICISTS
PSYCHOACOUSTIC
PSYCHOACOUSTICS
PSYCHOACTIVE
PSYCHOANALYSE
PSYCHOANALYSED
PSYCHOANALYSER
PSYCHOANALYSERS
PSYCHOANALYSES
PSYCHOANALYSING
PSYCHOANALYSIS
PSYCHOANALYST
PSYCHOANALYSTS
PSYCHOANALYTIC
PSYCHOANALYZE
PSYCHOANALYZED
PSYCHOANALYZER
PSYCHOANALYZERS
PSYCHOANALYZES
PSYCHOANALYZING
PSYCHOBABBLE
PSYCHOBABBLED
PSYCHOBABBLER
PSYCHOBABBLERS
PSYCHOBABBLES
PSYCHOBABBLING
PSYCHOBILLIES
PSYCHOBILLY
PSYCHOBIOGRAPHY
PSYCHOBIOLOGIC
PSYCHOBIOLOGIES
PSYCHOBIOLOGIST
PSYCHOBIOLOGY
PSYCHOCHEMICAL
PSYCHOCHEMICALS
PSYCHOCHEMISTRY
PSYCHODELIA
PSYCHODELIAS
PSYCHODELIC
PSYCHODELICALLY
PSYCHODRAMA
PSYCHODRAMAS
PSYCHODRAMATIC
PSYCHODYNAMIC
PSYCHODYNAMICS
PSYCHOGALVANIC
PSYCHOGASES
PSYCHOGENESES
PSYCHOGENESIS
PSYCHOGENETIC
PSYCHOGENETICAL
PSYCHOGENETICS
PSYCHOGENIC
PSYCHOGENICALLY
PSYCHOGERIATRIC
PSYCHOGNOSES
PSYCHOGNOSIS
PSYCHOGNOSTIC
PSYCHOGONIES
PSYCHOGONY
PSYCHOGRAM
PSYCHOGRAMS
PSYCHOGRAPH
PSYCHOGRAPHIC
PSYCHOGRAPHICAL
PSYCHOGRAPHICS
PSYCHOGRAPHIES
PSYCHOGRAPHS
PSYCHOGRAPHY
PSYCHOHISTORIAN
PSYCHOHISTORIES
PSYCHOHISTORY
PSYCHOKINESES
PSYCHOKINESIS
PSYCHOKINETIC
PSYCHOLINGUIST
PSYCHOLINGUISTS
PSYCHOLOGIC
PSYCHOLOGICAL
PSYCHOLOGICALLY
PSYCHOLOGIES
PSYCHOLOGISE
PSYCHOLOGISED
PSYCHOLOGISES
PSYCHOLOGISING
PSYCHOLOGISM
PSYCHOLOGISMS
PSYCHOLOGIST
PSYCHOLOGISTIC
PSYCHOLOGISTS
PSYCHOLOGIZE
PSYCHOLOGIZED
PSYCHOLOGIZES
PSYCHOLOGIZING
PSYCHOLOGY
PSYCHOMACHIA
PSYCHOMACHIAS
PSYCHOMACHIES
PSYCHOMACHY
PSYCHOMETER
PSYCHOMETERS
PSYCHOMETRIC
PSYCHOMETRICAL
PSYCHOMETRICIAN
PSYCHOMETRICS
PSYCHOMETRIES
PSYCHOMETRIST
PSYCHOMETRISTS
PSYCHOMETRY
PSYCHOMOTOR
PSYCHONEUROSES
PSYCHONEUROSIS
PSYCHONEUROTIC
PSYCHONEUROTICS
PSYCHONOMIC
PSYCHONOMICS
PSYCHOPATH
PSYCHOPATHIC
PSYCHOPATHICS
PSYCHOPATHIES
PSYCHOPATHIST
PSYCHOPATHISTS
PSYCHOPATHOLOGY
PSYCHOPATHS
PSYCHOPATHY
PSYCHOPHILIES
PSYCHOPHILY
PSYCHOPHYSICAL
PSYCHOPHYSICIST
PSYCHOPHYSICS
PSYCHOPOMP
PSYCHOPOMPS
PSYCHOSEXUAL
PSYCHOSEXUALITY
PSYCHOSEXUALLY
PSYCHOSOCIAL
PSYCHOSOCIALLY
PSYCHOSOCIOLOGY
PSYCHOSOMATIC
PSYCHOSOMATICS
PSYCHOSOMIMETIC
PSYCHOSURGEON
PSYCHOSURGEONS
PSYCHOSURGERIES
PSYCHOSURGERY
PSYCHOSURGICAL
PSYCHOSYNTHESES
PSYCHOSYNTHESIS
PSYCHOTECHNICS
PSYCHOTHERAPIES
PSYCHOTHERAPIST
PSYCHOTHERAPY
PSYCHOTICALLY
PSYCHOTICISM
PSYCHOTICISMS
PSYCHOTICS
PSYCHOTOMIMETIC
PSYCHOTOXIC
PSYCHOTROPIC
PSYCHOTROPICS
PSYCHROMETER
PSYCHROMETERS
PSYCHROMETRIC
PSYCHROMETRICAL
PSYCHROMETRIES
PSYCHROMETRY
PSYCHROPHILIC
PTARMIGANS
PTERANODON
PTERANODONS
PTERIDINES
PTERIDOLOGICAL
PTERIDOLOGIES
PTERIDOLOGIST
PTERIDOLOGISTS
PTERIDOLOGY
PTERIDOMANIA
PTERIDOMANIAS
PTERIDOPHILIST
PTERIDOPHILISTS
PTERIDOPHYTE
PTERIDOPHYTES
PTERIDOPHYTIC
PTERIDOPHYTOUS
PTERIDOSPERM
PTERIDOSPERMS
PTERODACTYL
PTERODACTYLE
PTERODACTYLES
PTERODACTYLS
PTEROSAURIAN
PTEROSAURIANS
PTEROSAURS
PTERYGIALS
PTERYGIUMS
PTERYGOIDS
PTERYLOGRAPHIC
PTERYLOGRAPHIES
PTERYLOGRAPHY
PTERYLOSES
PTERYLOSIS
PTOCHOCRACIES
PTOCHOCRACY
PTYALAGOGIC
PTYALAGOGUE
PTYALAGOGUES
PTYALISING
PTYALIZING

P

PUBCRAWLER
PUBCRAWLERS
PUBERULENT
PUBERULOUS
PUBESCENCE
PUBESCENCES
PUBLICALLY
PUBLICATION
PUBLICATIONS
PUBLICISED
PUBLICISES
PUBLICISING
PUBLICISTS
PUBLICITIES
PUBLICIZED
PUBLICIZES
PUBLICIZING
PUBLICNESS
PUBLICNESSES
PUBLISHABLE
PUBLISHERS
PUBLISHING
PUBLISHINGS
PUBLISHMENT
PUBLISHMENTS
PUCCINIACEOUS
PUCKERIEST
PUCKEROOED
PUCKISHNESS
PUCKISHNESSES
PUDDENINGS
PUDDINGIER
PUDDINGIEST
PUDGINESSES
PUDIBUNDITIES
PUDIBUNDITY
PUDICITIES
PUERILISMS
PUERILITIES
PUERPERALLY
PUERPERIUM
PUFFERFISH
PUFFERFISHES
PUFFINESSES
PUFFTALOONAS
PUFTALOONAS
PUFTALOONIES
PUFTALOONS
PUGGINESSES
PUGILISTIC
PUGILISTICAL
PUGILISTICALLY
PUGNACIOUS
PUGNACIOUSLY
PUGNACIOUSNESS
PUGNACITIES
PUISSANCES
PUISSANTLY
PUISSAUNCE
PUISSAUNCES
PULCHRITUDE
PULCHRITUDES
PULCHRITUDINOUS
PULLULATED
PULLULATES
PULLULATING
PULLULATION
PULLULATIONS
PULMOBRANCH
PULMOBRANCHIATE
PULMOBRANCHS
PULMONATES
PULMONOLOGIES
PULMONOLOGIST
PULMONOLOGISTS
PULMONOLOGY
PULPBOARDS
PULPIFYING
PULPINESSES
PULPITEERED
PULPITEERING
PULPITEERS
PULPITRIES
PULPSTONES
PULSATANCE
PULSATANCES
PULSATILITIES
PULSATILITY
PULSATILLA
PULSATILLAS
PULSATIONS
PULSATIVELY
PULSEBEATS
PULSELESSNESS
PULSELESSNESSES
PULSIMETER
PULSIMETERS
PULSOMETER
PULSOMETERS
PULTACEOUS
PULTRUDING
PULTRUSION
PULTRUSIONS
PULVERABLE
PULVERATION
PULVERATIONS
PULVERINES
PULVERISABLE
PULVERISATION
PULVERISATIONS
PULVERISED
PULVERISER
PULVERISERS
PULVERISES
PULVERISING
PULVERIZABLE
PULVERIZATION
PULVERIZATIONS
PULVERIZED
PULVERIZER
PULVERIZERS
PULVERIZES
PULVERIZING
PULVERULENCE
PULVERULENCES
PULVERULENT
PULVILISED
PULVILIZED
PULVILLIFORM
PULVILLING
PULVILLIOS
PULVINATED
PULVINULES
PUMICATING
PUMMELLING
PUMMELLINGS
PUMPERNICKEL
PUMPERNICKELS
PUMPHOUSES
PUMPKINSEED
PUMPKINSEEDS
PUNCHBALLS
PUNCHBOARD
PUNCHBOARDS
PUNCHBOWLS
PUNCHINELLO
PUNCHINELLOES
PUNCHINELLOS
PUNCHINESS
PUNCHINESSES
PUNCHLINES
PUNCTATION
PUNCTATIONS
PUNCTATORS
PUNCTILIOS
PUNCTILIOUS
PUNCTILIOUSLY
PUNCTILIOUSNESS
PUNCTUALIST
PUNCTUALISTS
PUNCTUALITIES
PUNCTUALITY
PUNCTUALLY
PUNCTUATED
PUNCTUATES
PUNCTUATING
PUNCTUATION
PUNCTUATIONIST
PUNCTUATIONISTS
PUNCTUATIONS
PUNCTUATIVE
PUNCTUATOR
PUNCTUATORS
PUNCTULATE
PUNCTULATED
PUNCTULATES
PUNCTULATING
PUNCTULATION
PUNCTULATIONS
PUNCTURABLE
PUNCTURATION
PUNCTURATIONS
PUNCTURERS
PUNCTURING
PUNDIGRION
PUNDIGRIONS
PUNDITRIES
PUNDONORES
PUNGENCIES
PUNICACEOUS
PUNINESSES
PUNISHABILITIES
PUNISHABILITY
PUNISHABLE
PUNISHINGLY
PUNISHMENT
PUNISHMENTS
PUNITIVELY
PUNITIVENESS
PUNITIVENESSES
PUNKINESSES
PUPIGEROUS
PUPILABILITIES
PUPILABILITY
PUPILARITIES
PUPILARITY
PUPILLAGES
PUPILLARITIES
PUPILLARITY
PUPILLATED
PUPILLATES
PUPILLATING
PUPILSHIPS
PUPIPAROUS
PUPPETEERED
PUPPETEERING
PUPPETEERS
PUPPETLIKE
PUPPETRIES
PUPPYHOODS
PURBLINDLY
PURBLINDNESS
PURBLINDNESSES
PURCHASABILITY
PURCHASABLE
PURCHASERS
PURCHASING
PURCHASINGS
PURDONIUMS
PUREBLOODS
PURENESSES
PURGATIONS
PURGATIVELY
PURGATIVES
PURGATORIAL
PURGATORIALLY
PURGATORIAN
PURGATORIANS
PURGATORIES
PURIFICATION

PURIFICATIONS
PURIFICATIVE
PURIFICATOR
PURIFICATORS
PURIFICATORY
PURISTICAL
PURISTICALLY
PURITANICAL
PURITANICALLY
PURITANICALNESS
PURITANISE
PURITANISED
PURITANISES
PURITANISING
PURITANISM
PURITANISMS
PURITANIZE
PURITANIZED
PURITANIZES
PURITANIZING
PURLICUING
PURLOINERS
PURLOINING
PUROMYCINS
PURPLEHEART
PURPLEHEARTS
PURPLENESS
PURPLENESSES
PURPORTEDLY
PURPORTING
PURPORTLESS
PURPOSEFUL
PURPOSEFULLY
PURPOSEFULNESS
PURPOSELESS
PURPOSELESSLY
PURPOSELESSNESS
PURPOSIVELY
PURPOSIVENESS
PURPOSIVENESSES
PURPRESTURE
PURPRESTURES
PURSERSHIP
PURSERSHIPS
PURSINESSES
PURSUANCES
PURSUANTLY
PURSUINGLY
PURSUIVANT
PURSUIVANTS
PURTENANCE
PURTENANCES
PURULENCES
PURULENCIES
PURULENTLY
PURVEYANCE
PURVEYANCES
PUSCHKINIA
PUSCHKINIAS
PUSHCHAIRS
PUSHFULNESS
PUSHFULNESSES
PUSHINESSES
PUSHINGNESS
PUSHINGNESSES
PUSILLANIMITIES
PUSILLANIMITY
PUSILLANIMOUS
PUSILLANIMOUSLY
PUSSYFOOTED
PUSSYFOOTER
PUSSYFOOTERS
PUSSYFOOTING
PUSSYFOOTINGS
PUSSYFOOTS
PUSTULANTS
PUSTULATED
PUSTULATES
PUSTULATING
PUSTULATION
PUSTULATIONS
PUTANGITANGI
PUTANGITANGIS
PUTATIVELY
PUTONGHUAS
PUTREFACIENT
PUTREFACTION
PUTREFACTIONS
PUTREFACTIVE
PUTREFIABLE
PUTREFIERS
PUTREFYING
PUTRESCENCE
PUTRESCENCES
PUTRESCENT
PUTRESCIBILITY
PUTRESCIBLE
PUTRESCIBLES
PUTRESCINE
PUTRESCINES
PUTRIDITIES
PUTRIDNESS
PUTRIDNESSES
PUTRIFICATION
PUTRIFICATIONS
PUTSCHISTS
PUTTYROOTS
PUZZLEDOMS
PUZZLEHEADED
PUZZLEMENT
PUZZLEMENTS
PUZZLINGLY
PUZZOLANAS
PYCNIDIOSPORE
PYCNIDIOSPORES
PYCNOCONIDIA
PYCNOCONIDIUM
PYCNODYSOSTOSES
PYCNODYSOSTOSIS
PYCNOGONID
PYCNOGONIDS
PYCNOGONOID
PYCNOGONOIDS
PYCNOMETER
PYCNOMETERS
PYCNOMETRIC
PYCNOSOMES
PYCNOSPORE
PYCNOSPORES
PYCNOSTYLE
PYCNOSTYLES
PYELITISES
PYELOGRAMS
PYELOGRAPHIC
PYELOGRAPHIES
PYELOGRAPHY
PYELONEPHRITIC
PYELONEPHRITIS
PYGARGUSES
PYGOSTYLES
PYKNODYSOSTOSES
PYKNODYSOSTOSIS
PYKNOMETER
PYKNOMETERS
PYKNOSOMES
PYLORECTOMIES
PYLORECTOMY
PYOGENESES
PYOGENESIS
PYORRHOEAL
PYORRHOEAS
PYORRHOEIC
PYRACANTHA
PYRACANTHAS
PYRACANTHS
PYRALIDIDS
PYRAMIDALLY
PYRAMIDICAL
PYRAMIDICALLY
PYRAMIDING
PYRAMIDION
PYRAMIDIONS
PYRAMIDIST
PYRAMIDISTS
PYRAMIDOLOGIES
PYRAMIDOLOGIST
PYRAMIDOLOGISTS
PYRAMIDOLOGY
PYRAMIDONS
PYRANOMETER
PYRANOMETERS
PYRANOSIDE
PYRANOSIDES
PYRARGYRITE
PYRARGYRITES
PYRENEITES
PYRENOCARP
PYRENOCARPS
PYRENOMYCETOUS
PYRETHRINS
PYRETHROID
PYRETHROIDS
PYRETHRUMS
PYRETOLOGIES
PYRETOLOGY
PYRETOTHERAPIES
PYRETOTHERAPY
PYRGEOMETER
PYRGEOMETERS
PYRHELIOMETER
PYRHELIOMETERS
PYRHELIOMETRIC
PYRIDOXALS
PYRIDOXAMINE
PYRIDOXAMINES
PYRIDOXINE
PYRIDOXINES
PYRIDOXINS
PYRIMETHAMINE
PYRIMETHAMINES
PYRIMIDINE
PYRIMIDINES
PYRITHIAMINE
PYRITHIAMINES
PYRITIFEROUS
PYRITISING
PYRITIZING
PYRITOHEDRA
PYRITOHEDRAL
PYRITOHEDRON
PYRITOHEDRONS
PYROBALLOGIES
PYROBALLOGY
PYROCATECHIN
PYROCATECHINS
PYROCATECHOL
PYROCATECHOLS
PYROCERAMS
PYROCHEMICAL
PYROCHEMICALLY
PYROCLASTIC
PYROCLASTICS
PYROCLASTS
PYROELECTRIC
PYROELECTRICITY
PYROELECTRICS
PYROGALLATE
PYROGALLATES
PYROGALLIC
PYROGALLOL
PYROGALLOLS
PYROGENETIC
PYROGENICITIES
PYROGENICITY
PYROGENOUS
PYROGNOSTIC
PYROGNOSTICS
PYROGRAPHER
PYROGRAPHERS
PYROGRAPHIC

PYROGRAPHIES
PYROGRAPHY
PYROGRAVURE
PYROGRAVURES
PYROKINESES
PYROKINESIS
PYROLATERS
PYROLATRIES
PYROLIGNEOUS
PYROLIGNIC
PYROLISING
PYROLIZING
PYROLOGIES
PYROLUSITE
PYROLUSITES
PYROLYSABLE
PYROLYSATE
PYROLYSATES
PYROLYSERS
PYROLYSING
PYROLYTICALLY
PYROLYZABLE
PYROLYZATE
PYROLYZATES
PYROLYZERS
PYROLYZING
PYROMAGNETIC
PYROMANCER
PYROMANCERS
PYROMANCIES
PYROMANIAC
PYROMANIACAL
PYROMANIACS
PYROMANIAS
PYROMANTIC
PYROMERIDE
PYROMERIDES
PYROMETALLURGY
PYROMETERS
PYROMETRIC
PYROMETRICAL
PYROMETRICALLY
PYROMETRIES
PYROMORPHITE
PYROMORPHITES
PYRONINOPHILIC
PYROPHOBIA
PYROPHOBIAS
PYROPHOBIC
PYROPHOBICS
PYROPHONES
PYROPHORIC
PYROPHOROUS
PYROPHORUS
PYROPHORUSES
PYROPHOSPHATE
PYROPHOSPHATES
PYROPHOSPHORIC
PYROPHOTOGRAPH
PYROPHOTOGRAPHS
PYROPHOTOGRAPHY
PYROPHOTOMETER
PYROPHOTOMETERS
PYROPHOTOMETRY
PYROPHYLLITE
PYROPHYLLITES
PYROSCOPES
PYROSTATIC
PYROSULFITE
PYROSULFITES
PYROSULPHATE
PYROSULPHATES
PYROSULPHURIC
PYROTARTARIC
PYROTARTRATE
PYROTARTRATES
PYROTECHNIC
PYROTECHNICAL
PYROTECHNICALLY
PYROTECHNICIAN
PYROTECHNICIANS
PYROTECHNICS
PYROTECHNIES
PYROTECHNIST
PYROTECHNISTS
PYROTECHNY
PYROVANADIC
PYROXENITE
PYROXENITES
PYROXENITIC
PYROXENOID
PYROXENOIDS
PYROXYLINE
PYROXYLINES
PYROXYLINS
PYRRHICIST
PYRRHICISTS
PYRRHOTINE
PYRRHOTINES
PYRRHOTITE
PYRRHOTITES
PYRRHULOXIA
PYRRHULOXIAS
PYRROLIDINE
PYRROLIDINES
PYTHOGENIC
PYTHONESSES
PYTHONOMORPH
PYTHONOMORPHS

Q

QABALISTIC
QINGHAOSUS
QUACKERIES
QUACKSALVER
QUACKSALVERS
QUACKSALVING
QUADCOPTER
QUADCOPTERS
QUADPLEXES
QUADRAGENARIAN
QUADRAGENARIANS
QUADRAGESIMAL
QUADRANGLE
QUADRANGLES
QUADRANGULAR
QUADRANGULARLY
QUADRANTAL
QUADRANTES
QUADRAPHONIC
QUADRAPHONICS
QUADRAPHONIES
QUADRAPHONY
QUADRAPLEGIA
QUADRAPLEGIAS
QUADRAPLEGIC
QUADRAPLEGICS
QUADRASONIC
QUADRASONICS
QUADRATICAL
QUADRATICALLY
QUADRATICS
QUADRATING
QUADRATRICES
QUADRATRIX
QUADRATRIXES
QUADRATURA
QUADRATURE
QUADRATURES
QUADRATUSES
QUADRELLAS
QUADRENNIA
QUADRENNIAL
QUADRENNIALLY
QUADRENNIALS
QUADRENNIUM
QUADRENNIUMS
QUADRICEPS
QUADRICEPSES
QUADRICIPITAL
QUADRICONE
QUADRICONES
QUADRIENNIA
QUADRIENNIAL
QUADRIENNIUM
QUADRIENNIUMS
QUADRIFARIOUS
QUADRIFOLIATE
QUADRIFORM
QUADRIGEMINAL
QUADRIGEMINATE
QUADRIGEMINOUS
QUADRILATERAL
QUADRILATERALS
QUADRILINGUAL
QUADRILITERAL
QUADRILITERALS
QUADRILLED
QUADRILLER
QUADRILLERS
QUADRILLES
QUADRILLING
QUADRILLION
QUADRILLIONS
QUADRILLIONTH
QUADRILLIONTHS
QUADRILOCULAR
QUADRINGENARIES
QUADRINGENARY
QUADRINOMIAL
QUADRINOMIALS
QUADRIPARTITE
QUADRIPARTITION
QUADRIPHONIC
QUADRIPHONICS
QUADRIPLEGIA
QUADRIPLEGIAS
QUADRIPLEGIC
QUADRIPLEGICS
QUADRIPOLE
QUADRIPOLES
QUADRIREME
QUADRIREMES
QUADRISECT
QUADRISECTED
QUADRISECTING
QUADRISECTION
QUADRISECTIONS
QUADRISECTS
QUADRISYLLABIC
QUADRISYLLABICS
QUADRISYLLABLE
QUADRISYLLABLES
QUADRIVALENCE
QUADRIVALENCES
QUADRIVALENCIES
QUADRIVALENCY
QUADRIVALENT
QUADRIVALENTS
QUADRIVIAL
QUADRIVIUM
QUADRIVIUMS
QUADROPHONIC
QUADROPHONICS
QUADROPHONIES
QUADROPHONY
QUADRUMANE
QUADRUMANES
QUADRUMANOUS
QUADRUMANS
QUADRUMVIR
QUADRUMVIRATE
QUADRUMVIRATES
QUADRUMVIRS
QUADRUPEDAL
QUADRUPEDS
QUADRUPLED
QUADRUPLES
QUADRUPLET
QUADRUPLETS
QUADRUPLEX
QUADRUPLEXED
QUADRUPLEXES
QUADRUPLEXING
QUADRUPLICATE
QUADRUPLICATED
QUADRUPLICATES
QUADRUPLICATING
QUADRUPLICATION
QUADRUPLICITIES
QUADRUPLICITY
QUADRUPLIES
QUADRUPLING
QUADRUPOLE
QUADRUPOLES
QUAESITUMS
QUAESTIONARIES
QUAESTIONARY
QUAESTORIAL
QUAESTORSHIP
QUAESTORSHIPS
QUAESTUARIES
QUAESTUARY
QUAGGINESS
QUAGGINESSES
QUAGMIRIER
QUAGMIRIEST
QUAGMIRING
QUAINTNESS
QUAINTNESSES
QUAKINESSES
QUALIFIABLE
QUALIFICATION
QUALIFICATIONS
QUALIFICATIVE
QUALIFICATIVES
QUALIFICATOR
QUALIFICATORS
QUALIFICATORY
QUALIFIEDLY
QUALIFIERS
QUALIFYING
QUALIFYINGS
QUALITATIVE
QUALITATIVELY
QUALMISHLY
QUALMISHNESS
QUALMISHNESSES
QUANDARIES
QUANGOCRACIES
QUANGOCRACY
QUANTIFIABLE
QUANTIFICATION
QUANTIFICATIONS
QUANTIFIED
QUANTIFIER
QUANTIFIERS
QUANTIFIES
QUANTIFYING
QUANTISATION
QUANTISATIONS
QUANTISERS
QUANTISING
QUANTITATE
QUANTITATED
QUANTITATES
QUANTITATING
QUANTITATION
QUANTITATIONS
QUANTITATIVE
QUANTITATIVELY
QUANTITIES
QUANTITIVE
QUANTITIVELY
QUANTIVALENCE
QUANTIVALENCES
QUANTIVALENT
QUANTIZATION
QUANTIZATIONS
QUANTIZERS
QUANTIZING

QUANTOMETER
QUANTOMETERS
QUAQUAVERSAL
QUAQUAVERSALLY
QUARANTINE
QUARANTINED
QUARANTINES
QUARANTINING
QUARENDENS
QUARENDERS
QUARRELERS
QUARRELING
QUARRELINGS
QUARRELLED
QUARRELLER
QUARRELLERS
QUARRELLING
QUARRELLINGS
QUARRELLOUS
QUARRELSOME
QUARRELSOMELY
QUARRELSOMENESS
QUARRENDER
QUARRENDERS
QUARRIABLE
QUARRINGTON
QUARRINGTONS
QUARRYINGS
QUARRYMASTER
QUARRYMASTERS
QUARTATION
QUARTATIONS
QUARTERAGE
QUARTERAGES
QUARTERBACK
QUARTERBACKED
QUARTERBACKING
QUARTERBACKINGS
QUARTERBACKS
QUARTERDECK
QUARTERDECKER
QUARTERDECKERS
QUARTERDECKS
QUARTERERS
QUARTERFINAL
QUARTERFINALIST
QUARTERFINALS
QUARTERING
QUARTERINGS
QUARTERLIES
QUARTERLIFE
QUARTERLIGHT
QUARTERLIGHTS
QUARTERMASTER
QUARTERMASTERS
QUARTERMISTRESS
QUARTEROON
QUARTEROONS
QUARTERSAW
QUARTERSAWED
QUARTERSAWING
QUARTERSAWN
QUARTERSAWS
QUARTERSTAFF
QUARTERSTAFFS
QUARTERSTAVES
QUARTETTES
QUARTODECIMAN
QUARTODECIMANS
QUARTZIEST
QUARTZIFEROUS
QUARTZITES
QUARTZITIC
QUASICRYSTAL
QUASICRYSTALS
QUASIPARTICLE
QUASIPARTICLES
QUASIPERIODIC
QUATERCENTENARY
QUATERNARIES
QUATERNARY
QUATERNATE
QUATERNION
QUATERNIONIST
QUATERNIONISTS
QUATERNIONS
QUATERNITIES
QUATERNITY
QUATORZAIN
QUATORZAINS
QUATREFEUILLE
QUATREFEUILLES
QUATREFOIL
QUATREFOILS
QUATTROCENTISM
QUATTROCENTISMS
QUATTROCENTIST
QUATTROCENTISTS
QUATTROCENTO
QUATTROCENTOS
QUAVERIEST
QUAVERINGLY
QUAVERINGS
QUEACHIEST
QUEASINESS
QUEASINESSES
QUEBRACHOS
QUEECHIEST
QUEENCAKES
QUEENCRAFT
QUEENCRAFTS
QUEENFISHES
QUEENHOODS
QUEENLIEST
QUEENLINESS
QUEENLINESSES
QUEENSHIPS
QUEENSIDES
QUEERCORES
QUEERITIES
QUEERNESSES
QUELQUECHOSE
QUELQUECHOSES
QUENCHABLE
QUENCHINGS
QUENCHLESS
QUENCHLESSLY
QUERCETINS
QUERCETUMS
QUERCITINS
QUERCITRON
QUERCITRONS
QUERIMONIES
QUERIMONIOUS
QUERIMONIOUSLY
QUERNSTONE
QUERNSTONES
QUERSPRUNG
QUERSPRUNGS
QUERULOUSLY
QUERULOUSNESS
QUERULOUSNESSES
QUERYINGLY
QUESADILLA
QUESADILLAS
QUESTINGLY
QUESTIONABILITY
QUESTIONABLE
QUESTIONABLY
QUESTIONARIES
QUESTIONARY
QUESTIONED
QUESTIONEE
QUESTIONEES
QUESTIONER
QUESTIONERS
QUESTIONING
QUESTIONINGLY
QUESTIONINGS
QUESTIONIST
QUESTIONISTS
QUESTIONLESS
QUESTIONLESSLY
QUESTIONNAIRE
QUESTIONNAIRES
QUESTORIAL
QUESTORSHIP
QUESTORSHIPS
QUESTRISTS
QUIBBLINGLY
QUIBBLINGS
QUICKBEAMS
QUICKENERS
QUICKENING
QUICKENINGS
QUICKLIMES
QUICKNESSES
QUICKSANDS
QUICKSILVER
QUICKSILVERED
QUICKSILVERIER
QUICKSILVERIEST
QUICKSILVERING
QUICKSILVERINGS
QUICKSILVERISH
QUICKSILVERS
QUICKSILVERY
QUICKSTEPPED
QUICKSTEPPING
QUICKSTEPS
QUICKTHORN
QUICKTHORNS
QUIDDANIED
QUIDDANIES
QUIDDANYING
QUIDDITATIVE
QUIDDITCHES
QUIDDITIES
QUIESCENCE
QUIESCENCES
QUIESCENCIES
QUIESCENCY
QUIESCENTLY
QUIETENERS
QUIETENING
QUIETENINGS
QUIETISTIC
QUIETNESSES
QUILLBACKS
QUILLWORKS
QUILLWORTS
QUINACRINE
QUINACRINES
QUINALBARBITONE
QUINAQUINA
QUINAQUINAS
QUINCENTENARIES
QUINCENTENARY
QUINCENTENNIAL
QUINCENTENNIALS
QUINCUNCIAL
QUINCUNCIALLY
QUINCUNXES
QUINCUNXIAL
QUINDECAGON
QUINDECAGONS
QUINDECAPLET
QUINDECAPLETS
QUINDECENNIAL
QUINDECENNIALS
QUINDECILLION
QUINDECILLIONS
QUINGENTENARIES
QUINGENTENARY
QUINIDINES
QUINOLINES
QUINOLONES
QUINQUAGENARIAN
QUINQUAGESIMAL
QUINQUECOSTATE

QUINQUEFARIOUS
QUINQUEFOLIATE
QUINQUENNIA
QUINQUENNIAD
QUINQUENNIADS
QUINQUENNIAL
QUINQUENNIALLY
QUINQUENNIALS
QUINQUENNIUM
QUINQUENNIUMS
QUINQUEPARTITE
QUINQUEREME
QUINQUEREMES
QUINQUEVALENCE
QUINQUEVALENCES
QUINQUEVALENCY
QUINQUEVALENT
QUINQUINAS
QUINQUIVALENCE
QUINQUIVALENCES
QUINQUIVALENCY
QUINQUIVALENT
QUINTESSENCE
QUINTESSENCES
QUINTESSENTIAL
QUINTESSENTIALS
QUINTETTES
QUINTILLION
QUINTILLIONS
QUINTILLIONTH
QUINTILLIONTHS
QUINTROONS
QUINTUPLED
QUINTUPLES
QUINTUPLET
QUINTUPLETS
QUINTUPLICATE
QUINTUPLICATED
QUINTUPLICATES
QUINTUPLICATING
QUINTUPLICATION
QUINTUPLIES
QUINTUPLING
QUIRISTERS
QUIRKINESS
QUIRKINESSES
QUISLINGISM
QUISLINGISMS
QUITCLAIMED
QUITCLAIMING
QUITCLAIMS
QUITTANCED
QUITTANCES
QUITTANCING
QUIVERFULS
QUIVERIEST
QUIVERINGLY
QUIVERINGS
QUIVERSFUL
QUIXOTICAL
QUIXOTICALLY
QUIXOTISMS
QUIXOTRIES
QUIZMASTER
QUIZMASTERS
QUIZZERIES
QUIZZICALITIES
QUIZZICALITY
QUIZZICALLY
QUIZZIFICATION
QUIZZIFICATIONS
QUIZZIFIED
QUIZZIFIES
QUIZZIFYING
QUIZZINESS
QUIZZINESSES
QUODLIBETARIAN
QUODLIBETARIANS
QUODLIBETIC
QUODLIBETICAL
QUODLIBETICALLY
QUODLIBETS
QUOTABILITIES
QUOTABILITY
QUOTABLENESS
QUOTABLENESSES
QUOTATIONS
QUOTATIOUS
QUOTATIVES
QUOTEWORTHIER
QUOTEWORTHIEST
QUOTEWORTHY
QUOTIDIANS
QUOTITIONS

R

RABATMENTS
RABATTEMENT
RABATTEMENTS
RABATTINGS
RABBINATES
RABBINICAL
RABBINICALLY
RABBINISMS
RABBINISTIC
RABBINISTS
RABBINITES
RABBITBRUSH
RABBITBRUSHES
RABBITFISH
RABBITFISHES
RABBITIEST
RABBITINGS
RABBITRIES
RABBLEMENT
RABBLEMENTS
RABIDITIES
RABIDNESSES
RACCAHOUTS
RACECOURSE
RACECOURSES
RACEGOINGS
RACEHORSES
RACEMATION
RACEMATIONS
RACEMISATION
RACEMISATIONS
RACEMISING
RACEMIZATION
RACEMIZATIONS
RACEMIZING
RACEMOSELY
RACEMOUSLY
RACETRACKER
RACETRACKERS
RACETRACKS
RACEWALKED
RACEWALKER
RACEWALKERS
RACEWALKING
RACEWALKINGS
RACHIOTOMIES
RACHIOTOMY
RACHISCHISES
RACHISCHISIS
RACHITIDES
RACHITISES
RACIALISED
RACIALISES
RACIALISING
RACIALISMS
RACIALISTIC
RACIALISTS
RACIALIZED
RACIALIZES
RACIALIZING
RACIATIONS
RACINESSES
RACKABONES
RACKETEERED
RACKETEERING
RACKETEERINGS
RACKETEERS
RACKETIEST
RACKETRIES
RACONTEURING
RACONTEURINGS
RACONTEURS
RACONTEUSE
RACONTEUSES
RACQUETBALL
RACQUETBALLS
RACQUETING
RACTOPAMINE
RACTOPAMINES
RADARSCOPE
RADARSCOPES
RADIALISATION
RADIALISATIONS
RADIALISED
RADIALISES
RADIALISING
RADIALITIES
RADIALIZATION
RADIALIZATIONS
RADIALIZED
RADIALIZES
RADIALIZING
RADIANCIES
RADIATIONAL
RADIATIONLESS
RADIATIONS
RADICALISATION
RADICALISATIONS
RADICALISE
RADICALISED
RADICALISES
RADICALISING
RADICALISM
RADICALISMS
RADICALISTIC
RADICALITIES
RADICALITY
RADICALIZATION
RADICALIZATIONS
RADICALIZE
RADICALIZED
RADICALIZES
RADICALIZING
RADICALNESS
RADICALNESSES
RADICATING
RADICATION
RADICATIONS
RADICCHIOS
RADICELLOSE
RADICICOLOUS
RADICIFORM
RADICIVOROUS
RADICULOSE
RADIESTHESIA
RADIESTHESIAS
RADIESTHESIST
RADIESTHESISTS
RADIESTHETIC
RADIOACTIVATE
RADIOACTIVATED
RADIOACTIVATES
RADIOACTIVATING
RADIOACTIVATION
RADIOACTIVE
RADIOACTIVELY
RADIOACTIVITIES
RADIOACTIVITY
RADIOAUTOGRAPH
RADIOAUTOGRAPHS
RADIOAUTOGRAPHY
RADIOBIOLOGIC
RADIOBIOLOGICAL
RADIOBIOLOGIES
RADIOBIOLOGIST
RADIOBIOLOGISTS
RADIOBIOLOGY
RADIOCARBON
RADIOCARBONS
RADIOCHEMICAL
RADIOCHEMICALLY
RADIOCHEMIST
RADIOCHEMISTRY
RADIOCHEMISTS
RADIOECOLOGIES
RADIOECOLOGY
RADIOELEMENT
RADIOELEMENTS
RADIOGENIC
RADIOGOLDS
RADIOGONIOMETER
RADIOGONIOMETRY
RADIOGRAMS
RADIOGRAPH
RADIOGRAPHED
RADIOGRAPHER
RADIOGRAPHERS
RADIOGRAPHIC
RADIOGRAPHIES
RADIOGRAPHING
RADIOGRAPHS
RADIOGRAPHY
RADIOIODINE
RADIOIODINES
RADIOISOTOPE
RADIOISOTOPES
RADIOISOTOPIC
RADIOLABEL
RADIOLABELED
RADIOLABELING
RADIOLABELLED
RADIOLABELLING
RADIOLABELS
RADIOLARIAN
RADIOLARIANS
RADIOLOCATION
RADIOLOCATIONAL
RADIOLOCATIONS
RADIOLOGIC
RADIOLOGICAL
RADIOLOGICALLY
RADIOLOGIES
RADIOLOGIST
RADIOLOGISTS
RADIOLUCENCIES
RADIOLUCENCY
RADIOLUCENT
RADIOLYSES
RADIOLYSIS
RADIOLYTIC
RADIOMETER
RADIOMETERS
RADIOMETRIC
RADIOMETRICALLY
RADIOMETRIES
RADIOMETRY
RADIOMICROMETER
RADIOMIMETIC
RADIONUCLIDE
RADIONUCLIDES

RADIOPACITIES
RADIOPACITY
RADIOPAGER
RADIOPAGERS
RADIOPAGING
RADIOPAGINGS
RADIOPAQUE
RADIOPHONE
RADIOPHONES
RADIOPHONIC
RADIOPHONICALLY
RADIOPHONICS
RADIOPHONIES
RADIOPHONIST
RADIOPHONISTS
RADIOPHONY
RADIOPHOSPHORUS
RADIOPHOTO
RADIOPHOTOS
RADIOPROTECTION
RADIOPROTECTIVE
RADIORESISTANT
RADIOSCOPE
RADIOSCOPES
RADIOSCOPIC
RADIOSCOPICALLY
RADIOSCOPIES
RADIOSCOPY
RADIOSENSITISE
RADIOSENSITISED
RADIOSENSITISES
RADIOSENSITIVE
RADIOSENSITIZE
RADIOSENSITIZED
RADIOSENSITIZES
RADIOSONDE
RADIOSONDES
RADIOSTRONTIUM
RADIOSTRONTIUMS
RADIOTELEGRAM
RADIOTELEGRAMS
RADIOTELEGRAPH
RADIOTELEGRAPHS
RADIOTELEGRAPHY
RADIOTELEMETER
RADIOTELEMETERS
RADIOTELEMETRIC
RADIOTELEMETRY
RADIOTELEPHONE
RADIOTELEPHONED
RADIOTELEPHONES
RADIOTELEPHONIC
RADIOTELEPHONY
RADIOTELETYPE
RADIOTELETYPES
RADIOTHERAPIES
RADIOTHERAPIST
RADIOTHERAPISTS
RADIOTHERAPY
RADIOTHERMIES
RADIOTHERMY
RADIOTHONS
RADIOTHORIUM
RADIOTHORIUMS
RADIOTOXIC
RADIOTRACER
RADIOTRACERS
RADULIFORM
RAFFINATES
RAFFINOSES
RAFFISHNESS
RAFFISHNESSES
RAFFLESIAS
RAFTERINGS
RAGAMUFFIN
RAGAMUFFINS
RAGGAMUFFIN
RAGGAMUFFINS
RAGGEDIEST
RAGGEDNESS
RAGGEDNESSES
RAGMATICAL
RAGPICKERS
RAILBUSSES
RAILLERIES
RAILROADED
RAILROADER
RAILROADERS
RAILROADING
RAILROADINGS
RAILWAYMAN
RAILWAYMEN
RAILWORKER
RAILWORKERS
RAINBOWIER
RAINBOWIEST
RAINBOWLIKE
RAINCHECKS
RAINFOREST
RAINFORESTS
RAININESSES
RAINMAKERS
RAINMAKING
RAINMAKINGS
RAINPROOFED
RAINPROOFING
RAINPROOFS
RAINSPOUTS
RAINSQUALL
RAINSQUALLS
RAINSTICKS
RAINSTORMS
RAINWASHED
RAINWASHES
RAINWASHING
RAINWATERS
RAISINIEST
RAISONNEUR
RAISONNEURS
RAIYATWARI
RAIYATWARIS
RAJAHSHIPS
RAJPRAMUKH
RAJPRAMUKHS
RAKEHELLIER
RAKEHELLIEST
RAKESHAMES
RAKISHNESS
RAKISHNESSES
RALLENTANDI
RALLENTANDO
RALLENTANDOS
RALLYCROSS
RALLYCROSSES
RALLYINGLY
RAMAPITHECINE
RAMAPITHECINES
RAMBLINGLY
RAMBOUILLET
RAMBOUILLETS
RAMBUNCTIOUS
RAMBUNCTIOUSLY
RAMENTACEOUS
RAMGUNSHOCH
RAMIFICATION
RAMIFICATIONS
RAMMISHNESS
RAMMISHNESSES
RAMOSITIES
RAMPACIOUS
RAMPAGEOUS
RAMPAGEOUSLY
RAMPAGEOUSNESS
RAMPAGINGS
RAMPALLIAN
RAMPALLIANS
RAMPANCIES
RAMPARTING
RAMPAUGING
RAMRODDING
RAMSHACKLE
RANCELLING
RANCHERIAS
RANCHERIES
RANCHETTES
RANCHLANDS
RANCIDITIES
RANCIDNESS
RANCIDNESSES
RANCOROUSLY
RANCOROUSNESS
RANCOROUSNESSES
RANDINESSES
RANDOMISATION
RANDOMISATIONS
RANDOMISED
RANDOMISER
RANDOMISERS
RANDOMISES
RANDOMISING
RANDOMIZATION
RANDOMIZATIONS
RANDOMIZED
RANDOMIZER
RANDOMIZERS
RANDOMIZES
RANDOMIZING
RANDOMNESS
RANDOMNESSES
RANDOMWISE
RANGATIRAS
RANGATIRATANGA
RANGATIRATANGAS
RANGEFINDER
RANGEFINDERS
RANGEFINDING
RANGEFINDINGS
RANGELANDS
RANGERSHIP
RANGERSHIPS
RANGINESSES
RANIVOROUS
RANKNESSES
RANKSHIFTED
RANKSHIFTING
RANKSHIFTS
RANSACKERS
RANSACKING
RANSACKINGS
RANSHACKLE
RANSHACKLED
RANSHACKLES
RANSHACKLING
RANSHAKLED
RANSHAKLES
RANSHAKLING
RANSOMABLE
RANSOMLESS
RANSOMWARE
RANSOMWARES
RANTERISMS
RANTIPOLED
RANTIPOLES
RANTIPOLING
RANUNCULACEOUS
RANUNCULUS
RANUNCULUSES
RAPACIOUSLY
RAPACIOUSNESS
RAPACIOUSNESSES
RAPACITIES
RAPIDITIES
RAPIDNESSES
RAPIERLIKE
RAPPELLING
RAPPELLINGS
RAPPORTAGE
RAPPORTAGES
RAPPORTEUR
RAPPORTEURS

R

RAPPROCHEMENT
RAPPROCHEMENTS
RAPSCALLION
RAPSCALLIONS
RAPTATORIAL
RAPTNESSES
RAPTURELESS
RAPTURISED
RAPTURISES
RAPTURISING
RAPTURISTS
RAPTURIZED
RAPTURIZES
RAPTURIZING
RAPTUROUSLY
RAPTUROUSNESS
RAPTUROUSNESSES
RAREFACTION
RAREFACTIONAL
RAREFACTIONS
RAREFACTIVE
RAREFIABLE
RAREFICATION
RAREFICATIONAL
RAREFICATIONS
RARENESSES
RASCAILLES
RASCALDOMS
RASCALISMS
RASCALITIES
RASCALLIER
RASCALLIEST
RASCALLION
RASCALLIONS
RASHNESSES
RASPATORIES
RASPBERRIES
RASPINESSES
RASTAFARIAN
RASTAFARIANS
RASTAFARIS
RASTERISED
RASTERISES
RASTERISING
RASTERIZED
RASTERIZES
RASTERIZING
RATABILITIES
RATABILITY
RATABLENESS
RATABLENESSES
RATAPLANNED
RATAPLANNING
RATATOUILLE
RATATOUILLES
RATBAGGERIES
RATBAGGERY
RATCHETING
RATEABILITIES
RATEABILITY
RATEABLENESS
RATEABLENESSES
RATEMETERS
RATEPAYERS
RATHERIPES
RATHSKELLER
RATHSKELLERS
RATIFIABLE
RATIFICATION
RATIFICATIONS
RATIOCINATE
RATIOCINATED
RATIOCINATES
RATIOCINATING
RATIOCINATION
RATIOCINATIONS
RATIOCINATIVE
RATIOCINATOR
RATIOCINATORS
RATIOCINATORY
RATIONALES
RATIONALISABLE
RATIONALISATION
RATIONALISE
RATIONALISED
RATIONALISER
RATIONALISERS
RATIONALISES
RATIONALISING
RATIONALISM
RATIONALISMS
RATIONALIST
RATIONALISTIC
RATIONALISTS
RATIONALITIES
RATIONALITY
RATIONALIZABLE
RATIONALIZATION
RATIONALIZE
RATIONALIZED
RATIONALIZER
RATIONALIZERS
RATIONALIZES
RATIONALIZING
RATIONALLY
RATIONALNESS
RATIONALNESSES
RATIONINGS
RATTENINGS
RATTINESSES
RATTLEBAGS
RATTLEBOXES
RATTLEBRAIN
RATTLEBRAINED
RATTLEBRAINS
RATTLEPODS
RATTLESNAKE
RATTLESNAKES
RATTLETRAP
RATTLETRAPS
RATTLINGLY
RATTOONING
RAUCOUSNESS
RAUCOUSNESSES
RAUNCHIEST
RAUNCHINESS
RAUNCHINESSES
RAUWOLFIAS
RAVAGEMENT
RAVAGEMENTS
RAVELLIEST
RAVELLINGS
RAVELMENTS
RAVENINGLY
RAVENOUSLY
RAVENOUSNESS
RAVENOUSNESSES
RAVIGOTTES
RAVISHINGLY
RAVISHMENT
RAVISHMENTS
RAWINSONDE
RAWINSONDES
RAWMAISHES
RAYGRASSES
RAYLESSNESS
RAYLESSNESSES
RAZMATAZES
RAZORBACKS
RAZORBILLS
RAZORCLAMS
RAZORFISHES
RAZZAMATAZZ
RAZZAMATAZZES
RAZZBERRIES
RAZZMATAZZ
RAZZMATAZZES
REABSORBED
REABSORBING
REABSORPTION
REABSORPTIONS
REACCEDING
REACCELERATE
REACCELERATED
REACCELERATES
REACCELERATING
REACCENTED
REACCENTING
REACCEPTED
REACCEPTING
REACCESSION
REACCESSIONS
REACCLAIMED
REACCLAIMING
REACCLAIMS
REACCLIMATISE
REACCLIMATISED
REACCLIMATISES
REACCLIMATISING
REACCLIMATIZE
REACCLIMATIZED
REACCLIMATIZES
REACCLIMATIZING
REACCREDIT
REACCREDITATION
REACCREDITED
REACCREDITING
REACCREDITS
REACCUSING
REACCUSTOM
REACCUSTOMED
REACCUSTOMING
REACCUSTOMS
REACQUAINT
REACQUAINTANCE
REACQUAINTANCES
REACQUAINTED
REACQUAINTING
REACQUAINTS
REACQUIRED
REACQUIRES
REACQUIRING
REACQUISITION
REACQUISITIONS
REACTANCES
REACTIONAL
REACTIONARIES
REACTIONARISM
REACTIONARISMS
REACTIONARIST
REACTIONARISTS
REACTIONARY
REACTIONARYISM
REACTIONARYISMS
REACTIONISM
REACTIONISMS
REACTIONIST
REACTIONISTS
REACTIVATE
REACTIVATED
REACTIVATES
REACTIVATING
REACTIVATION
REACTIVATIONS
REACTIVELY
REACTIVENESS
REACTIVENESSES
REACTIVITIES
REACTIVITY
REACTUATED
REACTUATES
REACTUATING
READABILITIES
READABILITY
READABLENESS
READABLENESSES
READAPTATION
READAPTATIONS
READAPTING
READDICTED

R

READDICTING
READDRESSED
READDRESSES
READDRESSING
READERLIER
READERLIEST
READERSHIP
READERSHIPS
READINESSES
READJUSTABLE
READJUSTED
READJUSTER
READJUSTERS
READJUSTING
READJUSTMENT
READJUSTMENTS
READMISSION
READMISSIONS
READMITTANCE
READMITTANCES
READMITTED
READMITTING
READOPTING
READOPTION
READOPTIONS
READORNING
READVANCED
READVANCES
READVANCING
READVERTISE
READVERTISED
READVERTISEMENT
READVERTISES
READVERTISING
READVERTIZE
READVERTIZED
READVERTIZEMENT
READVERTIZES
READVERTIZING
READVISING
READYMADES
REAEDIFIED
REAEDIFIES
REAEDIFYED
REAEDIFYES
REAEDIFYING
REAFFIRMATION
REAFFIRMATIONS
REAFFIRMED
REAFFIRMING
REAFFIXING
REAFFOREST
REAFFORESTATION
REAFFORESTED
REAFFORESTING
REAFFORESTS
REAGENCIES
REAGGREGATE
REAGGREGATED
REAGGREGATES
REAGGREGATING
REAGGREGATION
REAGGREGATIONS
REALIGNING
REALIGNMENT
REALIGNMENTS
REALISABILITIES
REALISABILITY
REALISABLE
REALISABLY
REALISATION
REALISATIONS
REALISTICALLY
REALIZABILITIES
REALIZABILITY
REALIZABLE
REALIZABLY
REALIZATION
REALIZATIONS
REALLOCATE
REALLOCATED
REALLOCATES
REALLOCATING
REALLOCATION
REALLOCATIONS
REALLOTMENT
REALLOTMENTS
REALLOTTED
REALLOTTING
REALNESSES
REALPOLITIK
REALPOLITIKER
REALPOLITIKERS
REALPOLITIKS
REALTERING
REAMENDING
REAMENDMENT
REAMENDMENTS
REANALYSED
REANALYSES
REANALYSING
REANALYSIS
REANALYZED
REANALYZES
REANALYZING
REANIMATED
REANIMATES
REANIMATING
REANIMATION
REANIMATIONS
REANNEXATION
REANNEXATIONS
REANNEXING
REANOINTED
REANOINTING
REANSWERED
REANSWERING
REAPPARELED
REAPPARELING
REAPPARELLED
REAPPARELLING
REAPPARELS
REAPPEARANCE
REAPPEARANCES
REAPPEARED
REAPPEARING
REAPPLICATION
REAPPLICATIONS
REAPPLYING
REAPPOINTED
REAPPOINTING
REAPPOINTMENT
REAPPOINTMENTS
REAPPOINTS
REAPPORTION
REAPPORTIONED
REAPPORTIONING
REAPPORTIONMENT
REAPPORTIONS
REAPPRAISAL
REAPPRAISALS
REAPPRAISE
REAPPRAISED
REAPPRAISEMENT
REAPPRAISEMENTS
REAPPRAISER
REAPPRAISERS
REAPPRAISES
REAPPRAISING
REAPPROPRIATE
REAPPROPRIATED
REAPPROPRIATES
REAPPROPRIATING
REAPPROVED
REAPPROVES
REAPPROVING
REARGUARDS
REARGUMENT
REARGUMENTS
REARHORSES
REARMAMENT
REARMAMENTS
REAROUSALS
REAROUSING
REARRANGED
REARRANGEMENT
REARRANGEMENTS
REARRANGER
REARRANGERS
REARRANGES
REARRANGING
REARRESTED
REARRESTING
REARTICULATE
REARTICULATED
REARTICULATES
REARTICULATING
REASCENDED
REASCENDING
REASCENSION
REASCENSIONS
REASONABILITIES
REASONABILITY
REASONABLE
REASONABLENESS
REASONABLY
REASONEDLY
REASONINGS
REASONLESS
REASONLESSLY
REASSAILED
REASSAILING
REASSEMBLAGE
REASSEMBLAGES
REASSEMBLE
REASSEMBLED
REASSEMBLES
REASSEMBLIES
REASSEMBLING
REASSEMBLY
REASSERTED
REASSERTING
REASSERTION
REASSERTIONS
REASSESSED
REASSESSES
REASSESSING
REASSESSMENT
REASSESSMENTS
REASSIGNED
REASSIGNING
REASSIGNMENT
REASSIGNMENTS
REASSORTED
REASSORTING
REASSORTMENT
REASSORTMENTS
REASSUMING
REASSUMPTION
REASSUMPTIONS
REASSURANCE
REASSURANCES
REASSURERS
REASSURING
REASSURINGLY
REASTINESS
REASTINESSES
REATTACHED
REATTACHES
REATTACHING
REATTACHMENT
REATTACHMENTS
REATTACKED
REATTACKING
REATTAINED
REATTAINING
REATTEMPTED
REATTEMPTING
REATTEMPTS
REATTRIBUTE

R

REATTRIBUTED
REATTRIBUTES
REATTRIBUTING
REATTRIBUTION
REATTRIBUTIONS
REAUTHORISATION
REAUTHORISE
REAUTHORISED
REAUTHORISES
REAUTHORISING
REAUTHORIZATION
REAUTHORIZE
REAUTHORIZED
REAUTHORIZES
REAUTHORIZING
REAVAILING
REAWAKENED
REAWAKENING
REAWAKENINGS
REBALANCED
REBALANCES
REBALANCING
REBAPTISED
REBAPTISES
REBAPTISING
REBAPTISMS
REBAPTIZED
REBAPTIZES
REBAPTIZING
REBARBATIVE
REBARBATIVELY
REBATEABLE
REBATEMENT
REBATEMENTS
REBBETZINS
REBEGINNING
REBELLIONS
REBELLIOUS
REBELLIOUSLY
REBELLIOUSNESS
REBELLOWED
REBELLOWING
REBIRTHERS
REBIRTHING
REBIRTHINGS
REBLENDING
REBLOCHONS
REBLOOMERS
REBLOOMING
REBLOSSOMED
REBLOSSOMING
REBLOSSOMS
REBOARDING
REBOATIONS
REBORROWED
REBORROWING
REBOTTLING
REBOUNDERS
REBOUNDING
REBOUNDINGS
REBRANCHED
REBRANCHES
REBRANCHING
REBRANDING
REBRANDINGS
REBREEDING
REBROADCAST
REBROADCASTED
REBROADCASTING
REBROADCASTS
REBUILDING
REBUILDINGS
REBUKEFULLY
REBUKINGLY
REBUTMENTS
REBUTTABLE
REBUTTONED
REBUTTONING
RECALCITRANCE
RECALCITRANCES
RECALCITRANCIES
RECALCITRANCY
RECALCITRANT
RECALCITRANTS
RECALCITRATE
RECALCITRATED
RECALCITRATES
RECALCITRATING
RECALCITRATION
RECALCITRATIONS
RECALCULATE
RECALCULATED
RECALCULATES
RECALCULATING
RECALCULATION
RECALCULATIONS
RECALESCED
RECALESCENCE
RECALESCENCES
RECALESCENT
RECALESCES
RECALESCING
RECALIBRATE
RECALIBRATED
RECALIBRATES
RECALIBRATING
RECALIBRATION
RECALIBRATIONS
RECALLABILITIES
RECALLABILITY
RECALLABLE
RECALLMENT
RECALLMENTS
RECALMENTS
RECANALISATION
RECANALISATIONS
RECANALISE
RECANALISED
RECANALISES
RECANALISING
RECANALIZATION
RECANALIZATIONS
RECANALIZE
RECANALIZED
RECANALIZES
RECANALIZING
RECANTATION
RECANTATIONS
RECAPITALISE
RECAPITALISED
RECAPITALISES
RECAPITALISING
RECAPITALIZE
RECAPITALIZED
RECAPITALIZES
RECAPITALIZING
RECAPITULATE
RECAPITULATED
RECAPITULATES
RECAPITULATING
RECAPITULATION
RECAPITULATIONS
RECAPITULATIVE
RECAPITULATORY
RECAPPABLE
RECAPTIONS
RECAPTURED
RECAPTURER
RECAPTURERS
RECAPTURES
RECAPTURING
RECARPETED
RECARPETING
RECARRYING
RECATALOGED
RECATALOGING
RECATALOGS
RECATALOGUE
RECATALOGUED
RECATALOGUES
RECATALOGUING
RECATCHING
RECAUTIONED
RECAUTIONING
RECAUTIONS
RECEIPTING
RECEIPTORS
RECEIVABILITIES
RECEIVABILITY
RECEIVABLE
RECEIVABLENESS
RECEIVABLES
RECEIVERSHIP
RECEIVERSHIPS
RECEIVINGS
RECEMENTED
RECEMENTING
RECENSIONS
RECENSORED
RECENSORING
RECENTNESS
RECENTNESSES
RECENTRIFUGE
RECENTRIFUGED
RECENTRIFUGES
RECENTRIFUGING
RECENTRING
RECEPTACLE
RECEPTACLES
RECEPTACULA
RECEPTACULAR
RECEPTACULUM
RECEPTIBILITIES
RECEPTIBILITY
RECEPTIBLE
RECEPTIONIST
RECEPTIONISTS
RECEPTIONS
RECEPTIVELY
RECEPTIVENESS
RECEPTIVENESSES
RECEPTIVITIES
RECEPTIVITY
RECERTIFICATION
RECERTIFIED
RECERTIFIES
RECERTIFYING
RECESSIONAL
RECESSIONALS
RECESSIONARY
RECESSIONISTA
RECESSIONISTAS
RECESSIONS
RECESSIVELY
RECESSIVENESS
RECESSIVENESSES
RECESSIVES
RECHALLENGE
RECHALLENGED
RECHALLENGES
RECHALLENGING
RECHANGING
RECHANNELED
RECHANNELING
RECHANNELLED
RECHANNELLING
RECHANNELS
RECHARGEABLE
RECHARGERS
RECHARGING
RECHARTERED
RECHARTERING
RECHARTERS
RECHARTING
RECHAUFFES
RECHEATING
RECHECKING
RECHIPPING
RECHIPPINGS
RECHOOSING

R

RECHOREOGRAPH
RECHOREOGRAPHED
RECHOREOGRAPHS
RECHRISTEN
RECHRISTENED
RECHRISTENING
RECHRISTENS
RECHROMATOGRAPH
RECIDIVISM
RECIDIVISMS
RECIDIVIST
RECIDIVISTIC
RECIDIVISTS
RECIDIVOUS
RECIPIENCE
RECIPIENCES
RECIPIENCIES
RECIPIENCY
RECIPIENTS
RECIPROCAL
RECIPROCALITIES
RECIPROCALITY
RECIPROCALLY
RECIPROCALS
RECIPROCANT
RECIPROCANTS
RECIPROCATE
RECIPROCATED
RECIPROCATES
RECIPROCATING
RECIPROCATION
RECIPROCATIONS
RECIPROCATIVE
RECIPROCATOR
RECIPROCATORS
RECIPROCATORY
RECIPROCITIES
RECIPROCITY
RECIRCLING
RECIRCULATE
RECIRCULATED
RECIRCULATES
RECIRCULATING
RECIRCULATION
RECIRCULATIONS
RECITALIST
RECITALISTS
RECITATION
RECITATIONIST
RECITATIONISTS
RECITATIONS
RECITATIVE
RECITATIVES
RECITATIVI
RECITATIVO
RECITATIVOS
RECKLESSLY
RECKLESSNESS
RECKLESSNESSES
RECKONINGS
RECLADDING
RECLAIMABLE
RECLAIMABLY
RECLAIMANT
RECLAIMANTS
RECLAIMERS
RECLAIMING
RECLAMATION
RECLAMATIONS
RECLASPING
RECLASSIFIED
RECLASSIFIES
RECLASSIFY
RECLASSIFYING
RECLEANING
RECLIMBING
RECLINABLE
RECLINATION
RECLINATIONS
RECLOSABLE
RECLOTHING
RECLUSENESS
RECLUSENESSES
RECLUSIONS
RECLUSIVELY
RECLUSIVENESS
RECLUSIVENESSES
RECLUSORIES
RECODIFICATION
RECODIFICATIONS
RECODIFIED
RECODIFIES
RECODIFYING
RECOGNISABILITY
RECOGNISABLE
RECOGNISABLY
RECOGNISANCE
RECOGNISANCES
RECOGNISANT
RECOGNISED
RECOGNISEE
RECOGNISEES
RECOGNISER
RECOGNISERS
RECOGNISES
RECOGNISING
RECOGNISOR
RECOGNISORS
RECOGNITION
RECOGNITIONS
RECOGNITIVE
RECOGNITORY
RECOGNIZABILITY
RECOGNIZABLE
RECOGNIZABLY
RECOGNIZANCE
RECOGNIZANCES
RECOGNIZANT
RECOGNIZED
RECOGNIZEE
RECOGNIZEES
RECOGNIZER
RECOGNIZERS
RECOGNIZES
RECOGNIZING
RECOGNIZOR
RECOGNIZORS
RECOILLESS
RECOINAGES
RECOLLECTED
RECOLLECTEDLY
RECOLLECTEDNESS
RECOLLECTING
RECOLLECTION
RECOLLECTIONS
RECOLLECTIVE
RECOLLECTIVELY
RECOLLECTS
RECOLONISATION
RECOLONISATIONS
RECOLONISE
RECOLONISED
RECOLONISES
RECOLONISING
RECOLONIZATION
RECOLONIZATIONS
RECOLONIZE
RECOLONIZED
RECOLONIZES
RECOLONIZING
RECOLORING
RECOLOURED
RECOLOURING
RECOMBINANT
RECOMBINANTS
RECOMBINATION
RECOMBINATIONAL
RECOMBINATIONS
RECOMBINED
RECOMBINES
RECOMBINING
RECOMFORTED
RECOMFORTING
RECOMFORTLESS
RECOMFORTS
RECOMFORTURE
RECOMFORTURES
RECOMMENCE
RECOMMENCED
RECOMMENCEMENT
RECOMMENCEMENTS
RECOMMENCES
RECOMMENCING
RECOMMENDABLE
RECOMMENDABLY
RECOMMENDATION
RECOMMENDATIONS
RECOMMENDATORY
RECOMMENDED
RECOMMENDER
RECOMMENDERS
RECOMMENDING
RECOMMENDS
RECOMMISSION
RECOMMISSIONED
RECOMMISSIONING
RECOMMISSIONS
RECOMMITMENT
RECOMMITMENTS
RECOMMITTAL
RECOMMITTALS
RECOMMITTED
RECOMMITTING
RECOMPACTED
RECOMPACTING
RECOMPACTS
RECOMPENCE
RECOMPENCES
RECOMPENSABLE
RECOMPENSE
RECOMPENSED
RECOMPENSER
RECOMPENSERS
RECOMPENSES
RECOMPENSING
RECOMPILATION
RECOMPILATIONS
RECOMPILED
RECOMPILES
RECOMPILING
RECOMPOSED
RECOMPOSES
RECOMPOSING
RECOMPOSITION
RECOMPOSITIONS
RECOMPRESS
RECOMPRESSED
RECOMPRESSES
RECOMPRESSING
RECOMPRESSION
RECOMPRESSIONS
RECOMPUTATION
RECOMPUTATIONS
RECOMPUTED
RECOMPUTES
RECOMPUTING
RECONCEIVE
RECONCEIVED
RECONCEIVES
RECONCEIVING
RECONCENTRATE
RECONCENTRATED
RECONCENTRATES
RECONCENTRATING
RECONCENTRATION
RECONCEPTION
RECONCEPTIONS
RECONCEPTUALISE
RECONCEPTUALIZE
RECONCILABILITY

RECONCILABLE
RECONCILABLY
RECONCILED
RECONCILEMENT
RECONCILEMENTS
RECONCILER
RECONCILERS
RECONCILES
RECONCILIATION
RECONCILIATIONS
RECONCILIATORY
RECONCILING
RECONDENSATION
RECONDENSATIONS
RECONDENSE
RECONDENSED
RECONDENSES
RECONDENSING
RECONDITELY
RECONDITENESS
RECONDITENESSES
RECONDITION
RECONDITIONED
RECONDITIONING
RECONDITIONS
RECONDUCTED
RECONDUCTING
RECONDUCTS
RECONFERRED
RECONFERRING
RECONFIGURATION
RECONFIGURE
RECONFIGURED
RECONFIGURES
RECONFIGURING
RECONFINED
RECONFINES
RECONFINING
RECONFIRMATION
RECONFIRMATIONS
RECONFIRMED
RECONFIRMING
RECONFIRMS
RECONNAISSANCE
RECONNAISSANCES
RECONNECTED
RECONNECTING
RECONNECTION
RECONNECTIONS
RECONNECTS
RECONNOISSANCE
RECONNOISSANCES
RECONNOITER
RECONNOITERED
RECONNOITERER
RECONNOITERERS
RECONNOITERING
RECONNOITERS
RECONNOITRE
RECONNOITRED
RECONNOITRER
RECONNOITRERS
RECONNOITRES
RECONNOITRING
RECONNOITRINGS
RECONQUERED
RECONQUERING
RECONQUERS
RECONQUEST
RECONQUESTS
RECONSECRATE
RECONSECRATED
RECONSECRATES
RECONSECRATING
RECONSECRATION
RECONSECRATIONS
RECONSIDER
RECONSIDERATION
RECONSIDERED
RECONSIDERING
RECONSIDERS
RECONSIGNED
RECONSIGNING
RECONSIGNS
RECONSOLED
RECONSOLES
RECONSOLIDATE
RECONSOLIDATED
RECONSOLIDATES
RECONSOLIDATING
RECONSOLIDATION
RECONSOLING
RECONSTITUENT
RECONSTITUENTS
RECONSTITUTABLE
RECONSTITUTE
RECONSTITUTED
RECONSTITUTES
RECONSTITUTING
RECONSTITUTION
RECONSTITUTIONS
RECONSTRUCT
RECONSTRUCTED
RECONSTRUCTIBLE
RECONSTRUCTING
RECONSTRUCTION
RECONSTRUCTIONS
RECONSTRUCTIVE
RECONSTRUCTOR
RECONSTRUCTORS
RECONSTRUCTS
RECONSULTED
RECONSULTING
RECONSULTS
RECONTACTED
RECONTACTING
RECONTACTS
RECONTAMINATE
RECONTAMINATED
RECONTAMINATES
RECONTAMINATING
RECONTAMINATION
RECONTEXTUALISE
RECONTEXTUALIZE
RECONTINUE
RECONTINUED
RECONTINUES
RECONTINUING
RECONTOURED
RECONTOURING
RECONTOURS
RECONVALESCE
RECONVALESCED
RECONVALESCENCE
RECONVALESCENT
RECONVALESCES
RECONVALESCING
RECONVENED
RECONVENES
RECONVENING
RECONVERSION
RECONVERSIONS
RECONVERTED
RECONVERTING
RECONVERTS
RECONVEYANCE
RECONVEYANCES
RECONVEYED
RECONVEYING
RECONVICTED
RECONVICTING
RECONVICTION
RECONVICTIONS
RECONVICTS
RECONVINCE
RECONVINCED
RECONVINCES
RECONVINCING
RECORDABLE
RECORDATION
RECORDATIONS
RECORDERSHIP
RECORDERSHIPS
RECORDINGS
RECORDISTS
RECOUNTALS
RECOUNTERS
RECOUNTING
RECOUNTMENT
RECOUNTMENTS
RECOUPABLE
RECOUPLING
RECOUPMENT
RECOUPMENTS
RECOURSING
RECOVERABILITY
RECOVERABLE
RECOVERABLENESS
RECOVEREES
RECOVERERS
RECOVERIES
RECOVERING
RECOVERORS
RECOWERING
RECREANCES
RECREANCIES
RECREANTLY
RECREATING
RECREATION
RECREATIONAL
RECREATIONALLY
RECREATIONIST
RECREATIONISTS
RECREATIONS
RECREATIVE
RECREATIVELY
RECREATORS
RECREMENTAL
RECREMENTITIAL
RECREMENTITIOUS
RECREMENTS
RECRIMINATE
RECRIMINATED
RECRIMINATES
RECRIMINATING
RECRIMINATION
RECRIMINATIONS
RECRIMINATIVE
RECRIMINATOR
RECRIMINATORS
RECRIMINATORY
RECROSSING
RECROWNING
RECRUDESCE
RECRUDESCED
RECRUDESCENCE
RECRUDESCENCES
RECRUDESCENCIES
RECRUDESCENCY
RECRUDESCENT
RECRUDESCES
RECRUDESCING
RECRUITABLE
RECRUITALS
RECRUITERS
RECRUITING
RECRUITINGS
RECRUITMENT
RECRUITMENTS
RECRYSTALLISE
RECRYSTALLISED
RECRYSTALLISES
RECRYSTALLISING
RECRYSTALLIZE
RECRYSTALLIZED
RECRYSTALLIZES
RECRYSTALLIZING
RECTANGLED
RECTANGLES
RECTANGULAR

RECTANGULARITY
RECTANGULARLY
RECTIFIABILITY
RECTIFIABLE
RECTIFICATION
RECTIFICATIONS
RECTIFIERS
RECTIFYING
RECTILINEAL
RECTILINEALLY
RECTILINEAR
RECTILINEARITY
RECTILINEARLY
RECTIPETALIES
RECTIPETALITIES
RECTIPETALITY
RECTIPETALY
RECTIROSTRAL
RECTISERIAL
RECTITISES
RECTITUDES
RECTITUDINOUS
RECTOCELES
RECTORATES
RECTORESSES
RECTORIALS
RECTORSHIP
RECTORSHIPS
RECTRESSES
RECTRICIAL
RECULTIVATE
RECULTIVATED
RECULTIVATES
RECULTIVATING
RECUMBENCE
RECUMBENCES
RECUMBENCIES
RECUMBENCY
RECUMBENTLY
RECUPERABLE
RECUPERATE
RECUPERATED
RECUPERATES
RECUPERATING
RECUPERATION
RECUPERATIONS
RECUPERATIVE
RECUPERATOR
RECUPERATORS
RECUPERATORY
RECURELESS
RECURRENCE
RECURRENCES
RECURRENCIES
RECURRENCY
RECURRENTLY
RECURRINGLY
RECURSIONS
RECURSIVELY
RECURSIVENESS
RECURSIVENESSES
RECURVIROSTRAL
RECUSANCES
RECUSANCIES
RECUSATION
RECUSATIONS
RECYCLABLE
RECYCLABLES
RECYCLATES
RECYCLEABLE
RECYCLEABLES
RECYCLINGS
RECYCLISTS
REDACTIONAL
REDACTIONS
REDACTORIAL
REDAMAGING
REDARGUING
REDBAITERS
REDBAITING
REDBELLIES
REDBREASTS
REDCURRANT
REDCURRANTS
REDDISHNESS
REDDISHNESSES
REDECIDING
REDECORATE
REDECORATED
REDECORATES
REDECORATING
REDECORATION
REDECORATIONS
REDECORATOR
REDECORATORS
REDECRAFTS
REDEDICATE
REDEDICATED
REDEDICATES
REDEDICATING
REDEDICATION
REDEDICATIONS
REDEEMABILITIES
REDEEMABILITY
REDEEMABLE
REDEEMABLENESS
REDEEMABLY
REDEEMLESS
REDEFEATED
REDEFEATING
REDEFECTED
REDEFECTING
REDEFINING
REDEFINITION
REDEFINITIONS
REDELIVERANCE
REDELIVERANCES
REDELIVERED
REDELIVERER
REDELIVERERS
REDELIVERIES
REDELIVERING
REDELIVERS
REDELIVERY
REDEMANDED
REDEMANDING
REDEMPTIBLE
REDEMPTION
REDEMPTIONAL
REDEMPTIONER
REDEMPTIONERS
REDEMPTIONS
REDEMPTIVE
REDEMPTIVELY
REDEMPTORY
REDEPLOYED
REDEPLOYING
REDEPLOYMENT
REDEPLOYMENTS
REDEPOSITED
REDEPOSITING
REDEPOSITS
REDESCENDED
REDESCENDING
REDESCENDS
REDESCRIBE
REDESCRIBED
REDESCRIBES
REDESCRIBING
REDESCRIPTION
REDESCRIPTIONS
REDESIGNED
REDESIGNING
REDETERMINATION
REDETERMINE
REDETERMINED
REDETERMINES
REDETERMINING
REDEVELOPED
REDEVELOPER
REDEVELOPERS
REDEVELOPING
REDEVELOPMENT
REDEVELOPMENTS
REDEVELOPS
REDIALLING
REDICTATED
REDICTATES
REDICTATING
REDIGESTED
REDIGESTING
REDIGESTION
REDIGESTIONS
REDIGRESSED
REDIGRESSES
REDIGRESSING
REDINGOTES
REDINTEGRATE
REDINTEGRATED
REDINTEGRATES
REDINTEGRATING
REDINTEGRATION
REDINTEGRATIONS
REDINTEGRATIVE
REDIRECTED
REDIRECTING
REDIRECTION
REDIRECTIONS
REDISBURSE
REDISBURSED
REDISBURSES
REDISBURSING
REDISCOUNT
REDISCOUNTABLE
REDISCOUNTED
REDISCOUNTING
REDISCOUNTS
REDISCOVER
REDISCOVERED
REDISCOVERER
REDISCOVERERS
REDISCOVERIES
REDISCOVERING
REDISCOVERS
REDISCOVERY
REDISCUSSED
REDISCUSSES
REDISCUSSING
REDISPLAYED
REDISPLAYING
REDISPLAYS
REDISPOSED
REDISPOSES
REDISPOSING
REDISPOSITION
REDISPOSITIONS
REDISSOLUTION
REDISSOLUTIONS
REDISSOLVE
REDISSOLVED
REDISSOLVES
REDISSOLVING
REDISTILLATION
REDISTILLATIONS
REDISTILLED
REDISTILLING
REDISTILLS
REDISTRIBUTE
REDISTRIBUTED
REDISTRIBUTES
REDISTRIBUTING
REDISTRIBUTION
REDISTRIBUTIONS
REDISTRIBUTIVE
REDISTRICT
REDISTRICTED
REDISTRICTING
REDISTRICTINGS
REDISTRICTS
REDIVIDING

R

REDIVISION
REDIVISIONS
REDIVORCED
REDIVORCES
REDIVORCING
REDLININGS
REDOLENCES
REDOLENCIES
REDOLENTLY
REDOUBLEMENT
REDOUBLEMENTS
REDOUBLERS
REDOUBLING
REDOUBTABLE
REDOUBTABLENESS
REDOUBTABLY
REDOUBTING
REDOUNDING
REDOUNDINGS
REDRAFTING
REDREAMING
REDRESSABLE
REDRESSALS
REDRESSERS
REDRESSIBLE
REDRESSING
REDRESSIVE
REDRESSORS
REDRILLING
REDRUTHITE
REDRUTHITES
REDSHIFTED
REDSHIRTED
REDSHIRTING
REDSTREAKS
REDUCIBILITIES
REDUCIBILITY
REDUCIBLENESS
REDUCIBLENESSES
REDUCTANTS
REDUCTASES
REDUCTIONAL
REDUCTIONISM
REDUCTIONISMS
REDUCTIONIST
REDUCTIONISTIC
REDUCTIONISTS
REDUCTIONS
REDUCTIVELY
REDUCTIVENESS
REDUCTIVENESSES
REDUCTIVES
REDUNDANCE
REDUNDANCES
REDUNDANCIES
REDUNDANCY
REDUNDANTLY
REDUPLICATE
REDUPLICATED
REDUPLICATES
REDUPLICATING
REDUPLICATION
REDUPLICATIONS
REDUPLICATIVE
REDUPLICATIVELY
REEDIFYING
REEDINESSES
REEDITIONS
REEDUCATED
REEDUCATES
REEDUCATING
REEDUCATION
REEDUCATIONS
REEDUCATIVE
REEFPOINTS
REEJECTING
REELECTING
REELECTION
REELECTIONS
REELEVATED
REELEVATES
REELEVATING
REELIGIBILITIES
REELIGIBILITY
REELIGIBLE
REEMBARKED
REEMBARKING
REEMBODIED
REEMBODIES
REEMBODYING
REEMBRACED
REEMBRACES
REEMBRACING
REEMBROIDER
REEMBROIDERED
REEMBROIDERING
REEMBROIDERS
REEMERGENCE
REEMERGENCES
REEMERGING
REEMISSION
REEMISSIONS
REEMITTING
REEMPHASES
REEMPHASIS
REEMPHASISE
REEMPHASISED
REEMPHASISES
REEMPHASISING
REEMPHASIZE
REEMPHASIZED
REEMPHASIZES
REEMPHASIZING
REEMPLOYED
REEMPLOYING
REEMPLOYMENT
REEMPLOYMENTS
REENACTING
REENACTMENT
REENACTMENTS
REENACTORS
REENCOUNTER
REENCOUNTERED
REENCOUNTERING
REENCOUNTERS
REENDOWING
REENERGISE
REENERGISED
REENERGISES
REENERGISING
REENERGIZE
REENERGIZED
REENERGIZES
REENERGIZING
REENFORCED
REENFORCES
REENFORCING
REENGAGEMENT
REENGAGEMENTS
REENGAGING
REENGINEER
REENGINEERED
REENGINEERING
REENGINEERS
REENGRAVED
REENGRAVES
REENGRAVING
REENJOYING
REENLARGED
REENLARGES
REENLARGING
REENLISTED
REENLISTING
REENLISTMENT
REENLISTMENTS
REENROLLED
REENROLLING
REENSLAVED
REENSLAVES
REENSLAVING
REENTERING
REENTHRONE
REENTHRONED
REENTHRONES
REENTHRONING
REENTRANCE
REENTRANCES
REENTRANTS
REEQUIPMENT
REEQUIPMENTS
REEQUIPPED
REEQUIPPING
REERECTING
REESCALATE
REESCALATED
REESCALATES
REESCALATING
REESCALATION
REESCALATIONS
REESTABLISH
REESTABLISHED
REESTABLISHES
REESTABLISHING
REESTABLISHMENT
REESTIMATE
REESTIMATED
REESTIMATES
REESTIMATING
REEVALUATE
REEVALUATED
REEVALUATES
REEVALUATING
REEVALUATION
REEVALUATIONS
REEVESHIPS
REEXAMINATION
REEXAMINATIONS
REEXAMINED
REEXAMINES
REEXAMINING
REEXECUTED
REEXECUTES
REEXECUTING
REEXHIBITED
REEXHIBITING
REEXHIBITS
REEXPELLED
REEXPELLING
REEXPERIENCE
REEXPERIENCED
REEXPERIENCES
REEXPERIENCING
REEXPLAINED
REEXPLAINING
REEXPLAINS
REEXPLORED
REEXPLORES
REEXPLORING
REEXPORTATION
REEXPORTATIONS
REEXPORTED
REEXPORTING
REEXPOSING
REEXPOSURE
REEXPOSURES
REEXPRESSED
REEXPRESSES
REEXPRESSING
REFASHIONED
REFASHIONING
REFASHIONMENT
REFASHIONMENTS
REFASHIONS
REFASTENED
REFASTENING
REFECTIONER
REFECTIONERS
REFECTIONS
REFECTORIAN
REFECTORIANS

REFECTORIES
REFEEDINGS
REFEREEING
REFEREEINGS
REFERENCED
REFERENCER
REFERENCERS
REFERENCES
REFERENCING
REFERENCINGS
REFERENDARIES
REFERENDARY
REFERENDUM
REFERENDUMS
REFERENTIAL
REFERENTIALITY
REFERENTIALLY
REFERRABLE
REFERRIBLE
REFIGHTING
REFIGURING
REFILLABLE
REFILTERED
REFILTERING
REFINANCED
REFINANCES
REFINANCING
REFINANCINGS
REFINEDNESS
REFINEDNESSES
REFINEMENT
REFINEMENTS
REFINERIES
REFINISHED
REFINISHER
REFINISHERS
REFINISHES
REFINISHING
REFITMENTS
REFITTINGS
REFLAGGING
REFLATIONARY
REFLATIONS
REFLECTANCE
REFLECTANCES
REFLECTERS
REFLECTING
REFLECTINGLY
REFLECTION
REFLECTIONAL
REFLECTIONLESS
REFLECTIONS
REFLECTIVE
REFLECTIVELY
REFLECTIVENESS
REFLECTIVITIES
REFLECTIVITY
REFLECTOGRAM
REFLECTOGRAMS
REFLECTOGRAPH
REFLECTOGRAPHS
REFLECTOGRAPHY
REFLECTOMETER
REFLECTOMETERS
REFLECTOMETRIES
REFLECTOMETRY
REFLECTORISE
REFLECTORISED
REFLECTORISES
REFLECTORISING
REFLECTORIZE
REFLECTORIZED
REFLECTORIZES
REFLECTORIZING
REFLECTORS
REFLEXIBILITIES
REFLEXIBILITY
REFLEXIBLE
REFLEXIONAL
REFLEXIONS
REFLEXIVELY
REFLEXIVENESS
REFLEXIVENESSES
REFLEXIVES
REFLEXIVITIES
REFLEXIVITY
REFLEXOLOGICAL
REFLEXOLOGIES
REFLEXOLOGIST
REFLEXOLOGISTS
REFLEXOLOGY
REFLOATING
REFLOODING
REFLOWERED
REFLOWERING
REFLOWERINGS
REFLOWINGS
REFLUENCES
REFOCILLATE
REFOCILLATED
REFOCILLATES
REFOCILLATING
REFOCILLATION
REFOCILLATIONS
REFOCUSING
REFOCUSSED
REFOCUSSES
REFOCUSSING
REFORESTATION
REFORESTATIONS
REFORESTED
REFORESTING
REFORMABILITIES
REFORMABILITY
REFORMABLE
REFORMADES
REFORMADOES
REFORMADOS
REFORMATES
REFORMATION
REFORMATIONAL
REFORMATIONIST
REFORMATIONISTS
REFORMATIONS
REFORMATIVE
REFORMATORIES
REFORMATORY
REFORMATTED
REFORMATTING
REFORMINGS
REFORMISMS
REFORMISTS
REFORMULATE
REFORMULATED
REFORMULATES
REFORMULATING
REFORMULATION
REFORMULATIONS
REFORTIFICATION
REFORTIFIED
REFORTIFIES
REFORTIFYING
REFOULEMENT
REFOULEMENTS
REFOUNDATION
REFOUNDATIONS
REFOUNDERS
REFOUNDING
REFRACTABLE
REFRACTARIES
REFRACTARY
REFRACTILE
REFRACTING
REFRACTION
REFRACTIONS
REFRACTIVE
REFRACTIVELY
REFRACTIVENESS
REFRACTIVITIES
REFRACTIVITY
REFRACTOMETER
REFRACTOMETERS
REFRACTOMETRIC
REFRACTOMETRIES
REFRACTOMETRY
REFRACTORIES
REFRACTORILY
REFRACTORINESS
REFRACTORS
REFRACTORY
REFRACTURE
REFRACTURED
REFRACTURES
REFRACTURING
REFRAINERS
REFRAINING
REFRAINMENT
REFRAINMENTS
REFRANGIBILITY
REFRANGIBLE
REFRANGIBLENESS
REFREEZING
REFRESHENED
REFRESHENER
REFRESHENERS
REFRESHENING
REFRESHENS
REFRESHERS
REFRESHFUL
REFRESHFULLY
REFRESHING
REFRESHINGLY
REFRESHMENT
REFRESHMENTS
REFRIGERANT
REFRIGERANTS
REFRIGERATE
REFRIGERATED
REFRIGERATES
REFRIGERATING
REFRIGERATION
REFRIGERATIONS
REFRIGERATIVE
REFRIGERATOR
REFRIGERATORIES
REFRIGERATORS
REFRIGERATORY
REFRINGENCE
REFRINGENCES
REFRINGENCIES
REFRINGENCY
REFRINGENT
REFRINGING
REFRONTING
REFUELABLE
REFUELINGS
REFUELLABLE
REFUELLING
REFUELLINGS
REFUGEEISM
REFUGEEISMS
REFULGENCE
REFULGENCES
REFULGENCIES
REFULGENCY
REFULGENTLY
REFUNDABILITIES
REFUNDABILITY
REFUNDABLE
REFUNDINGS
REFUNDMENT
REFUNDMENTS
REFURBISHED
REFURBISHER
REFURBISHERS
REFURBISHES
REFURBISHING
REFURBISHINGS
REFURBISHMENT
REFURBISHMENTS

REFURNISHED
REFURNISHES
REFURNISHING
REFUSENIKS
REFUTABILITIES
REFUTABILITY
REFUTATION
REFUTATIONS
REGAINABLE
REGAINMENT
REGAINMENTS
REGALEMENT
REGALEMENTS
REGALITIES
REGALNESSES
REGARDABLE
REGARDFULLY
REGARDFULNESS
REGARDFULNESSES
REGARDLESS
REGARDLESSLY
REGARDLESSNESS
REGATHERED
REGATHERING
REGELATING
REGELATION
REGELATIONS
REGENERABLE
REGENERACIES
REGENERACY
REGENERATE
REGENERATED
REGENERATELY
REGENERATENESS
REGENERATES
REGENERATING
REGENERATION
REGENERATIONS
REGENERATIVE
REGENERATIVELY
REGENERATOR
REGENERATORS
REGENERATORY
REGENTSHIP
REGENTSHIPS
REGGAETONS
REGIMENTAL
REGIMENTALLY
REGIMENTALS
REGIMENTATION
REGIMENTATIONS
REGIMENTED
REGIMENTING
REGIONALISATION
REGIONALISE
REGIONALISED
REGIONALISES
REGIONALISING
REGIONALISM
REGIONALISMS
REGIONALIST
REGIONALISTIC
REGIONALISTS
REGIONALIZATION
REGIONALIZE
REGIONALIZED
REGIONALIZES
REGIONALIZING
REGIONALLY
REGISSEURS
REGISTERABLE
REGISTERED
REGISTERER
REGISTERERS
REGISTERING
REGISTRABLE
REGISTRANT
REGISTRANTS
REGISTRARIES
REGISTRARS
REGISTRARSHIP
REGISTRARSHIPS
REGISTRARY
REGISTRATION
REGISTRATIONAL
REGISTRATIONS
REGISTRIES
REGLORIFIED
REGLORIFIES
REGLORIFYING
REGLOSSING
REGNANCIES
REGRAFTING
REGRANTING
REGRATINGS
REGREDIENCE
REGREDIENCES
REGREENING
REGREETING
REGRESSING
REGRESSION
REGRESSIONS
REGRESSIVE
REGRESSIVELY
REGRESSIVENESS
REGRESSIVITIES
REGRESSIVITY
REGRESSORS
REGRETFULLY
REGRETFULNESS
REGRETFULNESSES
REGRETTABLE
REGRETTABLY
REGRETTERS
REGRETTING
REGRINDING
REGROOMING
REGROOVING
REGROUPING
REGROUPINGS
REGUERDONED
REGUERDONING
REGUERDONS
REGULARISATION
REGULARISATIONS
REGULARISE
REGULARISED
REGULARISES
REGULARISING
REGULARITIES
REGULARITY
REGULARIZATION
REGULARIZATIONS
REGULARIZE
REGULARIZED
REGULARIZES
REGULARIZING
REGULATING
REGULATION
REGULATIONS
REGULATIVE
REGULATIVELY
REGULATORS
REGULATORY
REGULISING
REGULIZING
REGURGITANT
REGURGITANTS
REGURGITATE
REGURGITATED
REGURGITATES
REGURGITATING
REGURGITATION
REGURGITATIONS
REHABILITANT
REHABILITANTS
REHABILITATE
REHABILITATED
REHABILITATES
REHABILITATING
REHABILITATION
REHABILITATIONS
REHABILITATIVE
REHABILITATOR
REHABILITATORS
REHAMMERED
REHAMMERING
REHANDLING
REHANDLINGS
REHARDENED
REHARDENING
REHEARINGS
REHEARSALS
REHEARSERS
REHEARSING
REHEARSINGS
REHEATINGS
REHOSPITALISE
REHOSPITALISED
REHOSPITALISES
REHOSPITALISING
REHOSPITALIZE
REHOSPITALIZED
REHOSPITALIZES
REHOSPITALIZING
REHOUSINGS
REHUMANISE
REHUMANISED
REHUMANISES
REHUMANISING
REHUMANIZE
REHUMANIZED
REHUMANIZES
REHUMANIZING
REHYDRATABLE
REHYDRATED
REHYDRATES
REHYDRATING
REHYDRATION
REHYDRATIONS
REHYPNOTISE
REHYPNOTISED
REHYPNOTISES
REHYPNOTISING
REHYPNOTIZE
REHYPNOTIZED
REHYPNOTIZES
REHYPNOTIZING
REICHSMARK
REICHSMARKS
REIDENTIFIED
REIDENTIFIES
REIDENTIFY
REIDENTIFYING
REIFICATION
REIFICATIONS
REIFICATORY
REIGNITING
REIGNITION
REIGNITIONS
REILLUMINE
REILLUMINED
REILLUMINES
REILLUMING
REILLUMINING
REIMAGINED
REIMAGINES
REIMAGINING
REIMBURSABLE
REIMBURSED
REIMBURSEMENT
REIMBURSEMENTS
REIMBURSER
REIMBURSERS
REIMBURSES
REIMBURSING
REIMMERSED
REIMMERSES
REIMMERSING
REIMPLANTATION

REIMPLANTATIONS
REIMPLANTED
REIMPLANTING
REIMPLANTS
REIMPORTATION
REIMPORTATIONS
REIMPORTED
REIMPORTER
REIMPORTERS
REIMPORTING
REIMPOSING
REIMPOSITION
REIMPOSITIONS
REIMPRESSION
REIMPRESSIONS
REINCARNATE
REINCARNATED
REINCARNATES
REINCARNATING
REINCARNATION
REINCARNATIONS
REINCITING
REINCORPORATE
REINCORPORATED
REINCORPORATES
REINCORPORATING
REINCORPORATION
REINCREASE
REINCREASED
REINCREASES
REINCREASING
REINCURRED
REINCURRING
REINDEXING
REINDICTED
REINDICTING
REINDICTMENT
REINDICTMENTS
REINDUCING
REINDUCTED
REINDUCTING
REINDUSTRIALISE
REINDUSTRIALIZE
REINFECTED
REINFECTING
REINFECTION
REINFECTIONS
REINFESTATION
REINFESTATIONS
REINFLAMED
REINFLAMES
REINFLAMING
REINFLATED
REINFLATES
REINFLATING
REINFLATION
REINFLATIONS
REINFORCEABLE
REINFORCED
REINFORCEMENT
REINFORCEMENTS
REINFORCER
REINFORCERS
REINFORCES
REINFORCING
REINFORMED
REINFORMING
REINFUNDED
REINFUNDING
REINFUSING
REINHABITED
REINHABITING
REINHABITS
REINITIATE
REINITIATED
REINITIATES
REINITIATING
REINJECTED
REINJECTING
REINJECTION
REINJECTIONS
REINJURIES
REINJURING
REINNERVATE
REINNERVATED
REINNERVATES
REINNERVATING
REINNERVATION
REINNERVATIONS
REINOCULATE
REINOCULATED
REINOCULATES
REINOCULATING
REINOCULATION
REINOCULATIONS
REINSERTED
REINSERTING
REINSERTION
REINSERTIONS
REINSPECTED
REINSPECTING
REINSPECTION
REINSPECTIONS
REINSPECTS
REINSPIRED
REINSPIRES
REINSPIRING
REINSPIRIT
REINSPIRITED
REINSPIRITING
REINSPIRITS
REINSTALLATION
REINSTALLATIONS
REINSTALLED
REINSTALLING
REINSTALLS
REINSTALMENT
REINSTALMENTS
REINSTATED
REINSTATEMENT
REINSTATEMENTS
REINSTATES
REINSTATING
REINSTATION
REINSTATIONS
REINSTATOR
REINSTATORS
REINSTITUTE
REINSTITUTED
REINSTITUTES
REINSTITUTING
REINSTITUTION
REINSTITUTIONS
REINSURANCE
REINSURANCES
REINSURERS
REINSURING
REINTEGRATE
REINTEGRATED
REINTEGRATES
REINTEGRATING
REINTEGRATION
REINTEGRATIONS
REINTEGRATIVE
REINTERMENT
REINTERMENTS
REINTERPRET
REINTERPRETED
REINTERPRETING
REINTERPRETS
REINTERRED
REINTERRING
REINTERROGATE
REINTERROGATED
REINTERROGATES
REINTERROGATING
REINTERROGATION
REINTERVIEW
REINTERVIEWED
REINTERVIEWING
REINTERVIEWS
REINTRODUCE
REINTRODUCED
REINTRODUCES
REINTRODUCING
REINTRODUCTION
REINTRODUCTIONS
REINVADING
REINVASION
REINVASIONS
REINVENTED
REINVENTING
REINVENTION
REINVENTIONS
REINVESTED
REINVESTIGATE
REINVESTIGATED
REINVESTIGATES
REINVESTIGATING
REINVESTIGATION
REINVESTING
REINVESTMENT
REINVESTMENTS
REINVIGORATE
REINVIGORATED
REINVIGORATES
REINVIGORATING
REINVIGORATION
REINVIGORATIONS
REINVIGORATOR
REINVIGORATORS
REINVITING
REINVOKING
REINVOLVED
REINVOLVES
REINVOLVING
REIOYNDURE
REIOYNDURES
REISSUABLE
REISTAFELS
REITERANCE
REITERANCES
REITERATED
REITERATEDLY
REITERATES
REITERATING
REITERATION
REITERATIONS
REITERATIVE
REITERATIVELY
REITERATIVES
REJACKETED
REJACKETING
REJECTABLE
REJECTAMENTA
REJECTIBLE
REJECTINGLY
REJECTIONIST
REJECTIONISTS
REJECTIONS
REJIGGERED
REJIGGERING
REJOICEFUL
REJOICEMENT
REJOICEMENTS
REJOICINGLY
REJOICINGS
REJOINDERS
REJOINDURE
REJOINDURES
REJONEADOR
REJONEADORA
REJONEADORAS
REJONEADORES
REJOURNING
REJUGGLING
REJUSTIFIED
REJUSTIFIES
REJUSTIFYING
REJUVENATE

R

REJUVENATED
REJUVENATES
REJUVENATING
REJUVENATION
REJUVENATIONS
REJUVENATOR
REJUVENATORS
REJUVENESCE
REJUVENESCED
REJUVENESCENCE
REJUVENESCENCES
REJUVENESCENT
REJUVENESCES
REJUVENESCING
REJUVENISE
REJUVENISED
REJUVENISES
REJUVENISING
REJUVENIZE
REJUVENIZED
REJUVENIZES
REJUVENIZING
REKEYBOARD
REKEYBOARDED
REKEYBOARDING
REKEYBOARDS
REKINDLING
REKINDLINGS
REKNITTING
REKNITTINGS
REKNOTTING
REKNOTTINGS
RELABELING
RELABELLED
RELABELLING
RELACQUERED
RELACQUERING
RELACQUERS
RELANDSCAPE
RELANDSCAPED
RELANDSCAPES
RELANDSCAPING
RELATEDNESS
RELATEDNESSES
RELATIONAL
RELATIONALLY
RELATIONISM
RELATIONISMS
RELATIONIST
RELATIONISTS
RELATIONLESS
RELATIONSHIP
RELATIONSHIPS
RELATIVELY
RELATIVENESS
RELATIVENESSES
RELATIVISATION
RELATIVISATIONS
RELATIVISE
RELATIVISED
RELATIVISES
RELATIVISING
RELATIVISM
RELATIVISMS
RELATIVIST
RELATIVISTIC
RELATIVISTS
RELATIVITIES
RELATIVITIST
RELATIVITISTS
RELATIVITY
RELATIVIZATION
RELATIVIZATIONS
RELATIVIZE
RELATIVIZED
RELATIVIZES
RELATIVIZING
RELAUNCHED
RELAUNCHES
RELAUNCHING
RELAUNDERED
RELAUNDERING
RELAUNDERS
RELAXATION
RELAXATIONS
RELAXATIVE
RELAXATIVES
RELAXEDNESS
RELAXEDNESSES
RELEARNING
RELEASABLE
RELEASEMENT
RELEASEMENTS
RELEGATABLE
RELEGATING
RELEGATION
RELEGATIONS
RELENTINGS
RELENTLESS
RELENTLESSLY
RELENTLESSNESS
RELENTMENT
RELENTMENTS
RELETTERED
RELETTERING
RELEVANCES
RELEVANCIES
RELEVANTLY
RELIABILITIES
RELIABILITY
RELIABLENESS
RELIABLENESSES
RELICENSED
RELICENSES
RELICENSING
RELICENSURE
RELICENSURES
RELICTIONS
RELIEFLESS
RELIEVABLE
RELIEVEDLY
RELIGHTING
RELIGIEUSE
RELIGIEUSES
RELIGIONARIES
RELIGIONARY
RELIGIONER
RELIGIONERS
RELIGIONISE
RELIGIONISED
RELIGIONISES
RELIGIONISING
RELIGIONISM
RELIGIONISMS
RELIGIONIST
RELIGIONISTS
RELIGIONIZE
RELIGIONIZED
RELIGIONIZES
RELIGIONIZING
RELIGIONLESS
RELIGIOSELY
RELIGIOSITIES
RELIGIOSITY
RELIGIOSOS
RELIGIOUSES
RELIGIOUSLY
RELIGIOUSNESS
RELIGIOUSNESSES
RELINQUISH
RELINQUISHED
RELINQUISHER
RELINQUISHERS
RELINQUISHES
RELINQUISHING
RELINQUISHMENT
RELINQUISHMENTS
RELIQUAIRE
RELIQUAIRES
RELIQUARIES
RELIQUEFIED
RELIQUEFIES
RELIQUEFYING
RELIQUIFIED
RELIQUIFIES
RELIQUIFYING
RELISHABLE
RELISTENED
RELISTENING
RELIVERING
RELLISHING
RELOCATABLE
RELOCATEES
RELOCATING
RELOCATION
RELOCATIONS
RELOCATORS
RELUBRICATE
RELUBRICATED
RELUBRICATES
RELUBRICATING
RELUBRICATION
RELUBRICATIONS
RELUCTANCE
RELUCTANCES
RELUCTANCIES
RELUCTANCY
RELUCTANTLY
RELUCTATED
RELUCTATES
RELUCTATING
RELUCTATION
RELUCTATIONS
RELUCTIVITIES
RELUCTIVITY
RELUMINING
REMAILINGS
REMAINDERED
REMAINDERING
REMAINDERMAN
REMAINDERMEN
REMAINDERS
REMANDMENT
REMANDMENTS
REMANENCES
REMANENCIES
REMANUFACTURE
REMANUFACTURED
REMANUFACTURER
REMANUFACTURERS
REMANUFACTURES
REMANUFACTURING
REMARKABILITIES
REMARKABILITY
REMARKABLE
REMARKABLENESS
REMARKABLES
REMARKABLY
REMARKETED
REMARKETING
REMARRIAGE
REMARRIAGES
REMARRYING
REMASTERED
REMASTERING
REMATCHING
REMATERIALISE
REMATERIALISED
REMATERIALISES
REMATERIALISING
REMATERIALIZE
REMATERIALIZED
REMATERIALIZES
REMATERIALIZING
REMEASURED
REMEASUREMENT
REMEASUREMENTS
REMEASURES
REMEASURING
REMEDIABILITIES

REMEDIABILITY
REMEDIABLE
REMEDIABLY
REMEDIALLY
REMEDIATED
REMEDIATES
REMEDIATING
REMEDIATION
REMEDIATIONS
REMEDILESS
REMEDILESSLY
REMEDILESSNESS
REMEMBERABILITY
REMEMBERABLE
REMEMBERABLY
REMEMBERED
REMEMBERER
REMEMBERERS
REMEMBERING
REMEMBRANCE
REMEMBRANCER
REMEMBRANCERS
REMEMBRANCES
REMERCYING
REMIGATING
REMIGATION
REMIGATIONS
REMIGRATED
REMIGRATES
REMIGRATING
REMIGRATION
REMIGRATIONS
REMILITARISE
REMILITARISED
REMILITARISES
REMILITARISING
REMILITARIZE
REMILITARIZED
REMILITARIZES
REMILITARIZING
REMINERALISE
REMINERALISED
REMINERALISES
REMINERALISING
REMINERALIZE
REMINERALIZED
REMINERALIZES
REMINERALIZING
REMINISCED
REMINISCENCE
REMINISCENCES
REMINISCENT
REMINISCENTIAL
REMINISCENTLY
REMINISCENTS
REMINISCER
REMINISCERS
REMINISCES
REMINISCING
REMISSIBILITIES
REMISSIBILITY
REMISSIBLE
REMISSIBLENESS
REMISSIBLY
REMISSIONS
REMISSIVELY
REMISSNESS
REMISSNESSES
REMITMENTS
REMITTABLE
REMITTANCE
REMITTANCES
REMITTENCE
REMITTENCES
REMITTENCIES
REMITTENCY
REMITTENTLY
REMIXTURES
REMOBILISATION
REMOBILISATIONS
REMOBILISE
REMOBILISED
REMOBILISES
REMOBILISING
REMOBILIZATION
REMOBILIZATIONS
REMOBILIZE
REMOBILIZED
REMOBILIZES
REMOBILIZING
REMODELERS
REMODELING
REMODELINGS
REMODELLED
REMODELLER
REMODELLERS
REMODELLING
REMODELLINGS
REMODIFIED
REMODIFIES
REMODIFYING
REMOISTENED
REMOISTENING
REMOISTENS
REMONETISATION
REMONETISATIONS
REMONETISE
REMONETISED
REMONETISES
REMONETISING
REMONETIZATION
REMONETIZATIONS
REMONETIZE
REMONETIZED
REMONETIZES
REMONETIZING
REMONSTRANCE
REMONSTRANCES
REMONSTRANT
REMONSTRANTLY
REMONSTRANTS
REMONSTRATE
REMONSTRATED
REMONSTRATES
REMONSTRATING
REMONSTRATINGLY
REMONSTRATION
REMONSTRATIONS
REMONSTRATIVE
REMONSTRATIVELY
REMONSTRATOR
REMONSTRATORS
REMONSTRATORY
REMONTANTS
REMONTOIRE
REMONTOIRES
REMONTOIRS
REMORALISATION
REMORALISATIONS
REMORALISE
REMORALISED
REMORALISES
REMORALISING
REMORALIZATION
REMORALIZATIONS
REMORALIZE
REMORALIZED
REMORALIZES
REMORALIZING
REMORSEFUL
REMORSEFULLY
REMORSEFULNESS
REMORSELESS
REMORSELESSLY
REMORSELESSNESS
REMORTGAGE
REMORTGAGED
REMORTGAGES
REMORTGAGING
REMOTENESS
REMOTENESSES
REMOTIVATE
REMOTIVATED
REMOTIVATES
REMOTIVATING
REMOTIVATION
REMOTIVATIONS
REMOULADES
REMOULDING
REMOUNTING
REMOUNTINGS
REMOVABILITIES
REMOVABILITY
REMOVABLENESS
REMOVABLENESSES
REMOVALIST
REMOVALISTS
REMOVEABLE
REMOVEDNESS
REMOVEDNESSES
REMUNERABILITY
REMUNERABLE
REMUNERATE
REMUNERATED
REMUNERATES
REMUNERATING
REMUNERATION
REMUNERATIONS
REMUNERATIVE
REMUNERATIVELY
REMUNERATOR
REMUNERATORS
REMUNERATORY
REMURMURED
REMURMURING
REMYTHOLOGISE
REMYTHOLOGISED
REMYTHOLOGISES
REMYTHOLOGISING
REMYTHOLOGIZE
REMYTHOLOGIZED
REMYTHOLOGIZES
REMYTHOLOGIZING
RENAISSANCE
RENAISSANCES
RENASCENCE
RENASCENCES
RENATIONALISE
RENATIONALISED
RENATIONALISES
RENATIONALISING
RENATIONALIZE
RENATIONALIZED
RENATIONALIZES
RENATIONALIZING
RENATURATION
RENATURATIONS
RENATURING
RENCONTRED
RENCONTRES
RENCONTRING
RENCOUNTER
RENCOUNTERED
RENCOUNTERING
RENCOUNTERS
RENDERABLE
RENDERINGS
RENDEZVOUS
RENDEZVOUSED
RENDEZVOUSES
RENDEZVOUSING
RENDITIONED
RENDITIONING
RENDITIONS
RENEAGUING
RENEGADING
RENEGADOES
RENEGATION
RENEGATIONS
RENEGOTIABLE

RENEGOTIATE
RENEGOTIATED
RENEGOTIATES
RENEGOTIATING
RENEGOTIATION
RENEGOTIATIONS
RENEWABILITIES
RENEWABILITY
RENEWABLES
RENEWEDNESS
RENEWEDNESSES
RENFORCING
RENITENCES
RENITENCIES
RENOGRAPHIC
RENOGRAPHIES
RENOGRAPHY
RENOMINATE
RENOMINATED
RENOMINATES
RENOMINATING
RENOMINATION
RENOMINATIONS
RENORMALISATION
RENORMALISE
RENORMALISED
RENORMALISES
RENORMALISING
RENORMALIZATION
RENORMALIZE
RENORMALIZED
RENORMALIZES
RENORMALIZING
RENOSTERVELD
RENOSTERVELDS
RENOTIFIED
RENOTIFIES
RENOTIFYING
RENOUNCEABLE
RENOUNCEMENT
RENOUNCEMENTS
RENOUNCERS
RENOUNCING
RENOVASCULAR
RENOVATING
RENOVATION
RENOVATIONS
RENOVATIVE
RENOVATORS
RENSSELAERITE
RENSSELAERITES
RENTABILITIES
RENTABILITY
RENTALLERS
RENUMBERED
RENUMBERING
RENUNCIATE
RENUNCIATES
RENUNCIATION
RENUNCIATIONS
RENUNCIATIVE
RENUNCIATORY
RENVERSEMENT
RENVERSEMENTS
RENVERSING
REOBJECTED
REOBJECTING
REOBSERVED
REOBSERVES
REOBSERVING
REOBTAINED
REOBTAINING
REOCCUPATION
REOCCUPATIONS
REOCCUPIED
REOCCUPIES
REOCCUPYING
REOCCURRED
REOCCURRENCE
REOCCURRENCES
REOCCURRING
REOFFENDED
REOFFENDER
REOFFENDERS
REOFFENDING
REOFFERING
REOPENINGS
REOPERATED
REOPERATES
REOPERATING
REOPERATION
REOPERATIONS
REOPPOSING
REORCHESTRATE
REORCHESTRATED
REORCHESTRATES
REORCHESTRATING
REORCHESTRATION
REORDAINED
REORDAINING
REORDERING
REORDINATION
REORDINATIONS
REORGANISATION
REORGANISATIONS
REORGANISE
REORGANISED
REORGANISER
REORGANISERS
REORGANISES
REORGANISING
REORGANIZATION
REORGANIZATIONS
REORGANIZE
REORGANIZED
REORGANIZER
REORGANIZERS
REORGANIZES
REORGANIZING
REORIENTATE
REORIENTATED
REORIENTATES
REORIENTATING
REORIENTATION
REORIENTATIONS
REORIENTED
REORIENTING
REOUTFITTED
REOUTFITTING
REOVIRUSES
REOXIDATION
REOXIDATIONS
REOXIDISED
REOXIDISES
REOXIDISING
REOXIDIZED
REOXIDIZES
REOXIDIZING
REOXYGENATE
REOXYGENATED
REOXYGENATES
REOXYGENATING
REPACIFIED
REPACIFIES
REPACIFYING
REPACKAGED
REPACKAGER
REPACKAGERS
REPACKAGES
REPACKAGING
REPAGINATE
REPAGINATED
REPAGINATES
REPAGINATING
REPAGINATION
REPAGINATIONS
REPAINTING
REPAINTINGS
REPAIRABILITIES
REPAIRABILITY
REPAIRABLE
REPANELING
REPANELLED
REPANELLING
REPAPERING
REPARABILITIES
REPARABILITY
REPARATION
REPARATIONS
REPARATIVE
REPARATORY
REPARTEEING
REPARTITION
REPARTITIONED
REPARTITIONING
REPARTITIONS
REPASSAGES
REPASTURES
REPATCHING
REPATRIATE
REPATRIATED
REPATRIATES
REPATRIATING
REPATRIATION
REPATRIATIONS
REPATRIATOR
REPATRIATORS
REPATTERNED
REPATTERNING
REPATTERNS
REPAYMENTS
REPEALABLE
REPEATABILITIES
REPEATABILITY
REPEATABLE
REPEATEDLY
REPEATINGS
REPECHAGES
REPELLANCE
REPELLANCES
REPELLANCIES
REPELLANCY
REPELLANTLY
REPELLANTS
REPELLENCE
REPELLENCES
REPELLENCIES
REPELLENCY
REPELLENTLY
REPELLENTS
REPELLINGLY
REPENTANCE
REPENTANCES
REPENTANTLY
REPENTANTS
REPENTINGLY
REPEOPLING
REPERCUSSED
REPERCUSSES
REPERCUSSING
REPERCUSSION
REPERCUSSIONS
REPERCUSSIVE
REPERTOIRE
REPERTOIRES
REPERTORIAL
REPERTORIES
REPERUSALS
REPERUSING
REPETITEUR
REPETITEURS
REPETITEUSE
REPETITEUSES
REPETITION
REPETITIONAL
REPETITIONARY
REPETITIONS
REPETITIOUS
REPETITIOUSLY
REPETITIOUSNESS

REPETITIVE
REPETITIVELY
REPETITIVENESS
REPHOTOGRAPH
REPHOTOGRAPHED
REPHOTOGRAPHING
REPHOTOGRAPHS
REPHRASING
REPHRASINGS
REPIGMENTED
REPIGMENTING
REPIGMENTS
REPINEMENT
REPINEMENTS
REPININGLY
REPLACEABILITY
REPLACEABLE
REPLACEMENT
REPLACEMENTS
REPLANNING
REPLANTATION
REPLANTATIONS
REPLANTING
REPLASTERED
REPLASTERING
REPLASTERS
REPLEADERS
REPLEADING
REPLEDGING
REPLENISHABLE
REPLENISHED
REPLENISHER
REPLENISHERS
REPLENISHES
REPLENISHING
REPLENISHMENT
REPLENISHMENTS
REPLETENESS
REPLETENESSES
REPLETIONS
REPLEVIABLE
REPLEVINED
REPLEVINING
REPLEVISABLE
REPLEVYING
REPLICABILITIES
REPLICABILITY
REPLICABLE
REPLICANTS
REPLICASES
REPLICATED
REPLICATES
REPLICATING
REPLICATION
REPLICATIONS
REPLICATIVE
REPLICATOR
REPLICATORS
REPLOTTING
REPLOUGHED
REPLOUGHING
REPLUMBING
REPLUNGING
REPOINTING
REPOINTINGS
REPOLARISATION
REPOLARISATIONS
REPOLARISE
REPOLARISED
REPOLARISES
REPOLARISING
REPOLARIZATION
REPOLARIZATIONS
REPOLARIZE
REPOLARIZED
REPOLARIZES
REPOLARIZING
REPOLISHED
REPOLISHES
REPOLISHING
REPOPULARISE
REPOPULARISED
REPOPULARISES
REPOPULARISING
REPOPULARIZE
REPOPULARIZED
REPOPULARIZES
REPOPULARIZING
REPOPULATE
REPOPULATED
REPOPULATES
REPOPULATING
REPOPULATION
REPOPULATIONS
REPORTABLE
REPORTAGES
REPORTEDLY
REPORTINGLY
REPORTINGS
REPORTORIAL
REPORTORIALLY
REPOSEDNESS
REPOSEDNESSES
REPOSEFULLY
REPOSEFULNESS
REPOSEFULNESSES
REPOSITING
REPOSITION
REPOSITIONED
REPOSITIONING
REPOSITIONS
REPOSITORIES
REPOSITORS
REPOSITORY
REPOSSESSED
REPOSSESSES
REPOSSESSING
REPOSSESSION
REPOSSESSIONS
REPOSSESSOR
REPOSSESSORS
REPOTTINGS
REPOUSSAGE
REPOUSSAGES
REPOUSSOIR
REPOUSSOIRS
REPOWERING
REPREEVING
REPREHENDABLE
REPREHENDED
REPREHENDER
REPREHENDERS
REPREHENDING
REPREHENDS
REPREHENSIBLE
REPREHENSIBLY
REPREHENSION
REPREHENSIONS
REPREHENSIVE
REPREHENSIVELY
REPREHENSORY
REPRESENTABLE
REPRESENTAMEN
REPRESENTAMENS
REPRESENTANT
REPRESENTANTS
REPRESENTATION
REPRESENTATIONS
REPRESENTATIVE
REPRESENTATIVES
REPRESENTED
REPRESENTEE
REPRESENTEES
REPRESENTER
REPRESENTERS
REPRESENTING
REPRESENTMENT
REPRESENTMENTS
REPRESENTOR
REPRESENTORS
REPRESENTS
REPRESSERS
REPRESSIBILITY
REPRESSIBLE
REPRESSIBLY
REPRESSING
REPRESSION
REPRESSIONIST
REPRESSIONISTS
REPRESSIONS
REPRESSIVE
REPRESSIVELY
REPRESSIVENESS
REPRESSORS
REPRESSURISE
REPRESSURISED
REPRESSURISES
REPRESSURISING
REPRESSURIZE
REPRESSURIZED
REPRESSURIZES
REPRESSURIZING
REPRIEVABLE
REPRIEVALS
REPRIEVERS
REPRIEVING
REPRIMANDED
REPRIMANDING
REPRIMANDS
REPRINTERS
REPRINTING
REPRISTINATE
REPRISTINATED
REPRISTINATES
REPRISTINATING
REPRISTINATION
REPRISTINATIONS
REPRIVATISATION
REPRIVATISE
REPRIVATISED
REPRIVATISES
REPRIVATISING
REPRIVATIZATION
REPRIVATIZE
REPRIVATIZED
REPRIVATIZES
REPRIVATIZING
REPROACHABLE
REPROACHABLY
REPROACHED
REPROACHER
REPROACHERS
REPROACHES
REPROACHFUL
REPROACHFULLY
REPROACHFULNESS
REPROACHING
REPROACHINGLY
REPROACHLESS
REPROBACIES
REPROBANCE
REPROBANCES
REPROBATED
REPROBATER
REPROBATERS
REPROBATES
REPROBATING
REPROBATION
REPROBATIONARY
REPROBATIONS
REPROBATIVE
REPROBATIVELY
REPROBATOR
REPROBATORS
REPROBATORY
REPROCESSED
REPROCESSES
REPROCESSING
REPROCESSINGS
REPRODUCED

R

REPRODUCER
REPRODUCERS
REPRODUCES
REPRODUCIBILITY
REPRODUCIBLE
REPRODUCIBLES
REPRODUCIBLY
REPRODUCING
REPRODUCTION
REPRODUCTIONS
REPRODUCTIVE
REPRODUCTIVELY
REPRODUCTIVES
REPRODUCTIVITY
REPROGRAMED
REPROGRAMING
REPROGRAMMABLE
REPROGRAMME
REPROGRAMMED
REPROGRAMMES
REPROGRAMMING
REPROGRAMS
REPROGRAPHER
REPROGRAPHERS
REPROGRAPHIC
REPROGRAPHICS
REPROGRAPHIES
REPROGRAPHY
REPROOFING
REPROVABLE
REPROVINGLY
REPROVISION
REPROVISIONED
REPROVISIONING
REPROVISIONS
REPTATIONS
REPTILIANLY
REPTILIANS
REPTILIFEROUS
REPTILIFORM
REPTILIOUS
REPTILOIDS
REPUBLICAN
REPUBLICANISE
REPUBLICANISED
REPUBLICANISES
REPUBLICANISING
REPUBLICANISM
REPUBLICANISMS
REPUBLICANIZE
REPUBLICANIZED
REPUBLICANIZES
REPUBLICANIZING
REPUBLICANS
REPUBLICATION
REPUBLICATIONS
REPUBLISHED
REPUBLISHER
REPUBLISHERS
REPUBLISHES
REPUBLISHING
REPUDIABLE
REPUDIATED
REPUDIATES
REPUDIATING
REPUDIATION
REPUDIATIONIST
REPUDIATIONISTS
REPUDIATIONS
REPUDIATIVE
REPUDIATOR
REPUDIATORS
REPUGNANCE
REPUGNANCES
REPUGNANCIES
REPUGNANCY
REPUGNANTLY
REPULSIONS
REPULSIVELY
REPULSIVENESS
REPULSIVENESSES
REPUNCTUATION
REPUNCTUATIONS
REPURCHASE
REPURCHASED
REPURCHASES
REPURCHASING
REPURIFIED
REPURIFIES
REPURIFYING
REPURPOSED
REPURPOSES
REPURPOSING
REPURSUING
REPUTABILITIES
REPUTABILITY
REPUTATION
REPUTATIONAL
REPUTATIONLESS
REPUTATIONS
REPUTATIVE
REPUTATIVELY
REPUTELESS
REQUALIFIED
REQUALIFIES
REQUALIFYING
REQUESTERS
REQUESTING
REQUESTORS
REQUICKENED
REQUICKENING
REQUICKENS
REQUIESCAT
REQUIESCATS
REQUIGHTED
REQUIGHTING
REQUIRABLE
REQUIREMENT
REQUIREMENTS
REQUIRINGS
REQUISITELY
REQUISITENESS
REQUISITENESSES
REQUISITES
REQUISITION
REQUISITIONARY
REQUISITIONED
REQUISITIONING
REQUISITIONIST
REQUISITIONISTS
REQUISITIONS
REQUISITOR
REQUISITORIES
REQUISITORS
REQUISITORY
REQUITABLE
REQUITEFUL
REQUITELESS
REQUITEMENT
REQUITEMENTS
REQUITTING
REQUOYLING
RERADIATED
RERADIATES
RERADIATING
RERADIATION
RERADIATIONS
RERAILINGS
REREADINGS
REREBRACES
RERECORDED
RERECORDING
REREDORTER
REREDORTERS
REREDOSSES
REREGISTER
REREGISTERED
REREGISTERING
REREGISTERS
REREGISTRATION
REREGISTRATIONS
REREGULATE
REREGULATED
REREGULATES
REREGULATING
REREGULATION
REREGULATIONS
RERELEASED
RERELEASES
RERELEASING
REREMINDED
REREMINDING
REREPEATED
REREPEATING
REREVIEWED
REREVIEWING
REREVISING
REROUTEING
RESADDLING
RESALEABLE
RESALUTING
RESAMPLING
RESCHEDULE
RESCHEDULED
RESCHEDULES
RESCHEDULING
RESCHEDULINGS
RESCHOOLED
RESCHOOLING
RESCINDABLE
RESCINDERS
RESCINDING
RESCINDMENT
RESCINDMENTS
RESCISSIBLE
RESCISSION
RESCISSIONS
RESCISSORY
RESCREENED
RESCREENING
RESCRIPTED
RESCRIPTING
RESCRIPTION
RESCRIPTIONS
RESCULPTED
RESCULPTING
RESEALABLE
RESEARCHABLE
RESEARCHED
RESEARCHER
RESEARCHERS
RESEARCHES
RESEARCHFUL
RESEARCHING
RESEARCHIST
RESEARCHISTS
RESEASONED
RESEASONING
RESECTABILITIES
RESECTABILITY
RESECTABLE
RESECTIONAL
RESECTIONS
RESECURING
RESEGREGATE
RESEGREGATED
RESEGREGATES
RESEGREGATING
RESEGREGATION
RESEGREGATIONS
RESEIZURES
RESELECTED
RESELECTING
RESELECTION
RESELECTIONS
RESEMBLANCE
RESEMBLANCES
RESEMBLANT
RESEMBLERS
RESEMBLING

RESENSITISE
RESENSITISED
RESENSITISES
RESENSITISING
RESENSITIZE
RESENSITIZED
RESENSITIZES
RESENSITIZING
RESENTENCE
RESENTENCED
RESENTENCES
RESENTENCING
RESENTFULLY
RESENTFULNESS
RESENTFULNESSES
RESENTINGLY
RESENTMENT
RESENTMENTS
RESERPINES
RESERVABLE
RESERVATION
RESERVATIONIST
RESERVATIONISTS
RESERVATIONS
RESERVATORIES
RESERVATORY
RESERVEDLY
RESERVEDNESS
RESERVEDNESSES
RESERVICED
RESERVICES
RESERVICING
RESERVISTS
RESERVOIRED
RESERVOIRING
RESERVOIRS
RESETTABLE
RESETTLEMENT
RESETTLEMENTS
RESETTLING
RESHAPINGS
RESHARPENED
RESHARPENING
RESHARPENS
RESHINGLED
RESHINGLES
RESHINGLING
RESHIPMENT
RESHIPMENTS
RESHIPPERS
RESHIPPING
RESHOOTING
RESHOWERED
RESHOWERING
RESHOWINGS
RESHUFFLED
RESHUFFLES
RESHUFFLING
RESIDENCES
RESIDENCIES
RESIDENTER
RESIDENTERS
RESIDENTIAL
RESIDENTIALLY
RESIDENTIARIES
RESIDENTIARY
RESIDENTSHIP
RESIDENTSHIPS
RESIDUALLY
RESIGHTING
RESIGNATION
RESIGNATIONS
RESIGNEDLY
RESIGNEDNESS
RESIGNEDNESSES
RESIGNMENT
RESIGNMENTS
RESILEMENT
RESILEMENTS
RESILIENCE
RESILIENCES
RESILIENCIES
RESILIENCY
RESILIENTLY
RESILVERED
RESILVERING
RESINATING
RESINIFEROUS
RESINIFICATION
RESINIFICATIONS
RESINIFIED
RESINIFIES
RESINIFYING
RESINISING
RESINIZING
RESINOUSLY
RESINOUSNESS
RESINOUSNESSES
RESIPISCENCE
RESIPISCENCES
RESIPISCENCIES
RESIPISCENCY
RESIPISCENT
RESISTANCE
RESISTANCES
RESISTANTS
RESISTENTS
RESISTIBILITIES
RESISTIBILITY
RESISTIBLE
RESISTIBLY
RESISTINGLY
RESISTIVELY
RESISTIVENESS
RESISTIVENESSES
RESISTIVITIES
RESISTIVITY
RESISTLESS
RESISTLESSLY
RESISTLESSNESS
RESITTINGS
RESITUATED
RESITUATES
RESITUATING
RESKETCHED
RESKETCHES
RESKETCHING
RESKILLING
RESKILLINGS
RESKINNING
RESMELTING
RESMOOTHED
RESMOOTHING
RESNATRONS
RESOCIALISATION
RESOCIALISE
RESOCIALISED
RESOCIALISES
RESOCIALISING
RESOCIALIZATION
RESOCIALIZE
RESOCIALIZED
RESOCIALIZES
RESOCIALIZING
RESOFTENED
RESOFTENING
RESOLDERED
RESOLDERING
RESOLIDIFIED
RESOLIDIFIES
RESOLIDIFY
RESOLIDIFYING
RESOLUBILITIES
RESOLUBILITY
RESOLUBLENESS
RESOLUBLENESSES
RESOLUTELY
RESOLUTENESS
RESOLUTENESSES
RESOLUTEST
RESOLUTION
RESOLUTIONER
RESOLUTIONERS
RESOLUTIONIST
RESOLUTIONISTS
RESOLUTIONS
RESOLUTIVE
RESOLVABILITIES
RESOLVABILITY
RESOLVABLE
RESOLVABLENESS
RESOLVEDLY
RESOLVEDNESS
RESOLVEDNESSES
RESOLVENTS
RESONANCES
RESONANTLY
RESONATING
RESONATION
RESONATIONS
RESONATORS
RESORBENCE
RESORBENCES
RESORCINAL
RESORCINOL
RESORCINOLS
RESORPTION
RESORPTIONS
RESORPTIVE
RESOUNDING
RESOUNDINGLY
RESOURCEFUL
RESOURCEFULLY
RESOURCEFULNESS
RESOURCELESS
RESOURCING
RESOURCINGS
RESPEAKING
RESPECIFIED
RESPECIFIES
RESPECIFYING
RESPECTABILISE
RESPECTABILISED
RESPECTABILISES
RESPECTABILITY
RESPECTABILIZE
RESPECTABILIZED
RESPECTABILIZES
RESPECTABLE
RESPECTABLENESS
RESPECTABLES
RESPECTABLY
RESPECTANT
RESPECTERS
RESPECTFUL
RESPECTFULLY
RESPECTFULNESS
RESPECTING
RESPECTIVE
RESPECTIVELY
RESPECTIVENESS
RESPECTLESS
RESPELLING
RESPELLINGS
RESPIRABILITIES
RESPIRABILITY
RESPIRABLE
RESPIRATION
RESPIRATIONAL
RESPIRATIONS
RESPIRATOR
RESPIRATORS
RESPIRATORY
RESPIRITUALISE
RESPIRITUALISED
RESPIRITUALISES
RESPIRITUALIZE
RESPIRITUALIZED
RESPIRITUALIZES
RESPIROLOGIES

RESPIROLOGIST
RESPIROLOGISTS
RESPIROLOGY
RESPIROMETER
RESPIROMETERS
RESPIROMETRIC
RESPIROMETRIES
RESPIROMETRY
RESPITELESS
RESPLENDED
RESPLENDENCE
RESPLENDENCES
RESPLENDENCIES
RESPLENDENCY
RESPLENDENT
RESPLENDENTLY
RESPLENDING
RESPLICING
RESPLITTING
RESPONDENCE
RESPONDENCES
RESPONDENCIES
RESPONDENCY
RESPONDENT
RESPONDENTIA
RESPONDENTIAS
RESPONDENTS
RESPONDERS
RESPONDING
RESPONSELESS
RESPONSERS
RESPONSIBILITY
RESPONSIBLE
RESPONSIBLENESS
RESPONSIBLY
RESPONSIONS
RESPONSIVE
RESPONSIVELY
RESPONSIVENESS
RESPONSORIAL
RESPONSORIALS
RESPONSORIES
RESPONSORS
RESPONSORY
RESPONSUMS
RESPOOLING
RESPOTTING
RESPRAYING
RESPREADING
RESPRINGING
RESPROUTED
RESPROUTING
RESSALDARS
RESSENTIMENT
RESSENTIMENTS
RESTABILISE
RESTABILISED
RESTABILISES
RESTABILISING
RESTABILIZE
RESTABILIZED
RESTABILIZES
RESTABILIZING
RESTABLING
RESTACKING
RESTAFFING
RESTAMPING
RESTARTABLE
RESTARTERS
RESTARTING
RESTATEMENT
RESTATEMENTS
RESTATIONED
RESTATIONING
RESTATIONS
RESTAURANT
RESTAURANTEUR
RESTAURANTEURS
RESTAURANTS
RESTAURATEUR
RESTAURATEURS
RESTAURATION
RESTAURATIONS
RESTEMMING
RESTFULLER
RESTFULLEST
RESTFULNESS
RESTFULNESSES
RESTHARROW
RESTHARROWS
RESTIMULATE
RESTIMULATED
RESTIMULATES
RESTIMULATING
RESTIMULATION
RESTIMULATIONS
RESTITCHED
RESTITCHES
RESTITCHING
RESTITUTED
RESTITUTES
RESTITUTING
RESTITUTION
RESTITUTIONISM
RESTITUTIONISMS
RESTITUTIONIST
RESTITUTIONISTS
RESTITUTIONS
RESTITUTIVE
RESTITUTOR
RESTITUTORS
RESTITUTORY
RESTIVENESS
RESTIVENESSES
RESTLESSLY
RESTLESSNESS
RESTLESSNESSES
RESTOCKING
RESTORABLE
RESTORABLENESS
RESTORATION
RESTORATIONISM
RESTORATIONISMS
RESTORATIONIST
RESTORATIONISTS
RESTORATIONS
RESTORATIVE
RESTORATIVELY
RESTORATIVES
RESTRAINABLE
RESTRAINED
RESTRAINEDLY
RESTRAINEDNESS
RESTRAINER
RESTRAINERS
RESTRAINING
RESTRAININGS
RESTRAINTS
RESTRENGTHEN
RESTRENGTHENED
RESTRENGTHENING
RESTRENGTHENS
RESTRESSED
RESTRESSES
RESTRESSING
RESTRETCHED
RESTRETCHES
RESTRETCHING
RESTRICKEN
RESTRICTED
RESTRICTEDLY
RESTRICTEDNESS
RESTRICTING
RESTRICTION
RESTRICTIONISM
RESTRICTIONISMS
RESTRICTIONIST
RESTRICTIONISTS
RESTRICTIONS
RESTRICTIVE
RESTRICTIVELY
RESTRICTIVENESS
RESTRICTIVES
RESTRIKING
RESTRINGED
RESTRINGEING
RESTRINGENT
RESTRINGENTS
RESTRINGES
RESTRINGING
RESTRIVING
RESTRUCTURE
RESTRUCTURED
RESTRUCTURES
RESTRUCTURING
RESTRUCTURINGS
RESTUDYING
RESTUFFING
RESTUMPING
RESUBJECTED
RESUBJECTING
RESUBJECTS
RESUBMISSION
RESUBMISSIONS
RESUBMITTED
RESUBMITTING
RESULTANTLY
RESULTANTS
RESULTATIVE
RESULTATIVES
RESULTLESS
RESULTLESSNESS
RESUMMONED
RESUMMONING
RESUMPTION
RESUMPTIONS
RESUMPTIVE
RESUMPTIVELY
RESUPINATE
RESUPINATION
RESUPINATIONS
RESUPPLIED
RESUPPLIES
RESUPPLYING
RESURFACED
RESURFACER
RESURFACERS
RESURFACES
RESURFACING
RESURGENCE
RESURGENCES
RESURRECTED
RESURRECTING
RESURRECTION
RESURRECTIONAL
RESURRECTIONARY
RESURRECTIONISE
RESURRECTIONISM
RESURRECTIONIST
RESURRECTIONIZE
RESURRECTIONS
RESURRECTIVE
RESURRECTOR
RESURRECTORS
RESURRECTS
RESURVEYED
RESURVEYING
RESUSCITABLE
RESUSCITANT
RESUSCITANTS
RESUSCITATE
RESUSCITATED
RESUSCITATES
RESUSCITATING
RESUSCITATION
RESUSCITATIONS
RESUSCITATIVE
RESUSCITATOR
RESUSCITATORS
RESUSPENDED

RESUSPENDING
RESUSPENDS
RESVERATROL
RESVERATROLS
RESWALLOWED
RESWALLOWING
RESWALLOWS
RESYNCHRONISE
RESYNCHRONISED
RESYNCHRONISES
RESYNCHRONISING
RESYNCHRONIZE
RESYNCHRONIZED
RESYNCHRONIZES
RESYNCHRONIZING
RESYNTHESES
RESYNTHESIS
RESYNTHESISE
RESYNTHESISED
RESYNTHESISES
RESYNTHESISING
RESYNTHESIZE
RESYNTHESIZED
RESYNTHESIZES
RESYNTHESIZING
RESYSTEMATISE
RESYSTEMATISED
RESYSTEMATISES
RESYSTEMATISING
RESYSTEMATIZE
RESYSTEMATIZED
RESYSTEMATIZES
RESYSTEMATIZING
RETACKLING
RETAILINGS
RETAILMENT
RETAILMENTS
RETAILORED
RETAILORING
RETAINABLE
RETAINERSHIP
RETAINERSHIPS
RETAINMENT
RETAINMENTS
RETALIATED
RETALIATES
RETALIATING
RETALIATION
RETALIATIONIST
RETALIATIONISTS
RETALIATIONS
RETALIATIVE
RETALIATOR
RETALIATORS
RETALIATORY
RETALLYING
RETARDANTS
RETARDATES
RETARDATION
RETARDATIONS
RETARDATIVE
RETARDATORY
RETARDMENT
RETARDMENTS
RETARGETED
RETARGETING
RETEACHING
RETELLINGS
RETEMPERED
RETEMPERING
RETENTIONIST
RETENTIONISTS
RETENTIONS
RETENTIVELY
RETENTIVENESS
RETENTIVENESSES
RETENTIVES
RETENTIVITIES
RETENTIVITY
RETESTIFIED
RETESTIFIES
RETESTIFYING
RETEXTURED
RETEXTURES
RETEXTURING
RETHINKERS
RETHINKING
RETHINKINGS
RETHREADED
RETHREADING
RETICELLAS
RETICENCES
RETICENCIES
RETICENTLY
RETICULARLY
RETICULARY
RETICULATE
RETICULATED
RETICULATELY
RETICULATES
RETICULATING
RETICULATION
RETICULATIONS
RETICULOCYTE
RETICULOCYTES
RETICULUMS
RETIGHTENED
RETIGHTENING
RETIGHTENS
RETINACULA
RETINACULAR
RETINACULUM
RETINALITE
RETINALITES
RETINISPORA
RETINISPORAS
RETINITIDES
RETINITISES
RETINOBLASTOMA
RETINOBLASTOMAS
RETINOPATHIES
RETINOPATHY
RETINOSCOPE
RETINOSCOPES
RETINOSCOPIC
RETINOSCOPIES
RETINOSCOPIST
RETINOSCOPISTS
RETINOSCOPY
RETINOSPORA
RETINOSPORAS
RETINOTECTAL
RETIRACIES
RETIREDNESS
RETIREDNESSES
RETIREMENT
RETIREMENTS
RETIRINGLY
RETIRINGNESS
RETIRINGNESSES
RETORSIONS
RETORTIONS
RETOTALING
RETOTALLED
RETOTALLING
RETOUCHABLE
RETOUCHERS
RETOUCHING
RETOUCHINGS
RETRACEABLE
RETRACEMENT
RETRACEMENTS
RETRACKING
RETRACTABILITY
RETRACTABLE
RETRACTATION
RETRACTATIONS
RETRACTIBILITY
RETRACTIBLE
RETRACTILE
RETRACTILITIES
RETRACTILITY
RETRACTING
RETRACTION
RETRACTIONS
RETRACTIVE
RETRACTIVELY
RETRACTORS
RETRAINABLE
RETRAINEES
RETRAINING
RETRAININGS
RETRANSFER
RETRANSFERRED
RETRANSFERRING
RETRANSFERS
RETRANSFORM
RETRANSFORMED
RETRANSFORMING
RETRANSFORMS
RETRANSFUSE
RETRANSFUSED
RETRANSFUSES
RETRANSFUSING
RETRANSLATE
RETRANSLATED
RETRANSLATES
RETRANSLATING
RETRANSLATION
RETRANSLATIONS
RETRANSMISSION
RETRANSMISSIONS
RETRANSMIT
RETRANSMITS
RETRANSMITTED
RETRANSMITTING
RETREADING
RETREATANT
RETREATANTS
RETREATERS
RETREATING
RETRENCHABLE
RETRENCHED
RETRENCHES
RETRENCHING
RETRENCHMENT
RETRENCHMENTS
RETRIBUTED
RETRIBUTES
RETRIBUTING
RETRIBUTION
RETRIBUTIONS
RETRIBUTIVE
RETRIBUTIVELY
RETRIBUTOR
RETRIBUTORS
RETRIBUTORY
RETRIEVABILITY
RETRIEVABLE
RETRIEVABLENESS
RETRIEVABLY
RETRIEVALS
RETRIEVEMENT
RETRIEVEMENTS
RETRIEVERS
RETRIEVING
RETRIEVINGS
RETRIMMING
RETROACTED
RETROACTING
RETROACTION
RETROACTIONS
RETROACTIVE
RETROACTIVELY
RETROACTIVENESS
RETROACTIVITIES
RETROACTIVITY
RETROBULBAR
RETROCEDED
RETROCEDENCE

RETROCEDENCES
RETROCEDENT
RETROCEDES
RETROCEDING
RETROCESSION
RETROCESSIONS
RETROCESSIVE
RETROCHOIR
RETROCHOIRS
RETROCOGNITION
RETROCOGNITIONS
RETRODICTED
RETRODICTING
RETRODICTION
RETRODICTIONS
RETRODICTIVE
RETRODICTS
RETROENGINE
RETROENGINES
RETROFIRED
RETROFIRES
RETROFIRING
RETROFITTED
RETROFITTING
RETROFITTINGS
RETROFLECTED
RETROFLECTION
RETROFLECTIONS
RETROFLEXED
RETROFLEXES
RETROFLEXING
RETROFLEXION
RETROFLEXIONS
RETROGRADATION
RETROGRADATIONS
RETROGRADE
RETROGRADED
RETROGRADELY
RETROGRADES
RETROGRADING
RETROGRESS
RETROGRESSED
RETROGRESSES
RETROGRESSING
RETROGRESSION
RETROGRESSIONAL
RETROGRESSIONS
RETROGRESSIVE
RETROGRESSIVELY
RETROJECTED
RETROJECTING
RETROJECTION
RETROJECTIONS
RETROJECTS
RETROLENTAL
RETROMINGENCIES
RETROMINGENCY
RETROMINGENT
RETROMINGENTS
RETROPACKS
RETROPERITONEAL
RETROPHILIA
RETROPHILIAC
RETROPHILIACS
RETROPHILIAS
RETROPULSION
RETROPULSIONS
RETROPULSIVE
RETROREFLECTION
RETROREFLECTIVE
RETROREFLECTOR
RETROREFLECTORS
RETROROCKET
RETROROCKETS
RETRORSELY
RETROSEXUAL
RETROSEXUALS
RETROSPECT
RETROSPECTED
RETROSPECTING
RETROSPECTION
RETROSPECTIONS
RETROSPECTIVE
RETROSPECTIVELY
RETROSPECTIVES
RETROSPECTS
RETROUSSAGE
RETROUSSAGES
RETROVERSE
RETROVERSION
RETROVERSIONS
RETROVERTED
RETROVERTING
RETROVERTS
RETROVIRAL
RETROVIRUS
RETROVIRUSES
RETURNABILITIES
RETURNABILITY
RETURNABLE
RETURNABLES
RETURNLESS
RETWEETING
RETWISTING
REUNIFICATION
REUNIFICATIONS
REUNIFYING
REUNIONISM
REUNIONISMS
REUNIONIST
REUNIONISTIC
REUNIONISTS
REUNITABLE
REUPHOLSTER
REUPHOLSTERED
REUPHOLSTERING
REUPHOLSTERS
REUPTAKING
REUSABILITIES
REUSABILITY
REUTILISATION
REUTILISATIONS
REUTILISED
REUTILISES
REUTILISING
REUTILIZATION
REUTILIZATIONS
REUTILIZED
REUTILIZES
REUTILIZING
REUTTERING
REVACCINATE
REVACCINATED
REVACCINATES
REVACCINATING
REVACCINATION
REVACCINATIONS
REVALENTAS
REVALIDATE
REVALIDATED
REVALIDATES
REVALIDATING
REVALIDATION
REVALIDATIONS
REVALORISATION
REVALORISATIONS
REVALORISE
REVALORISED
REVALORISES
REVALORISING
REVALORIZATION
REVALORIZATIONS
REVALORIZE
REVALORIZED
REVALORIZES
REVALORIZING
REVALUATED
REVALUATES
REVALUATING
REVALUATION
REVALUATIONS
REVAMPINGS
REVANCHISM
REVANCHISMS
REVANCHIST
REVANCHISTS
REVARNISHED
REVARNISHES
REVARNISHING
REVEALABILITIES
REVEALABILITY
REVEALABLE
REVEALINGLY
REVEALINGNESS
REVEALINGNESSES
REVEALINGS
REVEALMENT
REVEALMENTS
REVEGETATE
REVEGETATED
REVEGETATES
REVEGETATING
REVEGETATION
REVEGETATIONS
REVELATION
REVELATIONAL
REVELATIONIST
REVELATIONISTS
REVELATIONS
REVELATIVE
REVELATORS
REVELATORY
REVELLINGS
REVELMENTS
REVENDICATE
REVENDICATED
REVENDICATES
REVENDICATING
REVENDICATION
REVENDICATIONS
REVENGEFUL
REVENGEFULLY
REVENGEFULNESS
REVENGELESS
REVENGEMENT
REVENGEMENTS
REVENGINGLY
REVENGINGS
REVERBATORIES
REVERBATORY
REVERBERANT
REVERBERANTLY
REVERBERATE
REVERBERATED
REVERBERATES
REVERBERATING
REVERBERATION
REVERBERATIONS
REVERBERATIVE
REVERBERATOR
REVERBERATORIES
REVERBERATORS
REVERBERATORY
REVERENCED
REVERENCER
REVERENCERS
REVERENCES
REVERENCING
REVERENTIAL
REVERENTIALLY
REVERENTLY
REVERENTNESS
REVERENTNESSES
REVERIFIED
REVERIFIES
REVERIFYING
REVERSEDLY
REVERSELESS
REVERSIBILITIES
REVERSIBILITY

R

REVERSIBLE
REVERSIBLES
REVERSIBLY
REVERSINGS
REVERSIONAL
REVERSIONALLY
REVERSIONARIES
REVERSIONARY
REVERSIONER
REVERSIONERS
REVERSIONS
REVERSISES
REVERTANTS
REVERTIBLE
REVESTIARIES
REVESTIARY
REVESTRIES
REVETMENTS
REVIBRATED
REVIBRATES
REVIBRATING
REVICTUALED
REVICTUALING
REVICTUALLED
REVICTUALLING
REVICTUALS
REVIEWABLE
REVILEMENT
REVILEMENTS
REVILINGLY
REVINDICATE
REVINDICATED
REVINDICATES
REVINDICATING
REVINDICATION
REVINDICATIONS
REVIOLATED
REVIOLATES
REVIOLATING
REVISIONAL
REVISIONARY
REVISIONISM
REVISIONISMS
REVISIONIST
REVISIONISTS
REVISITANT
REVISITANTS
REVISITATION
REVISITATIONS
REVISITING
REVISUALISATION
REVISUALIZATION
REVITALISATION
REVITALISATIONS
REVITALISE
REVITALISED
REVITALISES
REVITALISING
REVITALIZATION
REVITALIZATIONS
REVITALIZE
REVITALIZED
REVITALIZES
REVITALIZING
REVIVABILITIES
REVIVABILITY
REVIVALISM
REVIVALISMS
REVIVALIST
REVIVALISTIC
REVIVALISTS
REVIVEMENT
REVIVEMENTS
REVIVESCENCE
REVIVESCENCES
REVIVESCENCIES
REVIVESCENCY
REVIVESCENT
REVIVIFICATION
REVIVIFICATIONS
REVIVIFIED
REVIVIFIES
REVIVIFYING
REVIVINGLY
REVIVISCENCE
REVIVISCENCES
REVIVISCENCIES
REVIVISCENCY
REVIVISCENT
REVOCABILITIES
REVOCABILITY
REVOCABLENESS
REVOCABLENESSES
REVOCATION
REVOCATIONS
REVOCATORY
REVOKABILITIES
REVOKABILITY
REVOKEMENT
REVOKEMENTS
REVOLTINGLY
REVOLUTION
REVOLUTIONAL
REVOLUTIONARIES
REVOLUTIONARILY
REVOLUTIONARY
REVOLUTIONER
REVOLUTIONERS
REVOLUTIONISE
REVOLUTIONISED
REVOLUTIONISER
REVOLUTIONISERS
REVOLUTIONISES
REVOLUTIONISING
REVOLUTIONISM
REVOLUTIONISMS
REVOLUTIONIST
REVOLUTIONISTS
REVOLUTIONIZE
REVOLUTIONIZED
REVOLUTIONIZER
REVOLUTIONIZERS
REVOLUTIONIZES
REVOLUTIONIZING
REVOLUTIONS
REVOLVABLE
REVOLVABLY
REVOLVENCIES
REVOLVENCY
REVOLVINGLY
REVOLVINGS
REVULSIONARY
REVULSIONS
REVULSIVELY
REVULSIVES
REWAKENING
REWARDABLE
REWARDABLENESS
REWARDINGLY
REWARDLESS
REWATERING
REWEIGHING
REWIDENING
REWILDINGS
REWINDINGS
REWORDINGS
REWORKINGS
REWRAPPING
REWRITABLE
REWRITEABLE
RHABDOCOELE
RHABDOCOELES
RHABDOLITH
RHABDOLITHS
RHABDOMANCER
RHABDOMANCERS
RHABDOMANCIES
RHABDOMANCY
RHABDOMANTIST
RHABDOMANTISTS
RHABDOMERE
RHABDOMERES
RHABDOMYOMA
RHABDOMYOMAS
RHABDOMYOMATA
RHABDOSPHERE
RHABDOSPHERES
RHABDOVIRUS
RHABDOVIRUSES
RHACHIDIAL
RHACHILLAS
RHACHITISES
RHADAMANTHINE
RHAGADIFORM
RHAMNACEOUS
RHAMPHOTHECA
RHAMPHOTHECAE
RHAPONTICS
RHAPSODICAL
RHAPSODICALLY
RHAPSODIES
RHAPSODISE
RHAPSODISED
RHAPSODISES
RHAPSODISING
RHAPSODIST
RHAPSODISTIC
RHAPSODISTS
RHAPSODIZE
RHAPSODIZED
RHAPSODIZES
RHAPSODIZING
RHEOCHORDS
RHEOLOGICAL
RHEOLOGICALLY
RHEOLOGIES
RHEOLOGIST
RHEOLOGISTS
RHEOMETERS
RHEOMETRIC
RHEOMETRICAL
RHEOMETRIES
RHEOMORPHIC
RHEOMORPHISM
RHEOMORPHISMS
RHEOPHILES
RHEORECEPTOR
RHEORECEPTORS
RHEOSCOPES
RHEOSTATIC
RHEOTACTIC
RHEOTROPES
RHEOTROPIC
RHEOTROPISM
RHEOTROPISMS
RHETORICAL
RHETORICALLY
RHETORICIAN
RHETORICIANS
RHETORISED
RHETORISES
RHETORISING
RHETORIZED
RHETORIZES
RHETORIZING
RHEUMATEESE
RHEUMATEESES
RHEUMATICAL
RHEUMATICALLY
RHEUMATICKY
RHEUMATICS
RHEUMATISE
RHEUMATISES
RHEUMATISM
RHEUMATISMAL
RHEUMATISMS
RHEUMATIZE
RHEUMATIZES
RHEUMATOID
RHEUMATOIDALLY

R

RHEUMATOLOGICAL
RHEUMATOLOGIES
RHEUMATOLOGIST
RHEUMATOLOGISTS
RHEUMATOLOGY
RHIGOLENES
RHINENCEPHALA
RHINENCEPHALIC
RHINENCEPHALON
RHINENCEPHALONS
RHINESTONE
RHINESTONED
RHINESTONES
RHINITIDES
RHINITISES
RHINOCERICAL
RHINOCEROI
RHINOCEROS
RHINOCEROSES
RHINOCEROT
RHINOCEROTE
RHINOCEROTES
RHINOCEROTIC
RHINOLALIA
RHINOLALIAS
RHINOLITHS
RHINOLOGICAL
RHINOLOGIES
RHINOLOGIST
RHINOLOGISTS
RHINOPHONIA
RHINOPHONIAS
RHINOPHYMA
RHINOPHYMAS
RHINOPLASTIC
RHINOPLASTIES
RHINOPLASTY
RHINORRHAGIA
RHINORRHAGIAS
RHINORRHOEA
RHINORRHOEAL
RHINORRHOEAS
RHINOSCLEROMA
RHINOSCLEROMAS
RHINOSCLEROMATA
RHINOSCOPE
RHINOSCOPES
RHINOSCOPIC
RHINOSCOPIES
RHINOSCOPY
RHINOTHECA
RHINOTHECAE
RHINOVIRUS
RHINOVIRUSES
RHIPIDIONS
RHIPIDIUMS
RHIZANTHOUS
RHIZOCARPIC
RHIZOCARPOUS
RHIZOCARPS
RHIZOCAULS
RHIZOCEPHALAN
RHIZOCEPHALANS
RHIZOCEPHALOUS
RHIZOCTONIA
RHIZOCTONIAS
RHIZOGENETIC
RHIZOGENIC
RHIZOGENOUS
RHIZOMATOUS
RHIZOMORPH
RHIZOMORPHOUS
RHIZOMORPHS
RHIZOPHAGOUS
RHIZOPHILOUS
RHIZOPHORE
RHIZOPHORES
RHIZOPLANE
RHIZOPLANES
RHIZOPODAN
RHIZOPODANS
RHIZOPODOUS
RHIZOPUSES
RHIZOSPHERE
RHIZOSPHERES
RHIZOTOMIES
RHODAMINES
RHODANATES
RHODANISED
RHODANISES
RHODANISING
RHODANIZED
RHODANIZES
RHODANIZING
RHODOCHROSITE
RHODOCHROSITES
RHODODAPHNE
RHODODAPHNES
RHODODENDRA
RHODODENDRON
RHODODENDRONS
RHODOLITES
RHODOMONTADE
RHODOMONTADED
RHODOMONTADES
RHODOMONTADING
RHODONITES
RHODOPHANE
RHODOPHANES
RHODOPSINS
RHOEADINES
RHOICISSUS
RHOICISSUSES
RHOMBENCEPHALA
RHOMBENCEPHALON
RHOMBENPORPHYR
RHOMBENPORPHYRS
RHOMBENPORPHYRY
RHOMBOHEDRA
RHOMBOHEDRAL
RHOMBOHEDRON
RHOMBOHEDRONS
RHOMBOIDAL
RHOMBOIDEI
RHOMBOIDES
RHOMBOIDEUS
RHOMBPORPHYRIES
RHOMBPORPHYRY
RHOPALISMS
RHOPALOCERAL
RHOPALOCEROUS
RHOTACISED
RHOTACISES
RHOTACISING
RHOTACISMS
RHOTACISTIC
RHOTACISTS
RHOTACIZED
RHOTACIZES
RHOTACIZING
RHOTICITIES
RHUBARBIER
RHUBARBIEST
RHUBARBING
RHUBARBINGS
RHUMBATRON
RHUMBATRONS
RHYMESTERS
RHYNCHOCOEL
RHYNCHOCOELS
RHYNCHODONT
RHYNCHOPHORE
RHYNCHOPHORES
RHYNCHOPHOROUS
RHYPAROGRAPHER
RHYPAROGRAPHERS
RHYPAROGRAPHIC
RHYPAROGRAPHIES
RHYPAROGRAPHY
RHYTHMICAL
RHYTHMICALLY
RHYTHMICITIES
RHYTHMICITY
RHYTHMISATION
RHYTHMISATIONS
RHYTHMISED
RHYTHMISES
RHYTHMISING
RHYTHMISTS
RHYTHMIZATION
RHYTHMIZATIONS
RHYTHMIZED
RHYTHMIZES
RHYTHMIZING
RHYTHMLESS
RHYTHMOMETER
RHYTHMOMETERS
RHYTHMOPOEIA
RHYTHMOPOEIAS
RHYTHMUSES
RHYTIDECTOMIES
RHYTIDECTOMY
RHYTIDOMES
RIBALDRIES
RIBATTUTAS
RIBAUDRIES
RIBAVIRINS
RIBBONFISH
RIBBONFISHES
RIBBONIEST
RIBBONLIKE
RIBBONRIES
RIBBONWOOD
RIBBONWOODS
RIBGRASSES
RIBOFLAVIN
RIBOFLAVINE
RIBOFLAVINES
RIBOFLAVINS
RIBONUCLEASE
RIBONUCLEASES
RIBONUCLEIC
RIBONUCLEOSIDE
RIBONUCLEOSIDES
RIBONUCLEOTIDE
RIBONUCLEOTIDES
RICEFIELDS
RICEGRASSES
RICERCARES
RICERCATAS
RICHNESSES
RICINOLEIC
RICKBURNER
RICKBURNERS
RICKETIEST
RICKETINESS
RICKETINESSES
RICKETTIER
RICKETTIEST
RICKETTSIA
RICKETTSIAE
RICKETTSIAL
RICKETTSIAS
RICKSTANDS
RICKSTICKS
RICOCHETED
RICOCHETING
RICOCHETTED
RICOCHETTING
RIDABILITIES
RIDABILITY
RIDDLINGLY
RIDERSHIPS
RIDESHARING
RIDESHARINGS
RIDGEBACKS
RIDGELINES
RIDGELINGS
RIDGEPOLES
RIDGETREES

R

RIDICULERS
RIDICULING
RIDICULOUS
RIDICULOUSLY
RIDICULOUSNESS
RIEBECKITE
RIEBECKITES
RIFACIMENTI
RIFACIMENTO
RIFACIMENTOS
RIFAMPICIN
RIFAMPICINS
RIFAMYCINS
RIFENESSES
RIFLEBIRDS
RIGAMAROLE
RIGAMAROLES
RIGHTABLENESS
RIGHTABLENESSES
RIGHTENING
RIGHTEOUSLY
RIGHTEOUSNESS
RIGHTEOUSNESSES
RIGHTFULLY
RIGHTFULNESS
RIGHTFULNESSES
RIGHTNESSES
RIGHTSIZED
RIGHTSIZES
RIGHTSIZING
RIGHTSIZINGS
RIGHTWARDLY
RIGHTWARDS
RIGIDIFICATION
RIGIDIFICATIONS
RIGIDIFIED
RIGIDIFIES
RIGIDIFYING
RIGIDISING
RIGIDITIES
RIGIDIZING
RIGIDNESSES
RIGMAROLES
RIGORISTIC
RIGOROUSLY
RIGOROUSNESS
RIGOROUSNESSES
RIGSDALERS
RIGWIDDIES
RIGWOODIES
RIJKSDAALER
RIJKSDAALERS
RIJSTAFELS
RIJSTTAFEL
RIJSTTAFELS
RIMINESSES
RIMOSITIES
RINDERPEST
RINDERPESTS
RINFORZANDO
RINGBARKED
RINGBARKING
RINGHALSES
RINGLEADER
RINGLEADERS
RINGLETIER
RINGLETIEST
RINGMASTER
RINGMASTERS
RINGSIDERS
RINGSTANDS
RINGSTRAKED
RINGTOSSES
RINKHALSES
RINSABILITIES
RINSABILITY
RINSIBILITIES
RINSIBILITY
RINTHEREOUT
RINTHEREOUTS
RIOTOUSNESS
RIOTOUSNESSES
RIPENESSES
RIPIDOLITE
RIPIDOLITES
RIPIENISTS
RIPPLINGLY
RIPRAPPING
RIPSNORTER
RIPSNORTERS
RIPSNORTING
RIPSNORTINGLY
RISIBILITIES
RISIBILITY
RISKINESSES
RISORGIMENTO
RISORGIMENTOS
RISTRETTOS
RITARDANDI
RITARDANDO
RITARDANDOS
RITONAVIRS
RITORNELLE
RITORNELLES
RITORNELLI
RITORNELLO
RITORNELLOS
RITORNELLS
RITOURNELLE
RITOURNELLES
RITUALISATION
RITUALISATIONS
RITUALISED
RITUALISES
RITUALISING
RITUALISMS
RITUALISTIC
RITUALISTICALLY
RITUALISTS
RITUALIZATION
RITUALIZATIONS
RITUALIZED
RITUALIZES
RITUALIZING
RITUXIMABS
RITZINESSES
RIVALESSES
RIVALISING
RIVALITIES
RIVALIZING
RIVALSHIPS
RIVERBANKS
RIVERBOATS
RIVERCRAFT
RIVERCRAFTS
RIVERFRONT
RIVERFRONTS
RIVERHEADS
RIVERSCAPE
RIVERSCAPES
RIVERSIDES
RIVERWALKS
RIVERWARDS
RIVERWEEDS
RIVERWORTHIER
RIVERWORTHIEST
RIVERWORTHINESS
RIVERWORTHY
RIVETINGLY
ROADABILITIES
ROADABILITY
ROADBLOCKED
ROADBLOCKING
ROADBLOCKS
ROADCRAFTS
ROADHEADER
ROADHEADERS
ROADHOLDING
ROADHOLDINGS
ROADHOUSES
ROADMAKING
ROADMAKINGS
ROADMENDER
ROADMENDERS
ROADROLLER
ROADROLLERS
ROADRUNNER
ROADRUNNERS
ROADSTEADS
ROADWORTHIER
ROADWORTHIES
ROADWORTHIEST
ROADWORTHINESS
ROADWORTHY
ROBERDSMAN
ROBERDSMEN
ROBERTSMAN
ROBERTSMEN
ROBORATING
ROBOTICALLY
ROBOTISATION
ROBOTISATIONS
ROBOTISING
ROBOTIZATION
ROBOTIZATIONS
ROBOTIZING
ROBUSTIOUS
ROBUSTIOUSLY
ROBUSTIOUSNESS
ROBUSTNESS
ROBUSTNESSES
ROCAMBOLES
ROCKABILLIES
ROCKABILLY
ROCKBURSTS
ROCKCRESSES
ROCKETEERS
ROCKETRIES
ROCKETSONDE
ROCKETSONDES
ROCKFISHES
ROCKHOPPER
ROCKHOPPERS
ROCKHOUNDING
ROCKHOUNDINGS
ROCKHOUNDS
ROCKINESSES
ROCKSHAFTS
ROCKSLIDES
ROCKSTEADIES
ROCKSTEADY
ROCKWATERS
RODENTICIDE
RODENTICIDES
RODFISHERS
RODFISHING
RODFISHINGS
RODGERSIAS
RODOMONTADE
RODOMONTADED
RODOMONTADER
RODOMONTADERS
RODOMONTADES
RODOMONTADING
ROENTGENISATION
ROENTGENISE
ROENTGENISED
ROENTGENISES
ROENTGENISING
ROENTGENIUM
ROENTGENIUMS
ROENTGENIZATION
ROENTGENIZE
ROENTGENIZED
ROENTGENIZES
ROENTGENIZING
ROENTGENOGRAM
ROENTGENOGRAMS
ROENTGENOGRAPH
ROENTGENOGRAPHS

ROENTGENOGRAPHY
ROENTGENOLOGIC
ROENTGENOLOGIES
ROENTGENOLOGIST
ROENTGENOLOGY
ROENTGENOPAQUE
ROENTGENOSCOPE
ROENTGENOSCOPES
ROENTGENOSCOPIC
ROENTGENOSCOPY
ROGUESHIPS
ROGUISHNESS
ROGUISHNESSES
ROISTERERS
ROISTERING
ROISTERINGS
ROISTEROUS
ROISTEROUSLY
ROLLCOLLAR
ROLLCOLLARS
ROLLERBALL
ROLLERBALLS
ROLLERBLADE
ROLLERBLADED
ROLLERBLADER
ROLLERBLADERS
ROLLERBLADES
ROLLERBLADING
ROLLERBLADINGS
ROLLERCOASTER
ROLLERCOASTERED
ROLLERCOASTERS
ROLLERDROME
ROLLERDROMES
ROLLICKIER
ROLLICKIEST
ROLLICKING
ROLLICKINGS
ROLLOCKING
ROLLOCKINGS
ROMANCICAL
ROMANCINGS
ROMANESCOS
ROMANICITE
ROMANICITES
ROMANISATION
ROMANISATIONS
ROMANISING
ROMANIZATION
ROMANIZATIONS
ROMANIZING
ROMANTICAL
ROMANTICALITIES
ROMANTICALITY
ROMANTICALLY
ROMANTICISATION
ROMANTICISE
ROMANTICISED
ROMANTICISES
ROMANTICISING
ROMANTICISM
ROMANTICISMS
ROMANTICIST
ROMANTICISTS
ROMANTICIZATION
ROMANTICIZE
ROMANTICIZED
ROMANTICIZES
ROMANTICIZING
ROMELDALES
ROMPISHNESS
ROMPISHNESSES
RONDOLETTO
RONDOLETTOS
RONTGENISATION
RONTGENISATIONS
RONTGENISE
RONTGENISED
RONTGENISES
RONTGENISING
RONTGENIZATION
RONTGENIZATIONS
RONTGENIZE
RONTGENIZED
RONTGENIZES
RONTGENIZING
RONTGENOGRAM
RONTGENOGRAMS
RONTGENOGRAPH
RONTGENOGRAPHS
RONTGENOGRAPHY
RONTGENOLOGICAL
RONTGENOLOGIES
RONTGENOLOGIST
RONTGENOLOGISTS
RONTGENOLOGY
RONTGENOPAQUE
RONTGENOSCOPE
RONTGENOSCOPES
RONTGENOSCOPIC
RONTGENOSCOPIES
RONTGENOSCOPY
RONTGENOTHERAPY
ROOFLESSNESS
ROOFLESSNESSES
ROOFSCAPES
ROOMINESSES
ROOTEDNESS
ROOTEDNESSES
ROOTINESSES
ROOTLESSNESS
ROOTLESSNESSES
ROOTSERVER
ROOTSERVERS
ROOTSINESS
ROOTSINESSES
ROOTSTALKS
ROOTSTOCKS
ROPEDANCER
ROPEDANCERS
ROPEDANCING
ROPEDANCINGS
ROPEWALKER
ROPEWALKERS
ROPINESSES
ROQUEFORTS
ROQUELAURE
ROQUELAURES
ROSANILINE
ROSANILINES
ROSANILINS
ROSEBUSHES
ROSEFINCHES
ROSEFISHES
ROSEMALING
ROSEMALINGS
ROSEMARIES
ROSETTINGS
ROSEWATERS
ROSINESSES
ROSINWEEDS
ROSMARINES
ROSTELLATE
ROSTELLUMS
ROSTERINGS
ROSTROCARINATE
ROSTROCARINATES
ROTACHUTES
ROTAMETERS
ROTAPLANES
ROTATIONAL
ROTATIVELY
ROTAVATING
ROTAVATORS
ROTAVIRUSES
ROTGRASSES
ROTIFERANS
ROTIFEROUS
ROTISSERIE
ROTISSERIED
ROTISSERIEING
ROTISSERIES
ROTOGRAPHED
ROTOGRAPHING
ROTOGRAPHS
ROTOGRAVURE
ROTOGRAVURES
ROTORCRAFT
ROTORCRAFTS
ROTOSCOPED
ROTOSCOPES
ROTOSCOPING
ROTOTILLED
ROTOTILLER
ROTOTILLERS
ROTOTILLING
ROTOVATING
ROTOVATORS
ROTTENNESS
ROTTENNESSES
ROTTENSTONE
ROTTENSTONED
ROTTENSTONES
ROTTENSTONING
ROTTWEILER
ROTTWEILERS
ROTUNDITIES
ROTUNDNESS
ROTUNDNESSES
ROUGHBACKS
ROUGHCASTED
ROUGHCASTER
ROUGHCASTERS
ROUGHCASTING
ROUGHCASTS
ROUGHDRIED
ROUGHDRIES
ROUGHDRYING
ROUGHENING
ROUGHHEWED
ROUGHHEWING
ROUGHHOUSE
ROUGHHOUSED
ROUGHHOUSES
ROUGHHOUSING
ROUGHHOUSINGS
ROUGHNECKED
ROUGHNECKING
ROUGHNECKS
ROUGHNESSES
ROUGHRIDER
ROUGHRIDERS
ROULETTING
ROUNCEVALS
ROUNDABOUT
ROUNDABOUTATION
ROUNDABOUTED
ROUNDABOUTEDLY
ROUNDABOUTILITY
ROUNDABOUTING
ROUNDABOUTLY
ROUNDABOUTNESS
ROUNDABOUTS
ROUNDARCHED
ROUNDBALLS
ROUNDEDNESS
ROUNDEDNESSES
ROUNDELAYS
ROUNDHANDS
ROUNDHEADED
ROUNDHEADEDNESS
ROUNDHEELS
ROUNDHOUSE
ROUNDHOUSES
ROUNDNESSES
ROUNDTABLE
ROUNDTABLES
ROUNDTRIPPING
ROUNDTRIPPINGS
ROUNDTRIPS

R

ROUNDWOODS
ROUNDWORMS
ROUSEABOUT
ROUSEABOUTS
ROUSEDNESS
ROUSEDNESSES
ROUSEMENTS
ROUSSETTES
ROUSTABOUT
ROUSTABOUTS
ROUTEMARCH
ROUTEMARCHED
ROUTEMARCHES
ROUTEMARCHING
ROUTINEERS
ROUTINISATION
ROUTINISATIONS
ROUTINISED
ROUTINISES
ROUTINISING
ROUTINISMS
ROUTINISTS
ROUTINIZATION
ROUTINIZATIONS
ROUTINIZED
ROUTINIZES
ROUTINIZING
ROWANBERRIES
ROWANBERRY
ROWDINESSES
ROWDYDOWED
ROWDYDOWING
ROYALISING
ROYALISTIC
ROYALIZING
ROYALMASTS
ROYSTERERS
ROYSTERING
ROYSTEROUS
RUBBERIEST
RUBBERISED
RUBBERISES
RUBBERISING
RUBBERIZED
RUBBERIZES
RUBBERIZING
RUBBERLIKE
RUBBERNECK
RUBBERNECKED
RUBBERNECKER
RUBBERNECKERS
RUBBERNECKING
RUBBERNECKS
RUBBERWEAR
RUBBERWEARS
RUBBISHIER
RUBBISHIEST
RUBBISHING
RUBBISHLIER
RUBBISHLIEST
RUBBLEWORK
RUBBLEWORKS
RUBEFACIENT
RUBEFACIENTS
RUBEFACTION
RUBEFACTIONS
RUBELLITES
RUBESCENCE
RUBESCENCES
RUBIACEOUS
RUBICELLES
RUBICONING
RUBICUNDITIES
RUBICUNDITY
RUBIGINOSE
RUBIGINOUS
RUBRICALLY
RUBRICATED
RUBRICATES
RUBRICATING
RUBRICATION
RUBRICATIONS
RUBRICATOR
RUBRICATORS
RUBRICIANS
RUBYTHROAT
RUBYTHROATS
RUCTATIONS
RUDBECKIAS
RUDDERHEAD
RUDDERHEADS
RUDDERLESS
RUDDERPOST
RUDDERPOSTS
RUDDERSTOCK
RUDDERSTOCKS
RUDDINESSES
RUDENESSES
RUDIMENTAL
RUDIMENTALLY
RUDIMENTARILY
RUDIMENTARINESS
RUDIMENTARY
RUEFULNESS
RUEFULNESSES
RUFESCENCE
RUFESCENCES
RUFFIANING
RUFFIANISH
RUFFIANISM
RUFFIANISMS
RUGGEDISATION
RUGGEDISATIONS
RUGGEDISED
RUGGEDISES
RUGGEDISING
RUGGEDIZATION
RUGGEDIZATIONS
RUGGEDIZED
RUGGEDIZES
RUGGEDIZING
RUGGEDNESS
RUGGEDNESSES
RUGOSITIES
RUINATIONS
RUINOUSNESS
RUINOUSNESSES
RULERSHIPS
RUMBLEDETHUMP
RUMBLEDETHUMPS
RUMBLEGUMPTION
RUMBLEGUMPTIONS
RUMBLINGLY
RUMBULLION
RUMBULLIONS
RUMBUNCTIOUS
RUMBUSTICAL
RUMBUSTIOUS
RUMBUSTIOUSLY
RUMBUSTIOUSNESS
RUMELGUMPTION
RUMELGUMPTIONS
RUMFUSTIAN
RUMFUSTIANS
RUMGUMPTION
RUMGUMPTIONS
RUMINANTLY
RUMINATING
RUMINATINGLY
RUMINATION
RUMINATIONS
RUMINATIVE
RUMINATIVELY
RUMINATORS
RUMLEGUMPTION
RUMLEGUMPTIONS
RUMMELGUMPTION
RUMMELGUMPTIONS
RUMMINESSES
RUMMISHING
RUMMLEGUMPTION
RUMMLEGUMPTIONS
RUMORMONGER
RUMORMONGERING
RUMORMONGERINGS
RUMORMONGERS
RUMRUNNERS
RUNAROUNDS
RUNECRAFTS
RUNNINESSES
RUNTINESSES
RUPESTRIAN
RUPICOLINE
RUPICOLOUS
RUPTURABLE
RUPTUREWORT
RUPTUREWORTS
RURALISATION
RURALISATIONS
RURALISING
RURALITIES
RURALIZATION
RURALIZATIONS
RURALIZING
RURALNESSES
RURIDECANAL
RUSHINESSES
RUSHLIGHTS
RUSSETIEST
RUSSETINGS
RUSSETTING
RUSSETTINGS
RUSSIFYING
RUSTBUCKET
RUSTBUCKETS
RUSTICALLY
RUSTICATED
RUSTICATES
RUSTICATING
RUSTICATINGS
RUSTICATION
RUSTICATIONS
RUSTICATOR
RUSTICATORS
RUSTICISED
RUSTICISES
RUSTICISING
RUSTICISMS
RUSTICITIES
RUSTICIZED
RUSTICIZES
RUSTICIZING
RUSTICWORK
RUSTICWORKS
RUSTINESSES
RUSTLINGLY
RUSTPROOFED
RUSTPROOFING
RUSTPROOFINGS
RUSTPROOFS
RUTHENIOUS
RUTHENIUMS
RUTHERFORD
RUTHERFORDIUM
RUTHERFORDIUMS
RUTHERFORDS
RUTHFULNESS
RUTHFULNESSES
RUTHLESSLY
RUTHLESSNESS
RUTHLESSNESSES
RUTTINESSES
RUTTISHNESS
RUTTISHNESSES
RYBAUDRYES
RYEGRASSES

S

SABADILLAS
SABBATARIAN
SABBATICAL
SABBATICALS
SABBATISED
SABBATISES
SABBATISING
SABBATISMS
SABBATIZED
SABBATIZES
SABBATIZING
SABERMETRICIAN
SABERMETRICIANS
SABERMETRICS
SABLEFISHES
SABOTAGING
SABRETACHE
SABRETACHES
SABREWINGS
SABULOSITIES
SABULOSITY
SABURRATION
SABURRATIONS
SACAHUISTA
SACAHUISTAS
SACAHUISTE
SACAHUISTES
SACCADICALLY
SACCHARASE
SACCHARASES
SACCHARATE
SACCHARATED
SACCHARATES
SACCHARIDE
SACCHARIDES
SACCHARIFEROUS
SACCHARIFIED
SACCHARIFIES
SACCHARIFY
SACCHARIFYING
SACCHARIMETER
SACCHARIMETERS
SACCHARIMETRIES
SACCHARIMETRY
SACCHARINE
SACCHARINELY
SACCHARINES
SACCHARINITIES
SACCHARINITY
SACCHARINS
SACCHARISATION
SACCHARISATIONS
SACCHARISE
SACCHARISED
SACCHARISES
SACCHARISING
SACCHARIZATION
SACCHARIZATIONS
SACCHARIZE
SACCHARIZED
SACCHARIZES
SACCHARIZING
SACCHAROID
SACCHAROIDAL
SACCHAROIDS
SACCHAROMETER
SACCHAROMETERS
SACCHAROMETRIES
SACCHAROMETRY
SACCHAROMYCES
SACCHAROMYCETES
SACCHAROSE
SACCHAROSES
SACCHARUMS
SACCULATED
SACCULATION
SACCULATIONS
SACCULIFORM
SACERDOTAL
SACERDOTALISE
SACERDOTALISED
SACERDOTALISES
SACERDOTALISING
SACERDOTALISM
SACERDOTALISMS
SACERDOTALIST
SACERDOTALISTS
SACERDOTALIZE
SACERDOTALIZED
SACERDOTALIZES
SACERDOTALIZING
SACERDOTALLY
SACHEMDOMS
SACHEMSHIP
SACHEMSHIPS
SACKCLOTHS
SACRALGIAS
SACRALISATION
SACRALISATIONS
SACRALISED
SACRALISES
SACRALISING
SACRALITIES
SACRALIZATION
SACRALIZATIONS
SACRALIZED
SACRALIZES
SACRALIZING
SACRAMENTAL
SACRAMENTALISM
SACRAMENTALISMS
SACRAMENTALIST
SACRAMENTALISTS
SACRAMENTALITY
SACRAMENTALLY
SACRAMENTALNESS
SACRAMENTALS
SACRAMENTARIAN
SACRAMENTARIANS
SACRAMENTARIES
SACRAMENTARY
SACRAMENTED
SACRAMENTING
SACRAMENTS
SACRARIUMS
SACREDNESS
SACREDNESSES
SACRIFICEABLE
SACRIFICED
SACRIFICER
SACRIFICERS
SACRIFICES
SACRIFICIAL
SACRIFICIALLY
SACRIFICING
SACRIFYING
SACRILEGES
SACRILEGIOUS
SACRILEGIOUSLY
SACRILEGIST
SACRILEGISTS
SACRISTANS
SACRISTIES
SACROCOCCYGEAL
SACROCOSTAL
SACROCOSTALS
SACROILIAC
SACROILIACS
SACROILIITIS
SACROILIITISES
SACROSANCT
SACROSANCTITIES
SACROSANCTITY
SACROSANCTNESS
SADDLEBACK
SADDLEBACKED
SADDLEBACKS
SADDLEBAGS
SADDLEBILL
SADDLEBILLS
SADDLEBOWS
SADDLEBRED
SADDLEBREDS
SADDLECLOTH
SADDLECLOTHS
SADDLELESS
SADDLERIES
SADDLEROOM
SADDLEROOMS
SADDLETREE
SADDLETREES
SADISTICALLY
SADOMASOCHISM
SADOMASOCHISMS
SADOMASOCHIST
SADOMASOCHISTIC
SADOMASOCHISTS
SAFECRACKER
SAFECRACKERS
SAFECRACKING
SAFECRACKINGS
SAFEGUARDED
SAFEGUARDING
SAFEGUARDS
SAFEKEEPING
SAFEKEEPINGS
SAFELIGHTS
SAFENESSES
SAFFLOWERS
SAFFRONIER
SAFFRONIEST
SAFRANINES
SAGACIOUSLY
SAGACIOUSNESS
SAGACIOUSNESSES
SAGACITIES
SAGANASHES
SAGAPENUMS
SAGEBRUSHES
SAGENESSES
SAGINATING
SAGINATION
SAGINATIONS
SAGITTALLY
SAGITTARIES
SAGITTIFORM
SAILBOARDED
SAILBOARDER
SAILBOARDERS
SAILBOARDING

SAILBOARDINGS
SAILBOARDS
SAILBOATER
SAILBOATERS
SAILBOATING
SAILBOATINGS
SAILCLOTHS
SAILFISHES
SAILMAKERS
SAILMAKING
SAILMAKINGS
SAILORINGS
SAILORLESS
SAILORLIER
SAILORLIEST
SAILORLIKE
SAILPLANED
SAILPLANER
SAILPLANERS
SAILPLANES
SAILPLANING
SAILPLANINGS
SAINTESSES
SAINTFOINS
SAINTHOODS
SAINTLIEST
SAINTLINESS
SAINTLINESSES
SAINTLINGS
SAINTPAULIA
SAINTPAULIAS
SAINTSHIPS
SALABILITIES
SALABILITY
SALABLENESS
SALABLENESSES
SALACIOUSLY
SALACIOUSNESS
SALACIOUSNESSES
SALACITIES
SALAMANDER
SALAMANDERS
SALAMANDRIAN
SALAMANDRIANS
SALAMANDRINE
SALAMANDROID
SALAMANDROIDS
SALANGANES
SALBUTAMOL
SALBUTAMOLS
SALEABILITIES
SALEABILITY
SALEABLENESS
SALEABLENESSES
SALERATUSES
SALESCLERK
SALESCLERKS
SALESGIRLS
SALESLADIES
SALESMANSHIP
SALESMANSHIPS
SALESPEOPLE
SALESPERSON
SALESPERSONS
SALESROOMS
SALESWOMAN
SALESWOMEN
SALIAUNCES
SALICACEOUS
SALICETUMS
SALICIONAL
SALICIONALS
SALICORNIA
SALICORNIAS
SALICYLAMIDE
SALICYLAMIDES
SALICYLATE
SALICYLATED
SALICYLATES
SALICYLATING
SALICYLISM
SALICYLISMS
SALIENCIES
SALIENTIAN
SALIENTIANS
SALIFEROUS
SALIFIABLE
SALIFICATION
SALIFICATIONS
SALIMETERS
SALIMETRIC
SALIMETRIES
SALINISATION
SALINISATIONS
SALINISING
SALINITIES
SALINIZATION
SALINIZATIONS
SALINIZING
SALINOMETER
SALINOMETERS
SALINOMETRIC
SALINOMETRIES
SALINOMETRY
SALIVATING
SALIVATION
SALIVATIONS
SALIVATORS
SALLENDERS
SALLOWIEST
SALLOWNESS
SALLOWNESSES
SALLYPORTS
SALMAGUNDI
SALMAGUNDIES
SALMAGUNDIS
SALMAGUNDY
SALMANASER
SALMANASERS
SALMANAZAR
SALMANAZARS
SALMONBERRIES
SALMONBERRY
SALMONELLA
SALMONELLAE
SALMONELLAS
SALMONELLOSES
SALMONELLOSIS
SALMONIEST
SALMONOIDS
SALOMETERS
SALOPETTES
SALPIGLOSSES
SALPIGLOSSIS
SALPIGLOSSISES
SALPINGECTOMIES
SALPINGECTOMY
SALPINGIAN
SALPINGITIC
SALPINGITIS
SALPINGITISES
SALSOLACEOUS
SALSUGINOUS
SALTARELLI
SALTARELLO
SALTARELLOS
SALTATIONISM
SALTATIONISMS
SALTATIONIST
SALTATIONISTS
SALTATIONS
SALTATORIAL
SALTATORIOUS
SALTBUSHES
SALTCELLAR
SALTCELLARS
SALTCHUCKER
SALTCHUCKERS
SALTCHUCKS
SALTFISHES
SALTIGRADE
SALTIGRADES
SALTIMBANCO
SALTIMBANCOS
SALTIMBOCCA
SALTIMBOCCAS
SALTINESSES
SALTIREWISE
SALTISHNESS
SALTISHNESSES
SALTNESSES
SALTPETERS
SALTPETREMAN
SALTPETREMEN
SALTPETRES
SALTSHAKER
SALTSHAKERS
SALTWATERS
SALUBRIOUS
SALUBRIOUSLY
SALUBRIOUSNESS
SALUBRITIES
SALURETICS
SALUTARILY
SALUTARINESS
SALUTARINESSES
SALUTATION
SALUTATIONAL
SALUTATIONS
SALUTATORIAN
SALUTATORIANS
SALUTATORIES
SALUTATORILY
SALUTATORY
SALUTIFEROUS
SALVABILITIES
SALVABILITY
SALVABLENESS
SALVABLENESSES
SALVAGEABILITY
SALVAGEABLE
SALVARSANS
SALVATIONAL
SALVATIONISM
SALVATIONISMS
SALVATIONIST
SALVATIONISTS
SALVATIONS
SALVATORIES
SALVERFORM
SALVIFICAL
SALVIFICALLY
SALVINIACEOUS
SAMARIFORM
SAMARITANS
SAMARSKITE
SAMARSKITES
SAMENESSES
SAMEYNESSES
SAMNITISES
SAMPLERIES
SANATORIUM
SANATORIUMS
SANBENITOS
SANCTIFIABLE
SANCTIFICATION
SANCTIFICATIONS
SANCTIFIED
SANCTIFIEDLY
SANCTIFIER
SANCTIFIERS
SANCTIFIES
SANCTIFYING
SANCTIFYINGLY
SANCTIFYINGS
SANCTIMONIES
SANCTIMONIOUS
SANCTIMONIOUSLY
SANCTIMONY
SANCTIONABLE

SANCTIONED
SANCTIONEER
SANCTIONEERS
SANCTIONER
SANCTIONERS
SANCTIONING
SANCTIONLESS
SANCTITIES
SANCTITUDE
SANCTITUDES
SANCTUARIES
SANCTUARISE
SANCTUARISED
SANCTUARISES
SANCTUARISING
SANCTUARIZE
SANCTUARIZED
SANCTUARIZES
SANCTUARIZING
SANDALLING
SANDALWOOD
SANDALWOODS
SANDARACHS
SANDBAGGED
SANDBAGGER
SANDBAGGERS
SANDBAGGING
SANDBLASTED
SANDBLASTER
SANDBLASTERS
SANDBLASTING
SANDBLASTINGS
SANDBLASTS
SANDCASTLE
SANDCASTLES
SANDCRACKS
SANDERLING
SANDERLINGS
SANDERSWOOD
SANDERSWOODS
SANDFISHES
SANDGLASSES
SANDGROPER
SANDGROPERS
SANDGROUSE
SANDGROUSES
SANDINESSES
SANDLOTTER
SANDLOTTERS
SANDPAINTING
SANDPAINTINGS
SANDPAPERED
SANDPAPERIER
SANDPAPERIEST
SANDPAPERING
SANDPAPERINGS
SANDPAPERS
SANDPAPERY
SANDPIPERS
SANDSPOUTS
SANDSTONES
SANDSTORMS
SANDSUCKER
SANDSUCKERS
SANDWICHED
SANDWICHES
SANDWICHING
SANENESSES
SANGFROIDS
SANGUIFEROUS
SANGUIFICATION
SANGUIFICATIONS
SANGUIFIED
SANGUIFIES
SANGUIFYING
SANGUINARIA
SANGUINARIAS
SANGUINARILY
SANGUINARINESS
SANGUINARY
SANGUINELY
SANGUINENESS
SANGUINENESSES
SANGUINEOUS
SANGUINEOUSNESS
SANGUINING
SANGUINITIES
SANGUINITY
SANGUINIVOROUS
SANGUINOLENCIES
SANGUINOLENCY
SANGUINOLENT
SANGUIVOROUS
SANITARIAN
SANITARIANISM
SANITARIANISMS
SANITARIANS
SANITARIES
SANITARILY
SANITARINESS
SANITARINESSES
SANITARIST
SANITARISTS
SANITARIUM
SANITARIUMS
SANITATING
SANITATION
SANITATIONIST
SANITATIONISTS
SANITATIONS
SANITISATION
SANITISATIONS
SANITISERS
SANITISING
SANITIZATION
SANITIZATIONS
SANITIZERS
SANITIZING
SANITORIUM
SANITORIUMS
SANNYASINS
SANSCULOTTE
SANSCULOTTERIE
SANSCULOTTERIES
SANSCULOTTES
SANSCULOTTIC
SANSCULOTTIDES
SANSCULOTTISH
SANSCULOTTISM
SANSCULOTTISMS
SANSCULOTTIST
SANSCULOTTISTS
SANSEVIERIA
SANSEVIERIAS
SANTALACEOUS
SANTOLINAS
SANTONICAS
SAPANWOODS
SAPIDITIES
SAPIDNESSES
SAPIENCIES
SAPIENTIAL
SAPIENTIALLY
SAPINDACEOUS
SAPLESSNESS
SAPLESSNESSES
SAPODILLAS
SAPOGENINS
SAPONACEOUS
SAPONACEOUSNESS
SAPONARIAS
SAPONIFIABLE
SAPONIFICATION
SAPONIFICATIONS
SAPONIFIED
SAPONIFIER
SAPONIFIERS
SAPONIFIES
SAPONIFYING
SAPOTACEOUS
SAPPANWOOD
SAPPANWOODS
SAPPERMENT
SAPPHIRINE
SAPPHIRINES
SAPPINESSES
SAPRAEMIAS
SAPROBIONT
SAPROBIONTS
SAPROBIOTIC
SAPROBITIES
SAPROGENIC
SAPROGENICITIES
SAPROGENICITY
SAPROGENOUS
SAPROLEGNIA
SAPROLEGNIAS
SAPROLITES
SAPROLITIC
SAPROPELIC
SAPROPELITE
SAPROPELITES
SAPROPHAGOUS
SAPROPHYTE
SAPROPHYTES
SAPROPHYTIC
SAPROPHYTICALLY
SAPROPHYTISM
SAPROPHYTISMS
SAPROTROPH
SAPROTROPHIC
SAPROTROPHS
SAPSUCKERS
SARABANDES
SARBACANES
SARCASTICALLY
SARCENCHYMATOUS
SARCENCHYME
SARCENCHYMES
SARCOCARPS
SARCOCOLLA
SARCOCOLLAS
SARCOCYSTIS
SARCOCYSTISES
SARCOIDOSES
SARCOIDOSIS
SARCOLEMMA
SARCOLEMMAL
SARCOLEMMAS
SARCOLEMMATA
SARCOLOGIES
SARCOMATOID
SARCOMATOSES
SARCOMATOSIS
SARCOMATOUS
SARCOMERES
SARCOPENIA
SARCOPENIAS
SARCOPHAGAL
SARCOPHAGI
SARCOPHAGOUS
SARCOPHAGUS
SARCOPHAGUSES
SARCOPLASM
SARCOPLASMIC
SARCOPLASMS
SARCOSOMAL
SARCOSOMES
SARDONIANS
SARDONICAL
SARDONICALLY
SARDONICISM
SARDONICISMS
SARDONYXES
SARGASSOES
SARGASSUMS
SARKINESSES
SARMENTACEOUS
SARMENTOSE
SARMENTOUS

S

SARPANCHES
SARRACENIA
SARRACENIACEOUS
SARRACENIAS
SARRUSOPHONE
SARRUSOPHONES
SARSAPARILLA
SARSAPARILLAS
SARTORIALLY
SARTORIUSES
SASKATOONS
SASQUATCHES
SASSAFRASES
SASSARARAS
SASSINESSES
SASSOLITES
SASSYWOODS
SATANICALLY
SATANICALNESS
SATANICALNESSES
SATANITIES
SATANOLOGIES
SATANOLOGY
SATANOPHANIES
SATANOPHANY
SATANOPHOBIA
SATANOPHOBIAS
SATCHELFUL
SATCHELFULS
SATCHELLED
SATCHELSFUL
SATEDNESSES
SATELLITED
SATELLITES
SATELLITIC
SATELLITING
SATELLITISE
SATELLITISED
SATELLITISES
SATELLITISING
SATELLITIUM
SATELLITIUMS
SATELLITIZE
SATELLITIZED
SATELLITIZES
SATELLITIZING
SATIABILITIES
SATIABILITY
SATIATIONS
SATINETTAS
SATINETTES
SATINFLOWER
SATINFLOWERS
SATINWOODS
SATIRICALLY
SATIRICALNESS
SATIRICALNESSES
SATIRISABLE
SATIRISATION
SATIRISATIONS
SATIRISERS
SATIRISING
SATIRIZABLE
SATIRIZATION
SATIRIZATIONS
SATIRIZERS
SATIRIZING
SATISFACTION
SATISFACTIONS
SATISFACTORILY
SATISFACTORY
SATISFIABLE
SATISFICED
SATISFICER
SATISFICERS
SATISFICES
SATISFICING
SATISFICINGS
SATISFIERS
SATISFYING
SATISFYINGLY
SATURABILITIES
SATURABILITY
SATURATERS
SATURATING
SATURATION
SATURATIONS
SATURATORS
SATURNALIA
SATURNALIAN
SATURNALIANLY
SATURNALIAS
SATURNIIDS
SATURNINELY
SATURNINITIES
SATURNINITY
SATURNISMS
SATURNISTS
SATYAGRAHA
SATYAGRAHAS
SATYAGRAHI
SATYAGRAHIS
SATYRESQUE
SATYRESSES
SATYRIASES
SATYRIASIS
SAUCEBOATS
SAUCEBOXES
SAUCERFULS
SAUCERLESS
SAUCERLIKE
SAUCINESSES
SAUCISSONS
SAUERBRATEN
SAUERBRATENS
SAUERKRAUT
SAUERKRAUTS
SAUNTERERS
SAUNTERING
SAUNTERINGLY
SAUNTERINGS
SAURISCHIAN
SAURISCHIANS
SAUROGNATHOUS
SAUROPODOUS
SAUROPSIDAN
SAUROPSIDANS
SAUROPTERYGIAN
SAUROPTERYGIANS
SAUSSURITE
SAUSSURITES
SAUSSURITIC
SAVABLENESS
SAVABLENESSES
SAVAGEDOMS
SAVAGENESS
SAVAGENESSES
SAVAGERIES
SAVEABLENESS
SAVEABLENESSES
SAVEGARDED
SAVEGARDING
SAVINGNESS
SAVINGNESSES
SAVORINESS
SAVORINESSES
SAVOURIEST
SAVOURINESS
SAVOURINESSES
SAVOURLESS
SAVVINESSES
SAWBONESES
SAWDUSTIER
SAWDUSTIEST
SAWDUSTING
SAWGRASSES
SAWMILLERS
SAWTIMBERS
SAXICAVOUS
SAXICOLINE
SAXICOLOUS
SAXIFRAGACEOUS
SAXIFRAGES
SAXITOXINS
SAXOPHONES
SAXOPHONIC
SAXOPHONIST
SAXOPHONISTS
SCABBARDED
SCABBARDING
SCABBARDLESS
SCABBEDNESS
SCABBEDNESSES
SCABBINESS
SCABBINESSES
SCABERULOUS
SCABIOUSES
SCABRIDITIES
SCABRIDITY
SCABROUSLY
SCABROUSNESS
SCABROUSNESSES
SCAFFOLAGE
SCAFFOLAGES
SCAFFOLDAGE
SCAFFOLDAGES
SCAFFOLDED
SCAFFOLDER
SCAFFOLDERS
SCAFFOLDING
SCAFFOLDINGS
SCAGLIOLAS
SCAITHLESS
SCALABILITIES
SCALABILITY
SCALABLENESS
SCALABLENESSES
SCALARIFORM
SCALARIFORMLY
SCALATIONS
SCALDBERRIES
SCALDBERRY
SCALDFISHES
SCALDHEADS
SCALDSHIPS
SCALEBOARD
SCALEBOARDS
SCALENOHEDRA
SCALENOHEDRON
SCALENOHEDRONS
SCALETAILS
SCALEWORKS
SCALINESSES
SCALLAWAGS
SCALLOPERS
SCALLOPING
SCALLOPINGS
SCALLOPINI
SCALLOPINIS
SCALLYWAGS
SCALOGRAMS
SCALOPPINE
SCALOPPINES
SCALOPPINI
SCALPELLIC
SCALPELLIFORM
SCALPRIFORM
SCAMBAITING
SCAMBAITINGS
SCAMBLINGLY
SCAMBLINGS
SCAMMONIATE
SCAMMONIES
SCAMPERERS
SCAMPERING
SCAMPERINGS
SCAMPISHLY
SCAMPISHNESS
SCAMPISHNESSES
SCANDALING

S

SCANDALISATION
SCANDALISATIONS
SCANDALISE
SCANDALISED
SCANDALISER
SCANDALISERS
SCANDALISES
SCANDALISING
SCANDALIZATION
SCANDALIZATIONS
SCANDALIZE
SCANDALIZED
SCANDALIZER
SCANDALIZERS
SCANDALIZES
SCANDALIZING
SCANDALLED
SCANDALLING
SCANDALMONGER
SCANDALMONGERS
SCANDALOUS
SCANDALOUSLY
SCANDALOUSNESS
SCANSORIAL
SCANTINESS
SCANTINESSES
SCANTITIES
SCANTLINGS
SCANTNESSES
SCAPEGALLOWS
SCAPEGALLOWSES
SCAPEGOATED
SCAPEGOATING
SCAPEGOATINGS
SCAPEGOATISM
SCAPEGOATISMS
SCAPEGOATS
SCAPEGRACE
SCAPEGRACES
SCAPEMENTS
SCAPEWHEEL
SCAPEWHEELS
SCAPHOCEPHALI
SCAPHOCEPHALIC
SCAPHOCEPHALICS
SCAPHOCEPHALIES
SCAPHOCEPHALISM
SCAPHOCEPHALOUS
SCAPHOCEPHALUS
SCAPHOCEPHALY
SCAPHOPODS
SCAPIGEROUS
SCAPOLITES
SCAPULARIES
SCAPULATED
SCAPULIMANCIES
SCAPULIMANCY
SCAPULIMANTIC
SCAPULOMANCIES
SCAPULOMANCY
SCAPULOMANTIC
SCARABAEAN
SCARABAEANS
SCARABAEID
SCARABAEIDS
SCARABAEIST
SCARABAEISTS
SCARABAEOID
SCARABAEOIDS
SCARABAEUS
SCARABAEUSES
SCARABOIDS
SCARAMOUCH
SCARAMOUCHE
SCARAMOUCHED
SCARAMOUCHES
SCARAMOUCHING
SCARCEMENT
SCARCEMENTS
SCARCENESS
SCARCENESSES
SCARCITIES
SCARECROWS
SCAREHEADS
SCAREMONGER
SCAREMONGERING
SCAREMONGERINGS
SCAREMONGERS
SCAREWARES
SCARFISHES
SCARFSKINS
SCARIFICATION
SCARIFICATIONS
SCARIFICATOR
SCARIFICATORS
SCARIFIERS
SCARIFYING
SCARIFYINGLY
SCARINESSES
SCARLATINA
SCARLATINAL
SCARLATINAS
SCARLETING
SCARPERING
SCATHEFULNESS
SCATHEFULNESSES
SCATHELESS
SCATHINGLY
SCATOLOGIC
SCATOLOGICAL
SCATOLOGIES
SCATOLOGIST
SCATOLOGISTS
SCATOPHAGIES
SCATOPHAGOUS
SCATOPHAGY
SCATTERABLE
SCATTERATION
SCATTERATIONS
SCATTERBRAIN
SCATTERBRAINED
SCATTERBRAINS
SCATTEREDLY
SCATTERERS
SCATTERGOOD
SCATTERGOODS
SCATTERGRAM
SCATTERGRAMS
SCATTERGUN
SCATTERGUNS
SCATTERIER
SCATTERIEST
SCATTERING
SCATTERINGLY
SCATTERINGS
SCATTERLING
SCATTERLINGS
SCATTERMOUCH
SCATTERMOUCHES
SCATTEROMETER
SCATTEROMETERS
SCATTERSHOT
SCATTINESS
SCATTINESSES
SCATURIENT
SCAVENGERED
SCAVENGERIES
SCAVENGERING
SCAVENGERINGS
SCAVENGERS
SCAVENGERY
SCAVENGING
SCAVENGINGS
SCAZONTICS
SCELERATES
SCENARISATION
SCENARISATIONS
SCENARISED
SCENARISES
SCENARISING
SCENARISTS
SCENARIZATION
SCENARIZATIONS
SCENARIZED
SCENARIZES
SCENARIZING
SCENESHIFTER
SCENESHIFTERS
SCENESTERS
SCENICALLY
SCENOGRAPHER
SCENOGRAPHERS
SCENOGRAPHIC
SCENOGRAPHICAL
SCENOGRAPHIES
SCENOGRAPHY
SCENTLESSNESS
SCENTLESSNESSES
SCEPTERING
SCEPTERLESS
SCEPTICALLY
SCEPTICISM
SCEPTICISMS
SCEPTRELESS
SCEUOPHYLACIA
SCEUOPHYLACIUM
SCEUOPHYLACIUMS
SCEUOPHYLAX
SCEUOPHYLAXES
SCHADENFREUDE
SCHADENFREUDES
SCHALSTEIN
SCHALSTEINS
SCHAPPEING
SCHATCHENS
SCHECHITAH
SCHECHITAHS
SCHECHITAS
SCHECKLATON
SCHECKLATONS
SCHEDULERS
SCHEDULING
SCHEDULINGS
SCHEELITES
SCHEFFLERA
SCHEFFLERAS
SCHEMATICAL
SCHEMATICALLY
SCHEMATICS
SCHEMATISATION
SCHEMATISATIONS
SCHEMATISE
SCHEMATISED
SCHEMATISES
SCHEMATISING
SCHEMATISM
SCHEMATISMS
SCHEMATIST
SCHEMATISTS
SCHEMATIZATION
SCHEMATIZATIONS
SCHEMATIZE
SCHEMATIZED
SCHEMATIZES
SCHEMATIZING
SCHEMINGLY
SCHEMOZZLE
SCHEMOZZLED
SCHEMOZZLES
SCHEMOZZLING
SCHERZANDI
SCHERZANDO
SCHERZANDOS
SCHIAVONES
SCHILLERISATION
SCHILLERISE
SCHILLERISED
SCHILLERISES
SCHILLERISING
SCHILLERIZATION

SCHILLERIZE
SCHILLERIZED
SCHILLERIZES
SCHILLERIZING
SCHILLINGS
SCHINDYLESES
SCHINDYLESIS
SCHINDYLETIC
SCHIPPERKE
SCHIPPERKES
SCHISMATIC
SCHISMATICAL
SCHISMATICALLY
SCHISMATICALS
SCHISMATICS
SCHISMATISE
SCHISMATISED
SCHISMATISES
SCHISMATISING
SCHISMATIZE
SCHISMATIZED
SCHISMATIZES
SCHISMATIZING
SCHISTOSITIES
SCHISTOSITY
SCHISTOSOMAL
SCHISTOSOME
SCHISTOSOMES
SCHISTOSOMIASES
SCHISTOSOMIASIS
SCHIZAEACEOUS
SCHIZANTHUS
SCHIZANTHUSES
SCHIZOCARP
SCHIZOCARPIC
SCHIZOCARPOUS
SCHIZOCARPS
SCHIZOGENESES
SCHIZOGENESIS
SCHIZOGENETIC
SCHIZOGENIC
SCHIZOGNATHOUS
SCHIZOGONIC
SCHIZOGONIES
SCHIZOGONOUS
SCHIZOGONY
SCHIZOIDAL
SCHIZOMYCETE
SCHIZOMYCETES
SCHIZOMYCETIC
SCHIZOMYCETOUS
SCHIZOPHRENE
SCHIZOPHRENES
SCHIZOPHRENETIC
SCHIZOPHRENIA
SCHIZOPHRENIAS
SCHIZOPHRENIC
SCHIZOPHRENICS
SCHIZOPHYCEOUS
SCHIZOPHYTE
SCHIZOPHYTES
SCHIZOPHYTIC
SCHIZOPODAL
SCHIZOPODOUS
SCHIZOPODS
SCHIZOTHYMIA
SCHIZOTHYMIAS
SCHIZOTHYMIC
SCHIZZIEST
SCHLEMIELS
SCHLEMIHLS
SCHLEPPERS
SCHLEPPIER
SCHLEPPIEST
SCHLEPPING
SCHLIERENS
SCHLIMAZEL
SCHLIMAZELS
SCHLOCKERS
SCHLOCKEYS
SCHLOCKIER
SCHLOCKIEST
SCHLUMBERGERA
SCHLUMBERGERAS
SCHLUMPIER
SCHLUMPIEST
SCHLUMPING
SCHMALTZES
SCHMALTZIER
SCHMALTZIEST
SCHMALZIER
SCHMALZIEST
SCHMEARING
SCHMECKERS
SCHMECKING
SCHMEERING
SCHMICKEST
SCHMOOSING
SCHMOOZERS
SCHMOOZIER
SCHMOOZIEST
SCHMOOZING
SCHMUCKIER
SCHMUCKIEST
SCHMUCKING
SCHMUTTERS
SCHNAPPERS
SCHNAPPSES
SCHNAUZERS
SCHNITZELS
SCHNOODLES
SCHNORKELED
SCHNORKELING
SCHNORKELLED
SCHNORKELLING
SCHNORKELS
SCHNORRERS
SCHNORRING
SCHNOZZLES
SCHOLARCHS
SCHOLARLIER
SCHOLARLIEST
SCHOLARLINESS
SCHOLARLINESSES
SCHOLARSHIP
SCHOLARSHIPS
SCHOLASTIC
SCHOLASTICAL
SCHOLASTICALLY
SCHOLASTICATE
SCHOLASTICATES
SCHOLASTICISM
SCHOLASTICISMS
SCHOLASTICS
SCHOLIASTIC
SCHOLIASTS
SCHOOLBAGS
SCHOOLBOOK
SCHOOLBOOKS
SCHOOLBOYISH
SCHOOLBOYS
SCHOOLCHILD
SCHOOLCHILDREN
SCHOOLCRAFT
SCHOOLCRAFTS
SCHOOLDAYS
SCHOOLERIES
SCHOOLFELLOW
SCHOOLFELLOWS
SCHOOLGIRL
SCHOOLGIRLISH
SCHOOLGIRLS
SCHOOLGOING
SCHOOLGOINGS
SCHOOLHOUSE
SCHOOLHOUSES
SCHOOLINGS
SCHOOLKIDS
SCHOOLMAID
SCHOOLMAIDS
SCHOOLMARM
SCHOOLMARMISH
SCHOOLMARMS
SCHOOLMASTER
SCHOOLMASTERED
SCHOOLMASTERING
SCHOOLMASTERISH
SCHOOLMASTERLY
SCHOOLMASTERS
SCHOOLMATE
SCHOOLMATES
SCHOOLMISTRESS
SCHOOLMISTRESSY
SCHOOLROOM
SCHOOLROOMS
SCHOOLTEACHER
SCHOOLTEACHERS
SCHOOLTEACHING
SCHOOLTEACHINGS
SCHOOLTIDE
SCHOOLTIDES
SCHOOLTIME
SCHOOLTIMES
SCHOOLWARD
SCHOOLWARDS
SCHOOLWORK
SCHOOLWORKS
SCHOOLYARD
SCHOOLYARDS
SCHORLACEOUS
SCHORLOMITE
SCHORLOMITES
SCHOTTISCHE
SCHOTTISCHES
SCHRECKLICH
SCHTUPPING
SCHUSSBOOMER
SCHUSSBOOMERS
SCHVARTZES
SCHVITZING
SCHWARMEREI
SCHWARMEREIS
SCHWARMERISCH
SCHWARTZES
SCHWARZLOT
SCHWARZLOTS
SCIAENOIDS
SCIAMACHIES
SCIENTIFIC
SCIENTIFICAL
SCIENTIFICALLY
SCIENTIFICITIES
SCIENTIFICITY
SCIENTISED
SCIENTISES
SCIENTISING
SCIENTISMS
SCIENTISTIC
SCIENTISTS
SCIENTIZED
SCIENTIZES
SCIENTIZING
SCINCOIDIAN
SCINCOIDIANS
SCINDAPSUS
SCINDAPSUSES
SCINTIGRAM
SCINTIGRAMS
SCINTIGRAPHIC
SCINTIGRAPHIES
SCINTIGRAPHY
SCINTILLAE
SCINTILLANT
SCINTILLANTLY
SCINTILLAS
SCINTILLASCOPE
SCINTILLASCOPES
SCINTILLATE
SCINTILLATED
SCINTILLATES

SCINTILLATING
SCINTILLATINGLY
SCINTILLATION
SCINTILLATIONS
SCINTILLATOR
SCINTILLATORS
SCINTILLISCAN
SCINTILLISCANS
SCINTILLOMETER
SCINTILLOMETERS
SCINTILLON
SCINTILLONS
SCINTILLOSCOPE
SCINTILLOSCOPES
SCINTISCAN
SCINTISCANNER
SCINTISCANNERS
SCINTISCANS
SCIOLISTIC
SCIOMACHIES
SCIOMANCER
SCIOMANCERS
SCIOMANCIES
SCIOMANTIC
SCIOPHYTES
SCIOPHYTIC
SCIOSOPHIES
SCIRRHOSITIES
SCIRRHOSITY
SCIRRHUSES
SCISSIPARITIES
SCISSIPARITY
SCISSORERS
SCISSORING
SCISSORTAIL
SCISSORTAILS
SCISSORWISE
SCITAMINEOUS
SCLAUNDERS
SCLEREIDES
SCLERENCHYMA
SCLERENCHYMAS
SCLERENCHYMATA
SCLERIASES
SCLERIASIS
SCLERITISES
SCLEROCAULIES
SCLEROCAULOUS
SCLEROCAULY
SCLERODERM
SCLERODERMA
SCLERODERMAS
SCLERODERMATA
SCLERODERMATOUS
SCLERODERMIA
SCLERODERMIAS
SCLERODERMIC
SCLERODERMITE
SCLERODERMITES
SCLERODERMOUS
SCLERODERMS
SCLEROMALACIA
SCLEROMALACIAS
SCLEROMATA
SCLEROMETER
SCLEROMETERS
SCLEROMETRIC
SCLEROPHYLL
SCLEROPHYLLIES
SCLEROPHYLLOUS
SCLEROPHYLLS
SCLEROPHYLLY
SCLEROPROTEIN
SCLEROPROTEINS
SCLEROSING
SCLEROTALS
SCLEROTIAL
SCLEROTICS
SCLEROTINS
SCLEROTIOID
SCLEROTISATION
SCLEROTISATIONS
SCLEROTISE
SCLEROTISED
SCLEROTISES
SCLEROTISING
SCLEROTITIS
SCLEROTITISES
SCLEROTIUM
SCLEROTIZATION
SCLEROTIZATIONS
SCLEROTIZE
SCLEROTIZED
SCLEROTIZES
SCLEROTIZING
SCLEROTOMIES
SCLEROTOMY
SCOFFINGLY
SCOLDINGLY
SCOLECIFORM
SCOLECITES
SCOLLOPING
SCOLOPACEOUS
SCOLOPENDRA
SCOLOPENDRAS
SCOLOPENDRID
SCOLOPENDRIDS
SCOLOPENDRIFORM
SCOLOPENDRINE
SCOLOPENDRIUM
SCOLOPENDRIUMS
SCOLYTOIDS
SCOMBROIDS
SCOMFISHED
SCOMFISHES
SCOMFISHING
SCONCHEONS
SCOOTCHING
SCOOTERING
SCOOTERIST
SCOOTERISTS
SCOPELOIDS
SCOPOLAMINE
SCOPOLAMINES
SCOPOLINES
SCOPOPHILIA
SCOPOPHILIAC
SCOPOPHILIACS
SCOPOPHILIAS
SCOPOPHILIC
SCOPOPHOBIA
SCOPOPHOBIAS
SCOPTOPHILIA
SCOPTOPHILIAS
SCOPTOPHOBIA
SCOPTOPHOBIAS
SCORBUTICALLY
SCORCHINGLY
SCORCHINGNESS
SCORCHINGNESSES
SCORCHINGS
SCORDATURA
SCORDATURAS
SCOREBOARD
SCOREBOARDS
SCORECARDS
SCOREKEEPER
SCOREKEEPERS
SCORELINES
SCORESHEET
SCORESHEETS
SCORIACEOUS
SCORIFICATION
SCORIFICATIONS
SCORIFIERS
SCORIFYING
SCORNFULLY
SCORNFULNESS
SCORNFULNESSES
SCORODITES
SCORPAENID
SCORPAENIDS
SCORPAENOID
SCORPAENOIDS
SCORPIOIDS
SCORPIONIC
SCORZONERA
SCORZONERAS
SCOTODINIA
SCOTODINIAS
SCOTOMATOUS
SCOTOMETER
SCOTOMETERS
SCOUNDRELLIER
SCOUNDRELLIEST
SCOUNDRELLY
SCOUNDRELS
SCOURGINGS
SCOUTCRAFT
SCOUTCRAFTS
SCOUTHERED
SCOUTHERING
SCOUTHERINGS
SCOUTMASTER
SCOUTMASTERS
SCOWDERING
SCOWDERINGS
SCOWLINGLY
SCOWTHERED
SCOWTHERING
SCRABBLERS
SCRABBLIER
SCRABBLIEST
SCRABBLING
SCRABBLINGS
SCRAGGEDNESS
SCRAGGEDNESSES
SCRAGGIEST
SCRAGGINESS
SCRAGGINESSES
SCRAGGLIER
SCRAGGLIEST
SCRAGGLING
SCRAICHING
SCRAIGHING
SCRAMBLERS
SCRAMBLING
SCRAMBLINGLY
SCRAMBLINGS
SCRANCHING
SCRANNIEST
SCRAPBOOKED
SCRAPBOOKING
SCRAPBOOKINGS
SCRAPBOOKS
SCRAPEGOOD
SCRAPEGOODS
SCRAPEGUTS
SCRAPEPENNIES
SCRAPEPENNY
SCRAPERBOARD
SCRAPERBOARDS
SCRAPHEAPS
SCRAPPAGES
SCRAPPIEST
SCRAPPINESS
SCRAPPINESSES
SCRAPPINGS
SCRAPYARDS
SCRATCHBACK
SCRATCHBACKS
SCRATCHBOARD
SCRATCHBOARDS
SCRATCHBUILD
SCRATCHBUILDER
SCRATCHBUILDERS
SCRATCHBUILDING
SCRATCHBUILDS
SCRATCHBUILT
SCRATCHCARD

S

SCRATCHCARDS
SCRATCHERS
SCRATCHIER
SCRATCHIES
SCRATCHIEST
SCRATCHILY
SCRATCHINESS
SCRATCHINESSES
SCRATCHING
SCRATCHINGLY
SCRATCHINGS
SCRATCHLESS
SCRATCHPLATE
SCRATCHPLATES
SCRATTLING
SCRAUCHING
SCRAUGHING
SCRAVELING
SCRAVELLED
SCRAVELLING
SCRAWLIEST
SCRAWLINGLY
SCRAWLINGS
SCRAWNIEST
SCRAWNINESS
SCRAWNINESSES
SCREAKIEST
SCREAKINGS
SCREAMINGLY
SCREAMINGS
SCREECHERS
SCREECHIER
SCREECHIEST
SCREECHING
SCREEDINGS
SCREENABLE
SCREENAGER
SCREENAGERS
SCREENCAST
SCREENCASTS
SCREENCRAFT
SCREENCRAFTS
SCREENFULS
SCREENINGS
SCREENLAND
SCREENLANDS
SCREENLIKE
SCREENPLAY
SCREENPLAYS
SCREENSAVER
SCREENSAVERS
SCREENSHOT
SCREENSHOTS
SCREENSHOTTED
SCREENSHOTTING
SCREENWRITER
SCREENWRITERS
SCREENWRITING
SCREENWRITINGS
SCREEVINGS
SCREICHING
SCREIGHING
SCREWBALLS
SCREWBEANS
SCREWDRIVER
SCREWDRIVERS
SCREWHEADS
SCREWINESS
SCREWINESSES
SCREWWORMS
SCRIBACIOUS
SCRIBACIOUSNESS
SCRIBBLEMENT
SCRIBBLEMENTS
SCRIBBLERS
SCRIBBLIER
SCRIBBLIEST
SCRIBBLING
SCRIBBLINGLY
SCRIBBLINGS
SCRIECHING
SCRIEVEBOARD
SCRIEVEBOARDS
SCRIGGLIER
SCRIGGLIEST
SCRIGGLING
SCRIMMAGED
SCRIMMAGER
SCRIMMAGERS
SCRIMMAGES
SCRIMMAGING
SCRIMPIEST
SCRIMPINESS
SCRIMPINESSES
SCRIMPINGS
SCRIMPNESS
SCRIMPNESSES
SCRIMSHANDER
SCRIMSHANDERED
SCRIMSHANDERING
SCRIMSHANDERS
SCRIMSHANDIED
SCRIMSHANDIES
SCRIMSHANDY
SCRIMSHANDYING
SCRIMSHANK
SCRIMSHANKED
SCRIMSHANKER
SCRIMSHANKERS
SCRIMSHANKING
SCRIMSHANKS
SCRIMSHAWED
SCRIMSHAWING
SCRIMSHAWS
SCRIMSHONER
SCRIMSHONERS
SCRIPHOLDER
SCRIPHOLDERS
SCRIPOPHILE
SCRIPOPHILES
SCRIPOPHILIES
SCRIPOPHILIST
SCRIPOPHILISTS
SCRIPOPHILY
SCRIPPAGES
SCRIPTORIA
SCRIPTORIAL
SCRIPTORIUM
SCRIPTORIUMS
SCRIPTURAL
SCRIPTURALISM
SCRIPTURALISMS
SCRIPTURALIST
SCRIPTURALISTS
SCRIPTURALLY
SCRIPTURES
SCRIPTURISM
SCRIPTURISMS
SCRIPTURIST
SCRIPTURISTS
SCRIPTWRITER
SCRIPTWRITERS
SCRIPTWRITING
SCRIPTWRITINGS
SCRITCHING
SCRITCHINGS
SCRIVEBOARD
SCRIVEBOARDS
SCRIVENERS
SCRIVENERSHIP
SCRIVENERSHIPS
SCRIVENING
SCRIVENINGS
SCROBBLING
SCROBICULAR
SCROBICULATE
SCROBICULATED
SCROBICULE
SCROBICULES
SCROFULOUS
SCROFULOUSLY
SCROFULOUSNESS
SCROGGIEST
SCROLLABLE
SCROLLINGS
SCROLLWISE
SCROLLWORK
SCROLLWORKS
SCROOCHING
SCROOTCHED
SCROOTCHES
SCROOTCHING
SCROPHULARIA
SCROPHULARIAS
SCROUNGERS
SCROUNGIER
SCROUNGIEST
SCROUNGING
SCROUNGINGS
SCROWDGING
SCRUBBABLE
SCRUBBIEST
SCRUBBINESS
SCRUBBINESSES
SCRUBBINGS
SCRUBLANDS
SCRUBWOMAN
SCRUBWOMEN
SCRUFFIEST
SCRUFFINESS
SCRUFFINESSES
SCRUMDOWNS
SCRUMMAGED
SCRUMMAGER
SCRUMMAGERS
SCRUMMAGES
SCRUMMAGING
SCRUMMIEST
SCRUMPLING
SCRUMPOXES
SCRUMPTIOUS
SCRUMPTIOUSLY
SCRUMPTIOUSNESS
SCRUNCHEON
SCRUNCHEONS
SCRUNCHIER
SCRUNCHIES
SCRUNCHIEST
SCRUNCHING
SCRUNCHINGS
SCRUNCHINS
SCRUNCHION
SCRUNCHIONS
SCRUNTIEST
SCRUPLELESS
SCRUPULOSITIES
SCRUPULOSITY
SCRUPULOUS
SCRUPULOUSLY
SCRUPULOUSNESS
SCRUTABILITIES
SCRUTABILITY
SCRUTATORS
SCRUTINEER
SCRUTINEERS
SCRUTINIES
SCRUTINISE
SCRUTINISED
SCRUTINISER
SCRUTINISERS
SCRUTINISES
SCRUTINISING
SCRUTINISINGLY
SCRUTINIZE
SCRUTINIZED
SCRUTINIZER
SCRUTINIZERS
SCRUTINIZES
SCRUTINIZING
SCRUTINIZINGLY

SCRUTINOUS
SCRUTINOUSLY
SCRUTOIRES
SCUDDALERS
SCUFFLINGS
SCULDUDDERIES
SCULDUDDERY
SCULDUDDRIES
SCULDUDDRY
SCULDUGGERIES
SCULDUGGERY
SCULLERIES
SCULPTINGS
SCULPTRESS
SCULPTRESSES
SCULPTURAL
SCULPTURALLY
SCULPTURED
SCULPTURES
SCULPTURESQUE
SCULPTURESQUELY
SCULPTURING
SCULPTURINGS
SCUMBERING
SCUMBLINGS
SCUMFISHED
SCUMFISHES
SCUMFISHING
SCUNCHEONS
SCUNGILLIS
SCUNNERING
SCUPPERING
SCUPPERNONG
SCUPPERNONGS
SCURFINESS
SCURFINESSES
SCURRILITIES
SCURRILITY
SCURRILOUS
SCURRILOUSLY
SCURRILOUSNESS
SCURRIOURS
SCURVINESS
SCURVINESSES
SCUTATIONS
SCUTCHEONLESS
SCUTCHEONS
SCUTCHINGS
SCUTELLATE
SCUTELLATED
SCUTELLATION
SCUTELLATIONS
SCUTTERING
SCUTTLEBUTT
SCUTTLEBUTTS
SCUTTLEFUL
SCUTTLEFULS
SCUTTLINGS
SCUZZBALLS
SCYPHIFORM
SCYPHISTOMA
SCYPHISTOMAE
SCYPHISTOMAS
SCYPHOZOAN
SCYPHOZOANS
SCYTHELIKE
SDEIGNFULL
SDEIGNFULLY
SDRUCCIOLA
SEABEACHES
SEABORGIUM
SEABORGIUMS
SEABOTTLES
SEACHANGER
SEACHANGERS
SEACUNNIES
SEAFARINGS
SEAGRASSES
SEALIFTING
SEALPOINTS
SEAMANLIER
SEAMANLIEST
SEAMANLIKE
SEAMANSHIP
SEAMANSHIPS
SEAMINESSES
SEAMLESSLY
SEAMLESSNESS
SEAMLESSNESSES
SEAMSTRESS
SEAMSTRESSES
SEAMSTRESSIES
SEAMSTRESSY
SEANNACHIE
SEANNACHIES
SEAQUARIUM
SEAQUARIUMS
SEARCHABLE
SEARCHINGLY
SEARCHINGNESS
SEARCHINGNESSES
SEARCHINGS
SEARCHLESS
SEARCHLIGHT
SEARCHLIGHTS
SEAREDNESS
SEAREDNESSES
SEARNESSES
SEASICKEST
SEASICKNESS
SEASICKNESSES
SEASONABILITIES
SEASONABILITY
SEASONABLE
SEASONABLENESS
SEASONABLY
SEASONALITIES
SEASONALITY
SEASONALLY
SEASONALNESS
SEASONALNESSES
SEASONINGS
SEASONLESS
SEASTRANDS
SEAWEEDIER
SEAWEEDIEST
SEAWORTHIER
SEAWORTHIEST
SEAWORTHINESS
SEAWORTHINESSES
SEBIFEROUS
SEBORRHEAL
SEBORRHEAS
SEBORRHEIC
SEBORRHOEA
SEBORRHOEAL
SEBORRHOEAS
SEBORRHOEIC
SECERNENTS
SECERNMENT
SECERNMENTS
SECESSIONAL
SECESSIONISM
SECESSIONISMS
SECESSIONIST
SECESSIONISTS
SECESSIONS
SECLUDEDLY
SECLUDEDNESS
SECLUDEDNESSES
SECLUSIONIST
SECLUSIONISTS
SECLUSIONS
SECLUSIVELY
SECLUSIVENESS
SECLUSIVENESSES
SECOBARBITAL
SECOBARBITALS
SECONDARIES
SECONDARILY
SECONDARINESS
SECONDARINESSES
SECONDHAND
SECONDINGS
SECONDMENT
SECONDMENTS
SECRETAGES
SECRETAGOGIC
SECRETAGOGUE
SECRETAGOGUES
SECRETAIRE
SECRETAIRES
SECRETARIAL
SECRETARIAT
SECRETARIATE
SECRETARIATES
SECRETARIATS
SECRETARIES
SECRETARYSHIP
SECRETARYSHIPS
SECRETIONAL
SECRETIONARY
SECRETIONS
SECRETIVELY
SECRETIVENESS
SECRETIVENESSES
SECRETNESS
SECRETNESSES
SECRETORIES
SECTARIANISE
SECTARIANISED
SECTARIANISES
SECTARIANISING
SECTARIANISM
SECTARIANISMS
SECTARIANIZE
SECTARIANIZED
SECTARIANIZES
SECTARIANIZING
SECTARIANS
SECTILITIES
SECTIONALISE
SECTIONALISED
SECTIONALISES
SECTIONALISING
SECTIONALISM
SECTIONALISMS
SECTIONALIST
SECTIONALISTS
SECTIONALIZE
SECTIONALIZED
SECTIONALIZES
SECTIONALIZING
SECTIONALLY
SECTIONALS
SECTIONING
SECTIONISATION
SECTIONISATIONS
SECTIONISE
SECTIONISED
SECTIONISES
SECTIONISING
SECTIONIZATION
SECTIONIZATIONS
SECTIONIZE
SECTIONIZED
SECTIONIZES
SECTIONIZING
SECTORIALS
SECTORISATION
SECTORISATIONS
SECTORISED
SECTORISES
SECTORISING
SECTORIZATION
SECTORIZATIONS
SECTORIZED
SECTORIZES
SECTORIZING
SECULARISATION

SECULARISATIONS
SECULARISE
SECULARISED
SECULARISER
SECULARISERS
SECULARISES
SECULARISING
SECULARISM
SECULARISMS
SECULARIST
SECULARISTIC
SECULARISTS
SECULARITIES
SECULARITY
SECULARIZATION
SECULARIZATIONS
SECULARIZE
SECULARIZED
SECULARIZER
SECULARIZERS
SECULARIZES
SECULARIZING
SECUNDINES
SECUNDOGENITURE
SECURANCES
SECUREMENT
SECUREMENTS
SECURENESS
SECURENESSES
SECURIFORM
SECURITANS
SECURITIES
SECURITISATION
SECURITISATIONS
SECURITISE
SECURITISED
SECURITISES
SECURITISING
SECURITIZATION
SECURITIZATIONS
SECURITIZE
SECURITIZED
SECURITIZES
SECURITIZING
SECUROCRAT
SECUROCRATS
SEDATENESS
SEDATENESSES
SEDENTARILY
SEDENTARINESS
SEDENTARINESSES
SEDGELANDS
SEDIGITATED
SEDIMENTABLE
SEDIMENTARILY
SEDIMENTARY
SEDIMENTATION
SEDIMENTATIONS
SEDIMENTED
SEDIMENTING
SEDIMENTOLOGIC
SEDIMENTOLOGIES
SEDIMENTOLOGIST
SEDIMENTOLOGY
SEDIMENTOUS
SEDITIONARIES
SEDITIONARY
SEDITIOUSLY
SEDITIOUSNESS
SEDITIOUSNESSES
SEDUCEABLE
SEDUCEMENT
SEDUCEMENTS
SEDUCINGLY
SEDUCTIONS
SEDUCTIVELY
SEDUCTIVENESS
SEDUCTIVENESSES
SEDUCTRESS
SEDUCTRESSES
SEDULITIES
SEDULOUSLY
SEDULOUSNESS
SEDULOUSNESSES
SEECATCHES
SEECATCHIE
SEEDEATERS
SEEDINESSES
SEEDNESSES
SEEDSTOCKS
SEEMELESSE
SEEMINGNESS
SEEMINGNESSES
SEEMLIHEAD
SEEMLIHEADS
SEEMLIHEDS
SEEMLINESS
SEEMLINESSES
SEEMLYHEDS
SEERSUCKER
SEERSUCKERS
SEETHINGLY
SEGHOLATES
SEGMENTALLY
SEGMENTARY
SEGMENTATE
SEGMENTATION
SEGMENTATIONS
SEGMENTING
SEGREGABLE
SEGREGANTS
SEGREGATED
SEGREGATES
SEGREGATING
SEGREGATION
SEGREGATIONAL
SEGREGATIONIST
SEGREGATIONISTS
SEGREGATIONS
SEGREGATIVE
SEGREGATOR
SEGREGATORS
SEGUIDILLA
SEGUIDILLAS
SEIGNEURIAL
SEIGNEURIE
SEIGNEURIES
SEIGNIORAGE
SEIGNIORAGES
SEIGNIORALTIES
SEIGNIORALTY
SEIGNIORIAL
SEIGNIORIES
SEIGNIORSHIP
SEIGNIORSHIPS
SEIGNORAGE
SEIGNORAGES
SEIGNORIAL
SEIGNORIES
SEISMICALLY
SEISMICITIES
SEISMICITY
SEISMOGRAM
SEISMOGRAMS
SEISMOGRAPH
SEISMOGRAPHER
SEISMOGRAPHERS
SEISMOGRAPHIC
SEISMOGRAPHICAL
SEISMOGRAPHIES
SEISMOGRAPHS
SEISMOGRAPHY
SEISMOLOGIC
SEISMOLOGICAL
SEISMOLOGICALLY
SEISMOLOGIES
SEISMOLOGIST
SEISMOLOGISTS
SEISMOLOGY
SEISMOMETER
SEISMOMETERS
SEISMOMETRIC
SEISMOMETRICAL
SEISMOMETRIES
SEISMOMETRY
SEISMONASTIC
SEISMONASTIES
SEISMONASTY
SEISMOSCOPE
SEISMOSCOPES
SEISMOSCOPIC
SELACHIANS
SELAGINELLA
SELAGINELLAS
SELDOMNESS
SELDOMNESSES
SELECTABLE
SELECTIONIST
SELECTIONISTS
SELECTIONS
SELECTIVELY
SELECTIVENESS
SELECTIVENESSES
SELECTIVITIES
SELECTIVITY
SELECTNESS
SELECTNESSES
SELECTORATE
SELECTORATES
SELECTORIAL
SELEGILINE
SELEGILINES
SELENIFEROUS
SELENOCENTRIC
SELENODONT
SELENODONTS
SELENOGRAPH
SELENOGRAPHER
SELENOGRAPHERS
SELENOGRAPHIC
SELENOGRAPHICAL
SELENOGRAPHIES
SELENOGRAPHIST
SELENOGRAPHISTS
SELENOGRAPHS
SELENOGRAPHY
SELENOLOGICAL
SELENOLOGIES
SELENOLOGIST
SELENOLOGISTS
SELENOLOGY
SELFISHNESS
SELFISHNESSES
SELFLESSLY
SELFLESSNESS
SELFLESSNESSES
SELFNESSES
SELFSAMENESS
SELFSAMENESSES
SELLOTAPED
SELLOTAPES
SELLOTAPING
SELTZOGENE
SELTZOGENES
SELVEDGING
SEMAINIERS
SEMANTEMES
SEMANTICAL
SEMANTICALLY
SEMANTICIST
SEMANTICISTS
SEMANTIDES
SEMANTRONS
SEMAPHORED
SEMAPHORES
SEMAPHORIC
SEMAPHORICAL
SEMAPHORICALLY
SEMAPHORING
SEMASIOLOGICAL

S

SEMASIOLOGIES
SEMASIOLOGIST
SEMASIOLOGISTS
SEMASIOLOGY
SEMATOLOGIES
SEMATOLOGY
SEMBLABLES
SEMBLANCES
SEMBLATIVE
SEMEIOLOGIC
SEMEIOLOGICAL
SEMEIOLOGIES
SEMEIOLOGIST
SEMEIOLOGISTS
SEMEIOLOGY
SEMEIOTICALLY
SEMEIOTICIAN
SEMEIOTICIANS
SEMEIOTICS
SEMELPARITIES
SEMELPARITY
SEMELPAROUS
SEMESTERED
SEMESTERING
SEMESTERINGS
SEMESTRIAL
SEMIABSTRACT
SEMIABSTRACTION
SEMIANGLES
SEMIANNUAL
SEMIANNUALLY
SEMIAQUATIC
SEMIARBOREAL
SEMIARIDITIES
SEMIARIDITY
SEMIAUTOMATED
SEMIAUTOMATIC
SEMIAUTOMATICS
SEMIAUTONOMOUS
SEMIBASEMENT
SEMIBASEMENTS
SEMIBREVES
SEMICARBAZIDE
SEMICARBAZIDES
SEMICARBAZONE
SEMICARBAZONES
SEMICENTENNIAL
SEMICENTENNIALS
SEMICHORUS
SEMICHORUSES
SEMICIRCLE
SEMICIRCLED
SEMICIRCLES
SEMICIRCULAR
SEMICIRCULARLY
SEMICIRQUE
SEMICIRQUES
SEMICIVILISED
SEMICIVILIZED
SEMICLASSIC
SEMICLASSICAL
SEMICLASSICS
SEMICOLONIAL
SEMICOLONIALISM
SEMICOLONIES
SEMICOLONS
SEMICOLONY
SEMICOMATOSE
SEMICOMMERCIAL
SEMICONDUCTING
SEMICONDUCTION
SEMICONDUCTIONS
SEMICONDUCTOR
SEMICONDUCTORS
SEMICONSCIOUS
SEMICONSCIOUSLY
SEMICONSONANT
SEMICONSONANTS
SEMICRYSTALLIC
SEMICRYSTALLINE
SEMICYLINDER
SEMICYLINDERS
SEMICYLINDRICAL
SEMIDARKNESS
SEMIDARKNESSES
SEMIDEIFIED
SEMIDEIFIES
SEMIDEIFYING
SEMIDEPONENT
SEMIDEPONENTS
SEMIDESERT
SEMIDESERTS
SEMIDETACHED
SEMIDETACHEDS
SEMIDIAMETER
SEMIDIAMETERS
SEMIDIURNAL
SEMIDIVINE
SEMIDOCUMENTARY
SEMIDOMINANT
SEMIDRIEST
SEMIDRYING
SEMIDWARFS
SEMIDWARVES
SEMIELLIPTICAL
SEMIEMPIRICAL
SEMIEVERGREEN
SEMIFEUDAL
SEMIFINALIST
SEMIFINALISTS
SEMIFINALS
SEMIFINISHED
SEMIFITTED
SEMIFLEXIBLE
SEMIFLUIDIC
SEMIFLUIDITIES
SEMIFLUIDITY
SEMIFLUIDS
SEMIFORMAL
SEMIFREDDI
SEMIFREDDO
SEMIFREDDOS
SEMIGLOBES
SEMIGLOBULAR
SEMIGLOSSES
SEMIGROUPS
SEMIHOBOES
SEMILEGENDARY
SEMILETHAL
SEMILETHALS
SEMILIQUID
SEMILIQUIDS
SEMILITERATE
SEMILITERATES
SEMILOGARITHMIC
SEMILUCENT
SEMILUNATE
SEMILUSTROUS
SEMIMANUFACTURE
SEMIMENSTRUAL
SEMIMETALLIC
SEMIMETALS
SEMIMONASTIC
SEMIMONTHLIES
SEMIMONTHLY
SEMIMYSTICAL
SEMINALITIES
SEMINALITY
SEMINARIAL
SEMINARIAN
SEMINARIANS
SEMINARIES
SEMINARIST
SEMINARISTS
SEMINATING
SEMINATION
SEMINATIONS
SEMINATURAL
SEMINIFEROUS
SEMINOMADIC
SEMINOMADS
SEMINOMATA
SEMINUDITIES
SEMINUDITY
SEMIOCHEMICAL
SEMIOCHEMICALS
SEMIOFFICIAL
SEMIOFFICIALLY
SEMIOLOGIC
SEMIOLOGICAL
SEMIOLOGICALLY
SEMIOLOGIES
SEMIOLOGIST
SEMIOLOGISTS
SEMIOPAQUE
SEMIOTICALLY
SEMIOTICIAN
SEMIOTICIANS
SEMIOTICIST
SEMIOTICISTS
SEMIOVIPAROUS
SEMIPALMATE
SEMIPALMATED
SEMIPALMATION
SEMIPALMATIONS
SEMIPARASITE
SEMIPARASITES
SEMIPARASITIC
SEMIPARASITISM
SEMIPARASITISMS
SEMIPELLUCID
SEMIPERIMETER
SEMIPERIMETERS
SEMIPERMANENT
SEMIPERMEABLE
SEMIPLUMES
SEMIPOLITICAL
SEMIPOPULAR
SEMIPORCELAIN
SEMIPORCELAINS
SEMIPORNOGRAPHY
SEMIPOSTAL
SEMIPOSTALS
SEMIPRECIOUS
SEMIPRIVATE
SEMIPUBLIC
SEMIQUAVER
SEMIQUAVERS
SEMIREFINED
SEMIRELIGIOUS
SEMIRETIRED
SEMIRETIREMENT
SEMIRETIREMENTS
SEMIROUNDS
SEMISACRED
SEMISECRET
SEMISEDENTARY
SEMISHRUBBY
SEMISKILLED
SEMISOLIDS
SEMISOLUSES
SEMISUBMERSIBLE
SEMISYNTHETIC
SEMITERETE
SEMITERRESTRIAL
SEMITONALLY
SEMITONICALLY
SEMITRAILER
SEMITRAILERS
SEMITRANSLUCENT
SEMITRANSPARENT
SEMITROPIC
SEMITROPICAL
SEMITROPICS
SEMITRUCKS
SEMIVITREOUS
SEMIVOCALIC
SEMIVOWELS
SEMIWEEKLIES
SEMIWEEKLY

S

SEMIYEARLY
SEMPERVIVUM
SEMPERVIVUMS
SEMPITERNAL
SEMPITERNALLY
SEMPITERNITIES
SEMPITERNITY
SEMPITERNUM
SEMPITERNUMS
SEMPSTERING
SEMPSTERINGS
SEMPSTRESS
SEMPSTRESSES
SEMPSTRESSING
SEMPSTRESSINGS
SENARMONTITE
SENARMONTITES
SENATORIAL
SENATORIALLY
SENATORIAN
SENATORSHIP
SENATORSHIPS
SENECTITUDE
SENECTITUDES
SENESCENCE
SENESCENCES
SENESCHALS
SENESCHALSHIP
SENESCHALSHIPS
SENHORITAS
SENILITIES
SENIORITIES
SENNACHIES
SENSATIONAL
SENSATIONALISE
SENSATIONALISED
SENSATIONALISES
SENSATIONALISM
SENSATIONALISMS
SENSATIONALIST
SENSATIONALISTS
SENSATIONALIZE
SENSATIONALIZED
SENSATIONALIZES
SENSATIONALLY
SENSATIONISM
SENSATIONISMS
SENSATIONIST
SENSATIONISTS
SENSATIONLESS
SENSATIONS
SENSELESSLY
SENSELESSNESS
SENSELESSNESSES
SENSIBILIA
SENSIBILITIES
SENSIBILITY
SENSIBLENESS
SENSIBLENESSES
SENSIBLEST
SENSITISATION
SENSITISATIONS
SENSITISED
SENSITISER
SENSITISERS
SENSITISES
SENSITISING
SENSITIVELY
SENSITIVENESS
SENSITIVENESSES
SENSITIVES
SENSITIVITIES
SENSITIVITY
SENSITIZATION
SENSITIZATIONS
SENSITIZED
SENSITIZER
SENSITIZERS
SENSITIZES
SENSITIZING
SENSITOMETER
SENSITOMETERS
SENSITOMETRIC
SENSITOMETRIES
SENSITOMETRY
SENSOMOTOR
SENSORIALLY
SENSORIMOTOR
SENSORINEURAL
SENSORIUMS
SENSUALISATION
SENSUALISATIONS
SENSUALISE
SENSUALISED
SENSUALISES
SENSUALISING
SENSUALISM
SENSUALISMS
SENSUALIST
SENSUALISTIC
SENSUALISTS
SENSUALITIES
SENSUALITY
SENSUALIZATION
SENSUALIZATIONS
SENSUALIZE
SENSUALIZED
SENSUALIZES
SENSUALIZING
SENSUALNESS
SENSUALNESSES
SENSUOSITIES
SENSUOSITY
SENSUOUSLY
SENSUOUSNESS
SENSUOUSNESSES
SENTENCERS
SENTENCING
SENTENCINGS
SENTENTIAE
SENTENTIAL
SENTENTIALLY
SENTENTIOUS
SENTENTIOUSLY
SENTENTIOUSNESS
SENTIENCES
SENTIENCIES
SENTIENTLY
SENTIMENTAL
SENTIMENTALISE
SENTIMENTALISED
SENTIMENTALISES
SENTIMENTALISM
SENTIMENTALISMS
SENTIMENTALIST
SENTIMENTALISTS
SENTIMENTALITY
SENTIMENTALIZE
SENTIMENTALIZED
SENTIMENTALIZES
SENTIMENTALLY
SENTIMENTS
SENTINELED
SENTINELING
SENTINELLED
SENTINELLING
SEPALODIES
SEPARABILITIES
SEPARABILITY
SEPARABLENESS
SEPARABLENESSES
SEPARATELY
SEPARATENESS
SEPARATENESSES
SEPARATING
SEPARATION
SEPARATIONISM
SEPARATIONISMS
SEPARATIONIST
SEPARATIONISTS
SEPARATIONS
SEPARATISM
SEPARATISMS
SEPARATIST
SEPARATISTIC
SEPARATISTS
SEPARATIVE
SEPARATIVELY
SEPARATIVENESS
SEPARATORIES
SEPARATORS
SEPARATORY
SEPARATRICES
SEPARATRIX
SEPARATUMS
SEPIOLITES
SEPIOSTAIRE
SEPIOSTAIRES
SEPTATIONS
SEPTAVALENT
SEPTEMVIRATE
SEPTEMVIRATES
SEPTEMVIRI
SEPTEMVIRS
SEPTENARIES
SEPTENARII
SEPTENARIUS
SEPTENDECILLION
SEPTENNATE
SEPTENNATES
SEPTENNIAL
SEPTENNIALLY
SEPTENNIUM
SEPTENNIUMS
SEPTENTRIAL
SEPTENTRION
SEPTENTRIONAL
SEPTENTRIONALLY
SEPTENTRIONES
SEPTENTRIONS
SEPTICAEMIA
SEPTICAEMIAS
SEPTICAEMIC
SEPTICALLY
SEPTICEMIA
SEPTICEMIAS
SEPTICEMIC
SEPTICIDAL
SEPTICIDALLY
SEPTICITIES
SEPTIFEROUS
SEPTIFRAGAL
SEPTILATERAL
SEPTILLION
SEPTILLIONS
SEPTILLIONTH
SEPTILLIONTHS
SEPTIMOLES
SEPTIVALENT
SEPTUAGENARIAN
SEPTUAGENARIANS
SEPTUAGENARIES
SEPTUAGENARY
SEPTUPLETS
SEPTUPLICATE
SEPTUPLICATES
SEPTUPLING
SEPULCHERED
SEPULCHERING
SEPULCHERS
SEPULCHRAL
SEPULCHRALLY
SEPULCHRED
SEPULCHRES
SEPULCHRING
SEPULCHROUS
SEPULTURAL
SEPULTURED
SEPULTURES
SEPULTURING

SEQUACIOUS
SEQUACIOUSLY
SEQUACIOUSNESS
SEQUACITIES
SEQUELISED
SEQUELISES
SEQUELISING
SEQUELIZED
SEQUELIZES
SEQUELIZING
SEQUENCERS
SEQUENCIES
SEQUENCING
SEQUENCINGS
SEQUENTIAL
SEQUENTIALITIES
SEQUENTIALITY
SEQUENTIALLY
SEQUESTERED
SEQUESTERING
SEQUESTERS
SEQUESTRABLE
SEQUESTRAL
SEQUESTRANT
SEQUESTRANTS
SEQUESTRATE
SEQUESTRATED
SEQUESTRATES
SEQUESTRATING
SEQUESTRATION
SEQUESTRATIONS
SEQUESTRATOR
SEQUESTRATORS
SEQUESTRUM
SEQUESTRUMS
SERAPHICAL
SERAPHICALLY
SERAPHINES
SERASKIERATE
SERASKIERATES
SERASKIERS
SERENADERS
SERENADING
SERENATING
SERENDIPITIES
SERENDIPITIST
SERENDIPITISTS
SERENDIPITOUS
SERENDIPITOUSLY
SERENDIPITY
SERENENESS
SERENENESSES
SERENITIES
SERGEANCIES
SERGEANTIES
SERGEANTSHIP
SERGEANTSHIPS
SERIALISATION
SERIALISATIONS
SERIALISED
SERIALISES
SERIALISING
SERIALISMS
SERIALISTS
SERIALITIES
SERIALIZATION
SERIALIZATIONS
SERIALIZED
SERIALIZES
SERIALIZING
SERIATIONS
SERICICULTURE
SERICICULTURES
SERICICULTURIST
SERICITISATION
SERICITISATIONS
SERICITIZATION
SERICITIZATIONS
SERICTERIA
SERICTERIUM
SERICULTURAL
SERICULTURE
SERICULTURES
SERICULTURIST
SERICULTURISTS
SERIGRAPHER
SERIGRAPHERS
SERIGRAPHIC
SERIGRAPHIES
SERIGRAPHS
SERIGRAPHY
SERINETTES
SERIOCOMIC
SERIOCOMICAL
SERIOCOMICALLY
SERIOUSNESS
SERIOUSNESSES
SERJEANCIES
SERJEANTIES
SERJEANTRIES
SERJEANTRY
SERJEANTSHIP
SERJEANTSHIPS
SERMONEERS
SERMONETTE
SERMONETTES
SERMONICAL
SERMONINGS
SERMONISED
SERMONISER
SERMONISERS
SERMONISES
SERMONISING
SERMONISINGS
SERMONIZED
SERMONIZER
SERMONIZERS
SERMONIZES
SERMONIZING
SERMONIZINGS
SEROCONVERSION
SEROCONVERSIONS
SEROCONVERT
SEROCONVERTED
SEROCONVERTING
SEROCONVERTS
SERODIAGNOSES
SERODIAGNOSIS
SERODIAGNOSTIC
SEROGROUPS
SEROLOGICAL
SEROLOGICALLY
SEROLOGIES
SEROLOGIST
SEROLOGISTS
SERONEGATIVE
SERONEGATIVITY
SEROPOSITIVE
SEROPOSITIVITY
SEROPURULENT
SEROSITIES
SEROTAXONOMIES
SEROTAXONOMY
SEROTHERAPIES
SEROTHERAPY
SEROTINIES
SEROTINOUS
SEROTONERGIC
SEROTONINERGIC
SEROTONINS
SEROTYPING
SEROTYPINGS
SEROUSNESS
SEROUSNESSES
SERPENTIFORM
SERPENTINE
SERPENTINED
SERPENTINELY
SERPENTINES
SERPENTINIC
SERPENTINING
SERPENTININGLY
SERPENTININGS
SERPENTINISE
SERPENTINISED
SERPENTINISES
SERPENTINISING
SERPENTINITE
SERPENTINITES
SERPENTINIZE
SERPENTINIZED
SERPENTINIZES
SERPENTINIZING
SERPENTINOUS
SERPENTISE
SERPENTISED
SERPENTISES
SERPENTISING
SERPENTIZE
SERPENTIZED
SERPENTIZES
SERPENTIZING
SERPENTLIKE
SERPENTRIES
SERPIGINES
SERPIGINOUS
SERPIGINOUSLY
SERPULITES
SERRADELLA
SERRADELLAS
SERRADILLA
SERRADILLAS
SERRANOIDS
SERRASALMO
SERRASALMOS
SERRATIONS
SERRATIROSTRAL
SERRATULATE
SERRATURES
SERRATUSES
SERREFILES
SERRICORNS
SERRIEDNESS
SERRIEDNESSES
SERRULATED
SERRULATION
SERRULATIONS
SERTULARIAN
SERTULARIANS
SERVANTHOOD
SERVANTHOODS
SERVANTING
SERVANTLESS
SERVANTRIES
SERVANTSHIP
SERVANTSHIPS
SERVEWARES
SERVICEABILITY
SERVICEABLE
SERVICEABLENESS
SERVICEABLY
SERVICEBERRIES
SERVICEBERRY
SERVICELESS
SERVICEMAN
SERVICEMEN
SERVICEWOMAN
SERVICEWOMEN
SERVICINGS
SERVIETTES
SERVILENESS
SERVILENESSES
SERVILISMS
SERVILITIES
SERVITORIAL
SERVITORSHIP
SERVITORSHIPS
SERVITRESS
SERVITRESSES
SERVITUDES

SERVOCONTROL
SERVOCONTROLS
SERVOMECHANICAL
SERVOMECHANISM
SERVOMECHANISMS
SERVOMOTOR
SERVOMOTORS
SESQUIALTER
SESQUIALTERA
SESQUIALTERAS
SESQUIALTERS
SESQUICARBONATE
SESQUICENTENARY
SESQUIOXIDE
SESQUIOXIDES
SESQUIPEDAL
SESQUIPEDALIAN
SESQUIPEDALIANS
SESQUIPEDALITY
SESQUIPEDALS
SESQUIPLICATE
SESQUISULPHIDE
SESQUISULPHIDES
SESQUITERPENE
SESQUITERPENES
SESQUITERTIA
SESQUITERTIAS
SESSILITIES
SESSIONALLY
SESTERTIUM
SESTERTIUS
SETACEOUSLY
SETIFEROUS
SETIGEROUS
SETTERWORT
SETTERWORTS
SETTLEABLE
SETTLEDNESS
SETTLEDNESSES
SETTLEMENT
SETTLEMENTS
SEVENPENCE
SEVENPENCES
SEVENPENNIES
SEVENPENNY
SEVENTEENS
SEVENTEENTH
SEVENTEENTHLY
SEVENTEENTHS
SEVENTIETH
SEVENTIETHS
SEVERABILITIES
SEVERABILITY
SEVERALFOLD
SEVERALTIES
SEVERANCES
SEVERENESS
SEVERENESSES
SEVERITIES
SEWABILITIES
SEWABILITY
SEXAGENARIAN
SEXAGENARIANS
SEXAGENARIES
SEXAGENARY
SEXAGESIMAL
SEXAGESIMALLY
SEXAGESIMALS
SEXAHOLICS
SEXANGULAR
SEXANGULARLY
SEXAVALENT
SEXCAPADES
SEXCENTENARIES
SEXCENTENARY
SEXDECILLION
SEXDECILLIONS
SEXENNIALLY
SEXENNIALS
SEXERCISES
SEXINESSES
SEXIVALENT
SEXLESSNESS
SEXLESSNESSES
SEXLOCULAR
SEXOLOGICAL
SEXOLOGIES
SEXOLOGIST
SEXOLOGISTS
SEXPARTITE
SEXPLOITATION
SEXPLOITATIONS
SEXTARIUSES
SEXTILLION
SEXTILLIONS
SEXTILLIONTH
SEXTILLIONTHS
SEXTODECIMO
SEXTODECIMOS
SEXTONESSES
SEXTONSHIP
SEXTONSHIPS
SEXTUPLETS
SEXTUPLICATE
SEXTUPLICATED
SEXTUPLICATES
SEXTUPLICATING
SEXTUPLIED
SEXTUPLIES
SEXTUPLING
SEXTUPLYING
SEXUALISATION
SEXUALISATIONS
SEXUALISED
SEXUALISES
SEXUALISING
SEXUALISMS
SEXUALISTS
SEXUALITIES
SEXUALIZATION
SEXUALIZATIONS
SEXUALIZED
SEXUALIZES
SEXUALIZING
SFORZANDOS
SHABBINESS
SHABBINESSES
SHABRACQUE
SHABRACQUES
SHACKLEBONE
SHACKLEBONES
SHACKTOWNS
SHADBERRIES
SHADBUSHES
SHADCHANIM
SHADINESSES
SHADKHANIM
SHADOWBOXED
SHADOWBOXES
SHADOWBOXING
SHADOWCAST
SHADOWCASTED
SHADOWCASTING
SHADOWCASTINGS
SHADOWCASTS
SHADOWGRAPH
SHADOWGRAPHIES
SHADOWGRAPHS
SHADOWGRAPHY
SHADOWIEST
SHADOWINESS
SHADOWINESSES
SHADOWINGS
SHADOWLESS
SHADOWLIKE
SHAGGEDNESS
SHAGGEDNESSES
SHAGGINESS
SHAGGINESSES
SHAGGYMANE
SHAGGYMANES
SHAGREENED
SHAGTASTIC
SHAHTOOSHES
SHAKEDOWNS
SHAKINESSES
SHAKUHACHI
SHAKUHACHIS
SHALLOWEST
SHALLOWING
SHALLOWINGS
SHALLOWNESS
SHALLOWNESSES
SHAMANISMS
SHAMANISTIC
SHAMANISTS
SHAMATEURISM
SHAMATEURISMS
SHAMATEURS
SHAMBLIEST
SHAMBLINGS
SHAMBOLICALLY
SHAMEFACED
SHAMEFACEDLY
SHAMEFACEDNESS
SHAMEFASTNESS
SHAMEFASTNESSES
SHAMEFULLY
SHAMEFULNESS
SHAMEFULNESSES
SHAMELESSLY
SHAMELESSNESS
SHAMELESSNESSES
SHAMEWORTHIER
SHAMEWORTHIEST
SHAMEWORTHY
SHAMIANAHS
SHAMIYANAH
SHAMIYANAHS
SHAMMASHIM
SHAMOISING
SHAMPOOERS
SHAMPOOING
SHANACHIES
SHANDRYDAN
SHANDRYDANS
SHANDYGAFF
SHANDYGAFFS
SHANGHAIED
SHANGHAIER
SHANGHAIERS
SHANGHAIING
SHANKBONES
SHANKPIECE
SHANKPIECES
SHANTYTOWN
SHANTYTOWNS
SHAPELESSLY
SHAPELESSNESS
SHAPELESSNESSES
SHAPELIEST
SHAPELINESS
SHAPELINESSES
SHAPESHIFTER
SHAPESHIFTERS
SHAPESHIFTING
SHAPESHIFTINGS
SHAPEWEARS
SHARAWADGI
SHARAWADGIS
SHARAWAGGI
SHARAWAGGIS
SHAREABILITIES
SHAREABILITY
SHARECROPPED
SHARECROPPER
SHARECROPPERS
SHARECROPPING
SHARECROPPINGS
SHARECROPS

S

SHAREFARMER
SHAREFARMERS
SHAREHOLDER
SHAREHOLDERS
SHAREHOLDING
SHAREHOLDINGS
SHAREMILKER
SHAREMILKERS
SHARENTING
SHARENTINGS
SHAREWARES
SHARKSKINS
SHARKSUCKER
SHARKSUCKERS
SHARPBENDER
SHARPBENDERS
SHARPENERS
SHARPENING
SHARPENINGS
SHARPNESSES
SHARPSHOOTER
SHARPSHOOTERS
SHARPSHOOTING
SHARPSHOOTINGS
SHARPTAILS
SHASHLICKS
SHATOOSHES
SHATTERERS
SHATTERIER
SHATTERIEST
SHATTERING
SHATTERINGLY
SHATTERPROOF
SHAUCHLIER
SHAUCHLIEST
SHAUCHLING
SHAVASANAS
SHAVELINGS
SHAVETAILS
SHEARLINGS
SHEARWATER
SHEARWATERS
SHEATFISHES
SHEATHBILL
SHEATHBILLS
SHEATHFISH
SHEATHFISHES
SHEATHIEST
SHEATHINGS
SHEATHLESS
SHEATHLIKE
SHEBAGGING
SHEBAGGINGS
SHEBEENERS
SHEBEENING
SHEBEENINGS
SHECHITAHS
SHECKLATON
SHECKLATONS
SHEEPBERRIES
SHEEPBERRY
SHEEPCOTES
SHEEPFOLDS
SHEEPHEADS
SHEEPHERDER
SHEEPHERDERS
SHEEPHERDING
SHEEPHERDINGS
SHEEPISHLY
SHEEPISHNESS
SHEEPISHNESSES
SHEEPSHANK
SHEEPSHANKS
SHEEPSHEAD
SHEEPSHEADS
SHEEPSHEARER
SHEEPSHEARERS
SHEEPSHEARING
SHEEPSHEARINGS
SHEEPSKINS
SHEEPTRACK
SHEEPTRACKS
SHEEPWALKS
SHEERNESSES
SHEETROCKED
SHEETROCKING
SHEETROCKS
SHEIKHDOMS
SHELDDUCKS
SHELDRAKES
SHELFROOMS
SHELFTALKER
SHELFTALKERS
SHELLACKED
SHELLACKER
SHELLACKERS
SHELLACKING
SHELLACKINGS
SHELLBACKS
SHELLBARKS
SHELLBOUND
SHELLCRACKER
SHELLCRACKERS
SHELLDRAKE
SHELLDRAKES
SHELLDUCKS
SHELLFIRES
SHELLFISHERIES
SHELLFISHERY
SHELLFISHES
SHELLINESS
SHELLINESSES
SHELLPROOF
SHELLSHOCK
SHELLSHOCKED
SHELLSHOCKS
SHELLWORKS
SHELLYCOAT
SHELLYCOATS
SHELTERBELT
SHELTERBELTS
SHELTERERS
SHELTERIER
SHELTERIEST
SHELTERING
SHELTERINGS
SHELTERLESS
SHEMOZZLED
SHEMOZZLES
SHEMOZZLING
SHENANIGAN
SHENANIGANS
SHEPHERDED
SHEPHERDESS
SHEPHERDESSES
SHEPHERDING
SHEPHERDINGS
SHEPHERDLESS
SHEPHERDLING
SHEPHERDLINGS
SHERARDISATION
SHERARDISATIONS
SHERARDISE
SHERARDISED
SHERARDISES
SHERARDISING
SHERARDIZATION
SHERARDIZATIONS
SHERARDIZE
SHERARDIZED
SHERARDIZES
SHERARDIZING
SHEREEFIAN
SHERGOTTITE
SHERGOTTITES
SHERIFFALTIES
SHERIFFALTY
SHERIFFDOM
SHERIFFDOMS
SHERIFFSHIP
SHERIFFSHIPS
SHERLOCKED
SHERLOCKING
SHEWBREADS
SHIBBOLETH
SHIBBOLETHS
SHIBUICHIS
SHIDDUCHIM
SHIELDINGS
SHIELDLESS
SHIELDLIKE
SHIELDLING
SHIELDLINGS
SHIELDRAKE
SHIELDRAKES
SHIELDWALL
SHIELDWALLS
SHIFTINESS
SHIFTINESSES
SHIFTLESSLY
SHIFTLESSNESS
SHIFTLESSNESSES
SHIFTSTICK
SHIFTSTICKS
SHIFTWORKS
SHIGELLOSES
SHIGELLOSIS
SHIKARRING
SHILLABERS
SHILLALAHS
SHILLELAGH
SHILLELAGHS
SHILLELAHS
SHILLINGLESS
SHILLINGSWORTH
SHILLINGSWORTHS
SHILLYSHALLIED
SHILLYSHALLIER
SHILLYSHALLIERS
SHILLYSHALLIES
SHILLYSHALLY
SHILLYSHALLYING
SHIMMERIER
SHIMMERIEST
SHIMMERING
SHIMMERINGLY
SHIMMERINGS
SHIMOZZLES
SHINGLIEST
SHINGLINGS
SHINGUARDS
SHININESSES
SHININGNESS
SHININGNESSES
SHINLEAVES
SHINNERIES
SHINNEYING
SHINPLASTER
SHINPLASTERS
SHINSPLINTS
SHIPBOARDS
SHIPBROKER
SHIPBROKERS
SHIPBUILDER
SHIPBUILDERS
SHIPBUILDING
SHIPBUILDINGS
SHIPFITTER
SHIPFITTERS
SHIPLAPPED
SHIPLAPPING
SHIPLAPPINGS
SHIPMASTER
SHIPMASTERS
SHIPOWNERS
SHIPPOUNDS
SHIPWRECKED
SHIPWRECKING
SHIPWRECKS
SHIPWRIGHT

SHIPWRIGHTS
SHIRETOWNS
SHIRRALEES
SHIRTBANDS
SHIRTDRESS
SHIRTDRESSES
SHIRTFRONT
SHIRTFRONTED
SHIRTFRONTING
SHIRTFRONTS
SHIRTINESS
SHIRTINESSES
SHIRTLIFTER
SHIRTLIFTERS
SHIRTMAKER
SHIRTMAKERS
SHIRTSLEEVE
SHIRTSLEEVED
SHIRTSLEEVES
SHIRTTAILED
SHIRTTAILING
SHIRTTAILS
SHIRTWAIST
SHIRTWAISTED
SHIRTWAISTER
SHIRTWAISTERS
SHIRTWAISTS
SHITCANNED
SHITCANNING
SHITHOUSES
SHITSTORMS
SHITTIMWOOD
SHITTIMWOODS
SHITTINESS
SHITTINESSES
SHIVAREEING
SHIVERIEST
SHIVERINGLY
SHIVERINGS
SHLEMIEHLS
SHLEMOZZLE
SHLEMOZZLED
SHLEMOZZLES
SHLEMOZZLING
SHLEPPIEST
SHLIMAZELS
SHLOCKIEST
SHLUMPIEST
SHMALTZIER
SHMALTZIEST
SHMOOZIEST
SHMUCKIEST
SHOALINESS
SHOALINESSES
SHOALNESSES
SHOCKABILITIES
SHOCKABILITY
SHOCKHEADED
SHOCKINGLY
SHOCKINGNESS
SHOCKINGNESSES
SHOCKPROOF
SHOCKSTALL
SHOCKSTALLS
SHOCKUMENTARIES
SHOCKUMENTARY
SHODDINESS
SHODDINESSES
SHOEBLACKS
SHOEBRUSHES
SHOEHORNED
SHOEHORNING
SHOEMAKERS
SHOEMAKING
SHOEMAKINGS
SHOESHINES
SHOESTRING
SHOESTRINGS
SHOGGLIEST
SHOGUNATES
SHONGOLOLO
SHONGOLOLOS
SHOOGIEING
SHOOGLIEST
SHOOTAROUND
SHOOTAROUNDS
SHOOTDOWNS
SHOPAHOLIC
SHOPAHOLICS
SHOPAHOLISM
SHOPAHOLISMS
SHOPBOARDS
SHOPBREAKER
SHOPBREAKERS
SHOPBREAKING
SHOPBREAKINGS
SHOPFITTER
SHOPFITTERS
SHOPFRONTS
SHOPHOUSES
SHOPKEEPER
SHOPKEEPERS
SHOPKEEPING
SHOPKEEPINGS
SHOPLIFTED
SHOPLIFTER
SHOPLIFTERS
SHOPLIFTING
SHOPLIFTINGS
SHOPSOILED
SHOPWALKER
SHOPWALKERS
SHOPWINDOW
SHOPWINDOWS
SHOREBIRDS
SHOREFRONT
SHOREFRONTS
SHORELINES
SHORESIDES
SHOREWARDS
SHOREWEEDS
SHORTARSES
SHORTBOARD
SHORTBOARDS
SHORTBREAD
SHORTBREADS
SHORTCAKES
SHORTCHANGE
SHORTCHANGED
SHORTCHANGER
SHORTCHANGERS
SHORTCHANGES
SHORTCHANGING
SHORTCOMING
SHORTCOMINGS
SHORTCRUST
SHORTCUTTING
SHORTENERS
SHORTENING
SHORTENINGS
SHORTFALLS
SHORTGOWNS
SHORTHAIRED
SHORTHAIRS
SHORTHANDED
SHORTHANDS
SHORTHEADS
SHORTHORNS
SHORTLISTED
SHORTLISTING
SHORTLISTS
SHORTNESSES
SHORTSHEET
SHORTSHEETED
SHORTSHEETING
SHORTSHEETS
SHORTSIGHTED
SHORTSIGHTEDLY
SHORTSTOPS
SHORTSWORD
SHORTSWORDS
SHORTWAVED
SHORTWAVES
SHORTWAVING
SHOTCRETES
SHOTFIRERS
SHOTGUNNED
SHOTGUNNER
SHOTGUNNERS
SHOTGUNNING
SHOTMAKERS
SHOTMAKING
SHOTMAKINGS
SHOULDERED
SHOULDERING
SHOULDERINGS
SHOUTHERED
SHOUTHERING
SHOUTINGLY
SHOUTLINES
SHOVELBOARD
SHOVELBOARDS
SHOVELFULS
SHOVELHEAD
SHOVELHEADS
SHOVELLERS
SHOVELLING
SHOVELNOSE
SHOVELNOSES
SHOVELSFUL
SHOWBIZZES
SHOWBIZZIER
SHOWBIZZIEST
SHOWBOATED
SHOWBOATER
SHOWBOATERS
SHOWBOATING
SHOWBREADS
SHOWCASING
SHOWERHEAD
SHOWERHEADS
SHOWERIEST
SHOWERINESS
SHOWERINESSES
SHOWERINGS
SHOWERLESS
SHOWERPROOF
SHOWERPROOFED
SHOWERPROOFING
SHOWERPROOFINGS
SHOWERPROOFS
SHOWGROUND
SHOWGROUNDS
SHOWINESSES
SHOWJUMPED
SHOWJUMPER
SHOWJUMPERS
SHOWJUMPING
SHOWJUMPINGS
SHOWMANCES
SHOWMANLIER
SHOWMANLIEST
SHOWMANSHIP
SHOWMANSHIPS
SHOWPIECES
SHOWPLACES
SHOWROOMING
SHOWROOMINGS
SHOWSTOPPER
SHOWSTOPPERS
SHOWSTOPPING
SHREDDIEST
SHREDDINGS
SHREWDNESS
SHREWDNESSES
SHREWISHLY
SHREWISHNESS
SHREWISHNESSES
SHREWMOUSE
SHRIECHING

SHRIEKIEST
SHRIEKINGLY
SHRIEKINGS
SHRIEVALTIES
SHRIEVALTY
SHRILLIEST
SHRILLINGS
SHRILLNESS
SHRILLNESSES
SHRIMPIEST
SHRIMPINGS
SHRIMPLIKE
SHRINELIKE
SHRINKABLE
SHRINKAGES
SHRINKFLATION
SHRINKFLATIONS
SHRINKINGLY
SHRINKPACK
SHRINKPACKS
SHRITCHING
SHRIVELING
SHRIVELLED
SHRIVELLING
SHROFFAGES
SHROUDIEST
SHROUDINGS
SHROUDLESS
SHRUBBERIED
SHRUBBERIES
SHRUBBIEST
SHRUBBINESS
SHRUBBINESSES
SHRUBLANDS
SHTETELACH
SHTICKIEST
SHTREIMELS
SHUBUNKINS
SHUDDERIER
SHUDDERIEST
SHUDDERING
SHUDDERINGLY
SHUDDERINGS
SHUDDERSOME
SHUFFLEBOARD
SHUFFLEBOARDS
SHUFFLINGLY
SHUFFLINGS
SHUNAMITISM
SHUNAMITISMS
SHUNPIKERS
SHUNPIKING
SHUNPIKINGS
SHUTTERBUG
SHUTTERBUGS
SHUTTERING
SHUTTERINGS
SHUTTERLESS
SHUTTLECOCK
SHUTTLECOCKED
SHUTTLECOCKING
SHUTTLECOCKS
SHUTTLELESS
SHUTTLEWISE
SHYLOCKING
SIALAGOGIC
SIALAGOGUE
SIALAGOGUES
SIALOGOGIC
SIALOGOGUE
SIALOGOGUES
SIALOGRAMS
SIALOGRAPHIES
SIALOGRAPHY
SIALOLITHS
SIALORRHOEA
SIALORRHOEAS
SIBILANCES
SIBILANCIES
SIBILANTLY
SIBILATING
SIBILATION
SIBILATIONS
SIBILATORS
SIBILATORY
SICCATIVES
SICILIANAS
SICILIANOS
SICILIENNE
SICILIENNES
SICKENINGLY
SICKENINGS
SICKERNESS
SICKERNESSES
SICKISHNESS
SICKISHNESSES
SICKLEBILL
SICKLEBILLS
SICKLEMIAS
SICKLINESS
SICKLINESSES
SICKNESSES
SICKNURSED
SICKNURSES
SICKNURSING
SICKNURSINGS
SIDDHUISMS
SIDEARMERS
SIDEARMING
SIDEBOARDS
SIDEBURNED
SIDECHAIRS
SIDECHECKS
SIDEDNESSES
SIDEDRESSES
SIDELEVERS
SIDELIGHTS
SIDELINERS
SIDELINING
SIDEPIECES
SIDERATING
SIDERATION
SIDERATIONS
SIDEREALLY
SIDEROLITE
SIDEROLITES
SIDEROPENIA
SIDEROPENIAS
SIDEROPHILE
SIDEROPHILES
SIDEROPHILIC
SIDEROPHILIN
SIDEROPHILINS
SIDEROSTAT
SIDEROSTATIC
SIDEROSTATS
SIDESADDLE
SIDESADDLES
SIDESHOOTS
SIDESLIPPED
SIDESLIPPING
SIDESPLITS
SIDESPLITTING
SIDESPLITTINGLY
SIDESTEPPED
SIDESTEPPER
SIDESTEPPERS
SIDESTEPPING
SIDESTEPPINGS
SIDESTREAM
SIDESTROKE
SIDESTROKES
SIDESWIPED
SIDESWIPER
SIDESWIPERS
SIDESWIPES
SIDESWIPING
SIDETABLES
SIDETRACKED
SIDETRACKING
SIDETRACKS
SIDEWHEELER
SIDEWHEELERS
SIDEWHEELS
SIDEWINDER
SIDEWINDERS
SIEGECRAFT
SIEGECRAFTS
SIEGEWORKS
SIFFLEUSES
SIGHTLESSLY
SIGHTLESSNESS
SIGHTLESSNESSES
SIGHTLIEST
SIGHTLINES
SIGHTLINESS
SIGHTLINESSES
SIGHTSCREEN
SIGHTSCREENS
SIGHTSEEING
SIGHTSEEINGS
SIGHTSEERS
SIGHTWORTHIER
SIGHTWORTHIEST
SIGHTWORTHY
SIGILLARIAN
SIGILLARIANS
SIGILLARID
SIGILLARIDS
SIGILLATION
SIGILLATIONS
SIGMATIONS
SIGMATISMS
SIGMATRONS
SIGMOIDALLY
SIGMOIDECTOMIES
SIGMOIDECTOMY
SIGMOIDOSCOPE
SIGMOIDOSCOPES
SIGMOIDOSCOPIC
SIGMOIDOSCOPIES
SIGMOIDOSCOPY
SIGNALINGS
SIGNALISATION
SIGNALISATIONS
SIGNALISED
SIGNALISES
SIGNALISING
SIGNALIZATION
SIGNALIZATIONS
SIGNALIZED
SIGNALIZES
SIGNALIZING
SIGNALLERS
SIGNALLING
SIGNALLINGS
SIGNALMENT
SIGNALMENTS
SIGNATORIES
SIGNATURES
SIGNBOARDS
SIGNEURIES
SIGNIFIABLE
SIGNIFICANCE
SIGNIFICANCES
SIGNIFICANCIES
SIGNIFICANCY
SIGNIFICANT
SIGNIFICANTLY
SIGNIFICANTS
SIGNIFICATE
SIGNIFICATES
SIGNIFICATION
SIGNIFICATIONS
SIGNIFICATIVE
SIGNIFICATIVELY
SIGNIFICATOR
SIGNIFICATORS
SIGNIFICATORY
SIGNIFIEDS

SIGNIFIERS
SIGNIFYING
SIGNIFYINGS
SIGNIORIES
SIGNORINAS
SIGNPOSTED
SIGNPOSTING
SIGNPOSTINGS
SIKORSKIES
SILDENAFIL
SILDENAFILS
SILENTIARIES
SILENTIARY
SILENTNESS
SILENTNESSES
SILHOUETTE
SILHOUETTED
SILHOUETTES
SILHOUETTING
SILHOUETTIST
SILHOUETTISTS
SILICATING
SILICICOLOUS
SILICIFEROUS
SILICIFICATION
SILICIFICATIONS
SILICIFIED
SILICIFIES
SILICIFYING
SILICONISED
SILICONIZED
SILICOTICS
SILICULOSE
SILIQUACEOUS
SILKALENES
SILKALINES
SILKGROWER
SILKGROWERS
SILKINESSES
SILKOLINES
SILKSCREEN
SILKSCREENED
SILKSCREENING
SILKSCREENS
SILLIMANITE
SILLIMANITES
SILLINESSES
SILTATIONS
SILTSTONES
SILVERBACK
SILVERBACKS
SILVERBERRIES
SILVERBERRY
SILVERBILL
SILVERBILLS
SILVEREYES
SILVERFISH
SILVERFISHES
SILVERHORN
SILVERHORNS
SILVERIEST
SILVERINESS
SILVERINESSES
SILVERINGS
SILVERISED
SILVERISES
SILVERISING
SILVERIZED
SILVERIZES
SILVERIZING
SILVERLING
SILVERLINGS
SILVERPOINT
SILVERPOINTS
SILVERSIDE
SILVERSIDES
SILVERSKIN
SILVERSKINS
SILVERSMITH
SILVERSMITHING
SILVERSMITHINGS
SILVERSMITHS
SILVERTAIL
SILVERTAILS
SILVERTIPS
SILVERWARE
SILVERWARES
SILVERWEED
SILVERWEEDS
SILVESTRIAN
SILVICULTURAL
SILVICULTURALLY
SILVICULTURE
SILVICULTURES
SILVICULTURIST
SILVICULTURISTS
SILYMARINS
SIMAROUBACEOUS
SIMAROUBAS
SIMARUBACEOUS
SIMILARITIES
SIMILARITY
SIMILATIVE
SIMILISING
SIMILITUDE
SIMILITUDES
SIMILIZING
SIMILLIMUM
SIMILLIMUMS
SIMONIACAL
SIMONIACALLY
SIMONISING
SIMONIZING
SIMPERINGLY
SIMPERINGS
SIMPLEMINDED
SIMPLEMINDEDLY
SIMPLENESS
SIMPLENESSES
SIMPLESSES
SIMPLETONS
SIMPLICIAL
SIMPLICIALLY
SIMPLICIDENTATE
SIMPLICITER
SIMPLICITIES
SIMPLICITY
SIMPLIFIABLE
SIMPLIFICATION
SIMPLIFICATIONS
SIMPLIFICATIVE
SIMPLIFICATOR
SIMPLIFICATORS
SIMPLIFIED
SIMPLIFIER
SIMPLIFIERS
SIMPLIFIES
SIMPLIFYING
SIMPLISTES
SIMPLISTIC
SIMPLISTICALLY
SIMULACRES
SIMULACRUM
SIMULACRUMS
SIMULATING
SIMULATION
SIMULATIONS
SIMULATIVE
SIMULATIVELY
SIMULATORS
SIMULATORY
SIMULCASTED
SIMULCASTING
SIMULCASTS
SIMULTANEITIES
SIMULTANEITY
SIMULTANEOUS
SIMULTANEOUSES
SIMULTANEOUSLY
SIMVASTATIN
SIMVASTATINS
SINANTHROPUS
SINANTHROPUSES
SINARCHISM
SINARCHISMS
SINARCHIST
SINARCHISTS
SINARQUISM
SINARQUISMS
SINARQUIST
SINARQUISTS
SINCERENESS
SINCERENESSES
SINCERITIES
SINCIPITAL
SINDONOLOGIES
SINDONOLOGIST
SINDONOLOGISTS
SINDONOLOGY
SINDONOPHANIES
SINDONOPHANY
SINECURISM
SINECURISMS
SINECURIST
SINECURISTS
SINEWINESS
SINEWINESSES
SINFONIETTA
SINFONIETTAS
SINFULNESS
SINFULNESSES
SINGABLENESS
SINGABLENESSES
SINGALONGS
SINGLEDOMS
SINGLEHOOD
SINGLEHOODS
SINGLENESS
SINGLENESSES
SINGLESTICK
SINGLESTICKS
SINGLETONS
SINGLETRACK
SINGLETRACKS
SINGLETREE
SINGLETREES
SINGSONGED
SINGSONGIER
SINGSONGIEST
SINGSONGING
SINGSPIELS
SINGULARISATION
SINGULARISE
SINGULARISED
SINGULARISES
SINGULARISING
SINGULARISM
SINGULARISMS
SINGULARIST
SINGULARISTS
SINGULARITIES
SINGULARITY
SINGULARIZATION
SINGULARIZE
SINGULARIZED
SINGULARIZES
SINGULARIZING
SINGULARLY
SINGULARNESS
SINGULARNESSES
SINGULTUSES
SINICISING
SINICIZING
SINISTERITIES
SINISTERITY
SINISTERLY
SINISTERNESS
SINISTERNESSES
SINISTERWISE
SINISTRALITIES

SINISTRALITY
SINISTRALLY
SINISTRALS
SINISTRODEXTRAL
SINISTRORSAL
SINISTRORSALLY
SINISTRORSE
SINISTRORSELY
SINISTROUS
SINISTROUSLY
SINLESSNESS
SINLESSNESSES
SINNINGIAS
SINOATRIAL
SINOLOGICAL
SINOLOGIES
SINOLOGIST
SINOLOGISTS
SINOLOGUES
SINSEMILLA
SINSEMILLAS
SINTERABILITIES
SINTERABILITY
SINTERIEST
SINUATIONS
SINUITISES
SINUOSITIES
SINUOUSNESS
SINUOUSNESSES
SINUPALLIAL
SINUPALLIATE
SINUSITISES
SINUSOIDAL
SINUSOIDALLY
SIPHONAGES
SIPHONOGAM
SIPHONOGAMIES
SIPHONOGAMS
SIPHONOGAMY
SIPHONOPHORE
SIPHONOPHORES
SIPHONOPHOROUS
SIPHONOSTELE
SIPHONOSTELES
SIPHONOSTELIC
SIPHUNCLES
SIPUNCULID
SIPUNCULIDS
SIPUNCULOID
SIPUNCULOIDS
SIRENISING
SIRENIZING
SIRONISING
SIRONIZING
SISERARIES
SISSINESSES
SISSYNESSES
SISTERHOOD
SISTERHOODS
SISTERLESS
SISTERLIER
SISTERLIEST
SISTERLIKE
SISTERLINESS
SISTERLINESSES
SITATUNGAS
SITIOLOGIES
SITIOPHOBIA
SITIOPHOBIAS
SITOLOGIES
SITOPHOBIA
SITOPHOBIAS
SITOSTEROL
SITOSTEROLS
SITUATIONAL
SITUATIONALLY
SITUATIONISM
SITUATIONISMS
SITUATIONS
SITUTUNGAS
SITZKRIEGS
SIXPENNIES
SIXTEENERS
SIXTEENMOS
SIXTEENTHLY
SIXTEENTHS
SIZABLENESS
SIZABLENESSES
SIZARSHIPS
SIZEABLENESS
SIZEABLENESSES
SIZINESSES
SIZZLINGLY
SJAMBOKING
SJAMBOKKED
SJAMBOKKING
SKAITHLESS
SKALDSHIPS
SKANKINESS
SKANKINESSES
SKATEBOARD
SKATEBOARDED
SKATEBOARDER
SKATEBOARDERS
SKATEBOARDING
SKATEBOARDINGS
SKATEBOARDS
SKATEPARKS
SKATEPUNKS
SKEDADDLED
SKEDADDLER
SKEDADDLERS
SKEDADDLES
SKEDADDLING
SKELDERING
SKELETALLY
SKELETOGENOUS
SKELETONIC
SKELETONISE
SKELETONISED
SKELETONISER
SKELETONISERS
SKELETONISES
SKELETONISING
SKELETONIZE
SKELETONIZED
SKELETONIZER
SKELETONIZERS
SKELETONIZES
SKELETONIZING
SKELLOCHED
SKELLOCHING
SKELTERING
SKEPTICALLY
SKEPTICALNESS
SKEPTICALNESSES
SKEPTICISM
SKEPTICISMS
SKETCHABILITIES
SKETCHABILITY
SKETCHABLE
SKETCHBOOK
SKETCHBOOKS
SKETCHIEST
SKETCHINESS
SKETCHINESSES
SKETCHPADS
SKEUOMORPH
SKEUOMORPHIC
SKEUOMORPHISM
SKEUOMORPHISMS
SKEUOMORPHS
SKEWBACKED
SKEWNESSES
SKIAGRAPHS
SKIAMACHIES
SKIASCOPES
SKIASCOPIES
SKIBOBBERS
SKIBOBBING
SKIBOBBINGS
SKIDDOOING
SKIDOOINGS
SKIJORINGS
SKIJUMPERS
SKIKJORERS
SKIKJORING
SKIKJORINGS
SKILFULNESS
SKILFULNESSES
SKILLCENTRE
SKILLCENTRES
SKILLESSNESS
SKILLESSNESSES
SKILLFULLY
SKILLFULNESS
SKILLFULNESSES
SKILLIGALEE
SKILLIGALEES
SKILLIGOLEE
SKILLIGOLEES
SKIMBOARDED
SKIMBOARDER
SKIMBOARDERS
SKIMBOARDING
SKIMBOARDS
SKIMMINGLY
SKIMMINGTON
SKIMMINGTONS
SKIMOBILED
SKIMOBILES
SKIMOBILING
SKIMPINESS
SKIMPINESSES
SKIMPINGLY
SKINFLICKS
SKINFLINTIER
SKINFLINTIEST
SKINFLINTS
SKINFLINTY
SKINNINESS
SKINNINESSES
SKINTIGHTER
SKINTIGHTEST
SKINTIGHTS
SKIPPERING
SKIPPERINGS
SKIPPINGLY
SKIRMISHED
SKIRMISHER
SKIRMISHERS
SKIRMISHES
SKIRMISHING
SKIRMISHINGS
SKITTERIER
SKITTERIEST
SKITTERING
SKITTISHLY
SKITTISHNESS
SKITTISHNESSES
SKORDALIAS
SKREEGHING
SKREIGHING
SKRIECHING
SKRIEGHING
SKRIMMAGED
SKRIMMAGES
SKRIMMAGING
SKRIMSHANK
SKRIMSHANKED
SKRIMSHANKER
SKRIMSHANKERS
SKRIMSHANKING
SKRIMSHANKS
SKULDUDDERIES
SKULDUDDERY
SKULDUGGERIES
SKULDUGGERY
SKULKINGLY
SKULLDUGGERIES

S

SKULLDUGGERY
SKUMMERING
SKUNKBIRDS
SKUNKWEEDS
SKUTTERUDITE
SKUTTERUDITES
SKYBRIDGES
SKYDIVINGS
SKYJACKERS
SKYJACKING
SKYJACKINGS
SKYLARKERS
SKYLARKING
SKYLARKINGS
SKYLIGHTED
SKYROCKETED
SKYROCKETING
SKYROCKETS
SKYSCRAPER
SKYSCRAPERS
SKYSURFERS
SKYSURFING
SKYSURFINGS
SKYWATCHED
SKYWATCHES
SKYWATCHING
SKYWRITERS
SKYWRITING
SKYWRITINGS
SKYWRITTEN
SLABBERERS
SLABBERIER
SLABBERIEST
SLABBERING
SLABBINESS
SLABBINESSES
SLABSTONES
SLACKENERS
SLACKENING
SLACKENINGS
SLACKLINING
SLACKLININGS
SLACKNESSES
SLACKTIVISM
SLACKTIVISMS
SLACKTIVIST
SLACKTIVISTS
SLACTIVISM
SLACTIVISMS
SLACTIVIST
SLACTIVISTS
SLAISTERED
SLAISTERIES
SLAISTERING
SLALOMISTS
SLAMDANCED
SLAMDANCES
SLAMDANCING
SLAMMAKINS
SLAMMERKIN
SLAMMERKINS
SLANDERERS
SLANDERING
SLANDEROUS
SLANDEROUSLY
SLANDEROUSNESS
SLANGINESS
SLANGINESSES
SLANGINGLY
SLANGUAGES
SLANTENDICULAR
SLANTINDICULAR
SLANTINGLY
SLANTINGWAYS
SLAPDASHED
SLAPDASHES
SLAPDASHING
SLAPHAPPIER
SLAPHAPPIEST
SLAPSTICKS
SLASHFESTS
SLASHINGLY
SLATHERING
SLATINESSES
SLATTERING
SLATTERNLIER
SLATTERNLIEST
SLATTERNLINESS
SLATTERNLY
SLAUGHTERABLE
SLAUGHTERED
SLAUGHTERER
SLAUGHTERERS
SLAUGHTERHOUSE
SLAUGHTERHOUSES
SLAUGHTERIES
SLAUGHTERING
SLAUGHTERMAN
SLAUGHTERMEN
SLAUGHTEROUS
SLAUGHTEROUSLY
SLAUGHTERS
SLAUGHTERY
SLAVEHOLDER
SLAVEHOLDERS
SLAVEHOLDING
SLAVEHOLDINGS
SLAVERINGLY
SLAVERINGS
SLAVISHNESS
SLAVISHNESSES
SLAVOCRACIES
SLAVOCRACY
SLAVOCRATS
SLAVOPHILE
SLAVOPHILES
SLAVOPHILS
SLEAZEBAGS
SLEAZEBALL
SLEAZEBALLS
SLEAZINESS
SLEAZINESSES
SLEDGEHAMMER
SLEDGEHAMMERED
SLEDGEHAMMERING
SLEDGEHAMMERS
SLEECHIEST
SLEEKENING
SLEEKNESSES
SLEEKSTONE
SLEEKSTONES
SLEEPINESS
SLEEPINESSES
SLEEPLESSLY
SLEEPLESSNESS
SLEEPLESSNESSES
SLEEPOVERS
SLEEPSUITS
SLEEPWALKED
SLEEPWALKER
SLEEPWALKERS
SLEEPWALKING
SLEEPWALKINGS
SLEEPWALKS
SLEEPWEARS
SLEEPYHEAD
SLEEPYHEADED
SLEEPYHEADS
SLEETINESS
SLEETINESSES
SLEEVEHAND
SLEEVEHANDS
SLEEVELESS
SLEEVELETS
SLEEVELIKE
SLEIGHINGS
SLENDEREST
SLENDERISE
SLENDERISED
SLENDERISES
SLENDERISING
SLENDERIZE
SLENDERIZED
SLENDERIZES
SLENDERIZING
SLENDERNESS
SLENDERNESSES
SLEUTHHOUND
SLEUTHHOUNDS
SLEUTHINGS
SLICKENERS
SLICKENING
SLICKENSIDE
SLICKENSIDED
SLICKENSIDES
SLICKNESSES
SLICKROCKS
SLICKSTERS
SLICKSTONE
SLICKSTONES
SLIDDERIER
SLIDDERIEST
SLIDDERING
SLIDESHOWS
SLIGHTINGLY
SLIGHTNESS
SLIGHTNESSES
SLIMEBALLS
SLIMINESSES
SLIMNASTICS
SLIMNESSES
SLIMPSIEST
SLINGBACKS
SLINGSHOTS
SLINGSTONE
SLINGSTONES
SLINKINESS
SLINKINESSES
SLINKSKINS
SLINKWEEDS
SLIPCOVERED
SLIPCOVERING
SLIPCOVERS
SLIPDRESSES
SLIPFORMED
SLIPFORMING
SLIPNOOSES
SLIPPERIER
SLIPPERIEST
SLIPPERILY
SLIPPERINESS
SLIPPERINESSES
SLIPPERING
SLIPPERWORT
SLIPPERWORTS
SLIPPINESS
SLIPPINESSES
SLIPSHEETED
SLIPSHEETING
SLIPSHEETS
SLIPSHODDINESS
SLIPSHODNESS
SLIPSHODNESSES
SLIPSLOPPIER
SLIPSLOPPIEST
SLIPSLOPPY
SLIPSTREAM
SLIPSTREAMED
SLIPSTREAMING
SLIPSTREAMS
SLITHERIER
SLITHERIEST
SLITHERING
SLIVOVICAS
SLIVOVICES
SLIVOVITZES
SLIVOWITZES
SLOBBERERS
SLOBBERIER
SLOBBERIEST

SLOBBERING
SLOBBISHNESS
SLOBBISHNESSES
SLOCKDOLAGER
SLOCKDOLAGERS
SLOCKDOLIGER
SLOCKDOLIGERS
SLOCKDOLOGER
SLOCKDOLOGERS
SLOCKENING
SLOEBUSHES
SLOETHORNS
SLOGANEERED
SLOGANEERING
SLOGANEERINGS
SLOGANEERS
SLOGANISED
SLOGANISES
SLOGANISING
SLOGANISINGS
SLOGANIZED
SLOGANIZES
SLOGANIZING
SLOGANIZINGS
SLOMMOCKED
SLOMMOCKING
SLOPESIDES
SLOPINGNESS
SLOPINGNESSES
SLOPPINESS
SLOPPINESSES
SLOPWORKER
SLOPWORKERS
SLOTHFULLY
SLOTHFULNESS
SLOTHFULNESSES
SLOUCHIEST
SLOUCHINESS
SLOUCHINESSES
SLOUCHINGLY
SLOUGHIEST
SLOVENLIER
SLOVENLIEST
SLOVENLIKE
SLOVENLINESS
SLOVENLINESSES
SLOVENRIES
SLOWCOACHES
SLOWNESSES
SLUBBERING
SLUBBERINGLY
SLUBBERINGS
SLUGGABEDS
SLUGGARDISE
SLUGGARDISED
SLUGGARDISES
SLUGGARDISING
SLUGGARDIZE
SLUGGARDIZED
SLUGGARDIZES
SLUGGARDIZING
SLUGGARDLIER
SLUGGARDLIEST
SLUGGARDLINESS
SLUGGARDLY
SLUGGARDNESS
SLUGGARDNESSES
SLUGGISHLY
SLUGGISHNESS
SLUGGISHNESSES
SLUGHORNES
SLUICEGATE
SLUICEGATES
SLUICELIKE
SLUICEWAYS
SLUMBERERS
SLUMBERFUL
SLUMBERIER
SLUMBERIEST
SLUMBERING
SLUMBERINGLY
SLUMBERINGS
SLUMBERLAND
SLUMBERLANDS
SLUMBERLESS
SLUMBEROUS
SLUMBEROUSLY
SLUMBEROUSNESS
SLUMBERSOME
SLUMBROUSLY
SLUMBROUSNESS
SLUMBROUSNESSES
SLUMGULLION
SLUMGULLIONS
SLUMMOCKED
SLUMMOCKING
SLUMPFLATION
SLUMPFLATIONARY
SLUMPFLATIONS
SLUNGSHOTS
SLUSHINESS
SLUSHINESSES
SLUTCHIEST
SLUTTERIES
SLUTTINESS
SLUTTINESSES
SLUTTISHLY
SLUTTISHNESS
SLUTTISHNESSES
SMACKDOWNS
SMACKEROOS
SMACKHEADS
SMALLCLOTHES
SMALLHOLDER
SMALLHOLDERS
SMALLHOLDING
SMALLHOLDINGS
SMALLMOUTH
SMALLMOUTHS
SMALLNESSES
SMALLPOXES
SMALLSWORD
SMALLSWORDS
SMALMINESS
SMALMINESSES
SMARAGDINE
SMARAGDITE
SMARAGDITES
SMARMINESS
SMARMINESSES
SMARTARSED
SMARTARSES
SMARTASSES
SMARTENING
SMARTINGLY
SMARTMOUTH
SMARTMOUTHS
SMARTNESSES
SMARTPHONE
SMARTPHONES
SMARTWATCH
SMARTWATCHES
SMARTWEEDS
SMARTYPANTS
SMASHEROOS
SMASHINGLY
SMASHMOUTH
SMATTERERS
SMATTERING
SMATTERINGLY
SMATTERINGS
SMEARCASES
SMEARINESS
SMEARINESSES
SMELLINESS
SMELLINESSES
SMELTERIES
SMICKERING
SMICKERINGS
SMIERCASES
SMIFLIGATE
SMIFLIGATED
SMIFLIGATES
SMIFLIGATING
SMILACACEOUS
SMILINGNESS
SMILINGNESSES
SMIRKINGLY
SMITHCRAFT
SMITHCRAFTS
SMITHEREEN
SMITHEREENED
SMITHEREENING
SMITHEREENS
SMITHERIES
SMITHSONITE
SMITHSONITES
SMOKEBOARD
SMOKEBOARDS
SMOKEBOXES
SMOKEBUSHES
SMOKEHOODS
SMOKEHOUSE
SMOKEHOUSES
SMOKEJACKS
SMOKELESSLY
SMOKELESSNESS
SMOKELESSNESSES
SMOKEPROOF
SMOKESCREEN
SMOKESCREENS
SMOKESTACK
SMOKESTACKS
SMOKETIGHT
SMOKINESSES
SMOLDERING
SMOOCHIEST
SMOOTHABLE
SMOOTHBORE
SMOOTHBORED
SMOOTHBORES
SMOOTHENED
SMOOTHENING
SMOOTHINGS
SMOOTHNESS
SMOOTHNESSES
SMOOTHPATE
SMOOTHPATES
SMORGASBORD
SMORGASBORDS
SMORREBROD
SMORREBRODS
SMOTHERERS
SMOTHERIER
SMOTHERIEST
SMOTHERINESS
SMOTHERINESSES
SMOTHERING
SMOTHERINGLY
SMOTHERINGS
SMOULDERED
SMOULDERING
SMOULDERINGLY
SMOULDERINGS
SMOULDRIER
SMOULDRIEST
SMUDGELESS
SMUDGINESS
SMUDGINESSES
SMUGGERIES
SMUGGLINGS
SMUGNESSES
SMUTCHIEST
SMUTTINESS
SMUTTINESSES
SNACKETTES
SNAGGLETEETH
SNAGGLETOOTH
SNAGGLETOOTHED
SNAILERIES

SNAILFISHES
SNAKEBIRDS
SNAKEBITES
SNAKEBITTEN
SNAKEFISHES
SNAKEHEADS
SNAKEMOUTH
SNAKEMOUTHS
SNAKEROOTS
SNAKESKINS
SNAKESTONE
SNAKESTONES
SNAKEWEEDS
SNAKEWOODS
SNAKINESSES
SNAKISHNESS
SNAKISHNESSES
SNAPDRAGON
SNAPDRAGONS
SNAPHANCES
SNAPHAUNCE
SNAPHAUNCES
SNAPHAUNCH
SNAPHAUNCHES
SNAPPERING
SNAPPINESS
SNAPPINESSES
SNAPPINGLY
SNAPPISHLY
SNAPPISHNESS
SNAPPISHNESSES
SNAPSHOOTER
SNAPSHOOTERS
SNAPSHOOTING
SNAPSHOOTINGS
SNAPSHOTTED
SNAPSHOTTING
SNARLINGLY
SNATCHIEST
SNATCHINGLY
SNATCHINGS
SNAZZINESS
SNAZZINESSES
SNEAKBOXES
SNEAKINESS
SNEAKINESSES
SNEAKINGLY
SNEAKINGNESS
SNEAKINGNESSES
SNEAKISHLY
SNEAKISHNESS
SNEAKISHNESSES
SNEAKSBIES
SNEERINGLY
SNEESHINGS
SNEEZELESS
SNEEZEWEED
SNEEZEWEEDS
SNEEZEWOOD
SNEEZEWOODS
SNEEZEWORT
SNEEZEWORTS
SNICKERERS
SNICKERIER
SNICKERIEST
SNICKERING
SNICKERSNEE
SNICKERSNEED
SNICKERSNEEING
SNICKERSNEES
SNIDENESSES
SNIFFINESS
SNIFFINESSES
SNIFFINGLY
SNIFFISHLY
SNIFFISHNESS
SNIFFISHNESSES
SNIFFLIEST
SNIFTERING
SNIGGERERS
SNIGGERING
SNIGGERINGLY
SNIGGERINGS
SNIGGLINGS
SNIPEFISHES
SNIPERSCOPE
SNIPERSCOPES
SNIPPERSNAPPER
SNIPPERSNAPPERS
SNIPPETIER
SNIPPETIEST
SNIPPETINESS
SNIPPETINESSES
SNIPPINESS
SNIPPINESSES
SNITCHIEST
SNIVELIEST
SNIVELINGS
SNIVELLERS
SNIVELLIER
SNIVELLIEST
SNIVELLING
SNIVELLINGS
SNOBBERIES
SNOBBISHLY
SNOBBISHNESS
SNOBBISHNESSES
SNOBBOCRACIES
SNOBBOCRACY
SNOBOCRACIES
SNOBOCRACY
SNOBOGRAPHER
SNOBOGRAPHERS
SNOBOGRAPHIES
SNOBOGRAPHY
SNOCOACHES
SNOLLYGOSTER
SNOLLYGOSTERS
SNOOKERING
SNOOPERSCOPE
SNOOPERSCOPES
SNOOTINESS
SNOOTINESSES
SNORKELERS
SNORKELING
SNORKELINGS
SNORKELLED
SNORKELLER
SNORKELLERS
SNORKELLING
SNORKELLINGS
SNORTINGLY
SNOTTERIES
SNOTTERING
SNOTTINESS
SNOTTINESSES
SNOWBALLED
SNOWBALLING
SNOWBERRIES
SNOWBLADER
SNOWBLADERS
SNOWBLADES
SNOWBLADING
SNOWBLADINGS
SNOWBLINKS
SNOWBLOWER
SNOWBLOWERS
SNOWBOARDED
SNOWBOARDER
SNOWBOARDERS
SNOWBOARDING
SNOWBOARDINGS
SNOWBOARDS
SNOWBRUSHES
SNOWBUSHES
SNOWCAPPED
SNOWCLONES
SNOWCOACHES
SNOWDRIFTS
SNOWFIELDS
SNOWFLAKES
SNOWFLECKS
SNOWFLICKS
SNOWGLOBES
SNOWINESSES
SNOWMAKERS
SNOWMAKING
SNOWMOBILE
SNOWMOBILED
SNOWMOBILER
SNOWMOBILERS
SNOWMOBILES
SNOWMOBILING
SNOWMOBILINGS
SNOWMOBILIST
SNOWMOBILISTS
SNOWMOULDS
SNOWPLOUGH
SNOWPLOUGHED
SNOWPLOUGHING
SNOWPLOUGHS
SNOWPLOWED
SNOWPLOWING
SNOWSCAPES
SNOWSHOEING
SNOWSHOEINGS
SNOWSHOERS
SNOWSLIDES
SNOWSNAKES
SNOWSTORMS
SNOWSURFING
SNOWSURFINGS
SNOWTUBING
SNOWTUBINGS
SNUBBINESS
SNUBBINESSES
SNUBBINGLY
SNUBNESSES
SNUFFBOXES
SNUFFINESS
SNUFFINESSES
SNUFFLIEST
SNUFFLINGS
SNUGGERIES
SNUGGLIEST
SNUGNESSES
SOAPBERRIES
SOAPBOXING
SOAPDISHES
SOAPFISHES
SOAPFLAKES
SOAPINESSES
SOAPOLALLIE
SOAPOLALLIES
SOAPSTONES
SOAPSUDSIER
SOAPSUDSIEST
SOBERINGLY
SOBERISING
SOBERIZING
SOBERNESSES
SOBERSIDED
SOBERSIDEDNESS
SOBERSIDES
SOBOLIFEROUS
SOBRIETIES
SOBRIQUETS
SOCDOLAGER
SOCDOLAGERS
SOCDOLIGER
SOCDOLIGERS
SOCDOLOGER
SOCDOLOGERS
SOCIABILITIES
SOCIABILITY
SOCIABLENESS
SOCIABLENESSES
SOCIALISABLE
SOCIALISATION
SOCIALISATIONS

S

SOCIALISED
SOCIALISER
SOCIALISERS
SOCIALISES
SOCIALISING
SOCIALISINGS
SOCIALISMS
SOCIALISTIC
SOCIALISTICALLY
SOCIALISTS
SOCIALITES
SOCIALITIES
SOCIALIZABLE
SOCIALIZATION
SOCIALIZATIONS
SOCIALIZED
SOCIALIZER
SOCIALIZERS
SOCIALIZES
SOCIALIZING
SOCIALIZINGS
SOCIALNESS
SOCIALNESSES
SOCIATIONS
SOCIETALLY
SOCIOBIOLOGICAL
SOCIOBIOLOGIES
SOCIOBIOLOGIST
SOCIOBIOLOGISTS
SOCIOBIOLOGY
SOCIOCULTURAL
SOCIOCULTURALLY
SOCIOECONOMIC
SOCIOGRAMS
SOCIOHISTORICAL
SOCIOLECTS
SOCIOLINGUIST
SOCIOLINGUISTIC
SOCIOLINGUISTS
SOCIOLOGESE
SOCIOLOGESES
SOCIOLOGIC
SOCIOLOGICAL
SOCIOLOGICALLY
SOCIOLOGIES
SOCIOLOGISM
SOCIOLOGISMS
SOCIOLOGIST
SOCIOLOGISTIC
SOCIOLOGISTS
SOCIOMETRIC
SOCIOMETRIES
SOCIOMETRIST
SOCIOMETRISTS
SOCIOMETRY
SOCIOPATHIC
SOCIOPATHIES
SOCIOPATHS
SOCIOPATHY
SOCIOPOLITICAL
SOCIORELIGIOUS
SOCIOSEXUAL
SOCKDOLAGER
SOCKDOLAGERS
SOCKDOLIGER
SOCKDOLIGERS
SOCKDOLOGER
SOCKDOLOGERS
SODALITIES
SODBUSTERS
SODDENNESS
SODDENNESSES
SODICITIES
SODOMISING
SODOMITICAL
SODOMITICALLY
SODOMIZING
SOFTBALLER
SOFTBALLERS
SOFTBOUNDS
SOFTCOVERS
SOFTENINGS
SOFTHEADED
SOFTHEADEDLY
SOFTHEADEDNESS
SOFTHEARTED
SOFTHEARTEDLY
SOFTHEARTEDNESS
SOFTNESSES
SOFTSCAPES
SOFTSHELLS
SOGDOLAGER
SOGDOLAGERS
SOGDOLIGER
SOGDOLIGERS
SOGDOLOGER
SOGDOLOGERS
SOGGINESSES
SOILINESSES
SOJOURNERS
SOJOURNING
SOJOURNINGS
SOJOURNMENT
SOJOURNMENTS
SOKEMANRIES
SOLACEMENT
SOLACEMENTS
SOLANACEOUS
SOLARIMETER
SOLARIMETERS
SOLARISATION
SOLARISATIONS
SOLARISING
SOLARIZATION
SOLARIZATIONS
SOLARIZING
SOLDATESQUE
SOLDERABILITIES
SOLDERABILITY
SOLDERABLE
SOLDERINGS
SOLDIERIES
SOLDIERING
SOLDIERINGS
SOLDIERLIER
SOLDIERLIEST
SOLDIERLIKE
SOLDIERLINESS
SOLDIERLINESSES
SOLDIERSHIP
SOLDIERSHIPS
SOLECISING
SOLECISTIC
SOLECISTICAL
SOLECISTICALLY
SOLECIZING
SOLEMNESSES
SOLEMNIFICATION
SOLEMNIFIED
SOLEMNIFIES
SOLEMNIFYING
SOLEMNISATION
SOLEMNISATIONS
SOLEMNISED
SOLEMNISER
SOLEMNISERS
SOLEMNISES
SOLEMNISING
SOLEMNITIES
SOLEMNIZATION
SOLEMNIZATIONS
SOLEMNIZED
SOLEMNIZER
SOLEMNIZERS
SOLEMNIZES
SOLEMNIZING
SOLEMNNESS
SOLEMNNESSES
SOLENESSES
SOLENETTES
SOLENODONS
SOLENOIDAL
SOLENOIDALLY
SOLEPLATES
SOLEPRINTS
SOLFATARAS
SOLFATARIC
SOLFEGGIOS
SOLFERINOS
SOLICITANT
SOLICITANTS
SOLICITATION
SOLICITATIONS
SOLICITIES
SOLICITING
SOLICITINGS
SOLICITORS
SOLICITORSHIP
SOLICITORSHIPS
SOLICITOUS
SOLICITOUSLY
SOLICITOUSNESS
SOLICITUDE
SOLICITUDES
SOLIDARISM
SOLIDARISMS
SOLIDARIST
SOLIDARISTIC
SOLIDARISTS
SOLIDARITIES
SOLIDARITY
SOLIDATING
SOLIDIFIABLE
SOLIDIFICATION
SOLIDIFICATIONS
SOLIDIFIED
SOLIDIFIER
SOLIDIFIERS
SOLIDIFIES
SOLIDIFYING
SOLIDITIES
SOLIDNESSES
SOLIDUNGULATE
SOLIDUNGULATES
SOLIDUNGULOUS
SOLIFIDIAN
SOLIFIDIANISM
SOLIFIDIANISMS
SOLIFIDIANS
SOLIFLUCTION
SOLIFLUCTIONS
SOLIFLUXION
SOLIFLUXIONS
SOLILOQUIES
SOLILOQUISE
SOLILOQUISED
SOLILOQUISER
SOLILOQUISERS
SOLILOQUISES
SOLILOQUISING
SOLILOQUIST
SOLILOQUISTS
SOLILOQUIZE
SOLILOQUIZED
SOLILOQUIZER
SOLILOQUIZERS
SOLILOQUIZES
SOLILOQUIZING
SOLIPEDOUS
SOLIPSISMS
SOLIPSISTIC
SOLIPSISTICALLY
SOLIPSISTS
SOLITAIRES
SOLITARIAN
SOLITARIANS
SOLITARIES
SOLITARILY
SOLITARINESS
SOLITARINESSES

SOLITUDINARIAN
SOLITUDINARIANS
SOLITUDINOUS
SOLIVAGANT
SOLIVAGANTS
SOLLICKERS
SOLMISATION
SOLMISATIONS
SOLMIZATION
SOLMIZATIONS
SOLONCHAKS
SOLONETSES
SOLONETZES
SOLONETZIC
SOLONISATION
SOLONISATIONS
SOLONIZATION
SOLONIZATIONS
SOLSTITIAL
SOLSTITIALLY
SOLUBILISATION
SOLUBILISATIONS
SOLUBILISE
SOLUBILISED
SOLUBILISES
SOLUBILISING
SOLUBILITIES
SOLUBILITY
SOLUBILIZATION
SOLUBILIZATIONS
SOLUBILIZE
SOLUBILIZED
SOLUBILIZES
SOLUBILIZING
SOLUBLENESS
SOLUBLENESSES
SOLUTIONAL
SOLUTIONED
SOLUTIONING
SOLUTIONIST
SOLUTIONISTS
SOLVABILITIES
SOLVABILITY
SOLVABLENESS
SOLVABLENESSES
SOLVATIONS
SOLVENCIES
SOLVENTLESS
SOLVOLYSES
SOLVOLYSIS
SOLVOLYTIC
SOMAESTHESIA
SOMAESTHESIAS
SOMAESTHESIS
SOMAESTHESISES
SOMAESTHETIC
SOMASCOPES
SOMATICALLY
SOMATOGENIC
SOMATOLOGIC
SOMATOLOGICAL
SOMATOLOGICALLY
SOMATOLOGIES
SOMATOLOGIST
SOMATOLOGISTS
SOMATOLOGY
SOMATOMEDIN
SOMATOMEDINS
SOMATOPLASM
SOMATOPLASMS
SOMATOPLASTIC
SOMATOPLEURAL
SOMATOPLEURE
SOMATOPLEURES
SOMATOPLEURIC
SOMATOSENSORY
SOMATOSTATIN
SOMATOSTATINS
SOMATOTENSIC
SOMATOTONIA
SOMATOTONIAS
SOMATOTONIC
SOMATOTONICS
SOMATOTROPHIC
SOMATOTROPHIN
SOMATOTROPHINS
SOMATOTROPIC
SOMATOTROPIN
SOMATOTROPINE
SOMATOTROPINES
SOMATOTROPINS
SOMATOTYPE
SOMATOTYPED
SOMATOTYPES
SOMATOTYPING
SOMBERNESS
SOMBERNESSES
SOMBRENESS
SOMBRENESSES
SOMBRERITE
SOMBRERITES
SOMEBODIES
SOMEPLACES
SOMERSAULT
SOMERSAULTED
SOMERSAULTING
SOMERSAULTS
SOMERSETED
SOMERSETING
SOMERSETTED
SOMERSETTING
SOMESTHESIA
SOMESTHESIAS
SOMESTHESIS
SOMESTHESISES
SOMESTHETIC
SOMETHINGS
SOMEWHENCE
SOMEWHERES
SOMEWHILES
SOMEWHITHER
SOMMELIERS
SOMNAMBULANCE
SOMNAMBULANCES
SOMNAMBULANT
SOMNAMBULANTS
SOMNAMBULAR
SOMNAMBULARY
SOMNAMBULATE
SOMNAMBULATED
SOMNAMBULATES
SOMNAMBULATING
SOMNAMBULATION
SOMNAMBULATIONS
SOMNAMBULATOR
SOMNAMBULATORS
SOMNAMBULE
SOMNAMBULES
SOMNAMBULIC
SOMNAMBULISM
SOMNAMBULISMS
SOMNAMBULIST
SOMNAMBULISTIC
SOMNAMBULISTS
SOMNIATING
SOMNIATIVE
SOMNIATORY
SOMNIFACIENT
SOMNIFACIENTS
SOMNIFEROUS
SOMNIFEROUSLY
SOMNILOQUENCE
SOMNILOQUENCES
SOMNILOQUIES
SOMNILOQUISE
SOMNILOQUISED
SOMNILOQUISES
SOMNILOQUISING
SOMNILOQUISM
SOMNILOQUISMS
SOMNILOQUIST
SOMNILOQUISTS
SOMNILOQUIZE
SOMNILOQUIZED
SOMNILOQUIZES
SOMNILOQUIZING
SOMNILOQUOUS
SOMNILOQUY
SOMNOLENCE
SOMNOLENCES
SOMNOLENCIES
SOMNOLENCY
SOMNOLENTLY
SOMNOLESCENT
SONGCRAFTS
SONGFULNESS
SONGFULNESSES
SONGLESSLY
SONGOLOLOS
SONGSHEETS
SONGSMITHS
SONGSTRESS
SONGSTRESSES
SONGWRITER
SONGWRITERS
SONGWRITING
SONGWRITINGS
SONICATING
SONICATION
SONICATIONS
SONICATORS
SONIFEROUS
SONNETEERING
SONNETEERINGS
SONNETEERS
SONNETISED
SONNETISES
SONNETISING
SONNETIZED
SONNETIZES
SONNETIZING
SONNETTING
SONOFABITCH
SONOGRAPHER
SONOGRAPHERS
SONOGRAPHIES
SONOGRAPHS
SONOGRAPHY
SONOMETERS
SONORITIES
SONOROUSLY
SONOROUSNESS
SONOROUSNESSES
SOOTERKINS
SOOTFLAKES
SOOTHERING
SOOTHFASTLY
SOOTHFASTNESS
SOOTHFASTNESSES
SOOTHINGLY
SOOTHINGNESS
SOOTHINGNESSES
SOOTHSAYER
SOOTHSAYERS
SOOTHSAYING
SOOTHSAYINGS
SOOTINESSES
SOPAIPILLA
SOPAIPILLAS
SOPAPILLAS
SOPHISTERS
SOPHISTICAL
SOPHISTICALLY
SOPHISTICATE
SOPHISTICATED
SOPHISTICATEDLY
SOPHISTICATES
SOPHISTICATING
SOPHISTICATION
SOPHISTICATIONS

SOPHISTICATOR
SOPHISTICATORS
SOPHISTRIES
SOPHOMORES
SOPHOMORIC
SOPHOMORICAL
SOPORIFEROUS
SOPORIFEROUSLY
SOPORIFICALLY
SOPORIFICS
SOPPINESSES
SOPRANINOS
SOPRANISTS
SORBABILITIES
SORBABILITY
SORBEFACIENT
SORBEFACIENTS
SORBITISATION
SORBITISATIONS
SORBITISED
SORBITISES
SORBITISING
SORBITIZATION
SORBITIZATIONS
SORBITIZED
SORBITIZES
SORBITIZING
SORCERESSES
SORDAMENTE
SORDIDNESS
SORDIDNESSES
SOREHEADED
SOREHEADEDLY
SOREHEADEDNESS
SORENESSES
SORICIDENT
SORORIALLY
SORORICIDAL
SORORICIDE
SORORICIDES
SORORISING
SORORITIES
SORORIZING
SORRINESSES
SORROWFULLY
SORROWFULNESS
SORROWFULNESSES
SORROWINGS
SORROWLESS
SORTATIONS
SORTILEGER
SORTILEGERS
SORTILEGES
SORTILEGIES
SORTITIONS
SOSTENUTOS
SOTERIOLOGIC
SOTERIOLOGICAL
SOTERIOLOGIES
SOTERIOLOGY
SOTTISHNESS
SOTTISHNESSES
SOTTISIERS
SOUBRETTES
SOUBRETTISH
SOUBRIQUET
SOUBRIQUETS
SOULDIERED
SOULDIERING
SOULFULNESS
SOULFULNESSES
SOULLESSLY
SOULLESSNESS
SOULLESSNESSES
SOUNDALIKE
SOUNDALIKES
SOUNDBITES
SOUNDBOARD
SOUNDBOARDS
SOUNDBOXES
SOUNDCARDS
SOUNDINGLY
SOUNDLESSLY
SOUNDLESSNESS
SOUNDLESSNESSES
SOUNDNESSES
SOUNDPOSTS
SOUNDPROOF
SOUNDPROOFED
SOUNDPROOFING
SOUNDPROOFINGS
SOUNDPROOFS
SOUNDSCAPE
SOUNDSCAPES
SOUNDSTAGE
SOUNDSTAGES
SOUNDTRACK
SOUNDTRACKED
SOUNDTRACKING
SOUNDTRACKS
SOUPINESSES
SOUPSPOONS
SOURCEBOOK
SOURCEBOOKS
SOURCELESS
SOURDELINE
SOURDELINES
SOURDOUGHS
SOURNESSES
SOURPUSSES
SOUSAPHONE
SOUSAPHONES
SOUSAPHONIST
SOUSAPHONISTS
SOUTENEURS
SOUTERRAIN
SOUTERRAINS
SOUTHBOUND
SOUTHEASTER
SOUTHEASTERLIES
SOUTHEASTERLY
SOUTHEASTERN
SOUTHEASTERS
SOUTHEASTS
SOUTHEASTWARD
SOUTHEASTWARDS
SOUTHERING
SOUTHERLIES
SOUTHERLINESS
SOUTHERLINESSES
SOUTHERMOST
SOUTHERNER
SOUTHERNERS
SOUTHERNISE
SOUTHERNISED
SOUTHERNISES
SOUTHERNISING
SOUTHERNISM
SOUTHERNISMS
SOUTHERNIZE
SOUTHERNIZED
SOUTHERNIZES
SOUTHERNIZING
SOUTHERNLY
SOUTHERNMOST
SOUTHERNNESS
SOUTHERNNESSES
SOUTHERNWOOD
SOUTHERNWOODS
SOUTHLANDER
SOUTHLANDERS
SOUTHLANDS
SOUTHSAYING
SOUTHWARDLY
SOUTHWARDS
SOUTHWESTER
SOUTHWESTERLIES
SOUTHWESTERLY
SOUTHWESTERN
SOUTHWESTERS
SOUTHWESTS
SOUTHWESTWARD
SOUTHWESTWARDLY
SOUTHWESTWARDS
SOUVENIRED
SOUVENIRING
SOUVLAKIAS
SOVENANCES
SOVEREIGNLY
SOVEREIGNS
SOVEREIGNTIES
SOVEREIGNTIST
SOVEREIGNTISTS
SOVEREIGNTY
SOVIETISATION
SOVIETISATIONS
SOVIETISED
SOVIETISES
SOVIETISING
SOVIETISMS
SOVIETISTIC
SOVIETISTS
SOVIETIZATION
SOVIETIZATIONS
SOVIETIZED
SOVIETIZES
SOVIETIZING
SOVIETOLOGICAL
SOVIETOLOGIST
SOVIETOLOGISTS
SOVRANTIES
SOWBELLIES
SOYBURGERS
SPACEBANDS
SPACEBORNE
SPACECRAFT
SPACECRAFTS
SPACEFARING
SPACEFARINGS
SPACEFLIGHT
SPACEFLIGHTS
SPACEPLANE
SPACEPLANES
SPACEPORTS
SPACESHIPS
SPACESUITS
SPACETIMES
SPACEWALKED
SPACEWALKER
SPACEWALKERS
SPACEWALKING
SPACEWALKS
SPACEWOMAN
SPACEWOMEN
SPACINESSES
SPACIOUSLY
SPACIOUSNESS
SPACIOUSNESSES
SPADASSINS
SPADEFISHES
SPADEFOOTS
SPADEWORKS
SPADICEOUS
SPADICIFLORAL
SPADILLIOS
SPAGHETTIFIED
SPAGHETTIFIES
SPAGHETTIFY
SPAGHETTIFYING
SPAGHETTILIKE
SPAGHETTINI
SPAGHETTINIS
SPAGHETTIS
SPAGIRISTS
SPAGYRICAL
SPAGYRICALLY
SPAGYRISTS
SPALLATION
SPALLATIONS
SPANAEMIAS

SPANAKOPITA
SPANAKOPITAS
SPANCELING
SPANCELLED
SPANCELLING
SPANGHEWED
SPANGHEWING
SPANGLIEST
SPANGLINGS
SPANIELLED
SPANIELLING
SPANIOLATE
SPANIOLATED
SPANIOLATES
SPANIOLATING
SPANIOLISE
SPANIOLISED
SPANIOLISES
SPANIOLISING
SPANIOLIZE
SPANIOLIZED
SPANIOLIZES
SPANIOLIZING
SPANKINGLY
SPANOKOPITA
SPANOKOPITAS
SPARAGMATIC
SPARAGRASS
SPARAGRASSES
SPARAXISES
SPARENESSES
SPARGANIUM
SPARGANIUMS
SPARINGNESS
SPARINGNESSES
SPARKISHLY
SPARKLEBERRIES
SPARKLEBERRY
SPARKLESSLY
SPARKLIEST
SPARKLINGLY
SPARKLINGS
SPARKPLUGGED
SPARKPLUGGING
SPARKPLUGS
SPARROWFART
SPARROWFARTS
SPARROWGRASS
SPARROWGRASSES
SPARROWHAWK
SPARROWHAWKS
SPARROWLIKE
SPARSENESS
SPARSENESSES
SPARSITIES
SPARTEINES
SPARTERIES
SPARTICLES
SPASMATICAL
SPASMODICAL
SPASMODICALLY
SPASMODIST
SPASMODISTS
SPASMOLYTIC
SPASMOLYTICS
SPASTICALLY
SPASTICITIES
SPASTICITY
SPATANGOID
SPATANGOIDS
SPATCHCOCK
SPATCHCOCKED
SPATCHCOCKING
SPATCHCOCKS
SPATHACEOUS
SPATHIPHYLLUM
SPATHIPHYLLUMS
SPATHULATE
SPATIALISATION
SPATIALISATIONS
SPATIALITIES
SPATIALITY
SPATIALIZATION
SPATIALIZATIONS
SPATIOTEMPORAL
SPATTERDASH
SPATTERDASHES
SPATTERDOCK
SPATTERDOCKS
SPATTERING
SPATTERWORK
SPATTERWORKS
SPEAKEASIES
SPEAKERINE
SPEAKERINES
SPEAKERPHONE
SPEAKERPHONES
SPEAKERSHIP
SPEAKERSHIPS
SPEAKINGLY
SPEARCARRIER
SPEARCARRIERS
SPEARFISHED
SPEARFISHES
SPEARFISHING
SPEARHEADED
SPEARHEADING
SPEARHEADS
SPEARMINTS
SPEARWORTS
SPECIALEST
SPECIALISATION
SPECIALISATIONS
SPECIALISE
SPECIALISED
SPECIALISER
SPECIALISERS
SPECIALISES
SPECIALISING
SPECIALISM
SPECIALISMS
SPECIALIST
SPECIALISTIC
SPECIALISTS
SPECIALITIES
SPECIALITY
SPECIALIZATION
SPECIALIZATIONS
SPECIALIZE
SPECIALIZED
SPECIALIZER
SPECIALIZERS
SPECIALIZES
SPECIALIZING
SPECIALLED
SPECIALLING
SPECIALNESS
SPECIALNESSES
SPECIALOGUE
SPECIALOGUES
SPECIALTIES
SPECIATING
SPECIATION
SPECIATIONAL
SPECIATIONS
SPECIESISM
SPECIESISMS
SPECIESIST
SPECIESISTS
SPECIFIABLE
SPECIFICAL
SPECIFICALLY
SPECIFICATE
SPECIFICATED
SPECIFICATES
SPECIFICATING
SPECIFICATION
SPECIFICATIONS
SPECIFICATIVE
SPECIFICATORY
SPECIFICITIES
SPECIFICITY
SPECIFIERS
SPECIFYING
SPECIOCIDE
SPECIOCIDES
SPECIOSITIES
SPECIOSITY
SPECIOUSLY
SPECIOUSNESS
SPECIOUSNESSES
SPECKLEDNESS
SPECKLEDNESSES
SPECKSIONEER
SPECKSIONEERS
SPECKTIONEER
SPECKTIONEERS
SPECTACLED
SPECTACLES
SPECTACULAR
SPECTACULARITY
SPECTACULARLY
SPECTACULARS
SPECTATING
SPECTATORIAL
SPECTATORS
SPECTATORSHIP
SPECTATORSHIPS
SPECTATRESS
SPECTATRESSES
SPECTATRICES
SPECTATRIX
SPECTATRIXES
SPECTINOMYCIN
SPECTINOMYCINS
SPECTRALITIES
SPECTRALITY
SPECTRALLY
SPECTRALNESS
SPECTRALNESSES
SPECTROGRAM
SPECTROGRAMS
SPECTROGRAPH
SPECTROGRAPHIC
SPECTROGRAPHIES
SPECTROGRAPHS
SPECTROGRAPHY
SPECTROLOGICAL
SPECTROLOGIES
SPECTROLOGY
SPECTROMETER
SPECTROMETERS
SPECTROMETRIC
SPECTROMETRIES
SPECTROMETRY
SPECTROSCOPE
SPECTROSCOPES
SPECTROSCOPIC
SPECTROSCOPICAL
SPECTROSCOPIES
SPECTROSCOPIST
SPECTROSCOPISTS
SPECTROSCOPY
SPECULARITIES
SPECULARITY
SPECULARLY
SPECULATED
SPECULATES
SPECULATING
SPECULATION
SPECULATIONS
SPECULATIST
SPECULATISTS
SPECULATIVE
SPECULATIVELY
SPECULATIVENESS
SPECULATOR
SPECULATORS
SPECULATORY
SPECULATRICE

SPECULATRICES
SPECULATRIX
SPECULATRIXES
SPEECHCRAFT
SPEECHCRAFTS
SPEECHFULNESS
SPEECHFULNESSES
SPEECHIFICATION
SPEECHIFIED
SPEECHIFIER
SPEECHIFIERS
SPEECHIFIES
SPEECHIFYING
SPEECHIFYINGS
SPEECHLESS
SPEECHLESSLY
SPEECHLESSNESS
SPEECHMAKER
SPEECHMAKERS
SPEECHMAKING
SPEECHMAKINGS
SPEECHWRITER
SPEECHWRITERS
SPEEDBALLED
SPEEDBALLING
SPEEDBALLINGS
SPEEDBALLS
SPEEDBOATING
SPEEDBOATINGS
SPEEDBOATS
SPEEDFREAK
SPEEDFREAKS
SPEEDFULLY
SPEEDINESS
SPEEDINESSES
SPEEDOMETER
SPEEDOMETERS
SPEEDREADING
SPEEDREADS
SPEEDSKATING
SPEEDSKATINGS
SPEEDSTERS
SPEEDWALKS
SPEEDWELLS
SPELAEOLOGICAL
SPELAEOLOGIES
SPELAEOLOGIST
SPELAEOLOGISTS
SPELAEOLOGY
SPELAEOTHEM
SPELAEOTHEMS
SPELDERING
SPELDRINGS
SPELEOLOGICAL
SPELEOLOGIES
SPELEOLOGIST
SPELEOLOGISTS
SPELEOLOGY
SPELEOTHEM
SPELEOTHEMS
SPELEOTHERAPIES
SPELEOTHERAPY
SPELLBINDER
SPELLBINDERS
SPELLBINDING
SPELLBINDINGLY
SPELLBINDS
SPELLBOUND
SPELLCHECK
SPELLCHECKED
SPELLCHECKER
SPELLCHECKERS
SPELLCHECKING
SPELLCHECKS
SPELLDOWNS
SPELLICANS
SPELLINGLY
SPELLSTOPT
SPELUNKERS
SPELUNKING
SPELUNKINGS
SPENDTHRIFT
SPENDTHRIFTS
SPERMACETI
SPERMACETIS
SPERMADUCT
SPERMADUCTS
SPERMAGONIA
SPERMAGONIUM
SPERMAPHYTE
SPERMAPHYTES
SPERMAPHYTIC
SPERMARIES
SPERMARIUM
SPERMATHECA
SPERMATHECAE
SPERMATHECAL
SPERMATHECAS
SPERMATIAL
SPERMATICAL
SPERMATICALLY
SPERMATICS
SPERMATIDS
SPERMATIUM
SPERMATOBLAST
SPERMATOBLASTIC
SPERMATOBLASTS
SPERMATOCELE
SPERMATOCELES
SPERMATOCIDAL
SPERMATOCIDE
SPERMATOCIDES
SPERMATOCYTE
SPERMATOCYTES
SPERMATOGENESES
SPERMATOGENESIS
SPERMATOGENETIC
SPERMATOGENIC
SPERMATOGENIES
SPERMATOGENOUS
SPERMATOGENY
SPERMATOGONIA
SPERMATOGONIAL
SPERMATOGONIUM
SPERMATOPHORAL
SPERMATOPHORE
SPERMATOPHORES
SPERMATOPHYTE
SPERMATOPHYTES
SPERMATOPHYTIC
SPERMATORRHEA
SPERMATORRHEAS
SPERMATORRHOEA
SPERMATORRHOEAS
SPERMATOTHECA
SPERMATOTHECAE
SPERMATOTHECAS
SPERMATOZOA
SPERMATOZOAL
SPERMATOZOAN
SPERMATOZOANS
SPERMATOZOIC
SPERMATOZOID
SPERMATOZOIDS
SPERMATOZOON
SPERMICIDAL
SPERMICIDE
SPERMICIDES
SPERMIDUCT
SPERMIDUCTS
SPERMIOGENESES
SPERMIOGENESIS
SPERMIOGENETIC
SPERMOGONE
SPERMOGONES
SPERMOGONIA
SPERMOGONIUM
SPERMOPHILE
SPERMOPHILES
SPERMOPHYTE
SPERMOPHYTES
SPERMOPHYTIC
SPERRYLITE
SPERRYLITES
SPESSARTINE
SPESSARTINES
SPESSARTITE
SPESSARTITES
SPETSNAZES
SPETZNAZES
SPEWINESSES
SPHACELATE
SPHACELATED
SPHACELATES
SPHACELATING
SPHACELATION
SPHACELATIONS
SPHACELUSES
SPHAERIDIA
SPHAERIDIUM
SPHAERITES
SPHAEROCRYSTAL
SPHAEROCRYSTALS
SPHAEROSIDERITE
SPHAGNICOLOUS
SPHAGNOLOGIES
SPHAGNOLOGIST
SPHAGNOLOGISTS
SPHAGNOLOGY
SPHAIRISTIKE
SPHAIRISTIKES
SPHALERITE
SPHALERITES
SPHENDONES
SPHENODONS
SPHENODONT
SPHENODONTS
SPHENOGRAM
SPHENOGRAMS
SPHENOIDAL
SPHENOPSID
SPHENOPSIDS
SPHERELESS
SPHERELIKE
SPHERICALITIES
SPHERICALITY
SPHERICALLY
SPHERICALNESS
SPHERICALNESSES
SPHERICITIES
SPHERICITY
SPHERISTERION
SPHERISTERIONS
SPHEROCYTE
SPHEROCYTES
SPHEROCYTOSES
SPHEROCYTOSIS
SPHEROIDAL
SPHEROIDALLY
SPHEROIDICALLY
SPHEROIDICITIES
SPHEROIDICITY
SPHEROIDISATION
SPHEROIDISE
SPHEROIDISED
SPHEROIDISES
SPHEROIDISING
SPHEROIDIZATION
SPHEROIDIZE
SPHEROIDIZED
SPHEROIDIZES
SPHEROIDIZING
SPHEROMETER
SPHEROMETERS
SPHEROPLAST
SPHEROPLASTS
SPHERULITE
SPHERULITES
SPHERULITIC
SPHINCTERAL

SPHINCTERIAL
SPHINCTERIC
SPHINCTERS
SPHINGOMYELIN
SPHINGOMYELINS
SPHINGOSINE
SPHINGOSINES
SPHINXLIKE
SPHRAGISTIC
SPHRAGISTICS
SPHYGMOGRAM
SPHYGMOGRAMS
SPHYGMOGRAPH
SPHYGMOGRAPHIC
SPHYGMOGRAPHIES
SPHYGMOGRAPHS
SPHYGMOGRAPHY
SPHYGMOLOGIES
SPHYGMOLOGY
SPHYGMOMETER
SPHYGMOMETERS
SPHYGMOPHONE
SPHYGMOPHONES
SPHYGMOSCOPE
SPHYGMOSCOPES
SPHYGMUSES
SPICEBERRIES
SPICEBERRY
SPICEBUSHES
SPICILEGES
SPICINESSES
SPICULATED
SPICULATION
SPICULATIONS
SPIDERIEST
SPIDERLIKE
SPIDERWEBS
SPIDERWOOD
SPIDERWOODS
SPIDERWORK
SPIDERWORKS
SPIDERWORT
SPIDERWORTS
SPIEGELEISEN
SPIEGELEISENS
SPIFFINESS
SPIFFINESSES
SPIFFLICATE
SPIFFLICATED
SPIFFLICATES
SPIFFLICATING
SPIFFLICATION
SPIFFLICATIONS
SPIFLICATE
SPIFLICATED
SPIFLICATES
SPIFLICATING
SPIFLICATION
SPIFLICATIONS
SPIKEFISHES
SPIKENARDS
SPIKINESSES
SPILLIKINS
SPILLOVERS
SPILOSITES
SPINACENES
SPINACEOUS
SPINACHIER
SPINACHIEST
SPINACHLIKE
SPINARAMAS
SPINDLELEGS
SPINDLESHANKS
SPINDLIEST
SPINDLINGS
SPINDRIFTS
SPINELESSLY
SPINELESSNESS
SPINELESSNESSES
SPINESCENCE
SPINESCENCES
SPINESCENT
SPINIFEROUS
SPINIFEXES
SPINIGEROUS
SPINIGRADE
SPINIGRADES
SPININESSES
SPINMEISTER
SPINMEISTERS
SPINNAKERS
SPINNERETS
SPINNERETTE
SPINNERETTES
SPINNERIES
SPINNERULE
SPINNERULES
SPINOSITIES
SPINSTERDOM
SPINSTERDOMS
SPINSTERHOOD
SPINSTERHOODS
SPINSTERIAL
SPINSTERIAN
SPINSTERISH
SPINSTERLIER
SPINSTERLIEST
SPINSTERLY
SPINSTERSHIP
SPINSTERSHIPS
SPINSTRESS
SPINSTRESSES
SPINTHARISCOPE
SPINTHARISCOPES
SPINULESCENT
SPINULIFEROUS
SPIRACULAR
SPIRACULATE
SPIRACULUM
SPIRALIFORM
SPIRALISER
SPIRALISERS
SPIRALISMS
SPIRALISTS
SPIRALITIES
SPIRALIZER
SPIRALIZERS
SPIRALLING
SPIRASTERS
SPIRATIONS
SPIRIFEROUS
SPIRILLOSES
SPIRILLOSIS
SPIRITEDLY
SPIRITEDNESS
SPIRITEDNESSES
SPIRITINGS
SPIRITISMS
SPIRITISTIC
SPIRITISTS
SPIRITLESS
SPIRITLESSLY
SPIRITLESSNESS
SPIRITOUSNESS
SPIRITOUSNESSES
SPIRITUALISE
SPIRITUALISED
SPIRITUALISER
SPIRITUALISERS
SPIRITUALISES
SPIRITUALISING
SPIRITUALISM
SPIRITUALISMS
SPIRITUALIST
SPIRITUALISTIC
SPIRITUALISTS
SPIRITUALITIES
SPIRITUALITY
SPIRITUALIZE
SPIRITUALIZED
SPIRITUALIZER
SPIRITUALIZERS
SPIRITUALIZES
SPIRITUALIZING
SPIRITUALLY
SPIRITUALNESS
SPIRITUALNESSES
SPIRITUALS
SPIRITUALTIES
SPIRITUALTY
SPIRITUELLE
SPIRITUOSITIES
SPIRITUOSITY
SPIRITUOUS
SPIRITUOUSNESS
SPIRITUSES
SPIRKETTING
SPIRKETTINGS
SPIROCHAETAEMIA
SPIROCHAETAL
SPIROCHAETE
SPIROCHAETES
SPIROCHAETOSES
SPIROCHAETOSIS
SPIROCHETAL
SPIROCHETE
SPIROCHETES
SPIROCHETOSES
SPIROCHETOSIS
SPIROGRAMS
SPIROGRAPH
SPIROGRAPHIC
SPIROGRAPHIES
SPIROGRAPHS
SPIROGRAPHY
SPIROGYRAS
SPIROMETER
SPIROMETERS
SPIROMETRIC
SPIROMETRIES
SPIROMETRY
SPIRONOLACTONE
SPIRONOLACTONES
SPIROPHORE
SPIROPHORES
SPIRULINAE
SPIRULINAS
SPISSITUDE
SPISSITUDES
SPITBALLED
SPITBALLING
SPITCHCOCK
SPITCHCOCKED
SPITCHCOCKING
SPITCHCOCKS
SPITCHERED
SPITCHERING
SPITEFULLER
SPITEFULLEST
SPITEFULLY
SPITEFULNESS
SPITEFULNESSES
SPITSTICKER
SPITSTICKERS
SPITTLEBUG
SPITTLEBUGS
SPITTLIEST
SPIVVERIES
SPLANCHNIC
SPLANCHNOCELE
SPLANCHNOCELES
SPLANCHNOLOGIES
SPLANCHNOLOGY
SPLASHBACK
SPLASHBACKS
SPLASHBOARD
SPLASHBOARDS
SPLASHDOWN
SPLASHDOWNS
SPLASHIEST

S

SPLASHINESS
SPLASHINESSES
SPLASHINGS
SPLASHPROOF
SPLATCHING
SPLATTERED
SPLATTERING
SPLATTERPUNK
SPLATTERPUNKS
SPLATTINGS
SPLAYFOOTED
SPLAYFOOTEDLY
SPLEENFULLY
SPLEENIEST
SPLEENLESS
SPLEENLIKE
SPLEENSTONE
SPLEENSTONES
SPLEENWORT
SPLEENWORTS
SPLENATIVE
SPLENDIDER
SPLENDIDEST
SPLENDIDIOUS
SPLENDIDLY
SPLENDIDNESS
SPLENDIDNESSES
SPLENDIDOUS
SPLENDIFEROUS
SPLENDIFEROUSLY
SPLENDOROUS
SPLENDOURS
SPLENDROUS
SPLENECTOMIES
SPLENECTOMISE
SPLENECTOMISED
SPLENECTOMISES
SPLENECTOMISING
SPLENECTOMIZE
SPLENECTOMIZED
SPLENECTOMIZES
SPLENECTOMIZING
SPLENECTOMY
SPLENETICAL
SPLENETICALLY
SPLENETICS
SPLENISATION
SPLENISATIONS
SPLENITISES
SPLENIUSES
SPLENIZATION
SPLENIZATIONS
SPLENOMEGALIES
SPLENOMEGALY
SPLEUCHANS
SPLINTERED
SPLINTERIER
SPLINTERIEST
SPLINTERING
SPLINTLIKE
SPLINTWOOD
SPLINTWOODS
SPLITTINGS
SPLITTISMS
SPLITTISTS
SPLODGIEST
SPLODGINESS
SPLODGINESSES
SPLOOSHING
SPLOTCHIER
SPLOTCHIEST
SPLOTCHILY
SPLOTCHINESS
SPLOTCHINESSES
SPLOTCHING
SPLURGIEST
SPLUTTERED
SPLUTTERER
SPLUTTERERS
SPLUTTERIER
SPLUTTERIEST
SPLUTTERING
SPLUTTERINGLY
SPLUTTERINGS
SPODOGRAMS
SPODOMANCIES
SPODOMANCY
SPODOMANTIC
SPODUMENES
SPOILFIVES
SPOILSPORT
SPOILSPORTS
SPOKESHAVE
SPOKESHAVES
SPOKESMANSHIP
SPOKESMANSHIPS
SPOKESPEOPLE
SPOKESPERSON
SPOKESPERSONS
SPOKESWOMAN
SPOKESWOMEN
SPOLIATING
SPOLIATION
SPOLIATIONS
SPOLIATIVE
SPOLIATORS
SPOLIATORY
SPONDAICAL
SPONDOOLICKS
SPONDULICKS
SPONDYLITIC
SPONDYLITICS
SPONDYLITIDES
SPONDYLITIS
SPONDYLITISES
SPONDYLOLYSES
SPONDYLOLYSIS
SPONDYLOSES
SPONDYLOSIS
SPONDYLOSISES
SPONDYLOUS
SPONGEABLE
SPONGEBAGS
SPONGELIKE
SPONGEWARE
SPONGEWARES
SPONGEWOOD
SPONGEWOODS
SPONGICOLOUS
SPONGIFORM
SPONGINESS
SPONGINESSES
SPONGIOBLAST
SPONGIOBLASTIC
SPONGIOBLASTS
SPONGOLOGIES
SPONGOLOGIST
SPONGOLOGISTS
SPONGOLOGY
SPONSIONAL
SPONSORIAL
SPONSORING
SPONSORSHIP
SPONSORSHIPS
SPONTANEITIES
SPONTANEITY
SPONTANEOUS
SPONTANEOUSLY
SPONTANEOUSNESS
SPOOFERIES
SPOOKERIES
SPOOKINESS
SPOOKINESSES
SPOONBAITS
SPOONBILLS
SPOONDRIFT
SPOONDRIFTS
SPOONERISM
SPOONERISMS
SPOONHOOKS
SPOONWORMS
SPORADICAL
SPORADICALLY
SPORADICALNESS
SPORANGIAL
SPORANGIOLA
SPORANGIOLE
SPORANGIOLES
SPORANGIOLUM
SPORANGIOPHORE
SPORANGIOPHORES
SPORANGIOSPORE
SPORANGIOSPORES
SPORANGIUM
SPORICIDAL
SPORICIDES
SPORIDESMS
SPOROCARPS
SPOROCYSTIC
SPOROCYSTS
SPOROCYTES
SPOROGENESES
SPOROGENESIS
SPOROGENIC
SPOROGENIES
SPOROGENOUS
SPOROGONIA
SPOROGONIAL
SPOROGONIC
SPOROGONIES
SPOROGONIUM
SPOROPHORE
SPOROPHORES
SPOROPHORIC
SPOROPHOROUS
SPOROPHYLL
SPOROPHYLLS
SPOROPHYLS
SPOROPHYTE
SPOROPHYTES
SPOROPHYTIC
SPOROPOLLENIN
SPOROPOLLENINS
SPOROTRICHOSES
SPOROTRICHOSIS
SPOROZOANS
SPOROZOITE
SPOROZOITES
SPORTABILITIES
SPORTABILITY
SPORTANCES
SPORTBIKES
SPORTCASTER
SPORTCASTERS
SPORTCOATS
SPORTFISHERMAN
SPORTFISHERMEN
SPORTFISHING
SPORTFISHINGS
SPORTFULLY
SPORTFULNESS
SPORTFULNESSES
SPORTINESS
SPORTINESSES
SPORTINGLY
SPORTIVELY
SPORTIVENESS
SPORTIVENESSES
SPORTSCAST
SPORTSCASTER
SPORTSCASTERS
SPORTSCASTS
SPORTSMANLIER
SPORTSMANLIEST
SPORTSMANLIKE
SPORTSMANLY
SPORTSMANSHIP
SPORTSMANSHIPS
SPORTSPEOPLE
SPORTSPERSON

SPORTSPERSONS
SPORTSWEAR
SPORTSWEARS
SPORTSWOMAN
SPORTSWOMEN
SPORTSWRITER
SPORTSWRITERS
SPORTSWRITING
SPORTSWRITINGS
SPORULATED
SPORULATES
SPORULATING
SPORULATION
SPORULATIONS
SPORULATIVE
SPOTLESSLY
SPOTLESSNESS
SPOTLESSNESSES
SPOTLIGHTED
SPOTLIGHTING
SPOTLIGHTS
SPOTTEDNESS
SPOTTEDNESSES
SPOTTINESS
SPOTTINESSES
SPOUSELESS
SPOYLEFULL
SPRACHGEFUHL
SPRACHGEFUHLS
SPRACKLING
SPRADDLING
SPRANGLING
SPRATTLING
SPRAUCHLED
SPRAUCHLES
SPRAUCHLING
SPRAUNCIER
SPRAUNCIEST
SPRAWLIEST
SPREADABILITIES
SPREADABILITY
SPREADABLE
SPREADEAGLED
SPREADINGLY
SPREADINGS
SPREADSHEET
SPREADSHEETS
SPREAGHERIES
SPREAGHERY
SPREATHING
SPRECHERIES
SPRECHGESANG
SPRECHGESANGS
SPRECHSTIMME
SPRECHSTIMMES
SPREETHING
SPREKELIAS
SPRIGGIEST
SPRIGHTFUL
SPRIGHTFULLY
SPRIGHTFULNESS
SPRIGHTING
SPRIGHTLESS
SPRIGHTLIER
SPRIGHTLIEST
SPRIGHTLINESS
SPRIGHTLINESSES
SPRIGTAILS
SPRINGALDS
SPRINGBOARD
SPRINGBOARDS
SPRINGBOKS
SPRINGBUCK
SPRINGBUCKS
SPRINGEING
SPRINGHAAS
SPRINGHALT
SPRINGHALTS
SPRINGHASE
SPRINGHEAD
SPRINGHEADS
SPRINGHOUSE
SPRINGHOUSES
SPRINGIEST
SPRINGINESS
SPRINGINESSES
SPRINGINGS
SPRINGKEEPER
SPRINGKEEPERS
SPRINGLESS
SPRINGLETS
SPRINGLIKE
SPRINGTAIL
SPRINGTAILS
SPRINGTIDE
SPRINGTIDES
SPRINGTIME
SPRINGTIMES
SPRINGWATER
SPRINGWATERS
SPRINGWOOD
SPRINGWOODS
SPRINGWORT
SPRINGWORTS
SPRINKLERED
SPRINKLERING
SPRINKLERS
SPRINKLING
SPRINKLINGS
SPRINTINGS
SPRITEFULLY
SPRITEFULNESS
SPRITEFULNESSES
SPRITELIER
SPRITELIEST
SPRITSAILS
SPRITZIEST
SPROUTINGS
SPRUCENESS
SPRUCENESSES
SPRYNESSES
SPUILZIEING
SPULEBLADE
SPULEBLADES
SPULYIEING
SPULZIEING
SPUMESCENCE
SPUMESCENCES
SPUMESCENT
SPUNBONDED
SPUNKINESS
SPUNKINESSES
SPURGALLED
SPURGALLING
SPURIOSITIES
SPURIOSITY
SPURIOUSLY
SPURIOUSNESS
SPURIOUSNESSES
SPUTTERERS
SPUTTERIER
SPUTTERIEST
SPUTTERING
SPUTTERINGLY
SPUTTERINGS
SPYCATCHER
SPYCATCHERS
SPYGLASSES
SPYMASTERS
SQUABASHED
SQUABASHER
SQUABASHERS
SQUABASHES
SQUABASHING
SQUABBIEST
SQUABBLERS
SQUABBLING
SQUABBLINGS
SQUADOOSHES
SQUADRONAL
SQUADRONED
SQUADRONES
SQUADRONING
SQUAILINGS
SQUALIDEST
SQUALIDITIES
SQUALIDITY
SQUALIDNESS
SQUALIDNESSES
SQUALLIEST
SQUALLINGS
SQUAMATION
SQUAMATIONS
SQUAMELLAS
SQUAMIFORM
SQUAMOSALS
SQUAMOSELY
SQUAMOSENESS
SQUAMOSENESSES
SQUAMOSITIES
SQUAMOSITY
SQUAMOUSLY
SQUAMOUSNESS
SQUAMOUSNESSES
SQUAMULOSE
SQUANDERED
SQUANDERER
SQUANDERERS
SQUANDERING
SQUANDERINGLY
SQUANDERINGS
SQUANDERMANIA
SQUANDERMANIAS
SQUAREHEAD
SQUAREHEADS
SQUARENESS
SQUARENESSES
SQUAREWISE
SQUARISHLY
SQUARISHNESS
SQUARISHNESSES
SQUARSONAGE
SQUARSONAGES
SQUASHABLE
SQUASHIEST
SQUASHINESS
SQUASHINESSES
SQUATNESSES
SQUATTERED
SQUATTERING
SQUATTIEST
SQUATTINESS
SQUATTINESSES
SQUATTINGS
SQUATTLING
SQUATTOCRACIES
SQUATTOCRACY
SQUAWBUSHES
SQUAWFISHES
SQUAWKIEST
SQUAWKINGS
SQUAWROOTS
SQUEAKERIES
SQUEAKIEST
SQUEAKINESS
SQUEAKINESSES
SQUEAKINGLY
SQUEAKINGS
SQUEALINGS
SQUEAMISHLY
SQUEAMISHNESS
SQUEAMISHNESSES
SQUEEGEEING
SQUEEZABILITIES
SQUEEZABILITY
SQUEEZABLE
SQUEEZIEST
SQUEEZINGS
SQUEGGINGS
SQUELCHERS

SQUELCHIER
SQUELCHIEST
SQUELCHING
SQUELCHINGS
SQUETEAGUE
SQUETEAGUES
SQUIBBINGS
SQUIDGIEST
SQUIFFIEST
SQUIGGLERS
SQUIGGLIER
SQUIGGLIEST
SQUIGGLING
SQUILGEEING
SQUILLIONS
SQUINANCIES
SQUINCHING
SQUINNIEST
SQUINNYING
SQUINTIEST
SQUINTINGLY
SQUINTINGS
SQUIRALITIES
SQUIRALITY
SQUIRALTIES
SQUIRARCHAL
SQUIRARCHICAL
SQUIRARCHIES
SQUIRARCHS
SQUIRARCHY
SQUIREAGES
SQUIREARCH
SQUIREARCHAL
SQUIREARCHICAL
SQUIREARCHIES
SQUIREARCHS
SQUIREARCHY
SQUIREDOMS
SQUIREHOOD
SQUIREHOODS
SQUIRELIKE
SQUIRELING
SQUIRELINGS
SQUIRESHIP
SQUIRESHIPS
SQUIRESSES
SQUIRMIEST
SQUIRMINGLY
SQUIRRELED
SQUIRRELFISH
SQUIRRELFISHES
SQUIRRELIER
SQUIRRELIEST
SQUIRRELING
SQUIRRELLED
SQUIRRELLIER
SQUIRRELLIEST
SQUIRRELLING
SQUIRRELLY
SQUIRTINGS
SQUISHIEST
SQUISHINESS
SQUISHINESSES
SQUOOSHIER
SQUOOSHIEST
SQUOOSHING
STABBINGLY
STABILATES
STABILISATION
STABILISATIONS
STABILISATOR
STABILISATORS
STABILISED
STABILISER
STABILISERS
STABILISES
STABILISING
STABILITIES
STABILIZATION
STABILIZATIONS
STABILIZATOR
STABILIZATORS
STABILIZED
STABILIZER
STABILIZERS
STABILIZES
STABILIZING
STABLEBOYS
STABLEMATE
STABLEMATES
STABLENESS
STABLENESSES
STABLISHED
STABLISHES
STABLISHING
STABLISHMENT
STABLISHMENTS
STACATIONS
STACCATISSIMO
STACKROOMS
STACKYARDS
STACTOMETER
STACTOMETERS
STADDLESTONE
STADDLESTONES
STADHOLDER
STADHOLDERATE
STADHOLDERATES
STADHOLDERS
STADHOLDERSHIP
STADHOLDERSHIPS
STADIOMETER
STADIOMETERS
STADTHOLDER
STADTHOLDERATE
STADTHOLDERATES
STADTHOLDERS
STADTHOLDERSHIP
STAFFRIDER
STAFFRIDERS
STAFFROOMS
STAGECOACH
STAGECOACHES
STAGECOACHING
STAGECOACHINGS
STAGECOACHMAN
STAGECOACHMEN
STAGECRAFT
STAGECRAFTS
STAGEHANDS
STAGEHEADS
STAGESTRUCK
STAGFLATION
STAGFLATIONARY
STAGFLATIONS
STAGGERBUSH
STAGGERBUSHES
STAGGERERS
STAGGERIER
STAGGERIEST
STAGGERING
STAGGERINGLY
STAGGERINGS
STAGHOUNDS
STAGINESSES
STAGNANCES
STAGNANCIES
STAGNANTLY
STAGNATING
STAGNATION
STAGNATIONS
STAIDNESSES
STAINABILITIES
STAINABILITY
STAINLESSES
STAINLESSLY
STAINLESSNESS
STAINLESSNESSES
STAINPROOF
STAIRCASED
STAIRCASES
STAIRCASING
STAIRCASINGS
STAIRFOOTS
STAIRHEADS
STAIRLIFTS
STAIRSTEPPED
STAIRSTEPPING
STAIRSTEPS
STAIRWELLS
STAIRWORKS
STAKEHOLDER
STAKEHOLDERS
STAKHANOVISM
STAKHANOVISMS
STAKHANOVITE
STAKHANOVITES
STAKTOMETER
STAKTOMETERS
STALACTICAL
STALACTIFORM
STALACTITAL
STALACTITE
STALACTITED
STALACTITES
STALACTITIC
STALACTITICAL
STALACTITICALLY
STALACTITIFORM
STALACTITIOUS
STALAGMITE
STALAGMITES
STALAGMITIC
STALAGMITICAL
STALAGMITICALLY
STALAGMOMETER
STALAGMOMETERS
STALAGMOMETRIES
STALAGMOMETRY
STALEMATED
STALEMATES
STALEMATING
STALENESSES
STALKINESS
STALKINESSES
STALLENGER
STALLENGERS
STALLHOLDER
STALLHOLDERS
STALLINGER
STALLINGERS
STALLMASTER
STALLMASTERS
STALWARTLY
STALWARTNESS
STALWARTNESSES
STALWORTHS
STAMINEOUS
STAMINIFEROUS
STAMINODES
STAMINODIA
STAMINODIES
STAMINODIUM
STAMMERERS
STAMMERING
STAMMERINGLY
STAMMERINGS
STAMPEDERS
STAMPEDING
STAMPEDOED
STAMPEDOING
STANCHABLE
STANCHELLED
STANCHELLING
STANCHERED
STANCHERING
STANCHINGS
STANCHIONED
STANCHIONING
STANCHIONS

S

STANCHLESS
STANCHNESS
STANCHNESSES
STANDARDBRED
STANDARDBREDS
STANDARDISATION
STANDARDISE
STANDARDISED
STANDARDISER
STANDARDISERS
STANDARDISES
STANDARDISING
STANDARDIZATION
STANDARDIZE
STANDARDIZED
STANDARDIZER
STANDARDIZERS
STANDARDIZES
STANDARDIZING
STANDARDLESS
STANDARDLY
STANDDOWNS
STANDFASTS
STANDFIRST
STANDFIRSTS
STANDGALES
STANDISHES
STANDOFFISH
STANDOFFISHLY
STANDOFFISHNESS
STANDOVERS
STANDPATTER
STANDPATTERS
STANDPATTISM
STANDPATTISMS
STANDPIPES
STANDPOINT
STANDPOINTS
STANDSTILL
STANDSTILLS
STANNARIES
STANNATORS
STANNIFEROUS
STANNOTYPE
STANNOTYPES
STAPEDECTOMIES
STAPEDECTOMY
STAPEDIUSES
STAPHYLINE
STAPHYLINID
STAPHYLINIDS
STAPHYLITIS
STAPHYLITISES
STAPHYLOCOCCAL
STAPHYLOCOCCI
STAPHYLOCOCCIC
STAPHYLOCOCCUS
STAPHYLOMA
STAPHYLOMAS
STAPHYLOMATA
STAPHYLOPLASTIC
STAPHYLOPLASTY
STAPHYLORRHAPHY
STARBOARDED
STARBOARDING
STARBOARDS
STARBURSTS
STARCHEDLY
STARCHEDNESS
STARCHEDNESSES
STARCHIEST
STARCHINESS
STARCHINESSES
STARCHLIKE
STARDRIFTS
STARFISHED
STARFISHES
STARFLOWER
STARFLOWERS
STARFRUITS
STARFUCKER
STARFUCKERS
STARFUCKING
STARFUCKINGS
STARGAZERS
STARGAZING
STARGAZINGS
STARKENING
STARKNESSES
STARLIGHTED
STARLIGHTS
STARMONGER
STARMONGERS
STAROSTIES
STARRINESS
STARRINESSES
STARSHINES
STARSTONES
STARSTRUCK
STARTINGLY
STARTLEMENT
STARTLEMENTS
STARTLIEST
STARTLINGLY
STARTLINGS
STARVATION
STARVATIONS
STARVELING
STARVELINGS
STASIDIONS
STASIMORPHIES
STASIMORPHY
STATECRAFT
STATECRAFTS
STATEHOODS
STATEHOUSE
STATEHOUSES
STATELESSNESS
STATELESSNESSES
STATELIEST
STATELINESS
STATELINESSES
STATEMENTED
STATEMENTING
STATEMENTINGS
STATEMENTS
STATEROOMS
STATESMANLIER
STATESMANLIEST
STATESMANLIKE
STATESMANLY
STATESMANSHIP
STATESMANSHIPS
STATESPERSON
STATESPERSONS
STATESWOMAN
STATESWOMEN
STATICALLY
STATICKIER
STATICKIEST
STATIONARIES
STATIONARILY
STATIONARINESS
STATIONARY
STATIONERIES
STATIONERS
STATIONERY
STATIONING
STATIONMASTER
STATIONMASTERS
STATISTICAL
STATISTICALLY
STATISTICIAN
STATISTICIANS
STATISTICS
STATOBLAST
STATOBLASTS
STATOCYSTS
STATOLATRIES
STATOLATRY
STATOLITHIC
STATOLITHS
STATOSCOPE
STATOSCOPES
STATUARIES
STATUESQUE
STATUESQUELY
STATUESQUENESS
STATUETTES
STATUSIEST
STATUTABLE
STATUTABLY
STATUTORILY
STAUNCHABLE
STAUNCHERS
STAUNCHEST
STAUNCHING
STAUNCHINGS
STAUNCHLESS
STAUNCHNESS
STAUNCHNESSES
STAUROLITE
STAUROLITES
STAUROLITIC
STAUROSCOPE
STAUROSCOPES
STAUROSCOPIC
STAVESACRE
STAVESACRES
STAVUDINES
STAYCATION
STAYCATIONS
STAYMAKERS
STEADFASTLY
STEADFASTNESS
STEADFASTNESSES
STEADINESS
STEADINESSES
STEAKETTES
STEAKHOUSE
STEAKHOUSES
STEALINGLY
STEALTHFUL
STEALTHIER
STEALTHIEST
STEALTHILY
STEALTHINESS
STEALTHINESSES
STEALTHING
STEALTHINGS
STEAMBOATS
STEAMERING
STEAMFITTER
STEAMFITTERS
STEAMINESS
STEAMINESSES
STEAMPUNKS
STEAMROLLED
STEAMROLLER
STEAMROLLERED
STEAMROLLERING
STEAMROLLERS
STEAMROLLING
STEAMROLLS
STEAMSHIPS
STEAMTIGHT
STEAMTIGHTNESS
STEAROPTENE
STEAROPTENES
STEARSMATE
STEARSMATES
STEATOCELE
STEATOCELES
STEATOLYSES
STEATOLYSIS
STEATOMATOUS
STEATOPYGA
STEATOPYGAS
STEATOPYGIA
STEATOPYGIAS

S

STEATOPYGIC
STEATOPYGOUS
STEATORRHEA
STEATORRHEAS
STEATORRHOEA
STEATORRHOEAS
STEDFASTLY
STEDFASTNESS
STEDFASTNESSES
STEELHEADS
STEELINESS
STEELINESSES
STEELMAKER
STEELMAKERS
STEELMAKING
STEELMAKINGS
STEELWARES
STEELWORKER
STEELWORKERS
STEELWORKING
STEELWORKINGS
STEELWORKS
STEELYARDS
STEENBRASES
STEENBUCKS
STEENKIRKS
STEEPDOWNE
STEEPEDOWNE
STEEPENING
STEEPINESS
STEEPINESSES
STEEPLEBUSH
STEEPLEBUSHES
STEEPLECHASE
STEEPLECHASED
STEEPLECHASER
STEEPLECHASERS
STEEPLECHASES
STEEPLECHASING
STEEPLECHASINGS
STEEPLEJACK
STEEPLEJACKS
STEEPNESSES
STEERAGEWAY
STEERAGEWAYS
STEERLINGS
STEERSMATE
STEERSMATES
STEGANOGRAM
STEGANOGRAMS
STEGANOGRAPH
STEGANOGRAPHER
STEGANOGRAPHERS
STEGANOGRAPHIC
STEGANOGRAPHIES
STEGANOGRAPHIST
STEGANOGRAPHS
STEGANOGRAPHY
STEGANOPOD
STEGANOPODOUS
STEGANOPODS
STEGNOTICS
STEGOCARPOUS
STEGOCEPHALIAN
STEGOCEPHALIANS
STEGOCEPHALOUS
STEGODONTS
STEGOMYIAS
STEGOPHILIST
STEGOPHILISTS
STEGOSAURIAN
STEGOSAURIANS
STEGOSAURS
STEGOSAURUS
STEGOSAURUSES
STEINBOCKS
STEINKIRKS
STELLARATOR
STELLARATORS
STELLATELY
STELLERIDAN
STELLERIDANS
STELLERIDS
STELLIFEROUS
STELLIFIED
STELLIFIES
STELLIFORM
STELLIFYING
STELLIFYINGS
STELLIONATE
STELLIONATES
STELLULARLY
STELLULATE
STEMMATOUS
STEMMERIES
STEMWINDER
STEMWINDERS
STENCHIEST
STENCILERS
STENCILING
STENCILINGS
STENCILLED
STENCILLER
STENCILLERS
STENCILLING
STENCILLINGS
STENOBATHIC
STENOBATHS
STENOCARDIA
STENOCARDIAS
STENOCHROME
STENOCHROMES
STENOCHROMIES
STENOCHROMY
STENOGRAPH
STENOGRAPHED
STENOGRAPHER
STENOGRAPHERS
STENOGRAPHIC
STENOGRAPHICAL
STENOGRAPHIES
STENOGRAPHING
STENOGRAPHIST
STENOGRAPHISTS
STENOGRAPHS
STENOGRAPHY
STENOHALINE
STENOPAEIC
STENOPETALOUS
STENOPHAGOUS
STENOPHYLLOUS
STENOTHERM
STENOTHERMAL
STENOTHERMS
STENOTOPIC
STENOTROPIC
STENOTYPED
STENOTYPER
STENOTYPERS
STENOTYPES
STENOTYPIC
STENOTYPIES
STENOTYPING
STENOTYPIST
STENOTYPISTS
STENTMASTER
STENTMASTERS
STENTORIAN
STEPBAIRNS
STEPBROTHER
STEPBROTHERS
STEPCHILDREN
STEPDANCER
STEPDANCERS
STEPDANCING
STEPDANCINGS
STEPDAUGHTER
STEPDAUGHTERS
STEPFAMILIES
STEPFAMILY
STEPFATHER
STEPFATHERS
STEPHANITE
STEPHANITES
STEPHANOTIS
STEPHANOTISES
STEPLADDER
STEPLADDERS
STEPMOTHER
STEPMOTHERLIER
STEPMOTHERLIEST
STEPMOTHERLY
STEPMOTHERS
STEPPARENT
STEPPARENTING
STEPPARENTINGS
STEPPARENTS
STEPSISTER
STEPSISTERS
STEPSTOOLS
STERADIANS
STERCORACEOUS
STERCORANISM
STERCORANISMS
STERCORANIST
STERCORANISTS
STERCORARIES
STERCORARIOUS
STERCORARY
STERCORATE
STERCORATED
STERCORATES
STERCORATING
STERCORICOLOUS
STERCULIACEOUS
STERCULIAS
STEREOACUITIES
STEREOACUITY
STEREOBATE
STEREOBATES
STEREOBATIC
STEREOBLIND
STEREOCARD
STEREOCARDS
STEREOCHEMICAL
STEREOCHEMISTRY
STEREOCHROME
STEREOCHROMED
STEREOCHROMES
STEREOCHROMIES
STEREOCHROMING
STEREOCHROMY
STEREOGNOSES
STEREOGNOSIS
STEREOGRAM
STEREOGRAMS
STEREOGRAPH
STEREOGRAPHED
STEREOGRAPHIC
STEREOGRAPHICAL
STEREOGRAPHIES
STEREOGRAPHING
STEREOGRAPHS
STEREOGRAPHY
STEREOISOMER
STEREOISOMERIC
STEREOISOMERISM
STEREOISOMERS
STEREOISOMETRIC
STEREOLOGICAL
STEREOLOGICALLY
STEREOLOGIES
STEREOLOGY
STEREOMETER
STEREOMETERS
STEREOMETRIC
STEREOMETRICAL
STEREOMETRIES
STEREOMETRY
STEREOPHONIC

S

STEREOPHONIES
STEREOPHONY
STEREOPSES
STEREOPSIS
STEREOPTICON
STEREOPTICONS
STEREOPTICS
STEREOREGULAR
STEREOSCOPE
STEREOSCOPES
STEREOSCOPIC
STEREOSCOPICAL
STEREOSCOPIES
STEREOSCOPIST
STEREOSCOPISTS
STEREOSCOPY
STEREOSONIC
STEREOSPECIFIC
STEREOTACTIC
STEREOTACTICAL
STEREOTAXES
STEREOTAXIA
STEREOTAXIAS
STEREOTAXIC
STEREOTAXICALLY
STEREOTAXIS
STEREOTOMIES
STEREOTOMY
STEREOTROPIC
STEREOTROPISM
STEREOTROPISMS
STEREOTYPE
STEREOTYPED
STEREOTYPER
STEREOTYPERS
STEREOTYPES
STEREOTYPIC
STEREOTYPICAL
STEREOTYPICALLY
STEREOTYPIES
STEREOTYPING
STEREOTYPINGS
STEREOTYPIST
STEREOTYPISTS
STEREOTYPY
STEREOVISION
STEREOVISIONS
STERICALLY
STERIGMATA
STERILANTS
STERILISABLE
STERILISATION
STERILISATIONS
STERILISED
STERILISER
STERILISERS
STERILISES
STERILISING
STERILITIES
STERILIZABLE
STERILIZATION
STERILIZATIONS
STERILIZED
STERILIZER
STERILIZERS
STERILIZES
STERILIZING
STERLINGLY
STERLINGNESS
STERLINGNESSES
STERNALGIA
STERNALGIAS
STERNALGIC
STERNBOARD
STERNBOARDS
STERNEBRAE
STERNFASTS
STERNFOREMOST
STERNNESSES
STERNOCOSTAL
STERNOTRIBE
STERNPORTS
STERNPOSTS
STERNSHEET
STERNSHEETS
STERNUTATION
STERNUTATIONS
STERNUTATIVE
STERNUTATIVES
STERNUTATOR
STERNUTATORIES
STERNUTATORS
STERNUTATORY
STERNWARDS
STERNWORKS
STEROIDOGENESES
STEROIDOGENESIS
STEROIDOGENIC
STERTOROUS
STERTOROUSLY
STERTOROUSNESS
STETHOSCOPE
STETHOSCOPES
STETHOSCOPIC
STETHOSCOPIES
STETHOSCOPIST
STETHOSCOPISTS
STETHOSCOPY
STEVEDORED
STEVEDORES
STEVEDORING
STEVEDORINGS
STEVENGRAPH
STEVENGRAPHS
STEWARDESS
STEWARDESSES
STEWARDING
STEWARDRIES
STEWARDSHIP
STEWARDSHIPS
STEWARTRIES
STIACCIATO
STIACCIATOS
STIBIALISM
STIBIALISMS
STICCADOES
STICCATOES
STICHARION
STICHARIONS
STICHICALLY
STICHIDIUM
STICHOLOGIES
STICHOLOGY
STICHOMETRIC
STICHOMETRICAL
STICHOMETRIES
STICHOMETRY
STICHOMYTHIA
STICHOMYTHIAS
STICHOMYTHIC
STICHOMYTHIES
STICHOMYTHY
STICKABILITIES
STICKABILITY
STICKBALLS
STICKERING
STICKHANDLE
STICKHANDLED
STICKHANDLER
STICKHANDLERS
STICKHANDLES
STICKHANDLING
STICKHANDLINGS
STICKINESS
STICKINESSES
STICKLEADER
STICKLEADERS
STICKLEBACK
STICKLEBACKS
STICKLINGS
STICKSEEDS
STICKTIGHT
STICKTIGHTS
STICKWEEDS
STICKWORKS
STICKYBEAK
STICKYBEAKED
STICKYBEAKING
STICKYBEAKS
STIDDIEING
STIFFENERS
STIFFENING
STIFFENINGS
STIFFNESSES
STIFFWARES
STIFLINGLY
STIGMARIAN
STIGMARIANS
STIGMASTEROL
STIGMASTEROLS
STIGMATICAL
STIGMATICALLY
STIGMATICS
STIGMATIFEROUS
STIGMATISATION
STIGMATISATIONS
STIGMATISE
STIGMATISED
STIGMATISER
STIGMATISERS
STIGMATISES
STIGMATISING
STIGMATISM
STIGMATISMS
STIGMATIST
STIGMATISTS
STIGMATIZATION
STIGMATIZATIONS
STIGMATIZE
STIGMATIZED
STIGMATIZER
STIGMATIZERS
STIGMATIZES
STIGMATIZING
STIGMATOPHILIA
STIGMATOPHILIAS
STIGMATOPHILIST
STIGMATOSE
STILBESTROL
STILBESTROLS
STILBOESTROL
STILBOESTROLS
STILETTOED
STILETTOES
STILETTOING
STILLATORIES
STILLATORY
STILLBIRTH
STILLBIRTHS
STILLBORNS
STILLHOUSE
STILLHOUSES
STILLICIDE
STILLICIDES
STILLIFORM
STILLNESSES
STILLROOMS
STILPNOSIDERITE
STILTBIRDS
STILTEDNESS
STILTEDNESSES
STILTINESS
STILTINESSES
STIMPMETER
STIMPMETERS
STIMULABLE
STIMULANCIES
STIMULANCY
STIMULANTS
STIMULATED

STIMULATER
STIMULATERS
STIMULATES
STIMULATING
STIMULATINGLY
STIMULATION
STIMULATIONS
STIMULATIVE
STIMULATIVES
STIMULATOR
STIMULATORS
STIMULATORY
STINGAREES
STINGBULLS
STINGFISHES
STINGINESS
STINGINESSES
STINGINGLY
STINGINGNESS
STINGINGNESSES
STINKBIRDS
STINKEROOS
STINKHORNS
STINKINGLY
STINKINGNESS
STINKINGNESSES
STINKSTONE
STINKSTONES
STINKWEEDS
STINKWOODS
STINTEDNESS
STINTEDNESSES
STINTINGLY
STIPELLATE
STIPENDIARIES
STIPENDIARY
STIPENDIATE
STIPENDIATED
STIPENDIATES
STIPENDIATING
STIPITIFORM
STIPPLINGS
STIPULABLE
STIPULACEOUS
STIPULATED
STIPULATES
STIPULATING
STIPULATION
STIPULATIONS
STIPULATOR
STIPULATORS
STIPULATORY
STIRABOUTS
STIRPICULTURE
STIRPICULTURES
STIRRINGLY
STITCHCRAFT
STITCHCRAFTS
STITCHERIES
STITCHINGS
STITCHWORK
STITCHWORKS
STITCHWORT
STITCHWORTS
STOCCADOES
STOCHASTIC
STOCHASTICALLY
STOCKADING
STOCKBREEDER
STOCKBREEDERS
STOCKBREEDING
STOCKBREEDINGS
STOCKBROKER
STOCKBROKERAGE
STOCKBROKERAGES
STOCKBROKERS
STOCKBROKING
STOCKBROKINGS
STOCKFISHES
STOCKHOLDER
STOCKHOLDERS
STOCKHOLDING
STOCKHOLDINGS
STOCKHORNS
STOCKHORSE
STOCKHORSES
STOCKINESS
STOCKINESSES
STOCKINETS
STOCKINETTE
STOCKINETTES
STOCKINGED
STOCKINGER
STOCKINGERS
STOCKINGLESS
STOCKISHLY
STOCKISHNESS
STOCKISHNESSES
STOCKJOBBER
STOCKJOBBERIES
STOCKJOBBERS
STOCKJOBBERY
STOCKJOBBING
STOCKJOBBINGS
STOCKKEEPER
STOCKKEEPERS
STOCKLISTS
STOCKLOCKS
STOCKPILED
STOCKPILER
STOCKPILERS
STOCKPILES
STOCKPILING
STOCKPILINGS
STOCKPUNISHT
STOCKROOMS
STOCKROUTE
STOCKROUTES
STOCKTAKEN
STOCKTAKES
STOCKTAKING
STOCKTAKINGS
STOCKWORKS
STOCKYARDS
STODGINESS
STODGINESSES
STOECHIOLOGICAL
STOECHIOLOGIES
STOECHIOLOGY
STOECHIOMETRIC
STOECHIOMETRIES
STOECHIOMETRY
STOICALNESS
STOICALNESSES
STOICHEIOLOGIES
STOICHEIOLOGY
STOICHEIOMETRIC
STOICHEIOMETRY
STOICHIOLOGICAL
STOICHIOLOGIES
STOICHIOLOGY
STOICHIOMETRIC
STOICHIOMETRIES
STOICHIOMETRY
STOITERING
STOKEHOLDS
STOKEHOLES
STOLENWISE
STOLIDITIES
STOLIDNESS
STOLIDNESSES
STOLONIFEROUS
STOMACHACHE
STOMACHACHES
STOMACHALS
STOMACHERS
STOMACHFUL
STOMACHFULNESS
STOMACHFULS
STOMACHICAL
STOMACHICS
STOMACHIER
STOMACHIEST
STOMACHING
STOMACHLESS
STOMACHOUS
STOMATITIC
STOMATITIDES
STOMATITIS
STOMATITISES
STOMATODAEA
STOMATODAEUM
STOMATOGASTRIC
STOMATOLOGICAL
STOMATOLOGIES
STOMATOLOGIST
STOMATOLOGISTS
STOMATOLOGY
STOMATOPLASTIES
STOMATOPLASTY
STOMATOPOD
STOMATOPODS
STOMODAEAL
STOMODAEUM
STOMODAEUMS
STOMODEUMS
STONEBOATS
STONEBORER
STONEBORERS
STONEBRASH
STONEBRASHES
STONEBREAK
STONEBREAKER
STONEBREAKERS
STONEBREAKS
STONECASTS
STONECHATS
STONECROPS
STONECUTTER
STONECUTTERS
STONECUTTING
STONECUTTINGS
STONEFISHES
STONEFLIES
STONEGROUND
STONEHANDS
STONEHORSE
STONEHORSES
STONELESSNESS
STONELESSNESSES
STONEMASON
STONEMASONRIES
STONEMASONRY
STONEMASONS
STONESHOTS
STONEWALLED
STONEWALLER
STONEWALLERS
STONEWALLING
STONEWALLINGS
STONEWALLS
STONEWARES
STONEWASHED
STONEWASHES
STONEWASHING
STONEWORKER
STONEWORKERS
STONEWORKS
STONEWORTS
STONINESSES
STONISHING
STONKERING
STONYHEARTED
STOOLBALLS
STOOPBALLS
STOOPINGLY
STOPLIGHTS
STOPPERING
STOPWATCHES
STORECARDS

S

STOREFRONT
STOREFRONTS
STOREHOUSE
STOREHOUSES
STOREKEEPER
STOREKEEPERS
STOREKEEPING
STOREKEEPINGS
STOREROOMS
STORESHIPS
STORIETTES
STORIOLOGIES
STORIOLOGIST
STORIOLOGISTS
STORIOLOGY
STORKSBILL
STORKSBILLS
STORMBIRDS
STORMBOUND
STORMCOCKS
STORMFULLY
STORMFULNESS
STORMFULNESSES
STORMINESS
STORMINESSES
STORMPROOF
STORMSTAYED
STORYBOARD
STORYBOARDED
STORYBOARDING
STORYBOARDS
STORYBOOKS
STORYETTES
STORYLINES
STORYTELLER
STORYTELLERS
STORYTELLING
STORYTELLINGS
STORYTIMES
STOTTERING
STOUTENING
STOUTHEARTED
STOUTHEARTEDLY
STOUTHERIE
STOUTHERIES
STOUTHRIEF
STOUTHRIEFS
STOUTNESSES
STOVEPIPES
STOVEWOODS
STRABISMAL
STRABISMIC
STRABISMICAL
STRABISMOMETER
STRABISMOMETERS
STRABISMUS
STRABISMUSES
STRABOMETER
STRABOMETERS
STRABOTOMIES
STRABOTOMY
STRACCHINI
STRACCHINO
STRADDLEBACK
STRADDLERS
STRADDLING
STRAGGLERS
STRAGGLIER
STRAGGLIEST
STRAGGLING
STRAGGLINGLY
STRAGGLINGS
STRAICHTER
STRAICHTEST
STRAIGHTAWAY
STRAIGHTAWAYS
STRAIGHTBRED
STRAIGHTBREDS
STRAIGHTED
STRAIGHTEDGE
STRAIGHTEDGED
STRAIGHTEDGES
STRAIGHTEN
STRAIGHTENED
STRAIGHTENER
STRAIGHTENERS
STRAIGHTENING
STRAIGHTENS
STRAIGHTER
STRAIGHTEST
STRAIGHTFORTH
STRAIGHTFORWARD
STRAIGHTING
STRAIGHTISH
STRAIGHTJACKET
STRAIGHTJACKETS
STRAIGHTLACED
STRAIGHTLY
STRAIGHTNESS
STRAIGHTNESSES
STRAIGHTWAY
STRAIGHTWAYS
STRAINEDLY
STRAININGS
STRAITENED
STRAITENING
STRAITJACKET
STRAITJACKETED
STRAITJACKETING
STRAITJACKETS
STRAITLACED
STRAITLACEDLY
STRAITLACEDNESS
STRAITNESS
STRAITNESSES
STRAITWAISTCOAT
STRAMACONS
STRAMASHED
STRAMASHES
STRAMASHING
STRAMAZONS
STRAMINEOUS
STRAMONIES
STRAMONIUM
STRAMONIUMS
STRANDEDNESS
STRANDEDNESSES
STRANDFLAT
STRANDFLATS
STRANDLINE
STRANDLINES
STRANDWOLF
STRANDWOLVES
STRANGENESS
STRANGENESSES
STRANGERED
STRANGERING
STRANGLEHOLD
STRANGLEHOLDS
STRANGLEMENT
STRANGLEMENTS
STRANGLERS
STRANGLING
STRANGULATE
STRANGULATED
STRANGULATES
STRANGULATING
STRANGULATION
STRANGULATIONS
STRANGURIES
STRAPHANGED
STRAPHANGER
STRAPHANGERS
STRAPHANGING
STRAPHANGINGS
STRAPHANGS
STRAPLESSES
STRAPLINES
STRAPONTIN
STRAPONTINS
STRAPPADOED
STRAPPADOES
STRAPPADOING
STRAPPADOS
STRAPPIEST
STRAPPINGS
STRAPWORTS
STRATAGEMS
STRATEGETIC
STRATEGETICAL
STRATEGICAL
STRATEGICALLY
STRATEGICS
STRATEGIES
STRATEGISE
STRATEGISED
STRATEGISES
STRATEGISING
STRATEGIST
STRATEGISTS
STRATEGIZE
STRATEGIZED
STRATEGIZES
STRATEGIZING
STRATHSPEY
STRATHSPEYS
STRATICULATE
STRATICULATION
STRATICULATIONS
STRATIFICATION
STRATIFICATIONS
STRATIFIED
STRATIFIES
STRATIFORM
STRATIFYING
STRATIGRAPHER
STRATIGRAPHERS
STRATIGRAPHIC
STRATIGRAPHICAL
STRATIGRAPHIES
STRATIGRAPHIST
STRATIGRAPHISTS
STRATIGRAPHY
STRATOCRACIES
STRATOCRACY
STRATOCRAT
STRATOCRATIC
STRATOCRATS
STRATOCUMULI
STRATOCUMULUS
STRATOPAUSE
STRATOPAUSES
STRATOSPHERE
STRATOSPHERES
STRATOSPHERIC
STRATOSPHERICAL
STRATOTANKER
STRATOTANKERS
STRATOVOLCANO
STRATOVOLCANOES
STRATOVOLCANOS
STRAUCHTED
STRAUCHTER
STRAUCHTEST
STRAUCHTING
STRAUGHTED
STRAUGHTER
STRAUGHTEST
STRAUGHTING
STRAVAGING
STRAVAIGED
STRAVAIGER
STRAVAIGERS
STRAVAIGING
STRAWBERRIES
STRAWBERRY
STRAWBOARD
STRAWBOARDS
STRAWFLOWER
STRAWFLOWERS

S

STRAWWEIGHT
STRAWWEIGHTS
STRAWWORMS
STRAYLINGS
STREAKIEST
STREAKINESS
STREAKINESSES
STREAKINGS
STREAKLIKE
STREAMBEDS
STREAMERED
STREAMIEST
STREAMINESS
STREAMINESSES
STREAMINGLY
STREAMINGS
STREAMLESS
STREAMLETS
STREAMLIKE
STREAMLINE
STREAMLINED
STREAMLINER
STREAMLINERS
STREAMLINES
STREAMLING
STREAMLINGS
STREAMLINING
STREAMLININGS
STREAMSIDE
STREAMSIDES
STREETAGES
STREETBOYS
STREETCARS
STREETFULS
STREETIEST
STREETKEEPER
STREETKEEPERS
STREETLAMP
STREETLAMPS
STREETLIGHT
STREETLIGHTS
STREETROOM
STREETROOMS
STREETSCAPE
STREETSCAPES
STREETSMART
STREETWALKER
STREETWALKERS
STREETWALKING
STREETWALKINGS
STREETWARD
STREETWARDS
STREETWEAR
STREETWEARS
STREETWISE
STREIGNING
STRELITZES
STRELITZIA
STRELITZIAS
STRENGTHEN
STRENGTHENED
STRENGTHENER
STRENGTHENERS
STRENGTHENING
STRENGTHENINGS
STRENGTHENS
STRENGTHFUL
STRENGTHLESS
STRENUITIES
STRENUOSITIES
STRENUOSITY
STRENUOUSLY
STRENUOUSNESS
STRENUOUSNESSES
STREPEROUS
STREPHOSYMBOLIA
STREPITANT
STREPITATION
STREPITATIONS
STREPITOSO
STREPITOUS
STREPSIPTEROUS
STREPTOBACILLI
STREPTOBACILLUS
STREPTOCARPUS
STREPTOCARPUSES
STREPTOCOCCAL
STREPTOCOCCI
STREPTOCOCCIC
STREPTOCOCCUS
STREPTOKINASE
STREPTOKINASES
STREPTOLYSIN
STREPTOLYSINS
STREPTOMYCES
STREPTOMYCETE
STREPTOMYCETES
STREPTOMYCIN
STREPTOMYCINS
STREPTOSOLEN
STREPTOSOLENS
STREPTOTHRICIN
STREPTOTHRICINS
STRESSBUSTER
STRESSBUSTERS
STRESSBUSTING
STRESSFULLY
STRESSFULNESS
STRESSFULNESSES
STRESSIEST
STRESSLESS
STRESSLESSNESS
STRETCHABILITY
STRETCHABLE
STRETCHERED
STRETCHERING
STRETCHERS
STRETCHIER
STRETCHIEST
STRETCHINESS
STRETCHINESSES
STRETCHING
STRETCHINGS
STRETCHLESS
STRETCHMARKS
STREWMENTS
STRIATIONS
STRIATURES
STRICKENLY
STRICKLING
STRICTIONS
STRICTNESS
STRICTNESSES
STRICTURED
STRICTURES
STRIDDLING
STRIDELEGGED
STRIDELEGS
STRIDENCES
STRIDENCIES
STRIDENTLY
STRIDEWAYS
STRIDULANCE
STRIDULANCES
STRIDULANT
STRIDULANTLY
STRIDULATE
STRIDULATED
STRIDULATES
STRIDULATING
STRIDULATION
STRIDULATIONS
STRIDULATOR
STRIDULATORS
STRIDULATORY
STRIDULOUS
STRIDULOUSLY
STRIDULOUSNESS
STRIFELESS
STRIGIFORM
STRIKEBOUND
STRIKEBREAKER
STRIKEBREAKERS
STRIKEBREAKING
STRIKEBREAKINGS
STRIKELESS
STRIKEOUTS
STRIKEOVER
STRIKEOVERS
STRIKINGLY
STRIKINGNESS
STRIKINGNESSES
STRINGBOARD
STRINGBOARDS
STRINGCOURSE
STRINGCOURSES
STRINGENCIES
STRINGENCY
STRINGENDO
STRINGENTLY
STRINGENTNESS
STRINGENTNESSES
STRINGHALT
STRINGHALTED
STRINGHALTS
STRINGIEST
STRINGINESS
STRINGINESSES
STRINGINGS
STRINGLESS
STRINGLIKE
STRINGPIECE
STRINGPIECES
STRINGYBARK
STRINGYBARKS
STRINKLING
STRINKLINGS
STRIPAGRAM
STRIPAGRAMS
STRIPELESS
STRIPINESS
STRIPINESSES
STRIPLINGS
STRIPOGRAM
STRIPOGRAMS
STRIPPABLE
STRIPPAGRAM
STRIPPAGRAMS
STRIPPERGRAM
STRIPPERGRAMS
STRIPPINGS
STRIPTEASE
STRIPTEASER
STRIPTEASERS
STRIPTEASES
STRIVINGLY
STROBILACEOUS
STROBILATE
STROBILATED
STROBILATES
STROBILATING
STROBILATION
STROBILATIONS
STROBILIFORM
STROBILINE
STROBILISATION
STROBILISATIONS
STROBILIZATION
STROBILIZATIONS
STROBILOID
STROBILUSES
STROBOSCOPE
STROBOSCOPES
STROBOSCOPIC
STROBOSCOPICAL
STROBOTRON
STROBOTRONS
STRODDLING
STROGANOFF
STROGANOFFS

STROKEPLAY
STROLLINGS
STROMATOLITE
STROMATOLITES
STROMATOLITIC
STROMATOUS
STROMBULIFEROUS
STROMBULIFORM
STROMBUSES
STRONGARMED
STRONGARMING
STRONGARMS
STRONGBOXES
STRONGHOLD
STRONGHOLDS
STRONGNESS
STRONGNESSES
STRONGPOINT
STRONGPOINTS
STRONGROOM
STRONGROOMS
STRONGYLES
STRONGYLOID
STRONGYLOIDOSES
STRONGYLOIDOSIS
STRONGYLOIDS
STRONGYLOSES
STRONGYLOSIS
STRONTIANITE
STRONTIANITES
STRONTIANS
STRONTIUMS
STROPHANTHIN
STROPHANTHINS
STROPHANTHUS
STROPHANTHUSES
STROPHICAL
STROPHIOLATE
STROPHIOLATED
STROPHIOLE
STROPHIOLES
STROPHOIDS
STROPHULUS
STROPPIEST
STROPPINESS
STROPPINESSES
STROUDINGS
STROUPACHS
STRUCTURAL
STRUCTURALISE
STRUCTURALISED
STRUCTURALISES
STRUCTURALISING
STRUCTURALISM
STRUCTURALISMS
STRUCTURALIST
STRUCTURALISTS
STRUCTURALIZE
STRUCTURALIZED
STRUCTURALIZES
STRUCTURALIZING
STRUCTURALLY
STRUCTURATION
STRUCTURATIONS
STRUCTURED
STRUCTURELESS
STRUCTURES
STRUCTURING
STRUGGLERS
STRUGGLING
STRUGGLINGLY
STRUGGLINGS
STRUMITISES
STRUMPETED
STRUMPETING
STRUTHIOID
STRUTHIOIDS
STRUTHIOUS
STRUTTINGLY
STRUTTINGS
STRYCHNIAS
STRYCHNINE
STRYCHNINED
STRYCHNINES
STRYCHNINING
STRYCHNINISM
STRYCHNINISMS
STRYCHNISM
STRYCHNISMS
STUBBINESS
STUBBINESSES
STUBBLIEST
STUBBORNED
STUBBORNER
STUBBORNEST
STUBBORNING
STUBBORNLY
STUBBORNNESS
STUBBORNNESSES
STUCCOWORK
STUCCOWORKS
STUDDINGSAIL
STUDDINGSAILS
STUDENTIER
STUDENTIEST
STUDENTRIES
STUDENTSHIP
STUDENTSHIPS
STUDFISHES
STUDHORSES
STUDIEDNESS
STUDIEDNESSES
STUDIOUSLY
STUDIOUSNESS
STUDIOUSNESSES
STUFFINESS
STUFFINESSES
STULTIFICATION
STULTIFICATIONS
STULTIFIED
STULTIFIER
STULTIFIERS
STULTIFIES
STULTIFYING
STUMBLEBUM
STUMBLEBUMS
STUMBLIEST
STUMBLINGLY
STUMPINESS
STUMPINESSES
STUMPWORKS
STUNNINGLY
STUNTEDNESS
STUNTEDNESSES
STUNTWOMAN
STUNTWOMEN
STUPEFACIENT
STUPEFACIENTS
STUPEFACTION
STUPEFACTIONS
STUPEFACTIVE
STUPEFIERS
STUPEFYING
STUPEFYINGLY
STUPENDIOUS
STUPENDOUS
STUPENDOUSLY
STUPENDOUSNESS
STUPIDITIES
STUPIDNESS
STUPIDNESSES
STUPRATING
STUPRATION
STUPRATIONS
STURDINESS
STURDINESSES
STUTTERERS
STUTTERING
STUTTERINGLY
STUTTERINGS
STYLEBOOKS
STYLELESSNESS
STYLELESSNESSES
STYLIFEROUS
STYLISATION
STYLISATIONS
STYLISHNESS
STYLISHNESSES
STYLISTICALLY
STYLISTICS
STYLITISMS
STYLIZATION
STYLIZATIONS
STYLOBATES
STYLOGRAPH
STYLOGRAPHIC
STYLOGRAPHICAL
STYLOGRAPHIES
STYLOGRAPHS
STYLOGRAPHY
STYLOLITES
STYLOLITIC
STYLOMETRIES
STYLOMETRY
STYLOPHONE
STYLOPHONES
STYLOPISED
STYLOPISES
STYLOPISING
STYLOPIZED
STYLOPIZES
STYLOPIZING
STYLOPODIA
STYLOPODIUM
STYLOSTIXES
STYLOSTIXIS
STYPTICITIES
STYPTICITY
STYRACACEOUS
STYROFOAMS
SUABILITIES
SUASIVENESS
SUASIVENESSES
SUAVENESSES
SUAVEOLENT
SUBABDOMINAL
SUBACETATE
SUBACETATES
SUBACIDITIES
SUBACIDITY
SUBACIDNESS
SUBACIDNESSES
SUBACTIONS
SUBACUTELY
SUBADOLESCENT
SUBADOLESCENTS
SUBAERIALLY
SUBAFFLUENT
SUBAGENCIES
SUBAGGREGATE
SUBAGGREGATES
SUBAGGREGATION
SUBAGGREGATIONS
SUBAHDARIES
SUBAHSHIPS
SUBALLIANCE
SUBALLIANCES
SUBALLOCATION
SUBALLOCATIONS
SUBALTERNANT
SUBALTERNANTS
SUBALTERNATE
SUBALTERNATES
SUBALTERNATION
SUBALTERNATIONS
SUBALTERNITIES
SUBALTERNITY
SUBALTERNS
SUBANGULAR
SUBANTARCTIC

S

SUBAPOSTOLIC
SUBAPPEARANCE
SUBAPPEARANCES
SUBAQUATIC
SUBAQUEOUS
SUBARACHNOID
SUBARACHNOIDAL
SUBARACHNOIDS
SUBARBOREAL
SUBARBORESCENT
SUBARCTICS
SUBARCUATE
SUBARCUATION
SUBARCUATIONS
SUBARRATION
SUBARRATIONS
SUBARRHATION
SUBARRHATIONS
SUBARTICLE
SUBARTICLES
SUBASSEMBLE
SUBASSEMBLED
SUBASSEMBLES
SUBASSEMBLIES
SUBASSEMBLING
SUBASSEMBLY
SUBASSOCIATION
SUBASSOCIATIONS
SUBATMOSPHERIC
SUBATOMICS
SUBAUDIBLE
SUBAUDITION
SUBAUDITIONS
SUBAURICULAR
SUBAVERAGE
SUBAXILLARY
SUBBASEMENT
SUBBASEMENTS
SUBBITUMINOUS
SUBBRANCHES
SUBBUREAUS
SUBBUREAUX
SUBCABINET
SUBCABINETS
SUBCALIBER
SUBCALIBRE
SUBCANTORS
SUBCAPSULAR
SUBCARDINAL
SUBCARDINALS
SUBCARRIER
SUBCARRIERS
SUBCATEGORIES
SUBCATEGORISE
SUBCATEGORISED
SUBCATEGORISES
SUBCATEGORISING
SUBCATEGORIZE
SUBCATEGORIZED
SUBCATEGORIZES
SUBCATEGORIZING
SUBCATEGORY
SUBCAVITIES
SUBCEILING
SUBCEILINGS
SUBCELESTIAL
SUBCELESTIALS
SUBCELLARS
SUBCELLULAR
SUBCENTERS
SUBCENTRAL
SUBCENTRALLY
SUBCENTRES
SUBCEPTION
SUBCEPTIONS
SUBCHANTER
SUBCHANTERS
SUBCHAPTER
SUBCHAPTERS
SUBCHARTER
SUBCHARTERED
SUBCHARTERING
SUBCHARTERS
SUBCHASERS
SUBCHELATE
SUBCHLORIDE
SUBCHLORIDES
SUBCIRCUIT
SUBCIRCUITS
SUBCIVILISATION
SUBCIVILISED
SUBCIVILIZATION
SUBCIVILIZED
SUBCLASSED
SUBCLASSES
SUBCLASSIFIED
SUBCLASSIFIES
SUBCLASSIFY
SUBCLASSIFYING
SUBCLASSING
SUBCLAUSES
SUBCLAVIAN
SUBCLAVIANS
SUBCLAVICULAR
SUBCLIMACTIC
SUBCLIMAXES
SUBCLINICAL
SUBCLINICALLY
SUBCLUSTER
SUBCLUSTERED
SUBCLUSTERING
SUBCLUSTERS
SUBCOLLECTION
SUBCOLLECTIONS
SUBCOLLEGE
SUBCOLLEGES
SUBCOLLEGIATE
SUBCOLONIES
SUBCOMMISSION
SUBCOMMISSIONED
SUBCOMMISSIONER
SUBCOMMISSIONS
SUBCOMMITTEE
SUBCOMMITTEES
SUBCOMMUNITIES
SUBCOMMUNITY
SUBCOMPACT
SUBCOMPACTS
SUBCOMPONENT
SUBCOMPONENTS
SUBCONSCIOUS
SUBCONSCIOUSES
SUBCONSCIOUSLY
SUBCONSULS
SUBCONTIGUOUS
SUBCONTINENT
SUBCONTINENTAL
SUBCONTINENTS
SUBCONTINUOUS
SUBCONTRACT
SUBCONTRACTED
SUBCONTRACTING
SUBCONTRACTINGS
SUBCONTRACTOR
SUBCONTRACTORS
SUBCONTRACTS
SUBCONTRAOCTAVE
SUBCONTRARIES
SUBCONTRARIETY
SUBCONTRARY
SUBCOOLING
SUBCORDATE
SUBCORIACEOUS
SUBCORTEXES
SUBCORTICAL
SUBCORTICES
SUBCOSTALS
SUBCOUNTIES
SUBCRANIAL
SUBCRITICAL
SUBCRUSTAL
SUBCULTURAL
SUBCULTURALLY
SUBCULTURE
SUBCULTURED
SUBCULTURES
SUBCULTURING
SUBCURATIVE
SUBCUTANEOUS
SUBCUTANEOUSLY
SUBCUTISES
SUBDEACONATE
SUBDEACONATES
SUBDEACONRIES
SUBDEACONRY
SUBDEACONS
SUBDEACONSHIP
SUBDEACONSHIPS
SUBDEALERS
SUBDEANERIES
SUBDEANERY
SUBDEBUTANTE
SUBDEBUTANTES
SUBDECANAL
SUBDECISION
SUBDECISIONS
SUBDELIRIA
SUBDELIRIOUS
SUBDELIRIUM
SUBDELIRIUMS
SUBDEPARTMENT
SUBDEPARTMENTS
SUBDEPUTIES
SUBDERMALLY
SUBDEVELOPMENT
SUBDEVELOPMENTS
SUBDIACONAL
SUBDIACONATE
SUBDIACONATES
SUBDIALECT
SUBDIALECTS
SUBDIRECTOR
SUBDIRECTORS
SUBDISCIPLINE
SUBDISCIPLINES
SUBDISTRICT
SUBDISTRICTS
SUBDIVIDABLE
SUBDIVIDED
SUBDIVIDER
SUBDIVIDERS
SUBDIVIDES
SUBDIVIDING
SUBDIVISIBLE
SUBDIVISION
SUBDIVISIONAL
SUBDIVISIONS
SUBDIVISIVE
SUBDOMINANT
SUBDOMINANTS
SUBDUCTING
SUBDUCTION
SUBDUCTIONS
SUBDUEDNESS
SUBDUEDNESSES
SUBDUEMENT
SUBDUEMENTS
SUBDUPLICATE
SUBECONOMIC
SUBECONOMIES
SUBECONOMY
SUBEDITING
SUBEDITORIAL
SUBEDITORS
SUBEDITORSHIP
SUBEDITORSHIPS
SUBEMPLOYED
SUBEMPLOYMENT
SUBEMPLOYMENTS
SUBENTRIES

S

SUBEPIDERMAL
SUBEQUATORIAL
SUBERISATION
SUBERISATIONS
SUBERISING
SUBERIZATION
SUBERIZATIONS
SUBERIZING
SUBFACTORIAL
SUBFACTORIALS
SUBFAMILIES
SUBFERTILE
SUBFERTILITIES
SUBFERTILITY
SUBFEUDATION
SUBFEUDATIONS
SUBFEUDATORY
SUBFOLDERS
SUBFOSSILS
SUBFREEZING
SUBFUSCOUS
SUBGENERATION
SUBGENERATIONS
SUBGENERIC
SUBGENERICALLY
SUBGENUSES
SUBGLACIAL
SUBGLACIALLY
SUBGLOBOSE
SUBGLOBULAR
SUBGOVERNMENT
SUBGOVERNMENTS
SUBGROUPED
SUBGROUPING
SUBHARMONIC
SUBHARMONICS
SUBHASTATION
SUBHASTATIONS
SUBHEADING
SUBHEADINGS
SUBIMAGINAL
SUBIMAGINES
SUBIMAGOES
SUBINCISED
SUBINCISES
SUBINCISING
SUBINCISION
SUBINCISIONS
SUBINDEXES
SUBINDICATE
SUBINDICATED
SUBINDICATES
SUBINDICATING
SUBINDICATION
SUBINDICATIONS
SUBINDICATIVE
SUBINDICES
SUBINDUSTRIES
SUBINDUSTRY
SUBINFEUDATE
SUBINFEUDATED
SUBINFEUDATES
SUBINFEUDATING
SUBINFEUDATION
SUBINFEUDATIONS
SUBINFEUDATORY
SUBINFEUDED
SUBINFEUDING
SUBINFEUDS
SUBINHIBITORY
SUBINSINUATION
SUBINSINUATIONS
SUBINSPECTOR
SUBINSPECTORS
SUBINTELLECTION
SUBINTELLIGENCE
SUBINTELLIGITUR
SUBINTERVAL
SUBINTERVALS
SUBINTRANT
SUBINTRODUCE
SUBINTRODUCED
SUBINTRODUCES
SUBINTRODUCING
SUBINVOLUTION
SUBINVOLUTIONS
SUBIRRIGATE
SUBIRRIGATED
SUBIRRIGATES
SUBIRRIGATING
SUBIRRIGATION
SUBIRRIGATIONS
SUBITANEOUS
SUBITISING
SUBITIZING
SUBJACENCIES
SUBJACENCY
SUBJACENTLY
SUBJECTABILITY
SUBJECTABLE
SUBJECTIFIED
SUBJECTIFIES
SUBJECTIFY
SUBJECTIFYING
SUBJECTING
SUBJECTION
SUBJECTIONS
SUBJECTIVE
SUBJECTIVELY
SUBJECTIVENESS
SUBJECTIVES
SUBJECTIVISE
SUBJECTIVISED
SUBJECTIVISES
SUBJECTIVISING
SUBJECTIVISM
SUBJECTIVISMS
SUBJECTIVIST
SUBJECTIVISTIC
SUBJECTIVISTS
SUBJECTIVITIES
SUBJECTIVITY
SUBJECTIVIZE
SUBJECTIVIZED
SUBJECTIVIZES
SUBJECTIVIZING
SUBJECTLESS
SUBJECTSHIP
SUBJECTSHIPS
SUBJOINDER
SUBJOINDERS
SUBJOINING
SUBJUGABLE
SUBJUGATED
SUBJUGATES
SUBJUGATING
SUBJUGATION
SUBJUGATIONS
SUBJUGATOR
SUBJUGATORS
SUBJUNCTION
SUBJUNCTIONS
SUBJUNCTIVE
SUBJUNCTIVELY
SUBJUNCTIVES
SUBKINGDOM
SUBKINGDOMS
SUBLANCEOLATE
SUBLANGUAGE
SUBLANGUAGES
SUBLAPSARIAN
SUBLAPSARIANISM
SUBLAPSARIANS
SUBLATIONS
SUBLEASING
SUBLESSEES
SUBLESSORS
SUBLETHALLY
SUBLETTERS
SUBLETTING
SUBLETTINGS
SUBLIBRARIAN
SUBLIBRARIANS
SUBLICENSE
SUBLICENSED
SUBLICENSES
SUBLICENSING
SUBLIEUTENANCY
SUBLIEUTENANT
SUBLIEUTENANTS
SUBLIMABLE
SUBLIMATED
SUBLIMATES
SUBLIMATING
SUBLIMATION
SUBLIMATIONS
SUBLIMENESS
SUBLIMENESSES
SUBLIMINAL
SUBLIMINALLY
SUBLIMINALS
SUBLIMINGS
SUBLIMISED
SUBLIMISES
SUBLIMISING
SUBLIMITIES
SUBLIMIZED
SUBLIMIZES
SUBLIMIZING
SUBLINEATION
SUBLINEATIONS
SUBLINGUAL
SUBLITERACIES
SUBLITERACY
SUBLITERARY
SUBLITERATE
SUBLITERATES
SUBLITERATURE
SUBLITERATURES
SUBLITTORAL
SUBLITTORALS
SUBLUXATED
SUBLUXATES
SUBLUXATING
SUBLUXATION
SUBLUXATIONS
SUBMANAGER
SUBMANAGERS
SUBMANDIBULAR
SUBMANDIBULARS
SUBMANIFOLD
SUBMANIFOLDS
SUBMARGINAL
SUBMARGINALLY
SUBMARINED
SUBMARINER
SUBMARINERS
SUBMARINES
SUBMARINING
SUBMARKETS
SUBMATRICES
SUBMATRIXES
SUBMAXILLARIES
SUBMAXILLARY
SUBMAXIMAL
SUBMEDIANT
SUBMEDIANTS
SUBMENTUMS
SUBMERGEMENT
SUBMERGEMENTS
SUBMERGENCE
SUBMERGENCES
SUBMERGIBILITY
SUBMERGIBLE
SUBMERGIBLES
SUBMERGING
SUBMERSIBILITY
SUBMERSIBLE
SUBMERSIBLES
SUBMERSING

S

SUBMERSION
SUBMERSIONS
SUBMETACENTRIC
SUBMETACENTRICS
SUBMICROGRAM
SUBMICRONS
SUBMICROSCOPIC
SUBMILLIMETER
SUBMILLIMETERS
SUBMILLIMETRE
SUBMILLIMETRES
SUBMINIATURE
SUBMINIATURES
SUBMINIATURISE
SUBMINIATURISED
SUBMINIATURISES
SUBMINIATURIZE
SUBMINIATURIZED
SUBMINIATURIZES
SUBMINIMAL
SUBMINISTER
SUBMINISTERED
SUBMINISTERING
SUBMINISTERS
SUBMISSIBLE
SUBMISSION
SUBMISSIONS
SUBMISSIVE
SUBMISSIVELY
SUBMISSIVENESS
SUBMISSNESS
SUBMISSNESSES
SUBMITTABLE
SUBMITTALS
SUBMITTERS
SUBMITTING
SUBMITTINGS
SUBMOLECULE
SUBMOLECULES
SUBMONTANE
SUBMONTANELY
SUBMUCOSAE
SUBMUCOSAL
SUBMUCOSAS
SUBMULTIPLE
SUBMULTIPLES
SUBMUNITION
SUBMUNITIONS
SUBNASCENT
SUBNATIONAL
SUBNATURAL
SUBNETWORK
SUBNETWORKED
SUBNETWORKING
SUBNETWORKS
SUBNORMALITIES
SUBNORMALITY
SUBNORMALLY
SUBNORMALS
SUBNUCLEAR
SUBNUCLEUS
SUBNUCLEUSES
SUBOCCIPITAL
SUBOCEANIC
SUBOCTAVES
SUBOCTUPLE
SUBOFFICER
SUBOFFICERS
SUBOFFICES
SUBOPERCULA
SUBOPERCULAR
SUBOPERCULUM
SUBOPERCULUMS
SUBOPTIMAL
SUBOPTIMISATION
SUBOPTIMISE
SUBOPTIMISED
SUBOPTIMISES
SUBOPTIMISING
SUBOPTIMIZATION
SUBOPTIMIZE
SUBOPTIMIZED
SUBOPTIMIZES
SUBOPTIMIZING
SUBOPTIMUM
SUBOPTIMUMS
SUBORBICULAR
SUBORBITAL
SUBORDINAL
SUBORDINANCIES
SUBORDINANCY
SUBORDINARIES
SUBORDINARY
SUBORDINATE
SUBORDINATED
SUBORDINATELY
SUBORDINATENESS
SUBORDINATES
SUBORDINATING
SUBORDINATION
SUBORDINATIONS
SUBORDINATIVE
SUBORDINATOR
SUBORDINATORS
SUBORGANISATION
SUBORGANIZATION
SUBORNATION
SUBORNATIONS
SUBORNATIVE
SUBOSCINES
SUBPANATION
SUBPANATIONS
SUBPARAGRAPH
SUBPARAGRAPHS
SUBPARALLEL
SUBPENAING
SUBPERIODS
SUBPHRENIC
SUBPHYLUMS
SUBPOENAED
SUBPOENAING
SUBPOPULATION
SUBPOPULATIONS
SUBPOTENCIES
SUBPOTENCY
SUBPREFECT
SUBPREFECTS
SUBPREFECTURE
SUBPREFECTURES
SUBPRIMATE
SUBPRIMATES
SUBPRINCIPAL
SUBPRINCIPALS
SUBPRIORESS
SUBPRIORESSES
SUBPROBLEM
SUBPROBLEMS
SUBPROCESS
SUBPROCESSES
SUBPRODUCT
SUBPRODUCTS
SUBPROFESSIONAL
SUBPROGRAM
SUBPROGRAMS
SUBPROJECT
SUBPROJECTS
SUBPROLETARIAT
SUBPROLETARIATS
SUBRATIONAL
SUBREFERENCE
SUBREFERENCES
SUBREGIONAL
SUBREGIONS
SUBRENTING
SUBREPTION
SUBREPTIONS
SUBREPTITIOUS
SUBREPTITIOUSLY
SUBREPTIVE
SUBROGATED
SUBROGATES
SUBROGATING
SUBROGATION
SUBROGATIONS
SUBROUTINE
SUBROUTINES
SUBSAMPLED
SUBSAMPLES
SUBSAMPLING
SUBSATELLITE
SUBSATELLITES
SUBSATURATED
SUBSATURATION
SUBSATURATIONS
SUBSCAPULAR
SUBSCAPULARS
SUBSCHEMATA
SUBSCIENCE
SUBSCIENCES
SUBSCRIBABLE
SUBSCRIBED
SUBSCRIBER
SUBSCRIBERS
SUBSCRIBES
SUBSCRIBING
SUBSCRIBINGS
SUBSCRIPTION
SUBSCRIPTIONS
SUBSCRIPTIVE
SUBSCRIPTS
SUBSECRETARIES
SUBSECRETARY
SUBSECTION
SUBSECTIONS
SUBSECTORS
SUBSEGMENT
SUBSEGMENTS
SUBSEIZURE
SUBSEIZURES
SUBSELLIUM
SUBSENSIBLE
SUBSENTENCE
SUBSENTENCES
SUBSEQUENCE
SUBSEQUENCES
SUBSEQUENT
SUBSEQUENTIAL
SUBSEQUENTLY
SUBSEQUENTNESS
SUBSEQUENTS
SUBSERVIENCE
SUBSERVIENCES
SUBSERVIENCIES
SUBSERVIENCY
SUBSERVIENT
SUBSERVIENTLY
SUBSERVIENTS
SUBSERVING
SUBSESSILE
SUBSHRUBBY
SUBSIDENCE
SUBSIDENCES
SUBSIDENCIES
SUBSIDENCY
SUBSIDIARIAT
SUBSIDIARIATS
SUBSIDIARIES
SUBSIDIARILY
SUBSIDIARINESS
SUBSIDIARITIES
SUBSIDIARITY
SUBSIDIARY
SUBSIDISABLE
SUBSIDISATION
SUBSIDISATIONS
SUBSIDISED
SUBSIDISER
SUBSIDISERS
SUBSIDISES
SUBSIDISING

SUBSIDIZABLE
SUBSIDIZATION
SUBSIDIZATIONS
SUBSIDIZED
SUBSIDIZER
SUBSIDIZERS
SUBSIDIZES
SUBSIDIZING
SUBSISTENCE
SUBSISTENCES
SUBSISTENT
SUBSISTENTIAL
SUBSISTERS
SUBSISTING
SUBSOCIALLY
SUBSOCIETIES
SUBSOCIETY
SUBSOILERS
SUBSOILING
SUBSOILINGS
SUBSONICALLY
SUBSPECIALISE
SUBSPECIALISED
SUBSPECIALISES
SUBSPECIALISING
SUBSPECIALIST
SUBSPECIALISTS
SUBSPECIALITIES
SUBSPECIALITY
SUBSPECIALIZE
SUBSPECIALIZED
SUBSPECIALIZES
SUBSPECIALIZING
SUBSPECIALTIES
SUBSPECIALTY
SUBSPECIES
SUBSPECIFIC
SUBSPECIFICALLY
SUBSPINOUS
SUBSPONTANEOUS
SUBSTANCELESS
SUBSTANCES
SUBSTANDARD
SUBSTANTIAL
SUBSTANTIALISE
SUBSTANTIALISED
SUBSTANTIALISES
SUBSTANTIALISM
SUBSTANTIALISMS
SUBSTANTIALIST
SUBSTANTIALISTS
SUBSTANTIALITY
SUBSTANTIALIZE
SUBSTANTIALIZED
SUBSTANTIALIZES
SUBSTANTIALLY
SUBSTANTIALNESS
SUBSTANTIALS
SUBSTANTIATE
SUBSTANTIATED
SUBSTANTIATES
SUBSTANTIATING
SUBSTANTIATION
SUBSTANTIATIONS
SUBSTANTIATIVE
SUBSTANTIATOR
SUBSTANTIATORS
SUBSTANTIVAL
SUBSTANTIVALLY
SUBSTANTIVE
SUBSTANTIVELY
SUBSTANTIVENESS
SUBSTANTIVES
SUBSTANTIVISE
SUBSTANTIVISED
SUBSTANTIVISES
SUBSTANTIVISING
SUBSTANTIVITIES
SUBSTANTIVITY
SUBSTANTIVIZE
SUBSTANTIVIZED
SUBSTANTIVIZES
SUBSTANTIVIZING
SUBSTATION
SUBSTATIONS
SUBSTELLAR
SUBSTERNAL
SUBSTITUENT
SUBSTITUENTS
SUBSTITUTABLE
SUBSTITUTE
SUBSTITUTED
SUBSTITUTES
SUBSTITUTING
SUBSTITUTION
SUBSTITUTIONAL
SUBSTITUTIONARY
SUBSTITUTIONS
SUBSTITUTIVE
SUBSTITUTIVELY
SUBSTITUTIVITY
SUBSTRACTED
SUBSTRACTING
SUBSTRACTION
SUBSTRACTIONS
SUBSTRACTOR
SUBSTRACTORS
SUBSTRACTS
SUBSTRATAL
SUBSTRATES
SUBSTRATIVE
SUBSTRATOSPHERE
SUBSTRATUM
SUBSTRATUMS
SUBSTRUCTED
SUBSTRUCTING
SUBSTRUCTION
SUBSTRUCTIONS
SUBSTRUCTS
SUBSTRUCTURAL
SUBSTRUCTURE
SUBSTRUCTURES
SUBSULTIVE
SUBSULTORILY
SUBSULTORY
SUBSULTUSES
SUBSUMABLE
SUBSUMPTION
SUBSUMPTIONS
SUBSUMPTIVE
SUBSURFACE
SUBSURFACES
SUBSYSTEMS
SUBTACKSMAN
SUBTACKSMEN
SUBTANGENT
SUBTANGENTS
SUBTEMPERATE
SUBTENANCIES
SUBTENANCY
SUBTENANTS
SUBTENDING
SUBTENURES
SUBTERFUGE
SUBTERFUGES
SUBTERMINAL
SUBTERNATURAL
SUBTERRAIN
SUBTERRAINS
SUBTERRANE
SUBTERRANEAN
SUBTERRANEANLY
SUBTERRANEANS
SUBTERRANEOUS
SUBTERRANEOUSLY
SUBTERRANES
SUBTERRENE
SUBTERRENES
SUBTERRESTRIAL
SUBTERRESTRIALS
SUBTEXTUAL
SUBTHERAPEUTIC
SUBTHRESHOLD
SUBTILENESS
SUBTILENESSES
SUBTILISATION
SUBTILISATIONS
SUBTILISED
SUBTILISER
SUBTILISERS
SUBTILISES
SUBTILISIN
SUBTILISING
SUBTILISINS
SUBTILITIES
SUBTILIZATION
SUBTILIZATIONS
SUBTILIZED
SUBTILIZER
SUBTILIZERS
SUBTILIZES
SUBTILIZING
SUBTILTIES
SUBTITLING
SUBTITLINGS
SUBTITULAR
SUBTLENESS
SUBTLENESSES
SUBTLETIES
SUBTOTALED
SUBTOTALING
SUBTOTALLED
SUBTOTALLING
SUBTOTALLY
SUBTRACTED
SUBTRACTER
SUBTRACTERS
SUBTRACTING
SUBTRACTION
SUBTRACTIONS
SUBTRACTIVE
SUBTRACTOR
SUBTRACTORS
SUBTRAHEND
SUBTRAHENDS
SUBTREASURER
SUBTREASURERS
SUBTREASURIES
SUBTREASURY
SUBTRIANGULAR
SUBTRIPLICATE
SUBTROPICAL
SUBTROPICALLY
SUBTROPICS
SUBTRUDING
SUBTWEETED
SUBTWEETING
SUBTYPICAL
SUBUMBRELLA
SUBUMBRELLAR
SUBUMBRELLAS
SUBUNGULATE
SUBUNGULATES
SUBURBANISATION
SUBURBANISE
SUBURBANISED
SUBURBANISES
SUBURBANISING
SUBURBANISM
SUBURBANISMS
SUBURBANITE
SUBURBANITES
SUBURBANITIES
SUBURBANITY
SUBURBANIZATION
SUBURBANIZE
SUBURBANIZED
SUBURBANIZES
SUBURBANIZING
SUBURBICARIAN

S

SUBVARIETIES
SUBVARIETY
SUBVASSALS
SUBVENTION
SUBVENTIONARY
SUBVENTIONS
SUBVERSALS
SUBVERSING
SUBVERSION
SUBVERSIONARIES
SUBVERSIONARY
SUBVERSIONS
SUBVERSIVE
SUBVERSIVELY
SUBVERSIVENESS
SUBVERSIVES
SUBVERTEBRAL
SUBVERTERS
SUBVERTICAL
SUBVERTING
SUBVIRUSES
SUBVISIBLE
SUBVITREOUS
SUBVOCALISATION
SUBVOCALISE
SUBVOCALISED
SUBVOCALISES
SUBVOCALISING
SUBVOCALIZATION
SUBVOCALIZE
SUBVOCALIZED
SUBVOCALIZES
SUBVOCALIZING
SUBVOCALLY
SUBWARDENS
SUBWOOFERS
SUBWRITERS
SUCCEDANEA
SUCCEDANEOUS
SUCCEDANEUM
SUCCEDANEUMS
SUCCEDENTS
SUCCEEDABLE
SUCCEEDERS
SUCCEEDING
SUCCEEDINGLY
SUCCENTORS
SUCCENTORSHIP
SUCCENTORSHIPS
SUCCESSANTLY
SUCCESSFUL
SUCCESSFULLY
SUCCESSFULNESS
SUCCESSION
SUCCESSIONAL
SUCCESSIONALLY
SUCCESSIONIST
SUCCESSIONISTS
SUCCESSIONLESS
SUCCESSIONS
SUCCESSIVE
SUCCESSIVELY
SUCCESSIVENESS
SUCCESSLESS
SUCCESSLESSLY
SUCCESSLESSNESS
SUCCESSORAL
SUCCESSORS
SUCCESSORSHIP
SUCCESSORSHIPS
SUCCINATES
SUCCINCTER
SUCCINCTEST
SUCCINCTLY
SUCCINCTNESS
SUCCINCTNESSES
SUCCINCTORIA
SUCCINCTORIES
SUCCINCTORIUM
SUCCINCTORIUMS
SUCCINCTORY
SUCCINITES
SUCCINYLCHOLINE
SUCCORABLE
SUCCORLESS
SUCCOTASHES
SUCCOURABLE
SUCCOURERS
SUCCOURING
SUCCOURLESS
SUCCUBUSES
SUCCULENCE
SUCCULENCES
SUCCULENCIES
SUCCULENCY
SUCCULENTLY
SUCCULENTS
SUCCUMBERS
SUCCUMBING
SUCCURSALE
SUCCURSALES
SUCCURSALS
SUCCUSSATION
SUCCUSSATIONS
SUCCUSSING
SUCCUSSION
SUCCUSSIONS
SUCCUSSIVE
SUCHNESSES
SUCKERFISH
SUCKERFISHES
SUCKFISHES
SUCKHOLING
SUCKINESSES
SUCRALFATE
SUCRALFATES
SUCRALOSES
SUCTIONING
SUCTORIANS
SUDATORIES
SUDATORIUM
SUDATORIUMS
SUDDENNESS
SUDDENNESSES
SUDDENTIES
SUDORIFEROUS
SUDORIFICS
SUDORIPAROUS
SUEABILITIES
SUEABILITY
SUFFERABLE
SUFFERABLENESS
SUFFERABLY
SUFFERANCE
SUFFERANCES
SUFFERINGLY
SUFFERINGS
SUFFICIENCE
SUFFICIENCES
SUFFICIENCIES
SUFFICIENCY
SUFFICIENT
SUFFICIENTLY
SUFFICIENTS
SUFFICINGNESS
SUFFICINGNESSES
SUFFIGANCE
SUFFIGANCES
SUFFISANCE
SUFFISANCES
SUFFIXATION
SUFFIXATIONS
SUFFIXIONS
SUFFLATING
SUFFLATION
SUFFLATIONS
SUFFOCATED
SUFFOCATES
SUFFOCATING
SUFFOCATINGLY
SUFFOCATINGS
SUFFOCATION
SUFFOCATIONS
SUFFOCATIVE
SUFFRAGANS
SUFFRAGANSHIP
SUFFRAGANSHIPS
SUFFRAGETTE
SUFFRAGETTES
SUFFRAGETTISM
SUFFRAGETTISMS
SUFFRAGISM
SUFFRAGISMS
SUFFRAGIST
SUFFRAGISTS
SUFFRUTESCENT
SUFFRUTICOSE
SUFFUMIGATE
SUFFUMIGATED
SUFFUMIGATES
SUFFUMIGATING
SUFFUMIGATION
SUFFUMIGATIONS
SUFFUSIONS
SUGARALLIE
SUGARALLIES
SUGARBERRIES
SUGARBERRY
SUGARBUSHES
SUGARCANES
SUGARCOATED
SUGARCOATING
SUGARCOATS
SUGARHOUSE
SUGARHOUSES
SUGARINESS
SUGARINESSES
SUGARLOAVES
SUGARPLUMS
SUGGESTERS
SUGGESTIBILITY
SUGGESTIBLE
SUGGESTIBLENESS
SUGGESTIBLY
SUGGESTING
SUGGESTION
SUGGESTIONISE
SUGGESTIONISED
SUGGESTIONISES
SUGGESTIONISING
SUGGESTIONISM
SUGGESTIONISMS
SUGGESTIONIST
SUGGESTIONISTS
SUGGESTIONIZE
SUGGESTIONIZED
SUGGESTIONIZES
SUGGESTIONIZING
SUGGESTIONS
SUGGESTIVE
SUGGESTIVELY
SUGGESTIVENESS
SUICIDALLY
SUICIDOLOGIES
SUICIDOLOGIST
SUICIDOLOGISTS
SUICIDOLOGY
SUITABILITIES
SUITABILITY
SUITABLENESS
SUITABLENESSES
SUITRESSES
SULCALISED
SULCALISES
SULCALISING
SULCALIZED
SULCALIZES
SULCALIZING
SULCATIONS
SULFACETAMIDE

SULFACETAMIDES
SULFADIAZINE
SULFADIAZINES
SULFADIMIDINE
SULFADIMIDINES
SULFADOXINE
SULFADOXINES
SULFAMETHAZINE
SULFAMETHAZINES
SULFANILAMIDE
SULFANILAMIDES
SULFATASES
SULFATHIAZOLE
SULFATHIAZOLES
SULFATIONS
SULFHYDRYL
SULFHYDRYLS
SULFINPYRAZONE
SULFINPYRAZONES
SULFONAMIDE
SULFONAMIDES
SULFONATED
SULFONATES
SULFONATING
SULFONATION
SULFONATIONS
SULFONIUMS
SULFONMETHANE
SULFONMETHANES
SULFONYLUREA
SULFONYLUREAS
SULFOXIDES
SULFURATED
SULFURATES
SULFURATING
SULFURATION
SULFURATIONS
SULFUREOUS
SULFURETED
SULFURETING
SULFURETTED
SULFURETTING
SULFURIEST
SULFURISATION
SULFURISATIONS
SULFURISED
SULFURISES
SULFURISING
SULFURIZATION
SULFURIZATIONS
SULFURIZED
SULFURIZES
SULFURIZING
SULFUROUSLY
SULFUROUSNESS
SULFUROUSNESSES
SULKINESSES
SULLENNESS
SULLENNESSES
SULPHACETAMIDE
SULPHACETAMIDES
SULPHADIAZINE
SULPHADIAZINES
SULPHADOXINE
SULPHADOXINES
SULPHANILAMIDE
SULPHANILAMIDES
SULPHATASE
SULPHATASES
SULPHATHIAZOLE
SULPHATHIAZOLES
SULPHATING
SULPHATION
SULPHATIONS
SULPHHYDRYL
SULPHHYDRYLS
SULPHINPYRAZONE
SULPHINYLS
SULPHONAMIDE
SULPHONAMIDES
SULPHONATE
SULPHONATED
SULPHONATES
SULPHONATING
SULPHONATION
SULPHONATIONS
SULPHONIUM
SULPHONIUMS
SULPHONMETHANE
SULPHONMETHANES
SULPHONYLS
SULPHONYLUREA
SULPHONYLUREAS
SULPHOXIDE
SULPHOXIDES
SULPHURATE
SULPHURATED
SULPHURATES
SULPHURATING
SULPHURATION
SULPHURATIONS
SULPHURATOR
SULPHURATORS
SULPHUREOUS
SULPHUREOUSLY
SULPHUREOUSNESS
SULPHURETED
SULPHURETING
SULPHURETS
SULPHURETTED
SULPHURETTING
SULPHURIER
SULPHURIEST
SULPHURING
SULPHURISATION
SULPHURISATIONS
SULPHURISE
SULPHURISED
SULPHURISES
SULPHURISING
SULPHURIZATION
SULPHURIZATIONS
SULPHURIZE
SULPHURIZED
SULPHURIZES
SULPHURIZING
SULPHUROUS
SULPHUROUSLY
SULPHUROUSNESS
SULPHURWORT
SULPHURWORTS
SULPHURYLS
SULTANATES
SULTANESSES
SULTANSHIP
SULTANSHIPS
SULTRINESS
SULTRINESSES
SUMBITCHES
SUMMABILITIES
SUMMABILITY
SUMMARINESS
SUMMARINESSES
SUMMARISABLE
SUMMARISATION
SUMMARISATIONS
SUMMARISED
SUMMARISER
SUMMARISERS
SUMMARISES
SUMMARISING
SUMMARISTS
SUMMARIZABLE
SUMMARIZATION
SUMMARIZATIONS
SUMMARIZED
SUMMARIZER
SUMMARIZERS
SUMMARIZES
SUMMARIZING
SUMMATIONAL
SUMMATIONS
SUMMERHOUSE
SUMMERHOUSES
SUMMERIEST
SUMMERINESS
SUMMERINESSES
SUMMERINGS
SUMMERLESS
SUMMERLIER
SUMMERLIEST
SUMMERLIKE
SUMMERLONG
SUMMERSAULT
SUMMERSAULTED
SUMMERSAULTING
SUMMERSAULTS
SUMMERSETS
SUMMERSETTED
SUMMERSETTING
SUMMERTIDE
SUMMERTIDES
SUMMERTIME
SUMMERTIMES
SUMMERWEIGHT
SUMMERWOOD
SUMMERWOODS
SUMMITEERS
SUMMITLESS
SUMMITRIES
SUMMONABLE
SUMMONSING
SUMPHISHNESS
SUMPHISHNESSES
SUMPSIMUSES
SUMPTUOSITIES
SUMPTUOSITY
SUMPTUOUSLY
SUMPTUOUSNESS
SUMPTUOUSNESSES
SUNBATHERS
SUNBATHING
SUNBATHINGS
SUNBEAMIER
SUNBEAMIEST
SUNBERRIES
SUNBONNETED
SUNBONNETS
SUNBURNING
SUNDERABLE
SUNDERANCE
SUNDERANCES
SUNDERINGS
SUNDERMENT
SUNDERMENTS
SUNDOWNERS
SUNDOWNING
SUNDRENCHED
SUNDRESSES
SUNFLOWERS
SUNGAZINGS
SUNGLASSES
SUNLESSNESS
SUNLESSNESSES
SUNLOUNGER
SUNLOUNGERS
SUNNINESSES
SUNPORCHES
SUNRISINGS
SUNSCREENING
SUNSCREENINGS
SUNSCREENS
SUNSEEKERS
SUNSETTING
SUNSETTINGS
SUNSHINIER
SUNSHINIEST
SUNSPOTTED
SUNSTROKES
SUNTANNING

S

SUNTANNINGS
SUNWORSHIPPER
SUNWORSHIPPERS
SUOVETAURILIA
SUOVETAURILIAS
SUPERABILITIES
SUPERABILITY
SUPERABLENESS
SUPERABLENESSES
SUPERABOUND
SUPERABOUNDED
SUPERABOUNDING
SUPERABOUNDS
SUPERABSORBENT
SUPERABSORBENTS
SUPERABUNDANCE
SUPERABUNDANCES
SUPERABUNDANT
SUPERABUNDANTLY
SUPERACHIEVER
SUPERACHIEVERS
SUPERACTIVE
SUPERACTIVITIES
SUPERACTIVITY
SUPERACUTE
SUPERADDED
SUPERADDING
SUPERADDITION
SUPERADDITIONAL
SUPERADDITIONS
SUPERAGENCIES
SUPERAGENCY
SUPERAGENT
SUPERAGENTS
SUPERALLOY
SUPERALLOYS
SUPERALTAR
SUPERALTARS
SUPERALTERN
SUPERALTERNS
SUPERAMBITIOUS
SUPERANNUABLE
SUPERANNUATE
SUPERANNUATED
SUPERANNUATES
SUPERANNUATING
SUPERANNUATION
SUPERANNUATIONS
SUPERATHLETE
SUPERATHLETES
SUPERATING
SUPERATION
SUPERATIONS
SUPERATOMS
SUPERBANKS
SUPERBAZAAR
SUPERBAZAARS
SUPERBAZAR
SUPERBAZARS
SUPERBIKES
SUPERBITCH
SUPERBITCHES
SUPERBITIES
SUPERBLOCK
SUPERBLOCKS
SUPERBNESS
SUPERBNESSES
SUPERBOARD
SUPERBOARDS
SUPERBOMBER
SUPERBOMBERS
SUPERBOMBS
SUPERBRAIN
SUPERBRAINS
SUPERBRATS
SUPERBRIGHT
SUPERBUREAUCRAT
SUPERCABINET
SUPERCABINETS
SUPERCALENDER
SUPERCALENDERED
SUPERCALENDERS
SUPERCARGO
SUPERCARGOES
SUPERCARGOS
SUPERCARGOSHIP
SUPERCARGOSHIPS
SUPERCARRIER
SUPERCARRIERS
SUPERCAUTIOUS
SUPERCEDED
SUPERCEDES
SUPERCEDING
SUPERCELESTIAL
SUPERCELLS
SUPERCENTER
SUPERCENTERS
SUPERCHARGE
SUPERCHARGED
SUPERCHARGER
SUPERCHARGERS
SUPERCHARGES
SUPERCHARGING
SUPERCHERIE
SUPERCHERIES
SUPERCHURCH
SUPERCHURCHES
SUPERCILIARIES
SUPERCILIARY
SUPERCILIOUS
SUPERCILIOUSLY
SUPERCITIES
SUPERCIVILISED
SUPERCIVILIZED
SUPERCLASS
SUPERCLASSES
SUPERCLEAN
SUPERCLUBS
SUPERCLUSTER
SUPERCLUSTERS
SUPERCOILED
SUPERCOILING
SUPERCOILS
SUPERCOLLIDER
SUPERCOLLIDERS
SUPERCOLOSSAL
SUPERCOLUMNAR
SUPERCOMPUTER
SUPERCOMPUTERS
SUPERCOMPUTING
SUPERCOMPUTINGS
SUPERCONDUCT
SUPERCONDUCTED
SUPERCONDUCTING
SUPERCONDUCTION
SUPERCONDUCTIVE
SUPERCONDUCTOR
SUPERCONDUCTORS
SUPERCONDUCTS
SUPERCONFIDENCE
SUPERCONFIDENT
SUPERCONTINENT
SUPERCONTINENTS
SUPERCONVENIENT
SUPERCOOLED
SUPERCOOLING
SUPERCOOLS
SUPERCOVER
SUPERCOVERS
SUPERCRIMINAL
SUPERCRIMINALS
SUPERCRITICAL
SUPERCURRENT
SUPERCURRENTS
SUPERDAINTIER
SUPERDAINTIEST
SUPERDAINTY
SUPERDELEGATE
SUPERDELEGATES
SUPERDELUXE
SUPERDENSE
SUPERDIPLOMAT
SUPERDIPLOMATS
SUPERDOMINANT
SUPERDOMINANTS
SUPEREFFECTIVE
SUPEREFFICIENCY
SUPEREFFICIENT
SUPEREGOIST
SUPEREGOISTS
SUPERELASTIC
SUPERELEVATE
SUPERELEVATED
SUPERELEVATES
SUPERELEVATING
SUPERELEVATION
SUPERELEVATIONS
SUPERELITE
SUPERELITES
SUPEREMINENCE
SUPEREMINENCES
SUPEREMINENT
SUPEREMINENTLY
SUPEREROGANT
SUPEREROGATE
SUPEREROGATED
SUPEREROGATES
SUPEREROGATING
SUPEREROGATION
SUPEREROGATIONS
SUPEREROGATIVE
SUPEREROGATOR
SUPEREROGATORS
SUPEREROGATORY
SUPERESSENTIAL
SUPERETTES
SUPEREVIDENT
SUPEREXALT
SUPEREXALTATION
SUPEREXALTED
SUPEREXALTING
SUPEREXALTS
SUPEREXCELLENCE
SUPEREXCELLENT
SUPEREXPENSIVE
SUPEREXPRESS
SUPEREXPRESSES
SUPERFAMILIES
SUPERFAMILY
SUPERFARMS
SUPERFATTED
SUPERFECTA
SUPERFECTAS
SUPERFEMALE
SUPERFEMALES
SUPERFETATE
SUPERFETATED
SUPERFETATES
SUPERFETATING
SUPERFETATION
SUPERFETATIONS
SUPERFICIAL
SUPERFICIALISE
SUPERFICIALISED
SUPERFICIALISES
SUPERFICIALITY
SUPERFICIALIZE
SUPERFICIALIZED
SUPERFICIALIZES
SUPERFICIALLY
SUPERFICIALNESS
SUPERFICIALS
SUPERFICIES
SUPERFINENESS
SUPERFINENESSES
SUPERFIRMS
SUPERFIXES
SUPERFLACK
SUPERFLACKS
SUPERFLUID

S

SUPERFLUIDITIES
SUPERFLUIDITY
SUPERFLUIDS
SUPERFLUITIES
SUPERFLUITY
SUPERFLUOUS
SUPERFLUOUSLY
SUPERFLUOUSNESS
SUPERFLUXES
SUPERFOETATION
SUPERFOETATIONS
SUPERFOODS
SUPERFRONTAL
SUPERFRONTALS
SUPERFUNDS
SUPERFUSED
SUPERFUSES
SUPERFUSING
SUPERFUSION
SUPERFUSIONS
SUPERGENES
SUPERGIANT
SUPERGIANTS
SUPERGLACIAL
SUPERGLUED
SUPERGLUEING
SUPERGLUES
SUPERGLUING
SUPERGOVERNMENT
SUPERGRAPHICS
SUPERGRASS
SUPERGRASSES
SUPERGRAVITIES
SUPERGRAVITY
SUPERGROUP
SUPERGROUPS
SUPERGROWTH
SUPERGROWTHS
SUPERHARDEN
SUPERHARDENED
SUPERHARDENING
SUPERHARDENS
SUPERHEATED
SUPERHEATER
SUPERHEATERS
SUPERHEATING
SUPERHEATS
SUPERHEAVIES
SUPERHEAVY
SUPERHELICAL
SUPERHELICES
SUPERHELIX
SUPERHELIXES
SUPERHEROES
SUPERHEROINE
SUPERHEROINES
SUPERHETERODYNE
SUPERHIGHWAY
SUPERHIGHWAYS
SUPERHIVES
SUPERHUMAN
SUPERHUMANISE
SUPERHUMANISED
SUPERHUMANISES
SUPERHUMANISING
SUPERHUMANITIES
SUPERHUMANITY
SUPERHUMANIZE
SUPERHUMANIZED
SUPERHUMANIZES
SUPERHUMANIZING
SUPERHUMANLY
SUPERHUMANNESS
SUPERHUMANS
SUPERHUMERAL
SUPERHUMERALS
SUPERHYPED
SUPERHYPES
SUPERHYPING
SUPERIMPORTANT
SUPERIMPOSABLE
SUPERIMPOSE
SUPERIMPOSED
SUPERIMPOSES
SUPERIMPOSING
SUPERIMPOSITION
SUPERINCUMBENCE
SUPERINCUMBENCY
SUPERINCUMBENT
SUPERINDIVIDUAL
SUPERINDUCE
SUPERINDUCED
SUPERINDUCEMENT
SUPERINDUCES
SUPERINDUCING
SUPERINDUCTION
SUPERINDUCTIONS
SUPERINFECT
SUPERINFECTED
SUPERINFECTING
SUPERINFECTION
SUPERINFECTIONS
SUPERINFECTS
SUPERINSULATED
SUPERINTEND
SUPERINTENDED
SUPERINTENDENCE
SUPERINTENDENCY
SUPERINTENDENT
SUPERINTENDENTS
SUPERINTENDING
SUPERINTENDS
SUPERINTENSITY
SUPERIORESS
SUPERIORESSES
SUPERIORITIES
SUPERIORITY
SUPERIORLY
SUPERIORSHIP
SUPERIORSHIPS
SUPERJACENT
SUPERJOCKS
SUPERJUMBO
SUPERJUMBOS
SUPERKINGDOM
SUPERKINGDOMS
SUPERLARGE
SUPERLATIVE
SUPERLATIVELY
SUPERLATIVENESS
SUPERLATIVES
SUPERLAWYER
SUPERLAWYERS
SUPERLIGHT
SUPERLINER
SUPERLINERS
SUPERLOADS
SUPERLOBBYIST
SUPERLOBBYISTS
SUPERLOYALIST
SUPERLOYALISTS
SUPERLUMINAL
SUPERLUNAR
SUPERLUNARY
SUPERLUXURIES
SUPERLUXURIOUS
SUPERLUXURY
SUPERLYING
SUPERMACHO
SUPERMAJORITIES
SUPERMAJORITY
SUPERMALES
SUPERMARKET
SUPERMARKETS
SUPERMARTS
SUPERMASCULINE
SUPERMASSIVE
SUPERMAXES
SUPERMEMBRANE
SUPERMEMBRANES
SUPERMICRO
SUPERMICROS
SUPERMILITANT
SUPERMILITANTS
SUPERMINDS
SUPERMINIS
SUPERMINISTER
SUPERMINISTERS
SUPERMODEL
SUPERMODELS
SUPERMODERN
SUPERMOONS
SUPERMOTOS
SUPERMUNDANE
SUPERNACULA
SUPERNACULAR
SUPERNACULUM
SUPERNALLY
SUPERNANNIES
SUPERNANNY
SUPERNATANT
SUPERNATANTS
SUPERNATATION
SUPERNATATIONS
SUPERNATED
SUPERNATES
SUPERNATING
SUPERNATION
SUPERNATIONAL
SUPERNATIONALLY
SUPERNATIONS
SUPERNATURAL
SUPERNATURALISE
SUPERNATURALISM
SUPERNATURALIST
SUPERNATURALIZE
SUPERNATURALLY
SUPERNATURALS
SUPERNATURE
SUPERNATURES
SUPERNORMAL
SUPERNORMALITY
SUPERNORMALLY
SUPERNOVAE
SUPERNOVAS
SUPERNUMERARIES
SUPERNUMERARY
SUPERNURSE
SUPERNURSES
SUPERNUTRIENT
SUPERNUTRIENTS
SUPERNUTRITION
SUPERNUTRITIONS
SUPEROCTAVE
SUPEROCTAVES
SUPERORDER
SUPERORDERS
SUPERORDINAL
SUPERORDINARY
SUPERORDINATE
SUPERORDINATED
SUPERORDINATES
SUPERORDINATING
SUPERORDINATION
SUPERORGANIC
SUPERORGANICISM
SUPERORGANICIST
SUPERORGANISM
SUPERORGANISMS
SUPERORGASM
SUPERORGASMS
SUPEROVULATE
SUPEROVULATED
SUPEROVULATES
SUPEROVULATING
SUPEROVULATION
SUPEROVULATIONS
SUPEROXIDE
SUPEROXIDES
SUPERPARASITISM

S

SUPERPARTICLE
SUPERPARTICLES
SUPERPATRIOT
SUPERPATRIOTIC
SUPERPATRIOTISM
SUPERPATRIOTS
SUPERPEOPLE
SUPERPERSON
SUPERPERSONAL
SUPERPERSONS
SUPERPHENOMENA
SUPERPHENOMENON
SUPERPHONE
SUPERPHONES
SUPERPHOSPHATE
SUPERPHOSPHATES
SUPERPHYLA
SUPERPHYLUM
SUPERPHYSICAL
SUPERPIMPS
SUPERPLANE
SUPERPLANES
SUPERPLASTIC
SUPERPLASTICITY
SUPERPLASTICS
SUPERPLAYER
SUPERPLAYERS
SUPERPLUSES
SUPERPOLITE
SUPERPOLYMER
SUPERPOLYMERS
SUPERPORTS
SUPERPOSABLE
SUPERPOSED
SUPERPOSES
SUPERPOSING
SUPERPOSITION
SUPERPOSITIONS
SUPERPOWER
SUPERPOWERED
SUPERPOWERFUL
SUPERPOWERS
SUPERPRAISE
SUPERPRAISED
SUPERPRAISES
SUPERPRAISING
SUPERPREMIUM
SUPERPREMIUMS
SUPERPROFIT
SUPERPROFITS
SUPERQUALITIES
SUPERQUALITY
SUPERRACES
SUPERREALISM
SUPERREALISMS
SUPERREALIST
SUPERREALISTS
SUPERREFINE
SUPERREFINED
SUPERREFINES
SUPERREFINING
SUPERREGIONAL
SUPERREGIONALS
SUPERROADS
SUPERROMANTIC
SUPERSAFETIES
SUPERSAFETY
SUPERSALES
SUPERSALESMAN
SUPERSALESMEN
SUPERSALTS
SUPERSATURATE
SUPERSATURATED
SUPERSATURATES
SUPERSATURATING
SUPERSATURATION
SUPERSAURS
SUPERSAVER
SUPERSAVERS
SUPERSCALAR
SUPERSCALE
SUPERSCHOOL
SUPERSCHOOLS
SUPERSCOUT
SUPERSCOUTS
SUPERSCREEN
SUPERSCREENS
SUPERSCRIBE
SUPERSCRIBED
SUPERSCRIBES
SUPERSCRIBING
SUPERSCRIPT
SUPERSCRIPTION
SUPERSCRIPTIONS
SUPERSCRIPTS
SUPERSECRECIES
SUPERSECRECY
SUPERSECRET
SUPERSECRETS
SUPERSEDABLE
SUPERSEDEAS
SUPERSEDEASES
SUPERSEDED
SUPERSEDENCE
SUPERSEDENCES
SUPERSEDER
SUPERSEDERE
SUPERSEDERES
SUPERSEDERS
SUPERSEDES
SUPERSEDING
SUPERSEDURE
SUPERSEDURES
SUPERSELLER
SUPERSELLERS
SUPERSELLING
SUPERSELLS
SUPERSENSIBLE
SUPERSENSIBLY
SUPERSENSITIVE
SUPERSENSORY
SUPERSENSUAL
SUPERSESSION
SUPERSESSIONS
SUPERSEXES
SUPERSEXUALITY
SUPERSHARP
SUPERSHOWS
SUPERSINGER
SUPERSINGERS
SUPERSIZED
SUPERSIZES
SUPERSIZING
SUPERSLEUTH
SUPERSLEUTHS
SUPERSLICK
SUPERSMART
SUPERSMOOTH
SUPERSONIC
SUPERSONICALLY
SUPERSONICS
SUPERSOUND
SUPERSOUNDS
SUPERSPECIAL
SUPERSPECIALIST
SUPERSPECIALS
SUPERSPECIES
SUPERSPECTACLE
SUPERSPECTACLES
SUPERSPEED
SUPERSPEEDS
SUPERSPIES
SUPERSTARDOM
SUPERSTARDOMS
SUPERSTARS
SUPERSTATE
SUPERSTATES
SUPERSTATION
SUPERSTATIONS
SUPERSTIMULATE
SUPERSTIMULATED
SUPERSTIMULATES
SUPERSTITION
SUPERSTITIONS
SUPERSTITIOUS
SUPERSTITIOUSLY
SUPERSTOCK
SUPERSTOCKS
SUPERSTORE
SUPERSTORES
SUPERSTORM
SUPERSTORMS
SUPERSTRATA
SUPERSTRATUM
SUPERSTRATUMS
SUPERSTRENGTH
SUPERSTRENGTHS
SUPERSTRIKE
SUPERSTRIKES
SUPERSTRING
SUPERSTRINGS
SUPERSTRONG
SUPERSTRUCT
SUPERSTRUCTED
SUPERSTRUCTING
SUPERSTRUCTION
SUPERSTRUCTIONS
SUPERSTRUCTIVE
SUPERSTRUCTS
SUPERSTRUCTURAL
SUPERSTRUCTURE
SUPERSTRUCTURES
SUPERSTUDS
SUPERSUBTILE
SUPERSUBTLE
SUPERSUBTLETIES
SUPERSUBTLETY
SUPERSURGEON
SUPERSURGEONS
SUPERSWEET
SUPERSYMMETRIC
SUPERSYMMETRIES
SUPERSYMMETRY
SUPERSYSTEM
SUPERSYSTEMS
SUPERTANKER
SUPERTANKERS
SUPERTAXES
SUPERTEACHER
SUPERTEACHERS
SUPERTERRANEAN
SUPERTERRIFIC
SUPERTHICK
SUPERTHRILLER
SUPERTHRILLERS
SUPERTIGHT
SUPERTITLE
SUPERTITLES
SUPERTONIC
SUPERTONICS
SUPERTRAMS
SUPERTRUCK
SUPERTRUCKS
SUPERTWIST
SUPERTWISTS
SUPERUSERS
SUPERVENED
SUPERVENES
SUPERVENIENCE
SUPERVENIENCES
SUPERVENIENT
SUPERVENING
SUPERVENTION
SUPERVENTIONS
SUPERVIRILE
SUPERVIRTUOSI
SUPERVIRTUOSO
SUPERVIRTUOSOS
SUPERVIRULENT
SUPERVISAL

SUPERVISALS
SUPERVISED
SUPERVISEE
SUPERVISEES
SUPERVISES
SUPERVISING
SUPERVISION
SUPERVISIONS
SUPERVISOR
SUPERVISORS
SUPERVISORSHIP
SUPERVISORSHIPS
SUPERVISORY
SUPERVOLUTE
SUPERWAIFS
SUPERWAVES
SUPERWEAPON
SUPERWEAPONS
SUPERWEEDS
SUPERWIDES
SUPERWIVES
SUPERWOMAN
SUPERWOMEN
SUPINATING
SUPINATION
SUPINATIONS
SUPINATORS
SUPINENESS
SUPINENESSES
SUPPEAGOES
SUPPEDANEA
SUPPEDANEUM
SUPPERLESS
SUPPERTIME
SUPPERTIMES
SUPPLANTATION
SUPPLANTATIONS
SUPPLANTED
SUPPLANTER
SUPPLANTERS
SUPPLANTING
SUPPLEJACK
SUPPLEJACKS
SUPPLEMENT
SUPPLEMENTAL
SUPPLEMENTALLY
SUPPLEMENTALS
SUPPLEMENTARIES
SUPPLEMENTARILY
SUPPLEMENTARY
SUPPLEMENTATION
SUPPLEMENTED
SUPPLEMENTER
SUPPLEMENTERS
SUPPLEMENTING
SUPPLEMENTS
SUPPLENESS
SUPPLENESSES
SUPPLETION
SUPPLETIONS
SUPPLETIVE
SUPPLETIVES
SUPPLETORILY
SUPPLETORY
SUPPLIABLE
SUPPLIANCE
SUPPLIANCES
SUPPLIANTLY
SUPPLIANTS
SUPPLICANT
SUPPLICANTS
SUPPLICATE
SUPPLICATED
SUPPLICATES
SUPPLICATING
SUPPLICATINGLY
SUPPLICATION
SUPPLICATIONS
SUPPLICATORY
SUPPLICATS
SUPPLICAVIT
SUPPLICAVITS
SUPPLYMENT
SUPPLYMENTS
SUPPORTABILITY
SUPPORTABLE
SUPPORTABLENESS
SUPPORTABLY
SUPPORTANCE
SUPPORTANCES
SUPPORTERS
SUPPORTING
SUPPORTINGS
SUPPORTIVE
SUPPORTIVELY
SUPPORTIVENESS
SUPPORTLESS
SUPPORTMENT
SUPPORTMENTS
SUPPORTRESS
SUPPORTRESSES
SUPPORTURE
SUPPORTURES
SUPPOSABLE
SUPPOSABLY
SUPPOSEDLY
SUPPOSINGS
SUPPOSITION
SUPPOSITIONAL
SUPPOSITIONALLY
SUPPOSITIONARY
SUPPOSITIONLESS
SUPPOSITIONS
SUPPOSITIOUS
SUPPOSITIOUSLY
SUPPOSITITIOUS
SUPPOSITIVE
SUPPOSITIVELY
SUPPOSITIVES
SUPPOSITORIES
SUPPOSITORY
SUPPRESSANT
SUPPRESSANTS
SUPPRESSED
SUPPRESSEDLY
SUPPRESSER
SUPPRESSERS
SUPPRESSES
SUPPRESSIBILITY
SUPPRESSIBLE
SUPPRESSING
SUPPRESSION
SUPPRESSIONS
SUPPRESSIVE
SUPPRESSIVENESS
SUPPRESSOR
SUPPRESSORS
SUPPURATED
SUPPURATES
SUPPURATING
SUPPURATION
SUPPURATIONS
SUPPURATIVE
SUPPURATIVES
SUPRACHIASMIC
SUPRACHOROIDAL
SUPRACILIARY
SUPRACOSTAL
SUPRACRUSTAL
SUPRAGLOTTAL
SUPRALAPSARIAN
SUPRALAPSARIANS
SUPRALIMINAL
SUPRALIMINALLY
SUPRALUNAR
SUPRAMAXILLARY
SUPRAMOLECULAR
SUPRAMOLECULE
SUPRAMOLECULES
SUPRAMUNDANE
SUPRANATIONAL
SUPRANATIONALLY
SUPRAOPTIC
SUPRAORBITAL
SUPRAPUBIC
SUPRARATIONAL
SUPRARENAL
SUPRARENALS
SUPRASEGMENTAL
SUPRASENSIBLE
SUPRATEMPORAL
SUPRAVITAL
SUPRAVITALLY
SUPREMACIES
SUPREMACISM
SUPREMACISMS
SUPREMACIST
SUPREMACISTS
SUPREMATISM
SUPREMATISMS
SUPREMATIST
SUPREMATISTS
SUPREMENESS
SUPREMENESSES
SUPREMITIES
SURADDITION
SURADDITIONS
SURBASEMENT
SURBASEMENTS
SURBEDDING
SURCEASING
SURCHARGED
SURCHARGEMENT
SURCHARGEMENTS
SURCHARGER
SURCHARGERS
SURCHARGES
SURCHARGING
SURCINGLED
SURCINGLES
SURCINGLING
SURCULUSES
SUREFOOTED
SUREFOOTEDLY
SUREFOOTEDNESS
SURENESSES
SURETYSHIP
SURETYSHIPS
SURFACELESS
SURFACEMAN
SURFACEMEN
SURFACINGS
SURFACTANT
SURFACTANTS
SURFBOARDED
SURFBOARDER
SURFBOARDERS
SURFBOARDING
SURFBOARDINGS
SURFBOARDS
SURFCASTER
SURFCASTERS
SURFCASTING
SURFCASTINGS
SURFEITERS
SURFEITING
SURFEITINGS
SURFFISHES
SURFPERCHES
SURFRIDDEN
SURFRIDERS
SURFRIDING
SURFRIDINGS
SURGEONCIES
SURGEONFISH
SURGEONFISHES
SURGEONSHIP
SURGEONSHIPS
SURGICALLY
SURJECTION

S

SURJECTIONS
SURJECTIVE
SURLINESSES
SURMASTERS
SURMISABLE
SURMISINGS
SURMISTRESS
SURMISTRESSES
SURMOUNTABLE
SURMOUNTED
SURMOUNTER
SURMOUNTERS
SURMOUNTING
SURMOUNTINGS
SURMULLETS
SURNOMINAL
SURPASSABLE
SURPASSERS
SURPASSING
SURPASSINGLY
SURPASSINGNESS
SURPLUSAGE
SURPLUSAGES
SURPLUSING
SURPLUSSED
SURPLUSSES
SURPLUSSING
SURPRINTED
SURPRINTING
SURPRISALS
SURPRISEDLY
SURPRISERS
SURPRISING
SURPRISINGLY
SURPRISINGNESS
SURPRISINGS
SURPRIZING
SURQUEDIES
SURQUEDRIES
SURREALISM
SURREALISMS
SURREALIST
SURREALISTIC
SURREALISTS
SURREBUTTAL
SURREBUTTALS
SURREBUTTED
SURREBUTTER
SURREBUTTERS
SURREBUTTING
SURREJOINDER
SURREJOINDERS
SURREJOINED
SURREJOINING
SURREJOINS
SURRENDERED
SURRENDEREE
SURRENDEREES
SURRENDERER
SURRENDERERS
SURRENDERING
SURRENDEROR
SURRENDERORS
SURRENDERS
SURRENDRIES
SURREPTITIOUS
SURREPTITIOUSLY
SURROGACIES
SURROGATED
SURROGATES
SURROGATESHIP
SURROGATESHIPS
SURROGATING
SURROGATION
SURROGATIONS
SURROGATUM
SURROGATUMS
SURROUNDED
SURROUNDING
SURROUNDINGS
SURTARBRAND
SURTARBRANDS
SURTURBRAND
SURTURBRANDS
SURVEILING
SURVEILLANCE
SURVEILLANCES
SURVEILLANT
SURVEILLANTS
SURVEILLED
SURVEILLES
SURVEILLING
SURVEYABLE
SURVEYANCE
SURVEYANCES
SURVEYINGS
SURVEYORSHIP
SURVEYORSHIPS
SURVIEWING
SURVIVABILITIES
SURVIVABILITY
SURVIVABLE
SURVIVALISM
SURVIVALISMS
SURVIVALIST
SURVIVALISTS
SURVIVANCE
SURVIVANCES
SURVIVORSHIP
SURVIVORSHIPS
SUSCEPTANCE
SUSCEPTANCES
SUSCEPTIBILITY
SUSCEPTIBLE
SUSCEPTIBLENESS
SUSCEPTIBLY
SUSCEPTIVE
SUSCEPTIVENESS
SUSCEPTIVITIES
SUSCEPTIVITY
SUSCEPTORS
SUSCIPIENT
SUSCIPIENTS
SUSCITATED
SUSCITATES
SUSCITATING
SUSCITATION
SUSCITATIONS
SUSPECTABLE
SUSPECTEDLY
SUSPECTEDNESS
SUSPECTEDNESSES
SUSPECTERS
SUSPECTFUL
SUSPECTING
SUSPECTLESS
SUSPENDERED
SUSPENDERS
SUSPENDIBILITY
SUSPENDIBLE
SUSPENDING
SUSPENSEFUL
SUSPENSEFULLY
SUSPENSEFULNESS
SUSPENSELESS
SUSPENSERS
SUSPENSIBILITY
SUSPENSIBLE
SUSPENSION
SUSPENSIONS
SUSPENSIVE
SUSPENSIVELY
SUSPENSIVENESS
SUSPENSOID
SUSPENSOIDS
SUSPENSORIA
SUSPENSORIAL
SUSPENSORIES
SUSPENSORIUM
SUSPENSORS
SUSPENSORY
SUSPERCOLLATE
SUSPERCOLLATED
SUSPERCOLLATES
SUSPERCOLLATING
SUSPICIONAL
SUSPICIONED
SUSPICIONING
SUSPICIONLESS
SUSPICIONS
SUSPICIOUS
SUSPICIOUSLY
SUSPICIOUSNESS
SUSPIRATION
SUSPIRATIONS
SUSPIRIOUS
SUSTAINABILITY
SUSTAINABLE
SUSTAINABLY
SUSTAINEDLY
SUSTAINERS
SUSTAINING
SUSTAININGLY
SUSTAININGS
SUSTAINMENT
SUSTAINMENTS
SUSTENANCE
SUSTENANCES
SUSTENTACULA
SUSTENTACULAR
SUSTENTACULUM
SUSTENTATE
SUSTENTATED
SUSTENTATES
SUSTENTATING
SUSTENTATION
SUSTENTATIONS
SUSTENTATIVE
SUSTENTATOR
SUSTENTATORS
SUSTENTION
SUSTENTIONS
SUSTENTIVE
SUSURRATED
SUSURRATES
SUSURRATING
SUSURRATION
SUSURRATIONS
SUSURRUSES
SUTLERSHIP
SUTLERSHIPS
SUTTEEISMS
SUTTLETIES
SUTURATION
SUTURATIONS
SUZERAINTIES
SUZERAINTY
SVARABHAKTI
SVARABHAKTIS
SVELTENESS
SVELTENESSES
SWAGGERERS
SWAGGERING
SWAGGERINGLY
SWAGGERINGS
SWAINISHNESS
SWAINISHNESSES
SWALLOWABLE
SWALLOWERS
SWALLOWING
SWALLOWTAIL
SWALLOWTAILS
SWALLOWWORT
SWALLOWWORTS
SWAMPINESS
SWAMPINESSES
SWAMPLANDS
SWANKINESS
SWANKINESSES
SWANNERIES

SWANSDOWNS
SWARAJISMS
SWARAJISTS
SWARTHIEST
SWARTHINESS
SWARTHINESSES
SWARTHNESS
SWARTHNESSES
SWARTNESSES
SWASHBUCKLE
SWASHBUCKLED
SWASHBUCKLER
SWASHBUCKLERS
SWASHBUCKLES
SWASHBUCKLING
SWASHWORKS
SWATCHBOOK
SWATCHBOOKS
SWATHEABLE
SWATTERING
SWAYBACKED
SWEARWORDS
SWEATBANDS
SWEATBOXES
SWEATERDRESS
SWEATERDRESSES
SWEATINESS
SWEATINESSES
SWEATPANTS
SWEATSHIRT
SWEATSHIRTS
SWEATSHOPS
SWEATSUITS
SWEEPBACKS
SWEEPINGLY
SWEEPINGNESS
SWEEPINGNESSES
SWEEPSTAKE
SWEEPSTAKES
SWEETBREAD
SWEETBREADS
SWEETBRIAR
SWEETBRIARS
SWEETBRIER
SWEETBRIERS
SWEETCORNS
SWEETENERS
SWEETENING
SWEETENINGS
SWEETFISHES
SWEETHEART
SWEETHEARTED
SWEETHEARTING
SWEETHEARTINGS
SWEETHEARTS
SWEETIEWIFE
SWEETIEWIVES
SWEETISHLY
SWEETISHNESS
SWEETISHNESSES
SWEETMEATS
SWEETNESSES
SWEETSHOPS
SWEETVELDS
SWEETWATER
SWEETWATERS
SWEETWOODS
SWEIRNESSES
SWELLFISHES
SWELLHEADED
SWELLHEADEDNESS
SWELLHEADS
SWELLINGLY
SWELTERING
SWELTERINGLY
SWELTERINGS
SWELTRIEST
SWEPTWINGS
SWERVELESS
SWIFTNESSES
SWIMFEEDER
SWIMFEEDERS
SWIMMERETS
SWIMMINGLY
SWIMMINGNESS
SWIMMINGNESSES
SWINDLINGS
SWINEHERDS
SWINEHOODS
SWINEPOXES
SWINESTONE
SWINESTONES
SWINGBEATS
SWINGBOATS
SWINGEINGLY
SWINGINGER
SWINGINGEST
SWINGINGLY
SWINGLETREE
SWINGLETREES
SWINGLINGS
SWINGOMETER
SWINGOMETERS
SWINGTREES
SWINISHNESS
SWINISHNESSES
SWIRLINGLY
SWISHINGLY
SWITCHABLE
SWITCHBACK
SWITCHBACKED
SWITCHBACKING
SWITCHBACKS
SWITCHBLADE
SWITCHBLADES
SWITCHBOARD
SWITCHBOARDS
SWITCHEROO
SWITCHEROOS
SWITCHGEAR
SWITCHGEARS
SWITCHGIRL
SWITCHGIRLS
SWITCHGRASS
SWITCHGRASSES
SWITCHIEST
SWITCHINGS
SWITCHLIKE
SWITCHOVER
SWITCHOVERS
SWITCHYARD
SWITCHYARDS
SWITHERING
SWIVELBLOCK
SWIVELBLOCKS
SWIVELLING
SWOLLENNESS
SWOLLENNESSES
SWOONINGLY
SWOOPSTAKE
SWORDBEARER
SWORDBEARERS
SWORDBILLS
SWORDCRAFT
SWORDCRAFTS
SWORDFERNS
SWORDFISHES
SWORDPLAYER
SWORDPLAYERS
SWORDPLAYS
SWORDPROOF
SWORDSMANSHIP
SWORDSMANSHIPS
SWORDSTICK
SWORDSTICKS
SWORDSWOMAN
SWORDSWOMEN
SWORDTAILS
SYBARITICAL
SYBARITICALLY
SYBARITISH
SYBARITISM
SYBARITISMS
SYCOPHANCIES
SYCOPHANCY
SYCOPHANTIC
SYCOPHANTICAL
SYCOPHANTICALLY
SYCOPHANTISE
SYCOPHANTISED
SYCOPHANTISES
SYCOPHANTISH
SYCOPHANTISHLY
SYCOPHANTISING
SYCOPHANTISM
SYCOPHANTISMS
SYCOPHANTIZE
SYCOPHANTIZED
SYCOPHANTIZES
SYCOPHANTIZING
SYCOPHANTLIER
SYCOPHANTLIEST
SYCOPHANTLY
SYCOPHANTRIES
SYCOPHANTRY
SYCOPHANTS
SYLLABARIA
SYLLABARIES
SYLLABARIUM
SYLLABICAL
SYLLABICALLY
SYLLABICATE
SYLLABICATED
SYLLABICATES
SYLLABICATING
SYLLABICATION
SYLLABICATIONS
SYLLABICITIES
SYLLABICITY
SYLLABIFICATION
SYLLABIFIED
SYLLABIFIES
SYLLABIFYING
SYLLABISED
SYLLABISES
SYLLABISING
SYLLABISMS
SYLLABIZED
SYLLABIZES
SYLLABIZING
SYLLABLING
SYLLABOGRAM
SYLLABOGRAMS
SYLLABOGRAPHIES
SYLLABOGRAPHY
SYLLABUSES
SYLLEPTICAL
SYLLEPTICALLY
SYLLOGISATION
SYLLOGISATIONS
SYLLOGISED
SYLLOGISER
SYLLOGISERS
SYLLOGISES
SYLLOGISING
SYLLOGISMS
SYLLOGISTIC
SYLLOGISTICAL
SYLLOGISTICALLY
SYLLOGISTICS
SYLLOGISTS
SYLLOGIZATION
SYLLOGIZATIONS
SYLLOGIZED
SYLLOGIZER
SYLLOGIZERS
SYLLOGIZES
SYLLOGIZING
SYLPHIDINE
SYLVANITES

SYLVESTRAL
SYLVESTRIAN
SYLVICULTURAL
SYLVICULTURE
SYLVICULTURES
SYLVINITES
SYMBIONTIC
SYMBIONTICALLY
SYMBIOTICAL
SYMBIOTICALLY
SYMBOLICAL
SYMBOLICALLY
SYMBOLICALNESS
SYMBOLISATION
SYMBOLISATIONS
SYMBOLISED
SYMBOLISER
SYMBOLISERS
SYMBOLISES
SYMBOLISING
SYMBOLISMS
SYMBOLISTIC
SYMBOLISTICAL
SYMBOLISTICALLY
SYMBOLISTS
SYMBOLIZATION
SYMBOLIZATIONS
SYMBOLIZED
SYMBOLIZER
SYMBOLIZERS
SYMBOLIZES
SYMBOLIZING
SYMBOLLING
SYMBOLOGICAL
SYMBOLOGIES
SYMBOLOGIST
SYMBOLOGISTS
SYMBOLOGRAPHIES
SYMBOLOGRAPHY
SYMBOLOLATRIES
SYMBOLOLATRY
SYMBOLOLOGIES
SYMBOLOLOGY
SYMMETALISM
SYMMETALISMS
SYMMETALLIC
SYMMETALLISM
SYMMETALLISMS
SYMMETRIAN
SYMMETRIANS
SYMMETRICAL
SYMMETRICALLY
SYMMETRICALNESS
SYMMETRIES
SYMMETRISATION
SYMMETRISATIONS
SYMMETRISE
SYMMETRISED
SYMMETRISES
SYMMETRISING
SYMMETRIZATION
SYMMETRIZATIONS
SYMMETRIZE
SYMMETRIZED
SYMMETRIZES
SYMMETRIZING
SYMMETROPHOBIA
SYMMETROPHOBIAS
SYMPATHECTOMIES
SYMPATHECTOMY
SYMPATHETIC
SYMPATHETICAL
SYMPATHETICALLY
SYMPATHETICS
SYMPATHIES
SYMPATHINS
SYMPATHIQUE
SYMPATHISE
SYMPATHISED
SYMPATHISER
SYMPATHISERS
SYMPATHISES
SYMPATHISING
SYMPATHIZE
SYMPATHIZED
SYMPATHIZER
SYMPATHIZERS
SYMPATHIZES
SYMPATHIZING
SYMPATHOLYTIC
SYMPATHOLYTICS
SYMPATHOMIMETIC
SYMPATRICALLY
SYMPATRIES
SYMPETALIES
SYMPETALOUS
SYMPHILIES
SYMPHILISM
SYMPHILISMS
SYMPHILOUS
SYMPHONICALLY
SYMPHONIES
SYMPHONION
SYMPHONIONS
SYMPHONIOUS
SYMPHONIOUSLY
SYMPHONIST
SYMPHONISTS
SYMPHYLOUS
SYMPHYSEAL
SYMPHYSEOTOMIES
SYMPHYSEOTOMY
SYMPHYSIAL
SYMPHYSIOTOMIES
SYMPHYSIOTOMY
SYMPHYSTIC
SYMPIESOMETER
SYMPIESOMETERS
SYMPLASTIC
SYMPODIALLY
SYMPOSIACS
SYMPOSIARCH
SYMPOSIARCHS
SYMPOSIAST
SYMPOSIASTS
SYMPOSIUMS
SYMPTOMATIC
SYMPTOMATICAL
SYMPTOMATICALLY
SYMPTOMATISE
SYMPTOMATISED
SYMPTOMATISES
SYMPTOMATISING
SYMPTOMATIZE
SYMPTOMATIZED
SYMPTOMATIZES
SYMPTOMATIZING
SYMPTOMATOLOGIC
SYMPTOMATOLOGY
SYMPTOMLESS
SYMPTOMOLOGICAL
SYMPTOMOLOGIES
SYMPTOMOLOGY
SYNADELPHITE
SYNADELPHITES
SYNAERESES
SYNAERESIS
SYNAESTHESES
SYNAESTHESIA
SYNAESTHESIAS
SYNAESTHESIS
SYNAESTHETIC
SYNAGOGICAL
SYNAGOGUES
SYNALEPHAS
SYNALLAGMATIC
SYNALOEPHA
SYNALOEPHAS
SYNANDRIUM
SYNANDROUS
SYNANTHEROUS
SYNANTHESES
SYNANTHESIS
SYNANTHETIC
SYNANTHIES
SYNANTHOUS
SYNAPHEIAS
SYNAPOSEMATIC
SYNAPOSEMATISM
SYNAPOSEMATISMS
SYNAPTASES
SYNAPTICAL
SYNAPTICALLY
SYNAPTOSOMAL
SYNAPTOSOME
SYNAPTOSOMES
SYNARCHIES
SYNARTHRODIAL
SYNARTHRODIALLY
SYNARTHROSES
SYNARTHROSIS
SYNASTRIES
SYNAXARION
SYNBIOTICS
SYNCARPIES
SYNCARPOUS
SYNCHONDROSES
SYNCHONDROSIS
SYNCHORESES
SYNCHORESIS
SYNCHROFLASH
SYNCHROFLASHES
SYNCHROMESH
SYNCHROMESHES
SYNCHRONAL
SYNCHRONEITIES
SYNCHRONEITY
SYNCHRONIC
SYNCHRONICAL
SYNCHRONICALLY
SYNCHRONICITIES
SYNCHRONICITY
SYNCHRONIES
SYNCHRONISATION
SYNCHRONISE
SYNCHRONISED
SYNCHRONISER
SYNCHRONISERS
SYNCHRONISES
SYNCHRONISING
SYNCHRONISM
SYNCHRONISMS
SYNCHRONISTIC
SYNCHRONISTICAL
SYNCHRONIZATION
SYNCHRONIZE
SYNCHRONIZED
SYNCHRONIZER
SYNCHRONIZERS
SYNCHRONIZES
SYNCHRONIZING
SYNCHRONOLOGIES
SYNCHRONOLOGY
SYNCHRONOSCOPE
SYNCHRONOSCOPES
SYNCHRONOUS
SYNCHRONOUSLY
SYNCHRONOUSNESS
SYNCHROSCOPE
SYNCHROSCOPES
SYNCHROTRON
SYNCHROTRONS
SYNCLASTIC
SYNCLINALS
SYNCLINORIA
SYNCLINORIUM
SYNCOPATED
SYNCOPATES
SYNCOPATING
SYNCOPATION

SYNCOPATIONS
SYNCOPATIVE
SYNCOPATOR
SYNCOPATORS
SYNCRETISATION
SYNCRETISATIONS
SYNCRETISE
SYNCRETISED
SYNCRETISES
SYNCRETISING
SYNCRETISM
SYNCRETISMS
SYNCRETIST
SYNCRETISTIC
SYNCRETISTS
SYNCRETIZATION
SYNCRETIZATIONS
SYNCRETIZE
SYNCRETIZED
SYNCRETIZES
SYNCRETIZING
SYNDACTYLIES
SYNDACTYLISM
SYNDACTYLISMS
SYNDACTYLOUS
SYNDACTYLS
SYNDACTYLY
SYNDERESES
SYNDERESIS
SYNDESISES
SYNDESMOSES
SYNDESMOSIS
SYNDESMOTIC
SYNDETICAL
SYNDETICALLY
SYNDICALISM
SYNDICALISMS
SYNDICALIST
SYNDICALISTIC
SYNDICALISTS
SYNDICATED
SYNDICATES
SYNDICATING
SYNDICATION
SYNDICATIONS
SYNDICATOR
SYNDICATORS
SYNDICSHIP
SYNDICSHIPS
SYNDIOTACTIC
SYNDYASMIAN
SYNECDOCHE
SYNECDOCHES
SYNECDOCHIC
SYNECDOCHICAL
SYNECDOCHICALLY
SYNECDOCHISM
SYNECDOCHISMS
SYNECOLOGIC
SYNECOLOGICAL
SYNECOLOGICALLY
SYNECOLOGIES
SYNECOLOGIST
SYNECOLOGISTS
SYNECOLOGY
SYNECPHONESES
SYNECPHONESIS
SYNECTICALLY
SYNEIDESES
SYNEIDESIS
SYNERGETIC
SYNERGETICALLY
SYNERGICALLY
SYNERGISED
SYNERGISES
SYNERGISING
SYNERGISMS
SYNERGISTIC
SYNERGISTICALLY
SYNERGISTS
SYNERGIZED
SYNERGIZES
SYNERGIZING
SYNESTHESIA
SYNESTHESIAS
SYNESTHETIC
SYNGENESES
SYNGENESIOUS
SYNGENESIS
SYNGENETIC
SYNGNATHOUS
SYNKARYONIC
SYNKARYONS
SYNODICALLY
SYNOECETES
SYNOECIOSES
SYNOECIOSIS
SYNOECIOUS
SYNOECISED
SYNOECISES
SYNOECISING
SYNOECISMS
SYNOECIZED
SYNOECIZES
SYNOECIZING
SYNOECOLOGIES
SYNOECOLOGY
SYNOEKETES
SYNONYMATIC
SYNONYMICAL
SYNONYMICON
SYNONYMICONS
SYNONYMIES
SYNONYMISE
SYNONYMISED
SYNONYMISES
SYNONYMISING
SYNONYMIST
SYNONYMISTS
SYNONYMITIES
SYNONYMITY
SYNONYMIZE
SYNONYMIZED
SYNONYMIZES
SYNONYMIZING
SYNONYMOUS
SYNONYMOUSLY
SYNONYMOUSNESS
SYNOPSISED
SYNOPSISES
SYNOPSISING
SYNOPSIZED
SYNOPSIZES
SYNOPSIZING
SYNOPTICAL
SYNOPTICALLY
SYNOPTISTIC
SYNOPTISTS
SYNOSTOSES
SYNOSTOSIS
SYNOVIALLY
SYNOVITISES
SYNSEPALOUS
SYNTACTICAL
SYNTACTICALLY
SYNTACTICS
SYNTAGMATA
SYNTAGMATIC
SYNTAGMATITE
SYNTAGMATITES
SYNTECTICAL
SYNTENOSES
SYNTENOSIS
SYNTERESES
SYNTERESIS
SYNTEXISES
SYNTHESISATION
SYNTHESISATIONS
SYNTHESISE
SYNTHESISED
SYNTHESISER
SYNTHESISERS
SYNTHESISES
SYNTHESISING
SYNTHESIST
SYNTHESISTS
SYNTHESIZATION
SYNTHESIZATIONS
SYNTHESIZE
SYNTHESIZED
SYNTHESIZER
SYNTHESIZERS
SYNTHESIZES
SYNTHESIZING
SYNTHESPIAN
SYNTHESPIANS
SYNTHETASE
SYNTHETASES
SYNTHETICAL
SYNTHETICALLY
SYNTHETICISM
SYNTHETICISMS
SYNTHETICS
SYNTHETISATION
SYNTHETISATIONS
SYNTHETISE
SYNTHETISED
SYNTHETISER
SYNTHETISERS
SYNTHETISES
SYNTHETISING
SYNTHETISM
SYNTHETISMS
SYNTHETIST
SYNTHETISTS
SYNTHETIZATION
SYNTHETIZATIONS
SYNTHETIZE
SYNTHETIZED
SYNTHETIZER
SYNTHETIZERS
SYNTHETIZES
SYNTHETIZING
SYNTHRONUS
SYNTONICALLY
SYNTONISED
SYNTONISES
SYNTONISING
SYNTONIZED
SYNTONIZES
SYNTONIZING
SYPHERINGS
SYPHILISATION
SYPHILISATIONS
SYPHILISED
SYPHILISES
SYPHILISING
SYPHILITIC
SYPHILITICALLY
SYPHILITICS
SYPHILIZATION
SYPHILIZATIONS
SYPHILIZED
SYPHILIZES
SYPHILIZING
SYPHILOLOGIES
SYPHILOLOGIST
SYPHILOLOGISTS
SYPHILOLOGY
SYPHILOMAS
SYPHILOMATA
SYPHILOPHOBIA
SYPHILOPHOBIAS
SYPHONAGES
SYRINGITIS
SYRINGITISES
SYRINGOMYELIA
SYRINGOMYELIAS
SYRINGOMYELIC
SYRINGOTOMIES

SYRINGOTOMY
SYSSARCOSES
SYSSARCOSIS
SYSSARCOTIC
SYSTEMATIC
SYSTEMATICAL
SYSTEMATICALLY
SYSTEMATICIAN
SYSTEMATICIANS
SYSTEMATICNESS
SYSTEMATICS
SYSTEMATISATION
SYSTEMATISE
SYSTEMATISED
SYSTEMATISER
SYSTEMATISERS
SYSTEMATISES
SYSTEMATISING
SYSTEMATISM
SYSTEMATISMS
SYSTEMATIST
SYSTEMATISTS
SYSTEMATIZATION
SYSTEMATIZE
SYSTEMATIZED
SYSTEMATIZER
SYSTEMATIZERS
SYSTEMATIZES
SYSTEMATIZING
SYSTEMATOLOGIES
SYSTEMATOLOGY
SYSTEMICALLY
SYSTEMISATION
SYSTEMISATIONS
SYSTEMISED
SYSTEMISER
SYSTEMISERS
SYSTEMISES
SYSTEMISING
SYSTEMIZATION
SYSTEMIZATIONS
SYSTEMIZED
SYSTEMIZER
SYSTEMIZERS
SYSTEMIZES
SYSTEMIZING
SYSTEMLESS
SYZYGETICALLY

T

TABASHEERS
TABBOULEHS
TABBYHOODS
TABEFACTION
TABEFACTIONS
TABELLIONS
TABERNACLE
TABERNACLED
TABERNACLES
TABERNACLING
TABERNACULAR
TABESCENCE
TABESCENCES
TABLANETTE
TABLANETTES
TABLATURES
TABLECLOTH
TABLECLOTHS
TABLELANDS
TABLEMATES
TABLESPOON
TABLESPOONFUL
TABLESPOONFULS
TABLESPOONS
TABLESPOONSFUL
TABLETOPPED
TABLETTING
TABLEWARES
TABLOIDIER
TABLOIDIEST
TABOGGANED
TABOGGANING
TABOPARESES
TABOPARESIS
TABULARISATION
TABULARISATIONS
TABULARISE
TABULARISED
TABULARISES
TABULARISING
TABULARIZATION
TABULARIZATIONS
TABULARIZE
TABULARIZED
TABULARIZES
TABULARIZING
TABULATING
TABULATION
TABULATIONS
TABULATORS
TABULATORY
TACAMAHACS
TACHEOMETER
TACHEOMETERS
TACHEOMETRIC
TACHEOMETRICAL
TACHEOMETRIES
TACHEOMETRY
TACHISTOSCOPE
TACHISTOSCOPES
TACHISTOSCOPIC
TACHOGRAMS
TACHOGRAPH
TACHOGRAPHS
TACHOMETER
TACHOMETERS
TACHOMETRIC
TACHOMETRICAL
TACHOMETRICALLY
TACHOMETRIES
TACHOMETRY
TACHYARRHYTHMIA
TACHYCARDIA
TACHYCARDIAC
TACHYCARDIAS
TACHYGRAPH
TACHYGRAPHER
TACHYGRAPHERS
TACHYGRAPHIC
TACHYGRAPHICAL
TACHYGRAPHIES
TACHYGRAPHIST
TACHYGRAPHISTS
TACHYGRAPHS
TACHYGRAPHY
TACHYLITES
TACHYLITIC
TACHYLYTES
TACHYLYTIC
TACHYMETER
TACHYMETERS
TACHYMETRIC
TACHYMETRICAL
TACHYMETRICALLY
TACHYMETRIES
TACHYMETRY
TACHYPHASIA
TACHYPHASIAS
TACHYPHRASIA
TACHYPHRASIAS
TACHYPHYLAXES
TACHYPHYLAXIS
TACHYPNEAS
TACHYPNOEA
TACHYPNOEAS
TACITNESSES
TACITURNITIES
TACITURNITY
TACITURNLY
TACKBOARDS
TACKETIEST
TACKIFIERS
TACKIFYING
TACKINESSES
TACMAHACKS
TACTFULNESS
TACTFULNESSES
TACTICALLY
TACTICIANS
TACTICITIES
TACTILISTS
TACTILITIES
TACTLESSLY
TACTLESSNESS
TACTLESSNESSES
TACTUALITIES
TACTUALITY
TADALAFILS
TAEKWONDOS
TAENIACIDE
TAENIACIDES
TAENIAFUGE
TAENIAFUGES
TAFFETASES
TAFFETIEST
TAFFETISED
TAFFETIZED
TAGLIARINI
TAGLIARINIS
TAGLIATELLE
TAGLIATELLES
TAHSILDARS
TAIKONAUTS
TAILBOARDS
TAILCOATED
TAILENDERS
TAILGATERS
TAILGATING
TAILGATINGS
TAILHOPPING
TAILHOPPINGS
TAILLESSLY
TAILLESSNESS
TAILLESSNESSES
TAILLIGHTS
TAILORBIRD
TAILORBIRDS
TAILORESSES
TAILORINGS
TAILORMADE
TAILORMAKE
TAILORMAKES
TAILORMAKING
TAILPIECES
TAILPIPING
TAILPLANES
TAILSLIDES
TAILSPINNED
TAILSPINNING
TAILSTOCKS
TAILWATERS
TAILWHEELS
TAINTLESSLY
TAKINGNESS
TAKINGNESSES
TALBOTYPES
TALEBEARER
TALEBEARERS
TALEBEARING
TALEBEARINGS
TALEGALLAS
TALENTLESS
TALETELLER
TALETELLERS
TALETELLING
TALETELLINGS
TALISMANIC
TALISMANICAL
TALISMANICALLY
TALKABILITIES
TALKABILITY
TALKATHONS
TALKATIVELY
TALKATIVENESS
TALKATIVENESSES
TALKINESSES
TALLGRASSES
TALLIATING
TALLNESSES
TALLOWIEST
TALLYHOING
TALLYSHOPS
TALLYWOMAN
TALLYWOMEN
TALMUDISMS
TAMABILITIES
TAMABILITY
TAMABLENESS
TAMABLENESSES
TAMARILLOS

T

TAMBOURERS
TAMBOURINE
TAMBOURINES
TAMBOURING
TAMBOURINIST
TAMBOURINISTS
TAMBOURINS
TAMEABILITIES
TAMEABILITY
TAMEABLENESS
TAMEABLENESSES
TAMELESSNESS
TAMELESSNESSES
TAMENESSES
TAMOXIFENS
TAMPERINGS
TAMPERPROOF
TAMPONADES
TAMPONAGES
TANDEMWISE
TANGENCIES
TANGENTALLY
TANGENTIAL
TANGENTIALITIES
TANGENTIALITY
TANGENTIALLY
TANGERINES
TANGHININS
TANGIBILITIES
TANGIBILITY
TANGIBLENESS
TANGIBLENESSES
TANGINESSES
TANGLEFOOT
TANGLEFOOTS
TANGLEMENT
TANGLEMENTS
TANGLESOME
TANGLEWEED
TANGLEWEEDS
TANGLINGLY
TANISTRIES
TANKBUSTER
TANKBUSTERS
TANKBUSTING
TANKBUSTINGS
TANOREXICS
TANTALATES
TANTALISATION
TANTALISATIONS
TANTALISED
TANTALISER
TANTALISERS
TANTALISES
TANTALISING
TANTALISINGLY
TANTALISINGS
TANTALISMS
TANTALITES
TANTALIZATION
TANTALIZATIONS
TANTALIZED
TANTALIZER
TANTALIZERS
TANTALIZES
TANTALIZING
TANTALIZINGLY
TANTALIZINGS
TANTALUSES
TANTAMOUNT
TANTARARAS
TANZANITES
TAPERINGLY
TAPERNESSES
TAPERSTICK
TAPERSTICKS
TAPESCRIPT
TAPESCRIPTS
TAPESTRIED
TAPESTRIES
TAPESTRYING
TAPHEPHOBIA
TAPHEPHOBIAS
TAPHEPHOBIC
TAPHONOMIC
TAPHONOMICAL
TAPHONOMIES
TAPHONOMIST
TAPHONOMISTS
TAPHOPHOBIA
TAPHOPHOBIAS
TAPHROGENESES
TAPHROGENESIS
TAPOTEMENT
TAPOTEMENTS
TAPSALTEERIE
TAPSALTEERIES
TAPSIETEERIE
TAPSIETEERIES
TAPSTRESSES
TARABISHES
TARADIDDLE
TARADIDDLES
TARAMASALATA
TARAMASALATAS
TARANTARAED
TARANTARAING
TARANTARAS
TARANTASES
TARANTASSES
TARANTELLA
TARANTELLAS
TARANTISMS
TARANTISTS
TARANTULAE
TARANTULAS
TARATANTARA
TARATANTARAED
TARATANTARAING
TARATANTARAS
TARAXACUMS
TARBOGGINED
TARBOGGINING
TARBOGGINS
TARBOOSHES
TARBOUCHES
TARBOUSHES
TARDIGRADE
TARDIGRADES
TARDINESSES
TARGETABLE
TARGETEERS
TARGETINGS
TARGETITIS
TARGETITISES
TARGETLESS
TARIFFICATION
TARIFFICATIONS
TARIFFLESS
TARMACADAM
TARMACADAMS
TARMACKING
TARNATIONS
TARNISHABLE
TARNISHERS
TARNISHING
TARPAULING
TARPAULINGS
TARPAULINS
TARRADIDDLE
TARRADIDDLES
TARRIANCES
TARRINESSES
TARSALGIAS
TARSOMETATARSAL
TARSOMETATARSI
TARSOMETATARSUS
TARTANALIA
TARTANALIAS
TARTANRIES
TARTAREOUS
TARTARISATION
TARTARISATIONS
TARTARISED
TARTARISES
TARTARISING
TARTARIZATION
TARTARIZATIONS
TARTARIZED
TARTARIZES
TARTARIZING
TARTINESSES
TARTNESSES
TARTRAZINE
TARTRAZINES
TASEOMETER
TASEOMETERS
TASIMETERS
TASIMETRIC
TASIMETRIES
TASKMASTER
TASKMASTERS
TASKMISTRESS
TASKMISTRESSES
TASSELIEST
TASSELLIER
TASSELLIEST
TASSELLING
TASSELLINGS
TASTEFULLY
TASTEFULNESS
TASTEFULNESSES
TASTELESSLY
TASTELESSNESS
TASTELESSNESSES
TASTEMAKER
TASTEMAKERS
TASTINESSES
TATAHASHES
TATPURUSHA
TATPURUSHAS
TATTERDEMALION
TATTERDEMALIONS
TATTERDEMALLION
TATTERIEST
TATTERSALL
TATTERSALLS
TATTINESSES
TATTLETALE
TATTLETALED
TATTLETALES
TATTLETALING
TATTLINGLY
TATTOOISTS
TAUNTINGLY
TAUROBOLIA
TAUROBOLIUM
TAUROMACHIAN
TAUROMACHIES
TAUROMACHY
TAUROMORPHOUS
TAUTNESSES
TAUTOCHRONE
TAUTOCHRONES
TAUTOCHRONISM
TAUTOCHRONISMS
TAUTOCHRONOUS
TAUTOLOGIC
TAUTOLOGICAL
TAUTOLOGICALLY
TAUTOLOGIES
TAUTOLOGISE
TAUTOLOGISED
TAUTOLOGISES
TAUTOLOGISING
TAUTOLOGISM
TAUTOLOGISMS
TAUTOLOGIST
TAUTOLOGISTS
TAUTOLOGIZE

TAUTOLOGIZED
TAUTOLOGIZES
TAUTOLOGIZING
TAUTOLOGOUS
TAUTOLOGOUSLY
TAUTOMERIC
TAUTOMERISM
TAUTOMERISMS
TAUTOMETRIC
TAUTOMETRICAL
TAUTONYMIC
TAUTONYMIES
TAUTONYMOUS
TAUTOPHONIC
TAUTOPHONICAL
TAUTOPHONIES
TAUTOPHONY
TAWDRINESS
TAWDRINESSES
TAWHEOWHEO
TAWHEOWHEOS
TAWNINESSES
TAXABILITIES
TAXABILITY
TAXABLENESS
TAXABLENESSES
TAXAMETERS
TAXATIONAL
TAXIDERMAL
TAXIDERMIC
TAXIDERMIES
TAXIDERMISE
TAXIDERMISED
TAXIDERMISES
TAXIDERMISING
TAXIDERMIST
TAXIDERMISTS
TAXIDERMIZE
TAXIDERMIZED
TAXIDERMIZES
TAXIDERMIZING
TAXIMETERS
TAXIPLANES
TAXONOMERS
TAXONOMICAL
TAXONOMICALLY
TAXONOMIES
TAXONOMIST
TAXONOMISTS
TAXPAYINGS
TAYASSUIDS
TAYBERRIES
TCHOTCHKES
TCHOUKBALL
TCHOUKBALLS
TEABERRIES
TEACHABILITIES
TEACHABILITY
TEACHABLENESS
TEACHABLENESSES
TEACHERLESS
TEACHERLIER
TEACHERLIEST
TEACHERSHIP
TEACHERSHIPS
TEACUPFULS
TEACUPSFUL
TEAKETTLES
TEARFULNESS
TEARFULNESSES
TEARGASSED
TEARGASSES
TEARGASSING
TEARINESSES
TEARJERKER
TEARJERKERS
TEARLESSLY
TEARSHEETS
TEARSTAINED
TEARSTAINS
TEARSTRIPS
TEASELINGS
TEASELLERS
TEASELLING
TEASELLINGS
TEASPOONFUL
TEASPOONFULS
TEASPOONSFUL
TEATASTERS
TEAZELLING
TECHINESSES
TECHNETIUM
TECHNETIUMS
TECHNETRONIC
TECHNICALISE
TECHNICALISED
TECHNICALISES
TECHNICALISING
TECHNICALITIES
TECHNICALITY
TECHNICALIZE
TECHNICALIZED
TECHNICALIZES
TECHNICALIZING
TECHNICALLY
TECHNICALNESS
TECHNICALNESSES
TECHNICALS
TECHNICIAN
TECHNICIANS
TECHNICISE
TECHNICISED
TECHNICISES
TECHNICISING
TECHNICISM
TECHNICISMS
TECHNICIST
TECHNICISTS
TECHNICIZE
TECHNICIZED
TECHNICIZES
TECHNICIZING
TECHNICOLOUR
TECHNICOLOURED
TECHNIKONS
TECHNIQUES
TECHNOBABBLE
TECHNOBABBLES
TECHNOCRACIES
TECHNOCRACY
TECHNOCRAT
TECHNOCRATIC
TECHNOCRATS
TECHNOFEAR
TECHNOFEARS
TECHNOGRAPHIES
TECHNOGRAPHY
TECHNOJUNKIE
TECHNOJUNKIES
TECHNOLOGIC
TECHNOLOGICAL
TECHNOLOGICALLY
TECHNOLOGIES
TECHNOLOGISE
TECHNOLOGISED
TECHNOLOGISES
TECHNOLOGISING
TECHNOLOGIST
TECHNOLOGISTS
TECHNOLOGIZE
TECHNOLOGIZED
TECHNOLOGIZES
TECHNOLOGIZING
TECHNOLOGY
TECHNOMANIA
TECHNOMANIAC
TECHNOMANIACS
TECHNOMANIAS
TECHNOMUSIC
TECHNOMUSICS
TECHNOPHILE
TECHNOPHILES
TECHNOPHILIA
TECHNOPHILIAS
TECHNOPHOBE
TECHNOPHOBES
TECHNOPHOBIA
TECHNOPHOBIAS
TECHNOPHOBIC
TECHNOPHOBICS
TECHNOPOLE
TECHNOPOLES
TECHNOPOLIS
TECHNOPOLISES
TECHNOPOLITAN
TECHNOPOLITANS
TECHNOPOPS
TECHNOSPEAK
TECHNOSPEAKS
TECHNOSTRESS
TECHNOSTRESSES
TECHNOSTRUCTURE
TECTIBRANCH
TECTIBRANCHIATE
TECTIBRANCHS
TECTONICALLY
TECTONISMS
TECTRICIAL
TEDIOSITIES
TEDIOUSNESS
TEDIOUSNESSES
TEDIOUSOME
TEEMINGNESS
TEEMINGNESSES
TEENTSIEST
TEENYBOPPER
TEENYBOPPERS
TEETERBOARD
TEETERBOARDS
TEETHRIDGE
TEETHRIDGES
TEETOTALED
TEETOTALER
TEETOTALERS
TEETOTALING
TEETOTALISM
TEETOTALISMS
TEETOTALIST
TEETOTALISTS
TEETOTALLED
TEETOTALLER
TEETOTALLERS
TEETOTALLING
TEETOTALLY
TEGUMENTAL
TEGUMENTARY
TEHSILDARS
TEICHOPSIA
TEICHOPSIAS
TEINOSCOPE
TEINOSCOPES
TEKNONYMIES
TEKNONYMOUS
TELAESTHESIA
TELAESTHESIAS
TELAESTHETIC
TELANGIECTASES
TELANGIECTASIA
TELANGIECTASIAS
TELANGIECTASIS
TELANGIECTATIC
TELAUTOGRAPHIC
TELAUTOGRAPHIES
TELAUTOGRAPHY
TELEARCHICS
TELEBANKING
TELEBANKINGS
TELEBRIDGE
TELEBRIDGES
TELECAMERA

TELECAMERAS
TELECASTED
TELECASTER
TELECASTERS
TELECASTING
TELECHIRIC
TELECOMMAND
TELECOMMANDS
TELECOMMUTE
TELECOMMUTED
TELECOMMUTER
TELECOMMUTERS
TELECOMMUTES
TELECOMMUTING
TELECOMMUTINGS
TELECONFERENCE
TELECONFERENCES
TELECONNECTION
TELECONNECTIONS
TELECONTROL
TELECONTROLS
TELECONVERTER
TELECONVERTERS
TELECOPIES
TELECOTTAGE
TELECOTTAGES
TELECOTTAGING
TELECOTTAGINGS
TELECOURSE
TELECOURSES
TELEDILDONICS
TELEFACSIMILE
TELEFACSIMILES
TELEFAXING
TELEFERIQUE
TELEFERIQUES
TELEGENICALLY
TELEGNOSES
TELEGNOSIS
TELEGNOSTIC
TELEGONIES
TELEGONOUS
TELEGRAMMATIC
TELEGRAMMED
TELEGRAMMIC
TELEGRAMMING
TELEGRAPHED
TELEGRAPHER
TELEGRAPHERS
TELEGRAPHESE
TELEGRAPHESES
TELEGRAPHIC
TELEGRAPHICALLY
TELEGRAPHIES
TELEGRAPHING
TELEGRAPHIST
TELEGRAPHISTS
TELEGRAPHS
TELEGRAPHY
TELEHEALTH
TELEHEALTHS
TELEJOURNALISM
TELEJOURNALISMS
TELEJOURNALIST
TELEJOURNALISTS
TELEKINESES
TELEKINESIS
TELEKINETIC
TELEKINETICALLY
TELEMARKED
TELEMARKETER
TELEMARKETERS
TELEMARKETING
TELEMARKETINGS
TELEMARKING
TELEMATICS
TELEMEDICINE
TELEMEDICINES
TELEMEETING
TELEMEETINGS
TELEMESSAGE
TELEMESSAGES
TELEMETERED
TELEMETERING
TELEMETERS
TELEMETRIC
TELEMETRICAL
TELEMETRICALLY
TELEMETRIES
TELENCEPHALA
TELENCEPHALIC
TELENCEPHALON
TELENCEPHALONS
TELEOLOGIC
TELEOLOGICAL
TELEOLOGICALLY
TELEOLOGIES
TELEOLOGISM
TELEOLOGISMS
TELEOLOGIST
TELEOLOGISTS
TELEONOMIC
TELEONOMIES
TELEOSAURIAN
TELEOSAURIANS
TELEOSAURS
TELEOSTEAN
TELEOSTEANS
TELEOSTOME
TELEOSTOMES
TELEOSTOMOUS
TELEPATHED
TELEPATHIC
TELEPATHICALLY
TELEPATHIES
TELEPATHING
TELEPATHISE
TELEPATHISED
TELEPATHISES
TELEPATHISING
TELEPATHIST
TELEPATHISTS
TELEPATHIZE
TELEPATHIZED
TELEPATHIZES
TELEPATHIZING
TELEPHEMES
TELEPHERIQUE
TELEPHERIQUES
TELEPHONED
TELEPHONER
TELEPHONERS
TELEPHONES
TELEPHONIC
TELEPHONICALLY
TELEPHONIES
TELEPHONING
TELEPHONIST
TELEPHONISTS
TELEPHONITIS
TELEPHONITISES
TELEPHOTOGRAPH
TELEPHOTOGRAPHS
TELEPHOTOGRAPHY
TELEPHOTOS
TELEPOINTS
TELEPORTATION
TELEPORTATIONS
TELEPORTED
TELEPORTING
TELEPRESENCE
TELEPRESENCES
TELEPRINTED
TELEPRINTER
TELEPRINTERS
TELEPRINTING
TELEPRINTS
TELEPROCESSING
TELEPROCESSINGS
TELERECORD
TELERECORDED
TELERECORDING
TELERECORDINGS
TELERECORDS
TELERGICALLY
TELEROBOTS
TELESCIENCE
TELESCIENCES
TELESCOPED
TELESCOPES
TELESCOPIC
TELESCOPICAL
TELESCOPICALLY
TELESCOPIES
TELESCOPIFORM
TELESCOPING
TELESCOPIST
TELESCOPISTS
TELESCREEN
TELESCREENS
TELESELLING
TELESELLINGS
TELESERVICES
TELESHOPPED
TELESHOPPING
TELESHOPPINGS
TELESMATIC
TELESMATICAL
TELESMATICALLY
TELESOFTWARE
TELESOFTWARES
TELESTEREOSCOPE
TELESTHESIA
TELESTHESIAS
TELESTHETIC
TELESTICHS
TELESURGERIES
TELESURGERY
TELETYPESETTING
TELETYPEWRITER
TELETYPEWRITERS
TELETYPING
TELEUTOSPORE
TELEUTOSPORES
TELEUTOSPORIC
TELEVANGELICAL
TELEVANGELISM
TELEVANGELISMS
TELEVANGELIST
TELEVANGELISTS
TELEVERITE
TELEVERITES
TELEVIEWED
TELEVIEWER
TELEVIEWERS
TELEVIEWING
TELEVIEWINGS
TELEVISERS
TELEVISING
TELEVISION
TELEVISIONAL
TELEVISIONALLY
TELEVISIONARY
TELEVISIONS
TELEVISORS
TELEVISUAL
TELEVISUALLY
TELEWORKED
TELEWORKER
TELEWORKERS
TELEWORKING
TELEWORKINGS
TELEWRITER
TELEWRITERS
TELFERAGES
TELICITIES
TELIOSPORE
TELIOSPORES
TELLERSHIP
TELLERSHIPS

TELLURATES
TELLURETTED
TELLURIANS
TELLURIDES
TELLURIONS
TELLURISED
TELLURISES
TELLURISING
TELLURITES
TELLURIUMS
TELLURIZED
TELLURIZES
TELLURIZING
TELLUROMETER
TELLUROMETERS
TELNETTING
TELOCENTRIC
TELOCENTRICS
TELOMERASE
TELOMERASES
TELOMERISATION
TELOMERISATIONS
TELOMERIZATION
TELOMERIZATIONS
TELOPHASES
TELOPHASIC
TELPHERAGE
TELPHERAGES
TELPHERING
TELPHERLINE
TELPHERLINES
TELPHERMAN
TELPHERMEN
TELPHERWAY
TELPHERWAYS
TEMAZEPAMS
TEMERARIOUS
TEMERARIOUSLY
TEMERARIOUSNESS
TEMERITIES
TEMEROUSLY
TEMPERABILITIES
TEMPERABILITY
TEMPERABLE
TEMPERALITIE
TEMPERALITIES
TEMPERAMENT
TEMPERAMENTAL
TEMPERAMENTALLY
TEMPERAMENTFUL
TEMPERAMENTS
TEMPERANCE
TEMPERANCES
TEMPERATED
TEMPERATELY
TEMPERATENESS
TEMPERATENESSES
TEMPERATES
TEMPERATING
TEMPERATIVE
TEMPERATURE
TEMPERATURES
TEMPERINGS
TEMPESTING
TEMPESTIVE
TEMPESTUOUS
TEMPESTUOUSLY
TEMPESTUOUSNESS
TEMPOLABILE
TEMPORALISE
TEMPORALISED
TEMPORALISES
TEMPORALISING
TEMPORALITIES
TEMPORALITY
TEMPORALIZE
TEMPORALIZED
TEMPORALIZES
TEMPORALIZING
TEMPORALLY
TEMPORALNESS
TEMPORALNESSES
TEMPORALTIES
TEMPORALTY
TEMPORANEOUS
TEMPORARIES
TEMPORARILY
TEMPORARINESS
TEMPORARINESSES
TEMPORISATION
TEMPORISATIONS
TEMPORISED
TEMPORISER
TEMPORISERS
TEMPORISES
TEMPORISING
TEMPORISINGLY
TEMPORISINGS
TEMPORIZATION
TEMPORIZATIONS
TEMPORIZED
TEMPORIZER
TEMPORIZERS
TEMPORIZES
TEMPORIZING
TEMPORIZINGLY
TEMPORIZINGS
TEMPTABILITIES
TEMPTABILITY
TEMPTABLENESS
TEMPTABLENESSES
TEMPTATION
TEMPTATIONS
TEMPTATIOUS
TEMPTINGLY
TEMPTINGNESS
TEMPTINGNESSES
TEMPTRESSES
TEMULENCES
TEMULENCIES
TEMULENTLY
TENABILITIES
TENABILITY
TENABLENESS
TENABLENESSES
TENACIOUSLY
TENACIOUSNESS
TENACIOUSNESSES
TENACITIES
TENACULUMS
TENAILLONS
TENANTABLE
TENANTLESS
TENANTRIES
TENANTSHIP
TENANTSHIPS
TENDENCIAL
TENDENCIALLY
TENDENCIES
TENDENCIOUS
TENDENCIOUSLY
TENDENCIOUSNESS
TENDENTIAL
TENDENTIALLY
TENDENTIOUS
TENDENTIOUSLY
TENDENTIOUSNESS
TENDERABLE
TENDERFEET
TENDERFOOT
TENDERFOOTS
TENDERHEARTED
TENDERHEARTEDLY
TENDERINGS
TENDERISATION
TENDERISATIONS
TENDERISED
TENDERISER
TENDERISERS
TENDERISES
TENDERISING
TENDERIZATION
TENDERIZATIONS
TENDERIZED
TENDERIZER
TENDERIZERS
TENDERIZES
TENDERIZING
TENDERLING
TENDERLINGS
TENDERLOIN
TENDERLOINS
TENDERNESS
TENDERNESSES
TENDEROMETER
TENDEROMETERS
TENDINITIDES
TENDINITIS
TENDINITISES
TENDONITIDES
TENDONITIS
TENDONITISES
TENDOVAGINITIS
TENDRESSES
TENDRILLAR
TENDRILLED
TENDRILLIER
TENDRILLIEST
TENDRILLOUS
TENDRILOUS
TENEBRIFIC
TENEBRIONID
TENEBRIONIDS
TENEBRIOUS
TENEBRIOUSNESS
TENEBRISMS
TENEBRISTS
TENEBRITIES
TENEBROSITIES
TENEBROSITY
TENEBROUSNESS
TENEBROUSNESSES
TENEMENTAL
TENEMENTARY
TENEMENTED
TENESMUSES
TENIACIDES
TENIAFUGES
TENNANTITE
TENNANTITES
TENNESSINE
TENNESSINES
TENORRHAPHIES
TENORRHAPHY
TENOSYNOVITIS
TENOSYNOVITISES
TENOTOMIES
TENOTOMIST
TENOTOMISTS
TENOVAGINITIS
TENOVAGINITISES
TENPINNERS
TENPOUNDER
TENPOUNDERS
TENSENESSES
TENSIBILITIES
TENSIBILITY
TENSIBLENESS
TENSIBLENESSES
TENSILENESS
TENSILENESSES
TENSILITIES
TENSIMETER
TENSIMETERS
TENSIOMETER
TENSIOMETERS
TENSIOMETRIC
TENSIOMETRIES
TENSIOMETRY
TENSIONALLY

TENSIONERS
TENSIONING
TENSIONLESS
TENTACULAR
TENTACULATE
TENTACULIFEROUS
TENTACULITE
TENTACULITES
TENTACULOID
TENTACULUM
TENTATIONS
TENTATIVELY
TENTATIVENESS
TENTATIVENESSES
TENTATIVES
TENTERHOOK
TENTERHOOKS
TENTIGINOUS
TENTMAKERS
TENUIROSTRAL
TENUOUSNESS
TENUOUSNESSES
TENURIALLY
TEPEFACTION
TEPEFACTIONS
TEPHIGRAMS
TEPHROITES
TEPHROMANCIES
TEPHROMANCY
TEPIDARIUM
TEPIDITIES
TEPIDNESSES
TERAHERTZES
TERAMETERS
TERATOCARCINOMA
TERATOGENESES
TERATOGENESIS
TERATOGENIC
TERATOGENICIST
TERATOGENICISTS
TERATOGENICITY
TERATOGENIES
TERATOGENS
TERATOGENY
TERATOLOGIC
TERATOLOGICAL
TERATOLOGIES
TERATOLOGIST
TERATOLOGISTS
TERATOLOGY
TERATOMATA
TERATOMATOUS
TERATOPHOBIA
TERATOPHOBIAS
TERCENTENARIES
TERCENTENARY
TERCENTENNIAL
TERCENTENNIALS
TEREBINTHINE
TEREBINTHS
TEREBRANTS
TEREBRATED
TEREBRATES
TEREBRATING
TEREBRATION
TEREBRATIONS
TEREBRATULA
TEREBRATULAE
TEREBRATULAS
TEREPHTHALATE
TEREPHTHALATES
TEREPHTHALIC
TERGIVERSANT
TERGIVERSANTS
TERGIVERSATE
TERGIVERSATED
TERGIVERSATES
TERGIVERSATING
TERGIVERSATION
TERGIVERSATIONS
TERGIVERSATOR
TERGIVERSATORS
TERGIVERSATORY
TERMAGANCIES
TERMAGANCY
TERMAGANTLY
TERMAGANTS
TERMINABILITIES
TERMINABILITY
TERMINABLE
TERMINABLENESS
TERMINABLY
TERMINALLY
TERMINATED
TERMINATES
TERMINATING
TERMINATION
TERMINATIONAL
TERMINATIONS
TERMINATIVE
TERMINATIVELY
TERMINATOR
TERMINATORS
TERMINATORY
TERMINISMS
TERMINISTS
TERMINOLOGICAL
TERMINOLOGIES
TERMINOLOGIST
TERMINOLOGISTS
TERMINOLOGY
TERMINUSES
TERMITARIA
TERMITARIES
TERMITARIUM
TERMITARIUMS
TERNEPLATE
TERNEPLATES
TEROTECHNOLOGY
TERPENELESS
TERPENOIDS
TERPINEOLS
TERPOLYMER
TERPOLYMERS
TERPSICHOREAL
TERPSICHOREAN
TERRACELESS
TERRACETTE
TERRACETTES
TERRACINGS
TERRACOTTA
TERRACOTTAS
TERRAFORMED
TERRAFORMING
TERRAFORMINGS
TERRAFORMS
TERRAMARAS
TERRAMARES
TERRAQUEOUS
TERRARIUMS
TERREMOTIVE
TERREPLEIN
TERREPLEINS
TERRESTRIAL
TERRESTRIALLY
TERRESTRIALNESS
TERRESTRIALS
TERRIBILITIES
TERRIBILITY
TERRIBLENESS
TERRIBLENESSES
TERRICOLES
TERRICOLOUS
TERRIFICALLY
TERRIFIERS
TERRIFYING
TERRIFYINGLY
TERRIGENOUS
TERRITORIAL
TERRITORIALISE
TERRITORIALISED
TERRITORIALISES
TERRITORIALISM
TERRITORIALISMS
TERRITORIALIST
TERRITORIALISTS
TERRITORIALITY
TERRITORIALIZE
TERRITORIALIZED
TERRITORIALIZES
TERRITORIALLY
TERRITORIALS
TERRITORIED
TERRITORIES
TERRORISATION
TERRORISATIONS
TERRORISED
TERRORISER
TERRORISERS
TERRORISES
TERRORISING
TERRORISMS
TERRORISTIC
TERRORISTS
TERRORIZATION
TERRORIZATIONS
TERRORIZED
TERRORIZER
TERRORIZERS
TERRORIZES
TERRORIZING
TERRORLESS
TERSANCTUS
TERSANCTUSES
TERSENESSES
TERTIARIES
TERVALENCIES
TERVALENCY
TESCHENITE
TESCHENITES
TESSARAGLOT
TESSELATED
TESSELATES
TESSELATING
TESSELLATE
TESSELLATED
TESSELLATES
TESSELLATING
TESSELLATION
TESSELLATIONS
TESSERACTS
TESSITURAS
TESTABILITIES
TESTABILITY
TESTACEANS
TESTACEOUS
TESTAMENTAL
TESTAMENTAR
TESTAMENTARILY
TESTAMENTARY
TESTAMENTS
TESTATIONS
TESTATRICES
TESTATRIXES
TESTCROSSED
TESTCROSSES
TESTCROSSING
TESTERNING
TESTICULAR
TESTICULATE
TESTICULATED
TESTIFICATE
TESTIFICATES
TESTIFICATION
TESTIFICATIONS
TESTIFICATOR
TESTIFICATORS
TESTIFICATORY
TESTIFIERS
TESTIFYING

TESTIMONIAL
TESTIMONIALISE
TESTIMONIALISED
TESTIMONIALISES
TESTIMONIALIZE
TESTIMONIALIZED
TESTIMONIALIZES
TESTIMONIALS
TESTIMONIED
TESTIMONIES
TESTIMONYING
TESTINESSES
TESTOSTERONE
TESTOSTERONES
TESTUDINAL
TESTUDINARY
TESTUDINEOUS
TESTUDINES
TETANICALLY
TETANISATION
TETANISATIONS
TETANISING
TETANIZATION
TETANIZATIONS
TETANIZING
TETARTOHEDRAL
TETARTOHEDRALLY
TETARTOHEDRISM
TETARTOHEDRISMS
TETCHINESS
TETCHINESSES
TETHERBALL
TETHERBALLS
TETRABASIC
TETRABASICITIES
TETRABASICITY
TETRABORATE
TETRABORATES
TETRABRACH
TETRABRACHS
TETRABRANCHIATE
TETRACAINE
TETRACAINES
TETRACHLORIDE
TETRACHLORIDES
TETRACHORD
TETRACHORDAL
TETRACHORDS
TETRACHOTOMIES
TETRACHOTOMOUS
TETRACHOTOMY
TETRACTINAL
TETRACTINALS
TETRACTINE
TETRACTINES
TETRACYCLIC
TETRACYCLINE
TETRACYCLINES
TETRADACTYL
TETRADACTYLIES
TETRADACTYLOUS
TETRADACTYLS
TETRADACTYLY
TETRADITES
TETRADRACHM
TETRADRACHMS
TETRADYMITE
TETRADYMITES
TETRADYNAMOUS
TETRAETHYL
TETRAETHYLLEAD
TETRAETHYLLEADS
TETRAETHYLS
TETRAFLUORIDE
TETRAFLUORIDES
TETRAGONAL
TETRAGONALLY
TETRAGONALNESS
TETRAGONOUS
TETRAGRAMMATON
TETRAGRAMMATONS
TETRAGRAMS
TETRAGYNIAN
TETRAGYNOUS
TETRAHEDRA
TETRAHEDRAL
TETRAHEDRALLY
TETRAHEDRITE
TETRAHEDRITES
TETRAHEDRON
TETRAHEDRONS
TETRAHYDROFURAN
TETRAHYMENA
TETRAHYMENAS
TETRALOGIES
TETRAMERAL
TETRAMERIC
TETRAMERISM
TETRAMERISMS
TETRAMEROUS
TETRAMETER
TETRAMETERS
TETRAMETHYL
TETRAMETHYLLEAD
TETRAMORPHIC
TETRANDRIAN
TETRANDROUS
TETRAPLEGIA
TETRAPLEGIAS
TETRAPLEGIC
TETRAPLOID
TETRAPLOIDIES
TETRAPLOIDS
TETRAPLOIDY
TETRAPODIC
TETRAPODIES
TETRAPODOUS
TETRAPOLIS
TETRAPOLISES
TETRAPOLITAN
TETRAPTERAN
TETRAPTEROUS
TETRAPTOTE
TETRAPTOTES
TETRAPYRROLE
TETRAPYRROLES
TETRARCHATE
TETRARCHATES
TETRARCHIC
TETRARCHICAL
TETRARCHIES
TETRASEMIC
TETRASPORANGIA
TETRASPORANGIUM
TETRASPORE
TETRASPORES
TETRASPORIC
TETRASPOROUS
TETRASTICH
TETRASTICHAL
TETRASTICHIC
TETRASTICHOUS
TETRASTICHS
TETRASTYLE
TETRASTYLES
TETRASYLLABIC
TETRASYLLABICAL
TETRASYLLABLE
TETRASYLLABLES
TETRATHEISM
TETRATHEISMS
TETRATHLON
TETRATHLONS
TETRATOMIC
TETRAVALENCE
TETRAVALENCES
TETRAVALENCIES
TETRAVALENCY
TETRAVALENT
TETRAVALENTS
TETRAZOLIUM
TETRAZOLIUMS
TETRAZZINI
TETRODOTOXIN
TETRODOTOXINS
TETROTOXIN
TETROTOXINS
TETROXIDES
TEUTONISED
TEUTONISES
TEUTONISING
TEUTONIZED
TEUTONIZES
TEUTONIZING
TEXTBOOKISH
TEXTPHONES
TEXTSPEAKS
TEXTUALISM
TEXTUALISMS
TEXTUALIST
TEXTUALISTS
TEXTUARIES
TEXTURALLY
TEXTURELESS
TEXTURINGS
TEXTURISED
TEXTURISES
TEXTURISING
TEXTURIZED
TEXTURIZES
TEXTURIZING
THALAMENCEPHALA
THALAMICALLY
THALAMIFLORAL
THALASSAEMIA
THALASSAEMIAS
THALASSAEMIC
THALASSAEMICS
THALASSEMIA
THALASSEMIAS
THALASSEMIC
THALASSEMICS
THALASSIAN
THALASSIANS
THALASSOCRACIES
THALASSOCRACY
THALASSOCRAT
THALASSOCRATS
THALASSOGRAPHER
THALASSOGRAPHIC
THALASSOGRAPHY
THALASSOTHERAPY
THALATTOCRACIES
THALATTOCRACY
THALICTRUM
THALICTRUMS
THALIDOMIDE
THALIDOMIDES
THALLIFORM
THALLOPHYTE
THALLOPHYTES
THALLOPHYTIC
THANATISMS
THANATISTS
THANATOGNOMONIC
THANATOGRAPHIES
THANATOGRAPHY
THANATOLOGICAL
THANATOLOGIES
THANATOLOGIST
THANATOLOGISTS
THANATOLOGY
THANATOPHOBIA
THANATOPHOBIAS
THANATOPSES
THANATOPSIS
THANATOSES
THANATOSIS
THANEHOODS
THANESHIPS

T

THANKFULLER
THANKFULLEST
THANKFULLY
THANKFULNESS
THANKFULNESSES
THANKLESSLY
THANKLESSNESS
THANKLESSNESSES
THANKSGIVER
THANKSGIVERS
THANKSGIVING
THANKSGIVINGS
THANKWORTHIER
THANKWORTHIEST
THANKWORTHILY
THANKWORTHINESS
THANKWORTHY
THARBOROUGH
THARBOROUGHS
THATCHIEST
THATCHINGS
THATCHLESS
THATNESSES
THAUMASITE
THAUMASITES
THAUMATINS
THAUMATOGENIES
THAUMATOGENY
THAUMATOGRAPHY
THAUMATOLATRIES
THAUMATOLATRY
THAUMATOLOGIES
THAUMATOLOGY
THAUMATROPE
THAUMATROPES
THAUMATROPICAL
THAUMATURGE
THAUMATURGES
THAUMATURGIC
THAUMATURGICAL
THAUMATURGICS
THAUMATURGIES
THAUMATURGISM
THAUMATURGISMS
THAUMATURGIST
THAUMATURGISTS
THAUMATURGUS
THAUMATURGUSES
THAUMATURGY
THEANTHROPIC
THEANTHROPIES
THEANTHROPISM
THEANTHROPISMS
THEANTHROPIST
THEANTHROPISTS
THEANTHROPY
THEARCHIES
THEATERGOER
THEATERGOERS
THEATERGOING
THEATERGOINGS
THEATERLAND
THEATERLANDS
THEATREGOER
THEATREGOERS
THEATREGOING
THEATREGOINGS
THEATRELAND
THEATRELANDS
THEATRICAL
THEATRICALISE
THEATRICALISED
THEATRICALISES
THEATRICALISING
THEATRICALISM
THEATRICALISMS
THEATRICALITIES
THEATRICALITY
THEATRICALIZE
THEATRICALIZED
THEATRICALIZES
THEATRICALIZING
THEATRICALLY
THEATRICALNESS
THEATRICALS
THEATRICISE
THEATRICISED
THEATRICISES
THEATRICISING
THEATRICISM
THEATRICISMS
THEATRICIZE
THEATRICIZED
THEATRICIZES
THEATRICIZING
THEATROMANIA
THEATROMANIAS
THEATROPHONE
THEATROPHONES
THECODONTS
THEFTUOUSLY
THEGNLIEST
THEIRSELVES
THEISTICAL
THEISTICALLY
THELEMENTS
THELITISES
THELYTOKIES
THELYTOKOUS
THEMATICALLY
THEMATISATION
THEMATISATIONS
THEMATISED
THEMATISES
THEMATISING
THEMATIZATION
THEMATIZATIONS
THEMATIZED
THEMATIZES
THEMATIZING
THEMSELVES
THENABOUTS
THENARDITE
THENARDITES
THENCEFORTH
THENCEFORWARD
THENCEFORWARDS
THEOBROMINE
THEOBROMINES
THEOCENTRIC
THEOCENTRICISM
THEOCENTRICISMS
THEOCENTRICITY
THEOCENTRISM
THEOCENTRISMS
THEOCRACIES
THEOCRASIES
THEOCRATIC
THEOCRATICAL
THEOCRATICALLY
THEODICEAN
THEODICEANS
THEODICIES
THEODOLITE
THEODOLITES
THEODOLITIC
THEOGONICAL
THEOGONIES
THEOGONIST
THEOGONISTS
THEOLOGASTER
THEOLOGASTERS
THEOLOGATE
THEOLOGATES
THEOLOGERS
THEOLOGIAN
THEOLOGIANS
THEOLOGICAL
THEOLOGICALLY
THEOLOGIES
THEOLOGISATION
THEOLOGISATIONS
THEOLOGISE
THEOLOGISED
THEOLOGISER
THEOLOGISERS
THEOLOGISES
THEOLOGISING
THEOLOGIST
THEOLOGISTS
THEOLOGIZATION
THEOLOGIZATIONS
THEOLOGIZE
THEOLOGIZED
THEOLOGIZER
THEOLOGIZERS
THEOLOGIZES
THEOLOGIZING
THEOLOGOUMENA
THEOLOGOUMENON
THEOLOGUES
THEOMACHIES
THEOMACHIST
THEOMACHISTS
THEOMANCIES
THEOMANIAC
THEOMANIACS
THEOMANIAS
THEOMANTIC
THEOMORPHIC
THEOMORPHISM
THEOMORPHISMS
THEONOMIES
THEONOMOUS
THEOPATHETIC
THEOPATHIC
THEOPATHIES
THEOPHAGIES
THEOPHAGOUS
THEOPHANIC
THEOPHANIES
THEOPHANOUS
THEOPHOBIA
THEOPHOBIAC
THEOPHOBIACS
THEOPHOBIAS
THEOPHOBIST
THEOPHOBISTS
THEOPHORIC
THEOPHYLLINE
THEOPHYLLINES
THEOPNEUST
THEOPNEUSTIC
THEOPNEUSTIES
THEOPNEUSTY
THEORBISTS
THEOREMATIC
THEOREMATICAL
THEOREMATICALLY
THEOREMATIST
THEOREMATISTS
THEORETICAL
THEORETICALLY
THEORETICIAN
THEORETICIANS
THEORETICS
THEORIQUES
THEORISATION
THEORISATIONS
THEORISERS
THEORISING
THEORIZATION
THEORIZATIONS
THEORIZERS
THEORIZING
THEOSOPHER
THEOSOPHERS
THEOSOPHIC
THEOSOPHICAL
THEOSOPHICALLY

T

THEOSOPHIES
THEOSOPHISE
THEOSOPHISED
THEOSOPHISES
THEOSOPHISING
THEOSOPHISM
THEOSOPHISMS
THEOSOPHIST
THEOSOPHISTICAL
THEOSOPHISTS
THEOSOPHIZE
THEOSOPHIZED
THEOSOPHIZES
THEOSOPHIZING
THEOTECHNIC
THEOTECHNIES
THEOTECHNY
THERALITES
THERAPEUSES
THERAPEUSIS
THERAPEUTIC
THERAPEUTICAL
THERAPEUTICALLY
THERAPEUTICS
THERAPEUTIST
THERAPEUTISTS
THERAPISED
THERAPISES
THERAPISING
THERAPISTS
THERAPIZED
THERAPIZES
THERAPIZING
THERAPSIDS
THEREABOUT
THEREABOUTS
THEREAFTER
THEREAGAINST
THEREAMONG
THEREANENT
THEREBESIDE
THEREINAFTER
THEREINBEFORE
THERENESSES
THERETHROUGH
THERETOFORE
THEREUNDER
THEREWITHAL
THEREWITHIN
THERIANTHROPIC
THERIANTHROPISM
THERIOLATRIES
THERIOLATRY
THERIOMORPH
THERIOMORPHIC
THERIOMORPHISM
THERIOMORPHISMS
THERIOMORPHOSES
THERIOMORPHOSIS
THERIOMORPHOUS
THERIOMORPHS
THERMAESTHESIA
THERMAESTHESIAS
THERMALISATION
THERMALISATIONS
THERMALISE
THERMALISED
THERMALISES
THERMALISING
THERMALIZATION
THERMALIZATIONS
THERMALIZE
THERMALIZED
THERMALIZES
THERMALIZING
THERMESTHESIA
THERMESTHESIAS
THERMETTES
THERMICALLY
THERMIDORS
THERMIONIC
THERMIONICS
THERMISTOR
THERMISTORS
THERMOBALANCE
THERMOBALANCES
THERMOBARIC
THERMOBAROGRAPH
THERMOBAROMETER
THERMOCHEMICAL
THERMOCHEMIST
THERMOCHEMISTRY
THERMOCHEMISTS
THERMOCHROMIC
THERMOCHROMIES
THERMOCHROMISM
THERMOCHROMISMS
THERMOCHROMY
THERMOCLINE
THERMOCLINES
THERMOCOUPLE
THERMOCOUPLES
THERMODURIC
THERMODYNAMIC
THERMODYNAMICAL
THERMODYNAMICS
THERMOELECTRIC
THERMOELECTRON
THERMOELECTRONS
THERMOELEMENT
THERMOELEMENTS
THERMOFORM
THERMOFORMABLE
THERMOFORMED
THERMOFORMING
THERMOFORMS
THERMOGENESES
THERMOGENESIS
THERMOGENETIC
THERMOGENIC
THERMOGENOUS
THERMOGRAM
THERMOGRAMS
THERMOGRAPH
THERMOGRAPHER
THERMOGRAPHERS
THERMOGRAPHIC
THERMOGRAPHIES
THERMOGRAPHS
THERMOGRAPHY
THERMOHALINE
THERMOJUNCTION
THERMOJUNCTIONS
THERMOLABILE
THERMOLABILITY
THERMOLOGIES
THERMOLOGY
THERMOLYSES
THERMOLYSIS
THERMOLYTIC
THERMOMAGNETIC
THERMOMETER
THERMOMETERS
THERMOMETRIC
THERMOMETRICAL
THERMOMETRIES
THERMOMETRY
THERMOMOTOR
THERMOMOTORS
THERMONASTIES
THERMONASTY
THERMONUCLEAR
THERMOPERIODIC
THERMOPERIODISM
THERMOPHIL
THERMOPHILE
THERMOPHILES
THERMOPHILIC
THERMOPHILOUS
THERMOPHILS
THERMOPHYLLOUS
THERMOPILE
THERMOPILES
THERMOPLASTIC
THERMOPLASTICS
THERMORECEPTOR
THERMORECEPTORS
THERMOREGULATE
THERMOREGULATED
THERMOREGULATES
THERMOREGULATOR
THERMOREMANENCE
THERMOREMANENT
THERMOSCOPE
THERMOSCOPES
THERMOSCOPIC
THERMOSCOPICAL
THERMOSETS
THERMOSETTING
THERMOSIPHON
THERMOSIPHONS
THERMOSPHERE
THERMOSPHERES
THERMOSPHERIC
THERMOSTABILITY
THERMOSTABLE
THERMOSTAT
THERMOSTATED
THERMOSTATIC
THERMOSTATICS
THERMOSTATING
THERMOSTATS
THERMOSTATTED
THERMOSTATTING
THERMOTACTIC
THERMOTAXES
THERMOTAXIC
THERMOTAXIS
THERMOTENSILE
THERMOTHERAPIES
THERMOTHERAPY
THERMOTICAL
THERMOTICS
THERMOTOLERANT
THERMOTROPIC
THERMOTROPICS
THERMOTROPISM
THERMOTROPISMS
THEROLOGIES
THEROPHYTE
THEROPHYTES
THEROPODAN
THEROPODANS
THERSITICAL
THESAURUSES
THESMOTHETE
THESMOTHETES
THETICALLY
THEURGICAL
THEURGICALLY
THEURGISTS
THIABENDAZOLE
THIABENDAZOLES
THIAMINASE
THIAMINASES
THICKENERS
THICKENING
THICKENINGS
THICKETIER
THICKETIEST
THICKHEADED
THICKHEADEDNESS
THICKHEADS
THICKLEAVES
THICKNESSES
THICKSKINS
THIEVERIES
THIEVISHLY
THIEVISHNESS
THIEVISHNESSES

T

THIGHBONES
THIGMOTACTIC
THIGMOTAXES
THIGMOTAXIS
THIGMOTROPIC
THIGMOTROPISM
THIGMOTROPISMS
THIMBLEBERRIES
THIMBLEBERRY
THIMBLEFUL
THIMBLEFULS
THIMBLERIG
THIMBLERIGGED
THIMBLERIGGER
THIMBLERIGGERS
THIMBLERIGGING
THIMBLERIGGINGS
THIMBLERIGS
THIMBLESFUL
THIMBLEWEED
THIMBLEWEEDS
THIMBLEWIT
THIMBLEWITS
THIMBLEWITTED
THIMEROSAL
THIMEROSALS
THINGAMABOB
THINGAMABOBS
THINGAMAJIG
THINGAMAJIGS
THINGAMIES
THINGAMYBOB
THINGAMYBOBS
THINGAMYJIG
THINGAMYJIGS
THINGHOODS
THINGINESS
THINGINESSES
THINGLINESS
THINGLINESSES
THINGNESSES
THINGUMABOB
THINGUMABOBS
THINGUMAJIG
THINGUMAJIGS
THINGUMBOB
THINGUMBOBS
THINGUMMIES
THINGUMMYBOB
THINGUMMYBOBS
THINGUMMYJIG
THINGUMMYJIGS
THINKABLENESS
THINKABLENESSES
THINKINGLY
THINKINGNESS
THINKINGNESSES
THINKPIECE
THINKPIECES
THINNESSES
THIOALCOHOL
THIOALCOHOLS
THIOBACILLI
THIOBACILLUS
THIOBARBITURATE
THIOCARBAMIDE
THIOCARBAMIDES
THIOCYANATE
THIOCYANATES
THIOCYANIC
THIODIGLYCOL
THIODIGLYCOLS
THIOFURANS
THIOPENTAL
THIOPENTALS
THIOPENTONE
THIOPENTONES
THIOPHENES
THIORIDAZINE
THIORIDAZINES
THIOSINAMINE
THIOSINAMINES
THIOSULFATE
THIOSULFATES
THIOSULFURIC
THIOSULPHATE
THIOSULPHATES
THIOSULPHURIC
THIOURACIL
THIOURACILS
THIRDBOROUGH
THIRDBOROUGHS
THIRDSTREAM
THIRDSTREAMS
THIRSTIEST
THIRSTINESS
THIRSTINESSES
THIRSTLESS
THIRTEENTH
THIRTEENTHLY
THIRTEENTHS
THIRTIETHS
THIRTYFOLD
THIRTYSOMETHING
THISNESSES
THISTLEDOWN
THISTLEDOWNS
THISTLIEST
THITHERWARD
THITHERWARDS
THIXOTROPE
THIXOTROPES
THIXOTROPIC
THIXOTROPIES
THIXOTROPY
THOLEIITES
THOLEIITIC
THOLOBATES
THORACENTESES
THORACENTESIS
THORACICALLY
THORACOCENTESES
THORACOCENTESIS
THORACOPLASTIES
THORACOPLASTY
THORACOSCOPE
THORACOSCOPES
THORACOSTOMIES
THORACOSTOMY
THORACOTOMIES
THORACOTOMY
THORIANITE
THORIANITES
THORNBACKS
THORNBILLS
THORNBIRDS
THORNBUSHES
THORNHEDGE
THORNHEDGES
THORNINESS
THORNINESSES
THORNPROOF
THORNPROOFS
THORNTAILS
THORNTREES
THOROUGHBASS
THOROUGHBASSES
THOROUGHBRACE
THOROUGHBRACED
THOROUGHBRACES
THOROUGHBRED
THOROUGHBREDS
THOROUGHER
THOROUGHEST
THOROUGHFARE
THOROUGHFARES
THOROUGHGOING
THOROUGHGOINGLY
THOROUGHLY
THOROUGHNESS
THOROUGHNESSES
THOROUGHPACED
THOROUGHPIN
THOROUGHPINS
THOROUGHWAX
THOROUGHWAXES
THOROUGHWORT
THOROUGHWORTS
THOUGHTCAST
THOUGHTCASTS
THOUGHTFUL
THOUGHTFULLY
THOUGHTFULNESS
THOUGHTLESS
THOUGHTLESSLY
THOUGHTLESSNESS
THOUGHTWAY
THOUGHTWAYS
THOUSANDFOLD
THOUSANDFOLDS
THOUSANDTH
THOUSANDTHS
THRAIPINGS
THRALLDOMS
THRAPPLING
THRASHIEST
THRASHINGS
THRASONICAL
THRASONICALLY
THREADBARE
THREADBARENESS
THREADBARER
THREADBAREST
THREADFINS
THREADIEST
THREADINESS
THREADINESSES
THREADLESS
THREADLIKE
THREADMAKER
THREADMAKERS
THREADWORM
THREADWORMS
THREATENED
THREATENER
THREATENERS
THREATENING
THREATENINGLY
THREATENINGS
THREEFOLDNESS
THREEFOLDNESSES
THREENESSES
THREEPEATED
THREEPEATING
THREEPEATS
THREEPENCE
THREEPENCES
THREEPENCEWORTH
THREEPENNIES
THREEPENNY
THREEPENNYWORTH
THREEQUELS
THREESCORE
THREESCORES
THREESOMES
THREMMATOLOGIES
THREMMATOLOGY
THRENETICAL
THRENODIAL
THRENODIES
THRENODIST
THRENODISTS
THREONINES
THRESHINGS
THRESHOLDS
THRIFTIEST
THRIFTINESS
THRIFTINESSES
THRIFTLESS
THRIFTLESSLY

THRIFTLESSNESS
THRILLIEST
THRILLINGLY
THRILLINGNESS
THRILLINGNESSES
THRIVELESS
THRIVINGLY
THRIVINGNESS
THRIVINGNESSES
THROATIEST
THROATINESS
THROATINESSES
THROATLASH
THROATLASHES
THROATLATCH
THROATLATCHES
THROATWORT
THROATWORTS
THROBBINGLY
THROBBINGS
THROMBOCYTE
THROMBOCYTES
THROMBOCYTIC
THROMBOEMBOLIC
THROMBOEMBOLISM
THROMBOGEN
THROMBOGENS
THROMBOKINASE
THROMBOKINASES
THROMBOLYSES
THROMBOLYSIS
THROMBOLYTIC
THROMBOLYTICS
THROMBOPHILIA
THROMBOPHILIAS
THROMBOPLASTIC
THROMBOPLASTIN
THROMBOPLASTINS
THROMBOSED
THROMBOSES
THROMBOSING
THROMBOSIS
THROMBOTIC
THROMBOXANE
THROMBOXANES
THRONELESS
THRONGINGS
THROPPLING
THROTTLEABLE
THROTTLEHOLD
THROTTLEHOLDS
THROTTLERS
THROTTLING
THROTTLINGS
THROUGHFARE
THROUGHFARES
THROUGHGAUN
THROUGHGAUNS
THROUGHITHER
THROUGHOTHER
THROUGHOUT
THROUGHPUT
THROUGHPUTS
THROUGHWAY
THROUGHWAYS
THROWAWAYS
THROWBACKS
THROWDOWNS
THROWOVERS
THROWSTERS
THRUMMIEST
THRUMMINGLY
THRUMMINGS
THRUPENNIES
THRUPPENCE
THRUPPENCES
THRUPPENNIES
THRUPPENNY
THRUSHLIKE
THRUSTINGS
THRUTCHING
THUDDINGLY
THUGGERIES
THUMBHOLES
THUMBIKINS
THUMBLINGS
THUMBNAILS
THUMBPIECE
THUMBPIECES
THUMBPRINT
THUMBPRINTS
THUMBSCREW
THUMBSCREWS
THUMBSTALL
THUMBSTALLS
THUMBTACKED
THUMBTACKING
THUMBTACKS
THUMBWHEEL
THUMBWHEELS
THUMPINGLY
THUNBERGIA
THUNBERGIAS
THUNDERBIRD
THUNDERBIRDS
THUNDERBOLT
THUNDERBOLTS
THUNDERBOX
THUNDERBOXES
THUNDERCLAP
THUNDERCLAPS
THUNDERCLOUD
THUNDERCLOUDS
THUNDERERS
THUNDERFLASH
THUNDERFLASHES
THUNDERHEAD
THUNDERHEADS
THUNDERIER
THUNDERIEST
THUNDERING
THUNDERINGLY
THUNDERINGS
THUNDERLESS
THUNDEROUS
THUNDEROUSLY
THUNDEROUSNESS
THUNDERSHOWER
THUNDERSHOWERS
THUNDERSTONE
THUNDERSTONES
THUNDERSTORM
THUNDERSTORMS
THUNDERSTRICKEN
THUNDERSTRIKE
THUNDERSTRIKES
THUNDERSTRIKING
THUNDERSTROKE
THUNDERSTROKES
THUNDERSTRUCK
THURIFEROUS
THURIFICATION
THURIFICATIONS
THURIFYING
THUSNESSES
THWACKINGS
THWARTEDLY
THWARTINGLY
THWARTINGS
THWARTSHIP
THWARTSHIPS
THWARTWAYS
THWARTWISE
THYLACINES
THYLAKOIDS
THYMECTOMIES
THYMECTOMISE
THYMECTOMISED
THYMECTOMISES
THYMECTOMISING
THYMECTOMIZE
THYMECTOMIZED
THYMECTOMIZES
THYMECTOMIZING
THYMECTOMY
THYMELAEACEOUS
THYMIDINES
THYMIDYLIC
THYMOCYTES
THYRATRONS
THYRISTORS
THYROCALCITONIN
THYROGLOBULIN
THYROGLOBULINS
THYROIDECTOMIES
THYROIDECTOMY
THYROIDITIDES
THYROIDITIS
THYROIDITISES
THYROTOXICOSES
THYROTOXICOSIS
THYROTROPHIC
THYROTROPHIN
THYROTROPHINS
THYROTROPIC
THYROTROPIN
THYROTROPINS
THYROXINES
THYRSOIDAL
THYSANOPTEROUS
THYSANURAN
THYSANURANS
THYSANUROUS
TIBIOFIBULA
TIBIOFIBULAE
TIBIOFIBULAS
TIBIOTARSI
TIBIOTARSUS
TIBOUCHINA
TIBOUCHINAS
TICHORRHINE
TICHORRHINES
TICKETINGS
TICKETLESS
TICKETTYBOO
TICKLEASSES
TICKLISHLY
TICKLISHNESS
TICKLISHNESSES
TICKTACKED
TICKTACKING
TICKTACKTOE
TICKTACKTOES
TICKTOCKED
TICKTOCKING
TICTACKING
TICTOCKING
TIDDLEDYWINK
TIDDLEDYWINKS
TIDDLEYWINK
TIDDLEYWINKS
TIDDLYWINK
TIDDLYWINKS
TIDEWAITER
TIDEWAITERS
TIDEWATERS
TIDINESSES
TIDIVATING
TIDIVATION
TIDIVATIONS
TIEBREAKER
TIEBREAKERS
TIEMANNITE
TIEMANNITES
TIERCELETS
TIERCERONS
TIGERISHLY
TIGERISHNESS
TIGERISHNESSES
TIGERLIEST

TIGERWOODS
TIGGYWINKLE
TIGGYWINKLES
TIGHTASSED
TIGHTASSES
TIGHTENERS
TIGHTENING
TIGHTENINGS
TIGHTFISTED
TIGHTFISTEDNESS
TIGHTISHLY
TIGHTNESSES
TIGHTROPES
TIGHTWIRES
TIGRISHNESS
TIGRISHNESSES
TIKINAGANS
TIKOLOSHES
TIKTAALIKS
TILEFISHES
TILIACEOUS
TILLANDSIA
TILLANDSIAS
TILLERINGS
TILLERLESS
TILTMETERS
TILTROTORS
TIMBERDOODLE
TIMBERDOODLES
TIMBERHEAD
TIMBERHEADS
TIMBERIEST
TIMBERINGS
TIMBERLAND
TIMBERLANDS
TIMBERLINE
TIMBERLINES
TIMBERWORK
TIMBERWORKS
TIMBERYARD
TIMBERYARDS
TIMBRELLED
TIMBROLOGIES
TIMBROLOGIST
TIMBROLOGISTS
TIMBROLOGY
TIMBROMANIA
TIMBROMANIAC
TIMBROMANIACS
TIMBROMANIAS
TIMBROPHILIES
TIMBROPHILIST
TIMBROPHILISTS
TIMBROPHILY
TIMEFRAMES
TIMEKEEPER
TIMEKEEPERS
TIMEKEEPING
TIMEKEEPINGS
TIMELESSLY
TIMELESSNESS
TIMELESSNESSES
TIMELINESS
TIMELINESSES
TIMENOGUYS
TIMEPASSED
TIMEPASSES
TIMEPASSING
TIMEPIECES
TIMEPLEASER
TIMEPLEASERS
TIMESAVERS
TIMESAVING
TIMESCALES
TIMESERVER
TIMESERVERS
TIMESERVING
TIMESERVINGS
TIMESHARES
TIMESHIFTED
TIMESHIFTING
TIMESHIFTS
TIMESTAMPED
TIMESTAMPING
TIMESTAMPS
TIMETABLED
TIMETABLES
TIMETABLING
TIMETABLINGS
TIMEWORKER
TIMEWORKERS
TIMIDITIES
TIMIDNESSES
TIMOCRACIES
TIMOCRATIC
TIMOCRATICAL
TIMOROUSLY
TIMOROUSNESS
TIMOROUSNESSES
TIMPANISTS
TINCTORIAL
TINCTORIALLY
TINCTURING
TINDERBOXES
TINDERIEST
TINGLINGLY
TINGUAITES
TININESSES
TINKERINGS
TINKERTOYS
TINKLINGLY
TINNINESSES
TINNITUSES
TINPLATING
TINSELIEST
TINSELLIER
TINSELLIEST
TINSELLING
TINSELRIES
TINSMITHING
TINSMITHINGS
TINTINESSES
TINTINNABULA
TINTINNABULANT
TINTINNABULAR
TINTINNABULARY
TINTINNABULATE
TINTINNABULATED
TINTINNABULATES
TINTINNABULOUS
TINTINNABULUM
TINTOMETER
TINTOMETERS
TINTOOKIES
TIPPYTOEING
TIPSIFYING
TIPSINESSES
TIPTRONICS
TIRAILLEUR
TIRAILLEURS
TIREDNESSES
TIRELESSLY
TIRELESSNESS
TIRELESSNESSES
TIREMAKERS
TIRESOMELY
TIRESOMENESS
TIRESOMENESSES
TIROCINIUM
TIROCINIUMS
TITANESSES
TITANICALLY
TITANIFEROUS
TITANOSAUR
TITANOSAURS
TITANOTHERE
TITANOTHERES
TITARAKURA
TITARAKURAS
TITHINGMAN
TITHINGMEN
TITILLATED
TITILLATES
TITILLATING
TITILLATINGLY
TITILLATION
TITILLATIONS
TITILLATIVE
TITILLATOR
TITILLATORS
TITIPOUNAMU
TITIPOUNAMUS
TITIVATING
TITIVATION
TITIVATIONS
TITIVATORS
TITLEHOLDER
TITLEHOLDERS
TITLEHOLDING
TITRATABLE
TITRATIONS
TITRIMETRIC
TITTERINGLY
TITTERINGS
TITTIVATED
TITTIVATES
TITTIVATING
TITTIVATION
TITTIVATIONS
TITTIVATOR
TITTIVATORS
TITTLEBATS
TITTUPIEST
TITTUPPIER
TITTUPPIEST
TITTUPPING
TITUBANCIES
TITUBATING
TITUBATION
TITUBATIONS
TITULARIES
TITULARITIES
TITULARITY
TOADEATERS
TOADFISHES
TOADFLAXES
TOADGRASSES
TOADRUSHES
TOADSTONES
TOADSTOOLS
TOASTMASTER
TOASTMASTERS
TOASTMISTRESS
TOASTMISTRESSES
TOBACCANALIAN
TOBACCANALIANS
TOBACCOLESS
TOBACCONIST
TOBACCONISTS
TOBOGGANED
TOBOGGANER
TOBOGGANERS
TOBOGGANING
TOBOGGANINGS
TOBOGGANIST
TOBOGGANISTS
TOBOGGINED
TOBOGGINING
TOCCATELLA
TOCCATELLAS
TOCCATINAS
TOCHERLESS
TOCOLOGIES
TOCOPHEROL
TOCOPHEROLS
TOCOPHOBIA
TOCOPHOBIAS
TODDLERHOOD
TODDLERHOODS
TOENAILING

TOERAGGERS
TOFFISHNESS
TOFFISHNESSES
TOGAVIRUSES
TOGETHERNESS
TOGETHERNESSES
TOILETINGS
TOILETRIES
TOILFULNESS
TOILFULNESSES
TOILINETTE
TOILINETTES
TOILSOMELY
TOILSOMENESS
TOILSOMENESSES
TOKENISTIC
TOKOLOGIES
TOKOLOSHES
TOKOLOSHIS
TOKOPHOBIA
TOKOPHOBIAS
TOKTOKKIES
TOLBUTAMIDE
TOLBUTAMIDES
TOLERABILITIES
TOLERABILITY
TOLERABLENESS
TOLERABLENESSES
TOLERANCES
TOLERANTLY
TOLERATING
TOLERATION
TOLERATIONISM
TOLERATIONISMS
TOLERATIONIST
TOLERATIONISTS
TOLERATIONS
TOLERATIVE
TOLERATORS
TOLLBOOTHS
TOLLBRIDGE
TOLLBRIDGES
TOLLDISHES
TOLLGATING
TOLLHOUSES
TOLLKEEPER
TOLLKEEPERS
TOLUIDIDES
TOLUIDINES
TOMAHAWKED
TOMAHAWKING
TOMATILLOES
TOMATILLOS
TOMATOIEST
TOMBOYISHLY
TOMBOYISHNESS
TOMBOYISHNESSES
TOMBSTONES
TOMBSTONING
TOMBSTONINGS
TOMCATTING
TOMCATTINGS
TOMFOOLERIES
TOMFOOLERY
TOMFOOLING
TOMFOOLISH
TOMFOOLISHNESS
TOMOGRAPHIC
TOMOGRAPHIES
TOMOGRAPHS
TOMOGRAPHY
TONALITIES
TONALITIVE
TONELESSLY
TONELESSNESS
TONELESSNESSES
TONETICALLY
TONGUELESS
TONGUELETS
TONGUELIKE
TONGUESTER
TONGUESTERS
TONICITIES
TONISHNESS
TONISHNESSES
TONNISHNESS
TONNISHNESSES
TONOMETERS
TONOMETRIC
TONOMETRIES
TONOPLASTS
TONSILITIS
TONSILITISES
TONSILLARY
TONSILLECTOMIES
TONSILLECTOMY
TONSILLITIC
TONSILLITIDES
TONSILLITIS
TONSILLITISES
TONSILLOTOMIES
TONSILLOTOMY
TOOLCHESTS
TOOLHOLDER
TOOLHOLDERS
TOOLHOUSES
TOOLMAKERS
TOOLMAKING
TOOLMAKINGS
TOOLPUSHER
TOOLPUSHERS
TOOLPUSHES
TOOTHACHES
TOOTHBRUSH
TOOTHBRUSHES
TOOTHBRUSHING
TOOTHBRUSHINGS
TOOTHCOMBS
TOOTHFISHES
TOOTHINESS
TOOTHINESSES
TOOTHPASTE
TOOTHPASTES
TOOTHPICKS
TOOTHSHELL
TOOTHSHELLS
TOOTHSOMELY
TOOTHSOMENESS
TOOTHSOMENESSES
TOOTHWASHES
TOOTHWORTS
TOPAGNOSES
TOPAGNOSIA
TOPAGNOSIAS
TOPAGNOSIS
TOPARCHIES
TOPAZOLITE
TOPAZOLITES
TOPCROSSES
TOPDRESSING
TOPDRESSINGS
TOPECTOMIES
TOPGALLANT
TOPGALLANTS
TOPHACEOUS
TOPIARISTS
TOPICALITIES
TOPICALITY
TOPKNOTTED
TOPLESSNESS
TOPLESSNESSES
TOPLOFTICAL
TOPLOFTIER
TOPLOFTIEST
TOPLOFTILY
TOPLOFTINESS
TOPLOFTINESSES
TOPMAKINGS
TOPMINNOWS
TOPNOTCHER
TOPNOTCHERS
TOPOCENTRIC
TOPOCHEMISTRIES
TOPOCHEMISTRY
TOPOGRAPHER
TOPOGRAPHERS
TOPOGRAPHIC
TOPOGRAPHICAL
TOPOGRAPHICALLY
TOPOGRAPHIES
TOPOGRAPHS
TOPOGRAPHY
TOPOISOMERASE
TOPOISOMERASES
TOPOLOGICAL
TOPOLOGICALLY
TOPOLOGIES
TOPOLOGIST
TOPOLOGISTS
TOPOMETRIES
TOPONYMICAL
TOPONYMICS
TOPONYMIES
TOPONYMIST
TOPONYMISTS
TOPOPHILIA
TOPOPHILIAS
TOPSCORING
TOPSOILING
TOPSOILINGS
TOPSTITCHED
TOPSTITCHES
TOPSTITCHING
TOPWORKING
TORBANITES
TORBERNITE
TORBERNITES
TORCHBEARER
TORCHBEARERS
TORCHIERES
TORCHLIGHT
TORCHLIGHTS
TORCHWOODS
TORMENTEDLY
TORMENTERS
TORMENTILS
TORMENTING
TORMENTINGLY
TORMENTINGS
TORMENTORS
TORMENTUMS
TOROIDALLY
TOROSITIES
TORPEDINOUS
TORPEDOERS
TORPEDOING
TORPEDOIST
TORPEDOISTS
TORPEFYING
TORPESCENCE
TORPESCENCES
TORPESCENT
TORPIDITIES
TORPIDNESS
TORPIDNESSES
TORPITUDES
TORPORIFIC
TORREFACTION
TORREFACTIONS
TORREFYING
TORRENTIAL
TORRENTIALITIES
TORRENTIALITY
TORRENTIALLY
TORRENTUOUS
TORRIDITIES
TORRIDNESS
TORRIDNESSES
TORRIFYING
TORSIBILITIES

T

TORSIBILITY
TORSIOGRAPH
TORSIOGRAPHS
TORSIONALLY
TORTELLINI
TORTELLINIS
TORTFEASOR
TORTFEASORS
TORTICOLLAR
TORTICOLLIS
TORTICOLLISES
TORTILITIES
TORTILLONS
TORTIOUSLY
TORTOISESHELL
TORTOISESHELLS
TORTRICIDS
TORTUOSITIES
TORTUOSITY
TORTUOUSLY
TORTUOUSNESS
TORTUOUSNESSES
TORTUREDLY
TORTURESOME
TORTURINGLY
TORTURINGS
TORTUROUSLY
TOSSICATED
TOSTICATED
TOSTICATION
TOSTICATIONS
TOTALISATION
TOTALISATIONS
TOTALISATOR
TOTALISATORS
TOTALISERS
TOTALISING
TOTALISTIC
TOTALITARIAN
TOTALITARIANISE
TOTALITARIANISM
TOTALITARIANIZE
TOTALITARIANS
TOTALITIES
TOTALIZATION
TOTALIZATIONS
TOTALIZATOR
TOTALIZATORS
TOTALIZERS
TOTALIZING
TOTAQUINES
TOTEMICALLY
TOTEMISTIC
TOTIPALMATE
TOTIPALMATION
TOTIPALMATIONS
TOTIPOTENCIES
TOTIPOTENCY
TOTIPOTENT
TOTTERIEST
TOTTERINGLY
TOTTERINGS
TOUCHABLENESS
TOUCHABLENESSES
TOUCHBACKS
TOUCHDOWNS
TOUCHHOLES
TOUCHINESS
TOUCHINESSES
TOUCHINGLY
TOUCHINGNESS
TOUCHINGNESSES
TOUCHLINES
TOUCHMARKS
TOUCHPAPER
TOUCHPAPERS
TOUCHSCREEN
TOUCHSCREENS
TOUCHSTONE
TOUCHSTONES
TOUCHTONES
TOUCHWOODS
TOUGHENERS
TOUGHENING
TOUGHENINGS
TOUGHNESSES
TOURBILLION
TOURBILLIONS
TOURBILLON
TOURBILLONS
TOURISTICALLY
TOURISTIER
TOURISTIEST
TOURMALINE
TOURMALINES
TOURMALINIC
TOURNAMENT
TOURNAMENTS
TOURNEYERS
TOURNEYING
TOURNIQUET
TOURNIQUETS
TOURTIERES
TOVARICHES
TOVARISCHES
TOVARISHES
TOWARDLINESS
TOWARDLINESSES
TOWARDNESS
TOWARDNESSES
TOWELETTES
TOWELHEADS
TOWELLINGS
TOWERINGLY
TOWNHOUSES
TOWNSCAPED
TOWNSCAPES
TOWNSCAPING
TOWNSCAPINGS
TOWNSFOLKS
TOWNSPEOPLE
TOWNSPEOPLES
TOWNSWOMAN
TOWNSWOMEN
TOXALBUMIN
TOXALBUMINS
TOXAPHENES
TOXICATION
TOXICATIONS
TOXICITIES
TOXICOGENIC
TOXICOLOGIC
TOXICOLOGICAL
TOXICOLOGICALLY
TOXICOLOGIES
TOXICOLOGIST
TOXICOLOGISTS
TOXICOLOGY
TOXICOMANIA
TOXICOMANIAS
TOXICOPHAGOUS
TOXICOPHOBIA
TOXICOPHOBIAS
TOXIGENICITIES
TOXIGENICITY
TOXIPHAGOUS
TOXIPHOBIA
TOXIPHOBIAC
TOXIPHOBIACS
TOXIPHOBIAS
TOXOCARIASES
TOXOCARIASIS
TOXOPHILIES
TOXOPHILITE
TOXOPHILITES
TOXOPHILITIC
TOXOPLASMA
TOXOPLASMAS
TOXOPLASMIC
TOXOPLASMOSES
TOXOPLASMOSIS
TOYISHNESS
TOYISHNESSES
TRABEATION
TRABEATIONS
TRABECULAE
TRABECULAR
TRABECULAS
TRABECULATE
TRABECULATED
TRACASSERIE
TRACASSERIES
TRACEABILITIES
TRACEABILITY
TRACEABLENESS
TRACEABLENESSES
TRACELESSLY
TRACHEARIAN
TRACHEARIANS
TRACHEARIES
TRACHEATED
TRACHEATES
TRACHEIDAL
TRACHEIDES
TRACHEITIDES
TRACHEITIS
TRACHEITISES
TRACHELATE
TRACHEOLAR
TRACHEOLES
TRACHEOPHYTE
TRACHEOPHYTES
TRACHEOSCOPIES
TRACHEOSCOPY
TRACHEOSTOMIES
TRACHEOSTOMY
TRACHEOTOMIES
TRACHEOTOMY
TRACHINUSES
TRACHITISES
TRACHOMATOUS
TRACHYPTERUS
TRACHYPTERUSES
TRACHYTOID
TRACKBALLS
TRACKERBALL
TRACKERBALLS
TRACKLAYER
TRACKLAYERS
TRACKLAYING
TRACKLAYINGS
TRACKLEMENT
TRACKLEMENTS
TRACKLESSLY
TRACKLESSNESS
TRACKLESSNESSES
TRACKROADS
TRACKSIDES
TRACKSUITS
TRACKWALKER
TRACKWALKERS
TRACTABILITIES
TRACTABILITY
TRACTABLENESS
TRACTABLENESSES
TRACTARIAN
TRACTARIANS
TRACTATORS
TRACTILITIES
TRACTILITY
TRACTIONAL
TRACTORATION
TRACTORATIONS
TRACTORFEED
TRACTORFEEDS
TRACTRICES
TRADECRAFT
TRADECRAFTS
TRADEMARKED
TRADEMARKING

T

TRADEMARKS
TRADENAMES
TRADERSHIP
TRADERSHIPS
TRADESCANTIA
TRADESCANTIAS
TRADESFOLK
TRADESFOLKS
TRADESMANLIKE
TRADESPEOPLE
TRADESPEOPLES
TRADESPERSON
TRADESPERSONS
TRADESWOMAN
TRADESWOMEN
TRADITIONAL
TRADITIONALISE
TRADITIONALISED
TRADITIONALISES
TRADITIONALISM
TRADITIONALISMS
TRADITIONALIST
TRADITIONALISTS
TRADITIONALITY
TRADITIONALIZE
TRADITIONALIZED
TRADITIONALIZES
TRADITIONALLY
TRADITIONARILY
TRADITIONARY
TRADITIONER
TRADITIONERS
TRADITIONIST
TRADITIONISTS
TRADITIONLESS
TRADITIONS
TRADITORES
TRADUCEMENT
TRADUCEMENTS
TRADUCIANISM
TRADUCIANISMS
TRADUCIANIST
TRADUCIANISTIC
TRADUCIANISTS
TRADUCIANS
TRADUCIBLE
TRADUCINGLY
TRADUCINGS
TRADUCTION
TRADUCTIONS
TRADUCTIVE
TRAFFICABILITY
TRAFFICABLE
TRAFFICATOR
TRAFFICATORS
TRAFFICKED
TRAFFICKER
TRAFFICKERS
TRAFFICKIER
TRAFFICKIEST
TRAFFICKING
TRAFFICKINGS
TRAFFICLESS
TRAGACANTH
TRAGACANTHS
TRAGEDIANS
TRAGEDIENNE
TRAGEDIENNES
TRAGELAPHINE
TRAGELAPHS
TRAGICALLY
TRAGICALNESS
TRAGICALNESSES
TRAGICOMEDIES
TRAGICOMEDY
TRAGICOMIC
TRAGICOMICAL
TRAGICOMICALLY
TRAILBASTON
TRAILBASTONS
TRAILBLAZER
TRAILBLAZERS
TRAILBLAZING
TRAILBLAZINGS
TRAILBREAKER
TRAILBREAKERS
TRAILERABLE
TRAILERING
TRAILERINGS
TRAILERIST
TRAILERISTS
TRAILERITE
TRAILERITES
TRAILHEADS
TRAILINGLY
TRAINABILITIES
TRAINABILITY
TRAINBANDS
TRAINBEARER
TRAINBEARERS
TRAINEESHIP
TRAINEESHIPS
TRAINLOADS
TRAINSPOTTER
TRAINSPOTTERISH
TRAINSPOTTERS
TRAIPSINGS
TRAITORESS
TRAITORESSES
TRAITORHOOD
TRAITORHOODS
TRAITORISM
TRAITORISMS
TRAITOROUS
TRAITOROUSLY
TRAITOROUSNESS
TRAITORSHIP
TRAITORSHIPS
TRAITRESSES
TRAJECTILE
TRAJECTING
TRAJECTION
TRAJECTIONS
TRAJECTORIES
TRAJECTORY
TRALATICIOUS
TRALATITIOUS
TRAMELLING
TRAMMELERS
TRAMMELING
TRAMMELLED
TRAMMELLER
TRAMMELLERS
TRAMMELLING
TRAMONTANA
TRAMONTANAS
TRAMONTANE
TRAMONTANES
TRAMPETTES
TRAMPLINGS
TRAMPOLINE
TRAMPOLINED
TRAMPOLINER
TRAMPOLINERS
TRAMPOLINES
TRAMPOLINING
TRAMPOLININGS
TRAMPOLINIST
TRAMPOLINISTS
TRAMPOLINS
TRANCELIKE
TRANQUILER
TRANQUILEST
TRANQUILISATION
TRANQUILISE
TRANQUILISED
TRANQUILISER
TRANQUILISERS
TRANQUILISES
TRANQUILISING
TRANQUILISINGLY
TRANQUILITIES
TRANQUILITY
TRANQUILIZATION
TRANQUILIZE
TRANQUILIZED
TRANQUILIZER
TRANQUILIZERS
TRANQUILIZES
TRANQUILIZING
TRANQUILIZINGLY
TRANQUILLER
TRANQUILLEST
TRANQUILLISE
TRANQUILLISED
TRANQUILLISER
TRANQUILLISERS
TRANQUILLISES
TRANQUILLISING
TRANQUILLITIES
TRANQUILLITY
TRANQUILLIZE
TRANQUILLIZED
TRANQUILLIZER
TRANQUILLIZERS
TRANQUILLIZES
TRANQUILLIZING
TRANQUILLY
TRANQUILNESS
TRANQUILNESSES
TRANSACTED
TRANSACTING
TRANSACTINIDE
TRANSACTINIDES
TRANSACTION
TRANSACTIONAL
TRANSACTIONALLY
TRANSACTIONS
TRANSACTOR
TRANSACTORS
TRANSALPINE
TRANSALPINES
TRANSAMINASE
TRANSAMINASES
TRANSAMINATION
TRANSAMINATIONS
TRANSANDEAN
TRANSANDINE
TRANSATLANTIC
TRANSAXLES
TRANSCALENCIES
TRANSCALENCY
TRANSCALENT
TRANSCAUCASIAN
TRANSCEIVER
TRANSCEIVERS
TRANSCENDED
TRANSCENDENCE
TRANSCENDENCES
TRANSCENDENCIES
TRANSCENDENCY
TRANSCENDENT
TRANSCENDENTAL
TRANSCENDENTALS
TRANSCENDENTLY
TRANSCENDENTS
TRANSCENDING
TRANSCENDINGLY
TRANSCENDS
TRANSCODED
TRANSCODER
TRANSCODERS
TRANSCODES
TRANSCODING
TRANSCRANIAL
TRANSCRIBABLE
TRANSCRIBE
TRANSCRIBED
TRANSCRIBER
TRANSCRIBERS

T

TRANSCRIBES
TRANSCRIBING
TRANSCRIPT
TRANSCRIPTASE
TRANSCRIPTASES
TRANSCRIPTION
TRANSCRIPTIONAL
TRANSCRIPTIONS
TRANSCRIPTIVE
TRANSCRIPTIVELY
TRANSCRIPTOME
TRANSCRIPTOMES
TRANSCRIPTS
TRANSCULTURAL
TRANSCURRENT
TRANSCUTANEOUS
TRANSDERMAL
TRANSDUCED
TRANSDUCER
TRANSDUCERS
TRANSDUCES
TRANSDUCING
TRANSDUCTANT
TRANSDUCTANTS
TRANSDUCTION
TRANSDUCTIONAL
TRANSDUCTIONS
TRANSDUCTOR
TRANSDUCTORS
TRANSECTED
TRANSECTING
TRANSECTION
TRANSECTIONS
TRANSENNAS
TRANSEPTAL
TRANSEPTATE
TRANSEPTED
TRANSEXUAL
TRANSEXUALISM
TRANSEXUALISMS
TRANSEXUALITIES
TRANSEXUALITY
TRANSEXUALS
TRANSFECTED
TRANSFECTING
TRANSFECTION
TRANSFECTIONS
TRANSFECTS

TRANSFERABILITY
TRANSFERABLE
TRANSFERAL
TRANSFERALS
TRANSFERASE
TRANSFERASES
TRANSFEREE
TRANSFEREES
TRANSFERENCE
TRANSFERENCES
TRANSFERENTIAL
TRANSFEROR
TRANSFERORS
TRANSFERRABLE
TRANSFERRAL
TRANSFERRALS
TRANSFERRED
TRANSFERRER
TRANSFERRERS
TRANSFERRIBLE
TRANSFERRIN
TRANSFERRING
TRANSFERRINS
TRANSFIGURATION
TRANSFIGURE
TRANSFIGURED
TRANSFIGUREMENT
TRANSFIGURES
TRANSFIGURING
TRANSFINITE
TRANSFIXED
TRANSFIXES
TRANSFIXING
TRANSFIXION
TRANSFIXIONS
TRANSFORMABLE
TRANSFORMATION
TRANSFORMATIONS
TRANSFORMATIVE
TRANSFORMED
TRANSFORMER
TRANSFORMERS
TRANSFORMING
TRANSFORMINGS
TRANSFORMISM
TRANSFORMISMS
TRANSFORMIST
TRANSFORMISTIC

TRANSFORMISTS
TRANSFORMS
TRANSFUSABLE
TRANSFUSED
TRANSFUSER
TRANSFUSERS
TRANSFUSES
TRANSFUSIBLE
TRANSFUSING
TRANSFUSION
TRANSFUSIONAL
TRANSFUSIONIST
TRANSFUSIONISTS
TRANSFUSIONS
TRANSFUSIVE
TRANSFUSIVELY
TRANSGENDER
TRANSGENDERED
TRANSGENDERS
TRANSGENES
TRANSGENESES
TRANSGENESIS
TRANSGENIC
TRANSGENICS
TRANSGRESS
TRANSGRESSED
TRANSGRESSES
TRANSGRESSING
TRANSGRESSION
TRANSGRESSIONAL
TRANSGRESSIONS
TRANSGRESSIVE
TRANSGRESSIVELY
TRANSGRESSOR
TRANSGRESSORS
TRANSHIPMENT
TRANSHIPMENTS
TRANSHIPPED
TRANSHIPPER
TRANSHIPPERS
TRANSHIPPING
TRANSHIPPINGS
TRANSHISTORICAL
TRANSHUMANCE
TRANSHUMANCES
TRANSHUMANT
TRANSHUMANTS
TRANSHUMED

TRANSHUMES
TRANSHUMING
TRANSIENCE
TRANSIENCES
TRANSIENCIES
TRANSIENCY
TRANSIENTLY
TRANSIENTNESS
TRANSIENTNESSES
TRANSIENTS
TRANSILIENCE
TRANSILIENCES
TRANSILIENCIES
TRANSILIENCY
TRANSILIENT
TRANSILLUMINATE
TRANSISTHMIAN
TRANSISTOR
TRANSISTORISE
TRANSISTORISED
TRANSISTORISES
TRANSISTORISING
TRANSISTORIZE
TRANSISTORIZED
TRANSISTORIZES
TRANSISTORIZING
TRANSISTORS
TRANSITABLE
TRANSITING
TRANSITION
TRANSITIONAL
TRANSITIONALLY
TRANSITIONALS
TRANSITIONARY
TRANSITIONED
TRANSITIONING
TRANSITIONS
TRANSITIVE
TRANSITIVELY
TRANSITIVENESS
TRANSITIVES
TRANSITIVITIES
TRANSITIVITY
TRANSITORILY
TRANSITORINESS
TRANSITORY
TRANSLATABILITY
TRANSLATABLE

TRANSLATED
TRANSLATES
TRANSLATING
TRANSLATION
TRANSLATIONAL
TRANSLATIONALLY
TRANSLATIONS
TRANSLATIVE
TRANSLATIVES
TRANSLATOR
TRANSLATORIAL
TRANSLATORS
TRANSLATORY
TRANSLEITHAN
TRANSLITERATE
TRANSLITERATED
TRANSLITERATES
TRANSLITERATING
TRANSLITERATION
TRANSLITERATOR
TRANSLITERATORS
TRANSLOCATE
TRANSLOCATED
TRANSLOCATES
TRANSLOCATING
TRANSLOCATION
TRANSLOCATIONS
TRANSLUCENCE
TRANSLUCENCES
TRANSLUCENCIES
TRANSLUCENCY
TRANSLUCENT
TRANSLUCENTLY
TRANSLUCID
TRANSLUCIDITIES
TRANSLUCIDITY
TRANSLUMENAL
TRANSLUMINAL
TRANSLUNAR
TRANSLUNARY
TRANSMANCHE
TRANSMARINE
TRANSMEMBRANE
TRANSMEWED
TRANSMEWING
TRANSMIGRANT
TRANSMIGRANTS
TRANSMIGRATE

TRANSMIGRATED
TRANSMIGRATES
TRANSMIGRATING
TRANSMIGRATION
TRANSMIGRATIONS
TRANSMIGRATIVE
TRANSMIGRATOR
TRANSMIGRATORS
TRANSMIGRATORY
TRANSMISSIBLE
TRANSMISSION
TRANSMISSIONAL
TRANSMISSIONS
TRANSMISSIVE
TRANSMISSIVELY
TRANSMISSIVITY
TRANSMISSOMETER
TRANSMITTABLE
TRANSMITTAL
TRANSMITTALS
TRANSMITTANCE
TRANSMITTANCES
TRANSMITTANCIES
TRANSMITTANCY
TRANSMITTED
TRANSMITTER
TRANSMITTERS
TRANSMITTIBLE
TRANSMITTING
TRANSMITTIVITY
TRANSMOGRIFIED
TRANSMOGRIFIES
TRANSMOGRIFY
TRANSMOGRIFYING
TRANSMONTANE
TRANSMONTANES
TRANSMOUNTAIN
TRANSMOVED
TRANSMOVES
TRANSMOVING
TRANSMUNDANE
TRANSMUTABILITY
TRANSMUTABLE
TRANSMUTABLY
TRANSMUTATION
TRANSMUTATIONAL
TRANSMUTATIONS
TRANSMUTATIVE
TRANSMUTED
TRANSMUTER
TRANSMUTERS
TRANSMUTES
TRANSMUTING
TRANSNATIONAL
TRANSNATURAL
TRANSOCEANIC
TRANSONICS
TRANSPACIFIC
TRANSPADANE
TRANSPARENCE
TRANSPARENCES
TRANSPARENCIES
TRANSPARENCY
TRANSPARENT
TRANSPARENTISE
TRANSPARENTISED
TRANSPARENTISES
TRANSPARENTIZE
TRANSPARENTIZED
TRANSPARENTIZES
TRANSPARENTLY
TRANSPARENTNESS
TRANSPERSON
TRANSPERSONAL
TRANSPERSONS
TRANSPHOBIA
TRANSPHOBIAS
TRANSPHOBIC
TRANSPICUOUS
TRANSPICUOUSLY
TRANSPIERCE
TRANSPIERCED
TRANSPIERCES
TRANSPIERCING
TRANSPIRABLE
TRANSPIRATION
TRANSPIRATIONAL
TRANSPIRATIONS
TRANSPIRATORY
TRANSPIRED
TRANSPIRES
TRANSPIRING
TRANSPLACENTAL
TRANSPLANT
TRANSPLANTABLE
TRANSPLANTATION
TRANSPLANTED
TRANSPLANTER
TRANSPLANTERS
TRANSPLANTING
TRANSPLANTINGS
TRANSPLANTS
TRANSPOLAR
TRANSPONDER
TRANSPONDERS
TRANSPONDOR
TRANSPONDORS
TRANSPONTINE
TRANSPORTABLE
TRANSPORTAL
TRANSPORTALS
TRANSPORTANCE
TRANSPORTANCES
TRANSPORTATION
TRANSPORTATIONS
TRANSPORTED
TRANSPORTEDLY
TRANSPORTEDNESS
TRANSPORTER
TRANSPORTERS
TRANSPORTING
TRANSPORTINGLY
TRANSPORTINGS
TRANSPORTIVE
TRANSPORTS
TRANSPOSABILITY
TRANSPOSABLE
TRANSPOSAL
TRANSPOSALS
TRANSPOSED
TRANSPOSER
TRANSPOSERS
TRANSPOSES
TRANSPOSING
TRANSPOSINGS
TRANSPOSITION
TRANSPOSITIONAL
TRANSPOSITIONS
TRANSPOSITIVE
TRANSPOSON
TRANSPOSONS
TRANSPUTER
TRANSPUTERS
TRANSSEXUAL
TRANSSEXUALISM
TRANSSEXUALISMS
TRANSSEXUALITY
TRANSSEXUALS
TRANSSHAPE
TRANSSHAPED
TRANSSHAPES
TRANSSHAPING
TRANSSHIPMENT
TRANSSHIPMENTS
TRANSSHIPPED
TRANSSHIPPER
TRANSSHIPPERS
TRANSSHIPPING
TRANSSHIPPINGS
TRANSSHIPS
TRANSSONIC
TRANSTHORACIC
TRANSUBSTANTIAL
TRANSUDATE
TRANSUDATES
TRANSUDATION
TRANSUDATIONS
TRANSUDATORY
TRANSUDING
TRANSUMING
TRANSUMPTION
TRANSUMPTIONS
TRANSUMPTIVE
TRANSUMPTS
TRANSURANIAN
TRANSURANIC
TRANSURANICS
TRANSURANIUM
TRANSURETHRAL
TRANSVAGINAL
TRANSVALUATE
TRANSVALUATED
TRANSVALUATES
TRANSVALUATING
TRANSVALUATION
TRANSVALUATIONS
TRANSVALUE
TRANSVALUED
TRANSVALUER
TRANSVALUERS
TRANSVALUES
TRANSVALUING
TRANSVERSAL
TRANSVERSALITY
TRANSVERSALLY
TRANSVERSALS
TRANSVERSE
TRANSVERSED
TRANSVERSELY
TRANSVERSENESS
TRANSVERSES
TRANSVERSING
TRANSVERSION
TRANSVERSIONS
TRANSVERTER
TRANSVERTERS
TRANSVESTED
TRANSVESTIC
TRANSVESTING
TRANSVESTISM
TRANSVESTISMS
TRANSVESTIST
TRANSVESTISTS
TRANSVESTITE
TRANSVESTITES
TRANSVESTITISM
TRANSVESTITISMS
TRANSVESTS
TRANSWOMAN
TRANSWOMEN
TRAPANNERS
TRAPANNING
TRAPESINGS
TRAPEZIFORM
TRAPEZISTS
TRAPEZIUMS
TRAPEZIUSES
TRAPEZOHEDRA
TRAPEZOHEDRAL
TRAPEZOHEDRON
TRAPEZOHEDRONS
TRAPEZOIDAL
TRAPEZOIDS
TRAPNESTED
TRAPNESTING
TRAPPINESS
TRAPPINESSES
TRAPSHOOTER
TRAPSHOOTERS
TRAPSHOOTING

TRAPSHOOTINGS
TRASHERIES
TRASHINESS
TRASHINESSES
TRASHTRIES
TRATTORIAS
TRAUCHLING
TRAUMATICALLY
TRAUMATISATION
TRAUMATISATIONS
TRAUMATISE
TRAUMATISED
TRAUMATISES
TRAUMATISING
TRAUMATISM
TRAUMATISMS
TRAUMATIZATION
TRAUMATIZATIONS
TRAUMATIZE
TRAUMATIZED
TRAUMATIZES
TRAUMATIZING
TRAUMATOLOGICAL
TRAUMATOLOGIES
TRAUMATOLOGY
TRAUMATONASTIES
TRAUMATONASTY
TRAVAILING
TRAVELATOR
TRAVELATORS
TRAVELINGS
TRAVELLERS
TRAVELLING
TRAVELLINGS
TRAVELOGUE
TRAVELOGUES
TRAVERSABLE
TRAVERSALS
TRAVERSERS
TRAVERSING
TRAVERSINGS
TRAVERTINE
TRAVERTINES
TRAVERTINS
TRAVESTIED
TRAVESTIES
TRAVESTYING
TRAVOLATOR
TRAVOLATORS
TRAWLERMAN
TRAWLERMEN
TRAYCLOTHS
TRAYMOBILE
TRAYMOBILES
TRAZODONES
TREACHERER
TREACHERERS
TREACHERIES
TREACHEROUS
TREACHEROUSLY
TREACHEROUSNESS
TREACHETOUR
TREACHETOURS
TREACHOURS
TREACLIEST
TREACLINESS
TREACLINESSES
TREADLINGS
TREADMILLS
TREADWHEEL
TREADWHEELS
TREASONABLE
TREASONABLENESS
TREASONABLY
TREASONOUS
TREASURABLE
TREASURELESS
TREASURERS
TREASURERSHIP
TREASURERSHIPS
TREASURIES
TREASURING
TREATABILITIES
TREATABILITY
TREATMENTS
TREATYLESS
TREBBIANOS
TREBLENESS
TREBLENESSES
TREBUCHETS
TREBUCKETS
TRECENTIST
TRECENTISTS
TREDECILLION
TREDECILLIONS
TREDRILLES
TREEHOPPER
TREEHOPPERS
TREEHOUSES
TREELESSNESS
TREELESSNESSES
TREENWARES
TREGETOURS
TREHALOSES
TREILLAGED
TREILLAGES
TREKSCHUIT
TREKSCHUITS
TRELLISING
TRELLISWORK
TRELLISWORKS
TREMATODES
TREMATOIDS
TREMBLEMENT
TREMBLEMENTS
TREMBLIEST
TREMBLINGLY
TREMBLINGS
TREMENDOUS
TREMENDOUSLY
TREMENDOUSNESS
TREMOLANDI
TREMOLANDO
TREMOLANDOS
TREMOLANTS
TREMOLITES
TREMOLITIC
TREMORLESS
TREMULANTS
TREMULATED
TREMULATES
TREMULATING
TREMULOUSLY
TREMULOUSNESS
TREMULOUSNESSES
TRENCHANCIES
TRENCHANCY
TRENCHANTLY
TRENCHARDS
TRENCHERMAN
TRENCHERMEN
TRENDIFIED
TRENDIFIES
TRENDIFYING
TRENDINESS
TRENDINESSES
TRENDSETTER
TRENDSETTERS
TRENDSETTING
TRENDSETTINGS
TRENDYISMS
TREPANATION
TREPANATIONS
TREPANNERS
TREPANNING
TREPANNINGS
TREPHINATION
TREPHINATIONS
TREPHINERS
TREPHINING
TREPHININGS
TREPIDATION
TREPIDATIONS
TREPIDATORY
TREPONEMAL
TREPONEMAS
TREPONEMATA
TREPONEMATOSES
TREPONEMATOSIS
TREPONEMATOUS
TREPONEMES
TRESPASSED
TRESPASSER
TRESPASSERS
TRESPASSES
TRESPASSING
TRESTLETREE
TRESTLETREES
TRESTLEWORK
TRESTLEWORKS
TRETINOINS
TREVALLIES
TRIABLENESS
TRIABLENESSES
TRIACETATE
TRIACETATES
TRIACONTER
TRIACONTERS
TRIACTINAL
TRIADELPHOUS
TRIADICALLY
TRIALITIES
TRIALLINGS
TRIALLISTS
TRIALOGUES
TRIALWARES
TRIAMCINOLONE
TRIAMCINOLONES
TRIANDRIAN
TRIANDROUS
TRIANGULAR
TRIANGULARITIES
TRIANGULARITY
TRIANGULARLY
TRIANGULATE
TRIANGULATED
TRIANGULATELY
TRIANGULATES
TRIANGULATING
TRIANGULATION
TRIANGULATIONS
TRIAPSIDAL
TRIARCHIES
TRIATHLETE
TRIATHLETES
TRIATHLONS
TRIATOMICALLY
TRIAXIALITIES
TRIAXIALITY
TRIBADISMS
TRIBALISMS
TRIBALISTIC
TRIBALISTS
TRIBESPEOPLE
TRIBESWOMAN
TRIBESWOMEN
TRIBOELECTRIC
TRIBOLOGICAL
TRIBOLOGIES
TRIBOLOGIST
TRIBOLOGISTS
TRIBOMETER
TRIBOMETERS
TRIBRACHIAL
TRIBRACHIC
TRIBROMOETHANOL
TRIBROMOMETHANE
TRIBULATED
TRIBULATES
TRIBULATING

TRIBULATION
TRIBULATIONS
TRIBUNATES
TRIBUNESHIP
TRIBUNESHIPS
TRIBUNICIAL
TRIBUNICIAN
TRIBUNITIAL
TRIBUNITIAN
TRIBUTARIES
TRIBUTARILY
TRIBUTARINESS
TRIBUTARINESSES
TRICAMERAL
TRICARBOXYLIC
TRICARPELLARY
TRICENTENARIES
TRICENTENARY
TRICENTENNIAL
TRICENTENNIALS
TRICEPHALOUS
TRICERATOPS
TRICERATOPSES
TRICERIONS
TRICHIASES
TRICHIASIS
TRICHINELLA
TRICHINELLAE
TRICHINELLAS
TRICHINIASES
TRICHINIASIS
TRICHINISATION
TRICHINISATIONS
TRICHINISE
TRICHINISED
TRICHINISES
TRICHINISING
TRICHINIZATION
TRICHINIZATIONS
TRICHINIZE
TRICHINIZED
TRICHINIZES
TRICHINIZING
TRICHINOSE
TRICHINOSED
TRICHINOSES
TRICHINOSING
TRICHINOSIS
TRICHINOTIC
TRICHINOUS
TRICHLORACETIC
TRICHLORFON
TRICHLORFONS
TRICHLORIDE
TRICHLORIDES
TRICHLOROACETIC
TRICHLOROETHANE
TRICHLORPHON
TRICHLORPHONS
TRICHOBACTERIA
TRICHOCYST
TRICHOCYSTIC
TRICHOCYSTS
TRICHOGYNE
TRICHOGYNES
TRICHOGYNIAL
TRICHOGYNIC
TRICHOLOGICAL
TRICHOLOGIES
TRICHOLOGIST
TRICHOLOGISTS
TRICHOLOGY
TRICHOMONACIDAL
TRICHOMONACIDE
TRICHOMONACIDES
TRICHOMONAD
TRICHOMONADAL
TRICHOMONADS
TRICHOMONAL
TRICHOMONIASES
TRICHOMONIASIS
TRICHOPHYTON
TRICHOPHYTONS
TRICHOPHYTOSES
TRICHOPHYTOSIS
TRICHOPTERAN
TRICHOPTERANS
TRICHOPTERIST
TRICHOPTERISTS
TRICHOPTEROUS
TRICHOTHECENE
TRICHOTHECENES
TRICHOTOMIC
TRICHOTOMIES
TRICHOTOMISE
TRICHOTOMISED
TRICHOTOMISES
TRICHOTOMISING
TRICHOTOMIZE
TRICHOTOMIZED
TRICHOTOMIZES
TRICHOTOMIZING
TRICHOTOMOUS
TRICHOTOMOUSLY
TRICHOTOMY
TRICHROISM
TRICHROISMS
TRICHROMAT
TRICHROMATIC
TRICHROMATISM
TRICHROMATISMS
TRICHROMATS
TRICHROMIC
TRICHROMICS
TRICHRONOUS
TRICHURIASES
TRICHURIASIS
TRICKERIES
TRICKINESS
TRICKINESSES
TRICKISHLY
TRICKISHNESS
TRICKISHNESSES
TRICKLIEST
TRICKLINGLY
TRICKLINGS
TRICKSIEST
TRICKSINESS
TRICKSINESSES
TRICKSTERING
TRICKSTERINGS
TRICKSTERS
TRICKTRACK
TRICKTRACKS
TRICLINIUM
TRICLOSANS
TRICOLETTE
TRICOLETTES
TRICOLORED
TRICOLOURED
TRICOLOURS
TRICONSONANTAL
TRICONSONANTIC
TRICORNERED
TRICORPORATE
TRICORPORATED
TRICOSTATE
TRICOTEUSE
TRICOTEUSES
TRICOTINES
TRICROTISM
TRICROTISMS
TRICROTOUS
TRICUSPIDAL
TRICUSPIDATE
TRICUSPIDS
TRICYCLERS
TRICYCLICS
TRICYCLING
TRICYCLINGS
TRICYCLIST
TRICYCLISTS
TRIDACTYLOUS
TRIDENTATE
TRIDIMENSIONAL
TRIDOMINIA
TRIDOMINIUM
TRIDOMINIUMS
TRIDYMITES
TRIENNIALLY
TRIENNIALS
TRIENNIUMS
TRIERARCHAL
TRIERARCHIES
TRIERARCHS
TRIERARCHY
TRIETHIODIDE
TRIETHIODIDES
TRIETHYLAMINE
TRIETHYLAMINES
TRIFACIALS
TRIFARIOUS
TRIFFIDIAN
TRIFFIDIER
TRIFFIDIEST
TRIFLINGLY
TRIFLINGNESS
TRIFLINGNESSES
TRIFLUOPERAZINE
TRIFLURALIN
TRIFLURALINS
TRIFOLIATE
TRIFOLIATED
TRIFOLIOLATE
TRIFOLIUMS
TRIFURCATE
TRIFURCATED
TRIFURCATES
TRIFURCATING
TRIFURCATION
TRIFURCATIONS
TRIGAMISTS
TRIGEMINAL
TRIGEMINALS
TRIGEMINUS
TRIGGERFISH
TRIGGERFISHES
TRIGGERING
TRIGGERLESS
TRIGGERMAN
TRIGGERMEN
TRIGLYCERIDE
TRIGLYCERIDES
TRIGLYPHIC
TRIGLYPHICAL
TRIGNESSES
TRIGONALLY
TRIGONOMETER
TRIGONOMETERS
TRIGONOMETRIC
TRIGONOMETRICAL
TRIGONOMETRIES
TRIGONOMETRY
TRIGRAMMATIC
TRIGRAMMIC
TRIGRAPHIC
TRIHALOMETHANE
TRIHALOMETHANES
TRIHEDRALS
TRIHEDRONS
TRIHYBRIDS
TRIHYDRATE
TRIHYDRATED
TRIHYDRATES
TRIHYDROXY
TRIIODOMETHANE
TRIIODOMETHANES
TRILATERAL
TRILATERALISM
TRILATERALISMS

T

TRILATERALIST
TRILATERALISTS
TRILATERALLY
TRILATERALS
TRILATERATION
TRILATERATIONS
TRILINEATE
TRILINGUAL
TRILINGUALISM
TRILINGUALISMS
TRILINGUALLY
TRILITERAL
TRILITERALISM
TRILITERALISMS
TRILITERALS
TRILITHONS
TRILLIONAIRE
TRILLIONAIRES
TRILLIONTH
TRILLIONTHS
TRILOBATED
TRILOBITES
TRILOBITIC
TRILOCULAR
TRIMERISMS
TRIMESTERS
TRIMESTRAL
TRIMESTRIAL
TRIMETHADIONE
TRIMETHADIONES
TRIMETHOPRIM
TRIMETHOPRIMS
TRIMETHYLAMINE
TRIMETHYLAMINES
TRIMETHYLENE
TRIMETHYLENES
TRIMETRICAL
TRIMETROGON
TRIMETROGONS
TRIMMINGLY
TRIMNESSES
TRIMOLECULAR
TRIMONTHLY
TRIMORPHIC
TRIMORPHISM
TRIMORPHISMS
TRIMORPHOUS
TRIMPHONES
TRINACRIAN
TRINACRIFORM
TRINISCOPE
TRINISCOPES
TRINITARIAN
TRINITARIANS
TRINITRATE
TRINITRATES
TRINITRINS
TRINITROBENZENE
TRINITROCRESOL
TRINITROCRESOLS
TRINITROPHENOL
TRINITROPHENOLS
TRINITROTOLUENE
TRINITROTOLUOL
TRINITROTOLUOLS
TRINKETERS
TRINKETING
TRINKETINGS
TRINKETRIES
TRINOCULAR
TRINOMIALISM
TRINOMIALISMS
TRINOMIALIST
TRINOMIALISTS
TRINOMIALLY
TRINOMIALS
TRINUCLEOTIDE
TRINUCLEOTIDES
TRIOECIOUS
TRIOXOBORIC
TRIOXYGENS
TRIPALMITIN
TRIPALMITINS
TRIPARTISM
TRIPARTISMS
TRIPARTITE
TRIPARTITELY
TRIPARTITION
TRIPARTITIONS
TRIPEHOUND
TRIPEHOUNDS
TRIPERSONAL
TRIPERSONALISM
TRIPERSONALISMS
TRIPERSONALIST
TRIPERSONALISTS
TRIPERSONALITY
TRIPETALOUS
TRIPHAMMER
TRIPHAMMERS
TRIPHENYLAMINE
TRIPHENYLAMINES
TRIPHIBIOUS
TRIPHOSPHATE
TRIPHOSPHATES
TRIPHTHONG
TRIPHTHONGAL
TRIPHTHONGS
TRIPHYLITE
TRIPHYLITES
TRIPHYLLOUS
TRIPINNATE
TRIPINNATELY
TRIPITAKAS
TRIPLENESS
TRIPLENESSES
TRIPLETAIL
TRIPLETAILS
TRIPLEXING
TRIPLICATE
TRIPLICATED
TRIPLICATES
TRIPLICATING
TRIPLICATION
TRIPLICATIONS
TRIPLICITIES
TRIPLICITY
TRIPLOBLASTIC
TRIPLOIDIES
TRIPMETERS
TRIPPERIER
TRIPPERIEST
TRIPPERISH
TRIPPINGLY
TRIPTEROUS
TRIPTYQUES
TRIPUDIARY
TRIPUDIATE
TRIPUDIATED
TRIPUDIATES
TRIPUDIATING
TRIPUDIATION
TRIPUDIATIONS
TRIQUETRAE
TRIQUETRAL
TRIQUETRAS
TRIQUETROUS
TRIQUETROUSLY
TRIQUETRUM
TRIRADIATE
TRIRADIATELY
TRISACCHARIDE
TRISACCHARIDES
TRISAGIONS
TRISECTING
TRISECTION
TRISECTIONS
TRISECTORS
TRISECTRICES
TRISECTRIX
TRISKELION
TRISKELIONS
TRISOCTAHEDRA
TRISOCTAHEDRAL
TRISOCTAHEDRON
TRISOCTAHEDRONS
TRISTEARIN
TRISTEARINS
TRISTESSES
TRISTFULLY
TRISTFULNESS
TRISTFULNESSES
TRISTICHIC
TRISTICHOUS
TRISTIMULUS
TRISUBSTITUTED
TRISULCATE
TRISULFIDE
TRISULFIDES
TRISULPHIDE
TRISULPHIDES
TRISYLLABIC
TRISYLLABICAL
TRISYLLABICALLY
TRISYLLABLE
TRISYLLABLES
TRITAGONIST
TRITAGONISTS
TRITANOPES
TRITANOPIA
TRITANOPIAS
TRITANOPIC
TRITENESSES
TRITERNATE
TRITHEISMS
TRITHEISTIC
TRITHEISTICAL
TRITHEISTS
TRITHIONATE
TRITHIONATES
TRITHIONIC
TRITIATING
TRITIATION
TRITIATIONS
TRITICALES
TRITICALLY
TRITICALNESS
TRITICALNESSES
TRITICEOUS
TRITICISMS
TRITUBERCULAR
TRITUBERCULATE
TRITUBERCULIES
TRITUBERCULISM
TRITUBERCULISMS
TRITUBERCULY
TRITURABLE
TRITURATED
TRITURATES
TRITURATING
TRITURATION
TRITURATIONS
TRITURATOR
TRITURATORS
TRIUMPHALISM
TRIUMPHALISMS
TRIUMPHALIST
TRIUMPHALISTS
TRIUMPHALS
TRIUMPHANT
TRIUMPHANTLY
TRIUMPHERIES
TRIUMPHERS
TRIUMPHERY
TRIUMPHING
TRIUMPHINGS
TRIUMVIRAL
TRIUMVIRATE
TRIUMVIRATES
TRIUMVIRIES

TRIUNITIES
TRIVALENCE
TRIVALENCES
TRIVALENCIES
TRIVALENCY
TRIVALVULAR
TRIVIALISATION
TRIVIALISATIONS
TRIVIALISE
TRIVIALISED
TRIVIALISES
TRIVIALISING
TRIVIALISM
TRIVIALISMS
TRIVIALIST
TRIVIALISTS
TRIVIALITIES
TRIVIALITY
TRIVIALIZATION
TRIVIALIZATIONS
TRIVIALIZE
TRIVIALIZED
TRIVIALIZES
TRIVIALIZING
TRIVIALNESS
TRIVIALNESSES
TRIWEEKLIES
TROCHAICALLY
TROCHANTER
TROCHANTERAL
TROCHANTERIC
TROCHANTERS
TROCHEAMETER
TROCHEAMETERS
TROCHELMINTH
TROCHELMINTHS
TROCHILUSES
TROCHISCUS
TROCHISCUSES
TROCHLEARS
TROCHOIDAL
TROCHOIDALLY
TROCHOMETER
TROCHOMETERS
TROCHOPHORE
TROCHOPHORES
TROCHOSPHERE
TROCHOSPHERES
TROCHOTRON
TROCHOTRONS
TROCTOLITE
TROCTOLITES
TROGLODYTE
TROGLODYTES
TROGLODYTIC
TROGLODYTICAL
TROGLODYTISM
TROGLODYTISMS
TROLLEYBUS
TROLLEYBUSES
TROLLEYBUSSES
TROLLEYING
TROLLIUSES
TROLLOPEES
TROLLOPIER
TROLLOPIEST
TROLLOPING
TROLLOPISH
TROMBICULID
TROMBICULIDS
TROMBIDIASES
TROMBIDIASIS
TROMBONIST
TROMBONISTS
TROMOMETER
TROMOMETERS
TROMOMETRIC
TROOPSHIPS
TROOSTITES
TROPAEOLIN
TROPAEOLINS
TROPAEOLUM
TROPAEOLUMS
TROPARIONS
TROPEOLINS
TROPHALLACTIC
TROPHALLAXES
TROPHALLAXIS
TROPHESIAL
TROPHESIES
TROPHICALLY
TROPHOBIOSES
TROPHOBIOSIS
TROPHOBIOTIC
TROPHOBLAST
TROPHOBLASTIC
TROPHOBLASTS
TROPHOLOGIES
TROPHOLOGY
TROPHONEUROSES
TROPHONEUROSIS
TROPHOPLASM
TROPHOPLASMS
TROPHOTACTIC
TROPHOTAXES
TROPHOTAXIS
TROPHOTROPIC
TROPHOTROPISM
TROPHOTROPISMS
TROPHOZOITE
TROPHOZOITES
TROPICALISATION
TROPICALISE
TROPICALISED
TROPICALISES
TROPICALISING
TROPICALITIES
TROPICALITY
TROPICALIZATION
TROPICALIZE
TROPICALIZED
TROPICALIZES
TROPICALIZING
TROPICALLY
TROPICBIRD
TROPICBIRDS
TROPISMATIC
TROPOCOLLAGEN
TROPOCOLLAGENS
TROPOLOGIC
TROPOLOGICAL
TROPOLOGICALLY
TROPOLOGIES
TROPOMYOSIN
TROPOMYOSINS
TROPOPAUSE
TROPOPAUSES
TROPOPHILOUS
TROPOPHYTE
TROPOPHYTES
TROPOPHYTIC
TROPOSCATTER
TROPOSCATTERS
TROPOSPHERE
TROPOSPHERES
TROPOSPHERIC
TROPOTAXES
TROPOTAXIS
TROTHPLIGHT
TROTHPLIGHTED
TROTHPLIGHTING
TROTHPLIGHTS
TROUBADOUR
TROUBADOURS
TROUBLEDLY
TROUBLEFREE
TROUBLEMAKER
TROUBLEMAKERS
TROUBLEMAKING
TROUBLEMAKINGS
TROUBLESHOOT
TROUBLESHOOTER
TROUBLESHOOTERS
TROUBLESHOOTING
TROUBLESHOOTS
TROUBLESHOT
TROUBLESOME
TROUBLESOMELY
TROUBLESOMENESS
TROUBLINGS
TROUBLOUSLY
TROUBLOUSNESS
TROUBLOUSNESSES
TROUGHINGS
TROUGHLIKE
TROUNCINGS
TROUSERING
TROUSERINGS
TROUSERLESS
TROUSSEAUS
TROUSSEAUX
TROUTLINGS
TROUTSTONE
TROUTSTONES
TROUVAILLE
TROUVAILLES
TROWELLERS
TROWELLING
TRUANTINGS
TRUANTRIES
TRUANTSHIP
TRUANTSHIPS
TRUCKLINES
TRUCKLINGS
TRUCKLOADS
TRUCKMASTER
TRUCKMASTERS
TRUCKSTOPS
TRUCULENCE
TRUCULENCES
TRUCULENCIES
TRUCULENCY
TRUCULENTLY
TRUEHEARTED
TRUEHEARTEDNESS
TRUENESSES
TRUEPENNIES
TRUFFLINGS
TRUMPERIES
TRUMPETERS
TRUMPETING
TRUMPETINGS
TRUMPETLIKE
TRUMPETWEED
TRUMPETWEEDS
TRUNCATELY
TRUNCATING
TRUNCATINGS
TRUNCATION
TRUNCATIONS
TRUNCHEONED
TRUNCHEONER
TRUNCHEONERS
TRUNCHEONING
TRUNCHEONS
TRUNKFISHES
TRUNKSLEEVE
TRUNKSLEEVES
TRUNKWORKS
TRUNNIONED
TRUSTABILITIES
TRUSTABILITY
TRUSTAFARIAN
TRUSTAFARIANS
TRUSTBUSTER
TRUSTBUSTERS
TRUSTBUSTING
TRUSTBUSTINGS
TRUSTEEING
TRUSTEESHIP

TRUSTEESHIPS
TRUSTFULLY
TRUSTFULNESS
TRUSTFULNESSES
TRUSTINESS
TRUSTINESSES
TRUSTINGLY
TRUSTINGNESS
TRUSTINGNESSES
TRUSTLESSLY
TRUSTLESSNESS
TRUSTLESSNESSES
TRUSTWORTHIER
TRUSTWORTHIEST
TRUSTWORTHILY
TRUSTWORTHINESS
TRUSTWORTHY
TRUTHFULLY
TRUTHFULNESS
TRUTHFULNESSES
TRUTHINESS
TRUTHINESSES
TRUTHLESSNESS
TRUTHLESSNESSES
TRYINGNESS
TRYINGNESSES
TRYPAFLAVINE
TRYPAFLAVINES
TRYPANOCIDAL
TRYPANOCIDE
TRYPANOCIDES
TRYPANOSOMAL
TRYPANOSOME
TRYPANOSOMES
TRYPANOSOMIASES
TRYPANOSOMIASIS
TRYPANOSOMIC
TRYPARSAMIDE
TRYPARSAMIDES
TRYPSINOGEN
TRYPSINOGENS
TRYPTAMINE
TRYPTAMINES
TRYPTOPHAN
TRYPTOPHANE
TRYPTOPHANES
TRYPTOPHANS
TSAREVICHES
TSAREVITCH
TSAREVITCHES
TSCHERNOSEM
TSCHERNOSEMS
TSESAREVICH
TSESAREVICHES
TSESAREVITCH
TSESAREVITCHES
TSESAREVNA
TSESAREVNAS
TSESAREWICH
TSESAREWICHES
TSESAREWITCH
TSESAREWITCHES
TSOTSITAAL
TSOTSITAALS
TSUNAMIGENIC
TSUTSUGAMUSHI
TSUTSUGAMUSHIS
TUBBINESSES
TUBECTOMIES
TUBERACEOUS
TUBERCULAR
TUBERCULARLY
TUBERCULARS
TUBERCULATE
TUBERCULATED
TUBERCULATELY
TUBERCULATION
TUBERCULATIONS
TUBERCULES
TUBERCULIN
TUBERCULINS
TUBERCULISATION
TUBERCULISE
TUBERCULISED
TUBERCULISES
TUBERCULISING
TUBERCULIZATION
TUBERCULIZE
TUBERCULIZED
TUBERCULIZES
TUBERCULIZING
TUBERCULOID
TUBERCULOMA
TUBERCULOMAS
TUBERCULOMATA
TUBERCULOSE
TUBERCULOSED
TUBERCULOSES
TUBERCULOSIS
TUBERCULOUS
TUBERCULOUSLY
TUBERCULUM
TUBERIFEROUS
TUBERIFORM
TUBEROSITIES
TUBEROSITY
TUBICOLOUS
TUBIFICIDS
TUBIFLOROUS
TUBOCURARINE
TUBOCURARINES
TUBOPLASTIES
TUBOPLASTY
TUBULARIAN
TUBULARIANS
TUBULARITIES
TUBULARITY
TUBULATING
TUBULATION
TUBULATIONS
TUBULATORS
TUBULATURE
TUBULATURES
TUBULIFLORAL
TUBULIFLOROUS
TUBULOUSLY
TUCKAMORES
TUCKERBAGS
TUCKERBOXES
TUFFACEOUS
TUFFTAFFETA
TUFFTAFFETAS
TUFFTAFFETIES
TUFFTAFFETY
TUFTAFFETA
TUFTAFFETAS
TUFTAFFETIES
TUFTAFFETY
TUILLETTES
TUILYIEING
TUILZIEING
TUITIONARY
TULARAEMIA
TULARAEMIAS
TULARAEMIC
TULAREMIAS
TULIPOMANIA
TULIPOMANIAS
TULIPWOODS
TUMATAKURU
TUMATAKURUS
TUMBLEBUGS
TUMBLEDOWN
TUMBLEHOME
TUMBLEHOMES
TUMBLERFUL
TUMBLERFULS
TUMBLERSFUL
TUMBLESETS
TUMBLEWEED
TUMBLEWEEDS
TUMEFACIENT
TUMEFACTION
TUMEFACTIONS
TUMESCENCE
TUMESCENCES
TUMESCENTLY
TUMIDITIES
TUMIDNESSES
TUMORGENIC
TUMORGENICITIES
TUMORGENICITY
TUMORIGENESES
TUMORIGENESIS
TUMORIGENIC
TUMORIGENICITY
TUMULOSITIES
TUMULOSITY
TUMULTUARY
TUMULTUATE
TUMULTUATED
TUMULTUATES
TUMULTUATING
TUMULTUATION
TUMULTUATIONS
TUMULTUOUS
TUMULTUOUSLY
TUMULTUOUSNESS
TUNABILITIES
TUNABILITY
TUNABLENESS
TUNABLENESSES
TUNBELLIED
TUNBELLIES
TUNEFULNESS
TUNEFULNESSES
TUNELESSLY
TUNELESSNESS
TUNELESSNESSES
TUNESMITHS
TUNGSTATES
TUNGSTITES
TUNNELINGS
TUNNELLERS
TUNNELLIKE
TUNNELLING
TUNNELLINGS
TUPPENNIES
TUPTOWINGS
TURACOVERDIN
TURACOVERDINS
TURANGAWAEWAE
TURANGAWAEWAES
TURBELLARIAN
TURBELLARIANS
TURBIDIMETER
TURBIDIMETERS
TURBIDIMETRIC
TURBIDIMETRIES
TURBIDIMETRY
TURBIDITES
TURBIDITIES
TURBIDNESS
TURBIDNESSES
TURBINACIOUS
TURBINATED
TURBINATES
TURBINATION
TURBINATIONS
TURBOCHARGED
TURBOCHARGER
TURBOCHARGERS
TURBOCHARGING
TURBOCHARGINGS
TURBOELECTRIC
TURBOGENERATOR
TURBOGENERATORS
TURBOMACHINERY
TURBOPROPS
TURBOSHAFT

T

TURBOSHAFTS
TURBULATOR
TURBULATORS
TURBULENCE
TURBULENCES
TURBULENCIES
TURBULENCY
TURBULENTLY
TURCOPOLES
TURCOPOLIER
TURCOPOLIERS
TURDUCKENS
TURFGRASSES
TURFINESSES
TURFSKIING
TURFSKIINGS
TURGENCIES
TURGESCENCE
TURGESCENCES
TURGESCENCIES
TURGESCENCY
TURGESCENT
TURGIDITIES
TURGIDNESS
TURGIDNESSES
TURMOILING
TURNABOUTS
TURNAGAINS
TURNAROUND
TURNAROUNDS
TURNBROACH
TURNBROACHES
TURNBUCKLE
TURNBUCKLES
TURNIPIEST
TURNROUNDS
TURNSTILES
TURNSTONES
TURNTABLES
TURNTABLIST
TURNTABLISTS
TURNVEREIN
TURNVEREINS
TUROPHILES
TURPENTINE
TURPENTINED
TURPENTINES
TURPENTINIER
TURPENTINIEST
TURPENTINING
TURPENTINY
TURPITUDES
TURQUOISES
TURRIBANTS
TURRICULATE
TURRICULATED
TURTLEBACK
TURTLEBACKS
TURTLEDOVE
TURTLEDOVES
TURTLEHEAD
TURTLEHEADS
TURTLENECK
TURTLENECKED
TURTLENECKS
TUSSOCKIER
TUSSOCKIEST
TUTELARIES
TUTIORISMS
TUTIORISTS
TUTORESSES
TUTORIALLY
TUTORISING
TUTORIZING
TUTORSHIPS
TUTOYERING
TUTWORKERS
TUTWORKMAN
TUTWORKMEN
TWADDLIEST
TWADDLINGS
TWALPENNIES
TWANGINGLY
TWANGLINGLY
TWANGLINGS
TWATTLINGS
TWAYBLADES
TWEEDINESS
TWEEDINESSES
TWEEDLEDEE
TWEEDLEDEED
TWEEDLEDEEING
TWEEDLEDEES
TWEENAGERS
TWEENESSES
TWELVEFOLD
TWELVEMONTH
TWELVEMONTHS
TWENTIETHS
TWENTYFOLD
TWENTYFOLDS
TWICHILDREN
TWIDDLIEST
TWIDDLINGS
TWILIGHTED
TWILIGHTING
TWINBERRIES
TWINFLOWER
TWINFLOWERS
TWINKLIEST
TWINKLINGS
TWISTABILITIES
TWISTABILITY
TWITCHIEST
TWITCHINGS
TWITTERATI
TWITTERERS
TWITTERIER
TWITTERIEST
TWITTERING
TWITTERINGLY
TWITTERINGS
TWITTINGLY
TWOFOLDNESS
TWOFOLDNESSES
TWOPENCEWORTH
TWOPENCEWORTHS
TWOPENNIES
TWOSEATERS
TYCOONATES
TYCOONERIES
TYLECTOMIES
TYMPANIFORM
TYMPANISTS
TYMPANITES
TYMPANITESES
TYMPANITIC
TYMPANITIS
TYMPANITISES
TYNDALLIMETRIES
TYNDALLIMETRY
TYPECASTER
TYPECASTERS
TYPECASTING
TYPECASTINGS
TYPEFOUNDER
TYPEFOUNDERS
TYPEFOUNDING
TYPEFOUNDINGS
TYPEFOUNDRIES
TYPEFOUNDRY
TYPESCRIPT
TYPESCRIPTS
TYPESETTER
TYPESETTERS
TYPESETTING
TYPESETTINGS
TYPESTYLES
TYPEWRITER
TYPEWRITERS
TYPEWRITES
TYPEWRITING
TYPEWRITINGS
TYPEWRITTEN
TYPHACEOUS
TYPHLITISES
TYPHLOLOGIES
TYPHLOLOGY
TYPHLOSOLE
TYPHLOSOLES
TYPHOGENIC
TYPHOIDINS
TYPICALITIES
TYPICALITY
TYPICALNESS
TYPICALNESSES
TYPIFICATION
TYPIFICATIONS
TYPOGRAPHED
TYPOGRAPHER
TYPOGRAPHERS
TYPOGRAPHIA
TYPOGRAPHIC
TYPOGRAPHICAL
TYPOGRAPHICALLY
TYPOGRAPHIES
TYPOGRAPHING
TYPOGRAPHIST
TYPOGRAPHISTS
TYPOGRAPHS
TYPOGRAPHY
TYPOLOGICAL
TYPOLOGICALLY
TYPOLOGIES
TYPOLOGIST
TYPOLOGISTS
TYPOMANIAS
TYPOTHETAE
TYRANNESSES
TYRANNICAL
TYRANNICALLY
TYRANNICALNESS
TYRANNICIDAL
TYRANNICIDE
TYRANNICIDES
TYRANNISED
TYRANNISER
TYRANNISERS
TYRANNISES
TYRANNISING
TYRANNIZED
TYRANNIZER
TYRANNIZERS
TYRANNIZES
TYRANNIZING
TYRANNOSAUR
TYRANNOSAURS
TYRANNOSAURUS
TYRANNOSAURUSES
TYRANNOUSLY
TYRANNOUSNESS
TYRANNOUSNESSES
TYREMAKERS
TYROCIDINE
TYROCIDINES
TYROCIDINS
TYROGLYPHID
TYROGLYPHIDS
TYROPITTAS
TYROSINASE
TYROSINASES
TYROTHRICIN
TYROTHRICINS

U

UBERSEXUAL
UBERSEXUALS
UBIQUARIAN
UBIQUINONE
UBIQUINONES
UBIQUITARIAN
UBIQUITARIANISM
UBIQUITARIANS
UBIQUITARY
UBIQUITIES
UBIQUITINATION
UBIQUITINATIONS
UBIQUITINS
UBIQUITOUS
UBIQUITOUSLY
UBIQUITOUSNESS
UDOMETRIES
UFOLOGICAL
UFOLOGISTS
UGLIFICATION
UGLIFICATIONS
UGLINESSES
UGSOMENESS
UGSOMENESSES
UINTAHITES
UINTATHERE
UINTATHERES
UITLANDERS
ULCERATING
ULCERATION
ULCERATIONS
ULCERATIVE
ULCEROGENIC
ULCEROUSLY
ULCEROUSNESS
ULCEROUSNESSES
ULOTRICHIES
ULOTRICHOUS
ULSTERETTE
ULSTERETTES
ULTERIORLY
ULTIMACIES
ULTIMATELY
ULTIMATENESS
ULTIMATENESSES
ULTIMATING
ULTIMATUMS
ULTIMOGENITURE
ULTIMOGENITURES
ULTRABASIC
ULTRABASICS
ULTRACAREFUL
ULTRACASUAL
ULTRACAUTIOUS
ULTRACENTRIFUGE
ULTRACIVILISED
ULTRACIVILIZED
ULTRACLEAN
ULTRACOMMERCIAL
ULTRACOMPACT
ULTRACOMPETENT
ULTRACONVENIENT
ULTRACREPIDATE
ULTRACREPIDATED
ULTRACREPIDATES
ULTRACRITICAL
ULTRADEMOCRATIC
ULTRADENSE
ULTRADISTANCE
ULTRADISTANT
ULTRADRIER
ULTRADRIEST
ULTRADRYER
ULTRADRYEST
ULTRAEFFICIENT
ULTRAENERGETIC
ULTRAEXCLUSIVE
ULTRAFAMILIAR
ULTRAFASTIDIOUS
ULTRAFEMININE
ULTRAFICHE
ULTRAFICHES
ULTRAFILTER
ULTRAFILTERED
ULTRAFILTERING
ULTRAFILTERS
ULTRAFILTRATE
ULTRAFILTRATES
ULTRAFILTRATION
ULTRAGLAMOROUS
ULTRAHAZARDOUS
ULTRAHEATED
ULTRAHEATING
ULTRAHEATS
ULTRAHEAVIER
ULTRAHEAVIEST
ULTRAHEAVY
ULTRAHUMAN
ULTRAISTIC
ULTRALARGE
ULTRALEFTISM
ULTRALEFTISMS
ULTRALEFTIST
ULTRALEFTISTS
ULTRALEFTS
ULTRALIBERAL
ULTRALIBERALISM
ULTRALIBERALS
ULTRALIGHT
ULTRALIGHTS
ULTRAMAFIC
ULTRAMARATHON
ULTRAMARATHONER
ULTRAMARATHONS
ULTRAMARINE
ULTRAMARINES
ULTRAMASCULINE
ULTRAMICRO
ULTRAMICROMETER
ULTRAMICROSCOPE
ULTRAMICROSCOPY
ULTRAMICROTOME
ULTRAMICROTOMES
ULTRAMICROTOMY
ULTRAMILITANT
ULTRAMILITANTS
ULTRAMINIATURE
ULTRAMODERN
ULTRAMODERNISM
ULTRAMODERNISMS
ULTRAMODERNIST
ULTRAMODERNISTS
ULTRAMONTANE
ULTRAMONTANES
ULTRAMONTANISM
ULTRAMONTANISMS
ULTRAMONTANIST
ULTRAMONTANISTS
ULTRAMUNDANE
ULTRANATIONAL
ULTRAORTHODOX
ULTRAPATRIOTIC
ULTRAPHYSICAL
ULTRAPOWERFUL
ULTRAPRACTICAL
ULTRAPRECISE
ULTRAPRECISION
ULTRAPRECISIONS
ULTRAQUIET
ULTRARADICAL
ULTRARADICALS
ULTRARAPID
ULTRARAREFIED
ULTRARATIONAL
ULTRAREALISM
ULTRAREALISMS
ULTRAREALIST
ULTRAREALISTIC
ULTRAREALISTS
ULTRAREFINED
ULTRARELIABLE
ULTRARIGHT
ULTRARIGHTISM
ULTRARIGHTISMS
ULTRARIGHTIST
ULTRARIGHTISTS
ULTRARIGHTS
ULTRAROMANTIC
ULTRAROYALIST
ULTRAROYALISTS
ULTRASECRET
ULTRASENSITIVE
ULTRASENSUAL
ULTRASERIOUS
ULTRASHARP
ULTRASHORT
ULTRASIMPLE
ULTRASLICK
ULTRASMALL
ULTRASMART
ULTRASMOOTH
ULTRASONIC
ULTRASONICALLY
ULTRASONICS
ULTRASONOGRAPHY
ULTRASOUND
ULTRASOUNDS
ULTRASTRUCTURAL
ULTRASTRUCTURE
ULTRASTRUCTURES
ULTRATINIER
ULTRATINIEST
ULTRAVACUA
ULTRAVACUUM
ULTRAVACUUMS
ULTRAVIOLENCE
ULTRAVIOLENCES
ULTRAVIOLENT
ULTRAVIOLET
ULTRAVIOLETS
ULTRAVIRILE
ULTRAVIRILITIES
ULTRAVIRILITY
ULTRAVIRUS
ULTRAVIRUSES
ULTRAWIDEBAND
ULTRAWIDEBANDS
ULTRONEOUS
ULTRONEOUSLY
ULTRONEOUSNESS

ULULATIONS
UMBELLATED
UMBELLATELY
UMBELLIFER
UMBELLIFEROUS
UMBELLIFERS
UMBELLULATE
UMBELLULES
UMBILICALLY
UMBILICALS
UMBILICATE
UMBILICATED
UMBILICATION
UMBILICATIONS
UMBILICUSES
UMBILIFORM
UMBONATION
UMBONATIONS
UMBRACULATE
UMBRACULIFORM
UMBRACULUM
UMBRAGEOUS
UMBRAGEOUSLY
UMBRAGEOUSNESS
UMBRATICAL
UMBRATILES
UMBRATILOUS
UMBRELLAED
UMBRELLAING
UMBRELLOES
UMBRIFEROUS
UMPIRESHIP
UMPIRESHIPS
UMPTEENTHS
UNABASHEDLY
UNABATEDLY
UNABBREVIATED
UNABOLISHED
UNABRIDGED
UNABROGATED
UNABSOLVED
UNABSORBED
UNABSORBENT
UNACADEMIC
UNACADEMICALLY
UNACCENTED
UNACCENTUATED
UNACCEPTABILITY
UNACCEPTABLE
UNACCEPTABLY
UNACCEPTANCE
UNACCEPTANCES
UNACCEPTED
UNACCLIMATED
UNACCLIMATISED
UNACCLIMATIZED
UNACCOMMODATED
UNACCOMMODATING
UNACCOMPANIED
UNACCOMPLISHED
UNACCOUNTABLE
UNACCOUNTABLY
UNACCOUNTED
UNACCREDITED
UNACCULTURATED
UNACCUSABLE
UNACCUSABLY
UNACCUSTOMED
UNACCUSTOMEDLY
UNACHIEVABLE
UNACHIEVED
UNACKNOWLEDGED
UNACQUAINT
UNACQUAINTANCE
UNACQUAINTANCES
UNACQUAINTED
UNACQUAINTING
UNACQUAINTS
UNACTIVING
UNACTORISH
UNACTUATED
UNADAPTABLE
UNADDRESSED
UNADJUDICATED
UNADJUSTED
UNADMIRING
UNADMITTED
UNADMONISHED
UNADOPTABLE
UNADULTERATE
UNADULTERATED
UNADULTERATEDLY
UNADVENTROUS
UNADVENTUROUS
UNADVENTUROUSLY
UNADVERTISED
UNADVERTIZED
UNADVISABLE
UNADVISABLENESS
UNADVISABLY
UNADVISEDLY
UNADVISEDNESS
UNADVISEDNESSES
UNAESTHETIC
UNAFFECTED
UNAFFECTEDLY
UNAFFECTEDNESS
UNAFFECTING
UNAFFECTIONATE
UNAFFILIATED
UNAFFLUENT
UNAFFORDABLE
UNAGGRESSIVE
UNAGREEABLE
UNALIENABLE
UNALIENABLY
UNALIENATED
UNALLEVIATED
UNALLOCATED
UNALLOTTED
UNALLOWABLE
UNALLURING
UNALTERABILITY
UNALTERABLE
UNALTERABLENESS
UNALTERABLY
UNALTERING
UNAMBIGUOUS
UNAMBIGUOUSLY
UNAMBITIOUS
UNAMBITIOUSLY
UNAMBIVALENT
UNAMBIVALENTLY
UNAMENABLE
UNAMENDABLE
UNAMIABILITIES
UNAMIABILITY
UNAMIABLENESS
UNAMIABLENESSES
UNAMORTISED
UNAMORTIZED
UNAMPLIFIED
UNAMUSABLE
UNAMUSINGLY
UNANAESTHETISED
UNANAESTHETIZED
UNANALYSABLE
UNANALYSED
UNANALYTIC
UNANALYTICAL
UNANALYZABLE
UNANALYZED
UNANCHORED
UNANCHORING
UNANESTHETISED
UNANESTHETIZED
UNANIMATED
UNANIMITIES
UNANIMOUSLY
UNANIMOUSNESS
UNANIMOUSNESSES
UNANNEALED
UNANNOTATED
UNANNOUNCED
UNANSWERABILITY
UNANSWERABLE
UNANSWERABLY
UNANSWERED
UNANTICIPATED
UNANTICIPATEDLY
UNAPOLOGETIC
UNAPOLOGISING
UNAPOLOGIZING
UNAPOSTOLIC
UNAPOSTOLICAL
UNAPOSTOLICALLY
UNAPPALLED
UNAPPARELLED
UNAPPARELLING
UNAPPARELS
UNAPPARENT
UNAPPEALABLE
UNAPPEALABLY
UNAPPEALING
UNAPPEALINGLY
UNAPPEASABLE
UNAPPEASABLY
UNAPPEASED
UNAPPETISING
UNAPPETISINGLY
UNAPPETIZING
UNAPPETIZINGLY
UNAPPLAUSIVE
UNAPPLICABLE
UNAPPOINTED
UNAPPRECIATED
UNAPPRECIATION
UNAPPRECIATIONS
UNAPPRECIATIVE
UNAPPREHENDED
UNAPPREHENSIBLE
UNAPPREHENSIVE
UNAPPRISED
UNAPPROACHABLE
UNAPPROACHABLY
UNAPPROACHED
UNAPPROPRIATE
UNAPPROPRIATED
UNAPPROPRIATES
UNAPPROPRIATING
UNAPPROVED
UNAPPROVING
UNAPPROVINGLY
UNAPTNESSES
UNARGUABLE
UNARGUABLY
UNARMOURED
UNARRANGED
UNARROGANT
UNARTFULLY
UNARTICULATE
UNARTICULATED
UNARTIFICIAL
UNARTIFICIALLY
UNARTISTIC
UNARTISTLIKE
UNASCENDABLE
UNASCENDED
UNASCENDIBLE
UNASCERTAINABLE
UNASCERTAINED
UNASHAMEDLY
UNASHAMEDNESS
UNASHAMEDNESSES
UNASPIRATED
UNASPIRING
UNASPIRINGLY
UNASPIRINGNESS
UNASSAILABILITY
UNASSAILABLE

U

UNASSAILABLY
UNASSAILED
UNASSEMBLED
UNASSERTIVE
UNASSERTIVELY
UNASSIGNABLE
UNASSIGNED
UNASSIMILABLE
UNASSIMILATED
UNASSISTED
UNASSISTEDLY
UNASSISTING
UNASSOCIATED
UNASSUAGEABLE
UNASSUAGED
UNASSUMING
UNASSUMINGLY
UNASSUMINGNESS
UNATHLETIC
UNATONABLE
UNATTACHED
UNATTAINABLE
UNATTAINABLY
UNATTAINTED
UNATTEMPTED
UNATTENDED
UNATTENDING
UNATTENTIVE
UNATTENUATED
UNATTESTED
UNATTRACTIVE
UNATTRACTIVELY
UNATTRIBUTABLE
UNATTRIBUTED
UNAUGMENTED
UNAUSPICIOUS
UNAUTHENTIC
UNAUTHENTICATED
UNAUTHENTICITY
UNAUTHORISED
UNAUTHORITATIVE
UNAUTHORIZED
UNAUTOMATED
UNAVAILABILITY
UNAVAILABLE
UNAVAILABLENESS
UNAVAILABLY
UNAVAILING
UNAVAILINGLY
UNAVAILINGNESS
UNAVERTABLE
UNAVERTIBLE
UNAVOIDABILITY
UNAVOIDABLE
UNAVOIDABLENESS
UNAVOIDABLY
UNAVOWEDLY
UNAWAKENED
UNAWAKENING
UNAWARENESS
UNAWARENESSES
UNBAILABLE
UNBALANCED
UNBALANCES
UNBALANCING
UNBALLASTED
UNBANDAGED
UNBANDAGES
UNBANDAGING
UNBANNINGS
UNBAPTISED
UNBAPTISES
UNBAPTISING
UNBAPTIZED
UNBAPTIZES
UNBAPTIZING
UNBARBERED
UNBARRICADE
UNBARRICADED
UNBARRICADES
UNBARRICADING
UNBATTERED
UNBEARABLE
UNBEARABLENESS
UNBEARABLY
UNBEATABLE
UNBEATABLY
UNBEAUTIFUL
UNBEAUTIFULLY
UNBEAVERED
UNBECOMING
UNBECOMINGLY
UNBECOMINGNESS
UNBECOMINGS
UNBEDIMMED
UNBEDINNED
UNBEFITTING
UNBEFRIENDED
UNBEGETTING
UNBEGINNING
UNBEGOTTEN
UNBEGUILED
UNBEGUILES
UNBEGUILING
UNBEHOLDEN
UNBEKNOWNST
UNBELIEVABILITY
UNBELIEVABLE
UNBELIEVABLY
UNBELIEVED
UNBELIEVER
UNBELIEVERS
UNBELIEVES
UNBELIEVING
UNBELIEVINGLY
UNBELIEVINGNESS
UNBELLIGERENT
UNBENDABLE
UNBENDINGLY
UNBENDINGNESS
UNBENDINGNESSES
UNBENDINGS
UNBENEFICED
UNBENEFICIAL
UNBENEFITED
UNBENEFITTED
UNBENIGHTED
UNBENIGNANT
UNBENIGNLY
UNBESEEMED
UNBESEEMING
UNBESEEMINGLY
UNBESOUGHT
UNBESPEAKING
UNBESPEAKS
UNBESPOKEN
UNBESTOWED
UNBETRAYED
UNBETTERABLE
UNBETTERED
UNBEWAILED
UNBIASEDLY
UNBIASEDNESS
UNBIASEDNESSES
UNBIASINGS
UNBIASSEDLY
UNBIASSEDNESS
UNBIASSEDNESSES
UNBIASSING
UNBIASSINGS
UNBIBLICAL
UNBINDINGS
UNBIRTHDAY
UNBIRTHDAYS
UNBISHOPED
UNBISHOPING
UNBLAMABLE
UNBLAMABLY
UNBLAMEABLE
UNBLAMEABLY
UNBLEACHED
UNBLEMISHED
UNBLENCHED
UNBLENCHING
UNBLESSEDNESS
UNBLESSEDNESSES
UNBLESSING
UNBLINDFOLD
UNBLINDFOLDED
UNBLINDFOLDING
UNBLINDFOLDS
UNBLINDING
UNBLINKING
UNBLINKINGLY
UNBLISSFUL
UNBLOCKING
UNBLOODIED
UNBLOODIER
UNBLOODIEST
UNBLUSHING
UNBLUSHINGLY
UNBLUSHINGNESS
UNBOASTFUL
UNBONNETED
UNBONNETING
UNBORROWED
UNBOSOMERS
UNBOSOMING
UNBOTTLING
UNBOTTOMED
UNBOUNCIER
UNBOUNCIEST
UNBOUNDEDLY
UNBOUNDEDNESS
UNBOUNDEDNESSES
UNBOWDLERISED
UNBOWDLERIZED
UNBRACKETED
UNBRAIDING
UNBRANCHED
UNBREACHABLE
UNBREACHED
UNBREAKABLE
UNBREATHABLE
UNBREATHED
UNBREATHING
UNBREECHED
UNBREECHES
UNBREECHING
UNBRIBABLE
UNBRIDGEABLE
UNBRIDLEDLY
UNBRIDLEDNESS
UNBRIDLEDNESSES
UNBRIDLING
UNBRILLIANT
UNBROKENLY
UNBROKENNESS
UNBROKENNESSES
UNBROTHERLIKE
UNBROTHERLY
UNBUCKLING
UNBUDGEABLE
UNBUDGEABLY
UNBUDGETED
UNBUDGINGLY
UNBUFFERED
UNBUILDABLE
UNBUILDING
UNBULKIEST
UNBUNDLERS
UNBUNDLING
UNBUNDLINGS
UNBURDENED
UNBURDENING
UNBUREAUCRATIC
UNBURNABLE
UNBURNISHED
UNBURROWED
UNBURROWING

UNBURTHENED
UNBURTHENING
UNBURTHENS
UNBUSINESSLIKE
UNBUTTERED
UNBUTTONED
UNBUTTONING
UNCALCIFIED
UNCALCINED
UNCALCULATED
UNCALCULATING
UNCALIBRATED
UNCALLOUSED
UNCANCELED
UNCANCELLED
UNCANDIDLY
UNCANDIDNESS
UNCANDIDNESSES
UNCANDOURS
UNCANNIEST
UNCANNINESS
UNCANNINESSES
UNCANONICAL
UNCANONICALNESS
UNCANONISE
UNCANONISED
UNCANONISES
UNCANONISING
UNCANONIZE
UNCANONIZED
UNCANONIZES
UNCANONIZING
UNCAPITALISED
UNCAPITALIZED
UNCAPSIZABLE
UNCAPTIONED
UNCAPTIVATED
UNCAPTURABLE
UNCARPETED
UNCASTRATED
UNCATALOGED
UNCATALOGUED
UNCATCHABLE
UNCATCHIER
UNCATCHIEST
UNCATEGORISABLE
UNCATEGORIZABLE
UNCEASINGLY
UNCEASINGNESS
UNCEASINGNESSES
UNCELEBRATED
UNCENSORED
UNCENSORIOUS
UNCENSURED
UNCEREBRAL
UNCEREMONIOUS
UNCEREMONIOUSLY
UNCERTAINLY
UNCERTAINNESS
UNCERTAINNESSES
UNCERTAINTIES
UNCERTAINTY
UNCERTIFICATED
UNCERTIFIED
UNCHAINING
UNCHAIRING
UNCHALLENGEABLE
UNCHALLENGEABLY
UNCHALLENGED
UNCHALLENGING
UNCHANCIER
UNCHANCIEST
UNCHANGEABILITY
UNCHANGEABLE
UNCHANGEABLY
UNCHANGING
UNCHANGINGLY
UNCHANGINGNESS
UNCHANNELED
UNCHANNELLED
UNCHAPERONED
UNCHARGING
UNCHARIEST
UNCHARISMATIC
UNCHARITABLE
UNCHARITABLY
UNCHARITIES
UNCHARMING
UNCHARNELLED
UNCHARNELLING
UNCHARNELS
UNCHARTERED
UNCHASTELY
UNCHASTENED
UNCHASTENESS
UNCHASTENESSES
UNCHASTEST
UNCHASTISABLE
UNCHASTISED
UNCHASTITIES
UNCHASTITY
UNCHASTIZABLE
UNCHASTIZED
UNCHAUVINISTIC
UNCHECKABLE
UNCHECKING
UNCHEERFUL
UNCHEERFULLY
UNCHEERFULNESS
UNCHEWABLE
UNCHILDING
UNCHILDLIKE
UNCHIVALROUS
UNCHIVALROUSLY
UNCHLORINATED
UNCHOREOGRAPHED
UNCHRISTEN
UNCHRISTENED
UNCHRISTENING
UNCHRISTENS
UNCHRISTIAN
UNCHRISTIANED
UNCHRISTIANING
UNCHRISTIANISE
UNCHRISTIANISED
UNCHRISTIANISES
UNCHRISTIANIZE
UNCHRISTIANIZED
UNCHRISTIANIZES
UNCHRISTIANLIKE
UNCHRISTIANLY
UNCHRISTIANS
UNCHRONICLED
UNCHRONOLOGICAL
UNCHURCHED
UNCHURCHES
UNCHURCHING
UNCHURCHLY
UNCILIATED
UNCINARIAS
UNCINARIASES
UNCINARIASIS
UNCINEMATIC
UNCIPHERED
UNCIPHERING
UNCIRCULATED
UNCIRCUMCISED
UNCIRCUMCISION
UNCIRCUMCISIONS
UNCIRCUMSCRIBED
UNCIVILISED
UNCIVILISEDLY
UNCIVILISEDNESS
UNCIVILITIES
UNCIVILITY
UNCIVILIZED
UNCIVILIZEDLY
UNCIVILIZEDNESS
UNCIVILNESS
UNCIVILNESSES
UNCLAMPING
UNCLARIFIED
UNCLARITIES
UNCLASPING
UNCLASSICAL
UNCLASSIER
UNCLASSIEST
UNCLASSIFIABLE
UNCLASSIFIED
UNCLEANEST
UNCLEANLIER
UNCLEANLIEST
UNCLEANLINESS
UNCLEANLINESSES
UNCLEANNESS
UNCLEANNESSES
UNCLEANSED
UNCLEAREST
UNCLEARNESS
UNCLEARNESSES
UNCLENCHED
UNCLENCHES
UNCLENCHING
UNCLERICAL
UNCLESHIPS
UNCLIMBABLE
UNCLIMBABLENESS
UNCLINCHED
UNCLINCHES
UNCLINCHING
UNCLIPPING
UNCLOAKING
UNCLOGGING
UNCLOISTER
UNCLOISTERED
UNCLOISTERING
UNCLOISTERS
UNCLOTHING
UNCLOUDEDLY
UNCLOUDEDNESS
UNCLOUDEDNESSES
UNCLOUDIER
UNCLOUDIEST
UNCLOUDING
UNCLUBABLE
UNCLUBBABLE
UNCLUTCHED
UNCLUTCHES
UNCLUTCHING
UNCLUTTERED
UNCLUTTERING
UNCLUTTERS
UNCOALESCE
UNCOALESCED
UNCOALESCES
UNCOALESCING
UNCOATINGS
UNCODIFIED
UNCOERCIVE
UNCOERCIVELY
UNCOFFINED
UNCOFFINING
UNCOLLECTABLE
UNCOLLECTABLES
UNCOLLECTED
UNCOLLECTIBLE
UNCOLLECTIBLES
UNCOLOURED
UNCOMATABLE
UNCOMBATIVE
UNCOMBINED
UNCOMBINES
UNCOMBINING
UNCOMEATABLE
UNCOMELIER
UNCOMELIEST
UNCOMELINESS
UNCOMELINESSES
UNCOMFIEST
UNCOMFORTABLE

U

UNCOMFORTABLY
UNCOMFORTED
UNCOMMENDABLE
UNCOMMENDABLY
UNCOMMENDED
UNCOMMERCIAL
UNCOMMITTED
UNCOMMONER
UNCOMMONEST
UNCOMMONLY
UNCOMMONNESS
UNCOMMONNESSES
UNCOMMUNICABLE
UNCOMMUNICATED
UNCOMMUNICATIVE
UNCOMMUTED
UNCOMPACTED
UNCOMPANIED
UNCOMPANIONABLE
UNCOMPANIONED
UNCOMPASSIONATE
UNCOMPELLED
UNCOMPELLING
UNCOMPENSATED
UNCOMPETITIVE
UNCOMPLACENT
UNCOMPLAINING
UNCOMPLAININGLY
UNCOMPLAISANT
UNCOMPLAISANTLY
UNCOMPLETED
UNCOMPLIANT
UNCOMPLICATED
UNCOMPLIMENTARY
UNCOMPLYING
UNCOMPOSABLE
UNCOMPOUNDED
UNCOMPREHENDED
UNCOMPREHENDING
UNCOMPREHENSIVE
UNCOMPROMISABLE
UNCOMPROMISING
UNCOMPUTERISED
UNCOMPUTERIZED
UNCONCEALABLE
UNCONCEALED
UNCONCEALING
UNCONCEIVABLE
UNCONCEIVABLY
UNCONCEIVED
UNCONCERNED
UNCONCERNEDLY
UNCONCERNEDNESS
UNCONCERNING
UNCONCERNMENT
UNCONCERNMENTS
UNCONCERNS
UNCONCERTED
UNCONCILIATORY
UNCONCLUSIVE
UNCONCOCTED
UNCONDITIONAL
UNCONDITIONALLY
UNCONDITIONED
UNCONDUCIVE
UNCONFEDERATED
UNCONFESSED
UNCONFINABLE
UNCONFINED
UNCONFINEDLY
UNCONFINES
UNCONFINING
UNCONFIRMED
UNCONFORMABLE
UNCONFORMABLY
UNCONFORMING
UNCONFORMITIES
UNCONFORMITY
UNCONFOUNDED
UNCONFUSED
UNCONFUSEDLY
UNCONFUSES
UNCONFUSING
UNCONGEALED
UNCONGEALING
UNCONGEALS
UNCONGENIAL
UNCONGENIALITY
UNCONJECTURED
UNCONJUGAL
UNCONJUGATED
UNCONJUNCTIVE
UNCONNECTED
UNCONNECTEDLY
UNCONNECTEDNESS
UNCONNIVING
UNCONQUERABLE
UNCONQUERABLY
UNCONQUERED
UNCONSCIENTIOUS
UNCONSCIONABLE
UNCONSCIONABLY
UNCONSCIOUS
UNCONSCIOUSES
UNCONSCIOUSLY
UNCONSCIOUSNESS
UNCONSECRATE
UNCONSECRATED
UNCONSECRATES
UNCONSECRATING
UNCONSENTANEOUS
UNCONSENTING
UNCONSIDERED
UNCONSIDERING
UNCONSOLED
UNCONSOLIDATED
UNCONSTANT
UNCONSTRAINABLE
UNCONSTRAINED
UNCONSTRAINEDLY
UNCONSTRAINT
UNCONSTRAINTS
UNCONSTRICTED
UNCONSTRUCTED
UNCONSTRUCTIVE
UNCONSUMED
UNCONSUMMATED
UNCONTAINABLE
UNCONTAMINATED
UNCONTEMNED
UNCONTEMPLATED
UNCONTEMPORARY
UNCONTENTIOUS
UNCONTESTABLE
UNCONTESTED
UNCONTRACTED
UNCONTRADICTED
UNCONTRIVED
UNCONTROLLABLE
UNCONTROLLABLY
UNCONTROLLED
UNCONTROLLEDLY
UNCONTROVERSIAL
UNCONTROVERTED
UNCONVENTIONAL
UNCONVERSABLE
UNCONVERSANT
UNCONVERTED
UNCONVERTIBLE
UNCONVICTED
UNCONVINCED
UNCONVINCING
UNCONVINCINGLY
UNCONVOYED
UNCOOPERATIVE
UNCOOPERATIVELY
UNCOORDINATED
UNCOPYRIGHTABLE
UNCOQUETTISH
UNCORRECTABLE
UNCORRECTED
UNCORRELATED
UNCORROBORATED
UNCORRUPTED
UNCORSETED
UNCOSTLIER
UNCOSTLIEST
UNCOUNSELLED
UNCOUNTABLE
UNCOUPLERS
UNCOUPLING
UNCOURAGEOUS
UNCOURTEOUS
UNCOURTLIER
UNCOURTLIEST
UNCOURTLINESS
UNCOURTLINESSES
UNCOUTHEST
UNCOUTHNESS
UNCOUTHNESSES
UNCOVENANTED
UNCOVERING
UNCRAZIEST
UNCREATEDNESS
UNCREATEDNESSES
UNCREATING
UNCREATIVE
UNCREDENTIALED
UNCREDIBLE
UNCREDITABLE
UNCREDITED
UNCRIPPLED
UNCRITICAL
UNCRITICALLY
UNCROSSABLE
UNCROSSING
UNCROWNING
UNCRUMPLED
UNCRUMPLES
UNCRUMPLING
UNCRUSHABLE
UNCRYSTALLISED
UNCRYSTALLIZED
UNCTIONLESS
UNCTUOSITIES
UNCTUOSITY
UNCTUOUSLY
UNCTUOUSNESS
UNCTUOUSNESSES
UNCUCKOLDED
UNCULTIVABLE
UNCULTIVATABLE
UNCULTIVATED
UNCULTURED
UNCUMBERED
UNCURBABLE
UNCURTAILED
UNCURTAINED
UNCURTAINING
UNCURTAINS
UNCUSTOMARILY
UNCUSTOMARY
UNCUSTOMED
UNCYNICALLY
UNDANCEABLE
UNDAUNTABLE
UNDAUNTEDLY
UNDAUNTEDNESS
UNDAUNTEDNESSES
UNDAUNTING
UNDAZZLING
UNDEBARRED
UNDEBATABLE
UNDEBATABLY
UNDEBAUCHED
UNDECADENT
UNDECAGONS
UNDECEIVABLE
UNDECEIVED
UNDECEIVER

U

UNDECEIVERS
UNDECEIVES
UNDECEIVING
UNDECIDABILITY
UNDECIDABLE
UNDECIDEDLY
UNDECIDEDNESS
UNDECIDEDNESSES
UNDECIDEDS
UNDECILLION
UNDECILLIONS
UNDECIMOLE
UNDECIMOLES
UNDECIPHERABLE
UNDECIPHERED
UNDECISIVE
UNDECLARED
UNDECLINING
UNDECOMPOSABLE
UNDECOMPOSED
UNDECORATED
UNDEDICATED
UNDEFEATABLE
UNDEFEATED
UNDEFENDED
UNDEFINABLE
UNDEFOLIATED
UNDEFORMED
UNDEIFYING
UNDELAYING
UNDELECTABLE
UNDELEGATED
UNDELETING
UNDELIBERATE
UNDELIGHTED
UNDELIGHTFUL
UNDELIGHTS
UNDELIVERABLE
UNDELIVERED
UNDEMANDING
UNDEMARCATED
UNDEMOCRATIC
UNDEMONSTRABLE
UNDEMONSTRATED
UNDEMONSTRATIVE
UNDENIABLE
UNDENIABLENESS
UNDENIABLY
UNDEPENDABLE
UNDEPENDING
UNDEPLORED
UNDEPRAVED
UNDEPRECIATED
UNDEPRESSED
UNDEPRIVED
UNDERACHIEVE
UNDERACHIEVED
UNDERACHIEVER
UNDERACHIEVERS
UNDERACHIEVES
UNDERACHIEVING
UNDERACTED
UNDERACTING
UNDERACTION
UNDERACTIONS
UNDERACTIVE
UNDERACTIVITIES
UNDERACTIVITY
UNDERACTOR
UNDERACTORS
UNDERAGENT
UNDERAGENTS
UNDERBAKED
UNDERBAKES
UNDERBAKING
UNDERBEARER
UNDERBEARERS
UNDERBEARING
UNDERBEARINGS
UNDERBEARS
UNDERBELLIES
UNDERBELLY
UNDERBIDDER
UNDERBIDDERS
UNDERBIDDING
UNDERBITES
UNDERBITING
UNDERBITTEN
UNDERBLANKET
UNDERBLANKETS
UNDERBODIES
UNDERBORNE
UNDERBOSSES
UNDERBOUGH
UNDERBOUGHS
UNDERBOUGHT
UNDERBREATH
UNDERBREATHS
UNDERBREEDING
UNDERBREEDINGS
UNDERBRIDGE
UNDERBRIDGES
UNDERBRIMS
UNDERBRUSH
UNDERBRUSHED
UNDERBRUSHES
UNDERBRUSHING
UNDERBUDDED
UNDERBUDDING
UNDERBUDGET
UNDERBUDGETED
UNDERBUDGETING
UNDERBUDGETS
UNDERBUILD
UNDERBUILDER
UNDERBUILDERS
UNDERBUILDING
UNDERBUILDS
UNDERBUILT
UNDERBURNT
UNDERBUSHED
UNDERBUSHES
UNDERBUSHING
UNDERBUYING
UNDERCAPITALISE
UNDERCAPITALIZE
UNDERCARDS
UNDERCARRIAGE
UNDERCARRIAGES
UNDERCARTS
UNDERCASTS
UNDERCHARGE
UNDERCHARGED
UNDERCHARGES
UNDERCHARGING
UNDERCLASS
UNDERCLASSES
UNDERCLASSMAN
UNDERCLASSMEN
UNDERCLAYS
UNDERCLIFF
UNDERCLIFFS
UNDERCLOTHE
UNDERCLOTHED
UNDERCLOTHES
UNDERCLOTHING
UNDERCLOTHINGS
UNDERCLUBBED
UNDERCLUBBING
UNDERCLUBS
UNDERCOATED
UNDERCOATING
UNDERCOATINGS
UNDERCOATS
UNDERCOOKED
UNDERCOOKING
UNDERCOOKS
UNDERCOOLED
UNDERCOOLING
UNDERCOOLS
UNDERCOUNT
UNDERCOUNTED
UNDERCOUNTING
UNDERCOUNTS
UNDERCOVER
UNDERCOVERT
UNDERCOVERTS
UNDERCRACKERS
UNDERCREST
UNDERCRESTED
UNDERCRESTING
UNDERCRESTS
UNDERCROFT
UNDERCROFTS
UNDERCURRENT
UNDERCURRENTS
UNDERCUTTING
UNDERDAMPER
UNDERDAMPERS
UNDERDECKS
UNDERDELIVER
UNDERDELIVERED
UNDERDELIVERING
UNDERDELIVERS
UNDERDEVELOP
UNDERDEVELOPED
UNDERDEVELOPING
UNDERDEVELOPS
UNDERDOERS
UNDERDOING
UNDERDOSED
UNDERDOSES
UNDERDOSING
UNDERDRAIN
UNDERDRAINAGE
UNDERDRAINAGES
UNDERDRAINED
UNDERDRAINING
UNDERDRAINS
UNDERDRAWERS
UNDERDRAWING
UNDERDRAWINGS
UNDERDRAWN
UNDERDRAWS
UNDERDRESS
UNDERDRESSED
UNDERDRESSES
UNDERDRESSING
UNDERDRIVE
UNDERDRIVES
UNDEREARTH
UNDEREARTHS
UNDEREATEN
UNDEREATING
UNDEREDUCATED
UNDEREMPHASES
UNDEREMPHASIS
UNDEREMPHASISE
UNDEREMPHASISED
UNDEREMPHASISES
UNDEREMPHASIZE
UNDEREMPHASIZED
UNDEREMPHASIZES
UNDEREMPLOYED
UNDEREMPLOYMENT
UNDERESTIMATE
UNDERESTIMATED
UNDERESTIMATES
UNDERESTIMATING
UNDERESTIMATION
UNDEREXPLOIT
UNDEREXPLOITED
UNDEREXPLOITING
UNDEREXPLOITS
UNDEREXPOSE
UNDEREXPOSED
UNDEREXPOSES
UNDEREXPOSING
UNDEREXPOSURE
UNDEREXPOSURES

UNDERFEEDING
UNDERFEEDINGS
UNDERFEEDS
UNDERFELTS
UNDERFINANCED
UNDERFINISHED
UNDERFIRED
UNDERFIRES
UNDERFIRING
UNDERFISHED
UNDERFISHES
UNDERFISHING
UNDERFLOOR
UNDERFLOWS
UNDERFONGED
UNDERFONGING
UNDERFONGS
UNDERFOOTED
UNDERFOOTING
UNDERFOOTS
UNDERFULFIL
UNDERFULFILL
UNDERFULFILLED
UNDERFULFILLING
UNDERFULFILLS
UNDERFULFILS
UNDERFUNDED
UNDERFUNDING
UNDERFUNDINGS
UNDERFUNDS
UNDERGARMENT
UNDERGARMENTS
UNDERGIRDED
UNDERGIRDING
UNDERGIRDS
UNDERGLAZE
UNDERGLAZES
UNDERGOERS
UNDERGOING
UNDERGOWNS
UNDERGRADS
UNDERGRADUATE
UNDERGRADUATES
UNDERGRADUETTE
UNDERGRADUETTES
UNDERGROUND
UNDERGROUNDER
UNDERGROUNDERS
UNDERGROUNDS
UNDERGROVE
UNDERGROVES
UNDERGROWN
UNDERGROWTH
UNDERGROWTHS
UNDERHAIRS
UNDERHANDED
UNDERHANDEDLY
UNDERHANDEDNESS
UNDERHANDING
UNDERHANDS
UNDERHEATED
UNDERHEATING
UNDERHEATS
UNDERHONEST
UNDERINFLATED
UNDERINFLATION
UNDERINFLATIONS
UNDERINSURE
UNDERINSURED
UNDERINSURES
UNDERINSURING
UNDERINVEST
UNDERINVESTED
UNDERINVESTING
UNDERINVESTMENT
UNDERINVESTS
UNDERJAWED
UNDERKEEPER
UNDERKEEPERS
UNDERKEEPING
UNDERKEEPS
UNDERKILLS
UNDERKINGDOM
UNDERKINGDOMS
UNDERKINGS
UNDERLAPPED
UNDERLAPPING
UNDERLAYER
UNDERLAYERS
UNDERLAYING
UNDERLAYMENT
UNDERLAYMENTS
UNDERLEASE
UNDERLEASED
UNDERLEASES
UNDERLEASING
UNDERLEAVES
UNDERLETTER
UNDERLETTERS
UNDERLETTING
UNDERLETTINGS
UNDERLEVERAGED
UNDERLIERS
UNDERLINED
UNDERLINEN
UNDERLINENS
UNDERLINES
UNDERLINGS
UNDERLINING
UNDERLININGS
UNDERLOADED
UNDERLOADING
UNDERLOADS
UNDERLOOKER
UNDERLOOKERS
UNDERLYING
UNDERLYINGLY
UNDERMANNED
UNDERMANNING
UNDERMANNINGS
UNDERMASTED
UNDERMEANING
UNDERMEANINGS
UNDERMENTIONED
UNDERMINDE
UNDERMINDED
UNDERMINDES
UNDERMINDING
UNDERMINED
UNDERMINER
UNDERMINERS
UNDERMINES
UNDERMINING
UNDERMININGS
UNDERNAMED
UNDERNEATH
UNDERNEATHS
UNDERNICENESS
UNDERNICENESSES
UNDERNOTED
UNDERNOTES
UNDERNOTING
UNDERNOURISH
UNDERNOURISHED
UNDERNOURISHES
UNDERNOURISHING
UNDERNTIME
UNDERNTIMES
UNDERNUTRITION
UNDERNUTRITIONS
UNDEROCCUPIED
UNDERPAINTING
UNDERPAINTINGS
UNDERPANTS
UNDERPARTS
UNDERPASSES
UNDERPASSION
UNDERPASSIONS
UNDERPAYING
UNDERPAYMENT
UNDERPAYMENTS
UNDERPEEPED
UNDERPEEPING
UNDERPEEPS
UNDERPEOPLED
UNDERPERFORM
UNDERPERFORMED
UNDERPERFORMING
UNDERPERFORMS
UNDERPINNED
UNDERPINNING
UNDERPINNINGS
UNDERPITCH
UNDERPLANT
UNDERPLANTED
UNDERPLANTING
UNDERPLANTS
UNDERPLAYED
UNDERPLAYING
UNDERPLAYS
UNDERPLOTS
UNDERPOPULATED
UNDERPOWERED
UNDERPRAISE
UNDERPRAISED
UNDERPRAISES
UNDERPRAISING
UNDERPREPARED
UNDERPRICE
UNDERPRICED
UNDERPRICES
UNDERPRICING
UNDERPRICINGS
UNDERPRISE
UNDERPRISED
UNDERPRISES
UNDERPRISING
UNDERPRIVILEGED
UNDERPRIZE
UNDERPRIZED
UNDERPRIZES
UNDERPRIZING
UNDERPRODUCE
UNDERPRODUCED
UNDERPRODUCES
UNDERPRODUCING
UNDERPRODUCTION
UNDERPROOF
UNDERPROPPED
UNDERPROPPER
UNDERPROPPERS
UNDERPROPPING
UNDERPROPS
UNDERPUBLICISED
UNDERPUBLICIZED
UNDERQUALIFIED
UNDERQUOTE
UNDERQUOTED
UNDERQUOTES
UNDERQUOTING
UNDERRATED
UNDERRATES
UNDERRATING
UNDERREACT
UNDERREACTED
UNDERREACTING
UNDERREACTION
UNDERREACTIONS
UNDERREACTS
UNDERREPORT
UNDERREPORTED
UNDERREPORTING
UNDERREPORTS
UNDERRUNNING
UNDERRUNNINGS
UNDERSATURATED
UNDERSAYING
UNDERSCORE
UNDERSCORED
UNDERSCORES

U

UNDERSCORING
UNDERSCORINGS
UNDERSCRUB
UNDERSCRUBS
UNDERSEALED
UNDERSEALING
UNDERSEALINGS
UNDERSEALS
UNDERSECRETARY
UNDERSELLER
UNDERSELLERS
UNDERSELLING
UNDERSELLS
UNDERSELVES
UNDERSENSE
UNDERSENSES
UNDERSERVED
UNDERSETTING
UNDERSEXED
UNDERSHAPEN
UNDERSHERIFF
UNDERSHERIFFS
UNDERSHIRT
UNDERSHIRTED
UNDERSHIRTS
UNDERSHOOT
UNDERSHOOTING
UNDERSHOOTS
UNDERSHORTS
UNDERSHRUB
UNDERSHRUBS
UNDERSIDES
UNDERSIGNED
UNDERSIGNING
UNDERSIGNS
UNDERSIZED
UNDERSKIES
UNDERSKINKER
UNDERSKINKERS
UNDERSKIRT
UNDERSKIRTS
UNDERSLEEVE
UNDERSLEEVES
UNDERSLUNG
UNDERSOILS
UNDERSONGS
UNDERSOWED
UNDERSOWING
UNDERSPEND
UNDERSPENDING
UNDERSPENDINGS
UNDERSPENDS
UNDERSPENT
UNDERSPINS
UNDERSTAFFED
UNDERSTAFFING
UNDERSTAFFINGS
UNDERSTAND
UNDERSTANDABLE
UNDERSTANDABLY
UNDERSTANDED
UNDERSTANDER
UNDERSTANDERS
UNDERSTANDING
UNDERSTANDINGLY
UNDERSTANDINGS
UNDERSTANDS
UNDERSTATE
UNDERSTATED
UNDERSTATEDLY
UNDERSTATEMENT
UNDERSTATEMENTS
UNDERSTATES
UNDERSTATING
UNDERSTEER
UNDERSTEERED
UNDERSTEERING
UNDERSTEERS
UNDERSTOCK
UNDERSTOCKED
UNDERSTOCKING
UNDERSTOCKS
UNDERSTOOD
UNDERSTOREY
UNDERSTOREYS
UNDERSTORIES
UNDERSTORY
UNDERSTRAPPER
UNDERSTRAPPERS
UNDERSTRAPPING
UNDERSTRATA
UNDERSTRATUM
UNDERSTRATUMS
UNDERSTRENGTH
UNDERSTUDIED
UNDERSTUDIES
UNDERSTUDY
UNDERSTUDYING
UNDERSUBSCRIBED
UNDERSUPPLIED
UNDERSUPPLIES
UNDERSUPPLY
UNDERSUPPLYING
UNDERSURFACE
UNDERSURFACES
UNDERTAKABLE
UNDERTAKEN
UNDERTAKER
UNDERTAKERS
UNDERTAKES
UNDERTAKING
UNDERTAKINGS
UNDERTAXED
UNDERTAXES
UNDERTAXING
UNDERTENANCIES
UNDERTENANCY
UNDERTENANT
UNDERTENANTS
UNDERTHINGS
UNDERTHIRST
UNDERTHIRSTS
UNDERTHRUST
UNDERTHRUSTING
UNDERTHRUSTS
UNDERTIMED
UNDERTIMES
UNDERTINTS
UNDERTONED
UNDERTONES
UNDERTRICK
UNDERTRICKS
UNDERTRUMP
UNDERTRUMPED
UNDERTRUMPING
UNDERTRUMPS
UNDERUSING
UNDERUTILISE
UNDERUTILISED
UNDERUTILISES
UNDERUTILISING
UNDERUTILIZE
UNDERUTILIZED
UNDERUTILIZES
UNDERUTILIZING
UNDERVALUATION
UNDERVALUATIONS
UNDERVALUE
UNDERVALUED
UNDERVALUER
UNDERVALUERS
UNDERVALUES
UNDERVALUING
UNDERVESTS
UNDERVIEWER
UNDERVIEWERS
UNDERVOICE
UNDERVOICES
UNDERVOTES
UNDERWATER
UNDERWATERS
UNDERWEARS
UNDERWEIGHT
UNDERWEIGHTS
UNDERWHELM
UNDERWHELMED
UNDERWHELMING
UNDERWHELMS
UNDERWINGS
UNDERWIRED
UNDERWIRES
UNDERWIRING
UNDERWIRINGS
UNDERWOODS
UNDERWOOLS
UNDERWORKED
UNDERWORKER
UNDERWORKERS
UNDERWORKING
UNDERWORKS
UNDERWORLD
UNDERWORLDS
UNDERWRITE
UNDERWRITER
UNDERWRITERS
UNDERWRITES
UNDERWRITING
UNDERWRITINGS
UNDERWRITTEN
UNDERWROTE
UNDERWROUGHT
UNDESCENDABLE
UNDESCENDED
UNDESCENDIBLE
UNDESCRIBABLE
UNDESCRIBED
UNDESCRIED
UNDESERVED
UNDESERVEDLY
UNDESERVEDNESS
UNDESERVER
UNDESERVERS
UNDESERVES
UNDESERVING
UNDESERVINGLY
UNDESIGNATED
UNDESIGNED
UNDESIGNEDLY
UNDESIGNEDNESS
UNDESIGNING
UNDESIRABILITY
UNDESIRABLE
UNDESIRABLENESS
UNDESIRABLES
UNDESIRABLY
UNDESIRING
UNDESIROUS
UNDESPAIRING
UNDESPAIRINGLY
UNDESPATCHED
UNDESPOILED
UNDESTROYED
UNDETECTABLE
UNDETECTED
UNDETERMINABLE
UNDETERMINATE
UNDETERMINATION
UNDETERMINED
UNDETERRED
UNDEVELOPED
UNDEVIATING
UNDEVIATINGLY
UNDIAGNOSABLE
UNDIAGNOSED
UNDIALECTICAL
UNDIDACTIC
UNDIFFERENCED
UNDIGESTED
UNDIGESTIBLE
UNDIGHTING

U

UNDIGNIFIED
UNDIGNIFIES
UNDIGNIFYING
UNDIMINISHABLE
UNDIMINISHED
UNDIPLOMATIC
UNDIRECTED
UNDISAPPOINTING
UNDISCERNED
UNDISCERNEDLY
UNDISCERNIBLE
UNDISCERNIBLY
UNDISCERNING
UNDISCERNINGS
UNDISCHARGED
UNDISCIPLINABLE
UNDISCIPLINE
UNDISCIPLINED
UNDISCIPLINES
UNDISCLOSED
UNDISCOMFITED
UNDISCORDANT
UNDISCORDING
UNDISCOURAGED
UNDISCOVERABLE
UNDISCOVERABLY
UNDISCOVERED
UNDISCUSSABLE
UNDISCUSSED
UNDISCUSSIBLE
UNDISGUISABLE
UNDISGUISED
UNDISGUISEDLY
UNDISHONOURED
UNDISMANTLED
UNDISMAYED
UNDISORDERED
UNDISPATCHED
UNDISPENSED
UNDISPOSED
UNDISPUTABLE
UNDISPUTED
UNDISPUTEDLY
UNDISSEMBLED
UNDISSOCIATED
UNDISSOLVED
UNDISSOLVING
UNDISTEMPERED
UNDISTILLED
UNDISTINCTIVE
UNDISTINGUISHED
UNDISTORTED
UNDISTRACTED
UNDISTRACTEDLY
UNDISTRACTING
UNDISTRIBUTED
UNDISTURBED
UNDISTURBEDLY
UNDISTURBING
UNDIVERSIFIED
UNDIVERTED
UNDIVERTING
UNDIVESTED
UNDIVESTEDLY
UNDIVIDABLE
UNDIVIDEDLY
UNDIVIDEDNESS
UNDIVIDEDNESSES
UNDIVORCED
UNDIVULGED
UNDOCTORED
UNDOCTRINAIRE
UNDOCTRINAIRES
UNDOCUMENTED
UNDOGMATIC
UNDOGMATICALLY
UNDOMESTIC
UNDOMESTICATE
UNDOMESTICATED
UNDOMESTICATES
UNDOMESTICATING
UNDOUBLING
UNDOUBTABLE
UNDOUBTEDLY
UNDOUBTFUL
UNDOUBTING
UNDOUBTINGLY
UNDRAINABLE
UNDRAMATIC
UNDRAMATICALLY
UNDRAMATISED
UNDRAMATIZED
UNDREADING
UNDREAMING
UNDRESSING
UNDRESSINGS
UNDRINKABLE
UNDRIVEABLE
UNDROOPING
UNDROSSIER
UNDROSSIEST
UNDULANCES
UNDULANCIES
UNDULATELY
UNDULATING
UNDULATINGLY
UNDULATION
UNDULATIONIST
UNDULATIONISTS
UNDULATIONS
UNDULATORS
UNDULATORY
UNDUPLICATED
UNDUTIFULLY
UNDUTIFULNESS
UNDUTIFULNESSES
UNDYINGNESS
UNDYINGNESSES
UNEARMARKED
UNEARTHING
UNEARTHLIER
UNEARTHLIEST
UNEARTHLINESS
UNEARTHLINESSES
UNEASINESS
UNEASINESSES
UNEATABLENESS
UNEATABLENESSES
UNECCENTRIC
UNECLIPSED
UNECOLOGICAL
UNECONOMIC
UNECONOMICAL
UNEDIFYING
UNEDUCABLE
UNEDUCATED
UNEFFECTED
UNELABORATE
UNELABORATED
UNELECTABLE
UNELECTRIFIED
UNEMBARRASSED
UNEMBELLISHED
UNEMBITTERED
UNEMBODIED
UNEMOTIONAL
UNEMOTIONALLY
UNEMOTIONED
UNEMPHASISED
UNEMPHASIZED
UNEMPHATIC
UNEMPHATICALLY
UNEMPIRICAL
UNEMPLOYABILITY
UNEMPLOYABLE
UNEMPLOYABLES
UNEMPLOYED
UNEMPLOYEDS
UNEMPLOYMENT
UNEMPLOYMENTS
UNENCHANTED
UNENCLOSED
UNENCOURAGING
UNENCUMBERED
UNENDANGERED
UNENDEARED
UNENDEARING
UNENDINGLY
UNENDINGNESS
UNENDINGNESSES
UNENDURABLE
UNENDURABLENESS
UNENDURABLY
UNENFORCEABLE
UNENFORCED
UNENJOYABLE
UNENLARGED
UNENLIGHTENED
UNENLIGHTENING
UNENQUIRING
UNENRICHED
UNENSLAVED
UNENTAILED
UNENTERPRISING
UNENTERTAINED
UNENTERTAINING
UNENTHRALLED
UNENTHUSIASTIC
UNENTITLED
UNENVIABLE
UNENVIABLY
UNEQUALLED
UNEQUIPPED
UNEQUITABLE
UNEQUIVOCABLE
UNEQUIVOCABLY
UNEQUIVOCAL
UNEQUIVOCALLY
UNEQUIVOCALNESS
UNERASABLE
UNERRINGLY
UNERRINGNESS
UNERRINGNESSES
UNESCAPABLE
UNESCORTED
UNESSENCED
UNESSENCES
UNESSENCING
UNESSENTIAL
UNESSENTIALLY
UNESSENTIALS
UNESTABLISHED
UNESTHETIC
UNETHICALLY
UNEVALUATED
UNEVANGELICAL
UNEVENNESS
UNEVENNESSES
UNEVENTFUL
UNEVENTFULLY
UNEVENTFULNESS
UNEVIDENCED
UNEXACTING
UNEXAGGERATED
UNEXAMINED
UNEXAMPLED
UNEXCAVATED
UNEXCELLED
UNEXCEPTIONABLE
UNEXCEPTIONABLY
UNEXCEPTIONAL
UNEXCEPTIONALLY
UNEXCITABLE
UNEXCITING
UNEXCLUDED
UNEXCLUSIVE
UNEXCLUSIVELY
UNEXECUTED
UNEXEMPLIFIED
UNEXERCISED

UNEXHAUSTED
UNEXPANDED
UNEXPECTANT
UNEXPECTED
UNEXPECTEDLY
UNEXPECTEDNESS
UNEXPENDED
UNEXPENSIVE
UNEXPENSIVELY
UNEXPERIENCED
UNEXPERIENT
UNEXPIATED
UNEXPLAINABLE
UNEXPLAINED
UNEXPLODED
UNEXPLOITED
UNEXPLORED
UNEXPRESSED
UNEXPRESSIBLE
UNEXPRESSIVE
UNEXPUGNABLE
UNEXPURGATED
UNEXTENDED
UNEXTENUATED
UNEXTINGUISHED
UNEXTRAORDINARY
UNFADINGLY
UNFADINGNESS
UNFADINGNESSES
UNFAILINGLY
UNFAILINGNESS
UNFAILINGNESSES
UNFAIRNESS
UNFAIRNESSES
UNFAITHFUL
UNFAITHFULLY
UNFAITHFULNESS
UNFALLIBLE
UNFALSIFIABLE
UNFALTERING
UNFALTERINGLY
UNFAMILIAR
UNFAMILIARITIES
UNFAMILIARITY
UNFAMILIARLY
UNFANCIEST
UNFASHIONABLE
UNFASHIONABLY
UNFASHIONED
UNFASTENED
UNFASTENING
UNFASTIDIOUS
UNFATHERED
UNFATHERLIER
UNFATHERLIEST
UNFATHERLY
UNFATHOMABLE
UNFATHOMABLY
UNFATHOMED
UNFAULTIER
UNFAULTIEST
UNFAVORABLE
UNFAVORABLENESS
UNFAVORABLY
UNFAVORITE
UNFAVOURABLE
UNFAVOURABLY
UNFAVOURED
UNFAVOURITE
UNFEARFULLY
UNFEASIBLE
UNFEATHERED
UNFEATURED
UNFEELINGLY
UNFEELINGNESS
UNFEELINGNESSES
UNFEIGNEDLY
UNFEIGNEDNESS
UNFEIGNEDNESSES
UNFEIGNING
UNFELLOWED
UNFEMININE
UNFERMENTED
UNFERTILISED
UNFERTILIZED
UNFETTERED
UNFETTERING
UNFEUDALISE
UNFEUDALISED
UNFEUDALISES
UNFEUDALISING
UNFEUDALIZE
UNFEUDALIZED
UNFEUDALIZES
UNFEUDALIZING
UNFILIALLY
UNFILLABLE
UNFILLETED
UNFILTERABLE
UNFILTERED
UNFILTRABLE
UNFINDABLE
UNFINISHED
UNFINISHING
UNFINISHINGS
UNFITNESSES
UNFITTEDNESS
UNFITTEDNESSES
UNFITTINGLY
UNFIXEDNESS
UNFIXEDNESSES
UNFIXITIES
UNFLAGGING
UNFLAGGINGLY
UNFLAMBOYANT
UNFLAPPABILITY
UNFLAPPABLE
UNFLAPPABLENESS
UNFLAPPABLY
UNFLASHIER
UNFLASHIEST
UNFLATTERING
UNFLATTERINGLY
UNFLAVORED
UNFLAVOURED
UNFLESHING
UNFLESHLIER
UNFLESHLIEST
UNFLINCHING
UNFLINCHINGLY
UNFLUSHING
UNFLUSTERED
UNFOCUSSED
UNFOLDINGS
UNFOLDMENT
UNFOLDMENTS
UNFOLLOWED
UNFOLLOWING
UNFORBIDDEN
UNFORCEDLY
UNFORCIBLE
UNFORDABLE
UNFOREBODING
UNFOREKNOWABLE
UNFOREKNOWN
UNFORESEEABLE
UNFORESEEING
UNFORESEEN
UNFORESKINNED
UNFORESTED
UNFORETOLD
UNFOREWARNED
UNFORFEITED
UNFORGETTABLE
UNFORGETTABLY
UNFORGIVABLE
UNFORGIVABLY
UNFORGIVEN
UNFORGIVENESS
UNFORGIVENESSES
UNFORGIVING
UNFORGIVINGNESS
UNFORGOTTEN
UNFORMALISED
UNFORMALIZED
UNFORMATTED
UNFORMIDABLE
UNFORMULATED
UNFORSAKEN
UNFORTHCOMING
UNFORTIFIED
UNFORTUNATE
UNFORTUNATELY
UNFORTUNATENESS
UNFORTUNATES
UNFORTUNED
UNFORTUNES
UNFOSSILIFEROUS
UNFOSSILISED
UNFOSSILIZED
UNFOSTERED
UNFOUGHTEN
UNFOUNDEDLY
UNFOUNDEDNESS
UNFOUNDEDNESSES
UNFRANCHISED
UNFRAUGHTED
UNFRAUGHTING
UNFRAUGHTS
UNFREEDOMS
UNFREEZING
UNFREEZINGS
UNFREQUENT
UNFREQUENTED
UNFREQUENTING
UNFREQUENTLY
UNFREQUENTS
UNFRIENDED
UNFRIENDEDNESS
UNFRIENDING
UNFRIENDLIER
UNFRIENDLIEST
UNFRIENDLILY
UNFRIENDLINESS
UNFRIENDLY
UNFRIENDSHIP
UNFRIENDSHIPS
UNFRIGHTED
UNFRIGHTENED
UNFRIVOLOUS
UNFROCKING
UNFRUCTUOUS
UNFRUITFUL
UNFRUITFULLY
UNFRUITFULNESS
UNFULFILLABLE
UNFULFILLED
UNFULFILLING
UNFUNNIEST
UNFURNISHED
UNFURNISHES
UNFURNISHING
UNFURROWED
UNFUSSIEST
UNGAINLIER
UNGAINLIEST
UNGAINLINESS
UNGAINLINESSES
UNGAINSAID
UNGAINSAYABLE
UNGALLANTLY
UNGARMENTED
UNGARNERED
UNGARNISHED
UNGARTERED
UNGATHERED
UNGENEROSITIES
UNGENEROSITY
UNGENEROUS
UNGENEROUSLY

UNGENITURED
UNGENTEELLY
UNGENTILITIES
UNGENTILITY
UNGENTLEMANLIER
UNGENTLEMANLIKE
UNGENTLEMANLY
UNGENTLENESS
UNGENTLENESSES
UNGENTLEST
UNGENTRIFIED
UNGENUINENESS
UNGENUINENESSES
UNGERMINATED
UNGETATABLE
UNGHOSTLIER
UNGHOSTLIEST
UNGIMMICKY
UNGIRTHING
UNGLACIATED
UNGLAMORISED
UNGLAMORIZED
UNGLAMOROUS
UNGLITZIER
UNGLITZIEST
UNGODLIEST
UNGODLINESS
UNGODLINESSES
UNGOVERNABLE
UNGOVERNABLY
UNGOVERNED
UNGRACEFUL
UNGRACEFULLY
UNGRACEFULNESS
UNGRACIOUS
UNGRACIOUSLY
UNGRACIOUSNESS
UNGRAMMATIC
UNGRAMMATICAL
UNGRAMMATICALLY
UNGRASPABLE
UNGRATEFUL
UNGRATEFULLY
UNGRATEFULNESS
UNGRATIFIED
UNGREEDIER
UNGREEDIEST
UNGREENEST
UNGROUNDED
UNGROUNDEDLY
UNGROUNDEDNESS
UNGROUPING
UNGRUDGING
UNGRUDGINGLY
UNGUARDEDLY
UNGUARDEDNESS
UNGUARDEDNESSES
UNGUARDING
UNGUENTARIA
UNGUENTARIES
UNGUENTARIUM
UNGUENTARY
UNGUERDONED
UNGUESSABLE
UNGUICULATE
UNGUICULATED
UNGUICULATES
UNGUILTIER
UNGUILTIEST
UNGULIGRADE
UNHABITABLE
UNHABITUATED
UNHACKNEYED
UNHALLOWED
UNHALLOWING
UNHAMPERED
UNHANDIEST
UNHANDINESS
UNHANDINESSES
UNHANDSELLED
UNHANDSOME
UNHANDSOMELY
UNHANDSOMENESS
UNHAPPENED
UNHAPPENING
UNHAPPENINGS
UNHAPPIEST
UNHAPPINESS
UNHAPPINESSES
UNHAPPYING
UNHARBOURED
UNHARBOURING
UNHARBOURS
UNHARDENED
UNHARDIEST
UNHARMFULLY
UNHARMONIOUS
UNHARNESSED
UNHARNESSES
UNHARNESSING
UNHARVESTED
UNHASTIEST
UNHATTINGS
UNHAZARDED
UNHAZARDOUS
UNHEALABLE
UNHEALTHFUL
UNHEALTHFULLY
UNHEALTHFULNESS
UNHEALTHIER
UNHEALTHIEST
UNHEALTHILY
UNHEALTHINESS
UNHEALTHINESSES
UNHEARSING
UNHEARTING
UNHEEDEDLY
UNHEEDFULLY
UNHEEDIEST
UNHEEDINGLY
UNHELMETED
UNHELPABLE
UNHELPFULLY
UNHELPFULNESS
UNHELPFULNESSES
UNHERALDED
UNHEROICAL
UNHEROICALLY
UNHESITATING
UNHESITATINGLY
UNHIDEBOUND
UNHINDERED
UNHINGEMENT
UNHINGEMENTS
UNHISTORIC
UNHISTORICAL
UNHITCHING
UNHOARDING
UNHOLINESS
UNHOLINESSES
UNHOLSTERED
UNHOLSTERING
UNHOLSTERS
UNHOMELIER
UNHOMELIEST
UNHOMELIKE
UNHOMOGENISED
UNHOMOGENIZED
UNHONOURED
UNHOPEFULLY
UNHOSPITABLE
UNHOUSELED
UNHOUZZLED
UNHUMANISE
UNHUMANISED
UNHUMANISES
UNHUMANISING
UNHUMANIZE
UNHUMANIZED
UNHUMANIZES
UNHUMANIZING
UNHUMOROUS
UNHURRIEDLY
UNHURRYING
UNHURTFULLY
UNHURTFULNESS
UNHURTFULNESSES
UNHUSBANDED
UNHYDROLYSED
UNHYDROLYZED
UNHYGIENIC
UNHYPHENATED
UNHYSTERICAL
UNHYSTERICALLY
UNIAXIALLY
UNICAMERAL
UNICAMERALISM
UNICAMERALISMS
UNICAMERALIST
UNICAMERALISTS
UNICAMERALLY
UNICELLULAR
UNICELLULARITY
UNICENTRAL
UNICOLORATE
UNICOLORED
UNICOLOROUS
UNICOLOURED
UNICOSTATE
UNICYCLING
UNICYCLIST
UNICYCLISTS
UNIDEALISM
UNIDEALISMS
UNIDEALISTIC
UNIDENTIFIABLE
UNIDENTIFIED
UNIDEOLOGICAL
UNIDIMENSIONAL
UNIDIOMATIC
UNIDIOMATICALLY
UNIDIRECTIONAL
UNIFICATION
UNIFICATIONS
UNIFLOROUS
UNIFOLIATE
UNIFOLIOLATE
UNIFORMEST
UNIFORMING
UNIFORMITARIAN
UNIFORMITARIANS
UNIFORMITIES
UNIFORMITY
UNIFORMNESS
UNIFORMNESSES
UNIGENITURE
UNIGENITURES
UNIGNORABLE
UNILABIATE
UNILATERAL
UNILATERALISM
UNILATERALISMS
UNILATERALIST
UNILATERALISTS
UNILATERALITIES
UNILATERALITY
UNILATERALLY
UNILINGUAL
UNILINGUALISM
UNILINGUALISMS
UNILINGUALIST
UNILINGUALISTS
UNILINGUALS
UNILITERAL
UNILLUMINATED
UNILLUMINATING
UNILLUMINED
UNILLUSIONED
UNILLUSTRATED
UNILOBULAR

U

UNILOCULAR
UNIMAGINABLE
UNIMAGINABLY
UNIMAGINATIVE
UNIMAGINATIVELY
UNIMAGINED
UNIMMORTAL
UNIMMUNISED
UNIMMUNIZED
UNIMOLECULAR
UNIMPAIRED
UNIMPARTED
UNIMPASSIONED
UNIMPEACHABLE
UNIMPEACHABLY
UNIMPEACHED
UNIMPEDEDLY
UNIMPLORED
UNIMPORTANCE
UNIMPORTANCES
UNIMPORTANT
UNIMPORTUNED
UNIMPOSING
UNIMPREGNATED
UNIMPRESSED
UNIMPRESSIBLE
UNIMPRESSIVE
UNIMPRISONED
UNIMPROVED
UNIMPUGNABLE
UNINAUGURATED
UNINCHANTED
UNINCLOSED
UNINCORPORATED
UNINCUMBERED
UNINDEARED
UNINDENTED
UNINDICTED
UNINFECTED
UNINFLAMED
UNINFLAMMABLE
UNINFLATED
UNINFLECTED
UNINFLUENCED
UNINFLUENTIAL
UNINFORCEABLE
UNINFORCED
UNINFORMATIVE
UNINFORMATIVELY
UNINFORMED
UNINFORMING
UNINGRATIATING
UNINHABITABLE
UNINHABITED
UNINHIBITED
UNINHIBITEDLY
UNINHIBITEDNESS
UNINITIATE
UNINITIATED
UNINITIATES
UNINOCULATED
UNINQUIRING
UNINQUISITIVE
UNINSCRIBED
UNINSPECTED
UNINSPIRED
UNINSPIRING
UNINSTALLED
UNINSTALLING
UNINSTALLS
UNINSTRUCTED
UNINSTRUCTIVE
UNINSULATED
UNINSURABLE
UNINSUREDS
UNINTEGRATED
UNINTELLECTUAL
UNINTELLIGENCE
UNINTELLIGENCES
UNINTELLIGENT
UNINTELLIGENTLY
UNINTELLIGIBLE
UNINTELLIGIBLY
UNINTENDED
UNINTENTIONAL
UNINTENTIONALLY
UNINTEREST
UNINTERESTED
UNINTERESTEDLY
UNINTERESTING
UNINTERESTINGLY
UNINTERESTS
UNINTERMITTED
UNINTERMITTEDLY
UNINTERMITTING
UNINTERPRETABLE
UNINTERPRETED
UNINTERRUPTED
UNINTERRUPTEDLY
UNINTIMIDATED
UNINTOXICATING
UNINTRODUCED
UNINUCLEAR
UNINUCLEATE
UNINVENTIVE
UNINVESTED
UNINVIDIOUS
UNINVITING
UNINVOLVED
UNIONISATION
UNIONISATIONS
UNIONISERS
UNIONISING
UNIONISTIC
UNIONIZATION
UNIONIZATIONS
UNIONIZERS
UNIONIZING
UNIPARENTAL
UNIPARENTALLY
UNIPARTITE
UNIPERSONAL
UNIPERSONALITY
UNIPOLARITIES
UNIPOLARITY
UNIQUENESS
UNIQUENESSES
UNIRONICALLY
UNIRRADIATED
UNIRRIGATED
UNISEPTATE
UNISERIALLY
UNISERIATE
UNISERIATELY
UNISEXUALITIES
UNISEXUALITY
UNISEXUALLY
UNISONALLY
UNISONANCE
UNISONANCES
UNITARIANISM
UNITARIANISMS
UNITARIANS
UNITARITIES
UNITEDNESS
UNITEDNESSES
UNITHOLDER
UNITHOLDERS
UNITISATION
UNITISATIONS
UNITIZATION
UNITIZATIONS
UNIVALENCE
UNIVALENCES
UNIVALENCIES
UNIVALENCY
UNIVALENTS
UNIVALVULAR
UNIVARIANT
UNIVARIATE
UNIVERSALISABLE
UNIVERSALISE
UNIVERSALISED
UNIVERSALISES
UNIVERSALISING
UNIVERSALISM
UNIVERSALISMS
UNIVERSALIST
UNIVERSALISTIC
UNIVERSALISTS
UNIVERSALITIES
UNIVERSALITY
UNIVERSALIZABLE
UNIVERSALIZE
UNIVERSALIZED
UNIVERSALIZES
UNIVERSALIZING
UNIVERSALLY
UNIVERSALNESS
UNIVERSALNESSES
UNIVERSALS
UNIVERSITARIAN
UNIVERSITIES
UNIVERSITY
UNIVOCALLY
UNIVOLTINE
UNJAUNDICED
UNJOINTING
UNJUSTIFIABLE
UNJUSTIFIABLY
UNJUSTIFIED
UNJUSTNESS
UNJUSTNESSES
UNKEMPTNESS
UNKEMPTNESSES
UNKENNELED
UNKENNELING
UNKENNELLED
UNKENNELLING
UNKINDLIER
UNKINDLIEST
UNKINDLINESS
UNKINDLINESSES
UNKINDNESS
UNKINDNESSES
UNKINGLIER
UNKINGLIEST
UNKINGLIKE
UNKNIGHTED
UNKNIGHTING
UNKNIGHTLIER
UNKNIGHTLIEST
UNKNIGHTLINESS
UNKNIGHTLY
UNKNITTING
UNKNOTTING
UNKNOWABILITIES
UNKNOWABILITY
UNKNOWABLE
UNKNOWABLENESS
UNKNOWABLES
UNKNOWABLY
UNKNOWINGLY
UNKNOWINGNESS
UNKNOWINGNESSES
UNKNOWINGS
UNKNOWLEDGEABLE
UNKNOWNNESS
UNKNOWNNESSES
UNLABELLED
UNLABORING
UNLABORIOUS
UNLABOURED
UNLABOURING
UNLADYLIKE
UNLAMENTED
UNLATCHING
UNLAUNDERED
UNLAWFULLY
UNLAWFULNESS

U

UNLAWFULNESSES
UNLEARNABLE
UNLEARNEDLY
UNLEARNEDNESS
UNLEARNEDNESSES
UNLEARNING
UNLEASHING
UNLEAVENED
UNLEISURED
UNLEISURELY
UNLESSONED
UNLETTABLE
UNLETTERED
UNLEVELING
UNLEVELLED
UNLEVELLING
UNLIBERATED
UNLIBIDINOUS
UNLICENSED
UNLIFELIKE
UNLIGHTENED
UNLIGHTSOME
UNLIKEABLE
UNLIKELIER
UNLIKELIEST
UNLIKELIHOOD
UNLIKELIHOODS
UNLIKELINESS
UNLIKELINESSES
UNLIKENESS
UNLIKENESSES
UNLIMBERED
UNLIMBERING
UNLIMITEDLY
UNLIMITEDNESS
UNLIMITEDNESSES
UNLIQUEFIED
UNLIQUIDATED
UNLIQUORED
UNLISTENABLE
UNLISTENED
UNLISTENING
UNLITERARY
UNLIVEABLE
UNLIVELIER
UNLIVELIEST
UNLIVELINESS
UNLIVELINESSES
UNLOADINGS
UNLOCALISED
UNLOCALIZED
UNLOCKABLE
UNLOOSENED
UNLOOSENING
UNLORDLIER
UNLORDLIEST
UNLOVEABLE
UNLOVELIER
UNLOVELIEST
UNLOVELINESS
UNLOVELINESSES
UNLOVERLIKE
UNLOVINGLY
UNLOVINGNESS
UNLOVINGNESSES
UNLUCKIEST
UNLUCKINESS
UNLUCKINESSES
UNLUXURIANT
UNLUXURIOUS
UNMACADAMISED
UNMACADAMIZED
UNMAGNIFIED
UNMAIDENLY
UNMAILABLE
UNMAINTAINABLE
UNMAINTAINED
UNMALICIOUS
UNMALICIOUSLY
UNMALLEABILITY
UNMALLEABLE
UNMANACLED
UNMANACLES
UNMANACLING
UNMANAGEABLE
UNMANAGEABLY
UNMANFULLY
UNMANIPULATED
UNMANLIEST
UNMANLINESS
UNMANLINESSES
UNMANNERED
UNMANNEREDLY
UNMANNERLIER
UNMANNERLIEST
UNMANNERLINESS
UNMANNERLY
UNMANTLING
UNMANUFACTURED
UNMARKETABLE
UNMARRIABLE
UNMARRIAGEABLE
UNMARRIEDS
UNMARRYING
UNMASCULINE
UNMASKINGS
UNMASTERED
UNMATCHABLE
UNMATCHING
UNMATERIAL
UNMATERIALISED
UNMATERIALIZED
UNMATERNAL
UNMATHEMATICAL
UNMATRICULATED
UNMEANINGLY
UNMEANINGNESS
UNMEANINGNESSES
UNMEASURABLE
UNMEASURABLY
UNMEASURED
UNMEASUREDLY
UNMECHANIC
UNMECHANICAL
UNMECHANISE
UNMECHANISED
UNMECHANISES
UNMECHANISING
UNMECHANIZE
UNMECHANIZED
UNMECHANIZES
UNMECHANIZING
UNMEDIATED
UNMEDICATED
UNMEDICINABLE
UNMEDITATED
UNMEETNESS
UNMEETNESSES
UNMELLOWED
UNMELODIOUS
UNMELODIOUSNESS
UNMEMORABLE
UNMEMORABLY
UNMENTIONABLE
UNMENTIONABLES
UNMENTIONABLY
UNMENTIONED
UNMERCENARY
UNMERCHANTABLE
UNMERCIFUL
UNMERCIFULLY
UNMERCIFULNESS
UNMERITABLE
UNMERITEDLY
UNMERITING
UNMERRIEST
UNMETABOLISED
UNMETABOLIZED
UNMETALLED
UNMETAPHORICAL
UNMETAPHYSICAL
UNMETHODICAL
UNMETHODISED
UNMETHODIZED
UNMETRICAL
UNMILITARY
UNMINDFULLY
UNMINDFULNESS
UNMINDFULNESSES
UNMINGLING
UNMINISTERIAL
UNMIRACULOUS
UNMISSABLE
UNMISTAKABLE
UNMISTAKABLY
UNMISTAKEABLE
UNMISTAKEABLY
UNMISTRUSTFUL
UNMITERING
UNMITIGABLE
UNMITIGABLY
UNMITIGATED
UNMITIGATEDLY
UNMITIGATEDNESS
UNMODERATED
UNMODERNISED
UNMODERNIZED
UNMODIFIABLE
UNMODIFIED
UNMODULATED
UNMOISTENED
UNMOLESTED
UNMONITORED
UNMORALISED
UNMORALISING
UNMORALITIES
UNMORALITY
UNMORALIZED
UNMORALIZING
UNMORTGAGED
UNMORTIFIED
UNMORTISED
UNMORTISES
UNMORTISING
UNMOTHERLIER
UNMOTHERLIEST
UNMOTHERLY
UNMOTIVATED
UNMOULDING
UNMOUNTING
UNMOVEABLE
UNMOVEABLY
UNMUFFLING
UNMUNITIONED
UNMURMURING
UNMURMURINGLY
UNMUSICALLY
UNMUSICALNESS
UNMUSICALNESSES
UNMUTILATED
UNMUZZLING
UNMUZZLINGS
UNMYELINATED
UNNAMEABLE
UNNATIVING
UNNATURALISE
UNNATURALISED
UNNATURALISES
UNNATURALISING
UNNATURALIZE
UNNATURALIZED
UNNATURALIZES
UNNATURALIZING
UNNATURALLY
UNNATURALNESS
UNNATURALNESSES
UNNAVIGABLE
UNNAVIGATED
UNNECESSARILY
UNNECESSARINESS

UNNECESSARY
UNNEEDFULLY
UNNEGOTIABLE
UNNEIGHBORED
UNNEIGHBORLY
UNNEIGHBOURED
UNNEIGHBOURLY
UNNERVINGLY
UNNEUROTIC
UNNEWSWORTHIER
UNNEWSWORTHIEST
UNNEWSWORTHY
UNNILHEXIUM
UNNILHEXIUMS
UNNILPENTIUM
UNNILPENTIUMS
UNNILQUADIUM
UNNILQUADIUMS
UNNILSEPTIUM
UNNILSEPTIUMS
UNNOISIEST
UNNOTICEABLE
UNNOTICEABLY
UNNOTICING
UNNOURISHED
UNNOURISHING
UNNUMBERED
UNNURTURED
UNOBEDIENT
UNOBJECTIONABLE
UNOBJECTIONABLY
UNOBLIGING
UNOBNOXIOUS
UNOBSCURED
UNOBSERVABLE
UNOBSERVABLES
UNOBSERVANCE
UNOBSERVANCES
UNOBSERVANT
UNOBSERVED
UNOBSERVEDLY
UNOBSERVING
UNOBSTRUCTED
UNOBSTRUCTIVE
UNOBTAINABLE
UNOBTAINED
UNOBTRUSIVE
UNOBTRUSIVELY
UNOBTRUSIVENESS
UNOCCUPIED
UNOFFENDED
UNOFFENDING
UNOFFENSIVE
UNOFFICERED
UNOFFICIAL
UNOFFICIALLY
UNOFFICIOUS
UNOPENABLE
UNOPERATIVE
UNOPPOSING
UNOPPRESSIVE
UNORDAINED
UNORDERING
UNORDINARY
UNORGANISED
UNORGANIZED
UNORIGINAL
UNORIGINALITIES
UNORIGINALITY
UNORIGINALS
UNORIGINATE
UNORIGINATED
UNORNAMENTAL
UNORNAMENTED
UNORTHODOX
UNORTHODOXIES
UNORTHODOXLY
UNORTHODOXY
UNOSSIFIED
UNOSTENTATIOUS
UNOVERCOME
UNOVERTHROWN
UNOXIDISED
UNOXIDIZED
UNOXYGENATED
UNPACIFIED
UNPACKINGS
UNPAINTABLE
UNPAINTING
UNPALATABILITY
UNPALATABLE
UNPALATABLY
UNPAMPERED
UNPANELLED
UNPANELLING
UNPANNELLED
UNPANNELLING
UNPAPERING
UNPARADISE
UNPARADISED
UNPARADISES
UNPARADISING
UNPARAGONED
UNPARALLEL
UNPARALLELED
UNPARASITISED
UNPARASITIZED
UNPARDONABLE
UNPARDONABLY
UNPARDONED
UNPARDONING
UNPARENTAL
UNPARENTED
UNPARLIAMENTARY
UNPASSABLE
UNPASSABLENESS
UNPASSIONATE
UNPASSIONED
UNPASTEURISED
UNPASTEURIZED
UNPASTORAL
UNPASTURED
UNPATENTABLE
UNPATENTED
UNPATHETIC
UNPATHWAYED
UNPATRIOTIC
UNPATRIOTICALLY
UNPATRONISED
UNPATRONIZED
UNPATTERNED
UNPAVILIONED
UNPEACEABLE
UNPEACEABLENESS
UNPEACEFUL
UNPEACEFULLY
UNPEDANTIC
UNPEDIGREED
UNPEERABLE
UNPENSIONED
UNPEOPLING
UNPEPPERED
UNPERCEIVABLE
UNPERCEIVABLY
UNPERCEIVED
UNPERCEIVEDLY
UNPERCEPTIVE
UNPERCHING
UNPERFECTED
UNPERFECTION
UNPERFECTIONS
UNPERFECTLY
UNPERFECTNESS
UNPERFECTNESSES
UNPERFORATED
UNPERFORMABLE
UNPERFORMED
UNPERFORMING
UNPERFUMED
UNPERILOUS
UNPERISHABLE
UNPERISHED
UNPERISHING
UNPERJURED
UNPERPETRATED
UNPERPLEXED
UNPERPLEXES
UNPERPLEXING
UNPERSECUTED
UNPERSONED
UNPERSONING
UNPERSUADABLE
UNPERSUADED
UNPERSUASIVE
UNPERTURBED
UNPERVERTED
UNPERVERTING
UNPERVERTS
UNPHILOSOPHIC
UNPHILOSOPHICAL
UNPHONETIC
UNPICKABLE
UNPICTURESQUE
UNPIGMENTED
UNPILLARED
UNPILLOWED
UNPITIFULLY
UNPITIFULNESS
UNPITIFULNESSES
UNPITYINGLY
UNPLAITING
UNPLASTERED
UNPLASTICISED
UNPLASTICIZED
UNPLAUSIBLE
UNPLAUSIBLY
UNPLAUSIVE
UNPLAYABLE
UNPLEASANT
UNPLEASANTLY
UNPLEASANTNESS
UNPLEASANTRIES
UNPLEASANTRY
UNPLEASING
UNPLEASINGLY
UNPLEASURABLE
UNPLEASURABLY
UNPLOUGHED
UNPLUGGING
UNPLUMBING
UNPOETICAL
UNPOETICALLY
UNPOETICALNESS
UNPOISONED
UNPOISONING
UNPOLARISABLE
UNPOLARISED
UNPOLARIZABLE
UNPOLARIZED
UNPOLICIED
UNPOLISHABLE
UNPOLISHED
UNPOLISHES
UNPOLISHING
UNPOLITELY
UNPOLITENESS
UNPOLITENESSES
UNPOLITICAL
UNPOLLUTED
UNPOPULARITIES
UNPOPULARITY
UNPOPULARLY
UNPOPULATED
UNPOPULOUS
UNPORTIONED
UNPOSSESSED
UNPOSSESSING
UNPOSSIBLE
UNPOWDERED
UNPRACTICABLE

U

UNPRACTICAL
UNPRACTICALITY
UNPRACTICALLY
UNPRACTICALNESS
UNPRACTICED
UNPRACTISED
UNPRACTISEDNESS
UNPRAISEWORTHY
UNPRAISING
UNPREACHED
UNPREACHES
UNPREACHING
UNPRECEDENTED
UNPRECEDENTEDLY
UNPREDESTINED
UNPREDICTABLE
UNPREDICTABLES
UNPREDICTABLY
UNPREDICTED
UNPREDICTING
UNPREDICTS
UNPREFERRED
UNPREGNANT
UNPREJUDICED
UNPREJUDICEDLY
UNPRELATICAL
UNPREMEDITABLE
UNPREMEDITATED
UNPREMEDITATION
UNPREOCCUPIED
UNPREPARED
UNPREPAREDLY
UNPREPAREDNESS
UNPREPARES
UNPREPARING
UNPREPOSSESSED
UNPREPOSSESSING
UNPRESCRIBED
UNPRESENTABLE
UNPRESSURED
UNPRESSURISED
UNPRESSURIZED
UNPRESUMING
UNPRESUMPTUOUS
UNPRETENDING
UNPRETENDINGLY
UNPRETENTIOUS
UNPRETENTIOUSLY

UNPRETTIER
UNPRETTIEST
UNPRETTINESS
UNPRETTINESSES
UNPREVAILING
UNPREVENTABLE
UNPREVENTED
UNPRIESTED
UNPRIESTING
UNPRIESTLIER
UNPRIESTLIEST
UNPRIESTLY
UNPRINCELIER
UNPRINCELIEST
UNPRINCELY
UNPRINCIPLED
UNPRINTABLE
UNPRINTABLENESS
UNPRINTABLY
UNPRISABLE
UNPRISONED
UNPRISONING
UNPRIVILEGED
UNPRIZABLE
UNPROBLEMATIC
UNPROCEDURAL
UNPROCESSED
UNPROCLAIMED
UNPROCURABLE
UNPRODUCED
UNPRODUCTIVE
UNPRODUCTIVELY
UNPRODUCTIVITY
UNPROFANED
UNPROFESSED
UNPROFESSIONAL
UNPROFESSIONALS
UNPROFITABILITY
UNPROFITABLE
UNPROFITABLY
UNPROFITED
UNPROFITING
UNPROFITINGS
UNPROGRAMMABLE
UNPROGRAMMED
UNPROGRESSIVE
UNPROGRESSIVELY
UNPROHIBITED

UNPROJECTED
UNPROLIFIC
UNPROMISED
UNPROMISING
UNPROMISINGLY
UNPROMPTED
UNPRONOUNCEABLE
UNPRONOUNCED
UNPROPERLY
UNPROPERTIED
UNPROPHETIC
UNPROPHETICAL
UNPROPITIOUS
UNPROPITIOUSLY
UNPROPORTIONATE
UNPROPORTIONED
UNPROPOSED
UNPROPPING
UNPROSPEROUS
UNPROSPEROUSLY
UNPROTECTED
UNPROTECTEDNESS
UNPROTESTANTISE
UNPROTESTANTIZE
UNPROTESTED
UNPROTESTING
UNPROVABLE
UNPROVIDED
UNPROVIDEDLY
UNPROVIDENT
UNPROVIDES
UNPROVIDING
UNPROVISIONED
UNPROVOCATIVE
UNPROVOKED
UNPROVOKEDLY
UNPROVOKES
UNPROVOKING
UNPUBLICISED
UNPUBLICIZED
UNPUBLISHABLE
UNPUBLISHED
UNPUCKERED
UNPUCKERING
UNPUNCTUAL
UNPUNCTUALITIES
UNPUNCTUALITY
UNPUNCTUATED

UNPUNISHABLE
UNPUNISHABLY
UNPUNISHED
UNPURCHASABLE
UNPURCHASEABLE
UNPURCHASED
UNPURIFIED
UNPURPOSED
UNPURVAIDE
UNPURVEYED
UNPUTDOWNABLE
UNPUZZLING
UNQUALIFIABLE
UNQUALIFIED
UNQUALIFIEDLY
UNQUALIFIEDNESS
UNQUALIFIES
UNQUALIFYING
UNQUALITED
UNQUALITIED
UNQUANTIFIABLE
UNQUANTIFIED
UNQUANTISED
UNQUANTIZED
UNQUARRIED
UNQUEENING
UNQUEENLIER
UNQUEENLIEST
UNQUEENLIKE
UNQUENCHABLE
UNQUENCHABLY
UNQUENCHED
UNQUESTIONABLE
UNQUESTIONABLY
UNQUESTIONED
UNQUESTIONING
UNQUESTIONINGLY
UNQUICKENED
UNQUIETEST
UNQUIETING
UNQUIETNESS
UNQUIETNESSES
UNQUOTABLE
UNRANSOMED
UNRATIFIED
UNRAVELING
UNRAVELLED
UNRAVELLER

UNRAVELLERS
UNRAVELLING
UNRAVELLINGS
UNRAVELMENT
UNRAVELMENTS
UNRAVISHED
UNREACHABLE
UNREACTIVE
UNREADABILITIES
UNREADABILITY
UNREADABLE
UNREADABLENESS
UNREADABLY
UNREADIEST
UNREADINESS
UNREADINESSES
UNREALISABLE
UNREALISED
UNREALISES
UNREALISING
UNREALISMS
UNREALISTIC
UNREALISTICALLY
UNREALITIES
UNREALIZABLE
UNREALIZED
UNREALIZES
UNREALIZING
UNREASONABLE
UNREASONABLY
UNREASONED
UNREASONING
UNREASONINGLY
UNRECALLABLE
UNRECALLED
UNRECALLING
UNRECAPTURABLE
UNRECEIPTED
UNRECEIVED
UNRECEPTIVE
UNRECIPROCATED
UNRECKONABLE
UNRECKONED
UNRECLAIMABLE
UNRECLAIMABLY
UNRECLAIMED
UNRECOGNISABLE
UNRECOGNISABLY

U

UNRECOGNISED
UNRECOGNISING
UNRECOGNIZABLE
UNRECOGNIZABLY
UNRECOGNIZED
UNRECOGNIZING
UNRECOLLECTED
UNRECOMMENDABLE
UNRECOMMENDED
UNRECOMPENSED
UNRECONCILABLE
UNRECONCILABLY
UNRECONCILED
UNRECONCILIABLE
UNRECONSTRUCTED
UNRECORDED
UNRECOUNTED
UNRECOVERABLE
UNRECOVERABLY
UNRECOVERED
UNRECTIFIED
UNRECURING
UNRECYCLABLE
UNRECYCLABLES
UNREDEEMABLE
UNREDEEMED
UNREDRESSED
UNREDUCIBLE
UNREFLECTED
UNREFLECTING
UNREFLECTINGLY
UNREFLECTIVE
UNREFLECTIVELY
UNREFORMABLE
UNREFORMED
UNREFRACTED
UNREFRESHED
UNREFRESHING
UNREFRIGERATED
UNREGARDED
UNREGARDING
UNREGENERACIES
UNREGENERACY
UNREGENERATE
UNREGENERATED
UNREGENERATELY
UNREGENERATES
UNREGIMENTED
UNREGISTERED
UNREGRETTED
UNREGULATED
UNREHEARSED
UNREINFORCED
UNREJOICED
UNREJOICING
UNRELATIVE
UNRELEASED
UNRELENTING
UNRELENTINGLY
UNRELENTINGNESS
UNRELENTOR
UNRELENTORS
UNRELIABILITIES
UNRELIABILITY
UNRELIABLE
UNRELIABLENESS
UNRELIABLY
UNRELIEVABLE
UNRELIEVED
UNRELIEVEDLY
UNRELIGIOUS
UNRELIGIOUSLY
UNRELISHED
UNRELUCTANT
UNREMAINING
UNREMARKABLE
UNREMARKABLY
UNREMARKED
UNREMEDIED
UNREMEMBERED
UNREMEMBERING
UNREMINISCENT
UNREMITTED
UNREMITTEDLY
UNREMITTENT
UNREMITTENTLY
UNREMITTING
UNREMITTINGLY
UNREMITTINGNESS
UNREMORSEFUL
UNREMORSEFULLY
UNREMORSELESS
UNREMOVABLE
UNREMUNERATIVE
UNRENDERED
UNRENOWNED
UNREPAIRABLE
UNREPAIRED
UNREPEALABLE
UNREPEALED
UNREPEATABLE
UNREPEATED
UNREPELLED
UNREPENTANCE
UNREPENTANCES
UNREPENTANT
UNREPENTANTLY
UNREPENTED
UNREPENTING
UNREPENTINGLY
UNREPINING
UNREPININGLY
UNREPLACEABLE
UNREPLENISHED
UNREPORTABLE
UNREPORTED
UNREPOSEFUL
UNREPOSING
UNREPRESENTED
UNREPRESSED
UNREPRIEVABLE
UNREPRIEVED
UNREPRIMANDED
UNREPROACHED
UNREPROACHFUL
UNREPROACHING
UNREPRODUCIBLE
UNREPROVABLE
UNREPROVED
UNREPROVING
UNREPUGNANT
UNREPULSABLE
UNREQUESTED
UNREQUIRED
UNREQUISITE
UNREQUITED
UNREQUITEDLY
UNRESCINDED
UNRESENTED
UNRESENTFUL
UNRESENTING
UNRESERVED
UNRESERVEDLY
UNRESERVEDNESS
UNRESERVES
UNRESISTANT
UNRESISTED
UNRESISTIBLE
UNRESISTING
UNRESISTINGLY
UNRESOLVABLE
UNRESOLVED
UNRESOLVEDNESS
UNRESPECTABLE
UNRESPECTABLES
UNRESPECTED
UNRESPECTIVE
UNRESPITED
UNRESPONSIVE
UNRESPONSIVELY
UNRESTFULNESS
UNRESTFULNESSES
UNRESTINGLY
UNRESTINGNESS
UNRESTINGNESSES
UNRESTORED
UNRESTRAINABLE
UNRESTRAINED
UNRESTRAINEDLY
UNRESTRAINT
UNRESTRAINTS
UNRESTRICTED
UNRESTRICTEDLY
UNRETARDED
UNRETENTIVE
UNRETIRING
UNRETOUCHED
UNRETURNABLE
UNRETURNED
UNRETURNING
UNRETURNINGLY
UNREVEALABLE
UNREVEALED
UNREVEALING
UNREVENGED
UNREVENGEFUL
UNREVEREND
UNREVERENT
UNREVERSED
UNREVERTED
UNREVIEWABLE
UNREVIEWED
UNREVOLUTIONARY
UNREWARDED
UNREWARDEDLY
UNREWARDING
UNRHETORICAL
UNRHYTHMIC
UNRHYTHMICAL
UNRHYTHMICALLY
UNRIDDLEABLE
UNRIDDLERS
UNRIDDLING
UNRIDEABLE
UNRIGHTEOUS
UNRIGHTEOUSLY
UNRIGHTEOUSNESS
UNRIGHTFUL
UNRIGHTFULLY
UNRIGHTFULNESS
UNRIGHTING
UNRIPENESS
UNRIPENESSES
UNRIPPINGS
UNRIVALLED
UNRIVETING
UNRIVETTED
UNRIVETTING
UNROADWORTHY
UNROMANISED
UNROMANIZED
UNROMANTIC
UNROMANTICAL
UNROMANTICALLY
UNROMANTICISED
UNROMANTICIZED
UNROOSTING
UNROUNDING
UNRUFFABLE
UNRUFFLEDNESS
UNRUFFLEDNESSES
UNRUFFLING
UNRULIMENT
UNRULIMENTS
UNRULINESS
UNRULINESSES
UNRUPTURED
UNSADDLING
UNSAFENESS
UNSAFENESSES

UNSAFETIES
UNSAILORLIKE
UNSAINTING
UNSAINTLIER
UNSAINTLIEST
UNSAINTLINESS
UNSAINTLINESSES
UNSALABILITIES
UNSALABILITY
UNSALARIED
UNSALEABILITIES
UNSALEABILITY
UNSALEABLE
UNSALEABLY
UNSALVAGEABLE
UNSANCTIFIED
UNSANCTIFIES
UNSANCTIFY
UNSANCTIFYING
UNSANCTIONED
UNSANDALLED
UNSANITARY
UNSATIABLE
UNSATIATED
UNSATIATING
UNSATIRICAL
UNSATISFACTION
UNSATISFACTIONS
UNSATISFACTORY
UNSATISFIABLE
UNSATISFIED
UNSATISFIEDNESS
UNSATISFYING
UNSATURATE
UNSATURATED
UNSATURATES
UNSATURATION
UNSATURATIONS
UNSAVORIER
UNSAVORIEST
UNSAVORILY
UNSAVORINESS
UNSAVORINESSES
UNSAVOURIER
UNSAVOURIEST
UNSAVOURILY
UNSAVOURINESS
UNSAVOURINESSES
UNSAYABLES
UNSCABBARD
UNSCABBARDED
UNSCABBARDING
UNSCABBARDS
UNSCALABLE
UNSCARIEST
UNSCAVENGERED
UNSCEPTRED
UNSCHEDULED
UNSCHOLARLIKE
UNSCHOLARLY
UNSCHOOLED
UNSCIENTIFIC
UNSCISSORED
UNSCORCHED
UNSCOTTIFIED
UNSCRAMBLE
UNSCRAMBLED
UNSCRAMBLER
UNSCRAMBLERS
UNSCRAMBLES
UNSCRAMBLING
UNSCRATCHED
UNSCREENED
UNSCREWING
UNSCRIPTED
UNSCRIPTURAL
UNSCRIPTURALLY
UNSCRUPLED
UNSCRUPULOSITY
UNSCRUPULOUS
UNSCRUPULOUSLY
UNSCRUTINISED
UNSCRUTINIZED
UNSCULPTURED
UNSEALABLE
UNSEARCHABLE
UNSEARCHABLES
UNSEARCHABLY
UNSEARCHED
UNSEASONABLE
UNSEASONABLY
UNSEASONED
UNSEASONEDNESS
UNSEASONING
UNSEAWORTHINESS
UNSEAWORTHY
UNSECONDED
UNSECRETED
UNSECRETING
UNSECTARIAN
UNSECTARIANISM
UNSECTARIANISMS
UNSECTARIANS
UNSEEMINGS
UNSEEMLIER
UNSEEMLIEST
UNSEEMLINESS
UNSEEMLINESSES
UNSEGMENTED
UNSEGREGATED
UNSEISABLE
UNSEIZABLE
UNSELECTED
UNSELECTIVE
UNSELECTIVELY
UNSELFCONSCIOUS
UNSELFISHLY
UNSELFISHNESS
UNSELFISHNESSES
UNSELLABLE
UNSEMINARIED
UNSENSATIONAL
UNSENSIBLE
UNSENSIBLY
UNSENSITISED
UNSENSITIVE
UNSENSITIZED
UNSENSUALISE
UNSENSUALISED
UNSENSUALISES
UNSENSUALISING
UNSENSUALIZE
UNSENSUALIZED
UNSENSUALIZES
UNSENSUALIZING
UNSENTENCED
UNSENTIMENTAL
UNSEPARABLE
UNSEPARATED
UNSEPULCHRED
UNSERIOUSNESS
UNSERIOUSNESSES
UNSERVICEABLE
UNSETTLEDLY
UNSETTLEDNESS
UNSETTLEDNESSES
UNSETTLEMENT
UNSETTLEMENTS
UNSETTLING
UNSETTLINGLY
UNSETTLINGS
UNSHACKLED
UNSHACKLES
UNSHACKLING
UNSHADOWABLE
UNSHADOWED
UNSHADOWING
UNSHAKABLE
UNSHAKABLENESS
UNSHAKABLY
UNSHAKEABLE
UNSHAKEABLENESS
UNSHAKEABLY
UNSHAKENLY
UNSHAPELIER
UNSHAPELIEST
UNSHARPENED
UNSHEATHED
UNSHEATHES
UNSHEATHING
UNSHELLING
UNSHELTERED
UNSHIELDED
UNSHIFTING
UNSHINGLED
UNSHIPPING
UNSHOCKABLE
UNSHOOTING
UNSHOTTING
UNSHOUTING
UNSHOWERED
UNSHOWIEST
UNSHRINKABLE
UNSHRINKING
UNSHRINKINGLY
UNSHROUDED
UNSHROUDING
UNSHRUBBED
UNSHUNNABLE
UNSHUTTERED
UNSHUTTERING
UNSHUTTERS
UNSHUTTING
UNSIGHTEDLY
UNSIGHTING
UNSIGHTLIER
UNSIGHTLIEST
UNSIGHTLINESS
UNSIGHTLINESSES
UNSINEWING
UNSINKABLE
UNSINNOWED
UNSISTERED
UNSISTERLINESS
UNSISTERLY
UNSIZEABLE
UNSKILFULLY
UNSKILFULNESS
UNSKILFULNESSES
UNSKILLFUL
UNSKILLFULLY
UNSKILLFULNESS
UNSLAKABLE
UNSLEEPING
UNSLEEPINGS
UNSLINGING
UNSLIPPING
UNSLUICING
UNSLUMBERING
UNSLUMBROUS
UNSMILINGLY
UNSMIRCHED
UNSMOKABLE
UNSMOOTHED
UNSMOOTHING
UNSMOTHERABLE
UNSNAGGING
UNSNAPPING
UNSNARLING
UNSNECKING
UNSOBERING
UNSOCIABILITIES
UNSOCIABILITY
UNSOCIABLE
UNSOCIABLENESS
UNSOCIABLY
UNSOCIALISED
UNSOCIALISM
UNSOCIALISMS
UNSOCIALITIES

U

UNSOCIALITY
UNSOCIALIZED
UNSOCIALLY
UNSOCKETED
UNSOCKETING
UNSOFTENED
UNSOFTENING
UNSOLDERED
UNSOLDERING
UNSOLDIERLIKE
UNSOLDIERLY
UNSOLICITED
UNSOLICITOUS
UNSOLIDITIES
UNSOLIDITY
UNSOLVABLE
UNSONSIEST
UNSOPHISTICATE
UNSOPHISTICATED
UNSOUNDABLE
UNSOUNDEST
UNSOUNDNESS
UNSOUNDNESSES
UNSPARINGLY
UNSPARINGNESS
UNSPARINGNESSES
UNSPARRING
UNSPEAKABLE
UNSPEAKABLENESS
UNSPEAKABLY
UNSPEAKING
UNSPECIALISED
UNSPECIALIZED
UNSPECIFIABLE
UNSPECIFIC
UNSPECIFICALLY
UNSPECIFIED
UNSPECTACLED
UNSPECTACULAR
UNSPECULATIVE
UNSPELLING
UNSPHERING
UNSPIRITED
UNSPIRITUAL
UNSPIRITUALISE
UNSPIRITUALISED
UNSPIRITUALISES
UNSPIRITUALIZE
UNSPIRITUALIZED
UNSPIRITUALIZES
UNSPIRITUALLY
UNSPLINTERABLE
UNSPOOLING
UNSPORTING
UNSPORTSMANLIKE
UNSPOTTEDNESS
UNSPOTTEDNESSES
UNSPRINKLED
UNSTABLENESS
UNSTABLENESSES
UNSTABLEST
UNSTACKING
UNSTAIDNESS
UNSTAIDNESSES
UNSTAINABLE
UNSTANCHABLE
UNSTANCHED
UNSTANDARDISED
UNSTANDARDIZED
UNSTARCHED
UNSTARCHES
UNSTARCHING
UNSTARRIER
UNSTARRIEST
UNSTARTLING
UNSTATESMANLIKE
UNSTATUTABLE
UNSTATUTABLY
UNSTAUNCHABLE
UNSTAUNCHED
UNSTEADFAST
UNSTEADFASTLY
UNSTEADFASTNESS
UNSTEADIED
UNSTEADIER
UNSTEADIES
UNSTEADIEST
UNSTEADILY
UNSTEADINESS
UNSTEADINESSES
UNSTEADYING
UNSTEELING
UNSTEPPING
UNSTERCORATED
UNSTEREOTYPED
UNSTERILISED
UNSTERILIZED
UNSTICKING
UNSTIFFENED
UNSTIFFENING
UNSTIFFENS
UNSTIGMATISED
UNSTIGMATIZED
UNSTIMULATED
UNSTINTING
UNSTINTINGLY
UNSTITCHED
UNSTITCHES
UNSTITCHING
UNSTOCKING
UNSTOCKINGED
UNSTOOPING
UNSTOPPABLE
UNSTOPPABLY
UNSTOPPERED
UNSTOPPERING
UNSTOPPERS
UNSTOPPING
UNSTRAINED
UNSTRAPPED
UNSTRAPPING
UNSTRATIFIED
UNSTREAMED
UNSTRENGTHENED
UNSTRESSED
UNSTRESSES
UNSTRESSING
UNSTRIATED
UNSTRINGED
UNSTRINGING
UNSTRIPPED
UNSTRIPPING
UNSTRUCTURED
UNSTUFFIER
UNSTUFFIEST
UNSUBDUABLE
UNSUBJECTED
UNSUBJECTING
UNSUBJECTS
UNSUBLIMATED
UNSUBLIMED
UNSUBMERGED
UNSUBMISSIVE
UNSUBMITTING
UNSUBSCRIBE
UNSUBSCRIBED
UNSUBSCRIBER
UNSUBSCRIBERS
UNSUBSCRIBES
UNSUBSCRIBING
UNSUBSIDISED
UNSUBSIDIZED
UNSUBSTANTIAL
UNSUBSTANTIALLY
UNSUBSTANTIATED
UNSUBTLEST
UNSUCCEEDED
UNSUCCESSES
UNSUCCESSFUL
UNSUCCESSFULLY
UNSUCCESSIVE
UNSUCCOURED
UNSUFFERABLE
UNSUFFICIENT
UNSUITABILITIES
UNSUITABILITY
UNSUITABLE
UNSUITABLENESS
UNSUITABLY
UNSUMMERED
UNSUMMONED
UNSUNNIEST
UNSUPERFLUOUS
UNSUPERVISED
UNSUPPLENESS
UNSUPPLENESSES
UNSUPPLIED
UNSUPPORTABLE
UNSUPPORTED
UNSUPPORTEDLY
UNSUPPOSABLE
UNSUPPRESSED
UNSURFACED
UNSURMISED
UNSURMOUNTABLE
UNSURPASSABLE
UNSURPASSABLY
UNSURPASSED
UNSURPRISED
UNSURPRISING
UNSURPRISINGLY
UNSURVEYED
UNSUSCEPTIBLE
UNSUSPECTED
UNSUSPECTEDLY
UNSUSPECTEDNESS
UNSUSPECTING
UNSUSPECTINGLY
UNSUSPENDED
UNSUSPICION
UNSUSPICIONS
UNSUSPICIOUS
UNSUSPICIOUSLY
UNSUSTAINABLE
UNSUSTAINABLY
UNSUSTAINED
UNSUSTAINING
UNSWADDLED
UNSWADDLES
UNSWADDLING
UNSWALLOWED
UNSWATHING
UNSWAYABLE
UNSWEARING
UNSWEARINGS
UNSWEETENED
UNSWERVING
UNSWERVINGLY
UNSYLLABLED
UNSYMMETRICAL
UNSYMMETRICALLY
UNSYMMETRIES
UNSYMMETRISED
UNSYMMETRIZED
UNSYMMETRY
UNSYMPATHETIC
UNSYMPATHIES
UNSYMPATHISING
UNSYMPATHIZING
UNSYMPATHY
UNSYNCHRONISED
UNSYNCHRONIZED
UNSYSTEMATIC
UNSYSTEMATICAL
UNSYSTEMATISED
UNSYSTEMATIZED
UNSYSTEMIC
UNTACKLING
UNTAILORED
UNTAINTEDLY

UNTAINTEDNESS
UNTAINTEDNESSES
UNTAINTING
UNTALENTED
UNTAMABLENESS
UNTAMABLENESSES
UNTAMEABLE
UNTAMEABLENESS
UNTAMEABLY
UNTAMEDNESS
UNTAMEDNESSES
UNTANGIBLE
UNTANGLING
UNTARNISHED
UNTASTEFUL
UNTEACHABLE
UNTEACHABLENESS
UNTEACHING
UNTEARABLE
UNTECHNICAL
UNTELLABLE
UNTEMPERED
UNTEMPERING
UNTENABILITIES
UNTENABILITY
UNTENABLENESS
UNTENABLENESSES
UNTENANTABLE
UNTENANTED
UNTENANTING
UNTENDERED
UNTENDERLY
UNTENTIEST
UNTERMINATED
UNTERRESTRIAL
UNTERRIFIED
UNTERRIFYING
UNTESTABLE
UNTETHERED
UNTETHERING
UNTHANKFUL
UNTHANKFULLY
UNTHANKFULNESS
UNTHATCHED
UNTHATCHES
UNTHATCHING
UNTHEOLOGICAL
UNTHEORETICAL
UNTHICKENED
UNTHINKABILITY
UNTHINKABLE
UNTHINKABLENESS
UNTHINKABLY
UNTHINKING
UNTHINKINGLY
UNTHINKINGNESS
UNTHOROUGH
UNTHOUGHTFUL
UNTHOUGHTFULLY
UNTHREADED
UNTHREADING
UNTHREATENED
UNTHREATENING
UNTHRESHED
UNTHRIFTIER
UNTHRIFTIEST
UNTHRIFTIHEAD
UNTHRIFTIHEADS
UNTHRIFTILY
UNTHRIFTINESS
UNTHRIFTINESSES
UNTHRIFTYHEAD
UNTHRIFTYHEADS
UNTHRIFTYHED
UNTHRIFTYHEDS
UNTHRONING
UNTIDINESS
UNTIDINESSES
UNTILLABLE
UNTIMBERED
UNTIMELIER
UNTIMELIEST
UNTIMELINESS
UNTIMELINESSES
UNTIMEOUSLY
UNTINCTURED
UNTIRINGLY
UNTOCHERED
UNTOGETHER
UNTORMENTED
UNTORTURED
UNTOUCHABILITY
UNTOUCHABLE
UNTOUCHABLES
UNTOWARDLINESS
UNTOWARDLY
UNTOWARDNESS
UNTOWARDNESSES
UNTRACEABLE
UNTRACKING
UNTRACTABLE
UNTRACTABLENESS
UNTRADITIONAL
UNTRADITIONALLY
UNTRAMMELED
UNTRAMMELLED
UNTRAMPLED
UNTRANQUIL
UNTRANSFERABLE
UNTRANSFERRABLE
UNTRANSFORMED
UNTRANSLATABLE
UNTRANSLATABLY
UNTRANSLATED
UNTRANSMIGRATED
UNTRANSMISSIBLE
UNTRANSMITTED
UNTRANSMUTABLE
UNTRANSMUTED
UNTRANSPARENT
UNTRAVELED
UNTRAVELLED
UNTRAVERSABLE
UNTRAVERSED
UNTREADING
UNTREASURE
UNTREASURED
UNTREASURES
UNTREASURING
UNTREATABLE
UNTREMBLING
UNTREMBLINGLY
UNTREMENDOUS
UNTREMULOUS
UNTRENCHED
UNTRENDIER
UNTRENDIEST
UNTRESPASSING
UNTRIMMING
UNTROUBLED
UNTROUBLEDLY
UNTRUENESS
UNTRUENESSES
UNTRUSSERS
UNTRUSSING
UNTRUSSINGS
UNTRUSTFUL
UNTRUSTIER
UNTRUSTIEST
UNTRUSTINESS
UNTRUSTINESSES
UNTRUSTING
UNTRUSTWORTHILY
UNTRUSTWORTHY
UNTRUTHFUL
UNTRUTHFULLY
UNTRUTHFULNESS
UNTUCKERED
UNTUMULTUOUS
UNTUNABLENESS
UNTUNABLENESSES
UNTUNEABLE
UNTUNEFULLY
UNTUNEFULNESS
UNTUNEFULNESSES
UNTURNABLE
UNTWISTING
UNTWISTINGS
UNTYPICALLY
UNTYREABLE
UNUNUNIUMS
UNUPLIFTED
UNUSEFULLY
UNUSEFULNESS
UNUSEFULNESSES
UNUSUALNESS
UNUSUALNESSES
UNUTILISED
UNUTILIZED
UNUTTERABLE
UNUTTERABLENESS
UNUTTERABLES
UNUTTERABLY
UNVACCINATED
UNVALUABLE
UNVANQUISHABLE
UNVANQUISHED
UNVARIABLE
UNVARIEGATED
UNVARNISHED
UNVARYINGLY
UNVEILINGS
UNVENDIBLE
UNVENERABLE
UNVENTILATED
UNVERACIOUS
UNVERACITIES
UNVERACITY
UNVERBALISED
UNVERBALIZED
UNVERIFIABILITY
UNVERIFIABLE
UNVERIFIED
UNVIOLATED
UNVIRTUOUS
UNVIRTUOUSLY
UNVISITABLE
UNVISORING
UNVITIATED
UNVITRIFIABLE
UNVITRIFIED
UNVIZARDED
UNVIZARDING
UNVOCALISED
UNVOCALIZED
UNVOICINGS
UNVOYAGEABLE
UNVULGARISE
UNVULGARISED
UNVULGARISES
UNVULGARISING
UNVULGARIZE
UNVULGARIZED
UNVULGARIZES
UNVULGARIZING
UNVULNERABLE
UNWANDERING
UNWARENESS
UNWARENESSES
UNWARINESS
UNWARINESSES
UNWARRANTABLE
UNWARRANTABLY
UNWARRANTED
UNWARRANTEDLY
UNWASHEDNESS
UNWASHEDNESSES
UNWATCHABLE
UNWATCHFUL
UNWATCHFULLY

UNWATCHFULNESS
UNWATERING
UNWAVERING
UNWAVERINGLY
UNWEAKENED
UNWEAPONED
UNWEAPONING
UNWEARABLE
UNWEARABLES
UNWEARIABLE
UNWEARIABLY
UNWEARIEDLY
UNWEARIEDNESS
UNWEARIEDNESSES
UNWEARIEST
UNWEARYING
UNWEARYINGLY
UNWEATHERED
UNWEDGABLE
UNWEDGEABLE
UNWEETINGLY
UNWEIGHING
UNWEIGHTED
UNWEIGHTING
UNWEIGHTINGS
UNWELCOMED
UNWELCOMELY
UNWELCOMENESS
UNWELCOMENESSES
UNWELCOMING
UNWELLNESS
UNWELLNESSES
UNWESTERNISED
UNWESTERNIZED
UNWHISTLEABLE
UNWHOLESOME
UNWHOLESOMELY
UNWHOLESOMENESS
UNWIELDIER
UNWIELDIEST
UNWIELDILY
UNWIELDINESS
UNWIELDINESSES
UNWIELDLILY
UNWIELDLINESS
UNWIELDLINESSES
UNWIFELIER
UNWIFELIEST
UNWIFELIKE
UNWILLINGLY
UNWILLINGNESS
UNWILLINGNESSES
UNWINDABLE
UNWINDINGS
UNWINKINGLY
UNWINNABLE
UNWINNOWED
UNWISENESS
UNWISENESSES
UNWITCHING
UNWITHDRAWING
UNWITHERED
UNWITHERING
UNWITHHELD
UNWITHHOLDEN
UNWITHHOLDING
UNWITHSTOOD
UNWITNESSED
UNWITTIEST
UNWITTINGLY
UNWITTINGNESS
UNWITTINGNESSES
UNWOMANING
UNWOMANLIER
UNWOMANLIEST
UNWOMANLINESS
UNWOMANLINESSES
UNWONTEDLY
UNWONTEDNESS
UNWONTEDNESSES
UNWORKABILITIES
UNWORKABILITY
UNWORKABLE
UNWORKMANLIKE
UNWORLDLIER
UNWORLDLIEST
UNWORLDLINESS
UNWORLDLINESSES
UNWORSHIPFUL
UNWORSHIPPED
UNWORTHIER
UNWORTHIES
UNWORTHIEST
UNWORTHILY
UNWORTHINESS
UNWORTHINESSES
UNWOUNDABLE
UNWRAPPING
UNWREATHED
UNWREATHES
UNWREATHING
UNWRINKLED
UNWRINKLES
UNWRINKLING
UNYIELDING
UNYIELDINGLY
UNYIELDINGNESS
UPBRAIDERS
UPBRAIDING
UPBRAIDINGLY
UPBRAIDINGS
UPBREAKING
UPBRINGING
UPBRINGINGS
UPBUILDERS
UPBUILDING
UPBUILDINGS
UPBUOYANCE
UPBUOYANCES
UPBURSTING
UPCATCHING
UPCHEERING
UPCHUCKING
UPCLIMBING
UPCOUNTRIES
UPDATEABLE
UPDRAGGING
UPDRAGGINGS
UPDRAUGHTS
UPFILLINGS
UPFLASHING
UPFLINGING
UPFOLLOWED
UPFOLLOWING
UPGATHERED
UPGATHERING
UPGRADABILITIES
UPGRADABILITY
UPGRADABLE
UPGRADATION
UPGRADATIONS
UPGRADEABILITY
UPGRADEABLE
UPGROWINGS
UPHEAPINGS
UPHILLWARD
UPHOARDING
UPHOISTING
UPHOLDINGS
UPHOLSTERED
UPHOLSTERER
UPHOLSTERERS
UPHOLSTERIES
UPHOLSTERING
UPHOLSTERS
UPHOLSTERY
UPHOLSTRESS
UPHOLSTRESSES
UPHOORDING
UPKNITTING
UPLIFTINGLY
UPLIFTINGS
UPLIGHTERS
UPLIGHTING
UPLIGHTINGS
UPLINKINGS
UPMANSHIPS
UPMARKETED
UPMARKETING
UPPERCASED
UPPERCASES
UPPERCASING
UPPERCLASSMAN
UPPERCLASSMEN
UPPERCUTTING
UPPERPARTS
UPPERWORKS
UPPISHNESS
UPPISHNESSES
UPPITINESS
UPPITINESSES
UPPITYNESS
UPPITYNESSES
UPPROPPING
UPREACHING
UPRIGHTEOUSLY
UPRIGHTING
UPRIGHTNESS
UPRIGHTNESSES
UPROARIOUS
UPROARIOUSLY
UPROARIOUSNESS
UPROOTEDNESS
UPROOTEDNESSES
UPROOTINGS
UPSETTABLE
UPSETTINGLY
UPSETTINGS
UPSHIFTING
UPSHOOTING
UPSIDEOWNE
UPSITTINGS
UPSKILLING
UPSKIRTING
UPSKIRTINGS
UPSPEAKING
UPSPEARING
UPSPRINGING
UPSTANDING
UPSTANDINGNESS
UPSTARTING
UPSTEPPING
UPSTEPPINGS
UPSTIRRING
UPSTREAMED
UPSTREAMING
UPSTRETCHED
UPSURGENCE
UPSURGENCES
UPSWARMING
UPSWEEPING
UPSWELLING
UPSWINGING
UPTALKINGS
UPTHROWING
UPTHRUSTED
UPTHRUSTING
UPTHUNDERED
UPTHUNDERING
UPTHUNDERS
UPTIGHTEST
UPTIGHTNESS
UPTIGHTNESSES
UPTITLINGS
UPTRAINING
UPTURNINGS
UPVALUATION
UPVALUATIONS
UPWARDNESS
UPWARDNESSES

U

UPWELLINGS
UPWHIRLING
URALITISATION
URALITISATIONS
URALITISED
URALITISES
URALITISING
URALITIZATION
URALITIZATIONS
URALITIZED
URALITIZES
URALITIZING
URANALYSES
URANALYSIS
URANINITES
URANOGRAPHER
URANOGRAPHERS
URANOGRAPHIC
URANOGRAPHICAL
URANOGRAPHIES
URANOGRAPHIST
URANOGRAPHISTS
URANOGRAPHY
URANOLOGIES
URANOMETRIES
URANOMETRY
URANOPLASTIES
URANOPLASTY
URBANENESS
URBANENESSES
URBANISATION
URBANISATIONS
URBANISING
URBANISTIC
URBANISTICALLY
URBANITIES
URBANIZATION
URBANIZATIONS
URBANIZING
URBANOLOGIES
URBANOLOGIST
URBANOLOGISTS
URBANOLOGY
URCEOLUSES
UREDINIOSPORE
UREDINIOSPORES
UREDINIUMS
UREDIOSPORE
UREDIOSPORES
UREDOSORUS
UREDOSPORE
UREDOSPORES
UREOTELISM
UREOTELISMS
URETERITIS
URETERITISES
URETHANING
URETHRITIC
URETHRITIDES
URETHRITIS
URETHRITISES
URETHROSCOPE
URETHROSCOPES
URETHROSCOPIC
URETHROSCOPIES
URETHROSCOPY
URICOSURIC
URICOTELIC
URICOTELISM
URICOTELISMS
URINALYSES
URINALYSIS
URINATIONS
URINIFEROUS
URINIPAROUS
URINOGENITAL
URINOLOGIES
URINOMETER
URINOMETERS
URINOSCOPIES
URINOSCOPY
UROBILINOGEN
UROBILINOGENS
UROBOROSES
UROCHORDAL
UROCHORDATE
UROCHORDATES
UROCHROMES
URODYNAMICS
UROGENITAL
UROGENITALS
UROGRAPHIC
UROGRAPHIES
UROKINASES
UROLAGNIAS
UROLITHIASES
UROLITHIASIS
UROLOGICAL
UROLOGISTS
UROPOIESES
UROPOIESIS
UROPYGIUMS
UROSCOPIES
UROSCOPIST
UROSCOPISTS
UROSTEGITE
UROSTEGITES
UROSTHENIC
UROSTOMIES
URTICACEOUS
URTICARIAL
URTICARIAS
URTICARIOUS
URTICATING
URTICATION
URTICATIONS
USABILITIES
USABLENESS
USABLENESSES
USEABILITIES
USEABILITY
USEABLENESS
USEABLENESSES
USEFULNESS
USEFULNESSES
USELESSNESS
USELESSNESSES
USHERESSES
USHERETTES
USHERSHIPS
USQUEBAUGH
USQUEBAUGHS
USTILAGINEOUS
USTILAGINOUS
USTULATING
USTULATION
USTULATIONS
USUALNESSES
USUCAPIENT
USUCAPIENTS
USUCAPIONS
USUCAPTIBLE
USUCAPTING
USUCAPTION
USUCAPTIONS
USUFRUCTED
USUFRUCTING
USUFRUCTUARIES
USUFRUCTUARY
USURIOUSLY
USURIOUSNESS
USURIOUSNESSES
USURPATION
USURPATIONS
USURPATIVE
USURPATORY
USURPATURE
USURPATURES
USURPINGLY
UTERECTOMIES
UTERECTOMY
UTERITISES
UTEROGESTATION
UTEROGESTATIONS
UTEROTOMIES
UTILISABLE
UTILISATION
UTILISATIONS
UTILITARIAN
UTILITARIANISE
UTILITARIANISED
UTILITARIANISES
UTILITARIANISM
UTILITARIANISMS
UTILITARIANIZE
UTILITARIANIZED
UTILITARIANIZES
UTILITARIANS
UTILIZABLE
UTILIZATION
UTILIZATIONS
UTOPIANISE
UTOPIANISED
UTOPIANISER
UTOPIANISERS
UTOPIANISES
UTOPIANISING
UTOPIANISM
UTOPIANISMS
UTOPIANIZE
UTOPIANIZED
UTOPIANIZER
UTOPIANIZERS
UTOPIANIZES
UTOPIANIZING
UTRICULARIA
UTRICULARIAS
UTRICULATE
UTRICULITIS
UTRICULITISES
UTTERABLENESS
UTTERABLENESSES
UTTERANCES
UTTERMOSTS
UTTERNESSES
UVAROVITES
UVULITISES
UXORICIDAL
UXORICIDES
UXORILOCAL
UXORIOUSLY
UXORIOUSNESS
UXORIOUSNESSES

V

VACANTNESS
VACANTNESSES
VACATIONED
VACATIONER
VACATIONERS
VACATIONING
VACATIONIST
VACATIONISTS
VACATIONLAND
VACATIONLANDS
VACATIONLESS
VACCINATED
VACCINATES
VACCINATING
VACCINATION
VACCINATIONS
VACCINATOR
VACCINATORS
VACCINATORY
VACCINIUMS
VACILLATED
VACILLATES
VACILLATING
VACILLATINGLY
VACILLATION
VACILLATIONS
VACILLATOR
VACILLATORS
VACILLATORY
VACUATIONS
VACUOLATED
VACUOLATION
VACUOLATIONS
VACUOLISATION
VACUOLISATIONS
VACUOLIZATION
VACUOLIZATIONS
VACUOUSNESS
VACUOUSNESSES
VAGABONDAGE
VAGABONDAGES
VAGABONDED
VAGABONDING
VAGABONDISE
VAGABONDISED
VAGABONDISES
VAGABONDISH
VAGABONDISING
VAGABONDISM
VAGABONDISMS
VAGABONDIZE
VAGABONDIZED
VAGABONDIZES
VAGABONDIZING
VAGARIOUSLY
VAGILITIES
VAGINECTOMIES
VAGINECTOMY
VAGINICOLINE
VAGINICOLOUS
VAGINISMUS
VAGINISMUSES
VAGINITIDES
VAGINITISES
VAGOTOMIES
VAGOTONIAS
VAGOTROPIC
VAGRANCIES
VAGRANTNESS
VAGRANTNESSES
VAGUENESSES
VAINGLORIED
VAINGLORIES
VAINGLORIOUS
VAINGLORIOUSLY
VAINGLORYING
VAINNESSES
VAIVODESHIP
VAIVODESHIPS
VAJAZZLING
VAJAZZLINGS
VALEDICTION
VALEDICTIONS
VALEDICTORIAN
VALEDICTORIANS
VALEDICTORIES
VALEDICTORY
VALENTINES
VALERIANACEOUS
VALETUDINARIAN
VALETUDINARIANS
VALETUDINARIES
VALETUDINARY
VALIANCIES
VALIANTNESS
VALIANTNESSES
VALIDATING
VALIDATION
VALIDATIONS
VALIDATORS
VALIDATORY
VALIDITIES
VALIDNESSES
VALLATIONS
VALLECULAE
VALLECULAR
VALLECULAS
VALLECULATE
VALORISATION
VALORISATIONS
VALORISING
VALORIZATION
VALORIZATIONS
VALORIZING
VALOROUSLY
VALPOLICELLA
VALPOLICELLAS
VALPROATES
VALUABLENESS
VALUABLENESSES
VALUATIONAL
VALUATIONALLY
VALUATIONS
VALUELESSNESS
VALUELESSNESSES
VALVASSORS
VALVULITIS
VALVULITISES
VAMPIRISED
VAMPIRISES
VAMPIRISING
VAMPIRISMS
VAMPIRIZED
VAMPIRIZES
VAMPIRIZING
VANADIATES
VANADINITE
VANADINITES
VANASPATIS
VANCOMYCIN
VANCOMYCINS
VANDALISATION
VANDALISATIONS
VANDALISED
VANDALISES
VANDALISING
VANDALISMS
VANDALISTIC
VANDALIZATION
VANDALIZATIONS
VANDALIZED
VANDALIZES
VANDALIZING
VANGUARDISM
VANGUARDISMS
VANGUARDIST
VANGUARDISTS
VANISHINGLY
VANISHINGS
VANISHMENT
VANISHMENTS
VANITORIES
VANPOOLING
VANPOOLINGS
VANQUISHABLE
VANQUISHED
VANQUISHER
VANQUISHERS
VANQUISHES
VANQUISHING
VANQUISHMENT
VANQUISHMENTS
VANTAGELESS
VANTBRACES
VANTBRASSES
VAPIDITIES
VAPIDNESSES
VAPORABILITIES
VAPORABILITY
VAPORESCENCE
VAPORESCENCES
VAPORESCENT
VAPORETTOS
VAPORIFORM
VAPORIMETER
VAPORIMETERS
VAPORISABLE
VAPORISATION
VAPORISATIONS
VAPORISERS
VAPORISHNESS
VAPORISHNESSES
VAPORISING
VAPORIZABLE
VAPORIZATION
VAPORIZATIONS
VAPORIZERS
VAPORIZING
VAPOROSITIES
VAPOROSITY
VAPOROUSLY
VAPOROUSNESS
VAPOROUSNESSES
VAPORWARES
VAPOURABILITIES
VAPOURABILITY
VAPOURABLE
VAPOURIEST
VAPOURINGLY
VAPOURINGS

V

VAPOURISHNESS
VAPOURISHNESSES
VAPOURLESS
VAPOURWARE
VAPOURWARES
VAPULATING
VAPULATION
VAPULATIONS
VARIABILITIES
VARIABILITY
VARIABLENESS
VARIABLENESSES
VARIATIONAL
VARIATIONALLY
VARIATIONIST
VARIATIONISTS
VARIATIONS
VARICELLAR
VARICELLAS
VARICELLATE
VARICELLOID
VARICELLOUS
VARICOCELE
VARICOCELES
VARICOLORED
VARICOLOURED
VARICOSITIES
VARICOSITY
VARICOTOMIES
VARICOTOMY
VARIEDNESS
VARIEDNESSES
VARIEGATED
VARIEGATES
VARIEGATING
VARIEGATION
VARIEGATIONS
VARIEGATOR
VARIEGATORS
VARIETALLY
VARIFOCALS
VARIFORMLY
VARIOLATED
VARIOLATES
VARIOLATING
VARIOLATION
VARIOLATIONS
VARIOLATOR
VARIOLATORS
VARIOLISATION
VARIOLISATIONS
VARIOLITES
VARIOLITIC
VARIOLIZATION
VARIOLIZATIONS
VARIOLOIDS
VARIOMETER
VARIOMETERS
VARIOUSNESS
VARIOUSNESSES
VARISCITES
VARITYPING
VARITYPIST
VARITYPISTS
VARLETESSES
VARLETRIES
VARNISHERS
VARNISHIER
VARNISHIEST
VARNISHING
VARNISHINGS
VARSOVIENNE
VARSOVIENNES
VASCULARISATION
VASCULARISE
VASCULARISED
VASCULARISES
VASCULARISING
VASCULARITIES
VASCULARITY
VASCULARIZATION
VASCULARIZE
VASCULARIZED
VASCULARIZES
VASCULARIZING
VASCULARLY
VASCULATURE
VASCULATURES
VASCULIFORM
VASCULITIDES
VASCULITIS
VASCULITISES
VASECTOMIES
VASECTOMISE
VASECTOMISED
VASECTOMISES
VASECTOMISING
VASECTOMIZE
VASECTOMIZED
VASECTOMIZES
VASECTOMIZING
VASELINING
VASOACTIVE
VASOACTIVITIES
VASOACTIVITY
VASOCONSTRICTOR
VASODILATATION
VASODILATATIONS
VASODILATATORY
VASODILATION
VASODILATIONS
VASODILATOR
VASODILATORS
VASODILATORY
VASOINHIBITOR
VASOINHIBITORS
VASOINHIBITORY
VASOPRESSIN
VASOPRESSINS
VASOPRESSOR
VASOPRESSORS
VASOSPASMS
VASOSPASTIC
VASOTOCINS
VASOTOMIES
VASSALAGES
VASSALESSES
VASSALISED
VASSALISES
VASSALISING
VASSALIZED
VASSALIZES
VASSALIZING
VASSALLING
VASSALRIES
VASTIDITIES
VASTITUDES
VASTNESSES
VATICINATE
VATICINATED
VATICINATES
VATICINATING
VATICINATION
VATICINATIONS
VATICINATOR
VATICINATORS
VATICINATORY
VAUDEVILLE
VAUDEVILLEAN
VAUDEVILLEANS
VAUDEVILLES
VAUDEVILLIAN
VAUDEVILLIANS
VAUDEVILLIST
VAUDEVILLISTS
VAULTINGLY
VAUNTERIES
VAUNTINGLY
VAVASORIES
VECTOGRAPH
VECTOGRAPHS
VECTORIALLY
VECTORINGS
VECTORISATION
VECTORISATIONS
VECTORISED
VECTORISES
VECTORISING
VECTORIZATION
VECTORIZATIONS
VECTORIZED
VECTORIZES
VECTORIZING
VECTORSCOPE
VECTORSCOPES
VEDUTISTAS
VEGEBURGER
VEGEBURGERS
VEGETABLES
VEGETABLIER
VEGETABLIEST
VEGETARIAN
VEGETARIANISM
VEGETARIANISMS
VEGETARIANS
VEGETATING
VEGETATINGS
VEGETATION
VEGETATIONAL
VEGETATIONS
VEGETATIOUS
VEGETATIVE
VEGETATIVELY
VEGETATIVENESS
VEGGIEBURGER
VEGGIEBURGERS
VEHEMENCES
VEHEMENCIES
VEHEMENTLY
VEILLEUSES
VEINSTONES
VEINSTUFFS
VELARISATION
VELARISATIONS
VELARISING
VELARIZATION
VELARIZATIONS
VELARIZING
VELDSCHOEN
VELDSCHOENS
VELDSKOENS
VELITATION
VELITATIONS
VELLEITIES
VELLENAGES
VELLICATED
VELLICATES
VELLICATING
VELLICATION
VELLICATIONS
VELLICATIVE
VELOCIMETER
VELOCIMETERS
VELOCIMETRIES
VELOCIMETRY
VELOCIPEDE
VELOCIPEDEAN
VELOCIPEDEANS
VELOCIPEDED
VELOCIPEDER
VELOCIPEDERS
VELOCIPEDES
VELOCIPEDIAN
VELOCIPEDIANS
VELOCIPEDING
VELOCIPEDIST
VELOCIPEDISTS
VELOCIRAPTOR
VELOCIRAPTORS
VELOCITIES

VELODROMES
VELOUTINES
VELUTINOUS
VELVETEENED
VELVETEENS
VELVETIEST
VELVETINESS
VELVETINESSES
VELVETINGS
VELVETLIKE
VENALITIES
VENATICALLY
VENATIONAL
VENATORIAL
VENDETTIST
VENDETTISTS
VENDIBILITIES
VENDIBILITY
VENDIBLENESS
VENDIBLENESSES
VENDITATION
VENDITATIONS
VENDITIONS
VENEERINGS
VENEFICALLY
VENEFICIOUS
VENEFICIOUSLY
VENEFICOUS
VENEFICOUSLY
VENENATING
VENEPUNCTURE
VENEPUNCTURES
VENERABILITIES
VENERABILITY
VENERABLENESS
VENERABLENESSES
VENERABLES
VENERATING
VENERATION
VENERATIONAL
VENERATIONS
VENERATIVE
VENERATIVENESS
VENERATORS
VENEREALLY
VENEREOLOGICAL
VENEREOLOGIES
VENEREOLOGIST
VENEREOLOGISTS
VENEREOLOGY
VENESECTION
VENESECTIONS
VENGEANCES
VENGEFULLY
VENGEFULNESS
VENGEFULNESSES
VENGEMENTS
VENIALITIES
VENIALNESS
VENIALNESSES
VENIPUNCTURE
VENIPUNCTURES
VENISECTION
VENISECTIONS
VENOGRAPHIC
VENOGRAPHICAL
VENOGRAPHIES
VENOGRAPHY
VENOLOGIES
VENOMOUSLY
VENOMOUSNESS
VENOMOUSNESSES
VENOSCLEROSES
VENOSCLEROSIS
VENOSITIES
VENOUSNESS
VENOUSNESSES
VENTIDUCTS
VENTIFACTS
VENTILABLE
VENTILATED
VENTILATES
VENTILATING
VENTILATION
VENTILATIONS
VENTILATIVE
VENTILATOR
VENTILATORS
VENTILATORY
VENTOSITIES
VENTRICLES
VENTRICOSE
VENTRICOSITIES
VENTRICOSITY
VENTRICOUS
VENTRICULAR
VENTRICULE
VENTRICULES
VENTRICULI
VENTRICULUS
VENTRILOQUAL
VENTRILOQUIAL
VENTRILOQUIALLY
VENTRILOQUIES
VENTRILOQUISE
VENTRILOQUISED
VENTRILOQUISES
VENTRILOQUISING
VENTRILOQUISM
VENTRILOQUISMS
VENTRILOQUIST
VENTRILOQUISTIC
VENTRILOQUISTS
VENTRILOQUIZE
VENTRILOQUIZED
VENTRILOQUIZES
VENTRILOQUIZING
VENTRILOQUOUS
VENTRILOQUY
VENTRIPOTENT
VENTROLATERAL
VENTROMEDIAL
VENTURESOME
VENTURESOMELY
VENTURESOMENESS
VENTURINGLY
VENTURINGS
VENTUROUSLY
VENTUROUSNESS
VENTUROUSNESSES
VERACIOUSLY
VERACIOUSNESS
VERACIOUSNESSES
VERACITIES
VERANDAHED
VERAPAMILS
VERATRIDINE
VERATRIDINES
VERATRINES
VERBALISATION
VERBALISATIONS
VERBALISED
VERBALISER
VERBALISERS
VERBALISES
VERBALISING
VERBALISMS
VERBALISTIC
VERBALISTS
VERBALITIES
VERBALIZATION
VERBALIZATIONS
VERBALIZED
VERBALIZER
VERBALIZERS
VERBALIZES
VERBALIZING
VERBALLING
VERBARIANS
VERBASCUMS
VERBENACEOUS
VERBERATED
VERBERATES
VERBERATING
VERBERATION
VERBERATIONS
VERBICIDES
VERBIFICATION
VERBIFICATIONS
VERBIFYING
VERBIGERATE
VERBIGERATED
VERBIGERATES
VERBIGERATING
VERBIGERATION
VERBIGERATIONS
VERBOSENESS
VERBOSENESSES
VERBOSITIES
VERDANCIES
VERDIGRISED
VERDIGRISES
VERDIGRISING
VERDURELESS
VERGEBOARD
VERGEBOARDS
VERGENCIES
VERGERSHIP
VERGERSHIPS
VERIDICALITIES
VERIDICALITY
VERIDICALLY
VERIDICOUS
VERIFIABILITIES
VERIFIABILITY
VERIFIABLE
VERIFIABLENESS
VERIFIABLY
VERIFICATION
VERIFICATIONS
VERIFICATIVE
VERIFICATORY
VERISIMILAR
VERISIMILARLY
VERISIMILITIES
VERISIMILITUDE
VERISIMILITUDES
VERISIMILITY
VERISIMILOUS
VERITABLENESS
VERITABLENESSES
VERJUICING
VERKRAMPTE
VERKRAMPTES
VERMEILING
VERMEILLED
VERMEILLES
VERMEILLING
VERMICELLI
VERMICELLIS
VERMICIDAL
VERMICIDES
VERMICULAR
VERMICULARLY
VERMICULATE
VERMICULATED
VERMICULATES
VERMICULATING
VERMICULATION
VERMICULATIONS
VERMICULES
VERMICULITE
VERMICULITES
VERMICULOUS
VERMICULTURE
VERMICULTURES
VERMIFUGAL
VERMIFUGES
VERMILIONED
VERMILIONING

VERMILIONS
VERMILLING
VERMILLION
VERMILLIONS
VERMINATED
VERMINATES
VERMINATING
VERMINATION
VERMINATIONS
VERMINIEST
VERMINOUSLY
VERMINOUSNESS
VERMINOUSNESSES
VERMIVOROUS
VERNACULAR
VERNACULARISE
VERNACULARISED
VERNACULARISES
VERNACULARISING
VERNACULARISM
VERNACULARISMS
VERNACULARIST
VERNACULARISTS
VERNACULARITIES
VERNACULARITY
VERNACULARIZE
VERNACULARIZED
VERNACULARIZES
VERNACULARIZING
VERNACULARLY
VERNACULARS
VERNALISATION
VERNALISATIONS
VERNALISED
VERNALISES
VERNALISING
VERNALITIES
VERNALIZATION
VERNALIZATIONS
VERNALIZED
VERNALIZES
VERNALIZING
VERNATIONS
VERNISSAGE
VERNISSAGES
VERRUCIFORM
VERRUCOSITIES
VERRUCOSITY
VERSABILITIES
VERSABILITY
VERSATILELY
VERSATILENESS
VERSATILENESSES
VERSATILITIES
VERSATILITY
VERSICOLOR
VERSICOLORED
VERSICOLOUR
VERSICOLOURED
VERSICULAR
VERSIFICATION
VERSIFICATIONS
VERSIFICATOR
VERSIFICATORS
VERSIFIERS
VERSIFYING
VERSIONERS
VERSIONING
VERSIONINGS
VERSIONIST
VERSIONISTS
VERSLIBRIST
VERSLIBRISTE
VERSLIBRISTES
VERSLIBRISTS
VERTEBRALLY
VERTEBRATE
VERTEBRATED
VERTEBRATES
VERTEBRATION
VERTEBRATIONS
VERTICALITIES
VERTICALITY
VERTICALLY
VERTICALNESS
VERTICALNESSES
VERTICILLASTER
VERTICILLASTERS
VERTICILLATE
VERTICILLATED
VERTICILLATELY
VERTICILLATION
VERTICILLATIONS
VERTICILLIUM
VERTICILLIUMS
VERTICITIES
VERTIGINES
VERTIGINOUS
VERTIGINOUSLY
VERTIGINOUSNESS
VERTIPORTS
VERUMONTANA
VERUMONTANUM
VERUMONTANUMS
VESICATING
VESICATION
VESICATIONS
VESICATORIES
VESICATORY
VESICULARITIES
VESICULARITY
VESICULARLY
VESICULATE
VESICULATED
VESICULATES
VESICULATING
VESICULATION
VESICULATIONS
VESICULOSE
VESPERTILIAN
VESPERTILIONID
VESPERTILIONIDS
VESPERTILIONINE
VESPERTINAL
VESPERTINE
VESPIARIES
VESTIARIES
VESTIBULAR
VESTIBULED
VESTIBULES
VESTIBULING
VESTIBULITIS
VESTIBULITISES
VESTIBULUM
VESTIGIALLY
VESTIMENTAL
VESTIMENTARY
VESTIMENTS
VESTITURES
VESTMENTAL
VESTMENTED
VESUVIANITE
VESUVIANITES
VETCHLINGS
VETERINARIAN
VETERINARIANS
VETERINARIES
VETERINARY
VETTURINOS
VEXATIOUSLY
VEXATIOUSNESS
VEXATIOUSNESSES
VEXEDNESSES
VEXILLARIES
VEXILLATION
VEXILLATIONS
VEXILLOLOGIC
VEXILLOLOGICAL
VEXILLOLOGIES
VEXILLOLOGIST
VEXILLOLOGISTS
VEXILLOLOGY
VEXINGNESS
VEXINGNESSES
VIABILITIES
VIBRACULAR
VIBRACULARIA
VIBRACULARIUM
VIBRACULOID
VIBRACULUM
VIBRAHARPIST
VIBRAHARPISTS
VIBRAHARPS
VIBRANCIES
VIBRAPHONE
VIBRAPHONES
VIBRAPHONIST
VIBRAPHONISTS
VIBRATILITIES
VIBRATILITY
VIBRATINGLY
VIBRATIONAL
VIBRATIONLESS
VIBRATIONS
VIBRATIUNCLE
VIBRATIUNCLES
VIBRATOLESS
VIBROFLOTATION
VIBROFLOTATIONS
VIBROGRAPH
VIBROGRAPHS
VIBROMETER
VIBROMETERS
VICARESSES
VICARIANCE
VICARIANCES
VICARIANTS
VICARIATES
VICARIOUSLY
VICARIOUSNESS
VICARIOUSNESSES
VICARLIEST
VICARSHIPS
VICEGERENCIES
VICEGERENCY
VICEGERENT
VICEGERENTS
VICEREGALLY
VICEREGENT
VICEREGENTS
VICEREINES
VICEROYALTIES
VICEROYALTY
VICEROYSHIP
VICEROYSHIPS
VICHYSSOIS
VICHYSSOISE
VICHYSSOISES
VICINITIES
VICIOSITIES
VICIOUSNESS
VICIOUSNESSES
VICISSITUDE
VICISSITUDES
VICISSITUDINARY
VICISSITUDINOUS
VICOMTESSE
VICOMTESSES
VICTIMHOOD
VICTIMHOODS
VICTIMISATION
VICTIMISATIONS
VICTIMISED
VICTIMISER
VICTIMISERS
VICTIMISES
VICTIMISING
VICTIMIZATION
VICTIMIZATIONS
VICTIMIZED

VICTIMIZER
VICTIMIZERS
VICTIMIZES
VICTIMIZING
VICTIMLESS
VICTIMOLOGIES
VICTIMOLOGIST
VICTIMOLOGISTS
VICTIMOLOGY
VICTORESSES
VICTORIANA
VICTORIANAS
VICTORINES
VICTORIOUS
VICTORIOUSLY
VICTORIOUSNESS
VICTORYLESS
VICTRESSES
VICTUALAGE
VICTUALAGES
VICTUALERS
VICTUALING
VICTUALLAGE
VICTUALLAGES
VICTUALLED
VICTUALLER
VICTUALLERS
VICTUALLESS
VICTUALLING
VIDEOCASSETTE
VIDEOCASSETTES
VIDEOCONFERENCE
VIDEODISCS
VIDEODISKS
VIDEOGRAMS
VIDEOGRAPHER
VIDEOGRAPHERS
VIDEOGRAPHIES
VIDEOGRAPHY
VIDEOLANDS
VIDEOPHILE
VIDEOPHILES
VIDEOPHONE
VIDEOPHONES
VIDEOPHONIC
VIDEOTAPED
VIDEOTAPES
VIDEOTAPING
VIDEOTELEPHONE
VIDEOTELEPHONES
VIDEOTEXES
VIDEOTEXTS
VIDEOTHEQUE
VIDEOTHEQUES
VIDSCREENS
VIEWERSHIP
VIEWERSHIPS
VIEWFINDER
VIEWFINDERS
VIEWINESSES
VIEWLESSLY
VIEWPHONES
VIEWPOINTS
VIGILANCES
VIGILANTES
VIGILANTISM
VIGILANTISMS
VIGILANTLY
VIGILANTNESS
VIGILANTNESSES
VIGINTILLION
VIGINTILLIONS
VIGNETTERS
VIGNETTING
VIGNETTINGS
VIGNETTIST
VIGNETTISTS
VIGORISHES
VIGOROUSLY
VIGOROUSNESS
VIGOROUSNESSES
VIKINGISMS
VILDNESSES
VILENESSES
VILIFICATION
VILIFICATIONS
VILIPENDED
VILIPENDER
VILIPENDERS
VILIPENDING
VILLAGERIES
VILLAGIEST
VILLAGIOES
VILLAGISATION
VILLAGISATIONS
VILLAGIZATION
VILLAGIZATIONS
VILLAGREES
VILLAINAGE
VILLAINAGES
VILLAINESS
VILLAINESSES
VILLAINIES
VILLAINOUS
VILLAINOUSLY
VILLAINOUSNESS
VILLANAGES
VILLANELLA
VILLANELLAS
VILLANELLE
VILLANELLES
VILLANOUSLY
VILLEGGIATURA
VILLEGGIATURAS
VILLEINAGE
VILLEINAGES
VILLENAGES
VILLIACOES
VILLIAGOES
VILLICATION
VILLICATIONS
VILLOSITIES
VINAIGRETTE
VINAIGRETTES
VINBLASTINE
VINBLASTINES
VINCIBILITIES
VINCIBILITY
VINCIBLENESS
VINCIBLENESSES
VINCRISTINE
VINCRISTINES
VINDEMIATE
VINDEMIATED
VINDEMIATES
VINDEMIATING
VINDICABILITIES
VINDICABILITY
VINDICABLE
VINDICATED
VINDICATES
VINDICATING
VINDICATION
VINDICATIONS
VINDICATIVE
VINDICATIVENESS
VINDICATOR
VINDICATORILY
VINDICATORS
VINDICATORY
VINDICATRESS
VINDICATRESSES
VINDICTIVE
VINDICTIVELY
VINDICTIVENESS
VINEDRESSER
VINEDRESSERS
VINEGARETTE
VINEGARETTES
VINEGARIER
VINEGARIEST
VINEGARING
VINEGARISH
VINEGARRETTE
VINEGARRETTES
VINEGARROON
VINEGARROONS
VINEYARDIST
VINEYARDISTS
VINICULTURAL
VINICULTURE
VINICULTURES
VINICULTURIST
VINICULTURISTS
VINIFEROUS
VINIFICATION
VINIFICATIONS
VINIFICATOR
VINIFICATORS
VINOLOGIES
VINOLOGIST
VINOLOGISTS
VINOSITIES
VINTAGINGS
VINYLCYANIDE
VINYLCYANIDES
VINYLIDENE
VINYLIDENES
VIOLABILITIES
VIOLABILITY
VIOLABLENESS
VIOLABLENESSES
VIOLACEOUS
VIOLATIONS
VIOLENTING
VIOLINISTIC
VIOLINISTICALLY
VIOLINISTS
VIOLONCELLI
VIOLONCELLIST
VIOLONCELLISTS
VIOLONCELLO
VIOLONCELLOS
VIOSTEROLS
VIPASSANAS
VIPERFISHES
VIPERIFORM
VIPERISHLY
VIPEROUSLY
VIRAGINIAN
VIRAGINOUS
VIRALITIES
VIREONINES
VIRESCENCE
VIRESCENCES
VIRGINALIST
VIRGINALISTS
VIRGINALLED
VIRGINALLING
VIRGINALLY
VIRGINHOOD
VIRGINHOODS
VIRGINITIES
VIRGINIUMS
VIRIDESCENCE
VIRIDESCENCES
VIRIDESCENT
VIRIDITIES
VIRILESCENCE
VIRILESCENCES
VIRILESCENT
VIRILISATION
VIRILISATIONS
VIRILISING
VIRILITIES
VIRILIZATION
VIRILIZATIONS
VIRILIZING
VIROLOGICAL
VIROLOGICALLY

VIROLOGIES
VIROLOGIST
VIROLOGISTS
VIRTUALISATION
VIRTUALISATIONS
VIRTUALISE
VIRTUALISED
VIRTUALISES
VIRTUALISING
VIRTUALISM
VIRTUALISMS
VIRTUALIST
VIRTUALISTS
VIRTUALITIES
VIRTUALITY
VIRTUALIZATION
VIRTUALIZATIONS
VIRTUALIZE
VIRTUALIZED
VIRTUALIZES
VIRTUALIZING
VIRTUELESS
VIRTUOSITIES
VIRTUOSITY
VIRTUOSOSHIP
VIRTUOSOSHIPS
VIRTUOUSLY
VIRTUOUSNESS
VIRTUOUSNESSES
VIRULENCES
VIRULENCIES
VIRULENTLY
VIRULIFEROUS
VISAGISTES
VISCACHERA
VISCACHERAS
VISCERALLY
VISCERATED
VISCERATES
VISCERATING
VISCEROMOTOR
VISCEROPTOSES
VISCEROPTOSIS
VISCEROTONIA
VISCEROTONIAS
VISCEROTONIC
VISCIDITIES
VISCIDNESS
VISCIDNESSES
VISCOELASTIC
VISCOELASTICITY
VISCOMETER
VISCOMETERS
VISCOMETRIC
VISCOMETRICAL
VISCOMETRIES
VISCOMETRY
VISCOSIMETER
VISCOSIMETERS
VISCOSIMETRIC
VISCOSIMETRICAL
VISCOSIMETRIES
VISCOSIMETRY
VISCOSITIES
VISCOUNTCIES
VISCOUNTCY
VISCOUNTESS
VISCOUNTESSES
VISCOUNTIES
VISCOUNTSHIP
VISCOUNTSHIPS
VISCOUSNESS
VISCOUSNESSES
VISIBILITIES
VISIBILITY
VISIBLENESS
VISIBLENESSES
VISIOGENIC
VISIONALLY
VISIONARIES
VISIONARINESS
VISIONARINESSES
VISIONINGS
VISIONISTS
VISIONLESS
VISIOPHONE
VISIOPHONES
VISITATION
VISITATIONAL
VISITATIONS
VISITATIVE
VISITATORIAL
VISITATORS
VISITORIAL
VISITRESSES
VISUALISATION
VISUALISATIONS
VISUALISED
VISUALISER
VISUALISERS
VISUALISES
VISUALISING
VISUALISTS
VISUALITIES
VISUALIZATION
VISUALIZATIONS
VISUALIZED
VISUALIZER
VISUALIZERS
VISUALIZES
VISUALIZING
VITALISATION
VITALISATIONS
VITALISERS
VITALISING
VITALISTIC
VITALISTICALLY
VITALITIES
VITALIZATION
VITALIZATIONS
VITALIZERS
VITALIZING
VITALNESSES
VITAMINISE
VITAMINISED
VITAMINISES
VITAMINISING
VITAMINIZE
VITAMINIZED
VITAMINIZES
VITAMINIZING
VITASCOPES
VITATIVENESS
VITATIVENESSES
VITELLARIES
VITELLICLE
VITELLICLES
VITELLIGENOUS
VITELLINES
VITELLOGENESES
VITELLOGENESIS
VITELLOGENIC
VITELLUSES
VITIATIONS
VITICETUMS
VITICOLOUS
VITICULTURAL
VITICULTURALLY
VITICULTURE
VITICULTURER
VITICULTURERS
VITICULTURES
VITICULTURIST
VITICULTURISTS
VITIFEROUS
VITILITIGATE
VITILITIGATED
VITILITIGATES
VITILITIGATING
VITILITIGATION
VITILITIGATIONS
VITIOSITIES
VITRAILLED
VITRAILLIST
VITRAILLISTS
VITRECTOMIES
VITRECTOMY
VITREORETINAL
VITREOSITIES
VITREOSITY
VITREOUSES
VITREOUSLY
VITREOUSNESS
VITREOUSNESSES
VITRESCENCE
VITRESCENCES
VITRESCENT
VITRESCIBILITY
VITRESCIBLE
VITRIFACTION
VITRIFACTIONS
VITRIFACTURE
VITRIFACTURES
VITRIFIABILITY
VITRIFIABLE
VITRIFICATION
VITRIFICATIONS
VITRIFYING
VITRIOLATE
VITRIOLATED
VITRIOLATES
VITRIOLATING
VITRIOLATION
VITRIOLATIONS
VITRIOLING
VITRIOLISATION
VITRIOLISATIONS
VITRIOLISE
VITRIOLISED
VITRIOLISES
VITRIOLISING
VITRIOLIZATION
VITRIOLIZATIONS
VITRIOLIZE
VITRIOLIZED
VITRIOLIZES
VITRIOLIZING
VITRIOLLED
VITRIOLLING
VITUPERABLE
VITUPERATE
VITUPERATED
VITUPERATES
VITUPERATING
VITUPERATION
VITUPERATIONS
VITUPERATIVE
VITUPERATIVELY
VITUPERATOR
VITUPERATORS
VITUPERATORY
VIVACIOUSLY
VIVACIOUSNESS
VIVACIOUSNESSES
VIVACISSIMO
VIVACITIES
VIVANDIERE
VIVANDIERES
VIVANDIERS
VIVERRINES
VIVIANITES
VIVIDITIES
VIVIDNESSES
VIVIFICATION
VIVIFICATIONS
VIVIPARIES
VIVIPARISM
VIVIPARISMS
VIVIPARITIES
VIVIPARITY

VIVIPAROUS
VIVIPAROUSLY
VIVIPAROUSNESS
VIVISECTED
VIVISECTING
VIVISECTION
VIVISECTIONAL
VIVISECTIONALLY
VIVISECTIONIST
VIVISECTIONISTS
VIVISECTIONS
VIVISECTIVE
VIVISECTOR
VIVISECTORIA
VIVISECTORIUM
VIVISECTORIUMS
VIVISECTORS
VIVISEPULTURE
VIVISEPULTURES
VIXENISHLY
VIXENISHNESS
VIXENISHNESSES
VIZIERATES
VIZIERSHIP
VIZIERSHIPS
VIZIRSHIPS
VOCABULARIAN
VOCABULARIANS
VOCABULARIED
VOCABULARIES
VOCABULARY
VOCABULIST
VOCABULISTS
VOCALICALLY
VOCALISATION
VOCALISATIONS
VOCALISERS
VOCALISING
VOCALITIES
VOCALIZATION
VOCALIZATIONS
VOCALIZERS
VOCALIZING
VOCALNESSES
VOCATIONAL
VOCATIONALISM
VOCATIONALISMS
VOCATIONALIST
VOCATIONALISTS
VOCATIONALLY
VOCATIVELY
VOCICULTURAL
VOCIFERANCE
VOCIFERANCES
VOCIFERANT
VOCIFERANTS
VOCIFERATE
VOCIFERATED
VOCIFERATES
VOCIFERATING
VOCIFERATION
VOCIFERATIONS
VOCIFERATOR
VOCIFERATORS
VOCIFEROSITIES
VOCIFEROSITY
VOCIFEROUS
VOCIFEROUSLY
VOCIFEROUSNESS
VODCASTERS
VODCASTING
VODCASTINGS
VOETGANGER
VOETGANGERS
VOETSTOETS
VOETSTOOTS
VOGUISHNESS
VOGUISHNESSES
VOICEFULNESS
VOICEFULNESSES
VOICELESSLY
VOICELESSNESS
VOICELESSNESSES
VOICEMAILS
VOICEOVERS
VOICEPRINT
VOICEPRINTS
VOIDABLENESS
VOIDABLENESSES
VOIDNESSES
VOISINAGES
VOITURIERS
VOIVODESHIP
VOIVODESHIPS
VOLATILENESS
VOLATILENESSES
VOLATILISABLE
VOLATILISATION
VOLATILISATIONS
VOLATILISE
VOLATILISED
VOLATILISES
VOLATILISING
VOLATILITIES
VOLATILITY
VOLATILIZABLE
VOLATILIZATION
VOLATILIZATIONS
VOLATILIZE
VOLATILIZED
VOLATILIZES
VOLATILIZING
VOLCANICALLY
VOLCANICITIES
VOLCANICITY
VOLCANISATION
VOLCANISATIONS
VOLCANISED
VOLCANISES
VOLCANISING
VOLCANISMS
VOLCANISTS
VOLCANIZATION
VOLCANIZATIONS
VOLCANIZED
VOLCANIZES
VOLCANIZING
VOLCANOLOGIC
VOLCANOLOGICAL
VOLCANOLOGIES
VOLCANOLOGIST
VOLCANOLOGISTS
VOLCANOLOGY
VOLITATING
VOLITATION
VOLITATIONAL
VOLITATIONS
VOLITIONAL
VOLITIONALLY
VOLITIONARY
VOLITIONLESS
VOLITORIAL
VOLKSLIEDER
VOLKSRAADS
VOLLEYBALL
VOLLEYBALLS
VOLPLANING
VOLTAMETER
VOLTAMETERS
VOLTAMETRIC
VOLTAMMETER
VOLTAMMETERS
VOLTIGEURS
VOLTINISMS
VOLTMETERS
VOLUBILITIES
VOLUBILITY
VOLUBLENESS
VOLUBLENESSES
VOLUMENOMETER
VOLUMENOMETERS
VOLUMETERS
VOLUMETRIC
VOLUMETRICAL
VOLUMETRICALLY
VOLUMETRIES
VOLUMINOSITIES
VOLUMINOSITY
VOLUMINOUS
VOLUMINOUSLY
VOLUMINOUSNESS
VOLUMISERS
VOLUMISING
VOLUMIZERS
VOLUMIZING
VOLUMOMETER
VOLUMOMETERS
VOLUNTARIES
VOLUNTARILY
VOLUNTARINESS
VOLUNTARINESSES
VOLUNTARISM
VOLUNTARISMS
VOLUNTARIST
VOLUNTARISTIC
VOLUNTARISTS
VOLUNTARYISM
VOLUNTARYISMS
VOLUNTARYIST
VOLUNTARYISTS
VOLUNTATIVE
VOLUNTATIVES
VOLUNTEERED
VOLUNTEERING
VOLUNTEERISM
VOLUNTEERISMS
VOLUNTEERS
VOLUNTOURISM
VOLUNTOURISMS
VOLUPTUARIES
VOLUPTUARY
VOLUPTUOSITIES
VOLUPTUOSITY
VOLUPTUOUS
VOLUPTUOUSLY
VOLUPTUOUSNESS
VOLUTATION
VOLUTATIONS
VOLVULUSES
VOMERONASAL
VOMITORIES
VOMITORIUM
VOMITURITION
VOMITURITIONS
VOODOOISMS
VOODOOISTIC
VOODOOISTS
VOORKAMERS
VOORTREKKER
VOORTREKKERS
VORACIOUSLY
VORACIOUSNESS
VORACIOUSNESSES
VORACITIES
VORAGINOUS
VORTICALLY
VORTICELLA
VORTICELLAE
VORTICELLAS
VORTICISMS
VORTICISTS
VORTICITIES
VORTICULAR
VORTIGINOUS
VOTARESSES
VOTIVENESS
VOTIVENESSES
VOUCHERING
VOUCHSAFED
VOUCHSAFEMENT

V

VOUCHSAFEMENTS
VOUCHSAFES
VOUCHSAFING
VOUCHSAFINGS
VOUSSOIRED
VOUSSOIRING
VOUTSAFING
VOWELISATION
VOWELISATIONS
VOWELISING
VOWELIZATION
VOWELIZATIONS
VOWELIZING
VOWELLIEST
VOYAGEABLE
VOYEURISMS
VOYEURISTIC
VOYEURISTICALLY
VRAICKINGS
VRAISEMBLANCE
VRAISEMBLANCES
VRYSTATERS
VULCANICITIES
VULCANICITY
VULCANISABLE
VULCANISATE
VULCANISATES
VULCANISATION
VULCANISATIONS
VULCANISED
VULCANISER
VULCANISERS
VULCANISES
VULCANISING
VULCANISMS
VULCANISTS
VULCANITES
VULCANIZABLE
VULCANIZATE
VULCANIZATES
VULCANIZATION
VULCANIZATIONS
VULCANIZED
VULCANIZER
VULCANIZERS
VULCANIZES
VULCANIZING
VULCANOLOGIC
VULCANOLOGICAL
VULCANOLOGIES
VULCANOLOGIST
VULCANOLOGISTS
VULCANOLOGY
VULGARIANS
VULGARISATION
VULGARISATIONS
VULGARISED
VULGARISER
VULGARISERS
VULGARISES
VULGARISING
VULGARISMS
VULGARITIES
VULGARIZATION
VULGARIZATIONS
VULGARIZED
VULGARIZER
VULGARIZERS
VULGARIZES
VULGARIZING
VULNERABILITIES
VULNERABILITY
VULNERABLE
VULNERABLENESS
VULNERABLY
VULNERARIES
VULNERATED
VULNERATES
VULNERATING
VULNERATION
VULNERATIONS
VULPECULAR
VULPICIDES
VULPINISMS
VULPINITES
VULTURISMS
VULVITISES
VULVOVAGINAL
VULVOVAGINITIS

V

W

WACKINESSES
WADSETTERS
WADSETTING
WAFFLESTOMPER
WAFFLESTOMPERS
WAGELESSNESS
WAGELESSNESSES
WAGENBOOMS
WAGEWORKER
WAGEWORKERS
WAGGISHNESS
WAGGISHNESSES
WAGGLINGLY
WAGGONETTE
WAGGONETTES
WAGGONLESS
WAGGONLOAD
WAGGONLOADS
WAGHALTERS
WAGONETTES
WAGONLOADS
WAGONWRIGHT
WAGONWRIGHTS
WAINSCOTED
WAINSCOTING
WAINSCOTINGS
WAINSCOTTED
WAINSCOTTING
WAINSCOTTINGS
WAINWRIGHT
WAINWRIGHTS
WAISTBANDS
WAISTBELTS
WAISTCLOTH
WAISTCLOTHS
WAISTCOATED
WAISTCOATEER
WAISTCOATEERS
WAISTCOATING
WAISTCOATINGS
WAISTCOATS
WAISTLINES
WAITERAGES
WAITERHOOD
WAITERHOODS
WAITERINGS
WAITLISTED
WAITLISTING
WAITPEOPLE
WAITPERSON
WAITPERSONS
WAITRESSED
WAITRESSES
WAITRESSING
WAITRESSINGS
WAITSTAFFS
WAKEBOARDED
WAKEBOARDER
WAKEBOARDERS
WAKEBOARDING
WAKEBOARDINGS
WAKEBOARDS
WAKEFULNESS
WAKEFULNESSES
WALDFLUTES
WALDGRAVES
WALDGRAVINE
WALDGRAVINES
WALDSTERBEN
WALDSTERBENS
WALKABOUTS
WALKATHONS
WALKINGSTICK
WALKINGSTICKS
WALKSHORTS
WALLBOARDS
WALLCHARTS
WALLCLIMBER
WALLCLIMBERS
WALLCOVERING
WALLCOVERINGS
WALLFISHES
WALLFLOWER
WALLFLOWERS
WALLOPINGS
WALLOWINGS
WALLPAPERED
WALLPAPERING
WALLPAPERS
WALLPEPPER
WALLPEPPERS
WALLPOSTER
WALLPOSTERS
WALLYBALLS
WALLYDRAGS
WALLYDRAIGLE
WALLYDRAIGLES
WALNUTWOOD
WALNUTWOODS
WAMBENGERS
WAMBLINESS
WAMBLINESSES
WAMBLINGLY
WAMPISHING
WAMPUMPEAG
WAMPUMPEAGS
WANCHANCIE
WANDERINGLY
WANDERINGS
WANDERLUST
WANDERLUSTS
WANRESTFUL
WANTHRIVEN
WANTONISED
WANTONISES
WANTONISING
WANTONIZED
WANTONIZES
WANTONIZING
WANTONNESS
WANTONNESSES
WANWORDIER
WANWORDIEST
WAPENSCHAW
WAPENSCHAWS
WAPENSHAWS
WAPENTAKES
WAPINSCHAW
WAPINSCHAWS
WAPINSHAWS
WAPPENSCHAW
WAPPENSCHAWING
WAPPENSCHAWINGS
WAPPENSCHAWS
WAPPENSHAW
WAPPENSHAWING
WAPPENSHAWINGS
WAPPENSHAWS
WARBLINGLY
WARBONNETS
WARCHALKER
WARCHALKERS
WARCHALKING
WARCHALKINGS
WARDENRIES
WARDENSHIP
WARDENSHIPS
WARDERSHIP
WARDERSHIPS
WARDRESSES
WARDROBERS
WARDROBING
WAREHOUSED
WAREHOUSEMAN
WAREHOUSEMEN
WAREHOUSER
WAREHOUSERS
WAREHOUSES
WAREHOUSING
WAREHOUSINGS
WARFARINGS
WARGAMINGS
WARIBASHIS
WARINESSES
WARLIKENESS
WARLIKENESSES
WARLOCKRIES
WARLORDISM
WARLORDISMS
WARMBLOODS
WARMHEARTED
WARMHEARTEDNESS
WARMNESSES
WARMONGERING
WARMONGERINGS
WARMONGERS
WARRANDICE
WARRANDICES
WARRANDING
WARRANTABILITY
WARRANTABLE
WARRANTABLENESS
WARRANTABLY
WARRANTEES
WARRANTERS
WARRANTIED
WARRANTIES
WARRANTING
WARRANTINGS
WARRANTISE
WARRANTISED
WARRANTISES
WARRANTISING
WARRANTIZE
WARRANTIZED
WARRANTIZES
WARRANTIZING
WARRANTLESS
WARRANTORS
WARRANTYING
WARRIORESS
WARRIORESSES
WASHABILITIES
WASHABILITY
WASHATERIA
WASHATERIAS
WASHBASINS
WASHBOARDS
WASHCLOTHS
WASHERWOMAN

W

WASHERWOMEN
WASHETERIA
WASHETERIAS
WASHHOUSES
WASHINESSES
WASHINGTONIA
WASHINGTONIAS
WASHSTANDS
WASPINESSES
WASPISHNESS
WASPISHNESSES
WASSAILERS
WASSAILING
WASSAILINGS
WASSAILRIES
WASTEBASKET
WASTEBASKETS
WASTEFULLY
WASTEFULNESS
WASTEFULNESSES
WASTELANDS
WASTENESSES
WASTEPAPER
WASTEPAPERS
WASTERFULLY
WASTERFULNESS
WASTERFULNESSES
WASTEWATER
WASTEWATERS
WASTEWEIRS
WASTNESSES
WATCHABLES
WATCHBANDS
WATCHBOXES
WATCHCASES
WATCHCRIES
WATCHDOGGED
WATCHDOGGING
WATCHDOGGINGS
WATCHFULLY
WATCHFULNESS
WATCHFULNESSES
WATCHGLASS
WATCHGLASSES
WATCHGUARD
WATCHGUARDS
WATCHLISTS
WATCHMAKER
WATCHMAKERS
WATCHMAKING
WATCHMAKINGS
WATCHSPRING
WATCHSPRINGS
WATCHSTRAP
WATCHSTRAPS
WATCHTOWER
WATCHTOWERS
WATCHWORDS
WATERBIRDS
WATERBOARDING
WATERBOARDINGS
WATERBORNE
WATERBRAIN
WATERBRAINS
WATERBUCKS
WATERBUSES
WATERBUSSES
WATERCOLOR
WATERCOLORIST
WATERCOLORISTS
WATERCOLORS
WATERCOLOUR
WATERCOLOURIST
WATERCOLOURISTS
WATERCOLOURS
WATERCOOLER
WATERCOOLERS
WATERCOURSE
WATERCOURSES
WATERCRAFT
WATERCRAFTS
WATERCRESS
WATERCRESSES
WATERDRIVE
WATERDRIVES
WATERFALLS
WATERFINDER
WATERFINDERS
WATERFLOOD
WATERFLOODED
WATERFLOODING
WATERFLOODINGS
WATERFLOODS
WATERFOWLER
WATERFOWLERS
WATERFOWLING
WATERFOWLINGS
WATERFOWLS
WATERFRONT
WATERFRONTS
WATERGATES
WATERGLASS
WATERGLASSES
WATERHEADS
WATERHOLES
WATERINESS
WATERINESSES
WATERISHNESS
WATERISHNESSES
WATERLEAFS
WATERLEAVES
WATERLESSNESS
WATERLESSNESSES
WATERLILIES
WATERLINES
WATERLOGGED
WATERLOGGING
WATERLOGGINGS
WATERMANSHIP
WATERMANSHIPS
WATERMARKED
WATERMARKING
WATERMARKS
WATERMELON
WATERMELONS
WATERMILLS
WATERPOWER
WATERPOWERS
WATERPOXES
WATERPROOF
WATERPROOFED
WATERPROOFER
WATERPROOFERS
WATERPROOFING
WATERPROOFINGS
WATERPROOFNESS
WATERPROOFS
WATERQUAKE
WATERQUAKES
WATERSCAPE
WATERSCAPES
WATERSHEDS
WATERSIDER
WATERSIDERS
WATERSIDES
WATERSKIING
WATERSKIINGS
WATERSMEET
WATERSMEETS
WATERSPOUT
WATERSPOUTS
WATERTHRUSH
WATERTHRUSHES
WATERTIGHT
WATERTIGHTNESS
WATERWEEDS
WATERWHEEL
WATERWHEELS
WATERWORKS
WATERZOOIS
WATTLEBARK
WATTLEBARKS
WATTLEBIRD
WATTLEBIRDS
WATTLEWORK
WATTLEWORKS
WATTMETERS
WAULKMILLS
WAVEFRONTS
WAVEGUIDES
WAVELENGTH
WAVELENGTHS
WAVELESSLY
WAVELLITES
WAVEMETERS
WAVERINGLY
WAVERINGNESS
WAVERINGNESSES
WAVESHAPES
WAVETABLES
WAVINESSES
WAXBERRIES
WAXFLOWERS
WAXINESSES
WAXWORKERS
WAYFARINGS
WAYMARKING
WAYMENTING
WAYWARDNESS
WAYWARDNESSES
WAYZGOOSES
WEAKENINGS
WEAKFISHES
WEAKHEARTED
WEAKISHNESS
WEAKISHNESSES
WEAKLINESS
WEAKLINESSES
WEAKNESSES
WEALTHIEST
WEALTHINESS
WEALTHINESSES
WEALTHLESS
WEAPONEERED
WEAPONEERING
WEAPONEERINGS
WEAPONEERS
WEAPONISED
WEAPONISES
WEAPONISING
WEAPONIZED
WEAPONIZES
WEAPONIZING
WEAPONLESS
WEAPONRIES
WEARABILITIES
WEARABILITY
WEARIFULLY
WEARIFULNESS
WEARIFULNESSES
WEARILESSLY
WEARINESSES
WEARISOMELY
WEARISOMENESS
WEARISOMENESSES
WEARYINGLY
WEASELIEST
WEASELLERS
WEASELLIER
WEASELLIEST
WEASELLING
WEATHERABILITY
WEATHERABLE
WEATHERBOARD
WEATHERBOARDED
WEATHERBOARDING
WEATHERBOARDS
WEATHERCAST
WEATHERCASTER
WEATHERCASTERS

WEATHERCASTS
WEATHERCLOTH
WEATHERCLOTHS
WEATHERCOCK
WEATHERCOCKED
WEATHERCOCKING
WEATHERCOCKS
WEATHERERS
WEATHERGIRL
WEATHERGIRLS
WEATHERGLASS
WEATHERGLASSES
WEATHERING
WEATHERINGS
WEATHERISATION
WEATHERISATIONS
WEATHERISE
WEATHERISED
WEATHERISES
WEATHERISING
WEATHERIZATION
WEATHERIZATIONS
WEATHERIZE
WEATHERIZED
WEATHERIZES
WEATHERIZING
WEATHERLIER
WEATHERLIEST
WEATHERLINESS
WEATHERLINESSES
WEATHERMAN
WEATHERMEN
WEATHERMOST
WEATHEROMETER
WEATHEROMETERS
WEATHERPERSON
WEATHERPERSONS
WEATHERPROOF
WEATHERPROOFED
WEATHERPROOFING
WEATHERPROOFS
WEATHERWOMAN
WEATHERWOMEN
WEATHERWORN
WEAVERBIRD
WEAVERBIRDS
WEBCASTERS
WEBCASTING
WEBCASTINGS
WEBCHATTED
WEBCHATTING
WEBLIOGRAPHIES
WEBLIOGRAPHY
WEBLOGGERS
WEBLOGGING
WEBLOGGINGS
WEBMASTERS
WEEDICIDES
WEEDINESSES
WEEDKILLER
WEEDKILLERS
WEEKENDERS
WEEKENDING
WEEKENDINGS
WEEKNIGHTS
WEELDLESSE
WEEPINESSES
WEEVILIEST
WEEVILLIER
WEEVILLIEST
WEIGHBOARD
WEIGHBOARDS
WEIGHBRIDGE
WEIGHBRIDGES
WEIGHTAGES
WEIGHTIEST
WEIGHTINESS
WEIGHTINESSES
WEIGHTINGS
WEIGHTLESS
WEIGHTLESSLY
WEIGHTLESSNESS
WEIGHTLIFTER
WEIGHTLIFTERS
WEIGHTLIFTING
WEIGHTLIFTINGS
WEIMARANER
WEIMARANERS
WEIRDNESSES
WEISENHEIMER
WEISENHEIMERS
WELCOMENESS
WELCOMENESSES
WELCOMINGLY
WELDABILITIES
WELDABILITY
WELDMESHES
WELFARISMS
WELFARISTIC
WELFARISTS
WELFARITES
WELLBEINGS
WELLHOUSES
WELLINGTON
WELLINGTONIA
WELLINGTONIAS
WELLINGTONS
WELLNESSES
WELLSPRING
WELLSPRINGS
WELTANSCHAUUNG
WELTANSCHAUUNGS
WELTERWEIGHT
WELTERWEIGHTS
WELTSCHMERZ
WELTSCHMERZES
WELWITSCHIA
WELWITSCHIAS
WENSLEYDALE
WENSLEYDALES
WENTLETRAP
WENTLETRAPS
WEREWOLFERIES
WEREWOLFERY
WEREWOLFISH
WEREWOLFISM
WEREWOLFISMS
WEREWOLVES
WERNERITES
WERWOLFISH
WESTERINGS
WESTERLIES
WESTERLINESS
WESTERLINESSES
WESTERNERS
WESTERNISATION
WESTERNISATIONS
WESTERNISE
WESTERNISED
WESTERNISES
WESTERNISING
WESTERNISM
WESTERNISMS
WESTERNIZATION
WESTERNIZATIONS
WESTERNIZE
WESTERNIZED
WESTERNIZES
WESTERNIZING
WESTERNMOST
WESTWARDLY
WETTABILITIES
WETTABILITY
WHAIKORERO
WHAIKOREROS
WHAKAPAPAS
WHALEBACKS
WHALEBOATS
WHALEBONES
WHAREPUNIS
WHARFINGER
WHARFINGERS
WHARFMASTER
WHARFMASTERS
WHATABOUTERIES
WHATABOUTERY
WHATABOUTISM
WHATABOUTISMS
WHATABOUTS
WHATCHAMACALLIT
WHATNESSES
WHATSERNAME
WHATSERNAMES
WHATSHERNAME
WHATSHERNAMES
WHATSHISNAME
WHATSHISNAMES
WHATSISNAME
WHATSISNAMES
WHATSITSNAME
WHATSITSNAMES
WHATSOEVER
WHATSOMEVER
WHEATFIELD
WHEATFIELDS
WHEATGERMS
WHEATGRASS
WHEATGRASSES
WHEATLANDS
WHEATMEALS
WHEATWORMS
WHEEDLESOME
WHEEDLINGLY
WHEEDLINGS
WHEELBARROW
WHEELBARROWED
WHEELBARROWING
WHEELBARROWS
WHEELBASES
WHEELCHAIR
WHEELCHAIRS
WHEELHORSE
WHEELHORSES
WHEELHOUSE
WHEELHOUSES
WHEELSPINS
WHEELWORKS
WHEELWRIGHT
WHEELWRIGHTS
WHEESHTING
WHEEZINESS
WHEEZINESSES
WHEEZINGLY
WHENCEFORTH
WHENCESOEVER
WHENSOEVER
WHEREABOUT
WHEREABOUTS
WHEREAFTER
WHEREAGAINST
WHEREFORES
WHEREINSOEVER
WHERENESSES
WHERESOEVER
WHERETHROUGH
WHEREUNDER
WHEREUNTIL
WHEREWITHAL
WHEREWITHALS
WHEREWITHS
WHERRETING
WHERRITING
WHETSTONES
WHEWELLITE
WHEWELLITES
WHEYISHNESS
WHEYISHNESSES
WHICHSOEVER
WHICKERING
WHIDDERING

WHIFFLERIES
WHIFFLETREE
WHIFFLETREES
WHIFFLINGS
WHIGGAMORE
WHIGGAMORES
WHIGMALEERIE
WHIGMALEERIES
WHIGMALEERY
WHILLYWHAED
WHILLYWHAING
WHILLYWHAS
WHILLYWHAW
WHILLYWHAWED
WHILLYWHAWING
WHILLYWHAWS
WHIMBERRIES
WHIMPERERS
WHIMPERING
WHIMPERINGLY
WHIMPERINGS
WHIMSICALITIES
WHIMSICALITY
WHIMSICALLY
WHIMSICALNESS
WHIMSICALNESSES
WHIMSINESS
WHIMSINESSES
WHINBERRIES
WHINGDINGS
WHINGEINGLY
WHINGEINGS
WHININESSES
WHINSTONES
WHIPCORDIER
WHIPCORDIEST
WHIPCRACKS
WHIPLASHED
WHIPLASHES
WHIPLASHING
WHIPPERSNAPPER
WHIPPERSNAPPERS
WHIPPETING
WHIPPETINGS
WHIPPINESS
WHIPPINESSES
WHIPPLETREE
WHIPPLETREES
WHIPPOORWILL
WHIPPOORWILLS
WHIPSAWING
WHIPSNAKES
WHIPSTAFFS
WHIPSTALLED
WHIPSTALLING
WHIPSTALLS
WHIPSTITCH
WHIPSTITCHED
WHIPSTITCHES
WHIPSTITCHING
WHIPSTOCKS
WHIPTAILED
WHIRLABOUT
WHIRLABOUTS
WHIRLBLAST
WHIRLBLASTS
WHIRLIGIGS
WHIRLINGLY
WHIRLPOOLS
WHIRLWINDS
WHIRLYBIRD
WHIRLYBIRDS
WHIRRETING
WHISKERANDO
WHISKERANDOED
WHISKERANDOS
WHISKERIER
WHISKERIEST
WHISKEYFIED
WHISKIFIED
WHISPERERS
WHISPERIER
WHISPERIEST
WHISPERING
WHISPERINGLY
WHISPERINGS
WHISPEROUSLY
WHISTLEABLE
WHISTLEBLOWING
WHISTLEBLOWINGS
WHISTLINGLY
WHISTLINGS
WHITEBAITS
WHITEBASSES
WHITEBEAMS
WHITEBEARD
WHITEBEARDS
WHITEBOARD
WHITEBOARDS
WHITEBOYISM
WHITEBOYISMS
WHITECOATS
WHITECOMBS
WHITEDAMPS
WHITEFACES
WHITEFISHES
WHITEFLIES
WHITEHEADS
WHITELISTED
WHITELISTING
WHITELISTS
WHITENESSES
WHITENINGS
WHITESMITH
WHITESMITHS
WHITETAILS
WHITETHORN
WHITETHORNS
WHITETHROAT
WHITETHROATS
WHITEWALLS
WHITEWARES
WHITEWASHED
WHITEWASHER
WHITEWASHERS
WHITEWASHES
WHITEWASHING
WHITEWASHINGS
WHITEWATER
WHITEWINGS
WHITEWOODS
WHITEYWOOD
WHITEYWOODS
WHITHERING
WHITHERSOEVER
WHITHERWARD
WHITHERWARDS
WHITISHNESS
WHITISHNESSES
WHITLEATHER
WHITLEATHERS
WHITTAWERS
WHITTERICK
WHITTERICKS
WHITTERING
WHITTLINGS
WHIZZBANGS
WHIZZINGLY
WHODUNITRIES
WHODUNITRY
WHODUNNITRIES
WHODUNNITRY
WHODUNNITS
WHOLEFOODS
WHOLEGRAIN
WHOLEGRAINS
WHOLEHEARTED
WHOLEHEARTEDLY
WHOLEMEALS
WHOLENESSES
WHOLESALED
WHOLESALER
WHOLESALERS
WHOLESALES
WHOLESALING
WHOLESALINGS
WHOLESOMELY
WHOLESOMENESS
WHOLESOMENESSES
WHOLESOMER
WHOLESOMEST
WHOLESTITCH
WHOLESTITCHES
WHOLEWHEAT
WHOMSOEVER
WHOREHOUSE
WHOREHOUSES
WHOREMASTER
WHOREMASTERIES
WHOREMASTERLY
WHOREMASTERS
WHOREMASTERY
WHOREMISTRESS
WHOREMISTRESSES
WHOREMONGER
WHOREMONGERIES
WHOREMONGERS
WHOREMONGERY
WHORISHNESS
WHORISHNESSES
WHORTLEBERRIES
WHORTLEBERRY
WHOSESOEVER
WHUNSTANES
WHYDUNNITS
WICKEDNESS
WICKEDNESSES
WICKERWORK
WICKERWORKS
WICKETKEEPER
WICKETKEEPERS
WICKTHINGS
WIDDERSHINS
WIDEAWAKES
WIDEBODIES
WIDECHAPPED
WIDEMOUTHED
WIDENESSES
WIDERSHINS
WIDESCREEN
WIDESPREAD
WIDOWBIRDS
WIDOWERHOOD
WIDOWERHOODS
WIDOWHOODS
WIELDINESS
WIELDINESSES
WIENERWURST
WIENERWURSTS
WIFELINESS
WIFELINESSES
WIGWAGGERS
WIGWAGGING
WIKIALITIES
WIKITORIAL
WIKITORIALS
WILDCATTED
WILDCATTER
WILDCATTERS
WILDCATTING
WILDCATTINGS
WILDEBEEST
WILDEBEESTS
WILDERMENT
WILDERMENTS
WILDERNESS
WILDERNESSES
WILDFLOWER
WILDFLOWERS
WILDFOWLER

WILDFOWLERS
WILDFOWLING
WILDFOWLINGS
WILDGRAVES
WILDNESSES
WILFULNESS
WILFULNESSES
WILINESSES
WILLEMITES
WILLFULNESS
WILLFULNESSES
WILLIEWAUGHT
WILLIEWAUGHTS
WILLINGEST
WILLINGNESS
WILLINGNESSES
WILLOWHERB
WILLOWHERBS
WILLOWIEST
WILLOWLIKE
WILLOWWARE
WILLOWWARES
WILLPOWERS
WIMPINESSES
WIMPISHNESS
WIMPISHNESSES
WINCEYETTE
WINCEYETTES
WINCHESTER
WINCHESTERS
WINCOPIPES
WINDBAGGERIES
WINDBAGGERY
WINDBLASTS
WINDBREAKER
WINDBREAKERS
WINDBREAKS
WINDBURNED
WINDBURNING
WINDCHEATER
WINDCHEATERS
WINDCHILLS
WINDFALLEN
WINDFLOWER
WINDFLOWERS
WINDGALLED
WINDHOVERS
WINDINESSES

WINDJAMMER
WINDJAMMERS
WINDJAMMING
WINDJAMMINGS
WINDLASSED
WINDLASSES
WINDLASSING
WINDLESSLY
WINDLESSNESS
WINDLESSNESSES
WINDLESTRAE
WINDLESTRAES
WINDLESTRAW
WINDLESTRAWS
WINDMILLED
WINDMILLING
WINDOWIEST
WINDOWINGS
WINDOWLESS
WINDOWPANE
WINDOWPANES
WINDOWSILL
WINDOWSILLS
WINDPROOFED
WINDPROOFING
WINDPROOFS
WINDROWERS
WINDROWING
WINDSCREEN
WINDSCREENS
WINDSHAKES
WINDSHIELD
WINDSHIELDS
WINDSTORMS
WINDSUCKER
WINDSUCKERS
WINDSURFED
WINDSURFER
WINDSURFERS
WINDSURFING
WINDSURFINGS
WINDTHROWS
WINEBERRIES
WINEBIBBER
WINEBIBBERS
WINEBIBBING
WINEBIBBINGS
WINEGLASSES

WINEGLASSFUL
WINEGLASSFULS
WINEGROWER
WINEGROWERS
WINEGROWING
WINEGROWINGS
WINEMAKERS
WINEMAKING
WINEMAKINGS
WINEPRESSES
WINGCHAIRS
WINGLESSNESS
WINGLESSNESSES
WINGSPREAD
WINGSPREADS
WINNABILITIES
WINNABILITY
WINNINGEST
WINNINGNESS
WINNINGNESSES
WINNOWINGS
WINSOMENESS
WINSOMENESSES
WINTERBERRIES
WINTERBERRY
WINTERBOURNE
WINTERBOURNES
WINTERCRESS
WINTERCRESSES
WINTERFEED
WINTERFEEDING
WINTERFEEDS
WINTERGREEN
WINTERGREENS
WINTERIEST
WINTERINESS
WINTERINESSES
WINTERISATION
WINTERISATIONS
WINTERISED
WINTERISES
WINTERISING
WINTERIZATION
WINTERIZATIONS
WINTERIZED
WINTERIZES
WINTERIZING
WINTERKILL

WINTERKILLED
WINTERKILLING
WINTERKILLINGS
WINTERKILLS
WINTERLESS
WINTERLIER
WINTERLIEST
WINTERLINESS
WINTERLINESSES
WINTERTIDE
WINTERTIDES
WINTERTIME
WINTERTIMES
WINTERWEIGHT
WINTRINESS
WINTRINESSES
WIREDRAWER
WIREDRAWERS
WIREDRAWING
WIREDRAWINGS
WIREFRAMES
WIREGRASSES
WIREHAIRED
WIRELESSED
WIRELESSES
WIRELESSING
WIRELESSLY
WIREPHOTOS
WIREPULLER
WIREPULLERS
WIREPULLING
WIREPULLINGS
WIRETAPPED
WIRETAPPER
WIRETAPPERS
WIRETAPPING
WIRETAPPINGS
WIREWALKER
WIREWALKERS
WIREWORKER
WIREWORKERS
WIREWORKING
WIREWORKINGS
WIRINESSES
WISECRACKED
WISECRACKER
WISECRACKERS
WISECRACKING

WISECRACKS
WISENESSES
WISENHEIMER
WISENHEIMERS
WISHFULNESS
WISHFULNESSES
WISHTONWISH
WISHTONWISHES
WISPINESSES
WISTFULNESS
WISTFULNESSES
WITBLITSES
WITCHBROOM
WITCHBROOMS
WITCHCRAFT
WITCHCRAFTS
WITCHERIES
WITCHETTIES
WITCHGRASS
WITCHGRASSES
WITCHHOODS
WITCHINGLY
WITCHKNOTS
WITCHWEEDS
WITENAGEMOT
WITENAGEMOTE
WITENAGEMOTES
WITENAGEMOTS
WITGATBOOM
WITGATBOOMS
WITHDRAWABLE
WITHDRAWAL
WITHDRAWALS
WITHDRAWER
WITHDRAWERS
WITHDRAWING
WITHDRAWMENT
WITHDRAWMENTS
WITHDRAWNNESS
WITHDRAWNNESSES
WITHEREDNESS
WITHEREDNESSES
WITHERINGLY
WITHERINGS
WITHERITES
WITHERSHINS
WITHHOLDEN
WITHHOLDER

WITHHOLDERS
WITHHOLDING
WITHHOLDMENT
WITHHOLDMENTS
WITHINDOORS
WITHOUTDOORS
WITHSTANDER
WITHSTANDERS
WITHSTANDING
WITHSTANDS
WITHYWINDS
WITLESSNESS
WITLESSNESSES
WITNESSABLE
WITNESSERS
WITNESSING
WITTICISMS
WITTINESSES
WITWANTONED
WITWANTONING
WITWANTONS
WIZARDLIER
WIZARDLIEST
WIZARDRIES
WOADWAXENS
WOBBEGONGS
WOBBLINESS
WOBBLINESSES
WOEBEGONENESS
WOEBEGONENESSES
WOEFULLEST
WOEFULNESS
WOEFULNESSES
WOFULNESSES
WOLFBERRIES
WOLFFISHES
WOLFHOUNDS
WOLFISHNESS
WOLFISHNESSES
WOLFRAMITE
WOLFRAMITES
WOLFSBANES
WOLLASTONITE
WOLLASTONITES
WOLVERENES
WOLVERINES
WOMANFULLY
WOMANHOODS
WOMANISERS
WOMANISHLY
WOMANISHNESS
WOMANISHNESSES
WOMANISING
WOMANISINGS
WOMANIZERS
WOMANIZING
WOMANIZINGS
WOMANKINDS
WOMANLIEST
WOMANLINESS
WOMANLINESSES
WOMANNESSES
WOMANPOWER
WOMANPOWERS
WOMENFOLKS
WOMENKINDS
WOMENSWEAR
WOMENSWEARS
WONDERFULLY
WONDERFULNESS
WONDERFULNESSES
WONDERINGLY
WONDERINGS
WONDERKIDS
WONDERLAND
WONDERLANDS
WONDERLESS
WONDERMENT
WONDERMENTS
WONDERMONGER
WONDERMONGERING
WONDERMONGERS
WONDERSTRUCK
WONDERWORK
WONDERWORKS
WONDROUSLY
WONDROUSNESS
WONDROUSNESSES
WONKINESSES
WONTEDNESS
WONTEDNESSES
WOODBLOCKS
WOODBORERS
WOODBURYTYPE
WOODBURYTYPES
WOODCARVER
WOODCARVERS
WOODCARVING
WOODCARVINGS
WOODCHOPPER
WOODCHOPPERS
WOODCHUCKS
WOODCRAFTS
WOODCRAFTSMAN
WOODCRAFTSMEN
WOODCUTTER
WOODCUTTERS
WOODCUTTING
WOODCUTTINGS
WOODENHEAD
WOODENHEADED
WOODENHEADS
WOODENNESS
WOODENNESSES
WOODENTOPS
WOODENWARE
WOODENWARES
WOODGRAINS
WOODGROUSE
WOODGROUSES
WOODHORSES
WOODHOUSES
WOODINESSES
WOODLANDER
WOODLANDERS
WOODLESSNESS
WOODLESSNESSES
WOODNESSES
WOODPECKER
WOODPECKERS
WOODPRINTS
WOODREEVES
WOODRUSHES
WOODSCREWS
WOODSHEDDED
WOODSHEDDING
WOODSHEDDINGS
WOODSHOCKS
WOODSHRIKE
WOODSHRIKES
WOODSMOKES
WOODSPITES
WOODSTONES
WOODSTOVES
WOODSWALLOW
WOODSWALLOWS
WOODTHRUSH
WOODTHRUSHES
WOODWAXENS
WOODWORKER
WOODWORKERS
WOODWORKING
WOODWORKINGS
WOOLGATHERER
WOOLGATHERERS
WOOLGATHERING
WOOLGATHERINGS
WOOLGROWER
WOOLGROWERS
WOOLGROWING
WOOLGROWINGS
WOOLINESSES
WOOLLINESS
WOOLLINESSES
WOOLLYBACK
WOOLLYBACKS
WOOLLYBUTT
WOOLLYBUTTS
WOOLLYFOOT
WOOLLYFOOTS
WOOLSORTER
WOOLSORTERS
WOOMERANGS
WOOZINESSES
WORCESTERBERRY
WORCESTERS
WORDBREAKS
WORDCOUNTS
WORDINESSES
WORDISHNESS
WORDISHNESSES
WORDLESSLY
WORDLESSNESS
WORDLESSNESSES
WORDMONGER
WORDMONGERS
WORDSEARCH
WORDSEARCHES
WORDSMITHERIES
WORDSMITHERY
WORDSMITHS
WORKABILITIES
WORKABILITY
WORKABLENESS
WORKABLENESSES
WORKAHOLIC
WORKAHOLICS
WORKAHOLISM
WORKAHOLISMS
WORKAROUND
WORKAROUNDS
WORKBASKET
WORKBASKETS
WORKBENCHES
WORKERISTS
WORKERLESS
WORKFELLOW
WORKFELLOWS
WORKFORCES
WORKGROUPS
WORKHORSES
WORKHOUSES
WORKINGMAN
WORKINGMEN
WORKINGWOMAN
WORKINGWOMEN
WORKLESSNESS
WORKLESSNESSES
WORKMANLIER
WORKMANLIEST
WORKMANLIKE
WORKMANSHIP
WORKMANSHIPS
WORKMASTER
WORKMASTERS
WORKMISTRESS
WORKMISTRESSES
WORKPEOPLE
WORKPIECES
WORKPLACES
WORKPRINTS
WORKSHEETS
WORKSHOPPED
WORKSHOPPING
WORKSPACES
WORKSTATION
WORKSTATIONS
WORKSTREAM
WORKSTREAMS
WORKTABLES

WORKWATCHER
WORKWATCHERS
WORLDBEATS
WORLDLIEST
WORLDLINESS
WORLDLINESSES
WORLDLINGS
WORLDSCALE
WORLDSCALES
WORLDVIEWS
WORMINESSES
WORMWHEELS
WORNNESSES
WORRIMENTS
WORRISOMELY
WORRISOMENESS
WORRISOMENESSES
WORRYINGLY
WORRYWARTS
WORSENESSES
WORSENINGS
WORSHIPABLE
WORSHIPERS
WORSHIPFUL
WORSHIPFULLY
WORSHIPFULNESS
WORSHIPING
WORSHIPLESS
WORSHIPPED
WORSHIPPER
WORSHIPPERS
WORSHIPPING
WORTHINESS
WORTHINESSES
WORTHLESSLY
WORTHLESSNESS
WORTHLESSNESSES
WORTHWHILE
WORTHWHILENESS
WOUNDINGLY
WOUNDWORTS
WRAITHLIKE
WRANGLERSHIP
WRANGLERSHIPS
WRANGLESOME
WRANGLINGS
WRAPAROUND
WRAPAROUNDS
WRAPPERING
WRAPROUNDS
WRATHFULLY
WRATHFULNESS
WRATHFULNESSES
WRATHINESS
WRATHINESSES
WREATHIEST
WREATHLESS
WREATHLIKE
WRECKFISHES
WRECKMASTER
WRECKMASTERS
WRENCHINGLY
WRENCHINGS
WRESTLINGS
WRETCHEDER
WRETCHEDEST
WRETCHEDLY
WRETCHEDNESS
WRETCHEDNESSES
WRIGGLIEST
WRIGGLINGS
WRINKLELESS
WRINKLIEST
WRISTBANDS
WRISTLOCKS
WRISTWATCH
WRISTWATCHES
WRITEDOWNS
WRITERESSES
WRITERLIER
WRITERLIEST
WRITERSHIP
WRITERSHIPS
WRITHINGLY
WRONGDOERS
WRONGDOING
WRONGDOINGS
WRONGFULLY
WRONGFULNESS
WRONGFULNESSES
WRONGHEADED
WRONGHEADEDLY
WRONGHEADEDNESS
WRONGNESSES
WRONGOUSLY
WULFENITES
WUNDERKIND
WUNDERKINDER
WUNDERKINDS
WYANDOTTES
WYLIECOATS

W

XANTHATION
XANTHATIONS
XANTHOCHROIA
XANTHOCHROIAS
XANTHOCHROIC
XANTHOCHROID
XANTHOCHROIDS
XANTHOCHROISM
XANTHOCHROISMS
XANTHOCHROMIA
XANTHOCHROMIAS
XANTHOCHROOUS
XANTHOMATA
XANTHOMATOUS
XANTHOMELANOUS
XANTHOPHYL
XANTHOPHYLL
XANTHOPHYLLOUS
XANTHOPHYLLS
XANTHOPHYLS
XANTHOPSIA
XANTHOPSIAS
XANTHOPTERIN
XANTHOPTERINE
XANTHOPTERINES
XANTHOPTERINS
XANTHOXYLS
XENARTHRAL
XENOBIOTIC
XENOBIOTICS
XENOBLASTS
XENOCRYSTS
XENODIAGNOSES
XENODIAGNOSIS
XENODIAGNOSTIC
XENODOCHIUM
XENODOCHIUMS
XENOGAMIES
XENOGAMOUS
XENOGENEIC
XENOGENESES
XENOGENESIS
XENOGENETIC
XENOGENIES
XENOGENOUS
XENOGLOSSIA
XENOGLOSSIAS
XENOGLOSSIES
XENOGLOSSY
XENOGRAFTS
XENOLITHIC
XENOMANIAS
XENOMENIAS
XENOMORPHIC
XENOMORPHICALLY
XENOPHILES
XENOPHOBES
XENOPHOBIA
XENOPHOBIAS
XENOPHOBIC
XENOPHOBICALLY
XENOPHOBIES
XENOPLASTIC
XENOTRANSPLANT
XENOTRANSPLANTS
XENOTROPIC
XERANTHEMUM
XERANTHEMUMS
XERISCAPED
XERISCAPES
XERISCAPING
XEROCHASIES
XERODERMAE
XERODERMAS
XERODERMATIC
XERODERMATOUS
XERODERMIA
XERODERMIAS
XERODERMIC
XEROGRAPHER
XEROGRAPHERS
XEROGRAPHIC
XEROGRAPHICALLY
XEROGRAPHIES
XEROGRAPHY
XEROMORPHIC
XEROMORPHOUS
XEROMORPHS
XEROPHAGIES
XEROPHILES
XEROPHILIES
XEROPHILOUS
XEROPHTHALMIA
XEROPHTHALMIAS
XEROPHTHALMIC
XEROPHYTES
XEROPHYTIC
XEROPHYTICALLY
XEROPHYTISM
XEROPHYTISMS
XERORADIOGRAPHY
XEROSTOMAS
XEROSTOMATA
XEROSTOMIA
XEROSTOMIAS
XEROTHERMIC
XEROTRIPSES
XEROTRIPSIS
XIPHIHUMERALIS
XIPHIPLASTRA
XIPHIPLASTRAL
XIPHIPLASTRALS
XIPHIPLASTRON
XIPHISTERNA
XIPHISTERNUM
XIPHISTERNUMS
XIPHOPAGIC
XIPHOPAGOUS
XIPHOPAGUS
XIPHOPAGUSES
XIPHOPHYLLOUS
XIPHOSURAN
XIPHOSURANS
XYLOBALSAMUM
XYLOBALSAMUMS
XYLOCARPOUS
XYLOCHROME
XYLOCHROMES
XYLOGENOUS
XYLOGRAPHED
XYLOGRAPHER
XYLOGRAPHERS
XYLOGRAPHIC
XYLOGRAPHICAL
XYLOGRAPHIES
XYLOGRAPHING
XYLOGRAPHS
XYLOGRAPHY
XYLOIDINES
XYLOLOGIES
XYLOMETERS
XYLOPHAGAN
XYLOPHAGANS
XYLOPHAGES
XYLOPHAGOUS
XYLOPHILOUS
XYLOPHONES
XYLOPHONIC
XYLOPHONIST
XYLOPHONISTS
XYLOPYROGRAPHY
XYLORIMBAS
XYLOTOMIES
XYLOTOMIST
XYLOTOMISTS
XYLOTOMOUS
XYLOTYPOGRAPHIC
XYLOTYPOGRAPHY
XYRIDACEOUS

Y

YACHTSMANSHIP
YACHTSMANSHIPS
YACHTSWOMAN
YACHTSWOMEN
YAFFINGALE
YAFFINGALES
YAMMERINGS
YARBOROUGH
YARBOROUGHS
YARDLIGHTS
YARDMASTER
YARDMASTERS
YARDSTICKS
YATTERINGLY
YATTERINGS
YEARNINGLY
YEASTINESS
YEASTINESSES
YELLOCHING
YELLOWBACK
YELLOWBACKS
YELLOWBARK
YELLOWBARKS
YELLOWBIRD
YELLOWBIRDS
YELLOWCAKE
YELLOWCAKES
YELLOWFINS
YELLOWHAMMER
YELLOWHAMMERS
YELLOWHEAD
YELLOWHEADS
YELLOWIEST
YELLOWISHNESS
YELLOWISHNESSES
YELLOWLEGS
YELLOWNESS
YELLOWNESSES
YELLOWTAIL
YELLOWTAILS
YELLOWTHROAT
YELLOWTHROATS
YELLOWWARE
YELLOWWARES
YELLOWWEED
YELLOWWEEDS
YELLOWWOOD
YELLOWWOODS
YELLOWWORT
YELLOWWORTS
YEOMANRIES
YERSINIOSES
YERSINIOSIS
YESTERDAYS
YESTEREVEN
YESTEREVENING
YESTEREVENINGS
YESTEREVENS
YESTEREVES
YESTERMORN
YESTERMORNING
YESTERMORNINGS
YESTERMORNS
YESTERNIGHT
YESTERNIGHTS
YESTERYEAR
YESTERYEARS
YIELDABLENESS
YIELDABLENESSES
YIELDINGLY
YIELDINGNESS
YIELDINGNESSES
YOCTOSECOND
YOCTOSECONDS
YODELLINGS
YOHIMBINES
YOKEFELLOW
YOKEFELLOWS
YOTTABYTES
YOUNGBERRIES
YOUNGBERRY
YOUNGLINGS
YOUNGNESSES
YOUNGSTERS
YOURSELVES
YOUTHENING
YOUTHFULLY
YOUTHFULNESS
YOUTHFULNESSES
YOUTHHEADS
YOUTHHOODS
YOUTHQUAKE
YOUTHQUAKES
YPSILIFORM
YTHUNDERED
YTTERBITES
YTTERBIUMS
YTTRIFEROUS
YUCKINESSES
YUMBERRIES
YUMMINESSES
YUPPIEDOMS
YUPPIFICATION
YUPPIFICATIONS
YUPPIFYING

Z

ZABAGLIONE
ZABAGLIONES
ZALAMBDODONT
ZALAMBDODONTS
ZAMBOORAKS
ZAMINDARIES
ZAMINDARIS
ZANAMIVIRS
ZANINESSES
ZANTEDESCHIA
ZANTEDESCHIAS
ZANTEWOODS
ZANTHOXYLS
ZANTHOXYLUM
ZANTHOXYLUMS
ZAPATEADOS
ZAPOTILLAS
ZEALOTISMS
ZEALOTRIES
ZEALOUSNESS
ZEALOUSNESSES
ZEBRAFISHES
ZEBRAWOODS
ZEBRINNIES
ZEITGEBERS
ZEITGEISTIER
ZEITGEISTIEST
ZEITGEISTS
ZEITGEISTY
ZELATRICES
ZELATRIXES
ZELOPHOBIA
ZELOPHOBIAS
ZELOPHOBIC
ZELOPHOBICS
ZELOTYPIAS
ZEMINDARIES
ZEMINDARIS
ZEOLITIFORM
ZEPTOSECOND
ZEPTOSECONDS
ZESTFULNESS
ZESTFULNESSES
ZESTINESSES
ZETTABYTES
ZEUGLODONT
ZEUGLODONTS
ZEUGMATICALLY
ZIBELLINES
ZIDOVUDINE
ZIDOVUDINES
ZIGZAGGEDNESS
ZIGZAGGEDNESSES
ZIGZAGGERIES
ZIGZAGGERS
ZIGZAGGERY
ZIGZAGGIER
ZIGZAGGIEST
ZIGZAGGING
ZILLIONAIRE
ZILLIONAIRES
ZILLIONTHS
ZINCIFEROUS
ZINCIFICATION
ZINCIFICATIONS
ZINCIFYING
ZINCKENITE
ZINCKENITES
ZINCKIFICATION
ZINCKIFICATIONS
ZINCKIFIED
ZINCKIFIES
ZINCKIFYING
ZINCOGRAPH
ZINCOGRAPHER
ZINCOGRAPHERS
ZINCOGRAPHIC
ZINCOGRAPHICAL
ZINCOGRAPHIES
ZINCOGRAPHS
ZINCOGRAPHY
ZINCOLYSES
ZINCOLYSIS
ZINFANDELS
ZINGIBERACEOUS
ZINJANTHROPI
ZINJANTHROPUS
ZINJANTHROPUSES
ZINKENITES
ZINKIFEROUS
ZINKIFICATION
ZINKIFICATIONS
ZINKIFYING
ZINZIBERACEOUS
ZIPLOCKING
ZIPPINESSES
ZIRCALLOYS
ZIRCONIUMS
ZITHERISTS
ZIZYPHUSES
ZOANTHARIAN
ZOANTHARIANS
ZOANTHROPIC
ZOANTHROPIES
ZOANTHROPY
ZOECHROMES
ZOMBIELIKE
ZOMBIFICATION
ZOMBIFICATIONS
ZOMBIFYING
ZOOCEPHALIC
ZOOCHEMICAL
ZOOCHEMISTRIES
ZOOCHEMISTRY
ZOOCHORIES
ZOOCHOROUS
ZOOCULTURE
ZOOCULTURES
ZOODENDRIA
ZOODENDRIUM
ZOOGAMETES
ZOOGEOGRAPHER
ZOOGEOGRAPHERS
ZOOGEOGRAPHIC
ZOOGEOGRAPHICAL
ZOOGEOGRAPHIES
ZOOGEOGRAPHY
ZOOGLOEOID
ZOOGONIDIA
ZOOGONIDIUM
ZOOGRAFTING
ZOOGRAFTINGS
ZOOGRAPHER
ZOOGRAPHERS
ZOOGRAPHIC
ZOOGRAPHICAL
ZOOGRAPHIES
ZOOGRAPHIST
ZOOGRAPHISTS
ZOOKEEPERS
ZOOLATRIAS
ZOOLATRIES
ZOOLATROUS
ZOOLOGICAL
ZOOLOGICALLY
ZOOLOGISTS
ZOOMAGNETIC
ZOOMAGNETISM
ZOOMAGNETISMS
ZOOMANCIES
ZOOMETRICAL
ZOOMETRIES
ZOOMORPHIC
ZOOMORPHIES
ZOOMORPHISM
ZOOMORPHISMS
ZOONOMISTS
ZOOPATHIES
ZOOPATHOLOGIES
ZOOPATHOLOGY
ZOOPERISTS
ZOOPHAGANS
ZOOPHAGIES
ZOOPHAGOUS
ZOOPHILIAS
ZOOPHILIES
ZOOPHILISM
ZOOPHILISMS
ZOOPHILIST
ZOOPHILISTS
ZOOPHILOUS
ZOOPHOBIAS
ZOOPHOBOUS
ZOOPHYSIOLOGIES
ZOOPHYSIOLOGIST
ZOOPHYSIOLOGY
ZOOPHYTICAL
ZOOPHYTOID
ZOOPHYTOLOGICAL
ZOOPHYTOLOGIES
ZOOPHYTOLOGIST
ZOOPHYTOLOGISTS
ZOOPHYTOLOGY
ZOOPLANKTER
ZOOPLANKTERS
ZOOPLANKTON
ZOOPLANKTONIC
ZOOPLANKTONS
ZOOPLASTIC
ZOOPLASTIES
ZOOPSYCHOLOGIES
ZOOPSYCHOLOGY
ZOOSCOPIES
ZOOSPERMATIC
ZOOSPERMIA
ZOOSPERMIUM
ZOOSPORANGIA
ZOOSPORANGIAL
ZOOSPORANGIUM
ZOOSPOROUS
ZOOSTEROLS
ZOOTECHNICAL
ZOOTECHNICS
ZOOTECHNIES
ZOOTHAPSES
ZOOTHAPSIS
ZOOTHECIAL
ZOOTHECIUM
ZOOTHEISMS
ZOOTHEISTIC

ZOOTHERAPIES
ZOOTHERAPY
ZOOTOMICAL
ZOOTOMICALLY
ZOOTOMISTS
ZOOTROPHIC
ZOOTROPHIES
ZOOTSUITER
ZOOTSUITERS
ZOOXANTHELLA
ZOOXANTHELLAE
ZORBONAUTS
ZUCCHETTOS
ZUGZWANGED
ZUGZWANGING
ZUMBOORUKS
ZWANZIGERS
ZWISCHENZUG
ZWISCHENZUGS
ZWITTERION
ZWITTERIONIC
ZWITTERIONS
ZYGANTRUMS
ZYGAPOPHYSEAL
ZYGAPOPHYSES
ZYGAPOPHYSIAL
ZYGAPOPHYSIS
ZYGOBRANCH
ZYGOBRANCHIATE
ZYGOBRANCHIATES
ZYGOBRANCHS
ZYGOCACTUS
ZYGOCACTUSES
ZYGOCARDIAC
ZYGODACTYL
ZYGODACTYLIC
ZYGODACTYLISM
ZYGODACTYLISMS
ZYGODACTYLOUS
ZYGODACTYLS
ZYGOMATICS
ZYGOMORPHIC
ZYGOMORPHIES
ZYGOMORPHISM
ZYGOMORPHISMS
ZYGOMORPHOUS
ZYGOMORPHY
ZYGOMYCETE
ZYGOMYCETES
ZYGOMYCETOUS
ZYGOPHYLLACEOUS
ZYGOPHYTES
ZYGOPLEURAL
ZYGOSITIES
ZYGOSPERMS
ZYGOSPHENE
ZYGOSPHENES
ZYGOSPORES
ZYGOSPORIC
ZYGOTICALLY
ZYMOGENESES
ZYMOGENESIS
ZYMOLOGICAL
ZYMOLOGIES
ZYMOLOGIST
ZYMOLOGISTS
ZYMOMETERS
ZYMOSIMETER
ZYMOSIMETERS
ZYMOTECHNIC
ZYMOTECHNICAL
ZYMOTECHNICS
ZYMOTICALLY